INTERNATIONAL LITERARY MARKET PLACE™

ILMP
2019

International Literary Market Place™
52nd Edition

Publisher
Thomas H. Hogan

Vice President, Content
Dick Kaser

Senior Director, ITI Reference Group
Owen O'Donnell

Managing Editor
Karen Hallard

Assistant Editor
Karen DiDario

Tampa Operations:

Manager, Tampa Editorial Operations
Debra James

Project Coordinator, Tampa Editorial
Carolyn Victor

Graphics & Production:

Production Manager
Tiffany J. Chamenko

Production
Dana Stevenson
Jackie Crawford

INTERNATIONAL LITERARY MARKET PLACE™

ILMP 2019

The Directory of the
International Book Publishing Industry

OVER 175 COUNTRIES COVERED

Published by

Information Today, Inc.
143 Old Marlton Pike
Medford, NJ 08055-8750
Phone: (609) 654-6266
Fax: (609) 654-4309
E-mail (Orders): custserv@infotoday.com
Web site: http://www.infotoday.com

ISSN 0074-6827
ISBN 978-1-57387-547-9

Library of Congress Catalog Card Number 77-70295

Information Today, Inc. uses reasonable care to obtain accurate and timely information. However, Information Today, Inc. disclaims any liability to any party for any loss or damage caused by errors or omissions in *International Literary Market Place*™ whether or not such errors or omissions result from negligence, accident or any other cause.

Information Today, Inc.
143 Old Marlton Pike
Medford, NJ 08055-8750
Phone: 800-300-9868 (Customer Service)
              800-409-4929 (Editorial)
Fax: 609-654-4309
E-mail (Orders): custserv@infotoday.com
Web Site: www.infotoday.com

Printed in the United States of America

$349.50
ISBN 978-1-57387-547-9
34950

CONTENTS

CONTENTS

Preface

Since 1965, *International Literary Market Place (ILMP)* and its companion *Literary Market Place*, have covered the world of book publishing. These directories provide detailed information on the global book publishing industry. This edition of *ILMP* includes over 14,400 entries in over 175 countries. Publishers account for 9,403 of these entries.

Organization & Content

The six areas of coverage into which *ILMP* is arranged are as follows: Publishing, Manufacturing, Book Trade Information, Literary Associations & Prizes, Book Trade Calendar and Library Resources. Within most chapters, companies are sorted first by their country, then by key words in the company name. Sorting preference is determined by the entrant.

Pertinent information regarding each country represented - such as capital, language, population, currency, trade and copyright restrictions - can be found at the beginning of that country's listings in the Publishers section. The basic content of company entries includes - but is not limited to - address, telecommunications data, key personnel, a descriptive annotation and assorted statistics.

There are exceptions to this arrangement. Those U.S. and Canadian book manufacturing companies that do 10% or more of their business overseas are included in the appropriate sections within the Manufacturing chapter.

Compilation

ILMP is updated throughout the year via a number of methods. Most current entrants receive a request via e-mail asking them to corroborate and update the information contained in our database. All updates submitted are edited for the next product release. If a reply is not received, public sources are researched to determine the status of the listee.

Information on new listings is gathered using a similar method. *ILMP* editors identify possible new listings through their daily research or as a result of nominations from the organization itself or from third parties. In response to requested listings, a data collection form is sent to gather listing information.

An updating method using Internet technology is also available for *ILMP* listings:

You can use the *Literary Market Place* web site to update an *ILMP* listing. **Literarymarketplace.com** allows you the opportunity to provide new information for a listing by clicking on the option to Update or Correct Your Entry. The Feedback option on the home page of the web site can be used to suggest new entries as well.

Once information regarding a suggested new entry or a correction to an existing listing has been submitted, our editors verify the data with the organization to ensure the accuracy of the update.

Related Services

International Literary Market Place, along with its companion publication *Literary Market Place*, is also available online at **www.literarymarketplace.com**. Designed to give users simple, logical access to the information they require, the site offers the choice of searching for data alphabetically, geographically, by type, or by subject. Continuously updated by Information Today, Inc.'s team of editors, this is a truly enhanced version of the *ILMP* and *LMP* databases, incorporating features that make "must have" information easily available.

Your feedback is important to us. We strongly encourage you to contact us with comments on this 2019 edition of *ILMP*, as well as suggestions and comments for future editions. Our editorial office can be reached by phone at 1-800-409-4929 or 908-795-3755 or by e-mail at khallard@infotoday.com. Most importantly, thanks are due to those entrants who took the time to respond to our request for updated information.

Copyright Conventions

The Universal Copyright Convention was sponsored by UNESCO in 1952. It states that 'Each signatory country extends to foreign works covered by UCC the same protection which such country extends to works of its own nationals published within its own borders.'

The Berne Convention is a system of international copyright which is maintained among countries which have become signatories of the International Copyright Union for the Protection of Literary and Artistic Works. This Union plan, which was first agreed upon at Berne, Switzerland, in 1886, has been subject to later revisions.

The basic principle of the agreement is that any work properly copyrighted in its country of origin has protection in every Union country. Any work originating in a non-Union country, if it is simultaneously published in a Union country, has the same standing as it would if it had originated in a Union country. Different countries have different relationships under one or more of the revisions (Berlin, 1908; Rome, 1928; Brussels, 1948; Stockholm, 1968; and Paris, 1971).

The Florence Agreement, also known as 'free flow of ideas by word and image', is a UNESCO-sponsored international agreement aimed at easing the flow of books and other scientific, educational and cultural materials, through the elimination or reduction of tariffs and other barriers.

The Buenos Aires Convention: In most Latin-American countries, compliance with the copyright law of the country of first publication protects the work in other countries of the Buenos Aires Convention (1910). To secure copyright, each work must carry a notice to the effect that any use of the book or article will not be permitted without the consent of the copyright owner, and that copyright is reserved in English or any other language; for complete safety it is advised to add 'All rights reserved'. A later revision of the Buenos Aires Convention was made at the Washington Conference (Pan-American Copyright Convention) of 1946 which goes into greater detail than the Buenos Aires Convention.

See the General Information for each country in the Publishers Section for country specific copyright information.

The ISBN System

Background

The question of the need and feasibility of an international numbering system for books was first discussed at the third International Conference on Book Market Research and Rationalization in the Book Trade held in November 1966 in Berlin. At this time a number of publishers and book distributors in Europe were considering the use of computers in order processing and inventory control; and it was evident that a prerequisite of an efficient automated system was a unique and simple identification number for a published item.

The system which fulfilled this requirement and which became known as the International Standard Book Number (ISBN) System developed out of the book numbering system introduced into the United Kingdom in 1967.

In a report to the British Publishers Association, Professor F.G. Foster of the London School of Economics stated that there was '...a clear need of the introduction into the book trade of standard numbering...and substantial benefits would accrue to all parties therefrom'. After further study and deliberation, a detailed plan for standard numbering was produced. At the same time, the Technical Committee on Documentation of the International Standards Organization (ISO/TC 46) set up a working party (with the British Standards Institution acting as secretariat) to investigate the possibility of adapting the British system for international use. A meeting was held in London in 1968 with representatives from Denmark, France, Federal Republic of Germany, Eire, the Netherlands, Norway, the United Kingdom, the United States of America and an observer from Unesco. Other countries contributed written suggestions and expressions of interest. A report of the meeting was circulated to all countries belonging to the ISO. Comments on this report and subsequent proposals were considered at meetings held in Berlin and Stockholm in 1969.

As a result of these meetings there emerged The International Standard ISO 2108 which sets out the principles and procedures for international standard book numbering. The purpose of the ISO Recommendations is to coordinate and standardize internationally the use of book numbers so that an International Standard Book Number (ISBN) identifies one title or edition of a title from one specific publisher and is unique to that edition.

The ISBN applies in the main to books - for which the system was originally created - but, by extension, it may be used for any item produced by publishers or collected by libraries.

How the International Standard Book Number (ISBN) Is Built Up

Effective January 1, 2007, the publishing industry began using 13-digit ISBNs, phasing out the use of 10-digit ISBNs. The change was needed in order to expand the numbering capacity of the ISBN system and alleviate numbering shortages in certain areas of the world. Also, by changing the ISBN to 13 digits the book industry would be able to fully align the numbering system for books with the global EAN.UCC identification system that is widely used to identify most other consumer goods worldwide.

The 13-digit ISBNs are comprised of the following five elements:

Part 1. EAN Prefix
The first section of the ISBN consists of the numbers 978 or 979.

Part 2. Group Identifier
Identifies the national, geographic or other similar group of publishers.

Part 3. Publisher's Prefix
Identifies a particular publisher with a group.

Part 4. Title Identifier
This part identifies a particular title or edition of a title published by a particular publisher.

Part 5. Check Digit
This is a single digit at the end of the ISBN that provides an automatic check on the correctness of the ISBN.

The elements must be separated clearly by hyphens or spaces when displayed in human readable form. (Experience suggests that the hyphen is preferable to the space.) Of the five elements, the middle three will be of variable lengths; the EAN prefixes as currently defined (i.e., '978' or '979') and the check digit lengths will remain fixed.

Group Identifier
Group identifiers are allocated by the International ISBN Agency and a publisher wishing to participate in the ISBN system must belong to a recognized ISBN group. Groups are determined by national, geographic, language or other pertinent considerations. Experience has shown that groups based on national or geographic consideration are the most satisfactory. The following group identifiers are in use at present:

978-0 and 978-1	English-speaking countries including Anguilla, Australia, Bermuda, British Virgin Islands, Canada, Cayman Islands, Channel Islands, Gibraltar, Ireland, Isle of Man, Montserrat, New Zealand, Puerto Rico, South Africa, Swaziland, Turks and Caicos, United Arab Emirates (also 978-9948), UK, US, Virgin Islands, Zimbabwe
978-2	French-speaking countries including Belgium, Benin (also 978-99919), Canada, Congo (Democratic Republic of the), Cote d'Ivoire, France (also 979-10), French Polynesia, Gabon, Guadeloupe, Liechtenstein, Luxembourg (also 978-99959), Madagascar, Mali (also 978-99952), Martinique, Monaco, Reunion, Senegal, Switzerland, Togo
978-3	German-speaking countries including Austria, Belgium, Germany, Liechtenstein, Switzerland
978-4	Japan
978-5	Armenia (also 978-9939, 978-99930 and 978-99941), Azerbaijan (also 978-9952), Belarus (also 978-985), Estonia (also 978-9949 and 978-9985), Georgia (also 978-9941, 978-99928 and 978-99940), Kazakhstan (also 978-601 and 978-9965), Kyrgyzstan (also 978-9967), Latvia (also 978-9934 and 978-9984), Lithuania (also 978-609, 978-9955 and 978-9986), Moldova (also 978-9975), Russia, Tajikistan (also 978-99947 and 978-99975), Turkmenistan, Ukraine (also 978-617 and 978-966), Uzbekistan (also 978-9943)
978-7	China
978-80	Czechia, Slovakia
978-81	India (also 978-93)
978-82	Norway
978-83	Poland
978-84	Spain
978-85	Brazil
978-86	Bosnia and Herzegovina (also 978-9926 and 978-9958), Croatia (also 978-953), Kosovo (also 978-9951), Macedonia (also 978-608 and 978-9989), Montenegro (also 978-9940), Serbia, Slovenia (also 978-961)
978-87	Denmark, Greenland
978-88	Holy See, Italy (also 979-12)
978-89	South Korea (also 979-11)
978-90	Belgium (Flemish-speaking), Netherlands (both also 978-94)

978-91   Sweden

978-92   European Community Organizations and International NGO Publishers (also 978-99914)

978-93   India (also 978-81)

978-94   Belgium (Flemish-speaking), Netherlands (both also 978-90)

978-600   Iran (also 978-964)

978-601   Kazakhstan (also 978-5 and 978-9965)

978-602   Indonesia (also 978-979)

978-603   Saudi Arabia (also 978-9960)

978-604   Vietnam

978-605   Turkey (also 978-975 and 978-9944)

978-606   Romania (also 978-973)

978-607   Mexico (also 978-968 and 978-970)

978-608   Macedonia (also 978-86 and 978-9989)

978-609   Lithuania (also 978-5, 978-9955 and 978-9986)

978-611   Thailand (also 978-616 and 978-974)

978-612   Peru (also 978-9972)

978-613   Mauritius (also 978-620, 978-99903 and 978-99949)

978-614   Lebanon (also 978-9953)

978-615   Hungary (also 978-963)

978-616   Thailand (also 978-611 and 978-974)

978-617   Ukraine (also 978-5 and 978-966)

978-618   Greece (also 978-960)

978-619   Bulgaria (also 978-954)

978-620   Mauritius (also 978-613, 978-99903 and 978-99949)

978-621   Philippines (also 978-971)

978-950   Argentina (also 978-987)

978-951   Finland (also 978-952)

978-952   Finland (also 978-951)

978-953   Croatia (also 978-86)

978-954   Bulgaria (also 978-619)

978-955   Sri Lanka

978-956   Chile

978-957   Taiwan (also 978-986)

978-958   Colombia

978-959   Cuba

978-960   Greece (also 978-618)

978-961   Slovenia (also 978-86)

978-962   Hong Kong (also 978-988)

978-963   Hungary (also 978-615)

978-964   Iran (also 978-600)

978-965   Israel

978-966   Ukraine (also 978-5 and 978-617)

978-967   Malaysia (also 978-983)

978-968   Mexico (also 978-607 and 978-970)

978-969   Pakistan

978-970   Mexico (also 978-607 and 978-968)

978-971   Philippines (also 978-621)

978-972   Portugal (also 978-989)

978-973   Romania (also 978-606)

978-974   Thailand (also 978-611 and 978-616)

978-975   Turkey (also 978-605 and 978-9944)

978-976   Caribbean Community (CARICOM): Antigua and Barbuda, The Bahamas, Barbados, Belize, Dominica, Grenada, Guyana, Haiti (also 978-99935 and 978-99970), Jamaica, Montserrat, Saint Kitts and Nevis, Saint Lucia, Saint Vincent and the Grenadines, Suriname, Trinidad and Tobago

978-977   Egypt

978-978   Nigeria

978-979   Indonesia (also 978-602)

978-980   Venezuela

978-981   Singapore (also 978-9971)

978-982   South Pacific: American Samoa, Cook Islands, Fiji, Kiribati, Marshall Islands, Micronesia (Federated States of), Nauru, New Caledonia, Niue, Palau, Papua New Guinea (also 978-9980), Samoa, Solomon Islands, Tahiti, Timor Leste, Tokelau, Tonga, Tuvalu, Vanuatu

978-983   Malaysia (also 978-967)

978-984   Bangladesh

978-985   Belarus (also 978-5)

978-986   Taiwan (also 978-957)

978-987   Argentina (also 978-950)

978-988   Hong Kong (also 978-962)

978-989   Mozambique, Portugal (also 978-972)

978-9920 Morocco (also 978-9954 and 978-9981)

978-9921 Kuwait (also 978-99906 and 978-99966)

978-9922 Iraq

978-9923 Jordan (also 978-9957)

978-9924 Cambodia (also 978-99950 and 978-99963)

978-9925 Cyprus (also 978-9963)

978-9926 Bosnia and Herzegovina (also 978-86 and 978-9958)

978-9927 Qatar (also 978-99921)

978-9928 Albania (also 978-99927, 978-99943 and 978-99956)

978-9929 Guatemala (also 978-99922 and 978-99939)

978-9930 Costa Rica (also 978-9968 and 978-9977)

978-9931 Algeria (also 978-9947 and 978-9961)

978-9932 Laos

978-9933 Syria

978-9934 Latvia (also 978-5 and 978-9984)

978-9935 Iceland (also 978-9979)

978-9936 Afghanistan

978-9937 Nepal (also 978-99933 and 978-99946)

978-9938 Tunisia (also 978-9973)

978-9939 Armenia (also 978-5, 978-99930 and 978-99941)

978-9940 Montenegro (also 978-86)

978-9941 Georgia (also 978-5, 978-99928 and 978-99940)

978-9942 Ecuador (also 978-9978)

978-9943 Uzbekistan (also 978-5)

978-9944 Turkey (also 978-605 and 978-975)

978-9945 Dominican Republic (also 978-99934)

978-9946 North Korea

978-9947 Algeria (also 978-9931 and 978-9961)

978-9948 United Arab Emirates (also 978-0 and 978-1)

978-9949 Estonia (also 978-5 and 978-9985)

978-9950 Palestine

978-9951 Kosovo (also 978-86)

978-9952 Azerbaijan (also 978-5)

978-9953 Lebanon (also 978-614)

978-9954 Morocco (also 978-9920 and 978-9981)

978-9955 Lithuania (also 978-5, 978-609 and 978-9986)

978-9956 Cameroon

978-9957 Jordan (also 978-9923)

978-9958 Bosnia and Herzegovina (also 978-86 and 978-9926)

978-9959 Libya

978-9960 Saudi Arabia (also 978-603)

978-9961 Algeria (also 978-9931 and 978-9947)

978-9962 Panama

978-9963 Cyprus (also 978-9925)

978-9964 Ghana (also 978-9988)

978-9965 Kazakhstan (also 978-5 and 978-601)

978-9966 Kenya

978-9967 Kyrgyzstan (also 978-5)

978-9968 Costa Rica (also 978-9930 and 978-9977)

978-9970 Uganda

978-9971 Singapore (also 978-981)

978-9972 Peru (also 978-612)

978-9973 Tunisia (also 978-9938)

978-9974 Uruguay

978-9975 Moldova (also 978-5)

978-9976 Tanzania (also 978-9987)

978-9977 Costa Rica (also 978-9930 and 978-9968)

978-9978 Ecuador (also 978-9942)

978-9979 Iceland (also 978-9935)

978-9980 Papua New Guinea (also 978-982)

978-9981 Morocco (also 978-9920 and 978-9954)

978-9982 Zambia

978-9983 The Gambia

978-9984 Latvia (also 978-5 and 978-9934)

978-9985 Estonia (also 978-5 and 978-9949)

978-9986 Lithuania (also 978-5, 978-609 and 978-9955)

978-9987 Tanzania (also 978-9976)

978-9988 Ghana (also 978-9964)

978-9989 Macedonia (also 978-86 and 978-608)

978-99901 Bahrain (also 978-99958)

978-99903 Mauritius (also 978-613, 978-620 and 978-99949)

978-99904 Curacao

978-99905 Bolivia (also 978-99954 and 978-99974)

978-99906 Kuwait (also 978-9921 and 978-99966)

978-99908 Malawi (also 978-99960)

978-99909 Malta (also 978-99932 and 978-99957)

978-99910 Sierra Leone

978-99911 Lesotho

978-99912 Botswana (also 978-99968)

978-99913 Andorra (also 978-99920)

978-99914 International NGO Publishers (also 978-92)

978-99915 Maldives

978-99916 Namibia (also 978-99945)

978-99917 Brunei

978-99918 Faroe Islands (also 978-99972)

978-99919 Benin (also 978-2)

978-99920 Andorra (also 978-99913)

978-99921 Qatar (also 978-9927)

978-99922 Guatemala (also 978-9929 and 978-99939)

978-99923 El Salvador (also 978-99961)

978-99924 Nicaragua (also 978-99964)

978-99925 Paraguay (also 978-99953 and 978-99967)

978-99926 Honduras (also 978-99979)

978-99927 Albania (also 978-9928, 978-99943 and 978-99956)

978-99928 Georgia (also 978-5, 978-9941 and 978-99940)

978-99929 Mongolia (also 978-99962, 978-99973 and 978-99978)

978-99930 Armenia (also 978-5, 978-9939 and 978-99941)

978-99931 Seychelles

978-99932 Malta (also 978-99909 and 978-99957)

978-99933 Nepal (also 978-9937 and 978-99946)

978-99934 Dominican Republic (also 978-9945)

978-99935 Haiti (also 978-976 and 978-99970)

978-99936 Bhutan (also 978-99980)

978-99937 Macau (also 978-99965 and 978-99981)

978-99938 Srpska (also 978-99955 and 978-99976)

978-99939 Guatemala (also 978-9929 and 978-99922)

978-99940 Georgia (also 978-5, 978-9941 and 978-99928)

978-99941 Armenia (also 978-5, 978-9939 and 978-99930)

978-99942 Sudan

978-99943 Albania (also 978-9928, 978-99927 and 978-99956)

978-99944 Ethiopia

978-99945 Namibia (also 978-99916)

978-99946 Nepal (also 978-9937 and 978-99933)

978-99947 Tajikistan (also 978-5 and 978-99975)

978-99948 Eritrea

978-99949 Mauritius (also 978-613, 978-620 and 978-99903)

978-99950 Cambodia (also 978-9924 and 978-99963)

978-99952 Mali (also 978-2)

978-99953 Paraguay (also 978-99925 and 978-99967)

978-99954 Bolivia (also 978-99905 and 978-99974)

978-99955 Srpska (also 978-99938 and 978-99976)

978-99956 Albania (also 978-9928, 978-99927 and 978-99943)

978-99957 Malta (also 978-99909 and 978-99932)

978-99958 Bahrain (also 978-99901)

978-99959 Luxembourg (also 978-2)

978-99960 Malawi (also 978-99908)

978-99961 El Salvador (also 978-99923)

978-99962 Mongolia (also 978-99929, 978-978-99973 and 978-99978)

978-99963 Cambodia (also 978-9924 and 978-99950)

978-99964 Nicaragua (also 978-99924)

978-99965 Macau (also 978-99937 and 978-99981)

978-99966 Kuwait (also 978-9921 and 978-99906)

978-99967 Paraguay (also 978-99925 and 978-99953)

978-99968 Botswana (also 978-99912)

978-99969 Oman

978-99970 Haiti (also 978-976 and 978-99935)

978-99971 Myanmar

978-99972 Faroe Islands (also 978-99918)

978-99973 Mongolia (also 978-9929, 978-99962 and 978-99978)

978-99974 Bolivia (also 978-99905 and 978-99954)

978-99975 Tajikistan (also 978-5 and 978-99947)

978-99976 Srpska (also 978-99938 and 978-99955)

978-99977 Rwanda

978-99978 Mongolia (also 978-99929, 978-99962 and 978-99973)

978-99979 Honduras (also 978-99926)

978-99980 Bhutan (also 978-99936)

978-99981 Macau (also 978-99937 and 978-99965)

979-10 France (also 978-2)

979-11 South Korea (also 978-89)

979-12 Italy (also 978-88)

EAN Prefix
This element will consist of three digits, either 978 or 979.

Publisher's Prefix
The publisher's prefix designates the publisher of a given book. Publishers with a large output of books are assigned a short publisher's prefix; publishers with a small output of books are assigned a longer publisher's prefix.

Title Identifier
The title identifier is assigned to a particular title or edition of a title by the publisher from within the range of numbers assigned to him and which will depend upon the length of his publisher's prefix. Title identifiers are normally assigned by the publisher himself. Publishers who assign their own title identifiers may use them to identify titles in the publishing house throughout the planning stages.

Check Digit
The 'check digit' is the last digit in an ISBN and is computed as the result of an elaborate calculation on the other 12 digits. This calculation is performed almost instantaneously by an electronic computing device, and is a means of detecting incorrectly transcribed numbers. The check digit is calculated on a modulus 10 algorithm. Each of the first 12 digits of the ISBN - i.e. excluding the check digit itself - is multiplied alternately using weights 1 and 3. The check digit is equal to 10 minus the remainder resulting from dividing the sum of the weighted products of the first 12 digits by 10 with one exception. If the calculation results in an apparent check digit of 10, the check digit is 0.

The number of digits in each part, and how to recognize them in an ISBN
The number of digits in part 1 is always 3. Each of the identifying parts 2, 3 & 4 is variable, though the total number of digits contained in these four parts is always 12. These twelve digits together with the check digit bring the total number of digits in an ISBN to thirteen.

The number of digits in the group identifier will vary according to the likely output of books in a group. Thus, groups with an expected large output will get numbers of one or two digits; and publishers with an expected large output will get numbers of two or three digits.

Exceptionally, a one-digit number may be assigned to a publisher, but it will be appreciated that the assignment of one-digit publisher identifiers greatly reduces the range of possible identifiers in the group. For ease of reading, the four parts of the ISBN are divided by spaces or hyphens. These spaces or hyphens, however, are not retained in a computer which depends upon the special distribution of ranges of numbers for the recognition of the parts.

Scope of the ISBN

For the purposes of the ISBN system books and other items to be numbered include:

Printed books and pamphlets

Mixed media publications

Other similar media including educational films/ videos and transparencies

Electronic publications

Microcomputer software

Microform publications

Braille publications

Atlases & Maps

Except:
Ephemeral printed materials such as diaries, calendars, advertising matter and the like

Art prints and art folders without title page and text

Sound recordings

Principles and procedures to be observed by the publisher numbering his own publications

A publisher must ensure that a competent person is responsible for the assignment of ISBN and the application of the pertinent regulations. A publisher will be assigned a publisher identifier (publisher's prefix) by the group agency which will determine the range of title identifiers available to him. The number of title identifiers will depend upon the length of the publisher identifier assigned to him. The publisher should ensure that the group agency has as much information as possible about his back lists of books still available; and present and future publication programmes in order that a suitable publisher identifier can be assigned. A publisher is responsible for assigning title identifiers to the individual items he publishes.

A publisher may wish to incorporate an existing non-classifying identification system into his ISBN allocation. This may be arranged provided that such incorporation does not alter the fundamental characteristics of the ISBN system or reduce the amount of numbers available. For example: the publisher must not incorporate digits other than numerals which cause the resulting ISBN to be longer than or shorter than 13 digits, nor must the publisher attempt to build in special meanings or hierarchical order to groups of numbers, if by so doing he reduces the amount of available numbers in the range allocated to him.

Non-participating publishers

If by choice, or for any other reason, a publisher does not accept responsibility for assigning ISBN to his publications, two alternatives are open to the group agency.

1. The group agency can allocate a block of numbers for miscellaneous publishers and number all titles within that block irrespective of the publisher. In such a case the resulting ISBN will not identify the publisher of a specific title. (It is strongly recommended that this procedure should be reserved for publishers who only publish an occasional title and who are never likely to be in a position to assume the responsibility for numbering themselves.)

2. The group agency can assume responsibility for assigning a publisher identifier, a block of ISBNs associated with the publisher identifier and a number to each publication as well as informing the publisher before publication of the number assigned. In such a case, if the publisher agrees to do so, the ISBN can be printed in the book. It is expected that such a publisher will eventually assume full responsibility for assigning his own ISBN.

Application of ISBN

General
A separate ISBN must be assigned to every different edition of a book; but NOT to an unchanged impression or unchanged reprint of the same book in the same format and by the same publisher. Price changes do not need new ISBN.

Facsimile reprints
A separate ISBN must be assigned to a facsimile reprint produced by a different publisher.

Books in different formats
A separate ISBN must be assigned to the different formats in which a particular title is published. For example: a hardback edition and a paperback edition each receives a separate ISBN. On the same principle, a microform edition receives a separate ISBN.

Looseleaf publications
If a publication appears in looseleaf form, an ISBN is allocated to identify an edition at a given time. Individual issues of additions or replacement sheets will likewise be given an ISBN.

Multi-volume works
An ISBN must be assigned to the whole set of volumes of a multi-volume work, as well as to each individual volume in the set.

Back stock
A publisher is required to number his back stock and publish the ISBN in his catalogues. He must also print the ISBN in the first available reprint of an item from his back stock.

Collaborative publications
A publication issued as a coedition or joint imprint with other publishers is assigned an ISBN by the publisher in charge of distribution.

Books sold or distributed by agents
According to the principles of the ISBN system, a particular edition published by a particular publisher receives only one ISBN; this ISBN must be retained no matter where or by whom the book is distributed or sold.

A book imported by an exclusive distributor or sole agent from an area not yet in the ISBN system and for which, therefore, no ISBN has been assigned may be assigned an ISBN by the exclusive distributor.

A book imported by an exclusive distributor or sole agent to which a new title-page, bearing the imprint of the exclusive distributor, has been added in place of the title page of the original publisher, is to be given a new ISBN by the exclusive distributor or sole agent. The ISBN of the original publisher is also to be given as a related ISBN.

A book imported by several distributors from an area not yet in the ISBN system and for which, therefore, no ISBN has been assigned may be assigned an ISBN by the group agency responsible for those distributors.

Publishers with more than one place of publication
A publisher operating in a number of places which are listed together in the imprint of a book will assign only one ISBN to the book. A publisher operating separate and distinct offices or branches in different places may have a publisher identifier for each office or branch. Nevertheless, each book published is to be assigned only one ISBN, the assignment being made by the office or branch responsible for publication.

Register of ISBNs
Every publisher must keep a register of ISBNs that have been assigned to published and forthcoming books. The register is to be kept in numerical sequence giving ISBN, author, title and edition (where appropriate).

ISBNs are not to be re-used under any circumstances
An ISBN once allocated must not under any circumstances be re-used. This is of the utmost importance to avoid confusion. It is recognized that, owing to clerical errors, numbers will be incorrectly assigned. If this happens, the number must be deleted from the list of usable numbers and must not be assigned to another title. Every publisher will have sufficient numbers in his range for the loss of these numbers to be insignificant. Publishers should advise the group agency of the numbers thus deleted and of the titles to which they were erroneously assigned.

Guidelines for ISBN assignment to software

An ISBN is used to identify a specific software product. If there is more than one version (perhaps versions adapted for different machines, carrier media or language version), each version must have a different ISBN. When a software product is updated, revised or otherwise amended and the changes are sufficiently substantial for the product to be called a new edition (and thus probably the subject of a new launch, or marketing push), then a new ISBN must be allocated. A relaunch of an existing product, even in new packaging, where there is no basic difference in the performance of the new and the old product, does NOT justify a new ISBN, and the original ISBN must be used.

When software is accompanied by a manual, useful only as an adjunct to the software, and the

software needs the manual before it can be operated, and the two items are always sold as a package, one ISBN must be used to cover both items. When two or more items in a software package (as above) can be used separately, or are sold separately as well as together, then
(i) the package as a whole must have an ISBN
(ii) each item in the package must have its own ISBN.

ISBNs should be allocated to a software product independent of its physical form, e.g., if software is only available from a remote database form whence it is downloaded to the customer.

As well as identifying the product itself, an ISBN identifies the publisher or manufacturer; it should not be used to identify a distributor or wholesaler.

Printing of the ISBN

General
The ISBN must appear on the item itself. This is essential for the efficient running of the system.

Printing of ISBN on books: In the case of books, the ISBN must appear whenever possible:

On the reverse of the title page, or, if this is not possible, on the base of the title page, or, if this too is not possible, at some other conspicuous location in the book.

On the base of the spine.

On the back of the cover in 9-point type or larger.

On the back of the dust jacket, and on the back of any other protective case or wrapper.

The ISBN should always be printed in type large enough to be easily legible (i.e. not smaller than 9 point).

Printing of ISBN on books in machine readable coding
An agreement between the International Article Numbering Association (EAN) and the International ISBN Agency permits the conversion of the ISBN into EAN bar code (European Article Number). All EAN bar codes start with a national identifier except those on books and periodicals. The agreement replaces the usual national identifier with a special "Bookland" identifier represented by the digits 978 for books and 977 for periodicals. The 978 Bookland/EAN prefix is followed by the first nine digits of the ISBN. The check digit of the ISBN is dropped and replaced by a check digit calculated according to the EAN rules.

For more information on the ISBN and how to convert an ISBN to ISBN-13, visit www. isbn.org.

Optional 5-digit add-on code
There is an optional 5-digit add-on code which can be used for additional information. In the publishing industry it can be used for price information which may have the following formats:
a) Five-digit bar code indicating the price with human readable numbers above the bar code or
b) Five-digit bar code indicating the price with no human readable numbers.

Administration of the ISBN System

General
The administration of the ISBN system is carried on at three levels. These are the international, group and publisher levels.

International administration
The international administration of the system is in the hands of the International Standard Book Number Agency which has an Advisory Panel representing the ISO and the publishing and library world. The address of the International Agency is:

International ISBN Agency
48-49 Russell Square
London WC1B 4JP
United Kingdom

The principal functions of the International Agency are:

To supervise the use of the system

To approve the definition and structure of groups

To allocate identifiers to groups

To advise groups on the setting up and functioning of group agencies

To advise group agencies on the allocation of publisher identifiers

To promote the worldwide use of the system

In addition, the International Agency also offers the following services. It will:

Provide a group agency with lists of ISBNs (with computer-generated check digits) for the use of publishers in the group

Provide international registers of publishers, prefixes and publishers' names

Provide from information supplied by group agencies a computer printout of lists of publishers' prefixes, names and locations

Provide from information supplied by group agencies a computer printout of invalid or duplicate ISBNs

Group administration
Groups are administered by Group Agencies. Within the group there may be several national agencies, e.g. group 0/1 has separate agencies in USA, United Kingdom, Canada, Australia, etc, with the main agency for the whole group in the UK.

The functions of a group agency are:

To manage and administer the affairs of the group

To handle relations with the International ISBN Agency on behalf of all the publishers in the group

To decide, in consultation with trade organizations and publishers, the publisher identifier ranges required

To allocate publishers' prefixes to publishers eligible to join the group and to maintain a register of publishers and their prefixes

To decide, in consultation with trade organizations and publishers, which publishers shall assign numbers to their own titles and which publishers shall have numbers assigned to their titles by the group agency

To provide technical advice and assistance to the publishers and to ensure that standards and approved procedures are observed in the group

To make available a manual of instruction for publishers

To make available computer printouts of ISBNs to publishers numbering their own books with check digits already calculated (such printouts may be obtained from the International Agency on request)

To validate all ISBNs assigned by publishers numbering their own books and keep a register of them

To inform publishers of any invalid or duplicate ISBNs assigned by them

To assign numbers to all publications from those publishers who do not assign their own ISBNs and advise the publishers concerned of ISBNs assigned upon request

To achieve, thereby, total numbering in the group

To arrange with book listing and bibliographic agencies for the publication of ISBNs with the titles to which they refer

To arrange with publishers for the numbering of their back lists and for the publication of these in appropriate trade lists and bibliographies

To maintain liaison with all elements of the book trade and introduce new publishers to the system

To assist the trade in the use of the ISBN in computer systems

ISBN and ISSN

In addition to the International Standard Book Number System, a complementary numbering system for serial publications has also been established.

A serial is defined as any publication issued in successive parts, usually bearing numerical or chronological designations and intended to be continued indefinitely.

Serials include periodicals, yearbooks and monographic series.

The International Standard Serial Number system (ISSN) is administered by the ISSN International Centre, whose address is:

Centre International de l'ISSN
45 rue de Turbigo
75003 Paris
France

Publishers of serials should apply to the ISSN International Centre or to their National Serials Data Centre, if there is one, for ISSNs for their serial publications.

Certain publications, such as yearbooks, annuals, monographic series, etc, should be assigned an ISSN for the serial title (which will remain the same for all the parts or individual volumes of the serial) and an ISBN for each individual volume.

Both ISSN and ISBN, when they are assigned, must be given on the publication and clearly identified.

(The preceding information is mainly from the ISBN User's Manual, compiled by the former International ISBN Agency, Staatsbibliothek zu Berlin, Preussischer Kulturbesitz, Berlin, Germany.)

Abbreviations

+	Publisher's indication of interest in buying/selling international rights or editions
†	Organizations that are international in scope
§	Publications that are international in scope
◇	Organizations with publishing activities
‡	United nations agencies with publishing activities
*	Prizes with no geographical restriction placed upon recipients
AB	aktiebolag (=public limited company)
AE	anonymous etaireia
AG	Aktiengesellschaft (=public limited company)
al	aleja
Apdo	apartado (=post-box)
ApS	anpartsselskab (=private limited company)
A/S	(Norwegian) aksjeselskap. (Swedish) aaktieselskab (=limited company)
AS	anonim sirketi
ASBL	association sans but lucratif (=non-profit-making society)
Av	(Spanish) avenida
Ave	(English, French) avenue. (Portuguese) avenida
Bldg	Building
Blvd	(Bulgarian, Romanian) bulevard. (English, French) boulevard
BP	boite postale (=post-box)
BV	besloten vennootschap (=private limited company)
C	compagnia (=company)
CA	compania anonima (=public limited company)
CEDEX	Courrier d'enterpise a distribution exceptionnelle
CFA	Communaute financiere africaine
CFP	comptoirs fracais du Pacifique
Cia	companhia, compania (=company)
Cie	compagnie (=company)
Co	(English) company, county. (German) Kompanie
c/o	care of
Corp	Corporation
CP	(Italian) casetta postale. (Portuguese) caixa postal, (=post-box)
CV	commanditaire vennootschap (=limited partnership)
Dept	department
Dir	Director
Dr	Drive
EE	eterorruthmos etaireia
eV	einetragener Verein (=registered society)
ext	extension
GmbH	Gesellschaft mit beschrankter Haftung (=private limited company)
Inc	incorporated
ISBN	international standard book number
Jl	jalan (=street)
KG	Kommanditgesellschaft (=partnership)
KK	kabushiki kaisha (=public limited company)
Lda	limitada (=limited)
Ltd	limited
Ltda	limitada (=limited)
Mng	Managing
Nachf	Nachfolger(s) (=successor(s))
nam	namesti (=square)
NV	naamloze vennootschap (=public limited company)
OE	omorruthmos etaireia of oficina (=office)

Off	office
Oy	osakeyhitio (=limited company)
pA	per Adresse (=care of)
Pl	(Bulgarian) ploshtad. (English, French) place. (Polish) plac. (Russian) ploshchad. (Spanish) plaza
PL	postriokero (=post-box)
PLC	public limited company
PMB	private mail bag
PO	Post Office
Prof	Professor
Pty	proprietary
PVBA	personenvennootschap met beperkte aansprakelijkheid (=private limited company)
Pvt	private
Rd	Road
SA	(French) societe anonyyme. (Portuguese) sociedade anonima.(Spanish) sociedad anonima (=public limited company)
Sarl	societe a responsabilite limitee (=private limited company)
SAS	societa in accomandita semplice (=limited partnership)
SCA	sociedad en comandita por acciones (=limited partnership)
S de RL	sociedad de responsabilidad limitada (=private limited company)
Sdn Bhd	sendirian berhad (=private limited company)
SL	sociedad de responsabilidad limitada (=private limited company)
SNC	societa in nome collettivo (=partnership)
SpA	societa per azioni (=public limited company)
SPRL	societe de personnes a responsabilite (=private limited company)
Sq	square
SRL	(Italian) societa a responsabilita limita. (Spanish) sociedad de responsabilida limitada (=private limited company)
St	Saint, street
STD	subscriber trunk dialing
Str	(Danish) straede. (Dutch) straat. (German) Strasse. (Icelandic) straeti. (Italian) strada. (Romanian) strada. (=street)
Tel	telephone number
u	utca (=street)
UCC	Universal Copyright Convention
ul	(Bulgarian) ulitsa. (Czech) ulice. (Polish) ulica. (Romanian) ulita. (Russian) ulitsa. (Serbocroatian, Slovak, Slovene) ulica (=street)
UK	United Kingdom
USA	United States of America
VEB	volkseigener Betrieb (=people's enterprise)
VZW	vereniging zonder winstoogmerk (=non-profit-making society)

A limited company is a corporation owned by shareholders (or stockholders) who may contribute capital to the company but are not otherwise generally liable for its debts.

A public company may invite anyone to become a shareholder, and its shares (or stock) are usually traded on a stock exchange.

A private, or proprietary, company has a restricted number of shareholders and its shares are not traded on a stock exchange.

The owners of a partnership or proprietorship are generally liable for its debts, but a limited partnership has some owners who only contribute capital and are not otherwise liable for debts.

Publishing

Publishers

This section covers book publishers throughout the world, with the exception of U.S. and Canadian publishers, which can be found in the companion publication, *Literary Market Place*. Publishers and their imprints are listed alphabetically within their country of business. General information for each country can be found preceding the entries for that country.

+ following a publisher's name indicates those who are involved in the buying or selling of international rights.

Immediately following this section are indexes that list publishers by type of publication and by subjects.

Albania

General Information

Capital: Tirane
Language: Albanian
Religion: Islamic, Orthodox, Roman Catholic
Population: 3.3 million
Bank Hours: 0730-2330 Monday-Saturday
Shop Hours: 0900-1200 and 1600-2000; one day per week is holiday
Currency: 100 qintars = 1 lek
Export/Import Information: Importation of books is through State Trading Organization, Nd. Shperndarjes Te (or NST) Librit, Blvd K e Pezes, Tirana. Correspondence should be in English, French, German or Italian. Copies of correspondence to Albanian Legation in Rome. Some import licenses but no strict exchange controls.
Copyright: Berne (see Copyright Conventions, pg viii)

Shtepia Botuese Albas (Albas Publishing House)
Rr Budit, Pallati Klasik konstruksioni zyra nr 2, Tirana
Tel: (04) 2379184 *Fax:* (04) 2379184
E-mail: info@albas.al
Web Site: www.albas.al
Key Personnel
Manager: Artin Cili *E-mail:* a.cili@albas.al
Founded: 2000
Subjects: Biological Sciences, Chemistry, Chemical Engineering, History, Language Arts, Linguistics, Mathematics, Philosophy, Physics, Science (General), Social Sciences, Sociology
Branch Office(s)
Rr Muharrem Fejza, 10000 Pristina, Kosovo, Manager: Fatlum Hetemi *Tel:* (045) 999 770 *E-mail:* albas_pr@yahoo.com
Rr Ilindenit, nr 105, 1200 Tetovo, Macedonia, Manager: Nehat Havziu *Tel:* (044) 344047 *Fax:* (044) 344047 *E-mail:* albas_te@yahoo.com

Algeria

General Information

Capital: Algiers (El Djazair)
Language: Arabic. French is the language of business and administration
Religion: Islamic
Population: 26.7 million
Bank Hours: 0900-1500 or 1600 Saturday-Wednesday
Shop Hours: 0900-1200, 1500-1900 Monday-Saturday
Currency: 100 centimes = 1 Algerian dinar
Export/Import Information: Books may be imported or exported only by or with permission of SNED State Monopoly, 3 blvd Zirout Yousef, BP 49, Alger Strasbourg. There are also quota restrictions. Permission to import usually entitles holder to obtain necessary foreign exchange; strict controls are in effect. Documentation formalities are rigidly enforced.
Copyright: UCC (see Copyright Conventions, pg viii)

Editions Chihab
11, Ave Brahim Gharafa, 16009 Bab El Oued, Algiers
Tel: (021) 97 54 54 *Fax:* (021) 97 51 91
E-mail: chihab@chihab.com
Web Site: www.chihab.com
Key Personnel
Dir: Azeddine Guerfi
Founded: 1989
Subjects: Government, Political Science, History, Regional Interests
ISBN Prefix(es): 978-9961-63
Subsidiaries: Chihab 2000
Bookshop(s): 10, Ave Brahim Gharafa, 16009 Bab El Oued, Algiers *Tel:* (021) 97 54 53

Dar el Afaq Sarl
10 rue Mustapha Khalef, 16606 El Biar
Tel: (021) 79 16 44 *Fax:* (021) 79 16 44
E-mail: afaq.edition@gmail.com
Key Personnel
Contact: Mostefa Harkat
Founded: 1989
Subjects: Science (General)
ISBN Prefix(es): 978-9961-57

Andorra

General Information

Capital: Andorra la Vella
Language: French & Catalan
Religion: Roman Catholic
Population: 65,780 million
Currency: 100 Eurocents = 1 Euro
Copyright: UCC (see Copyright Conventions, pg viii)

Editorial Andorra
C/Les Canals 21, Andorra la Vella
Tel: 802925; 328175 (cell)
E-mail: editorialand@andorra.ad
Web Site: www.editorialandorra.com
Subjects: Art, Biography, Memoirs, Drama, Theater, History, Poetry
ISBN Prefix(es): 978-99920-53; 978-99913-33

Angola

General Information

Capital: Luanda
Language: Portuguese (official), several African languages also in common use
Religion: Christian (mainly Roman Catholic)
Population: 8.9 million
Currency: 100 iwei = 1 new kwanza
Export/Import Information: No tariff on books and advertising. Very restricted issuance of import licenses. Advertising matter is currently given considerably lower priority. Exchange controls.

Plural Editores
Rua Lucrecia Paim, 16-A, (ex-Marques de Minas), Bairro Maculusso, Luanda
Tel: 924 351990
E-mail: plural@pluraleditores.co.ao
Web Site: www.pluraleditores.co.ao
Publish educational & technical materials.
Subjects: Education
Parent Company: Grupo Porto Editora

Argentina

General Information

Capital: Buenos Aires
Language: Spanish
Religion: Roman Catholic
Population: 33 million
Bank Hours: 1000-1500 Monday-Friday
Shop Hours: 0900-1900 Monday-Saturday
Currency: 100 centavos = 1 nuevo peso argentino
Export/Import Information: No import licenses required. Import duties are assessed ad valorem. However, no import duties on books or similar material.
Copyright: UCC, Berne, Buenos Aires (see Copyright Conventions, pg viii)

A-Z Editora SA+
Paraguay 2351, C1121ABK Buenos Aires
Tel: (011) 4961-4036 *Fax:* (011) 4961-0089
E-mail: contacto@az.com.ar
Web Site: www.az.com.ar
Key Personnel
Dir: Dr Eugenio Miguel Arceo; Ramiro Villalba Garibaldi; Rodrigo Villalba Garibaldi
Founded: 1976
This publisher has indicated that 30% of its product line is author subsidized.
Membership(s): Camara Argentina de Publicaciones (CAP).
Subjects: Accounting, Aeronautics, Aviation, Agriculture, Alternative, Americana, Regional, Anthropology, Art, Behavioral Sciences, Biography, Memoirs, Biological Sciences, Career Development, Chemistry, Chemical Engineering, Child Care & Development, Communications, Computer Science, Crafts, Games, Hobbies, Developing Countries, Drama, Theater, Earth Sciences, Economics, Education, Environmental Studies, Ethnicity, Fiction, Finance, Foreign Countries, Geography, Geology, Government, Political Science, Health, Nutrition, History, How-to, Human Relations, Language Arts, Linguistics, Law, Literature, Literary Criticism, Essays, Mathematics, Mysteries, Suspense, Native American Studies, Natural History, Nonfiction (General), Outdoor Recreation, Philosophy, Physics, Poetry, Psychology, Psychiatry, Public Administration, Romance, Science (General), Science Fiction, Fantasy, Social Sciences, Sociology, Sports, Athletics, Technology
ISBN Prefix(es): 978-950-534
Number of titles published annually: 40 Print
Total Titles: 600 Print
Branch Office(s)
Sarmiento 871, X5004EYG Cordoba *Tel:* (0351) 421-8273 *E-mail:* cordoba@az.com.ar
Buenos Aires 222, T4000IJF Tucuman
Tel: (0381) 4215899 *E-mail:* tucuman@az.com.ar

Editorial Abaco de Rodolfo Depalma SRL
Viamonte 1336, 4° piso, C1053ACB Buenos Aires
Tel: (011) 4371-1675 *Fax:* (011) 4371-1675
E-mail: info@abacoeditorial.com.ar
Web Site: www.abacoeditorial.com.ar
Key Personnel
Editor: Hernan Biscayart
Founded: 1975
Subjects: Economics, History, Journalism, Law, Philosophy, Psychology, Psychiatry, Public Administration, Social Sciences, Sociology
ISBN Prefix(es): 978-950-569
Number of titles published annually: 20 Print
Total Titles: 250 Print

ABAP, see Asociacion Bautista Argentina de Publicaciones (ABAP)

Abeledo-Perrot SA+
Lavalle 1280, C1048AAF Buenos Aires
Tel: (011) 5235-5400; (011) 4883-0492; (011) 5236-8886 (orders); (011) 5236-8888 (customer service)
Key Personnel
Founder: Emilio Jose Perrot
Online Sales: Sergio Terziotti
Founded: 1956
Subjects: Criminology, Law, Philosophy, Public Administration
ISBN Prefix(es): 978-950-20
Total Titles: 17 CD-ROM
Parent Company: Legal Publishing Netherlands
Ultimate Parent Company: Palmfund LLC

Academia Argentina de Letras (Argentine Academy of Letters)
Subsidiary of Ministerio de Ciencia, Tecnologia e Innovacion Productiva
Sanchez de Bustamante 2663, Boedo, C1425DVA Buenos Aires
Tel: (011) 4802-3814; (011) 4802-7509 (ext 5) *Fax:* (011) 4802-7509
E-mail: administracion@aal.edu.ar; publicaciones@aal.edu.ar; biblioteca@aal.edu.ar; secretaria.general@aal.edu.ar
Web Site: www.aal.edu.ar
Key Personnel
President: Jose Luis Moure *Tel:* (011) 4802-3814 ext 6 *E-mail:* presidencia@aal.edu.ar
Vice President: Alicia Maria Zorrilla
Dir, Division of Communication & Publications: Mariano Leopoldo Tielens
Dir, Bookstore: Alejandro E Parada *E-mail:* a.parada@aal.edu.ar
Head, Administration: Estela Adamo
Founded: 1931
Specialize in literature, philology & linguistics. Has published literary essays (about works, authors, epochs & places), linguistic studies, dictionaries & lexical works, publication of works & poems of Argentine diverse authors, etc & the official & periodic (four-month) publication that is the Boletin de la Academia Argentina de Letras, that contains, generally, articles of literary analysis, honorings to Spanish or Latin writers & notes about the Academy activities & academicians activities, agreements about the language, record of the Argentine words, etc.
Membership(s): Asociacion de Academias de la Lengua Espanola (ASALE).
Subjects: Language Arts, Linguistics, Literature, Literary Criticism, Essays, Poetry
ISBN Prefix(es): 978-950-585
Number of titles published annually: 6 Print
Total Titles: 399 Print; 3 CD-ROM
Distribution Center: Libreria Garcia Cambeiro, Pasaje Gallegos 3570, C1240ACD Buenos Aires, Contact: Marcos Galeano *E-mail:* marcosgaleano@cambeiro.com.ar *Web Site:* www.latbook.com/sp/home.html

Aique Grupo Editor SRL
Francisco Acuna de Figueroa, 352, C1181AAF Buenos Aires
Tel: (011) 4867-7000
E-mail: centrodocente@aique.com.ar
Web Site: www.aique.com.ar
Founded: 1976
Subjects: Education, Literature, Literary Criticism, Essays
ISBN Prefix(es): 978-950-701; 978-950-9003; 978-987-06

Libreria Akadia Editorial+
Paraguay 2065, C1121ABE Buenos Aires
Tel: (011) 4962-4258 *Fax:* (011) 4962-4258
E-mail: ventas@editorialakadia.com; editorialakadia@gmail.com; akadia@arnet.com.ar
Web Site: www.editorialakadia.com.ar

Key Personnel
President: Jose F Patlallan
Dir: Daniel Patlallan
Founded: 1967
Specialize in medical books.
Subjects: Biological Sciences, Health, Nutrition, Library & Information Sciences, Medicine, Nursing, Dentistry, Psychology, Psychiatry, Science (General), Social Sciences, Sociology, Veterinary Science
ISBN Prefix(es): 978-950-9020; 978-987-570
Number of titles published annually: 30 Print
Total Titles: 150 Print
Branch Office(s)
Paraguay 2078, C1121ABF Buenos Aires
Tel: (011) 4961-8614 *Fax:* (011) 4964-2230

Editorial Albatros SACI+
Torre Las Plazas, J Salguero 2745-5° Off 51, C1425DEL Buenos Aires
Tel: (011) 4807-2030 *Fax:* (011) 4807-2010
E-mail: info@albatros.com.ar; ventas@albatros.com.ar; edicion@albatros.com.ar
Web Site: www.albatros.com.ar
Key Personnel
President: Andrea Ines Canevaro
Vice President: Gustavo Gabriel Canevaro
Founded: 1950
Subjects: Agriculture, Animals, Pets, Astrology, Occult, Economics, Electronics, Electrical Engineering, Environmental Studies, Gardening, Plants, Health, Nutrition, Medicine, Nursing, Dentistry, Social Sciences, Sociology, Sports, Athletics, Veterinary Science
ISBN Prefix(es): 978-950-24; 978-987-1195; 978-987-1088
Foreign Rep(s): Abastanza (Colombia); Aparicio Distribuidores (Puerto Rico); Libreria Armonia (Bolivia); Artemis Distribuciones (Guatemala); Libreria Ateneo (Bolivia); Baker & Taylor (USA); The Bilingual Publications Co (USA); Litexsa Boliviana (Bolivia); Books SRL (Paraguay); Brodart Co (USA); Libreria La Casita (El Salvador); Editorial La Ceiba (El Salvador); Centro Cuesta Nacional (Dominican Republic); Grupo Editorial Circulo (Puerto Rico); Disa Libros (Honduras); Distril (Uruguay); Edarsi Cia Ltda (Ecuador); Libreria Espanola (Ecuador); La Familia Distribuidora de Libros SA (Peru); Fausto Cultural (Paraguay); Fi-Rex 21 SL (Spain); Distribuidora Garden Book, CA (Venezuela); Hispamer (Nicaragua); Libreria Internacional (Costa Rica); El Lector (Paraguay); Lectorum Publications (USA); Distribuidora Lewis SA (Panama); Libri Mundi Libreria Internacional SA (Ecuador); Liser (Honduras); Mr Books (Ecuador); Libreria Navarro (Honduras); Grupo Corporativo New Horizons (Dominican Republic); Libreria Olimpia (Bolivia); Panamericana Libreria y Papeleria SA (Colombia); Quijote SRL (Paraguay); Sophos (Guatemala); Sur (Brazil); Tecni-Ciencia Libros (Venezuela); Ediciones Tecnicas Paraguayas SRL (Paraguay); Thesaurus (Dominican Republic); Tinta y Cafe (Ecuador); Libreria Vida Nueva (Ecuador); Ediciones y Distribuciones Zeus (Mexico); Empresa Editora ZIG-ZAG SA (Chile)

Alfagrama Ediciones SRL
Zapata 160, C1426AEB Buenos Aires
Tel: (011) 4772-0995
E-mail: info@alfagrama.com.ar
Web Site: alfagrama.com.ar
Key Personnel
Contact: Facundo Nunez *E-mail:* facundo@alfagrama.com.ar; Matias Nunez
Founded: 1991
Specialize in science, archivology & education books.

Subjects: Disability, Special Needs, Education, Environmental Studies, LGBTQ, Library & Information Sciences, Publishing & Book Trade Reference, Science (General), Social Sciences, Sociology, Technology, Women's Studies, Conservation, Museology
ISBN Prefix(es): 978-987-1305

Amorrortu Editores SA+
Paraguay 1225, 7° piso, C1057AAS Buenos Aires
Tel: (011) 4816-5812; (011) 4816-5869
Fax: (011) 4816-3321
E-mail: info@amorrortueditores.com
Web Site: www.amorrortueditores.com
Key Personnel
President: Horacio de Amorrortu
Founded: 1967
Publisher of academic, social science & humanities books.
Subjects: Anthropology, Economics, Education, Philosophy, Psychology, Psychiatry, Regional Interests, Religion - Other, Social Sciences, Sociology
ISBN Prefix(es): 978-950-518; 978-84-610
Branch Office(s)
Amorrortu Editores Espana SL, C/Lopez de Hoyos, 15-3ra Izda, 28006 Madrid, Spain
Tel: 91 187 75 68 *E-mail:* info_madrid@ amorrortueditores.com

Libros de la Araucaria SA
Chacabuco 1421, C1140AAE Buenos Aires
Tel: (011) 43058058 *Fax:* (011) 43058058
E-mail: info@librosaraucaria.com
Web Site: www.librosaraucaria.com
Key Personnel
President & Publisher: Hector E Dinsmann
E-mail: dinsmann@librosaraucaria.com
Founded: 2004
Subjects: Anthropology, Literature, Literary Criticism, Essays, Philosophy, Photography, Religion - Other, Social Sciences, Sociology
ISBN Prefix(es): 978-987-21406
Foreign Rep(s): Catalonia (Chile); Libreria Cientifica (Colombia); Distribuciones Cifuentes SA de CV (Mexico); Ediciones Continente (Argentina); Dedalo SRL (Argentina); Edarsi Ltda (Ecuador); Euroamericana de Ediciones (Venezuela); Libreria Norberto Gonzalez (Puerto Rico); Gussi Libros (Uruguay); El Hombre de la Mancha (Panama); Libreria y Distribuidora Lerner Ltda (Colombia); Editorial Nueva Decada SA (Costa Rica); La Odisea Ediciones SA de CV (El Salvador); Promolibro (Colombia); Servicios Libreros (Ecuador); Sophos (Guatemala); UDL Libros (Spain); Distribuidora de Libros El Virrey SAC (Peru)

Editorial Artemisa SA
Av Belgrano 687, piso 11°, C1092AAG Buenos Aires
Tel: (011) 4331-5823; (011) 4331-5839
E-mail: administracion@editorialartemisasa.com.ar
Web Site: www.editorialartemisasa.com.ar
Founded: 2010
ISBN Prefix(es): 978-987-674

Asociacion Bautista Argentina de Publicaciones (ABAP)+
Ave Benardino Rivadavia 3474, C1203AAT Buenos Aires
Tel: (011) 4863-8924 *Fax:* (011) 4863-6745
Founded: 1911
Subjects: Religion - Other
ISBN Prefix(es): 978-950-9074

Asociacion Educacionista Argentina, see Editorial Stella

Asociacion para la Promocion de los Estudios Territoriales y Ambientales, see Oikos

Editorial Astrea de Alfredo y Ricardo Depalma SRL+
Lavalle 1208, C1048AAF Buenos Aires
Tel: (011) 4382-1880 *Fax:* (011) 4382-1880
E-mail: info@astrea.com.ar; libreria@astrea.com.ar (bookshop)
Web Site: www.astrea.com.ar
Key Personnel
Mng Dir: Alfredo Depalma; Ricardo Depalma
Founded: 1968
Subjects: Economics, Government, Political Science, History, Law, Philosophy, Social Sciences, Sociology
ISBN Prefix(es): 978-950-508
Number of titles published annually: 65 Print
Total Titles: 1,000 Print

Editorial Atlantida SA+
Subsidiary of Editorial Televisa SA de CV
Azopardo 565, C1107ADG Buenos Aires
Tel: (011) 4346-0100 *Fax:* (011) 4331-3272
Web Site: www.atlantida.com.ar
Founded: 1918
Subjects: Cookery, Fiction, Nonfiction (General), Self-Help
ISBN Prefix(es): 978-950-08
Number of titles published annually: 150 Print

La Azotea Editorial Fotografica SRL
Paraguay 1480, C1061ABB Buenos Aires
Tel: (011) 4811 0931 *Fax:* (011) 4811 0931
E-mail: azotea@laazotea.com.ar
Web Site: www.laazotea.com.ar
Key Personnel
Dir: Sara Facio; Maria Cristina Orive
Founded: 1973
Subjects: Photography
ISBN Prefix(es): 978-950-9536
Distributed by Galerna SRL (Argentina)

Jorge Baudino Ediciones
Fray Cayetano Rodriguez 885, C1406AWM Buenos Aires
Tel: (011) 4632-0054
E-mail: info@baudinoediciones.com.ar
Web Site: www.baudinoediciones.com.ar
Key Personnel
Founder: Jorge Baudino; Maria Clotilde Frigo Comelian
Founded: 1991
Subjects: Economics, Education, History, Medicine, Nursing, Dentistry, Philosophy, Social Sciences, Sociology, Ecology
ISBN Prefix(es): 978-950-99748; 978-987-9020

Beas Ediciones SRL+
Inclan 3945, C1258ABG Buenos Aires
Tel: (011) 4923-4030; (011) 4924-5337
Fax: (011) 4924-0217
Founded: 1992
Subjects: Fiction, Humor, Nonfiction (General), Self-Help
ISBN Prefix(es): 978-950-834
Parent Company: Circulo del Buen Lector SRL

Beatriz Viterbo Editora+
Sargento Cabral 74, 2000 Rosario
Tel: (0341) 4256909 *Fax:* (0341) 4256909
E-mail: info@beatrizviterbo.com.ar
Web Site: www.beatrizviterbo.com.ar
Key Personnel
Dir: Adriana Astutti; Sandra Contreras
Founded: 1991
Subjects: Drama, Theater, Fiction, Literature, Literary Criticism, Essays, Nonfiction (General), Poetry
ISBN Prefix(es): 978-950-845

Foreign Rep(s): Latin American Book Source Inc (USA); Tarahumara Libros SL (Spain)
Distribution Center: Waldhuter Libros *Tel:* (011) 6091-4786; (011) 3221-5195 *Web Site:* www.waldhuter.com.ar
Latin American Book Source Inc, 681 Anita St, Suite 102, Chula Vista, CA 91911, United States *Fax:* 619-426-0212 *E-mail:* sales@latambooks.com *Web Site:* www.latambooks.com

Editorial Beeme
Av Warnes 596, C1414AAS Buenos Aires
Tel: (011) 4854-4200 *Fax:* (011) 4854-4200
Key Personnel
Editorial Dir: Jose Dahir
Sales & Dir, Production: Nicolas Arfeli
ISBN Prefix(es): 978-987-669; 978-987-24256; 978-987-1594

Editorial Biblos
Pasaje Jose Maria Giuffra 324, C1064ADD Buenos Aires
Tel: (011) 4361-0522 *Fax:* (011) 4361-0522
E-mail: info@editorialbiblos.com
Web Site: www.editorialbiblos.com
Key Personnel
Dir: Javier Riera
Editorial Dir: Veronica Riera *E-mail:* veronica@editorialbiblos.com
Sales & Distribution: Alicia Bureau
E-mail: ventas@editorialbiblos.com
Educational Sales: Silvia Licht *E-mail:* silvia@editorialbiblos.com
Founded: 1980
Subjects: Communications, Economics, Education, Government, Political Science, Social Sciences, Sociology, Culture, Humanities, Immigration
ISBN Prefix(es): 978-950-786; 978-950-9316
Foreign Rep(s): Axolotl Libros (Mexico); Editorial Byblos Ltda (Uruguay); Canoa Editorial (Spain); Catalonia Ltda (Chile); Catriel SL (Spain); Compania Caribena de Libros (Puerto Rico); Dedalo SRL (Argentina); Libreria Espanola/Libresa SA (Ecuador); El Hombre de la Mancha (Panama); Libreria Nueva Decada (Costa Rica); Promolibro (Colombia); Libreria La Sasita (El Salvador); Sophos SA (Guatemala); Thesaurus (Dominican Republic); Libreria del Virrey (Peru); Libreria Yachaywasi (Bolivia)

Bonum Editorial SACI+
Av Corrientes 6687, CP1427BPE Buenos Aires
Tel: (011) 4554-1414 / (011) 4554-1414
E-mail: edicion@editorialbonum.com.ar; ventas@editorialbonum.com.ar; autores@editorialbonum.com.ar
Web Site: www.editorialbonum.com.ar
Key Personnel
President: Martin Gremmelspacher
Vice President: Ursula Gremmelspacher
Rights & Permissions: Vanessa Della Casa
Founded: 1960
Membership(s): Camara Argentina del Libro.
Subjects: Drama, Theater, Education, Literature, Literary Criticism, Essays, Music, Dance, Nonfiction (General), Philosophy, Psychology, Psychiatry, Religion - Catholic, Religion - Other, Securities, Self-Help, Theology
ISBN Prefix(es): 978-950-507; 978-987-667
Bookshop(s): Maipu 869, 1006 Buenos Aires
Fax: (011) 4314-0888

Ediciones Botella al Mar
Luis Maria Agote 2280, 7° piso, 1425 Buenos Aires
Tel: (011) 4803-8246 *Fax:* (011) 4803-8246
E-mail: edicionesbotellaalmar@yahoo.com.ar
Subjects: Fiction, Poetry
ISBN Prefix(es): 978-950-513

Editorial Brujas
Pasaje Espana 1485, X5000ISC Cordoba
Tel: (0351) 460-6044 *Fax:* (0351) 469-1616
E-mail: publicaciones@editorialbrujas.com.ar
Web Site: www.editorialbrujas.com.ar
Key Personnel
Chief Executive Officer: German Marcelo Ferrero
Founded: 1999
Membership(s): Camara Argentina del Libro.
Subjects: Architecture & Interior Design, Art, Communications, Education, Geography, Geology, Health, Nutrition, History, Inspirational, Spirituality, Law, Literature, Literary Criticism, Essays, Management, Philosophy, Social Sciences, Sociology
ISBN Prefix(es): 978-987-591; 978-987-1142; 978-987-9452; 978-987-97763

Osmar D Buyatti Libreria Editorial
Viamonte 1509, C1055ABC Buenos Aires
Tel: (011) 4371-2512; (011) 4812-5492; (011) 4811-6173 *Fax:* (011) 4371-2512; (011) 4812-5492; (011) 4811-6173
E-mail: info@osmarbuyatti.com; ventas@osmarbuyatti.com
Web Site: www.osmarbuyatti.com
Key Personnel
Dir General: Osmar Buyatti
Subjects: Accounting, Economics, Marketing, Public Administration, Science (General), Social Sciences, Sociology, Commerce
ISBN Prefix(es): 978-950-99861; 978-987-1140; 978-987-9156
Foreign Rep(s): AB Representaciones Gerenciales SRL (Peru); Libreria Alvaro Nora CA (Venezuela); American Book Store (Guatemala); Juridica Cevallos (Ecuador); El Foro SA (Paraguay); Fundacion De Cultura Universitaria (Uruguay); Distribuidora Garden Book CA (Venezuela); Distribuciones Intermilenio Ltda (Colombia); Libreria y Editorial Juricentro SA (Costa Rica); Libreria San Cristobal SAC (Peru); Libun (Peru); Libros Tecnicos Profesionales Limerin (Ecuador); Lyber E-Books (Honduras); Master Bolivia Libros (Bolivia); Libreria Especializada Olejnik (Chile); Panamericana Libreria y Papeleria SA (Colombia); Ediciones Tecnicas Paraguayas (Paraguay); Libreria San Cristobal SAC (Peru); Ediciones de la "U" (Colombia)

Calibroscopio Ediciones
Aguirre 458, C1414ASJ Buenos Aires
Tel: (011) 4855-8657 *Fax:* (011) 4855-8657
E-mail: editorial@calibroscopio.com.ar
Web Site: www.calibroscopio.com.ar
Key Personnel
Dir General: Walter Binder
Editorial Dir: Judith Wilheim
Founded: 2005
ISBN Prefix(es): 978-987-22204
Foreign Rep(s): Babel Libros (Colombia); Cuatro Azules (Spain); Ediciones Ekare (Venezuela); Barbara Fiore Editora (Spain); Kokinos (Spain); Editorial Loquez (Spain); Tandem Edicions (Spain)

Ediciones Abran Cancha
Gorriti 3909, C1172ACK Buenos Aires
Tel: (011) 4864-0267 *Fax:* (011) 4864-0267
E-mail: info@abrancancha.com; tuopinioncuenta@abrancancha.com (sales)
Web Site: www.abrancancha.com
Key Personnel
Dir General: Adela Basch
Editor: Luciana Murzi *E-mail:* lucianamurzi@abrancancha.com
Founded: 2002
Subjects: Fiction, Literature, Literary Criticism, Essays
ISBN Prefix(es): 978-987-20309; 978-987-23451; 978-987-25708

Editorial Capital Intelectual SA
Paraguay 1535, C1061ABC Buenos Aires
Tel: (011) 4872-1300 *Fax:* (011) 4872-1300
E-mail: info@capin.com.ar; pedidos@capin.com.ar; exterior@capin.com.ar
Web Site: www.editorialcapin.com.ar
Key Personnel
Editorial Dir: Jorge Sigal
General Editor: Daniel Gonzalez
Press & Marketing: Nicolas Abreu
Sales Manager: Jorge Eduardo Vanzulli
Sales: Esteban Zabaljauregui
Subjects: Biography, Memoirs, Geography, Geology, History, Literature, Literary Criticism, Essays, Science (General), Social Sciences, Sociology
ISBN Prefix(es): 978-950-99670; 978-987-1181; 978-987-98731

Catapulta Editores
Av Donado 4694, C14300TP Buenos Aires
Tel: (011) 4547 2780 *Fax:* (011) 4544 1276
E-mail: info@catapulta.net
Web Site: www.catapulta.net
Key Personnel
Vice President: Rodolfo Reyna
Founded: 2001
Co-edition partner of the Quarto Group in London.
Subjects: Art, Cookery, Crafts, Games, Hobbies, Fiction, Gardening, Plants, Nonfiction (General)
ISBN Prefix(es): 978-987-637
Imprints: Catapulta Junior
Branch Office(s)
Rua Jose Felix de Oliveira, 834, Sala 7C, 06708-645 Cotia-SP, Brazil *Tel:* (011) 4612 6116 *E-mail:* faleconosco@catapulta.net
Distribution Center: Penguin Random House, Merced 280, Piso 6, 8320000 Santiago, Chile *Tel:* (02) 2782 82 00 *E-mail:* editorial@rhm.cl
UDL Libros, Av del Acero 4, PI Miralcampo, 19200 Azuqueca de Henares, Guadalajara, Spain *Tel:* 949 267 648 (Madrid); 932 262 764 (Barcelona) *E-mail:* info@udllibros.com *Web Site:* www.udllibros.com

Catapulta Junior, *imprint of* Catapulta Editores

Editorial Caymi SACI
15 de Noviembre de 1889 N° 1149, C1130ABA Buenos Aires
Tel: (011) 4304-2474 *Fax:* (011) 4304-2474
Founded: 1945
Subjects: Animals, Pets, Astrology, Occult, Automotive, Cookery, Gardening, Plants, Medicine, Nursing, Dentistry, Science Fiction, Fantasy, Self-Help, Sports, Athletics, Chess, Esoterism
ISBN Prefix(es): 978-950-501

Cesarini Hermanos+
Sarmiento 3213 1° A°, C1196AAI Buenos Aires
Tel: (011) 4861-1152 *Fax:* (011) 4863-8753
Founded: 1931
Membership(s): Camara Argentina del Libro.
Subjects: Environmental Studies, Music, Dance, Nonfiction (General), Technology
ISBN Prefix(es): 978-950-526

Editorial Cesarini Hnos, see Cesarini Hermanos

CICCUS, see Ediciones Ciccus

Ediciones Ciccus
Medrano 288, C1179AAB Buenos Aires
Tel: (011) 4981 6318; (011) 4958 0991 *Fax:* (011) 4981 6318; (011) 4958 0991
E-mail: ciccus@ciccus.org.ar
Web Site: www.ciccus.org.ar
Key Personnel
President & Editorial Dir: Juan Carlos Manoukian

Administration: Eliana Fiorito
Press & Communications: Jose Ignacio Sanchez Duran
Sales: Ariel Schafran
Subjects: Anthropology, Art, Economics, Education, Health, Nutrition, History, Literature, Literary Criticism, Essays, Social Sciences, Sociology, Travel & Tourism, Ecology
ISBN Prefix(es): 978-987-9355; 978-987-95631

Editorial Ciudad Argentina
Av Cordoba 1255, C1055AAC Buenos Aires
Tel: (011) 4811 4250; (011) 4813 0390
E-mail: editorial@ciudadargentina.com.ar
Web Site: www.ciudadargentina.com.ar
Subjects: Economics, Environmental Studies, History, Law, Literature, Literary Criticism, Essays, Philosophy, Social Sciences, Sociology, Integration, Public Policy, Public Services, Urbanism
ISBN Prefix(es): 978-84-923011; 978-84-95823; 978-950-9385; 978-987-507; 978-84-16083
Branch Office(s)
Velazquez, 75 2° Izq, 28006 Madrid, Spain *Tel:* 91 577 0195 *Fax:* 91 575 6639

Editorial Ciudad Nueva+
Lezica 4358, C1202AAJ Buenos Aires
Tel: (011) 4981-4885 *Fax:* (011) 4981-4885
E-mail: libros@ciudadnueva.org.ar; ventas@ciudadnueva.org.ar (sales); info@ciudadnueva.org.ar
Web Site: www.ciudadnueva.org.ar
Key Personnel
Editor: Damian L Garcia
Sales: Sergio Tripodi
Founded: 1964
Subjects: Biography, Memoirs, Education, Religion - Catholic, Securities, Theology
ISBN Prefix(es): 978-950-586
Parent Company: Grupo Editorial Ciudad Nueva

CLACSO, see Consejo Latinoamericano de Ciencias Sociales (CLACSO)

Editorial Claretiana+
Lima 1360, C1138ACD Buenos Aires
Tel: (011) 4305-9597; (011) 4305-9510 *Fax:* (011) 4305-6552
E-mail: editorial@editorialclaretiana.com.ar; ventas@editorialclaretiana.com.ar; contacto@editorialclaretiana.com.ar
Web Site: www.editorialclaretiana.com.ar
Founded: 1956
Subjects: Religion - Catholic, Theology
ISBN Prefix(es): 978-950-512

Editorial Claridad SA+
Subsidiary of Editorial Heliasta SRL
Juncal 3451, C1425AYT Buenos Aires
Tel: (011) 4804-0472; (011) 4804-8757; (011) 4804-0119 *Fax:* (011) 4804-0472; (011) 4804-8757; (011) 4804-0119
E-mail: editorial@heliasta.com.ar; web@heliasta.com.ar
Web Site: www.editorialclaridad.com.ar
Key Personnel
President: Dr Ana Maria Cabanellas
Bookstore Sales: Carlos Domingo *E-mail:* cdomingo@heliasta.com.ar
Press & Promotions: Monica Dombrover
Founded: 1922
Subjects: Biography, Memoirs, Economics, Government, Political Science, History, Literature, Literary Criticism, Essays, Philosophy, Poetry, Classic Literature
ISBN Prefix(es): 978-950-620

Club de Lectores+
Suipacha 211, 24 F, C1008AAE Buenos Aires

Tel: (011) 4327-2253
E-mail: tpignataro1@hotmail.com
Web Site: www.clubdelectores.com.ar
Founded: 1938
Subjects: History, Philosophy, Psychology, Psychiatry, Religion - Other, Social Sciences, Sociology, Theology
ISBN Prefix(es): 978-950-9034
Bookshop(s): Av de Mayo 624, C1084AAO Buenos Aires *Tel:* (011) 4342-6251

Coleccion Juridica Bco de Datos en Computacion, *imprint of* Editorial Zeus SRL

Ediciones Colihue SRL
Av Diaz Velez 5125, C1405DCG Buenos Aires
Tel: (011) 4958-4442 *Fax:* (011) 4958-5673
E-mail: ecolihue@colihue.com.ar
Web Site: www.colihue.com.ar
Founded: 1981
Subjects: Art, Drama, Theater, Economics, Fiction, Government, Political Science, Language Arts, Linguistics, Law, Literature, Literary Criticism, Essays, Nonfiction (General), Philosophy, Physical Sciences, Poetry, Science (General), Social Sciences, Sociology, Narrative, Natural Science
ISBN Prefix(es): 978-950-581; 978-950-563

Colision Libros
Junin 1616 6°, C1113AAR Buenos Aires
Tel: (011) 4807 8611
E-mail: colisionlibros@gmail.com
Web Site: www.lacolision.com.ar
Key Personnel
Mng Dir: Cristina Witt *E-mail:* cristinawitt@lacolision.com.ar
Subjects: Literature, Literary Criticism, Essays, Poetry, Romance, Crime, Narrative, Prose
ISBN Prefix(es): 978-987-25151; 978-987-24358; 978-987-22198; 978-987-1804

Editorial Comunicarte
Ituzaingo 882, Planta Alta, X5000IJR Cordoba
Tel: (0351) 468 43 42 *Fax:* (0351) 468 34 60
E-mail: editorial@comunicarteweb.com.ar
Web Site: www.comunicarteweb.com.ar
Founded: 1993
Subjects: Communications, Education, Fiction, Language Arts, Linguistics, Literature, Literary Criticism, Essays, Didactics, Pedagogy, Theory
ISBN Prefix(es): 978-987-602; 978-987-1151; 978-987-96384; 978-987-9280

Consejo Latinoamericano de Ciencias Sociales (CLACSO)
Av Callao 875, 4° G, C1023AAB Buenos Aires
Tel: (011) 4811-2301; (011) 4811-6588
Fax: (011) 4812-8459
E-mail: biblioteca@clacso.edu.ar; clacso@clacso.edu.ar; clacsoinst@clacso.edu.ar
Web Site: www.clacso.org.ar; www.clacso.edu.ar
Key Personnel
Coordinator: Emir Sader
Founded: 1971
Subjects: Social Sciences, Sociology
ISBN Prefix(es): 978-950-9231; 978-987-1183
Distribution Center: Prometeo, Pringles 519/521, 1047 Buenos Aires *Tel:* (011) 4864-3297 *Web Site:* www.prometeolibros.com.ar
HomoSapiens Ediciones, Sarmiento 825, S200CMM Rosario, Santa Fe *Tel:* (0341) 424-3399; (0341) 425-3852 *Web Site:* www.homosapiens.com.ar

Ediciones Continente
Pavon 2229, C1248AAE Buenos Aires
Tel: (011) 4308-3535 *Fax:* (011) 4308-4800
E-mail: info@edicontinente.com.ar
Web Site: www.edicontinente.com.ar

Key Personnel
Dir General: Jorge Gurbanov
Editorial Dir: Andres Gurbanov
Subjects: Art, Biography, Memoirs, Fiction, Geography, Geology, Government, Political Science, History, Literature, Literary Criticism, Essays, Social Sciences, Sociology
ISBN Prefix(es): 978-950-754; 978-950-99666
Distributed by Brosquil Edicions; Combel Editorial; Editorial Corimbo; Editorial De Vecchi; Editorial Juventud; Editorial Kairos; Jose J de Olaneta Editor; Libros del Zorro Rojo
Foreign Rep(s): Editorial Dilema (Spain); Empresa Editora Zig Zag (Chile); Gussi Libros (Uruguay); Ibero Librerias (Peru); Jupiter Editores (Venezuela); Panamericana Editorial (Colombia); Editorial Pax (Mexico)

Cooperativa de Trabajo Cultura y Educativa Cefomar Ltda+
Chile 1432, 1098 Buenos Aires
Tel: (011) 4382-0312
E-mail: soporte@cefomar.com.ar
Web Site: cefomar.com.ar
Founded: 1960
Subjects: Government, Political Science, Mathematics, Self-Help, Patagonia
ISBN Prefix(es): 978-950-503

Corpus Libros
Suipacha 581, S2000LRK Rosario
Tel: (0341) 439-4978 *Fax:* (0341) 437-1327
E-mail: rosario@corpuslibros.com.ar
Web Site: www.corpuslibros.com.ar
Key Personnel
General Manager: Esteban Oscar Mestre *E-mail:* emestre@corpuslibros.com
Head of Administration & Sales: Gabriela Ines Nerbutti *E-mail:* gnerbutti@corpuslibros.com
Foreign Trade: Julia Mestre *E-mail:* jmestre@corpuslibros.com
Subjects: Education, Health, Nutrition, History, Law, Literature, Literary Criticism, Essays, Medicine, Nursing, Dentistry, Psychology, Psychiatry, Social Sciences, Sociology, Veterinary Science
ISBN Prefix(es): 978-950-9030; 978-950-99001; 978-987-20292
Branch Office(s)
Tucuman 2120, C1050AAR Buenos Aires
Tel: (011) 4373-5128 *Fax:* (011) 4373-5128
E-mail: capital@corpuslibros.com.ar

Ediciones Corregidor+
Rodriguez Pena 452, C1020ADJ Buenos Aires
Tel: (011) 4374-5000; (011) 4374-4959
Fax: (011) 4374-5000; (011) 4374-4959
E-mail: corregidor@corregidor.com; info@corregidor.com
Web Site: www.corregidor.com
Key Personnel
Dir: Manuel Pampin *E-mail:* manuel.pampin@corregidor.com
Sales Manager: Juan M Pampin *E-mail:* jmp@corregidor.com
Foreign Rights: Maria Fernanda Pampin *E-mail:* mfp@corregidor.com
Founded: 1970
Membership(s): Alianza de Editores Independientes de la Argentina por la Bibliodiversidad.
Subjects: Drama, Theater, Economics, Literature, Literary Criticism, Essays, Music, Dance, Poetry, Cinema
ISBN Prefix(es): 978-950-05
Number of titles published annually: 50 Print
Total Titles: 3,000 Print
Foreign Rep(s): Libreria El Ateneo (Bolivia); Distribuidora Bibliografica (Colombia); The Bilingual Publications Co (USA); Brodart Co Books & Automation (USA); Libreria Calle Corrientes (Brazil); Editorial Canoa (Spain); Libreria La Casita (El Salvador); Catalonia (Chile); Catriel

SL (Spain); Libreria El Condor (Switzerland); Libreria Espagnole (France); Librerias Gandhi (Mexico); Gussi Libros (Uruguay); L'Harmattan, Librairie Centre (France); Libreria Hispanoamericana (France); Ibero A&G (Peru); Ideal Foreign Books Inc (USA); Libreria Internacional (Costa Rica); Howard Karno Books Inc (USA); Lectorum SA de CV (Mexico); Lectorum Publications Inc (USA); Letraviva (Brazil); Distribuidora Lewis (Panama); Libreria Libromania (Switzerland); Litexsa Boliviana SRL (Bolivia); Libri Mundi (Ecuador); Pan American Books (USA); Libreria Quijote (Paraguay); SBS Special Book Service (Peru); Sur Distribuidora De Livros, Jomais e Revistas Ltda (Brazil); La Tertulia Inc (Puerto Rico); Klaus Dieter Vervuert (Germany)

Cosmopolita SRL
Piedras 744, C1070AAP Buenos Aires
Tel: (011) 4361-8049
Founded: 1942
Subjects: Automotive, Auto Mechanics
ISBN Prefix(es): 978-950-9069

Studia Croatica
Matienzo 2532, 1426 Buenos Aires
Tel: (011) 4771-4954 *Fax:* (011) 4771-4954
E-mail: studiacroatica@gmail.com
Web Site: www.studiacroatica.org
Key Personnel
Dir: Joza Vrljicak *E-mail:* joza.vrljicak@gmail.com
Founded: 1960
Subjects: History, Croatia, Croatian History
ISBN Prefix(es): 978-987-95467

Editorial Croquis
Viamonte 947 1°A, 1053 Buenos Aires
Tel: (011) 4393 1194
E-mail: info@editorialcroquis.com
Web Site: www.editorialcroquis.com
Key Personnel
Mng Dir: Martin Enrique Gil
Subjects: Art, Drama, Theater, Education, Fiction, Literature, Literary Criticism, Essays, Psychology, Psychiatry, Religion - Other, Sports, Athletics, Digital Art
ISBN Prefix(es): 978-987-96450

La Crujia Ediciones
Tucuman 1999, C1050AAM Buenos Aires
Tel: (011) 4375 0376; (011) 4375 0664
Founded: 1999
Subjects: Communications, Education, Culture
ISBN Prefix(es): 978-987-601

Cute Ediciones
Aguero 148, 4 B, C1425EHG Bueno Aires
Tel: (011) 4824 5694
E-mail: info@cuteediciones.com.ar
Web Site: www.cuteediciones.com.ar
Founded: 2009
Subjects: Cookery
ISBN Prefix(es): 978-987-27297; 978-987-25829

de Dios Editores+
Tacuari 131 1° piso, B, C1071AAC Buenos Aires
Tel: (011) 4334-0235 *Fax:* (011) 4342-0029
E-mail: info@dediosonline.com
Web Site: www.dediosonline.com
Key Personnel
Publishing Dir: Horacio de Dios; Julian de Dios *E-mail:* julian@dediosonline.com
Commercial Dir: Carla D'Elia *E-mail:* cdelia@dediosonline.com
Founded: 1993
Specialize in travel guides & guide maps for major South American travel destinations.
Membership(s): Camara Argentina del Libro (CAL).

Subjects: Outdoor Recreation, Travel & Tourism
ISBN Prefix(es): 978-987-9445; 978-987-96719
Number of titles published annually: 50 Print
Total Titles: 98 Print
Foreign Rep(s): Map Iberia (Spain); Sur Livro (Brazil)

Ediciones de la Flor SRL+
Gorriti 3695, C1172ACE Buenos Aires
Tel: (011) 4963-7950 *Fax:* (011) 4963-5616
E-mail: delaflor@edicionesdelaflor.com.ar; edic-flor@datamarkets.com.ar
Web Site: www.edicionesdelaflor.com.ar
Key Personnel
Dir: Daniel Divinsky; Ana Maria T Miler
Founded: 1966
Membership(s): Camara Argentina del Libro.
Subjects: Biography, Memoirs, Drama, Theater, Fiction, History, Humor, Literature, Literary Criticism, Essays, Philosophy, Psychology, Psychiatry, Social Sciences, Sociology
ISBN Prefix(es): 978-950-515
Number of titles published annually: 30 Print
Total Titles: 700 Print
Foreign Rep(s): Libreria Artemis (Guatemala); Libreria Ateneo (Bolivia); Baker & Taylor (USA); The Bilingual Publications Co (USA); Books on Wings (USA); Libreria La Casita (El Salvador); Catalonia (Chile); La Ceiba (El Salvador); Compania Caribena de Libros (Puerto Rico); Cuesto Nacional (Puerto Rico); Editorial Cultural Inc (Puerto Rico); D H Libros CA (Venezuela); Librairie Espagnole (France); La Familia Distribuidora (Peru); Fi-Rex 21 SL (Spain); Livraria Martins Fontes Ltda (Brazil); Librerias Gandhi (Mexico); Grant & Cutler at Foyles (UK); Gussi Libros (Uruguay); Libreria Hispanoamericana (France); El Hombre de la Mancha (Panama); Mariuccia Iaconi Book Imports (USA); Ibero A&G (Peru); Ideal Foreign Books Inc (USA); Libreria Internacional (Costa Rica); Latin American Book Source Inc (USA); Lectorum Publications Inc (USA); Lectorum SA de CV (Mexico); Distribuidora Lewis (Ecuador); Mr Books (Ecuador); Libri Mundi (Ecuador); Libros 1000 (Bolivia); Plaza & James (Colombia); Libreria Quijote (Paraguay); El Regalo Universal CA (Venezuela); Schoenhof's Foreign Books (USA); Sophos (Guatemala); Sur Distribuidora De Livros, Jornaise e Revistas Ltda (Brazil); Tecni-Ciencia-Libros (Venezuela); La Tertulia Inc (Puerto Rico); Thesaurus (Dominican Republic); V&D Distribuidores SA (Peru); Klaus Dieter Vervuert (Germany); Libreria El Virrey (Peru)

Del Nuevo Extremo Grupo Editorial
Angel J Carranza 1852, C1414COV Buenos Aires
Tel: (011) 4773 3228
E-mail: info@dnxlibros.com
Web Site: www.delnuevoextremo.com
Subjects: Cookery, Fiction, Health, Nutrition, Literature, Literary Criticism, Essays, Photography, Self-Help
ISBN Prefix(es): 978-950-9681; 978-987-1068; 978-987-1427; 978-987-609
Distribution Center: IPG Spanish Books, 814 N Franklin St, Chicago, IL 60610, United States

Editorial Depalma SRL+
Talcahuano 494, C1013AAJ Buenos Aires
Tel: (011) 4371-7306 *Fax:* (011) 4371-6913
Founded: 1944
Subjects: Business, History, Law, Social Sciences, Sociology
ISBN Prefix(es): 978-950-14
Distributor for Iberiamerican Juridical Books
Showroom(s): Lavalle 1302, Buenos Aires

Editorial Diana Argentina SA
Jorge Beauchef 559, C1424BDK Buenos Aires

Tel: (011) 4922-5035 *Fax:* (011) 4922-5036
Subjects: Accounting, Animals, Pets, Art, Biography, Memoirs, Business, Communications, Computer Science, Economics, Education, Engineering (General), History, Journalism, Language Arts, Linguistics, Literature, Literary Criticism, Essays, Marketing, Medicine, Nursing, Dentistry, Music, Dance, Philosophy, Photography, Religion - Other, Self-Help, Sports, Athletics, Travel & Tourism
ISBN Prefix(es): 978-987-96980

Editorial Ruy Diaz SA+
Elpidio Gonzalez 5562, C1407GBT Buenos Aires
Tel: (011) 4567-4918; (011) 4567-2865
    Fax: (011) 4567-4918
E-mail: editorial@ruydiaz.com.ar
Web Site: www.ruydiaz.com.ar
Key Personnel
Founder: Rafael Zuccotti
Founded: 1963
Subjects: Cookery, Education, Law
ISBN Prefix(es): 978-950-9023; 978-987-516

Editorial Dunken
Ayacucho 357, C1025AAG Buenos Aires
Tel: (011) 4954 7700
E-mail: info@dunken.com.ar
Web Site: www.dunken.com.ar
Key Personnel
Dir: Guillermo A de Urquiza
Founded: 1988
ISBN Prefix(es): 978-987-518; 978-987-9123; 978-987-95041; 978-987-95089; 978-987-02

Ediciones del Eclipse+
Julian Alvarez 843, C1414DRQ Buenos Aires
Tel: (011) 4771-3583 *Fax:* (011) 4771-3583
E-mail: edicionesdeleclipse@gmail.com
Web Site: www.deleclipse.com
Founded: 1989
Subjects: Literature, Literary Criticism, Essays, Mathematics, Poetry, Psychology, Psychiatry, Travel & Tourism
ISBN Prefix(es): 978-987-9011; 978-950-99530

Edebe SA+
Don Bosco 4069, C1206ABM Buenos Aires
Tel: (011) 4883-0111; (011) 4883-0112
    Fax: (011) 4883-0115
Web Site: edebe.com.ar
Key Personnel
President: P Roque Sella
Editorial Dir: Juan L Rodriguez
Founded: 1993
Membership(s): Camara Argentina del Libro.
Subjects: Accounting, Drama, Theater, Education, History, Journalism, Radio, TV, Religion - Catholic
ISBN Prefix(es): 978-950-514
Parent Company: Grupo Edebe, Barcelona, Spain
Distributed by Centro Salesiano de Estudios
Distributor for Edebe

Edicial SA+
Ave Rivadavia 739, C1002AAF Buenos Aires
Tel: (011) 4342-8481 *Fax:* (011) 4343-1151
Founded: 1931
Subjects: Communications, Government, Political Science, History, Language Arts, Linguistics, Literature, Literary Criticism, Essays, Philosophy, Regional Interests
ISBN Prefix(es): 978-950-506
Showroom(s): Palacio del Libro International, Suipacha 1136, 1008 Buenos Aires

Editorial Universitaria de Buenos Aires, see EUDEBA (Editorial Universitaria de Buenos Aires)

EDIUM, see Editorial Idearium de la Universidad de Mendoza (EDIUM)

Editorial Educa, see Fundacion Universidad Catolica Argentina

EDUNLa, see Editorial de la Universidad Nacional de Lanus (EDUNLa)

EDUNTREF, see Editorial de la Universidad de Tres de Febrero (EDUNTREF)

Eduvim
Chile 251, X5900JKE Villa Maria
Tel: (0353) 453-9145
E-mail: eduvimprensa@gmail.com; foreign.rights. eduvim@gmail.com
Web Site: www.eduvim.com.ar
Key Personnel
Publisher: Carlos Gazzera *E-mail:* cgazzera@ gmail.com
Editorial Coordinator: Emanuel Molina
    E-mail: emanuel.molina@gmail.com
Foreign Rights: Luis Seia
Founded: 2008
ISBN Prefix(es): 978-987-699

Errepar SA+
Parana 725, C1017AAO Buenos Aires
Tel: (011) 4370-2002
E-mail: clientes@errepar.com
Web Site: www.errepar.com
Key Personnel
Dir: Dr Francisco Canada
Subjects: Astrology, Occult, Cookery, Economics, Education, Religion - Catholic, Religion - Hindu, Religion - Other, Self-Help
ISBN Prefix(es): 978-950-739; 978-950-9524; 978-987-01; 978-987-9088

Espacio Editorial
Simon Bolivar 547, 3° piso Off 1, C1066AAK Buenos Aires
Tel: (011) 4331-1945 *Fax:* (011) 4331-1945
E-mail: espacioedit@ciudad.com.ar
Web Site: www.espacioeditorial.com.ar
Key Personnel
Dir General: Osvaldo Dubini
Founded: 1977
Membership(s): Camara Argentina del Libro.
Subjects: Education, Social Sciences, Sociology, Ecology
ISBN Prefix(es): 978-950-802

Angel Estrada y Cia SA
Maipu 116, 8° piso, C1084ABD Buenos Aires
Tel: (011) 4344-5500 *Fax:* (011) 4344-5555
E-mail: info@estrada.com.ar
Web Site: www.angelestrada.com.ar; www.estrada. com.ar
Key Personnel
Dir: Tomas de Estrada
General Manager: Fernando Bidegain
Founded: 1869
Subjects: Education, How-to
ISBN Prefix(es): 978-950-01
Branch Office(s)
Ruta Nac 38, km 1,555, F5302EIA La Rioja *Tel:* (03822) 42 8215; (03822) 42 8217 *Fax:* (03822) 42 8087
Distribution Center: Ruta 205 km 42,180, B1812GXA Buenos Aires *Tel:* (011) 4234 9370 *Fax:* (011) 4234 9374

Eterna Cadencia Editora
Honduras 5574, C1414BND Buenos Aires
Tel: (011) 4774-4100
E-mail: info@eternacadencia.com.ar
Web Site: www.eternacadencia.com
Key Personnel
Dir General: Pablo Braun
Editorial Dir: Leonora Djament

Press: Claudia Ramon
Founded: 2008
Subjects: Literature, Literary Criticism, Essays, Chronicles, Narrative
ISBN Prefix(es): 978-987-1673
Distribution Center: Distribuidora Waldhuter, Pavon 2636, C1248AAV Buenos Aires *Tel:* (011) 6091-4786 *E-mail:* jwalibros@ciudad.com.ar *Web Site:* www.waldhuter.com.ar

EUDEBA (Editorial Universitaria de Buenos Aires)+
Av Rivadavia 1571, C1033AAF Buenos Aires
Tel: (011) 4383-8025 *Fax:* (011) 4383-2202
E-mail: pedidos@eudeba.com.ar
Web Site: www.eudeba.com.ar
Key Personnel
President: Gonzalo Alvarez
Vice President: Santos Lopez Uriburu
General Manager: Luis Quevedo
Sales Manager: Marcelo Poretti
Founded: 1958
Subjects: Accounting, Archaeology, Architecture & Interior Design, Art, Astrology, Occult, Chemistry, Chemical Engineering, Drama, Theater, Economics, Education, Geography, Geology, Health, Nutrition, History, Law, Literature, Literary Criticism, Essays, Mathematics, Medicine, Nursing, Dentistry, Music, Dance, Philosophy, Physics, Psychology, Psychiatry, Science (General), Theology, Veterinary Science
ISBN Prefix(es): 978-950-23
Number of titles published annually: 150 Print; 5 CD-ROM

Fundacion Editorial de Belgrano
Zabala 1837, C1426DQG Buenos Aires
Tel: (011) 4788-5400 *Fax:* (011) 4775-8788
Subjects: Architecture & Interior Design, Economics, Government, Political Science, Law, Literature, Literary Criticism, Essays, Psychology, Psychiatry, Radio, TV, Social Sciences, Sociology
ISBN Prefix(es): 978-950-577

Fundacion Universidad Catolica Argentina
Av Alicia M de Justo 1400-PB Contrafrente, Edif Santo Tomas Moro, C1107AFD Buenos Aires
Tel: (011) 4349 0200 (ext 1177)
E-mail: educa@uca.edu.ar
Web Site: www.uca.edu.ar; www.editorialeduca.com.ar
Key Personnel
Dir General: Ezequiel Obiglio Pena
Sales: Maria Guillermina Celeri
    E-mail: guillermina_celeri@uca.edu.ar
Membership(s): Camara Argentino del Libro.
Subjects: Art, Geography, Geology, History, Philosophy, Religion - Other, Science (General), Social Sciences, Sociology
ISBN Prefix(es): 978-987-1190; 978-987-21544; 978-950-523; 978-987-620

Galerna SRL+
Lambare 893, C1185ABA Buenos Aires
Tel: (011) 4867-1661 *Fax:* (011) 4862-5031
E-mail: contacto@galerna.net; info@galerna.net
Web Site: shop.galerna.net
Key Personnel
President: Matias Sanabria
Vice President: Daniel Jorge Razzetto
Executive Dir: Hugo Benjamin Levin
    E-mail: hl1@galerna.net
Press & Public Relations: Salvador Biedma
    E-mail: salvador@galerna.net
Founded: 1967
Membership(s): Camara Argentina del Libro.
Subjects: Drama, Theater, History, Humor, Literature, Literary Criticism, Essays, Poetry, Social Sciences, Sociology, Theology
ISBN Prefix(es): 978-950-556

Subsidiaries: Librogal SRL
Branch Office(s)
Av Cabildo 1852, Buenos Aires *Tel:* (011) 4788-6201 *E-mail:* cabildo@galerna.net
Uruguay 1049, Buenos Aires *Tel:* (011) 4813-5513 *E-mail:* uruguay@galerna.net
Hipolito Yrigoyen 1719, Mar del Plata *Tel:* (023) 493-1545 *E-mail:* mardelplata@galerna.net
La Anonima Paseo de Compras, Antartida Argentina 1111 - Local 2A, Neuquen *Tel:* (0299) 443-7249 *E-mail:* neuquen@galerna.net

Editorial Gradifco
Viamonte 2632, B1678DWB Caseros, Buenos Aires
Tel: (011) 4750-5688; (011) 4759-0286
    Fax: (011) 4759-0286
E-mail: info@gradifco.com.ar
Web Site: www.gradifco.com.ar
Key Personnel
Account Executive: Sergio A Paolini
Founded: 1999
Also a distributor.
Subjects: Biography, Memoirs, Fiction, Literature, Literary Criticism, Essays, Science Fiction, Fantasy
ISBN Prefix(es): 978-987-1093; 978-987-571
Associate Companies: Gradifco SRL

Gram Editora
Cochabamba 1652, C1148ABF Buenos Aires
Tel: (011) 4304-4833; (011) 4305-8397
    Fax: (011) 4304-5692
E-mail: grameditora@infovia.com.ar
Web Site: www.grameditora.com.ar
Key Personnel
Dir: Manuel Herrero Montes
Founded: 1925
Subjects: Computer Science, Education, Religion - Catholic, Religion - Other
ISBN Prefix(es): 978-950-530
Branch Office(s)
Libreria Marista, Av Callao 226, 1022 Buenos Aires *Tel:* (011) 4374-3114; (011) 4374-3125; (011) 4374-3135 *Fax:* (011) 4374-3146 *E-mail:* libreriamarista@infovia.com.ar *Web Site:* www.facebook.com/libreriamarista

Gran Aldea Editores
Camarones 1762, C1416ECH Buenos Aires
Tel: (011) 4585-2241 *Fax:* (011) 4584-5803
E-mail: info@granaldeaeditores.com.ar
Web Site: www.granaldeaeditores.com.ar
Key Personnel
President: Estela Falicov
Art Dir & Foreign Rights: Michelle Kenigstein
National Marketing Manager: Maximiliano Piris
Subjects: Education, Health, Nutrition, Medicine, Nursing, Dentistry, Science (General)
ISBN Prefix(es): 978-987-21834; 978-987-98678
Foreign Rep(s): Fundacion Libro Universitario (Peru); Librerias Gandhi SA de CV (Mexico); Ediciones Granica SA (Uruguay); Panamericana Libreria y Papeleria SA (Colombia); Quijote SRL (Paraguay); Tarahumara (Spain); Tecni-Ciencia-Libros (Venezuela); Unilibros SA (Dominican Republic)

Ediciones Granica SA
Lavalle 1634, 3° piso, C1048AAN Buenos Aires
Tel: (011) 4374-1456 *Fax:* (011) 4373-0669
E-mail: granica.ar@granicaeditor.com; prensa@granicaeditor.com
Web Site: www.granicaeditor.com
Key Personnel
General Manager: Claudio Iannini
Head, Press & Promotion: Carina Durnhofer
Subjects: Cookery, Education, Management, Marketing, Travel & Tourism, Human Resources
ISBN Prefix(es): 978-84-7577; 978-950-641

Grito Sagrado Editorial
11 de Septiembre 992, 7° piso, C1426BFK Buenos Aires
Tel: (011) 4775-9228 *Fax:* (011) 4777-6765
E-mail: ventas@gritosagrado.com.ar
Web Site: www.gritosagrado.com.ar
Key Personnel
Manager: Dr Rosa Pelz Galperin *E-mail:* rpg@gritosagrado.com.ar
Subjects: History, Management, Philosophy, Freedom, Natural Healing
ISBN Prefix(es): 978-987-1239; 978-987-20951
Imprints: GS Junior
Foreign Rep(s): The Ayn Rand Institute (USA); CEDICE AC (Venezuela); Firex 21 SL (Barcelona) (Spain); Firex 21 SL (Madrid) (Spain); Universidad Francisco Marroquin (Guatemala); Librerias Gandhi (Mexico); Distribuidora de Libros Hidalgo Ltda (Colombia); Instituto de Estudios para una Sociedad Abierta (Panama); Walter Puelles Navarrete (Bolivia, Ecuador, Peru); Togus Distribuidora (Uruguay)

GS Junior, *imprint of* Grito Sagrado Editorial

Editorial Guadal SA
Av de Mayo 1209 2°D, C1085ABC Buenos Aires
Tel: (011) 5278-7000 *Fax:* (011) 5278-7000
E-mail: info@editorialguadal.com.ar
Web Site: www.editorialguadal.com.ar
ISBN Prefix(es): 978-987-579; 978-987-1134; 978-987-1175; 978-987-20661
Foreign Rep(s): Editorial Pomaire Ltda (Uruguay); Vergara & Riba Editoras SA (Federico Catalano) (Mexico); Zig Zag SA (Ramon Olaciregui) (Chile)

Editorial Guadalupe+
Subsidiary of Editorial Verbo Divino
Mansilla 3865, C1425BPZ Buenos Aires
Tel: (011) 4826-8587 *Fax:* (011) 4826-8587
E-mail: ventas@editorialguadalupe.com.ar; gerencia@editorialguadalupe.com.ar; edicion@editorialguadalupe.com.ar
Web Site: www.editorialguadalupe.com.ar
Key Personnel
Sales Manager: Agustin Grizzuti *E-mail:* agustin.grizzuti@editorialguadalupe.com.ar
Editorial: Liliana Ferreiros *E-mail:* liliana.ferreiros@editorialguadalupe.com.ar
Sales: Jorge Ontivero *E-mail:* jorge.ontivero@editorialguadalupe.com.ar
Founded: 1894
Membership(s): Camara Argentina de Publicaciones.
Subjects: Anthropology, Education, History, Language Arts, Linguistics, Literature, Literary Criticism, Essays, Music, Dance, Philosophy, Psychology, Psychiatry, Religion - Catholic, Social Sciences, Sociology, Theology
ISBN Prefix(es): 978-950-500
Bookshop(s): Libreria Guadalupe, Mansilla 3865, 1425 Buenos Aires *Tel:* (011) 4826-8587; Libreria Verbo Divino, Velez Sarsfield 66, 5000 Cordoba *Tel:* (0351) 424-3229 *E-mail:* libreverbo@hotmail.com; Libreria San Jose, Colon y La Rioja, 3300 Posadas, Misiones *Tel:* (0376) 422-2445 *E-mail:* ventas@libreriasanjose.com.ar; Libreria del Salvador, Ave Cordoba 1437, 4600 San Salvador de Jujuy *Tel:* (0388) 423-5454

Editorial Heliasta SRL
Juncal 3451, C1425AYT Buenos Aires
Tel: (011) 4804-0472; (011) 4804-8757; (011) 4804-0119 *Fax:* (011) 4804-0472; (011) 4804-8757; (011) 4804-0119
E-mail: editorial@heliasta.com.ar
Web Site: www.heliasta.com.ar
Key Personnel
Mng Partner: Ana Maria Cabanellas de las Cuevas *E-mail:* amc@heliasta.com.ar; Guillermo Cabanellas de las Cuevas

Subjects: Business, Economics, Labor, Industrial
  Relations, Law
ISBN Prefix(es): 978-950-9065; 978-950-885
Subsidiaries: Editorial Claridad SA; Una Luna

Editorial Hemisferio Sur SA+
Pasteur 743, 1028 Buenos Aires
Tel: (011) 4952-9825; (011) 4952-8454
  Fax: (011) 4952-8454
E-mail: informe@hemisferiosur.com.ar
Web Site: www.hemisferiosur.com.ar
Key Personnel
President & Mng Dir, Licensing: Adolfo Julian
  Pena
Founded: 1966
Membership(s): Camara Argentina de Publica-
  ciones.
Subjects: Agriculture, Animals, Pets, Biological
  Sciences, Gardening, Plants, Science (General),
  Veterinary Science, Wine & Spirits, Ecology,
  Zoology
ISBN Prefix(es): 978-950-504

Adriana Hidalgo Editora
Francisco de Vittoria 2324, Planta baja,
  C1426ENB Buenos Aires
Tel: (011) 4800-1900
E-mail: info@adrianahidalgo.com
Web Site: www.adrianahidalgo.com
Key Personnel
Dir General: Adriana Hidalgo Sola
Editorial Dir: Fabian Lebenglik
Subjects: Biography, Memoirs, History, Language
  Arts, Linguistics, Philosophy
ISBN Prefix(es): 978-987-9396; 978-987-1156
Foreign Rep(s): Catalonia (Chile); Fondo de Cul-
  tura Economica (Colombia); Gussi Libros
  (Uruguay); Proculmex SA de CV (Mexico);
  Tusquets Editores (Argentina); UDL Libros
  (Spain)

Editorial Hispania Libros, see Editorial Ciudad
  Argentina

Editorial Hola Chicos
Av Callao 1121, 4° D, C1023AAE Buenos Aires
Tel: (011) 4812-1800 *Fax:* (011) 4815-1998
Web Site: www.holachicos.com.ar
Key Personnel
Mng Editor: Patricia Repetto
Subjects: Education
ISBN Prefix(es): 978-987-1061; 978-987-97282;
  978-987-98346; 978-987-1561

HomoSapiens Ediciones
Sarmiento 825, S2000CMM Rosario, Santa Fe
Tel: (0341) 4243399 *Fax:* (0341) 4253852
E-mail: editorial@homosapiens.com.ar
Web Site: www.homosapiens.com.ar
Subjects: Education, Psychology, Psychiatry, So-
  cial Sciences, Sociology
ISBN Prefix(es): 978-950-808

Ediciones Iamique
Guatemala 6013, C1425BVQ Buenos Aires
Tel: (011) 4779 0809 *Fax:* (011) 4779 0809
E-mail: info@iamique.com.ar; ventas@iamique.
  com.ar
Web Site: www.iamique.com.ar
Key Personnel
Co-Mng Dir: Carla Baredes; Ileana Lotersztain
Founded: 2000
Subjects: Language Arts, Linguistics, Mathemat-
  ics, Social Sciences, Natural Science
ISBN Prefix(es): 978-987-1217
Foreign Rep(s): Libreria America Latina
  (Uruguay); Baker & Taylor (USA); Brodart
  & Co (USA); Editorial Cordillera de los Andes
  SA de CV (Mexico); Coservisa (Nicaragua);

Libri Mundi (Ecuador); Siglo del Hombre Editores (Colombia); Libreria El Virrey (Peru);
  Empresa Editorial Zig-Zag SA (Chile)

**Editorial Idearium de la Universidad de
  Mendoza (EDIUM)**
Boulogne Sur Mer 683, M5502BZG Mendoza
Tel: (0261) 420 2017; (0261) 420 0740
  Fax: (0261) 420 1100
E-mail: rectorado@um.edu.ar
Web Site: www.um.edu.ar
Key Personnel
Dir: Dr Juan Carlos Menghini
Founded: 1979
Subjects: Architecture & Interior Design, Com-
  puter Science, Economics, Education, Electron-
  ics, Electrical Engineering, Engineering (Gen-
  eral), Environmental Studies, History, Language
  Arts, Linguistics, Law, Mathematics, Medicine,
  Nursing, Dentistry, Philosophy, Physics, Social
  Sciences, Sociology, Technology
ISBN Prefix(es): 978-950-624
Distributed by Abeledo-Perrot

Grupo Imaginador de Ediciones SA
Bartolome Mitre 3749, C1201AAS Buenos Aires
Tel: (011) 4958-4111 *Fax:* (011) 4958-4111
E-mail: editorial@imaginador.com.ar
Web Site: www.imaginador.com.ar
Key Personnel
Dir General: Luis Hernan Rodriguez Felder
Founded: 1991
Subjects: Cookery, Education, Government, Po-
  litical Science, Health, Nutrition, Inspirational,
  Spirituality, Literature, Literary Criticism, Es-
  says, Music, Dance, Philosophy, Romance,
  Travel & Tourism, Esoteric, Parenting
ISBN Prefix(es): 978-950-768
Distributor for Edris; G Division Libros; Grulla;
  Larsen; Ediciones Ruz; Ziel

INA, see Instituto Nacional de Agua

Ediciones Infinito
Ave Callao 2001, 3° piso, C1024AAG Buenos
  Aires
Tel: (011) 4816 9004; (011) 4814 4546
E-mail: info@edicionesinfinito.com; ventas@
  edicionesinfinito.com
Web Site: www.edicionesinfinito.com
Key Personnel
Mng Dir: Cristina Lafiandra
Founded: 1954
Subjects: Architecture & Interior Design, Envi-
  ronmental Studies, Graphic & Industrial De-
  sign, Planning, Visual Arts
ISBN Prefix(es): 978-987-9393

Instituto de Publicaciones Navales+
Division of Centro Naval - Argentina
Florida 801, 3° piso, C1005AAQ Buenos Aires
Tel: (011) 4311-1011 (ext 621); (011) 4312-2598
  Fax: (011) 4311-5443
E-mail: instituto.publicaciones@centronaval.org.
  ar; gerente.ipn@centronaval.org.ar
Web Site: www.ipn.centronaval.org.ar/ipn/
  publicaciones.html
Key Personnel
President: Carlos L Mazzoni
Vice President: Guillermo Montenegro
Founded: 1961
Specialize in strategy, naval history, international
  relations & maritime issues.
Membership(s): Camara Argentino del Libro.
Subjects: Biography, Memoirs, Maritime, Mili-
  tary Science, Sports, Athletics, International
  Relations, Narrative, Nautical Sports, Sailing,
  Strategics
ISBN Prefix(es): 978-950-9016; 978-950-899
Number of titles published annually: 7 Print

Total Titles: 155 Print
Orders to: Galeria Larreta Local 28, Florida 971,
  C100AAG Buenos Aires *Tel:* (011) 4311-0042
  Fax: (011) 4311-0043

Instituto Nacional de Agua (National Water
  Institute)
AU Ezeiza-Canuelas, Tramo Jorge Newbery Km
  1.620, 1802 Ezeiza, Buenos Aires
Tel: (011) 4480-4500 *Fax:* (011) 4480-0094
E-mail: ina@ina.gov.ar
Web Site: www.ina.gov.ar
Key Personnel
President: Dr Raul A Lopardo *Tel:* (011) 4480-
  9162
Vice President: Oscar N Bronzina
Subjects: Computer Science, Earth Sciences, Ge-
  ography, Geology, Law, Library & Information
  Sciences, Mathematics, Technology
ISBN Prefix(es): 978-950-634

Instituto Torcuato Di Tella
Minones 2159/77 1° Piso, C1428ATG Buenos
  Aires
Tel: (011) 5169-7000
Web Site: www.itdt.edu
Key Personnel
Chief Executive Officer: Salvador Orsini
  E-mail: salvadororsini@fibertel.com.ar
Founded: 1958
Subjects: Economics, Government, Political Sci-
  ence, History, Social Sciences, Sociology
ISBN Prefix(es): 978-950-621

Editorial Inter-Medica SA+
Junin 917 1°A, C1113ACC Buenos Aires
Tel: (011) 4961-9234 *Fax:* (011) 4961-5572
E-mail: info@inter-medica.com.ar
Web Site: www.inter-medica.com.ar
Key Personnel
President: Jorge Modyeievsky
Vice President: Sonia M B de Modyeievsky
  E-mail: soniam@inter-medica.com.ar
Founded: 1959
Membership(s): Camara Argentino del Libro.
Subjects: Veterinary Science
ISBN Prefix(es): 978-950-555

Interzona Editora
Pasaje Rivarola 115, C1015AAA Buenos Aires
Tel: (011) 4383 6262
E-mail: info@interzonaeditora.com; edicion@
  interzonaeditora.com
Web Site: www.interzonaeditora.com
Key Personnel
Editorial Dir: Guido Indij
Editorial Coordinator: Cecilia Esposito
Founded: 2002
Subjects: Literature, Literary Criticism, Essays
ISBN Prefix(es): 978-987-1180; 978-987-20677;
  978-987-21014
Distribution Center: Asunto Impreso, Pasaje Ri-
  varola 169, C1015AAA Buenos Aires, Con-
  tact: Juan Montes de Oca *Tel:* (011) 4383-6262
  E-mail: ventas@asuntoimpreso.com
Tarahumara Libros, C/ Angel, 14-Local izdo,
  28005 Madrid, Spain *Tel:* 91 365 62 21
  Fax: 91 354 01 48 *E-mail:* tarahumara@
  tarahumaralibros.com

Ediciones Journal SA
Viamonte 2146 1° A, C1056ABH Buenos Aires
Tel: (011) 5277 4444 *Fax:* (011) 5277 3095
E-mail: ediciones@journal.com.ar; info@journal.
  com.ar
Web Site: www.journal.com.ar
Subjects: Medicine, Nursing, Dentistry, Cardiol-
  ogy, Dermatology, Neonatology, Nephrology,
  Obstetrics, Oncology, Pediatrics, Radiology,
  Urology
ISBN Prefix(es): 978-987-97739

Juegos & Co SRL+
Corrientes 1312, piso 8, C1043ABN Buenos
  Aires
Tel: (011) 4374-7903 *Fax:* (011) 4372-3829
Web Site: www.demente.com
Key Personnel
Dir: Jaime Poniachik; Daniel Samoilovich
Founded: 1980
Membership(s): Argentine Association of Maga-
  zine Publishers.
Subjects: Mathematics
ISBN Prefix(es): 978-950-765
Associate Companies: Zugarto Ediciones, Madrid,
  Spain
Distribution Center: Distrimachi SA, Av Indepen-
  dencia 2744, Buenos Aires

Editorial Juris+
Moreno 1580, S2000DLF Rosario
Tel: (0341) 4267301; (0341) 4267302 *Fax:* (0341)
  4267301; (0341) 4267302
E-mail: editorial@editorialjuris.com; libreria@
  editorialjuris.com
Web Site: www.editorialjuris.com
Key Personnel
Owner: Luis Maesano
Founded: 1952
Subjects: Criminology, Law
ISBN Prefix(es): 978-950-817; 978-950-99649;
  978-987-1539
Number of titles published annually: 25 Print; 5
  CD-ROM
Total Titles: 400 Print; 20 CD-ROM

Kapelusz Editora SA
San Jose 831, C1076AAQ Buenos Aires
Tel: (011) 5236-5000 *Fax:* (011) 5236-5005
E-mail: contacto@kapelusznorma.com.ar
Web Site: www.kapelusznorma.com.ar
Key Personnel
Sales Executive & Editor: Carlos Sebastian
  Anselmo
Founded: 1905
Membership(s): Camara Argentina de Publica-
  ciones.
Subjects: Art, Business, Cookery, Education, Hu-
  mor, Literature, Literary Criticism, Essays, Psy-
  chology, Psychiatry, Science (General), Self-
  Help, Family
ISBN Prefix(es): 978-950-13
Parent Company: Grupo Editorial Norma
Ultimate Parent Company: Carvajal SA

Katz Editores SA
Charlone 216, C1427BXF Buenos Aires
Tel: (011) 4554 6754
E-mail: info@katzeditores.com
Web Site: www.katzeditores.com
Key Personnel
Dir: Alejandro Katz
Founded: 2006
Membership(s): Camara Argentina de Publica-
  ciones.
Subjects: Geography, Geology, History, Philoso-
  phy, Science (General), Social Sciences, Soci-
  ology
ISBN Prefix(es): 978-84-96859
Branch Office(s)
Calle del Barco 40, 3° D esc ext, 28004 Madrid,
  Spain *Tel:* 91 522 9857
Foreign Rep(s): Modesto Alonso Estravis Dis-
  tribuidora (Spain); Azeta Distribuciones
  (Spain); Contratiempo (Spain); Cuspide Dis-
  tribuidora (Argentina); Difusio General de Lli-
  breria (Spain); Gaia Libros (Spain); Gussi Libros (Uruguay); Lidiza (Spain); Libros Nova
  Terrae SA (Chile); Sexto Piso (Mexico); Siglo
  del Hombre Editores (Colombia); Troquel Li-
  bros (Spain); UDL Libros (Spain)

Editorial Kier+
Ave Santa Fe 1260, C1059ABT Buenos Aires

Tel: (011) 4811-0507 *Fax:* (011) 4811-3395
E-mail: ventadirecta@kier.com.ar; info@kier.com.
  ar
Web Site: www.kier.com.ar
Key Personnel
President: Hector Pibernus
Mng Dir: Osvaldo Pibernus
Publishing Dir: Cristina Grigna
Founded: 1907
Specialize in esoteric books.
Subjects: Anthropology, Astrology, Occult,
  Health, Nutrition, Parapsychology, Religion -
  Buddhist, Religion - Hindu, Religion - Islamic,
  Religion - Jewish, Religion - Other, Self-Help,
  Martial Arts
ISBN Prefix(es): 978-950-17
Number of titles published annually: 40 Print
Total Titles: 800 Print

Laffont Ediciones Electronicas SA
Av Reg Patricios 929 3° piso, C1265AEC Buenos
  Aires
Tel: (011) 4302-8668 *Fax:* (011) 4302-8668
E-mail: info@laffont.com.ar
Web Site: www.laffont.com.ar
Key Personnel
Dir: Dr Julio Laffont
Membership(s): Camara Argentina del Libro.
Subjects: Art, Education, Geography, Geology,
  History, Humor, Law, Literature, Literary Crit-
  icism, Essays, Religion - Other, Science (Gen-
  eral), Ecology, Grammar
ISBN Prefix(es): 978-987-9220; 978-987-95410

Ediciones Larousse Argentina SA
Francisco Acuna de Figueroa 352, C1180AAF
  Buenos Aires
Tel: (011) 4865-9581; (011) 4865-9582; (011)
  4865-9583 *Toll Free Tel:* 0800-333-5757
  Fax: (011) 4865-9581; (011) 4865-9582; (011)
  4865-9583
Web Site: www.aique.com.br/catalogo/larousse
Founded: 1963
Subjects: English as a Second Language, Lan-
  guage Arts, Linguistics, Spanish Language
ISBN Prefix(es): 978-950-538
Parent Company: Aique Grupo Editor SA

Ediciones LEA SA
Av Dorrego 330, C1440FOA Buenos Aires
Tel: (011) 4846-9056
E-mail: info@edicioneslea.com; ventas@
  edicioneslea.com
Web Site: www.edicioneslea.com
Key Personnel
Editorial Dir: Pedro Ferrantelli
Sales Manager: Mariana Vidakovicks De Victor
  E-mail: mariana@edicioneslea.com
Editor: Adrian Rimondino *E-mail:* adrianr@
  edicioneslea.com
Editorial Production: Cecilla Garcia Ussher
International Sales: Miriam Alvarez
  E-mail: miriam@edicioneslea.com
Founded: 2003
Subjects: Cookery, Health, Nutrition, Literature,
  Literary Criticism, Essays, Psychology, Psychi-
  atry, Science (General), Self-Help, Alternative
  Medicine, Argentine Culture
ISBN Prefix(es): 978-987-1257; 978-987-21776;
  978-987-22032; 978-987-22079; 978-987-634
Distribution Center: IPG Spanish Books, 814 N
  Franklin St, Chicago, IL 60610, United States

Lenguaje Claro Editora
Portugal 2951, B1606EFA Carapachay, Buenos
  Aires
Tel: (011) 5955-3151
E-mail: info@lenguajeclaro.com
Web Site: www.lenguajeclaro.com
Founded: 2007

Subjects: Economics, Government, Political Science, Argentina
ISBN Prefix(es): 978-987-23627; 978-987-3764

Letra Impresa Grupo Editor
Palpa 3672, C1427EBD Buenos Aires
Tel: (011) 4552-9533; (011) 4553-0155
E-mail: contacto@letraimpresa.com.ar
Web Site: letraimpresa.com.ar
Key Personnel
Editor: Elsa Pizzi; Patricia Roggio
  E-mail: roggio@letraimpresa.com.ar
Marketing: Diego Medina *E-mail:* medina@
  letraimpresa.com.ar
Founded: 2007
Subjects: Language Arts, Linguistics, Literature,
  Literary Criticism, Essays
ISBN Prefix(es): 978-987-1565; 978-987-2414

Editorial Leviatan
Adolfo Alsina 1170, 5° piso, Off 511, C1088AAF
  Buenos Aires
Tel: (011) 4381-7947; (011) 4381-0453
E-mail: editorial@e-leviatan.com.ar
Web Site: www.e-leviatan.com.ar
Key Personnel
Dir: Gerardo Manfredi; Claudia Schvartz
Founded: 1983
Subjects: Art, Drama, Theater, History, Literature,
  Literary Criticism, Essays, Philosophy, Poetry,
  Social Sciences, Sociology
ISBN Prefix(es): 978-950-9546; 978-987-514

La Ley SA Editora e Impresora+
Tucuman 1471, C1050AAC Buenos Aires
Tel: (011) 4378-4733 *Fax:* (011) 4378-4723
E-mail: consultas@laley.com.ar;
  atencionalcliente@laley.com.ar
Web Site: www.laley.com.ar
Key Personnel
President: Juan C Milberg
General Dir: Enrique J Algorta Gaona
Founded: 1935
Subjects: Economics, History, Law, Philosophy
ISBN Prefix(es): 978-950-527; 978-987-03

Librograf Editora SRL+
Chacabuco 1185/87, C1069AAW Buenos Aires
Tel: (011) 4300-1466; (011) 4300-3670
  Fax: (011) 4300-1466
Founded: 1968
Subjects: Cookery, Education
ISBN Prefix(es): 978-950-848; 978-950-99827

Editorial Losada SA+
Moreno 3362, C1209ABL Buenos Aires
Tel: (011) 43 75 50 01 *Fax:* (011) 43 73 40 06
E-mail: administra@editoriallosada.com
Web Site: www.editoriallosada.com
Key Personnel
President: Jose Juan Fernandez Reguera
Founded: 1938
Membership(s): Camara Argentina del Libro.
Subjects: Biography, Memoirs, Drama, Theater,
  Education, Fiction, History, Law, Philosophy,
  Poetry, Psychology, Psychiatry
ISBN Prefix(es): 978-950-03

Lugar Editorial SA
Castro Barros 1754, C1237ABN Buenos Aires
Tel: (011) 4921-5174; (011) 4924-1555; (011)
  4922-3175 *Fax:* (011) 4921-5174; (011) 4924-
  1555; (011) 4922-3175
E-mail: lugar@lugareditorial.com.ar; info@
  lugareditorial.com.ar
Web Site: www.lugareditorial.com.ar
Key Personnel
Dir General: Jose Rosenberg
Dir: Graciela Rosenberg *E-mail:* grosenberg@
  lugareditorial.com.ar
Founded: 1991

Subjects: Education, Health, Nutrition, Literature, Literary Criticism, Essays, Medicine, Nursing, Dentistry, Psychology, Psychiatry, Science (General), Psychoanalysis
ISBN Prefix(es): 978-950-9129; 978-950-892

Macmillan Publishers SA
Av Blanco Encalada 104, B1609EEO San Isidro, Buenos Aires
Tel: (011) 4708 8000 *Fax:* (011) 4708 8158
E-mail: argentina.eltinfo@macmillaneducation. com
Web Site: www.macmillan.com.ar
Founded: 1998
Subjects: Education, English Language Teaching (ELT), Grammar, Methodology, Vocabulary
ISBN Prefix(es): 978-987-9401
Parent Company: Macmillan Group
Ultimate Parent Company: Holtzbrinck Publishing Group
Warehouse: Gurruchaga 2374, B1778ETA Ciudad Evita, Buenos Aires *Tel:* (011) 4487 7200
Fax: (011) 4487 7200

Ediciones Madres de Plaza de Mayo
Hipolito Yrigoyen 1432, C1089AAB Buenos Aires
Tel: (011) 4383-4188 *Fax:* (011) 4383-4188
E-mail: editorial@madres.org
Web Site: madres.org
Subjects: Government, Political Science, Social Sciences, Sociology
ISBN Prefix(es): 978-987-99610; 978-987-1231; 978-950-99969

Editorial Maipue
Zufriategui 1153, B1714GDQ Ituzaingo
Tel: (011) 4624 9370 *Fax:* (011) 4458 0259
E-mail: promocion@maipue.com.ar; ventas@ maipue.com.ar
Web Site: www.maipue.com.ar
Founded: 1997
Subjects: Communications, Education, Government, Political Science, History, Law, Literature, Literary Criticism, Essays, Social Sciences, Sociology, Technology, Ecology
ISBN Prefix(es): 978-987-9493; 978-987-96871

Maizal Ediciones
Francisco J Muniz 438, B1640FDB Martinez, Buenos Aires
Tel: (011) 47 92 94 96
E-mail: info@maizal.com
Web Site: www.maizal.com
Subjects: History, Regional Interests, Travel & Tourism, Argentinian Culture
ISBN Prefix(es): 978-987-9479; 978-987-97899

Ediciones Manantial
Av de Mayo 1365 6to piso, C1085ADB Buenos Aires
Tel: (011) 4383-6059; (011) 4383-7350
Fax: (011) 4383-7350
E-mail: info@emanantial.com.ar; ventas@ emanantial.com.ar; prensa@emanantial.com.ar
Web Site: www.emanantial.com.ar
Key Personnel
Dir General: Carlos A de Santos
Sales Manager: Leonardo Lanzani
Press: Malena La Rocca
Founded: 1984
Subjects: Education, Government, Political Science, Literature, Literary Criticism, Essays, Social Sciences, Sociology, Psychoanalysis
ISBN Prefix(es): 978-987-500; 978-950-9515

Editorial Marea SRL
Pico 1850, C1429EFD Buenos Aires
Tel: (011) 4703-0464 *Fax:* (011) 4703-0464
E-mail: marea@editorialmarea.com.ar
Web Site: www.editorialmarea.com.ar

Key Personnel
Editorial Dir: Constanza Brunet *E-mail:* cbrunet@ editorialmarea.com.ar
Editor: Virginia Ruano *E-mail:* vruano@ editorialmarea.com.ar
Founded: 2003
Membership(s): Editores Independientes de la Argentina (EDINAR).
Subjects: Fiction, History, Journalism, Literature, Literary Criticism, Essays, Investigative Journalism
ISBN Prefix(es): 978-987-21109; 978-987-22181; 978-987-1307
Distribution Center: Grupal SA, Solis 2045, C1134ADQ Buenos Aires *Tel:* (011) 4306-2444 *E-mail:* ventas@grupaldistribuidora.com. ar
Distribuidora El Placard, Calle 168 a No 54 d61-Torre 4-502, Bogota, Colombia *E-mail:* info@ elplacard.net *Web Site:* www.elplacard.net
Distribuidora de Libros Pablo Ameneiros, Uruguayana 3223, 11800 Montevideo, Uruguay *Tel:* 22042756 *Fax:* 22042756
E-mail: info@pabloameneiros.com *Web Site:* www.pabloameneiros.com

Melos Ediciones Musicales SA
Tte Gral Juan D Peron 1560, C1037ACD Buenos Aires
Tel: (011) 4371-9842; (011) 4371-9843
Fax: (011) 4372-3452; (011) 4372-3453
E-mail: info@melos.com.ar; ventas@melos.com. ar
Web Site: www.melos.com.ar
Key Personnel
President: Gaston Larcade
Vice President: Ernesto R Larcade
Founded: 1924
Subjects: Education, Music, Dance
ISBN Prefix(es): 978-950-22
Branch Office(s)
Dean Funes 163, Pasaje Santa Catalina, local 9, Cordoba *Tel:* (0351) 425-1921

Editorial Nazhira+
Catamarca 972, C1231AAJ Buenos Aires
Tel: (011) 4308-1521
E-mail: info@nazhira.com
Web Site: www.editorialnazhira.com.ar
Key Personnel
Dir: Bettina Cositorto
Subjects: Education
ISBN Prefix(es): 978-987-20905

Ediciones Novedades Educativas (Noveduc)
Av Corrientes 4345, C1195AAC Buenos Aires
Tel: (011) 5278-2200
E-mail: contacto@noveduc.com
Web Site: www.noveduc.com.ar
Subjects: Education, Health, Nutrition, Philosophy, Psychology, Psychiatry, Social Sciences, Sociology
ISBN Prefix(es): 978-987-9116; 978-987-95294

Nueva Libreria
Estados Unidos 301, C1101AAG San Telmo, Buenos Aires
Tel: (011) 4362-9266 *Fax:* (011) 4362-6887
E-mail: libros@nuevalibreria.com.ar
Web Site: www.nuevalibreria.com.ar
Key Personnel
Dir General: Jorge Lopez Montero
Manager: Fabiola Sanchez
Subjects: Architecture & Interior Design, Art, Biological Sciences, Economics, Engineering (General), Fiction, Geography, Geology, History, Literature, Literary Criticism, Essays, Mathematics, Medicine, Nursing, Dentistry, Music, Dance, Nonfiction (General), Philosophy, Administration, Botany, Ecology
ISBN Prefix(es): 978-950-9088; 978-987-1104

Bookshop(s): Libreria Rector Juan Sabato, Universidad Tecnologica Nacional, Sede Medrano, calle Medrano 951, Hall Central, Buenos Aires
Tel: (011) 4867-2772; Libreria Rector Juan Sabato, Universidad Tecnologica Nacional, Sede Campus, calle Mozart 2300, Hall Central, Buenos Aires *Tel:* (011) 4602-4020

Ediciones Nueva Vision+
Tucuman 3748, C1189AAV Buenos Aires
Tel: (011) 4863-1461; (011) 4864-5050
E-mail: ventas@nuevavisionedic.com.ar; administracion@nuevavisionedic.com.ar
Web Site: www.facebook.co/Ediciones-Nueva-Vision-746426855417742
Key Personnel
President: Haydee Perez de Giacone
Vice President: Javier Ernesto Giacone
Founded: 1954
Subjects: Architecture & Interior Design, Art, Drama, Theater, Psychology, Psychiatry, Social Sciences, Sociology
ISBN Prefix(es): 978-950-602

Oikos+
Rivadavia 1823, piso 9, 1033 Buenos Aires
Tel: (011) 4951-9489; (011) 4951-8129
Founded: 1975
Subjects: Earth Sciences, Geography, Geology, Social Sciences, Sociology
ISBN Prefix(es): 978-950-601
Bookshop(s): Hipolito Yrigoyen 1970, 1089 Buenos Aires

Editorial Paidos SAICF
Member of Grupo Planeta
Av Independencia 1682/1686, C1100ABQ Buenos Aires
Tel: (011) 4124-9100 *Fax:* (011) 4124-9100
E-mail: paidos@paidos.com
Founded: 1945
Membership(s): Camara Argentina de Publicaciones.
Subjects: Art, Biography, Memoirs, Business, Child Care & Development, Communications, Education, Environmental Studies, Geography, Geology, Government, Political Science, Health, Nutrition, Philosophy, Psychology, Psychiatry, Science (General), Science Fiction, Fantasy, Self-Help, Social Sciences, Sociology, Travel & Tourism, Women's Studies
ISBN Prefix(es): 978-950-12

Paradiso Ediciones
Fco Acuna de Figueroa 786, C1180AAN Buenos Aires
Tel: (011) 4862-9167
E-mail: info@paradisoediciones.com.ar
Web Site: www.paradisoediciones.com.ar
Subjects: Literature, Literary Criticism, Essays, Poetry
ISBN Prefix(es): 978-987-9409; 978-987-99242; 978-987-99867

Editora Patria Grande Ltda
Rivadavia 6369, G1406GLG Buenos Aires
Tel: (011) 4631-6446; (011) 4631-6577
Fax: (011) 4631-6577
E-mail: edpatria@infovia.com.ar
Web Site: www.editorapatriagrande.com
Key Personnel
Vice President: Ignacio Pacho
Publishing: Sergio Avasolo
Sales & Publishing: Elsa Soto
Founded: 1973
Subjects: Poetry, Religion - Other
ISBN Prefix(es): 978-950-546
Distributed by Paradiso Ediciones (worldwide exc Argentina)

Pearson Educacion SA
Av Belgrano 615, piso 11, C1092AAG Buenos
   Aires
Tel: (011) 4309-6100 *Fax:* (011) 4309-6199
E-mail: argentina@pearson.com; universit@
   pearson.com
Web Site: www.pearsoneducacion.net
Membership(s): Camara Argentina de Publica-
   ciones.
Subjects: Business, Computer Science, Eco-
   nomics, Engineering (General), English as a
   Second Language, Geography, Geology, Math-
   ematics, Science (General), Social Sciences,
   Sociology, Business Administration, Humani-
   ties
ISBN Prefix(es): 978-987-615
Parent Company: Pearson Education SA, Madrid,
   Spain
Ultimate Parent Company: Pearson PLC

Pequeno Editor
Charlone 978, C1427BXT Buenos Aires
Tel: (011) 4554-8192 *Fax:* (011) 4554-8192
E-mail: news@pequenoeditor.com; comercial@
   pequenoeditor.com
Web Site: www.pequenoeditor.com
Key Personnel
Editorial Dir: Raquel Franco
Artistic Dir: Diego Bianchi
Literary Editor: Ruth Kaufman *E-mail:* ruth@
   pequenoeditor.com
Business Coordinator: Maria Emilia Sanchez
Founded: 2002
ISBN Prefix(es): 978-987-1374; 978-987-22094;
   978-987-20847

Editorial Planeta Argentina SAIC+
Member of Grupo Planeta
Av Independencia 1668, C1100ABQ Buenos
   Aires
Tel: (011) 4124-9100 *Fax:* (011) 4124-9190
E-mail: info@ar.planetadelibros.com
Web Site: www.planetadelibros.com.ar
Key Personnel
Editorial Dir: Alberto Diaz
Editorial Dir, International Division: Ricardo Sa-
   banes
Founded: 1983
Membership(s): Camara Argentina de Publica-
   ciones.
Subjects: Biography, Memoirs, Environmental
   Studies, Fiction, Health, Nutrition, History,
   How-to, Literature, Literary Criticism, Essays,
   Nonfiction (General), Parapsychology, Psychol-
   ogy, Psychiatry, Religion - Other
ISBN Prefix(es): 978-950-742; 978-950-9216;
   978-950-49

Planta Editora
Tronador 2051, C1430AM Buenos Aires
Tel: (011) 4552-4380
E-mail: hola@plantaeditora.net
Web Site: www.plantaeditora.net
Key Personnel
Art Dir: Ana Armendariz
Editorial Dir: Luciana Delfabro *E-mail:* luciana.
   delfabro@gmail.com
Production: Marina Lazo *E-mail:* marina.
   plantaeditora@gmail.com
ISBN Prefix(es): 978-987-24546

Plaza & Janes
Imprint of Penguin Random House Grupo Edito-
   rial
Humbero Primo 555, C1103ACK Buenos Aires
Tel: (011) 5235-4400
E-mail: recepcion@penguinrandomhouse.com
Web Site: www.megustaleer.com.ar/editoriales/
   plaza-janes/050
Subjects: Fiction, Nonfiction (General)
ISBN Prefix(es): 978-950-644

Editorial Plus Ultra SA
Av Callao 575, C1022AAF Buenos Aires
Tel: (011) 4374-2973; (011) 4374-5092
   Fax: (011) 4374-2973
Founded: 1964
Subjects: Economics, Education, Government, Po-
   litical Science, History, Law, Literature, Liter-
   ary Criticism, Essays, Philosophy, Psychology,
   Psychiatry, Social Sciences, Sociology
ISBN Prefix(es): 978-950-21

Editorial Polemos SA+
Moreno 1785 5º piso, C1093ABG Buenos Aires
Tel: (011) 4383-5291 *Fax:* (011) 4382-4181
E-mail: informes@polemos.com.ar; editorial@
   polemos.com.ar
Web Site: www.editorialpolemos.com.ar
Key Personnel
President: Juan Carlos Stagnaro
Founded: 1990
Subjects: Behavioral Sciences, Health, Nutrition,
   Medicine, Nursing, Dentistry, Psychology, Psy-
   chiatry, Science (General), Social Sciences,
   Sociology, Psychoanalysis, Wellness
ISBN Prefix(es): 978-987-9165; 978-987-99545
Foreign Rep(s): Axolotl Libros (Mexico); Bib-
   liomedica Ediciones (Uruguay); Compania
   Caribena de Libros Inc (Puerto Rico); Importa-
   ciones PH Lugo Libros CA (Venezuela); Edi-
   torial Nueva Decada SA (Costa Rica); Libreria
   y Distribuidora Olejnik (Chile); Paradox Libros
   SL (Spain); Promolibro (Colombia); Libreria
   San Critobal SAC (Peru)

Producciones Mawis SRL
Emilio Lamarca 1917, C1407DGM Buenos Aires
Tel: (011) 4567-0625 *Fax:* (011) 4567-0625
E-mail: info@produccionesmawis.com.ar
Web Site: www.produccionesmawis.com.ar
Founded: 1970
Subjects: Fiction, Literature, Literary Criticism,
   Essays
ISBN Prefix(es): 978-950-99783; 978-987-586;
   978-987-9166

Quipu
Jose Bonifacio 2434, C1406GYB Buenos Aires
Tel: (011) 4612 3440; (011) 4611 3939
E-mail: info@quipu.com.ar
Web Site: quipu.com.ar
Founded: 1992
ISBN Prefix(es): 978-987-5040

RiderChail Editions SRL
Hortiguera 172, piso 8A, 1406 Buenos Aires
Tel: (011) 44 31 91 07
E-mail: contacto@riderchail.com
Web Site: www.riderchail.com
Key Personnel
Publishing Manager: Gabriela A Perez
Founded: 2007
Subjects: Humor
ISBN Prefix(es): 978-987-1603

Ediciones La Rocca SRL+
Talcahuano 458, C1013AAI Buenos Aires
Tel: (011) 4382-8526 *Fax:* (011) 4384-5774
Web Site: www.edicioneslarocca.com
Key Personnel
Dir: Alfonso La Rocca
Founded: 1985
Membership(s): Camara Argentino del Libro.
Subjects: Law, Criminalistics, Forensics
ISBN Prefix(es): 978-950-9714; 978-987-517

Ediciones Libreria Rodriguez SA+
Sarmiento 835, C1041AAQ Buenos Aires
Tel: (011) 4326-1959
Founded: 1981
Membership(s): Camara Argentina de Publica-
   ciones.

ISBN Prefix(es): 978-950-604
Associate Companies: LR Distribuidora SA

San Pablo+
Riobamba 230, C1025ABF Buenos Aires
Tel: (011) 5555-2400; (011) 5555-2416 (sales)
   Fax: (011) 5555-2425
E-mail: ventas@san-pablo.com.ar; director.
   editorial@san-pablo.com.ar; contacto@san-
   pablo.com.ar
Web Site: www.san-pablo.com.ar
Founded: 1931
A multimedia international Catholic publisher,
   whose publications are intended primarily for
   children, youth, families, parish communities &
   pastoral agents.
Subjects: Biblical Studies, Education, Health, Nu-
   trition, Human Relations, Language Arts, Lin-
   guistics, Psychology, Psychiatry, Religion -
   Catholic, Self-Help, Theology
ISBN Prefix(es): 978-950-861

Editorial Santa Maria
Av Directoria 3755/59, C1407HFE Buenos Aires
Tel: (011) 4671-0110
E-mail: info@editorialsantamaria.com
Web Site: www.editorialsantamaria.com
Key Personnel
Dir General: Fernando Perfetti
Founded: 1997
Subjects: Religion - Other
ISBN Prefix(es): 978-987-9405; 978-987-96863;
   978-987-616

Santiago Arcos Editor
Puan 481, C1406CQI Buenos Aires
Tel: (011) 4432-3107
E-mail: santiagoarcoseditor@uolsinectis.com.ar
Key Personnel
Editor: Miguel Angel Villafane
Founded: 2002
Subjects: Fiction, Literature, Literary Criticism,
   Essays, Argentina, Spanish Language
ISBN Prefix(es): 978-987-1240; 978-987-20374;
   978-987-21493

Enrique Santiago Rueda Editor
Humberto I 1274, 1103 Buenos Aires
Tel: (011) 4305-0745
Key Personnel
Mng Dir: Enrique S Rueda
Founded: 1940
Subjects: Literature, Literary Criticism, Essays
ISBN Prefix(es): 978-950-564; 978-987-98745

Sessa Editores
Pasaje Bollini 2234, C1425ECD Buenos Aires
Tel: (011) 4804-6700
Web Site: www.sessaeditores.com
Key Personnel
Dir General: Luis Sessa
Founded: 1976
Subjects: Art, Geography, Geology, History
ISBN Prefix(es): 978-950-9140
Branch Office(s)
Pasaje Bollini 2241, C1425ECD Buenos Aires
   Tel: (011) 4806-3796

Editorial Sigmar SACI+
Av Belgrano 1580, 7º piso, C1093AAQ Buenos
   Aires
Tel: (011) 4381-2510; (011) 4381-1715
   Fax: (011) 4383-5633
E-mail: editorial@sigmar.com.ar
Web Site: www.sigmar.com.ar
Key Personnel
President & Mng Dir: Robert G Chwat
Founded: 1941
Membership(s): Camara Argentina de Publica-
   ciones; Camara Argentina del Libro.
Subjects: Fiction, Ecology

ISBN Prefix(es): 978-950-11
Number of titles published annually: 100 Print
Total Titles: 1,200 Print
Distributor for Albatros (Argentina & Latin America)

Ediciones del Signo
Julian Alvarez 2844 1º A, C1425DHT Buenos Aires
Tel: (011) 4804-4147 *Fax:* (011) 4782-1836
E-mail: contactodelsigno@gmail.com
Web Site: www.edicionesdelsigno.com.ar
Key Personnel
Dir General: Beatriz Gercman
Founded: 1995
Subjects: Business, Communications, Education, Government, Political Science, History, Literature, Literary Criticism, Essays, Philosophy, Psychology, Psychiatry, Social Sciences, Sociology
ISBN Prefix(es): 978-987-96575; 978-987-98166

Sociedad Biblica Argentina+
Tucuman 352/58, G4230XAI Buenos Aires
Tel: (011) 4312-3400
E-mail: info@biblica.org; microcentro@biblica.org
Web Site: www.sba.org.ar; www.unitedbiblesocieties.org
Founded: 1966
Subjects: Biblical Studies
ISBN Prefix(es): 978-950-711; 978-950-99044
Branch Office(s)
Ave Rivadavia 3402, C1413AAT Buenos Aires
  Tel: (011) 4861-5589
Saavedra 44, B8000DDB Bahia Blanca
  Tel: (0291) 452-2020 *E-mail:* bahiablanca@biblica.org
Obispo Salguero 141, X5000IAC Cordoba
  Tel: (0351) 422-9014 *E-mail:* cordoba@biblica.org
Av Colon 3524, B7600FZP Mar del Plata
  Tel: (0223) 492-4862 *E-mail:* mardelplata@biblica.org
San Martin 2650, S3004CVJ Rosario, Santa Fe
  Tel: (0341) 607-2911 *E-mail:* rosario@biblica.org

Eduardo Sohns+
Dr Luis Belaustegui 1310, C1416CXR Buenos Aires
Tel: (011) 4585-2791 *Fax:* (011) 4585-2791
E-mail: info@eduardosohns.com.ar
Web Site: www.eduardosohns.com.ar
Key Personnel
Contact: Eduardo Sohns *E-mail:* eduardosohns@mail.com
Specialize in music editions, Renaissance music & choral/instrumental.
Subjects: Education, History, Music, Dance, Music Theory
ISBN Prefix(es): 978-987-97071

Editorial Stella
Viamonte 1984, C1056AAM Buenos Aires
Tel: (011) 4374-0346 *Fax:* (011) 4374-8719
Web Site: www.editorialstella.com.ar
Founded: 1941
Membership(s): Asociacion Educacionista Argentina.
Subjects: Education, Nonfiction (General), Religion - Catholic
ISBN Prefix(es): 978-950-525; 978-987-1004

Editorial Sudamericana SA+
Imprint of Penguin Random House Grupo Editorial
Humberto 1º 555, C1103ACK Buenos Aires
Tel: (011) 5235-4400; (011) 5235-4450
  Fax: (011) 5235-4468; (011) 5235-4407; (011) 5235-4451

E-mail: info@rhm.com.ar; aclientes@rhm.com.ar
Web Site: www.rhm.com.ar
Key Personnel
General Manager: Olaf Hantel
Publicity: Florencia Ure *E-mail:* fure@rhm.com.ar
Rights & Permissions: Susana Kaluzynski
Founded: 1939
Subjects: Biography, Memoirs, Fiction, History, Literature, Literary Criticism, Essays, Nonfiction (General), Philosophy, Psychology, Psychiatry
ISBN Prefix(es): 978-950-07; 978-950-37
Associate Companies: Penguin Random House Grupo Editorial, Merced Nº 280 piso 6 Centro, Santiago, Chile *Tel:* (02) 782 8200 *Fax:* (02) 782 8210 *E-mail:* editorial@rhm.cl *Web Site:* www.rhm.cl; Editorial Sudamericana Uraguaya, Yaguaron 1568, 11100 Montevideo, Uruguay *Tel:* 29013668 *E-mail:* ventas@rhm.com.uy
Subsidiaries: Editorial Sudamericana Chilena

Editorial Teseo
Tucuman 3350 PB A, 1189 Buenos Aires
E-mail: info@editorialteseo.com
Web Site: www.editorialteseo.com
Founded: 2007
Subjects: Agriculture, Anthropology, Archaeology, Biography, Memoirs, Communications, Education, Government, Political Science, Health, Nutrition, History, Law, Philosophy, Psychology, Psychiatry, Social Sciences, Sociology, Historical Archeology, International Relations, Nautilus, Public Health
ISBN Prefix(es): 978-987-1354

Ediciones Theoria SRL+
Av Rivadavia 1255, piso 4 407, G4230XAI Buenos Aires
Tel: (011) 4381-0131 *Fax:* (011) 4381-0131
Key Personnel
Mng Dir: Jorge O Orus
Founded: 1954
Subjects: Anthropology, Biography, Memoirs, Genealogy, Government, Political Science, History, Literature, Literary Criticism, Essays, Military Science, Religion - Catholic
ISBN Prefix(es): 978-950-99711; 978-987-9048

Editorial Troquel SA+
Olleros 1818, Depto I, C1426CRH Buenos Aires
Tel: (011) 4779-9444
E-mail: info@troquel.com.ar
Web Site: www.troquel.com.ar
Founded: 1954
Subjects: Education, History, Literature, Literary Criticism, Essays, Psychology, Psychiatry, Religion - Other, Technology
ISBN Prefix(es): 978-950-16

UNDAV Ediciones (Universidad Nacional de Avellaneda)
F Ameghino 838, 3 piso, Avellaneda, B1870CVR Buenos Aires
Tel: (011) 5436-7550
Web Site: ediciones.undav.edu.ar
Key Personnel
Publisher & Dir: Carlos Zelarayan
  E-mail: czelarayan@undav.edu.ar
Editorial Coordinator: Julia Aibar
  E-mail: jaibar@undav.edu.ar
Subjects: Environmental Studies, Labor, Industrial Relations, Sports, Athletics, Technology, Humanities
ISBN Prefix(es): 978-987-630

Ediciones UNGS, see Universidad Nacional de General Sarmiento (Ediciones UNGS)

UNIPE: Editorial Universitaria
Camino Centenario No 2565, entre 506 y 507, La Plata, B1897AVA Buenos Aires
Tel: (011) 48611963
E-mail: editorial.universitaria@unipe.edu.ar
Web Site: unipe.edu.ar
Key Personnel
Editorial Dir: Flavia Costa
Editorial Coordinator: Maria Teresa D'Meza
Founded: 2010
ISBN Prefix(es): 978-987-26468

Editorial de la Universidad de Tres de Febrero (EDUNTREF)
Mosconi 2736, B1674AHF Saenz Pena
Tel: (011) 4519-6010
E-mail: rectorado@untref.edu.ar
Web Site: www.untref.edu.ar
Subjects: Art, Business, Communications, Economics, Education, Government, Political Science, History, Law, Philosophy, Social Sciences, Sociology, Administration
ISBN Prefix(es): 978-987-1172; 978-987-20509; 978-987-98300

Universidad Nacional de Avellaneda, see UNDAV Ediciones (Universidad Nacional de Avellaneda)

Universidad Nacional de Cordoba-Editorial Universitaria
Pabellon Agustin Tosco, Primer piso, Ciudad Universitaria, X5000GYA Cordoba
Tel: (0351) 462-9526
E-mail: info@editorial.unc.edu.ar; editorial@editorial.unc.edu.ar
Web Site: editorial.unc.edu.ar
Key Personnel
Dir: Carlos Longhini
Founded: 2007
Subjects: Architecture & Interior Design, Art, History, Literature, Literary Criticism, Essays, Science (General), Social Sciences, Sociology, Natural Science
ISBN Prefix(es): 978-950-33

Editorial de la Universidad Nacional de Cuyo (EDIUNC)
Edificio CICUNC, planta baja, Centro Universitario, Universidad Nacional de Cuyo, M5502JMA Mendoza
Tel: (0261) 413 5202
E-mail: ediunc@uncu.edu.ar
Web Site: www.ediunc.uncu.edu.ar
Key Personnel
Editorial Management: Pilar Pineyrua
Administration: Sandra Nieto
Marketing: Sandra Xenia Bueno
Subjects: Art, Health, Nutrition, Science (General), Technology
ISBN Prefix(es): 978-950-39

Universidad Nacional de General Sarmiento (Ediciones UNGS)
Juan Maria Gutierrez 1150, Los Palvorines, B1613GSX Buenos Aires
Tel: (011) 4469-7578
E-mail: ediciones@ungs.edu.ar
Web Site: www.ungs.edu.ar/areas/publicaciones/n/.html
ISBN Prefix(es): 978-987-630; 978-987-574; 978-987-96252

Universidad Nacional de la Patagonia San Juan Bosco
Ciudad Universitaria, Km 4, 9005 Comodoro Rivadavia-Chubut
Tel: (0297) 4557453; (0297) 4557856 *Fax:* (0297) 4557453
E-mail: dzonal@unpata.edu.ar
Web Site: www.unp.edu.ar

Key Personnel
President: Alberto Cesar Ayape
Founded: 1993
Subjects: Agriculture, Biological Sciences, Fiction, Geography, Geology, History, Philosophy
ISBN Prefix(es): 978-950-763

Editorial de la Universidad Nacional de Lanus (EDUNLa)
Libreria Rodolfo Walsh, 29 de Septembre 3901, B1826GLC Remedios de Escalada, Lanus
Tel: (011) 5533-5600 (ext 5727)
E-mail: edunla@unla.edu.ar
Web Site: www.unla.edu.ar/index.php/ediciones-de-la-unla
Key Personnel
President: Hector Perillo
Vice President: Jorge Bragulat
Subjects: Art, Fiction, Social Sciences, Sociology, Humanities
ISBN Prefix(es): 978-987-1987; 978-987-1326
Number of titles published annually: 30 Print

Editorial de la Universidad Nacional de Mar del Plata (EUDEM)
Formosa 3485, Mar del Plata
E-mail: secretariaeudem@gmail.com
Web Site: www.eudem.mdp.edu.ar
Key Personnel
Dir: Prof Osvaldo Picardo
Founded: 1981
Subjects: Biography, Memoirs, Communications, Poetry
ISBN Prefix(es): 978-987-1371

Editorial Universidad Nacional de Quilmes
Roque Saenz Pena 352, Bernal, B1876BXD Buenos Aires
Tel: (011) 4365 7184 *Fax:* (011) 4365 7101
E-mail: editorial@unq.edu.ar
Web Site: www.unq.edu.ar
Key Personnel
Chief Executive Officer: Anna Monica Aguilar
   E-mail: anna.aguilar@unq.edu.ar
Editorial Dir: Rafael Centeno *E-mail:* rcenteno@unq.edu.ar
Administration: Amorina Albanese
   E-mail: amorina.albanese@unq.edu.ar
Founded: 1996
ISBN Prefix(es): 978-987-558; 978-987-9173

Universidad Nacional de San Martin, see UNSAM EDITA (Universidad Nacional de San Martin)

Universidad Nacional del Litoral
9 de Julio 3563, S3002EXA Santa Fe
Tel: (0342) 4571194 (ext 112); (0342) 4571194 (ext 103)
E-mail: editorial@unl.edu.ar
Web Site: www.unl.edu.ar/editorial
Subjects: Geography, Geology, History, Literature, Literary Criticism, Essays, Science (General), Technology
ISBN Prefix(es): 978-950-9840; 978-987-508

Universidad Nacional Rosario Editora, see UNR Editora

UNR Editora
Urquiza 2050, S2000A0B Rosario
Tel: (0341) 480 2687
E-mail: info-editora@unr.edu.ar
Web Site: www.unreditora.unr.edu.ar
Founded: 1989
ISBN Prefix(es): 978-87-702

UNSAM EDITA (Universidad Nacional de San Martin)
25 de Mayo 1779, B1650HMK San Martin, Buenos Aires
Tel: (011) 4512 6360
E-mail: unsamedita@unsam.edu.ar; prensaeditorial@unsam.edu.ar; ventas@unsam.edu.ar
Web Site: unsamedita.unsam.edu.ar
Key Personnel
Public Relations: Deborah Lapidus
Subjects: Art, Science (General), Social Sciences, Sociology, Technology, Humanities
ISBN Prefix(es): 978-987-1435

V & R Editoras SA
Demaraa 4412, C1425AEB Buenos Aires
Tel: (011) 4778-9444 *Fax:* (011) 4778-9444
E-mail: info@vreditoras.com
Web Site: www.vreditoras.com
Key Personnel
Chief Executive Officer: Maria Ines Redoni
Dir: Lidia Maria Riba; Trini Vergara
Founded: 1996
Subjects: Cookery, Fiction
ISBN Prefix(es): 978-987-9201; 978-987-9338; 978-987-95816
Branch Office(s)
Vergara & Riba Editoras Ltda, Rua Capital Federal, 263, Sumar, 01259-010 Sao Paulo-SP, Brazil *Tel:* (011) 4612-2866 *E-mail:* editoras@livropresente.com.br
Vergara & Riba Editoras SA de CV, Av Tamaulipas 145, Col Hipodromo Condesa, Delegacion Cuauhtemoc, 06170 Mexico, DF, Mexico *Tel:* (0155) 5211-5714; (0155) 5211-5415 *Toll Free Tel:* 01800-543-4995 *E-mail:* editoras@vergarariba.com.mx
Foreign Rep(s): Distribuidora America Latina (Uruguay); Libreria Artemis Edinter SA (Guatemala); Editoriales La Ceiba SA de CV (El Salvador); Desarrollos Culturales Costarricenses DCC SA (Costa Rica, Nicaragua); Fi-Rex 21 SL (Spain); Distribuciones Impart (Honduras); Distribuidora Inca SAC (Peru); JRBL Management (Puerto Rico); Lectorum Publications Inc (USA); Distribuidora Lewis SA (Panama); Litexsa Boliviana SRL (Bolivia); Editorial Oceano de Venezuela SA (Venezuela); Editorial Oceano Ecuatoriana SA (Ecuador); Quijote SRL (Paraguay); Ediciones Urano Colombia Ltda (Colombia); Empresa Editora Zig-Zag SA (Chile)

Valletta Ediciones SRL
Francisco Laprida 1780, Florida, Vicente Lopez, B1602EFF Buenos Aires
Tel: (011) 4796-5244; (011) 4718-1172
Fax: (011) 4796-5244; (011) 4718-1172
Web Site: vallettaediciones.com
Key Personnel
Dir General: Orlando Valletta
Founded: 1984
Membership(s): Camara Argentina del Libro.
Subjects: Economics, Law, Literature, Literary Criticism, Essays, Nonfiction (General)
ISBN Prefix(es): 978-950-743; 978-950-99209; 978-950-99599

Vergara+
Imprint of Ediciones B
Ave Paseo Colon 221 6° piso, C1063ACC Buenos Aires
Tel: (011) 4343-7510; (011) 4343-7706
Fax: (011) 4334-0173
E-mail: prensa@edicionesb.com.ar
Web Site: www.edicionesb.com.ar; www.edicionesb-argentina.com
Founded: 1975
Subjects: Biography, Memoirs, Fiction, History, Nonfiction (General), Self-Help, Women's Literature
ISBN Prefix(es): 978-950-15

Grupo Editorial Vestales
Cantilo 946, San Martin, Buenos Aires
Tel: (011) 4713 1606
E-mail: contacto@vestales.com.ar; distribucion@vestales.com.ar
Web Site: www.vestales.com.ar
Founded: 2006
Subjects: Mysteries, Suspense, Parapsychology, Romance, Anthologies, Historical Romance, Paranormal, Vampires, Women's Literature
ISBN Prefix(es): 978-987-21470
Distribution Center: Editorial Catalonia Ltda
   Tel: (02) 2099407 *Fax:* (02) 2255948
   E-mail: contacto@catalonia.cl (Chile)
Distribuciones Alfaomega SL *Tel:* 91 614 58 49 *Fax:* 91 618 40 12 *E-mail:* alfaomega@alfaomega.es (Spain)

Villa Maria University Press, see Eduvim

Victor P de Zavalia SA+
Alberti 835, C1223AAG Buenos Aires
Tel: (011) 4942-1274 *Fax:* (011) 4942-2421
E-mail: correo@zavalia.com.ar
Web Site: www.zavalia.com.ar
Key Personnel
Dir: Dr Ricardo de Zavalia
Founded: 1951
Subjects: Government, Political Science, Law, Politics
ISBN Prefix(es): 978-950-572

Editorial Zeus SRL+
San Lorenzo 1329, S2000ARM Rosario, Santa Fe
Tel: (0341) 449 5585 *Fax:* (0341) 425 4259
E-mail: zeus@zeus.com.ar
Web Site: www.zeus.com.ar
Key Personnel
Dir & Editor: Gustavo Luis Caviglia
   E-mail: gcaviglia@zeus.com.ar
Editorial Dir: Jorge Raul Murillo
Founded: 1970
Subjects: Law
ISBN Prefix(es): 978-950-664
Imprints: Coleccion Juridica Bco de Datos en Computacion

Libros del Zorzal
Tucuman 3350, PB A, C1189AAN Buenos Aires
E-mail: info@delzorzal.com.ar
Web Site: www.delzorzal.com
Key Personnel
Dir: Leopoldo Kulesz; Octavio Kulesz
Editorial: Carolina Uribe
Press: Carolina Salvini
Founded: 2000
Subjects: Education, Fiction, Government, Political Science, Language Arts, Linguistics, Literature, Literary Criticism, Essays, Mathematics, Philosophy, Psychoanalysis
ISBN Prefix(es): 978-987-1081; 978-987-599; 978-987-98068
Total Titles: 250 Print
Distributed by Galerna

Armenia

General Information

Capital: Yerevan
Language: Armenian (official) and Kurdish
Religion: Predominantly Christian (Armenian Apostolic Church)
Population: 3.4 million
Bank Hours: Generally open for short hours between 0930-1230 Monday-Friday
Shop Hours: Generally 0900-1800 Monday-Friday; often open weekends
Currency: 100 kopeks = 1 rubl

Export/Import Information: According to Ukrainian quotas and customs duties, companies engaged in trade should register with the Ukraine Ministry of Foreign Economic Relations. Licenses for export and import are also required for trade with Russia.

Ankyunacar Press
34-36, Babaian St, 0037 Yerevan
Tel: (010) 253784
E-mail: info@ankyunacar.com
Web Site: ankyunacar.com/booksfromarmenia; www.booksfromarmenia.com
Subjects: Archaeology, Fiction, Geography, Geology, Government, Political Science, History, Language Arts, Linguistics, Psychology, Psychiatry, Religion - Other, Science (General), Sports, Athletics, Folklore
ISBN Prefix(es): 978-99930-809; 978-99941-949; 978-99941-800

Antares Ltd
50a/1 Mashtots Ave, 0009 Yerevan
Tel: (010) 58 10 59; (010) 58 76 69; (010) 58 09 59; (010) 56 15 26 *Fax:* (010) 58 76 69
E-mail: antares@antares.am
Web Site: antares.am
Founded: 1992
Subjects: Art, Fiction, Literature, Literary Criticism, Essays, Poetry, Specialized Literature
ISBN Prefix(es): 978-99930-839; 978-99930-881; 978-99930-924; 978-99930-948; 978-99941-32; 978-99941-57; 978-9939-51
Parent Company: Antares Media Holding

Arevik Publishing House (Little Sun)+
Teryan St 91, 375009 Yerevan
Tel: (010) 524561 *Fax:* (010) 520536
E-mail: arevikbooks@gmail.com
Web Site: www.arevik.am
Key Personnel
Chairman: David Hovhannes
Dir: Sabet Hovhannisyan
Vice Dir: Smbat Gyurgyan *Tel:* (010) 520773
Founded: 1986
Subjects: Chemistry, Chemical Engineering, Crafts, Games, Hobbies, Education, English as a Second Language, Fiction, Gardening, Plants, Geography, Geology, History, Humor, Language Arts, Linguistics, Mathematics, Natural History, Poetry, Science Fiction, Fantasy
ISBN Prefix(es): 978-5-8077
Number of titles published annually: 28 Print
Total Titles: 2,000 Print

Collage Ltd
4 Sarian St, 0002 Yerevan
Tel: (010) 520217 *Fax:* (010) 584693
E-mail: collageltd@gmail.com
Web Site: collage.am
Founded: 1995

Edit Print Publishing House
12 Toumanyan, 375001 Yerevan
Tel: (010) 520 848; (010) 614 327 (sales)
Fax: (010) 543 620
E-mail: webshop@editprint.am
Web Site: www.editprint.am
Founded: 1993
Since establishment, over 3,000 books released & 2 popular magazines founded for primary & middle school-age children, *Happy train* & *My planet.* Leading Armenian publisher in the disciplines of education, children's, young adult & adult literature. Ebooks & ebook library. Publishing & printing activities. Participates & promotes reading competitions & literacy among the Armenian population.

Subjects: Art, Biography, Memoirs, Education, Fiction, Language Arts, Linguistics, Travel & Tourism, Foreign Languages
ISBN Prefix(es): 978-99930-821; 978-99930-876; 978-99930-935; 978-99930-950; 978-99941-36; 978-9939-52

Grakan Hayrenik CJSC+
28, Isahakyan St, 375009 Erevan
Tel: (010) 528520; (010) 524496 *Fax:* (010) 528520
Founded: 1921
Subjects: Agriculture, Government, Political Science, Law, Literature, Literary Criticism, Essays, Military Science, Science (General)
ISBN Prefix(es): 978-5-540

Lingua
42 Tumanyan St, 0002 Yerevan
Tel: (010) 530552
E-mail: info@brusov.am
Web Site: www.brusov.am
ISBN Prefix(es): 978-9939-56
Parent Company: Yerevan State Linguistic University (named after Valery Brusov)

RAU Publishing House
Hovsep Emin 123, 0051 Yerevan
Tel: (010) 27 70 52 (ext 112) *Fax:* (010) 27 70 52
E-mail: publish@rau.am
Web Site: www.rau.am
Key Personnel
Head, Publishing: Minasian Paruir Minasovich
Editor-in-Chief: Mariam Torgomyan
Translator & Editor: Alla Gevorkyan
  E-mail: webeditor@rau.am
Founded: 2002
ISBN Prefix(es): 978-99930-843; 978-99930-928; 978-99930-989; 978-99941-919; 978-99941-952; 978-99941-966
Total Titles: 120 Print
Parent Company: Russian Armenian (Slavonic) University

Zangak Publishing House
49/2 Komitas Ave, 375051 Yerevan
Tel: (010) 232528 *Fax:* (010) 232529
E-mail: info@zangak.am
Web Site: www.zangak.am
Key Personnel
President: Sokrat Mkrtchyan *E-mail:* sokrat@zangak.am
Mng Dir: Emin Mkrtchyan *E-mail:* emin@zangak.am
Founded: 1997
Subjects: Fiction, History, Psychology, Psychiatry, Ecology
ISBN Prefix(es): 978-99930-2; 978-99941-1

Australia

General Information

Capital: Canberra
Language: English
Religion: Predominantly Christian
Population: 22.5 million
Bank Hours: 1000-1500 Monday-Thursday; 1000-1700 Friday
Shop Hours: 0900-1700 Monday-Saturday
Currency: 100 cents = 1 Australian dollar
Export/Import Information: No tariffs on books. Most books, especially of literary or educational nature, free of sales tax. No import li-

censes for books; no seditious literature permitted.
Copyright: UCC, Berne (see Copyright Conventions, pg viii)

A K A Publishing Pty Ltd
46-58 Holt St, Surry Hills, NSW 2010
Toll Free Tel: 1300 697 867 *Toll Free Fax:* 1300 554 461
E-mail: admin@akapublishing.com.au
Web Site: akapublishing.com.au
Key Personnel
Editor-in-Chief: Graeme Brosnan
Subjects: Biography, Memoirs, Fiction, Nonfiction (General)
ISBN Prefix(es): 978-0-9752147; 978-0-9803494; 978-0-9804530; 978-0-9804531

A+A Publishing
Imprint of Art + Australia
234 St Kilda Rd, Southbank, Victoria 3006
Tel: (03) 9035 9463
E-mail: art-australia@unimelb.edu.au
Web Site: www.artandaustralia.com
Key Personnel
Mng Editor: Vikki McInnes *E-mail:* vmcinnes@unimelb.edu.au
Publisher of *Art + Australia* biannual journal.
Subjects: Art
ISBN Prefix(es): 978-0-9953925

ABARES, see Australian Bureau of Agricultural & Resource Economics (ABARES)

ABC Audiobooks, *imprint of* Bolinda Publishing Pty Ltd

ABC Books+
Level 8, Ultimo B, 700 Harris St, Ultimo, NSW 2007
Mailing Address: GPO Box 9994, Sydney, NSW 2001
Tel: (02) 8333 1500; (02) 8333 5666 (orders) *Toll Free Tel:* 1300 360 111 *Fax:* (02) 8333 1051; (02) 8333 5622 *Toll Free Fax:* 1300 360 150 (orders)
Web Site: abccommercial.com/abc-books; shop.abc.net.au
Subjects: Fiction, Nonfiction (General)
ISBN Prefix(es): 978-0-7333; 978-1-74086
Number of titles published annually: 180 Print; 50 Audio
Parent Company: ABC Commercial
Ultimate Parent Company: Australian Broadcasting Corp
Distributed by Allen & Unwin Pty Ltd
Orders to: Allen & Unwin Pty Ltd, 83 Alexander St, Crows Nest, NSW 2065 *Tel:* (02) 8425 0100 *Fax:* (02) 9906 2218

Aboriginal Studies Press+
Lawson Crescent, Canberra, ACT 2600
Tel: (02) 6246 1183 *Fax:* (02) 6261 4288
E-mail: asp@aiatsis.gov.au; commsmedia@aiatsis.gov.au; sales@aiatsis.gov.au
Web Site: www.aiatsis.gov.au
Key Personnel
Principal: Russell Taylor
Specialize in Australian indigenous cultures.
Subjects: Anthropology, Archaeology, Art, Biography, Memoirs, Education, Health, Nutrition, History, Language Arts, Linguistics, Music, Dance, Regional Interests, Social Sciences, Sociology, Women's Studies, Cultural Studies, Native Title/Land Rights
ISBN Prefix(es): 978-0-85575
Number of titles published annually: 8 Print; 5 E-Book

Total Titles: 120 Print
Parent Company: Australian Institute of Aboriginal & Torres Strait Islander Studies (AIATSIS), GPO Box 553, Canberra, ACT 2601

Academic Press, *imprint of* Elsevier Australia

ACE Open
Lion Arts Centre North Terrace (West End), Kaurna Yarta, Adelaide, SA 5000
Mailing Address: PO Box 10114, Kaurna Yarta, Adelaide, SA 5000
Tel: (08) 8211 7505
E-mail: admin@aceopen.art
Web Site: www.aceopen.art
Key Personnel
Chief Executive Officer: Liz Nowell
Founded: 2017
Publisher of art books & *Broadsheet Journal.*
Subjects: Art, Contemporary Art
ISBN Prefix(es): 978-0-9750239
Number of titles published annually: 6 Print

ACER Press+
19 Prospect Hill Rd, Private Bag 55, Camberwell, Victoria 3124
Tel: (03) 9277 5555; (03) 9277 5447
Toll Free Tel: 1800 338 402 *Fax:* (03) 9277 5500; (03) 9277 5499
E-mail: sales@acer.edu.au
Web Site: www.acer.edu.au/publications/press-education
Key Personnel
General Manager: Annemarie Rolls
Publishing Manager: Steve Holden
Mng Editor: Debbie Lee
Founded: 1930
Subjects: Behavioral Sciences, Career Development, Disability, Special Needs, Education, Human Relations, Psychology, Psychiatry, Self-Help, Parenting
ISBN Prefix(es): 978-0-86431; 978-0-85563; 978-1-74286
Foreign Rep(s): Eurospan Group (Europe, Middle East, North Africa); Ingenio (Southeast Asia); ISBS (North America); South Pacific Books (New Zealand)

ACHPER (The Australian Council for Health, Physical Education & Recreation Inc)
184a Grange Rd, Flinders Park, SA 5025
Tel: (08) 8352 3288 *Fax:* (08) 8352 4099
E-mail: custserv@achper.org.au; membership@achper.org.au
Web Site: www.achper.org.au
Key Personnel
National Executive Dir: Alison Turner
E-mail: alison.turner@achper.org.au
Event & Communications Coordinator: Chelsea Modra *E-mail:* chelsea.modra@achper.org.au
Finance Officer: Lorraine Ottanelli
E-mail: lorraine.ottanelli@achper.org.au
Founded: 1955
Specialize in community fitness & movement sciences, dance, health education, physical education, recreation & sports.
Also publish subscription & mail order books.
Subjects: Education, Health, Nutrition, Outdoor Recreation, Sports, Athletics
ISBN Prefix(es): 978-1-86352; 978-0-9871109
Branch Office(s)
105 King William St, Kent Town, SA 5067, Executive Dir: Matt Schmidt *Tel:* (08) 8363 5700 *Fax:* (08) 8362 9800 *E-mail:* info@achpersa.com.au *Web Site:* www.achpersa.com.au
PO Box 58, Belmore, NSW 2192, Executive Officer: Julie Percival *Tel:* (02) 9787 5142 *Fax:* (02) 9572 8603 *E-mail:* julie@achper.com.au *Web Site:* www.achpernsw.com.au
PO Box 2331, Darwin, NT 0801, Executive Officer: Jac Stirrat *Tel:* (08) 8999 4252 *Fax:* (08)

8999 4222 *E-mail:* achper.nt@gmail.com *Web Site:* www.achpernt.com.au
Sports House South, 14/866 Main St, Woolloongabba, Qld 4102, Executive Officer: Linda Marsden *Tel:* (07) 3895 8383 *Fax:* (07) 3895 8166 *E-mail:* executiveofficer@achperqld.org.au *Web Site:* www.achperqld.org.au
PO Box 454, Devonport, Tas 7310, Secretary: Angela Sheahen *E-mail:* achpertas@gmail.com *Web Site:* www.achpertas.org.au
Suite 1, 651 Victoria St, Abbotsford, Victoria 3067, Chief Executive Officer: Hilary Shelton *Tel:* (03) 9274 8900 *Fax:* (03) 9429 4176 *E-mail:* achper@achper.vic.edu.au *Web Site:* www.achper.vic.edu.au
PO Box 57, Claremont, WA 6010, Executive Officer: Denyse Passmore *Tel:* (04) 6610 0049 *E-mail:* info@achperwa.asn.au *Web Site:* www.achperwa.asn.au
Bookshop(s): Healthy Lifestyles Bookshop *E-mail:* sales@healthylifestylesbookshop.com.au *Web Site:* www.healthylifestylesbookshop.com.au

ACMA, see Australian Communications & Media Authority (ACMA)

Acorns, *imprint of* Pearson Library

ACP Books, see ACP Publishing Pty Ltd

ACP Publishing Pty Ltd+
54 Park St, Level 1, Sydney, NSW 2000
Mailing Address: GPO Box 4088, Sydney, NSW 2001
Tel: (02) 9282 8618 *Fax:* (02) 9126 3702
E-mail: acpbooks@acpmagazines.com.au
Web Site: www.acpbooks.com.au; www.acpmagazines.com.au
Key Personnel
General Manager: Christine Whiston
Tel: (02) 9282 8863 *Fax:* (02) 9267 9438 *E-mail:* cwhiston@acpmagazines.com.au
Editor-in-Chief: Susan Tomnay *Tel:* (02) 9282 8685 *Fax:* (02) 9267 9438 *E-mail:* stomnay@acpmagazines.com.au
Dir, Sales & Rights: Brian Cearnes *Tel:* (02) 9282 8414 *Fax:* (02) 9267 9438 *E-mail:* bcearnes@acpmagazines.com.au
Marketing Manager: Bridget Cody *Tel:* (02) 9282 8552 *Fax:* (02) 9267 9438 *E-mail:* bcody@acpmagazines.com.au
Production Manager: Victoria Jefferys *Tel:* (02) 9282 8916 *Fax:* (02) 9267 9438 *E-mail:* vjefferys@acpmagazines.com.au
Subjects: Cookery
ISBN Prefix(es): 978-0-949892; 978-1-86396; 978-0-949128; 978-1-74245
Distribution Center: Network Services Co (Australia) *Toll Free Tel:* 1300 131 169 *Toll Free Fax:* 1300 360 165 *E-mail:* networkcontactus@networkservicecompany.com.au *Web Site:* www.netonline.com.au
Pansing IMM Pty Ltd, Unit 9, Discovery Cove, 1801 Botany Rd, Bandsmeadow, NSW 2019 *Tel:* (012) 8304 5902 *Fax:* (012) 9666 7843 *E-mail:* natasha@pansingimm.com *Web Site:* www.pansingimm.com
Double & Newman Pty Ltd, 171 Pittwater Rd, Hunters Hill, NSW 2110 *Tel:* (02) 9879 7891 *E-mail:* bembo@bigpond.com (Asia)
Random House Australia, Level 3, 100 Pacific Highway, North Sydney, NSW 2060 *Tel:* (02) 9954 9966 *Fax:* (02) 9954 4562 *E-mail:* random@randomhouse.com.au *Web Site:* www.randomhouse.com.au
Southern Publishers Group, c/o Bookreps NZ Ltd, Unit 2/39, Woodside Ave, Northcote, Auckland, New Zealand *Tel:* (09) 419 2635 *Fax:* (09) 419 2634 *E-mail:* hub@spg.co.nz
Netlink Distribution Co, ACP Media Centre, Corner of Fanshawe & Beaumont Sts, Westhaven,

Auckland, New Zealand *Tel:* (09) 366 9966 *Toll Free Fax:* 0800 277 412 *E-mail:* ask@ndc.co.nz
PSD Promotions, PO Box 1175 Isando, 1600 Guateng, Johannesburg, South Africa *Tel:* (011) 392 6065; (011) 392 6066; (011) 392 6067 *Fax:* (011) 392 6079; (011) 392 6080 *Web Site:* www.psdpromotions.com

Aeolian Press
22 Brassey St, Swanbourne, WA 6010
Founded: 1985
Subjects: Art, Poetry, Australian Art, Italian Classic Text & Illustration
ISBN Prefix(es): 978-1-875306
Distributor for Edizioni Tallone (Australia only); Edizioni Valdonega (Australia only)

Affirm Press
28 Thistlethwaite St, South Melbourne, Victoria 3205
Tel: (03) 8695 9623 *Fax:* (03) 8256 0114
E-mail: info@affirmpress.com.au
Web Site: affirmpress.com.au
Key Personnel
Publisher: Martin Hughes
Associate Publisher: Rebecca Starford
Sales & Marketing Dir: Keiran Rogers *Tel:* (03) 8695 9639 *E-mail:* keiran.rogers@affirmpress.com.au
Publicity & Marketing Manager: Grace Breen *Tel:* (03) 8695 9619 *E-mail:* grace.breen@affirmpress.com.au
Founded: 2007
Subjects: Fiction, Nonfiction (General)
ISBN Prefix(es): 978-0-9803746; 978-0-9806378; 978-0-9807904
Distributed by Hardie Grant Books
Foreign Rights: Kaplan/DeFiore Rights (worldwide)
Distribution Center: United Book Distributors *Tel:* (03) 8537 4400 *Fax:* (03) 8537 4497 *E-mail:* orders@unitedbookdistributors.com.au

Affirmations Australia Pty Ltd
34 Hyde St, Bellingen, NSW 2454
Mailing Address: PO Box 189, Bellingen, NSW 2454
Tel: (02) 6655 2350 *Toll Free Tel:* 0800 222 254 *Fax:* (02) 6655 2634
E-mail: sales@affirmations.com.au
Web Site: affirmations.com.au
Key Personnel
Principal: Dan Maher *E-mail:* dan@affirmations.com.au; Suzi Maher
Founded: 1988
Subjects: Inspirational, Spirituality, Motivational
ISBN Prefix(es): 978-0-9757703; 978-0-9804060; 978-0-9805377; 978-0-9808150
Branch Office(s)
2 Rugby Rd, PO Box 34388, Birkenhead, Auckland 0726, New Zealand, Contact: Alison Shepherd *Tel:* (09) 419 6988 *Toll Free Tel:* 0800 444 224 *Fax:* (09) 419 0976 *E-mail:* sales@affirmations.co.nz

AIFS, see Australian Institute of Family Studies (AIFS)

Aladdin, *imprint of* Simon & Schuster (Australia) Pty Ltd

Aletheia Publishing
Box 641, Albany Creek, Qld 4035
Web Site: www.defenceofthefaith.org
Key Personnel
Contact: David Holden
Founded: 1992
Subjects: Biblical Studies, Religion - Protestant, Theology
ISBN Prefix(es): 978-0-9578052
Total Titles: 3 Print

Alicat Publishing
16 Sandilands St, South Melbourne, Victoria 3205
Tel: (03) 9188 3650
E-mail: publishing@alicat.com.au
Web Site: www.alicat.com.au
Key Personnel
Chief Executive Officer: David Horgan
 E-mail: david@alicat.com.au
Chief Financial Officer: Alan Reynolds
 E-mail: alan@alicat.com.au
Publisher: Ali Horgan *E-mail:* ali@alicat.com.au
ISBN Prefix(es): 978-1-921708; 978-1-921847;
 978-1-921969; 978-1-74340

Allen & Unwin+
83 Alexander St, Crows Nest, NSW 2065
Mailing Address: PO Box 8500, St Leonards,
 NSW 1590
Tel: (02) 8425 0100 *Fax:* (02) 9906 2218
E-mail: vogel@allenandunwin.com;
 internationalsales@allenandunwin.com
Web Site: www.allenandunwin.com
Key Personnel
Executive Chairman: Patrick Gallagher
Chief Executive Officer: Robert Gorman
Executive Dir: Paul Donovan
Children's Publisher: Erica Wagner
Academic & Digital Publishing Dir: Elizabeth
 Weiss
Children's Books Dir: Liz Bray
Children's Rights Dir: Angela Namoi
Editorial Dir: Rebecca Kaiser
Finance & Administration Dir: David Martin
Production Dir: Lou Playfair
Publicity Dir: Andy Palmer
Trade Marketing Dir: Karen Williams
Professional & Reference Manager: Fiona Wilson
Rights Manager: Wenona Byrne
Founded: 1976
Membership(s): Australian Multimedia Industry
 Association (AMIA); Australian Publishers As-
 sociation (APA); Publish Australia (PA).
Subjects: Alternative, Art, Asian Studies, Behav-
 ioral Sciences, Biography, Memoirs, Business,
 Cookery, Earth Sciences, Economics, Educa-
 tion, Ethnicity, Fiction, Government, Political
 Science, Health, Nutrition, History, Labor, In-
 dustrial Relations, LGBTQ, Literature, Literary
 Criticism, Essays, Natural History, Nonfiction
 (General), Science (General)
ISBN Prefix(es): 978-1-86448; 978-1-86508; 978-
 1-74114
Number of titles published annually: 250 Print
Imprints: Arena; Crows Nest; Inspired Living;
 Jacana Books; Murdoch Books
Branch Office(s)
406 Albert St, East Melbourne, Victoria 3002
 Tel: (03) 9665 5000 *Fax:* (03) 9665 5050
HB Bldg, Off 3, Level 3, 228 Queen St, Auck-
 land, New Zealand *Tel:* (09) 377 3800
 Fax: (09) 377 3811
Ormond House, 26-27 Boswell St, London
 WC1N 3JZ, United Kingdom *Tel:* (020) 7269
 1610 *E-mail:* uk@allenandunwin.com
Distributed by ADP Singapore Pte Ltd (Singa-
 pore, Malaysia, Indonesia, Thailand, Philip-
 pines, Vietnam); Asia Publishers Services
 (Hong Kong, Korea, Taiwan & People's Re-
 public of China); Independent Publisher's
 Group (USA & Canada trade); Francis Lin-
 coln Publishers Ltd (UK & Europe children's);
 Roundhouse Group (UK & Europe); Viva
 Books Pvt Ltd (Bangladesh, India, Pakistan
 & Sri Lanka); Wild Dog Press (South Africa)
Distributor for A&C Black; Atlantic Books;
 Bloomsbury; Nicholas Brealey; Corvus; Faber
 & Faber; Granta; Icon Books; Murdoch Books;
 Nosy Crow; Portobello; Profile; Quarto Group
 (Australia & New Zealand); Serpent's Tail;
 Short Books; V&A
Foreign Rights: Ia Atterholm Agency (Scandi-
 navia); Authors Rights Agency (Russia); Bar-
 don Chinese Media Agency (China, Taiwan);

Bernabo (Italy); Bookcosmos Agency (Korea);
Lora Fountain & Associates (France); Agencja
Literacka Graal (Poland); The Deborah Harris
Agency (Israel); InterAustralia/The Choice-
maker Korea Co (Korea); International Editors
Co (Argentina, Brazil, Portugal, Spain); Japan
UNI (Japan); Maxima Creative Agency (In-
donesia); Mo Literary Services (Netherlands);
Mohrbooks AG Literary Agency (Germany);
NIKA Literary Agency (Bulgaria); OA Liter-
ary Agency (Greece); Kristin Olson Literary
Agency SRO (Czechia); Plima Literary Agency
(Albania, Bosnia and Herzegovina, Bulgaria,
Croatia, Greece, Kosovo, Macedonia, Montene-
gro, Romania, Serbia, Slovenia); Miles Stott
Literary Agency (UK)
Distribution Center: United Book Distributors
 (UBD), 30 Centre Rd, Scoresby, Victoria 3179
 Tel: (03) 9811 2555 *Fax:* (03) 9811 2403

AMCS, see Australian Marine Conservation
Society Inc (AMCS)

AMPCo, see Australasian Medical Publishing Co
Pty Ltd (AMPCo)

Anchor, *imprint of* Random House Books
 Australia, A Penguin Random House Company

Anchor Books Australia
PO Box 4, Spit Junction, NSW 2088
E-mail: sales@anchorbooksaustralia.com.au
Web Site: www.anchorbooksaustralia.com.au
Subjects: History, Nonfiction (General), Colonial
 History
ISBN Prefix(es): 978-0-9803354

Michelle Anderson Publishing+
PO Box 6032, Chapel St North, South Yarra, Vic-
 toria 3141
Tel: (03) 9826 9028 *Fax:* (03) 9826 8552
E-mail: mapubl@bigpond.net.au
Web Site: www.michelleandersonpublishing.com
Key Personnel
Publisher, Rights & Permissions: Michelle Ander-
 son
Founded: 1965
Membership(s): Australian Publishers Association
 (APA).
Subjects: Health, Nutrition, Medicine, Nursing,
 Dentistry, Philosophy, Psychology, Psychiatry
ISBN Prefix(es): 978-0-85572
Number of titles published annually: 15 Print
Total Titles: 70 Print
Distributed by Deep Books UK (UK)

Anderson Press, *imprint of* Random House
 Books Australia, A Penguin Random House
 Company

Anglican Press Australia, *imprint of* Youthworks

**ANZAC Day Commemoration Committee Inc
(Queensland)**
21 Wolverhampton St, Stafford, Qld 4053
Mailing Address: PO Box 3246, Stafford, Qld
 4053
Tel: (07) 3263 7118 *Fax:* (07) 3175 0608
E-mail: office.adcc@anzacday.org.au
Web Site: anzacday.org.au
Key Personnel
Publications Officer: Peter Collins
Subjects: Education, History
ISBN Prefix(es): 978-0-9577957; 978-0-9580273;
 978-0-9581625; 978-0-9804480; 978-0-
 9757123

Apace WA
One Johannah St, North Fremantle, WA 6159
Tel: (08) 9336 1262 *Fax:* (08) 9430 5729

E-mail: admin@apacewa.org.au; apace@apacewa.
 org.au
Web Site: www.apacewa.org.au
Key Personnel
Coordinator: Tony Freeman
Founded: 1983
Not-for-profit environmental community group.
Subjects: Alternative, Environmental Studies,
 Technology, Appropriate Technology, Bush
 Regeneration, Revegetation
ISBN Prefix(es): 978-0-9590309
Number of titles published annually: 5 Print

Aquila Press, *imprint of* Youthworks

Arcadia, *imprint of* Australian Scholarly
 Publishing Pty Ltd (ASP)

Archaeological Publications Inc+
PO Box 216, Caulfield South, Victoria 3162
Tel: (03) 9523 0549 *Fax:* (03) 9523 0549
E-mail: robertbednarik@hotmail.com
Web Site: www.ifrao.com/robert-g-bednarik/;
 semioticon.com/pool/robert-g-bednarik/
Key Personnel
Mng Dir: Robert G Bednarik
Founded: 1983
Books, periodicals, academic textbooks & confer-
 ence proceedings.
Subjects: Anthropology, Archaeology, Art
ISBN Prefix(es): 978-0-9586802
Number of titles published annually: 4 Print
Distributed by ANH Publications (Australia);
 Piedra Pintada Books (USA)

Arena, *imprint of* Allen & Unwin

Argyle-Pacific, *imprint of* Austed Publishing Co

Arrow, *imprint of* Random House Books
 Australia, A Penguin Random House Company

Art Gallery of New South Wales
Art Gallery Rd, The Domain, Sydney, NSW 2000
Tel: (02) 9225 1744; (02) 9225 1718 (shop)
 Toll Free Tel: 1800-NSW-ART (679 278)
 Fax: (02) 9225 1701; (02) 9225 1630 (shop)
E-mail: artmail@ag.nsw.gov.au; galleryshop@ag.
 nsw.gov.au
Web Site: www.artgallery.nsw.gov.au
Subjects: Architecture & Interior Design, Art,
 Fashion, Photography
ISBN Prefix(es): 978-0-7347; 978-1-74174

Art Gallery of Western Australia+
Perth Cultural Centre, Perth, WA 6000
Mailing Address: Perth Business Centre, PO Box
 8363, Perth, WA 6849
Tel: (08) 9492 6600 *Fax:* (08) 9492 6655
E-mail: admin@artgallery.wa.gov.au
Web Site: www.artgallery.wa.gov.au
Key Personnel
Dir: Dr Stefano Carboni
Deputy Dir & Chief Operating Officer: Brian
 Stewart
Founded: 1895
Exhibition catalogues.
Subjects: Art
ISBN Prefix(es): 978-0-7309; 978-0-7244; 978-0-
 7307
Total Titles: 22 Print

Art on the Move
71 Boulder Rd, Malaga, WA 6090
Mailing Address: Malaga LPO, PO Box 1731,
 Malaga, WA 6944
Tel: (08) 9249 3479 *Fax:* (08) 9248 3698
E-mail: artmoves@artonthemove.com.au
Web Site: www.artonthemove.com.au
Key Personnel
Executive Dir: Paul Thompson

Founded: 1986
Subjects: Architecture & Interior Design, Art, Marketing
ISBN Prefix(es): 978-0-9585326; 978-0-9578242; 978-0-9581859

Artand Publishing Pty Ltd+
PO Box 1074, Double Bay, Sydney, NSW 2028
Tel: (02) 9328 5222
E-mail: projects@artandfoundation.com
Web Site: www.artandfoundation.com
Key Personnel
Chairman & Publisher: Eleonora Triguboff
Subjects: Art
ISBN Prefix(es): 978-0-9943535
Imprints: Dott Publishing

Artists Associated Pty Ltd, see Boolarong Press

Artmoves Inc+
27 Burwood Ave, Hawthorn East, Victoria 3123
Tel: (03) 9882 8116
E-mail: artmoves@bigpond.com
Key Personnel
Dir: Helen Vivian
Founded: 1987
Subjects: Art, History, Women's Studies

Arts Centre Melbourne
100 St Kilda Rd, Melbourne, Victoria 3004
Mailing Address: PO Box 7585, Melbourne, Victoria 8004
Tel: (03) 9281 8000 *Toll Free Tel:* 1300 182 183
Fax: (03) 9281 8282
E-mail: info@artscentremelbourne.com.au
Web Site: www.artscentremelbourne.com.au
Key Personnel
Chief Executive: Judith Isherwood
Marketing & Communications: Melindy Green
Subjects: Art, Drama, Theater, Music, Dance
ISBN Prefix(es): 978-0-7241

Ashling Books+
26 Hewlett Circuit, Florey, ACT 2615
Tel: (02) 6259 1027
Key Personnel
Mng Dir & International Rights: Edward J Murtagh
Founded: 1992
Subjects: Fiction, How-to, Poetry, Religion - Catholic, Self-Help
ISBN Prefix(es): 978-0-9585244

ASP, see Australian Scholarly Publishing Pty Ltd (ASP)

ATF Asia, *imprint of* ATF Press

ATF Press
Imprint of ATF Ltd & the ATF Literary Fund
Level 1, 26 Moore St, Adelaide, SA 5000
Mailing Address: PO Box 504, Hindmarsh, SA 5007
Tel: (08) 8232 2093 *Fax:* (08) 8223 5643
Web Site: atfpress.com
Key Personnel
Executive Officer: Mr Hilary Regan
General Editor: Dr Alan Cadwallader
Membership(s): Australian Publishers Association (APA).
Subjects: Theology
ISBN Prefix(es): 978-0-9586399; 978-1-920691; 978-1-921511; 978-1-922239; 978-1-921816 (ATF Asia); 978-1-921817 (ATF Theology)
Imprints: ATF Asia; ATF Theology

ATF Theology, *imprint of* ATF Press

Atheneum Books for Young Readers, *imprint of* Simon & Schuster (Australia) Pty Ltd

Atria Books, *imprint of* Simon & Schuster (Australia) Pty Ltd

AURA, see Archaeological Publications Inc

AuSIL, see Australian Society for Indigenous Languages Inc

Ausmed Education Pty Ltd+
275-277 Mount Alexander Rd, Ascot Vale, Victoria 3032
Mailing Address: PO Box 4086, Melbourne University, Parkville, Victoria 3052
Tel: (03) 9326 8101 *Fax:* (03) 9326 8179
E-mail: ausmed@ausmed.com.au
Web Site: www.ausmed.com.au
Key Personnel
Chief Executive Officer, Publisher & Commissioning Editor: Cynthea Wellings
E-mail: cwelling@ausmed.com.au
General Manager: Natalie Angove
E-mail: nangove@ausmed.com.au
Founded: 1987
Specialize in books & conferences for nurses & other workers in related health fields.
Subjects: Behavioral Sciences, Ethnicity, Health, Nutrition, Medicine, Nursing, Dentistry, Social Sciences, Sociology, Allied Health, Clinical Issues
ISBN Prefix(es): 978-0-9587171; 978-0-9577988; 978-0-9750445; 978-0-9579876; 978-0-9751585; 978-0-9752018; 978-0-9803662
Total Titles: 24 Print
Orders to: Trans Middle East International Distribution Co Ltd, Jordan Trade Center, Queen Rania Al-Abdullah St, PO Box 2376, Amman 11953, Jordan *Tel:* (06) 5153467 *Fax:* (06) 5153472 *E-mail:* info@kasha.cc *Web Site:* www.kashaonline.com (Middle East)
Medical Books (NZ) Ltd, Symonds St, PO Box 8565, Auckland 1150, New Zealand *Tel:* (09) 3733772 *Fax:* (09) 3733282 *E-mail:* medbooks@iprolink.co.nz *Web Site:* www.medical-books.co.nz (New Zealand)
ChoiceTEXTS (Asia) Pte Ltd, 7 Kampong Bahru Rd 123, Singapore 169342, Singapore, Contact: Phillip Ang *Tel:* 6324 3616 *Fax:* 6324 5669 *E-mail:* phillip_ang@choicetexts.com.sg *Web Site:* choicetexts.com.sg (Asia)
Baker & Taylor Publisher Services, 30 Amberwood Parkway, Ashland, OH 44805, United States *Tel:* 567-215-0030 *E-mail:* info@btpubservices.com *Web Site:* www.btpubservices.com (USA)

Aussie Books
Division of Treasure Enterprises of Australia
Unit 6/30 Lensworth St, Coopers Plains, Qld 4108
Mailing Address: PO Box 383, Archerfield, Qld 4108
Tel: (07) 3345 4253 *Fax:* (07) 3344 1582
E-mail: sildale@yahoo.com
Web Site: www.treasureenterprises.com
Key Personnel
Dir: David A Cooper
Founded: 1988
Subjects: Earth Sciences, Geography, Geology, History
ISBN Prefix(es): 978-0-947336
Ultimate Parent Company: Sildale Pty Ltd
Distributor for Hesperian Press

Austed Publishing Co+
PO Box 8025, Subiaco East, WA 6008
Tel: (08) 9203 6044 *Fax:* (08) 9203 6055
E-mail: admin@austed.com.au
Web Site: www.austed.com.au

Founded: 1983
Subjects: Accounting, Animals, Pets, Education, Fiction, Mathematics, Nonfiction (General)
ISBN Prefix(es): 978-1-86307; 978-0-9592597
Imprints: Argyle-Pacific; Churchill House

Australasian Medical Publishing Co Pty Ltd (AMPCo)+
Subsidiary of Australian Medical Association
AMPCo House, 277 Clarence St, Sydney, NSW 2000
Mailing Address: Locked Bag 3030, Strawberry Hills, NSW 2012
Tel: (02) 9562 6666 *Fax:* (02) 9562 6600
E-mail: sales@ampco.com.au
Web Site: www.ampco.com.au
Key Personnel
Publishing Dir: Catherine Godfrey
Commercial Manager: Delores D'Costa
Digital Media Manager: Peter Rodrigues
Sales & Marketing Manager: David Kelly
Founded: 1914
Publisher & distributor of medical publications. Also publishes *The Medical Journal of Australia & Medical Directory of Australia.*
Subjects: History, Medicine, Nursing, Dentistry
ISBN Prefix(es): 978-0-85557

Australian Academic Press+
32 Jeays St, Bowen Hills, Qld 4006
Tel: (07) 3257 1176 *Fax:* (07) 3252 5908
E-mail: aap@australianacademicpress.com.au
Web Site: www.australianacademicpress.com.au
Key Personnel
Owner, Editor & Publisher: Stephen May
Marketing & Sales Manager: Amanda Hearn
Rights & Journal Sales Manager: Karita Guiney
Founded: 1987
Specialize in book production; also book packager. Academic publisher for the behavioral sciences.
Membership(s): The Association of Learned and Professional Society Publishers (ALPSP).
Subjects: Behavioral Sciences, Psychology, Psychiatry, Social Sciences, Sociology
ISBN Prefix(es): 978-1-875378; 978-1-921513

Australian Academy of Science
Ian Potter House, Gordon St, Canberra, ACT 2601
Mailing Address: GPO Box 783, Canberra, ACT 2601
Tel: (02) 6201 9400 *Fax:* (02) 6201 9494
E-mail: eb@science.org.au; aas@science.org.au
Web Site: www.science.org.au
Founded: 1956
Subjects: Biological Sciences, Chemistry, Chemical Engineering, Environmental Studies, Geography, Geology, Mathematics
ISBN Prefix(es): 978-0-85847

Australian Bureau of Agricultural & Resource Economics (ABARES)
18 Marcus Clarke St, Canberra, ACT 2601
Mailing Address: GPO Box 858, Canberra, ACT 2601
Tel: (02) 6272 2000 *Fax:* (02) 6272 2104
Web Site: www.agriculture.gov.au/abares
Key Personnel
Executive Dir: Karen Schneider *Tel:* (02) 6272 4636
Founded: 1992
Research arm of the Australian Government Department of Agriculture & Water Resources.
Subjects: Agriculture, Biological Sciences, Science (General), Veterinary Science
ISBN Prefix(es): 978-0-9750443; 978-1-921192; 978-1-920925; 978-1-921448; 978-1-74323

Australian Chart Book Pty Ltd
PO Box 148, Turramurra, NSW 2074
Tel: (02) 9489 4786 *Fax:* (02) 9487 2089
Web Site: www.austchartbook.com.au

Key Personnel
Contact: David Kent *E-mail:* davidkent@bigpond.com
Founded: 1970
Publisher of Australian chart books, historical reference books based on Australia's National Charts of singles & albums.
This publisher has indicated that 100% of their product line is author subsidized.
Subjects: History, Music, Dance
Total Titles: 5 Print

Australian Communications & Media Authority (ACMA)
Level 5, The Bay Centre, 65 Pirrama Rd, Pyrmont, NSW 2009
Mailing Address: PO Box Q500, Queen Victoria Bldg, Sydney, NSW 1230
Tel: (02) 9334 7700 *Fax:* (02) 9334 7799
Web Site: www.acma.gov.au
Key Personnel
Chairman: Chris Chapman *E-mail:* chris.chapman@acma.gov.au
Deputy Chair: Richard Bean
Media Manager: Emma Rossi *Tel:* (02) 9334 7719 *E-mail:* emma.rossi@acma.gov.au
Founded: 1992
Subjects: Communications, Broadcasting
Branch Office(s)
Purple Bldg, Benjamin Offices, Chan St, PO Box 78, Belconnen, ACT 2616 *Tel:* (02) 6219 5555 *Fax:* (02) 6219 5353
Level 44, Melbourne Central Tower, 360 Elizabeth St, PO Box 13112, Melbourne, Victoria 3000 *Tel:* (03) 9963 6800 *Fax:* (03) 9963 6899

Australian Council for Education Research, see ACER Press

The Australian Council for Health, Physical Education & Recreation Inc, see ACHPER (The Australian Council for Health, Physical Education & Recreation Inc)

Australian Film Television & Radio School
The Entertainment Quarter, Bldg 130, Moore Park, NSW 2021
Mailing Address: PO Box 2286, Strawberry Hills, NSW 2012
Tel: (02) 9805 6611 *Toll Free Tel:* 1300 13 14 61 *Fax:* (02) 9887 1030
E-mail: info@aftrs.edu.au; infonsw@aftrs.edu.au
Web Site: www.aftrs.edu.au
Key Personnel
Chief Executive Officer: Sandra Levy *Tel:* (02) 9805 6410
Founded: 1973
Subjects: Film, Video, Radio, TV
ISBN Prefix(es): 978-1-876351

Australian Institute of Criminology
74 Leichhardt St, Griffith, ACT 2603
Mailing Address: GPO Box 2944, Canberra, ACT 2601
Tel: (02) 6260 9200; (02) 6260 9221 (orders) *Fax:* (02) 6260 9201; (02) 6260 9299 (orders)
E-mail: aicpress@aic.gov.au
Web Site: www.aic.gov.au
Key Personnel
Dir: Adam Tomison *Fax:* (02) 6260 9205 *E-mail:* adam.tomison@aic.gov.au
Deputy Dir, Research: Rick Brown *Tel:* (02) 6260 9231
Communications Manager: Colin Campbell *Tel:* (02) 6260 9244
Research Manager: Laura Beacroft *Tel:* (02) 6260 9254; Peter Homel; Russell Smith *E-mail:* russell.smith@aic.gov.au
Founded: 1973
Subjects: Criminology, Law

ISBN Prefix(es): 978-1-921185; 978-1-921532; 978-1-922009
Number of titles published annually: 25 Print; 75 Online

Australian Institute of Family Studies (AIFS)
485 La Trobe St, Level 20, South Tower, Melbourne, Victoria 3000
Tel: (03) 9214 7888 *Fax:* (03) 9214 7839
E-mail: publications@aifs.gov.au
Web Site: www.aifs.gov.au
Key Personnel
Dir: Prof Alan Hayes
Founded: 1980
Undertake research & factors affecting family stability & well-being; Australian government statutory authority.
Subjects: Behavioral Sciences, Criminology, Disability, Special Needs, Economics, Human Relations, Social Sciences, Sociology, Women's Studies
ISBN Prefix(es): 978-1-876513
Number of titles published annually: 3 Print; 1 CD-ROM
Total Titles: 12 Print; 4 CD-ROM

Australian Marine Conservation Society Inc (AMCS)
Level 4/145 Melbourne St, South Brisbane, Qld 4101
Mailing Address: PO Box 5815, West End, Qld 4101
Tel: (07) 3846 6777 *Toll Free Tel:* 1800 066 299 *Fax:* (07) 3846 6788
E-mail: amcs@amcs.org.au
Web Site: www.amcs.org.au
Key Personnel
Dir: Darren Kindleysides
Communications & Fundraising Manager: Ingrid Neilson *E-mail:* ingridneilson@amcs.org.au
Subjects: Biological Sciences, Earth Sciences, Environmental Studies, Geography, Geology, Maritime, Natural History
Branch Office(s)
GPO Box 2120, Darwin, NT 0801, Contact: Jess Abrahams *Tel:* (08) 8941 7461 *Fax:* (08) 8941 0387

Australian Rock Art Research Association, see Archaeological Publications Inc

Australian Scholarly Publishing Pty Ltd (ASP)+
7 Little Lothian St North, North Melbourne, Victoria 3051
Mailing Address: PO Box 299, Kew, Victoria 3101
Tel: (03) 9329 6963 *Fax:* (03) 9329 5452
E-mail: enquiry@scholarly.info
Web Site: www.scholarly.info
Key Personnel
Dir: Nick Walker
Publicist: Terryn Whiteoak
Trade Manager: Helen Latemore
Graphic Designer: Art Rowlands
Founded: 1991
Subjects: Environmental Studies, Fiction, Geography, Geology, Government, Political Science, History, Nonfiction (General), Publishing & Book Trade Reference, Social Sciences, Sociology, Wine & Spirits
ISBN Prefix(es): 978-1-875606; 978-1-74097; 978-1-921509
Number of titles published annually: 50 Print
Total Titles: 3 E-Book
Imprints: Arcadia
Distribution Center: Australian Book Marketing *E-mail:* aspic@ozemail.com.au

Australian Society for Indigenous Languages Inc
Shop 13, Gray Shopping Centre, 20 Essington Ave, Gray, NT 0830
Mailing Address: PO Box 3575, Palmerston, NT 0831
Tel: (08) 8931 3133
E-mail: ausil@sil.org
Web Site: www.ausil.org.au
Founded: 1961
Subjects: Anthropology, Education, Language Arts, Linguistics, Australian Aboriginal & Torres Strait Islander Languages
ISBN Prefix(es): 978-0-86892
Branch Office(s)
3/38 Elder St, PO Box 8794, Alice Springs, NT 0871 *Tel:* (08) 8953 3057 *Fax:* (08) 8953 3047 *E-mail:* silalice@sil.org

Avon, *imprint of* Random House Books Australia, A Penguin Random House Company

Axiom Publishing
One Union St, Unit 2, Stepney, SA 5069
Tel: (08) 8362 7052 *Fax:* (08) 8362 9430
E-mail: axiom@axiomdist.com.au
Web Site: www.axiompublishing.com.au
Key Personnel
Mng Dir: John Gallehawk *E-mail:* john@axiomdist.com.au
Publishing: Greg Willson *E-mail:* greg@axiomdist.com.au
Also publishes gift books.
Subjects: Art, Biography, Memoirs, Cookery, Fiction, Health, Nutrition, History, Humor, Inspirational, Spirituality, Literature, Literary Criticism, Essays, Nonfiction (General), Outdoor Recreation, Philosophy, Religion - Other, Social Sciences, Sociology, Travel & Tourism, Wine & Spirits, Australia, Family, Mind, Body & Spirit, Recreation, Self-Development, Social History
ISBN Prefix(es): 978-0-947338; 978-0-9594164; 978-1-86476

Baird Publications
20 Cato St, Suite 3, Hawthorne East, Victoria 3123
Tel: (03) 9824 6055 *Fax:* (03) 9824 6588
E-mail: marinfo@baird.com.au
Web Site: www.bairdmaritime.com
Key Personnel
Chairman: Neil Baird
Founded: 1978
Subjects: Maritime
ISBN Prefix(es): 978-0-9577279; 978-0-9587013

Ballantine, *imprint of* Random House Books Australia, A Penguin Random House Company

Ballistic, *imprint of* Ballistic Media Pty Ltd

Ballistic Media Pty Ltd
134 Gilbert St, Adelaide, SA 5000
Tel: (08) 8463 1866 *Fax:* (08) 8212 8255
E-mail: info@ballisticpublishing.com
Web Site: www.ballisticpublishing.com
Key Personnel
Chief Executive Officer: Andrew F Plumer *E-mail:* andrew@ballisticmedia.net
Dir, Chief Financial Officer & Chief Operating Officer: Garth S Hammet
Founded: 2003
Independent publisher of books for the digital arts industry.
Subjects: 2D & 3D Digital Art
ISBN Prefix(es): 978-0-9750965; 978-1-921002; 978-1-921828
Imprints: Ballistic
Foreign Rep(s): Peter Couzens (Asia)

Ballistic Publishing, see Ballistic Media Pty Ltd

Bandicoot Books
PO Box 50, Margate, Tas 7054
Tel: (03) 6267 2530
Web Site: www.bandicootbooks.com
Key Personnel
Publisher: Marion Isham; Steve Isham
   E-mail: steve.isham@gmail.com
Founded: 1992
Home & school educational resources.
Subjects: Animals, Pets, Fiction, Foreign Coun-
   tries, History, Language Arts, Linguistics, Mys-
   teries, Suspense, Poetry
ISBN Prefix(es): 978-0-9586536

Bantam, *imprint of* Random House Books
   Australia, A Penguin Random House Company

Batchelor Press
Imprint of Batchelor Institute of Indigenous Ter-
   tiary Education
c/o Post Office, Batchelor, NT 0845
Tel: (08) 8939 7352 *Fax:* (08) 8939 7354
E-mail: orders@batchelorpress.com
Web Site: batchelorpress.com
Subjects: Education, Culture, Ethnoecology
ISBN Prefix(es): 978-0-7245; 978-1-74131

Bay Books, *imprint of* Murdoch Books Pty Ltd
   Australia

Bayda Books
PO Box 178, East Brunswick, Victoria 3057
Tel: (03) 9380 2988
Key Personnel
Manager: Yuri Tkacz *E-mail:* ytkacz@gmail.com
Founded: 1976
Specialize in books in Russian & Ukrainian &
   books in English on Ukraine.
Also mail order book supplier & library supplier.
Subjects: Fiction, Nonfiction (General)
ISBN Prefix(es): 978-0-908480
Total Titles: 1,000 Print

BBC, *imprint of* Random House Books Australia,
   A Penguin Random House Company

BBC Chidren's Books, *imprint of* Penguin
   Group (Australia)

Beach Lane, *imprint of* Simon & Schuster
   (Australia) Pty Ltd

Barbara Beckett Publishing Pty Ltd
14 Hargrave St, Paddington, NSW 2021
Tel: (02) 9331 2871
Key Personnel
Publisher: Barbara Beckett
Founded: 1994
Subjects: Art, Cookery
ISBN Prefix(es): 978-1-875891
Book Club(s): Doubleday Australia

Beri Publishing+
36 Alfred Rd, Burwood, Victoria 3125
Tel: (03) 9809 1434 *Fax:* (03) 9809 1434
Key Personnel
Head of Company: Nola Schlegel
Founded: 1991
Subjects: Education
ISBN Prefix(es): 978-0-9577233

Bernal Publishing+
4 Frank St, Box Hill South, Victoria 3128
Tel: (03) 9808 3775 *Fax:* (03) 9808 3775
Key Personnel
Mng Editor: Robert Martin

Founded: 1991
Subjects: Agriculture, Biography, Memoirs, History, Nonfiction (General), Farming (Commercial Chick Sexing)

Bible Society Australia+
30 York Rd, Ingleburn, NSW 2565
Tel: (02) 9829 9000 *Toll Free Tel:* 1300 242 537
   (bookshop) *Fax:* (02) 9829 9040; (02) 9829
   4685 (bookshop)
E-mail: bsdirect@bible.org.au (bookshop);
   bibles@biblesociety.org.au
Web Site: www.biblesociety.org.au
Key Personnel
Head, Content & Publishing: John Sandeman
Head, Marketing & Communications: Damian
   Fisher
Founded: 1817
Specialize in Bibles & related publications.
Membership(s): United Bible Societies.
Subjects: Biblical Studies, Religion - Catholic,
   Religion - Protestant, Theology
ISBN Prefix(es): 978-0-647
Branch Office(s)
5 Byfield St, Macquarie Park, NSW 2113
   Tel: (02) 9888 6588 *Toll Free Tel:* 1300 552
   537 *Fax:* (02) 9888 7820 *E-mail:* sydney@
   biblesociety.org.au *Web Site:* www.
   biblesocietynsw.com.au
213 Clarence St, Sydney, NSW 2000
   Tel: (02) 9262 6355 *Fax:* (02) 9267 7415
   E-mail: shopnsw@biblesociety.org.au
GPO Box 9874, Darwin, NT 0801 *Tel:* (08) 8927
   3056 *Fax:* (08) 8927 2794 *E-mail:* darwin@
   biblesociety.org.au
Level 4, 126 Barry Parade, Fortitude Valley, Qld
   4006 *Tel:* (07) 3112 6500 *Fax:* (07) 3112 6595
   E-mail: brisbane@biblesociety.org.au *Web
   Site:* www.bsqld.org.au
770 South Rd, Glandore, SA 5037 *Tel:* (08) 8292
   4888 *Fax:* (08) 8292 4899 *E-mail:* adelaide@
   biblesociety.org.au
GPO Box 9874, Hobart, Tas 7001 *Tel:* (03) 6331
   0248 *Fax:* (03) 6331 0249 *E-mail:* hobart@
   biblesociety.org.au
2-6 Albert St, Blackburn, Victoria 3130
   Tel: (03) 9877 9277 *Fax:* (03) 9877 8399
   E-mail: melbourne@biblesociety.org.au
23 Belgravia St, Suite 1, Belmont, WA 6104
   Tel: (08) 9479 6711 *Fax:* (08) 9479 6733
   E-mail: perth@biblesociety.org.au *Web
   Site:* www.biblesocietywa.com.au
Bookshop(s): 213 Clarence St, Sydney, NSW
   2000 *Tel:* (02) 9262 6355 *Fax:* (02) 9267
   7415 *E-mail:* shopnsw@biblesociety.org.au
   Web Site: www.bibleshop.com.au; 770 South
   Rd, Glandore, SA 5037 *Tel:* (08) 8292 4888
   Fax: (08) 8292 4899 *E-mail:* shopsa@bible.
   com.au

Bideena Publishing Co Pty Ltd+
180 Phillip St, 8th floor, Sydney, NSW 2000
Tel: (02) 9233 6300 *Fax:* (02) 9233 7416
E-mail: goannapress@bideenapublishingco.com
Web Site: www.bideenapublishingco.com
Key Personnel
Publisher: Jennifer Bingham
Publishing Manager: Cathy Phillips
Founded: 2010
Specialize in Australian fiction.
Membership(s): Australian Publishers Association
   (APA).
Subjects: Fiction
ISBN Prefix(es): 978-0-9808157
Number of titles published annually: 1 Print; 1
   CD-ROM; 1 Online; 1 E-Book
Total Titles: 3 Print; 2 CD-ROM; 2 Online; 2 E-
   Book
Imprints: Goanna Press
Warehouse: Peribo Pty Ltd, 58 Beaumont Rd,
   Mount Kuring-gai, NSW 2080
Distribution Center: Peribo Pty Ltd, 58 Beaumont
   Rd, Mount Kuring-gai, NSW 2080

Bio Concepts Pty Ltd
783 Kingsford Smith Dr, Unit 9, Eagle Farm, Qld
   4009
Mailing Address: PO Box 1492, Eagle Farm, Qld
   4009
Tel: (07) 3868 0699 *Fax:* (07) 3868 0612
E-mail: info@bioconcepts.com.au
Web Site: www.bioconcepts.com.au
Key Personnel
Founder & Dir: Henry Osiecki
Subjects: Alternative, Health, Nutrition, Self-
   Help, Sports, Athletics
ISBN Prefix(es): 978-1-875239

Black Dog Books, *imprint of* Walker Books
   Australia

Black Dog Books+
Imprint of Walker Books Australia
1-15 Wilson St, Level 2, Locked Bag 22, New-
   town, NSW 2042
Tel: (02) 9517 9577 *Fax:* (02) 9517 9997
E-mail: sales@walkerbooks.com.au
Web Site: www.walkerbooks.com.au
Key Personnel
Publishing Dir: Maryann Ballantyne
ISBN Prefix(es): 978-1-876372; 978-1-74259;
   978-1-74203; 978-1-921167
Distribution Center: Harper Entertainment Dis-
   tribution Services, PO Box 264, Moss Vale,
   NSW 2577 *Toll Free Tel:* 1300 551 721 *Toll
   Free Fax:* 1800 645 547 *E-mail:* orders@
   harpercollins.com.au (Australia & New
   Zealand)

Black Inc Agenda, *imprint of* Black Inc

Black Inc
37-39 Langridge St, Collingwood, Victoria 3066
Tel: (03) 9486 0288 *Fax:* (03) 9486 0244
E-mail: enquiries@blackincbooks.com
Web Site: www.blackincbooks.com
Key Personnel
Chief Executive Officer & Rights Dir: Sophy
   Williams
Publisher: Chris Feik
Dir: Morry Schwartz
General Manager: Caitlin Yates
Subjects: Biography, Memoirs, Fiction, History,
   Nonfiction (General)
ISBN Prefix(es): 978-1-86395; 978-0-9750769;
   978-1-921825; 978-1-921866; 978-1-921870;
   978-1-922231; 978-1-925203; 978-1-925435
Imprints: Black Inc Agenda; Nero; Quarterly Es-
   say; Redbacks; Schwartz Business; Schwartz
   City
Distribution Center: Penguin Random House,
   30 Centre Rd, Scoresby, Victoria 3179
   Tel: (03) 8537 4400 *Fax:* (03) 8537 4497
   E-mail: orders@unitedbookdistributors.com.au
Consortium Book Sales & Distribution, The Keg
   House, 34 13 Ave NE, Suite 101, Minneapolis,
   MN 55413-1007, United States *Tel:* 612-746-
   2600 *Fax:* 612-746-2606 *E-mail:* info@cbsd.
   com *Web Site:* www.cbsd.com SAN: 200-6049

Black Swan, *imprint of* Random House Books
   Australia, A Penguin Random House Company

Blake Education
108 Main Rd, Clayton South, Victoria 3169
Tel: (03) 9558 4433 *Fax:* (03) 9558 5433
E-mail: accounts@blake.com.au;
   customerservice@blake.com.au; info@blake.
   com.au; vip@blake.com.au (marketing)
Web Site: www.blake.com.au
Key Personnel
International Sales Manager: Nadeem Ansari
   Tel: (02) 8585 4013 *Fax:* (02) 8585 4087
   E-mail: nadeem@blake.com.au

Specialize in educational resources for teachers & students.
Subjects: Economics, Education, English as a Second Language, Geography, Geology, Health, Nutrition, History, Law, Mathematics, Music, Dance, Science (General), Technology, Civics, English, Information Technology, Legal Studies, Literary Education, Materials & Technology, Personal Development
ISBN Prefix(es): 978-1-876133; 978-1-86441; 978-1-86509; 978-1-74164; 978-1-921367; 978-1-921403; 978-1-920826; 978-1-921143; 978-1-921631; 978-1-921680; 978-1-921852
Branch Office(s)
655 Parramatta Rd, Leichhardt, NSW 2040

Blue Angel Gallery Pty Ltd
80 Glen Tower Dr, Glen Waverley, Victoria 3150
Tel: (03) 9574 7776 Fax: (03) 9574 7772
E-mail: info@blueangelonline.com
Web Site: www.blueangelonline.com; www. tonicarminesalerno.com
Key Personnel
Contact: Toni Carmine Salerno
E-mail: tonicarmine@optusnet.com.au
Founded: 2001
Subjects: Self-Help, Meditation, New Age, Personal Development, Well-being
ISBN Prefix(es): 978-0-9579149; 978-0-9752166; 978-0-9757683; 978-0-9802865; 978-0-9803983; 978-0-9805550; 978-0-9807406; 978-0-9808719

Blue Bottle Books, imprint of Youthworks

Board of Studies NSW
117 Clarence St, Sydney, NSW 2000
Mailing Address: GPO Box 5300, Sydney, NSW 2001
Tel: (02) 9367 8111 Fax: (02) 9367 8484
E-mail: information@bos.nsw.edu.au; service@bos.nsw.edu.au
Web Site: www.boardofstudies.nsw.edu.au
Key Personnel
President: Tom Alegounarias Tel: (02) 9367 8176
Chief Executive: Carol Taylor Tel: (02) 9367 8169 E-mail: carol.taylor@bos.nsw.edu.au
Established to serve government & non-government schools in the development of school education for years K-12.
Subjects: Education
ISBN Prefix(es): 978-0-7305; 978-0-7313; 978-1-74099; 978-1-74147; 978-1-74301

Boat Books Australia
31 Albany St, Crows Nest, NSW 2065
Tel: (02) 9439 1133 Toll Free Tel: 1300 2628 2665 Fax: (02) 9439 8517
E-mail: boatbooks@boatbooks-aust.com.au
Web Site: www.boatbooks-aust.com.au
Key Personnel
Dir: Christian Brook
Founded: 1973
Subjects: Nautical (Recreational & Professional)
Branch Office(s)
214 St Kilda Rd, St Kilda, Victoria 3182
Tel: (03) 9525 3444 Fax: (03) 9525 3355
E-mail: melbourne@boatbooks-aust.com.au

Boden Books Pty Ltd, see Science Press

Bolinda Audio, imprint of Bolinda Publishing Pty Ltd

Bolinda Publishing Pty Ltd+
17 Mohr St, Tullamarine, Victoria 3043
Mailing Address: Locked Bag 1315, Tullamarine, Victoria 3043
Tel: (03) 9338 0666 Toll Free Tel: 1300 782 547 (Australia) Fax: (03) 9335 1903
Toll Free Fax: 1800 671 411 (Australia)

E-mail: info@bolinda.com; sales@bolinda.com
Web Site: www.bolinda.com
Key Personnel
Founder & Co-Chief Executive Officer: Rebecca Herrmann E-mail: rebecca@bolinda.com
Founded: 1985
World leading audiobook & technology company.
Membership(s): Audio Publishers Association; Australian Publishers Association (APA).
Subjects: Fiction, Nonfiction (General)
ISBN Prefix(es): 978-0-947072; 978-1-86340; 978-1-74030; 978-1-876584; 978-1-74093; 978-1-74094; 978-1-4893
Number of titles published annually: 300 Audio
Total Titles: 4,000 Audio
Imprints: ABC Audiobooks; Bolinda Audio

Book Agencies of Tasmania+
5 Cleve Court, Howrah, Tas 7018
Tel: (03) 6247 7405 Fax: (03) 6247 1116
Founded: 1982
Subjects: Regional Interests
ISBN Prefix(es): 978-0-9757199
Number of titles published annually: 2 Print
Total Titles: 15 Print

Bookman Health
337A Lennox St, Suite 7, Richmond, Victoria 3121
Tel: (03) 9428 8633 Toll Free Tel: 1800 060 555
E-mail: sales@bookman.com.au; bookman@bookman.com.au
Web Site: www.bookman.com.au
Key Personnel
Manager: Leon Ridge-Cooke
Subjects: Health, Nutrition, Self-Help

Boolarong Press
1/655 Toohey Rd, Salisbury, Qld 4107
Mailing Address: PO Box 308, Moorooka, Qld 4105
Tel: (07) 3373 7855 Fax: (07) 3373 8611
E-mail: publish@boolarongpress.com.au
Web Site: www.boolarongpress.com.au
Founded: 1977
Subjects: Art, Biography, Memoirs, Business, History, Management, Nonfiction (General)
ISBN Prefix(es): 978-0-86439; 978-0-908175; 978-1-86252; 978-1-86439; 978-1-921054; 978-0-9587365; 978-1-921555; 978-1-921920

Bower Bird Books
PO Box 4104, Winmalee, NSW 2777
Key Personnel
Principal Officer: Margaret Baker
Founded: 1983
Subjects: Archaeology, Biological Sciences, Gardening, Plants, Geography, Geology, History, Natural History
ISBN Prefix(es): 978-0-9590203
Parent Company: Three Sisters Productions Pty Ltd

Boyce's Automotive Data Pty Ltd+
PO Box 1035, Strawberry Hills, NSW 2012
Tel: (02) 9319 7484 Fax: (02) 9698 7346
E-mail: support@boyce.com.au; sales@boyce.com.au
Web Site: www.boyce.com.au
Key Personnel
Mng Dir: Mark Boyce
Founded: 1975
Specialize in automotive manuals for workshops & software.
Subjects: Automotive, Technology
ISBN Prefix(es): 978-0-909682; 978-1-920991

Louis Braille Audio
454 Glenferrie Rd, Kooyong, Victoria 3144
Tel: (03) 8378 1259 Toll Free Tel: 1300 84 74 66 Fax: (03) 9747 5993

E-mail: library@visionaustralia.org
Web Site: www.visionaustralia.org
Founded: 1993
Subjects: Biography, Memoirs, Fiction, History, Literature, Literary Criticism, Essays, Nonfiction (General), Travel & Tourism, Military History, Self-Development, Social History
ISBN Prefix(es): 978-0-7320; 978-0-86764
Number of titles published annually: 95 Print
Total Titles: 600 Print; 600 Audio
Parent Company: Vision Australia

Brandl & Schlesinger Pty Ltd
PO Box 127, Blackheath, NSW 2785
Tel: (02) 4787 5848 Fax: (02) 4787 5672
E-mail: books@brandl.com.au (orders)
Web Site: www.brandl.com.au
Key Personnel
Owner & Publisher: Andras Berkes
E-mail: andras@brandl.com.au
Publishing Dir: Veronica Sumegi
E-mail: vsumegi@brandl.com.au
Founded: 1994
Membership(s): Australian Publishers Association (APA).
Subjects: Biography, Memoirs, Fiction, Literature, Literary Criticism, Essays, Nonfiction (General), Poetry
ISBN Prefix(es): 978-1-876040; 978-1-921556
Imprints: Verand Press
Foreign Rep(s): Agencja AKF (Anna Kolendarska-Fidyk) (Poland); Amo Agency (Korea); AnatoliaLit Agency (Amy Spangler) (Turkey); Book Publishers Association of Israel (Shoshi Grajower) (Israel); Lora Fountain Agent Litteraire (France); Iris Agency (Catherine Fragou) (Greece); Japan Uni Agency (Japan); Katai & Bolza Literary Agency (Hungary); Mo Literary Services (Monique Oosterhof) (Netherlands); Andrew Nurnberg Associates (Jackie Huang) (Mainland China); Pan Macmillan Asia (China, India); Pansing Distribution (Brunei, Indonesia, Malaysia, Singapore); Svetlana Pironko (Russia); Cristina Tatareanu (Romania); Agenzia Thesis Contents (Maria Cristina Guerra) (Italy); Eric Yang Agency (Korea)
Distribution Center: Macmillan Distribution Services, 15-19 Claremont St, Level 1, South Yarra, Victoria 3141 Tel: (03) 9825 1000 Toll Free Tel: 1300 135 113 Fax: (03) 9825 1010 Toll Free Fax: 1300 135 103 E-mail: customer.service@macmillan.com.au Web Site: www.macmillan.com.au

Brio Books
Formerly Xoum
307/4-14 Buckingham St, Surrey Hills, NSW 2010
Mailing Address: PO Box Q324, QVB Post Office, NSW 1230
Tel: (02) 8399 1850
Web Site: www.xoum.com.au
Key Personnel
Owner & Publisher: Rod Morrison
E-mail: rmorrison@xoum.com.au
Associate Publisher, Brio: Alice Grundy
Subjects: Fiction, Health, Nutrition, History, Nonfiction (General), Science (General), Science Fiction, Fantasy, Travel & Tourism, Popular Science
ISBN Prefix(es): 978-1-921134; 978-1-925143
Imprints: Fantastica; Seizure
Distributed by Hardie Grant Books (Australia & New Zealand)

Broadway Books, imprint of Random House Books Australia, A Penguin Random House Company

Brolga Publishing
GPO Box 12544, A'Beckett St, Melbourne 8006

Tel: (03) 9614 3209
Web Site: www.brolgapublishing.com.au
Key Personnel
Founding Dir: Mark Zocchi
   E-mail: markzocchi@brolgapublishing.com.au
Associate Publisher: Vern Beasley; David Conners
Founded: 1994
Membership(s): Australian Publishers Association (APA).
Subjects: Biography, Memoirs, Fiction, History, Inspirational, Spirituality, Mysteries, Suspense, Nonfiction (General)
ISBN Prefix(es): 978-0-909608; 978-1-920785; 978-1-921221; 978-1-921596; 978-1-922036
Distributed by Pan Macmillan

Brolly Books
Imprint of Borghesi & Adam Publishers Pty Ltd
Unit 2, 35 Progress St, Mornington, Victoria 3931
Tel: (03) 5975 5414
Web Site: www.brollybooks.com
Key Personnel
Founder: Andrew Adam *E-mail:* andrew@brollybooks.com; Emma Borghesi
   E-mail: emma@brollybooks.com
Founded: 1997
ISBN Prefix(es): 978-0-9577403; 978-1-877035; 978-0-9775720; 978-0-9802892
Number of titles published annually: 15 Print
Distribution Center: Scholastic New Zealand, 21 Lady Ruby Dr, East Tamaki, Auckland, New Zealand *Tel:* (09) 2748 8112

Brooks Waterloo, *imprint of* John Wiley & Sons Australia Ltd

Broughton Publishing Pty Ltd+
32 Glenvale Crescent, Mulgrave, Victoria 3170
Tel: (03) 9560 7077 *Fax:* (03) 8545 2922
Web Site: www.broughtonpublishing.com.au
Key Personnel
Company Secretary & Manager: Katherine Blyth
   E-mail: katherine.blyth@broughtonpublishing.com.au
Founded: 2001
Publisher of print & electronic liturgical & other materials for the Anglican Church of Australia.
Membership(s): Australian Publishers Association (APA); Australian Religious Press Association (ARPA).
Subjects: History, Religion - Protestant
ISBN Prefix(es): 978-0-9750866; 978-0-9806634; 978-0-9807244; 978-0-9870458
Distributed by John Garratt Publishing Pty Ltd

CalorieKing, see Family Health Publications

Cambridge University Press
477 Williamstown Rd, Port Melbourne, Victoria 3207
Mailing Address: Private Bag 31, Port Melbourne, Victoria 3207
Tel: (03) 8671 1400; (03) 8671 1411 *Fax:* (03) 9676 9966
E-mail: enquiries@cambridge.edu.au
Web Site: www.cambridge.org/aus
Key Personnel
President: Stephen Bourne
Permissions: Kate Buskes *Tel:* (03) 8671 1421 *Fax:* (03) 9676 9955 *E-mail:* kbuskes@cambridge.edu.au
Founded: 1969
Subjects: Education
ISBN Prefix(es): 978-0-521
Parent Company: Cambridge University Press (UK), University Printing House, Shaftebury Rd, Cambridge CB2 8RU, United Kingdom

Branch Office(s)
Suite 3.1, 3rd floor, 64 Talavera Rd, North Ryde, NSW 2113
U.S. Office(s): 32 Avenue of the Americas, New York, NY 10013-2473, United States *Tel:* 212-924-3900 *Fax:* 212-691-3239

Candlelight Farm
4110 Phillips Rd, Mundaring, WA 6073
Tel: (08) 9295 1933 *Fax:* (08) 9295 1933
Web Site: www.cfpermaculture.com.au
Key Personnel
Editorial Manager: Ross Mars *E-mail:* rossmars@waterinstallations.com
Subjects: Agriculture, Education, Environmental Studies, Gardening, Plants
ISBN Prefix(es): 978-0-9587626
Total Titles: 4 Print

CARTER'S Publications
PO Box 8464, Armadale, Victoria 3143
Toll Free Tel: 1800 670 630 (orders) *Fax:* (02) 8850 4100
E-mail: info@carters.com.au
Web Site: www.carters.com.au
Key Personnel
General Manager: Trent McVey
Founded: 1985
Online collector's price guides including art, antiquities, antiques, collectibles, retro, vintage & 20th century design.
Subjects: Antiques, Collectibles
ISBN Prefix(es): 978-1-876079
Number of titles published annually: 4 Online
Total Titles: 4 Online
Subsidiaries: Carter's Publications - New Zealand Ltd

Catchfire Press Inc
PO Box 72, Wallsend, NSW 2287
Web Site: www.catchfirepress.com.au
Key Personnel
President: Don Cohen *Tel:* (02) 4955 8924
Vice President: Zeny Giles
Secretary: Margaret Gibberd
Treasurer: Ross Edmonds
Founded: 1998
Not-for-profit publisher located in Newcastle representing the Hunter Valley community.
Subjects: Literature, Literary Criticism, Essays, Poetry
ISBN Prefix(es): 978-0-9577330

CCEAM, see Commonwealth Council for Educational Administration & Management

CDU Press, see Charles Darwin University Press

Central Queensland University Press
PO Box 1615, Rockhampton, Qld 4700
Tel: (07) 4923 2520 *Fax:* (07) 4923 2525
Web Site: www.cqunipress.com.au
Founded: 1993
Specialize in subjects about country heritage, regional history, South Pacific & Australiana.
Subjects: Biography, Memoirs, History, Nonfiction (General), Regional Interests
ISBN Prefix(es): 978-1-875998; 978-1-876780; 978-1-921274; 978-0-908140; 978-1-875902; 978-1-876674
Imprints: Outback Books
Bookshop(s): Level 7, 160 Ann St, Brisbane, Qld 4000 *Tel:* (07) 3295 1112; University Dr, Bundaberg, Qld 4670 *Tel:* (07) 4150 7073 *Fax:* (07) 4150 7120; Bldg 607, Bryan Jordan Dr, Gladstone, Qld 4680 *Tel:* (07) 4970 7230; Planlands, Mackay, Qld 4740 *Tel:* (07) 4940 7438 *Fax:* (07) 4940 7594; Bruce Highway, Bldg 35, North Rockhampton, Qld 4701 *Tel:* (07) 4930 9421; (07) 4930 9609 *Fax:* (07) 4930 9454; 60 Marine Parade, Southport, Qld

4215 *Tel:* (07) 5552 4965 *Fax:* (07) 5503 0447; 400 Kent St, Sydney, NSW 2000 *Tel:* (02) 9324 5713 *Fax:* (02) 9324 5178; Level 1, 108 Lonsdale St, Melbourne, Victoria 3000 *Tel:* (03) 9663 9728 *Fax:* (03) 9663 9728

Centre for Information Studies
Charles Sturt University, Locked Bag 660, Wagga Wagga, NSW 2678
Tel: (02) 6933 2325 *Fax:* (02) 6933 2733
E-mail: cis@csu.edu.au
Web Site: www.csu.edu.au
Key Personnel
Executive Officer: Chelsea Kovacs
   E-mail: ckovacs@csu.edu.au
Senior Public Relations Officer: Fiona Halloran
   Tel: (02) 6933 2207 *E-mail:* fhalloran@csu.edu.au
Aims to support & commission high quality research, publications & continuing professional development in library & information science, teacher librarianship & Australian literature for young people.
Subjects: Library & Information Sciences
ISBN Prefix(es): 978-0-949060; 978-1-876938

Century, *imprint of* Random House Books Australia, A Penguin Random House Company

Chalkface Press Pty Ltd+
PO Box 23, Cottesloe, Perth, WA 6011
Tel: (08) 9385 1923
E-mail: chalk@chalkface.net.au
Web Site: www.chalkface.net.au
Key Personnel
Publisher & Editorial Dir: Dr Bronwyn Mellor
Dir: Stephen Mellor
Founded: 1987
Publish textbooks for students & teachers in the area of subject English, at secondary & tertiary level.
Membership(s): Australian Publishers Association (APA).
ISBN Prefix(es): 978-1-875136; 978-0-9587924
Foreign Rep(s): English & Media Centre (UK); National Council of English Teachers (Canada, USA)
Distribution Center: Campion Education Pty Ltd, 7 Oxleigh Dr, Malaga, WA 6090 *Tel:* (08) 6240 2700 *Fax:* (08) 6240 2799 *E-mail:* chalkface@campion.com.au *Web Site:* www.campion.com.au

Chapter & Verse, *imprint of* Wellington Lane Press Pty Ltd

Charles Darwin University Press
Charles Darwin University Bookshop, Red Bldg 1, Casuarina Campus, Casuarina, NT 0815
Mailing Address: Charles Darwin University Bookshop, PO Box U476, Darwin, NT 0810
Tel: (08) 8946 7625 *Fax:* (08) 8946 6656
E-mail: bookshop@cdu.edu.au
Web Site: bookshop.cdu.edu.au
Key Personnel
Manager: Margaret Waterson-James
Communications Officer: Sarah Price
Subjects: Accounting, Architecture & Interior Design, Art, Business, Computers, Cookery, Economics, Education, Engineering (General), Gardening, Plants, Government, Political Science, History, Language Arts, Linguistics, Law, Literature, Literary Criticism, Essays, Marketing, Mathematics, Medicine, Nursing, Dentistry, Psychology, Psychiatry, Regional Interests, Social Sciences, Sociology
ISBN Prefix(es): 978-1-876248; 978-1-9758356; 978-1-9806650; 978-1-9808641

Chatto & Windus, *imprint of* Random House Books Australia, A Penguin Random House Company

Cherrytree, *imprint of* Pearson Library

Childerset Pty Ltd+
67b Katrina St, Blackburn, Victoria 3130
Tel: (03) 8776191
Founded: 1970
ISBN Prefix(es): 978-0-909404; 978-0-949130
Distributed by Scholastic Australia

China Books
234 Swanston St, 2nd floor, Melbourne, Victoria 3000
Tel: (03) 9663 8822 *Toll Free Tel:* 1800 44 88 55 (Australia only) *Fax:* (03) 9663 8821
E-mail: info@chinabooks.com.au
Web Site: www.chinabooks.com.au
Key Personnel
Mng Dir: Tony McGlinchey
Founded: 1989
Book importer, wholesaler & retailer/specialist.
Subjects: Asian Studies, Business, Government, Political Science, History, Language Arts, Linguistics, Philosophy, Women's Studies, China, Chinese Studies
ISBN Prefix(es): 978-0-7100
Branch Office(s)
Shop F7, Level 1, Citymark Bldg, 683 George St, Sydney, NSW 2000 *Tel:* (02) 9280 1885 *Fax:* (02) 9280 1887 *E-mail:* info@ chinabookssydney.com.au

Ching Chic Publishers
83 River Walk Ave, Robina, Qld 4226
Tel: (07) 5575 8572
E-mail: chingchic@winshop.com.au
Web Site: www.chingchic.com
Key Personnel
Proprietor: Judy Eather
Manager, Author & Historian: Charles E Eather
Founded: 1993
Subjects: Aeronautics, Aviation
ISBN Prefix(es): 978-0-9586746; 978-0-949756
Total Titles: 3 CD-ROM

Christian Education Publications, *imprint of* Youthworks

Churchill House, *imprint of* Austed Publishing Co

Churchill Livingstone, *imprint of* Elsevier Australia

Claremont, *imprint of* Penguin Group (Australia)

Commonwealth Council for Educational Administration & Management
86 Ellison Rd, Springwood, NSW 2777
Tel: (02) 4751 7974 *Fax:* (02) 4751 7974
E-mail: admin@cceam.org
Web Site: www.cceam.org
Key Personnel
Executive Dir: Jenny Lewis *E-mail:* jennylewis@ cceam.org
Founded: 1970
Publisher of International Studies in Educational Administration.
Subjects: Education, Management

Commonwealth Scientific & Industrial Research Organisation, see CSIRO Publishing

Coolabah Publishing
Division of The Narnia Group
Unit 9, 6 Frost Dr, Mayfield West, NSW 2304

Tel: (04) 2865 9693 *Fax:* (02) 4967 2336
Key Personnel
Sales: Patrick O'Connor
Founded: 1991
Also distributor.
Subjects: Education, Aboriginal
ISBN Prefix(es): 978-1-876400

Corgi, *imprint of* Random House Books Australia, A Penguin Random House Company

Country Bumpkin Publications
916 South Rd, Edwardstown, SA 5039
Tel: (08) 8293 8600 *Toll Free Tel:* 1800 033 371 *Fax:* (08) 8293 8733
E-mail: admin@countrybumpkin.com.au
Web Site: www.countrybumpkin.com.au
Key Personnel
Dir: Fiona Fagan *E-mail:* fiona@countrybumpkin. com.au
Founded: 1987
Specialize in craft books & magazines.
Subjects: Crafts, Games, Hobbies, How-to, Embroidery
ISBN Prefix(es): 978-0-9577159; 978-0-9579069; 978-0-9750920; 978-0-9757094; 978-0-9775476; 978-0-9804359; 978-0-9805753; 978-0-9756854; 978-0-9808767
Imprints: Inspirations Books

Covenanter Press
PO Box 8480, Kooringal, NSW 2650
Tel: (02) 4257 9188
Key Personnel
Sales Manager: Rev Don Burgess
Founded: 1967
Publisher of Christian books.
Subjects: History, Religion - Protestant, Theology
ISBN Prefix(es): 978-0-908189
Number of titles published annually: 2 Print
Total Titles: 50 Print
Parent Company: Presbyterian Reformed Church of Australia
Orders to: 159 Burke St, Dapto, NSW 2530, Contact: Dick McKay

CQUni Press, see Central Queensland University Press

Crawford House Publishing Pty Ltd+
34 Kingdon Pl, Unit 2, Goolwa, SA 5214
Tel: (08) 8555 0667
Web Site: www.crawfordhouse.com.au
Key Personnel
Mng Dir: Anthony L Crawford
   E-mail: tonycraw@bigpond.net.au
Founded: 1989
Specialize in human & natural sciences of the Pacific Island nations, Papua New Guinea & Southeast Asia.
Subjects: Anthropology, Art, Asian Studies, Biography, Memoirs, Government, Political Science, History, Maritime, Natural History, Social Sciences, Sociology, Australiana, Ethnology, Marine Life Identification
ISBN Prefix(es): 978-1-86333
Number of titles published annually: 4 Print
Total Titles: 123 Print

Creative House, *imprint of* Sally Milner Publishing Pty Ltd

Crossing Press
PO Box 1137, Darlinghurst, NSW 1300
Tel: (02) 4782 4984 *Fax:* (02) 4782 4984
E-mail: sales@crossingpress.com.au
Web Site: www.crossingpress.com.au
Key Personnel
Mng Editor & Founder: Peter Moore
   E-mail: plm@crossingpress.com.au
Founded: 1992

Specialize in multicultural Australian history & legal history.
Subjects: Biography, Memoirs, History, Law, Australian & Irish-Australian, Legal Profession
ISBN Prefix(es): 978-0-9586713; 978-0-9578291; 978-1-876906
Number of titles published annually: 4 Print
Total Titles: 38 Print

Crown Publishing Group, *imprint of* Random House Books Australia, A Penguin Random House Company

Crows Nest, *imprint of* Allen & Unwin

CSIRO Publishing+
Unipark, Bldg 1, Level 1, 195 Wellington Rd, Clayton, Victoria 3168
Mailing Address: Locked Bag 10, Clayton, South Victoria 3169
Tel: (03) 9545 8400 *Fax:* (03) 9545 8555
E-mail: publishing@csiro.au; publishing.sales@ csiro.au
Web Site: www.publish.csiro.au
Founded: 1926
Subjects: Agriculture, Biological Sciences, Chemistry, Chemical Engineering, Environmental Studies, Natural History, Physical Sciences, Physics, Science (General), Technology
ISBN Prefix(es): 978-0-643
Number of titles published annually: 50 Print
Distributor for Earthscan; Island Press; Manaaki Whenua Press; Manson Publishing; Natural History Museum, London; Roberts & Company Publishers
Warehouse: Bldg 13, Gate 6, 71 Normanby Rd, Clayton, Victoria 3168

Currency Press+
164 James St, (rear, 201 Cleveland St), Redfern, NSW 2016
Mailing Address: PO Box 2287, Strawberry Hills, NSW 2012
Tel: (02) 9319 5877 *Fax:* (02) 9319 3649
E-mail: enquiries@currency.com.au; orders@ currency.com.au
Web Site: www.currency.com.au
Key Personnel
Chairman: Nicholas Parsons
Publisher: Victoria Chance
Sales & Marketing Dir: Deborah Franco
Founded: 1971
Specialize in Australian performing arts.
Subjects: Drama, Theater, Film, Video, Music, Dance
ISBN Prefix(es): 978-0-86819
Number of titles published annually: 30 Print
Total Titles: 450 Print
Distributor for Nick Hern Books (Australia); Oberon Books (Australia)
Foreign Rep(s): Antipodes Books & Beyond Ltd (Canada, USA); Gazelle Book Services Ltd (Europe, UK); NewSouth Books (Australia); Resource Room (New Zealand)

Curriculum Press+
Imprint of Education Services Australia Ltd
Level 5, 440 Collins St, Melbourne, Victoria 3000
Mailing Address: PO Box 177, Carlton South, Victoria 3053
Tel: (03) 9207 9600 *Toll Free Tel:* 1300 780 545 (within Australia) *Fax:* (03) 9910 9800
E-mail: sales@esa.edu.au
Web Site: www.curriculumpress.edu.au
Key Personnel
Chief Executive Officer: Susan Mann
   E-mail: susan.mann@esa.edu.au
Founded: 2010
Specialize in curriculum & education support material.
Subjects: Education
ISBN Prefix(es): 978-1-86366

Eleanor Curtain Publishing+
Level 1, Suite 3, 102 Toorak Rd, South Yarra, Victoria 3141
Tel: (03) 9867 4880 *Fax:* (03) 9820 4696
E-mail: info@ecpublishing.com.au; orders@ecpublishing.com.au
Web Site: www.ecpublishing.com.au
Key Personnel
Mng Dir: Eleanor Curtain
Dir: Andrew Curtain
Publish reference & professional development books for primary teachers.
Subjects: Education, Elementary Reading Books
ISBN Prefix(es): 978-1-875327; 978-1-876917; 978-1-876975; 978-1-920877; 978-1-74148; 978-1-74234; 978-1-74235; 978-1-74320
Distributed by AgaWorld Co Ltd (Republic of Korea); Gardner Education Ltd (UK); Giant Management Consulting Co Ltd (Taiwan); Kiwik International (Hong Kong); Lioncrest Education (Australia & New Zealand); Macmillan South Africa (Pty) Ltd (South Africa); Okapi Educational Publishing Inc (USA); Scholastic Canada Ltd (Canada); Sundance Publishing (USA)

Cygnet Books, *imprint of* University of Western Australia Publishing

Dagraja Press+
3 Verco St, Hackett, ACT 2602
Tel: (02) 6247 0782; (02) 6262 7533
Key Personnel
Owner: Graeme Barrow
Founded: 1977
Specialize in bushwalking guides & local history.
Subjects: History
ISBN Prefix(es): 978-0-9587552; 978-0-9596877; 978-0-9775328
Number of titles published annually: 1 Print
Total Titles: 5 Print
Distributed by ABC Maps; MacStyle Media; Tabletop Press

Daw, *imprint of* Penguin Group (Australia)

Del Rey, *imprint of* Random House Books Australia, A Penguin Random House Company

Dell Publishing, *imprint of* Random House Books Australia, A Penguin Random House Company

Department of Environment & Heritage (OEH)+
Level 14, 59-61 Goulburn St, Sydney, NSW 2000
Mailing Address: PO Box A290, Sydney, NSW 1232
Tel: (02) 9995 5000 *Toll Free Tel:* 1300 361 967
Fax: (02) 9995 5999
E-mail: info@environment.nsw.gov.au
Web Site: www.environment.nsw.gov.au
Key Personnel
Chief Executive: Lisa Corbyn
Subjects: Earth Sciences
ISBN Prefix(es): 978-1-74232; 978-1-74293

Desert Pea Press, *imprint of* The Federation Press

Deva Wings Publications+
PO Box 200, Daylesford, Victoria 3460
Tel: (03) 5348 1414 *Fax:* (03) 5348 1411
E-mail: info@devawings.com
Web Site: devawings.com
Key Personnel
Contact: Arjuna Govindamurti; Shanti Dass Portia
Founded: 1994 (Right Human Relations Day)
Provide materials related to spiritual psychology, theosophy & spiritual healing. The materials are by the author Tarajyoti Govinda with the purpose of making Spirit & Divine Wisdom comprehensible to all.
Subjects: Inspirational, Spirituality, Religion - Buddhist, Self-Help
ISBN Prefix(es): 978-0-9587202

Dial, *imprint of* Penguin Group (Australia)

Discovery Press
18 Myers St, Geelong, Victoria 3220
Toll Free Tel: 1300 361 680
Key Personnel
Publisher & Manager: Juliet Williams
Publisher: Bruce du Vergier
Desktop Publisher: Ruben Shannon
Editor: Megan Frazer
Commissioning Editor: Claire Jennings
Founded: 2007
ISBN Prefix(es): 978-0-9804701

Dorling Kindersley, *imprint of* Penguin Group (Australia)

Dott Publishing, *imprint of* Artand Publishing Pty Ltd

Doubleday, *imprint of* Random House Books Australia, A Penguin Random House Company

Dunmore Press, *imprint of* Social Science Press

Dutton, *imprint of* Penguin Group (Australia)

Dynamo House Pty Ltd+
22-26 Joseph St, Blackburn North, Victoria 3130
Tel: (03) 8892 4844 *Fax:* (03) 9429 8036
E-mail: customerservice@dynamoh.com.au
Web Site: www.dynamohouse.com.au
Key Personnel
Mng Dir: David Plush
Founded: 1975
Subjects: Astrology, Occult, Health, Nutrition, Humor, Alternative Therapies & Philosophies, Aromatherapy, Reflexology
ISBN Prefix(es): 978-0-949266; 978-1-876100; 978-0-949383
Subsidiaries: Dynamo Press
Distributed by Aromaland Inc (USA); Asiapac Books (Singapore); Milk & Honey, Inc. (USA)

Ebury Press, *imprint of* Random House Books Australia, A Penguin Random House Company

Echidna Books, *imprint of* Pearson Library

The Educational Advantage Pty Ltd
5 Echuca St, Shop 4, Moama, NSW 2731
Mailing Address: PO Box 1068, Echuca, Victoria 3564
Tel: (03) 5480 9466 *Fax:* (03) 5480 9462
E-mail: info@mathsmate.net
Web Site: www.mathsmate.net
Key Personnel
Project Management & Curriculum Alignment: Joanna Tutos *E-mail:* joanna@mathsmate.net
Program Development & Business Management: Joseph B Wright *E-mail:* joe@mathsmate.net
Publishing & Design: Lou McKenna *E-mail:* lou@mathsmate.net
Founded: 1995
Subjects: Education, Mathematics
ISBN Prefix(es): 978-1-876081
Total Titles: 44 Print; 2 CD-ROM; 9 Online
Associate Companies: Math's Mate USA, PO Box 1050, Morrison, CO 80465-1050, United States, Educational Representative: Kathy Frick *Tel:* 303-697-2073 *Fax:* 303-697-8609
E-mail: mathsmate@me.com *Web Site:* www.mathsmate.com
Foreign Rep(s): Kathy Frick (USA); Trish Kidd (New Zealand)

Educational Supplies Pty Ltd
Division of Dominie Group
23 Cross St, Brookvale, NSW 2100
Mailing Address: PO Box 33, Brookvale, NSW 2100
Tel: (02) 9938 8699 *Fax:* (02) 9938 8695
Key Personnel
Mng Dir: Ross Martin
Founded: 1951
Educational publisher & distributor.
Subjects: Art, Mathematics, Religion - Other, Science (General), Technology
ISBN Prefix(es): 978-1-86251; 978-0-909268; 978-0-949029

Ek Books, *imprint of* Exisle Publishing Ltd

Elsevier Australia+
Division of Reed International Books Australia Pty Ltd
Level 12, Tower 1, 475 Victoria Ave, Chatswood, NSW 2067
Mailing Address: Locked Bag 7500, Chatswood DC, NSW 2067
Tel: (02) 9422 8500 *Toll Free Tel:* 1800 263 951 (within Australia); 0800 170 165 (to Australia from New Zealand) *Fax:* (02) 9422 8501
Toll Free Fax: 0800 170 160 (to Australia from New Zealand)
E-mail: customerserviceau@elsevier.com
Web Site: www.elsevierhealth.com.au
Key Personnel
Mng Dir: Rob Kolkman
Founded: 1972
Also college, medical, psychological testing & professional/trade divisions.
Subjects: Business, Education, Mathematics, Medicine, Nursing, Dentistry, Psychology, Psychiatry, Science (General), Social Sciences, Sociology, Veterinary Science
ISBN Prefix(es): 978-0-7295
Total Titles: 8,000 Print; 65 CD-ROM
Associate Companies: Academic Press Ltd, Harcourt Place, 32 Jamestown Rd, London NW1 7BY, United Kingdom; Bailliere Tindall Ltd, Harcourt Place, 32 Jamestown Rd, London NW1 7BY, United Kingdom; Harcourt Publishers Ltd, Harcourt Place, 32 Jamestown Rd, London NW1 7BY, United Kingdom; Academic Press Inc, 1250 Sixth Ave, San Diego, CA 92101, United States; W B Saunders Co, The Curtis Center, Independence Sq, Philadelphia, PA 19106-3399, United States; Holt Rinehart & Winston Inc, 1627 Woodland Ave, Austin, TX 78741, United States; Harcourt College Publishers, 301 Commerce St, Suite 3700, Fort Worth, TX 78741, United States; The Psychological Corp, 555 Academic Court, San Antonio, TX 78204-0952, United States
Imprints: Academic Press; Churchill Livingstone; Holt, Rinehart and Winston; Industrial Press; Mayfield Publishing; Morgan Kaufmann; Mosby; The Psychological Corp; W B Saunders/Bailliere Tindall; Saunders College; Singular Press; Technomic Publishing
Branch Office(s)
461 Bourke St, 13th floor, Melbourne, Victoria 3000 *Tel:* (03) 9691 3344 *Fax:* (03) 9691 3313
236 Dominion Rd, Mount Eden, Auckland 3, New Zealand
Distributor for Mayfield (Australia & New Zealand); Technomic Publishing (Australia & New Zealand)
Warehouse: 1/18 Shale Pl, Eastern Creek, Sydney, NSW 2766 *Tel:* (02) 9620 2284

Elton Publications+
57 Camden St, Wembly Downs, WA 6019
Tel: (08) 9446 1328 *Fax:* (08) 9445 8229
E-mail: elton@iinet.net.au
Web Site: www.elton.iinet.net.au
Key Personnel
Contact: Richard Lyon; Hilaire Lyon
Founded: 1994
Specializes in supplying Blackline Masters books
   to primary school teachers.
Membership(s): Copyright Agency Ltd.
Subjects: History, Regional Interests, Aboriginal
   Australians, Culture, Internet, Wildlife
ISBN Prefix(es): 978-1-876486; 978-0-9587567;
   978-0-9587025
Number of titles published annually: 8 Print; 1 E-
   Book
Total Titles: 49 Print; 6 E-Book
Distributed by The Dominie Group; Educa-
   tion World; Holding Educational Aids; Nar-
   nia Bookshop; Nepean Educational Supplies;
   Wooldridges

Encyclopaedia Britannica (Australia) Ltd
90 Mount St, Level 1, North Sydney, NSW 2060
Mailing Address: PO Box 5608, Chatswood West,
   NSW 1515
Tel: (02) 9915 8800 *Toll Free Tel:* 1800 000 060
   Fax: (02) 9419 5247
E-mail: sales@britannica.com.au
Web Site: www.britannica.com.au
Key Personnel
Executive Dir: Roland Smith
Mng Dir: James Buckle
Subjects: Art, Biological Sciences, Geography,
   Geology, Science (General)
ISBN Prefix(es): 978-0-86741
Parent Company: Encyclopaedia Britannica Inc,
   311 North LaSalle St, Chicago, IL 60610,
   United States
Associate Companies: Encyclopaedia Britannica
   International Ltd UK

Envirobook
182a River Rd, Sussex Inlet, NSW 2540
Tel: (0402) 361 424 (cell) *Fax:* (0402) 361 424
   (cell)
E-mail: sales@envirobook.com.au
Web Site: www.envirobook.com.au
Key Personnel
Mng Dir: Patrick Thompson *E-mail:* pat@
   envirobook.com.au
Specialize in natural science, travel, Aboriginal &
   Australiana.
Subjects: Environmental Studies, Natural History,
   Outdoor Recreation, Aboriginal Children
ISBN Prefix(es): 978-0-85881
Number of titles published annually: 2 Print
Total Titles: 60 Print

Era Publications
220-222 Grange Rd, Flinders Park, SA 5025
Mailing Address: PO Box 231, Brooklyn Park,
   SA 5032
Tel: (08) 8352 4122 *Fax:* (08) 8219 0180
E-mail: service@erapublications.com
Web Site: www.erapublications.com
Key Personnel
Export, Marketing & Professional Development:
   Rod Martin *E-mail:* rod@erapublications.com
Financial Controller: Lina D'Amico
   E-mail: lina@erapublications.com
Art Dir: Ann Lewis *E-mail:* ann@erapublications.
   com
Administration Coordinator: Joseph Lia
   E-mail: joe@erapublications.com
Senior Editor: Nicole Dent *E-mail:* nicole@
   erapublications.com
Graphic Design: Nathan Kolic *E-mail:* nathan@
   erapublications.com

Trade Sales: Sandra Martin *E-mail:* sandra@
   erapublications.com; Tania Martin
   E-mail: tania@erapublications.com
Founded: 1971
Primary & elementary school educational materi-
   als.
Membership(s): Australian Literacy Educators
   Association; Australian Publishers Association
   (APA); Club NW Adelaide; English Associa-
   tion; Family Business Australia; International
   Literacy Association.
Subjects: Education, Fiction, Language Arts, Lin-
   guistics, Literature, Literary Criticism, Essays,
   Nonfiction (General)
ISBN Prefix(es): 978-1-86374; 978-1-74120; 978-
   0-947212; 978-0-908507; 978-1-74144; 978-1-
   74049
Number of titles published annually: 50 Print; 90
   Online; 2 E-Book; 30 Audio
Total Titles: 1,000 Print; 90 Online; 4 E-Book;
   400 Audio
Foreign Rep(s): AH2 International (Norway);
   All Prints Distributors & Publishers (United
   Arab Emirates); Beaver Books (Canada); BRIC
   (Brunei, Malaysia); The Choicemaker (South
   Korea); English Language Services (Colom-
   bia); Essential Resources (New Zealand);
   ETA/Cuisenaire (USA); GAN Ascheoug (Nor-
   way); Gardner Education (UK); Horizon Books
   (Southern Africa); Learning Needs Centre (Sin-
   gapore); B K Norton Pty Ltd (China, Japan,
   Taiwan); SchoolSupport (Austria, Belgium,
   Germany, Netherlands, Switzerland); Stanford
   House (Hong Kong); Studentlitteratur (Finland,
   Sweden); WB Promotions (Vietnam)

eScholarship Research Centre
Thomas Cherry Bldg, Level 2, The University of
   Melbourne, Parkville, Victoria 3010
Tel: (03) 8344 3659 *Fax:* (03) 9347 4803
Web Site: www.esrc.unimelb.edu.au
Key Personnel
Dir: Gavan McCarthy *E-mail:* gavan.mccarthy@
   unimelb.edu.au
Founded: 1985 (as the Australian Science
   Archives Project & then the Australian Science
   & Technology Heritage Centre in 1999)
Specialize in history & archives of Australian
   science, technology & medicine. Also broader
   interests in digital scholarly practice & infor-
   mation infrastructure.
Subjects: Biography, Memoirs, History, Science
   (General), Social Sciences, Sociology, Technol-
   ogy, Women's Studies
Number of titles published annually: 5 Print; 5
   Online
Total Titles: 50 Print; 50 Online
Parent Company: The University of Melbourne

Essien, *imprint of* Hudson Publishing Services
Pty Ltd

Evans Publishing, *imprint of* Pearson Library

Even Before Publishing, *imprint of* Wombat
Books

Exisle Publishing Ltd+
2884 Wollombi Rd, Wollombi 2325
Mailing Address: 226 High St, Dunedin 9016,
   New Zealand
Tel: (03) 477 1615
E-mail: sales@exislepublishing.com
Web Site: exislepublishing.com
Key Personnel
Chief Executive, Publisher & Foreign Rights
   Dir: Gareth St John Thomas *E-mail:* gareth@
   exislepublishing.com
General Manager & Production Manager: Carole
   Doesburg *E-mail:* carole@exisle.co.nz

Media Relations, Sales & Marketing (New
   Zealand): Jane Dennis *E-mail:* jane@
   exislepublishing.co.nz
Publisher, Ek Books: Anouska Jones
   E-mail: anouska@exislepublishing.com
Publicist, Australia: Alison Worrad
   E-mail: alison@exislepublishing.com
Publicist, UK: Hannah Corbett *E-mail:* hannah@
   hannahcorbett.co.uk
Publicist, USA: Jennifer Prost *E-mail:* jprostpr@
   comcast.net
Digital Affairs Manager: James Elms
   E-mail: james@exislepublishing.com
Sales, Australia: Siobhan Dillon
   E-mail: siobhan@exislepublishing.com
Founded: 1993
Membership(s): Book Publishers of New Zealand.
Subjects: Animals, Pets, Biography, Memoirs,
   Business, Health, Nutrition, Inspirational, Spir-
   ituality, Language Arts, Linguistics, Maritime,
   Natural History, Nonfiction (General), Outdoor
   Recreation, Self-Help, Social Sciences, Sociol-
   ogy, Pacific Studies
ISBN Prefix(es): 978-0-908988; 978-1-921966;
   978-1-877568; 978-1-877437; 978-1-927147;
   978-1-927187; 978-1-77559
Number of titles published annually: 25 Print; 25
   E-Book
Total Titles: 300 Print; 200 E-Book
Parent Company: Exisle Holdings Ltd
Imprints: Ek Books (children's list); Hourglass
   (memoir)
Distributed by Quarto

Explore Australia, *imprint of* Hardie Grant
Travel

Extraordinary People Press+
c/o Australian Health & Education Centre, 3
   Glebe Pl, 131-145 Glebe Point Rd, Glebe,
   NSW 2037
Tel: (02) 9571 4333
Key Personnel
Commissions Editor: Katrina Fox
Founded: 1997
Subjects: Behavioral Sciences, Health, Nutrition,
   Human Relations, LGBTQ, Nonfiction (Gen-
   eral), Psychology, Psychiatry, Self-Help, Social
   Sciences, Sociology
ISBN Prefix(es): 978-0-9529482
Distribution Center: Turnaround Publisher Ser-
   vices, Unit 3, Olympia Trading Estate, Coburg
   Rd, Wood Green, London N22 6TZ, United
   Kingdom *Tel:* (020) 8829 3000 *Fax:* (020)
   8881 5088 *E-mail:* orders@turnaround-uk.com

JB Fairfax Craft, *imprint of* Sally Milner
Publishing Pty Ltd

Family Health Publications+
88 Broadway, Suite 1, Nedlands, WA 6009
Mailing Address: PO Box 3100, Nedlands, WA
   6009
Tel: (08) 9389 8777 *Fax:* (08) 9389 8444
Web Site: www.calorieking.com.au
Key Personnel
Owner: Allan Borushek
Dir: Aston David Borushek
Founded: 1972
Software developer & applications service
   provider producing innovative solutions for
   health & wellness related software & services.
Subjects: Health, Nutrition
ISBN Prefix(es): 978-0-947091
U.S. Office(s): Allan Borushek & Associates
   Inc, 1001 W 17 St, No M, Costa Mesa, CA
   92627-4512, United States *Tel:* 949-642-8500
   Fax: 949-642-8900

Fantastica, *imprint of* Brio Books

Fawcett, *imprint of* Random House Books Australia, A Penguin Random House Company

The Federation Press+
71 John St, Leichhardt, NSW 2040
Mailing Address: PO Box 45, Annandale, NSW 2038
Tel: (02) 9552 2200 *Fax:* (02) 9552 1681
E-mail: info@federationpress.com.au; sales@federationpress.com.au
Web Site: www.federationpress.com.au
Key Personnel
Publisher & Dir: Christopher Holt
Editorial Dir: Kathryn Fitzhenry
Dir, Marketing: Diane Young
Founded: 1987
Specialize in legal, social & academic books.
Subjects: Business, Environmental Studies, Law
ISBN Prefix(es): 978-1-86287
Total Titles: 300 Print
Imprints: Desert Pea Press (non-law); Hawkins Press (criminology); Themis Press (legal research)
Distributed by Gaunt Inc (USA); Irwin Law (North America); Taylor & Francis (Africa, Europe, Israel, Middle East & UK); Yushodo Co Ltd (Japan)
Distributor for Australian Institute of Criminology; Barr Smith Press-The University of Adelaide; BJU (Boom Juridische Uitgevers); The Centre for Independent Studies; Crime Research Centre, University of Western Australia; The Francis Forbes Society for Australian Legal History; Institute of Criminology, Sydney; Irwin Law; Kingsford Legal Centre; Siber Ink; Unidroit; The Victoria Law Foundation; Zed Books
Foreign Rep(s): China Publishers Services Ltd (Edwin Chu) (China, Hong Kong, Macau, Taiwan); Greene Phoenix Marketing (Paul Greenberg) (New Zealand); Edwin Makabenta (Philippines); Publishers Marketing Services Pte Ltd (Brunei, Malaysia, Singapore); Sara Books Pvt Ltd (Bangladesh, India, Pakistan, Sri Lanka)

Fig Tree, *imprint of* Penguin Group (Australia)

Finch Publishing+
1A 64 Darley St, Mona Vale, NSW 2103
Tel: (02) 9418 6247 *Fax:* (02) 9418 8878
Web Site: finch.com.au
Key Personnel
Publisher & Dir: Rex Finch *E-mail:* rex@finch.com.au
Editor: Samantha Miles *E-mail:* samantha@finch.com.au
Founded: 1992
Specialize in books on family, health, memoirs, relationships, society & social ecology.
Subjects: Biography, Memoirs, Child Care & Development, Communications, Education, Government, Political Science, Health, Nutrition, Human Relations, Nonfiction (General), Philosophy, Psychology, Psychiatry, Self-Help, Social Sciences, Sociology, Women's Studies, Children's Health, Men's Studies, Parenting, Social Issues
ISBN Prefix(es): 978-1-876451; 978-1-921462
Number of titles published annually: 10 Print; 1 Audio
Total Titles: 100 Print
Distributed by Deep Books (UK); HarperCollins (Australia); Southern Publishers Group (New Zealand); Trafalgar Square Publishing (North America)

Fireside, *imprint of* Simon & Schuster (Australia) Pty Ltd

Five Islands Press
University of Melbourne, PO Box 4429, Parkville, Victoria 3052
Tel: (03) 8344 9727
E-mail: contact@fiveislandspress.com; orders@fiveislandspress.com
Web Site: fiveislandspress.com
Key Personnel
Mng Editor: Kevin Brophy
Founded: 1986
Subjects: Poetry
ISBN Prefix(es): 978-1-875604; 978-1-7340; 978-0-9587972

Fodor, *imprint of* Random House Books Australia, A Penguin Random House Company

Forge, *imprint of* Pan Macmillan Australia Pty Ltd

Free Press, *imprint of* Simon & Schuster (Australia) Pty Ltd

Fremantle Press
25 Quarry St, Fremantle, WA 6160
Mailing Address: PO Box 158, North Fremantle, WA 6159
Tel: (08) 9430 6331 *Fax:* (08) 9430 5242
E-mail: admin@fremantlepress.com.au
Web Site: www.fremantlepress.com.au
Key Personnel
Media & Publicity: Claire Miller *Tel:* (0419) 837 841 *E-mail:* cmiller@fremantlepress.com.au
Founded: 1976
Subjects: Art, Biography, Memoirs, Cookery, Education, Fiction, History, Literature, Literary Criticism, Essays, Nonfiction (General), Photography, Poetry, Food
ISBN Prefix(es): 978-1-86368; 978-0-949144; 978-0-949206; 978-1-920731; 978-1-92106
Number of titles published annually: 24 Print
Total Titles: 300 Print
Orders to: Wilmot Book Agencies, Contact: Jenny Gillam *Toll Free Tel:* 0400 920 440 (Western Australia)
Penguin Books (other states & New Zealand)
Independent Publishers Group *Tel:* 312-337-0747 *Fax:* 312-337-1807 *Web Site:* www.ipgbook.com (North America)

Gallery, *imprint of* Simon & Schuster (Australia) Pty Ltd

Garratt Publishing+
32 Glenvale Crescent, Private Bag 400, Mulgrave, Victoria 3170
Tel: (03) 8545 2911 *Toll Free Tel:* 1300 650 878 *Fax:* (03) 8545 2922
E-mail: sales@garrattpublishing.com.au
Web Site: www.garrattpublishing.com.au
Founded: 1995
Also importation & marketing of overseas religious titles.
Membership(s): Christian Bookselling Association of Australia (CBAA).
Subjects: Religion - Catholic, Religion - Other
ISBN Prefix(es): 978-1-875938; 978-1-920682; 978-1-920721; 978-1-921946
Number of titles published annually: 15 Print
Total Titles: 90 Print
Distributor for General Synod of the Anglican Church of Australia

GHR Press
30 Lynwood Ave, Killara, NSW 2071
Mailing Address: PO Box 612, Brookvale, NSW 2100
Tel: (02) 9418 4518
E-mail: andi@ghrpress.com
Web Site: ghrpress.com

Key Personnel
Dir: Dale Druckman; Katherine Owen; Michael Rakusin
Subjects: Biography, Memoirs, Fiction, Genealogy, Labor, Industrial Relations, Women's Studies
ISBN Prefix(es): 978-0-86806; 978-0-908094; 978-0-949818; 978-0-9578081; 978-0-9757723; 978-0-9806324
Imprints: Goko Publishing; Hale & Iremonger; Krinos

Ginninderra Press
PO Box 3461, Port Adelaide, SA 5015
Tel: (08) 7005 0370
Web Site: www.ginninderrapress.com.au
Key Personnel
Publisher: Stephen Matthews *E-mail:* stephen@ginninderrapress.com.au
Founded: 1996
Accepts manuscripts from residents of Australia only.
Membership(s): Small Press Underground Network Community (SPUNC).
Subjects: Biography, Memoirs, Child Care & Development, Disability, Special Needs, Education, Fiction, Health, Nutrition, History, Literature, Literary Criticism, Essays, Nonfiction (General), Poetry
ISBN Prefix(es): 978-1-876259; 978-0-9586825; 978-1-74027
Number of titles published annually: 40 Print
Total Titles: 400 Print
Imprints: Mockingbird
Orders to: East Avenue Books, 53 East Ave, Clarence Park, SA 5034 *Tel:* (08) 7226 6753 *E-mail:* info@eastavenuebooks.com

Giramondo Publishing Co
Imprint of University of Western Sydney, Writing & Society Research Centre
PO Box 752, Artarmon, NSW 1570
Tel: (02) 9772 6350 *Fax:* (02) 9419 7934
E-mail: books@giramondopublishing.com
Web Site: giramondopublishing.com
Founded: 1995
Subjects: Fiction, Nonfiction (General), Poetry
ISBN Prefix(es): 978-0-9578311; 978-1-920882; 978-1-925336; 978-1-922146

Goanna Press, *imprint of* Bideena Publishing Co Pty Ltd

Goko Publishing, *imprint of* GHR Press

Gould Genealogy & History
4/247 Milne Rd, Modbury North, SA 5092
Mailing Address: PO Box 675, Modbury, SA 5092
Tel: (08) 8396 1110 *Fax:* (08) 8396 1163
E-mail: inquiries@gould.com.au; orders@gould.com.au
Web Site: www.gould.com.au
Key Personnel
Manager: Alan Phillips *E-mail:* alan@gould.com.au
Business Manager: Stephen Phillips *E-mail:* stephen@gould.com.au
Sales: Beth Langdon *E-mail:* beth@gould.com.au
Founded: 1976
Subjects: Genealogy, History
ISBN Prefix(es): 978-0-947284; 978-0-9595446; 978-1-921807; 978-0-9807760; 978-0-9808746; 978-1-921956
Total Titles: 4,000 Print; 4,000 CD-ROM; 5 Online

Graffiti Publications Pty Ltd+
69 Forest St, Castlemaine, Victoria 3450
Mailing Address: PO Box 232, Castlemaine, Victoria 3450

Tel: (03) 5472 3805; (03) 5472 3653
E-mail: info@graffitipub.com.au; sales@
graffitipub.com.au
Web Site: www.graffitipub.com.au
Key Personnel
Dir: Larry O'Toole
Founded: 1977
Publish magazines & books which promote street
rodding as a hobby & business.
Subjects: Automotive, Crafts, Games, Hobbies
ISBN Prefix(es): 978-0-949398
Total Titles: 16 Print
Distributed by Motorbooks International; South
Pacific Books (New Zealand)
Distributor for The Rodder's Journal; Tex Smith
Library
Foreign Rep(s): Motorbooks International (North
America)

Grainger Museum
University of Melbourne, Melbourne, Victoria
3010
Tel: (03) 8344 5270 *Fax:* (03) 8344 5221
E-mail: grainger@unimelb.edu.au
Web Site: www.lib.unimelb.edu.au/collections/
grainger
Key Personnel
Curator, Exhibitions & Public Programs: Brian
Allison *Tel:* (03) 8344 8822 *E-mail:* ballison@
unimelb.edu.au
Manager, Marketing & Communications: Eliza-
beth Cashen *E-mail:* ecashen@unimelb.edu.au
Founded: 1938
Subjects: Music, Dance

Grass Roots Publishing Pty Ltd
Shop 4/55 Anzac Ave, Seymour, Victoria 3660
Mailing Address: PO Box 117, Seymour, Victoria
3661
Tel: (03) 5792 4000 *Fax:* (03) 5792 4222
E-mail: grp@eck.net.au
Founded: 1973
Subjects: Agriculture, Crafts, Games, Hobbies,
Gardening, Plants, Health, Nutrition, How-to
ISBN Prefix(es): 978-0-9595244; 978-0-9590152;
978-0-947065; 978-0-9580894

Greater Glider Productions Australia Pty Ltd+
Book Farm, 8 Rees Lane, Maleny, Qld 4552
Tel: (07) 5494 3000 *Fax:* (07) 5494 3284
Web Site: www.greaterglider.com.au
Key Personnel
Contact: Jill Morris
Founded: 1983
Membership(s): Australian Publishers Association
(APA).
Subjects: Education, Health, Nutrition, Natural
History, Science (General)
ISBN Prefix(es): 978-0-947304

Griffin, *imprint of* Pan Macmillan Australia Pty
Ltd

Grosset & Dunlap, *imprint of* Penguin Group
(Australia)

H & H Publishing
6 Southern Court, Forest Hill, Victoria 3131
Tel: (03) 9877 4428
Founded: 1981
Subjects: Civil Engineering, Mechanical Engi-
neering

Hachette Australia+
Division of Hachette UK
207 Kent St, Level 17, Sydney, NSW 2000
Tel: (02) 8248 0800; (02) 4390 1300 (customer
service) *Fax:* (02) 8248 0810
E-mail: auspub@hachette.com.au (Australian
publishing); hsales@hachette.com.au; adscs@

alliancedist.com.au (customer service); rights@
hachette.com.au
Web Site: www.hachette.com.au
Key Personnel
Chief Executive Officer: Louise Sherwin-Stark
Mng Dir: Justin Ractliffe
Australian Publishing Dir: Fiona Hazard
Head, Children's Publishing: Jeanmarie Morosin
Dir, Hachette Children's Books: Chris Raine
Head, Fiction: Rebecca Saunders
Head, Literary & Illustrated: Robert Watkins
Head, Nonfiction: Vanessa Radnidge
Nonfiction Publisher: Sophie Hamley
Publishing & Production Manager: Anne
Macpherson
Junior Commissioning Editor: Kate Stevens
Founded: 1958
Membership(s): Australian Booksellers Associa-
tion; Australian Publishers Association (APA).
ISBN Prefix(es): 978-0-7499 (Piatkus); 978-0-
340; 978-0-7267; 978-0-7472 (Headline Re-
view); 978-0-7553 (Headline Review); 978-0-
412 (Hodder Arnold); 978-0-7336; 978-0-450
Number of titles published annually: 120 Print
Total Titles: 1,500 Print
Ultimate Parent Company: Lagardere

Hale & Iremonger, *imprint of* GHR Press

Hamish Hamilton, *imprint of* Penguin Group
(Australia)

Margaret Hamilton Books, *imprint of* Scholastic
Australia Pty Ltd

Hardie Grant, *imprint of* Hardie Grant Travel

Hardie Grant Books
658 Church St, Ground floor, Bldg 1, Richmond
3121
Mailing Address: Private Bag 1600, South Yarra,
Victoria 3141
Tel: (03) 8520 6444 *Fax:* (03) 8520 6422
E-mail: info@hardiegrant.com.au
Web Site: www.hardiegrant.com.au
Key Personnel
Chief Executive: Sandy Grant
E-mail: sandygrant@hardiegrant.com.au
Publishing Administrator: Jodie Martin
E-mail: jodiemartin@hardiegrant.com.au
Founded: 1997
Subjects: Biography, Memoirs, Cookery, Fiction,
Humor, Pop Culture, Social Sciences, Sociol-
ogy, Sports, Athletics, Travel & Tourism, Wine
& Spirits, Designs, Food, Mind, Body & Spirit,
Social Issues, True Crime
ISBN Prefix(es): 978-1-86498; 978-1-876719;
978-1-74066; 978-1-74270; 978-1-74273
Branch Office(s)
Hardie Grant Books UK, 52-54 Southwark St,
5th & 6th floors, London SE1 1UN, United
Kingdom *Tel:* (020) 7601 7500 *E-mail:* info@
hardiegrant.co.uk
Distributor for Brio Books; Carlton Books;
Chronicle Books; Cico Books; Hardie Grant
London; Andrews McMeel Publishing; Michael
O'Mara; Paperblanks; Quadrille; Rizzoli New
York; Ryland Peters & Small; Workman
Orders to: United Book Distributors, 30 Cen-
tre Rd, Scoresby, Victoria 3179 *Tel:* (03) 9811
2555 *Fax:* (03) 9811 2403 *E-mail:* orders@
unitedbookdistributors.com.au *Web Site:* www.
unitedbookdistributors.com.au

Hardie Grant Travel+
Division of Hardie Grant Publishing Pty Ltd
658 Church St, Ground floor, Bldg 1, Richmond,
Victoria 3121
Tel: (03) 8520 6444 *Fax:* (03) 8520 6422
E-mail: info@exploreaustralia.net.au

Web Site: www.hardiegrant.com/au/travel; www.
exploreaustralia.net.au
Founded: 1950
Diverse range of street directories, travel guides,
books, maps & atlases.
Subjects: Automotive, Travel & Tourism
ISBN Prefix(es): 978-0-7261; 978-0-85566; 978-
0-7319; 978-0-949164; 978-1-86939; 978-1-
86949
Imprints: Explore Australia; Hardie Grant; UBD
Gregory's
Distributor for Bradt Travel Guides; Marco Polo;
Michelin; National Geographic

Hargreen Publishing Co
430 William St, Melbourne, Victoria 3000
Tel: (03) 9329 9714
Founded: 1972
Specialize in Australian history.
Subjects: Education, History, Nonfiction (General)
ISBN Prefix(es): 978-0-949905; 978-0-9596696
Parent Company: Scotshouse Corp Pty Ltd

HarperCollins Publishers Australia+
Division of HarperCollins Publishers
201 Elizabeth St, Sydney, NSW 2000
Mailing Address: PO Box A565, Sydney South,
NSW 2000
Tel: (02) 9952 5000 *Fax:* (02) 9952 5555
E-mail: publicity@harpercollins.com.au
Web Site: www.harpercollins.com.au
Key Personnel
Chief Executive Officer: James Kellow
Art Dir: Matt Stanton
Finance Dir: Malcolm Boyd
Marketing, Digital & Communications Dir: Si-
mon Milne
Dir, People & Technology: Jonathan Connolly
Rights & Co-editions Manager: Elizabeth
O'Donnell
Production Manager: Janelle Garside
Publicity: Shontell Samuels
Founded: 1888
Subjects: Biography, Memoirs, Business, Cook-
ery, Fiction, History, Inspirational, Spirituality,
Literature, Literary Criticism, Essays, Manage-
ment, Nonfiction (General), Religion - Other,
Science Fiction, Fantasy, Self-Help, Social Sci-
ences, Sociology
ISBN Prefix(es): 978-0-7322
Ultimate Parent Company: News Corp
Associate Companies: Angus & Robertson Pub-
lishers; Bartholomew, United Kingdom; Bay
Books; Collins Dove; Collins Inc; Fontana,
United Kingdom; Scott Foresman; Golden
Press, New Zealand; Grafton Books, United
Kingdom; HarperCollins, 2 Bloor St E, 20th
floor, Toronto, ON M4W 1A8, Canada; Harper-
Collins General Books, United Kingdom;
HarperCollins Ltd, Hong Kong; HarperCollins
Publishers, 31 View Rd, Glenfield, Auckland,
New Zealand; HarperCollins Publishers Asia
Pte Ltd; HarperCollins Publishers India (P)
Ltd, 1A Connaught Pl, New Delhi 110 001, In-
dia; HarperCollins Publishers (SA) (Pty) Ltd,
South Africa; Marshall Pickering, United King-
dom; Thorsons Times Books, United Kingdom;
Zondervan
Distribution Center: Yarrawa Rd, PO Box 264,
Moss Vale, NSW 2577 *Tel:* (02) 4860 2900
Fax: (02) 4860 2990

Hawker Brownlow Education+
Factory 2/47 Wangara Rd, Cheltenham, Victoria
3192
Mailing Address: PO Box 580, Moorabbin, Victo-
ria 3189
Tel: (03) 8558 2444 *Toll Free Tel:* 1800 334 603
(Australia); 0800 501 019 (New Zealand)
Fax: (03) 8558 2400 *Toll Free Fax:* 1800 150
445 (Australia)
E-mail: orders@hbe.com.au
Web Site: www.hbe.com.au

Key Personnel
Publishing Dir: Elaine Brownlow
 E-mail: ebrownlow@hbe.com.au
Founded: 1981
Subjects: Asian Studies, Human Relations, Mathematics, Technology
ISBN Prefix(es): 978-1-86299; 978-1-86401; 978-0-947326; 978-1-74025; 978-1-74101

Hawkins Press, *imprint of* The Federation Press

Hay House Australia Pty Ltd
18/36 Ralph St, Alexandria, NSW 2015
Mailing Address: PO Box 515, Brighton-Le-Sands, NSW 2216
Tel: (02) 9669 4299 *Fax:* (02) 9669 4299
Web Site: www.hayhouse.com.au
Founded: 1999
Subjects: Astrology, Occult, Business, Cookery, Environmental Studies, Finance, Health, Nutrition, Inspirational, Spirituality, Philosophy, Psychology, Psychiatry, Self-Help, Social Sciences, Sociology, Alternative Health, Food, New Age
ISBN Prefix(es): 978-1-877087
Parent Company: Hay House Inc, PO Box 5100, Carlsbad, CA 92018-5100, United States
Branch Office(s)
Hay House Publications (India) Pvt Ltd, Muskaan Complex, Plot No 3, B-2, Vasant Kunj, New Delhi 110 070, India *Tel:* (011) 4176 1620 *Fax:* (011) 4716 1630 *Web Site:* www.hayhouse.co.in
Hay House SA (Pty) Ltd, PO Box 990, Witkoppen 2068, South Africa *Tel:* (011) 326 3449 *Fax:* (011) 326 3449 *Web Site:* www.hayhouse.co.za
Hay House Publishers (UK), 33 Notting Hill Gate, London W11 3JQ, United Kingdom *Tel:* (020) 3675 2450 *Fax:* (020) 3675 2451 *Web Site:* www.hayhouse.co.uk
U.S. Office(s): 665 Broadway, Suite 1200, New York, NY 10012, United States *Tel:* 646-484-4950 *Fax:* 646-484-4956

Hayward Books, *imprint of* In-Tune Books

Heinemann First Library, *imprint of* Pearson Library

Heinemann Library, see Pearson Library

Heinemann Library (UK), *imprint of* Pearson Library

Heinemann-Raintree (USA), *imprint of* Pearson Library

William Heinemann, *imprint of* Random House Books Australia, A Penguin Random House Company

Hema Maps Pty Ltd+
25 McKechnie Dr, Eight Mile Plains, Qld 4113
Mailing Address: PO Box 4365, Eight Mile Plains, Qld 4113
Tel: (07) 3340 0000; (07) 3340 0075 (customer service) *Fax:* (07) 3340 0099
E-mail: sales.hema@clear.net.nz
Web Site: www.hemamaps.com
Key Personnel
Mng Dir: Robert Boegheim
Founded: 1983
Membership(s): International Map Industry Association (IMIA).
Subjects: Travel & Tourism
ISBN Prefix(es): 978-1-875610; 978-1-875992; 978-1-86500; 978-1-876413
Branch Office(s)
Hema Maps NZ, 10 Cryers Rd, Unit 2, East Tamaki 2013, New Zealand *Tel:* (09) 273 6459

Fax: (09) 273 6479 *E-mail:* sales.hema@clear.net.nz
U.S. Office(s): Hema Maps North America Inc, 921 E 86 St, Suite 107, Indianapolis, IN 46240, United States *Tel:* 317-257-4362 *Fax:* 317-257-5362
Foreign Rep(s): Liberia Altair (Spain); Apple Globes (South Korea); Australia Travel (Italy); La Cartotheque (France); Craenen BVBA (Belgium); Freytag & Berndt (Austria); Geobuch (Germany); GeoCenter Touristik Medienservice (Germany); Il Giramondo (Italy); Intelligent Turisticke Mapy (Czechia); Interkart (Germany); ITMB (Canada); Jana Seta (Latvia); Kartcentrum (Sweden); Landkarten-Versand.de (Germany); Magellan Buchversand (Germany); Map Co Trading (Singapore); Map House (Japan); Nilsson & Lamm (Netherlands); Nordisk Korthandel (Denmark); Norstedts Kartbutiken (Sweden); Olf centre de Distribution (Switzerland); Olf Travelmaps (Canada); Omni Resources (USA); Avigdor Orgad (Israel); Scanvik Books (Denmark)

Hinkler Books Pty Ltd
44-55 Fairchild St, Heatherton, Victoria 3202
Tel: (03) 9552 1333 *Fax:* (03) 9558 2566
E-mail: enquiries@hinkler.com.au; sales@hinkler.com.au
Web Site: www.hinkler.com.au
Key Personnel
Chief Executive Officer & Publisher: Stephen Ungar
Mng Dir: Nadika Garber
International Sales Dir: Gary Coppen
Founded: 1994
Subjects: Cookery, Nonfiction (General), Lifestyle
ISBN Prefix(es): 978-1-86515; 978-1-74121; 978-1-875980; 978-1-74157; 978-1-74181; 978-1-74182; 978-1-74183; 978-1-74184; 978-1-74185
Branch Office(s)
Hinkler Books UK, The Johnsons Group Ltd, James St West, Green Park, Bath BA1 2BU, United Kingdom *Tel:* (01225) 320 837 *Fax:* (01225) 320 880
Foreign Rep(s): Bookreps (New Zealand); Elmtree Books (Singapore); Wilco International (India)

Holt, Rinehart and Winston, *imprint of* Elsevier Australia

Hospitality Books
PO Box 3007, Putney, NSW 2112
Tel: (02) 9809 5793 *Fax:* (02) 9809 4884
E-mail: sales@hospitalitybooks.com.au
Web Site: www.hospitalitybooks.com.au
Key Personnel
Manager: Jeffrey Puckeridge
Founded: 1987
Specialize in how-to books on professional bartending & waiting. Publisher of the *Australian Wine Guide & Hospitality Core Units*.
Membership(s): Copyright Agency Ltd.
Subjects: How-to, Self-Help, Travel & Tourism, Wine & Spirits, Food & Beverage Service, Hospitality Industry, Wine Appreciation
ISBN Prefix(es): 978-0-9775912
Total Titles: 4 Print

Hospitality Press, *imprint of* Pearson Australia Group Pty Ltd

Hourglass, *imprint of* Exisle Publishing Ltd

Howard, *imprint of* Simon & Schuster (Australia) Pty Ltd

Hudson Publishing Services Pty Ltd+
7 Panmure St, Newstead, Victoria 3462

Tel: (03) 5476 2795
Web Site: www.hudson-publishing.com
Key Personnel
Owner: Nick Hudson
Founded: 1985
Membership(s): Australian Publishers Association (APA).
Subjects: Literature, Literary Criticism, Essays, Nonfiction (General)
ISBN Prefix(es): 978-0-949873
Total Titles: 50 Print
Imprints: Essien
Distributed by Dennis Jones & Associates (Australia & New Zealand)

Hungry Minds Australia, *imprint of* John Wiley & Sons Australia Ltd

Hutchinson, *imprint of* Random House Books Australia, A Penguin Random House Company

Hyland House Publishing Pty Ltd+
PO Box 1116, Carlton, Victoria 3053
Tel: (03) 9347 5715
E-mail: info@hylandhouse.com.au
Web Site: www.hylandhouse.com.au
Key Personnel
Mng Dir: Michael Schoo
Founded: 1976
Subjects: Animals, Pets, Cookery, Gardening, Plants, How-to, Organisational Histories
ISBN Prefix(es): 978-0-908090; 978-0-947062; 978-1-875657; 978-1-86447
Imprints: Manna Press
Distribution Center: Dennis Jones & Associates *Tel:* (03) 9762 9100 *Fax:* (03) 9762 9200 *E-mail:* theoffice@dennisjones.com.au *Web Site:* www.dennisjones.com.au

IAD Press+
3 South Terrace, Alice Springs, NT 0870
Mailing Address: PO Box 2531, Alice Springs, NT 0871
Tel: (08) 8951 1334 *Fax:* (08) 8951 1381
E-mail: sales@iad.edu.au
Web Site: www.iadpress.com
Key Personnel
Press Manager: Jeanette Wormald *Tel:* (08) 8951 1335 *E-mail:* press.manager@iad.edu.au
Customer Service Officer: Gina Campbell *Tel:* (08) 8951 1337
Production/Designer: Tina Tilhard *Tel:* (08) 8951 1336 *E-mail:* production@iad.edu.au
Coordinating Editor: Margaret McDonell *Tel:* (08) 8951 1332 *E-mail:* press.editor@iad.edu.au
Editor: Seona Galbally *Tel:* (08) 8951 1330 *E-mail:* editor@iad.edu.au
Media & Marketing: Marion Erlich *Tel:* (08) 8951 1333 *E-mail:* marketing@iad.edu.au
Indigenous publishing house producing works by Aboriginal & Torres Strait Islander peoples of Australia.
Membership(s): Australian Publishers Association (APA); Publish Australia.
Subjects: Anthropology, Art, Biography, Memoirs, Education, Fiction, History, Language Arts, Linguistics, Literature, Literary Criticism, Essays, Natural History, Nonfiction (General), Regional Interests
ISBN Prefix(es): 978-0-949659; 978-1-86465; 978-1-9596206
Number of titles published annually: 10 Print; 1 E-Book; 1 Audio
Total Titles: 55 Print; 1 CD-ROM; 3 E-Book; 3 Audio
Parent Company: Institute of Aboriginal Development
Imprints: Jukurrpa Books
Foreign Rep(s): International Specialized Book Services (North America)
Distribution Center: JB Books, PO Box 118, Marleston, SA 5033 *Tel:* (08) 8351 1688

Fax: (08) 8351 1699 *E-mail:* jbbooks@
internode.on.net *Web Site:* www.jbbooks.com.
au
Dennis Jones & Associates, Unite 1/10 Melrich
Rd, Bayswater, Victoria 3153 *Tel:* (03) 9762
9100 *Fax:* (03) 9762 9200 *E-mail:* theoffice@
dennisjones.com.au *Web Site:* www.
dennisjones.com.au

The Images Publishing Group Pty Ltd+
Images House, 6 Bastow Pl, Mulgrave, Victoria
3170
Tel: (03) 9561 5544 *Fax:* (03) 9561 4860
E-mail: books@imagespublishing.com
Web Site: www.imagespublishinggroup.com;
imagespublishing.com
Key Personnel
Joint Mng Dir: Paul Alan Latham
Founded: 1983
Subjects: Accounting, Advertising, Animals, Pets,
Architecture & Interior Design, Art, Automo-
tive, Biography, Memoirs, Business, Civil Engi-
neering, Crafts, Games, Hobbies, Drama, The-
ater, Education, Engineering (General), Envi-
ronmental Studies, Fashion, Gardening, Plants,
House & Home, Photography, Pop Culture,
Religion - Jewish, Religion - Other, Travel &
Tourism, Wine & Spirits
ISBN Prefix(es): 978-1-875498; 978-0-9589598;
978-1-876907; 978-1-920744; 978-1-86470
Number of titles published annually: 50 Print
Total Titles: 475 Print
Parent Company: Images Australia Pty Ltd
Imprints: Peleus Press
Foreign Rep(s): ACC Distribution (Africa,
Canada, Central America, Europe, Ireland,
Mexico, Middle East, South America, UK,
USA); Alpha Books Pty Ltd (Australia); APD
Singapore (Southeast Asia); Azur Corp (Asia);
Beijing Designer Books (China); Bookreps
New Zealand Ltd (New Zealand); BookWorld
Enterprises (India)

In-Tune Books+
PO Box 193, Avalon Beach, NSW 2107
Tel: (02) 9974 5981 *Fax:* (02) 9974 4552
Founded: 1984
Subjects: Alternative, Art, Philosophy, Self-Help
ISBN Prefix(es): 978-0-9577024; 978-0-9577025;
978-0-9590439; 978-0-9752291
Imprints: Hayward Books
Distributed by Alternate Books (South Africa)
Distribution Center: Words Distributing Co, 7900
Edgewater Dr, Oakland, CA 94621, United
States
World Leisure Marketing, Unit 11, Newmar-
ket Court, Newmarket Dr, Derby DE24
8NW, United Kingdom *Tel:* (01332) 573 737
Fax: (01332) 573 399

Indra Publishing+
PO Box 7, Briar Hill, Victoria 3088
Tel: (03) 8704 3575 *Fax:* (03) 8704 3575
Web Site: indrabooks.com
Key Personnel
Publisher: Ian James Fraser *E-mail:* ian@
indrabooks.com
Founded: 1987
Membership(s): Australian Publishers Association
(APA).
Subjects: Asian Studies, Disability, Special
Needs, Literature, Literary Criticism, Essays,
Philosophy, Religion - Other, Asia, Australia,
Pacific
ISBN Prefix(es): 978-0-9587718; 978-0-9585805;
978-0-9578735; 978-1-9207870
Number of titles published annually: 3 Print
Total Titles: 47 Print; 3 Audio
Foreign Rep(s): Australian Book Group (Aus-
tralia, New Zealand); Double & Newman
(Asia); Gazelle Book Services Ltd (Europe,
Iceland, Ireland, UK)

Industrial Press, *imprint of* Elsevier Australia

Infosearch, *imprint of* Pearson Library

Insight Publications Pty Ltd
3/350 Charman Rd, Cheltenham, Victoria 3192
Tel: (03) 8571 4950 *Fax:* (03) 8571 0257
E-mail: sales@insightpublications.com.au
Web Site: www.insightpublications.com.au
Subjects: Education, English as a Second Lan-
guage, Literature, Literary Criticism, Essays
ISBN Prefix(es): 978-1-875882; 978-1-920693;
978-1-921088; 978-1-921411
Distribution Center: Ingram Publisher Services

Inspirations Books, *imprint of* Country Bumpkin
Publications

Inspired Living, *imprint of* Allen & Unwin

Inwardpath Publishers
76 McArthur Rd, East Ivanhoe, Victoria 3079
Tel: (03) 9499 3405
Web Site: inwardpath.com.au
Subjects: Philosophy, Esoteric, New Age
ISBN Prefix(es): 978-0-9585722

Island Press Co-operative
29 Park Rd, Woodford, NSW 2778
Tel: (02) 4758 6635
E-mail: awphaw@bigpond.com
Web Site: islandpress.tripod.com/ISLAND.htm
Key Personnel
Mng Dir: Philip Hammial
Founded: 1970
Subjects: Poetry
ISBN Prefix(es): 978-0-909771
Number of titles published annually: 4 Print
Total Titles: 47 Print

J L Publications, see Submariner Publications
P/L

The Jabiru Press
13 Ferdinand Ave, North Balwyn, Victoria 3104
Tel: (03) 9857 7362 *Fax:* (03) 9857 9110
Key Personnel
Publisher & Mng Dir: Dick Johnson
Publish activity books for young Australians.
ISBN Prefix(es): 978-0-908104

Jacana Books, *imprint of* Allen & Unwin

The Jacaranda Press, *imprint of* John Wiley &
Sons Australia Ltd

James Nicholas Publishers Pty Ltd
PO Box 5179, South Melbourne, Victoria 3205
Tel: (03) 9690 5955 (customer service); (03) 9696
5545 (editorial off) *Fax:* (03) 9699 2040
E-mail: custservice@jnponline.com; orders@
jnponline.com
Web Site: www.jamesnicholaspublishers.com.au;
www.jnponline.com
Key Personnel
Dir: Rea Zajda
Founded: 1978
Publish journals & books in education & social
sciences.
Subjects: Business, Communications, Education,
Government, Political Science, Health, Nutri-
tion, Management, Marketing, Medicine, Nurs-
ing, Dentistry, Social Sciences, Sociology
ISBN Prefix(es): 978-1-875408
Total Titles: 10 Print; 7 Online

Jarrah Publications+
42 Chisholm Circle, Armadale, WA 6112

Founded: 1987
Partnership specializing in fantasy & contempo-
rary issues.
Subjects: Fiction, Human Relations, Romance,
Science Fiction, Fantasy
Total Titles: 2 Print

Jesuit Communications+
Unit of Australian Province of the Society of Je-
sus
PO Box 553, Richmond, Victoria 3121
Tel: (03) 9421 9611
E-mail: info@jesuit.org.au
Web Site: www.jesuit.org.au
Key Personnel
Advertising Manager: Camille Collins
Communications Officer: Michael McVeigh
Founded: 1988
Subjects: Poetry, Religion - Catholic, Religion -
Protestant, Religion - Other, Theology
ISBN Prefix(es): 978-0-9586796

John Furphy Pty Ltd, see CARTER'S
Publications

Michael Joseph, *imprint of* Penguin Group
(Australia)

Jukurrpa Books, *imprint of* IAD Press

Gregory Kefalas Publishing
5A Byron St, Campsie, NSW 2194
Tel: (02) 9789 6049 *Fax:* (02) 9787 6181
Subjects: Automotive
ISBN Prefix(es): 978-0-9586798

Kingsclear Books+
PO Box 335, Alexandria, Sydney, NSW 1435
Tel: (02) 9557 4367 *Fax:* (02) 9557 2337
E-mail: kingsclearbooks@gmail.com
Web Site: www.kingsclearbooks.com.au
Key Personnel
Mng Dir: Catherine Warne
Founded: 1983
Specialize in local history, alternative health,
tourism & true crime.
Subjects: Criminology, Health, Nutrition, History,
Travel & Tourism
ISBN Prefix(es): 978-0-908272; 978-0-9871840;
978-0-9807255
Number of titles published annually: 6 Print
Total Titles: 60 Print

Knopf, *imprint of* Random House Books
Australia, A Penguin Random House Company

Koala Books, *imprint of* Scholastic Australia Pty
Ltd

Koala Books
Imprint of Scholastic Australia Pty Ltd
76-80 Railway Crescent, Lisarow, NSW 2250
Mailing Address: PO Box 579, Gosford, NSW
2250
Tel: (02) 4328 3555
E-mail: customer_service@scholastic.com.au
Web Site: www.koalabooks.com.au
Key Personnel
State Sales Manager: David Livy
E-mail: david_livy@scholastic.com.au
ISBN Prefix(es): 978-1-875354; 978-1-875846;
978-0-86461; 978-1-74276
Number of titles published annually: 70 Print
Distributed by Scholastic Australia Pty Ltd;
Scholastic NZ

Krinos, *imprint of* GHR Press

Ladybird, *imprint of* Penguin Group (Australia)

Laguna Bay Publishing Pty Ltd
PO Box 260, Mosman, NSW 2088
Tel: (02) 9660 5420 *Fax:* (02) 9660 5346
E-mail: lagunabaypublish@bigpond.com
Web Site: www.lagunabaypublishing.com
Key Personnel
Mng Dir: Kaye Richards
Financial Controller & Production Manager:
  Barry Richards
Founded: 2002
Subjects: Fiction, Nonfiction (General)
ISBN Prefix(es): 978-0-9805664
Total Titles: 200 Print
Distributed by Macmillan Education Australia;
  Marshall Cavendish Asia; McGraw-Hill/Wright
  Group (USA); Pearson Australia; Scholastic ·
  (Australia, Canada & UK)
Distribution Center: Dennis Jones & Associates,
  Unit 1/10 Merlich Rd, Bayswater, Victoria
  3153 *Tel:* (03) 9762 9100 *Fax:* (03) 9762 9200
  E-mail: theoffice@dennisjones.com.au (trade
  sales)

Lake Press
5 Burwood Rd, Hawthorn, Victoria 3122
Tel: (03) 9188 3650
E-mail: publishing@lakepress.com.au
Web Site: lakepress.com.au
Key Personnel
Publisher: Sarah Mumme *E-mail:* sarah@
  lakepress.com.au
Asia Sales: Shannon Ryan *E-mail:* shannon@
  lakepress.com.au
Australian Sales: Scott Barry *E-mail:* scott@
  lakepress.com.au
Foreign Language Sales: Mark Mobsby
  E-mail: mark@lakepress.com.au
USA/UK Sales: Sarah Tanner *E-mail:* saraht@
  lakepress.com.au
Founded: 2009
Specialize in illustrated books primarily for chil-
  dren 0-8 years of age.
ISBN Prefix(es): 978-1-76045
Foreign Rights: Arika Interrights Agency (Kate
  Thammano, translations) (Indonesia, Thai-
  land, Vietnam); BookBug (Teresa Mendonca)
  (Portugal); Eric Chiu (English language) (In-
  dia, Indonesia, Malaysia, Philippines, Singa-
  pore); Japan UNI Agency Inc (Takeshi Oyama)
  (Japan); Korea Copyright Center Inc (Korea);
  BK Norton Agency (Lillian Hsiao) (China, Tai-
  wan)

Allen Lane, *imprint of* Penguin Group (Australia)

Mitchell Lane Publishers, *imprint of* Pearson
  Library

Lansdowne Publishing Pty Ltd+
3A Grandview St, Naremburn, NSW 2065
Mailing Address: PO Box 1669, Crows Nest,
  NSW 1585
Tel: (04) 1745 4615 *Fax:* (02) 9436 2974
E-mail: info@lansdownepublishing.com.au
Web Site: www.lansdownepublishing.com.au
Key Personnel
Owner: Steven Morris
Specialize in cooking, New Age, interior design,
  gardening, health, history & spirituality.
Subjects: Animals, Pets, Architecture & Interior
  Design, Cookery, Gardening, Plants, Health,
  Nutrition, History, Inspirational, Spirituality,
  Mythology, New Age
ISBN Prefix(es): 978-1-86302; 978-0-947116;
  978-0-949708; 978-0-7018
Parent Company: Kirin Publishing Pty Ltd

Lantern, *imprint of* Penguin Group (Australia)

Laurel Press+
850 Huon Rd, Ferntree, Tas 7054

Mailing Address: PO Box 132, Sandy Bay, Tas
  7006
Tel: (03) 6239 1139
Key Personnel
Head of Company: Chris Bell
  E-mail: chrisbell63@bigpond.com
Founded: 1990
Publisher of ongoing large format fine editions.
Subjects: Natural History, Photography
Total Titles: 2 Print

LCP, see Local Consumption Publications (LCP)

LexisNexis Australia
Division of Reed International Books Australia
  Pty Ltd
Tower 2, 475-495 Victoria Ave, Chatswood, NSW
  2067
Mailing Address: Level 9, Locked Bag 2222,
  Chatswood Delivery Centre, Chatswood, NSW
  2067
Tel: (02) 9422 2174 *Toll Free Tel:* 1800 772 772
  Fax: (02) 9422 2405
E-mail: customer.relations@lexisnexis.com.au
Web Site: www.lexisnexis.com.au
Key Personnel
Chief Executive Officer: Theuns Viljoen
Chief Financial Officer: Dev Mahendran
Chief Marketing Officer: Jen Armstrong
Dir, Technology & Business Development: Marc
  K Peter *E-mail:* marc.peter@lexisnexis.com.au
Human Resources Dir: Josephine Simeone
Research Solutions Dir: Daemoni Bishop
Sales Dir: Simon Wilkins *Tel:* (02) 9422 2333
  E-mail: simon.wilkins@lexisnexis.com.au
Founded: 1910
Subjects: Accounting, Business, Law
ISBN Prefix(es): 978-0-409
Ultimate Parent Company: Reed Elsevier plc, 1-3
  Strand, London WC2N 5JR, United Kingdom
Associate Companies: LexisNexis CZ sro, Czech
  Republic; LexisNexis Juris Classeur, France;
  LexisNexis Deutschland GmbH, Germany;
  Guiffre Editore, Italy; LexisNexis Malaysia
  Sdn Bhd, Malaysia; Wydawnictwo Prawnicze,
  Poland
U.S. Office(s): 201 Mission St, 26th floor, San
  Francisco, CA 94105, United States *Tel:* 415-
  781-1707

Little Hills Press Pty Ltd+
12/103 Kurrajong Ave, Mount Druitt, NSW 2770
SAN: 901-7682
Tel: (02) 9677 9658 *Fax:* (02) 9677 9152
E-mail: info@littlehills.com; sales@littlehills.com
Web Site: www.littlehills.com; www.lhdistribution.
  com
Key Personnel
Owner: Charles C Burfitt
Founded: 1981
Publishing & distribution company specializing in
  travel.
Membership(s): Australian Booksellers Associa-
  tion.
Subjects: Business, Cookery, Crafts, Games, Hob-
  bies, Fashion, Fiction, Inspirational, Spiritu-
  ality, Nonfiction (General), Religion - Other,
  Travel & Tourism
ISBN Prefix(es): 978-0-949773; 978-1-86315
Total Titles: 59 Print

Little Nippers, *imprint of* Pearson Library

Little Red Apple Publishing+
PO Box K152 Haymarket, Sydney, NSW 1240
Tel: (02) 9430 6867 (leave message)
E-mail: littleredapplepublishing520@yahoo.com.
  au; littleredapple3@hotmail.com (book club)
Web Site: www.littleredapplepublishing.net.au
Key Personnel
Contact: Rose Solomon *Tel:* (04) 5025 9923

Founded: 1988
Network for author, editors & illustrators. Publish
  works that make the world's understanding of
  life as a better place. Books in Italian or about
  Italian migration around the world. Also stories
  of survival due to war displacement. $300 read-
  ing fee. Editorial office located in Thornleigh.
Subjects: Biography, Memoirs, Child Care & De-
  velopment, Disability, Special Needs, Educa-
  tion, Fiction, History, Human Relations, Hu-
  mor, Nonfiction (General), Poetry, Religion -
  Catholic, Religion - Other, Romance
ISBN Prefix(es): 978-1-875329
Number of titles published annually: 8 Print; 1
  CD-ROM; 8 Online
Total Titles: 70 Print; 8 Online
Bookshop(s): Abbey's Bookshop, York St,
  Sydney, NSW 2000 *Tel:* (02) 9264 3111
  E-mail: info@abbeys.com.au

Little Simon, *imprint of* Simon & Schuster
  (Australia) Pty Ltd

Local Consumption Publications (LCP)
32 Rochford St, Erskineville, NSW 2043
Tel: (02) 9590 8051
Founded: 2004
Subjects: Literature, Literary Criticism, Essays
ISBN Prefix(es): 978-0-949793

Lonestone Press, *imprint of* Oceans Enterprises

Lost the Plot, *imprint of* Pantera Press Pty Ltd

Lowden Publishing Co
29 Lisbeth Ave, Donvale, Victoria 3111
Tel: (03) 9873 7202 *Fax:* (03) 9873 0542
E-mail: theruralstore@bigpond.com
Web Site: www.theruralstore.com.au
Key Personnel
Mng Dir: Jim Lowden
Founded: 1969
Subjects: Biography, Memoirs, History, Religion -
  Other, Transportation
ISBN Prefix(es): 978-0-909706; 978-1-920753
Number of titles published annually: 2 Print
Total Titles: 30 Print
Associate Companies: The Rural Store (agricul-
  tural booksellers)

Lyrebird Press
Melbourne Conservatorium of Music, University
  of Melbourne, Parkville, Victoria 3010
Tel: (03) 9035 8671 *Fax:* (03) 8344 5346
E-mail: lyrebirdpress-info@unimelb.edu.au
Web Site: vca-mcm.unimelb.edu.au/lyrebirdpress
Founded: 2006
Subjects: Music, Dance
ISBN Prefix(es): 978-0-7340

MAAS Media, see Museum of Applied Arts &
  Sciences Media

Macmillan, *imprint of* Pan Macmillan Australia
  Pty Ltd

Macmillan Education Australia Pty Ltd+
1-3/15-19 Claremont St, South Yarra, Victoria
  3141
Tel: (03) 9825 1000 *Toll Free Tel:* 1300 135 113
  Fax: (03) 9825 1010 *Toll Free Fax:* 1300 135
  103
E-mail: mea@macmillan.com.au
Web Site: www.macmillan.com.au; www.
  macmillaneducation.com.au
Key Personnel
Mng Dir: Peter Saffin *E-mail:* peter.saffin@
  macmillan.com.au
Sales & Marketing Dir: Peter Huntley *Tel:* (03)
  9825 1095 *E-mail:* peter.huntley@macmillan.
  com.au

Marketing Manager: Christine Powers *Tel:* (03) 9825 1153 *E-mail:* christine.powers@ macmillan.com.au

National Sales Manager, Primary: Carol Baker *Tel:* (03) 9825 1146 *E-mail:* carol.baker@ macmillan.com.au

National Sales Manager, Secondary: Jodie Fitz *E-mail:* jodie.fitz@macmillan.com.au

Founded: 1896

Subjects: Accounting, Behavioral Sciences, Economics, Education, Geography, Geology, Government, Political Science, History, Management, Mathematics, Physics, Science (General), Social Sciences, Sociology

ISBN Prefix(es): 978-0-333; 978-0-7329; 978-0-86859; 978-0-7330; 978-1-4202; 978-1-4586

Parent Company: Macmillan Publishers Australia Pty Ltd

Branch Office(s)

One Market St, Level 25, Sydney, NSW 2000 *Fax:* (02) 9285 9290

Warehouse: Macmillan Distribution Services Pty Ltd, 56 Park West Dr, Derrimut, Victoria 3030 *E-mail:* customer.service@macmillan.com.au

Macquarie Dictionary Publishers, *imprint of* Pan Macmillan Australia Pty Ltd

Macquarie Dictionary Publishers Pty Ltd+
Level 25, One Market St, Sydney, NSW 2000
Toll Free Tel: 1800 645 349; 1300 135 113 (orders)
E-mail: macquarie@macmillan.com.au; customer. service@macmillan.com.au
Web Site: www.macquariedictionary.com.au
Founded: 1981
ISBN Prefix(es): 978-0-949757; 978-1-876429
Total Titles: 5 Online
Parent Company: Macmillan Publishers Australia
Distributed by Pan Macmillan Australia Pty Ltd; John Wiley & Sons Australia Ltd

Magabala Books+
One Bagot St, Broome, WA 6725
Mailing Address: PO Box 668, Broome, WA 6725
Tel: (08) 9192 1991 *Fax:* (08) 9193 5254
E-mail: sales@magabala.com
Web Site: www.magabala.com
Key Personnel
Chief Executive Officer: Suzie Haslehurst
Management Committee Chairperson: Coco Yu
Publishing Manager: Rachael Christensen
Founded: 1987
Specialize in indigenous publishing.
Subjects: Anthropology, Art, Biography, Memoirs, Drama, Theater, Fiction, Human Relations, Literature, Literary Criticism, Essays, Natural History, Nonfiction (General), Philosophy, Religion - Other
ISBN Prefix(es): 978-1-875641; 978-0-9588101
Number of titles published annually: 6 Print; 6 Online
Total Titles: 100 Print; 100 Online
Distribution Center: UNIREPS

Magpies Magazine Pty Ltd
PO Box 7128, Leura, NSW 2780
Tel: (02) 4784 1453 *Fax:* (02) 4784 1806
E-mail: james@magpies.net.au
Web Site: www.magpies.net.au
Founded: 1986
Subjects: Library & Information Sciences
ISBN Prefix(es): 978-1-875249

MAI Press, see Monash Asia Institute Press

Malthouse Theatre Co+
113 Sturt St, Southbank, Victoria 3006
Tel: (03) 9685 5100; (03) 9685 5111 *Fax:* (03) 9685 5112

E-mail: admin@malthousetheatre.com.au
Web Site: www.malthousetheatre.com.au
Key Personnel
Company Manager: Julian Hobba
E-mail: companymanager@malthousetheatre. com.au
Development, presentation & promotion of new Australian plays & playwrights.
Subjects: Drama, Theater
ISBN Prefix(es): 978-0-7326
Number of titles published annually: 12 Print
Distributed by Currency Press
Distributor for Currency Press

Manna Press, *imprint of* Hyland House Publishing Pty Ltd

Marie Claire, *imprint of* Murdoch Books Pty Ltd Australia

Marketing Focus
26 Central Rd, Kalamunda, WA 6076
Tel: (08) 9257 1777 *Fax:* (08) 9257 1888
Web Site: www.marketingfocus.net.au
Key Personnel
Head of Company & Mng Dir: Barry Ross Urquhart *E-mail:* urquhart@marketingfocus. net.au
Founded: 1978
Marketing & strategic planning consultant.
Subjects: Business, Marketing
ISBN Prefix(es): 978-0-9586558

Marque Publishing Co Pty Ltd
15 Belina Ave, Wyoming, NSW 2250
Mailing Address: PO Box 1896, Gosford, NSW 2250
Tel: (02) 4322 4803; (02) 4329 4637 *Fax:* (02) 4322 4803
Key Personnel
Editorial Dir: Ewan Kennedy
Business Manager: Alistair Kennedy
Founded: 1987
Specialize in motoring books, collectible books, DVDs & videos.
Subjects: Automotive, Transportation, Travel & Tourism
ISBN Prefix(es): 978-0-947079
Distributed by Bookworks Pty Ltd

Tracy Marsh Publications Pty Ltd+
312A Unley Rd, Hyde Park, SA 5061
Tel: (08) 8272 0001
E-mail: admin@tracymarsh.com
Web Site: www.tracymarsh.com
Key Personnel
Chief Executive: Tracy Marsh
Founded: 1984
Subjects: Crafts, Games, Hobbies, Travel & Tourism
ISBN Prefix(es): 978-1-875899; 978-0-9590174

Mason Crest, *imprint of* Pearson Library

Matthias Media
42 Gardeners Rd, Suite 1, Kingsford, NSW 2032
Mailing Address: PO Box 225, Kingsford, NSW 2032
Tel: (02) 9663 1478 *Toll Free Tel:* 1800 814 360 (Australia) *Fax:* (02) 9663 3265
E-mail: info@matthiasmedia.com.au; sales@ matthiasmedia.com.au
Web Site: www.matthiasmedia.com.au
Key Personnel
Founder: Phillip Jensen
Publishing Dir: Tony Payne
Business Growth Dir: Ian Carmichael
Founded: 1988
Subjects: Education, Religion - Protestant, Bible, Christianity, Evangelicalism, Ministry

ISBN Prefix(es): 978-1-876326; 978-1-875245; 978-1-921441
U.S. Office(s): Matthias Media (USA), 97 Karago Ave, Suite 5, Youngstown, OH 44512, United States *Tel:* 330-953-1702 *Fax:* 330-953-1712

Mayfield Publishing, *imprint of* Elsevier Australia

Mayne Publishing Pty Ltd+
Level 1, Unit E, 5 Skyline Pl, Frenchs Forest, NSW 2086
Mailing Address: PO Box 489, Dee Why, NSW 2099
Tel: (02) 9452 4517 *Fax:* (02) 9452 5319
E-mail: reception@trademags.com.au
Web Site: www.trademags.com.au
Key Personnel
Founder & Chief Executive Officer: Kurt Quambusch
Founded: 1995
Subjects: Behavioral Sciences, Cookery, Crafts, Games, Hobbies, Fiction, Government, Political Science, Health, Nutrition, How-to, Self-Help
ISBN Prefix(es): 978-0-9578142

Margaret K McElderry, *imprint of* Simon & Schuster (Australia) Pty Ltd

McGraw-Hill Australia Pty Ltd+
Subsidiary of The McGraw-Hill Companies Inc
Level 2, The Everglade Bldg, 82 Waterloo Rd, North Ryde, NSW 2113
Mailing Address: Locked Bag 2233, North Ryde, NSW 1670
Tel: (02) 9900 1800 (customer service)
Toll Free Tel: 1800 646 572 (in Australia)
Fax: (02) 9900 1980 (customer service)
E-mail: cservice_sydney@mheducation.com
Web Site: www.mheducation.com
Key Personnel
Publishing Dir: Nicole Meehan
Finance & Operations Dir: Kevin Camilleri
Executive General Manager, Schools & Professional Division: Cindy Jones
General Manager, Higher Education & Medical Divisions: Cath Godfrey
Media Services Manager: James Herd
Founded: 1964
Subjects: Accounting, Advertising, Aeronautics, Aviation, Anthropology, Architecture & Interior Design, Art, Automotive, Behavioral Sciences, Biological Sciences, Chemistry, Chemical Engineering, Child Care & Development, Computer Science, Criminology, Disability, Special Needs, Earth Sciences, Economics, Education, Electronics, Electrical Engineering, Engineering (General), English as a Second Language, Environmental Studies, Film, Video, Geography, Geology, Health, Nutrition, Journalism, Labor, Industrial Relations, Language Arts, Linguistics, Management, Maritime, Marketing, Mathematics, Mechanical Engineering, Medicine, Nursing, Dentistry, Philosophy, Photography, Physical Sciences, Physics, Psychology, Psychiatry, Social Sciences, Sociology, Sports, Athletics
ISBN Prefix(es): 978-0-07; 978-0-697; 978-0-256
Associate Companies: McGraw-Hill Book Co New Zealand Ltd
Imprints: PressXpress
Distributed by Active Path (Wrox); Amacom (American Management); American Education Publishing; Appleton & Lange; ASQ (American Society of Quality); Barnell Loft Ltd; Benziger Publishing Co; Brown & Benchmark; William C Brown; Business Week Books; Certification Press; Citrix Press; Clearway Exam Questions (HSC); Clearway Textbooks; CommerceNet Press; Computing McGraw-Hill; Contemporary Publications/NTC; Corel Press; Custom Publications; Dushkin Publishing Group; J D Edwards; Fine Arts Press; Friends

of Ed; Glencoe/McGraw; Harvard Business School Press; International Marine; Irwin Publishers; Richard D Irwin; James Town Publishers/NTC; Keats Publishing/NTC; Learning Triangle Press; London House; Macmillan/McGraw-Hill School; Mayfield Publishing Co; McGraw-Hill Canada; McGraw-Hill Italy; McGraw-Hill Microsoft Press; McGraw-Hill Singapore; McGraw-Hill UK; McGraw-Hill USA; Charles E Merrill; Metric Schaum; New Holland Publishers; NTC (National Textbook Co); Oracle Press; Osborne; Platts (USA); Possum Press; Primis; Quicken Press; Quilt Digest Press/NTC; Ragged Mountain Press; Rebol Press; Republic of Texas Press; RSA Press; Sapphire Books; Schaum; Science Research Associates (SRA); Tab Books; Tata McGraw-Hill India; Terrific Science Press; Visual Education Corp (School); Webster Publishing; Windcrest; Wordware Publishing; Wright Group/McGraw-Hill; Wrox Press; Xebec/McGraw-Hill
Distributor for Amacom (American Management); Barnell Loft Ltd (USA); Benziger Publishing Co (USA); Brown & Benchmark; William C Brown; Clearway Textbooks; Custom Publications; Clearway Exam Questions-HSC; Dushkin Publishing Group; Glencoe/McGraw (USA); Harvard Business School Press (USA); International Marine (USA); Irwin Professional PRO (USA); Irwin Publishers (USA); Richard D Irwin (USA); London House (USA); Macmillan/McGraw-Hill School; McGraw-Hill (UK); McGraw-Hill Canada (Canada); McGraw-Hill Italy (Italy); McGraw-Hill Singapore (Singapore); McGraw-Hill USA (USA); Charles E Merrill (USA); Metric Schaum (Singapore); Osborne (USA); Possum Press (Australia); Primis; Ragged Mountain Press; Republic of Texas Press (Australia); Sapphire Books (USA); Schaum (USA); Science Research Associates SRA (USA); Tab Books (USA); Tata McGraw-Hill India (India); Alfred Waller (UK); Webster Publishing; Wordware Publishing (USA); Wrox Press; Windcrest

Melbourne University Press, *imprint of* Melbourne University Publishing Ltd

Melbourne University Publishing Ltd+
187 Grattan St, Carlton, Victoria 3053
Tel: (03) 9342 0300 *Fax:* (03) 9342 0399
E-mail: mup-info@unimelb.edu.au
Web Site: www.mup.com.au
Key Personnel
Chief Executive Officer & Publisher-in-Chief: Louise Adler
Chief Operating Officer: Richard Tegoni
Executive Publisher: Colette Vella
National Sales & Marketing Manager: Jacqui Gray
Mng Editor: Diane Leyman
Senior Editor: Cathy Smith
Editor: Lily Keil
Founded: 1922
Subjects: Biography, Memoirs, History, Literature, Literary Criticism, Essays, Natural History, Nonfiction (General), Psychology, Psychiatry, Travel & Tourism
ISBN Prefix(es): 978-0-522
Number of titles published annually: 50 Print; 2 CD-ROM; 10 E-Book
Total Titles: 600 Print; 3 CD-ROM; 1 E-Book
Imprints: Melbourne University Press; Miegunyah Press; Victory Books
Foreign Rep(s): The Eurospan Group (Europe, UK); Independent Publishers Group (North America); Macmillan Publishers New Zealand Ltd (New Zealand); Macmillan Publishing Services (Australia)

Melbournestyle Books
155 Clarendon St, South Melbourne, Victoria 3205
Tel: (03) 9696 8445
E-mail: mca@melbournestyle.com.au
Web Site: www.melbournestyle.com.au
Key Personnel
Publisher: Maree Coote
Founded: 2003
Membership(s): Australian Publishers Association (APA).
Subjects: Art, History, Regional Interests
ISBN Prefix(es): 978-0-9757047
Distribution Center: Trafalgar Square Publishing, c/o Independent Publishers Group (IPG), 814 N Franklin St, Chicago, IL 60610, United States

Melting Pot Press+
173-179 Broadway, Suite 4, Level 3, Broadway, NSW 2007
SAN: 901-1005
Tel: (02) 9212 1882 *Fax:* (02) 9211 1868
E-mail: books@elt.com.au
Web Site: www.elt.com.au
Key Personnel
Dir: Ronald J Wood
Founded: 1983
Specialize in publishing & distribution of English Language Teaching (ELT) titles.
Subjects: English as a Second Language
ISBN Prefix(es): 978-0-947103
Total Titles: 3 Print; 3 Audio
Distributor for Academic English Press; Dubois Publishing; Martha Lam & Stanley Po; Leigh Salter; R A Thompson

Melway Publishing Pty Ltd+
32 Ricketts Rd, Mount Waverley 3149
Mailing Address: PO Box 737, Mount Waverley 3149
Toll Free Tel: 1300 MELWAY (1300 676776) *Fax:* (03) 9585 9800 *Toll Free Fax:* 1800 638648
E-mail: reception@ausway.com
Web Site: www.melway.com.au
Key Personnel
Dir: Murray Godfrey *E-mail:* murray.godfrey@ausway.com
Founded: 1966
Producers of street directories & maps (hard copy & digital).
This publisher has indicated that 100% of their product line is author subsidized.
Membership(s): International Map Industry Association (IMIA).
Subjects: Publishing & Book Trade Reference, Travel & Tourism
ISBN Prefix(es): 978-0-909439 (Melway)
Total Titles: 12 Print; 2 CD-ROM; 23 Online; 8 E-Book
Parent Company: Ausway Publishing Pty Ltd
Ultimate Parent Company: Ausway Group of Companies
Associate Companies: Ausway Digital Pty Ltd; Sydway Publishing Pty Ltd, PO Box 693, Coogee 2034 *Tel:* (03) 9585 9806 *Toll Free Tel:* 1300 676776 *Fax:* (03) 9585 9807 *Toll Free Fax:* 1800 638648; Brisway Publishing Pty Ltd, PO Box 1155, Eagle Farm 4009 *Tel:* (03) 9585 9833 *Toll Free Tel:* 1300 274799 *Fax:* (03) 9585 9800 *Toll Free Fax:* 1300 274792
Distribution Center: Gordon & Gotch, The Equinox Centre, 18 Rodborough Rd, Frenchs Forest 2086
Waymore Distributors, 39 Parkhurst Dr, Knoxfield 3180

Mentor, *imprint of* Penguin Group (Australia)

Mercury Ink, *imprint of* Simon & Schuster (Australia) Pty Ltd

Meridian, *imprint of* Penguin Group (Australia)

Miegunyah Press, *imprint of* Melbourne University Publishing Ltd

Millennium House
4 Barons Crescent, Hunters Hill, NSW 2110
Tel: (02) 9817 4971
Web Site: www.millenniumhouse.com.au
Key Personnel
Mng Dir: Gordon Cheers
Publisher: Janet Parker
Art Dir: Stan Lamond
Production Manager: Simone Coupland
Editor: Kate Etherington
Media & Public Relations: Jannine Doyle
Founded: 2005
Subjects: Architecture & Interior Design, Geography, Geology, History, Natural History, Pop Culture, Science (General), Cartography
ISBN Prefix(es): 978-1-921209; 978-1-921811

The Milner Craft Series, *imprint of* Sally Milner Publishing Pty Ltd

The Milner Health Series, *imprint of* Sally Milner Publishing Pty Ltd

Sally Milner Publishing Pty Ltd
734 Woodville Rd, Binda, NSW 2583
Mailing Address: PO Box 30, Crookwell, NSW 2583
Tel: (02) 4835 6212
E-mail: info@sallymilner.com.au
Web Site: www.sallymilner.com.au
Key Personnel
Mng Dir: Ian Webster
Publishing Dir: Libby Renney
Subjects: Crafts, Games, Hobbies, Health, Nutrition, History
ISBN Prefix(es): 978-1-86351; 978-1-877080
Number of titles published annually: 12 Print
Total Titles: 180 Print
Imprints: Creative House; JB Fairfax Craft; The Milner Craft Series; The Milner Health Series
Foreign Rep(s): Ascot Lane Distributors (NZ) Ltd (New Zealand); David Bateman Ltd (New Zealand); Sales East (Thailand); Search Press (Europe, UK); Sterling Publishing Co Inc (Canada, USA)
Distribution Center: Gary Allen Pty Ltd, PO Box 6640, Wetherill Park BC, NSW 1851 *Tel:* (02) 9725 2933 *E-mail:* orders@garyallen.com.au
Web Site: www.garyallen.com.au

Mission Publications of Australia (MPA)
Subsidiary of Australian Indigenous Ministries
PO Box 579, Springwood, NSW 2777
Tel: (02) 4754 3833 *Fax:* (02) 4754 3822
E-mail: aim@aimpa.com
Web Site: www.aimpa.com/Publications.htm
Key Personnel
General Dir: Rev Trevor Leggott
Field Dir: Rev Cliff Letcher
Administrator: Pamela Leggott
Founded: 1960
Specialize in easy English Christian literature.
Subjects: Religion - Other
ISBN Prefix(es): 978-0-909448; 978-1-86288

Mockingbird, *imprint of* Ginninderra Press

Monash Asia Institute Press
Imprint of Monash University Press
Monash University, H Bldg, 5th floor, 900 Dandenong Rd, Caulfield East, Victoria 3145
Mailing Address: PO Box 197, Caulfield East, Victoria 3145
Tel: (03) 9903 5043 *Fax:* (03) 9905 5370
E-mail: mai-enquiries@monash.edu

Web Site: ecommerce.arts.monash.edu.au/
categories.asp?cID=48
Subjects: Ethnicity, Literature, Literary Criticism,
Essays, Asia, Asian Studies
ISBN Prefix(es): 978-0-86746
Foreign Rep(s): Eurospan Group (Africa, Central
Asia, Europe, Middle East, UK); Inbooks (Aus-
tralia, New Zealand); International Specialised
Book Services (North America); ISEAS Publi-
cations Unit (Asia)

Moonlight Publishing
PO Box 187, Frankston, Victoria 3199
Tel: (03) 5447 8221
E-mail: moonlight@impulse.net.au;
moonlightau@gmail.com
Key Personnel
Manager: Chris Spencer
Founded: 1989
Subjects: Music, Dance
ISBN Prefix(es): 978-1-876187; 978-0-9586515
Total Titles: 60 Print; 1 Audio
Orders to: PO Box 5, Golden Square, Victoria
3555

Morgan Kaufmann, *imprint of* Elsevier Australia

Mosby, *imprint of* Elsevier Australia

Mostly for Mothers, *imprint of* Wombat Books

Mostly Unsung+
PO Box 7020, Gardenvale, Victoria 3186
Tel: (03) 5971 5565
Web Site: mostlyunsung.com.au
Key Personnel
Head, Company: Neil C Smith
Founded: 1991
Subjects: History, Military Science, Regional In-
terests
ISBN Prefix(es): 978-1-876179
Total Titles: 50 Print
U.S. Office(s): c/o Anzar Services Inc, PO Box
274, Lexington, VA 24450, United States

MPA, see Mission Publications of Australia
(MPA)

Murdoch Books, *imprint of* Allen & Unwin

Murdoch Books Pty Ltd Australia+
Imprint of Allen & Unwin
Pier 8/9, 23 Hickson Rd, Millers Point, Sydney,
NSW 2000
Mailing Address: GPO Box 4115, Sydney, NSW
2001
Tel: (02) 8220 2000 *Fax:* (02) 8220 2558
E-mail: enquiries@murdochbooks.com.au
Web Site: www.murdochbooks.com.au
Key Personnel
Chief Executive Officer: Robert Gorman
Chief Financial Officer: David Martin
Creative Dir: Deborah Brash
International Sales Dir: Amanda Maclean
Marketing Dir: Mark Ashbridge
Publishing Dir: Sue Hines
Sales & Marketing Dir: Jim Demetriou
International Sales Manager: Cara Codemo
National Marketing Manager: Mary-Jayne House
Production Manager: Karen Small
Sales Development Manager: Noel Hammond
Publisher, Lifestyle: Lynn Lewis
Publisher, Pier 9: Melanie Ostell
Founded: 1989
General nonfiction illustrated publisher.
Subjects: Biography, Memoirs, Cookery, Crafts,
Games, Hobbies, Fiction, Gardening, Plants,
History, Domestic & Decorative Arts, Human
Interest

ISBN Prefix(es): 978-0-86411; 978-1-74045; 978-
1-921259; 978-1-921208; 978-1-74196; 978-1-
74266; 978-1-74325; 978-1-74336
Total Titles: 800 Print
Imprints: Bay Books; Marie Claire; Pier 9
Distributor for Black Dog & Leventhal
Distribution Center: Harper Entertainment
Distribution Services (HEDS) *Toll Free
Tel:* 1300 551 721 *Toll Free Fax:* 1800 645
547 *E-mail:* orders@harpercollins.com.au

Murray Books
21 Waverley Ridge Rd, Crafers West, Adelaide,
SA 5152
Mailing Address: PO Box 1047, Stirling, Ade-
laide, SA 5152
Web Site: www.murraybooks.com.au
Key Personnel
Chief Executive: Peter Murray
Mng Dir: Lorraine Lynn *E-mail:* lorraine@
murraybooks.com
International Rights Dir: Kim Edwards
E-mail: kim@murraybooks.com
Retail Sales Manager: Sonia Hein *E-mail:* sonia@
murraybooks.com
Founded: 2006
Subjects: Cookery, Sports, Athletics, Lifestyle
ISBN Prefix(es): 978-0-9580348; 978-0-9757455;
978-0-9803131; 978-0-9803829; 978-0-
9803830
Branch Office(s)
26 Beeleigh Rd, Maldon, Essex CM9 5QH,
United Kingdom, Editorial Dir: Michelle Bra-
chet *E-mail:* michelle@murraybooks.com

Museum of Applied Arts & Sciences Media
500 Harris St, Ultimo, NSW 2007
Tel: (02) 9217 0129 *Fax:* (02) 9217 0434
E-mail: powerhousepublishing@maas.museum
Web Site: maas.museum/maas-media
Subjects: Architecture & Interior Design, Art,
Asian Studies, Astronomy, Fashion, History,
Science (General), Technology, Transportation,
Museology, Textiles
ISBN Prefix(es): 978-1-86317
Distributed by Lund Humphries
Distribution Center: NewSouth Books, 45
Beach St, Coogee, NSW 2034 *Tel:* (02) 9664
0912 *Fax:* (02) 9664 5420 *Web Site:* www.
newsouthbooks.com.au (Australia & New
Zealand)

Museum of Victoria
11 Nicholson St, Carlton, Victoria 3053
Mailing Address: GPO Box 666E, Melbourne,
Victoria 3001
Tel: (03) 8341 7574 *Fax:* (03) 8341 7573
E-mail: publications@museum.vic.gov.au
Web Site: museumvictoria.com.au
Subjects: Education, History
Distribution Center: NewSouth Books
Tel: (02) 8778 9999 *Fax:* (02) 8778 9944
E-mail: orders@tldistribution.com.au (Aus-
tralian wholesale orders)

National Archives of Australia
Canberra Business Centre, PO Box 7425, Can-
berra, ACT 2610
Tel: (02) 6212 3600; (02) 6212 3659 (sales)
E-mail: archives@naa.gov.au; naasales@naa.gov.
au
Web Site: www.naa.gov.au/about-us/publications/
index.aspx; eshop.naa.gov.au
Subjects: Anthropology, History, Photography,
Archives, Family History, Foreign Relations,
Immigration, Military History
ISBN Prefix(es): 978-1-920807

National Gallery of Australia+
Parkes Pl, Parkes, ACT 2600

Mailing Address: GPO Box 1150, Canberra, ACT
2601
Tel: (02) 6240 6438; (02) 6240 6411; (02) 6240
6420 (orders) *Fax:* (02) 6240 6628 (orders);
(02) 6240 6529
E-mail: ecom@nga.gov.au
Web Site: www.nga.gov.au
Key Personnel
Executive Dir: Maryanne Voyazis
Dir: Ron Radford *E-mail:* ron.radford@nga.gov.
au
Deputy Dir: Alan Froud *E-mail:* alan.froud@nga.
gov.au
Rights & Permissions Officer: Nick Nicholson
E-mail: copyright@nga.gov.au
Marketing & Communications: Ashley Zmijewski
E-mail: ashley.zmijewski@nga.gov.au
Founded: 1982
Subjects: Art, Photography, American, Australian,
Asian, European, Indigenous & Pacific Art,
Decorative Arts

National Gallery of Victoria
180 St Kilda Rd, Melbourne, Victoria 3004
Mailing Address: PO Box 7259, Melbourne, Vic-
toria 8004
Tel: (03) 8620 2222; (03) 8620 2243 (bookshop)
Fax: (03) 8620 2535
E-mail: enquiries@ngv.vic.gov.au; gallery.shop@
ngv.vic.gov.au (bookshop)
Web Site: www.ngv.vic.gov.au
Key Personnel
Dir & Chief Executive Officer: Dr Gerard
Vaughan
Founded: 1861
Specialize in large collections of art for the state
of Victoria, Australia.
Subjects: Art, Fashion
ISBN Prefix(es): 978-0-7241
Number of titles published annually: 25 Print
Total Titles: 85 Print

National Library of Australia
Parkes Pl, Canberra, ACT 2600
Tel: (02) 6262 1111 *Fax:* (02) 6257 1703
E-mail: nlasales@nla.gov.au
Web Site: www.nla.gov.au/publications
Key Personnel
Dir General: Anne-Marie Schwirtlich *Tel:* (02)
6262 1262 *E-mail:* aschwirtlich@nla.gov.au
Assistant Dir General, Executive & Pub-
lic Programs Division: Jasmine Cameron
E-mail: jcameron@nla.gov.au
Manager, Publications & Production: Susan Hall
Tel: (02) 6262 1593 *E-mail:* shall@nla.gov.au
Founded: 1960

Navarine Publishing
GPO Box 2178, Hobart, Tas 7001
Tel: (03) 6236 9445
Key Personnel
Founder & Publisher: Graeme Broxam
Founded: 1992
Subjects: Genealogy, History, Maritime, Nonfic-
tion (General), Regional Interests, Transporta-
tion
ISBN Prefix(es): 978-0-9586561; 978-0-9751331;
978-0-9923660
Number of titles published annually: 1 Print
Total Titles: 15 Print
Distributor for The Roebuck Society

Nelson Cengage Learning+
Imprint of Cengage Learning Australia Pty Ltd
80 Dorcas St, Level 7, South Melbourne, Victoria
3205
Tel: (03) 9685 4111 *Toll Free Tel:* 1300 790 853;
0800 449 725 (New Zealand) *Fax:* (03) 9685
4199 *Toll Free Fax:* 1300 790 852; 0800 442
104 (New Zealand)
E-mail: anz.customerservice@cengage.com
Web Site: cengage.com.au; cengage.co.nz

Key Personnel
Pres, Asia Pacific: Tat Chu Tan
Vice President, Higher Education: Paul Petrulis
Vice President, International GPMS: Barbara
  Stephan
Vice President, School Division: David O'Brien
Finance Dir: John Durow
Head, Production: Nigel Matai
General Manager, International: Nicole McCarten
Human Resources Manager: Tamara Silver
Marketing Manager: Elizabeth Dilevska
Operations Manager: Sandra Hamilton
Founded: 1957
Subjects: Accounting, Biological Sciences, Busi-
  ness, Chemistry, Chemical Engineering, Child
  Care & Development, Communications, Com-
  puter Science, Drama, Theater, Economics,
  Education, Electronics, Electrical Engineering,
  Finance, Geography, Geology, Health, Nutri-
  tion, History, Language Arts, Linguistics, Law,
  Management, Marketing, Mathematics, Outdoor
  Recreation, Physical Sciences, Physics, Poetry,
  Science (General), Social Sciences, Sociology,
  Sports, Athletics, Technology
ISBN Prefix(es): 978-0-17

Nero, *imprint of* Black Inc

New American Library, *imprint of* Penguin
  Group (Australia)

New Creation Publications Inc
268 Ackland Hill Rd, Coromandel East, SA 5157
Mailing Address: PO Box 403, Blackwood, SA
  5051
Tel: (08) 8270 1861 *Fax:* (08) 8270 4003
Web Site: www.newcreationlibrary.net
Key Personnel
Dir, Ministry: Andrew Klynsmith
General Manager: John David Skewes
Founded: 1974
Christian publishing.
Subjects: Biblical Studies, Fiction, Human Rela-
  tions, Theology
ISBN Prefix(es): 978-0-86408; 978-0-949851;
  978-0-9597018
Number of titles published annually: 6 Print; 20
  CD-ROM
Total Titles: 422 Print; 138 CD-ROM
Imprints: Troubadour Press

New Endeavour Press+
3 Bournemouth St, Bundeena, NSW 2230
Tel: (02) 9544 5813
Founded: 1989
Specialize in quality Australian fiction, poetry &
  art books.
Subjects: Anthropology, Art, Fiction, Humor,
  Journalism, Language Arts, Linguistics, Poetry
ISBN Prefix(es): 978-1-875505
Associate Companies: New South Wales Univer-
  sity Press

New Frontier Publishing
48 Ross St, Glebe, NSW 2037
Tel: (02) 9660 4614 *Fax:* (02) 9571 5952
E-mail: info@newfrontier.com.au
Web Site: www.newfrontier.com.au
Founded: 2002
Subjects: Fiction, Nonfiction (General)
ISBN Prefix(es): 978-0-9581463; 978-0-9750907;
  978-0-9750896; 978-1-921042; 978-0-9579884
Distribution Center: Scholastic Australia Pty Ltd,
  76-80 Railway Crescent, Lisarow, NSW 2250
  E-mail: customer_service@scholastic.com.au

Newman Centre Publications
One Chetwynd Rd, Merrylands, NSW 2160
Tel: (02) 9637 3351
Founded: 1974

Subjects: Education, Fiction, Philosophy, Religion
  - Catholic, Catholic Catechism
ISBN Prefix(es): 978-0-9587535; 978-0-9751678

NewSouth, *imprint of* University of New South
  Wales Press Ltd

NSW Department of Primary Industries
161 Kite St, Orange, NSW 2800
Mailing Address: Locked Bag 21, Orange, NSW
  2800
Tel: (02) 6391 3100 *Fax:* (02) 6391 3336
E-mail: nsw.agriculture@dpi.nsw.gov.au
Web Site: www.dpi.nsw.gov.au
Key Personnel
Dir General: R F Sheldrake
Founded: 2004
Subjects: Agriculture, Business, Environmental
  Studies, Health, Nutrition, Law
ISBN Prefix(es): 978-0-7347

Ocean Press Pty Ltd+
PO Box 1015, North Melbourne, Victoria 3051
Tel: (03) 9326 4280 *Fax:* (03) 9329 5040
E-mail: info@oceanbooks.com.au
Web Site: www.oceanbooks.com.au
Key Personnel
President: David Deutschmann
Founded: 1989
Subjects: Biography, Memoirs, Developing Coun-
  tries, Environmental Studies, Government, Po-
  litical Science, History, Social Sciences, Sociol-
  ogy, Women's Studies
ISBN Prefix(es): 978-1-875284; 978-1-876175;
  978-1-920888; 978-1-921235 (Ocean Sur)
Total Titles: 150 Print
Imprints: Ocean Sur (Spanish language)
U.S. *Office(s):* 511 Avenue of the Americas, No
  96, New York, NY 10011-8436, United States
Foreign Rep(s): Consortium Book Sales & Dis-
  tribution (Canada, USA); Ocean Sur (Cuba,
  Latin America); Palgrave Macmillan (Australia,
  New Zealand); Turnaround Publisher Services
  Ltd (Europe, UK); Two Rivers Distribution
  (Canada, USA)

Ocean Sur, *imprint of* Ocean Press Pty Ltd

Oceans Enterprises+
303 Commercial Rd, Yarram, Victoria 3971
Tel: (03) 5182 5108 *Fax:* (03) 5182 5823
E-mail: oceans@netspace.net.au (orders)
Web Site: www.oceans.com.au
Key Personnel
Manager: Peter Stone *E-mail:* peter@oceans.com.
  au
Founded: 1982
Specialize in marine, military & history publica-
  tions, commercial & sport scuba diving.
Subjects: History, Maritime, Military Science,
  Photography, Sports, Athletics, Travel &
  Tourism
ISBN Prefix(es): 978-0-9586657
Imprints: Lonestone Press

OEH, see Department of Environment &
  Heritage (OEH)

Of Primary Importance
PO Box 1001, Horsham, Victoria 3402
Tel: (03) 5382 1010 *Fax:* (03) 5382 4014
E-mail: opi@opi.com.au
Web Site: www.opi.com.au
Subjects: Education, Fiction, Mathematics, Read-
  ing
ISBN Prefix(es): 978-1-876573; 978-0-9587111;
  978-1-74015; 978-1-876298

Off the Shelf Publishing+
9 Silver Strand Circle, Hyams Beach, NSW 2540

Tel: (02) 4443 7555 *Fax:* (02) 4443 7666
E-mail: info@offtheshelf.com.au
Web Site: www.offtheshelf.com.au
Key Personnel
Publisher: Gillian Souter
Co-Proprietor: John Souter
Founded: 1991
Specialize in illustrated international craft &
  leisure books.
Subjects: Crafts, Games, Hobbies, Travel &
  Tourism
ISBN Prefix(es): 978-0-9586682; 978-1-876779
Total Titles: 20 Print
Distribution Center: Australian Book Group,
  PO Box 130, Drouin, Victoria 3818 *Tel:* (03)
  5625 4290 *Fax:* (03) 5625 3756 *E-mail:* book.
  distribution@elandmark.com.au *Web
  Site:* www.australianbookgroup.com.au

Omnibus Books, *imprint of* Scholastic Australia
  Pty Ltd

Omnibus Books+
Imprint of Scholastic Australia Pty Ltd
175-177 Young St, Parkside, SA 5063
Tel: (08) 8425 8300 *Fax:* (08) 8425 8304
E-mail: customer_service@scholastic.com.au
Web Site: www.scholastic.com.au
Key Personnel
Publisher: Dyan Blacklock
Senior Editor: Celia Jellett
Founded: 1983
Subjects: Fiction
ISBN Prefix(es): 978-0-86896; 978-1-86291; 978-
  0-949641
Number of titles published annually: 30 Print
Ultimate Parent Company: Scholastic Inc
Shipping Address: Scholastic Australia Pty Ltd,
  76-80 Railway Crescent, Lisarow, NSW 2250
Warehouse: Scholastic Australia Pty Ltd, 76-80
  Railway Crescent, Lisarow, NSW 2250

Onyx, *imprint of* Penguin Group (Australia)

Orin Books
25 Barkly St, St Kilda, Victoria 3182
Tel: (03) 9534 5680
Membership(s): Australian Publishers Association
  (APA).
Subjects: Humor
ISBN Prefix(es): 978-1-875230; 978-0-9588190;
  978-0-9588648; 978-0-9592263
Orders to: PO Box 2089, St Kilda, West Victoria
  3182

Outback Books, *imprint of* Central Queensland
  University Press

Outdoor Press Pty Ltd+
380 High St, Kew, Victoria 3101
Tel: (03) 9852 8400 *Fax:* (03) 9852 8400
Founded: 1976
Specialize in gold & gemstone guides to Aus-
  tralia.
Subjects: Gemstones, Gold
ISBN Prefix(es): 978-0-9596392
Total Titles: 4 Print

Owl Publishing
22 Rooding St, Brighton, Victoria 3186
Tel: (03) 9596 6064 *Fax:* (03) 9596 6942
E-mail: owlbooks@bigpond.com
Web Site: www.owlpublishing.com.au
Key Personnel
Publisher: Helen Nickas
Founded: 1992
Subjects: Biography, Memoirs, Ethnicity, Fiction,
  Literature, Literary Criticism, Essays, Poetry,
  Women's Studies
ISBN Prefix(es): 978-0-9586390; 978-0-9805321
Number of titles published annually: 1 Print
Total Titles: 18 Print

Oxfam Australia
Affiliate of Oxfam International
132 Leicester St, Carlton, Victoria 3053
Tel: (03) 9289 9444 *Toll Free Tel:* 1800 088 110
 Fax: (03) 9347 1983
E-mail: enquire@oxfam.org.au
Web Site: www.oxfam.org.au
Founded: 1953
Specialize in overseas aid & development.
Subjects: Economics, Education, Environmental
 Studies, Foreign Countries, Genealogy, Gov-
 ernment, Political Science, Health, Nutrition,
 Women's Studies
ISBN Prefix(es): 978-0-9587791; 978-0-9599636;
 978-1-875870; 978-0-9806661

Oxford University Press
253 Normanby Rd, South Melbourne, Victoria
 3205
Mailing Address: GPO Box 2784, Melbourne,
 Victoria 3001
Tel: (03) 9934 9123 *Fax:* (03) 9934 9100
E-mail: cs.au@oup.com
Web Site: www.oup.com.au
Key Personnel
Schools Publishing Dir: Lee Walker
Rights & Permissions Manager: Gillian Cardinal
Subjects: Business, Education, Journalism,
 Law, Management, Marketing, Mathematics,
 Medicine, Nursing, Dentistry, Science (Gen-
 eral), Social Sciences, Sociology
ISBN Prefix(es): 978-0-7253; 978-0-7255; 978-0-
 19

Jill Oxton Publications Pty Ltd+
PO Box 283, Park Holme, SA 5043
Tel: (08) 8276 2722
E-mail: jill@jilloxtonxstitch.com
Web Site: www.jilloxtonxstitch.com
Key Personnel
Publisher: Jill Oxton
Founded: 1990
Publishing cross stitch & beading charted designs.
Subjects: Crafts, Games, Hobbies
ISBN Prefix(es): 978-0-9587576
Number of titles published annually: 4 Print
Total Titles: 50 Print
Foreign Rep(s): Gordon & Gotch (New Zealand);
 Miyuki Co Ltd (Japan); Needlecraft Distribu-
 tors Ltd (New Zealand); Pineapple Media Via
 Comag (UK); Source Interlink (Canada, USA);
 Wichelt Imports (Canada, USA)
Distribution Center: Craft Book Wholesalers,
 3/18-20 Steele Court, Tullamarine, Victo-
 ria 3043 *Tel:* (03) 9336 4822 *Fax:* (03) 9335
 5399 *E-mail:* info@craftbooks.com.au *Web
 Site:* www.craftbooks.com.au

Pademelon Press Pty Ltd+
7/3 Packard Ave, Castle Hill, NSW 2154
Mailing Address: PO Box 6500, Baulkham Hills
 BC, NSW 2153
Tel: (02) 9634 4655 *Fax:* (02) 9680 4634
E-mail: enquiry@pademelonpress.com.au
Web Site: www.pademelonpress.com.au
Key Personnel
Dir & International Rights: Rodney Kenner
 E-mail: rodneyk@pademelonpress.com.au
Founded: 1990
Specialize in early childhood teacher resource &
 reference books.
Subjects: Child Care & Development, Education
ISBN Prefix(es): 978-1-876138
Number of titles published annually: 4 Print
Total Titles: 22 Print
Distributor for Bright Ring Publishing; Building
 Blocks (Australia & New Zealand); Exchange;
 Gryphon House (Australia & New Zealand);
 HighScope Press (Australia & New Zealand);
 Ideals Books; MindStretchers; National Asso-
 ciation for the Education of Young Children
 (Australia & New Zealand); New Horizons

(Australia & New Zealand); Peppinot Press
(Australia); Redleaf Press (Australia & New
Zealand); School-Age NOTES Inc (Australia
& New Zealand); Siren Films Ltd; Teachers
College Press (Australia & New Zealand)

Palms Press
190 Boomerang Dr, Pacific Palms, NSW 2428
Tel: (061) 6554 0512
Subjects: Environmental Studies, History, How-to,
 Humor, Public Administration
ISBN Prefix(es): 978-0-9593041

Pan, *imprint of* Pan Macmillan Australia Pty Ltd

Pan Macmillan Australia Pty Ltd+
Publishing Dept, Level 25, One Market St, Syd-
 ney, NSW 2000
Tel: (02) 9285 9100 *Fax:* (02) 9285 9190
E-mail: pansyd@macmillan.com.au; enquiries@
 macmillan.com.au
Web Site: www.panmacmillan.com.au
Key Personnel
Manager, Global Trade Division: John Sargent
Publisher: Mary Small
Publishing Dir, Nonfiction: Tom Gilliatt
Program Manager: Praveen Naidoo
Digital Marketing Executive: Hayley Crandell
Founded: 1983
Subjects: Biography, Memoirs, Cookery, Fiction,
 Health, Nutrition, History, Humor, Literature,
 Literary Criticism, Essays, Nonfiction (Gen-
 eral), Regional Interests, Self-Help, Sports,
 Athletics, Travel & Tourism, Australiana, Cur-
 rent Affairs, Thrillers, True Crime
ISBN Prefix(es): 978-0-330; 978-0-7329; 978-0-
 7251; 978-1-4050; 978-1-74198; 978-1-74197;
 978-1-74261; 978-1-74262; 978-1-74303; 978-
 1-74328; 978-1-74329; 978-1-74334
Imprints: Forge; Griffin; Macmillan; Macquarie
 Dictionary Publishers; Pan; Pancake; Picador;
 Plum; St Martin's Press; Sidgwick & Jackson;
 Tor
Branch Office(s)
Level 1-3, 15-19 Claremont St, South Yarra, Vic-
 toria 3141 *Tel:* (03) 9825 1000 *Fax:* (03) 9825
 1015

Pancake, *imprint of* Pan Macmillan Australia Pty
Ltd

Pantera Press Pty Ltd
PO Box 1989, Neutral Bay, NSW 2089
E-mail: info@panterapress.com
Web Site: www.panterapress.com.au
Key Personnel
Co-Founder & Chief Executive Officer: Alison
 Green
Co-Founder: John Green
Public Relations & Marketing Manager: Susan
 Hando *E-mail:* susan.hando@panterapress.com
Rights Manager: Katy McEwen *E-mail:* katy.
 mcewen@panterapress.com
Founded: 2008
Subjects: Criminology, Fiction, Government, Po-
 litical Science, History, Nonfiction (General),
 Romance, Science Fiction, Fantasy, Children's
 Literacy
ISBN Prefix(es): 978-0-9807418; 978-0-9870685
Imprints: Lost the Plot
Distributed by Simon & Schuster
Distribution Center: United Book Distributors
 Tel: (03) 8537 4499 *Toll Free Tel:* 1800 338
 836 *Fax:* (03) 8537 4497 *E-mail:* orders@
 unitedbookdistributors.com.au

Pantheon, *imprint of* Random House Books
 Australia, A Penguin Random House Company

Papyrus Publishing+
c/o Post Office, Smythesdale, Victoria 3351

Tel: (03) 5342 2263 *Fax:* (03) 5342 2423
E-mail: editor@papyrus.com.au; orders@papyrus.
 com
Web Site: www.papyrus.com.au
Key Personnel
Technical Dir: Herbert Stein *E-mail:* h.stein@
 papyrus.com.au
Chief Editor: Clariss Stein
Founded: 1991
Multiculture literature.
Membership(s): Australian Publishers Association
 (APA).
Subjects: Ethnicity, Fiction, Literature, Literary
 Criticism, Essays, Poetry, Science (General)
ISBN Prefix(es): 978-1-875934
Number of titles published annually: 8 Print
Total Titles: 50 Print

Particular Books, *imprint of* Penguin Group
 (Australia)

Pascal Press+
PO Box 250, Glebe, NSW 2037
Tel: (02) 8585 4044 *Fax:* (02) 8585 4001
E-mail: contact@pascalpress.com.au
Web Site: www.pascalpress.com.au
Key Personnel
Publisher: Matthew Blake *E-mail:* matthew@
 pascalpress.com.au
Marketing Manager: Lynda Pendino
National Trade Manager: David Duyker
 E-mail: david@pascalpress.com.au
International Sales Manager: Nadeem Ansari
 E-mail: nadeem@pascalpress.com.au
Founded: 1989
Specialize in education publishing.
Membership(s): Australian Publishers Association
 (APA).
Subjects: Education
ISBN Prefix(es): 978-1-74020; 978-1-74125; 978-
 1-875312; 978-1-875777; 978-1-877085; 978-1-
 920728
Total Titles: 1,000 Print; 16 CD-ROM; 50 Online;
 50 E-Book; 20 Audio
Associate Companies: Blake Education Pty Ltd
Distributed by Nelson Thornes (UK); Sundance
 (USA)
Distributor for Wild Daisies (New Zealand)
Shipping Address: TLD Distribution, 15-
 23 Helles Ave, Moorebank, NSW 2170
Tel: (02) 8778 9999 *Fax:* (02) 8778 9944
E-mail: orders@tldistribution.com.au *Web
 Site:* www.tldistribution.com.au

Pascoe Publishing Pty Ltd+
30 Gambier St, Apollo Bay, Victoria 3233
Tel: (03) 5237 9227
Web Site: brucepascoe.com.au
Key Personnel
Dir: Bruce Pascoe *E-mail:* brucepascoe@westnet.
 com.au
Dir & International Rights: Lyn Harwood
Founded: 1983
Subjects: Fiction, History, Literature, Literary
 Criticism, Essays, Social Sciences, Sociology,
 Australian Literary Fiction
ISBN Prefix(es): 978-0-947087; 978-0-9592104
Number of titles published annually: 4 Print
Total Titles: 110 Print
Imprints: Seaglass
Orders to: PO Box 42, Apollo Bay, Victoria 3233

Pavillion, *imprint of* Random House Books
 Australia, A Penguin Random House Company

PCS Publications
PO Box 600, Darling Heights, Qld 4530
Tel: (07) 4630 9921
E-mail: sales@pcspublications.com.au
Web Site: pcspublications.com.au
Founded: 1986

Subjects: Engineering (General), Construction, Furnishing
ISBN Prefix(es): 978-0-9587787; 978-0-947225; 978-1-876135

Pearson Addison-Wesley, *imprint of* Pearson Australia Group Pty Ltd

Pearson Allyn & Bacon, *imprint of* Pearson Australia Group Pty Ltd

Pearson Australia Group Pty Ltd+
Unit 4, Level 3, 14 Aquatic Dr, Frenchs Forest, NSW 2086
Mailing Address: Locked Bag 507, Frenchs Forest, NSW 1640
Tel: (02) 9454 2200; (02) 9454 2222 (customer service) *Fax:* (02) 9453 0089; (02) 9453 0093 (customer service)
E-mail: customer.service@pearson.com.au
Web Site: www.pearson.com.au
Key Personnel
Chief Executive Officer: David Barnett
Global Chief Executive: Marjorie Scardina
Senior Marketing Manager: David Hobson
Educational publishers.
Subjects: Accounting, Anthropology, Behavioral Sciences, Biological Sciences, Business, Child Care & Development, Communications, Computer Science, Criminology, Economics, Education, Engineering (General), Fiction, Government, Political Science, Health, Nutrition, History, Journalism, Labor, Industrial Relations, Language Arts, Linguistics, Law, Library & Information Sciences, Management, Mathematics, Medicine, Nursing, Dentistry, Science (General), Social Sciences, Sociology
ISBN Prefix(es): 978-1-74091; 978-1-74103
Number of titles published annually: 500 Print
Parent Company: Pearson Plc
Imprints: Hospitality Press; Pearson Addison-Wesley; Pearson Allyn & Bacon; Pearson Benjamin Cummings; Pearson Longman; Pearson NCS; Pearson Prentice Hall
Divisions: Pearson Library
Branch Office(s)
32 Robinson Ave, Belmont, WA 6104 *Tel:* (08) 9477 1539 *Fax:* (08) 9477 1547
Suite A, Level 2, 57 Coronation Dr, Brisbane, Qld 4000 *Fax:* (07) 3016 7333
170 Green Hill Rd, Box 7, Parkside, SA 5063
20 Thackray Rd, PO Box 460, Port Melbourne, Victoria 3207 *Tel:* (03) 9245 7111 *Fax:* (03) 9245 7333

Pearson Benjamin Cummings, *imprint of* Pearson Australia Group Pty Ltd

Pearson Library
Division of Pearson Australia Group Pty Ltd
20 Thackray Rd, Port Melbourne, Victoria 3207
Mailing Address: PO Box 460, Port Melbourne, Victoria 3207
Tel: (03) 9245 7111 *Toll Free Tel:* 1800 656 685
Fax: (03) 9245 7333 *Toll Free Fax:* 1800 642 270
E-mail: schools@pearson.com.au
Web Site: www.heinemannlibrary.com.au; www.pearsonplaces.com.au/library.aspx
Founded: 1996
Pearson Library now incorporates Heinemann Library & includes nonfiction & fiction library titles from imprints such as Heinemann, Echidna, Raintree, Evans & Mason Crest. Titles cover a wide variety of subjects from science, technology & the arts, to literacy & religious studies.
ISBN Prefix(es): 978-1-86391; 978-1-74070
Ultimate Parent Company: Pearson Plc
Imprints: Acorns; Cherrytree; Echidna Books; Evans Publishing; Heinemann First Library;

Heinemann Library (UK); Heinemann-Raintree (USA); Infosearch; Mitchell Lane Publishers; Little Nippers; Mason Crest; Raintree; Young Explorer; Zero to Ten
Distributor for Atlantic Europe; Barrington Stoke; Chrysalis; Evans Publishing Group; Heinemann Library UK; Heinemann Library US; Marshall Cavendish (children's list); Mason Crest Publishers; Mitchell Lane Publishing; QED; Raintree; Gareth Stevens

Pearson Longman, *imprint of* Pearson Australia Group Pty Ltd

Pearson NCS, *imprint of* Pearson Australia Group Pty Ltd

Pearson Prentice Hall, *imprint of* Pearson Australia Group Pty Ltd

Peleus Press, *imprint of* The Images Publishing Group Pty Ltd

Penguin, *imprint of* Penguin Group (Australia)

Penguin Classics, *imprint of* Penguin Group (Australia)

Penguin Group (Australia)+
250 Camberwell Rd, Camberwell, Victoria 3124
Mailing Address: PO Box 701, Hawthorn, Victoria 3122
Tel: (03) 9811 2400 *Fax:* (03) 9811 2620
E-mail: sales@au.penguingroup.com
Web Site: penguin.com.au
Key Personnel
Chief Executive Officer: Julie Burland
Publisher: P Blake
Publishing Dir, Penguin Young Readers: Laura Harris
General Manager, Brands & Licensing: Troy Lewis
Founded: 1946
Subjects: Biography, Memoirs, Cookery, Fiction, Humor, Literature, Literary Criticism, Essays, Nonfiction (General), Science Fiction, Fantasy, Self-Help, Travel & Tourism
ISBN Prefix(es): 978-0-14; 978-0-670; 978-1-872031; 978-0-86914; 978-1-920
Parent Company: Penguin Australia Group Pty Ltd
Ultimate Parent Company: Pearson Plc (London)
Associate Companies: Pearson Education; Penguin Group (Canada), 90 Eglinton Ave E, Suite 700, Toronto, ON M4P 2Y3, Canada *E-mail:* online@penguin.ca *Web Site:* www.penguin.ca; Penguin Group (China), B1525 Nan Xin Cang, 22 Dongsi Shi Tiao, Dongcheng District, Beijing 100007, China *Web Site:* www.penguin.com.cn; Penguin Books India Pvt Ltd, 11 Community Centre, Panchsheel Park, New Delhi 110 017, India *E-mail:* customer.service@penguin-india.com *Web Site:* www.penguinbooksindia. com; Penguin Ireland, 25 St Stephen's Green, Dublin 2, Ireland *E-mail:* info@penguin.ie *Web Site:* www.penguin.ie; Penguin Books New Zealand, Private Bag 102 902, North Shore Mail Centre, Auckland 0745, New Zealand *E-mail:* orders@penguin.co.nz *Web Site:* www. penguin.co.nz; Penguin Books (South Africa) (Pty) Ltd, 24 Sturdee Ave, Rosebank 2196, South Africa *E-mail:* info@za.penguingroup. com *Web Site:* www.penguinbooks.co.za; Penguin Books Ltd, 80 Strand, London WC2R 0RL, United Kingdom; Penguin Group (USA) Inc, 375 Hudson St, New York, NY 10014, United States *Tel:* 212-366-2000 *Fax:* 212-366-2666 *Web Site:* www.penguin.com
Imprints: BBC Chidren's Books; Claremont; Daw; Dial; Dorling Kindersley; Dutton; Gros-

set & Dunlap; Fig Tree; Hamish Hamilton; Michael Joseph; Ladybird; Allen Lane; Lantern; Mentor; Meridian; New American Library; Onyx; Particular Books; Penguin; Penguin Classics; Penguin Ireland; Penguin Press; Picture Puffin; Plume; Portfolio; Price Stern Sloan; Puffin; Puffin Baby; Razorbill; Rough Guides; Signet; Sunbird; Viking; Frederick Warne
Divisions: Penguin Adult, Penguin Children
Distribution Center: 30 Centre Rd, Scoresby, Victoria 3179
Trafalgar Square Publishing (USA)

Penguin Ireland, *imprint of* Penguin Group (Australia)

Penguin Press, *imprint of* Penguin Group (Australia)

PETAA, see The Primary English Teaching Association Australia

Phoenix Education Pty Ltd+
PO Box 3141, Putney, NSW 2112
Tel: (02) 9809 3579 *Fax:* (02) 9808 1430
E-mail: service@phoenixeduc.com
Web Site: www.phoenixeduc.com
Key Personnel
Contact: David Stewart *E-mail:* david@phoenixeduc.com
Founded: 1992
Subjects: Language Arts, Linguistics, Mathematics
ISBN Prefix(es): 978-1-875695; 978-1-876580
Number of titles published annually: 20 Print
Total Titles: 200 Print
Parent Company: Five Senses Education

Picador, *imprint of* Pan Macmillan Australia Pty Ltd

Picture Puffin, *imprint of* Penguin Group (Australia)

Pier 9, *imprint of* Murdoch Books Pty Ltd Australia

Pimlico, *imprint of* Random House Books Australia, A Penguin Random House Company

Pinchgut Press
11 Bates St Dickson, Dickson, ACT 2602
Tel: (04) 0407 2753
E-mail: books@pinchgut-press.com.au
Web Site: www.pinchgut-press.com.au
Key Personnel
Dir: Kim Holburn
Founded: 1947
Subjects: Fiction, Poetry, Science Fiction, Fantasy, Self-Help, Australian Poetry, Young Adult Fantasy
ISBN Prefix(es): 978-0-9598913; 978-0-949625; 978-0-9808056; 978-0-9871191; 978-0-9870607
Total Titles: 18 Print; 10 E-Book
Bookshop(s): Lulu Enterprises Inc, 3131 RDU Center Dr, Suite 210, Morrisville, NC 27560, United States *Tel:* 919-459-5858 *Fax:* 919-459-5867 *Web Site:* www.lulu.com

Playlab Press
Metro Arts Bldg, Level 2, 109 Edward St, Brisbane City, Qld 4000
Tel: (07) 3220 0841 *Fax:* (07) 3220 0828
E-mail: info@playlab.org.au
Web Site: www.playlab.org.au
Key Personnel
Acting Executive Dir: Ian Lawson
Marketing & Press Coordinator: Alana Tierney

Graphic Designer: Christine Sharp
Founded: 1972
Subjects: Drama, Theater, History, Humor, Litera-
ture, Literary Criticism, Essays, Music, Dance,
Women's Studies, Australiana, Comedy, Youth
ISBN Prefix(es): 978-0-908156
Parent Company: Playlab Inc

Plum, *imprint of* Pan Macmillan Australia Pty
Ltd

Plum Press+
PO Box 419, Toowong, Qld 4066
Tel: (0419) 729 202
Key Personnel
Head of Company: Neil Flanagan *E-mail:* neil@
neil.com.au
Founded: 1989
Subjects: Management
ISBN Prefix(es): 978-0-9577362

Plume, *imprint of* Penguin Group (Australia)

Pluto Press Australia Pty Ltd+
PO Box 617, North Melbourne, Victoria 3051
Tel: (03) 9328 3811
E-mail: pluto@plutoaustralia.com; gellery@
plutoaustralia.com
Web Site: www.plutoaustralia.com
Key Personnel
Publishing Manager: Sarah Crisp *E-mail:* scrisp@
plutoaustralia.com
Founded: 1984
Subjects: Communications, Environmental Stud-
ies, Government, Political Science, History,
House & Home, Human Relations, Labor, In-
dustrial Relations, Nonfiction (General), Re-
gional Interests, Social Sciences, Sociology,
Women's Studies
ISBN Prefix(es): 978-1-86403; 978-0-9802924
Distributed by Macmillan Publishing Services
(Australia)
Orders to: Pan Macmillan Australia, 15-19
Claremont St, Level 1-3, South Yarra, Vic-
toria 3141 *Toll Free Tel:* 1300 135 113 *Toll
Free Fax:* 1300 135 103 *E-mail:* pansyd@
macmillan.com.au

Pocket Books, *imprint of* Simon & Schuster
(Australia) Pty Ltd

The Polding Press+
322 Lonsdale St, Melbourne, Victoria 3000
Tel: (03) 9639 0844 *Fax:* (03) 9639 0879
Founded: 1968
Subjects: Biography, Memoirs, History, Religion -
Other
ISBN Prefix(es): 978-0-85884
Bookshop(s): Central Catholic Bookshop

Pollitecon Publications
PO Box 3411, Wareemba, NSW 2046
Tel: (02) 9705 0578; (02) 9705 0578 (orders)
Fax: (02) 9705 0685
E-mail: info@pollitecon.com
Web Site: www.pollitecon.com
Key Personnel
Editor & Publisher: Victor Bivell
Founded: 1992
Subjects: Anthropology, Ethnicity, Foreign Coun-
tries, History, Literature, Literary Criticism, Es-
says, Regional Interests, Social Sciences, Soci-
ology, Human Rights, Macedonians of Greece,
Bulgaria & Albania
ISBN Prefix(es): 978-0-9586789
Total Titles: 13 Print; 2 E-Book

Portfolio, *imprint of* Penguin Group (Australia)

Power Publications+
RC Mills Bldg, A26, University of Sydney, Syd-
ney, NSW 2006
Tel: (02) 9351 7234 *Fax:* (02) 9351 7323
E-mail: power.publications@sydney.edu.au
Web Site: sydney.edu.au/arts/power/publications
Key Personnel
Dir: Prof Mark Ledbury
Publications Officer: Emma White *Tel:* (02) 9351
7324 *E-mail:* emma.white@sydney.edu.au
Founded: 1986
Subjects: Art, Film, Video
ISBN Prefix(es): 978-0-909952; 978-1-86467
Distribution Center: NewSouth Books, Uni-
versity of New South Wales, Sydney, NSW
2052 *Tel:* (02) 8778 9999 *E-mail:* orders@
tldistribution.com.au
Turnaround Publisher Services Ltd, Unit 3,
Olympia Trading Estate, Coburg Rd, Wood
Green, London N22 6TZ, United Kingdom
Tel: (020) 8829 3000 *Fax:* (020) 8881 5088
E-mail: enquires@turnaround-uk.com
University of Washington Press, c/o Hopkins Ful-
fillment Services, PO Box 50370, Baltimore,
MD 21211-4370, United States *Tel:* 410-516-
6956 *Fax:* 410-516-6998 *E-mail:* hfscustserv@
press.jhu.edu

PressXpress, *imprint of* McGraw-Hill Australia
Pty Ltd

Price Stern Sloan, *imprint of* Penguin Group
(Australia)

**The Primary English Teaching Association
Australia**
Camdenville School, Laura St, Newtown, NSW
2042
Mailing Address: PO Box 3106, Marrickville
Metro, NSW 2204
Tel: (02) 8020 3900 *Fax:* (02) 8020 3933
E-mail: info@petaa.edu.au
Web Site: www.petaa.edu.au
Key Personnel
Dir: Ian Hardy
Founded: 1972
Subjects: Education
ISBN Prefix(es): 978-0-909955; 978-1-875622

Protestant Publications
11 Callistemon Close, North Epping, NSW 2121
Tel: (02) 9868 4591
E-mail: bisden@pnc.com.au
Key Personnel
Contact: D Shelton
Founded: 1945
Subjects: History, Religion - Catholic, Religion -
Protestant
ISBN Prefix(es): 978-0-949926
Orders to: PO Box 551, Epping, NSW 1710

The Psychological Corp, *imprint of* Elsevier
Australia

Puffin, *imprint of* Penguin Group (Australia)

Puffin Baby, *imprint of* Penguin Group
(Australia)

Wendy Pye Publishing Ltd, see Sunshine
Multimedia (Australia) Pty Ltd

Quarterly Essay, *imprint of* Black Inc

**Queen Victoria Museum & Art Gallery
Publications**
Division of Launceston City Council
2 Invermay Rd, Launceston, Tas 7248

Tel: (03) 6323 3728; (03) 6323 3742; (03) 6323
3777
E-mail: enquiries@qvmag.tas.gov.au; shop@
qvmag.tas.gov.au
Web Site: www.qvmag.tas.gov.au
Key Personnel
Media & Communications Officer: Tamara Clark
Tel: (03) 6323 3702 *E-mail:* tamara.clark@
launceston.tas.gov.au
Founded: 1891
Operated as a department of the Launceston City
Council.
Subjects: Anthropology, Archaeology, Art, Bio-
logical Sciences, Earth Sciences, History, Natu-
ral History, Physical Sciences
ISBN Prefix(es): 978-0-7246; 978-0-9494
Number of titles published annually: 1 Print
Total Titles: 27 Print

Queensland Art Gallery
Stanley Pl, South Bank, Qld
Mailing Address: PO Box 3686, South Brisbane,
Qld 4101
Tel: (07) 3840 7309; (07) 3840 7303 *Fax:* (07)
3844 8865; (07) 3840 7042
E-mail: gallery@qagoma.qld.gov.au
Web Site: www.qagoma.qld.gov.au
Key Personnel
Dir: Tony Elwood
Senior Editor: Ian Were
Founded: 1895
Subjects: Art, Asian Studies
ISBN Prefix(es): 978-0-7242; 978-1-876509; 978-
1-921503
Number of titles published annually: 6 Print
Total Titles: 15 Print
Foreign Rep(s): James Bennett Pty Ltd (Aus-
tralia); DAP (Distributed Art Publishers Inc)
(USA); GOBI® Library Solutions (USA);
Idea Books Inc (Europe); Thames & Hudson
Australia Pty Ltd (New Zealand); Timezone 8
(Asia); Worldwide Books (USA)
Orders to: Gallery Shop, South Brisbane, Qld,
Contact: Peter Beiers *Tel:* (07) 3840 7290
Fax: (07) 3840 7149 *E-mail:* peter.beiers@qag.
qld.gov.au *Web Site:* www.gallerystore.com.au

Radge Publishing
PO Box 721, Noosa Heads, Qld 4567
Tel: (07) 5473 5743
Web Site: www.radgepublishing.com
Key Personnel
Publisher: Trish Radge *E-mail:* trish@
radgepublishing.com
Subjects: Business, Finance, Investment & Trad-
ing
ISBN Prefix(es): 978-0-9806372; 978-0-9808128;
978-0-9808712
Distribution Center: Australian Book Group

Raintree, *imprint of* Pearson Library

The Rams Skull Press
PO Box 142, Esk, Qld 4312
Tel: (04) 9825 7239
E-mail: info@ramsskullpress.com
Web Site: www.ramsskullpress.com
Key Personnel
Contact: David Edwards
Founded: 1950
Subjects: Alternative, Art, Cookery, Crafts,
Games, Hobbies, Poetry, Travel & Tourism,
Australian Bush Culture, Folklore
Number of titles published annually: 20 Print
Total Titles: 230 Print

Random House, *imprint of* Random House
Books Australia, A Penguin Random House
Company

Random House Books Australia, A Penguin Random House Company+
100 Pacific Highway, Level 3, North Sydney, NSW 2060
Tel: (02) 9954 9966 *Fax:* (02) 9954 4562
E-mail: random@randomhouse.com.au; corporatesales@randomhouse.com.au; customerservice@randomhouse.com.au
Web Site: www.randomhouse.com.au
Key Personnel
Chief Executive Officer: Julie Burland
Chief Financial Officer: Richard Alweyn
Mng Dir: Andrew Davis; Karen Ferns
Publishing Dir: Nikki Christer
Human Resources Dir: Belinda Hansen
Marketing Dir: Alysha Farry
Publicity & Communications Dir: Karen Reid
Sales & Operations Dir: Gavin Schwarcz
Business Development Executive: Holly Toohey
  Tel: (02) 8923 9950
Head, Children's Publicity & Marketing: Dorothy Tonkin
Head, Digital: Brett Osmond
Rights Manager: Nerrilee Weir
Subjects: Fiction, Nonfiction (General)
Associate Companies: Random House of Canada Ltd, 2775 Matheson Blvd E, Mississauga, Ontario, Canada *Tel:* 905-624-0672 *Fax:* 905-624-6217; Verlagsgruppe Random House GmbH, Neumarkter Str 28, 81673 Munich, Germany *Tel:* (089) 4372-0 *Fax:* (089) 431-2837; Random House Publishers India Pvt Ltd, 301-A, World Trade Tower, Adjacent to Hotel Intercontinental Grand, Barakhamba Lane, New Delhi 110 001, India *Tel:* (011) 4152 8305 *Fax:* (011) 4152 8307 *Web Site:* www.randomhouse.co.in; Random House Books New Zealand, 18 Poland Rd, Wairau Valley, Auckland 0627, New Zealand *Tel:* (09) 444 7197 *Fax:* (09) 444 7524 *Web Site:* www.randomhouse.co.nz; Random House South Africa, Isle of Houghton, Boundary Rd, Corner of Carse O'Gowrie, Gauteng 2198, South Africa *Tel:* (011) 484-3538 *Fax:* (011) 484-6180 *Web Site:* www.umuzi-randomhouse.co.za; Penguin Random House Grupo Editorial, Travessera de Gracia 47-49, 08021 Barcelona, Spain *Tel:* 93 366 03 00 *Fax:* 93 366 04 49 *Web Site:* www.randomhousemondadori.com; Random House UK Ltd, 20 Vauxhall Bridge Rd, London SW1V 2SA, United Kingdom *Tel:* (020) 7840 8400 *Fax:* (020) 7828 6681 *Web Site:* www.randomhouse.co.uk; Transworld Publishing Ltd (UK), 61-63 Uxbridge Rd, Ealing, London W5 5SA, United Kingdom *Tel:* (020) 8579 2652 *Fax:* (020) 8579 5479 *Web Site:* www.booksattransworld.co.uk; Random House Inc, 1745 Broadway, New York, NY 10019, United States *Tel:* 212-782-9000
Imprints: Anchor; Anderson Press; Arrow; Avon; Ballantine; Bantam; BBC; Black Swan; Broadway Books; Century; Chatto & Windus; Corgi; Crown Publishing Group; Dell Publishing; Del Rey; Doubleday; Ebury Press; Fawcett; Fodor; William Heinemann; Hutchinson; Knopf; Pantheon; Pavillion; Pimlico; Random House; Red Fox; Rider; Secker & Warburg; Vermillion; Vintage; Virgin; Windmill Books; Woolshed Press
Distributor for ACP Books; Hardi Grant Publishing
Foreign Rights: AnatoliaLit Agency (Amy Spangler) (Turkey); Bardon-Chinese Media Agency (Joanne Yang) (China, Taiwan); Agencja Literacka Graal (Magda Koceba) (Poland); Katai & Bolza Literary Agents (Peter Bolza) (Hungary); Simona Kessler International Copyright Agency (Adriana Marina) (Romania); Maxima Creative Agency (Santo Manurung) (Indonesia); Michael Meller Literary Agency (Regina Seitz & Cristina Bernadi) (Germany); MO Literary Services (Monique Oosterhof) (Netherlands); Piergiorgio Nicolazzinni Literary Agency (Italy); La Nouvelle Agence (Vanessa Kling

& Michele Kanonidis) (France); Kristin Olson Literary Agency SRO (Czechia); I Pikarski Ltd Literary Agency (Gabrielle Hertzmann) (Israel); RDC Agencia Literaria (Beatriz Coll) (Latin America, Portugal, Spain); Synopsis Literary Agency (Olga Zasetskaya) (Russia)
Shipping Address: 16 Dalmore Dr, Scoresby, Victoria 3179 *Tel:* (03) 9753 4511 *Fax:* (03) 9753 3944 *E-mail:* customerservice@randomhouse.com.au
Warehouse: 16 Dalmore Dr, Scoresby, Victoria 3179 *Tel:* (03) 9753 4511 *Fax:* (03) 9753 3944 *E-mail:* customerservice@randomhouse.com.au
Orders to: 16 Dalmore Dr, Scoresby, Victoria 3179 *Tel:* (03) 9753 4511 *Fax:* (03) 9753 3944 *E-mail:* customerservice@randomhouse.com.au

R&R Publications Pty Ltd+
12 Edward St, Brunswick, Victoria 3056
Mailing Address: PO Box 254, Carlton North, Victoria 3054
Tel: (03) 9381 2199 *Toll Free Tel:* 1800 063 296 (Australia only) *Fax:* (03) 9381 2689
Founded: 1989
Specialize in cooking, drinking & lifestyles. Also book packagers.
Subjects: Cookery, Crafts, Games, Hobbies, Gardening, Plants, Health, Nutrition, How-to, Sports, Athletics, Wine & Spirits, Lifestyle
ISBN Prefix(es): 978-1-875655; 978-1-74022
Number of titles published annually: 60 Print
Total Titles: 140 Print; 4 CD-ROM

Rankin Publishers
PO Box 500, Sumner Park, Qld 4074
Tel: (07) 3376 9115 *Fax:* (07) 3376 9360
E-mail: info@rankin.com.au
Web Site: www.rankin.com.au
Key Personnel
Founder: Robert Rankin
Founded: 1980
Subjects: Outdoor Recreation, Photography, Physics, Regional Interests, Science (General), Australiana
ISBN Prefix(es): 978-0-9592418

Rawlinsons Publishing+
16 Tanunda Dr, Rivervale, WA 6103
Mailing Address: PO Box 670, Belmont, WA 6984
Tel: (08) 9424 5800 *Toll Free Tel:* 1300 730 117 *Fax:* (08) 9277 9065
E-mail: info@rawlhouse.com; orders@rawlhouse.com
Web Site: www.rawlhouse.com
Key Personnel
Dir: Christine Morriss *E-mail:* cmorriss@rawlhouse.com
Founded: 1983
Construction cost reference books.
Subjects: Australian Construction Costs & Data
ISBN Prefix(es): 978-0-9587406; 978-0-9587853
Total Titles: 2 Print

Razorbill, *imprint of* Penguin Group (Australia)

RD Press, *imprint of* Reader's Digest (Australia) Pty Ltd

Reader's Digest (Australia) Pty Ltd+
80 Bay St, Ultimo, NSW 2007
Mailing Address: PO Box 262, Surry Hills, NSW 2010
Tel: (02) 9018 6273 *Fax:* (02) 9018 7290
E-mail: customerservice.au@readersdigest.com
Web Site: www.readersdigest.com.au
Founded: 1946
Subjects: Education
ISBN Prefix(es): 978-0-86438; 978-0-909486; 978-0-949819; 978-0-86449; 978-0-9577023; 978-1-876691; 978-1-921077; 978-0-86450;

978-1-876689; 978-1-921344; 978-1-921569; 978-1-921743; 978-1-921744
Parent Company: Trusted Media Brands Inc, 750 Third Ave, 3rd floor, New York, NY 10017, United States
Imprints: RD Press; Reader's Digest Select Editions
Orders to: GPO Box 3548, Sydney NSW 1149

Reader's Digest Select Editions, *imprint of* Reader's Digest (Australia) Pty Ltd

Ready-Ed Publications+
11/17 Foley St, Balcatta, WA 6021
Tel: (08) 9349 6111 *Fax:* (08) 9349 7222
Web Site: readyed.net
Key Personnel
International Rights: Tim Lowson *E-mail:* tim@readyed.com.au
Founded: 1984
Subjects: Education
ISBN Prefix(es): 978-1-83697; 978-1-875268

Red Fox, *imprint of* Random House Books Australia, A Penguin Random House Company

Redbacks, *imprint of* Black Inc

Rhiza Press, *imprint of* Wombat Books

RIC Publications Pty Ltd+
5 Bendsten Pl, Balcatta, WA 6021
Tel: (08) 9240 9888 *Fax:* (08) 9240 1513
E-mail: mail@ricgroup.com.au
Web Site: www.ricgroup.com.au
Founded: 1986
Educational publishers of textbooks & teacher resource/reference books.
Subjects: Education
ISBN Prefix(es): 978-1-86311; 978-1-74126
Number of titles published annually: 90 Print
Total Titles: 1,000 Print
Branch Office(s)
Prim-Ed Publishing Ltd, Bosheen, New Ross, Co Wexford, Ireland *Tel:* (0890) 929 959 *E-mail:* sales@prim-ed.com *Web Site:* www.prim-ed.com
Orders to: PO Box 332, Greenwood, Perth, WA 6924

Rider, *imprint of* Random House Books Australia, A Penguin Random House Company

RMIT Publishing+
Unit of RMIT Training Pty Ltd
Level 9, 501 Swanston St, Melbourne, Victoria 3000
Mailing Address: PO Box 12058, A'Beckett St, Melbourne, Victoria 8006
Tel: (03) 9925 8100; (03) 9925 8210 (sales) *Fax:* (03) 9925 8134
E-mail: publish@rmitpublishing.com.au; info@rmitpublishing.com.au; sales@rmitpublishing.com.au
Web Site: www.informit.com.au
Founded: 1989
Also distributor.
Membership(s): Australian Publishers Association (APA); National Book Council.
Subjects: Accounting, Business, Child Care & Development, Engineering (General), Fashion, Language Arts, Linguistics, Management, Travel & Tourism
ISBN Prefix(es): 978-0-7241; 978-0-7306
Ultimate Parent Company: RMIT University
Imprints: RMIT University Press; TAFE Publications
Foreign Rep(s): Rod Crowley (Ireland, UK); Gibson Library Connections (Canada, USA); In-

formatics (India) Ltd (India); Thompson Henry Ltd (Europe); World Wide Information Services (South Africa)

RMIT University Press, *imprint of* RMIT Publishing

Rockpool Publishing
24 Constitution Rd, Dulwich Hill, NSW 2203
Mailing Address: PO Box 252, Summer Hill, NSW 2130
Tel: (01) 9327 7150; (02) 9560 1280
Web Site: www.rockpoolpublishing.com.au
Key Personnel
Owner: Paul Dennett; Lisa Hanrahan
Subjects: Health, Nutrition, Nonfiction (General), Family
ISBN Prefix(es): 978-1-921295; 978-1-921878
Distribution Center: Herron Book Distributors, 23 Archimedes Pl, Murarrio, Qld 4172 *Tel:* (07) 3399 8799 *Fax:* (07) 3399 3255 *E-mail:* sales@herronbooks.com *Web Site:* www.herronbooks.com
David Bateman Ltd, 30 Tarndale Grove, Albany, Auckland 0632, New Zealand *Tel:* (09) 415 7664 *Fax:* (09) 415 8892 *E-mail:* bateman@bateman.co.nz *Web Site:* www.batemanpublishing.co.nz
Blue Weaver, PO Box 30370, Tokai 7966, South Africa *Tel:* (021) 701 4477 *E-mail:* marketing@blueweaver.co.za *Web Site:* www.blueweaver.co.za
Deep Books Ltd, Unit 3, Goose Green Trading Estate, 47 E Dulwich Rd, London SE22 9BN, United Kingdom *Tel:* (020) 8693 0234 *Fax:* (020) 8693 1400 *E-mail:* sales@deep-books.co.uk *Web Site:* www.deep-books.co.uk (UK & Europe)
Trafalgar Square Publishing, c/o Independent Publishers Group (IPG), 814 N Franklin St, Chicago, IL 60610, United States *Tel:* 312-337-0747 *Fax:* 312-337-1807 *E-mail:* orders@ipgbook.com *Web Site:* www.ipgbook.com (USA, Canada, Southeast Asia & Far East)

Rosenberg Publishing+
3 Whitehall Rd, Kenthurst, NSW 2156
Mailing Address: PO Box 6125, Dural Delivery Centre, NSW 2158
Tel: (02) 9654 1502 *Fax:* (02) 9654 1338
E-mail: sales@rosenbergpub.com.au
Web Site: www.rosenbergpub.com.au
Key Personnel
Dir: David Rosenberg *E-mail:* rosenbergpub@smartchat.net.au
Founded: 2000
Small nonfiction publisher.
Membership(s): Australian Publishers Association (APA).
Subjects: Earth Sciences, Gardening, Plants, History, Maritime, Natural History, Nonfiction (General), Transportation
ISBN Prefix(es): 978-1-877058; 978-1-921719
Number of titles published annually: 12 Print
Total Titles: 200 Print; 50 E-Book
Foreign Rep(s): Gazelle (Europe, UK); ISBS (Canada, USA)

Rough Guides, *imprint of* Penguin Group (Australia)

St Martin's Press, *imprint of* Pan Macmillan Australia Pty Ltd

St Pauls Publications+
35 Meredith St, Strathfield, NSW 2135
Mailing Address: PO Box 906, Strathfield, NSW 2135
Tel: (02) 9394 3400 *Fax:* (02) 9746 1140
E-mail: publications@stpauls.com.au; info@stpauls.com.au; sales@stpauls.com.au

Web Site: www.stpauls.com.au
Key Personnel
Publishing Dir: Fr Michael Goonan
 E-mail: mgoonan@stpauls.com.au
Marketing Dir: Fr Francis Kochupaliyathil
 E-mail: francis@stpauls.com.au
Production & IT Dir: Fr Joselito Layug
 E-mail: jlayug@stpauls.com.au
Regional Superior: Fr Nestor Candado
 E-mail: ncandado@stpauls.com.au
Founded: 1953
Subjects: Biblical Studies, Biography, Memoirs, Education, Human Relations, Inspirational, Spirituality, Nonfiction (General), Philosophy, Religion - Catholic, Social Sciences, Sociology, Theology
ISBN Prefix(es): 978-0-949080; 978-0-909986; 978-1-875570; 978-1-876295; 978-1-921032; 978-1-921472; 978-1-921963
Distributed by Alba House (USA); Editions Mediaspaul (Canada); St Pauls Distribution (Ireland); St Pauls Publishing (UK)
Bookshop(s): St Pauls Book Centre, 277 Elizabeth St, Brisbane, Qld 4000 *Tel:* (07) 3336 9236 *Fax:* (07) 3221 9122 *E-mail:* bookcentre@stpauls.com.au; St Pauls Book Centre, 502 Ruthven St, Toowoomba, Qld 4350 *Tel:* (07) 4638 4649 *Fax:* (07) 4638 0796 *E-mail:* bookcentretwb@stpauls.com.au

W B Saunders/Bailliere Tindall, *imprint of* Elsevier Australia

Saunders College, *imprint of* Elsevier Australia

Scholastic Australia Pty Ltd
76-80 Railway Crescent, Lisarow, NSW 2250
Mailing Address: PO Box 579, Gosford, NSW 2250
Tel: (02) 4328 3555 *Toll Free Tel:* 1800 021 233 *Toll Free Fax:* 1800 789 948
E-mail: customer_service@scholastic.com.au
Web Site: www.scholastic.com.au
Key Personnel
Chairman: Ken Jolly
Mng Dir: David Peagram
General Manager, Publishing: Andrew Berkhut
Founded: 1968
Subjects: Education
ISBN Prefix(es): 978-0-86896; 978-1-86388; 978-1-86504; 978-0-9689600
Parent Company: Scholastic Inc, 557 Broadway, New York, NY 10012, United States
Imprints: Margaret Hamilton Books; Koala Books; Omnibus Books; Scholastic Press
Branch Office(s)
345 Pacific Highway, Lindfield, NSW 2070
2/350 Lytton Rd, Morningside, Qld 4170
39-41 King St, Norwood, SA 5067
9-11 Northern Rd, West Heidelberg, Victoria 3081
70 Beringarra Ave, Malaga, WA 6090
Bookshop(s): Scholastic, Niagara Park Shopping Centre, Washington Ave, Niagara Park, NSW 2250
Book Club(s): Arrow; Lucky; Star; TBS; Wombat
Distribution Center: Trafalgar Square Publishing, c/o Independent Publishers Group (IPG), 814 N Franklin St, Chicago, IL 60610, United States (USA & Canada)

Scholastic Press, *imprint of* Scholastic Australia Pty Ltd

Schwartz Business, *imprint of* Black Inc

Schwartz City, *imprint of* Black Inc

Science Press+
Bag 7023, Marrickville, NSW 1475

Tel: (02) 9516 1122 *Toll Free Tel:* 1800 225 031 *Fax:* (02) 9550 1915
E-mail: sales@sciencepress.com.au
Web Site: www.sciencepress.com.au
Key Personnel
Mng Dir: William Boden
Founded: 1948
Educational publisher.
Subjects: Education
ISBN Prefix(es): 978-0-85583
Warehouse: 16/102 Edinburgh Rd, Marrickville, NSW 2204

Scribe Publications Pty Ltd+
18-20 Edward St, Brunswick, Victoria 3056
Tel: (03) 9388 8780 *Fax:* (03) 9388 8787
E-mail: info@scribepub.com.au
Web Site: www.scribepublications.com.au
Key Personnel
Founder & Publisher: Henry Rosenbloom
Marketing Manager: Marika Webb-Pullman
 E-mail: marika@scribepub.com.au
Publicity Manager: Anna Lensky *E-mail:* anna@scribepub.com.au
Rights Manager: Amanda Tokar
 E-mail: amandatokar@scribepub.com.au
Sales & Distribution Manager: Roger Horton
 E-mail: rogerhorton@scribepub.com.au
Founded: 1976
Subjects: Fiction, Nonfiction (General)
ISBN Prefix(es): 978-0-908011; 978-1-920769; 978-1-921215; 978-1-921372; 978-1-921640; 978-1-921753; 978-1-921844; 978-1-921863; 978-1-921864; 978-1-921942; 978-1-922070; 978-1-922072; 978-1-922247; 978-1-925106; 978-1-925113; 978-1-925228; 978-1-925292; 978-1-925293; 978-1-925307; 978-1-925321; 978-1-925322
Number of titles published annually: 60 Print
Branch Office(s)
Scribe UK, 2 John St, London WC1N 2ES, United Kingdom, Publicity & Operations Manager: Sarah Braybrooke *Tel:* (020) 3405 4218 *E-mail:* sarah@scribepub.co.uk *Web Site:* scribepublications.co.uk
Foreign Rights: Eliane Benisti Agency (Eliane Benisti) (France); Big Apple Agency Inc (Lily Chen) (China, Indonesia); Big Apple Agency Inc (Chris Lin) (Taiwan); Paul & Peter Fritz AG (Christian Dittus) (Germany); Graal Literary Agency (Marcin Biegaj) (Poland); Laura Grandi & Associates (Alessandra Mele) (Italy); The Deborah Harris Agency (Efrat Lev) (Israel); InkWell Management LLC (Catherine Drayton & George Lucas) (USA); JLM Literary Agency (Nelly Moukakou) (Greece); Katai & Bolza Literary Agency (Peter Bolza) (Hungary); Nurcihan Kesim Literary Agency Inc (Filiz Karaman) (Turkey); Korea Copyright Center Inc (KCC) (Jieun Jeong) (Korea); Mo Literary Services (Monique Oosterhof) (Netherlands, Scandinavia); Andrew Nurnberg Associates (Ludmilla Sushkova) (Russia); Andrew Nurnberg Associates Sofia (Mira Droumeva) (Bulgaria, Romania, Serbia); Kristin Olson Literary Agency SRO (Kristin Olson) (Czechia, Slovakia); Riff Agency (Laura Riff) (Brazil, Portugal); Silkroad Publishers Agency (Jane Vejjajiva) (Thailand); Abner Stein Agency (Arabella Stein) (UK); Tuttle-Mori Agency (Manami Tamaoki) (Japan)
Distribution Center: Penguin Books/United Book Distributors *Toll Free Tel:* 1800 33 1015 *Fax:* (03) 9811 2405 *Web Site:* www.penguin.com.au
Penguin Group (NZ), 67 Apollo Dr Rosedale, Private Bag 102 902, North Shore Mail Centre, Auckland 0745, New Zealand *Tel:* (09) 442 7400 *Fax:* (09) 442 7401
Pansing Distribution Pty Ltd, 438 Ang Mo Kio Industrial Park 1, off Ang Mo Kio Ave 10, Singapore 569619, Singapore *Tel:* 6319 9939 *Fax:* 6459 4930 (Singapore, Brunei, Indonesia & Malaysia)

Independent Publishers Group, Chicago, IL, United States *Tel:* 312-337-0747 *Fax:* 312-337-5985 *E-mail:* frontdesk@ipgbook.com (North America)

Scribner, *imprint of* Simon & Schuster (Australia) Pty Ltd

Seaglass, *imprint of* Pascoe Publishing Pty Ltd

Secker & Warburg, *imprint of* Random House Books Australia, A Penguin Random House Company

See Australia Guides Pty Ltd+
13 Orchid Grove, Warrandyte, Victoria 3113
Tel: (0417) 540 942
Key Personnel
Contact: Greg Dunnett
Founded: 1990
Subjects: Travel & Tourism
ISBN Prefix(es): 978-0-9586439

Seizure, *imprint of* Brio Books

Sidgwick & Jackson, *imprint of* Pan Macmillan Australia Pty Ltd

Signet, *imprint of* Penguin Group (Australia)

Simon & Schuster, *imprint of* Simon & Schuster (Australia) Pty Ltd

Simon & Schuster (Australia) Pty Ltd
Division of Simon & Schuster, Inc
Suite 19A, Level 1, Bldg C, 450 Miller St, Cammeray, NSW 2062
Tel: (02) 9983 6600 *Fax:* (02) 9988 4232 (editorial, sales & marketing)
E-mail: pr@simonandschuster.com.au
Web Site: www.simonandschuster.com.au
Key Personnel
Mng Dir: Dan Ruffino *E-mail:* dan.ruffino@simonandschuster.com.au
Founded: 1987
Subjects: Alternative, Animals, Pets, Anthropology, Art, Behavioral Sciences, Biography, Memoirs, Business, Career Development, Child Care & Development, Cookery, Crafts, Games, Hobbies, Fashion, Fiction, Film, Video, Gardening, Plants, Health, Nutrition, History, House & Home, How-to, Humor, Inspirational, Spirituality, LGBTQ, Literature, Literary Criticism, Essays, Management, Marketing, Mysteries, Suspense, Natural History, Nonfiction (General), Outdoor Recreation, Philosophy, Photography, Poetry, Pop Culture, Psychology, Psychiatry, Radio, TV, Romance, Science (General), Science Fiction, Fantasy, Self-Help, Sports, Athletics, Western Fiction, Women's Studies
ISBN Prefix(es): 978-0-7318; 978-0-949924; 978-0-86417; 978-1-921470
Ultimate Parent Company: CBS Corporation, 51 W 52 St, New York, NY 10019-6188, United States
Associate Companies: Simon & Schuster UK Ltd, 222 Grays Inn Rd, 1st floor, London WC1X 8HB, United Kingdom *Tel:* (020) 7316 1900 *Fax:* (020) 7316 0332 *E-mail:* enquiries@simonandschuster.co.uk *Web Site:* www.simonandschuster.co.uk
Imprints: Aladdin; Atheneum Books for Young Readers; Atria Books; Beach Lane; Fireside; Free Press; Gallery; Howard; Little Simon; Margaret K McElderry; Mercury Ink; Pocket Books; Scribner; Simon & Schuster; Simon451; Simon Pulse; Simon Spotlight; Touchstone; Paula Wiseman

U.S. Office(s): Simon & Schuster, Inc, 1230 Avenue of the Americas, New York, NY 10020, United States *Web Site:* www.simonandschuster.com
Distributor for Cider Mill Press; Elliott & Thompson; 4 Ingredients; Fox Chapel Publishing; Gallup Press; Hunter Publishers; Insight Editions; Manuscript Publishing; Regan Arts; Smith Street Books; Ventura Press; Viz Media; Watkins Publishing
Distribution Center: Harper Entertainment Distribution Services, Yarrawa Rd, PO Box 264, Moss Vale, NSW 2577 *Toll Free Tel:* 1300 551 721 *Toll Free Fax:* 1800 645 547 *E-mail:* orders@harpercollins.com.au *Web Site:* www.harpercollins.com.au/customer-service/contactus
Orders to: Harper Entertainment Distribution Services, Yarrawa Rd, PO Box 264, Moss Vale, NSW 2577 *Toll Free Tel:* 1300 551 721 *Toll Free Fax:* 1800 645 547 *E-mail:* orders@harpercollins.com.au *Web Site:* www.harpercollins.com.au/customer-service/contactus
Returns: Harper Entertainment Distribution Services, Yarrawa Rd, PO Box 264, Moss Vale, NSW 2577 *Toll Free Tel:* 1300 551 721 *Toll Free Fax:* 1800 645 547 *E-mail:* orders@harpercollins.com.au *Web Site:* www.harpercollins.com.au/customer-service/contactus

Simon Pulse, *imprint of* Simon & Schuster (Australia) Pty Ltd

Simon Spotlight, *imprint of* Simon & Schuster (Australia) Pty Ltd

Simon451, *imprint of* Simon & Schuster (Australia) Pty Ltd

Singular Press, *imprint of* Elsevier Australia

Sisters of St Joseph+
St Joseph's Regional Centre, 5 Alexandra Ave, Croydon, NSW 2132
Mailing Address: Locked Bag 3031, Burwood, NSW 1805
Tel: (02) 8741 2300 *Fax:* (02) 8741 2399
E-mail: communications@sosj.org.au
Web Site: www.sosj.org.au
Key Personnel
Contact: Steph Walker
Founded: 1981
Subjects: Education, History, Music, Dance, Religion - Catholic
ISBN Prefix(es): 978-0-9579976; 978-0-9808389
Total Titles: 30 Print
Distributed by St Pauls Publications
Showroom(s): Mary MacKillop Pl, 7 Mount St, North Sydney, NSW 2060 *Tel:* (02) 8912 4894 *Fax:* (02) 8912 4835 *E-mail:* mmp.shop@sosj.org.au *Web Site:* www.marymackillopplace.org.au

Skills Publishing
8 Livingstone St, Lawson, NSW 2783
Mailing Address: PO Box 514, Hazelbrook, NSW 2779
Tel: (02) 4759 2844 *Fax:* (02) 4759 3721
E-mail: administration@skillspublish.com.au
Web Site: www.skillspublish.com.au
Key Personnel
Publisher: Art Burrows
Mng Editor: Steven Burrows
Founded: 1985
Publisher of books & magazines in woodworking, metalworking, home construction & renovation.
Subjects: Crafts, Games, Hobbies, House & Home, How-to

Sleepers Publishing
PO Box 1204, Collingwood, Victoria 3066

Web Site: sleeperspublishing.com
Key Personnel
Editorial Dir: Louise Swinn *E-mail:* louise@sleeperspublishing.com
Creative Dir: Zoe Dattner *E-mail:* zoe@sleeperspublishing.com
Founded: 2003
Subjects: Fiction
ISBN Prefix(es): 978-0-9756991

Slouch Hat Publications+
PO Box 174, McCrae, Victoria 3938
Tel: (03) 5986 6437 *Fax:* (03) 5986 6312
E-mail: slouchhatbooks@gmail.com
Web Site: www.slouch-hat.com.au
Key Personnel
Contact: Michelle Walters
Founded: 1989
Subjects: History, Military Science, Australian Military History
ISBN Prefix(es): 978-0-9585296; 978-0-9579752

Richard Smart Publishing
1/5a Courland St, Randwick, NSW 2031
Tel: (02) 9398 7094 *Fax:* (02) 9398 7094
E-mail: rsppublish@primusonline.com.au
Web Site: richardsmartpublishing.wordpress.com
Founded: 1975
Subjects: Art, Business, Cookery, Finance, Gardening, Plants, Government, Political Science, Humor, Sports, Athletics, Australiana, Current Affairs, Lifestyle, Media, Military History
ISBN Prefix(es): 978-0-9589038

Smink Works Books+
PO Box 2154, Fitzroy BC, Victoria 3065
Tel: (03) 9018 7732 *Fax:* (03) 9428 5101
E-mail: books@sminkworks.com
Web Site: www.sminkworks.com; kids.sminkworks.com
Key Personnel
Publisher: Suzanne Male
Founded: 2002
Independent book & ebook publisher.
Membership(s): Small Press Underground Networking Community (SPUNC)
Subjects: Fiction, How-to, Nonfiction (General)
ISBN Prefix(es): 978-1-920936
Number of titles published annually: 3 Print; 1 CD-ROM; 5 Online; 5 E-Book
Total Titles: 7 Print; 2 CD-ROM; 15 Online; 15 E-Book

Social Science Press+
Imprint of Cengage Learning Australia
Level 7, 80 Dorcas St, South Melbourne, Victoria 3205
Tel: (03) 9685 4111 *Fax:* (03) 9685 4199
E-mail: anz.customerservice@cengage.com; anz.permissions@cengage.com
Web Site: www.cengage.com.au
Key Personnel
Vice President, Higher Education Division: Paul Petrulis
Founded: 1980
Subjects: Education
ISBN Prefix(es): 978-0-949218; 978-1-876033; 978-1-876633
Imprints: Dunmore Press

Spectrum Publications+
PO Box 75, Richmond, Victoria 3121
Tel: (03) 0054 0736 *Fax:* (03) 0054 0737
E-mail: spectrum@spectrumpublications.com.au
Web Site: www.spectrumpublications.com.au
Key Personnel
Mng Dir: Peter Henry Rohr
Founded: 1974
Membership(s): Australian Publishers Association (APA).
Subjects: Biography, Memoirs, Education, History, Inspirational, Spirituality, LGBTQ, Music, Dance, Nonfiction (General), Psychology, Psy-

chiatry, Regional Interests, Religion - Buddhist, Religion - Catholic, Religion - Hindu, Religion - Islamic, Religion - Jewish, Religion - Protestant, Religion - Other, Self-Help, Theology, Australiana, Grief
ISBN Prefix(es): 978-0-86786; 978-0-909837
Number of titles published annually: 10 Print
Total Titles: 70 Print

Spineless Wonders
PO Box 220, Strawberry Hills, NSW 2012
E-mail: info@shortaustralianstories.com.au
Web Site: shortaustralianstories.com.au
Subjects: Fiction, Poetry
ISBN Prefix(es): 978-0-9870897; 978-0-9872546; 978-0-9874479; 978-0-9875355; 978-1-925052
Distribution Center: Dennis Jones & Associates, Unit 1/10 Melrich Rd, Bayswater, Victoria 3153 *Tel:* (03) 9762 9100 *Fax:* (03) 9762 9200 *E-mail:* theoffice@dennisjones.com.au *Web Site:* www.dennisjones.com.au (Australia & New Zealand)
Trafalgar Square Publishing, c/o Independent Publishers Group (IPG), 814 N Franklin St, Chicago, IL 60610, United States *Tel:* 312-337-0747 (trade inquiries) *Fax:* 312-337-5985 *E-mail:* orders@ipgbook.com (North America)

Spinifex Press+
PO Box 5270, North Geelong, Victoria 3215
SAN: 908-0627
Mailing Address: PO Box 105, Mission Beach, Qld 4852
Tel: (0490) 151 560 (orders, customer service); (0418) 506 645 (editorial, rights, permissions)
E-mail: women@spinifexpress.com.au
Web Site: www.spinifexpress.com.au
Key Personnel
Owner: Susan Hawthorne *E-mail:* hawsu@spinifexpress.com.au; Renate Klein
Founded: 1991
Specialize in feminist publishing.
Membership(s): Alliance of Independent Publishers; Australian Publishers Association (APA); Small Press Network (SPN).
Subjects: Alternative, Animals, Pets, Anthropology, Archaeology, Art, Asian Studies, Astrology, Occult, Astronomy, Biography, Memoirs, Developing Countries, Disability, Special Needs, Drama, Theater, Economics, Education, Environmental Studies, Ethnicity, Fiction, Foreign Countries, Health, Nutrition, History, Human Relations, Humor, Journalism, Labor, Industrial Relations, LGBTQ, Literature, Literary Criticism, Essays, Medicine, Nursing, Dentistry, Music, Dance, Nonfiction (General), Philosophy, Photography, Poetry, Publishing & Book Trade Reference, Religion - Hindu, Religion - Other, Science Fiction, Fantasy, Self-Help, Social Sciences, Sociology, Technology, Travel & Tourism, Women's Studies, Feminism
ISBN Prefix(es): 978-1-875559; 978-1-876756; 978-0-908205 (Sybylla); 978-1-742199; 978-1-925581
Number of titles published annually: 6 Print; 30 E-Book
Total Titles: 220 Print; 150 E-Book
Imprints: Sybylla
Foreign Rights: Agencja AKF (Poland); Imprima Korea Agency (Joseph Lee) (Korea); International Editor's Co (Isabel Monteagudo) (Spain); Natoli, Stefan & Oliva (Italy); Tuttle Mori Agency (Yuji Takeda) (Japan)
Distribution Center: Missing Link, Westerstr 114-116, 28199 Bremen, Germany *Tel:* (0421) 50 43 48 *Fax:* (0421) 50 43 16 *E-mail:* info@missing-link.de *Web Site:* www.missing-link.de
Gazelle Book Services Ltd, White Cross Mills, High Town, South Rd, Lancaster, Lancs LA1 4XS, United Kingdom *Tel:* (01524) 68765 *Fax:* (01524) 63232 *E-mail:* sales@gazellebooks.co.uk *Web Site:* www.gazellebooks.co.uk

Independent Publishers Group, Order Dept, 814 N Franklin St, Chicago, IL 60610, United States *Fax:* 312-337-5985 *E-mail:* orders@ipgbook.com *Web Site:* www.ipgbook.com

The Spinney Press
PO Box 438, Thirroul, NSW 2515
Tel: (02) 4268 5600 *Fax:* (02) 4268 5611
E-mail: enquiries@spinneypress.co.au
Web Site: spinneypress.com.au
Subjects: Communications, Economics, Science (General), Social Sciences, Sociology, Children's Issues, HIV & AIDS, National Security, Poverty, Terrorism
ISBN Prefix(es): 978-1-876811; 978-1-920801; 978-1-875682; 978-1-921507

Standards Australia Ltd
Level 10, The Exchange Centre, 20 Bridge St, Sydney, NSW 2001
Mailing Address: GPO Box 476, Sydney, NSW 2001
Tel: (02) 8206 6000; (02) 9237 6000
Toll Free Tel: 1800 035 822 (Australia only)
Fax: (02) 8206 6020; (02) 9237 6010
E-mail: mail@standards.org.au
Web Site: www.standards.org.au
Key Personnel
Chairman: Dr Alan Morrison
Chief Executive Officer: Colin Blair
Public Affairs Officer: Torrin Marquardt *E-mail:* torrin.marquardt@standards.org.au
Founded: 1922
Develops Australian Standards® of public benefit & national interest & supports excellence in design & innovation through the Australian Design Awards.
Membership(s): International Council of Societies of International Design (ICSID); International Electrotechnical Commission (IEC); International Organization for Standardization; Pacific Area Standards Congress (PASC).
Subjects: Business, Chemistry, Chemical Engineering, Civil Engineering, Communications, Education, Electronics, Electrical Engineering, Energy, Engineering (General), Environmental Studies, Finance, Health, Nutrition, House & Home, Management, Marketing, Mechanical Engineering, Medicine, Nursing, Dentistry, Outdoor Recreation, Technology, Transportation

Staples, *imprint of* University of Western Australia Publishing

Starfish Bay Children's Books
PO Box 1058, Unley, SA 5061
E-mail: enquiries@starfishbaypublishing.com.au; books@starfishbaypublishing.com.au
Web Site: starfishbaypublishing.com.au
Key Personnel
Dir: Luke Hou
ISBN Prefix(es): 978-1-76036; 978-0-9941002; 978-0-9941003; 978-0-9941007
Branch Office(s)
PO Box 35760, Browns Bay, Auckland 0753, New Zealand *E-mail:* enquiries@starfishbaypublishing.com *Web Site:* starfishbaypublishing.co.nz
Distribution Center: NewSouth Books, 45 Beach St, Cogee, NSW 2034 *Tel:* (02) 8936 0100 *Fax:* (02) 8936 0040 (trade sales)
NewSouth Books, c/o TL Distribution, 15-23 Helles Ave, Moorebank, NSW 2170 *Tel:* (02) 8778 9999 *Fax:* (02) 8778 9944 *E-mail:* orders@tldistribution.com.au (trade orders)
David Bateman Ltd, 30 Tarndale Grove, Albany, Auckland 0632, New Zealand *Tel:* (09) 415 7664 *Fax:* (09) 415 8892 *E-mail:* bateman@bateman.co.nz

Independent Publishers Group, 814 N Franklin St, Chicago, IL 60610, United States *Tel:* 312-337-0747 *Fax:* 312-337-5985 *E-mail:* frontdesk@ipgbook.com (USA & Canada)

Submariner Publications P/L+
PO Box 387, Ashburton, Victoria 3147
Tel: (03) 9886 0200 *Fax:* (03) 9886 0200
E-mail: jlpubs@bigpond.net.au
Web Site: www.submarinerpublications.com
Key Personnel
Mng Dir: John Lippmann
Founded: 1983
Specialize in publishing & distributing scuba diving medical & safety texts, as well as general first aid publications.
Subjects: Sports, Athletics, Scuba Diving Safety
ISBN Prefix(es): 978-0-9752290; 978-0-9587118; 978-0-9590306; 978-0-9586452
Total Titles: 15 Print
Distributed by Aqua Quest Publications (USA)

Sunbird, *imprint of* Penguin Group (Australia)

Sunshine Multimedia (Australia) Pty Ltd
2/71 Northgate Dr, Thomastown, Victoria 3074
Mailing Address: PO Box 139, Thomastown, Victoria 3074
Tel: (03) 9464 7422 *Toll Free Tel:* 1800 244 542 *Fax:* (03) 9464 2226 *Toll Free Fax:* 1800 684 528
E-mail: info@sunshinebooks.com.au; sales@sunshinebooks.com.au
Web Site: sunshinebooks.com.au
Founded: 1986
Subjects: Fiction, Mathematics, Nonfiction (General), Regional Interests
ISBN Prefix(es): 978-1-927148; 978-1-877559; 978-1-877482; 978-1-877508; 978-1-877456
Bookshop(s): Sunshine Book Shop, 413 Great South Rd, Ellerslie, Auckland 1051, New Zealand *Tel:* (09) 525 3575 *Toll Free Tel:* 0800 500 130 *Fax:* (09) 525 4205 *E-mail:* sales@sunshine.co.nz
Orders to: Wendy Pye Publishing, Private Bag 17 905, Greenlane, Auckland 1546, New Zealand, Contact: Gill Protheroe *Tel:* (09) 525 3575 *Fax:* (09) 525 4205 *E-mail:* sales@sunshine.co.nz

Sybylla, *imprint of* Spinifex Press

Sydney University Press
University of Sydney, Fisher Library F03, Level 5, Sydney, NSW 2006
Tel: (02) 9036 9958 *Fax:* (02) 9114 0620
E-mail: info@sup.usyd.edu.au
Web Site: sydney.edu.au/sup
Key Personnel
Business Manager: Susan Murray-Smith *Tel:* (02) 9036 6442
Founded: 2003
ISBN Prefix(es): 978-0-424; 978-0-909798; 978-1-921634; 978-0-9750860; 978-1-920897; 978-1-920898; 978-1-920899

TAFE Publications, *imprint of* RMIT Publishing

Technomic Publishing, *imprint of* Elsevier Australia

Terania Rainforest Publishing
391 The Channon Rd, The Channon, Lismore, NSW 2480
Tel: (02) 6688 6204 *Fax:* (02) 6688 6227
E-mail: terania@rainforestpublishing.com.au
Web Site: www.rainforestpublishing.com.au
Key Personnel
Owner: Nan J Nicholson
Founded: 1985
Subjects: Environmental Studies, Gardening, Plants, Natural History, Botany, Rainforest

ISBN Prefix(es): 978-0-9589436
Total Titles: 7 Print; 1 CD-ROM

The Text Publishing Co+
Swann House, 22 William St, Melbourne, Victoria 3000
Tel: (03) 8610 4500 *Fax:* (03) 9629 8621
E-mail: books@textpublishing.com.au
Web Site: www.textpublishing.com.au
Key Personnel
Publisher: Michael Heyward
Rights: Anne Beilby *E-mail:* anne.beilby@textpublishing.com.au
Founded: 1990
Subjects: Biography, Memoirs, Fiction, Government, Political Science, History, Humor, Literature, Literary Criticism, Essays, Nonfiction (General)
ISBN Prefix(es): 978-1-875847; 978-1-876485; 978-1-877008; 978-1-86372; 978-1-920885; 978-1-921145
Number of titles published annually: 40 Print
Total Titles: 105 Print
Distributed by Penguin Books Australia; Penguin Books NZ Ltd
Foreign Rep(s): Consortium Book Sales & Distribution (USA)
Foreign Rights: AnatoliaLit Agency (Amy Spangler) (Turkey); Antonella Antonelli Agencia Letteraria (Italy); Carmen Balcells Agencia Literaria SA (Maribel Luque) (Portugal, Spain); Bardon-Chinese Media Agency (Luisa Yeh) (China, Taiwan); Eliane Benisti Agency (France); The English Agency Japan (Junzo Sawa) (Japan); Paul & Peter Fritz AG (Christian Dittus & Antonia Fritz) (Germany); Agencja Literacka Graal (Marcin Biegaj) (Poland); I Pikarski Ltd (Gabi Hertzmann) (Israel); InkWell Management (David Forrer & Kim Witherspoon) (Canada, USA); International Copyright Agency Ltd (Marina Adriana) (Romania); Japan Uni Agency Inc (Takeshi Oyama) (Japan); Katai & Bolza Literary Agency (Peter Bolza) (Hungary); Korea Copyright Center (MiSook Hong) (Korea); Leonhardt & Hoier Literary Agency ApS (Anneli Hoier) (Scandinavia); Lutyens & Rubinstein (Sarah Lutyens) (UK); Andrew Nurnberg Associates (Tatjana Zoldnere) (Baltic States); Kristin Olson Literary Agency SRO (Czechia, Slovakia); The Riff Agency (Laura Riff) (Brazil); Sebes & Bisseling Literary Agency (Netherlands); Synopsis Literary Agency (Natalia Sanina) (Russia); The Van Lear Agency (Elizabeth Van Lear) (Russia)
Warehouse: Penguin Books Australia, 250 Camberwell Rd, Camberwell, Victoria 3124 *Tel:* (03) 9811 2555 *Toll Free Tel:* 1800 338 836 *Fax:* (03) 9811 2403
Orders to: Penguin Books Australia, 250 Camberwell Rd, Camberwell, Victoria 3124 *Tel:* (03) 9811 2555 *Toll Free Tel:* 1800 338 836 *Fax:* (03) 9811 2403

Thames & Hudson Australia Pty Ltd
Subsidiary of Thames & Hudson Ltd
Portside Business Park, 11 Central Blvd, Fishermans Bend, Melbourne, Victoria 3207
Tel: (03) 9646 7788 *Fax:* (03) 9646 8790
E-mail: enquiries@thaust.com.au
Web Site: www.thameshudson.com.au
Key Personnel
Mng Dir: Jodie Mann
Sales & Marketing Manager: Saraid Banahan *E-mail:* s.banahan@thaust.com.au
Publicity & Events Manager: Michelle Brasington *E-mail:* m.brasington@thaust.com.au
Founded: 1969
Subjects: Archaeology, Architecture & Interior Design, Art, Fashion, Foreign Countries, History, Literature, Literary Criticism, Essays, Music, Dance, Natural History, Photography, Travel & Tourism, Visual Arts

ISBN Prefix(es): 978-0-500
Distributor for Harry N Abrams; Aperture; Art Gallery of New South Wales; Art Gallery of Queensland; Art Gallery of South Australia; Australian Galleries; AVA Publishing; Mark Batty Publisher; Bloomings Books; Bois de Chesne; Chris Boot Ltd; Boothe-Clibborn Editions; Braun; British Museum Press; Rory Burke; Contrasto; Craftsman House; DAP Guggenheim; Five Continents; Flammarion; Historic Houses Trust of NSW; Ilex; J B Books; Kaldor Project; Laurence King Publishing; Frances Lincoln; McCulloch & McCulloch; Editions Didier Millet; MoMA; National Gallery of Australia; National Portrait Gallery; Object Gallery NSW; Outre Gallery; Quintus Publishing; RotoVision; Royal Academy; The Royal Collection; Schilt Publishing; Scriptum Editions; Sherman Galleries; Skira; Steidl; Tate Gallery; Vendome Press; Violette Editions; War Memorial; John Wardle
Orders to: Macmillan Distribution Services *Toll Free Tel:* 1300 135 113 *Toll Free Fax:* 1300 135 103 *E-mail:* orders@macmillan.com.au

Themis Press, *imprint of* The Federation Press

Caroline Thornton+
43 Edward St, North Sydney, NSW 2060
Tel: (02) 9955 7375
Founded: 1988
Subjects: History

Thorpe-Bowker+
Division of R R Bowker LLC
Level 1, 607 St Kilda Rd, Melbourne, Victoria 3004
Mailing Address: PO Box 6509, Central Victoria 8008
Tel: (03) 8517 8333 *Fax:* (03) 8517 8399
E-mail: subscriptions@thorpe.com.au
Web Site: www.thorpe.com.au
Key Personnel
Publisher: Tim Coronel *Tel:* (03) 8517 8343 *E-mail:* tim.coronel@thorpe.com.au
General Manager: Gary Pengelly *Tel:* (03) 8517 8345 *E-mail:* gary.pengelly@thorpe.com.au
Founded: 1921
Bibliographic & library reference publisher.
Membership(s): Australian Booksellers Association Inc (ABA); Australian Library & Information Association Ltd (ALIA); Australian Publishers Association (APA).
Subjects: Business, Library & Information Sciences, Publishing & Book Trade Reference
ISBN Prefix(es): 978-0-909532; 978-1-875589; 978-1-86452
Distributor for Bowker; R R Bowker; Whitaker

Tilde Business, *imprint of* Tilde Publishing Pty Ltd

Tilde Language, *imprint of* Tilde Publishing Pty Ltd

Tilde Publishing Pty Ltd
2/2 Queens Parade, Ashwood, Victoria 3147
Mailing Address: PO Box 72, Prahran, Victoria 3181
Tel: (03) 9807 1031
E-mail: orders@tilde.com.au
Web Site: bkbpress.com
Key Personnel
Publisher: Rick Ryan
Subjects: Accounting, Business, Finance, Law, Management, Marketing, Psychology, Psychiatry
ISBN Prefix(es): 978-0-7346

Imprints: Tilde Business; Tilde Language; Tilde Skills; Tilde University Press; TUP Business
Foreign Rep(s): Eurospan Group (Asia, China, Europe, India, UK); International Publishers Marketing (IPM) (Canada, USA)

Tilde Skills, *imprint of* Tilde Publishing Pty Ltd

Tilde University Press, *imprint of* Tilde Publishing Pty Ltd

Tirian Publications
813 Pacific Highway, Level 2, Suite 255, Chatsworth 2067
Tel: (02) 8003 3410
E-mail: info@tirian.com; enquiries@tirian.com
Web Site: www.tirian.com
Key Personnel
Dir: Andrew Grant *E-mail:* agrant@tirian.com; Gaia Grant *E-mail:* ggrant@tirian.com
Manager: Grant Henderson
Subjects: Education
ISBN Prefix(es): 978-0-9580144
Foreign Rep(s): Ajyal-Hr (Oman); AME Consultancy (Saudi Arabia); APM Group (Thailand); People Inc (FZ-LLC) (Saudi Arabia, United Arab Emirates); PT Antara Bintang Jaya (Indonesia); Synapses On-Life (Anastasia Moira) (Greece); Tirian International (Pty) (China, Hong Kong); Tirian (London) (Europe); Tirian Pte Ltd (Singapore); Tirian Pty Ltd Australia (Australia); Turnaround (Rob Day) (United Arab Emirates)

Tor, *imprint of* Pan Macmillan Australia Pty Ltd

Touchstone, *imprint of* Simon & Schuster (Australia) Pty Ltd

Transit Lounge Publishing
95 Stephen St, Yarraville, Victoria 3013
Fax: (03) 9689 8100
E-mail: info@transitlounge.com.au
Web Site: www.transitlounge.com.au
Key Personnel
Contact: Tess Rice *Tel:* (03) 9808 5693; Barry Scott *Tel:* (03) 9332 7847
Membership(s): Australian Publishers Association (APA); Small Press Underground Networking Community (SPUNC).
Subjects: Fiction, Nonfiction (General), Travel & Tourism
ISBN Prefix(es): 978-0-9750228; 978-0-9804616; 978-0-9805717; 978-0-9808462; 978-1-921924
Orders to: NewSouth Books, c/o TL Distribution, 15-23 Helles Ave, Moorebank, NSW 2170 *Tel:* (02) 8778 9999 *Fax:* (02) 8778 9944 *E-mail:* orders@tldistribution.com.au (Australia & New Zealand)

Troubadour Press, *imprint of* New Creation Publications Inc

TUP Business, *imprint of* Tilde Publishing Pty Ltd

UBD Gregory's, *imprint of* Hardie Grant Travel

University of New South Wales Press Ltd+
Cliffbrook Campus, 45 Beach St, Coogee, NSW 2034
Mailing Address: University of New South Wales, Sydney, NSW 2052
Tel: (02) 8936 0100
E-mail: enquiries@newsouthpublishing.com
Web Site: www.unswpress.com
Key Personnel
Chairman: Merlin Crossley

Chief Executive Officer: Kathy Bail
  E-mail: kathy.bail@unswpress.com.au
Chief Operating Officer & Finance Dir: David
  Moody
Executive Publisher, NewSouth Publishing:
  Phillipa McGuinness
NewSouth Books Dir: Nella Soeterboek
Founded: 1962
Membership(s): Australian Publishers Association
  (APA).
Subjects: Architecture & Interior Design, Biog-
  raphy, Memoirs, Biological Sciences, Earth
  Sciences, Engineering (General), Environmental
  Studies, Gardening, Plants, Government, Polit-
  ical Science, History, Natural History, Nonfic-
  tion (General), Public Administration, Science
  (General), Social Sciences, Sociology, Technol-
  ogy, Women's Studies
ISBN Prefix(es): 978-0-86840; 978-0-947205;
  978-1-74223
Number of titles published annually: 50 Print
Total Titles: 1,300 Print
Imprints: NewSouth; UNSW Press
Distributed by Eurospan (UK, Continental Eu-
  rope, Middle East and Africa); Independent
  Publishers Group (USA, Canada and Asia);
  NewSouth Books (Australia & New Zealand)
Distributor for Aboriginal Studies Press; ACER
  Books; Arsenal Pulp Press; Australian Aca-
  demic Press; Beacon Press; Birlinn; Broad-
  view; Brookings Institution Press; Career
  FAQs; CSIRO Publishing; Currency Press;
  ECW Press; Edinburgh University Press; Eland
  Books; Hackett Publishing; Hordern House; C
  Hurst & Co; Indiana University Press; Insight;
  Magasala Books; Museum of Victoria; National
  Library of Australia; National Museum of Aus-
  tralia; Rosenberg Publishing; Signal Books;
  University of Minnesota Press; University of
  Western Australia Press
Bookshop(s): UNSW Bookshop, Quadrangle
  Bldg, College Rd, Kensington, NSW 2033,
  Dir: Mark Halladay *Tel:* (02) 9385 6622
  E-mail: orders@bookshop.unsw.edu.au *Web
  Site:* www.bookshop.unsw.edu.au
Warehouse: NewSouth Books, c/o TL Distribu-
  tion Pty Ltd, 15-23 Helles Ave, Moorebank
  2170 *Tel:* (02) 8778 9999 *Fax:* (02) 8778 9944
  E-mail: orders@tldistribution.com.au

University of Newcastle
Callaghan Campus, University Dr, Callaghan,
  NSW 2308
Tel: (02) 4921 5000 *Fax:* (02) 4985 4200
E-mail: publications@newcastle.edu.au
Web Site: www.newcastle.edu.au
Subjects: Accounting, Aeronautics, Aviation, An-
  thropology, Architecture & Interior Design, Bi-
  ological Sciences, Business, Chemistry, Chem-
  ical Engineering, Civil Engineering, Commu-
  nications, Computer Science, Economics, Ed-
  ucation, Electronics, Electrical Engineering,
  Energy, Environmental Studies, Film, Video,
  Finance, Geography, Geology, Government,
  Political Science, Health, Nutrition, History,
  Journalism, Language Arts, Linguistics, Law,
  Management, Marketing, Mathematics, Mechanical Engineering, Medicine, Nursing, Dentistry, Music, Dance, Natural History, Philosophy, Physics, Psychology, Psychiatry, Religion
  - Other, Social Sciences, Sociology, Technol-
  ogy, Travel & Tourism
ISBN Prefix(es): 978-0-7259; 978-1-920701

University of Queensland Press+
PO Box 6042, St Lucia, Qld 4067
Tel: (07) 3365 7244 *Fax:* (07) 3365 7579
E-mail: uqp@uqp.uq.edu.au
Web Site: www.uqp.uq.edu.au
Key Personnel
Chief Executive Officer: Greg Bain
Head of Publishing: Madonna Duffy
Nonfiction Publisher: Alexandra Payne

Marketing Manager: Meredene Hill
Founded: 1948
Publisher of quality literary works of fiction &
  nonfiction. Also specialize in Black Australian
  writings, Aboriginal studies & social & politi-
  cal issues, reference books & picture books.
Subjects: Architecture & Interior Design, Art,
  Biography, Memoirs, Fiction, Government,
  Political Science, History, Literature, Literary
  Criticism, Essays, Nonfiction (General), Poetry,
  Social Sciences, Sociology, Sports, Athletics,
  Travel & Tourism, Culture Studies, Current Af-
  fairs
ISBN Prefix(es): 978-0-7022
Number of titles published annually: 60 Print
Distributed by Penguin Group (Australia) (or-
  ders@au.penguingroup.com); Penguin Books
  (NZ) (orders@penguin.co.nz)
Distribution Center: Roundhouse Group, 18
  Marine Gardens, Unit B, Brighton BN2
  1AH, United Kingdom *Tel:* (01273) 603 717
  E-mail: orders@roundhousegroup.co.uk *Web
  Site:* www.roundhousegroup.co.uk (Europe in-
  cluding the UK)
Independent Publishers Group, 814 N Franklin
  St, Chicago, IL 60610, United States *Tel:* 312-
  337-0747 *E-mail:* frontdesk@ipgbook.com *Web
  Site:* www.ipgbook.com (North America)

University of Western Australia Publishing+
Division of The University of Western Australia
M419, University of Western Australia, 35 Stir-
  ling Highway, Crawley, WA 6009
Tel: (08) 6488 3670 *Fax:* (08) 6488 1027
E-mail: admin-uwap@uwa.edu.au; marketing-
  uwap@uwa.edu.au
Web Site: www.uwap.uwa.edu.au; www.facebook.
  com/uwapublishing
Key Personnel
Dir: Terri-ann White
Publisher: Kate Pickard
Editor: Linda Martin; Anne Ryden
Design Manager: Anna Maley-Fadgyas
Sales, Rights & Marketing Coordinator: Kiri Falls
Publishing Assistant: Britt Ingerson
Founded: 1935
Subjects: Art, Biography, Memoirs, Fiction, His-
  tory, Literature, Literary Criticism, Essays, Nat-
  ural History, Nonfiction (General), Photogra-
  phy, Poetry, Regional Interests, Social Sciences,
  Sociology, Wine & Spirits, Women's Studies
ISBN Prefix(es): 978-1-875560; 978-1-876268;
  978-1-920694; 978-0-85564; 978-0-86422;
  978-0-909751; 978-0-9802694; 978-0-9802965;
  978-1-921401; 978-1-920964; 978-1-74258
Number of titles published annually: 22 Print
Imprints: Cygnet Books; Staples; UWA Publishing Custom; UWA Publishing Scholarly
Orders to: NewSouth Books, c/o TL Distribu-
  tion Pty Ltd, 15-23 Helles Ave, Moorebank,
  NSW 2170 *Tel:* (02) 8778 9999 *Fax:* (02) 8778
  9944 *E-mail:* orders@tldistribution.com.au *Web
  Site:* www.newsouthbooks.com.au (Australia)
Roundhouse Group, Unit B, 18 Marine Gar-
  dens, Brighton BN2 1AH, United Kingdom
  Tel: (01273) 603 717 *Fax:* (01273) 697 494
  E-mail: sandy@roundhousegroup.co.uk *Web
  Site:* www.roundhousegroup.co.uk (UK & Eu-
  rope)
International Specialized Book Services (ISBS),
  920 NE 58 Ave, Suite 300, Portland, OR
  97213-3786, United States *Tel:* 503-287-3093
  Fax: 503-280-8832 *E-mail:* orders@isbs.com
  Web Site: www.isbs.com (North America)

Unlock the Past, see Gould Genealogy &
  History

UNSW Press, *imprint of* University of New
  South Wales Press Ltd

UNSW Press Ltd, see University of New South
  Wales Press Ltd

UQP, see University of Queensland Press

UWA Publishing, see University of Western
  Australia Publishing

UWA Publishing Custom, *imprint of* University
  of Western Australia Publishing

UWA Publishing Scholarly, *imprint of*
  University of Western Australia Publishing

VCTA Publishing+
Carringbush Business Centre, 134-136 Cambridge
  St, Suite 201, Level 2, Collingwood, Victoria
  3066
Mailing Address: PO Box 361, Abbotsford, Vic-
  toria 3067
Tel: (03) 9419 9622 *Fax:* (03) 9419 1205
E-mail: vcta@vcta.asn.au
Web Site: www.vcta.asn.au
Key Personnel
Executive Officer: Leonie Swarbrick
  E-mail: leonie.swarbrick@vcta.asn.au
Executive Dir: Christine Reid *E-mail:* christine.
  reid@vcta.asn.au
Dir: Sandra Brogden
Manager, Publications: Lyn Thane
Founded: 1953
An independent organization which exists to pro-
  vide leadership, support services, programs &
  resources to educators.
Subjects: Accounting, Business, Career Develop-
  ment, Communications, Economics, Finance,
  Law, Regional Interests
ISBN Prefix(es): 978-0-86859; 978-0-909715

Ventura Press
2 Macdonald St, Paddington, NSW 2021
Mailing Address: PO Box 780, Edgecliff, NSW
  2027
Tel: (02) 8060 9191
E-mail: info@venturapress.com.au
Web Site: www.venturapress.com.au
Key Personnel
Owner & Mng Dir: Jane Curry
Media & Marketing: Eleanor Reader
  E-mail: ereader@venturapress.com.au
Founded: 2002
Subjects: Fiction, Health, Nutrition, Nonfiction
  (General), Psychology, Psychiatry, Self-Help,
  Ethics, Family, Parenting
ISBN Prefix(es): 978-1-925183; 978-1-922190

Verand Press, *imprint of* Brandl & Schlesinger
  Pty Ltd

Vermillion, *imprint of* Random House Books
  Australia, A Penguin Random House Company

Victorian Commercial Teachers Association,
  see VCTA Publishing

Victory Books, *imprint of* Melbourne University
  Publishing Ltd

Viking, *imprint of* Penguin Group (Australia)

Villamanta Publishing Services+
Division of Villamanta Disability Rights Legal
  Service Inc
44 Bellerine St, Geelong, Victoria 3220
Tel: (03) 5229 2925 *Fax:* (03) 5229 3354
E-mail: publishing@villamanta.org.au
Web Site: www.villamanta.org.au
Founded: 1993
Subjects: Disability, Special Needs, Law

ISBN Prefix(es): 978-0-9587635; 978-1-876493; 978-0-9871576
Total Titles: 14 Print

Vintage, *imprint of* Random House Books Australia, A Penguin Random House Company

Virgin, *imprint of* Random House Books Australia, A Penguin Random House Company

Wakefield Crime Classics, *imprint of* Wakefield Press Pty Ltd

Wakefield Press Pty Ltd+
One The Parade West, Kent Town, SA 5067
Mailing Address: PO Box 2266, Kent Town, SA 5071
Tel: (08) 8362 8800 *Fax:* (08) 8362 7592
E-mail: orders@wakefieldpress.com.au
Web Site: www.wakefieldpress.com.au
Key Personnel
Dir: Michael Bollen *E-mail:* michael@wakefieldpress.com.au
Founded: 1989
Subjects: Art, Biography, Memoirs, Cookery, Fiction, Gardening, Plants, History, Humor, Language Arts, Linguistics, Literature, Literary Criticism, Essays, Mysteries, Suspense, Nonfiction (General), Poetry, Travel & Tourism
ISBN Prefix(es): 978-1-86254; 978-0-949268
Number of titles published annually: 50 Print
Total Titles: 1,000 Print
Imprints: Wakefield Crime Classics
Distributor for AATE Interface Series; Bookends Books; Bookhappy Books; City of Adelaide; Conway's Collectables; Davam Place; Department of Environment & Heritage; DFK Management; Dilettante Press; E&E Productions; Girl Press Books; The Gerald & Mark Hoberman Collection; Kensington West Productions; Key Porter Books; Lythrum Press; Prospect Books; Barbara Santich; Select Books; Serif; State Records of South Australia; Still Life Cards; Suhas; Tomahawk Press; Wakefield Press; Welcome Rain Publishers
Foreign Rep(s): Greene Phoenix Marketing (Paul Greenberg) (New Zealand)
Foreign Rights: Eliane Benisti Literary Agency (Eliane Benisti) (France); Big Apple Agency Inc (Erica Zhou) (China); Big Apple Agency Inc (Chris Lin) (Taiwan); Bookpack (Agata Radkiewicz) (Poland); DMM Literary Management (Dominique Massessoria) (Brazil); EntersKorea Agency (Lauren Kim) (Korea); The Fritz Agency (Christian Dittus) (Germany); International Editors' Co (Maru de Monserrat & Isabel Monteagudo) (Spain); International Editors' Co (Nicolas Costa) (Argentina); Nurcihan Kesim Literary Agency Inc (Filiz Karaman) (Turkey); Kristin Olson Literary Agency SRO (Czechia); Tuttle Mori Agency Inc (Asako Kawachi) (Japan); Adrian Weston Literary Agency (Adrian Weston) (UK); The Writers House (Michele Rubin) (North America)

Walker Books Australia
Level 2, 1-15 Wilson St, Locked Bag 22, Newtown, NSW 2042
Tel: (02) 9517 9577 *Fax:* (02) 9517 9997
E-mail: sales@walkerbooks.com.au; marketingwba@walkerbooks.com.au; permissionswba@walkerbooks.com.au
Web Site: www.walkerbooks.com.au
Key Personnel
Mng Dir & Publisher: Sarah Foster
Group Trade Publishing Dir: Liz Bicknell
Chief Global Development Officer, Walker Books Group: Helen McAleer
Publicist: Jaclyn Prescott
Founded: 1993

ISBN Prefix(es): 978-1-921150; 978-1-921529; 978-1-921720; 978-1-921977
Parent Company: Walker Books Ltd, 87 Vauxhall Walk, London SE11 5HJ, United Kingdom
Associate Companies: Candlewick Press
Imprints: Black Dog Books
Distributor for Lerner Publishing (trade imprints)
Distribution Center: TL Distribution, 15-23 Helles Ave, Moorebank, NSW 2170
Tel: (02) 8778 9900 *Fax:* (02) 8778 9944
E-mail: walkerbooks@tldistribution.com.au

Frederick Warne, *imprint of* Penguin Group (Australia)

The Watermark Press+
44-48 Farm St, Boorowa, NSW 2586
Mailing Address: PO Box 141, Boorowa, NSW 2586
Tel: (02) 6385 1111 *Fax:* (02) 6385 1900
E-mail: books@bigpond.net.au
Web Site: www.watermarkpress.com.au
Key Personnel
Head of Company: Simon Blackall
Founded: 1983
Subjects: Animals, Pets, Architecture & Interior Design, Cookery, Crafts, Games, Hobbies, Gardening, Plants, Humor, Military Science, Nonfiction (General), Travel & Tourism, Wine & Spirits
ISBN Prefix(es): 978-0-949284
Foreign Rep(s): Antique Collectors' Club (North America); Roundhouse Group (Europe, UK)

Wellington Lane Press Pty Ltd+
120 Wycombe Rd, Neutral Bay, NSW 2089
Mailing Address: PO Box 603, Neutral Bay, NSW 2089
Tel: (02) 9904 0962 *Fax:* (02) 9904 0962
Key Personnel
Publisher: Carol Dettmann
Founded: 1976
Subjects: Art, Photography, Regional Interests
ISBN Prefix(es): 978-0-908022; 978-0-947322
Imprints: Chapter & Verse

John Wiley & Sons, *imprint of* John Wiley & Sons Australia Ltd

John Wiley & Sons Australia Ltd+
42 McDougall St, Milton, Qld 4064
Tel: (07) 3859 9755 *Fax:* (07) 3859 9715
E-mail: brisbane@wiley.com
Web Site: www.wiley.com
Key Personnel
Executive Dir, John Wiley & Sons Australia Ltd & Wiley Japan, Vice President & Publishing Dir, Wiley Blackwell Asia-Pacific: Mark Robertson
Dir, Finance & Off Services: Scott Menzies
General Manager, Professional/Trade: Maria Hendriks
Founded: 1954
Membership(s): Australian Publishers Association (APA).
Subjects: Education, Nonfiction (General)
ISBN Prefix(es): 978-0-395; 978-0-471; 978-0-393; 978-1-740; 978-1-876; 978-0-7314; 978-0-7016
Parent Company: John Wiley & Sons Inc, 111 River St, Hoboken, NJ 07030-5774, United States
Associate Companies: John Wiley & Sons (Asia) Pte Ltd; John Wiley & Sons Canada Ltd, 90 Eglinton Ave E, Suite 300, Toronto, Ontario M4P 2Y3, Canada *Tel:* 416-236-4433 *Fax:* 416-236-8743 *E-mail:* canada@wiley.com; John Wiley & Sons Ltd, The Atrium, Southern Gate, Chichester, West Sussex PO19 8SQ, United Kingdom *Tel:* (01243) 779777

Fax: (01243) 775878 *E-mail:* customer@wiley.co.uk
Imprints: Brooks Waterloo; Hungry Minds Australia; The Jacaranda Press; John Wiley & Sons; Wrightbooks
Branch Office(s)
155 Cremorne St, Richmond, Victoria 3121
Tel: (03) 9274 3100 *Fax:* (03) 9274 3101
E-mail: melbourne@wiley.com
Distributor for Houghton Mifflin Harcourt; W W Norton & Company Inc
Warehouse: Australian Distribution Center, Keppel Logistics, 33 Windorah St, Stafford, Qld 4053 *Tel:* (07) 3859 9611 *Fax:* (07) 3859 9627
Distribution Center: Australian Distribution Center, Keppel Logistics, 33 Windorah St, Stafford, Qld 4053 *Tel:* (07) 3959 9611 *Fax:* (07) 3959 9627 *E-mail:* brisbane@wiley.com

Wilkinson Publishing
Alcaston House, Level 4, 2 Collins St, Melbourne, Victoria 3000
Tel: (03) 9654 5446
E-mail: sales@wilkinsonpublishing.com.au
Web Site: www.wilkinsonpublishing.com.au
Subjects: Biography, Memoirs, Business, Criminology, Environmental Studies, Finance, Health, Nutrition, Humor, Management, Sports, Athletics, Comics, Entertainment, Graphic Novels, Lifestyle, True Crime
ISBN Prefix(es): 978-0-9775457; 978-0-9802818; 978-1-921332; 978-1-921667; 978-1-921804

Windmill Books, *imprint of* Random House Books Australia, A Penguin Random House Company

Windward Publications Pty Ltd+
464 Woodhill Mountain Rd, Berry, NSW 2535
Mailing Address: PO Box 361, Berry, NSW 2535
Tel: (02) 4464 1977 *Fax:* (02) 4464 1906
E-mail: sales@windward.com.au
Web Site: www.windward.com.au
Key Personnel
Contact: David Colfelt *E-mail:* dc@windward.com.au
Founded: 1984
Subjects: Maritime, Regional Interests, Travel & Tourism, Great Barrier Reef, Whitsunday Islands
ISBN Prefix(es): 978-0-9590830; 978-0-9586989

Windy Hollow Books
PO Box 265, Kew East, Victoria 3102
E-mail: info@windyhollowbooks.com.au; sales@windyhollowbooks.com.au
Web Site: www.windyhollowbooks.com.au
ISBN Prefix(es): 978-1-921136
Orders to: Peribo, 58 Beaumont Rd, Mount Kuring-gai, NSW 2080 *Tel:* (02) 9457 0011 *Fax:* (02) 9457 0022 *E-mail:* info@peribo.com.au *Web Site:* www.peribo.com.au (Australia & New Zealand)

Winetitles Media Pty Ltd
Division of Provincial Press Group
630 Regency Rd, Broadview, SA 5083
Mailing Address: PO Box 1006, Prospect East, SA 5082
Tel: (08) 8369 9500 *Fax:* (08) 8369 9501
E-mail: info@winetitles.com.au; editorial@winetitles.com.au; orders@winetitles.com.au
Web Site: www.winetitles.com.au; www.winebiz.com.au
Key Personnel
Publisher: Hartley Higgins
General Manager: Elizabeth Bouzoudis
Sales Manager: Nicole Evans *Tel:* (08) 8369 9515
Also publishes magazines: *Australian & New Zealand Grapegrower & Winemaker; Australian Viticulture; Australian & New Zealand*

Wine Industry Journal. In addition *Australian & New Zealand Wine Industry Directory* published annually, daily enewsletter *Daily Wine News* & books on viticulture & oenology.
Subjects: Agriculture, Wine & Spirits, Wine & Viticulture Industries
ISBN Prefix(es): 978-1-875130; 978-0-9756850

Paula Wiseman, *imprint of* Simon & Schuster (Australia) Pty Ltd

Wombat Books
PO Box 1519, Capalaba BC, Qld 4157
Tel: (07) 3245 1938
E-mail: wombat@wombatbooks.com.au
Web Site: www.wombatbooks.com.au
Key Personnel
Dir & Publisher: Rochelle Manners
Founded: 2009
Subjects: Fiction, Nonfiction (General), Christian, Family, Parenting
ISBN Prefix(es): 978-0-9752321; 978-1-921632; 978-1-921633
Imprints: Even Before Publishing; Mostly for Mothers; Rhiza Press
Distribution Center: Novella Distribution, PO Box 2707, Mansfield, Qld 4122 *Tel:* (07) 3167 6519 *E-mail:* sales@novelladistribution.com.au *Web Site:* www.novelladistribution.com.au

Woodslane Press, *imprint of* Woodslane Pty Ltd

Woodslane Pty Ltd
10 Apollo St, Warriewood, NSW 2102
Tel: (02) 8445 2300 *Fax:* (02) 9997 5850
E-mail: info@woodslane.com.au
Web Site: www.woodslane.com.au
Key Personnel
Mng Dir: David Scott
Founded: 1989
Subjects: Biography, Memoirs, Business, Computer Science, Cookery, History, Music, Dance, Poetry, Sports, Athletics, Travel & Tourism, Lifestyle, Military, Popular Science, Technical
ISBN Prefix(es): 978-1-875680; 978-0-7299; 978-1-875889; 978-1-921203; 978-1-921606; 978-1-921683; 978-1-921874
Imprints: Woodslane Press

Woolshed Press, *imprint of* Random House Books Australia, A Penguin Random House Company

Working Title Press
9 Harriett St, Adelaide, SA 5000
Tel: (08) 8232 0226
Web Site: www.workingtitlepress.com.au
Key Personnel
Dir: Jane Covernton *E-mail:* jane@workingtitlepress.com
Subjects: Fiction, Nonfiction (General)
ISBN Prefix(es): 978-1-876288; 978-1-921504
Distribution Center: Penguin Group (Australia) *Tel:* (03) 8537 4499 *Toll Free Tel:* 1800 338 836 *Fax:* (03) 8537 4497 *E-mail:* orders@unitedbookdistributors.com.au *Web Site:* www.penguin.com.au (Australia & New Zealand)

Wrightbooks, *imprint of* John Wiley & Sons Australia Ltd

Xoum, see Brio Books

Young Explorer, *imprint of* Pearson Library

Youthworks
Level 1, St Andrews House, 464 Kent St, Sydney South, NSW 2000

Mailing Address: PO Box A287, Sydney South, NSW 1235
Tel: (02) 8268 3344 *Fax:* (02) 8268 3357
E-mail: info@youthworks.net; sales@youthworks.net
Web Site: cep.youthworks.net
Key Personnel
Chief Executive Officer: Zachary Veron
Founded: 1994
Subjects: Biblical Studies, Religion - Protestant
ISBN Prefix(es): 978-1-875861; 978-0-909827; 978-1-875650; 978-1-875596; 978-0-908089; 978-1-86459; 978-0-949108; 978-0-949038; 978-1-876960; 978-1-920935; 978-1-921137; 978-1-921460; 978-1-922000
Imprints: Anglican Press Australia; Aquila Press; Blue Bottle Books; Christian Education Publications
Branch Office(s)
118 King St, Palmerston North 4440, New Zealand *Tel:* (06) 355 2317 *Fax:* (06) 357 0281 *E-mail:* cep@clcnewzealand.com

Zero to Ten, *imprint of* Pearson Library

Austria

General Information

Capital: Vienna
Language: German, small Croat & Slovene speaking minorities
Religion: Predominantly Roman Catholic, some Protestant and Muslim
Population: 8.1 million
Bank Hours: 0800-1230, 1330-1500 Monday-Wednesday, Friday; 0800-1230, 1300-1730 Thursday
Shop Hours: 0800-1800 Monday-Friday; 0800-1200 or 1300 Saturday
Currency: 100 Eurocents = 1 Euro
Export/Import Information: Import licenses not required for books. No exchange controls. 10% VAT on books.
Copyright: UCC, Berne, Florence (see Copyright Conventions, pg viii)

Aarachne Verlag+
Bergengasse 6, RH 14, 1220 Vienna
Tel: (01) 285 53 53 *Fax:* (01) 285 53 53
Founded: 1992
Subjects: Drama, Theater, Ethnicity, Fiction, Human Relations, Journalism, Literature, Literary Criticism, Essays, Mysteries, Suspense, Science Fiction, Fantasy
ISBN Prefix(es): 978-3-85255

Abakus Verlag GesmbH+
Pezoltgasse 50, 5020 Salzburg
Tel: (0662) 632076
Founded: 1979
Subjects: Environmental Studies, Language Arts, Linguistics, Mathematics
ISBN Prefix(es): 978-3-7044

ADEVA (Akademische Druck-u Verlagsanstalt)
(Academic Printing & Publishing House)
St Peter Hauptstr 98, 8042 Graz
Mailing Address: Postfach 598, 8011 Graz
Tel: (0316) 46 3003 *Fax:* (0316) 46 3003-24
E-mail: info@adeva.com
Web Site: www.adeva.com
Key Personnel
Chief Executive Officer & Dir, Marketing & Sales: Dr Paul Struzl *E-mail:* pstruzl@adeva.com
President: Dr Michael Struzl *E-mail:* struzl@adeva.com

Program Dir: Christopher Schaffer *Tel:* (0316) 3644-45 *E-mail:* schaffer@adeva.com
Editor: Dr Christine Brandstaetter *Tel:* (0316) 3644-34 *E-mail:* brandstaetter@adeva.com
Founded: 1950
Specialize in facsimile edition true-to-original reproductions of ancient & medieval manuscripts.
Subjects: Art, Film, Video, History, Literature, Literary Criticism, Essays, Music, Dance, Science (General), Cultural History
ISBN Prefix(es): 978-3-201; 978-3-900144
Number of titles published annually: 10 Print
Total Titles: 2,000 Print
Orders to: Musikverlag Doblinger, Dorotheergasse 10, 1010 Vienna *Tel:* (01) 515 03-0 *Fax:* (01) 515 03-51 (music titles-International)
Buch- und Medienvertriebs AG, Hochstr 357, 8200 Schaffhausen, Switzerland *Tel:* (052) 643 54 30 *Fax:* (052) 643 54 35 *E-mail:* info@buch-medien.ch (booksellers in Switzerland)

Verlag Adinkra
Harterfeldstr 2A, 4060 Leonding
Tel: (0732) 673229 *Fax:* (0732) 67460623
E-mail: verlag@adinkra.at
Web Site: www.adinkra.at
Key Personnel
Publisher: Patrick K Addai
Subjects: Fiction
ISBN Prefix(es): 978-3-9501083

Verlagshaus der Aerzte
Nibelungengasse 13, 1010 Vienna
Tel: (01) 512 44 86 *Fax:* (01) 512 44 86-24
E-mail: buch.medien@aerzteverlagshaus.at; office@aerzteverlagshaus.at
Web Site: www.aerzteverlagshaus.at
Key Personnel
Dir: Martin Stickler
Publishing Dir: Hagen Schaub *Tel:* (01) 512 44 86-15 *E-mail:* h.schaub@aerzteverlagshaus.at
Marketing & Sales: Michael Hlatky *Tel:* (01) 512 44 86-43 *E-mail:* m.hlatky@aerzteverlagshaus.at
Public Relations: Andrea Karall *Tel:* (01) 512 44 86-22 *E-mail:* a.karall@aerzteverlagshaus.at
Subjects: Cookery, Health, Nutrition, History, Medicine, Nursing, Dentistry, Health Facility Management, Medical History
ISBN Prefix(es): 978-3-901488
Distribution Center: Mohr Morawa Buchvertrieb GmbH, Sulzengasse 2, 1230 Vienna *Tel:* (01) 680 14-0 *Fax:* (01) 688 71 30 *E-mail:* momo@mohrmorawa.at *Web Site:* www.mohrmorawa.at
Herold Verlagsauslieferung & Logistik GmbH, Raiffeisenallee 10, 82041 Oberhaching, Germany *Tel:* (089) 61 38 71-0 *Fax:* (089) 61 38 71-20 *E-mail:* herold@herold-va.de *Web Site:* www.herold-va.de

Agens-Werk, Geyer+Reisser, Druck- und Verlagsgesellschaft mbH
Arbeitergasse 1-7, 1050 Vienna
Tel: (01) 5445641-0 *Fax:* (01) 5445641-66
Subjects: Art
ISBN Prefix(es): 978-3-7033; 978-3-85202

Akademische Druck- u Verlagsanstalt, see ADEVA (Akademische Druck-u Verlagsanstalt)

Amalthea Signum Verlag GmbH
Am Heumarkt 19, 1030 Vienna
Tel: (01) 7 12 35 60 *Fax:* (01) 7 12 89 95
E-mail: verlag@amalthea.at
Web Site: www.amalthea.at
Key Personnel
Mng Dir: Dr Herbert Fleissner
Publishing Dir: Dr Brigitte-Sinhuber Harenberg *E-mail:* brigitte.sinhuber@amalthea.at
Sales: Ingeborg Lux *Tel:* (01) 7 12 35 60-12 *E-mail:* ingeborg.lux@amalthea.at

Founded: 1917
Subjects: Art, Biography, Memoirs, Business, Cookery, Fiction, Government, Political Science, History, Humor, Music, Dance, Nonfiction (General)
ISBN Prefix(es): 978-3-85002; 978-3-85436; 978-3-902313
Associate Companies: Herbig; LangenMueller; LangenMueller Hoerbuch; nymphenburger; terra magica; Universitas
Distribution Center: Mohr Morawa Buchvertrieb GmbH, Sulzengasse 2, 1230 Vienna *Tel:* (01) 68 01 40 *Fax:* (01) 688 71 30 *E-mail:* momo@mohrmorawa.at *Web Site:* www.mohrmorawa.at
VVA, An der Autobahn, Postfach 77 77, 33310 Guetersloh, Germany *Tel:* (05241) 80 88 077 *Fax:* (05241) 80 66 43 *E-mail:* langen-mueller-herbig@bertelsmann.de
Buchzentrum AG, Industriestr Ost 10, 4614 Haegendorf, Switzerland *Tel:* (062) 209 26 26 *Fax:* (062) 209 26 27 *E-mail:* kundendienst@sbz.ch

Andreas & Andreas Verlagsbuchhandel+
Hans-Seebach-Str 10, 5020 Salzburg
Tel: (0664) 15 65 357 (cell)
E-mail: office@andreasverlag.at
Web Site: www.andreasverlag.at
Founded: 1956
Subjects: Fiction
ISBN Prefix(es): 978-3-85012

Verlag Der Apfel+
Schottenfeldgasse 24/13, 1070 Vienna
Tel: (01) 52 661 52 *Fax:* (01) 52 287 18
E-mail: office@verlagderapfel.at
Web Site: www.verlagderapfel.at
Key Personnel
Publisher: Thomas C Cubasch
Founded: 1984
Subjects: Art, History, Literature, Literary Criticism, Essays, Music, Dance, Arts Restoration & Conservation, Musicology
ISBN Prefix(es): 978-3-85450
Number of titles published annually: 20 Print
Total Titles: 80 Print

Ares Verlag, *imprint of* Leopold Stocker Verlag GmbH

Ares Verlag GmbH
Imprint of Leopold Stocker Verlag GmbH
Hofgasse 5, 8011 Graz
Mailing Address: Postfach 438, 8011 Graz
Tel: (0316) 82 16 36 *Fax:* (0316) 83 56 12
E-mail: office@ares-verlag.com
Web Site: www.ares-verlag.com
Key Personnel
Publishing Dir: Wolfgang Dvorak-Stocker
Marketing & Sales: Franz Koiner *E-mail:* franz.koiner@ares-verlag.com
Press: Carina Spielberger *E-mail:* carina.spielberger@ares-verlag.com
Subjects: Government, Political Science, History, Nonfiction (General)
ISBN Prefix(es): 978-3-902475

Arovell Verlag
Vordertal 660, 4824 Gosau
Tel: (061) 368430
E-mail: office@arovell.at
Web Site: www.arovell.at
Key Personnel
Dir: Paul Jaeg
Founded: 1991
Subjects: Computers, Literature, Literary Criticism, Essays, Poetry, Romance
ISBN Prefix(es): 978-3-902808; 978-3-902547
Number of titles published annually: 20 Print

Astor-Verlag, Willibald Schlager+
Weyringergasse 35/DG, 1040 Vienna
Tel: (01) 9144281 *Fax:* (01) 9144281
E-mail: astor-media@chello.at
Web Site: www.astormedia.at
Key Personnel
Owner: Willi Schlager *E-mail:* willi.schlager@chello.at
Founded: 1975
Subjects: Biography, Memoirs, Fiction, Humor, Literature, Literary Criticism, Essays, Regional Interests
ISBN Prefix(es): 978-3-900277
Orders to: Mohr Morawa Buchvertrieb GmbH, Sulzengasse 2, 1230 Vienna *Tel:* (01) 680 14-5 *Fax:* (01) 688 71 30 *E-mail:* momo@mohrmorawa.at *Web Site:* www.mohrmorawa.at

Edition Atelier
Schwarzspanierstr 12/2, 1090 Vienna
Tel: (01) 907 34 10
E-mail: office@editionatelier.at; presse@editionatelier.at
Web Site: www.editionatelier.at
Key Personnel
Editorial: Jorghi Poll *E-mail:* jorghi.poll@editionatelier.at
Sales & Press: Sarah Legler *E-mail:* sarah.legler@editionatelier.at
Founded: 1985
Subjects: Drama, Theater, Fiction, History, Literature, Literary Criticism, Essays
ISBN Prefix(es): 978-3-902498
Distribution Center: Hain Verlagsauslieferung GmbH, Dr-Otto-Neurath-Gasse 5, 1220 Vienna *Tel:* (01) 282 65 65-77 *Fax:* (01) 282 52 82 *E-mail:* bestell@hain.at
GVA Gemeinsame Verlagsauslieferung, Postfach 2021, 37010 Goettingen, Germany *Tel:* (0551) 48 71 77 *Fax:* (0551) 413 92 *E-mail:* bestellungen@gva-verlage.de

Autorensolidaritaet-Verlag der Interessengemeinschaft oesterreichischer autorinnen und Autoren, see IG Autorinnen Autoren

Verlag Ferdinand Berger & Soehne GesmbH
Wiener Str 21-23, 3580 Horn
Tel: (02982) 4161-332 *Fax:* (02982) 4161-268
E-mail: druckerei.office@berger.at
Web Site: www.verlag-berger.at
Key Personnel
Publishing Manager: Michaela Jungwirth *Tel:* (02982) 4161-341 *E-mail:* jungwirth.michaela@berger.at
Founded: 1868
Subjects: Anthropology, Archaeology, Art, Natural History
ISBN Prefix(es): 978-3-85028
Branch Office(s)
Pulverturmgasse 3, 1090 Vienna *Tel:* (01) 31335-0 *Fax:* (01) 31335-19

Verlag Alexander Bernhardt
Vomperberg 14, 6134 Vomperberg/Tirol
Tel: (05242) 62131-0 *Fax:* (05242) 72801
E-mail: verlag@alexander-bernhardt.com; shop@alexander-bernhardt.com
Web Site: www.alexander-bernhardt.com
Key Personnel
Contact: Siegfried Bernhardt
Founded: 1945
Subjects: Philosophy
ISBN Prefix(es): 978-3-85029
Associate Companies: Grailland Publishers, Grailland, Iju Hills, PO Box 4157, Lagos, Nigeria *Tel:* (01) 853 6730 *E-mail:* graillandpublishers@yahoo.com; Grail Acres Publishing Co, 23 Hamilton Rd, Sidcup, Kent DA15 7HB, United Kingdom *Tel:* (0208) 308 9575 *E-mail:* info@grailmessage.org.uk;

Grail Publications Inc, Grail Acres, 3103 High Falls Rd, Jackson, GA 30233, United States *Tel:* 770-775-5720 *E-mail:* grailacres@gmail.com
Branch Office(s)
Alexander Bernhardt Grail Publishing Canada, PO Box 3572, Cheneville, QC J0V 1E0, Canada *Tel:* 819-428-2219 *E-mail:* info@alexander-bernhardt-canada.com *Web Site:* www.alexander-bernhardt-canada.com
Editions Alexander Bernhardt France, 15 rue Leon Blum, Actipole La Neuvillette, 51100 Reims, France *Tel:* (03) 26 82 58 26 *E-mail:* contact@alexander-bernhardt-france.com *Web Site:* www.alexander-bernhardt-france.com

Bethania Verlag+
Theresiengasse 33, 1180 Vienna
Tel: (01) 4793559; (01) 6672216
Key Personnel
Editor: Helene Mirtl
Founded: 1982
Subjects: Biological Sciences, Chemistry, Chemical Engineering, Philosophy, Physical Sciences, Science (General)
ISBN Prefix(es): 978-3-900085

Annette Betz Verlag, *imprint of* Verlag Carl Ueberreuter GmbH

Annette Betz Verlag+
Imprint of Verlag Carl Ueberreuter GmbH
Alser Str 24, 1090 Vienna
Tel: (01) 40 444-0 *Fax:* (01) 40 444-5
E-mail: office@ueberreuter.at
Web Site: www.ueberreuter.at
Key Personnel
Mng Dir: Klaus Kaempfe-Burghardt *Tel:* (01) 40 444-171 *E-mail:* kkb@ueberreuter.at
Sales Manager: Saskia Mekul *Tel:* (01) 40 444-196 *Fax:* (01) 40 444-330 *E-mail:* mekul@ueberreuter.at
Marketing: Katrin Hehberger *Tel:* (030) 65 21 623-31 *E-mail:* katrin.hehberger@ueberreuter.de
Rights & Licenses: Julia Balogh *Tel:* (030) 652 16 23-25 *E-mail:* julia.balogh@ueberreuter.de
Founded: 1962
ISBN Prefix(es): 978-3-219; 978-3-8000
Distribution Center: Medienlogistik-Pichler OEBZ GmbH & Co KG, IZ NOE Sued, Str 1, Objekt 34, 2355 Wiener Neudorf *Tel:* (02236) 63535 236 *Fax:* (02236) 63535 243 *E-mail:* mlo@medien-logistik.at *Web Site:* www.medien-logistik.at
arvato media GmbH, An der Autobahn 100, 33333 Guetersloh, Germany *Tel:* (05241) 80-3877 *Fax:* (05241) 80-66959 *E-mail:* gisela.mense@bertelsmann.de
Buchzentrum AG, Industriestr Ost 10, 4614 Haegendorf, Switzerland *Tel:* (062) 209 26 26 *Fax:* (062) 209 26 27 *E-mail:* kundendienst@buchzentrum.ch

Bibliothek der Provinz, see Richard Pils Bibliothek der Provinz

Bohmann Druck & Verlag GmbH & Co KG
Leberstr 122, 1110 Vienna
Tel: (01) 740 95-0 *Fax:* (01) 740 95-183
E-mail: office.gl@bohmann.at; kontakt@bohmann.at
Web Site: www.bohmann.at
Key Personnel
Publishing Dir: Dr Gabriele Susanne Ambros
Editor-in-Chief: George Karp *Tel:* (01) 740 95-464 *Fax:* (01) 74 95-491 *E-mail:* karp.zv@bohmann.at
Founded: 1936

Subjects: Automotive, Business, Computer Science, Environmental Studies, Transportation, Travel & Tourism
ISBN Prefix(es): 978-3-7002; 978-3-901983

Braintrust GmbH
Dornbacher Str 59, 1170 Vienna
Tel: (01) 40416-0 *Fax:* (01) 40416-33
E-mail: office@braintrust.at
Web Site: www.braintrust.at
Key Personnel
Chief Executive Officer: Thomas Stern
   E-mail: stern@braintrust.at
Founded: 1989
Subjects: Career Development, Education, Management
ISBN Prefix(es): 978-3-901116

Christian Brandstaetter Verlag GmbH & Co KG+
Wickenburggasse 26, 1080 Vienna
Tel: (01) 512 15 43-0 *Fax:* (01) 512 15 43-231
E-mail: info@cbv.at
Web Site: www.brandstaetter-verlag.at; www.cbv.at
Key Personnel
Chief Executive Officer & Publishing Dir: Nicholas Brandstaetter *E-mail:* n.brandstaetter@cbv.at
Publisher: Dr Christian Brandstaetter *E-mail:* ch.brandstaetter@cbv.at
Head, Press & Public Relations: Friederike Harr *E-mail:* f.harr@cbv.at
Head, Sales & Marketing: Horst Grabensberger *E-mail:* h.grabensberger@cbv.at
Program Management & Licenses: Elisabeth Hoelzl *E-mail:* e.hoelzl@cbv.at
Founded: 1982
Subjects: Architecture & Interior Design, Art, Biography, Memoirs, Cookery, History, Photography, Regional Interests
ISBN Prefix(es): 978-3-85447; 978-3-206; 978-3-85498; 978-3-902510; 978-3-85033
Total Titles: 236 Print
Distribution Center: Medienlogistik Pichler-OEBZ GmbH & Co KG, IZ-NOE Sued, Str 1, Objekt 34, Postfach 133, 2355 Wiener Neudorf *Tel:* (02236) 63535-290 *Fax:* (02236) 63535-243 *E-mail:* mlo@medien-logistik.at *Web Site:* www.medien-logistik.at
Leipziger Kommissions- und Grossbuchhandelsgesellschaft mbH (LKG), An der Suedspitze 1-12, 04571 Roetha, Germany, Contact: Kathrin Obarski *Tel:* (034206) 65-106 *Fax:* (034206) 65-1741 *E-mail:* kobarski@lkg-service.de *Web Site:* www.lkg-va.de
Buchzentrum AG (BIZ), Industriestr Ost 10, 4614 Haegensdorf, Switzerland *Tel:* (062) 209 26 26 *Fax:* (062) 209 26 27 *E-mail:* kundendienst@buchzentrum.ch

Wilhelm Braumueller Universitaets-Verlagsbuchhandlung GmbH
Servitengasse 5, 1090 Vienna
Tel: (01) 319 11 59 *Fax:* (01) 310 28 05
E-mail: office@braumueller.at; bestellung@braumueller.at; presse@braumueller.at
Web Site: www.braumueller.at
Key Personnel
Publishing Dir: Bernhard Borovansky
Manager: Konstanze Borovansky
Press & Public Relations: Dr Elisabeth Siegel *Tel:* (01) 319 11 59 14
Founded: 1783
Subjects: Art, Government, Political Science, Law, Philosophy, Psychology, Psychiatry, Science (General)
ISBN Prefix(es): 978-3-7003; 978-3-99100
Imprints: Lesethek

Verlagsbuchhandlung Julius Breitschopf GmbH & Co KG
Hauptstr 104/19, 3420 Klosterneuburg-Kritzendorf
Tel: (02243) 36868-0; (0664) 4502116 (cell) *Fax:* (02243) 36868-20
E-mail: breitschopf.verlag@utanet.at
Web Site: www.breitschopf-verlag.com
Key Personnel
Contact: Julius Peter Breitschopf
Founded: 1947
Subjects: Cookery, Crafts, Games, Hobbies, Fiction, Fairy Tales, Family
ISBN Prefix(es): 978-3-7004

BSE Verlag Dr Bernhard Schuettengruber+
Wiesenweg 4, 8054 Pirka
Tel: (0316) 283170
Founded: 1984
Subjects: History, Poetry
ISBN Prefix(es): 978-3-900542

Bucher Verlag GmbH
Diepoldsauer Str 41, 6845 Hohenems
Tel: (05576) 7118-0 *Fax:* (05576) 7118-44
Web Site: www.bucherverlag.com
Key Personnel
Distribution/Sales, Finance & Personnel: Dr Michelle Bucher *Tel:* (05576) 7118-42 *E-mail:* m.bucher@bucherverlag.com
Editorial, Production & Marketing: Robert Lackner *Tel:* (05576) 7118-13 *E-mail:* lackner@bucherverlag.com
Subjects: Architecture & Interior Design, Art, Literature, Literary Criticism, Essays, Nonfiction (General), Photography
ISBN Prefix(es): 978-3-99018; 978-3-902679
Distribution Center: Mohr Morawa Buchvertrieb GmbH, Sulzengasse 2, 1230 Vienna *Tel:* (01) 680 14 5 *Fax:* (01) 689 68 00 *E-mail:* bestellung@mohrmorawa.at
LIBRI GmbH, Europaallee 1, 36244 Bad Hersfeld, Germany *Tel:* (06621) 89-0 *Fax:* (06621) 89-1313 *E-mail:* libri@libri.de *Web Site:* www.home.libri.de
Leipziger Kommissions- und Grossbuchhandelsgesellschaft mbH (LKG), An der Suedspitze 1-12, 04571 Roetha, Germany *Tel:* (034206) 65-100 *Fax:* (034206) 65-110 *E-mail:* lkg@lkg-service.de *Web Site:* www.lkg-va.de
AVA Verlagsauslieferung AG, Centralweg 16, 8910 Affoltern am Albis, Switzerland *Tel:* (044) 762 42 01 *Fax:* (044) 762 42 10 *E-mail:* avainfo@ava.ch

Buchkultur Verlagsgesellschaft mbH
Huetteldorfer Str 26, 1150 Vienna
Tel: (01) 7863380-0 *Fax:* (01) 7863380-10
E-mail: office@buchkultur.net
Web Site: www.buchkultur.net
Key Personnel
Mng Dir & Editor: Michael Schnepf *E-mail:* schnepf@buchkultur.net
Executive Editor: Hans Lerchbacher *E-mail:* lerchbacher@buchkultur.net
Chief Editor: Dr Tobias Hierl *E-mail:* hierl@buchkultur.net
Editor: Nils Jensen *E-mail:* jensen@buchkultur.net
Founded: 1989
Subjects: Communications, Journalism, Literature, Literary Criticism, Essays, Publishing & Book Trade Reference, Regional Interests
ISBN Prefix(es): 978-3-901052
Branch Office(s)
Birkenstr 7, 85774 Unterfoehring, Germany *Fax:* (089) 958216-92

Fachverlag fuer Buergerinformation+
Grabenstr 117, 8010 Graz
Tel: (0316) 686727 *Fax:* (0316) 686727-4
Key Personnel
Manager: Alfred Steingruber

Founded: 1986
Subjects: Public Administration
ISBN Prefix(es): 978-3-85363

Camera Austria+
Lendkai 1, 8020 Graz
Tel: (0316) 81 55 500 *Fax:* (0316) 81 55 509
E-mail: office@camera-austria.at; distribution@camera-austria.at (sales)
Web Site: www.camera-austria.at
Key Personnel
Dir & Editor: Reinhard Braun
Editor-in-Chief: Maren Luebbke-Tidow
Advertising Manager: Barbara Stoecker
Public Relations: Tanja Gassler
Sales: Michaela Puffer-Sand
Founded: 1980
Subjects: Art, Photography
ISBN Prefix(es): 978-3-900508; 978-3-9501098
Number of titles published annually: 5 Print
Distributed by Vice Versa Vertrieb (Germany & Switzerland)

Communicatio Kommunikations- und Publications GmbH
Steinfeldgasse 5, 1190 Vienna
Tel: (01) 370 33 02 *Fax:* (01) 370 59 34
E-mail: pr@communicatio.cc
Web Site: www.communicatio.cc
Key Personnel
Contact: Dr Verena Hofstaetter
Subjects: Communications, Film, Video, Marketing, Social Sciences, Sociology
ISBN Prefix(es): 978-3-85495

Compass-Verlag GmbH
Matznergasse 17, 1141 Vienna
Mailing Address: Postfach 160, 1141 Vienna
Tel: (01) 981 16-0 *Fax:* (01) 981 16-118; (01) 981 16-148 (sales)
E-mail: office@compass.at
Web Site: www.compass.at
Key Personnel
Mng Dir: Hermann Futter *Tel:* (01) 981 16-113 *E-mail:* hermann.futter@compass.at; Nikolaus Futter
Founded: 1867
Specialize in Internet databases.
Membership(s): EAVV; OeAVV.
Subjects: Business, Economics, Finance
ISBN Prefix(es): 978-3-85041
Number of titles published annually: 4 Print; 2 CD-ROM
Total Titles: 4 Print
Subsidiaries: Comp Almanach Kft

Czernin Verlags GmbH+
Kupkagasse 4, 1080 Vienna
Tel: (01) 403 35 63 *Fax:* (01) 403 35 63-15
E-mail: office@czernin-verlag.com
Web Site: www.czernin-verlag.com
Key Personnel
Mng Dir: Benedikt Foeger *E-mail:* foeger@czernin-verlag.com
Contracts, License & Promotions: Barbara Blaha *Tel:* (01) 403 35 63-80 *E-mail:* blaha@czernin-verlag.com
Production: Burghard List
Sales & Marketing: Karl Bichler *Tel:* (01) 403 35 63-80 *E-mail:* bichler@czernin-verlag.com
Founded: 1999
Subjects: Cookery, Film, Video, History, Law, Literature, Literary Criticism, Essays, Poetry
ISBN Prefix(es): 978-3-7076
Number of titles published annually: 15 Print
Total Titles: 120 Print
Distribution Center: Mohr Morawa Buchvertrieb GmbH, 1230 Vienna *Tel:* (01) 680 14-5 *Fax:* (01) 688 71 30 *E-mail:* momo@mohrmorawa.at *Web Site:* www.mohrmorawa.at

**dbv-Verlag Druck-, Beratungs- und
Verlagsgesellschaft mbH+**
Geidorfguertel 20, 8010 Graz
Tel: (0316) 38 30 33-0 *Fax:* (0316) 38 30 43
E-mail: office@dbv.at
Web Site: www.dbv.at
Key Personnel
Mng Dir: Gerald Muther
Manager: Herbert Klein
Project Manager/Editor: Patricia Egger
Tel: (0316) 38 30 33-14
Marketing/Public Relations: Johannes Reinprecht
Tel: (0316) 38 30 33-13
Founded: 1977
Subjects: Law, Tax & Business Law
ISBN Prefix(es): 978-3-7041

Denzel-Verlag+
Amraser Str 90b, 6020 Innsbruck
Tel: (0512) 586880 *Fax:* (0512) 586880
E-mail: denzel-verlag@web.de; denzel.verlag@
yahoo.de
Web Site: www.denzel-verlag.de
Key Personnel
Contact: Harald Denzel
Founded: 1952
Subjects: Geography, Geology, Outdoor Recreation, Travel & Tourism, Illustrated Guide
Books
ISBN Prefix(es): 978-3-85047
Distribution Center: Freytag-Berndt und Artaria
KG, Brunner Str 69, 1231 Vienna *Tel:* (01)
8699090 *Fax:* (01) 8698855 *E-mail:* sales@
freytagberndt.at
GeoCenter T + M Touristik und Medien GmbH,
Schockenriedstr 44, 70565 Stuttgart, Germany
Tel: (0711) 781946-10 *Fax:* (0711) 782437-5
E-mail: vertrieb@geocenter.de
Buchzentrum AG, Industriestr Ost 10, 4614
Haegendorf, Switzerland *Tel:* (062) 209-
2525 *Fax:* (062) 209-2627 *Web Site:* www.
buchzentrum.ch

Deuticke, *imprint of* Paul Zsolnay Verlag GmbH

Deuticke Verlag+
Imprint of Paul Zsolnay Verlag
Prinz-Eugen-Str 30, 1040 Vienna
Tel: (01) 505 76 61-0 *Fax:* (01) 505 76 61-10
E-mail: info@zsolnay.at
Web Site: www.hanser-literaturverlage.de
Key Personnel
Publishing Dir: Michael Kruger
Program Manager: Dr Martina Schmidt
E-mail: schmidt@zsolnay.at
Foreign Rights: Annette Lechner *E-mail:* annette.
lechner@zsolnay.at
Press: Susanne Roessler *Tel:* (01) 505 76 61-28
E-mail: susanne.roessler@zsolnay.at
Founded: 1878
Subjects: Literature, Literary Criticism, Essays,
Mysteries, Suspense, Nonfiction (General), Regional Interests
ISBN Prefix(es): 978-3-552
Ultimate Parent Company: Carl Hanser Verlag
GmbH
Orders to: A Stein'schen Buchhandlung GmbH,
Steinerstr 10, 59457 Werl, Germany, Contact:
Reinhard Stein

Atelier Diotima+
Bachgasse 22, 3200 Obergrafendorf
Tel: (043) 2747-8528
E-mail: mail@atelier-diotima.com
Web Site: www.atelier-diotima.com
Key Personnel
Owner: Roman Baumgartner; Charlotte Karner
Founded: 2000
Handcrafted books with mainly original illustrations.
Subjects: Philosophy, Poetry

Number of titles published annually: 3 Print
Total Titles: 35 Print

**Ludwig Doblinger (Bernhard Herzmansky)
GmbH & Co KG,** see Musikverlag -
Musikhaus Doblinger

Musikverlag - Musikhaus Doblinger (Doblinger
Music Publishers & Music Shop)+
Dorotheergasse 10, 1010 Vienna
Tel: (01) 51503-0; (01) 51503-15 (music shop)
Fax: (01) 51503-51
E-mail: info@doblinger.at; webshop@doblinger.at
(music shop)
Web Site: www.doblinger.at
Key Personnel
Owner & Mng Dir: Peter Pany *Tel:* (01) 515 03
50 *E-mail:* peter.pany@doblinger.at
Rights & Licensing: Martin Sima *Tel:* (01) 515
03 13 *E-mail:* martin.sima@doblinger.at
Founded: 1876
Specialize in music notes & books.
Subjects: Music, Dance
ISBN Prefix(es): 978-3-900695; 978-3-900035
Number of titles published annually: 50 Print
Total Titles: 10,000 Print; 6,000 Online
Bookshop(s): Doblinger Music Shop
Warehouse: MDS - Music Distribution Services GmbH, Carl-Zeiss-Str 1, 55129 Mainz,
Germany *Tel:* (06131) 505100 *Fax:* (06131)
505115 *E-mail:* order@mds-partner.com *Web
Site:* www.mds-partner.com
Distribution Center: MDS - Music Distribution Services GmbH, Carl-Zeiss-Str 1,
55129 Mainz, Germany *Tel:* (06131) 505100
Fax: (06131) 505115 *E-mail:* order@mds-
partner.com *Web Site:* www.mds-partner.com
Orders to: MDS - Music Distribution Services
GmbH, Carl-Zeiss-Str 1, 55129 Mainz, Germany *Tel:* (06131) 505100 *Fax:* (06131)
505115 *E-mail:* order@mds-partner.com *Web
Site:* www.mds-partner.com

Drava Verlag
Tarviser Str 16, 9020 Klagenfurt/Celovec
Tel: (0463) 501 099 *Fax:* (0463) 501 099-20
E-mail: office@drava.at
Web Site: www.drava.at
Key Personnel
Mng Dir: Marjan Verdel
Publishing Dir: Peter Wieser *E-mail:* peter.
wieser@drava.at
Sales: Thomas Busch *E-mail:* thomas.busch@
drava.at
Subjects: Fiction, History, Language Arts, Linguistics, Nonfiction (General), Poetry
ISBN Prefix(es): 978-3-85435
Distribution Center: Mohr Morawa Buchvertrieb
GmbH, Sulzengasse 2, 1230 Vienna *Tel:* (01)
680 14-0 *Fax:* (01) 688 71 30 *E-mail:* momo@
mohrmorawa.at *Web Site:* www.mohrmorawa.at
(Austria)
GVA Goettingen (Germany)
Herder AG Basel (Switzerland)

Literaturverlag Droschl GmbH+
Stenggstr 33, 8043 Graz
Tel: (0316) 32-64-04 *Fax:* (0316) 32-40-71
E-mail: literaturverlag@droschl.com
Web Site: www.droschl.com
Key Personnel
Contact: Annette Knoch *E-mail:* annette.knoch@
droschl.com
Founded: 1978
Subjects: Art, Drama, Theater, Literature, Literary Criticism, Essays, Poetry, Contemporary
European Literature
ISBN Prefix(es): 978-3-85420
Number of titles published annually: 18 Print
Total Titles: 300 Print; 5 Audio
Imprints: Edition Neue Text

Distribution Center: Mohr Morawa Buchvertrieb
GmbH, Sulzengasse 2, 1230 Vienna *Tel:* (01)
680 14-0 *Fax:* (01) 688 71 30 *E-mail:* momo@
mohrmorawa.at *Web Site:* www.mohrmorawa.at
PROLIT Verlagsauslieferung, Siemensstr 16,
35463 Fernwald, Germany, Contact: Rainer
Eckert *Tel:* (0641) 94393-33 *Fax:* (0641)
94393-199
Buchzentrum AG, Industriestr Ost 10, 4614 Haegendorf, Switzerland *Tel:* (062) 209 25 25
E-mail: kundendienst@buchzentrum.ch

Ecowin Verlag GmbH
Lessingstr 6, 5020 Salzburg
Tel: (0662) 2240 21581 *Fax:* (0662) 2240 28312
E-mail: info@ecowin.at
Web Site: ecowin.at
Key Personnel
Publisher: Dr Hannes Steiner
Communications Manager: Sarah Hyden
E-mail: sarah.hyden@beneventobooks.com
Sales: Florian Poetzelsberger
Subjects: Nonfiction (General)
ISBN Prefix(es): 978-3-7110; 978-3-902404
Parent Company: Red Bull Media House GmbH
Associate Companies: Benevento Publishing
Distribution Center: Mohr Morawa Buchvertrieb GmbH, Sulzengasse 2, 1230 Vienna
Tel: (01) 680 140 *Fax:* (01) 689 6800
E-mail: bestellung@mohrmorawa.at *Web
Site:* www.mohrmorawa.at (Austria & South
Tyrol)
Arvato Media GmbH-Vereinigte Verlagsauslieferung, Abt D6F5, An der Autobahn 100,
33333 Guetersloh, Germany *Tel:* (05241)
80-88280 *Fax:* (05241) 49014 *E-mail:* vva-
auftragsservice@bertelsmann.de

editio historiae
Leopoldauerplatz 42, 1210 Vienna
Tel: (0676) 518 85 20 *Fax:* (01253) 30 33 67 80
E-mail: verlagsleitung@editiohistoriae.at
Web Site: www.editiohistoriae.at
Key Personnel
Publishing Dir: Dr Marianne Acquarelli
Subjects: Fiction, History, Historical Fiction
ISBN Prefix(es): 978-3-9502862

Edition Atelier, see Edition Atelier

egoth Verlag GmbH
Untere Weissgerberstr 63/12, 1030 Vienna
Tel: (0699) 123 31 960 (cell)
Web Site: www.egoth.at
Key Personnel
Management: Egon Theiner *E-mail:* egon.
theiner@egoth.at
Founded: 2004
Subjects: Sports, Athletics
ISBN Prefix(es): 978-3-902480

Ennsthaler Gesellschaft mbH & Co KG+
Stadtplatz 26, 4400 Steyr
Tel: (07252) 52053-10; (07252) 52053-50;
(07252) 52053-21 (distribution) *Fax:* (07252)
52053-16; (07252) 52053-55; (07252) 52053-
22 (distribution)
E-mail: verlag@ennsthaler.at; buchhandlung@
ennsthaler.at; buero@ennsthaler.at;
auslieferung@ennsthaler.at
Web Site: www.ennsthaler.at
Key Personnel
Mng Dir: Christoph Ennsthaler *Tel:* (07252)
52053-53 *E-mail:* christoph@ennsthaler.at;
Gottfried Ennsthaler
Editorial: Sabine Thoene *Tel:* (07252) 52053-20
Sales: Geraldine Schirl-Ennsthaler *Tel:* (07252)
52053-20 *E-mail:* geraldine@ennsthaler.at
Founded: 1880
Subjects: Cookery, Health, Nutrition, History,
Medicine, Nursing, Dentistry, Poetry, Regional
Interests, Religion - Catholic, Theology
ISBN Prefix(es): 978-3-85068

Foreign Rights: Buechercoach Austria (Ingrid Fuehrer)
Distribution Center: SuedOst Service GmbH, Am Steinfeld 4, 94065 Waldkirchen, Germany, Contact: Carola Eibl *Tel:* (08581) 9605-0 *Fax:* (08581) 754 *E-mail:* info@suedost-service.de
Buchzentrum AG, Industriestr Ost 10, 4614 Haegendorf, Switzerland *Tel:* (062) 2092626 *Fax:* (062) 2092627 *E-mail:* kundendienst@buchzentrum.ch
Deep Books Ltd, Green Trading Estate, Unit 3, 47 E Dulwich Rd, London SE22 QBN, United Kingdom *Tel:* (020) 8693 0234 *Fax:* (020) 8693 1400 *E-mail:* sales@deep-books.co.uk

eoVision GmbH
Franz-Josef-Str 19, 5020 Salzburg
Tel: (0662) 243217-0 *Fax:* (0662) 243217-11
E-mail: office@eovision.at
Web Site: www.eovision.at
Subjects: Environmental Studies, Geography, Geology, Sustainability
ISBN Prefix(es): 978-3-902834

Verlag Esterbauer GmbH
Haupstr 31, 3751 Rodingersdorf
Tel: (02983) 28982-0 *Fax:* (02983) 28982-500
E-mail: bikeline@esterbauer.com; marketing@esterbauer.com
Web Site: www.esterbauer.com
Key Personnel
Publishing Dir & Mng Dir: Roland Esterbauer
Marketing: Claudia Retzer *Tel:* (02983) 28982-313
Founded: 1987
Subjects: Outdoor Recreation, Cycling, Hiking
ISBN Prefix(es): 978-3-85000
Distribution Center: Freytag & Berndt, Industrastr 10, 2120 Wolkersdorf *Tel:* (01) 8699090-85 *Fax:* (01) 8698855 *E-mail:* sales@freytagberndt.at *Web Site:* www.freytagberndt.at
Craenen BVBA, Mechelsesteenweg 633, 3020 Herent, Belgium *Tel:* (016) 239090 *Fax:* (016) 239711 *E-mail:* sales@craenen.be *Web Site:* www.craenen.be (Belgium, Netherlands & UK)
GoTrekkers Ltd, 61342 Brentwood, Calgary, AB T2L 2K6, Canada *Tel:* 403-289-6983 *E-mail:* info@gotrekkers.com *Web Site:* www.gotrekkers.com
GeoCenter - ILH, Schockenriedstr 44, 70565 Stuttgart, Germany *Tel:* (0711) 781946-10 *Fax:* (0711) 781946-54 *E-mail:* vertrieb@geocenter.de *Web Site:* www.geocenter.de
AVA Verlagsauslieferung AG, Centralweg 16, Postfach 119, 8910 Affoltern, Switzerland *Tel:* (044) 7624250 *Fax:* (044) 7624210 *E-mail:* verlagservice@ava.ch *Web Site:* www.ava.ch

Evangelischer Presseverband in Oesterreich
Ungargasse 9, 1030 Vienna
Tel: (01) 712 54 61; (01) 712 54 61-0 *Fax:* (01) 712 54 61-50
E-mail: epv@evang.at; info@evang.at
Web Site: www.evang.at/buecher/buchkatalog
Key Personnel
Mng Dir: Thomas Dasek
Founded: 1925
Subjects: Education, Religion - Protestant, Religion - Other, Theology
ISBN Prefix(es): 978-3-85073
Warehouse: Ungargasse 12, 1030 Vienna

facultas.wuv Universitatsverlag, see Facultas Verlags- und Buchhandels AG

Facultas Verlags- und Buchhandels AG+
Stolberggasse 26, 1050 Vienna
Tel: (01) 310 53 56 *Fax:* (01) 319 70 50

E-mail: verlag@facultas.at
Web Site: www.facultas.at/verlag
Key Personnel
Head, Sales: Daniela Neundlinger-Schalleschak *Tel:* (01) 310 53 56-62 *E-mail:* daniela.neundlinger-schalleschak@facultas.at
Founded: 1981
Subjects: Accounting, Art, Behavioral Sciences, Business, Career Development, Communications, Economics, Finance, History, Language Arts, Linguistics, Law, Management, Marketing, Medicine, Nursing, Dentistry, Nonfiction (General), Philosophy, Psychology, Psychiatry, Science (General), Social Sciences, Sociology, Women's Studies
ISBN Prefix(es): 978-3-8252; 978-3-7089
Divisions: Maudrich
Distribution Center: Mohr Morawa Buchvertrieb GmbH, Sulzengasse 2, 1230 Vienna *Tel:* (01) 680 14-0 *Fax:* (01) 688 71 30 *E-mail:* momo@mohrmorawa.at *Web Site:* www.mohrmorawa.at
Brockhaus/Commission, Kreidlerstr 9, 70806 Kornwestheim, Germany *Tel:* (07154) 13 27-74 *Fax:* (07154) 13 27-13 *E-mail:* facultas@brocom.de
AVA Verlagsauslieferung AG, Centralweg 16, 8910 Affoltern am Albis, Switzerland *Tel:* (044) 762 42 00 *Fax:* (044) 762 42 10 *E-mail:* e.bachofner@ava.ch

Falter Verlagsgesellschaft mbH
Marc-Aurel-Str 9, 1011 Vienna
Tel: (01) 536 60-0 *Fax:* (01) 536 60-935
E-mail: service@falter.at
Web Site: www.falter.at
Key Personnel
Publishing Dir: Susanne Schwameis *Tel:* (01) 536 60-938 *E-mail:* schwameis@falter.at
Head, Sales: Christa Thurnher *Tel:* (01) 536 60-929 *E-mail:* christa.thurnher@falter.at
Marketing: Lukas Winkelmeier *Tel:* (01) 536 60-947 *E-mail:* winkelmeier@falter.at
Subjects: Criminology, Government, Political Science, Regional Interests, Travel & Tourism
ISBN Prefix(es): 978-3-85439

Verlag Fassbaender
Lichtgasse 10, 1150 Vienna
Tel: (01) 892-35-46
E-mail: office@fassbaender.com
Web Site: www.fassbaender.com
Key Personnel
Executive: Ernst Becvar
Founded: 1987
Specialize in literature, literary criticism.
Subjects: Antiques, Astronomy, Genealogy, History, Language Arts, Linguistics, Literature, Literary Criticism, Essays, Maritime, Psychology, Psychiatry, Religion - Catholic, Science (General)
ISBN Prefix(es): 978-3-900538; 978-3-902575; 978-3-902984 (Bernest)
Number of titles published annually: 7 Print
Total Titles: 125 Print
Parent Company: Buchdruckerei Ernst Becvar GmbH

Fischer & Gann Publishing
Imprint of Aumayer Druck & Verlag
Gewerbegebiet Nord 3, 5222 Munderfing
Tel: (07744) 200 80-0
E-mail: office@fischerundgann.com
Web Site: fischerundgann.com
Key Personnel
Publisher: Dr Mathilde Fischer *E-mail:* m.fischer@fischerundgann.com
Mng Dir: Christine Gann *E-mail:* c.gann@fischerundgann.com; Heiner Gann
Subjects: Health, Nutrition, Nonfiction (General), Psychology, Psychiatry
ISBN Prefix(es): 978-3-903072

Foreign Rep(s): Prolit Verlagsauslieferung GmbH (Germany); Schweizer Buchzentrum AG (Switzerland)
Distribution Center: Mohr Morawa Buchvertrieb GmbH, Sulzengasse 2, 1230 Vienna *Tel:* (01) 680 14-5 *Fax:* (01) 688 71 30 *E-mail:* momo@mohrmorawa.at *Web Site:* www.mohrmorawa.at

Folio Verlagsgesellschaft mbH+
Schoenbrunnerstr 31, 1050 Vienna
Tel: (01) 5813708-0 *Fax:* (01) 5813708-20
E-mail: office@folioverlag.com
Web Site: www.folioverlag.com
Key Personnel
Mng Dir: Hermann Gummerer *E-mail:* gummerer@folioverlag.com; Dr Ludwig Paulmichl *E-mail:* paulmichl@folioverlag.com
Sales & Licensing: Doris Schrenk *E-mail:* schrenk@folioverlag.com
Founded: 1994
Subjects: Art, Fiction, Nonfiction (General), Poetry
ISBN Prefix(es): 978-3-85256
Number of titles published annually: 30 Print
Total Titles: 200 Print
Branch Office(s)
Pfarrhofstr 2d, 39100 Bozen, Italy *Tel:* (0471) 971323 *Fax:* (0471) 971603 *E-mail:* office.bz@folioverlag.com

Fotohof Edition
Inge-Morath-Platz 3, 5020 Salzburg
Tel: (0662) 84 92 96 *Fax:* (0662) 84 92 96 4
E-mail: fotohof@fotohof.at
Web Site: www.fotohof.at
Key Personnel
Publisher: Rainer Iglar; Michael Mauracher
Public Relations: Martin Mlineritsch
Subjects: Photography
ISBN Prefix(es): 978-3-901756; 978-3-902675
Distribution Center: Vice Versa Vertrieb, Immanuelkirchstr, 12, 10405 Berlin, Germany *Tel:* (030) 61609236 *Fax:* (030) 61609238 *E-mail:* info@vice-versa-vertrieb.de (Germany & Switzerland)
art data, 12 Bell Industrial Estate, 50 Cunnington St, London W4 5HB, United Kingdom *Tel:* (0208) 747 1061 *Fax:* (0208) 742 2319 *E-mail:* orders@artdata.co.uk *Web Site:* www.artdata.co.uk (Great Britain & France)
ram publications + distributions, 2525 Michigan Ave, Bldg A2, Santa Monica, CA 90404, United States *Tel:* 310-453-0043 *Fax:* 310-264-4888 *E-mail:* info@rampub.com *Web Site:* www.rampub.com

Freya Verlag GmbH
Industriezeile 36a, 4020 Linz
Tel: (0732) 781108-0 *Fax:* (0732) 781108-18
E-mail: office@freya.at
Web Site: shop.freya.at
Founded: 1991
Subjects: Architecture & Interior Design, Biography, Memoirs, Cookery, Economics, Fiction, Health, Nutrition, Nonfiction (General), Poetry, Self-Help, Ancient Herbs, Folk Medicine
ISBN Prefix(es): 978-3-99025; 978-3-2540; 978-3-902540; 978-3-902134
Number of titles published annually: 50 Print

Freytag-Berndt und Artaria KG+
Brunner Str 69, 1230 Vienna
Tel: (01) 869 90 90-0 *Fax:* (01) 869 90 90-61
E-mail: office@freytagberndt.at
Web Site: www.freytagberndt.at
Key Personnel
General Manager: Dr Christian Halbwachs *Tel:* (01) 869 90 90-17 *Fax:* (01) 869 90 90-72 *E-mail:* halbwachs@freytagberndt.at
Sales & Marketing: Melanie Grotter *Tel:* (01) 869 90 90-41 *E-mail:* grotter@freytagberndt.at

Founded: 1770
Subjects: Geography, Geology
ISBN Prefix(es): 978-3-85084; 978-3-7079
Foreign Rep(s): Freytag & Berndt (Czechia, Hungary, Slovakia); Mapiberia F&B (Spain); Bergverlag Rother (Germany)
Bookshop(s): Kohlmarkt 9, 1010 Vienna, Contact: Dieter Grabenauer *Tel:* (01) 533 86 85 *Fax:* (01) 533 86 85-86 *E-mail:* shop@ freytagberndt.at; Herrengasse 28, 8010 Graz, Contact: Niku Aschdjai *Tel:* (0316) 81 82 30 *Fax:* (0316) 81 82 30-30 *E-mail:* shopgraz@ freytagberndt.at; Karlsplatz 5 (Stachus), 80335 Munich, Germany, Contact: Sabine von Grolman *Tel:* (089) 660 59 71 *Fax:* (089) 660 59 72 *E-mail:* shopmuenchen@ freytagberndt.de; Koenigstr 85, 90402 Nuenberg, Germany, *Tel:* (0911) 202 97 09 *Fax:* (0911) 211 04 19 *E-mail:* shopnuernberg@freytagberndt. de; Kohlenmarket 1, 93047 Regensburg, Germany, Contact: Evelyn Bachl *Tel:* (0941) 584 08 32 *Fax:* (0941) 584 08 33 *E-mail:* shopregensburg@freytagberndt.de

Galerie + Edition Thurnhof KEG
Muehlfeld 43, 3580 Horn
Tel: (02982) 3333 *Fax:* (02982) 3333
Web Site: www.thurnhof.at
Key Personnel
Publisher: Toni Kurz *E-mail:* toni.kurz@thurnhof. at
Founded: 1983
Subjects: Art, Poetry
ISBN Prefix(es): 978-3-900678

G&G Verlagsgesellschaft mbH
Frankgasse 4, 1090 Vienna
Tel: (01) 494 96 99 0 *Fax:* (01) 494 96 99 420
E-mail: office@ggverlag.at
Web Site: www.ggverlag.at
Key Personnel
Publisher: Georg Gloeckler
Mng Dir: Christian Drozda
Sales Manager: Isabella Scheuringer *E-mail:* isabella.scheuringer@ggverlag.at
Foreign Rights: Ursula Holler
Founded: 1998
ISBN Prefix(es): 978-3-7074
Associate Companies: Verlag Carl Ueberreuter GmbH
Foreign Rights: A R T Dialog (Daniela Vranovska) (Czechia); Alp Arts Co (Sandy Fuller) (Canada, USA); Bestun (Hyeyoung Lee) (Korea); Borobudur Agency (Nung Atasana) (Indonesia); Bruecke Agency (Young Sun Park) (Korea); Agency Chang (Heaza Yu) (Korea); English Agency Japan (Corinne Shoij) (Japan); Himmer Winco Co Ltd (Andreas Zhao) (China, Taiwan); Japan Uni Agency (Maiko Fujinaga) (Japan); Natoli Stefan & Oliva SAS (Roberta Oliva) (Italy); Propons Agency (Miran Suh) (Korea); Shinwon Agency (Nayoung Lee) (Korea); Eric Yang Agency (Nari Shin) (Korea)
Distribution Center: Mohr Morawa Buchvertrieb GmbH *Tel:* (01) 680 140 *Fax:* (01) 688 71 30 *E-mail:* momo@mohrmorawa.at *Web Site:* www.mohrmorawa.at
Sigloch Verlagsservice, Germany *Tel:* (07953) 71 89 052 *Fax:* (07953) 71 89 080 *E-mail:* verlagservice@sigloch.de

Alois Goeschl & Co
Trummelhofgasse 12/2, 1190 Vienna
Tel: (01) 3201080
Key Personnel
Owner: Friedrich Lechner
Founded: 1949
Subjects: Health, Nutrition, Psychology, Psychiatry, Veterinary Science

Goldegg Verlag GmbH
Mommsengasse 4/2, 1040 Vienna
Tel: (01) 505 43 76-0 *Fax:* (01) 505 43 76-20
E-mail: office@goldegg-verlag.at
Web Site: www.goldegg-verlag.at
Key Personnel
Publishing Dir: Verena Minoggio-Weixlbaumer *Tel:* (01) 505 43 76-43
Editing & Head, Press: Maria Schlager *Tel:* (01) 505 43 76-46 *E-mail:* maria.schlager@goldegg-verlag.at
Subjects: Business, Government, Political Science, Health, Nutrition, Management, Travel & Tourism, Organization, Society, Training
ISBN Prefix(es): 978-3-902729; 978-3-901880
Branch Office(s)
Friedrichstr 191, 10117 Berlin, Germany *Web Site:* www.goldegg-verlag.de
Distribution Center: Mohr Morawa Buchvertrieb GmbH, Postfach 260, 1101 Vienna *Tel:* (01) 680 14-0 *Fax:* (01) 688 71 30 *E-mail:* bestellung@mohrmorawa.at *Web Site:* www.mohrmorawa.at
Brockhaus Commission, Kreidlerstr 9, 70806 Kornwestheim, Germany *Tel:* (07154) 1327-0 *Fax:* (07154) 1327-13 *E-mail:* info@brocom.de
Verlags-Service Ernst Imfeld, Bruenigstr 40, 6055 Alpnach, Switzerland *Tel:* (041) 660 34 81 *Fax:* (041) 660 32 63 *E-mail:* redaktion@ luuboks.ch

Verlag Guthmann-Peterson+
Esslergasse 17, 1130 Vienna
Tel: (01) 877 04 26 *Fax:* (01) 876 40 04
E-mail: verlag@guthmann-peterson.de
Web Site: www.guthmann-peterson.de
Key Personnel
Mng Dir: Wolf Peterson
Founded: 1988
Subjects: Agriculture, Art, Biography, Memoirs, Economics, Government, Political Science, Literature, Literary Criticism, Essays, Science (General), Social Sciences, Sociology
ISBN Prefix(es): 978-3-900782; 978-3-85306; 978-3-85481
Divisions: Edition Garamond; Edition Liber Libri

Hermann Hakel Gesellschaft+
Traisengasse 17/28, 1200 Vienna
Tel: (01) 7342294
Key Personnel
Mng Dir: Emmerich Kolovic
Founded: 1988
Subjects: Biography, Memoirs, Fiction, Humor, Literature, Literary Criticism, Essays, Poetry
ISBN Prefix(es): 978-3-900924

Hannibal-Verlag+
Falkstr 25, 6020 Innsbruck
Tel: (0512) 570 345-0 *Fax:* (0512) 570 345-11
E-mail: info@hannibal-verlag.de
Web Site: www.hannibal-verlag.de
Key Personnel
Mng Dir & Publisher: Dr Monika Koch *E-mail:* monika.koch@kochint.at
Founded: 1986
Subjects: Literature, Literary Criticism, Essays, Musical Biographies
ISBN Prefix(es): 978-3-85445
Number of titles published annually: 12 Print
Total Titles: 240 Print
Parent Company: KOCH International GmbH/ Hannibal
Foreign Rep(s): AVA Verlagsauslieferung AG (Switzerland); Mohr Morawa Buchvertrieb GmbH (Austria, Italy); Prolit Verlagsauslieferung GmbH (Germany, Luxembourg)

Hanreich Verlag
Esterhazygasse 7/2, 1060 Vienna
Tel: (01) 504 28 29-1 *Fax:* (01) 504 28 29-4

E-mail: office@hanreich-verlag.at; bestellung@ hanreich-verlag.at
Web Site: www.hanreich-verlag.at; www. kinderkost.com
Key Personnel
Publisher: Ingeborg Hanreich *Tel:* (01) 504 28 29-2 *E-mail:* ingeborg.hanreich@hanreich-verlag.at
Administration: Cornelia Krisper *Tel:* (01) 504 28 29-3 *E-mail:* cornelia.krisper@hanreich-verlag. at
Founded: 1994
Subjects: Cookery, Health, Nutrition, Baby Food Cookbooks, Infant Nutrition
ISBN Prefix(es): 978-3-901518

Haymon Verlag GesmbH+
Erlerstr 10, 6020 Innsbruck
Tel: (0512) 576300 *Fax:* (0512) 576300 14
E-mail: office@haymonverlag.at
Web Site: www.haymonverlag.at
Key Personnel
Publisher: Markus Hatzer *E-mail:* markus. hatzer@haymonverlag.at
Commercial Administration: Stephanie Gogl *Tel:* (0512) 576300 26 *E-mail:* stephanie.gogl@ haymonverlag.at
Editor: Georg Hasibeder *Tel:* (0512) 576300 17 *E-mail:* georg.hasibeder@haymonverlag.at
Licenses: Anna Stock *Tel:* (0512) 567300 21 *E-mail:* anna.stock@haymonverlag.at
Marketing: Marion Bernhard *Tel:* (0512) 576300 38 *E-mail:* marion.bernhard@haymonverlag.at
Press: Gerlinde Tamerl *Tel:* (0512) 576300 20 *E-mail:* gerlinde.tamerl@haymonverlag.at
Sales: Dr Ute Steiner *Tel:* (0512) 576300 40 *E-mail:* ute.steiner@haymonverlag.at
Founded: 1982
Subjects: Architecture & Interior Design, Art, Biography, Memoirs, Cookery, Criminology, Fiction, History, Literature, Literary Criticism, Essays, Mysteries, Suspense, Nonfiction (General), Philosophy, Social Sciences, Sociology
ISBN Prefix(es): 978-3-85218
Number of titles published annually: 25 Print
Total Titles: 350 Print
Distribution Center: Mohr Morawa Buchvertrieb GmbH, Sulzengasse 2, 1230 Vienna, Contact: Guenther Kramer *Tel:* (01) 680 14-0 *Fax:* (01) 688 71 30 *E-mail:* guenther.kramer@ mohrmorawa.at *Web Site:* www.mohrmorawa.at
SVK Stuttgarter Verlagskontor, Rotebuehlstr 77, 70049 Stuttgart, Germany, Contact: Brunhilde Haist *Tel:* (0711) 6672 1426 *Fax:* (0711) 6672 1974 *E-mail:* b.haist@svk.de
Buch 2000, c/o AVA, Centralweg 16, 8910 Affoltern, Switzerland, Contact: Karin Zgraggen *Tel:* (044) 762 42 60 *Fax:* (044) 762 42 10 *E-mail:* k.zgraggen@ava.ch

Helbling Languages GmbH+
Kaplanstr 9, 6063 Rum/Innsbruck
Tel: (0512) 26 23 33-0 *Fax:* (0512) 26 23 33-111
E-mail: e.amjad@helblinglanguages.com; office@ helbling.co.at
Web Site: www.helblinglanguages.at
Key Personnel
President & General Manager: Lucia Astuti
International Rights: Elisa Pasqualini *E-mail:* e. pasqualini@helblinglanguages.com
Founded: 2004
Specialize in languages (English).
Also publish software & audio CDs.
Subjects: Education, English as a Second Language, Language Arts, Linguistics
ISBN Prefix(es): 978-3-902504; 978-3-85272; 978-3-99045

Helbling Verlagsgesellschaft mbH
Kaplanstr 9, 6063 Rum/Innsbruck
Tel: (0512) 26 23 33-0 *Fax:* (0512) 26 23 33-111
E-mail: office@helbling.co.at
Web Site: www.helbling.com

Key Personnel
President: Markus Spielmann
International Rights: Klaus Mayerl *E-mail:* k.
  mayerl@helbling.co.at
Founded: 1946
Specialize in choral music books.
Subjects: Education, English as a Second Language, Music, Dance, Choral Music
ISBN Prefix(es): 978-3-85061; 978-3-900590;
  978-3-86227; 978-3-99035
Branch Office(s)
Helbling Verlag GmbH, Martinstr 42-44, Esslingen 73728, Germany, Contact: Alwin Wollinger
  Tel: (0711) 75 87 01-0 *Fax:* (0711) 75 87
  01-11 *E-mail:* service@helbling.com *Web
  Site:* www.helbling-verlag.de
Helbling Verlag AG, Aemmenmattstr 43, 3123
  Belp b Bern, Switzerland, Contact: Kurt
  Rohrbach *Tel:* (031) 812 22 28 *Fax:* (031) 812
  22 27 *E-mail:* service@helbling-verlag.ch

Hermagoras Verlag, see Mohorjeva druzba v
  Celovcu - Hermagoras Verein

HEROLD Business Data GmbH+
Guntramsdorfer Str 105, 2340 Moedling
Tel: (02236) 401-8; (02236) 401-38133 (customer
  service) *Fax:* (02236) 401-8; (02236) 401-8
  (customer service)
E-mail: office@herold.at; kundenservice@herold.
  at (customer service)
Web Site: www.herold.at
Key Personnel
Mng Dir: Thomas Friess
Founded: 1919
Subjects: Marketing
ISBN Prefix(es): 978-3-85110

Verlag Johannes Heyn GesmbH & Co KG
Friedensgasse 23, 9020 Klagenfurt
Tel: (0463) 33 631 *Fax:* (0463) 33 631-33
E-mail: office@verlagheyn.at
Web Site: www.verlagheyn.at
Key Personnel
Publishing Dir: Achim Zechner
Founded: 1868
Subjects: Art, Biography, Memoirs, Cookery, Fiction, History, How-to, Music, Dance, Poetry,
  Science (General)
ISBN Prefix(es): 978-3-85366; 978-3-7084
Distribution Center: Dr Franz Hain Verlagsauslieferungen GmbH, Dr-Otto-Neurath-Gasse 5,
  1220 Vienna *Tel:* (01) 282 6565-77 *Fax:* (01)
  282 5282 *E-mail:* bestell@hain.at
Suedost Verlags Service GmbH, Am Steinfeld
  4, 94065 Waldkirchen, Germany *Tel:* (08581)
  9605-0 *Fax:* (08581) 754 *E-mail:* info@
  suedost-verlags-service.de *Web Site:* www.
  suedostverlagsservice.de

Galerie Ernest Hilger GesmbH
Dorotheergasse 5, 1010 Vienna
Tel: (01) 512 53 15 *Fax:* (01) 513 91 26
E-mail: ernst.hilger@hilger.at
Web Site: www.hilger.at
Key Personnel
Owner: Ernst Hilger
Founded: 1973
Subjects: Art
ISBN Prefix(es): 978-3-900318

Verlag Brueder Hollinek & Co GesmbH+
Luisenstr 20, 3002 Purkersdorf
Tel: (02231) 67365 *Fax:* (02231) 67365
E-mail: office@hollinek.at
Web Site: www.hollinek.at
Key Personnel
Mng Dir: Richard Hollinek
Marketing: Richard Hollinek, Jr
Founded: 1872

Subjects: Law
ISBN Prefix(es): 978-3-85119

Verlag Holzhausen GmbH
Leberstr 122, 1110 Vienna
Tel: (01) 74 095-452; (01) 74 095-222 *Fax:* (01)
  74 095-111
E-mail: office@verlagholzhausen.at
Web Site: www.verlagholzhausen.at
Key Personnel
Publishing Dir: Robert Lichtner *Tel:* (01) 74 095-
  119 *E-mail:* robert.lichtner@verlagholzhausen.
  at
Project Manager: Helga Nesselberger
  E-mail: helga.nesselberger@verlagholzhausen.at
Subjects: Accounting, Architecture & Interior Design, Art, Biography, Memoirs, Business, Government, Political Science, Health, Nutrition,
  History, Law, Nonfiction (General), Science
  (General), Social Sciences, Sociology
ISBN Prefix(es): 978-3-85117; 978-3-900518;
  978-3-85493

IAEA, see International Atomic Energy Agency
  (IAEA)

Ibera Verlag+
Hegelgasse 15, 1010 Vienna
Tel: (01) 513 19 72 *Fax:* (01) 513 19 72-28
E-mail: office@ibera.at; buchhandel@ibera.at
Web Site: www.ibera.at
Key Personnel
Mng Dir: Brigitte Strobele *E-mail:* strobele@
  ibera.at
Sales: Matthias Strobele
Subjects: Nonfiction (General)
ISBN Prefix(es): 978-3-900436; 978-3-85052
Distribution Center: Mohr Morawa Buchvertrieb
  GmbH, Sulzengasse 2, 1230 Vienna *Tel:* (01)
  680 14-0 *Fax:* (01) 688 71 30 *E-mail:* momo@
  mohrmorawa.at *Web Site:* www.mohrmorawa.at
HEROLD Verlagsauslieferung, Raiffeisenallee
  10, Oberhaching, 82041 Munich, Germany
  Tel: (089) 613871-0 *E-mail:* herold@herold-
  va.de

IG Autorinnen Autoren (Austrian Author's
  Association)
im Literaturhaus, Seidengasse 13, 1070 Vienna
Tel: (01) 526 20 44-13 *Fax:* (01) 526 20 44-55
E-mail: ig@literaturhaus.at
Web Site: www.literaturhaus.at
Key Personnel
President: Renate Welsh
Mng Dir: Gerhard Ruiss *Tel:* (01) 526 20 44-35
  E-mail: gr@literaturhaus.at
Founded: 1971
Subjects: Publishing & Book Trade Reference
ISBN Prefix(es): 978-3-900419

IIASA, see International Institute for Applied
  Systems Analysis (IIASA)

Ilsinger editions
Seegasse 8/14, 1090 Vienna
Tel: (0316) 323028
E-mail: ilsinger@ilsingereditions.com; werkstatt@
  ilsingereditions.com
Web Site: www.ilsingereditions.com
Key Personnel
Owner: Renate Ilsinger
Distribution, Public Relations & Marketing: Tanja
  Gurke *Tel:* (0664) 7345 8326 (cell)
Founded: 2005
Subjects: Art, Culture
ISBN Prefix(es): 978-3-901959

edition innsalz
Ranshofnerstr 24a, 5282 Ranshofen
Tel: (07722) 64666 *Fax:* (07722) 64666-4
E-mail: info@edition-innsalz.at

Web Site: edition-innsalz.at
Key Personnel
Contact: Wolfgang Maxlmoser
Subjects: Literature, Literary Criticism, Essays,
  Nonfiction (General), Religion - Other
ISBN Prefix(es): 978-3-903126
Imprints: Edition Irrsee

Innsbruck University Press (IUP)
Universitaet Innsbruck, ICT-Technologiepark,
  Technikerstr 21a, 6020 Innsbruck
Fax: (0512) 507-31799
E-mail: iup@uibk.ac.at
Web Site: www.uibk.ac.at/iup
Key Personnel
Publishing Dir: Dr Birgit Holzner *Tel:* (0512)
  507-31700 *E-mail:* birgit.holzner@uibk.ac.at
Sales: Sonja Kabiczek *Tel:* (0512) 507-31704
  E-mail: sonja.kabiczek@uibk.ac.at
Founded: 2005
ISBN Prefix(es): 978-3-902936; 978-3-903122
Number of titles published annually: 50 Print
Total Titles: 450 Print

Innverlag Lehr- und Lernsystem GmbH+
Egger-Lienz-Str 130, 6020 Innsbruck
Tel: (0512) 345 331; (05238) 20 7000
  Fax: (0512) 341 290; (05238) 20 7000-40
E-mail: info@innverlag.at
Web Site: www.innverlag.at; www.innlibri.at
Key Personnel
Mng Dir: Roland Gatt *E-mail:* r.gatt@innverlag.at
Publishing Dir: Gerti Neuhauser *E-mail:* g.
  neuhauser@innverlag.at
Founded: 1947
Subjects: History, Public Administration, Sports,
  Athletics
ISBN Prefix(es): 978-3-85123; 978-3-9501975

**Interessengemeinschaft oesterreichischer
  Autorinnen und Autoren,** see IG Autorinnen
  Autoren

International Atomic Energy Agency (IAEA)
Vienna International Centre, Wagramer Str 5,
  1400 Vienna
Mailing Address: PO Box 100, 1400 Vienna
Tel: (01) 2600-0; (01) 2600-21273; (01) 2600-
  21279 *Fax:* (01) 2600-7; (01) 2600-29610
E-mail: official.mail@iaea.org; info@iaea.org
Web Site: www.iaea.org
Key Personnel
Dir General: Yukiya Amano
Dir, Office of Public Information & Communication: Serge Gas *Tel:* (01) 2600-21279
Press & Public Information Officer: Susanna Loof
Founded: 1957
Serves as the world's central intergovernmental
  forum for scientific & technical cooperation in
  the nuclear field.
Subjects: Agriculture, Biological Sciences, Chemistry, Chemical Engineering, Energy, Environmental Studies, Geography, Geology, Health,
  Nutrition, Law, Physical Sciences, Physics,
  Technology, Veterinary Science, Nuclear Science
ISBN Prefix(es): 978-92-0
Number of titles published annually: 40 Print
Total Titles: 2,000 Print
Branch Office(s)
United Nations, Room B 426, Palais des Nations,
  1211 Geneva 10, Switzerland *Tel:* (022) 917-
  3632 *Fax:* (022) 917-0066 *E-mail:* iaeage@
  unog.ch
U.S. Office(s): One United Nations Plaza, Room
  DC-1-1155, New York, NY 10017, United
  States *Tel:* 212-963-6010; 212-963-6011
  Fax: 917-367-4046 *E-mail:* iaeany@un.org

**International Institute for Applied Systems
  Analysis (IIASA)**
Schlossplatz 1, 2361 Laxenburg
Tel: (02236) 807 342 *Fax:* (02236) 71313

E-mail: publications@iiasa.ac.at
Web Site: www.iiasa.ac.at
Key Personnel
Head, Communications Dept: Iain Stewart
  Tel: (02236) 807 433 *E-mail:* stewart@iiasa.ac.at
Founded: 1972
Subjects: Computer Science, Energy, Environmental Studies, Management, Mathematics, Science (General)
ISBN Prefix(es): 978-3-7045

Edition Irrsee, *imprint of* edition innsalz

IUP, see Innsbruck University Press (IUP)

Jung und Jung Verlag GmbH
Hubert-Sattler-Gasse 1, 5020 Salzburg
Tel: (0662) 88 50 48 *Fax:* (0662) 88 50 48-20
E-mail: office@jungundjung.at
Web Site: www.jungundjung.at
Key Personnel
Mng Dir: Dr Jochen Jung
Sales & Advertising: Regina Rumpold-Kunz
Founded: 2000
Subjects: Art, Language Arts, Linguistics, Literature, Literary Criticism, Essays, Music, Dance
ISBN Prefix(es): 978-3-902144; 978-3-902497
Foreign Rep(s): AVA Verlagsauslieferung AG (Switzerland); Buchnetzwerk Verlagsvertretungen (Austria)

Verlag Jungbrunnen GmbH+
Rauhensteingasse 5, 1010 Vienna
Tel: (01) 5121299 *Fax:* (01) 5121299-75
E-mail: office@jungbrunnen.co.at
Web Site: www.jungbrunnen.co.at
Key Personnel
Mng Dir, Editorial: Hildegard Gaertner
Press & Advertising: Gunde Dorner
Rights & Permissions: Martina Moosleitner
Founded: 1923
Subjects: Developing Countries, Fiction, Human Relations
ISBN Prefix(es): 978-3-7026

Edition Juridica
Subsidiary of MANZ'sche Verlags- und Universitaetsbuchhandlung GmbH
Kohlmarkt 16, 1010 Vienna
Tel: (01) 531-61-0 *Fax:* (01) 531-61-181
E-mail: verlag@manz.at; verlagsleitung@manz.at
Web Site: www.manz.at
Key Personnel
Mng Dir: Susanne Stein-Pressl
Publishing Dir: Dr Wolfgang Pichler
Sales Manager: Peter Guggenberger
Founded: 1968
Subjects: Accounting, Law, Literature, Literary Criticism, Essays, Nonfiction (General)
ISBN Prefix(es): 978-3-85131
Orders to: MANZ-Auslieferung, Gutheil-Schoder-Gasse 17 Halle C 3, 1230 Vienna *Tel:* (01) 66 28 675-5677 *Fax:* (01) 66 28 675-5687
  E-mail: auslieferung@manz.at

Karolinger Verlag+
Kutschkergasse 12/7, 1180 Vienna
Tel: (01) 409 22 79 *Fax:* (01) 409 22 79
E-mail: verlag@karolinger.at
Web Site: www.karolinger.at
Key Personnel
Mng Dir, Sales: Jean-Jacques Langendorf
Editorial: Dr Peter Weiss
Publicity: Cornelia Langendorf
Founded: 1980
Subjects: Fiction, Government, Political Science, History, Literature, Literary Criticism, Essays
ISBN Prefix(es): 978-3-85418
Number of titles published annually: 6 Print
Total Titles: 110 Print

Distribution Center: AS Hoeller GmbH, Schrackengasse 11a, 8650 Kindberg *Tel:* (03865) 44880 *Fax:* (03865) 44880-77
Brockhaus/Commission, Kreidlerstr 9, 70806 Kornwestheim, Germany *Tel:* (07154) 13270 *Fax:* (07154) 1327 13
Buch- und Medienvertriebs AG, Hochstr 357, 8200 Schaffhausen, Switzerland *Tel:* (052) 643 5430 *Fax:* (052) 643 5435

Edition Keiper
Puchstr 17, 8020 Graz
Tel: (0316) 269298 *Fax:* (0316) 269299
E-mail: office@editionkeiper.at; office@textzentrum.at
Web Site: www.editionkeiper.at
Key Personnel
Publisher: Anita Keiper
Founded: 2008
Subjects: Art, Nonfiction (General), Poetry, Science (General), Thriller
ISBN Prefix(es): 978-3-902901; 978-3-9503343

Kitab-Verlag
Deutenhofenstr 26, 9020 Klagenfurt
Tel: (0463) 592174-11 *Fax:* (0463) 592174-44
E-mail: office@kitab-verlag.com
Web Site: www.kitab-verlag.com
Key Personnel
Mng Dir: Dr Wilhelm Baum
Founded: 1998
Subjects: Business, Literature, Literary Criticism, Essays, Science (General)
ISBN Prefix(es): 978-3-902005
Distribution Center: Medienlogistik Pichler-OEBZ GmbH & Co KG, IZ-NOE Sued, Str 1, Obj 34, 2355 Wiener Neudorf *Tel:* (02236) 63535236 *E-mail:* oebz@oebz.co.at (Austria & South Tyrol)
Servicevermittlung Revilak, Gutenbergstr 5, 82205 Gilching, Germany *Tel:* (08105) 5051 *E-mail:* info@revilakservice.de (Germany, Netherlands & Switzerland)

Kitzler Verlag GesmbH
Uraniastr 4, 1010 Vienna
Tel: (01) 713 53 34 *Fax:* (01) 713 53 34-85
E-mail: office@kitzler-verlag.at
Web Site: www.kitzler-verlag.at
Key Personnel
Mng Dir: Walter Loeffler *Tel:* (01) 713 53 34-0
  E-mail: walter.loeffler@kitzler-verlag.at
Sales Manager: Wolfgang Goeth *Tel:* (01) 713 53 34-12 *E-mail:* wolfgang.goeth@kitzler-verlag.at
Founded: 1923
Subjects: Foreign Countries, Transportation, Chemicals, Customs, Dangerous Goods, Foreign Trade
ISBN Prefix(es): 978-3-902586

Klever Verlag
Hochstettergasse 4/1, 1020 Vienna
Tel: (01) 522 10 43
E-mail: office@klever-verlag.com
Web Site: klever-verlag.com
Key Personnel
Mng Dir: Ralph Klever
Founded: 2008
Subjects: Fiction, Language Arts, Linguistics, Literature, Literary Criticism, Essays, Poetry
ISBN Prefix(es): 978-3-902665
Distribution Center: Dr Franz Hain Verlagsauslieferungen GmbH, Dr-Otto-Neurath-Gasse 5, 1220 Vienna *Tel:* (01) 2826565-77 *Fax:* (01) 2825282 *E-mail:* bestell@hain.at
GVA Gemeinsame Verlagsauslieferung Goettingen GmbH & Co KG, Postfach 2021, 37010 Goettingen, Germany *Tel:* (0551) 487177 *Fax:* (0551) 41392 *E-mail:* order@gva-verlage.de

Musikverlag Johann Kliment KG
Kolingasse 15, 1090 Vienna
Tel: (01) 317 5147-0 *Fax:* (01) 317 5147-20
E-mail: office@kliment.at
Web Site: www.kliment.at
Key Personnel
Contact: Juliana Puehrer-Kliment
Founded: 1928
Subjects: Music, Dance
ISBN Prefix(es): 978-3-85139

Kneipp Verlag GmbH und Co KG+
Lobkowitzplatz 1, 1010 Vienna
Tel: (01) 203 28 88-0 *Fax:* (01) 23 28 88-6885
E-mail: office@kneippverlag.com
Web Site: www.kneippverlag.com
Key Personnel
Mng Dir & Sales (Austria): Anneliese Paulhart
  Tel: (01) 203 28 88-6878 *E-mail:* anneliese.paulhart@kneippverlag.com
Mng Dir: Gerda Schaffelhofer
Editorial: Eva Manhardt *Tel:* (01) 203 28 88-6882
  E-mail: eva.manhardt@kneippverlag.com
Press: Ina Tuerk *Tel:* (01) 203 28 88-6879
  E-mail: ina.tuerk@kneippverlag.com
Founded: 1985
Specializing in health & medicine.
Subjects: Alternative, Child Care & Development, Cookery, Health, Nutrition, Medicine, Nursing, Dentistry, Outdoor Recreation, Philosophy, Psychology, Psychiatry, Sports, Athletics
ISBN Prefix(es): 978-3-901794; 978-3-902191; 978-3-7088
Distribution Center: Medienlogistik Pichler-OEBZ GmbH & Co Kg, IZ-NOE Sued, Str 1, Objekt 34, 2355 Wiener Neudorf, Contact: Sabine Heinrich *Tel:* (02236) 635 35-290 *Fax:* (02236) 635 35-243 *E-mail:* bestellen@medien-logistik.at *Web Site:* www.medien-logistik.at
Brockhaus/Commission, Kreidlerstr 9, 70806 Kornwestheim, Germany, Contact: Petra Brandt *Tel:* (07154) 1327-71 *Fax:* (07154) 1327-13 *E-mail:* p.brandt@brocom.de
Buchzentrum AG, Industriestr Ost 10, 4614 Haegendorf, Switzerland *Tel:* (062) 209 26 26 *Fax:* (062) 209 26 27 *E-mail:* kundendienst@buchzentrum.ch *Web Site:* www.buchzentrum.ch

Edition Koenigstein+
Anzengrubergasse 50, 3400 Klosterneuburg
Tel: (02243) 26046
E-mail: office@koenigsteinkunst.com
Web Site: www.koenigsteinkunst.com
Key Personnel
Publisher: Georg Koenigstein
Editor & Marketing: Christine Koenigstein
Founded: 1987
Specialize in fine editions & poetry.
Subjects: Art, Erotica, Music, Dance, Poetry
ISBN Prefix(es): 978-3-901495
Number of titles published annually: 5 Print
Total Titles: 55 Print

Kompass Karten GmbH
Karl-Kapfererstr 5, 6020 Innsbruck
Tel: (0512) 265561-0 *Fax:* (0512) 265561-8
E-mail: info@kompass.at
Web Site: www.kompass.at
Key Personnel
Mng Dir: Walter Scheran
Subjects: Outdoor Recreation, Sports, Athletics
ISBN Prefix(es): 978-3-85491

Edition Konturen Mediendesign GmbH
Alliiertenstr 3/16, 1020 Vienna
Tel: (0699) 1714 9790
E-mail: mail@konturen.cc
Web Site: www.konturen.cc
Key Personnel
Contact: Georg Hauptfeld *E-mail:* gh@konturen.cc
ISBN Prefix(es): 978-3-902968

Branch Office(s)
Schmarjestr 42, 22767 Hamburg, Germany
Distribution Center: Mohr Morawa Buchvertrieb GmbH, Sulzengasse 2, 1230 Vienna *Tel:* (01) 680 14-0 *E-mail:* momo@mohrmorawa.at
Brockhaus Kommissionsgeschaeft GmbH, Kreidlerstr 9, 70806 Kornwestheim, Germany *Tel:* (07154) 1327-0 *E-mail:* info@brocom.de

Edition Korrespondenzen
Mollardgasse 2/16, 1060 Vienna
Tel: (01) 3151409 *Fax:* (01) 3151409
E-mail: edition@korrespondenzen.at
Web Site: www.korrespondenzen.at
Key Personnel
Publisher: Reto Ziegler
Subjects: Language Arts, Linguistics, Poetry
ISBN Prefix(es): 978-3-902113
Distribution Center: Mohr Morawa Buchvertrieb GmbH, Sulzengasse 2, 1230 Vienna *Tel:* (01) 680 14-0 *Fax:* (01) 688 71 30 *E-mail:* momo@mohrmorawa.at *Web Site:* www.mohrmorawa.at
GVA Gemeinsame Verlagsauslieferung, Postfach 2021, 37073 Goettingen, Germany *Tel:* (0551) 487177 *Fax:* (0551) 41392 *E-mail:* bestellung@gva-verlage.de
AVA Verlagsauslieferung AG, Centralweg 16, 8910 Affoltern am Albis, Switzerland *Tel:* (044) 7624260 *Fax:* (044) 7624210 *E-mail:* verlagsservice@ava.ch *Web Site:* www.ava.ch

KRAL-Verlag
John F Kennedy-Platz 2, 2560 Berndorf
Tel: (02672) 82236 *Fax:* (02672) 82236-4
E-mail: office@kral-verlag.at
Web Site: www.kral-verlag.at
Key Personnel
Owner: Robert Ivancich *E-mail:* ivancich@kral-berndorf.at
Subjects: Biography, Memoirs, Cookery, Fiction, Gardening, Plants, History, Music, Dance, Nonfiction (General), Travel & Tourism
ISBN Prefix(es): 978-3-902447

Buchverlage Kremayr & Scheriau/Orac, see Verlag Kremayr & Scheriau KG

Verlag Kremayr & Scheriau KG+
Waehringerstr 76/8, 1090 Vienna
Tel: (01) 713 87 70-0 *Fax:* (01) 713 87 70-20
E-mail: office@kremayr-scheriau.at
Web Site: www.kremayr-scheriau.at
Key Personnel
Mng Dir: Martin Scheriau *E-mail:* m.scheriau@kremayr-scheriau.at
Program Management: Barbara Koeszegi *E-mail:* b.koeszegi@kremayr-scheriau.at
Marketing/Advertising & Events: Tanja Raich *E-mail:* t.raich@kremayr-scheriau.at
Press & Public Relations: Vanja Rusnov *E-mail:* v.rusnov@kremayr-scheriau.at
Sales & Administration: Werner Scheucher *E-mail:* w.scheucher@kremayr-scheriau.at
Founded: 1950
Subjects: Art, History, Music, Dance, Nonfiction (General)
ISBN Prefix(es): 978-3-218; 978-3-7015; 978-3-85368; 978-3-204; 978-3-85356; 978-3-7077
Bookshop(s): Buchhandlung und Zeitschriftenvertrieb Kremayr und Scheriau, Niederhofstr 37, 1121 Vienna
Book Club(s): Buchgemeinschaft Donauland, Kremayr & Scheriau, Mariahilfer Str 22-24, 1070 Vienna
Distribution Center: Dr Franz Hain Verlagsauslieferungen GmbH, Dr-Otto-Neurath-Gasse 5, 1220 Vienna *Tel:* (01) 282 65 65-77 *Fax:* (01) 282 52 82 *E-mail:* bestell@hain.at
Prolit Verlagsauslieferung, Siemensstr 16, 35463 Fernwald (Annerod), Germany, Contact: Jens

Vogt *Tel:* (0641) 943 93 31 *Fax:* (0641) 943 93 39 *E-mail:* j.vogt@prolit.de (Germany & Luxembourg)

Hubert Krenn Verlag GmbH
Gusshausstr 18, 1040 Vienna
Tel: (01) 585 34 72 *Fax:* (01) 585 04 83
E-mail: hwk@buchagentur.at
Web Site: www.hubertkrenn.at
Key Personnel
Mng Dir: Hubert W Krenn
Founded: 2002
Subjects: Cookery, Education, Health, Nutrition
ISBN Prefix(es): 978-3-902532; 978-3-9501316; 978-3-902351
Number of titles published annually: 30 Online
Total Titles: 160 Print

Verlag Lafite, Musikzeit Edition+
Castellezgasse 25/3/14, 1020 Vienna
Tel: (01) 5126869
E-mail: redaktion@musikzeit.at
Web Site: www.musikzeit.at
Key Personnel
Owner: Dr Marion Diederichs-Lafite
Founded: 1962
Specialize in music.
Publisher of *Austrian Music Magazine.*
Subjects: Journalism, Music, Dance
ISBN Prefix(es): 978-3-85151
Associate Companies: Internationale Schonberg Gesellschaft, Vienna

Edition Lammerhuber
Dumbagasse 9, 2500 Baden
Tel: (02252) 42 269 *Fax:* (02252) 85 938
E-mail: edition@lammerhuber.at
Web Site: www.edition.lammerhuber.at
Key Personnel
Publisher: Lois Lammerhuber *E-mail:* lois.lammerhuber@lammerhuber.at
Management, Marketing & Public Relations: Silvia Lammerhuber *E-mail:* silvia.lammerhuber@lammerhuber.at
ISBN Prefix(es): 978-3-901753

Edition Laurin
Universitaet Innsbruck, Technikerstr 21a, 6020 Innsbruck
Tel: (0512) 507 9098 *Fax:* (0512) 507 9812
E-mail: office@editionlaurin.at
Web Site: www.editionlaurin.at
Key Personnel
Publishing Dir: Dr Birgit Holzner *Tel:* (0512) 507 9096 *E-mail:* birgit.holzner@editionlaurin.at
Sales: Claudia Wallner-Heuschneider *E-mail:* claudia.wallner.heuschneider@editionlaurin.at
Subjects: Drama, Theater, Fiction
ISBN Prefix(es): 978-3-902866; 978-3-902719

Lesethek, *imprint of* Wilhelm Braumueller Universitaets-Verlagsbuchhandlung GmbH

edition lex liszt 12
Raingasse 9b, 7400 Oberwart
Tel: (03352) 33940 *Fax:* (03352) 34685
E-mail: info@lexliszt12.at
Web Site: www.lexliszt12.at
Subjects: Art, Education, Literature, Literary Criticism, Essays, Nonfiction (General)
ISBN Prefix(es): 978-3-99016; 978-3-901757; 978-3-9500185

Leykam Buchverlagsgesellschaft mbH Nfg & Co KG
Karlauerguertel 1/2, Stock, 8020 Graz
Tel: (05) 0109-6530 *Fax:* (05) 0109-6539
E-mail: verlag@leykam.com
Web Site: www.leykamverlag.at

Key Personnel
Mng Dir: Klaus Brunner *Tel:* (05) 0109-5300 *E-mail:* klaus.brunner@leykamverlag.at
Publishing Dir: Dr Wolfgang Hoelzl *E-mail:* wolfgang.hoelzl@leykamverlag.at
Editorial/Production: Elisabeth Kloeckl-Stadler *Tel:* (05) 0109-6534 *E-mail:* elisabeth.kloeckl-stadler@leykamverlag.at
Marketing: Dagmar Holzmann *Tel:* (05) 0109-6535 *E-mail:* dagmar.holzmann@leykamverlag.at
Founded: 1585
Subjects: Art, Education, Fiction, Literature, Literary Criticism, Essays, Nonfiction (General), Science (General)
ISBN Prefix(es): 978-3-7011
Distribution Center: Mohr Morawa Buchvertrieb GmbH, Sulzengasse 2, 1230 Vienna *Tel:* (01) 680 14-0 *Fax:* (01) 688 17 30 *E-mail:* momo@mohrmorawa.at *Web Site:* www.mohrmorawa.at (book trade)
Leykam Alpina Verlags- und VertriebsgmbH Nfg & Co KG, Gewerbepark 5, 8402 Werndorf *Tel:* (05) 0109-5520 *Fax:* (05) 0109-5710 *E-mail:* alpina.buchauslieferung@leykam.com
Suedost Verlags Service GmbH, Am Steinfeld 4, 94065 Waldkirchen, Germany *Tel:* (08581) 9605-0 *Fax:* (08581) 754 *E-mail:* info@suedost-verlags-service.de

Limbus Verlag
Pradlerstr 41, 6020 Innsbruck
Tel: (0650) 350 7050 (cell) *Fax:* (0720) 883 206
E-mail: buero@limbusverlag.at; lektorat@limbusverlag.at
Web Site: www.limbusverlag.at
Key Personnel
Publisher: Bernd Schuchter
Editorial: Merle Ruedisser
Founded: 2005
Subjects: Fiction, Literature, Literary Criticism, Essays
ISBN Prefix(es): 978-3-902534

Linde Verlag Wien GesmbH+
Scheydgasse 24, 1210 Vienna
Tel: (01) 24 630-0 *Fax:* (01) 24 630-23
E-mail: office@lindeverlag.at; redaktion@lindeverlag.at; presse@lindeverlag.at
Web Site: www.lindeverlag.at
Key Personnel
Mng Dir: Dr Eleonore Breitegger; Dr Oskar Mennel *Tel:* (01) 24 630-43 *E-mail:* oskar.mennel@lindeverlag.at
Head, Marketing & Sales: Thomas Jentzsch *Fax:* (01) 24 630-53 *E-mail:* thomas.jentzsch@lindeverlag.at
Press & Public Relations: Sabine Brozek *Tel:* (01) 24 630-30 *Fax:* (01) 24 630-53
Sales: Antje Lutz
Founded: 1925
Subjects: Accounting, Business, Communications, Economics, How-to, Labor, Industrial Relations, Law, Management, Marketing
ISBN Prefix(es): 978-3-85122; 978-3-7073; 978-3-7093; 978-3-7143
Number of titles published annually: 120 Print; 3 CD-ROM
Total Titles: 300 Print; 20 CD-ROM

Literas Universitaetsverlag GmbH
Fischerstrand 9, 1220 Vienna
Tel: (01) 269 22 07 *Fax:* (01) 269 22 07
Founded: 1981
Subjects: Psychology, Psychiatry
ISBN Prefix(es): 978-3-85429

Literaturedition Niederoesterreich Amt de NOE Landesregierung Abteilung Kultur und Wissenschaft
Landhausplatz 1, 3109 St Poelten
Tel: (02742) 9005 15538 *Fax:* (02742) 9005 15585

E-mail: noe-literaturedition@noel.gv.at; post.
internetk1@noel.gv.at
Web Site: www.literaturedition-noe.at
Key Personnel
Mng Dir: Gabriele Ecker *E-mail:* gabriele.ecker@
noel.gv.at
Editor: Christa Haitzer *Tel:* (02742) 9005 13234;
Karin Wagisreither *Tel:* (02742) 9005 13101
Founded: 1991
Subjects: Fiction, Poetry, Prose
ISBN Prefix(es): 978-3-901117; 978-3-902717

Loecker Verlag+
Annagasse 3a/21, 1010 Vienna
Tel: (01) 512 02 82 *Fax:* (01) 512 02 82-15
E-mail: lverlag@loecker.at
Web Site: www.loecker-verlag.at
Key Personnel
General Manager: Erhard Loecker
Rights & Permissions: Dr Alexander Lellek
Founded: 1974
Subjects: Architecture & Interior Design, Art,
History, Literature, Literary Criticism, Essays,
Music, Dance, Philosophy, Photography, Cul-
tural Studies, Pedagogy
ISBN Prefix(es): 978-3-85409
Bookshop(s): Antiquariat Loecker, Annagasse 5,
1015 Vienna *Tel:* (01) 512 73 44 *Fax:* (01) 512
73 44 15 *E-mail:* loecker@loecker.at; Arca-
dia Opera Shop, Kaerntnerstr 40, 1015 Vienna
Tel: (01) 513 95 68 *Fax:* (01) 513 98 86 *Web
Site:* www.arcadia.at
Distribution Center: Mohr Morawa Buchvertrieb
GmbH, Sulzengasse 2, 1230 Vienna *Tel:* (01)
680 14-0 *Fax:* (01) 688 71 30 *E-mail:* momo@
mohrmorawa.at *Web Site:* www.mohrmorawa.at
GVA Gemeinsame Verlagsauslieferung Goettin-
gen GmbH & Co KG, Postfach 2021, 37073
Goettingen, Germany *Tel:* (0551) 48 71 77
Fax: (0551) 4 13 92

**Loewenzahn Verlag in der Studienverlag
GesmbH**
Erlerstr 10, 6020 Innsbruck
Tel: (0512) 395045 *Fax:* (0512) 395045 15
E-mail: loewenzahn@studienverlag.at
Web Site: www.loewenzahn.at
Key Personnel
Mng Dir: Markus Hatzer
Marketing: Marion Bernhard *E-mail:* m.
bernhard@studienverlag.at
Press Relations: Gerlinde Tamerl *E-mail:* g.
tamerl@studienverlag.at
Subjects: Agriculture, Art, Cookery, Fiction, Gar-
dening, Plants, Health, Nutrition, Nature
ISBN Prefix(es): 978-3-7066; 978-3-920521
Foreign Rep(s): GVA Goettingen GmbH & Co
KG (Germany); Mohr Morawa Buchvertrieb
GmbH (Austria, Switzerland)
Distribution Center: Mohr Morawa Buchvertrieb
GmbH, Sulzengasse 2, 1230 Vienna *Tel:* (01)
680 14-0 *Fax:* (01) 688 71 30 *E-mail:* momo@
mohrmorawa.at *Web Site:* www.mohrmorawa.at

Luftschacht Verlag OG
Malzgasse 12/2°, 1020 Vienna
Tel: (01) 2197303-23 *Fax:* (01) 2197303-38
E-mail: office@luftschacht.com
Web Site: www.luftschacht.com
Key Personnel
Press & Public Relations: Stefan Buchberger
E-mail: buchberger@luftschacht.com
Sales & Production: Juergen Lagger
E-mail: lagger@luftschacht.com
Subjects: Fiction, Language Arts, Linguistics
ISBN Prefix(es): 978-3-902373
Distribution Center: Dr Franz Hain Verlagsaus-
lieferung GmbH, Dr-Otto-Neurath-Gasse 5,
1220 Vienna *Tel:* (01) 2826565-77 *Fax:* (01)
2825282 *E-mail:* bestell@hain.at

GVA Gemeinsame Verlagsauslieferung Goettin-
gen GmbH & Co KG, Postfach 2021, 37010
Goettingen, Germany *Tel:* (0551) 487177
Fax: (0551) 41392

Mandelbaum Verlag
Wipplingerstr 23, 1010 Vienna
Tel: (01) 53 53 477-0 *Fax:* (01) 53 53 477-12
E-mail: office@mandelbaum.at
Web Site: www.mandelbaum.at
Key Personnel
Publishing Dir: Michael Baiculescu
Press & Public Relations: Kathrin Konrad
Sales & Finance: Elizabeth Baumhoefer
Subjects: Economics, Government, Political Sci-
ence, History, Literature, Literary Criticism,
Essays, Psychology, Psychiatry, Science (Gen-
eral), Travel & Tourism
ISBN Prefix(es): 978-3-85476
Foreign Rep(s): Indie Book (Nicole Grabert, Ju-
dith Heckel, Christiane Krause) (Germany);
Michael Orou (Eastern Austria); Guenther
Thiel (Western Austria)
Distribution Center: Mohr Morawa Buchvertrieb
GmbH, Sulzengasse 2, 1230 Vienna *Tel:* (01)
68 14-0 *Fax:* (01) 688 71 30 *E-mail:* momo@
mohrmorawa.at *Web Site:* www.mohrmorawa.at
GVA Joint Publishers Distribution, PO Box
2021, 37010 Goettingen, Germany *Tel:* (0551)
487177 *Fax:* (0551) 41392 *E-mail:* order@gva-
verlage.de

**MANZ'sche Verlags- und
Universitaetsbuchhandlung GmbH**
Kohlmarkt 16, 1010 Vienna
Tel: (01) 531 61-0 *Fax:* (01) 531 61-181
E-mail: verlag@manz.at
Web Site: www.manz.at
Key Personnel
Mng Partner: Susanne Stein-Pressl *Tel:* (01) 531
61-124 *E-mail:* susanne.stein@manz.at
Mng Dir: Peter Guggenberger *Tel:* (01) 531 61-
681 *E-mail:* peter.guggenberger@manz.at
Business Development: Dr Wolfgang Pichler
Tel: (01) 531 61-112 *E-mail:* wolfgang.
pichler@manz.at
Public Relations & Media Relations: Dr Christo-
pher Dietz *Tel:* (01) 531 61-364
Founded: 1849
Specialize in law books in Europe.
Subjects: Economics, Law, Tax
ISBN Prefix(es): 978-3-214; 978-3-7067
Subsidiaries: Edition Juridica
Distributor for Amt der Europaeischen Gemein-
schaften

Maudrich+
Division of Facultas Verlags- und Buchhandels
AG
Stolberggasse 26, 1050 Vienna
Tel: (01) 310 53 56 *Fax:* (01) 319 70 50
E-mail: office@facultas.at; maudrich@maudrich.
com
Web Site: www.maudrich.com
Founded: 1929
Subjects: Health, Nutrition, Medicine, Nursing,
Dentistry, Psychology, Psychiatry
ISBN Prefix(es): 978-3-85175
Total Titles: 250 Print
Bookshop(s): Universitaetsbuchhandlung Mau-
drich, Spitalgasse 21a, 1090 Vienna *Tel:* (01)
402 47 12 *Fax:* (01) 408 50 80

Medien und Recht Verlags GmbH (Media &
Law Publishers Inc)+
Danhausergasse 6, 1040 Vienna
Tel: (01) 505 27 66 *Fax:* (01) 505 27 66-15
E-mail: verlag@medien-recht.ccom
Web Site: www.medien-recht.com
Key Personnel
Mng Dir: Dr Heinz Wittmann *E-mail:* h.
wittmann@medien-recht.com

Founded: 1985
Specialize in Austrian & European media &
telecommunication law. Offer a variety of pub-
lications in German & English.
Subjects: Communications, Computer Science,
Journalism, Law
ISBN Prefix(es): 978-3-900741; 978-3-939438
Branch Office(s)
Schellingstr 113, 80798 Munich, Germany
Tel: (089) 543 566 31 *Fax:* (089) 543 566 59

Milena Verlag+
Wickenburgg 21/1-2, 1080 Vienna
Tel: (01) 402 59 90 *Fax:* (01) 408 88 58
E-mail: office@milena-verlag.at
Web Site: www.milena-verlag.at
Key Personnel
Publishing Manager: Vanessa Wieser
E-mail: wieser@milena-verlag.at
Assistant Publisher: George Holeschofsky
Press: Evelyn Steinthalar *E-mail:* steinthalar@
milena-verlag.at
Founded: 1980
Subjects: Biography, Memoirs, Fiction, History,
LGBTQ, Library & Information Sciences, Lit-
erature, Literary Criticism, Essays, Nonfiction
(General), Philosophy, Social Sciences, Sociol-
ogy, Women's Studies
ISBN Prefix(es): 978-3-900399; 978-3-85286
Total Titles: 160 Print
Foreign Rep(s): Book Network (Guenther
Staudinger) (Austria); Nicole Grabert Pub-
lishing Agencies (Judith Heckel & Christian
Krause) (Germany); Leipziger Kommissions-
und Grossbuchhandelsgesellschaft mbH (LKG)
(Germany)
Orders to: Mohr Morawa Buchvertrieb GmbH,
Sulzengasse 2, 1230 Vienna *Tel:* (01) 680
14-0 *Fax:* (01) 688 71 30 *E-mail:* momo@
mohrmorawa.at *Web Site:* www.mohrmorawa.at
Leipziger Kommissions- und Grossbuchhandelsgesellschaft mbH (LKG), An der Suedspitze 1-
12, 04571 Roetha, Germany *Tel:* (034206) 65-
100 *Fax:* (034206) 65-110 *E-mail:* lkg@lkg-
service.de *Web Site:* www.lkg-va.de

Thomas Mlakar Verlag
Michlbauerweg 1, 8755 St Peter ob Judenburg
Tel: (03579) 2258; (0664) 357 71 73
Fax: (03579) 2258
E-mail: mlakar-media@gmx.at
Web Site: www.mlakar-media.at
Key Personnel
Founder & Senior Partner: Erich Mlakar
Mng Dir: Thomas Mlakar
Founded: 1970
Subjects: Fashion, History, Literature, Literary
Criticism, Essays, Natural History
ISBN Prefix(es): 978-3-900289

**Mohorjeva druzba v Celovcu - Hermagoras
Verein+**
Viktringer Ring 26, 9020 Klagenfurt
Tel: (0463) 56 515 *Fax:* (0463) 56 515-12
E-mail: direktion@mohorjeva.at
Web Site: www.mohorjeva.at
Key Personnel
Publishing Dir: Franz Kelih *Tel:* (0463) 56 515
36 *E-mail:* franz.kelih@mohorjeva.at
Mng Editor: Hanzi Filipic *Tel:* (0463) 56 515 26
E-mail: hanzi.filipic@mohorjeva.at
Editor & Consultant: Franc Kattnig *Tel:* (0463)
56 515 20 *E-mail:* franc.kattnig@mohorjeva.at
Marketing/Editorial: Adrian Kert *Tel:* (0463) 56
515 27 *E-mail:* adrian.kert@mohorjeva.at; Ro-
man Till *Tel:* (0463) 56 515 15 *E-mail:* roman.
till@mohorjeva.at
Founded: 1851
Specialize in books in Slovenian & German.
Subjects: Art, Biological Sciences, Fiction, History, Regional Interests, Religion - Other, Science (General)

ISBN Prefix(es): 978-3-85013; 978-3-900119; 978-3-7086
Subsidiaries: Korotan Import-Export GmbH

Edition moKKa
Floridsdorfer Hauptstr 36/2/12, 1210 Vienna
Tel: (0660) 490 55 61 (cell) *Fax:* (01) 270 21 56
E-mail: office@edition-mokka.eu
Web Site: www.edition-mokka.eu
Key Personnel
Owner: Harald Reiter
Program Management, Advertising, Press: Angelika Herburger
Editing, Content Consulting: Traude Korosa
Subjects: Cookery, History, Literature, Literary Criticism, Essays, Travel & Tourism
ISBN Prefix(es): 978-3-902693

Molden Verlag, *imprint of* Verlagsgruppe Styria GmbH & Co KG

Otto Mueller Verlag
Ernest-Thun-Str 11, 5020 Salzburg
Tel: (0662) 881974-0 *Fax:* (0662) 872387
E-mail: info@omvs.at; presse@omvs.at; vertrieb@omvs.at
Web Site: www.omvs.at
Key Personnel
Publisher: Arno Kleibel *E-mail:* kleibel@omvs.at
Editorial: Astrid Treusch
Press & Public Relations: Tanja Karlsboeck
Sales: Volker Maria Rechberger
Founded: 1937
Subjects: History, Literature, Literary Criticism, Essays, Poetry, Psychology, Psychiatry, Religion - Other, Theology
ISBN Prefix(es): 978-3-7013
Distribution Center: Mohr Morawa Buchvertrieb GmbH, Sulzengasse 2, 1230 Vienna *Tel:* (01) 680 14-0 *Fax:* (01) 688 71 30 *E-mail:* momo@mohrmorawa.at *Web Site:* www.mohrmorawa.at
Leipziger Kommissions- und Grossbuchhandelsges mbH (LKG), An der Suedspitze 1-12, 04571 Roetha, Germany *Tel:* (034206) 65-100 *Fax:* (034206) 65-110 *E-mail:* lkg@lkg-service.de *Web Site:* www.lkg-va.de
Herder AG Basel, Muttenzenstr, 109, Postfach, 4133 Pratteln 1, Switzerland *Tel:* (061) 8279060 *Fax:* (061) 8279067 *E-mail:* verkauf@herder.ch

Mueller-Speiser Wissenschaftlicher Verlag
Mitterweg 6, 5081 Anif/Salzburg
Tel: (06246) 7 31 66 *Fax:* (06246) 7 31 66
E-mail: verlag@mueller-speiser.at
Web Site: www.mueller-speiser.at
Key Personnel
Contact: Ursula Mueller-Speiser
Founded: 1989
Subjects: Drama, Theater, Music, Dance, Philosophy, Religion - Other, Theology, General Religion, Music Science/Music Ethnology
ISBN Prefix(es): 978-3-85145; 978-3-902537
Total Titles: 78 Print

Muery Salzmann Verlag Gesellschaft mbH
Faberstr 7A, 5020 Salzburg
Tel: (0662) 873721 *Fax:* (0662) 873942
E-mail: office@muerysalzmann.at
Web Site: www.muerysalzmann.at
Key Personnel
Publisher: Mona Muery *E-mail:* mmuery@muerysalzmann.at
Editing & Project Management: Dr Silke Duernberger *E-mail:* duernberger@muerysalzmann.at
Founded: 2009
Subjects: Architecture & Interior Design, Art, Drama, Theater, History, Literature, Literary Criticism, Essays, Photography, Culture, Lifestyle

ISBN Prefix(es): 978-3-9901400; 978-3-9901402; 978-3-9901403
Foreign Rep(s): Hans Frieden (Germany); Joachim Klinger (Austria)
Distribution Center: Medienlogistik Pichler-OEBZ GmbH & Co KG, IZ-NOE Sued, Str 1, Objekt 34, 2355 Weiner Nuedorf *Tel:* (02236) 63 535-290 *Fax:* (02236) 63 535-243 *E-mail:* mlo@medien-logistik.at *Web Site:* www.medien-logistik.at
Sigloch Distribution GmbH & Co KG, Am Buchberg 8, 74572 Blaufelden, Germany *Tel:* (07953) 7189 052 *Fax:* (07953) 7189 080 *E-mail:* verlagservice@sigloch.de

Musikwissenschaftlicher Verlag
Schwedenplatz 3-4/2/19, 1010 Vienna
Tel: (01) 5322483 *Fax:* (01) 2533033
E-mail: office@mwv.at
Web Site: www.mwv.at
Key Personnel
Dir: Dr Angela Pachovsky
Mng Dir: Tilly Eder
Subjects: Music, Dance
ISBN Prefix(es): 978-3-902681; 978-3-900270

Edition Neue Text, *imprint of* Literaturverlag Droschl GmbH

Neuer Wissenschaftlicher Verlag GmbH
Faradaygasse 6, 1030 Vienna
Tel: (01) 796 35 62-24 *Fax:* (01) 796 35 62-25
E-mail: office@nwv.at
Web Site: www.nwv.at
Founded: 2001
Subjects: Architecture & Interior Design, Business, Economics, Environmental Studies, History, Law, Social Sciences, Sociology, Technology, Tax Law
ISBN Prefix(es): 978-3-7083
Branch Office(s)
Geidorfguertel 24, 8010 Graz
Orders to: Medien-Logistik Pichler OEBZ GmbH & Co KG, IZ NOE Sued, Str 1, Objekt 34, 2355 Wiener Neudorf *Tel:* (02236) 63535-246 *Fax:* (02236) 63535-243 *E-mail:* gabriela.atlas@medien-logistik.at

Wolfgang Neugebauer Verlag GmbH
Duens 134, 6822 Satteins
Fax: (05524) 5199
E-mail: wnverlag@aon.at
Web Site: www.wnverlag.com
Key Personnel
Dir: Irmgard Neugebauer
Founded: 1975
Subjects: History, Language Arts, Linguistics, Library & Information Sciences, Literature, Literary Criticism, Essays, Theology
ISBN Prefix(es): 978-3-85376
Total Titles: 250 Print

Dr Waltraud Neuwirth Selbstverlag (Dr Waltraud Neuwirth Self Publishing House)
Weinzingergasse 10/18, 1190 Vienna
Tel: (01) 3207323 *Fax:* (01) 3200225
Key Personnel
Contact: Dr Waltraud Neuwirth
Founded: 1976
Subjects: Art, Biography, Memoirs
ISBN Prefix(es): 978-3-900282

NOI-Verlag
Morrestr 13, 9020 Klagenfurt
Tel: (0463) 224742 *Fax:* (0463) 224744
Key Personnel
Owner: Dr Dietfried Schoenemann
Subjects: Education, Environmental Studies, Ethnicity, Health, Nutrition, History, Social Sciences, Sociology
ISBN Prefix(es): 978-3-900453

Novum Publishing GmbH
Rathausgasse 73, 7311 Neckenmarkt
Tel: (02610) 431 11 *Fax:* (02610) 431 11 28
E-mail: office@novumverlag.com
Web Site: www.novumverlag.at
Key Personnel
Head of Publishing: Wolfgang Bader
Mng Dir: Sabine Bader
Sales Manager: Beate Krug
Founded: 1997
This publisher has indicated that 95% of its product line is author subsidized.
Membership(s): Hauptverband des Oesterreichischen Buchhandels; Oesterreichischer Verlegerverband; Wirtschaftskammer Burgenland.
Subjects: Art, Biography, Memoirs, Cookery, Crafts, Games, Hobbies, Erotica, Government, Political Science, History, Humor, Mysteries, Suspense, Photography, Science Fiction, Fantasy
ISBN Prefix(es): 978-3-900693; 978-3-902057; 978-3-902324; 978-3-902514; 978-3-99026; 978-3-99003
Number of titles published annually: 600 Print
Branch Office(s)
Kurfuerstendamm 21, 10719 Berlin, Germany
Novum Publishing kft, Varkereulet 1-3 II em 6, Sopron 9400, Hungary
Novum Publishing SL, C/ del Ter 27, 1a Plta, 07009 Palma de Mallorca, Spain
Thurgauerstr 40, 8050 Zurich, Switzerland

Obelisk Verlag+
Falkstr 1, 6020 Innsbruck
Tel: (0512) 580733 *Fax:* (0512) 580733 13
E-mail: obelisk-verlag@utanet.at; info@obelisk-verlag.at
Web Site: www.obelisk-verlag.at
Key Personnel
Editorial Dir: Helga Buchroithner *E-mail:* helga.buchroithner@obelisk-verlag.at
Children's Book Editor: Dr Inge Auboeck *E-mail:* inge.auboeck@obelisk-verlag.at
Rights & Permissions: Georg Buchroithner *E-mail:* georg.buchroithner@obelisk-verlag.at
Founded: 1967
Publisher has indicated that 65% of its product line is author subsidized.
ISBN Prefix(es): 978-3-85197
Number of titles published annually: 20 Print
Total Titles: 165 Print
Distribution Center: Medienlogistik-Pichler OEBZ, IZ Noe Sued Str 1, Objekt 34, 2355 Wiener Neudorf, Contact: Eva Prinz *Tel:* (02236) 63535 245 *Fax:* (02236) 63 535 243 *E-mail:* order@medien-logistik.at
Runge Verlagsauslieferung, Bergstr 2, 33803 Steinhagen, Germany, Contact: Pia Flesken *Tel:* (05204) 998 123 *Fax:* (05204) 998 114 *E-mail:* info@rungeva.de
AVA Umbreit Barsortiment, Centralweg 16, 8910 Affoltern am Albis, Switzerland *Tel:* (044) 762 42 00 *Fax:* (044) 762 42 10 *E-mail:* avainfo@ava.ch

OEAW, see Verlag der Oesterreichischen Akademie der Wissenschaften (OEAW)

Verlag Oesterreich GmbH+
Subsidiary of Wissenschaftlichen Verlagsgesellschaft
Baeckerstr 1, 1010 Vienna
Tel: (01) 610 77-0 *Fax:* (01) 610 77-419
E-mail: office@verlagoesterreich.at; office@voe.at
Web Site: www.verlagoesterreich.at
Key Personnel
Mng Dir: Andre Caro
Sales & Key Account Manager: Marcus Dalfen *Tel:* (01) 610 77-123 *Fax:* (01) 610 77-589 *E-mail:* m.dalfen@verlagoesterreich.at
Founded: 1804

Membership(s): Boersenverein des Deutschen Buchhandels; Hauptverband des Oesterreichischen Buchhandels.
Subjects: Law
ISBN Prefix(es): 978-3-7046; 978-3-85201
Number of titles published annually: 60 Print; 5 CD-ROM; 4 Online
Total Titles: 2,600 Print; 20 CD-ROM; 5 Online
Distribution Center: Mohr Morawa Buchvertrieb GmbH *Tel:* (01) 680 14-0 *Fax:* (01) 688 71 30 *E-mail:* momo@mohrmorawa.at *Web Site:* www.mohrmorawa.at

Verlag der Oesterreichischen Akademie der Wissenschaften (OEAW) (Austrian Academy of Sciences Press)
Dr Ignaz Seipel Platz 2, 1011 Vienna
Tel: (01) 512 9050; (01) 51581-3402; (01) 51581-3406 *Fax:* (01) 51581-3400
E-mail: verlag@oeaw.ac.at
Web Site: verlag.oeaw.ac.at
Key Personnel
Manager: Herwig Stoeger *Tel:* (01) 51581-3405 *E-mail:* herwig.stoeger@oeaw.ac.at
Founded: 1973
Membership(s): Association of Learned & Professional Society Publishers; Hauptverband des Oesterreichischen Buchhandels; PILA/Crossref; Portico.
Subjects: Archaeology, Asian Studies, Biography, Memoirs, Biological Sciences, History, Language Arts, Linguistics, Law, Physical Sciences, Science (General), Social Sciences, Sociology
ISBN Prefix(es): 978-3-7001
Number of titles published annually: 100 Print; 2 CD-ROM; 70 Online; 3 Audio
Total Titles: 3,400 Print; 50 CD-ROM; 600 Online; 30 Audio
Distribution Center: Casemate | academic (USA)

Verlag des Oesterreichischen Gewerkschaftsbundes GmbH
Johann-Boehm-Platz 1, 1020 Vienna
Tel: (01) 662 32 96-0 *Fax:* (01) 662 32 96-39793
E-mail: office@oegbverlag.at
Web Site: www.oegbverlag.at
Key Personnel
Chief Executive Officer: Gerhard Broethaler *Tel:* (01) 662 32 96-39701 *E-mail:* gerhard.broethaler@oegbverlag.at
Mng Dir: Gerald Woedl *E-mail:* gerald.woedl@oegbverlag.at
Publisher: Dr Peter Autengruber *Tel:* (01) 662 32 96-39711 *E-mail:* peter.autengruber@oegbverlag.at
Marketing: Oliver Avanzini *Tel:* (01) 662 32 96-39712 *E-mail:* oliver.avanzini@oegbverlag.at
Founded: 1947
Subjects: Career Development, Government, Political Science, History, Labor, Industrial Relations, Law
ISBN Prefix(es): 978-3-7035
Subsidiaries: EDV GmbH; Elbemuhl GmbH; Pichler GmbH; Printex GmbH
Bookshop(s): Rathaus Str 21, 1010 Vienna *Tel:* (01) 405 49 98-132 *Fax:* (01) 405 49 98-136 *E-mail:* fachbuchhandlung@oegbverlag.at
Book Club(s): Buechergilde Gutenberg

Oesterreichischer Agrarverlag, Druck- und Verlagsges mbH Nfg KG+
Sturzgasse 1a, 1140 Vienna
Tel: (01) 98 177-0
E-mail: office@agrarverlag.at
Web Site: www.agrarverlag.at
Key Personnel
Publishing Dir: Winfried Eberl *Tel:* (01) 98 133-112 *Fax:* (01) 98 133-276 *E-mail:* w.eberl@agrarverlag.at

Assistant Dir, Publishing: Johanna Kolbert *Tel:* (01) 98 177-103 *Fax:* (01) 98 177-111 *E-mail:* j.kolbert@agrarverlag.at
Founded: 1945
Subjects: Agriculture, Environmental Studies, Fiction
ISBN Prefix(es): 978-3-7040
Parent Company: AV Holding
Subsidiaries: Hugo H Hitschmann Verlag
Warehouse: Hennersdorfer Str 32/6, 2333 Leopoldsdorf
Orders to: Ing H Fischer/AV Buchhandlung, Linzerstr 32, 1141 Vienna *Fax:* (01) 951501-289

Oesterreichischer Bundesverlag Schulbuch GmbH & Co KG
Frankgasse 4, 1090 Vienna
Tel: (01) 401 36-0 *Fax:* (01) 401 36-185
E-mail: office@oebv.at; service@oebv.at
Web Site: www.oebv.at
Key Personnel
Mng Dir: Jens Kapitzky
Editor: Karin Mayr; Gregor Wieser-Gmainer
Founded: 1772
Subjects: Biological Sciences, Career Development, Chemistry, Chemical Engineering, Education, English as a Second Language, History, Language Arts, Linguistics, Music, Dance, Nonfiction (General), Philosophy, Sports, Athletics
ISBN Prefix(es): 978-3-215

Oesterreichischer Jagd -und Fischerei-Verlag
Wickenburggasse 3, 1080 Vienna
Tel: (01) 405 16 36-39 *Fax:* (01) 405 16 36-59
E-mail: verlag@jagd.at
Web Site: www.jagd.at
Key Personnel
Publishing Dir: Dr Michael Sternath *Tel:* (01) 405 16 36-37
Sales Manager: Hermann Striednig
Founded: 1928
Subjects: Animals, Pets, Art, Cookery, History, Nonfiction (General)
ISBN Prefix(es): 978-3-85208

Oesterreichischer Kunst und Kulturverlag+
Freundgasse 11, 1040 Vienna
Tel: (01) 587 85 51 *Fax:* (01) 587 85 52
E-mail: office@kunstundkulturverlag.at
Web Site: www.kunstundkulturverlag.at
Key Personnel
Contact: Dr Michael Martischnig
Founded: 1981
Subjects: Antiques, Architecture & Interior Design, Communications, Engineering (General), History, Nonfiction (General), Regional Interests, Social Sciences, Sociology
ISBN Prefix(es): 978-3-85437
Number of titles published annually: 10 CD-ROM
Total Titles: 480 Print; 40 CD-ROM; 3 Audio

Oesterreichisches Katholisches Bibelwerk (Austrian Catholic Biblical Association)
Stiftsplatz 8, 3400 Klosterneuburg
Tel: (02243) 32938 *Fax:* (02243) 32938 (ext 39)
E-mail: sekretariat@bibelwerk.at; auslieferung@bibelwerk.at
Web Site: www.bibelwerk.at
Key Personnel
Dir: Dr Wolfgang Schwarz
Sales: Sabine Niedl *Tel:* (02243) 32938 ext 83
Founded: 1966
Membership(s): Catholic Biblical Federation (CBF); Forum Katholischer Erwachsenenbildung in Oesterreich.
Subjects: Religion - Other
ISBN Prefix(es): 978-3-85396

Osterreichischer Wirtschaftsverlag GmbH
Wiedner Hauptstr 120-124, 1051 Vienna

Tel: (01) 546 64-0 *Fax:* (01) 546 64-511
E-mail: office@wirtschaftsverlag.at
Web Site: www.wirtschaftsverlag.at
Key Personnel
Mng Dir: Thomas Zembacher
Subjects: Advertising, Automotive, Business, Economics, Transportation
ISBN Prefix(es): 978-3-85212
Parent Company: Sueddeutscher Verlag Huethig Factinformationen GmbH (SVHFI)

Passagen Verlag GmbH+
Walfischgasse 15/14, 1010 Vienna
Tel: (01) 513 77 61 *Fax:* (01) 512 63 27
E-mail: office@passagen.at
Web Site: www.passagen.at
Key Personnel
Publisher: Dr Peter Engelmann
Founded: 1987
Subjects: Architecture & Interior Design, Art, Economics, Government, Political Science, Literature, Literary Criticism, Essays, Philosophy, Social Sciences, Sociology, Theology
ISBN Prefix(es): 978-3-900767; 978-3-85165
Total Titles: 700 Print
Orders to: Runge Verlagsauslieferung GmbH, Bergstr 2, 33803 Steinhagen, Germany, Contact: Team 3 *Tel:* (05204) 998 123 *Fax:* (05204) 998 114 *E-mail:* msr@rungeva.de *Web Site:* rungeva.de (Austria & Germany)
Herder AG Basel, Muttenzerstr 109, 4133 Pratteln 1, Switzerland *Tel:* (061) 827 90 *Fax:* (061) 827 90 67 *E-mail:* sales@herder.ch

Phoibos Verlag+
Anzengrubergasse 16, 1050 Vienna
Tel: (01) 544 03 191 *Fax:* (01) 544 03 199
E-mail: office@phoibos.at
Web Site: www.phoibos.at
Key Personnel
Mng Dir: Roman Jacobek
Founded: 1992
Subjects: Antiques, Archaeology, Art, Biblical Studies, History, Library & Information Sciences, Transportation, Travel & Tourism
ISBN Prefix(es): 978-3-901232; 978-3-85161

Pichler Verlag, *imprint of* Verlagsgruppe Styria GmbH & Co KG

Picus Verlag GesmbH
Friedrich Schmidt Platz 4, 1080 Vienna
Tel: (01) 408 18 21 *Fax:* (01) 408 18 216
E-mail: info@picus.at; presse@picus.at; vertrieb@picus.at
Web Site: www.picus.at
Key Personnel
Publishing Dir & Program Management: Dorothea Loecker *E-mail:* loecker@picus.at; Alexander Potyka *E-mail:* potyka@picus.at
Licensing & Sales: Barbara Giller *Tel:* (01) 408 18 21 14
Press & Events: Helene Griendl *Tel:* (01) 408 18 21 12
Founded: 1984
Subjects: Architecture & Interior Design, Biography, Memoirs, Fiction, History, Literature, Literary Criticism, Essays, Nonfiction (General), Travel & Tourism
ISBN Prefix(es): 978-3-85452
Number of titles published annually: 40 Print

Richard Pils Bibliothek der Provinz+
Grosswolfgers 29, 3970 Weitra
Tel: (02856) 37 94 *Fax:* (02856) 37 92
E-mail: verlag@bibliothekderprovinz.at
Web Site: www.bibliothekderprovinz.at
Key Personnel
Publisher: Richard Pils
Editing: Barbara Fink *Tel:* (02856) 37 94-12
Founded: 1989

Subjects: Art, Cookery, Drama, Theater, Fiction, Literature, Literary Criticism, Essays, Music, Dance, Photography, Poetry
ISBN Prefix(es): 978-3-900878; 978-3-85252; 978-3-900000; 978-3-901862; 978-3-902414; 978-3-902415; 978-3-902416
Number of titles published annually: 50 Print
Total Titles: 700 Print

plattform Johannes Martinek Verlag
Herzogbergstr 210, 2380 Perchtoldsdorf
Tel: (01) 923 56 59; (0650) 865 53 95 (cell)
Fax: (01) 923 56 59
E-mail: office@plattform-martinek.at
Web Site: www.plattform-martinek.at
Key Personnel
Publisher: Ingrid Martinek; Dr Johannes Martinek
Subjects: Biography, Memoirs, Fiction, History, Poetry, Culture, Social Policy
ISBN Prefix(es): 978-3-9503295; 978-3-9502885

Promedia Verlag+
Wickenburggasse 5/12, 1080 Vienna
Tel: (01) 405 27 02 *Fax:* (01) 405 27 02 22
E-mail: promedia@mediashop.at
Web Site: www.mediashop.at/typolight/index.php/home.html
Key Personnel
Mng Dir: Erich Ertl
Founded: 1983
Subjects: Anthropology, Architecture & Interior Design, Biography, Memoirs, Developing Countries, Foreign Countries, Government, Political Science, History, Nonfiction (General), Travel & Tourism, Women's Studies
ISBN Prefix(es): 978-3-900478; 978-3-85371
Number of titles published annually: 20 Print
Total Titles: 300 Print
Distribution Center: Mohr Morawa Buchvertrieb GmbH, Sulzengasse 2, 1230 Vienna *Tel:* (01) 680 14-0 *Fax:* (01) 688 71 30 *E-mail:* momo@mohrmorawa.at *Web Site:* www.mohrmorawa.at
Prolit Verlagsauslieferung, Siemensstr 16, 35463 Fernwald, Germany *Tel:* (0641) 94393-23; (0641) 94393-26 *Fax:* (0641) 94393-29 *E-mail:* g.hoerr@prolit.de
AVA Verlagsauslieferung AG, Centralweg 16, 8910 Affoltern am Albis, Switzerland *Tel:* (044) 762 42 00 *Fax:* (044) 762 42 10 (orders) *E-mail:* avainfo@ava.ch

PROverbis eU+
Obere Donaustr 21/1/8, 1020 Vienna
Tel: (01) 2763593 *Fax:* (01) 276359315
E-mail: office@proverbis.at; verlag@proverbis.at
Web Site: www.proverbis.at
Key Personnel
Owner: Andreas Schinko *Tel:* (0676) 9446020 (cell) *E-mail:* schinko@proverbis.at
Founded: 2007
Membership(s): Fachverband der Buch- und Medienwirtschaft; Hauptverband des Oesterreichischen Buchhandels.
ISBN Prefix(es): 978-3-9502506 (2008-2010); 978-3-9502912 (2010-2011); 978-3-902838 (2011-)
Number of titles published annually: 5 Print
Total Titles: 50 Print
Distribution Center: Medienlogistik Pichler-OEBZ GmbH & Co KG, IZ-NOE Sued, Str 1, Objekt 34, 2355 Wiener Neudorf, Contact: Eva Prinz *Tel:* (02236) 63 535-290 *Fax:* (02236) 63 535-243 *E-mail:* mlo@medien-logistik.at *Web Site:* www.medien-logistik.at
GVA Gemeinsame Verlagsauslieferung Gottingen GmbH & Co KG, Postfach 2021, 37010 Goettingen, Germany, Contact: Anja Klimaschewski *Tel:* (0551) 384200-27 *E-mail:* klimaschewski@gva-verlage.de

Verlag Anton Pustet+
Bergstr 12, 5020 Salzburg

Tel: (0662) 873507-0 *Fax:* (0662) 873507-79
E-mail: buch@spv-verlage.at
Web Site: www.pustet.at
Key Personnel
Publishing Dir: Gerald Klonner *Tel:* (0662) 873507-20 *E-mail:* gerald.klonner@spv-verlage.at
Marketing & Sales: Katrin Lackner *Tel:* (0662) 873507-55 *E-mail:* katrin.lackner@spv-verlage.at
Founded: 1592
Subjects: Architecture & Interior Design, Art, Cookery, Fiction, History, Philosophy, Psychology, Psychiatry, Regional Interests, Theology, Travel & Tourism
ISBN Prefix(es): 978-3-7025
Number of titles published annually: 20 Print
Total Titles: 180 Print; 2 CD-ROM
Distribution Center: Art Stock Books/Independent Publishers Group (IPG), 814 N Franklin St, Chicago, IL 60610, United States

Redelsteiner Dahimene Verlag
Zirkusgasse 27/9, 1020 Vienna
Key Personnel
Founder & Manager: Ilias Dahimene *E-mail:* dahimene@rdedition.com; Stefan Redelsteiner *E-mail:* redelsteiner@rdedition.com
Founded: 2013
Subjects: Literature, Literary Criticism, Essays, Nonfiction (General)
ISBN Prefix(es): 978-3-9503359

Resch Verlag Innsbruck+
Maximilianstr 8, 6020 Innsbruck
Mailing Address: Postfach 8, 6010 Innsbruck
Tel: (0512) 574772 *Fax:* (0512) 574772-16
E-mail: info@igw-resch-verlag.at
Web Site: www.igw-resch-verlag.at
Key Personnel
Publisher: Andreas Resch
Founded: 1974
Subjects: Parapsychology, Physics, Science (General), Theology, Ethics
ISBN Prefix(es): 978-3-85382
Parent Company: Institut fuer Grenzgebiete der Wissenschaft (IGW)

Residenz Verlag im Niederosterreichische Pressehaus Druck- und Verlagsgesellschaft mbH+
Muehlstr 7, 5023 Salzburg-Gnigl
Tel: (0662) 641 900-0 *Fax:* (0662) 641 900-150
E-mail: info@residenzverlag.at
Web Site: www.residenzverlag.at
Key Personnel
Mng Dir: Claudia Romeder *Tel:* (0512) 13 33 -200 *E-mail:* c.romeder@residenzverlag.at; Roswitha Wonka *Tel:* (0662) 0641 900-100 *E-mail:* r.wonka@residenzverlag.at
Foreign Rights: Nina Stren *E-mail:* n.stren@residenzverlag.at
Marketing & Sales Management: Roland Tomrle *Tel:* (0662) 0641 900-101 *E-mail:* r.tomrle@residenzverlag.at
Press & Public Relations: Heidi Selbach *Tel:* (0512) 13 33-203 *E-mail:* h.selbach@residenzverlag.at
Founded: 1956
Subjects: Animals, Pets, Architecture & Interior Design, Art, Biography, Memoirs, Cookery, Criminology, Drama, Theater, Fiction, Gardening, Plants, Health, Nutrition, History, House & Home, Human Relations, Humor, Literature, Literary Criticism, Essays, Nonfiction (General), Outdoor Recreation, Poetry, Sports, Athletics, Travel & Tourism, Wine & Spirits
ISBN Prefix(es): 978-3-7017
Number of titles published annually: 50 Print
Total Titles: 400 Print
Foreign Rep(s): Agentur Gudrun Hebel (Germany); Balla & Tsa Irodalmi Uegynoekseg

(Catherina Balla) (Hungary); Donzelli Fietta Agency Srls (Stefania Fietta) (Italy); Graal Literary Agency (Tomasz Berezinski) (Poland); Hercules Business & Culture Development (Hongjun Cai) (China, Taiwan); ICSTI (Tatjana Vaniat) (Russia); Internationaal Literatuur Bureau (Linda Kohn) (Netherlands); International Editors (Henriette Hubacher) (Latin America, Portugal, Spain); International Editors (Flavia Sala) (Brazil); L'Autre agence (Marie Lannurien) (France); Jennifer Lyons Literary Agency (USA); Meike Marx Literary Agency (Japan); Momo Agency (Geenie Han) (China, Taiwan); Onk Agency (Idil Pisgin) (Turkey); Katia Schumer (Turkey); Shin Won Agency (Nayoung Lee) (China, Taiwan)
Distribution Center: Mohr Morawa Buchvertrieb GmbH, Sulzengasse 2, 1232 Vienna *Tel:* (01) 680 14-0 *Fax:* (01) 688 71 30 *E-mail:* bestellung@mohrmorawa.at
Leipziger Kommissions- und- Grossbuchhandelsgesellschaft mbH (LKG), An der Suedspitze 1-12, 04571 Roetha, Germany, Contact: Ursula Fritzsche *Tel:* (034206) 65-100 *Fax:* (034206) 65-110 *E-mail:* ursula.fritzsche@lkg-service.de *Web Site:* www.lkg-va.de
AVA Verlagsauslieferung AG, Centralweg 16, 8910 Affoltern am Albis, Switzerland *Tel:* (01) 762 42 00 *Fax:* (01) 762 42 10 *E-mail:* verlagservice@ava.ch

Rhombus Verlag GmbH
Schottenfeldgasse 24, 1070 Vienna
Tel: (01) 52 661 52 *Fax:* (01) 52 287 18
Subjects: Literature, Literary Criticism, Essays, Avant Garde & Experimental Literature
ISBN Prefix(es): 978-3-85394
Number of titles published annually: 1 Print
Total Titles: 20 Print

edition riedenburg
Anton-Hochmuth-Str 8, 5020 Salzburg
Tel: (0664) 12 43 193 *Fax:* (0662) 234 663 234
E-mail: verlag@editionriedenburg.at
Web Site: www.editionriedenburg.at
Key Personnel
Publishing Dir: Dr Caroline Oblasser *E-mail:* co@editionriedenburg.at
Founded: 2007
Subjects: Child Care & Development, Education, Parenting
ISBN Prefix(es): 978-3-902943; 978-3-902647; 978-3-903085; 978-3-9502357

Ritter Verlag KG+
Hagenstr 3, 9020 Klagenfurt
Tel: (0463) 42631 *Fax:* (0463) 42631-37
E-mail: office@ritterbooks.com
Web Site: www.ritterbooks.com
Key Personnel
Owner: Karin Ritter
Publisher: Helmut Ritter
Editor: Martina Mosebach-Ritter
Founded: 1980
Subjects: Architecture & Interior Design, Art, Literature, Literary Criticism, Essays, Music, Dance, Art Theory, Exhibition
ISBN Prefix(es): 978-3-85415
Distribution Center: Dr Franz Hain, Dr-Otto-Neurathgasse 5, 1220 Vienna *Tel:* (01) 282 65 65 77 *Fax:* (01) 282 52 82
Runge Verlagsauslieferung GmbH, Bergstr 2, 33803 Steinhagen, Germany, Contact: Team 3 *Tel:* (05204) 998 123 *Fax:* (05204) 998 114 *E-mail:* msr@rungeva.de *Web Site:* rungeva.de

Edition Roesner
Bad Str 3/6, 2340 Moedling
Tel: (02236) 23 5 40; (0664) 234 44 67 (cell)
Fax: (02236) 23 5 40
E-mail: office@edition-roesner.at
Web Site: www.edition-roesner.at

Key Personnel
Publishing Management & Editing: Nadja Roesner-Krisch
Public Relations & Editing: Laura Roesner
Founded: 2002
Subjects: Art, Fiction, Literature, Literary Criticism, Essays, Philosophy, Poetry
ISBN Prefix(es): 978-3-902300

Roetzer Druck GmbH
Joseph Haydngasse 32, 7000 Eisenstadt
Tel: (02682) 624 94 *Fax:* (02682) 624 94 4
E-mail: office@roetzerdruck.at
Web Site: www.roetzerdruck.at
Key Personnel
Mng Dir: Rainer Roetzer *E-mail:* rainer.roetzer@roetzerdruck.at
Founded: 1969
Subjects: Physics
ISBN Prefix(es): 978-3-85253

Zeitschriftenverlag St Gabriel+
Gabrielerstr 171, 2340 Maria Enzersdorf
Tel: (02236) 803 859; (0664) 621 6934
Fax: (02236) 24483
E-mail: presse@steyler.at
Web Site: www.steyler.at/svd/medien/zeitschriftenverlage
Key Personnel
Press: P Christian Tauchner
Founded: 1901
Subjects: Religion - Catholic, Theology
ISBN Prefix(es): 978-3-85264; 978-3-901781
Number of titles published annually: 8 Print
Total Titles: 40 Print
Parent Company: Steyler Missionare eV, Bahnhofstr 9, 41334 Nettetal, Germany
Distributed by Rex-Verlag (Switzerland); Steyler Verlag (Germany)
Bookshop(s): St Gabriel Missionsbuchhandlung, Stephansplatz 6, 1010 Vienna *Tel:* (01) 5122105 *Fax:* (01) 5122105

Verlag St Peter GmbH
Erzabtei St Peter, St Peter-Bezirk 1, 5010 Salzburg
Mailing Address: Postfach 113, 5010 Salzburg
Tel: (0662) 842166-82 *Fax:* (0662) 842166-80
E-mail: info@verlag-st-peter.at
Web Site: www.stift-stpeter.at
Key Personnel
Editor & Production: Dr Elisabeth Nowak
Founded: 1946
Subjects: Art, Regional Interests, Religion - Other
ISBN Prefix(es): 978-3-900173

Verlag fuer Sammler+
Hofgasse 5, 8010 Graz
Mailing Address: Postfach 438, 8011 Graz
Tel: (0316) 82 16 36 *Fax:* (0316) 83 56 12
E-mail: stocker-verlag@stocker-verlag.com
Web Site: www.stocker-verlag.com/stocker/buch_sammler.htm
Founded: 1968
Subjects: Art, History, Natural History, Social Sciences, Sociology
ISBN Prefix(es): 978-3-85365
Parent Company: Leopold Stocker Verlag GmbH

Dr A Schendl GmbH & Co KG
Geblergasse 95/8, 1170 Vienna
Tel: (01) 906 80-12 *Fax:* (01) 906 80-91299
E-mail: info@schendl.at
Web Site: www.schendl.at
Key Personnel
Publisher: Dr A Schendl
Founded: 1965
Also packager, warehouse, promoter.
Subjects: Economics, Ethnicity, Geography, Geology, History, Literature, Literary Criticism, Essays, Music, Dance, Natural History
ISBN Prefix(es): 978-3-85268

Schlager Verlag, see Astor-Verlag, Willibald Schlager

Schnider Verlag
Peterstalstr 127, 8042 Graz
Tel: (0664) 3575444
E-mail: office@schnider.at
Web Site: www.schnider.at
Key Personnel
Owner: Dr Andreas Schnider
Founded: 1989
Subjects: Archaeology, Architecture & Interior Design, Art, Computer Science, Education, Electronics, Electrical Engineering, Fiction, Government, Political Science, History, Law, Literature, Literary Criticism, Essays, Photography, Poetry, Psychology, Psychiatry, Religion - Catholic, Religion - Other, Theology, Veterinary Science
ISBN Prefix(es): 978-3-900993; 978-3-902020; 978-3-901902

Schubert & Franzke GesmbH Kartografischer Verlag
Kranzbichlerstr 57, 3100 St Poelten
Tel: (02742) 785 01-0 *Fax:* (02742) 785 01-15
E-mail: office@schubert-franzke.com
Web Site: www.schubert-franzke.com
Key Personnel
Mng Partner: Josef Scheibenreif *E-mail:* j.scheibenreif@schubert-franzke.com
Project Manager: Albert Seltenheim *Tel:* (02742) 785 01-84 *E-mail:* a.seltenheim@schubert-franzke.com
Production: Christian Schirmbrand *Tel:* (02742) 785 01-77 *E-mail:* c.schirmbrand@schubert-franzke.com
Subjects: Geography, Geology, Regional Interests
ISBN Prefix(es): 978-3-7056; 978-3-900938
Branch Office(s)
S C Schubert & Franzke SRL Editura Cartografica, Str Plopilor nr 83, 400383 Cluj-Napoca, Romania *Tel:* (0364) 10 39 31 *Fax:* (0264) 428 611

Verlagsbuero Schwarzer
Ziegelofengasse 27/1/2, 1050 Vienna
Tel: (01) 548 13 15 *Fax:* (01) 548 13 15-39
E-mail: verlagsbuero@schwarzer.at
Web Site: www.schwarzer.at
Key Personnel
Mng Dir: Oskar Hejlek *Tel:* (01) 548 13 15-34 *E-mail:* oskar.hejlek@schwarzer.at
Deputy Mng Dir: Christine Kollegger *Tel:* (01) 548 13 15-38 *E-mail:* christine.kollegger@schwarzer.at
Sales Manager: Sonja Ueberhuber *E-mail:* sonja.ueberhuber@schwarzer.at
Marketing & Sales: Roland Tomrie *Tel:* (01) 548 13 15-13 *E-mail:* roland.tomrie@schwarzer.at
Public Relations: Petra Kern *Tel:* (01) 548 13 15-34 *E-mail:* petra.kern@schwarzer.at
Subjects: Fiction, Nonfiction (General)
ISBN Prefix(es): 978-3-900392

Seifert Verlag GmbH
Ungargasse 45/13, 1030 Vienna
Tel: (01) 712 79 55-0 *Fax:* (01) 712 79 55-25
E-mail: office@seifertverlag.at
Web Site: www.seifertverlag.at
Key Personnel
Publishing Dir: Dr Maria Seifert *Tel:* (01) 712 79 55-21 *E-mail:* maria.seifert@seifertverlag.at
Administration & Public Relations: Laura Seifert *Tel:* (01) 712 79 55-22 *E-mail:* laura.seifert@seifertverlag.at
Subjects: Fiction, Nonfiction (General)
ISBN Prefix(es): 978-3-902406
Distribution Center: Mohr Morawa Buchvertrieb GmbH, Sulzengasse 2, 1230 Vienna *Tel:* (01) 680 14-0 *Fax:* (01) 688 71 30 *E-mail:* momo@mohrmorawa.at *Web Site:* www.mohrmorawa.at

Herold Verlagsauslieferung und Logistik GmbH, Raiffeisenalle 10, 82041 Oberhaching, Germany *Tel:* (089) 61 38 71-24 *Fax:* (089) 61 38 71-5524 *E-mail:* m.spielhaupter@herold-va.de
Web Site: www.herold-va.de

Septime Verlag eU
Johannagasse 15-17/18, 1050 Vienna
Tel: (01) 664 164 28 92
E-mail: office@septime-verlag.at
Web Site: www.septime-verlag.at
Key Personnel
Manager: Juergen Schuetz *E-mail:* js@septime-verlag.at
Public Relations & Licenses: Sabrina Gmeiner *E-mail:* sg@septime-verlag.at
Founded: 2008
Subjects: Fiction, Mysteries, Suspense
ISBN Prefix(es): 978-3-902711

Verlag Sisyphus
Bahnstr 25, 9020 Klagenfurt
Tel: (0650) 7779122 *Fax:* (0463) 242246
E-mail: kontakt@sisyphus.at
Web Site: www.sisyphus.at
Founded: 1987
Subjects: Fiction, Poetry
ISBN Prefix(es): 978-3-901960; 978-3-9500149

Solaris Edition
Helferstorferstr 4, 1010 Vienna
Tel: (01) 689 75 66 *Fax:* (01) 689 75 66-4
E-mail: office@solarisweb.at
Web Site: www.solarisedition.at
Key Personnel
Mng Dir: E Strauss
Founded: 1998
Subjects: Inspirational, Spirituality
ISBN Prefix(es): 978-3-901975; 978-3-901971
Parent Company: LAST&CO Verlag

Sonderzahl Verlagsgesellschaft mbH
Grosse Neugasse 35/15, 1040 Vienna
Tel: (01) 586 80 70 *Fax:* (01) 586 80 70
E-mail: sonderzahl-verlag@chello.at
Web Site: www.sonderzahl.at
Key Personnel
Publisher: Dieter Bandhauer
Editorial: Dr Wolfgang Straub
Membership(s): Association of Austrian Private Publishing Houses; Austrian Chamber of Commerce; Federation of Austrian Book Trade.
Subjects: Architecture & Interior Design, History, Literature, Literary Criticism, Essays, Poetry
ISBN Prefix(es): 978-3-85449

Springer-Verlag GmbH+
Sachsenplatz 4-6, 1201 Vienna
Mailing Address: PO Box 89, 1201 Vienna
Tel: (01) 330 24 15 *Fax:* (01) 330 24 26
E-mail: springer@springer.at; books@springer.at (orders); journals@springer.com (orders)
Web Site: www.springer.com/de
Key Personnel
Editorial Rights: Levente Istvan Koltai *Tel:* (01) 330 24 15-512 *E-mail:* levente.koltai@springer.at
Founded: 1924
Subjects: Anthropology, Architecture & Interior Design, Art, Biological Sciences, Business, Chemistry, Chemical Engineering, Civil Engineering, Communications, Computer Science, Economics, Education, Electronics, Electrical Engineering, Engineering (General), Environmental Studies, Law, Mathematics, Mechanical Engineering, Medicine, Nursing, Dentistry, Philosophy, Physics, Psychology, Psychiatry, Science (General), Technology
ISBN Prefix(es): 978-3-211; 978-3-7091

Associate Companies: Springer-Verlag New York Inc, 233 Spring St, New York, NY 10013, United States *Tel:* 212-460-1500 *Fax:* 212-460-1700 *E-mail:* customerservice@springer.com
Distributor for Springer; Steinkopff

Stadtmuseum Graz GmbH
Sackstr 18, 8010 Graz
Tel: (0316) 872-7600
E-mail: stadtmuseum@stadt.graz.at
Web Site: www.stadtmuseumgraz.at
Key Personnel
Dir: Otto Hochreiter *Tel:* (0316) 872-7605
Commercial Manager: Sibylle Dienesch *Tel:* (0316) 872-7601
Subjects: Art, History, Regional Interests
ISBN Prefix(es): 978-3-900764
Total Titles: 275 Print

J Steinbrener KG+
Im Eichbuechl 1, 4780 Schaerding
Tel: (07712) 20 38 *Fax:* (07712) 203820
E-mail: steinbrener@aon.at
Web Site: www.steinbrener.at
Founded: 1855
Subjects: Religion - Other
ISBN Prefix(es): 978-3-85296
Branch Office(s)
Wagnerstr 21, 94152 Neuhaus, Germany
Tel: (08503) 341

STEINVERLAG OG
Oberer Markt 7, 3632 Bad Traunstein
Tel: (0664) 13 003 31 (cell) *Fax:* (02742) 222 3333236
E-mail: office@steinverlag.at
Web Site: www.steinverlag.at
Subjects: Art, Biography, Memoirs, Gardening, Plants, Government, Political Science
ISBN Prefix(es): 978-3-901392

Leopold Stocker Verlag GmbH+
Hofgasse 5, 8011 Graz
Mailing Address: Postfach 438, 8011 Graz
Tel: (0316) 82 16 36 *Fax:* (0316) 83 56 12
E-mail: stocker-verlag@stocker-verlag.com
Web Site: www.stocker-verlag.com
Key Personnel
Publishing Dir: Wolfgang Dvorak-Stocker
Marketing & Sales: Franz Koiner *E-mail:* franz.koiner@stocker-verlag.com
Press: Carina Spielberger *E-mail:* carina.spielberger@stocker-verlag.com
Production: Bernhard Stroissnigg *E-mail:* bernhard.stroissnigg@stocker-verlag.com
Founded: 1917
Subjects: Agriculture, Cookery, Crafts, Games, Hobbies, Gardening, Plants, Government, Political Science, Health, Nutrition, History, Military Science, Nonfiction (General), Wine & Spirits, Beekeeping, Hiking, Hunting, Nature
ISBN Prefix(es): 978-3-7020; 978-3-85365; 978-3-902475
Imprints: Ares Verlag

Dr Paul Struzl GmbH, see ADEVA (Akademische Druck-u Verlagsanstalt)

StudienVerlag GesmbH+
Erlerstr 10, 6020 Innsbruck
Tel: (0512) 395045 *Fax:* (0512) 395045 15
E-mail: order@studienverlag.at
Web Site: www.studienverlag.at
Key Personnel
Publisher: Markus Hatzer *Tel:* (0512) 395045 11 *E-mail:* m.hatzer@studienverlag.at
Licenses: Anna Stock *Tel:* (0512) 395045 21 *E-mail:* a.stock@studienverlag.at
Marketing: Marion Bernhard *Tel:* (0512) 395045 38 *E-mail:* m.bernhard@studienverlag.at

Founded: 1990
Subjects: Architecture & Interior Design, Communications, Education, History, Journalism, Language Arts, Linguistics, Literature, Literary Criticism, Essays, Music, Dance, Philosophy, Science (General), Social Sciences, Sociology, Women's Studies, Cultural Science, Media
ISBN Prefix(es): 978-3-901160; 978-3-7065
Number of titles published annually: 80 Print
Total Titles: 1,500 Print
Distribution Center: Mohr Morawa Buchvertrieb GmbH, Sulzengasse 2, 1230 Vienna *Tel:* (01) 680 14-0 *Fax:* (01) 688 71 30 *E-mail:* momo@mohrmorawa.at *Web Site:* www.mohrmorawa.at (Austria & Europe)
Transaction Publishers Distribution, Dept CAT64 2005, 390 Campus Dr, Somerset, NJ 08873, United States *Tel:* 732-445-1245 *Fax:* 732-748-9801 (UK & USA, English titles)

Styria Premium, *imprint of* Verlagsgruppe Styria GmbH & Co KG

Styria Regional (Carinthia Verlag, Edition Oberoesterreich), *imprint of* Verlagsgruppe Styria GmbH & Co KG

Verlagsgruppe Styria GmbH & Co KG+
Lobkowitzplatz 1, 1010 Vienna
Tel: (01) 512 8808-0 *Fax:* (01) 512 8808-75
E-mail: office@styriabooks.at
Web Site: www.verlagsgruppestyria.at
Key Personnel
Publishing Dir: Gerda Schaffelhofer *E-mail:* gerda.schaffelhofer@styriabooks.at
Marketing Dir: Reinhard Deutsch *Tel:* (01) 512 8808-51 *E-mail:* reinhard.deutsch@styriabooks.at
Mng Editor: Dr Johannes Sachslehner *Tel:* (01) 512 8808-50 *E-mail:* johannes.sachslehner@styriabooks.at
Assistant Manager, Rights & Licensing: Alexander Zwickl *Tel:* (01) 512-8808-84 *E-mail:* alexander.zwickl@styriabooks.at
Press & Public Relations: Catharina Rosenauer *Tel:* (01) 512 8808-83 *E-mail:* catharina.rosenauer@styriabooks.at
Founded: 1793
Subjects: Biography, Memoirs, Cookery, Government, Political Science, Health, Nutrition, Inspirational, Spirituality, Literature, Literary Criticism, Essays, Poetry, Sports, Athletics, Theology, Travel & Tourism
ISBN Prefix(es): 978-3-85431 (Pichler); 978-3-85378 (Carinthia); 978-3-7012 (Oberoesterreich); 978-3-85485 (Molden)
Number of titles published annually: 80 Print
Total Titles: 600 Print
Imprints: Molden Verlag; Pichler Verlag; Styria Premium; Styria Regional (Carinthia Verlag, Edition Oberoesterreich)
Subsidiaries: Kneipp Verlag
Branch Office(s)
Schoenaugasse 64, 8010 Graz *Tel:* (0316) 8063-7601 *Fax:* (0316) 8063-7004
Voelkermarkter Ring 25, 9020 Klagenfurt *Tel:* (0463) 501 220-212 *Fax:* (0463) 501 220-214

Suedwind-Buchwelt Buchhandelsges mbH
Schwarzpanierstr 15, 1090 Vienna
Tel: (01) 405 44 34; (01) 798 83 49-0 *Fax:* (01) 798 83 75-15
Web Site: www.suedwind-buchwelt.at
Founded: 1984
Subjects: Government, Political Science, Nonfiction (General)
ISBN Prefix(es): 978-3-900592
Total Titles: 25 Print

Edition Tandem
Michael-Pacher-Str 25A, 5020 Salzburg

Tel: (0662) 634220; (0664) 1605141 (cell) *Fax:* (0662) 634870
E-mail: verlag@edition-tandem.at; lektorat@edition-tandem.at
Web Site: www.edition-tandem.at
Key Personnel
Owner: Ludwig Volker Toth
Subjects: Education, Nonfiction (General), Poetry, Science (General)
ISBN Prefix(es): 978-3-902932; 978-3-902606

Verlag der Technischen Universitaet Graz
Technikerstr 4, 8010 Graz
Tel: (0316) 873 6157
E-mail: verlag@tugraz.at
Web Site: www.ub.tugraz.at/verlag
Key Personnel
Contact: Gabriele Gross
ISBN Prefix(es): 978-3-901351; 978-3-902465; 978-3-85125

Edition Thanhaeuser
Wallseerstr 6, 4100 Ottensheim an der Donau
Tel: (07234) 83800 *Fax:* (07234) 83800
E-mail: thanhaeuser@ottensheim.at
Web Site: www.thanhaeuser.at
Key Personnel
Contact: Christian Thanhaeuser
Founded: 1989
Subjects: Poetry
ISBN Prefix(es): 978-3-900986
Total Titles: 40 Print

Trauner Verlag + Buchservice GmbH
Koeglstr 14, 4020 Linz
Tel: (0732) 77 82 41-0 *Fax:* (0732) 77 82 41-400
E-mail: office@trauner.at
Web Site: www.trauner.at
Key Personnel
Mng Dir: Ingrid Trauner *Tel:* (0732) 77 82 41-203 *E-mail:* i.trauner@trauner.at; Dr Rudolf Trauner *Tel:* (0732) 77 82 41-212 *E-mail:* rudolf.trauner@trauner.at
Founded: 1946
Subjects: Cookery, Medicine, Nursing, Dentistry, Science (General)
ISBN Prefix(es): 978-3-85320; 978-3-85487; 978-3-85499; 978-3-9500931

Verlag Turia + Kant
Schottengasse 3A/5/DG 1, 1010 Vienna
Tel: (01) 925 16 05 *Fax:* (01) 923 09 76
E-mail: info@turia.at
Web Site: www.turia.at
Key Personnel
Publisher: Ingo Vavra *E-mail:* ingo.vavra@turia.at
Founded: 1989
Subjects: Government, Political Science, Literature, Literary Criticism, Essays, Philosophy, Psychology, Psychiatry
ISBN Prefix(es): 978-3-85132
Branch Office(s)
Crellestr 14/Remise, 10827 Berlin, Germany, Contact: Olga von Schubert *Tel:* (030) 612 963 74 *Fax:* (030) 612 936 78 *E-mail:* berlin@turia.at
Distribution Center: Mohr Morawa Buchvertrieb GmbH, Sulzengasse 2, 1230 Vienna *Tel:* (01) 680 14-0 *Fax:* (01) 688 71 30 *E-mail:* momo@mohrmorawa.at *Web Site:* www.mohrmorawa.at
Runge Verlagsauslieferung GmbH, Bergstr 2, 33803 Steinhagen, Germany, Contact: Team 3 *Tel:* (05204) 998 123 *Fax:* (05204) 998 114 *E-mail:* msr@rungeva.de *Web Site:* rungeva.de

Tyrolia Verlag
Exlgasse 20, 6020 Innsbruck
Tel: (0512) 2233-202; (0512) 2233-211 (ordering) *Fax:* (0512) 2233-206
E-mail: buchverlag@tyrolia.at; auslieferung@tyrolia.at
Web Site: www.tyrolia-verlag.at

Key Personnel
Publishing Dir: Gottfried Kompatscher *E-mail:* g.
kompatscher@tyrolia.at
Marketing: Gerhard Roedlach *Tel:* (0512) 2233-
143 *E-mail:* gerhard.roedlach@tyrolia.at
Press & Foreign Rights: Monika Resler
Tel: (0512) 2233-213 *E-mail:* monika.resler@
tyrolia.at
Sales & Distribution: Gabriela Exel *Tel:* (0512)
2233-211 *E-mail:* gabriela.exel@tyrolia.at
Founded: 1888
Subjects: Mysteries, Suspense, Nonfiction (General), Religion - Other, Theology, Travel &
Tourism
ISBN Prefix(es): 978-3-7022
Orders to: Mohr Morawa Buchvertrieb GmbH,
Sulzengasse 2, 1230 Vienna *Tel:* (01) 680
14-0 *Fax:* (01) 688 71 30 *E-mail:* momo@
mohrmorawa.at *Web Site:* www.mohrmorawa.at
Auslieferungszentrum Niederrhein (AZN),
Hoogeweg 71, 47623 Kevelaer, Germany,
Contact: Helga Behr *Tel:* (02832) 929-290
Fax: (02832) 929-211 *E-mail:* helga.behr@
azn.de
Athesiabuch GmbH, Buchauslieferung, Weinbergweg 1, 39100 Bozen, Italy, Contact: Igor
Planinschek *Tel:* (0471) 927620 *Fax:* (0471)
927431 *E-mail:* buchauslieferung.buch@
athesia.it
Herder AG Basel, Muttenzerstr 109, 4133 Pratteln
1, Switzerland *Tel:* (061) 8279060 *Fax:* (061)
8279067 *E-mail:* verkauf@herder.ch

Verlag Carl Ueberreuter GmbH+
Alser Str, 1090 Vienna
Tel: (01) 40 444-0 *Fax:* (01) 40 444-5
E-mail: office@ueberreuter.at
Web Site: www.ueberreuter.at
Key Personnel
Mng Dir: Klaus Kaempfe-Burghardt *Tel:* (01) 40
444-175 *E-mail:* kkb@ueberreuter.de
Marketing Manager: Katrin Hehberger *Tel:* (030)
65 21 623-31 *Fax:* (030) 65 21 623-66
E-mail: katrin.hehberger@ueberreuter.de
Foreign Rights: Julia Balogh *Tel:* (030) 65 21
623-25 *E-mail:* julia.balogh@ueberreuter.de
Founded: 1946
Subjects: Animals, Pets, Art, Astrology, Occult,
Biography, Memoirs, Child Care & Development, Economics, Fiction, Government, Political Science, Health, Nutrition, History, Humor,
Music, Dance, Nonfiction (General), Science
(General), Science Fiction, Fantasy, Self-Help,
Cartoons
ISBN Prefix(es): 978-3-219
Number of titles published annually: 300 Print; 5
CD-ROM; 8 Audio
Total Titles: 1,500 Print; 20 CD-ROM; 20 Audio
Associate Companies: G&G Verlagsgesellschaft
mbH
Imprints: Annette Betz Verlag
Subsidiaries: Lappan Verlag GmbH
Branch Office(s)
Ueberreuter Verlag GmbH, Prinzenstr 85D,
10969 Berlin, Germany *Tel:* (030) 65 21 623
10 *Fax:* (030) 65 21 623 66 *E-mail:* office@
ueberreuter.de
Foreign Rights: Agente Literaria (Martina Nommel) (Latin America, Spain); Akcali Copyright
Agency (Bengu Ayfer) (Turkey); ART Dialog (Daniela Vranovska) (Czechia); English
Agency (Corinne Shoij) (Japan); Agencja Literacka Graal (Joanna Maciuk) (Poland); Hercules
Business & Culture Development (Hongjun
Cai) (China); Internationaal Literatuur Bureau (Linda Kohn) (Netherlands); Iris Literary
Agency (Catherine Fragou) (Greece); Japan
Uni Agency (Maiko Fujinaga) (Japan); Nurcihan Kesim Literary Agency Inc (Filiz Karaman) (Turkey); Marx Agency (Meike Marx)
(Japan); Motovun (Mari Koga) (Japan); Natoli
Stefan & Oliva (Roberta Oliva) (Italy); ONK
Agency Ltd (Hatice Gok) (Turkey); Pikarski

(Gabi Hertzmann) (Israel); ZNN Agency (Nurgul Senefe) (Turkey)
Distribution Center: arvato media GmbH, Vereinigte Verlagsauslieferung, An der Autobahn
100, 33333 Guetersloh, Germany *Tel:* (05241)
80-3877 *Fax:* (05241) 80-66959
Medien-Logistik Pichler OEBZ GmbH & Co KG,
IZ NOE Sued, Str 1, Objekt 34, 2355 Wiener
Neudorf *Tel:* (02236) 63535 290 *Fax:* (02236)
63535 243 *Web Site:* www.medien-logistik.at
Buchzentrum AG, Industriestr Ost 10, 4614 Haegendorf, Switzerland *Tel:* (062) 209 26 26
Fax: (062) 209 26 27

unartproduktion
Wallenmahd 23, C1, 2nd floor, 6850 Dornbirn
Tel: (05572) 23019
E-mail: office@unartproduktion.at
Web Site: www.unartproduktion.at
Key Personnel
Publisher: Ulrich Gabriel *E-mail:* unart@
unartproduktion.at
Founded: 1984
Subjects: Art, Culture
ISBN Prefix(es): 978-3-901325
Branch Office(s)
Schlager Gasse 7/13, 1090 Vienna, Contact: Dr Lucia Mennel *Tel:* (01) 799 4447
E-mail: officewein@unartproduktion.at
Distribution Center: Barsortiment G Umbreit
GmbH & Co KG, Mundelsheimer Str 3, 74321
Bietigheim-Bissingen, Germany *Tel:* (07142)
596-0 *Fax:* (07142) 596-200
Runge Verlagsauslieferung, Bergstr 2, 33803
Steinhagen, Germany *Tel:* (05204) 998-0
Fax: (05204) 998-11 *E-mail:* info@rungeva.de
Web Site: www.rungeva.de

Universal Edition AG
Forsthausgasse 9, 1200 Vienna
Tel: (01) 337 23-218 *Fax:* (01) 337 23-420
E-mail: publishing@universaledition.com;
vertrieb@universaledition.com
Web Site: www.universaledition.com
Key Personnel
Marketing & Sales Promotion Manager: Monika
Stricker
Publishing Manager: Christina Meglitsch-Kopacek
Public Relations: Kerstin Schwager
Founded: 1901
Subjects: Music, Dance
ISBN Prefix(es): 978-3-7024
Subsidiaries: Wiener Urtext Edition-Musikverlag
GmbH KG
Distributor for Editions Durand-Salabert-Eschig;
European American Music Distributors LLC;
Editio Musica Budapest; Oxford University
Press; PWM; Rai Trade; Schott Music; Edizioni Suvini Zerboni (Sugar Music); Universal
Music Publishing Ricordi
Foreign Rep(s): Accent Music Publishers & Distributors (Annette Emdon) (South Africa);
Albersen Verhuur BV (Netherlands); ALMO
Musikabteilung (Anja van Gysegem) (Belgium,
Luxembourg); Atlantis Musikbuch-Verlag AG
(Nicole Froidevaux) (Switzerland); Dilia (Jan
Rychta) (Czechia); Durand-Salabert-Eschig
(Marjorie Sarthou) (Belgium, France, Luxembourg); Edition DSS (Klemen Weiss) (Slovenia); European American Music (Amy Dickinson, Caroline Kane & Norman Ryan) (Canada,
Mexico, USA); Hal Leonard Australia Pty Ltd
(Megan Stapleton) (Australia, New Zealand);
Hartai Agentur Fuer Musik (Hungary); HDS
- ZAMP (Suzana Markovic) (Croatia); Hudobny fond (Slovakia); KMS - Korea Music
Service (Jung-eun Park) (South Korea); Samuel
Lewis (Israel); LITA (Lucia Vicianova) (Slovakia); LM Edition AB (Peter Magro) (Denmark, Estonia, Finland, Iceland, Latvia, Lithuania, Sweden); MDS (Hire & Copyright) Ltd
(Deirdre Bates & Rod Taylor) (Ireland, UK);
Melos Ediciones Musicales SA (Argentina);

Norsk Musikforlag AS (Lisbet Froystadvag)
(Norway); PMPH - People's Music Publishing House (China); PWM Edition (Justyna
Luboradzka-Neuer & Krystyna Mardarowicz) (Poland); Schott Music Co Ltd (Japan);
Schott Music Panton sro (Alena Dvorakova)
(Czechia); Schott Music (Susanne Krichbaum
& Annegret Strehle) (Germany); SEEMSA
(Portugal, Spain); SO PE Hellas (Greece); Universal Music Publishing (Italy)

Edition Va Bene
Max Kahrer Gasse 32, 3400 Klosterneuburg
Tel: (0664) 16 16 356 (cell) *Fax:* (02243) 22 159
E-mail: edition@vabene.at
Web Site: www.vabene.at
Key Personnel
Publishing Dir: Dr Walter Weiss
Sales & Advertising: Susanne Lurf
Founded: 1990
Subjects: Anthropology, Asian Studies, Biography, Memoirs, Communications, Developing
Countries, Ethnicity, Foreign Countries, Health,
Nutrition, History, Humor, Literature, Literary
Criticism, Essays, Philosophy, Physical Sciences, Poetry, Religion - Catholic, Religion -
Jewish, Romance, Science (General), Sports,
Athletics, Theology, Travel & Tourism
ISBN Prefix(es): 978-3-85167
Number of titles published annually: 10 Print
Total Titles: 297 Print
Branch Office(s)
Reichstratsstr 17, 1010 Vienna
Distribution Center: Dr Franz Hain, Dr-Otto-
Neurath-Gasse 5, 1220 Vienna *Tel:* (01) 282
65 65-0 *Fax:* (01) 282 52 82
Herold Verlagsauslieferung, Raiffeisenallee 10,
82041 Oberhaching, Germany *Tel:* (089) 61 38
71-0 *Fax:* (089) 61 38 71-20 *E-mail:* herold@
herold-va.de *Web Site:* www.herold-va.de

Vehling Medienservice und Verlag GmbH
Reninghausstr 29, 8020 Graz
Tel: (0664) 84 96 922
E-mail: verlag@vehling.at
Web Site: www.vehling.at
Subjects: Military Science, Nonfiction (General),
Regional Interests, Travel & Tourism
ISBN Prefix(es): 978-3-85333

Verband der Wissenschaftlichen Gesellschaften Oesterreichs (VWGOe) (Federation of Austrian Scientific Societies)
c/o Zentrum fuer Pathophysiologie, Infektiologie
& Immunologie, der Medizinischen Universitaet Wien, Kinderspitalgasse 15, 1090 Vienna
Tel: (0650) 544 8086 (cell) *Fax:* (01) 40160
933002
E-mail: office@vwgoe.at
Web Site: www.vwgoe.at
Key Personnel
President: Prof Hannes Stockinger
Secretary: Michaela Pinkawa
Founded: 1954
Subjects: Archaeology, Business, Education, History, Mathematics, Music, Dance, Philosophy,
Physical Sciences
ISBN Prefix(es): 978-3-85369

Veritas Verlags- und HandelsgesmbH & Co OHG+
Hafenstr 2a, 4020 Linz
Tel: (0732) 776451-0 *Fax:* (0732) 776451-2239
E-mail: veritas@veritas.at; kundenberatung@
veritas.at
Web Site: www.veritas.at
Key Personnel
Mng Dir: Manfred Christl *Tel:* (0732) 776451-
2233 *E-mail:* m.christl@veritas.at
Chief Editor: Martina Griessner *Tel:* (0732)
776451-2232 *E-mail:* m.griessner@veritas.at
Head, Production: Martin Grasl *Tel:* (0732)
776451-2238 *E-mail:* m.grasl@veritas.at

Marketing & Sales Manager: Reinhard Gassner *Tel:* (0732) 776451-2265 *E-mail:* r.gassner@veritas.at
Founded: 1945
Membership(s): Wirtschaftskammern Oesterreichs Fachgruppe Buch- und Medienwirtschaft.
Subjects: Education
ISBN Prefix(es): 978-3-85329; 978-3-7058; 978-3-7060; 978-3-85204
Total Titles: 1,000 Print; 140 CD-ROM; 50 Audio
Parent Company: Cornelsen, Germany
Bookshop(s): Buchhandlung Veritas, Harrachstr 5, 4010 Linz *Tel:* (0732) 776401-0 *Fax:* (0732) 776401-2633 *E-mail:* handel@veritas-buch.at *Web Site:* www.veritas-buch.at

Verlag OUPS GmbH & Co KG
Volksfeststr 16/EG, 4910 Ried im Innkreis
Tel: (07752) 82 966-0 *Fax:* (07752) 82 966-4
E-mail: office@oups.com; office@werteart.com
Web Site: www.oups.com
Key Personnel
Chief Executive Officer: Kurt Hoertenhuber
Sales Manager: Christoph Holly *E-mail:* c.holly@oups.com
Subjects: Art
ISBN Prefix(es): 978-3-902763
Foreign Rights: Agentur im Medien- und Verlagswesen (Dr Ivana Beil) (Bosnia and Herzegovina, Bulgaria, Croatia, Czechia, Estonia, Hungary, Latvia, Lithuania, Poland, Romania, Russia, Serbia, Slovakia, Slovenia, Ukraine); Book Cosmos Agency (Richard Hong) (Korea); Hercules Business & Culture Development GmbH (Hongjun Cai) (China); Inter Rights Agency (Jun Hasebe) (Japan)
Distribution Center: Mohr Morawa Buchvertrieb GmbH, Sulzengasse 2, 1230 Vienna *Tel:* (01) 680 14-0 *Fax:* (01) 688 71 30 *E-mail:* momo@mohrmorawa.at *Web Site:* www.mohrmorawa.at
Vull Service GmbH, August-Borsig-Str 11, 24783 Osterronfeld, Germany *Tel:* (04331) 8095-781 *Fax:* (04331) 8095-777

Vorarlberger Verlagsanstalt GmbH
Schwefel 81, 6850 Dornbirn
Tel: (05572) 24697-0 *Fax:* (05572) 24697-78
E-mail: office@vva.at
Web Site: www.vva.at
Key Personnel
Mng Partner: Karl-Heinz Milz *Tel:* (05572) 24697-18 *Fax:* (05572) 24697-7818 *E-mail:* kh.milz@vva.at
Manager: Herbert Gaechter *Tel:* (05572) 24697-28 *Fax:* (05572) 24697-7828 *E-mail:* h.gaechter@vva.at
Sales Manager: Alexander Richl *Tel:* (05572) 24697-19 *Fax:* (05572) 24697-7819 *E-mail:* a.richl@vva.at
Founded: 1920
Subjects: Geography, Geology, History, Regional Interests
ISBN Prefix(es): 978-3-85430

VWGOe, see Verband der Wissenschaftlichen Gesellschaften Oesterreichs (VWGOe)

Universitaetsverlag Wagner GesmbH
Erlerstr 10, 6020 Innsbruck
Tel: (0512) 395045-23 *Fax:* (0512) 395045-15
E-mail: mail@uvw.at
Web Site: www.uvw.at
Key Personnel
Management: Markus Hatzer
Programming, Editorial & Production: Dr Mercedes Blaas
Sales: Ida Hoertnagl
Founded: 1554
Subjects: Archaeology, Geography, Geology, History, Language Arts, Linguistics, Science (General)
ISBN Prefix(es): 978-3-7030

Verlag Mag Johann Wanzenboeck+
Landstr Hauptstr 88/6, 1030 Vienna
Tel: (01) 7148542 *Fax:* (01) 7135814
Key Personnel
Dir: Johann Wanzenboeck *E-mail:* johann.wanzenboeck@chello.at
Founded: 1990
Subjects: English as a Second Language
ISBN Prefix(es): 978-3-901682
Number of titles published annually: 2 Print; 1 CD-ROM
Total Titles: 20 Print; 1 CD-ROM

Weishaupt Verlag
Hauptplatz 27, 8342 Gnas
Tel: (03151) 8487 *Fax:* (03151) 84874
E-mail: verlag@weishaupt.at
Web Site: www.weishaupt.at
Key Personnel
Contact: Annemarie Weishaupt; Herbert Weishaupt
Founded: 1980
Subjects: Aeronautics, Aviation, Maritime, Military Science, Natural History, Nonfiction (General), Regional Interests, Travel & Tourism
ISBN Prefix(es): 978-3-7059; 978-3-900310
Number of titles published annually: 30 Print; 1 CD-ROM; 1 Audio
Total Titles: 420 Print

Verlag Galerie Welz
Sigmund-Haffner-Gasse 16, 5020 Salzburg
Tel: (0662) 841771 *Fax:* (0662) 841771-20
E-mail: office@galerie-welz.at
Web Site: www.galerie-welz.at
Subjects: Art
ISBN Prefix(es): 978-3-85349

Wiener Dom-Verlag GmbH
Stephansplatz 4/VI/DG, 1010 Vienna
Tel: (01) 512 35 03-3964 *Fax:* (01) 512 35 03-3960
E-mail: office@domverlag.at
Web Site: www.domverlag.at
Key Personnel
Dir: Anton F Gatnar
Publishing Dir: Inge Cevela *Tel:* (01) 512 35 03-3968 *E-mail:* cevela@domverlag.at
Press & Events: Barbara Kornherr *E-mail:* kornherr@domverlag.at
Founded: 1946
Subjects: Religion - Catholic
ISBN Prefix(es): 978-3-85351

Wieser Verlag GmbH+
Ebentaler Str 34B, 9020 Klagenfurt/Celovec
Tel: (0463) 37036 *Fax:* (0463) 37635
E-mail: office@wieser-verlag.com
Web Site: www.wieser-verlag.com
Key Personnel
Publisher: Prof Lojze Wieser
Program & Production: Jakob Grollitsch *E-mail:* jakob.grollitsch@wieser-verlag.com
Founded: 1987
Subjects: Biography, Memoirs, Drama, Theater, Fiction, Government, Political Science, Literature, Literary Criticism, Essays, Poetry, Science (General)
ISBN Prefix(es): 978-3-85129
Total Titles: 900 Print
Distribution Center: Mohr Morawa Buchvertrieb GmbH, Sulzengasse 2, 1230 Vienna *Tel:* (01) 680 14-0 *Fax:* (01) 688 71 30 *E-mail:* momo@mohrmorawa.at *Web Site:* www.mohrmorawa.at
Runge Verlagsauslieferung GmbH, Bergstr 2, 33803 Steinhagen, Germany, Contact: Team 3 *Tel:* (05204) 998 123 *Fax:* (05204) 998 114 *E-mail:* msr@rungeva.de *Web Site:* rungeva.de
Scheidegger & Co AG, c/o AVA Verlagsauslieferung AG, Centralweg 16, 8910 Affoltern am Albis, Switzerland *Tel:* (044) 762 42 50 *Fax:* (044) 762 42 10 *E-mail:* scheidegger@ava.ch *Web Site:* www.ava.ch

Kunstverlag Wolfrum
Augustinerstr 10, 1010 Vienna
Tel: (01) 512 53 98-0 *Fax:* (01) 512 53 98-57
E-mail: wolfrum@wolfrum.at
Web Site: www.wolfrum.at
Key Personnel
Owner & Publisher: Hubert Wolfrum
Founded: 1850
Subjects: Art
ISBN Prefix(es): 978-3-900178

Zirkular - Verlag der Dokumentationsstelle fuer neuere oesterreichische Literatur
Seidengasse 13, 1070 Vienna
Tel: (01) 526 20 44-0 *Fax:* (01) 526 20 44-30
E-mail: info@literaturhaus.at
Web Site: www.literaturhaus.at
Key Personnel
Mng Dir: Dr Heinz Lunzer *Tel:* (01) 526 20 44-17 *E-mail:* huez@literaturhaus.at
Deputy Mng Dir: Dr Anne Zauner *Tel:* (01) 526 20 44-45 *E-mail:* az@literaturhaus.at
Founded: 1979
Subjects: Biography, Memoirs, Literature, Literary Criticism, Essays
ISBN Prefix(es): 978-3-900467

Paul Zsolnay Verlag GmbH+
Subsidiary of Carl Hanser Verlag GmbH & Co
Prinz-Eugen-Str 30, 1040 Vienna
Tel: (01) 505 76 61-0 *Fax:* (01) 505 76 61-10
E-mail: info@zsolnay.at
Web Site: www.hanser-literaturverlage.de/verlage/zsolnay-deuticke
Key Personnel
Publishing Dir: Michael Krueger
Program Management: Herbert Ohrlinger
Sales Manager: Felicitas Feilhauer
Production: Stefanie Schelleis
Rights & Permissions: Annette Lechner *E-mail:* annette.lechner@zsolnay.at
Founded: 1923
Subjects: Biography, Memoirs, Fiction, History, Nonfiction (General), Poetry
ISBN Prefix(es): 978-3-552; 978-3-223; 978-3-85190
Number of titles published annually: 40 Print
Total Titles: 500 Print
Imprints: Deuticke
Orders to: Dr Franz Hain, Dr-Otto-Neurath-Gasse 5, 1220 Vienna *Tel:* (01) 2826565-77 *Fax:* (01) 2825282

Bahrain

General Information

Capital: Manama
Language: Arabic (English also widely spoken)
Religion: Muslims of the Shiite & Sunni sects
Population: 551,000
Bank Hours: 0730-1200 Saturday-Wednesday; 0730-1100 Thursday
Currency: 1000 Fils = 1 Bahrain dinar
Export/Import Information: Generally books dutied at 10%, most schoolbooks free of duty; none on advertising matter. No import license required but no obscene literature permitted & for books (not for advertising) a Chamber of Commerce certificate is mandatory. No exchange controls.

Al Hilal Publishing & Marketing Group
PO Box 1100, Manama
Tel: 17 29 31 31 *Fax:* 17 29 34 00

E-mail: hilalad@tradearabia.net
Web Site: www.alhilalgroup.com
Key Personnel
Mng Dir: Ronnie Middleton
Founded: 1978
Subjects: Business, Regional Interests, Travel &
Tourism
Parent Company: Al Hilal Group
Foreign Rep(s): Auslandswerbung Stelmaszyk
(Germany); Echo Japan Corp (Japan); Edicon-
sult Internazionale (Italy); Medialink (India);
Tit Ajans Dis Tanitim Ltd Sti (Hilmi Z Erdem)
(Turkey)

Bangladesh

General Information

Capital: Dhaka
Language: Bengali (English widely used commer-
cially)
Religion: Predominantly Muslim with some
Hindu
Population: 129.2 million
Bank Hours: 0900-330 Saturday-Wednesday;
0900-1100 Thursday
Shop Hours: 1000-2030 Saturday-Thursday
Currency: 100 pisha = 1 taka (Tk)
Export/Import Information: No tariff on books
and advertising matter. Import licenses required
for all imports.
Copyright: UCC (see Copyright Conventions, pg
viii)

Academic Press & Publishers Library+
Prantik Apartment, Apartment D2, House 70/1,
Rd 6, Dhanmondi, Dhaka 1209
Tel: (02) 8125394 *Fax:* (02) 8117277
E-mail: applbooks@gmail.com
Web Site: www.applbooks.com
Key Personnel
Chairman: Dr Mizanur Rahman Shelley
Mng Dir: Shahina Rahman
Deputy Mng Dir: Ahmed Sarwerruddawla
Founded: 1982
Subjects: Engineering (General), Fiction, Geog-
raphy, Geology, Government, Political Science,
History, Literature, Literary Criticism, Essays,
Music, Dance, Poetry, Religion - Other, Sci-
ence (General), Social Sciences, Sociology,
Women's Literature
ISBN Prefix(es): 978-984-08

Agamee Prakashani (Agamee Publication)+
36 Bangla Bazar, Dhaka 1100
Tel: (02) 7192160; (02) 7110021 *Fax:* (02)
7110021
E-mail: info@agameeprakashani-bd.com
Web Site: www.agameeprakashani-bd.com; www.
facebook.com/AgameePrakashani
Key Personnel
Chief Executive Officer: Osman Gani *Tel:* (01)
819219024 (cell)
Founded: 1986
Renowned for publishing a large number of
books based on the 1971 liberation war of
Bangladesh. The slogan of this organization
is "Moktijodhu o Muktochinta Amader Proka-
sona".
Membership(s): Academic & Creative Publish-
ers Association of Bangladesh; Bangladesh
Publishers & Book Sellers Association; Dhaka
Chamber of Commerce & Industry; FBCCI.
Subjects: Fiction, Government, Political Science,
Journalism, Literature, Literary Criticism, Es-
says, Music, Dance, Philosophy, Poetry, Sci-
ence (General), Social Sciences, Sociology,
Women's Studies

ISBN Prefix(es): 978-984-401
Number of titles published annually: 90 Print
Total Titles: 2,030 Print
Distributed by Phuthipatra (Kolkata, India)
Distributor for Muktadhara (USA)

Ankur Prakashani+
40/1 Purana Paltan, Dhaka 1000
Tel: (02) 9564799; (02) 7176126 *Fax:* (02)
9553635; (02) 7410986
Web Site: www.ankur-prakashani.com
Key Personnel
Publisher: Mesbahuddin Ahmed
Founded: 1984
Also a library supplier & importer of reference
books.
Subjects: Anthropology, Asian Studies, Eco-
nomics, Education, Fiction, Government, Polit-
ical Science, Health, Nutrition, Literature, Lit-
erary Criticism, Essays, Nonfiction (General),
Social Sciences, Sociology, Women's Studies,
Childrens Literature, Youth Literature
ISBN Prefix(es): 978-984-464; 978-984-8010
Distributor for Narosa; Prints India

Bangladesh Government Press
Tejgaon, Dhaka 1208
Tel: (02) 9117415
Web Site: www.dpp.gov.bd/bgpress
Key Personnel
Deputy Dir: Nazrul Islam
Assistant Dir: Alamgir Hossian
E-mail: alamgirbgp@gmail.com
Subjects: Regional Interests
ISBN Prefix(es): 978-984-01

BG Press, see Bangladesh Government Press

Gatidhara+
38/2-ka Banglabazar, Dhaka 1100
Tel: (02) 7392077 (press); (02) 7117515 (show-
room); (02) 7118273 (showroom); 01552-
385784 (cell); 01711-053196 (cell); 0171-
1602442 (cell); 01552-337280 (cell) *Fax:* (02)
7123472
E-mail: info@gatidhara.com; gatidhara2008@
yahoo.com; gatidhara2008@gmail.com
Web Site: www.gatidhara.com
Key Personnel
Chief Executive: Ahamed Kawser
Publisher: Sikdar Abul Bashar
Founded: 1988
Also a distributor & exporter.
Membership(s): Publishers Association; Publish-
ers Guild.
Subjects: Behavioral Sciences, Child Care & De-
velopment, Drama, Theater, Education, Fiction,
Health, Nutrition, Humor, Literature, Literary
Criticism, Essays, Poetry, Religion - Islamic
ISBN Prefix(es): 978-984-461
Subsidiaries: Gatidhara Computers

Mullick & Brothers
160-161, Dhaka New Market, Dhaka 1205
Tel: (02) 8619125; (02) 8625386 *Fax:* (02)
8610562
E-mail: mullick_161@yahoo.com
Subjects: Education
ISBN Prefix(es): 978-984-411; 978-984-8272

The University Press Ltd (UPL)+
Red Crescent House, 61 Motijheel C/A, Dhaka
1000
Mailing Address: GPO Box 2611, Dhaka 1000
Tel: (02) 9565441; (02) 9565444 *Fax:* (02)
9565443
E-mail: info@uplbooks.com.bd
Web Site: www.uplbooks.com
Key Personnel
Mng Dir & Publisher: Mohiuddin Ahmed

Consulting Editor & Acting Sales Manager: Badi-
uddin Nazir
IT Manager: Babul Chandra Dhar
Founded: 1974
Specialize in publishing, selling, importing & exporting.
Subjects: Agriculture, Anthropology, Archaeology, Architecture & Interior Design, Art, Biography, Memoirs, Communications, Economics,
Education, Environmental Studies, Fiction, Fi-
nance, Geography, Geology, Government, Po-
litical Science, Health, Nutrition, History, Law,
Literature, Literary Criticism, Essays, Manage-
ment, Military Science, Nonfiction (General),
Philosophy, Photography, Poetry, Public Ad-
ministration, Publishing & Book Trade Refer-
ence, Religion - Islamic, Social Sciences, Soci-
ology, Technology, Travel & Tourism, Women's
Studies, Ethics, Media
ISBN Prefix(es): 978-984-05
Number of titles published annually: 50 Print
Total Titles: 600 Print
Branch Office(s)
Rumi Market, 1st floor, 68-69 Paridas Rd, Dhaka
1100
73 Shahi Jame Masjid, Super Market Complex,
Anderkilla, Chittagong
Distributed by DK Agencies (P) Ltd (New
Delhi, India); Intermediate Technology (UK);
Manohar Publishers & Distributors (New Delhi,
India); Oxford University Press (Pakistan);
Paragon Enterprise (India); ZED Books (UK)
Distributor for Indiana University Press; Interme-
diate Technology (UK); Manohar Publishers &
Distributors (New Delhi, India); ZED Books
(UK)
Showroom(s): Highway Homes, 5th floor, Ka-
32/6 Pragati Sarani (Bishwa Rd), Shaljadpur,
Gulshan, Dhaka 1212 *E-mail:* showroom@
uplbooks.com.bd

UPL, see The University Press Ltd (UPL)

Belarus

General Information

Capital: Minsk
Language: Belarusian
Religion: Predominantly Christian (mostly Roman
Catholic & Eastern Orthodox)
Population: 10.4 million
Bank Hours: Generally open for short hours be-
tween 0930-1230 Monday-Friday
Shop Hours: Generally 0900-1800 Monday-
Friday; often open weekends
Currency: 100 kopeks = 1 rubl
Export/Import Information: According to
Ukrainian quotas & customs duties, compa-
nies engaged in trade should register with the
Ukraine Ministry of Foreign Economic Rela-
tions. Licenses for export & import are also
required for trade with Russia.
Copyright: UCC (see Copyright Conventions, pg
viii)

Belarus Vydavectva
Prospect Maserova, 11, 220600 Minsk
Tel: (017) 2238742 *Fax:* (017) 2238731
Founded: 1921
Subjects: Art, Economics, Government, Political
Science, Medicine, Nursing, Dentistry, Music,
Dance
ISBN Prefix(es): 978-5-338; 978-985-01

Belaruskaja Encyklapedyja (Byelorussian
Encyclopaedia)
pr F Skaryny 15A, 220072 Minsk
Tel: (017) 2323433 *Fax:* (017) 2393144

Founded: 1967
Subjects: Agriculture, Archaeology, Architecture & Interior Design, Art, Biography, Memoirs, Biological Sciences, Cookery, Crafts, Games, Hobbies, Drama, Theater, Education, Fiction, Finance, Health, Nutrition, History, House & Home, Language Arts, Linguistics, Law, Literature, Literary Criticism, Essays, Mathematics, Medicine, Nursing, Dentistry, Natural History, Parapsychology, Photography, Physics, Poetry, Religion - Other, Science (General), Sports, Athletics
ISBN Prefix(es): 978-5-85700; 978-985-11

Kavaler Publishers+
Pobediteley Ave, 11-1222, 220004 Minsk
Tel: (017) 203 80 41 *Fax:* (017) 203 80 41
E-mail: info@kavaler.by; kavaler-design@yandex.ru
Web Site: www.kavaler.by
Founded: 1991
All editions are prize winners of the annual national contests *Art of the Book*.
Membership(s): Belarusian Association of Book Publishers & Book Distributors; Belarusian Union of Artists.
Subjects: Advertising, Business, English as a Second Language, Fiction, History, Nonfiction (General), Poetry, Wine & Spirits, German as a Second Language
ISBN Prefix(es): 978-985-6427; 978-985-6748
Number of titles published annually: 8 Print
Total Titles: 70 Print
Book Club(s): Minsk Book Exhibition-Sale Club Belakk

Vydavectva Mastackaja Litaratura
Maserava prospect 11, 220600 Minsk
Tel: (017) 2235809; (017) 2238664
Founded: 1972
Subjects: Fiction, Literature, Literary Criticism, Essays
ISBN Prefix(es): 978-5-340; 978-985-02

Narodnaya Asveta Publishing House+
11 Pobediteli Ave, 220004 Minsk
Tel: (017) 203-61-84
E-mail: narasveta@narasveta.by; marketing@narasveta.by
Web Site: www.narasveta.by
Key Personnel
Dir: Victoria Viktorovna Kalistratova
    E-mail: director@narasveta.by
Head, Sales & Advertising: Zhanna Petrovna Reznik *Tel:* (017) 203-84-44
Chief Editor: Elena Vladimirovna Litvinovich
    Tel: (017) 203-99-44 *E-mail:* editor@narasveta.by
Founded: 1951
Subjects: Biological Sciences, Economics, Education, Environmental Studies, Fiction, Geography, Geology, History, Mathematics, Poetry, Science (General)
ISBN Prefix(es): 978-5-341; 978-985-03; 978-985-12

Belgium

General Information

Capital: Brussels
Language: Dutch in the north, French in the south. Brussels is officially bilingual. German in eastern Belgium
Religion: Predominantly Roman Catholic, some Protestant
Population: 10.2 million

Bank Hours: Main towns: 0900-1200/1300 & 1400-1530/1600: Monday-Friday
Shop Hours: 0900-1900 with variations
Currency: 100 Eurocents = 1 Euro
Export/Import Information: Member of the European Union. No import license required, just Model A form of notice declaration of payment. No exchange controls. 6% VAT on books.
Copyright: UCC, Berne, Florence (see Copyright Conventions, pg viii)

AAM, see Archives d'Architecture Moderne

Uitgeverij Abimo+
Hubert Frere Orbanlaan 48, 9000 Gent
Tel: (03) 660 27 20 *Fax:* (03) 660 27 01
E-mail: info@abimo.be
Web Site: www.abimo.net
Key Personnel
Assistant Dir, Foreign Rights: Inne van den Bossche *E-mail:* inne.van.den.bossche@abimo.net
Educational Publisher: Rene De Cock
    E-mail: rene@abimo.net; Sarah Kumar
    E-mail: sarah@abimo.net
Educational Publisher & International Rights: Jef Goedeme *E-mail:* jef@abimo.net
Press & Promotion: Katrien Borms
    E-mail: promotie@abimo.net
Production: Klaas Demeulemeester
    E-mail: klaas@abimo.net
Founded: 1993
Membership(s): Vlaamse Uitgevers Vereniging.
Subjects: Drama, Theater, Earth Sciences, Education, Fiction, Foreign Countries, Geography, Geology
ISBN Prefix(es): 978-90-75905; 978-90-801767; 978-90-5932

Editions Academia+
Rue Charlemagne 6/203, 1348 Louvain-la-Neuve
Tel: (010) 45 36 93 *Fax:* (010) 45 44 80
E-mail: contact@editions-academia.be
Web Site: www.editions-academia.be
Key Personnel
Mng Dir: Yves Wellemans *E-mail:* direction@editions-academia.be
Public Relations: Sidonie Maissin *E-mail:* s.maissin@editions-academia.be
Founded: 1987
Membership(s): Association des Editeurs Belges (ADEB).
Subjects: Accounting, Anthropology, Journalism, Law, Physical Sciences, Religion - Islamic, Social Sciences, Sociology
ISBN Prefix(es): 978-2-87209
Total Titles: 500 Print

Academia Press+
Subsidiary of Uitgeverij Lannoo NV
Prudens Van Duyseplein 8, 9000 Ghent
Tel: (09) 233 80 88 *Fax:* (09) 233 14 09
E-mail: info@academiapress.be
Web Site: www.academiapress.be
Key Personnel
Publisher: Lies Poignie *E-mail:* lies.poignie@academiapress.be
Founded: 1989
Scientific publishers.
Membership(s): The Association of Learned and Professional Society Publishers (ALPSP).
Subjects: Agriculture, Archaeology, Art, Business, Communications, Economics, Environmental Studies, Government, Political Science, History, Journalism, Medicine, Nursing, Dentistry, Psychology, Psychiatry, Science (General), Social Sciences, Sociology, Environment
ISBN Prefix(es): 978-90-382

Acco Uitgeverij
Blijde Inkomststr 22, 3000 Leuven
Tel: (016) 62 80 00 *Fax:* (016) 62 80 01

E-mail: uitgeverij@acco.be
Web Site: www.acco.be/nl-be/publisher
Key Personnel
Publishing Manager: Deborah Bicke *Tel:* (016) 62 80 39 *E-mail:* deborah.bicke@acco.be
Editor: Nancy Derboven *Tel:* (016) 62 80 38
    E-mail: nancy.derboven@acco.be
Marketing: Greet Coenegrachts *Tel:* (016) 62 80 33 *E-mail:* greet.coenegrachts@acco.be; An Puissant *Tel:* (016) 62 80 32 *E-mail:* an.puissant@acco.be
Founded: 1960
Subjects: Behavioral Sciences, Cookery, Criminology, Economics, Education, Government, Political Science, History, Language Arts, Linguistics, Law, Literature, Literary Criticism, Essays, Management, Mathematics, Medicine, Nursing, Dentistry, Philosophy, Psychology, Psychiatry, Religion - Other, Science (General), Social Sciences, Sociology, Travel & Tourism
ISBN Prefix(es): 978-90-334
Imprints: De Horstink
Subsidiaries: Acco (Netherlands); Broadcast Book Services (UK & Ireland)
Branch Office(s)
Acco Nederland, Westvlietweg 67 F, 2495 AA Den Haag, Netherlands *Tel:* (070) 386 88 54 *Fax:* (070) 386 14 98 *E-mail:* info@uitgeverijacco.nl
Foreign Rep(s): Quantum Publishing Solutions Ltd (worldwide)
Foreign Rights: Quantum Publishing Solutions Ltd
Distribution Center: York Publishing Services Ltd, 64 Hallfield Rd, Layerthorpe, York YO31 7ZQ, United Kingdom *Tel:* (01904) 431 213 *Fax:* (01904) 430 868 *E-mail:* engs@yps-publishing.co.uk

Editions Aden
rue Antoine Breart 44, 1060 Brussels
Tel: (02) 5370062 *Fax:* (02) 5344662
Web Site: www.aden.be
Key Personnel
Publisher: Gilles Martin
Subjects: Government, Political Science, History, Religion - Other, Social Sciences, Sociology
ISBN Prefix(es): 978-2-930402; 978-2-9600273
Foreign Rep(s): Les Belles Lettres (France)

Centre Aequatoria
Stationsstr 48, 3360 Lovenjoel
Tel: (016) 46 44 84 *Fax:* (016) 46 44 84
Web Site: www.aequatoria.be; www.abbol.com
Key Personnel
Editor-in-Chief: Honore Vinck *E-mail:* vinck.aequatoria@skynet.be
Founded: 1980
Promotes research on Central African humanities preference for Central African authors.
Subjects: Anthropology, Biography, Memoirs, Ethnicity, History, Language Arts, Linguistics, Regional Interests, Social Sciences, Sociology
Branch Office(s)
Maison MSC, 3ieme Rue, BP 779, Limete, Kinshasa 1, Democratic Republic of the Congo
BP 276, Mbandaka, Democratic Republic of the Congo
U.S. Office(s): The Missionaries of the Sacred Heart (Aequatoria), 305 S Lake St, PO Box 270, Aurora, IL 60507, United States *Fax:* 630-892-3071 *E-mail:* mscusafin@ibm.net (for payments of subscriptions to Annales Aequatoria only)
Distributed by Editions St Paul (Zaire)

Alamire Music Publishers+
Toekomstlaan 5 B, 3910 Neerpelt
Tel: (011) 610 510 *Fax:* (011) 610 511
E-mail: info@alamire.com
Web Site: www.alamire.com

Key Personnel
Dir: Herman Baeten
Founded: 1984
Specialize in early music facsimiles.
Subjects: Music, Dance
ISBN Prefix(es): 978-90-6853

Alice Editions+
Rue Beckers, 17, 1040 Brussels
Tel: (02) 660 10 45
E-mail: info@alice-editions.be; communication@
  alice-editions.be
Web Site: www.alice-editions.be; www.facebook.
  com/aliceeditions
Key Personnel
Editor & Foreign Rights: Melanie Roland
Assistant Editor/Media: Virginie Bassanello
Founded: 1995
Subjects: Architecture & Interior Design, Art,
  Fiction, Gardening, Plants, House & Home,
  Science Fiction, Fantasy
ISBN Prefix(es): 978-2-87426; 978-2-930182
Number of titles published annually: 25 Print
Total Titles: 300 Print
Foreign Rep(s): Dimedia (Canada); Servidis
  (Switzerland); Le Seuil - Volumen (France)
Distribution Center: SDL Caravelle, Rue Pre-aux-
  Oies, 303, 1130 Brussels *Tel:* (02) 240 93 00
  Fax: (02) 216 35 98 *E-mail:* info@sdlcaravelle.
  com

Amnesty International Vlaanderen VZW
156 Kerkstr, 2060 Antwerp
Tel: (03) 271 16 16 *Fax:* (03) 235 78 12
E-mail: amnesty@aivl.be
Web Site: www.amnesty.be
Key Personnel
Coordinator: Staf Coertjens
Subjects: Human Relations
ISBN Prefix(es): 978-90-70895

Editions Amyris SPRL
Rue Lannoy, 22, 1050 Brussels
Tel: (02) 660 51 01 *Fax:* (02) 660 51 01
E-mail: info.commande@editionsamyris.com
Web Site: www.editionsamyris.com
Key Personnel
Dir: B Depatoul
Founded: 1996
Subjects: Health, Nutrition, Aromatherapy, Holis-
  tic Medicine, Hydrotherapy
ISBN Prefix(es): 978-2-9303
Distribution Center: D G Diffusion, ZI des
  Bogues F, 31750 Escalquens, France *Tel:* 05
  61 00 09 99 (Belgium & France)
Diffusion Transat, Chemin des Chalets, 1279
  Chavannes de Bogis, Switzerland *Tel:* (022)
  342 77 40 *Fax:* (022) 343 46 46

Anthemis SA
Place Albert 1, 9, 1300 Limal
Tel: (010) 42 02 90 *Fax:* (010) 40 21 84
E-mail: info@anthemis.be
Web Site: www.anthemis.be
Key Personnel
Publisher: Olivier Cruysmans; Anne Eloy; Patri-
  cia Keunings
Subjects: Economics, Law, Management,
  Medicine, Nursing, Dentistry
ISBN Prefix(es): 978-2-87455
Distribution Center: Patrimoine sprl, 168, rue
  du Noyer, 1030 Brussels *Tel:* (02) 736 68 47
  E-mail: patrimoine@telenet.be (Belgium &
  Luxembourg)
Parc Scientifique Einstein, Chemin du Cyclotron
  6, 1348 Louvain-la-Neuve *Tel:* (010) 39 00 70
  Fax: (010) 39 00 01

Les editions de l'arbre
Rue de Nieuwenhove, 41, 1180 Brussels
Tel: (02) 626 06 70

Subjects: Fiction, History, How-to, Nonfiction
  (General), Lifestyle
ISBN Prefix(es): 978-2-87462
Branch Office(s)
Rue du Docteur Paul Brouse, 75017 Paris, France
  Tel: 01 42 28 98 03

Archives d'Architecture Moderne
Rue de l'Ermitage 55, 1050 Brussels
Tel: (02) 642 24 62
E-mail: info@aam.be
Web Site: aam.be
Key Personnel
President: Maurice Culot
Mng Dir: Yaron Pesztat
Founded: 1968
Subjects: Architecture & Interior Design, Gar-
  dening, Plants, Photography, Garden Design,
  Urban Planning
ISBN Prefix(es): 978-2-87143; 978-2-930037
Distribution Center: ADY Books, Rue de Rot-
  terdam 20, 4000 Liege, Contact: Andre Del-
  ruelle *Tel:* (04) 223 18 28 *Fax:* (04) 223 18
  29 *E-mail:* andre.delruelle@adybooks.be *Web
  Site:* www.adybooks.com (Benelux)
Belles Lettres, 25 rue du General Leclerc, 94270
  Le Kremlin Bicetre, France *Tel:* 01 45 15 19
  70 *Fax:* 01 45 15 19 80 *Web Site:* bldd.fr

Uitgeverij Averbode NV (Averbode Publishers)+
Abdijstr 1, 3271 Averbode
Mailing Address: Postbus 54, 3271 Averbode
Tel: (013) 780 111 *Fax:* (013) 780 183
E-mail: info@verbode.be
Web Site: www.averbode.com
Key Personnel
Foreign Rights: Sonja Wuytens *E-mail:* prod@
  verbode.be
Founded: 1993
Educational books & magazines for children to
  18 years, teacher support materials & religious
  books.
Subjects: Education, Religion - Catholic, Theol-
  ogy
ISBN Prefix(es): 978-90-317; 978-2-87394
Number of titles published annually: 40 Print
Total Titles: 250 Print
Subsidiaries: Editions Sedrap SAS
Branch Office(s)
Editions Averbode Sarl, Le Turenne 2, rue Icare,
  67960 Entzheim, France *Tel:* 03 88 22 04 49
  Fax: 03 88 22 43 33 *E-mail:* abonnements@
  averbode.fr *Web Site:* www.averbode.fr
Uitgeverij Averbode BV, De Maas 9, Postbus 248,
  5680 Best, Netherlands *Tel:* (0499) 330103
  Fax: (0499) 329328 *E-mail:* info@averbode.nl

Maison d'Editions Baha'ies
Rue Henri Evenepoel St 52, 1030 Schaarbeek
Tel: (02) 647 07 49
Founded: 1970
Subjects: Biography, Memoirs, History, Law, Phi-
  losophy, Religion - Other
ISBN Prefix(es): 978-2-87203

BAI
Herentalsebaan 406, 2160 Wommelgem
Mailing Address: Schijnparklaan 14, 2900
  Schoten
Tel: (03) 320 95 95 *Fax:* (03) 320 95 69
E-mail: ria@baipublishers.be; kathleen@
  baipublishers.be
Web Site: www.baipublishers.be
Subjects: Art, Cookery
ISBN Prefix(es): 978-90-8586
Distribution Center: Exhibitions International,
  Kol Begaultlaan 17, 3012 Leuven *Tel:* (016) 29
  69 00 *Fax:* (016) 29 61 29 *E-mail:* orders@

exhibitionsinternational.be *Web Site:* www.
  exhibitionsinternational.be
EF & EF, Eind 36, 6017 BH Thorn, Netherlands *Tel:* (0475) 561501 *Fax:* (0475) 561660
  E-mail: ef-ef.in.boeken@wxs.nl

Uitgeverij Bakermat
Maanstr 9 A & B, 2800 Mechelen
Tel: (015) 71 56 53 *Fax:* (015) 71 56 54
E-mail: info@baeckensbooks.be; info@bakermat.
  com
Web Site: www.bakermat.be
Key Personnel
Publisher: Jos Baeckens *E-mail:* jos.baeckens@
  baeckensbooks.be
Foreign Rights: Kathleen Van Steenwinkel
Marketing & Foreign Rights: Stijn Baeckens
  E-mail: stijn.baeckens@baeckensbooks.be
Founded: 1991
ISBN Prefix(es): 978-90-5461; 978-90-5924
Parent Company: Baeckens Book BVBA

Ballon Kids
Franklin Rooseveltplaats 12, 2060 Antwerp
Tel: (03) 294 15 00 *Fax:* (03) 294 15 01
E-mail: info@ballonmedia.com
Web Site: www.ballonmedia.com
Key Personnel
Mng Dir: Alexis Dragonetti
Sales Manager: Herve Quillot *E-mail:* h.quillot@
  ballonmedia.com
Foreign Rights: Stijn Mertens
Founded: 2008
ISBN Prefix(es): 978-90-374
Parent Company: Ballon Media
Branch Office(s)
Ballon Media France, 15-27 rue Moussorgski,
  75018 Paris, France *Tel:* 01 70 38 56 00
  Fax: 01 70 38 56 02

Bartleby & Co
19, Blvd Jamar, Boite 7.01, 1060 Brussels
Tel: (02) 538 10 51
Web Site: www.bartlebybooks.eu
Key Personnel
President: Thorsten Baensch
Founded: 1996
Specialize in artist books in limited editions.
Subjects: Art
ISBN Prefix(es): 978-2-930279
Number of titles published annually: 3 Print
Total Titles: 75 Print

Beta-Plus Publishing
Ave Louise 367, 1050 Brussels
Tel: (02) 395 90 20 *Fax:* (02) 395 90 21
E-mail: info@betaplus.com
Web Site: www.betaplus.com
Founded: 1996
Subjects: Architecture & Interior Design, Garden-
  ing, Plants
ISBN Prefix(es): 978-2-930367; 978-2-9600168;
  978-90-77213; 978-90-802216; 978-90-806114;
  978-90-8944

Editions Beya ASBL
Chavee Boulanger 20, 1390 Grez Doiceau
Tel: (010) 84 14 30 *Fax:* (010) 84 14 30
E-mail: info@beyaeditions.com
Web Site: www.beyaeditions.com
Subjects: Hermeticism
ISBN Prefix(es): 978-2-9600575; 978-2-9600364
Distribution Center: ARCHE-EDIDIT Sarl, 4,
  rue Basfroi, 75011 Paris, France *Tel:* 01 48 87
  42 98 *Fax:* 01 48 87 42 98 *E-mail:* diffusion.
  arche@gmail.com (France & Italy)

De Boeck Universite+
Fond Jean-Paques, 4, 1348 Louvain-la-Neuve
Tel: (010) 48 25 11 *Fax:* (010) 48 26 93
E-mail: info@superieur.deboeck.com

Web Site: superieur.deboeck.com
Key Personnel
Dir (Professional): Marc-Oliver Lifrange
Editorial Dir (Primary & Secondary): Francoise Goethals
Editorial Dir (College): Frederic Jongen
Founded: 1918
Subjects: Education, English as a Second Language, Language Arts, Linguistics, Literature, Literary Criticism, Essays
ISBN Prefix(es): 978-2-8041; 978-2-7445
Parent Company: Groupe de Boeck SA
Branch Office(s)
2 ter, rue des Chantiers, 75005 Paris, France
  Tel: 01 72 36 41 75 *Fax:* 01 72 36 41 74
Distributed by Afrique-Editions (The Democratic Republic of the Congo); ERPI (Canada); Servidis (Switzerland)
Showroom(s): Rue des Minimes, 39, 1000 Brussels *Tel:* (02) 548 07 11 *Fax:* (02) 513 90 09

Uitgeverij De Boeck, see Uitgeverij Van In

Brepols, *imprint of* Brepols Publishers NV

Brepols Publishers NV+
Member of Brepols Group NV
Begijnhof 67, 2300 Turnhout
Tel: (014) 44 80 20; (014) 44 80 30 (sales)
  Fax: (014) 42 89 19
E-mail: info@brepols.net; orders@brepols.net
Web Site: www.brepols.net
Key Personnel
Mng Dir: Paul De Jongh *Tel:* (014) 44 80 21
  E-mail: paul.de.jongh@brepols.net
Publishing Manager: Johan Van Der Beke
  Tel: (212) 288 40 90 *E-mail:* johan.
  vanderbeke@brepols.net; Simon Forde
  Tel: (014) 44 80 25 *E-mail:* simon.forde@
  brepols.net; Luc Jocque *Tel:* (014) 71
  10 54 *E-mail:* luc.jocque@brepols.net;
  Christophe Lebbe *Tel:* (014) 44 80 26
  E-mail: christophe.lebbe@brepols.net; Chris
  VandenBorre *Tel:* (014) 44 80 27 *E-mail:* chris.
  vandenborre@brepols.net
Administration & Information Technology Manager: Wim Borgers *Tel:* (014) 44 80 39
  E-mail: wim.borgers@brepols.net
Commercial Manager: Hans Deraeve *Tel:* (014)
  44 80 22 *E-mail:* hans.deraeve@brepols.net
Customer Care Manager: Ann Duchene *Tel:* (014)
  44 80 34 *E-mail:* ann.duchene@brepols.net
Marketing Manager: Patrick Daemen *Tel:* (014)
  44 80 31 *E-mail:* patrick.daemen@brepols.net
Production & Logistics Manager: Jean Verstraete
  Tel: (014) 44 80 28 *E-mail:* jean.verstraete@
  brepols.net
Founded: 1796
International academic publishers.
Subjects: Archaeology, Architecture & Interior Design, Art, Asian Studies, Biblical Studies, History, Language Arts, Linguistics, Literature, Literary Criticism, Essays, Native American Studies, Philosophy, Religion - Other
ISBN Prefix(es): 978-2-503; 978-90-5622; 978-2-85006; 978-90-72100
Number of titles published annually: 240 Print; 5 CD-ROM; 5 Online
Total Titles: 5,000 Print
Imprints: Brepols; Corpus Christianorum; Harvey Miller
Warehouse: Tieblokkenlaan 2, Gate C, 2300 Turnhout
Distribution Center: Casemate | academic (USA)
Marston Book Services Ltd (UK)
Sotedis/Sodis (France)

Etablissements Emile Bruylant SA+
Rue des Minimes, 39, Brussels
Tel: (02) 548 07 11 *Fax:* (02) 513 90 09
E-mail: contact@bruylant.be
Web Site: www.bruylant.be

Key Personnel
Editorial Dir: Michel Jezierski *Tel:* (010) 48 26 19
Marketing Manager: Dimitri Grollemund
  E-mail: dimitri.grollemund@larciergroup.com
Sales Manager: Jean-Raymond Jehu *Tel:* (010) 48 26 25 *E-mail:* jean-raymond.jehu@deboeck.com
Rights: Camille Delacroix *Tel:* (010) 48 26 14
  E-mail: camille.delacroix@deboeck.com
Founded: 1838
Publisher & bookseller of law books & journals.
Subjects: Government, Political Science, Law
ISBN Prefix(es): 978-2-8027
Number of titles published annually: 90 Print
Total Titles: 1,600 Print
Parent Company: Editions Larcier
Ultimate Parent Company: Groupe De Boeck
Distribution Center: De Boeck Services (DBS), Fond Jean-Paques 4, 1348 Louvain-la-Neuve *Tel:* (010) 48 25 00 *Toll Free Tel:* 0800 99 613 *Fax:* (010) 48 25 19 *Toll Free Fax:* 0800 99 614 *E-mail:* commande@deboeckservices.com (Belgium & Luxembourg)
De Boeck Diffusion, 2 ter, rue des Chantiers, 75005 Paris, France *Tel:* 01 72 36 41 75 *Fax:* 01 72 36 41 74 *E-mail:* commande@deboeckdiffusion.com (rest of world)
Lextenso Editions, 33 rue du mail, 75081 Paris Cedex 02, France, Contact: Isabelle Cadilhac *Tel:* 01 56 54 16 26 *Fax:* 01 56 54 16 47 *E-mail:* isabelle.cadilhac@lextenso-editions.fr
Volumen, 25 Blvd Romain Rolland, CS21418, 75993 Paris Cedex 14, France *Tel:* 01 41 48 80 80 *Fax:* 01 41 48 84 81 *E-mail:* commandes@volumen.fr
La Librairie Nationale, El Farah II lot nº3, Quartier industriel, Mohammedia, Morocco *Tel:* (0523) 31 96 30 *Fax:* (0523) 31 10 99 *E-mail:* librairienationale@librairienationale.co.ma
Servidis, Chemin des Chalets 7, 1279 Chavannes de Bogis, Switzerland *Tel:* (022) 960 95 25 *Fax:* (022) 960 95 77 *E-mail:* commande@servidis.ch

Campinia Media cvba-vso+
Kleinhoefstr 4, 2440 Geel
Tel: (014) 59 09 59 *Fax:* (014) 59 03 44
E-mail: info@campiniamedia.be
Web Site: www.campiniamedia.be
Key Personnel
Dir: Erik Borgmans *E-mail:* erik.borgmans@campiniamedia.be
Production: Anja Breugelmans *E-mail:* anjab@campiniamedia.be
Administration: Eveline Loos *E-mail:* eveline.loos@campiniamedia.be
Founded: 1983
Subjects: Agriculture, Behavioral Sciences, Biological Sciences, Computer Science, Language Arts, Linguistics, Physics, Science (General), Social Sciences, Sociology
ISBN Prefix(es): 978-90-356

Editions Les Capucines
Ave des Capucines 15, 1342 Limelette
Tel: (010) 41 13 47 *Fax:* (010) 41 13 47
Web Site: www.editions-lescapucines.be
Key Personnel
Publisher: Nicole Darchambeau *E-mail:* nicole.darchambeau@skynet.be
Founded: 1994
Subjects: Cookery, History
ISBN Prefix(es): 978-2-930629; 978-2-9600836; 978-2-9600846
Number of titles published annually: 5 Print
Total Titles: 8 Print
Distributed by Editions de l'Ocean Indien; Editions Le Printemps
Distributor for Editions de l'Ocean Indien

Caramel, *imprint of* Uitgeverij Caramel

Uitgeverij Caramel+
Otto de Mentockplein 19, 1853 Strombeek-Bever
Tel: (02) 263 20 40 *Fax:* (02) 263 20 50
Web Site: www.caramel.be
Key Personnel
Chief Executive Officer: Jean-Michel d'Oultremont *E-mail:* jmdoultremont@caramel.be
Head, Commercial Dept: Jean-Luc Dubois
  E-mail: jeanluc.dubois@caramel.be
Head, Production Dept: Dirk Mennes
  E-mail: dirk.mennes@caramel.be
Export Sales Mgr: Valerie Colin
Editorial Dept: Galia van der Kar *E-mail:* galia.vanderkar@caramel.be
Founded: 1993
Also packager.
Subjects: Crafts, Games, Hobbies, Fiction
ISBN Prefix(es): 978-90-5562; 978-90-5828
Number of titles published annually: 250 Print
Imprints: Caramel

Carmelitana+
Burgstr 92, 9000 Ghent
Tel: (09) 225 48 36 *Fax:* (09) 224 06 01
E-mail: boekhandel@carmelitana.be
Web Site: www.carmelitana.be
Key Personnel
President: Jos Rymen
Editor: F Lodewijckx
Founded: 1941
Subjects: Religion - Other
ISBN Prefix(es): 978-90-70092; 978-90-76671

Carto Uitgeverij bvba
Pagodenlaan 241, 1020 Brussels
Tel: (02) 268 03 45 *Fax:* (02) 268 58 16
E-mail: uitgeverij@carto.be
Web Site: www.carto.be
Founded: 1950
Subjects: Education, Geography, Geology, History, Travel & Tourism
ISBN Prefix(es): 978-90-74437
Subsidiaries: Carpress, International Press Agency; Cremers Cartographic Institute; Cremers (Schoollandkaarten) PVBA; European Cartographic Institute

Editions Casterman SA+
Imprint of Flammarion Groupe
47 Cantersteen, 1000 Brussels
Tel: (02) 209 83 00 *Fax:* (02) 209 83 01
Web Site: www.casterman.com
Key Personnel
Dir General: Louis Delas
Dir: Willy Fadeur
Dir, Production: France Moline
Marketing Dir: Simon Casterman
International Rights Manager: Fabiana Angelini
  Tel: (02) 209 83 68 *E-mail:* f.angelini@casterman.com
Founded: 1780
Subjects: Graphic Novels
ISBN Prefix(es): 978-2-203; 978-2-542
Ultimate Parent Company: RCS MediaGroup
Branch Office(s)
87, quai Panhard et Levassor, 75647 Paris Cedex 13, France

Editions du CEFAL+
Affiliate of UDC Consortium
31, Blvd Frere Orban, 4000 Liege
Tel: (04) 254 25 20 *Fax:* (04) 254 24 40
E-mail: cefal@skynet.be
Web Site: www.cefal.com
Key Personnel
Dir: Jacques Burlet
Founded: 1993
Specialize in para-literary school books.
Membership(s): Editions de l'Universite de Liege; French Editor UDC Consortium.

Subjects: Library & Information Sciences
ISBN Prefix(es): 978-2-87130
Number of titles published annually: 30 Print
Total Titles: 80 Print
Distributor for Editions de l'Universite de Liege
(Belgium)
Distribution Center: Edipresse, 945 ave Beaumont, Montreal, QC H3N 1W3, Canada
Tel: 514-273-6141 *Fax:* 514-273-7021
E-mail: information@edipresse.ca *Web
Site:* www.edipresse.ca
Alterdis, 5, rue du Marechal Leclerc, 28600
Luisant, France

**Centrale d'Impression et d'Achat en
Cooperative,** see CIACO

Centre de Recherches Culturelles Africanistes,
see Centre Aequatoria

Centre d'etude des Primitifs Flamands, see
Studiecentrum Vlaamse Primitieven

Chantecler, *imprint of* Zuidnederlandse
Uitgeverij NV

Editions Chantecler+
Imprint of Zuidnederlandse Uitgeverij NV
Vluchtenburgstr 7, 2630 Aartselaar
Tel: (03) 870 44 05 *Fax:* (03) 877 21 15
Founded: 1947
Subjects: Fiction, Nonfiction (General)
ISBN Prefix(es): 978-2-8034; 978-90-243; 978-
90-447
Imprints: Pre-Ecole

La Charte Editions Juridiques
rue Guimard 19/2, 1040 Brussels
Tel: (02) 512 29 49 *Fax:* (02) 512 26 93
E-mail: info@lacharte.be
Web Site: juridischeuitgaven.diekeure.be/nl-be
Founded: 1948
Subjects: Government, Political Science, Language Arts, Linguistics, Law, Social Sciences,
Sociology
ISBN Prefix(es): 978-2-87403

CIACO+
Grand Rue 2-14, 1348 Louvain-la-Neuve
Tel: (010) 45 30 97 *Fax:* (010) 45 73 50
E-mail: print@ciaco.com
Web Site: www.ciaco.com
Founded: 1983
Subjects: Economics, Education, History, Literature, Literary Criticism, Essays, Management,
Medicine, Nursing, Dentistry, Philosophy, Psychology, Psychiatry, Religion - Other, Science
(General), Social Sciences, Sociology
ISBN Prefix(es): 978-2-87085
Subsidiaries: Artel SC

Clavis Uitgeverij BVBA+
Vooruitzichtstr 42, 3500 Hasselt
Tel: (011) 28 68 68 *Fax:* (011) 28 68 69
E-mail: info@clavisbooks.com
Web Site: www.clavisbooks.com
Key Personnel
Publisher & CEO: Philippe Werck
E-mail: philippe@clavisbooks.com
Commercial Dir: Anthony Vavrinek
E-mail: anthony@clavisbooks.com
General Manager: Leon Kustermans
Foreign Rights: Irina Grabinova *Tel:* (011) 28 68
62 *E-mail:* irina@clavisbooks.com
Marketing & Promotion: Tanja Appelants
Tel: (011) 28 68 63 *E-mail:* tanja@clavisbooks.
com
Founded: 1981
Subjects: Fiction, Nonfiction (General)

ISBN Prefix(es): 978-90-6822; 978-90-5933; 978-
90-77106; 978-90-448; 978-90-77060
Number of titles published annually: 150 Print
Total Titles: 806 Print
Imprints: Facet NV
U.S. Office(s): Clavis Publishing Inc, 575 Madison Ave, New York, NY 10022, United
States *E-mail:* info-us@clavisbooks.com *Web
Site:* usa.clavisbooks.com

**Coalition of the Flemish North South
Movement,** see Koepel van de Vlaamse Noord
- Zuidbewegingen 11.11.11

Editions Complexe+
24, Rue de Bosnie, 1060 Brussels
Tel: (02) 538 88 46 *Fax:* (02) 538 88 42
Web Site: www.editionscomplexe.com
Key Personnel
Production Manager: Anne Van Hees-Mertens
Rights: Yang Chen
Founded: 1971
Subjects: Biography, Memoirs, Geography, Geology, Government, Political Science, History,
Literature, Literary Criticism, Essays, Poetry,
Science (General)
ISBN Prefix(es): 978-2-87027; 978-2-8048
Number of titles published annually: 50 Print
Total Titles: 1,000 Print
Branch Office(s)
25, rue Ginoux, 75015 Paris, France, Press:
Elodie d'Athis *Tel:* 01 45 77 85 92 *Fax:* 01
45 79 97 15 *E-mail:* elodiedathis@
editionscomplexe.com

Concraid SA+
rue de la Licorne, 52, 7022 Hyon/Mons
Tel: (065) 221307 *Fax:* (065) 221306
Key Personnel
Owner: Francois Preud'homme
Founded: 1983
Specialize in finance, stock market & health.
Membership(s): Association des Editeurs Belges
(ADEB).
Subjects: Finance, Health, Nutrition
ISBN Prefix(es): 978-2-87189

Conservart+
Chaussee d'Alsemberg, 975, 1180 Brussels
Tel: (02) 332 25 38 *Fax:* (02) 375 40 40
E-mail: conservart@skynet.be
Web Site: www.conservart.be
Subjects: Architecture & Interior Design, Art,
Chemistry, Chemical Engineering, Literature,
Literary Criticism, Essays, Photography
ISBN Prefix(es): 978-2-930022

Corpus Christianorum, *imprint of* Brepols
Publishers NV

Editions Couleur Livres
4, rue Lebeau, 6000 Charleroi
Tel: (071) 32 63 22 *Fax:* (071) 32 63 22
E-mail: couleurlivres@skynet.be; commandes@
couleurlivres.be; presse@couleurlivres.be
Web Site: www.couleurlivres.be
Key Personnel
Dir: Pierre Bertrand
Press & Production: Joelle Salmon
Founded: 1958
Subjects: Economics, History, Photography, Psychology, Psychiatry, Religion - Other, Social
Sciences, Sociology
ISBN Prefix(es): 978-2-87003
Foreign Rep(s): Albert-le-Grand (Switzerland);
Diffusion CED (France); Daudin Distribution
(France); Interforum Benelux (Belgium)

Creadif
Rue de la Regence, 67, 1000 Brussels
Tel: (02) 512 98 45 *Fax:* (02) 511 72 02

Founded: 1974
Specialize in law books.
Subjects: Business, Economics, Ethnicity, Geography, Geology, History, Law, Travel & Tourism
ISBN Prefix(es): 978-2-8022

Creations for Children International
Gustaaf Callierlaan 232, Apartment 304, 9000
Gent
Tel: (09) 395 04 40
Web Site: c4ci.assist.be
Imprints: Inky Press

Le Cri Edition+
Ave Leopold Wiener 18, 1170 Brussels
Tel: (02) 646 65 33 *Fax:* (02) 646 66 07
E-mail: lecri@skynet.be
Web Site: www.lecri.be
Key Personnel
Editor: Christian Lutz
Founded: 1981
Subjects: Biography, Memoirs, History, Literature,
Literary Criticism, Essays
ISBN Prefix(es): 978-2-87106
Distribution Center: Interforum Benelux, Fond
Jean-Paques, 6 b, 1348 Louvain-la-Neuve
Tel: (010) 42 03 20 *Fax:* (010) 41 20 24
Afrique Editions, Ave de Livre 51, Kinshasa-
Gombe, Democratic Republic of the Congo
Daudin Distribution, One, Rue Guynemer, 78771
Magny Les Hameaux Cedex, France *Tel:* 01 30
48 74 74 *Fax:* 01 34 98 02 44

Le Daily-Bul
Rue Daily-Bul 29, 7100 La Louviere
Tel: (064) 22 29 73 *Fax:* (064) 22 29 73
E-mail: dailybulandco@lalouviere.be
Web Site: www.dailybulandco.be
Key Personnel
Dir: Nicolas Balthazar
Founded: 1957
Also bookseller.
Subjects: Art, Literature, Literary Criticism, Essays, Poetry
ISBN Prefix(es): 978-2-930136
Parent Company: Centre Daily-Bul & Co, Rue de
loi 14, 7100 La Louviere

Daphne Distributie NV
Poortakkerstr 29, 9051 Ghent
Tel: (09) 221 45 91 *Fax:* (09) 220 16 12
E-mail: info@daphne.be
Web Site: www.daphne.be
Key Personnel
Dir: Pierre Dubrulle
Founded: 1962
Subjects: Cookery, Fiction, Travel & Tourism
ISBN Prefix(es): 978-2-504

Davidsfonds Uitgeverij+
Blijde-Inkomststr 79-81, 3000 Leuven
Tel: (016) 310 600 *Fax:* (016) 310 608
E-mail: info@davidsfonds.be
Web Site: www.davidsfonds.be
Key Personnel
Dir: Katrien De Vreese
Publisher, Children's Books: Veerle Moureau
Publisher, Nonfiction: Dirk Remmerie
Editor: Caroline Van Godtsenhoven; Griet Vandewalle
Production: Peter Frison
Subjects: Art, Fiction, History
ISBN Prefix(es): 978-90-6152; 978-90-6565; 978-
90-6306; 978-90-5826; 978-90-5908; 978-90-
76827; 978-90-76830; 978-90-77241; 978-90-
806759; 978-90-806883; 978-90-808290
Number of titles published annually: 110 Print
Distributor for NBCC (Netherlands)
Warehouse: Distributiecentrum AGORA, De Vunt
5, 3220 Holsbeek

Editions Delta SA (Delta Publications)
64-66 rue du Tabellion, 1050 Brussels
Tel: (02) 217 55 55
E-mail: editions.delta@gmail.com
Web Site: www.delta-europe.be
Key Personnel
Mng Dir: Georges-Francis Seingry
Founded: 1976
Specialize in European public affairs & art books.
Subjects: Art, Biography, Memoirs, Cookery,
    Public Administration, European Public Affairs
ISBN Prefix(es): 978-2-8029
Number of titles published annually: 8 Print
Total Titles: 185 Print
Parent Company: EuroReferences
Distributed by Bernan (USA)

Deltas, *imprint of* Zuidnederlandse Uitgeverij NV

Derouck Geocart Edition+
Division of Derouck Geomatics SA
Breedstr 94, 9100 Sint-Niklaas
Tel: (03) 760 14 60 *Fax:* (03) 760 15 29
E-mail: carto@derouckgeocart.com
Web Site: www.derouckgeocart.com
Key Personnel
Chief Executive Officer: Mr Alain van Gelderen
    Tel: (02) 354 69 95 *E-mail:* a.vangelderen@
    derouckgeomatics.com
Founded: 1972
Specialize in digital cartography.
ISBN Prefix(es): 978-90-5208
Number of titles published annually: 60 Print
Total Titles: 145 Print
Associate Companies: La Renaissance du Livre,
    Av du Chateau Jaco 1, 1410 Waterloo, Chief
    Executive Officer: Mr Alain van Gelderen
    Tel: (02) 210 89 12 *Fax:* (02) 210 89 15
    E-mail: a.vangelderen@derouckgeomatics.com
    Web Site: www.renaissancedulivre.be

Editions Dupuis SA+
rue Destree, 52, 6001 Marcinelle
Tel: (071) 600 500 *Fax:* (071) 600 599
E-mail: info@dupuis.com; dupuis@dupuis.com;
    licensing@dupuis.com
Web Site: www.dupuis.com
Key Personnel
Dir, Audiovisual: Leon Perahia
Founded: 1898
Subjects: Humor
ISBN Prefix(es): 978-2-8001; 978-90-314; 978-
    90-6574
Parent Company: Groupe Dupuis SA
Associate Companies: Mediatoon SA
Branch Office(s)
Dupuis France SAS, 15-27 rue Moussorgski,
    75895 Paris Cedex 18, France *Tel:* 01 70 38
    56 00 *Fax:* 01 70 38 56 01
Distribution Center: Media Deffusion, Av P H
    Spaak 7, 1060 Brussels *Tel:* (02) 526 68 11
    Fax: (02) 526 68 40
Diffusion du livre Mirabel, 5757 rue Cypihot, St
    Laurent, QC H4S 1R2, Canada *Tel:* 514-334-
    2690 *Fax:* 514-334-8289

Easy Computing Publishing NV
Horzelstr 100, 1180 Brussels
Tel: (02) 346 52 52 *Fax:* (02) 346 01 20
E-mail: info@easycomputing.com
Web Site: www.easycomputing.com
Founded: 1989
Subjects: Computer Science, Computers, Elec-
    tronics, Electrical Engineering
ISBN Prefix(es): 978-90-5167; 978-90-456; 978-
    2-87208
Total Titles: 100 Print; 70 CD-ROM
Divisions: Easy Computing BV
Distributor for Micro Application
Distribution Center: Multidis NV

Ecobooks
Heerbaan 132, 1840 Londerzeel
Tel: (052) 37 11 38 *Fax:* (052) 37 11 51
E-mail: ecobooks@scarlet.be
Web Site: www.ecobooks.be
Key Personnel
Contact: Hugo Vanderstadt
Subjects: Ecology, Sustainability
ISBN Prefix(es): 978-90-75855

**Edi.pro - Editions de Chambre de Commerce
et d'Industrie SA+**
Esplanade de l'Europe 2, Boite 5, 4020 Liege
Tel: (04) 344 50 88 *Fax:* (04) 343 05 53
Web Site: www.edipro.info
Key Personnel
Mng Dir & Editor: Luca Venanzi
    E-mail: lvenanzi@edipro.info
Project Manager: Isabella Fanara
    E-mail: ifanara@edipro.info
Editor: Isabelle Mintkewicz *E-mail:* isabelle.m@
    edipro.info
Founded: 1998
Subjects: Accounting, Business, Career Develop-
    ment, Communications, Economics, Finance,
    Law, Management, Marketing, Real Estate
ISBN Prefix(es): 978-2-930287; 978-90-76924;
    978-2-87496
Number of titles published annually: 40 Print
Total Titles: 150 Print
Foreign Rep(s): DPLU (Canada, USA); Albert Le
    Grand SA (Switzerland); Horizon-Education
    (all other territories); Loglibris-Volumen
    (France); Maison du Livre (Tunisia); Librairie
    Nationale (Morocco); Patrimoine (Belgium,
    Luxembourg)

**Editions de Chambre de Commerce et
d'Industrie SA**, see Edi.pro - Editions de
Chambre de Commerce et d'Industrie SA

Uitgeverij de Eenhoorn+
Vlasstr 17, 8710 Wielsbeke
Tel: (056) 60 54 60 *Fax:* (056) 61 69 81
E-mail: info@eenhoorn.be; rights@eenhoorn.be
Web Site: www.eenhoorn.be
Key Personnel
Dir & Editor: Bart Desmyter *Tel:* (056) 62 77 32
    E-mail: bart.desmyter@eenhoorn.be
Publisher: Marita Vermeulen *Tel:* (056) 62 77 31
    E-mail: marita.vermeulen@eenhoorn.be
Press, Promotion & Foreign Rights: Sarah Claeys
    E-mail: sarah.claeys@eenhoorn.be
Press & Promotion: Nele Declercq *E-mail:* nele.
    declercq@eenhoorn.be
Founded: 1990
Subjects: Fiction
ISBN Prefix(es): 978-90-73913; 978-90-5838
Number of titles published annually: 50 Print

**EGMONT-Institut Royal des Relations
Internationales** (Egmont Royal Institute for
International Relations)
Rue de Namur 69, 1000 Brussels
Tel: (02) 223 41 14 *Fax:* (02) 223 41 16
E-mail: info@egmontinstitute.be
Web Site: www.egmontinstitute.be
Key Personnel
President: Etienne Davignon
Vice President: Dirk Achten
Executive Dir: M Cruysmans *Tel:* (02) 213 40 26
    E-mail: m.cruysmans@egmontinstitute.be
Dir General: Marc Trenteseau *E-mail:* director.
    general@egmontinstitute.be
Editor-in-Chief, Studia Diplomatica: Sven Biscop,
    PhD *E-mail:* s.biscop@egmontinstitute.be
Founded: 1947
Research institute.
Subjects: Developing Countries, Foreign Coun-
    tries, Government, Political Science
ISBN Prefix(es): 978-2-9600353; 978-2-930432

Number of titles published annually: 5 Print
Total Titles: 20 Print

EHMA, see European Health Management
Association (EHMA)

Uitgeverij EPO+
Lange Pastoorstr 25-27, 2600 Berchem, Antwerp
Tel: (03) 239 68 74 *Fax:* (03) 218 46 04
E-mail: uitgeverij@epo.be
Web Site: www.epo.be
Key Personnel
Publisher: Jos Hennes *Tel:* (03) 287 08 75
    E-mail: jos.hennes@epo.be
Editor: Hugo Franssen
Management & Planning: Martine Uytterhoeven
    E-mail: martine.uytterhoeven@epo.be
Marketing: Tim Vermast *E-mail:* tim.vermast@
    epo.be
Press & Marketing: Lotte Lemoine *E-mail:* lotte.
    lemoine@epo.be
Founded: 1978
Subjects: Anthropology, Biography, Memoirs,
    Communications, Developing Countries, Fic-
    tion, History, Journalism, Literature, Literary
    Criticism, Essays, Nonfiction (General), Psy-
    chology, Psychiatry, Social Sciences, Sociology
ISBN Prefix(es): 978-90-6445; 978-2-87262
Distributed by Centraal Boekhuis BV Culemborg
    (Netherlands)
Distributor for Uitgeverij Jan Van Arkel; The bal-
    ancing model; Bas Lubberhuizen Uitgeverij;
    Bebuquin; Benerus; Books @ Home; Bulaaq;
    The Contrabass; Coppens & Frenks; Coutinho
    (Netherlands); Demos association; The Dragon;
    Etnicom; From Gruting; Gawain; GetBasic; de
    Graaf; Les iles; Indymedia; Iron; KIT Publish-
    ers; Lavita Publishing; Maope Books; Maven
    Publishing; NCOS; Nieuwezijds; Nino (imprint
    of SWP); Note; NTR; Octavo; Paper Tiger;
    Pels & Kemper; Perdido; Pereboom; Pirola;
    Recreational Cycling; reverie; Serena Libri;
    Solidarity Fund; SWP; T Change; Themes; The
    Torch; Tornado Editions; Troth; XOI; Zirimiri
    Press
Bookshop(s): Groene Waterman, Wolstr 7, 2000
    Antwerp; Librairie Internationale, Ave LeMon-
    nier 171, 1000 Brussels
Book Club(s): Komma's en Punten

Espace de Libertes+
Campus de la Plane ULB, CP-236, Acces 2, Ave
    Arnaud Fraiteur, 1050 Brussels
Tel: (02) 627 68 60; (02) 627 68 11 *Fax:* (02)
    626 68 01
E-mail: editions@laicite.net; cal@laicite.net
Web Site: www.laicite.be
Founded: 1979
Membership(s): Association des Editeurs Belges
    (ADEB)
Subjects: Biography, Memoirs, Government, Po-
    litical Science, History, Philosophy, Religion -
    Other, Social Sciences, Sociology
ISBN Prefix(es): 978-2-930001; 978-2-875040
Number of titles published annually: 7 Print
Total Titles: 108 Print

**European Health Management Association
(EHMA)**
Rue Belliard 15-17, 6th floor, 1040 Brussels
Tel: (02) 502 65 25 *Fax:* (02) 503 10 07
E-mail: joinehma@ehma.org
Web Site: www.ehma.org
Key Personnel
Interim Dir: Usman Khan *E-mail:* usman.khan@
    ehma.org
Health Services Management Research is an au-
    thoritative international peer-reviewed journal
    which exists to publish theoretically & empir-
    ically rigorous research on questions of endur-
    ing interest & concern to health-care organiza-
    tions & systems throughout the world.
Subjects: Health, Nutrition, Management

Facet NV, *imprint of* Clavis Uitgeverij BVBA

Facet NV+
Imprint of Clavis Uitgeverij BVBA
Vooruitzichtstr 42, 3500 Hasselt
Tel: (011) 28 68 68 *Fax:* (011) 28 68 69
E-mail: info@clavisbooks.com
Web Site: www.clavisbooks.com
Founded: 1986
Specialize in children's books.
ISBN Prefix(es): 978-90-5016

Fidelite, *imprint of* Editions Jesuites

Fonds Mercator, see Mercatorfonds NV

Garant-Uitgevers NV
Somersstr 13-15, 2018 Antwerp
Tel: (03) 231 29 00 *Fax:* (03) 233 26 59
E-mail: uitgeverij@garant.be; info@garant.be
Web Site: www.maklu.be
Key Personnel
Chairman: Huug Van Gompel *E-mail:* huug.
vangompel@garant.be
Publisher: Lieve De Witte
Editorial & Production Manager: Theo Kengen
Founded: 1990
Subjects: Economics, Education, Psychology, Psychiatry, Social Sciences, Sociology
ISBN Prefix(es): 978-90-441; 978-90-5350
Number of titles published annually: 200 Print
Total Titles: 2,500 Print
Associate Companies: Maklu Uitgevers NV
Branch Office(s)
Koninginnelaan 96, 7315 EB Apeldoorn, Netherlands *Tel:* (055) 522 06 25 *Fax:* (055) 522 56 94 *E-mail:* info@garant-uitgevers.nl
Distribution Center: University Book House, 130 Planning St, Box 16983, Al Ain, United Arab Emirates *Tel:* (03) 755 82 29 *Fax:* (03) 755 69 11 *E-mail:* bookhous@emirates.net.ae *Web Site:* www.universitybookhouse.com
Central Books Ltd, One Heath Park Industrial Estate, Freshwater Rd, Dagenham RM8 1RX, United Kingdom *Tel:* (020) 8525 8800 *Fax:* (020) 8599 2694 *E-mail:* bill@centralbooks.com *Web Site:* www.centralbooks.com
Coronet Books, 311 Bainbridge St, Philadelphia, PA 19147, United States *Tel:* 215-925-2762 *Fax:* 215-925-1912 *E-mail:* jeffgolds@comcast.net

Georeto-Geogidsen
Rozenstr 11, 3723 Kortessem
Tel: (011) 37 52 54 *Fax:* (011) 37 52 54
E-mail: info@geogidsen.be
Web Site: www.geogidsen.be
Key Personnel
Contact: Pierre Diriken
Founded: 1991
Subjects: Geography, Geology, History, Outdoor Recreation, Travel & Tourism
Number of titles published annually: 4 Print
Total Titles: 45 Print

Glenat Benelux NV+
Member of Groupe Glenat
Sint Lambertusstr 131, 1200 Brussels
Tel: (02) 761 26 40 *Fax:* (02) 761 26 45
Web Site: www.glenat.be
Key Personnel
Publisher & Public Relations: Paul Herman
Marketing: Cedric Goujon-Dubois
Founded: 1985
Subjects: Antiques, Art, Automotive, Crafts, Games, Hobbies, Humor, Regional Interests, Wine & Spirits, Comics
ISBN Prefix(es): 978-2-87176; 978-90-6969
Subsidiaries: Glenat France
Distributor for Vent D'Ouest

Distribution Center: SDL Caravelle, Ganzenweidstr 303, 1130 Haren *Tel:* (02) 240 93 15 *Fax:* (02) 216 35 98 (Belgium, Luxembourg & Netherlands)

Globe, *imprint of* Roularta Books NV

Graton Editeur+
1487 Chaussee de Waterloo, 1180 Brussels
Tel: (02) 675 66 66 *Fax:* (02) 675 63 63
E-mail: info@michelvaillant.be
Web Site: www.michelvaillant.com; vaillantfanclub.free.fr
Key Personnel
Executive: Philippe Graton
Founded: 1981
Subjects: Film, Video, Journalism, Photography, Sports, Athletics, Comic Strips, Motor Racing
ISBN Prefix(es): 978-90-70816; 978-2-87098
Distributed by Diffulivre (Switzerland); Dupuis (Belgium); Hachette (France); Mosaik (Germany)

Uitgeverij Groeninghe Drukkerij BVBA
President Rooseveltplein, Belfaststr 12, 8500 Kortrijk
Tel: (056) 22 40 77 *Fax:* (056) 22 82 86
E-mail: info@groeninghedrukkerij.be
Web Site: www.groeninghedrukkerij.be
Key Personnel
Manager: Robert Timperman
Founded: 1839
Subjects: Archaeology, Art, Economics, Gardening, Plants, Government, Political Science, History, Literature, Literary Criticism, Essays, Photography, Poetry, Sports, Athletics, Cycle Racing, Enterpreneurs, Heritage, Nature, War History
ISBN Prefix(es): 978-90-71868; 978-90-77723
Associate Companies: Groeninghe Bookbinders

Uitgeverij Van Halewyck
Diestsesteenweg 71 A, 3010 Leuven
Web Site: www.vanhalewyck.be
Key Personnel
Chief Executive Officer & Publisher: Andre Van Halewyck *Tel:* (016) 359317 *E-mail:* andre@vanhalewyck.be
Publisher: Lut Raymaekers *Tel:* (016) 359317 *E-mail:* lut@vanhalewyck.be
Public Relations: Elien Delaere *Tel:* (016) 468481 *E-mail:* elien@vanhalewyck.be
Subjects: Cookery, Fiction, Nonfiction (General)
ISBN Prefix(es): 978-94-6131
Distributor for Cossee; Erven J Bijleveld; Van Gennep; Historische Uitgeverij; Librero; Oogachtend; Pegasus; Plint; Poeaziecentrum; Rubinstein; Taschen; Uitgeverij Vantilt

Van Hemeldonck BVBA+
Emiel Van Hemeldonckstr 5, 2350 Vosselaar
Tel: (014) 611034
Founded: 1932
Specialize in large prints.
ISBN Prefix(es): 978-90-5274

Editions Hemma+
106, rue de Chevron, 4987 Chevron
Tel: (086) 43 01 01 *Fax:* (086) 43 36 40
E-mail: hemma@hemma.be
Web Site: www.hemma.be
Key Personnel
Dir: Albert Hemmerlin
Founded: 1952
Subjects: Crafts, Games, Hobbies, Fiction, Mysteries, Suspense, Science Fiction, Fantasy
ISBN Prefix(es): 978-2-8006; 978-90-6804; 978-90-380; 978-90-412
Subsidiaries: Editions Diffusion Hemma; Hemma Joven SA; Hemma Verlag GmbH

Foreign Rep(s): Dar Almoufid (Lebanon); Diffusion Transat SA (Switzerland); Impato (Switzerland); Messageries du Livre (Luxembourg); Les Presses D-Or (Canada) Inc (Canada); Socadis Inc (Canada)

De Horstink, *imprint of* Acco Uitgeverij

Uitgeverij Houtekiet
Imprint of Linkeroever Uitgevers
Katwilgweg 2, 2050 Antwerp
Tel: (03) 210 30 50 *Fax:* (03) 238 80 41
E-mail: info@houtekiet.com; info@linkeroeveruitgevers.be
Web Site: www.houtekiet.com
Key Personnel
Press & Promotion: Ann Horsten *Tel:* (03) 210 30 59 *E-mail:* ahorsten@linkeroeveruitgevers.be
Production & Marketing: Mathieu Morret *E-mail:* mmorret@vbku.be
Founded: 1986
ISBN Prefix(es): 978-90-5240; 978-90-70876; 978-90-5067
Ultimate Parent Company: Veen Bosch & Keuning Uitgeversgroep BV

Huis Van Het Boek
Te Boelaerlei 37, 2140 Borgerhout
Tel: (03) 230 89 23 *Fax:* (03) 281 22 40
E-mail: info@boek.be
Web Site: www.boek.be
Key Personnel
General Dir: Geert Joris
Founded: 1929
Publisher & professional organization for booksellers, distributors & editors.
Subjects: Literature, Literary Criticism, Essays, Publishing & Book Trade Reference
ISBN Prefix(es): 978-90-72103; 978-90-77165

Les Impressions Nouvelles
84 ave Albert, 1190 Brussels
Tel: (02) 503 30 95 *Fax:* (02) 503 30 33
E-mail: info@lesimpressionsnouvelles.com
Web Site: www.lesimpressionsnouvelles.com
Key Personnel
Dir: Benoit Peeters
Founded: 1985
Subjects: Drama, Theater, Poetry, Cartoon, Humanities
ISBN Prefix(es): 978-2-906131; 978-2-87449
Distribution Center: Caravelle, Rue du Pre aux Oies, 303, 1130 Brussels *Tel:* (02) 240 93 00 *Fax:* (02) 216 35 98 *E-mail:* info@sdlcaravelle.com
Dimedia, Canada *Web Site:* www.dimedia.qc.ca
Harmonia Mundi, Mas de Vert, Petite route de St Gilles, BP 20150, 13631 Arles Cedex, France *Tel:* 04 90 49 58 05 *Fax:* 04 90 49 58 35 *E-mail:* adv-livre@harmoniamundi.com
Diffusion Zoe, 11, rue des Moraines, 1227 Carouge, Geneva, Switzerland *Tel:* (022) 309 36 00 *Fax:* (022) 309 36 03 *E-mail:* commandes@editionszoe.ch

Imprimerie Hayez SPRL
Rue Fernand Brunfaut 19, 1080 Brussels
Tel: (02) 413 02 00 *Fax:* (02) 411 23 78
E-mail: info@hayez.be
Web Site: www.hayez.be
Key Personnel
Chief Executive Officer & Dir: Maximilien Hayez *E-mail:* mh@hayez.be
Mng Dir: Serge Hayez *E-mail:* sh@hayez.be
Technical Dir: Michel Bouhon *E-mail:* mb@hayez.be
Founded: 1780
Subjects: History, Medicine, Nursing, Dentistry, Philosophy, Poetry, Religion - Other, Science (General), Sports, Athletics
ISBN Prefix(es): 978-2-87126

Infor Jeunes Namur ASBL
Rue du Beffroi, 4, 5000 Namur
Tel: (081) 22 38 12 *Fax:* (081) 22 41 22
E-mail: namur@inforjeunes.be
Web Site: www.inforjeunesnamur.be
Key Personnel
Dir: Lillo Canta
Publisher: Fabian Martin
Membership(s): European Youth Information &
Counselling Agency (ERYICA).
Subjects: Education

Inky Press, *imprint of* Creations for Children
International

Intersentia NV
Groenstr 31, 2640 Mortsel-Antwerp
Tel: (03) 680 15 50 *Fax:* (03) 658 71 21
E-mail: mail@intersentia.be
Web Site: www.intersentia.be
Key Personnel
Publisher: Hans Kluwer *Tel:* (03) 680 15 57
Publisher, Law: Kris Moeremans *E-mail:* k.
moeremans@intersentia.be
Founded: 1996
Academic publishing house. Specialize in Bel-
gian, Dutch, European & international law &
economics.
Subjects: Accounting, Business, Economics, Fi-
nance, Law, Human Rights, European Law
ISBN Prefix(es): 978-90-5095; 978-94-000
Number of titles published annually: 70 Print; 3
CD-ROM
Total Titles: 420 Print; 2 Online
Distributor for Hart Publishing
Foreign Rep(s): Aditya Books Pvt Ltd (Kailash
Balani) (India); James Bennett Pty Ltd (Aus-
tralia); Booknet Co Ltd (Suphaluck Sattabuz)
(Cambodia, Laos, Myanmar, Thailand, Viet-
nam); ChoiceTEXTS (Asia) Pte Ltd (Phillip
Ang) (Indonesia, Singapore); Hart Publishing
Ltd (UK); IG Knowledge Services Ltd (Grace
Wang) (Taiwan); iGroup Press Co Ltd (Frank
Wang) (China); International Specialized Book
Services Inc (Canada, USA); D J Kim (Ko-
rea); Eddy Lam (Hong Kong); Liang-Hoe Lee
(Brunei, Malaysia); Mare Nostrum (France,
Italy); MegaTEXTS Phil Inc (Jean Tiu Lim)
(Philippines); Schulthess Verlag (Switzerland)

Invader, *imprint of* Zuidnederlandse Uitgeverij
NV

Toneelfonds J Janssens+
Te Boelaerlei 107, 2140 Borgerhout, Antwerp
Tel: (03) 366 44 00 *Fax:* (03) 366 45 01
E-mail: info@toneelfonds.be
Web Site: www.toneelfonds.be
Key Personnel
Dir: Jessica Janssens
Founded: 1880
Publisher of theatre plays.
Also literary agent for playwrights.
Subjects: Drama, Theater
ISBN Prefix(es): 978-90-385
Number of titles published annually: 100 Print

Editions Jesuites
7, rue Blondeau, 5000 Namur
Tel: (081) 22 15 51 *Fax:* (081) 22 08 97
E-mail: info@editionsjesuites.com; contact@
editionsjesuites.com
Web Site: www.editionsjesuites.com
Key Personnel
Administrative Dir: Jean Hanotte *E-mail:* jean.
hanotte@editionsjesuites.com
Dir General: Pierre Sauvage *E-mail:* pierre.
sauvage@editionsjesuites.com
Subjects: Inspirational, Spirituality, Philosophy,
Theology, Christian, Faith, Pastoral Liturgy,
Prayer, Social Issues

ISBN Prefix(es): 978-2-87324 (Lumen Vitae);
978-2-87299 (Lessius); 978-2-87356 (Fidelite)
Imprints: Fidelite; Lessius; Lumen Vitae
Branch Office(s)
14, Rue d'Assas, 75006 Paris, France

Editions Jourdan
Ave Paul de Lorraine, 5, 1410 Waterloo
Tel: (02) 626 06 70 *Fax:* (02) 626 06 79
E-mail: editorial@editionsjourdan.com; info@
editionsjourdan.com; presse@editionsjourdan.
com
Web Site: www.editionsjourdan.com
Founded: 1999
Subjects: Art, Criminology, Fiction, History
ISBN Prefix(es): 978-2-87466; 978-2-930359
Number of titles published annually: 60 Print
Branch Office(s)
Rue de Penthievre 10, 75008 Paris, France
Tel: 09 72 54 51 61
Distribution Center: Interforum Editis, Fond Jean
Paques, 6, 1348 Louvain-La-Neuve *Tel:* (010)
42 03 20 *Fax:* (010) 41 20 24 *E-mail:* info@
interforum.be
Interforum Canada, 1055 blvd Rene Levesque E,
Montreal H2L 4S5, Canada
Interforum, Bldg Paryseine, 3 Alley de la Seine,
94854 Ivry Cedex, France
Interforum Switzerland, 33A Route Andre Piller
Givisiez, 1701 Fribourg, Switzerland

Kate'Art Edition
Rue de l'Automne 56, 1050 Brussels
Tel: (02) 648 68 58
E-mail: info@kateart.com
Web Site: www.kateart.com
Founded: 2000
Subjects: Art, History
ISBN Prefix(es): 978-2-93038; 978-2-9600406

Die Keure NV+
Kleine Pathoekeweg 3, 8000 Brugge
Tel: (050) 47 12 72 *Fax:* (050) 34 37 68
E-mail: info@diekeure.be
Web Site: www.diekeure.be
Key Personnel
Publisher: Bart Vandenbussche *Tel:* (050) 47 12
88 *Fax:* (050) 47 12 87
Marketing: Gisele Quenis *Fax:* (050) 47 12 87
Founded: 1948
Subjects: Education
ISBN Prefix(es): 978-90-6200; 978-90-5751; 978-
90-5958; 978-90-486; 978-90-8661

King Baudouin Foundation
Brederodestr 21, 1000 Brussels
Tel: (02) 511 18 40; (070) 233 065 *Fax:* (02) 511
52 21
E-mail: proj@kbs-frb.be; info@kbs-frb.be
Web Site: www.kbs-frb.be
Key Personnel
Mng Dir: Luc Tayart de Borms *E-mail:* tayart.l@
kbs-frb.be
Founded: 1976
Improve living conditions for the population tak-
ing economic, social, scientific & cultural fac-
tors into account.
Subjects: Agriculture, Architecture & Interior De-
sign, Economics, Labor, Industrial Relations,
Social Sciences, Sociology
ISBN Prefix(es): 978-90-5130; 978-2-87212

Editions Kluwer
Ragheno Business Park, Motstr 30, 2800 Meche-
len
Tel: (015) 36 10 00 *Toll Free Tel:* 0800 94 571
Fax: (015) 36 11 91 *Toll Free Fax:* 0800 17
529
E-mail: klant.be@wolterskluwer.com
Web Site: www.wolterskluwer.be/corporate/nl

Key Personnel
Dir: Guy VanPeel
Founded: 1977
Subjects: Economics, Law
ISBN Prefix(es): 978-90-6321; 978-90-5583; 978-
90-6716; 978-90-5928; 978-90-5062; 978-90-
5938; 978-90-465; 978-2-87377
Parent Company: Wolters Kluwer Belgie NV
Ultimate Parent Company: Wolters Kluwer NV,
Apollolaan 153, PO Box 75248, 1077 AE Am-
sterdam, Netherlands

KnackBibliotheek/Radio 1, *imprint of* Roularta
Books NV

**Koepel van de Vlaamse Noord -
Zuidbewegingen 11.11.11** (Coalition of the
Flemish North South Movement)+
Vlasfabriekstr 11, 1060 Brussels
Tel: (02) 536 11 11 *Fax:* (02) 536 19 10
E-mail: info@11.be
Web Site: www.11.be
Key Personnel
Education Coordinator: Bart Demedts *Tel:* (02)
536 11 14 *E-mail:* bart.demedts@11.be
Founded: 1966
Specialize in Third World affairs.
Subjects: Anthropology, Child Care & Develop-
ment, Cookery, Developing Countries, Eco-
nomics, Geography, Geology, Government, Po-
litical Science, Health, Nutrition, Journalism,
Labor, Industrial Relations, Literature, Literary
Criticism, Essays, Travel & Tourism
ISBN Prefix(es): 978-90-71665
Distributed by Jan Van Arkel (Netherlands); Van
Haelewyck-Uitgeverij (Belgium)
Distributor for Kit (Netherlands); Jan Mets
(Netherlands); Novib (Netherlands)

**Koninklijke Vlaamse Academie van Belgie
voor Wetenschappen en Kunsten (KVAB)**
(Royal Flemish Academy of Belgium for
Sciences & Arts)
Paleis der Academien, Hertogsstr 1, 1000 Brus-
sels
Tel: (02) 550 23 23 *Fax:* (02) 550 23 25
E-mail: publicaties@kvab.be
Web Site: www.kvab.be
Key Personnel
Chairman: Pierre Jacobs
Permanent Secretary: Gery Van Outryve
d'Ydewalle
Founded: 1938
Membership(s): International Academic Associa-
tion.
Subjects: Art, Music, Dance, Philosophy, Science
(General)
ISBN Prefix(es): 978-90-6569

La Charte
Kleine Pathoekeweg 3, 8000 Bruges
Tel: (05) 0471272 *Fax:* (05) 0343768
E-mail: info@lacharte.be
Web Site: www.diekeure.be/fr-be/la-charte
Key Personnel
Chief Executive Officer: Alexis Bogaert
Subjects: Education, Law, Management
ISBN Prefix(es): 978-90-4860
Parent Company: Die Keure Printing & Publish-
ing

Uitgeverij Lannoo NV (Lannoo Publishers)+
Kasteelstr 97, 8700 Tielt
Tel: (051) 42 42 11 *Fax:* (051) 40 11 52
E-mail: lannoo@lannoo.be
Web Site: www.lannoo.com
Key Personnel
Mng Dir: Matthias Lannoo
Editorial Dir: Lieven Sercu
Founded: 1909

Subjects: Architecture & Interior Design, Art, Biography, Memoirs, Cookery, Economics, Gardening, Plants, Government, Political Science, Health, Nutrition, History, House & Home, Management, Nonfiction (General), Photography, Poetry, Religion - Catholic, Self-Help, Travel & Tourism
ISBN Prefix(es): 978-90-209; 978-94-014
Associate Companies: DistriMedia NV, Meulebeeksesteenweg 20, 8700 Tielt *Tel:* (051) 42 38 60; Meulenhoff Boekerij BV, Herengracht 507, 1017 BV Amsterdam, Netherlands *Tel:* (020) 535 31 35; TerraLannoo BV, Papiermolen 14-24, 3994 DK Houten, Netherlands *Tel:* (030) 300 04 00; Unieboek|Het Spectrum BV, Papiermolen 14-24, 3994 DK Houten, Netherlands *Tel:* (030) 799 83 00
Subsidiaries: Academia Press; LannooCampus Uitgeverij; Editions Racine
Divisions: Lannoo Graphics
Distributed by TerraLannoo (Netherlands)
Distributor for ANWB (Netherlands); Baeckens Books (Belgium); Beta-Plus (Belgium); Van Duuren (Netherlands); Forte (Netherlands); LannooCampus (Belgium & Netherlands); Meulenhoff Boekerij (Netherlands); Michelin Distributie (Belgium); Editions Moulinsart (Belgium); Racine (Belgium); TerraLannoo (Netherlands); Unieboek|Het Spectrum BV (Netherlands)
Warehouse: DistriMedia NV, Meulebeeksesteenweg 20, 8700 Tielt *Tel:* (051) 42 38 60
Distribution Center: ACC Distribution (UK & USA)
Edigroup/Vilo (France)
La Generale du Livre (France)
OLF (Switzerland)

Lansman Editeur (Lansman Publisher)+
EMILE&CIE-Rue Royale, 63-65, 7141 Carnieres/Morlanwelz
Tel: (064) 23 78 40 *Fax:* (064) 23 78 49
E-mail: info.lansman@gmail.com
Web Site: www.lansman.org
Key Personnel
Dir: Emile Lansman
Press, Bookshop: Caroline Cullus
Founded: 1989
Specialize in theatre in French language (plays & research books).
Subjects: Art, Drama, Theater, Education, Literature, Literary Criticism, Essays
ISBN Prefix(es): 978-2-87282
Number of titles published annually: 40 Print
Total Titles: 700 Print
Distribution Center: Prothedis, Espace Culture Provincial, 19, Pl de la Hestre, bte 3, 7170 Manage *E-mail:* prothedis@promotion-theatre.org
Diffusion Dimedia Inc, 539, blvd Lebeau, St-Laurent, QC H4N 1S2, Canada *Tel:* 514-336-3941 *Fax:* 514-331-3916 *E-mail:* general@dimedia.qc.ca
Daudin Distribution, One, rue Guynemer, CS 30504, 78771 Magny-les-Hameaux Cedex, France *Tel:* 01 30 48 74 50 *E-mail:* commandes@daudin.fr

Editions Larcier
Rue Haute, 139, Loft 6, 1000 Brussels
Tel: (02) 548 07 13 *Fax:* (02) 548 07 14
E-mail: marketing@larciergroup.com; press@larciergroup.com; contact@larciergroup.com
Web Site: editionslarcier.larciergroup.com
Key Personnel
Chief Executive Officer: Marc Olivier Lifrange
Chief Publishing Officer: Anne Jacobs
Marketing Dir: Elisabeth Courtens
Press & Public Relations: Charlotte Claes
Editor: Nicolas Cassart; Roxane Jungbluth; Evelyne Vannoote
Founded: 1839
Subjects: Law

ISBN Prefix(es): 978-2-8044
Parent Company: Groupe Larcier
Foreign Rep(s): Lextenso Editions (France); NBN International (Ireland, UK); Librairie Papeterie Nationale (Morocco); Servidis (Switzerland)
Distribution Center: Larcier Distribution Services SPRL, Blvd Baudouin 1er, 25, 1348 Louvain-la-Neuve *E-mail:* commande@larciergroup.com (worldwide exc France, Ireland, Morocco, Switzerland & UK)

Claude Lefrancq Editeur+
Alsembergse Steenweg 386, 1180 Brussels
Tel: (02) 344 49 34 *Fax:* (02) 347 55 34
Founded: 1995
Subjects: Anthropology, Biography, Memoirs, Film, Video, Humor, Literature, Literary Criticism, Essays, Mysteries, Suspense, Romance
ISBN Prefix(es): 978-2-87153; 978-90-71987; 978-90-75388

Lessius, *imprint of* Editions Jesuites

La Lettre volee
146 ave Coghen, 1180 Brussels
Tel: (02) 512 02 88 *Fax:* (02) 512 02 88
E-mail: lettre.volee@skynet.be
Web Site: www.lettrevolee.com
Key Personnel
Dir: Daniel Vander Gucht; Pierre-Yves Soucy
Founded: 1989
Subjects: Architecture & Interior Design, Art, Literature, Literary Criticism, Essays, Social Sciences, Sociology
ISBN Prefix(es): 978-2-87317
Distribution Center: Exhibitions International, Kol Begaultlaan 17, 3012 Leuven *Tel:* (016) 29 69 00 *Fax:* (016) 29 61 29 *E-mail:* orders@exhibitionsinternational.be (Europe exc France & French-speaking Switzerland)
Les Belles Lettres, 25, rue du General Leclerc, 94270 Le Kremlin-Bicetre, France *Tel:* 01 45 15 19 90 *Fax:* 01 45 15 19 99 *E-mail:* bldd@lesbelleslettres.com (France & French-speaking Switzerland)

Leuven University Press (Universitaire Pers Leuven)+
Division of KU Leuven
Minderbroedersstr 4, 3000 Leuven
Tel: (016) 32 53 45 *Fax:* (016) 32 53 52
E-mail: info@lup.be
Web Site: www.upers.kuleuven.be
Key Personnel
Dir: Veerle De Laet *E-mail:* veerle.delaet@lup.be
Editor: Beatrice Van Eeghem *E-mail:* beatrice.vaneeghem@lup.be
Acquisitions Editor: Viktor Emonds
   E-mail: viktor.emonds@upl.be
Finance Manager: Margreet Meijer
   E-mail: margreet.meijer@lup.be
Marketing Manager: Annemie Vandezande
   E-mail: annemie.vandezande@lup.be
Production Coordinator: Patricia Di Costanzo
   E-mail: patricia.dicostanzo@lup.be
Founded: 1971
Membership(s): Association of European University Presses (AEUP); Association of University Presses (AUPresses).
Subjects: Agriculture, Archaeology, Art, Biological Sciences, Criminology, Economics, Education, Environmental Studies, Geography, Geology, Government, Political Science, History, Language Arts, Linguistics, Law, Literature, Literary Criticism, Essays, Mathematics, Medicine, Nursing, Dentistry, Music, Dance, Philosophy, Physical Sciences, Physics, Psychology, Psychiatry, Religion - Other, Science (General), Social Sciences, Sociology, Theology
ISBN Prefix(es): 978-90-6186; 978-90-5867

Number of titles published annually: 40 Print; 1 Audio
Total Titles: 1,000 Print; 5 CD-ROM; 3 Audio
Imprints: Lipsius Leuven
Foreign Rep(s): University Presses Marketing (Denmark, Finland, France, Greece, Ireland, Norway, Sweden, UK)
Distribution Center: Centraal Boekhuis, Erasmusweg 10, 4104 AK Culemborg, Netherlands *Tel:* (0345) 47 59 11 *Fax:* (0345) 47 53 43 *E-mail:* info@centraalboekhuis.nl
NBN International, 10 Thornbury Rd, Plymouth PL6 7PP, United Kingdom *Tel:* (01752) 202301 *Fax:* (01752) 202333 *E-mail:* orders@nbninternational.com *Web Site:* www.nbninternational.com (UK, Ireland, Denmark, Sweden, Norway, Finland, France & Greece)
Cornell University Press, 750 Cascadilla St, PO Box 6525, Ithaca, NY 14851-6525, United States *Tel:* 607-277-2211 *Fax:* 607-277-6292 *E-mail:* cupress-sales@cornell.edu *Web Site:* www.cornellpress.cornell.edu (USA & Canada)
Orders to: NBN International, 10 Thornbury Rd, Plymouth PL6 7PP, United Kingdom *Tel:* (01752) 202301 *Fax:* (01752) 202333 *E-mail:* orders@nbninternational.com *Web Site:* www.nbninternational.com
Cornell University Press, 750 Cascadilla St, PO Box 6525, Ithaca, NY 14851-6525, United States *Tel:* 607-277-2211 *Fax:* 607-277-6292 *E-mail:* cupress-sales@cornell.edu *Web Site:* www.cornellpress.cornell.edu (USA & Canada)

Liberica, *imprint of* Zuidnederlandse Uitgeverij NV

Ligue pour la Lecture de la Bible+
Subsidiary of Scripture Union
Ave Giele 23, 1090 Brussels
Tel: (02) 427 92 77 *Fax:* (02) 428 82 06
E-mail: info@ligue.be
Web Site: www.ligue.be
Key Personnel
National Secretary: Jean-Pierre Frere
Head of Administration: Annabel Jourez
Founded: 1955
Subjects: Religion - Other
ISBN Prefix(es): 978-2-87001
Number of titles published annually: 3 Print
Distributed by Ligue pour la Lecture de la Bible Quebec, Canada; Ligue pour la Lecture de la Bible France; Maison de la Bible Suisse
Distributor for Ligue pour la Lecture de la Bible France; Maison de la Bible Suisse

Lipsius Leuven, *imprint of* Leuven University Press

Les Editions du Lombard SA+
Ave Paul-Henri Spaak, 7, 1060 Brussels
Tel: (02) 526 68 11 *Fax:* (02) 520 44 05
E-mail: info@lombard.be
Web Site: www.lelombard.com
Key Personnel
Dir General: Francois Pernot
Founded: 1946
Subjects: Fiction, History, Humor, Science Fiction, Fantasy
ISBN Prefix(es): 978-2-8036; 978-90-6421
Parent Company: Groupe Dargaud
Subsidiaries: Citel & Dargaud; Dargaud Benelux; Dargaud Marina; Dargaud Suisse
Branch Office(s)
15-27, rue Moussorgski, 75018 Paris, France
   Tel: 01 53 26 32 32 *Fax:* 01 53 26 32 00

Uitgeverij Ludion+
Imprint of Uitgeverij De Bezige Bij BV
Mechelsesteenweg 203, 2000 Antwerp
Tel: (03) 285 72 00 *Fax:* (03) 285 72 99
E-mail: info@wpg.be

Web Site: www.ludion.be
Key Personnel
Publisher: Peter Ruyffelaere *E-mail:* peter.
  ruyffelaere@wpg.be
Editor: Sandra Darbe *E-mail:* sandra.darbe@wpg.
  be
Press & Promotion: Michele Meermans
  E-mail: michele.meermans@wpg.be
Subjects: Architecture & Interior Design, Art,
  Fashion, Film, Video, Music, Dance, Photogra-
  phy
ISBN Prefix(es): 978-90-5544
Ultimate Parent Company: WPG Uitgevers Belgie
  NV
Branch Office(s)
Uitgeverij Ludion/De Bezige Bij, Van Mierev-
  eldstr 1, Postbus 75184, 1071 DW Amster-
  dam *Tel:* (020) 3059810 *Fax:* (020) 3059824
  E-mail: info@debezigebij.nl *Web Site:* www.
  debezigebij.nl
Orders to: WPG Uitgevers Belgie *Tel:* (03)
  2059400 *Fax:* (03) 2339569 *E-mail:* orders@
  ludion.be *Web Site:* www.wpg.be

Lumen Vitae, *imprint of* Editions Jesuites

Uitgeverij Luster
Hopland 33 bus 4.2, 2000 Antwerp
Tel: (03) 298 37 23 *Fax:* (03) 298 37 24
E-mail: info@lusterweb.com
Web Site: www.uitgeverijluster.be
Key Personnel
Mng Dir: Tania Van de Vondel *E-mail:* tania@
  lusterweb.com
Founded: 2009
Subjects: Architecture & Interior Design, Cook-
  ery, Photography, Travel & Tourism, Culture,
  Lifestyle
ISBN Prefix(es): 978-94-6058

Maklu-Uitgevers NV+
Somersstr 13-15, 2018 Antwerp
Tel: (03) 231 29 00 *Fax:* (03) 233 26 59
E-mail: info@maklu.be
Web Site: www.maklu.be
Founded: 1972
Specialize in law books & dictionaries.
Also wholesaler (Dutch books).
Subjects: Criminology, Economics, Government,
  Political Science, Law, Management, Social
  Sciences, Sociology
ISBN Prefix(es): 978-90-6215; 978-90-466
Number of titles published annually: 80 Print
Total Titles: 1,052 Print
Associate Companies: Garant Uitgevers NV
Branch Office(s)
Koninginnelaan 96, 7315 EB Apeldoorn, Nether-
  lands *Tel:* (055) 522 06 25 *Fax:* (055) 522 56
  94 *E-mail:* info@maklu.nl
Distribution Center: ISBS, 920 NE 58 Ave,
  Suite 300, Portland, OR 97213, United
  States *Tel:* 503-287-3093 *Fax:* 503-280-8832
  E-mail: info@isbs.com (USA & Canada)

Manteau, *imprint of* Standaard Uitgeverij

Editions Mardaga
Rue du College, 27, 1050 Brussels
Tel: (02) 894 09 40 *Fax:* (02) 894 09 48
E-mail: info@editionsmardaga.com
Web Site: www.editionsmardaga.com
Key Personnel
Dir: Clotilde Guislain *Tel:* (02) 894 09 41
  E-mail: clotilde.guislain@editionsmardaga.com
Editor: Andre Querton *E-mail:* andre.querton@
  editionsmardaga.com; Brigitte de Ter-
  wange *Tel:* (02) 894 09 44 *E-mail:* brigitte.
  deterwangne@editionsmardaga.com
Founded: 1938
1600 titles available.

Subjects: Architecture & Interior Design, Art,
  Education, Language Arts, Linguistics, Mu-
  sic, Dance, Philosophy, Psychology, Psychiatry,
  Social Sciences, Sociology, Humanities
ISBN Prefix(es): 978-2-87009; 978-2-8047
Number of titles published annually: 45 Print
Total Titles: 1,600 Print

Editions Masoin+
Ave Masoin 15, 1090 Brussels
Tel: (02) 478 37 06 *Fax:* (02) 478 64 29
Web Site: www.editions-masoin.be
Key Personnel
President & Administrator: Charles Blanchart
  E-mail: charles.blanchart@scarlet.be
Founded: 2008
Also distributor.
Subjects: Transportation, Central Africa, Railways
ISBN Prefix(es): 978-2-87202
Number of titles published annually: 2 Print
Total Titles: 11 Print
Distributor for George Antippas; ARBAC; Edi-
  tions G Blanchart & Co; Publishing Cabri;
  Heritage Railway & Tourism; Light Rail Tran-
  sit Association; Of Alk; Presses & Publishing
  Railway; Robert Schwandl Verlag; The Train;
  Tram 2000; Uquilair Uitgeverij; La Vie du Rail

Mercatorfonds NV+
Rue du Midi 2, 1000 Brussels
Tel: (02) 548 25 35 *Fax:* (02) 502 16 28
E-mail: kunstboeken@mercatorfonds.be
Web Site: www.mercatorfonds.be
Founded: 1965
Publisher of fine art books & illustrated historical
  studies.
Subjects: Archaeology, Architecture & Interior
  Design, Art, History, Music, Dance, Photogra-
  phy, Contemporary Art, Cultural History, Mod-
  ern Art
ISBN Prefix(es): 978-90-6153
Number of titles published annually: 30 Print
Foreign Rep(s): Actes Sud (Canada, France,
  Switzerland); Exhibitions International (world-
  wide exc Canada, France & Switzerland)

Meulenhoff/Manteau, *imprint of* Standaard
Uitgeverij

Editions Mijade
18, rue de l'Ouvrage, 5000 Namur
Tel: (081) 26 22 97 *Fax:* (081) 23 18 98
Web Site: www.mijade.be
Key Personnel
Dir: Michel Demeulenaere
Editor: Muriel Molhant
Marketing/Communications: Gaetane Ponet
Founded: 1993
Subjects: Fiction
ISBN Prefix(es): 978-2-87142
Foreign Rep(s): Gallimard (Switzerland); Pro-
  logue (Canada); Sofedis (France)
Distribution Center: SDLC-La Caravelle, 303,
  Rue du Pre aux Oies, 1130 Brussels *Tel:* (02)
  240 93 00 *Fax:* (02) 216 35 98 *E-mail:* info@
  sdlcaravelle.com *Web Site:* www.sdlcaravelle.
  com

Harvey Miller, *imprint of* Brepols Publishers NV

Harvey Miller Publishers+
Imprint of Brepols Publishers NV
Begijnhof 67, 2300 Turnhout
Tel: (014) 44 80 30 *Fax:* (014) 42 89 19
E-mail: info@brepols.net
Web Site: www.harveymillerpublishers.com; www.
  brepols.net
Key Personnel
Publishing Manager: Johan Van der Beke
  E-mail: johan.vanderbeke@brepols.net
Founded: 1968

Subjects: Art, History
ISBN Prefix(es): 978-0-905203; 978-1-872501;
  978-0-85602; 978-1-905375
Associate Companies: G+B Arts International
U.S. Office(s): PO Box 58070, Lenox Hill Sta-
  tion, Washington, DC 20037, United States
  Tel: 212-288-4090
Distributed by International Publishers Distributor
Distribution Center: Casemate | academic, 20
  Main St, PO Box 511, Oakville, CT 06779,
  United States *Tel:* 860-945-9329 *Fax:* 860-945-
  9468 *Web Site:* www.oxbowbooks.com/dbbc/
  (Canada & USA)
Marston Book Services Ltd, 160 Eastern
  Ave, Milton Park, Abingdon, Oxon OX14
  4SB, United Kingdom *Tel:* (01235) 465500
  Fax: (01235) 465555 *E-mail:* direct.orders@
  marston.co.uk *Web Site:* www.marston.co.uk
  (UK)

Editions Mols
tienne de la Petite Bilande, 67, 1300 Wavre
Tel: (010) 86 28 00; 32 475 735 800 (cell)
  Fax: (010) 24 58 17
E-mail: mols@skynet.be
Web Site: www.editions-mols.eu
Key Personnel
Mng Dir: Philippe Comeliau *E-mail:* philippe.
  comeliau@editions-mols.eu
Founded: 1994
Subjects: Fiction, Government, Political Science,
  History, Inspirational, Spirituality, Literature,
  Literary Criticism, Essays, Nonfiction (Gen-
  eral), Philosophy, Religion - Other, Self-Help,
  Theology
ISBN Prefix(es): 978-2-87402
Number of titles published annually: 15 Print
Total Titles: 200 Print
Foreign Rep(s): Nord-Sud (Belgium); OLF
  (Switzerland); Socadis (Canada); Sodis
  (France)

Moneta
Hoenderstr 22, 9230 Wetteren
Tel: (09) 369 15 95 *Fax:* (09) 369 59 25
E-mail: info@moneta.be
Web Site: www.moneta.be
Key Personnel
Contact: Georges Depeyrot
Founded: 1894
Specialize in numismatic publications.
Subjects: Art, Economics, History, Literature, Lit-
  erary Criticism, Essays, Photography, Poetry
ISBN Prefix(es): 978-90-74623; 978-94-91384;
  978-90-77297

Nauwelaerts Editions SA+
19, Rue de l'Eglise-St-Sulpice, 1320 Beauvechain
Tel: (010) 86 67 37 *Fax:* (010) 86 16 55
Key Personnel
Mng Dir: Stephane Rouget
Founded: 1934
Subjects: Economics, History, Literature, Literary
  Criticism, Essays, Medicine, Nursing, Den-
  tistry, Philosophy, Psychology, Psychiatry, So-
  cial Sciences, Sociology, Theology
ISBN Prefix(es): 978-2-8038

Editions Nevicata
42 Ave du General de Gaulle, 1050 Brussels
Tel: (02) 647 83 78
E-mail: info@editionsnevicata.be
Web Site: editionsnevicata.be
Founded: 2008
Subjects: Biography, Memoirs, History, Nonfic-
  tion (General), Travel & Tourism
ISBN Prefix(es): 978-2-87523; 978-2-9600255
Distribution Center: Adybooks Diffusion, Rue
  de Rotterdam 20, 4000 Liege, Contact: Andre
  Delruelle *Tel:* (04) 223 18 28 *E-mail:* andre.
  delruelle@adybooks.be (Belgium & Luxem-
  bourg)

L'Arche du Livre Inc, 1740 rue du College, St-Laurent, Quebec H4L 2M7, Canada *Tel:* 514-744-7396 *E-mail:* archedulivre@hotmail.com
CED Diffusion, 128 bis ave Jean Jaures, 94200 Ivry-sur-Seine, France *Tel:* 01 46 58 38 40 *E-mail:* societe@ced-cedif.fr
Albert le Grand, Route de Beaumont, 20, 1701 Fribourg, Switzerland *Tel:* (026) 425 85 95 *E-mail:* diffusion@albert-le-grand.ch

Editions NordSud (NorthSouth Editions)
Subsidiary of NordSud Verlag AG (Switzerland)
18 rue de l'ouvrage, 5000 Namur
Tel: (081) 26 22 97
E-mail: info@editionsnordsud.com
Web Site: www.editionsnordsud.com
Key Personnel
Dir, Editor: Michel Demeulenaere
Editor (novels): Muriel Molhant
Marketing/Communication: Gaetane Ponet
Founded: 1981
ISBN Prefix(es): 978-3-314
Associate Companies: NorthSouth Books Inc, 11 E 26 St, New York, NY 10010, United States *Tel:* 212-706-4545 *Fax:* 212-706-4545

Nova Vista Publishing+
Imprint of Kathe Grooms BVBA
Fraikinstr 43D, 2200 Herentals
Tel: (0476) 360 989
E-mail: kgrooms@novavistapub.com
Web Site: www.novavistapub.com
Subjects: Business, Career Development, Communications, Environmental Studies, Management, Music, Dance, Change, Conservation, Customer Service, Entrepreneurship, Innovation, Leadership, Nature, Sales, Sales Management, Social Styles, Wildlife Management
ISBN Prefix(es): 978-90-77256
U.S. Office(s): 5910 SE Rhone St, Portland, OR 97206, United States
Distribution Center: Career Press, Pompton Plains, NJ, United States *Web Site:* www.careerpress.com
Baker & Taylor Publisher Services, 30 Amberwood Pkwy, Ashland, OH 44805, United States *Tel:* 567-215-0030 *E-mail:* info@btpubservices.com *Web Site:* www.btpubservices.com

Ons Erfdeel VZW
Murissonstr 260, 8930 Rekkem
Tel: (056) 411201 *Fax:* (056) 414707
E-mail: info@onserfdeel.be; adm@onserfdeel.be
Web Site: www.onserfdeel.be
Key Personnel
President: Herman Balthazar
Mng Dir & Chief Editor: Luc Devoldere
    E-mail: luc.devoldere@onserfdeel.be
Head, Administration: Kevin Vandenbussche
Founded: 1970
Specialize in promoting cultural cooperation among all speakers of the Dutch language & increase awareness of Flemish & Dutch culture abroad. Publish & distribute a range of periodicals & other publications, both in Dutch & other languages.
Subjects: Art, Ethnicity, Language Arts, Linguistics, Literature, Literary Criticism, Essays, Regional Interests
ISBN Prefix(es): 978-90-70831; 978-90-75862
Branch Office(s)
Rijvoortshoef 265, 4941 VJ Raamsdonksveer, Netherlands *Tel:* (0162) 513425

Pandora Publishers NV+
Van Praetlei 145, 2170 Merksem
Tel: (03) 2338770 *Fax:* (03) 2333399
Web Site: www.pandorapublishers.eu
Founded: 1988
Also publishes catalogs & monographs.
Subjects: Architecture & Interior Design, Art, History, Literature, Literary Criticism, Essays,

Music, Dance, Photography, Sports, Athletics, Travel & Tourism
ISBN Prefix(es): 978-90-5325
Number of titles published annually: 30 Print
Total Titles: 220 Print
Foreign Rep(s): Antique Collectors Club (UK, USA)

Editions La Part de L'Oeil+
144, rue du Midi, 1000 Brussels
Tel: (02) 514 18 41 *Fax:* (02) 514 18 41
E-mail: info@lapartdeloeil.be
Web Site: www.lapartdeloeil.be
Key Personnel
Contact: Karine Barbareau; Lucien Massaert
Founded: 1985
Also publishes *La Part de L'Oeil,* a theoretical arts review published in French.
Subjects: Art, Language Arts, Linguistics, Literature, Literary Criticism, Essays, Philosophy, Poetry, Psychology, Psychiatry
ISBN Prefix(es): 978-2-930174
Number of titles published annually: 3 Print
Total Titles: 41 Print
Distribution Center: Pollen Diffusion, 81 rue Romain Rolland, 93260 Les Lilas, France *Tel:* 01 43 62 08 07 *Fax:* 01 72 71 84 51 *Web Site:* www.pollen-diffusion.com

Uitgeverij Peeters Leuven (Belgie) (Peeters Publishers & Booksellers)+
Bondgenotenlaan 153, 3000 Leuven
Tel: (016) 23 51 70 *Fax:* (016) 22 85 00
E-mail: peeters@peeters-leuven.be
Web Site: www.peeters-leuven.be
Founded: 1857
Publish books & journals in English, French, German & Dutch. Publish original research as well as bibliographic data, reviews & reference material.
Subjects: Archaeology, Art, Asian Studies, Biblical Studies, History, Language Arts, Linguistics, Literature, Literary Criticism, Essays, Philosophy, Religion - Other, Theology, Classical Studies, Ethics, History of Art, Medieval Studies, Oriental Studies
ISBN Prefix(es): 978-2-87723; 978-90-6831; 978-90-429; 978-2-8017
Number of titles published annually: 150 Print; 2 CD-ROM; 55 Online
Total Titles: 4,000 Print; 55 Online
Branch Office(s)
52, Blvd St-Michel, 75006 Paris, France, Editor: Vladimir Randa *Tel:* 01 40 51 89 20 *Fax:* 01 40 51 81 05
U.S. Office(s): 141 Endean Dr, Walpole, MA 02032, United States *E-mail:* peeters@peeters-us.com
Warehouse: Kolonel Begaultlaan 61, 3012 Wilsele (Leuven)
Distribution Center: John Garratt Publishing, Private Bag 400, Mulgrave, Victoria 3170, Australia *Tel:* (03) 8545 2905 *Fax:* (03) 6545 3222
VRIN, 6 Place de la Sorbonne, 75005 Paris, France *Tel:* 01 43 54 03 47 *Fax:* 01 43 54 48 18 *E-mail:* contact@vrin.fr *Web Site:* www.vrin.fr
ISD, 70 Enterprise Dr, Suite 2, Bristol, CT 06010, United States *Tel:* 860-584-6546 *Fax:* 860-516-4873 *E-mail:* orders@isdistribution.com *Web Site:* www.isdistribution.com (USA & Canada)

Uitgeverij Pelckmans NV
Kapelsestr 222, 2950 Kapellen
Tel: (03) 660 27 00 *Fax:* (03) 660 27 01
E-mail: uitgeverij@pelckmans.be
Web Site: www.pelckmans.be
Key Personnel
Publisher: Thom Pelckmans
Founded: 1892

Subjects: History, Philosophy, Religion - Other, Social Sciences, Sociology
ISBN Prefix(es): 978-90-289
Associate Companies: Uitgeverij Helios; Uitgeverij Patmos
Bookshop(s): Sint Jacobsmarkt 7, 2000 Antwerp

Editions Luc Pire
Rue Cesar Franck, 26, 4000 Liege
Tel: (04) 220 96 50 *Fax:* (04) 222 30 45
E-mail: editions@lucpire.be
Web Site: www.lucpire.be
Key Personnel
Mng Dir: Luc Pire
Editorial Dir & Foreign Rights: Laurence Waterkeyn
Subjects: Government, Political Science, History, Humor, Travel & Tourism
ISBN Prefix(es): 978-2-87415; 978-2-930088; 978-2-930240

Editions Plantyn
Waterloo Off Park, Dreve Richelle, 161 bat.L, 1410 Waterloo
Tel: (02) 427 42 47 *Fax:* (02) 425 79 03
E-mail: editions.plantyn@plantyn.com
Web Site: www.plantyn.com
Founded: 1959
Educational publishers.
Subjects: Computer Science, Economics, Education, Geography, Geology, Language Arts, Linguistics, Mathematics, Physics, Psychology, Psychiatry, Science (General), Dutch, English, French, Latin, Pedagogy
ISBN Prefix(es): 978-2-8010; 978-90-309; 978-90-301
Parent Company: Infinitas Learning, Het Spoor 8-14, 3994 AK Houten, Netherlands

Poeziecentrum VZW+
Vrijdagmarkt 36, 9000 Ghent
Tel: (09) 225 22 25 *Fax:* (09) 225 90 54
Web Site: www.poeziecentrum.be
Key Personnel
Dir: Carl De Strycker *E-mail:* carl.destrycker@poeziecentrum.be
Founded: 1980
Subjects: Poetry
ISBN Prefix(es): 978-90-5655; 978-90-70968
Number of titles published annually: 10 Print

Le Pole Nord ASBL
rue du Nord, 66, 1000 Brussels
E-mail: pole.nord@skynet.be
Web Site: www.metavolution.org
Key Personnel
Coordinator: Charlotte Goetz
Founded: 1983
Also a scientific research association.
Subjects: History, French Revolution, Jean-Paul Marat
ISBN Prefix(es): 978-2-930040
Total Titles: 18 Print

Pre-Ecole, *imprint of* Editions Chantecler

Preschool, *imprint of* Zuidnederlandse Uitgeverij NV

Presses agronomiques de Gembloux ASBL+
Passage des Deportes, 2, 5030 Gembloux
Tel: (081) 62 22 42 *Fax:* (081) 62 25 52
E-mail: pressesagro.gembloux@ulg.ac.be
Web Site: www.pressesagro.be
Key Personnel
President: Daniel Portetelle
Mng Dir: Bernard Pochet *E-mail:* bernard.pochet@ulg.ac.be
Founded: 1964
Specialize also in chemistry & the food industry.
Subjects: Agriculture, Art, Biological Sciences, Economics, Environmental Studies, Mathemat-

ics, Technology, Culture, Ecology, Forestry, Society
ISBN Prefix(es): 978-2-87016
Number of titles published annually: 3 Print
Total Titles: 30 Print
Distribution Center: Librarie Lavoisier, Rue de Provigny, 14, 94236 Cachan Cedex, France
Tel: 01 47 40 67 00 *Fax:* 01 47 40 67 02
E-mail: info@lavoisier.fr *Web Site:* www.lavoisier.fr (Algeria, Canada, France, Morocco & Switzerland)

Presses Universitaires de Bruxelles ASBL (PUB)
Campus Solbosch, batiment V (2e etage), Ave Paul Heger 42, CP 149, 1000 Brussels
Tel: (02) 641 14 46; (02) 649 97 80 *Fax:* (02) 647 79 62
E-mail: pub@ulb.ac.be
Web Site: www.ulb.ac.be/ulb/pub
Key Personnel
President: Eric Gouder de Beauregard
Dir: Jeannine De Backer *E-mail:* jdbacker@ulb.ac.be
Manager: Emilienne Pizzolon *E-mail:* epizzolo@ulb.ac.be
Founded: 1958
Subjects: Architecture & Interior Design, Economics, Engineering (General), Medicine, Nursing, Dentistry, Philosophy, Science (General)
ISBN Prefix(es): 978-2-500
Branch Office(s)
Campus Erasme, Route de Linnik 808, bat C, 1070 Brussels *Tel:* (02) 555 64 29 *Fax:* (02) 555 64 28

Presses Universitaires de Louvain
Promenade de l'Alma, 31, bte B1, 41.03, 1200 Brussels
Tel: (02) 764 41 72 *Fax:* (02) 764 41 58
Web Site: pul.uclouvain.be
Key Personnel
Contact: Berengere Deprez *E-mail:* berengere.deprez@uclouvain.be
Founded: 2000
Membership(s): Association des Editeurs Belges (ADEB).
Subjects: Economics, Education, History, Language Arts, Linguistics, Law, Literature, Literary Criticism, Essays, Management, Medicine, Nursing, Dentistry, Philosophy, Psychology, Psychiatry, Religion - Other, Science (General), Social Sciences, Sociology, Applied Sciences, Ethics, Natural Science
ISBN Prefix(es): 978-2-87200; 978-90-06; 978-2-930344
Parent Company: Universite catholique de Louvain UCL, Pl de l'Universite 1, 1348 Louvain-la-Neuve

Presses Universitaires de Namur
Rempart de la Vierge 13, 5000 Namur
Mailing Address: rue de Bruxelles 61, 5000 Namur
Tel: (081) 72 48 84 *Fax:* (081) 72 49 12
E-mail: info@pun.be
Web Site: www.fundp.ac.be/asbl/pun
Key Personnel
Dir: Rene Robaye *E-mail:* rene.robaye@fundp.ac.be
Public Relations: Stephanie Herfurth *Tel:* (081) 72 48 85 *E-mail:* stephanie.herfurth@fundp.ac.be
Founded: 1972
Membership(s): Association des Editeurs Belges (ADEB).
ISBN Prefix(es): 978-2-87037
Number of titles published annually: 15 Print
Distribution Center: Librairie Wallonie-Bruxelle, 46 rue Quin campoix, 75004 Paris, France

Tel: 01 42 71 58 03 *Fax:* 01 42 71 58 09
E-mail: librairie.wb@orange.fr *Web Site:* www.librairiewb.com

Prisme Editions
Ave Wielemans Ceuppens 45/2, 1190 Brussels
Tel: (02) 346 13 19 *Fax:* (02) 346 13 03
E-mail: contact@prisme-editions.be
Web Site: www.prisme-editions.be
Key Personnel
Founder & Dir: Liliane Knopes *E-mail:* lk@prisme-editions.be
Founded: 1995
Subjects: Architecture & Interior Design, Art, Photography, Urban Planning
ISBN Prefix(es): 978-2-9600103; 978-2-930451
Distribution Center: Exhibitions International, 17 Kol Begaultlaan, 3012 Leuven *Tel:* (016) 296 900 *Fax:* (016) 296 129 *E-mail:* orders@exhibitionsinternational.be *Web Site:* www.exhibitionsinternational.be
Sofedis, 11 Rue Soufflot, 75005 Paris, France *Tel:* 01 53 10 25 25 *Fax:* 01 53 10 25 26 *E-mail:* info@sofedis.fr *Web Site:* www.sofedis.fr
Idea Books, Nieuwe Herengracht 11, 1011 RK Amsterdam, Netherlands *Tel:* (020) 6226154; (020) 6247376 *Fax:* (020) 6209299 *E-mail:* idea@ideabooks.nl *Web Site:* www.ideabooks.nl

Prodim SPRL+
184, blvd General Jacques, 1050 Brussels
Tel: (02) 640 59 70 *Fax:* (02) 640 59 91
E-mail: prodim.books@prodim.be; prodim.editeur@prodim.be; prodim.journals@prodim.be
Web Site: www.prodim.be
Founded: 1968
Specialize in medicine, science & technology.
Membership(s): Association des Editeurs Belges (ADEB).
Subjects: Biological Sciences, Health, Nutrition, Medicine, Nursing, Dentistry, Psychology, Psychiatry, Science (General), Sports, Athletics, Technology, Veterinary Science
ISBN Prefix(es): 978-2-87017
Subsidiaries: de Visscher

Production et Diffusion de Medias sprl, see Prodim SPRL

PUB, see Presses Universitaires de Bruxelles ASBL (PUB)

Publications des Facultes Universitaires Saint-Louis+
43 Blvd du Jardin Botanique, 1000 Brussels
Tel: (02) 211 78 94 *Fax:* (02) 211 79 97
Web Site: www.fusl.ac.be
Key Personnel
Mng Dir: Francois Ost *Tel:* (02) 211 78 76 ext 12876 *E-mail:* francois.ost@fusl.ac.be
Founded: 1973
Subjects: Economics, History, Law, Philosophy, Psychology, Psychiatry, Social Sciences, Sociology, Theology
ISBN Prefix(es): 978-2-8028
Number of titles published annually: 5 Print
Total Titles: 187 Print
Foreign Rep(s): Albert le Grand Diffusion (Switzerland); DPLU (Canada, USA); Interforum Benelux (Belgium); Librairie Wallonie-Bruxelles (France)

PUL, see Presses Universitaires de Louvain

Editions Racine+
Subsidiary of Uitgeverij Lannoo NV
Ave du Port, 86C/bte 104A, 1000 Brussels
Tel: (02) 646 44 44 *Fax:* (02) 646 55 70

E-mail: info@racine.be
Web Site: www.racine.be
Key Personnel
Manager: Michelle Poskin *Tel:* (02) 645 18 94 *E-mail:* michelle.poskin@racine.be
Marketing & Sales: Pascale Stavaux *Tel:* (02) 645 18 91 *E-mail:* pascale.stavaux@racine.be
Press: Sandrine Thys *E-mail:* sandrine.thys@racine.be
Founded: 1993
Specialize medicine, science & technology.
Subjects: Architecture & Interior Design, Art, Economics, Gardening, Plants, History, Inspirational, Spirituality, Literature, Literary Criticism, Essays, Nonfiction (General), Science (General), Sports, Athletics, Technology, Travel & Tourism, Nature
ISBN Prefix(es): 978-2-87386
Total Titles: 160 Print

Rainbow Grafics International-Baronian Books+
63, rue Charles Legrelle, 1040 Brussels
Tel: (02) 7348114 *Fax:* (02) 7325764
Key Personnel
Publisher & Rights: Anne Lous Baronian
Specialize in international co-production.

La Renaissance du Livre (RL)+
Ave du Chateau Jaco, 1, 1410 Waterloo
Tel: (02) 210 89 14 *Fax:* (02) 210 89 15
E-mail: editions@renaissancedulivre.be
Web Site: www.renaissancedulivre.be
Key Personnel
Head, Publishing: Geraldine Henry
General Manager: Alain van Gelderen
Sales Manager: Therese Clotuche
Editor: Ariane Coquelet; Stephanie Dubois
Marketing & Communication: Joelle Reeners
Founded: 1926
Membership(s): Association of Belgian Publishers.
Subjects: Art, History, Humor, Literature, Literary Criticism, Essays, Sports, Athletics, Travel & Tourism, Lifestyle, Society
ISBN Prefix(es): 978-2-87148; 978-2-8046
Distributed by Exhibitions International (Dutch-speaking Belgium & Netherlands); Vivendi Universal Publishing (French-speaking Belgium & Grand Duchy)
Distribution Center: SDLCaravelle SA, 303 rue de pre aux oies, 1130 Brussels *Tel:* (02) 240 93 00 *Fax:* (02) 216 35 98 *E-mail:* info@sdlcaravelle.com (Belgium)
Sodis, 128 ave de Marechal-de-Lattre-de-Tassigny, 77403 Lagney Cedex, France *Tel:* 01 60 07 82 00 *Fax:* 01 64 30 32 27 (worldwide exc Belgium)
CDE, Rue de Tournon 17, 75006 Paris, France *Tel:* 01 44 41 19 19 *Fax:* 01 44 41 19 14 (worldwide exc Belgium)

RL, see La Renaissance du Livre (RL)

Roularta Books NV+
Meiboomlaan 33, 8800 Roeselare
Tel: (051) 266 111 *Fax:* (051) 266 866
E-mail: info@roularta.be; roulartabooks@roularta.be
Web Site: www.roularta.be
Key Personnel
Executive Dir: Lieve Claeys
Editor: Jan Ingelbeen *E-mail:* jan.ingelbeen@roularta.be
Founded: 1988
Subjects: Architecture & Interior Design, Art, Business, Economics, Finance, Gardening, Plants, Literature, Literary Criticism, Essays, Management, Marketing, Nonfiction (General), Sports, Athletics, Travel & Tourism
ISBN Prefix(es): 978-90-5466; 978-90-72411
Parent Company: Roularta Media Group
Imprints: Globe; KnackBibliotheek/Radio 1

Uitgeverij Snoeck
Molenstr 152, 8501 Heule
Tel: (056) 36 35 35 *Fax:* (056) 35 79 04
E-mail: info@snoeckpublishers.be
Web Site: www.snoeckpublishers.be
Key Personnel
Publisher: Philip Van Bost *E-mail:* philip@
snoeckpublishers.be; Hans Devisscher
E-mail: hans@snoeckpublishers.be
Press & Promotion Manager: Caroline Vanden-
heede *E-mail:* caroline@snoeckpublishers.be
Founded: 1782
Subjects: Archaeology, Architecture & Interior
Design, Art, Cookery, Drama, Theater, Film,
Video, Health, Nutrition, History, Literature,
Literary Criticism, Essays, Music, Dance, Pho-
tography, Science (General), Contemporary Art,
History & Heritage
ISBN Prefix(es): 978-90-70481; 978-90-5349
Foreign Rep(s): DPLU (Diffusion et Promotion
du Livre Universitaire); Hudson Hills Press
LLC; Schuyt & Co (Netherlands); Sofedis
(France)
Bookshop(s): Distriboek, De Vunt 5, 3220 Hols-
beek *E-mail:* verkoop@davisfonds.be

Stafeto, *imprint of* Vlaamse Esperantobond VZW

Standaard Uitgeverij+
Subsidiary of WPG Uitgevers
Mechelsesteenweg 203, 2018 Antwerp
Tel: (03) 285 72 00 *Fax:* (03) 285 72 99
E-mail: info@wpg.be
Web Site: www.wpg.be
Key Personnel
Publishing Dir: Johan de Koning *Tel:* (03) 285 72
35
Publisher: Geert Cortebeeck; Patricia Defour;
Wim Verheije
Marketing Dir: Lude Stroobants
Rights & Export Manager: Bieke Van Duppen
Tel: (03) 285 73 79 *E-mail:* bieke.vanduppen@
wpg.be
Founded: 1919
Subjects: Biography, Memoirs, Cookery, Fiction,
Humor, Nonfiction (General), Poetry, Lifestyle
ISBN Prefix(es): 978-90-02
Parent Company: WPG Uitgevers Belgie NV
Imprints: Manteau; Meulenhoff/Manteau
Warehouse: Centraal Boekhuis, Erasmusweg 10,
4104 AK Aulemborg, Netherlands *Tel:* (0345)
475800 *Fax:* (0345) 475575
Orders to: Centraal Boekhuis, Erasmusweg 10,
4104 AK Aulemborg, Netherlands *Tel:* (0345)
475800 *Fax:* (0345) 475575

Stichting Kunstboek bvba (Foundation
Kunstboek bvba)+
Legeweg 165, 8020 Oostkamp
Tel: (050) 46 19 10 *Fax:* (050) 46 19 18
E-mail: info@stichtingkunstboek.com; orders@
stichtingkunstboek.com
Web Site: www.stichtingkunstboek.com
Key Personnel
Publisher & Chief Executive Officer: Jaak Van
Damme
Publisher: Karel Puype
Editor: Katrien Van Moerbeke
Administration & Orders: Mieke Byttebier
Finance: Jos Leupe
Founded: 1992
Subjects: Architecture & Interior Design, Art,
Crafts, Games, Hobbies, Gardening, Plants,
History, Music, Dance, Photography, Travel &
Tourism, Floral Design, Food
ISBN Prefix(es): 978-90-74377; 978-90-5856;
978-90-73408
Distribution Center: Exhibitions International,
Kol Begaultlaan 17, 3020 Leuven *Tel:* (016) 29
69 00 *Fax:* (016) 29 61 29 *E-mail:* orders@
exhibitionsinternational.be *Web Site:* www.
exhibitionsinternational.be

ImageBooks Factory, Doornhoek 3742,
5465 TA Veghel, Netherlands *Tel:* (0413)
387272 *Fax:* (0413) 387271 *E-mail:* info@
imagegroupholland.nl *Web Site:* www.
imagegroupholland.nl
Antique Collectors' Club, Sandy Lane, Old
Martlesham, Woodbridge, Suffolk IP12
4SD, United Kingdom *Tel:* (01394) 389950
Fax: (01394) 389999 *E-mail:* sales@antique-
acc.com
Antique Collectors' Club Inc, 6 W 18 St,
Suite 4B, New York, NY 10011, United
States *Tel:* 212-645-1111 *Fax:* 212-989-3205
E-mail: sales@antiquecc.com

Studiecentrum Vlaamse Primitieven (Centre for
the Study of the Flemish Primitives)+
Koninklijk Instituut voor het Kunstpartimonium,
Jubelpark 1, 1000 Brussels
Tel: (02) 739 68 66 *Fax:* (02) 732 01 05
Web Site: xv.kikirpa.be
Key Personnel
Coordinator: Bart Fransen *E-mail:* bart.fransen@
kikirpa.be
Founded: 1949
Specialize in XV century Flemish painting.
Subjects: Art
ISBN Prefix(es): 978-2-87033
Orders to: Brepols Publishers, Order Dept, Be-
gijnhof 67, 2300 Turnhout *Tel:* (01) 444 80 20
Fax: (01) 442 89 19 *E-mail:* info@brepols.net
Web Site: www.brepols.net

Editions UGA (Uitgeverij)+
Division of Continuga NV
Stijn Streuvelslaan 73, 8501 Kortrijk-Heul
Tel: (056) 36 32 00 *Fax:* (056) 35 60 96
E-mail: publ@uga.be; sales@uga.be
Web Site: www.uga.be
Key Personnel
Publisher, Dir & Editorial, Sales: Bruno Scheers
E-mail: bruno.scheers@uga.be
Founded: 1948
Also packager.
Subjects: History, Language Arts, Linguistics,
Law, Public Administration, Social Sciences,
Sociology
ISBN Prefix(es): 978-90-6768; 978-90-8977
Number of titles published annually: 120 Print; 8
CD-ROM; 2 Online
Branch Office(s)
Guimardstr 19, bus 2, 1040 Brussels *Tel:* (02) 512
09 75 *Fax:* (02) 512 26 93

Editions de l'Universite de Bruxelles+
ave Paul Heger 26, 1000 Brussels
Tel: (02) 650 37 97 *Fax:* (02) 650 37 94
E-mail: editions@ulb.ac.be
Web Site: www.editions-universite-bruxelles.be
Key Personnel
Dir, Foreign Rights: Michele Mat
E-mail: michele.mat@ulb.ac.be
Founded: 1972
Subjects: Architecture & Interior Design, Eco-
nomics, Geography, Geology, Government,
Political Science, History, Law, Literature, Lit-
erary Criticism, Essays, Management, Math-
ematics, Philosophy, Religion - Other, Social
Sciences, Sociology
ISBN Prefix(es): 978-2-8004
Number of titles published annually: 20 Print
Total Titles: 260 Print
Foreign Rep(s): Interforum (Belgium, Luxem-
bourg, Netherlands); Servidis (Switzerland);
Sodis (France); Somabec (Canada)

Uitgeverij Van In (Van In Publishing House)
Nijverheidsstr 92/5, 2160 Wommelgem
Tel: (03) 480 55 11
E-mail: uitgeverij@vanin.be; editions@vanin.be;
informations@vanin.be
Web Site: www.vanin.be

Key Personnel
Head, Publishing: Patrick Hermans
E-mail: patrick.hermans@vanin.be
Founded: 1833
Educational publishing, mainly for primary &
secondary education for the Flanders & Wallo-
nia regions.
Subjects: Education, Language Arts, Linguistics,
Law
ISBN Prefix(es): 978-90-306
Parent Company: Sanoma
Subsidiaries: J Van In Editions
Branch Office(s)
Editions Van In, Ave Jean Monnet, 1, 1348
Wavre, Louvain-la-Neuve

Uitgeverij Vanden Broele+
Stationslaan 23, 8200 Brugge
Tel: (050) 642 800 *Fax:* (050) 642 808
E-mail: uitgeverij@vandenbroele.be; info@
uitgeverij.vandenbroele.be
Web Site: www.uitgeverij.vandenbroele.be
Key Personnel
Chief Executive Officer: Tom Van den Broele
E-mail: tom.vanden.broele@vandenbroele.be
Chief Operating Officer: Bram Van Impe
E-mail: bram.van.impe@vandenbroele.be
Chief Financial Officer: Dieter Vanreybrouck
E-mail: dieter.vanreybrouck@vandenbroele.be
Publishing Dir: Bart Keirse *E-mail:* bart.keirse@
vandenbroele.be
Publisher: Stefanie Vanacker *E-mail:* stefanie.
vanacker@vandenbroele.be; Steven Houbrechts
E-mail: steven.houbrechts@vandenbroele.be
Founded: 1957
Subjects: Government, Political Science, Law,
Public Administration, Social Sciences, Sociol-
ogy
ISBN Prefix(es): 978-90-5753; 978-90-6267; 978-
90-5946; 978-90-8584; 978-90-496
Number of titles published annually: 20 CD-
ROM; 20 Online; 2 E-Book
Total Titles: 20 CD-ROM; 20 Online; 2 E-Book

VBVB, see Huis Van Het Boek

Editions Versant Sud
blvd General Jacques 20, 1050 Brussels
Tel: (02) 646 08 90 *Fax:* (02) 646 21 68
Web Site: www.versant-sud.com
Key Personnel
Editor: Elisabeth Jongen *E-mail:* elisabeth.
jongen@versant-sud.com
Production Manager: Sebastien Vellut *Tel:* (0496)
23 27 52 *E-mail:* sebastien.vellut@versant-sud.
com
Founded: 2001
Subjects: History, Music, Dance, Travel &
Tourism, Wine & Spirits
ISBN Prefix(es): 978-2-930358
Foreign Rep(s): ADL Agence Du Livre (Canada);
CED (France); Interforum Benelux SA (Bel-
gium, Luxembourg, Netherlands); Servidis
(Switzerland)

Vlaamse Esperantobond VZW+
Frankrijklei 140, 2000 Antwerp
Tel: (03) 234 34 00 *Fax:* (03) 233 54 33
E-mail: info@fel.esperanto.be
Web Site: www.esperanto.be
Key Personnel
General Dir: Paul Peeraerts
Founded: 1979
Subjects: Education, Fiction, Language Arts, Lin-
guistics, Poetry
ISBN Prefix(es): 978-90-71205; 978-90-77066
Total Titles: 10 Print
Imprints: Stafeto
U.S. Office(s): Esperanto League of North Amer-
ica, PO Box 1129, El Cerrito, CA 94530-1129,
United States *Tel:* 510-653-0998 *E-mail:* info@
esperanto-usa.org *Web Site:* www.esperanto-
usa.org

Uitgeverij de Vries & Brouwers
Haantjeslei 80, 2018 Antwerp
Tel: (03) 237 41 80 *Fax:* (03) 237 70 01
E-mail: dvbkantoor@skynet.be
Web Site: www.devries-brouwers.be
Key Personnel
Publisher: Isi de Vries
Founded: 1946
Subjects: Architecture & Interior Design, Cookery, Crafts, Games, Hobbies, Education, Health, Nutrition, History, Philosophy, Psychology, Psychiatry, Sports, Athletics, Animal & Plant Science, Culture, Ecology, Folk Art, Mediation
ISBN Prefix(es): 978-90-6174; 978-90-5927

Uitgeverij Vrijdag NV
Jodenstr 16, 2000 Antwerp
Tel: (03) 345 60 40
E-mail: info@uitgeverijvrijdag.be; mail@uitgeverijvrijdag.be
Web Site: www.uitgeverijvrijdag.be
Subjects: Fiction, Nonfiction (General)
ISBN Prefix(es): 978-94-6001

VUB Brussels University Press (Vrije Universiteit Brussel Press)+
Imprint of ASP (Academic & Scientific Publishers)
Ravensteingalerij 28, 1000 Brussels
Tel: (02) 289 26 50 *Fax:* (02) 289 26 59
E-mail: info@aspeditions.be
Web Site: www.aspeditions.be
Key Personnel
Dir: Stefaan Janssens *E-mail:* stefaan.janssens@aspeditions.be
Publisher: Gert De Nutte *Tel:* (02) 289 26 51
E-mail: gert.denutte@aspeditions.be
Founded: 1987
Specialize in scientific publications in Dutch, English & French.
Subjects: Communications, Criminology, Environmental Studies, Government, Political Science, History, Mathematics, Philosophy, Science (General), Social Sciences, Sociology, Women's Studies
ISBN Prefix(es): 978-90-5487; 978-90-70289
Number of titles published annually: 30 Print
Total Titles: 400 Print

VUB Press, see VUB Brussels University Press

Wereldmediahuis VZW+
Vlasfabriekstr 11, 1060 Brussels
Tel: (02) 536 19 77 *Fax:* (02) 536 19 34
E-mail: info@mo.be
Web Site: www.mo.be
Key Personnel
Mng Dir: Jan Lamers *Tel:* (02) 536 19 78
E-mail: jan.lamers@mo.be
Editor-in-Chief: Gie Goris *Tel:* (02) 536 19 64
E-mail: gie.goris@mo.be
Communications: Jan Buelinckx *E-mail:* jan.buelinckx@mo.be
Founded: 1970
Membership(s): VBVB.
Subjects: Developing Countries
ISBN Prefix(es): 978-90-76421

Van de Wiele bvba+
Jakobinessenstr 5, 8000 Brugge
Tel: (050) 490769 *Fax:* (050) 346457
E-mail: uitgeverij.vandewiele@proximus.be
Web Site: www.marcvandewiele.com
Key Personnel
Contact: Frederick Moyaert
Founded: 1979
Subjects: Art, History
ISBN Prefix(es): 978-90-6966; 978-90-76297
Number of titles published annually: 5 Print
Bookshop(s): Antiquariaat Marc Van de Wiele, St Salvatorkerkhof 7, 8000 Brugge

Editions Luce Wilquin+
Rue d'Atrive 48, 4280 Avin
Tel: (019) 69 98 13 *Fax:* (019) 69 98 13
E-mail: editions@wilquin.com
Web Site: www.wilquin.com
Founded: 1992
Subjects: Art, Fiction, History, Literature, Literary Criticism, Essays, Romance
ISBN Prefix(es): 978-2-88161; 978-2-88253
Number of titles published annually: 20 Print
Total Titles: 170 Print
Foreign Rep(s): ADL-Agency Book (Canada); SDLCaravelle SA (Belgium); Zoe (Switzerland)

Yoyo Books
Hagelberg 33, 2250 Olen
Tel: (014) 28 23 40 *Fax:* (014) 28 23 49
E-mail: editorial@yoyo-books.com
Web Site: www.yoyo-books.com
Key Personnel
Mng Dir & International Sales: Jo Dupre
Editorial: Ester Heylen
Production: Elise De Fre; Tamara Viskens
Subjects: Fiction, Nonfiction (General)
ISBN Prefix(es): 978-90-5843; 978-90-8622

ZNU, see Zuidnederlandse Uitgeverij NV

Zuidnederlandse Uitgeverij NV+
Vluchtenburgstr 7, 2630 Aartselaar
Tel: (03) 8704400 *Fax:* (03) 8772115
Key Personnel
Mng Dir: Jan Vande Velden
Editorial Dir: Christophe Iserentant
Sales Manager: Pieter Gladinez
Founded: 1946
Subjects: Animals, Pets, Child Care & Development, Crafts, Games, Hobbies, English as a Second Language, Gardening, Plants, Humor
ISBN Prefix(es): 978-2-8034; 978-90-243; 978-90-447
Imprints: Chantecler; Deltas; Invader; Liberica; Preschool
Subsidiaries: Editions Chantecler; Centrale Uitgeverij; Invader Ltd; Liberica

Uitgeverij Zwijsen
Subsidiary of WPG Uitgevers
Nassaustr 37-41, 2000 Antwerp
Tel: (03) 205 94 94 *Toll Free Tel:* 0800 94362
Fax: (03) 205 94 99
E-mail: info@uitgeverijzwijsen.be
Web Site: www.uitgeverijzwijsen.be
Key Personnel
Dir: Bart Vandenbussche *Tel:* (0487) 48 70 83
E-mail: bart.vandenbussche@uitgeverijzwijsen.be
Publishing Manager: Patrick Vandevelde *Tel:* (03) 205 94 80 *E-mail:* patrick.vandevelde@uitgeverijzwijsen.be
Founded: 1971
Subjects: Crafts, Games, Hobbies, Education, Language Arts, Linguistics, Literature, Literary Criticism, Essays, Music, Dance, Philosophy, Religion - Other, Sports, Athletics
ISBN Prefix(es): 978-90-5535

Belize

General Information

Capital: Belmopan
Language: English (official) & Spanish
Religion: Roman Catholic & various Protestant denominations
Population: 189,000

Bank Hours: 0800-1300 Monday-Thursday; 0800-1200, 1500-1800 Friday
Shop Hours: 0730-1130, 1300-1600 Monday-Saturday (some open 0800-2100 daily, some open Sunday); generally early closing Wednesday
Currency: 100 cents = 1 Belizian dollar
Export/Import Information: No tariff on books. General license. Nominal exchange controls.
Copyright: UCC (see Copyright Conventions, pg viii)

Cubola Productions
35 Elizabeth St, Benque Viejo del Carmen
Tel: 823 2083 *Fax:* 823 2240
E-mail: cubolabz@btl.com; sales@cubola.com
Web Site: www.cubola.com
Founded: 1973
Subjects: Cookery, Education, Fiction, Nonfiction (General)
ISBN Prefix(es): 978-976-8161

Producciones de la Hamaca
PO Box 6, Caye Caulker
Tel: 600-4710
E-mail: producciones.hamaca@gmail.com
Web Site: producciones-hamaca.com
Key Personnel
Editor: Judy Lumb *E-mail:* judylumb@btl.net
Author: Dorothy Beveridge *Tel:* 623-7182
E-mail: bzvisuals@yahoo.com
Founded: 1992 (2009 as a nongovernmental organization in Belize & a nonprofit in Georgia, USA)
Publish nonfiction spiritual, environmental & culture books both in Belize & with Quakers in the USA, Canada & Kenya.
Subjects: Environmental Studies, Inspirational, Spirituality, Nonfiction (General)
ISBN Prefix(es): 978-976-8142
Number of titles published annually: 5 Print
Total Titles: 13 Print; 9 Online

Benin

General Information

Capital: Porto-Novo
Language: French
Religion: About 15% Christian (mostly Roman Catholic), 13% Islamic, remainder traditional beliefs
Population: 4.5 million
Bank Hours: 0800-1000, 1500-1600 Monday-Friday
Shop Hours: 0800-1300, 1500-1900 Monday-Saturday. Larger ones close Monday, some open for a few hours Sunday morning
Currency: 100 centimes = CFA franc
Export/Import Information: Import license required but issued automatically for imports from European Union countries.
Copyright: Berne (see Copyright Conventions, pg viii)

Les Editions du Flamboyant
08 BP 271, Cotonou
Tel: 21 31 02 20 *Fax:* 90 91 57 27
Key Personnel
Contact: Mr Dorothee Gerard Houessou
Founded: 1989
Membership(s): Alliance Internationale des Editeurs Independants.
ISBN Prefix(es): 978-2-909130; 978-99919-41; 978-99919-5

Office National d'Edition de Presse et d'Imprimerie (ONEPI)
Rue de L'archeveche, 01 BP 1210, Cotonou

Tel: 21 30 11 52
E-mail: quotidienlanation@yahoo.fr
Key Personnel
Dir: M Assevi Akuete
Founded: 1975

ONEPI, see Office National d'Edition de Presse et d'Imprimerie (ONEPI)

Editions Ruisseaux d'Afrique
C/ 2186, 04 BP 1154, Kindonou
Tel: 21 38 31 86 *Fax:* 21 38 34 61
E-mail: contact@ruisseauxdafrique.com
Web Site: www.ruisseauxdafrique.com
ISBN Prefix(es): 978-99919-63

Bolivia

General Information

Capital: Sucre
Language: Spanish, Quechua, Aymara
Religion: Predominantly Roman Catholic
Population: 7.3 million
Bank Hours: 0900-1200, 1400-1630 Monday-
Friday
Shop Hours: 0900-1200, 1400-1800 Monday-
Friday; 0900-1200 Saturday
Currency: 100 centavos = 1 Boliviano
Export/Import Information: Member of the Latin
American Free Trade Association. No tariffs
on books, except for 10% luxury bindings. No
import licenses, except for textbooks, but no
pornography allowed. No advertising that in-
cludes imitation money, stamps, etc, allowed.
No exchange controls.
Copyright: UCC, Berne, Buenos Aires (see Copy-
right Conventions, pg viii)

Los Amigos del Libro Ltda+
Calle Espana 0-153 Edif Alba 1, Cochabamba
Tel: (04) 4256005
Key Personnel
Manager: Ingrid Guttentag
Founded: 1945
Subjects: Regional Interests, Bolivia
ISBN Prefix(es): 978-99905-45
Number of titles published annually: 600 Print
Total Titles: 1,250 Print
Subsidiaries: Bio Bibliografia Boliviana
Bookshop(s): Torres Sofer, Cochabamba *Tel:* (04)
4504151; Calle Ballivian 145, Santa Cruz de la
Sierra *Tel:* (03) 3327937

Editorial Gisbert y Cia SA
Calle Comercio 1270, La Paz
Tel: (02) 220 2626 *Fax:* (02) 220 2911
E-mail: info@libreriagisbert.com
Web Site: libreriagisbert.com
Key Personnel
General Manager: Antonio Schulczewskila
Promotion & Sales Manager: Maria del Carmen
Schulczewski
Founded: 1907
Subjects: History, Law
ISBN Prefix(es): 978-99905-800
Number of titles published annually: 2 Print
Distributor for Pearson Education

Grupo Editorial La Hoguera
Calle Beni 678, 2nd floor, Santa Cruz de la Sierra
Tel: (03) 335-4426; (03) 337-5169
E-mail: lahoguera@lahoguera.com
Web Site: www.lahoguera.com
Key Personnel
General Dir: Mauricio Mendez
Regional Manager: Andres Aguilera *Tel:* (03)
364-5080 *E-mail:* aaguilera@lahoguera.com

Founded: 1989
Subjects: Fiction, Poetry, Sports, Athletics
ISBN Prefix(es): 978-99954-51; 978-99954-801;
978-99905-76

UATF, see Universidad Autonoma "Tomas Frias",
Division de Extension Universitaria

**Universidad Autonoma "Tomas Frias",
Division de Extension Universitaria**
Av del Maestro y Av Civica y Serrudo, Casilla
36, Potosi
Tel: (02) 6227300; (02) 6227301 *Fax:* (02)
6226663
Web Site: www.uatf.edu.bo
Subjects: History, Literature, Literary Criticism,
Essays

Bosnia and Herzegovina

General Information

Capital: Sarajevo
Language: Bosnian, Serbian, Croatian
Religion: Predominantly Sunni Muslim, also Ser-
bian Orthodox & Roman Catholic
Population: 4.4 million
Currency: 100 convertible pfenniga = 1 convert-
ible marka (KM)
Copyright: UCC, Berne (see Copyright Conven-
tions, pg viii)

BTC Sahinpasic, see Sahinpasic Publishing

Sahinpasic Publishing
Vreoca bb, 71210 Ilidza
Tel: 33 77 11 80 *Fax:* 33 77 11 88
E-mail: info@btcsahinpasic.com; mensura@
btcsahinpasic.com
Web Site: www.btcsahinpasic.com
Key Personnel
Owner: Tajib Sahinpasic *E-mail:* tajib@
btcsahinpasic.com
Founded: 1989
Subjects: Fiction, Literature, Literary Criticism,
Essays, Poetry
ISBN Prefix(es): 978-9958-41

Sarajevo Publishing
Obala Kulina bana 4, 71000 Sarajevo
Tel: (033) 220 809
Web Site: www.sarajevopublishing.ba
Key Personnel
Editor: Amra Mekic *E-mail:* redakcija@
sarajevopublishing.ba
Marketing: Nerma Sakic *E-mail:* marketing@
sarajevopublishing.ba
Founded: 1950
Subjects: Fiction, Government, Political Science,
Philosophy, Science (General)
ISBN Prefix(es): 978-86-21; 978-86-25; 978-
9958-21

Sluzbeni List
Dz Bijedica 39/III, 71000 Sarajevo
Tel: (033) 722-030; (033) 722-051; (033) 722-061
(editorial)
E-mail: info@sllist.ba; redakcija@sllist.ba
Web Site: www.sluzbenilist.ba
Subjects: Law
ISBN Prefix(es): 978-86-355

Botswana

General Information

Capital: Gaborone
Language: English (official), Setswana (national)
Religion: Traditional African
Population: 1.3 million
Bank Hours: 0830-1300 Monday-Friday; 0830-
1100 Saturday
Shop Hours: 0800-1300, 1400-1700 or 1800
Monday-Saturday
Currency: 100 thebe = 1 pula
Export/Import Information: No import license
required; no obscene literature. Exchange con-
trols.

The Botswana Society
Plto 2704 Phala Crescent, Gaborone
Mailing Address: PO Box 71, Gaborone
Tel: 391-9745 *Fax:* 391-9745
E-mail: botsoc@info.bw
Web Site: www.botsoc.org.bw; www.
botswanabeckons.com
Key Personnel
President: Festus G Mogae
Editor, Botswana Notes & Records: Prof C J
Makgala *E-mail:* makgalac@mopipi.ub.bw
Founded: 1969
National Learned Society: nonprofit, non-
government.
Publisher of *Botswana Notes & Records.*
Subjects: Archaeology, Biography, Memoirs, De-
veloping Countries, Earth Sciences, Environ-
mental Studies, Ethnicity, Government, Political
Science, History, Language Arts, Linguistics,
Natural History, Nonfiction (General), Public
Administration, Science (General), Social Sci-
ences, Sociology, Travel & Tourism
ISBN Prefix(es): 978-99912-60
Number of titles published annually: 2 Print; 1
Online
Total Titles: 48 Print; 3 Online

Morula Press, Business School of Botswana
Plot 222, Independence Ave, Broadhurst,
Gaborone
Mailing Address: PO Box 402492, Gaborone
Tel: 390-6134 *Fax:* 390-4809
E-mail: admin@briscoe.co.bw
Founded: 1994
Subjects: Business, Law
ISBN Prefix(es): 978-99912-902; 978-99912-912;
978-99912-952; 978-99912-968; 978-99912-
969; 978-99912-991; 978-99912-992

Pearson Botswana (Pty) Ltd
Plot 14386, New Lobatse Rd, West Industrial
Site, Gaborone
Tel: 392-2969 *Fax:* 392-2682
E-mail: pearsonza.enquiries@pearson.com;
pearsonza.orders@pearson.com
Web Site: za.pearson.com; www.
pearsonschoolsandfecolleges.co.uk
Key Personnel
Mng Dir: Joe Chalashika *E-mail:* joe.chalashika@
pearson.com
Subjects: English as a Second Language, Fiction,
Geography, Geology, History, Language Arts,
Linguistics, Literature, Literary Criticism, Es-
says, Poetry, Travel & Tourism
ISBN Prefix(es): 978-99912-66; 978-99912-73;
978-99912-501; 978-99912-502; 978-99912-
503; 978-99912-504; 978-99912-505; 978-
99912-568; 978-99912-569; 978-99912-570;
978-99912-571; 978-99912-578; 978-99912-
579; 978-99912-580; 978-99912-581; 978-
99912-583; 978-99912-584; 978-99912-594;
978-99912-595; 978-99912-599
Parent Company: Pearson South Africa
Ultimate Parent Company: Pearson Education

Brazil

General Information

Capital: Brasilia
Language: Portuguese
Religion: Predominantly Roman Catholic
Population: 157 million
Bank Hours: Generally 1000-1500 Monday-Friday
Shop Hours: 0900-1700 Monday-Friday (many open much later); 0900-1400 Saturday
Currency: 100 centavos = 1 real
Export/Import Information: Member of the Latin American Free Trade Association. No tariffs on books & advertising, but luxury bindings & children's picture books are dutied. Import licenses & deposits required; exchange controls operate.
Copyright: UCC, Berne, Buenos Aires, Florence (see Copyright Conventions, pg viii)

A&A&A Edicoes e Promocoes Internacionais Ltda+
Rua Jose Lemos, 8, Bonsucesso, 25725-170 Petropolis-RJ
Tel: (024) 2221-8643; (024) 2221-2740
 Fax: (024) 2221-8643; (024) 2221-2740
Web Site: www.criancascriativas.com.br
Key Personnel
General Dir: Lucila Martinez
Editor: Gian Calvi
Founded: 1988
Membership(s): National Syndication of Book Publishers.
Subjects: Child Care & Development, Cookery, Education, Library & Information Sciences, Public Administration, Science Fiction, Fantasy
ISBN Prefix(es): 978-85-7210
Subsidiaries: IPE Amarelo Criacao Multimidia Ltda
Branch Office(s)
Gian Calvi Asun Balzola y Asociados SL, Calle de Clara del Rey, 39 Off 708, 28002 Madrid, Spain
Showroom(s): Livraria Amais, Rua Real Grandeza 314, Botafogo-RJ

Editora Abril
Av das Nacoes Unidas, 7221, 20th floor, Pinheiros, 05425-902 Sao Paulo-SP
Tel: (011) 3037-2000 *Fax:* (011) 3037-5638
E-mail: publiabril@abril.com.br
Web Site: www.abril.com.br; www.grupoabril.com.br
Key Personnel
Dir, Planning, Control & Administration: Fabio d'Avila Carvalho *E-mail:* fabio.carvalho@abril.com.br
Regional Offices Contact: Marcia Viana
 E-mail: marcia.viana@abril.com.br
Founded: 1983
Subjects: Cookery, Science (General)
ISBN Prefix(es): 978-85-86476
Parent Company: Abril SA

Action Editora Ltda+
Av das Americas, 3333 sala 817, 22631-003 Rio de Janeiro-RJ
Tel: (021) 3325-7229 *Fax:* (021) 3325-7229
E-mail: loja@actioneditora.com.br
Web Site: loja.actioneditora.com.br
Key Personnel
Dir: Carlos Lorch
Founded: 1986
Specialize in military history, natural history & aviation.
Subjects: Aeronautics, Aviation, History, Military Science, Sports, Athletics, Transportation, Brazil, Military Defense
ISBN Prefix(es): 978-85-85654

Number of titles published annually: 8 Print
Total Titles: 60 Print
Distributed by Howell Press (USA)

Addison Wesley, *imprint of* Pearson Education do Brasil Ltda

Editora Agalma+
Av Garibaldi, Centro Medico Empresarial, bloco B, Sala 401, 40170-130 Salvador-BA
Tel: (071) 3332-8776 *Fax:* (071) 3245-7883
E-mail: pedidos@agalma.com.br
Web Site: www.agalma.com.br
Key Personnel
Contact: Marcus Do Rio Teixeira
Founded: 1991
Membership(s): Sindicato Nacional dos Editores de Livros (SNEL).
Subjects: Anthropology, Child Care & Development, Nonfiction (General), Philosophy, Psychology, Psychiatry, Romance
ISBN Prefix(es): 978-85-85458
Distributor for Editions De L'Association Freudienne

AGIR+
Rua Nova Jerusalem, 345, Bonsucesso, 21042-901 Rio de Janeiro-RJ
Tel: (021) 3882-8200; (021) 3882-8323 (sales)
Web Site: www.ediouro.com.br/novo; www.facebook.com.AgirEditora
Founded: 1944
Subjects: Architecture & Interior Design, Art, Biography, Memoirs, Communications, Cookery, Drama, Theater, Education, Fiction, History, Literature, Literary Criticism, Essays, Philosophy, Social Sciences, Sociology
ISBN Prefix(es): 978-85-220
Parent Company: Ediouro Publicacoes

AgirEditora, see AGIR

Editora Agora Ltda+
Division of Grupo Editorial Summus
Rua Itapicuru, 613-7° andar, Perdizes, 05006-000 Sao Paulo-SP
Tel: (011) 3872-3322 *Fax:* (011) 3872-7476
E-mail: agora@editoraagora.com.br; editora@editoraagora.com.br
Web Site: www.grupposummus.com.br/agora
Key Personnel
Editor: Edith M Elek
Founded: 1979
Subjects: Astrology, Occult, Biography, Memoirs, Communications, Cookery, Economics, Education, Health, Nutrition, Inspirational, Spirituality, Literature, Literary Criticism, Essays, Philosophy, Psychology, Psychiatry, Religion - Other, Self-Help, Social Sciences, Sociology, Travel & Tourism
ISBN Prefix(es): 978-85-7183

Aide Editora e Comercio de Livros Ltda
Rua Bela, 740, Sao Cristovao, 20930-380 Rio de Janeiro-RJ
Founded: 1976
Subjects: Law
ISBN Prefix(es): 978-85-321; 978-85-85797
Total Titles: 5 Print

Editora Alfa-Omega Ltda+
Rua Lisboa, 489, 05413-000 Sao Paulo-SP
Tel: (011) 3062-6400; (011) 3062-6690
 Fax: (011) 3083-0746
E-mail: alfaomega@alfaomega.com.br
Web Site: www.alfaomega.com.br
Key Personnel
Editorial Dir: Fernando Mangarielo
Founded: 1973
Subjects: Anthropology, Behavioral Sciences, Biography, Memoirs, Economics, History, Law,

Management, Philosophy, Social Sciences, Sociology
ISBN Prefix(es): 978-85-295
Divisions: Alfa Omega Data; Distribuidora Alfa Omega e Disque Livros; Estudio Alfa Omega

Livraria Francisco Alves Editora SA+
Praca Mahatma Gandhi, 2 Sala 1201, Cinelandia, 20031-100 Rio de Janeiro-RJ
Tel: (021) 2240-7987; (021) 2240-7988; (021) 2240-7989
Key Personnel
Owner: Carlos Leal
Founded: 1854
Also a bookseller.
Subjects: Astrology, Occult, Criminology, Fiction, Literature, Literary Criticism, Essays, Nonfiction (General), Science (General), Science Fiction, Fantasy
ISBN Prefix(es): 978-85-265

Amadio, *imprint of* Editora Rideel Ltda

Amarilys Editora, *imprint of* Editora Manole Ltda

Organizacao Andrei Editora Ltda+
Rua Conselheiro Nebias, 1.071, Campos Eliseos, 01203-002 Sao Paulo-SP
Tel: (011) 3223-5111 *Fax:* (011) 3221-0246
E-mail: vendas@editora-andrei.com.br; diretoria@editora-andrei.com.br
Web Site: www.editora-andrei.com.br
Founded: 1955
Subjects: Medicine, Nursing, Dentistry, Veterinary Science, Acupuncture, Homeopathy
ISBN Prefix(es): 978-85-7476
Number of titles published annually: 30 Print; 4 CD-ROM
Total Titles: 700 Print; 4 CD-ROM

Antenna Edicoes Tecnicas Ltda+
PO Box 1131, 20010-974 Rio de Janeiro-RJ
Tel: (021) 25573960
E-mail: antenna@anep.com.br
Web Site: www.anep.com.br
Founded: 1926
Subjects: Computer Science, Computers, Electronics, Electrical Engineering, Technology
ISBN Prefix(es): 978-85-7036
Number of titles published annually: 5 Print
Total Titles: 60 Print

Editora Antroposofica Ltda+
Rua da Fraternidade, 174/180, Santo Amaro, 04738-020 Sao Paulo-SP
Tel: (011) 5686 4550 *Fax:* (011) 5687 9714
E-mail: editora@antroposofica.com.br
Web Site: www.antroposofica.com.br; www.facebook.com/EditoraAntroposofica; www.sab.org.br
Founded: 1981
Specializes in therapy & anthroposophy.
Membership(s): Brazilian House of Books.
Subjects: Agriculture, Art, Biography, Memoirs, Child Care & Development, Cookery, Disability, Special Needs, Economics, Education, Health, Nutrition, History, Literature, Literary Criticism, Essays, Medicine, Nursing, Dentistry, Music, Dance, Philosophy, Psychology, Psychiatry, Science (General), Anthroposophy, Ecology, Therapy
ISBN Prefix(es): 978-85-7122
Number of titles published annually: 15 Print
Total Titles: 140 Print
Parent Company: Livraria Antroposofica
Ultimate Parent Company: Sociedade Antroposofica no Brasil

Ao Livro Tecnico Industria e Comercio Ltda+
Rua Sa Freire, 40, Sao Cristovao, 20930-430 Rio
de Janeiro-RJ
Tel: (021) 2580-1168 *Fax:* (021) 2580-9955
Web Site: www.aolivrotecnicolivros.com.br
Founded: 1933
Membership(s): IPA.
Subjects: Education, Language Arts, Linguistics,
Sports, Athletics
ISBN Prefix(es): 978-85-215; 978-85-87970; 978-
85-87988
Associate Companies: Sociedade Distribuidora de
Livros Ltda (Sodilivro)
Subsidiaries: DISAL (Distribuidores Associados
de Livros Ltda); SODILIVRO (Sociedade Dis-
tribuidora de Livros Ltda)

Editora Aquariana Ltda+
Rua Lacedemonia, 85, 04634-020 Sao Paulo-SP
Tel: (011) 5031-1500 *Fax:* (011) 5031-3462
Web Site: www.aquariana.com.br
Key Personnel
Dir: Jose Carlos Venancio
Founded: 1989
Subjects: Alternative, Art, Astrology, Occult,
Biography, Memoirs, Environmental Studies,
Health, Nutrition, Literature, Literary Criticism,
Essays, Management, Marketing, Self-Help,
New Science
ISBN Prefix(es): 978-85-7217; 978-85-7287
Parent Company: Editora Ground Ltda
Imprints: DeLeitura

Arquivo Nacional (National Archives)
Praca da Republica, 173, 20211-350 Rio de
Janeiro-RJ
Tel: (021) 2179-1228; (021) 2179-1273
E-mail: pi@arquivonacional.gov.br
Web Site: www.arquivonacional.gov.br
Key Personnel
General Dir: Jose Ricardo Marques *Tel:* (021)
2179-1313 *E-mail:* ricardo.marques@
arquivonacional.gov.br
Subjects: Geography, Geology, History, Photogra-
phy
ISBN Prefix(es): 978-85-7009

Artes e Oficios Editora Ltda+
Rua Almirante Barroso, 215, Barrio Floresta,
90220-021 Porto Alegre-RS
Tel: (051) 3311-0832
E-mail: arteseoficios@arteseoficios.com.br
Web Site: www.arteseoficios.com.br
Founded: 1991
Subjects: Biography, Memoirs, Fiction, Human
Relations, Humor, Journalism, Psychology,
Psychiatry, Romance, Travel & Tourism
ISBN Prefix(es): 978-85-85418; 978-85-7421;
978-85-87239

Artes Medicas+
Imprint of Grupo A Editoras
Ave Jeronimo de Ornelas, 670, 90040-340 Porto
Alegre-RS
Tel: (051) 3027-7000 *Fax:* (051) 3027-7070
E-mail: grupoa@grupoaeditoras.com.br
Web Site: www.grupoa.com.br
Key Personnel
Manager: Michael Menta
Founded: 1962
Subjects: Medicine, Nursing, Dentistry
ISBN Prefix(es): 978-85-367

Artmed Editora SA+
Imprint of Grupo A Editoras
Av Jeronimo de Ornelas, 670, Bairro Santana,
90040-340 Porto Alegre-RS
Tel: (051) 3027 7000 *Fax:* (051) 3027 7070
E-mail: grupoa@grupoaeditoras.com.br
Web Site: www.grupoa.com.br

Key Personnel
Founder: Henrique L Kiperman
Dir: Celso Kiperman
International Rights Manager & Permissions: An-
gelo I Castrogiovanni
Founded: 1973
Membership(s): Brazilian Book Association; Pub-
lishers Club of Southern Rio Grande.
Subjects: Architecture & Interior Design, Behav-
ioral Sciences, Biological Sciences, Chemistry,
Chemical Engineering, Child Care & Devel-
opment, Civil Engineering, Computer Science,
Economics, Education, Electronics, Electrical
Engineering, Health, Nutrition, Management,
Marketing, Mathematics, Medicine, Nursing,
Dentistry, Photography, Psychology, Psychiatry,
Science (General), Sports, Athletics, Technol-
ogy, Travel & Tourism, Veterinary Science
ISBN Prefix(es): 978-85-7307; 978-85-363
Number of titles published annually: 90 Print; 3
CD-ROM
Total Titles: 893 Print; 11 CD-ROM
Associate Companies: Bookman Companhia Edi-
tora Ltda
Branch Office(s)
Artmed Minas Gerais, Rua Pouso Alegre, 1084,
Bairro Floresta, 31015-030 Belo Horizonte-MG
Tel: (031) 3213 1443 *Fax:* (031) 3213 7499
E-mail: minasgerais@grupoaeditoras.com.br
Artmed Centro-Oeste, SHIN CA 05 - Conj L-
4, Loja 1, Lago Norte, 71505-000 Brasilia-
DF *Tel:* (061) 3468 2852 *E-mail:* brasilia@
grupoaeditoras.com.br
Artmed Parana, Rua Alferes Poli, 2722, Bairro
Parolin, 80220-051 Curitiba-PR *Tel:* (041) 3026
4232; (041) 3026 4242 *Fax:* (041) 3026 4232;
(041) 3026 4242 *E-mail:* falecom@smlivros.
com.br
Artmed Nordeste, Rua Osvaldo Cruz, 2780,
Bairro Dionisio Torres, 60125-151 Fortaleza-
CE *Tel:* (085) 3224 9171; (085) 3264 7098;
(085) 3264 7099 *E-mail:* zorrercom@webcabo.
com.br
Artmed Rio Grande Do Sul, Rua Ernesto Alves,
150, Bairro Floresta, 90220-190 Porto Alegre-
RS *Tel:* (051) 3221 8999 *Fax:* (051) 3221 8999
Artmed Rio de Janeiro, Rua Mesquitela, 34,
Bairro Bonsucesso, 21032-100 Rio de Janeiro-
RJ *Tel:* (021) 3976 2960; (021) 3976 3152
Fax: (021) 3976 3190 *E-mail:* lbtlivros@
lbtlivros.com.br
Artmed Sao Paulo, Av Embaixador Macedo
Soares 10735 - Galpao 5 - Cond Espace Cen-
ter, Vila Ribeiro de Barros, 01277-100 Sao
Paulo-SP *Tel:* (011) 3665 1100 *Fax:* (011)
3667 1333 *E-mail:* saopaulo@grupoaeditores.
com.br
Distributed by Dinalivro (Portugal)
Bookshop(s): Rua General Vitorino, 277, 90020
Porto Alegre-RS, Dir: Celso Kiperman
Tel: (051) 3225 1579

Editora Arvore da Vida (Tree of Life Publishing
Co)
Av Corifeu Azevedo Marques, 137, Butanta,
05581-000 Sao Paulo-SP
Toll Free Tel: 0800 555 123
E-mail: editora@arvoredavida.org.br
Web Site: www.arvoredavida.org.br
Founded: 1978
Subjects: Biblical Studies
ISBN Prefix(es): 978-85-7304

ASE - Associacao Sinodal de Editoracao, see
Editora Sinodal

Editora Atheneu Ltda+
Rua Jesuino Pascoal, 30, Santa Cecilia, 01224-
050 Sao Paulo-SP
Tel: (011) 6858-8750 *Toll Free Tel:* 0800-
0267753 *Fax:* (011) 6858-8765

E-mail: seditorial@atheneu.com.br; sal@atheneu.
com.br
Web Site: www.atheneu.com.br
Key Personnel
Mng Dir & Editorial Dir: Dr Paulo Rzezinski
Publishing Dir: Alexandre Massa
Founded: 1928
Subjects: Biological Sciences, Health, Nutrition,
Medicine, Nursing, Dentistry, Psychology, Psy-
chiatry, Veterinary Science
ISBN Prefix(es): 978-85-7379
Subsidiaries: Editora Atheneu Cultura
Branch Office(s)
Rua Bambina, 74 A/B, 22251-050 Botafogo, Rio
de Janeiro-RJ

Editora Atica Ltda
Ave Otaviano Alves de Lima, 4400, Freguesa do
O, 02909-900 Sao Paulo-SP
Tel: (011) 3990-2100 *Toll Free Tel:* 0800 115 152
Fax: (011) 3990-1784
E-mail: atendimento@atica.com.br
Web Site: www.atica.com.br
Key Personnel
General Dir: Vera Balhestero
Commercial Dir: Magda Ottani
Dir, Marketing: Elisha Urban
Founded: 1965
Subjects: Literature, Literary Criticism, Essays,
Regional Interests
ISBN Prefix(es): 978-85-08
Ultimate Parent Company: Abril Educacao

Atlas, *imprint of* Grupo Editorial Nacional (GEN)

Autentica Editora
Rua Aimores, 981, 8° andar, Funcionarios, Belo
Horizonte-MG 30140-071
Tel: (031) 3214-5700 *Toll Free Tel:* 0800 28 31
322
E-mail: vendas@autenticaeditora.com.br
Web Site: grupoautentica.com.br
Founded: 1997
Subjects: Anthropology, Drama, Theater, Edu-
cation, Language Arts, Linguistics, Literature,
Literary Criticism, Essays, Philosophy, Social
Sciences, Sociology, Humanities
ISBN Prefix(es): 978-85-7526; 978-85-86583;
978-85-89239
Imprints: Gutenberg; Nemo; Vestigio
Branch Office(s)
Av Paulista, 2073, Conjunto Nacional, Horsa I,
23° andar, Conj 2301 Cerqueira Cesar, Sao
Paulo-SP 01311-940 *Tel:* (011) 3034-4468

Editora Autores Associados Ltda
Av Albino J B de Oliveira, 901, Barao Geraldo,
13084-008 Campinas-SP
Tel: (019) 3289 5930
E-mail: coordenacao@autoresassociados.com.br
Web Site: www.autoresassociados.com.br
Key Personnel
Editorial Coordinator & Foreign Rights: Erica
Bombardi
Founded: 1976
Subjects: Education, Sports, Athletics, Physical
Education
ISBN Prefix(es): 978-85-7496; 978-85-85701

Editora Ave-Maria
Rua Martim Francisco, 636, Santa Cecilia, 01226-
000 Sao Paulo-SP
Tel: (011) 3823-1060
E-mail: vendas@avemaria.com.br
Web Site: www.avemaria.com.br
Founded: 1898
Subjects: Education, Inspirational, Spirituality,
Religion - Catholic, Religion - Other, Self-
Help, Theology
ISBN Prefix(es): 978-85-276

Barleu Edicoes Ltda
Praca Mahatma Gandhi 2/1202, Cinelandia,
20031-100 Rio de Janeiro-RJ
Tel: (021) 2240-7988
E-mail: editora@barleu.com; barleu@globo.com;
comercialfalves@gmail.com (sales)
Web Site: www.barleu.com
Founded: 2002
Subjects: Architecture & Interior Design, Art,
Photography
ISBN Prefix(es): 978-85-89365

Editora Bertrand Brasil Ltda+
Imprint of Grupo Editorial Record
Rua Argentina, 171, Sao Cristovao, 20921-380
Rio de Janeiro-RJ
Tel: (021) 2585-2070 *Fax:* (021) 2585-2087
E-mail: marketing@record.com.br; record@
record.com.br
Web Site: www.record.com.br
Key Personnel
President: Sonia Machado Jardim
Founded: 1953
Subjects: Anthropology, Astrology, Occult, Be-
havioral Sciences, Biography, Memoirs, Cook-
ery, Drama, Theater, Education, Fiction, Geog-
raphy, Geology, Government, Political Science,
Literature, Literary Criticism, Essays, Non-
fiction (General), Poetry, Religion - Buddhist,
Religion - Hindu, Religion - Jewish, Romance,
Self-Help, Women's Studies
ISBN Prefix(es): 978-85-286
Number of titles published annually: 80 Print
Total Titles: 1,000 Print
Branch Office(s)
Rua do Paraiso 139/7° andar, conj 71, 04103-000
Sao Paulo-SP *Tel:* (011) 3171-1540 *Fax:* (011)
3285-0251 *E-mail:* bertrand@bertrandbrasil.
com.br

Best Business, *imprint of* Grupo Editorial Record

Edicoes BestBolso, *imprint of* Grupo Editorial
Record

Editora Betania S/C+
Rua 1° de Marco, 125, Centro, 20010-000 Rio de
Janeiro-RJ
Tel: (021) 2233-5144
E-mail: contato@editorabetania.com.br
Web Site: www.editorabetania.com.br
Founded: 1966
Subjects: Religion - Other
Imprints: Temos Grafica Propria

Editora Bezerra de Araujo
Rua Viuva Dantas, n° 501, Campo Grande,
23052-090 Rio de Janeiro-RJ
Tel: (021) 2413-1017
E-mail: comunicacao@bezerradearaujo.com.br
Key Personnel
Dir & President: Maria Jose Bezerra de Araujo
Subjects: Health, Nutrition, Medicine, Nursing,
Dentistry, Pharmacy, Physical Therapy
ISBN Prefix(es): 978-85-85767

M J Bezerra de Araujo Editora Ltda, see
Editora Bezerra de Araujo

Editora Biruta Ltda
Rua Joao Moura 166, 05412-000 Sao Paulo-SP
Tel: (011) 3081-5741 (sales); (011) 3081-5739
E-mail: biruta@editorabiruta.com.br
Web Site: www.editorabiruta.com.br
Key Personnel
Foreign Rights: Carolina Maluf
Founded: 2000
ISBN Prefix(es): 978-85-7848; 978-85-88159

Editora Edgard Blucher Ltda
Rua Pedroso Alvarenga 1245 4° andar, 04531-012
Sao Paulo-SP
Tel: (011) 3078-5366 *Fax:* (011) 3079-2707
Web Site: www.blucher.com.br
Key Personnel
Founder: Edgard Blucher
Publisher: Eduardo Blucher
Founded: 1957
Subjects: Biological Sciences, Earth Sciences,
Electronics, Electrical Engineering, Engineering
(General), Management, Mathematics, Physics,
Science (General), Technology
ISBN Prefix(es): 978-85-212

Editora do Brasil SA+
Rua Conselheiro Nebias, 887, Campos Eliseos,
01203-001 Sao Paulo-SP
Tel: (011) 3226-0211 *Fax:* (011) 3223-7709
Web Site: www.editoradobrasil.com.br
Key Personnel
President: Dr Carlos Costa
Founded: 1943
Subjects: Education, History, Psychology, Psychi-
atry, Social Sciences, Sociology
ISBN Prefix(es): 978-85-10
Branch Office(s)
Rua do Resende 89, 20231-090 Rio de Janeiro-RJ
Tel: (021) 2224-6942 *Fax:* (021) 2224-6942

Editora Brasiliense SA+
R Mourato Coelho 111, Pinheiros, 05417-010 Sao
Paulo-SP
Tel: (011) 3087-0000 *Fax:* (011) 3087-0000
E-mail: editorabrasiliense@editorabrasiliense.com.
br; editorabrasiliense@gmail.com
Web Site: www.editorabrasiliense.com.br
Founded: 1943
Subjects: Education, Literature, Literary Criti-
cism, Essays, Social Sciences, Sociology, Hu-
manities
ISBN Prefix(es): 978-85-11; 978-85-206
Bookshop(s): Livraria Brasiliense Editora SA, Av
Azevedo, 484-Tatuape, 03308-000 Sao Paulo-
SP *Tel:* (011) 6197-0054 *Fax:* (011) 6675-0188
E-mail: livrariasbrasiliense@editorabrasiliense.
com.br

Brinque Book Editora de Livros Ltda+
Rua Mourato Coehlo, 1215, Vila Madelena,
05417-012 Sao Paulo-SP
Tel: (011) 3032-6436 *Fax:* (011) 3032-6436
E-mail: brinquebook@brinquebook.com.br;
vendas@brinquebook.com.br; editorial@
brinquebook.com.br
Web Site: www.brinquebook.com.br
Key Personnel
President: Suzana Taves David Sanson
Founded: 1990
Specialize in children's literature.
Membership(s): Camara Brasileira do Livro
(CBL); Fundacao do Livro Infantil y Juvenil
(FNLIJ); Sindicato Nacional dos Editores de
Livros (SNEL).
Subjects: Cookery, Music, Dance
ISBN Prefix(es): 978-85-7412

Cadence Publicacoes Ltda+
Rua Clarimundo Melo 432, 20740-323 Rio de
Janeiro-RJ
Tel: (021) 2269-5459
Founded: 1980
Subjects: Science (General), Technology

Callis Editora Ltda+
Rua Oscar Freire, 379, 6° andar, 01426-001 Sao
Paulo-SP
Tel: (011) 3068 5600 *Fax:* (011) 3088 3133
E-mail: editorial@callis.com.br; info@callis.com.
br; comunicacao@callis.com.br
Web Site: www.callis.com.br

Key Personnel
President: Miriam Gabbai
Editorial: Idonize Alvez; Ricardo Barreiros; Thi-
ago Nieri
Press: Ailton Guedes
Founded: 1987
Subjects: Art, Computer Science, Computers,
Cookery, Military Science, Nonfiction (Gen-
eral)
ISBN Prefix(es): 978-85-85642; 978-85-7416
Distributed by Jacaranda Ediciones (Mexico)

Edicoes Camara (Chamber of Deputies)
Division of Camara dos Deputadoe
Centro de Documentacao e Informacao-cedi,
Anexo II-Pracados Tres Poderes, 70160-900
Brasilia-DF
Tel: (061) 3216-5809 *Fax:* (061) 3216-5810
E-mail: edicoes.cedi@camara.gov.br
Web Site: www2.camara.gov.br/internet/
publicacoes/edicoes
Key Personnel
Dir: Dr Maria Clara Bicudo Cesar
Founded: 1971
Produces & distributes Chamber of Deputies
printed publications. Created primarily to sat-
isfy the printing needs of Chamber of Deputies,
today has contributed to disseminate Brazilian
legislative information around the country &
the world.
Subjects: Government, Political Science, Public
Administration
ISBN Prefix(es): 978-85-7365
Number of titles published annually: 60 Print
Total Titles: 781 Print

Editora Campus Ltda+
Rua Sete de Setembro, 111/16° andar, 20050-006
Rio de Janeiro-RJ
Tel: (021) 3970-9300 *Fax:* (021) 2507-1991
Web Site: www.elsevier.com.br
Founded: 1976
Subjects: Art, Civil Engineering, Communica-
tions, Computer Science, Computers, Eco-
nomics, Electronics, Electrical Engineering,
Engineering (General), Environmental Studies,
Government, Political Science, Health, Nutri-
tion, History, Nonfiction (General), Physics,
Psychology, Psychiatry, Science (General), So-
cial Sciences, Sociology, Travel & Tourism
ISBN Prefix(es): 978-85-7001; 978-85-352
Number of titles published annually: 190 Print
Parent Company: Elsevier Science
Ultimate Parent Company: RELX Group PLC
Branch Office(s)
Rua Quintana, 753/8° andar, Brooklin, 04569-011
Sao Paulo-SP *Tel:* (011) 5105-8555 *Fax:* (011)
5505-5564 *E-mail:* comercialsp@elsevier.com.
br

Editora Cancao Nova
Rua Joao Paulo II, 12630-000 Cachoeira Paulista-
SP
Mailing Address: CP 57, 12630-000 Cachoeira
Paulista-SP
Tel: (012) 3186-2600
E-mail: editorial@cancaonova.com
Web Site: www.cancaonova.com
Key Personnel
Manager: Osvaldo Luiz *E-mail:* oswaldo@
cancaonova.com
Contact: Magda Ishikawa *E-mail:* direcaoartistica.
editorial@cancaonova.com
Founded: 1996
Subjects: Religion - Catholic, Catechesis, Prayer
ISBN Prefix(es): 978-85-7677; 978-85-150

Capivara Editora (Capivara Publishing House)+
Rua Sao Luiz Gonzaga 731, sala 204, 20910-060
Rio de Janeiro-RJ
Tel: (021) 2512-2612; (021) 2540-6954
Fax: (021) 2511-3918

E-mail: atendimento@editoracapivara.com.br
Web Site: www.editoracapivara.com.br
Founded: 2001
Membership(s): Liga Brasileira de Editoras (LI-BRE).
Subjects: Art, Photography, 19th Century Brazilian Art
ISBN Prefix(es): 978-85-89063
Total Titles: 20 Print
Distributed by Dina Livros (Portugal)
Bookshop(s): Librairie Portugaise, Paris, France

Casa da Palavra
Member of Grupo LeYa
Av Calogeras, 6, sala 1001, Rio de Janeiro-RJ 20030-070
Tel: (021) 2222 3167 *Fax:* (021) 2224 7461
Web Site: www.casadapalavra.com.br
Subjects: Art, Biography, Memoirs, Cookery, Fashion, Inspirational, Spirituality, Music, Dance, Romance, Science Fiction, Fantasy, Self-Help, Travel & Tourism
ISBN Prefix(es): 978-85-7734; 978-85-87220

Casarao do Verbo
Rua Landulfo Alves, 113-cj 1, 45180-000 Anaje-BA
Tel: (077) 3435 2674
Web Site: www.casaraodoverbo.com.br; www.facebook.com/casaraodoverboeditora
Founded: 2007
Subjects: Fiction, Poetry, Comics
ISBN Prefix(es): 978-85-61878

CEDIC - Centro Difusor de Cultura
Rua Batista Pereira, 137, 11015-100 Macuco-Santos-SP
Tel: (013) 3301-5333
E-mail: contato@cedicbrasil.com.br
Web Site: cedicbrasil.com.br
Founded: 1984
Subjects: Art, Biblical Studies, Education, Literature, Literary Criticism, Essays, Pedagogy
ISBN Prefix(es): 978-85-7530

Editora Cejup+
Travessa Alenquer nº 99-B, Cidade Velha, 66020-020 Belem-PA
Tel: (091) 3222-6995; (091) 3230-0537
Founded: 1979
Membership(s): Associacao Nacional de Livrarias (ANL); Sindicato Nacional de Livrarias (SNL).
Subjects: Biological Sciences, Criminology, Drama, Theater, Education, Fiction, Law, Science Fiction, Fantasy, Social Sciences, Sociology
ISBN Prefix(es): 978-85-338
Bookshop(s): Assis de Vasconcelos, n 498, 66017-070 Belem-PA

Celebris, *imprint of* Editora Rideel Ltda

Cengage Learning+
Condominio E-Business Park, Rua Werner Siemens, 111-Predio 20-Espaco 04, Lapa de Baixo, 05069-900 Sao Paulo-SP
Tel: (011) 3665-9900 *Fax:* (011) 3665-9901
Web Site: www.cengage.com.br
Founded: 1960
Subjects: Accounting, Advertising, Agriculture, Architecture & Interior Design, Astrology, Occult, Behavioral Sciences, Business, Computer Science, Economics, Education, History, Language Arts, Linguistics, Management, Mysteries, Suspense, Photography, Psychology, Psychiatry, Social Sciences, Sociology
ISBN Prefix(es): 978-85-221

CEPA - Centro de Psicologia Aplicada
Rua Evaristo da Veiga 16, Cobertura - Centro (Cinelandia), 20031-040 Rio de Janeiro-RJ

Tel: (021) 2220-6545; (021) 2220-5545
E-mail: psicocepa@psicocepa.com.br
Web Site: www.psicocepa.com.br
Key Personnel
Mng Dir: Antonio Rodrigues, Jr
Founded: 1952
Subjects: Psychology, Psychiatry
ISBN Prefix(es): 978-85-7043

Editora Cidade Nova (Editora New City)+
Rua Jose Ernesto Tozzi, 198, Mariapolis Ginetta, 06730-000 Vargem Grande Paulista-SP
Tel: (011) 4158-8890 *Toll Free Tel:* 0800 724 2252 (subscriptions)
E-mail: vendas@cidadenova.org.br
Web Site: www.cidadenova.org.br
Key Personnel
Chief Editor: Luis Henrique Marques
   E-mail: luismarques@cidadenova.org.br
Editorial Coordinator: Adelmo Galindo
   E-mail: adelmo@cidadenova.org.br
Founded: 1960
Subjects: Biblical Studies, Child Care & Development, Economics, Education, Human Relations, Psychology, Psychiatry, Religion - Catholic, Social Sciences, Sociology, Theology
ISBN Prefix(es): 978-85-7112; 978-85-89736; 978-85-7821
Parent Company: Citta Nuova Editrice, Italy
U.S. Office(s): New City Press, 202 Comforter Blvd, Hyde Park, NY 12538, United States *E-mail:* info@newcitypress.com *Web Site:* www.newcitypress.com

Ciranda Cultural Editora e Distribuidora Ltda
Alameda Rio Negro, 585, Alphaville, bloco B, 4º andar, Cj 42, 06454-000 Baruer-SP
Tel: (011) 3761-9500
E-mail: sales@cirandaculturalpub.com
Web Site: www.cirandaculturalpublishing.com
ISBN Prefix(es): 978-85-380; 978-85-7520
Branch Office(s)
Ciranda Cultural Publishing Ltd, Bolney Business Park, One Stairbridge Court, Haywards Heath, West Sussex RH17 5PA, United Kingdom

Civilizacao Brasileira, *imprint of* Grupo Editorial Record

CNEN, see Comissao Nacional de Energia Nuclear (CNEN)

Comissao Nacional de Energia Nuclear (CNEN)
Rua Gal Severiano, 90, 22290-901 Rio de Janeiro-RJ
Tel: (021) 2173-2000; (021) 2173-2001
   Fax: (021) 2173-2003
Web Site: www.cnen.gov.br
Key Personnel
President: Angelo Fernando Padilha
   Tel: (021) 2173-2101 *Fax:* (021) 2173-2103
   E-mail: presidencia@cnen.gov.br
Founded: 1970
Also is the Brazilian national center for the International Nuclear Information System (INIS) & the Energy Technology Data Exchange (ETDE).
Subjects: Energy, Engineering (General), Environmental Studies, Nuclear Energy
ISBN Prefix(es): 978-85-344

Editora Companhia das Letras/Editora Schwarcz Ltda+
Rua Bandeira Paulista, 702, cj 32, 04532-002 Sao Paulo-SP
Tel: (011) 3707-3500 *Fax:* (011) 3707-3501
E-mail: pedidos@companhiadasletras.com.br
Web Site: www.companhiadasletras.com.br
Key Personnel
Chief Executive Officer: Luiz Schwarcz

Founded: 1986
Subjects: Anthropology, Biblical Studies, Biography, Memoirs, Cookery, Fiction, History, Humor, Literature, Literary Criticism, Essays, Philosophy, Photography, Poetry
ISBN Prefix(es): 978-85-7164; 978-85-85095; 978-85-85466
Number of titles published annually: 150 Print
Distributed by Jorge Zahar (Rio de Janeiro)
Distributor for Jorge Zahar (Sao Paulo)
Foreign Rep(s): Atlantico Book Importer Inc (USA); Dinalivro National Book Distributor Ltda (Portugal); JB Communication (Japan)
Foreign Rights: Carmen Balcells Agencia Literaria SA (Europe); Melanie Jackson (USA); Ray-Guede Mertin (Europe); Anne Marie Vallat (Spain)

Editora Concordia Ltda
Av Sao Pedro, 633, Bairro Sao Geraldo, 90230-120 Porto Alegre-RS
Tel: (051) 3272-3456 *Fax:* (051) 3272-3482
E-mail: comercial@editoraconcordia.com.br; editora@editoraconcordia.com.br
Web Site: www.editoraconcordia.com.br
Founded: 1923
Subjects: Music, Dance, Religion - Other, Theology
ISBN Prefix(es): 978-85-89258
Parent Company: Igreja Evangelica Luterana do Brasil (IELB)
Branch Office(s)
Ave Getulio Vargas, 4388, Sao Leopoldo-RS

Conex, *imprint of* Livraria Nobel SA

Conquista Empresa de Publicacoes Ltda
av 28 de Setembro 174, Vila Isabel, 20551-030 Rio de Janeiro-RJ
Founded: 1951
Subjects: Art, Cookery, Literature, Literary Criticism, Essays
ISBN Prefix(es): 978-85-7066

Conrad Editora
Av Alexandre Mackenzie, 619-Jaguare, 05322-000 Sao Paulo-SP
Tel: (011) 2799-7799
E-mail: imprensa@conradeditora.com.br; vendas@conradeditora.com.br
Web Site: www.lojaconrad.com.br
Subjects: Fiction, Music, Dance, Nonfiction (General), Science Fiction, Fantasy, Manga
ISBN Prefix(es): 978-85-7616; 978-85-87193

Consultor Assessoria Planejamentos Ltda
R General Gurjao 479, 20931-040 Rio de Janeiro-RJ
Tel: (021) 2589-3030
Founded: 1988
Subjects: Education, Literature, Literary Criticism, Essays
ISBN Prefix(es): 978-85-85206; 978-85-7434

Editora Contexto (Editora Pinsky Ltda)+
Rua Dr Jose Elias, 520, 05083-030 Sao Paulo-SP
Tel: (011) 3832-5838 *Fax:* (011) 3832-1043
E-mail: contexto@editoracontexto.com.br
Web Site: www.editoracontexto.com.br
Key Personnel
Editorial & Production: Jaime Pinsky
Marketing: Diego Jock
Founded: 1987
Membership(s): Camara Brasileina do Livro.
Subjects: Anthropology, Economics, Education, Environmental Studies, Geography, Geology, Government, Political Science, Health, Nutrition, History, Journalism, Language Arts, Linguistics, Philosophy, Social Sciences, Sociology, Travel & Tourism
ISBN Prefix(es): 978-85-7244; 978-85-85134

Number of titles published annually: 20 Print; 20
E-Book
Total Titles: 165 Print; 165 E-Book

Cortez Editora
Rua Monte Alegre, 1074, Perdizes, 05014-001
Sao Paulo-SP
Tel: (011) 3611-9616; (011) 3864-0111
E-mail: mkt@cortezeditora.com.br; sac@
cortezeditora.com.br
Web Site: www.cortezeditora.com.br
Key Personnel
Proprietor: Jose Xavier Cortez
Dir, Foreign Rights: Antonio Erivan Gomes
E-mail: erivan@cortezeditora.com.br
Coordinator: Elaine Nunes
Founded: 1980
Subjects: Economics, Education, Government, Po-
litical Science, Psychology, Psychiatry, Social
Sciences, Sociology
ISBN Prefix(es): 978-85-249
Bookshop(s): Livraria Cortez, Rua Bartira, 317,
Perdizes, 05009-000 Sao Paulo-SP *Tel:* (011)
3873-7111

Editora Crescer+
Rua do Ouro, 104, Conj 501, Serra, 30220-000
Belo Horizonte-MG
Tel: (031) 3221-9235 *Fax:* (031) 3227-0729
E-mail: editoracrescer@editoracrescer.com.br
Web Site: www.editoracrescer.com.br
Key Personnel
Dir: Clara Feldman
Founded: 1983
Subjects: Human Relations, Self-Help
ISBN Prefix(es): 978-85-85615

Editora Cultura Crista+
Rua Miguel Telles Junior, 382/394, Cambuci,
01540-040 Sao Paulo-SP
Mailing Address: CP 15136, 01599-970 Sao
Paulo-SP
Tel: (011) 3207-7099 *Toll Free Tel:* 0800 014
1963 (sales) *Fax:* (011) 3209-1255
E-mail: cep@cep.org.br
Web Site: www.editoraculturacrista.com.br
Key Personnel
Editor: Claudio A B Marra
Founded: 1948
Subjects: History, Religion - Other

Editora Cultura Medica Ltda+
Rua Gonzaga Bastos, 163, Vila Isabel, 20541-000
Rio de Janeiro-RJ
Tel: (021) 2567-3888 *Fax:* (021) 3259-5443
E-mail: cultura@culturamedica.com.br
Web Site: culturamedica.com.br/wp/
Key Personnel
Mng Dir: Ezequiel Feldman
Founded: 1966
Subjects: Medicine, Nursing, Dentistry,
Biomedicine
ISBN Prefix(es): 978-85-7006
Orders to: Rua Lucio de Mendonca, 37, Apart-
ment 401, 20470-040 Rio de Janeiro-RJ

DBA Editora, see Dorea Books & Art

Editora DCL
New Worker Tower, Ave Marques de Sao Vi-
cente, 446 18º andar, 01139-000 Sao Paulo-SP
Tel: (011) 3932-5222
E-mail: sac@editoradcl.com.br
Web Site: www.editoradcl.com.br
Subjects: Cookery, Education, Environmental
Studies, Health, Nutrition, Literature, Liter-
ary Criticism, Essays, Religion - Other, Beauty,
Disney
ISBN Prefix(es): 978-85-368

DeLeitura, *imprint of* Editora Aquariana Ltda

Difel, *imprint of* Grupo Editorial Record

Editorial Dimensao Ltda+
Rua Rosinha Sigaud 201, Caicara, 30770-560
Belo Horizonte-MG
Tel: (031) 3527-8000 *Fax:* (031) 3411-2427
E-mail: dimensao@editoradimensao.com.br
Web Site: www.editoradimensao.com.br
Key Personnel
Executive Chairman & General Editor: Zelia
Almeida
Founded: 1986
Membership(s): Brazilian House of Books.
Subjects: Law, Psychology, Psychiatry
ISBN Prefix(es): 978-85-7319

Dorea Books & Art
Al Franca 1185 cj 31 Cerqueira Cesar, 01422-001
Sao Paulo-SP
Tel: (011) 3062 1643 *Fax:* (011) 3088 3361
E-mail: dba@dbaeditora.com.br; faleconosco@
dbaeditora.com.br
Web Site: www.dbaeditora.com.br
Key Personnel
Press: Andrea M Santos
Subjects: Art, Biography, Memoirs, Cookery, Lit-
erature, Literary Criticism, Essays, Photogra-
phy, Sports, Athletics
ISBN Prefix(es): 978-85-7234; 978-85-85628

Editora DSOP
Al Santos, 2326, cj 86, Jardim Paulista, 01418-
200 Sao Paulo-SP
Tel: (011) 3660-5400; (011) 3177-7800 (sales)
E-mail: contato@editoradsop.com.br
Web Site: www.editoradsop.com.br
ISBN Prefix(es): 978-85-63680

Livraria Duas Cidades
Rua Doutor Emilio Ribas, 89, 05006-020 Sao
Paulo-SP
Tel: (011) 3668-2160
Founded: 1956
Subjects: Literature, Literary Criticism, Essays,
Philosophy, Psychology, Psychiatry, Religion -
Other, Social Sciences, Sociology
ISBN Prefix(es): 978-85-235

Editora Dublinense Ltda
Av Augusto Meyer, 163 conj 605, Porto Alegre-
RS 90550-110
Tel: (051) 3024-0787
E-mail: editorial@dublinense.com.br
Web Site: www.dublinense.com.br
Key Personnel
Publisher: Gustavo Faraon; Rodrigo Rosp
Founded: 2007
Subjects: Biography, Memoirs, Business, Fic-
tion, Government, Political Science, Poetry,
Romance, Sports, Athletics, Travel & Tourism
ISBN Prefix(es): 978-85-62757

Edicon Editora e Consultorial Ltda
Rua Herculano de Freitas, 181, Cerqueira Cesar,
01308-020 Sao Paulo-SP
Tel: (011) 3255-1002 *Fax:* (011) 3255-1002
E-mail: vendas@edicon.com.br
Web Site: www.edicon.com.br
Founded: 1981
Subjects: Animals, Pets, Antiques, Architecture &
Interior Design, Art, Astrology, Occult, Biogra-
phy, Memoirs, Communications, Drama, The-
ater, Earth Sciences, Education, Government,
Political Science, LGBTQ, Literature, Liter-
ary Criticism, Essays, Mathematics, Medicine,
Nursing, Dentistry, Music, Dance, Philosophy,
Physics, Poetry, Psychology, Psychiatry, Re-
ligion - Other, Romance, Science (General),
Science Fiction, Fantasy, Social Sciences, Soci-
ology, Ecology
ISBN Prefix(es): 978-85-290

Edipro-Edicoes Profissionais Ltda+
R Marcondes Salgado, 21-21, Vila Cardia, 17013-
231 Bauru-SP
Tel: (014) 3234 4121
E-mail: edipro@edipro.com.br; pedidos@edipro.
com.br (sales)
Web Site: www.edipro.com.br
Founded: 1977
Subjects: Law, Philosophy, Social Sciences, Soci-
ology
ISBN Prefix(es): 978-85-7283; 978-85-89987;
978-85-89988
Total Titles: 350 Print
Branch Office(s)
R Conde de Sao Joaquim, 332, Liberdade, 01324-
001 Sao Paulo-SP *Tel:* (011) 3107 4788

EDIPUCRS (Editora Universitaria de PUCRS)
Av Ipiranga 6681, Bldg 33, 90619-900 Porto
Alegre-RS
Tel: (051) 3320 3711
E-mail: editora.vendas@pucrs.br
Web Site: livrariaedipucrs.pucrs.br
Key Personnel
President: Jorge Luis Nicolas Audy
Executive Dir: Jeronimo Carlos Santos Braga
Chief Editor: Jorge Campos da Costa
Founded: 1988
Subjects: Advertising, Aeronautics, Aviation, An-
thropology, Archaeology, Architecture & Inte-
rior Design, Biography, Memoirs, Biological
Sciences, Communications, Economics, Edu-
cation, Engineering (General), Fiction, Geog-
raphy, Geology, History, Language Arts, Lin-
guistics, Literature, Literary Criticism, Essays,
Management, Mathematics, Medicine, Nursing,
Dentistry, Music, Dance, Philosophy, Physics,
Poetry, Psychology, Psychiatry, Social Sciences,
Sociology, Theology, Travel & Tourism, Ad-
ministration, Aeronautical Sciences, Botany,
Physical Education
ISBN Prefix(es): 978-85-7430

Editora da Unicamp
Rua Caio Graco Prado, 50, Cidade Universitaria,
13083-892 Campinas-SP
Tel: (019) 3521-7787
E-mail: vendas@editora.unicamp.br
Web Site: www.editora.unicamp.br
Key Personnel
Dir: Marcia Abreu *E-mail:* diretor@editora.
unicamp.br
Production Manager: Ricardo Lima *Tel:* (019)
3521-7077 *E-mail:* ricardo@editora.unicamp.br
Founded: 1982
Subjects: Art, Literature, Literary Criticism, Es-
says, Technology
ISBN Prefix(es): 978-85-268
Parent Company: Universidade de Campinas

Editora Positivo Ltda
Rua Major Heitor Guimaraes, 174, 80440-120
Curibita-PR
Tel: (041) 3312-3500 *Toll Free Tel:* 0800 724
4241
E-mail: vendaspublicas@positivo.com.br
Web Site: www.editorapositivo.com.br
Subjects: Art, Fiction, Geography, Geology, His-
tory, Language Arts, Linguistics, Mathematics,
Music, Dance, Nonfiction (General), Science
(General), Portuguese Language
ISBN Prefix(es): 978-85-7472
Parent Company: Grupo Positivo
Branch Office(s)
11 de Fevereiro, 187/189, Sao Paulo-SP
Tel: (041) 5588-9500 *Fax:* (041) 5588-9501

Editora Universidade Estadual de Ponta Grossa (UEPG)
Praca Santos Andrade, 01, Sala A-28, Centro, 84010-790 Ponta Grossa-PR
Tel: (042) 3220-3362
E-mail: editora@uepg.br; vendas.editora@uepg.br
Web Site: www.uepg.br/editora
Key Personnel
President & Editorial Coordinator: Lucia Cortes da Costa
Distribution & Sales: Margarete Simioni
Tel: (042) 3220-3306
Subjects: Agriculture, Art, Biological Sciences, Engineering (General), Health, Nutrition, Language Arts, Linguistics, Social Sciences, Sociology, Humanities
ISBN Prefix(es): 978-85-86941
Bookshop(s): Av Carlos Cavalcanti, 4748, 84030-900 Ponta Grossa-PR, Contact: Luiza Helena Costa Neves *Tel:* (042) 3220-3058; Praca Santos Andrade, 1, 84010-790 Ponta Grossa-PR, Contact: Wilson Jose Nascimento *Tel:* (042) 3220-3369

Editora Universitaria de PUCRS, see EDIPUCRS (Editora Universitaria de PUCRS)

Editus, see Editora da Universidade Estadual de Santa Cruz (UESC)

EDUC+
Rua Monte Alegre, 984, Sala S16, Perdizes, 05014-901 Sao Paulo-SP
Tel: (011) 3670-8085 *Fax:* (011) 3670-8558
E-mail: educ@pucsp.br
Web Site: www.pucsp.br/educ
Key Personnel
Dir: Prof Miguel Chaia
Founded: 1984
Membership(s): Associacao Brasileira das Editoras Universitaries (ABEU); Associacao Brasileira de Editores Cientificos (ABEC); Camara Brasileira do Livro (CBL).
Subjects: Anthropology, Biological Sciences, Communications, Disability, Special Needs, Economics, Education, English as a Second Language, Geography, Geology, Government, Political Science, History, Humor, Language Arts, Linguistics, Law, Literature, Literary Criticism, Essays, Mathematics, Medicine, Nursing, Dentistry, Music, Dance, Philosophy, Psychology, Psychiatry, Social Sciences, Sociology, Theology
ISBN Prefix(es): 978-85-283
Total Titles: 230 Print; 1 Audio
Parent Company: Pontificia Universidade Catolica de Sao Paulo
Ultimate Parent Company: Fundacao Cultural Sao Paulo

EDUFPE, see Editora da Universidade Federal de Pernambuco (UFPE)

EDUSC - Editora da Universidade do Sagrado Coracao (Sacred Heart University Press)+
Rua Irma Arminda, 10-50, Jardim, 17011-160 Bauru-SP
Tel: (014) 2107-7220
E-mail: eduscp@edusc.com.br; vendasedusc@edusc.com.br
Web Site: www.edusc.com.br
Key Personnel
Chairman of Executive Board: Prof Alexandre Oliveira
President: Irma Susana de Jesus Fadel
Editor: Prof Jose Jobson de Andrade Arruda
Editorial Coordinator: Prof Carina Nascimento
Marketing & Finance: Celia Quintanilha
Tel: (014) 2107-7390
Marketing & Sales: Marcos Goulart *Tel:* (014) 2107-7252

International Relations: Marili Ferreira Cariadade
Tel: (014) 2107-7251 *E-mail:* mferreira@edusc.com.br
Founded: 1996
Subjects: Anthropology, Art, Biography, Memoirs, Biological Sciences, Child Care & Development, Communications, Economics, Education, Health, Nutrition, History, Journalism, Law, Literature, Literary Criticism, Essays, Medicine, Nursing, Dentistry, Philosophy, Psychology, Psychiatry, Religion - Catholic, Science (General), Social Sciences, Sociology, Travel & Tourism, Brazilian Originals, Politics
ISBN Prefix(es): 978-85-7460; 978-85-86259
Number of titles published annually: 80 Print
Distribution Center: Rio de Janeiro
Sao Paulo

EDUSP, see Editora da Universidade de Sao Paulo (EDUSP)

Editora Elementar
Rua Bernardino Fanganiello, 543, Casa Verde, 02512-000 Sao Paulo-SP
Tel: (011) 3857-0740; (011) 3951-9302; (011) 3856-7571; (011) 3856-9206 *Fax:* (011) 3857-0740; (011) 3951-9302; (011) 3856-7571; (011) 3856-9206
E-mail: administrativo@editoraelementar.com.br; editorial@editoraelementar.com.br
Web Site: www.editoraelementar.com.br
Founded: 2000
ISBN Prefix(es): 978-85-99306

Editora Elevacao+
Affiliate of Fundacao Jose de Paiva Netto
Rua Doraci, 90, Bom Retiro, 01134-050 Sao Paulo-SP
Tel: (011) 2836-6478
Founded: 1998
Subjects: Biblical Studies, Biography, Memoirs, Business, Communications, Education, Health, Nutrition, History, Human Relations, Inspirational, Spirituality, Management, Parapsychology, Philosophy, Poetry, Religion - Other, Romance, Self-Help, Sports, Athletics, Theology
ISBN Prefix(es): 978-85-7513; 978-85-86623
Number of titles published annually: 13 Print; 2 Audio
Total Titles: 37 Print; 2 Audio
Distribution Center: Distribooks International Inc, 8120 N Ridgeway, Skokie, IL 60076, United States, Manager: Elizabeth Mitas *Tel:* 847-676-1596 *Fax:* 847-676-1195 *E-mail:* distribooks@mepnet.com

Embrapa Informacao Tecnologica (Embrapa Technological Information)+
Parque Estacao Biologica - PqEB - Av W3 Norte (final), 70770-901 Brasilia-DF
Mailing Address: CP 040315, 70770-901 Brasilia-DF
Tel: (061) 3448-4162; (061) 3448-4155 *Fax:* (061) 3272-4168
E-mail: sac@sct.embrapa.br
Web Site: www.sct.embrapa.br
Key Personnel
General Manager: Fernando do Amaral Pereira
E-mail: chefia.dtt@embrapa.br
Founded: 1991
Subjects: Agriculture, Animals, Pets, Biological Sciences, Earth Sciences, Economics, Environmental Studies, Geography, Geology, Journalism, Social Sciences, Sociology, Technology, Veterinary Science
ISBN Prefix(es): 978-85-7383
Number of titles published annually: 70 Print; 2 CD-ROM; 30 Online; 2 E-Book
Total Titles: 103 Online; 2 E-Book
Parent Company: Empresa Brasileira de Pesquisa Agropecuaria - Embrapa

EPU - Editora Pedagogica e Universitaria Ltda
Rua Joaquim Floriano 72-6° andar, Conjuntos 65/68, 04534-000 Sao Paulo-SP
Tel: (011) 3168-6077 *Fax:* (011) 3078-5803
Web Site: www.grupogen.com.br
Key Personnel
Manager: Wolfgang Knapp
Founded: 1952
Subjects: Education, Medicine, Nursing, Dentistry, Philosophy, Psychology, Psychiatry
ISBN Prefix(es): 978-85-12; 978-85-202
Parent Company: Grupo Editorial Nacional (GEN)

Editora Escala Educacional
Rua Professora Ida Kolb, 551-Casa Verde, 02518-000 Sao Paulo-SP
Tel: (011) 3855-2201 *Fax:* (011) 3855-2189
E-mail: atendimento@escalaeducacional.com.br
Web Site: www.escalaeducacional.com.br
Subjects: Art, Education, Literacy
ISBN Prefix(es): 978-85-377

Escrituras Editora e Distribuidora de Livros Ltda+
Rua Maestro Callia, 123, Vila Mariana, 04012-100 Sao Paulo-SP
Tel: (011) 5904-4499 *Fax:* (011) 5904-4495
E-mail: vendas@escrituras.com.br
Web Site: www.escrituras.com.br
Key Personnel
Executive Editor: Raimundo Nonato Rocha Gadelha
Founded: 1994
Specialize in works from Brazilian & international literature & photography.
Subjects: Environmental Studies, Cinema, Contemporary Portuguese Literature, Culture
ISBN Prefix(es): 978-85-86303; 978-85-7531

Editora Evora
Rua Sergipe 401-cj 1310, Higienopolis, Sao Paulo-SP
Tel: (011) 3562-7815
E-mail: contato@editoraevora.com.br
Web Site: www.editoraevora.com.br
Key Personnel
Publisher: Henrique Farinha
Founded: 2010
Subjects: Biography, Memoirs, Fiction, Sports, Athletics
ISBN Prefix(es): 978-85-63993

Editora Expressao e Cultura-Exped Ltda
Estrada dos Bandeirantes, 1700 bloco B, Jacarepagua, 22710-113 Rio de Janeiro-RJ
Founded: 1967
Subjects: Education, Literature, Literary Criticism, Essays
ISBN Prefix(es): 978-85-208

Fantastica Rocco, *imprint of* Editora Rocco Ltda

FEI, *imprint of* Editora Gaia Ltda

Editora FGV+
Rua Jornalista Orlando Dantas, 37, Botafogo, 22231-010 Rio de Janeiro-RJ
Tel: (021) 3799-4426; (021) 3799-4427; (021) 3799-4228; (021) 3799-4429
Toll Free Tel: 0800 021 7777 *Fax:* (021) 3799-4430
E-mail: editora@fgv.br
Web Site: www.editora.fgv.br; www.fgv.br
Founded: 1974
Subjects: Accounting, Anthropology, Biography, Memoirs, Business, Communications, Economics, Education, Government, Political Science, Marketing, Philosophy, Psychology, Psychiatry, Public Administration, Science (Gen-

eral), Social Sciences, Sociology, Technology, Ecology
ISBN Prefix(es): 978-85-225

Forense, *imprint of* Grupo Editorial Nacional (GEN)

Editora Forense+
Imprint of Grupo Editorial Nacional (GEN)
Travessa do Ouvidor, 11, 20040-040 Rio de Janeiro-RJ
Tel: (021) 3543-0770; (021) 3543-0780 (sales)
E-mail: diretoria@grupogen.com.br; vendas@grupogen.com.br
Web Site: www.grupogen.com.br
Founded: 1904
Subjects: Biography, Memoirs, Cookery, Criminology, Education, Health, Nutrition, History, Law, Music, Dance, Nonfiction (General), Philosophy, Psychology, Psychiatry, Religion - Buddhist, Romance, Self-Help, Social Sciences, Sociology, Sports, Athletics, Travel & Tourism, Women's Studies
ISBN Prefix(es): 978-85-309
Number of titles published annually: 360 Print

Forense Universitaria, *imprint of* Grupo Editorial Nacional (GEN)

Forense Universitaria+
Imprint of Grupo Editorial Nacional (GEN)
Travessa do Ouvidor, 11, 20040-040 Rio de Janeiro-RJ
Tel: (021) 3543-0770; (021) 3543-0780 (sales)
E-mail: diretoria@grupogen.com.br; vendas@grupogen.com.br
Web Site: www.grupogen.com.br
Founded: 1973
Membership(s): National Book Publishers of Rio de Janeiro, Brazil; Sindicato Nacional dos Editores de Livros (SNEL).
Subjects: Economics, Government, Political Science, History, Language Arts, Linguistics, Law, Philosophy, Psychology, Psychiatry, Social Sciences, Sociology
ISBN Prefix(es): 978-85-218

Scott Foresman, *imprint of* Pearson Education do Brasil Ltda

Livraria Freitas Bastos Editora SA+
Rua Beneditinos nº 16, Sala 902, 20081-050 Rio de Janeiro-RJ
Tel: (021) 2276-4500 *Fax:* (021) 2276-4500
E-mail: freitasbastos@freitasbastos.com.br
Web Site: www.freitasbastos.com.br
Key Personnel
Editor: Isaac Delgado Abulafia
Founded: 1917
Membership(s): The Association of Brazilian Publishers.
Subjects: Accounting, Law, Administration
ISBN Prefix(es): 978-85-353

Editora FTD SA
Rua Manuel Dutra, 225, Bela Vista, 01328-010 Sao Paulo-SP
Tel: (011) 3284-8500 *Toll Free Tel:* 0800 772 2300 *Fax:* (011) 3283-8500
E-mail: central.atendimento@ftd.com.br
Web Site: www.ftd.com.br
Key Personnel
President: Joao Tissi
Founded: 1902
ISBN Prefix(es): 978-85-322
Branch Office(s)
Av Ermano Marchetti, 974, Lapa de Baixo, 05038-001 Sao Paulo-SP *Tel:* (011) 3598-6200 *Fax:* (011) 3611-7075
Rua Primeiro de Agosto, 12-63, 17013-010 Bauru-SP *Tel:* (014) 3232-8540

Rua Ana Eufrosina, 60, Guanabara, 130753-023 Campinas-SP *Tel:* (019) 3242-3822 *Fax:* (019) 3242-3493
Rua Sao Jose, 123, Centro, 14010-160 Ribeirao Preto-SP *Tel:* (016) 3797-0777 *Fax:* (016) 3797-0753
R Dr Samuel Baccarat, 70, Boqueirao, 11055-040 Santos-SP *Tel:* (013) 3221-8707
Rua Vilaca, 201, Centro, 12210-000 Sao Jose Dos Campos-SP *Tel:* (012) 3941-6584
Floriano Peixoto St, 407, Centro, 69908-030 Rio Branco-AC *Tel:* (068) 3224-8363
Av Andre Araujo, 85, Neighborhood Alexis, 69060-000 Manaus-AM *Tel:* (092) 3663-6595 *Fax:* (092) 3664-6840
Rua Padre July, 3960, Santa Rita, 68900-030 Macapa-AP *Tel:* (091) 4006-5606
Av Amelia Amado, 926, 45600-000 Itabuna-BA *Tel:* (073) 3613-1049
Luz Gonzaga St - Soldier of Virgins, 156, Pituba, 41820-560 Salvador-BA *Tel:* (071) 2101-4200
Ave Luciano Carneiro, 841, Fatima, 60410-690 Fortaleza-CE *Tel:* (085) 3066-8585 *Fax:* (085) 3066-8599
Sector Chart (GIS), Block 08 - Lots 2266/2277, 70610-480 Brasilia-DF *Tel:* (061) 3343-2555 *Fax:* (061) 3343-2455
Rua Eng Fabio Ruschi, 398, Bento Ferreira, 29050-670 Vitoria-ES *Tel:* (027) 3227-6044 *Fax:* (027) 3227-6857
Rua 68, 710, Centro, 74055-100 Goiania-GO *Tel:* (062) 3605-5200 *Fax:* (062) 3605-5212
Rua Teixeira de Freitas, 325, Centro, 65700-000 Bacabal-MA *Tel:* (099) 3621-1612
Rua Godofredo Viana, 565, 65900-100 Imperatriz-MA *Tel:* (099) 3525-1085; (099) 9524-1599
Rua da Bacabeira, 136, Centro, 65300-000 Santa Ines-MA *Tel:* (098) 3653-2347
Av Getulio Vargas, 36, Apeadouro, 65030-000 Sao Luis-MA *Tel:* (098) 3232-3021; (098) 3232-1331 *Fax:* (098) 3231-2886
Av Cristiano Machado, 2860, Uniao, 31160-380 Belo Horizonte-MG *Tel:* (031) 3057-4800 *Fax:* (031) 3057-4831
Rua Francisco Sales, 1065, Osvaldo, 38400-440 Uberlandia-MG *Tel:* (034) 3236-2818
Av Mato Grosso, 773, Centro, 79002-231 Campo Grande-MS *Tel:* (067) 3324-2561 *Fax:* (067) 3384-2424
Rua Pedro Celestino, 225, Centro, 78005-010 Cuiaba-MT *Tel:* (065) 3624-2464 *Fax:* (065) 3262-2464
Travessa Sao Pedro, 406, 66023-570 Belem-PA *Tel:* (091) 3081 7766
Rua Pedro Americo, 52, Centro, 58100-000 Campina Grande-PB *Tel:* (083) 3322-7260
Av Dom Pedro I, 882, Centro, 58013-020 Joao Pessoa-PB *Tel:* (083) 3221-1635 *Fax:* (083) 3221-1635
Rua Manoel Clementino, 1374 A, Centro, 56302-170 Petrolina-PE *Tel:* (087) 3861-1901
Rua Barao de Igarassu, 35, Santo Amaro, 50110-410 Recife-PE *Tel:* (081) 2128-5555 *Fax:* (081) 2128-5572
Ave Prof Valter Alencar, 1714, Macauba, 64019-625 Teresina-PL *Tel:* (086) 3229-3202 *Fax:* (086) 3229-3203
Rua Joao Negrao, 2720, Prado Velho, 80230-150 Curitiba-PR *Tel:* (041) 3208-8400 *Fax:* (041) 3208-8430
Ave Rio Branco, 173, Shangri-La, 86070-010 Londrina-PR *Tel:* (043) 2104-4700 *Fax:* (043) 2104-4710
Rua Comendador Jose Francisco Sanguedo, 107, Centro, 28010-235 Campos Dos Goytacazes-RJ *Tel:* (022) 2722-3799
Rua Vandenkolk, 137, Olaria, 21073-290 Rio de Janeiro-RJ *Tel:* (021) 2127-9700 *Fax:* (021) 2127-9724
Rua dos Calcos, 1321, Alecrim, 59034-700 Natal-RN *Tel:* (084) 3213-6654 *Fax:* (084) 3213-0492

Rua Ramiro Barcelos, 334, Floresta, 90035-000 Porto Alegre-RS *Tel:* (051) 3204-8100 *Fax:* (051) 3204-8135
Rua Santos Saraiva, 732 loja 02, Estreito, 88070-100 Florianopolis-SC *Tel:* (048) 3248-4140 *Fax:* (048) 3244-9200
Rua Riachuelo, 550, Sao Jose, 49015-160 Aracaju-SE *Tel:* (079) 3211-9941 *Fax:* (079) 3211-8010
Quadra 104 sul SE 02, conjunto 4, lote 11, sala 05, 0, Centro, 77020-026 Palmas-TO *Tel:* (063) 3225-1639

Fundacao Cultural Avatar
Rua Pereira Nunes, 141 - Inga, 24210-430 Niteroi-RJ
Tel: (021) 2621-0217; (021) 3587-3463 *Fax:* (021) 2721-0033
E-mail: fcavatar@nitnet.com.br; fc.avatar@hotmail.com
Web Site: www.nitnet.com.br/~fcavatar
Key Personnel
President: Dr Maria Elisa de Mattos Treiger
Dir, Administration & Financial: Prof Ruth Machado Barbosa
Dir, Culture: Lija Nogueira de Faria
Founded: 1973
Subjects: Asian Studies, Astrology, Occult, Biography, Memoirs, Education, Philosophy, Psychology, Psychiatry, Religion - Other
ISBN Prefix(es): 978-85-7104

Fundacao Getulio Vargas, see Editora FGV

Fundacao Joaquim Nabuco-Editora Massangana+
Av 17 de Agosto, 2187, Casa Forte, 52061-540 Recife-PE
Tel: (081) 3073-6232 *Fax:* (081) 3073-6351
E-mail: editora@fundaj.gov.br; cpl@fundaj.gov.br
Web Site: www.fundaj.gov.br
Key Personnel
Dir General: Leonardo Dantas Silva
Founded: 1980
Subjects: Anthropology, Economics, Education, History, Social Sciences, Sociology
ISBN Prefix(es): 978-85-7019

Fundacao Palavra Magica (Magic Word Foundation)+
Rua Americo Brasiliense, 1205 - Casa 2, Centro, 14015-050 Ribeirao Preto-SP
Tel: (016) 3610-0204
E-mail: fundacao@palavramagica.org.br
Web Site: www.palavramagica.org.br; www.facebook.com/fundpalavramagica/
Key Personnel
Chairman: Paulo Marcos de R Ramos
Treasurer: Pietro Fornitano Roveri
Secretary: Desiree Albuquerque Biasoli Correa
Founded: 1995
Subjects: Behavioral Sciences, Earth Sciences, Human Relations, Regional Interests, Religion - Catholic, Religion - Other, Romance, Social Sciences, Sociology
ISBN Prefix(es): 978-85-85997

Editora Gaia Ltda+
Rua Pirapitingui, 111, Liberdade, 01508-020 Sao Paulo-SP
Tel: (011) 3277-7999 *Fax:* (011) 3277-8141
E-mail: global@globaleditora.com.br
Web Site: www.editoragaia.com.br
Key Personnel
Commercial Dir: Richard A Alves
Founded: 1989
Subjects: Cookery, Environmental Studies, Health, Nutrition, Self-Help
ISBN Prefix(es): 978-85-85351; 978-85-7555
Parent Company: Gaia Global Group
Associate Companies: Editora Ground Ltda
Imprints: FEI

Galera Record, *imprint of* Grupo Editorial Record

Galerinha Record, *imprint of* Grupo Editorial Record

Editora Gente Livraria e Editora Ltda+
Rua Pedro Soares de Almeida, 114, 05029-030 Sao Paulo-SP
Tel: (011) 3670-2500
E-mail: marketing@editoragente.com.br; vendas@editoragente.com.br
Web Site: www.editoragente.com.br
Founded: 1984
Subjects: Education, Management, Philosophy, Psychology, Psychiatry, Self-Help
ISBN Prefix(es): 978-85-7312; 978-85-85247; 978-85-87881

Global Editora e Distribuidora Ltda+
Rua Pirapitingui, 111, Liberdade, 01508-020 Sao Paulo-SP
Tel: (011) 3277-7999 *Fax:* (011) 3277-8141
E-mail: global@globaleditora.com.br
Web Site: www.globaleditora.com.br
Key Personnel
Mng Dir, Sales: Luis Alves, Jr
Commercial Dir: Richard A Alves
Editorial Dir: Jefferson L Alves
Founded: 1973
Subjects: Anthropology, Biography, Memoirs, Education, Fashion, Health, Nutrition, History, Music, Dance, Poetry, Romance, Social Sciences, Sociology
ISBN Prefix(es): 978-85-260
Associate Companies: Editora Gaia Ltda; Editora Ground Ltda
Imprints: Parma; Prol; Sao Paulo Editora
Subsidiaries: Centro Editorial Latino Americano Ltda

Editora Globo SA+
Av Jaguare, 1485, 05346-902 Sao Paulo-SP
Tel: (011) 3767-7000
Web Site: editoraglobo.globo.com
Key Personnel
Editorial Dir: Flavio Barros Pinto
Founded: 1952
Subjects: Biography, Memoirs, Business, Cookery, Drama, Theater, Economics, Education, Environmental Studies, Fiction, History, Howto, Humor, Journalism, Language Arts, Linguistics, Law, Literature, Literary Criticism, Essays, Medicine, Nursing, Dentistry, Music, Dance, Mysteries, Suspense, Poetry, Science (General), Self-Help, Sports, Athletics, Travel & Tourism
ISBN Prefix(es): 978-85-250; 978-85-217
Branch Office(s)
SRTVS 701 - Centro Empresarial Assis Chateaubriant, Bloco 2 - Salas 701/716 - Asa Sul, Brasilia-DF *Tel:* (061) 3316-9501
Rua Hortencio Ribeiro de Luna, 333, Distrito Industrial, Joao Pessoa-PB *Tel:* (083) 3233-2600
Praca Floriano, 19-8 Andar, Centro, 20031-050 Rio de Janeiro-RJ *Tel:* (021) 3380 5900
Warehouse: Alameda Tocantins, 679 Alphaville, Barueri, Sao Paulo-SP

Edicoes Graal Ltda, *imprint of* Editora Paz e Terra Ltda

Edicoes Graal Ltda+
Imprint of Editora Paz e Terra Ltda
Rua do Triunfo, 177, Sta Ifigenia, 01212-010 Sao Paulo-SP
Tel: (011) 3337-8399 *Fax:* (011) 3223-6290
E-mail: divulgacao@pazeterra.com.br; editorial@pazeterra.com.br
Web Site: www.pazeterra.com.br

Key Personnel
Dir: Marcus Gasparian *E-mail:* diretoria@pazeterra.com.br
Editorial Production: Katia Halbe *E-mail:* producao@pazeterra.com.br; Cleber Paes *E-mail:* cleber@pazeterra.com.br
Founded: 1976
Subjects: Art, Biography, Memoirs, Business, Communications, Developing Countries, Drama, Theater, Economics, Education, Fiction, Government, Political Science, Health, Nutrition, History, Literature, Literary Criticism, Essays, Nonfiction (General), Philosophy, Psychology, Psychiatry, Science (General), Social Sciences, Sociology, Culture
ISBN Prefix(es): 978-85-7038

Ordem do Graal na Terra
Rua Sete de Setembro, 29.200, Chacaras Bartira, 06845-000 Embu das Artes-SP
Tel: (011) 4781-0006
E-mail: graal@graal.org.br
Web Site: www.graal.org.br
Founded: 1947
Subjects: Inspirational, Spirituality, Philosophy, Religion - Other, Self-Help, New-Age
ISBN Prefix(es): 978-85-7279
Number of titles published annually: 3 Print
Total Titles: 55 Print
Bookshop(s): Av Sao Luiz, 192-lj14, 01046-000 Sao Paulo-SP *Tel:* (011) 259-7646
Orders to: Buch Vertrieb Liane Buchheister, Schulstr 11a, 38126 Braunschweig, Germany *Tel:* (0531) 69 59 56 *Fax:* (0531) 69 58 56 *E-mail:* buchvertriebbuchheister@alice.de (Europe)
Nobre Books Distributor, 5117 Black Diamond Court, Raleigh, NC 27604, United States *Tel:* 919-212-6211 *E-mail:* nobrebooks@graal.org.br (USA & Canada)

Editora Ground Ltda+
Rua Lacedemonia, 85, 04634-020 Sao Paulo-SP
Tel: (011) 5031-1500 *Fax:* (011) 5031-3462
E-mail: vendas@ground.com.br
Web Site: www.ground.com.br
Founded: 1972
Subjects: Asian Studies, Astrology, Occult, Environmental Studies, Health, Nutrition, Literature, Literary Criticism, Essays, Philosophy, Self-Help, Food, Massage, Natural Medicine, Yoga
ISBN Prefix(es): 978-85-7187
Associate Companies: Editora Aquariana Ltda

Grupo Editorial Nacional (GEN)
Travessa do Ouvidor, 11, 20040-040 Rio de Janeiro-RJ
Tel: (021) 3543-0770
Web Site: www.grupogen.com.br
Key Personnel
Chief Executive Officer: Mauro Koogan Lorch
Founded: 2007
Scientific, technical & professional publishing & content.
Subjects: Health, Nutrition, Law, Social Sciences, Sociology
ISBN Prefix(es): 978-85-970018
Imprints: Atlas; Forense; Forense Universitaria; Guanabara Koogan; LTC; Metodo; Roca; Santos
Branch Office(s)
Rua Dona Brigida, 701, Vila Mariana, 04111-081 Sao Paulo-SP *Tel:* (011) 5080-0770
Rua Eugenio de Castro Rodrigues, 7A, 1700-183 Lisbon, Portugal *Tel:* (021) 840 50 66; (021) 840 50 67

Guanabara Koogan, *imprint of* Grupo Editorial Nacional (GEN)

Guanabara Koogan+
Imprint of Grupo Editorial Nacional (GEN)

Travessa do Ouvidor, 11, 20040-040 Rio de Janeiro-RJ
Tel: (021) 3970-9450 *Fax:* (021) 2221-5744
E-mail: vendas@grupogen.com.br
Web Site: www.grupogen.com.br
Key Personnel
Dir: Mauro Koogan Lorch
Rights & Permissions: Christina Noren
Founded: 1930
Subjects: Biological Sciences, Environmental Studies, Medicine, Nursing, Dentistry, Veterinary Science
ISBN Prefix(es): 978-85-277

Gutenberg, *imprint of* Autentica Editora

Editora Harbra Ltda+
Rua Joaquim Tavora, 779, Vila Mariana, 04015-001 Sao Paulo-SP
Tel: (011) 5084-2403; (011) 5084-2482; (011) 5571-1122; (011) 5549-2244; (011) 5571-0276 *Fax:* (011) 5575-6876; (011) 5571-9777 (sales)
E-mail: editorial@harbra.com.br; vendas@harbra.com.br; administracao@harbra.com.br
Web Site: www.harbra.com.br
Key Personnel
Mng Dir: Julio Esteban Emod-Eghy *E-mail:* emod@harbra.com.br
Founded: 1986
Subjects: Behavioral Sciences, Biography, Memoirs, Biological Sciences, Computer Science, Earth Sciences, Management, Physical Sciences, Science (General), Self-Help, Social Sciences, Sociology
ISBN Prefix(es): 978-85-294
Total Titles: 250 Print; 1 CD-ROM; 1 Audio
Branch Office(s)
Rua Maura, 512, Bairro Ipiranga, 31160-260 Belo Horizonte-MG *Tel:* (031) 3285-2977; (031) 3221-1904 *Fax:* (031) 3285-1704 *E-mail:* filialminas@harbra.com.br
Rua 70, No 687 Qd 127 Lt 75, 74055-120 Goiania-GO *Tel:* (062) 3212-9875; (062) 3225-8632 *Fax:* (062) 3212-9874 *E-mail:* filialgoias@harbra.com.br
Rua Riachuelo 453, Loja 7, Boa Vista, 50050-400 Recife-PE *Tel:* (081) 3221-0700; (081) 3222-2808 *Fax:* (081) 3221-3655 *E-mail:* filialrecife@harbra.com.br
Distributor for editora Edgard Blucher; editora Universidade de Brasilia

Hemus Editora Ltda+
Ave Divino Salvador, 736-Moema, 04078-012 Sao Paulo-SP
Tel: (011) 5093-7822 *Fax:* (011) 5044-6366
E-mail: atendimento@leopardoeditora.com.br
Web Site: www.hemus.com.br; www.leopardoeditora.com.br
Key Personnel
Executive Publisher: Maxim Behar
Founded: 1963
Subjects: Archaeology, Architecture & Interior Design, Astrology, Occult, Career Development, Civil Engineering, Electronics, Electrical Engineering, Fiction, Health, Nutrition, Law, Philosophy, Sports, Athletics, Leisure, Naturalism, Puzzles
ISBN Prefix(es): 978-85-289
Distributed by Leopardo Editora

Horus Editora Ltda+
R Ribeiro de Lima, 531 cj 51, 01122-000 Sao Paulo-SP
Tel: (011) 3288-7681 *Fax:* (011) 3288-7681
E-mail: horus@horuseditora.com.br
Web Site: www.horuseditora.com.br
Founded: 1996
Also distributor.
Subjects: Astrology, Occult, Music, Dance, Psychology, Psychiatry, Religion - Buddhist, Religion - Catholic, Religion - Hindu, Religion

- Islamic, Religion - Jewish, Religion - Other, Theology
ISBN Prefix(es): 978-85-86204

IBEP
Ave Alexandre Mackenzie, 619, Jaguare, 05322-000 Sao Paulo-SP
Tel: (011) 2799-7799 *Toll Free Tel:* 08000-175678 *Fax:* (011) 2799-7799
E-mail: atendimento@editoraibep.com.br
Web Site: www.ibep-nacional.com.br
Key Personnel
Mng Dir, Rights & Permissions: Jorge Antonio Miguel Yunes
Editorial: Paulo Marti
Founded: 1965
Subjects: Business, Education, Fiction, History, Philosophy, Psychology, Psychiatry, Science (General), Social Sciences, Sociology, Technology
ISBN Prefix(es): 978-85-04
Branch Office(s)
Al Carrara, 186, Pituba, 41830-590 Salvador-BA
Tel: (071) 3346-5200 *Fax:* (071) 3345-0086
E-mail: filial.ba@ibep-nacional.com.br
Rua Teodora da Silva, 1004/1006, Vila Isabel, 20560-001 Rio de Janeiro-RJ *Tel:* (021) 3539-7700 *E-mail:* filial.rj@ibep-nacional.com.br

Livro Ibero-Americano Ltda
Rua Hermenegildo de Barros, 40, 20241-040 Rio de Janeiro-RJ
Tel: (021) 4105-4590 *Fax:* (021) 4105-4590
E-mail: livro-ibero@oi.com.br
Founded: 1946
Subjects: Agriculture, Art, Electronics, Electrical Engineering, History, Language Arts, Linguistics, Philosophy, Photography, Psychology, Psychiatry, Religion - Other
ISBN Prefix(es): 978-85-7032

IBGE, see Instituto Brasileiro de Geografia e Estatistica (IBGE)

IBICT, see Instituto Brasileiro de Informacao em Ciencia e Tecnologia

Editora IBPEX, see Editora InterSaberes

IBRASA (Instituicao Brasileira de Difusao Cultural Ltda)+
Rua Treze de Maio, 446, Bela Vista, 01327-000 Sao Paulo-SP
Tel: (011) 3284-8382
Web Site: www.ibrasa.com.br
Founded: 1958
Subjects: Art, Crafts, Games, Hobbies, Economics, Education, Government, Political Science, Health, Nutrition, History, Literature, Literary Criticism, Essays, Medicine, Nursing, Dentistry, Parapsychology, Philosophy, Psychology, Psychiatry, Science (General), Social Sciences, Sociology, Sports, Athletics, Administration, Physical Education, Spiritism
ISBN Prefix(es): 978-85-348

ICEA, see Instituto Campineiro de Ensino Agricola (ICEA)

Icone Editora Ltda
Rua das Palmeiras, 213, Santa Cecilia, 01226-010 Sao Paulo-SP
Tel: (011) 3392-7771
E-mail: sac@iconeeditora.com.br
Web Site: www.iconeeditora.com.br
Founded: 1985
Also acts as distributor.
Membership(s): Brazilian Association of Books & Collections; Brazilian House of Books; National Syndication of Books.

Subjects: Agriculture, Astrology, Occult, Biography, Memoirs, Cookery, Crafts, Games, Hobbies, Economics, Education, History, Law, Literature, Literary Criticism, Essays, Mathematics, Medicine, Nursing, Dentistry, Music, Dance, Philosophy, Psychology, Psychiatry, Science (General), Self-Help, Sports, Athletics, Technology, Veterinary Science, Martial Arts, Physiotherapy
ISBN Prefix(es): 978-85-274; 978-85-85503
Number of titles published annually: 70 Print
Total Titles: 680 Print

Iglu Editora Ltda
Rua Duilio 386, Lapa, 05043-020 Sao Paulo-SP
Tel: (011) 3873-0227 *Fax:* (011) 3873-0227
E-mail: iglueditora@uol.com.br
Web Site: www.iglueditora.com.br
Founded: 1987
Subjects: Economics, Education, Health, Nutrition, Law
ISBN Prefix(es): 978-85-7494; 978-85-85631

Editora Iluminuras Ltda+
Rua Inacio Pereira da Rocha, 389, 05432-011 Sao Paulo-SP
Tel: (011) 3031-6161 *Fax:* (011) 3031-6161
Web Site: www.iluminuras.com.br
Key Personnel
Contact: Beatriz Costa; Sir Samuel Leon
Founded: 1987
Subjects: Anthropology, Biography, Memoirs, Communications, Drama, Theater, Education, Film, Video, History, Literature, Literary Criticism, Essays, Philosophy, Poetry, Religion - Other, Social Sciences, Sociology
ISBN Prefix(es): 978-85-85219; 978-85-7321

Imago Editora Ltda+
Rua da Quitanda nº 52/8º andar, Centro, 20011-030 Rio de Janeiro-RJ
Tel: (021) 2242-0627 *Fax:* (021) 2224-8359
E-mail: imago@imagoeditora.com.br
Web Site: www.imagoeditora.com.br
Key Personnel
President: Jayme Salomao
Executive Dir: Eduardo Salomao
Founded: 1967
Membership(s): Camara Brasileira do Livro (CBL); Sindicato Nacional dos Editores de Livros (SNEL).
Subjects: Biblical Studies, Biography, Memoirs, Drama, Theater, Fiction, Film, Video, Health, Nutrition, History, How-to, Language Arts, Linguistics, Literature, Literary Criticism, Essays, Mysteries, Suspense, Nonfiction (General), Philosophy, Psychology, Psychiatry, Religion - Other, Romance, Science Fiction, Fantasy, Self-Help
ISBN Prefix(es): 978-85-312

IMESP, see Imprensa Oficial do Estado SA (IMESP)

Imprensa Oficial do Estado SA (IMESP)
Rua da Mooca, 1921, 03103-902 Sao Paulo-SP
Toll Free Tel: 0800 0123401
E-mail: assessoriadeimprensa@imprensaoficial.com.br
Web Site: www.imprensaoficial.com.br; www.facebook.com/imprensaoficial
Key Personnel
Manager, Publications: Vera Wey
Subjects: Art, Biography, Memoirs, Geography, Geology, History
ISBN Prefix(es): 978-85-7060

Editora Index Ltda+
Av Rio Branco, 45 - S1 1707, 20090-003 Rio de Janeiro-RJ

Key Personnel
President: Jose Paulo M Soares; Christina Ferrao
Founded: 1982
Subjects: Art, Environmental Studies, History
ISBN Prefix(es): 978-85-7083
Associate Companies: Editora Libris
Imprints: Editora Kapa

Instituicao Brasileira de Difusao Cultural Ltda, see IBRASA (Instituicao Brasileira de Difusao Cultural Ltda)

Instituto Brasileiro de Edicoes Pedagogicas, see IBEP

Instituto Brasileiro de Geografia e Estatistica (IBGE) (Brasilian Institute of Geography & Statistics)
Rua General Canabarro 706, terreo, Bairro Maracana, 20271-201 Rio de Janeiro-RJ
Tel: (021) 2142-4780 *Toll Free Tel:* 0800 721 8181
E-mail: ibge@ibge.gov.br
Web Site: www.ibge.gov.br
Key Personnel
Coordinator: David Wu Tai
Coordinator, Integrated Service: Paulo Cesar De Sousa Quintslr
Coordinator, Marketing: Carmen Danielle Lins Mendes Macedo
Coordinator, Production: Marise Maria Ferreira
Founded: 1936
Subjects: Economics, Geography, Geology, Mathematics
ISBN Prefix(es): 978-85-240
Bookshop(s): Av Franklin Roosevelt, 146 lj.A, 20021-112 Castelo-RJ
Orders to: IBGE - CDDI/DECOP/DICOM, Rua General Canabarro 666, Bloco B - 2/Andar, 20271-200 Rio de Janeiro-RJ, Contact: Carlos Lessa *Tel:* (021) 569-2043 *Fax:* (021) 234-8480
E-mail: atandicddi@ibge.gov.br

Instituto Brasileiro de Informacao em Ciencia e Tecnologia
Setor de Autarquias Sul (SAUS), Quadra 05 Lote 06 Bloco H, 70070-912 Brasilia-DF
Tel: (061) 3217-6360; (061) 3217-6350
Fax: (061) 3217-6490
Web Site: www.ibict.br
Subjects: Science (General), Technology
ISBN Prefix(es): 978-85-7013

Instituto Campineiro de Ensino Agricola (ICEA)
Rua Romoaldo Andreazzi, 425, Jd do Trevo, 13036-100 Campinas-SP
Tel: (019) 3258-8225; (019) 9791-6629 (cell)
Fax: (019) 3258-8225
E-mail: icea@icea.com.br
Web Site: www.icea.com.br
Key Personnel
Dir: Gervasio de Souza Cavalcanti
Founded: 1955
Subjects: Agriculture, Veterinary Science, Ecology, Horticulture
ISBN Prefix(es): 978-85-7121

Editora Interciencia Ltda+
Rua Verna Magalhaes, 66, Engenho Novo, 20710-290 Rio de Janeiro-RJ
Tel: (021) 2581-9378; (021) 2241-6916; (021) 2501-4635
E-mail: vendas@editorainterciencia.com.br
Web Site: www.editorainterciencia.com.br
Key Personnel
Mng Dir, Publicity, Rights & Permissions: Rodrigo Nascimento
Founded: 1969 (1975 as publisher)
Subjects: Science (General)
ISBN Prefix(es): 978-85-7193; 978-85-63960; 978-85-89116

Interlivros Edicoes Ltda
Rua Comandante Coelho 1085, 21250-510 Rio de Janeiro-RJ
Tel: (021) 3913134
Subjects: Biological Sciences, Health, Nutrition, Medicine, Nursing, Dentistry, Psychology, Psychiatry
ISBN Prefix(es): 978-85-85891

Editora InterSaberes
Formerly Editora IBPEX
Rua Clara Vendramin, 58, 81200-170 Curibita-PR
Tel: (041) 2106-4170
E-mail: contato@editoraintersaberes.com.br
Web Site: www.intersaberes.com
Founded: 2005
Subjects: Business, Education, Government, Political Science, Language Arts, Linguistics, Management, Marketing, Mathematics, Music, Dance, Social Sciences, Sociology
ISBN Prefix(es): 978-85-8212

Editora Intrinseca
Rua Marques de Sao Vicente, 99, 3° andar-Gavea, Rio de Janeiro-RJ 22451-041
Tel: (021) 3206-7400
E-mail: contato@intrinseca.com.br
Web Site: www.intrinseca.com.br/a-editora
Founded: 2003
Subjects: Fiction, Nonfiction (General)
ISBN Prefix(es): 978-85-8057

Irmaos Vitale SA
Rua Franca Pinto, 42, 04016-000 Sao Paulo-SP
Tel: (011) 5081-9499 *Fax:* (011) 5574-7388
E-mail: virtual@vitale.com.br
Web Site: www.vitale.com.br
Key Personnel
Dir: Fernando Vitale
Founded: 1923
Subjects: Music, Dance
ISBN Prefix(es): 978-85-7407; 978-85-85188
Parent Company: Irmaos Vitale SA Industria E Comercio
Subsidiaries: Casa Vitale
Divisions: Edicoes musicais e Instrumentos musicais (Nacionais e importados)

JUERP, see Junta de Educacao Religiosa e Publicacoes da Convencao Batista Brasileira (JUERP)

Junta de Educacao Religiosa e Publicacoes da Convencao Batista Brasileira (JUERP)+
CP 320, 20001-970 Rio de Janeiro-RJ
Tel: (021) 2104-0044 *Toll Free Tel:* 0800 0216768 *Fax:* (021) 2104-0044
Key Personnel
Dir General: Almir dos Santos Goncalves, Jr
Coordinator: Solange Cardoso A d'Almeida
Founded: 1907
Membership(s): Association of Brazilian Baptist Publishers; Association of Brazilian Christian Publishers.
Subjects: Religion - Other
ISBN Prefix(es): 978-85-350

Editora Kapa, *imprint of* Editora Index Ltda

Komedi Editora
Rua Alvares Machado, 460-3° e 4° andares, Campinas-SP 13013-070
Tel: (019) 3234-4864
Web Site: www.komedi.com.br/editora
Founded: 1992
Subjects: Business, Computer Science, English as a Second Language, Fiction, History, Literature, Literary Criticism, Essays, Photography, Pop Culture, Self-Help, Technology
ISBN Prefix(es): 978-85-7582; 978-85-86569

Branch Office(s)
Alameda Madiera, 162, sala 308, Alphaville, 06453-057 Baruei-SP *Tel:* (011) 4195-2077
Av Presidente Wilson, 165-Sala 1202, 20030-020 Rio de Janeiro-RJ *Tel:* (021) 2240-1486
Rua Imperatriz Leopoldina, 263, sala 23, Nova Petropolis, Sao Bernardo do Campo-SP
Tel: (011) 4941-5058

Livraria Kosmos Editora SA
Rua do Rosario, 155, 20050-092 Rio de Janeiro-RJ
Tel: (021) 2221-4582
Founded: 1935
Subjects: Engineering (General), History, Language Arts, Linguistics, Music, Dance, Travel & Tourism
ISBN Prefix(es): 978-85-7096

LAKE-Livraria Editora Allan Kardec+
Rua do Lucas n° 84/86, 03005-000 Sao Paulo-SP
Tel: (011) 3229-1227 *Fax:* (011) 3227-5714
E-mail: lakelivraria@uol.com.br
Web Site: www.lake.com.br
Key Personnel
Dir: Roberto Francisco Ferrero
Founded: 1936
Subjects: Inspirational, Spirituality, Religion - Other, Romance
ISBN Prefix(es): 978-85-7360

Editora Leitura Ltda
Rua Euclides da Cunha, 70 - Prado, 30410-010 Belo Horizonte-MG
Tel: (031) 3292-8300; (031) 2519-8100; (031) 3379-0620
Founded: 1994
Subjects: Education
ISBN Prefix(es): 978-85-7358; 978-85-85807

LEUD, see Livraria e Editora Universitaria de Direito Ltda (LEUD)

LGE Editora+
SIG Quadra 4 Lote 283, 70610-440 Brasilia-DF
Tel: (061) 3362 0008 *Fax:* (061) 3233 3771
Founded: 1999
Membership(s): Camara Brasileira do Livro (CBL); Sindicato Nacional dos Editores de Livros (SNEL).
Subjects: Fiction, History, Journalism, Religion - Other
ISBN Prefix(es): 978-85-7238
Parent Company: Ler Editora

Libreria Editora Ltda+
Rua Taquaritinga, 139, Mooca, 03170-010 Sao Paulo-SP
Tel: (011) 2618-5411 *Fax:* (011) 2618-5411
E-mail: libreria@libreria.com.br; atendimento@libreria.com.br
Web Site: www.libreria.com.br
Key Personnel
General Manager: Mario Fiorentino
Development: Alessandra Fiorentino
Production & Quality Control: Antonio de Jesus
Sales: Roseli Ferreira; Clodoaldo Soares
Founded: 1974
Also producer of globes.
Membership(s): Association of Brazilian Distributors; The Association of Brazilian Publishers.
Subjects: Cookery, English as a Second Language, Geography, Geology, Language Arts, Linguistics, Natural History
ISBN Prefix(es): 978-85-85900

Editora Lidador Ltda+
Rua Hilario Ribeiro 154, Pca da Bandeira, 20270-180 Rio de Janeiro-RJ
Tel: (021) 2569-0594 *Fax:* (021) 2204-0684
Founded: 1960

Subjects: Communications, Economics, Education, Erotica, Fiction, Human Relations, Music, Dance, Parapsychology, Social Sciences, Sociology
ISBN Prefix(es): 978-85-7003
Number of titles published annually: 9 Print
Distributed by Topbook

Waldyr Lima Editora Ltda
Rua 24 de Maio, 347, 20950-090 Rio de Janeiro-RJ
Tel: (021) 3982-5050
Founded: 1961
Specialize in English, Portuguese & Spanish language instruction.
Subjects: Education, English as a Second Language, Language Arts, Linguistics
ISBN Prefix(es): 978-85-341; 978-85-340
U.S. Office(s): CCLS Publishing House, 3181 Coral Way, Miami, FL 33145, United States
Orders to: CCLS Publishing House, 3181 Coral Way, Miami, FL 33145, United States

Livraria e Editora Infobook SA+
Ave Marechal Camara, 160 Grupos 231 A 233, 20024-970 Rio de Janeiro-RJ
Founded: 1993
Subjects: Computer Science, Management
ISBN Prefix(es): 978-85-85588; 978-85-7331

Livros Tecnicos e Cientificos Editora Ltda, see LTC Editora

Editora Logosofica
Rua Coronel Oscar Porto, 818 - Paraiso, 04003-004 Sao Paulo-SP
Tel: (011) 3804 1640 *Fax:* (011) 3804 1640
E-mail: sp-editora@logosofia.org.br
Web Site: www.editoralogosofica.com.br
Key Personnel
Mng Dir, Editorial: Paulo Mauricio de Moraes
Author: Carlos Bernardo Gonzalez Pecotche
Founded: 1964
Logosophy science books.
Membership(s): Camara Brasileira do Livro.
Subjects: Behavioral Sciences, Education, Philosophy
ISBN Prefix(es): 978-85-7097
U.S. Office(s): Logosophy Center of Study, 2640 Hollywood Blvd, Suite 112, Hollywood, FL 33020, United States *Web Site:* www.logosophy.net
Logosophy Center of Study, 304 Park Ave S, 11th floor, New York, NY 10010, United States *E-mail:* info@logosophy-nyc.org *Web Site:* www.logosophy-nyc.org
Bookshop(s): Fundacao Logosofica, Rua Piaui 74 2, 30150-320 Belo Horizonte-MG; Fundacao Logosofica, SHCG - Norte-Area de Escolas Q704, 70730-730 Brasilia-DF; Fundacao Logosofica, Rua General Polidoro 36, 22280-001 Rio de Janeiro-RJ

Longman, *imprint of* Pearson Education do Brasil Ltda

Edicoes Loyola SA+
Rua Mil Oitocentos e Vinte e Dois, N° 341, 04216-000 Sao Paulo-SP
Tel: (011) 3385-8500; (011) 3385-8501 *Fax:* (011) 2063-4275
E-mail: marketing@loyola.com.br
Web Site: www.loyola.com.br
Founded: 1965
Also acts as book packager.
Subjects: Anthropology, Art, Biblical Studies, Communications, Computer Science, Economics, Education, History, Law, Literature, Literary Criticism, Essays, Management, Philosophy, Psychology, Psychiatry, Religion - Other, Self-Help, Social Sciences, Sociology
ISBN Prefix(es): 978-85-15

Number of titles published annually: 150 Print
Total Titles: 3,000 Print
Parent Company: AJEAS-Edicoes Loyola

LTC, *imprint of* Grupo Editorial Nacional (GEN)

LTC Editora+
Imprint of Grupo Editorial Nacional (GEN)
Travessa do Ouvidor, 11, 20040-040 Rio de
Janeiro-RJ
Tel: (021) 3970-9480 *Fax:* (021) 2221-3202
E-mail: vendas@grupogen.com.br; ltc@ltceditora.
com.br
Web Site: www.grupogen.com.br
Key Personnel
Dir: Mauro Koogan Lorch
Rights & Permissions: Christina Noren
E-mail: norenltc@uninet.com.br
Founded: 1968
Subjects: Chemistry, Chemical Engineering, Com-
puter Science, Economics, Engineering (Gen-
eral), Management, Mathematics, Physics,
Technology
ISBN Prefix(es): 978-85-216

LTR Editora Ltda
Rua Jaguaribe, 571, 01224-001 Sao Paulo-SP
Tel: (011) 2167-1101 *Fax:* (011) 2167-1131
E-mail: ltr@ltr.com.br
Web Site: www.ltr.com.br
Founded: 1937
Subjects: Law
ISBN Prefix(es): 978-85-7322; 978-85-361
Branch Office(s)
Rua Guajajaras, 880-Sala 701, 30180-100 Belo
Horizonte-MG *Tel:* (031) 3295-7050 *Fax:* (031)
3295-6160 *E-mail:* polobh@ltr.com.br
Brasilia-DF *Tel:* (061) 9946-2030; (061) 3242-
7570 *E-mail:* alfredo.venturoli@ltr.com.br
Rua Cerqueira Cesar, 481-Cj 1200-12º
andar, 14010-130 Ribeirao Preto-SP
Tel: (016) 3967-7000 *Fax:* (016) 3967-7200
E-mail: poloribeiraopto@ltr.com.br
Rua Anfilofio de Carvalho, 29-6º andar-Cjs 601/2,
20030-060 Rio de Janeiro-RJ *Tel:* (021) 2220-
4744 *Fax:* (021) 2533-1393 *E-mail:* polorio@
ltr.com.br

Lute Editorial Ltda
Rua Hildebrando Thomaz de Carvalho, 60, Vila
Mariana, 04012-120 Sao Paulo-SP
Tel: (011) 5572-9474; (011) 5579-6757
Fax: (011) 5572-9474; (011) 5579-6757
E-mail: alaude@alaude.com.br
Web Site: www.alaude.com.br
Founded: 2004
Subjects: Business, Health, Nutrition, Marketing,
Philosophy, Sports, Athletics, Cuisine, Infant &
Youth, Motorsports, Personal Development
ISBN Prefix(es): 978-85-7881

M.Books do Brasil Editora Ltda
Rua Jorge Americano, 61, Alto da Lapa, 05083-
130 Sao Paulo-SP
Tel: (011) 3645-0409 *Fax:* (011) 3832-0335
Web Site: www.mbooks.com.br
Key Personnel
President: Milton Mira de Assumpcao Filho
Founded: 2002
Subjects: Business, Child Care & Development,
Economics, Health, Nutrition, History, Man-
agement, Marketing, Psychology, Psychiatry,
Information Technology
ISBN Prefix(es): 978-85-7680

Madras Editora+
Rua Paulo Goncalves, 88, 02403-020 Sao Paulo-
SP
Tel: (011) 2281-5555 *Fax:* (011) 2959-3090
E-mail: vendas@madras.com.br
Web Site: www.madras.com.br

Key Personnel
President: Wagner Veneziani Costa
E-mail: wagner@madras.com.br
Founded: 1991
Produces & sells books for university students,
professionals & esoteric individuals. Distributes
for publishing houses throughout Brazil.
Subjects: Animals, Pets, Archaeology, Asian
Studies, Astrology, Occult, Crafts, Games,
Hobbies, Fashion, Genealogy, Health, Nutri-
tion, Mysteries, Suspense, Nonfiction (General),
Philosophy, Religion - Buddhist, Religion -
Hindu, Religion - Islamic, Romance, Self-Help,
Theology
ISBN Prefix(es): 978-85-7374; 978-85-85505
Number of titles published annually: 100 Print
Total Titles: 1,500 Print
Imprints: WVC (law)

Editora Manole Ltda+
Av Ceci, 672, 06460-120 Barueri-SP
Tel: (011) 4196 6000
E-mail: falecom@manole.zendesk.com;
secretaria@manole.com.br
Web Site: www.manole.com.br
Key Personnel
Editor, Publisher Administration: Amarylis
Manole
Editor: Daniela Manole
Founded: 1966
Subjects: Cookery, Crafts, Games, Hobbies,
Health, Nutrition, Law, Medicine, Nursing,
Dentistry, Sports, Athletics, Veterinary Sci-
ence, Alternative Medicine, Anatomy, Physical
Education, Physical Therapy, Research
ISBN Prefix(es): 978-85-204
Total Titles: 120 Print
Imprints: Amarilys Editora; Minha Editora

Editora Mantiqueira de Ciencia e Arte Ltda+
Av Eduardo Moreira da Cruz, 295, 12460-000
Campos do Jordao-SP
Mailing Address: CP 42, 12460-000 Campos do
Jordao-SP
Tel: (012) 3662-1832 *Fax:* (012) 3662-1832
E-mail: editora@editoramantiqueira.com.br
Web Site: www.editoramantiqueira.com.br
Key Personnel
Dir: Antonio Fernando Costella
Founded: 1977
Subjects: Animals, Pets, Art, Communications,
Fiction, History, Journalism, Poetry, Travel &
Tourism
ISBN Prefix(es): 978-85-85681

Editora Manuais Tecnicos de Seguros Ltda
R Brig Galvao, 288, Barra Funda, 01151-000 Sao
Paulo-SP
Tel: (011) 50835587
Founded: 1970
Subjects: Securities
ISBN Prefix(es): 978-85-85549

Marco Zero, *imprint of* Livraria Nobel SA

Marco Zero+
Imprint of Livraria Nobel SA
Rua Pedroso Alvarenga 1046, Itaim Bibi, 04531-
004 Sao Paulo-SP
Tel: (011) 3706-1466
Web Site: www.editoranobel.com.br
Founded: 1980
Subjects: Biography, Memoirs, Child Care & De-
velopment, Cookery, How-to, Literature, Lit-
erary Criticism, Essays, Mysteries, Suspense,
Nonfiction (General), Travel & Tourism
ISBN Prefix(es): 978-85-279
Ultimate Parent Company: Nobel Franquias S/A
Associate Companies: Conex; Studio Nobel

Martins Editora Livraria Ltda+
Av Dr Arnaldo, 2076, 01255-000 Sao Paulo-SP
Tel: (011) 3116-0000 *Fax:* (011) 3116-0000
E-mail: info@emartinsfontes.com.br
Web Site: www.emartinsfontes.com.br
Founded: 1960
Subjects: Art, Education, English as a Second
Language, History, Law, Nonfiction (General),
Philosophy, Psychology, Psychiatry, Social Sci-
ences, Sociology
ISBN Prefix(es): 978-85-336
Bookshop(s): Livraria Martins Fontes-Patriarca,
Praca do Patriarca, 78, 01002-010 Sao Paulo-
SP *Tel:* (011) 3106-9133 *E-mail:* livraria@
martinseditora.com.br; Livraria Martins
Fontes-Jardins, Alameda Jau, 1742, 01420-
002 Sao Paulo-SP *Tel:* (011) 3061-0250
E-mail: livraria@martinseditora.com.br;
Livraria Martins Fontes-Rio, Rua Dias Fer-
reira, 135 Loja A, 22431-050 Rio de Janeiro-
RJ *Tel:* (021) 2221-2823 *E-mail:* livraria@
martinseditora.com.br

Matrix Editora
Rua Heitor Penteado, 103, 05347-000 Sao Paulo-
SP
Tel: (011) 3868-2863
E-mail: editor@matrixeditora.com.br
Web Site: www.matrixeditora.com.br
Key Personnel
Publisher: Paulo Tadeu Vieira
Manager: Nice Vieira
Membership(s): Sindicato Nacional dos Editores
de Livros (SNEL).
Subjects: Advertising, Biography, Memoirs, Busi-
ness, Career Development, Health, Nutrition,
History, Humor, Literature, Literary Criticism,
Essays, Religion - Other, Self-Help, Sports,
Athletics, Children & Youth
ISBN Prefix(es): 978-85-87431
Number of titles published annually: 36 Print; 3
Audio
Total Titles: 3 Audio

Editora Meca Ltda
Rua Araujo 81, Vila Buarque, 01220-020 Sao
Paulo-SP
Tel: (011) 3259 9034; (011) 3259 9049
E-mail: editora_meca@uol.com.br
Web Site: www.editorameca.com.br
Key Personnel
Mng Dir & Editor: Cosmo Juvela
Editorial Dir: Marcos Juvela
Founded: 1963
Subjects: English as a Second Language, Environ-
mental Studies, Literature, Literary Criticism,
Essays, Parapsychology, Psychology, Psychia-
try, Religion - Other
ISBN Prefix(es): 978-85-88579
Warehouse: 51 Campos Eliseos, Sao Paulo-SP

Editora Melhoramentos Ltda+
Subsidiary of Cia Melhoramentos
Rua Tito, 479, Vila Romana (Lapa), 05051-000
Sao Paulo-SP
Tel: (011) 3874-0854 *Fax:* (011) 3874-0855
Web Site: www.melhoramentos.com.br
Key Personnel
Publishing Dir: Breno Lerner *E-mail:* blerner@
melhoramentos.com.br
Editor: Walter Weiszflog
Founded: 1915
Specialize in reference books.
Subjects: Archaeology, Art, Cookery, English as a
Second Language, History, Literature, Literary
Criticism, Essays
ISBN Prefix(es): 978-85-06
Total Titles: 1,200 Print; 20 CD-ROM; 8 Audio
Distributed by Dinapress; Dipon; Lectorum;
Piedra Santa; SEP; Volcano Press
Distributor for Disney

Memorias Futuras Edicoes Ltda+
Rua Pereira da Silva 444 s 401, Laranjeiras,
22221-140 Rio de Janeiro-RJ
Tel: (021) 2557-0861
Founded: 1982
Subjects: Fiction
ISBN Prefix(es): 978-85-287

Editora Mercado Aberto Ltda+
Rua Dona Margarida 894, Navegantes, 90240-160
Porto Alegre-RS
Tel: (051) 337-4833 *Fax:* (051) 337-4905
Founded: 1977
Subjects: Anthropology, Education, Fiction,
Health, Nutrition, History, Literature, Literary
Criticism, Essays, Romance
ISBN Prefix(es): 978-85-280; 978-85-86829; 978-
85-86840

Editora Mercuryo Ltda+
Alameda dos Guaramomis, 1267 Moema, 04076-
012 Sao Paulo-SP
Tel: (011) 5531-8222 *Fax:* (011) 5093-3265
E-mail: vendas@mercuryo.com.br
Web Site: www.mercuryo.com.br
Founded: 1986
Subjects: Architecture & Interior Design, Art,
Astrology, Occult, Automotive, Biblical Stud-
ies, Biography, Memoirs, Education, Fiction,
Health, Nutrition, History, Human Relations,
Inspirational, Spirituality, Literature, Literary
Criticism, Essays, Mysteries, Suspense, Non-
fiction (General), Parapsychology, Psychology,
Psychiatry, Religion - Other, Science Fiction,
Fantasy, Self-Help, Horses
ISBN Prefix(es): 978-85-7272; 978-85-86052
Number of titles published annually: 10 Print
Total Titles: 190 Print
Imprints: Mercuryo Jovem; Unicornio Azul

Mercuryo Jovem, *imprint of* Editora Mercuryo
Ltda

Editora Meridional Ltda+
Av Oswaldo Aranha, 440 Conj 101 - Bom Fim,
90035-190 Porto Alegre-RS
Tel: (051) 3311 4082 *Fax:* (051) 3264 4194
E-mail: sulina@editorasulina.com.br
Web Site: www.editorasulina.com.br
Key Personnel
Editor: Luis Gomes
Founded: 1946
Subjects: Architecture & Interior Design, Bio-
logical Sciences, Communications, Education,
Geography, Geology, Health, Nutrition, History,
Law, Psychology, Psychiatry, Religion - Other,
Science (General), Self-Help, Social Sciences,
Sociology, Ecology
ISBN Prefix(es): 978-85-205
Imprints: Sulina
Showroom(s): Rua Deuetrio Ribeiro, 990 202
Porto Alegre-RS
Bookshop(s): Livraria Sulina, Rua Riachuelo,
1218 Porta Alegre-RS

Metodo, *imprint of* Grupo Editorial Nacional
(GEN)

MG Editores
Division of Grupo Editorial Summus
Rua Itapicuru, 613-7° andar, Perdizes, 05006-000
Sao Paulo-SP
Tel: (011) 3872-3322 *Fax:* (011) 3872-7476
E-mail: mg@mgeditores.com.br; editor@
mgeditores.com.br
Web Site: www.gruposummus.com.br/mgeditores/
mg_fale.php
Key Personnel
Executive Dir: Soraia Bini Cury

Subjects: Behavioral Sciences, Education, Health,
Nutrition
ISBN Prefix(es): 978-85-7255

Minas Editora e Distribuidora Ltda+
Rua Wenceslau Braz, 276-Centro, 38440-216
Araguari-MG
Tel: (034) 3246 0093
E-mail: atendimento@minaseditora.com
Web Site: www.minaseditora.com
Key Personnel
Editor: Publio Carisio de Paula
Founded: 1984
Subjects: Fiction, Religion - Other, Self-Help
ISBN Prefix(es): 978-85-86030; 978-85-87538

Minha Editora, *imprint of* Editora Manole Ltda

**Ministerio da Marinha Diretoria de
Hidrografia e Navegacao**
Rua Barao de Jaceguay, s/n Ponta da Armacao,
24048-900 Niteroi-RJ
Tel: (021) 2189-3387
E-mail: dhn.ouvidoria@marinha.mil.br; dhn.
comunicacaosocial@marinha.mil.br
Web Site: www.marinha.mil.br/dhn
Subjects: Maritime, Transportation, Marine mete-
orology, navigation & oceanography
ISBN Prefix(es): 978-85-7293

Editora Moderna Ltda+
Rua Padre Adelino, 758, Belenzinho, 03303-904
Sao Paulo-SP
Tel: (011) 2790-1300 *Fax:* (011) 2790-1454
E-mail: moderna@moderna.com.br
Web Site: www.moderna.com.br
Founded: 1968
Subjects: Education, Fiction, Health, Nutrition,
History, Literature, Literary Criticism, Es-
says, Mathematics, Social Sciences, Sociology,
Women's Studies
ISBN Prefix(es): 978-85-16
Total Titles: 1,515 Print; 12 CD-ROM
Branch Office(s)
Av Vereador Abel Ferreira, 374-V, Regente Feijo,
03340-000 Sao Paulo-SP *Tel:* (011) 2076-7900
SAAN Quadra 1 Lote 400/410-Zona Industrial,
70632-100 Brasilia-DF *Tel:* (061) 3701-9000;
(061) 3701-9009
Av Oliveira Paiva, 233, Cidade dos Funcionarios,
60822-131 Fortaleza-CE *Tel:* (085) 3115-5111
Fax: (085) 3115-5150
Rua 74, n° 601-Quadra 133, Lote 67 Setor Cen-
tral, 74045-020 Goiania-GO *Tel:* (062) 3225-
0646; (062) 3213-5710
Av Farrapos, 2.840, Sao Geraldo, 90220-002
Porto Alegre-RS *Tel:* (051) 3535-1600
Av Marechal Mascarenhas de Moraes, 5.855,
Imbiribeira, 51210-001 Recife-PE *Tel:* (081)
3366-1700 *Fax:* (081) 3366-1712
Rua Drumond, 93, Olaria, 21031-460 Rio de
Janeiro-RJ *Tel:* (021) 3535-1900 *Fax:* (021)
3535-1990
Rua Luis Viana Filho, 2192, 41720-200 Salvador-
BA *Tel:* (071) 3111-2300 *Fax:* (071) 3366-
3468

**Modulo Editora e Desenvolvimento
Educacional**
Rua Albano Reis, 1093, Bom Retiro, 80520-530
Curitiba-PR
Tel: (041) 3253-0077 *Fax:* (041) 3253-0103
Web Site: www.moduloeditora.com.br
Founded: 1991
Subjects: Education, Geography, Geology, His-
tory, Mathematics, Science (General), Sports,
Athletics
ISBN Prefix(es): 978-85-7397; 978-85-85764

Editora Mundo Cristao (Christian World
Publishing)+
Rua Antonio Carlos Tacconi n° 79, Cidade Dutra,
04810-020 Sao Paulo-SP
Tel: (011) 2127-4147 *Fax:* (011) 2127-4128
E-mail: site_editorial@mundocristao.com.br
Web Site: www.mundocristao.com.br
Key Personnel
President: Mark L Carpenter
Founded: 1965
Subjects: Biblical Studies, Biography, Memoirs,
Child Care & Development, Fiction, Religion -
Protestant, Theology
ISBN Prefix(es): 978-85-7325
Number of titles published annually: 50 Print; 50
E-Book
Total Titles: 700 Print; 100 E-Book

Musa Editora Ltda
Rua Cardoso de Almeida 985, 05013-001 Sao
Paulo-SP
Mailing Address: Rua Bartira 62/21, 05009-000
Sao Paulo-SP
Tel: (011) 9354-3700 *Fax:* (011) 3862-6435
E-mail: musaeditora@uol.com.br;
musacomercial@uol.com
Web Site: www.musaeditora.com.br
Key Personnel
Executive: Ana Candida Costa
Subjects: Art, Behavioral Sciences, Drama, The-
ater, Education, Literature, Literary Criticism,
Essays, Mathematics, Music, Dance, Religion
- Other, Science Fiction, Fantasy, Social Sci-
ences, Sociology, Technology, Classics, Cul-
ture & Society, Digital Media Arts & Culture,
Ecology, General Affairs, Innovation, National
Literature
ISBN Prefix(es): 978-85-85653

Musimed Edicoes Musicais Ltda+
SDS Ed Vanancio IV Terreo Loja 14, 70393-903
Brasilia-DF
Tel: (061) 3225-6820 *Fax:* (061) 3321-3673
E-mail: contato@livrariamusimed.com.br
Web Site: www.musimed.com.br
Key Personnel
Contact: Joselita Soares
Founded: 1982
Specialize in sheet music & music books.
Subjects: Music, Dance
ISBN Prefix(es): 978-85-7092; 978-85-85886
Total Titles: 23 Print

Companhia Editora Nacional
Rua Funchal, 263, 04551-060 Sao Paulo-SP
Tel: (011) 2799-7799 *Toll Free Tel:* 0800-
0175678
E-mail: atendimento@editoraibep.com.br
Web Site: editoranacional.com.br
Founded: 1925
ISBN Prefix(es): 978-85-342; 978-85-04
Number of titles published annually: 50 Print
Total Titles: 500 Print
Parent Company: Instituto Brasileiro de Edicoes
Pedagogicas (IBEP)

Editora Napoleao
Rua Prof Carlos Liepin, 534, 13460-000 Nova
Odessa-SP
Tel: (019) 3466 2063; (019) 3498 2339
E-mail: comunicacao@editoranapoleao.com.br
Web Site: www.editoranapoleao.com.br
Key Personnel
Manager: Ana Maria Napoleao; Guilherme
Napoleao; Leonardo Napoleao
Subjects: Health, Nutrition
ISBN Prefix(es): 978-85-60842

Nemo, *imprint of* Autentica Editora

Nobel, *imprint of* Livraria Nobel SA

Nobel
Imprint of Livraria Nobel SA
Av Sagiario, 138, Torre London, 25º andar, Alpha
Sq, Alphaville, 06473-073 Barueri-SP
Tel: (011) 3706-1466
Web Site: www.editoranobel.com.br
Subjects: Crafts, Games, Hobbies, Gardening,
Plants, History
ISBN Prefix(es): 978-85-213; 978-85-86466; 978-
88-97502
Associate Companies: Conex; Marco Zero; Studio
Nobel

Nobel Franquias, see Livraria Nobel SA

Livraria Nobel SA
Rua Pedroso Alvarenga, 1046 9º andar, 04531-
004 Sao Paulo-SP
Tel: (011) 3706-1469; (011) 3706-1466
Toll Free Tel: 0800 160018 *Fax:* (011) 3706-
1462
E-mail: sac@livrarianobel.com.br
Web Site: www.livrarianobel.net.br
Key Personnel
Publisher: Ary Kuflik Benclowicz
Founded: 1943
Subjects: Advertising, Agriculture, Animals,
Pets, Architecture & Interior Design, Biogra-
phy, Business, Cookery, Economics,
Gardening, Plants, Health, Nutrition, House &
Home, Romance, Self-Help, Sports, Athletics,
Technology, Travel & Tourism
ISBN Prefix(es): 978-85-213; 978-85-7471
Number of titles published annually: 80 Print
Total Titles: 1,200 Print
Parent Company: Nobel Franquias
Imprints: Conex; Marco Zero; Studio Nobel; No-
bel

Editora Nova Aguilar+
Member of Grupo Editorial Global
Rua Pirapitingui, 111, Liberdade, 01508-020 Sao
Paulo-SP
Tel: (011) 3277-7999 *Fax:* (011) 3277-8141
E-mail: globaleditora@globaleditora.com.br
Web Site: www.globaleditora.com.br
Founded: 1950
Subjects: Fiction, Poetry, Prose
ISBN Prefix(es): 978-85-210; 978-85-7384

Editora Nova Alexandria Ltda+
Av Dom Pedro I, 840, Vila Monumento, 01552-
000 Sao Paulo-SP
Tel: (011) 2215-6252 *Fax:* (011) 2215-6252
E-mail: novaalexandria@novaalexandria.com.br
Web Site: www.novaalexandria.com.br
Founded: 1992
Subjects: Art, Biography, Memoirs, Cookery, Ed-
ucation, Fiction, History, Humor, Literature,
Literary Criticism, Essays, Philosophy, Poetry,
Romance, Social Sciences, Sociology, Sports,
Athletics
ISBN Prefix(es): 978-85-86075; 978-85-7492
Number of titles published annually: 18 Print
Total Titles: 136 Print

Nova Era, *imprint of* Grupo Editorial Record

Nova Fronteira+
Rua Nova Jerusalem, 345, Bonsucesso, 21042-
901 Rio de Janeiro-RJ
Tel: (021) 3882-8200; (021) 3882-8323 (sales)
E-mail: novafronteira@ediouro.com.br
Web Site: ediouro.com.br/novo/
Key Personnel
General Manager: Antonio Araujo
Founded: 1965
Subjects: Art, Astrology, Occult, Astronomy, Bi-
ography, Memoirs, Biological Sciences, Busi-
ness, Education, Fiction, Health, Nutrition, His-
tory, Language Arts, Linguistics, Literature,

Literary Criticism, Essays, Mysteries, Suspense,
Natural History, Nonfiction (General), Philoso-
phy, Poetry, Psychology, Psychiatry, Publishing
& Book Trade Reference, Regional Interests,
Romance, Science (General), Self-Help, Social
Sciences, Sociology, Theology
ISBN Prefix(es): 978-85-209
Number of titles published annually: 90 Print
Total Titles: 1,200 Print
Parent Company: Ediouro Publicacoes

Novas Ideias, *imprint of* Grupo Editorial Novo
Conceito

Novas Paginas, *imprint of* Grupo Editorial Novo
Conceito

Grupo Editorial Novo Conceito
Rua Dr Hugo Fortes, 1885, Pq Industrial
Lagoinha, 14095-260 Ribeirao Preta-SP
Tel: (016) 3512-5500
E-mail: contato@grupoeditorialnovoconceito.com.
br
Web Site: www.editoranovoconceito.com.br
Founded: 2004
Subjects: Biography, Memoirs, Drama, Theater,
Romance, Science Fiction, Fantasy
ISBN Prefix(es): 978-858-163
Imprints: Novas Ideias; Novas Paginas; Novo
Concieto

Novo Concieto, *imprint of* Grupo Editorial Novo
Conceito

Olho d'Agua, Editora e Livraria+
Rua Dr Homem de Melo, 1036, Perdizes, 05007-
002 Sao Paulo-SP
Tel: (011) 3673-1287 *Fax:* (011) 3673-1287
E-mail: editora@olhodagua.com.br
Web Site: www.olhodagua.com.br
Key Personnel
Publisher: Jorge Claudio Noel Ribeiro, Jr
Founded: 1991
Subjects: Behavioral Sciences, Education, Jour-
nalism, Literature, Literary Criticism, Essays,
Psychology, Psychiatry, Social Sciences, Soci-
ology, Theology
ISBN Prefix(es): 978-85-85428

**Oliveira Rocha-Comercio e Servicos Ltda
Dialetica+**
Rua Sena Madureira, 34, Sleaford, 04021-000
Sao Paulo-SP
Tel: (011) 5084-4544 *Fax:* (011) 5084-4544
Key Personnel
Coordinator: Valdir Oliveira Rocha
Founded: 1995
Subjects: Law
ISBN Prefix(es): 978-85-86208; 978-85-7500;
978-85-89288

Editora Original, see Panda Books/Editora
Original

Outras Letras Editora
Rua Almirante Goncalves 15-302, 22060-040 Rio
de Janeiro-RJ
Tel: (021) 2267 6627
E-mail: contato@outrasletras.com.br
Web Site: www.outrasletras.com.br
Subjects: Art, Literature, Literary Criticism, Es-
says, Social Sciences, Sociology
ISBN Prefix(es): 978-85-88642

Associacao Palas Athena do Brasil+
Alameda Lorena 355, Jardim Paulista, 01424-001
Sao Paulo-SP
Tel: (011) 3266-6188; (011) 3289-5426
Fax: (011) 3287-8941
E-mail: editora@palasathena.org.br

Web Site: www.palasathena.org.br
Key Personnel
Co-Founder: Basilio Pawlowicz
Founded: 1975
Subjects: Anthropology, Philosophy, Psychology,
Psychiatry, Religion - Other
ISBN Prefix(es): 978-85-7242

Pallas Editora+
Rua Frederico de Albuquerque, 56, Higienopolis,
21050-840 Rio de Janeiro-RJ
Tel: (021) 2270-0186 *Fax:* (021) 2270-0186
E-mail: pallas@pallaseditora.com.br
Web Site: www.pallaseditora.com.br
Key Personnel
Publisher, Editorial, Rights & Permis-
sions: Cristina Fernandes Warth
E-mail: cristinawarth@pallaseditora.com.br
Editor: Mariana Warth
Founded: 1975
Membership(s): Alliance Internationale des Edi-
teurs Independants; Liga Brasileira de Editoras
(LIBRE).
Subjects: African American Studies, Anthropol-
ogy, Art, Biography, Memoirs, Cookery, Eth-
nicity, History, Human Relations, Literature,
Literary Criticism, Essays, Music, Dance, Phi-
losophy, Religion - Catholic, Religion - Other,
Self-Help, Social Sciences, Sociology, Theol-
ogy, Afro-Brazilian Religions, Culture, Magic,
Romance
ISBN Prefix(es): 978-85-347
Number of titles published annually: 30 Print
Total Titles: 200 Print

Panda Books/Editora Original
Rua Henrique Schaumann, 286 cj 41, Cerqueira
Cesar, 05413-010 Sao Paulo-SP
Tel: (011) 3088-8444
E-mail: edoriginal@pandabooks.com.br;
editorial@pandabooks.com.br; impresa@
pandabooks.com.br; vendas@pandabooks.com.
br (sales)
Web Site: www.pandabooks.com.br
Founded: 1999
ISBN Prefix(es): 978-85-7888

Parma, *imprint of* Global Editora e Distribuidora
Ltda

Paulinas Editorial+
Av Indianopolis, 2752, 04062-003 Sao Paulo-SP
Tel: (011) 3276-5566 *Fax:* (011) 3275-0255
E-mail: livirtual@paulinas.com.br
Web Site: www.paulinas.org.br/institucional/
editora.aspx
Subjects: Biblical Studies, Biography, Memoirs,
Child Care & Development, Communications,
Education, Health, Nutrition, Human Rela-
tions, Inspirational, Spirituality, Literature, Lit-
erary Criticism, Essays, Medicine, Nursing,
Dentistry, Psychology, Psychiatry, Religion -
Catholic, Self-Help, Social Sciences, Sociology,
Theology
ISBN Prefix(es): 978-85-356; 978-85-7311

Paulus Editora+
Rua Francisco Cruz, 229, Vila Mariana, 04117-
091 Sao Paulo-SP
Tel: (011) 3789-4119; (011) 3789-4000 (sales)
Toll Free Tel: 0800 16 40 11 *Fax:* (011) 570-
3627
E-mail: editorial@paulus.com.br
Web Site: www.paulus.com.br
Key Personnel
Mng Dir, Publicity & Production: Arno Brustolin
Editorial Dir: Paulo Bazajlia
Sales: Valdecir Uveda
Founded: 1931
Subjects: Biblical Studies, Communications, Ed-
ucation, Health, Nutrition, How-to, Music,
Dance, Philosophy, Psychology, Psychiatry, Re-

ligion - Catholic, Religion - Other, Self-Help, Social Sciences, Sociology, Theology
ISBN Prefix(es): 978-85-05; 978-85-349
Number of titles published annually: 100 Print
Bookshop(s): Rua Mexico 111-B, Castle, 20031-145 Rio de Janeiro-RJ *Tel:* (021) 2240-1303; (021) 2240-1356 *E-mail:* riodejaneiro@paulus.com.br

Editora Paz e Terra Ltda+
Rua do Triunfo, 177, Santa Ifigenia, 01212-010 Sao Paulo-SP
Tel: (011) 3337-8399 *Fax:* (011) 3223-6290
E-mail: vendas@pazeterra.com.br (sales); editorial@pazeterra.com.br; divulgacao@pazeterra.com.br
Web Site: www.pazeterra.com.br
Key Personnel
Dir: Marcus Gasparian *E-mail:* diretoria@pazeterra.com.br
Editorial Production: Katia Halbe *E-mail:* producao@pazeterra.com.br; Cleber Paes *E-mail:* cleber@pazeterra.com.br
Founded: 1966
Subjects: Drama, Theater, Government, Political Science, Literature, Literary Criticism, Essays, Philosophy, Regional Interests, Social Sciences, Sociology
ISBN Prefix(es): 978-85-219
Imprints: Edicoes Graal Ltda

Pearson Education do Brasil Ltda
Rua Nelson Francisco, 26, Limao, 02712-100 Sao Paulo-SP
Tel: (011) 2178-8686; (011) 2178-8613 (sales) *Fax:* (011) 2178-8688
Web Site: www.pearson.com.br
Founded: 1996
Subjects: Accounting, Behavioral Sciences, Biological Sciences, Business, Economics, Engineering (General), Marketing, Technology
ISBN Prefix(es): 978-85-7054; 978-85-87675; 978-85-87214; 978-85-87918; 978-85-88317; 978-85-88639
Number of titles published annually: 20 Print
Parent Company: Pearson Plc
Imprints: Addison Wesley; Scott Foresman; Longman; Pearson Makron Books; Prentice Hall
Foreign Rights: Roger Trimer

Pearson Makron Books, *imprint of* Pearson Education do Brasil Ltda

Pearson Makron Books+
Imprint of Pearson Education do Brasil Ltda
Rua Nelson Francisco, 26, Limao, 02712-100 Sao Paulo-SP
Tel: (011) 2178-8686; (011) 2178-8613 (sales) *Fax:* (011) 2178-8688
Web Site: www.pearson.com.br
Key Personnel
President: Milton Assumpcao
Founded: 1985
Subjects: Business, Computer Science
ISBN Prefix(es): 978-85-346

Editora Pedagogica e Universitaria Ltda, see EPU - Editora Pedagogica e Universitaria Ltda

Editora Pensamento-Cultrix Ltda
Rua Dr Mario Vicente, 368, 04270-000 Sao Paulo-SP
Tel: (011) 2066-9000 *Fax:* (011) 2066-9008
E-mail: atendimento@pensamento-cultrix.com.br (sales & service); imprensa@pensamento-cultrix.com.br
Web Site: www.pensamento-cultrix.com.br
Key Personnel
Publisher: Ricardo Riedel
Contact: Mayara Volpe *Tel:* (011) 2066-9000 ext 231

Founded: 1907
Subjects: Advertising, Astrology, Occult, Biography, Memoirs, Economics, Health, Nutrition, History, Humor, Inspirational, Spirituality, Journalism, Language Arts, Linguistics, Literature, Literary Criticism, Essays, Management, Marketing, Psychology, Psychiatry, Romance, Science (General), Self-Help, Social Sciences, Sociology, Sports, Athletics, Administration, Esoteric, Humanities, Journalism, Numerology, Oriental Wisdom, Professional Development, Reincarnation
ISBN Prefix(es): 978-85-316; 978-85-315
Foreign Rep(s): Dinalivro Distribuidora Nacional de Livros Ltda (Portugal)
Bookshop(s): Rua Dr Mario Vicente, 374-Ipiranga, 04270-000 Sao Paulo-SP
E-mail: livraria@pensamento-cultrix.com.br

Editora Perspectiva
Av Brigadeiro Luis Antonio, 3025, 01401-000 Sao Paulo-SP
Tel: (011) 3885-8388 *Fax:* (011) 3885-8388
E-mail: editora@editoraperspectiva.com.br
Web Site: www.editoraperspectiva.com.br
Key Personnel
Mng Dir: Jaco Guinsburg
Founded: 1965
Subjects: Drama, Theater, Economics, Education, History, Human Relations, Music, Dance, Philosophy, Psychology, Psychiatry, Religion - Other, Social Sciences, Sociology
ISBN Prefix(es): 978-85-273
Distribution Center: Acre Nacional, Rua 24 de Maio, 415, 69010-080 Manaus-AM
Tel: (092) 3234-4617 *Fax:* (092) 3234-4617
E-mail: livrarianacionalam@vivax.com.br

Petit Editora e Distribuidora Ltda+
Rua Atuai 383, Vila Esperance, 03646-000 Sao Paulo-SP
Tel: (011) 2684-6000
Web Site: www.petit.com.br
Key Personnel
Dir & Founder: Llaguno Carmen; Flavio Machado
Founded: 1982
Subjects: Religion - Other
ISBN Prefix(es): 978-85-7253
Foreign Rep(s): Bertrand (Portugal); Jose Ricardo Canelossi (USA); Dina Books (Portugal); Sekai Corp Ltda (Japan)

Petra Editora
Rua Nova Jerusalem, 345, Bonsucesso, 21042-901 Rio de Janeiro-RJ
Tel: (021) 3882-8200
E-mail: livros@petraeditora.com.br
Web Site: www.petraeditora.com.br
Key Personnel
General Manager: Antonio Araujo
Subjects: Inspirational, Spirituality, Religion - Catholic
ISBN Prefix(es): 978-85-8278

Pia Sociedade Filhas de Sao Paulo, see Paulinas Editorial

Editora Pini Ltda
Rua Anhaia, 964, Born Retiro, 01130-900 Sao Paulo-SP
Tel: (011) 4001-6400; (011) 2173-2300
E-mail: construcao@pini.com.br; vendas@pini.com.br (sales)
Web Site: www.piniweb.com
Key Personnel
Dir: Mario Sergio Pini *Tel:* (011) 2173-2368 *E-mail:* mariosergio@pini.com.br
Publisher: Renato Evangelho
Editorial Dir: Eric Cozza
Founded: 1948

Subjects: Architecture & Interior Design, Engineering (General)
ISBN Prefix(es): 978-85-7266
Bookshop(s): Rua Vitoria, 486/496, 01210-000 Sao Paulo-SP; Rua Gentil de Moura, 128, 04278-000 Sao Paulo-SP

Editora Planeta de Livros Brasil
Member of Grupo Planeta
Av Matarazzo 1500, 3° andar, conjunto 32B, edificio New York, 05001-100 Sao Paulo-SP
Tel: (011) 3087-8888 *Fax:* (011) 3898-2039
E-mail: info@planetadelivros.com.br
Web Site: www.planeta.es/es/editora-planeta-do-brasil (Spanish); www.planeta.es/en/editora-planeta-do-brasil (English); www.planetadelivros.com.br
Founded: 2003
Subjects: Fiction, Nonfiction (General), Self-Help
ISBN Prefix(es): 978-85-7665; 978-85-87097; 978-85-89885

Prentice Hall, *imprint of* Pearson Education do Brasil Ltda

Grafica e Editora Primor Ltda+
Rua Joao Goulart, 3216, Sao Joao Bosco, 78902-600 Porto Velho-RO
Tel: (069) 3224-6756
Subjects: Fiction, Humor, Nonfiction (General)
ISBN Prefix(es): 978-85-7024

Prol, *imprint of* Global Editora e Distribuidora Ltda

Proton Editora Ltda
Ave Reboucas, 3819, 05401-450 Sao Paulo-SP
Tel: (011) 3032-3616 *Fax:* (011) 3815-9920
E-mail: proton@editoraproton.com.br
Web Site: www.editoraproton.com.br; www.keppepacheco.com
Key Personnel
President: Norberto R Keppe
Mng Dir: Claudia S Pacheco
Founded: 1976
Subjects: Medicine, Nursing, Dentistry, Psychology, Psychiatry, Science (General)
ISBN Prefix(es): 978-85-7072; 978-85-85001

Ediouro Publicacoes SA+
Rua Nova Jerusalem, 345, Bonsucesso, 21042-235 Rio de Janeiro-RJ
Tel: (021) 3882-8200 *Fax:* (021) 3882-8200
Web Site: www.ediouro.com.br
Key Personnel
President: Jorge Carneiro
Subjects: Animals, Pets, Biography, Memoirs, How-to, Journalism, Literature, Literary Criticism, Essays, Mysteries, Suspense, Science Fiction, Fantasy
ISBN Prefix(es): 978-85-00

Editora da PUC-SP, see EDUC

Qualitymark Editora Ltda+
R Teixeira Junior, 441, Sao Cristovao, 20921-405 Rio de Janeiro-RJ
Tel: (021) 3295-9800 *Fax:* (021) 3295-9824
E-mail: quality@qualitymark.com.br
Web Site: www.qualitymark.com.br
Key Personnel
Editor: Saidul Rahman Mahomed
Founded: 1990
Promote events dealing with seminars & lectures.
Subjects: Business, Career Development, Communications, Economics, Education, Environmental Studies, Finance, Labor, Industrial Relations, Management, Medicine, Nursing, Dentistry, Nonfiction (General), Public Administration, Self-Help, Travel & Tourism
ISBN Prefix(es): 978-85-7303; 978-85-85360; 978-85-86558; 978-85-88979

Raboni Editora Ltda+
CP 140, 13001-970 Campinas-SP
Tel: (019) 3242-8433 *Fax:* (019) 3242-8505
E-mail: raboni@raboni.com.br
Web Site: www.raboni.com.br; www.raboni.net
Key Personnel
President & Co-Founder: Maisa Castro; Regis
  Castro
Founded: 1991
Publish & distribute Catholic books worldwide.
Subjects: Religion - Catholic
ISBN Prefix(es): 978-85-7345

Grupo Editorial Record+
Rua Argentina 171, Sao Cristovao, 20921-380
  Rio de Janeiro-RJ
Tel: (021) 2585-2000 *Fax:* (021) 2580-4911
E-mail: record@record.com.br
Web Site: www.record.com.br
Key Personnel
President: Sonia Machado Jardim
Founded: 1942
Subjects: Biography, Memoirs, Business, Fiction,
  History, Nonfiction (General), Philosophy
ISBN Prefix(es): 978-85-01; 978-85-03 (Editora
  Jose Olympio Ltda); 978-85-20 (Civilizacao
  Brasileira)
Number of titles published annually: 600 Print;
  50 E-Book
Total Titles: 7,000 Print; 100 E-Book
Parent Company: Distribuidora Record SA
Associate Companies: DLD-Distribuidora de
  Livros Digitais Ltda; Editora HR Ltda
Imprints: Edicoes BestBolso; Best Business; Civi-
  lizacao Brasileira; Difel; Galera Record; Galer-
  inha Record; Nova Era
Subsidiaries: Editora Bertrand Brasil Ltd; Edi-
  tora BestSeller Ltda; Editora Jose Olympio Ltda;
  Editora Paz e Terra Ltd; Editora Record Ltd;
  Verus Editora Ltda
Branch Office(s)
Paraiso 139, 10 andar, 04103-000 Sao Paulo-SP,
  Contact: Roberta Machado *Tel:* (011) 3286-
  0802 *Toll Free Tel:* (011) 0800-212380

Relume Dumara+
Rua Nova Jerusalem, 345, 21042-235
  Bonsucesso-RJ
Tel: (021) 2564-6869 *Fax:* (021) 2564-6869
Web Site: www.relumedumara.com.br
Key Personnel
Contact: Alberto Jak Schprejer
Founded: 1989
Subjects: Anthropology, Drama, Theater, Fiction,
  Social Sciences, Sociology
ISBN Prefix(es): 978-85-7316; 978-85-85427
Parent Company: Ediouro Publicacoes

Editora Revan Ltda+
Av Paulo de Frontin, 163, Rio Comprido, 20260-
  010 Rio de Janeiro-RJ
Tel: (021) 2502-7495 *Fax:* (021) 2273-6873
E-mail: vendas@revan.com.br
Web Site: www.revan.com.br
Key Personnel
Dir: Dr Renato Guimaraes
Founded: 1983
Subjects: Anthropology, Art, Behavioral Sciences,
  Biography, Memoirs, Computer Science, Crim-
  inology, Economics, Fiction, History, Military
  Science, Psychology, Psychiatry, Science (Gen-
  eral), Self-Help, Social Sciences, Sociology
ISBN Prefix(es): 978-85-7106
Number of titles published annually: 40 Print
Total Titles: 300 Print

Livraria e Editora Revinter Ltda+
Rua do Matoso, 170, Tijuca, 20270-131 Rio de
  Janeiro-RJ
Tel: (021) 2563-9700 *Fax:* (021) 2563-9701
E-mail: livraria@revinter.com.br
Web Site: www.revinter.com.br

Key Personnel
Chief Executive Officer: Sergio Duarte Dortas
Subjects: Medicine, Nursing, Dentistry
ISBN Prefix(es): 978-85-7309; 978-85-85228
Branch Office(s)
Rua Amarai Gurgel, 127/8 andar, Vila Buarque,
  01221-001 Sao Paulo-SP *Tel:* (011) 3362-2464
  Fax: (011) 3362-2465 *E-mail:* revintersp@
  revinter.com.br
Distributor for Churchill Livingstone; Lippincott
  Williams & Wilkins; Mosby; W B Saunders;
  Georg Thieme

Editora RHJ+
Rua Cuiaba, 415, Prado, 30411-180 Belo
  Horizonte-MG
Tel: (031) 3334-1566 *Fax:* (031) 3332-5823
E-mail: editorarhj@editorarhj.com.br
Web Site: www.editorarhj.com.br
Founded: 1987
Membership(s): Sindicato Nacional dos Editores
  de Livros (SNEL).
Subjects: Literature, Literary Criticism, Essays
ISBN Prefix(es): 978-85-7153

Editora Rideel Ltda+
Avda Casa Verde, 455, Casa Verde, 02519-000
  Sao Paulo-SP
Tel: (011) 2238-5100
E-mail: sac@rideel.com.br
Web Site: www.rideel.com.br
Key Personnel
Publisher: Mario Amadio
Founded: 1970
Subjects: Cookery, History, Language Arts, Lin-
  guistics, Medicine, Nursing, Dentistry, Religion
  - Other
ISBN Prefix(es): 978-85-339; 978-85-89219; 978-
  85-89259
Imprints: Amadio; Celebris
Bookshop(s): Al Afonso Schmidt, No 877, Santa
  Terezinha, 02450-001 Sao Paulo-SP

Roca, *imprint of* Grupo Editorial Nacional (GEN)

Roca+
Imprint of Grupo Editorial Nacional (GEN)
Rua Dona Brigida, 701, Vila Mariana, 04111-081
  Sao Paulo-SP
Tel: (011) 5080-0770
Web Site: www.grupogen.com.br
Founded: 1977
Subjects: Health, Nutrition, History, Journalism,
  Medicine, Nursing, Dentistry, Social Sciences,
  Sociology, Travel & Tourism, Veterinary Sci-
  ence, Social Services
ISBN Prefix(es): 978-85-7241

Editora Rocco Ltda+
Av Pres Wilson, 231 - 8° andar, 20030-021 Rio
  de Janeiro-RJ
Tel: (021) 3525-2000 *Fax:* (021) 3525-2001
E-mail: rocco@rocco.com.br
Web Site: www.rocco.com.br
Key Personnel
Manager: Cintia Borges *Tel:* (021) 3525-2016
  E-mail: cborges@rocco.com.br
Editor: Danielle Borges *E-mail:* dborges@rocco.
  com.br
Founded: 1975
Subjects: Anthropology, Biography, Memoirs,
  Communications, Fiction, Management, Sci-
  ence (General), Self-Help, Social Sciences, So-
  ciology, Women's Studies
ISBN Prefix(es): 978-85-325
Imprints: Fantastica Rocco

Salamandra Editorial Ltda+
Rua Padre Adelino, 758, Belenzinho, 03303-904
  Sao Paulo-SP

Tel: (011) 2790-1300 *Toll Free Tel:* 0800 17 20
  02 *Fax:* (011) 2790-1454
E-mail: moderna@moderna.com.br
Web Site: www.salamandra.com.br
Founded: 1982
Subjects: Art
ISBN Prefix(es): 978-85-281; 978-85-7568
Parent Company: Editora Moderna

Santos, *imprint of* Grupo Editorial Nacional
  (GEN)

Santos Editora+
Imprint of Grupo Editorial Nacional (GEN)
Travessa do Ouvidor, 11, 20040-040 Rio de
  Janeiro-RJ
Tel: (021) 3543-0770
E-mail: vendas@grupogen.com.br
Web Site: www.grupogen.com.br
Founded: 1974
Subjects: Medicine, Nursing, Dentistry, Veterinary
  Science
ISBN Prefix(es): 978-85-7288
Number of titles published annually: 60 Print
Total Titles: 700 Print

Editora Santuario+
Rua Padre Claro Monteiro 342, 12570-000
  Aparecida-SP
Tel: (012) 3104-2000 *Toll Free Tel:* 0800 16 00
  04 *Fax:* (012) 3104-2036
Web Site: www.editorasantuario.com.br
Key Personnel
Marketing Manager: Guto Kater
Founded: 1900
Specialize in graphic services.
Subjects: Literature, Literary Criticism, Essays,
  Religion - Catholic
ISBN Prefix(es): 978-85-7200; 978-85-7265
Parent Company: Congregacao do Santissimo Re-
  dentor
Bookshop(s): Praca Nossa Senhora Aparecida,
  292, 12570-000 Aparecida-SP *Tel:* (012) 3108-
  1553 *E-mail:* livraria@editorasantuario.com.br;
  Praca Nossa Senhora Aparecida, 141, 12570-
  000 Aparecida-SP *Tel:* (012) 3108-1532; Cen-
  tro de Apoio ao Romeiro, Asa leste 59/60/64,
  12570-000 Aparecida-SP *Tel:* (012) 3104-
  1363; Subsolo do Santuario Nacional, Av Dr
  Julio Prestes s/no, 12570-000 Aparecida-SP
  Tel: (012) 3104-1552

Sao Paulo Editora, *imprint of* Global Editora e
  Distribuidora Ltda

Saraiva SA Livreiros Editores+
Rua Henrique Schaumann, 270, Cerqueira Cesar,
  05413-909 Sao Paulo-SP
Tel: (011) 3613-3212 *Toll Free Tel:* 0800-754-
  4000
E-mail: falecomri@saraiva.com.br
Web Site: www.saraiva.com.br; www.saraivari.
  com.br
Key Personnel
Chief Executive Officer & Investor Relations Of-
  ficer: Jorge Saraiva Neto
Chief Financial Officer: Marcus Mingoni
Chief Information Officer: Luis Claudio Correa
  Villani
Vice President & Dir: Ruy Mendes Gonalves
Vice President, Retail: Marcelo Ubriaco
E-Publishing Dir: Nilson Lepera
Law Publishing Dir: Antonio Luiz Toledo Pinto
Founded: 1914
17 Branches in Sao Paulo.
Subjects: Accounting, Business, Economics, Edu-
  cation, Finance, Law, Management, Marketing,
  Mathematics, Philosophy, Psychology, Psychia-
  try, Securities, Administration
ISBN Prefix(es): 978-85-02; 978-85-357; 978-85-
  7056
Subsidiaries: Saraiva Data-Informatica

Branch Office(s)
Travessa Apinages, 186, Batista Campos, 66025-080 Belem-PA *Tel:* (091) 3222-9034; (091) 3224-9038 *Fax:* (091) 3241-0499
Rua Alem Paraiba, 449, Lagoinha, 31210-120 Belo Horizonte-MG *Tel:* (031) 3429-8300 *Fax:* (031) 3429-8310
Rua 14 de Julho, 3148, Centro, 79002-335 Campo Grande-MS *Tel:* (067) 3382-3682 *Fax:* (067) 3382-0112
Rua Conselheiro Laurindo, 2895, Prado Velho, 80230-180 Curitiba-PR *Tel:* (041) 3332-4894
Av Independencia, 5330, Setor Aeroporto, 74070-010 Goiania-TO *Tel:* (062) 3225-2882; (062) 3212-2806 *Fax:* (062) 3224-3016
Rua Costa Azevedo, 56, Centro, 69010-230 Manaus-AM *Tel:* (092) 3633-4227 *Fax:* (092) 3633-4782
Av A J Renner, 231, Farrapos, 90245-000 Porto Alegre-RS *Tel:* (051) 3371-4001; (051) 3371-1467; (051) 3371-1567
Rua Corredor do Bispo, 185, Boa Vista, 50050-090 Recife-PE *Tel:* (081) 3421-4246 *Fax:* (081) 3421-4510
Rua Visconde de Santa Isabel, 113 ao 119, Vila Isabel, 20560-121 Rio de Janeiro-RJ *Tel:* (021) 2577-9494 *Fax:* (021) 2577-8867
Rua Agripino Dorea, 23, Brotas, 40255-430 Salvador-BA *Tel:* (071) 3381-5854; (071) 3381-5895 *Fax:* (071) 3381-0959

Editora Scipione Ltda+
Rua Cenno Sbrighi, loja e sobreloja, 25, 05036-010 Sao Paulo-SP
Tel: (011) 3611-1695; (011) 3611-4847
Toll Free Tel: 0800-161700
E-mail: atendimento@scipione.com.br
Web Site: www.scipione.com.br
Founded: 1983
Specialize in books preschool to second grade & also in technical & professional books.
Membership(s): Brazilian Book Association; National Book Foundation for Children & Juveniles.
Subjects: Astronomy, Biological Sciences, Chemistry, Chemical Engineering, Education, Environmental Studies, Fiction, Geography, Geology, History, Literature, Literary Criticism, Essays, Mathematics, Mysteries, Suspense, Nonfiction (General), Physics, Religion - Other, Romance, Science (General)
ISBN Prefix(es): 978-85-262
Branch Office(s)
Rua Felipe Schmidt, 60, Centro, 88075-000 Florianapolis-SC *Tel:* (048) 3223-1015 *E-mail:* aticasc@livrariascuritiba.com.br
Av Visconde de Suassuna, 634, Santo Amaro, 50050-540 Recife-PE *Tel:* (081) 3321-6200 *Fax:* (081) 3312-6201 *E-mail:* cp.recife@scipione.com.br
Av Dorival Caymmi, 1080, Sao Cristavao, 41635-150 Salvador-BA *Tel:* (071) 3612-8300 *Fax:* (071) 3612-8301 *E-mail:* alex.miyazaki@abrileducacao.com.br
Distributor for Allca XX/Scipione Culture - Collection Archivos (South America)
Showroom(s): Rua Felipe Schmidt, 60, Centro, 88075-000 Florianapolis-SC *Tel:* (048) 3223-1015 *E-mail:* aticasc@livrariascuritiba.com.br; Av Macrana, 592, 20511-001 Rio de Janeiro-RJ *Tel:* (021) 2587-4300 *Fax:* (021) 2587-4339 *E-mail:* vendas.rio@scipione.com.br; Rua Ipiranga, 35, Jd Maringa, 12243-280 Sao Jose dos Campos-SP *Tel:* (012) 3941-6637 *Fax:* (012) 3922-6549 *E-mail:* salasjcampos@abril.com.br

Editora Seculo XXI Ltda
Av Dos Autonomistas 5781, Km 18, Osasco, 06194-050 Sao Paulo-SP
Tel: (011) 3608-1294; (011) 3695-1273
E-mail: wilmrc@yahoo.com.br
Web Site: www.editorasseculo21.com.br
Founded: 1992

Subjects: Astrology, Occult, Religion - Other, Self-Help, Kabbalah, Motivation, Numerology, Tarot
ISBN Prefix(es): 978-85-86371

Selinunte Editora Ltda+
Av Miguel Estefno, 183-Conj 01, Saude, 04301-010 Sao Paulo-SP
Founded: 1987
Subjects: Literature, Literary Criticism, Essays
ISBN Prefix(es): 978-85-85538

Editora Senac Rio
Rua Marques de Abrantes, 99/2º andar, Flamengo, 22230-060 Rio de Janeiro-RJ
Tel: (021) 2536-3900 *Fax:* (021) 2536-3933
E-mail: comercial.editora@rj.senac.br
Web Site: www.rj.senac.br; www.senac.br
Founded: 2000
Subjects: Communications, Computer Science, Cookery, Education, Fashion, Health, Nutrition, Language Arts, Linguistics, Travel & Tourism, Administration, Commerce, Culture
ISBN Prefix(es): 978-85-7458; 978-85-85746; 978-85-87864

Editora Senac Sao Paulo
Rua Rui Barbosa 377, 1 Andar, Bela Vista, 01326-010 Sao Paulo-SP
Tel: (011) 2187-4450; (011) 2187-4496 *Fax:* (011) 2187-4486
E-mail: editora@sp.senac.br
Web Site: www.editorasenacsp.com.br
Key Personnel
Publisher: Jeane Passos Santana
Editor: Luiz Carlos Dourado; Luiz Francisco de A Salgado
Founded: 1995
Subjects: Art, Biography, Memoirs, Computer Science, Computers, Education, Environmental Studies, Fashion, Film, Video, Health, Nutrition, Journalism, Language Arts, Linguistics, Literature, Literary Criticism, Essays, Management, Marketing, Photography, Design
ISBN Prefix(es): 978-85-7359; 978-85-85578; 978-85-98694; 978-85-7756; 978-85-7558
Associate Companies: Editora Senac Rio

Editora Sextante
Rua Voluntarios da Patria, 45, sala 1404, Botafogo, 22270-000 Rio de Janeiro-RJ
Tel: (021) 2538-4100
E-mail: atendimento@esextante.com.br
Web Site: www.esextante.com.br
Founded: 1998
Subjects: Art, Biography, Memoirs, Business, Fiction, Health, Nutrition, Inspirational, Spirituality, Management, Nonfiction (General), Self-Help, Meditation
ISBN Prefix(es): 978-85-7542

Editora Sinodal+
Rua Amadeo Rossi, 467, 93030-220 Sao Leopoldo-RS
Tel: (051) 3037-2366 *Fax:* (051) 3037-2366
E-mail: vendas@editorasinodal.com.br; pedidos@editorasinodal.com.br
Web Site: www.editorasinodal.com.br
Key Personnel
Mng Dir: Eloy Teckemeier *E-mail:* diretor@editorasinodal.com.br
Editorial Dir: Robson Luis Neu *E-mail:* editor@editorasinodal.com.br
Sales & Marketing Manager: Eliseu da Cunha *E-mail:* gerenciavendas@editorasinodal.com.br
Founded: 1927
Subjects: Education, Music, Dance, Psychology, Psychiatry, Religion - Other, Social Sciences, Sociology, Theology
ISBN Prefix(es): 978-85-233

Parent Company: Instituicao Sinodal de Assistencia, Educacao e Cultura (ISAEC)
Associate Companies: Colegio Sinodal
Subsidiaries: Escola Superior de Teologia
Showroom(s): Rua Buenos Aires, 123 Sao Paulo-SP
Bookshop(s): Editora Sinodal-Livraria; Livraria Volante

Studio Nobel, *imprint of* Livraria Nobel SA

Sulina, *imprint of* Editora Meridional Ltda

Summus Editorial Ltda+
Division of Grupo Editorial Summus
Rua Itapicuru, 613-7º andar, Perdizes, 05006-000 Sao Paulo-SP
Tel: (011) 3872-3322 *Fax:* (011) 3872-7476
E-mail: marketing@summus.com.br; summus@summus.com.br; vendas@summus.com.br
Web Site: www.summus.com.br; www.gruposummus.com.br/summus
Key Personnel
Dir: Raul Wassermann
Founded: 1974
Subjects: Advertising, Astrology, Occult, Behavioral Sciences, Biography, Memoirs, Business, Communications, Cookery, Economics, Education, Film, Video, Human Relations, Journalism, Literature, Literary Criticism, Essays, Marketing, Music, Dance, Psychology, Psychiatry, Radio, TV, Religion - Other, Self-Help, Social Sciences, Sociology, Sports, Athletics, Travel & Tourism, Women's Studies
ISBN Prefix(es): 978-85-323
Number of titles published annually: 100 Print
Total Titles: 1,100 Print; 10 E-Book

Temos Grafica Propria, *imprint of* Editora Betania S/C

Oficina de Textos
Rua Cubatao, 959, 04013-043 Sao Paulo-SP
Tel: (011) 3085-7933
Web Site: www.ofitexto.com.br
Key Personnel
Dir: Shoshana Signer
Founded: 1996
Subjects: Architecture & Interior Design, Civil Engineering, Energy, Environmental Studies, Geography, Geology, Literature, Literary Criticism, Essays, Physics, Psychology, Psychiatry, Agronomy, Meteorology, Oceanography
ISBN Prefix(es): 978-85-86238
Parent Company: Signer Editora Ltda

Thex Editora e Distribuidora Ltda+
Rua da Lapa, 180, Conj 804/805, 20021-180 Rio de Janeiro-RJ
Tel: (021) 2221-4458 *Fax:* (021) 2252-9338
E-mail: atendimento@thexeditora.com.br
Web Site: www.thexeditora.com.br
Key Personnel
Founder: Thex Correa da Silva
Founded: 1992
Subjects: Earth Sciences, Economics, Education, Fiction, Human Relations, Literature, Literary Criticism, Essays, Marketing, Mysteries, Suspense, Poetry, Self-Help, Social Sciences, Sociology
ISBN Prefix(es): 978-85-85575; 978-85-7603
Number of titles published annually: 10 Print
Total Titles: 50 Print

34 Literatura Ltda+
Rua Hungria, 592, Jardim Europa, 01455-000 Sao Paulo-SP
Tel: (011) 3816-6777; (011) 3032-6755 (sales) *Fax:* (011) 3816-6777; (011) 3815-9977 (sales)
E-mail: vendas@editora34.com.br; editora34@editora34.com.br; rights@editora34.com.br

Web Site: www.editora34.com.br
Founded: 1992
Subjects: Anthropology, Art, Drama, Theater, Economics, Fiction, History, Literature, Literary Criticism, Essays, Music, Dance, Philosophy, Poetry, Psychology, Psychiatry, Romance, Science Fiction, Fantasy, Social Sciences, Sociology, Technology, Psychoanalysis
ISBN Prefix(es): 978-85-85490; 978-85-7326
Branch Office(s)
Rua Massaca, 276 Alto de Pinheiros, 05465-050 Sao Paulo-SP *Tel:* (011) 2609738 *Fax:* (011) 8321041

Editora 34, see 34 Literatura Ltda

Editora Todavia
Rua Luis Anhaia, 44, 05433-00 Sao Paulo-SP
Tel: (011) 30940500
E-mail: contato@todavialivros.com.br
Web Site: www.todavialivros.com.br
Key Personnel
Communications: Bruna Eduarda Brito; Cica Pinheiro; Clarissa Wolff
Editorial: Andre Conti; Flavio Moura; Leandro Sarmatz; Alfredo Nugent Setubal
Subjects: Biography, Memoirs, Fiction, Nonfiction (General), Poetry, Romance
ISBN Prefix(es): 978-85-93828

Todolivro Distribuidora Ltda+
Rua das Missoes-Ponta Aguda, 89051-000 Blumenau-SC
Tel: (047) 3221-2235; (047) 3221-2222
E-mail: atendimento@todolivro.com.br
Web Site: www.todolivro.com.br
Key Personnel
Dir: Juergen Konig
Founded: 1989
Subjects: Anthropology, Medicine, Nursing, Dentistry, Music, Dance, Self-Help, Travel & Tourism, Advocacy, Drawing, Painting, Terror
ISBN Prefix(es): 978-85-85415; 978-85-7324; 978-85-7398
Subsidiaries: Editora EKO/Distribuidora Alema

Totalidade Editora Ltda+
Rua Eng Alcides Barbosa 29, 01430-010 Sao Paulo-SP
Tel: (011) 3064-3688
Founded: 1989
Membership(s): Astrological-Psychological Institute; Brazilian House of Books; English Huber School of Astrology; Meditation Mount; National Syndication of Book Publishers; Seven Ray Institute; University of the Seven Rays.
Subjects: Art, Astrology, Occult, Psychology, Psychiatry, Self-Help
ISBN Prefix(es): 978-85-85293

Triom Editora e Centro de Estudos+
Rua Aracari, 218, Itaim Bibi, 01453-020 Sao Paulo-SP
Tel: (019) 3272-7344
E-mail: info@triom.com.br; editora@triom.com.br
Web Site: www.triom.com.br
Founded: 1991
Bookstore, publishing house.
Subjects: Alternative, Astrology, Occult, Music, Dance, Women's Studies
ISBN Prefix(es): 978-85-85464
Number of titles published annually: 5 Print
Total Titles: 40 Print; 2 Audio

Editora UEPG, see Editora Universidade Estadual de Ponta Grossa (UEPG)

Edicoes UESB, see Editora da Universidade Estadual do Sudoeste da Bahia (UESB)

Editora da UESC, see Editora da Universidade Estadual de Santa Cruz (UESC)

Editora UFG, see Editora da Universidade Federal de Goias (UFG)

Editora UFPR, see Editora da Universidade Federal do Parana (UFPR)

Editora UNESP+
Praca Da Se, 108, 01001-900 Sao Paulo-SP
Tel: (011) 3242-7171; (011) 3107-2623 (bookshop) *Fax:* (011) 3242-7172
E-mail: feu@editora.unesp.br; livraria@editora.unesp.br (bookshop)
Web Site: www.editoraunesp.br
Key Personnel
Dir & President: Jose Castilho Marques Neto
E-mail: castilho@editora.unesp.br
Executive Editor: Jezio H B Gutierre
E-mail: jezio@editora.unesp.br
Founded: 1987
Membership(s): Asociacion de Editoriales de America Latina y el Caribe; Associacao Brasileira das Editoras Universitarias; Associacao Brasileira de Direitos Reprograficos; Camara Brasileira do Livro.
Subjects: Anthropology, Education, Government, Political Science, History, Philosophy, Psychology, Psychiatry, Social Sciences, Sociology
ISBN Prefix(es): 978-85-7139; 978-85-87361
Number of titles published annually: 100 Print
Parent Company: State University of Sao Paulo

Uni Duni Editora
Rua Antonio de Albuquerque, 247, Salas 402/403, funcionarios, 30112-010 Minas Gerais-BH
Tel: (031) 3309-4272 *Fax:* (031) 2514-4272
E-mail: comunicacao@uniduni.com.br; unidunieditora@hotmail.com
Web Site: www.uniduni.com.br
Founded: 2006
ISBN Prefix(es): 978-85-60276

UNICENTRO - Universidade Estadual do Centro Oeste
Rua Pres Zacarias 875, CP 3010, 85015-430 Guarapuava-PR
Tel: (042) 3621-1019 *Fax:* (042) 3621-1090
E-mail: editora@unicentro.br
Web Site: www2.unicentro.br/editora
Subjects: Science (General), Humanities
ISBN Prefix(es): 978-85-7891

Unicornio Azul, *imprint of* Editora Mercuryo Ltda

Editora Unisinos
Av Unisinos, 950, 93022-000 Sao Leopoldo-RS
Tel: (051) 3590-8239
E-mail: editora@unisinos.br
Web Site: www.edunisinos.com.br
Founded: 1993
Subjects: Philosophy, Theology
ISBN Prefix(es): 978-85-7431

Editora Universidade de Brasilia
SCS, quadra 2, bloco C, no 78, Edificio OK, 2º andar, 70302-907 Brasilia-DF
Tel: (061) 3035-4200; (061) 3035-4248 (sales) *Fax:* (061) 3035-4230
E-mail: contatoeditora@unb.br; vendaseditora@unb.br
Web Site: www.editora.unb.br
Key Personnel
Pres: Germana Henriques Pereira
Secretary, Editorial Board: Fabio Henrique Estival
Commercial Manager: Elizania de Araujo Goncalves

Editorial Production Manager: Nathalie Letouze Moreira
Finance Manager: Adriana Rodrigues de Moraes
Information Technology Manager: Jeronimo Felipe da Silva
Founded: 1962
Subjects: Government, Political Science, Human Relations, Physical Sciences, Social Sciences, Sociology
ISBN Prefix(es): 978-85-230
Parent Company: Livraria Universidade
Branch Office(s)
Escritorio de Representacao da Universidade de Brasilia, Ave Presidente Vargas 542 - 1309, 20210 Rio de Janeiro-RJ *Tel:* (021) 2636959
Rua Joao Adolfo 118 - 6º andar - sala 608, 01050-020 Sao Paulo-SP *Tel:* (011) 321413
Bookshop(s): Livrarias Universidade-Loja Aeroporto, Aeroporto Internacional Juscelino Kubitschek, 70300 Brasilia-DF *Tel:* (061) 3364-9145 *E-mail:* livrariaaero@editora.unb.br; Livrarias Universidade-Loja Centro de Vivencia, Campus Universitario Darcy Ribeiro *Tel:* (061) 3307-2221 *E-mail:* livrariacampus@editora.unb.br; Livrarias Universidade-Loja ICC Norte, Campus Universitario Darcy Ribeiro *Tel:* (061) 3307-2578 *E-mail:* livrariaiccnorte@editora.unb.br
Book Club(s): Clube do Livro da Universidade de Brasilia
Warehouse: Subsolo ICC-SUL, CP 04551, 70919 Brasilia-DF

Editora da Universidade de Sao Paulo (EDUSP)+
Av Corifeu de Azevedo, 1975-Butana, 05581-001 Sao Paulo-SP
Tel: (011) 3091-4008; (011) 3091-4007 *Fax:* (011) 3091-4169
E-mail: edusp@usp.br; assessoria.edusp@edu.usp.br
Web Site: www.edusp.com.br
Key Personnel
Dir & President: Plinio Martins Filho
Dir, Editorial: Cristiane Tonon Silvestrin
Dir, Marketing: Cinzia de Araujo
Founded: 1963
Specialize in academic text.
Subjects: Anthropology, Art, Literature, Literary Criticism, Essays, Medicine, Nursing, Dentistry, Philosophy, Science (General), Social Sciences, Sociology
ISBN Prefix(es): 978-85-314
Total Titles: 7,000 Print
Bookshop(s): Livraria Joao Alexandre Barbosa, Edificio da Reitoria-Terreo, Rua da Reitoria, 374, 05508-010 Sao Paulo-SP *Tel:* (011) 3091-4156; (011) 3091-4157 *E-mail:* jab-edusp@usp.br; Livraria Educacao, Predio da Faculdade de Educacao, Bldg B, Av da Universidade, Trav 11, 251, 05508-900 Sao Paulo-SP, Manager: Ailton de Vieira *Tel:* (011) 3091-3545 *E-mail:* educacao-edusp@usp.br; Livraria Geografia/Historia, Predio da Historia e Geografia da FFLCH, Av Prof Lineu Prestes 338, 05508-900 Sao Paulo-SP, Manager: Marta Pereira *Tel:* (011) 3091-3896 *E-mail:* geo-edusp@usp.br; Livraria Politecnica, Predio do Bienio da Poli, Av Prof Almeida Prado, Trav 2, 128, 05508-900 Sao Paulo-SP, Manager: Marco Antonio Amorin *Tel:* (011) 3091-5103 *E-mail:* poli-edusp@usp.br; Livraria Bauru, Campus da USP-Faculdade de Odontologia, Predio de Biblioteca Central, Al Otavio Pinheiro Brisola, 9-75, 17043-101 Bauru-SP, Manager: David Fernandes *Tel:* (014) 3235-8395 *E-mail:* bauru-edusp@usp.br; Livraria Piracicaba, Campus da USP-ESALQ Agronomia, Predio da Biblioteca Central, Av Padua Dias, 11, 13418-900 Piracicabra-SP, Manager: Lidia Medeiros *Tel:* (019) 3429-4335 *E-mail:* piracicaba-edusp@usp.br; Livraria Pirassununga, Campus da USP-Faculdade de Zootecnia e Engenharia de Alimentos,

Predio da Biblioteca, Av Duque de Caxias-Norte, 225 CP 23, 13630-000 Pirassununga-SP, Manager: Edson Reche *Tel:* (019) 3565-4126 *E-mail:* pirassununga-edusp@usp.br; Livraria Ribeirao Preto, Rua Clovis Vieira, caso 25, 14040-900 Ribeirao Preto-SP, Manager: Reginaldo Lincoln *Tel:* (016) 3602-3568 *E-mail:* ribpreto-edusp@usp.br; Livraria Sao Carlos, Campus da USP (ao lado da Biblioteca), Av do Trabalhador Saocarlense, 400, 13566-590 Sao Carlos-SP, Manager: Erika Lemes de Aquino *Tel:* (016) 3373-8018 *E-mail:* scarlos-edusp@usp.br

Editora da Universidade do Sagrado Coracao, see EDUSC - Editora da Universidade do Sagrado Coracao

Editora Universidade do Vale do Rio dos Sinos, see Editora Unisinos

Editora da Universidade Estadual de Santa Cruz (UESC)
Rodovia Jorge Amado, km 16, Bairro Salobrinho, 45662-900 Ilheus-BA
Tel: (073) 3680-5028
E-mail: editus@uesc.br
Web Site: www.uesc.br/editora
Key Personnel
Dir: Rita Virginia Argolio
Production Manager: Jose Montival de Alencar, Jr
Founded: 1996
Subjects: Agriculture, Education, Environmental Studies, Geography, Geology, Health, Nutrition, History, Law, Philosophy
ISBN Prefix(es): 978-85-7455

Universidade Estadual do Centro Oeste, see UNICENTRO - Universidade Estadual do Centro Oeste

Editora da Universidade Estadual do Sudoeste da Bahia (UESB)
Estrada do Bem Querer, km 4, 45083-900 Vitoria da Conquista-BA
Tel: (077) 3424-8716 *Fax:* (077) 3424-8716
E-mail: edicoesuesb@uesb.edu.br
Web Site: www2.uesb.br/editora
Founded: 1999
This publisher has indicated that 30% of their product line is author subsidized.
Subjects: Agriculture, Art, Biological Sciences, Health, Nutrition, Journalism, Language Arts, Linguistics, Literature, Literary Criticism, Essays, Science (General), Social Sciences, Sociology, Humanities
ISBN Prefix(es): 978-85-88505; 978-85-7985

Editora da Universidade Federal de Goias (UFG)
Campus Samambaia, CP 131, 74001-970 Goiania-GO
Tel: (062) 3521-1107; (062) 3521-1352
Fax: (062) 3521-1814
E-mail: comercial.editora@ufg.br
Web Site: www.editora.ufg.br
Key Personnel
Dir General: Maria das Gracas Monteiro Castro
Editorial Advisor: Andre Barcellos Carlos de Souza
Founded: 1977
Subjects: Agriculture, Art, Biological Sciences, Engineering (General), Health, Nutrition, Language Arts, Linguistics, Earth Science, Humanities
ISBN Prefix(es): 978-85-7274; 978-85-85003

Editora da Universidade Federal de Pernambuco (UFPE)
Av Academcio Helio Ramos, 20, 50740-530 Recife-PE

Tel: (081) 2126 8397; (081) 2126 8930
Fax: (081) 2126 8395
E-mail: ufpebooks@edufpe.com.br
Web Site: www.ufpe.br/edufpe
Key Personnel
Dir: Maria Jose de Matos Luna
Commercial Manager: Eduardo Malta
Founded: 1955
ISBN Prefix(es): 978-85-7315

Editora da Universidade Federal do Parana (UFPR)
Rua Joao Negrao, 280, 2° andar, Centro, 80010-200 Curitiba-PR
Tel: (041) 3360 7487 *Fax:* (041) 3360 7486
E-mail: editora@ufpr.br
Web Site: www.editora.ufpr.br
Key Personnel
Dir: Gilberto de Castro
Deputy Dir: Suzete de Paula Bornatto
Editorial Coordinator: Daniele Carneiro *Tel:* (041) 3360 7490 *E-mail:* dscarneiro@gmail.com
Communications & Marketing: Michael Schaffer *Tel:* (041) 3360 7488 *E-mail:* maycom@ufpr.br
Founded: 1987
Subjects: Agriculture, Anthropology, Architecture & Interior Design, Art, Biological Sciences, Earth Sciences, Law, Library & Information Sciences, Literature, Literary Criticism, Essays, Music, Dance, Philosophy, Physical Sciences, Psychology, Psychiatry, Social Sciences, Sociology
ISBN Prefix(es): 978-85-7335; 978-85-85132

Editora Universidade Federal do Rio de Janeiro (UFRJ)+
Predio do Forum de Ciencia e Cultura Av Pasteur, 250, Praia Vermelha, 22290-902 Rio de Janeiro-RJ
Tel: (021) 2542-7646 *Fax:* (021) 2295-0346
E-mail: administrador@editora.ufrj.br
Web Site: www.editora.ufrj.br; www.ufrj.br
Founded: 1986
Subjects: Anthropology, Architecture & Interior Design, Art, Economics, Education, History, Language Arts, Linguistics, Library & Information Sciences, Management, Physical Sciences, Social Sciences, Sociology
ISBN Prefix(es): 978-85-7108

Livraria e Editora Universitaria de Direito Ltda (LEUD)
Rua Santo Amaro, 586, Bela Vista, 01315-000 Sao Paulo-SP
Tel: (011) 3105-6374 *Fax:* (011) 3104-0317
E-mail: leud@leud.com.br
Web Site: www.leud.com.br; www.editoraleud.com.br
Key Personnel
Mng Dir, Production: Armando Luiz Almeida Martins
Sales Dir: Armando des Santos Mesquita Martins
Founded: 1968
Subjects: Law
ISBN Prefix(es): 978-85-7456

Universo dos Livros Editora Ltda
Rua do Bosque, 1589, Conjunto 603/605, Barra Funda, 01136-001 Sao Paulo-SP
Tel: (011) 3392-3336
E-mail: editor@universodoslivros.com.br; relacionamento@universodoslivros.com.br; vendas@universodoslivros.com.br
Web Site: www.universodoslivros.com.br
Founded: 2006
Subjects: Biography, Memoirs, Health, Nutrition, Language Arts, Linguistics, Religion - Other, Romance, Self-Help, Technology, Culture
ISBN Prefix(es): 978-85-99187; 978-85-7930

Editora Vale das Letras Ltda
Rua Bahia, no 5129, Salto Weissbach, 89032-001 Blumenau-SC
Tel: (047) 3340-7045
E-mail: editora@valedasletras.com.br
Web Site: www.valedasletras.com.br
ISBN Prefix(es): 978-85-410

Editora Verbo Ltda
Rua Figueira, 203, 03003-000 Sao Paulo-SP
Tel: (011) 3228-9230
Founded: 1966
Subjects: Art, Education, Geography, Geology, History, Psychology, Psychiatry, Religion - Other, Social Sciences, Sociology
ISBN Prefix(es): 978-85-7230
Parent Company: Editorial Verbo SA

Verus Editora Ltda
Subsidiary of Grupo Editorial Record
Rua Benedicto Aristides Ribeiro, 41, Jd Santa Genebra II, 13084-753 Campinas-SP
E-mail: verus@veruseditora.com.br
Web Site: www.veruseditora.com.br
Founded: 2000
Subjects: Biography, Memoirs, Cookery, Education, History, Inspirational, Spirituality, Philosophy, Poetry, Psychology, Psychiatry, Religion - Other, Romance, Self-Help, Travel & Tourism, Entertainment
ISBN Prefix(es): 978-85-7686; 978-85-87795

Vestigio, *imprint of* Autentica Editora

Editora Vida Crista Ltda (Christian Life Publishing Co)+
CP 60.161, 05391-970 Sao Paulo-SP
Tel: (011) 3923-0009 *Toll Free Tel:* 800-11-5074
Fax: (011) 6647-7125
Key Personnel
Founder: Dr Alaor Leite
Chief Executive Officer: Sidney Leite
Founded: 1977
Subjects: Religion - Protestant
ISBN Prefix(es): 978-85-7163

Editora Vozes Ltda
Rua Frei Luis, 100 - Centro, 25689-900 Petropolis-RJ
Mailing Address: CP 90023, 25689-900 Petropolis-RJ
Tel: (024) 2233-9000 *Fax:* (024) 2231-4676
E-mail: editorial@vozes.com.br; vendas@vozes.com.br; marketing@vozes.com.br
Web Site: www.universovozes.com.br
Founded: 1901
Subjects: Communications, Language Arts, Linguistics, Philosophy, Psychology, Psychiatry, Public Administration, Religion - Other, Social Sciences, Sociology
ISBN Prefix(es): 978-85-326
Branch Office(s)
Rua Ourissanga, 114, 30150-200 Belo Horizonte-MG *Tel:* (031) 3048-2100 *Fax:* (031) 3048-2121 *E-mail:* vendas.04@vozes.com.br
SCLRN 704, Bloco A, Asa Norte, 70730-516 Brasilia-DF *Tel:* (061) 3326-2436 *Fax:* (061) 3326-2282 *E-mail:* vendas.09@vozes.com.br
Rua Antonio Maria Coelho, 197 A, 78005-970 Cuiaba-MT *Tel:* (065) 3623-5307 *Fax:* (065) 3623-5186 *E-mail:* vendas.54@vozes.com.br
Rua Pamphilo D'Assumpcao, 554, Reboucas, 80220-040 Curitiba-PR *Tel:* (041) 3333-9812 *Fax:* (041) 3013-7712 *E-mail:* vendas.21@vozes.com.br
Rua Jeronimo Coelho, 308, Centro, 88010-030 Florianopolis-SC *Tel:* (048) 3222-4112 *Fax:* (048) 3222-1052 *E-mail:* vendas.45@vozes.com.br
Rua Major Facundo 730, Centro, 60025-100 Fortaleza-CE *Tel:* (085) 3231-9321 *Fax:* (085) 3221-4238 *E-mail:* vendas.23@vozes.com.br

Rua Tres 291, Centro, 74023-010 Goiania-GO
Tel: (062) 3225-3077 *Fax:* (062) 3225-3994
E-mail: vendas.27@vozes.com.br
Rua Costa Azevedo, 105, Centro, 69010-230
Manaus-AM *Tel:* (092) 3232-5777 *Fax:* (092)
3233-0154 *E-mail:* varejo.61@vozes.com.br
Rua Riachuelo, 1280, Porto Alegre-RS 90010-273
Tel: (051) 3226-3911 *Fax:* (051) 3226-3710
E-mail: vendas.05@vozes.com.br
Rua do Principe, 482, Boa Vista, 50050-410
Recife-PE *Tel:* (081) 3423-4100 *Fax:* (081)
3423-7575 *E-mail:* vendas.10@vozes.com.br
Rua 7 de Setembro, 132, Centro, 20050-002 Rio
de Janeiro-RJ *Tel:* (021) 2526-8310 *Fax:* (021)
2526-8315 *E-mail:* vendas.58@vozes.com.br
Rua Carlos Gomes, 698-A, Dois de Julho,
40060-410 Salvador-BA *Tel:* (071) 3329-5466
Fax: (071) 3329-4749 *E-mail:* vendas.20@
vozes.com.br
Rua dos Trilhos, 627, Mooca, 01527-030 Sao
Paulo-SP *Tel:* (011) 2081-7944 *Fax:* (011)
2081-7940 *E-mail:* vendas.37@vozes.com.br

White Balloon Books
Imprint of Lemos Editorial
Rua Issac de Azevedo, 716, 45988-054 Teixeira
de Freitas-BA
ISBN Prefix(es): 978-85-63698
Branch Office(s)
Rheinstr 87, 1 stock, 65185 Weisbaden, Germany
Tel: (0151) 2196 0682

WVC, *imprint of* Madras Editora

Yendis Editora
Estrada das Lagrimas, 105, Bairro Jardim Sao
Caetano, 09581-300 Sao Caetano do Sul-SP
Tel: (011) 4224-9400 *Fax:* (011) 4224-9400
E-mail: marketing@yendis.com.br
Web Site: www.yendis.com.br
Founded: 2004
Subjects: Health, Nutrition, History, Literature,
Literary Criticism, Essays, Humanities
ISBN Prefix(es): 978-85-98859

Jorge Zahar Editor+
Rua Marques de Sao Vicente 99-1° andar, Gavea,
22451-041 Rio de Janeiro-RJ
Tel: (021) 2529-4750
E-mail: sac@zahar.com.br
Web Site: www.zahar.com.br
Key Personnel
Executive Dir: Mariana Zahar Ribeiro
E-mail: mariana@zahar.com.br
Manager: Isabela Santiago *E-mail:* isabela.
santiago@zahar.com.br
Founded: 1956
Subjects: Anthropology, Art, Behavioral Sciences,
Biography, Memoirs, Drama, Theater, Eco-
nomics, Education, Finance, Geography, Ge-
ology, History, Human Relations, Literature,
Literary Criticism, Essays, Management, Mar-
keting, Music, Dance, Nonfiction (General),
Philosophy, Psychology, Psychiatry, Science
(General), Social Sciences, Sociology, Cinema
ISBN Prefix(es): 978-85-7110; 978-85-85061
Number of titles published annually: 40 Print
Total Titles: 600 Print
Warehouse: Rua Cotia 35 (Rocha), 20960-
100 Rio de Janeiro-RJ *Tel:* (021) 2108-0800
Fax: (021) 2108-0809 *E-mail:* comercial@
zahar.com.br
Distribution Center: Catavento Distribuidora
de Livros SA, Rua Conselheiro Ramalho
928, Bela Vista, 01325-000 Sao Paulo-SP
Tel: (011) 3289-0811 *Fax:* (011) 3251-3756
E-mail: compras@cataventobr.com.br

Brunei

General Information

Capital: Bandar Seri Begawan
Language: Malay, English & Chinese
Religion: Predominantly Sunni Muslim
Population: 369,000
Bank Hours: 0900-1200, 1400-1500 Monday-
Friday; 0900-1100 Saturday
Shop Hours: 0730-1930 or 2000 Monday-
Saturday in Bandar Seri Begawan, Tuesday-
Sunday in Seria, Wednesday-Monday in Kuala
Belait
Currency: 100 sen = 1 Brunei dollar
Export/Import Information: No tariff on books.
No obscene literature allowed. Import licenses
not required. No exchange controls.

Brunei Press Sdn Bhd
Lot 8 & 11, Perindustrian Beribi II, Gadong BE
1118
Mailing Address: Locked Bag No 2, MPC Be-
rakas, Bandar Seri Begawan BB 3510
Tel: 2451468; 2451460 *Fax:* 2451460
E-mail: brupress@bruneipress.com.bn;
marketing@bruneipress.com.bn
Web Site: www.bruneipress.com.bn
Founded: 1953
Also offers printing, binding, colour separation,
finishing & distribution services.
Subjects: Business, Economics, Regional Inter-
ests, Technology
ISBN Prefix(es): 978-99917-32
Branch Office(s)
Unit 8B, Supasave Panaga, Lorong 14 Barat,
Seria KB 4533 *Tel:* 3334344; 3334345
Fax: 3334346
Brunei Press Sales (M) Sdn Bhd, No 8-1-6, 1st
floor, Menara Mutiara Bangsar, Jl Liku Off
Jl Bangsar, 59100 Kuala Lumpur, Malaysia
Tel: (03) 22876623 *Fax:* (03) 22870093
E-mail: brupress@tm.net.my
Brunei Press Sales (S) Pte Ltd, Pico Creative
Centre, 20 Kallang Ave, No 03-00, Singapore
339411, Singapore *Tel:* 6297 9622 *Fax:* 6297
9633 *E-mail:* brupress@singnet.com.sg

Bulgaria

General Information

Capital: Sofia
Language: Bulgarian
Religion: Bulgarian Orthodox & Islamic
Population: 8.9 million
Bank Hours: 0800-1200 Monday-Friday
Shop Hours: 0900-1230, 1300-1800 Monday-
Saturday
Currency: 100 stotinki = 1 lev
Export/Import Information: Exchange controls.
18% VAT on books.
Copyright: UCC, Berne (see Copyright Conven-
tions, pg viii)

Abagar JSC+
98 Nikola Gabrovski Str, 5000 Veliko Tarnovo
Tel: (062) 643936; (062) 647814 *Fax:* (062)
646993
E-mail: abagar@dir.bg
Web Site: www.abagar.net
Key Personnel
Executive Dir: Marian Kenarov
Founded: 1991
Membership(s): Bulgarian Book Publishers Asso-
ciation.

Subjects: Art, Education, Fiction, Health, Nu-
trition, History, Literature, Literary Criticism,
Essays, Science (General)
ISBN Prefix(es): 978-954-427
Distributed by Damian Jacob (Sofia); Hermes
(Plovdiv)
Showroom(s): 47N Tzarigradsko shose Str, Sofia

AECD, *imprint of* Agencija Za ikonomimeski
analizi i prognozi

Agencija Za ikonomimeski analizi i prognozi+
31 Aksakov Str, 1000 Sofia
Tel: (02) 98595601 *Fax:* (02) 9813358
Web Site: www.minfin.bg
Founded: 1991
Subjects: Economics
ISBN Prefix(es): 978-954-567
Imprints: AECD

Agency for Economic Analysis & Forecasting,
see Agencija Za ikonomimeski analizi i
prognozi

Aratron Publishing House+
PO Box 1587, 1000 Sofia
Tel: (02) 9807455
E-mail: aratron@mail.bg
Web Site: www.aratron.org; www.aratronbooks.
info
Founded: 1993
Specialize in New Age books.
Subjects: Astrology, Occult, Business, Health,
Nutrition, How-to, Nonfiction (General), Para-
psychology, Psychology, Psychiatry, Self-Help,
New Age
ISBN Prefix(es): 978-954-626

Bulgarski Houdozhnik Publishers+
6 Shipka St, et 1, 1504 Sofia
Fax: (02) 8467285
Key Personnel
Dir: Bouyan Filchev
Founded: 1952 (reformation 1991)
ISBN Prefix(es): 978-954-406
Subsidiaries: Union of Bulgarian Artists

Bulgarski Pisatel+
6 ti Septemvri 35, 1000 Sofia
Tel: (02) 987-35-01
E-mail: izdatelstvo_bulgarskipisatel@abv.bg
Key Personnel
Dir: Valerie Karadjinova
Publishing House of the Union of Bulgarian Writ-
ers.
Subjects: Fiction
ISBN Prefix(es): 978-954-443

Bulvest 2000 Ltd+
ul Vasil Drumev 36, 1505 Sofia
Tel: (02) 8061 300; (02) 8061 301; (02) 8061 302
Fax: (02) 8061 313
E-mail: administration@bulvest2000.com;
bulvest@bulvest2000.com
Web Site: www.bulvest.com
Key Personnel
President: Vladimir Topencharov
Founded: 1990
Subjects: Education, Fiction, Science (General)
ISBN Prefix(es): 978-954-18; 978-954-8112

Ciela Ltd Publishing House+
Blvd Vladimir Vazov 9, 1510 Sofia
Tel: (02) 90300 00 *Fax:* (02) 90301 00
E-mail: books@ciela.net
Web Site: www.ciela.bg
Key Personnel
Publishing Dir: Svetlozar Zhelev *Tel:* (02) 90300
90 *E-mail:* svetlyo@ciela.net

Editor-in-Chief: Natalia Petrova *Tel:* (02) 90300
68 *E-mail:* natalia_petrova@ciela.net
Head of Publicity: Elitsa Penova *Tel:* (02) 90300
62 *E-mail:* elica@ciela.net
Sales Manager: Borislav Gurov *Tel:* (02) 90300
26
Founded: 1991
Membership(s): Bulgarian Book Publishers Asso-
ciation.
Subjects: Accounting, Business, Economics, Edu-
cation, Fiction, Finance, Law, Medicine, Nurs-
ing, Dentistry, Nonfiction (General), Psychol-
ogy, Psychiatry, Publishing & Book Trade Ref-
erence, Technology
ISBN Prefix(es): 978-954-649
Number of titles published annually: 39 Print
Total Titles: 487 Print
Associate Companies: Ciela Consultancy, Ciela
Printing House
Distributed by New Star; Sofi-R

Colibri Publishing Group
Ul Ivan Vazov 36, 1000 Sofia
Tel: (02) 987 48 10 (off); (02) 988 87 81
E-mail: colibri@colibri.org
Web Site: www.colibri.bg
Key Personnel
Executive Dir: Zlatka Popova *E-mail:* zpopova@
colibri.bg
General Manager: Raymond Wagenstein
E-mail: rwagenstein@colibri.bg
Editor-in-Chief, English: Jechka Georgieva
E-mail: jgeorgieva@colibri.bg
Editor-in-Chief, Romance Languages: Sylvia Wa-
genstein *E-mail:* swagenstein@colibri.bg
Public Relations & Foreign Rights: Jacqueline
Wagenstein *E-mail:* jwagenstein@colibri.bg
Founded: 1990
Subjects: Crafts, Games, Hobbies, Fashion, Fic-
tion, Health, Nutrition, History, Humor, In-
spirational, Spirituality, Literature, Literary
Criticism, Essays, Nonfiction (General), Po-
etry, Psychology, Psychiatry, Travel & Tourism,
Crime, Humanities, Thrillers
ISBN Prefix(es): 978-954-529
Distributor for Abrams; Larousse; Random
House; Taschen; Thames & Hudson
Bookshop(s): 2 Dyakon Ignatiy St, 1000 Sofia
Tel: (02) 937 79 19 *Fax:* (02) 981 50 47; 57
Vasil Levski Blvd, 1000 Sofia *Tel:* (02) 981 19
12

Hristo G Danov EOOD+
ul Stojan Chalykov 1, 4025 Plovdiv
Tel: (032) 632552
Founded: 1855
Subjects: Fiction, Poetry
ISBN Prefix(es): 978-954-442

DataMap Europe Ltd+
44, Cherni Vrah Blvd, 1407 Sofia
Tel: (02) 951 54 50 *Toll Free Tel:* (0888) 492 172
Fax: (02) 951 58 24
E-mail: office@datamap.bg
Web Site: www.datamap.bg
Founded: 1991
Specialize in digital & printed maps, atlases &
catalogues.
Total Titles: 25 Print; 2 CD-ROM

Marin Drinov Academic Publishing House
Acad G Bonchev St, Bldg 6, 1113 Sofia
Tel: (02) 72 09 22; (02) 979 34 49 *Fax:* (02) 870
40 54
E-mail: baspress@abv.bg
Web Site: m-drinov.bas.bg
Key Personnel
Dir: Prof Yatchko Ivanov
Editor-in-Chief: Margarita Mihaylova *Tel:* (02) 72
24 66; (02) 979 34 41
Founded: 1869

Drinov Publishing House of the Bulgarian
Academy of Sciences.
Subjects: Science (General)
ISBN Prefix(es): 978-954-430; 978-954-322
Distribution Center: Bulgarian Book, Blvd
Serdika block 12, floor 52, 1379 Sofia *Web
Site:* www.bgbook.dir.bg

Fama Publishers+
23 Z Zerkovsky Str, 1164 Sofia
Tel: (02) 418 41 34; (02) 416 24 62
E-mail: famapublishers@famapublishers.com
Web Site: famapublishers.com
Key Personnel
Editor: Maria Koeva *E-mail:* mariakoeva@
famapublishers.com; Igor Shemtov
E-mail: igorshemtov@famapublishers.com
Founded: 1992
Subjects: History, Literature, Literary Criticism,
Essays, Poetry, Classic Literature, Contempo-
rary Literature
ISBN Prefix(es): 978-954-597
Branch Office(s)
11 Slaveikov Sq, 1000 Sofia

Gea Libris Publishing House+
PO Box 365, 1000 Sofia
Tel: (02) 9867131 *Fax:* (02) 9866900
E-mail: book@gealibris.com; info@gealibris.com
Web Site: www.gealibris.com
Key Personnel
Dir: Emil Krastev
Founded: 1991
Publish in Bulgarian, English, German & Rus-
sian.
Subjects: Animals, Pets, Biological Sciences,
Chemistry, Chemical Engineering, Crafts,
Games, Hobbies, Economics, Environmental
Studies, Fiction, Gardening, Plants, Geogra-
phy, Geology, Health, Nutrition, Mathematics,
Physical Sciences, Science (General), Botany,
Culture, Nature, Zoology
ISBN Prefix(es): 978-954-300; 978-954-8232;
978-954-9550
Total Titles: 2,000 Print
Branch Office(s)
Boucher Str No 5, Varna, Contact: Anton Apos-
tolov *Tel:* (052) 250452; (052) 824369
Bookshop(s): 52 Thessaloniki, Sofia *Tel:* (02)
4654258

Heliopol
yn Xah Kpym 7a, 1000 Sofia
Tel: (02) 9867773
E-mail: heliopol@abv.bg
Web Site: www.heliopol.com
ISBN Prefix(es): 978-954-578

Hermes Publishing House+
59 Bogomil Str, floor 3, 4000 Plovdiv
Mailing Address: PO Box 4077, 4000 Plovdiv
Tel: (032) 630 630; (032) 608 100 *Fax:* (032) 608
199
E-mail: info@hermesbooks.com
Web Site: hermesbooks.com
Key Personnel
Sales Manager: Stoyan Drinov *Tel:* (032) 608 107
E-mail: stoyan@hermesbooks.com
Founded: 1991
Membership(s): Bulgarian Book Publishers Asso-
ciation.
Subjects: Cookery, Education, Fiction, Health,
Nutrition, Nonfiction (General), Philosophy,
Romance
ISBN Prefix(es): 978-954-459; 978-954-26
Subsidiaries: Hermes Publishers
Book Club(s): Connoisseurs of the Book; Friends
of Hermes

Heron Press+
ul Oborishte 18, 1504 Sofia

Tel: (02) 9443368
Key Personnel
Contact: Ilya Vassilev Petrov
Founded: 1993
Subjects: Fiction, Geography, Geology, History,
Mathematics, Medicine, Nursing, Dentistry,
Natural History, Nonfiction (General), Physical
Sciences, Physics, Science (General)
ISBN Prefix(es): 978-954-580

Janet-45 Print & Publishing
Blvd Al Stambolijski 9, 4004 Plovdiv
Tel: (032) 609090; (032) 609099 *Fax:* (032)
677723
E-mail: books@janet45.com
Web Site: books.janet45.com
Key Personnel
Chief Executive Officer: Bozhana Apostolova
Mng Partner: Manol Peykov
Founded: 1989
ISBN Prefix(es): 978-954-491

Kibea Publishing Co+
u Lulin bl 329 ent J ap 130, 1336 Sofia
Mailing Address: PO Box 161, 1000 Sofia
Tel: (02) 980 50 63; (02) 980 01 69 *Fax:* (02)
980 46 98
E-mail: office@kibea.net
Web Site: www.kibea.net
Key Personnel
Dir: Mariana Zlatarev
Founded: 1991
Subjects: Alternative, Anthropology, Art, Astrol-
ogy, Occult, Biography, Memoirs, Cookery,
Fiction, Foreign Countries, Health, Nutrition,
History, How-to, Human Relations, Nonfiction
(General), Parapsychology, Philosophy, Poetry,
Psychology, Psychiatry, Religion - Buddhist,
Religion - Other, Self-Help
ISBN Prefix(es): 978-954-474
Total Titles: 350 Print
Bookshop(s): Kibea Books & Health Centre,
Dr G Valkovich St 2A, 1000 Sofia, Con-
tact: Maria Ignatova *Tel:* (02) 988 01 93
E-mail: bookstore@kibea.net
Book Club(s): Friends of Kibea Club

Kralica MAB (Queen Mab)
Mladost 1, bl 29A, tel B, ap 21, 1784 Sofia
Web Site: www.queenmab.eu
Key Personnel
President: Mariana Aretova
Editor-in-Chief: Dr Nikolay Aretov, PhD *Tel:* (02)
876 73 57 *E-mail:* mab@queenmab.eu
Founded: 1992
Membership(s): Bulgarian Book Association.
Subjects: Astrology, Occult, Cookery, Literature,
Literary Criticism, Essays, Mysteries, Suspense,
Parapsychology, Philosophy, Psychology, Psy-
chiatry, Theology
ISBN Prefix(es): 978-954-533
Number of titles published annually: 20 Print
Total Titles: 230 Print

Izdatelstvo Lettera (Lettera Publishers)+
62, Rhodope Str, 4000 Plovdiv
Mailing Address: PO Box 802, 4000 Plovdiv
Tel: (032) 600 941; (032) 600 943 *Fax:* (032) 600
940
E-mail: office@lettera.bg
Web Site: www.lettera.bg
Key Personnel
Owner & Manager: Nadya Ivanova Furnadjieva
Tel: (032) 600 930
Founded: 1991
Membership(s): BBA (Bulgarian Book Associ-
ation); ICC (International Certificate Confer-
ence).
Subjects: Education, English as a Second Lan-
guage, Fiction, History, Humor, Language Arts,
Linguistics, Mathematics, Medicine, Nurs-

ing, Dentistry, Nonfiction (General), Travel & Tourism
ISBN Prefix(es): 978-954-516
Showroom(s): 10 Svetoslav Terter Str, 1124 Sofia, Contact: Sashka Todorova *Tel:* (02) 944 16 07; (02) 944 14 52 *Fax:* (02) 944 14 52
E-mail: lettera_sofia@abv.bg
Bookshop(s): 10 Svetoslav Terter Str, 1124 Sofia, Contact: Sashka Todorova *Tel:* (02) 944 16 07; (02) 944 14 52 *Fax:* (02) 944 14 52
E-mail: lettera_sofia@abv.bg

LIK Izdanija+
ul Gogol 19, 1504 Sofia
Tel: (02) 943 44 00; (02) 943 47 48 *Fax:* (02) 943 44 00; (02) 943 47 48
Key Personnel
President: Liuben Kosarev
Founded: 1993
Subjects: Anthropology, Art, Biography, Memoirs, Business, Education, Health, Nutrition, History, Literature, Literary Criticism, Essays, Mathematics, Philosophy, Psychology, Psychiatry, Social Sciences, Sociology, Humanities, Parenting, Psychoanalysis
ISBN Prefix(es): 978-954-607; 978-954-8945

Litera Prima Publishing+
117 Tsarigradsko shose Blvd, 1784 Sofia
Tel: (02) 974 55 75
Key Personnel
Founder & Editor: Marin Naydenov
Founded: 1989
Subjects: Anthropology, Archaeology, Astronomy, Mysteries, Suspense, Natural History, Parapsychology, Physical Sciences, Science (General)
ISBN Prefix(es): 978-954-8163; 978-954-738

Makros 2001 - Plovdiv+
Village of Markovo, 2 Loznitsa St, 4108 Plovdiv
Tel: (032) 677845; (089) 8645424 (cell); (089) 8641484 (cell)
E-mail: makros@makros.net
Web Site: makros.net
Key Personnel
President & Owner: Georgi Stanchev Nikolov
Founded: 1991
Subjects: Art, Astronomy, Biography, Memoirs, Biological Sciences, Business, Chemistry, Chemical Engineering, Computer Science, Computers, Economics, Education, Electronics, Electrical Engineering, Geography, Geology, History, Literature, Literary Criticism, Essays, Management, Mathematics, Medicine, Nursing, Dentistry, Music, Dance, Philosophy, Physical Sciences, Physics, Psychology, Psychiatry, Science (General), Social Sciences, Sociology
ISBN Prefix(es): 978-954-561
Bookshop(s): 70 Rodopi Str, 4000 Plovdiv
Tel: (032) 642900 *Fax:* (032) 642900

Izdatelstvo Meditsina i Fizkultura EOOD
pl Slavejkov 11, et 6, 1000 Sofia
Tel: (02) 987 99 75 *Fax:* (02) 987 13 08
E-mail: medpubl@abv.bg
Web Site: www.medpubl.com
Founded: 1956
Membership(s): Bulgarian Book Association.
Subjects: Biological Sciences, Geography, Geology, Health, Nutrition, Medicine, Nursing, Dentistry, Sports, Athletics
ISBN Prefix(es): 978-954-420

Izdatelstvo Naouka i Izkoustvo OOD+
pl Slavejkov 11, et 5, 1000 Sofia
Tel: (02) 9874790; (02) 9872496 *Fax:* (02) 9872496
E-mail: nauk_izk@sigma-bg.com
Founded: 1948
Bulgarian & foreign scientific literature in the fields of philosophy, psychology, linguisitics,

history, dictionaries & language learning materials.
Subjects: Art, Business, Economics, History, Language Arts, Linguistics, Law, Mathematics, Philosophy, Physics, Psychology, Psychiatry, Science (General), Social Sciences, Sociology
ISBN Prefix(es): 978-954-02

Narodna Kultura Publishing
ul Angel Kanchev 1, 1000 Sofia
Tel: (02) 981 4739 *Fax:* (02) 981 4739
Key Personnel
Contact: Ivan Esenski
Founded: 1945
Subjects: Art, Fiction, Government, Political Science, History, Literature, Literary Criticism, Essays, Poetry, Social Sciences, Sociology, International Affairs
ISBN Prefix(es): 978-954-04

Nov Covek Publishing (New Man Publishing)+
ul Antim I 28, 1303 Sofia
Tel: (02) 9863772 (off); (02) 9863766 (orders)
E-mail: offis@novchovek.com; purchase@novchovek.com
Web Site: www.novchovek.com
Key Personnel
President: Rumen Papratilov
Founded: 1990
Produces & distributes theological, reference & sociological literature.
Membership(s): Bulgarian Book Association; International Literature Association.
Subjects: Biblical Studies, Child Care & Development, History, Human Relations, Philosophy, Psychology, Psychiatry, Social Sciences, Sociology, Theology
ISBN Prefix(es): 978-954-407

Pensoft Publishers+
Geo Milev Str, No 13a, 1111 Sofia
Tel: (02) 8704281 *Fax:* (02) 8704282
E-mail: pensoft@mbox.infotel.bg; orders@pensoft.net; info@pensoft.net
Web Site: www.pensoft.net
Key Personnel
Mng Dir: Dr Lyubomir D Penev, PhD
  E-mail: penev@pensoft.net
Editor-in-Chief: Sergei I Golovatch
  E-mail: sgolovatch@yandex.ru
Founded: 1993
Also acts as book supplier for East European books.
Subjects: Agriculture, Archaeology, Biological Sciences, Business, Earth Sciences, Environmental Studies, Finance, History, Language Arts, Linguistics, Mathematics, Natural History, Physics, Religion - Other, Science (General), Botany, Zoology
ISBN Prefix(es): 978-954-642
Number of titles published annually: 60 Print
Total Titles: 160 Print
Distributed by Coronet Books Inc (USA); Goecke & Evers Antiquariat (Germany); Kabourek; NHBS-Natural History Book Service
Distributor for Academic Publishing House-Sofia; Heron Press

Prosveta Publishing House+
2 Zemedelska Str, 1618 Sofia
Tel: (02) 8182020 *Fax:* (02) 8182019
E-mail: prosveta@prosveta.bg
Web Site: www.prosveta.bg
Key Personnel
Chairman: Joana Tomova
  Fax: joana.tomova@prosveta.bg
Dir, Marketing: Emil Mihajlov *E-mail:* emil.mihajlov@prosveta.bg
Dir, Production: Veska Popova *E-mail:* veska.popova@prosveta.bg
Editor-in-Chief: Sofia Dimitrova *E-mail:* sofia.dimitrova@prosveta.bg

Founded: 1945
Specialize in school textbooks.
Membership(s): Bulgarian Book Association.
Subjects: Education
ISBN Prefix(es): 978-954-01
Bookshop(s): 45 Dondukov, Sofia *Tel:* (02) 987 16 67; 39 Ivan Assen II Str, Sofia *Tel:* (02) 944 18 50
Warehouse: Hostile Sq, farmyard, Botevgradso shose, 1839 Sofia *Tel:* (02) 483 00 96 *Fax:* (02) 945 61 84 *E-mail:* realizacia@prosveta.bg

Prozoretz Ltd Publishing House (Izdatelsica Kushta Prozoretz)+
7 Tulovo St, 1504 Sofia
Tel: (02) 983-04-85 *Fax:* (02) 983-04-86
E-mail: office@prozoretz.com
Web Site: www.prozoretz.com
Key Personnel
Literary Rights Manager: Kaloyan Ignatovski
  E-mail: kaloyanski@abv.bg
Editor: Luboslava Ruseva
  E-mail: liuboslavaruseva17@gmail.com; Aneta Panteleeva *E-mail:* aneta.panteleeva@gmail.com; Gergana Nenovski *E-mail:* gerracheva@yahoo.com
Founded: 1991
Subjects: English as a Second Language, Fiction, Health, Nutrition, Philosophy, Poetry, Religion - Other, Self-Help
ISBN Prefix(es): 978-954-733

Regalia 6 Publishing House+
Akad Georgi Bonchev St, Bldg 8, floor 2, Apartment 220, 1113 Sofia
Tel: (02) 9793842
E-mail: regalia@abv.bg
Web Site: www.regalia.bg; www.regalia6.com/books
Founded: 1991
Publication of school aids & supplementary materials for all levels of education, compiled by the specialists in the corresponding areas.
Subjects: Biological Sciences, Career Development, Chemistry, Chemical Engineering, Computer Science, Crafts, Games, Hobbies, Education, English as a Second Language, Geography, Geology, Mathematics, Science (General)
ISBN Prefix(es): 978-954-745

Reporter Publishing Co Ltd+
Blvd Tzarigradsko Shosse 113, 1784 Sofia
Tel: (02) 975 23 82 *Fax:* (02) 975 23 84
E-mail: reporter7@abv.bg
Web Site: www.reporter-foundation.net
Key Personnel
Manager: Krum Blagov
Founded: 1990
Nonfiction & fiction Bulgarian & foreign literature, planners & calendars.
Subjects: Advertising, Biography, Memoirs, Child Care & Development, Fiction, Health, Nutrition, Nonfiction (General)
ISBN Prefix(es): 978-954-8102
Number of titles published annually: 12 Print
Total Titles: 30 Print

Sanra Book Trust
ul Vezen 14, 1421 Sofia
Tel: (02) 8659594
E-mail: sanra@abv.bg
Key Personnel
Editor: Sasho Ranguelov
Founded: 1993
Subjects: English as a Second Language
ISBN Prefix(es): 978-954-662

SIBI, see Sibi Ltd

Sibi Ltd+
4 Slaveikov Sq, 4th floor, 1000 Sofia

Tel: (02) 9870141; (02) 9814598; (02) 9873609
 Fax: (02) 9875709
E-mail: sibi@sibi.bg
Web Site: www.sibi.bg
Founded: 1990
Publishing house for legal literature with book-shops in major Bulgarian cities.
Subjects: Labor, Industrial Relations, Law, Publishing & Book Trade Reference, Science (General), Social Sciences, Sociology
ISBN Prefix(es): 978-954-8150; 978-954-730
Shipping Address: 3 Reka Osam Str, 1124 Sofia
Warehouse: 3 Reka Osam Str, 1124 Sofia
Orders to: 3 Reka Osam Str, 1124 Sofia, Contact: Svetlana Tasheva *Tel:* (07) 0017424
 E-mail: sales@sibi.bg

Slance, see Sluntse Publishing House

Slavena Ltd+
Radko Dimitriev 59A, 9018 Varna
Tel: (052) 602 465 *Fax:* (052) 603 054
E-mail: books@slavena.net
Web Site: www.slavena.net; www.nazz.bg
Key Personnel
Chief Executive Officer: Vitaly Zarkov
Manager: Nasko Yakimov
Founded: 1990
Subjects: Art, Crafts, Games, Hobbies, Economics, Education, History, Law, Literature, Literary Criticism, Essays, Science (General), Cultural Heritage; Tourism
ISBN Prefix(es): 978-954-579

Sluntse Publishing House+
11, Slaveykov Sq, 1000 Sofia
Mailing Address: PO Box 694, 1000 Sofia
Tel: (02) 988 37 97 *Fax:* (02) 987 14 05
E-mail: sluntse@dir.bg
Web Site: www.sluntse.com
Key Personnel
Mng Dir: Nadejda Kabakchieva
Founded: 1937
Subjects: Astrology, Occult, Biography, Memoirs, Child Care & Development, Education, Fiction, Foreign Countries, Gardening, Plants, Health, Nutrition, House & Home, Human Relations, Marketing, Native American Studies, Nonfiction (General), Publishing & Book Trade Reference, Romance, Beauty, Letters
ISBN Prefix(es): 978-954-8023; 978-954-742

Srebaren lav+
ul Plovdivsko pole, bl2 vhA ap3, 1756 Sofia
Tel: (02) 752298
Key Personnel
Contact: Mariya Ivanova Markovska
Founded: 1991
Subjects: Literature, Literary Criticism, Essays
ISBN Prefix(es): 978-954-571

Tangra TanNakRa Publishing House+
Subsidiary of Tangra TanNakRa All Bulgarian Foundation
PO Box 1832, 1000 Sofia
Tel: (02) 986 4419 *Fax:* (02) 986 6945
E-mail: mail@tangra-bg.org
Web Site: www.tangra-bg.org
Founded: 1999
Editing history books & textbooks; Support of research work in the field of history.
Subjects: Archaeology, Education, Government, Political Science, History, Travel & Tourism
ISBN Prefix(es): 978-954-9942; 978-954-9717; 978-954-378
Number of titles published annually: 10 Print
Total Titles: 60 Print
Distribution Center: 11, Nicolai Rakitin Str, Sofia
 Tel: (02) 943 7788; (02) 943 7782

Technica Publishing House+
Slaveikov One Sq, 1000 Sofia
Tel: (02) 987 1283 *Fax:* (02) 987 4906
E-mail: office@technica-bg.com
Web Site: www.technica-bg.com
Key Personnel
Manager: Maria Tcankova *E-mail:* upravitel@technica-bg.com
Marketing: Tereza Evtimova *Tel:* (02) 987 4936
 E-mail: sales@technica-bg.com
Founded: 1958
Subjects: Science (General)
ISBN Prefix(es): 978-954-03
Warehouse: 18 Momina Cheshma Str, 1000 Sofia
 Tel: (02) 978 3691

TEMTO+
Bul Gen Skobelev 35, ap 26, 1463 Sofia
Tel: (02) 8524-924
E-mail: temtomail@yahoo.com
Web Site: www.temto.eu
Key Personnel
Manager: Temenuga Todorova Zhivkova
Founded: 1991
This publisher has indicated that 90% of their product line is author subsidized.
Subjects: Advertising, Agriculture, Architecture & Interior Design, Computer Science, Computers, Health, Nutrition, Mathematics, Poetry, Psychology, Psychiatry, Publishing & Book Trade Reference, Programming
ISBN Prefix(es): 978-954-9566
Number of titles published annually: 8 Print

Todor Kableshkov University of Transport+
158 Geo Milev St, 1574 Sofia
Tel: (02) 9709-211 *Fax:* (02) 9709-242
E-mail: office@vtu.bg
Web Site: www.vtu.bg
Key Personnel
Deputy Editor-in-Chief: Dr Daniela Todorova
 Tel: (02) 9709-335 *E-mail:* dtodorova@vtu.bg
Editor: Dr Petar Kolev *E-mail:* petarkolev@vtu.bg
Founded: 1922
Subjects: Advertising, Behavioral Sciences, Business, Civil Engineering, Communications, Economics, Electronics, Electrical Engineering, Engineering (General), Mechanical Engineering, Transportation
ISBN Prefix(es): 978-954-12
Number of titles published annually: 45 Print
Parent Company: Ministry of Education & Science

Trud Izd kasta (TRUD Publishing House)+
47 Tsarigrasko Shose Str, 1st floor, 1124 Sofia
Tel: (02) 942 43 71; (02) 942 43 73; (02) 942 43 75; (02) 942 43 76
E-mail: sales@trud.cc; office@trud.cc
Web Site: www.trud.cc
Key Personnel
Owner: Lyubomir Pavlov
Chief Editor: Nadejda Deleva *Tel:* (02) 942 23 75
 E-mail: nadya@trud.cc
Sales Manager: Nelly Toneva *E-mail:* nelly@trud.cc
Founded: 1992
Subjects: Biography, Memoirs, Fiction, History, Humor, Mysteries, Suspense, Nonfiction (General), Western Fiction
ISBN Prefix(es): 978-954-528
Number of titles published annually: 40 Print; 1 CD-ROM; 100 Online; 10 E-Book
Total Titles: 600 Print; 5 CD-ROM; 150 Online; 10 E-Book
Parent Company: Media Holding, 119 Ekzarh Joseph, 1000 Sofia
Ultimate Parent Company: WAZ- Germany

Universitetsko Izdatelstvo 'Kliment Ochridski'
 (St Kliment Ohridski University)
30 Zlatovrah St, Lozenets District, 1164 Sofia

Tel: (02) 9308200 *Fax:* (02) 9460255
E-mail: unipress@press.uni-sofia.bg; marketing@press.uni-sofia.bg
Web Site: www.uni-sofia.bg
Key Personnel
Dir: Dimitar Radichkov *Tel:* (02) 8161601
Deputy Dir: Valya Ilieva *Tel:* (02) 8161287
Editor-in-Chief: Margarita Krumova *Tel:* (02) 8161231 *E-mail:* krumova_margy@abv.bg
Marketing: Irena Tsanova
Founded: 1986
Subjects: Science (General)
ISBN Prefix(es): 978-954-07
Bookshop(s): 15 Tsar Osvoboditel Blvd, 1504 Sofia *Tel:* (02) 9308453

Voenno Izdatelstvo (Military Publishing)
ul Ivan Vazov 12, 1080 Sofia
Tel: (02) 987 80 92
E-mail: info@vi-books.com; vi_books@abv.bg (book store)
Web Site: www.vi-books.com
Key Personnel
Manager: Dragomir Petkov *Tel:* (02) 987 39 34
 E-mail: d.petkov@vi-books.com
Administrative Dir: Valentin Nikolov *E-mail:* v.nikolov@vi-books.com
Dir, Production: Tatiana Nenkova-Levi *E-mail:* t.nenkova@vi-books.com
Editor: Georgi Rachev *E-mail:* g.rachev@vi-books.com
Advertising & Sales: Valia Kostova; Teodora Petkova
Head of Sales: Kalin Rushkov
Subjects: Fiction, History, Military Science, Psychology, Psychiatry, Social Sciences, Sociology
ISBN Prefix(es): 978-954-509

Cameroon

General Information

Capital: Yaounde
Language: French & English (officially bilingual)
Religion: Christian, Islamic, traditional
Population: 12.7 million
Bank Hours: East: 0800-1130, 1430-1630 Monday-Friday; West: 0800-1330 Monday-Friday
Shop Hours: 0800-1200, 1430-1730 (earlier closing in West) Monday-Friday; 0800-1200 Saturday
Currency: 100 centimes = 1 CFA franc
Export/Import Information: Member of Customs & Economic Union of Central Africa. Import license, entitling holder to provision for necessary foreign exchange, required if value of import is over 500,000 CFA francs.
Copyright: UCC, Berne, Florence (see Copyright Conventions, pg viii)

Centre de Litterature Evangelique, see Editions CLE

Editions CLE+
Ave Foch, face credit foncier, Agence du centre, Yaounde
Mailing Address: BP 1501, Yaounde
Tel: 222 22 35 54 *Fax:* 222 23 27 09
E-mail: editionscle@yahoo.fr
Key Personnel
Dir: Marcellin Vounda Etoa
Founded: 1962
Subjects: Drama, Theater, Fiction, How-to, Literature, Literary Criticism, Essays, Poetry, Religion - Protestant, Social Sciences, Sociology
ISBN Prefix(es): 978-2-7235; 978-9956-0

Branch Office(s)
c/o Mille Laurette Tango, BP 1256, Bafoussam
Tel: 699 53 94 78 *Fax:* 233 44 66 69
BP 13079, Douala
Distributed by CEC (Brussels); Editions ZOE (Geneva); L'Harmattan (Paris); Presence Africaine (Paris)
Distributor for CEDA (Ivory Coast); Editions Reynald Goulet (Quebec, Canada); Modulo Editeur (Quebec, Canada)

Presses Universitaires d'Afrique+
1077 rue Mballa eloumden, Bastos, Yaounde
Mailing Address: BP 8106, Yaounde
Tel: 2222-026-95 *Fax:* 2222-026-98
E-mail: contact@aes-pua.com
Web Site: www.aes-pua.com
Key Personnel
Contact: Serge Dontchueng Kouam
Founded: 1986
Membership(s): Cameroon Publishers Association.
Subjects: Economics, Education, Finance, Law, Literature, Literary Criticism, Essays, Public Administration, Social Sciences, Sociology, Theology
ISBN Prefix(es): 978-2-912086; 978-9956-444
Parent Company: L'Africaine D'Edition et de Services (AES)
Distributed by Editions CLE (West Africa); Librarie de France

Chile

General Information

Capital: Santiago
Language: Spanish
Religion: Roman Catholic
Population: 14 million
Bank Hours: 0900-1400 Monday-Friday
Shop Hours: 1000-1900 Monday-Friday; 1000-1800 Saturday-Sunday
Currency: 100 centavos = 1 Chilean peso
Export/Import Information: Member of Latin American Integration Association (ALADI). 19% VAT on books, 11% tariff.
Copyright: UCC, Berne, Buenos Aires (see Copyright Conventions, pg viii)

Bibliografica Internacional Ltda
Monjitas 308, Casillas 1371, 8320113 Santiago
Tel: (02) 2639-4057 *Fax:* (02) 2639-7693
Web Site: www.bibliografica.com
Key Personnel
Dir: Ana Maria Trepat Miranda; Jaime Nino Trepat; Norgia Nino Trepat
Commercial Manager: Paula Soto Landa
Founded: 1958
Subjects: Architecture & Interior Design, Art, Business, Computers, Cookery, Economics, Education, Engineering (General), Management, Music, Dance, Technology
ISBN Prefix(es): 978-956-7240; 978-956-8090

Cesoc Ltda - Centro de Estudios Sociales+
Carlos Autunez No 1843, dept 215, Providencia, Santiago
Tel: (02) 501 89 01
E-mail: contacto@cesoc.cl
Web Site: www.cesoc.cl
Key Personnel
Manager: Julio Silva Solar
Founded: 1983
Subjects: Biography, Memoirs, Government, Political Science, History, Nonfiction (General), Poetry

ISBN Prefix(es): 978-956-211
U.S. Office(s): Para Textor, 6 Avery St, Saratoga Springs, NY 12866, United States *Tel:* 518-587-3774 *Fax:* 518-581-1859

Ediciones Cieplan
Dag Hammarskjoeld 3269, Piso 3, Vitacura, 7630412 Santiago
Tel: (02) 2796 56 60
E-mail: contacto@cieplan.org
Web Site: www.cieplan.cl
Key Personnel
Administration & Finance: Jorge Olave
   E-mail: jorge.olave@cieplan.org
Coordinator, Communications & Press: Cecilia Barria *E-mail:* cecilia.barria@cieplan.org
Founded: 1976
Subjects: Developing Countries, Economics, Public Administration, Technology
ISBN Prefix(es): 978-956-204

Corporacion de Promocion Universitaria (CPU)
Almirante Pastene 7, Depto 5, 7500535 Providencia, Santiago
Tel: (02) 22369612; (02) 22369329; (02) 23468320 *Fax:* (02) 22369008
E-mail: cpu@cpu.cl
Web Site: www.cpu.cl
Founded: 1968
Subjects: Education, Science (General), Technology
ISBN Prefix(es): 978-956-229

CPU, see Corporacion de Promocion Universitaria (CPU)

Editorial Cuarto Propio
Valenzuela Castillo 990, 7500719 Providencia, Santiago
Tel: (02) 279 265 18 *Fax:* (02) 279 265 20
E-mail: produccioneditorial@tie.cl
Web Site: www.cuartopropio.cl
Key Personnel
Editor: Paloma Bravo
   E-mail: palomacuartopropio@gmail.com
Founded: 1984
Membership(s): Chilean Chamber of the Book.
Subjects: Drama, Theater, Fiction, Government, Political Science, Literature, Literary Criticism, Essays, Nonfiction (General), Philosophy, Poetry, Women's Studies, Anthologies
ISBN Prefix(es): 978-956-260
Distributed by Paratextos (USA)
Distributor for Editorial Biblos (Argentina); Editorial La Marca (Argentina)
Foreign Rep(s): La Asociacion Latinoamericana de Libreria SA de CV (USA); El Libro de fuentes de America Latina Inc (USA); Ideal Exterior del Libro Inc (USA); Libreria Otra Lluvia (Argentina)
Bookshop(s): Libros sin Frontera, PO Box 2085, Olympia, WA 98507-2085, United States
Orders to: Paratextos, 6 Avery St, Saratoga Springs, NY 12866, United States, Contact: Patricia Rubio *Tel:* 518-581-1859
   E-mail: prubio@scottskidmore.edu (USA)

Editorial Cuatro Vientos (Cuatro Vientos Publishing House)+
Maturana 19, 8340608 Santiago Centro
Tel: (02) 2672 9226; (02) 2695 4477 *Fax:* (02) 2673 2153
E-mail: editorial@cuatrovientos.cl
Web Site: www.cuatrovientos.cl
Key Personnel
Founder & Manager: Dr Francisco Huneeus
Founded: 1974
Membership(s): The Chilean Association of Publishers.

Subjects: Drama, Theater, Economics, Education, Human Relations, Inspirational, Spirituality, Music, Dance, Nonfiction (General), Philosophy, Psychology, Psychiatry, Sports, Athletics, Ecology, Sexuality
ISBN Prefix(es): 978-84-89333; 978-956-242
Number of titles published annually: 12 Print
Total Titles: 120 Print
Distributed by Edin (Argentina); Editorial Andres Bello (Chile); Editorial Universitaria (Chile)
Distributor for Be-Uve-Drais Editores (Chile); Luz De Luna (Argentina); Editorial Nuevo Extremo (Argentina); Editorial Troquel (Argentina)

EDEVAL
Imprint of University of Valparaiso School of Law
Escuela de Derecho, Facultad de Derecho y Ciencias Sociales, Av Errazuriz 2120, 2362736 Valparaiso
Tel: (032) 2507014; (032) 2507015 *Fax:* (032) 2507046
E-mail: direccion.derecho@uv.cl
Web Site: www.derechouv.cl
Founded: 1961
Subjects: Criminology, Economics, Government, Political Science, History, Human Relations, Labor, Industrial Relations, Law, Maritime, Philosophy, Publishing & Book Trade Reference, Social Sciences, Sociology
ISBN Prefix(es): 978-956-200

Ediciones Mil Hojas Ltda (Editions Thousand Leaves)
Antonio Varas 1480, Providencia, Santiago
Tel: (02) 22743172
Key Personnel
Contact: Manuel Parrao Gacitua
   E-mail: manuelparrao@milhojas.cl
Founded: 1991
Subjects: Anthropology, Architecture & Interior Design, Art, Astrology, Occult, Education, Health, Nutrition, Management, Medicine, Nursing, Dentistry, Psychology, Psychiatry, Religion - Other, Science (General), Self-Help, Social Sciences, Sociology, Sports, Athletics, Travel & Tourism, Beauty
ISBN Prefix(es): 978-956-7741
Subsidiaries: Abanico Libros Ltda

IGM, see Instituto Geografico Militar (IGM)

Instituto Geografico Militar (IGM)
Nueva Santa Isabel 1640, Santiago
Tel: (02) 24109300; (02) 24104109 *Fax:* (02) 24109320; (02) 24109430
E-mail: ventas@igm.cl
Web Site: www.igm.cl
Key Personnel
Dir: Colonel Rony Jara Lecanda
Founded: 1992
Specialized in cartography & topography of national territory.
Subjects: Earth Sciences, Geography, Geology
ISBN Prefix(es): 978-956-202
Total Titles: 30 Print; 2 CD-ROM

Libertad SA
Jorge Alessandri N° 101, Parque Industrial de La Reina, Santiago
Tel: (02) 28160700
E-mail: liber@libertadsa.cl; ventas@libertadsa.cl
Web Site: www.libertadsa.cl
Founded: 1967
Subjects: Art, Crafts, Games, Hobbies, Mathematics
ISBN Prefix(es): 978-956-7348

Editorial Mediterraneo Ltda+
Av Andres Bello Nº 1587-1591, 7500031 Providencia, Santiago
Tel: (02) 2351 0600; (02) 2351 0606 *Fax:* (02) 2351 0644
E-mail: ventas@mediterraneo.cl; contacto@mediterraneo.cl
Web Site: www.mediterraneo.cl
Key Personnel
President: Ramon Alvarez Minder
Founded: 1981
Membership(s): Chilean Book Association.
Subjects: Medicine, Nursing, Dentistry, Psychology, Psychiatry
ISBN Prefix(es): 978-956-220
Foreign Rep(s): Cuadrado-Libros Medicos (Uruguay); Edidac SA (Ecuador); Elsevier Espana SL (Spain); Fundacion del Libro Universitario-Libun (Peru); Libreria Gonvill SA de CV (Mexico); Editorial El Manual Moderno Ltda (Colombia); Editorial El Manual Moderno SA de CV (Mexico); Meditec (Panama); Ediciones Tecnicas Paraguayas SRL (Paraguay)

Editorial Metales Pesados
Jose Miguel de la Barra Nº 460, 8320110 Santiago
Tel: (02) 26387597
E-mail: mpesados@metalespesados.cl
Web Site: www.metalespesados.cl
Subjects: Art, Literature, Literary Criticism, Essays, Religion - Other, Science (General)
ISBN Prefix(es): 978-956-8415

Museo Chileno de Arte Precolombino
Bandera 361, 8320298 Santiago
Tel: (02) 2928 1500; (02) 2928 1510; (02) 2928 1522 *Fax:* (02) 2697 2779
E-mail: mmarin@museoprecolombino.cl
Web Site: www.precolombino.cl
Key Personnel
Public Relations: Luisa Eyzaguirre
  E-mail: leyzaguirre@museoprecolombino.cl
Specialize in pre-Colombian art.
Subjects: Archaeology, Art
ISBN Prefix(es): 978-84-89332; 978-956-243

Nadar Ediciones Ltda
Av Salvadore 1319, 7501355 Santiago
Tel: (09) 745 69 24
E-mail: contacto@nadarediciones.cl
Web Site: nadarediciones.cl
Key Personnel
Editorial Dir: Diego Mellado
Administration: David Bascur
Founded: 2014
Subjects: Anthropology, Education, Geography, Geology, Literature, Literary Criticism, Essays, Philosophy
ISBN Prefix(es): 978-956-9552

Grupo Editorial Norma Chile
Av Monjitas 527, piso 17, Santiago
Tel: (02) 731 7500 *Fax:* (02) 632 2079
E-mail: servicliente@norma.com
Subjects: Art, Business, Crafts, Games, Hobbies, Health, Nutrition, Literature, Literary Criticism, Essays, Management, Marketing, Photography, Science (General), Science Fiction, Fantasy, Self-Help, Travel & Tourism, Family
ISBN Prefix(es): 978-956-7250; 978-956-300
Parent Company: Carvajal SA

Editora Nueva Generacion+
Via Gris 9425, Vitacura, Santiago
Tel: (02) 2183974 *Fax:* (02) 2182281
Founded: 1982
Subjects: Cookery, Human Relations, Humor, Social Sciences, Sociology
ISBN Prefix(es): 978-956-226

Editorial Nueva Patris S A+
Jose Manuel Infante 132, 7500641 Providencia, Santiago
Tel: (02) 22351343 *Fax:* (02) 22358674
E-mail: gerencia@patris.cl
Web Site: www.patris.cl
Founded: 1982
Subjects: Inspirational, Spirituality, Religion - Other, Self-Development
ISBN Prefix(es): 978-956-246
Distributor for Edit Patris (Argentina)
Bookshop(s): Libreria Patris (Nazareth), Providencia, Santiago

Origo Ediciones
Alonso de Ovalle 748, 8330169 Santiago
Tel: (02) 2480 9800
E-mail: info@origo.cl
Web Site: www.origo.cl
Founded: 2000
Subjects: Art, Cookery, Geography, Geology, Wine & Spirits
ISBN Prefix(es): 978-956-8077

Paulinas OTEC Ltda
Ave Colombia 7648, 8240590 La Florida, Santiago
Tel: (02) 2255 07 02
E-mail: libreriavirtual@paulinas.cl; inquietudvocacional@gmail.com
Web Site: www.paulinas.cl
Key Personnel
Dir: Zoila Guzman Vega; Veronica Pinto Pasten; Carlos Pino
Founded: 1948
Subjects: Religion - Catholic, Theology
ISBN Prefix(es): 978-956-7433
Bookshop(s): Libreria San Pablo; Centro Catequistico, Cienfuegos 60, Casilla, Santiago
Orders to: Centro Catequistico, Cienfuegos 60, Casilla, Santiago *Tel:* (02) 26964650 *Fax:* (02) 26990327

Pehuen Editores SA+
Brown Norte 417, 7790670 Nunoa, Santiago
Tel: (02) 27957133
E-mail: editorial@pehuen.cl
Web Site: www.pehuen.cl
Key Personnel
Dir: Sebastian Barros Cerda
  E-mail: sebastianbarros@pehuen.cl
Founded: 1983
Subjects: Biography, Memoirs, Literature, Literary Criticism, Essays, Philosophy, Poetry, Social Sciences, Sociology
ISBN Prefix(es): 978-956-16
Subsidiaries: Temuco

Penguin Random House Grupo Editorial
Merced 280, Piso 6º, Santiago
Tel: (02) 782-8200
Web Site: www.megustaleer.cl
Key Personnel
Sales Manager: Sebastian Rodriguez-Pena
  E-mail: srodriguez-pena@rhm.cl
Subjects: Art, Education, Fiction, Government, Political Science, Mysteries, Suspense, Romance
Parent Company: Penguin Random House

Editorial Planeta Chilena SA+
Member of Grupo Planeta
Av Andres Bello 2115, Piso 8, 7500000 Providencia, Santiago
Tel: (02) 26522927 *Fax:* (02) 26522912
Web Site: www.editorialplaneta.cl
Founded: 1968
Subjects: Biography, Memoirs, Fiction, History, Journalism, Literature, Literary Criticism, Essays, Nonfiction (General), Culture, Entertainment, News

ISBN Prefix(es): 978-956-247
Subsidiaries: Inversiones Planeta SA

Publicaciones Lo Castillo SA
Cerro Colorado 5240, Torre 2, Piso 8, Las Condes, 7560995 Santiago
Tel: (02) 27514800
E-mail: contacto@plc.cl
Web Site: www.plc.cl
Key Personnel
Dir: Maria Olga Delpiano
Founded: 1982
Subjects: Education, House & Home, Journalism, Travel & Tourism
ISBN Prefix(es): 978-956-237
Imprints: Revista DATO

Publicaciones Nuevo Extremo SA
Bombero A Ossa 1067, 8320245 Santiago
Tel: (02) 6979749
E-mail: publicacionesnextremo@tie.cl
Founded: 1981
Subjects: Art, Biography, Memoirs, Education, History, Literature, Literary Criticism, Essays, Philosophy, Psychology, Psychiatry, Religion - Other, Theology
ISBN Prefix(es): 978-956-7063; 978-956-2170

Random House Mondadori, see Penguin Random House Grupo Editorial

Red Internacional Del Libro Ltda (RIL Editores)+
Los Leones 2258, 7511055 Providencia, Santiago
Tel: (02) 22238100 *Fax:* (02) 22238100
E-mail: ril@rileditores.com; comunicacions@rileditores.com; ventas@rileditores.com
Web Site: www.rileditores.com
Key Personnel
Publisher: Daniel Calabrese *E-mail:* dcalabrese@rileditores.com; Eleonora Finkelstein
  E-mail: efinkelstein@rileditores.com
Public Relations & Marketing: Luisa Jaimovich
Distribution Bookstores: Emilio Campos
Founded: 1991
Subjects: Anthropology, Drama, Theater, Education, Fiction, History, Literature, Literary Criticism, Essays, Philosophy, Poetry, Social Sciences, Sociology, Academic
ISBN Prefix(es): 978-956-284; 978-956-7159

Ediciones Rehue Ltda
Centro Ecumenico Diego de Medellin, Argomedo 40, 8330398 Santiago
Tel: (02) 26341804; (02) 26344653 *Fax:* (02) 26341804
E-mail: secretaria@cedmchile.org
Web Site: www.diegodemedellin.cl
Subjects: Theology
ISBN Prefix(es): 978-956-228

Revista DATO, *imprint of* Publicaciones Lo Castillo SA

RIL Editores, see Red Internacional Del Libro Ltda (RIL Editores)

J C Saez Editor+
Mac Iver 125, Oficina 1601, 8320218 Santiago
Tel: (02) 26333239
E-mail: jcsaezeditor@gmail.com
Web Site: www.jcsaezeditor.blogspot.com
Key Personnel
Dir General: Juan Carlos Saez
Founded: 2002
Subjects: Art, Biological Sciences, Drama, Theater, Economics, Education, Fiction, Literature, Literary Criticism, Essays, Management, Music, Dance, Poetry, Social Sciences, Sociology, Comics

ISBN Prefix(es): 978-956-7802; 978-956-306
Foreign Rep(s): Ediciones Granica (Argentina, Spain); Ediciones Granica Mexico de CV (Mexico)

Editorial Texido SA+
Manuel Antonio Tocornal 1487, Santiago
Tel: (02) 5555534; (02) 5555544 *Fax:* (02) 5555466
Founded: 1969
Subjects: Gardening, Plants, Human Relations, Nonfiction (General)
ISBN Prefix(es): 978-956-273
Associate Companies: Comercial Distribuidora Librimundi Ltda; Altima Ltda

Ediciones UC, see Ediciones Universidad Catolica de Chile

UFRO Editions, see Ediciones Universidad de la Frontera

Ediciones Universidad Catolica de Chile+
Alameda 390, piso 3, Santiago
Tel: (02) 2354 2417; (02) 2345 6544
E-mail: editaledicionesuc@uc.cl; edicionesuc@uc.cl
Web Site: ediciones.uc.cl
Key Personnel
Dir: Maria Angelica Zegers Vial
    E-mail: mazegers@uc.cl
Mng Editor: Patricia Corona *E-mail:* pcorona@uc.cl
Founded: 1975
Also publishes preparation manuals for university entrance examinations.
50% of titles published are university textbooks & 50% all reader.
Subjects: Anthropology, Art, Biological Sciences, Chemistry, Chemical Engineering, Economics, Education, Engineering (General), Environmental Studies, History, Law, Literature, Literary Criticism, Essays, Philosophy, Poetry, Psychology, Psychiatry, Religion - Other, Science (General), Social Sciences, Sociology, Agronomy, Social Work
ISBN Prefix(es): 978-956-14
Number of titles published annually: 55 Print
Total Titles: 600 Print
Foreign Rep(s): Alfaomega Grupo Editor S A de C V (Mexico); Apuntes Libro SH (Argentina); Aquileo Libros (Uruguay); Libreria Cientifica SA (Peru); Jose Dibarbera (Argentina); Dolmen Ediciones SA (Uruguay); Edarsi-Milton Arias Larenas (Ecuador); Fausto SRL (Paraguay); Vidal Marquez Flores (Bolivia); Grupo Editor SA de CV (Mexico); Distribuidora Lianed SA (Panama); Manuel Zalazar Principe (Peru); Editiorial Nueva Decada-End (Costa Rica)
Bookshop(s): Libreria UC Campus San Joaquin, Av Vicuna Mackenna 4860, Santiago *Tel:* (02) 2354 5305 *E-mail:* libreriasuc@uc.cl; Libreria UC del Centro de Extension, Alameda 390, primer Piso, Santiago *Tel:* (02) 2354 6524 *E-mail:* liberiasuc@uc.cl; Libreria UC Campus Oriente, Av Jaime Guzman Errazuriz 3300, Santiago *Tel:* (02) 2354 5153 *E-mail:* liberiasuc@uc.cl; Libreria UC Lo Contador, Av El Comendador 1916, Santiago *Tel:* (02) 2354 5521; Libreria UC Derecho, Alameda 340, Santiago *Tel:* (02) 2354 1829; Libreria UC Villarica, Calle O'Higgins 501, Villarica *Tel:* (045) 2411830

Ediciones Universidad de la Frontera
Av Arturo Prat 321, 4790888 Temuco
Tel: (045) 2592117
Web Site: www.extension.ufro.cl
Key Personnel
Coordinator: Luis Alberto Abarzua Guzman
    E-mail: luis.abarzua@ufrontera.cl
ISBN Prefix(es): 978-956-236

Editorial Universitaria+
Av Libertador Bernardo O'Higgins 1050, Santiago
Tel: (02) 2896 89 60 *Fax:* (02) 2896 89 69
E-mail: comunicaciones@universitaria.cl
Web Site: www.universitaria.cl
Key Personnel
General Manager: Jose Santiago Arellano
Founded: 1947
Subjects: Art, Drama, Theater, Education, Literature, Literary Criticism, Essays, Medicine, Nursing, Dentistry, Music, Dance, Philosophy, Poetry, Psychology, Psychiatry, Science (General), Social Sciences, Sociology, Humanities
ISBN Prefix(es): 978-84-8340; 978-956-11
Subsidiaries: Talleres Graficos; Texto Libro
Distributed by Axius (Argentina); Ediciones Coliguee (Argentina); Contemporanea de Ediciones (Venezuela); Ericiencia (Ecuador); Librerias Faustos (Argentina); Maria Ester Garcia (Paraguay); Zulema Medina (Uruguay)

Ediciones Universitarias de Valparaiso SA+
Calle Doce de Febrero 187, Casilla 1415, 2340026 Valparaiso
Tel: (032) 2227 30 87 *Fax:* (032) 2227 34 29
E-mail: euvsa@ucv.cl
Web Site: www.euv.cl
Key Personnel
Manager: Maria Teresa Vega Segovia
Marketing & Finance: Carla Martinez Leon
Founded: 1970
Subjects: Art, Education, Engineering (General), History, Law, Literature, Literary Criticism, Essays, Music, Dance, Philosophy, Science (General), Social Sciences, Sociology, Technology
ISBN Prefix(es): 978-956-17
Parent Company: Pontificia Universidad Catolica de Valparaiso
Branch Office(s)
Moneda 673 - 8 piso, Santiago

Editorial UV
Av Errazuriz 1108, 2361910 Valparaiso
Tel: (032) 2507652; (032) 2507645; (032) 2507643
E-mail: editorial@uv.cl
Web Site: editorial.uv.cl
Founded: 1991
Subjects: Poetry
ISBN Prefix(es): 978-956-214
Distribution Center: La Komuna, Pedro Leon Ugalde 1433, 8360288, Santiago *Tel:* (022) 5441234 *E-mail:* contacto@lakomuna.cl

Empresa Editora Zig-Zag SA+
Los Conquistadores 1700, Piso 10, 7520282 Providencia, Santiago
Tel: (02) 2810 7400 *Fax:* (02) 2810 7452
E-mail: contacto@zigzag.cl
Web Site: www.zigzag.cl
Key Personnel
Mng Editor: Jose Manuel Zanartu
Founded: 1905
Distribuidor en Chile de otros sellos editoriales.
Subjects: Cookery, Education, Literature, Literary Criticism, Essays, Self-Help
ISBN Prefix(es): 978-956-12
Parent Company: Grupo Educaria
Distributor for Aique; Editorial Albatros (Argentina); Anaya; Editorial Bonum; Ediciones Continente; Editorial iamique; Longseller Editions; Macmillan; MP Ediciones; Mundo Cartografico; Una Luna; Ediciones VerEdit; Vergara & Reba Editores
Showroom(s): Compania 2752, Santiago
Orders to: Compania 2752, Santiago

China

General Information

Capital: Beijing
Language: Principally Northern Chinese (Mandarin). Local dialects spoken in the south & southeast
Religion: Confucianism, Buddhism & Daoism with small Muslim & Christian minorities
Population: 1.2 billion
Shop Hours: Generally 0900-1900 every day
Currency: 100 fen = 10 jiao = 1 yuan
Copyright: UCC, Berne (see Copyright Conventions, pg viii)

Agricultural Publishing House, see China Agriculture Press

Anhui Children's Publishing House (Anhui Shaoer Chubanshe)
11-12F, Chuban Chuanmei Guangchang, Feicui Rd, No 1118, Zhengwu Wenhua Xinqu, Hefei, Anhui Province 230071
Tel: (0551) 3533566 *Fax:* (0551) 3533566
Web Site: www.ahse.cn
Key Personnel
Rights: Ms Hongxia Gu *E-mail:* ahsegu@gmail.com; Ms Jia Rui *E-mail:* ahserui@gmail.com; Ms Li Wang *E-mail:* ahsewl@gmail.com
Founded: 1984
Publishes a wide range of quality books created to uplift, inspire & entertain children of all ages.
Subjects: Child Care & Development, Crafts, Games, Hobbies, Fiction, Literature, Literary Criticism, Essays, Nonfiction (General)
ISBN Prefix(es): 978-7-5397
Number of titles published annually: 400 Print
Total Titles: 4,420 Print
Parent Company: Time Publishing & Media Co Ltd
Ultimate Parent Company: Anhui Publishing Group

Anhui People Publishing House (Anhui Renmin Chubanshe)+
Publishing & Media Plaza, No 1118 Sheng Quan Rd, Hefei, Anhui Province 230071
Tel: (0551) 63533112; (0551) 63533114
Key Personnel
President: Zhengyi Hu
Founded: 1952
Subjects: Accounting, Advertising, Behavioral Sciences, Economics, Government, Political Science, History, Law, Philosophy, Social Sciences, Sociology
ISBN Prefix(es): 978-7-212
Parent Company: Time Publishing & Media Co Ltd

Artpower International Publishing Co Ltd (Yili Guoji Chuban Youxian Gongsi)
G009, 17F, Bldg 807-808, Yimao Zhongxin, Meiyuanlu Rd, Luohu District, Shenzhen 518048
Tel: (0755) 82913355
E-mail: artpower@artpower.com.cn; press@artpower.com.cn; editor@artpower.com.cn
Web Site: www.artpower.com.cn
Founded: 2004
Subjects: Architecture & Interior Design, Art, Graphic Design
ISBN Prefix(es): 978-988-17684; 978-988-18893
Branch Office(s)
21/F, Skyline Commercial Centre, 71-77 Wing Lok St, Sheung Wan, Hong Kong *Tel:* 3184 0676 *Fax:* 2543 2396

Baihuazhou Literature & Art Publishing House Co Ltd (Baihuazhou Wenyi Chubanshe Youxian Zeren Gongsi)
9F Lou, A Zuo, Bonengzhongxin, No 898, Shimaolu Rd, Honggutan District, Nanchang, Jiangxi 330038
Tel: (0791) 6894790 *Fax:* (0791) 6894790
E-mail: bhzwy0791@163.com
Web Site: www.bhzwy.com
Founded: 1990
Subjects: Art, Fiction, Literature, Literary Criticism, Essays, Poetry, Art & Literature Theory, Prose, Satire
ISBN Prefix(es): 978-7-80742

Beijing Arts & Photography Publishing House (Beijing Meishu Sheying Chubanshe)+
No 6 Beisanhuan Zhonglu, Beijing 100120
Tel: (010) 58572216; (010) 58572600 *Fax:* (010) 58572220
Web Site: www.bph.com.cn; www.bphg.com.cn
Key Personnel
Chairman: Zhixian Zhong
General Manager: Fen Qiao
Editor-in-Chief: Zhong Qu
Founded: 1983
Subjects: Art, Photography, Regional Interests
ISBN Prefix(es): 978-7-80501
Parent Company: Beijing Publishing House Group

Beijing Children & Juvenile Publishing House (Beijing Shaonian Ertong Chubanshe)+
No 6 Beisanhuan Zhonglu, Beijing 100120
Tel: (010) 58572216; (010) 58572600 *Fax:* (010) 58572220
E-mail: xiongyn@bphg.com.cn
Web Site: www.bph.com.cn; www.bphg.com.cn
Key Personnel
Chairman: Zhixian Zhong
General Manager: Fen Qiao
Editor-in-Chief: Zhong Qu
Founded: 1983
Subjects: Child Care & Development, Education, Literature, Literary Criticism, Essays, Self-Help, Cartoons, Classics, Family
ISBN Prefix(es): 978-7-5301
Parent Company: Beijing Publishing House Group

Beijing Education Publishing House (Beijing Jiaoyu Chubanshe)+
No 6 Beisanhuan Zhonglu, Beijing 100120
Tel: (010) 58572216; (010) 58572253 *Fax:* (010) 58572220
E-mail: bjkgedu@163.com
Web Site: www.bjkgedu.com; www.bphg.com.cn; www.bph.com.cn
Founded: 1983
Subjects: Education
ISBN Prefix(es): 978-7-5303
Parent Company: Beijing Publishing House Group

Beijing Fine Arts Publishing House (Beijing Gongyi Meishu Chubanshe Youxian Zeren Gongsi)
No 16 Hepingli 7 Qu, Dongcheng District, Beijing 100013
Tel: (010) 84255105; (010) 84257032 *Fax:* (010) 84255105
E-mail: gms0000@126.com
Web Site: www.gmcbs.cn
Key Personnel
Contact: Gaochao Chen
Founded: 1985
Subjects: Art
ISBN Prefix(es): 978-7-80526
Subsidiaries: Beijing Stars Advertisement Co

Beijing Normal University Press
No 19 Xinjiekoudajie, Haidian District, Beijing 100875
Tel: (010) 58808015 *Fax:* (010) 58806196; (010) 58807664
Web Site: www.bnup.com
Key Personnel
President: Lv Jiansheng
Vice President, Deputy Editor: Ma Zhaoyang
Editor-in-Chief: Ye Zi
Founded: 1980
Subjects: Education, Language Arts, Linguistics, Psychology, Psychiatry, Humanities, Natural Science
ISBN Prefix(es): 978-7-303; 978-7-900649

Beijing Publishing House (Beijing Chubanshe)+
No 6 Beisanhuan Zhonglu, Beijing 100120
Tel: (010) 58572216; (010) 58572600 *Fax:* (010) 58572220
Web Site: www.bph.com.cn; www.bphg.com.cn
Key Personnel
Chairman: Zhixian Zhong
General Manager: Fen Qiao
Editor-in-Chief: Zhong Qu
Founded: 1956
Subjects: Agriculture, Antiques, Architecture & Interior Design, Art, Behavioral Sciences, Biography, Memoirs, Business, Child Care & Development, Computer Science, Cookery, Drama, Theater, Economics, Education, Engineering (General), English as a Second Language, Fiction, Finance, History, How-to, Human Relations, Language Arts, Linguistics, Law, Literature, Literary Criticism, Essays, Management, Marketing, Medicine, Nursing, Dentistry, Nonfiction (General), Philosophy, Physics, Poetry, Science (General), Self-Help, Social Sciences, Sociology, Western Fiction, Women's Studies
ISBN Prefix(es): 978-7-200

Beijing University Press, see Peking University Press

Beijing World Publishing Corp (BWPC) (Shijie Tushu Chuban Gongsi)+
137 Chaoneidajie, Beijing 100010
Tel: (010) 64015659; (010) 64073770; (010) 64015580
Web Site: www.wpcbj.com.cn
Founded: 1986
Subjects: Language Arts, Linguistics, Social Sciences, Sociology, Technology
ISBN Prefix(es): 978-7-5062

CABP, see China Architecture & Building Press

CAMG, see China Aviation Media Group (CAMG)

CBPH, see China Braille Publishing House

Chemical Industry Press (Huaxue Gongye Chubanshe)+
No 13 Qingnianhu South St, Dongcheng District, Beijing 100011
Tel: (010) 64518888; (010) 64519478; (010) 64519483; (010) 64519685 *Fax:* (010) 64519686; (010) 64519392
E-mail: rights@cip.com.cn; wssd@cip.com.cn; cipedu@cip.com.cn
Web Site: www.cip.com.cn
Key Personnel
Manager: Xu Zhou
Founded: 1953
Subjects: Agriculture, Biological Sciences, Chemistry, Chemical Engineering, Civil Engineering, Communications, Education, Electronics, Electrical Engineering, Energy, Engineering (General), Environmental Studies, Health, Nutrition,

Mechanical Engineering, Medicine, Nursing, Dentistry, Technology, Transportation, Computer Technology, Pharmacy, Safety
ISBN Prefix(es): 978-7-5025
Number of titles published annually: 1,000 Print
Total Titles: 10,000 Print
Divisions: Beijing Progress Periodicals; Biology & Pharmacy Publishing Department; Chemical Technology & Material Publishing Department; Computer Technology Publishing Department; Education Publishing Department; Environment & Architecture Publishing Department; Machinery & Electrical Engineering Publishing Department; Popular Science & Medical Publishing Department
Bookshop(s): Chemical Bookstore

Chengdu Cartographic Publishing House (Chengdu Ditu Chubanshe)+
One Jianshe Rd, Longquanyi District, Chengdu, Sichuan 610100
Tel: (028) 84884820; (028) 84884916 *Fax:* (028) 84884820
Web Site: www.ccph-map.com
Founded: 1984
Membership(s): Sichuan News Publishing Bureau; Sichuan Surveying & Mapping Bureau.
Subjects: Advertising, Communications, Computer Science, Earth Sciences, Education, Foreign Countries, Geography, Geology, Travel & Tourism
ISBN Prefix(es): 978-7-80544; 978-7-80704
Distributor for China Cartography Publishing House
Bookshop(s): 198 Renmin Beilu Rd, 2nd Section, Wholesale Dept, Chengdu, Sichuan *Tel:* (028) 83191070

China Agriculture Press (Zhongguo Nongye Chubanshe)+
18, Maizidian St, Chaoyang District, Beijing 100125
Tel: (010) 65083260; (010) 59194918; (010) 59191580
E-mail: capassistant@126.com
Web Site: www.ccap.com.cn
Key Personnel
President: Zengsheng Liu
Editor-in-Chief: Huimin Yuan
Founded: 1958
Specialize in agricultural, scientific & technological books.
Subjects: Agriculture, Animals, Pets, Biological Sciences, Gardening, Plants, Technology, Veterinary Science
ISBN Prefix(es): 978-7-109
Subsidiaries: Rural Readings Press

China Architecture & Building Press (Zhongguo Jianzhu Gongye Chubanshe)+
Affiliate of Ministry of Housing & Urban-Rural Development of the People's Republic of China
Baiwanzhuang, Beijing 100037
Tel: (010) 58337142; (010) 58337147 *Fax:* (010) 58337413
E-mail: dn.cabp@gmail.com; ydn@cabp.com.cn
Web Site: www.cabp.com.cn; en.cabp.cn
Key Personnel
President & Editor-in-Chief: Yuanqin Shen
Founded: 1954
Applied & academic books, reference books, art albums, dictionaries, yearbooks, textbooks, standards & norms.
Subjects: Architecture & Interior Design, Art, Civil Engineering, Economics, Engineering (General), Environmental Studies, Gardening, Plants, Real Estate, Transportation, Travel & Tourism, Building Economics & Management, Building Materials, Building Structure, Construction, Furnishing & Decoration, Geo-engineering, Heating/Ventilation & Air Conditioning, Industrial Design, Roads & Bridges,

Urban Planning & Design, Water Supply &
Drainage
ISBN Prefix(es): 978-7-112; 978-7-900046; 978-
7-900189; 978-7-900232
Number of titles published annually: 1,000 Print;
100 CD-ROM; 500 E-Book
Total Titles: 10,000 Print; 400 CD-ROM; 1,000
E-Book

China Aviation Media Group (CAMG)
(Zhonghang Chuban Chuanmei Youxian Zeren
Gongsi)+
Keyanlou, 2 Yuan, Beiyuanlu Rd, Andingmenwai,
Chaoyang District, Beijing 100012
Tel: (010) 84936540; (010) 84936262
E-mail: chengkun@aviationnow.com.cn (public
relations & marketing)
Web Site: www.aviationnow.com.cn
Key Personnel
President: Xin Liu
Database Consultant: Fan Dandan
E-mail: fandd@iag.cn
Founded: 1985
Subjects: Aeronautics, Aviation, Computer Sci-
ence, Economics, English as a Second Lan-
guage, Mechanical Engineering
ISBN Prefix(es): 978-7-80134; 978-7-80046; 978-
7-80183; 978-7-0243

China Braille Publishing House (Zhongguo
Mangwen Chubanshe)
No 6 Taipingjie Jia, Xicheng District, Beijing
Tel: (010) 83892479; (010) 83891763
E-mail: hjjm8389@163.com
Web Site: www.cbph.org.cn; www.cbp.org.cn
Key Personnel
President & Editor-in-Chief: Wei Zhang
Vice President: Zhongyi Han
Founded: 1953
Production of books & magazines in Braille &
tapes for the blind.
Also acts as China Library for the Blind.
Membership(s): Press & Publication Administra-
tion.
Subjects: Animals, Pets, Art, Child Care & De-
velopment, Crafts, Games, Hobbies, Disability,
Special Needs, Economics, Education, English
as a Second Language
ISBN Prefix(es): 978-7-5002; 978-7-88754
Subsidiaries: Beijing Hengji Co
Book Club(s): China Library for the Blind Read-
ing Club

China Children's Press & Publication Group
Bing 12, Jianguomenwai St, Chaoyang District,
Beijing 100022
Tel: (010) 5752 6080 *Fax:* (010) 5752 6075
E-mail: rights@ccppg.com.cn
Web Site: www.ccppg.com.cn
Key Personnel
President: Li Xueqian
Subjects: Fiction, History, Science (General)
ISBN Prefix(es): 978-7-5007
Number of titles published annually: 1,500 Print

China Commerce & Trade Press (Zhongguo
Shangwu Chubanshe)+
28 Houxiang Anwaidajie Dong, Beijing
Tel: (010) 64212247
E-mail: cctp@cctpress.com
Web Site: www.cctpress.com
Key Personnel
President: Weijing Yan
Vice President: Dongjin Song
Editor-in-Chief: Jianchu Qian
Founded: 1980
Business books & magazines.
Subjects: Accounting, Business, Economics, En-
glish as a Second Language, Finance, Govern-
ment, Political Science, Management, Market-
ing
ISBN Prefix(es): 978-7-80004; 978-7-80181

China CRITIC Press, see CITIC Publishing
House

China Film Press (Zhongguo Dianying
Chubanshe)+
22 Beisanhuan Donglu, Chaoyang District, Bei-
jing 100013
Tel: (010) 64216278; (010) 64296664 (editorial);
(010) 64296742
E-mail: tougao@chinafilmpress.com; cfpygb@
126.com; ygb@chinafilmpress.com
Web Site: www.chinafilmpress.com
Founded: 1956
Specialize in film.
Membership(s): International Film Exchange.
Subjects: Advertising, Art, Biography, Memoirs,
Career Development, Crafts, Games, Hobbies,
Drama, Theater, Fashion, Fiction, Film, Video,
History, Law, Literature, Literary Criticism,
Essays, Marketing, Outdoor Recreation, Pho-
tography
ISBN Prefix(es): 978-7-106; 978-7-88734
Parent Company: Chinese Film Association
Subsidiaries: Beijing Film Book; Shanghai Film
Services Co
Bookshop(s): China Film Bookshop

China Forestry Publishing House (Zhongguo
Linye Chubanshe)+
7 Liuhai Hutong, Deshengmennei, Xichengqu
District, Beijing 100009
Tel: (010) 83227529; (010) 83220373; (010)
83224477
Key Personnel
President: Hao Jin
Dir, Sales: Yuejin Li *Tel:* (010) 83225597
Fax: (010) 83224477
Founded: 1953
Subjects: Agriculture, Animals, Pets, Biological
Sciences, Chemistry, Chemical Engineering,
Computers, Economics, Education, Environ-
mental Studies, Gardening, Plants, Law, Sci-
ence (General), Technology, Construction/De-
velopment, Forestry
ISBN Prefix(es): 978-7-5038
Distributed by University of British Columbia
Press (UBC Press) (North America)

China Fortune Press (Zhongguo Caifu
Chubanshe)+
No 20 Lou 5 Qu, 188 Nansihua Xilu, Fengtai
District, Beijing 100070
Tel: (010) 52227588; (010) 52227566
E-mail: zgcfcbs@126.com
Web Site: www.cfpress.com.cn
Key Personnel
President: Bo Wang
Founded: 1981
Subjects: Automotive, Behavioral Sciences, Busi-
ness, Economics, Human Relations, Manage-
ment, Marketing
ISBN Prefix(es): 978-7-5047
Book Club(s): China Copyright Association

**China Human Resources & Social Security
Publishing Group Co Ltd** (Zhongguo
Renliziyuan He Shehuibaozhang Chubanjituan
Youxian Gongsi)+
Subsidiary of Ministry of Human Resources &
Social Security of China
One Huixin East St, Chaoyang District, Beijing
100029
Tel: (010) 64929196
Web Site: www.class.com.cn
Key Personnel
President: Mengxin Zhang
Vice President & Deputy Editor-in-Chief: Ling
Jin
Editor-in-Chief: Shuguo Zhao
Founded: 1980
Subjects: Business, Labor, Industrial Relations
ISBN Prefix(es): 978-7-5045

China International Culture Press Ltd
(Zhongguo Guoji Wenhua Chubanshe)+
No 3 Balizhuang Dongli, Chaoyang District,
Mailbox 654, Beijing 100025
Tel: (010) 57733086; (010) 57733087; (010)
57733088 *Fax:* (010) 89506878
E-mail: book@bookhk.com; book9@bookhk.com;
bookbj@bookhk.com
Web Site: www.bookhk.com
Founded: 1984
Subjects: Art, Biography, Memoirs, Business,
Economics, Education, Fiction, Finance,
Health, Nutrition, History, Literature, Literary
Criticism, Essays, Management, Philosophy,
Social Sciences, Sociology, Travel & Tourism
ISBN Prefix(es): 978-7-80105; 978-7-80049; 978-
7-80173; 978-7-88706
Branch Office(s)
Shanghai, Contact: Zhicheng Yu
Tel: 13301809608 (cell) *E-mail:* bookhs@126.
com
Room C, 15/F Hua Chiao Commercial Cen-
tre, 678 Nathan Rd, Mongkok, Hong Kong
Tel: 6062 4867 *Fax:* 3078 5638

China Light Industry Press (Zhongguo
Qinggongye Chubanshe)+
6 Dongchang'an St, Beijing 100740
Tel: (010) 65241695; (010) 85119752; (010)
85009896 *Fax:* (010) 65128352
E-mail: faxing@vip.163.com
Web Site: www.chlip.com.cn
Key Personnel
Dir, Sales: Leiguang Wang
Founded: 1954
Subjects: Art, Cookery, Fashion, Film, Video,
House & Home, Language Arts, Linguistics,
Wine & Spirits
ISBN Prefix(es): 978-7-5019

China Machine Press (CMP) (Jixie Gongye
Chubanshe)+
22 Baiwanzhuang Rd, Xicheng District, Beijing
100037
Tel: (010) 88361066; (010) 88379977; (010)
88379973 (overseas) *Fax:* (010) 88379345;
(010) 68320405 (overseas)
Web Site: www.cmpbook.com
Key Personnel
President: Wenbin Wang
Vice President: Qi Li
Dir, Sales: Xiaoming Tang
Founded: 1952
Subjects: Architecture & Interior Design, Automotive, Business, Computer Science, Comput-
ers, Electronics, Electrical Engineering, Lan-
guage Arts, Linguistics, Management, Mechan-
ical Engineering, Science (General), Technol-
ogy, Foreign Languages, Telecommunications
ISBN Prefix(es): 978-7-111; 978-7-88709; 978-7-
900066; 978-7-89492
Number of titles published annually: 3,000 Print;
130 CD-ROM
Associate Companies: Jingfeng Printing Com-
pany of China Machine Press, 88 Liuzhuangzi,
Fengtai District, Beijing 100071 *Tel:* (010)
63793671; The Printing Company of China
Machine Press, 4 Ganjiakou, Haidian District,
Beijing 100037 *Tel:* (010) 68353476
Subsidiaries: Huazhang Graphics & Information
Co
Warehouse: Huaxiang, Beijing 100071

China Ocean Press (Zhongguo Haiyang
Chubanshe)+
Subsidiary of State Oceanic Administration
No 8 Da Hui Si Rd, Haidian District, Beijing
100081
Tel: (010) 62114335; (010) 62100963; (010)
62100075 *Fax:* (010) 62100074

Web Site: www.oceanpress.com.cn
Key Personnel
President: Jixue Sui
Editor-in-Chief: Miss Suihua Yang
Contact: Ang Deng; Jianwei Zhu
Founded: 1978
Publish mainly in English, other languages available. Specialize in marine science & technology.
Subjects: Biography, Memoirs, Biological Sciences, Chemistry, Chemical Engineering, Civil Engineering, Computer Science, Earth Sciences, Environmental Studies, Geography, Geology, Management, Maritime, Mechanical Engineering, Physical Sciences, Physics, Real Estate, Religion - Buddhist, Religion - Islamic, Religion - Jewish, Science (General), Social Sciences, Sociology, Technology, Marine Biology, Oceanography
ISBN Prefix(es): 978-7-5027
Number of titles published annually: 10 Print
Total Titles: 300 Print

China Pictorial Publishing House (Zhongguo Huabao Chubanshe)
33 Chegongzhuang Xilu, Haidian District, Beijing 100048
Tel: (010) 88417359; (010) 88417358; (010) 68469053 *Fax:* (010) 88417359
E-mail: cpph1985@126.com
Web Site: www.zghbcbs.com
Founded: 1985
Subjects: Business, Economics, Regional Interests, Sports, Athletics, Travel & Tourism
ISBN Prefix(es): 978-7-80024; 978-7-80220

China Renmin University Press Co Ltd
Zhongguancun St, No 31, Haidian District, Beijing 100080
Tel: (010) 62510566 *Fax:* (010) 62514760
E-mail: club@crup.com.cn
Web Site: www.crup.com.cn
Founded: 1982
Subjects: Art, Economics, Education, Government, Political Science, History, Law, Mathematics, Philosophy, Social Sciences, Sociology
ISBN Prefix(es): 978-7-300; 978-7-88702; 978-7-900646; 978-7-900693

China Social Sciences Press (Zhongguo Shehui Kexue Chubanshe)+
Jia 158 Gulouxi Dajie, Xicheng District, Beijing 100720
Tel: (010) 84029453; (010) 61294748 *Fax:* (010) 84002041
E-mail: duzhe_cbs@cass.org.cn
Web Site: www.csspw.com.cn
Key Personnel
President & Editor-in-Chief: Jianying Zhao
Founded: 1978
Specialize in the task of editing & publishing monographs, reference books, teaching materials & basic reading materials in the fields of philosophy & social sciences as well as Chinese translations of major foreign works. Publisher for Social Sciences in China (Journal of Cass) & periodicals for several research institutes.
Subjects: Philosophy, Social Sciences, Sociology
ISBN Prefix(es): 978-7-5097
Bookshop(s): 5 Jianguomen Nei Ave, Beijing 100005, Contact: Huang Zhi *Tel:* (010) 65133190; 31 Book-Town Haidian Dajie, Beijing 100080

China Textile & Apparel Press (Zhongguo Fangzhi Chubanshe)+
Subsidiary of China National Textile & Apparel Council (CNTAC)
A407 Baiziwan Dongli, Chaoyang District, Beijing 100124

Tel: (010) 67004461; (010) 67004471; (010) 87155800 (rights) *Fax:* (010) 87155801 (rights)
E-mail: zongbianshi8240@c-textilep.com (rights)
Web Site: www.c-textilep.com
Key Personnel
President: Weiliang Zheng
Editor-in-Chief: Binghua Li
Founded: 1953
Arts & Crafts, Business & Management, Culture & Lifestyle, Textile & Clothing Technology.
Membership(s): The Publishers Association of China.
Subjects: Accounting, Art, Business, Chemistry, Chemical Engineering, Cookery, Crafts, Games, Hobbies, Health, Nutrition, Management, Marketing, Nonfiction (General)
ISBN Prefix(es): 978-7-5064
Number of titles published annually: 600 Print; 100 CD-ROM
Total Titles: 4,000 Print; 500 CD-ROM

China Tibetology Publishing House (Zhongguo Zangxue Chubanshe)+
131 Beisihuan Donglu, Beijing 100101
Tel: (010) 64917618; (010) 64937991 *Fax:* (010) 64917619
Key Personnel
President: Hua Zhou
Editor-in-Chief: Hua Bi
Founded: 1986
Specialize in Tibetan studies.
Subjects: Anthropology, Archaeology, Asian Studies, Economics, Education, Religion - Buddhist, Social Sciences, Sociology
ISBN Prefix(es): 978-7-80057
Parent Company: China Tibetology Research Center
Orders to: China International Book Trading Corp, PO Box 399, Beijing 100080

China Translation & Publishing Corp
(Zhongguo Duiwai Fanyi Chuban Youxian Gongsi)+
Floor 6, Wuhua Bldg, 4A Chegongzhuang St, Xicheng District, Beijing 100044
Tel: (010) 68359725; (010) 68005858 *Fax:* (010) 53223646
Founded: 1973
Subjects: Economics, Education, Management
ISBN Prefix(es): 978-7-5001
Parent Company: China Publishing Group Corp

China Water & Power Press (CWPP)
(Zhongguo Shuili Shuidian Chubanshe)+
D Zuo, No 1, Yuyuantan Nanlu Rd, Haidian District, Beijing 100038
Tel: (010) 68317638; (010) 68367658 (marketing) *Fax:* (010) 68353010; (010) 68331835 (marketing)
E-mail: info@waterpub.com.cn; cwpp@waterpub.com.cn; sales@waterpub.com.cn
Web Site: www.waterpub.com.cn
Key Personnel
President: Xinhua Tang
Dir: Lijuan Xu *E-mail:* xlj@waterpub.com.cn
Founded: 1956
Subjects: Civil Engineering, Electronics, Electrical Engineering, Energy, Engineering (General), Environmental Studies
ISBN Prefix(es): 978-7-120

China Youth Publishing House (Zhongguo Qingnian Chubanshe)+
No 21 Dong Si 12 Tiao, Beijing 100708
Tel: (010) 57350300; (010) 57350312 *Fax:* (010) 57350313
E-mail: cypzbs@126.com
Web Site: www.cyp.com.cn
Key Personnel
Dir: Zhi Yang *Tel:* (010) 57350350
Deputy Dir: Kefeng Zhang *Tel:* (010) 57350351

Founded: 1950
Subjects: Education, Language Arts, Linguistics, Literature, Literary Criticism, Essays, Science (General), Social Sciences, Sociology, Comics
ISBN Prefix(es): 978-7-5006
Parent Company: China Youth Publishing Group

Chinese Drama Press, see Chinese Theatre Publishing House

Chinese Theatre Publishing House (Zhongguo Xiju Chubanshe)+
Jiahao International Centre, Room 1010, Block A, 116 Zizhuyuan Rd, Haidian, Beijing 100097
Tel: (010) 58930235; (010) 58930238 (orders) *Fax:* (010) 58930242 (orders)
Key Personnel
President & Editor-in-Chief: Guobin Fan
Dir, Sales: Guangcai Fu
Founded: 1957
Subjects: Crafts, Games, Hobbies, Drama, Theater, Education, Fiction, History, Literature, Literary Criticism, Essays, Nonfiction (General)
ISBN Prefix(es): 978-7-104

Chongqing University Press (Chongqing Daxue Chubanshe)+
21 Daxuecheng Xilu Rd, Shapingbei District, Chongqing 400030
Tel: (023) 88617009 *Fax:* (023) 88617014
E-mail: office@cqup.com.cn; wangbin@cqup.com.cn; liuxj@cqup.com.cn
Web Site: www.cqup.com.cn
Key Personnel
President: Xiaoyi Deng *Tel:* (023) 88617009
Editor-in-Chief: Banghua Rao *Tel:* (023) 88617008 *E-mail:* raobh@cqup.edu.cn
General Manager, Marketing: Jiaying Mao *Tel:* (023) 88617199 *E-mail:* maojy@cqup.com.cn
International Cooperation Dept: Mr Tiantong Fang *E-mail:* fangtt@cqup.com.cn
Founded: 1985
Subjects: Architecture & Interior Design, Art, Economics, Health, Nutrition, Language Arts, Linguistics, Law, Management, Medicine, Nursing, Dentistry, Science (General), Social Sciences, Sociology, Technology, Humanity
ISBN Prefix(es): 978-7-5624
Number of titles published annually: 500 Print
Total Titles: 4,000 Print

CHSPG, see China Human Resources & Social Security Publishing Group Co Ltd

CITIC Publishing House (Zhongxin Chuban Jituan)+
No 14 Liangmahe South Rd, Chaoyang District, Beijing 100029
Tel: (010) 84849555 *Fax:* (010) 84849000
E-mail: author@citicpub.com
Web Site: www.publish.citic.com
Founded: 1988
Specialize in both copyright transactions & co-publication of books with foreign publishers, bookdealers or any other relevant groups or individuals & launching joint ventures on business in publication & distribution.
Subjects: Accounting, Business, Economics, Finance, How-to, Law, Management, Marketing, Nonfiction (General)
ISBN Prefix(es): 978-7-80073; 978-7-5086
Parent Company: CITIC Press Group
Associate Companies: CITIC Representative Office in Japan, 3/F, The Landic Third Akasaka Bldg, 2-3-2, Akasaka, Minato-ku, Tokyo 107-0052, Japan *Tel:* (03) 35842635 *Fax:* (03) 35056235 *E-mail:* citic.tyo@nifty.com; CITIC Representative Office in Kazakhstan, 135 Abylaikhan Ave, 5th floor, Almaty, Kazakhstan *Tel:* (072) 2583823 *Fax:* (072) 2581315; CITIC Representative Office in New York, 100 Wall

St, Suite 603, New York, NY 10005, United States *Tel:* 212-363-8060 *Fax:* 212-363-8062
E-mail: citicny@msn.com

CMP, see China Machine Press (CMP)

The Commercial Press (Shangwu Yinshuguan)+
No 36 Wangfujing Ave, Beijing 100710
Tel: (010) 65252026 (editorial); (010) 65135899 (rights); (010) 65253913 (sales) *Fax:* (010) 65134942
E-mail: gaoshan@cp.com.cn
Web Site: www.cp.com.cn
Founded: 1897
Publisher of children's books, bilingual dictionaries, Chinese language dictionaries & textbooks.
Subjects: Art, Asian Studies, Economics, Education, Geography, Geology, Government, Political Science, History, Language Arts, Linguistics, Law, Management, Philosophy, Public Administration, Religion, Religion - Buddhist, Religion - Catholic, Religion - Hindu, Religion - Islamic, Social Sciences, Sociology, Technology, Natural Sciences
ISBN Prefix(es): 978-7-100
Number of titles published annually: 700 Print
Total Titles: 40,000 Print

CQUP, see Chongqing University Press

CSSP, see China Social Sciences Press

CTPC, see China Translation & Publishing Corp

Cultural Relics Press (Wenwu Chubanshe)+
Affiliate of Chinese Administration for Cultural Heritage
Dongzhimennei, Bldg 2, Beixiaojie, Beijing 100007
Tel: (010) 64029006; (010) 64027424 *Fax:* (010) 64010698
E-mail: club@wenwu.com (sales); honglou800@ aliyun.com
Web Site: www.wenwu.com
Key Personnel
President: Zicheng Zhang
Editor-in-Chief: Chengyong Ge
Founded: 1957
Specializes in cultural relics & archeology publications. Also publishes catalogs.
Subjects: Anthropology, Antiques, Archaeology, Art, Asian Studies, History
ISBN Prefix(es): 978-7-5010

CWPP, see China Water & Power Press (CWPP)

Dalian Maritime University Press LLC (Dalian Haishi Daxue Chubanshe Youxian Zeren Gongsi)+
One Linghai Rd, Dalian, Liaoning Province 116026
Tel: (0411) 84728394; (0411) 84729665; (0411) 84723216 *Fax:* (0411) 84727996
E-mail: dmupress@163.com
Web Site: www.dmupress.com
Key Personnel
Marketing Dir: Ruiguo Wang
Founded: 1986
Subjects: Communications, Computer Science, Economics, Electronics, Electrical Engineering, English as a Second Language, Management, Maritime, Science (General)
ISBN Prefix(es): 978-7-5632

Dolphin Books (Haitun Chubanshe)+
24 Baiwanzhuang Rd, Beijing 100037
Tel: (010) 68997468; (010) 68998879 *Fax:* (010) 68993503
E-mail: dolphin_books@163.com
Founded: 1986

Specialize in illustrated children's books.
ISBN Prefix(es): 978-7-80051; 978-7-80138
Parent Company: Foreign Languages Press
Ultimate Parent Company: China International Publishing Group
Shipping Address: China International Book Trading Corp, 35 Chegong-zhuang Xilu, Beijing 100044
Warehouse: China International Book Trading Corp, 35 Chegong-zhuang Xilu, Beijing 100044
Orders to: Cypress Book Co (UK) Ltd, 10 Swinton St, London WC1X 9NX, United Kingdom
Cypress Book (US) Co Inc, 3450 Third St, Unit 4B, San Francisco, CA 94124, United States
Tel: 415-821-3582

East China Normal University Press (Huadong Shifan Daxue Chubanshe)+
14F Shendasha Bldg, 3663 Zhongshan Beilu Rd, Shanghai 200062
Tel: (021) 60821616; (021) 62869887 *Fax:* (021) 60821717
E-mail: ecnup@ecnupress.com.cn
Web Site: www.ecnupress.com.cn; www.ecnup-dayu.com.cn
Key Personnel
Chairman: Prof Jieren Zhu
President: Yan Wang
Editor-in-Chief: Prof Guangye Yuan
Founded: 1957
Subjects: Education, Psychology, Psychiatry, Science (General), Self-Help, Social Sciences, Sociology, Humanities
ISBN Prefix(es): 978-7-5617
Subsidiaries: Da Hua Industry & Trade Co

East China University of Science & Technology Press (Huadong Ligong Daxue Chubanshe)
130 Meilong Rd, Shanghai 200237
Tel: (021) 64253300; (021) 64251231 *Fax:* (021) 64252280
E-mail: xiaoban@ecust.edu.cn
Web Site: www.ecust.edu.cn
Key Personnel
President: Xuhong Qian *Tel:* (021) 64251181
E-mail: liuliu@ecust.edu.cn
Founded: 1952
Subjects: Agriculture, Computer Science, Education, Engineering (General), English as a Second Language, Environmental Studies, Finance, Technology
ISBN Prefix(es): 978-7-5628

ECNUP, see East China Normal University Press

ECPH, see Encyclopedia of China Publishing House (ECPH)

Educational Science Publishing House (ESPH) (Jiaoyu Kexue Chubanshe)
Jia No 9, Anyuan Anhuibeili, Chaoyang District, Beijing 100101
Tel: (010) 64989234 (rights & permissions) *Fax:* (010) 64891839
E-mail: copyright@esph.com.cn
Web Site: www.esph.com.cn
Founded: 1980
Subjects: Education, English as a Second Language, Human Relations, Military Science, Natural History, Science Fiction, Fantasy
ISBN Prefix(es): 978-7-5041
Total Titles: 1,866 Print; 12 Audio
Parent Company: China National Institute for Educational Research
Ultimate Parent Company: Ministry of Education

Encyclopedia of China Publishing House (ECPH) (Zhongguo Da Baike Quanshu Chubanshe)+
Subsidiary of China Publishing Group

17 Fuchengmen Beidajie, Beijing 100037
Tel: (010) 88390601; (010) 88390732 *Fax:* (010) 68316510
E-mail: 522060247@qq.com
Web Site: www.ecph.com.cn/main
Key Personnel
Deputy Editor-in-Chief: Yijun Ma
Founded: 1978
Subjects: Art, Education, Fiction, Science (General), Technology, Culture
ISBN Prefix(es): 978-7-5000; 978-7-900006; 978-7-900179
Subsidiaries: Knowledge Publishing House

ESPH, see Educational Science Publishing House (ESPH)

The Ethnic Publishing House (Minzu Chubanshe)+
14 Hepingli Beijie, Dongcheng District, Beijing 100013
Tel: (010) 64212794; (010) 58130000; (010) 58130363 *Fax:* (010) 64211734; (010) 64284284; (010) 64228007
E-mail: e56@e56.com.cn
Web Site: www.e56.com.cn
Key Personnel
Contact: Rong Chen *Tel:* (010) 64285364
Founded: 1953
Subjects: Chinese Ethnic Groups, Ethnic Minorities
ISBN Prefix(es): 978-7-105
Bookshop(s): The Nationalities Culture Bookshop, 5 Hepingli Beijie, Beijing 100013

First Edition, *imprint of* Publishing House of Jinan

FLP, see Foreign Languages Press

FLTRP, see Foreign Language Teaching & Research Press

Foreign Language Teaching & Research Press (Waiyu Jiaoxue Yu Yanjiu Chubanshe)+
No 19 Xisanhuan Beilu, Beijing 100089
Tel: (010) 88819000; (010) 88819476 (orders) *Fax:* (010) 88819433
E-mail: international@fltrp.com; sales@fltrp.com; overseas@fltrp.com; service@fltrp.com
Web Site: www.fltrp.com
Key Personnel
Dir, Sales: Yang Zhou *Tel:* (010) 88819818
Founded: 1979
Subjects: Education, English as a Second Language, Foreign Countries, History, Language Arts, Linguistics, Literature, Literary Criticism, Essays, Social Sciences, Sociology, Western Fiction
ISBN Prefix(es): 978-7-5600; 978-7-900626

Foreign Languages Press (Waiwen Chubanshe)+
Member of China International Publishing Group
24 Baiwanzhuang Rd, Xicheng District, Beijing 100037
Tel: (010) 68320579; (010) 68326853; (010) 68996138; (010) 68997794 *Fax:* (010) 68326642; (010) 68993501
E-mail: flprights@yahoo.com.cn
Web Site: www.flp.com.cn
Key Personnel
President & Editor-in-Chief: Bu Xu
Dir, Sales: Gang Xiao
Founded: 1952
Published languages (in addition to Chinese): Arabic, English, French, German, Japanese, Portuguese, Russian & Spanish.
Subjects: Anthropology, Archaeology, Art, Biography, Memoirs, Cookery, Drama, Theater, Economics, Geography, Geology, Government, Political Science, History, Law, Literature,

Literary Criticism, Essays, Medicine, Nursing, Dentistry, Philosophy, Science (General), Sports, Athletics, Travel & Tourism
ISBN Prefix(es): 978-7-119
Total Titles: 1,500 Print; 40 Audio
Orders to: Cypress Book Co (UK) Ltd, Unit 6, Provident Industrial Estate, Pump Lane, Hayes, London UB3 3NE, United Kingdom, Mng Dir: Jing Ru *Tel:* (020) 8453 0687 *Fax:* (020) 8561 1062 *E-mail:* info@cypressbooks.com *Web Site:* www.cypressbooks.com
Cypress Book (US) Co Inc, 360 Swift Ave, Units 42 & 48, South San Francisco, CA 94080, United States, President: Du Wei *Tel:* 650-872-7718 *Fax:* 650-872-7808 *E-mail:* mqxu@pacbell.net *Web Site:* www.chinabookmart.com

FSTPH, see Fujian Science & Technology Publishing House

Fudan University Press (Fudan Daxue Chubanshe)+
579 GuoQuan Rd, Shanghai 200433
Tel: (021) 65642854 *Fax:* (021) 65104812
Web Site: www.fudanpress.com; www.fudanpress.com.cn
Founded: 1981
Subjects: Accounting, Advertising, Art, Asian Studies, Behavioral Sciences, Biography, Memoirs, Biological Sciences, Business, Chemistry, Chemical Engineering, Communications, Computer Science, Computers, Economics, Education, Electronics, Electrical Engineering, English as a Second Language, Finance, Genealogy, Geography, Geology, Government, Political Science, Health, Nutrition, History, How-to, Human Relations, Language Arts, Linguistics, Law, Library & Information Sciences, Literature, Literary Criticism, Essays, Management, Marketing, Mathematics, Natural History, Philosophy, Photography, Physical Sciences, Physics, Poetry, Psychology, Psychiatry, Public Administration, Regional Interests, Religion - Buddhist, Science (General), Securities, Social Sciences, Sociology, Technology, Women's Studies
ISBN Prefix(es): 978-7-309; 978-7-900606

Fujian Children's Publishing House (Fujian Shaonian Ertong Chubanshe)+
76, Dongshui Rd, F1 17, Fujian Province, Fuzhou 350001
Tel: (0591) 87539030; (0591) 87606554; (0591) 87625183 *Fax:* (0591) 87606554
E-mail: fcph@fjcp.com
Web Site: www.fjcp.com
Founded: 1984
Subjects: Art, Education, Humor, Literature, Literary Criticism, Essays
ISBN Prefix(es): 978-7-5395
Total Titles: 320 Print

Fujian Science & Technology Publishing House (Fujian Kexue Jishu Chubanshe)+
15/F, Fujian Publishing Center Bldg, 76 Dongshui Rd, Fuzhou, Fujian 350001
Tel: (0591) 87600084; (0591) 87602964 *Fax:* (0591) 87602907
E-mail: office@fjstp.com
Web Site: www.fjstp.com
Key Personnel
President & Editor-in-Chief: Jie He
Founded: 1979
Provider of scientific & technological books & magazines.
Subjects: Agriculture, Architecture & Interior Design, Communications, Computer Science, Electronics, Electrical Engineering, Health, Nutrition, Medicine, Nursing, Dentistry, Science (General), Technology, Transportation
ISBN Prefix(es): 978-7-5335

Number of titles published annually: 400 Print; 100 CD-ROM
Total Titles: 4,000 Print; 300 CD-ROM

Geological Publishing House (GPH) (Dizhi Chubanshe)+
No 31 Xueyuan Lu, Haidian District, Beijing 100083
Tel: (010) 82324519; (010) 82324537 *Fax:* (010) 82328538
Web Site: www.gph.com.cn
Founded: 1954
Subjects: Geography, Geology, Science (General), Technology
ISBN Prefix(es): 978-7-116; 978-7-900140
Bookshop(s): Geological Bookshop, Beijing *Tel:* (010) 82324508; (010) 82324512 *E-mail:* shw82324512@163.com

GPH, see Geological Publishing House (GPH)

Graphic Communications Press (Yinshua Gongye Chubanshe)+
2 Cuiwei Rd, Haidian District, Beijing 100036
Tel: (010) 88275709; (010) 88275602 (sales); (010) 88275706 *Fax:* (010) 88275711; (010) 88275707
E-mail: book@keyin.cn; luguihua@keyin.cn
Web Site: www.keyinmedia.com; www.keyin.cn
Founded: 1981
Subjects: Chemistry, Chemical Engineering, Electronics, Electrical Engineering, Engineering (General), Management, Mechanical Engineering, Photography, Technology
ISBN Prefix(es): 978-7-80000
Parent Company: KeyinPrint Media

Guangdong Science & Technology Press (Guangdong Keji Chubanshe)+
9-10 F, 11 Shuiyinlu, Huanshi Donglu, Yuexiu District, Guangzhou 510075
Tel: (020) 37607770 *Fax:* (020) 37606412
E-mail: gdkjzbb@gdstp.com.cn
Web Site: www.gdstp.com.cn
Key Personnel
President: Bing Chen
Editor-in-Chief: Chunling Ding
Sales Manager: Yanchun Shen *Tel:* (020) 37592148
Rights: Connie Yang *Tel:* (020) 37606412 *E-mail:* ylq5460@163.com
Founded: 1978
Subjects: Agriculture, Architecture & Interior Design, Computer Science, Cookery, English as a Second Language, Gardening, Plants, Mathematics, Medicine, Nursing, Dentistry, Science (General), Technology
ISBN Prefix(es): 978-7-5359; 978-7-900341

Guangxi Normal University Press
22 Zhonghua Rd, Guilin, Guangxi 541001
Tel: (0773) 2808798 *Fax:* (0773) 2809979
E-mail: abg@bbtpress.com
Web Site: www.bbtpress.com
Key Personnel
President: He Lin Xia
Founded: 1986
ISBN Prefix(es): 978-7-5495

Guizhou Education Publishing House (Guizhou Jiaoyu Chubanshe)
Member of Guizhou Publishing Group
289 Zhonghua North Rd, Guiyang, Guizhou 550004
Tel: (0851) 6828337
Key Personnel
Chairman: Xiaoyong Peng
General Manager: Jian Song
Founded: 1990
Subjects: Art, Chemistry, Chemical Engineering, Child Care & Development, Economics, Ed-

ucation, Gardening, Plants, History, Human Relations
ISBN Prefix(es): 978-7-80583; 978-7-80650

Haitian Publishing House (Haitian Chubanshe)
Room 710, Haitian Zonghe Dasha, Caitian South Rd, Futian District, Shenzhen, Guangdong Province 518033
Tel: (0755) 83460914; (0755) 83460397; (0755) 83460234 (editorial)
E-mail: jj@htph.com.cn; szhtph@qq.com
Web Site: www.htph.com.cn
Key Personnel
President: Xinliang Chen
Editor-in-Chief: Shiping Mao
Dir, Publishing: Jong Chen
Dir, Sales: Hui Yu *Tel:* (0755) 83460003 *Fax:* (0755) 83461113
Founded: 1984
Book & magazine publishing.
Subjects: Accounting, Business, Economics, Fashion, Finance, Health, Nutrition, Management, Marketing, Travel & Tourism
ISBN Prefix(es): 978-7-80697; 978-7-80542; 978-7-80615; 978-7-80654; 978-7-80747

Heilongjiang Science & Technology Press (Heilongjiang Kexue Jishu Chubanshe)+
Member of Heilongjiang Publishing Group
66 Youyilu Rd, Nangang District, Harbin, Heilongjiang Province 150001
Tel: (0451) 58855674; (0451) 58930235 *Fax:* (0451) 53642143
E-mail: zbs53635613@163.com
Web Site: science.ebook.dbw.cn
Subjects: Advertising, Agriculture, Architecture & Interior Design, Business, Communications, Economics, Electronics, Electrical Engineering, Health, Nutrition, How-to, Management, Marketing, Medicine, Nursing, Dentistry, Photography, Physical Sciences, Science (General), Technology, Transportation, Veterinary Science
ISBN Prefix(es): 978-7-5388

Henan Science & Technology Press (Henan Kexue Jishu Chubanshe)+
No 66 Jingwu Rd, Zhengzhou, Henan 450002
Tel: (0371) 65788613 *Fax:* (0371) 65726941 (sales); (0371) 65725195; (0371) 65736917
Web Site: www.hnstp.cn
Key Personnel
Dir, Sales: Ruiguang Guo
Founded: 1980
Specialize in scientific & technological subjects.
Subjects: Architecture & Interior Design, Biological Sciences, Chemistry, Chemical Engineering, Gardening, Plants, Mechanical Engineering, Medicine, Nursing, Dentistry, Physical Sciences, Living
ISBN Prefix(es): 978-7-5349
Total Titles: 300 Print
Parent Company: News & Publishing Bureau of Henan Province

HEP, *imprint of* Higher Education Press

Higher Education Press (Gaodeng Jiaoyu Chubanshe)+
Subsidiary of China Education Publishing & Media Group Co Ltd
No 4 DeWai DaJie Ave, Xicheng District, Beijing 100120
Tel: (010) 58581118 *Toll Free Tel:* 800-8100598 *Fax:* (010) 82085552
E-mail: gjdzfwb@pub.hep.cn
Web Site: www.hep.edu.cn; www.hep.com.cn; www.hep.cn
Key Personnel
President: Yuheng Su
Foreign Rights: Mr Yunpeng Sun; Ms Xueying Zou
Founded: 1954

Publications for textbooks & references in higher education, vocational & adult educational.
Subjects: Agriculture, Architecture & Interior Design, Biological Sciences, Civil Engineering, Computer Science, Cookery, Education, Engineering (General), English as a Second Language, Finance, Gardening, Plants, Geography, Geology, History, Language Arts, Linguistics, Management, Psychology, Psychiatry, Science (General), Social Sciences, Sociology, Technology, Travel & Tourism, Women's Studies
ISBN Prefix(es): 978-7-04; 978-7-900076
Number of titles published annually: 4,000 Print
Total Titles: 12,000 Print
Ultimate Parent Company: Ministry of Education
Imprints: HEP
Branch Office(s)
No 4 Huixin Dongjie, Chaoyang District, Beijing 100029
No 848 Baoshan Rd, Zhabei District, Shanghai 200081

Huazhong University of Science & Technology Press
1037 Luoyu Rd, Wuhan, Hubei 430074
Tel: (027) 87547172 *Fax:* (027) 87542324
E-mail: service@hustp.com
Web Site: www.hustp.com
Key Personnel
President: Haihong Ruan
Founded: 1980
Subjects: Economics, Engineering (General), Mathematics, Photography
ISBN Prefix(es): 978-7-5609

Hunan Science & Technology Press
276 Xiangya Rd, Changsha 410008
Tel: (0731) 84375806 *Fax:* (0731) 84375800
E-mail: hnkjliujing@163.com
Web Site: www.hnstp.com
Founded: 1979
Subjects: Agriculture, Fiction, Health, Nutrition, Medicine, Nursing, Dentistry, Science (General)
ISBN Prefix(es): 978-7-5357
Number of titles published annually: 600 Print

HUST Press, see Huazhong University of Science & Technology Press

Tianjin Ifengspace Media Co Ltd
Imprint of Phoenix Publishing & Media Group (PPMG)
3rd floor, No 240 Baidi Rd, Nankai District, Tianjin 300192
Tel: (022) 60262226 *Fax:* (022) 60266199
E-mail: info@ifengspace.cn; ifengspace@hotmail.com (international sales)
Web Site: www.ifengspace.com
Subjects: Architecture & Interior Design, Landscape Design, Urban Design
ISBN Prefix(es): 978-7-5537
Branch Office(s)
16th floor, Bldg 5, Qianhe Home, N 4th Ring E Rd, Chaoyang District, Beijing 100000
Tel: (010) 64933786 *Fax:* (010) 64933786-8010
16c3, The Central Mansion, Zhongshan District, Dalian, Liaoning Province 116000
Room 3201, Wufu Bldg, Liehe Garden, No 9 Haiwen Rd, Tianhe District, Guangzhou 510000 *Tel:* (020) 85219519 *Fax:* (020) 37303738

Inner Mongolia Science & Technology Press (Neimenggu Keji Chubanshe)+
No 4 Nanyiduan, Hadajie, Hongshan District, Chifeng, Neimenggu 024000
Tel: (0476) 8224547; (0476) 8221347; (0476) 8226769 *Fax:* (0476) 8231843
Toll Free Fax: (0476) 8231924
Web Site: www.nm-kj.com

Key Personnel
Editor-in-Chief: Mei Xiang
Founded: 1982
Subjects: Agriculture, Astronomy, Computers, Electronics, Electrical Engineering, Mathematics, Physics, Publishing & Book Trade Reference, Science (General), Veterinary Science
ISBN Prefix(es): 978-7-5380

Intellectual Property Publishing House LLC (Zhishi Chanquan Chubanshe Youxian Zeren Gongsi)
No 1 Madian Nancun, Haidian District, Beijing 100088
Tel: (010) 82000373; (010) 82000860; 4001880860 (cell) *Fax:* (010) 82000905; (010) 82000373
E-mail: yanjiang@cnipr.com; patentservice@cnipr.com
Web Site: www.ipph.cn
Key Personnel
President: Guangqing Bai
Founded: 1980
Subjects: Law, Science (General), Technology, Intellectual Property, Patent
ISBN Prefix(es): 978-7-80011; 978-7-80198; 978-7-900018

IPPH, see Intellectual Property Publishing House LLC

Jiangsu Juveniles & Children's Publishing House (Jiangsu Shaonian Ertong Chubanshe)+
14-15F, Fenghuangtai Fandian Hotel, 47 Hunan Rd, Nanjing, Jiangsu 210012
Tel: (025) 83242508; (025) 83242350
E-mail: sushao@163.com
Web Site: www.jsfxw.com
Founded: 1984
Publish books for children under 15 years old including picture books, literature & parenting books.
Subjects: Child Care & Development, Literature, Literary Criticism, Essays
ISBN Prefix(es): 978-7-5346

Jiangsu People's Publishing House (Jiangsu Renmin Chubanshe)+
8F-9F Lou, A Zuo, Fenghuangguangchang, No 1 Huan Rd, Nanjing, Jiangsu 210009
Tel: (025) 83658113; (025) 83658045 *Fax:* (025) 83658119
E-mail: jsppright@gmail.com
Web Site: www.jspph.com
Key Personnel
President: Jianbing Liu
Copyright Manager: Yan Liu *Tel:* (025) 83658048 *Fax:* (025) 83658094
Founded: 1953
Subjects: Art, Government, Political Science, Health, Nutrition, History, Literature, Literary Criticism, Essays, Philosophy, Religion - Buddhist, Social Sciences, Sociology
ISBN Prefix(es): 978-7-214

Jiangxi Education Publishing House (Jiangxi Jiaoyu Chubanshe)
Member of Jiangxi Publishing Group
291 Fuhebeilu Rd, Nanchang, Jiangxi 330008
Tel: (0791) 86710875; (0791) 86711067; (0791) 86705909 *Fax:* (0791) 86710460; (0791) 86711067; (0791) 86710461
E-mail: jxeph@jxeph.com
Web Site: www.jxeph.com
Founded: 1985
Subjects: Education
ISBN Prefix(es): 978-7-5392

Jiangxi Fine Arts Publishing House (Jiangxi Meishu Chubanshe)
Member of Jiangxi Publishing Group

Jiangmei Tower, 66 Zi'an Rd, Nanchang, Jiangxi 330025
Tel: (0791) 86565661 *Fax:* (0791) 86565770; (0791) 86565274
E-mail: jxms@jxfinearts.com; faxing@jxfinearts.com
Web Site: www.jxfinearts.com
Founded: 1990
Subjects: Art
ISBN Prefix(es): 978-7-80580; 978-7-80690

Jilin Fine Arts Publishing House
4646 Renmin St, Changchun City 130021
Tel: (0431) 85651156 *Fax:* (0431) 85637195
E-mail: zb@jlmspress.com
Web Site: www.jlmspress.com
Founded: 1984
Subjects: Art, Fiction, Photography
ISBN Prefix(es): 978-7-5386
Parent Company: Jilin Publishing Group Co Ltd

Jilin Publishing Group Co Ltd
No 4646 Renmin St, Changchun 130021
Tel: (0431) 85618706 *Fax:* (0431) 85621745
Web Site: www.jlpg.cn
Founded: 2003
Subjects: Art, Geography, Geology, History, Literature, Literary Criticism, Essays, Philosophy, Science (General), Social Sciences, Sociology, Transportation
ISBN Prefix(es): 978-7-80720; 978-7-5463; 978-7-80762

Jilin Science & Technology Publishing House (Jilin Kexue Jishu Chubanshe)+
4646 Renmin St, Changchun, Jilin 130021
Fax: (0431) 85635177
E-mail: editor@vip.126.com
Web Site: www.jlstp.net; www.jlpg.cn; www.weibo.com/jlstp
Key Personnel
Contact: Lei Ding *Tel:* 013904334883 (cell)
Founded: 1984
Subjects: Accounting, Advertising, Agriculture, Animals, Pets, Anthropology, Architecture & Interior Design, Astronomy, Automotive, Biography, Memoirs, Biological Sciences, Business, Career Development, Chemistry, Chemical Engineering, Child Care & Development, Civil Engineering, Computer Science, Computers, Cookery, Electronics, Electrical Engineering, Engineering (General), English as a Second Language, Environmental Studies, Health, Nutrition, House & Home, How-to, Management, Marketing, Mathematics, Mechanical Engineering, Medicine, Nursing, Dentistry, Outdoor Recreation, Photography, Physical Sciences, Physics, Science (General), Science Fiction, Fantasy, Sports, Athletics, Technology, Travel & Tourism, Veterinary Science
ISBN Prefix(es): 978-7-5384; 978-7-900379
Number of titles published annually: 200 Print
Total Titles: 500 Print
Parent Company: Jilin Publishing Group Co Ltd

Publishing House of Jinan (Jinan Chubanshe)+
No 1 Erhuannanlu Rd, Jinan, Shandong 250002
Tel: (0531) 86131709; (0531) 86922073 (orders)
Key Personnel
Chairman: Gang Cui
Founded: 1988
Subjects: Agriculture, Cookery, Economics, Education, Medicine, Nursing, Dentistry, Nonfiction (General), Social Sciences, Sociology
ISBN Prefix(es): 978-7-80572; 978-7-80629; 978-7-80710
Number of titles published annually: 200 Print
Imprints: First Edition

JTart Publishing & Media Group
Room 309, Bldg No 18, VTREK Innovation Industry Park, 644 Shibei Industrial Rd, Dashi Town, Panyu District, Guangzhou 511400

Tel: (020) 89090386; (020) 89090342 *Fax:* (020) 89090386; (020) 89091650
E-mail: jtart@jtart.com
Web Site: www.jtart.com; book.jtart.com
Subjects: Architecture & Interior Design, Landscaping, Urban Planning
ISBN Prefix(es): 978-7-5623

Juvenile & Children's Publishing House (Shaonian Ertong Chubanshe)
1538 Yan An Xi Rd, Shanghai 200052
Tel: (021) 62823025; (021) 62949970 *Fax:* (021) 62826241; (021) 62815625
Web Site: www.jcph.com
Founded: 1952
Subjects: Language Arts, Linguistics, Literature, Literary Criticism, Essays, Science (General), Humanities, Natural Sciences
ISBN Prefix(es): 978-7-5324

Knowledge Press (Zhishi Chubanshe)+
Subsidiary of Encyclopedia of China Publishing House (ECPH)
17 Fuchengmen Beidajie, Beijing 100037
Tel: (010) 88390601; (010) 88390732 *Fax:* (010) 68316510
E-mail: 522060247@qq.com
Web Site: www.ecph.com.cn/main
Key Personnel
Deputy Editor-in-Chief: Yijun Ma
Subjects: Civil Engineering, Health, Nutrition, Human Relations, Science (General), Social Sciences, Sociology
ISBN Prefix(es): 978-7-5015
Ultimate Parent Company: China Publishing Group

Kunlun Press (Kunlun Chubanshe)+
40 Di An Men Xi Dajie, Xicheng District, Beijing 100035
Tel: (010) 66730373
E-mail: conan9586@163.com
Web Site: tp.chinamil.com.cn
Founded: 1951
Subjects: Biography, Memoirs, Literature, Literary Criticism, Essays, Military Science, Nonfiction (General), Social Sciences, Sociology
ISBN Prefix(es): 978-7-80040
Parent Company: PLA Publishing House
Bookshop(s): 36 Middle North Sanhuan Rd, Beijing 100084

Language Publishing House (Yuwen Chubanshe)+
51 Chaoyangmen Neinanxiaojie, Beijing 100010
Tel: (010) 65283384
E-mail: fxzx2@sina.com; ywcbsywp@163.com
Founded: 1956
Subjects: Communications
ISBN Prefix(es): 978-7-80126; 978-7-80184

Lanzhou University Press (Lanzhou Daxue Chubanshe)+
No 222 Tianshuinanlu Rd, Lanzhou City, Gansu Province 730000
Tel: (0931) 8912613; (0931) 8617156
E-mail: press@lzu.edu.cn
Web Site: www.onbook.com.cn
Key Personnel
President: Ming Cui
Editor-in-Chief: Mr Hongchang Lei *Tel:* (0931) 8912611
Dir, Marketing: Feng Ge *Tel:* (0931) 8914219
Founded: 1985
Subjects: Behavioral Sciences, Biography, Memoirs, Economics, Education, Government, Political Science, History, Law, Philosophy, Physics, Psychology, Psychiatry, Science (General), Social Sciences, Sociology
ISBN Prefix(es): 978-7-311
Bookshop(s): 268 Tianshui Rd, Lanzhou University, Lanzhou, Gansu 730000

The Law Publishing House (Falu Chubanshe)
7 Lianhuachi Xili, Fengtai District, Beijing 100073
Tel: (010) 63939796; (010) 63939792 *Fax:* (010) 63939622
E-mail: info@lawpress.com.cn
Web Site: www.lawpress.com.cn
Key Personnel
President: Huang Min
Editor-in-Chief: Shan Lu
Founded: 1954
Also acts as book packager.
Subjects: Law
ISBN Prefix(es): 978-7-5036; 978-7-5118

Liaoning People's Publishing House (Liaoning Renmin Chubanshe)+
No 25 Shiyiweilu Rd, Heping District, Shenyang City, Liaoning 110003
Tel: (024) 23284321
E-mail: xchen@mail.lnpgc.com.cn
Key Personnel
President & Editor-in-Chief: Dongping Zhang
Founded: 1951
Subjects: Economics, History
ISBN Prefix(es): 978-7-205
Subsidiaries: Liao-Shen Publishing House

Liaoning Science & Technology Publishing House (Liaoning Kexue Jishu Chubanshe)
Member of Liaoning Publishing Group
No 29 Shiyiwei Rd, Heping District, Shenyang 110003
Tel: (024) 23284360; (024) 23284367 *Fax:* (024) 23284365
Web Site: www.lnkj.com.cn
Key Personnel
President & Editor-in-Chief: Chunzhi Song
Founded: 1982
Subjects: Architecture & Interior Design, Art, Automotive, Crafts, Games, Hobbies, Health, Nutrition, Management, Medicine, Nursing, Dentistry, Science (General), Technology
ISBN Prefix(es): 978-7-5381
Subsidiaries: Design Media Ltd

Metallurgical Industry Press (MIP) (Yejin Gongye Chubanshe)+
No 39 Songzhuyuan Beixiang, Shatan, Dongcheng District, Beijing 100009
Tel: (010) 64044283 *Fax:* (010) 64027893
E-mail: yjcbs@cnmip.com.cn; fxb@cnmip.com.cn
Web Site: www.cnmip.com.cn
Key Personnel
President: Tan Xueyu *E-mail:* txy@cnmip.com.cn
Editor-in-Chief: Ren Jingbo *E-mail:* rjb@cnmip.com.cn
Founded: 1953
Subjects: Chemistry, Chemical Engineering, Computer Science, Earth Sciences, Electronics, Electrical Engineering, Engineering (General), Environmental Studies, Geography, Geology, Management, Mathematics, Mechanical Engineering, Technology
ISBN Prefix(es): 978-7-5024

MIP, see Metallurgical Industry Press (MIP)

Modern Education Press Co (Xiandai Jiaoyu Chubanshe)
504 Anhuali, floor 4, Chaoyang District, Beijing 100011
Tel: (010) 88624956; (010) 64251256
E-mail: 470360744@qq.com
Web Site: www.chinamep.com.cn
Key Personnel
President: Yifu Song
Founded: 2004
Subjects: Education, History, Social Sciences, Sociology

ISBN Prefix(es): 978-7-80028; 978-7-80188
Parent Company: China Publishing Group Corp

Morning Glory Publishers (Zhaohua Chubanshe)+
Subsidiary of China International Publishing Group
No 24 Baiwanzhuang Dajie Ave, Bldg 4, Xicheng District, Beijing 100037
Tel: (010) 68995510
Founded: 1982
Copyright transfer; purchase of entire editions.
Subjects: Art, Career Development, Cookery, Education, Fashion, Fiction, History, Literature, Literary Criticism, Essays, Photography, Self-Help, Social Sciences, Sociology
ISBN Prefix(es): 978-7-5054

Nanjing University Press (Nanjing Daxue Chubanshe)+
22 Hankou Rd, Nanjing, Jiangsu 210093
Tel: (025) 83601783; (025) 83594756 *Fax:* (025) 83686347
Web Site: www.njupco.com
Key Personnel
President: Jian Zuo
Editor-in-Chief: Xinrong Jin
Founded: 1984
Also publishes monographs.
Subjects: Biography, Memoirs, Biological Sciences, Chemistry, Chemical Engineering, Computer Science, Earth Sciences, Economics, English as a Second Language, Environmental Studies
ISBN Prefix(es): 978-7-305

National Defense Industry Press (Guofang Gongye Chubanshe)+
23 Zizhuyuan South Rd, Haidian District, Beijing 100048
Tel: (010) 88540777; (010) 88540559 (editorial) *Fax:* (010) 88540776
Web Site: www.ndip.cn
Key Personnel
President: Zongxin Yang
Founded: 1954
Subjects: Aeronautics, Aviation, Automotive, Business, Computer Science, Computers, Education, Electronics, Electrical Engineering, Military Science, Science (General), Technology
ISBN Prefix(es): 978-7-118; 978-7-88704
Imprints: New Era Publishing

New Era Publishing, *imprint of* National Defense Industry Press

New Era Publishing (Xinshidai Chubanshe)+
Imprint of National Defense Industry Press
23 Zizhuyuan South Rd, Haidian District, Beijing 100048
Tel: (010) 88540777 (sales); (010) 88540559 (editorial) *Fax:* (010) 88540776
Web Site: www.ndip.cn
Founded: 1980
ISBN Prefix(es): 978-7-5042

New World Press (Xinshijie Chubanshe)
24 Baiwanzhuang St, Xicheng District, Beijing 100037
Tel: (010) 68995424 *Fax:* (010) 68998733
Key Personnel
Rights Manager: Hanzhong Jiang
Founded: 1951
Subjects: Art, Education, Finance, History, Language Arts, Linguistics, Literature, Literary Criticism, Essays, Social Sciences, Sociology, Chinese History & Culture, Investment
ISBN Prefix(es): 978-7-80005; 978-7-80187; 978-7-88717

Peking University Press+
205 Chengfu Rd, Haidian District, Beijing
100871
Tel: (010) 62752036; (010) 62752015; (010)
62752033; (010) 62754697 *Fax:* (010)
62765015
E-mail: zpup@pup.cn; marketing@pup.cn;
rights@pup.cn
Web Site: www.pup.cn
Key Personnel
President: Mingzhou Wang
Editor-in-Chief: Liming Zhang
Founded: 1902
Subjects: Biological Sciences, Chemistry, Chemical Engineering, Computer Science, Economics, Education, English as a Second Language, Finance, Science (General), Social Sciences, Sociology, Humanities
ISBN Prefix(es): 978-7-301; 978-7-900620; 978-
7-900632

**The People's Communications Publishing
House** (Renmin Jiaotong Chubanshe)+
No 3, WaiGuanXieJie, Andingmenwai, ChaoYang
District, Beijing 100011
Tel: (010) 59757908 (sales) *Fax:* (010) 85285392
E-mail: ccpress@ccpress.com.cn; jtbook@ccpress.
com.cn (sales)
Web Site: www.ccpress.com.cn
Key Personnel
President: Jialin Zhu *E-mail:* shezhang@ccpress.
com.cn
Editor-in-Chief: Min Han
Founded: 1952
Subjects: Automotive, Civil Engineering, Com-
munications, Film, Video, Transportation, Ship-
building & Repair
ISBN Prefix(es): 978-7-114

People's Education Press (Renmin Jiaoyu
Chubanshe)+
17 Zhongguancun Nandajie Rd, Bldg 1, Haidian
District, Beijing 100081
Tel: (010) 58758866 *Fax:* (010) 58758877
E-mail: pep@pep.com.cn
Web Site: www.pep.com.cn
Key Personnel
President: Zhongmin Yin
Editor-in-Chief: Zhirong Wei
Founded: 1950
Subjects: Disability, Special Needs, Education
ISBN Prefix(es): 978-7-900055; 978-7-107
Number of titles published annually: 300 Print
Total Titles: 1,400 Print

People's Fine Arts Publishing House (Renmin
Meishu Chubanshe)+
Subsidiary of China Fine Arts Publishing Group
No 63 Dongsanhuan Zhonglu Rd, Chaoyang Dis-
trict, Beijing 100022
Tel: (010) 5669200
Web Site: en.cnpubg.com/enabout/2015/0812/
24203.shtml
Founded: 1951
Membership(s): China Publishing Association.
Subjects: Art, Biography, Memoirs, History, Pho-
tography
ISBN Prefix(es): 978-7-102
Ultimate Parent Company: China Publishing
Group
Book Club(s): Art Books Research Association

People's Health Publishing House, see People's
Medical Publishing House Co Ltd

People's Literature Publishing House (Renmin
Wenxue Chubanshe)+
Member of China Publishing Group
166 Chaonei St, Dongcheng District, Beijing
100705
Web Site: www.weibo.com/renwenshe

Founded: 1951
Subjects: Literature, Literary Criticism, Essays,
Nonfiction (General), Poetry, Cultural History
& Studies, Current Events
ISBN Prefix(es): 978-7-02; 978-7-5016
Number of titles published annually: 600 Print
Branch Office(s)
Shanghai

People's Medical Publishing House Co Ltd
(Renmin Weisheng Chubanshe)+
Shijie Yiyao Tushudasha B Zuo, No 19, Pan-
jiayuan Nanli, Chaoyang District, Beijing
100021
Tel: (010) 59780011 *Fax:* (010) 59787588
E-mail: pmph@pmph.com
Web Site: www.pmph.com
Key Personnel
Chairman: Xianyi Chen
General Manager: Yang He
Editor-in-Chief: Xian Du
Founded: 1953
Division of Ministry of Public Health.
Subjects: Health, Nutrition, Medicine, Nursing,
Dentistry
ISBN Prefix(es): 978-7-117
Bookshop(s): 92 Dongdan Beidajie, Beijing

People's Sports Publishing House (Renmin Tiyu
Chubanshe)+
8 Tiyuguan Rd, Chongwen District, Beijing
100061
Tel: (010) 67118491; (010) 67152966 *Fax:* (010)
67138489; (010) 67155616
E-mail: renmintiyu@126.com
Web Site: www.sportspublish.cn
Key Personnel
Dir, Editorial: He Yang
Contact: Jun Zhao
Founded: 1954
Subjects: Crafts, Games, Hobbies, Sports, Athlet-
ics
ISBN Prefix(es): 978-7-5009; 978-7-88721
Number of titles published annually: 440 Print;
70 Audio
Bookshop(s): Wu Huan Bookshops

Petroleum Industry Press (Shiyou Gongye
Chubanshe)+
No 1 Bilg, 2 Qu, Anhuali, Chaoyanganwai, Bei-
jing 100011
Tel: (010) 6421 8729
Web Site: www.petropub.com
Key Personnel
General Manager: Yubao Zheng
Editor-in-Chief: Zhen Zhang
Founded: 1994
Subjects: Energy
ISBN Prefix(es): 978-7-5021

PHEI, see Publishing House of Electronics
Industry (PHEI)

Phoenix Publishing & Media Inc (Fenghuang
Chuban Chuanmei Gufen Youxian Gongsi)
165 Zhongyang Rd, Nanjing 210009
Tel: (025) 83247221 *Fax:* (025) 83247221
E-mail: phoenixmedia@ppm.cn
Web Site: www.ppm.cn; www.ppmg.cn
Key Personnel
Chairman: Haiyan Chen
General Manager: Bin Zhou
Founded: 2001
Subjects: Art, Child Care & Development, Litera-
ture, Literary Criticism, Essays, Science (Gen-
eral), Technology
ISBN Prefix(es): 978-7-80643; 978-7-80729
Orders to: Phoenix Publishing & Media Group

Phoenix Science Press (Jiangsu Fenghuang
Kexue Jishu Chubanshi)+
No 1 Hunan Rd, 18F, Fenghuang Guangchang,
Nanjing 210009
Tel: (025) 86633229; (025) 86634269 *Fax:* (025)
83273111
Web Site: www.pspress.cn
Key Personnel
General Manager: Guohua Jin
Founded: 1978
Subjects: Agriculture, Chemistry, Chemical En-
gineering, Computer Science, Earth Sciences,
Education, Engineering (General), Environmen-
tal Studies, Geography, Geology, Health, Nu-
trition, Medicine, Nursing, Dentistry, Physical
Sciences, Science (General), Technology
ISBN Prefix(es): 978-7-5345

PMPH, see People's Medical Publishing House
Co Ltd

Popular Science Press (Kexue Puji Chubanshe)
16 Zhongguancun Nandajie, Haidian District, Bei-
jing 100081
Tel: (010) 62103158; (010) 62103349; (010)
62176522 (editorial); (010) 62103354 (orders)
Fax: (010) 62103109
E-mail: huping-kjp@cast.org.cn (editorial)
Web Site: www.cspbooks.com.cn
Key Personnel
President: Qing Su
Copyright: Ting Shan *E-mail:* shanting-kjp@cast.
org.cn
Founded: 1956
Subjects: Astronomy, Economics, Government,
Political Science, Medicine, Nursing, Dentistry,
Science (General), Technology
ISBN Prefix(es): 978-7-110
Parent Company: China Science & Technology
Press

Posts & Telecom Press (Renmin Youdian
Chubanshe)
No 11 Chengshousilu Rd, Fengdai District, Bei-
jing 100164
Tel: (010) 81055410 *Fax:* (010) 81055055
Web Site: www.ptpress.com.cn
Key Personnel
Administration: Yi Liu *Tel:* (010) 81055043
Editorial: Yaming Wang *Tel:* (010) 81055106
Sales: Hua Hu *Tel:* (010) 81055075
Founded: 1953
Subjects: Business, Communications, Computer
Science, Crafts, Games, Hobbies, Economics,
Electronics, Electrical Engineering, Manage-
ment, Psychology, Psychiatry
ISBN Prefix(es): 978-7-115; 978-7-88745; 978-7-
89497
Parent Company: Ministry of Information Indus-
try of the People's Republic of China (PRC)

Printing Industry Publishing House, see
Graphic Communications Press

PTPress, see Posts & Telecom Press

Publishing House of Electronics Industry
(PHEI) (Dianzi Gongye Chubanshe)
No 288 Jin Jia Cun, Huaxin Bldg, Wanshou Rd
S, Beijing 100036
Tel: (010) 88258888; (010) 88254114
E-mail: duca@phei.com.cn
Web Site: www.phei.com.cn
Key Personnel
Editorial Dir: Yanbo Shen *Tel:* (010) 88254400
E-mail: syb@phei.com.cn
International Rights: Ms Sunny Tian *Tel:* (010)
88254398 *E-mail:* sunny_tian@phei.com.cn
Founded: 1982

Subjects: Communications, Computer Science, Computers, Electronics, Electrical Engineering, Radio, TV
ISBN Prefix(es): 978-7-5053

Qilu Press (Qilu Shushe)
Subsidiary of Shandong Publishing Group (SDPG)
189 Yingxiongshanlu Rd, Jinan, Shandong 250002
Tel: (0531) 82098520; (0531) 82098522; (0531) 82098512 (chief editor) *Fax:* (0531) 82098517; (0531) 82098519; (0531) 82098521; (0531) 82906811 (chief editor)
E-mail: qlss@sdpress.com.cn; qilupress@126.com
Web Site: www.qlss.com.cn
Founded: 1979
Specialize in ancient books.
Subjects: Biography, Memoirs, Education, Geography, Geology, Philosophy, Religion - Buddhist
ISBN Prefix(es): 978-7-5333

Qingdao Publishing Group (Qingdao Chuban Jituan)+
182 Hai'er Rd, Qingdao, Shandong 266071
Tel: (0532) 68068026; (0532) 68068800
Fax: (0532) 85815240
E-mail: sdqingdaozxy@163.com
Web Site: www.qdpub.com
Key Personnel
Chairman: Mingfei Meng
General Manager: Bao'an Wu
Editor-in-Chief: Yachuan Li
Founded: 2004
Subjects: Accounting, Advertising, Aeronautics, Aviation, Agriculture, Alternative, Animals, Pets, Anthropology, Antiques, Archaeology, Architecture & Interior Design, Art, Asian Studies, Astrology, Occult, Astronomy, Automotive, Behavioral Sciences, Biblical Studies, Biography, Memoirs, Biological Sciences, Business
ISBN Prefix(es): 978-7-5436
Showroom(s): Cui Zifan Art Gallery

Sandu Cultural Media, see Sandu Publishing Co Ltd

Sandu Publishing Co Ltd
3rd floor, Design Bldg, Guangzhou Academy of Fine Arts, No 257 Changgang East Rd, Haizhu District, Guangzhou, Guangdong 510260
Tel: (020) 84344460
E-mail: info@sandupublishing.com; sales@sandupublishing.com (sales & distribution); editorial@sandupublishing.com (editorial submissions)
Web Site: www.sandupublishing.com
Key Personnel
Senior Editor: Daniela Huang
Acquisitions Editor: Matt Guo
Founded: 2001
Subjects: Advertising, Architecture & Interior Design, Fashion, Design Theory, Lifestyle
ISBN Prefix(es): 978-988-98566

Science Press (Kexue Chubanshe)+
16 Donghuangchenggen North St, Beijing 100717
Tel: (010) 64034541; (010) 64010628
E-mail: office@mail.sciencep.com; webmaster@mail.sciencep.com
Web Site: www.sciencep.com
Key Personnel
President: Mr Jixiang Wang
Chairman: Peng Lin
Founded: 1954
Subjects: Animals, Pets, Archaeology, Biological Sciences, Chemistry, Chemical Engineering, Computer Science, Earth Sciences, Electronics, Electrical Engineering, Environmental Studies, Gardening, Plants, Law, Mathematics,

Medicine, Nursing, Dentistry, Natural History, Physics, Science (General), Technology
ISBN Prefix(es): 978-7-03; 978-7-88730; 978-7-900146; 978-7-900185
Number of titles published annually: 500 Print; 20 Audio
Total Titles: 5,000 Print
Subsidiaries: Science Press New York Ltd
U.S. Office(s): 84-04 58 Ave, Elmhurst, NY 11373, United States, Contact: Mr Zhang Ju
Tel: 718-476-0238 *Fax:* 718-476-0273

SDX (Shenghuo-Dushu-Xinzhi) Joint Publishing Co (Shenghuo Dushu Xinzhi Sanlian Shudian)+
Member of China Publishing Group
China Art Museum, 22 East St, Beijing 100010
Tel: (010) 64001122; (010) 64020511 (editorial); (010) 64008687 (marketing); (010) 84010544 (rights) *Fax:* (010) 64002729
Web Site: www.sdxjpc.com
Founded: 1948
Subjects: Anthropology, Archaeology, Architecture & Interior Design, Art, Asian Studies, Biography, Memoirs, Developing Countries, Economics, History, Literature, Literary Criticism, Essays, Management, Philosophy, Psychology, Psychiatry, Social Sciences, Sociology
ISBN Prefix(es): 978-7-108
Number of titles published annually: 200 Print

SendPoints Publishing Co Ltd (Shanben Chuban Gongsi)
7/F, 10 Anningjie St, Jinshazhou, Baiyun District, Guangzhou, Guangdong 510280
Tel: (020) 89095121
E-mail: zhangjuan@sendpoints.cn
Web Site: www.sendpoints.cn
Founded: 2006
Subjects: Architecture & Interior Design, Art, Fashion, Real Estate, Animation, Culture, Graphic Design, Landscape, Product Design
ISBN Prefix(es): 978-988-17933; 978-988-15624; 978-988-19610; 978-988-16834; 978-988-12943
Branch Office(s)
Room 107, Bldg 1, No 9 Yuan, Andelu Xiyingfang Hutong, Dongcheng District, Beijing
Tel: (010) 84139071 *E-mail:* yan@sendpoints.cn
Room 307, Bldg 1, 1481 Gonghexinlu, Hongqiangchuangyiyuan, Shanghai *Tel:* (021) 63523469 *E-mail:* cui@sendpoints.cn

SEP, see Shandong Education Press (SEP)

SEPH, see Shanghai Educational Publishing House (SEPH)

SFLEP, see Shanghai Foreign Language Education Press (SFLEP)

Shandong Education Press (SEP) (Shandong Jiaoyu Chubanshe)+
Subsidiary of Shandong Publishing Group (SDPG)
No 321 Weiyi Rd, Jinan City, Shandong 250001
Tel: (0531) 82092612; (0531) 82092600; (0531) 82092689 *Fax:* (0531) 82092661
E-mail: rights@sjs.com.cn; faxing@sjs.com.cn; zongbianshi@sjs.com.cn
Web Site: www.sjs.com.cn
Key Personnel
General Manager: Fei Qi *Tel:* (0531) 82092695 *Fax:* (0531) 82092625
Founded: 1982
Subjects: Child Care & Development, Education, Fiction
ISBN Prefix(es): 978-7-5328

Shandong Fine Arts Publishing House+
Subsidiary of Shandong Publishing Group (SDPG)
39 Shengli St, Jinan, Shandong 250001
Tel: (0531) 82098268 *Fax:* (0531) 82066185
E-mail: sdmscbs@163.com
Web Site: www.sdmspub.com
Key Personnel
President: Liu Chuanxi
Editor: Wang Kai
Founded: 1983
Books, commercial printing, engineering & architectural services, newspapers.
Subjects: Fine Arts
ISBN Prefix(es): 978-7-5330
Bookshop(s): Fine Arts Bookshop, Bldg No 1, Shunhe Commercial St, Jinan
Tel: (0531) 86193020 *Fax:* (0531) 86193029
E-mail: sdmeishu@126.com

Shandong Friendship Publishing House (Shandong Youyi Chubanshe)+
Subsidiary of Shandong Publishing Group (SDPG)
14F Shandong Xinhuashudiandasha Bldg, 189 Yingxiongshanlu Rd, Jinan, Shandong 250002
Tel: (0531) 82098752; (0531) 82098037; (0531) 82098756 *Fax:* (0531) 82098140; (0531) 82098035
E-mail: youyisd@126.com
Web Site: www.sdyouyi.com.cn
Key Personnel
President: Wenrui Yao
Founded: 1986
Specialize in education, travel, foreign & Chinese culture exchange with an international emphasis.
Subjects: Art, Fashion, Fiction, Travel & Tourism, Comics/Cartoons, Culture, Lifestyle
ISBN Prefix(es): 978-7-80551; 978-7-80642

Shandong People's Publishing House (Shandong Renmin Chubanshe)+
Subsidiary of Shandong Publishing Group (SDPG)
39 Shengli St, Jinan, Shandong 250001
Tel: (0531) 82098914; (0531) 82098016; (0531) 82098027 (sales) *Fax:* (0531) 82069396
E-mail: sdrmpress@126.com
Web Site: www.sd-book.com.cn
Key Personnel
President: Haitao Guo
Editor-in-Chief: Changqing Hu
Founded: 1951
Subjects: Economics, Government, Political Science, History, Law, Philosophy, Social Sciences, Sociology
ISBN Prefix(es): 978-7-209

Shandong Science & Technology Press Co Ltd (Shandong Kexue Jishu Chubanshe)+
Subsidiary of Shandong Publishing Group (SDPG)
16 Yuhan Rd, Jinan, Shandong Province 250002
Tel: (0531) 82098073 (orders); (0531) 82098088; (0531) 82098090
E-mail: sdkj@sdpress.com.cn; 263871875@qq.com
Web Site: www.lkj.com.cn
Founded: 1978
Subjects: Agriculture, Architecture & Interior Design, Business, Computers, Earth Sciences, Economics, Education, Electronics, Electrical Engineering, Energy, Engineering (General), English as a Second Language, Environmental Studies, Language Arts, Linguistics, Mechanical Engineering, Medicine, Nursing, Dentistry, Technology, Foreign Language Study
ISBN Prefix(es): 978-7-5331

Shandong University Press Co Ltd (Shandong
Daxue Chubanshe)+
No 27 Shanda Nanlu Rd, Jinan, Shandong
250100
Tel: (0531) 88364701; (0531) 88364702
Fax: (0531) 88365167; (0531) 88565657
E-mail: ipo@sdu.edu.cn
Web Site: en.sdu.edu.cn
Key Personnel
President: Prof Rong Zhang
Founded: 1983
Subjects: Accounting, Architecture & Interior
Design, Behavioral Sciences, Business, Chem-
istry, Chemical Engineering, Communications,
Computer Science, Computers, Economics,
Electronics, Electrical Engineering, Energy,
Engineering (General), English as a Second
Language, Environmental Studies, Finance, Ge-
ography, Geology, History, Human Relations,
Library & Information Sciences, Management,
Mathematics, Mechanical Engineering, Philoso-
phy, Physical Sciences, Physics, Public Admin-
istration, Science (General), Technology
ISBN Prefix(es): 978-7-5607

**Shanghai Calligraphy & Painting Publishing
House** (Shanghai Shuhua Chubanshe)+
593 Yan'an Xi Rd, Changning District, Shanghai
200050
Tel: (021) 61229008; (021) 61229010; (021)
61229020
E-mail: shcpph@online.sh.cn
Web Site: www.shshuhua.com; www.duoyunxuan.
com
Key Personnel
President: Lixiang Wang
Editor-in-Chief: Fusheng Lu
Founded: 1960
Subjects: Antiques, Art, Biography, Mem-
oirs, Fashion, Photography, Culural Studies,
Lifestyles
ISBN Prefix(es): 978-7-80635; 978-7-80512; 978-
7-80672; 978-7-80725

Shanghai Educational Publishing House
(SEPH) (Shanghai Jiaoyu Chubanshe)+
123 Yongfu Rd, Shanghai 200031
Tel: (021) 64377165; (021) 64319241 (editorial)
Fax: (021) 64339995
E-mail: sephbgs@seph.sh.cn
Web Site: www.seph.com.cn
Founded: 1958
Subjects: Child Care & Development, Comput-
ers, Education, English as a Second Language,
History, Physics, Science (General), Social Sci-
ences, Sociology, Technology, Academics
ISBN Prefix(es): 978-7-5320; 978-7-5444; 978-7-
88843
Distributor for Xin Hua Book Store (Peoples Re-
public of China)

Shanghai Far East Publishers (SFEP)
(Shanghai Yuandong Chubanshe)+
10F Chubandalou, No 81 Qinzhou Nanlu, Shang-
hai 200235
Tel: (021) 62347733; (021) 62594457; (021)
63914066 (orders) *Fax:* (021) 62594779
E-mail: ydbook100@sina.com
Web Site: www.ydbook.com
Founded: 1983
Subjects: Accounting, Animals, Pets, Art, Biogra-
phy, Memoirs, Business, Career Development,
Child Care & Development, Communications,
Economics, Education, English as a Second
Language, Film, Video, Health, Nutrition, Hu-
mor, Literature, Literary Criticism, Essays,
Management, Nonfiction (General), Psychol-
ogy, Psychiatry, Social Sciences, Sociology,
Technology, Travel & Tourism, Women's Stud-
ies

ISBN Prefix(es): 978-7-80514; 978-7-80706
Parent Company: Shanghai Century Publishing
Group

**Shanghai Foreign Language Education Press
(SFLEP)** (Shinghai Waiyu Jiaoyu Chubanshe)+
Affiliate of Shanghai International University
558 Dalian Xi Rd, Hongkou District, Shanghai
200083
Tel: (021) 65425300; (021) 65424871; (021)
35051290 (editorial); (021) 65422896 (publishing) *Fax:* (021) 65422956; (021) 35051287
(editorial); (021) 65425300-4044 (publishing)
E-mail: editorial@sflep.com.cn; marketing@sflep.
com.cn; sales@sflep.com.cn
Web Site: www.sflep.com
Founded: 1979
Subjects: Business, Education, English as a Second Language, Language Arts, Linguistics, Literature, Literary Criticism, Essays
ISBN Prefix(es): 978-7-81046; 978-7-81009; 978-
7-5446; 978-7-81095; 978-7-900653
Bookshop(s): 564 Dalian Xi Rd, Shanghai 200083

Shanghai Jiao Tong University Press
951 Panyu Rd, Xuhui District, Shanghai 200030
Tel: (021) 61675298 *Fax:* (021) 64073126
E-mail: sjtop@sjtu.edu.cn
Web Site: jiaodapress.com.cn
Key Personnel
President: Dr Jianmin Han
Dir: Guangliang Li *Tel:* (021) 61675193
E-mail: liguangliang@gmail.com
Copyright Licensing: Dan Li *Tel:* (021) 6167296
E-mail: liwwo@hotmail.com
Subjects: Economics, Education, Engineering
(General), Medicine, Nursing, Dentistry, Sci-
ence (General), Social Sciences, Sociology
ISBN Prefix(es): 978-7-313; 978-7-900624
Number of titles published annually: 800 Print

Shanghai Lexicographical Publishing House
(Shanghai Cishu Chubanshe)
Member of Shanghai Century Publishing Group
457 North Shanxi Rd, Shanghai 200040
Tel: (021) 62472088 *Fax:* (021) 62676853
E-mail: cishuyougou@sina.com
Founded: 1978
Subjects: Art, Business, Economics, History, Phi-
losophy, Poetry
ISBN Prefix(es): 978-7-5326

Shanghai People's Fine Arts Publishing House
(Shanghai Renmin Meishu Chubanshe)
No 33 Lane 672, Bldg D, Changle Rd, Shanghai
200040
Tel: (021) 54044520; (021) 64668747 *Fax:* (021)
54032331; (021) 64668747
E-mail: all@artchinanet.com
Web Site: www.shrmms.com
Key Personnel
President: Haiyan Gai
Founded: 1952
Established publisher with 50 years publishing
history on fine arts, visual arts (architecture,
design, photography) & children's books.
Subjects: Architecture & Interior Design, Art,
Photography, Travel & Tourism, Comic Books
ISBN Prefix(es): 978-7-5322

Shanghai People's Publishing House (Shanghai
Renmin Chubanshe)+
Member of Shanghai Century Publishing Group
193 Fujianzhong Rd, 19F-21F, Shanghai 200001
Tel: (021) 53594508 *Fax:* (021) 63914796; (021)
63507653
E-mail: spphmb@online.sh.cn; b2c@ewen.cc
Web Site: www.spph.com.cn
Founded: 1951
Subjects: Anthropology, Biography, Memoirs,
Business, Economics, Fiction, Finance, Govern-

ment, Political Science, History, Law, Manage-
ment, Marketing, Nonfiction (General), Philos-
ophy, Psychology, Psychiatry, Social Sciences,
Sociology
ISBN Prefix(es): 978-7-208
Number of titles published annually: 400 Print
Total Titles: 600 Print

Shanghai Scientific & Technical Publishers
(Shanghai Kexue Jishu Chubanshe)+
Member of Shanghai Century Publishing Group
71 Qinzhou Nanlu Rd, Shanghai 200235
Tel: (021) 64089888; (021) 64085630; (021)
64845386; (021) 64845328 *Fax:* (021)
64845082
E-mail: sstp@sstp.cn; english-c@sstp.cn; sstp-c@
sstp.cn; zbb-c@sstp.cn; rights@sstp.cn
Web Site: www.sstp.com.cn; www.sstp.cn; www.
sstp-china.com
Key Personnel
President: Wentao Mao
Founded: 1956
Subjects: Agriculture, Engineering (General),
Medicine, Nursing, Dentistry, Science (Gen-
eral), Technology
ISBN Prefix(es): 978-7-5323
Bookshop(s): SSTP Bookshop, 50 Ruijin Rd,
Shanghai 200020

**Shanghai Scientific & Technological Literature
Publishing House Co Ltd** (Shanghai Kexue
Jishu Wenxian Chubanshe Youxian Gongsi)
746 Changlelu Rd, Jingan District, Shanghai
200040
Tel: (021) 54036563; (021) 54037397 *Fax:* (021)
54033023
Web Site: www.sstlp.com
Key Personnel
Dir, Sales: Minghai Wang *Tel:* (021) 54032190
Fax: (021) 64374078 *E-mail:* mhwang@libnet.
sh.cn
Founded: 1978
Subjects: Agriculture, Engineering (General),
Medicine, Nursing, Dentistry, Science (Gen-
eral)
ISBN Prefix(es): 978-7-5439
Parent Company: Science & Technology Com-
mission of Shanghai Municipality, 30 Fu Zhou
Rd, Shanghai

Shanghai Translation Publishing House
(Shanghai Yiwen Chubanshe)+
Member of Shanghai Century Publishing Group
193 Fujianzhong Rd, Shanghai 200001
Tel: (021) 53594508; (021) 61914803 (rights)
Fax: (021) 63914291
E-mail: info@yiwen.com.cn; rights@yiwen.com.
cn
Web Site: www.yiwen.com.cn
Key Personnel
Rights Dept: Ms Pinxuan Jiang; Mr Wuping Zhao
Founded: 1978
Subjects: Biography, Memoirs, Business, Eco-
nomics, English as a Second Language, Fic-
tion, Finance, History, Inspirational, Spiritual-
ity, Language Arts, Linguistics, Literature, Lit-
erary Criticism, Essays, Nonfiction (General),
Philosophy, Psychology, Psychiatry, Romance,
Science Fiction, Fantasy, Social Sciences, Soci-
ology, Suspense
ISBN Prefix(es): 978-7-5327; 978-7-900325; 978-
7-88841
Number of titles published annually: 700 Print
Total Titles: 10,000 Print

**Shanghai University of Traditional Chinese
Medicine Press** (Shanghai Zhongyiyao Daxue
Chubanshe)+
1200 Cai lun Lu, Pudong, Shanghai 201203
Tel: (021) 51322222; (021) 51322548; (021)
51322549
Web Site: www.shutcm.com/shutcm/zzcbs

Key Personnel
President: Weiguo Hua
Founded: 1985
Specialize in Chinese traditional medicine.
Subjects: Asian Studies, Behavioral Sciences, Health, Nutrition, Science (General), Alternative Medicine
ISBN Prefix(es): 978-7-81010; 978-7-81121

Sichuan Renmin Chubanshe (Sichuan People's Publishing House)
No 2 Huaishu St, Qingyang District, Chengdu, Sichuan 610031
Tel: (028) 86250877 *Fax:* (028) 86259529
E-mail: scrmcbs@sina.com
Web Site: www.scpph.com
Founded: 1952
Subjects: Art, Economics, Government, Political Science, History, Law, Literature, Literary Criticism, Essays, Philosophy, Religion - Other, Social Sciences, Sociology, Travel & Tourism
ISBN Prefix(es): 978-7-220
Number of titles published annually: 400 Print
Total Titles: 3,000 Print

Sichuan University Press Co Ltd (Sichuan Daxue Chubanshe)+
No 141 Kehuabeilu Rd Fusanhao, Chengdu, Sichuan 610065
Tel: (028) 85460736; (028) 85401107 *Fax:* (028) 85461699
E-mail: copyright@scupress.net; editor@scupress.net
Web Site: www.scupress.cn; www.scupress.net
Key Personnel
President: Yu Xiong
Founded: 1985
Subjects: Accounting, Antiques, Computer Science, Economics, History, Marketing, Mathematics
ISBN Prefix(es): 978-7-5614; 978-7-900678
Parent Company: Ministry of Education

Sinolingua Co Ltd (Huayu Jiaoxue Chubanshe)+
Member of China International Publishing Group
24 Baiwanzhuanglu St, Xicheng District, Beijing 100037
Tel: (010) 68997826; (010) 68320585 *Fax:* (010) 68326333
E-mail: hyjx@sinolingua.com.cn; fxb@sinolingua.com.cn
Web Site: www.sinolingua.com.cn
Founded: 1986
Specialize in teaching Chinese as a foreign language.
Subjects: Education, Language Arts, Linguistics
ISBN Prefix(es): 978-7-80052; 978-7-80200
Total Titles: 300 Print; 30 Audio
Associate Companies: China International Book Trading Corp, 35 Chegong-zhuang Xilu, Beijing 100044 *Tel:* (010) 68412045 *Fax:* (010) 68412023 *E-mail:* cibtc@mail.cibtc.com.cn
Distributed by China Books & Periodicals
Shipping Address: China International Book Trading Corp, 35 Chegong-zhuang Xilu, Beijing 100044 *Tel:* (010) 68412045 *Fax:* (010) 68412023 *E-mail:* cibtc@mail.cibtc.com.cn; CBT China Book Trading GmbH, Max-Planck Str 6-A, 63322 Rodermark, Germany *Tel:* (06074) 95564 *Fax:* (06074) 95271 *E-mail:* post@cbt-chinabook.de
Warehouse: China International Book Trading Corp, 35 Chegong-zhuang Xilu, Beijing 100044 *Tel:* (010) 68412045 *Fax:* (010) 68412023 *E-mail:* cibtc@mail.cibtc.com.cn
CBT China Book Trading GmbH, Max-Planck Str 6-A, 63322 Rodermark, Germany *Tel:* (06074) 95564 *Fax:* (06074) 95271 *E-mail:* post@cbt-chinabook.de
Orders to: CBT China Book Trading GmbH, Max-Planck Str 6-A, 63322 Rodermark, Ger-

many *Tel:* (06074) 95564 *Fax:* (06074) 95271
E-mail: post@cbt-chinabook.de
Cypress Book Co (UK) Ltd, Unit 13/Park Royal Metro Centre, Britannia Way, London NW10 7PA, United Kingdom *Tel:* (020) 8838 2491 *Fax:* (020) 8453 0709 *E-mail:* sales@cypressbooks.com

SinoMaps Press (Zhongguo Ditu Chubanshe)+
3 Baizhifang Xijie, Xuanwuqu, Beijing 100054
Tel: (010) 83543969; (010) 83543970; (010) 83543971
Web Site: www.sinomaps.com
Key Personnel
President: Xiaoming Zhao
General Manager: Qinghua Ni
Founded: 1954
Subjects: Earth Sciences, Geography, Geology, Transportation, Travel & Tourism
ISBN Prefix(es): 978-7-5031; 978-7-900048

Social Sciences Academic Press
Division of Chinese Academy of Social Sciences
13/F, 15/F, A/B Tower of Hua Long Plaza, Bldg 3, Jia No 29, Beisanhuan Zhonglu, Xicheng District, Beijing 100029
Tel: (010) 59367190 *Fax:* (010) 59367198
E-mail: guoji@ssap.cn
Web Site: www.ssapchina.com
Key Personnel
President: Li Yanling *Tel:* (010) 59367270 *E-mail:* liyanling@ssap.cn
Editor & Book Sales: Zhao Ran *Tel:* (010) 59367197 *E-mail:* zhaoran@ssap.cn
Copyright Manager: Li Yang *Tel:* (010) 59367270 *E-mail:* ssapcopyright@ssap.cn
Founded: 1985
Subjects: Economics, Finance, Government, Political Science, History, Journalism, Language Arts, Linguistics, Law, Medicine, Nursing, Dentistry, Social Sciences, Sociology
ISBN Prefix(es): 978-7-5097
Number of titles published annually: 200 Print

South China University of Technology Press (Huanan Ligong Daxue Chubanshe)+
Wushan Lu, 17 Bldg, Guangzhou, Guangdong 510640
Tel: (020) 87113489 *Fax:* (020) 87113489
E-mail: z2cb@scut.edu.cn
Web Site: www.scutpress.com
Key Personnel
Vice President: Yiling Pan *Tel:* (020) 22236186
Deputy Editor-in-Chief: Li Qiao *Tel:* (020) 22236187
Founded: 1985
Subjects: Agriculture, Biological Sciences, Chemistry, Chemical Engineering, Civil Engineering, Computer Science, Economics, Education, Electronics, Electrical Engineering
ISBN Prefix(es): 978-7-5623
Total Titles: 4,000 Print

Southwest Jiaotong University Press (Xinan Jiaotong Daxue Chubanshe)+
No 111 Erhuanlu Beiyiduan, Chengdu, Sichuan 610031
Tel: (028) 8700533; (028) 87600562 *Fax:* (028) 87600502
E-mail: cbsxx@swjtu.edu.cn
Web Site: press.swjtu.edu.cn
Key Personnel
President: Xiao Yang
Vice President: Ting Wang *Tel:* (028) 876309161 *E-mail:* wangtina@sohu.com
Dir, Rights: Mei Li *E-mail:* 13881863330@163.com
Founded: 1985
Also has an audiovisual publication division.
Membership(s): Sichuan Publishers Association.
Subjects: Aeronautics, Aviation, Agriculture, Architecture & Interior Design, Civil Engineer-

ing, Communications, Computer Science, Economics, Electronics, Electrical Engineering, Engineering (General), English as a Second Language, Environmental Studies, History, Language Arts, Linguistics, Law, Literature, Literary Criticism, Essays, Management, Mathematics, Mechanical Engineering, Medicine, Nursing, Dentistry, Science (General), Technology, Transportation
ISBN Prefix(es): 978-7-81057; 978-7-81022; 978-7-81104
Bookshop(s): SWJUP Readers Service, Chengdu, Sichuan

Tianjin Education Publishing House
No 35 Xikang Rd, Heping District, Tianjin 300051
Tel: (022) 23332306 *Fax:* (022) 23332306
Web Site: www.tjeph.com.cn
Key Personnel
President: Hu Zhentai
Founded: 1983
Subjects: Art, Economics, Education, Literature, Literary Criticism, Essays, Management, Psychology, Psychiatry, Science (General), Social Sciences, Sociology, Popular Science
ISBN Prefix(es): 978-7-5309

Tianjin Science & Technology Press (Tianjin Kexue Jishu Chubanshe Youxian Gongsi)+
Unit of Bureau of Publications
10-11, Kangyue dasha, 35 Xikanglu, Hepingqu, Heping District, Tianjin 300051
Tel: (022) 23332402 *Fax:* (022) 23332392
E-mail: tjkjcbs@sina.com
Web Site: www.tjkjcbs.com.cn
Key Personnel
President & Editor-in-Chief: Hao Cai
Founded: 1979
Subjects: Agriculture, Architecture & Interior Design, Biological Sciences, Chemistry, Chemical Engineering, Child Care & Development, Computer Science, Computers, Cookery, Electronics, Electrical Engineering, Engineering (General), English as a Second Language, Gardening, Plants, Health, Nutrition, Mathematics, Medicine, Nursing, Dentistry, Physical Sciences, Science (General), Technology
ISBN Prefix(es): 978-7-5308
Number of titles published annually: 300 Print

Tomorrow Publishing House (Mingtian Chubanshe)+
Subsidiary of Shandong Publishing Group (SDPG)
39 Shengli St, Jinan, Shandong 250001
Tel: (0531) 8209 8215 *Fax:* (0531) 8206 3583
Web Site: www.tomorrowpub.com; www.sdpress.com.cn
Key Personnel
President & Editor-in-Chief: Peng Hu
Editor-in-Chief: David Fu
Founded: 1984
Subjects: Art, Education, Literature, Literary Criticism, Essays, Science (General)
ISBN Prefix(es): 978-7-5332
Associate Companies: Shandong Xinhua Book Store

Tsinghua University Press (TUP) (Qinghua Daxue Chubanshe)+
5-7 Ceng, A Zuo, Xueyandasha, Shuangqinglu Rd, Haidian District, Beijing 100084
Tel: (010) 62793001; (010) 62781733; (010) 62772014; (010) 62776969; (010) 62786544 (orders) *Fax:* (010) 62770278
E-mail: c-service@tup.tsinghua.edu.cn; e-sale@tup.tsinghua.edu.cn; zhilang@tup.tsinghua.edu.cn
Web Site: www.tup.edu.cn
Key Personnel
President: Junfeng Zong

Editor-in-Chief: Peihua Wu
Founded: 1980
Subjects: Architecture & Interior Design, Chemistry, Chemical Engineering, Civil Engineering, Computer Science, Education, Electronics, Electrical Engineering, Engineering (General), English as a Second Language, Management, Mathematics, Medicine, Nursing, Dentistry, Physics, Social Sciences, Sociology, Technology
ISBN Prefix(es): 978-7-302
Number of titles published annually: 250 Print
Total Titles: 700 Print

TUP, see Tsinghua University Press (TUP)

21st Century Publishing House
75 Zi'an Rd, Nanchang 330009
Tel: (0791) 86516175 *Fax:* (0791) 86516280
E-mail: 21cccc@21cccc.com
Web Site: www.21cccc.com
Key Personnel
Copyright: Lin Shan
Founded: 1985
Subjects: Health, Nutrition, Literature, Literary Criticism, Essays, Culture
ISBN Prefix(es): 978-7-5391; 978-7-88861; 978-7-900386

World Knowledge Publishing House (Shijie Zhishi Chubanshi)+
51 Ganmian Hutong, Dongcheng District, Beijing 100010
Tel: (010) 65232695 *Fax:* (010) 65233645
E-mail: 274271772@qq.com; wapnet_cn@sina.com
Key Personnel
President: Mr Yongnian Min
Editor-in-Chief: Jianmin Fan
Dir, Sales: Qin Wang *Tel:* (010) 65265923
Contact: Jun Dai
Founded: 1934
Subjects: Biography, Memoirs, Developing Countries, Fiction, Foreign Countries, Government, Political Science, History, Journalism, Social Sciences, Sociology
ISBN Prefix(es): 978-7-5012

The Writers Publishing House (Zuojia Chubanshe)+
10 Wenliandalou Nongzhanguan Nanli, Chaoyang District, Beijing 100125
Tel: (010) 65389156 *Fax:* (010) 65389156
E-mail: haozuojia@163.com
Web Site: www.zuojiachubanshe.com
Founded: 1953
A state enterprise publishing reprints of Chinese literature.
Subjects: Fiction, Literature, Literary Criticism, Essays, Poetry, Romance
ISBN Prefix(es): 978-7-5063
Number of titles published annually: 200 Print

Wuhan University Press (Wuhan Daxue Chubanshe)+
S-1F Lou, B Zuo, Kailequiyuan, No 108 Zhuodaoquanlu, Hongshan District, Wuhan, Hubei 430079
Tel: (027) 87215593; (027) 87215822 *Fax:* (027) 87215541
Web Site: www.wdp.com.cn
Key Personnel
President: Qinghui Chen
Founded: 1981
Subjects: Biological Sciences, Chemistry, Chemical Engineering, Computer Science, Economics, English as a Second Language, Government, Political Science, History, Law, Library & Information Sciences, Mathematics, Social Sciences, Sociology

ISBN Prefix(es): 978-7-307; 978-7-900634; 978-7-900673
Subsidiaries: Edit Computer Company

Xiamen University Press (Xiamen Daxue Chubanshe)
6F, 39 Wanghailu Rd, Erqi Ruanjianyuan, Xiamen, Fujian 361005
Tel: (0592) 2181111; (0592) 2182177 *Fax:* (0592) 2181406
E-mail: xmup@xmupress.com
Web Site: www.xmupress.com
Key Personnel
President: Dongming Jiang
Editor-in-Chief: Wenyan Song
Contact: Chengzhong Hui *Tel:* (0592) 2186128
Founded: 1985
ISBN Prefix(es): 978-7-5615

Xinhua Publishing House (Xinhua Chubanshe)+
Division of Xinhua News Agency
8 Jingyuan Lu, Shijingshan District, Beijing 100040
Tel: (010) 63073021; (010) 63077116 (editorial) *Fax:* (010) 63073880
E-mail: xh_zb@xinhuanet.com; ra98@xinhuanet.com
Web Site: www.xinhuapub.com
Key Personnel
President: Baixin Zhang
Vice President: Lishi Yao
Founded: 1979
Also publisher of People's Republic of China Year Book.
Subjects: Biography, Memoirs, Economics, Ethnicity, Government, Political Science, Journalism, Social Sciences, Sociology
ISBN Prefix(es): 978-7-5011
Bookshop(s): China News Bookstore

Yunnan University Press (Yunnan Daxue Chubanshe)+
Yunnan Daxue Yinghua Yuannei, 182 Yi'eryidajie, Wuhua District, Kunming, Yunan 650091
E-mail: 627137729@qq.com
Web Site: www.ynup.com
Key Personnel
Dir, Sales: Yinfeng Sun *Tel:* (0871) 65033244
Founded: 1988
Publishing house of Yunnan University. Over 1,700 titles published covering a wide variety of academic fields.
Subjects: Anthropology, Art, Business, Career Development, English as a Second Language, Ethnicity, Management, Marketing, Outdoor Recreation, Photography, Public Administration, Self-Help, Social Sciences, Sociology, Travel & Tourism
ISBN Prefix(es): 978-7-81068; 978-7-81025
Number of titles published annually: 125 Print; 10 CD-ROM
Total Titles: 150 Print; 10 CD-ROM
Parent Company: Yunnan University

ZheJiang Education Publishing House (Zhejiang Jiaoyu Chubanshe)+
Subsidiary of ZheJiang Publishing United Group Co Ltd
No 40 Tianmushan Rd, Hangzhou 310013
Tel: (0571) 88908755; (0571) 88909753; (0571) 88909727 *Fax:* (0571) 88909717
E-mail: zjjy@zjcb.com; jys@zjcb.com
Web Site: www.zjeph.com
Key Personnel
Dir, Sales: Ding Zhou *Tel:* (0571) 88909715
Deputy Dir: Jianming Zhou *Tel:* (0571) 88909710
Founded: 1983
Subjects: Education, English as a Second Language
ISBN Prefix(es): 978-7-5338

Zhejiang University Press (Zhejiang Daxue Chubanshe)+
Xixi Campus of Zhejiang University, No 148 Tianmushanlu Rd, Hangzhou, Zhejiang 310028
Tel: (0571) 88215650; (0571) 88273066 *Fax:* (0571) 88215650; (0571) 88273066
E-mail: zupress@zju.edu.cn; zup_hr@126.com
Web Site: www.zjupress.com
Founded: 1984
Subjects: Accounting, Agriculture, Art, Biological Sciences, Business, Chemistry, Chemical Engineering, Civil Engineering, Computer Science, Education, Engineering (General), History, How-to, Medicine, Nursing, Dentistry, Science (General), Social Sciences, Sociology, Technology, Electronic Media, Natural Sciences, Teaching Methods & Materials
ISBN Prefix(es): 978-7-308

Zhonghua Book Co (Zhonghua Shuju)
38 Taipingqiao xili, Fengtai District, Beijing 100073
Tel: (010) 63458236; (010) 63311241
E-mail: zhbc@zhbc.com.cn
Web Site: www.zhbc.com.cn
Key Personnel
Copyright Manager: Ruiling Wang
Tel: (010) 63395419 *Fax:* (010) 63395419
E-mail: lindawrl@126.com
Founded: 1912
Also distribution.
Subjects: Anthropology, Fiction, History, Language Arts, Linguistics, Literature, Literary Criticism, Essays, Philosophy, Poetry, Travel & Tourism, Classics, Texts
ISBN Prefix(es): 978-7-101
Number of titles published annually: 800 Print
Total Titles: 20,000 Print
Parent Company: China Publishing Group
Orders to: 36 Wangfujing Dajie, Beijing 100710
Tel: (010) 65140650 *Fax:* (010) 65140650
E-mail: zhsj1234@163.com

ZUP, see Zhejiang University Press

Colombia

General Information

Capital: Bogota
Language: Spanish (English widely used in business)
Religion: Roman Catholic
Population: 34.3 million
Bank Hours: 0900-1500 Monday-Friday
Shop Hours: 0900-1230, 1430-1830 Monday-Saturday
Currency: 100 centavos = 1 Colombian peso
Export/Import Information: Member of Latin American Free Trade Association. Value added taxes on all imports; no sales tax on books. Ad valorem: none generally on books except on books bound in leather or similar materials, on photonovels of thrillers, detective stories, etc, on horoscopes, children's picture books, atlases & advertising catalogues. No import license for books. Exchange license from Banco de la Republica required.
Copyright: UCC, Berne, Buenos Aires (see Copyright Conventions, pg viii)

La Carreta Editores
Calle 32D No 81 B-99 apto 301, Nueva Villa de Aburra, Medellin
Tel: (04) 2500684
E-mail: lacarretaeditores@muine.net; lacarreta.ed@gmail.com; lacarretaeditores@gmail.com
Web Site: www.lacarretaeditores.com

Subjects: Art, History, Language Arts, Linguistics, Literature, Literary Criticism, Essays, Outdoor Recreation, Social Sciences, Sociology
ISBN Prefix(es): 978-958-97664; 978-958-97811

Casa Editorial Escala SA
Calle 30 No 17-52, Bogota
Tel: (01) 232 0482 *Fax:* (01) 285 9882
E-mail: escala@revistaescala.com
Web Site: www.revistaescala.com
Founded: 1962
Subjects: Architecture & Interior Design, Art, Engineering (General)
ISBN Prefix(es): 978-958-9082; 978-958-97473
Branch Office(s)
Cr No 53 No 13E-31 Ap 301C, Cali *Tel:* (023) 3335506
Cr 5, No 13-51, Manizales *Tel:* (069) 8778133; (069) 8771978 *E-mail:* felipe27697@hotmail.com
Cr 37 No 12-20, Pasto *Tel:* (027) 7231268
E-mail: jezam_olgajar@hotmail.com
Ecuador, Contact: Mariana Criollo *Tel:* (02) 433047; (02) 368750 *E-mail:* marianacriollo@hotmail.com
Cuenca, Ecuador, Contact: Rolando Peralta *Tel:* (07) 2839485; (07) 2839484
E-mail: roloparq@hotmail.com
Huizucar 7, Altos de Vista Hermosa, El Salvador *Tel:* 2422614 *E-mail:* avigar.dc@integra.com.sv
Calle 15, No 26 Col Espartaco, Coyoacan, Mexico *Tel:* (052) 56173287; (052) 53385751
E-mail: revista_escala@hotmail.com
6 Bajo, 28005 La Paloma, Spain *Tel:* 913656221
E-mail: tarahumara@telefonica.net

CELAM, see Consejo Episcopal Latinoamericano (CELAM)

Centro de Investigacion y Educacion Popular (CINEP) (Center for Research & Popular Education)+
Carrera 5 No 33B-02, Bogota
Tel: (01) 245 61 81 *Fax:* (01) 287 90 89
E-mail: cinep@cinep.org.co; administrativa@cinep.org.co
Web Site: www.cinep.org.co
Key Personnel
Contact: Maria Salas
Founded: 1972
Specialize in social science.
Subjects: Economics, Regional Interests, Social Sciences, Sociology
ISBN Prefix(es): 978-958-644; 978-958-9027

Centro Regional para el Fomento del Libro en America Latina y el Caribe (CERLALC) (Regional Center for the Promotion of Books in Latin America & the Caribbean)
Calle 70 No 9-52, Bogota
Tel: (01) 540 20 71 *Fax:* (01) 541 63 98
E-mail: libro@cerlalc.org
Web Site: cerlalc.org/es
Key Personnel
Dir: Marianne Ponsford *E-mail:* mponsford@cerlalc.org
Secretary General: Alba Dolores Lopez Hoyos
Dir, Publications: Jose Diego Gonzalez
E-mail: jgonzalez@cerlalc.org
Founded: 1971
Also offers editing, lecture promotion, production & circulation services.
Subjects: Law, Literature, Literary Criticism, Essays
ISBN Prefix(es): 978-92-9057; 978-958-671
Parent Company: UNESCO

CERLALC, see Centro Regional para el Fomento del Libro en America Latina y el Caribe (CERLALC)

CIAT
Km 17, Recta Cali-Palmira, Cali
Mailing Address: Apdo Aereo 6713, Cali
Tel: (023) 4450000 *Fax:* (023) 4450073
E-mail: ciat@cgiar.org
Web Site: ciat.cgiar.org
Key Personnel
Dir General: Dr Ruben Echeverria
Founded: 1967
Specialize in investigation of tropical agriculture.
Subjects: Agriculture
Branch Office(s)
Edifico de DICTA/SAG, Blvd Centroamerica 2 do Piso, Oficina 225, Apdo No 15159, Tegucigalpa, Honduras *Tel:* 2213-1669 *E-mail:* v.escober@cgiar.org
c/o International Centre of Insect Physiology & Ecology (ICIPE), Duduville Campus Off Kasarani Rd, CIAT Africa Coordination, PO Box 823-00621, Nairobi 00100, Kenya *Tel:* (020) 8632800 *Fax:* (020) 8632001
E-mail: r.buruchara@cgiar.org
Residencial San Juan de Los Robles, Casa No 303, Apdo LM-172, Managua, Nicaragua
Tel: 22709965 *Fax:* 22709963 *E-mail:* m.e.baltodano@cgiar.org
c/o Agricultural Genetics Institute (AGI), Pham Van Dong St, Tu Liem District, Hanoi, Vietnam *E-mail:* r.lefroy@cgiar.org

CINEP, see Centro de Investigacion y Educacion Popular (CINEP)

Consejo Episcopal Latinoamericano (CELAM) (Latin American Episcopal Council)+
Centro de Publicaciones, Av Boyaca Nº 169D-75, Bogota, DC
Tel: (01) 587 97 10 (ext 307); (01) 587 97 10 (ext 562) *Fax:* (01) 587 97 12
E-mail: celam@celam.org
Web Site: www.celam.org/publicaciones
Founded: 1970
Subjects: Biblical Studies, Child Care & Development, Education, Nonfiction (General), Philosophy, Regional Interests, Religion - Catholic, Theology
ISBN Prefix(es): 978-958-625
Number of titles published annually: 30 Print; 2 CD-ROM; 5 Online
Total Titles: 460 Print
Distributed by Agape Libros; Paulinas

Derecho Penal y Criminologia, *imprint of* Universidad Externado de Colombia

Ecoe Ediciones
Carrera 19 No 63C-32 PBX, Bogota
Tel: (01) 2481449 *Fax:* (01) 3461741
E-mail: info@ecoediciones.com; internacional@ecoediciones.com
Web Site: www.ecoediciones.com
Key Personnel
General Manager: Alvaro Carvajal
E-mail: alvaro@ecoediciones.com
Dir, Commercial: Nydia Patricia Gutierrez
Subjects: Business, Engineering (General), Health, Nutrition, Law, Science (General), Human Science, Natural Science, Pedagogy
ISBN Prefix(es): 978-958-648
Foreign Rep(s): Libreria Artemis Edinter (Guatemala); Cientifica Libreria y Papeleria (Ecuador); CODEU (Corporacion para el desarrollo de la educacion Universitaria) (Ecuador); Miguel Concha SA (Chile); Cydma (Peru); EDISA (Costa Rica); Educativa (Ecuador); Fundacion del Libro Universitario, Libun (Peru); Global Ediciones SA (Venezuela); Libreria Hispamer (Nicaragua); Libreria Lehmann SA (Costa Rica); Libros y Libros (Bolivia); Limerin SA (Ecuador); Editorial Master (Bolivia); Multilibro (Ecuador); Representaciones Nacional Book SA (Panama); Negocios Multiples SA (NEMUSA) (Nicaragua); Libreria Papiros (Ecuador); Probooks (Mexico); Prolibros (El Salvador); San Cristobal Libros SAC (Peru); Sodilibrio Cia Ltda (Ecuador); Ediciones Tecnicas Paraguayas SRL (Paraguay); Tecnilibro (Ecuador); Unilibros (Dominican Republic)

El Ancora Editores (Anchor Publishing)+
Av-Calle 26 Nº 6-91 (802), Bogota
Tel: (01) 2415270; (01) 3348486; (01) 2828445
Key Personnel
Founder & Editorial Dir: Felipe Escobar
Founded: 1980
Subjects: Art, Drama, Theater, Economics, History, Humor, Journalism, Literature, Literary Criticism, Essays, Poetry, Social Sciences, Sociology
ISBN Prefix(es): 978-958-9044; 978-84-8277; 978-958-36; 978-958-96577; 978-958-8048; 978-958-95646; 978-958-96050; 978-958-96201; 978-958-96244

Eurolibros Ltda+
Calle 40, No 20-27, Bogota
Tel: (01) 2886400 *Fax:* (01) 3401811
E-mail: eurolibros@gmail.com
Key Personnel
Contact: Carlos Roberto Jimenez
Founded: 1983
Membership(s): Camara Colombiana de la Industria Editorial.
Subjects: Education, Outdoor Recreation, Religion - Catholic
ISBN Prefix(es): 978-958-9417
Number of titles published annually: 2 Print
Total Titles: 12 Print
Distributed by Oriente (Argentina)

Europea de Libros Ltda, see Eurolibros Ltda

Fondo Editorial EAFIT
Carrera 48A-10 Sur 107, Medellin
Tel: (04) 261 9271
E-mail: fonedit@eafit.edu.co
Web Site: www.eafit.edu.co/cultura-eafit/fondo-editorial
Key Personnel
Head, Editorial: Nathalia Franco *Tel:* (04) 261 9271 ext 9462 *E-mail:* nafranco@eafit.edu.co
Editorial Coordinator: Claudia I Giraldo
Administration & Finance: Gilberto Valencia
Tel: (04) 261 9271 ext 9271 *E-mail:* gvalenci@eafit.edu.co
Subjects: Art, History, Literature, Literary Criticism, Essays, Music, Dance, Poetry, Administration
ISBN Prefix(es): 978-958-720

Fundacion Universidad de la Sabana Ediciones INSE+
Campus del Puente del Comun, Km 7 Autopista Norte de Bogota, Chia, Cundinamarca
Tel: (01) 2699950; (01) 8615555; (01) 8616666
Fax: (01) 3440351
E-mail: publicaciones@unisabana.edu.co; sandra.casto1@unisabana.edu.co
Web Site: publicaciones.unisabana.edu.co; www.unisabana.edu.co
Key Personnel
Dir, Publications: Elsa Cristina Robayo Ruiz
E-mail: elsa.robayo@unisabana.edu.co
Head, Editorial: Diego Esteban Romero Varon
E-mail: diego.romero@unisabana.edu.co
Coordinator, Distribution & Sales: Nubia Esperanza Cortes Forero *E-mail:* nubia.cortes@unisabana.edu.co
Founded: 1987
Subjects: Biological Sciences, Economics, Management, Philosophy, Religion - Catholic

ISBN Prefix(es): 978-958-12
Bookshop(s): Sede del Puente del Comon-Chia-cundina-marca

Ediciones Gamma SA+
Calle 85 No 18-32, Bogota
Tel: (01) 593 08 77 (ext 521); (01) 593 08 77
(ext 531); (01) 593 08 77 (ext 553) *Fax:* (01)
593 08 67
Web Site: www.edicionesgamma.com
Key Personnel
Commercial Dir: Alvaro Mesa Plazas
E-mail: amesa@revistadiners.com.co
Founded: 1978
Subjects: Architecture & Interior Design, Art, Literature, Literary Criticism, Essays, Travel &
Tourism
ISBN Prefix(es): 978-958-95108; 978-958-95237;
978-958-8177; 978-958-9308
Parent Company: Banco Davivienda

Editorial GatoMalo
Calle 5, No 78 B-04, Bogota
Tel: (01) 264 2587 *Fax:* (01) 264 2587
E-mail: editorialgatomalo@yahoo.com
Web Site: www.editorialgatomalo.com
ISBN Prefix(es): 978-958-57365
Foreign Rights: Abiali Afidi Literary Agency

Editora Guadalupe Ltda
Carrera 42 B 10 A-57, Bogota DC
Tel: (01) 2690788; (01) 2690211 *Fax:* (01)
2685308
Founded: 1969
Membership(s): The Colombian Booksellers Association.
Subjects: Literature, Literary Criticism, Essays,
Science (General), Technology
ISBN Prefix(es): 978-958-608

Editorial Hispanoamerica Ltda+
Cra 67B No 45-25, Bogota DC
Tel: (01) 2216694; (01) 3155587; (01) 2213020
Fax: (01) 3155813
E-mail: info@hispanoamerica.com.co
Web Site: hispanoamerica.com.co
Key Personnel
Editor: Alvaro Pinzon Escamilla
Subjects: Language Arts, Linguistics, Mathematics, Science (General)
ISBN Prefix(es): 978-958-9104; 978-958-658

Icono Editorial
Carrera 10A, No 70-62, Bogota
Tel: (01) 3178905 *Fax:* (01) 3178898
Web Site: www.iconoeditorial.com
Subjects: Fiction, Nonfiction (General)
ISBN Prefix(es): 978-958-8461; 978-958-97842

Informativo, *imprint of* Universidad Externado de
Colombia

INSE, see Fundacion Universidad de la Sabana
Ediciones INSE

Instituto Caro y Cuervo+
Calle 10 N° 4-69, Bogota
Tel: (01) 342 2121
E-mail: contactenos@caroycuervo.gov.co
Web Site: www.caroycuervo.gov.co
Key Personnel
Dir: Carmen Millan de Benavides
Founded: 1942
Subjects: Education, Language Arts, Linguistics,
Literature, Literary Criticism, Essays, Cultural
History, Philology
ISBN Prefix(es): 978-958-611
Bookshop(s): Libreria Cuervo; Libreria
Yerbabuena

Instituto Misionero Hijas De San Pablo+
Calle 161A No 15-50, Bogota DC
Tel: (01) 528 74 44 *Fax:* (01) 671 09 92
E-mail: centrodecomunicacion@paulinas.org.co
Web Site: www.libreriapaulinas.com
Key Personnel
Superior Provincial: Yermy Castano
Dir: Gloria Ines Canas Arroyave
E-mail: giarroyave1@gmail.com
Founded: 1948
Subjects: Communications, Education, Philosophy, Women's Studies
ISBN Prefix(es): 978-958-669
Branch Office(s)
Barranquilla (two)
Bogota
Cali
Cucuta
Manizales
Medellin
Bookshop(s): Carrera 13 No 72-41, Bogota

International Center for Tropical Agriculture,
see CIAT

Juridica, *imprint of* Universidad Externado de
Colombia

Editorial Kinesis
Carrera 25, 18-12, Armenia
Tel: (06) 7401584; (06) 7409155 *Fax:* (06)
7401584
E-mail: atencion@kinesis.com.co
Web Site: kinesis.com.co
Subjects: Education, Sports, Athletics, Physical
Education
ISBN Prefix(es): 978-958-9401
Foreign Rep(s): Libreria Deportiva Agmex/
Podium Editores (Mexico); Biblio Informatica 2000 (Puerto Rico); EDISA - Ediciones y
Distribuciones del Istmo (Costa Rica); Global
Ediciones SA (Venezuela); Importadora Centrolibros Ltda (Chile); Internacional Libros
(Chile); Librerias Libun (Peru); Limerin SA
(Ecuador); Maracaibo Lib Europe Costa Verde
(Venezuela); Mr Books (Ecuador); Libreria deportiva Esteban Sanz (Spain)

LEGIS - Editores SA+
Ave Calle 26 No 82-70, Bogota
Tel: (01) 425-5255
E-mail: webmaster@legis.com.co
Web Site: www.legis.com.co
Founded: 1952
Subjects: Economics, Law, Management, Marketing
ISBN Prefix(es): 978-958-653
Subsidiaries: Legislacion Economica SRL; URB
Industrial la Urbina

Leyer Editores Ltda
Carrera 4a, No 16-51, Bogota
Tel: (01) 2821903 *Fax:* (01) 2822373
E-mail: contacto@edileyer.com
Web Site: www.edileyer.com
Founded: 1991
Subjects: Law
ISBN Prefix(es): 978-958-690; 978-958-769
Bookshop(s): Carrera 7 No 12-15, Bogota
Tel: (01) 3429097; (01) 3364200 *Fax:* (01)
2822373; Calle 40 No 44-69, Barranquilla
Tel: (05) 3406061; Carrera 13 No 35-22 Edificio El Plaza, Bucaramanga *Tel:* (076) 6521055;
Carrera 7 No 11-46, Cali *Tel:* (023) 8881530;
Calle del Porvenir No 35-76 Centro, Cartagena
Tel: (053) 6642062; Carrera 23 No 26-60, Edificio Camara de Comercio Local 8 y 9, Manizales *Tel:* (06) 8831370; Av La Playa (Calle
52) No 45-50, Edificio Los Bucaros Local 5,
Medellin *Tel:* (04) 5112926; (04) 5134983;
Carrera 10 No 19-52 Local 41, Complejo Diario del Otun, Pereira *Tel:* (06) 3257391

Editorial Libros & Libros SA (Books &
Books)+
Calle 15 No 68D-52, Zona Industrial Motevideo,
Bogota
Tel: (01) 7050265; (01) 7050266; (01) 7050267
Web Site: www.librosylibros.com.co
Founded: 1985
Specialize in writing & publishing textbooks for
elementary & high school education.
Subjects: Education, Publishing & Book Trade
Reference
ISBN Prefix(es): 978-958-9253; 978-958-8270;
978-958-8147; 978-958-724
Number of titles published annually: 50 Print
Total Titles: 50 Print
Associate Companies: Hillman Publicaciones

McGraw-Hill Education+
Carrera 85D No 46A-65, Bodegas 9, 10 y 11,
Complejo Logistico San Cayetano, Bogota
Tel: (01) 600-3800 *Fax:* (01) 600-3855
Web Site: www.mheducationcolombia.com
Key Personnel
Division Manager: Jorge Ospina *E-mail:* jorge.
ospina@mheducation.com
Founded: 1974
Subjects: Accounting, Biological Sciences, Business, Chemistry, Chemical Engineering, Economics, Engineering (General), Physics, Psychology, Psychiatry, Social Sciences, Sociology,
Technology
ISBN Prefix(es): 978-958-600; 978-84-8278; 978-958-41
Parent Company: The McGraw-Hill Companies,
1221 Avenue of the Americas, New York, NY
10020, United States
Subsidiaries: McGraw-Hill Interamericana de
Venezuela
Distributor for Harvard Business; Houghton Mifflin Harcourt; Microsoft Press

Editorial Migema SA
Calle 32A, No 19-22, Barrio Teusaquillo, Bogota
DC
Tel: (01) 2858538 *Fax:* (01) 2873204
E-mail: apamigema2@gmail.com
Key Personnel
Administrative Manager: Hayde Torres
Subjects: Mathematics
ISBN Prefix(es): 978-958-681; 978-958-921
Orders to: Calle 33A N 18-2D, Bogota

Ediciones Monserrate Ltda+
Member of Grupo Editorial Monserrate
Av Carrera 40 N° 20A-89, Bogota
Tel: (01) 269 51 37 *Fax:* (01) 269 51 37
E-mail: comercial@edimonserrate.com;
edimonse@cable.net.co
Web Site: www.edimonserrate.com
Key Personnel
Mng Dir & Editorial: Pablo Enrique Fajardo
Founded: 1977
Subjects: Cookery, Law, Travel & Tourism
ISBN Prefix(es): 978-958-95014
Warehouse: Calle 21 N° 40-13, Bodega

Norma SA
Av El Dorado No 90-10, Bogota
Tel: (01) 41004000
E-mail: servicliente@norma.com
Web Site: www.norma.com; www.librerianorma.
com
Founded: 1985
ISBN Prefix(es): 978-958-04; 978-958-45
Parent Company: Carvajal Educacion
Ultimate Parent Company: Carvajal SA

Editorial Oveja Negra+
Carrera 14 N° 47-39, Oficina 205, Bogota DC
Tel: (01) 302 06 22

E-mail: info@editorialovejanegra.com
Web Site: www.editorialovejanegra.com
Founded: 1969
Subjects: Biography, Memoirs, Business, Humor, Literature, Literary Criticism, Essays, Poetry, Social Sciences, Sociology
ISBN Prefix(es): 978-958-06; 978-84-8280
Number of titles published annually: 40 Print; 10 Audio
Total Titles: 20 Audio

Panamericana Editorial (Panamericana Publishing)+
Calle 12 No 34-20, Bogota
Mailing Address: Apdo Aereo No 6210, Bogota
Tel: (01) 360 30 77; (01) 277 01 00 *Fax:* (01) 237 38 05
Web Site: www.panamericanaeditorial.com
Key Personnel
General Manager: Fernando Rojas
Editor: Monica Laverde Henao; Luisa Noquera
Founded: 1993
Publish books of science & culture.
Subjects: Architecture & Interior Design, Art, Biography, Memoirs, Business, Communications, Cookery, Crafts, Games, Hobbies, Drama, Theater, English as a Second Language, Fashion, Health, Nutrition, History, Literature, Literary Criticism, Essays, Poetry, Religion - Other, Self-Help, Social Sciences, Sociology, Sports, Athletics
ISBN Prefix(es): 978-958-30
Number of titles published annually: 180 Print
Total Titles: 2,100 Print
Parent Company: Panamericana Editorial Ltda

Pearson Educacion de Colombia Ltda+
Carrera 7 No 156-78, piso 26, Bogota
Tel: (01) 294 0800 *Fax:* (01) 655 2871
E-mail: pearsonstore@pearson.com
Web Site: www.pearsoneducacion.net; www.pearsoncolombia.com
Founded: 1995
Educational texts in Spanish language.
Subjects: Computer Science, Education
ISBN Prefix(es): 978-958-9498
Number of titles published annually: 40 Print
Parent Company: Pearson Education

Editorial Planeta Colombia SA
Member of Grupo Planeta
Calle 73 No 7-60, floors 7-11, Bogota
Tel: (01) 607-9997 *Fax:* (01) 607-9976
E-mail: info@planeta.com.co
Web Site: www.planetadelibros.com.co; www.facebook.com/planetadelibrosco
Founded: 1966
Subjects: Architecture & Interior Design, Art, Biography, Memoirs, Fiction, History, Mysteries, Suspense, Nonfiction (General), Regional Interests, Self-Help
ISBN Prefix(es): 978-958-42; 978-958-614

Pontifica Universidad Javeriana
Carrera 7 N° 37-25, Oficina 1301, Edificio Lutaima, Bogota
Tel: (01) 3208320 (ext 4752)
E-mail: editorialpuj@javeriana.edu.co
Web Site: www.javeriana.edu.co/editorial
Key Personnel
Dir: Nicolas Morales *Tel:* (01) 2870715
Editorial Coordinator, Books: John Meza *Tel:* (01) 3208320 ext 4753
Marketing Coordinator: Rafael Alejandro Nieto *Tel:* (01) 3208320 ext 4207
Founded: 1992
ISBN Prefix(es): 978-958-683; 978-958-716; 978-958-97533

Sociedad de San Pablo
Carrera 46 No 22A-90, Bogota

Tel: (01) 3682099 *Fax:* (01) 2444957
E-mail: direcciongeneral@sanpablo.com.co; ventas@sanpablo.com.co
Web Site: www.sanpablo.com.co
Key Personnel
Dir General: Ciro Monroy
Editorial Dir: Vicente Miotto
Founded: 1914
Subjects: Philosophy, Religion - Other
ISBN Prefix(es): 978-958-607

Santillana Colombia+
Member of Grupo Santillana SA
Carrera 11 A, N° 98-50, Oficina 501, Bogota
Tel: (01) 705 77 77
Web Site: www.santillana.com.co
Key Personnel
General Manager: Alberto Polanco Blanco
Founded: 1988
Also distributor.
Membership(s): Colombia Book Association.
Subjects: Animals, Pets, Antiques, Art, Cookery, Management, Science Fiction, Fantasy, Self-Help
ISBN Prefix(es): 978-958-24

Siglo del Hombre Editores Ltda
Carrera 31A, No 25B-50, Bogota
Tel: (01) 337 7700 *Fax:* (01) 337 7665
E-mail: info@siglodelhombre.com
Web Site: www.siglodelhombre.com
Key Personnel
Dir General: Emilia Franco de Arcila
Editorial Dir: Angel Nogueira
Subjects: Art, Education, Engineering (General), Government, Political Science, Literature, Literary Criticism, Essays, Medicine, Nursing, Dentistry, Philosophy, Religion - Other, Science (General), Social Sciences, Sociology, Ecology, Humanities
ISBN Prefix(es): 978-958-665

Tragaluz Editores
Calle 6 Sur No 43A-200, Edificio Lugo Oficina 1108, Medellin
Tel: (04) 448 02 95 *Fax:* (04) 448 02 95
E-mail: info@tragaluzeditores.com
Web Site: www.tragaluzeditores.com
Key Personnel
Editorial Dir: Pilar Gutierrez Llano
E-mail: pgutierrez@tragaluzeditores.com
Distribution & Communications: Daniela Gomez
E-mail: danielagomez@tragaluzeditores.com
Founded: 2005
ISBN Prefix(es): 978-958-8845; 978-958-8562
Foreign Rights: Abiali Afidi Literary Agency

Editorial UN, see Editorial Universidad Nacional de Colombia

UNAD, see Universidad Nacional Abierta y a Distancia (UNAD)

Ediciones Uniandes
Carrera 1 No 19-27, Edificio Aulas, piso 2, Bogota
SAN: 005-2027
Tel: (01) 339 49 49 (ext 2133); (01) 339 49 49 (ext 2181, bookshop) *Fax:* (01) 339 49 49 (ext 3177, bookshop)
E-mail: infeduni@uniandes.edu.co; libreria@uniandes.edu.co (bookshop)
Web Site: ediciones.uniandes.edu.co
Key Personnel
General Editor: Julio Paredes *Tel:* (01) 339 49 49 ext 2159 *E-mail:* j.paredes189@uniandes.edu.co
Founded: 1958
Subjects: Accounting, Architecture & Interior Design, Art, Biological Sciences, Chemistry, Chemical Engineering, Economics, History,

Literature, Literary Criticism, Essays, Mathematics, Music, Dance, Philosophy, Science (General)
ISBN Prefix(es): 978-958-695; 978-958-9057; 978-958-95572
Distributed by Siglo del Hombre Editors; Editorial Temis SA

Editorial Universidad de Antioquia, Division Publicaciones (University of Antioquia Publisher, Publications Division)
Ciudad Universitaria, Calle 67 N° 53-108, Bloque 28, of 233, Medellin
Mailing Address: Calle 70 No 52-21, Apdo Aereo 1226, Medellin
Tel: (04) 219 5010 *Fax:* (04) 219 5012
E-mail: editorial@udea.edu.co
Web Site: www.udea.edu.co
Key Personnel
Dir: Jorge Ivan Franco Giraldo
E-mail: dpublica@arhuaco.udea.edu.co
Founded: 1984
Specialize in scientific & cultural texts, not only from the institution, but also from other intellectual & academic environments.
Membership(s): The Asociacion of Editorials; The University Editorial Association of Colombia (ASEUC).
Subjects: Art, Drama, Theater, Education, Health, Nutrition, History, Journalism, Literature, Literary Criticism, Essays, Medicine, Nursing, Dentistry, Music, Dance, Philosophy, Poetry, Science (General), Social Sciences, Sociology
ISBN Prefix(es): 978-958-9021; 978-958-655
Number of titles published annually: 50 Print; 1 CD-ROM
Total Titles: 46 Print
Foreign Rep(s): Siglo XXI de Espana Editores SA (Spain); Siglo XXI Editores de Mexico (Mexico); Libreria la Tertulia (Puerto Rico); Jorge Waldhuter (Argentina)

Universidad de los Andes, see Ediciones Uniandes

Editorial Universidad del Norte
Km 5 Via Puerto Colombia, Barranquilla
Tel: (05) 3509509
E-mail: edicionesun@uninorte.edu.co
Web Site: www.uninorte.edu.co/web/publicaciones-uninorte
Key Personnel
Editorial Dir: Sandra Alvarez *E-mail:* sanalvar@uninorte.edu.co
Editorial Coordinator: Zoila Sotomayor *Tel:* (05) 3509509 ext 4334 *E-mail:* zsotomay@uninorte.edu.co
Subjects: Architecture & Interior Design, Economics, Education, Engineering (General), History, Literature, Literary Criticism, Essays, Mathematics, Music, Dance, Philosophy, Science (General)
ISBN Prefix(es): 978-958-741

Universidad del Rosario
Carrera 7, No 12 B-41, Oficina 501, Bogota
Tel: (01) 2970200
E-mail: editorial@urosario.edu.co
Web Site: editorial.urosario.edu.co
Key Personnel
Dir, Publications: Juan Felipe Cordoba *Tel:* (01) 2970200 ext 3110 *E-mail:* juan.cordoba@urosario.edu.co
Mng Editor: Ingrith Torres *Tel:* (01) 2970200 ext 3119 *E-mail:* ingrith.torres@urosario.edu.co
Administrative & Commercial Coordinator: Juan Carlos Ruiz *Tel:* (01) 2970200 ext 3113 *E-mail:* juanc.ruiz@urosario.edu.co
Subjects: Economics, Government, Political Science, Law, Medicine, Nursing, Dentistry, Administration
ISBN Prefix(es): 978-958-738
Total Titles: 800 Print

Universidad Externado de Colombia+
Departamento de Publicaciones, Calle 12 no 1-17, Bogota
Tel: (01) 3537000; (01) 3420288; (01) 3419900
E-mail: sitioweb@uexternado.edu.co
Web Site: www.uexternado.edu.co/publicaciones
Key Personnel
Dir: Dr Jorge Sanchez
Founded: 1886
Subjects: Criminology, Education, Finance, Government, Political Science, Law, Management, Mathematics, Social Sciences, Sociology
ISBN Prefix(es): 978-958-616; 978-958-710
Imprints: Derecho Penal y Criminologia; Informativo; Juridica

Universidad Nacional Abierta y a Distancia (UNAD)
Calle 14 Sur No 14-23, Bogota
Tel: (01) 344 3700
E-mail: atencionalusuario@unad.edu.co
Web Site: www.unad.edu.co
Founded: 1981
Subjects: Accounting, Agriculture, Biological Sciences, Business, Chemistry, Chemical Engineering, Communications, Computer Science, Economics, Environmental Studies, Film, Video, Finance, Management, Mathematics, Philosophy, Physics, Science (General), Social Sciences, Sociology
ISBN Prefix(es): 978-958-651
U.S. Office(s): 1820 N Corporate Lakes Blvd, Off 203, Weston, FL, United States *Tel:* 954-389-2277; 954-389-4528 *Fax:* 954-389-0506
E-mail: contact@unad.us
Bookshop(s): Cread Jose Acevedo y Gomex, Autopista Sur No 16-38, Bogota

Editorial Universidad Nacional de Colombia
Av el Dorado, No 44A-40, Hemeroteca Universitaria Nacional, primer piso, ala oriental, Bogota DC
Tel: (01) 3165000 (ext 20046)
E-mail: direditorial@unal.edu.co
Web Site: www.editorial.unal.edu.com
ISBN Prefix(es): 978-958-17

Ediciones USTA
Carrera 13 No 54-39, Bogota
Tel: (01) 587 8797 (ext 2991)
E-mail: editorial@usantotomas.edu.co
Web Site: ediciones.usta.edu.co
Key Personnel
Dir: Daniel Mauricio Blanco
Secretary: Gina Andrea Alvarez
Subjects: Accounting, Architecture & Interior Design, Economics, Education, History, Law, Literature, Literary Criticism, Essays, Psychology, Psychiatry, Science (General), Social Sciences, Sociology, Sports, Athletics, Humanities
ISBN Prefix(es): 978-958-631
Number of titles published annually: 100 Print

Villegas Editores Ltda
Av 82 No 11-50, Interior 3, Bogota
Tel: (01) 616 1788; (01) 616 0306 (warehouse)
Fax: (01) 616 0020
E-mail: informacion@villegaseditores.com
Web Site: www.villegaseditores.com
Key Personnel
President & Editor: Benjamin Villegas Jimenez
Founded: 1986
Subjects: Architecture & Interior Design, Art, Cookery, Drama, Theater, History, Humor, Literature, Literary Criticism, Essays, Philosophy, Photography, Poetry, Self-Help, Sports, Athletics, Travel & Tourism
ISBN Prefix(es): 978-958-8160; 978-958-9393; 978-958-9138

Editorial Voluntad SA+
Av El Dorado No 90-10, Bogota

Tel: (01) 410 63 55
Web Site: www.voluntad.com.co
Founded: 1930
Subjects: Art, Communications, Cookery, Crafts, Games, Hobbies, Journalism, Language Arts, Linguistics, Music, Dance, Sports, Athletics
ISBN Prefix(es): 978-958-02
Branch Office(s)
Via 40 No 65-101, Barranquilla *Tel:* (095) 330 98 00
Kra 34, No 52-38 Cabecera, Bucaramanga *Tel:* (097) 657 55 00
Calle 15, No 32-234, Acopi Yumbo, Cali *Tel:* (092) 666 83 00
Los Angeles Kra 60A, No 30-47, Cartagena *Tel:* (095) 653 12 96
Ave 0A, No 3-51, Barrio Lleras Restrepo, Cucuta *Tel:* (097) 574 19 98
Calle 16, No 7-53, Ibague *Tel:* (098) 261 43 12
Kra 42, No 85A-95, Autopista Sur, Medellin *Tel:* (094) 384 56 14
Calle 25 No 7-59, Monteria *Tel:* (094) 782 61 66
Kra 13, No 5-14, Barrio El Altico, Neiva *Tel:* (0988) 872 03 37
Manzana 18 Casa 2 La Florida, Pasto *Tel:* (0927) 272 93 54
Kra 12 Bis, No 8-64, Barrio Rosales, Pereira *Tel:* (0963) 335 62 26; (0963) 335 61 49
Calle 11D, No 17A-154, Urbanizacion Riascos, Santa Marta *Tel:* (0954) 434 96 52
Kra 12 No 11-65, Int 217, Segundo Piso, Sogamoso *Tel:* (098) 770 17 78
Kra 12, No 18-24, Apto 101, La Granja, Valledupar *Tel:* (0955) 571 21 56
Calle 20 No 37 M-42, Villavicencio *Tel:* (09866) 665 30 09
Foreign Rep(s): Carvajal SA de CV (El Salvador); Dislivenca Editorial Excelencia (Venezuela); Ediciones Farben SA (Costa Rica); Kapelusz Editora SA (Argentina); Editorial Norma de Panama SA (Panama); Distribuidora Norma Inc (Puerto Rico); Norma Ediciones SA de CV (Mexico); Grupo Editorial Norma (Chile, Dominican Republic, Ecuador, Guatemala); Grupo Editorial Norma SAC (Peru); Parramon Ediciones SA (Spain)

Democratic Republic of the Congo

General Information

Capital: Kinshasa
Language: French (official)
Religion: Most follow traditional African beliefs; some Catholic and Protestant
Population: 39 million
Shop Hours: 0800-1200, 1500-1800 Monday-Friday; 0800-1200 Saturday
Currency: 100 makuta = 1 zaire
Export/Import Information: No tariff, but for books not of educational, scientific or cultural use there is a revenue tax; children's picture books and atlases are also taxed. Small quantities of advertising matter free. Statistical tax on all imports. Goods subject to duty also subject to turnover tax of percentage of CIF value and customs and statistical tax. No import licences for books. Exchange controls.
Copyright: Berne, Florence (see Copyright Conventions, pg viii)

Editions Mediaspaul ASBL+
10eme Rue N° 18 Limete Industriel, BP 127, Kinshasa

Tel: (089) 8218984; (099) 9509598 (cell)
E-mail: info@mediaspaul.cd; diffusion@mediaspaul.cd; marketing.msp@mediaspaul.cd; service.clients@mediaspaul.cd
Web Site: www.mediaspaul.cd
Founded: 1957
Subjects: African American Studies, Communications, Drama, Theater, Fiction, Health, Nutrition, Literature, Literary Criticism, Essays, Religion-Christian
ISBN Prefix(es): 978-2-7414
Branch Office(s)
Av Usoke prol, Quartier Kigoma
Distributed by Mediaspaul
Bookshop(s): Librarie Mediaspaul Gombe, Ab Haut-Congo N° 17, Kinshasa *Tel:* (081) 6917292; Librarie Mediaspaul Kimwenza, Paroisse St Marie, Kinshasa *Tel:* (097) 7664974 (cell); Librarie Mediaspaul Kintambo, Av Kasa-vubu N° 2, Kinshasa *Tel:* (097) 1485782 (cell); Librairie Mediaspaul Masina, Av Force Nationale n° 10, Kinshasa *Tel:* (097) 1485783 (cell); Librarie Mediaspaul Victoire, Av Victoire N°15, Kinshasa *Tel:* (097) 1485781 (cell); Librarie Mediaspaul Kikwit, Blvd national n° 47, Kikwit *Tel:* (081) 3618790; Librairie Mediaspaul Lubumbashi, Route Kasapa, Carrefour, Lubumbasi *Tel:* (099) 5454006 (cell); Librairie Mediaspaul Matadi, Route de Kinshasa, Rd Point n° 2415, Matadi *Tel:* (099) 7751031 (cell); Librairie Mediaspaul Mbujimayi, Av Cathedrale n° 1, Mbuji-Mayi

Costa Rica

General Information

Capital: San Jose
Language: Spanish
Religion: Roman Catholic
Population: 3.2 million
Bank Hours: 0900-1500 Monday-Friday
Shop Hours: 0800-1200, 1400-1800 Monday-Saturday (some close Saturday afternoon)
Currency: 100 centimos = 1 Costa Rican colon
Export/Import Information: No import licenses, but statistical recording prior to importation necessary. Imports over a certain value must be registered with Banco Central to be eligible for foreign exchange allocation.
Copyright: Berne, UCC, Buenos Aires (see Copyright Conventions, pg viii)

Academia de Centroamerica (Academy of Central America)+
100 este y 325 sur de Universidad Veritas, Barrio Montealegre, Zapote, San Jose
Mailing Address: Apdo 6347, 1000 San Jose
Tel: 2283-1847 *Fax:* 2283-1848
E-mail: academia@academiaca.or.cr
Web Site: www.academiaca.or.cr
Key Personnel
President: Edna Camacho
Founded: 1969
Subjects: Agriculture, Business, Economics, Environmental Studies, Finance, Health, Nutrition, Labor, Industrial Relations
ISBN Prefix(es): 978-9977-21
U.S. Office(s): 7311 NW 12 St, Suite 12, Miami, FL 33126, United States

Asamblea Legislativa de la Republica de Costa Rica
Relaciones Publicas, Prensa y Protocolo, Ave Central y Primera entre calles 15 y 17, San Jose
Tel: 2243-2000
Web Site: www.asamblea.go.cr

Key Personnel
Dir: Karla Granados Brenes *Tel:* 2243-2546
  E-mail: kgranados@asamblea.go.cr
Subjects: Economics, Education, Social Sciences,
  Sociology
ISBN Prefix(es): 978-9977-916; 978-9968-35

CATIE, see Centro Agronomico Tropical de
  Investigacion y Ensenanza (CATIE)

CCC-CA, see Confederacion de Cooperativas del
  Caribe, Centro y Suramerica (CCC-CA)

**Centro Agronomico Tropical de Investigacion y
  Ensenanza (CATIE)** (Tropical Agricultural
  Research & Higher Education Center)
Sede Central CATIE, 7170 Cartago, Turrialba
  30501
Tel: 2558-2000
E-mail: comunica@catie.ac.cr; catie@catie.ac.cr
Web Site: www.catie.ac.cr
Key Personnel
Dir General: Dr Jose Joaquin Campos
Founded: 1942
Research & higher educational center specializing
  in scientific investigation & techniques of trop-
  ical America, research & training of tropical
  agriculture & natural resouces.
Subjects: Agriculture, Biological Sciences, De-
  veloping Countries, Economics, Education,
  Engineering (General), Environmental Stud-
  ies, Gardening, Plants, How-to, Natural History,
  Social Sciences, Sociology, Technology
ISBN Prefix(es): 978-9977-57; 978-9977-951;
  978-9977-51

**Confederacion de Cooperativas del Caribe,
  Centro y Suramerica (CCC-CA)+**
Apdo 3658, 1000 San Jose
Tel: 2240-4641 *Fax:* 2240-4284
E-mail: info@ccc-ca.com
Web Site: www.ccc-ca.com
Key Personnel
Executive Dir: Felix J Cristia *E-mail:* fcristia@
  ccc-ca.com
Founded: 1980
Subjects: Finance, Public Administration
ISBN Prefix(es): 978-9977-82
Subsidiaries: Sistema de Informacion Cooperativa
  (REDI-COOP)
Branch Office(s)
CCC-CA/Oficina Subregional, PO Box 360707,
  San Juan 00936-0707, Puerto Rico

Editorial Costa Rica
Apdo 10010, 1000 San Jose
Tel: 2233-0812 *Fax:* 2233-1949
E-mail: ventas@editorialcostarica.com;
  difusion@editorialcostarica.com; produccion@
  editorialcostarica.com
Web Site: www.editorialcostarica.com
Key Personnel
General Manager: Maria Isabel Brenes Alvarado
  E-mail: gerenciageneral@editorialcostarica.com
Assistant Manager: Carlos Calvo Castro
  E-mail: asistegerencia@editorialcostarica.com
Head, Production: Marianela Camacho
Founded: 1959
Subjects: Regional Interests
ISBN Prefix(es): 978-84-8361; 978-9977-23

**DEI (Departamento Ecumenico de
  Investigaciones)+**
Apdo 389-2070, Sabanilla, Montes de Oca, 1000
  San Jose
Tel: 2253-0229
E-mail: contactenos@deicr.org
Web Site: www.deicr.org
Founded: 1977
Subjects: Economics, Government, Political Sci-
  ence, History, Theology, Women's Studies

ISBN Prefix(es): 978-9977-904; 978-9977-83
Imprints: Revista Pasos

Departamento Ecumenico de Investigaciones,
  see DEI (Departamento Ecumenico de
  Investigaciones)

ECR, see Editorial Costa Rica

Editorama SA
Apdo Postal 2171-1002, San Jose
Tel: 2255-0202; 2233-8645 (marketing & sales)
  Fax: 2222-7878
Key Personnel
President/General Manager: Delio Sanchez
  Cordero
Manager: Eduardo Cisneros Sanchez
  E-mail: financierocontable@editorama.
  net; Leonardo Sanchez Orozco
  E-mail: mercadeoyventas@editorama.net;
  Adrian Sanchez Cordero *E-mail:* produccion@
  editorama.net
Founded: 1970
ISBN Prefix(es): 978-9977-88

EDNASSS, see Editorial Nacional de Salud y
  Seguridad Social (EDNASSS)

EUNA, see Editorial Universidad Nacional
  (EUNA)

EUNED, see Editorial Universidad Estatal a
  Distancia (EUNED)

**Facultad Latinoamericana de Ciencias Sociales
  - Sede Academica de Costa Rica**, see
  Ediciones FLACSO Costa Rica

Ediciones FLACSO Costa Rica
De Plaza del Sol en Curridabat, 200 metros sur y
  25 metros este, 1000 San Jose
Tel: 2224-8059 *Fax:* 2224-2638
E-mail: dalfaro@flacso.or.cr; eazofeifa@flacso.or.
  cr
Web Site: www.flacso.or.cr
Key Personnel
Dir: Jorge Mora *E-mail:* jmora@flasco.or.cr
Founded: 1957
Subjects: Social Sciences, Sociology, Cross-
  Border Migration, Decentralization & Munic-
  ipal Management, Democratic Governance &
  Political Institutions, Food Security & Rural
  Development, Globalization, Labor Markets
  & Inequality, Population & Territory, Social
  Development & Public Policies, Sustainable
  Tourism
ISBN Prefix(es): 978-9977-68; 978-84-89401

Fundacion Omar Dengo
Barrio Francisco Peralta, Av 10 y 12, Calle 25,
  1000 San Jose
Mailing Address: Apdo 1032-2050, 1000 San
  Jose
Tel: 2527-6000 *Fax:* 2527-6010
E-mail: info@fod.ac.cr
Web Site: www.fod.ac.cr
Key Personnel
Contact: Alfonso Gutierrez Cerdas
Founded: 1987
Subjects: Career Development, Education, Mathe-
  matics, Science (General)
ISBN Prefix(es): 978-9977-11

IICA, see Instituto Interamericano de
  Cooperacion para la Agricultura (IICA)

INCAE, see Insituto Centroamericano de
  Administracion de Empresas (INCAE)

**Insituto Centroamericano de Administracion
  de Empresas (INCAE)**
2 Km al Oeste del Vivero Procesa No 1, 4050 La
  Garita, Alajuela
Mailing Address: Apdo 960, La Garita, Alajuela
Tel: 2437-2200 *Fax:* 2433-9101
E-mail: incae-costarica@incae.edu
Web Site: www.incae.edu
Key Personnel
President: Arturo Condo *E-mail:* rectoria@incae.
  edu
Administrator: Yenory Salazar *E-mail:* yenory.
  salazar@incae.edu
Founded: 1964
Subjects: Business, Economics, Finance, Manage-
  ment, Marketing
ISBN Prefix(es): 978-9977-71

**Instituto Interamericano de Cooperacion para
  la Agricultura (IICA)** (Inter-American
  Institute for Cooperation on Agriculture)
600 m Norte del Cruce Ipis-Coronado, San Isidro
  de Coronado, 2200 San Jose
Mailing Address: Apdo 55, San Isidro de Coron-
  ado, 2200 San Jose
Tel: 2216-0222 *Fax:* 2216-0233
E-mail: iicahq@iica.int
Web Site: www.iica.int
Key Personnel
Dir General: Dr Victor M Villalobos
Representative: Diego Montenegro *E-mail:* diego.
  montenegro@iica.int
Founded: 1942
Subjects: Agriculture, Computer Science, Devel-
  oping Countries, Earth Sciences, Environmental
  Studies, Marketing, Technology, Veterinary Sci-
  ence, Women's Studies
ISBN Prefix(es): 978-92-9248

Libreria Lehmann SA
Av Central, Calles 1 y 3, 10011 San Jose
Tel: 2522-4848
E-mail: sac@librerialehmann.com; servicio@
  librerialehmann.com
Web Site: www.librerialehmann.com
Founded: 1896
Subjects: Art, Biography, Memoirs, Cookery,
  Drama, Theater, Fiction, Health, Nutrition,
  Inspirational, Spirituality, Literature, Literary
  Criticism, Essays, Nonfiction (General), Poetry,
  Self-Help, Sports, Athletics, Travel & Tourism
ISBN Prefix(es): 978-9977-949

Museo Historico Cultural Juan Santamaria
Ave tercera, Calle central y segunda, Frente al
  norte del Parque Central, Alajuela
Mailing Address: Apdo 785, 4050 Alajuela
Tel: 2441-4775; 2442-1838 *Fax:* 2441-6926
E-mail: info@mhcjs.go.cr; junta@mhcjs.go.cr
Web Site: www.museojuansantamaria.go.cr
Key Personnel
Dir General: Maria Elena Masis Munoz
  E-mail: direccion@mhcjs.go.cr
Founded: 1981
Subjects: Genealogy, History
ISBN Prefix(es): 978-9977-953

**Editorial Nacional de Salud y Seguridad Social
  (EDNASSS)**
Hospital San Juan de Dios, frente al Paseo Colon,
  Apdo 10105, 1000 San Jose
Tel: 2221-6193 *Fax:* 2233-8359
E-mail: ednasss@ns.binasss.sa.cr
Web Site: www.cendeisss.sa.cr/ednasss
Founded: 1974
Subjects: Behavioral Sciences, Biological Sci-
  ences, Health, Nutrition, Medicine, Nursing,
  Dentistry, Public Administration, Social Sci-
  ences, Sociology
ISBN Prefix(es): 978-9977-984; 978-9968-916
Number of titles published annually: 10 Print
Total Titles: 2 Print

Revista Pasos, *imprint of* DEI (Departamento Ecumenico de Investigaciones)

Ediciones Promesa+
Edificio Electronic Engineering, 200 N Del Mall San Pedro, San Jose
Tel: 2283-3033 *Fax:* 2225-1286
E-mail: administracion@promesacultural.com; editorialpromesa@gmail.com
Web Site: www.promesacultural.com
Key Personnel
Dir: Helena Ospina de Fonseca *E-mail:* ospina@promesacultural.com
Sales: Leslie Bonilla
Founded: 1982
Publishing, video, CD & documentation cultural center. Cultural project interrelating the arts.
Membership(s): Camara Costarricense del Libro.
Subjects: Anthropology, Art, Behavioral Sciences, Biography, Memoirs, Child Care & Development, Drama, Theater, Education, Fashion, Fiction, Film, Video, History, Human Relations, Inspirational, Spirituality, Language Arts, Linguistics, LGBTQ, Literature, Literary Criticism, Essays, Music, Dance, Nonfiction (General), Philosophy, Poetry, Psychology, Psychiatry, Religion - Catholic, Social Sciences, Sociology, Theology, Western Fiction, Women's Studies, Family
ISBN Prefix(es): 978-9977-947; 978-9968-41
Number of titles published annually: 24 Print; 1 CD-ROM; 6 Audio
Total Titles: 150 Print; 1 CD-ROM; 2 E-Book; 20 Audio
Parent Company: Promotora de Medios de Comunicacion SA
Associate Companies: Electronic Engineering, PO Box 4300, 1000 San Jose, Contact: Helena Maria Fonseca
U.S. Office(s): Ma Antonia Ospina, PO Box 491-050, Key Biscayne, FL 33149-7050, United States *Tel:* 305-361-0442
Showroom(s): Edificio Electronic Engineering, Frente a Rectoria, Universidad de Costa Rica, Carretera a Sabanilla, 1000 San Jose, Contact: Helena Maria Fonseca *Tel:* (305) 283-3033 *Fax:* (305) 225-1286 *E-mail:* hf@eecr.net *Web Site:* www.eecrica.com
Bookshop(s): Libreria Lehmann, San Jose; Libreria Universal, San Jose; Libreria Universitaria, San Pedro de Montes de Oca, San Jose

Editorial Tecnologica de Costa Rica+
Apdo 159, 7050 Cartagp
Tel: 2550-2297; 2550-2336 *Fax:* 2552-5354
E-mail: editorial@tec.ac.cr
Web Site: www.editorialtecnologica.tec.ac.cr
Key Personnel
Chairman, Editorial Board: Mario Castillo Mendez *E-mail:* mariocastillo@tec.ac.cr
Dir: Ana Ruth Vilchez Rodriguez *Tel:* 2550-2753 *E-mail:* avilchez@tec.ac.cr
Founded: 1978
Membership(s): Association of University Publishers of Latin American & the Caribbean (EULAC).
Subjects: Science (General), Technology
ISBN Prefix(es): 978-9977-66; 978-84-89400

Trejos Hermanos Sucesores SA
Apdo 10096, 1000 San Jose
Tel: 2224-2411 *Fax:* 2224-1528
Key Personnel
Founder: Alvaro Trejos
Subjects: Biography, Memoirs, Geography, Geology, History
ISBN Prefix(es): 978-9977-54

UICN, see Union Mundial para la Naturaleza (UICN), Oficina Regional para Mesoamerica y Caribe

Union Mundial para la Naturaleza (UICN), Oficina Regional para Mesoamerica y Caribe
Los Yoses, del Automercado 50 metros Sur, San Pedro de Montes de Oca, San Jose 11501
Mailing Address: Apdo 146-2150, San Pedro de Montes de Oca, San Jose 11501
Tel: 2283-8449
E-mail: mesoamerica@iucn.org
Web Site: www.iucn.org/mesoamerica
Key Personnel
Regional Dir: Grethel Aguilar
Founded: 1988
Subjects: Biological Sciences, Developing Countries, Environmental Studies, Coastal Zone Management, Forest Management, Gender & Development, Nature Conservation, Sustainable Development, Wetlands, Wildlife Management
ISBN Prefix(es): 978-9968-743

Editorial Universidad de Costa Rica+
Imprint of University of Costa Rica
Codigo Postal 2060, 11501 San Jose
Tel: 2511-5310 *Fax:* 2511-5257
E-mail: direccion.siedin@ucr.ac.cr
Web Site: www.editorial.ucr.ac.cr
Key Personnel
Administrative Coordinator: Ruben Chacon *E-mail:* administracion.siedin@editorial.ucr.ac.cr
Founded: 1975
Subjects: Agriculture, Anthropology, Archaeology, Architecture & Interior Design, Art, Behavioral Sciences, Biological Sciences, Career Development, Civil Engineering, Computer Science, Cookery, Earth Sciences, Economics, Education, Energy, Engineering (General), English as a Second Language, Environmental Studies, Government, Political Science, Health, Nutrition, History, Language Arts, Linguistics, Law, Management, Natural History, Physical Sciences, Poetry, Public Administration, Science (General), Social Sciences, Sociology, Sports, Athletics
ISBN Prefix(es): 978-9977-67; 978-9968-936
Total Titles: 40 Print; 1 CD-ROM

Editorial Universidad Estatal a Distancia (EUNED)
Apdo 474, 2050 San Jose
Tel: 2234-7954; 2527-2440; 2527-2638 *Fax:* 2234-9138
E-mail: euned@uned.ac.cr
Web Site: sanpedro.uned.ac.cr/editoria
Key Personnel
President: Dr Luis Alberto Canas Escalante
Executive Dir: Rene Muinos Gual
Founded: 1978
Subjects: Agriculture, Art, Biological Sciences, Computer Science, Economics, Education, Government, Political Science, Health, Nutrition, History, Library & Information Sciences, Literature, Literary Criticism, Essays, Mathematics, Medicine, Nursing, Dentistry, Philosophy, Psychology, Psychiatry, Religion - Catholic, Science (General), Social Sciences, Sociology, Theology
ISBN Prefix(es): 978-9977-64; 978-84-8362; 978-9968-31
Showroom(s): Calle 11, Ave 12-14, San Jose *Fax:* 331601
Bookshop(s): Libreria UNED; Calle 11, Ave 12-14, San Jose

Editorial Universidad Nacional (EUNA)
(National University of Costa Rica Press)
Apdo 86, 3000 Heredia
Tel: 2261-7017
E-mail: euna@una.ac.cr; publica@una.cr
Web Site: www.una.ac.cr/euna

Key Personnel
Dir, Publications & Printing: Erick Alvarez Ramirez *Tel:* 2562-4036
Founded: 1976
Subjects: Art, Education, Environmental Studies, Literature, Literary Criticism, Essays, Philosophy, Science (General), Social Sciences, Sociology
ISBN Prefix(es): 978-9977-65
Number of titles published annually: 40 Print; 2 Online
Total Titles: 300 Print; 2 Online
Parent Company: Universidad Nacional (Costa Rica)

Universidad para la Paz (University for Peace)
Campus Rodrigo Carazo, El Rodeo de Mora, San Jose
Tel: 2205-9000 *Fax:* 2249-1929
E-mail: info@upeace.org
Web Site: www.upeace.org
Founded: 1980
Subjects: Environmental Studies, Human Relations
ISBN Prefix(es): 978-9977-925

Uruk Editores SA
100 m al este y 15 al sur de municipalidad, Curridabat, San Jose
Tel: 2271 4824
E-mail: info@urukeditores.com
Web Site: www.urukeditores.com; www.facebook.com/Uruk.Editores/
Key Personnel
Dir: Oscar Castillo Rojas
Subjects: Fiction
ISBN Prefix(es): 978-9977-952; 978-9968-664; 978-9930-526

Cote d'Ivoire

General Information

Capital: Yamoussoukro
Language: French (officially) and several African languages
Religion: Traditional, 20% Islamic, 20% Christian (mostly Roman Catholic)
Population: 13.5 million
Bank Hours: 0800-1200, 1500-1900 Monday-Friday
Shop Hours: 0800-1200, 1530-1830 or 1900 Monday-Friday; 0800-1200, 1430-1730 Saturday
Currency: 100 centimes = 1 CFA franc
Export/Import Information: Member of West African Economic Community. No tariff on books; single copies free but most advertising subject to customs duty, fiscal duty and VAT. No import licenses required for imports from European Union.
Copyright: Berne, Florence (see Copyright Conventions, pg viii)

Centre de Publications Evangeliques
08 BP 900, Abidjan 08
Tel: 22 44 48 05 *Fax:* 22 44 58 17
E-mail: cpe@aviso.ci
Web Site: www.editionscpe.com
Founded: 1969
Subjects: Biblical Studies, Nonfiction (General), Religion - Protestant, Religion - Other
ISBN Prefix(es): 978-2-910307; 978-2-35686

INADES-Formation (Institut Africain pour le Developpment Economique et Social)
Rue C13 Brooker Washington, Cocody, Abidjan 08

Mailing Address: BP 8, Abidjan 08
Tel: 22 40 02 16 *Fax:* 22 40 02 30
E-mail: ifsiege@inadesfo.net
Web Site: www.inadesfo.net
Founded: 1975
Subjects: Agriculture, Literature, Literary Criticism, Essays, Regional Interests, Religion - Other, Social Sciences, Sociology

Institut Africain pour le Developpment Economique et Social, see INADES-Formation (Institut Africain pour le Developpment Economique et Social)

NEI/CEDA Editions+
One Blvd de Marseille, Abidjan 01
Mailing Address: BP 1818, Abidjan 01
Tel: 21 21 64 70 *Fax:* 21 21 64 86
E-mail: info@nei-ceda.com
Web Site: www.nei-ceda.com/fr/
Key Personnel
Relations Coordinator: Miriam Moro
Founded: 1972
Subjects: Art, Drama, Theater, History, Literature, Literary Criticism, Essays, Poetry, Religion - Other, Romance, Social Sciences, Sociology
ISBN Prefix(es): 978-2-910190; 978-2-911725; 978-2-84487

Nouvelles Editions Ivoiriennes/Centre d'Edition et de Diffusion Africaines, see NEI/CEDA Editions

Croatia

General Information

Capital: Zagreb
Language: Croatian
Religion: Predominantly Roman Catholic & Eastern Orthodox
Population: 4.8 million
Bank Hours: 0700-1900 Monday-Friday; 0700-1200 Saturday; 0800-1600 in the small towns
Shop Hours: 0800-1900 Monday-Friday & 0800-1300 Saturday
Currency: kuna, divisible into 100 lipa
Export/Import Information: Firms trade freely with foreign partners in accordance with international agreements & treaties, and with measures which are in line with the principles & demands of the World Trade Organization.
Copyright: UCC, Berne (see Copyright Conventions, pg viii)

AGM doo+
Mihanoviceva 28, 10000 Zagreb
Tel: (01) 4856 307; (01) 4856 309; (01) 4854 980
  Fax: (01) 4856 316
E-mail: agm@agm.hr
Web Site: www.agm.hr
Key Personnel
Dir: Svjetlana Dizdar *E-mail:* svjetlana.dizdar@agm.hr; Daniela Franici
Chief Editor: Grozdana Cvitan *E-mail:* grozdana.cvitan@agm.hr
Commercial Manager: Branka Jaksic
  E-mail: branka@agm.hr
Subjects: Art, Drama, Theater, History, Literature, Literary Criticism, Essays, Nonfiction (General), Philosophy, Social Sciences, Sociology
ISBN Prefix(es): 978-953-174
Parent Company: Zagrebacki Holding doo

ALFA dd+
Nova Ves 23A, 10000 Zagreb
Tel: (01) 4698 555; (01) 4698 512 (bookshop)
  Fax: (01) 4666 258

E-mail: info@alfa.hr
Web Site: www.alfa.hr
Key Personnel
Dir: Miro Petric
Founded: 1971
Subjects: Cookery, Education, Fiction, Gardening, Plants, Government, Political Science, Literature, Literary Criticism, Essays, Poetry, Religion - Catholic
ISBN Prefix(es): 978-953-168; 978-86-409
Bookshop(s): Importanne Centar, Starcevicev trg bb, 10000 Zagreb *Tel:* (01) 4573 079
Shipping Address: Jankomir Vucak 4, 10000 Zagreb
Warehouse: Jankomir Vucak 4, 10000 Zagreb
  Tel: (01) 2864 470; (01) 2923 953 *Fax:* (01) 2992 199

Algoritam doo
Harambasiceva 19, 10000 Zagreb
Tel: (01) 2359-333 *Fax:* (01) 2335-956
E-mail: info@algoritam.hr
Web Site: www.algoritam.hr
ISBN Prefix(es): 978-953-220; 978-953-6166; 978-953-6450

ArTresor naklada+
Sulekova 4a, 10000 Zagreb
Tel: (01) 2335 365 *Fax:* (01) 2335 300
E-mail: kontakt@artresor.hr
Web Site: www.artresor.hr
Key Personnel
Dir: Silva Tomanic Kis
Founded: 1996
Subjects: Art, Fiction, History, Language Arts, Linguistics, Literature, Literary Criticism, Essays, Philosophy, Poetry, Social Sciences, Sociology, Humanities
ISBN Prefix(es): 978-953-6522

Biblijski Institut
Kuslanova 21, 10000 Zagreb
Tel: (01) 23 38 638 *Fax:* (01) 23 08 188
E-mail: bizg@bizg.hr
Web Site: www.bizg.hr
Key Personnel
Dir: Thomas Sibley *E-mail:* tsibley@bizg.hr
Academic Dean & Editor: Stanko Jambrek
  E-mail: sjambrek@bizg.hr
Administrative Secretary: Marina Karadza
  E-mail: mkaradza@bizg.hr
Subjects: Philosophy, Religion - Protestant
ISBN Prefix(es): 978-953-8003

Centar tehnicke kulture Rijeka
Skoljic 6/1, 51000 Rijeka
Tel: (051) 327 155; (051) 327 183; (051) 320 281
  Fax: (051) 338 531
E-mail: info@ctk-rijeka.hr
Web Site: www.ctk-rijeka.hr
Key Personnel
President: Marko Sokolic
Secretary: Olivera Stanic
Founded: 1993
Nonprofit organization formed to encourage & promote technical culture & information science. Created to foster interest in the fields of scientific, technical & information technology education & to promote scientific, technical, information & cultural achievements.
Subjects: Education
ISBN Prefix(es): 978-953-99150

Centar za politoloska istrazivanja (CPI)
  (Political Science Research Center)
Gupceva 14a, 10000 Zagreb
Tel: (01) 3863 113 *Fax:* (01) 3863 113
E-mail: cpi@cpi.hr
Web Site: www.cpi.hr
Key Personnel
Dir: Andelko Milardovic *E-mail:* anmilard@gmail.com

Founded: 2001
Subjects: Social Sciences, Sociology
ISBN Prefix(es): 978-953-7022
Number of titles published annually: 3 Print
Total Titles: 8 Print

CPI, see Centar za politoloska istrazivanja (CPI)

CTK Rijeka, see Centar tehnicke kulture Rijeka

Cvor
Matice hrvatske 43, 43000 Bjelovar
Tel: (043) 244 572; (043) 244 050; (043) 221 773
  Fax: (043) 243 337
E-mail: cvor@cvor.hr
Web Site: www.cvor.hr
Key Personnel
Dir: Hrvoje Horvat *Tel:* (043) 243 042
  E-mail: hrvoje@cvor.hr
Marketing: Vesna Grandverger *Tel:* (098) 9271 555 (cell) *E-mail:* vesna@cvor.hr
Founded: 1968
Subjects: Cookery, Humor, Marketing, Outdoor Recreation
ISBN Prefix(es): 978-86-7303; 978-953-6254
Number of titles published annually: 11 Print

Durieux doo+
Sulekova 23, 10000 Zagreb
Tel: (01) 23 00 337 *Fax:* (01) 23 00 337
E-mail: prodaja@durieux.hr
Web Site: www.durieux.hr
Key Personnel
President: Drazen Toncic
Co-Founder & Editor: Nenad Popovic
  E-mail: nenad.popovic@durieux.hr
Founded: 1990
Subjects: Drama, Theater, Fiction, History, Literature, Literary Criticism, Essays, Philosophy, Poetry
ISBN Prefix(es): 978-953-188

Edit (Edizioni Italiane) (Italian Editions)+
Via Re Zvonimir 20a, 51000 Fiume
Tel: (051) 672-153 *Fax:* (051) 672-151
E-mail: editoria@edit.hr
Web Site: www.edit.hr; editfiume.com
Key Personnel
Editor-in-Chief: Silvio Forza *E-mail:* direttore@edit.hr
Founded: 1952
Publisher of newspapers & books.
Subjects: Art, Fiction, Health, Nutrition, Literature, Literary Criticism, Essays, Poetry
ISBN Prefix(es): 978-953-6150; 978-953-230
Number of titles published annually: 15 Print
Total Titles: 203 Print
Associate Companies: Il Ramo D'oro Editore, Via Duca d'Aosta 6, 34123 Trieste, Italy, Contact: Francesco Cenetiempo *Tel:* (040) 640 568 *Fax:* (040) 310 670 *E-mail:* info@ilramodoroeditore.it *Web Site:* www.ilramodoroeditore.it
Distributed by Il Ramo D'oro Editore
Bookshop(s): EDIT, Korzo 37, 51000 Rijeka, Bookshop Manager: Ester Ujeiae *Tel:* (051) 333-427

EDO doo+
89 Sv Ane St, 10430 Samobor, Hrvatska
Mailing Address: PO Box 72, 10430 Samobor, Hrvatska
Tel: (01) 33 61 044 *Fax:* (01) 33 60 585
E-mail: edo@edo.hr
Web Site: www.edo.hr
Key Personnel
President: Eduard E Osredecki, MA
Founded: 1984
Publishing, business seminars & business conferences.

Membership(s): HUOJ (The Croatian Association for Public Relations).
Subjects: Behavioral Sciences, Business, Education, Human Relations, Management, Marketing, Nonfiction (General), Public Administration
ISBN Prefix(es): 978-953-6094; 978-86-7425; 978-86-7697
Number of titles published annually: 5 Print
Total Titles: 14 Print

Egmont doo Hrvatska
Visnjevac 3, 10000 Zagreb
Tel: (01) 3040 555 *Fax:* (01) 3091 713
E-mail: info@cro.egmont.com
Web Site: www.egmont.hr
Founded: 1994

Fakultet Gradevinarstva Arhitekture I Geodezue (Faculty of Engineering & Architecture)
Matice hrvatske 15, 21000 Split
Tel: (021) 303 333 *Fax:* (021) 465 117
Web Site: www.gradst.hr
Key Personnel
Dean: Prof Alen Harapin *Tel:* (021) 303 351
  E-mail: alen.harapin@gradst.hr
Founded: 1977
Specialize in education, civil engineering, architecture & interior design, urbanism.
Subjects: Architecture & Interior Design, Civil Engineering, Education, Engineering (General), Management, Mathematics, Mechanical Engineering, Science (General), Technology
ISBN Prefix(es): 978-953-6116
Parent Company: Sveueiliste u Splitu

Filozofski Fakultet Sveucilista u Zagrebu (Faculty of Philosophy University of Zagreb)
Ivana Lucica 3, 10000 Zagreb
Tel: (01) 6120-111 *Fax:* (01) 6156-879
Web Site: www.ffzg.unizg.hr
Key Personnel
Secretary: Nada Cutic *Tel:* (01) 6120-175
  Fax: (01) 6120-125 *E-mail:* ncutic@ffzg.hr
Subjects: History, Language Arts, Linguistics, Literature, Literary Criticism, Essays, Social Sciences, Sociology
ISBN Prefix(es): 978-86-80279; 978-953-175

Fraktura doo
PP 102, 10290 Zapresic
Tel: (01) 335 78 63 *Fax:* (01) 335 83 20
E-mail: fraktura@fraktura.hr
Web Site: www.fraktura.hr
Key Personnel
Board: Sibila Serdarevic
Founded: 2002
Subjects: Literature, Literary Criticism, Essays, Nonfiction (General), Culture, Fine Arts, Literary Fiction
ISBN Prefix(es): 978-953-266

Golden Marketing/Tehnicka Knjiga
Jurisiceva 10, 10000 Zagreb
Tel: (01) 4810 820 *Fax:* (01) 4810 821
E-mail: gmtk@gmtk.net
Web Site: www.gmtk.net
Key Personnel
Dir: Ana Resetar
Editor: Omer Rak *E-mail:* orak@gmtk.net
Children's Editor: Natasa Maletic
  E-mail: nmaletic@gmtk.net
Founded: 1947
Subjects: Engineering (General), Literature, Literary Criticism, Essays, Science (General)
ISBN Prefix(es): 978-86-7059; 978-953-172; 978-953-6168; 978-953-212
Bookshop(s): Antikvarijat, Gunduliceva 19, Zagreb; Knjizara Tehnicka Knjia, Masarykova 17, Zagreb

Graficki zavod Hrvatske doo
Radnicka cesta 210, 10000 Zagreb
Tel: (01) 2499 000 *Fax:* (01) 2407 166
E-mail: info@gzh.hr
Web Site: www.gzh.hr
Key Personnel
Dir: Gordan Miler *Tel:* (01) 2407 159
  E-mail: gordan.miler@gzh.hr
Executive Dir of Production: Ivan Cvirn *Tel:* (01) 6410 660 *E-mail:* ivan.cvirn@gzh.hr
Head, Sales: Ognjen Bojanac *Tel:* (01) 2404 761 *E-mail:* ognjen.bojanac@gzh.hr; Katja Krizmanic *Tel:* (01) 6399 531 *E-mail:* katja.krizmanic@gzh.hr
Founded: 1874
Subjects: Art, Biography, Memoirs, Fiction
ISBN Prefix(es): 978-86-399; 978-953-6009

Graphis doo
Jurjevska 20, 10000 Zagreb
Mailing Address: Maksimirska 88, 10000 Zagreb
Tel: (01) 2322 975 *Fax:* (01) 2322 975; (01) 4668 204
E-mail: graphis1@inet.hr
Web Site: www.graphis.hr
Key Personnel
Dir: Elizabeta Sunde
Founded: 1994
Subjects: Electronics, Electrical Engineering, Government, Political Science, Medicine, Nursing, Dentistry, Sports, Athletics, Technology
ISBN Prefix(es): 978-953-6647; 978-953-96399
Number of titles published annually: 7 Print
Total Titles: 60 Print; 60 Online

Hrvatska akademija znanosti i umjetnosti (Croatian Academy of Sciences & Arts)
Hebrangova 1, 10000 Zagreb
Tel: (01) 48 95 178 *Fax:* (01) 48 95 178
E-mail: naklada@hazu.hr
Web Site: info.hazu.hr/hr/nakladnistvo/o_nakladnistvu/; info.hazu.hr
Key Personnel
Secretary General: Pavao Rudan *Tel:* (01) 48 95 122 *Fax:* (01) 48 19 979
Manager: Mr Aco Zrnic *Tel:* (01) 48 95 173
Founded: 1861
Subjects: Art, Science (General)
ISBN Prefix(es): 978-86-407; 978-953-154
Number of titles published annually: 100 Print; 5 CD-ROM
Total Titles: 4,800 Print; 20 CD-ROM
Bookshop(s): Prirucna knjizara HAZU, Contact: Mr Inoslav Tompak *Tel:* (01) 48 95 174 *E-mail:* inoslav@hazu.hr

Hrvatski centar ITI-International Theatre Institute (Croatian Centre of ITI)+
Basaricekova 24, 10000 Zagreb
Tel: (01) 4920 667 *Fax:* (01) 4920 668
E-mail: hc-iti@zg.t-com.hr
Web Site: www.hciti.hr
Key Personnel
President & Editor: Zeljka Turcinovic
  E-mail: zeljka.turcinovic@zg.t-com.hr
Founded: 1994
International theatre organization.
Membership(s): UNESCO.
Subjects: Drama, Theater, Music, Dance
ISBN Prefix(es): 978-953-6343
Number of titles published annually: 6 Print
Total Titles: 43 Print

Hrvatsko filolosko drustvo (Croatian Philological Society)+
Ivana Lucica 3, Room B-115, 10000 Zagreb
Tel: (01) 6120 119
E-mail: hfd@hfiloloskod.hr
Web Site: www.hfiloloskod.hr
Key Personnel
President: Ivana Vidovic Bolt
Vice President: Ida Raffaeli

Founded: 1952
Subjects: Fiction, Literature, Literary Criticism, Essays, Humanities
ISBN Prefix(es): 978-86-81173; 978-953-164
Number of titles published annually: 15 Print
Total Titles: 75 Print

Hrvatsko filozofsko Drustvo (Croatian Philosophical Society)+
Filozofski Fakultet, Ivana Lucica 3, 10000 Zagreb
Tel: (01) 6111 808 *Fax:* (01) 6170 682
E-mail: hrfd@hrfd.hr
Web Site: www.hrfd.hr
Key Personnel
President: Nada Gosic
Vice President: Milana Funduk
Founded: 1957
Subjects: Ethnicity, Philosophy, Psychology, Psychiatry, Social Sciences, Sociology
ISBN Prefix(es): 978-86-81173; 978-953-164
Warehouse: Krcka 1, 10000 Zagreb

Kasmir Promet doo
Andrije Hebranga 22, 10000 Zagreb
Tel: (01) 4553805; (01) 4553806; (01) 4553807 *Fax:* (01) 4553805; (01) 4553806; (01) 4553807
E-mail: kasmir@kasmir-promet.hr
Web Site: www.kasmir-promet.hr
Key Personnel
Publisher & Dir: Dr Kasmir Huseinovic
ISBN Prefix(es): 978-953-6613

Kastrapeli doo+
Tomasevica 7, 10410 Velika Gorica
Tel: (01) 888 9798
E-mail: info@kastrapeli.hr
Web Site: kastrapeli.hr
Key Personnel
Owner & Manager: Gordana Kastrapeli
Founded: 1991
Subjects: Behavioral Sciences, Disability, Special Needs, Human Relations, Self-Help
ISBN Prefix(es): 978-953-6604
Number of titles published annually: 1 Print
Total Titles: 4 Print

Knjizevni Krug Split
Ispod ure 3, 21000 Split
Tel: (021) 346-801; (021) 361-081; (021) 346-802; (021) 339-755 (editorial) *Fax:* (021) 344-711
E-mail: knjizevni-krug-split@st.t-com.hr
Web Site: www.knjizevni-krug.hr
Key Personnel
President: Prof Nenad Cambi, PhD
Vice President: Prof Ivo Grabovac; Prof Ivan Mimica
Editor: Prof Bratislav Lucin
Founded: 1979
Subjects: Archaeology, Drama, Theater, History, Language Arts, Linguistics, Law, Literature, Literary Criticism, Essays, Maritime, Poetry
ISBN Prefix(es): 978-86-7397; 978-953-163

Krscanska sadasnjost doo
Marulicev trg 14 pp 434, 10001 Zagreb
Tel: (01) 63 49 010; (01) 63 49 050 (editorial) *Fax:* (01) 46 66 815; (01) 48 28 227 (editorial)
E-mail: uprava@ks.hr; ks@zg.t-com.hr
Web Site: www.ks.hr
Founded: 1968
Also acts as a press agency.
Subjects: Art, Biblical Studies, Religion - Other, Theology
ISBN Prefix(es): 978-86-397; 978-953-151; 978-953-11
Bookshop(s): Knjizara Krscanska Sadasnjost, Kaptol 1, 10000 Zagreb *Tel:* (01) 48 14 931; Knjizara Krscanska Sadasnjost, Kaptol 29, 10000 Zagreb *Tel:* (01) 48 14 714;

Knjizara Krscanska Sadasnjost, Radiceva 4, 47000 Karlovac *Tel:* (047) 601 643; Knjizara Krscanske Sadasnjosti, Trg Ivana Pavla II 32, 49246 Marija Bistrica *Tel:* (049) 468 050; Prodavaonica "Dr Josip Turcinovic", Trg slobde bb, 31000 Osijek *Tel:* (031) 201 565; Knjizara "Krscanske Sadasnjosti", Fiorella La Guardie 10c, 51000 Rijeka *Tel:* (051) 321 648; Knjizara "Sveta Klara", Kralja Zvonimira 18, 21000 Split *Tel:* (021) 482 316 *E-mail:* knjizara. split@ks.hr

Leksikografski Zavod Miroslav Krleza (The Miroslav Krleza Institute of Lexicographic)
Frankopanska 26, 10000 Zagreb
Tel: (01) 4800 333; (01) 4800 300 *Fax:* (01) 4800 399
E-mail: lzmk@lzmk.hr
Web Site: www.lzmk.hr
Key Personnel
General Dir: Antun Vujic, PhD *E-mail:* antun. vujic@lzmk.hr
Dir: Bruno Kragic *E-mail:* ravnatelj@lzmk.hr
Advisor: Bogisic Vlaho *E-mail:* vlaho.bogisic@ lzmk.hr
Head Finance: Ankica Karacic *Tel:* (01) 4800 319 *E-mail:* ankica.karacic@lzmk.hr
Head, Sales & Promotion: Dubravka Lukic *Tel:* (01) 4800 327 *E-mail:* dubravka.lukic@ lzmk.hr
Founded: 1950
ISBN Prefix(es): 978-953-268

Masmedia doo+
Subsidiary of Styria Medien International
Baruna Trenka 13, 10000 Zagreb
Tel: (01) 45 77 400 *Toll Free Tel:* 0800 300 000 *Fax:* (01) 45 77 769
E-mail: info@masmedia.hr; informacije@ masmedia.hr
Web Site: www.masmedia.hr
Key Personnel
Dir: Stjepan Andrasic *E-mail:* stjepan@ masmedia.hr
Mng Dir: Vjeran Andrasic
Founded: 1990
Specialize in business & professional books, magazines & electronic publications.
Subjects: Business, Economics, Finance, Management, Marketing, Construction, Electricity
ISBN Prefix(es): 978-953-157
Associate Companies: Andratom; Creditreform; GBMA; Rimedia
Subsidiaries: Masmedia-Split
U.S. Office(s): Associated Book Publishers Inc, PO Box 5657, Scottsdale, AZ 85261-5657, United States
Distributed by Associated Book Publishers
Distributor for Braun Verlag; Euredit (Europages) BDI; Gentner Verlag; Herold
Bookshop(s): Masmedia Rijeka, Dolac 9A, 51000 Rijeka
Book Club(s): Croatian Book Clubs

Matica hrvatska+
Matice hrvatske 2, Strossmayerov trg 4, 10000 Zagreb
Tel: (01) 4878-360; (01) 4819-318 (bookshop); (01) 4878-374 (bookshop) *Fax:* (01) 4819-319
E-mail: matica@matica.hr; knjizara@matica.hr (bookshop)
Web Site: www.matica.hr
Key Personnel
President: Igor Zidic
Vice President: Stjepan Damjanovic; Ante Stamac; Stjepan Sucic
Founded: 1842
Also publisher of biweekly newspaper *Vijenac*.
Subjects: Agriculture, Archaeology, Art, Chemistry, Chemical Engineering, Drama, Theater, Geography, Geology, History, Language Arts, Linguistics, Literature, Literary Criticism, Es-

says, Medicine, Nursing, Dentistry, Natural History, Nonfiction (General), Philosophy, Physics, Poetry, Regional Interests, Science (General), Social Sciences, Sociology, Art History, Electricity
ISBN Prefix(es): 978-86-401; 978-86-7807; 978-953-150; 978-953-185; 978-953-6014; 978-953-96033

Meandar Media doo
Petrinjska 51/3, 10000 Zagreb
Tel: (01) 481 30 22 *Fax:* (01) 481 33 23
E-mail: prodaja@meandar.hr
Web Site: www.meandar.hr
Key Personnel
Dir & Editor: Branko Cegec *Tel:* (01) 4680 500
Dir, Sales: Ivana Plejic *Tel:* (01) 481 30 39 *E-mail:* ivana.plejic@meandar.hr
Founded: 1992
Subjects: Art, Drama, Theater, Film, Video, Literature, Literary Criticism, Essays, Music, Dance, Poetry
ISBN Prefix(es): 978-953-206; 978-953-6181

Medicinska Naklada doo
Cankarova 13, 10000 Zagreb
Tel: (01) 3779 444 *Fax:* (01) 3907 041
Web Site: www.medicinskanaklada.hr
Subjects: Medicine, Nursing, Dentistry, Veterinary Science, Pharmacy
ISBN Prefix(es): 978-86-7111; 978-953-176
Bookshop(s): Vaska 90, Zagreb *Tel:* (01) 4640 647 *E-mail:* prodaja@medicinskanaklada.hr

Ministarstvo Zastite Okolisa i Prirode (Ministry of Environmental & Nature Protection)
ul Republike Austrije 14, 10000 Zagreb
Tel: (01) 3717-111 *Fax:* (01) 3717-149
E-mail: ministar@mzoe.hr
Web Site: www.mzoip.hr
Founded: 1991
Subjects: Environmental Studies
ISBN Prefix(es): 978-953-97087; 978-953-6793

Mozaik Knjiga doo (Mosaic Books Ltd)
Karlovacka cesta 24A, 10020 Zagreb
Tel: (01) 6315 101; (01) 6315 124 *Fax:* (01) 6315 222
E-mail: info@mozaik-knjiga.hr
Web Site: www.mozaik-knjiga.hr
Key Personnel
Dir: Bojan Vidmar
Founded: 1991
Subjects: Child Care & Development, Cookery, Education, Fiction, Philosophy
ISBN Prefix(es): 978-86-457; 978-953-173; 978-953-223; 978-953-196
Bookshop(s): Arena Center, Laniste Jaruscica bb, Zagreb *Tel:* (01) 2068 816 *E-mail:* arena@ profil-mozaik.hr; Megastore, Bogoviceva 7, Zagreb *Tel:* (01) 4877 309 *E-mail:* megastore@ profil-mozaik.hr; Branimir Centar, Branimirova 29, Zagreb *Tel:* (01) 4554 385 *E-mail:* branimir-centar@profil-mozaik.hr; City Center One, Jankomir 33, Zagreb *Tel:* (01) 3878 789 *E-mail:* citycenter@profil-mozaik. hr; Garden Mall, Oporovecka 14, Zagreb *Tel:* (01) 6408 350 *E-mail:* dubrava@profil-mozaik.hr; Shopping City West Gate, Zapresicka 2, Jablanovec, 10298 Zagreb *Tel:* (01) 6394 235; (01) 3692 865 *E-mail:* westgate@ profil-mozaik.hr; Zagreb Kaptol, Kaptol 4, Zagreb *Tel:* (01) 4814 955 *E-mail:* kczagreb. kub@profil-mozaik.hr; Gunduliceva 6, Bjelovar *Tel:* (043) 221 112 *E-mail:* bjelovar@ mozaik-knjiga.hr; Minceta P-30, Nikole Tesle 2, Dubrovnik *Tel:* (020) 356 600 *E-mail:* pm. minceta@profil-mozaik.hr; Obala kraija Tomislava 12, Makarska *Tel:* (021) 678 824 *E-mail:* makarska@profil-mozaik.hr; Fosal 12, Omis *Tel:* (021) 757 924 *E-mail:* omis-fosal@profil-mozaik.hr; Trg I Raosa 1, Omis

Tel: (021) 757 938 *E-mail:* omis-punta@profil-mozaik.hr; Kapucinska 33, Osijek *Tel:* (031) 205 063 *E-mail:* osijek@profil-mozaik.hr; Giardini 4, Pula *Tel:* (052) 210 816 *E-mail:* pula@ profil-mozaik.hr; Rijeka Centar, Uzarska 1, Rijeka *Tel:* (051) 315 526; (051) 315 525; (051) 315 519 *E-mail:* rijeka-korzo@profil-mozaik. hr; J Sizgorica 2, Sibenik *Tel:* (022) 214 441 *E-mail:* sibenik@profil-mozaik.hr; SIA Radica 5, Sisak *Tel:* (044) 521 126 *E-mail:* sisak@ profil-mozaik.hr; Trg I B Mazuranic bb, SL Brod *Tel:* (035) 411 335 *E-mail:* slbrod@ profil-mozaik.hr; Kraj Sv Marije 1, Split *Tel:* (021) 317 806 *E-mail:* st.krleza@profil-mozaik.hr; Morpurgo Split, Narodni trg 16, Split *Tel:* (021) 346 843 *E-mail:* st.morpurgo@ profil-mozaik.hr; Subiceva 7, Split *Tel:* (021) 360 050 *E-mail:* split-center@profil-mozaik. hr; Gajeva 17, Varazdin *Tel:* (042) 200 580 *E-mail:* varazdin@profil-mozaik.hr; Trg bana J Sokcevica 1, Vinkovci *Tel:* (032) 338 102 *E-mail:* vinkovci@profil-mozaik.hr; Knezova Subica Bribirskih 11, Zadar *Tel:* (023) 254 518 *E-mail:* zadar@profil-mozaik.hr

Naklada Ljevak doo
Kopacevski put 1c, 10000 Zagreb
Tel: (01) 4804-000; (01) 4804-007 (sales) *Fax:* (01) 4804-001
E-mail: skole@naklada-ljevak.hr; prodaja@ naklada-ljevak.hr; marketing@naklada-ljevak.hr
Web Site: www.naklada-ljevak.hr
Key Personnel
Executive Dir: Petra Ljevak
Dir, Marketing: Lidija Krvaric *Tel:* (01) 4804-021 *E-mail:* lidija.krvaric@naklada-ljevak.hr
Dir, Sales: Mirko Loncar *E-mail:* mirko.loncar@ naklada-ljevak.hr
Head, Direct Sales: Magdalena Margeta Kusulja *E-mail:* magdalena.kusulja@naklada-ljevak.hr
Founded: 1957
Subjects: Art, Economics, Fiction, Government, Political Science, History, Philosophy, Psychology, Psychiatry, Science (General), Social Sciences, Sociology
ISBN Prefix(es): 978-86-349; 978-953-178
Total Titles: 2,500 Print
Bookshop(s): Trg bana Jelacica 17, 10000 Zagreb *Tel:* (01) 4812-992 *Fax:* (01) 4812-970 *E-mail:* knjizara-ljevak@knjizara-ljevak.hr

Naklada Pavicic doo
Sv Mateja 81, 10010 Zagreb
Tel: (01) 66 01 993; (01) 66 23 749 *Fax:* (01) 66 23 748
E-mail: naklada-pavicic@zg.t-com.hr
Web Site: www.naklada-pavicic.hr
Key Personnel
Member of the Board: Josip Pavicic
Founded: 1993
Subjects: Biography, Memoirs, Fiction, History, Humor, Literature, Literary Criticism, Essays, Medicine, Nursing, Dentistry, Science (General)
ISBN Prefix(es): 978-953-6308

Nakladni zavod Globus doo
pp232, Vlaska 109, 10000 Zagreb
Tel: (01) 46 28 400; (01) 46 28 404; (01) 46 28 407 *Fax:* (01) 45 51 146
E-mail: globus@globus.hr
Web Site: www.globus.hr
Founded: 1969
Subjects: Art, Fiction, Government, Political Science, History, Philosophy, Social Sciences, Sociology
ISBN Prefix(es): 978-86-343; 978-953-167

Narodne Novine dd
Savski gaj, XIII put 6, 10020 Zagreb
Tel: (01) 6652-888 *Fax:* (01) 6652-851
E-mail: e-pretplata@nn.hr
Web Site: www.nn.hr

Key Personnel
Dir: Prof Sanja Peric *Tel:* (01) 6652-852
 E-mail: speric@nn.hr
Board Member: Nikola Sila *Tel:* (01) 6652-703
 Fax: (01) 6652-774 *E-mail:* nsila@nn.hr
Executive Editor: Dane Bicanic *Tel:* (01) 6652-855 *Fax:* (01) 6652-879 *E-mail:* dbicanic@nn.hr
Head, Advertising & Subscriptions: Ivica Sabo
 Tel: (01) 6652-865 *E-mail:* isabo@nn.hr
Subjects: Career Development, Law, Science
 (General)
ISBN Prefix(es): 978-86-337; 978-953-6053; 978-953-234

Nasa Djeca doo+
Velika cesta 90, 10020 Zagreb
Tel: (01) 39 09 460 *Fax:* (01) 39 09 468
E-mail: nasa-djeca@nasa-djeca.hr; prodaja@nasa-djeca.hr (sales)
Web Site: www.nasa-djeca.hr
Founded: 1951
Also publish children's periodical *Radost*.
Subjects: Literature, Literary Criticism, Essays, Poetry
ISBN Prefix(es): 978-86-7037; 978-953-171
Number of titles published annually: 30 Print

Novi Informator doo
Kneza Mislava 7/I, 10000 Zagreb
Tel: (01) 45 55 454 *Fax:* (01) 46 12 553
E-mail: info@novi-informator.net
Web Site: www.novi-informator.net
Key Personnel
President: Mladen Zuvela
Dir: Marina Surbek
Editor: Davorka Foretic *E-mail:* davorka.foretic@novi-informator.net
Head, Sales: Snjezana Vlaovic
Subjects: Economics, Law
ISBN Prefix(es): 978-953-7327; 978-953-7812; 978-953-99385

Otokar Kersovani doo
Janeza Trdine 2/II, 51000 Rijeka
Tel: (051) 338 558 *Fax:* (051) 331 690
E-mail: otokar-kersovani@ri.htnet.hr
Key Personnel
Contact: Valter Lisica
Founded: 1954
Subjects: Biography, Memoirs, Fiction
ISBN Prefix(es): 978-86-385; 978-953-153
Branch Office(s)
Slavise Vajiera-Cice 3, Rijeka
Biankinijeva 11, Zagreb
Mehmed-pase Soholovica 24, Sarajevo, Bosnia
 and Herzegovina
Zrmanjska 2/a, Belgrade, Serbia
Nade Tomic 15, Nis, Serbia

Institut drustvenih znanosti Ivo Pilar (Institute
 of Social Sciences Ivo Pilar)
Marulicev trg 19/I, 10000 Zagreb
Mailing Address: PO Box 277, 10000 Zagreb
Tel: (01) 4886-800 *Fax:* (01) 4828-296
E-mail: ured@pilar.hr
Web Site: www.pilar.hr
Key Personnel
Dir: Dr Vlado Sakic *E-mail:* vlado.sakic@pilar.hr
Assistant Dir: Ljiljana Kaliterna Lipovcan
 Tel: (01) 4886 820 *E-mail:* ljiljana.kaliterna@pilar.hr
Head, Publishing Services: Mirjana Paic Jurinic
 E-mail: mirjana.paic-jurinic@pilar.hr
Founded: 1991
Research institute & publisher of the journal
 Drustvend Istrazivanja.
Subjects: Behavioral Sciences, History, Philosophy, Psychology, Psychiatry, Social Sciences, Sociology
ISBN Prefix(es): 978-953-6666
Number of titles published annually: 11 Print

Total Titles: 108 Print
Branch Office(s)
Trg Stjepana Radica 4/1, 53000 Gospic, Contact: Zeljko Holjevac *Tel:* (053) 741-140
 E-mail: zeljko.holjevac@gmail.com
Samacka 9/II, 31000 Osijek, Contact: Miljenko
 Brekalo *Tel:* (031) 207-294; (031) 207-285
 Fax: (031) 202-067 *E-mail:* miljenko.brekalo@os.t-com.hr
Leharoval, 52100 Pula, Contact: Stipan Trogrlic *Tel:* (052) 210 499 *Fax:* (052) 210 499
 E-mail: stipan.trogrlic@pilar.hr
Polijana Kraljice Jelene 1, 21000 Split, Contact:
 Sasa Mrduljas *Tel:* (021) 314-30 *Fax:* (021)
 344-154 *E-mail:* sasa.mrduljas@pilar.hr
204 vukovarske brigade 6 pp 58, 32000 Vukovar, Contact: Drazen Zivic *Tel:* (032) 450-323
 Fax: (032) 450-348 *E-mail:* drazen.zivic@pilar.hr
Distributed by Erasmus Naklada doo

Planetopija doo+
Ilica 70, 10000 Zagreb
Tel: (01) 4851 557; (01) 4883 370 *Fax:* (01) 4883 371
E-mail: planetopija@planetopija.hr
Web Site: www.planetopija.hr
Key Personnel
Dir: Marina Kralj Vidacak *E-mail:* marina@planetopija.hr
Sales Manager: Andrea Bertol Komadina
 E-mail: andrea@planetopija.hr
Public Relations & Marketing: Vlasta Prohaska
 Jarec *E-mail:* vlasta@planetopija.hr
Subjects: Alternative, Biography, Memoirs, Cookery, Health, Nutrition, Humor, Nonfiction (General), Parapsychology, Philosophy, Psychology, Psychiatry, Self-Help, Women's Studies
ISBN Prefix(es): 978-953-257
Number of titles published annually: 35 Print
Total Titles: 150 Print
Bookshop(s): Ilica 72, 10000 Zagreb, Manager: Kristina Kvastek *Tel:* (01) 4846 197
 E-mail: kristina@planetopija.hr

Politicka Kultura
Amruseva 8, 10000 Zagreb
Tel: (01) 4817 648 *Fax:* (01) 4817 648
Key Personnel
Dir: Ruzica Jakesevic
Subjects: Economics, Government, Political Science, History, Philosophy
ISBN Prefix(es): 978-953-6213

Privlacica doo+
Trg Franje Tudmana 2, 32100 Vinkovci
Tel: (032) 306 068; (032) 306 069 *Fax:* (032) 306 070
Founded: 1980
Subjects: Regional Interests, Social Sciences, Sociology
ISBN Prefix(es): 978-953-156
Total Titles: 350 Print

Profil Klett doo
Petra Hektorovica 2, 4th floor, 10000 Zagreb
Tel: (01) 4724 824 (management); (01) 4724 805
 (sales); (01) 4724 803 (editorial); (01) 4724
 809 (marketing)
E-mail: uprava@profil-klett.hr; prodaja@profil-klett.hr; marketing@profil-klett.hr
Web Site: www.profil-klett.hr
Key Personnel
Chairman of the Board: Dalibor Greganic
School textbook publisher.
Subjects: Art, Biological Sciences, Chemistry, Chemical Engineering, Geography, Geology, History, Mathematics, Music, Dance, Physics, Technology
ISBN Prefix(es): 978-953-200; 978-953-12; 978-953-6011

Prosvjeta doo
D Golika 32, 10000 Zagreb
Tel: (01) 4872-477 *Fax:* (01) 3665-309
E-mail: prosvjeta@inet.hr
Web Site: www.prosvjeta.hr
Founded: 1944
Publish scientific & popular scientific texts from
 the history of the Serbs in Croatia, as well as
 historiographic texts in general.
Subjects: Business, Journalism
ISBN Prefix(es): 978-86-353; 978-953-6279; 978-953-7130
Bookshop(s): Trg P Preradovica 5, 10000 Zagreb *Tel:* (01) 4830-115 *Fax:* (01) 4833-697
 E-mail: prosvjeta1@zg.t-com.hr; Drvingje 32,
 10000 Zagreb *Tel:* (01) 3665-141

Skolska Knjiga dd (School Book Inc)
Masarykova 28, 10000 Zagreb
Tel: (01) 4830 491 (administration); (01) 4830
 511 *Fax:* (01) 4830 506
E-mail: skolska@skolskaknjiga.hr; press@skolskaknjiga.hr
Web Site: www.skolskaknjiga.hr
Key Personnel
Dir: Prof Ante Zuzul *E-mail:* ante.zuzul@skolskaknjiga.hr
President: Mihovil Zuzul
Dir, Publishing: Martina Zuzul *E-mail:* martina.zuzul@skolskaknjiga.hr
Dir, Marketing: Sanja Aralica *Tel:* (01) 4830 508
 E-mail: sanja.aralica@skolskaknjiga.hr
Founded: 1950
Subjects: Art, Biography, Memoirs, Education, Engineering (General), History, How-to, Medicine, Nursing, Dentistry, Music, Dance, Philosophy, Poetry, Psychology, Psychiatry, Science (General), Social Sciences, Sociology
ISBN Prefix(es): 978-86-03; 978-953-0
Bookshop(s): Bogoviceva 1a, 41000 Zagreb
Tel: (01) 4810 989 *Fax:* (01) 4926 549
 E-mail: skolskabogoviceva@skolskaknjiga.hr; Ivana Lucica 3 (Filozofski fakultet), Zagreb *Tel:* (01) 5393 855; (01) 5393 856
 Fax: (01) 6120 093 *E-mail:* skolskafilozofski@skolskaknjiga.hr; Trg bana Josipa Jelacica 14, Arkadija *Tel:* (01) 644 1845; (01) 644 1846; (01) 644 1847 *Fax:* (01) 644 1848 *E-mail:* skolskatrg@skolskaknjiga.hr; Kvaternikov trg 12, Arkadija *Tel:* (01) 6441 861; (01) 6441 860 *Fax:* (01) 6441 862 *E-mail:* skolskakvatric@skolskaknjiga.hr; Gunduliceva 8, Bjelovar *Tel:* (043) 638 775; (043) 638 776 *Fax:* (043) 638 777
 E-mail: skolskabjelovar@skolskaknjiga.hr; Kralja Tomislava 6, 40000 Cakovec
Tel: (040) 638 090 *Fax:* (040) 638 093
 E-mail: skolskacakovec@skolskaknjiga.hr; Poljana Paska Milicevica 1, 20000 Dubrovnik
Tel: (020) 638 655 *Fax:* (020) 638 657
 E-mail: skolskadubrovnik@skolskaknjiga.hr; Dr Ante Starcevica 17, 53000 Gospic *Tel:* (053) 658 995; (053) 658 996 *Fax:* (053) 658 997
 E-mail: skolskagospic@skolskaknjiga.hr; Glavina Donja 336, Imotski *Tel:* (021) 670 904
 Fax: (021) 670 905 *E-mail:* skolskamotski@skolskaknjiga.hr; Stjepana Radica 7, 47000 Karlovac *Tel:* (047) 601 439; (047) 804 043
 Fax: (047) 804 044 *E-mail:* skolskakarlovac@skolskaknjiga.hr; Ante Starcevica bb, 20350 Metkovic *Tel:* (020) 690 629 *Fax:* (020) 690 629 *E-mail:* skolskametkovic@skolskaknjiga.hr; B Frankopana 8, Ogulin *Tel:* (047) 525 364
 Fax: (047) 525 096 *E-mail:* skolskaogulin@skolskaknjiga.hr; Trg A Starcevica 12, 31000 Osijek *Tel:* (031) 212 025; (031) 212 024
 Fax: (031) 215 096 *E-mail:* skolskaosijek@skolskaknjiga.hr; Trg Sv Trojstva 7, Pozega
Tel: (034) 638 950; (034) 638 951 *Fax:* (034) 638 956 *E-mail:* skolskapozega@skolskaknjiga.hr; Forum 6, Pula *Tel:* (052) 217 150
 Fax: (052) 210 026 *E-mail:* skolskapula@skolskaknjiga.hr; Ignacija Henckea 1B, 51000 Rijeka *Tel:* (051) 211 119 *Fax:* (051) 211

121 *E-mail:* skolskarijeka@skolskaknjiga.
hr; Trg kralja Tomislava 3, 21230 Sinj
Tel: (021) 821 077 *Fax:* (021) 821 077
E-mail: skolskasinj@skolskaknjiga.hr; Trg bana
Josipa Jelacica 6, 44000 Sisak *Tel:* (044) 524
300 *Fax:* (044) 524 303 *E-mail:* skolskasisak@
skolskaknjiga.hr; Trg brace Radica 7,
Split *Tel:* (021) 688 680; (021) 688 681
Fax: (021) 688 682 *E-mail:* skolskasplit@
skolskaknjiga.hr; Janka Draskovica 2, 42000
Varazdin *Tel:* (042) 200 539 *Fax:* (042)
200 565 *E-mail:* skolskavarazdin1@
skolskaknjiga.hr; Stanka Vraza 8, 42000
Varazdin *Tel:* (042) 659 100; (042) 659 104
Fax: (042) 659 103 *E-mail:* skolskavarazdin2@
skolskaknjiga.hr; Duga ul 27, 32100 Vinkovci
Tel: (032) 336 000 *Fax:* (032) 336 014
E-mail: skolskavinkovci@skolskaknjiga.
hr; Dr Franje Tudmana 13, Vukovar
Tel: (032) 638 972 *Fax:* (032) 632 971
E-mail: skolskavukovar@skolskaknjiga.hr; Bra-
nimirova obala 2, Zadar *Tel:* (023) 628
Fax: (023) 628 299 *E-mail:* skolskazadar@
skolskaknjiga.hr; Trg Mladosti 1, Zapresic
Tel: (01) 6438 931 *Fax:* (01) 6438 938
E-mail: skolskazapresic@skolskaknjiga.hr

Skorpion d o o+
Baboniceva 44, 10000 Zagreb
Tel: (01) 4635 341 *Fax:* (01) 4635 342
E-mail: itp-skorpion@zg.htnet.hr; info@
kupiknjigu.com
Web Site: www.kupiknjigu.com
Founded: 1990
Specialize in publishing & trade; also acts as
    agent of buying or selling international rights
    & editions.
Membership(s): Association of Pubishers.
Subjects: Animals, Pets, Crafts, Games, Hobbies,
    Health, Nutrition, Philosophy, Theology, Veteri-
    nary Science
ISBN Prefix(es): 978-953-289
Distributed by Solutions Ltd (Western Europe)

Sveucilisna Tiskara
Trg marsala Tita 14, 10000 Zagreb
Tel: (01) 45 64 430; (01) 45 64 428 *Fax:* (01) 45
    64 427
E-mail: info@sveucilisnatiskara.hr; sveucilisna@
net.hr
Web Site: www.sveucilisnatiskara.hr
Founded: 1990
Publishing service of Zagreb University.
Subjects: Ethnicity, Language Arts, Linguistics,
    Literature, Literary Criticism, Essays, Science
    (General)
ISBN Prefix(es): 978-86-7819; 978-86-329; 978-
    953-6231

Znaci Vremena, Institut Za Istrazivanje Biblije
Prilaz Gjure Dezelica 75, 10000 Zagreb
E-mail: knjizara@znaci-vremena.com
Web Site: www.znaci-vremena.com
Founded: 1969
Subjects: Archaeology, Biblical Studies, Health,
    Nutrition, Human Relations, Religion - Protes-
    tant, Theology
ISBN Prefix(es): 978-953-183

Znanje doo (Knowledge Inc)+
Mandiceva 2, 10000 Zagreb
Tel: (01) 3689-535 *Fax:* (01) 3689-531; (01)
    3638-477
E-mail: znanje@znanje.hr; znanje-tiskara@znanje.
hr
Web Site: znanje.hr
Key Personnel
Dir: Zvonimir Cimic *E-mail:* zvonimir.cimic@
znanje.hr
Vice President: Ivancica Blazanin *Tel:* (01) 3689-
    534 *E-mail:* ivancica.blazanin@znanje.hr

Editor-in-Chief & Head, Marketing: Silvia
    Sinkovic *Tel:* (01) 3689-545 *E-mail:* silvia.
    sinkovic@znanje.hr
Founded: 1925
ISBN Prefix(es): 978-86-313; 978-953-195; 978-
    953-6124; 978-953-6473
Branch Office(s)
Vukovarska 71, 31000 Osijek *Fax:* (031) 504-495
Riva 8, Rijeka
Znanje d o o Mostar, Kralja Tomislava 1, 88000
    Mostar, Bosnia and Herzegovina *Tel:* (036)
    317-680 *Fax:* (063) 313-504
Showroom(s): Zvonimirova, 17 Zagreb

Zrinski
Dr Ivana Novaka 13, 40000 Cakovec
Tel: (040) 37 22 22; (040) 37 22 77 (sales)
    Fax: (040) 37 22 12
E-mail: zrinski@zrinski.hr
Web Site: www.zrinski.com
Subjects: Agriculture, Animals, Pets, Cookery,
    Fiction
ISBN Prefix(es): 978-86-7003; 978-953-155
Branch Office(s)
Unska 2/b, 10000 Zagreb *Tel:* (01) 61 71 467
    Fax: (01) 61 71 273

Cuba

General Information

Capital: Havana
Language: Spanish
Religion: Predominantly Roman Catholic
Population: 10.8 million
Bank Hours: 0800-1200, 1415-1615 Monday-
    Friday; 0800-1200 Saturday
Currency: 100 centavos = 1 Cuban peso
Export/Import Information: Control of all import
    & export by Ministry of Foreign Trade; books
    imported & exported by Ediciones Cubanas,
    Apdo 605, Havana. No commercial advertis-
    ing permitted in Cuba; brochures etc must be
    sent to the appropriate foreign trade organiza-
    tion. Exchange controlled by National Bank of
    Cuba.
Copyright: UCC, Florence (see Copyright Con-
    ventions, pg viii)

Editorial Capitan San Luis+
Calle 38 No 4717 el 40 y 47 Playa, Havana
Tel: (07) 203-0926; (07) 203-4917 *Fax:* (07) 204-
    9931
E-mail: editorial@ecsanluis.rem.cu
Web Site: www.capitansanluis.cu
Founded: 1989
Subjects: Government, Political Science, Litera-
    ture, Literary Criticism, Essays
ISBN Prefix(es): 978-959-211
Warehouse: Ave 41 No 1410 entre 14 y 18,
    Playa, Havana

Casa Editora Abril+
Prado 553 esquina A Tte Rey, CP 10200 Old Ha-
vana
Tel: (07) 862-5031
Web Site: www.editoraabril.cu
Key Personnel
Dir: Niurka Dumenigo Garcia *Tel:* (07) 862-7871
Public Relations: Irenia Gonzalez Cela *Tel:* (07)
    862-3187
Founded: 1980
Subjects: Advertising, Computers, Film, Video,
    History, Humor, Journalism, Literature, Literary
    Criticism, Essays, Philosophy, Poetry, Science
    Fiction, Fantasy
ISBN Prefix(es): 978-959-210

Centro de Estudios Martianos
Calzada No 807, esquina a 4, El Vedado, Plaza
    de la Revolucion, CP 10400 Havana
Tel: (07) 836-4966; (07) 836-4969 *Fax:* (07) 833-
    3721
E-mail: cem@josemarti.co.cu
Web Site: www.josemarti.cu
Key Personnel
Dir General: Ana Sanchez Collazo
Founded: 1977
Subjects: Literature, Literary Criticism, Essays,
    Social Sciences, Sociology
ISBN Prefix(es): 978-959-271; 978-959-7006

**Centro de Informacion y Gestion Technologica
(CIGET)**
Ave 52 No 2316 e/23 y 25, CP 55100 Cienfuegos
Tel: (043) 51 9732; (043) 51 8486
Web Site: www.cienfuegos.cu/ciget
Key Personnel
Dir: Alayn A Alonso Gonzalez-Abreu
    E-mail: aleman@ciget.cienfuegos.cu
Founded: 1963
Subjects: Career Development, Library & Infor-
    mation Sciences, Technology
ISBN Prefix(es): 978-959-234

Editorial Ciencias Medicas (ECIMED)
Calle 23 No 654 entre D y E, Vedado Pl, CP
    10400 Havana
Tel: (07) 8330311
E-mail: ecimed@infomed.sld.cu
Web Site: www.ecimed.sld.cu
Key Personnel
Head of Dept, Books: Yudexy Pacheco Perez
    E-mail: yudexi@infomed.sld.cu
Subjects: Medicine, Nursing, Dentistry
ISBN Prefix(es): 978-959-212; 978-959-7132

Editorial de Ciencias Sociales
Calle 14, No 4104, e/ 41 y 43, Playa, CP 11300
    Havana
Tel: (07) 203 60 90; (07) 203 48 01
Key Personnel
Dir: Ernesto Escobar Soto
Founded: 1967
Subjects: Social Sciences, Sociology
ISBN Prefix(es): 978-959-06
Orders to: Ediciones Cubanas, Obispo y Bernaza,
    Havana Vieja

Editorial Cientifico-Tecnica+
Calle 14, No 4104 entre 41 y 43, Playa, CP
    10400 Havana
Tel: (07) 203 6090; (07) 203 3959; (07) 203
    4801; (07) 333 441 *Fax:* (07) 833 3441
Key Personnel
Dir: Ernesto Escobar Soto
Founded: 1967
Subjects: Engineering (General), Science (Gen-
    eral)
ISBN Prefix(es): 978-959-05

CIGET, see Centro de Informacion y Gestion
    Technologica (CIGET)

Editora Cultura Popular, *imprint of* Editora
    Politica

ECIMED, see Editorial Ciencias Medicas
    (ECIMED)

Fondo Editorial Casa de las Americas
3ra y G, El Vedado, CP 10500 Havana
Tel: (07) 8382706; (07) 8382707; (07) 8382708;
    (07) 8382709
Web Site: www.casa.cult.cu/editorial.php
Key Personnel
Dir: Caridad Fernandez Tamayo
Editor-in-Chief: Nisleidys Flores Carmona
Founded: 1960

Subjects: Art, Ethnicity, Social Sciences, Sociology
ISBN Prefix(es): 978-959-04

Editorial Gente Nueva+
O'Reilly no 4, esquina a tacon, CP 10100 Havana Vieja
Tel: (07) 624753 *Fax:* (07) 338187
Web Site: www.gentenueva.cult.cu
Key Personnel
Dir: Hermes Jesus Moreno
Founded: 1967
ISBN Prefix(es): 978-959-08

Ediciones Holguin
7 Callejon del Mercado 1, CP 80100 Holguin
Key Personnel
Dir: Lourdes Gonzalez Herrero
Founded: 1986
Subjects: Art, Biography, Memoirs, Drama, Theater, History, Literature, Literary Criticism, Essays, Poetry
ISBN Prefix(es): 978-959-221
Book Club(s): SCAL (Sociedad Cabana de Amigos del Libro)

Editorial Letras Cubanas+
Obispo No 302 esquina a Aguiar, CP 10100 Havana
Tel: (07) 862 43 78; (07) 862 80 91 *Fax:* (07) 66 81 87
E-mail: elc@icl.cult.cu
Web Site: www.letrascubanas.cult.cu
Key Personnel
Dir: Rogelio Riveron
Founded: 1977
Membership(s): Instituto Cubano del Libro.
Subjects: Art, Drama, Theater, Fiction, Literature, Literary Criticism, Essays, Poetry, Romance, Science Fiction, Fantasy
ISBN Prefix(es): 978-959-10
Number of titles published annually: 70 Print
Total Titles: 70 Print
Distribution Center: Ediciones Cubanas, 527 esquina a Bernaza, CP 10100 Havana *Tel:* (07) 863-1989 *Fax:* (07) 866-8943 *E-mail:* libro@edicuba.artex.cu
Distribuidora Nacional del Libro, Ave 23 esquina a 250, CP 10200 Playa *Tel:* (07) 272-5278; (07) 272-5266; (07) 272-5249 *E-mail:* dnl@ceniai.inf.cu

Editorial Oriente+
J Castillo Duany 356, CP 90100 Santiago de Cuba
Tel: (022) 622496; (022) 628096
E-mail: edoriente@cultstgo.cult.cu
Web Site: www.editorialoriente.cult.cu
Key Personnel
Dir: Aimara Vera
Founded: 1971
Subjects: African American Studies, Cookery, Crafts, Games, Hobbies, Fiction, Health, Nutrition, History, House & Home, Literature, Literary Criticism, Essays, Poetry, Self-Help, Sports, Athletics
ISBN Prefix(es): 978-959-11
Total Titles: 821 Print
Parent Company: Instituto Cubano del Libro

Editora Politica+
Calle Belascoain No 864, esquina a Desague, Municipio Centro Habana, CP 10300 Havana
Tel: (07) 879 8553; (07) 879 2910 *Fax:* (07) 556836; (07) 556896
E-mail: editora@epol.cc.cu; comercialep@epol.cc.cu
Web Site: www.editpolitica.cu
Key Personnel
Dir General: Santiago Dorquez Perez
Founded: 1963

Subjects: Biography, Memoirs, Economics, Education, Government, Political Science, Health, Nutrition, History, Human Relations, Law, Philosophy, Poetry, Psychology, Psychiatry, Religion - Catholic, Religion - Other, Science (General), Social Sciences, Sociology
ISBN Prefix(es): 978-959-01
Imprints: Editora Cultura Popular
Showroom(s): Pabelloo Medios de Difusion EX-POCUBA, Tienda 11 y Paseo
Bookshop(s): Centro Internacional de Prensa, Calle 23 esquina O Vedado

Editorial Pueblo y Educacion (PE)+
Avda 3a, No 4605, entre 46 y 60, Playa, Havana
Tel: (07) 202 14 90; (07) 209 37 08; (07) 204 08 44 *Fax:* (07) 204 08 44; (07) 206 15 94
Key Personnel
Dir: Catalina Lajud Herrera
Founded: 1971
Subjects: Computer Science, Education, Literature, Literary Criticism, Essays, Psychology, Psychiatry, Science (General), Social Sciences, Sociology, Sports, Athletics, Technology
ISBN Prefix(es): 978-959-13
Number of titles published annually: 8 Print
Total Titles: 476 Print
Distributed by Ediciones Cubanas Empresa de Comercio Exterior de Publicaciones

Casa Editorial Tablas-Alarcos
Esquina B, El Vedado, Plaza de la Revolucion, CP 10400 Havana
Tel: (07) 8330214
E-mail: revistatablas@cubarte.cult.cu
Web Site: www.eltandem.cult.cu
Subjects: Art, Drama, Theater, Performing Arts
ISBN Prefix(es): 978-959-7154

Cyprus

General Information

Capital: Nicosia
Language: Greek & Turkish (English widely spoken)
Religion: Greek Orthodox & Islamic (among Turks)
Population: 716,000
Bank Hours: 0830-1200 Monday-Saturday
Shop Hours: Winter: 0800-1300, 1430-1700 Monday-Friday; 0730-1300 Saturday. Summer: 0730-1300, 1600-1830 Monday-Friday. Closed Wednesday afternoon (both winter & summer)
Currency: 100 Eurocents = 1 Euro
Export/Import Information: Member of the European Union. No tariffs on books or advertising matter. No import license specially required. Exchange control administered by Central Bank of Cyprus.
Copyright: UCC, Berne, Florence (see Copyright Conventions, pg viii)

Alithia Publishing Co Ltd
Tseriou Ave, 2238 Latsia
Tel: 22487966
ISBN Prefix(es): 978-9963-586

Andreou Chr Publishers
67a Rigainis St, 1010 Nicosia
Tel: 22666877 *Fax:* 22666878
E-mail: andreou2@cytanet.com.cy
Founded: 1979
Subjects: Biography, Memoirs, History, Literature, Literary Criticism, Essays, Regional Interests, Bibliographies, Cypress History
ISBN Prefix(es): 978-9963-563

Associate Companies: Practorion Vivliou; Chr Andreou Co Ltd
Bookshop(s): Rigenis 64a, Nicosia

The House of Cyprus & Cyprological Publications, see MAM (The House of Cyprus & Cyprological Publications)

Human Resource Development Authority of Cyprus (HRDA)
Anavyssou 2, 2025 Strovolos
Mailing Address: PO Box 25431, 1392 Nicosia
Tel: 22515000 *Fax:* 22496949
E-mail: hrda@hrdauth.org.cy
Web Site: www.anad.org.cy
Subjects: Labor, Industrial Relations
ISBN Prefix(es): 978-9963-43

Kyrenia Municipality+
8 Markou Drakou Av, 1102 Nicosia
Mailing Address: PO Box 25572, 1310 Nicosia
Tel: 22818040 *Fax:* 22818228
E-mail: kyreniamunicipality@cytanet.com.cy
Web Site: www.kyreniamunicipality.com
Subjects: Regional Interests
ISBN Prefix(es): 978-9963-559
Showroom(s): 9 Othello's St, Nicosia
Bookshop(s): Kypriaka Themata, PO Box 3835, Nicosia

MAM (The House of Cyprus & Cyprological Publications)+
PO Box 21722, 1512 Nicosia
Tel: 22753536 *Fax:* 22375802
E-mail: mam@mam.com.cy
Web Site: www.mam.com.cy
Key Personnel
Manager: Alexandros Michaelidou; Fryni Michaelidou
Founded: 1965
Specialize in publications on Cyprus & by Cypriots.
Subjects: Archaeology, Economics, History, Literature, Literary Criticism, Essays, Culture, Cyprus
ISBN Prefix(es): 978-9963-625
Bookshop(s): 19 Konstantinou Palaiologou Ave, 1015 Nicosia

Moufflon Publications
Agiou Kassianou St, Old Nicosia
Mailing Address: PO Box 22375, 1521 Nicosia
Tel: 22665155 *Fax:* 22668703
E-mail: distribution@moufflon.com.cy
Web Site: www.moufflonpublications.com
Subjects: Art, History, Regional Interests
ISBN Prefix(es): 978-9963-642
Bookshop(s): One Bopholuis St, PO Box 2375, Nicosia

Pierides Foundation
19 Apostolou Varnava St, 1500 Nicosia
Mailing Address: PO Box 21015, 1500 Nicosia
Tel: 22432577 *Fax:* 22432531
Web Site: www.pieridesfoundation.com.cy
Key Personnel
Curator: Peter H Ashdjian
Founded: 1974
Subjects: Art, History
ISBN Prefix(es): 978-9963-9071

Rimal Publications+
PO Box 57017, 3311 Limassol
Tel: 25580029 *Fax:* 25580039
E-mail: info@rimalbooks.com; order@rimalbooks.com
Web Site: www.rimalbooks.com
Key Personnel
Publisher: Nora Shawwa *E-mail:* nora@rimalbooks.com
Founded: 1993

Membership(s): Cyprus Publisher's Association; Independent Publishers Guild.
Subjects: Art, Travel & Tourism
ISBN Prefix(es): 978-9963-610
Associate Companies: Melisende, United Kingdom

SELAS Publications Ltd
51, RIK Ave, 2122 Nicosia
Tel: 22336633 *Fax:* 22337033
E-mail: info@selas.com.cy
Web Site: www.selas.com.cy
Founded: 1992
Specialize in maps & travel books.
Subjects: Geography, Geology, Travel & Tourism, Cartography
ISBN Prefix(es): 978-9963-566

Czech Republic

General Information

Capital: Prague
Language: Czech (official)
Religion: Predominantly Christian (mostly Roman Catholic)
Population: 10.4 million
Currency: 100 halerue = 1 koruna
Export/Import Information: 5% VAT on books.
Copyright: UCC, Berne (see Copyright Conventions, pg viii)

Nakladatelstvi Academia
Vodickova 40, 110 00 Prague 1
Fax: 224 941 982
E-mail: eshop@academia.cz
Web Site: www.academia.cz; www.academiabooks.com
Key Personnel
Dir: Jiri Padevet *E-mail:* padevet@academia.cz
Assistant Dir: Jana Halaskova
    E-mail: halaskova@academia.cz
Production Manager: Milan Bobek *Tel:* 221 403 846 *E-mail:* bobek@academia.cz
Retail Manager: Sarka Hakenova *Tel:* 221 403 841 *E-mail:* hakenova@academia.cz
Wholesale Manager: Viktoria Gjurisicova *Tel:* 221 403 823 *E-mail:* gjurisicova@academia.cz
Founded: 1953
Publisher of the Academy of Sciences of the Czech Republic.
Subjects: Archaeology, Chemistry, Chemical Engineering, Economics, Engineering (General), Geography, Geology, History, Language Arts, Linguistics, Mathematics, Philosophy, Physics
ISBN Prefix(es): 978-80-200
Bookshop(s): Hybernska 8, 110 00 Prague, Head: Marie Pankova *Tel:* 221 403 829 *E-mail:* hybernska@academia.cz; Na Florenci 3, 110 00 Prague 1, Head: Petr Franek *Tel:* 224 814 621 *E-mail:* knihy.naflorenci@academia.cz; Narodni 7, 110 00 Prague 1, Head: Jana Vavrova *Tel:* 221 403 856 *Fax:* 221 403 541 *E-mail:* knihy.narodni@academia.cz; Vaclavske namesti 34, 110 00 Prague 1 *Tel:* 224 223 511 *Fax:* 224 223 520 *E-mail:* knihy.vaclavskenam@academia.cz; nam Svobody 13, 602 00 Brno, Head: Jiri Svoboda *Tel:* 221 403 879 *E-mail:* knihy.brno@academia.cz; Zamecka 2, 702 00 Ostrava 1, Head: Anna Swiatkova *Tel:* 596 114 580 *E-mail:* knihy.ostrava@academia.cz
Orders to: Expedice Academia, Rozvojova 135, 160 00 Prague 6 *E-mail:* expedice@academia.cz

Nakladatelstvi Akropolis
Severozapadni IV, 16/433, 141 00 Prague 41

Tel: 222 360 991; 251 560 042
Web Site: www.akropolis.info
Key Personnel
Publisher: Filip Tomas *E-mail:* filiptomas@akropolis.info; Jiriho Tomas *Tel:* 724 751 042 *E-mail:* tomas.akropolis@tiscali.cz
Founded: 1990
Subjects: Art, Fiction, History, Science Fiction, Fantasy
ISBN Prefix(es): 978-80-903417; 978-80-901020; 978-80-7304; 978-80-85770
Branch Office(s)
Na Belidle 1, 150 00 Prague 5

Albatros, *imprint of* Albatros Media AS

Albatros Media AS+
Na Pankraci 30/1618, 140 00 Prague 4
Tel: 261 397 201
E-mail: info@albatrosmedia.cz
Web Site: www.albatrosmedia.cz
Key Personnel
Mng Dir: Vaclav Kadlec
Editorial Dir: Ondrej Muller *E-mail:* ondrej.muller@albatrosmedia.cz
Foreign Sales Manager: Jana Cieslarova
    Tel: 234 633 298 *E-mail:* jana.cieslarova@albatrosmedia.cz
Founded: 1949
ISBN Prefix(es): 978-80-00
Number of titles published annually: 1,000 Print
Total Titles: 16,000 Print
Imprints: Albatros; Bizbooks; Computer Press; CooBoo; CPress; Edika; Motto; Plus; XYZ

ARGO spol sro
Milicova 13, 130 00 Prague 3
Tel: 222 782 262
E-mail: argo@argo.cz; rights@argo.cz
Web Site: www.argo.cz
Key Personnel
Dir: Milan Gelnar *Tel:* 222 781 361
    E-mail: milan.gelnar@argo.cz
Mng Dir: Hana Gelnarova *Tel:* 222 782 261
    E-mail: hana.gelnarova@argo.cz; Jiri Michek *Tel:* 222 782 147 *E-mail:* jiri.michek@kosmas.cz
Foreign Rights: Marketa Matuskova *Tel:* 734 336 067
Sales: Pavel Krummer *Tel:* 222 783 512
    E-mail: pavel.krummer@argo.cz
Founded: 1992
Subjects: Art, Fiction, History, Nonfiction (General), Science Fiction, Fantasy
ISBN Prefix(es): 978-80-257; 978-5-85956; 978-80-85794; 978-3-937987; 978-3-941800; 978-3-9807812; 978-3-9807917; 978-3-9808206; 978-3-9808745; 978-88-8234; 978-88-86211; 978-9949-415; 978-9949-438; 978-80-7203
Distribution Center: Kosmas spol sro, Za Halami 877, 252 62 Horomerice *Tel:* 226 519 383 *Fax:* 226 519 387 *E-mail:* sklad.horomerice@kosmas.cz *Web Site:* www.firma.kosmas.cz

Atlantis Spol sro+
PS 374, Ceska 15, 602 00 Brno
Tel: 542 213 221; 549 255 884 (sales) *Fax:* 542 213 221; 549 255 884 (sales)
E-mail: atlantis-brno@volny.cz
Web Site: www.atlantis-brno.cz
Founded: 1989
Subjects: Biography, Memoirs, History, Literature, Literary Criticism, Essays
ISBN Prefix(es): 978-80-7108

AULOS sro
Michalaska 21, 110 00 Prague 1
Tel: 732 504 098 (cell)
E-mail: info@aulos.cz
Web Site: www.aulos.cz
Founded: 1992

Subjects: Fiction, Literature, Literary Criticism, Essays, Philosophy, Poetry
ISBN Prefix(es): 978-80-901261; 978-80-901895; 978-80-86184

Nakladatelstvi Aurora (Aurora Publishing House)
Spalena 53, 110 00 Prague 1
Tel: 224 214 326
E-mail: eaurora@eaurora.cz
Web Site: www.eaurora.cz
Key Personnel
Owner: Eva Michalkova
Founded: 1993
Subjects: Art, Fiction, Humor, Military Science, Nonfiction (General), Outdoor Recreation, Philosophy, Poetry
ISBN Prefix(es): 978-80-85974; 978-80-901603; 978-80-7299
Number of titles published annually: 50 Print
Total Titles: 75 Print

Aventinum sro+
Tolsteho 22, 101 00 Prague 10
Tel: 732 801 905 *Fax:* 272 735 387
E-mail: info@aventinum.cz
Web Site: www.aventinum.cz
Founded: 1990
Specialize in illustrated books.
Subjects: Animals, Pets, Art, Astrology, Occult, Biological Sciences, Gardening, Plants, Natural History
ISBN Prefix(es): 978-80-7151; 978-80-85277

Editio Baerenreiter Praha spol sro
Division of Baerenreiter Verlag
Nam Jiriho z Podebrad 112/19, 130 00 Prague 3
Tel: 274 001 911; 274 781 006 *Fax:* 222 220 829
E-mail: info@baerenreiter.cz; order@baerenreiter.cz
Web Site: www.sheetmusic.cz
Key Personnel
Mng Dir: Lukas Ptak *E-mail:* ptak@baerenreiter.cz
Distribution Manager: Dalibor Loter *Tel:* 274 001 912 *E-mail:* loter@baerenreiter.cz
Founded: 1923
Subjects: Biography, Memoirs, Education, History, Music, Dance, Science (General)
ISBN Prefix(es): 978-80-86385
Distributor for Alkor-Edition Kassel; Boosey & Hawkes; Bote & Bock; DSCH Publishers
Orders to: Baerenreiter Ltd, Burnt Mill, Elizabeth Way, Harlow, Essex CM20 2HX, United Kingdom *Tel:* (01279) 82 89 30 *Fax:* (01279) 82 89 31 *E-mail:* info@baerenreiter.co.uk (Australia, Hong Kong, Ireland, Malaysia, New Zealand, Singapore, South Africa & UK)
KGA Verlags-Service GmbH & Co KG, Postfach 10 21 80, 34021 Kassel, Germany *Tel:* (0561) 3105 320 *Fax:* (0561) 3105 310 (all other countries)

Baobab & GplusG sro
Plavecka 14, 128 00 Prague 2
Tel: 737 774 538
E-mail: gplusg@gplusg.cz
Web Site: www.baobab-books.net
Key Personnel
Contact: Barbora Cermakova *E-mail:* bara@gplusg.cz
ISBN Prefix(es): 978-80-87060
Bookshop(s): Krymska 29, 101 00 Prague, Contact: Kristyna Svata *Tel:* 739 261 971 *E-mail:* baobab.praha@gmail.com; Zizkova 250, 390 01 Tabor, Contact: Lenka Vocilkova *Tel:* 721 909 599 *E-mail:* baobab.tabor@gmail.com

Baronet AS+
Kvetnoveho vitezstvi 332/31, 149 00 Prague 4
Tel: 222 310 115
E-mail: info@baronet.cz

Web Site: www.baronet.cz
Founded: 1993
Specialize in historical romances, horoscopes &
English/American fiction.
Subjects: Fiction, Military Science, Nonfiction
(General), Romance, Science Fiction, Fantasy
ISBN Prefix(es): 978-80-7214; 978-80-85621;
978-80-85890; 978-80-900765; 978-80-901068

Barrister & Principal os+
Martinkova 7, 602 00 Brno
Tel: 545 211 015
E-mail: distribuce@barrister.cz
Web Site: www.barrister.cz
Key Personnel
Dir: Ivo Lukas *E-mail:* lukas@barrister.cz
Editor-in-Chief: Frantisek Miks *E-mail:* miks@
barrister.cz
Founded: 1994
Publish book & study materials for high school &
university students.
Subjects: Archaeology, Economics, Education,
Government, Political Science, History, Jour-
nalism, Language Arts, Linguistics, Philoso-
phy, Poetry, Psychology, Psychiatry, Religion -
Catholic, Social Sciences, Sociology, Theology
ISBN Prefix(es): 978-80-85947; 978-80-86598
Number of titles published annually: 15 Print
Total Titles: 226 Print
Orders to: Capkova 31, 602 00 Brno, Con-
tact: Lev Dolezal *Tel:* 774 422 121
E-mail: obchod@barrister.cz

B4U Publishing sro
Minska 13, 616 00 Brno
Mailing Address: Purkynova 108, 612 00 Brno
Tel: 511 112 199 *Fax:* 537 036 844
Web Site: www.b4upublishing.com
Key Personnel
Publisher: Oldrich Ruzicka *E-mail:* oldrich.
ruzicka@b4upublishing.com
Foreign Rights Manager: Jitka Albrechtova
E-mail: jitka.albrechtova@b4upublishing.com
Graphics & Design: Veronika Kopeckova
E-mail: veronika.kopeckova@b4upublishing.
com
Subjects: Animals, Pets, Fiction, Nonfiction (Gen-
eral)
ISBN Prefix(es): 978-80-87222

Bizbooks, *imprint of* Albatros Media AS

Nakladatelstvi BRANA AS
Jankovcova 18/938, 170 37 Prague 7
Tel: 220 191 313
E-mail: info@brana-knihy.cz
Web Site: brana-knihy.cz
Key Personnel
Editorial Manager: Dana Bryndova *Tel:* 220 191
323 *E-mail:* bryndova@brana-knihy.cz
Marketing: Hedvika Mojzisova
Production: Vlasta Machova *Tel:* 220 191 311
E-mail: vyroba@brana-knihy.cz
Founded: 1994
Subjects: Criminology, Education, Fiction, His-
tory, Literature, Literary Criticism, Essays,
Mysteries, Suspense, Nonfiction (General),
Travel & Tourism
ISBN Prefix(es): 978-80-7243; 978-80-85946;
978-80-901783

Nakladatelstvi Brio
Oderska 333, 196 03 Prague 9
Tel: 266 177 141 *Fax:* 266 177 147
Web Site: www.slovart.cz
Subjects: Fables, Fairy Tales, Nature
ISBN Prefix(es): 978-80-86113; 978-80-902209
Parent Company: Nakladatelstvi Slovart sro

CANIS-Media+
Korunni 9, 120 00 Prague 2

Tel: 222 522 457
E-mail: media@canis-media.cz
Web Site: www.canis-media.cz
Key Personnel
Owner: Dr M Cisarovsky
Founded: 1990
Subjects: Animals, Pets
ISBN Prefix(es): 978-80-900820

Ceska Biblicka Spolecnost os (Czech Bible
Society)
Nahorni 1816/12, 182 00 Prague 8
Tel: 284 693 925 *Fax:* 284 693 912
E-mail: info@dumbible.cz
Web Site: www.dumbible.cz; www.bibleshop.cz
(online store)
Key Personnel
Dir: Pavel Novak *Tel:* 284 693 924
E-mail: novak@dumbible.cz
Sales Manager: Marta Pumrova *Tel:* 284 693 926
E-mail: pumrova@dumbible.cz
Editor: Pavel Napravnik *Tel:* 284 693 927
E-mail: napravnik@dumbible.cz
Founded: 1990
Membership(s): United Bible Societies.
Subjects: Biblical Studies, Theology
ISBN Prefix(es): 978-80-85810; 978-80-900881

Ceska geologicka sluzba (Czech Geological
Survey)
Klarov 3, 118 21 Prague 1
Tel: 257 089 411; 257 089 500 *Fax:* 257 531 376
E-mail: secretar@geology.cz
Web Site: www.geology.cz
Key Personnel
Dir, Publishing: Patrik Fiferna *Tel:* 257 089 433
E-mail: patrik.fiferna@geology.cz
Founded: 1919
Subjects: Chemistry, Chemical Engineering, Earth
Sciences, Geography, Geology, Physical Sci-
ences
ISBN Prefix(es): 978-80-7075
Branch Office(s)
Geologicka 6, 152 00 Prague 5 *Tel:* 251 085 111
Fax: 251 818 748
Kotlarska 2, 611 37 Brno *Tel:* 541 129 496
Fax: 541 211 214
Leitnerova 22, 658 69 Brno *Tel:* 543 429 200
Fax: 543 212 370
Erbenova 348, 790 01 Jesenik *Tel:* 584 412 081
Fax: 584 412 081
CP 432, 270 51 Luzna u Rakovnika *Tel:* 602 191
529

Chvojkovo nakladatelstvi
Hlvicka 427, 181 00 Prague 8
Tel: 606 358 389
E-mail: chvojkovo@seznam.cz
Key Personnel
Contact: Milada Mala
Founded: 2002
Subjects: Alternative, Astrology, Occult, History,
Parapsychology, Psychology, Psychiatry
ISBN Prefix(es): 978-80-900239; 978-80-901270;
978-80-901622; 978-80-86183

Nakladatelstvi Columbus SRO+
Nad Kolcavkou 8, 190 00 Prague 9
Mailing Address: U Milosrdnych 10, 110 00
Prague, Stare Mesto 1
Tel: 284 820 446
Founded: 1993
Subjects: Biography, Memoirs, Cookery, Fiction,
Geography, Geology, History, Nonfiction (Gen-
eral), Parapsychology
ISBN Prefix(es): 978-80-85928; 978-80-901578;
978-80-901696; 978-80-901727; 978-80-7249
Distribution Center: Hornatecka 18a, 182 00
Prague 8 *Tel:* 284 681 710 *Fax:* 284 681 710
E-mail: sklad@columbus.cz

Computer Press, *imprint of* Albatros Media AS

Computer Press
Imprint of Albatros Media AS
Na Pankraci 30/1618, 140 00 Prague 4
Toll Free Tel: 800 555 513
E-mail: eshop@cpress.cz
Web Site: www.cpress.cz
Founded: 1994
Subjects: Automotive, Business, Computer Sci-
ence, Crafts, Games, Hobbies, Economics,
Health, Nutrition, Language Arts, Linguistics,
Literature, Literary Criticism, Essays, Sports,
Athletics, Travel & Tourism, Slovak Literature
ISBN Prefix(es): 978-80-251; 978-80-7226; 978-
80-85896

Nakladatelstvi Concordia+
Belohorska 99, 169 00 Prague 6
Tel: 233 357 280
Web Site: www.nakladatelstviconcordia.cz
Key Personnel
Contact: Magdalena Pechova
E-mail: magdalenapechova@atlas.cz
Founded: 1990
Subjects: Literature, Literary Criticism, Essays
ISBN Prefix(es): 978-80-900124; 978-80-901389;
978-80-85997
Bookshop(s): Luzicka 31, 120 00 Prague 2

CooBoo, *imprint of* Albatros Media AS

CPress, *imprint of* Albatros Media AS

Dimenze 2+2 (Dimension 2+2)+
Soukenicka 21, 110 00 Prague 1
Tel: 222 311 141
E-mail: info@dub.cz
Web Site: www.dub.cz
Key Personnel
Honourary President: Tomas Pfeiffer
Founded: 1990
Subjects: Film, Video, Health, Nutrition, Philoso-
phy, Theology
ISBN Prefix(es): 978-80-85238
Number of titles published annually: 4 Print; 2
CD-ROM; 3 Online; 2 Audio
Total Titles: 30 Print; 3 CD-ROM; 14 Online; 5
Audio
Associate Companies: Biotronic Centre of Social
Help; The Foundation of Being for Life Philos-
ophy & Biotronic Healing; SANATOR

Divadelni ustav (Arts & Theatre Institute)+
Subsidiary of Ministry of Culture, Czech Repub-
lic
Celetna 17, 110 00 Prague 1
Tel: 224 809 111 *Fax:* 224 809 226
E-mail: info@idu.cz; du@divadlo.cz; publik@
divadlo.cz; book@theatre.cz
Web Site: www.idu.cz/en
Key Personnel
Head, Publishing Dept: Kamila Cerna *Tel:* 224
809 170 *E-mail:* kamila.cerna@divadlo.cz
Founded: 1960
Subjects: Drama, Theater, Theatre Plays
ISBN Prefix(es): 978-80-7008
Number of titles published annually: 10 Print
Distribution Center: Kosmas sro, Lublanska
34, 120 00 Prague 2 *Tel:* 222 510 749; 222
515 407 *Fax:* 222 510 749; 222 515 407
E-mail: sklad.lublanska@kosmas.cz *Web
Site:* www.kosmas.cz/kosmas
Sklad Ruzyne, Kralupska 2, 161 00 Prague
6 *Tel:* 235 313 255 *Fax:* 235 316 362
E-mail: skald.kralupska@kosmas.cz
Artforum, Kozia 20, 811 03 Bratislava, Slovakia
Tel: 75311746 *Fax:* 75311746 *E-mail:* kozia@
artforum.sk

Nakladatelstvi Domino
Na Hradbach 3, 702 00 Ostrava

Tel: 596 127 644 *Fax:* 596 127 571
E-mail: domino@dominoknihy.cz
Web Site: www.dominoknihy.cz
Key Personnel
Owner & Publisher: Karin Lednicka
Editor: Dana Konvickova *E-mail:* dana@
dominoknihy.cz
Founded: 1997
Subjects: Fiction, Mysteries, Suspense, Romance
ISBN Prefix(es): 978-80-7498

Nakladatelstvi Doplnek+
Antonina Slavika 7, 602 00 Brno
Tel: 545 242 455; 731 507 666 (cell)
E-mail: doplnek@doplnek.cz; objednavky@
doplnek.cz (orders)
Web Site: www.doplnek.cz
Founded: 1991
Specialize in publishing of books with subject
specialties.
Membership(s): Association of Czech Booksellers
& Publishers (ACBP).
Subjects: Biography, Memoirs, Economics, Edu-
cation, Environmental Studies, History, Humor,
Journalism, Law, Literature, Literary Criticism,
Essays, Psychology, Psychiatry, Science Fic-
tion, Fantasy, Social Sciences, Sociology
ISBN Prefix(es): 978-80-7239; 978-80-85765;
978-80-901102
Number of titles published annually: 35 Print
Total Titles: 200 Print
Subsidiaries: Jan Sabata
Distributor for Jan Sabata
Bookshop(s): Zerotinovo nam 9, 602 00 Brno
Tel: 542 128 382
Distribution Center: Kosmas sro, Za Halami 877,
252 62 Horomerice *Tel:* 226 519 400 *Fax:* 226
519 387 *E-mail:* sklad.horomerice@kosmas.cz
Ales Cenek sro, K Cervenemu dvoru 24, 130 00
Prague 3 *Tel:* 222 311 629 *E-mail:* distribuce@
alescenek.cz *Web Site:* www.alascenek.cz
Sabata & Sabata Sro, Naskove 3, 150 00
Prague 5 *Tel:* 251 564 612 *Fax:* 251 561 256
E-mail: distribuce@knihsabata.cz

Edika, *imprint of* Albatros Media AS

EMG, see Euromedia Group ks (EMG)

Euromedia Group ks (EMG)+
Nadrazni 896/32, 150 00 Prague 5
Tel: 296 536 111 *Fax:* 296 536 935
E-mail: knizni.klub@euromedia.cz
Web Site: www.euromedia.cz
Key Personnel
Chief Executive Officer: Andreas Kaulfuss
Founded: 1953
Publishing house of literature & art.
Subjects: Art, Biography, Memoirs, Fiction, Po-
etry
ISBN Prefix(es): 978-80-207
Imprints: Ikar; Knizni klub; Odeon; Universum
Bookshop(s): Wilsonova 1618, 110 00 Prague 1
Tel: 224 242 915 *E-mail:* hln@euromedia.cz;
patro -1, stanice metra Budejovicka, Prague 4
Tel: 296 825 313 *E-mail:* dbk@euromedia.cz;
Plzenska 8, 150 00 Prague 5 *Tel:* 251 510 831
E-mail: novysmichov@euromedia.cz; Vaclavske
nam 41, 110 00 Prague 1 *Tel:* 221 111 314;
221 111 311 *E-mail:* svetkk@euromedia.cz;
Starobrnenska 16/18, 602 00 Brno *Tel:* 542
214 742 *E-mail:* brno@euromedia.cz; U Cerne
veze 15, Ceske Budejovice *Tel:* 386 322 064
E-mail: budejovice@euromedia.cz; Svehlova
393, 500 02 Hradec Kralove *Tel:* 495 511 421
E-mail: hradec@euromedia.cz; Knihkupectvi
OP, Masarykovo nam 47, Jihlava *Tel:* 567
308 158 *E-mail:* jihlava@euromedia.cz;
Zelezna 245, 460 01 Liberec *Tel:* 485 102
462 *E-mail:* liberec@euromedia.cz; Horni namesti 25, 771 11 Olomouc *Tel:* 585 242 445
E-mail: olomouc@euromedia.cz; Mezi Trhy

1-3, Opava *Tel:* 553 650 260 *E-mail:* opava@
euromedia.cz; Masarykovo nam 15, 701 00
Ostrava 1 *Tel:* 596 273 225 *E-mail:* ostrava@
euromedia.cz; Sedlackova 22, 301 11 Plzen
Tel: 377 222 844 *E-mail:* plzen@euromedia.
cz; Knihkupectvi Orion, 9 kvetna 618, Tabor
Tel: 381 253 549 *E-mail:* tabor@euromedia.
cz; Knihkupectvi Beran, Revolucni 179/7,
400 01 Usti nad Labem *Tel:* 475 205 513
E-mail: usti@euromedia.cz; tr T Bati 193, Zlin
Tel: 577 019 090 *E-mail:* archa@euromedia.
cz; nam Miru 174, Zlin *Tel:* 571 817 328
E-mail: jablko@euromedia.cz
Book Club(s): Odeon Book Club (Klub Ctenaru)
Distribution Center: u Rybnika 1161, 271 01
Nove Straseci, Logistics Manager: Kamil
Kidon *Tel:* 314 502 110; 731 451 340
E-mail: objednavky-vo@euromedia.cz

Exemplare, *imprint of* Nakladatelstvi Granit sro

Fortuna Libri spol sro
Vodickova 791/41, 112 09 Prague 1
Tel: 267 911 813
E-mail: fortuna@fortunalibri.cz
Web Site: www.fortunaprint.cz
Subjects: Art, Cookery, Fiction, History, Non-
fiction (General), Travel & Tourism, Canine
Literature
ISBN Prefix(es): 978-80-86144; 978-80-85873;
978-80-7321
Branch Office(s)
Fortuna Libri SK spol sro, Zadunajska cesta 8,
851 01 Bratislava, Slovakia *Tel:* (02) 6820
4700; (02) 6820 4701 *Fax:* (02) 6820 4740
E-mail: fortuna@fortuna.sk *Web Site:* www.
fortunalibri.sk

Nakladatelstvi Fragment sro
Pujmanove 1221/4, 140 00 Prague 4
Tel: 241 004 011 *Fax:* 241 004 071
E-mail: fragment@fragment.cz
Web Site: www.fragment.cz
Key Personnel
Co-Owner/Production Manager: Jan Eisler
E-mail: eisler@fragment.cz
Co-Owner/Business Dir: Pavel Nyc *E-mail:* nyc@
fragment.cz
Foreign Rights Manager: Sarka Vojtechova
Tel: 241 004 028 *E-mail:* vojtechova@
fragment.cz
Founded: 1991
Subjects: Animals, Pets, Fiction, Literature, Liter-
ary Criticism, Essays, Nonfiction (General)
ISBN Prefix(es): 978-80-7200; 978-80-901070;
978-80-85768
Branch Office(s)
Vydavatelstvo Fragment sro, Kominarska 2,4,
831 04 Bratislava 3, Slovakia, Dir: Iveta Cer-
nakova *Tel:* 250 234 583 *Fax:* 255 573 151
E-mail: fragment@fragment.sk

Nakladatelstvi Fraus sro
Edvarda Benese 72, 301 00 Plzen
Tel: 377 226 102 *Fax:* 377 224 594
E-mail: info@fraus.cz
Web Site: www.fraus.cz; www.fraus.com
Founded: 1991
Specialize in educational books.
Subjects: Chemistry, Chemical Engineering, Edu-
cation, History, Mathematics, Nonfiction (Gen-
eral), Physics, Science (General), Social Sci-
ences, Sociology, Nature
ISBN Prefix(es): 978-80-7238; 978-80-900619;
978-80-85784

Galerie Hlavniho Mesta Prahy (City Gallery
Prague)
Staromestske nam 605/13, 110 00 Prague 1
Tel: 224 826 391; 725 818 722
E-mail: pr@ghmp.cz

Web Site: www.ghmp.cz
Key Personnel
Dir: Magdalena Jurikova
Sales & Marketing: Miroslav Kolacek
E-mail: miroslav.kolacek@ghmp.cz
Public Relations: Alice Lenska *E-mail:* alice.
lenska@ghmp.cz
Founded: 1963
Subjects: Architecture & Interior Design, Art,
History, Literature, Literary Criticism, Essays,
Photography
ISBN Prefix(es): 978-80-7010
Bookshop(s): Staromestske nam 13, 110 00
Prague 1 *Tel:* 224 827 526 *Fax:* 222 327 851
E-mail: lekt-ghmp@volny.cz

Grada Publishing AS+
U Pruhonu 22, 170 00 Prague 7
Tel: 234 264 401; 234 264 402 *Fax:* 234 264 400
E-mail: info@grada.cz
Web Site: www.grada.cz
Key Personnel
Dir: Milan Brunat *Tel:* 234 264 411
Marketing: Zdenek Jaros *Tel:* 234 264 514
Foreign Rights: Magdalena Brenkova *Tel:* 234
264 412
Founded: 1991
Subjects: Computer Science, Economics, Law,
Medicine, Nursing, Dentistry, Technology
ISBN Prefix(es): 978-80-7169; 978-80-85424;
978-80-85623; 978-80-900250; 978-80-247
Total Titles: 850 Print

Nakladatelstvi Granit sro+
Novorossijska 16, 100 00 Prague 10
Tel: 271 752 381 *Fax:* 245 008 229
E-mail: obchod@granit-publishing.cz
Web Site: www.granit-publishing.cz
Founded: 1991
Specialize in natural history publications.
Subjects: Animals, Pets, Biological Sciences,
Crafts, Games, Hobbies, Education, Gardening,
Plants, Geography, Geology, Health, Nutrition,
Natural History, Science (General)
ISBN Prefix(es): 978-80-85805; 978-80-7296;
978-80-901195; 978-80-901443
Number of titles published annually: 12 Print
Total Titles: 80 Print
Imprints: Exemplare

**Historicky Ustav Akademie ved Ceske
Republiky vvi** (Institute of History, Academy
of Sciences of the Czech Republic vvi)
Prosecka 809/76, 190 00 Prague 9
Tel: 286 882 121 *Fax:* 286 887 513
Web Site: www.hiu.cas.cz
Key Personnel
Dir: Dr Eva Semotanova *Tel:* 286 882 121 ext
251 *E-mail:* semotanova@hiu.cas.cz
Assistant Dir: Martina Volesakova *Tel:* 286 890
189 *E-mail:* volesakova@hiu.cas.cz
Founded: 1921
Subjects: History
ISBN Prefix(es): 978-80-85268; 978-80-7286
Branch Office(s)
Veveri 97, 602 00 Brno, Head: Dr Radomir
Vlcek *Tel:* 532 290 500 *Fax:* 532 290 511
E-mail: stefanova@brno.avcr.cz

HOST-vydavatelstvi sro
Radlas 5, 602 00 Brno
Tel: 545 212 747; 733 715 765 (cell); 725 606
146 *Fax:* 545 212 747
E-mail: redakce@hostbrno.cz
Web Site: www.hostbrno.cz
Key Personnel
Dir: Tomas Reichel *E-mail:* reichel@hostbrno.cz
Foreign Rights: Jana Liskova *E-mail:* liskova@
hostbrno.cz
Founded: 1990
Subjects: Fiction, Mysteries, Suspense, Nonfiction
(General), Poetry

ISBN Prefix(es): 978-80-7294; 978-80-85233; 978-80-86055; 978-80-902127
Number of titles published annually: 50 Print

Ikar, *imprint of* Euromedia Group ks (EMG)

INFOA International sro+
Nova 141, 789 72 Dubicko
Tel: 583 456 810
E-mail: infoa@infoa.cz
Web Site: www.infoa.cz
Key Personnel
Executive Officer: Stanislav Sojak
Consultant: Martina Kutalova *E-mail:* kutalova.infoa@seznam.cz
Founded: 1992
Private company with its own distribution network in the Czech Republic, Slovakia & Poland.
Specialize in foreign languages.
Subjects: Language Arts, Linguistics
ISBN Prefix(es): 978-80-7240; 978-80-85836; 978-80-901005
Total Titles: 250 Print
Branch Office(s)
Hurbanova 10, 909 01 Skalica, Slovakia, Branch Manager: Pavol Rehus *Tel:* 905 314 342 *E-mail:* infoa@infoa.sk
Distributed by Arkadiusz Wingert (Poland); Bay Foreign Language Books (UK); Book-X-Press Bt (Hungary); INFOA (Slovakia)
Distributor for Cambridge University Press; Express Publishing (Czech Republic & Slovakia); Mary Glasgow Magazine; Longman; Macmillan Heinemann; Oxford University Press
Showroom(s): Druzstevni 5, 789 72 Dubicko
Shipping Address: Druzstevni 5, 789 72 Dubicko
Warehouse: Druzstevni 5, 789 72 Dubicko

Nakladatelstvi Jan Vasut+
Pod Vodovodem 4, 158 00 Prague 5
Tel: 222 319 319 *Fax:* 224 811 059
E-mail: nakladatelstvi@vasut.cz
Web Site: www.vasut.cz
Key Personnel
Owner & Publisher: Jan Vasut *Tel:* 222 318 707 *E-mail:* jan.vasut@vasut.cz
Sales Manager: Petr Vrana *E-mail:* vrana@vasut.cz
Founded: 1990
Subjects: Cookery, Crafts, Games, Hobbies, Humor, Sports, Athletics
ISBN Prefix(es): 978-80-7236
Total Titles: 350 Print
Warehouse: Grada Bohemia sro, Luzna 591, Prague 6 *Tel:* 220 121 360

Jednota ceskych matematiku a fysiku (Union of Czech Mathematicians & Physicists)
Zitna 25, 117 10 Prague 1
Tel: 222 211 100; 222 090 709; 222 090 708
E-mail: jcmf@jcmf.cz; predseda@jcmf.cz (chairman); tajemnik@jcmf.cz (secretary)
Web Site: www.jcmf.cz
Founded: 1862
Book & journal publisher.
Subjects: Mathematics, Physics, Basic Research & Education
ISBN Prefix(es): 978-80-7015
Total Titles: 5 Print
Bookshop(s): Celetna 18, 116 36 Prague 1 *Tel:* 224 491 448 *Fax:* 224 491 671

Nakladatelstvi JOTA sro+
Skarova 16, 612 00 Brno
Tel: 539 086 580
E-mail: jota@jota.cz
Web Site: www.jota.cz
Founded: 1990
Subjects: Alternative, Biography, Memoirs, Crafts, Games, Hobbies, Health, Nutrition, History,
Military Science, Outdoor Recreation, Science Fiction, Fantasy
ISBN Prefix(es): 978-80-85617; 978-80-900281; 978-80-7217

Kalich
Jungmannova 9, 110 00 Prague 1
Tel: 224 947 844 (editor); 224 947 505 (orders) *Fax:* 224 947 845
E-mail: kalich@ekalich.cz (orders); kalichpub@ekalich.cz (editor)
Web Site: www.ekalich.cz
Key Personnel
Mng Dir & Chief Editor: Michal Plzak
Founded: 1921
Subjects: History, Philosophy, Religion - Catholic, Religion - Jewish, Religion - Protestant, Religion - Other, Social Sciences, Sociology, Theology
ISBN Prefix(es): 978-80-7017; 978-80-7072

Kanzelsberger AS
4D Office Center, Kodanska 46, 100 00 Prague 10
Tel: 234 064 211
E-mail: info@kanzelsberger.cz
Web Site: www.kanzelsberger.cz
Founded: 1990
Subjects: Biography, Memoirs, Language Arts, Linguistics
ISBN Prefix(es): 978-80-900095; 978-80-85387; 978-80-900184
Bookshop(s): Lodzska 850, 181 00 Prague 8, Head: Kristyna Kucharova *Tel:* 605 440 887; Vaclavske nam 42, Prague 1, Head: Lenka Kristinova *Tel:* 224 217 335 *E-mail:* orbis@kanzelsberger.cz; Starostrasnicka 56, 101 00 Prague 10, Head: Dana Hoschlova *Tel:* 274 777 374 *E-mail:* strasnice@kanzelsberger.cz; Svehlova 32, 102 00 Prague 10, Head: Katerina Beerova *Tel:* 271 752 223 *E-mail:* hostivar@kanzelsberger.cz; U Slavie 1527, 101 33 Prague 10, Head: Zuzana Slechtova *Tel:* 272 731 985 *E-mail:* eden@kanzelsberger.cz; Chlumeoka 756, 198 19 Prague 9, Head: Jana Kmunickova *Tel:* 605 020 403; Cs armady 31, 160 00 Prague 6, Head: Vit Pulda *Tel:* 233 323 509 *E-mail:* dejvice@kanzelsberger.cz; Freyova 35, 190 00 Prague 9, Head: Lenka Trousilova *Tel:* 211 138 401 *E-mail:* vysocany@kanzelsberger.cz; Palackeho 96, 266 01 Beroun, Head: Zuzana Muricova *Tel:* 311 611 244 *E-mail:* beroun@kanzelsberger.cz; JP Koubka 99, 388 01 Blatna, Head: Aneta Kvardova *Tel:* 383 380 152 *E-mail:* blatna@kanzelsberger.cz; Masarykova 6, 602 00 Brno, Head: Lucie Nemcova *Tel:* 542 212 275 *E-mail:* brno_mas@kanzelsberger.cz; Videnska 100, 619 00 Brno, Head: Marcela Halickova *Tel:* 547 213 181 *E-mail:* brno_fut@kanzelsberger.cz; J Palacha 3152, 690 02 Breclav, Head: Marketa Miklova *Tel:* 519 323 703 *E-mail:* breclav@kanzelsberger.cz; Sedlackova 109, 250 88 Celakovice, Head: Alena Vrana *Tel:* 326 921 547 *E-mail:* celakovice@kanzelsberger.cz; Kanovnicka 3, 370 01 Ceske Budejovice, Head: Petr Pistulka *Tel:* 387 201 317 *E-mail:* cbud@kanzelsberger.cz; Prokopa Holeho 15, 405 02 Decin, Head: Alena Rihova *Tel:* 412 530 245 *E-mail:* decin@kanzelsberger.cz; Dolni Valy 3940/2, 695 01 Hodonin, Head: Radim Hudec *Tel:* 518 325 415 *E-mail:* hodonin@kanzelsberger.cz; Celakovskeho 488/10, 500 02 Hradec Kralove, Head: Renata Jansova *Tel:* 495 514 407; Cs armady 216, 500 03 Hradec Kralove, Head: Sona Ornostova *Tel:* 495 518 454; Dukelska tr 3, 500 02 Hradec Kralove, Head: Martina Kavkova *Tel:* 495 523 909 *E-mail:* hk_duk@kanzelsberger.cz; nam Svobody 822/1, 790 01 Jesenik, Head: Monika Rosenbergova *Tel:* 584 412 214 *E-mail:* jesenik@kanzelsberger.cz; Hradebni 1, 586 01 Jihlava, Head: Michaela
Sera *Tel:* 567 213 929 *E-mail:* jihlava@kanzelsberger.cz; Panska 132/l, 377 01 Jindrichuv Hradec, Head: Regina Liskova *Tel:* 384 361 745 *E-mail:* j_hradec@kanzelsberger.cz; Kpt Jarose 375/31, 360 06 Karlovy Vary, Head: Anna Remlova *Tel:* 353 221 238; T G Masaryka 253, 272 01 Kladno, Head: Radka Haskova *Tel:* 312 249 765 *E-mail:* kladno@kanzelsberger.cz; nam Miru 169, 339 01 Klatovy, Head: Katerina Suldova *Tel:* 376 311 529 *E-mail:* klatovy@kanzelsberger.cz; Hlavni namesti 25, 794 01 Krnov, Head: Karin Pobucka *Tel:* 554 620 095 *E-mail:* krnov@kanzelsberger.cz; Vodni 61, 767 01 Kromeriz, Head: Jaroslava Zabloudilova *Tel:* 573 339 286 *E-mail:* kromeriz@kanzelsberger.cz; Jicinska 1350/3, 293 01 Mlada Boleslav, Head: Vera Brodska *Tel:* 326 330 291 *E-mail:* ml_boleslav@kanzelsberger.cz; Palackeho trida 118/21, 288 02 Nymburk, Head: Dita Drimalova *Tel:* 325 546 210 *E-mail:* nymburk@kanzelsberger.cz; Kafkova 8, 779 00 Olomouc, Head: Marcela Hofirkova *Tel:* 585 319 427 *E-mail:* olomouc@kanzelsberger.cz; Novinarska 6A, 702 00 Ostrava, Head: Tatiana Prosilova *Tel:* 596 617 692 *E-mail:* ostrava_fut@kanzelsberger.cz; tr Miru 2670, 530 02 Pardubice, Head: Martina Jelinkova *Tel:* 466 510 288 *E-mail:* pardubice@kanzelsberger.cz; Nerudova 88, 397 01 Pisek, Head: Lenka Paskova *Tel:* 382 213 442 *E-mail:* pisek@kanzelsberger.cz; Pisecka 972, 326 00 Plzen, Head: Ladislava Kotesovcova *Tel:* 377 458 137 *E-mail:* plzen_oc@kanzelsberger.cz; Turinskeho 44, 290 01 Podebrady, Head: Marketa Simonova *Tel:* 325 532 956 *E-mail:* podebrady@kanzelsberger.cz; Wilsonova 6, 750 00 Prerov, Head: Alena Mozisova *Tel:* 581 219 764 *E-mail:* prerov@kanzelsberger.cz; Milinska 134, 261 01 Pribram 3, Head: Jana Sadilkova *Tel:* 318 590 606 *E-mail:* pribram@kanzelsberger.cz; Husovo nam 34, 269 01 Rakovnik, Head: Romana Engelova *Tel:* 313 512 775 *E-mail:* rakovnik@kanzelsberger.cz; Husova 94, 274 01 Slany, Head: Marketa Vinceova *Tel:* 312 521 403 *E-mail:* slany@kanzelsberger.cz; Velke nam 215, 386 01 Strakonice, Head: Marcela Paskova *Tel:* 383 321 744 *E-mail:* strakonice@kanzelsberger.cz; tr 9 kvetna 2886, 390 01 Tabor, Head: Ivan Kubat *Tel:* 381 253 972 *E-mail:* tabor@kanzelsberger.cz; 28 rijna 1/419, 415 01 Teplice, Head: Helena Koptova *Tel:* 417 534 299 *E-mail:* teplice@kanzelsberger.cz; Srbicka 464, 415 01 Teplice, Head: Nikola Havlickova *Tel:* 417 563 566 *E-mail:* teplice_oc@kanzelsberger.cz; Krakonosovo nam 19, 541 00 Trutnov, Head: Jirina Milova *Tel:* 499 819 183 *E-mail:* trutnov@kanzelsberger.cz; nam Svobody 52, 438 01 Zatec, Head: Lenka Roubikova *Tel:* 415 212 677 *E-mail:* zatec@kanzelsberger.cz; nam Republiky 147, 591 01 Zd'ar nad Sazavou, Head: Radka Kalova *Tel:* 566 524 714 *E-mail:* zdar@kanzelsberger.cz; nam Miru 2/488, 760 01 Zlin, Head: Martina Vecerova *Tel:* 577 213 474 *E-mail:* zlin@kanzelsberger.cz; Obrokova 93/16, 669 01 Znojmo, Head: Zuzana Chudobova *Tel:* 515 223 970 *E-mail:* znojmo@kanzelsberger.cz

Karmelitanske Nakladatelstvi Sro (Carmelite Publishing House Ltd)+
Thakurova 3, 160 00 Prague 6
Tel: 220 181 350; 230 233 140 (foreign rights) *Fax:* 220 181 390
E-mail: secretariat@kna.cz; rights@kna.cz
Web Site: www.kna.cz
Key Personnel
Mng Dir: Dr Zuzana Jelenova, PhD *Tel:* 220 181 247 *E-mail:* jelenova@kna.cz
Editor-in-Chief: Katerina Lachmanova *E-mail:* lachmanova@kna.cz

Editorial Manager: Pavel Kindermann *Tel:* 220 181 379 *E-mail:* kindermann@kna.cz
Founded: 1991
Subjects: Biblical Studies, Biography, Memoirs, History, Poetry, Religion - Catholic, Theology
ISBN Prefix(es): 978-80-7192; 978-80-7195; 978-80-85527
Total Titles: 530 Print; 150 Audio
Bookshop(s): Jindrisska 23, 110 00 Prague 1, Head: Pavel Sana *Tel:* 224 212 376 *E-mail:* sv.jindrich@kna.cz; Kolejni 4, 160 00 Prague 6, Dir: Josef Lacman *Tel:* 220 181 714 *E-mail:* sv.vojtech@kna.cz; Masarykovo nam 8/6, 680 01 Boskovice, Head: Jana Horakova *Tel:* 731 604 040 *E-mail:* boskovice@kna.cz; Dominikanske nam 8, 602 00 Brno, Head: Ondrej Matal *Tel:* 542 213 140 *E-mail:* michal@kna.cz; Knezska 21, 370 01 Ceske Budejovice, Head: Veronika Kucerova *Tel:* 386 321 426 *E-mail:* mikulas@kna.cz; Kostelni Vydri 58, 380 01 Dacice, Head: Lukas Malotin *Tel:* 384 420 295 *E-mail:* zasilky@kna.cz; Velke nam 36, 500 01 Hradec Kralove, Head: Benedikt Krizan *Tel:* 495 063 173 *E-mail:* hradec@kna.cz; Chelcickeho 8, 506 01 Jicin, Head: Bohuslava Korbelarova *Tel:* 493 721 967 *E-mail:* jicin@kna.cz; Pivovarska 12/3, 733 01 Karvina, Head: Emilie Steffanova *Tel:* 596 311 399 *E-mail:* karvina@kna.cz; Kostelni 7, 460 59 Liberec, Head: Veronika Francova *Tel:* 485 104 064 *E-mail:* liberec@kna.cz; Mirove nam 15, 412 01 Litomerice, Head: Blanka Tomasova *Tel:* 416 732 458 *E-mail:* jonas@kna.cz; Kateriny Militke 54, 293 01 Mlada Boleslav, Head: Alena Nemeckova *Tel:* 572 557 842 *E-mail:* boleslav@kna.cz; Pekarska 4, 779 00 Olomouc, Head: Jan Pilar *Tel:* 583 033 390 *E-mail:* olomouc@kna.cz; Puchmajerova 10, 702 00 Ostrava, Head: Alena Svechova *Tel:* 596 121 463 *E-mail:* caritas@kna.cz; Frantiskanska 9, 301 12 Plzen, Head: Hana Prokopova *Tel:* 377 323 615 *E-mail:* plzen@kna.cz; Marianske nam 200, 686 01 Uherske Hradiste *Tel:* 572 557 842 *E-mail:* uh.hradiste@kna.cz; ul U lipy 302, 687 06 Velehrad, Head: Pavla Zakova Supakova *Tel:* 573 034 150 *E-mail:* poutini.prodejna@kna.cz; Sadova ul, 760 01 Zlin, Head: Marie Hrdlickova *Tel:* 577 219 451 *E-mail:* zlin@kna.cz; Zupne nam 10, 811 01 Bratislava, Slovakia *Tel:* 233 002 739 *E-mail:* kapucini@kna.sk
Web Site: www.kna.sk
Distribution Center: Kolejni 4, 160 00 Prague 6, Head: Iveta Souckova *Tel:* 224 316 157; 220 181 715 *Fax:* 224 316 160 *E-mail:* souckova@kna.cz
Dukelska 103, 614 00 Brno-Husovice, Head: Eva Tacchinardi *Tel:* 543 237 064 *E-mail:* tacchinardi@kna.cz

Nakladatelstvi Karolinum, see Univerzita Karlova v Praze, Nakladatelstvi Karolinum

Kartografie PRAHA AS
Ostrovni 30, 110 00 Prague 1
Tel: 221 969 446
E-mail: info@kartografie.cz
Web Site: www.kartografie.cz
Key Personnel
Dir: Milada Svobodova *Tel:* 221 969 445 *E-mail:* svobodova@kartografie.cz
Sales: Miroslava Basarova *Tel:* 221 969 446 *E-mail:* basarova@kartografie.cz; Ivana Novakova *Tel:* 221 969 433 *E-mail:* novakova@kartografie.cz
Founded: 1954
Geodetic & cartographic enterprise in Prague.
ISBN Prefix(es): 978-80-7011
Bookshop(s): Centrum Ucebnic CZ sro, Ostrovni 30, 110 00 Prague 1 *Tel:* 224 931 451; KIWI svet map a pruvodcu sro, Jungmannova 23, Prague 1 *Tel:* 224 948 455; Knihkupectvi Sevcik, Solni 5-7, Plzen *Tel:* 377 236 336

Shipping Address: Cestlice 108, 251 70 Prague *Tel:* 272 680 978 *Fax:* 272 680 976
Warehouse: Cestlice 108, 251 70 Prague *Tel:* 272 680 978 *Fax:* 272 680 976

Knizni klub, *imprint of* Euromedia Group ks (EMG)

Svet Kridel+
Chebska 146, 350 02 Cheb-Podhrad
Tel: 604 109 456
E-mail: redakce@svetkridel.cz
Web Site: www.svetkridel.cz
Founded: 1990
Air war & literature & professional publications for air sports.
Subjects: Aeronautics, Aviation
ISBN Prefix(es): 978-80-86808; 978-80-85280
Total Titles: 150 Print
Associate Companies: Magnet Press

Labyrint+
Dittrichova 5, 120 00 Prague 2
Mailing Address: PO Box 52, Jablonecka 715, 190 00 Prague 9
Tel: 224 922 422 *Fax:* 224 922 422
E-mail: labyrint@labyrint.net
Web Site: www.labyrint.net
Founded: 1992
Subjects: Art, Fiction, Library & Information Sciences, Poetry
ISBN Prefix(es): 978-80-85935; 978-80-901289
Number of titles published annually: 20 Print; 1 E-Book; 2 Audio
Total Titles: 200 Print; 2 E-Book; 5 Audio
Subsidiaries: RAKETA (Children's books)

Nakladatelstvi Librex
Raisova 1066/6, 709 00 Ostrava-Marianske Hory
Tel: 735 491 701
E-mail: librex.cz@gmail.com; prace.librex@gmail.com
Web Site: www.librex.eu
Key Personnel
Mng Dir: Dana Becherova *Tel:* 724 091 885 *E-mail:* becherova.dana@gmail.com
Sales: Lenka Tvrzova *E-mail:* tvrzova.librex@gmail.com
Founded: 1992
ISBN Prefix(es): 978-80-7228; 978-80-85987

Nakladatelstvi Libri sro+
Neklanova 109/27, 128 00 Prague 2
Tel: 251 541 632
E-mail: libri@libri.cz
Web Site: www.libri.cz
Key Personnel
Publishing Dir: Dr Karel Zaloudek
Sales: Blanka Bobokova
Founded: 1993
Original Czech encyclopedia, popularization.
Membership(s): Federation of Czech Publishers & Booksellers.
Subjects: Archaeology, Architecture & Interior Design, Economics, Foreign Countries, Geography, Geology, History, Literature, Literary Criticism, Essays, Social Sciences, Sociology
ISBN Prefix(es): 978-80-901579; 978-80-85983; 978-80-7277
Number of titles published annually: 50 Print
Total Titles: 300 Print; 3 CD-ROM; 25 E-Book
Foreign Rep(s): Artforum (Slovenia)

Nakladatelstvi Lidove noviny+
Dykova 15, 101 00 Prague 10
Tel: 222 522 350; 222 510 843
E-mail: nln@nln.cz
Web Site: www.nln.cz
Key Personnel
Dir: Eva Pleskova *E-mail:* pleskova@nln.cz
Founded: 1993

Subjects: Archaeology, Art, Biography, Memoirs, Fiction, History, Language Arts, Linguistics, Nonfiction (General), Poetry, Science (General), Social Sciences, Sociology, Travel & Tourism
ISBN Prefix(es): 978-80-7106
Number of titles published annually: 5 Print
Total Titles: 10 Print; 10 E-Book
Bookshop(s): Jana Masaryka 58, 120 00 Prague 2, Head: Alena Jelinkova *Tel:* 224 250 365 *E-mail:* knihkupectvi@nln.cz

Luxpress spol sro+
Malirska 6, 170 00 Prague 7
Tel: 242 412 704; 721 981 836 (cell)
Web Site: www.luxpress.cz
Key Personnel
Contact: Jiri Drejnar
Founded: 1990
Subjects: Health, Nutrition, Human Relations, Religion - Other
ISBN Prefix(es): 978-80-7130
Bookshop(s): Medena 17, 811 02 Bratislava, Slovakia *Tel:* (02) 5463 0661 *Fax:* (02) 5443 2245 *E-mail:* medena@kna.sk

Knihovna a tiskarna pro nevidome K E Macana (K E Macana Library & Printing House for the Blind)
Ve Smeckach 15, 115 17 Prague 1
Tel: 222 210 492; 222 211 523 *Fax:* 222 210 494
E-mail: ktn@ktn.cz
Web Site: www.ktn.cz
Key Personnel
Dir: Bohdan Roule *Tel:* 296 326 121
Deputy Dir & Head, Economic Dept: Miloslava Kourimska *Tel:* 296 326 120
Founded: 1918
Subjects: Biography, Memoirs, Fiction, Humor, Mysteries, Suspense, Poetry, Psychology, Psychiatry, Religion - Other, Science Fiction, Fantasy
ISBN Prefix(es): 978-80-7061

Masaryk University Press
Rybkova 987/19, Bldg T, Complex Kravi hora, veveri, 602 00 Brno
Tel: 549 491 170; 549 491 171
E-mail: munipress@press.muni.cz; redakce@press.muni.cz
Web Site: www.muni.cz/press
Key Personnel
Dir: Dr Alena Mizerova *E-mail:* mizerova@rect.muni.cz
Manager: Radka Vyskocilova
Subjects: Economics, Law, Medicine, Nursing, Dentistry, Philosophy, Science (General)
ISBN Prefix(es): 978-80-210

Maxdorf sro+
Na Sejdru 247/6a, 142 00 Prague 4
Tel: 241 011 681 *Fax:* 241 710 245
E-mail: info@maxdorf.cz; knihy@maxdorf.cz (orders)
Web Site: www.maxdorf.cz
Founded: 1993
Publishing house of scientific & professional literature specializing in medicine, monographies & handbooks.
Subjects: Art, Health, Nutrition, History, Medicine, Nursing, Dentistry, Science (General)
ISBN Prefix(es): 978-80-85800; 978-80-85912; 978-80-7345
Number of titles published annually: 40 Print
Total Titles: 105 Print; 1 E-Book

Medica Publishing, Pavla Momcilova+
V Zahradach 146, 251 01 Cestlice
Tel: 272 680 919 *Fax:* 272 680 919
E-mail: momcilova@volny.cz

Web Site: www.medicapublishing.cz; www.
facebook.com/medicapublishing
Key Personnel
Publisher: Mrs Pavla Momcilova
Founded: 1990
Subjects: Child Care & Development, Cookery,
Education, Fiction, Health, Nutrition, Medicine,
Nursing, Dentistry, Poetry, Science (General),
Self-Help, Technology
ISBN Prefix(es): 978-80-900140; 978-80-901137;
978-80-85936
Number of titles published annually: 5 Print
Total Titles: 60 Print
Distribution Center: Pemic Books AS, Vrati-
movska 703/101, 719 00 Ostrava-Kuncice
Euromedia Group ks, Nadrazni 869/32, 150 00
Prague 5
Pavel Dobrovsky-BETA SRO, Kvetnoveho
vitezstvi 332, 149 00 Prague 415

Mendelova univerzita v Brne (Mendel
University in Brno)
Zemedelska 1/1665, 613 00 Brno
Tel: 545 131 111 *Fax:* 545 211 128
E-mail: info@mendelu.cz
Web Site: www.mendelu.cz
Key Personnel
Head: Prof Jaroslav Hlusek *E-mail:* hlusek@
mendelu.cz
Founded: 1992
Subjects: Agriculture, Animals, Pets, Biological
Sciences, Earth Sciences, Economics, Physical
Sciences
ISBN Prefix(es): 978-80-7157
Number of titles published annually: 70 Print; 30
Audio
Total Titles: 400 Print; 2,000 Audio

Mlada fronta AS+
Mezi Vodami 1952/9, 143 00 Prague 4
Tel: 225 276 111
E-mail: mf@mf.cz
Web Site: www.mf.cz
Key Personnel
Chairman & Chief Executive Officer: Karel Pol-
car *Tel:* 225 276 380 *E-mail:* polcar@mf.cz
Dir, Books Division: Tomas Cerny *Tel:* 225 347
324 *E-mail:* cerny@mf.cz
Dir, Magazines Division: Jan Martinek
Head, Marketing & Public Relations, Books Divi-
sion: Magdalena Potmesilova *Tel:* 225 347 302
E-mail: potmesilova@mf.cz
Dir, Marketing & Distribution: David Svanda
Tel: 225 276 495 *E-mail:* svanda@mf.cz
Public Relations Manager: Pavlina Micova
Tel: 225 276 484 *E-mail:* micova@mf.cz
Founded: 1945
Subjects: Art, Astronomy, Biography, Memoirs,
Fiction, History, Nonfiction (General), Philoso-
phy, Poetry, Science (General), Science Fiction,
Fantasy, Travel & Tourism
ISBN Prefix(es): 978-80-204
Number of titles published annually: 100 Print
Total Titles: 6,500 Print

Editio Moravia Hudebni Nakladatelstvi+
Hvozdec 55, 664 71 Veverska Bityska
Tel: 549 420 675 *Fax:* 549 420 675
Web Site: www.editiomoravia.cz
Founded: 1990
Specialize in music literature for schools.
Subjects: Education, Music, Dance
ISBN Prefix(es): 978-80-85322; 978-80-86565

Moravska Galerie v Brne (Moravian Gallery in
Brno)
Husova 18, 662 26 Brno
Tel: 532 169 111 *Fax:* 532 169 181
E-mail: info@moravska-galerie.cz
Web Site: www.moravska-galerie.cz
Key Personnel
Dir: Jan Press

Deputy Dir: Katerina Tlachova *Tel:* 532 169 131
E-mail: katerina.tlachova@moravska-galerie.cz
Head, Marketing: Adela Biravska *Tel:* 532 169
175 *E-mail:* adela.biravska@moravska-galerie.
cz
Founded: 1873
Subjects: Architecture & Interior Design, Art,
Photography, Applied Art, Design, Fine Art
ISBN Prefix(es): 978-80-7027
Number of titles published annually: 6 Print; 1
CD-ROM
Total Titles: 30 Print; 2 CD-ROM
Distributed by Kosmas cz

Motto, *imprint of* Albatros Media AS

MU Press, see Masaryk University Press

Nakladatelski A Vydavatelska Agentura, see
NAVA (Nakladatelski A Vydavatelska
Agentura)

Narodni filmovy archiv (National Film
Archive)+
Malesicka 12 & 14, 130 00 Prague 3
Tel: 271 770 500 *Fax:* 271 770 501
E-mail: nfa@nfa.cz
Web Site: www.nfa.cz
Key Personnel
Chief Executive Officer: Michal Bregant
E-mail: michal.bregant@nfa.cz
Researcher: Ivan Klimes *E-mail:* ivan.klimes@
nfa.cz
Founded: 1943
Subjects: Film, Video
ISBN Prefix(es): 978-80-7004
Branch Office(s)
Bartolomejska 11, 110 00 Prague 1

Narodni Knihovna Ceske republiky (National
Library of the Czech Republic)+
Central Depository, Publishing Division,
Sodomkova 2/1146, 102 00 Prague 10
Tel: 281 013 317; 281 013 230 *Fax:* 281 013 333
E-mail: vydavatelstvi@nkp.cz
Web Site: www.nkp.cz
Key Personnel
Dir, Publishing Division: Milena Redinova, PhD
E-mail: milena.redinova@nkp.cz
The publishing division manages & coordinates
publishing activities of the National Library in
the areas of librarianship, bibliography & sci-
entific information. The division is responsible
for editorial planning, production, sales & ship-
ping.
Membership(s): Conference of European Na-
tional Librarians (CENL); Czech Association
of Booksellers & Publishers; Czech Association
of Librarian & Information Professionals; In-
ternational Federation of Library Associations
& Institutions (IFLA); Lique des Bibliotheques
Europeennes de Recherche (LIBER).
Subjects: Library & Information Sciences
ISBN Prefix(es): 978-80-7050
Number of titles published annually: 32 Print; 2
CD-ROM; 1 Online
Total Titles: 94 Print; 2 CD-ROM; 1 Online

Narodni Muzeum (National Museum)
Vaclavske nam 68, 115 79 Prague 1
Tel: 224 497 111; 224 497 159 (publications)
Fax: 224 226 488
E-mail: nm@nm.cz; publikace@nm.cz
Web Site: www.nm.cz
Key Personnel
Dir General: Dr Michal Lukes *Tel:* 224 497 310
E-mail: lukes_michal@nm.cz
Founded: 1818
General museum.
Subjects: African American Studies, Animals,
Pets, Anthropology, Archaeology, Art, Asian

Studies, Biological Sciences, Drama, Theater,
Earth Sciences, History, Music, Dance, Native
American Studies, Natural History, Science
(General), Sports, Athletics
ISBN Prefix(es): 978-80-7036
Number of titles published annually: 15 Print; 3
CD-ROM; 2 Online; 3 Audio
Total Titles: 5,000 Print; 15 CD-ROM; 10 Online;
10 Audio
Distributed by Myris Trade spol sro

Nase vojsko - Knizni Distribuce sro+
Masovicka 202/8, 142 00 Prague 4
Tel: 224 313 071; 224 224 662 *Fax:* 224 311 204
E-mail: info@nasevojsko.eu
Web Site: www.nasevojsko.eu
Founded: 1945
Subjects: History, Humor, Maritime, Military Sci-
ence, Mysteries, Suspense, Nonfiction (Gen-
eral), Philosophy
ISBN Prefix(es): 978-80-206
Bookshop(s): Stefanikova 235, 150 00 Prague
Tel: 257 326 457 *E-mail:* andel@nasevojsko.eu

**NAVA (Nakladatelski A Vydavatelska
Agentura)+**
nam Republiky 17, 301 00 Plzen
Tel: 377 324 189 (editor); 377 235 721 (sales)
Fax: 377 324 189 (editor); 377 235 721 (sales)
E-mail: nakladatelstvi@nava.cz; marketing@nava.
cz; sekretariat@nava.cz
Web Site: www.nava.cz
Founded: 1990
Publishes Czech translation & literature for chil-
dren & youth.
Subjects: Fiction, History, Humor, Crime Stories,
Leisure Time, Women's Literature
ISBN Prefix(es): 978-80-85254; 978-80-7211
Total Titles: 250 Print

NLN sro, see Nakladatelstvi Lidove noviny

NOXI sro
Grosslingova 50, 811 09 Bratislava
Web Site: www.noxi.cz
Key Personnel
Marketing Dir: Martin Vydra *Tel:* 918 326 599
Sales Dir: Kristina Kralova *Tel:* 917 536 354
Marketing Manager: Pavel Zuska *Tel:* 773 993
275 *E-mail:* zuska@noxi.cz
Editor: Maria Stankova *Tel:* 902 560 500
Founded: 2004
Subjects: Fiction, Health, Nutrition
ISBN Prefix(es): 978-80-8111

Odeon, *imprint of* Euromedia Group ks (EMG)

Nakladatelstvi Oeconomica
Vysoke Skoly Ekonomicke v Praze, Nam W
Churchilla 4, 130 67 Prague 3
Tel: 224 095 554
Web Site: nakladatelstvi.vse.cz
Key Personnel
Dir, Publishing: Libuse Doubravova *Tel:* 224 095
727 *Fax:* 224 095 674 *E-mail:* doubrav@vse.cz
Editor: Marie Skalicka *Tel:* 224 095 676
E-mail: skalicma@vse.cz
Production: Jaroslav Loncak *Tel:* 224 095 543
E-mail: loncakj@vse.cz
Founded: 2003
ISBN Prefix(es): 978-80-245

Nakladatelstvi Olympia sro+
Werichova 973, 252 67 Velke Prilepy
Tel: 233 089 999
E-mail: info@iolympia.cz; olysklad@volny.cz
(sales)
Web Site: www.iolympia.cz
Key Personnel
Mng Dir & Editor-in-Chief: Jaroslav Kotouc
Tel: 233 089 984 *E-mail:* jkotouc@iolympia.cz

Sales: Marie Saldova *Tel:* 274 822 902
Founded: 1954
Publishing house of sports & tourism.
Subjects: Sports, Athletics, Travel & Tourism
ISBN Prefix(es): 978-80-7033
Bookshop(s): Opletalova 59, Prague 1

Ottovo Nakladatelstvi sro
Kristanova 675/3, 130 00 Prague 3
Tel: 221 424 111
E-mail: info@ottovo.eu
Web Site: www.ottovo.cz
Subjects: Nonfiction (General)
ISBN Prefix(es): 978-80-7360
Branch Office(s)
Grosslingova 2465/45, 811 09 Bratislava, Slo-
vakia *Tel:* (02) 57 202 111 *E-mail:* info.sk@
ottovo.eu

Nakladatelstvi Paseka
Chopinova 4, 120 00 Prague 2
Tel: 222 710 751; 222 710 753
E-mail: paseka@paseka.cz
Web Site: www.paseka.cz
Key Personnel
Owner: Ladislav Horacek
Dir, Publishing: Anna Horackova
    E-mail: horackova@paseka.cz
Marketing: Marie Bohmova *E-mail:* bohmova@
    paseka.cz
Sales: Filip Mikes *E-mail:* mikes@paseka.cz
Founded: 1989
Subjects: Art, Biography, Memoirs, Fiction, His-
tory, Literature, Literary Criticism, Essays, Po-
etry
ISBN Prefix(es): 978-80-85192; 978-80-7185
Bookshop(s): Hyblova 51, 560 02 Ceska Tre-
bova *Tel:* 465 534 551 *E-mail:* ceska.trebova@
paseka.cz

Pierot spol sro
Stefanikova 29, 150 00 Prague 5
Tel: 257 328 476; 736 620 254 *Fax:* 257 328
478; 257 329 990
E-mail: pierot@pierot.biz
Web Site: www.pierot.biz
Key Personnel
Dir: Petr Sulc *E-mail:* ps@pierot.biz
Founded: 1993
Specialize in educational titles for children &
youth.
Subjects: Fiction, Nonfiction (General)
ISBN Prefix(es): 978-80-7353; 978-80-86272
Branch Office(s)
6 rue Scipion, 75005 Paris, France, Dir: Eliska
Sulcova *Tel:* 06 42 39 32 19 *E-mail:* eliska.
sulcova@gmail.com

Plus, *imprint of* Albatros Media AS

Portal sro+
Klapkova 2, 182 00 Prague 8
Tel: 283 028 111; 283 028 203 (bookshop); 283
028 204 (bookshop)
E-mail: naklad@portal.cz; obchod@portal.cz
(bookshop)
Web Site: www.portal.cz
Key Personnel
Mng Dir & Ed-in-Chief: Martin Bedrich, PhD
Tel: 283 028 600 *E-mail:* bedrich@portal.cz
Head, Marketing: Katerina Kokesova *Tel:* 283
028 503 *E-mail:* kokesova@portal.cz
Head, Operations: Eva Jarosova *Tel:* 283 028 113
E-mail: jarosova@portal.cz
Head, Production: Katerina Tvrda *Tel:* 283 028
602 *E-mail:* tvrda@portal.cz
Head, Sales: Milan Miskarik *Tel:* 283 028 200
E-mail: miskarik@portal.cz
Founded: 1990
Membership(s): Association of Catholic Publish-
ers & Booksellers.

Subjects: Child Care & Development, Commu-
nications, Crafts, Games, Hobbies, Disability,
Special Needs, Economics, Education, Fic-
tion, Government, Political Science, Health,
Nutrition, Human Relations, Inspirational, Spir-
ituality, Management, Nonfiction (General),
Philosophy, Psychology, Psychiatry, Religion -
Catholic, Social Sciences, Sociology, Antropol-
ogy, Ecology, Exercise, Lifestyle, Media, Social
Work
ISBN Prefix(es): 978-80-7178; 978-80-85282;
978-80-7367; 978-80-262
Number of titles published annually: 90 Print
Total Titles: 450 Print
Foreign Rep(s): Artforum sro (Slovakia)
Bookshop(s): Jindrisska 30, 110 00 Prague
1 *Tel:* 224 213 415 *Fax:* 224 213 415
E-mail: knpraha@portal.cz

Nakladatelstvi Pragma+
V Hodkovickach 2/20, 147 00 Prague 4
Tel: 241 768 565; 241 768 566; 603 205 099
E-mail: pragma@pragma.cz
Web Site: www.pragma.cz
Key Personnel
Contact: Robert Nemec
Founded: 1989
Subjects: Business, Cookery, Fiction, Health, Nu-
trition, Philosophy, Religion - Buddhist, Self-
Help, Sports, Athletics
ISBN Prefix(es): 978-80-7205; 978-80-85213;
978-80-7349
Total Titles: 480 Print; 20 Audio
Distributed by Kanzelsberger

Prostor, nakladatelstvi sro (Prostor, Publishing
House Ltd)+
Nad Spadem 649/10, 147 00 Prague 4
Tel: 224 826 688
E-mail: prostor@eprostor.com
Web Site: www.prostor-nakladatelstvi.cz
Founded: 1990
Specialize in Czech & German history.
Membership(s): Association of Czech Booksellers
& Publishers (ACBP).
Subjects: Biography, Memoirs, Fiction, Govern-
ment, Political Science, History, Nonfiction
(General), Philosophy, Photography
ISBN Prefix(es): 978-80-7260
Number of titles published annually: 25 Print
Total Titles: 300 Print

Psychoanalyticke Nakladatelstvi+
Vitezne nam 10, 160 00 Prague 6
Tel: 233 340 305
Web Site: www.iapsa.cz
Key Personnel
Dir: Jiri Kocourek, PhD *E-mail:* kocourek.jiri@
upcmail.cz
Founded: 1992
Subjects: Education, Medicine, Nursing, Den-
tistry, Psychology, Psychiatry, Psychoanalysis,
Psychotherapy, Scientific & Popular
ISBN Prefix(es): 978-80-901601; 978-80-86123
Number of titles published annually: 10 Print
Total Titles: 40 Print
Parent Company: Institut Aplikovane Psychoana-
lyzy (IAPSA)
Distributed by Grada, Mata, Kolporter

Verlag Harry Putz+
Houbraska 327, 460 07 Liberec
Tel: 485 152 120 *Fax:* 485 152 120
E-mail: harry.putz@volny.cz
Web Site: www.courseczech.com
Subjects: Language Arts, Linguistics
ISBN Prefix(es): 978-80-901119; 978-80-902165;
978-80-86727

Severoceska vedecka knihovna (The North
Bohemian Research Library)
W Churchilla 3, 401 34 Usti Nad Labem

Tel: 475 209 126 *Fax:* 475 200 045
E-mail: knihovna@svkul.cz
Web Site: www.svkul.cz
Founded: 1945
Subjects: Library & Information Sciences
ISBN Prefix(es): 978-80-7055
Orders to: PO Box 134, 401 34 Usti Nad Labem

SEVT AS
Pekarova 4, 181 06 Prague 8
Tel: 283 090 352; 283 090 354 *Fax:* 233 553 422
(orders)
E-mail: objednavky@sevt.cz
Web Site: www.sevt.cz
Key Personnel
Dir: Petr Kulhanek *E-mail:* reditel@sevt.cz
Sales & Marketing Dir: Milan Zwiefelhofer
E-mail: zwiefelhofer@sevt.cz
Founded: 1954
Publishing House of Statistics & Data.
Subjects: Animals, Pets, Architecture & Inte-
rior Design, Art, Computer Science, Cookery,
Crafts, Games, Hobbies, Economics, Education,
Erotica, Fashion, Fiction, Finance, Gardening,
Plants, Health, Nutrition, History, Humor, In-
spirational, Spirituality, Language Arts, Lin-
guistics, Medicine, Nursing, Dentistry, Military
Science, Music, Dance, Mysteries, Suspense,
Outdoor Recreation, Philosophy, Photogra-
phy, Psychology, Psychiatry, Science (General),
Social Sciences, Sociology, Sports, Athletics,
Technology
ISBN Prefix(es): 978-80-7049
Bookshop(s): Pekarova 4, 181 06 Prague 8,
Contact: Zuzana Sablerova *Tel:* 283 090 349
Fax: 233 553 422 *E-mail:* praho8@sevt.cz;
Ceska 14, 602 00 Brno, Contact: Vendulka
Navratilova *Tel:* 542 211 427 *Fax:* 542 213
962 *E-mail:* navratilova@sevt.cz; Ceska 3, 370
01 Ceske Budejovice, Head: Romana Kolarova
Tel: 387 312 087; 387 319 045 *Fax:* 387 319
045 *E-mail:* cb@sevt.cz

Vydavatelstvi SHOCart spol sro
Zadverice 48, 763 12 Vizovice
Tel: 577 105 911
E-mail: mapy@shocart.cz
Web Site: www.shocart.cz
Key Personnel
Dir: Karel Krsak *E-mail:* eko@shocart.cz
Subjects: Outdoor Recreation, Sports, Athletics,
Travel & Tourism, Canoeing, Cycling, Fishing,
Hiking, Skiing
ISBN Prefix(es): 978-80-85781
Distribution Center: Freytag-Berndt spol s
ro, Sodomkova 1558/12, 102 00 Prague
10 *Tel:* 603 856 723 *E-mail:* obchod@
freytagberndt.cz
fb geoclub.sk sro, Stara Vajnorska 11/25, 831 04
Bratislava, Slovakia *Tel:* 243 191 718 *Fax:* 243
191 718 *E-mail:* fbgeoclub@fbgeoclub.sk

Rysavy Simon
Ceska 31, 602 00 Brno
Tel: 542 216 633 *Fax:* 542 216 633
E-mail: info@rysavy.cz
Web Site: www.rysavy.cz
Subjects: Biography, Memoirs, Computer Science,
Fiction, Poetry, Travel & Tourism
ISBN Prefix(es): 978-80-86137; 978-80-902143;
978-80-7354
Bookshop(s): nam Svobody 8, 602 00 Brno
Tel: 542 212 052 *E-mail:* svobodak@rysavy.cz

SLON, see Sociologicke Nakladatelstvi (SLON)

Nakladatelstvi Slovart sro
Oderska 333, 196 00 Prague 9
Tel: 266 177 141 *Fax:* 266 177 147
E-mail: slovart@slovart.cz
Web Site: www.slovart.cz
Founded: 1991

Subjects: Architecture & Interior Design, Fiction, Photography, Science Fiction, Fantasy, Graphic Design, Visual Arts
ISBN Prefix(es): 978-80-7209; 978-80-85871
Distribution Center: Euromedia Group ks, Nadrazni 896/32, 150 00 Prague 5 *Toll Free Tel:* 800 103 203 *E-mail:* objednavky.vo@euromedia.cz
Kosmas sro, Lublanska 34, 120 00 Prague 2 *Tel:* 226 519 397 *E-mail:* kosmas@kosmas.cz
Pemic Books AS, Vratimovska 709/101, 719 00 Ostrava-Kuncice *Tel:* 597 490 436 *E-mail:* nakup@pemic.cz
Nakladatelsky Servis sro, Kladenska 117, 252 68 Stredokluky *Tel:* 233 900 784 *E-mail:* nsdistri@mbox.vol.cz

Sociologicke Nakladatelstvi (SLON)+
Jilska 1, 110 00 Prague 1
Tel: 222 220 025; 221 183 241 *Fax:* 222 220 025
E-mail: slon@slon-knihy.cz
Web Site: www.slon-knihy.cz
Key Personnel
Contact: Alena Miltova
Founded: 1991
This publisher has indicated that 33% of its product line is author subsidized.
Subjects: Anthropology, Government, Political Science, History, Philosophy, Psychology, Psychiatry, Public Administration, Social Sciences, Sociology, Women's Studies
ISBN Prefix(es): 978-80-85850; 978-80-901059; 978-80-901424; 978-80-86429; 978-80-7419
Number of titles published annually: 25 Print
Total Titles: 280 Print
Distribution Center: Kosmas sro, Lublanska 34, 120 00 Prague 2, Contact: Pan Vejrosta *Tel:* 222 510 749 *E-mail:* kosmas@kosmas.cz *Web Site:* www.kosmas.cz
PEMIC BOOKS AS, Vratimovska 703/101, 719 00 Ostrava-Kuncice *Tel:* 597 490 411 *Fax:* 597 490 499 *E-mail:* knizni.velkoobchod@pemic.cz *Web Site:* www.pemic.cz
Vydavatelstvi a nakladatelstvi Ales Cenek sro, Kardinala Berana 1157/32, 301 00 Plzen, Contact: Ales Cenek *Tel:* 222 311 629 *Fax:* 222 311 629 *E-mail:* distribuce@alescenek.cz *Web Site:* www.alescenek.cz
ELITA spol sro, Klincova 35, 821 08 Bratislava, Slovakia *Tel:* (02) 555 717 97; (02) 555 623 51 *Fax:* (02) 554 213 88 *E-mail:* info@elita.sk *Web Site:* www.elita.sk
Partner Technic spol sro, Nam slobody 17, 811 06 Bratislava, Slovakia, Contact: Gabriel Repka *Tel:* (02) 62410904 *E-mail:* gabriel.repka@partnertechnic.sk *Web Site:* www.partnertechnic.sk
Knizny vel'koobchod PEMIC sro, Padlych hrdinov 60, 821 06 Bratislava, Slovakia *Tel:* (02) 3388 8296; (02) 3388 8299 *E-mail:* knizny.velkoobchod@pemic.sk *Web Site:* www.pemic.sk
Inform lib sro, Bratislavska 14, 010 01 Zilina, Slovakia, Contact: Alan Michna *Tel:* (041) 500 1118; (041) 500 1119 *Fax:* (041) 562 3950 *E-mail:* inform@inform-za.sk *Web Site:* www.inform-za.sk
Sirion Group sro, Studentska 30, 960 01 Zvolen, Slovakia *Tel:* (0905) 553 000 *E-mail:* info@sirion.sk *Web Site:* www.sirion.sk

NS Svoboda sro+
Na Cervene 726, 103 00 Prague 10
Tel: 777 230 614; 777 067 868
E-mail: nssvoboda@centrum.cz
Web Site: www.nssvoboda.cz
Founded: 1970
Publishing house in state ownership.
Subjects: Finance, History, Management, Marketing, Mysteries, Suspense, Nonfiction (General)
ISBN Prefix(es): 978-80-205

Bookshop(s): Samova 1476/1, 101 00 Prague 10
Book Club(s): Friends of Antiquity; Readers Club of Svoboda

SystemConsult+
Bartolomejska 89-90, 530 02 Pardubice
Tel: 466 501 585; 603 336 685 *Fax:* 466 501 585
E-mail: system.consult@tiscali.cz (orders)
Web Site: www.systemconsult.cz
Key Personnel
Contact: Ivo Machacka
Founded: 1990
Specialize in computer dictionaries (German-Czech, English-Czech), road transport techniques & automotive industry dictionaries (German-English-Czech), travel dictionaries (English & German) & road transport, traffic signs in Europe.
Subjects: Business, Computer Science, History, Transportation, Travel & Tourism
ISBN Prefix(es): 978-80-900344; 978-80-85629
Number of titles published annually: 5 Print; 5 CD-ROM
Total Titles: 70 Print; 7 CD-ROM

T&M, see Nakladatelstvi Touzimsky & Moravec

Nakladatelstvi Touzimsky & Moravec
Pod Lazni 12, 140 00 Prague 4
Tel: 261 212 458 *Fax:* 261 212 458
E-mail: touzimskyamoravec@seznam.cz
Web Site: www.touzimskyamoravec.cz
Key Personnel
Contact: Michal Moravec
Founded: 1990
Subjects: Poetry, Science Fiction, Fantasy, Western Fiction
ISBN Prefix(es): 978-80-900955; 978-80-900137; 978-80-85773; 978-80-7264

Universum, *imprint of* Euromedia Group ks (EMG)

Univerzita Karlova v Praze, Nakladatelstvi Karolinum (Charles University in Prague, The Karolinum Press)+
Ovocny trh 3/5, 116 36 Prague 1
Tel: 224 491 276 *Fax:* 224 212 041
E-mail: cupress@cuni.cz
Web Site: www.cupress.cuni.cz
Key Personnel
Dir: Petr Valo *E-mail:* petr.valo@ruk.cuni.cz
Editorial Manager: Renata Camska *Tel:* 224 491 266 *E-mail:* renata.camska@ruk.cuni.cz
Distribution Manager: Jaroslava Stribrska *Tel:* 224 491 275 *E-mail:* jaroslava.stribrska@ruk.cuni.cz
Head Editor: Milada Motlova *Tel:* 224 491 631 *E-mail:* milada.motlova@ruk.cuni.cz
Deputy Dir, Production: Milan Susta *Tel:* 222 539 250 *E-mail:* milan.susta@ruk.cuni.cz
Deputy Dir, Foreign Rights: Martin Janecek *Tel:* 224 491 269 *E-mail:* martin.janecek@ruk.cuni.cz
Production: Nadezda Lemochova *Tel:* 222 539 252 *E-mail:* nadezda.lemochova@ruk.cuni.cz
Founded: 1990
Subjects: Anthropology, Archaeology, Architecture & Interior Design, Art, Biological Sciences, Business, Economics, Education, Fiction, Foreign Countries, Government, Political Science, History, Language Arts, Linguistics, Law, Mathematics, Medicine, Nursing, Dentistry, Philosophy, Physical Sciences, Religion - Other, Science (General), Social Sciences, Sociology
ISBN Prefix(es): 978-80-7066; 978-80-7184; 978-80-246
Number of titles published annually: 300 Print
Total Titles: 4,000 Print

Distributed by University of Chicago Press, Chicago Distribution Center (North America)
Bookshop(s): Celetna 18, 116 36 Prague 1, Contact: Jana Padevetova *Tel:* 224 491 448 *Fax:* 224 491 671 *E-mail:* jana.padevetova@ruk.cuni.cz

Univerzita Palackeho v Olomouci Vydavatelstvi
Krizkovskeho 8, 771 47 Olomouc
Tel: 585 631 111; 585 631 783 (bookshop) *Fax:* 585 631 012; 585 631 786 (bookshop)
E-mail: prodejna.vup@upol.cz
Web Site: www.upol.cz/vup
Key Personnel
Dir: Hana Dzikova *Tel:* 585 631 704 *E-mail:* hana.dzikova@upol.cz
Assistant Dir: Radka Voborska *Tel:* 585 631 710 *E-mail:* radka.voborska@upol.cz
Head, Technical Editors: Helena Hladisova *Tel:* 585 631 724 *E-mail:* helena.hladisova@upol.cz
Founded: 1573
ISBN Prefix(es): 978-80-244; 978-80-7067

UNMZ, see Urad pro Technickou Normalizaci, Metrologii a Statni Zkusebnictvi

Urad pro Technickou Normalizaci, Metrologii a Statni Zkusebnictvi (Czech Office for Standards, Metrology & Testing)
Biskupsky dvur, 110 00 Prague 1
Tel: 221 802 111; 221 802 802
E-mail: info@unmz.cz
Web Site: www.unmz.cz
Key Personnel
President: Victor Pokorny *Tel:* 224 907 162 *Fax:* 224 907 154 *E-mail:* pokorny@unmz.cz
Founded: 1922
Membership(s): CEN; CENELEC; ETSi; IEC; ISO.
Subjects: Automotive, Chemistry, Chemical Engineering, Electronics, Electrical Engineering, Engineering (General), Environmental Studies, Mechanical Engineering, Medicine, Nursing, Dentistry
ISBN Prefix(es): 978-80-85111; 978-80-7283

Vitalis sro+
Ke Klimentce 1867/43, 150 00 Prague 5
Tel: 257 181 660 *Fax:* 257 181 670
E-mail: info@vitalis-verlag.com
Web Site: www.vitalis-verlag.com
Founded: 1993
Specialize in Bohemian literary culture.
Subjects: Biography, Memoirs, Cookery, Fiction, Foreign Countries, Medicine, Nursing, Dentistry, Nonfiction (General), Poetry
ISBN Prefix(es): 978-80-85938; 978-80-901621; 978-80-901370; 978-80-7253
Number of titles published annually: 40 Print
Total Titles: 300 Print
Bookshop(s): Zlata ul 22, Prager Burg, 119 08 Prague 1

Nakladatelstvi Vodnar
Kosicka 34, 101 00 Prague 10
Tel: 604 674 633
E-mail: naklvodnar@volny.cz
Web Site: vodnar.eu
Key Personnel
Contact: Vladimir Kvasnicka
Founded: 1990
Subjects: Astrology, Occult, Philosophy
ISBN Prefix(es): 978-80-85255; 978-80-86226; 978-80-7439
Number of titles published annually: 15 Print

Volvox Globator Nakladatelstvi & vydavatelstvi
Stitneho 17, 130 00 Prague 3
Tel: 224 236 268 *Fax:* 224 217 721

E-mail: volvox@volvox.cz
Web Site: www.volvox.cz
Key Personnel
Contact: Vit Houska
Founded: 1990
Subjects: Cookery, Fiction, History, Literature,
Literary Criticism, Essays, Philosophy, Science
Fiction, Fantasy, Prose
ISBN Prefix(es): 978-80-7207; 978-80-85769;
978-80-900906; 978-80-901226
Distributed by Artforum-Slovakia
Bookshop(s): Stitneho 16, 130 00 Prague 3
Tel: 222 781 970

Nakladatelstvi Vysehrad spol sro+
Vita Nejedleho 15, 130 00 Prague 3
Tel: 224 221 703 *Fax:* 224 221 703
E-mail: info@ivysehrad.cz
Web Site: www.ivysehrad.cz
Key Personnel
Dir: Pravomil Novak *Tel:* 777 710 690 (cell)
E-mail: novak@ivysehrad.cz
Editor-in-Chief: Marie Valkova *Tel:* 777 710 696
(cell) *E-mail:* valkova@ivysehrad.cz
Marketing: Jitka Sucha *Tel:* 777 710 694 (cell)
E-mail: sucha@ivysehrad.cz
Founded: 1934
Specialize in Christian-oriented books.
Subjects: Biblical Studies, Cookery, Ethnicity,
Fiction, Health, Nutrition, History, Human Re-
lations, Humor, Nonfiction (General), Philos-
ophy, Poetry, Public Administration, Religion
- Buddhist, Religion - Catholic, Religion -
Hindu, Religion - Islamic, Religion - Jewish,
Religion - Protestant, Religion - Other, Science
(General), Theology
ISBN Prefix(es): 978-80-7021
Shipping Address: Sterboholska 44/1307, 102
00 Prague 10 *Tel:* 271 961 380; 271 962
474 *Fax:* 271 961 380 *E-mail:* distribuce@
ivysehrad.cz
Warehouse: Sterboholska 44/1307, 102 00 Prague
10 *Tel:* 271 961 380; 271 962 474 *Fax:* 271
961 380 *E-mail:* distribuce@ivysehrad.cz
Distribution Center: Sterboholska 44/1307,
102 00 Prague 10, Contact: Jana Ko-
houtova *Tel:* 271 961 380 *Fax:* 271 961 380
E-mail: distribuce@ivysehrad.cz
Beta, Kvetnoveho vitezstvi 332, Prague 4
Tel: 272 910 733 *E-mail:* info@dobrovsky.cz
Karmelitanske Nakladatelstvi Knizni Distribuce,
Kolejni 4, 160 00 Prague 6 *Tel:* 224 316 157
E-mail: souckova@kna.cz
Kosmas, Za Halami 8, 252 62 Horomerice
Tel: 226 519 400 *E-mail:* odbyt@kosmas.cz
Pemic Books as, Vratimovska 703/101, 719
00 Ostrava-Kuncice *Tel:* 597 490 494
E-mail: obchod@pemic.cz
Artforum, Kozia 20, 811 03 Bratislava, Slovakia
Tel: (02) 5441 1898 *E-mail:* is-objednavky@
artforum.sk
Inform, Bratislavska 14, 010 01 Zilina, Slo-
vakia *Tel:* (041) 500 111 8; (041) 500 111 9
E-mail: odbyt@inform-za.sk

XYZ, *imprint of* Albatros Media AS

Denmark

General Information

Capital: Copenhagen
Language: Danish (English and German widely
spoken). Faeroese in the Faroes. Greenlandic in
Greenland
Religion: Evangelical Lutheran
Population: 5.2 million
Bank Hours: 0930-1600 Monday-Friday; open
until 1800 Thursday

Shop Hours: 0800 or 0900-1700 or 1730
Monday-Thursday; open until 1900 Friday;
open until 1300 or 1700 Saturday
Currency: 100 ore = 1 krone
Export/Import Information: Denmark is a member
of the European Union, Faroes and Greenland
are not. No tariff on books except children's
picture-books from non-EU. No import licenses
required. Importers must use longest of alternative credit terms in contract, otherwise no
exchange controls. 25% VAT on books.
Copyright: UCC, Berne, Florence (see Copyright
Conventions, pg viii)

Aarhus Universitetsforlag (Aarhus University
Press)+
Langelandsgade 177, 8200 Aarhus N
Tel: 87 15 39 63
E-mail: unipress@au.dk
Web Site: www.unipress.dk
Key Personnel
Dir: Carsten Fenger-Grondahl *Tel:* 87 15 39 74
E-mail: cfg@unipress.au.dk
Editor: Sanne Lind Hansen *Tel:* 87 15 39 71
E-mail: slh@unipress.au.dk
Founded: 1985
Membership(s): International Association of
Scholarly Publishers.
Subjects: Anthropology, Archaeology, Asian Stud-
ies, Biblical Studies, Drama, Theater, History,
Language Arts, Linguistics, Literature, Liter-
ary Criticism, Essays, Philosophy, Psychology,
Psychiatry, Religion - Other, Social Sciences,
Sociology, Theology, Classical Studies
ISBN Prefix(es): 978-87-7288; 978-87-7934
Number of titles published annually: 60 Print; 30
E-Book
Total Titles: 1,000 Print; 50 E-Book
Distributor for Jutland Archaeological Society
Foreign Rep(s): Casemate Academic (North
America); Gazelle Book Services Ltd (Ireland,
UK)

ABC Forlag
Sct Olaigade 34, 3000 Helsingor
Tel: 49263773
E-mail: info@abc-forlag.dk
Web Site: www.abc-forlag.dk
Key Personnel
Owner: Flemming Moldrup
Founded: 2006 (originally 1998; 1999-2006 part
of Gyldendal)
ISBN Prefix(es): 978-87-7916

Academic Press, see Akademisk Forlag

Academic Publishers, *imprint of* Lindhardt og
Ringhof

Akademisk Forlag+
Vognmagergade 11, 4th floor, 1148 Copenhagen
K
Tel: 36 15 66 10 *Fax:* 36 15 67 26
E-mail: info@akademisk.dk
Web Site: www.akademisk.dk
Founded: 1962
Subjects: Economics, Education, Health, Nu-
trition, History, Language Arts, Linguistics,
Medicine, Nursing, Dentistry, Philosophy, Psy-
chology, Psychiatry, Science (General), Social
Sciences, Sociology, Humanities
ISBN Prefix(es): 978-87-500
Parent Company: Lindhardt & Ringhof Forlag A/
S
Ultimate Parent Company: Egmont

Alfabeta, *imprint of* Lindhardt og Ringhof

Alinea, *imprint of* Lindhardt og Ringhof

Alinea+
Vognemagergade 11, 2 sal, 1148 Copenhagen K
Tel: 33 69 46 66 *Fax:* 33 69 46 60
E-mail: info@alinea.dk
Web Site: www.alinea.dk
Key Personnel
Dir: Ebbe Dam Nielsen *Tel:* 33 69 46 78
E-mail: edn@alinea.dk
Deputy Dir: Lars Tindholt *Tel:* 43 50 30 50
E-mail: lti@alinea.dk
Publishing Dir: Cliff Hansen *Tel:* 20 78 71 70
E-mail: cliff.hansen@alinea.dk
Marketing Manager: Christine Lego Boye *Tel:* 21
14 93 30 *E-mail:* clb@alinea.dk
Production Manager: Christian Davidsen *Tel:* 36
15 66 70 *E-mail:* christian.davidsen@lrforlag.
dk
Sales Manager: Mette Boye *Tel:* 40 22 04 67
E-mail: mbo@alinea.dk
Founded: 1996
ISBN Prefix(es): 978-87-23; 978-87-7993
Parent Company: Lindhardt & Ringhof Forlag A/
S
Ultimate Parent Company: Egmont

Forlaget alma+
Kaalundsvej 13, 3400 Hillerod
Tel: 48 25 54 41 *Fax:* 48 25 20 41
E-mail: almadk@hotmail.com
Web Site: www.alma.dk
Key Personnel
Publisher: Susanne Vebel
Founded: 1983
Specialize in picture books.
Subjects: Fiction
ISBN Prefix(es): 978-87-7243; 978-87-985145

Forlaget alokke A/S+
Porskaervej 15, Nim, 8740 Braedstrup
Tel: 7567 1119 *Fax:* 7567 1074
E-mail: alokke@get2net.dk
Web Site: www.alokke.dk; www.alokkedigital.com
(online portal)
Key Personnel
President: Bertil Toft Hansen
Founded: 1977
Publish & import digital & analogue educational
books, aids & materials.
Membership(s): BFU.
Subjects: Archaeology, English as a Second Lan-
guage, Foreign Countries, History, Language
Arts, Linguistics, Natural History
ISBN Prefix(es): 978-87-592; 978-87-87777
Number of titles published annually: 15 Print; 5
CD-ROM; 5 Online; 5 E-Book
Total Titles: 150 Print; 20 CD-ROM; 10 Online;
5 E-Book

Forlaget Alvilda ApS
Affiliate of Forlaget Modtryk
Bredgade 23B, 3 th, 1260 Copenhagen K
Tel: 33 17 98 00 *Fax:* 33 17 98 09
E-mail: forlaget@alvilda.dk
Web Site: www.alvilda.dk
Key Personnel
Publishing Dir: Jens Trasborg *Tel:* 33 17 98 01
E-mail: jt@alvilda.dk
Editorial Dir: Jonas Holm Hansen *Tel:* 33 17 98
02 *E-mail:* jhh@alvilda.dk
Founded: 2009
ISBN Prefix(es): 978-87-7105

Carit Andersens Forlag A/S
Subsidiary of Mercantila Publishers A/S
Strandlodsvej 1C, 2300 Copenhagen
Tel: 3543 6222
E-mail: info@caritandersen.dk
Web Site: www.caritandersen.dk
Key Personnel
Publisher: Erik Albrechtsen
Founded: 1940

Subjects: Biography, Memoirs, Drama, Theater, Artist Portraits, Bibliographies, Drama Documentary Books
ISBN Prefix(es): 978-87-424

Apollo Books+
Aamosen 1, 5762 Vester Skerninge
Tel: 62263737 *Fax:* 62263780
E-mail: info@apollobooks.dk
Web Site: www.apollobooks.com
Founded: 1984
Publishers of books & CD-ROMs specializing on insects.
Subjects: Natural History, Insects
ISBN Prefix(es): 978-87-88757
Number of titles published annually: 8 Print
Total Titles: 170 Print; 1 CD-ROM
Distributor for Entomological Press; Harley Books; SLU Press
Foreign Rep(s): International Specialized Book Services (North America)

Forlaget Apostrof+
Vognmagergade II, 1148 Copenhagen K
Tel: 33 69 50 00 *Fax:* 36 15 67 26
E-mail: kundeservice@lindhardtogringhof.dk
Web Site: www.apostrof.dk
Founded: 1980
Specialize in psychology books, children's books & quality children's books.
Subjects: Psychology, Psychiatry
ISBN Prefix(es): 978-87-591; 978-87-88002
Number of titles published annually: 30 Print
Total Titles: 400 Print
Parent Company: Forlaget Carlsen A/S
Ultimate Parent Company: Lindhardt & Ringhof
Warehouse: Dbks Forlagsekspedition, Mimersuej 4, 4600 Koge

Arkitektens Forlag (The Danish Architecture Press)
Pasteursvej 14, 4 tv (6 etage), 1799 Copenhagen V
Tel: 3283 6970 *Fax:* 3283 6941
E-mail: eksp@arkfo.dk (sales); arkfo@arkfo.dk
Web Site: www.arkfo.dk
Key Personnel
Dir: Kim Dirckinck-Holmfeld
Founded: 1949
Subjects: Architecture & Interior Design, Gardening, Plants, Landscaping, Urban Planning
ISBN Prefix(es): 978-87-7407; 978-87-87136
Total Titles: 100 Print

Athene, *imprint of* Lindhardt og Ringhof

Bibelselskabet (The Danish Bible Society)+
Frederiksborggade 50, 1360 Copenhagen K
Tel: 33 12 78 35 *Fax:* 33 93 21 50
E-mail: bibelselskabet@bibelselskabet.dk
Web Site: www.bibelselskabet.dk
Key Personnel
Secretary General: Birgitte Stoklund Larsen
Tel: 29 42 05 21 *E-mail:* bsl@bibelselskabet.dk
Publishing Manager: Lisbeth Elkjaer Oland
Tel: 61 78 19 80 *E-mail:* lisbeth.elkjaer.oeland@bibelselskabet.dk
Editor: Karen Karmark Kristensen *Tel:* 26 36 43 47 *E-mail:* kk@bibelselskabet.dk
Sales & Marketing Manager: Morten Predstrup
Tel: 22 72 41 05 *E-mail:* mp@bibelselskabet.dk
Founded: 1814
Also publish hymn books & Christian knowledge school books.
Membership(s): United Bible Societies.
Subjects: Theology
ISBN Prefix(es): 978-87-7523; 978-87-7524

Bogans Forlag+
Egholmvej 5A, 8883 Gjern

Tel: 86 27 65 00 *Fax:* 86 27 65 37
E-mail: mail@hovedland.dk
Web Site: www.hovedland.dk/om_bogan.htm
Key Personnel
Dir, Forlaget Hovedland: Steen Piper
Founded: 1974
Subjects: Astrology, Occult, Health, Nutrition, Humor, Nonfiction (General), Religion - Other, Science (General)
ISBN Prefix(es): 978-87-87533; 978-87-7466; 978-87-7525
Number of titles published annually: 30 Print
Total Titles: 250 Print
Parent Company: Forlaget Hovedland
Imprints: My Best Book

Bogfabrikken Fakta ApS
Egholmvej 5A, 8883 Gjern
Tel: 86 27 65 00
Subjects: Crafts, Games, Hobbies, Environmental Studies, Fashion, Nonfiction (General), Science (General), Transportation
ISBN Prefix(es): 978-87-7771
Parent Company: Forlaget Hovedland A/S

Forlaget Bolden ApS
Frederiksberg Runddel 3F, 2000 Fredericksberg
Web Site: www.forlagetbolden.dk
Key Personnel
Production: Ulrikke Juul Bondo *Tel:* 26120393
E-mail: ulrikke@forlagetbolden.dk
Sales: Lone Ibsen *Tel:* 28820430 *E-mail:* lone@forlagetbolden.dk
Founded: 2009
ISBN Prefix(es): 978-87-7106

Bonnier Publications A/S+
Strandboulevarden 130, 2100 Copenhagen O
Tel: 39 17 20 00; 3910 3000 (customer service)
Fax: 3917 2300
E-mail: bonnierpublications@bonnier.dk
Web Site: bonnierpublications.com; www.bonnier.dk
Key Personnel
President & Chief Executive Officer: Michael Cordsen
Executive Vice President & Editorial Dir: Jens Henneberg *Tel:* 3917 2003 *E-mail:* jens.henneberg@bonnier.dk
Vice President, Finance: Morten Kaiser
Vice President, Marketing: Jesper Buchvald
Founded: 1959
Subjects: Criminology, Fiction, Military Science, Western Fiction
ISBN Prefix(es): 978-82-535
Parent Company: Bonnier AB
Branch Office(s)
Bonnier Publications Oy, Vilhonvuorenkatu 11 A, 3rd floor, 00500 Helsinki, Finland *Tel:* (020) 7608 500 *E-mail:* bonnierpublications@bonnier.fi *Web Site:* www.bonnierpublications.fi
Bonnier Publications International AS, Ovre Vollgate 6, 0158 Oslo, Norway *Tel:* 22 40 72 00 *E-mail:* post@bonnier.no *Web Site:* www.bonniermedia.no
Bonnier Publications AB, Bodalsvagen 2 A, 181 04 Lidingo, Sweden *Tel:* (08) 731 29 00 *E-mail:* bp.bonnier@bp.bonnier.se *Web Site:* www.bonnierpublications.se
Bonnier Publications, Volokolamskoye shosse 2, 125993 Moscow, Russia *Tel:* (495) 725 1070 *E-mail:* info@phbp.ru *Web Site:* www.gastronom.ru

Borgens Forlag+
Klareboderne 3, 1001 Copenhagen K
Tel: 3375 5555
E-mail: salg@borgen.dk; borgen_post@gyldendal.dk
Web Site: www.borgen.dk

Key Personnel
Information & Sales: Jacob Mahler *Tel:* 3375 5793 *E-mail:* jacob_mahler@gyldendal.dk
Founded: 1948
Subjects: Alternative, Animals, Pets, Art, Astrology, Occult, Behavioral Sciences, Child Care & Development, Crafts, Games, Hobbies, Education, Environmental Studies, Fiction, Health, Nutrition, How-to, Human Relations, Humor, Literature, Literary Criticism, Essays, Music, Dance, Nonfiction (General), Philosophy, Poetry, Psychology, Psychiatry, Regional Interests, Religion - Other, Self-Help
ISBN Prefix(es): 978-87-418; 978-87-21; 978-87-7895; 978-87-982973
Number of titles published annually: 250 Print; 5 Audio
Total Titles: 2,000 Print; 10 Audio
Parent Company: Gyldendal
Imprints: Hekla; Sommer & Sorensen; Forlaget Vindrose A/S
Orders to: DBK-Logistik Service, Mimersvej 4, 4600 Koge

Borsen Forlag, see Dagbladet Borsen A/S

Buster Nordic A/S
Mindevej 45, 2870 Dyssegaard
Tel: 2844 8311 *Fax:* 3967 9096
E-mail: publisher@busternordic.com
Web Site: www.busternordic.com
Key Personnel
Chief Executive Officer & Publisher: Knud Pilegaard *E-mail:* knud@busternordic.com
Editor: Maria Wittendorff *Tel:* 2990 0875
E-mail: maria@busternordic.com
ISBN Prefix(es): 978-87-90399; 978-87-985509; 978-87-91971

Ca' Luna-Bogforlag-Feng Shui-radgivning-Helsemesser+
Skejbytoften 122, 8200 Aarhus N
Tel: 86 82 86 88; 26 39 60 88 *Fax:* 86 82 86 64
E-mail: caluna@caluna.dk
Web Site: www.caluna.dk
Key Personnel
Publisher: Maianne L Petersen
Founded: 1995
Specialize in New Age books.
Subjects: Feng Shui, New Age
ISBN Prefix(es): 978-87-90312
Total Titles: 10 Print

C&K Forlag, *imprint of* JP/Politikens Forlag

Carlsen, *imprint of* Lindhardt og Ringhof

Carlsen Comics, *imprint of* Forlaget Carlsen A/S

Forlaget Carlsen A/S+
Vognmagergade 11, 1148 Copenhagen K
Tel: 33 69 50 00 *Fax:* 36 16 04 27
E-mail: kundeservice@carlsen.dk; carlsen@carlsen.dk
Web Site: www.carlsen.dk
Key Personnel
Editor & Foreign Rights Manager: Lotte Kjeldskouv *E-mail:* lkj@carlsen.dk
Founded: 1940
Subjects: Humor
ISBN Prefix(es): 978-87-562; 978-87-456; 978-87-7529; 978-87-90008; 978-87-626
Number of titles published annually: 300 Print; 3 CD-ROM; 75 Audio
Total Titles: 2,000 Print; 8 CD-ROM; 120 Audio
Parent Company: Lindhardt & Ringhof Forlag A/S
Ultimate Parent Company: Egmont
Imprints: Carlsen Comics
Subsidiaries: Carlsen Book Production
Book Club(s): Bogklubben Rasmus & Den Faktyrlige Boklub

Warehouse: Holme Forlags Service, Lise Lundvej 4, 4791 Borre *Tel:* 55812252 *Fax:* 55 812078
Holme Forlag Service APS
Semil Forlag NE A/S

CBS Press, see Copenhagen Business School Press

Cicero-Chr Erichsen, *imprint of* Rosinante & Co

Cicero-Chr Erichsen
Imprint of Rosinante & Co
Kobmagergade 62, 4 sal, 1019 Copenhagen K
Mailing Address: Postboks 2252, 1019 Copenhagen K
Tel: 3341 1800 *Fax:* 3341 1801
E-mail: info@rosinante-co.dk
Web Site: www.cicero.dk
Founded: 1990
Subjects: Fiction, Mysteries, Suspense
ISBN Prefix(es): 978-87-7714; 978-87-555
Ultimate Parent Company: Gyldendal

Copenhagen Business School Press, *imprint of* Samfundslitteratur

Copenhagen Business School Press+
Imprint of Samfundslitteratur
Rosenorns Alle 9, 1970 Frederiksberg C
Tel: 3815 3880
E-mail: slforlagene@samfundslitteratur.dk
Web Site: www.cbspress.dk
Key Personnel
Publisher: Birgit Vra *E-mail:* bv@samfundslitteratur.dk
Chief Editor: Kristian Kreiner *E-mail:* kk.ioa@cbs.dk
Public Relations & Marketing: Poul Kragh Jensen *E-mail:* pj@samfundslitteratur.dk
Founded: 1967
Specialized academic publisher of books on management, economics & organization.
Membership(s): University Presses of Denmark.
Subjects: Economics, Management, Organization
ISBN Prefix(es): 978-87-630
Orders to: DBK Logistik Service, Mimersvej 4, 4600 Koge, Dir: Peter Johnsen *Tel:* 32 69 77 89 *Fax:* 32 69 77 89 *E-mail:* personale@dbk.dk (Scandinavian countries)
International Specialized Book Services, 920 NE 58 Ave, Suite 300, Portland, OR 97213, United States *Tel:* 503-287-3093 *Fax:* 503-280-8832 *Web Site:* www.isbs.com (USA & Canada)
Marston Book Services, 160 Eastern Ave, Milton Park, Abingdon, Oxon OX14 4SB, United Kingdom *Tel:* (01235) 465500 *Fax:* (01235) 465555 *E-mail:* direct.orders@marston.co.uk *Web Site:* www.marston.co.uk (outside North America & Scandinavia)

Copenhagen Publishing House ApS (CPH)
Eskildstrupvej 2, 2700 Copenhagen
Tel: 3146 4060; 2620 4060 (cell)
E-mail: info@copenhagenpublishing.com
Web Site: www.copenhagenpublishing.com
Key Personnel
Publishing Dir & Theologian: Michael Berghof
Founded: 2007
Subjects: Religion - Other
ISBN Prefix(es): 978-87-92105

CPH, see Copenhagen Publishing House ApS (CPH)

Dafolo Forlag+
Division of Dafolo A/S
Suderbovej 24, 9900 Frederikshavn
Tel: 9620 6666 *Fax:* 9842 9711
E-mail: lkm@dafolo.dk; dafolo@dafolo.dk
Web Site: www.dafolo.dk

Key Personnel
Mng Dir: Michael Schelde *Tel:* 2080 2808 *E-mail:* ms@dafolo.dk
General Manager: Hans Christian Hojslet *Tel:* 2080 2850 *E-mail:* hch@dafolo.dk
Marketing Manager: Birgit Bogvad *Tel:* 2199 7518 *E-mail:* bb@dafolo.dk; Jan Kroll *Tel:* 4139 4505 *E-mail:* jk@dafolo.dk
Founded: 1957
Specialize in elementary textbooks.
Subjects: Education, Foreign Countries, History
ISBN Prefix(es): 978-87-7794; 978-87-7281; 978-87-7320; 978-87-7846; 978-87-89460; 978-87-982569; 978-87-984669
Branch Office(s)
Havnegade 39, 3 sal, 1058 Copenhagen K
Videnpark Trekantom radet, Vesterballevej 5, 7000 Fredericia

Dagbladet Borsen A/S
Montergade 19, 1140 Copenhagen K
Tel: 33 32 01 02; 72 42 34 00 (editorial) *Fax:* 33 12 24 45
E-mail: redaktionen@borsen.dk
Web Site: www.borsen.dk
Key Personnel
Chief Executive Officer & Editor-in-Chief: Anders Krab Johansen
Editorial Manager: Jens Kristian Lai
Founded: 1996
Subjects: Management
ISBN Prefix(es): 978-87-7553; 978-87-7664; 978-87-7901; 978-87-88184; 978-87-90790; 978-87-91157
Parent Company: Bonnier AB

Danmarks Forvaltningshojskole (Danish School of Public Administration)
Lindevangs Alle 6-12, 2000 Frederiksberg
Tel: 38 14 52 00 *Fax:* 38 14 53 45
Key Personnel
Head, International Relations: Lisa Bronnum
Founded: 1963
Subjects: Business, Economics, Management, Public Administration
ISBN Prefix(es): 978-87-7392
Parent Company: Professionshojskolen Metropol

Dansk Biblioteks Center A/S (DBC) (Danish Bibliographic Centre)+
Tempovej 7-11, 2750 Ballerup
Tel: 44 86 77 77
E-mail: dbc@dbc.dk
Web Site: www.dbc.dk
Founded: 1991
Subjects: Library & Information Sciences
ISBN Prefix(es): 978-87-552

Dansk Psykologisk Forlag A/S (Danish Psychological Publishers)+
Knabrostr 3, 1st floor, 1210 Copenhagen
Tel: 4546 0050
E-mail: info@dpf.dk
Web Site: www.dpf.dk
Key Personnel
Mng Dir: Henrik Skovdahl Hansen *Tel:* 8880 2350 *E-mail:* hsh@dpf.dk
Editorial Dir/Chief Editor: Signe Lindskov Hansen *Tel:* 8880 2358 *E-mail:* slh@dpf.dk
Founded: 1949
Membership(s): European Test Publishers Group.
Subjects: Business, Career Development, Education, Health, Nutrition, Human Relations, Management, Psychology, Psychiatry, Self-Help
ISBN Prefix(es): 978-87-7706; 978-87-7158; 978-87-7185

Dansk Teknologisk Institut, Forlaget (Danish Technological Institute)
Gregersensvej 1, 2630 Taastrup
Tel: 72 20 20 00 *Fax:* 72 20 20 19

E-mail: info@teknologisk.dk
Web Site: www.teknologisk.dk; www.dti.dk
Key Personnel
President: Soren Stjernqvist *Tel:* 72 20 20 01 *E-mail:* st@teknologisk.dk
Subjects: Crafts, Games, Hobbies, Labor, Industrial Relations
ISBN Prefix(es): 978-87-7511; 978-87-7756
Branch Office(s)
Dancert A/S, Gregersensvej, 2630 Taastrup *Tel:* 72 20 21 60
Danfysik A/S, Gregersensvej 8, 2630 Taastrup *Tel:* 72 20 24 00 *Fax:* 72 20 24 10 *E-mail:* sales@danfysik.dk
Teknologiparken, Kongsvang Alle 29, 8000 Aarhus *E-mail:* info@teknologisk.dk
Nordsocentret, Postboks 104, 9850 Hirtshals *Tel:* 72 20 39 30 *Fax:* 72 20 39 44
Forskerparken Fyn, Forskerparken 10F, 5230 Odense M *Fax:* 72 2039 70
Maglegaardsvej 2, 4000 Roskilde *Fax:* 72 20 27 44
Gammel Albovej 1, 6092 Sonder Stenderup *Tel:* 75 57 10 10 *Fax:* 75 57 10 29
Ipark, Prof Olav Hanssensvej 7A, 4068 Stavanger, Norway *Tel:* 51 87 42 02
DTI Polska, Ul Krolowej Marysienki 90, 02-954 Warsaw, Poland *Tel:* (22) 642 58 72 *Fax:* (22) 642 58 73 *E-mail:* dti@dtipolska.com.pl *Web Site:* www.dtipolska.com.pl
Teknologisk Institut AB, Vallgatan 14, 411 16 Gothenburg, Sweden *Tel:* (031) 350 55 00 *Fax:* (031) 350 55 10 *E-mail:* info@teknologiskinstitut.se *Web Site:* www.teknologiskinstitut.se
U.S. Office(s): DTI Robotics US Inc, 75 Fifth St NW, Suite 236, Atlanta, GA 30308, United States *Tel:* 404-692-1888 *E-mail:* info@dtirobotics.com

DBC, see Dansk Biblioteks Center A/S (DBC)

DJOF Publishing
Gothersgade 137, 1123 Copenhagen K
Mailing Address: Postboks 2702, 2100 Copenhagen O
Tel: 3913 5500 *Fax:* 3913 5555
E-mail: forlag@djoef.dk
Web Site: www.djoef-forlag.dk
Key Personnel
Publishing Dir: Anette Wad *Tel:* 3913 5522 *E-mail:* awad@djoef.dk
Editorial Manager: Torben W Nielson *Tel:* 3913 5521 *E-mail:* twn@djoef.dk
Production Manager: Christian Soltoft *Tel:* 3913 5530 *E-mail:* cst@djoef.dk
Sales Manager: Tanja Verbik *Tel:* 3913 5516 *E-mail:* tav@djoef.dk
Founded: 1959
Membership(s): IUS-Nordica, Nordic Legal Publishers Group.
Subjects: Business, Communications, Economics, Finance, Law, Management, Public Administration, Social Sciences, Sociology, Legal History
ISBN Prefix(es): 978-87-574; 978-87-629; 978-87-7673
Subsidiaries: Handelshojskolens Forlag; Nyt Juridisk Forlag
Distribution Center: Marston Book Services Ltd, 160 Eastern Ave, Milton Park, Abingdon, Oxon OX14 4SB, United Kingdom *Tel:* (01235) 465500 *Fax:* (01235) 465555 *E-mail:* trade.orders@marston.co.uk *Web Site:* www.marston.co.uk (worldwide exc North America)
International Specialized Book Services, 920 NE 58 Ave, Suite 300, Portland, OR 97213, United States *Fax:* 503-280-8832 *E-mail:* orders@isbs.com *Web Site:* www.isbs.com (North America)

Don Max, *imprint of* JP/Politikens Forlag

Forlaget DRAMA ApS
Jernbanegade 5, 6230 Rodekro

Tel: 70 25 11 41 *Fax:* 74 65 20 93
E-mail: drama@drama.dk
Web Site: www.drama.dk
Key Personnel
Dir: Liselotte Lunding *E-mail:* ll@drama.dk
Founded: 1977
Specialize in drama & theatre, books &
   manuscripts.
Subjects: Drama, Theater
ISBN Prefix(es): 978-87-7419; 978-87-7865
Branch Office(s)
Teaterhjornet, Vesterbrogade 175, 1800 Frederiks-
   berg *Tel:* 70 25 11 41

Egmont International Holding A/S
Vognmagergade 11, 1148 Copenhagen K
Tel: 33 30 55 50 *Fax:* 33 32 19 02
Web Site: www.egmont.com
Key Personnel
President & Chief Executive Officer: Steffen
   Kragh
Founded: 1878
ISBN Prefix(es): 978-87-982380
Parent Company: Egmont Foundation

Egmont Kids Media A/S
Vognmagergade 11, 1148 Copenhagen K
Tel: 3945 7545 (customer service)
E-mail: info@egmont.com
Web Site: www.serieforlaget.dk
Key Personnel
Publishing Dir: Tony Jorgensen
Marketing Manager: Gitte Hoffmann *Tel:* 3945
   7582 *E-mail:* gitte.hoffmann.hansen@egmont.
   dk
Production Manager: Morten Ladewig *Tel:* 3945
   7687 *E-mail:* morten.ladewig@egmont.dk
Founded: 1920
Subjects: Fiction, Human Relations, Cartoons,
   Comics
ISBN Prefix(es): 978-87-89601
Parent Company: Egmont
Associate Companies: Ehapa-Verlag GmbH, Ger-
   many

Ekstra Bladets Forlag, *imprint of* JP/Politikens
   Forlag

Ekstra Bladets Forlag
Imprint of JP/Politikens Forlag
Vestergade 26, 1456 Copenhagen K
Tel: 33 47 07 07
E-mail: info@jppol.dk
Web Site: www.ekstrabladetsforlag.dk
Key Personnel
Chief Executive Officer: Karsten Blauert
Dir: Lene Juul *Tel:* 33 47 07 01 *E-mail:* lene.
   juul@jppol.dk
Foreign Rights Manager: Nya Guldberg
   E-mail: nya.guldberg@jppol.dk
Marketing Manager: Pernille Engelbert Weil
   Tel: 33 47 07 41 *E-mail:* pernille.e.weil@jppol.
   dk
Publishing Manager: Kim Hundevadt
   E-mail: kim.hundevadt@jppol.dk
Sales Manager: Pernille Hjorth *Tel:* 33 47 07 57
   E-mail: pernille.hjorth@jppol.dk
Founded: 1998
Subjects: Biography, Memoirs, Cookery, Crafts,
   Games, Hobbies, Erotica, Fiction, Health, Nu-
   trition, Humor, Mysteries, Suspense, Travel &
   Tourism
ISBN Prefix(es): 978-87-7731; 978-87-980579
Ultimate Parent Company: JP/Politikens Hus A/S

Erhvervsstyrelsen (Danish Business Authority)
Langelinie Alle 17, 2100 Copenhagen
Tel: 35 29 10 00 *Fax:* 35 46 60 01
E-mail: erst@erst.dk
Web Site: erhvervsstyrelsen.dk

Subjects: Business, Government, Political Science
ISBN Prefix(es): 978-87-90774

FADL's Forlag A/S+
Blegdamsvej 26, Baghuset, 1 sal, 2200 Copen-
   hagen N
Tel: 35 35 62 87 *Fax:* 35 36 62 29
E-mail: kundeservice@fadlsforlag.dk; redaktion@
   fadlsforlag.dk
Web Site: fadlforlag.dk
Key Personnel
Manager: Rikke Sommer *E-mail:* rikke@
   fadlsforlag.dk
Editor: Thomas Bo Thomsen *E-mail:* thomas@
   fadlsforlag.dk; Carl-Albert Demidoff
   E-mail: carl-albert@fadlsforlag.dk; Kristoffer
   Flakstad *E-mail:* kristoffer@fadlsforlag.dk
Editoral Assistant: Soren Hundahl Bislev
Founded: 1962
Membership(s): International Association of STM
   Publishers.
Subjects: Biological Sciences, Medicine, Nursing,
   Dentistry
ISBN Prefix(es): 978-87-7437; 978-87-7749

Faktor Funf, *imprint of* Kaleidoscope Publishers
   Ltd

Ficcion Espanola, *imprint of* Kaleidoscope
   Publishers Ltd

Fiction Factory, *imprint of* Kaleidoscope
   Publishers Ltd

Fiction Francaise, *imprint of* Kaleidoscope
   Publishers Ltd

**Foreningen af danske Laegestuderendes
   Forlag**, see FADL's Forlag A/S

Forum, *imprint of* Rosinante & Co

Forlaget Forum (Forum Publishers)
Imprint of Rosinante & Co
Kobmagergade 62, 4 sal, 1019 Copenhagen K
Mailing Address: Postbox 2252, 1019 Copen-
   hagen K
Tel: 3341 1800 *Fax:* 3341 1801
E-mail: info@rosinante-co.dk
Web Site: www.forlagetforum.dk
Founded: 1940
Subjects: Fiction, History, Humor, Mysteries, Sus-
   pense
ISBN Prefix(es): 978-87-553; 978-87-6380
Ultimate Parent Company: Gyldendal
Divisions: Spektrum Publishers

Frydenlund Academic, *imprint of* Bogforlaget
   Frydenlund

Bogforlaget Frydenlund (Frydenlund Publishers)
Alhambravej 6, 1826 Frederiksberg C
Tel: 3393 2212
E-mail: post@frydenlund.dk
Web Site: www.frydenlund.dk
Key Personnel
Publisher: Henning Lund *Tel:* 3318 8132
   E-mail: henning@frydenlund.dk
Founded: 1990
Subjects: Communications, Criminology, Drama,
   Theater, Education, Fiction, Film, Video, Gov-
   ernment, Political Science, Health, Nutrition,
   History, Psychology, Psychiatry, Social Sci-
   ences, Sociology, Travel & Tourism
ISBN Prefix(es): 978-87-7887; 978-87-88762;
   978-87-90053
Imprints: Frydenlund Academic
Book Club(s): Frydenlunds Bogklub

Gads Forlag
Fiolstr 31-33, 1171 Copenhagen K
Tel: 77 66 60 00 *Fax:* 77 66 60 01
E-mail: reception@gad.dk
Web Site: gad.dk
Key Personnel
Mng Dir: Ulrik Hvilshoj *E-mail:* uh@gad.dk
Publishing & Development Manager: Susanne
   Svendsen *Tel:* 77 66 60 20 *E-mail:* sus@gad.dk
Editorial Manager: Hanne Dal *Tel:* 77 66 60 31
   E-mail: hda@gad.dk
Marketing Manager: Rebecca Scavenius *Tel:* 77
   66 60 72 *E-mail:* rs@gad.dk
Production Manager: Bo Borum *Tel:* 77 66 60 57
   E-mail: borum@gad.dk
Sales Manager: Tina Fossing *Tel:* 77 66 60 10
   E-mail: tf@gad.dk
Founded: 1855
Subjects: Art, Biography, Memoirs, Biological
   Sciences, Cookery, Crafts, Games, Hobbies,
   Economics, Education, English as a Second
   Language, Environmental Studies, Fiction, Gar-
   dening, Plants, Health, Nutrition, History, Law,
   Mathematics, Medicine, Nursing, Dentistry,
   Natural History, Nonfiction (General), Phi-
   losophy, Physics, Religion - Other, Travel &
   Tourism, Culture, Occupational Therapy, Per-
   sonal Development, Popular Science
ISBN Prefix(es): 978-87-12; 978-87-13; 978-87-
   557
Number of titles published annually: 40 Print
Parent Company: GEC Gads Fond
Associate Companies: Alinea A/S; Systime A/S
Bookshop(s): G E C Gads Boglader A/S GADs,
   Antikuariat Fiolstr 31-33, Copenhagen

Forlaget Globe A/S
Skodsborgvej 305 D, 2850 Naerum
Tel: 70151400 *Fax:* 70151410
E-mail: info@globe.dk
Web Site: www.globe.dk
Subjects: Animals, Pets, Career Development,
   Cookery, Crafts, Games, Hobbies, Health, Nu-
   trition, History, Travel & Tourism
ISBN Prefix(es): 978-87-7900; 978-87-7884; 978-
   87-90069; 978-87-983645

Gyldendal
Klareboderne 3, 1001 Copenhagen K
Tel: 33 75 55 55 *Fax:* 33 75 55 56
E-mail: gyldendal@gyldendal.dk; kundeservice@
   gyldendal.dk
Web Site: www.gyldendal.dk
Key Personnel
Dir: Bjarne Ponikowski
Publishing Dir: Tine Smedegaard Andersen
Mng Dir: Stig Andersen
Literary Dir: Johannes Riis
Sales Dir: Jan H Schmith
Founded: 1770
Subjects: Art, Biography, Memoirs, Education,
   Fiction, History, How-to, Medicine, Nursing,
   Dentistry, Music, Dance, Philosophy, Poetry,
   Psychology, Psychiatry, Science (General), So-
   cial Sciences, Sociology
ISBN Prefix(es): 978-87-01; 978-87-00; 978-87-
   02
Subsidiaries: Cicero/Chr Erichsen; Krea Media
   A/S; Nordisk Bog Center A/S; Hans Reitzels
   Forlag; Rosinante & Co; Systime A/S
Book Club(s): Bolig & Livsstil; Gyldendals
   Bogklub; Gyldendals Bornebogklub; Krimi
   & Spaending; Laererbogklubben; Paedagogisk
   Bogklub; The Piccadilly Book Club; Psyke
   & Sjael; Samlerens Bogklub; Bogklubben for
   Sundhedsprofessionelle

Haase & Sons Forlag A/S+
Lovstr 8, 2 tv, 1152 Copenhagen K
Tel: 3314 4175 *Fax:* 3311 5959
E-mail: haase@haase.dk
Web Site: www.haase.dk

Key Personnel
Mng Dir: Michael Haase *Tel:* 2167 8232
  E-mail: mh@haase.dk
Editorial: Mette Viking *Tel:* 2683 8016
  E-mail: mv@haase.dk
Production: Dennis Stovring *E-mail:* ds@
  bogfremstilling.dk
Founded: 1877
Subjects: Biography, Memoirs, Education, Health,
  Nutrition, Humor, Maritime, Medicine, Nurs-
  ing, Dentistry, Music, Dance, Nonfiction (Gen-
  eral), Psychology, Psychiatry, Science (Gen-
  eral), Sports, Athletics, Anthopologies
ISBN Prefix(es): 978-87-559
Imprints: Rasmus Naver

Edition Wilhelm Hansen AS
Bornholmsgade 1A, 1266 Copenhagen K
Tel: 33 11 78 88 *Fax:* 33 14 81 78
E-mail: ewh@ewh.dk; salg@ewh.dk (sales)
Web Site: www.ewh.dk
Key Personnel
Executive Dir: Loui Tornquist *E-mail:* lt@ewh.dk
Copyright: Marianne Rottboll *Tel:* 33 70 15 10
  E-mail: mrp@ewh.dk
Editorial: Michael Rehder *Tel:* 33 70 15 13
  E-mail: mr@ewh.dk
Promotion: Hjarne Fessel *Tel:* 33 70 15 11
  E-mail: hf@ewh.dk
Sales: Frances Fridan *Tel:* 33 70 15 16
Founded: 1857
Subjects: Art, Education, Music, Dance, Contem-
  porary Composition, Pop Music
ISBN Prefix(es): 978-87-7455; 978-87-598
Parent Company: Music Sales Group, 8/9 Frith
  St, London W1V 5TZ, United Kingdom

Hekla, *imprint of* Borgens Forlag

Hekla Forlag+
Imprint of Borgens Forlag
c/o Gyldendal, Klareboderne 3, 1001 Copenhagen
  K
Tel: 3375 5555 *Fax:* 3615 3616
E-mail: salg@borgen.dk; borgen_post@gyldendal.
  dk
Web Site: www.borgen.dk
Key Personnel
Information & Sales: Jacob Mahler *Tel:* 3375
  5793 *E-mail:* jacob_mahler@gyldendal.dk
Founded: 1979
Subjects: Fiction, Nonfiction (General)
ISBN Prefix(es): 978-87-7474
Number of titles published annually: 5 Print
Total Titles: 20 Print
Ultimate Parent Company: Gyldendal
Orders to: DBK-Logistik Service, Mimersvej 4,
  4600 Koge

Hernovs Forlag+
Ordrup Vaenge 94, 2920 Charlottenlund
Tel: 3296 3314 *Fax:* 3296 0446
Web Site: www.hernovsforlag.dk
Founded: 1941
Subjects: Fiction, Nonfiction (General)
ISBN Prefix(es): 978-87-7215; 978-87-590
Warehouse: Nordisk Bog Center - NBC, Boekvej
  10-12, 4690 Haslev
Distribution Center: Nordisk Bog Center - NBC,
  Boekvej 10-12, 4690 Haslev

Forlaget Hjulet+
Brydegardsvej 17A, 2760 Malov
Tel: 4497 7664
E-mail: mail@hjulet.nu
Web Site: www.forlagethjulet.nu
Key Personnel
Publisher: Vagn Plenge
Founded: 1976
Subjects: Developing Countries, Fiction
ISBN Prefix(es): 978-87-87403; 978-87-89213

Subsidiaries: Hjulet, Sweden
Distribution Center: Sorlins Forlag AB, Tor-
  shagshuset, 616 33 Aby, Sweden *Tel:* (011)
  64170 *Fax:* (011) 64172 *E-mail:* info@
  bokcentralen.se

Host & Son, *imprint of* Rosinante & Co

Host & Son+
Imprint of Rosinante & Co
Kobmagergade 62, 4 sal, 1150 Copenhagen K
Mailing Address: Postbox 2252, 1019 Copen-
  hagen K
Tel: 3341 1800 *Fax:* 3341 1801
E-mail: info@rosinante-co.dk
Web Site: www.hoest.dk/hostogson.aspx
Key Personnel
Editorial, Young Adults: Nanna Gyldenkaerne
Founded: 1836
Subjects: Crafts, Games, Hobbies, Environmental
  Studies, Fiction, History, Regional Interests
ISBN Prefix(es): 978-87-14; 978-87-7545; 978-
  87-87581; 978-87-638
Ultimate Parent Company: Gyldendal
Foreign Rep(s): Gyldendal Group Agency
Warehouse: NBC, Bokvej 10-12, 4690 Haslev

Forlaget Hovedland+
Egholmvej 5A, 8883 Gjern
Tel: 86 27 65 00 *Fax:* 86 27 65 37
E-mail: mail@hovedland.dk
Web Site: hovedland.dk
Key Personnel
Publisher: Steen Piper
Founded: 1984
Subjects: Biography, Memoirs, Crafts, Games,
  Hobbies, Economics, Environmental Studies,
  Fiction, History, Humor, Literature, Literary
  Criticism, Essays, Mysteries, Suspense, Non-
  fiction (General), Philosophy, Self-Help, Social
  Sciences, Sociology, Sports, Athletics, Theol-
  ogy
ISBN Prefix(es): 978-87-7739; 978-87-88589

Hr Ferdinand, *imprint of* JP/Politikens Forlag

Hr Ferdinand
Imprint of JP/Politikens Forlag
Radhuspladsen 37, 1785 Copenhagen V
Tel: 51 28 41 46
E-mail: info@hrferdinand.dk
Web Site: hrferdinand.dk
Key Personnel
Editorial Dir: Line Miller *E-mail:* line.miller@
  jppol.dk
Press & Public Relations: Mette C Konig *Tel:* 26
  27 21 66 *E-mail:* mette.c.konig@jppol.dk
Founded: 2003
Subjects: Mysteries, Suspense
ISBN Prefix(es): 978-87-91746; 978-87-990157;
  978-87-92639
Ultimate Parent Company: JP/Politikens Hus A/S

IBIS
Vesterbrogade 2B, 1620 Copenhagen V
Tel: 35 35 87 88 *Fax:* 35 35 06 96
E-mail: ibis@ibis.dk
Web Site: www.ibis.dk; ibis-global.org
Key Personnel
Controller: Niels Svensson *Tel:* 35 20 05 17
  E-mail: ns@ibis.dk
Dir, Finance: Peter Bro Jorgensen *Tel:* 35 20 05
  20 *E-mail:* pbj@ibis.dk
Head, Communication & Fundraising: Annelie
  Abildgaard *Tel:* 35 20 05 31 *E-mail:* aa@ibis.
  dk
Founded: 1972
ISBN Prefix(es): 978-87-87804
Parent Company: International Children's Book
  Service (ICBS)

Branch Office(s)
Klosterport 4C, 3 sal, 8000 Aarhus, Contact: Angelika Marning *Tel:* 30 28 02 93 *E-mail:* asm@
  ibis.dk

Jensen og Dalgaard
Vesterfaelledvej 15, 1750 Copenhagen V
E-mail: forlaget@jensenogdalgaard.dk
Web Site: www.jensenogdalgaard.dk
Key Personnel
Partner: Jeanne Dalgaard *Tel:* 42442070
  E-mail: dalgaard@jensenogdalgaard.dk; Bjarne
  Michael Jensen *Tel:* 42442080 *E-mail:* jensen@
  jensenogdalgaard.dk
ISBN Prefix(es): 978-87-7151

JENTAS A/S
Folfodvej 202, 2300 Copenhagen
Tel: 35 81 35 00 *Fax:* 35 81 37 00
E-mail: info@jentas.dk
Web Site: www.jentas.dk
Key Personnel
Dir: Sigrun Halldors *E-mail:* sigrun@jentas.com
Subjects: Biography, Memoirs, Cookery, Crafts,
  Games, Hobbies, Criminology, Fiction, Myster-
  ies, Suspense
ISBN Prefix(es): 978-87-7677

JP/Politikens Forlag+
Vestergade 26, 1456 Copenhagen K
Mailing Address: Radhuspladsen 37, 1785 Copen-
  hagen K
Tel: 33 47 07 07
E-mail: info@jppol.dk
Web Site: www.politikensforlag.dk
Key Personnel
Dir: Lene Juul *Tel:* 33 47 07 01 *E-mail:* lene.
  juul@jppol.dk
Head, Fiction: Charlotte Weiss *E-mail:* charlotte.
  weiss@pol.dk
Head, Foreign Rights: Sofie Voller *Tel:* 33 47 07
  93 *E-mail:* sofie.voller@jppol.dk
Head, Nonfiction: Kim Hundevadt *E-mail:* kim.
  hundevadt@jppol.dk
Commercial Manager: Jakob Harden *Tel:* 33 47
  07 40 *E-mail:* jakob.harden@jppol.dk
Finance Manager: Anette Whitt *Tel:* 33 47 07 77
  E-mail: anette.whitt@jppol.dk
Marketing Manager: Pernille Engelbert Weil
  Tel: 33 47 07 41 *E-mail:* pernille.e.weil@jppol.
  dk
Production Manager, Fiction: Tomas Henriksen
  Tel: 33 47 07 11 *E-mail:* tomas.henriksen@pol.
  dk
Production Manager, Nonfiction: Peter Wrang
  Tel: 33 47 07 10 *E-mail:* peter.wrang@jppol.dk
Sales Manager: Pernille Hjorth *Tel:* 33 47 07 57
  E-mail: pernille.hjorth@jppol.dk
Press Officer: Camilla Hoy *Tel:* 30 38 28 12
  E-mail: camilla.hoy@jppol.dk
Founded: 1946
Subjects: Alternative, Biography, Memoirs, Cook-
  ery, Crafts, Games, Hobbies, Fiction, Health,
  Nutrition, Humor, Psychology, Psychiatry, Self-
  Help, Travel & Tourism
ISBN Prefix(es): 978-87-89019; 978-87-90181;
  978-87-567; 978-87-7963; 978-87-400
Number of titles published annually: 80 Print
Parent Company: JP/Politikens Hus A/S
Imprints: C&K Forlag; Don Max; Ekstra Bladets
  Forlag; Hr Ferdinand; Jyllands-Postens Forlag;
  Polaris; Bokforlaget Polaris i Sverige; Politiken
  Books; Politikens Boghal
Warehouse: D B K Bogdistribution, Siljangade 2-
  8, 2300 Copenhagen S

Jyllands-Postens Forlag, *imprint of* JP/Politikens
  Forlag

Kaleidoscope Publishers Ltd+
Division of Gyldendal Education
3 Klareboderne, 1001 Copenhagen K
Tel: 33 75 55 55 *Fax:* 33 75 55 44

Key Personnel
Publisher: Jens Bendtsen
Founded: 1983
Subjects: Education, English as a Second Language, Film, Video, Language Arts, Linguistics, Literature, Literary Criticism, Essays
ISBN Prefix(es): 978-87-7565; 978-87-431
Imprints: Faktor Funf; Ficcion Espanola; Fiction Factory; Fiction Francaise
Subsidiaries: Fiction Factory International Ltd/APS

Forlaget Klematis A/S+
Ostre Skovvej 1, 8240 Risskov
Tel: 8617 5455 *Fax:* 8617 5959
E-mail: klematis@klematis.dk; bogholderi@klematis.dk
Web Site: www.klematis.dk
Key Personnel
Founder, Owner & Publisher: Claus Dalby
Founder & Chief Executive Officer: Jaume Ferrer
Founded: 1987
Specialize in children's books, craft, fiction & nonfiction.
Subjects: Crafts, Games, Hobbies, Fiction, Nonfiction (General)
ISBN Prefix(es): 978-87-7721; 978-87-7905; 978-87-641
Shipping Address: Jeuro Danmark, Baggeskaervej 6, 7400 Herning, Contact: M Stausholm
Warehouse: D B K, Siljangade 6-8, 2300 Copenhagen S

Forlaget Klim
Ny Tjornegade 19, 8200 Arhus N
Tel: 86 10 37 00 *Fax:* 86 10 30 45
E-mail: forlaget@klim.dk; bestillinger@klim.dk (orders)
Web Site: www.klim.dk
Key Personnel
Editor: Karen Lise Sondergaard Brandt *Tel:* 72 34 45 16 *E-mail:* karenlise@klim.dk
Sales & Marketing Manager: Helle Brandenborg *Tel:* 72 34 45 14 *E-mail:* helle@klim.dk
Founded: 1984
Subjects: Fiction, Nonfiction (General), Philosophy, Psychology, Psychiatry, Pedagogy
ISBN Prefix(es): 978-87-7724; 978-87-7955; 978-87-88727
Book Club(s): Klims Bogklub

Forlaget Klingbjerg I/S
Torvet 5, 6100 Haderslev
Tel: 7453 1500 *Fax:* 7453 1508
E-mail: klempaa@klingbjerg.dk
Web Site: www.klingbjerg.dk
Key Personnel
Dir: Thomas Klemann; Christa Palsson
Founded: 1978
Glossaries.
Subjects: English as a Second Language
ISBN Prefix(es): 978-87-87764
Number of titles published annually: 3 Print
Total Titles: 40 Print

L & R Business, *imprint of* Lindhardt og Ringhof

Lindhardt og Ringhof+
Division of Egmont
Vognmagergade 11, 1148 Copenhagen K
Tel: 33695000
E-mail: info@lindhardtogringhof.dk
Web Site: www.aschehoug.dk; www.lindhardtogringhof.dk
Key Personnel
Chief Executive Dir: Lars Boesgaard *E-mail:* lars.boesgaard@lindhardtogringhof.dk
Dir, Business Development: Cliff Hansen *E-mail:* cliff.hansen@lindhardtogringhof.dk

Head, Press & Marketing: Soren Anker Madsen *E-mail:* soren.anker.madsen@lindhardtogringhof.dk
Sales Manager: Joel Haviv *E-mail:* joel.haviv@lindhardtogringhof.dk
Editor & Foreign Rights, Non Fiction: Lone Selfort *Tel:* 36156743
Editor & Foreign Rights, Children's Books: Lotte Kjeldskouv *Tel:* 36156781
Founded: 1971
Subjects: Biography, Memoirs, Cookery, Fiction, Health, Nutrition, How-to, Maritime
ISBN Prefix(es): 978-87-11; 978-87-15; 978-87-632; 978-87-429; 978-87-7512
Total Titles: 900 Print
Imprints: Academic Publishers; Alfabeta; Alinea; Athene; Carlsen; L & R Business
Book Club(s): Bogklubben 12 Boger; Bogsamleren; Rasmus og Romanbogklubben

Forlagsgruppen Lohse+
Korskaervej 25, 7000 Fredericia
Tel: 7593 4455 *Fax:* 7592 4275
E-mail: info@lohse.dk
Web Site: www.lohse.dk
Founded: 1868
Specialize in Christian books & music.
Subjects: Biblical Studies, Fiction, Religion - Protestant
ISBN Prefix(es): 978-87-564
Associate Companies: J Frimodts Forlag
Book Club(s): Lohses Bogklub

Magnus Informatik A/S
Subsidiary of Wolters Kluwer
Nyhavn 16, 1051 Copenhagen K
Tel: 70 20 33 14
E-mail: magnus@magnus.dk; salg@magnus.dk
Web Site: www.magnus.dk
Founded: 1962
Production & distribution of law materials.
Subjects: Law, Public Administration
ISBN Prefix(es): 978-87-87451; 978-87-7762
Branch Office(s)
Soren Frichs Vej 25, 1 Sal, 8000 Aarhus C *Tel:* 70 20 33 14 *Fax:* 87 32 14 01 *E-mail:* aarhus@magnus.dk

Mercantila Publishers A/S
Kirke Vaerlosevej 38, 3500 Vaerlose
Tel: 3543 6222
E-mail: info@gtft.dk
Web Site: www.gtft.dk
Key Personnel
Partner: Erik Albrechtsen
Founded: 1986
The guides to food transport are reference books with basic information about transporting perishables.
Subjects: Transportation, Food & Perishable Transport
ISBN Prefix(es): 978-87-89010
Subsidiaries: Carit Andersens Forlag A/S

Forlaget Modtryk+
Anholtsgade 4-6, 8000 Aarhus C
Tel: 8731 7600 *Fax:* 8619 9138
E-mail: forlaget@modtryk.dk
Web Site: www.modtryk.dk
Key Personnel
Mng Dir: Ilse Norr *Tel:* 8731 7603 *E-mail:* in@modtryk.dk
Sales Manager: Malene Schioldan *Tel:* 8731 7608 *E-mail:* ms@modtryk.dk
Production: Henning Morck Jensen *Tel:* 8731 7605 *E-mail:* hmj@modtryk.dk
Founded: 1972
Subjects: Fiction, Humor, Mysteries, Suspense, Nonfiction (General)
ISBN Prefix(es): 978-87-87458; 978-87-7394; 978-87-87620; 978-87-87817; 978-87-88135

Munksgaard Danmark
Klareboderne 5, 1001 Copenhagen K
Tel: 3375 5560
Web Site: www.munksgaarddanmark.dk
Key Personnel
Mng Dir: Hanne Salomonsen *Tel:* 3375 5535 *E-mail:* hanne_salomonsen@gyldendal.dk
Founded: 1917
Specialize in medical & scientific publishing.
Subjects: Health, Nutrition, Medicine, Nursing, Dentistry, Odontology, Physiotherapy
ISBN Prefix(es): 978-87-628
Parent Company: Gyldendal Akademisk A/S

Museum Tusculanum Press
University of Copenhagen, Birketinget 6, 2300 Copenhagen S
Tel: 32 34 14 14 *Fax:* 32 58 14 88
E-mail: info@mtp.dk
Web Site: www.mtp.dk
Key Personnel
Mng Dir & Editor-in-Chief: Marianne Alenius, PhD *Tel:* 32 34 14 22 *E-mail:* alenius@mtp.dk
Deputy Dir: Julie Bjorchmar Kolle *Tel:* 32 34 14 47 *E-mail:* julie@mtp.dk
Founded: 1975
Independent scholarly press based at the University of Copenhagen.
Subjects: Anthropology, Antiques, Archaeology, Art, Asian Studies, Foreign Countries, History, Language Arts, Linguistics, Literature, Literary Criticism, Essays, Philosophy, Religion - Other, Social Sciences, Sociology, Women's Studies
ISBN Prefix(es): 978-87-980131; 978-87-88073; 978-87-7289; 978-87-635
Number of titles published annually: 60 Print; 1 CD-ROM; 40 Online; 20 E-Book
Total Titles: 1,100 Print; 3 CD-ROM; 550 Online; 100 E-Book
Distributed by Editions Picard (France); University of Chicago Press (Canada & USA)
Foreign Rep(s): Gazelle Book Services Ltd (UK); Edition Picard (France); University of Chicago Press (Canada, USA)

My Best Book, *imprint of* Bogans Forlag

Rasmus Naver, *imprint of* Haase & Sons Forlag A/S

New Era Publications International ApS+
Smedeland 20, 2600 Glostrup
Tel: 33 73 66 66 *Toll Free Tel:* 800-808-8-8008 *Fax:* 33 73 66 89
E-mail: books@newerapublications.com
Web Site: www.newerapublications.com
Key Personnel
Senior Vice President: Brian Hickey *E-mail:* bhickey@newerapub.com
Vice President, Export Sales: Thomas Goeldenitz *E-mail:* tgoeldenitz@newerapub.com
Founded: 1969
Publisher of L Ron Hubbard's fiction & nonfiction books outside of America.
Subjects: Art, Education, Inspirational, Spirituality, Management, Philosophy, Religion - Other, Science Fiction, Fantasy, Self-Help, Dianetics & Scientology, Personal Development
ISBN Prefix(es): 978-87-7336; 978-87-87347; 978-87-7816; 978-87-7968; 978-87-7989; 978-87-7687; 978-87-7688
Subsidiaries: N E Publications (India) Pvt Ltd; New Era Publications Group; New Era Publications Italia SRL; New Era Publications UK Ltd

NIAS Press
Oster Farimagsgade 5, 1353 Copenhagen K
Tel: 3532 9500 *Fax:* 3532 9549
E-mail: books@nias.ku.dk
Web Site: www.niaspress.dk
Key Personnel
Editor-in-Chief: Gerald Jackson

Subjects: Asian Studies
ISBN Prefix(es): 978-87-87062; 978-87-91114;
978-87-7694
Parent Company: Nordic Institute of Asian Studies
Foreign Rep(s): InBooks (James Bennett) (Australia, New Zealand); Institute of Southeast Asian Studies (Asia exc Burma, Cambodia, Japan, Laos, Thailand & Vietnam); Marston Book Services Ltd (Africa, Europe, Middle East); Silkworm Books (Cambodia, Laos, Myanmar, Thailand, Vietnam); United Publishers Service Ltd (Japan); University of Hawaii Press (Latin America, North America)

Nordic Council of Ministers Publications
Ved Stranden 18, 1061 Copenhagen K
Tel: 33 96 02 00; 33 96 04 00
E-mail: nmr@norden.org; nordisk-rad@norden.org
Web Site: www.norden.org
Key Personnel
Head, Communications: Mary Gestrin
  E-mail: mage@norden.org
Founded: 1971
This publisher has indicated that 90% of their product line is author subsidized.
Subjects: Economics, Environmental Studies, Government, Political Science, Health, Nutrition, Travel & Tourism, Public Health
ISBN Prefix(es): 978-92-893; 978-92-9120
Number of titles published annually: 200 Print; 200 Online; 200 E-Book

Forlaget Palle Fogtdal A/S
Ostergade 22, 1100 Copenhagen K
Tel: 3315 3915 *Fax:* 3393 3505
E-mail: pallefogtdal@pallefogtdal.dk
Web Site: www.pallefogtdal.dk
Key Personnel
Mng Dir: Palle Fogtdal
Founded: 1984
Subjects: Art, Biography, Memoirs, History
ISBN Prefix(es): 978-87-7248

Paludan Forlag ApS+
Egevej 19, 2970 Horsholm
Tel: 4975-1536 *Fax:* 4975-1537
E-mail: paludans.forlag@newmail.dk
Key Personnel
Mng Dir: Joergen Viggo Paludan
Subjects: Cookery, Economics, Education, Government, Political Science, History, Nonfiction (General), Psychology, Psychiatry, Self-Help
ISBN Prefix(es): 978-87-7230
Warehouse: Nordisk Bog Center, 4690 Hastev
Distribution Center: Nordisk Bog Center, 4690 Hastev

People's Press
ArtPeople, Orstedhus, Vester Farimagsgade 41, 1606 Copenhagen V
Tel: 3311 3311
E-mail: info@peoplespress.dk
Web Site: www.peoplespress.dk
Key Personnel
Dir: Jan Degner *Tel:* 7221 5232 *E-mail:* jan.degner@peoplespress.dk
Creative Dir: Jakob Kvist *Tel:* 2265 5233
  E-mail: kvist@peoplespress.dk
Rights Dir: Louise Langhoff Koch *Tel:* 2265 5368
  E-mail: louise.langhoff@peoplespress.dk
Founded: 2002
Subjects: Art, Biography, Memoirs, Fiction, Music, Dance, Nonfiction (General)
ISBN Prefix(es): 978-87-91693; 978-87-91293; 978-87-91518; 978-87-91812

Polaris, *imprint of* JP/Politikens Forlag

Bokforlaget Polaris i Sverige, *imprint of* JP/Politikens Forlag

Politiken Books, *imprint of* JP/Politikens Forlag

Politikens Boghal, *imprint of* JP/Politikens Forlag

Forlaget Politisk Revy+
Nansensgade 70, 1366 Copenhagen K
Tel: 33 91 41 41 *Fax:* 33 91 51 15
E-mail: politiskrevy@forlagene.dk
Web Site: www.forlagene.dk/politiskrevy
Key Personnel
Publisher: Johannes Sohlman
Founded: 1963
Independent small press.
Subjects: Fiction, Government, Political Science, Literature, Literary Criticism, Essays, Nonfiction (General), Philosophy, Photography, Poetry, Psychology, Psychiatry, Social Sciences, Sociology
ISBN Prefix(es): 978-87-7378; 978-87-85186
Number of titles published annually: 12 Print
Total Titles: 250 Print
Warehouse: Nordisk Bogcenter A/S, Baekvej 2, 4690 Haslev

Polyteknisk Boghandel & Forlag+
Anker Engelunds Vej 1, 2800 Lyngby
Tel: 77 42 43 44
E-mail: poly@polyteknisk.dk
Web Site: www.polyteknisk.dk
Key Personnel
Administrative Dir: Lise Scharff *Tel:* 77 42 43 22
  E-mail: lise@polyteknisk.dk
Founded: 1960
Subjects: Engineering (General), Science (General)
ISBN Prefix(es): 978-87-502; 978-87-769; 978-87-990

PRAXIS-Nyt Teknisk Forlag (Danish Technical Press)+
Munkehatten 28, 5220 Odense
Tel: 6315 1700 *Fax:* 6315 1733
E-mail: info@praxis.dk
Web Site: ntf.praxis.dk
Key Personnel
Editor: Thomas Rump
Founded: 1948
Subjects: Business, Computer Science, Engineering (General)
ISBN Prefix(es): 978-87-571; 978-87-89535
Number of titles published annually: 80 Print; 4 CD-ROM; 3 E-Book

Pretty Ink, *imprint of* Rosinante & Co

Forlaget Punktum
Industriparken 23, 2750 Ballerup
Tel: 88 82 65 82
Web Site: www.forlagetpunktum.dk
Key Personnel
Public Relations: Katrine Sandbjerg *Tel:* 28 45 16 13 *E-mail:* katrine@forlagetpunktum.dk
Founded: 2010
Subjects: Fiction
ISBN Prefix(es): 978-87-92621

Hans Reitzel Forlag+
Klarebodernes, 1001 Copenhagen K
Tel: 3375 5560
E-mail: hrf@hansreitzel.dk
Web Site: hans.gyldendal-uddannelse.dk
Key Personnel
Dir: Hanne Salomonsen *Tel:* 33 75 59 10
  E-mail: hs@ga-forlagene.dk
Publishing Dir: Henriette Thiesen *Tel:* 3375 5985
  E-mail: ht@hansreitzel.dk
Founded: 1949

Subjects: Business, Communications, Education, Philosophy, Psychology, Psychiatry, Public Administration, Social Sciences, Sociology
ISBN Prefix(es): 978-87-628
Number of titles published annually: 60 Print; 40 E-Book
Total Titles: 350 Print
Parent Company: Gyldendalske Akademisk AS
Warehouse: Nordisk Bog Center, Bcekvej 10-12, 4690 Haslev

Hans Reitzels Forlag
Subsidiary of Gyldendal
Klareboderne 5, 1001 Copenhagen K
Tel: 33 75 55 60
E-mail: hrf@hansreitzel.dk
Web Site: hansreitzel.dk
Key Personnel
Dir: Hanne Salomonsen *Tel:* 33 75 59 10
  E-mail: hs@ga-forlagene.dk
Publishing Dir: Henriette Thiesen *Tel:* 33 75 59 85 *E-mail:* ht@hansreitzel.dk
Communications & Marketing Manager: Anne Charlotte Storm *Tel:* 33 75 59 76 *E-mail:* acs@gyldendalakademisk.dk
Publishing Coordinator: Lise Lotte Hansen *Tel:* 33 75 59 51 *E-mail:* llh@hansreitzel.dk
Founded: 1949
Subjects: Communications, Economics, Law, Psychology, Psychiatry, Social Sciences, Sociology, Humanities, Pedagogy
ISBN Prefix(es): 978-87-412

Forlaget Rhodos A/S (Rhodos Publishers A/S)
Horsholmvej 17, Holtegaard, 3050 Humlebaek
Tel: 32 54 30 20 *Fax:* 32 54 30 22
E-mail: rhodos@rhodos.dk
Web Site: www.rhodos.dk
Key Personnel
Owner: Gertrud Jensen
Mng Dir: Ruben Blaedel
Founded: 1959
Subjects: Architecture & Interior Design, Art, History, Science (General)
ISBN Prefix(es): 978-87-7245; 978-87-7496; 978-87-7999

Forlaget Ries
Robert Jacobsens Vej 64, 3 T2, 8tallet-Orestad, 2300 Copenhagen S
Tel: 3963 3205; 2424 1263 (cell)
E-mail: mr@riesforlag.dk
Web Site: www.riesforlag.dk
Key Personnel
Owner: Merete Ries
Founded: 2004
Subjects: Criminology, Fiction, Mysteries, Suspense, Nonfiction (General)
ISBN Prefix(es): 978-87-91318

Rosinante, *imprint of* Rosinante & Co

Rosinante & Co
Subsidiary of Gyldendal
Kobmagergade 62, 1150 Copenhagen K
Mailing Address: Postboks 2252, 1919 Copenhagen K
Tel: 3341 1800 *Fax:* 3341 1801
E-mail: info@rosinante-co.dk
Web Site: www.rosinante-co.dk
Subjects: Fiction
ISBN Prefix(es): 978-87-638; 978-87-621; 978-87-7357
Imprints: Cicero-Chr Erichsen; Forum; Host & Son; Pretty Ink; Rosinante
Foreign Rights: Rogers Coleridge & White

Samfundslitteratur+
Rosenorns Alle 9, 1970 Frederiksberg C
Tel: 38 15 38 80 *Fax:* 35 35 78 22
E-mail: slforlagene@samfundslitteratur.dk
Web Site: www.samfundslitteratur.dk

Key Personnel
Publishing Manager: Birgit Vra *Tel:* 38 15 38 77
  E-mail: bv@samfundslitteratur.dk
Marketing: Poul Kragh Jensen *Tel:* 38 15 38 82
  E-mail: pj@samfundslitteratur.dk
Founded: 1967
Publishers at Copenhagen Business School.
Subjects: Accounting, Advertising, Agriculture, Business, Communications, Economics, Education, English as a Second Language, Environmental Studies, Film, Video, Finance, Government, Political Science, History, Journalism, Language Arts, Linguistics, Literature, Literary Criticism, Essays, Management, Marketing, Philosophy, Psychology, Psychiatry, Public Administration, Social Sciences, Sociology, Veterinary Science
ISBN Prefix(es): 978-87-593; 978-87-7313; 978-87-87322
Total Titles: 600 Print; 3 CD-ROM
Imprints: Copenhagen Business School Press
Distributor for The World Bank (Denmark)
Bookshop(s): Okonomi-bogladen, Solberg Plads 3, 2000 Frederiksberg C; Samfundslitteratur - Life Sciences, Thorvaldsensvej 40, 1871 Frederiksberg C; Sprog-bogladen, Dalgas Have 15, 2000 Frederiksberg C; IT-bogladen, Rued Langgaardsvej 7, 2300 Copenhagen S; RUC - bogladen, Bygn 01, Universitetsvej 1, 4000 Roskilde

Scandinavia Publishing House+
Drejervej 15, 3rd floor, 2400 Copenhagen NV
Tel: 3123 3380 *Fax:* 3531 0334
E-mail: info@scanpublishing.dk
Web Site: www.scanpublishing.dk
Key Personnel
President & Publisher: Jorgen Vium Olesen
  Tel: 2258 9420 *E-mail:* jvo@scanpublishing.dk
Production Manager: Filip Lindell *E-mail:* fl@scanpublishing.dk
Sales Manager: Jacob Vium *E-mail:* jv@scanpublishing.dk
Founded: 1973
Specialize in illustrated children's books & bibles.
Subjects: Biblical Studies, Biography, Memoirs, Education, Theology
ISBN Prefix(es): 978-87-7247; 978-87-87732
Total Titles: 323 Print
Branch Office(s)
Scandinavia Hong Kong Ltd, China Insurance Bldg, Rooms 2101-3, 141 Des Voeux Rd Central, Hong Kong, Hong Kong
The 401 Centre, 302 Regent St, London W1B 3HH, United Kingdom
Foreign Rep(s): The Bible Society in Australia (Australia); The Bible Society in New Zealand (New Zealand); The Bible Society of India (India); Faithworks (USA); Foundation Distributing Inc (Canada); Horizons Distributors (UK); National Book Network Inc (USA); WORD Group Australia (Australia)
Book Club(s): Den Kristne Bogklub, Contact: Bo Nielsen *Tel:* 35 31 03 36

Schultz Information+
Annexstr 5, 2500 Valby
Tel: 72 28 28 27; 72 28 28 26 (customer service)
  Fax: 43 63 56 15
E-mail: schultz@schultz.dk; kundeservice@schultz.dk
Web Site: www.schultz.dk
Key Personnel
Chief Executive Officer: Mette Kaagaard *Tel:* 61 62 83 73 *E-mail:* mk@schultz.dk
Chief Editor: Erik Nielsen *Tel:* 41 95 47 10
  E-mail: en@schultz.dk
Sales Dir: Eskil Thygesen *Tel:* 41 95 47 40
  E-mail: et@schultz.dk
Founded: 1661
Specialize in law information.
Subjects: Business, Environmental Studies, Law, Nonfiction (General)

ISBN Prefix(es): 978-87-569; 978-87-609
Parent Company: J H Schultz Holding A/S
Ultimate Parent Company: J H Schultz-Fonden
Associate Companies: Synergi Data A/S

Sommer & Sorensen, *imprint of* Borgens Forlag

Sommer & Sorensen
Imprint of Borgens Forlag
Klareboderne 3, 1001 Copenhagen K
Tel: 3375 5555
E-mail: salg@borgen.dk; borgen_post@gyldendal.dk
Web Site: www.borgen.dk
Key Personnel
Information & Sales: Jacob Mahler *Tel:* 3375 5793 *E-mail:* jacob_mahler@gyldendal.dk
Subjects: Fiction
ISBN Prefix(es): 978-87-7499; 978-87-90189
Number of titles published annually: 5 Print
Total Titles: 10 Print
Ultimate Parent Company: Gyldendal

Strandbergs Forlag A/S+
Viggo Rothes Vej 23, 2920 Charlottenlund
Tel: 4589 4760
Web Site: www.strandbergsforlag.dk
Key Personnel
Publisher: Niels Norgaard *Tel:* 4052 0021
  E-mail: niels@strandbergsforlag.dk
Founded: 1861
Also book packager.
Subjects: Ethnicity, Humor
ISBN Prefix(es): 978-87-7717; 978-87-87200

Syddansk Universitetsforlag (University Press of Southern Denmark)+
Campusvej 55, 5230 Odense M
Tel: 6550 1740
E-mail: press@forlag.sdu.dk
Web Site: www.universitypress.dk
Key Personnel
Dir: Martin Lindo Westergaard *Tel:* 6550 1740 ext 1744 *E-mail:* mw@forlag.sdu.dk
Founded: 1966
Subjects: Archaeology, Art, Fiction, History, Literature, Literary Criticism, Essays, Medicine, Nursing, Dentistry, Philosophy, Social Sciences, Sociology, Sports, Athletics, Technology
ISBN Prefix(es): 978-87-7492; 978-87-7838; 978-87-7674

Systime A/S+
Subsidiary of Gyldendal
Sankt Pauls Gade 25, 8000 Aarhus C
Tel: 70 12 11 00
E-mail: systime@systime.dk
Web Site: www.systime.dk
Key Personnel
Dir: Poul Henrik Mikkelsen *Tel:* 86 20 31 86
  E-mail: phm@systime.dk
Sales Manager: Gitte Faerch Nielsen *Tel:* 86 20 31 51 *E-mail:* gfn@systime.dk
Project Manager & Dir of Marketing: Lene Fischer-Mogensen *Tel:* 86 20 31 83
  E-mail: lfm@systime.dk
Founded: 1980
Specialize in educational materials.
Subjects: Accounting, Astronomy, Biological Sciences, Chemistry, Chemical Engineering, Communications, Computer Science, Drama, Theater, Economics, English as a Second Language, Film, Video, Finance, Geography, Geology, History, Marketing, Mathematics, Music, Dance, Philosophy, Physics, Psychology, Psychiatry, Religion - Other, Technology
ISBN Prefix(es): 978-87-616; 978-87-7351; 978-87-7783; 978-87-87454
Total Titles: 100 Print

Thaning & Appel
Klareboderne 3, 1001 Copenhagen K
Tel: 33 75 55 55
E-mail: gyldendal@gyldendal.dk
Web Site: www.gyldendal.dk
Subjects: Art, Biography, Memoirs, Business, Cookery, Fiction, Health, Nutrition, History, Literature, Literary Criticism, Essays, Mysteries, Suspense, Nonfiction (General), Philosophy, Poetry
ISBN Prefix(es): 978-87-02; 978-87-413
Parent Company: Gyldendal

Forlaget Thomson A/S+
Sankt Petri Passage 5, 1165 Copenhagen K
Tel: 33 74 07 00
E-mail: post.dk@karnovgroup.com
Web Site: www.karnovgroup.dk
Subjects: Accounting, Business, Education, Law
ISBN Prefix(es): 978-87-619; 978-87-7747; 978-87-88109; 978-87-980953
Parent Company: Karnov Group Denmark A/S

Tiderne Skifter Forlag A/S+
Laederstr 5, 1 sal, 1201 Copenhagen K
Tel: 33 18 63 90 *Fax:* 33 18 63 91
E-mail: tiderneskifter@tiderneskifter.dk
Web Site: www.tiderneskifter.dk
Key Personnel
Founder & Mng Dir: Claus Clausen
Founded: 1973
Subjects: Ethnicity, Fiction, Government, Political Science, Literature, Literary Criticism, Essays, Photography, Poetry, Gender
ISBN Prefix(es): 978-87-7445; 978-87-7973
Number of titles published annually: 40 Print
Total Titles: 1,000 Print
Orders to: Nordisk Bog Center, Baekvej 10-12, 4690 Haslev *Tel:* 56364000 *Fax:* 56384038

TURBINE forlaget A/S
Balticagade 10, 2 sal, 8000 Aarhus C
Tel: 86 12 79 16 *Fax:* 86 12 73 16
E-mail: post@turbine.dk
Web Site: www.turbineforlaget.dk
Key Personnel
Mng Dir: Ulrik T Skafte *E-mail:* ulrik@turbine.dk
Dir & Editor: Jesper Tolstrup *E-mail:* jesper@turbine.dk
Founded: 2004
Subjects: Biography, Memoirs, Cookery, Crafts, Games, Hobbies, Education, Fiction
ISBN Prefix(es): 978-87-7090; 978-87-91926; 978-87-92208; 978-87-92389
Number of titles published annually: 200 Print

Unitas Forlag+
Frederiksberg Alle 10, 1820 Frederiksberg
Tel: 33 24 92 50 *Fax:* 38 25 06 07
E-mail: info@unitasforlag.dk
Web Site: www.unitasforlag.dk; www.kirkebogladen.dk (bookshop)
Key Personnel
Dir: Henrik Brandt-Pedersen
Publishing Editor: Niels Roesgaard Mose
  E-mail: nrm@unitasforlag.dk
Sales: Anette Thorup Lange *E-mail:* atl@unitasforlag.dk; Birthe Spendrup Pedersen
  E-mail: bsp@unitasforlag.dk
Founded: 1914
Subjects: Biblical Studies, Biography, Memoirs, Education, Fiction, Religion - Protestant, Theology
ISBN Prefix(es): 978-87-7517
Number of titles published annually: 30 Print
Total Titles: 300 Print
Parent Company: YMCA/YWCA

Vandrer mod Lysets Forlag ApS (Toward the Light Publishing House)
Bredgade 36 C, st th, 1260 Copenhagen K
Tel: 33 15 78 15

E-mail: vml@vandrer-mod-lyset.dk; forlag@vml. nu
Web Site: www.vandrer-mod-lyset.dk; www. toward-the-light.com/html/fond.php
Key Personnel
Chairman: Ole Enghave
Publisher: Mrs Konny Falck
Founded: 1974
Subjects: Inspirational, Spirituality
ISBN Prefix(es): 978-87-87871; 978-87-980350

Forlaget Vindrose A/S, *imprint of* Borgens Forlag

Forlaget Vindrose A/S+
Imprint of Borgens Forlag
Klareboderne 3, 1001 Copenhagen K
Tel: 3375 5555
E-mail: borgen_post@gyldendal.dk; salg@borgen. dk
Web Site: www.borgen.dk
Key Personnel
Information & Sales: Jacob Mahler *Tel:* 3375 5793 *E-mail:* jacob_mahler@gyldendal.dk
Founded: 1980
Subjects: Fiction, Poetry, Science (General), Social Sciences, Sociology
ISBN Prefix(es): 978-87-7456
Number of titles published annually: 20 Print
Total Titles: 200 Print
Ultimate Parent Company: Gyldendal
Warehouse: DBK-Logistik Service, Mimersvej 4, 4600 Koge
Orders to: DBK-bogdistribution, Mimersvej 4, 4600 Koge

Wisby & Wilkens+
Vesterled 45, 8300 Odder
Tel: 64 67 08 64
E-mail: mail@bogshop.dk
Web Site: www.bogshop.dk
Founded: 1986
Membership(s): Danish Publishers Association.
Subjects: Crafts, Games, Hobbies, Fiction, Humor, Literature, Literary Criticism, Essays, Nonfiction (General), Outdoor Recreation, Science Fiction, Fantasy
ISBN Prefix(es): 978-87-89190; 978-87-89191; 978-87-7046; 978-87-70461
Number of titles published annually: 24 Print
Total Titles: 200 Print
Parent Company: Forlagsgruppen BOGSHOP
Associate Companies: MIKRO, Vestergade 6, Box 98, 8464 Galten; Limbo
Distributor for Grandview USA (Scandinavia)
Warehouse: DBK, Siljangade 2, 2300 Copenhagen S

Dominican Republic

General Information

Capital: Santo Domingo
Language: Spanish
Religion: Predominantly Roman Catholic
Population: 7.5 million
Bank Hours: 0830-1230 Monday-Friday; some open 0830-1130 Saturday
Shop Hours: 0800-1200, 1400 or 1500-1800 Monday-Friday; some open Saturday
Currency: 100 centavos = 1 Dominican peso. US currency is widely used

Export/Import Information: No import licenses required for books. Exchange license and approval from Central Bank required.
Copyright: UCC, Berne, Buenos Aires (see Copyright Conventions, pg viii)

Fundacion Corripio
Ave Nunez de Caceres casi esquina, Ave J F Kennedy, Edificio Distribuidora Corripio II, 10513 Santo Domingo
Tel: (809) 227-3000 (ext 3276) *Fax:* (809) 567-5915
E-mail: fcorripio@corripio.com.do
Web Site: fundacioncorripio.org
Key Personnel
President: Jose L Corripio Estrada
Chief Executive Officer: Jacinto Gimbernard Pellerano
Founded: 1986
Subjects: History, Literature, Literary Criticism, Essays
ISBN Prefix(es): 978-84-89752; 978-84-921628

Fundacion Global Democracia y De Sarrollo, see Editorial FUNGLODE

Editorial FUNGLODE
Calle Pedro Henriquez Urena No 58, La Esperilla, 10107 Santo Domingo
Tel: (809) 685-9966; (809) 730-9910 *Fax:* (809) 685-9927
E-mail: administracion@editorialfunglode.com
Web Site: www.editorialfunglode.com
Key Personnel
Dir: Noris Eusebio-Pol *E-mail:* noris.eusebiopol@ gmail.com
Communications & Public Relations: Elaine Hernandez Pion *E-mail:* e.hernandez@funglode.org
Subjects: Government, Political Science, History
ISBN Prefix(es): 978-9945-412; 978-99934-879

Pontificia Universidad Catolica Madre y Maestra+
Autopista Duarte Km 1 1/2, Santiago
SAN: 004-5527
Tel: (809) 200-1962; (809) 535-0111; (809) 580-1962 *Fax:* (809) 582-4549
E-mail: info@pucmm.edu.do
Web Site: www.pucmm.edu.do
Founded: 1962
Membership(s): University Editorial Association of Latin America & the Caribbean.
Subjects: Accounting, Agriculture, Archaeology, Architecture & Interior Design, Biblical Studies, Biography, Memoirs, Biological Sciences, Business, Career Development, Chemistry, Chemical Engineering, Civil Engineering, Communications, Developing Countries, Drama, Theater, Economics, Education, Electronics, Electrical Engineering, Energy, Engineering (General), English as a Second Language, Environmental Studies, Geography, Geology, Government, Political Science, Health, Nutrition, History, Language Arts, Linguistics, Law, Library & Information Sciences, Literature, Literary Criticism, Essays, Management, Marketing, Mathematics, Mechanical Engineering, Medicine, Nursing, Dentistry, Philosophy, Physical Sciences, Physics, Poetry, Regional Interests, Religion - Catholic, Social Sciences, Sociology, Technology, Theology
ISBN Prefix(es): 978-84-89548; 978-99934-832; 978-99934-870
Warehouse: Economato Universitario, PUCMM

PUCMM, see Pontificia Universidad Catolica Madre y Maestra

Editora Taller CxA+
Zona Industrial de Herrera, Juan Vallenilla No 1 esquina Dolores, Santo Domingo

SAN: 002-2136
Tel: (809) 531-7975 *Fax:* (809) 531-7979
E-mail: editora.taller@codetel.net.do
Founded: 1971
Subjects: Economics, History, Literature, Literary Criticism, Essays
ISBN Prefix(es): 978-84-8400; 978-99934-846
Distributor for Editora Vicens Vives
Orders to: Vicente Celestino Duarte, No 2, Santo Domingo

Ecuador

General Information

Capital: Quito
Language: Spanish
Religion: Predominantly Roman Catholic
Population: 10.9 million
Bank Hours: 0900-1330 Monday-Friday
Shop Hours: 0930-1300, 1500-1900 Monday-Friday; 0930-1300 Saturday
Currency: 100 centavos = 1 sucre
Export/Import Information: Member of the Latin American Free Trade Association. Books and most advertising catalogues not dutiable. No import licenses or exchange controls for books.
Copyright: UCC, Buenos Aires (see Copyright Conventions, pg viii)

Editorial Abya Yala+
Unit of Universidad Politenica Salesiana (UPS)
Av 12 de Octubre N2422 y Wilson, Bloque A UPS, Quito
Mailing Address: Casilla Postal 17-12-719, Quito
Tel: (02) 3962800 (ext 2638); (02) 2506255 *Fax:* (02) 2506267
E-mail: webmaster@abyayala.org
Web Site: www.abyayala.org
Key Personnel
President: Padre Juan Bottasso
Rector UPS: Padre Javier Herran Gomez
Founded: 1975
Specialize in social sciences.
Membership(s): Quito Book Association.
Subjects: Anthropology, Environmental Studies, Language Arts, Linguistics, Theology
ISBN Prefix(es): 978-9978-04; 978-9978-22
Total Titles: 1,060 Print; 2 CD-ROM; 900 E-Book
Imprints: Andean World; Mondo Shuar

Andean World, *imprint of* Editorial Abya Yala

Centro Interamericano de Artesanias y Artes Populares, see CIDAP (Centro Interamericano de Artesanias y Artes Populares)

Centro Internacional de Estudios Superiores de Comunicacion para America Latina, see Ediciones CIESPAL

CEP, see Corporacion de Estudios y Publicaciones

CIDAP (Centro Interamericano de Artesanias y Artes Populares)
Hermano Miguel 3-23 y Paseo Tres de Noviembre (Escalinatas), Cuenca
Mailing Address: EC 010111, Cuenca
Tel: (07) 2829 451; (07) 2840 919; (07) 2850 516 *Fax:* (07) 2831 450
Web Site: www.cidap.gob.ec
Key Personnel
Executive Dir: Juan Pablo Serrano
Founded: 1975
Subjects: Art, Crafts, Games, Hobbies
ISBN Prefix(es): 978-84-89420; 978-9978-85

Ediciones CIESPAL (International Centre for Advanced Studies in Communication for Latin America)
Av Diego de Almagro N32-133, Andrade Marin, Quito
Tel: (02) 2548011 *Fax:* (02) 2502487
E-mail: info@ciespal.org
Web Site: ediciones.ciespal.org
Key Personnel
Dir General: Francisco Sierra Caballero
 E-mail: franciscosierra@ciespal.org
Dir, Research: Javier Moreno
Publications Coordinator: Pablo Escandon
Founded: 1959 (as an initiative of the Regional Seminar on Education)
Training, research, publications, CHASQUI magazine, television, radio, documentation center, media oversight, audiovisual & multimedia center.
Subjects: Biography, Memoirs, Communications, Journalism, Publishing & Book Trade Reference, Radio, TV, Technology
ISBN Prefix(es): 978-9978-55
Number of titles published annually: 12 Print; 50 Online
Total Titles: 300 Print; 120 Online

Corporacion de Estudios y Publicaciones
Acuna E2-02 y Juan Agama, Quito, Casilla
Tel: (02) 2221-711; (02) 2232-694 *Fax:* (02) 2226-256
E-mail: ventas@cep.org.ec
Web Site: www.cep.org.ec
Founded: 1965
Subjects: Law, Public Administration
ISBN Prefix(es): 978-9978-86

Corporacion Editora Nacional
Roca E-9-59 y Tamayo, Quito
Tel: (02) 2554358; (02) 2554658
E-mail: cen@cenlibrosecuador.org; ventas@cenlibrosecuador.org
Web Site: www.cenlibrosecuador.org
Key Personnel
Founder & President: Dr Hernan Malo Gonzalez
Founded: 1978
Editorial corporation with nonprofits.
Subjects: Archaeology, Biography, Memoirs, Economics, Education, Geography, Geology, Government, Political Science, History, Law, Literature, Literary Criticism, Essays, Philosophy, Social Sciences, Sociology
ISBN Prefix(es): 978-9978-84; 978-9978-958
Total Titles: 332 Print

Facultad Latinoamericana de Ciencias Sociales (FLACSO)
La Pradera E7-174 y Av Diego de Almagro, Quito
Tel: (02) 3238888 *Fax:* (02) 3237960
E-mail: flacso@flacso.org.ec
Web Site: www.flacso.org.ec
Key Personnel
Dir: Juan Ponce *Tel:* (02) 3238888 ext 2902
 E-mail: jponce@flacso.org.ec
Editorial Dir: Alicia Torres *Tel:* (02) 3238888 ext 2804 *E-mail:* atorres@flacso.org.ec
Founded: 1956
Subjects: Social Sciences, Sociology
ISBN Prefix(es): 978-9978-67

FLACSO, see Facultad Latinoamericana de Ciencias Sociales (FLACSO)

Ediciones Legales SA
Unit of Corporacion Myl
Los Cipreses N65-149 y los Eucaliptos, Quito
Tel: (02) 248 0800; (02) 223 9470
E-mail: edicioneslegales@corpmyl.com
Web Site: www.edicioneslegales.com.ec

Key Personnel
President: Dr Ernesto Alban Gomez
Founded: 1989
Subjects: Law
ISBN Prefix(es): 978-9978-81
Total Titles: 28 Print; 2 CD-ROM
Branch Office(s)
Av 6 de Diciembre N 23-49 y Baquedano, Quito
 Tel: (02) 224 0589; (02) 223 6881 *E-mail:* lbc.q.edle@corpmyl.com
Av Rodrigo Pachano y Calle Juan Montalvo, Edificio FICOAPARK, Oficina 209 Segundo Piso, Ambato *Tel:* (03) 242 5697
 E-mail: edicioneslegales@corpmyl.com
Av Jorge Perez Concha N 504 entre Ebanos y Las Monjas, Circuvalacion Sur, Urdesa Central, Guayaguil *Tel:* (04) 238 7265
 E-mail: edicioneslegales@corpmyl.com

Libresa SA+
Murgeon Oe3-10, entre Jorge Juan y Ulloa, Quito
Tel: (02) 2230925; (02) 2525581 *Fax:* (02) 2502992
E-mail: libresa@libresa.com
Web Site: www.libresa.com
Founded: 1927
Subjects: Education, Literature, Literary Criticism, Essays, Philosophy
ISBN Prefix(es): 978-9978-80; 978-9978-952

Mondo Shuar, *imprint of* Editorial Abya Yala

Pontificia Universidad Catolica del Ecuador, Centro de Publicaciones
Av 12 de Octubre, entre Patria y Veintimilla, Quito
Tel: (02) 2991711
E-mail: webmaster@puce.edu.ec; promocion@puce.edu.ec
Web Site: www.puce.edu.ec
Founded: 1974
Subjects: Anthropology, Archaeology, Art, Economics, Government, Political Science, History, Law, Literature, Literary Criticism, Essays, Philosophy, Science (General), Social Sciences, Sociology, Theology
ISBN Prefix(es): 978-9978-77

Pudeleco Editores SA/Publicaciones de Legislacion
Reina Victoria N21-141 entre Robles y Roca, Edif Proinco II, Quito
Tel: (02) 254 3273; (02) 252 9246
E-mail: principal@pudeleco.com
Web Site: www.comercioexteriorecuador.com
Key Personnel
Manager: Enrique Arias Angel Barriga
Founded: 1979
Provide books that help manage economic & legal issues in the areas of foreign trade activities, business taxation & labor relations. Print, digital & online.
Subjects: Economics, Labor, Industrial Relations, Law
ISBN Prefix(es): 978-9978-966

SECAP
Jose Arizaga E3-24 y Londres, Quito
Tel: (02) 3944000 *Toll Free Tel:* 1800073227
Web Site: www.secap.gob.ec
Key Personnel
Dir, Communication: Marcia Villafuerte *Tel:* (02) 3944000 ext 206 *E-mail:* m.villafuerte@secap.gob.ec
Founded: 1966
Subjects: Agriculture, Automotive, Education, Library & Information Sciences, Public Administration
ISBN Prefix(es): 978-9978-64

Servicio Ecuatoriano de Capacitacion Profesional, see SECAP

Egypt

General Information

Capital: Cairo
Language: Arabic (English and French widely used)
Religion: Predominantly Muslim (of the Sunni sect)
Population: 56.4 million
Bank Hours: Generally 0830-1230 Monday-Thursday; 1000-1200 Saturday
Shop Hours: 0830-1330, 1630-1900 Monday-Saturday
Currency: 1,000 milliemes = 100 piastres = 5 tallaris = 1 Egyptian pound
Export/Import Information: Exchange rate set by individual banks. No longer government monopoly but some book importing done by Foreign Trade Company, Misr Import & Export Co, 6 Adly St, Cairo.
Copyright: Berne, Florence (see Copyright Conventions, pg viii)

Al-Dar Al Masriah Al-Lubnaniah
16 Abdel Khalek Tharwat St, Cairo 11511
Tel: (02) 3910250 *Fax:* (02) 3909618
E-mail: info@almasriah.com; orders@almasriah.com
Web Site: www.almasriah.com
Key Personnel
Publisher: Mohamed Rashad
Founded: 1985
Subjects: Art, Astronomy, Biography, Memoirs, Economics, Education, Geography, Geology, Government, Political Science, Health, Nutrition, History, Language Arts, Linguistics, Law, Library & Information Sciences, Literature, Literary Criticism, Essays, Philosophy, Poetry, Psychology, Psychiatry, Science (General), Social Sciences, Sociology, Technology
ISBN Prefix(es): 978-977-427

The American University in Cairo Press+
113 Kasr el Aini St, Cairo 11511
Mailing Address: PO Box 2511, Cairo 11511
Tel: (02) 2797 6926; (02) 2797 6895 (orders) *Fax:* (02) 2794 1440
E-mail: aucpress@aucegypt.edu
Web Site: aucpress.com
Key Personnel
Dir: Dr Nigel Fletcher-Jones *Tel:* (02) 2797 6888
 E-mail: nigel@aucegypt.edu
Associate Dir, Editorial Programs: Neil Hewison
 Tel: (02) 2797-6892 *E-mail:* rnh@aucegypt.edu
Associate Dir, Sales & Marketing: Trevor Naylor
 Tel: (02) 2797 5759 *E-mail:* trevornaylor@aucegypt.edu
Marketing Manager: Basma El Manialawi
 Tel: (02) 2615 3973 *E-mail:* basma.manialawi@aucegypt.edu
General Sales Manager: Tahany El Shammaa
 Tel: (02) 2797-6895 *E-mail:* tahany@aucegypt.edu
Production & Purchasing: Miriam Fahmi
 E-mail: miriam@aucegypt.edu
Founded: 1960
Leading English-language publisher in Egypt & the Middle East.
Membership(s): Association of University Presses (AUPresses)
Subjects: Anthropology, Archaeology, Architecture & Interior Design, Art, Biography, Memoirs, Business, Earth Sciences, Economics, Environmental Studies, Government, Political

Science, History, Language Arts, Linguistics,
Literature, Literary Criticism, Essays, Regional
Interests, Religion - Islamic, Religion - Other,
Social Sciences, Sociology, Travel & Tourism
ISBN Prefix(es): 978-977-424; 978-977-416; 978-
1-936190; 978-1-936481; 978-1-61797
Number of titles published annually: 80 Print
Total Titles: 800 Print
U.S. Office(s): 420 Fifth Ave, New York, NY
10018, United States *Tel:* 212-730-8800
Fax: 212-730-1600 *E-mail:* ct_aucpress@
aucnyo.edu
Distributed by Oxford University Press (Canada
& USA)
Shipping Address: Eurospan, c/o Turpin Distribu-
tion, Stratton Business Park, Pegasus Dr, Big-
gleswade, Beds SG18 8TQ, United Kingdom
Tel: (0176) 760 4972 *Fax:* (0176) 760 1640
E-mail: eurospan@turpin-distribution.com (UK
& continental Europe)
Distribution Center: Auc Press Distribution
Center, New Cairo, Manager: Cherif Samaan
Tel: (02) 2615 4711 *Fax:* (02) 2615 6005
E-mail: csamaan@aucegypt.edu
Oxford University Press, 8 Sampson Mews,
Suite 204, Don Mills, ON M3C 0H5, Canada
E-mail: customer.service.ca@oup.com
Macmillan Distribution Ltd, United Kingdom
Tel: (01256) 302692 *Fax:* (01256) 812558
E-mail: orders@macmillan.co.uk (worldwide
exc Egypt & North America)
Oxford University Press, Customer Service Dept,
2001 Evans Rd, Cary, NC 27513, United States
Fax: 919-677-1303 *E-mail:* custserv.us@oup.
com

Arab Group for Training & Publishing
8A Ahmed Fakhry St, Nasr City, Cairo
Tel: (02) 22739110; (02) 22759945
E-mail: info@arabgroup.net.eg
Web Site: www.arabgroup.net.eg
Subjects: Communications, Education, Engi-
neering (General), Management, Marketing,
Physics, Psychology, Psychiatry
ISBN Prefix(es): 978-977-6298

Cairo University
Giza, Cairo 12613
Tel: (02) 35726595 (publications)
Web Site: cu.edu.eg
Key Personnel
President: Dr Gaber Nassar
Founded: 1908
ISBN Prefix(es): 978-977-223

CEDEJ, see Centre d'Etudes et de
Documentation Economiques, Juridiques et
Sociales (CEDEJ)

**Centre d'Etudes et de Documentation
Economiques, Juridiques et Sociales
(CEDEJ)** (Centre for Social, Judicial &
Economic Documentation & Study)
One, rue Madrasset El Huquq El Frinsiya, El
Mounira, Cairo
Mailing Address: PO Box 392, Muhhamad Farid,
Cairo
Tel: (02) 27 93 03 50; (02) 27 93 03 51; (02) 27
93 03 52; (02) 27 93 03 54; (02) 27 93 03 55
Fax: (02) 27 93 03 53
E-mail: cedej@cedej-eg.org
Web Site: www.cedej-eg.org
Key Personnel
Dir: Karine Bennafla *E-mail:* karine.bennafla@
cedej-eg.org
Communication & Publishing Officer: Clemence
Curty *E-mail:* communication@cedej-eg.org
Founded: 1970
Subjects: Economics, Government, Political Sci-
ence, Social Sciences, Sociology
ISBN Prefix(es): 978-2-905838

Dar Al Hilal Publishing Institution
16 Mohamed Ezz El-Arab St, Cairo 11511
Tel: (02) 3625450; (02) 3625451
Founded: 1892
Subjects: Fiction, Nonfiction (General)
ISBN Prefix(es): 978-977-07

Dar Al-Kitab Al-Masri+
33 Kasr El Nile St, Cairo 11511
Tel: (02) 3922168 *Fax:* (02) 3924657
E-mail: info@daralkitabalmasri.com
Web Site: www.daralkitabalmasri.com
Founded: 1929
Also distributor & printer.
Subjects: Education, Regional Interests
ISBN Prefix(es): 978-977-238
Associate Companies: Dar Al-Kitab Al-Lubnani,
Madame Kuri St in front of Bristol Hotel,
PO Box 11, Beirut 8330, Lebanon *Tel:* (01)
735731, (01) 735732 *Fax:* (01) 351433
Branch Office(s)
Cairo
Paris, France
Beirut, Lebanon
Casablanca, Morocco
Madrid, Spain
Geneva, Switzerland

Dar Al Maaref+
1119 Corniche El Nile St, Cairo
Tel: (02) 25777077 *Fax:* (02) 25744999
E-mail: info@daralmaaref.com
Web Site: www.daralmaaref.com
Founded: 1890
Also co-publishers, importers & exporters.
Subjects: Education, Regional Interests, Science
(General)
ISBN Prefix(es): 978-977-02
Subsidiaries: Dar Al-Maaref Liban Sarl
Bookshop(s): Alexandria; El Arish; Assiut; Ass-
wan; Cairo; Ismailia; Mansoura; Qena; Shebin
El kom; Sohage; Suez; Tanta; Zagazig

Dar alnahda alarabia (fb)
32, Abdel-Khalik Tharwat St, Cairo
Tel: (02) 392 6931 *Fax:* (02) 395 6150
E-mail: info@daralnahda.com
Web Site: www.daralnahda.com
Founded: 1960
Also distributor.
Subjects: Law, Literature, Literary Criticism, Es-
says
ISBN Prefix(es): 978-977-04

Dar El Shorouk (Sunrise House)+
8 Sibaweh El Masry St, Nasr City, Cairo
Tel: (02) 24023399 *Fax:* (02) 24037567
E-mail: dar@shorouk.com
Web Site: www.shorouk.com
Key Personnel
General Manager: Ahmed Bedeir
Art Dir: Hisham El Feky
Founded: 1968
Subjects: Art, Biography, Memoirs, Cookery, Fic-
tion, History, Humor, Nonfiction (General),
Religion - Islamic
ISBN Prefix(es): 978-977-09
Number of titles published annually: 170 Print
Total Titles: 3,500 Print
Associate Companies: Clip Solutions; Egyptian
Company for Publishing; E-Kotob; Shorouk
Press; United Media Production
Bookshop(s): 26 Mohamed Karmel Morsy,
Cairo *Tel:* (02) 33361774; One Taalat Harb
Sq, Cairo *Tel:* (02) 23930643; Cairo Alexan-
dria Desert: Oasis Omar, Cairo *Tel:* (010)
16337711; San Stefano Mall, Alexandria
Tel: (03) 4690370; First Mall, 35 Giza St,
Giza *Tel:* (02) 35685187; 15 Baghdad St, Ko-
rba, Heliopolis *Tel:* (02) 24172945; City Stars
Mall, 1st floor, entrance 7, Nasr City *Tel:* (02)
24802544

Elias Modern Publishing House+
One, Kenisset El Rum El Kathulik St, Daher,
Cairo 11271
Tel: (02) 2590 3756; (02) 2593 9544 *Fax:* (02)
2588 0091
E-mail: info@eliaspublishing.com; publishing@
eliaspublishing.com
Web Site: www.eliaspublishing.com
Key Personnel
Chairman: Nadim Elias
Mng Dir: Laura Kfoury *E-mail:* laura.kfoury@
eliaspublishing.com
Founded: 1913
Publishing & printing of monolingual & bilin-
gual dictionaries, children's fiction & nonfiction
books (3-16 years), educational books, trans-
lated from Arabic to English & from European
languages to Arabic.
Membership(s): Arab Publishers Association;
Egyptian Canadian Businessmen Association;
Egyptian Publishers Association.
Subjects: Fiction, Language Arts, Linguistics, Lit-
erature, Literary Criticism, Essays, Nonfiction
(General), Poetry
ISBN Prefix(es): 978-977-5028; 978-977-304
Subsidiaries: Elias Modern Press; Sahara Printing
Co

GEBO, see General Egyptian Book Organization
(GEBO)

**General Egyptian Book Organization
(GEBO)+**
1193 Cornich el Nil, Boulaq, Cairo 11511
Mailing Address: PO Box 235, Cairo 11794
Tel: (02) 25775646; (02) 25775109; (02)
25775371; (02) 25775228 *Fax:* (02) 25789316;
(02) 25754213
E-mail: info@gebo.gov.eg
Web Site: www.gebo.gov.eg
Key Personnel
Chairman: Dr Haytham El Hajaly
Founded: 1961
26 branches throughout Egypt.
ISBN Prefix(es): 978-977-01

Sphinx Publishing Co
3 Shawarby St, apartment 305, Cairo
Tel: (02) 392 4616 *Fax:* (02) 391 8002
Founded: 1958
Part of Librairie du Liban Group, Lebanon.
Subjects: Education
Branch Office(s)
Zahra's St, Al Dokki *Tel:* (02) 7494998 *Fax:* (02)
3389595 *E-mail:* zahraasp@intouch.com
127 Horriya St, Al-Shallalat, Alexandria *Tel:* (03)
4940539; (03) 4930356 *Fax:* (03) 4924839
E-mail: sphinx@internetalex.com

El Salvador

General Information

Capital: San Salvador
Language: Spanish
Religion: Predominantly Roman Catholic
Population: 5.6 million
Bank Hours: 0900-1200, 1345-1530 Monday-
Friday
Shop Hours: 0800-1200, 1400-1800 Monday-
Friday; 0800-1200 Saturday
Currency: 100 centavos = 1 Salvadorean colon
Export/Import Information: Member of the Cen-
tral American Common Market. No import
licenses but exchange license from Exchange
Control Department of Central Reserve Bank
required, if goods coming from outside Central

America. Commercial banks authorize certain import payments.
Copyright: UCC, Berne, Buenos Aires, Florence (see Copyright Conventions, pg viii)

Clasicos Roxsil SA de CV+
4 Ave Sur No 2-3, La Libertad, Santa Tecla
Tel: 2228-1832; 2200-5209; 2228-1212
E-mail: clasicosroxsil@yahoo.es
Web Site: ww.facebook.com/Clasicos-Roxsil-331476613687219/
Key Personnel
Dir: Roxana Beatriz Lopez *E-mail:* roxanabe@navegante.com.sv
Founded: 1976
Subjects: Biography, Memoirs, Literature, Literary Criticism, Essays, Poetry
ISBN Prefix(es): 978-84-89541; 978-84-89899; 978-99923-24
Number of titles published annually: 10 Print
Total Titles: 183 Print
Distributor for Fondo Editorial UNESCO (El Salvador)
Book Club(s): Club de Lectores de Clasicos Roxsil, Contact: Marco Antonio Barraza

Direccion de Publicaciones e Impresos (DPI)
17 Ave Sur No 430, San Salvador
Tel: 2222 9152
E-mail: direcciondepublicaciones@culture.gob.sv
Web Site: www.facebook.com/dpi.elsalvador
Founded: 1953
Subjects: Anthropology, Fiction, History, Music, Dance
ISBN Prefix(es): 978-99923-0

DPI, see Direccion de Publicaciones e Impresos (DPI)

UCA Editores+
PO Box 01-575, San Salvador
Tel: 22 10 66 50; 22 10 66 00 (ext 240) *Fax:* 22 10 66 50
E-mail: ucaeditores@gmail.com; distpubli@ued.uca.edu.sv
Web Site: www.ucaeditores.com.sv
Founded: 1975
Subjects: Architecture & Interior Design, Biography, Memoirs, Communications, Computer Science, Economics, Education, Electronics, Electrical Engineering, Engineering (General), Finance, Government, Political Science, History, Literature, Literary Criticism, Essays, Mathematics, Medicine, Nursing, Dentistry, Philosophy, Psychology, Psychiatry, Regional Interests, Religion - Other, Science (General), Social Sciences, Sociology, Theology
ISBN Prefix(es): 978-99923-34
Number of titles published annually: 10 Print
Total Titles: 400 Print
Bookshop(s): Libreria UCA (under Major Booksellers)

Universidad Centroamericana, see UCA Editores

Estonia

General Information

Capital: Tallinn
Language: Estonian, Russian, Finnish & English
Religion: Evangelical Lutheran
Population: 1.5 million
Currency: 100 Eurocents = 1 Euro

Export/Import Information: No export/import duties. 18% VAT on books (except educational & medical).
Copyright: Berne (see Copyright Conventions, pg viii)

Ajakirjade Kirjastus AS
Niine 11, 10414 Tallinn
Tel: 666 2600 *Fax:* 666 2557
E-mail: sekr@kirjastus.ee
Web Site: www.kirjastus.ee
Key Personnel
Chairman of the Board: Tonu Vaat *E-mail:* tonu.vaat@kirjastus.ee
Head, Publishing: Rain Siemer *Tel:* 666 2687
E-mail: rain.siemer@kirjastus.ee
Advertising Dir: Nele Laev *Tel:* 666 2605
E-mail: nele.laev@kirjastus.ee
Marketing & Distribution Dir: Sigrid Kupenko
Tel: 666 2684 *E-mail:* sigrid.kupenko@kirjastus.ee
Founded: 2000
Subjects: Biography, Memoirs, Cookery, Crafts, Games, Hobbies, Economics, Fiction, Gardening, Plants, Health, Nutrition, House & Home, Inspirational, Spirituality, Outdoor Recreation, Poetry, Psychology, Psychiatry, Social Sciences, Sociology, Sports, Athletics, Travel & Tourism
ISBN Prefix(es): 978-9985-9303; 978-9985-9536; 978-9985-9590; 978-9985-9633

Kirjastus Argo
Ravala pst 8, C114, 10143 Tallinn
Tel: 688 86 80 *Fax:* 688 86 81
E-mail: argokirjastus@argokirjastus.ee
Web Site: www.argokirjastus.ee
Subjects: Art, Education, Fiction, History, Language Arts, Linguistics, Literature, Literary Criticism, Essays, Mathematics, Music, Dance, Social Sciences, Sociology, Foreign Language
ISBN Prefix(es): 978-9985-9382; 978-9985-9407; 978-9985-9495

Atlex AS
Kivi 23, 51009 Tartu
Tel: 7 349 099 *Fax:* 7 348 915
E-mail: atlex@atlex.ee
Web Site: www.atlex.ee
Key Personnel
Contact: Kairi Saag *E-mail:* kairi.saag@atlex.ee
Founded: 1992
Subjects: Economics, Education, Fiction, History, Medicine, Nursing, Dentistry, Philosophy, Psychology, Psychiatry, Sports, Athletics, Forestry
ISBN Prefix(es): 978-9985-864; 978-9985-863; 978-9985-9335; 978-9985-9389; 978-9985-9417; 978-9985-9470; 978-9985-9489; 978-9985-9551; 978-9985-9574; 978-9985-9617

Kirjastus Avita
Pikk 68, 10133 Tallinn
Tel: 6275401; 6275403 (sales) *Fax:* 6411340
E-mail: info@avita.ee
Web Site: www.avita.ee
Key Personnel
Mng Dir: Marko Usler *E-mail:* marko@avita.ee
Founded: 1988
Subjects: Art, Chemistry, Chemical Engineering, Cookery, Education, Fiction, Geography, Geology, History, Language Arts, Linguistics, Literature, Literary Criticism, Essays, Mathematics, Music, Dance, Physics
ISBN Prefix(es): 978-9985-2; 978-9985-825

Kirjastus Canopus
Kihnu 2-52, 13913 Tallinn
Tel: 5543680; 6373663
E-mail: tonu.lember@canopus.ee
Web Site: www.canopus.ee
Subjects: Biography, Memoirs, Fiction, History
ISBN Prefix(es): 978-9985-9306; 978-9985-9548

Eesti Keele Sihtasutus (Estonian Language Institute)
Roosikrantsi 6, 10119 Tallinn
Tel: 6449271 *Fax:* 6449271
E-mail: eksa@eki.ee; ateena@eki.ee (sales)
Web Site: www.eksa.ee
Key Personnel
Chairman of the Board: Toomas Valjataga
E-mail: toomas@eki.ee
Technical Editor: Merle Moorlat *E-mail:* merle@eki.ee
Sales Manager: Sirje Hiie; Tiia Varol
Founded: 1993
Subjects: Language Arts, Linguistics, Literature, Literary Criticism, Essays
ISBN Prefix(es): 978-9985-79; 978-9985-811; 978-9985-851; 978-9985-9002; 978-9985-9218; 978-9985-9236; 978-9985-9245; 978-9985-9260; 978-9985-9284; 978-9985-9291; 978-9985-9313; 978-9985-9332

Eesti Piibliselts (Estonian Bible Society)+
Kaarli pst 9, 10119 Tallinn
Tel: 6311 671 *Fax:* 6311 438
E-mail: eps@eps.ee
Web Site: www.piibliselts.ee
Key Personnel
Secretary General: Jaan Barenson *Tel:* 509 4034
E-mail: jaan@eps.ee
Founded: 1813
Specialize in Estonian Bibles, New Testaments & portions, Bible related literature.
Membership(s): United Bible Societies.
Subjects: Biblical Studies, History
ISBN Prefix(es): 978-9985-889; 978-9985-9027
Number of titles published annually: 4 Print; 1 CD-ROM

Eesti Raamat Ou (Estonian Book)
Laki 26, 12915 Tallinn
Tel: 6587 889 *Fax:* 6587 889
E-mail: eestiraamat@gmail.com
Web Site: www.eestiraamat.ee
Founded: 1940
Subjects: Biography, Memoirs, Fiction, History, Literature, Literary Criticism, Essays, Poetry, Psychology, Psychiatry, Romance, Science Fiction, Fantasy, Estonian & World Literature Classics, Modern Estonian & Reference Literature
ISBN Prefix(es): 978-9985-65
Number of titles published annually: 50 Print
Total Titles: 932 Print

Eesti Rahvusraamatukogu (National Library of Estonia)
Tonismagi 2, 15189 Tallinn
Tel: 630 7611 *Fax:* 631 1410
E-mail: nlib@nlib.ee; info@nlib.ee
Web Site: www.nlib.ee
Key Personnel
Dir General: Janne Andresoo *Tel:* 630 7600
E-mail: janne.andresoo@nlib.ee
Dir, Library Services: Kristel Veimann *Tel:* 630 7416 *E-mail:* kristel.veimann@nlib.ee
Founded: 1918
Information services on humanities & social sciences; exhibition & conference service; book binding & conservation; photocopying; publishing.
Specialize in information services, exhibition & conference services, preservation, publishing for Parliament & other libraries.
Membership(s): CDNL; CENL; EIA; IALL; IAML; International Council of Archives; International Federation of Library Associations & Institutions (IFLA); LIBER.
Subjects: Art, History, Law, Library & Information Sciences, Music, Dance
ISBN Prefix(es): 978-9985-803; 978-9985-9217; 978-9985-9265; 978-9985-9334

Number of titles published annually: 50 Print; 13
CD-ROM; 2 E-Book
Total Titles: 13 CD-ROM; 8 E-Book

Egmont Estonia AS
Laki 26, 12915 Tallinn
Tel: 646 12 14 *Fax:* 646 00 23
E-mail: info@egmont.ee
Web Site: www.egmont.ee
Key Personnel
Chief Executive Officer: Svea Uusen
Editor-in-Chief: Tiit Heidmets
Sales Manager: Mihkel Reimaa
ISBN Prefix(es): 978-9985-53

EKSA, see Eesti Keele Sihtasutus

ELIC, see Estonian Literature Center (ELIC)

Kirjastus Elmatar AS
Viljandi mnt 11, 50412 Tartu
Tel: 5227188
E-mail: kirjastus@elmatar.ee
Web Site: www.elmatar.ee
Key Personnel
President: Alo Murutar *Tel:* 7409700
E-mail: alo@elmatar.ee
Editor: Katre Talviste *E-mail:* katre@elmatar.ee
Subjects: Literature, Literary Criticism, Essays,
Poetry, Science Fiction, Fantasy
ISBN Prefix(es): 978-9985-9354; 978-9985-832;
978-9985-9222; 978-9985-9238; 978-9985-
9248; 978-9985-9266; 978-9985-9292; 978-
9985-9325; 978-9985-9376; 978-9985-9405

Kirjastuse Ersen
Tartu mnt 84a-111, 10112 Tallinn
Tel: 6023086; 53924601 (cell) *Fax:* 6023085
E-mail: info@ersen.ee; rkaup@ersen.ee
Web Site: www.ersen.ee
Founded: 2000
Subjects: Crafts, Games, Hobbies, Criminology,
Health, Nutrition, Inspirational, Spirituality,
Medicine, Nursing, Dentistry, Romance, Sci-
ence Fiction, Fantasy, Alternative Medicine,
Horror, Parenting
ISBN Prefix(es): 978-9985-864; 978-9985-76

Estonian Academy Publishers (Eesti Teaduste
Akadeemia Kirjastus)
Unit of Estonian Academy of Sciences
Kohtu 6, 10130 Tallinn
Fax: 646 6026
Web Site: www.kirj.ee
Key Personnel
Dir: Ulo Niine *Tel:* 645 4504 *E-mail:* niine@kirj.
ee
Executive Editor: Virve Kurnitski *Tel:* 645 4156
E-mail: virve@kirj.ee
Sales Manager: Asta Tikerpae *Tel:* 645 4106
E-mail: asta@kirj.ee
Founded: 1994
Subjects: Archaeology, Biological Sciences,
Chemistry, Chemical Engineering, Civil En-
gineering, Computer Science, Earth Sciences,
Economics, Education, Energy, Engineering
(General), English as a Second Language, En-
vironmental Studies, Geography, Geology, His-
tory, Maritime, Mathematics, Mechanical En-
gineering, Natural History, Philosophy, Science
(General)
ISBN Prefix(es): 978-9985-50
Number of titles published annually: 30 Print
Total Titles: 388 Print

Estonian ISBN Agency
Tonismaegi 2, 15189 Tallinn
Tel: 630 7372 *Fax:* 631 1200
E-mail: isbn@nlib.ee
Web Site: www.nlib.ee

Key Personnel
Dir: Mai Valtna
Subjects: Architecture & Interior Design, Art,
Economics, Government, Political Science, His-
tory, Law, Social Sciences, Sociology
ISBN Prefix(es): 978-9949-10; 978-9985-60; 978-
9985-78; 978-9949-13; 978-9949-15; 978-9949-
18; 978-9949-30; 978-9949-21; 978-9949-33;
978-9949-38; 978-9949-81; 978-9949-88
Number of titles published annually: 500 Print;
100 Online; 100 E-Book
Parent Company: National Library of Estonia

Estonian Literature Center (ELIC) (Eesti
Kirjanduse Teabekeskus)
Sulevimagi 2-5, 10123 Tallinn
Fax: 6 314 871
E-mail: estlit@estlit.ee
Web Site: www.estlit.ee
Key Personnel
Dir: Ilvi Liive *Tel:* 6 314 870 *E-mail:* ilvi@estlit.
ee
Dir of Foreign Affairs: Kerti Tergem *Tel:* 6 314
872 *E-mail:* kerti@estlit.ee
Project Manager: Elle-Mari Talivee *E-mail:* elle-
mari.talivee@estlit.ee
Founded: 2001
Subjects: Literature, Literary Criticism, Essays,
Poetry, Regional Interests
ISBN Prefix(es): 978-9985-9368

Grenader Publishing House
Kopli 29, 10412 Tallin
Tel: 6 817 200 (marketing); 53 477 777
(Grenader Grupp OU); 6 817 201 (management
& editorial) *Fax:* 6 817 201
E-mail: info@phototour.ee; info@grenader.ee
Web Site: www.grenader.ee; www.phototour.ee
Key Personnel
Manager: Aimur Kruuse *E-mail:* aimur@grenader.
ee
Sales Manager: Kristina Grepp *E-mail:* kristina@
grenader.ee
Founded: 2003
Specialize in guide books & history books.
Subjects: History, Travel & Tourism
ISBN Prefix(es): 978-9949-411; 978-9949-422
Parent Company: Grenader Grupp OU
Imprints: PhotoTour

Hea Lugu
Narva mnt 11e, 10151 Tallinn
Tel: 661 3390
Web Site: www.healugu.ee
Key Personnel
Editor: Annika Reiljan *E-mail:* annika@healugu.
ee
Founded: 1994
Subjects: Cookery, Economics, Gardening, Plants,
Health, Nutrition, Home Economics
ISBN Prefix(es): 978-9985-64
Number of titles published annually: 30 Print

UU Kirjastus Ilmamaa+
Vanemuise 19, 51014 Tartu
Tel: 7427 290 *Fax:* 7427 320
E-mail: ilmamaa@ilmamaa.ee
Web Site: www.ilmamaa.ee
Key Personnel
Chairman: Hando Runnel
Dir: Mart Jagomagi *E-mail:* mj@ilmamaa.ee
Mng Editor: Liis Vaher *E-mail:* liis@ilmamaa.ee
Founded: 1993
Subjects: Fiction, History, Literature, Literary
Criticism, Essays, Nonfiction (General), Philos-
ophy, Poetry
ISBN Prefix(es): 978-9985-821; 978-9985-878;
978-9985-77; 978-9949-11
Number of titles published annually: 30 Print; 6
Online
Total Titles: 320 Print; 23 Online

Kirjastus Ilo
Paavli 1/Kopli 33, 10412 Tallinn
Tel: 6161 022; 6161 006 (sales) *Fax:* 6161 008
E-mail: info@tea.eu
Web Site: kirjastus.tea.ee
Key Personnel
President: Silva Tomingas *E-mail:* silva.
tomingas@tea.eu
Vice President & Art Dir: Kalev Tomingas
E-mail: kalev.tomingas@tea.eu
Foreign Rights: Kristel Klaar *E-mail:* kristel.
klaar@tea.eu
Founded: 1991
Subjects: Biography, Memoirs, Child Care & De-
velopment, Cookery, Crafts, Games, Hobbies,
Education, History, How-to, Human Relations,
Humor, Law, Nonfiction (General), Philoso-
phy, Psychology, Psychiatry, Self-Help, Social
Sciences, Sociology, Travel & Tourism
ISBN Prefix(es): 978-9985-57
Number of titles published annually: 100 Print
Total Titles: 1,000 Print
Parent Company: Tea Kirjastus

Kirjastus Koolibri (Koolibri Publishers Ltd)+
PO Box 1793, 11615 Tallin
Tel: 6515 300 *Fax:* 6515 301
E-mail: koolibri@koolibri.ee
Web Site: www.koolibri.ee
Key Personnel
Mng Dir: Kalle Kaljurand *Tel:* 6515 325
E-mail: kalle@koolibri.ee
Founded: 1991
Membership(s): European Educational Publishers
Group (EEPG).
Subjects: Chemistry, Chemical Engineering, Fic-
tion, Geography, Geology, History, Litera-
ture, Literary Criticism, Essays, Mathematics,
Physics, Science Fiction, Fantasy
ISBN Prefix(es): 978-9985-0
Number of titles published annually: 200 Print
Total Titles: 300 Print

Kirjastus Kunst (Kunst Publishers)+
Mustamae tee 5, 10616 Tallinn
Tel: 6411764 (editorial); 6411766 (sales)
E-mail: tellimused@kirjastuskunst.ee
Web Site: www.kirjastuskunst.ee
Founded: 1957
Specialize in art.
Subjects: Architecture & Interior Design, Art, Bi-
ography, Memoirs, Fiction, History, Social Sci-
ences, Sociology, Travel & Tourism, Culture,
Society
ISBN Prefix(es): 978-5-89920; 978-9949-407;
978-9949-437
Number of titles published annually: 40 Print

Medicina AS+
Laki 26, 12915 Tallinn
Tel: 6567660; 6567620 *Fax:* 6567620
Founded: 1993
Membership(s): Estonian Book Publishers Associ-
ation.
Subjects: Medicine, Nursing, Dentistry
ISBN Prefix(es): 978-9985-829
Parent Company: Kustannus Oy Duodecim, Kale-
vankatu 11A, PL 713, 00101 Helsinki, Finland

Menu Kirjastus
Tartu mnt 74, 10144 Tallinn
Tel: 670 0555
E-mail: info@menuk.ee
Web Site: menuk.ee
Key Personnel
Chief Executive Officer: Ain Lausmaa *Tel:* 504
9094 *E-mail:* ain@menuk.ee
Marketing & Advertising Sales: Helina Ounapuu
Tel: 516 6996 *E-mail:* helina@menuk.ee
Marketing & Sales, Books: Urvi Kaljas *Tel:* 534
93406 *E-mail:* urvi@menuk.ee
Founded: 2008

Subjects: Biography, Memoirs, Cookery, Health, Nutrition, History, Medicine, Nursing, Dentistry, Travel & Tourism
ISBN Prefix(es): 978-9949-470; 978-9949-495; 978-9949-9011

PhotoTour, *imprint of* Grenader Publishing House

Kirjastus Pilgrim (Pilgrim Publishing House)
Tonismagi 2, 10122 Tallinn
Tel: 600 6604; 528 7380; 501 9787 *Fax:* 600 6604
E-mail: info@pilgrimbooks.ee
Web Site: www.pilgrimbooks.ee
Founded: 2003
Subjects: Biography, Memoirs, Cookery, Economics, Fiction, Health, Nutrition, Inspirational, Spirituality, Philosophy, Poetry, Psychology, Psychiatry, Science (General), Travel & Tourism, Blog, Mythology
ISBN Prefix(es): 978-9985-9569; 978-9985-9532

Regio AS
Riia 24, 51010 Tartu
Tel: 738 7300 *Fax:* 737 7301
E-mail: regio@regio.ee
Web Site: www.regio.ee
Key Personnel
Chairman of the Board: Teet Jagomagi
    E-mail: teet.jagomagi@regio.ee
Chief Financial Officer: Aivar Parnpuu
    E-mail: aivar.parnpuu@regio.ee
Head of Dept: Leida Lepik *Tel:* 738 7320
    E-mail: leida.lepik@regio.ee
Production Manager & Cartographer: Merle Annov *Tel:* 661 3145 *E-mail:* merle.annov@regio.ee
Sales Manager: Erki Kokkota *Tel:* 738 7303
    E-mail: erki.kokkota@regio.ee
ISBN Prefix(es): 978-9985-817

Kirjastus SE&JS
Endla 3, 10122 Tallinn
Tel: 660 1894 *Fax:* 661 6262
E-mail: sejs@sejs.ee
Web Site: www.sejs.ee
Key Personnel
Publisher: Sirje Endre
Marketing Manager: Elle Veermae
Founded: 1992
Subjects: Biography, Memoirs, History, Music, Dance, Poetry
ISBN Prefix(es): 978-9985-854

Sinisukk AS+
Betooni 14, 11415 Tallinn
Tel: 602 5950 *Fax:* 602 5950
E-mail: sinisukk@sinisukk.ee
Web Site: www.sinisukk.ee
Key Personnel
President: Marie Edala *E-mail:* marie@sinisukk.ee
Founded: 1992
Subjects: Animals, Pets, Astrology, Occult, Biography, Memoirs, Child Care & Development, Cookery, Crafts, Games, Hobbies, Fiction, Film, Video, Gardening, Plants, Health, Nutrition, House & Home, How-to, Nonfiction (General), Psychology, Psychiatry, Self-Help
ISBN Prefix(es): 978-9985-73; 978-9985-812; 978-9949-14
Number of titles published annually: 180 Print
Total Titles: 212 Print

Tallinn Ulikooli Kirjastus (Tallinn University Press)
Division of Tallinn University
Narva mnt 29, 10120 Tallinn
Tel: 640 9124
E-mail: tlupress@tlu.ee

Web Site: www.tlupress.com
Key Personnel
Editor-in-Chief: Rebekka Lotman *Tel:* 640 9243
    E-mail: rebekka.lotman@tlu.ee
Customer Service Manager: Liina Paroll
    E-mail: liina.paroll@tlu.ee
ISBN Prefix(es): 978-9985-58

Tallinna Tehnikaulikooli Raamatukogu (Tallinn University of Technology Library)
Akadeemia tee 1, 12618 Tallinn
Tel: 620 3556 *Fax:* 620 3561
E-mail: kontakt@lib.ttu.ee
Web Site: www.ttu.ee/en/?id=24873
Key Personnel
Dir: Juri Jars *Tel:* 620 3564 *E-mail:* juri.jars@ttu.ee
Deputy Dir: Gerda Koidla *Tel:* 620 3550
    E-mail: gerda.koidla@ttu.ee
Founded: 1919
Also a research library.
Membership(s): IATUL; UNICA.
Subjects: Biography, Memoirs, Chemistry, Chemical Engineering, Civil Engineering, Earth Sciences, Economics, Electronics, Electrical Engineering, Engineering (General), Library & Information Sciences, Physical Sciences, Science (General)
ISBN Prefix(es): 978-9949-23
Number of titles published annually: 100 Print; 3,000 Online
Parent Company: Tallinna Tehnikaulikool, Ehitajate tee 5, 19086 Tallinn

Tanapaev Publishers
Parnu mnt 20, 10141 Tallinn
Tel: 6691 890 *Fax:* 6691 891
E-mail: tnp@tnp.ee
Web Site: www.tnp.ee
Key Personnel
Chairman of the Board: Toomas Leito *Tel:* 6691 897 *E-mail:* toomas@tnp.ee
Editor-in-Chief: Tauno Vahter *Tel:* 6691 894
    E-mail: tauno@tnp.ee
Marketing & Sales Manager: Cia-Helena Meldo
    E-mail: cia@tnp.ee
Founded: 1999
Subjects: Biography, Memoirs, Fiction, Government, Political Science, Health, Nutrition, History, Humor, Social Sciences, Sociology, Current Events, Popular Science
ISBN Prefix(es): 978-9985-62; 978-9985-9212; 978-9985-9243; 978-9985-9254; 978-9985-9269; 978-9985-9273; 978-9985-9288; 978-9985-9312; 978-9985-9327; 978-9985-9329

Tartu Ulikooli Kirjastus (University of Tartu Press)
W Struve 1, 50091 Tartu
Tel: 737 5945 *Fax:* 737 5944
E-mail: tyk@ut.ee
Web Site: www.tyk.ee
Key Personnel
Mng Dir: Ulle Ergma *Tel:* 737 5961 *E-mail:* ulle.ergma@ut.ee
Editor-in-Chief: Ivo Volt *Tel:* 737 5946
    E-mail: ivo.volt@ut.ee
Subjects: Art, Economics, Language Arts, Linguistics, Law, Mathematics, Medicine, Nursing, Dentistry, Philosophy, Theology
ISBN Prefix(es): 978-9949-11; 978-9949-32; 978-9949-19

Kirjastus TEA AS (TEA Publishers)+
Paavli 1/Kopli 33, 10412 Tallinn
Tel: 616 1022; 616 1006 (sales); 616 1024 (editorial) *Fax:* 616 1008
E-mail: info@tea.eu
Web Site: kirjastus.tea.ee
Key Personnel
Chairman: Silva Tomingas *Tel:* 6161 015
    E-mail: silva.tomingas@tea.eu

Sales Manager: Riinalt Hanson *Tel:* 6677 852
    E-mail: riinalt.hanson@tea.eu
Founded: 1991
Publishing & design of books & dictionaries on diskettes. Specialties include textbooks, practice books & grammar books.
Subjects: Guide Books
ISBN Prefix(es): 978-9985-71; 978-9985-843; 978-9985-9003; 978-9985-9029
Number of titles published annually: 50 Print; 1 CD-ROM; 3 Audio
Total Titles: 130 Print; 1 CD-ROM; 10 Audio
Branch Office(s)
Parnu, Contact: Sirje Manna *Tel:* 4476303
Betooni 9, 51014 Tartu *Tel:* 7307959
    Fax: 7307970
Bookshop(s): 27 Narva mnt, Tallinn, Contact: Mrs Ene Tiidelepp *Tel:* 6426019

Kirjastus Tiritamm (Tiritamm Publishing)
Endla 3, 10122 Tallinn
Tel: 6563 570
E-mail: info@tiritamm.ee
Web Site: www.tiritamm.ee
Founded: 1991
Subjects: Literature, Literary Criticism, Essays, Folklore
ISBN Prefix(es): 978-9985-55

Tuum+
Harju 1, 10146 Tallinn
Tel: 627 6427
E-mail: info@tuum.ee
Web Site: www.tuum.ee
Key Personnel
Chief Executive Officer: Britta Korzets
Founded: 1992
Subjects: Human Relations, Literature, Literary Criticism, Essays, Natural History, Philosophy, Poetry, Psychology, Psychiatry, Science Fiction, Fantasy
ISBN Prefix(es): 978-9985-802

Kirjastus Valgus+
Tonismagi 3A, 10119 Tallinn
Tel: 6 177 015
E-mail: info@kirjastusvalgus.ee
Web Site: www.kirjastusvalgus.ee
Key Personnel
Editor-in-Chief: Madli Vallikivi-Pats
    E-mail: madli@kirjastusvalgus.ee
Founded: 1965
Subjects: Agriculture, Animals, Pets, Archaeology, Architecture & Interior Design, Biological Sciences, Child Care & Development, Cookery, Crafts, Games, Hobbies, Electronics, Electrical Engineering, Engineering (General), English as a Second Language, Gardening, Plants, Geography, Geology, Health, Nutrition, History, Medicine, Nursing, Dentistry, Philosophy, Psychology, Psychiatry, Science (General), Handbooks, Healthcare, Popular Science
ISBN Prefix(es): 978-5-440; 978-9985-68

Varrak AS
Parnu mnt 67a, 7 Korrus, 10134 Tallinn
Tel: 6161 035 *Fax:* 6161 030
E-mail: varrak@varrak.ee
Web Site: www.varrak.ee
Key Personnel
Dir: Priit Maide *E-mail:* priit@varrak.ee
Production Dir: Andrus Maide *E-mail:* andrus@varrak.ee
Editor-in-Chief: Krista Kaer *Tel:* 6161 038
    E-mail: krista@varrak.ee
Founded: 1991
Subjects: Cookery, Criminology, Fiction, History, Philosophy, Poetry, Science Fiction, Fantasy
ISBN Prefix(es): 978-9985-3; 978-9985-807
Number of titles published annually: 200 Print

Bookshop(s): Kristiine Kaubanduskeskus, Endla
45, 10615 Tallinn; Ravala 6, 10143 Tallinn
Warehouse: Tiigi 26, Juri, Rae vald, Harjumaa, Contact: Thea Truverk *Tel:* 6018 091
E-mail: thea@varrak.ee

Ethiopia

General Information

Capital: Addis Ababa
Language: Amharic (official), English also widely
used
Religion: Ethiopian Orthodox
Population: 51.1 million
Bank Hours: 0830-1230, 1430-1730 Monday-
Friday; 0830-1230 Saturday
Shop Hours: Addis Ababa: 0900-1300, 1500-
2000 Monday-Saturday. Asmara: 0800-1300,
1600-2000 Monday-Friday
Currency: 100 cents = 1 birr
Export/Import Information: No tarriff on books,
but additional taxes. Advertising subject to cus-
toms and same taxes. No import license re-
quired but Exchange Payment License neces-
sary.
Copyright: No copyright conventions signed

Addis Ababa University Press
PO Box 1176, Addis Ababa University, Addis
Ababa
Tel: (011) 1239746
E-mail: infolib@lib.aau.edu.et
Web Site: www.aau.edu.et
Key Personnel
Dir: Dr Yacob Arsano *Tel:* 920192191 (cell)
E-mail: yacob.arsano@aau.edu.et
Editor: Ato Berhanu Debotch *Tel:* 911678904
(cell) *E-mail:* bahruuuu@gmail.com
Founded: 1968
Publishing house of Addis Ababa University.
Membership(s): ABC; African Association of Sci-
ence Editors; APNET; Ethiopian Publishers
Association.
Subjects: Biography, Memoirs, Chemistry, Chem-
ical Engineering, Geography, Geology, Health,
Nutrition, History, Language Arts, Linguistics,
Literature, Literary Criticism, Essays, Science
(General), Technology, Botany, Climatology,
Diary, Hydrology, Public Health
ISBN Prefix(es): 978-99944-52
Total Titles: 18 Print
Associate Companies: Norwegian University of
Science & Technology, Norway; Lund Univer-
sity Press, Sweden; James Currey Publishers,
United Kingdom; Illinois University Press, IL,
United States

**Organization for Social Science Research in
Eastern & Southern Africa (OSSREA)**
PO Box 31971, Addis Ababa
Tel: (011) 123 94 84 *Fax:* (011) 122 39 21
E-mail: info@ossrea.net
Web Site: www.ossrea.net
Key Personnel
Editor: Mr Matebu Tadesse
Founded: 1980
Subjects: Anthropology, Education, Social Sci-
ences, Sociology, Women's Studies
ISBN Prefix(es): 978-99944-55
Number of titles published annually: 15 Print; 5
Online
Total Titles: 500 Print

OSSREA, see Organization for Social Science
Research in Eastern & Southern Africa
(OSSREA)

Faroe Islands

General Information

Capital: Torshavn
Language: Faroese, Danish
Religion: Predominantly Evangelical Lutheran
Population: 48,856
Currency: Danish Kroner

BFL, see Bokadeild Foroya Laerarafelags (BFL)

Bokadeild Foroya Laerarafelags (BFL)
Pedda vid Steingota 9, FO100 Torshavn
Tel: 61 76 44 *Fax:* 31 96 44
E-mail: bfl@bfl.fo
Web Site: www.bfl.fo
Key Personnel
Mng Dir: Niels Jakup Thomsen
E-mail: nielsjakup@bfl.fo
Editor: Marna Jacobsen *E-mail:* marna@bfl.fo;
Turid Kjolbro *E-mail:* turid@bfl.fo
Magazine Editor & Marketing: Beinta Johannesen
E-mail: beinta@bfl.fo
Founded: 1956
Specialize in children's & youth literature.
ISBN Prefix(es): 978-99918-1

Faroe University Press
JC Svabos Gota 14, FO100 Torshavn
Mailing Address: PO Box 272, FO110 Torshavn
Tel: 352500 *Fax:* 352501
E-mail: frodskapur@setur.fo; setur@setur.fo
Web Site: www.setur.fo/frodskapur
Key Personnel
Dir: Annika Solvara
Founded: 2005
Specialize in scientific publications.
Subjects: Humanities, Natural Sciences
ISBN Prefix(es): 978-99918-65; 978-99918-41

Fiji

General Information

Capital: Suva
Language: Fijian & Hindi. English widely spoken
Religion: Christian (mainly Methodist) with large
minority of Hindus
Population: 800,000
Bank Hours: 1000-1500 Monday-Thursday; 1000-
1600 Friday
Shop Hours: 0800-1630 or later Monday-Friday;
early closing Wednesday or Saturday
Currency: 100 cents = 1 Fiji dollar
Export/Import Information: No tariffs on books
and advertising. No import licenses. Exchange
control by Reserve Bank of Fiji; no specific
Exchange license required and authorized
banks perform transaction upon application.
Copyright: Berne, UCC (see Copyright Conventions, pg viii)

Islands Business International
PO Box 12718, Suva
Tel: 330 3108 *Fax:* 330 1423
E-mail: editor@ibi.com.fj
Web Site: www.islandsbusiness.com
Key Personnel
Mng Dir & Publisher: Godfrey Scoullar
Group Advertising & Marketing Manager: Sharon
Stretton
Editor: Dev Nadkarni
Writer: Dionisia Tabureguci

Subjects: Aeronautics, Aviation, Agriculture,
Business, Education, Government, Political Sci-
ence, Sports, Athletics, Technology
ISBN Prefix(es): 978-982-206

The University of the South Pacific+
Marketing, Development, Communications &
Alumni Off, Laucala Campus, Suva
Tel: 323 2148 *Fax:* 323 1551
Web Site: www.usp.ac.fj
Key Personnel
Dir: Jaindra Karan *Tel:* 323 2226
E-mail: karan_j@usp.ac.fj
Founded: 1968
Subjects: Education, Environmental Studies, Nat-
ural History, Regional Interests
ISBN Prefix(es): 978-982-02; 978-982-03; 978-
982-01

USP, see The University of the South Pacific

Finland

General Information

Capital: Helsinki
Language: Finnish and Swedish (officially bilin-
gual); English and German spoken widely
Religion: Predominantly Evangelical Lutheran
Population: 5.2 million
Bank Hours: 0915-1615 Monday-Friday
Shop Hours: 0900-1700 or later Monday-Friday;
0900-1600 (1400 in summer) Saturday
Currency: 100 Eurocents = 1 Euro
Export/Import Information: Member of the Eu-
ropean Union. 12% VAT on books. No import
licenses required on books. No exchange con-
trols.
Copyright: UCC, Berne, Florence (see Copyright
Conventions, pg viii)

Aalto-yliopisto, Taideteollinen korkeakoulu
(Aalto University School of Arts Design &
Architecture)
PL 31000, 00076 Aalto
Tel: (050) 431 8135
E-mail: artbooks@aalto.fi
Web Site: www.taik.fi/kirjakauppa
Key Personnel
Publishing Editor & Marketing: Sanna Tyyri-
Pohjonen
Mng Editor: Annu Ahonen *E-mail:* annu.
ahonen@aalto.fi
Publication Coordinator: Pia Alapeteri
E-mail: pia.alapeteri@aalto.fi
Subjects: Architecture & Interior Design, Art,
Education, Fashion, Film, Video, History, Pho-
tography, Art Education, Ceramics & Glass,
Fashion & Textiles, Graphic Art, History of
Art, Industrial Art History & Theory
ISBN Prefix(es): 978-951-558; 978-951-9384
Bookshop(s): Hameentie 135 C, 6 kerros, 00560
Helsinki

**Abo Akademis forlag - Abo Akademi
University Press**
Tavastgatan 13, 20500 Abo
Tel: (02) 215 3478
E-mail: forlaget@abo.fi
Web Site: www.abo.fi/forskning/en/publikationer
Key Personnel
Executive Officer: Inger Hassel *E-mail:* inger.
hassel@abo.fi
Founded: 1987
Also publish doctoral dissertations.
Subjects: Science (General)
ISBN Prefix(es): 978-951-9498; 978-952-9616;
978-951-765
Number of titles published annually: 25 Print

Aikamedia Oy (Aikamedia Ltd)
Heikkilantie 177, 42700 Keuruu
Mailing Address: PL 99, 42701 Keuruu
Tel: (020) 7619 800 *Fax:* (014) 7514 757
E-mail: asiakaspalvelu@aikamedia.fi
Web Site: www.aikamedia.fi
Key Personnel
President: Jari Vieltojarvi *Tel:* (040) 0533 036
  E-mail: jari.vieltojarvi@aikamedia.fi
Publishing Manager: Outi M Katto *Tel:* (040)
  0618 601 *E-mail:* outi.katto@aikamedia.fi
Production: Pertti Lukkarila *Tel:* (050) 0663 987
  E-mail: pertti.lukkarila@aikamedia.fr
Founded: 1995
Christian books, music & periodicals.
Subjects: Biography, Memoirs, Fiction, History,
  Inspirational, Spirituality
ISBN Prefix(es): 978-951-605; 978-951-606
Branch Office(s)
Jaspilankatu 2, 04250 Kerava

Alma Talent Oy
Alvar Aallon katu 3C, 00100 Helsinki
Mailing Address: PL 830, 00101 Helsinki
Tel: (010) 665 101
Web Site: www.almatalent.fi
Key Personnel
Chief Executive Officer: Juha-Petri Loimovuori
  E-mail: juha-petri.loimovuori@almatalent.fi
Editor-in-Chief: Arno Ahosniemi *E-mail:* arno.
  ahosniemi@almatalent.fi
Founded: 1938
Subjects: Business, Law
ISBN Prefix(es): 978-951-640; 978-952-14; 978-
  951-8986; 978-951-762
Parent Company: Alma Media Corp

Art House Oy
Blvd 19, 1 & 2 kerros, 00120 Helsinki
Tel: (09) 694 0752 *Fax:* (09) 693 3762
E-mail: info@arthouse.fi; myynti@arthouse.fi
Web Site: arthouse.fi; kauppa.tietosanoma.fi
Key Personnel
President: Heikki Haavikko *Tel:* (050) 582 8261
Publishing Manager: Urpu Strellman *Tel:* (09)
  694 6501
Mng Editor: Nana Sironen *Tel:* (09) 694 6500
Marketing: Tuija Lappalainen
Founded: 1975
Publish Finnish & translated literature, science
  books, health books, cookbooks & Roald
  Dahl's children's books. Specialize in histori-
  cal books.
Subjects: Biological Sciences, Chemistry, Chemi-
  cal Engineering, Cookery, Fiction, Film, Video,
  Health, Nutrition, History, Mathematics, Music,
  Dance, Nonfiction (General), Physics, Religion
  - Other, Science (General), Science Fiction,
  Fantasy, Comics, Horror
ISBN Prefix(es): 978-951-884; 978-951-96086;
  978-951-96135; 978-952-481

Atena Kustannus Oy+
Nikolainkulma Asemakatu 6, 2 kerros, 40100 Jy-
  vaskyla
Mailing Address: PL 436, 40101 Jyvaskyla
Tel: (010) 4214 200
E-mail: atena@atena.fi
Web Site: www.atenakustannus.fi
Key Personnel
Publisher: Ville Rauvola *Tel:* (010) 4214 204
  E-mail: ville.rauvola@atena.fi
Marketing & Sales: Minna Vepsalainen *Tel:* (010)
  4214 203 *E-mail:* minna.vepsalainen@atena.fi
Founded: 1986
Subjects: Biography, Memoirs, Cookery, Crafts,
  Games, Hobbies, Fiction, History, Humor, Lit-
  erature, Literary Criticism, Essays, Nonfiction
  (General), Cultural History, Current Affairs,
  Popular Science
ISBN Prefix(es): 978-951-9362; 978-951-796

Basam Books Oy+
Hameentie 155 A 6, 00561 Helsinki
Mailing Address: PL 42, 00561 Helsinki
Tel: (09) 7579 3839 *Fax:* (09) 7579 3839
E-mail: info@basambooks.com
Web Site: www.basambooks.com
Key Personnel
Publisher: Batu Samaletdin *E-mail:* batu.
  samaletdin@basambooks.com
Foreign Rights: Tuomas Lojamo *E-mail:* tuomas.
  lojamo@basambooks.com
Founded: 1993
Subjects: Fiction, Literature, Literary Criticism,
  Essays, Nonfiction (General), Philosophy, Po-
  etry, Psychology, Psychiatry
ISBN Prefix(es): 978-952-9842; 978-952-5534;
  978-952-5734
Number of titles published annually: 25 Print

Kustannus Oy Duodecim (Duodecim Medical
  Publications Ltd)+
Kaivokatu 10 A, 00100 Helsinki
Mailing Address: PL 874, 00101 Helsinki
Tel: (09) 618 851 *Fax:* (09) 6188 5400
Web Site: www.duodecim.fi
Key Personnel
Mng Dir: Pekka Mustonen *Tel:* (09) 6188 5411
  E-mail: pekka.mustonen@duodecim.fi
Administrative Manager: Sari Saarijarvi
  E-mail: sari.saarijarvi@duodecim.fi
Business Manager: Timo Haikonen *E-mail:* timo.
  haikonen@duodecim.fi
Marketing Manager: Liisa Snicker *E-mail:* liisa.
  snicker@duodecim.fi
Founded: 1984
Membership(s): Finnish Book Publishers Associa-
  tion.
Subjects: Health, Nutrition, Medicine, Nursing,
  Dentistry, Psychology, Psychiatry
ISBN Prefix(es): 978-951-656; 978-951-8917;
  978-951-9347
Number of titles published annually: 15 Print
Parent Company: Suomalainen Laakariseura
  Duodecim, Kalevankatu 11 A, 00100 Helsinki

Edita Publishing Oy+
Subsidiary of Nordic Morning
Porkkalankatu 22 A, 00043 Helsinki
Mailing Address: PL 700, 00043 Edita
Tel: (020) 450 00; (020) 450 05 (customer ser-
  vice) *Fax:* (020) 450 2380
E-mail: asiakaspalvelu.publishing@edita.fi
  (customer service)
Web Site: www.editapublishing.fi
Key Personnel
Mng Dir: Paivi Hietanen *E-mail:* paivi.hietanen@
  edita.fi
Founded: 1859
Subjects: Chemistry, Chemical Engineering,
  Health, Nutrition, History, Mathematics, Non-
  fiction (General), Philosophy, Psychology, Psy-
  chiatry, Religion - Other
ISBN Prefix(es): 978-951-37; 978-951-859; 978-
  951-860; 978-951-861
Bookshop(s): Annankatu 44, 00100 Helsinki

Egmont Kustannus Oy AB
Vuorikatu 14 A, 4 kerros, 00100 Helsinki
Mailing Address: PL 1269, 00100 Helsinki
Tel: (0201) 332 222 *Fax:* (0201) 332 360
E-mail: tilaajapalvelu@egmont.fi; palaute@
  egmont.fi
Web Site: www.egmontkustannus.fi
Key Personnel
Publishing Dir: Jukka Torvinen *Tel:* (0201) 332
  244 *E-mail:* jukka.torvinen@egmont.fi
Founded: 1971
ISBN Prefix(es): 978-951-9112; 978-951-876;
  978-951-95793; 978-951-95794; 978-951-
  95231; 978-951-95232; 978-952-469

Fenix-Kustannus Oy+
PL 14, 02201 Espoo
Tel: (050) 0448146
E-mail: tilaus@fenixkustannus.fi
Founded: 1993
Subjects: Nonfiction (General)
ISBN Prefix(es): 978-951-862

Oy Finn Lectura AB
Italahdenkatu 18 A, 00210 Helsinki
Tel: (09) 74151 005 *Fax:* (09) 1464 370
E-mail: info@finnlectura.fi
Web Site: www.finnlectura.fi
Key Personnel
Customer & Communications Officer: Jenni
  Honkonen *E-mail:* jenni.honkonen@finnlectura.
  fi
Founded: 1986
Subjects: Child Care & Development, Education,
  Language Arts, Linguistics, Psychology, Psy-
  chiatry, Foreign Language, Social Skills
ISBN Prefix(es): 978-951-792; 978-951-8905
Distributed by Kustannustaito

Fontana Media Ab+
Sandvikskajen 13, 00180 Helsinki
Tel: (09) 612 615 30 *Fax:* (09) 278 4138
E-mail: redaktionen@fontanamedia.fi; info@
  fontanamedia.fi
Web Site: www.fontanamedia.fi
Key Personnel
Publishing Dir: Pian Wistbacka *Tel:* (040)
  8315797 *E-mail:* pian.wistbacka@
  fontanamedia.fi
Editor: Ulrika Hansson *Tel:* (040) 8316322
Founded: 1920
Subjects: Biblical Studies, Psychology, Psychiatry,
  Religion - Protestant
ISBN Prefix(es): 978-951-550
Distributor for Verbum-Sweden; Libris, Sweden

Gaudeamus Oy
Fabianinkatu 28, 2 kerros, 00100 Helsinki
Tel: (09) 50 540 1303
E-mail: info@gaudeamus.fi
Web Site: www.gaudeamus.fi
Key Personnel
Publisher: Leena Kaakinen *E-mail:* leena.
  kaakinen@gaudeamus.fi
Marketing Manager: Riitta Korpipaa *Tel:* (09) 050
  386 4462 *E-mail:* riitta.korpipaa@gaudeamus.fi
Subjects: Art, Education, Health, Nutrition, His-
  tory, Literature, Literary Criticism, Essays, Phi-
  losophy, Religion - Other, Science (General)
ISBN Prefix(es): 978-951-662; 978-952-495
Number of titles published annually: 50 Print
Bookshop(s): Vuorikatu 7, 00100 Helsinki
  Tel: (09) 50 466 1012

Gummerus Publishing Co+
Lapinlahdenkatu 1 C, 7 kerros, 00180 Helsinki
Mailing Address: PL 749, 00101 Helsinki
Tel: (010) 6836 200
E-mail: info@gummerus.fi
Web Site: www.gummerus.fi
Key Personnel
President: Mikko Meronen *Tel:* (010) 6836 220
Publishing Dir: Anna Baijars *Tel:* (010) 6836 207
Chief Financial Officer: Esa Pikkarainen
  Tel: (010) 6836 638
Communications & Marketing: Katja Leino
  Tel: (010) 6836 204
Founded: 1872
Subjects: Fiction, Nonfiction (General)
ISBN Prefix(es): 978-951-20; 978-951-95447;
  978-952-06
Number of titles published annually: 160 Print

Helsinki University Press, see Gaudeamus Oy

Herattaja-Yhdistys
Kosolankatu 1, 62100 Lapua
Mailing Address: PL 21, 62101 Lapua
Tel: (06) 433 5700 Fax: (06) 438 7430
E-mail: hy@h-y.fi
Web Site: www.h-y.fi
Key Personnel
Executive Dir: Simo Juntunen Tel: (050) 337
1535 E-mail: simo.juntunen@h-y.fi
Mng Editor: Johanna Sointula Tel: (040) 719
7664 E-mail: johanna.sointula@h-y.fi
Founded: 1892
Subjects: Biblical Studies, History, Literature,
Literary Criticism, Essays, Poetry, Religion -
Protestant, Theology
ISBN Prefix(es): 978-951-878; 978-951-9012;
978-951-9013; 978-951-9014
Branch Office(s)
Ratakatu 1a A 3, 00120 Helsinki

Into Kustannus Oy
Kalevankatu 43, 00180 Helsinki
Tel: (040) 179 5297
E-mail: myynti@intokustannus.fi
Web Site: intokustannus.fi
Key Personnel
Publisher & Chief Executive Officer: Jaana
Airaksinen Tel: (045) 633 4495 E-mail: jaana.
airaksinen@intokustannus.fi
Publisher: Mika Ronkko Tel: (050) 436 2170
E-mail: mika.ronkko@intokustannus.fi
Dir, Sales: Antti Kurko Tel: (040) 834 0286
E-mail: antti.kurko@intokustannus.fi
Marketing & Communications Manager: Nora
Varjama Tel: (050) 547 6868 E-mail: nora.
varjama@intokustannus.fi
Founded: 2007
Subjects: Biography, Memoirs, Economics, Fic-
tion, Government, Political Science, History,
Music, Dance, Mysteries, Suspense, Nonfiction
(General), Science Fiction, Fantasy
ISBN Prefix(es): 978-952-264
Number of titles published annually: 70 Print

K-kauppiasliitto ry+
Kruunuvuorenkatu 5A, 00160 Helsinki
Tel: (010) 53010 Fax: (010) 533 6238
Web Site: www.k-kauppiasliitto.fi
Key Personnel
President: Joana Hertsberg Tel: (010) 533 6289
E-mail: joana.hertsberg@k-kauppiasliitto.fi
Marketing: Tommi Tanhuanpaa Tel: (010)
53 36218 E-mail: tommi.tanhuanpaa@k-
kauppiasliitto.fi
Founded: 1912
Publishing House of the Finnish Retailers Associ-
ation.
Subjects: Cookery, Crafts, Games, Hobbies,
House & Home
ISBN Prefix(es): 978-951-635; 978-952-204

Karas-Sana Oy+
PL 48, 08101 Lohja
Tel: (0207) 681 610 Fax: (0420) 793 435
E-mail: krs@sana.fi
Web Site: www.kansanraamattuseura.fi
Key Personnel
Mng Dir: Terhi Rajala Tel: (0207) 681 614
E-mail: terhi.rajala@sana.fi
Founded: 1974
Subjects: Human Relations, Religion - Protestant,
Self-Help
ISBN Prefix(es): 978-951-655
Number of titles published annually: 15 Print; 2
CD-ROM
Total Titles: 172 Print; 12 CD-ROM; 1 Audio
Parent Company: Kansan Raamattuseura

Karisto Oy+
Paroistentie 2, 13600 Hameenlinna
Mailing Address: PL 102, 13101 Hameenlinna
Tel: (03) 63 151 Fax: (03) 616 1565
E-mail: kustannusliike@karisto.fi
Web Site: www.karisto.fi
Key Personnel
Mng Dir: Mika Kotilainen Tel: (03) 631 5220
E-mail: mika.kotilainen@karisto.fi
Publishing Dir: Sanna Vartiainen Tel: (03) 631
5211 E-mail: sanna.vartiainen@karisto.fi
Founded: 1900
Subjects: Fiction, Nonfiction (General)
ISBN Prefix(es): 978-951-23
Warehouse: Kirjavalitys Oy, Hakakalliontie 10,
05800 Hyvinkaeae

Kirjatoimi+
Ketarantie 4, 33680 Tampere
Mailing Address: PL 94, 33101 Tampere
Tel: (03) 361 1200 Fax: (03) 360 0454
Key Personnel
Acting Vice President: Timo Flink Tel: (03) 361
1233
Marketing Manager: Hannu Kinnunen Tel: (03)
361 1242 E-mail: hannu.kinnunen@sdafin.fi
Founded: 1897
Specialize in Christian children's books.
Subjects: Health, Nutrition, Religion - Protestant
ISBN Prefix(es): 978-951-629
Parent Company: Suomen Adventtikirkko

Koala-Kustannus Oy+
Kulosaarentie 8 C 20, 00570 Helsinki
Tel: (050) 408 1590 Fax: (09) 684 5034
E-mail: info@koalakustannus.fi
Web Site: www.koalakustannus.fi
Founded: 1997
Membership(s): Finnish Book Publishers Associa-
tion.
Subjects: Aeronautics, Aviation, Film, Video, His-
tory, Maritime, Military Science, Music, Dance,
Nonfiction (General), Sports, Athletics
ISBN Prefix(es): 978-952-5186
Number of titles published annually: 20 Print; 1
CD-ROM
Total Titles: 40 Print

Kustannusosakeyhtio Tammi (Tammi
Publishers)
Korkeavuorenkatu 37, 00130 Helsinki
Mailing Address: PL 410, 00101 Helsinki
Tel: (010) 5060 300 Fax: (010) 5060 399
Web Site: www.tammi.fi
Key Personnel
Dir: Outi Makinen Tel: (010) 5060 323
E-mail: outi.makinen@tammi.fi
Publishing Dir, Non-Fiction: Tuija Nurmiranta
Tel: (010) 5060 324 E-mail: tuija.nurmiranta@
tammi.fi
Sales & Marketing Dir: Anne-Marie Suomalainen
Tel: (010) 5060 330
Communications: Satu-Maria Rastas E-mail: satu-
maria.rastas@tammi.fi
Founded: 1943
Subjects: Fiction, Nonfiction (General)
ISBN Prefix(es): 978-951-30; 978-951-31
Number of titles published annually: 400 Print
Parent Company: Bonnier Group
Bookshop(s): Tammikauppa
Book Club(s): Lasten Parhaat Kirjat, PL 314,
00101 Helsinki Tel: (09) 6937 6600 Fax: (09)
6944 186 E-mail: lastenparhaatkirjat@tammi.fi;
Unelmakerho, PL 314, 00101 Helsinki
Warehouse: WSOY Kirjakeskus, Teollisuustie 4,
06100 Porvoo
Orders to: WSOY Kirjakeskus, Teollisuustie 4,
06100 Porvoo

Kuva ja Sana Oy+
Pajuniityntie 1, 00320 Helsinki
Mailing Address: PL 86, 00381 Helsinki
Tel: (09) 85674999 Fax: (09) 85674950
E-mail: tilaukset@kuvajasana.fi
Web Site: www.kuvajasana.fi

Key Personnel
Chief Executive Officer & President: Pekka Haa-
pasaari E-mail: pekka.haapasaari@kuvajasana.fi
Founded: 1942
Subjects: Government, Political Science, Religion
- Other, Social Sciences, Sociology
ISBN Prefix(es): 978-951-9204; 978-951-9072;
978-951-9073; 978-951-9203; 978-951-585
Associate Companies: Patmos International
Subsidiaries: Ideakustannus
Bookshop(s): Christian Center, Harjukatu 2,
00500 Helsinki

Lasten Keskus ja Kirjapaja Oy (Children's
Centre Ltd)
Italahdenkatu 27 A, 3 kerros, 00210 Helsinki
Tel: (09) 6877 450 Fax: (09) 6877 4545
E-mail: tilaukset@lastenkeskus.fi
Web Site: www.lastenkeskus.fi
Key Personnel
President: Juha-Pekka Heinonen Tel: (09) 6877
4540
Publishing Manager: Eeva Johansson Tel: (09)
6877 4515
Sales & Marketing Coordinator: Sari Rautanen
Tel: (09) 6877 4563
Communications: Marja-Liisa Saraste Tel: (09)
6877 4568
Founded: 1974
Subjects: Biblical Studies, Child Care & Devel-
opment, Crafts, Games, Hobbies, Education,
Human Relations, Religion - Protestant
ISBN Prefix(es): 978-951-627; 978-951-626; 978-
951-607; 978-951-621; 978-951-625
Associate Companies: Suomen Kirkko-Mediat Oy
Subsidiaries: Pentella Oy
Bookshop(s): Lasten Kirjakauppa, Fredrikinkatu
61, 00100 Helsinki (Children's Bookstore)

Like Kustannus Oy (Like Publishing Ltd)+
Subsidiary of Kustannusosakeyhtio Otava
PL 37, 00521 Helsinki
Tel: (09) 622 9970 Fax: (09) 135 1372
E-mail: like@like.fi
Web Site: www.like.fi
Key Personnel
Publishing Manager: Paivi Paappanen
E-mail: paivi.paappanen@like.fi
Financial Manager: Merja Leisso Tel: (050) 389
6525
Communications: Nora Varjama Tel: (050) 547
6868 E-mail: nora.varjama@like.fi
Sales, Marketing & Advertising: Timo Taussi
Tel: (041) 511 0302
Founded: 1987
Also publishes a cultural magazine, circulation
700,000 copies.
Subjects: Fiction, Nonfiction (General), Science
Fiction, Fantasy
ISBN Prefix(es): 978-951-578; 978-951-8929;
978-951-96078; 978-952-471
Number of titles published annually: 100 Print
Total Titles: 600 Print
Bookshop(s): Like Kirjakauppe, Vuorikatu
5, 00100 Helsinki, Contact: Otto Sallinen
Tel: (09) 260 0288 E-mail: likekauppa@like.fi

Minerva Kustannus Oy
Lastenkodinkuja 1 A, 4 kerros, 00180 Helsinki
Tel: (050) 556 7654 Fax: (050) 7830 1697
Web Site: www.minervakustannus.fi
Key Personnel
Chief Executive Officer: Juhani Korolainen
Tel: (040) 556 7654 E-mail: juhani.
korolainen@minervakustannus.fi
Publishing Manager: Pekka Saarainen
Tel: (040) 537 7114 E-mail: pekka.saarainen@
minervakustannus.fi
Sales & Marketing Manager: Jorma Mahlanen
Tel: (044) 567 8072 E-mail: jorma.mahlanen@
minervakustannus.fi
Founded: 1991

Subjects: Biography, Memoirs, Cookery, Fiction, Health, Nutrition, History, Nonfiction (General), Sports, Athletics
ISBN Prefix(es): 978-951-95466; 978-952-5092; 978-952-492; 978-952-5478; 978-952-482

Kustannusosakeyhtio Nemo
Uudenmaankatu 10, 00120 Helsinki
Tel: (09) 15661 (Otava)
E-mail: info@nemokustannus.fi
Web Site: www.nemokustannus.fi
Key Personnel
Publisher: Nina Karjalainen *E-mail:* nina. karjalainen@nemokustannus.fi; Mika Siimes *E-mail:* mika.siimes@nemokustannus.fi
Editor: Nina Tarvainen *E-mail:* nina.tarvainen@ nemokustannus.fi
Founded: 1997
Subjects: Fiction
ISBN Prefix(es): 978-952-5180; 978-952-240

Kustannusosakeyhtio Otava (Otava Publishing Co Ltd)+
Member of Otava Group
Uudenmaankatu 10, 00120 Helsinki
Mailing Address: PL 134, 00121 Helsinki
Tel: (09) 19961 *Fax:* (09) 643 136
Web Site: www.otava.fi
Key Personnel
Mng Dir: Pasi Vainio *Tel:* (09) 1996 240
  E-mail: pasi.vainio@otava.fi
Publishing Dir: Minna Castren *Tel:* (09) 1996 250
  E-mail: minna.castren@otava.fi; Teuvo Sankila
  Tel: (09) 1996 280 *E-mail:* teuvo.sankila@ otava.fi
Communications Dir: Liisa Riekki *Tel:* (09) 1996
  340 *E-mail:* liisa.riekki@otava.fi
Editorial Dir, Children's & Young Adult:
  Heli Hottinen-Puukko *Tel:* (09) 1996 455
  E-mail: heli.hottinen-puukko@otava.fi
Editorial Dir, Fiction: Antti Kasper *Tel:* (09) 1996
  441 *E-mail:* antti.kasper@otava.fi
Editorial Dir, Nonfiction: Eva Reenpaa *Tel:* (09)
  1996 459 *E-mail:* eva.reenpaa@otava.fi
Rights Dir: Emma Alftan *Tel:* (050) 5286881
  (cell) *E-mail:* emma.alftan@otava.fi
Sales & Marketing Dir: Maija Kuusi *Tel:* (09)
  1996 330 *E-mail:* maija.kuusi@otava.fi
Publishing Manager, Adult & Vocational Education: Jarmo Lindroos *Tel:* (0500) 202 385
  E-mail: jarmo.lindroos@otava.fi
Publishing Manager, E-Learning: Frederik Rahka
  Tel: (09) 1996 585 *E-mail:* frederik.rahka@ otava.fi
Publishing Manager, Fiction: Jaana Koistinen
  Tel: (09) 1996 421 *E-mail:* jaana.koistinen@ otava.fi
Publishing Manager, Humanities: Selja Saarialho
  Tel: (09) 1996 518 *E-mail:* selja.saarialho@ otava.fi
Publishing Manager, Modern Language: Mika
  Perttola *Tel:* (09) 1996 569 *E-mail:* mika. perttola@otava.fi
Publishing Manager, Sciences: Mervi Korhonen
  Tel: (09) 1996 544 *E-mail:* mervi.korhonen@ otava.fi
Publishing Manager, Swedish Educational Publishing: Magdalena Lindberg *Tel:* (09) 1996
  470 *E-mail:* magdalena.lindberg@otava.fi
Founded: 1890
Subjects: Architecture & Interior Design, Art, Cookery, Fiction, History, How-to, Nonfiction (General), Travel & Tourism, Nature
ISBN Prefix(es): 978-951-1
Subsidiaries: Like Kustannus Oy; Otavan Kirjapaino Oy (Otava Book Printing Ltd); Suuri Suomalainen Kirjakerho Oy (The Great Finnish Book Club Ltd); Yhtyneet Kuvalehdet Oy (United Magazines Ltd)

Paiva Osakeyhtio+
Lukiokatu 15, 13101 Hameenlinna

Mailing Address: PL 10, 13101 Hameenlinna
E-mail: paiva@paiva.fi
Web Site: www.paiva.fi
Key Personnel
Mng Dir: Merja Pitkanen *Tel:* (010) 3288 100
  E-mail: merja.pitkanen@paiva.fi
Editor-in-Chief: Hanno Lahtinen *Tel:* (010) 3288
  110 *E-mail:* hanno.lahtinen@paiva.fi
Marketing: Harri Gronqvist *Tel:* (0400) 476 899
  E-mail: harri.gronqvist@paiva.fi
Founded: 1962
Subjects: Religion - Protestant, Religion - Other
ISBN Prefix(es): 978-951-622

Parvs Publishing
Koskelantie 33B, 00610 Helsinki
Tel: (0400) 262 853
E-mail: info@parvspublishing.com
Web Site: www.parvspublishing.com
Founded: 2006
Subjects: Architecture & Interior Design, Art, Photography
ISBN Prefix(es): 978-952-5654
Number of titles published annually: 10 Print

Rakennustieto Oy (Building Information Ltd)+
Malminkatu 16 A, 00100 Helsinki
Mailing Address: PL 1004, 00101 Helsinki
Tel: (0207) 476 400 *Fax:* (0207) 476 320
E-mail: rts@rakennustieto.fi; rakennustieto@ rakennustieto.fi
Web Site: www.rakennustieto.fi/publishing
Key Personnel
Vice President, Business Development: Heimo
  Salo *Tel:* (0207) 476 395 *E-mail:* heimo.salo@ rakennustieto.fi
Publishing Manager & Rights: Tiina Heloma
  Tel: (0207) 476 402 *E-mail:* tiina.heloma@ rakennustieto.fi
Mng Editor: Kristiina Bergholm *E-mail:* kristiina. bergholm@rakennustieto.fi
Founded: 1974
Subjects: Architecture & Interior Design
ISBN Prefix(es): 978-951-682; 978-952-967
Parent Company: Rakennustietosaeaetio - Building Information Foundation RTS
Bookshop(s): Runeberginkatu 5, 00100 Helsinki
  Tel: (0207) 476 366 *Fax:* (0207) 476 340
  E-mail: bookshop@rakennustieto.fi *Web Site:* www.rakennustietoshop.fi

Recallmed Oy+
Valkjarventie 45, 01800 Klaukkala
Tel: (09) 879 7177
E-mail: recallmed@recallmed.fi
Web Site: www.recallmed.fi
Founded: 1981
Subjects: Biography, Memoirs, Medicine, Nursing, Dentistry, Music, Dance, Sports, Athletics
ISBN Prefix(es): 978-951-9221; 978-951-847

REUNA Kustantamo ja Kirjakauppa Oy
Rusutjarventie 125, 04370 Rusutjarvi
Tel: (09) 7268 9910
E-mail: info@reunalla.fi
Web Site: reunalla.fi
Key Personnel
Publisher: Tarja Tornaeus *E-mail:* tarja.tornaeus@ reunalla.fi
Sales Manager: Sami Mahonen *Tel:* (045) 646
  4966 *E-mail:* sami.mahonen@reunalla.fi
Marketing & Foreign Rights: Anna Toni
  Tel: (050) 531 1796 *E-mail:* anna.toni@ reunalla.fi
Founded: 2013
Subjects: Biography, Memoirs, Fiction, History, Nonfiction (General), Poetry, Science Fiction, Fantasy, Travel & Tourism
ISBN Prefix(es): 978-952-6762; 978-952-7028

Sanoma Pro Ltd+
Annankatu 15, 00121 Helsinki

Tel: (0203) 91000 (customer service); (020) 11 611
E-mail: asiakaspalvelu@sanomapro.fi
Web Site: www.sanomapro.fi
Key Personnel
Publishing Editor: Vuokko Lipponen
  E-mail: vuokko.lipponen@sanomapro.fi
Founded: 1990
Subjects: Art, Biological Sciences, Chemistry, Chemical Engineering, Civil Engineering, Computer Science, Computers, Crafts, Games, Hobbies, Engineering (General), Environmental Studies, History, Mathematics, Music, Dance, Physics, Religion - Other, Science (General)
ISBN Prefix(es): 978-952-63

Kustantajat Sarmala Oy (Sarmala Publishers Ltd)+
Metsapurontie 26, 00630 Helsinki
Toll Free Tel: 0400 703838
Key Personnel
Publisher: Kalevi Sarmala
Founded: 1991
Subjects: Agriculture, Architecture & Interior Design, Environmental Studies
ISBN Prefix(es): 978-952-9687; 978-951-664

Schildts & Soderstroms+
Bulevarden 7, 8th floor, 00120 Helsinki
Mailing Address: PO Box 870, 00121 Helsinki
Tel: (09) 6841 860
E-mail: info@sets.fi
Web Site: www.sets.fi
Key Personnel
Executive Vice President: Stefan Kajanus
  E-mail: stefan.kajanus@sets.fi
Publishing Dir: Mari Koli *E-mail:* mari.koli@sets. fi
Marketing: Susanna Sucksdorff *E-mail:* susanna. sucksdorff@sets.fi
Founded: 1913
Subjects: Art, Biography, Memoirs, Fiction, History, Music, Dance, Philosophy, Poetry
ISBN Prefix(es): 978-951-52; 978-951-50
Associate Companies: Pagina
Distribution Center: Kirjavalitys, Hakakalliontie 10, 05460 Hyvinge *Tel:* (010) 345 15 30
  E-mail: kvtilaus@kirjavalitys.fi *Web Site:* www. kirjavalitys.fi
Orders to: Foerlagssystem Finland Ab *Tel:* (09)
  88 70 40 52 *Fax:* (09) 88 70 40 55

Forlags AB Scriptum
Handelsesplanaden 23 A, 4th floor, 65100 Vasa
Tel: (045) 175 7454 (cell)
E-mail: scriptum@scriptum.fi
Web Site: www.scriptum.fi
Founded: 1987
Subjects: Archaeology, Fiction, Literature, Literary Criticism, Essays, Poetry
ISBN Prefix(es): 978-951-8902; 978-952-5496; 978-952-7005
Number of titles published annually: 9 Print
Total Titles: 100 Print
Orders to: Porvon Kirjakeskus, Teolisuustie 4, 06150 Porvo *Tel:* (020) 16 620 *Fax:* (020) 16
  62291 *E-mail:* tilakuset@kirjakeskus.fi (for books published 2008 or later)

Kustannusosakeyhtio Siltala
Suvilahdenkatu 7, 00500 Helsinki
E-mail: info@siltalapublishing.fi
Web Site: www.siltalapublishing.fi
Key Personnel
Publisher: Aleksi Siltala *Tel:* (09) 407 329435
  E-mail: aleksi@siltalapublishing.fi; Touko
  Siltala *Tel:* (09) 400 548403 *E-mail:* touko@ siltalapublishing.fi
Mng Editor: Sari Lindsten *Tel:* (09) 400 828732
  E-mail: sari@siltalapublishing.fi
Press Officer: Reetta Ravi *E-mail:* reetta@ siltalapublishing.fi
Founded: 2008

Subjects: Fiction, Literature, Literary Criticism, Essays, Nonfiction (General), Design
ISBN Prefix(es): 978-952-234
Number of titles published annually: 30 Print

Suomalaisen Kirjallisuuden Seura (SKS)
(Finnish Literature Society)
Mariankatu 7 A, 4th floor, 00170 Helsinki
E-mail: books@finlit.fi
Web Site: www.finlit.fi
Key Personnel
Publishing Dir: Tero Norkola *Tel:* (040) 088 2700
E-mail: tero.norkola@finlit.fi
Publishing Manager: Rauno Enden *Tel:* (040) 534 2675 *E-mail:* rauno.enden@finlit.fi
Editor: Aino Rajala *Tel:* (040) 534 2480
E-mail: aino.rajala@finlit.fi; Pauliina Rihto *Tel:* (040) 534 2704 *E-mail:* pauliina.rihto@finlit.fi
Founded: 1834
Publisher of arts related nonfiction.
Subjects: Anthropology, History, Language Arts, Linguistics, Literature, Literary Criticism, Essays, Women's Studies, Monography
ISBN Prefix(es): 978-951-717; 978-951-746; 978-952-222
Number of titles published annually: 80 Print
Total Titles: 2,000 Print
Bookshop(s): Mariankatu 7, 00170 Helsinki, France

Suomen Pipliaseura RY+
Maistraatinportti 2A, 00241 Helsinki
Mailing Address: PL 54, 00241 Helsinki
Tel: (010) 838 6500 *Fax:* (010) 838 6511
E-mail: info@piplia.fi
Web Site: www.piplia.fi
Key Personnel
Secretary General: Markku Kotila *Tel:* (010) 838 6512
Program Dir: Martti Asikainen *Tel:* (010) 838 6530
Founded: 1812
Specialize in Bibles, fundraising for Bible Society & development of teaching methods of the Bible.
Subjects: Biblical Studies
ISBN Prefix(es): 978-951-9010; 978-951-577

Tahtitieteellinen Yhdistys Ursa ry (Ursa Astronomical Association)+
Kopernikuksentie 1, 00130 Helsinki
Tel: (09) 684 0400
E-mail: ursa@ursa.fi
Web Site: www.ursa.fi
Key Personnel
Executive Dir: Markku Sarimaa *Tel:* (09) 6840 4060 *E-mail:* markku.sarimaa@ursa.fi
Editor-in-Chief: Marko Pekkola *Tel:* (09) 6840 4050 *E-mail:* marko.pekkola@ursa.fi
Founded: 1921
Subjects: Earth Sciences, Physical Sciences, Science (General)
ISBN Prefix(es): 978-951-9269; 978-952-5329

Talentum Media Oyj, see Alma Talent Oy

Kustannusosakeyhtio Teos (Teos Publishers)
Blvd 12, 3 kerros, 00120 Helsinki
Tel: (020) 743 1250
Web Site: www.teos.fi
Key Personnel
Chief Executive Officer: Nina Paavolainen
Tel: (040) 500 8342 *E-mail:* nina.paavolainen@teos.fi
Mng Editor: Elia Lennes *Tel:* (040) 720 6310
E-mail: elia.lennes@teos.fi
Founded: 2003
Independent publisher focusing on works of Finnish literature & nonfiction.

Subjects: Fiction, Literature, Literary Criticism, Essays, Nonfiction (General), Poetry
ISBN Prefix(es): 978-951-851
Number of titles published annually: 40 Print

Kustannus Oy Uusi Tie+
Opistotie 1, 12310 Ryttyla
Tel: (019) 7792307 *Fax:* (019) 7792300
E-mail: asiakaspalvelu@nettikirjakauppa.com
Web Site: www.nettikirjakauppa.com
Founded: 1965
Subjects: Fiction, Religion - Other, Theology
ISBN Prefix(es): 978-951-619

Osuuskunta Vastapaino+
Yliopistonkatu 60 A, 4 kerros, 33100 Tampere
Tel: (03) 3141 3501 *Fax:* (03) 3141 3550
E-mail: vastapaino@vastapaino.fi
Web Site: www.vastapaino.fi
Key Personnel
Mng Dir: Kimmo Jylhamo *Tel:* (03) 3141 3500
E-mail: kimmo.jylhamo@vastapaino.fi
Publishing Editor: Irina Kyllonen *Tel:* (03) 3141 3502 *E-mail:* irina.kyllonen@vastapaino.fi
Founded: 1981
Subjects: Behavioral Sciences, Education, History, Journalism, Literature, Literary Criticism, Essays, Philosophy, Social Sciences, Sociology, Women's Studies
ISBN Prefix(es): 978-951-9066; 978-951-768
Number of titles published annually: 25 Print
Total Titles: 180 Print

Werner Soderstrom Osakeyhtio (WSOY)+
Korkeavuorenkatu 37, 00130 Helsinki
Mailing Address: PL 314, 00101 Helsinki
Tel: (010) 5060 200; (020) 16 6222 2 (bookshop) *Fax:* (010) 5060 287; (020) 16 6229 1 (bookshop)
E-mail: tilaukset@kirjakeskus.fi
Web Site: www.wsoy.fi
Key Personnel
Chairman of the Board: Jacob Dahlborg
E-mail: jacob.dahlborg@wsoy.fi
President: Timo Julkunen *E-mail:* timo.julkunen@wsoy.fi
Executive Vice President & Publisher: Leena Majander *E-mail:* leena.majander@wsoy.fi
Rights Manager: Anna Suominen *E-mail:* anna.suominen@wsoy.fi
Marketing & Communications: Satu-Maria Rastas
Tel: (050) 3617 980 *E-mail:* satu-maria.rastas@wsoy.fi
Founded: 1878
Also literary agent.
Subjects: Education, Fiction, Literature, Literary Criticism, Essays, Nonfiction (General)
ISBN Prefix(es): 978-951-0
Parent Company: Bonnier AB
Book Club(s): JUJU; Lasten Parhaat Kirjat; Muumikirjasto; Satuklassikot; Tyyli ja Koti; Uudet Kirjat

WSOY, see Werner Soderstrom Osakeyhtio (WSOY)

France

General Information

Capital: Paris
Language: French (official), with regional dialects & languages rapidly declining
Religion: Predominantly Roman Catholic
Population: 59.3 million
Bank Hours: 0900-1200, 1400-1600 Monday-Friday. Some closed Monday.

Shop Hours: 0900-1930 Monday-Saturday. Many closed Monday
Currency: 100 Eurocents = 1 Euro
Export/Import Information: Member of the European Union. 5.5% VAT on books. Import licenses not required. There is a control of the book trade based on a number of legal and regulating provisions applying to the import of pirated publications, articles and writings that offend against morality and public order, publications harmful to youth, writings forbidden by the Minister for the Interior; the customs official must submit articles subject to control for examination by the General Information Service of the Ministry of the Interior.
Copyright: UCC, Berne, Buenos Aires, Florence (see Copyright Conventions, pg viii)

editions A dos d'ane
8 rue Littre, 75006 Paris
Tel: 06 85 36 93 29
E-mail: contact@adosdane.com
Web Site: www.adosdane.com
Subjects: Art, Biography, Memoirs, Film, Video, Literature, Literary Criticism, Essays, Music, Dance
ISBN Prefix(es): 978-2-9193721

ABC Melody Editions
26 rue Liancourt, 75014 Paris
Tel: 01 44 78 92 43 *Fax:* 01 70 24 76 03
E-mail: info@abcmelody.com
Web Site: www.abcmelody.com
Key Personnel
Dir: Stephane Husar *Tel:* 06 28 60 25 77 (cell)
E-mail: stef@abcmelody.com
Founded: 2000
Subjects: Language Arts, Linguistics, Culture
ISBN Prefix(es): 978-2-916947

ABES, see Agence Bibliographique de l'Enseignement Superieur

Academie Nationale de Reims
17 rue du Jard, 51100 Reims
Tel: 03 26 91 04 49; 09 60 52 19 03 *Fax:* 03 26 91 04 49
E-mail: academie.nationale.reims@wanadoo.fr
Web Site: academie-nationale-reims.fr
Key Personnel
Secretary General: Patrick Demouy
E-mail: patrick.demouy@laposte.net
Founded: 1841 (by Cardinal Gousset, archeveque de Reims)
Subjects: Biography, Memoirs, Communications, History
Total Titles: 500 Print
Foreign Rep(s): Champagne-Ardenne

Editions Accarias L'Originel+
5 passage de la Folie-Regnault, 75011 Paris
Tel: 01 43 48 73 07
E-mail: accarias@orange.fr
Web Site: originel-accarias.com
Key Personnel
Dir: Jean-Louis Accarias
Founded: 1980
Subjects: Philosophy, Religion - Buddhist, Religion - Hindu, Religion - Other, Social Sciences, Sociology
ISBN Prefix(es): 978-2-86316
Total Titles: 220 Print; 2 E-Book
Shipping Address: Dilisco, 128 bis ave Jean Jaures, 94200 Ivry-sur-Seine
Orders to: Dilisco, 128 bis ave Jean Jaures, 94200 Ivry-sur-Seine

ACR Edition
20ter, rue de Bezons, Les Poissons 1193, 92400 Courbevoie, Paris
Tel: 01 47 88 14 92

E-mail: acredition@acr-edition.com
Web Site: www.acr-edition.com
Founded: 1983
This publisher has indicated that 50% of their
product line is author subsidized.
Membership(s): Syndicat de L'Edition Groupe
Art.
Subjects: Art
ISBN Prefix(es): 978-2-86770
Number of titles published annually: 3 Print; 5
Online
Total Titles: 230 Print; 150 Online
Foreign Rep(s): Antique Collector Club (UK &
Commonwealth)

Editions Acropole
12, Ave d'Italie, 75627 Paris Cedex 13
Tel: 01 44 16 05 00
E-mail: acropole@placedesediteurs.com
Web Site: www.editions-acropole.com
Key Personnel
Publication Dir: Jean Arcache
Subjects: History, Inspirational, Spirituality, Cur-
rent Affairs
ISBN Prefix(es): 978-2-7357
Parent Company: Place des editeurs

Actes-Graphiques+
67 ter Cours Fauriel, 42100 St-Etienne Cedex 2
Tel: 06 09 42 21 13 (cell) *Fax:* 04 77 25 39 28
Key Personnel
Dir: Georges Callet *E-mail:* georges.callet@
orange.fr
Founded: 1994
Subjects: Architecture & Interior Design, Biog-
raphy, Memoirs, Gardening, Plants, Geogra-
phy, Geology, Government, Political Science,
Humor, Literature, Literary Criticism, Essays,
Mysteries, Suspense, Photography, Regional In-
terests, Religion - Catholic, Religion - Other,
Science (General), Social Sciences, Sociology
ISBN Prefix(es): 978-2-910868
Subsidiaries: Action Graphique; Cosmo; Le
Henaff
Distributor for Action Graphique; Le Henaff

Editions Actes Sud+
Place Nina-Berberova, 13200 Arles Cedex
Mailing Address: BP 90038, 13633 Arles Cedex
Tel: 04 90 49 86 91 *Fax:* 04 90 96 95 25
Web Site: www.actes-sud.fr
Key Personnel
Editorial Dir: Bertrand Py
Commercial Dir & Development: Jean-Paul Capi-
tani
Rights: Laurence Caillieret
Foreign Rights: Claire Teeuwissen
Founded: 1978
Subjects: Art, Biography, Memoirs, Drama, The-
ater, Literature, Literary Criticism, Essays, Po-
etry, Nature
ISBN Prefix(es): 978-2-7427; 978-2-86869; 978-
2-86943; 978-2-7274; 978-2-85376; 978-2-
901567
Number of titles published annually: 300 Print
Imprints: Babel (paperback)
Subsidiaries: Actes Sud BD; Actes Sud Junior
(children's books & literature); Actes Sud-
Papiers; L'An2; Editions Dis Voir; Editions Er-
rance; Helium Editions; Imprimerie Nationale
Editions; Editions Jacquelin Chambon; Photo
poche; Sinbad (Arab literature & Islam); Solin
(nonfiction: essays, biographies & foreign liter-
ature)
Branch Office(s)
18, rue Seguier, 75006 Paris *Tel:* 01 55 42 63 00
Fax: 01 55 42 63 01
Distributor for Andre Dimanche; Lemeac; Paris-
Musees
Bookshop(s): Librairie du Channel, 173 bd, Gambetta, BP 77, 62102 Calais Cedex *Tel:* 03 21
96 46 03; Librairie Maupetit, 128 & 142, La

Canebiere, 13001 Marseille *Tel:* 04 91 48 30
30; 04 91 36 50 50 *Fax:* 04 91 36 50 79; Li-
brairie du MuCEM, Esplanade du J4, 13002
Marseille *Tel:* 04 84 35 14 95; Librairie du
Rond-Point, 2 bis Ave Roosevelt, 75008 Paris
Tel: 01 44 95 98 22 *Fax:* 01 44 95 98 43; Li-
brairie du Parc, Grande Halle du Parc de la
Villette, 211, ave Jean Jaures, 75019 Paris
Tel: 01 42 38 37 52 *Fax:* 01 42 38 00 72;
Librairie Picard & Epona, 82, rue Bonaparte,
75006 Paris *Tel:* 01 43 26 40 41; 01 43 26 96
73 *Fax:* 01 43 29 34 88; Chaine d'Encre//Chez
Hermes, 17, rue de Sevres, 75006 Paris *Tel:* 01
42 84 41 57

Editions Ad Solem
37, rue Barbet-de-Jouy, 75007 Paris
Tel: 01 44 18 39 77 *Fax:* 06 73 03 28 59
Web Site: www.editions-adsolem.fr
Key Personnel
Editorial Dir: Gregory Solari
Subjects: Inspirational, Spirituality, Literature,
Literary Criticism, Essays, Philosophy, Poetry,
Theology, Christian Literature, Culture, Mysti-
cism
ISBN Prefix(es): 978-2-88482; 978-2-940090
Distribution Center: SOFEDIS, 11, rue Soufflot,
75005 Paris *Tel:* 01 53 10 25 25 *Fax:* 01 53
10 25 26 *E-mail:* info@sofedis.fr (France, Bel-
gium & Canada)
Albert-le-Grand, 20, route de Beaumont,
Box 928, 1701 Fribourg, Switzerland
Tel: (026) 425 85 95 *Fax:* (026) 425 85 90
E-mail: diffusion@albert-le-grand.ch

Adverbum+
Batiment La Belle Aureille, Micropolis, 05000
Gap
Tel: 04 92 81 28 81 *Fax:* 04 92 81 37 11
E-mail: info@adverbum.fr
Web Site: www.adverbum.fr
Key Personnel
Manager: Michel Mirale *E-mail:* michel-mirale@
adverbum.fr
Production: Christophe Boulage *E-mail:* chb@
adverbum.fr
Founded: 1989
Subjects: Anthropology, Behavioral Sciences,
Biblical Studies, Health, Nutrition, How-to,
Language Arts, Linguistics, Medicine, Nursing,
Dentistry, Religion - Catholic
ISBN Prefix(es): 978-2-907653; 978-2-911328;
978-2-914338; 978-2-911220
Number of titles published annually: 18 Print
Total Titles: 120 Print
Imprints: Editions Desiris; Editions Gregori-
ennes; Atelier Perrousseaux Editeur; Editions
le Sureau

Editions Aedis
72 Ave Raymond-Poincare, 03200 Vichy Cedex
Mailing Address: BP 12324, 03200 Vichy Cedex
Tel: 04 70 97 69 81 *Fax:* 04 73 61 67 65
E-mail: contact@aedis-editions.fr
Web Site: www.aedis-editions.fr
Founded: 1988
Subjects: Cookery, Education, Genealogy, History,
Language Arts, Linguistics
ISBN Prefix(es): 978-2-84259

AFNOR, see Association Francaise de
Normalisation

**Agence Bibliographique de l'Enseignement
Superieur** (Bibliographic Agency for Higher
Education)
Unit of French Ministry for Higher Education
227, av du Prof Jean-Louis Viala, CS 84308,
34193 Montpellier Cedex 5
Tel: 04 67 54 84 10 *Fax:* 04 67 54 84 14
Web Site: www.abes.fr

Key Personnel
Dir: David Aymonin *E-mail:* david.aymonin@
abes.fr
Founded: 1994
Membership(s): The Association of Informa-
tion & Documentation Professionals (ADBS);
Association of European Research Libraries
(LIBER); Association of French Libraries
(ABF); International Federation of Library As-
sociations & Institutions (IFLA).
Subjects: Library & Information Sciences
ISBN Prefix(es): 978-2-912292
Total Titles: 2 CD-ROM
Imprints: CCNPS
Branch Office(s)
Repertoire des bibliotheque
Distributed by Bibliopolis

**Agence Rhone-Alpes pour le livre et la
documentation (ARALD)**
Parc de la Cerisaie, Villa Gillet, 25 rue Chaziere,
69004 Lyon
Tel: 04 78 39 58 87 *Fax:* 04 78 39 57 46
E-mail: contact@arald.org
Web Site: www.arald.org
Key Personnel
Publishing Dir: Gilles Eboli
Mng Editor: Laurent Bonzon *E-mail:* l.bonzon@
arald.org
Subjects: Library & Information Sciences, Book
Industry
ISBN Prefix(es): 978-2-913384

Editions Agone
BP 70072, 13192 Marseille Cedex 20
Tel: 04 91 64 38 07
E-mail: editions@agone.org
Web Site: agone.org
Subjects: Fiction, Geography, Geology, History,
Language Arts, Linguistics, Literature, Literary
Criticism, Essays, Philosophy, Social Sciences,
Sociology
ISBN Prefix(es): 978-2-7489; 978-2-910846

Editions Al Liamm
14 rue du Muguet, 22300 Lannuon
E-mail: sekretourva@alliamm.bzh
Web Site: alliamm.bzh
Key Personnel
President: Mr Tudual Huon
Founded: 1949
This is a noncommercial organization specializing
in the Breton language.
Subjects: Drama, Theater, Education, Fiction, Lit-
erature, Literary Criticism, Essays, Poetry
ISBN Prefix(es): 978-2-7368
Number of titles published annually: 4 Print
Total Titles: 120 Print
Parent Company: Association Al Liamm (Breizh
- Brittany)
Orders to: 7 Bel Air, 29460 Dirinonn

Editions Al Manar
96, bd Maurice Barres, 92200 Neuilly
Tel: 09 53 09 50 74 *Fax:* 01 46 41 04 32
E-mail: editmanar@free.fr
Web Site: www.editmanar.com
Subjects: Art, Literature, Literary Criticism, Es-
says, South Mediterranean
ISBN Prefix(es): 978-2-913896

Alain Thomas Editeur+
18 passage Foubert, 75013 Paris
Tel: 01 45 88 28 03
Web Site: www.alainthomasimages.com
Key Personnel
Editor: Alain Thomas *E-mail:* alain-thomas@
wanadoo.fr
Founded: 1991
Subjects: Photography, Travel & Tourism, Ameri-
can West Nature/Parks
ISBN Prefix(es): 978-2-9503864; 978-2-9527891

Total Titles: 4 Print; 1 CD-ROM; 5 Online
Parent Company: Alain Thomas Images

Alliance Biblique Universelle, *imprint of* Societe
Biblique Francaise

Editions Alternatives+
Subsidiary of Editions Gallimard
5 rue Gaston Gallimard, 75007 Paris
Tel: 01 46 33 47 33; 01 49 54 42 00
E-mail: info@editionsalternatives.com
Web Site: www.editionsalternatives.com
Key Personnel
Co-Founder: Gerard Aime *E-mail:* aime@
  editionsalternatives.com; Patrice Aoust
Editorial: Sabine Bledniak *E-mail:* bledniak@
  editionsalternatives.com; Charlotte Gallimard
Foreign Rights: Helene Clastres *E-mail:* helene.
  clastres@gallimard-loisirs.fr
Manufacturing: Cecile Lebreton *E-mail:* cecile.
  lebreton@gallimard.fr
Press & Public Relations: Sophie Gallet
  E-mail: sophie.gallet@gallimard.fr
Founded: 1975
Subjects: Alternative, Architecture & Interior De-
  sign, Art, House & Home, How-to, Music,
  Dance, Photography
ISBN Prefix(es): 978-2-86227
Foreign Rep(s): Gallimard Ltd (Joelle Gagnon)
  (Canada); Pascal Sauve (Switzerland); SDLC la
  Caravelle (Rodolphe Dondeyne) (Belgium)
Distribution Center: Sodis, 128 Ave du Marechal
  de Lattre de Tassigny, 77400 Lagny sur Marne
  Tel: 01 60 07 82 99

Editions ALTESS+
Praly, 07360 Les Ollieres-sur-Eyrieux
Tel: 04 75 66 24 48
Key Personnel
Contact: Alain-Rene Gelineau
Founded: 1990
Subjects: Art, Biography, Memoirs, Health, Nu-
  trition, Inspirational, Spirituality, Literature,
  Literary Criticism, Essays, Poetry, Psychology,
  Psychiatry, Religion - Other, Personal Develop-
  ment
ISBN Prefix(es): 978-2-84243; 978-2-905219
Number of titles published annually: 15 Print
Total Titles: 160 Print
Distributed by LAVAL Distribution (Quebec,
  Canada)
Distributor for Editions Voici la Clef (Here's the
  Key) (France)
Orders to: ALTESS-AR Gelineau, PO Box 8,
  07360 Les Ollieres-Sur-Eyrieux *Tel:* 04 75 66
  24 48 *Fax:* 04 75 66 32 43

Alzabane Edtions
46 bis, rue des Vignes, 92140 Clamart
Tel: 01 46 48 72 21
E-mail: contact@alzabane-editions.com
Web Site: www.alzabane-editions.com
Key Personnel
Dir: Jean-Sebastien Blanck
Press & Public Relations: Helen Broustet *Tel:* 06
  20 45 31 61
Founded: 2007
ISBN Prefix(es): 978-2-9528192; 978-2-35920

Editions Alzieu+
One rue du Mouline, 38120 Fontanil Cornillon
Mailing Address: BP 232, 38522 Saint Egreve
  Cedex
Tel: 04 76 75 33 76; 06 67 49 03 72 *Fax:* 04 76
  75 33 76
E-mail: admin@editions-alzieu.com
Web Site: www.editions-alzieu.com
Key Personnel
Dir: Claude Alzieu *E-mail:* claude@editions-
  alzieu.com
Founded: 1991

Subjects: Art, Biography, Memoirs, History, Poetry, Regional Interests, Religion - Other
ISBN Prefix(es): 978-2-910717; 978-2-914093;
  978-2-35022
Distributed by Brepols

Les Editions de l'Amandier
56 Blvd Davout, 75020 Paris
Tel: 01 55 25 80 82 *Fax:* 01 55 25 20 12
E-mail: editionsdelamandier@wanadoo.fr
Web Site: www.editionsamandier.fr
Founded: 1988
Subjects: Art, Drama, Theater, History, Literature,
  Literary Criticism, Essays, Photography, Poetry,
  French Theater, Nature, Novels
ISBN Prefix(es): 978-2-35516; 978-2-907649;
  978-2-915695

Editions Amaterra
6C, rue de Capucins, 69001 Lyon
Tel: 09 50 60 52 50 *Fax:* 09 55 60 52 50
E-mail: contact@amaterra.fr
Web Site: www.amaterra.fr
Key Personnel
Creative Dir: Eric Andre
Editorial Dir: Andre Guenolee
Literary Editor: Sylvie Misslin
Foreign Rights: Daniela Bonerba
  E-mail: daniela@amaterra.fr
ISBN Prefix(es): 978-2-354
Foreign Rep(s): Dimedia (Canada); Servidis
  (Switzerland)

Les Editions de l'Amateur+
17-19, rue Visconti, 75006 Paris
Tel: 01 44 41 19 79 *Fax:* 01 43 29 87 11
E-mail: contact@editionsdelamateur.fr
Web Site: www.editionsdelamateur.fr
Subjects: Art
ISBN Prefix(es): 978-2-85917
Total Titles: 100 Print
Parent Company: JNF Productions

Editions Amphora SAS+
27, rue St-Andre des Arts, 75006 Paris
Tel: 01 43 29 03 04 *Fax:* 01 43 29 49 49
Web Site: www.ed-amphora.fr/fr
Key Personnel
President & Dir General: Bernard Dubois
Dir General & Editorial Dir: Renaud Dubois
  E-mail: r.dubois@ed-amphora.fr
Dir, Marketing & Sales: Gregorie Lartigot
Founded: 1954
Subjects: Crafts, Games, Hobbies, Health, Nutri-
  tion, Sports, Athletics, Fitness, Wellness
ISBN Prefix(es): 978-2-85180
Branch Office(s)
6, zone d'activites "Le Revol", 84240 La Tour
  d'Aigues *Tel:* 04 90 07 39 56 *Fax:* 04 90 07 25
  30
Distributed by Dimedia (Canada); Interforum
  Benelux (Belgium); OLF Diffusion (Switzer-
  land)
Distributor for Editions Actio

Editions de L'Anabase
BP 50028, 78511 Rambouillet
Tel: 01 30 41 07 47 *Fax:* 01 34 85 80 73
Founded: 1991
Subjects: Literature, Literary Criticism, Essays,
  Philosophy, Psychology, Psychiatry, Social Sci-
  ences, Sociology
ISBN Prefix(es): 978-2-909535

Anako Editions+
236, ave Victor Hugo, 94120 Fontenay-sous-Bois
Tel: 01 43 94 92 88 *Fax:* 01 43 94 02 45
E-mail: planete.anako@free.fr
Web Site: www.anako.com
Key Personnel
Dir: Patrick Bernard

Founded: 1988
Subjects: Anthropology, Photography, Travel &
  Tourism
ISBN Prefix(es): 978-2-907754
Parent Company: Planete Anako

Editions l'Ancre de Marine+
2, rue des Quatre Moulins, 27400 Louviers
Tel: 02 32 25 45 97
E-mail: service-clients@ancre-de-marine.com
Web Site: www.ancre-de-marine.com
Key Personnel
Head: Franck Martin
Founded: 1985
Subjects: Fiction, History, Humor, Maritime, Re-
  gional Interests, Adventure
ISBN Prefix(es): 978-2-905970; 978-2-84141
Number of titles published annually: 20 Print
Total Titles: 200 Print
Parent Company: Syndicat National de l'edition
Imprints: Cifonit Figle
Distributed by Edilarge Ouest France

Annales du Bac, *imprint of* Editions Vuibert

Editions Anthese+
32 ave Jean-Jaures, 94110 Arcueil
Tel: 01 46 56 06 67 *Fax:* 01 49 56 06 67
E-mail: editions@editions-anthese.com
Web Site: www.anthese.fr
Key Personnel
Dir: Nicolas Draeger
Founded: 1984
Subjects: Architecture & Interior Design, Art, Bi-
  ography, Memoirs
ISBN Prefix(es): 978-2-904420; 978-2-912257
Distribution Center: Sodis, 128, av du Marechal
  de Lattre de Tassigny, 77400 Lagny sur Marne
  Tel: 01 60 07 82 00 *Fax:* 01 64 30 92 22
  E-mail: portail@sodis.fr *Web Site:* www.sodis.
  fr
CDE-Centre de Diffusion de L'Edition, 17 rue
  de Tournon, 75006 Paris *Tel:* 01 44 41 19 19
  Fax: 01 44 41 19 14

ARALD, see Agence Rhone-Alpes pour le livre
  et la documentation (ARALD)

L'Arche Editeur
86, rue Bonaparte, 75006 Paris
Tel: 01 46 33 46 45 *Fax:* 01 46 33 56 40
E-mail: contact@arche-editeur.com
Web Site: www.arche-editeur.com
Key Personnel
Dir: Rudolf Rach
Stage Rights: Katharina von Bismarck
Founded: 1949
Publishes some of the most famous dramatic au-
  thors of the 19th & 20th centuries, also con-
  temporary texts. Essays on art, music, cinema
  & philosophy.
Membership(s): Syndicat National de l'Edition
  (SNE).
Subjects: Art, Biography, Memoirs, Drama, The-
  ater, Literature, Literary Criticism, Essays, Mu-
  sic, Dance, Philosophy, Psychology, Psychiatry,
  Social Sciences, Sociology
ISBN Prefix(es): 978-2-85181
Number of titles published annually: 15 Print
Total Titles: 436 Print
Distribution Center: UD-Union Distribution, 106
  rue Petit Leroy, 94550 Chevilly-Larue *Web
  Site:* www.ud-net.com

Editions de l'Archipel+
34, rue des Bourdonnais, 75001 Paris
Tel: 01 55 80 77 40 *Fax:* 01 55 80 77 41
E-mail: ecricom@wanadoo.fr
Web Site: www.editionsarchipel.com
Key Personnel
Dir: Jean-Daniel Belfond
Foreign Rights: Sandrine Robinet

Founded: 1991
Subjects: Biography, Memoirs, Fiction, Literature, Literary Criticism, Essays
ISBN Prefix(es): 978-2-84187; 978-2-909241; 978-2-8098
Number of titles published annually: 100 Print
Total Titles: 500 Print
Divisions: Archipoche; Editions Ecriture; Presses du Chatelet
Distributed by Hachette
Foreign Rep(s): Diffulivre (Switzerland); Dilibel (Belgium); Edipresse (Canada)

Archipoche+
Division of Editions de l'Archipel
34, rue des Bourdonnais, 75001 Paris
Tel: 01 55 80 77 40 *Fax:* 01 55 80 77 41
E-mail: ecricom@wanadoo.fr
Web Site: www.archipoche.com
Key Personnel
Dir: Jean-Daniel Belfond
Foreign Rights: Sandrine Robinet
Founded: 2005
Subjects: Fiction, Nonfiction (General)
ISBN Prefix(es): 978-2-35287
Number of titles published annually: 40 Print
Total Titles: 100 Print
Distributed by Hachette
Foreign Rep(s): Diffulivre (Switzerland); Dilibel (Belgium); Edipresse (Canada)

Architecture-Modelisme, *imprint of* Editions l'Instant Durable

Editions des Arenes
27 rue Jacob, 75006 Paris
Tel: 01 42 17 47 80 *Fax:* 01 43 31 77 97
E-mail: arenes@arenes.fr
Web Site: www.arenes.fr
Key Personnel
Dir: Laurent Beccaria *E-mail:* l.beccaria@arenes.fr
Secretary General: Jean-Baptiste Bourrat *Tel:* 01 42 17 47 85 *E-mail:* jb.bourrat@arenes.fr
Press: Isabelle Mazzaschi *E-mail:* i.mazza@arenes.fr
Subjects: History, Humor, Psychology, Psychiatry
ISBN Prefix(es): 978-2-912485; 978-2-35204

Editions Arfuyen
35, rue Le Marois, 75016 Paris
E-mail: contact@arfuyen.com
Web Site: www.arfuyen.fr
Key Personnel
Contact: Anne Pfister; Gerard Pfister
Founded: 1975
Subjects: Inspirational, Spirituality, Literature, Literary Criticism, Essays
ISBN Prefix(es): 978-2-84590; 978-2-903941; 978-2-908825

Editions de l'Armancon+
24, rue de l'Hotel-de-Ville, 21390 Precy-sous-Thil
Mailing Address: BP 14, 21390 Precy-sous-Thil
Tel: 03 80 64 41 87 *Fax:* 03 80 64 46 96
E-mail: contact@editions-armancon.fr; editions-armancon@wanadoo.fr
Web Site: www.editions-armancon.fr
Key Personnel
Dir: Gerard Gautier
Founded: 1987
Subjects: Art, Biography, Memoirs, Cookery, History, Literature, Literary Criticism, Essays, Photography, Regional Interests, Wine & Spirits, Entertainment
ISBN Prefix(es): 978-2-906594; 978-2-84479
Number of titles published annually: 10 Print
Total Titles: 110 Print

Armand Colin Drott, *imprint of* Editions Dalloz

Art Creation Realisation, see ACR Edition

Editions Artege
11 rue du Bastion St-Francois, 66000 Perpignan
Tel: 04 34 88 14 00
Web Site: www.editionsartege.fr
Key Personnel
General Dir: Bruno Nougayrede
Editor: Florence Buck
Communication & Press: Laurence Angebault
Subjects: Government, Political Science, History, Inspirational, Spirituality, Culture, Geopolitics, Humanities
ISBN Prefix(es): 978-2-360
Divisions: Editions du Rocher

Editions Artemis+
ZA des Vignettes, 2 rue du Colombier, 63400 Chamalieres
Tel: 04 73 19 58 80 *Fax:* 04 73 19 58 99
Web Site: www.editions-artemis.com
Key Personnel
Dir: Herve Chaumeton
Founded: 1984
Subjects: Aeronautics, Aviation, Animals, Pets, Archaeology, Art, Astronomy, Automotive, Cookery, Crafts, Games, Hobbies, Earth Sciences, Gardening, Plants, Health, Nutrition, History, House & Home, Natural History, Outdoor Recreation, Science (General), Wine & Spirits, Ecology, Fishing, Hunting, Nature
ISBN Prefix(es): 978-2-84550; 978-2-84416
Number of titles published annually: 100 Print
Foreign Rep(s): Daphne Distributie NV (Belgium); Diffusion Nord-Sud SPRL (Belgium); Diffusion Dimedia Inc (Canada); Losange Diffusion (Belgium, France); SCAR (Graineterie de Wallonie) (Belgium); Transat SA (Switzerland)

Arthaud, *imprint of* Flammarion Groupe

Artprice+
Subsidiary of Groupe Serveur
Domaine de la Source, BP 69, 69270 Saint-Romain-au-Mont-D'or
Tel: 04 72 42 17 06 *Fax:* 04 78 22 06 06
E-mail: artinvestment@artprice.com
Web Site: www.artprice.com
Key Personnel
Press: Josette Mey *Tel:* 04 78 22 00 00 *E-mail:* ir@artprice.com
Subjects: Art
ISBN Prefix(es): 978-2-909711; 978-2-907129

L'Asiatheque-Maison des langues du monde+
11, Cite Veron, 75018 Paris
Tel: 01 42 62 04 00 *Fax:* 01 42 62 12 34
E-mail: info@asiatheque.com
Web Site: www.asiatheque.com
Key Personnel
Dir: Philippe Thiollier *E-mail:* philippe.thiollier@asiatheque.com
Founded: 1973
Specialize in material for learning of foreign languages & books about cultures & civilizations of the whole world.
Subjects: Asian Studies, Cookery, Education, Foreign Countries, Language Arts, Linguistics, Literature, Literary Criticism, Essays, Religion - Buddhist, Religion - Hindu, Self-Help
ISBN Prefix(es): 978-2-911053; 978-2-901795; 978-2-915255
Total Titles: 130 Print; 23 Audio
Distributor for Presses Universitaires de France (PUF); Union Distribution Flammarion (UD)

Assimil
13, rue Gay-Lussac, 94431 Chennevieres-sur-Marne Cedex

Mailing Address: BP 25, 94431 Chennevieres-sur-Marne Cedex
Tel: 01 45 76 87 37 *Fax:* 01 45 94 06 55
E-mail: contact@assimil.com; marketing@assimil.com
Web Site: fr.assimil.com
Key Personnel
Publisher: Christine Rosengard
Dir & Editorial: Yannick Cherel
Dir, Development: Nicolas Ragonneau
Export & Corporate Manager: Oliver Sartoux
Founded: 1929
Publisher in self-study courses.
Subjects: Language Arts, Linguistics
ISBN Prefix(es): 978-2-7005
Associate Companies: AFAT/Selectour
Bookshop(s): 11, rue des Pyramides, 75001 Paris *Tel:* 01 42 60 40 66 *Fax:* 01 40 20 02 17 *E-mail:* admventes@assimil.com *Web Site:* www.assimil75.fr

L'Association a la Pulpe
104 Rue Ordener, 75018 Paris
Tel: 01 43 55 85 87 *Fax:* 01 43 55 86 21
E-mail: lhydre@lassociation.fr
Web Site: www.lassociation.fr
Key Personnel
Press & Foreign Rights: Sarah Lapalu *Tel:* 01 43 55 96 86 *E-mail:* sarah@lassociation.fr
Founded: 1990
Subjects: Fiction, Humor
ISBN Prefix(es): 978-2-909020; 978-2-84414
Foreign Rep(s): BLDD (Belgium, France); Dimedia (Canada); Servidis (Switzerland)

Editions L'Atalante
11 & 15 rue des Vieilles-Douves, 44000 Nantes
Tel: 02 40 89 14 41; 02 40 47 54 77 (bookshop); 02 40 20 56 23 (editorial) *Fax:* 02 40 47 56 69
Web Site: www.l-atalante.com
Key Personnel
Manager: Mireille Michaut Rivalland; Pierre Michaut Rivalland
Communications: Soledad Ottone
Foreign Rights: Annette Werther-Medou
Subjects: Drama, Theater, Film, Video, Literature, Literary Criticism, Essays, Science Fiction, Fantasy, Humanities
ISBN Prefix(es): 978-2-84172; 978-2-905158

Les Editions de l'Atelier+
51-55 rue Hoche, Bat B Hall 1 Etage 3, 94200 Ivry-sur-Seine
Tel: 01 45 15 20 20 *Fax:* 01 45 15 20 22
E-mail: contact@editionsatelier.com
Web Site: www.editionsatelier.com
Key Personnel
General Dir: Bernard Stephan *E-mail:* bernard.stephan@editionsatelier.com
Editorial Manager: Camille Deltombe *Tel:* 01 45 15 20 27 *E-mail:* camille.deltombe@editionsatelier.com
Head, Communications & Digital: Delphine Richard *Tel:* 01 45 15 20 21 *E-mail:* delphine.richard@editionsatelier.com
Head, Promotions & Press: Carole Lozano *Tel:* 01 45 15 20 25 *E-mail:* carole.lozano@editionsatelier.com
Foreign Rights: Arielle Corbani *Tel:* 01 45 15 20 26 *E-mail:* arielle.corbani@editionsatelier.com; Lan-Hanh Do *E-mail:* lan-hanh.do@editionsatelier.com
Founded: 1929
Subjects: Biblical Studies, Biography, Memoirs, Economics, Education, Government, Political Science, History, Religion - Catholic, Social Sciences, Sociology
ISBN Prefix(es): 978-2-7082

Ateliers et Presses de Taize+
Communaute de Taize, 71250 Taize
Tel: 03 85 50 30 30 *Fax:* 03 85 50 30 15
E-mail: editions@taize.fr

Web Site: www.taize.fr
Key Personnel
Contact: Brother Alois
Founded: 1959
Subjects: Religion - Catholic, Religion - Protestant
ISBN Prefix(es): 978-2-85040
Number of titles published annually: 2 Print
Imprints: Les Presses de Taize

Editions Atlantica+
18, allee Marie-Politzer, 64200 Biarritz Cedex
Mailing Address: BP 30229, 64205 Biarritz
  Cedex
Tel: 05 59 52 84 00; 05 59 52 84 01 *Fax:* 05 59
  52 84 01
E-mail: contact@atlantica.fr
Web Site: www.atlantica.fr
Key Personnel
Chief Executive Officer: Jean Le Gall
Editorial: Sylvie Poupart *E-mail:* s.poupart@
  atlantica.fr
Founded: 1983
Subjects: Art, Biography, Memoirs, Drama, Theater, Fiction, Literature, Literary Criticism, Essays
ISBN Prefix(es): 978-2-84394; 978-2-7588
Parent Company: La Societe Ariegeoise de Participation
Branch Office(s)
3, rue Seguier, 75006 Paris *Tel:* 01 55 42 61 40
  Fax: 01 55 42 61 41

Les Editions Atlas
Subsidiary of Groupe de Agostini
Batiment ADAM ZI n° 2, 23 rue Lavoisier, 27000
  Evreux
Tel: 09 70 82 01 01
Web Site: www.editionsatlas.fr
Key Personnel
Dir, Publishing: Olivier Izard
Founded: 1975
Subjects: Animals, Pets, Art, Cookery, History,
  Science (General)
ISBN Prefix(es): 978-2-7234; 978-2-7312; 978-2-
  87687

Editions de l'Aube+
Rue Amedee Ginies, 84240 La-Tour-d'Aigues
Tel: 04 90 07 46 60
E-mail: contact@editionsdelaube.com
Web Site: editionsdelaube.fr
Key Personnel
Founder: Marion Hennebert; Jean Viard
Founded: 1987
Subjects: Cookery, Economics, Environmental
  Studies, Foreign Countries, Literature, Literary
  Criticism, Essays, Mysteries, Suspense, Philosophy, Social Sciences, Sociology
ISBN Prefix(es): 978-2-87678; 978-2-7526
Distributed by Editions Zoe (Switzerland)

Editions Aubier, *imprint of* Flammarion Groupe

Editions Aubier
Imprint of Flammarion Groupe
87 quai Panhard et Levassor, 75647 Paris Cedex
  13
Tel: 01 40 51 31 00
Web Site: editions.flammarion.com
Key Personnel
Publishing Dir: Teressa Cremisi
Founded: 1925
Subjects: Education, History, Language Arts, Linguistics, Philosophy, Poetry, Psychology, Psychiatry, Religion - Other, Social Sciences, Sociology, Humanities
ISBN Prefix(es): 978-2-7007

Etudes Augustiniennes, see Institut d'Etudes
  Augustiniennes (IEA)

Aurore Editions D'Art, *imprint of* Editions
  Cercle d'Art

Autrement, *imprint of* Flammarion Groupe

Editions Autrement
Imprint of Flammarion Groupe
17 rue de l'Universite, 75007 Paris
Tel: 01 44 73 80 00 *Fax:* 01 44 73 00 12
E-mail: contact@autrement.com
Web Site: www.autrement.com
Key Personnel
Publishing Dir: Emmanuelle Vial
  E-mail: emmanuelle.vial@autrement.com
Founded: 1975
Subjects: Anthropology, Behavioral Sciences, Fiction, Foreign Countries, History, Literature,
  Literary Criticism, Essays, Natural History,
  Nonfiction (General), Philosophy, Psychology,
  Psychiatry, Regional Interests, Social Sciences,
  Sociology, Travel & Tourism
ISBN Prefix(es): 978-2-86260; 978-2-7467
Total Titles: 700 Print
Distributed by Editions du le Seuil

Editions Auzou+
24/32 rue des Amandiers, 75020 Paris
Tel: 01 40 33 84 00 *Fax:* 01 47 97 20 08
E-mail: editions@auzou.com
Web Site: auzou.fr
Key Personnel
President & Dir General: M Philippe Auzou
Administrative Dir: Michele Halimi
Founded: 1978
Subjects: Art
ISBN Prefix(es): 978-2-7338
Subsidiaries: Editions & Diffusions Internationales
Distribution Center: SODIS, 128 Ave du
  Marechal de Lattre de Tassigny, 77400 Lagny
  sur Marne *Tel:* 01 60 07 82 99 *Fax:* 01 64 30
  32 27 *E-mail:* saisie@sodis.fr *Web Site:* www.
  sodis.fr

Editions l'Avant-Scene Theatre+
75, rue des Saints-Peres, 75006 Paris
Tel: 01 53 63 80 60 *Fax:* 01 53 63 88 75
E-mail: contact@avant-scene-theatre.com;
  commercial@avant-scene-theatre.com
Web Site: www.avant-scene-theatre.com
Key Personnel
President & Dir General: Philippe Tesson
Editor-in-Chief: Anne-Claire Boumendil; Olivier
  Celik
Sales: Emilie Delaporte *Tel:* 01 53 63 88 77
Founded: 1949
Subjects: Drama, Theater, Film, Video, Music,
  Dance
ISBN Prefix(es): 978-2-907468; 978-2-7498; 978-
  2-900130
Imprints: Editions des Quatre-Vents
Warehouse: 6 Mail Nord, 5350 Boynes

AVM-Editions de l'Emmanuel Sarl
89 blvd Auguste Blanqui, 75013 Paris
Tel: 01 58 10 74 90 *Fax:* 01 58 10 74 99
E-mail: communication@editions-emmanuel.fr
Web Site: www.editions-emmanuel.com
Key Personnel
Dir: Louis-Etienne de Labarthe
  E-mail: ledelabarthe@editions-emmanuel.fr
Press Relations: Marie Bletry *E-mail:* mbletry@
  editions-emmanuel.fr
Subjects: Humor, Inspirational, Spirituality, Family, Human Development, Liturgy, Prayer,
  Saints, Society, Testimonies, Training
ISBN Prefix(es): 978-2-905995; 978-2-911036;
  978-2-35389; 978-2-914083; 978-2-915313

Babel, *imprint of* Editions Actes Sud

Bac en Poche, *imprint of* Editions Vuibert

Editions Stephane Baches
17, rue Rene Leynaud, 69001 Lyon
Tel: 04 78 28 18 18 *Fax:* 04 72 00 88 02
E-mail: contact@editionstephanebaches.com
Web Site: www.editionstephanebaches.com
Key Personnel
Press Relations: Camille Carlier *Tel:* 06 60 67 52
  76 *E-mail:* camille.carlier@questiondegout.net
Founded: 1999
Subjects: Architecture & Interior Design, Art,
  Cookery, Lifestyle, Painting
ISBN Prefix(es): 978-2-915266; 978-2-9511985;
  978-2-9516680
Distribution Center: Cap Diffusion, 13, rue du
  Breil, 35063 Rennes Cedex *Tel:* 02 99 32 58
  23 *Fax:* 02 99 32 58 18 *E-mail:* commercial@
  capdiffusion.fr *Web Site:* www.capdiffusion.fr
SDL Caravelle, 303, rue du pre aux oies,
  1130 Brussels, Belgium *Tel:* (02) 240 93 00
  Fax: (02) 216 35 98 *E-mail:* info@sdlcaravelle.
  com
Ulysse, 4176 Rue Saint-Denis, Montreal, QC
  H2W 2M5, Canada *Tel:* 514-843-9882
  Fax: 514-843-9448 *E-mail:* info@ulysse.ca
  Web Site: www.ulyssesguides.com
Servidis, Switzerland *Tel:* (022) 960 95 37
  Fax: (022) 776 35 44 *E-mail:* commercial@
  servidis.ch *Web Site:* www.servidis.ch

Balivernes Editions
16, rue de la Doulline, 69340 Francheville
Tel: 06 76 21 32 10 *Fax:* 04 26 29 90 34
E-mail: presse@balivernes.com; editions@
  balivernes.com
Web Site: www.balivernes.com
Key Personnel
Dir: Pierre Crooks *E-mail:* pcrooks@balivernes.
  com
Founded: 2004
ISBN Prefix(es): 978-2-35067
Foreign Rep(s): Caravelle (Belgium); Edipresse
  (Canada); Servidis (Switzerland)

Bamboo Edition
116, rue des Joncheres, 71012 Charnay les Macon
  Cedex
Mailing Address: BP 3, 71850 Charnay les Macon Cedex
Tel: 03 85 34 99 09 *Fax:* 03 85 34 47 55
Web Site: www.bamboo.fr
Key Personnel
Licensing: Catherine Loiselet *E-mail:* c.loiselet@
  bamboo.fr
Subjects: Fiction, Humor, Sports, Athletics
ISBN Prefix(es): 978-2-35078; 978-2-8189
Foreign Rep(s): Diffulivre (Switzerland); Dilibel
  (Belgium)
Distribution Center: Hachette Livres, Av Gutenberg, 78316 Maurepas Cedex *Tel:* 01 30 66 20
  66 *Fax:* 01 30 66 24 39

Editions Le Baron Perche
30 rue Jacob, 75006 Paris
Fax: 01 83 64 07 89
E-mail: infolivre@editionslebaronperche.com
Web Site: www.editionslebaronperche.com
Key Personnel
Dir: Brigitte Stephan *Tel:* 01 83 64 07 80
  E-mail: b.stephan@editionslebaronperche.com
Editor: Celine Ottenwaelter *Tel:* 01 83 64 07 81
  E-mail: c.ottenwaelter@editionslebaronperche.
  com
Foreign Rights: Christian Voges
  E-mail: vogesforeignrights@free.fr
Founded: 2004
ISBN Prefix(es): 978-2-36080
Distribution Center: Sodis, 128 Ave du Marechal
  de Lattre de Tassigny, 77400 Lagny sur Marne

Editions Xavier Barral
42, rue Sedaine, 75011 Paris
Tel: 01 48 05 73 01
E-mail: exb@xavierbarral.fr
Web Site: www.exb.fr
Key Personnel
Chief Executive Officer: Xavier Barral
Subjects: Art
ISBN Prefix(es): 978-2-36511

La Bartavelle
8, rue des Tanneries, 42190 Charlieu
Tel: 04 77 60 11 94 *Fax:* 04 77 60 11 94
E-mail: caruslocus@aol.com
Web Site: www.la-bartavelle-editeur.com
Key Personnel
Publications Dir: Eric Ballandras
Founded: 1985
Subjects: Literature, Literary Criticism, Essays,
Photography
ISBN Prefix(es): 978-2-87744; 978-2-84414

Editions A Barthelemy+
Domaine de Fontvert, 84132 Le Pontet Cedex
Mailing Address: BP 50050, 84132 Le Pontet
Cedex
Tel: 04 90 03 60 00 *Fax:* 04 90 03 60 09
E-mail: infos@editions-barthelemy.com
Web Site: www.editions-barthelemy.com
Founded: 1978
Subjects: Art, Cookery, Health, Nutrition, Humor,
Photography, Regional Interests, Sports, Athlet-
ics, Travel & Tourism, Nature
ISBN Prefix(es): 978-2-87923
Foreign Rep(s): Memograms Directe Diffusion
(Belgium); Ulysse Distribution (Canada)
Distribution Center: Daudin Distribution, One
rue Guynemr, CS 30504, 78771 Magny les
Hameaux Cedex *Tel:* 01 30 48 74 74 *Fax:* 01
34 98 02 44

Bayard Editions+
18 rue Barbes, 92128 Montrouge Cedex
Tel: 01 74 31 60 60
E-mail: contact@editions-bayard.com; foreign.
rights@editions-bayard.com
Web Site: www.editions-bayard.com; www.
groupebayard.com
Key Personnel
Dir: Franck Girard
Foreign Rights Dir: Emmanuelle Marie
E-mail: emmanuelle.marie@groupebayard.com
Chief Communication Officer: Corinne Vorms
E-mail: corinne.vorms@bayard-presse.com
Founded: 1870
Subjects: Art, Education, History, Religion -
Other, Social Sciences, Sociology, Humanities
ISBN Prefix(es): 978-2-227; 978-2-7009; 978-2-
915480; 978-2-9518356; 978-2-7470
Number of titles published annually: 60 Print
Parent Company: Groupe Bayard
Associate Companies: Bayard Jeunesse; Editions
Milan; Twenty Third
Orders to: Sofedis, The Soufflot, 75005 Paris

Bayard Presse SA, see Bayard Editions

Editions des Beatitudes+
Burtin, 41600 Nouan le Fuzelier
Tel: 02 54 88 21 18 *Fax:* 02 54 88 97 73
Web Site: www.editions-beatitudes.com
Key Personnel
Foreign Rights Manager: Sr Faustine de Jesus
Founded: 1984
Subjects: Religion - Catholic
ISBN Prefix(es): 978-2-905480; 978-2-84024;
978-2-85847
Distributed by Editions Mediaspaul (Canada);
Editions Salvator (France)

Beauchesne Editeur+
7, cite du Cardinal-Lemoine, 75005 Paris
Tel: 01 53 10 08 18 *Fax:* 01 53 10 85 19
Web Site: www.editions-beauchesne.com
Key Personnel
President: Jean-Etienne Mittlelmann
Founded: 1851
Subjects: Art, Biography, Memoirs, Government,
Political Science, History, Human Relations,
Inspirational, Spirituality, Journalism, Litera-
ture, Literary Criticism, Essays, Music, Dance,
Philosophy, Religion - Other, Science (Gen-
eral), Social Sciences, Sociology, Theology
ISBN Prefix(es): 978-2-7010
Total Titles: 800 Print; 1 CD-ROM; 1 Audio
Distributor for Anne Sigier Canada (Canada);
Anne Sigier France (Belgium & Luxembourg)
Distribution Center: OLF SA, ZI3, Corminboeuf,
PO Box 1152, 1701 Fribourg, Switzerland

Le Bec en l'Air Editions
Friche La Belle de Mai, 41, rue Jobin, 13003
Marseille
Tel: 04 91 50 29 88 *Fax:* 09 74 53 17 90
E-mail: contact@becair.com; projets@becair.com
(editorial)
Web Site: www.becair.com
Key Personnel
Editorial: Fabienne Pavia
Subjects: Architecture & Interior Design, Art,
Photography, Social Sciences, Sociology, Travel
& Tourism, Contemporary Art, Heritage
ISBN Prefix(es): 978-2-9521472; 978-2-916073;
978-2-9516595

Editions Belfond
12, ave d'Italie, 75627 Paris Cedex 13
Tel: 01 44 16 05 00 *Fax:* 01 44 16 05 01
Web Site: www.belfond.fr
Key Personnel
Chief Executive Officer: Jean Arcache
Rights Dir, Fiction & Nonfiction: Alexan-
dra Buchman *Tel:* 01 44 16 05 76
E-mail: alexandra.buchman@placedesediteurs.
com
Rights Dir, Illustrated Books & Children's Books:
Paul Bernard *Tel:* (086) 43 01 44 *E-mail:* paul.
bernard@hemma.de
Founded: 1963
Subjects: History, Literature, Literary Criticism,
Essays, Science Fiction, Fantasy
ISBN Prefix(es): 978-2-84228; 978-2-7144
Parent Company: Place des editeurs
Distribution Center: Interforum - Immeuble Pary-
seine, 3, allee de la Seine, 94854 Ivry Cedex
Tel: 01 49 59 10 10
Interforum Benelux SA, 117 bd de l'Europe,
1301 Wavre, Belgium *Tel:* (010) 420 320
Interforum Canada Inc, 1001, boul de Maison-
neuve Est, 10th floor, Suite 1001, Montreal,
QC H2X 4P9, Canada *Tel:* 514-281-1050
Interforum Suisse SA, Route Andre Piller, 33, A
Givisiez, CP 69, 1701 Fribourg, Switzerland
Tel: (026) 460 80 60

Editions Belin+
8, rue Ferou, 75278 Paris Cedex 06
Tel: 01 55 42 84 00 *Fax:* 01 43 25 18 29
E-mail: enseignants@editions-belin.fr
Web Site: www.editions-belin.com
Key Personnel
Mng Dir: Sylvie Marce
Founded: 1777
Subjects: Art, Education, Gardening, Plants, Lit-
erature, Literary Criticism, Essays, Poetry, Sci-
ence (General)
ISBN Prefix(es): 978-2-7011
Number of titles published annually: 150 Print; 5
CD-ROM; 10 Audio
Total Titles: 2,000 Print; 40 Audio

Subsidiaries: Herscher; Les Editions du Pommier;
Pour la Science Sarl
Foreign Rep(s): La Caravelle (Belgium); Edi-
presse (Canada); El Maarif (Morocco); Servidis
SA (Switzerland)

Societe d'Edition Les Belles Lettres+
95 Blvd Raspail, 75006 Paris
Tel: 01 44 39 84 21 *Fax:* 01 45 44 92 88
E-mail: courrier@lesbelleslettres.com
Web Site: www.lesbelleslettres.com
Key Personnel
President & Mng Dir: Michel Desgranges
E-mail: m.desgranges@lesbelleslettres.com
Foreign Rights: Marie-Pierre Ciric
Founded: 1919
Subjects: Art, Drama, Theater, Education, Fiction,
History, Language Arts, Linguistics, Literature,
Literary Criticism, Essays, Philosophy, Religion
- Other, Science (General), Theology, Classical
Studies. Humanities, Mythology
ISBN Prefix(es): 978-2-251
Imprints: Manitoba; Sortileges
Bookshop(s): Librairie Guillaume Bude, Paris
Tel: 01 44 39 84 21 *E-mail:* librairie@
lesbelleslettres.com

Berg International Editeur+
129, blvd Saint-Michel, 75005 Paris
Tel: 01 43 26 72 73 *Fax:* 01 46 33 94 99
E-mail: berg.international@wanadoo.fr
Web Site: www.berg-international.fr
Key Personnel
Mng Dir: Georges Nataf
Founded: 1969
Subjects: Anthropology, History, Literature, Lit-
erary Criticism, Essays, Philosophy, Religion
- Islamic, Religion - Jewish, Religion - Other,
Humanities
ISBN Prefix(es): 978-2-900269; 978-2-911289

Berger-Levrault Editions SAS
104 ave du President Kennedy, 75016 Paris
Web Site: boutique.berger-levrault.fr
Key Personnel
Publishing Dir: Pierre-Marie Lehucher
Founded: 1676
Subjects: Architecture & Interior Design, Art,
Education, Ethnicity, History, Law, Social Sci-
ences, Sociology
ISBN Prefix(es): 978-2-7013
Bookshop(s): Librairie Berger-Levrault, 23 pl
Broglie, 67000 Strasbourg

Editions Bertrand-Lacoste
36 rue St-Germain-l'Auxerrois, 75041 Paris
Cedex 01
Tel: 01 53 40 53 53 *Fax:* 01 42 33 82 47
E-mail: contact@bertrand-lacoste.fr
Web Site: www.bertrand-lacoste.fr
Key Personnel
Mng Dir: Denis Deslogis
Founded: 1980
Subjects: Accounting, Computer Science, Eco-
nomics, Law
ISBN Prefix(es): 978-2-7399; 978-2-7352

Bibliotheque Nationale de France (National
Library of France)+
Quai Francois-Mauriac, 75706 Paris Cedex 13
Tel: 01 53 79 59 59 *Fax:* 01 47 03 81 72
E-mail: reproduction@bnf.fr
Web Site: www.bnf.fr
Key Personnel
President: Laurence Engel
Publishing department of the French National Li-
brary.
Subjects: History, Library & Information Sci-
ences, Literature, Literary Criticism, Essays
ISBN Prefix(es): 978-2-7177
Number of titles published annually: 30 Print
Total Titles: 500 Print
Foreign Rep(s): Sevil (worldwide)

Bibliotheque pour l'Ecole (BPE)+
Bernardan Cherbois RD 912, 87890 Jouac
Tel: 05 55 60 17 57 *Fax:* 05 55 60 17 74
E-mail: infos@b-p-e.com.fr
Web Site: bpe.pemf.fr
Founded: 1986
ISBN Prefix(es): 978-2-87785; 978-2-84526
Associate Companies: CELF, 9, rue de Toul,
75589 Paris Cedex 12 *Tel:* 01 44 67 83 83
Fax: 01 43 47 59 43
Distribution Center: Education Populaire ASBL,
Maison de la Francite, 19F, Ave des Arts, 1000
Brussels, Belgium, Contact: Mr Jean Dumont
Tel: (0486) 90 59 89 *E-mail:* mat.educpop@
gmail.com

**BIEF (Bureau International de l'Edition
Francaise)** (French Publishers International
Office)
Association d'editeurs, 115, Blvd Saint-Germain,
75006 Paris
Tel: 01 44 41 13 13 *Fax:* 01 46 34 63 83
E-mail: info@bief.org
Web Site: www.bief.org
Key Personnel
Dir: Jean-Guy Boin *Tel:* 01 44 41 13 08
Assistant Dir: Catherine Leprovost *Tel:* 01 44 41
13 21 *E-mail:* c.leprovost@bief.org
Publishes titles in all subjects.
Subjects: Architecture & Interior Design, Art,
Humor, Literature, Literary Criticism, Essays,
Nonfiction (General), Publishing & Book Trade
Reference, Social Sciences, Sociology
U.S. Office(s): The French Publishers' Agency,
39 W 59 St, Suite 804, New York, NY 10018,
United States, Dir: Lucinda Karter *Tel:* 212-
254-4540 *Fax:* 212-979-6229 *E-mail:* lucinda@
frenchrights.com *Web Site:* www.frenchrights.
com

Biro Editeur+
2 rue des 4 Fils, 75003 Paris
Tel: 01 49 96 43 92
Key Personnel
Editorial Dir & Manager: Stephane Cohen
Editorial Advisor: Adam Biro
Founded: 1987
Subjects: Antiques, Architecture & Interior De-
sign, Art, Fashion, Photography
ISBN Prefix(es): 978-2-87660; 978-2-35119
Number of titles published annually: 20 Print
Total Titles: 285 Print
Orders to: Les Belles Lettres

Editions William Blake & Co+
BP 4, 33037 Bordeaux Cedex
Fax: 05 56 31 45 47
E-mail: editions.william.blake@wanadoo.fr
Web Site: www.editions-william-blake-and-co.com
Key Personnel
Founder & Publisher: Jean-Paul Michel
Founded: 1976
Subjects: Architecture & Interior Design, Art,
Drama, Theater, History, Literature, Literary
Criticism, Essays, Philosophy, Photography,
Poetry
ISBN Prefix(es): 978-2-84103; 978-2-905810
Imprints: L'Invention du Lecteur; La Pharmacie
de Platon
Distributor for Arts & Arts
Distribution Center: Societe de diffusion Les
Belles Lettres, 25 rue du General Leclerc,
94270 Le Kremlin Bicetre *Tel:* 01 45 15 19
70 *Fax:* 01 45 15 19 80 *Web Site:* www.bldd.fr

Editions Albert Blanchard
9, rue de Medicis, 75006 Paris
Tel: 01 43 26 90 34 *Fax:* 01 43 29 90 34
E-mail: librairie.blanchard@wanadoo.fr
Web Site: www.blanchard75.fr

Subjects: Astronomy, Chemistry, Chemical Engi-
neering, Earth Sciences, Mathematics, Natural
History, Philosophy, Physics, Science (General)
ISBN Prefix(es): 978-2-85367
Number of titles published annually: 3 Print
Total Titles: 1,721 Print

Blay-Foldex
Member of Groupe Artique
149 ave du General de Gaulle, 37230 Fondettes
(Tours)
Tel: 02 47 49 90 49 *Fax:* 02 47 79 91 49
E-mail: info@blayfoldex.com
Web Site: www.blayfoldex.com
Key Personnel
Founder & President: Georges-Antoine Strauch
E-mail: gas@articque.com
Founded: 1934
Publisher of maps & atlases.
Subjects: How-to
ISBN Prefix(es): 978-2-400200

Editions Bleu autour
11 Ave Pasteur, Saint-Pourcain-sur-Sioule 03500
Tel: 04 70 45 72 45 *Fax:* 04 70 45 72 54
E-mail: dialogue@bleu-autour.com
Web Site: www.bleu-autour.com
Key Personnel
Editorial Dir: Patrice Rotig *E-mail:* patrice.rotig@
bleu-autour.com
Events & Press: Simon Rotig *E-mail:* simon.
rotig@bleu-autour.com
Subjects: Art, Biography, Memoirs, Literature,
Literary Criticism, Essays
ISBN Prefix(es): 978-2-35848; 978-2-912019
Distribution Center: La Canopee diffusion,
109, chemin du Sphinx, Saint-Armand, QC
JOJ 1TO, Canada, Contact: John Davis
E-mail: lacanopee@primus.ca
Editions Porte d'Anfa, Residence Pavillon d'or,
Angle des rues Ahmed Charsi et Ali Abder-
razak, 21100 Casablanca, Morocco, Contact:
Amina Masnaoui *Tel:* 22 36 60 34 *Fax:* 22 26
60 39 *E-mail:* librairieporteanfa@hotmail.com

BNF, see Bibliotheque Nationale de France

Editions De Boccard
11, rue de Medicis, 75006 Paris
Tel: 01 43 26 00 37
E-mail: info@deboccard.com
Web Site: www.deboccard.com
Founded: 1866
Subjects: Archaeology, Art, Asian Studies, His-
tory, Religion - Other
ISBN Prefix(es): 978-2-7018

La Boite a bulles
5 Villa do Petit Valet, 92160 Antony
Tel: 01 42 37 86 80
E-mail: projet@la-boite-a-bulles.com
Web Site: www.la-boite-a-bulles.com
Key Personnel
Rights: Vincent Henry *E-mail:* vincent@la-boite-
a-bulles.com
Founded: 2003
Subjects: Art, Drama, Theater, Fiction
ISBN Prefix(es): 978-2-84953

Bordas, *imprint of* Les Editions Bordas

Les Editions Bordas+
31 ave Pierre de Coubertin, 75013 Paris
Tel: 01 53 55 26 23; 01 53 55 26 15; 01 72 36
40 08 (press)
E-mail: contactnumerique@bordas.tm.fr
Web Site: www.editions-bordas.fr
Key Personnel
Publications Dir: Catherine Lucet
Public Relations: Guillaume Piettre
E-mail: gpiettre@bordas.tm.fr

Founded: 1946
Subjects: Drama, Theater, Education, History,
Literature, Literary Criticism, Essays, Music,
Dance, Nonfiction (General)
ISBN Prefix(es): 978-2-04; 978-2-7294; 978-2-
7109
Imprints: Bordas; Pedagogie Modern; Technique
et Vulgarisation
Subsidiaries: Societe Gauthier-Villars; Privat SA
Foreign Rep(s): Interforum Benelux (Belgium,
Luxembourg); Interforum Canada Inc (Canada);
Interforum Suisse (Switzerland); Messageries
ADP (Canada)
Distribution Center: Interforum, Immeuble Pary-
seine, 3 allee de la Seine, 94854 Ivry-sur-Seine
Cedex *Tel:* 01 49 59 10 10 *Fax:* 01 49 59 10
72 *Web Site:* www.interforum.fr

Presses Universitaires de Bordeaux (PUB)+
Domaine Universitaire, Universite Michel de
Montaigne Bordeaux 3, 33607 Pessac
Tel: 05 57 12 46 60
E-mail: pub@u-bordeaux3.fr
Web Site: pub.u-bordeaux3.fr
Key Personnel
Dir: Bernadette Rigal-Cellard *Tel:* 05 57 12 44 21
E-mail: bernadette.rigal-cellard@u-bordeaux3.fr
Editor: Antoine Poli *Tel:* 05 57 12 46 34
E-mail: antoine.poli@u-bordeaux-montaigne.fr
Founded: 1983
Subjects: Anthropology, Education, Environmen-
tal Studies, Geography, Geology, History, Law,
Literature, Literary Criticism, Essays, Philoso-
phy, Wine & Spirits
ISBN Prefix(es): 978-2-86781
Distribution Center: Sodis, 128, Ave du Marechal
Lattre de Tassigny, BP 142, 77403 Lagny-sur-
Marne Cedex *Tel:* 01 60 07 82 99 *Fax:* 01 64
30 32 27
SLU, 131, blvd Saint-Michel, 75005 Paris *Tel:* 01
53 10 53 95 *Fax:* 01 40 51 02 80 *E-mail:* slu@
msh-paris.fr (worldwide exc France)

Bornemann
15 rue Mansart, 75009 Paris
Tel: 01 48 78 40 74 *Fax:* 01 48 78 40 77
E-mail: contact@ulisseditions.com
Web Site: www.ulisseditions.com
Founded: 1829
Subjects: Animals, Pets, Crafts, Games, Hob-
bies, Gardening, Plants, How-to, Music, Dance,
Sports, Athletics
ISBN Prefix(es): 978-2-85182
Parent Company: Groupe Ulisse

Christian Bourgois Editeur
116 rue du Bac, 75007 Paris
Tel: 01 45 44 09 13 *Fax:* 01 45 44 87 86
Web Site: www.christianbourgois-editeur.com;
www.facebook.com/EditionsChristianBourgois
Founded: 1966
Specialize in foreign literature.
Subjects: Fiction, Literature, Literary Criticism,
Essays, Music, Dance
ISBN Prefix(es): 978-2-267

BPE, see Bibliotheque pour l'Ecole (BPE)

Editions Bragelonne+
60/62 rue d'Hauteville, 75010 Paris
Tel: 01 56 88 20 90
Web Site: www.bragelonne.fr
Key Personnel
Publishing Dir: Stephane Marsan *E-mail:* s.
marsan@bragelonne.fr
Art Dir: David Oghia *E-mail:* d.oghia@
bragelonne.fr
Rights Manager: Yolanda Rochat de la Valle
E-mail: y.rochat@bragelonne.fr
Founded: 2000
Specialize in science fiction & fantasy.
Subjects: Crafts, Games, Hobbies, Fiction, Film,
Video, History, Humor, Literature, Literary

Criticism, Essays, Mysteries, Suspense, Radio,
TV, Science Fiction, Fantasy
ISBN Prefix(es): 978-2-914370
Number of titles published annually: 50 Print
Total Titles: 170 Print
Imprints: Milady
Foreign Rep(s): Patricia Pasqualini Literary
Agency (worldwide)
Foreign Rights: Patricia Pasqualini Literary
Agency (worldwide)

Editions Breal
24/38 rue Camille Pelletan, 92309 Levallois-
Perret Cedex
Tel: 01 41 06 64 99; 01 41 06 59 17
Web Site: www.editions-breal.fr
Key Personnel
Contact: Cecile Colonna
Founded: 1969
Subjects: Accounting, Advertising, Biological Sci-
ences, Communications, Computer Science,
Economics, Electronics, Electrical Engineering,
History, Language Arts, Linguistics, Law, Man-
agement, Marketing, Mathematics, Philosophy,
Physical Sciences, Physics
ISBN Prefix(es): 978-2-85394; 978-2-84291; 978-
2-7495
Parent Company: Groupe Studyrama
Associate Companies: ABC Editions
Foreign Rep(s): Al Madariss (Morocco); Dif-
fulivre SA (Switzerland); Diffusion-Service
Export (all other territories); Jourdan-Le-Clercq
Editions (Belgium); Somabec (Canada)
Bookshop(s): Librairie Des Prepas, 34 rue Ser-
pente, 75006 Paris *Tel:* 01 43 26 85 04 *Fax:* 01
46 33 98 15
Warehouse: Diffusion Breal, 2 rue des Vieilles
Vignes, 77183 Croissy Beaubourg *Tel:* 01 64
61 80 80 *Fax:* 01 64 61 80 86
Distribution Center: Dilisco, Rue de Limousin,
BP 25, 23220 Cheniers *Tel:* 05 55 51 80 00
Fax: 05 55 62 17 39 *E-mail:* relation.client@
dilisco.fr

Les Editions Emgleo Breiz+
2 bis rue Prof Chretien, 29200 Brest
Tel: 02 98 02 68 17
E-mail: emgleo.breiz@wanadoo.fr
Web Site: www.emgleobreiz.com
Key Personnel
President: Fanch Broudig
Founded: 1955
Subjects: Biography, Memoirs, Fiction, Literature,
Literary Criticism, Essays, Poetry, Travel &
Tourism
ISBN Prefix(es): 978-2-900828; 978-2-911210
Number of titles published annually: 12 Print
Total Titles: 250 Print; 20 Audio
Divisions: Ar Skol Vrezoneg; Brud Nevez

Editions Jacques Bremond+
Le Clos de la Cournilhe, 30210 Remoulins-sur-
Gardon
Tel: 04 66 57 45 61 *Fax:* 04 66 37 27 40
E-mail: editions-jacques-bremond@wanadoo.fr
Key Personnel
Chairman: Jacques Bremond
Founded: 1975
Typographie:
Subjects: Drama, Theater, Literature, Literary
Criticism, Essays, Poetry
ISBN Prefix(es): 978-2-910063; 978-2-903108;
978-2-915519
Number of titles published annually: 10 Print
Total Titles: 300 Print

Editions BRGM+
3 ave Claude-Guillemin, 45060 Orleans Cedex 02
Mailing Address: BP 36009, 45060 Orleans
Cedex 02
Tel: 02 38 64 34 34
E-mail: contact-brgm@brgm.fr

Web Site: editions.brgm.fr/editions.jsp
Founded: 1962
BRGM is the Office of Geological & Mineral Re-
search in France & French Geological Survey.
Subjects: Earth Sciences, Environmental Studies,
Geography, Geology
ISBN Prefix(es): 978-2-7159; 978-2-901709
Number of titles published annually: 20 Print
Total Titles: 800 Print; 80 E-Book; 3 Audio
Parent Company: BRGM, 39-43 quai Andre Cit-
roen, 75739 Paris Cedex 15

Galerie Michele Broutta, see OGC Michele
Broutta Editeur

Editions Buchet/Chastel+
Imprint of Libella Publishing Group
7 rue des Canettes, 75006 Paris
Tel: 01 44 32 05 60 *Fax:* 01 44 32 05 61
E-mail: informations@libella.fr
Web Site: www.buchetchastel.fr
Key Personnel
President: Vera Michalski
Foreign Rights: Christine Legrand
E-mail: christine.legrand@libella.fr
Founded: 1986
Subjects: Art, Biblical Studies, Crafts, Games,
Hobbies, Education, Literature, Literary Criti-
cism, Essays, Music, Dance, Photography, Po-
etry, Religion - Catholic, Theology, Ecology
ISBN Prefix(es): 978-2-7020; 978-2-283
Number of titles published annually: 60 Print
Total Titles: 700 Print

Editions Bulles de Savon
Bas de Rochefort, 69850 St Martin-en-Haut
Tel: 09 86 20 31 13
E-mail: contact@editions-bullesdesavon.com
Web Site: www.editions-bullesdesavon.com
Key Personnel
Publisher: Jean Rene *E-mail:* jeanrene@editions-
bullesdesavon.com
Founded: 2011
ISBN Prefix(es): 979-10-90597
Distribution Center: Flammarion, 87 quai Pan-
hard et Levassor, 75647 Paris Cedex 13 *Tel:* 01
40 51 31 00 *Web Site:* www.flammarion-
diffusion.fr

Bureau des Longitudes
23 quai de Conti, 75006 Paris
Mailing Address: 3 rue Mazarine, 75006 Paris
Tel: 01 43 26 59 02 *Fax:* 01 43 26 80 90
E-mail: renseignements@bureau-des-longitudes.fr
Web Site: www.bureau-des-longitudes.fr
Key Personnel
President: Pierre Bauer
Secretary: Pascal Willis
Contact: Nicole Capitaine
Founded: 1795
Subjects: Astronomy, Earth Sciences, Science
(General), Space Science
ISBN Prefix(es): 978-2-910015

Bureau International de l'Edition Francaise,
see BIEF (Bureau International de l'Edition
Francaise)

Le Buveur D'encre
14 rue Charles V, 75004 Paris
Tel: 01 43 71 34 67
Web Site: lebuveurdencre.fr
Founded: 2001
ISBN Prefix(es): 978-2-914686

Editions ca et la
6, rue Jean Baptiste Vacher, 77600 Bussy Saint-
Georges
Tel: 06 14 83 60 42
Web Site: www.caetla.fr

Key Personnel
Editor & Press: Serge Ewenczyk *E-mail:* serge@
caetla.fr
Artistic Dir: Helene Duhamel *E-mail:* helene@
caetla.fr
Founded: 2005
Subjects: Fiction, Science Fiction, Fantasy,
Graphic Novels
ISBN Prefix(es): 978-2-916207
Foreign Rep(s): Dimedia (Canada); Servidis
(Switzerland)
Distribution Center: Belles Lettres Diffusion Dis-
tribution, 25, rue du General Leclerc, 94270 Le
Kremlin-Bicetre *Tel:* 01 45 15 19 73 *Fax:* 01
45 15 19 81 *E-mail:* m.herve@lesbelleslettres.
com *Web Site:* www.bldd.fr (France & Bel-
gium)

Editions du Cadratin+
6 quai de l'Ource, 10360 Essoyes
Tel: 03 25 38 60 24 *Fax:* 03 25 38 60 24
Web Site: www.editions-du-cadratin.com
Founded: 1979
Subjects: Art, History, Literature, Literary Criti-
cism, Essays
ISBN Prefix(es): 978-2-86549

Editions des Cahiers Bourbonnais+
rue de l'Horloge, 03140 Charroux-en-
Bourbonnais
Tel: 04 70 56 80 61 *Fax:* 04 70 56 80 80
Web Site: www.cahiers-bourbonnais.com
Key Personnel
Dir: Jean-Pierre Petit *E-mail:* j-p.petit@cahiers-
bourbonnais.com
Editor: Jean-Paul Perrin
Founded: 1957
Subjects: Agriculture, Archaeology, Art, Business,
History, Literature, Literary Criticism, Essays,
Poetry, Publishing & Book Trade Reference
ISBN Prefix(es): 978-2-85370

Editions Cahiers d'Art
14 rue du Dragon, 75006 Paris
Tel: 01 45 48 76 73
E-mail: info@cahiersdart.fr
Web Site: www.cahiersdart.fr
Founded: 1926
Subjects: Art, Photography
ISBN Prefix(es): 978-2-85117

Cahiers du Cinema+
18-20, rue Claude Tillier, 75012 Paris
Tel: 01 53 44 75 75
Web Site: www.cahiersducinema.com
Key Personnel
Publishing Dir: Jerome Cuzol *E-mail:* jcuzol@
cahiersducinema.com
Executive Dir: Catherine Laulhere-Vigneau
E-mail: claulhere@cahiersducinema.com
Editor-in-Chief: Stephane Delorme
E-mail: sdelorme@cahiersducinema.com
Associate Editor: Jean-Philippe Tesse
E-mail: jptesse@cahiersducinema.com
Founded: 1951
Subjects: Art, Drama, Theater, Religion - Other,
Social Sciences, Sociology, Human Sciences
ISBN Prefix(es): 978-2-86642
Number of titles published annually: 25 Print
Total Titles: 2,000 Print
Parent Company: Phaidon Press
Distribution Center: Sodis, 128 Ave du Marechal
de Lattre de Tassigny, 77400 Lagny-sur-Marne
Tel: 01 60 07 82 00

Les Cahiers Fiscaux Europeens Sarl+
51 Ave Reine Victoria, 06000 Nice
Tel: 04 93 53 89 39 *Fax:* 04 93 53 66 28
E-mail: cfe@fontaneau.com
Web Site: www.fontaneau.com
Key Personnel
Dir, Publication: Pierre Marie Fontaneau
Founded: 1968

Subjects: Economics, Taxation
ISBN Prefix(es): 978-2-85444
Parent Company: Societe d'Etudes Juridiques Internationales et Fiscales
Subsidiaries: CFE Belgique

Editions Calmann-Levy SA+
Subsidiary of Hachette Livre
31 rue de Fleurus, 75006 Paris Cedex 06
Tel: 01 49 54 36 00; 01 49 54 36 48 (rights)
Fax: 01 49 54 36 40
E-mail: cessionscl@calmann-levy.fr (rights)
Web Site: calmann-levy.fr
Key Personnel
Mng Dir: Mdme Florence Sultan
Subsidiary Rights Manager: Patricia Roussel
    E-mail: proussel@calmann-levy.fr
Subsidiary Rights Assistant: Julia Balcells
    E-mail: jbalcells@calmann-levy.fr
Founded: 1836
Subjects: Biography, Memoirs, Economics, Fiction, History, Humor, Literature, Literary Criticism, Essays, Nonfiction (General), Philosophy, Psychology, Psychiatry, Science Fiction, Fantasy, Social Sciences, Sociology, Sports, Athletics
ISBN Prefix(es): 978-2-7021
Foreign Rep(s): Diffulivre (Switzerland); Dilibel (Belgium); Hachette Canada (Canada)
Foreign Rights: AMV Agencia Literaria (Eduardo Melon Vallet) (Portugal, Spain); Luigi Bernabo & Associates (Luigi Bernabo) (Italy); Niki Douge (Greece); Liepman Agentur (Eva Koralnik) (Germany)
Distribution Center: Hachette Livre Distribution, One Ave Gutenberg, 78316 Maurepas Cedex
    Tel: 01 30 66 20 66

Editions Cambourakis
24, rue Voltaire, 75011 Paris
Tel: 09 81 02 10 92
E-mail: editions@cambourakis.com
Web Site: www.cambourakis.com
Key Personnel
Publishing Dir: Frederic Cambourakis
Editorial: Geraldine Chognard; Levente Selaf
Public Relations & Press: Chiara Gennaretri
Founded: 2006
Subjects: Literature, Literary Criticism, Essays, Poetry
ISBN Prefix(es): 978-2-916589
Distribution Center: Prologue (Canada)
Servidis (Switzerland)
UD-Union Distribution Flammarion (France & Belgium)

Captures Editions
One rue Gutenberg, 26000 Valencia
Tel: 04 75 78 45 14 *Fax:* 06 33 56 50 26
E-mail: contact@captures-editions.com
Web Site: www.captures-editions.com
Key Personnel
Founder & Mng Dir: Valerie Cudel
Founded: 2008
Subjects: Art
ISBN Prefix(es): 978-2-9531889
Distribution Center: Les Presses du Reel, 35 rue Colson, 21000 Dijon *Tel:* 03 80 30 75 23 *Fax:* 03 80 30 59 74 *E-mail:* info@lespressesdureel.com *Web Site:* www.lespressesdureel.com

Editions Caracteres+
7 rue de l'Arbalete, 75005 Paris
Tel: 01 43 37 96 98 *Fax:* 01 43 37 26 10
E-mail: contact@editions-caracteres.fr
Web Site: www.editions-caracteres.fr
Founded: 1950
Subjects: Art, Drama, Theater, Philosophy, Poetry
ISBN Prefix(es): 978-2-85446

Parent Company: TC Media Livres, 5800, rue Saint-Denis, 9e etage, Montreal, QC H2S 3L5, Canada
Distributed by Alterdis
Distribution Center: Casteilla, 10 rue Leon-Foucault, 78184 Saint-Quentin-en-Yveline
    Tel: 01 30 14 19 30 *Fax:* 01 30 14 19 46
    E-mail: casteilla@wanadoo.fr

Editions Carpentier
22, rue d'Aumale, 75009 Paris
Tel: 01 48 78 00 72 *Fax:* 01 48 78 86 25
E-mail: editions@editions-carpentier.fr
Web Site: www.editions-carpentier.fr
Key Personnel
Manager: Didier Carpentier
Founded: 1982
Subjects: Biography, Memoirs, Cookery, Crafts, Games, Hobbies, House & Home, Literature, Literary Criticism, Essays, Music, Dance
ISBN Prefix(es): 978-2-84167; 978-2-906962
Total Titles: 400 Print
Distribution Center: Volumen, 69 Bis rue de Vaugirard, 75006 Paris

Editions Casteilla+
Route du Limousin, BP 22, 23220 Cheniers
Web Site: www.casteilla.fr
Founded: 1950
Specialize in textbooks, vocational training.
Subjects: Art, Economics, Law, Vocational Training
ISBN Prefix(es): 978-2-7135
Number of titles published annually: 100 Print
Total Titles: 800 Print
Parent Company: Delagrave

Castelmore
60-62 rue d'hauteville, 75010 Paris
Tel: 01 56 88 20 90
Web Site: www.castelmore.fr
Key Personnel
Publishing Dir: Alain Nevant
Founded: 2010
Subjects: Drama, Theater, Fiction, Science Fiction, Fantasy
ISBN Prefix(es): 978-2-36231

Casterman, *imprint of* Flammarion Groupe

Le Castor Astral Editeur+
27, rue Jules Auffret, 93500 Pantin
Mailing Address: 52, rue des Grilles, 93500 Pantin
Tel: 01 48 40 14 95 *Fax:* 01 48 45 97 52
E-mail: castor.astral@wanadoo.fr; castor.editeur@wanadoo.fr
Web Site: www.castorastral.com
Key Personnel
Dir General & Administration: Marc Torralba
    Tel: 05 56 85 23 51
Editorial Dir: Jean-Yves Reuzeau
    E-mail: jyreuzeau@wanadoo.fr
Assistant Editorial Dir: Benedicte Perot
Founded: 1975
Subjects: Art, Literature, Literary Criticism, Essays, Music, Dance, Poetry
ISBN Prefix(es): 978-2-85920
Foreign Rep(s): Dimedia (Canada); Servidis (Switzerland)
Distribution Center: Volumen, 25, Blvd Romain Rolland, 75014 Paris *Tel:* 01 41 48 84 60 *E-mail:* volumen@volumen.fr (France & Belgium)

CCNPS, *imprint of* Agence Bibliographique de l'Enseignement Superieur

Editions Celse
10 rue Leon Cogniet, 75821 Paris Cedex 17
Mailing Address: BP 106, 75821 Paris Cedex 17

Tel: 01 42 67 41 23 *Fax:* 01 42 27 40 20
E-mail: celse@celsedit.com
Web Site: www.celsedit.com
Key Personnel
President: Marie-Francoise Courtin
Dir General: Isabelle Dekeukelaere
Founded: 1957
Specialize in transportation & logistics.
Subjects: Transportation
ISBN Prefix(es): 978-2-85009
Total Titles: 75 Print

Editions Cenomane+
59, rue Henry-Delageniere, 72000 Le Mans
Tel: 02 43 24 21 57
Web Site: www.editions-cenomane.fr
Key Personnel
Dir General: Alain Mala
Founded: 1986
Subjects: Art, History, Literature, Literary Criticism, Essays, Military Science, Regional Interests, Transportation
ISBN Prefix(es): 978-2-905596; 978-2-916329
Number of titles published annually: 8 Print
Total Titles: 130 Print

Editions Cent Pages
BP 291, 38009 Grenoble Cedex
Tel: 04 38 12 16 20 *Fax:* 04 38 12 16 29
E-mail: centpages@wanadoo.fr
Web Site: centpages.atheles.org
ISBN Prefix(es): 978-2-906724
Distributed by Les Belles Lettres

Centre de Formation et de Perfectionnement des Journalistes, see Les Editions du CFPJ (Centre de Formation et de Perfectionnement des Journalistes)

Centre International de Poesie Marseille (Marseille International Poetry Center)
Centre de la Veille Charite, 2, rue de la Charite, 13236 Marseille Cedex 2
Tel: 04 91 91 26 45 *Fax:* 04 91 90 99 51
E-mail: cipm@cipmarseille.com
Web Site: www.cipmarseille.com
Key Personnel
Literature Dir: Emmanuel Ponsart
    E-mail: ponsart@cipmarseille.com
Subjects: Literature, Literary Criticism, Essays, Poetry
ISBN Prefix(es): 978-2-909097; 978-2-909857; 979-10-91991

Centre National de Documentation Pedagogique (CNDP)+
BP 80158, 86961 Futuroscope Cedex
Tel: 05 49 49 78 78 *Fax:* 05 49 49 78 16
Web Site: www2.cndp.fr/accueil.htm
Key Personnel
General Dir: Jean-Marc Merriaux
    E-mail: directeur.general@cndp.fr
Head, International Relations: Sylvie Lamy
    Tel: 05 49 49 78 05 *E-mail:* sylvie.lamy@cndp.fr
Dir, Communications: Delphine Groux
    E-mail: delphine.groux@cndp.fr
Foreign Rights: Maxime Bissonet *Tel:* 01 46 12 84 31 *E-mail:* maxime.bissonet@cndp.fr
Founded: 1932
Publisher of multimedia educational material for teachers (as part of the French Ministry of Education).
Membership(s): International Council for Educational Media (ICEM).
Subjects: Archaeology, Architecture & Interior Design, Art, Behavioral Sciences, Biological Sciences, Business, Chemistry, Chemical Engineering, Child Care & Development, Communications, Computer Science, Developing Countries, Disability, Special Needs, Drama,

Theater, Earth Sciences, Economics, Education, Electronics, Electrical Engineering, Energy, Environmental Studies, Ethnicity, Film, Video, Foreign Countries, Geography, Geology, Government, Political Science, Health, Nutrition, History, Human Relations, Journalism, Language Arts, Linguistics, Library & Information Sciences, Literature, Literary Criticism, Essays, Management, Mathematics, Music, Dance, Philosophy, Photography, Physical Sciences, Physics, Poetry, Public Administration, Regional Interests, Science (General), Social Sciences, Sociology, Technology, Transportation
ISBN Prefix(es): 978-2-240
Parent Company: Ministry of Education France
Associate Companies: CRDP
Bookshop(s): 13, rue du Four, 75006 Paris, Dir: Odile Mandalian *Toll Free Tel:* 0800 008212 *Fax:* 01 46 34 82 01 *E-mail:* librairie@cndp.fr

Editions du Centre Pompidou+
Centre Pompidou, 75191 Paris Cedex 04
Tel: 01 44 78 12 33
E-mail: cahiers.musee@centrepompidou.fr
Web Site: www.centrepompidou.fr/editions
Key Personnel
President & Publishing Dir: Alain Seban
Dir, Publishing: Nicholas Roche
Deputy Dir, Publishing: Jean-Christophe Claude
Editor-in-Chief: Jean-Pierre Criqui
Editorial: Gonzague Gauthier
Communications: Stephanie Hussonnois
Founded: 1977
Subjects: Architecture & Interior Design, Art, Film, Video, LGBTQ
ISBN Prefix(es): 978-2-85850; 978-2-84426
Distributed by Art Data (Great Britain); Flammarion (Canada); Flammarion Export (Austria, Egypt, Germany, Greece, Israel, Italy, Jordan, Lebanon, Portugal, Scandinavia, Spain, Syria, Turkey); Idea Books (Netherlands); Union Distribution (France, Belgium & Switzerland); Yohan (Japan)
Distributor for BPI
Foreign Rep(s): Richard Bowen (Denmark, Finland, Norway, Sweden); Phillip Galgiani (USA)
Orders to: Service Commercial, 75191 Paris Cedex 04

Centre Technique des Industries de la Fonderie-Service Edition
44 ave de la Division Leclerc, 92318 Sevres Cedex
Tel: 01 41 14 63 82 *Fax:* 01 41 14 63 91
Web Site: www.ctif.com
Key Personnel
Mng Dir: Phillipe Malle
Dir, Administrative Services: Jean-Yves Lejeune
Founded: 1950
Subjects: Engineering (General), Technology, French Foundry, Manufacturing, Metallurgy
ISBN Prefix(es): 978-2-7119

Cepadues Editions SA+
111, rue Nicholas Vauquelin, 31100 Toulouse
Tel: 05 61 40 57 36 *Fax:* 05 61 41 79 89
E-mail: cepadues@cepadues.com
Web Site: www.cepadues.com
Key Personnel
President: Jean-Claude Joly
Publishing Dir: Jean-Pierre Marson
   E-mail: jpmarson@cepadues.com
Founded: 1967
Specialize in scientific & technical books.
Subjects: Aeronautics, Aviation, Computer Science, Education, Mathematics, Mechanical Engineering, Science (General), Technology, Transportation
ISBN Prefix(es): 978-2-85428
Total Titles: 200 Print

Editions Cercle d'Art+
10, Rue Sainte-Anastase, 75003 Paris
Tel: 01 48 87 92 12
E-mail: info@cercledart.com
Web Site: www.cercledart.com/editions_cercle_art
Key Personnel
Chief Executive Officer: Philippe Monsel
Founded: 1949
Subjects: Art, Biography, Memoirs, History, Literature, Literary Criticism, Essays, Art History, Picasso
ISBN Prefix(es): 978-2-7022
Imprints: Aurore Editions D'Art; Diagonales
Foreign Rep(s): Caravelle (Belgium); DPLU (Canada); Horizon Education (all other territories); Zoe Diffusion (Switzerland)
Distribution Center: Harmonia Mundi, BP 150, 13631 Arles *Tel:* 04 90 49 90 49 *E-mail:* info@harmoniamundi.com

Les Editions du Cerf
24 rue des Tanneries, 75013 Paris
Tel: 01 80 05 36 36 *Fax:* 01 80 05 36 10
Web Site: www.editionsducerf.fr
Key Personnel
Mng Dir: Eric T de Clermont-Tonnerre
Founded: 1929
Subjects: Art, Biblical Studies, History, Inspirational, Spirituality, Philosophy, Religion - Other, Social Sciences, Sociology, Theology
ISBN Prefix(es): 978-2-204
Distributed by Fides; Labor & Fides Medialogue; Novalis; Saint Paul

Les Editions de la Cerise
54 rue de la Rousselle, 33000 Bordeaux
Tel: 05 56 44 11 01; 06 85 35 56 73
E-mail: editionsdelacerise@gmail.com
Web Site: www.editionsdelacerise.com
Subjects: Cookery, Drama, Theater, Fiction, Nonfiction (General)
ISBN Prefix(es): 978-2-9519498; 978-2-918596
Distributed by Makassar

Editions Jacqueline Chambon+
Imprint of Editions Actes Sud
18, rue Seguier, 75006 Paris
E-mail: contact@jacquelinechambon.fr; communication@actes-sud.fr
Web Site: www.jacquelinechambon.fr
Key Personnel
Contact: Jacqueline Chambon
Founded: 1987
Subjects: Art, Literature, Literary Criticism, Essays, Philosophy, Photography
ISBN Prefix(es): 978-2-7427; 978-2-87711
Number of titles published annually: 20 Print
Total Titles: 250 Print

Champ Libre, *imprint of* Editions Ivrea

Editions Champ Vallon+
56 Route Ardosset, 01350 Ceyzerieu
Tel: 04 79 81 47 66
E-mail: info@champ-vallon.com
Web Site: www.champ-vallon.com
Key Personnel
Editor: Patrick Beaune
International Rights: Myriam Monteiro-Braz
   E-mail: myriam.monteiro@champ-vallon.com
Founded: 1980
Subjects: Biography, Memoirs, Fiction, History, Literature, Literary Criticism, Essays, Philosophy, Poetry, Psychology, Psychiatry, Social Sciences, Sociology
ISBN Prefix(es): 978-2-87673; 978-2-903528
Total Titles: 440 Print
Distributed by Presses Universitaires de France
Foreign Rights: Marion Colas
Distribution Center: Harmonia Mundi, BP 150, Le Mas de Vert, 13631 Arles Cedex *Tel:* 04 90 49 90 49 *Fax:* 04 90 49 96 14

Caravelle, 303 rue du Pre aux Oies, 1130 Brussels, Belgium *Tel:* (02) 240 93 00 *Fax:* (02) 216 35 98
Diffusion Dimedia Inc, 539, Blvd Lebeau, Ville Saint-Laurent, QC, Canada *Tel:* 514-336-3941 *Fax:* 514-331-3916
Zoe, 11, rue des Moraines, 1227 Carouge, Geneva, Switzerland *Tel:* (022) 3 09 36 00 *Fax:* (022) 3 09 36 03

Champs, *imprint of* Flammarion Groupe

Editions Chandeigne
10 rue Tournefort, 75005 Paris
Tel: 01 43 36 78 47
E-mail: editionschadeigne@orange.fr
Web Site: www.editions-chandeigne.fr
Key Personnel
Co-Founder & Mng Dir: Michel Chandeigne; Anne Lima *E-mail:* annelima@wanadoo.fr
Founded: 1992
Membership(s): Alliance des Editeurs Independants; Editeurs Associes.
Subjects: Fiction, History, Religion - Other, Iberian Peninsula, Judaica
ISBN Prefix(es): 978-2-915540; 978-2-906462; 978-2-9526550
Foreign Rep(s): Dimedia (Canada); Servidis (Switzerland)
Distribution Center: Volumen, 25 Blvd Romain Rolland, CS 21418, 75993 Paris Cedex 14 *Tel:* 01 41 48 84 60 *Fax:* 01 41 48 81 32 *E-mail:* volumen@volumen.fr (France, Belgium, Brazil & Luxembourg)

Editions du Chariot+
7 rte de St Georges, 28120 Pont-Tranchefetu
Tel: 02 37 25 84 42; 06 20 54 50 68 (cell) *Fax:* 02 37 25 89 00 *Toll Free Fax:* 0811 38 1951
E-mail: edchariot@aol.com; infos@editions-du-chariot.com
Web Site: www.editions-du-chariot.com
Key Personnel
Publisher & Editor: Liliane Genin-Muchery
Founded: 1927
Subjects: Astrology, Occult, Parapsychology
ISBN Prefix(es): 978-2-85371

Editions Chasse-Maree
51 rue Henri Barbusse, 29177 Douarnenez Cedex
Tel: 02 98 92 66 33 *Fax:* 02 98 92 04 34
E-mail: contact@chasse-maree.fr
Web Site: www.chasse-maree.com
Key Personnel
Founder: Bernard Cadoret
Publishing Dir: Rodolphe de Lyones
Mng Dir: Stephane Cossart
Editor-in-Chief: Gwendal Jaffry
Founded: 1981
Subjects: Art, Crafts, Games, Hobbies, History, How-to, Maritime, Music, Dance
ISBN Prefix(es): 978-2-903708; 978-2-914208

Editions du Chene+
43 Quai de Grenelle, 75905 Paris Cedex 15
Tel: 01 43 92 30 00 *Fax:* 01 43 92 33 81
Web Site: www.editionsduchene.fr
Key Personnel
Mng Dir: Fabienne Kriegel
Rights & Co-Editions: Beatrice de Verdiere *Tel:* 01 43 92 33 90 *E-mail:* bdverdiere@hachette-livre.fr
Press: Helene Maurice *Tel:* 01 43 92 33 87 *E-mail:* hmaurice@hachette-livre.fr
Founded: 1941
Specializes in illustrated books.
Subjects: Architecture & Interior Design, Art, Cookery, History, Photography, Travel & Tourism
ISBN Prefix(es): 978-2-85108; 978-2-84277
Number of titles published annually: 70 Print

Parent Company: Hachette Livre SA
Imprints: Editions du Chene EPA
Orders to: Hachette Livre SA

Editions du Chene EPA, *imprint of* Editions du Chene

Le Cherche Midi Editeur+
23, rue du Cherche-Midi, 75006 Paris
Tel: 01 42 22 71 20 *Fax:* 01 45 44 08 38
E-mail: infos@cherche-midi.com
Web Site: www.cherche-midi.com
Key Personnel
Chief Executive Officer & Publisher: Philippe Heracles
Editorial Dir: Pierre Drachline
Dir, Marketing & Communications: Nicolas Watrin
Production Manager: Brigitte Trichet
Sales Manager: Xavier Belrose
Foreign Rights: Cristina Prepelita Chiarasini
Founded: 1978
Subjects: Aeronautics, Aviation, Animals, Pets, Art, Astrology, Occult, Biography, Memoirs, Cookery, Fiction, History, Humor, Journalism, Literature, Literary Criticism, Essays, Mysteries, Suspense, Nonfiction (General), Poetry, Romance, Science (General), Social Sciences, Sociology, Sports, Athletics, Transportation
ISBN Prefix(es): 978-2-86274; 978-2-7491
Parent Company: Editis

Les Editions Chiron+
155, rue de Fontenay, 94300 Vincennes
Tel: 01 30 48 74 50 *Fax:* 01 34 98 02 44
E-mail: contact@editionschiron.com
Web Site: www.editionschiron.com
Key Personnel
Publishing Dir: Thierry Heuninck
Founded: 1911
Subjects: Aeronautics, Aviation, Automotive, Health, Nutrition, How-to, Music, Dance, Outdoor Recreation, Psychology, Psychiatry, Sports, Athletics
ISBN Prefix(es): 978-2-7027
Bookshop(s): 50 bd Saint-Germain, 75005 Paris
Tel: 01 46 34 61 57

Chronique Sociale+
One, rue Vaubecour, 69002 Lyon
Tel: 04 78 37 22 12 *Fax:* 04 78 42 03 18
E-mail: secretariat@chroniquesociale.com
Web Site: www.chroniquesociale.com
Key Personnel
Mng Dir: Andre Soutrenon
Founded: 1892
Subjects: History, Human Relations, Philosophy, Psychology, Psychiatry, Religion - Other, Self-Help, Social Sciences, Sociology, Social History
ISBN Prefix(es): 978-2-85008
Number of titles published annually: 40 Print
Total Titles: 700 Print
Distributor for Beauchemin (Canada); Couleurs Savoirs (Brussels); Presses Universite Laval (PUL) (Canada)

Cifonit Figle, *imprint of* Editions l'Ancre de Marine

Editions CILF, see Conseil International de la Langue Francaise

Les Editions Circe+
Circe 18, Grand Rue, 88210 Belval
Tel: 03 29 41 02 15 *Fax:* 03 29 41 02 15
E-mail: contact@editions-circe.fr
Web Site: www.editions-circe.fr
Key Personnel
Dir: Claude Lutz
Founded: 1989

Subjects: Drama, Theater, Fiction, Literature, Literary Criticism, Essays, Nonfiction (General), Philosophy, Poetry, Humanities
ISBN Prefix(es): 978-2-908024; 978-2-84242
Number of titles published annually: 4 Print
Total Titles: 1,500 Print
Orders to: Harmonia Mundi, Le Mas de Vert, 13200 Arles

Editions Circonflexe+
2 ter, rue des Chantiers, 75005 Paris
Tel: 01 46 34 78 78 *Fax:* 01 46 34 77 82
E-mail: info@circonflexe.fr
Web Site: www.circonflexe.fr
Key Personnel
Chief Executive Officer & Publishing Dir: Philippe Sylvestre
Editorial Manager: Fatiha Djiaba *E-mail:* fatiha.djiaba@circonflexe.fr
Founded: 1989
Subjects: Art, Education, Fiction, History, Humor, Language Arts, Linguistics
ISBN Prefix(es): 978-2-87833
Parent Company: Info Media Communication
Orders to: Dilisco, Rue du Limousin, BP 25, 23220 Cheniers *Tel:* 05 55 51 80 00 *Fax:* 05 55 62 17 39

Editions Citadelles & Mazenod+
8, rue Gaston de St-Paul, 75116 Paris
Tel: 01 53 04 30 60; 01 53 04 30 66 (sales)
Fax: 01 53 04 30 61
E-mail: info@citadelles-mazenod.com; commercial@citadelles-mazenod.com
Web Site: www.citadelles-mazenod.com
Key Personnel
President & Dir General: Francois de Waresquiel *E-mail:* f.dewaresquiel@citadelles-mazenod.com
Dir General: Matthieu de Waresquiel *E-mail:* m.dewaresquiel@citadelles-mazenod.com
Editorial Dir: Genevieve Rudolf *Tel:* 01 53 04 30 64 *E-mail:* g.rudolf@citadelles-mazenod.com
Founded: 1936
Specialize in architecture & art.
Subjects: Architecture & Interior Design, Art
ISBN Prefix(es): 978-2-85088
Number of titles published annually: 12 Print
Total Titles: 80 Print
Foreign Rep(s): CELF (all other territories); Diffulivre (Switzerland); Dilibel (Belgium); Hachette Canada Inc (Canada); Hachette Diffusion Internationale (all other territories)
Distribution Center: Hachette Livre/CDL, One ave Gutenberg, ZA Coignieres-Maurepas-BP 154, 78316 Maurepas Cedex *Tel:* 01 30 66 20 66 *Fax:* 01 30 62 28 02

Editions de la Cite, *imprint of* Editions Ouest-France

Editions CLD+
33, avenue du Maine, 75015 Paris
Web Site: www.editionscld.fr
Founded: 1961
Subjects: Architecture & Interior Design, Ethnicity, History, Regional Interests, Religion - Other, Travel & Tourism
ISBN Prefix(es): 978-2-85443
Total Titles: 300 Print

CLE International+
9 bis, rue Abel Hovelacque, 75013 Paris
Tel: 01 45 87 44 00; 01 72 36 30 53 *Fax:* 01 45 87 44 10
E-mail: info@cle-inter.com; marketing@cle-inter.com
Web Site: www.cle-inter.com
Key Personnel
Chief Executive Officer: Jean-Luc Wollensack
Editorial Dir: Michele Grandmangin

Sales Dir: Evelyne Mazallon *Tel:* 01 72 36 30 56
E-mail: emazallon@cle-inter.com
Founded: 1975
Subjects: Education, Language Arts, Linguistics, French Language Education
ISBN Prefix(es): 978-2-19; 978-2-09
Showroom(s): Espace Luxembourg, 103 Blvd Saint-Michel, 75005 Paris *Tel:* 01 53 10 41 20 *Fax:* 01 45 87 44 25

Climapoche, *imprint of* COSTIC

Climats, *imprint of* Flammarion Groupe

Editions Climats+
Imprint of Flammarion Groupe
87 quai Panhard et Levassor, 75647 Paris Cedex 13
Tel: 01 40 51 31 00
Web Site: editions.flammarion.com
Key Personnel
Head, Communications: Vivien Boyer *Tel:* 01 40 51 30 16 *E-mail:* vboyer@flammarion.fr
Founded: 1988
Subjects: Film, Video, Literature, Literary Criticism, Essays, Music, Dance, Mysteries, Suspense
ISBN Prefix(es): 978-2-84158; 978-2-907563

CNDP, see Centre National de Documentation Pedagogique (CNDP)

CNRS Editions
15 rue Malebranche, 75005 Paris
Tel: 01 53 10 27 00
E-mail: cnrseditions@cnrseditions.fr
Web Site: www.cnrseditions.fr
Key Personnel
Dir: Jacques Baudouin
Editorial Dir: Bladine Genthon
Foreign Rights: Martine Bertea *Tel:* 01 53 10 27 14 *E-mail:* martine.bertea@cnrseditions.fr
Press: Christelle Voisin *Tel:* 01 53 10 27 13 *E-mail:* christelle.voisin@cnrseditions.fr
Subjects: Anthropology, Art, Biological Sciences, Geography, Geology, History, Language Arts, Linguistics, Mathematics, Philosophy, Social Sciences, Sociology
ISBN Prefix(es): 978-2-222; 978-2-271

Codes Rousseau SAS
135, rue des Plesses, Chateau d'Olonne, 85109 Les Sables d'Olonne Cedex
Mailing Address: BP 80093, 85109 Les Sables d'Olonne Cedex
Tel: 02 51 23 11 00; 02 51 23 11 31 *Fax:* 02 51 23 11 31
E-mail: service.commercial@codes-rousseau.fr
Web Site: www.codes-rousseau.fr
Key Personnel
President: Michel Goepp *Tel:* 02 51 23 11 17 *Fax:* 02 51 22 05 25 *E-mail:* michel.goepp@codes-rousseau.fr
Founded: 1937
Subjects: Education, Electronics, Electrical Engineering, Law, Transportation, Driving Licenses, Driving School, Road Safety Education
ISBN Prefix(es): 978-2-7095
Parent Company: Springer Science + Business Media
Subsidiaries: Les Editions du Bateau; Les Editions La Baule
Branch Office(s)
31 rue la Quintinie, 75015 Paris *Tel:* 01 48 28 57 57 *Fax:* 01 45 30 15 84
E-mail: agencedeparis@codes-rousseau.fr

Armand Colin+
Subsidiary of Hachette Livre
11 rue Paul Bert, CS 30024, 92247 Malakoff Cedex
Toll Free Tel: 0820 065 095 *Fax:* 01 41 23 67 35

E-mail: infos@armand-colin.fr; revues@armand-colin.com; infos@dunod.com
Web Site: www.armand-colin.com; www.revues.armand-colin.com
Founded: 1870
Incorporates publications of former separate company, Editions Armand.
Subjects: Behavioral Sciences, Communications, Drama, Theater, Earth Sciences, Economics, Film, Video, Geography, Geology, Government, Political Science, History, Language Arts, Linguistics, Literature, Literary Criticism, Essays, Philosophy, Psychology, Psychiatry, Regional Interests, Social Sciences, Sociology
ISBN Prefix(es): 978-2-200
Number of titles published annually: 130 Print
Total Titles: 1,500 Print
Distribution Center: Interforum

Editions du Comite des Travaux Historiques et Scientifiques (CTHS)+
110, rue de Grenelle, 75357 Paris Cedex 07
E-mail: ventes@cths.fr; service.presse@cths.fr; actes.congres@cths.fr
Web Site: www.cths.fr
Key Personnel
President: Dominique Poulot *Tel:* 01 47 03 84 90 *E-mail:* president@cths.fr
Publishing Manager: David Simon *Tel:* 01 55 95 89 11
Sales & Inventory Manager: Antoine Dorizon *Tel:* 01 55 95 89 67
Press & Communication: Stephanie Henry *Tel:* 01 55 95 89 62
Founded: 1834
Subjects: Archaeology, Art, Ethnicity, Geography, Geology, History
ISBN Prefix(es): 978-2-7355

Comite Scientifique et Technique des Industries Climatiques, see COSTIC

Editions du Conseil de l'Europe, see Council of Europe Publishing

Conseil International de la Langue Francaise
11, rue de Navarin, 75009 Paris
Tel: 01 48 78 73 95 *Fax:* 01 48 78 49 28
E-mail: cilf@cilf.org
Web Site: www.cilf.org
Key Personnel
President: Andre Goosse
Secretary-General: Hubert Joly
Treasurer: Christian Begin
Founded: 1968
Specialize in multilingual scientific dictionaries.
Subjects: Agriculture, Architecture & Interior Design, Language Arts, Linguistics, Medicine, Nursing, Dentistry, Public Administration
ISBN Prefix(es): 978-2-85319

Le Conseiller Juridique Pour Tous, *imprint of* Les Editions du Puits Fleuri

Cooperative Regionale de l'Enseignement Religieux (CRER)
19, rue de la Saillerie, CS 10 002, 49184 Saint-Barthelemy d'Anjou Cedex
Tel: 02 41 68 91 40 *Fax:* 02 41 68 91 41
E-mail: relations.commerciales@editions-crer.fr
Web Site: www.editions-crer.fr
Founded: 1968
Subjects: Religion - Other, Catechism
ISBN Prefix(es): 978-2-85733
Number of titles published annually: 20 Print; 5 CD-ROM
Total Titles: 200 Print; 50 CD-ROM

Editions Coprur, see Les Editions du Quotidien

Corsaire Editions+
11, rue de Chateaudun, 45000 Orleans
Tel: 02 38 53 15 00 *Fax:* 02 38 54 08 92
E-mail: corsaire.editions@orange.fr
Web Site: www.corsaire-editions.com; www.journaldunsein.com
Key Personnel
President: Gilbert Trompas
Founded: 1994
Subjects: Biography, Memoirs, History, Humor, Literature, Literary Criticism, Essays, Maritime, Regional Interests
ISBN Prefix(es): 978-2-910475
Number of titles published annually: 10 Print
Total Titles: 40 Print
Foreign Rep(s): La Canopee (North America); Diffusion Transat (Switzerland)

Editions Jose Corti+
60, rue Monsieur-Le-Prince, 75006 Paris
Tel: 01 43 26 63 00
E-mail: librairie-corti@orange.fr
Web Site: www.jose-corti.fr
Key Personnel
Editorial & Foreign Rights: Bertrand Fillaudeau
Editorial: Fabienne Raphoz
Founded: 1938
Subjects: Fiction, Literature, Literary Criticism, Essays, Poetry, Romance
ISBN Prefix(es): 978-2-7143
Number of titles published annually: 30 Print
Total Titles: 907 Print
Bookshop(s): 11, rue Medicis, 75006 Paris
Orders to: Volumen, 25 Blvd Romain Rolland, CS 21418, 75993 Paris Cedex 14 *Tel:* 01 41 48 84 60 *E-mail:* volumen@volumen.fr *Web Site:* www.volumen.fr

Editions du Cosmogone
6, rue Salomon Reinach, 69007 Lyon
Tel: 04 72 72 92 51; 06 80 63 84 88 (cell)
E-mail: edcosmogone@orange.fr
Web Site: www.cosmogone.com
Key Personnel
Contact: Evelyne Penisson
Founded: 1990
Subjects: Alternative, Architecture & Interior Design, Biography, Memoirs, Drama, Theater, Inspirational, Spirituality, Literature, Literary Criticism, Essays, Social Sciences, Sociology
ISBN Prefix(es): 978-2-909781; 978-2-914238
Number of titles published annually: 10 Print
Total Titles: 215 Print
Bookshop(s): 47, rue Pasteur, 69007 Lyon

COSTIC
Centre de St-Remy-les-Chevreuse, Domaine de St-Paul, 78471 St-Remy-les-Chevreuse Cedex
Tel: 01 30 85 20 10 *Fax:* 01 30 85 20 38
Web Site: www.costic.com
Key Personnel
Contact: Carole Martinet
Founded: 1968
Subjects: Civil Engineering, Energy, Engineering (General), Technology
ISBN Prefix(es): 978-2-236
Imprints: Climapoche; Refclim

Council of Europe Publishing+
Division of Directorate of Communication
Palais de l'Europe, 67075 Strasbourg Cedex
Tel: 03 88 41 25 81; 03 88 41 25 60 (communication) *Fax:* 03 88 41 39 10; 03 88 41 39 11 (communication)
E-mail: publishing@coe.int; pressunit@coe.int
Web Site: book.coe.int
Key Personnel
Communications Officer: Sophie Lobey *Tel:* 03 88 41 22 63 *E-mail:* sophie.lobey@coe.int
Founded: 1949
Official publisher of the Council of Europe & reflects many different aspects of the Council's work, addressing the main challenges facing European society & the world today. Catalogue of over 1,500 titles in French & English includes topics ranging from international law, human rights, ethical & moral issues, society, environment, health, education & culture.
Subjects: Criminology, Education, Law, Medicine, Nursing, Dentistry, Social Sciences, Sociology, Sports, Athletics, Consumer Protection, Culture, Human Rights, Local Authorities, Nature, Social Security, Youth
ISBN Prefix(es): 978-92-871
Number of titles published annually: 120 Print
Total Titles: 1,500 Print
Distributed by Manhattan Publishing Co (USA)
Foreign Rep(s): Akademika A/S Universitetsbokhandel (Norway); Akateeminen Kirjakauppa (Finland); Ars Polona JSC (Poland); Libreria Commissionaria Sansoni (Italy); Euro Info Service (Hungary); La Librairie Europeenne SA (Belgium); Documentation Francaise (France); GAD Direct (Denmark); Librairie Kauffmann (Greece); Librairie Jean de Lannoy (Belgium); Manhattan Publishing Co (USA); Mundi-Prensa Libros SA (Spain); Mundi Prensa Mexico (Mexico); Planetis Sarl (Switzerland); Renouf Publishing Co Ltd (Canada); Robert's Plus doo (Bosnia and Herzegovina, Croatia); The Stationery Office Ltd (UK); SUWECO CZ spol sro (Czechia); UNO GmbH (Austria, Germany); Ves Mir (Russia)
Returns: Mundi-Prensa Libros SA, Castello 37, 28001 Madrid, Spain *Tel:* 914 36 37 00 *Fax:* 915 75 39 98 *E-mail:* libreria@mundiprensa.es *Web Site:* www.mundiprensa.es

Editions Courtes et Longues
16, rue St-Paul, 75004 Paris
Tel: 01 48 87 16 35
E-mail: info@cleditions.com
Web Site: www.cleditions.com
Key Personnel
Foreign Rights: Hannele Legras *Tel:* 06 10 52 55 73
Founded: 2005
Specialize in art books for children & adults.
Subjects: Art, Fiction, History, Science (General), Art History, Culture, World Arts
ISBN Prefix(es): 978-2-35290
Distribution Center: CDE-Sodis

Editions Crepin-Leblond
14 rue du Patronage Laique, 52000 Chaumont
Tel: 03 25 03 87 48 *Fax:* 03 25 03 87 40
Web Site: www.crepin-leblond.fr
Key Personnel
Publishing Dir: Laurent Picart *Tel:* 03 25 03 87 41 *E-mail:* lp@graphycom.com
Founded: 1952
Subjects: Animals, Pets, Environmental Studies, Sports, Athletics
ISBN Prefix(es): 978-2-7030
Parent Company: Groupe Graphycom
Orders to: PO Box 2057, 52902 Chaumont

CRER, see Cooperative Regionale de l'Enseignement Religieux (CRER)

Editions du CTHS, see Editions du Comite des Travaux Historiques et Scientifiques (CTHS)

CTIF, see Centre Technique des Industries de la Fonderie-Service Edition

Editions Cujas+
4/8, rue de la Maison Blanche, 75013 Paris
Mailing Address: BP 20417, 75626 Paris Cedex 13
Tel: 01 44 24 24 36 *Fax:* 01 44 24 24 38
Web Site: www.cujas.fr
Founded: 1946

Subjects: Economics, Education, Government, Political Science, History, Law, Social Sciences, Sociology
ISBN Prefix(es): 978-2-254
Bookshop(s): Cujas Librairie, 2 rue de Rouen, 92000 Nanterre

Dalloz, *imprint of* Editions Dalloz

Editions Dalloz+
31-35, rue Froidevaux, 75685 Paris Cedex 14
Tel: 01 40 64 54 54 *Fax:* 01 40 64 54 97
E-mail: ventes@dalloz.fr
Web Site: editions-dalloz.fr; www.dalloz.fr
Key Personnel
Chief Executive Officer & President: Sylvie Faye
Press: Julie Loreille *Tel:* 01 40 64 54 22
   E-mail: j.loreille@dalloz.fr
Customer Relations: Marie-Helene Tylman
   Tel: 08 20 80 00 17
Founded: 1845
Subjects: Advertising, Economics, Finance, Law, Marketing
ISBN Prefix(es): 978-2-247; 978-2-248
Total Titles: 2,000 Print; 50 CD-ROM; 10 E-Book
Imprints: Armand Colin Drott; Dalloz; Editions Delmas; Sirey
Distributor for Groupe Revue Fiduciaire
Bookshop(s): 22, rue Soufflot, 75005 Paris
   Tel: 01 40 64 54 44 *Fax:* 01 40 64 54 42
   E-mail: librairie@dalloz.fr *Web Site:* www.librairiedalloz.fr
Distribution Center: Livredis, 11-15 Rue Pierre Rig-Aud, 94854 Ivry-sur-Seine

Editions Dangles+
Imprint of Groupe Editorial Piktos
Z I de Bogues, rue Gutenberg, 31750 Escalquens
Tel: 05 61 00 09 86 *Fax:* 05 61 00 09 83
E-mail: contact@piktos.fr
Web Site: editions-dangles.fr; www.piktos.fr
Key Personnel
Dir General, Groupe Piktos: Jacques Gruszewski
   E-mail: j.gruszewski@piktos.fr
Publishing Manager: Philippe Lahille *E-mail:* p.lahille@piktos.fr
Head, Media Relations: Florence Vaillant
   E-mail: f.vaillant@piktos.fr
Founded: 1926
Subjects: Art, Astrology, Occult, Health, Nutrition, Medicine, Nursing, Dentistry, Parapsychology, Psychology, Psychiatry, Religion - Other, Esotericism
ISBN Prefix(es): 978-2-7033
Foreign Rep(s): DG Diffusion (Benelux, France); Messageries de Presse Benjamin Inc (Canada); Distribution Servidis SA (Switzerland)

Dargaud+
15/27 rue Moussorgski, 75018 Paris
E-mail: contact@dargaud.fr
Web Site: www.dargaud.com
Key Personnel
Dir General: Philippe Osterman
Marketing Manager: Frederic Schwamberger
Press: Helene Werle *E-mail:* werle@dargaud.fr
Founded: 1947
Subjects: Fiction, Humor, Mysteries, Suspense, Science Fiction, Fantasy, Western Fiction, Comics
ISBN Prefix(es): 978-2-205; 978-0-917201
Subsidiaries: Editions Blake et mortimer; Citel Video; Dargaud Benelux; Dargaud Publishing International; Dargard Suisse; Delta Verlag; Grijalbo-Dargaud; Hodder-Dargaud; Editions du Lombard; Marina Productions; Millesime Productions
Branch Office(s)
Ave PH Spaak, 7, 1060 Brussels, Belgium
   Tel: (02) 526 68 11 *Fax:* (02) 526 68 89
   E-mail: info@lombard.be

5757, rue Cypihot, Saint-Laurent, QC H4S 1X4, Canada *Tel:* 514-334-2690 *Fax:* 514-334-8289
   E-mail: karine.halle@erpi.com
En Budron B, 13, 1052 Le Mont/Lausanne, Switzerland *Tel:* (021) 651 64 64 *Fax:* (021) 651 64 65 *E-mail:* bdinfo@dargargudsuisse.ch
Distributor for Blake et Mortimer; Lombard
Foreign Rights: Mediatoon Foreign Rights (Sophie Castille) (worldwide)
Orders to: MDS, ZI de la Gaudree, 91417 Dourdan Cedex *Tel:* 01 60 81 87 00 *Fax:* 01 64 59 30 63

Editions du Dauphin+
43-45, rue de la tombe-lssoire, 75014 Paris
Tel: 01 43 27 79 00 *Fax:* 01 43 27 76 31
E-mail: contact@editionsdudauphin.com
Web Site: www.editionsdudauphin.com
Key Personnel
Dir, Publications: Gabrielle Tromelin
Founded: 1935
Subjects: Animals, Pets, Art, Cookery, Environmental Studies, Fiction, Film, Video, Gardening, Plants, Health, Nutrition, History, How-to, Inspirational, Spirituality, Literature, Literary Criticism, Essays, Music, Dance, Psychology, Psychiatry, Religion - Other, Science (General), Self-Help, Technology, Travel & Tourism, Wine & Spirits, Ecology, Nature, Personal Growth
ISBN Prefix(es): 978-2-7163
Number of titles published annually: 30 Print
Total Titles: 200 Print
Subsidiaries: Editions Jacqueline Renard
Foreign Rep(s): Dimedia (Canada); SDLC Caravelle (Belgium, Luxembourg); Servidis (Switzerland)
Distribution Center: Volumen, 13 rue du General Leclerc, 91165 Ballainvilliers Cedex
   Tel: 01 69 10 89 09 *Fax:* 01 64 48 49 63
   E-mail: volumen@volumen.fr *Web Site:* www.volumen.fr

DDB, see Editions Desclee de Brouwer

Editions Decanord
30 rue de Verlinghem, 59832 Lambersart Cedex
Mailing Address: BP 40139, 59832 Lambersart Cedex
Tel: 03 20 09 90 60
E-mail: renseignements@decanord.fr; contact@decanord.fr
Web Site: www.decanord.fr
Key Personnel
Publishing Dir: Luc Jonghmans
Founded: 1948
Subjects: Religion - Catholic
ISBN Prefix(es): 978-2-903898

Editions La Decouverte+
9 bis, rue Abel-Hovelacque, 75013 Paris
Tel: 01 44 08 84 01 *Fax:* 01 44 08 84 39
E-mail: ladecouverte@editionsladecouverte.com
Web Site: www.editionsladecouverte.fr
Key Personnel
Chairman & Chief Executive Officer: Hugues Jallon
Deputy Dir General: Emmanuelle Bagneris
Commercial Dir: Bruno Gendre
Head, Press: Pascale Iltis *Tel:* 01 44 08 84 21
   E-mail: p.iltis@editionsladecouverte.com
Foreign Rights Manager: Delphine Ribouchon
   Tel: 01 44 08 84 35 *Fax:* 01 44 08 84 05
   E-mail: d.ribouchon@editionsladecouverte.com
Production Manager: Caroline Robert
Founded: 1959
Membership(s): Syndicat National de l'Edition (SNE).
Subjects: Communications, Developing Countries, Economics, Foreign Countries, History, Nonfiction (General), Philosophy, Social Sciences, Sociology

ISBN Prefix(es): 978-2-7071
Number of titles published annually: 135 Print; 1 Online; 60 E-Book
Total Titles: 1,500 Print; 1 Online; 400 E-Book
Parent Company: Editis
Imprints: Collection Reperes; Les Empecheurs de Penser en Rond; Encyclopedie de L'Etat du Monde; Les Revues de La Decouverte; Zones
Distribution Center: Interforum, Immeuble Paryseine, 3, allee de la Seine, 94854 Ivry-sur-Seine Cedex *Tel:* 01 49 59 10 10 *Fax:* 01 49 59 10 72; 01 49 59 10 94 *Web Site:* www.interforum.fr
Interforum Benelux SA, Fond Jean-Paques, 6, 1348 Louvain-la-Neuve, Belgium *Tel:* (010) 42 03 30; (010) 42 03 60 *Web Site:* www.interforum.be
Interforum Canada, 1055, Blvd Rene Levesque Est, Bureau 1100, Montreal, QC H2L 4S5, Canada *Tel:* 514-281-1050 *Web Site:* interforumcanadapresse.qc.ca
Interforum Suisse SA, Route Andre Piller 33A, Givisiez, 1701 Fribourg, Switzerland *Tel:* (026) 480 80 60 *Web Site:* www.interforumsuisse.ch
Orders to: 46, route de Sermaises, BP 11, 45331 Malesherbes Cedex *Tel:* 02 38 32 78 88 *Web Site:* www.interforum.fr
Returns: Route d'Etampes, 45331 Malesherbes Cedex

Defrenois, *imprint of* Lextenso Editions

Editions Delachaux et Niestle+
Subsidiary of La Martiniere Groupe
25, blvd Romain Rolland, 75014 Paris
Tel: 01 41 48 80 00
E-mail: delachaux@lamartiniere.fr; contact@lamartiniere.fr
Web Site: www.delachauxetniestle.com
Key Personnel
Foreign Rights Manager: Marianne Lassandro
Founded: 1885
Subjects: Earth Sciences, Education, Environmental Studies, Geography, Geology, Medicine, Nursing, Dentistry, Psychology, Psychiatry, Science (General), Social Sciences, Sociology, Biodiversity, Ecology, Natural Sciences
ISBN Prefix(es): 978-2-603; 978-2-8255; 978-2-242
Number of titles published annually: 50 Print
Total Titles: 300 Print
Foreign Rep(s): Dimedia (Canada); Loglibris (Belgium, France); Servidis (Switzerland)

Delagrave Edition
5, allee de la 2e DB, 75015 Paris
E-mail: service.enseignant@editions-delagrave.fr
Web Site: www.editions-delagrave.fr
Key Personnel
Publishing Dir: Guillaume Dervieux
Subjects: Education
ISBN Prefix(es): 978-2-206

Editions Delcourt+
54, rue d'Hauteville, 75010 Paris
Tel: 01 56 03 92 20 *Fax:* 01 56 03 92 30
Web Site: www.editions-delcourt.fr
Key Personnel
Editorial Manager: Francois Capuron
Foreign Rights & Permissions: Lucie Massena
   E-mail: lmassena@groupedelcourt.com
Founded: 1986
Children's & comic books.
ISBN Prefix(es): 978-2-906187; 978-2-84055; 978-2-84789
Distributed by Hachette
Foreign Rep(s): Diffulivre (Switzerland); Dilibel (Benelux)

La Delirante
112, rue Rambuteau, 75001 Paris
Tel: 01 45 08 42 58

E-mail: contact@ladelirante.fr; commandes@
ladelirante.fr
Web Site: www.ladelirante.fr
Key Personnel
President: Patrick Genevaz
Literary Dir: Fouad El-Etr
Editorial Secretary: Edwig Dulac
Founded: 1967
Subjects: Drama, Theater, Literature, Literary
Criticism, Essays, Poetry
ISBN Prefix(es): 978-2-85745

Delizon Publications, *imprint of* Delizon
Publishers

Delizon Publishers+
Division of Delizon SARL
19 rue des Allies, 64000 Pau
Tel: 05 59 12 24 09
E-mail: info@delizonpublishers.com; europe@
delizonpublishers.com
Web Site: www.delizon.fr; www.delizonpublishers.
com
Founded: 2011
Aim is to publish books that will sell where
people want to read them, where there is the
highest demand & to convert potential books
to other entertainment products, CDs, plays,
books, films, music & more. Objective is to
make publishing a means of exchange - arrange
for authors to give talks in different commu-
nities & to participate in broadening people's
opinions.
Subjects: Biography, Memoirs, Computer Science,
Developing Countries, Education, Environmen-
tal Studies, Fiction, Foreign Countries, Human
Relations, Inspirational, Spirituality, Nonfiction
(General), Philosophy, Pop Culture, Regional
Interests, Religion - Other, Romance, Science
(General), Science Fiction, Fantasy, Self-Help,
Western Fiction, Women's Studies
ISBN Prefix(es): 978-2-36523
Number of titles published annually: 30 Print; 30
Online; 30 E-Book
Imprints: Delizon Publications
Foreign Rights: Big Apple Agency (China)

Editions Delmas, *imprint of* Editions Dalloz

Editions Delmas
Imprint of Editions Dalloz
31-35 rue Froidevaux, 75685 Paris Cedex 14
Tel: 08 20 80 00 17 Fax: 01 40 64 89 90
Web Site: www.editions-dalloz.fr
Founded: 1947
Subjects: Accounting, Business, Economics, Law,
Management, Public Administration, Real Es-
tate, Securities
ISBN Prefix(es): 978-2-247; 978-2-7034

Editions Delville+
Imprint of Groupe Editorial Piktos
Z I de Bogues, rue Gutenberg, 31750 Escalquens
Tel: 05 61 00 09 86 Fax: 05 61 00 09 83
E-mail: contact@piktos.fr
Web Site: www.editions-delville.fr; www.piktos.fr
Key Personnel
Dir General, Groupe Editoral Piktos: Jacques
Gruszewski E-mail: j.gruszewski@piktos.fr
Publishing Manager: Philippe Lahille E-mail: p.
lahille@piktos.fr
Head, Media Relations: Florence Vaillant
E-mail: f.vaillant@piktos.fr
Founded: 1976
Subjects: Aeronautics, Aviation, Automotive,
Cookery, History, How-to
ISBN Prefix(es): 978-2-85922
Distributed by Editions De Vecchi
Foreign Rep(s): DG Diffusion (Benelux, France);
Messageries de Presse Benjamin Inc (Canada);
Servidis SA (Switzerland)

Editions Denoel+
Subsidiary of Editions Gallimard
33, rue St-Andre des Arts, 75278 Paris Cedex 06
Tel: 01 44 39 73 73 Fax: 01 44 39 73 90
E-mail: denoel@denoel.fr; rights@denoel.fr;
presse@denoel.fr
Web Site: www.denoel.fr
Key Personnel
Rights Manager: Judith Becqueriaux
Founded: 1930
Subjects: Art, Economics, Fiction, Government,
Political Science, History, Philosophy, Psychol-
ogy, Psychiatry, Science Fiction, Fantasy
ISBN Prefix(es): 978-2-207
Associate Companies: Mercure de France

Editions Dervy+
19 rue St Severin Medici, 75005 Paris
Tel: 01 43 36 41 05
Web Site: www.dervy-medicis.fr
Key Personnel
Publishing Dir: Guy Tredaniel
Press: Isabelle Laurand Tel: 01 43 36 73 62
E-mail: isabelle.laurand@dervy.fr
Founded: 1946
Subjects: History, Human Relations, Psychology,
Psychiatry, Religion - Buddhist, Religion -
Hindu, Religion - Islamic, Religion - Jewish,
Religion - Other, Social Sciences, Sociology,
Free Masonry, Personal Development, Spiritu-
ality
ISBN Prefix(es): 978-2-85076; 978-2-84454
Number of titles published annually: 40 Print
Total Titles: 772 Print
Parent Company: Groupe Guy Tredaniel
Foreign Rep(s): Nord-Sud (Benelux); Prologue
(Canada); Transat-Servidis (Switzerland)
Warehouse: Dilisco, Parc Carre Ivry, Batiment J4,
128 Ave Jean Jaures, CS 20065, 94208 Ivry-
sur-Seine
Distribution Center: Dilisco, Rue du Limousin,
BP 25, 23220 Cheniers Tel: 05 55 51 80 00
Fax: 05 55 62 17 39

Editions Desclee de Brouwer+
10, rue Mercoeur, 75011 Paris
Tel: 01 40 46 54 00 Fax: 01 58 51 10 48
Web Site: www.editionsddb.fr
Key Personnel
Editorial Dir: Marc Larive
Marketing: Odile Tequi
Press: Jean-Philippe Bertrand Tel: 01 40 46 54 30
Founded: 1877
Subjects: History, Inspirational, Spirituality, Lit-
erature, Literary Criticism, Essays, Religion -
Other, Social Sciences, Sociology, Theology,
Humanities
ISBN Prefix(es): 978-2-220; 978-2-7045
Number of titles published annually: 30 Print
Total Titles: 1,900 Print
Parent Company: Groupe Artege
Foreign Rep(s): Gallimard Export SDLC (Bel-
gium); Gallimard Export Socadis (Canada);
OLF (Switzerland)
Distribution Center: Sofedis-Sodis

Editions Desiris, *imprint of* Adverbum

Dessain et Tolra SA+
21, rue du Montparnasse, 75006 Paris
Tel: 01 44 39 44 00
E-mail: livres-larousse@larousse.fr
Web Site: www.editions-larousse.fr/catalogue/
dessain-tolra.asp
Key Personnel
Publication Dir: Isabelle Jeuge-Maynart
Deputy General Manager: Ghislaine Stora
Founded: 1964
Subjects: Architecture & Interior Design, Art,
Crafts, Games, Hobbies, How-to
ISBN Prefix(es): 978-2-249; 978-2-04; 978-2-295
Parent Company: Editions Larousse

Ultimate Parent Company: Hachette Livre
Distributed by Hachette
Bookshop(s): Diff-edi, 96 BD DU Montparnasse,
75680 Paris Cedex 14

Les Editions des Deux Coqs d'Or+
Imprint of Hachette Jeunesse
43, quai de Grenelle, 75905 Paris Cedex 15
Tel: 01 43 92 34 55
E-mail: cbenhamou@hachette-livre.fr
Web Site: www.deux-coqs-dor.com; www.
hachette.com/en/maison/editions-deux-coqs-d-or
Key Personnel
Publishing Dir: Frederique de Buron
Editor: Sarah Koegler-Jacquet
Founded: 1949
Membership(s): Syndicate National de l'Edition
(SNE).
Subjects: Animals, Pets, Fiction, History, Religion
- Catholic, Religion - Other
ISBN Prefix(es): 978-2-01; 978-2-7192
Number of titles published annually: 130 Print
Total Titles: 350 Print
Ultimate Parent Company: Hachette Livre
Warehouse: Hachette Livre Distribution, One, Ave
Gutenberg, 78316 Maurepas Cedex Tel: 01 30
66 20 66 (France, Belgium, Canada & Switzer-
land)

Deux Coqs d'Or, *imprint of* Hachette Jeunesse

Institut pour le Developpement Forestier
(Institute for Forestry Development)
47 rue de Chaillot, 75116 Paris
Tel: 01 47 20 68 15; 01 47 20 68 39 (bookshop)
Fax: 01 47 23 49 20
E-mail: idf@cnpf.fr; cnpf@cnpf.fr; idf-librairie@
cnpf.fr (bookshop)
Web Site: www.foretpriveefrancaise.com
Key Personnel
President: Alain de Montgascon
Publications, Distribution & Communication:
Samuel Six
Founded: 1960
Subjects: Agriculture, Earth Sciences, Environ-
mental Studies
ISBN Prefix(es): 978-2-904740
Parent Company: Centre National de la Propriete
Forestiere

Les Devenirs Visuels+
65, rue du Faubourg-St-Denis, 75010 Paris
Tel: 01 47 70 60 02; 01 47 70 11 30
E-mail: info@devenirvisuel.com; info@devenirs.
eu
Web Site: devenirvisuel.com; devenirs.eu
Key Personnel
Manager: Claire Rius
Founded: 1987
Also specializes in packaging.
Subjects: Economics, Geography, Geology, Physi-
cal Sciences
ISBN Prefix(es): 978-2-910745

DHP, see Disney Hachette Presse

Au Diable Vauvert
La Laune, 30600 Vauvert
Tel: 04 66 73 16 56
E-mail: contact@audiable.com
Web Site: www.audiable.com
Founded: 2000
Subjects: Erotica, History, Humor, Literature, Lit-
erary Criticism, Essays, Music, Dance, Poetry
ISBN Prefix(es): 978-2-84626

Diagonales, *imprint of* Editions Cercle d'Art

Les Editions Diateino
57 bis Blvd Exelmans, 75016 Paris

Tel: 01 46 51 62 44
E-mail: contact@diateino.com
Web Site: www.diateino.com
Key Personnel
Founder: Dominique Gibert
Editor-in-Chief: Claire Gautier
Founded: 2002
Subjects: Business, Career Development, Humor, Management, Marketing, Entrepreneurship, Social Media
ISBN Prefix(es): 978-2-915142
Distribution Center: Courses Livres, 105, rue de Tolbiac, 75013 Paris *Tel:* 01 44 06 64 64 *Fax:* 01 44 06 64 68
Patrimoine, 168 rue du Noyer, 1030 Brussels, Belgium *Tel:* (02) 73668 47 *Fax:* (02) 73668 47 (Belgium & Luxembourg)
La Canopee, 109 chemin du Sphinx, Saint-Armand, QC J0J 1T0, Canada *E-mail:* lacanopee_1@sympatico.ca
OLF, Zl 3, Corminboeuf, PO Box 1152, 1701 Fribourg, Switzerland, Representative: Dominique Tinguely *Tel:* (026) 467 51 11 *Fax:* (026) 467 54 66 *E-mail:* information@olf.ch

Editions Didier
13, rue de l'Odeon, 75006 Paris
Tel: 01 44 41 31 31 *Fax:* 01 44 41 31 48
E-mail: contact@editions-didier.fr
Web Site: www.editionsdidier.com
Key Personnel
Publishing Dir: Isabelle Louviot
Manufacturing Manager: Bernard Rivol
Production Manager: Florence Pedretti
Rights: Maria Mora Fontanilla
Specialize in teaching & learning of languages.
Subjects: Education, Language Arts, Linguistics, Pedagogy
ISBN Prefix(es): 978-2-278
Orders to: HLI, 58, rue Jean Bleuzen, 92178 Vanves Cedex *Tel:* 01 55 00 11 00 *Fax:* 01 55 00 11 20 (international)

Didier Jeunesse
8, rue d'Assas, 75006 Paris
Tel: 01 49 54 48 30 *Fax:* 01 49 54 48 31
Web Site: www.didier-jeunesse.com
Key Personnel
Dir: Michele Moreau
Foreign Rights Manager: Anne Risaliti *Tel:* 01 49 54 48 99 *E-mail:* arisaliti@editions-didier.fr
Press: Laure-Anne Le Coat *Tel:* 01 49 54 48 68 *E-mail:* lalecoat@editions-hatier.fr
Founded: 1988
Subjects: Art, Literature, Literary Criticism, Essays, Music, Dance
ISBN Prefix(es): 978-2-278
Parent Company: Groupe Alexandre Hatier
Ultimate Parent Company: Hachette Livre
Distributed by Hachette Canada; Hachette Livre; Hachette Livre International

Edition Diffusion Presse Sciences, see EDP Sciences

Editions Dilecta+
4, rue de Capri, 75012 Paris
Tel: 01 43 40 28 10 *Fax:* 01 43 40 28 62
E-mail: contact@editions-dilecta.com; presse@editions-dilecta.com
Web Site: www.editions-dilecta.com
Key Personnel
Dir: Gregoire Robinne
Founded: 2005
Art & cultural history.
Subjects: Art, Literature, Literary Criticism, Essays, Social Sciences, Sociology, Entertainment
ISBN Prefix(es): 978-2-916275
Number of titles published annually: 15 Print
Total Titles: 30 Print
Foreign Rep(s): Cornerhouse Publications (Ireland, UK); DAP-Distributed Art Publishers Inc

(worldwide exc Europe); Garzon Diffusion Internationale (Europe, South America); Buchhandlung Walter Koenig (Europe)
Distribution Center: Belles Lettres Diffusion Distribution SAS, 25, rue du General Leclerc, 94270 Le Kremlin-Bicetre *Tel:* 01 45 15 19 70 *Fax:* 01 45 15 19 80 *Web Site:* www.bldd.fr

Editions Le Dilettante+
19, rue Racine, 75006 Paris
Tel: 01 43 37 98 98 *Fax:* 01 43 37 06 10
E-mail: info@ledilettante.com
Web Site: www.ledilettante.com
Key Personnel
Publisher: Dominique Gaultier *E-mail:* gaultier@ledilettante.com
Founded: 1985
Specialize in 20th century literature & rare books.
Subjects: Art, Literature, Literary Criticism, Essays, Music, Dance, Science (General)
ISBN Prefix(es): 978-2-84263; 978-2-905344
Foreign Rep(s): Flammarion Limitee (Canada); OLF (Switzerland); Union Distribution (Belgium, France)
Bookshop(s): Impasse du Ferradou, 11170 Montolieu (specialize in books for young people); 7, pl de l'Odeon, 75006 Paris

Editions Dis Voir+
Imprint of Editions Actes Sud
One Cite Riverin, 75010 Paris
E-mail: contact@disvoir.com
Web Site: www.disvoir.com
Key Personnel
Dir General & Editor: Daniele Riviere *Tel:* 09 51 17 07 39 *E-mail:* daniele@disvoir.com
Founded: 1986
Subjects: Architecture & Interior Design, Art, Fiction, Film, Video, Language Arts, Linguistics, Literature, Literary Criticism, Essays, Music, Dance, Philosophy, Contemporary Art, English Language, French Language
ISBN Prefix(es): 978-2-906571; 978-2-914563
Total Titles: 125 Print; 65 Online
Distributed by Art Data (UK); CELF (Germany, Greece, Italy, Japan, Portugal, South America & Spain); DAP (USA); Manic Ex-Poseur/BAM (Australia); UD Flammarion (France)

Disney Hachette Presse+
124, rue Danton, 92538 Levallois-Perret Cedex
Tel: 02 77 63 11 15 (subscription service)
E-mail: abonnementsmickey@cba.fr
Web Site: www.dhpregie.com
Key Personnel
Commercial & Marketing Dir: Marion Stastny *Tel:* 01 41 34 87 36 *E-mail:* marion.stastny@lagardere-active.com
Dir, Customer Service: Barbara Valdes Le Franc *Tel:* 01 41 34 92 65 *E-mail:* barbara.valdes@lagardere-active.com
Founded: 1991
Subjects: Child Care & Development
ISBN Prefix(es): 978-2-230
Parent Company: The Walt Disney Company France/Hachette Livre
Shipping Address: Centre de distribution du Livre, One ave Gutenberg, 78316 Maurepas
Warehouse: Centre de distribution du Livre, One ave Gutenberg, 78316 Maurepas
Orders to: Hachette - Service Commercial, 79 blvd St Germain, 75006 Paris

La Documentation Francaise+
29 Quai Voltaire, 75007 Paris
Tel: 01 40 15 70 00; 01 40 15 71 10 (bookshop) *Fax:* 01 40 15 67 83
Web Site: www.ladocumentationfrancaise.fr
Founded: 1945
Publications of DILA-Direction de l'Information Legale et Administrative.

Membership(s): Syndicat National de l'Edition (SNE).
Subjects: Art, Economics, Environmental Studies, Government, Political Science, Law, Management, Technology
ISBN Prefix(es): 978-2-11
Number of titles published annually: 600 Print; 3 CD-ROM
Total Titles: 7,000 Print; 5 CD-ROM
Foreign Rep(s): DPLU Inc (Canada); Librairie Kauffmann SA (Greece); Jean de Lannoy (Belgium, Luxembourg); Librairie Nationale (Morocco); Licosa (Italy); Maruzen Co Ltd (Japan); Mundi Prensa Libros SA (Spain); RMR & Associes (Tunisia); Servidis SA (Switzerland)
Orders to: 124 rue Henri-Barbusse, 93308 Aubervilliers Cedex, Contact: Catherine Percik *Tel:* 01 40 15 67 73 *Fax:* 01 40 15 70 01 *E-mail:* commande@ladocumentationfrancaise.fr

Doin Editeurs+
One rue Eugene et Armand Peugeot, 92856 Rueil-Malmaison
Tel: 01 76 73 37 26
Founded: 1874
Subjects: Biological Sciences, Chemistry, Chemical Engineering, Earth Sciences, Education, Health, Nutrition, How-to, Medicine, Nursing, Dentistry, Psychology, Psychiatry, Science (General), Social Sciences, Sociology
ISBN Prefix(es): 978-2-7040
Parent Company: Wolters Kluwer

Les Dossiers d'Aquitaine
7 impasse Bardos, 33800 Bordeaux
Tel: 05 56 91 84 98 *Fax:* 05 56 91 64 92
E-mail: ddabordeaux@gmail.com; ddabx.info@gmail.com
Web Site: www.ddabordeaux.com
Key Personnel
President: Andre Desforges
Founded: 1978
Subjects: Biography, Memoirs, Drama, Theater, History, How-to, Humor, Literature, Literary Criticism, Essays, Poetry, Publishing & Book Trade Reference
ISBN Prefix(es): 978-2-905212; 978-2-84622
Number of titles published annually: 50 Print
Total Titles: 200 Print

Draeger Editeur, see Editions Anthese

Editions Du May+
18/20, rue de la Saussiere, 92100 Boulogne Billancourt
Tel: 01 46 99 24 12
Founded: 1986
ISBN Prefix(es): 978-2-84102
Returns: 65, rue Etienne-Bezout Zl du chateau d'eau, 77550 Moissy-Cramayel *Tel:* 01 64 88 75 10 *Fax:* 01 64 88 76 18

Lec Alain Ducasse Editions
84, Ave Victor Cresson, 92130 Issy-les-Moulineaux
Tel: 01 58 00 21 95 *Fax:* 01 58 00 21 96
Web Site: www.alain-ducasse.com
Founded: 1999
Subjects: Cookery
ISBN Prefix(es): 978-2-84123

Dunod Editeur+
Subsidiary of Hachette Livre
5 rue Laromiguiere, 75005 Paris
Tel: 01 40 46 35 00 *Fax:* 01 40 46 49 95
E-mail: infos@dunod.com
Web Site: www.dunod.com
Key Personnel
Dir, Publications: Pierre-Andre Michel
Rights & Permissions: Maryvonne Vitry
Founded: 1800

Subjects: Computer Science, Computers, Eco-
nomics, Education, Electronics, Electrical En-
gineering, Film, Video, Language Arts, Lin-
guistics, Literature, Literary Criticism, Essays,
Management, Photography, Psychology, Psychi-
atry, Science (General)
ISBN Prefix(es): 978-2-10
Imprints: Ediscience; InterEditions; Microsoft
Press; Editions Techniques et Scientifiques
Francaises (ETSF)
Distributed by Hachette Livre International
Foreign Rep(s): Diffulivre SA (Switzerland);
Somabec (Canada)
Distribution Center: Dilibel, Ave Louise 130 A,
1050 Brussels, Belgium, Contact: Samuel Hen-
naut *Tel:* (02) 508 04 51 *Fax:* (02) 502 02 89
E-mail: diffusion@dilibel.be *Web Site:* www.
dilibel.be (Belgium, Luxembourg & Nether-
lands)
Somabec, 2475 Sylva Clapin, BP 295, Saint-
Hyacinthe, QC J2S 7B6, Canada *Tel:* 450-
774-8118 *Fax:* 450-774-3017 *E-mail:* ventes@
somabec.com *Web Site:* www.somabec.com

Duo, Harlequin, *imprint of* Editions Harlequin

Dupuis France SAS+
15-27 rue Moussorgski, 75895 Paris Cedex 18
Tel: 01 70 38 56 00 *Fax:* 01 70 38 56 01
E-mail: infos@dupuis.com; edito@dupuis.com
Web Site: www.dupuis.com
Key Personnel
Dir General: Olivier Perrard
Editor: Louis-Atoine Dujardin
Press Relations: Mathieu Poulhalec *Tel:* 01 70 38
56 40 *E-mail:* poulhalec@dupuis.com
Founded: 1938
Subjects: Humor
ISBN Prefix(es): 978-2-8001; 978-90-314; 978-
90-6574
Parent Company: Editions Dupuis SA, Rue De-
stree, 52, 6001 Marcinelle, Belgium

Editions de l'eclat+
41, rue Basfroi, 75011 Paris
Tel: 06 45 75 75 34
E-mail: contact@lyber-eclat.net
Web Site: www.lyber-eclat.net
Founded: 1985
Subjects: Literature, Literary Criticism, Essays,
Philosophy, Religion - Islamic, Religion - Jew-
ish, Humanities
ISBN Prefix(es): 978-2-84162; 978-2-905372
Total Titles: 160 Print
Foreign Rep(s): Dimedia (Canada); Hamonia
Mundi (Belgium, France); Zoe (Switzerland)

**Editions de l'Ecole des Hautes Etudes en
Sciences Sociales**, see Editions de l'EHESS

L'ecole des Loisirs
11, rue de Sevres, 75006 Paris
Tel: 01 42 22 94 10
E-mail: edl@ecoledesloisirs.com
Web Site: www.ecoledesloisirs.fr
Key Personnel
Mng Dir: Jean-Louis Fabre
Foreign Rights Manager: Isabelle Darthy
E-mail: idarthy@ecoledesloisirs.com
Subjects: Education
ISBN Prefix(es): 978-2-211
Branch Office(s)
79, blvd Louis Schmidt, 1040 Brussels, Belgium
Tel: 02 736 44 62 *E-mail:* edl@ecoleloisirs.be

**Editions et Publications de l'Ecole Lacanienne
(EPEL)+**
110 blvd Raspail, 75006 Paris
Tel: 01 45 44 24 00
E-mail: epel.paris@wanadoo.fr
Web Site: www.epel-edition.com

Key Personnel
Dir General: Thierry Marchaisse *Tel:* 06 70 49 95
73 *E-mail:* tmarchaisse@gmail.com
Dir, Collections: Jean Allouch *E-mail:* jean.
allouch@wanadoo.fr
Founded: 1990
Subjects: Philosophy, Psychology, Psychiatry
ISBN Prefix(es): 978-2-35427

Ecole Nationale Superieure des Beaux-Arts+
14 rue Bonaparte, 75006 Paris Cedex
Tel: 01 47 03 50 00 *Fax:* 01 47 03 50 80
E-mail: info@beauxartsparis.fr
Web Site: www.beauxartsparis.com
Key Personnel
President: Frederic Jousset
Dir: Nicolas Bourriaud
Communication: Tanguy Grard *Tel:* 01 47 03 50
05 *E-mail:* tanguy.grard@beauxartsparis.fr
Editor: Pascale Le Thorel *Tel:* 01 47 03 50 55
E-mail: pascale.lethorel@beauxartsparis.fr
Press: Isabelle Reye *E-mail:* isabelle.reye@
beauxartsparis.fr
Subjects: Architecture & Interior Design, Art,
Performing Arts
ISBN Prefix(es): 978-2-84056; 978-2-903639
Number of titles published annually: 15 Print; 1
CD-ROM
Total Titles: 100 Print
Parent Company: Ministry of Culture & Commu-
nication
Bookshop(s): 13, quai Malaquais, 75006 Paris

Ecole Normale Superieure de Lyon, see ENS
Editions

Editions Ecriture+
Division of Editions de l'Archipel
34 rue des Bourdonnais, 75001 Paris
Tel: 01 55 80 77 40 *Fax:* 01 55 80 77 41
E-mail: ecricom@wanadoo.fr
Web Site: www.editionsecriture.com
Key Personnel
Dir: Jean-Daniel Belfond
Founded: 1992
Subjects: Literature, Literary Criticism, Essays
ISBN Prefix(es): 978-2-909240
Number of titles published annually: 5 Print
Total Titles: 40 Print
Foreign Rep(s): Anna Droumeva (Bulgaria, Mon-
tenegro, Romania, Serbia); Catherine Fragou-
Rassinier (Greece); Laura Grandi (Italy); Judit
Hermann (Croatia, Hungary); Jackie Huang
(China); Didier Imbot (USA); Asli Karasuil
(Turkey); Eva Koralnik (Germany); Efrat Lev
(Israel); Muriel Park (Korea); Corinne Quentin
(Japan); Marianne Schoenbach (Netherlands,
Scandinavia); Maria Strarz-Kanska (Poland);
Ludmilla Sushkova (Russia); Petra Tobiskova
(Czechia, Slovenia); Anne-Marie Vallat (Spain);
Tatjana Zoldnere (Baltic States)
Distribution Center: Hachette, ZI, One ave
Gutenberg, 78316 Maurepas Cedex *Tel:* 01 30
66 20 66 *E-mail:* cbru@hachette-livre.fr
Dilibel, Ave Louise 130A, 1050 Brussels, Bel-
gium *Tel:* (02) 508 04 51 *E-mail:* bernadette.
gildemyn@dilibel.be
Edipresse, 945, av Beaumont, Montreal, QC
H3N 1W3, Canada *Tel:* 514-273-6141
E-mail: information@edipresse.ca
Diffulivre, Jordils, 41, 1025 Saint-Sulpice,
Switzerland *Tel:* (021) 691 53 31 37
E-mail: diffusion@diffulivre.ch

EDICEF, *imprint of* Hachette Livre International

Edilarge SA, see Editions Ouest-France

Ediscience, *imprint of* Dunod Editeur

Les Editeurs Reunis+
Division of Editions YMCA-Press
11, rue de la Montagne Ste Genevieve, 75005
Paris
Tel: 01 43 54 74 46
E-mail: ed.reunis@wanadoo.fr
Web Site: www.editeurs-reunis.fr
Founded: 1932
The company acts as sole agent for YMCA Press
in publishing a comprehensive list of Russian
books in the original Russian.
Subjects: Art, Biography, Memoirs, History, Lit-
erature, Literary Criticism, Essays, Philosophy,
Religion - Other, Theology
ISBN Prefix(es): 978-2-85065

**Les Editions du CFPJ (Centre de Formation et
de Perfectionnement des Journalistes)+**
Affiliate of CFPJ
35 rue du Louvre, 75002 Paris
Tel: 01 44 82 20 00; 01 44 09 22 28
E-mail: cfpj@cfpj.com; editions@cfpj.com
Web Site: www.cfpj.com
Key Personnel
Dir General: Fabrice Daverio *E-mail:* fdaverio@
cfpj.com
Dir: Marie Ducastel *E-mail:* mducastel@cfpj.com
Head, Print & Mutimedia: Valerie Pailler
E-mail: vpailler@cfpj.com
Assistant, Press Dept: Carole Boyer
E-mail: cboyer@cfpj.com
Founded: 1988
Subjects: Communications, Journalism
ISBN Prefix(es): 978-2-85900; 978-2-902734
Imprints: Presse et Formation

**Editions Litteraires et Linguistiques de
l'Universite de Grenoble**, see ELLUG
(Editions Litteraires et Linguistiques de
l'Universite de Grenoble)

Editions1+
Subsidiary of Hachette Livre
31, rue du Montparnasse, 75298 Paris
Tel: 01 49 54 36 00
E-mail: commercial@calmann-levy.fr
Web Site: calmann-levy.fr
Key Personnel
Dir General: Philippe Robinet *Tel:* 01 49 54 36
43 *E-mail:* probinet@calmann-levy.fr
Head, Foreign Rights: Patricia Roussel
E-mail: proussel@calmann-levy.fr
Founded: 1979
Subjects: Biography, Memoirs, Literature, Lit-
erary Criticism, Essays, Nonfiction (General),
Self-Help, Sports, Athletics
ISBN Prefix(es): 978-2-86391; 978-2-84612
Ultimate Parent Company: Lagardere Publishing
Associate Companies: Calmann-Levy

Editions EDK, *imprint of* EDP Sciences

EDP Dentaire, *imprint of* EDP Sciences

EDP Sante, *imprint of* EDP Sciences

EDP Sciences+
17, ave du Hoggar, Parc d'Activities de
Courtaboeuf, 91944 Les Ulis Cedex
Tel: 01 69 18 75 75 *Fax:* 01 69 28 84 91; 01 69
86 06 78 (orders)
E-mail: contact-edps@edpsciences.org; editorial@
edpsciences.org; books@edpsciences.org
(orders)
Web Site: www.edpsciences.org
Key Personnel
Mng Dir & Publications Manager: Jean-Marc
Quilbe *E-mail:* jean-marc.quilbe@edpsciences.
org
Founded: 1920
Scientific, technical & medical publisher (jour-
nals, books, trade magazines).

Subjects: Astronomy, Chemistry, Chemical Engineering, Earth Sciences, Energy, Engineering (General), Environmental Studies, Mathematics, Mechanical Engineering, Medicine, Nursing, Dentistry, Physical Sciences, Physics, Psychology, Psychiatry, Science (General), Technology
ISBN Prefix(es): 978-2-86883; 978-2-902731
Number of titles published annually: 50 Print; 20 E-Book
Total Titles: 400 Print; 200 E-Book
Imprints: Editions EDK; EDP Dentaire; EDP Sante
Distribution Center: Sofedis, 11 Rue Soufflot, 75006 Paris, Dir General: Marc Galitzky
Tel: 01 53 10 25 25 *E-mail:* info@sofedis.fr
Web Site: www.sofedis.fr

Editions de l'EHESS+
190-198 ave de France, 75013 Paris
Tel: 01 49 54 24 75
E-mail: editionsdirection@ehess.fr
Web Site: editions.ehess.fr
Key Personnel
Dir: Emmanuel Desveaux
Coordinator: Guillaume Dervieux
Head, Publications: Jean-Baptiste Boyer *Tel:* 01 53 10 53 65
International Development & Foreign Rights: Anne Madelain *Tel:* 01 53 10 53 85
   E-mail: madelain@ehess.fr
Founded: 1975
Subjects: Anthropology, Asian Studies, Economics, History, Social Sciences, Sociology
ISBN Prefix(es): 978-2-7132; 978-2-85783
Number of titles published annually: 15 Print
Total Titles: 650 Print
Branch Office(s)
131 blvd Saint-Michel, 75005 Paris *Tel:* 01 53 10 53 55 *Fax:* 01 44 07 08 89 *E-mail:* editions@ehess.fr
Distributed by CID; Seuil; Vrin
Foreign Rep(s): OLF (Switzerland); Socadis (Canada)
Distribution Center: Sodis, 128 Ave du Marechal de Lattre de Rassigny, 7740 Lagny-sur-Marne *Tel:* 01 60 07 82 99; 01 60 07 82 00 *Fax:* 01 64 30 32 27

Eho, see Editions Heloise d'Ormesson (Eho)

ELAH, see Editions Lyonnaises d'Art et d'Histoire

Editions de L'Elan Vert
64 ave Guy Leroux, 37700 Saint-Pierre des Corps
E-mail: courrier@elanvert.fr
Web Site: www.elanvert.fr
Key Personnel
Founder: Jean-Rene Gombert
Founder & Editorial Dir: Amelie Leveille
Editor: Chloe Laborde
Founded: 1998
ISBN Prefix(es): 978-2-84455
Foreign Rep(s): ADL (Canada); La Caravelle (Belgium); Servidis (Switzerland)
Distribution Center: Sodis, 128 ave du Marechal de Lattre de Tassigny, 77400 Lagny sur Marne *Tel:* 01 60 07 82 99 *Fax:* 01 64 30 32 27
E-mail: saisie@sodis.fr

Electre, Editions du Cercle de la Librairie+
35, rue Gregoire de Tours, 75006 Paris Cedex
Tel: 01 44 41 28 00 *Fax:* 01 44 41 28 65
E-mail: librairie@electre.com
Web Site: www.electre.com; www.electrelaboutique.com
Key Personnel
Dir: Philippe Beauvillard
Dir, Development: Pascal Fouche
Founded: 1983
Subjects: Library & Information Sciences

ISBN Prefix(es): 978-2-7654
Number of titles published annually: 10 Print

Ellebore Editions
91 ave de la Republique, 75011 Paris
Tel: 01 77 13 03 77
Web Site: www.ellebore.com
Key Personnel
Dir: Edouard Frison-Roche
Founded: 1980
Subjects: Health, Nutrition, Psychology, Psychiatry
ISBN Prefix(es): 978-2-86898

Les Editions Ellipses
8/10 rue de la Quintinie, 75740 Paris Cedex 15
Tel: 01 56 56 64 10 *Fax:* 01 45 31 07 67
E-mail: editorial@editions-ellipses.fr; contact@editions-ellipses.fr; presse@editions-ellipses.fr
Web Site: www.editions-ellipses.fr
Key Personnel
Mng Dir: Jean-Pierre Benezet
Founded: 1973
Subjects: Medicine, Nursing, Dentistry, Science (General)
ISBN Prefix(es): 978-2-7298

ELLUG (Editions Litteraires et Linguistiques de l'Universite de Grenoble)+
BP 25, 38040 Grenoble Cedex 9
Tel: 04 76 82 43 72 *Fax:* 04 76 82 41 12
E-mail: ellug@u-grenoble3.fr
Web Site: www.u-grenoble3.fr/ellug
Key Personnel
Editorial Dir: Daniel Lancon *E-mail:* daniel.lancon@u-grenoble3.fr
Founded: 1978
Membership(s): International Association of Scholarly Publishers.
Subjects: Antiques, Communications, Language Arts, Linguistics, Literature, Literary Criticism, Essays
ISBN Prefix(es): 978-2-902709; 978-2-84310
Number of titles published annually: 10 Print
Total Titles: 120 Print
Distribution Center: FMSH-Diffusion, 18-20, rue Robert-Schuman, 94220 Charenton-le-Pont *Tel:* 01 53 48 56 30 *Fax:* 01 53 48 20 95

ELOR Editions
10 rue du Chandelier, 56350 Saint-Vincent-sur-Oust
Tel: 02 99 91 22 80 *Fax:* 02 99 91 34 45
E-mail: edit.elor@wanadoo.fr
Web Site: www.livre-achat.com/eloreditions
Founded: 1976
Subjects: Crafts, Games, Hobbies, Fiction, Religion - Catholic
ISBN Prefix(es): 978-2-907524; 978-2-912214
Imprints: Editions de Iorme Rond

Elsevier Masson SAS+
62, rue Camille Desmoulins, 92442 Issy-les-Moulineaux Cedex
Tel: 01 71 16 55 00; 01 71 16 55 99 (customer relations) *Fax:* 01 71 16 55 88
E-mail: relclients@elsevier-masson.fr
Web Site: www.elsevier-masson.fr
Key Personnel
Dir, Sales: Mr Jean-Marie Pinson
Founded: 1804
Publish medicine & health care-related subjects & 50 journals in print & online versions; dictionaries.
Subjects: Medicine, Nursing, Dentistry, Psychology, Psychiatry, Veterinary Science
ISBN Prefix(es): 978-2-10; 978-2-225; 978-2-294
Number of titles published annually: 200 Print
Total Titles: 3,000 Print
Parent Company: Elsevier

Editions de l'Emmanuel, see AVM-Editions de l'Emmanuel Sarl

Les Empecheurs de Penser en Rond, *imprint of* Editions La Decouverte

Encres Vives
2, allee des Allobroges, 31770 Colomiers
Tel: 05 62 74 07 87
Key Personnel
Dir: Michel Cosem *E-mail:* michelcosem@wanadoo.fr
Founded: 1960
Subjects: Poetry
ISBN Prefix(es): 978-2-85550

Encyclopaedica Universalis+
62 bis ave Andre Morizet, 92100 Boulogne Billancourt
Tel: 01 75 60 43 13; 01 75 60 43 17
E-mail: contact@universalis.fr
Web Site: www.universalis.fr
Key Personnel
President: Dominique Liardet
Dir General: Herve Rouanet
Editorial: Bernard Couvelaire
Founded: 1968
ISBN Prefix(es): 978-2-85229

Encyclopedie de L'Etat du Monde, *imprint of* Editions La Decouverte

ENS Editions
15, parvis Rene Descartes, 69342 Lyon Cedex 07
Mailing Address: BP 7000, 69342 Lyon Cedex 07
Tel: 04 26 73 11 91; 04 26 73 11 98 *Fax:* 04 26 73 12 68
E-mail: editions@ens-lyon.fr
Web Site: www.ens-lyon.fr/editions/catalogue
Key Personnel
Head, Publishing: Denise Pierrot
Founded: 1993
Subjects: Art, Economics, Education, Geography, Geology, Government, Political Science, History, Literature, Literary Criticism, Essays, Philosophy, Science (General), Social Sciences, Sociology
ISBN Prefix(es): 978-2-84788; 978-2-902126
Bookshop(s): ENS de Lyon, Institut francais de l'Education, Batiment Ferdinand-Buisson, 19, allee de Fontenay, 69007 Lyon *Tel:* 04 26 73 12 70; 04 26 73 12 03 *Fax:* 04 26 73 12 68
Orders to: Comptoil des Presses d'universites, 18 rue Robert-Schuman, CS 90003, 94227 Charenton-le-Pont Cedex *Tel:* 01 53 48 56 30 *Fax:* 01 53 48 20 95 *Web Site:* www.lcdpu.fr

Editions L'Entretemps
264 rue du capitaine Pierre Pontal, 34000 Montpellier
Tel: 04 99 53 09 75 *Fax:* 09 58 09 15 14
E-mail: info@entretemps.org; administration@entretemps.org
Web Site: www.entretemps.org
Key Personnel
President: Jean-Charles Gerard
Assistant Dir: Elodie Dombre *E-mail:* elodie.dombre@entretemps.org
Editorial Manager: Christophe Bara
   E-mail: christophebara@claranet.fr
Administration: Rosalie Mathevet
Production: Marie Mougnaud
   E-mail: mariemougnaud@entretemps.org
Founded: 1997
Subjects: Art, Drama, Theater, Literature, Literary Criticism, Essays, Music, Dance
ISBN Prefix(es): 978-2-912877

Editions EP&S+
11, ave du Tremblay, 75571 Paris Cedex 12
Tel: 01 41 74 82 82 *Fax:* 01 43 98 37 38
E-mail: revue@revue-eps.com

Web Site: www.revue-eps.com
Key Personnel
President & Dir of Publication: Yves Touchard
 E-mail: yves.touchard@orange.fr
Vice President: Gilles Klein
Dir: Pierre-Philippe Bureau
Founded: 1950
Subjects: Education, Sports, Athletics
ISBN Prefix(es): 978-2-86713

Epanouissement, *imprint of* Editions Jouvence
 Sarl

Les Editions de l'Epargne SA+
24, Blvd de l'Hopital, 75005 Paris
Tel: 01 45 87 76 76
Web Site: www.editions-epargne.fr
Key Personnel
Dir General: Albert Pinto
Founded: 1957
Subjects: Architecture & Interior Design, Art,
 Economics, Finance, History, How-to, Law
ISBN Prefix(es): 978-2-85015
Parent Company: Groupe BPCE

EPEL, see Editions et Publications de l'Ecole
 Lacanienne (EPEL)

Editions Equinoxe/Edisud+
La Massane, Les joncades Basses, 13210 St-
 Remy-de-Provence
Tel: 04 90 90 21 10
E-mail: contact@editions-equinoxe.com
Web Site: www.edisud.com
Founded: 1971
Subjects: Agriculture, Anthropology, Archaeol-
 ogy, Architecture & Interior Design, Art, Cook-
 ery, Energy, Environmental Studies, Ethnicity,
 Gardening, Plants, Geography, Geology, His-
 tory, How-to, Music, Dance, Outdoor Recre-
 ation, Regional Interests, Sports, Athletics,
 Wine & Spirits
ISBN Prefix(es): 978-2-85744; 978-2-7449; 978-
 2-85459

L'Ere Nouvelle (The New Era)+
BP 171, 06407 Cannes Cedex
Tel: 04 93 99 30 13
E-mail: lerenouvelle@wanadoo.fr
Web Site: lerenouvelle.pagespro-orange.fr/pub
Key Personnel
Dir & Editor-in-Chief: Pierre Lance
Founded: 1980
Subjects: Energy, Health, Nutrition, Philosophy,
 Psychology, Psychiatry, Social Sciences, Soci-
 ology
ISBN Prefix(es): 978-2-905825

Editions Eres+
33 ave Marcel Dassault, 31500 Toulouse
Tel: 05 61 75 15 76 *Fax:* 05 61 73 52 89
E-mail: eres@editions-eres.com
Web Site: www.editions-eres.com
Key Personnel
Founder: Jean Sacrispeyre
Publishing Dir: Marie-Francoise Dubois-
 Sacrispeyre
Marketing Dir: Liliane Gestermann
Founded: 1980
Subjects: Criminology, Education, Law, Philoso-
 phy, Psychology, Psychiatry, Social Sciences,
 Sociology, Childhood & Parenting, Gerontol-
 ogy, Humanities, Mental Health, Psychoanaly-
 sis
ISBN Prefix(es): 978-2-86586; 978-2-7492
Number of titles published annually: 60 Print
Foreign Rep(s): Servidis (Switzerland); Somabec
 (Canada)
Distribution Center: Volumen, 25 blvd Romain
 Rolland, 75014 Paris *Tel:* 01 44 10 75 75
 Fax: 01 44 10 75 80 (France & Benelux)

Editions Errance
Imprint of Editions Actes Sud
Pl Nina-Berberova, BP 90038, 13633 Arles
Tel: 04 88 65 92 05 *Fax:* 04 88 65 92 09
Key Personnel
Editorial Dir: Romain Pigeaud
Founded: 1982
Subjects: Archaeology, History
ISBN Prefix(es): 978-2-87772; 978-2-903442
Number of titles published annually: 25 Print
Total Titles: 250 Print

Editions Les Escales
12 Ave d'Italie, 75013 Paris
Tel: 01 44 16 09 36
E-mail: contact@lesescales.fr
Web Site: www.lesescales.fr; www.facebook.com/
 editionslesescales/
Key Personnel
Editorial Dir: Sarah Rigaud *E-mail:* sarah.
 rigaud@edi8.fr
Press Officer: Charlotte Rousseau
 E-mail: charlotte.rousseau@edi8.fr
Sales Manager & Marketing: Damien Naddeo
Sales Manager: Marie Potdevin
Editor: Constance Trapenard
Founded: 2012
ISBN Prefix(es): 978-2-365
Parent Company: Edi8
Ultimate Parent Company: Editis Group

Les Editions ESF+
Forum 52, 52 Rue Camille Desmoulins, 92448
 Issy-les-Moulineaux Cedex
Tel: 01 46 29 46 29; 02 37 29 69 20 (customer
 service)
E-mail: info@esf-editeur.fr
Web Site: www.esf-editeur.fr
Key Personnel
President: Alexandre Sidommo
Marketing Manager: Veronique Brossier
Founded: 1928
Subjects: Business, Communications, Computers,
 Economics, Education, Finance, Law, Man-
 agement, Marketing, Psychology, Psychiatry,
 Technology
ISBN Prefix(es): 978-2-7101
Parent Company: Intescia
Warehouse: PRAT, Zi de Comhre, 28481 Thiron
Orders to: CDE, 17 rue de Tournon, 75006 Paris
Presses de Belgique, Belgium
Dimedia, Canada
Servidis, Switzerland

Editions ESKA
12, rue du Quatre-Septembre, 75002 Paris
Tel: 01 42 86 55 65 *Fax:* 01 42 60 45 35
E-mail: congres@eska.fr
Web Site: www.eska.fr
Subjects: Aeronautics, Aviation, Economics, En-
 gineering (General), Labor, Industrial Relations,
 Law, Management, Medicine, Nursing, Den-
 tistry
ISBN Prefix(es): 978-2-86911; 978-2-7472
Distributor for Presses Universitaires du Quebec
 (Canada)

Editions Espaces 34+
5, place du Chateau, 34270 Les Matelles
Tel: 09 52 44 58 17
E-mail: editions.espaces34@free.fr
Web Site: www.editions-espaces34.fr
Key Personnel
Editorial Dir: Sabine Chevallier
Collection Dir: Francoise Rubellin
Financial Dir: Francois Girard
Subjects: Biological Sciences, Drama, The-
 ater, Literature, Literary Criticism, Essays,
 Medicine, Nursing, Dentistry
ISBN Prefix(es): 978-2-907293; 978-2-84705
Total Titles: 150 Print

Distribution Center: Diffusion Tec & Doc,
 Lavoisier 14, rue de Provigny, 94236 Cachan
 Cedex *Tel:* 01 47 40 67 00 *Fax:* 01 47 40 67
 02 *E-mail:* info@lavoisier.fr *Web Site:* www.
 lavosier.fr

Editions L'Esprit Du Temps+
115 rue Anatole France, 33491 Le Bouscat Cedex
Mailing Address: BP 107, 33491 Le Bouscat
 Cedex
Tel: 05 56 02 84 19 *Fax:* 05 56 02 91 31
E-mail: espritemp@aol.com; info@
 lespritdutemps.com
Web Site: www.lespritdutemps.com
Key Personnel
Dir: Patrick Baradeau
Literary Dir: Philippe Brenot; Laetitia Devaux
Press: Maurice Cadart
Founded: 1989
Subjects: Literature, Literary Criticism, Essays,
 Medicine, Nursing, Dentistry, Psychology, Psy-
 chiatry, Psychoanalysis, Sexology
ISBN Prefix(es): 978-2-908206; 978-2-913062;
 978-2-84795
Number of titles published annually: 30 Print
Total Titles: 250 Print
Orders to: PUF, 6 ave Reille, 75104 Paris

Editions Esprit Ouvert+
142 ave des Champs Elysees, 75008 Paris
Tel: 06 08 61 43 88
Web Site: www.espritouvert.fr
Founded: 1988
Subjects: Biography, Memoirs, Film, Video, His-
 tory, Literature, Literary Criticism, Essays, Po-
 etry, European Literature
ISBN Prefix(es): 978-2-88329
Foreign Rep(s): Diffusion Nord-Sud (Belgium);
 Servidis SA (Switzerland)
Distribution Center: Daudin Distribution, 628 ave
 du Grain d'Or, 41350 Vineuil *Tel:* 01 30 48 74
 74 *Web Site:* www.daudin.fr

Etonnants Classiques, *imprint of* Flammarion
 Groupe

ETSF, see Editions Techniques et Scientifiques
 Francaises

Institut d'Etudes Augustiniennes (IEA)
3 rue de l'Abbaye, 75006 Paris
Tel: 01 43 54 80 25 *Fax:* 01 43 54 39 55
E-mail: etudes.augustiniennes@gmail.com
Web Site: www.etudes-augustiniennes.paris-
 sorbonne.fr
Key Personnel
Dir: Frederic Chapot *E-mail:* chapot@unistra.fr
Librarian: Claudine Croyere *E-mail:* claudine.
 croyere@paris-sorbonne.fr
Founded: 1955
Subjects: Antiques, Archaeology, History, Philos-
 ophy, Religion - Catholic, Theology
ISBN Prefix(es): 978-2-85121
Shipping Address: Brepols Publishers NV, Begijn-
 hof 67, 2300 Turnhout, Belgium *Tel:* 14 40 27
 00 *Fax:* 14 42 89 19 *E-mail:* info@brepols.com
 Web Site: www.brepols.net
Warehouse: Brepols Publishers NV, Begijnhof
 67, 2300 Turnhout, Belgium *Tel:* 14 40 27 00
 Fax: 14 42 89 19 *E-mail:* info@brepols.com
 Web Site: www.brepols.net
Orders to: Brepols Publishers NV, Begijnhof
 67, 2300 Turnhout, Belgium *Tel:* 14 44 80 30
 Fax: 14 42 89 19 *E-mail:* orders@brepols.net
 Web Site: www.brepols.net

Institut d'etudes slaves+
9, rue Michelet, 75006 Paris
Tel: 01 42 02 27 54 *Fax:* 01 43 26 16 23
E-mail: ies.paris@orange.fr
Web Site: institut-etudes-slaves.fr

Key Personnel
President: Pierre Gonneau
Founded: 1920
Subjects: Anthropology, History, Language Arts, Linguistics, Literature, Literary Criticism, Essays, Slavic Studies
ISBN Prefix(es): 978-2-7204

L'Expansion Scientifique Francaise (French Scientific Development Co)
31 Blvd de la Tour Maubourg, 75007 Paris 07
Tel: 01 45 48 42 60 *Fax:* 01 45 44 81 55
Key Personnel
Chief Executive Officer: Denis Paul Justin Besancon
Founded: 1925
Subjects: Biological Sciences, Medicine, Nursing, Dentistry
ISBN Prefix(es): 978-2-7046
Subsidiaries: Expansion Formation et Editions
Bookshop(s): L'Ecume des Pages, 174 blvd St-Germain, 75006 Paris Cedex 06 *Tel:* 01 45 48 54 48 *Fax:* 01 45 48 84 10

Editions Eyrolles+
61 blvd St-Germain, 75240 Paris Cedex 05
Tel: 01 44 41 11 11 *Fax:* 01 44 41 11 85
E-mail: info@eyrolles.com; foreignrights@eyrolles.com
Web Site: www.editions-eyrolles.com
Founded: 1918
Subjects: Architecture & Interior Design, Computer Science, Crafts, Games, Hobbies, Earth Sciences, Electronics, Electrical Engineering, Management, Mechanical Engineering, Physical Sciences
ISBN Prefix(es): 978-2-212
Parent Company: Groupe Eyrolles SA
Associate Companies: Editions d'Organisation
Distributor for Microsoft Press France

Editions Fabert
107 rue de l'Universite, 75007 Paris
Tel: 01 47 05 32 68 *Fax:* 01 47 05 05 61
E-mail: editions@fabert.com
Web Site: www.fabert.com
Key Personnel
Dir: Thomas Jallaud
Founded: 2004
Subjects: Pedagogy
ISBN Prefix(es): 978-2-84922; 978-2-907164
Imprints: Editions Souffles
Branch Office(s)
20 rue Fabert, 75007 Paris
15 rue des Capuchins, 69001 Lyon *Tel:* 04 37 28 96 17

Fage Editions
3, rue Camille Jordan, 69001 Lyon
Tel: 04 72 07 70 98
E-mail: fage.editions@free.fr
Web Site: www.fage-editions.com
Key Personnel
Dir: Gilles Fage
Subjects: Art, History, Social Sciences, Sociology
ISBN Prefix(es): 978-2-84975
Distribution Center: Interforum, Immeuble Paryseine, 3 allee de la Seine, 94854 Ivry-sur-Seine *Tel:* 01 49 59 10 10 *Fax:* 01 49 59 10 72

Editions de Fallois
22 rue La Boetie, 75008 Paris
Tel: 01 42 66 91 95 *Fax:* 01 49 24 06 37
Key Personnel
Chief Executive Officer: Bernard de Fallois
Founded: 1987
Subjects: Literature, Literary Criticism, Essays
ISBN Prefix(es): 978-2-87706
Orders to: Hachette Export, 58 rue Jean Bleuzen, 92178 Vanves Cedex

Editions Fanlac+
12, rue du Prof Peyrot, 24002 Perigueux Cedex
Mailing Address: BP 60043, 24002 Perigueux Cedex
Tel: 05 53 53 41 90 *Fax:* 05 53 08 05 85
E-mail: info@fanlac.com
Web Site: www.fanlac.com
Founded: 1943
Subjects: Art, Cookery, Literature, Literary Criticism, Essays, Photography, Poetry, Regional Interests, Travel & Tourism
ISBN Prefix(es): 978-2-86577; 978-2-85122
Number of titles published annually: 10 Print
Branch Office(s)
31 rue Faidherbe, 75011 Paris *Tel:* 06 08 98 33 17

Editions Farel+
19 rue Georges Bidault, Croissy Beauborg, 77435 Marne-la-Vallee Cedex 2
Tel: 01 64 68 46 44 *Fax:* 01 64 68 39 90
E-mail: lire@editionsfarel.com; english@editionsfarel.com
Web Site: www.editionsfarel.com
Key Personnel
Dir: Joel Short
Founded: 1978
Subjects: Religion - Protestant
ISBN Prefix(es): 978-2-86314
Number of titles published annually: 20 Print
Total Titles: 220 Print
Distributed by Le Bon Livre (Belgium); Diffusion Emmaues (Switzerland); Diffusion Inter-Livres (Canada)
Distributor for G-Lu Publishing House; Janz Team/Peniel
Distribution Center: Diffusion Excelsis, 385 chemin du Clos, 26450 Charols *Tel:* 04 75 91 81 81 *Fax:* 04 75 90 43 18 *E-mail:* contact@xl6.com

Editions Fata Morgana+
Fontfroide le Haut, 34980 Saint-Clement de riviere
Tel: 04 67 54 40 40
E-mail: fatamorgana@wanadoo.fr
Web Site: www.fatamorgana.fr
Key Personnel
President & Editor: Bruno Roy
Dir: David Massabuau
Founded: 1966
Subjects: Art, Asian Studies, Literature, Literary Criticism, Essays, Philosophy, Religion - Catholic, Religion - Hindu, Religion - Islamic, Religion - Jewish, Religion - Other
ISBN Prefix(es): 978-2-85194
Subsidiaries: A Bastiano; Bibliotheque Artistique & Litteraire; Fakir Press
Foreign Rep(s): L'Age d'Homme (Switzerland); Les Belles Lettres (France); DPLU (Canada); Nouvelle Diffusion (Belgium)
Distribution Center: Librairie Nicaise, 145 blvd Saint Germain, 75006 Paris, Contact: Pierre Walusinski *Tel:* 01 43 26 62 38 *Fax:* 01 44 07 34 80 (France, Belgium & Switzerland)
La Canopee, 109 chemin du Sphinx, Saint-Armand, QC J0J 1T0, Canada
Orders to: Les Belles Lettres, 25 rue du General Leclerc, 94270 Le Kremlin Bicetre *Tel:* 01 45 15 19 70 *Fax:* 01 45 15 19 80

Editions Faton+
25, rue Berbisey, 21017 Dijon Cedex
Mailing Address: BP 669, 21017 Dijon Cedex
Tel: 03 80 40 41 00 *Fax:* 03 80 30 15 37
E-mail: infos@faton.fr
Web Site: www.faton.fr; www.art-metiers-du-livre.com
Key Personnel
Sales Manager: Olivier Fabre *Tel:* 03 80 40 41 21 *Fax:* 03 80 40 41 29 *E-mail:* olivier-fabre@faton.fr

Founded: 1994
Subjects: Archaeology, Art, Crafts, Games, Hobbies, History, Literature, Literary Criticism, Essays, Religion - Other, Science (General), Sports, Athletics
ISBN Prefix(es): 978-2-87844
Total Titles: 3 Print
Orders to: One, rue des Artisans, BP 90, 21003 Quetigny Cedex *Tel:* 03 80 48 98 48 *Fax:* 03 80 48 98 46

Librairie Artheme Fayard+
Subsidiary of Hachette Livre
13, rue du Montparnasse, 75006 Paris
Tel: 01 45 49 82 00
Web Site: www.fayard.fr
Key Personnel
Publishing Dir: Sophie de Closets
Rights Dir: Carole Saudejaud *E-mail:* rights@editions-fayard.fr
Press: Caroline Gutmann *E-mail:* presse@editions-fayard.fr
Founded: 1854
Subjects: Biography, Memoirs, Fiction, History, Music, Dance, Philosophy, Religion - Other, Science (General), Social Sciences, Sociology, Technology
ISBN Prefix(es): 978-2-213

Federation Francaise de la Randonnee Pedestre+
64 rue du Dessous des Berges, 75013 Paris
Tel: 01 44 89 93 93; 01 44 89 93 90 *Fax:* 01 40 35 85 67
E-mail: info@ffrandonnee.fr; e-publicite@ffrandonnee.fr (advertising)
Web Site: www.ffrandonnee.fr
Founded: 1947
Subjects: Outdoor Recreation, Sports, Athletics
ISBN Prefix(es): 978-2-85699
Shipping Address: IGN, lamp des Landes, 41200 Villefranche-sur-Cher
Warehouse: IGN, lamp des Landes, 41200 Villefranche-sur-Cher
Orders to: IGN, lamp des Landes, 41200 Villefranche-sur-Cher

Editions des Femmes+
35, rue Jacob, 75006 Paris
Tel: 01 42 22 60 74; 01 42 60 93 76 *Fax:* 01 42 22 62 73; 01 58 62 20 13
E-mail: contact@desfemmes.fr; librairie@desfemmes.fr
Web Site: www.desfemmes.fr; www.alliancedesfemmes.fr
Key Personnel
Proprietor & Mng Dir: Antoinette Fouque
Founded: 1973
Subjects: Art, Biography, Memoirs, Drama, Theater, Fiction, History, Literature, Literary Criticism, Essays, Photography, Poetry
ISBN Prefix(es): 978-2-7210
Number of titles published annually: 5 Print; 2 Audio
Total Titles: 450 Print; 100 Audio
Distributor for Sonjis

Editions Feret+
24, allees de Tourny, 33000 Bordeaux
Tel: 05 56 13 79 95 *Fax:* 05 56 13 79 96
E-mail: feret@feret.com
Web Site: www.feret.com
Key Personnel
Dir: Bruno Boidron
Founded: 1813
Subjects: Wine & Spirits
ISBN Prefix(es): 978-2-902416; 978-2-35156
Number of titles published annually: 10 Print
Total Titles: 75 Print
Foreign Rep(s): Dimedia (Canada); Servidis (Switzerland)

Distribution Center: Volumen, 69 bis rue de
Vaugirard, 75006 Paris *Tel:* 01 44 10 75 75
Fax: 01 44 10 75 80 *Web Site:* www.volumen.
fr

Groupe Revue Fiduciaire+
100, rue La Fayette, 75485 Paris Cedex 10
Tel: 08 26 80 52 52; 01 41 83 62 58
E-mail: src@grouperf.com; courrier@grouperf.
com
Web Site: corporate.grouperf.com
Founded: 1919
Subjects: Accounting, Business
ISBN Prefix(es): 978-2-86521
Associate Companies: Societe Europeenne de
Presse Fiscale, Juridique
Orders to: 45 rue Victor Hugo, 93507 Pantin
Tel: 01 48 40 01 11

Editions First & First Interactive+
12 ave d'Italie, 75013 Paris
Tel: 01 45 49 60 00 *Fax:* 01 45 49 60 01
E-mail: firstinfo@efirst.com; foreign.rights@
grund.fr
Web Site: www.editionsfirst.fr
Key Personnel
Dir: Vincent Barbare
Dir, Communications & Head, Press: Caro-
line Destais-Brochain *Tel:* 01 44 16 09 04
E-mail: cdestais@efirst.com
Foreign Rights Manager: Sarah Rigaud *Tel:* 01 44
16 09 61 *E-mail:* srigaud@efirst.com
Founded: 1992
Subjects: Computer Science, Cookery, Fiction,
Health, Nutrition, Humor, Marketing, Self-Help
ISBN Prefix(es): 978-2-87691; 978-2-7540
Parent Company: Edi8
Ultimate Parent Company: Editis Group
Associate Companies: Editions Grund; Grund Je-
unesse; Livres du Dragon d'Or; Pour les Nuls
Foreign Rep(s): Interforum (Belgium, Canada,
Switzerland)
Distribution Center: Interforum, 3, allee de la
Seine, Immeuble Paris Seine, 94854 Ivry
Cedex *Tel:* 01 49 59 10 10 *Web Site:* www.
interforum.fr
Interforum Benelux, Fond Jean - Paques, 6, 1348
Louvain-la-nueve, Belgium *Tel:* (010) 42 03 20
Web Site: www.interforum.be
Interforum Canada, 1001, boul de Maisonneuve
Est, Montreal, QC H2L 4P9, Canada *Tel:* 514-
281-1050 *E-mail:* info@interforum.qc.ca
Interforum Suisse, Route Andre Piller, 33A,
Giviziez, CP 69, 1701 Fribourg, Switzer-
land *Tel:* (026) 46 080 60 *Web Site:* www.
interforumsuisse.ch

Les Editions Fischbacher (Fischbacher
Publishing)
5, rue Barbette, 75003 Paris
Tel: 01 44 54 55 11 *Fax:* 01 44 54 55 15
E-mail: info@editionsfischbacher.com
Web Site: www.editionsfischbacher.com
Key Personnel
Dir, Production, Publicity, Rights & Permissions:
Catherine Aflalo
Founded: 1872
Subjects: Alternative, Art, Drama, Theater, Edu-
cation, History, Inspirational, Spirituality, Liter-
ature, Literary Criticism, Essays, Music, Dance,
Nonfiction (General), Philosophy, Photography,
Religion - Protestant, Social Sciences, Sociol-
ogy, Theology
ISBN Prefix(es): 978-2-7179
Associate Companies: Onciale *Web Site:* www.
onciale.fr
Distributed by Les Belles Lettres
Distribution Center: CED, 73 quai Auguste
Deshaies, 94854 Ivry-sur-Seine Cedex
E-mail: ced.societe@wanadoo.fr

Flammarian Quebec, *imprint of* Flammarion
Groupe

Flammarion, *imprint of* Flammarion Groupe

Flammarion Groupe+
Subsidiary of Editions Gallimard
87, quai Panhard et Levassor, 75647 Paris Cedex
13
Tel: 01 40 51 31 00 *Fax:* 01 43 29 21 48
Web Site: editions.flammarion.com
Key Personnel
Chief Executive Officer & Publishing Dir: Teresa
Cremisi
Chief Financial Officer: Thierry Capot
Vice President: Alain Flammarion
Dir, Human Resources & Operations: Olivier
Randon
Founded: 1876
Subjects: Architecture & Interior Design, Art, Ed-
ucation, Fiction, Gardening, Plants, House &
Home, Humor, Literature, Literary Criticism,
Essays, Medicine, Nursing, Dentistry, Non-
fiction (General), Science (General), Wine &
Spirits, Humanities
ISBN Prefix(es): 978-2-257
Imprints: Arthaud; Editions Aubier; Autrement;
Casterman; Champs; Climats; Etonnants Clas-
siques; Flammarion; Flammarion Jeunesse;
Flammarian Quebec; Fluide Glacial; GF; J'ai
lu; Jungle; Librio; Ombres Noires; Pere Castor;
Pygmalion; Sakka
Distributor for Arthaud; Editions Aubier;
Autrement; Beaux Arts Editions; Editions des
Bulles dans l'ocean; Casterman; Cavatines;
Centre Pompidou; Centre Pompidou Metz; Cli-
mats; Al Dante; Delagrave (exc school); Ego
comme X; 84 Editions; Encyclopaedia Univer-
salis (exc encyclopedias); Farrago; Flammarion;
Fluide Glacial; Helium; L'Herne; Horay; J'ai
lu; Jungle; Kameleo; Librio; Ludetis; Le Lu-
dion; Musee du Quai Branly; Nova; Paquet;
Pere Castor; Petit Fute; Plume; Pygmalion;
Rizzoli New York; Leo Scheer; Skira; Somogy;
Tabary; La Tengo; Editions de la 13eme note;
de la Tour; Via Valeriano; Vidal; Vie et Cie;
White Star; Zagat
Distribution Center: 6, rue Europe, 45300 Ser-
maises du Loiret *Tel:* 02 38 39 00 43
Orders to: UD-Union Distribution, 106 rue du
Lieutenant Petit Le Roy, 94669 Chevilly-Larue
Cedex *Tel:* 01 41 80 20 20 *Fax:* 01 46 87 51
80

Flammarion Jeunesse, *imprint of* Flammarion
Groupe

Fleurus, *imprint of* Fleurus Editions

Fleurus Editions+
15/27, rue Moussorgski, 75895 Paris Cedex 18
E-mail: fleuruseditions@fleuruseditions.com;
foreignrights@fleuruseditions.com
Web Site: www.fleuruseditions.com
Key Personnel
Publishing Dir: Hilaire de Laage
Foreign Rights Manager, Adult Books: Marion
Girona *E-mail:* m.girona@fleuruseditions.com
Foreign Rights Manager, Children's Books: Anne
Desrame *Tel:* 01 40 83 82 73 *Fax:* 01 40 83 82
71 *E-mail:* a.desrame@fleuruseditions.com
Founded: 1944
Subjects: Architecture & Interior Design, Art,
Cookery, Crafts, Games, Hobbies, Fiction, Gar-
dening, Plants, Psychology, Psychiatry, Reli-
gion - Other, Social Sciences, Sociology, The-
ology, Home Improvement, Parenting
ISBN Prefix(es): 978-2-215
Imprints: Fleurus; Mame; Mango; Rustica
Foreign Rep(s): La Caravelle SDL (Belgium);
Dargaud Suisse (Switzerland); IRIS Diffusion
(Canada); MDS (France); Prologue (Canada)

Fleuve Editions
12, ave d'Italie, 75627 Paris Cedex 13
Tel: 01 44 16 05 00
E-mail: foreignrights@universpoche.com
Web Site: www.fleuve-editions.fr
Key Personnel
Publishing Dir: Marie-Christine Conchon
Founded: 1949
Subjects: Literature, Literary Criticism, Essays,
Science Fiction, Fantasy, Popular Fiction, TV
Series, Women's Literature
ISBN Prefix(es): 978-2-265
Parent Company: Univers Poche SA

Fluide Glacial, *imprint of* Flammarion Groupe

Editions Folies d'Encre
9, Ave Resistance, 93100 Montreuil
Tel: 01 49 20 80 00; 01 49 20 80 06
E-mail: folies@nerim.fr; editionsfoliesdencre@
yahoo.fr
Web Site: www.foliesdencre.com
Key Personnel
Contact: Jean Marie Ozanne
Founded: 1981
Subjects: Fiction
ISBN Prefix(es): 978-2-907337

Folklore Comtois Editions
Musee des Maisons Comtoises, 25360 Nancray
Tel: 03 81 55 87 60
E-mail: folklore-comtois@orange.fr
Web Site: www.folklore-comtois.fr
Key Personnel
President: Maurice Colette
Publishing & Advertising: Michele Gaiffe
Subjects: Agriculture, Architecture & Interior
Design, History, House & Home, Literature,
Literary Criticism, Essays, Regional Interests,
Culture, Folklore, Regional Ethnology
ISBN Prefix(es): 978-2-9524096
Parent Company: Association Folklore Comtois

Fondation Presses Universitaires de Strasbourg
5, Allee du General Rouvillois, CS 50008, 67083
Strasbourg Cedex
Tel: 03 68 85 60 15 *Fax:* 03 68 85 62 85
E-mail: lapierre@unistra.fr
Web Site: www.unistra.fr
Key Personnel
Dir: Cecile Geiger *E-mail:* cecile.geiger@unistra.
fr
Founded: 1920
Subjects: Art, History, Law, Literature, Literary
Criticism, Essays, Philosophy, Poetry, Social
Sciences, Sociology, Theology
ISBN Prefix(es): 978-2-86820
Distribution Center: CID, 131 bd Saint-Michel,
75005 Paris *Tel:* 01 53 10 53 95

Les Editions Foucher
Subsidiary of Hachette Livre
11 rue Paul Bert, 92247 Malakoff Cedex
Tel: 01 41 23 65 60; 01 41 23 65 65 *Fax:* 01 41
23 65 03
E-mail: fouchercontact@editions-foucher.fr
Web Site: www.editions-foucher.fr
Key Personnel
Publishing Dir: Olivier Jaoui
Founded: 1936
Subjects: Accounting, Economics, Education,
Medicine, Nursing, Dentistry, Public Admin-
istration
ISBN Prefix(es): 978-2-216
Total Titles: 1,000 Print

Les Fourmis Rouges
32 ave du President Wilson, 93100 Montreuil
Tel: 01 70 24 18 38
E-mail: manuscrits@fourmisrouges.fr (manuscript
submission)

Web Site: editionslesfourmisrouges.com; www.
facebook.com/EditionsLesFourmisRouges
Key Personnel
Publisher: Valerie Cussaguet *E-mail:* v.
cussaguet@fourmisrouges.fr
Press & Marketing: Brune Bottero *E-mail:* b.
bottero@fourmisrouges.fr
Founded: 2013
We accept manuscripts preferably by e-mail or
mail. We return the manuscripts sent by mail if
they are accompanied by a stamped envelope.
ISBN Prefix(es): 978-2-36902
Foreign Rep(s): Zoe Diffusion (Switzerland)
Foreign Rights: Hannele & Associates
Distribution Center: Harmonia mundi, Mas de
vert, BP 150, 13631 Arles Cedex *Tel:* 04 90 49
90 49; 04 90 49 58 05 *Fax:* 04 90 49 96 14;
04 90 49 58 35

Association Francaise de Normalisation+
11, rue Francis de Pressense, 93571 La Plaine
Saint-Denis Cedex
Tel: 01 41 62 80 00 *Fax:* 01 49 17 90 00
E-mail: info.formation@afnor.org; norminfo@
afnor.org; presse@afnor.org
Web Site: www.afnor.org
Key Personnel
Dir General: Olivier Peyrat
President: Claude Satinet
Vice President: Henri Halna du Fretay; Do-
minique Hoestland
Press: Olivier Gibert *Tel:* 01 41 62 85 55; Daniele
Klein *Tel:* 06 76 73 66 20 *E-mail:* kleinrp@
orange.fr
Subjects: Management
ISBN Prefix(es): 978-2-12

Editions France-Empire+
41, rue Copernic, 75116 Paris
Tel: 01 40 67 72 90 *Fax:* 01 40 67 74 18
Key Personnel
Publishing Manager: Clotilde James
Founded: 1945
Subjects: Biography, Memoirs, Government, Po-
litical Science, History
ISBN Prefix(es): 978-2-7048
Parent Company: Desquenne et Giral
Bookshop(s): Librairie France-Empire, 30 rue
Washington, 75008 Paris

France Loisirs SAS
123 blvd de Grenelle, 75015 Paris Cedex 15
Mailing Address: Vepex 5000, 62070 Arras
Cedex 9
Tel: 08 92 70 06 05 *Fax:* 03 21 79 56 50
E-mail: serviceclub@france-loisirs.com
Web Site: www.franceloisirs.com
Key Personnel
Dir: Jorg Hagen
Founded: 1970
Subjects: Art, Literature, Literary Criticism, Es-
says
ISBN Prefix(es): 978-2-7242; 978-2-7441

Les Editions Franciscaines
9, rue Marie-Rose, 75014 Paris
Tel: 01 45 40 73 51 *Fax:* 01 40 44 75 04
E-mail: contact@editions-franciscaines.com
Web Site: www.editions-franciscaines.com
Founded: 1932
Subjects: Religion - Catholic, Theology, Francis-
can Spirituality
ISBN Prefix(es): 978-2-85020
Number of titles published annually: 8 Print; 3
CD-ROM
Total Titles: 105 Print
Distributor for Franciscan Printing Press
Foreign Rep(s): Interforum-WAVRE (Belgium);
Socadis-Fides (Canada)

Futuribles Sarl+
47, rue de Babylone, 75007 Paris

Tel: 01 53 63 37 70 *Fax:* 01 42 22 65 54
Web Site: www.futuribles.com
Key Personnel
Publishing Dir: Hugues de Jouvenel
E-mail: hjouvenel@futuribles.com
Secretary General: Corinne Roels *Tel:* 01 53 63
37 71 *E-mail:* croels@futuribles.com
Manager: Francois de Jouvenel
Subcription Manager: Benjamin Privey *Tel:* 01 53
63 37 73 *E-mail:* bprivey@futuribles.com
Founded: 1975
Publish a monthly independent transdisciplinary
policy oriented journal.
Subjects: Developing Countries, Economics, En-
vironmental Studies, Government, Political Sci-
ence, Labor, Industrial Relations, Management,
Social Sciences, Sociology, Technology
ISBN Prefix(es): 978-2-84387
Number of titles published annually: 11 Print; 11
Online
Total Titles: 350 Print; 45 Online
Parent Company: Futuribles International

Editions Jacques Gabay
151 bis, rue St-Jacques, 75005 Paris
Tel: 01 43 54 64 64 *Fax:* 01 43 54 87 00
E-mail: infos@gabay.com
Web Site: www.gabay.com
Key Personnel
Mng Dir: Jacques Gabay
Founded: 1987
This publisher has indicated that 40% of their
product line is author subsidized.
Subjects: Astronomy, Chemistry, Chemical Engi-
neering, Economics, Mathematics, Philosophy,
Physical Sciences, Physics, Science (General)
ISBN Prefix(es): 978-2-87647
Total Titles: 310 Print
Imprints: Oblong

Galaade Editions
108, rue Damremont, 75018 Paris
Tel: 01 42 23 56 02 *Fax:* 01 42 23 56 21
E-mail: lire@galaade.com
Web Site: www.galaade.com
Key Personnel
President & Publisher: Emmanuelle Collas
E-mail: emmanuelle@galaade.com
Foreign Rights: Cecile Magne *E-mail:* cecile@
galaade.com
Press, Festivals & Foreign Rights: Romaric Vinet-
Kammerer *E-mail:* romaric@galaade.com
Founded: 2005
Subjects: Fiction, Nonfiction (General)
ISBN Prefix(es): 978-2-35176

Editions Galilee+
9, rue Linne, 75005 Paris
Tel: 01 47 07 85 11 *Fax:* 01 45 35 53 68
E-mail: info@editions-galilee.com
Web Site: www.editions-galilee.fr
Key Personnel
Mng Dir: Michel Delorme
Founded: 1971
Subjects: Art, History, Literature, Literary Criti-
cism, Essays, Philosophy, Poetry, Psychology,
Psychiatry, Social Sciences, Sociology
ISBN Prefix(es): 978-2-7186
Number of titles published annually: 20 Print
Total Titles: 900 Print
Shipping Address: 128 ave du Marechalde Laltre-
de-Tattiguy, 77400 Lagny
Warehouse: 128 ave du Marechalde Laltre-de-
Tattiguy, 77400 Lagny
Orders to: Sodis, BP 142, 77403 Lagny sur
Marne *Tel:* 01 45 31 16 06

Editions Gallimard
5, rue Gaston-Gallimard, 75328 Paris Cedex 07
Tel: 01 49 54 42 00 *Fax:* 01 45 44 94 03
E-mail: catalogue@gallimard.fr; droits-
entrangers@gallimard.fr

Web Site: www.gallimard.fr
Key Personnel
President: Antoine Gallimard
Editorial Dir: Teresa Cremisi
Founded: 1911
Subjects: Art, Biography, Memoirs, Fiction, His-
tory, Music, Dance, Philosophy, Poetry
ISBN Prefix(es): 978-2-07
Subsidiaries: Editions Alternatives; Editions De-
noel; Flammarion Groupe; Editions Futuropo-
lis; Editions Gallimard Jeunesse; Editions Gal-
limard Loisirs; Editions des Grandes Person-
nes; Editions Hoebeke; Editions du Mercure
de France; Editions POL; Editions de la Table
Ronde
Distributed by Editions des Cinq Frontieres
(Switzerland); Editions Foliade (Belgium)
Bookshop(s): Librairie Delamain, 155, rue Saint
Honore, 75001 Paris *Tel:* 01 42 61 48 78
Fax: 01 40 15 91 69 *E-mail:* delamain@
librairie-delamain.com; Librairie Le Di-
van, 203, rue la convention, 75015 Paris
Tel: 01 53 68 90 68 *Fax:* 01 42 50 84 68
E-mail: ledivan@ledivan.com; Librairie Gallimard, 15 blvd Raspail, 75007 Paris, Contact:
Paul Derieux *Tel:* 01 45 48 24 84 *Fax:* 01
42 84 16 97 *E-mail:* gallimard@librairie-
gallimard.com *Web Site:* www.librairie-
gallimard.com; Librairie de Paris, 7-11 pl
de Clichy, 75017 Paris *Tel:* 01 45 22 47
81 *Fax:* 01 40 08 08 50 *E-mail:* lib.paris@
librairie-de-paris.fr; Librairie Kleber, One
rue des Francs-Bourgeois, 67000 Strasbourg
Tel: 03 88 15 78 88 *Fax:* 03 88 15 78 80
E-mail: commandes@librairie-kleber.fr
Distribution Center: CDE (Centre de diffusion de
l'edition)
FED (France Editions Diffusion)
Sodis
Sofedis

Guides Gallimard, *imprint of* Les Editions
Gallimard Loisirs

Editions Gallimard-Jeunesse
Subsidiary of Editions Gallimard
5, rue Gaston Gallimard, 75328 Paris
Tel: 01 49 54 42 00 *Fax:* 01 45 44 39 46
E-mail: marketing@gallimard-jeunesse.fr;
foreignrights@gallimard-jeunesse.fr; presse@
gallimard-jeunesse.fr
Web Site: www.gallimard-jeunesse.fr
Key Personnel
Dir, Foreign Rights & Licenses: Anne Bouteloup
E-mail: anne.bouteloup@gallimard-jeunesse.fr
Subjects: Fiction, Literature, Literary Criticism,
Essays, Music, Dance
ISBN Prefix(es): 978-2-07
Foreign Rights: Bardon Chinese Media Agency
(Jian-Mei Wang) (China); Bardon Chinese Me-
dia Agency (Cynthia Chang) (Taiwan); DS Bu-
dapest (Margit Gruber) (Hungary); ICSTI (Ta-
tiana Vaniat) (Belarus, Russia, Ukraine); Kolar
Rights & Translation (Lynne Kolar-Thompson)
(Baltic States, Czechia, Slovakia); Motovun
Tokyo (Mari Koga) (Japan); Nika Literary
Agency (Vania Kadiyska) (Bulgaria); Patricial
Seibel (Brazil); Sibylle Books Agency (Young
Sun Choi) (South Korea); Livia Stoia Agency
(Livia Stoia) (Albania, Bosnia and Herzegov-
ina, Bulgaria, Croatia, Greece, Macedonia,
Montenegro, Poland, Romania, Serbia, Slove-
nia)

Les Editions Gallimard Loisirs+
Subsidiary of Editions Gallimard
5, rue Sebastien Bottin, 75328 Paris Cedex 07
Tel: 01 49 54 42 00
E-mail: coedition@guides.gallimard.tm.fr
Web Site: www.gallimard-loisirs.fr
Founded: 1989
Specialize in travel guides.

Subjects: Architecture & Interior Design, Art, Environmental Studies, Geography, Geology, History, How-to, Regional Interests, Travel & Tourism
ISBN Prefix(es): 978-2-7424
Associate Companies: Gallimard Jeunesse
Imprints: Guides Gallimard
Distributed by Dohosna (Japan); Dumont (Germany); Everytian (UK); Knopf (USA); Owl Publishing (China, Taiwan); SM-Acento (Spain); Standard (Netherlands); TCI (Italy)

Editions Ganymede+
BP 50013, 77221 Tournan Cedex
Fax: 01 64 42 86 68
E-mail: rozeille.hatem@wanadoo.fr
Web Site: www.hatem.com/books.htm; editions-ganymede.wix.com/editionsganymede
Key Personnel
Dir & International Rights: Frank Hatem
Founded: 2005
Subjects: Philosophy, Physics, Psychology, Psychiatry, Science (General), Holistic Psychology, Metaphysics
ISBN Prefix(es): 978-2-9500999

Gautier Languereau, *imprint of* Hachette Jeunesse

Gazette du Palais, *imprint of* Lextenso Editions

Librairie Generale Francaise+
31, rue de Fleurus, 75278 Paris
Tel: 01 49 54 37 00 *Fax:* 01 49 54 37 01
E-mail: contact-ldp@livredepoche.com
Web Site: www.livredepoche.com
Key Personnel
Editorial Dir: Laura Behn
Founded: 1953
Subjects: Biography, Memoirs, Drama, Theater, Environmental Studies, Fiction, Government, Political Science, History, Language Arts, Linguistics, Literature, Literary Criticism, Essays, Mysteries, Suspense, Philosophy, Poetry, Science (General), Science Fiction, Fantasy, Social Sciences, Sociology
ISBN Prefix(es): 978-2-253
Parent Company: Hachette Livre

Editions Geuthner+
16 rue de la Grande Chaumiere, 75006 Paris
Tel: 01 46 34 71 30 *Fax:* 01 43 29 75 64
E-mail: geuthner@geuthner.com
Web Site: www.geuthner.com
Key Personnel
Publisher & Editor: Myra Prince
Founded: 1901
Subjects: Anthropology, Antiques, Archaeology, Architecture & Interior Design, Art, Biblical Studies, Biography, Memoirs, Foreign Countries, Geography, Geology, History, Language Arts, Linguistics, Law, Literature, Literary Criticism, Essays, Music, Dance, Philosophy, Religion - Buddhist, Religion - Catholic, Religion - Hindu, Religion - Islamic, Religion - Jewish, Religion - Protestant, Science (General), Social Sciences, Sociology, Technology
ISBN Prefix(es): 978-2-7053

GF, *imprint of* Flammarion Groupe

Editions Gilletta
5, rue Michel-Ange, 06100 Nice
Tel: 04 92 07 94 94 *Fax:* 04 92 07 94 92
E-mail: edgilletta@nicematin.fr
Web Site: www.editionsgilletta.com
Key Personnel
Dir: Valerie Castera
Founded: 1880
Subjects: Architecture & Interior Design, Art, Cookery, Health, Nutrition, History, Literature,

Literary Criticism, Essays, Travel & Tourism, Fine Arts, Nature, Local History, Wellness
ISBN Prefix(es): 978-2-915606
Parent Company: Nice-Matin

Bernard Giovanangeli Editeur
22, rue Carducci, 75019 Paris
E-mail: bged@wanadoo.fr
Web Site: www.bgedition.com
Key Personnel
Independent Editor: Bernard Giovanangeli
Specialize in books on Napoleon.
Subjects: Biography, Memoirs, History
ISBN Prefix(es): 978-2-909034
Number of titles published annually: 3 Print

GIPPE, see Groupement d'Information Promotion Presse Edition (GIPPE)

Gippe-Les Amoureux des Livres, *imprint of* Groupement d'Information Promotion Presse Edition (GIPPE)

Editions Jean-Paul Gisserot+
10, rue Gracieuse, 75005 Paris
Tel: 01 43 31 80 04; 01 43 31 88 24 *Fax:* 01 43 31 88 15
E-mail: editions@editions-gisserot.com
Web Site: www.editions-gisserot.com
Key Personnel
President: Jean-Paul Gisserot *E-mail:* gisserot@editions-gisserot.eu
Dir General: Thibault Chattard *E-mail:* thibault.chattard@editions-gisserot.eu
Publishing: Christophe Renault
  E-mail: christophe.renault@editions-gisserot.eu
Production Manager: Nelson Martinez
  E-mail: nelson.martinez@editions-gisserot.eu
Sales Manager: Philippe Dinam *E-mail:* philippe.dinam@editions-gisserot.eu
Founded: 1988
Subjects: Aeronautics, Aviation, Animals, Pets, Anthropology, Archaeology, Architecture & Interior Design, Art, Astronomy, Biography, Memoirs, Cookery, Education, English as a Second Language, Fiction, Foreign Countries, Gardening, Plants, Genealogy, History, How-to, Humor, Maritime, Music, Dance, Natural History, Regional Interests, Religion - Catholic, Religion - Protestant, Travel & Tourism, Wine & Spirits
ISBN Prefix(es): 978-2-87747; 978-2-7558
Number of titles published annually: 50 Print
Total Titles: 700 Print
Subsidiaries: Telegiss Distribution/Editions Gisserot Diffusion (France)
Shipping Address: Editions Gisserot Diffusion, ZI de Saint Eloi, route de Plouedern, 29800 Plouedern *Tel:* 02 98 21 36 63 *Fax:* 02 98 21 56 31
Orders to: Editions Gisserot Diffusion, ZI de Saint Eloi, route de Plouedern, 29800 Plouedern *Tel:* 02 98 21 36 63 *Fax:* 02 98 21 56 31 *E-mail:* telegiss@wanadoo.fr
Returns: Editions Gisserot Diffusion, ZI de Saint Eloi, route de Plouedern, 29800 Plouedern *Tel:* 02 98 21 36 63 *Fax:* 02 98 21 56 31

Glenat Editions SA+
37 rue Servan, 38008 Grenoble
Tel: 04 76 88 75 75 *Fax:* 04 76 88 75 70
Web Site: www.glenat.com
Key Personnel
President: Jacques Glenat
Founded: 1969
Subjects: Cookery, Fiction, Humor, Science Fiction, Fantasy, Sports, Athletics, Travel & Tourism, Comics, Leisure
ISBN Prefix(es): 978-2-7234
Subsidiaries: Editions Glenat Benelux; Editions Glenat Suisse SA

Showroom(s): 22, rue de Picardie, 75003 Paris *Tel:* 01 42 71 46 86 *Web Site:* www.galerie-glenat.com
Bookshop(s): 19 av Alsace Lorraine, 38000 Grenoble *Tel:* 04 76 46 34 60 *Fax:* 04 76 85 06 57 *Web Site:* librairiegrenoble.glenat.com; Centre Commercial de la Part-Dieu, aile Oxygene, Niveau 3, Boutique B14A, 12 Blvd Vivier Merle, 69003 Lyon *Tel:* 04 78 95 49 79 *Fax:* 04 78 60 17 57 *Web Site:* librairielyon.glenat.com

Editions Graine 2
43 rue Taitbout, 75009 Paris
Tel: 01 47 42 48 76 *Fax:* 09 72 15 75 49
Web Site: www.graine2-editions.com
Key Personnel
Executive & Sales Manager: Emilie Hourtoulle
  E-mail: e.hourtoulle@graine2-editions.com
Associate Dir, Editorial: Stephanie Guillaume
Editorial Projects: Marie Lemaire
Founded: 2007
Subjects: Art, Cookery, Crafts, Games, Hobbies, Travel & Tourism
ISBN Prefix(es): 978-2-917537

Les Editions Grancher+
Imprint of Group Editorial Piktos
ZI de Bogues, 31750 Escalquens
Tel: 06 49 99 23 27
E-mail: contact@grancher.com
Web Site: www.grancher.com
Key Personnel
Editor: Michel Grancher *E-mail:* michel@grancher.com; Philippe Grancher *E-mail:* pg@grancher.com
Press: Florence Vaillant *E-mail:* f.vaillant@piktos.fr
Founded: 1952
Subjects: Astrology, Occult, Cookery, Health, Nutrition, How-to, Humor, Military Science, Nonfiction (General), Parapsychology, Psychology, Psychiatry, Religion - Catholic, Religion - Islamic, Religion - Jewish, Religion - Protestant, Religion - Other, Travel & Tourism
ISBN Prefix(es): 978-2-7339
Number of titles published annually: 40 Print
Total Titles: 400 Print
Distributed by Hachette
Foreign Rep(s): Flammarion-Socadis (Canada); OLF SA (Switzerland); SDL Caravelle (Belgium); Transat SA (Switzerland)
Foreign Rights: Agence Litteraire Galtier Roussel (Cristina Prepelita Chiarasini)
Distribution Center: DG Diffusion, ZI de Boques, rue Gutenberg, 31750 Escalquens, Contact: Sophie Barthelemy *Tel:* 05 61 00 09 99 *Fax:* 05 61 00 23 12 *E-mail:* info@dgdiffusion.com (France & Benelux)

Grand Angle, *imprint of* Editions l'Instant Durable

Editions des Grandes Personnes
Subsidiary of Editions Gallimard
63, blvd de Menilmontant, 75011 Paris
Tel: 01 77 16 71 35
E-mail: editionsdesgrandespersonnes@gmail.com
Web Site: www.editionsdesgrandespersonnes.com
Key Personnel
Foreign Rights: Sabine Louali *E-mail:* sabine.louali@gmail.com
Subjects: Fiction
ISBN Prefix(es): 978-2-36

Editions Grandir (To Grow)+
2 Impasse des Soucis, 30000 Nimes
Tel: 04 66 84 01 19 *Fax:* 04 66 26 14 50
E-mail: editions-grandir@orange.fr
Web Site: www.editionsgrandir.fr
Key Personnel
Manager: Rene Turc

Founded: 1978
Subjects: Art, Fiction, Geography, Geology, Physical Sciences
ISBN Prefix(es): 978-2-84166; 978-2-904292
Number of titles published annually: 215 Print; 5 CD-ROM
Total Titles: 450 Print; 5 CD-ROM
Parent Company: Lirabelle

Editions Grasset et Fasquelle+
Subsidiary of Hachette Livre
61, rue des Saints-Peres, 75006 Paris
Tel: 01 44 39 22 00 *Fax:* 01 42 22 64 18
Web Site: www.grasset.fr
Key Personnel
Chief Executive Officer: Olivier Nora
Dir, Foreign Literature: Fasquelle Ariane
Executive Editor, Foreign Literature: Jean Mattern
Acquisitions Editor, Foreign Literature: Joachim Schnerf
Editor: Christophe Bataille
Press Officer: Elodie Deglaire
Public Relations: Aline Gurdiel
Founded: 1907
Subjects: Fiction, History, Literature, Literary Criticism, Essays, Nonfiction (General), Philosophy, Social Sciences, Sociology, Western Fiction
ISBN Prefix(es): 978-2-246
Number of titles published annually: 200 Print
Ultimate Parent Company: Lagardere

Editions Gregoriennes, *imprint of* Adverbum

GRET
Campus du Jardin d'Agronomie Tropicale de Paris, 45 bis avenue de la Belle Gabrielle, 94736 Nogent-sur-Marne
Tel: 01 70 91 92 00 *Fax:* 01 70 91 92 01
E-mail: gret@gret.org
Web Site: www.gret.org
Key Personnel
Chairman: Pierre Jacquemot
Dir: Olivier Bruyeron
Publishing Manager: Daniele Ribier
  E-mail: ribier@gret.org
Communications: Claire Labat *E-mail:* labat@gret.org
Founded: 1976
Subjects: Agriculture, Anthropology, Developing Countries, Finance, Journalism, Technology
ISBN Prefix(es): 978-2-86844
Total Titles: 110 Print

Groupement d'Information Promotion Presse Edition (GIPPE)
51, rue Santos Dumont, 75015 Paris
Tel: 01 42 50 80 25
E-mail: gippe@wanadoo.fr
Web Site: www.gippe.org
Founded: 1987
Subjects: Literature, Literary Criticism, Essays
ISBN Prefix(es): 978-2-9508635
Imprints: Gippe-Les Amoureux des Livres

Editions Grund+
12 ave d'Italie, 75627 Paris Cedex 13
Tel: 01 44 16 09 00
E-mail: foreign.rights@grund.fr
Web Site: www.grund.fr
Key Personnel
Publishing Dir: Vincent Barbare
Dir, Communications: Caroline Destais-Brochain
  Tel: 01 44 16 09 04 *E-mail:* cdestais@efirst.com
Foreign Rights Manager: Sarah Rigaud
  Tel: 01 44 16 09 61 *Fax:* 01 44 16 09 01
  E-mail: srigaud@edi8.fr
Sales Manager: Yannick Lemonnier *Tel:* 01 44 16 09 24 *E-mail:* yannick.lemonnier@grund.fr
Founded: 1880

Subjects: Animals, Pets, Art, Environmental Studies, How-to, Travel & Tourism
ISBN Prefix(es): 978-2-7000
Number of titles published annually: 180 Print
Parent Company: Edi8
Ultimate Parent Company: Editis Group
Associate Companies: Livres du Dragon d'Or; Editions First & First Interactive; Grund Jeunesse; Pour les Nuls
Foreign Rep(s): Sophie Godefroy (Italy, Lebanon, Morocco, Portugal, Spain, Tunisia); Marie Ratti (Mauritius)

Gualino, *imprint of* Lextenso Editions

Librairie Guenegaud
Subsidiary of P M C
10, rue de l'Odeon, 75006 Paris
Tel: 01 43 26 07 91 *Fax:* 01 40 46 88 72
Web Site: www.guenegaud.fr
Key Personnel
Mng Dir: Philippe Barrault
Founded: 1912
Subjects: Biography, Memoirs, Genealogy, History, Outdoor Recreation, Regional Interests, Romance
ISBN Prefix(es): 978-2-85023
Number of titles published annually: 10 Print
Total Titles: 95 Print
Associate Companies: La Societe et le High Life

Editions Guerin
BP 153, 74404 Chamonix Cedex
Tel: 04 50 53 74 74 *Fax:* 04 50 53 61 49
E-mail: ecrire@editionsguerin.com
Web Site: www.editionsguerin.com
Key Personnel
Dir: Marie-Christine Guerin *E-mail:* mc@editionsguerin.com
Founded: 1995
Subjects: Biography, Memoirs, Outdoor Recreation, Sports, Athletics, Mountaineering
ISBN Prefix(es): 978-2-911755; 978-2-35221
Distribution Center: SODIS, 128 Ave du Marechal de Lattre de Tassigny, 77400 Lagny sur Marne *Tel:* 01 60 07 82 00

Gulf Stream Editeur
Impasse du Forgeron, CP 910, 44806 Saint-Herblain cedex
Tel: 02 40 48 06 68 *Fax:* 02 40 48 74 69
E-mail: contact@gulfstream.fr
Web Site: www.gulfstream.fr
Key Personnel
Chief Executive Officer: Luc Brossier
Executive Dir: Berenice Hupel
Editorial Dir: Paola Grieco
Subjects: Fiction, Nonfiction (General)
ISBN Prefix(es): 978-2-909421; 978-2-35488

Hachette Education+
Subsidiary of Hachette Livre
43, quai de Grenelle, 75905 Paris Cedex 15
Tel: 01 43 92 30 00
E-mail: relations-enseignants.hachette-education@lpc.fr
Web Site: www.hachette-education.com
Key Personnel
Publishing Dir: Isabelle Jeuge-Maynart
Mng Editor: Sophie Corvi
Founded: 1826
Specialize in CD-ROMs & reference books.
Subjects: Education, French as a Second Language
ISBN Prefix(es): 978-2-01
Total Titles: 4,000 Print
Ultimate Parent Company: Lagardere Groupe
Subsidiaries: Edicef; Sylemma-Andrieu; Hachette Diffusion Internationale
Showroom(s): Espace Enseignant, 8 rue Haute Jenille, 75006 Paris

Hachette FLE, see Hachette Francais Langue Etrangere - FLE

Hachette Francais Langue Etrangere - FLE+
Subsidiary of Hachette Livre
43, quai de Grenelle, 75905 Paris Cedex 15
Tel: 01 43 92 30 00
E-mail: relations-enseignants.hachette-education@lpc.fr
Web Site: www.hachettefle.com
Key Personnel
Publishing Dir: Isabelle Jeuge-Maynart
Mng Editor: Sophie Corvi
Commercial Dir: Robert Menand
Subjects: Education, Language Arts, Linguistics
ISBN Prefix(es): 978-2-01
Number of titles published annually: 50 Print; 4 Audio
Total Titles: 50 Print
Ultimate Parent Company: Lagardere Groupe

Hachette Jeunesse+
Subsidiary of Hachette Livre
43, quai de Grenelle, 75905 Paris Cedex 15
Tel: 01 43 92 30 00
Web Site: www.hachette-jeunesse.com/livres-illustres/accueil.html
Key Personnel
Senior Rights Manager: Mathilde Jablonski
  E-mail: mjablonski@hachette-livre.fr
Founded: 1852
Also publisher of picture & character books.
Subjects: Nonfiction (General)
ISBN Prefix(es): 978-2-01; 978-2-217
Ultimate Parent Company: Lagardere Groupe
Imprints: Deux Coqs d'Or; Gautier Languereau
Distribution Center: Centre de Distribution du Livre, ave Gutenberg, 78316 Maurepas Cedex
  Tel: 01 30 66 20 66

Hachette Livre+
43, quai de Grenelle, 75905 Paris Cedex 15
Tel: 01 43 92 30 00
Web Site: www.hachette.com
Key Personnel
Chairman & Chief Executive Officer: Arnaud Nourry
Chief Innovation Officer: Maja Thomas
Deputy Secretary General & Deputy Chief Financial Officer: Fabrice Bakhouche
Senior Vice President, Corporate Communications: Ronald Blunden
Group Chief Customer Relationship Management & Digital Marketing Officer: Guillaume Pech-Gourg
Group Chief Digital Innovator: Pierre Danet
Innovation Project Manager: Eva Dunoyer
International Consultant & Editor-at-Large: Leonello Brandolini
Founded: 1826
Subjects: Architecture & Interior Design, Art, Economics, Education, Engineering (General), Fiction, Government, Political Science, History, Language Arts, Linguistics, Literature, Literary Criticism, Essays, Nonfiction (General), Philosophy, Science (General), Self-Help, Social Sciences, Sociology, Sports, Athletics, Travel & Tourism
ISBN Prefix(es): 978-2-01
Number of titles published annually: 5,000 Print
Parent Company: Lagardere Groupe
Subsidiaries: Audiolib; La Bibliotheque Rose; Calmann-Levy; Editions du Chene; Editions Chene EPA; Armand Colin; Dessain et Tolra; Les Editions Deux Coqs d'Or; Editions des Deux Terres; Editions Didier; Didier Jeunesse; Dunod; Edicef; Fayard; Foucher; Gautier Languereau; Grasset; Grasset Jeunesse; Hachette Education; Hachette Francais Langue Etrangere; Hachette Jeunesse; Hachette Jeunesse Collection Disney; Hachette Livre International; Hachette Pratique; Hachette Romans; Hachette Tourisme; Hachette UK; Edi-

tions Harlequin; Harrap's; Hatier; Hatier International; Hatier Jeunesse; Hazan; Istra; Larousse; JC Lattes; Le Livre de Poche; Le Livre de Poche Jeunesse; Marabout; Editions du Masque; Pika; Rageot; Stock
Distribution Center: Hachette Livre International, 11 rue Paul Bert, 92247 Malakoff Cedex *Tel:* 01 55 00 11 00 *Web Site:* hachette-livre-international.com.fr
Hachette Livre Distribution, One Ave Gutenberg, 78316 Maurepas Cedex *Tel:* 01 30 66 20 66 (France, Belgium, Canada & Switzerland)
Alliance Distribution Services, 9 Pioneer Ave, Tuggerah, NSW 2259, Australia *Tel:* (02) 4390 1300 *E-mail:* adscs@alliancedist.com.au *Web Site:* www.alliancedist.com.au (Australia & New Zealand)
Comercial Grupo Anaya, C/ Juan Ignacio Luca de Tena, 15, 28027 Madrid, Spain *Tel:* 91 393 88 00; 91 393 87 00 (export)
Bookpoint, 130 Milton Park, Abingdon, Oxon OX14 4SE, United Kingdom *Tel:* (012) 35 400 400 *Web Site:* bookpoint.wp.hachette.co.uk
Hachette Book Group Distribution Center, 121 N Enterprise Dr, Lebanon, IN 46052, United States *Tel:* 765-483-9900 *Fax:* 765-483-0706 *Web Site:* www.hachettebookgroup.com
LBS, Faraday Close, Durrington, Worthing, West Sussex BN13 3RB, United Kingdom *Tel:* (019) 0382 8500 *Web Site:* www.lbsltd.co.uk

Hachette Livre International+
Subsidiary of Hachette Livre
11, rue Paul Bert, 92247 Malakoff Cedex
Tel: 01 55 00 11 00 *Fax:* 01 55 00 11 20
E-mail: hli@hachette-livre-intl.com
Web Site: www.editions-hachette-livre-international.com; www.hachette-livre-international.com
Key Personnel
Mng Dir: Patrick C Dubs
Founded: 2002
Subjects: Economics, Education, English as a Second Language, Environmental Studies, Law, Literature, Literary Criticism, Essays, Mathematics, Physics
ISBN Prefix(es): 978-2-84129; 978-2-85069
Number of titles published annually: 120 Print
Total Titles: 900 Print
Imprints: EDICEF; Hatier International
Distributor for EDICEF; Hatier International

Hachette Pratique+
Subsidiary of Hachette Livre
43, quai de Grenelle, 75905 Paris Cedex 15
Tel: 01 43 92 30 30
Web Site: www.hachette-pratique.com
Key Personnel
Publishing Dir: Catherine Saunier-Talec
Mng Editor: Sophie Perfus-Mousselon
Head, Communications: Johanna Rodrigue *Tel:* 01 43 92 32 46 *E-mail:* jrodrigue@hachette-livre.fr
Rights: Pierre-Jean Furet *E-mail:* pjfuret@hachette-livre.fr; Morgane Planchon *E-mail:* mplanchon@hachette-livre.fr
Founded: 1826
Subjects: Animals, Pets, Astrology, Occult, Biography, Memoirs, Cookery, Crafts, Games, Hobbies, Fashion, Gardening, Plants, Health, Nutrition, Management, Sports, Athletics, Wine & Spirits
ISBN Prefix(es): 978-2-01
Ultimate Parent Company: Lagardere Groupe
Warehouse: Hachette Livre Distribution, One ave Gutenberg, 78316 Maurepas Cedex *Tel:* 01 30 66 20 66

Hachette Romans+
Subsidiary of Hachette Livre
58, rue Jean-Bleuzen, CS 70007, 92178 Vanves Cedex

Tel: 01 43 92 30 00 *Fax:* 01 43 92 30 30
Web Site: www.lecture-academy.com; www.livredepochejeunesse.com
Key Personnel
Dir: Cecile Terouanne *Tel:* 01 43 92 34 35 *E-mail:* cterouanne@hachette-livre.fr
Founded: 1852
ISBN Prefix(es): 978-2-01
Associate Companies: Le Livre de Poche Jeunesse
Distribution Center: Hachette Livre Distribution, One Ave Gutenberg, 78316 Maurepas Cedex *Tel:* 01 30 66 20 66

Les Editions Viviane Hamy+
Cour de la Maison Brulee, 89, rue du Faubourg-Saint-Antoine, 75011 Paris
Tel: 01 53 17 16 00
Web Site: www.viviane-hamy.fr
Key Personnel
Contact: Maylis Vauterin *Tel:* 01 53 17 16 03 *E-mail:* maylis.vauterin@viviane-hamy.fr
Founded: 1990
Subjects: Literature, Literary Criticism, Essays
ISBN Prefix(es): 978-2-87858
Number of titles published annually: 12 Print
Total Titles: 120 Print
Distributed by Flammarion
Foreign Rep(s): Acer (Catherine Passion) (Spain); Niki Douge (Greece); The Grayhawk Agency (Chung Sen Wu) (Taiwan); Anastasia Lester (Georgia, Russia, Ukraine); Sibylle Books (Young Sun Choi) (South Korea); Anna Spadolini (Italy); 2 Seas Agency (Netherlands)

Harlequin, *imprint of* HarperCollins France

Editions Harlequin
Subsidiary of Hachette Livre
83-85, blvd Vincent Auriol, 75646 Paris Cedex 13
Mailing Address: BP 20008, 59718 Lille Cedex 9
Tel: 01 42 16 63 63; 01 45 82 47 47 (orders) *Fax:* 01 45 82 86 94
Web Site: www.harlequin.fr
Key Personnel
Publishing Dir: Emmanuelle Bucco-Cances *Tel:* 01 42 16 63 33 *E-mail:* ebuccocances@harlequin.fr
Founded: 1978
Subjects: Astrology, Occult, Romance
ISBN Prefix(es): 978-2-280; 978-2-86259
Imprints: Duo, Harlequin

L'Harmattan+
5-7 rue de l'Ecole Polytechnique, 75005 Paris
Tel: 01 40 46 79 22; 01 40 46 79 20 (sales) *Fax:* 01 43 25 82 03 (sales)
E-mail: diffusion.harmattan@wanadoo.fr
Web Site: www.editions-harmattan.fr
Key Personnel
Dir: Denis Pryen
Foreign Relations: Alessandra Fra *E-mail:* alessandra.fra@harmattan.fr
Founded: 1975
Subjects: African American Studies, Asian Studies, Developing Countries, Foreign Countries, History, Human Relations, Language Arts, Linguistics, Literature, Literary Criticism, Essays, Science (General), Social Sciences, Sociology
ISBN Prefix(es): 978-2-7384; 978-2-85802; 978-2-7475; 978-2-296
Total Titles: 1,400 Print
Parent Company: Groupe L'Harmattan
Bookshop(s): 16 rue des Ecoles, 75005 Paris *Tel:* 01 40 46 79 11 *E-mail:* librairie.harmattan@orange.fr *Web Site:* www.librairieharmattan.com; 21 bis rue des Ecoles, 75005 Paris *Tel:* 01 46 34 13 71 *E-mail:* harmattan.sh@gmail.com *Web Site:* www.librairieharmattansh.com; 21 bis rue des Ecoles (M° Maubert Mutu-

alite), 75005 Paris *Tel:* 01 43 29 49 42 *E-mail:* lesalizes4@free.fr; 24 rue des Ecoles, 75005 Paris *Tel:* 01 46 34 03 36 *E-mail:* boutiquehistoire.harmattan@gmail.com *Web Site:* www.boutique-histoire.fr; 25 rue des Ecoles, 75005 Paris *Tel:* 01 78 11 88 20 *E-mail:* boutiquevideo@harmattantv.com *Web Site:* www.harmattantv.com; Ave Mohamar Kadhafi (Ouaga 2000), A 200m du pont echangeur - 12 BP 226, Ouagadougou 12, Burkina Faso *Tel:* 50 37 54 36 *E-mail:* infos@harmattanburkina.com; BP 11486, Yaounde, Cameroon, Manager: Jacques Deboheur Koukam *Tel:* 699198028; 670420431 *E-mail:* harmattancam@yahoo.fr; 67 ave Emery Patrice Lumumba, Batiment - Congo pharmacie (Bibliotheque nationale), BP 2874, Brazzaville, Congo (Brazzaville) *Tel:* 5713723 *E-mail:* harmattan.congo@yahoo.fr; Residence Karl / Cite des arts Abidjan-Cocody 03, BP 1588, Abidjan 03, Cote d'Ivoire *Tel:* 05 77 87 31 *E-mail:* espace_harmattan.ci@hotmail.fr; 185 rue Nyangwe - Commune de Lingwala, Kinshasa, Democratic Republic of the Congo, Dir: Leon Matangila Musadila *Tel:* 99 86 97 603 *E-mail:* matangilamusadila@yahoo.fr; Almamya Rue KA 028 En face du restaurant Le Cedre OKB agency, BP 3470, Conakry, Guinea *E-mail:* harmattanguinea@yahoo.fr; Kossuth L u 14-16, Budapest 1053, Hungary *Tel:* (01) 267-59-79 *Fax:* (01) 328-09-19; Via Di Santa Cecilia 1/A, 00153 Rome, Italy *Tel:* (06) 58334116; Editrice L'Harmattan Italia Srl, Via Degli Artisti 15, 10124 Turin TO, Italy *Tel:* (011) 817 13 88; (011) 348 39 89 198 *Fax:* (011) 817 13 88 *E-mail:* harmattan.italia@agora.it; Rue 58, Porte 203, face au Palais de la culture, Badalabougou-Bamako, Mali *Tel:* 20 22 57 24; 76 37 80 82 *E-mail:* poudiougopaul@yahoo.fr; Espace El Kettab du livre francophone N°472 ave Palais des Congres, BP 316, Nouakchott, Mauritania, Manager: Mouhamed Lemine Ould El Kettab *Tel:* 632 59 80 *E-mail:* mdlemkettab@yahoo.com; Association Senegalais Des Economistes (ASE), "Villa Rose" Rue Diourbel X Rue G, Point e - En Face, BP 45034, Dakar-Fann, Senegal, Contact: Abdoulaye Diallo *Tel:* 33 825 98 58; 77 242 25 08 *E-mail:* senharmattan@gmail.com

Harmonia Mundi, *imprint of* Les Editions Lettres Vives

HarperCollins, *imprint of* HarperCollins France

HarperCollins France
83-85 Blvd Vincent Auriol, 75646 Paris Cedix 13
Tel: 01 42 16 63 63; 01 45 82 44 26 (customer service)
Web Site: www.harpercollins.fr
Key Personnel
Mng Dir: Emmanuelle Bucco-Cances
Dir, Operations & Finance: Thierry Cavel
Editorial Dir: Anne Coquet
Marketing & Communication Dir: Antoine Duquesne
Sales Dir: Thierry Gonthier
Editorial Manager, General Literature: Sabrina Arab
Editorial Manager, Romance: Karine Lanini
Founded: 2016
Subjects: Literature, Literary Criticism, Essays, Romance
ISBN Prefix(es): 978-2-280; 979-10-339
Imprints: Harlequin; HarperCollins

Editions Hatier SA+
Subsidiary of Hachette Livre
8, rue d'Assas, 75278 Paris Cedex 06
Mailing Address: BP 60076, 86501 Montmorillon Cedex
Tel: 01 49 91 87 67 *Fax:* 05 49 91 87 68

E-mail: infoprofs@editions-hatier.fr
Web Site: www.editions-hatier.fr
Key Personnel
Dir General: Celia Rosentraub
Foreign Rights: Anne Risaliti *Tel:* 01 49 54 48 99
Fax: 01 49 54 47 30 *E-mail:* arisaliti@editions-hatier.fr
Founded: 1880
Subjects: Architecture & Interior Design, Biological Sciences, Economics, Education, English as a Second Language, Environmental Studies, Self-Help
ISBN Prefix(es): 978-2-218
Subsidiaries: Rageot Editeur
Bookshop(s): 59 blvd Raspail, 75006 Paris, Contact: Christian Reynaud *Tel:* 05 49 91 80 50
E-mail: creynaud@editions-hatier.fr

Hatier International, *imprint of* Hachette Livre International

Hatier International+
Imprint of Hachette Livre International
11, rue Paul Bert, 92247 Malakoff Cedex
Tel: 01 55 00 11 00 *Fax:* 01 55 00 11 20
E-mail: hli@hachette-livre-intl.com
Web Site: www.editions-hachette-livre-international.com
Key Personnel
Mng Dir: Patrick C Dubs
Founded: 2000
Specialize in export & textbook publishing for French & Arabic speaking countries, educational materials & maps.
ISBN Prefix(es): 978-2-7473
Number of titles published annually: 30 Print
Total Titles: 600 Print
Ultimate Parent Company: Hachette Livre
Distributor for Editions Didier

Editions Monelle Hayot
Chateau de Saint-Remy-en-l'Eau, 60130 Saint-Remy-en-l'Eau
Tel: 03 44 78 79 61 *Fax:* 03 44 78 78 59
E-mail: contact@editions-monelle-hayot.com
Web Site: www.editions-monelle-hayot.com
Key Personnel
Owner: Monelle Hayot
Subjects: Art, Gardening, Plants, Ceramics, French Art
ISBN Prefix(es): 978-2-903824
Distributed by Vilo Groupe

Editions Hazan+
Subsidiary of Hachette Livre
11, rue Paul Bert, 92247 Malakoff Cedex
Tel: 01 41 23 67 44 *Fax:* 01 41 23 64 37
Web Site: www.editions-hazan.fr
Key Personnel
Dir: Jean-Francois Barrielle
Mng Editor: Marie-Helene Durand de Corbiac
E-mail: mhdecorbiac@hachette-livre.fr
Rights & Co-Editions Manager: Jerome Gille
Tel: 01 41 23 64 13
Founded: 1945
Subjects: Architecture & Interior Design, Art
ISBN Prefix(es): 978-2-85025
Ultimate Parent Company: Lagardere
Foreign Rep(s): Diffulivre SA (Switzerland); Dilibel (Belgium); Hachette Canada (Canada)
Distribution Center: Hachette Distribution, CDL Ave Gutenberg, 78316 Maurepas Cedex *Tel:* 01 30 66 20 66
Hachette Livre International, 58, rue Jean Bleuzen, 92178 Vanves Cedex *Tel:* 01 55 00 11 00 *Fax:* 01 55 00 11 20 *E-mail:* hli@hachette-livre.intl.com

Editions Helium
Imprint of Editions Actes Sud
18, rue Seguier, 75006 Paris

Tel: 01 45 87 99 15
E-mail: info@helium-editions.fr
Web Site: www.helium-editions.fr
ISBN Prefix(es): 978-2-35851

Les Editions Herault
BP 14, 49360 Maulevrier
Tel: 02 41 55 45 90
E-mail: editions.herault@orange.fr
Web Site: www.editionsherault.com
Key Personnel
General Manager: Andre Hubert Herault
Founded: 2007
Subjects: Biography, Memoirs, Genealogy, History, Regional Interests
ISBN Prefix(es): 978-2-7407; 978-2-903851

Hermann Editeurs des Sciences et des Arts SA+
6 Rue Labrouste, 75015 Paris
Tel: 01 45 57 45 40
Web Site: www.editions-hermann.fr
Key Personnel
Chief Executive Officer: Arthur Cohen
Deputy Dir General: Philippe Fauvernier
Founded: 1876
Subjects: Art, Chemistry, Chemical Engineering, Economics, Mathematics, Medicine, Nursing, Dentistry, Music, Dance, Philosophy, Physics, Psychology, Psychiatry, Religion - Other, Science (General), Technology
ISBN Prefix(es): 978-2-7056
Number of titles published annually: 50 Print
Total Titles: 1,000 Print
Subsidiaries: Pierre Beres; La Palme

Hermes Science, *imprint of* Editions Lavoisier

Editions Hermes Science Publications+
Imprint of Editions Lavoisier
14 rue de Provigny, 94230 Cachan
Tel: 01 47 40 67 00 *Fax:* 01 47 40 67 02
E-mail: editionslavoisier@lavoisier.fr
Web Site: editions.lavoisier.fr
Key Personnel
Editorial Dir: Emmanuel Leclerc
Founded: 1981
Membership(s): French Publishers Association.
Subjects: Chemistry, Chemical Engineering, Civil Engineering, Communications, Computer Science, Electronics, Electrical Engineering, Engineering (General), Geography, Geology, Health, Nutrition, Language Arts, Linguistics, Law, Management, Marketing, Mechanical Engineering, Medicine, Nursing, Dentistry, Social Sciences, Sociology, Technology
ISBN Prefix(es): 978-2-86601; 978-2-7462
Number of titles published annually: 300 Print; 150 Online; 150 E-Book
Total Titles: 1,200 Print; 1 CD-ROM; 15 Online; 15 E-Book
Imprints: ISTE Editions
Distributed by Editions Lavoisier
Bookshop(s): Librairie Lavoisier, 14 rue de Provigny, 94236 Cachan Cedex *Tel:* 01 47 40 67 00 *Fax:* 01 47 40 67 02 *E-mail:* service.client@lavoisier.fr *Web Site:* www.lavoisier.fr

Editions de l'Herne+
22, rue Mazarine, 75006 Paris
Tel: 01 46 33 03 00 *Fax:* 01 46 33 03 01
E-mail: lherne@lherne.com; lherne@wanadoo.fr
Web Site: www.lherne.com; www.editionsdelherne.com
Key Personnel
Dir & Chairman, Rights & Permissions: Laurence Tacou
Foreign Rights Manager: Nataly Villena
E-mail: natalyvillena@lherne.com
Editorial: Pascale de Langautier

Press: Lucie Lallier *E-mail:* lucielallier@lherne.com
Founded: 1962
Subjects: Art, Fiction, Government, Political Science, Philosophy, Poetry, Social Sciences, Sociology
ISBN Prefix(es): 978-2-85197
Number of titles published annually: 45 Print; 40 Online
Distributed by Flammarion
Foreign Rep(s): La Caravelle (Belgium); Gallimard Export (worldwide exc Belgium, Canada, France & Switzerland); OLF (Switzerland); Socadis (Canada)
Foreign Rights: Astiere-Pecher Literary & Film Agency (Pierre Astiere) (worldwide)
Distribution Center: UD-Union Distribution, 106, Rue du Petit Le Roy, 94550 Chevilly Larue, Contact: Orielle Rayner *Tel:* 01 41 80 20 70

Herscher+
Subsidiary of Editions Belin
8, rue Ferou, 75278 Paris Cedex 6
Tel: 08 25 82 01 11 *Fax:* 01 43 25 18 29
E-mail: enseignants@editions-belin.fr; droitsetrangers@editions-belin.fr
Web Site: www.editions-belin.fr
Key Personnel
President & Dir General: Marie-Claude Brossollet
Founded: 1981
Subjects: Art
ISBN Prefix(es): 978-2-7335
Total Titles: 1,200 Print; 50 Audio
Shipping Address: 4 rue Ferdinand de Lesseps, 91420 Morangis
Warehouse: 4 rue Ferdinand de Lesseps, 91420 Morangis

Histoire & Collections SA
5, ave de la Republique, 75011 Paris, Cedex 11
Tel: 01 40 21 18 20 *Fax:* 01 47 00 51 11
E-mail: vpc@histecoll.com
Web Site: www.histoireetcollections.com
Key Personnel
President & Publishing Dir: Francois Vauvillier
Editorial Dir: Jean-Marie Mongin
Founded: 1984
Subjects: Crafts, Games, Hobbies, History, Military Science, Transportation, Strategy
ISBN Prefix(es): 978-2-915239; 978-2-908182; 978-2-913903; 978-2-35250

Editions Hoebeke+
Subsidiary of Editions Gallimard
7, rue d'Assas, 75006 Paris
Tel: 01 42 22 83 81 *Fax:* 01 45 44 04 96
E-mail: contact@hoebeke.fr
Web Site: www.hoebeke.fr
Key Personnel
Dir: Lionel Hoebeke
Foreign Rights: Audrey Demarre
E-mail: audreydemarre@hoebeke.fr
Press: Isabelle Nardari *E-mail:* isabellenardari@hoebeke.fr
Founded: 1984
Subjects: Art, Fiction, Humor, Photography
ISBN Prefix(es): 978-2-905292; 978-2-84230
Distribution Center: Flammarion Diffusion, 87, quai Panhard et Levassor, 75647 Paris Cedex 13 *Tel:* 01 40 51 31 00
UD-Union Distribution, 106, rue Petit Leroy, 94550 Chevilly-Larue

Les Editions de l'Homme
c/o Messageries ADP, Immeuble Paryseine, 3, Allee de la Seine, 94854 Ivry Cedex
Fax: 01 49 59 11 33
Web Site: www.editions-homme.com
Key Personnel
Dir: Helene Murphy-Aubry *E-mail:* hmurphy-aubry@sogides.com
Press: Cecilia Castagne *Tel:* 01 49 59 11 91

Subjects: Cookery, History, Music, Dance, Non-fiction (General), Self-Help, Travel & Tourism
ISBN Prefix(es): 978-2-7619; 978-0-7759
Parent Company: Groupe Sogides Inc
Ultimate Parent Company: Quebecor Media
Branch Office(s)
955, rue Amherst, Montreal, QC H2L 3K4,
  Canada *Tel:* 514-523-1182 *Fax:* 514-597-0370
  E-mail: adpcommandes@messageries-adp.com
Foreign Rights: Groupe Homme (Florence Bisch)

HongFei Cultures Sarl
73 ave de Tours, 37400 Amboise
Tel: 02 47 79 39 30
E-mail: contact@hongfei-cultures.com; rights@
  hongfei-cultures.com
Web Site: www.hongfei-cultures.com
Key Personnel
Owner: Loic Jacob; Chun-Liang Yeh
Founded: 2007
Subjects: Literature, Literary Criticism, Essays,
  Poetry, Chinese Literature
ISBN Prefix(es): 978-2-35558

Editions Honore Champion
3, rue Corneille, 75006 Paris
Tel: 01 46 34 07 29 *Fax:* 01 46 34 64 06
E-mail: champion@honorechampion.com
Web Site: www.honorechampion.com
Key Personnel
Press Relations: Sylvie Duhamel
  E-mail: sduhamel@honorechampion.com
Founded: 1874
Subjects: History, Language Arts, Linguistics,
  Literature, Literary Criticism, Essays, Music,
  Dance, Religion - Jewish, Comparative Litera-
  ture, Freemasonry, French Literature, Grammar,
  Lexicography, Human Sciences, Jewish Studies
ISBN Prefix(es): 978-2-85203; 978-2-7453
Distributor for Archives Nationales de France;
  Ecole des Chartes; Ecole Pratique des Hautes
  Etudes; Societe de l'Histoire de France; Societe
  des literatures classiques

Editions Horay SAS
22 bis, passage Dauphine, 75006 Paris
Tel: 01 43 54 53 90
E-mail: editions@horay-editeur.fr
Web Site: editions-horay.pagesperso-orange.fr
Key Personnel
Mng Dir & Rights & Permissions: Sophie Horay
Founded: 1946
Subjects: Art, Biography, Memoirs, Fiction, His-
  tory, How-to, Music, Dance
ISBN Prefix(es): 978-2-7058
Orders to: Flammarion, 26 rue Racine, 75006
  Paris

Editions Hors Collection
12, Ave d'Italie, 75627 Paris Cedex 13
Tel: 01 44 16 05 00
E-mail: horscollection@placedesediteurs.com
Web Site: www.horscollection.com
Key Personnel
Publication Dir: Jean Arcache
Press: Mona Fatouhi *Tel:* 06 29 60 51 45
  E-mail: mona.fatouhi@wanadoo.fr
Founded: 1991
Subjects: Astrology, Occult, Film, Video, Humor,
  Music, Dance, Photography, Pop Culture, Ra-
  dio, TV, Nostalgia, Sexuality
ISBN Prefix(es): 978-2-258
Foreign Rights: Place des editeurs (Paul Bernard)

Les Humanoides Associes
24, ave Philippe Auguste, 75011 Paris
Tel: 01 49 29 88 88 *Fax:* 09 56 92 12 34
E-mail: editorial@humano.com; presse@humano.
  com; licensing@humano.com; contact@
  humano.com
Web Site: www.humano.com

Key Personnel
Foreign, Press & Merchandise Rights: Edmond
  Lee *Tel:* 01 49 29 89 18
Comic publisher.
Subjects: Erotica, History, Humor, Science Fic-
  tion, Fantasy
ISBN Prefix(es): 978-2-7316
U.S. Office(s): Humanoids Inc, 8033 Sunset
  Blvd, No 628, Hollywood, CA, United States
  Tel: 323-522-5466 *Fax:* 323-892-2848

IBE, *imprint of* Editions UNESCO

ICC Services/Publications
Affiliate of International Chamber of Commerce
33-43 ave du President Wilson, 75116 Paris
Tel: 01 49 53 30 56 *Fax:* 01 49 53 29 02
E-mail: publications@iccwbo.org
Web Site: www.iccwbo.org; www.storeiccwbo.org
Founded: 1919
Books & reference materials on global trade.
Subjects: Business, Finance, Law, International
  Business, Finance & Law
ISBN Prefix(es): 978-92-842
Number of titles published annually: 10 Print; 5
  E-Book
Total Titles: 100 Print; 60 E-Book
U.S. Office(s): USCIB, 1212 Avenue of the Amer-
  icas, New York, NY 10036, United States
  Tel: 212-354-4480 *Fax:* 212-575-0327 *Web
  Site:* www.uscib.org

IDF, see Institut pour le Developpement Forestier

IEA, see Institut d'Etudes Augustiniennes (IEA)

IGN, see Institut National de l'Information
  Geographique et Forestiere (IGN)

IIEP, *imprint of* Editions UNESCO

Images en Manoeuvres Editions
14, rue des trois Freres Barthelemy, 13006 Mar-
  seille
Tel: 04 91 92 15 30 *Fax:* 04 91 42 97 58
Web Site: www.iemeditions.com
Key Personnel
Contact: Arnaud Bizalion; Andre Frere
Founded: 1990
Subjects: Art
ISBN Prefix(es): 978-2-84995; 978-2-908445
Distribution Center: Pollen Diffusion, 101 rue
  des Moines, 75017 Paris, Contact: Benoit Vail-
  lant *Tel:* 01 43 58 74 11 *Fax:* 01 72 71 84 51
  E-mail: contact@pollen-diffusion.com *Web
  Site:* www.pollen-diffusion.com

Editions Imago+
7, rue Suger, 75006 Paris
Tel: 01 46 33 15 33
E-mail: info@editions-imago.fr
Web Site: www.editions-imago.fr
Key Personnel
Dir General: Thierry Auzas *E-mail:* auzas@
  editions-imago.fr
Founded: 1977
Subjects: Anthropology, History, Literature, Liter-
  ary Criticism, Essays, Philosophy, Psychology,
  Psychiatry, Religion - Other, Romance, Social
  Sciences, Sociology, Ethnology, Fine Arts
ISBN Prefix(es): 978-2-902702; 978-2-911416;
  978-2-84952
Number of titles published annually: 20 Print
Total Titles: 240 Print
Distribution Center: Presses Universitaires de
  France, 6 Ave Reille, 75685 Paris Cedex 14
  Tel: 01 58 10 31 00 *Fax:* 01 58 10 31 82
  E-mail: verstraete@puf.com (Belgium)

Union-Distribution, 6 ave de l'Europe, 45300 Sermaises *Tel:* 02 38 39 00 43 *Fax:* 02 38 39 03
  08
Diffusion Dimedia Inc, 539 Blvd Lebeau, Saint-
  Laurent, QC H4N 1S2, Canada *Tel:* 514-336-
  3941 *Fax:* 514-331-3916 *E-mail:* general@
  dimedia.qc.ca
Office Du Livre, Z1 3 Corninboeuf, CP 1061,
  1701 Fribourg, Switzerland *Tel:* (026) 467 51
  11 *Fax:* (026) 467 54 44 *E-mail:* information@
  aol.ch

IMEC+
174 rue de Rivoli, 75001 Paris
Tel: 01 53 34 23 23 *Fax:* 01 53 34 23 00
E-mail: presse@imec-archives.com; editions@
  imec-archives.com; communication@imec-
  archives.com
Web Site: www.imec-archives.com
Key Personnel
Chairman of the Board: Pierre Leroy
Chief Executive Officer: Nathalie Leger
Founded: 1989
Preserves & manages archives & studies linked to
  the writing & book world of the 20th century
  allowing academic researches in intellectual,
  artistic & literary domains.
Subjects: History, Literature, Literary Criticism,
  Essays, History of Literature & Publications
ISBN Prefix(es): 978-2-908295
Number of titles published annually: 4 Print
Total Titles: 70 Print
Branch Office(s)
l'abbaye d'Ardenne, 14280 St Germain-La-
  Blanche-Herbe *Tel:* 02 31 29 37 37 *Fax:* 02
  31 29 37 36

Indigo & Cote-Femmes Editions+
55 rue des Petites Ecuries, 75010 Paris
Founded: 1989
Subjects: Anthropology, Art, Biography, Memoirs,
  Literature, Literary Criticism, Essays, Poetry,
  Women's Studies, Latin American Literature,
  Women's Literature
ISBN Prefix(es): 978-2-907883; 978-2-911571;
  978-2-914378; 978-2-35260
Number of titles published annually: 20 Print; 20
  E-Book
Total Titles: 370 Print; 370 E-Book
Distributed by Editions L'Harmattan

Editions Infrarouge+
7 rue du Capitaine Ferber, 75020 Paris
Tel: 01 44 93 45 64; 06 66 77 34 20
E-mail: editionsinfrarouge@aliceadsl.fr
Web Site: www.editionsinfrarouge.com; www.
  monartisabelledrouin.com
Key Personnel
Dir: Yves Soubrillard *E-mail:* yvessoubrillard@
  aliceadsl.fr
Literature Dir: Isabelle Soubrillard
Founded: 1996
Specialize in titles by Isabelle Drouin.
Subjects: Alternative, Art, Behavioral Sciences,
  Drama, Theater, Environmental Studies, Fic-
  tion, Humor, Literature, Literary Criticism,
  Essays, Medicine, Nursing, Dentistry, Para-
  psychology, Psychology, Psychiatry, Religion -
  Catholic, Religion - Other, Romance, Science
  (General), Science Fiction, Fantasy, Social Sci-
  ences, Sociology, Theology, Novels
ISBN Prefix(es): 978-2-908614
Number of titles published annually: 4 Print
Total Titles: 50 Print; 3 E-Book

Editions INSERM+
101, rue de Tolbiac, 75654 Paris Cedex 13
Tel: 01 44 23 60 00
E-mail: siteinserm@inserm.fr
Web Site: www.inserm.fr
Key Personnel
Dir of Publications, Chairman & Chief Executive

Officer: Andre Syrota *E-mail:* andre.syrota@
inserm.fr
Founded: 1970
Subjects: Biological Sciences, Health, Nutrition,
Medicine, Nursing, Dentistry, Social Sciences,
Sociology, Biomedical Research, Public Health
ISBN Prefix(es): 978-2-85598
Total Titles: 2 Print
Parent Company: Institut National de la Sante et
de la Recherche Medicale
Distributed by Lavoisier (France)

Editions l'Instant Durable+
PO Box 234, 63007 Clermont-Ferrand Cedex 1
Tel: 04 73 92 07 89 *Fax:* 04 73 91 13 87
E-mail: art@instantdurable.com
Web Site: www.instantdurable.com
Founded: 1983
Membership(s): Syndicat National de l'Edition
(SNE).
Subjects: Architecture & Interior Design, Art,
History, Literature, Literary Criticism, Essays
ISBN Prefix(es): 978-2-86404
Imprints: Architecture-Modelisme; Grand Angle
Distributor for PALEO Editions

**Institut de Recherche et Documentation en
Economie de la Sante,** see IRDES - Institut de
Recherche et Documentation en Economie de
la Sante

Institut de Recherche pour le Developpement,
see IRD Editions

Institut Francais
8-14 rue du Capitaine Scott, 75015 Paris
Tel: 01 53 69 83 00 *Fax:* 01 53 69 33 00
E-mail: info@institutfrancais.com
Web Site: www.institutfrancais.com
Key Personnel
Executive Chairman: Xavier Darcos
Secretary General: Pierre Colliot
Communications Dir: Caroline Cesbron
Founded: 2011
Subjects: Art, Biography, Memoirs, Literature,
Literary Criticism, Essays, Philosophy, Photog-
raphy, Poetry

Institut Memoires de l'edition contemporaine,
see IMEC

**Institut National de l'Information
Geographique et Forestiere (IGN)** (National
Institute of Geographic & Forest Information)
73, ave de Paris, 94165 Saint-Mande Cedex
Tel: 01 43 98 80 00
E-mail: communication@ign.fr
Web Site: www.ign.fr
Key Personnel
Publications Dir: Benedicte Dussert
Press: Sophie Couturier *Tel:* 01 43 98 83 05
Fax: 06 85 31 34 90 *E-mail:* sophie.couturier@
ign.fr
Founded: 1940
ISBN Prefix(es): 978-2-85595

InterEditions, *imprint of* Dunod Editeur

InterEditions+
Imprint of Dunod Editeur
5, rue Laromiguiere, 75005 Paris
Tel: 01 40 46 35 00 *Fax:* 01 40 46 49 95
E-mail: infos@intereditions.com; crea@dunod.
com
Web Site: www.dunod.com
Key Personnel
Publisher: Helene de Castilla
Founded: 1976

Subjects: How-to, Human Relations, Inspirational,
Spirituality, Management, Psychology, Psychia-
try, Self-Help, Personal Development
ISBN Prefix(es): 978-2-10; 978-2-7296; 978-2-
225
Ultimate Parent Company: Hachette Livre

Les Editions Interferences
4 rue Cesar Franck, 75015 Paris
Tel: 01 45 67 33 56; 06 31 75 87 20; 06 14 15
18 62
E-mail: interferences@editions-interferences.com
Web Site: www.editions-interferences.com
Key Personnel
Publisher-Bookseller: Alain Benech
Translator: Sophie Benech
Founded: 1992
Subjects: Literature, Literary Criticism, Essays
ISBN Prefix(es): 978-2-909589
Distribution Center: Les Editions Belin, 8
rue Ferou, 75006 Paris *Tel:* 01 55 42 84 00
Fax: 01 55 42 84 30 *Web Site:* www.editions-
belin.com

Institut International de la Marionnette
7 pl Winston Churchill, 08000 Charleville-
Mezieres
Tel: 03 24 33 72 50 *Fax:* 03 24 33 72 69
E-mail: institut@marionnette.com
Web Site: www.marionnette.com
Key Personnel
President: Raymond Weber
Dir: Lucile Bodson
Communications & Public Relations: Sophie
Wathle
Founded: 1981
Subjects: Art, Drama, Theater
ISBN Prefix(es): 978-2-9505282

L'Invention du Lecteur, *imprint of* Editions
William Blake & Co

Editions de Iorme Rond, *imprint of* ELOR
Editions

Editions Ipagine
86 rue du Rocher, 75008 Paris
Tel: 01 44 01 66 22 *Fax:* 08 26 42 48 57
E-mail: contact@ipagine.com
Web Site: www.ipagine.com
Subjects: Literature, Literary Criticism, Essays,
Social Sciences, Sociology
ISBN Prefix(es): 978-2-9533549; 979-10-9174

IRD Editions+
Centre IRD de Montepellier, 911 ave Angropolis,
34394 Montpellier Cedex 5
Mailing Address: BP 64501, 34394 Montpellier
Cedex 5
Tel: 01 48 03 56 49 *Fax:* 01 48 02 79 09
E-mail: editions@ird.fr; diffusion@ird.fr
Web Site: www.editions.ird.fr
Key Personnel
Dir: Thomas Mourier *E-mail:* thomas.mourier@
ird.fr
Editorial: Elisabeth Lorne *E-mail:* elisabeth.
lorne@ird.fr
Founded: 1962
Scientific publisher.
Subjects: Archaeology, Biological Sciences, De-
veloping Countries, Earth Sciences, Environ-
mental Studies, Geography, Geology, Health,
Nutrition, History, Science (General), Social
Sciences, Sociology, Technology, Ecology
ISBN Prefix(es): 978-2-7099
Number of titles published annually: 35 Print; 6
CD-ROM
Total Titles: 830 Print; 30 CD-ROM

**IRDES - Institut de Recherche et
Documentation en Economie de la Sante**
10 rue Vauvenargues, 75018 Paris
Tel: 01 53 93 43 00 *Fax:* 01 53 93 43 50
E-mail: presse@irdes.fr
Web Site: www.irdes.fr
Key Personnel
President: Francois Joliclerc
Dir: Yann Bourgueil *Tel:* 01 53 93 43 20
E-mail: bourgueil@irdes.fr
Deputy Dir: Catherine Sermet
Press: Anne Evans *Tel:* 01 53 93 43 02
Founded: 1985
Subjects: Economics, Health, Nutrition, Medicine,
Nursing, Dentistry
ISBN Prefix(es): 978-2-87812

Editions Isoete
24 rue Emmanuel Liais, 50100 Cherbourg-
Octeville
Tel: 02 33 43 36 64 *Fax:* 02 33 43 37 13
E-mail: editions.isoete@wanadoo.fr
Web Site: isoete.over-blog.fr
Founded: 1984
Subjects: Art, History, Humor, Literature, Liter-
ary Criticism, Essays, Photography, Regional
Interests, Travel & Tourism, ContemporaryLit-
erature
ISBN Prefix(es): 978-2-905385; 978-2-913920
Distributor for Distique

ISTE Editions, *imprint of* Editions Hermes
Science Publications

Editions Ivoire-Clair
BP 24, 85270 Saint-Hilaire-de-Riez
Tel: 02 51 68 58 33
E-mail: service.clients@ivoire-clair.com
Web Site: www.ivoire-clair.com
Founded: 1999
Subjects: Criminology, Drama, Theater, History,
Inspirational, Spirituality, Literature, Literary
Criticism, Essays, Philosophy, Science Fiction,
Fantasy, Social Sciences, Sociology, Culture,
Nature
ISBN Prefix(es): 978-2-913882

Editions Ivrea+
One, place Paul Painleve, 75005 Paris
Tel: 01 43 26 06 21
E-mail: editionsivrea@wanadoo.fr
Web Site: www.editions-ivrea.fr
Key Personnel
Contact: Valentin Lorenzo
International Rights: Jacques Dodart
Founded: 1970
Subjects: History, Literature, Literary Criticism,
Essays, Military Science, Poetry, Social Sci-
ences, Sociology
ISBN Prefix(es): 978-2-85184
Imprints: Champ Libre
Bookshop(s): 27, rue du Sommerard, 75005 Paris
Warehouse: BLDD, 4, route du Plan d'eau, 27600
Gaillon *Tel:* 02 32 21 86 55 *Fax:* 02 32 21 86
60 *Web Site:* www.bldd.fr
Orders to: BLDD, 25, rue du General Leclerc,
94270 Le Kremlin-Bicetre *Tel:* 01 45 15 19 70
Fax: 01 45 15 19 80 *Web Site:* www.bldd.fr

Editions Odile Jacob+
15, rue Soufflot, 75240 Paris Cedex 05
Tel: 01 44 41 64 84 *Fax:* 01 44 41 64 99; 01 43
29 88 77 (foreign rights)
Web Site: www.odilejacob.fr
Key Personnel
President: Odile Jacob
Rights Manager: Marie Morvan *E-mail:* morvan.
rights@odilejacob.fr
Founded: 1986
Subjects: Biography, Memoirs, Economics, Fic-
tion, Government, Political Science, Health,

Nutrition, History, How-to, Law, Literature, Literary Criticism, Essays, Medicine, Nursing, Dentistry, Philosophy, Psychology, Psychiatry, Science (General), Social Sciences, Sociology
ISBN Prefix(es): 978-2-7381
Number of titles published annually: 120 Print
Imprints: Poches Odile Jacob (Pocket Series)
Distribution Center: Centre de Diffusion de l'Edition, 17 rue de Tournan, 75006 Paris
Tel: 01 44 41 19 19 *Fax:* 01 46 34 56 33

Les Editions du Jaguar
57 bis, rue d'Auteuil, 75016 Paris
Tel: 01 40 71 71 92 *Fax:* 01 40 71 71 91
E-mail: jaguar@jeuneafrique.com
Web Site: leseditionsdujaguar.com
Key Personnel
Deputy Dir: Nicole Houstin *E-mail:* n.houstin@jeuneafrique.com
Founded: 1967
Subjects: Art, Cookery, Geography, Geology, Government, Political Science, Health, Nutrition, History, How-to, Human Relations, Regional Interests, Religion - Islamic, Social Sciences, Sociology, Travel & Tourism, Africa
ISBN Prefix(es): 978-2-86950; 978-2-85258
Foreign Rep(s): Nord-Sud (Belgium); OLF (Switzerland); Ulysse (Canada)
Distribution Center: Cap Diffusion, 4 rue de Maye Lanne, 65420 Ibos *Tel:* 05 62 90 09 96
E-mail: accueil@rando-diffusion.com

J'ai lu, *imprint of* Flammarion Groupe

Editions J'ai Lu
Imprint of Flammarion Groupe
87, quai Panhard et Levassor, 75013 Paris
E-mail: contact@jailu.com
Web Site: www.jailu.com
Key Personnel
Editorial Dir: Anna Pavlowitch
Founded: 1958
Subjects: Fiction, Science Fiction, Fantasy
ISBN Prefix(es): 978-2-277; 978-2-290
Number of titles published annually: 460 Print
Total Titles: 3,000 Print

Editions Jannink
127, rue de la Galciere, 75013 Paris
Tel: 01 45 89 14 02 *Fax:* 01 45 89 14 02
Web Site: www.editionsjannink.com
Founded: 1978
Subjects: Art, History, Contemporary Art
ISBN Prefix(es): 978-2-902462; 978-2-916067
Number of titles published annually: 6 Print
Total Titles: 70 Print
Associate Companies: SIPEL

Editions du Jasmin
4, rue Valiton, 92110 Clichy
Tel: 01 41 27 04 48 *Fax:* 01 42 70 11 59
E-mail: saad.bouri@wanadoo.fr
Web Site: editions-du-jasmin.com
Founded: 1987
Subjects: Biography, Memoirs, Criminology, Fiction, Language Arts, Linguistics, Mysteries, Suspense, Poetry, Travel & Tourism
ISBN Prefix(es): 978-2-35284; 978-2-912080
Number of titles published annually: 20 Print
Total Titles: 200 Print

Editions du Jeu de Paume
One Place de la Concorde, Jardin des Tuileries, 75008 Paris
Tel: 01 47 03 12 50
E-mail: info@jeudepaume.org
Web Site: www.jeudepaume.org
Key Personnel
Dir General: Marta Gili

Administration & Finance: Claude Bocage
E-mail: claude.bocage@jeudepaume.org
Founded: 1991
Specialize in exhibitions catalogues.
Subjects: Art, Film, Video, Photography
ISBN Prefix(es): 978-2-915704
Number of titles published annually: 5 Print
Total Titles: 80 Print

Nouvelles Editions JMP, see Nouvelles Editions Jean-Michel Place

Joly, *imprint of* Lextenso Editions

Joly Editions+
Imprint of Lextenso Editions
70, rue du Gouverneur General Felix Eboue, 92131 Issy-les-Moulineaux Cedex
Tel: 01 40 93 40 40 *Fax:* 01 41 09 92 14
Web Site: www.editions-joly.com
Subjects: Law, Securities
ISBN Prefix(es): 978-2-907512

Editions Le Jour+
c/o Messageries ADP, Immeuble Paryseine, 3, Alle de la Seine, 94854 Ivry Cedex
Fax: 01 49 59 11 33
Web Site: www.edjour.com
Key Personnel
Press: Cecilia Castagne *Tel:* 01 49 59 11 91
Subjects: Animals, Pets, Astrology, Occult, Career Development, Health, Nutrition, How-to, Medicine, Nursing, Dentistry, Psychology, Psychiatry, Women's Studies
ISBN Prefix(es): 978-0-7760; 978-2-89044
Parent Company: Groupe Sogides Inc
Ultimate Parent Company: Quebecor Media
Branch Office(s)
955, rue Amherst, Montreal, QC H2L 3K4, Canada *Tel:* 514-523-1182 *Fax:* 514-597-0370
E-mail: adpcommandes@messageries-adp.com
Foreign Rights: Groupe Homme (Florence Bisch)

Editions Jouvence Sarl+
BP 90107, 74161 St Julien-en-Genevois Cedex
Tel: 04 50 43 28 60 *Fax:* 04 50 43 29 24
E-mail: info@editions-jouvence.com
Web Site: www.editions-jouvence.com
Key Personnel
Dir: Jacques Maire *E-mail:* j2.maire@editions-jouvence.com
Sales Manager: Aurore Guignard
Foreign Rights: Annick Maziers *Tel:* 04 50 43 38 40 *E-mail:* a.maziers@editions-jouvence.com
Founded: 1989
Subjects: Cookery, Earth Sciences, Education, Health, Nutrition, How-to, Human Relations, Medicine, Nursing, Dentistry, Philosophy, Psychology, Psychiatry, Self-Help, Social Sciences, Sociology, Sports, Athletics
ISBN Prefix(es): 978-2-88353; 978-2-909206
Imprints: Epanouissement; Pratique Sante; Sante Spiritualite
Branch Office(s)
Av Adrien Jeandin nr 1, CP 89, 1226 Thonex, Switzerland *Tel:* (022) 757 62 20 *Fax:* (022) 348 37 66
Distributor for Carthame editions
Foreign Rights: Julio F-Yanez (Latin America, Portugal, Spain); Agence Litteraire Iris (Catherine Fragou) (Greece); Anastasia Lester (Russia, Ukraine)

Editions du Jubile+
4 rue Chopin, 92120 Montrouge
Tel: 01 49 85 85 90 *Fax:* 01 49 12 55 34
E-mail: contact@editionsdujubile.com
Web Site: editionsdujubile.com
Key Personnel
Founder & Dir: Jean-Claude Didelot
Founded: 2001

Subjects: Religion - Catholic
ISBN Prefix(es): 978-2-86679
Number of titles published annually: 30 Print
Distributed by Hachette Livre
Distribution Center: AVM Distribution, BP 49, 71601 Paray Le Monial Cedex
Tel: 03 85 81 95 95 *Fax:* 03 85 81 95 96
E-mail: contactlibraires@avm-diffusion.com

Editions Julliard
30 Pl d'Italie, 75013 Paris
Tel: 01 53 67 14 00
Web Site: www.julliard.fr
Key Personnel
President & Dir General: Cecile Boyer-Runge
Deputy Dir General: Antoine Caro
Dir: Bernard Barrault; Betty Mialet
Founded: 1942
Specialize in contemporary French literature.
Subjects: Anthropology, Biography, Memoirs, Drama, Theater, Fiction, Film, Video, History, Literature, Literary Criticism, Essays, Photography, Poetry, Science Fiction, Fantasy, Sports, Athletics, Folklore
ISBN Prefix(es): 978-2-260
Parent Company: Groupe Robert Laffont
Associate Companies: Bouquins; Editions Robert Laffont; NiL Editions; Seghers

Jungle, *imprint of* Flammarion Groupe

Jurif (Societe d' Etudes Juridiques Internationales et Fiscales), see Les Cahiers Fiscaux Europeens Sarl

Juris Editions
75 bis rue de Seze, 69006 Lyon
Tel: 04 72 98 18 40 *Fax:* 04 78 28 93 83
E-mail: infojuris@dalloz.fr; serviceclient@dalloz.fr
Web Site: www.juriseditions.fr
Key Personnel
President: Sylvie Faye
Editorial Dir: Pascal Remillieux
Publication Dir: Renaud Lefebvre
Founded: 1983
Specialize in tourism & law, nonprofit sector, real estate joint ownership, liberal professions.
Subjects: Communications, Law, Management, Real Estate
ISBN Prefix(es): 978-2-907648; 978-2-910992
Number of titles published annually: 5 Print
Total Titles: 70 Print; 2 CD-ROM
Parent Company: Editions Dalloz, 31-35, rue Froidevaux, 75685 Paris Cedex 14

JurisClasseur Groupe LexisNexis
141, rue de Javel, 75747 Paris Cedex 15
Tel: 08 21 20 07 00 *Fax:* 01 45 58 94 00
E-mail: relation.client@lexisnexis.fr
Web Site: www.lexisnexis.fr; www.juris-classeur.com
Key Personnel
Dir: Philippe Carillon
Founded: 1907
Subjects: Law
ISBN Prefix(es): 978-2-7110
Parent Company: LexisNexis Group
Ultimate Parent Company: Reed Elsevier PLC
Warehouse: 14 rue de la Passerelle, 31200 Toulouse Cedex

Editions Kaleidoscope+
11, rue de Sevres, 75006 Paris
Tel: 01 45 44 07 08 *Fax:* 01 45 44 53 71
E-mail: infos@editions-kaleidoscope.com
Web Site: www.editions-kaleidoscope.com
Key Personnel
President: Isabel Finkenstaedt
Foreign Rights: Juliet Quarini
Founded: 1989

Specialize in upmarket picture books for ages 0-7.
ISBN Prefix(es): 978-2-87767
Number of titles published annually: 30 Print
Total Titles: 350 Print
Parent Company: Kaleidoscope SAS
Warehouse: Ecole des loisirs, Lotissment de la Butte, 11 rue Gutenberg, 91620 Nozay
Orders to: L'Ecole des Loisirs *Tel:* 01 42 22 94 10 *Fax:* 01 45 48 04 99 *E-mail:* edl@ecoledesloisirs.com

KANJIL Editeur
2 rue des Fosses St Jacques, 75005 Paris
Tel: 01 44 27 01 04; 06 13 26 61 96
E-mail: kanjilediteur@gmail.com
Web Site: www.kanjil.com
Key Personnel
Editor: Lise Bourquin Mercade
ISBN Prefix(es): 978-2-916046

Les Editions Karthala+
22-24, blvd Arago, 75013 Paris
Tel: 01 43 31 15 59 *Fax:* 01 45 35 27 05
E-mail: karthala@orange.fr
Web Site: www.karthala.com
Key Personnel
Mng Dir: Robert Ageneau
Founded: 1980
Subjects: Anthropology, Asian Studies, Developing Countries, Economics, Education, Geography, Geology, Literature, Literary Criticism, Essays, Religion - Catholic, Religion - Islamic, Religion - Protestant, Social Sciences, Sociology, Travel & Tourism
ISBN Prefix(es): 978-2-86537; 978-2-84586; 978-2-8111
Number of titles published annually: 110 Print
Total Titles: 2,400 Print
Distribution Center: Nord-Sud Diffusion, 150, rue Berthelot, 1190 Brussels, Belgium *Tel:* (02) 343 10 13 *Fax:* (02) 343 42 91 *E-mail:* info@diffusionnord-sud.be (Benelux)
Somabec, 2475, Sylva Clapin, St-Hyacinthe, QC J2S 7B6, Canada *Tel:* 450-774-8118 *Fax:* 450-774-3017 *E-mail:* info@somabec.qc.ca *Web Site:* www.somabec.com

Editions Kero
14, bis rue des Minimes, 75003 Paris
Tel: 01 53 01 01 75
E-mail: contact@editionskero.com; editorial@editionskero.com
Web Site: www.editionskero.com
Key Personnel
Chief Executive Officer: Philippe Robinet *E-mail:* phrobinet@editionskero.com
Assistant Dir General: Camille Lucet *E-mail:* clucet@editionskero.com
Dir, Communications: Catherine Bourgey *E-mail:* cbourgey@editionskero.com
Editor: Marine Montegut *E-mail:* mmontegut@editionskero.com
Marketing: Lisa Parrod *Tel:* 01 53 01 21 62 *E-mail:* lparrod@editionskero.com
Subjects: Fiction, Nonfiction (General)
ISBN Prefix(es): 978-2-36658
Parent Company: Hachette Livre

Editions Klincksieck
95, blvd Raspail, 75006 Paris
Tel: 01 43 54 47 57 *Fax:* 01 45 44 92 88
E-mail: courrier@klincksieck.com
Web Site: www.klincksieck.com
Key Personnel
Publishing Dir: Caroline Noirot
Founded: 1842
Subjects: Archaeology, Art, Drama, Theater, History, Language Arts, Linguistics, Literature, Literary Criticism, Essays, Music, Dance, Philosophy, Science (General), Social Sciences, Sociology

ISBN Prefix(es): 978-2-252
Associate Companies: Aux Amateurs De Livres

Editions Eric Koehler+
16, rue Arthur-Groussier, 75010 Paris 10
Tel: 01 49 27 06 37 *Fax:* 01 47 03 39 86
Key Personnel
Owner: Lydia Rolland
Manager: Guillaume Dopffer
Founded: 1988
Subjects: Photography
ISBN Prefix(es): 978-2-7107; 978-2-907220

Editions Lacour-Olle+
25 bd Amiral Courbet, 30000 Nimes
Tel: 04 66 67 30 30 *Fax:* 04 66 21 11 23; 04 66 29 74 91
E-mail: colpmaud@bbox.fr
Web Site: www.editions-lacour.com
Key Personnel
Dir: Christian Lacour *E-mail:* c.lacour@editions-lacour.com
Founded: 1791
Subjects: Astrology, Occult, Cookery, Parapsychology, Regional Interests, Religion - Catholic, Religion - Protestant, Religion - Other
ISBN Prefix(es): 978-2-86971; 978-2-84149; 978-2-84406; 978-2-84692; 978-2-84691; 978-2-7504
Total Titles: 7,300 Print

Les Editions Jeanne Laffitte
25, cours d'Estienne d'Orves, 13001 Marseille
Tel: 04 91 59 80 37; 04 91 59 80 43 (editorial); 04 91 59 80 49 (bookstore)
E-mail: editions@jeanne-laffitte.com; librairie@jeanne-laffitte.com (bookstore)
Web Site: www.jeanne-laffitte.com/editions
Key Personnel
President: Jeanne Laffitte
Founded: 1978
Subjects: Ethnicity, History, Regional Interests
ISBN Prefix(es): 978-2-85203; 978-2-86276; 978-2-7348; 978-2-86604
Distributed by Centre d'Exportation du Livre Francais (CELF)

Editions Robert Laffont+
30 pl d'Italie, 75013 Paris
Mailing Address: CS 51391, 75627 Paris Cedex 13
Tel: 01 53 67 14 00
Web Site: www.laffont.fr
Key Personnel
President & Dir General: Cecile Boyer-Runge
Foreign Rights: Benita Edzard *E-mail:* bedzard@robert-laffont.fr; Judith Temmam *E-mail:* jtemmam@robert-laffont.fr
Founded: 1941
Subjects: Biography, Memoirs, Fiction, Inspirational, Spirituality, Literature, Literary Criticism, Essays
ISBN Prefix(es): 978-2-221; 978-2-87645
Number of titles published annually: 200 Print
Total Titles: 4,500 Print
Associate Companies: Bellitz Fixot
Branch Office(s)
955 Amherst, Montreal, QC H2L 3K4, Canada *Tel:* 514-282-1012

Editions Lafitte-Hebrard - Who's Who in France
16, rue Camille Pelletan, 92300 Levallois-Perret
Tel: 01 41 27 28 30 *Fax:* 01 41 27 28 40
E-mail: whoswho@whoswho.fr
Web Site: www.whoswho.fr
Key Personnel
President: Antoine Hebrard
Dir General: Etienne Prevost

Contact: Julie Jamgotchian *E-mail:* julie.jamgotchian@whoswho.fr
Founded: 1953
Subjects: Biography, Memoirs, Biographical Dictionary
ISBN Prefix(es): 978-2-85784
Number of titles published annually: 1 Print; 1 Online

Michel Lafon Publishing+
118 ave Achille Peretti, 92521 Neuilly-sur-Seine Cedex
Mailing Address: CS 70024, 92521 Neuilly-sur-Seine Cedex
Tel: 01 41 43 85 85 *Fax:* 01 46 24 00 95
E-mail: contact@michel-lafon.fr; presse@michel-lafon.fr
Web Site: www.michel-lafon.fr
Key Personnel
Marketing Dir: Florian Lafani
Foreign Rights Manager: Roxana Jamet *Tel:* 01 41 43 09 79 *E-mail:* roxana@michel-lafon.com
Founded: 1980
Subjects: Biography, Memoirs, Cookery, Drama, Theater, Fiction, Film, Video, History, Humor, Mysteries, Suspense, Sports, Athletics, Comics, Testimony
ISBN Prefix(es): 978-2-84098; 978-2-908652; 978-2-7499

Editions Lamarre SA
One rue Eugene et Armand Peugeot, 92856 Rueil-Malmaison
Tel: 01 76 73 30 00; 08 25 08 08 00
Key Personnel
Press: Sylvie Caron *Tel:* 01 76 73 41 51 *E-mail:* scaron@wolters-kluwer.fr
Founded: 1957
Subjects: Medicine, Nursing, Dentistry
ISBN Prefix(es): 978-2-85030
Parent Company: Wolters Kluwer France
Ultimate Parent Company: Wolters Kluwer Group

Editions Lamy
One, rue Eugene et Armand Peugeot, 92856 Rueil-Malmaison Cedex
Tel: 08 25 08 08 00 *Fax:* 01 76 73 48 09
E-mail: contact@wkf.fr
Web Site: www.wkf.fr
Key Personnel
President: Hubert Chemla *Tel:* 01 76 73 30 00
Founded: 1949
Subjects: Law, Social Sciences, Sociology
ISBN Prefix(es): 978-2-7212
Parent Company: Wolters Kluwer France
Ultimate Parent Company: Wolters Kluwer NV
Associate Companies: Editions Dalian; Groupe Liaisons

Editions Fernand Lanore+
6 rue de Vaugirard, 75006 Paris
Tel: 01 43 25 66 61 *Fax:* 01 43 29 69 81
E-mail: contact@editionslanore.com
Web Site: www.fernand-lanore.com
Key Personnel
Dir: Francois-Xavier Sorlot
Founded: 1910
Subjects: Astrology, Occult, Education, Health, Nutrition, History, Inspirational, Spirituality, Language Arts, Linguistics, Literature, Literary Criticism, Essays, Music, Dance, Outdoor Recreation, Philosophy, Poetry, Religion - Other, Science (General), Travel & Tourism, Humanities
ISBN Prefix(es): 978-2-85157
Number of titles published annually: 25 Print
Total Titles: 450 Print
Foreign Rep(s): Agence du Livre (Canada); La Caravelle (Belgium); Servidis (Switzerland)

Distribution Center: Dilisco, 128 bis, ave Jean-Jaures, Parc Mure 2, 94208 Ivry-sur-Seine
Tel: 01 49 59 50 50
Orders to: rue du Limousin, BP 25, 23220 Cheniers *Tel:* 05 55 51 80 00 *Fax:* 05 55 62 17 39

Les Editions Larousse+
Subsidiary of Hachette Livre
21, rue du Montparnasse, 75006 Paris Cedex 06
Tel: 01 44 39 44 00
E-mail: livres-larousse@larousse.fr
Web Site: www.larousse.fr; www.editions-larousse.fr
Key Personnel
Publishing Dir: Isabelle Jeuge-Maynart
Foreign Rights Dir: Evelyne Le Bourse *Tel:* 01 44 39 44 11 *E-mail:* elebourse@larousse.fr
Press: Therese Leridon *Tel:* 01 44 39 43 92 *E-mail:* tleridon@larousse.fr
Founded: 1852
Subjects: Animals, Pets, Art, Child Care & Development, Cookery, Gardening, Plants, History, Language Arts, Linguistics, Medicine, Nursing, Dentistry, Music, Dance, Psychology, Psychiatry, Regional Interests, Science (General), Self-Help, Social Sciences, Sociology, Sports, Athletics, Technology
ISBN Prefix(es): 978-2-03
Subsidiaries: Editions Francaises Inc; Ediciones Larousse Argentina SA; Larousse-Belgique; Editora Larousse do Brazil; Ediciones Larousse Colombiana Ltda; Ediciones Larousse SA; Larousse (Suisse) SA

Editions JC Lattes+
Subsidiary of Hachette Livre
17 rue Jacob, 75006 Paris
Tel: 01 44 41 74 00 *Fax:* 01 43 25 30 47; 01 43 26 91 04
Web Site: www.editions-jclattes.fr
Key Personnel
General Dir: Isabelle Laffont
Editorial Dir: Laurent Laffont
Literary Dir: Karina Hocine
Rights Dir: Eva Bredin-Wachter *Tel:* 01 44 41 74 30 *E-mail:* ebredin@editions-jclattes.fr
Sales Dir: Philippe Dorey
Communications Officer: Laurence Barrere
Founded: 1968
Subjects: Fiction, Nonfiction (General)
ISBN Prefix(es): 978-2-7096
Number of titles published annually: 100 Print
Total Titles: 1,250 Print
Ultimate Parent Company: Lagardere

Editions Le Laurier
26 rue Pierre Joigneaux, 92270 Bois Colombes
Tel: 01 45 51 55 08 *Fax:* 01 45 51 81 83
E-mail: contact@editions-lelaurier.com
Web Site: editions-lelaurier.com
Founded: 1981
Subjects: Religion - Catholic
ISBN Prefix(es): 978-2-86495; 978-2-910095

Les Editions Lavauzelle SA+
Le Prouet, BP 8, 87350 Panazol
Tel: 05 55 58 45 00
E-mail: editions@lavauzelle.com
Web Site: www.lavauzelle.com/keops/edition
Founded: 1830
Subjects: Law, Military Science, Sports, Athletics
ISBN Prefix(es): 978-2-7025
Branch Office(s)
20 rue de Saint Petersbourg, 75008 Paris Cedex
Tel: 01 43 87 42 30

Editions Lavoisier+
14, rue de Provigny, 94230 Cachan
Tel: 01 47 40 67 00 *Fax:* 01 47 40 67 02
E-mail: editionslavoisier@lavoisier.fr
Web Site: editions.lavoisier.fr

Key Personnel
Editorial Dir: Fabienne Roulleaux
Publisher Services Manager: Agnes Fleury
Founded: 1947
Subjects: Agriculture, Biological Sciences, Chemistry, Chemical Engineering, Cookery, Electronics, Electrical Engineering, Energy, Engineering (General), Environmental Studies, Geography, Geology, Health, Nutrition, Labor, Industrial Relations, Maritime, Medicine, Nursing, Dentistry, Physical Sciences, Physics, Science (General), Technology, Veterinary Science, New Communication & Information Technologies
ISBN Prefix(es): 978-2-85206 (Tec & Doc); 978-2-7430 (Tec & Doc); 978-2-7462 (Hermes Science); 978-2-257
Number of titles published annually: 100 Print
Imprints: Hermes Science; Medecine Sciences; Tec & Doc
Bookshop(s): Librairie Lavoisier, 14 rue de Provigny, 94236 Cachan Cedex *Tel:* 01 47 40 67 00 *Fax:* 01 47 40 67 02 *E-mail:* service.client@lavoisier.fr *Web Site:* www.lavoisier.fr

LCD Mediation
2, rue de la Chancellerie, 41400 Montrichard
Tel: 02 54 32 37 90 *Fax:* 02 54 32 37 90
Key Personnel
President: Brigitte Kissel
Subjects: Fiction, Inspirational, Spirituality, Social Sciences, Sociology
ISBN Prefix(es): 978-2-909539

Editions Musicales Alphonse Leduc
85, rue Gabriel Peri, 92120 Montrouge
Tel: 01 42 96 89 11 *Fax:* 01 42 86 02 83
E-mail: alphonseleduc@wanadoo.fr
Web Site: www.alphonseleduc.com
Founded: 1841
Specialize in printed music & notes.
Subjects: Music, Dance
ISBN Prefix(es): 978-2-85689
Subsidiaries: Alphonse Leduc-Robert King Inc

Editions Francis Lefebvre
42 rue de Villiers, 92532 Levallois, Perret Cedex
Tel: 01 41 05 22 00; 08 20 71 00 51 *Fax:* 01 41 05 22 30
Web Site: www.efl.fr
Key Personnel
Communications Manager: Nathalie Le Garff *Tel:* 01 41 05 22 77 *Fax:* 01 41 05 22 23 *E-mail:* n.le_garff@efl.fr
Communications Officer: Emmanuelle Carrat *Tel:* 01 41 05 22 70 *Fax:* 01 41 05 22 23 *E-mail:* e.carrat@efl.fr
Founded: 1930
Subjects: Law
ISBN Prefix(es): 978-2-85115; 978-2-85786
Number of titles published annually: 40 Print; 10 CD-ROM; 10 Online
Total Titles: 120 Print
Parent Company: Lefebvre-Sarrut

Editions Legislatives+
80, ave de la Marne, 92546 Montrouge Cedex
Tel: 01 40 92 36 36; 08 10 00 45 19 (customer service)
E-mail: sav@convention-collective.fr
Web Site: www.editions-legislatives.fr
Key Personnel
Publication Dir: Philippe Deroche
Founded: 1947
Subjects: Agriculture, Business, Career Development, Economics, Environmental Studies, Labor, Industrial Relations, Law, Library & Information Sciences, Medicine, Nursing, Dentistry, Real Estate
ISBN Prefix(es): 978-2-85086

Editions Dominique Leroy+
3, rue Docteur Ragot, 89100 Sens
Mailing Address: BP 313, 89103 Sens Cedex
Tel: 03 86 64 15 24
E-mail: contact@dominiqueleroy.fr
Web Site: www.dominiqueleroy.fr; www.enfer.com
Key Personnel
Mng Dir: Dominique Leroy *E-mail:* domleroy@enfer.com
Founded: 1970
Subjects: Art, Erotica, Fiction, Humor, Literature, Literary Criticism, Essays
ISBN Prefix(es): 978-2-86688
Number of titles published annually: 4 CD-ROM; 12 E-Book
Total Titles: 110 Print; 10 CD-ROM; 42 E-Book
Imprints: Vertiges Bulles
Bookshop(s): Librairie Curiosa - MBD, Contact: Daniele Masson *E-mail:* curiosa@enfer.com

Letouzey et Ane Editeurs
87, blvd Raspail, 75006 Paris
Tel: 01 45 48 80 14 *Fax:* 01 45 49 03 43
E-mail: letouzey@free.fr
Web Site: www.letouzey.com
Key Personnel
General Dir: Florence Letouzey-Dumont
Founded: 1885
Subjects: Biblical Studies, Biography, Memoirs, History, Religion - Catholic, Religion - Islamic, Religion - Other
ISBN Prefix(es): 978-2-7063
Number of titles published annually: 10 Print
Distributor for L'Annee Canonique

Lettres Modernes Minard
6, rue de la Sorbonne, 75005 Paris
Tel: 09 61 34 43 02 *Fax:* 01 46 33 28 90
Web Site: www.lettresmodernesminard.org
Key Personnel
President: Patrick Marot
Vice President: Philippe Antoine; Christian Chelebourg
Secretary: Julien Roumette
Editorial: Llewellyn Brown; Johan Faerber
Founded: 1954
Subjects: Film, Video, Literature, Literary Criticism, Essays
ISBN Prefix(es): 978-2-256
Number of titles published annually: 20 Print

Les Editions Lettres Vives+
Campu Magnu, 20213 Castellare-di-Casinca
Mailing Address: BP 7, 20213 Folelli
Tel: 04 95 36 40 93
Web Site: www.editions-lettresvives.com
Key Personnel
Founder: Michel Camus; Claire Tievant
Founded: 1981
Subjects: Literature, Literary Criticism, Essays, Poetry
ISBN Prefix(es): 978-2-903721; 978-2-914577
Number of titles published annually: 5 Print
Total Titles: 120 Print
Imprints: Harmonia Mundi

Editions Liana Levi+
One, Place Paul-Painleve, 75005 Paris
Tel: 01 44 32 19 30 *Fax:* 01 46 33 69 56
E-mail: editions@lianalevi.fr
Web Site: www.lianalevi.fr
Key Personnel
Communications & Rights: Amelie Dor
Editorial & Foreign Rights: Sylvie Mouches
Founded: 1982
Subjects: Art, Fiction, History, Nonfiction (General)
ISBN Prefix(es): 978-2-86746

LexisNexis+
141, rue de Javel, 75747 Paris Cedex 15
Tel: 08 21 20 07 00 *Fax:* 01 45 58 94 00
E-mail: relation.client@lexisnexis.fr

Web Site: www.lexisnexis.fr
Founded: 1927
Subjects: Accounting, Government, Political Science, Labor, Industrial Relations, Law
ISBN Prefix(es): 978-2-7110
Parent Company: LexisNexis
Ultimate Parent Company: Reed Elsevier PLC
Branch Office(s)
26 rue Soufflot, 75005 Paris *Tel:* 01 43 29 07 71
  Fax: 01 40 51 83 72 *E-mail:* librairie.soufflot@
  lexisnexis.fr
27 Pl Dauphine, 75001 Paris *Tel:* 01 43 26 60
  90 *Fax:* 01 46 34 22 98 *E-mail:* librairie.
  dauphine@lexisnexis.fr
Warehouse: Zone Artisanale-Route de Niort,
  85205 Fontenay le Comte Cedex

Lextenso Editions+
70, rue du Gouverneur General Felix Eboue,
  92131 Issy-les-Moulineaux Cedex
Tel: 01 40 93 40 00
E-mail: info@lextenso-editions.fr
Web Site: www.lextenso-editions.fr
Key Personnel
President & Dir General: Emanuelle Filiberti
Founded: 1836
Subjects: Economics, Government, Political Science, History, Law, Public Administration, Social Sciences, Sociology
ISBN Prefix(es): 978-2-275; 978-2-35971
Imprints: Defrenois; Gazette du Palais; Gualino;
  Joly; LGDJ; Montchrestien; Petites Affiches
Distributed by Bruylant; Patrimoine
Distributor for AENGDE; Alpha (Liban); Anthemis; ATOL; Bibliotheque de l'Institut Andre Tunc; Bruylant; City & York; Comite
  pour l'histoire economique et financiere de la
  France; La croisee des chemins; Edipro; Europolitique; Faculte de droit et des sciences
  sociales de Poitiers; Edition Formation Entreprise; Georg; Helbing & Lichtenhahn; Institut Federatif de Recherche "Mutation des
  normes juridiques" - Universite Toulouse; MB
  Edition; Imprimerie Nationale; Pantheon-Assas
  Paris II; Presses Universitaires de la Faculte de
  droit de Clermont; Promoculture; Schulthess;
  Staempfli; UNICOMM; Universite de Cergy-
  Pontoise/LEJEP; Universite de Savoie; Fondation Varenne
Bookshop(s): 20, rue Soufflot, 75005 Paris
  Tel: 01 46 33 89 85 *Fax:* 01 40 51 81 85
  E-mail: librairie@lgdj.fr
Orders to: 160 rue Saint-Jacques, 75005 Paris

LGDJ, *imprint of* Lextenso Editions

LGF, see Librairie Generale Francaise

LGR, see Editions Librairie-Galerie Racine
  (LGR)

Editions John Libbey Eurotext+
Subsidiary of John Libbey Eurotext Ltd
127, ave de la Republique, 92120 Montrouge
Tel: 01 46 73 06 60 *Fax:* 01 40 84 09 99
E-mail: contact@jle.com
Web Site: www.jle.com
Key Personnel
Publications Dir: Gilles Cahn
Foreign Rights: Anne Chevalier *Tel:* 01 46 73 06
  73 *E-mail:* anne.chevalier@jle.com
Founded: 1986
Specialize in all areas of medical & scientific
  subjects in both French & English.
Subjects: Agriculture, Economics, Environmental
  Studies, Health, Nutrition, Medicine, Nursing,
  Dentistry, Life Sciences
ISBN Prefix(es): 978-2-7420
Number of titles published annually: 60 Print
Total Titles: 600 Print

Foreign Rep(s): All Things Medical (Australia,
  New Zealand); Gazelle (Europe, UK); Geodif
  (France); Nankodo Co Ltd (Japan); Probooks
  (Central America, South America)

La Librairie des Ecoles Sarl
Subsidiary of Albin-Michel/Magnard/vuibert
26 rue Vercingetorix, 75014 Paris
Tel: 01 84 16 99 05 *Fax:* 01 84 16 99 05
E-mail: contact@lalibrairiedesecoles.com
Web Site: www.lalibrairiedesecoles.com
Founded: 2007
Subjects: Education, History, Language Arts,
  Linguistics, Mathematics, Science (General),
  French Language, Morals, Pedagogy, Reading
ISBN Prefix(es): 978-2-916788
Distribution Center: Dilisco, Parc Mure 2 - Bat
  4.4 - 128 bis, ave Jean Jaures, BP 102, 94208
  Ivry-sur-Seine *Tel:* 01 49 59 50 17; 01 49 59
  50 40 *Fax:* 01 46 71 05 06 *Web Site:* www.
  dilisco.fr

Editions Librairie-Galerie Racine (LGR)+
23 rue Racine, 75006 Paris
Tel: 01 43 26 97 24
E-mail: contact@editions-lgr.fr
Web Site: www.editions-lgr.fr/fr_FR/
Key Personnel
Dir: Alain Breton; Claudia Sperry
Founded: 1969
Subjects: Poetry
ISBN Prefix(es): 978-2-243; 978-2-84328

Librio, *imprint of* Flammarion Groupe

Editions Les Liens qui Liberent
2, Impasse de Conti, 75006 Paris
Web Site: www.editionslesliensquiliberent.fr
Key Personnel
Editorial & Commercial Coordinator: Nicolas
  Deschamps *Tel:* 06 79 49 19 20 *E-mail:* n.
  deschamps@editionslll.fr
Communication & Partnerships: Antoine Naitab-
  dullah *Tel:* 09 72 99 10 28 *E-mail:* antoine@
  editionslll.fr
Subjects: Economics, Government, Political Science, Psychology, Psychiatry, Science (General), Psychoanalysis
ISBN Prefix(es): 979-10-209
Foreign Rep(s): Prologue (Canada); Servidis
  (Switzerland)
Foreign Rights: L'Autre Agence (Marie Lannurien
  & Corinne Marotte)
Distribution Center: UD-Union Distribution SAS,
  106 rue Petit Leroy, 94550 Chevilly-Larue

Editions Lieux Dits
17 rue Rene Leynaud, 69001 Lyon
Tel: 04 72 00 94 20 *Fax:* 04 72 07 97 64
E-mail: contact@lieuxdits.fr
Web Site: www.lieuxdits.fr
Key Personnel
Publications: Alain Franchella
Founded: 2000
Subjects: Architecture & Interior Design, Art,
  Photography, Heritage
ISBN Prefix(es): 978-2-914528; 978-2-36219
Foreign Rep(s): ADL (Canada); Caravelle (Belgium); Servidis (Switzerland)
Distribution Center: Rando Diffusion, 4, rue
  Maye Lane, 65420 Ibos *Tel:* 05 62 90 09 96
  Fax: 05 62 90 09 91 *E-mail:* accueil@rando-
  diffusion.com

**La Ligue France (Ligue pour la Lecture de la
  Bible) (Scripture Union France)+**
51 Blvd Gustave Andre, 26000 Valence
Mailing Address: CS 50728, 26007 Valence
  Cedex
Tel: 04 75 55 95 00 *Fax:* 04 75 56 02 97
Web Site: www.editions-llb.fr; laligue.net

Key Personnel
Chairperson: Daniel Agopian
Dir: Jean-Daniel Linsig
Founded: 1945
Membership(s): Association des Libraires et des
  Editeurs Protestants, Evangeliques Francophones (ALEPEF).
Subjects: Archaeology, Biblical Studies, Fiction,
  How-to, Religion - Protestant, Theology
ISBN Prefix(es): 978-2-85031
Number of titles published annually: 20 Print; 1
  Audio
U.S. Office(s): Scripture Union, Suite 115, 150
  Shafford Ave, Wayne, PA 19087, United States
Distributed by Cedis; CLC; Maison de la Bible;
  Salvator Diffusions

Lirabelle
2 Impasse des Soucis, 30000 Nimes
Tel: 04 66 80 23 65 *Fax:* 08 11 48 93 68
E-mail: lirabelle-olivierayme@wanadoo.fr
Web Site: www.lirabelle.fr
ISBN Prefix(es): 978-2-914216

Editions Lito
41 rue de Verdun, 94503 Champigny-sur-Marne
Tel: 01 45 16 17 00 *Fax:* 01 48 82 42 00
E-mail: commercial@editionslito.com;
  foreignrights@editionslito.com
Web Site: www.editionslito.com
Key Personnel
Mng Dir, Editorial, Rights & Permissions: Pierre
  Rosdahl
Founded: 1951
Subjects: Crafts, Games, Hobbies, Nonfiction
  (General)
ISBN Prefix(es): 978-2-244
Subsidiaries: Lito Editrice
Foreign Rep(s): Daphne (Belgium); OLF
  (Switzerland); Prologue (Canada)

Le Livre de Poche, see Librairie Generale
  Francaise

Livre des Vacances, *imprint of* Editions Vuibert

Les Livres du Dragon d'Or+
60, rue Mazarine, 75006 Paris
Tel: 01 53 10 36 00 *Fax:* 01 45 49 60 61
E-mail: foreign.rights@grund.fr
Web Site: www.grund.fr
Key Personnel
Dir: Vincent Barbare
Foreign Rights Manager: James Elliott *Tel:* 01 44
  16 09 61 *E-mail:* james.elliott@edi8.fr
Founded: 1989
Specialize in license publishing & book packaging for the international market.
ISBN Prefix(es): 978-2-87881
Number of titles published annually: 10 Print
Total Titles: 100 Print
Parent Company: Edi8
Ultimate Parent Company: Editis Group

Editions LLB, see La Ligue France (Ligue pour
  la Lecture de la Bible)

Lonely Planet
12, ave d'Italie, 75627 Paris Cedex 13
Tel: 01 44 16 05 00 *Fax:* 01 44 08 84 02
E-mail: lonelyplanet@placesdesediteurs.com
Web Site: www.lonelyplanet.fr
Key Personnel
Publishing Dir: Jean Arcache
Rights Dir: Alexandra Buchman *Tel:* 01 44
  16 05 76 *E-mail:* alexandra.buchman@
  placesdesediteurs.com
Founded: 1992
Subjects: Travel & Tourism
ISBN Prefix(es): 978-2-84070
Parent Company: Place des editeurs

Branch Office(s)
186 City Rd, 2nd floor, London EC1V
2NT, United Kingdom *Tel:* (020) 7106
2101 *Fax:* (020) 7106 2101 *E-mail:* go@
lonelyplanet.co.uk
U.S. Office(s): 150 Linden St, Oakland, CA
94607-2538, United States *Tel:* 510-893-8555
Fax: 510-893-8563 *E-mail:* info@lonelyplanet.
com *Web Site:* www.lonelyplanet.com
Orders to: Vilo Diffusion, 25 rue Ginoux, 75015
Paris

Editions LT Jacques Lanore+
Rute du Limonsin, BP 22, 23220 Cheniers
Tel: 05 55 51 80 00
E-mail: service.enseignant@editions-delagrave.fr
Web Site: www.editions-delagrave.fr
Founded: 1865
Subjects: Architecture & Interior Design, Career
Development, Child Care & Development,
Cookery, Health, Nutrition, House & Home,
Law, Technology, Travel & Tourism
ISBN Prefix(es): 978-2-86268
Parent Company: Delagrave Edition
Bookshop(s): Librarie-Editions J Lanore, 4 rue de
Tournon, 75006 Paris *Tel:* 01 43 29 43 50

Editions Josette Lyon+
19, rue St-Severin, 75005 Paris
Tel: 01 43 36 41 05 *Fax:* 01 43 31 07 45
Web Site: www.editions-tredaniel.com/josette-
lyon-editeur-8.html
Key Personnel
Contact: Sophie Gillot
Founded: 1986
Subjects: Health, Nutrition
ISBN Prefix(es): 978-2-906757; 978-2-84319
Parent Company: Guy Tredaniel Editeur

Editions Lyonnaises d'Art et d'Histoire
2, quai Claude Bernard, 69007 Lyon
Tel: 04 78 72 49 00 *Fax:* 04 78 69 00 48
E-mail: contact@editions-lyonnaises.fr
Web Site: www.editions-lyonnaises.fr
Founded: 1995
Subjects: Archaeology, Biography, Memoirs, Ge-
nealogy, History, How-to, Literature, Literary
Criticism, Essays, Regional Interests
ISBN Prefix(es): 978-2-84147
Distributor for Ed Nichel Chomarer; Ed Nichel
Repnier

Editions Macula+
8, rue St-Bon, 75004 Paris
Tel: 01 58 30 39 35 *Fax:* 01 45 44 45 89
E-mail: macula@editionsmacula.com
Web Site: www.editionsmacula.com
Key Personnel
Dir: Veronique Yersin *E-mail:* vyersin@
editionsmacula.com
Founded: 1980
Specialize in history books & art theory.
Subjects: Antiques, Art, Film, Video, History,
Literature, Literary Criticism, Essays, Photogra-
phy, Psychology, Psychiatry, Art Theory
ISBN Prefix(es): 978-2-86589
Total Titles: 60 Print
Distribution Center: Volumen, 25 blvd Romain-
Rolland, 75014 Paris *Tel:* 01 41 48 80 00 *Web
Site:* www.volumen.fr

Magnard
Subsidiary of Groupe Albin Michel
5, allee de la 2eme DB, 75726 Paris Cedex 15
Mailing Address: CS 11531, Paris Cedex 15
E-mail: service.enseignant@magnard.fr
Web Site: www.magnard.fr
Key Personnel
Dir: Guillaume Dervieux
Founded: 1933
Subjects: Education

ISBN Prefix(es): 978-2-210
Number of titles published annually: 150 Print
Total Titles: 2,000 Print
Foreign Rep(s): ERPI/Diffusion du Livre Mirabel
(Canada); Sophie Godefroy (Lebanon); Georges
Haddad (Tunisia); Al Madariss (Morocco);
SDLC Caravelle SA (Belgium, Luxembourg);
Servidis SA (Switzerland); Sogere (Eric Buc-
quet) (Africa)
Distribution Center: Dilisco, BP 22, 23220 Bon-
nat *Tel:* 05 55 51 80 00 *Fax:* 05 55 62 17 39

Editions Thierry Magnier
18 rue Seguier, 75006 Paris
Tel: 01 44 83 80 00
E-mail: etm@editions-thierry-magnier.com
Web Site: www.editions-thierry-magnier.com
Key Personnel
Dir: Thierry Magnier
Communications Officer: Amelie Annoni *Tel:* 01
44 83 80 06
Press Officer: Amandine Lefebvre *Tel:* 01 44 83
80 05
Foreign Rights: Johanna Brock Lacassin
Editor: Soazig Le Bail; Angele Cambournac
ISBN Prefix(es): 978-2-84420
Foreign Rep(s): Lemeac (Canada); Servidis
(Switzerland)
Distribution Center: UD-Union Distribution, 106
rue Petit Leroy, 94550 Chevilly-Larue

La Maison des Instituteurs, see Editions MDI
(La Maison des Instituteurs)

Editions Maison des Langues
78, rue de Turbigo, 75003 Paris
Tel: 01 46 33 85 59 *Fax:* 01 71 19 97 11
E-mail: info@emdl.fr; fle@emdl.fr
Web Site: www.emdl.fr
Key Personnel
Publishing Dir: Katia Coppola
Subjects: Education, Language Arts, Linguistics,
French as a Foreign Language
ISBN Prefix(es): 978-2-35685
Parent Company: Klett Gruppe

**Les Editions de la Maison des Sciences de
l'Homme** (Publishing House of the Human
Sciences)
18 rue Robert Schuman, CS 90003, 94227
Charenton-le Pont Cedex
Web Site: www.editions.msh-paris.fr
Key Personnel
Dir, Publications: Jean-Michel Henry
Head, Editorial Dept: Emmanuelle Corne
Founded: 1975
Specialize in French-German Programs.
Subjects: Anthropology, Archaeology, Economics,
Geography, Geology, Government, Political
Science, History, Language Arts, Linguistics,
Literature, Literary Criticism, Essays, Music,
Dance, Philosophy, Psychology, Psychiatry, So-
cial Sciences, Sociology
ISBN Prefix(es): 978-2-7351; 978-2-901725
Number of titles published annually: 30 Print
Foreign Rep(s): DPLU (Canada); SLU (Belgium,
Switzerland); Sodis (France)
Orders to: Le Comptoir des Presses
d'Universites, 131 blvd St-Michel, 75005 Paris
E-mail: contact@lcdpu.fr

La Maison du Dictionnaire+
98 Blvd du Montparnasse, 75014 Paris
Tel: 01 43 22 12 93 *Fax:* 01 43 22 01 77
E-mail: service-client@dicoland.com
Web Site: www.dicoland.com
Founded: 1976
Specialize in software aides, electronic dictionar-
ies & CD-ROMs.
ISBN Prefix(es): 978-2-85608

Editions A Maisonneuve+
3 bis, place de la Sorbonne, 75005 Paris
Tel: 01 43 26 19 50 *Fax:* 01 43 54 59 54
E-mail: maisonneuve@maisonneuve-adrien.com
Web Site: www.maisonneuve-adrien.com
Key Personnel
Mng Dir: Jean Maisonneuve
Founded: 1959
Subjects: Art, Ethnicity, History, Philosophy, Reli-
gion - Other, Social Sciences, Sociology
ISBN Prefix(es): 978-2-7200; 978-2-7160

Editions Maloine+
23-27, rue de l'Ecole de Medecine, 75006 Paris
Tel: 01 43 29 54 50 *Fax:* 01 43 29 56 12 (orders)
E-mail: vpc@vigot.fr
Web Site: www.maloine.fr
Key Personnel
President: Daniel Vigot
Founded: 1881
Subjects: Medicine, Nursing, Dentistry, Sports,
Athletics, Veterinary Science, Pharmacy
ISBN Prefix(es): 978-2-224
Foreign Rep(s): Prologue Inc (Canada); SDL Car-
avelle SA (Belgium); Servidis SA (Switzer-
land)

Mame, *imprint of* Fleurus Editions

Mame Desclee
Imprint of Mame
15/27 rue Moussorgski, 75018 Paris
E-mail: boutique.mame@mdsfrance.fr (customer
service)
Web Site: www.mameeditions.com
Founded: 1872
Subjects: Literature, Literary Criticism, Essays,
Philosophy, Religion - Other
ISBN Prefix(es): 978-2-7189
Ultimate Parent Company: Fleurus Editions

Mango, *imprint of* Fleurus Editions

Editions Mango+
Imprint of Fleurus Editions
15-27 rue Moussorgski, 75895 Paris Cedex 17
E-mail: fleuruseditions@fleuruseditions.com;
foreignrights@fleuruseditions.com
Web Site: www.fleuruseditions.com/mango
Key Personnel
Chief Executive Officer: Hilaire de Laage
Foreign Rights Manager, Adult Books: Marion
Girona *Tel:* 01 53 26 34 46 *Fax:* 01 53 26 33
41 *E-mail:* m.girona@fleuruseditions.com
Foreign Rights Manager, Children's Books: Anne
Desrame
Founded: 1990
Subjects: Art, Child Care & Development, Com-
puters, Cookery, Crafts, Games, Hobbies, Fic-
tion, Gardening, Plants, Health, Nutrition,
House & Home, How-to, Outdoor Recreation,
Sports, Athletics, Travel & Tourism, Wine &
Spirits
ISBN Prefix(es): 978-2-7404; 978-2-84270

Manitoba, *imprint of* Societe d'Edition Les
Belles Lettres

Marabout+
Subsidiary of Hachette Livre
Hachette Livre, Dept Marabout, 43 Quai de
Grenelle, 75905 Paris Cedex 15
Tel: 01 43 92 30 00 *Fax:* 01 43 92 32 99
E-mail: contact@marabout.com;
pressemarabout@hachette-livre.fr
Web Site: www.marabout.com
Key Personnel
Publications Dir: Elisabeth Darets-Chochod
Dir, Communications: Anne Bonvoisin
Dir, Marketing: Geraldine Barral
Editorial Dir: Helene Gedouin; Emmanuel Le
Vallois

International Rights Dir: Pixie Shields
Finance & Administration: Dominique Saitcevsky
Founded: 1949
Subjects: Animals, Pets, Astrology, Occult, Be-
havioral Sciences, Career Development, Child
Care & Development, Computer Science,
Cookery, Crafts, Games, Hobbies, English as
a Second Language, Gardening, Plants, Ge-
nealogy, Health, Nutrition, History, Human
Relations, Humor, Inspirational, Spirituality,
Medicine, Nursing, Dentistry, Psychology, Psy-
chiatry, Self-Help
ISBN Prefix(es): 978-2-501
Distributed by Diffulivre Suisse; Hachette
Canada; Hachette Livre France; Tous Pays

Editions Marcus
17, rue Pascal, 75005 Paris
Tel: 01 45 77 04 04
E-mail: contact@guidesmarcus.com
Web Site: www.guidesmarcus.com
Key Personnel
Mng Dir: Patrick Arfi *E-mail:* patrickarfi@
guidesmarcus.com
Founded: 1963
Subjects: Travel & Tourism
ISBN Prefix(es): 978-2-7131

Librairie Maritime Outremer
Le Yacht, 26 rue Jocob, 75006 Paris
Tel: 01 42 34 96 60
E-mail: librairieoutremer@wanadoo.fr
Web Site: www.librairie-outremer.com
Founded: 1839
Subjects: Maritime, Sports, Athletics
ISBN Prefix(es): 978-2-7070
Bookshop(s): Le Yacht, 55 ave de la Grande
Armee, 75116 Paris *Tel:* 01 45 00 17 99
Fax: 01 45 00 10 02

Editions Maritimes et D'Outremer, *imprint of*
Editions Ouest-France

Marsu Productions
15-27 rue Moussorgski, 75018 Paris
E-mail: marsu@marsuproductions.com
Web Site: www.marsupro.com; www.marsupilami.
com
Founded: 1987
Specialize in comic collector editions with pri-
mary focus on the work of Andre Franquin.
Subjects: Humor
ISBN Prefix(es): 978-2-9502211; 978-2-912536;
978-2-908462

Editions Martelle
3 rue des Vergeaux, 80000 Amiens
Tel: 03 22 71 54 54 *Fax:* 03 22 92 89 33
E-mail: serviceclients@librairiemartelle.com
Web Site: www.librairiemartelle.com
Key Personnel
Publication Dir: Francoise Gaudefroy
E-mail: francoise.gaudefroy@librairiemartelle.
com
Founded: 1990
Subjects: Regional Interests
ISBN Prefix(es): 978-2-87890

Editions de la Martiniere
Subsidiary of La Martiniere Groupe
25, blvd Romain Rolland, 75014 Paris
Tel: 01 41 48 80 00
E-mail: contact@lamartiniere.fr; rights@
lamartiniere.fr
Web Site: www.editionsdelamartiniere.fr
Key Personnel
Chief Executive Officer: Herve de La Martiniere
Sales Dir: Jean-Luc Labourdette
Foreign Rights: Marianne Lassandro
Founded: 1992

Subjects: Art, Cookery, Fashion, History, Litera-
ture, Literary Criticism, Essays, Photography
ISBN Prefix(es): 978-2-7324; 978-2-84675
Number of titles published annually: 70 Print
Total Titles: 400 Print

Marval Editions+
17-19, Rue Visconti, 75006 Paris
Tel: 01 44 41 19 79 *Fax:* 01 43 29 87 11
E-mail: contact@marval.fr
Web Site: www.marval.fr
Founded: 1969
Subjects: Art, History, Literature, Literary Criti-
cism, Essays, Photography
ISBN Prefix(es): 978-2-86234
Total Titles: 180 Print
Parent Company: JNF Productions
Distribution Center: Nord Sud, rue Berthelot
150, 1190 Brussels, Belgium *Tel:* (02) 343
10 13 *Fax:* (02) 343 42 91 *E-mail:* info@
diffusionnord-sud.be
OLF, ZI 3, Corminboeuf, PO Box 1152, 1701
Fribourg, Switzerland *Tel:* (026) 467 51 11
Fax: (026) 467 54 66 *E-mail:* information@olf.
ch *Web Site:* www.olf.ch

Editions du Masque+
Subsidiary of Hachette Livre
17 rue Jacob, 75006 Paris
Tel: 01 44 41 74 00 *Fax:* 01 43 25 30 47; 01 43
26 91 04
Web Site: www.editions-jclattes.fr/le-masque
Key Personnel
Editorial Dir: Laurent Laffont
Foreign Rights: Joan Peguillan-Schlottenmeier
Sales Manager: Philippe Dorey
Founded: 1927
Subjects: Criminology, Mysteries, Suspense
ISBN Prefix(es): 978-2-7024
Number of titles published annually: 40 Print
Total Titles: 600 Print

Charles Massin Editions
10, blvd des Frers Voisin, 92130 Issy-les-
Moulineaux Cedex 9
Tel: 02 41 32 40 91 (orders)
E-mail: info@massin.fr
Web Site: www.massin.fr
Key Personnel
Marketing & Purchases Dir: Florence
Prud'homme *Tel:* 01 41 46 88 69
Head, Sales: Laurence Degirardier *Tel:* 01 41 46
80 88
Founded: 1910
Subjects: Architecture & Interior Design, Art,
House & Home
ISBN Prefix(es): 978-2-7072
Parent Company: Groupe Marie Claire

Editions Matrice
71, rue des Camelias, 91270 Vigneux
Tel: 01 69 42 13 02 *Fax:* 01 69 40 21 57
E-mail: edition.matrice@wanadoo.fr
Web Site: pig.asso.free.fr/Matrice.dir/Matrice.htm
Key Personnel
Dir: Danial David; Jacques Pain; Christine Vander
Borght
Founded: 1984
Subjects: Education, Human Relations, Institu-
tional Pedagogy
ISBN Prefix(es): 978-2-905642
Showroom(s): Casteilla, 10, rue Leon-Foucault,
78180 Montigny le Bretonneux *Tel:* 01 30 14
19 30
Distribution Center: 628, ave du Grain-d'Or,
41350 Vineuil *Tel:* 02 54 55 50 50 *Fax:* 02
54 55 50 55

Editions Michel De Maule+
41 rue de Richelieu, 75001 Paris

Tel: 01 42 97 93 56; 01 42 97 93 48 *Fax:* 01 42
97 94 90
E-mail: studio@micheldemaule.com
Web Site: www.micheldemaule.com
Founded: 1997
Specialize in Latin & Greek publications.
Subjects: History, Law, Literature, Literary Criti-
cism, Essays, Music, Dance, Religion - Other
ISBN Prefix(es): 978-2-87623
Parent Company: Editions Tum
Foreign Rep(s): Gallimard Export (all other ter-
ritories); Gallimard Limitee (Canada); OLF
(Switzerland); SDLC (Belgium, Luxembourg,
Netherlands)
Distribution Center: Sodis, 128 Ave du Marechal
de Lattre de Tassigny, 77400 Lagny-sur-Marne
Tel: 01 60 07 95 32 *Fax:* 01 60 07 86 89
E-mail: portail@sodis.fr *Web Site:* www.sodis.
fr

Maxima Laurent du Mesnil Editeur SA+
8, rue Pasquier, 75008 Paris
Tel: 01 44 39 74 00 *Fax:* 01 45 48 46 88
E-mail: info@maxima.fr
Web Site: www.maxima.fr
Key Personnel
Editor: Stephane Derville
Communications Manager: Laurence Bucher
Founded: 1990
Subjects: Business, Career Development, Eco-
nomics, Finance, Human Relations, Law, Man-
agement, Marketing
ISBN Prefix(es): 978-2-84001; 978-2-81880 (e-
isbn)
Number of titles published annually: 30 Print; 20
E-Book
Total Titles: 400 Print; 250 E-Book; 3 Audio
Distributed by Interforum-Editis

Editions MDI (La Maison des Instituteurs)
30 Pl d'Italie, 75702 Paris
Tel: 01 53 55 26 15; 01 53 55 26 21 *Fax:* 01 45
87 56 54
E-mail: service.clients@mdi-editions.com
Web Site: www.mdi-editions.com
Key Personnel
Publishing Dir: Catherine Lucet
Founded: 1952
Subjects: Education, Geography, Geology, His-
tory, Mathematics, Science (General), French
Language
ISBN Prefix(es): 978-2-223
Parent Company: Editions Nathan
Foreign Rep(s): Au Gai Savoir (Belgium); Inter-
forum Diffusion Internationale (Africa, Alge-
ria, Guyana, Libya, Mauritania, Middle East,
Morocco, The Pacific, Tunisia); Interforum Su-
isse SA (Switzerland); Editions Marie-France
(Canada); Editions MDI Export (all other terri-
tories)

Medecine Sciences, *imprint of* Editions Lavoisier

Editions Medianes+
72 rue d'Amiens, 76000 Rouen
Tel: 02 35 88 85 71; 02 35 98 06 82 *Fax:* 02 35
15 28 44
E-mail: medianesconseil@wanadoo.fr
Key Personnel
Dir: Christian de Chanteloup
Founded: 1989
Membership(s): Syndicat National de l'Edition
(SNE).
Subjects: Art, Biography, Memoirs, Drama, The-
ater, History, Literature, Literary Criticism, Es-
says, Photography, Regional Interests
ISBN Prefix(es): 978-2-908345

Editions Mediaspaul+
48 rue du Four, 75006 Paris
Tel: 01 45 48 21 31 *Fax:* 01 42 22 47 46

E-mail: editeur@mediaspaul.fr; presse@
mediaspaul.fr; production.mediaspaul@
mediaspaul.fr
Web Site: mediaspaul.fr
Key Personnel
Deputy Dir General: Dominique le Blon
E-mail: dominique.leblon@mediaspaul.fr
General Manager: Ignace Cau *E-mail:* ignace.
cau@mediaspaul.fr
Editorial Dir: Gilles Collicelli
Deputy Editorial Dir: Bertrand Revillion
E-mail: bertrand.revillion@mediaspaul.fr
Production Manager: Michael Leone
Press: Helene Rousselot Daigremont
Founded: 1981
Subjects: Biblical Studies, Religion - Catholic,
Theology
ISBN Prefix(es): 978-2-7122
Bookshop(s): 16 rue de la Visitation, 71600 Paray
Le Monial *Tel:* 03 85 81 08 93 *Fax:* 03 85 81
08 93 *E-mail:* librairiesaintpaul.paray@orange.
fr
Warehouse: 62 rue de Chanteloup, St Germain les
Arpajon, BP 26, 91291 Arpajon Cedex *Tel:* 01
64 90 76 77; 01 64 90 87 40 *Fax:* 01 64 90 96
09 *E-mail:* distribution@mediaspaul.fr
Distribution Center: Sodis, 128 Ave du Mal de
Lattre de Tassigny, 77400 Lagny-Sur-Marne
Tel: 01 60 07 82 89 *Fax:* 01 64 30 32 37 *Web
Site:* www.sodis.fr
3965 blvd Henri-Bourassa Est, Montreal, QC
H1H 1L1, Canada *Tel:* 514-322-7341 *Fax:* 514-
322-4281 *E-mail:* sylvie.rheault@mediaspaul.ca

Editions Medicis
19 rue St Severin Medici, 75005 Paris
Tel: 01 43 36 41 05
Web Site: www.dervy-medicis.fr
Key Personnel
Publishing Dir: Guy Tredaniel
Press: Isabelle Laurand *Tel:* 01 43 36 73 62
E-mail: isabelle.laurand@dervy.fr
Subjects: Astrology, Occult, Psychology, Psy-
chiatry, Bach Flowers, Feng Shui, Reiki, Self-
Medicine, Yi King Chakras
ISBN Prefix(es): 978-2-85327
Number of titles published annually: 12 Print
Total Titles: 213 Print
Parent Company: Groupe Guy Tredaniel
Foreign Rep(s): Nord-Sud (Benelux); Prologue
(Canada); Transat-Servidis (Switzerland)
Warehouse: Dilisco, Rue du Limousin, BP 25,
23220 Cheniers *Tel:* 05 55 51 80 00 *Fax:* 05
55 62 17 39

Editions MeMo+
5 Passage Douard, 44000 Nantes
Tel: 02 40 47 98 19
E-mail: editionsmemo@editionsmemo.fr
Web Site: www.editions-memo.fr
Key Personnel
Founder: Yves Mestrallet; Mdme Christine
Morault
Founded: 1993
Subjects: Art, Geography, Geology, History, Liter-
ature, Literary Criticism, Essays
ISBN Prefix(es): 978-2-910391
Foreign Rights: Hannele & Associates
Distribution Center: Harmonia Mundi Mas de
vert, BP 150, 13631 Arles Cedex *Tel:* 04 90 49
90 49 *Fax:* 04 90 49 96 14
Garzon Diffusion Internationale, 10, rue de la
Maison Blanche, 75013 Paris *Tel:* 01 45 82 01
14 *E-mail:* emonsallier@garzondi.com
Zoe Diffusion, 11, rue des Moraines, 1221
Carouge-Geneva, Switzerland *Tel:* (022) 309
36 00 *Fax:* (022) 309 36 03

Editions Memoire des Arts+
BP 4553, 69244 Lyon Cedex 04
Tel: 04 74 01 05 45; 09 64 43 02 38 *Fax:* 04 72
19 48 74

E-mail: contact@memoire-des-arts.com
Web Site: www.memoire-des-arts.com
Key Personnel
General Dir: Alain Vollerin *E-mail:* alain.
vollerin@wanadoo.fr
Founded: 1986
Subjects: Art
ISBN Prefix(es): 978-2-912544

Editions Menges+
6, rue du Mail, 75002 Paris
Tel: 01 44 55 37 50 *Fax:* 01 40 20 99 74
E-mail: info@editions-menges.com
Web Site: www.editions-menges.com; www.
victoires.com
Key Personnel
Chairman: Carl Van Eiszner
Chief Editor: Isabelle de Tinguy
Production Editor: Mathilde Decorbez
Subjects: Architecture & Interior Design, Art,
Astrology, Occult, Biography, Memoirs, Cook-
ery, Film, Video, Gardening, Plants, Health,
Nutrition, History, Inspirational, Spirituality,
Medicine, Nursing, Dentistry, Music, Dance,
Philosophy, Photography, Psychology, Psychia-
try, Sports, Athletics, Nature
ISBN Prefix(es): 978-2-85620
Foreign Rep(s): Afrique Culture (Tunisia);
Agence du Livre (ADL) (Canada); Interforum
Benelux (Benelux); Interforum Suisse (Switzer-
land)
Distribution Center: Interforum, Paryseine Bldg,
3, allee de la Seine, 94854 Ivry-sur-Seine
Cedex *Tel:* 01 49 59 10 10 *Fax:* 01 49 59 10
72 (France, Algeria & Morocco)

Mercure de France SA
Subsidiary of Editions Gallimard
26, rue de Conde, 75006 Paris
Tel: 01 55 42 61 90
E-mail: mercure@mercure.fr
Web Site: www.mercuredefrance.fr
Key Personnel
Chief Executive Officer: Isabelle Gallimard
Foreign Rights: Genevieve Lebrun-Taugourdeau
Tel: 01 55 42 61 95 *E-mail:* genevieve.lebrun-
taugourdeau@mercure.fr
Founded: 1825
Subjects: Astrology, Occult, Biography, Memoirs,
Fiction, History, Literature, Literary Criticism,
Essays, Philosophy, Poetry
ISBN Prefix(es): 978-2-7152
Associate Companies: Editions Denoel Sarl
Distribution Center: CDE, 17, rue de Tournon,
75006 Paris
Sodis, 128 Ave du Marechel de Lattre de Tas-
signy, 77403 Lagny-sur-Marne Cedex

Editions Metailie+
20 rue des Grands Augustins, 75006 Paris
Tel: 01 56 81 02 45
E-mail: presse@metailie.fr; secretariat@metailie.
fr
Web Site: www.editions-metailie.fr
Key Personnel
Mng Dir & Editor: Anne Marie Metailie
Communications & Press: Julia Polack-de Chau-
mont *Tel:* 01 56 81 02 46 *E-mail:* julia.
polack@metailie.fr
Rights: Catherine de Leobardy *Tel:* 01 56 81 02
51
Founded: 1979
Subjects: Anthropology, Fiction, Literature, Lit-
erary Criticism, Essays, Mysteries, Suspense,
Social Sciences, Sociology
ISBN Prefix(es): 978-2-86424
Number of titles published annually: 34 Print
Total Titles: 700 Print
Distribution Center: Volumen *Tel:* 01 69 10 89
09 *Fax:* 01 64 48 49 63

Les Editions Albin Michel+
22 rue Huyghens, 75014 Paris
Tel: 01 42 79 10 00 *Fax:* 01 43 27 21 58
Web Site: www.albin-michel.fr
Key Personnel
President: Francis Esmenard
Vice President: Guillaume Dervieux
Secretary General: Agnes Fruman *Tel:* 01 42 79
10 60
Dir, Communications & Press: Florence Godfer-
naux *Tel:* 01 42 79 10 12
Administrative & Finance Dir: Guy Maucollot
Tel: 01 42 79 46 09
License Dir: Lise Boell *Tel:* 01 42 79 19 01
Foreign Rights Manager: Solene Chabanais
Tel: 01 42 79 10 79
Founded: 1900
Membership(s): Bureau International de l'Edition
Francaise (BIEF).
Subjects: Art, Biography, Memoirs, Child Care
& Development, Cookery, Fiction, History,
How-to, Humor, Literature, Literary Criticism,
Essays, Music, Dance, Nonfiction (General),
Philosophy, Religion - Other, Social Sciences,
Sociology
ISBN Prefix(es): 978-2-226

Editions Yves Michel
5, Allee du Torrent, 05000 Gap
Tel: 04 92 65 52 24
E-mail: contact@yvesmichel.org; presse@
yvesmichel.org
Web Site: www.yvesmichel.org
Key Personnel
President & Editor: Yves Michel *E-mail:* ym@
yvesmichel.org
Subjects: Economics, Health, Nutrition, Ecology
ISBN Prefix(es): 978-2-913492
Foreign Rep(s): Nord-Sud (Belgium); Servidis
(Switzerland); Transat (Switzerland)
Distribution Center: Dilisco, Rue du Limousin,
23220 Chenniers *Tel:* 05 55 51 80 00 *Fax:* 05
55 62 17 39 *E-mail:* relation.client@dilisco.fr
Web Site: www.dilisco-diffusion-distribution.fr

Michelin
27, cours de l'ile Seguin, 92100 Boulogne Billan-
court
Tel: 01 55 19 57 00
Web Site: www.viamichelin.com
Key Personnel
Publication Manager: Mr Alain Cuq
Founded: 1900
Subjects: Travel & Tourism, Home & Leisure
ISBN Prefix(es): 978-2-06
Associate Companies: Michelin Reifenwerke,
Austria; S A Belge du Pneumatique Michelin,
Belgium; Ste Canadienne des Pneus Miche-
lin, Canada; Michelin Reifenwerke, Germany;
Elastika Michelin, Greece; Michelin Asia Ltd,
Hong Kong; S P A Michelin Italiana, Italy; Ni-
hon Michelin Tire KK, Japan; Michelin Com-
panhia Luso - Pneu Lda, Portugal; Michelin
Asia Co PTE Ltd, Singapore; SAFE de Neu-
maticos Michelin, Spain; SA des Pneumatiques
Michelin, Switzerland; Michelin Tyre PLC,
United Kingdom; Michelin Travel Publications,
United States

Microsoft Press, *imprint of* Dunod Editeur

Microsoft Press
Imprint of Dunod Editeur
5 rue Laromiguiere, 75005 Paris
Tel: 01 40 46 35 00 *Fax:* 01 40 46 49 95
E-mail: infos@dunod.com
Web Site: www.dunod.com
Founded: 1992
Subjects: Computer Science
ISBN Prefix(es): 978-2-84082
Ultimate Parent Company: Hachette Livre

Mila Editions
2 ter, rue des Chantiers, 75005 Paris
Tel: 01 46 34 77 70 *Fax:* 01 43 25 34 67
E-mail: info@mila-editions.fr
Web Site: www.mila-editions.fr
Key Personnel
Founder: Mila Boutan
Contact: Benoit Rouillard
Founded: 1984
ISBN Prefix(es): 978-2-84006
Foreign Rep(s): Agence du Livre (Canada); Servidis (Switzerland)
Distribution Center: Dilisco, Rue du Limousin, BP 25, 23220 Cheniers (France & Belgium)

Milady, *imprint of* Editions Bragelonne

Milady
Imprint of Editions Bragelonne
60-62 rue d'Hauteville, 75010 Paris
E-mail: info@milady.fr
Web Site: www.milady.fr
Key Personnel
Publication Dir: Alain Nevant
Subjects: Romance, Science Fiction, Fantasy, Horror, Paranormal Romance
ISBN Prefix(es): 978-2-8112
Foreign Rep(s): La Boite de Diffusion (Canada); Dargaude Suisse (Switzerland); Media Diffusion (Belgium, France)

Editions Milan
300, rue Leon Joulin, 31101 Toulouse Cedex 9
Tel: 05 61 76 64 64
Web Site: www.editionsmilan.com
Key Personnel
President: Franck Girard
Sales Management: Louis-Pascal Deforges
International Rights & Co-editions Sales: Sybille Le Maire
Subjects: Regional Interests, Travel & Tourism
ISBN Prefix(es): 978-2-7459; 978-2-84113; 978-2-86726
Number of titles published annually: 350 Print
Total Titles: 2,700 Print
Parent Company: Groupe Bayard

Editions Mille et Une Nuits+
Subsidiary of Editions Fayard
13, rue du Montparnasse, 75006 Paris Cedex 06
Tel: 01 45 49 82 00
Web Site: www.fayard.fr
Key Personnel
President: Sophie de Closets
International Rights Dir: Carole Saudejaud
    Fax: 01 45 49 82 54 *E-mail:* csaudejaud@editions-fayard.fr
Founded: 1993
Subjects: Literature, Literary Criticism, Essays
ISBN Prefix(es): 978-2-84205; 978-2-910233; 978-2-7555

Les Editions de Minuit SA+
7, rue Bernard-Palissy, 75006 Paris
Tel: 01 44 39 39 20 *Fax:* 01 44 39 39 23
E-mail: contact@leseditionsdeminuit.fr; commercial@leseditionsdeminuit.fr; presse@leseditionsdeminuit.fr
Web Site: www.leseditionsdeminuit.fr
Key Personnel
President & Dir General: Irene Lindon
Founded: 1942
Subjects: Fiction, Literature, Literary Criticism, Essays, Philosophy, Social Sciences, Sociology
ISBN Prefix(es): 978-2-7073
Number of titles published annually: 20 Print
Total Titles: 600 Print
Distributed by La Cite - L'Age d'Homme (Switzerland); Dimedia Inc (Canada)
Foreign Rights: Georges Borchardt Inc (North America)

Bookshop(s): Compagnie, 58 rue des Ecoles, 75005 Paris
Orders to: Le Seuil/Volumen, 27 rue Jacob, 75006 Paris *Tel:* 01 43 54 74 86

Editions du Moniteur+
Case 61, 17, rue d'Uzes, 75108 Paris Cedex 02
Tel: 01 40 13 30 30; 01 40 13 50 65; 01 40 13 37 52 *Fax:* 01 40 13 51 21; 01 40 13 51 77
E-mail: contact@groupemoniteur.fr; abonnerment@groupemoniteur.fr
Web Site: www.editionsdumoniteur.com
Key Personnel
President & Dir, Publications: Christophe Czajka
Founded: 1981
Subjects: Architecture & Interior Design, Environmental Studies, Law, Real Estate, Technology, Construction/Building
ISBN Prefix(es): 978-2-281; 978-2-7327; 978-2-902302; 978-2-86282
Number of titles published annually: 50 Print; 1 CD-ROM
Total Titles: 250 Print; 10 CD-ROM; 15 Online
Foreign Rep(s): Diffulivre SA (Switzerland); Dilibel (Belgium, Luxembourg); Hachette Livre International (all other territories); Somabec (Canada)
Bookshop(s): 7 pl de l'Odeon, 75006 Paris
Distribution Center: Hachette Livre, One ave Gutenberg, 78316 Maurepas *Toll Free Tel:* 01 30 66 23 45 *Fax:* 01 39 26 47 02 *Web Site:* www.hachette-diffusion.fr

Montchrestien, *imprint of* Lextenso Editions

Editions Le Mot et le Reste
BP 34, 13244 Marseille Cedex 01
Tel: 09 75 28 42 27 *Fax:* 09 75 28 42 27
E-mail: ed.mr@wanadoo.fr
Web Site: lemotetlereste.com
Key Personnel
Dir: Yves Jolivet
Press Relations: Pierre Suchaud
Founded: 1996
Subjects: Music, Dance, Aesthetics, Counterculture
ISBN Prefix(es): 978-2-36054; 978-2-915378
Distribution Center: Harmonia Mundi, Mas de vert, BP 150, 13631 Arles *Tel:* 04 90 49 58 05 *Fax:* 04 90 49 58 35 *E-mail:* adv-livre@harmoniamundi.com

Muller Edition+
3, rue de l'Arrivee, 75015 Paris
Web Site: www.muller-edition.com
Key Personnel
Contact: Guillaume de Thieulloy
Founded: 1990
Subjects: Archaeology, Economics, Government, Political Science, History, How-to, Literature, Literary Criticism, Essays, Military Science, Social Sciences, Sociology
ISBN Prefix(es): 978-2-904255
Total Titles: 1,000 Print; 600 E-Book
Distributed by Editions Picard
Distributor for Editions Domens; Ecrivains Societe des Ecrivains; Editions Grancher; Editions L' Harmattan; Editions Charles Lavauzelle; Martelle; Editions Ouest-France; Editions Publisud

Musee du Louvre Editions
Direction de la Production Culturelle, 75058 Paris Cedex 01
Tel: 01 40 20 84 80; 01 40 20 53 53 (bookshop)
E-mail: client.louvre@rmn.fr (orders)
Web Site: editions.louvre.fr
Key Personnel
Publications Dir: Violaine Bouvet-Lanselle
Founded: 1992
Subjects: Art, Art Collections

ISBN Prefix(es): 978-2-35031; 978-2-901785
Total Titles: 700 Print
Distributed by Academie des Inscriptions et Belles-Lettres (AIBL); Actes Sud; Actes Sud Junior; Artlys; Editions Les Arts Decoratifs; L'atelier du Poisson Soluble; Editions Le Baron Perche; Les Editions Beaux-Arts de Paris; Beaux Arts Editions; Christian Bourgois; Editions Casterman; Centre Pompidou; Chandeigne; Nicholas Chaudun Editions; Bernard Chauveau Editeur; Citadells et Mazenod; Editions du Comitedes Travaux Historiques et Scientifiques (CTHS); Connaissance des Arts; Editions Dilecta; La Documentation Francaise; Fage Editions; Fayard; 5 Continents Editions; Editions First; Fonds Mercator; Flammarion; Futuropolis; Gallimard; Gourcuff Gradenigo/Papier & Co; Editions du Gram; Hachette Jeunesse; Editions Monelle Hayot; Hatier; Hazan; Institut Fransais de Recherche en Iran; Editions du Jasmin; Editions Kheops; Klincksieck; Editions Thierry Magnier; Editions de la Martiniere; Editions Marval; Mer Paper Kunsthalle; Mondadori Electa SpA; Moneta; Norma; Oxbow Books; Officina Libraria; Editions du Patrimoine; Palette; Editions Parigramme; Paris Musees; Editions Le Passage; Peeters Publishers; Editions Picard; Place des Victoires; Presses de l'Universite de Paris-Sorbonne (PUPS); Prestel Verlag; Editions du Regard; Reunion des Musees Nationaux; Rmn-Grand Palais; Le Seuil; Schirmer/Mosel; Skira; Snoeck Editions; Somogy; Steidl; Thames & Hudson; Editions 365; Librairie Vrin

Editions du Musee Rodin
19, Blvd des Invalides, 75007 Paris
Tel: 01 44 18 61 10; 01 44 18 61 24 *Fax:* 01 44 18 65 65
E-mail: servcom@musee-rodin.fr
Web Site: www.musee-rodin.fr
Key Personnel
Dir: Dominique Vieville
Head, Editorial: Edwige Ridel *E-mail:* ridel@musee-rodin.fr
Subjects: Antiques, Art, Photography, Sculptures
ISBN Prefix(es): 978-2-901428

Editions de la Reunion des Musees Nationaux-Grand Palais+
254/256 rue de Bercy, 75577 Paris Cedex 12
Tel: 01 40 13 48 00 *Fax:* 01 40 13 44 00
E-mail: editions@rmn.fr
Web Site: www.rmn.fr
Key Personnel
Publishing Dir: Valerie Vesque-Jeancard
Founded: 1931
Subjects: Antiques, Archaeology, Architecture & Interior Design, Art, Ethnicity, History
ISBN Prefix(es): 978-2-7118
Distributed by Editions du Seuie
Bookshop(s): Musee du Louvre, 75001 Paris *Tel:* 01 40 20 68 84 *Fax:* 01 40 20 53 53; Librairie du Musee d'Orsay, 60, rue de Lille, 75343 Paris
Warehouse: Centre de Distribution de la RMN, 1-31, allee du 12 fevrier 1934, 77186 Noisiel

Editions Maurice Nadeau-Les Lettres Nouvelles+
145 rue Raymond Losserand, 75014 Paris
Tel: 01 46 34 30 42
E-mail: editions.mauricenadeau@orange.fr
Web Site: www.quinzaine-litteraire.presse.fr
Key Personnel
Contact: Gilles Nadeau *E-mail:* gilles.nadeau@orange.fr
Founded: 1966
Subjects: Literature, Literary Criticism, Essays
ISBN Prefix(es): 978-2-86231
Parent Company: Societe D'Editions Litteraires et Scientifiques (SELIS)
Orders to: Harmonia Mundi, 13200 Arles

Nanga Editions
56 bis rue de Locqueran, 29780 Plouhinec
Mailing Address: BP 10048, 29770 Audierne
Tel: 06 11 19 47 53
Web Site: www.revuenanga.com
Key Personnel
Editor: Jerome Feugereux
Founded: 1991
Subjects: Art, Earth Sciences, Literature, Literary Criticism, Essays, Poetry
ISBN Prefix(es): 978-2-909152
Number of titles published annually: 4 Print; 2 E-Book
Total Titles: 20 Print; 3 E-Book

Les Editions Nathan
25 ave Pierre de Coubertin, 75211 Paris Cedex 13
Tel: 01 53 55 26 62 *Fax:* 01 45 87 53 43
E-mail: export@nathan.fr
Web Site: www.nathan.fr
Key Personnel
President: Catherine Lucet
Rights & Permissions: Marie Dessaix
  Tel: 01 45 87 50 00 *Fax:* 01 45 87 57 80
  E-mail: mdessaix@nathan.fr
Communications: Fabienne Rubert *Tel:* 01 45 87 53 64 *Fax:* 01 45 87 57 84 *E-mail:* frubert@nathan.fr
Founded: 1881
Specialize in children's books & pedagogy.
Subjects: Child Care & Development, Education, History, Philosophy, Psychology, Psychiatry, Science (General), Social Sciences, Sociology
ISBN Prefix(es): 978-2-09
Parent Company: Editis
Subsidiaries: CLE; Retz; Le Robert

NEL, *imprint of* Nouvelles Editions Latines

NiL Editions+
Editions Robert Laffont, 30, place d'Italie, 75627 Paris Cedex 13
Tel: 01 53 67 14 00
E-mail: web@robert-laffont.fr
Web Site: www.nil-editions.fr
Key Personnel
President-Dir General: Cecile Boyer-Runge
Dir: Guillaume Allary
Foreign Rights: Benita Edzard *E-mail:* bedzard@robert-laffont.fr; Judith Temmam
  E-mail: jtemmam@robert-laffont.fr
Founded: 1993
Subjects: Biography, Memoirs, Fiction, Human Relations, Inspirational, Spirituality, Literature, Literary Criticism, Essays, Mysteries, Suspense, Nonfiction (General), Philosophy, Pop Culture
ISBN Prefix(es): 978-2-84111
Parent Company: Groupe Robert Laffont
Branch Office(s)
Robert Laffont Canada, 955 Amherst, Montreal, QC, Canada *Tel:* 514-282-1012

Librairie de Nobele
35, rue Bonaparte, 75006 Paris
Tel: 01 43 26 08 62 *Fax:* 01 40 46 85 96
E-mail: librairie.f.de.nobele@wanadoo.fr
Web Site: www.denobele.fr; librairiedenobele.blogspot.com
Key Personnel
President: Francoise de Nobele-Smilenko
Founded: 1920
Subjects: Art
ISBN Prefix(es): 978-2-85189

Les Editions Noir sur Blanc+
Imprint of Libella Publishing Group
7, rue des Canettes, 75006 Paris
Tel: 01 44 32 05 60 *Fax:* 01 44 32 05 61
E-mail: informations@libella.fr; foreignrights@libellagroup.com

Web Site: www.leseditionsnoirsurblanc.fr; www.libella.fr
Key Personnel
Chief Executive Officer: Vera Michalski
Dir General: Michel Boutinard-Rouelle
Foreign Rights: Christine Legrand
  E-mail: christine.legrand@libella.fr
Founded: 1987
Subjects: Biography, Memoirs, Cookery, Drama, Theater, Fiction, History, Humor, Literature, Literary Criticism, Essays, Poetry, Travel & Tourism
ISBN Prefix(es): 978-2-88250
Number of titles published annually: 10 Print
Total Titles: 170 Print
Branch Office(s)
18 ave de la Gare, 1003 Lausanne, Switzerland
  Tel: (021) 614 77 44 *Fax:* (021) 614 77 40
Foreign Rep(s): Servidis (Switzerland); Socadis (Canada)
Distribution Center: Sodis, 128 Ave du Marechal de Lattre de Tassigny, 77400 Lagny-sur-Marne

Editions Non Lieu
224, rue des Pyrenees, 75020 Paris
Tel: 01 40 29 04 80
E-mail: edsnonlieu@yahoo.fr
Web Site: www.editionsnonlieu.fr
Founded: 2005
Subjects: Drama, Theater, Fiction, Medicine, Nursing, Dentistry, Poetry, Social Sciences, Sociology, Alternative Medicine, Humanities
ISBN Prefix(es): 978-2-35270
Total Titles: 130 Print

Editions Norma+
3 rue Milton, 75009 Paris
Tel: 01 45 48 70 96 *Fax:* 01 45 48 05 84
E-mail: editionsnorma@wanadoo.fr
Web Site: www.editions-norma.com
Key Personnel
Manager: Maite Hudry
Founded: 1991
Subjects: Architecture & Interior Design, Art, Drama, Theater, Foreign Countries, History, House & Home, Literature, Literary Criticism, Essays, Regional Interests, 20th Century Decorative Arts
ISBN Prefix(es): 978-2-909283; 978-2-915542
Number of titles published annually: 10 Print
Total Titles: 120 Print
Distribution Center: Vilo, 91 bis, rue du Cherche-Midi, 75006 Paris *Web Site:* www.vilo-groupe.com

Editions Mare Nostrum
One rue des Varietes, 66000 Perpignan
Tel: 04 68 51 17 50 *Fax:* 04 68 51 17 50
E-mail: marenostrum@orange.fr
Web Site: www.marenostrumedition.com
Key Personnel
Manager: Philippe Salus
Founded: 1990
Subjects: Fiction, History, Literature, Literary Criticism, Essays, Mysteries, Suspense, Philosophy, Poetry, Religion - Jewish
ISBN Prefix(es): 978-2-908476
Distribution Center: Soleils Diffusion, 23, rue de Fleurus, 75006 Paris *Tel:* 01 45 48 84 62 *Web Site:* www.soleils-diffusion.com
Le Comptoir du Livre, 10 bis blvd de l'Europe, 31120 Portet-sur-Garonne *Tel:* 05 62 11 73 33 *Web Site:* www.comptoirdulivre.fr
Nordest Llibres, C/Alemanya, 19, 17600 Figueres, Spain *Tel:* 972 67 23 54 *Fax:* 972 50 36 29

Nous
4 chemin de Fleury, 14000 Caen
Tel: 02 31 72 66 21
E-mail: nous@editions-nous.com
Web Site: www.editions-nous.com

Key Personnel
Editorial, Foreign Rights Manager: Patrizia Atzei
  Tel: 06 63 55 33 05
Subjects: Government, Political Science, Philosophy, Photography, Poetry
ISBN Prefix(es): 978-2-913549
Total Titles: 70 Print

Nouveau Monde Editions
44 quai Henri IV, 75004 Paris
Tel: 01 43 54 67 43 *Fax:* 01 43 54 03 60
E-mail: info@nouveau-monde.net
Web Site: www.nouveau-monde.net
Key Personnel
Press: Frederic Durand *Tel:* 01 46 34 42 32
  E-mail: fdurand@nouveau-monde.net
Founded: 2000
Subjects: History, Culture, Humanities
ISBN Prefix(es): 978-2-84736

Le Nouvel Attila
127 ave Parmentier, 75011 Paris
E-mail: contact@lenouvelattila.fr; attila@lenouvelattila.fr
Web Site: www.lenouvelattila.fr
Key Personnel
Owner: Benoit Virot
Press & Communications: Elsa Pierrot
  E-mail: elsa@lenouvelattila.fr
Founded: 2013
Subjects: Fiction
ISBN Prefix(es): 978-2-917084; 978-2-37100
Distributed by Editions Anne Carriere
Foreign Rights: Mon Agent et Cie (Nickie Athanassi & Emmanuel Bonnet)

Editions Nouvelle Cite+
Domaine d'Arny, 91680 Bruyeres-le-Chatel
Tel: 01 69 17 10 06 *Fax:* 01 69 17 13 04
E-mail: commercial@nouvellecite.fr; rights@nouvellecite.fr
Web Site: www.nouvellecite.fr
Key Personnel
Assistant Editor: Emilie Tevane *E-mail:* emilie.tevane@nouvellecite.fr
Founded: 1957
Subjects: Biography, Memoirs, Education, Inspirational, Spirituality, Religion - Other
ISBN Prefix(es): 978-2-85313

Nouvelles Editions Latines+
rue Moulin Vieux, 60590 Le Vaumain
Tel: 01 43 54 77 42 *Fax:* 01 43 29 69 81
E-mail: info@editions-nel.com
Web Site: www.editions-nel.com
Founded: 1928
Subjects: Aeronautics, Aviation, Art, Drama, Theater, Fiction, History, Inspirational, Spirituality, Poetry, Religion - Other, Science (General), Travel & Tourism
ISBN Prefix(es): 978-2-7233
Imprints: NEL
Bookshop(s): 6 rue de Vaugirard, 75006 Paris
  Fax: 29 69 81 01 43

Nouvelles Editions Loubatieres+
10 bis blvd de l'Europe, 31122 Portet-sur-Garonne
Mailing Address: BP 50014, 31122 Portet-sur-Garonne Cedex
Tel: 05 61 72 83 53; 05 61 98 94 10 *Fax:* 05 61 72 83 50
E-mail: contact@loubatieres.fr
Web Site: www.loubatieres.fr
Key Personnel
Dir: Maxence Fabiani *Tel:* 05 61 72 83 52
  E-mail: maxence.fabiani@loubatieres.fr
Administration & Communication: Maryline Garrabos *E-mail:* line.garrabos@loubatieres.fr
Founded: 1970

Subjects: Art, Geography, Geology, History, Regional Interests, Travel & Tourism
ISBN Prefix(es): 978-2-7165
Distribution Center: Union Distribution, 106 rue Petit Leroy, 94550 Chevilly-Larue

Editions La Nuee Bleue
3, rue St Pierre le Jeune, 67000 Strasbourg
Tel: 03 88 15 77 27 *Fax:* 03 88 75 16 21
E-mail: dnanueebleue@dna.fr
Web Site: www.nueebleue.com
Founded: 1920
Subjects: Cookery, History, Literature, Literary Criticism, Essays, Travel & Tourism, Lifestyle, Nature
ISBN Prefix(es): 978-2-7165
Parent Company: Editions des Dernieres Nouvelles d'Alsace

Oblong, *imprint of* Editions Jacques Gabay

Editions de l'Observatoire
170 bis rue du Montparnasse, 75014 Paris
Tel: 01 55 42 72 56
E-mail: contact@editions-observatoire.com
Web Site: editions-observatoire.com
Subjects: Biography, Memoirs, Fiction, Mysteries, Suspense, Romance
ISBN Prefix(es): 979-10-329
Distribution Center: Union Distribution, 106 rue Petit Leroy, 94550 Chevilly-Larue
Tel: 01 41 80 20 20 *Fax:* 01 41 80 20 75
E-mail: commandesclients@union-distribution. fr *Web Site:* ud.centprod.com

Editions Obsidiane+
18 chemin du camp gaulois, Chateau, 89500 Bussy-le-Repos
Tel: 03 86 96 52 18 *Fax:* 03 86 87 01 12
Web Site: perso.numericable.com/editions-obsidiane
Key Personnel
Founder & Manager: Francois Boddaert
E-mail: f.boddaert@orange.fr
Founded: 1978
Subjects: Literature, Literary Criticism, Essays, Poetry
ISBN Prefix(es): 978-2-904469; 978-2-911914; 978-2-916447
Number of titles published annually: 10 Print
Total Titles: 220 Print
Distributed by Les Belles-Lettres
Distribution Center: Farandole Diffusion (Belgium)

OECD Publishing+
2, rue Andre Pascal, 75775 Paris Cedex 16
Tel: 01 45 24 82 00 *Fax:* 01 45 24 85 00
E-mail: sales@oecd.org; rights@oecd.org
Web Site: www.oecd.org/publishing
Key Personnel
Head, Publishing: Toby Green *E-mail:* toby. green@oecd.org
Deputy Head, Publishing & Head, Editorial: Catherine Candea *E-mail:* catherine.candea@ oecd.org
Head, Marketing: Francois Barnaud
E-mail: francois.barnaud@oecd.org
Head, Production: Marion Desmartin
E-mail: marion.desmartin@oecd.org
Founded: 1960
OECD is the forum where the governments of 30 democracies work together to address the economic, social & environmental challenges of our times. OECD Publishing disseminates the results of the Organization's statistics gathering & research on economic, social & environmental issues, as well as the conventions, guidelines & standards agreed by its members.
Subjects: Agriculture, Business, Child Care & Development, Communications, Developing

Countries, Economics, Education, Energy, Environmental Studies, Government, Political Science, Labor, Industrial Relations, Management, Public Administration, Science (General), Social Sciences, Sociology, Technology, Transportation
ISBN Prefix(es): 978-92-64; 978-92-821
Number of titles published annually: 250 Print; 12 CD-ROM; 250 Online; 250 E-Book
Total Titles: 12 CD-ROM; 250 Online; 250 E-Book
Branch Office(s)
OECD Berlin Centre, Schumannstr 10, 10117 Berlin, Germany *Tel:* (030) 2888 353
Fax: (030) 2888 3545 *E-mail:* berlin.centre@ oecd.org *Web Site:* www.oecd.org/berlin
OECD Tokyo Centre, Nippon Press Center Bldg, 3rd floor, 2-2-1, Uchisaiwaicho, Chiyoda-ku, Tokyo 100-0011, Japan *Tel:* (03) 5532 0021
Fax: (03) 5532 0035 *E-mail:* tokyo.contact@ oecd.org *Web Site:* www.oecd.org/tokyo
OECD Mexico Centre, Av Presidente Mazaryk 526, Piso 1, Colonia Polanco, 11560 Mexico, DF, Mexico, Dir: Eugenia Garduno
Tel: (0155) 91386230 *Fax:* (0155) 91387096
E-mail: mexico.contact@oecd.org *Web Site:* www.oecd.org/centrodemexico
U.S. Office(s): OECD Washington Center, 1776 "I" St NW, Suite 450, Washington, DC 20006, United States, Head: Carol Guthrie
Tel: 202-785-6323 *Fax:* 202-315-2508
E-mail: washington.contact@oecd.org *Web Site:* www.oecd.org/washington
Distributor for European Conference of Ministers of Transport; International Energy Agency; Nuclear Energy Agency
Foreign Rep(s): Access Dunia Sdn Bhd (Malaysia); Accucoms (Argentina, Chile, Paraguay, Uruguay); Akademika AS (Norway); Akme Archive Sp zo o (Poland); Albertina icome Bratislava sro (Slovakia); Albertina icome Praha sro (Czechia); ANACO (Greece); Ars Polona (Poland); Balani Intech (India); Bernan Associates (USA); Book Promotion & Service Ltd (Thailand); Booknet Co Ltd (Thailand); Books Around the Corner Lda (Portugal); Bookwell (India); CADOC (Algeria); Charlesworth China (China); Dandy Booksellers (UK); Databeuro Ltd (Ireland, UK); DEA Mediagroup SpA (Italy); Diyar Publishers-Qeshm (Iran); La Documentation Francaise (France); Dynapresse Marketing SA (Switzerland); EBSCO Korea (Korea); Euro Info Service (Hungary); Far Eastern Booksellers Import Division (Japan); Federal Publications Inc (Canada); Greendata (Spain); GV Zalozba doo (Slovenia); iGroup (Asia Pacific) Ltd (Indonesia, Philippines, Vietnam); iGroup Taiwan (China); IMC Services (United Arab Emirates); Infile (Spain); Info Access & Distribution (HK) Ltd (Hong Kong); Infoenlace Ltda (Colombia); Infoenlace Peru SAC (Peru); Info-Host Pte Ltd (Singapore); Informa Management (Romania); Informacion Cientifica Internacional (Mexico); International Tax Institute (Canada, USA); JSC MK-Periodica (Russia); Kinokuniya Co Ltd (Japan); KONEK Ltd (Russia); Jean De Lannoy (Belgium, Luxembourg); Latin Knowledge Consulting Group LLC (Aruba, Barbados, Puerto Rico, Trinidad and Tobago, Venezuela); Legislation Direct (New Zealand); Les Editions La Liberte Inc (Canada); Librotrade Kft (Hungary); Marka Lda (Portugal); Maruzen Co Ltd (Japan); MegaTEXTS Phil (Philippines); MERIC-Middle East Readers' Information Center (Egypt); Miller Distributors Ltd (Malta); Osiris Libros y Revistas SL (Spain); Librairie Payot SA (Switzerland); Planetis (Switzerland); PrioInfo AB (Sweden); Prior & Books (Romania); Les Publications Gouvernementales (Canada); Renouf Publishing Co Ltd (Canada, USA); Roodveldt Import BV (Netherlands); Rosendahls - Schultz Grafisk A/S (Denmark); Libreria Commissionaria Sansoni (Italy); Slo-

vart GTG sro (Slovakia); The Stationery Office (UK); STM Info (Turkey); Suomalainen Kirjakauppa Oy (Finland); Swindon Book Co Ltd (Hong Kong); Systematics Studies Ltd (Trinidad and Tobago); TechKnowledge (United Arab Emirates); Teldan Info Systems (Israel); Tmecca (Korea); Izdatelstvo VES MIR (Russia); Wize Nordic AB (Denmark, Finland, Netherlands, Norway, Sweden, UK); Worldwide Information Services (South Africa)
Distribution Center: Turpin Distribution Services Ltd, Stratton Business Park, Pegasus Dr, Biggleswade, Beds SG18 8TQ, United Kingdom *Tel:* (01767) 604960 *Fax:* (01767) 601640
E-mail: oecdrow@turpin-distribution.com *Web Site:* www.turpin-distribution.com
Turpin Distribution, The Bleachery, 143 West St, New Milford, CT 06776, United States *Tel:* 860-350-0041 (from Canada)
E-mail: oecdna@turpin-distribution.com *Web Site:* www.turpin-distribution.com

OGC Michele Broutta Editeur
31 rue des Bergers, 75015 Paris
Tel: 01 45 77 93 71
Web Site: www.galerie-broutta.com
Key Personnel
Mng Dir: Michele Broutta *E-mail:* m.broutta@ wanadoo.fr
Founded: 1970
Subjects: Art, Library & Information Sciences
ISBN Prefix(es): 978-2-9510380

OH ! Editions
Subsidiary of XO Editions
Tour Maine Montparnasse, 33, ave du Maine, 75755 Paris Cedex 15
Mailing Address: BP 34, 75755 Paris Cedex 15
Tel: 01 56 54 27 30 *Fax:* 01 56 54 27 38
E-mail: xoeditions@xoeditions.com
Web Site: www.xoeditions.com
Key Personnel
Dir: Bernard Fixot; Edith Leblond; Philippe Robinet
Communications Dir: Valerie Taillefer *Tel:* 01 56 80 26 81
Press: Stephanie Le Foll *Tel:* 01 56 80 34 82
Founded: 2002
Subjects: Fiction, Nonfiction (General), Women's Studies
ISBN Prefix(es): 978-2-915056

Editions de l'Olivier
Subsidiary of La Martiniere Groupe
96, blvd du Montparnass, 75014 Paris
Tel: 01 41 48 84 76
E-mail: editionsdelolivier@editionsdelolivier.fr
Web Site: www.editionsdelolivier.fr
Founded: 1991
Subjects: Literature, Literary Criticism, Essays, French & Foreign Literature
ISBN Prefix(es): 978-2-87929

Ombres Noires, *imprint of* Flammarion Groupe

Editions Omnibus+
12, Ave d'Italie, 75627 Paris Cedex 13
Tel: 01 44 16 05 00
E-mail: omnibus@psb-editions.com
Web Site: www.omnibus.tm.fr
Key Personnel
Publishing Dir: Jean Arcache
Founded: 1988
Subjects: Drama, Theater, Humor, Literature, Literary Criticism, Essays, Poetry, Science Fiction, Fantasy, Popular & Classical Literature
ISBN Prefix(es): 978-2-258; 978-2-84119
Number of titles published annually: 250 Print
Total Titles: 370 Print
Parent Company: Place des editeurs
Ultimate Parent Company: Editis

Editions Ophrys+
25, rue Ginoux, 75015 Paris
Tel: 01 45 78 33 80 *Fax:* 01 45 75 37 11
E-mail: info@ophrys.fr
Web Site: www.ophrys.fr
Founded: 1934
Specialize in foreign language teaching books for pupils in middle school, students at the university or teachers; English literature, French language study, old languages, research in linguistics, history, geography, sociology & history of art. Also distributes dictionaries in foreign languages.
Subjects: Earth Sciences, Education, English as a Second Language, Genealogy, Geography, Geology, History, Language Arts, Linguistics, Regional Interests, Self-Help, Social Sciences, Sociology, Travel & Tourism
ISBN Prefix(es): 978-2-7080
Number of titles published annually: 20 Print
Total Titles: 500 Print; 1 CD-ROM; 3 Audio
Foreign Rep(s): Servidis (Switzerland)
Distribution Center: Daudin Distribution, One, rue Guynemer, CS 30504, 78771 Magny-les-Hameaux Cedex *Tel:* 01 30 48 74 50 *Fax:* 01 34 98 02 44 *E-mail:* info@daudin.fr

Editions d'Organisation+
61 bd St-Germain, 75240 Paris Cedex 05
Tel: 01 44 41 11 11 *Fax:* 01 44 41 11 44
E-mail: editeurs_entreprise@eyrolles.com; foreignrights@eyrolles.com
Web Site: www.editions-organisation.com
Key Personnel
President: Serge Eyrolles
Founded: 1952
Subjects: Business, Computer Science, Electronics, Electrical Engineering, Engineering (General), House & Home, How-to, Law, Management, Social Sciences, Sociology
ISBN Prefix(es): 978-2-7081
Number of titles published annually: 550 Print
Parent Company: Groupe Eyrolles SA, 57 bd St-Germain, 75240 Paris Cedex 05
Bookshop(s): Librairie Eyrolles, 79 ave de la Republique, 75011 Paris *Tel:* 01 43 38 26 71 *Fax:* 01 48 07 89 59 *E-mail:* librairie-paris11@wanadoo.fr; Librairie Eyrolles, One rue Thenard, 75005 Paris *Tel:* 01 44 41 11 74 *E-mail:* librairie@eyrolles.com; Librairie de Provence, 31 Cours Mirabeau, 13100 Aix-en-Provence *Tel:* 04 42 26 07 23 *Fax:* 04 42 26 89 47 *E-mail:* contact@librairie-provence.com; Librairie de l'Universite, 12 rue Nazareth, 13100 Aix-en-Provence *Tel:* 04 42 26 18 08 *Fax:* 04 42 26 63 26; Librairie Eyrolles, Ave Bernard Hirsch, BP 105, 95021 Cergy Pontoise *Tel:* 01 30 38 14 52 *Fax:* 01 30 32 58 90 *E-mail:* librairie@essec.fr; Librairie Eyrolles, One rue de la Liberation, 78350 Jouy-en-Josas *Tel:* 01 39 67 94 59 *Fax:* 01 39 67 70 91 *E-mail:* librairie.hec@hotmail.fr

Organisation for Economic Co-operation & Development, see OECD Publishing

Editions Oriane+
173, Wood Chapelet, 44430 Le Loroux-Bottereau
Tel: 02 40 77 34 20
E-mail: editions.oriane@gmail.com
Web Site: www.editionsoriane.com
Key Personnel
Editor: Alain Brethes
Founded: 2001
Subjects: Astrology, Occult, Health, Nutrition, Human Relations, Philosophy, Psychology, Psychiatry
ISBN Prefix(es): 978-2-906803; 978-2-912662
Number of titles published annually: 2 Print
Total Titles: 16 Print

Librairie Orientaliste, see Editions Geuthner

Editions Heloise d'Ormesson (Eho)
3, rue Rollin, 75005 Paris
Tel: 01 56 81 30 70
Web Site: www.editions-heloisedormesson.com
Key Personnel
Dir: Heloise d'Ormesson
Editorial & Rights: Sarah Hirsch *Tel:* 01 56 81 30 73
Press & Public Relations: Audrey Siourd *Tel:* 01 56 81 30 75
Subjects: Literature, Literary Criticism, Essays, Nonfiction (General)
ISBN Prefix(es): 978-2-35087

Editions de l'Ouest
10 rue de Terre Nueve, 49300 Cholet
Tel: 02 41 55 19 62
Founded: 1989
Subjects: Accounting, Biological Sciences, Chemistry, Chemical Engineering, Civil Engineering, Earth Sciences, Economics, Geography, Geology, History, Regional Interests
ISBN Prefix(es): 978-2-908261
Distributed by Alena Libert Inc (Canada); Boinemouth (UK); Chinon Diffusion (Europe); Continental Books
Bookshop(s): Centre Chretien des familles de l'Quest, One pl Louis-Marie Grignion de Montfort, 85290 St Laurent-Sur-Sevre *Tel:* 02 51 92 36 17

Editions Ouest-France+
13, rue du Breil, 35063 Rennes Cedex
Mailing Address: CS 26339, 35063 Rennes Cedex
Tel: 02 99 32 58 23
E-mail: commercial@edilarge.fr; editorial@edilarge.fr; press@edilarge.fr
Web Site: www.editionsouestfrance.eu
Key Personnel
Dir General: Servane Biguais
Press: Catherine Jolivet-Goarin *Tel:* 02 99 32 58 29 *E-mail:* cgoarin@editionsouestfrance.fr; Delphine Monneraye *Tel:* 02 99 32 58 67 *E-mail:* dmonneraye@edilarge.fr
Founded: 1975
Subjects: Cookery, History, Science (General), Travel & Tourism, Creative Leisures
ISBN Prefix(es): 978-2-7373; 978-2-85882
Number of titles published annually: 150 Print
Total Titles: 1,800 Print
Imprints: Editions de la Cite; Editions Maritimes et D'Outremer

Les Editions du Pacifique
5 rue St-Romain, 75006 Paris
Tel: 01 42 22 48 63 *Fax:* 01 42 22 12 69
E-mail: contact@leseditionsdupacifique.com
Web Site: leseditionsdupacifique.com
Subjects: Architecture & Interior Design, Art, Cookery, Health, Nutrition, Photography, Travel & Tourism
ISBN Prefix(es): 978-2-87868
Distributor for Editions Didier Millet

Editions Pardes+
44, rue Wilson, 77880 Grez-sur-Loing
Tel: 01 04 45 67 23; 01 64 28 53 38 *Fax:* 01 64 45 67 25
E-mail: sarl.pardes@orange.fr
Founded: 1982
Subjects: Archaeology, Astrology, Occult, Health, Nutrition, History, Religion - Buddhist, Religion - Hindu, Social Sciences, Sociology
ISBN Prefix(es): 978-2-86714

Editions Parentheses+
72, cours Julien, 13006 Marseille
Tel: 04 95 08 18 20 *Fax:* 04 95 08 18 24
E-mail: info@editionsparentheses.com
Web Site: www.editionsparentheses.com

Key Personnel
General Dir: Varoujan Arzoumanian
Dir: Patrick Bardou
Founded: 1978
Subjects: Anthropology, Architecture & Interior Design, Art, Ethnicity, Music, Dance, Photography, Urbanisme
ISBN Prefix(es): 978-2-86364
Number of titles published annually: 18 Print
Total Titles: 250 Print
Bookshop(s): 13, rue Andre Masson, 75013 Paris *Tel:* 01 53 80 02 23 *E-mail:* comptoir@harmoniamundi.com
Distribution Center: Harmonia Mundi, BP 20150, 13631 Arles Cedex *Tel:* 04 90 49 90 49 *E-mail:* adv-livre@harmonium.com
Harmonia Mundi, Rue de pre aux Oies, 303, 1130 Brussels, Belgium *Tel:* (02) 240 93 00 *Fax:* (02) 216 35 98 *E-mail:* info@sdlcaravelle.com *Web Site:* www.sdlcaravelle.com
Diffusion Dimedia, 539 blvd Lebeau, St-Laurent, QC N4N 1S2, Canada
Office du Livre (OLF), Route de Villars 101, 1701 Fribourg, Switzerland

Editions Paris-Musees+
27, rue des Petites-Ecuries, 75010 Paris
Tel: 01 80 05 41 11
Web Site: www.parismusees.paris.fr
Key Personnel
Publishing Dir: Olivier Donat *E-mail:* olivier.donat@paris.fr
Editorial Dir: Isabelle Jendron *E-mail:* isabelle.jendron@paris.fr
Founded: 1985
Specialize in art exhibition catalogues.
Subjects: Architecture & Interior Design, Art, Fashion, History, Photography
ISBN Prefix(es): 978-2-87900; 978-2-7596
Number of titles published annually: 30 Print
Total Titles: 300 Print
Parent Company: Association Paris-Musees
Distribution Center: UD-Union Distribution, 6, rue de l'Europe, 45300 Sermaises *Tel:* 02 28 39 00 43

Editions du Patrimoine
Hotel de Sully, 62, rue St-Antoine, 75004 Paris
Tel: 01 44 54 95 20; 01 44 61 21 75 (bookshop) *Fax:* 01 44 54 95 21; 01 44 61 22 10 (bookshop)
Web Site: www.editions.monuments-nationaux.fr
Key Personnel
Publishing Dir: Jocelyn Bouraly *E-mail:* jocelyn.bouraly@monuments-nationaux.fr
Head, Editorial Dept: Catherine Donzel *E-mail:* catherine.donzel@monuments-nationaux.fr
Communications & Press: Clair Morizet *Tel:* 01 44 61 95 23 *E-mail:* clair.morizet@monuments-nationaux.fr
Marketing & Sales: Anne Alligorides
Publishing department of the Centre des Monuments Nationaux & the appointed publisher for the heritage services of the Ministry of Culture & Communications.
Subjects: Archaeology, Architecture & Interior Design, Art, History, Science (General)
ISBN Prefix(es): 978-2-85822
Number of titles published annually: 30 Print
Total Titles: 400 Print
Distribution Center: Seuil-Volumen, 25, blvd Romain-Rolland, 75993 Paris Cedex 14 *Tel:* 01 41 48 84 60 *Fax:* 01 41 48 81 35

Editions Payot & Rivages+
106, Blvd St-Germain, 75006 Paris
Tel: 01 44 41 39 90 *Fax:* 01 44 41 39 89
E-mail: editions@payotrivages.com
Web Site: www.payot-rivages.net
Key Personnel
President: Jean-Francois Lamuniere

Foreign Rights Dir: Marie-Martine Serrano
    E-mail: mmserrano@payotrivages.com
Editorial Dir: Helene Fiamma
Founded: 1984
Subjects: Anthropology, Biography, Memoirs,
    Cookery, Fiction, Government, Political Sci-
    ence, History, Humor, Language Arts, Lin-
    guistics, Literature, Literary Criticism, Essays,
    Mysteries, Suspense, Nonfiction (General), Phi-
    losophy, Religion - Other, Science Fiction, Fan-
    tasy, Social Sciences, Sociology, Technology,
    Transportation, Travel & Tourism, Contem-
    porary History, Cultural Studies, Ethnology,
    Modern History, Sexuality Short Stories
ISBN Prefix(es): 978-2-228; 978-2-86930; 978-2-
    7436; 978-2-903059
Number of titles published annually: 100 Print
Total Titles: 2,000 Print
Distribution Center: Hachette Livre, One Ave
    Gutenberg, 78316 Maurepas Cedex Tel: 01 30
    66 20 66
Orders to: Le Seuil, 27 rue Jacod, 75006 Paris

Pearson Education/CampusPress, imprint of
Pearson Education France

Pearson Education France+
Immeuble Terra Nova II, 74 rue de Lagny, 5e
    etage gauche, 93100 Montreuil
Tel: 01 43 62 31 00 Fax: 01 43 62 30 80
Web Site: www.pearson.fr
Key Personnel
President: Helene Dennery
Founded: 1995
Subjects: Business, Computer Science, Comput-
    ers, Economics, Education, Finance, Health,
    Nutrition, Language Arts, Linguistics, Science
    (General), Humanities
ISBN Prefix(es): 978-2-7440
Total Titles: 300 Print
Parent Company: Pearson Education
Ultimate Parent Company: Pearson PLC
Imprints: Pearson Education/CampusPress; Pear-
    son Education/Les Echos; Pearson Educa-
    tion/Les Echos.fr Press

Pearson Education/Les Echos, imprint of
Pearson Education France

Pearson Education/Les Echos.fr Press, imprint
of Pearson Education France

Pedagogie Modern, imprint of Les Editions
Bordas

Editions A Pedone+
13 rue Soufflot, 75005 Paris
Tel: 01 43 54 05 97 Fax: 01 46 34 07 60
E-mail: editions-pedone@wanadoo.fr
Web Site: www.pedone.info
Key Personnel
Editor: Benedicte Pedone-Ribot; Marc Pedone
    E-mail: marc@apedone.net
Founded: 1837
Subjects: Agriculture, Earth Sciences, Economics,
    Engineering (General), Law, Management,
    Maritime, Air Law, Criminal Philosophy,
    Diplomatic History, International Law, Inter-
    national Relations, Penal Sciences, Philosophy
    of the Right, Right European, Right of the Sea
ISBN Prefix(es): 978-2-233

Peeters-France
52, Blvd St-Michel, 75006 Paris
Tel: 01 40 51 89 20 Fax: 01 40 51 81 05
E-mail: peeters.publish@free.fr
Web Site: www.peeters-leuven.be
Key Personnel
Editor: Vladimir Randa

Specialize in classical studies, Eastern studies,
    Egyptology, history of art, medicine, Oriental
    studies & ethics, patristics.
Subjects: Anthropology, Archaeology, Art, Bib-
    lical Studies, History, Language Arts, Lin-
    guistics, Literature, Literary Criticism, Essays,
    Medicine, Nursing, Dentistry, Philosophy, The-
    ology
ISBN Prefix(es): 978-2-87723; 978-90-6831; 978-
    90-429
Number of titles published annually: 120 Print; 2
    CD-ROM
Parent Company: Peeters, Bondgenotenlaan 153,
    3000 Leuven, Belgium
U.S. Office(s): Peeters Academic Publishers Inc,
    70 Enterprise Dr, Suite 2, Bristol, CT 06010,
    United States E-mail: peeters@peeters-us.com
Warehouse: Kolonel Begaultlaan 61, 3012
    Wilsele, Belgium Tel: (016) 23 51 70
    Fax: (016) 22 85 00

PEMF, see Bibliotheque pour l'Ecole (BPE)

Pere Castor, imprint of Flammarion Groupe

Editions Perrin
76, rue de Bonaparte, 75006 Paris
Tel: 01 44 41 35 00
Web Site: www.editions-perrin.fr
Key Personnel
Publication Dir: Benoit Yvert
Sales Dir: Stephane Billerey Fax: 01 44 41 35 64
Foreign Rights Manager: Florence Maletrez
    E-mail: florence.maletrez@editions-perrin.com
Press: Florence Millard Tel: 01 44 41 30 58
    E-mail: florence.millard@editions-perrin.com
Subjects: Biography, Memoirs, Cookery, Fiction,
    History, Current Affairs, Historical Fiction
ISBN Prefix(es): 978-2-262
Parent Company: Edi8
Ultimate Parent Company: Editis Group

Atelier Perrousseaux Editeur, imprint of
Adverbum

Editions Petite Plume
Division of Editions Plume de Carotte
28 impasse des Bons Amis, 31200 Toulouse
Tel: 05 34 43 17 59; 05 62 72 08 76 Fax: 05 62
    87 59 14
E-mail: petiteplume@plumedecarotte.com
Web Site: www.plumedecarotte.com
Key Personnel
Dir: Frederic Lisak E-mail: f.lisak@
    plumedecarotte.com
Manager: Frederique Bousque-Villechenon
    E-mail: f.villechenon@plumedecarotte.com
Founded: 2010
Subjects: Education, Fiction
ISBN Prefix(es): 978-2-36154
Distribution Center: Distribution Volumen, 25
    blvd Romain Rolland, CS 21418, 75014 Paris
    Tel: 01 41 48 80 89 Fax: 01 41 48 81 36
    E-mail: commandes@volumen.fr

Petites Affiches, imprint of Lextenso Editions

Les petits matins (The Little Mornings)+
31, rue Faidherbe, 75011 Paris
Tel: 01 46 59 11 73
E-mail: lespetitsmatins@wanadoo.fr
Web Site: www.lespetitsmatins.fr
Key Personnel
Founder & Editor: Marie-Edith Alouf; Olivier
    Szulzynger
Head, Communications: Macha Dvinina Tel: 01
    43 48 77 27 E-mail: macha@lespetitsmatins.
    com
Editor: Stephanie Lebassard
Founded: 2005

Subjects: Economics, Environmental Studies, Po-
    etry, Social Sciences, Sociology
ISBN Prefix(es): 978-2-915879; 978-2-36383
Foreign Rep(s): La Caravelle/Volumen (Belgium);
    Dimedia (Canada); Servidis (Switzerland)
Distribution Center: Volumen, 25 blvd Romain-
    Rolland, CS 21418, 75993 Paris Cedex
    14 Tel: 01 41 48 80 80 Fax: 01 41 48 81
    32 E-mail: commandes@volumen.fr Web
    Site: www.volumen.fr

Les Petits Platons
21 bis rue d'Armaille, 75017 Paris
Mailing Address: 89-91 blvd Auguste Blanqui,
    75013 Paris
Tel: 06 98 35 59 40; 09 70 46 94 14
E-mail: contact@lespetitsplatons.com
Web Site: www.lespetitsplatons.com
Key Personnel
President: Jean Paul Mongin
Head, Communications: Aurore Champavere
    E-mail: a.champavere@lespetitsplatons.com
Founded: 2010
Specialize in illustrated books by great philoso-
    phers for children.
Subjects: Philosophy
ISBN Prefix(es): 978-2-36165
Distribution Center: Dilisco, Rue du Limousin,
    BP n°25, 23223 Cheniers Tel: 05 55 51 80 00
    Fax: 05 55 62 17 39 E-mail: relation.client@
    dilisco.fr
CED, 73, quai Auguste Deshaies, 94854 Ivry-sur-
    Seine Cedex Tel: 01 46 58 38 40 Fax: 01 46
    71 25 59 E-mail: secretariat@ced-cedif.fr

La Pharmacie de Platon, imprint of Editions
William Blake & Co

Editions Phebus
Imprint of Libella Publishing Group
7, rue des Canettes, 75006 Paris
Tel: 01 44 32 05 60 Fax: 01 44 32 05 61
E-mail: informations@libella.fr; foreignrights@
    libellagroup.com
Web Site: www.editionsphebus.fr
Key Personnel
Commercial & Promotion: Eric Lahirigoyen
Press: Blandine de Caunes
Founded: 1976
Subjects: Art, Literature, Literary Criticism, Es-
    says
ISBN Prefix(es): 978-2-85940; 978-2-7529
Number of titles published annually: 55 Print
Total Titles: 1,260 Print
Foreign Rep(s): Servidis (Switzerland); Socadis
    (Canada)
Distribution Center: Sodis, 128 Ave du Marechal
    de Lattre de Tassigny, 77400 Lagny-sur-Marne
    Web Site: www.sodis.fr

Editions A et J Picard SA
82, rue Bonaparte, 75006 Paris
Tel: 01 43 26 96 73 Fax: 01 43 26 42 64; 01 43
    30 85 45
E-mail: commercial@editions-picard.com
Web Site: www.editions-picard.com
Key Personnel
Mng Dir: Chantal Pasini-Picard
Founded: 1869
Subjects: Antiques, Archaeology, Architecture &
    Interior Design, Art, Education, Ethnicity, His-
    tory, Language Arts, Linguistics, Literature,
    Literary Criticism, Essays, Music, Dance, Phi-
    losophy, Fine Arts, France, Religion
ISBN Prefix(es): 978-2-7084

Editions Piccolia
Imprint of Bonnier Publishing
5, rue d'Alembert, 91240 St-Michel-sur-Orge
Tel: 01 69 02 60 30 Fax: 01 60 15 19 31
E-mail: info@editions-piccolia.fr; piccolia@
    piccolia.fr
Web Site: www.editions-piccolia.fr

Key Personnel
International Sales Manager: Prudence Mukendi
E-mail: prudence@piccolia.fr
Founded: 1991
Subjects: Nonfiction (General)
ISBN Prefix(es): 978-2-7530
Number of titles published annually: 250 Print
Total Titles: 700 Print
Ultimate Parent Company: Bonnier AB

Editions Jean Picollec+
47, rue Auguste Lancon, 75013 Paris
Tel: 01 45 89 73 04 *Fax:* 01 45 89 40 72
Key Personnel
Editorial Dir: Jean Picollec
Founded: 1978
Specialize in reference books & documents - Celtic world.
Subjects: Biography, Memoirs, Ethnicity, Fiction, Government, Political Science, History, Literature, Literary Criticism, Essays, Nonfiction (General), Regional Interests, Travel & Tourism
ISBN Prefix(es): 978-2-86477
Number of titles published annually: 12 Print
Total Titles: 220 Print
Distributed by L'Age d'Homme (Switzerland)
Foreign Rep(s): L'Age d'Homme (Switzerland)
Foreign Rights: Arabella Cruse (Scandinavia); Catherine Fragou (Greece); Chantal Galtier Roussel (all other territories); Anastasia Lester (Russia & former USSR); Anna Spadolini (Italy)
Distribution Center: Dilisco, Rue du Limousin, BP 25, 23220 Cheniers *Tel:* 05 55 51 80 00 *Fax:* 05 55 62 17 39 *E-mail:* relation.client@dilisco.fr *Web Site:* www.dilisco.fr
Orders to: CED, 73 quai Auguste Deshaies, 94200 Ivry-sur-Seine *Tel:* 01 46 58 38 40 *Fax:* 01 46 71 25 59 *E-mail:* ced.societe@wanadoo.fr

Editions Philippe Picquier+
Le Mas De Vert, 13631 Arles
Mailing Address: BP 20150, 13631 Arles Cedex
Tel: 04 90 49 61 56 *Fax:* 04 90 49 91 95
Web Site: www.editions-picquier.fr
Key Personnel
Foreign Rights: Antonia Bou
Founded: 1986
Specialize in Asian Literature.
Subjects: Asian Studies, Erotica, Literature, Literary Criticism, Essays
ISBN Prefix(es): 978-2-87730; 978-2-8097
Total Titles: 400 Print
Foreign Rep(s): Caravelle (Belgium); Dimedia (Canada); Zoe (Switzerland)
Orders to: Harmonia Mundi Diffusion Livres
Tel: 04 90 49 90 49 *Fax:* 04 90 49 96 14
E-mail: editions-philippepicquier@picquier.com

Editions Pierron Sarl+
2, rue Gutenberg, 57200 Sarreguemines Cedex
Mailing Address: BP 80609, 57206 Sarreguemines Cedex
Tel: 03 87 95 10 89 *Fax:* 03 87 95 60 95
Key Personnel
Dir: Matthieu Biberon *Tel:* 01 46 22 17 83
Subjects: Education, History
ISBN Prefix(es): 978-2-7085
Parent Company: Pierron Entreprise SA

Nouvelles Editions Jean-Michel Place+
12, rue Pierre et Marie Curie, 75005 Paris
Tel: 06 80 63 43 53; 09 63 63 35 90 *Fax:* 01 46 33 54 11
E-mail: contact@jeanmichelplace.com
Web Site: www.jeanmichelplace.com
Key Personnel
Editorial Dir: Jean-Michel Place
E-mail: jeanmichelplace@gmail.com
Founded: 1975

Subjects: Anthropology, Architecture & Interior Design, Art, Film, Video, Literature, Literary Criticism, Essays, Music, Dance, Philosophy, Photography, Publishing & Book Trade Reference
ISBN Prefix(es): 978-2-85893

Editions Places des Victoires, see Editions Menges

Editions La Plage Sarl
60 rue Monsieur-le-prince, 75006 Paris
Tel: 01 43 29 56 85 *Fax:* 01 72 70 50 70
E-mail: presse@laplage.fr; info@laplage.fr; edition@laplage.fr
Web Site: www.laplage.fr
Key Personnel
Editorial Dir: Laurence Auger *E-mail:* laurence@laplage.fr
Management, Sales & Production: Jean-Luc Ferrante *E-mail:* jlf@laplage.fr
Founded: 1993
Membership(s): Les editeurs ecolo-compatibles.
Subjects: Cookery, Health, Nutrition, Ecology, Natural Health & Nutrition, Organic Cooking
ISBN Prefix(es): 978-2-84221; 978-2-914369
Number of titles published annually: 12 Print
Total Titles: 100 Print
Foreign Rep(s): La Caravelle (Belgium); Interforum Canada (Canada); Interforum Suisse SA (Switzerland)
Foreign Rights: Abiali Afidi (Ximena Renjifo)
Distribution Center: Interforum Editis, 44 route de Sermaises, BP 11, 45331 Malesherbes Cedex *Tel:* 02 38 32 71 00 *Fax:* 02 38 32 71 28 *E-mail:* cdes-excel.clientes@interforum.fr

Editions Play Bac
33 rue du Petit-Musc, 75004 Paris
Tel: 01 53 01 24 00 *Fax:* 01 53 01 24 31
Web Site: www.playbac.fr
Key Personnel
Chief Executive Officer: Anne-Lous Plantinga
Tel: 01 53 01 24 57
Production Manager: Christophe Guerin
Foreign Rights: Louise Barber *E-mail:* l.barber@playbac.fr
Founded: 1986
ISBN Prefix(es): 978-2-8096
Distributed by Hachette Canada; Hachette Livre International

Editions Plon
12, ave d'Italie, 75627 Paris Cedex 13
Tel: 01 44 16 09 00
Web Site: www.plon.fr
Key Personnel
President & Chief Executive Officer: Vincent Barbare
Foreign Rights Sales Manager: Florence Maletrez *Tel:* 01 44 16 09 30 *E-mail:* florence.maletrez@plon-perrin.com
Founded: 1852
Subjects: Literature, Literary Criticism, Essays
ISBN Prefix(es): 978-2-259
Parent Company: Edi8
Ultimate Parent Company: Editis Group
Distribution Center: Interforum, Immeuble Paryseine, 3, allee de la Seine, 94854 Ivry Cedex *Tel:* 01 49 59 10 10 (worldwide exc Belgium, Canada & Switzerland)
Interforum Benelux SA, 117 bd de l'Europe, 1301 Wavre, Belgium *Tel:* (010) 420 320
Interforum Canada Inc, 1055 bd Rene Levesque Est, Montreal, Quebec H2L 4S5, Canada *Tel:* 514-281-1050
Interforum Suisse SA, Route Andre Piller, 33, A Givisiez, CP 69, 1701 Fribourg, Switzerland *Tel:* (026) 460 80 60

Editions Plume de Carotte
28 impasse des Bons Amis, 31200 Toulouse

Tel: 05 62 72 08 76 *Fax:* 05 62 87 59 14
E-mail: contact@plumedecarotte.com
Web Site: www.plumedecarotte.com
Key Personnel
Dir: Frederick Lisak *E-mail:* f.lisak@plumedecarotte.com
Editor: Audrey Calvo-Guiochet *E-mail:* a.calvo@plumedecarotte.com
Foreign Rights: Laura Puechberty *E-mail:* l.puechberty@plumedecarotte.com
Founded: 2001
Subjects: Animals, Pets, Art, Cookery, Crafts, Games, Hobbies, Environmental Studies, Gardening, Plants, Science (General), Travel & Tourism, Nature
ISBN Prefix(es): 978-2-915810
Divisions: Editions Petite Plume
Distribution Center: Distribution Volumen, 25 bld Romain Rolland, CS21418, 75014 Paris *Tel:* 01 41 48 80 89 *Fax:* 01 41 48 81 36 *E-mail:* commandes@volumen.fr

Poches Odile Jacob (Pocket Series), *imprint of* Editions Odile Jacob

Pocket Jeunesse, *imprint of* Pocket Press

Pocket Press
Subsidiary of Univers Poche AS
12 ave d'Italie, 75627 Paris Cedex 13
Tel: 01 44 16 05 00
Web Site: www.pocket.fr
Key Personnel
Publishing Dir: Marie-Christine Conchon
Foreign Rights Manager: Julie Buffaud
Founded: 1962
Subjects: Art, Fiction, Inspirational, Spirituality, Nonfiction (General), Science Fiction, Fantasy, Classics, Entertainment, Humanities, Personal Development
ISBN Prefix(es): 978-2-266
Imprints: Pocket Jeunesse
Foreign Rights: Intercontinental Literary Agency; Lucas Alexander Whitley

Les Editions du Point Veterinaire+
10 ave de l'Arche, 92419 Courbevoie Cedex
Toll Free Tel: 0800 94 98 89
Web Site: www.lepointveterinaire.fr
Key Personnel
Publisher: Thierry Renaud *E-mail:* thierry.renaud@lepointveterinaire.fr
Product Manager: Thomas Kassab
E-mail: thomas.kassab@lepointveterinaire.fr
Subjects: Animals, Pets, Veterinary Science
ISBN Prefix(es): 978-2-86326
Parent Company: Wolters Kluwer NV

L'Atelier du Poisson Soluble
35, blvd Carnot, 43000 Le-Puy-en-Velay
Tel: 04 71 02 81 75 *Fax:* 04 71 02 81 60
E-mail: poissonsoluble@wanadoo.fr; rights@poissonsoluble.com
Web Site: www.poissonsoluble.com
Key Personnel
Foreign Rights: Daniela Bonerba
Contact: Claire Bretin *E-mail:* claire@poissonsoluble.com
ISBN Prefix(es): 978-2-913741; 978-2-9504568; 978-2-35871
Foreign Rep(s): Esperluete (Belgium); Agence du Livre (Canada); Maria Pages (Spain); Servidis SA (Switzerland)
Distribution Center: Generale Librest, 8-10 rue Robert Schuman, 94220 Charenton-le-Pont *Tel:* 01 58 94 56 00 *Fax:* 01 58 94 56 56

Editions POL+
Subsidiary of Editions Gallimard
33, rue St-Andre-des-Arts, 75006 Paris
Tel: 01 43 54 21 20 *Fax:* 01 43 54 11 31
E-mail: polediteur@pol-editeur.fr

Web Site: www.pol-editeur.com
Key Personnel
President: Paul Otchakovsky-Laurens
   E-mail: otchakov@pol-editeur.fr
Foreign Rights: Vibeke Madsen
   E-mail: madsen@pol-editeur.fr
Founded: 1983
Subjects: Drama, Theater, Fiction, Literature, Literary Criticism, Essays, Poetry
ISBN Prefix(es): 978-2-86744; 978-2-84682
Number of titles published annually: 44 Print
Total Titles: 1,000 Print
Foreign Rep(s): Gallimard/La Caravelle (Belgium); Gallimard Limitee (Canada); Gallimard/Office du Livre (Switzerland)
Distribution Center: Sodis, 128 Ave du Marechal de Lattre de Tassigny, 77400 Lagny-sur-Marne

Pole de Recherche pour l'Organisation et la Diffusion de l'Information Geographique, see PRODIG

Editions le Pommier
8, rue Ferou, 75278 Paris Cedex 6
Tel: 01 53 10 24 60 *Fax:* 01 53 10 24 67
E-mail: le.pommier@editions-lepommier.fr
Web Site: www.editions-lepommier.fr
Key Personnel
Dir: Sophie Bancquart
Editor: Marie-Agathe Le Gueut; Juliette Thomas
Marketing: Camille Cheroux
Press: Celine Sinson
Founded: 1999
Subjects: Astronomy, Earth Sciences, Mathematics, Philosophy, Physics, Science (General), Astrophysics, Life Sciences
ISBN Prefix(es): 978-2-7465

Pratique Sante, *imprint of* Editions Jouvence Sarl

Editions Le Pre Aux Clercs+
12, Ave d'Italie, 75627 Paris Cedex 13
Tel: 01 44 16 05 00
E-mail: lepreauxclercs@placedesediteurs.com
Web Site: www.lepreauxclercs.com
Key Personnel
Editorial Dir: Carola Strang
Publishing Dir: Jean Arcache
Founded: 1963
Subjects: Art, Biography, Memoirs, Fiction, Health, Nutrition, History, How-to, Human Relations, Literature, Literary Criticism, Essays, Music, Dance, Mysteries, Suspense, Nonfiction (General), Poetry, Romance
ISBN Prefix(es): 978-2-84228
Parent Company: Place des editeurs
Ultimate Parent Company: Editis

Presence Africaine Editions+
25 bis, rue des Ecoles, 75005 Paris
Tel: 01 43 54 13 74; 01 43 54 15 88 *Fax:* 01 43 25 96 67
E-mail: presaf@club-internet.fr
Web Site: www.presenceafricaine.com
Key Personnel
Dir: Suzanne Diop
Founded: 1947
Subjects: Fiction, History, Philosophy, Poetry, Religion - Other
ISBN Prefix(es): 978-2-7087
Distributed by Nord-Sud (Benelux); Zoe (Switzerland)

Presse et Formation, *imprint of* Les Editions du CFPJ (Centre de Formation et de Perfectionnement des Journalistes)

Editions Presses de la Cite+
12, Ave d'Italie, 75627 Paris Cedex 13
Tel: 01 44 16 05 00

E-mail: pressesdelacite-fr@placedesediteurs.com
Web Site: www.pressesdelacite.com
Key Personnel
Publishing Dir: Jean Arcache
Press Dir: Sophie Thiebaut *Tel:* 01 44 16 06 80
   E-mail: sophie.thiebaut@placedesediteurs.com
Editorial Dir: Frederique Polet *E-mail:* frederique.polet@placedesediteurs.com
Founded: 1944
Subjects: Biography, Memoirs, Fiction, History, Humor, Mysteries, Suspense, Nonfiction (General), Romance, Science Fiction, Fantasy
ISBN Prefix(es): 978-2-258
Total Titles: 300 Print
Parent Company: Place des editeurs
Ultimate Parent Company: Editis
Foreign Rep(s): Interforum Benelux SA (Belgium); Interforum Canada Inc (Canada); Interforum Suisse SA (Switzerland)
Distribution Center: Interforum, Immeuble Paryseine, 3, allee de la Seine, 94854 Ivry Cedex
Tel: 01 49 59 10 10

Presses de la Renaissance SA+
12, ave d'Italie, 75627 Paris Cedex 13
Tel: 01 44 16 09 00; 01 44 16 09 30 (rights)
Web Site: www.plon.fr
Key Personnel
Rights Sales Manager: Florence Maletrez
   E-mail: florence.maletrez@plon-perrin.com
Founded: 1998
Subjects: Biography, Memoirs, Philosophy, Spirituality, Novels, Documents & Testimonials
ISBN Prefix(es): 978-2-85616; 978-2-7509
Number of titles published annually: 50 Print
Total Titles: 400 Print
Parent Company: Edi8
Ultimate Parent Company: Editis Group

Presses de l'Ecole Nationale des Ponts et Chaussees+
Unit of Ponts Formation Edition SA
15, rue de la Fontaine au Roi, 75127 Paris Cedex 11
Tel: 01 44 58 27 40 *Fax:* 01 44 58 27 44
E-mail: presses.ponts@mail.enpc.fr
Web Site: www.presses-des-ponts.fr
Key Personnel
Chief Executive Officer: Bruno Bieder
Publishing Dir: Armel de la Bourdonnaye
Founded: 1977
Specialize in scientific, technical & professional subjects.
Membership(s): Syndicat National de l'Edition (SNE).
Subjects: Civil Engineering, Earth Sciences, Environmental Studies, Real Estate, Science (General), Technology, Transportation, Urban Planning
ISBN Prefix(es): 978-2-85978
Number of titles published annually: 20 Print
Total Titles: 300 Print; 2 CD-ROM
Distributed by Geodif

Presses de Sciences Po+
117, blvd St-Germain, 75006 Paris
Tel: 01 45 49 83 64 *Fax:* 01 45 49 83 34
E-mail: info.presses@sciences-po.fr
Web Site: www.pressesdesciencespo.fr
Key Personnel
Executive Dir: Marie-Genevieve Vandesande
   E-mail: mariegenevieve.vandesande@sciences-po.fr
Foreign Rights Manager: Sandrine Boisard
   Tel: 01 45 49 83 30 *E-mail:* sandrine.boisard@sciences-po.fr
Founded: 1975
Specialize in European issues & questions. Publishes advanced research on its specialist areas thus contributing to current debate in both the public & private sectors: geopolitics, globalisation & governance, changes in political life,

societal changes & developments, economics, 20th century history, sustainable development, geography, health.
Subjects: Economics, Environmental Studies, Government, Political Science, History, Social Sciences, Sociology
ISBN Prefix(es): 978-2-7246
Number of titles published annually: 40 Print; 30 E-Book
Total Titles: 1,200 Print; 500 E-Book
Bookshop(s): Librairie des sciences politiques, 30 rue St Guillaume, 75007 Paris, Contact: Stephane Derreumaux *Tel:* 01 45 49 86 86 *Fax:* 01 42 22 56 89 *E-mail:* librairie@sciences-po.fr

Les Presses de Taize, *imprint of* Ateliers et Presses de Taize

Presses des Ponts, see Presses de l'Ecole Nationale des Ponts et Chaussees

Les Presses d'Ile-de-France+
65, rue de la Glaciere, 75013 Paris
Tel: 01 44 52 37 24 *Fax:* 01 44 52 37 62
E-mail: contact@presses-idf.fr
Web Site: www.presses-idf.fr
Founded: 1929
Subjects: Crafts, Games, Hobbies, Music, Dance, Outdoor Recreation, Religion - Catholic
ISBN Prefix(es): 978-2-7088

Presses du Chatelet+
Division of Editions de l'Archipel
34 rue des Bourdonnais, 75001 Paris
Tel: 01 55 80 77 40 *Fax:* 01 55 80 77 41
E-mail: ecricom@wanadoo.fr
Web Site: www.pressesduchatelet.com
Key Personnel
Dir: Jean-Daniel Belfond
Founded: 1995
Subjects: Health, Nutrition, Inspirational, Spirituality, Self Development
ISBN Prefix(es): 978-2-911217; 978-2-84592
Number of titles published annually: 30 Print
Total Titles: 150 Print
Distributed by Hachette Livre
Foreign Rep(s): Diffulivre (Switzerland); Dilibel (Belgium); Edipresse (Canada)

Presses Universitaires de Caen
Universite de Caen Basse-Normandie/MRSH, Esplanade de la Paix, CS 14032, 14032 Caen Cedex 5
Tel: 02 31 56 62 20 *Fax:* 02 31 56 62 25
E-mail: puc@unicaen.fr
Web Site: www.unicaen.fr/puc
Key Personnel
Dir, University Press: Antoine Foucher
   E-mail: puc.direction@unicaen.fr
Administrative Officer: Sandrine Menil *Tel:* 02 31 56 64 89 *E-mail:* puc.gestion@unicaen.fr
Technical Dir: Dominique Roux *Tel:* 02 31 56 62 22 *E-mail:* puc.technique@unicaen.fr
Founded: 1984
Subjects: Antiques, Biological Sciences, Drama, Theater, Education, Gardening, Plants, Geography, Geology, History, Language Arts, Linguistics, Literature, Literary Criticism, Essays, Philosophy, Psychology, Psychiatry, Regional Interests, Social Sciences, Sociology, Sports, Athletics
ISBN Prefix(es): 978-2-84133; 978-2-904461

Presses Universitaires de France (PUF)+
6, ave Reille, 75685 Paris Cedex 14
Tel: 01 58 10 31 00 *Fax:* 01 58 10 31 82
Web Site: www.puf.com
Key Personnel
Chairman & Editorial Dir: Monique Labrune
Dir, Foreign Rights: Maria Vlachou *Tel:* 01 58 10 31 55 *E-mail:* vlachou@puf.com

Sales Dir: Christophe Jeancourt-Galignani
Editor: Paul Garapon
Press: Doris Audoux *E-mail:* audoux@puf.com
Founded: 1921
Administration & Editorial offices are located
  at the above main address; Public Relations
  & Publicity departments are at 90 Blvd St-
  Germain, 75005 Paris.
Subjects: Art, Biography, Memoirs, Engineering
  (General), Geography, Geology, Government,
  Political Science, History, Human Relations,
  Law, Medicine, Nursing, Dentistry, Music,
  Dance, Philosophy, Psychology, Psychiatry,
  Religion - Other, Social Sciences, Sociology
ISBN Prefix(es): 978-2-13
Bookshop(s): Librairie Generale des PUF, 49,
  blvd St Michel, 75005 Paris, Contact: Do-
  minique Morel *Tel:* 01 44 41 81 20 *Fax:* 01
  43 54 64 81; La Pochotheque, 17 rue Soufflot,
  75005 Paris *Tel:* 01 43 26 77 41 *Fax:* 01 46 33
  21 96
Orders to: 14 Ave du Bois de l'Epine, BP 90,
  91003 Evry Cedex, Contact: Jean-Pierre
  Giband *Tel:* 01 60 87 30 00 *Fax:* 01 60 79 20
  45

Presses Universitaires de Grenoble+
5, place Robert-Schuman, 38025 Grenoble Cedex
  1
Tel: 04 76 29 43 09 *Fax:* 04 76 44 64 31
E-mail: editorial@pug.fr; presse@pug.fr
Web Site: www.pug.fr
Key Personnel
Chief Executive Officer & President: Sylvie Bigot
Editorial Manager: Segolene Marbach
Finance Manager: Sophie Rochville
Communications Officer: Lucile Pajot
Editor: Rose Mognard
Founded: 1972
Subjects: Accounting, Art, Communications, Eco-
  nomics, Education, Government, Political Sci-
  ence, History, Language Arts, Linguistics, Law,
  Literature, Literary Criticism, Essays, Man-
  agement, Marketing, Psychology, Psychiatry,
  Social Sciences, Sociology, Sports, Athletics,
  Technology, Culture, Europe, French Language
ISBN Prefix(es): 978-2-7061
Number of titles published annually: 45 Print
Total Titles: 1,000 Print
Imprints: PUG
Orders to: Sofedis, 11 rue Soufflot, 75005 Paris
  Tel: 01 53 10 25 26

Presses Universitaires de Lyon (PUL)+
86, rue Pastuer, 69365 Lyon Cedex 07
Tel: 04 78 69 76 48 *Fax:* 04 78 69 76 51
E-mail: pul@univ-lyon2.fr
Web Site: presses.univ-lyon2.fr
Key Personnel
Dir: Delphine Hautois *Tel:* 04 78 69 76 50
  E-mail: delphine.hautois@univ-lyon2.fr
Editor: Sandy Remy *E-mail:* s.remy@univ-lyon2.
  fr; Francois Tison *E-mail:* francois.tison@univ-
  lyon2.fr
Sales & Communication: Hugo Ferrante
  E-mail: h.ferrante@univ-lyon2.fr; Delphine
  Giard *E-mail:* delphine.giard@univ-lyon2.fr
Founded: 1976
Specialize in humanities & social sciences.
Membership(s): Syndicat National de l'Edition
  (SNE).
Subjects: Economics, Government, Political Sci-
  ence, History, Human Relations, Language
  Arts, Linguistics, Law, Literature, Literary Crit-
  icism, Essays, Management, Aesthetics, Episte-
  mology, Gender Studies
ISBN Prefix(es): 978-2-7297
Distributor for Editions W a Macon; Editions Ly-
  onnaises d'Art et d'Histoire a'Lyon
Distribution Center: Sodis, 128 ave du Marechal
  de lattre de Tassigny, BP 142, 77403 Lagny
  Cedex

Gallimard Export, 5, rue Sebastien Bot-
  tin, 75007 Paris *Tel:* 01 49 54 14 53
  E-mail: international@gallimard.fr (worldwide
  exc Canada & USA)
La Canopee, 109, chemin du Sphinx, St Ar-
  mand, QC J0J 1T0, Canada *Tel:* 450-248-9084
  Fax: 450-248-0681 *E-mail:* lacanopee@bell.net
  (Canada & USA)

Presses Universitaires de Nancy, see Editions
Universitaires de Lorraine

**Presses Universitaires de Pau et des Pays de
l'Adour**
Institut Claude Laugenie, Domaine Universitaire,
  Ave du Doyen Poplawski, 64000 Pau
Tel: 05 59 40 79 15
E-mail: contact@presses-univ-pau.fr
Web Site: www.presses-univ-pau.fr
Key Personnel
Dir: Victor Pereira
Founded: 1992
Subjects: Art, Geography, Geology, Language
  Arts, Linguistics, Law, Literature, Literary Crit-
  icism, Essays, Photography, Poetry, Social Sci-
  ences, Sociology
ISBN Prefix(es): 978-2-908930; 978-2-35311

Presses Universitaires de Vincennes (PUV)
2, rue de la Liberte, 93526 St-Denis Cedex 02
Tel: 01 49 40 67 50 *Fax:* 01 49 40 67 53
E-mail: puv@univ-paris8.fr
Web Site: www.puv-univ-paris8.org
Key Personnel
Dir: Paul-Louis Rinwy *E-mail:* direction.puv@
  univ-paris8.fr
Production Manager: Laurence Hallouin
  E-mail: lhallouin@univ-paris8.fr
Founded: 1982
Subjects: Language Arts, Linguistics, Literature,
  Literary Criticism, Essays, Philosophy, Science
  (General), Culture
ISBN Prefix(es): 978-2-84292; 978-2-903981;
  978-2-910381

Presses Universitaires du Mirail (PUM)+
Division of Universite de Toulouse-Le Mirail
c/o Universite Toulouse-Le Mirail, 5 alles Anto-
  nio Machado, 31058 Toulouse Cedex 9
Tel: 05 61 50 38 10 *Fax:* 05 61 50 38 00
E-mail: pum@univ-tlse2.fr
Web Site: pum.univ-tlse2.fr
Key Personnel
Administrative Dir: Dalila Mechitoua
Marketing & Distribution: Vanessa Gordo-
  Finestres
Founded: 1987
University press that publishes books written
  mainly by academics.
Subjects: Anthropology, Archaeology, Drama,
  Theater, Education, English as a Second Lan-
  guage, Geography, Geology, History, Language
  Arts, Linguistics, Literature, Literary Criticism,
  Essays, Philosophy, Psychology, Psychiatry,
  Social Sciences, Sociology, Women's Studies
ISBN Prefix(es): 978-2-85816
Number of titles published annually: 30 Print
Total Titles: 600 Print; 1 CD-ROM; 1 E-Book
Imprints: PUM Toulouse
Foreign Rep(s): La Canopee (Canada); Gallimard
  Export (worldwide exc Canada & Spain); Por-
  tico Librerias SA (Spain)
Distribution Center: Sodis, 128 Ave Marechal
  de Lattre de Tassigny, BP 142, 77403 Lagny-
  sur-Marne Cedex *Tel:* 01 60 07 82 00 *Fax:* 01
  64 30 92 22 *E-mail:* portail@sodis.fr *Web
  Site:* www.sodis.fr

Presses Universitaires du Septentrion+
Universite de Lille 3, rue du Barreau, 59654 Villeneuve d'Ascq Cedex

Mailing Address: BP 30199, 59654 Villeneuve
  d'Ascq Cedex
Tel: 03 20 41 66 80 *Fax:* 03 20 41 66 90
E-mail: contact@septentrion.com
Web Site: www.septentrion.com
Key Personnel
Executive Dir: Jerome Valiant *Tel:* 03 20 41 66
  81
Administrative Dir: Nicolas Delargilliere *Tel:* 03
  20 41 66 83
Founded: 1971
Subjects: History, Language Arts, Linguistics,
  Law, Literature, Literary Criticism, Essays, Phi-
  losophy, Psychology, Psychiatry, Social Sci-
  ences, Sociology
ISBN Prefix(es): 978-2-284; 978-2-85939; 978-2-
  86531; 978-2-907170; 978-2-7574

Editions Privat SAS+
10, rue des Arts, 31000 Toulouse
Mailing Address: BP 38028, 31080 Toulouse
  Cedex 6
Tel: 05 61 33 77 00 *Fax:* 05 34 31 64 44
E-mail: info@editions-privat.com
Web Site: www.editions-privat.com
Key Personnel
President: M Olivier Lamarque
Publisher: Aude Babin *Tel:* 05 61 33 77 08
  E-mail: aude.babin@editions-privat.com
Dir: Philippe Terrancle *E-mail:* philippe.
  terrancle@editions-privat.com
Foreign Rights: Elisabeth Knebelmann
Founded: 1839
Subjects: Aeronautics, Aviation, Health, Nutrition,
  History
ISBN Prefix(es): 978-2-7089
Number of titles published annually: 70 Print
Total Titles: 300 Print
Parent Company: Laboratories Pierre Fabre, Le
  Carla-Burlats, 81106 Castres Cedex
Foreign Rights: Chantal Galtier-Roussez (France)
Distribution Center: Sodis, 128 Ave du Marechal
  de Lattre de Tassigny, 77400 Lagny-sur-Marne
  Tel: 01 60 07 82 73 *Fax:* 01 60 07 82 44
Sofedis, 11, rue Soufflot, 75005 Paris *Tel:* 01 53
  10 25 25 *Fax:* 01 53 10 25 26

PRODIG+
2 rue Valette, 75005 Paris
Tel: 01 44 07 75 99 *Fax:* 01 44 07 75 63
E-mail: prodig@univ-paris.fr
Web Site: www.prodig.cnrs.fr; www.univ-paris1.fr
Key Personnel
Dir: Jerome Lombard; Thierry Sanjuan
Founded: 1947
Subjects: Geography, Geology, Library & Infor-
  mation Sciences
ISBN Prefix(es): 978-2-901560
Parent Company: Centre national de la recherche
  scientifique (CNRS)
Associate Companies: Universite de Paris One;
  Universite de Paris Four; Universite de Paris
  Seven

Propos 2 Editions+
MJC-allee de Provence, 04100 Manosque
Tel: 06 07 41 17 70 (cell) *Toll Free Tel:* 0877 180
  615
E-mail: courrier@propos2editions.net
Web Site: www.propos2editions.net
Key Personnel
Publications Dir: Jacques Norigeon
Founded: 1993
Subjects: Art, Poetry
ISBN Prefix(es): 978-2-912144

Editions Prosveta SA
ZA du Capitou, 1277 Ave Lachenaudm, 83601
  Frejus Cedex
Mailing Address: CS 30012, 83601 Frejus Cedex
Tel: 04 94 19 33 33 *Fax:* 04 94 19 33 34
E-mail: international@prosveta.com
Web Site: www.prosveta.fr

Key Personnel
Chief Executive Officer: Jean-Robert Taro
Founded: 1972
Subjects: Education, Philosophy, Religion - Other
ISBN Prefix(es): 978-2-85566
U.S. Office(s): Prosveta USA, 29781 Shenan-doah Lane, Canyon Country, CA 91387, United States *Tel:* 661-252-9090 *E-mail:* prosveta@ sbcglobal.net *Web Site:* www.prosveta-usa.com
Foreign Rep(s): Asociacion Prosveta Espanola (Spain); Harmoniequell Versand (Austria); Publicacoes Maitreya (Brazil, Portugal); Prosveta (Colombia, Czechia, Ireland); Prosveta Australia (Australia); Prosveta Belgique (Belgium, Luxembourg); Prosveta Books (Eastern USA); Prosveta Congo (Congo (Brazzaville)); Prosveta Coop (Italy); Prosveta Depot Haiti (Haiti); Editions Prosveta (Africa); Editura Prosveta Srl (Romania); Prosveta Inc (Canada); Prosveta Liban (Lebanon); Librairie Prosveta (Benin, Cote d'Ivoire (Ivory Coast), Togo); Prosveta New Zealand Ltd (New Zealand); Prosveta Norden (Norway); Prosveta Russie (Russia); Editions Prosveta Societe Cooperative (Switzerland); Prosveta UK (UK); Prosveta US Distribution (Western USA); Prosveta Venezuela CA (Venezuela); Prosveta Verlag GmbH (Germany); Pyrinos Kosmos (Greece); The Solar Civilisation Bookshop (Cyprus); Stichting Prosveta Nederland (Netherlands); Surya (Bolivia); Zohar (Israel)

PUB, see Presses Universitaires de Bordeaux (PUB)

Publi Union, *imprint of* Editions Village Mondial

Editions Publisud+
15 rue des Cinq-Diamants, 75013 Paris
Tel: 01 45 85 78 50 *Fax:* 01 45 89 94 15
E-mail: publisud.editions@cegetel.net
Web Site: editionspublisud.hautetfort.com
Founded: 1981
Subjects: Architecture & Interior Design, Art, Cookery, Drama, Theater, Economics, Geography, Geology, Government, Political Science, History, Inspirational, Spirituality, Literature, Literary Criticism, Essays, Music, Dance, Philosophy, Poetry, Religion - Other, Social Sciences, Sociology, Ethnology
ISBN Prefix(es): 978-2-86600

PUF, see Presses Universitaires de France (PUF)

PUG, *imprint of* Presses Universitaires de Grenoble

Les Editions du Puits Fleuri+
22 ave de Fontainebleau, 77850 Hericy
Tel: 01 64 23 61 46 *Fax:* 01 64 23 69 42
E-mail: puitsfleuri@wanadoo.fr
Web Site: www.puitsfleuri.com
Key Personnel
Publisher: Emile Guchet
Founded: 1981
Subjects: How-to, Law
ISBN Prefix(es): 978-2-86739; 978-2-84486
Imprints: Le Conseiller Juridique Pour Tous
Distribution Center: Sodis, 128 Ave du Marechal de Lattre de Tassigny, 77400 Lagny sur Marne

PUL, see Presses Universitaires de Lyon (PUL)

PUM, see Presses Universitaires du Mirail (PUM)

PUM Toulouse, *imprint of* Presses Universitaires du Mirail (PUM)

PUN, see Editions Universitaires de Lorraine

PUPPA, see Presses Universitaires de Pau et des Pays de l'Adour

PURH, see Presses Universites de Rouen et du Havre (PURH)

PUS, see Presses Universitaires du Septentrion

PUV, see Presses Universitaires de Vincennes (PUV)

PYC Edition+
16-18 Place de La Chapelle, 75018 Paris
Tel: 01 53 26 48 00 *Fax:* 01 53 26 48 01
E-mail: info@pyc.fr
Web Site: www.pyc.fr
Key Personnel
President: Jean-Christophe Raveau
Founded: 1934
Subjects: Energy, Mechanical Engineering
ISBN Prefix(es): 978-2-85330; 978-2-911008; 978-2-84651

Pygmalion, *imprint of* Flammarion Groupe

Editions Pygmalion+
Imprint of Flammarion Groupe
87, quai Panhard et Levassor, 75647 Paris Cedex 13
Tel: 01 40 51 31 00
Web Site: www.groupe-flammarion.com
Key Personnel
Press Contact: Remy Verne *Tel:* 01 40 51 33 88 *E-mail:* remy.verne@flammarion.fr
Founded: 1975
Specialize in history & fantasy.
Subjects: Archaeology, Art, Biography, Memoirs, Fiction, History, Literature, Literary Criticism, Essays, Parapsychology, Science Fiction, Fantasy
ISBN Prefix(es): 978-2-85704; 978-2-7564
Total Titles: 500 Print
Ultimate Parent Company: Madrigall Group
Warehouse: Union Distribution, 106 rue Petit Leroy, Cherilly-La rue, 94152 Rungis Cedex
Distribution Center: Flammarion, 26 rue Racine, 75278 Paris Cedex 06, Marketing Dir: Patrick Du Fant *Tel:* 01 40 51 31 00

Editions Quae+
RD 10, 78026 Versailles Cedex
Tel: 01 30 83 34 06 *Fax:* 01 30 83 34 49
E-mail: serviceclients@quae.fr
Web Site: www.quae.com
Key Personnel
Mng Dir: Jean Arbeille *E-mail:* jean.arbeille@ quae.fr
Foreign Rights: Christiane Colon *E-mail:* christiane.colon@quae.fr
Editorial: Martine Seguier-Guis *E-mail:* martine. seguier-guis@quae.fr
Founded: 2006
Covers four research organizations: Cemagref, Cirad, Ifremer & Inra.
Subjects: Agriculture, Biological Sciences, Earth Sciences, Environmental Studies, Geography, Geology, Health, Nutrition, Maritime, Science (General), Social Sciences, Sociology
ISBN Prefix(es): 978-2-7592
Number of titles published annually: 60 Print
Total Titles: 1,000 Print; 10 E-Book
Foreign Rep(s): DPLU (Canada); Albert le Grand (Switzerland); Librairie Internationale & Le Triangle Universitaire (Morocco); Interscientia (Italy); Patrimoine & Jean de Lannoy (Benelux); Mundi-Prensa Libros (Spain)

Editions des Quatre-Vents, *imprint of* Editions l'Avant-Scene Theatre

Don Quichotte, *imprint of* Editions du Seuil

Les Editions du Quotidien
34 rue du Wacken, 67913 Strasbourg Cedex 9
Tel: 03 10 36 02 20 *Fax:* 03 10 36 02 22
E-mail: commandes-lcv@orange.fr
Web Site: www.lelivrechezvous.fr
Founded: 1871
Subjects: History, Natural History, Regional Interests
ISBN Prefix(es): 978-2-84208; 978-2-903297
Number of titles published annually: 20 Print
Total Titles: 800 Print

Rageot Editeur+
Subsidiary of Editions Hatier
6, rue d'Assas, 75006 Paris
Tel: 01 45 48 07 31 *Fax:* 01 42 22 68 01
E-mail: rageotediteur@editions-hatier.fr
Web Site: www.rageot.fr; www.livre-attitude.fr
Key Personnel
Dir: Caroline Westberg
Foreign Rights: Claire Billaud *E-mail:* cbillaud@ rageotediteur.fr
Press: Axelle Gaulupeau *E-mail:* agaulupeau@ rageotediteur.fr
Founded: 1945
Subjects: Science Fiction, Fantasy
ISBN Prefix(es): 978-2-7002
Ultimate Parent Company: Hachette Livre
Distributed by Hachette Canada Inc; Hachette Livre
Foreign Rep(s): Nathalie Moreau
Orders to: Hachette Livre International, 58 rue Jean Bleuzen, 92178 Vanves Cedex *Tel:* 01 55 00 11 00 *Fax:* 01 55 00 11 20 *Web Site:* www. hachette-livre-international.com (orders abroad)
Hatier Diffusion, 8 rue d'Assas, 75006 Paris *Tel:* 01 49 54 49 54 *Fax:* 01 49 54 49 71 *E-mail:* ffera@editions-hatier.com *Web Site:* www.editions-hatier.com (orders within France)

Editions Ramsay
91 bis rue du Cherche-Midi, 75006 Paris
Tel: 01 53 10 02 80 *Fax:* 01 53 10 02 88
Founded: 1976
Subjects: Drama, Theater, Fiction, History, Literature, Literary Criticism, Essays, Nonfiction (General)
ISBN Prefix(es): 978-2-84114
Parent Company: Vilo Groupe

Les Editions Raphael
7 pl Gambetta, 19400 Argentat
Tel: 05 55 28 61 20
E-mail: info@editionsraphael.com
Web Site: www.editionsraphael.com
Founded: 1990
Subjects: Inspirational, Spirituality, Literature, Literary Criticism, Essays, Philosophy, Psychology, Psychiatry, Religion - Protestant, Christian
ISBN Prefix(es): 978-2-88417
Number of titles published annually: 3 Print
Total Titles: 42 Print
Foreign Rep(s): La Centrale biblique (Belgium); Interlivres (North America); Maison de la Bible (Switzerland); Librairie 7ICI (France)

Refclim, *imprint of* COSTIC

Regain de lecture
11, rue de Chateaudun, 45000 Orleans
Tel: 02 38 53 15 00 *Fax:* 01 76 50 35 93
E-mail: regaindelecture@laposte.net
Web Site: www.regaindelecture.com
Key Personnel
President: Gilbert Trompas
Founded: 2007

Subjects: Biography, Memoirs, Fiction, Health,
Nutrition, History, Humor, Literature, Literary
Criticism, Essays, Social Sciences, Sociology
ISBN Prefix(es): 978-2-35391
Parent Company: Corsaire Editions
Foreign Rep(s): La Canopee (North America);
Daudin (France)

Les Editions du Regard
One rue du Delta, 75009 Paris
Tel: 01 53 21 86 80 *Fax:* 01 53 21 86 90
E-mail: info@editions-du-regard.com
Web Site: www.editions-du-regard.com
Key Personnel
Dir: Jose Alvarez *E-mail:* j.alvarez@editions-du-
regard.com
Sales Dir: Christine Simon *Tel:* 06 76 81 50 48
(cell) *E-mail:* c.simon@editions-du-regard.com
Press: Catherine Philippot *E-mail:* cathphilippot@
photographie.com
Founded: 1979
Subjects: Architecture & Interior Design, Art,
Fashion, Photography, Contemporary Culture
ISBN Prefix(es): 978-2-903370; 978-2-84105

Collection Reperes, *imprint of* Editions La
Decouverte

Editions Retz
9 bis, rue Abel Hovelacque, 75013 Paris
Tel: 01 72 36 48 58 *Fax:* 01 72 36 48 65
E-mail: info@editions-retz.com
Web Site: www.editions-retz.com
Key Personnel
Dir General: Philippe Champy
Dir, Publication: Catherine Lucet
Editorial Dir: Sylvie Cuchin
Dir, Sales & Promotion: Annik Chailan
Foreign Rights: Laurence Beauchee *Tel:* 01 72 36
30 58 *E-mail:* lbeauchee@sejer.fr
Founded: 1975
Subjects: Education, Pedagogy
ISBN Prefix(es): 978-2-7256
Number of titles published annually: 85 Print
Total Titles: 700 Print
Distribution Center: Interforum, Immeuble Pary-
seine, 3, allee de la seine, 94854 Ivry-sur-Seine
Tel: 01 49 59 10 10 *Web Site:* www.interforum.
fr

Les Revues de La Decouverte, *imprint of*
Editions La Decouverte

Les Editions du Ricochet
One, rue Spitalieri, 06000 Nice
Tel: 01 40 33 84 16
Web Site: ricochet-livres-jeunesse.fr; ricochet.
over-blog.net
Key Personnel
Dir, Foreign Rights & Editor: Natalie Vock-Verley
Tel: 06 99 55 19 90 *E-mail:* ricochet.nvv@
orange.fr
Editor: Marguerite Tiberti *Tel:* 04 93 13 04 00
E-mail: ricochet.mt@orange.fr
Founded: 1995
Membership(s): Editeurs sans Frontieres; Jedi
Paca.
Subjects: Fiction, Literature, Literary Criticism,
Essays, Poetry
ISBN Prefix(es): 978-2-35263; 978-2-911013
Foreign Rep(s): ADL (Canada); Dargaud Suisse
(Switzerland); SDL Caravelle (Belgium)
Distribution Center: SODIS *Tel:* 01 60 07 82 99
Fax: 01 64 30 32 27 *E-mail:* saisie@sodis.fr

RMN-Grand Palais, see Editions de la Reunion
des Musees Nationaux-Grand Palais

Le Robert
Subsidiary of Les Editions Nathan

25, ave Pierre de Coubertin, 75211 Paris Cedex
13
Tel: 01 53 55 26 25
E-mail: commercial.numerique@lerobert.com
Web Site: www.lerobert.com
Key Personnel
President & Mng Dir: Bertrand Eveno
Publishing Dir: Catherine Lucet
Founded: 1951
ISBN Prefix(es): 978-2-85036; 978-2-84902

Editions du Rouergue+
47 rue du Docteur Fanton, 13633 Arles Cedex
Mailing Address: BP 90038, 13633 Arles Cedex
Tel: 05 65 77 73 70 *Fax:* 05 65 77 73 71
E-mail: info@lerouergue.com
Web Site: www.lerouergue.com
Key Personnel
Press: Brigitte Reydel *E-mail:* brigitte.reydel@
lerouergue.com
Sales & Promotion: Adele Leproux *E-mail:* adele.
leproux@lerouergue.com
Founded: 1986
Subjects: Cookery, Fiction, Gardening, Plants,
Health, Nutrition, How-to, Romance, Wine &
Spirits
ISBN Prefix(es): 978-2-84156; 978-2-905209
Foreign Rep(s): Servidis (Canada, Switzerland)
Distribution Center: UD-Union Distribution, 106
rue Petit Leroy, 94550 Chevilly-Larue

Rue du Monde
5 rue de Port-Royal, 78960 Voisins-le-Bretonneux
Tel: 01 30 48 08 38 *Fax:* 01 30 57 90 82
E-mail: contact@ruedumonde.fr
Web Site: ruedumonde.fr
Key Personnel
Publisher: Alain Serres
Founded: 1996
ISBN Prefix(es): 978-2-912084; 978-2-915569

Editions Rue d'Ulm
45, rue d'Ulm, 75005 Paris
Tel: 01 44 32 36 80; 01 44 32 36 83
E-mail: ulm-editions@ens.fr
Web Site: www.presses.ens.fr
Key Personnel
Dir: Lucie Marignac *E-mail:* lucie.marignac@ens.
fr
Communication, Rights & Website: Dominique
Michel *E-mail:* dominique.michel@ens.fr
Editorial & Production: Marie-Helene Ravenel
Tel: 01 44 32 36 83 *E-mail:* marie-helene.
ravenel@ens.fr
Founded: 1975
Subjects: Anthropology, Antiques, Archaeology,
Art, Economics, Geography, Geology, History,
Language Arts, Linguistics, Literature, Literary
Criticism, Essays, Music, Dance, Native Amer-
ican Studies, Nonfiction (General), Philosophy,
Science (General), Social Sciences, Sociology,
Ecography
ISBN Prefix(es): 978-2-7288
Number of titles published annually: 20 Print; 2
Online
Total Titles: 300 Print; 50 Online

Rustica, *imprint of* Fleurus Editions

Editions Rustica
Imprint of Fleurus Editions
15-27, rue Moussorgski, 75018 Paris
Tel: 01 53 26 33 00 *Fax:* 01 53 26 33 36
E-mail: editions-web@rustica.fr
Web Site: www.rustica.fr; www.fleuruseditions.
com/rustica
Key Personnel
Dir General: Hilaire de Laage
Dir, Publications: Vincent Montagne
Founded: 1928
Subjects: Cookery, Gardening, Plants

ISBN Prefix(es): 978-2-84038; 978-2-8153
Foreign Rep(s): Dargaud Suisse (Switzerland);
Media Diffusion Belgique (Belgium); Prologue
(Canada)
Distribution Center: MDS, ZA des Jalots, 91417
Dourdan Cedex *Tel:* 01 60 81 87 00 *Fax:* 01
64 59 30 63

Le Sablier Editions
8 Pl du Bourguet, 04300 Forcalquier
Tel: 04 92 79 40 00 *Fax:* 04 92 79 40 01
E-mail: contact@lesablier-editions.com
Web Site: www.lesablier-editions.com
Key Personnel
Chief Executive Officer: Helene Bonis
E-mail: hbonis@lesablier-editions.com
Subjects: Art, Fiction, Geography, Geology, His-
tory
ISBN Prefix(es): 978-2-84390
Foreign Rep(s): Benjamin (Canada); La Caravelle
(Belgium); Heidiffusion (Switzerland); Sodis
(France)

Sakka, *imprint of* Flammarion Groupe

Editions Salvator+
103 rue Notre-Dame des Champs, 75006 Paris
Tel: 01 53 10 38 38 *Fax:* 01 53 10 38 39
E-mail: contact@editions-salvator.com
Web Site: www.editions-salvator.com
Key Personnel
Dir General: Yves Briend *E-mail:* briend.yves@
wanadoo.fr
Commercial Dir: Francois-Rene Charles
E-mail: frcharles@editions-salvator.com
Commercial: Francois de Bayser
E-mail: fdebayser@editions-salvator.com
Press: Thomine Josseaume *E-mail:* tjosseaume@
editions-salvator.com
Founded: 1924
Subjects: Human Relations, Religion - Other
ISBN Prefix(es): 978-2-7067

Editions Sand & Tchou+
6, rue du Mail, 75002 Paris
Tel: 01 44 55 37 50 *Fax:* 01 40 20 99 74
Key Personnel
Mng Dir: Carl van Eiszner
Founded: 1979
Subjects: Astrology, Occult, Biography, Memoirs,
Health, Nutrition, How-to, Psychology, Psychi-
atry, Social Sciences, Sociology
ISBN Prefix(es): 978-2-7107
Subsidiaries: Editions Menges
Distribution Center: Interforum Editis, 46 Route
de Sermaises, 45330 Malesherbes

Editions Sang de la Terre+
4 rue d'Alesia, 75014 Paris
Tel: 08 91 67 00 08; 01 40 47 79 14
E-mail: info@ellebore.com
Web Site: www.sangdelaterre.fr
Key Personnel
Publishing Dir: Edouard Frison-Roche
Founded: 1986
Subjects: Agriculture, Animals, Pets, Cookery,
Crafts, Games, Hobbies, Environmental Stud-
ies, Gardening, Plants, Health, Nutrition, How-
to
ISBN Prefix(es): 978-2-86985
Subsidiaries: 670 Bornemann

Sante Spiritualite, *imprint of* Editions Jouvence
Sarl

Editions Sarbacane
35, rue d'Hauteville, 75010 Paris
Tel: 01 42 46 24 00 *Fax:* 01 42 46 28 15
E-mail: contacts@sarbacane.net
Web Site: www.editions-sarbacane.com

Key Personnel
Dir: Frederic Lavabre *E-mail:* frederic.lavabre@
  sarbacane.net
Editorial Dir: Emmanuelle Beulque *E-mail:* e.
  beulque@sarbacane.net
ISBN Prefix(es): 978-2-84865
Foreign Rep(s): OLF SA (Switzerland); Socadis
  (Canada)
Distribution Center: UD-Union Distribution, 106
  rue Petit Leroy, 94550 Chevilly-Larue (France,
  Belgium & other countries exc Canada &
  Switzerland)

Sauramps Medical+
11 bd Henri IV, 34000 Montpellier
Tel: 04 67 63 68 80; 04 67 63 62 19 *Fax:* 04 67
  52 59 05
Web Site: www.sauramps-medical.com; www.
  livres-medicaux.com
Key Personnel
Mng Dir: Dominique Torreilles
Founded: 1977
Subjects: Medicine, Nursing, Dentistry,
  Gynecology-Obstetrics, Orthopaedic Surgery,
  Radiology
ISBN Prefix(es): 978-2-905030; 978-2-84023
Number of titles published annually: 35 Print
Total Titles: 500 Print
Distributed by Lidel (Portugal); Somabec
  (Canada); Vivendi (Belgium)
Bookshop(s): 8 rue Primatice, 75013 Paris, Con-
  tact: Anelia Andonova *Tel:* 01 40 09 27 71
  Fax: 01 40 03 80 71
Distribution Center: Sodis, 128 Ave du Marechal
  de Lattre de Tassigny, 77400 Lagny sur Marne
  Tel: 01 60 07 82 00 *Fax:* 01 64 30 92 22
  E-mail: portail@sodis.fr *Web Site:* www.sodis.
  fr

Sciences Humaines Editions
38, rue Rantheaume, 89004 Auxerre Cedex
Mailing Address: BP 256, 89004 Auxerre Cedex
Tel: 03 86 72 07 00 *Fax:* 03 86 52 53 26
Web Site: editions.scienceshumaines.com; www.
  scienceshumaines.com
Key Personnel
Publishing Dir: Veronique Bedin *Tel:* 03 86 72 17
  34 *E-mail:* veronique.bedin@scienceshumaines.
  com
Dir, Sales & Marketing: Nadia Latreche
  Tel: 03 86 72 07 08 *E-mail:* nadia.latreche@
  scienceshumaines.fr
Production: Natacha Reverre *Tel:* 03 86 72 07 11
  E-mail: natacha.reverre@scienceshumaines.fr
Subjects: Anthropology, Communications, Eco-
  nomics, Education, Geography, Geology, Gov-
  ernment, Political Science, History, Philosophy,
  Psychology, Psychiatry, Social Sciences, Soci-
  ology, Humanities
ISBN Prefix(es): 978-2-912601

Editions Seghers+
Imprint of Editions Robert Laffont
24 Ave Marceau, 75381 Paris Cedex 08
Tel: 01 53 67 14 00
Web Site: www.editions-seghers.tm.fr
Key Personnel
Publishing Dir: Alain Kouck
Foreign Rights: Benita Edzard *E-mail:* bedzard@
  robert-laffont.fr; Judith Temmam
  E-mail: jtemmam@robert-laffont.fr
Founded: 1944
Subjects: Poetry
ISBN Prefix(es): 978-2-232

Editions Seguier
3, rue Seguier, 75006 Paris
Tel: 01 55 42 61 40 *Fax:* 01 55 42 61 41
E-mail: contact@editions-seguier.fr
Web Site: www.editions-seguier.fr
Key Personnel
Dir: Jean Le Gall

Subjects: Art, Drama, Theater, Literature, Literary
  Criticism, Essays, Music, Dance, Photography,
  Cinema
ISBN Prefix(es): 978-2-84049

Selection du Reader's Digest SA
191, ave Aristide Briand, 94230 Cachan
Web Site: www.selectionclic.com
Key Personnel
Chief Executive Officer: Hanno Schwarzenegger
Founded: 1947
Subjects: Architecture & Interior Design, Art,
  Economics, Environmental Studies, Fiction,
  History, How-to, Literature, Literary Criticism,
  Essays, Medicine, Nursing, Dentistry, Science
  (General), Social Sciences, Sociology, Technol-
  ogy, Travel & Tourism
ISBN Prefix(es): 978-2-7098

Editions Diane de Selliers
20, rue d'Anjou, 75008 Paris
Tel: 01 42 68 09 00 *Fax:* 01 42 68 11 50
E-mail: contact@dianedeselliers.com
Web Site: www.editionsdianedeselliers.com
Key Personnel
Publisher: Diane de Selliers
Founded: 1991
Subjects: Art, Literature, Literary Criticism, Es-
  says, Fine Art
ISBN Prefix(es): 978-2-903656

Editions Le Seneve+
10 Rue Mercoeur, 75011 Paris
Tel: 01 40 46 54 00 *Fax:* 01 58 51 10 48
E-mail: contact@editionsleseneve.fr
Web Site: www.editionsleseneve.fr
Key Personnel
Press: Jean-Philippe Bertrand *Tel:* 01 40 46 54 30
  E-mail: jeanphilippe.bertrand@artege.fr
Founded: 1950
Subjects: Education, Religion - Catholic, Theol-
  ogy
ISBN Prefix(es): 978-2-283
Number of titles published annually: 10 Print
Total Titles: 130 Print
Parent Company: Artege, 9 Espace Mediterranee,
  6600 Perpignan
Distribution Center: Sodis, 128 Ave du Marechal
  de Lattre de Tassigny, 77400 Lagny-sur-Marne
  Tel: 01 60 07 82 00 *E-mail:* portail@sodis.fr

Editions Sepia
6 Ave du Gouverneur General Binger, 94100 St-
  Maur-des-Fosses
Tel: 01 43 97 22 14 *Fax:* 01 43 97 32 62
E-mail: sepia@editions-sepia.com
Web Site: www.editions-sepia.com
Founded: 1986
Specialize in Africa.
Subjects: Archaeology, Art, Ethnicity, Fiction,
  Foreign Countries, Social Sciences, Sociology
ISBN Prefix(es): 978-2-84280; 978-2-907888

Le Serpent a Plumes
2, rue de la Mairie, La Madeleine-De-
  Nonancourt, 27320 Haute-Normandie
E-mail: contact@leserpentaplumes.com
Web Site: www.facebook.com/leserpentaplumes
Key Personnel
Contact: Xavier Belrose; Pierre Bisiou
Founded: 1988
Subjects: Fiction, Foreign Countries, Literature,
  Literary Criticism, Essays
ISBN Prefix(es): 978-2-908957; 978-2-84261

**Service Hydrographique et Oceanographique
  de la Marine (SHOM)** (Navy Hydrographic &
  Oceangraphic Service)
CS 92803, 29228 Brest Cedex 2
Tel: 02 98 22 17 47
Web Site: www.shom.fr

Key Personnel
Executive Dir: Bruno Frachon
Founded: 1720
Charts & nautical books.
Membership(s): International Hydrographic Orga-
  nization.
Subjects: Maritime
ISBN Prefix(es): 978-2-218

Editions du Seuil+
Subsidiary of La Martiniere Groupe
25, bd Romain Rolland, 75014 Paris
Tel: 01 41 48 80 00 *Fax:* 01 41 48 83 89
E-mail: contact@seuil.com; commercial@seuil.
  com; droitsetrangers@seuil.com
Web Site: www.seuil.com; www.editions-seuil-
  paris.fr
Key Personnel
President: Olivier Betourne
Founded: 1935
Also distributor.
Subjects: Art, Biography, Memoirs, Fiction, Gov-
  ernment, Political Science, History, How-to,
  Literature, Literary Criticism, Essays, Music,
  Dance, Philosophy, Photography, Poetry, Psy-
  chology, Psychiatry, Religion - Other, Science
  (General), Social Sciences, Sociology
ISBN Prefix(es): 978-2-02; 978-2-35949 (Don
  Quichotte)
Total Titles: 500 Print
Imprints: Don Quichotte
Distributor for Alliage; L'Ane; Arlea; Autrement;
  Baleine; Belin; Bibliotheque Nationale de
  France; Boreal; Bourgois; Cahiers du Cin-
  ema; Callicephale; Cause Freudienne; Corti;
  Esprit; Les 400 coups; Genre Humain; Hoe-
  beke; L'Homme; O Jacob; Liana Levi; Mai-
  son des Roches; A M Metailie; Milan; Minuit;
  Mollat; Montparnasse Editions Video; Navarin;
  Noir sur Blanc; Olivier; Panoramiques; Payot-
  Rivages; Phebus; Raisons d'Agir; Regard;
  RMN; Sept Video Arte; Taize; Textuel; Thames
  & Hudson; Verticales
Foreign Rep(s): Dimedia (Canada); Loglibris
  (Belgium, France); Servidis (Switzerland)

SHOM, see Service Hydrographique et
  Oceanographique de la Marine (SHOM)

Editions La Simarre+
24 rue Joseph Cugnot, 37300 Joue-les-Tours
  Cedex
Mailing Address: BP 10407, 37304 Joue-les-
  Tours Cedex
Tel: 02 47 53 53 66 *Fax:* 02 47 67 45 05
E-mail: la-simarre@wanadoo.fr
Web Site: www.lasimarre.com; www.
  christianpirot.com
Founded: 1967
Subjects: Archaeology, Biography, Memoirs,
  Cookery, Fiction, History, Literature, Literary
  Criticism, Essays, Medicine, Nursing, Den-
  tistry, Music, Dance, Poetry, Science (General),
  Travel & Tourism
ISBN Prefix(es): 978-2-86808; 978-2-36536
Total Titles: 46 Print
Associate Companies: Friendship-First, 40 rue de
  Vincennes, 33000 Bordeaux *Web Site:* www.
  friendship-first.com
Orders to: Les Belles Lettres, 25, rue du general
  Leclerc, 94270 Le Kremlin-Bicetre *Tel:* 01 45
  15 19 70 *Fax:* 01 45 15 19 80 *Web Site:* www.
  bldd.fr

Sirey, *imprint of* Editions Dalloz

Slavonic, see Institut d'etudes slaves

SN Editions Anne Carriere
39 rue de Mathurins, 75008 Paris
Tel: 01 44 07 47 57 *Fax:* 01 44 07 47 58
Web Site: www.anne-carriere.fr

Key Personnel
Publisher: Anne Carriere
Editorial & Production: Sophie Bagur
Rights: Yasmina Urien
Press: Anne-Sophie Naudin *Tel:* 01 44 07 47 53
Founded: 1994
Subjects: Fiction, Literature, Literary Criticism,
Essays, Nonfiction (General)
ISBN Prefix(es): 978-2-84337; 978-2-910188

Societe Biblique Francaise+
5 Ave des Erables, 95400 Villiers-le-Bel
Mailing Address: BP 47, 95400 Villiers-le-Bel
Tel: 01 39 94 50 51 *Fax:* 01 39 90 53 51
E-mail: alliance.biblique@sbf.fr
Web Site: www.la-bible.net
Key Personnel
President: Christian Megrelis
Acting Secretary General: Elsbeth Scherrer
  E-mail: elsbeth.scherrer@sbf.fr
Founded: 1818
Membership(s): United Bible Societies/Alliance
  Biblique Universelle.
Subjects: Religion - Catholic, Religion - Protes-
  tant
ISBN Prefix(es): 978-2-85300
Number of titles published annually: 4 CD-ROM
Total Titles: 140 Print; 14 CD-ROM
Imprints: Alliance Biblique Universelle
U.S. Office(s): American Bible Society, 1865
  Broadway, New York, NY 10023-7505, United
  States *Tel:* 212-408-1200
Distributed by CERF; Oberlin
Distributor for Brepols; CERF; CLC; Desclee de
  Brower; Farel; Vie et Sante

**Societe d'Etudes Juridiques Internationales et
Fiscales**, see Les Cahiers Fiscaux Europeens
Sarl

**Societe Francaise des Imprimeries
  Administratives Centrales**, see Sofiac (Societe
Francaise des Imprimeries Administratives
Centrales)

**Societe Mathematique de France - Institut
  Henri Poincare**
11 rue Pierre-et-Marie-Curie, 75231 Paris Cedex
05
Tel: 01 44 27 67 96 *Fax:* 01 40 46 90 96
E-mail: smf@dma.ens.fr
Web Site: smf.emath.fr
Key Personnel
President: Marc Peigne *Tel:* 01 44 27 67 77
  E-mail: smfpre@dma.ens.fr
Secretary General: Claire Ropartz *Tel:* 01 44 27
  67 96
Publications: Nathalie Christiansen *Tel:* 01 44 27
  67 99 *E-mail:* christia@dma.ens.fr
Founded: 1872
Subjects: Mathematics
ISBN Prefix(es): 978-2-85629
Number of titles published annually: 20 Print
Bookshop(s): Maison de la SMF, Case 916-
  Luminy, 13288 Marseille Cedex 9, Contact:
  Christian Munusami *Tel:* 04 91 26 74 64
  Fax: 04 91 41 17 51 *E-mail:* smf@smf.univ-
  mrs.fr

**Sofiac (Societe Francaise des Imprimeries
  Administratives Centrales)+**
104 ave du President Kennedy, 75016 Paris
Tel: 03 83 38 83 83
E-mail: courrier@berger-levrault.fr
Web Site: www.berger-levrault.com
Subjects: Accounting, Business, Law, Public Ad-
  ministration
ISBN Prefix(es): 978-2-85130
Parent Company: Groupe Berger-Levrault

Editions Solar
12, Ave d'Italie, 75627 Paris Cedex 13
Tel: 01 44 16 05 00
E-mail: contact_solar@placedeseediteurs.com
Web Site: www.solar.fr
Key Personnel
Publishing Dir: Jean Arcache
Founded: 1999
Subjects: Cookery, Crafts, Games, Hobbies, Gar-
  dening, Plants, Health, Nutrition, Nonfiction
  (General), Photography, Sports, Athletics,
  Transportation, Wine & Spirits, Fitness, Nature,
  Performing Arts
ISBN Prefix(es): 978-2-263
Parent Company: Place des editeurs
Ultimate Parent Company: Editis
Foreign Rep(s): Interforum Benelux SA (Bel-
  gium); Interforum Canada Inc (Canada); Inter-
  forum Suisse SA (Switzerland)
Foreign Rights: Editions Hemma (Paul Bernard)
Distribution Center: Interforum, Immeuble Pary-
  seine, 3, allee de la Seine, 94854 Ivry Cedex
  Tel: 01 49 59 10 10

Somogy Editions d'art+
57, rue de la Roquette, 75011 Paris
Tel: 01 48 05 70 10 *Fax:* 01 48 05 71 70
Web Site: www.somogy.fr
Key Personnel
Editorial Dir: Nicolas Neumann
Dir, Commercial & Marketing: Marc-Alexis
  Baranes
Founded: 1937
Subjects: Antiques, Archaeology, Architecture &
  Interior Design, Art, Biography, Memoirs, Pho-
  tography
ISBN Prefix(es): 978-2-84598; 978-2-85056; 978-
  2-7572

Sonatine Editions
32, rue Washington, 75008 Paris
Tel: 01 45 00 13 63 *Fax:* 01 45 00 13 09
Web Site: www.sonatine-editions.fr
Key Personnel
Manager: Francois Verdoux
Literary Dir: Arnaud Hofmarcher
Deputy Dir: Anne-France Hubau-Nicolas
Editorial Coordinator & Sales Manager: Leonore
  Dauzier *E-mail:* l.dauzier@sonatine-editions.fr
Editorial Coordinator & Bookseller Relations:
  Marie Labonne
Administrator: Valentine Gressel
Press & Public Relations: Muriel Poletti-Arles
  Tel: 06 63 68 24 43 *E-mail:* murielpoletti.
  arles@gmail.com
Subjects: Biography, Memoirs, Fiction, Mysteries,
  Suspense
ISBN Prefix(es): 978-2-35584
Foreign Rep(s): Interforum Benelux (Belgium);
  Interforum Canada (Canada); Interforum Suisse
  (Switzerland)
Distribution Center: Interforum, 46, route de
  Sermaises, BP 11, 45331 Malesherbes Cedex
  Tel: 02 38 32 71 00 *Fax:* 02 38 32 71 28

Presses Sorbonne Nouvelle
Universite Paris III, 8 rue de la Sorbonne, 75005
Paris
Tel: 01 40 46 48 02 *Fax:* 01 40 46 48 04
E-mail: psn@univ-paris3.fr
Web Site: psn.univ-paris3.fr
Key Personnel
Dir: Nathalie Dauvois
Administrative, Technique & Finance: Michele
  Leprettre *Tel:* 01 45 87 40 27 *E-mail:* michele.
  leprettre@univ-paris3.fr
Promotion & Distribution: Corinne Luc
Founded: 1982
Subjects: Drama, Theater, History, Language
  Arts, Linguistics, Literature, Literary Criticism,
  Essays
ISBN Prefix(es): 978-2-87854; 978-2-903019

Number of titles published annually: 20 Print
Bookshop(s): CID, 131 Blvd St Michel, 75005
  Paris, Contact: Michel Zumkir *Tel:* 01 43 54
  47 45 *Fax:* 01 43 54 80 73 *E-mail:* cid@msh-
  paris.fr

Publications de la Sorbonne
212, rue St-Jacques, 75005 Paris
Tel: 01 43 25 80 15 *Fax:* 01 43 54 03 24
E-mail: rapubsor@univ-paris1.fr
Web Site: www.univ-paris1.fr/services/
  publications-de-la-sorbonne; www.publications-
  sorbonne.fr
Founded: 1971
Subjects: Anthropology, Archaeology, Art, Eco-
  nomics, Geography, Geology, Government,
  Political Science, History, Language Arts, Lin-
  guistics, Law, Literature, Literary Criticism,
  Essays, Philosophy, Social Sciences, Sociology
ISBN Prefix(es): 978-2-85944
Number of titles published annually: 30 Print
Total Titles: 600 Print
Distribution Center: Sodis, 128 Ave du Marechel
  de Lattre de Tassigny, 77403 Lagny-sur-Marne
  Tel: 01 60 07 82 00

Sortileges, *imprint of* Societe d'Edition Les
Belles Lettres

Editions Le Souffle d'Or
5, Allee du Torrent, 05000 Gap
Tel: 04 92 65 52 24
E-mail: contact@souffledor.fr
Web Site: www.souffledor.fr
Key Personnel
President & Editor: Yves Michel
  E-mail: ymichel@souffledor.fr
Founded: 1983
Subjects: Crafts, Games, Hobbies, Education,
  Health, Nutrition, Inspirational, Spirituality,
  Literature, Literary Criticism, Essays, Music,
  Dance, Nonfiction (General), Self-Help, Ecol-
  ogy, Humanities
ISBN Prefix(es): 978-2-84058; 978-2-904670
Foreign Rep(s): Nord-Sud (Belgium); Prologue
  (Canada); Servidis (Switzerland); Transat
  (Switzerland)
Distribution Center: Dilisco, Rue de Limousin,
  23220 Chenniers *Tel:* 05 55 51 80 00 *Fax:* 05
  55 62 17 39 *E-mail:* relation.client@dilisco.fr
Web Site: www.dilisco-diffusion-distribution.fr

Editions Souffles, *imprint of* Editions Fabert

Editions Souffles+
Imprint of Editions Fabert
107 rue de la Universite, 75007 Paris
Tel: 01 47 05 32 68 *Fax:* 01 47 05 05 61
Key Personnel
President: Thomas Jallaud
Founded: 1987
Subjects: Literature, Literary Criticism, Essays
ISBN Prefix(es): 978-2-87658

Springer-Verlag France SAS+
Subsidiary of Springer-Verlag GmbH
22, rue de Palestro, 75002 Paris
Tel: 01 53 00 98 60 *Fax:* 01 53 00 98 61
Web Site: www.springer.com/?SGWID=7-102-12-
  173889-0
Key Personnel
Dir General: Guido Zosimo-Landolfo
Founded: 1986
Subjects: Astronomy, Chemistry, Chemical En-
  gineering, Civil Engineering, Computer Sci-
  ence, Earth Sciences, Economics, Electron-
  ics, Electrical Engineering, Engineering (Gen-
  eral), Mathematics, Mechanical Engineering,
  Medicine, Nursing, Dentistry, Physics, Psychol-
  ogy, Psychiatry
ISBN Prefix(es): 978-2-287; 978-88-470

STIL Editions Paris
22, bd St-Denis, 75010 Paris
Tel: 01 48 00 92 24 *Fax:* 01 48 00 93 36
E-mail: info@stileditions.com
Web Site: www.stileditions.com
Key Personnel
Editor: Alain Villain
Founded: 1971
Subjects: Art, Literature, Literary Criticism, Essays, Music, Dance
ISBN Prefix(es): 978-2-85254

Editions Stock+
Subsidiary of Hachette Livre
31 rue de Fleurus, 75006 Paris
Tel: 01 49 54 36 55; 01 49 54 36 75 (rights)
    Fax: 01 49 54 36 62; 01 49 54 36 67 (rights)
Web Site: www.editions-stock.fr
Key Personnel
Publishing Dir: Manuel Carcassonne
Foreign Rights Dir: Maylis Vauterin
    E-mail: mvauterin@editions-stock.fr
Founded: 1708
Subjects: Biography, Memoirs, Child Care & Development, Fiction, Film, Video, Literature, Literary Criticism, Essays, Nonfiction (General), Poetry, Social Sciences, Sociology
ISBN Prefix(es): 978-2-234

Editions Sud Ouest
Subsidiary of Groupe Sud Ouest
23, quai de Queyries, 33094 Bordeaux Cedex
Mailing Address: CS 20001, 33094 Bordeaux Cedex
Tel: 05 35 31 21 35 *Fax:* 05 35 31 21 39
E-mail: contact@editions-sudouest.com
Web Site: www.editions-sudouest.com
Key Personnel
Publisher: Marie Cardinaud *E-mail:* m.cardinaud@editions-sudouest.com
Press: Maria Darribere *E-mail:* m.darribere@editions-sudouest.com
Founded: 1988
Subjects: Cookery, History, How-to, Outdoor Recreation, Regional Interests
ISBN Prefix(es): 978-2-87901; 978-2-902083
Number of titles published annually: 60 Print
Total Titles: 500 Print
Subsidiaries: Rando Editions SA
Distributor for Editions Jean Paul Gisserot
Foreign Rep(s): Caravelle (Belgium, Luxembourg); Craenen (Belgium, Luxembourg); Servidis (Switzerland); Ulysse (Canada)
Distribution Center: Cap Diffusion, 13, rue de Breil, 35000 Rennes *Tel:* 02 99 32 58 23 *Fax:* 02 99 32 58 18 *E-mail:* commercial@capdiffusion.fr

Editions le Sureau, *imprint of* Adverbum

Editions SW Telemaque
7, rue Perignon, 75015 Paris
Tel: 01 56 58 69 99 *Fax:* 01 56 58 26 00
E-mail: sw@editionstelemaque.com (foreign rights)
Web Site: www.editionstelemaque.com
Key Personnel
Editor: Stephane Watelet
Press: Chantal Pelletier *E-mail:* cp@editionstelemaque.com
Founded: 2004
Subjects: Biography, Memoirs, Fiction, History, Mysteries, Suspense, Romance, Science Fiction, Fantasy
ISBN Prefix(es): 978-2-7533

Editions Syros
25, ave Pierre de Coubertin, 75211 Paris Cedex 13
Tel: 01 45 87 50 55 *Fax:* 01 45 87 50 70
E-mail: contact@syros.fr

Web Site: www.syros.fr
Key Personnel
Foreign Rights: Marie Dessaix *Tel:* 01 45 87 53 71 *Fax:* 01 45 87 57 80 *E-mail:* mdessaix@nathan.fr
Press: Veronique Delisle-Guijarro *Tel:* 01 45 87 50 10 *E-mail:* vdelisle@syros.fr
Founded: 1972
Subjects: Fiction, Nonfiction (General)
ISBN Prefix(es): 978-2-7485
Foreign Rep(s): Interforum Benelux SA (Belgium); Interforum Canada (Canada); Interforum Suisse SA (Switzerland)
Distribution Center: Interforum, 46, route de Sermaises, BP 11, 45331 Malesherbes Cedex *Tel:* 02 38 32 71 00 *Fax:* 02 38 32 71 28

Editions de la Table Ronde
Subsidiary of Editions Gallimard
26, rue de Conde, 75006 Paris
Tel: 01 40 46 70 70
E-mail: editionslatableronde@editionslatableronde.fr
Web Site: www.editionslatableronde.fr
Key Personnel
Dir General: Alice Deon *E-mail:* alicedeon@editionslatableronde.fr
Editorial Dir: Francoise de Maulde *E-mail:* francoise.demaulde@editionslatableronde.fr
Press: Nadine Straub *Tel:* 01 40 46 70 73 *E-mail:* n.straub@editionslatableronde.fr
Founded: 1944
Subjects: Biography, Memoirs, Drama, Theater, Fiction, History, Inspirational, Spirituality, Literature, Literary Criticism, Essays, Nonfiction (General), Philosophy, Poetry, Psychology, Psychiatry, Religion - Buddhist, Religion - Other, Sports, Athletics, French Literature
ISBN Prefix(es): 978-2-7103
Number of titles published annually: 55 Print
Total Titles: 3,500 Print
Associate Companies: Editione la Palatine

Editions Talents Hauts
8 rue Charles Pathe, 94300 Vincennes
Tel: 01 41 93 16 64
E-mail: contact@talentshauts.fr; information@talentshauts.fr
Web Site: www.talentshauts.fr
Key Personnel
Founder: Melanie Decourt; Laurence Faron
Founded: 2005
Subjects: Education, Fiction, Mysteries, Suspense
ISBN Prefix(es): 978-2-36266
Total Titles: 150 Print
Distribution Center: Volumen, 25 blvd Romain Rolland, 75014 Paris *Tel:* 01 41 48 84 60 *Fax:* 01 41 48 81 32 (France & Belgium)
Le Forum, 3 Westgate Mall, Fremantle, WA 6160, Australia *Tel:* (08) 9335 5730 *Fax:* (08) 9335 5731 *E-mail:* info@leforum.com.au
Dimedia, 539 Blvd Lebeau, St Laurent, QC H4N 1S2, Canada *Tel:* 514-336-3941 *Fax:* 514-331-3916 *E-mail:* general@dimedia.qc.ca
Servidis, Chemin des Chalets n 7, 1279 Chavannes de Bogis, Switzerland *Tel:* (022) 960 95 10 *Fax:* (022) 776 35 27 *E-mail:* admin@servidis.ch

Editions Tallandier+
2, rue Rotrou, 75006 Paris
Tel: 01 40 46 43 88 *Fax:* 01 40 46 43 98
E-mail: info@tallandier.com; rights@tallandier.com
Web Site: www.tallandier.com
Key Personnel
Commercial: Baptiste Renault *Tel:* 01 40 46 43 87
Foreign Rights: Marie Lannurien
Press: Isabelle Bouche *Tel:* 01 40 46 43 97
Founded: 1865

Specialize in history.
Subjects: Art, Fiction, Geography, Geology, History
ISBN Prefix(es): 978-2-235
Foreign Rep(s): Dimedia (Canada); SDLC La Caravelle (Belgium); Servidis (Switzerland); Volumen (France)

Editions Tana
12, ave d'Italie, 75627 Paris
Tel: 01 44 16 09 04
Web Site: www.tana.fr
Key Personnel
Dir, Communications: Caroline Destais-Brochain *E-mail:* cdestais@efirst.com
Subjects: Cookery, Crafts, Games, Hobbies, Sports, Athletics
ISBN Prefix(es): 978-2-84567; 979-10-301
Parent Company: Edi8
Ultimate Parent Company: Editis Group

Editions Tardy+
Imprint of Fleurus Editions
15-27, rue Moussorgski, 75018 Paris
E-mail: fleuruseditions@fleuruseditions.com; foreignrights@fleuruseditions.com
Web Site: www.fleuruseditions.com
Key Personnel
Foreign Rights Manager: Anne Desrame *Tel:* 01 40 83 82 73 *Fax:* 01 40 83 82 71 *E-mail:* a.desrame@fleuruseditions.com
Founded: 1938
Subjects: Religion - Catholic, Religion - Other
ISBN Prefix(es): 978-2-7105
Ultimate Parent Company: Media-Participations

Taride Editions+
15 rue Mansart, 75009 Paris
Tel: 01 48 78 40 74 *Fax:* 01 48 78 40 77
E-mail: contact@ulisseditions.com; ulisseditions@orange.fr
Web Site: www.ulisseditions.com
Founded: 1852
Subjects: Cookery, Geography, Geology, Travel & Tourism
ISBN Prefix(es): 978-2-7106
Parent Company: Groupe Ulisse

Edition Tawhid
6 impasse Victor Hugo, 69003 Lyon
Tel: 04 72 74 06 46
E-mail: info@edition-tawhid.com
Web Site: www.edition-tawhid.com
Founded: 1990
Subjects: Religion - Islamic, Muslim
ISBN Prefix(es): 978-2-84862; 978-2-909087; 978-2-9782923

Tec & Doc, *imprint of* Editions Lavoisier

Editions Technip SA+
One rue du Bac, 75007 Paris
Tel: 01 45 78 33 80 *Fax:* 01 45 75 37 11
E-mail: info@editionstechnip.com
Web Site: www.editionstechnip.com
Key Personnel
Dir: Paul-Francois Trioux *E-mail:* pft@to-groupe.com
Manager: Sasan Mottaghian *E-mail:* smottaghian@to-groupe.com
Advertising & Press: Annick Deniel *E-mail:* adeniel@to-groupe.com
Founded: 1956
Specialize in the publishing of scientific & technical books on the oil & gas industry.
Subjects: Automotive, Chemistry, Chemical Engineering, Computer Science, Earth Sciences, Electronics, Electrical Engineering, Energy, Engineering (General), Environmental Studies, Mathematics, Technology
ISBN Prefix(es): 978-2-7108

Number of titles published annually: 20 Print
Total Titles: 700 Print; 3 CD-ROM
Distribution Center: Presses Internationales Polytechnique, CP 6079 Succursale Centre-ville,
Montreal, QC H3C 3A7, Canada *Tel:* 514-
340-2835 *Fax:* 514-340-5882 *Web Site:* www.
presses-polytechnique.ca
Servidis, Chemin des Chalets, 1279 Chavannes-
de-Bogis, Switzerland *Tel:* (022) 960 95 25
Fax: (022) 776 63 64 *Web Site:* www.servidis.
ch
Baker & Taylor Publisher Services, 30 Amberwood Parkway, Ashland, OH 44805, United
States *Tel:* 567-215-0030 *E-mail:* info@
btpubservices.com *Web Site:* www.
btpubservices.com

Technique et Vulgarisation, *imprint of* Les
Editions Bordas

Editions Techniques et Scientifiques Francaises
Imprint of Dunod Editeur
5 rue Laromiguiere, 75005 Paris
Tel: 01 40 46 35 00 *Fax:* 01 40 46 49 95
E-mail: infos@dunod.com
Web Site: www.dunod.com
Key Personnel
Dir: Pierre-Andre Michel
ISBN Prefix(es): 978-2-10; 978-2-85535
Ultimate Parent Company: Groupe Hachette Livre

**Editions Techniques et Scientifiques Francaises
(ETSF)**, *imprint of* Dunod Editeur

Le Temps Apprivoise
Imprint of Libella Publishing Group
7, rue des Canettes, 75006 Paris
Tel: 01 44 32 05 60 *Fax:* 01 44 32 05 61
E-mail: informations@libella.fr
Web Site: www.letempsapprivoise.fr
Key Personnel
Press: Stephanie Sanchez
Founded: 2000
Subjects: Crafts, Games, Hobbies, Home Decor,
Needlework
ISBN Prefix(es): 978-2-299
Foreign Rep(s): Interforum Editis (Belgium,
Canada, France, Luxembourg, Switzerland)

Editions 10/18+
Imprint of Univers Poche
12, ave d'Italie, 75013 Paris
Tel: 01 44 16 05 00
E-mail: foreignrights@universpoche.com
Web Site: www.10-18.fr
Key Personnel
Chief Executive Officer: Marie Christine Conchon
Deputy Mng Dir: Francois Laurent
Editorial Dir: Carine Fannius
Commercial Dir: Thierry Diaz
Communications Dir: Sabrina Ananna
Marketing Dir: Veronique Ferrandez
Press: Marie-Laure Pascaud *E-mail:* ml.pascaud@
universpoche.com
Founded: 1962
Subjects: Fiction, Government, Political Science,
Literature, Literary Criticism, Essays, Myster-
ies, Suspense, Historical Crime, International
Fiction
ISBN Prefix(es): 978-2-264
Number of titles published annually: 114 Print
Total Titles: 1,086 Print
Ultimate Parent Company: Editis

Librairie Pierre Tequi et Editions Tequi
8, rue de Mezieres, 75006 Paris
Tel: 01 42 22 70 40
E-mail: contact@editionstequi.com
Web Site: www.librairietequi.com
Key Personnel
Dir: Francois Lemaire

Founded: 1865
Subjects: Education, Philosophy, Religion -
Catholic, Social Sciences, Sociology, Theology
ISBN Prefix(es): 978-2-7403; 978-2-85244
Bookshop(s): Le Roc St-Michel, 53150 St-Cenere
Tel: 02 43 01 01 81 *Fax:* 02 43 02 25 52
Distribution Center: AVM Diffusion, BP 49,
ZA des Charmes, 71601 Paray-le-Monial
Tel: 03 85 81 95 95 *Fax:* 03 85 81 95 96
E-mail: librairie@avm-diffusion.com *Web
Site:* www.avm-diffusion.com
Alliance Services, rue de Hal 46A, 1421 Orphain
Bois Seigneur Isaac, Belgium
Librairie Saint Jospeh, 1313 route de
l'Eglise, Quebec, QC G1W 3P3, Canada
E-mail: distribution@librairiesaintjoseph.com
Web Site: www.librairiesaintjoseph.com

Terre Vivante+
Domaine de Raud, 38710 Mens
Tel: 04 76 34 80 80 *Fax:* 04 76 34 84 02
E-mail: info@terrevivante.org
Web Site: www.terrevivante.org
Key Personnel
Publishing Dir: Benoit Richard
Editor: Marie Arnould
Founded: 1979
Subjects: Agriculture, Cookery, Energy, Garden-
ing, Plants, Health, Nutrition, House & Home,
Technology
ISBN Prefix(es): 978-2-904082; 978-2-914717
Total Titles: 2 Print; 60 Audio

Tertium Editions
38 ave Charles de Verninac, 46100 Vayrac
Tel: 09 62 03 18 96 *Fax:* 05 65 41 24 63
E-mail: contact@tertium-editions.fr
Web Site: www.tertium-editions.fr
Key Personnel
Dir: Mireille Veyssiere
Founded: 1995
Subjects: Cookery, Drama, Theater, Environmen-
tal Studies, Literature, Literary Criticism, Es-
says, Management, Poetry
ISBN Prefix(es): 978-2-916132

Editions Theatrales+
20, rue Voltaire, 93100 Montreuil-Sous-Bois
Tel: 01 56 93 36 70 *Fax:* 01 56 93 36 71
E-mail: info@editionstheatrales.fr; catajeunesse@
editionstheatrales.fr
Web Site: www.editionstheatrales.fr
Key Personnel
Founder & Manager: Jean-Pierre Engelbach
Dir: Pierre Banos *E-mail:* pbanos@
editionstheatrales.fr
Commercial Service: Renaud Lopes
E-mail: rlopes@editionstheatrales.fr
Founded: 1988
Subjects: Drama, Theater
ISBN Prefix(es): 978-2-907810; 978-2-84260
Distributed by CDE/Sodis
Distributor for CNDP collection Theatre Aujourd-
hui; Theatre du Soleil

Editions Tiresias+
21, rue Letort, Hall 1, 75018 Paris
Tel: 01 42 23 47 27 *Fax:* 01 42 23 73 27
E-mail: contact@editionstiresias.com
Web Site: www.editionstiresias.com
Key Personnel
Contact: Michel Reynaud
Founded: 1989
Subjects: Biography, Memoirs, History, Literature,
Literary Criticism, Essays
ISBN Prefix(es): 978-2-908527

Editions Tourbillon
10 rue Remy Dumoncel, 75014 Paris
Tel: 01 43 21 24 84 *Fax:* 01 43 21 34 85
Web Site: www.editions-tourbillon.fr

ISBN Prefix(es): 978-2-84801
Imprints: Twirl

Editions Tournez La Page
27, rue Jean Claret, 63000 Clermont-Ferrand
Tel: 09 80 37 62 47
E-mail: communication@editions-tlp.fr; rights@
editions-tlp.fr
Web Site: www.editions-tlp.fr
Key Personnel
Publisher: Christel Durantin *E-mail:* cdurantin@
editions-tlp.fr
Editorial & Production Manager: Marc Pinard
E-mail: mpinard@editions-tlp.fr
Foreign Rights: Tery Bourdon
Press Service & Communication: Severine Le
Goff *Tel:* 06 33 57 17 30
Founded: 2010
Subjects: Education, Health, Nutrition, Humor,
Psychology, Psychiatry, Travel & Tourism,
Coaching, Personal Development
ISBN Prefix(es): 978-2-36483

Editions Tredaniel, see Guy Tredaniel Editeur le
Courrier du Livre

Guy Tredaniel Editeur le Courrier du Livre
19 rue St Severin, 75005 Paris
Tel: 01 43 36 41 05
E-mail: tredaniel-courrier@wanadoo.fr
Web Site: www.editions-tredaniel.com
Key Personnel
Dir: Guy Tredaniel
Founded: 1974
Subjects: Environmental Studies, Gardening,
Plants, Health, Nutrition, Philosophy, Religion -
Other, Sports, Athletics, Personal Development
ISBN Prefix(es): 978-2-7029; 978-2-84445; 978-
2-85707

Editions Le Tripode
16, rue Charlemagne, 75004 Paris
Tel: 01 48 87 67 07
E-mail: info@le-tripode.net
Web Site: le-tripode.net
Key Personnel
Owner: Frederic Martin
Founded: 2013
Subjects: Fiction
ISBN Prefix(es): 978-2-37055

Les Trois Ourses
2/6, passage Rauch, 75011 Paris
Tel: 01 43 79 07 35 *Fax:* 01 43 79 07 42
E-mail: troisourses@wanadoo.fr
Web Site: lestroisourses.com
Founded: 1988
Subjects: Art, Education
ISBN Prefix(es): 978-2-9513083; 978-2-9518639

Editions Turquoise
12, rue Anatole France, 92300 Levallois-Perret
Tel: 01 41 05 08 35 *Fax:* 01 41 05 08 37
E-mail: contact@editions-turquoise.com
Web Site: www.editions-turquoise.com
Key Personnel
General Manager: Erhan Turgut
Founded: 2000
This publisher has indicated that 30% of their
product line is author subsidized.
Subjects: Fiction, History, Nonfiction (General),
Photography, Poetry, Ankara (Yakup Kadri
Karaosmanoglu), Armenia (1915 Massacre,
Manuel Kirkyacharian, Baski Oran), Euro-
pean Union, Istanbul, Le Mont des Oliviers
(Zeytindagi, Grande Guerre, Falih Rifki Atay),
Mustafa Kemal Ataturk, Nazim Hikmet (Po-
etry), Non a la Guerre (Peace, War, Anthology,
Photography), Turkey
ISBN Prefix(es): 978-2-9514448; 978-2-918823
Number of titles published annually: 3 Print
Total Titles: 8 Print

Twirl, *imprint of* Editions Tourbillon

Ulisse Editions+
15 rue Mansart, 75009 Paris
Tel: 01 48 78 40 74 *Fax:* 01 48 78 40 77
E-mail: contact@ulisseditions.com
Web Site: www.ulisseditions.com
Key Personnel
Mng Editor: Gerard Boulanger
Founded: 1990
Subjects: Architecture & Interior Design, Art,
    Crafts, Games, Hobbies, House & Home,
    Sports, Athletics, Travel & Tourism
ISBN Prefix(es): 978-2-907601; 978-2-84415
Parent Company: Groupe Ulisse

Editions UNESCO+
7, place de Fontenoy, 75352 Paris 07
Tel: 01 45 68 03 70; 01 45 68 10 00 (rights)
    Fax: 01 45 67 16 90; 01 45 68 56 54 (rights)
E-mail: publishing.promotion@unesco.org;
    publication.copyright@unesco.org; unesco.
    courier@unesco.org
Web Site: publishing.unesco.org
Key Personnel
Dir General: Irina Bokova
Founded: 1946
Subjects: Art, Communications, Education, Hu-
    man Relations, Science (General), Social Sci-
    ences, Sociology
ISBN Prefix(es): 978-92-3
Imprints: IBE; IIEP

**United Nations Educational, Scientific &
    Cultural Organization**, see Editions UNESCO

Editions Universitaires de Lorraine+
42-44 ave de la Liberation, 54014 Nancy Cedex
Mailing Address: BP 3347, 54014 Nancy Cedex
Tel: 03 54 50 46 90 *Fax:* 03 54 50 46 94
E-mail: edulor-edition@univ-lorraine.fr
Web Site: www.univ-lorraine.fr
Key Personnel
Dir: Ferri Briquet
Administrative Manager: Maurice Rausch
Founded: 1982
Subjects: Anthropology, Archaeology, Art, Com-
    munications, Drama, Theater, Economics, Edu-
    cation, Geography, Geology, Government, Po-
    litical Science, History, Language Arts, Lin-
    guistics, Law, Literature, Literary Criticism,
    Essays, Philosophy, Psychology, Psychiatry,
    Religion - Other, Social Sciences, Sociology
ISBN Prefix(es): 978-2-86480; 978-2-8143
Orders to: CID/FMSH-Diffusion, 18, rue Robert
    Schuman, CS 90003, 94227 Charenton-le-Pont
    Cedex *Tel:* 01 53 48 56 30 *Fax:* 01 53 48 20
    95 *E-mail:* cid@msh-paris.fr

**Presses Universites de Rouen et du Havre
    (PURH)**
Rue Lavoisier, 76821 Mont-St-Aignan Cedex
Tel: 02 35 14 61 82 *Fax:* 02 35 14 63 47
Web Site: purh.univ-rouen.fr
Key Personnel
Dir: Francois Bessire *Tel:* 02 35 14 63 45
    E-mail: francois.bessire@univ-rouen.fr
Administrative Manager: Patricia Lanoe *Tel:* 02
    35 14 63 43 *E-mail:* patricia.lanoe@univ-
    rouen.fr
Sales Manager: Martine Amourette *Tel:* 02 35 14
    65 31 *E-mail:* martine.amourette@univ-rouen.fr
Press: Anais Lebreton
Founded: 1968
Subjects: Geography, Geology, History, Law, Lit-
    erature, Literary Criticism, Essays, Psychology,
    Psychiatry
ISBN Prefix(es): 978-2-87775
Orders to: CID, 131 Blvd St-Michel, 75005 Paris

Editions d'Utovie
402 route des Pyrenees, 40320 Bats
Tel: 05 58 79 17 93
E-mail: utovie@utovie.com
Web Site: www.utovie.com
Key Personnel
Dir: Mauve Carite *E-mail:* mauve@utovie.com
Editorial Dir: Jean-Marc Carite; Marie Fougere
    E-mail: marie@utovie.com
Founded: 1971
Subjects: Government, Political Science, Liter-
    ature, Literary Criticism, Essays, Social Sci-
    ences, Sociology, Ecology
ISBN Prefix(es): 978-2-86819

Editions la Vague verte (Green Wave
    Publishing)+
25, rue du Marais, 80430 Inval-Boiron
Tel: 03 22 31 90 36 *Fax:* 03 22 31 90 36
E-mail: edlavagueverte@wanadoo.fr
Web Site: editionslavagueverte.pagesperso-orange.
    fr
Founded: 1989
Subjects: Art, Biography, Memoirs, Earth Sci-
    ences, Environmental Studies, History, Liter-
    ature, Literary Criticism, Essays, Mysteries,
    Suspense, Natural History, Poetry, Regional
    Interests, Travel & Tourism
ISBN Prefix(es): 978-2-908227; 978-2-913924
Number of titles published annually: 25 Print
Total Titles: 135 Print

Editions Van de Velde+
27 blvd Beaumarchais, 75004 Paris
Tel: 01 56 68 86 64 *Fax:* 01 56 68 90 66
E-mail: info@van-de-velde.fr
Web Site: www.van-de-velde.fr
Key Personnel
Dir: Pierre H Lemoine
Founded: 1899
Subjects: Music, Dance
ISBN Prefix(es): 978-2-85868; 978-2-86299
Number of titles published annually: 20 Print
Total Titles: 197 Print
Distribution Center: Hexamusic, 246 Ave de la
    Couronne des Pres, CS 10604, 78147 Auber-
    genville Cedex *Tel:* 01 30 90 20 02 *Fax:* 01
    30 90 10 23 *E-mail:* hexamusic@wanadoo.fr
    (music stores)
Daudin Distribution, One rue Guynemer, CS
    30504, 78771 Magny Les Hameaux Cedex
    Tel: 01 30 48 74 50 *Fax:* 01 34 98 02 44
    E-mail: info@daudin.fr (libraries)

Editions De Vecchi
164, rue Ambroise Pare, ZI St Cesaire, 30900
    Nimes
Tel: 04 66 62 98 27; 04 66 62 98 43 *Fax:* 04 66
    62 98 42
E-mail: contact@de-vecchi.fr
Web Site: www.de-vecchi.fr
Founded: 1962
Subjects: Animals, Pets, Art, Astrology, Oc-
    cult, Business, Cookery, Gardening, Plants,
    Health, Nutrition, How-to, Outdoor Recreation,
    Parapsychology, Sports, Athletics, Alternative
    Medicine, Entertainment
ISBN Prefix(es): 978-2-7328; 978-2-85177
Foreign Rep(s): Interforum Editis (Belgium); Pro-
    logue (Canada); Transat Diffusion SA (Switzer-
    land)

Vents d'ailleurs
11, route de Ste-Anne, 13640 La Roque
    d'Antheron
Tel: 04 42 50 59 92 *Fax:* 04 42 50 58 03
E-mail: info@ventsdailleurs.com
Web Site: www.ventsdailleurs.fr
Key Personnel
Publisher: Jutta Hepke *E-mail:* jhepke@
    ventsdailleurs.com

Editor: Gilles Colleu *E-mail:* gcolleu@
    ventsdailleurs.com
Founded: 1994
Publisher of African & Caribbean literature, chil-
    dren's & art books.
Membership(s): l'Alliance de editeurs indepen-
    dants; l'association Editeurs sans frontieres.
Subjects: Art, Literature, Literary Criticism, Es-
    says
ISBN Prefix(es): 978-2-911412; 978-2-36413
Foreign Rep(s): Book'in (The Pacific); La Car-
    avelle (Belgium); Communication Plus (Haiti);
    Dimedia (Canada); Servidis (Switzerland)
Distribution Center: Pollen Diffusion, 101 rue
    des Moines, 75017 Paris *Tel:* 01 43 58 74 11
    Fax: 01 72 71 84 51

Editions Vents d'Ouest+
Member of Groupe Glenat
39, rue du Gouverneur-General-Eboue, 92130
    Issy-les-Moulineaux
Tel: 01 41 46 11 11 *Fax:* 01 41 46 11 00
Web Site: www.ventsdouest.com
Key Personnel
President: Jacques Glenat
Subjects: Humor, Science Fiction, Fantasy
ISBN Prefix(es): 978-2-86967; 978-2-7493

Editions Verdier+
17-19, rue Houdart, 75020 Paris
Tel: 04 68 24 05 75; 01 43 79 20 45
E-mail: contact@editions-verdier.fr
Web Site: www.editions-verdier.fr
Key Personnel
Manager: Colette Olive; Michele Planel
Press: Gwenaelle Dream *Tel:* 06 72 70 68 14
    E-mail: gwenaelle.drean@lanavire.net
Founded: 1979
Subjects: Art, Inspirational, Spirituality, Litera-
    ture, Literary Criticism, Essays, Philosophy,
    Religion - Islamic, Religion - Jewish, Humani-
    ties
ISBN Prefix(es): 978-2-86432
Number of titles published annually: 25 Print
Total Titles: 700 Print
Distribution Center: Sodis, 128 Ave du Marechal
    de Lattre de Tassigny, 77400 Lagny sur Marne
    Tel: 01 60 07 82 00 *Fax:* 01 64 30 92 22
    E-mail: portail@sodis.fr *Web Site:* www.sodis.
    fr

Vertiges Bulles, *imprint of* Editions Dominique
Leroy

Editions Vial
BP 90087, 91416 Dourdan Cedex
Tel: 01 64 59 70 48 *Fax:* 01 64 59 52 96
E-mail: info@editionsvial.com
Web Site: www.editionsvial.com
Key Personnel
Contact: Veronique Lavastrou; Olivier Wittwer
Founded: 1910
Subjects: Architecture & Interior Design, Art,
    Crafts, Games, Hobbies, Cabinet Making, Car-
    pentry/Woodworking, Design, Furniture, Sculp-
    ture
ISBN Prefix(es): 978-2-85101
Foreign Rep(s): Librairie l'Art du Livre (Bel-
    gium); DPLU (Canada); Pierre Finkelstein
    Institute of Decorative Painting Inc (USA);
    Langevin & Forest (Canada); OLF (Switzer-
    land); Ruth Schouwey (Switzerland)

Editions Vigot
23-27 rue de l'ecole de Medecine, 75006 Paris
Tel: 01 43 29 54 50 *Fax:* 01 43 29 56 12
E-mail: ventelibraires@vigot.fr
Web Site: www.vigot.fr
Founded: 1890
Subjects: Health, Nutrition, Medicine, Nursing,
    Dentistry, Sports, Athletics, Veterinary Science
ISBN Prefix(es): 978-2-7114
Parent Company: Groupe Vigot Maloine

Foreign Rep(s): Horizon Education (worldwide exc Belgium, Canada & Switzerland); Prologue Inc (Canada); Sdl Caravelle (Belgium); Servidis SA (Switzerland)

Editions Village Mondial+
Immeuble Terra Nova II, 74 rue de Lagny, 5e etage gauche, 93100 Montreuil
Tel: 01 43 62 31 00 *Fax:* 01 43 62 30 80
Web Site: www.pearson.fr/collections/ villagemondial
Founded: 1995
Specialize in higher education textbooks.
Subjects: Business, Economics, Finance, Human Relations, Management, Marketing, Psychology, Psychiatry
ISBN Prefix(es): 978-2-84211; 978-2-7440
Total Titles: 100 Print
Parent Company: Pearson Education France
Imprints: Publi Union
Distribution Center: MDS, ZA des Jalots, 22 rue Robert Benoist, 91417 Dourdan Cedex *Tel:* 01 60 81 87 00 *Fax:* 01 64 59 30 63

Editions de la Villette
144, ave de Flandre, 75019 Paris
Tel: 01 44 65 23 58; 01 44 65 23 59 *Fax:* 01 44 65 23 28
E-mail: editions@paris-lavillette.archi.fr
Web Site: www.paris-lavillette.archi.fr
Key Personnel
Editorial Manager: Marc Bedarida *E-mail:* marc. bedarida@paris-lavillette.archi.fr
Management: Philippe Foos
Editorial Assistant: Brankica Radic
Founded: 1980
Subjects: Architecture & Interior Design, Landscape, Spatial Art House, Urbanism
ISBN Prefix(es): 978-2-903539; 978-2-915456
Parent Company: Ecole Nationale Superieure d'Architecture de Paris la Villette

Editions Gerard de Villiers
15 Chemin des Courtilles, 92600 Asnieres-sur-Seine
Tel: 01 41 21 37 88
E-mail: contact@editionssas.com
Web Site: www.editionssas.com
Founded: 1988
Subjects: Erotica, Fiction, Mysteries, Suspense, Science Fiction, Fantasy, Detective
ISBN Prefix(es): 978-2-36053

Editions Vilo SA
116 rue de la Tour, 75116 Paris
Tel: 01 45 77 08 05 *Fax:* 01 45 75 75 53
Web Site: www.vilo-groupe.com
Subjects: Architecture & Interior Design, Art, Automotive, History, Language Arts, Linguistics, Literature, Literary Criticism, Essays, Nonfiction (General), Religion - Other, Sports, Athletics, Travel & Tourism
ISBN Prefix(es): 978-2-7191
Parent Company: Groupe Vilo
Foreign Rep(s): CELF (worldwide exc Belgium, Canada & Switzerland); Edipresse (Canada); Nouvelle Diffusion (Belgium); OLF (Switzerland)

Editions VM+
61 Blvd St-Germain, 75240 Paris Cedex 05
E-mail: editeurs-enterprise@eyrolles.com; foreignrights@eyrolles.com
Web Site: www.editions-vm.com
Key Personnel
Press: Sabine Jacquier *Tel:* 01 44 41 46 03
E-mail: sjacquier@eyrolles.com
Founded: 1965
Subjects: Photography
ISBN Prefix(es): 978-2-86258
Parent Company: Groupe Eyrolles

Foreign Rep(s): Flammarion Ltee (Canada); Diffusion Nord-Sud (Belgium, Luxembourg); Servidis (Switzerland)
Bookshop(s): Librairie Eyrolles *Tel:* 01 44 41 11 74
Distribution Center: Sodis, 128 Ave du Marechal de Lattre de Tassigny, 77400 Lagny-sur-Marne *Tel:* 01 60 07 82 00 *Fax:* 01 64 30 92 22
E-mail: portail@sodis.fr *Web Site:* www.sodis. fr

Librairie Philosophique J Vrin+
6, place de la Sorbonne, 75005 Paris
Tel: 01 43 54 03 47 *Fax:* 01 43 54 48 18
E-mail: contact@vrin.fr
Web Site: www.vrin.fr
Key Personnel
Publishing Dir: Denis Arnaud
Rights: Gael Kervoas
Founded: 1920
Also bookseller, new & secondhand books.
Specialize in philosophy.
Subjects: History, Philosophy, Psychology, Psychiatry, Religion - Other
ISBN Prefix(es): 978-2-7116
Number of titles published annually: 50 Print; 1 CD-ROM
Total Titles: 1,500 Print

Editions Vuibert+
5, allee de la 2e DB, 75726 Paris Cedex 15
Mailing Address: CS 11531, 75726 Paris Cedex 15
Tel: 01 42 79 44 53
E-mail: relations.presse@vuibert.fr
Web Site: www.vuibert.fr
Key Personnel
Publishing Dir: Guillaume Dervieux
Founded: 1877
Subjects: Biological Sciences, Chemistry, Chemical Engineering, Earth Sciences, Economics, Law, Mathematics, Physics
ISBN Prefix(es): 978-2-7117
Imprints: Annales du Bac; Bac en Poche; Livre des Vacances
Distribution Center: Dilisco, Rte du Limousin, BP 23, 23220 Bonnat *Tel:* 05 55 51 80 00 *Fax:* 05 55 62 17 39

Editions WEKA SAS
249, rue de Crimee, 75019 Paris
Tel: 01 53 35 17 17
E-mail: relation.clientele@weka.fr
Web Site: www.weka.fr
Key Personnel
Dir: Andre Blanc
Founded: 1979
Subjects: Computer Science, Electronics, Electrical Engineering, Labor, Industrial Relations, Law, Management, Social Sciences, Sociology
ISBN Prefix(es): 978-2-7337
Parent Company: WEKA Media GmbH & Co KG, Roemerstr 4, 86438 Kissing, Germany
Associate Companies: Weka Presse, 82 rue Curial, 75935 Paris
U.S. Office(s): Weka Publishing Inc, 97 Indian Field Rd, Greenwich, CT 06830, United States
50 Main St, Suite 1000, White Plains, NY 10606, United States

Sabine Wespieser editeur
13, rue Seguier, 75006 Paris
Tel: 01 44 07 59 59 *Fax:* 01 42 71 21 67
E-mail: contact@swediteur.com
Web Site: www.swediteur.com
Key Personnel
Editor & Manager: Sabine Wespieser
Foreign Rights: Joschi Guitton
Subjects: Literature, Literary Criticism, Essays
ISBN Prefix(es): 978-2-84805

Foreign Rep(s): Dimedia (Canada); Servidis (Switzerland)
Distribution Center: Seuil/Volumen, 25 blvd Romain Rolland, 75993 Paris Cedex 14 *Tel:* 01 41 48 84 60 *E-mail:* volumen@volumen.fr

XO Editions
33 ave du Maine, 75755 Paris Cedex 15
Mailing Address: BP 142, 75755 Paris Cedex 15
Tel: 01 56 80 26 80; 01 56 80 26 81 (press)
Fax: 01 56 80 26 72
E-mail: press@xoeditions.com; edito@ xoeditions.com; commercial@xoeditions.com; foreignrights@xoeditions.com
Web Site: www.xoeditions.com
Key Personnel
Founder, Chairman & Publisher: Bernard Fixot
Dir, Communications: Valerie Taillefer
Founded: 2000
Subjects: Fiction
ISBN Prefix(es): 978-2-84563

Editions YMCA-Press
11, rue de la Montagne-Ste-Genevieve, 75005 Paris
Tel: 01 43 54 74 46 *Fax:* 01 43 25 34 79
E-mail: ed.reunis@wanadoo.fr
Web Site: www.editeurs-reunis.fr
Founded: 1925
Subjects: Literature, Literary Criticism, Essays, Religion - Other
ISBN Prefix(es): 978-2-85065
Divisions: Les Editeurs Reunis

Editions Yvert et Tellier
2, rue de l'Etoile, 80094 Amiens Cedex 03
Tel: 03 22 71 71 71 *Fax:* 03 22 71 71 89
E-mail: contact@yvert.com
Web Site: www.editons-yvert-tellier.com
Key Personnel
Dir: Benoit Gervais *E-mail:* bgervais@yvert.com
Subjects: Crafts, Games, Hobbies, Philately
ISBN Prefix(es): 978-2-86814

Zellige
15, rue des Pres - Lunay, 77171 Lechelle
Tel: 01 64 00 86 92 *Fax:* 01 64 00 86 92
E-mail: zellige.edition@orange.fr
Web Site: www.zellige.eu
Key Personnel
Dir: Roger Tavernier
Founded: 2001
Subjects: History, Language Arts, Linguistics, Caribbean, Haiti
ISBN Prefix(es): 978-2-914773

Zones, *imprint of* Editions La Decouverte

Editions Zulma
18, rue du Dragon, 75006 Paris
Tel: 01 58 22 19 90 *Fax:* 01 58 22 19 99
E-mail: zulma@zulma.fr
Web Site: www.zulma.fr
Key Personnel
Dir & Foreign Rights: Laure Leroy
Founded: 1991
Subjects: Literature, Literary Criticism, Essays
ISBN Prefix(es): 978-2-84304
Foreign Rep(s): Dimedia (Canada); Servidis (Switzerland)
Distribution Center: Volumen, 25 blvd Romain Rolland, CS 21418, 75993 Paris Cedex 14 *Tel:* 01 41 48 84 60 *E-mail:* volumen@ volumen.fr

French Polynesia

General Information

Capital: Papeete
Language: French (official) & Polynesian languages
Religion: Mainly Protestant & Roman Catholic
Population: 199,031
Bank Hours: 0730-1530 Monday-Friday; some 0730-1130 Saturday
Shop Hours: 0730-1100, 1400-1700 Monday-Friday; 0730-1130 Saturday
Currency: 100 centimes = 1 CFA franc
Export/Import Information: No tariff on books other than children's picture books; advertising matter subject to customs duty, import duty, although catalogues generally considered printed books. Advertising subject to statistical tax. Miscellaneous tax of 2% of customs value on books and advertising. No import license required. Exchange controls.

Editions Haere Po+
BP 1958, 98713 Papeete Tahiti
Tel: 58 26 36; 77 23 46 (cell); 71 85 00 (cell)
Fax: 58 04 01
E-mail: haerepotahiti@mail.pf
Web Site: www.haerepo.com
Founded: 1981
Subjects: Anthropology, Earth Sciences, Ethnicity, History, Language Arts, Linguistics, Natural History, Travel & Tourism
ISBN Prefix(es): 978-2-904171

Nouvelles du Pacifique, *imprint of* Scoop/Au Vent des Iles

Scoop, see Scoop/Au Vent des Iles

Scoop/Au Vent des Iles+
BP 5670, 98716 Pirae, Tahiti
Tel: 50 95 95 *Fax:* 50 95 97
Web Site: www.auventdesiles.pf
Key Personnel
Manager: Christian Robert *E-mail:* christian@auventdesiles.pf
Founded: 1991
Subjects: Biography, Memoirs, Cookery, Fiction, Geography, Geology, History, How-to, Literature, Literary Criticism, Essays, Mysteries, Suspense, South Pacific
ISBN Prefix(es): 978-2-909790
Imprints: Nouvelles du Pacifique
Distribution Center: One rue Guynemer, CS 30504, 78771 Magny Les Hameaux, France
Tel: 01 30 48 74 50 *Fax:* 01 34 98 02 44
E-mail: commandes@daudin.fr

Georgia

General Information

Capital: Tbilisi
Language: Georgian
Religion: Predominantly Georgian Orthodox
Population: 5.6 million
Currency: 100 tetri = 1 lari; 1 dollar = 2.23 lari
Export/Import Information: Customs duty for import, 12% to 20% of VAT.

Artanuji Publishing House
Chavchavadze Ave, N5, 0179 Tbilisi
Tel: (032) 2 25 05 22 *Fax:* (032) 2 25 05 22
E-mail: info.artanuji@gmail.com
Web Site: www.artanuji.ge
Key Personnel
Founder: Buba Kudava
Founded: 2000
Subjects: History, Literature, Literary Criticism, Essays, Science (General)
ISBN Prefix(es): 978-99928-826; 978-99928-973; 978-99928-940; 978-99928-991; 978-99928-993; 978-99940-11; 978-99940-55

Bakur Sulakauri Publishing
150 Agmashenebeli Ave, 0112 Tbilisi
Tel: (032) 91 09 54 *Fax:* (032) 91 11 65
E-mail: info@sulakauri.ge
Web Site: www.sulakauri.ge
Founded: 1999
ISBN Prefix(es): 978-9941-15

Diogene Ltd
9, Apakidze St, 0171 Tbilisi
Tel: (032) 2213321
E-mail: adm@diogene.ge
Web Site: www.diogene.ge
Founded: 1995
Membership(s): Georgian Publishers & Booksellers Association.
Subjects: Fiction, Poetry, Science (General)
ISBN Prefix(es): 978-99928-59; 978-99928-953; 978-99928-954; 978-99928-994; 978-99940-16; 978-99940-45

Elf Publishing House
8 Kartozia St, 2nd floor, Bldg 9, 0177 Tbilisi
Tel: (032) 292 35 70 *Fax:* (032) 292 35 70
E-mail: office@elf.ge; right@elf.ge
Web Site: elf.ge
Key Personnel
Founder & Dir: Tina Didebulidze
Foreign Rights Manager: Tamta Grigolia
Founded: 1996
Subjects: Computer Science, Psychology, Psychiatry, Science (General)
ISBN Prefix(es): 978-99928-61

Intelekti Publishing
Chavchavadze Ave 5, 0179 Tbilisi
Tel: (032) 2250522 *Fax:* (032) 2250522
E-mail: inteleqti@caucasus.net
Web Site: www.intelekti.ge
Founded: 1994
Subjects: Fiction, Literature, Literary Criticism, Essays, Poetry
ISBN Prefix(es): 978-9941-458; 978-9941-446; 978-9941-420; 978-9941-430
Number of titles published annually: 300 Print

Karchkhadze Publishing
Vazha-Pshavela VII kV, N17/6, 0186 Tbilisi
Tel: (032) 2514527
E-mail: info@karchkhadze.ge
Web Site: karchkhadze.ge
Founded: 2004
Subjects: Art, Fiction, Literature, Literary Criticism, Essays, Nonfiction (General), Georgian Cultural Heritage
ISBN Prefix(es): 978-99940-34

Klio Publishing House
D Agmashenebeli Ave, 191, 0112 Tbilisi
Tel: (032) 340430 *Fax:* (032) 340430
E-mail: book@klio.ge; kliopublishing@gmail.com
Web Site: www.klio.ge
Key Personnel
Publisher & Dir: Zaza Khidureli *Tel:* (099) 5033 76
Manager: Tamara Nachkebia *E-mail:* tamara@klio.ge

Founded: 2003
Subjects: Government, Political Science, Health, Nutrition, Literature, Literary Criticism, Essays, Poetry, Social Sciences, Sociology, Georgian Classical Literature, World Literature
ISBN Prefix(es): 978-9941-415

Logos Press Ltd
Mitropane Lagidze St 8, 0108 Tbilisi
Tel: (032) 243 03 02
E-mail: info@logospress.ge
Web Site: www.logospress.ge
Key Personnel
Dir & Chief Editor: Mr Lasha Beraia
Sales Manager: Teona Tabatadze
E-mail: tabatadzeteko@yahoo.com
Founded: 2000
Subjects: Fiction, Literature, Literary Criticism, Essays
ISBN Prefix(es): 978-99928-883; 978-99928-924; 978-99928-926; 978-99928-927; 978-99928-928

Merani
42, Rustaveli Ave, 0108 Tbilisi
Tel: (032) 996492
Founded: 1925
Subjects: Regional Interests
ISBN Prefix(es): 978-5-515; 978-99928-946; 978-99928-16; 978-99928-948; 978-99940-769; 978-99940-817

Shemetsneba
3 Kavsadze str, 0177 Tbilisi
Tel: (032) 21-01-54
E-mail: info@shemetsneba.ge
Web Site: www.shemetsneba.ge
Key Personnel
Founder & Dir: Lia Shalvashvili
Founded: 2005
Subjects: Education, Literature, Literary Criticism, Essays, Poetry, Travel & Tourism, Scientific Popular Literature
ISBN Prefix(es): 978-9941-910

Tsigni+Eri
Revaz Lagidze St 2, 0108 Tbilisi
Tel: (032) 2180332
E-mail: contact@tsignieri.ge
Web Site: books.tsignieri.ge
Founded: 2012
ISBN Prefix(es): 978-9941-24; 978-9941-9302; 978-9941-9349

Germany

General Information

Capital: Berlin
Language: German. Sorbian speaking minority. Danish spoken by a Danish minority in South Schleswig, North Frisian in North Frisian Islands
Religion: Predominantly Protestant and Roman Catholic
Population: 82.7 million
Bank Hours: 0900-1300, 1430-1600 Monday-Friday
Shop Hours: 0900-1830 Monday-Friday; 0900-1400 Saturday
Currency: 100 Eurocents = 1 Euro
Export/Import Information: Member of the European Union. No tariff on books except children's picture books from non-EU. None on advertising to be distributed free, if exporter's country grants reciprocal treatment, otherwise charged. Import turnover tax on books and ad-

vertising. Also, 7% VAT on books. No import license required. No exchange controls.
Copyright: UCC, Berne, Florence (see Copyright Conventions, pg viii)

ABAKUS Musik Barbara Fietz
Haversbach 1, 35753 Greifenstein
Tel: (06478) 2774-0; (06478) 2250 *Fax:* (06478) 1355; (06478) 2774-19
E-mail: info@abakus-musik.de
Web Site: www.abakus-musik.de
Key Personnel
Mng Dir: Barbara Fietz *Tel:* (06478) 2774-11
   E-mail: bf@abakus-musik.de
Marketing: Oliver Fietz *Tel:* (06478) 2744-15
   E-mail: of@abakus-musik.de
Sales: Sandra Oberbeck *E-mail:* so@abakus-musik.de
Founded: 1974
Specialize in Christian musical & notebook publications.
Subjects: Music, Dance, Religion - Other
ISBN Prefix(es): 978-3-88124
Total Titles: 100 E-Book; 250 Audio
Distributed by BMK Wartburg Vertriebsges mbH (Austria); Herder AG Basel (Switzerland)

Abentheuer Verlag UG
Allerstr 18, 12049 Berlin
Tel: (030) 80575445
E-mail: info@abentheuerverlag.de
Web Site: www.abentheuerverlag.de
Key Personnel
Owner: Karl Ernst Horbol *E-mail:* keh@abentheuerverlag.de
ISBN Prefix(es): 978-3-940650

absolut MEDIEN GmbH
Am Hasenbergl 12, 83413 Friddfing
Tel: (030) 285 39 87-0 *Fax:* (030) 285 39 87-2
E-mail: info@absolutmedien.de
Web Site: absolutmedien.de
Key Personnel
Mng Dir: Molto Menz *E-mail:* moltomenz@absolutmedien.de
Subjects: Architecture & Interior Design, Art, Cookery, Film, Video, History, Literature, Literary Criticism, Essays, Music, Dance, Philosophy, Photography, Religion - Other, Science (General), Social Sciences, Sociology, Technology
ISBN Prefix(es): 978-3-89848
Distribution Center: Prolit Verlagsauslieferung GmbH, Siemensstr 16, 35463 Fernwald (Annerod), Contact: Inge Peters *Tel:* (0641) 943 93-25 *Fax:* (0641) 943 93-89 *E-mail:* i.peters@prolit.de

ABW Wissenschaftsverlag GmbH (ABW Science Publishers GmbH)
Altensteinstr 42, 14195 Berlin
Tel: (030) 308 316 0 *Fax:* (030) 308 316 79
E-mail: zentrale@abw-verlag.de
Web Site: www.abw-verlag.de
Key Personnel
Mng Partner: Axel Beduerftig
Subjects: Medicine, Nursing, Dentistry
ISBN Prefix(es): 978-3-936072

Accedo Verlagsgesellschaft mbH+
Gnesener Str 1, 81929 Munich
Tel: (089) 935714 *Fax:* (089) 9294109
E-mail: accedoverlag@web.de
Web Site: www.accedoverlag.de
Key Personnel
Manager: Dr Manfred Holler *E-mail:* holler@econ.uni-hamburg.de; Dr Barbara Klose-Ullmann
Founded: 1988
Subjects: Art, Economics, Geography, Geology, Government, Political Science, History, Management, Medicine, Nursing, Dentistry, Phi-

losophy, Science (General), Social Sciences, Sociology, Art History
ISBN Prefix(es): 978-3-89265
Total Titles: 60 Print
Associate Companies: Verlag Holler
Distributor for Verlag Holler

Achter Verlag
Klosterhofstr 24, 69469 Weinheim
Tel: (06201) 9597767
E-mail: achter-verlag@t-online.de
Web Site: www.achter-verlag.de
Key Personnel
Contact: Wolfgang Orians
Founded: 2007
Membership(s): Verlags-Karree eV
Subjects: Biography, Memoirs, Fiction, Travel & Tourism, Corporate Communications, Human Resources, Knowledge Management
ISBN Prefix(es): 978-3-9812372

Achterbahn, *imprint of* Lappan Verlag GmbH

Achterbahn+
Imprint of Lappan Verlag GmbH
Wuerzburger Str 14, 26121 Oldenburg
Mailing Address: Postfach 3407, 26024 Oldenburg
Tel: (0441) 980 66-0 *Fax:* (0441) 980 66-34
E-mail: bilderbuchprogramm@lappan.de; info@lappan.de; presse@lappan.de; programm@lappan.de
Web Site: www.lappan.de/Cartoons.Comic.Achterbahn.html; www.drive-in-cartoons.de
Key Personnel
Mng Dir: Dieter Schwalm
Publishing Dir: Constanze Steindamm
Press: Ulrike Renneberg
Sales: Heike Kroner *E-mail:* h.kroner@lappan.de; Juergen Schulz *E-mail:* j.schulz@lappan.de
Founded: 1991
Subjects: Humor
ISBN Prefix(es): 978-3-89982
Distribution Center: Koepenicker Cartoon Gesellschaft GmbH, Birkenstr 32, 12559 Berlin *E-mail:* info@cartoonkarten.de *Web Site:* www.cartoonkaufhaus.de

Joh van Acken GmbH & Co KG
Magdeburger Str 5, 47800 Krefeld
Mailing Address: Postfach 100105, 47701 Krefeld
Tel: (02151) 44 00-0 *Fax:* (02151) 44 00-11
E-mail: info@van-acken.de
Web Site: www.van-acken.de
Key Personnel
Mng Dir: Ulrich Kaltenmeier
Founded: 1890
Subjects: Regional Interests
ISBN Prefix(es): 978-3-923140

Acolada GmbH
Wallensteinstr 61-63, 90431 Nuremberg
Tel: (0911) 37 66 75-0 *Fax:* (0911) 37 66 75-29
E-mail: info@acolada.de
Web Site: www.acolada.de
Key Personnel
Mng Dir: Torsten Kuprat
Founded: 2001
Subjects: Architecture & Interior Design, Automotive, Chemistry, Chemical Engineering, Economics, Government, Political Science, Law, Mechanical Engineering, Medicine, Nursing, Dentistry, Real Estate, Technology
ISBN Prefix(es): 978-3-936022

Verlag und Vertrieb der Action 365 GmbH
Kennedyallee 111a, 60596 Frankfurt am Main
Tel: (069) 68 09 12 33 *Fax:* (069) 68 09 12 12
E-mail: verlag@action365.de
Web Site: www.action365.de

Key Personnel
Mng Dir: Mattias Copray; Stefan Mook
Subjects: Inspirational, Spirituality, Religion - Catholic, Religion - Protestant, Public Relations
ISBN Prefix(es): 978-3-925138

ADAC Verlag GmbH+
Hansastr 19, 80686 Munich
Tel: (089) 7676-0 *Fax:* (089) 7676-2925
E-mail: verlag@adac.de
Web Site: www.adac.de
Key Personnel
Mng Dir: Dr Carsten C Huebner
Founded: 1958
Also carry magazines & travel guides.
Subjects: Automotive, Travel & Tourism
ISBN Prefix(es): 978-3-87003; 978-3-8264; 978-3-89905
Distributed by TRAVEL HOUSE MEDIA GmbH

ADDISON, *imprint of* Wolters Kluwer Deutschland GmbH

Addison-Wesley, *imprint of* Pearson Deutschland GmbH

adeo, *imprint of* Gerth Medien GmbH

adeo, *imprint of* Verlagsgruppe Random House Bertelsmann

Adobe Press, *imprint of* Pearson Deutschland GmbH

Adyar Edition, *imprint of* Aquamarin Verlag GmbH

Adyar Verlag, *imprint of* Aquamarin Verlag GmbH

Aethera, *imprint of* Verlag Freies Geistesleben

Editions AfricAvenir/Exchange & Dialogue
c/o AfricAvenir, Kamerunerstr 1, 13351 Berlin
Tel: (030) 26934764; (01766) 3228341 *Fax:* (03212) 1258815
E-mail: info@africavenir.org
Web Site: www.africavenir.com
Key Personnel
Mng Dir: Prof Kum'a Ndumbe, III
Founded: 2005
Subjects: Drama, Theater, Government, Political Science, History, Literature, Literary Criticism, Essays
ISBN Prefix(es): 978-3-939313

AG SPAK Buecher
Holzheimer Str 7, 89233 Neu-Ulm
Tel: (07308) 919261 *Fax:* (07308) 919095
E-mail: spak-buecher@leibi.de
Web Site: www.agspak-buecher.de
Key Personnel
Contact: Waldemar Schindowski
Subjects: Criminology, Economics, Education, Social Sciences, Sociology
ISBN Prefix(es): 978-3-930830

agenda Verlag GmbH & Co KG+
Drubbel 4, 48143 Muenster
Tel: (0251) 79 96 10 *Fax:* (0251) 79 95 19
E-mail: info@agenda.de
Web Site: www.agenda.de
Key Personnel
Owner & Mng Dir: Dr Bernhard Schneeberger
Publishing Dir: Dr Frank Haettich
Press & Marketing: Irina Templin, MA
Founded: 1992
Membership(s): Boersenverein des Deutschen Buchhandels.

Subjects: Art, Biography, Memoirs, Developing Countries, Environmental Studies, Fiction, Government, Political Science, History, Journalism, Law, Music, Dance, Nonfiction (General), Philosophy, Regional Interests, Science (General), Social Sciences, Sociology, Women's Studies
ISBN Prefix(es): 978-3-929440; 978-3-89688

Agentur des Rauhen Hauses Hamburg GmbH
Beim Bruederhof 8, 22844 Norderstedt
Tel: (040) 53 53 88 0 *Fax:* (040) 53 53 88 43
E-mail: kundenservice@agentur-rauhes-haus.de
Web Site: www.agentur-rauhes-haus.de
Key Personnel
Mng Dir: Dr Martin Sterr
Program Management: Dr Britta Fuchs
   E-mail: dr.fuchs@agentur-rauhes-haus.de
Rights & Permissions: Gabriele Schneider
   E-mail: schneider@agentur-rauhes-haus.de
Sales: Kirsten Lenz *E-mail:* lenz@agentur-rauhes-haus.de
Founded: 1842
Specialize in Christian & non-denominational literature & materials for parish work.
Subjects: Biography, Memoirs, Religion - Protestant, Religion - Other, Theology
ISBN Prefix(es): 978-3-7600
Divisions: Reise-und Versandbuchhandlung des Rauhen Hauses
Foreign Rep(s): BMK Wartburg Vertriebsges mbH (Austria); Dessauer (Switzerland); Horst Grueneis & Claudia Grueneis-Labourne (Austria)

Edition Aglaia, *imprint of* Bookspot Verlag GmbH

Agon Sportverlag
Frankfurter Str 92a, 34131 Kassel
Tel: (0561) 927 98 27 *Fax:* (0561) 28 34 39
E-mail: agon@agon-online.de
Web Site: www.agon-shop.de
Key Personnel
Mng Dir: Wolfgang Fuhr
Subjects: Sports, Athletics, Olympics, Soccer, Winter Sports
ISBN Prefix(es): 978-3-928562; 978-3-89609; 978-3-89784

Agora Verlag+
Nollendorfstr 28, 10777 Berlin
Tel: (030) 8 545372 *Fax:* (030) 8 545372
Web Site: www.agora-verlag.de
Key Personnel
Mng Dir: Manfred Schloesser
   E-mail: schloesser@agora-verlag.de
Sales & Publicity: Monika Schloesser-Fischer
Founded: 1960
Subjects: Fiction, Literature, Literary Criticism, Essays, Music, Dance, Poetry, Religion - Jewish
ISBN Prefix(es): 978-3-87008
Total Titles: 140 Print
Subsidiaries: Erato-Presse

Ahead and Amazing Verlag fuer Grenzueberschreitungen eK
Magnussenstr 8, 25872 Ostenfeld
Tel: (0485) 1291 *Fax:* (0485) 1486
E-mail: info@aheadandamazing.de
Web Site: www.aheadandamazing.de
Key Personnel
Owner: Kristina Jelinski; Manfred Jelinski
Subjects: Mysteries, Suspense, Nonfiction (General), Science Fiction, Fantasy
ISBN Prefix(es): 978-3-933305

Ahriman-Verlag GmbH+
Stuebeweg 60, 79108 Freiburg
Mailing Address: Postfach 6569, 79041 Freiburg

Tel: (0761) 502303 *Fax:* (0761) 502247
E-mail: ahriman@t-online.de
Web Site: www.ahriman.com
Key Personnel
Mng Dir: Ingrid Karfich
Founded: 1983
Subjects: Government, Political Science, History, Psychology, Psychiatry, Religion - Other, Science (General)
ISBN Prefix(es): 978-3-922774; 978-3-89484
Total Titles: 74 Print; 1 CD-ROM; 20 Audio
Distribution Center: Thanilo Verlags- und Vertriebs-GmbH, Postfach 710, 79007 Freiburg
   Tel: (0761) 502247 *E-mail:* thanilo@t-online.de

aid infodienst - Verbraucherschst, Ernaehrung, Landwirtschaft eV
Heilsbachstr 16, 53123 Bonn
Tel: (0228) 8499-0 *Fax:* (0228) 8499-177
E-mail: aid@aid.de
Web Site: www.aid.de
Key Personnel
Mng Dir: Dr Margret Buening-Fesel
Subjects: Agriculture, Economics, Education, Energy, Environmental Studies, Gardening, Plants, Health, Nutrition, Law, Social Sciences, Sociology, Technology

Aisthesis Verlag+
Oberntorwall 21 (Eingang Mauerstr), 33602 Bielefeld
Mailing Address: Postfach 100427, 33504 Bielefeld
Tel: (0521) 172604 *Fax:* (0521) 172812
E-mail: info@aisthesis.de
Web Site: www.aisthesis.de
Key Personnel
Mng Dir, Rights & Permissions: Dr Detlev Kopp; Dr Michael Vogt
Founded: 1985
Subjects: Art, Biography, Memoirs, History, Literature, Literary Criticism, Essays, Philosophy, Science (General)
ISBN Prefix(es): 978-3-925670; 978-3-89528

AKA Verlag, see Akademische Verlagsgesellschaft AKA GmbH

Akademie Schloss Solitude, see merz&solitude

Akademie Verlag+
Genthiner Str 13, 10785 Berlin
Tel: (030) 260 05-0 *Fax:* (030) 260 05-251
E-mail: info@degruyter.com
Web Site: www.degruyter.com
Key Personnel
Marketing Dir: Ralf Gruemme *Tel:* (030) 260 05-148 *Fax:* (030) 260 05-322 *E-mail:* ralf.gruemme@degruyter.com
Editor: Mischka Dammaschke *Tel:* (030) 260 05-117 *E-mail:* mischka.dammaschke@degruyter.com; Peter Heyl *Tel:* (030) 260 05-213 *E-mail:* peter.heyl@degruyter.com; Manfred Karras *Tel:* (030) 260 05-113 *E-mail:* manfred.karras@degruyter.com; Katja Leuchtenberger *Tel:* (030) 260 05-163 *E-mail:* katja.leuchtenberger@degruyter.com
Project Editor: Christina Gericke *Tel:* (030) 260 05-167 *E-mail:* christina.gericke@degruyter.com
Founded: 1946
Subjects: History, Language Arts, Linguistics, Literature, Literary Criticism, Essays, Philosophy, Social Sciences, Sociology
ISBN Prefix(es): 978-3-05; 978-3-922251
Parent Company: Walter de Gruyter GmbH
Distribution Center: Cornelsen Verlagskontor GmbH, 33598 Bielefeld *Tel:* (0521) 9719-323 *E-mail:* oldenbourg@cvk.de (for shipment to Germany, Austria & Switzerland)

Akademische Arbeitsgemeinschaft Verlag, *imprint of* Wolters Kluwer Deutschland GmbH

Akademische Verlagsgesellschaft AKA GmbH (Academic Publishing Co AKA GmbH)
Saknower Landstr 122, 14089 Berlin
Tel: (030) 36430164
E-mail: info@aka-verlag.de
Web Site: www.aka-verlag.com
Key Personnel
Mng Dir: Dr Einar H Fredriksson; Arnoud de Kemp
Founded: 1906
Subjects: Computer Science, Health, Nutrition, Medicine, Nursing, Dentistry, Social Sciences, Sociology, E-Health, Gerontology, Humanities, Life Science, Media Studies, Nanotechnology, Robotics
ISBN Prefix(es): 978-3-89838
Distribution Center: Suedost Service GmbH, Am Steinfeld 4, 94065 Waldkirchen *Tel:* (08581) 96050 *Fax:* (08581) 754 *E-mail:* service@suedorst-service.de

Akademisher Verlag Muenchen, see Christoph Hofbauer, Ilija Trojanow & Berthold Klewing

akg-images gmbh+
Teutonenstr 22, 14129 Berlin
Tel: (030) 80485-0 *Fax:* (030) 80485-500
E-mail: info@akg-images.de
Web Site: www.akg-images.de
Key Personnel
Management: Friedrich Goepel
Founded: 1945
Picture library, collection, documentation.
Subjects: Art, History, Photojournalism
ISBN Prefix(es): 978-3-88912
Associate Companies: akg-images Paris, 67, rue Notre-Dame des Champs, 75006 Paris, France, Dir: Thomas Pey *Tel:* 01 44 41 99 88 *Fax:* 01 44 41 99 99 *E-mail:* thomas@akg-images.fr *Web Site:* www.akg-images.fr; akg-images Ltd, 5 Melbray Mews, 158 Hurlingham Rd, London SW6 3NS, United Kingdom *Tel:* (020) 7610 6103 *Fax:* (020) 7610 6125 *E-mail:* enquiries@akg-images.co.uk *Web Site:* www.akg-images.co.uk

AKSE-Verlag Wolfgang Gerz
Lanzenhaarer Str 2, 82041 Oberhaching
Tel: (089) 6252397 *Fax:* (089) 6252291
E-mail: akse@akse.de
Web Site: www.akse-verlag.de
Key Personnel
Contact: Wolfgang Gerz
Subjects: Biological Sciences, Health, Nutrition, Medicine, Nursing, Dentistry
ISBN Prefix(es): 978-3-9805706

Aktive Musik Verlagsgesellschaft mbH
Poststr 6, 44137 Dortmund
Tel: (0231) 9142497 *Fax:* (0231) 9143213
E-mail: info@aktive-musik.de
Web Site: www.igel-records.de
Key Personnel
Mng Dir: Mira Brinkschulte; Rudi Mika
ISBN Prefix(es): 978-3-89353

Aladin Verlag GmbH
Erdmanstr 10-12, 22765 Hamburg
Tel: (040) 558 91 56-20 *Fax:* (040) 558 91 56-21
E-mail: info@aladin-verlag.de
Web Site: www.aladin-verlag.de
Key Personnel
Mng Dir: Klaus Humann
Public Relations: Anna Helbling *Tel:* (040) 558 91 56-22 *E-mail:* anna.helbling@aladin-verlag.de
Founded: 2013
ISBN Prefix(es): 978-3-8489
Number of titles published annually: 40 Print

Alawi Verlag
Finkenstr 11, 50858 Cologne
Tel: (0221) 9483756 *Fax:* (0221) 9483757
E-mail: info@alawi-verlag.de
Web Site: www.alawi-verlag.de
Key Personnel
Publisher: Abdul-Rahman Alawi
Membership(s): Boersenverein des Deutschen
    Buchhandels.
Subjects: Literature, Literary Criticism, Essays,
    Arabic Literature
ISBN Prefix(es): 978-3-941822

Alb-Fils Verlag
Muehlwiesenstr 15, 73342 Bad Ditzenbach
Tel: (07335) 924110 *Fax:* (07335) 924135
Key Personnel
Publisher: Claudia Ruckdaeschel, MA
Subjects: Biography, Memoirs, Travel & Tourism
ISBN Prefix(es): 978-3-938108

Alba Fachverlag GmbH & Co KG+
Am Meerkamp 20, 40667 Meerbusch
Tel: (02132) 91395-0 *Fax:* (02132) 91395-28
E-mail: info@alba-verlag.de
Web Site: www.alba-publikation.de
Key Personnel
Publisher: Alf Teloeken *Tel:* (02132) 91395-10
Mng Dir: Tim Teloeken *Tel:* (02132) 91395-12
Production: Peter Gerens *Tel:* (02132) 91395-60
Sales: Harald Sager *Tel:* (02132) 91395-51
Founded: 1951
Subjects: Crafts, Games, Hobbies, Film, Video,
    Outdoor Recreation, Transportation
ISBN Prefix(es): 978-3-87094

**Alba Publikation Alf Teloeken GmbH & Co
KG**, see Alba Fachverlag GmbH & Co KG

Albarello Verlag GmbH+
Bahnstr 17a, 42781 Haan
Tel: (02104) 817233 *Fax:* (02104) 817234
E-mail: email@albarello.de
Web Site: www.albarello.de
Key Personnel
Mng Dir: Frank Zimmermann
Founded: 2001
ISBN Prefix(es): 978-3-930299; 978-3-9801855;
    978-3-86559
Foreign Rep(s): Michael Beranek (Austria);
    Guenther Lintschinger (Austria)
Distribution Center: Leipziger Kommissions-
    und Grossbuchhandels-gesellschaft mbH
    (LKG), An der Suedspitze 1-12, 04571 Roetha
Tel: (034206) 65-100 *Fax:* (034206) 65-110
E-mail: lkg@lkg-service.de *Web Site:* www.
    lkg-va.de

Albatross, *imprint of* Bibliographisches Institut
GmbH

Verlag Karl Alber, *imprint of* Verlag Herder
GmbH

Verlag Karl Alber GmbH+
Imprint of Verlag Herder GmbH
Hermann-Herder-Str 4, 79104 Freiburg
Tel: (0761) 2717-436 *Fax:* (0761) 2717-212
E-mail: info@verlag-alber.de
Web Site: www.verlag-alber.de
Key Personnel
Publishing Dir: Lukas Trabert *Tel:* (0761) 2712-
    213 *E-mail:* trabert@verlag-alber.de
Production: Martin Pauls *Tel:* (0761) 2717-410
    E-mail: pauls@verlag-alber.de
Marketing & Editorial: Angela Haury
    E-mail: haury@verlag-alber.de
Sales: Julia Pirschl *Tel:* (0761) 2717-315
    E-mail: pirschl@verlag-alber.de
Founded: 1939

Subjects: History, Literature, Literary Criticism,
    Essays, Philosophy, Science (General)
ISBN Prefix(es): 978-3-7820; 978-3-495
Number of titles published annually: 30 Print
Total Titles: 400 Print
Foreign Rep(s): Joe A Fuchs (Switzerland); Ver-
    lagsagentur Erich Neuhold (Erich Neuhold &
    William Platzer) (Austria); Harald Rumpold
    (Austria, Italy, South Tyrol, Italy)
Distribution Center: Koch, Neff & Oetinger Ver-
    lagsauslieferung GmbH, Industriestr 23, 70565
    Stuttgart (Germany & Austria)
Herder AG Basel Verlagsauslieferungen, Mut-
    tenzerstr 109, 4133 Pratteln 1, Switzerland
Tel: (061) 827-9060 *Fax:* (061) 827-9067
    E-mail: verkauf@herder.ch

Antiquariat und Verlag Frank Albrecht
Mozartstr 62, 69198 Schriesheim
Tel: (06203) 65713 *Fax:* (06203) 65311
E-mail: albrecht@antiquariat.com
Web Site: www.antiquariat.com
Key Personnel
Publisher: Frank Albrecht
Founded: 1985
Membership(s): PEN International; Verband
    Deutscher Antiquare eV.
Subjects: Art, Government, Political Science, His-
    tory, Literature, Literary Criticism, Essays, Cul-
    tural History
ISBN Prefix(es): 978-3-926360
Total Titles: 16 Print

Albrecht Golf Verlags GmbH+
Am Schnepfenweg 153, 80995 Munich
Tel: (089) 85 85 30 *Fax:* (089) 85 85 3-197
E-mail: golf@albrecht.de
Web Site: www.1golf.eu
Key Personnel
Mng Dir: Oliver Albrecht
Chief Editor: Elsa-Maria Honecker
Founded: 1927
Subjects: Career Development, Sports, Athletics
ISBN Prefix(es): 978-3-87014

Alert-Verlag
Rheinstr 46, 12161 Berlin
Tel: (030) 76 69 99 80 *Fax:* (030) 76 69 99 40
E-mail: info@alertverlag.de
Web Site: www.alert-verlag.de
Key Personnel
Owner & Mng Dir: Dr Johann-Friedrich Huff-
    mann
Subjects: Finance, Law, Management
ISBN Prefix(es): 978-3-941136

Alexander Verlag Berlin+
Fredericiastr 8, 14050 Berlin
Mailing Address: Postbox 19 18 24, 14008 Berlin
Tel: (030) 302 18 26 *Fax:* (030) 302 94 08
E-mail: info@alexander-verlag.com; presse@
    alexander-verlag.com; vertrieb@alexander-
    verlag.com
Web Site: www.alexander-verlag.com
Key Personnel
Publisher: Alexander Wewerka
    E-mail: wewerka@alexander-verlag.com
Press/Public Relations: Marilena Savino
Sales: Peter Walter *Tel:* (030) 91 68 10 12
Founded: 1983
Subjects: Drama, Theater, Film, Video, Literature,
    Literary Criticism, Essays, Music, Dance
ISBN Prefix(es): 978-3-923854; 978-3-89581
Number of titles published annually: 10 E-Book
Total Titles: 160 Print; 8 CD-ROM; 40 E-Book; 5
    Audio
Foreign Rep(s): Beat Eberle (Switzerland); Helga
    Schuster (Austria)
Distribution Center: PROLIT Verlagsausliefer-
    ungs GmbH, Siemensstr 16, 35463 Fernwald
    Annerod, Contact: Gabriele Lemuth *Tel:* (0641)

943 93 209 *Fax:* (0641) 943 95 29 *E-mail:* g.
    lemuth@prolit.de (Germany & Austria)
AVA/Buch 2000, Centralweg 16, 8910 Affoltern
    am Albis, Switzerland, Contact: Barbara Joss
    Tel: (044) 762 42 60 *Fax:* (044) 762 42 10
    E-mail: b.joss@ava.ch

Alibri Verlag GmbH
Ernsthofstr 12, 63739 Aschaffenburg
Tel: (06021) 581 734 *Fax:* (03212) 119 89 72
E-mail: verlag@alibri.de
Web Site: www.alibri-buecher.de; www.facebook.
    com/alibri.verlag
Key Personnel
Mng Dir: Gunnar Schedel
Subjects: Cookery, Fiction, History, Philosophy,
    Science (General), Religious Skepticism
ISBN Prefix(es): 978-3-86569; 978-3-932710;
    978-3-9804386
Foreign Rep(s): Seth Meyer-Bruhns (Austria)
Orders to: sova, Philipp-Reis-Str 17, 63477 Main-
    tal *Tel:* (06181) 90 880 72 *Fax:* (06181) 90 880
    73 *E-mail:* sovaffm@t-online.de (Germany &
    Austria)
Balmer Buecherdienst AG, Kobiboden, 8840
    Einsiedeln, Switzerland *Tel:* (0848) 840 820
    Fax: (0848) 840 830 *E-mail:* info@balmer-
    bd.ch

Alkor-Edition Kassel GmbH+
Division of Baerenreiter-Verlag Karl Voetterle
    GmbH & Co KG
Heinrich-Schuetz-Allee 35, 34131 Kassel
Tel: (0561) 3105-282 *Fax:* (0561) 37755
E-mail: info.alkor@baerenreiter.com
Web Site: www.alkor-edition.com
Key Personnel
Mng Dir: Barbara Scheuch-Voetterle
    E-mail: bscheuch@baerenreiter.com
Founded: 1934
Subjects: Music, Dance
Distributor for Editio Baerenreiter Praha (Ger-
    many, Austria & Switzerland); Baerenreiter
    Verlag Kassel (worldwide); Gustav Bosse
    Verlag Kassel (worldwide); Dilia Prag (Ger-
    many, Austria, Benelux countries, Scandi-
    navia, Switzerland); Faber Music London (Ger-
    many, Austria & Switzerland); Henle Verlag
    Muenchen (worldwide); Henschel Verlag fuer
    Musik Berlin (worldwide); Editions Henry
    Lemoine Paris (Germany, Austria & Switzer-
    land); Musikwissenschaftlicher Verlag Wien
    (worldwide exc Austria); Slowakischer Musik-
    fonds Bratislava (Germany, Austria, Benelux
    countries, Switzerland); Strauss Edition Wien
    (worldwide); Sueddeutscher Musikverlag Hei-
    delberg (worldwide); Tschechischer Musik-
    fonds Praha (Germany, Austria, Benelux coun-
    tries, Portugal, Scandinavia, Spain & Switzer-
    land)
Foreign Rep(s): Albersen Verhuur bv (Nether-
    lands); Baerenreiter Praha spol sro (Czechia,
    Slovakia); Casa Musicale Sonzogno (Italy);
    Faber Music Ltd (Australia, Ireland, New
    Zealand, UK); Hartai Music Agency (Hun-
    gary); Hrvatsko Drustvo Skladatelja (Croatia,
    Slovenia); Schott Music Corp & European
    American Music Distributors (Canada, USA);
    SEEMSA (Sociedad Espanola de Ediciones
    Musicales SA) (Portugal, Spain)

Allegria, *imprint of* Ullstein Buchverlage GmbH

Allegria Verlag
Imprint of Ullstein Buchverlage GmbH
Friedrichstr 126, 10117 Berlin
Tel: (030) 23456-300 *Fax:* (030) 23456-303
E-mail: info@allegria-verlag.de
Web Site: www.ullsteinbuchverlage.de/nc/verlage/
    allegria.html
Key Personnel
Press & Public Relations: Christine Heinrich
    Tel: (030) 23456-433 *Fax:* (030) 23456-445

E-mail: christine.heinrich@ullstein-buchverlag.
de
Founded: 2004
Subjects: Literature, Literary Criticism, Essays,
Nonfiction (General), Entertainment, New Age
ISBN Prefix(es): 978-3-548; 978-3-7934

AlohaIpo Verlag
Anton-Braith-Str 1, 83026 Rosenheim
Tel: (08031) 2479800 *Fax:* (08031) 2479798
E-mail: verlag@alohaipo.com; presse@alohaipo.
de
Web Site: www.alohaipo.de
Key Personnel
Publisher: Robert Schmoeller
Founded: 2008
Subjects: Animals, Pets
ISBN Prefix(es): 978-3-9811146

Alouette Verlag+
Uferstr 41, 22113 Oststeinbek
Tel: (040) 712 23 53 *Fax:* (040) 713 41 88
E-mail: webmaster@alouette-verlag.de
Web Site: www.alouette-verlag.de
Key Personnel
President & Publisher: Juergen F Boden
    E-mail: juergen.boden@alouette-verlag.de
Art Dir: Petra Horn
Editor: Elke Emshoff
Founded: 1983
Book & film publishers. Specialize in nature-
    oriented picture & textbooks (pictorials with
    profound text matter) mainly about North
    America, the Arctic & Siberia, TV documen-
    taries & cultural books.
Subjects: Anthropology, Asian Studies, Native
    American Studies, Natural History, Travel &
    Tourism, Foreign Cultures
ISBN Prefix(es): 978-3-924324
Number of titles published annually: 1 Print; 1
    Audio
Total Titles: 27 Print; 5 Audio

ALS-Verlag GmbH+
Voltastr 3, 63128 Dietzenbach
Mailing Address: Postfach 14 40, 63114 Dietzen-
    bach
Tel: (06074) 82 16-0 *Fax:* (06074) 82 16-75
E-mail: info@als-verlag.de
Web Site: www.als-verlag.de
Key Personnel
Mng Dir: Juergen Hils
Founded: 1967
Subjects: Art, Crafts, Games, Hobbies, Educa-
    tion, Environmental Studies, How-to, Outdoor
    Recreation
ISBN Prefix(es): 978-3-89135; 978-3-921366

Verlag Alte Uni
Brettener Str 30, 75031 Eppingen
Tel: (07262) 4417 *Fax:* (07262) 7942
E-mail: alteuni@aol.com
Key Personnel
Owner: Karl Knoll
Founded: 1986
Subjects: Art, Cookery, Medicine, Nursing, Den-
    tistry, Music, Dance, Regional Interests
ISBN Prefix(es): 978-3-926315

Verlag Haus Altenberg GmbH
Carl-Mosterts-Platz 1, 40477 Duesseldorf
Tel: (0211) 4693-160 *Fax:* (0211) 4693-172
E-mail: bestellung@jugendhaus-duesseldorf.de
Web Site: www.verlaghausaltenberg.de
Key Personnel
Mng Dir: Markus Hoffmann *Tel:* (0211) 4693-114
    E-mail: hoffmann@jugendhaus-duesseldorf.
    de; Stephan Jentgens *Tel:* (0211) 4693-114
    Fax: (0211) 4693-120 *E-mail:* sjentgens@
    jugendhaus-duesseldorf.de

Publishing Dir: Rainer Schute *Tel:* (0211) 4693-
    138 *E-mail:* rschute@jugendhaus-duesseldorf.
    de
Rights & Licenses: Hermann Giesen
    E-mail: ngiesen@jugendhaus-duesseldorf.de
Sales: Martina Kaczmarczyk *Tel:* (0211) 4693-
    129
Founded: 1946
Subjects: Education, Inspirational, Spirituality,
    Religion - Catholic
ISBN Prefix(es): 978-3-7761

AMA Verlag GmbH
Uhlstr 19-23, 50321 Bruehl
Mailing Address: Postfach 1168, 50301 Bruehl
Tel: (02232) 9693 0 *Fax:* (02232) 9693 66
E-mail: mail@ama-verlag.de
Web Site: www.ama-verlag.de
Key Personnel
Mng Dir: Detlef Kessler
Subjects: Music, Dance
ISBN Prefix(es): 978-3-89922; 978-3-927190;
    978-3-932587

AMBERPRESS
Chausseestr 116, 10115 Berlin
Tel: (030) 9789 43-30 *Fax:* (030) 9789 43-33
E-mail: info@amberpress.eu
Web Site: amberpress.eu
Key Personnel
Owner: Malgorzata Karolina Warrink
Founded: 2007
Subjects: Architecture & Interior Design, Art
ISBN Prefix(es): 978-3-9809655

Ambro Lacus, Buch- und Bildverlag
Betzenweg 60, 81247 Munich
Tel: (089) 8112768
Web Site: kremnitz.com/ambrolacus
Key Personnel
Owner: Gisela M Schinzel
    E-mail: gschinzelpenth@gmx.de
Founded: 1974
Subjects: Earth Sciences, Gardening, Plants, Law,
    Nonfiction (General), Science (General), Travel
    & Tourism
ISBN Prefix(es): 978-3-921445
Number of titles published annually: 1 Print

AMRA Publishing & Records
Auf der Reitbahn 8, 63452 Hanau
Tel: (06181) 18 93 92 *Fax:* (03212) 174 03 23
E-mail: info@amraverlag.de
Web Site: amraverlag.de
Key Personnel
Dir: Michael Nagula
Founded: 2005
Subjects: Art, Health, Nutrition, Literature, Liter-
    ary Criticism, Essays, Romance, Children
ISBN Prefix(es): 978-3-939373; 978-3-95447

Anabas-Verlag GmbH & Co KG+
c/o Majuskel Medienproduktion GmbH, Schulstr
    20, 35579 Wetzlar
Mailing Address: c/o Majuskel Medienproduktion
    GmbH, Postfach 2820, 35538 Wetzlar
Tel: (041) 91 13 18 *Fax:* (041) 91 13 12
E-mail: anabas.vlg@googlemail.com
Web Site: www.anabas-verlag.de
Key Personnel
Mng Dir: Peter Grosshaus
Founded: 1966
Membership(s): Borsenverein des Deutschen
    Buchandles, Hessischer Buchhandler- und Ver-
    legerverband.
Subjects: Art, History, Poetry, Travel & Tourism
ISBN Prefix(es): 978-3-87038
Number of titles published annually: 10 Print
Total Titles: 355 Print
Foreign Rep(s): Pierre Bachofner (Switzerland);
    Seth Meyer-Bruhns (Austria)

Anaconda Verlag GmbH
Subbelrather Str 543a, 50827 Cologne
Tel: (0221) 589604-0 *Fax:* (0221) 589604-29
E-mail: info@anacondaverlag.de
Web Site: www.anacondaverlag.de
Key Personnel
Contact: Hansjoerg Kohl
Founded: 2004
Subjects: Antiques, Art, History, Language Arts,
    Linguistics, Literature, Literary Criticism, Es-
    says, Nonfiction (General), Philosophy, Psy-
    chology, Psychiatry, Religion - Other, Science
    (General)
ISBN Prefix(es): 978-3-86647; 978-3-938484

Andrea Verlags GmbH
Schwanebecker Chaussee 12, 16321 Bernau
Tel: (03338) 75 29 94 *Fax:* (03338) 75 29 96
E-mail: info@andrea-verlag.de
Web Site: www.andrea-verlag.de
Key Personnel
Management: Andrea Bigalke *E-mail:* a.bigalke@
    andrea-verlag.de
Production: Carmen Lang *E-mail:* c.lang@andrea-
    verlag.de
Wholesale: Michael Bigalke *Tel:* (03338) 5489
    Fax: (03338) 5485 *E-mail:* m.bigalke@mb-
    kontakt.de
Subjects: Cookery, Crafts, Games, Hobbies, Hu-
    mor, Poetry
ISBN Prefix(es): 978-3-9807951; 978-3-9808877;
    978-3-9809890; 978-3-9810368

Angkor Verlag
Foockenstr 5, 65933 Frankfurt
E-mail: webmaster@angkor-verlag.de
Web Site: www.angkor-verlag.de
Key Personnel
Contact: Guido Keller
Subjects: Philosophy, Religion - Buddhist,
    Japanese Culture, Oriental Studies, Samurai,
    Zen
ISBN Prefix(es): 978-3-936018

animal learn Verlag
Am Anger 36, 83233 Bernau
Tel: (08051) 961 71-0 *Fax:* (08051) 961 71-17
E-mail: animal.learn@t-online.de
Web Site: www.animal-learn.de
Key Personnel
Contact: Clarissa von Reinhardt
    E-mail: vonreinhardt@animal-learn.de
Founded: 1993
Subjects: Animals, Pets, Dog Training
ISBN Prefix(es): 978-3-936188

AnNo Text, *imprint of* Wolters Kluwer
    Deutschland GmbH

Ansata, *imprint of* Verlagsgruppe Random House
    Bertelsmann

Ansata
Imprint of Verlagsgruppe Random House Bertels-
    mann
Bayerstr 71-73, 80335 Munich
Tel: (089) 4136-0 *Fax:* (089) 4136-3333
E-mail: kundenservice@randomhouse.de
Web Site: www.randomhouse.de
Key Personnel
Events: Carolin Assmann *Tel:* (089) 4136-3915
    E-mail: carolin.assmann@randomhouse.de
Press: Claudia Grab *Tel:* (089) 4136-3131
    Fax: (089) 4136-3507 *E-mail:* claudia.grab@
    randomhouse.de
Subjects: Inspirational, Spirituality
ISBN Prefix(es): 978-3-7787

AnTex Verlag+
Sanderhoehe 13, 51688 Wipperfuerth
Tel: (02267) 82 85 19; (02267) 659922

Key Personnel
Contact: Martina Hermann
Founded: 1988
ISBN Prefix(es): 978-3-9801871; 978-3-9809302
Distribution Center: Leipziger Kommissions
  und- Grossbuchhandelsgesellschaft mbH
  (LKG), An der Suedspitze 1-12, 04571 Roetha
  Tel: (034206) 65-100 *Fax:* (034206) 65-110
  E-mail: lkg@lkg-service.de *Web Site:* www.
  lkg-va.de

Antiqua-Verlag GmbH
Dorneckstr 3a, 79793 Wutoeschingen-Horheim
Tel: (07746) 2260; (07746) 2273 *Fax:* (07746)
  2260
Key Personnel
Manager: Ottfried Ludwig *E-mail:* ottfried-
  ludwig@t-online.de
Founded: 1977
Subjects: Geography, Geology, Medicine, Nurs-
  ing, Dentistry
ISBN Prefix(es): 978-3-88210

Antiquariats-Union Vertriebs GmbH & Co KG
Luener Rennbahn 14, 21339 Lueneburg
Tel: (04131) 983504 *Fax:* (04131) 9835595
Number of titles published annually: 15 Print
Total Titles: 70 Print

Anzeigenverwaltung & Herstellung, *imprint of*
Johann Wolfgang Goethe-Universitaet Frankfurt
am Main

AOL-Verlag GmbH
Bahnhofstra 21-25, 21614 Buxtehude
Mailing Address: Postfach 1656, 21606 Buxte-
  hude
Tel: (04161) 7 49 60-0; (04161) 7 49 60-60 (or-
  ders) *Fax:* (04161) 7 49 60-50; (04161) 7 49
  60-65 (orders)
E-mail: info@aol-verlag.de; bestellung@aol-
  verlag.de
Web Site: www.aol-verlag.de
Key Personnel
Mng Dir: Christian Glaser
Head, Marketing: Ursula Herrmann
Program Dir: Dr Kristina Poncin *E-mail:* k.
  poncin@yahoo.verlag.de
Press: Daniel Voelzow *Tel:* (04161) 7 49 60-26
  E-mail: d.voelzow@lehrerfachverlage.de
Focus on education & tools.
Subjects: Advertising, Art, Biological Sciences,
  Career Development, Chemistry, Chemical En-
  gineering, Child Care & Development, Com-
  puter Science, Drama, Theater, Education,
  Energy, English as a Second Language, En-
  vironmental Studies, Fiction, Film, Video, For-
  eign Countries, Government, Political Science,
  Health, Nutrition, History, Literature, Literary
  Criticism, Essays, Management, Mathematics,
  Natural History, Nonfiction (General), Outdoor
  Recreation, Physical Sciences, Physics, Science
  (General), Sports, Athletics, Transportation
ISBN Prefix(es): 978-3-89111
Parent Company: AAP Lehrerfachverlag GmbH
Ultimate Parent Company: Klett Gruppe
Orders to: AAP Lehrerfachverlag GmbH
  Verlagsvertretung Schweiz

A1 Verlag GmbH
Hippmannstr 11, 80639 Munich
Tel: (089) 1711928-0 *Fax:* (089) 1711928-8
E-mail: info@a1-verlag.de
Web Site: www.a1-verlag.de
Key Personnel
Dir: Inge Holzheimer *E-mail:* holzheimer@a1-
  verlag.de; Albert Voelkmann
Subjects: Literature, Literary Criticism, Essays,
  Nonfiction (General)
ISBN Prefix(es): 978-3-927743; 978-3-940666

APHAIA Verlag+
Franz Wolter Str 2, 81925 Munich
Tel: (089) 8151 277844 *Fax:* (089) 8151 277846
E-mail: team@aphaia-verlag.de
Web Site: www.aphaia.de
Key Personnel
Editor: Dr Harald Ernst Albrecht *E-mail:* harald.
  albrecht@amcomedia.de
Founded: 1986
Subjects: Art, Literature, Literary Criticism, Es-
  says, Music, Dance, Poetry, Bookart, Lyrics
ISBN Prefix(es): 978-3-946574
Number of titles published annually: 8 Print; 2
  CD-ROM
Total Titles: 160 Print; 10 CD-ROM

Apollo-Verlag Paul Lincke GmbH
Weihergarten 5, 55116 Mainz
Tel: (06131) 246300 *Fax:* (06131) 246823
Subjects: Music, Dance
ISBN Prefix(es): 978-3-920030

E Appelhans Verlag GmbH & Co
Jasperallee 18, 38102 Braunschweig
Tel: (0531) 349 60333 *Fax:* (0531) 349 60334
E-mail: info@appelhans-verlag.de
Web Site: www.appelhans-verlag.de
Key Personnel
Mng Dir: Oliver Ruth
Subjects: History, Regional Culture
ISBN Prefix(es): 978-3-930292; 978-3-937664
Parent Company: Ruth Printmedien

Apprimus
Steinbachstr 25, 52074 Aachen
Tel: (0241) 80 2071 4 *Fax:* (0241) 80 20 6010
E-mail: info@apprimus-verlag.de
Web Site: www.apprimus-verlag.de
Key Personnel
Mng Dir: Kristin Marso-Walbeck
Founded: 2008
Scientific publisher of the Institute for Industrial
  Communication & Professional Media (IIF).
Subjects: Engineering (General), Medicine, Nurs-
  ing, Dentistry, Psychology, Psychiatry, Science
  (General), Anthologies, Humanities, Natural
  Science
ISBN Prefix(es): 978-3-86359

Aquamarin Verlag GmbH+
Vogelherd 1, 85567 Grafing
Tel: (08075) 913274 *Fax:* (08075) 913275
E-mail: info@aquamarin-verlag.de
Web Site: www.aquamarin-verlag.de
Key Personnel
Mng Dir: Peter Michel
Founded: 1981
Subjects: Art, Astrology, Occult, Inspirational,
  Spirituality, Parapsychology, Philosophy, Reli-
  gion - Buddhist, Religion - Hindu, Religion -
  Other, Science (General), World Religion
ISBN Prefix(es): 978-3-922936; 978-3-89427
Imprints: Adyar Edition; Adyar Verlag; Sulamith
  Wulfing Edition; Sulamith Wulfing Verlag
Foreign Rep(s): Dr Fiuliana Bernardi (Italy)
Foreign Rights: Katia Schume (Portugal, South
  America, Spain)
Distribution Center: Alexander Herrmann
  Vertrieb & Beratung, Eversbuschstr 40a,
  80999 Munich *Tel:* (089) 38 38 06 90
  Fax: (089) 38 38 06 910 *E-mail:* a.herrmann@
  vertriebundberatung.de *Web Site:* www.
  vertriebundberatung.de

Aragon GmbH+
Amselstr 8, 47445 Moers
Mailing Address: Postfach 10 11 06, 47401 Mo-
  ers
Tel: (02841) 1 65 61 *Fax:* (02841) 2 43 36
E-mail: info@aragon-verlag.de
Web Site: www.aragon-verlag.de

Key Personnel
Mng Dir: Karin Low
Founded: 1984
Subjects: Art, Drama, Theater, Travel & Tourism
ISBN Prefix(es): 978-3-89535
Distributed by AVA b+i (Switzerland)
Orders to: Prolit, Siemensstr 18a, 35463 Fern-
  wald/Annerod

Arbor Verlag GmbH
Alice-Salomon-Str 4, 79111 Freiburg
Tel: (0761) 40140930
Web Site: www.arbor-verlag.de
Key Personnel
Mng Dir: Dirk Henn; Ulrich Lienhard Valentin
Founded: 1985
Subjects: Child Care & Development, Education,
  Health, Nutrition, Inspirational, Spirituality,
  Medicine, Nursing, Dentistry, Psychology, Psy-
  chiatry, Meditation
ISBN Prefix(es): 978-3-86781; 978-3-936855;
  978-3-924195

Arcadia Verlag GmbH+
Johnsallee 23, 20148 Hamburg
Tel: (040) 41 41 00-0; (040) 41 41 00-34 (ed-
  itorial) *Fax:* (040) 41 41 00-40; (040) 41 41
  00-60 (editorial)
E-mail: contact@sikorski.de; editorial@sikorski.
  de
Web Site: www.sikorski.de
Key Personnel
Mng Dir: Dr Axel Sikorski; Dagmar Sikorski
Founded: 1935
Subjects: Drama, Theater, Music, Dance
ISBN Prefix(es): 978-3-920880; 978-3-935196
Parent Company: Internationale Musikverlage
  Hans Sikorski GmbH & Co KG

Arche Literatur Verlag AG+
Max-Brauer-Allee 34, 22765 Hamburg
E-mail: info@arche-verlag.com
Web Site: www.arche-verlag.com
Key Personnel
Mng Dir: Tim Jung *E-mail:* t.jung@vgo-arche-
  atrium.de
Marketing: Ute Hollmann *Tel:* (040) 607909-929
  Fax: (040) 607909-629 *E-mail:* u.hollmann@
  vgo-arche-atrium.de
Press: Frauke Jansen *Tel:* (060) 79 09-931
  Fax: (060) 79 09-631 *E-mail:* f.jansen@vgo-
  arche-atrium.de
Rights & Licenses: Kristine Buchholz *Tel:* (060)
  79 09-932 *Fax:* (060) 79 09-632 *E-mail:* k.
  buchholz@vgo-arche-atrium.de
Sales: Anke Strunz *Tel:* (040) 607909-929
  Fax: (040) 607909-630 *E-mail:* a.strunz@vgo-
  arche-atrium.de
Founded: 1944
Subjects: Biography, Memoirs, Fiction, Litera-
  ture, Literary Criticism, Essays, Music, Dance,
  Mysteries, Suspense, Poetry, Travel & Tourism
ISBN Prefix(es): 978-3-7160
Branch Office(s)
Heinrichstr 249, 8005 Zurich, Switzerland
Foreign Rep(s): Wolfgang Habenschuss (Austria);
  Annelies Hohl (Switzerland); Martin Schlieber
  (Austria); Dietmar Vorderwinkler (Austria)
Distribution Center: Prolit Verlagsausliefer-
  ung GmbH, Siemensstr 16, 35463 Fernwald,
  Contact: Jens Vogt *Tel:* (0641) 9 43 93 31
  Fax: (0641) 9 43 93 39 *E-mail:* j.vogt@prolit.
  de *Web Site:* www.prolit.de
Dr Franz Hain, Dr-Otto-Neurath-Gasse 5, 1220
  Vienna, Austria *Tel:* (01) 282 65 65 77
  Fax: (01) 282 52 82 *E-mail:* bestell@hain.at
Scheidegger & Co AG, Obere Bahnhofstr
  10A, 8910 Affoltern am Albis, Switzerland
  Tel: (044) 762 42 42 *Fax:* (044) 762 42 49
  E-mail: info@scheidegger-buecher.ch *Web
  Site:* www.scheidegger-buecher.ch

Arche Noah Verlag
Ammergauer Str 80, 86971 Peiting
Tel: (08861) 59018 *Fax:* (08861) 67091
E-mail: info@michaelsverlag.de
Web Site: arche-noah-verlag.com; www.
michaelsverlag.de
Key Personnel
Mng Dir: Petra Otto
Subjects: Inspirational, Spirituality, Meditation,
Reiki, Wellness
ISBN Prefix(es): 978-3-931721; 978-3-86733
Parent Company: Michaels Verlag & Vertrieb
GmbH

Archiati Verlag eK, see Rudolf Steiner
Ausgaben eK

archimappublishers
c/o Kaiser Peters Wormuth GbR, Weimarer Str
32, 10625 Berlin
Tel: (030) 88624111 *Fax:* (030) 88624113
E-mail: info@archipendium.com
Web Site: www.archipendium.com
Subjects: Architecture & Interior Design, Travel
& Tourism, European Travel
ISBN Prefix(es): 978-3-940874

Arco Verlag GmbH
Krautstr 64, 42289 Wuppertal
Tel: (0202) 623382 *Fax:* (0202) 2634000
E-mail: service@arco-verlag.com
Web Site: www.arco-verlag.com
Key Personnel
Dir: Christoph Haacker
Founded: 2002
Subjects: Literature, Literary Criticism, Essays,
Science (General)
ISBN Prefix(es): 978-3-938375

ARCult Media GmbH+
Ulmenallee 24 A, 50999 Cologne
Tel: (02236) 5097972
E-mail: info@arcultmedia.de
Web Site: www.arcultmedia.de; www.kulturpreise.
de; www.ericarts.org; www.culture-rights.net
Key Personnel
Dir: Dr Andreas Joh Wiesand *E-mail:* wroclaw@
arcultmedia.de
Project Dir: Regina Wyrwoll *E-mail:* wyrwoll@
arcultmedia.de
Founded: 1969
Publications & research documents in all fields
of the arts & culture industries; international &
European cooperation projects.
Subjects: Art, Developing Countries, Drama, The-
ater, Journalism, Management, Music, Dance,
Outdoor Recreation, Publishing & Book Trade
Reference, Radio, TV, Social Sciences, Soci-
ology, Women's Studies, Arts Management,
Cultural Policies, Heritage, Human Rights
ISBN Prefix(es): 978-3-930395
Total Titles: 62 Print; 2 CD-ROM; 5 Online
Branch Office(s)
Berlin
Vienna, Austria
Distributed by De Gruyter (Berlin); Leske & Bu-
drich (Opladen); Sam's Books (Services for
Arts Management)

Ardey-Verlag GmbH
An den Speichern 6, 48157 Muenster
Tel: (0251) 4132-0 *Fax:* (0251) 4132-20
E-mail: info@ardey-verlag.de
Web Site: www.ardey-verlag.de
Key Personnel
Mng Dir: Bodo Strototte
Founded: 1951
Subjects: Art, Genealogy, Geography, Geology,
Government, Political Science, History, Liter-
ature, Literary Criticism, Essays, Nonfiction

(General), Regional Interests, Technology, Culture
ISBN Prefix(es): 978-3-87023
Distribution Center: Runge Verlagsauslieferung, Bergstr 2, 33803 Steinhagen *Tel:* (05204)
998-442 *Fax:* (05204) 998-116 *E-mail:* msr@
rungeva.de

Arena Verlag GmbH+
Rottendorfer Str 16, 97074 Wuerzburg
Tel: (0931) 79644-0 *Fax:* (0931) 79644-13
E-mail: info@arena-verlag.de
Web Site: www.arena-verlag.de
Key Personnel
Mng Dir: Albrecht Oldenbaurg
Foreign Rights: Tanja Dziewior *Tel:* (0931)
73644-62 *E-mail:* tanja.dziewior@arena-verlag.
de
Press: Susanne Baumann *Tel:* (0931) 79644-20
E-mail: susanne.baumann@arena-verlag.de
Founded: 1949
Subjects: Fiction, Nonfiction (General)
ISBN Prefix(es): 978-3-401; 978-3-88155
Number of titles published annually: 500 Print
Total Titles: 2,000 Print
Parent Company: Georg Westermann GmbH &
Co, Georg-Westermann-Allee 66, 38104 Braun-
schweig
Imprints: Edition Buecherbar im Arena Verlag;
Ensslin Verlag im Arena Verlag
Foreign Rep(s): Verlagsgentur Kager & Treml
(Austria); Scheidegger & Co AG (Switzerland)
Foreign Rights: Agency TEXT (Charubhas-
tra Meyhoefer-Talayasut) (Thailand); Ana-
toliaLit Agency (Dilek Akdemir) (Turkey);
Balla-Sztojkov Literary Agency (Catherine
Balla) (Hungary); Dr Ivana Beil (Czechia, Slo-
vakia); Eliane Benisti Agency (France); Giu-
liana Bernardi (Italy); Agencja Literacka Graal
(Maria Strarz-Kanska) (Poland); Hercules Busi-
ness & Culture GmbH (Hongjun Cai) (China,
Hong Kong, Taiwan); Internationaal Literatuur
Bureau (Linda Kohn) (Netherlands); Interna-
tional Copyright Agency Ltd (Simona Kessler)
(Romania); Ute Koerner Literary Agent SL
(Raquel Riu) (Spanish & Portuguese); Meike
Marx Literary Agent (Japan); Momo Agency
(Geenie Han) (Korea); I Pikarski Literary
Agency (Gabrielle Hertzmann) (Israel); Mar-
git Schaleck (Denmark)
Warehouse: VSB Verlagsservice Braunschweig
GmbH, Georg-Westermann-Allee 66, 38104
Braunschweig

Argon Verlag GmbH+
Neue Gruenstr 17, 10179 Berlin
Tel: (030) 257 620 60 *Fax:* (030) 257 620 620
E-mail: info@argon-verlag.de
Web Site: www.argon-verlag.de
Key Personnel
Mng Dir: Christian Doettinger
Publishing Dir: Heike Schmidtke *Tel:* (030) 257
620 624 *E-mail:* heike.schmidtke@argon-
verlag.de
Manager, Sales & Marketing: Kilian Kissling
Tel: (030) 257 620 621 *E-mail:* kilian.
kissling@argon-verlag.de
Press: Katja Wanoth *Tel:* (030) 267 620 630
E-mail: katja.wanoth@argon-verlag.de
Rights: Margot Kaiser *Tel:* (030) 257 620 622
E-mail: margot.kaiser@argon-verlag.de
Founded: 1952
Subjects: Fiction, Nonfiction (General)
ISBN Prefix(es): 978-3-87024; 978-3-930088;
978-3-86610; 978-3-8398
Parent Company: Verlagsgruppe Georg von
Holtzbrinck GmbH
Foreign Rep(s): Hans Jobst (Austria, South Tyrol,
Italy); Ulrich Nebroj (Switzerland)
Orders to: HGV, Weidestr 122 A, 22083 Ham-
burg *Tel:* (040) 84000888 *Fax:* (040) 84000855
E-mail: bestellung@hgv-online.de

Argument-Verlag GmbH+
Glashuettenstr 28, 20357 Hamburg
Tel: (040) 40 18 00-0 *Fax:* (040) 40 18 00-20
E-mail: verlag@argument.de; presse@argument.
de
Web Site: www.argument.de
Key Personnel
Mng Dir: Prof Frigga Haug; Marion Laudan
Editing & Production: Dr Iris Konopik *Tel:* (040)
40 18 00-13 *E-mail:* i.konopik@argument.de
Press & Public Relations: Doerte Graul *Tel:* (040)
40 18 00-15
Founded: 1959
Subjects: Fiction, Government, Political Science,
LGBTQ, Mysteries, Suspense, Philosophy, Psy-
chology, Psychiatry, Science Fiction, Fantasy,
Social Sciences, Sociology, Women's Studies,
Critical Science
ISBN Prefix(es): 978-3-88619; 978-3-920037
Foreign Rep(s): Elisabeth Anintah-Hirt (Austria);
Richard Bhend (Switzerland)
Shipping Address: Reichenberger Str 150, 10999
Berlin *Tel:* (030) 6113983 *Fax:* (030) 6114270
E-mail: versand-argument@t-online.de *Web
Site:* www.argument-buchhandlung.de
Distribution Center: Prolit, Siemensstr 16, 35463
Fernwald (Annerod), Contact: Nina Kallweit
Tel: (0641) 943 93 24 *Fax:* (0641) 943 93 89
E-mail: n.kallweit@prolit.de *Web Site:* www.
prolit.de
Hain Verlagsauslieferung, Dr-Otto-Neurath-Gasse
5, 1220 Vienna, Austria *Tel:* (01) 282 65 65
Fax: (01) 282 52 82 *E-mail:* bestell@hain.at
AVA Verlagsauslieferung AG, Centralweg
16, 8910 Affoltern am Albis, Switzerland
Tel: (044) 762 42 50 *Fax:* (044) 762 42 10
E-mail: verlagsservice@ava.ch

Ariston, *imprint of* Verlagsgruppe Random House
Bertelsmann

Ariston Editions+
Imprint of Verlagsgruppe Random House Bertels-
mann
Bayer Str 71-73, 80335 Munich
Tel: (089) 4136-0 *Toll Free Tel:* 0800 500 33 22
Fax: (089) 4136-3333
E-mail: kundenservice@randomhouse.de
Web Site: www.randomhouse.de/ariston
Key Personnel
Head, Corporate Communications: Claudia Lim-
mer *Tel:* (089) 4136-3130 *Fax:* (089) 4136-
3507 *E-mail:* claudia.limmer@randomhouse.de
Founded: 1964
Subjects: How-to, Medicine, Nursing, Dentistry,
Nonfiction (General), Parapsychology, Psychol-
ogy, Psychiatry, Self-Help
ISBN Prefix(es): 978-3-424

Arkana, *imprint of* Verlagsgruppe Random House
Bertelsmann

Arkana Verlag+
Imprint of Verlagsgruppe Random House Bertels-
mann
Neumarkter Str 28, 81673 Munich
Tel: (089) 4136-0 *Toll Free Tel:* (0800) 500 33 22
Fax: (089) 4136-3333
E-mail: kundenservice@randomhouse.de
Web Site: www.randomhouse.de/arkana
Key Personnel
Foreign Rights Dir: Gesche Wendebourg
Tel: (089) 4136-3313 *E-mail:* gesche.
wendebourg@randomhouse.de
Press Dir: Claudia Hanssen *Tel:* (089) 4136-
3569 *Fax:* (089) 4136-3723 *E-mail:* claudia.
hanssen@randomhouse.de
Founded: 1981
Subjects: Health, Nutrition, Inspirational, Spiri-
tuality, Self-Help, Body-Mind-Spirit, Holistic
Healing
ISBN Prefix(es): 978-3-923257; 978-3-442

Arnoldsche Verlagsanstalt GmbH (Arnoldsche Art Publishers)+
Olgastr 137, 70180 Stuttgart
Tel: (0711) 64 56 18 0 *Fax:* (0711) 64 56 18 79
E-mail: art@arnoldsche.com
Web Site: www.arnoldsche.com
Key Personnel
Mng Dir: Dirk Allgaier *Tel:* (0711) 64 56 18 20
  E-mail: allgaier@arnoldsche.com
Production & Product Management: Marion Boschka *Tel:* (0711) 64 56 18 15
  E-mail: boschka@arnoldsche.com
Press & Public Relations: Winfried Stuerzl
  E-mail: stuerzl@arnoldsche.com
Project Assistant: Sarah Guese *Tel:* (0711) 64 56 18 30 *E-mail:* guese@arnoldsche.com
Founded: 1988
Specialize in jewelry, glass, porcelain, Asian art & non-European art.
Subjects: Antiques, Architecture & Interior Design, Art, Fashion, Photography
ISBN Prefix(es): 978-3-925369; 978-3-89790
Number of titles published annually: 15 Print
Total Titles: 80 Print
Associate Companies: Forum fuer Europaeische Kunst und Kultur, Stuttgart
Foreign Rep(s): ACC Ltd (Canada, USA); Bookport Associates (Joe Portelli) (Southern Europe); China Publishers Marketing (Benjamin Pan) (China); Elisabeth Harder-Kreimann (Scandinavia); Josef Kolar (Eastern Europe); Martin Schnetzer (Switzerland); Ralph & Sheila Summers (Asia); TowerToo Pty Ltd (Dale Druckman) (Australia, New Zealand); Yasmy International Marketing (Yasy Murayama) (Japan)
Distribution Center: SVK-Stuttgarter Verlagskontor Verlagsbetreuerin, Postfach 10 60 16, 70049 Stuttgart, Contact: Heike Bauer *Tel:* (0711) 66 72-12 16 *Fax:* (0711) 66 72-19 74 *E-mail:* h.bauer@svk.de
NewSouth Books, University of New South Wales, Sydney, NSW 2052, Australia *Tel:* (02) 8936 0190 *Fax:* (02) 8936 0400 *E-mail:* orders@tldistribution.com.au (Australia & New Zealand)
NBN Canada, 67 Mowat Ave, Suite 241, Toronto, ON, Canada *E-mail:* lpetriw@nbnbooks.com
Coen Sligting Bookimport, Groot Nieuwland 27, 1811 ET Alkmaar, Netherlands *Tel:* (072) 511 92 20 *Fax:* (072) 511 70 29 *E-mail:* sligting@xs4all.nl (Benelux)
MAGMA, PO Box 451, 119296 Moscow, Russia *Tel:* (495) 205 64 19 *Fax:* (495) 205 64 19 *E-mail:* magmabooks@mail.ru
OLF SA, ZI 3 Corminboeuf, 1701 Fribourg, Switzerland *Tel:* (026) 467 51 11 *Fax:* (026) 467 54 66 *E-mail:* information@olf.ch
Paragon Asia Co Ltd, 687 Taksin Rd, Bukkalo, Thonburi, Bangkok 10600, Thailand *Tel:* (02) 877-77 55 *Fax:* (02) 468-96 36 *E-mail:* rapeepan@paragonasia.com
ACC GB, Sandy Lane, Old Martlesham, Woodbridge, Suffolk IP12 4SD, United Kingdom *Tel:* (01394) 38 99 50 *Fax:* (01394) 38 99 99 *E-mail:* sales@accdistribution.com (France, Great Britain & South America)
ACC Distribution, 6 W 18 St, 4th floor, New York, NY 10011, United States *Fax:* 212-989-3205 *E-mail:* sales@antiquecc.com

Ars liturgica eK
c/o Buch- und Kunstverlag Maria Laach, 56653 Maria Laach
Tel: (02652) 59 360; (02652) 59 381 (orders) *Fax:* (02652) 59 383; (02652) 59 386 (orders)
E-mail: verlag@maria-laach.de; versand@maria-laach.de
Web Site: www.ars-liturgica.de/verlag
Key Personnel
Mng Dir: P Drutmar Cremer; Br Norbert Frings; Dr Stefan Ohnesorge

Subjects: Inspirational, Spirituality, Religion - Other
ISBN Prefix(es): 978-3-86534

edition ars porcellana
Birnauer Str 6, 80809 Munich
Tel: (089) 6 88 27 50 *Fax:* (089) 4543 9098
Web Site: www.edition-ars-porcellana.de
Key Personnel
Owner & Publisher: Andrea Hoelzl
  E-mail: hoelzl@edition-ars-porcellana.de
Subjects: Porcelain Painting
ISBN Prefix(es): 978-3-938532

arsEdition GmbH+
Friedrichstr 9, 80801 Munich
Mailing Address: Postfach 40 14 52, 80714 Munich
Tel: (089) 38 10 06-0 *Fax:* (089) 38 10 06-58
E-mail: marketing@arsedition.de; presse@arsedition.de; verlag@arsedition.de; vertrieb@arsedition.de
Web Site: www.arsedition.de
Key Personnel
Mng Dir: Michael Schweins
Head, Communications: Britta Kierdorf *E-mail:* b.kierdorf@arsedition.de
Rights Dir: Angela Schaaf de Lavado *Tel:* (089) 38 10 06-43 *E-mail:* a.schaaf@arsedition.de
Marketing Manager: Andrea Lederer *E-mail:* a.lederer@arsedition.de
Production Manager: Harald Meyer
Rights Manager: Dr Sandra Ebert *E-mail:* s.ebert@arsedition.de
Founded: 1896
Subjects: Art, Child Care & Development, Cookery, Crafts, Games, Hobbies, Fiction, House & Home, Nonfiction (General), Romance
ISBN Prefix(es): 978-3-7607
Parent Company: Bonnier Media Deutschland GmbH
Ultimate Parent Company: The Bonnier Group
Imprints: bloomoon

ArtEdition, *imprint of* Bookspot Verlag GmbH

Artemis & Winkler, *imprint of* Bibliographisches Institut GmbH

Artenic Verlag
Kirchweg 65, 34119 Kassel
Tel: (0561) 15273; (0561) 2020628 (sales) *Fax:* (0561) 7397587
E-mail: hallo@artenic.de; mail@artenic.de
Web Site: artenic.de
Key Personnel
Mng Dir: Sebastian von Roos
Subjects: Literature, Literary Criticism, Essays, Regional Interests
ISBN Prefix(es): 978-3-932817
U.S. Office(s): artenic, 7154 Fenwick St, Tujunga, CA 91042, United States, Contact: Luisa V Ashley *Tel:* 818-353-2077 *Fax:* 818-353-0237 *E-mail:* la@artenic.de

Arun Verlag+
Engerda 28, 07407 Uhlstaedt-Kirchhasel
Tel: (036743) 2330 *Fax:* (036743) 23317
E-mail: info@arun-verlag.de
Web Site: www.arun-verlag.de
Key Personnel
Publisher: Stefan Ulbrich
Founded: 1989
Subjects: Astrology, Occult, Native American Studies, Philosophy, Religion - Other
ISBN Prefix(es): 978-3-927940; 978-3-935581; 978-3-86663
Total Titles: 50 Print
Parent Company: Stefan Ulbrich eK

Roland Asanger Verlag GmbH
Boedldorf 3, 84178 Kroening
Tel: (08744) 7262 *Fax:* (08744) 967755
E-mail: verlag@asanger.de
Web Site: www.asanger.de
Key Personnel
Mng Dir: Dr Gerd Wenninger
Founded: 1987
Subjects: Environmental Studies, Health, Nutrition, Psychology, Psychiatry, Self-Help, Social Sciences, Sociology
ISBN Prefix(es): 978-3-89334
Distributed by Herder AG Basel
Distribution Center: PVS Verlags-Service GmbH, Boschstr 2, 68753 Waghaeusel *Tel:* (07254) 507 0 *Fax:* (07254) 507 24 *E-mail:* info@pvs-vs.com
Orders to: PVS Verlags-Service GmbH, Boschstr 2, 68753 Waghaeusel *Tel:* (07254) 507 0 *Fax:* (07254) 507 24 *E-mail:* info@pvs-vs.com

Aschendorff Verlag GmbH & Co KG+
Soester Str 13, 48155 Muenster
Tel: (0251) 690-131 *Fax:* (0251) 690-143
E-mail: buchverlag@aschendorff.de
Web Site: www.aschendorff-buchverlag.de
Key Personnel
Mng Dir: Dr Benedikt Hueffer; Dr Eduard Hueffer
Publishing Dir: Dr Dirk F Passmann *Tel:* (0251) 690-120 *E-mail:* dirk.passmann@aschendorff.de
Licenses/Foreign Rights: Sabine Aberdiek
  E-mail: sabine.averdiek@aschendorff.de
Marketing & Sales: Silke Haunfelder *Tel:* (0251) 690-184 *E-mail:* silke.haunfelder@aschendorff.de
Press: Petra Landsknecht *Tel:* (0251) 690-133
  E-mail: petra.landsknecht@aschendorff.de
Founded: 1720
Membership(s): VGS - Verlagsgesellschaft mbH & Co KG.
Subjects: History, Language Arts, Linguistics, Philosophy, Psychology, Psychiatry, Regional Interests, Religion - Other, Theology
ISBN Prefix(es): 978-3-402
Number of titles published annually: 80 Print; 2 CD-ROM

Asclepios Edition Lothar Baus+
Zum Lappentascher Hof 65, 66424 Homburg/Saar
Tel: (06841) 71863
Web Site: www.asclepiosedition.de
Key Personnel
Contact: Lothar Baus *E-mail:* lotharbaus@web.de
Founded: 1985
Specialize in Goethe studies, Friedrich Nietzsche & Stoic philosophy.
Subjects: Biography, Memoirs, Literature, Literary Criticism, Essays, Philosophy, Indian Samkhya, Stoic Philosophy
ISBN Prefix(es): 978-3-925101; 978-3-935288

Asgard-Verlag Dr Werner Hippe GmbH
Einsteinstr 10, 53757 Sankt Augustin
Tel: (02241) 3164-0 *Fax:* (02241) 3164-36
E-mail: info@asgard.de
Web Site: www.asgard.de
Key Personnel
Mng Dir: Stefan Maus; Uwe Schliebusch
Marketing: Anke Boelmann *Tel:* (02241) 3164-33
Sales: Anna-Maria Velder *Tel:* (02241) 3164-27
  E-mail: anna-maria.velder@asgard.de
Founded: 1947
Subjects: Government, Political Science, Health, Nutrition, Medicine, Nursing, Dentistry, Public Administration, Social Sciences, Sociology
ISBN Prefix(es): 978-3-537
Subsidiaries: Siegler & Co Verlag fuer Zeitarchive GmbH

Edition Assemblage
Niederdingshstr 8, 48155 Muenster
Mailing Address: Postfach 2746, 48014 Muenster
Tel: (0251) 1491256
E-mail: info@edition-assemblage.de; presse@
edition-assemblage.de
Web Site: www.edition-assemblage.de
Key Personnel
Editorial & Sales: Willi Bischot
Subjects: Government, Political Science, Social
Sciences, Sociology
ISBN Prefix(es): 978-3-942885

Assimil GmbH
Beekmanns Hof 3, 45439 Muelheim
Tel: (0208) 49504-0; (0221) 40 28 20 *Fax:* (0208)
49504-95
E-mail: kontakt@assimil.com
Web Site: www.assimilwelt.com
Key Personnel
Mng Dir, Sales & Marketing: Philippe Gagneur
Founded: 1988
Specialize in textbooks-foreign languages.
Subjects: Language Arts, Linguistics
ISBN Prefix(es): 978-3-89625

assoverlag+
Hasenstr 15, 46119 Oberhausen
Tel: (0208) 62 900-32 *Fax:* (0208) 62 900-33
E-mail: info@assoverlag.de
Web Site: www.assoverlag.de
Key Personnel
Contact: Ingrid Gerlach
Founded: 1970
Subjects: Fiction, Labor, Industrial Relations,
Nonfiction (General), Poetry, Regional Inter-
ests, Social Sciences, Sociology
ISBN Prefix(es): 978-3-921541; 978-3-938834
Distribution Center: Runge Verlagsausliefer-
ung GmbH, Bergstr 2, 33803 Steinhagen
Tel: (05204) 998-441 *Fax:* (05204) 998-114
E-mail: info@rungeva.de *Web Site:* www.
rungeva.de

Assoziation A
Gneisenaustr 2a, 10961 Berlin
Tel: (030) 69582971 *Fax:* (030) 69582973
E-mail: berlin@assoziation-a.de
Web Site: www.assoziation-a.de
Key Personnel
Board of Directors: Reiner Wendling
Subjects: Fiction, Government, Political Science,
History, Anti-fascism, Biopolitics, Racial Mi-
gration, Urban Development
ISBN Prefix(es): 978-3-922611; 978-3-935936;
978-3-86241

Verlag Atelier im Bauernhaus+
In der Bredenau, 6, 28870 Fischerhude
Tel: (04293) 491; (04293) 493; (04293) 492
(bookstore) *Fax:* (04293) 1238
E-mail: bestellung@atelierbauernhaus.de
Web Site: www.atelierbauernhaus.de
Key Personnel
Publisher: Wolf-Dietmar Stock
Founded: 1976
Subjects: Art, Fiction, Regional Interests
ISBN Prefix(es): 978-3-88132

Atelier Verlag Ursula Fritzsche KG+
Hospeltstr 47, 50825 Cologne
Tel: (0221) 9545858 *Fax:* (0221) 9545860
E-mail: info@atelier-verlag.de
Web Site: www.atelier-verlag.de
Subjects: Art, Poetry
ISBN Prefix(es): 978-3-921042

Atrium Verlag AG+
Max-Brauer-Allee 34, 22765 Hamburg
Tel: (040) 60 79 09-04 *Fax:* (040) 60 79 09-557
E-mail: info@vgo-atrium.de

Web Site: www.atrium-verlag.com
Key Personnel
Publishing Dir: Tim Jung
Marketing: Dana Kabbani *Tel:* (060) 79 09-719
E-mail: d.kabbani@verlagsgruppe-oetinger.de
Production: Birgit Henningsen *Tel:* (060) 79 09-
737 *E-mail:* b.henningsen@vgo-oetinger.de
Rights & Licenses: Renate Reichstein *Tel:* (060)
79 09-713 *E-mail:* r.reichstein@verlagsgruppe-
oetinger.de
Sales: Ute Hollmann *Tel:* (060) 79 09-704
E-mail: u.hollmann@verlagsgruppe-oetinger.de
Founded: 1936
Subjects: Fiction, Literature, Literary Criticism,
Essays
ISBN Prefix(es): 978-3-85535
Branch Office(s)
Heinrichstr 249, 8005 Zurich, Switzerland
Distribution Center: Runge Verlagsausliefer-
ung GmbH, Bergstr 2, 33803 Steinhagen
Tel: (05204) 998121 *Fax:* (05204) 998111
E-mail: vgo@rungeva.de (Austria & Germany)
AVA Verlagsauslieferung AG, Centralweg
16, 8910 Affoltern am Albis, Switzerland
Tel: (044) 7624261 *Fax:* (044) 7624210
E-mail: verlagsservice@ava.ch

Aue-Verlag GmbH+
Korber Str 20, 74219 Moeckmuehl
Tel: (06298) 1328 *Fax:* (06298) 4298
E-mail: info@aue-verlag.de
Web Site: www.aue-verlag.de
Key Personnel
Manager: Thomas Gauger
Founded: 1919
Subjects: Crafts, Games, Hobbies, Education, Re-
ligion - Protestant, Religion - Other
ISBN Prefix(es): 978-3-87029
Orders to: Neuhaldenstr 42/1, 70825 Ko-
rntal *Fax:* (06298) 4298 *Web Site:* www.
modellbogen-versand.de

Auer Verlag GmbH+
Heilig-Kreuz-Str 16, 86609 Donauwoerth
Mailing Address: Postfach 11 52, 86601 Donau-
woerth
Tel: (0906) 73-240 *Fax:* (0906) 73-177; (0906)
73-178 (orders)
E-mail: info@auer-verlag.de; sekretariat@auer-
verlag.de
Web Site: www.auer-verlag.de
Key Personnel
Mng Dir: Christian Glaser
Founded: 1875
Membership(s): TR-Verlagsunion GmbH.
Subjects: Education, History, Mathematics, Mu-
sic, Dance, Psychology, Psychiatry, Religion -
Catholic, Science (General), Sports, Athletics,
Theology
ISBN Prefix(es): 978-3-403; 978-3-87904
Number of titles published annually: 50 Print; 20
CD-ROM; 5 Audio
Total Titles: 2,100 Print; 60 CD-ROM; 20 Audio
Parent Company: Klett Gruppe
Branch Office(s)
Westenhellweg 126, 44137 Dortmund
Tel: (0231) 584483-0 *Fax:* (0231) 584483-20
E-mail: dortmund@auer-verlag.de

Aufbau Taschenbuch Verlag GmbH
Imprint of Aufbau Verlag GmbH & Co KG
Prinzenstr 85, 10969 Berlin
Tel: (030) 283 94-0 *Fax:* (030) 283 94-100
E-mail: info@bau-verlag.de
Web Site: www.aufbau-verlag.de
Key Personnel
Mng Dir: Matthias Koch
Head, Press & Public Relations: Silke Ohlenforst
Tel: (030) 283 94-231 *E-mail:* ohlenforst@
aufbau-verlag.de

Press & Public Relations: Andrea Doberenz
Tel: (030) 283 94-233 *E-mail:* doberenz@
aufbau-verlag.de
Foreign Rights: Inka Ihmels *Tel:* (030) 283 94-
123 *E-mail:* ihmels@aufbau-verlag.de
Marketing: Christine Seiler *Tel:* (030) 283 94-230
E-mail: seiler@aufbau-verlag.de
Founded: 1994
Subjects: Fiction, Film, Video, Government, Po-
litical Science, Literature, Literary Criticism,
Essays, Poetry, Romance
ISBN Prefix(es): 978-3-7466
Number of titles published annually: 150 Print
Total Titles: 500 Print
Distribution Center: VVA-Vereinigte Verlagsaus-
lieferung, Betreuung Aufbau Verlag, An der
Autobahn 100, 33333 Guetersloh *Fax:* (05241)
80 88 077 *E-mail:* vva-d6f3.bestellungen@
bertelsmann.de
Mohr Morawa Buchvertrieb GmbH, Sulzen-
gasse 2, 1230 Vienna, Austria *Tel:* (01) 680
14-5 *E-mail:* bestellung@mohrmorawa.at *Web
Site:* www.mohrmorawa.at
Buchzentrum AG, Industriestr Ost 10, 4614 Hae-
gendorf, Switzerland *Tel:* (062) 209 26 26
Fax: (062) 206 26 27 *E-mail:* kundendienst@
buchzentrum.ch

Aufbau Tashenbuch Verlag GmbH, *imprint of*
Aufbau Verlag GmbH & Co KG

Aufbau Verlag GmbH & Co KG+
Imprint of Aufbau Verlagsgruppe GmbH & Co
KG
Prinzenstr 85, 10969 Berlin
Tel: (030) 283 94-0 *Fax:* (030) 283 94-100
E-mail: info@bau-verlag.de
Web Site: www.aufbau-verlag.de
Key Personnel
Mng Dir: Matthias Koch
Editor-in-Chief, Literary Fiction: Constanze Neu-
mann
Head, Press & Public Relations: Silke Ohlenforst
Tel: (030) 283 94-231 *E-mail:* ohlenforst@
aufbau-verlag.de
Press & Public Relations: Andrea Doberenz
Tel: (030) 283 94-233 *E-mail:* doberenz@
aufbau-verlag.de
Foreign Rights: Inka Ihmels *Tel:* (030) 283 94-
123 *E-mail:* ihmels@aufbau-verlag.de
Marketing: Christine Seiler *Tel:* (030) 283 94-230
E-mail: seiler@aufbau-verlag.de
Founded: 1945
Subjects: Fiction, Film, Video, Government, Po-
litical Science, Literature, Literary Criticism,
Essays, Mysteries, Suspense, Poetry, Romance
ISBN Prefix(es): 978-3-351
Number of titles published annually: 80 Print; 20
Audio
Total Titles: 400 Print
Imprints: Aufbau Taschenbuch Verlag GmbH; Blu-
menbar
Foreign Rep(s): Johann Czap (Eastern Austria);
Michael Hipp (Western Austria); Verlagsaus-
lieferung Scheidegger & Co AG (Ruedi Am-
rhein) (Switzerland)
Distribution Center: VVA-Vereinigte Verlagsaus-
lieferung, Betruung Aufbau Verlag, An der Au-
tobahn 100, 33333 Guetersloh *Fax:* (05241)
80 88 077 *E-mail:* vva-d6f3.bestellungen@
bertelsmann.de
Mohr Morawa Buchvertrieb GmbH, Sulzengasse 2, 1230 Vienna, Austria *Tel:* (01) 680
14-5 *E-mail:* bestellung@mohrmorawa.at *Web
Site:* www.mohrmorawa.at
Buchzentrum AG, Industriestr Ost 10, 4614 Haegendorf, Switzerland *Tel:* (062) 209 26 26
Fax: (062) 209 26 27 *E-mail:* kundendienst@
buchzentrum.ch

Aufstieg Verlag GmbH
Isarweg 37, 84028 Landshut

Tel: (0871) 54112 *Fax:* (0871) 4710831
E-mail: aufstieg-verlag@gmx.de
Web Site: www.aufstieg-verlag.de
Key Personnel
Mng Dir: Gisela Werner
Founded: 1947
Subjects: Cookery, Fiction, Foreign Countries,
History, Humor
ISBN Prefix(es): 978-3-7612; 978-3-920235

August Dreesbach Verlag
Viktoriastr 5, 80803 Munich
Tel: (089) 95449845 *Fax:* (089) 38989169
E-mail: info@augustdreesbachverlag.de
Web Site: www.augustdreesbachverlag.de
Key Personnel
Mng Dir: Dr Anne Dreesbach *E-mail:* anne.
dreesbach@augustdreesbachverlag.de
Press & Marketing: Ramona Feilke *E-mail:* r.
feilke@augustdreesbachverlag.de
Subjects: Art, Biography, Memoirs, Economics,
Fiction, History, Science (General)
ISBN Prefix(es): 978-3-940061
Branch Office(s)
Heinrichstr 73, 40223 Duesseldorf *Tel:* (0211)
61019925
Rosenthaler Str 36, 10178 Berlin *Tel:* (030) 9559
8823

Verlag J J Augustin GmbH
Am Fleth 36-37, 25348 Glueckstadt
Tel: (04124) 2044 *Fax:* (04124) 4709
E-mail: augustinverlag@t-online.de
Founded: 1920
Subjects: Asian Studies, Literature, Literary Criti-
cism, Essays, Religion - Islamic, Science (Gen-
eral)
ISBN Prefix(es): 978-3-87030

Aulis, *imprint of* Friedrich Verlag GmbH

Aulis im Friedrich Verlag+
Formerly Aulis Verlag in der STARK Verlagsge-
sellschaft mbH & Co KG
Imprint of Friedrich Verlag GmbH
Im Brande 17, 30926 Seelze
Tel: (0511) 400 04-150 *Fax:* (0511) 400 04-170
Web Site: friedrich-verlag.de/aulis-bei-friedrich
Founded: 1950
Subjects: Biological Sciences, Chemistry, Chemi-
cal Engineering, Geography, Geology, History,
Mathematics, Nonfiction (General), Physics,
Science (General)
ISBN Prefix(es): 978-3-7614

**Aulis Verlag in der STARK Verlagsgesellschaft
mbH & Co KG**, see Aulis im Friedrich Verlag

Verlag der Autoren GmbH & Co KG+
Taunusstr 19, 60329 Frankfurt am Main
Mailing Address: Postfach 111963, 60054 Frank-
furt am Main
Tel: (069) 23 85 74 0 *Fax:* (069) 24 27 76 44
E-mail: buch@verlag-der-autoren.de
Web Site: www.verlag-der-autoren.de; www.
verlagderautoren.de
Key Personnel
Mng Dir: Thomas Maagh *E-mail:* maagh@
verlagderautoren.de; RA Oliver Schlecht;
Dr Marion Victor *E-mail:* victor@
verlagderautoren.de
Publisher: Brigitte Pfannmoeller
E-mail: pfannmoeller@verlagderautoren.de
Founded: 1969
One of Germany's theatre & film agencies, pub-
lishing a line of titles on theatre & film.
Subjects: Art, Drama, Theater, Fiction, Film,
Video, Literature, Literary Criticism, Essays,
Nonfiction (General)
ISBN Prefix(es): 978-3-920983; 978-3-88661
Number of titles published annually: 8 Print

Total Titles: 190 Print
Foreign Rep(s): Rosica Colin Ltd (Canada, London); International Editors (Argentina, South
America, Spain); Marton Agency of New York
(USA)
Foreign Rights: AAS - Avtorska agencija za
Slovenijo (Vera Bozic) (Slovenia); Auteurs-
bureau Almo BVBA (Brenda Ongena) (Bel-
gium); AO International (Antje Oegel) (USA);
Arcadia & Ricono SRL (Anna Ashton Par-
nanzini) (Italy); L'Arche Editeur (Katharina
von Bismarck) (France); AURA-PONT (Anna
Pychova) (Czechia); Autorenagentur Hart-
mut Becher (Latin America); Bookmark Ko-
rea Agency (Byeong-Suh Lee) (South Ko-
rea); Rosica Colin Ltd (Joanna Marston) (UK);
Eesti Teatri Agentuur (Ott Karulin) (Estonia);
Hofra Theatrical & Literary Agency (Judit
Zadori) (Hungary); IBVA Holland BV (Am-
ateur Toneel) (Netherlands); Internationaal
Literatuur Bureau ILB (Linda Kohn) (Nether-
lands); International Editors Co (Henriette
Hubacher) (Spain); International Editors Co
Literary Agency (Latin America); LITA Soci-
ety of Authors (Veronika Baliova) (Slovakia);
Naytelmakulma - Nordic Drama Corner (Ri-
itta Pohjola) (Finland); Nordiska ApS (Patric
Maury) (Denmark, Norway, Sweden); ONK
Agency Ltd (Aslihan Gulay) (Turkey); Rus-
sian Author's Society (Elena Orlowa) (Russia);
Sakai Agency Inc (Tatemi Sakai) (Japan); SO
PE Hellas - C Samaras & Cie (Greece); SPA
- Sociedade Portuguesa de Autores (Portu-
gal); Stowarzyszeniu Autorow ZAiKS (Aida
Jordan) (Poland); UACRR Ukrainian Agency
of Copyright & Related Rights (Tatiana Ver-
noslov) (Ukraine)
Distribution Center: edition text+kritik im
Richard Boorberg Verlag, Levelingstr 6a, 81673
Munich *Tel:* (089) 43 60 00 12 *Fax:* (089) 43
60 00 19 *E-mail:* info@etk-muenchen.de *Web
Site:* www.etk-muenchen.de (Germany & Austria)
Buch 2000 AVA Verlagsauslieferungen, Centralweg 16, 8910 Affoltern am Albis, Switzerland, Contact: Beat Eberle *Tel:* (044) 86 91
706 *Fax:* (044) 86 90 982 *E-mail:* be_eberle@
bluewin.at *Web Site:* www.ava.ch

Autorenhaus Verlag GmbH
Karmeliterweg 116, 13465 Berlin
Tel: (030) 40 10 30 90
E-mail: autoren@autorenhaus-verlag.de
Web Site: www.autorenhaus-verlag.de
Key Personnel
Mng Dir: Gerhild Tieger
Membership(s): Association of German Publishers
& Booksellers
Subjects: Film, Video, Journalism, Literature, Lit-
erary Criticism, Essays, Publishing & Book
Trade Reference
ISBN Prefix(es): 978-3-932909; 978-3-9804980

av edition GmbH
Senefelderstr 109, 70176 Stuttgart
Tel: (0711) 220 22 79-0
E-mail: sales@avedition.de; presse@avedition.de
Web Site: www.avedition.de
Key Personnel
Mng Dir: Norbert W Daldrop *Tel:* (0711) 220
22 79-12 *E-mail:* n.dalrop@avedition.de; Dr
Petra Kiedaisch *Tel:* (0711) 220 22 79-13
E-mail: p.kiedaisch@avedition.de; Bettina Klett
Tel: (0711) 220 22 79-12 *E-mail:* b.klett@
avedition.de
Sales: Sophia Wittwer *E-mail:* s.wittwer@
avedition.de
Founded: 1992
Subjects: Advertising, Architecture & Interior De-
sign, Photography, Travel & Tourism
ISBN Prefix(es): 978-3-89986
Foreign Rep(s): China Publishers Marketing
(Benjamin Pan) (China, Indonesia, Singapore,

Taiwan, Thailand); Continental Sales Inc (CSI)
(USA); Sebastian Graf (Switzerland); Elisabeth
Harder-Kreimann (Scandinavia); IMA Interme-
diaamericana Ltd (David Williams) (Caribbean,
Latin America); Marcello SAS (Flavio Mar-
cello) (France, Greece, Italy, Portugal, Spain);
National Book Network (NBN) (Canada)
Distribution Center: SVK - Stuttgarter Verlagskontor, Rotebuehlstr 77, 70178 Stuttgart,
Contact: Heike Bauer *Tel:* (0711) 6672-1924
Fax: (0711) 6672-1974 *E-mail:* h.bauer@svk.
de *Web Site:* www.svk.de
buch 2000, c/o AVA, Centralweg 16, 8910 Affoltern, Switzerland *Tel:* (01) 762 42 60
Fax: (01) 762 42 10 *E-mail:* verlagsservice@
ava.ch *Web Site:* www.ava.ch
National Book Network (NBN)/CSI Group,
15200 NBN Way, Blue Ridge Summit, PA
17214, United States *E-mail:* custserv@
nbnbooks.com (North America & Canada)

avant-verlag
Weichselplatz 3-4, 12045 Berlin
Tel: (030) 806 147 70 *Fax:* (030) 806 147 71
E-mail: info@avant-verlag.de
Web Site: www.avant-verlag.de
Key Personnel
Publisher: Johann Ulrich
Founded: 2001
Subjects: Art, Government, Political Science, Hu-
mor, Comics
ISBN Prefix(es): 978-3-939080; 978-3-9807725;
978-3-9809428

Aviatic Verlag GmbH+
Kolpingring 16, 82041 Oberhaching
Tel: (089) 61 38 90-0 *Fax:* (089) 61 38 90-10
E-mail: aviatic@aviatic.de
Web Site: www.aviatic.de
Key Personnel
Manager: Peter Pletschacher
Founded: 1985
Specialize in aeronautics.
Subjects: Aeronautics, Aviation
ISBN Prefix(es): 978-3-925505
Total Titles: 35 Print
Distributed by Schiffer Publishing (USA)

AivvA Verlag
Emdener Str 33, 10551 Berlin
Tel: (030) 39 73 13 72 *Fax:* (030) 39 73 13 71
E-mail: info@aviva-verlag.de
Web Site: www.aviva-verlag.de
Key Personnel
Publisher: Britta Juergs
Founded: 1997
Subjects: Art, Literature, Literary Criticism, Es-
says, Women's Studies
ISBN Prefix(es): 978-3-932338
Foreign Rep(s): Andreas Meisel (Switzerland);
Elisabeth Anintah-Hirt (Austria)
Distribution Center: Leipziger Kommissions- und
Grossbuchhandelsgesellschaft mbH (LKG),
An der Suedspitze 1-12, 04571 Roetha, Con-
tact: Elisabeth Kaiser *Tel:* (034206) 65-107
Fax: (034206) 65-1740 *E-mail:* ekaiser@lkg-
service.de *Web Site:* www.lkg.va.de
Medienlogistik Pichler OEBZ GmbH & Co KG,
IZ NOE Sued, Str 1, Objekt 34, 2355 Wiener
Neudorf, Austria *Tel:* (02236) 63535-290
Fax: (02236) 63535-243 *E-mail:* bestellen@
medien-logistik.at *Web Site:* www.medien-
logistik.at
Kaktus Verlagsauslieferung, Langfeldstr 54,
Postfach 459, 8501 Frauenfeld, Switzerland
Tel: (052) 722 31 90 *Fax:* (052) 722 17 82
E-mail: kaktus@solnet.ch *Web Site:* www.
kaktus.net

AXENT - Verlag+
Steinerne Furt 78, 86167 Augsburg
Tel: (0821) 70 50 11 *Fax:* (0821) 70 50 08
E-mail: info@axent-verlag.de

Web Site: www.axent-verlag.de
Key Personnel
Owner: Antony Fedrigotti
Founded: 1982
Subjects: Health, Nutrition, Nonfiction (General), Self-Help
ISBN Prefix(es): 978-3-925557; 978-3-928086; 978-3-89647

AZ Direct GmbH
Subsidiary of arvato Bertelsmann
Carl-Bertelsmann-Str 161 S, 33311 Guetersloh
Tel: (05241) 80-5438 *Fax:* (05241) 80-66962
E-mail: az@bertelsmann.de
Web Site: www.az-direct.com
Key Personnel
Mng Dir: Dirk Kemmerer; Thomas Wonnemann
Founded: 1966
A full service provider for successful worldwide direct marketing.
Subjects: Advertising, Business, Marketing
ISBN Prefix(es): 978-3-573
Ultimate Parent Company: Bertelsmann SE & Co KGaA
Foreign Rep(s): arvato-AZ Direct GmbH (Austria); AZ Direct AG (Switzerland)

Babel Verlag
Lorenz-Paul-Str 4, 86920 Denklingen
Mailing Address: Postfach 1, 86925 Denklingen
Tel: (08243) 961691
E-mail: info@babel-verlag.de
Web Site: www.babel-verlag.de
Key Personnel
Publisher: Kevin Perryman
Founded: 1983
Specializes in poetry, bilingual poetry & translations.
Subjects: Poetry
ISBN Prefix(es): 978-3-931798
Number of titles published annually: 3 Print
Total Titles: 50 Print
Distribution Center: GVA, Postfach 2021, 37010 Goettingen *Tel:* (0551) 487177 *Fax:* (0551) 41392 *E-mail:* bestellungen@gva-verlage.de

J P Bachem Verlag GmbH+
Ursulaplatz 1, 50668 Cologne
Tel: (0221) 161 99-00 *Fax:* (0221) 161 99-09
E-mail: verlag@bachem.de
Web Site: www.bachem-verlag.de
Key Personnel
Mng Dir: Claus Bachem; Lambert Bachem
Sales Manager: Philipp Mainzer *Tel:* (0221) 161 99-20 *E-mail:* philipp.mainzer@bachem.de
Chief Editor: Detlef Reich *Tel:* (0221) 161 99-30 *E-mail:* detlef.reich@bachem.de
Press & Public Relations: Carolin Thissen *Tel:* (0221) 161 99-40 *E-mail:* carolin.thissen@bachem.de
Founded: 1818
Subjects: Regional Interests
ISBN Prefix(es): 978-3-7616

Dr Bachmaier Verlag GmbH+
Kagerstr 8B, 81669 Munich
Tel: (089) 685120 *Fax:* (089) 685120
Key Personnel
Mng Dir: Dr Peter Bachmaier
Also acts as bookseller.
Subjects: History, Literature, Literary Criticism, Essays, Poetry, Science (General), Science Fiction, Fantasy
ISBN Prefix(es): 978-3-931680; 978-3-88605
Number of titles published annually: 7 Print
Total Titles: 34 Print
Foreign Rights: Dr Doglioli (Italy)

Badischer Landwirtschafts-Verlag GmbH
Merzhauserstr 111, 79100 Freiburg im Breisgau
Tel: (0761) 27133400 *Fax:* (0761) 27133401

E-mail: verlag@blv-freiburg.de; redaktion@blv-freiburg.de
Web Site: www.badische-bauern-zeitung.de
Key Personnel
Mng Dir: Barbara Sester *E-mail:* sester@blv-freiburg.de
Editor-in-Chief: Walter Eberenz *Tel:* (0761) 27133403 *E-mail:* eberenz@blv-freiburg.de
Deputy Chief Editor: Rene Bossert *Tel:* (0761) 27133408 *E-mail:* bossert@blv-freiburg.de
Advertising Manager: Karin Wirbals-Langner *Tel:* (0761) 27133453 *E-mail:* langner@blv-freiburg.de
Sales Manager: Sonja Wahl *Tel:* (0761) 27133432 *E-mail:* wahl@blv-freiburg.de
Founded: 1947
Subjects: Agriculture
ISBN Prefix(es): 978-3-9801818

Hans A Baensch, see Mergus Verlag GmbH Hans A Baensch

Baerenreiter-Spieltexte, *imprint of* Otto Teich Verlag

Baerenreiter-Verlag Karl Voetterle GmbH & Co KG+
Member of Baerenreiter Verlagsgruppe
Heinrich-Schuetz-Allee 35-37, 34131 Kassel
Tel: (0561) 3105-0 *Fax:* (0561) 3105-240
E-mail: info@baerenreiter.com
Web Site: www.baerenreiter.com
Key Personnel
Chief Executive Officer: Leonhard Scheuch *E-mail:* lscheuch@baerenreiter.com; Prof Barbara Scheuch-Voetterle *E-mail:* bscheuch@baerenreiter.com
Publishing Dir: Dr Wendelin Goebel *E-mail:* goebel@baerenreiter.com
Head, Finances & Human Resources: Anne Schaefer *E-mail:* schaefer@baerenreiter.com
Dir, Editorial Dept-Books: Dr Jutta Schmoll-Barthel *Tel:* (0561) 3105-144 *E-mail:* schmoll-barthel@baerenreiter.com
Dir, Editorial Dept-Music: Dr Wolfgang Thein *Tel:* (0561) 3105-137 *E-mail:* wthein@baerenreiter.com
Dir, Promotion & Public Relations: Georg Hammann *Tel:* (0561) 3105-151 *E-mail:* hammann@baerenreiter.com
Dir, Sales & Marketing, Germany, Austria & Switzerland: Ivan Dorenburg *Tel:* (0561) 3105-162 *E-mail:* dorenburg@baerenreiter.com
Dir, Sales & Marketing, International & Sales & Marketing, Asia & Belgium: Corinne Votteler *Tel:* (0561) 3105-175 *E-mail:* votteler@baerenreiter.com
Foreign Rights: Bianca Trennheuser *Tel:* (0561) 3105-155 *E-mail:* trennheuser@baerenreiter.com
Founded: 1923
Subjects: Music, Dance
ISBN Prefix(es): 978-3-7618
Divisions: Alkor-Edition Kassel GmbH; Baerenreiter Music Corp New York; Baerenreiter Verlag Basel AG (Switzerland); Baerenreiter Praha; Gustav Bosse GmbH & Co KG; Henschel Verlag fuer Musik GmbH; Icebear Music GmbH; Joh Philipp Hinnenthal-Verlag; KGA Verlag-Service GmbH & Co KG; Nagels Verlag; Neuwerk Buch- und Musikalienhandlung GmbH; Willy Mueller Sueddeutscher Musikverlag GmbH
Distributed by Baerenreiter Ltd London (UK); Baerenreiter Verlag Basel AG (Switzerland)
Shipping Address: KGA Verlags-Service GmbH & Co KG, Brandaustr 10, 34127 Kassel
Warehouse: KGA Verlags-Service GmbH & Co KG, Brandaustr 10, 34127 Kassel
Distribution Center: Baerenreiter Ltd London (UK)
Orders to: KGA Verlags-Service GmbH & Co KG, Brandaustr 10, 34127 Kassel

Baha'i-Verlag GmbH+
Eppsteiner Str 89, 65719 Hofheim am Taunus
Tel: (06192) 992926; (06151) 9517140 (orders) *Fax:* (06151) 9517299 (orders)
E-mail: office@bahai-verlag.de; vertrieb@bahai-verlag.de (orders)
Web Site: www.bahai-verlag.de
Key Personnel
Chief Executive Officer: Dr Shamim Rafat
Founded: 1946
Publishes Baha'i religious literature in German.
Subjects: Religion - Other, Baha'i
ISBN Prefix(es): 978-3-87037

Bajazzo Verlag
Imprint of Verlagsgruppe Beltz
Werderstr 10, 69469 Weinheim
Mailing Address: Postfach 100154, 69441 Weinheim
Tel: (06201) 6007-0 *Fax:* (06201) 6007-310
E-mail: info@beltz.de
Web Site: www.bajazzoverlag.ch; www.beltz.de
Founded: 1998
ISBN Prefix(es): 978-3-907588; 978-3-905871

BALANCE buch + medien verlag, *imprint of* Psychiatrie-Verlag GmbH

Verlag Dr Thomas Balistier
Egartstr 19, 72127 Maehringen
Tel: (07071) 368018; (0172) 7321899 (cell) *Fax:* (07071) 368018
E-mail: info@balistier.de
Web Site: www.kreta-buch.de
Key Personnel
Publisher: Dr Thomas Balistier
Founded: 1998
Specialize in travel literature of Greece & Crete.
Subjects: Architecture & Interior Design, Poetry, Travel & Tourism, Crete, Greece
ISBN Prefix(es): 978-3-9806168; 978-3-937108

B&L MedienGesellschaft mbH & Co KG
Max-Volmer-Str 28, 40724 Hilden
Mailing Address: Postfach 100220, 40702 Hilden
Tel: (02103) 204-0 *Fax:* (02103) 204-204
E-mail: muc@blmedien.de; info@blmedien.de
Web Site: www.blmedien.de
Key Personnel
Mng Dir: Harry Lietzenmayer
Editor-in-Chief: Annemarie Heinrichsdobler *Tel:* (089) 370 60-100
Editorial: Daniela Mueller *Tel:* (089) 370 60-165
Founded: 1950
Subjects: Business, Food Trade
ISBN Prefix(es): 978-3-928709
Branch Office(s)
Ridlerstr 37, 80339 Munich *Tel:* (089) 37060-0 *Fax:* (089) 37060-111

C Bange Verlag GmbH+
Marienplatz 12, 96142 Hollfeld
Mailing Address: Postfach 1160, 96139 Hollfeld
Tel: (09274) 80899-0 *Fax:* (09274) 80899-10
E-mail: service@bange-verlag.de
Web Site: www.bange-verlag.de
Key Personnel
Mng Dir: Thomas Appel *E-mail:* thomas.appel@bange-verlag.de
Marketing: Sebastian Kaas *Tel:* (09274) 80899-14 *E-mail:* sebastian.kaas@bange-verlag.de
Accounting: Sabine Weggel *Tel:* (09274) 80899-11 *E-mail:* sabine.weggel@bange-verlag.de
Rights & Licenses: Helga Weggel *Tel:* (09274) 80899-13 *E-mail:* helga.weggel@bange-verlag.de
Founded: 1871
Specialize in learning & teaching German language.
Subjects: Education, Fiction, Language Arts, Linguistics

ISBN Prefix(es): 978-3-8044
Number of titles published annually: 30 Print
Total Titles: 300 Print
Imprints: Koenigs Abi-Trainer; Koenigs Er-
laeuterungen; Koenigs Kopiervorlagen; Koenigs
Lernhilfen; Koenigs Uebersetzungen

Bank-Verlag GmbH+
Subsidiary of Bundesverbands Deutscher Banken
Wendelinstr 1, 50933 Cologne
Tel: (0221) 5490-0 *Fax:* (0221) 5490-120
E-mail: bank-verlag@bank-verlag.de
Web Site: www.bank-verlag.de
Key Personnel
Mng Dir: Wilhelm Niehoff; Michael Eichler;
Matthias Strobel
Founded: 1961
Subjects: Business, Economics, Finance, Law,
Management, Securities
ISBN Prefix(es): 978-3-86556

Verlag Dr Albert Bartens KG
Lueckhoffstr 16, 14129 Berlin
Tel: (030) 803 56 78 *Fax:* (030) 804 74 74 23
E-mail: info@bartens.com
Web Site: www.bartens.com
Key Personnel
Contact: Dr Juergen Bruhns
Founded: 1951
Specialize in the technology & economics of the
sugar industry.
Subjects: Agriculture, Economics, Energy, Tech-
nology
ISBN Prefix(es): 978-3-87040

Bartkowiaks Forum Book Art
Koernerstr 24, 22301 Hamburg
Tel: (040) 279 36 74 *Fax:* (040) 270 43 97
Web Site: www.forumbookart.de
Key Personnel
Owner & Mng Dir: Heinz Stefan Bartkowiak
Founded: 1988
Subjects: Art, Biography, Memoirs, Poetry, Pub-
lishing & Book Trade Reference, Calligraphy,
Graphic Techniques, Printing, Typography
ISBN Prefix(es): 978-3-9802035; 978-3-935462;
978-3-9803534

Basilisken-Presse+
Friedensallee 21, 15834 Rangsdorf
Tel: (033708) 20431 *Fax:* (033708) 20433
E-mail: info@naturundtext.de; shop@
naturundtext.de
Web Site: www.basilisken-presse.de
Key Personnel
Editor: Dr Armin Geus
Founded: 1976
Specialize in medicine, nursing & history of sci-
ence.
Subjects: Art, Biological Sciences, History, Lit-
erature, Literary Criticism, Essays, Medicine,
Nursing, Dentistry, Science (General), Humani-
ties
ISBN Prefix(es): 978-3-925347; 978-3-9800020;
978-3-941365
Parent Company: Natur+Text GmbH

BasisDruck Verlag GmbH
Prenzlauer Promenade 4, 13086 Berlin
Tel: (030) 473 083 60; (030) 473 083 61
Fax: (030) 473 083 62
E-mail: infomail@basisdruck.de; bestellung@
basisdruck.de
Web Site: www.basisdruck.de
Key Personnel
Mng Dir: Stefan Ret
Mng Dir & Editor: Hugo Velarde
Founded: 1989
Subjects: Government, Political Science, History,
Literature, Literary Criticism, Essays
ISBN Prefix(es): 978-3-86163

Bassermann, *imprint of* Verlagsgruppe Random
House Bertelsmann

Verlag Bassermann+
Imprint of Verlagsgruppe Random House Bertels-
mann
Bayerstr 71-73, 80335 Munich
Tel: (089) 4136-0 (headquarters) *Fax:* (089) 4136-
3333; (089) 4136-3721 (headquarters)
E-mail: kundenservice@randomhouse.de
Web Site: www.randomhouse.de/bassermann
Key Personnel
Foreign Rights: Dr Gesche Wendebourg
Tel: (089) 4136-3313 *E-mail:* gesche.
wendebourg@randomhouse.de
Founded: 1843
Subjects: Art, Cookery, Crafts, Games, Hobbies,
Fiction, Gardening, Plants, Health, Nutrition,
Nonfiction (General), Outdoor Recreation
ISBN Prefix(es): 978-3-8094
Number of titles published annually: 130 Print

Battenberg Gietl Verlag GmbH+
Pfaelzer Str 11, 93128 Regenstauf
Mailing Address: Postfach 166, 93122 Regenstauf
Tel: (09402) 93 37-0 *Fax:* (09402) 93 37-24
E-mail: info@gietl-verlag.de
Web Site: www.gietl-verlag.de
Key Personnel
Mng Dir & Publishing Dir: Josef Roidl
Advertising Manager: Sandra Penar *Tel:* (09402)
93 37-18 *E-mail:* sandra.penar@gietl-verlag.de
Press & Public Relations: Verena Roesch
Tel: (09402) 93 37-20 *E-mail:* verena.roesch@
gietl-verlag.de
Proofreader: Manuela Bonfissuto *Tel:* (09402) 93
37-19 *E-mail:* manuela.bonfissuto@gietl-verlag.
de
Sales & Marketing: Andrea Krampfl *Tel:* (09402)
93 37-11 *E-mail:* andrea.krampfl@gietl-verlag.
de
Assistant: Martina Singruen *Tel:* (09402) 93 37-
28 *E-mail:* martina.singruen@gietl-verlag.de
Special publishing house for numismatic litera-
ture.
Subjects: Antiques, Crafts, Games, Hobbies, His-
tory
ISBN Prefix(es): 978-3-89441; 978-3-924861;
978-3-86646; 978-3-938614
Total Titles: 70 Print
Imprints: Battenberg Verlag; Buch- und Kunstverlag Oberpfalz; Gietl Verlag; MZ-Buchverlag;
Muenzen & Sammeln; MuenzenRevue;
SuedOst-Verlag

Battenberg Verlag, *imprint of* Battenberg Gietl
Verlag GmbH

Verlagsbereich Bau, *imprint of* Verlagshaus
Wohlfarth

Baumhaus Verlag, *imprint of* Bastei Luebbe
GmbH & Co KG

Baumhaus Verlag+
Imprint of Bastei Luebbe GmbH & Co KG
Schanzenstr 6-20, 51063 Cologne
Tel: (0221) 8200 0
E-mail: webmaster@luebbe.de
Web Site: www.luebbe.de
Founded: 1986
Publisher of books for children 3-15 years of age.
Board books, picture books, cinema & TV tie-ins,
gift books, didactic games, records & tapes,
video, fiction, novels & CD-ROMs.
Membership(s): Arbeitsgemeinschaft von Ju-
gendbuchverlagen; Arbeitskreis Hoerbuchver-
lage des Boersenvereins; Boersenverein des
Deutschen Buchhandels.
Subjects: Fiction, Kid's Factual
ISBN Prefix(es): 978-3-8339

Number of titles published annually: 200 Print;
10 CD-ROM; 1 Online; 1 E-Book; 30 Audio
Total Titles: 1,252 Print; 10 CD-ROM; 1 Online;
1 E-Book; 500 Audio

Verlag Traugott Bautz GmbH
Ellernstr 1, 99734 Nordhausen
Tel: (03631) 466710 *Fax:* (03631) 466711
E-mail: bautz@bautz.de
Web Site: www.bautz.de
Key Personnel
Manager: Uta Timpe-Bautz
Editor: Traugott Bautz *Tel:* (05521) 5588
Fax: (05521) 1673
Founded: 1969
Subjects: Regional Interests, Theology
ISBN Prefix(es): 978-3-88309

Bauverlag BV GmbH+
Avenwedder Str 55, 33311 Guetersloh
Tel: (05241) 802476 *Fax:* (05241) 809582
E-mail: info@bauverlag.de
Web Site: www.bauverlag.de
Key Personnel
Mng Dir: Karl-Heinz Mueller *Tel:* (05241)
802476 *E-mail:* karl-heinz.mueller@bauverlag.
de
Sales Dir: Erdal Top *Tel:* (05241) 8089452
E-mail: erdal.top@bauverlag.de
Founded: 1929
Subjects: Architecture & Interior Design, Civil
Engineering, Energy, Environmental Studies,
Real Estate
ISBN Prefix(es): 978-3-7625
Parent Company: Docu Group
Imprints: LBO-Dienst
Branch Office(s)
Nikolsburger Str 11, 10717 Berlin

Bayerische Akademie der Wissenschaften
(Bavarian Academy of Sciences & Humanities)
Alfons-Goppel-Str 11, 80539 Munich
Tel: (089) 23031-0 *Fax:* (089) 23031-1100
E-mail: info@badw.de
Web Site: www.badw.de
Key Personnel
President: Dr Karl-Heinz Hoffmann *Tel:* (089)
23031-1135 *E-mail:* praesident@badw.de
Press & Public Relations: Janina Amendt
Tel: (089) 23031-1141 *E-mail:* amendt@badw.
de; Dr Ellen Latzin *Tel:* (089) 23031-1141
E-mail: latzin@badw.de
Founded: 1759
Subjects: Science (General), Humanities, Natural
Science, Social Science
ISBN Prefix(es): 978-3-7696
Number of titles published annually: 130 Print
Orders to: CH Beck'sche Verlags Buchhand-
lung, Postfach 400340, 80703 Munich, Con-
tact: Oscar Beck *Tel:* (089) 381890 *Fax:* (089)
38189/381398

**Druckerei und Verlagsanstalt Bayerland
GmbH**
Konrad-Adenauer-Str 19, 85221 Dachau
Mailing Address: Postfach 1868, 85208 Dachau
Tel: (08131) 7 20 66 *Fax:* (08131) 73 53 99
E-mail: zentrale@bayerland-amperbote.de
Web Site: www.bayerland.de
Key Personnel
Mng Dir: Karin Kiermeier
Subjects: Cookery, Fiction, Humor, Regional In-
terests, Travel & Tourism
ISBN Prefix(es): 978-3-89251; 978-3-922394;
978-3-9800040
Number of titles published annually: 20 Print
Total Titles: 250 Print

BC Publications GmbH
Behringstr 10, 82152 Planegg
Tel: (089) 318905-0 *Fax:* (089) 318905-86

E-mail: info@bc-publications.de
Web Site: bc-e-edition.de
Key Personnel
Publisher & Mng Dir: Burkhard P Bierschenck
Public Relations & Press: Martina Kliem
Founded: 2010
Subjects: Art, Health, Nutrition, Inspirational, Spirituality, Psychology, Psychiatry, Technology, Nature
ISBN Prefix(es): 978-3-941717

bd-edition, *imprint of* Wochenschau Verlag

BdWi-Studienhefte, *imprint of* BdWi-Verlag

BdWi-Verlag+
Gisselberger Str 7, 35037 Marburg
Tel: (06421) 21395
E-mail: verlag@bdwi.de
Web Site: www.bdwi.de
Key Personnel
Publishing: Werner Zentner
Founded: 1993
Subjects: Government, Political Science, Psychology, Psychiatry, Social Sciences, Sociology, Women's Studies
ISBN Prefix(es): 978-3-924684; 978-3-939864
Associate Companies: Informationsstelle Wissenschaft und Frieden (IWIF), Beringstr 14, 53113 Bonn *Tel:* (0170) 2156346
Imprints: BdWi-Studienhefte; Forum Wissenschaft Studien; Reihe Hochschule

be.bra verlag GmbH+
KulturBrauerei Haus 2, Schoenhauser Allee 37, 10435 Berlin
Tel: (030) 440 23 810 *Fax:* (030) 440 23 819
E-mail: post@bebraverlag.de
Web Site: www.bebraverlag.de
Key Personnel
Mng Dir: Ulrich Hopp *E-mail:* ulrich.hopp@bebraverlag.de
Program Dir: Dr Robert Zagolla *Tel:* (030) 490 23 816 *E-mail:* r.zagolla@bebraverlag.de
Press Manager: Ingrid Kirschey-Feix *Tel:* (030) 440 23 812 *E-mail:* i.kirschey-feix@bebraverlag.de
Sales Manager: Ingo Halscheidt *Tel:* (030) 440 23 813 *E-mail:* i.halscheidt@bebraverlag.de
Founded: 1994
Membership(s): Borsenverein des Deutschen Buchhandels.
Subjects: Architecture & Interior Design, Government, Political Science, Regional Interests
ISBN Prefix(es): 978-3-930863; 978-3-89809
Number of titles published annually: 20 Print
Total Titles: 46 Print
Foreign Rep(s): Richard Bhend (Switzerland); Dr Winfried Plattner (Austria); Margaret Sacher-Koczewska (Poland); Regine Zschernig (Australia)

Bechtle, Graphische Betriebe und Verlagsgesellschaft GmbH & Co KG
Zeppelinstr 116, 73730 Esslingen
Tel: (0711) 93 10 0 *Fax:* (0711) 93 10 400
E-mail: info@bechtle-online.de
Web Site: www.bechtle-online.de
Key Personnel
Mng Dir: Dr Werner Schumacher *Tel:* (0711) 93 10 340 *E-mail:* werner.schumacher@bechtle-online.de
Publisher: Dr Christine Bechtle-Kobarg *Tel:* (0711) 93 10 207 *Fax:* (0711) 31 69 488 *E-mail:* christine.bechtlekobarg@ez-online.de
Marketing Manager: Dieter Meyer *Tel:* (0711) 93 10 234 *Fax:* (0711) 93 10 197 *E-mail:* dieter.meyer@bechtle-online.de
Founded: 1868
Subjects: Biography, Memoirs, Regional Interests

ISBN Prefix(es): 978-3-7628
Subsidiaries: Bechtle Druck & Service

Verlag C H Beck oHG+
Wilhelmstr 9, 80801 Munich
Mailing Address: Postfach 400340, 80703 Munich
Tel: (089) 38189-0 *Fax:* (089) 38189-402
E-mail: kundenservice@beck-shop.de; beck-online@beck.de; info@beck-online.de
Web Site: www.chbeck.de
Key Personnel
Dir: Dr Hans Dieter Beck
Head, Press/Licenses: Mathias Bruchmann *Tel:* (089) 38189-266 *Fax:* (089) 38189-480 *E-mail:* mathias.bruchmann@beck.de
Foreign Rights: Susanne Simor *Tel:* (089) 38189-228 *Fax:* (089) 38189-699 *E-mail:* susanne.simor@beck.de
Founded: 1763
Subjects: Anthropology, Archaeology, Art, Economics, History, Language Arts, Linguistics, Law, Literature, Literary Criticism, Essays, Management, Music, Dance, Nonfiction (General), Philosophy, Social Sciences, Sociology, Theology
ISBN Prefix(es): 978-3-406
Subsidiaries: Verlag Franz Vahlen GmbH
Branch Office(s)
Palmengartenstr 14, 60325 Frankfurt am Main
Distribution Center: Mohr Morawa Buchvertrieb GmbH, Sulzengasse 2, 1230 Vienna, Austria *Tel:* (01) 680 14-0 *Fax:* (01) 688 71 30 *E-mail:* momo@mohrmorawa.at *Web Site:* www.mohrmorawa.at
Schweizer Buchzentrum Haegendorf, Postfach, 4601 Olten 1, Switzerland *Tel:* (062) 2092525

edition m beck
Schwedenhof/Am Roemermuseum/Am Schwedenhof 4, 66424 Homburg/Saar-Schwarzenacker
Tel: (0700) 26632325; (06848) 72152
E-mail: ger@comebeck.com
Web Site: www.comebeck.com
Key Personnel
Mng Dir & Proprietor: Mathias Beck
Mng Dir & Editorial & Publicity: Susanna Beck
Mng Dir: Dr Christopher Naumann
Chief Editor: Gerald A W Hunze
    E-mail: geraldhunze@comebeck.com
Founded: 1967
Subjects: Art
ISBN Prefix(es): 978-3-924360; 978-3-939755
Number of titles published annually: 8 Print
Total Titles: 248 Print
Parent Company: comebeck ltd .ca

Verlag Hartmut Becker
In den Borngaerten 9, 35274 Kirchhain
Tel: (06427) 930455 *Fax:* (06427) 930457
E-mail: verlag-hartmut-becker@t-online.de
Web Site: www.verlag-hartmut-becker.de
Key Personnel
Publisher: Hartmut Becker
Founded: 1992
Membership(s): Boersenverein des Deutschen Buchhandels eV.
Subjects: Human Relations
ISBN Prefix(es): 978-3-929480

Becker Joest Volk Verlag GmbH & Co KG
Bahnhofsallee 5, 40721 Hilden
Tel: (02103) 9 07 88 0 *Fax:* (02103) 9 07 88 28
E-mail: info@bjvv.de
Web Site: bjvv.de
Key Personnel
Owner: Juergen Becker *E-mail:* jb@bjvv.de; Ralf Joest *E-mail:* rj@bjvv.de; Hans-Eckehard Volk *E-mail:* hv@bjvv.de
Founded: 2003
Subjects: Cookery, Gardening, Plants, Photography, Design

ISBN Prefix(es): 978-3-938100; 978-3-9808977
Distribution Center: Leipziger Kommissions- und Grossbuchhandelsgesellschaft mbH (LKG), An der Suedspitze 1-12, 04571 Roetha, Contact: Kathrin Obarski *Tel:* (034206) 65106 *Fax:* (034206) 651741 *E-mail:* bjvv@lkg-service.de *Web Site:* www.lkg-va.de
Mohr Morawa Buchvertrieb GmbH, Sulzengasse 2, 1230 Vienna, Austria *Tel:* (01) 680 14-0 *Fax:* (01) 689 68 00 *E-mail:* bestellung@mohrmorawa.at *Web Site:* www.mohrmorawa.at
Buchzentrum AG (BZ), Industriestr Ost 10, 4614 Haegendorf, Switzerland *Tel:* (062) 2 09 26 26 *Fax:* (062) 2 09 26 27 *E-mail:* kundendienst@buchzentrum.ch

Bede Verlag, *imprint of* Verlag Eugen Ulmer KG

Beerenverlag
Wilhelmshoeher Str 200F, 60389 Frankfurt am Main
Tel: (069) 610 095 51 *Fax:* (069) 242 491 92
E-mail: info@beerenverlag.de; buchhandel@beerenverlag.de
Web Site: www.beerenverlag.de
Key Personnel
Manager: Bernard Rensinghoff
Press: Dorthea Volke *Tel:* (0176) 616 590 71 *E-mail:* dorothea.volke@beerenverlag.de
Founded: 1992
Subjects: Fiction, Humor, Literature, Literary Criticism, Essays, Poetry, Travel & Tourism
ISBN Prefix(es): 978-3-929198
Distributed by Harrassourk Verlag

M P Belaieff, *imprint of* Musia International Musikalien-Handelsgesellschaft Ehrlich GmbH & Co KG

Verlag Beleke GmbH+
Kronprinzenstr 13, 45128 Essen
Tel: (0201) 8130-0 *Fax:* (0201) 8130-108
E-mail: info@beleke.de
Web Site: www.beleke.de
Key Personnel
Owner & Mng Dir: Norbert Beleke
Mng Dir: Stephanie Beleke-Wesskamp
Mng Dir & International Rights: Dr Michael Platzkoester *Tel:* (0201) 8130-118 *E-mail:* mplatzkoester@beleke.de
Founded: 1964
Membership(s): Boersenverein des Deutschen Buchhandels eV; European Association of Directory & Database Publishers; Verband Deutscher Auskunfts und Verzeichnismedien eV.
Subjects: Biography, Memoirs, Business, Criminology, Medicine, Nursing, Dentistry, Nonfiction (General), Regional Interests
ISBN Prefix(es): 978-3-8215; 978-3-922785
Associate Companies: Elvikom Film-Verlag GmbH, Essen; ntv neue television FILM-TV-PRODUKTION GmbH, Essen; Das Rathaus Verlagsgesellschaft mbH & Co KG, Essen; Verlag Wendler GmbH, Vereinsstr 4-6, 52062 Aachen *Tel:* (0241) 47 08 20 *Fax:* (0241) 47 08-236 *E-mail:* info@verlag-wendler.de; Max Schmidt-Roemhild Verlagsgesellschaft mbH Leipzig, Coppistr 2, 04129 Leipzig *Tel:* (0341) 9 04 85-0 *Fax:* (0341) 9 04 85-20 *E-mail:* info@schmidt-roemhild.de; Hansisches Verlagskontor GmbH, Mengstr 16, 23552 Luebeck *Tel:* (0451) 70 31-01 *Fax:* (0451) 70 31-253 *E-mail:* hansisches-verlagskontor@t-online.de; Schmidt-Roemhild Kongressgesellschaft mbH, Mengstr 16, 23552 Luebeck *Tel:* (0451) 70 31-01 *Fax:* (0451) 70 31-253 *E-mail:* info@schmidt-roemhild.de; Max Schmidt-Roemhild KG, Mengstr 16, 23552 Luebeck *Tel:* (0451) 70 31-01 *Fax:* (0451) 70 31-253 *E-mail:* info@schmidt-roemhild.de; Max Schmidt-Roemhild Verlagsgesellschaft mbH Schwerin, Graf-Schack-Allee 6, 19053

Schwerin *Tel:* (0385) 5 91 88-0 *Fax:* (0385) 5 91 88-10 *E-mail:* info@schmidt-roemhild.de
Branch Office(s)
Ruhralle 9, 44139 Dortmund *Tel:* (0231) 12 10 08 *Fax:* (0231) 12 10 00

belleville Verlag Michael Farin
Hormayrstr 15, 80997 Munich
Tel: (089) 1492799 *Fax:* (089) 1404585
E-mail: belleville@t-online.de
Web Site: www.belleville-verlag.de
Key Personnel
Owner: Michael Farin
Founded: 1982
Subjects: Art, Criminology, Erotica, Fiction, Film, Video, Literature, Literary Criticism, Essays, Philosophy, Psychology, Psychiatry, Libya
ISBN Prefix(es): 978-3-923646

Verlag Beltz & Gelberg+
Subsidiary of Julius Beltz GmbH & Co KG
Werderstr 10, 69469 Weinheim
Mailing Address: Postfach 10 01 54, 69441 Weinheim
Tel: (06201) 6007-0 *Fax:* (06201) 6007-310
E-mail: info@beltz.de
Web Site: www.beltz.de
Key Personnel
Publisher & Chief Executive Officer: Marianne Ruebelmann
Head, Press & Public Relations: Bettina Schaub *Tel:* (06201) 6007-443 *Fax:* (06201) 6007-9443 *E-mail:* b.schaub@beltz.de
Sales Manager: Andrea Foelster *Tel:* (06201) 6007-431 *E-mail:* a.foelster@beltz.de
Marketing & Sales: Andreas Horn *Tel:* (06201) 6007-440 *E-mail:* a.horn@beltz.de
Rights: Kerstin Michaelis *Tel:* (06201) 6007-327 *Fax:* (06201) 6007-338 *E-mail:* k.michaelis@beltz.de
Founded: 1971
ISBN Prefix(es): 978-3-407; 978-3-621
Ultimate Parent Company: Beltz Ruebelmann Holding
Foreign Rep(s): Ruedi Amrhein (Switzerland); Guenther Raunjak (Austria)
Distribution Center: Rhenus Medien Logistik, Justus-von-Liebig Str 1, 86899 Landsberg am Lech *Tel:* (08191) 97000-0 *E-mail:* beltz@de.rhenus.com
Mohr Morawa Buchvertrieb GmbH, Sulzengasse 2, 1230 Vienna, Austria *Tel:* (01) 680 14-0 *Fax:* (01) 688 71 30 *E-mail:* momo@mohrmorawa.at *Web Site:* www.mohrmorawa.at
AVA Verlagsauslieferung AG, Centralweg 16, 8910 Affoltern am Albis, Switzerland *Tel:* (044) 762 42 50 *Fax:* (044) 762 42 49 *E-mail:* verlagsservice@ava.ch *Web Site:* www.ava.ch

Julius Beltz GmbH & Co KG+
Werderstr 10, 69469 Weinheim
Mailing Address: Postfach 10 01 54, 69441 Weinheim
Tel: (06201) 6007-0 *Fax:* (06201) 6007-310
E-mail: info@beltz.de
Web Site: www.beltz.de
Key Personnel
Publisher & Chief Executive Officer: Marianne Ruebelmann
Head, Press & Public Relations: Bettina Schaub *Tel:* (06201) 6007-443 *Fax:* (06201) 6007-9443 *E-mail:* b.schaub@beltz.de
Sales Manager: Andrea Foelster *Tel:* (06201) 6007-431 *E-mail:* a.foelster@beltz.de
Marketing & Sales: Andreas Horn *Tel:* (06201) 6007-440 *E-mail:* a.horn@beltz.de
Rights: Kerstin Michaelis *Tel:* (06201) 6007-327 *Fax:* (06201) 6007-338 *E-mail:* k.michaelis@beltz.de
Founded: 1841

Membership(s): VGS - Verlagsgessellschaft mbH & Co KG.
Subjects: Science (General)
ISBN Prefix(es): 978-3-407; 978-3-621
Subsidiaries: Anrich Verlag; Verlag Beltz & Gelberg; Beltz Athenaeum Verlag; Deutscher Studien Verlag; Juventa Verlag GmbH; Psychologie Verlags Union GmbH
Distribution Center: Rhenus Medien Logistik GmbH & Co KG, Justus-von-Liebig-Str 1, 86899 Landsberg am Leche *Tel:* (08191) 97000-0 *E-mail:* beltz@de.rhenus.com
Mohr Morawa Buchvertrieb GmbH, Sulzengasse 2, 1230 Vienna, Austria *Tel:* (01) 680 14-0 *Fax:* (01) 688 71 30 *E-mail:* momo@mohrmorawa.at *Web Site:* www.mohrmorawa.at
AVA Verlagsauslieferung AG, Centralweg 16, 8910 Affoltern am Albis, Switzerland *Tel:* (044) 762 42 50 *Fax:* (044) 762 42 49 *E-mail:* verlagsservice@ava.ch *Web Site:* www.ava.ch

Bender Verlag
Boppstr 25, 55118 Mainz
Tel: (06131) 226078 *Fax:* (06131) 226079
E-mail: mail@ventil-verlag.de; bender@bender-verlag.de; presse@ventil-verlag.de
Web Site: www.bender-verlag.de
Key Personnel
Publisher: Theo Bender; Jens Neumann; Oliver Schmitt
Subjects: Art, Fiction, Literature, Literary Criticism, Essays, Music, Dance, Nonfiction (General), Pop Culture
ISBN Prefix(es): 978-3-936497; 978-3-9806528
Parent Company: Ventil Verlag KG
Foreign Rep(s): Andreas Meisel (Switzerland); Seth Meyer-Bruhns (Austria)
Distribution Center: SoVa, Friesstr 20-24, 60388 Frankfurt *Tel:* (069) 41 02 11 *Fax:* (069) 41 02 80 (Germany & Austria)
Kaktus Verlagsauslieferung, Thundorferstr 15, 8501 Frauenfeld, Switzerland *Tel:* (052) 722 31 90 *Fax:* (052) 722 17 82

Anton J Benjamin GmbH, see Boosey & Hawkes Bote & Bock GmbH

Berenberg Verlag
Sophienstr 28, 10178 Berlin
Tel: (030) 21 91 63 60 *Fax:* (030) 21 91 63 61
E-mail: info@berenberg-verlag.de
Web Site: www.berenberg-verlag.de
Key Personnel
Mng Dir: Heinrich von Berenberg *E-mail:* hb@berenberg-verlag.de
Dir: Petra von Berenberg
Founded: 2004
Subjects: Biography, Memoirs, Literature, Literary Criticism, Essays
ISBN Prefix(es): 978-3-937834
Distribution Center: Leipziger Kommissions- und Grossbuchhandelsgesellschaft mbH (LKG), An der Suedspitze 1-12, 04571 Roetha, Contact: Ursula Fritzsche *Tel:* (034206) 6 51 35 *Fax:* (034206) 6 51 10 *E-mail:* ufritzsche@lkg-service.de *Web Site:* www.lkg-va.de

J Berg Verlag
Infanteriestr 11a, 80797 Munich
Tel: (089) 1306-99-0 *Fax:* (089) 1306-99-100
E-mail: info@bruckmann.de
Web Site: www.j-berg-verlag.de
Key Personnel
Product Management: Sabine Klingan *Tel:* (089) 1306-99-615 *Fax:* (089) 1306-99-600 *E-mail:* sabine.klingan@bruckmann.de; Marianne Huber *Tel:* (089) 1306-99-635 *Fax:* (089) 1306-99-600 *E-mail:* marianne.huber@bruckmann.de
Subjects: Art, Automotive, History, Inspirational, Spirituality, Sports, Athletics, Cycling, Hiking,

Motorcycles, Mountain Climbing, People & Nature, Regional History, Winter Sports
ISBN Prefix(es): 978-3-7658; 978-3-86246
Parent Company: Bruckmann Verlag GmbH
Ultimate Parent Company: GeraNova Bruckmann Verlagshaus GmbH
Orders to: Justus-von-Liebig-Str One, 86899 Landsberg *Tel:* (0180) 5 32 16 17 *Fax:* (0180) 5 32 16 20 *E-mail:* rml@verlaghaus.com

Bergkristall Verlag GmbH
Krumme Weide 30, 32108 Bad Salzuflen
Tel: (05222) 92 34 51 *Fax:* (05222) 92 34 52
E-mail: info@bergkristall-verlag.de
Web Site: www.bergkristall-verlag.de
Key Personnel
Owner & Mng Dir: Martin Fieber
Founded: 2000
Subjects: Inspirational, Spirituality, Literature, Literary Criticism, Essays
ISBN Prefix(es): 978-3-935422

Bergmoser + Hoeller Verlag AG
Karl-Friedrich-Str 76, 52072 Aachen
Tel: (0241) 93888-123 *Fax:* (0241) 93888-188
E-mail: kontakt@buhv.de
Web Site: www.buhv.de
Key Personnel
Commercial Dir: Andreas Bergmoser *Tel:* (0241) 93888-117 *E-mail:* gf@buhv.de
Program Manager: Peter Tiarks *Tel:* (0241) 93888-132 *E-mail:* gf@buhv.de
Press & Public Relations: Anne Weinmann *Tel:* (0241) 93888-120 *E-mail:* aweinmann@buhv.de
Founded: 1970
Subjects: Art, English as a Second Language, Mathematics, Music, Dance
ISBN Prefix(es): 978-3-88997
U.S. Office(s): C I Publishing Inc, 230 Fifth Ave NE, Hickory, NC 28601, United States
Orders to: Postfach 50 04 04, 52088 Aachen

Bergverlag Rother GmbH+
Keltenring 17, 82041 Oberhaching
Tel: (089) 608669-0 *Fax:* (089) 608669-69
E-mail: bergverlag@rother.de
Web Site: www.rother.de
Key Personnel
Press: Bettina Loeneke *Tel:* (089) 608669-23 *E-mail:* loeneke@rother.de
Founded: 1920
Specialize in Alpine literature, documents & guidebooks.
Subjects: Nonfiction (General), Outdoor Recreation, Sports, Athletics, Travel & Tourism
ISBN Prefix(es): 978-3-7633
Number of titles published annually: 25 Print
Total Titles: 500 Print
Distributed by Cordee (UK); Travel House Media GmbH
Foreign Rep(s): AlpenBooks (USA); Cartotheque - EGG (France); Cordee (UK); Craenen bvba (Belgium); Freytag & Berndt Praha (Czechia); Freytag-Berndt Budapest Kft (Hungary); Freytag-Berndt sro (Slovakia); Freytag-Berndt u Artaria KG (Austria); Libridis (Netherlands); MapIberia-Freytag & Berndt SL (Spain); Photoglob AG (Switzerland)
Distribution Center: GeoCenter Touristik Medienservice GmbH, Postfach 80 08 30, 70508 Stuttgart *Tel:* (0711) 781 946 10 *Fax:* (0711) 782 43 75 *E-mail:* vertrieb@geocenter.de *Web Site:* www.geocenter.de
Koch, Neff & Oetinger Verlagsauslieferung GmbH, Industriestr 23, 70565 Stuttgart *E-mail:* travel-house-media@kno-va.de
Freytag-Bernet & Artaria KG, Brunner Str 69, 1230 Vienna, Austria *Tel:* (01) 869 90 90 *Fax:* (01) 869 88 55 *E-mail:* sales@freytagberndt.at *Web Site:* www.freytagberndt.at
Baumgartner Buecher AG, c/o AVA Verlagsauslieferung AG, Centralweg 16, 8910 Affoltern

am Albis, Switzerland *Tel:* (044) 762 42 80
Fax: (044) 762 42 85 *E-mail:* baumgartner@
ava.ch *Web Site:* www.ava.ch

Verlag fuer Berlin-Brandenburg
Binzstr 19, 13189 Berlin
Tel: (030) 70 22 34 06 *Fax:* (030) 70 22 34 26
Web Site: www.verlagberlinbrandenburg.de
Key Personnel
Publisher: Andre Foerster *E-mail:* foerster@
verlagberlinbrandenburg.de
Sales: Cornelia Lange *E-mail:* lange@
verlagberlinbrandenburg.de
Subjects: History, Nonfiction (General), Culture
ISBN Prefix(es): 978-3-945256

berlin.krimi.verlag
Imprint of be.bra verlag GmbH
KulturBrauerei Haus 2, Schoenhauser Allee 37,
10435 Berlin
Tel: (030) 440 23 810 *Fax:* (030) 440 23 819
E-mail: post@bebraverlag.de; presse@
bebraverlag.de
Web Site: www.bebraverlag.de
Key Personnel
Mng Dir: Ulrich Hopp *E-mail:* ulrich.hopp@
bebraverlag.de
Sales Manager: Ingo Halscheidt *Tel:* (030) 440 23
813 *E-mail:* i.halscheidt@bebraverlag.de
Editorial: Ingrid Kirschey-Feix *Tel:* (030) 440 23
812 *E-mail:* i.kirschey-feix@bebraverlag.de
Press: Eileen Janiszewski *Tel:* (030) 440 23 815
E-mail: e.janiszewski@bebraverlag.de
Founded: 2001
Subjects: Criminology, Fiction, History, Historical
Crime
ISBN Prefix(es): 978-3-89809

Berlin University Press, *imprint of* Verlagshaus
Roemerweg GmbH

Berlin University Press
Imprint of Verlagshaus Roemerweg GmbH
Roemerweg 10, 65187 Wiesbaden
Tel: (0611) 986 98 0 *Fax:* (0611) 986 98 26
E-mail: info@verlagshaus-roemerweg.de
Web Site: www.verlagshaus-roemerweg.de
Key Personnel
Publishing Dir: Lothar Wekel *E-mail:* wekel@
verlagshaus-roemerweg.de
Sales & Marketing: Fabian Reinecke *Tel:* (0611)
986 98 15 *E-mail:* reinecke@verlagshaus-
roemerweg.de
ISBN Prefix(es): 978-3-940432; 978-3-86280;
978-3-7374
Foreign Rep(s): Buchzentrum AG (Switzerland);
Mohr Morawa Buchvertrieb GmbH (Austria)
Distribution Center: Sigloch Distribution
GmbH & Co KG, Am Buchberg 8, Tor
6-10, 74572 Blaufelden *Tel:* (07953)
718 90 69 *Fax:* (07953) 883 16 0
E-mail: verlagshausroemerweg@sigloch.de *Web
Site:* www.sigloch.de

Berlin Verlag
Damaschkestr 4, 10711 Berlin
Tel: (030) 44 38 45 90 *Fax:* (030) 44 38 45 95
E-mail: info@piper.de
Web Site: www.piper.de/berlin-verlag
Founded: 1994
Subjects: Art, Biography, Memoirs, Cookery,
Erotica, Fiction, Government, Political Science,
Health, Nutrition, Humor, Literature, Literary
Criticism, Essays, Philosophy, Religion - Other,
Romance, Science Fiction, Fantasy, Travel &
Tourism
ISBN Prefix(es): 978-3-8270
Number of titles published annually: 4 Print
Parent Company: Bonnier Media Deutschland
Ultimate Parent Company: Bonnier AB
Divisions: Berlin Academic

Verlagshaus Berlin
Chodowieckistr 2, 10405 Berlin
Tel: (030) 675 155 00 *Fax:* (030) 675 155 01
E-mail: post@verlagshaus-berlin.de
Web Site: verlagshaus-berlin.de
Key Personnel
Partner: Johannes C S Frank; Andrea Schmidt;
Dominik Ziller
Subjects: Fiction, Poetry
ISBN Prefix(es): 978-3-940249

Berliner Wissenschafts-Verlag GmbH (BWV)+
Markgrafenstr 12-14, 10969 Berlin
Tel: (030) 84 17 70-0 *Fax:* (030) 84 17 70-21
E-mail: bwv@bwv-verlag.de
Web Site: www.bwv-verlag.de
Key Personnel
Publishing Dir: Dr Thomas Schaber
E-mail: schaber@bwv-verlag.de
Program Manager: Jessica Gutsche *Tel:* (030) 87
17 70-18 *E-mail:* gutsche@bwv-verlag.de
Marketing: Franziska Fiebig *Tel:* (030) 87 17 70-
26 *E-mail:* fiebig@bwv-verlag.de
Founded: 1962
Subjects: Business, Economics, Education, Envi-
ronmental Studies, Government, Political Sci-
ence, History, Law, Library & Information Sci-
ences, Management, Marketing, Mathematics,
Medicine, Nursing, Dentistry, Music, Dance,
Philosophy, Psychology, Psychiatry, Public Ad-
ministration, Publishing & Book Trade Reference, Real Estate, Science (General), Technology, Theology, Culture
ISBN Prefix(es): 978-3-87061; 978-3-8305
Imprints: Ostrecht

Bernard und Graefe Verlag GmbH & Co KG+
Heilsbachstr 26, 53123 Bonn
Tel: (0228) 6483-0; (0228) 6483-116; (0228)
6483-142 *Fax:* (0228) 6483-109
E-mail: info@mpgbonn.de
Web Site: www.mpgbonn.de; www.monch.com
Key Personnel
Chief Executive Officer & President: Manfred
Sadlowski
Project Leader: Volker Schwichtenberg
E-mail: volker.schwichtenberg@mpgbonn.de
Founded: 1918
Subjects: Military Science
ISBN Prefix(es): 978-3-7637
Parent Company: Moench Publishing Group

A Bernecker Verlag GmbH
Unter dem Schoeneberg 1, 34212 Melsungen
Tel: (05661) 731-0 *Fax:* (05661) 731-111
E-mail: info@bernecker.de; verlag@bernecker.de
Web Site: www.bernecker.de
Key Personnel
Mng Dir: Conrad Fischer *Tel:* (05661) 731-101
Founded: 1869
Subjects: Business, Cookery, History, Law, Re-
gional Interests
ISBN Prefix(es): 978-3-87064
Parent Company: Bernecker Mediagruppe
Associate Companies: Bernecker MediaWare AG

Bernstein Verlag GbR
Holzgasse 45, 53721 Siegburg
Mailing Address: Postfach 1753, 53707 Siegburg
Tel: (02241) 8667170 *Fax:* (02241) 8668266
E-mail: bernstein@bernstein-verlag.de
Web Site: www.bernstein-verlag.de
Key Personnel
Mng Dir: Andreas Remmel *E-mail:* ar@bernstein-
verlag.de; Paul Remmel *E-mail:* pr@bernstein-
verlag.de
Founded: 2002
Subjects: Economics, History, Law, Literature,
Literary Criticism, Essays, Philosophy, Theol-
ogy, Classical Studies, Cultural Studies
ISBN Prefix(es): 978-3-9809762; 978-3-939431;
978-3-945426

C Bertelsmann, *imprint of* Verlagsgruppe
Random House Bertelsmann

C Bertelsmann Verlag GmbH
Imprint of Verlagsgruppe Random House Bertels-
mann
Neumarkterstr 28, 81673 Munich 80
Tel: (089) 4136-0 *Toll Free Tel:* (0800) 500 33 22
Fax: (089) 4136-3333
E-mail: kundenservice@randomhouse.de
Web Site: www.randomhouse.de/cbertelsmann
Key Personnel
Foreign Rights Dir: Gesche Wendebourg
Tel: (089) 4136-3313 *E-mail:* gesche.
wendebourg@randomhouse.de
Press Dir: Heidrun Gebhardt *Tel:* (089) 4136-
3454 *Fax:* (089) 4136-3474 *E-mail:* heidrun.
gebhardt@randomhouse.de
Founded: 1835
Membership(s): TR-Verlagsunion GmbH.
Subjects: Art, Biography, Memoirs, Fiction, Gov-
ernment, Political Science, History, Nonfiction
(General)
ISBN Prefix(es): 978-3-570

Verlag Bertelsmann Stiftung (Bertelsmann
Foundation Publishers)+
Carl-Bertelsmann-Str 256, 33311 Guetersloh
Mailing Address: Postfach 103, 33311 Guetersloh
Tel: (05241) 810 *Fax:* (05241) 81681396; (05241)
81681175
E-mail: info@bertelsmann-stiftung.de
Web Site: www.bertelsmann-stiftung.de/verlag
Key Personnel
Publisher: Sabine Reimann *Tel:* (05241) 81-81175
E-mail: sabine.reimann@bertelsmann.de
Internet Publishing Program: Elisabeth Menke
Tel: (05241) 81-81308
Production: Christiane Raffel *Tel:* (05241) 81-
81256
Subjects: Economics, Education, Government,
Political Science, Health, Nutrition, Social Sci-
ences, Sociology
ISBN Prefix(es): 978-3-89204
Number of titles published annually: 50 Print
Total Titles: 308 Print
Branch Office(s)
Residence Palace, Rue de la Loi 155, 1040 Brus-
sels, Belgium *Tel:* (02) 280-2830 *Fax:* (02) 280
3221
Fundacion Bertelsmann, Pg de Picasso,
16, baixos, 08003 Barcelona, Spain
Tel: 932687444 *Fax:* 932687173 *Web
Site:* fundacionbertelsmann.org
U.S. Office(s): Bertelsmann Foundation North
America, 1101 New York Ave NW, Suite 901,
Washington, DC 20005, United States *Tel:* 202-
384-1980 *Fax:* 202-384-1984
Distribution Center: VVA-arvato media GmbH,
Warenannahme 100, An der Autobahn 120,
33333 Guetersloh
Orders to: Brookings Institution Press, 1775
Massachusetts Ave NW, Washington, DC
20036, United States, Contact: Jessica
Howard *Tel:* 202-797-6468 *Fax:* 202-797-
6195 *E-mail:* hfscustserv@press.jhu.edu *Web
Site:* www.brookings.edu/press

W Bertelsmann Verlag GmbH & Co KG
Auf dem Esch 4, 33619 Bielefeld
Mailing Address: Postfach 100633, 33506 Biele-
feld
Tel: (0521) 911-01-0 *Fax:* (0521) 911 01-79
E-mail: service@wbv.de
Web Site: www.wbv.de; www.berufsbildung.de;
www.berufe.net
Key Personnel
Mng Dir: W Arndt Bertelsmann *Tel:* (0521) 911
01-10
Founded: 1864

Subjects: Career Development, Education, Foreign
Countries, Labor, Industrial Relations, Law,
Management, Public Administration, Science
(General), Social Sciences, Sociology, Voca-
tional Training
ISBN Prefix(es): 978-3-7639
Distributor for Bundesanstalt fuer Arbeit; Bun-
desinstitut fuer Berufsbildung; Deutsches Insti-
tute fuer Erwachsenenbildung

Bertz + Fischer GbR
Wrangelstr 67, 10997 Berlin
Tel: (030) 6128 67 41
E-mail: mail@bertz-fischer.de
Web Site: www.bertz-fischer.de
Key Personnel
Mng Dir & Press: Dieter Bertz *E-mail:* dbertz@
bertz-fischer.de
Mng Dir & Sales: Katrin Fischer
E-mail: kfischer@bertz-fischer.de
Founded: 1997
Subjects: Film, Video, Government, Political Sci-
ence, Literature, Literary Criticism, Essays,
Culture
ISBN Prefix(es): 978-3-86505; 978-3-929470
Foreign Rep(s): Elisabeth Anintah-Hirt (Austria)
Distribution Center: Prolit Verlagsauslieferung
GmbH, Siemensstr 16, 35463 Fernwald, Con-
tact: Ulrike Schmidt *Tel:* (0641) 943 93 28
Fax: (0641) 943 93 29 *E-mail:* u.schmidt@
prolit.de *Web Site:* www.prolit.de
Dr Franz Hain Verlagsauslieferungen GmbH,
Dr-Otto-Neurath-Gasse 5, 1220 Vienna, Aus-
tria *Tel:* (01) 282 65 65-0 *Fax:* (01) 282 52 82
E-mail: bestell@hain.at

Verlag Beruf + Schule+
Albert-Schweitzer-Ring 45, 25524 Itzehoe
Mailing Address: Postfach 2008, 25510 Itzehoe
Tel: (04821) 40140 *Fax:* (04821) 4941
E-mail: vbus@online.de
Web Site: www.vbus.de
Key Personnel
Publishing Dir: Renate Golpon *E-mail:* renate@
golpon.de
Founded: 1970
Specialize in teaching & training materials in the
printing & media field.
Membership(s): Association of German Publishers
& Booksellers.
Subjects: Career Development, Chemistry, Chem-
ical Engineering, Computer Science, Humor,
Mathematics, Poetry, Publishing & Book Trade
Reference, Printing Industry
ISBN Prefix(es): 978-3-88013
Imprints: Edition Heitere Poetik
Divisions: Buchdienst B & S
Orders to: VVA arvato media GmbH, Postfach
7600, 7600 Guetersloh *Tel:* (05241) 802895
Fax: (05241) 809352

Beuroner Kunstverlag+
Abteistr 2, 88631 Beuron
Tel: (07466) 17-228 *Fax:* (07466) 17-209
E-mail: info@beuroner-kunstverlag.de
Web Site: www.klosterkunst.de
Key Personnel
Publishing Dir: P Mauritius Sauerzapf
E-mail: leitung@beuroner-kunstverlag.de
Founded: 1898
Subjects: Art, Biblical Studies, Humor, Religion
- Catholic, Religion - Protestant, Religion -
Other
ISBN Prefix(es): 978-3-87071
Imprints: Monastica

Beuth Verlag GmbH
Subsidiary of DIN Deutsches Institut fuer Nor-
mung eV
Burggrafenstr 6, 10787 Berlin
Tel: (030) 2601-0; (030) 2601-2260 *Fax:* (030)
2601-1260

E-mail: kundenservice@beuth.de
Web Site: www.beuth.de
Key Personnel
Mng Dir: Mario Schacht *E-mail:* mario.schacht@
beuth.de; Marion Winkenbach
Founded: 1924
Specialize in technical & scientific literature.
Subjects: Architecture & Interior Design, Chem-
istry, Chemical Engineering, Communications,
Electronics, Electrical Engineering, Energy, En-
gineering (General), Environmental Studies,
Health, Nutrition, Management, Mathematics,
Mechanical Engineering, Physics, Securities,
Technology, Theology, Transportation
ISBN Prefix(es): 978-3-410
Orders to: Osterreichisches Normungsinstitut,
Heinestr 38, 1020 Vienna 2, Austria
Schweizerische Normenvereinigung, Buerglistr
29, Winterthur 8400, Switzerland

Joachim Beyer Verlag, see Schachversand
Ullrich

Bezugsbedingungen, *imprint of* Johann Wolfgang
Goethe-Universitaet Frankfurt am Main

Biblio Verlag
Subsidiary of Zeller Verlag GmbH & Co
Auf dem Busch 2, 49143 Bissendorf
Tel: (05402) 64 17 20 *Fax:* (05402) 64 17 22
E-mail: biblio-verlag@t-online.de; info@militaria-
biblio.de
Web Site: www.militaria-biblio.de
Key Personnel
Mng Dir: Wolfram Zeller
Subjects: Archaeology, Art, History, Language
Arts, Linguistics, Law, Military Science, Phi-
losophy, Religion - Other
ISBN Prefix(es): 978-3-7648

Bibliographisches Institut GmbH+
Dudenstr 6, 68167 Mannheim
Mailing Address: Postfach 10 03 11, 68003
Mannheim
Tel: (0621) 3901-01 *Fax:* (0621) 3901-391
Key Personnel
Mng Dir: Timo Bluemer; Marion Winkenbach
Sales Manager: Carsten Hiller
Press: Dr Nicole Weiffen-Aumann *Tel:* (0621)
3901-366 *Fax:* (0621) 3901-395 *E-mail:* nicole.
weiffen@dudenverlag.de
Founded: 1826
Publishers of the Duden Series of Dictionaries &
Meyer Series of Encyclopedias.
Subjects: Education, Engineering (General), Ge-
ography, Geology, Language Arts, Linguis-
tics, Literature, Literary Criticism, Essays,
Medicine, Nursing, Dentistry, Nonfiction (Gen-
eral), Science (General)
ISBN Prefix(es): 978-3-411; 978-3-323
Parent Company: Cornelsen Schulverlage
Associate Companies: Thueringer Verlagsaus-
lieferung Langenscheidt KG, Langenschei-
dtstr 10, 99867 Gotha *Tel:* (03621) 71 22-
0 *Fax:* (03621) 71 22-44 *E-mail:* info@tva-
logistik.de *Web Site:* www.tva-logistik.de
Imprints: Albatross; Artemis & Winkler; Duden;
Harenberg; Meyers; Sauerlaender; Sauerlaender
Audio
Subsidiaries: Duden Schulbuchverlag (Berlin);
KV&H Verlag GmbH; wissenswert24 Buch &
Medien GmbH (Mannheim)

**Bibliomed Medizinische Verlagsgesellschaft
mbH**
Subsidiary of B Braun Melsungen AG
Stadtwaldpark 10, 34201 Melsungen
Mailing Address: Postfach 1150, 34201 Melsun-
gen
Tel: (05661) 73440 *Fax:* (05661) 8360
E-mail: info@bibliomed.de

Web Site: www.bibliomed.de
Key Personnel
Mng Dir & Editor-in-Chief: Stefan Deges
Tel: (05661) 7344-99 *Fax:* (05661) 7344-44
E-mail: stefan.deges@bibliomed.de
Sales: Petra Volk *Tel:* (05661) 7344-79
E-mail: petra.volk@bibliomed.de
Founded: 1977
Subjects: Health, Nutrition, Law, Management,
Medicine, Nursing, Dentistry, Family Care,
Health Care, Hospital Law, Hospital Manage-
ment, Intensive Care
ISBN Prefix(es): 978-3-89556; 978-3-921958
Total Titles: 8 CD-ROM
Imprints: Krankenpflegeforschung; Melsunger
Medizinische Mitteilungen

Bibliothek Natur & Wissenschaft, *imprint of*
Verlag Natur & Wissenschaft Harro
Hieronimus & Dr Juergen Schmidt GbR

Verlag BibSpider
Reichsstr 28a, 14052 Berlin
Tel: (030) 401 04 354 *Fax:* (030) 401 04 407
E-mail: mail@bibspider.de
Web Site: www.bibspider.de
Key Personnel
Owner: Dr Walburga Loesch
Specialize in information sciences for libraries,
archives & museums.
Subjects: Library & Information Sciences, In-
formation Science, Knowledge & Information
Management
ISBN Prefix(es): 978-3-936960

Edition Bielefelden Kunstverein, *imprint of*
Pendragon Verlag

Bielefelder Verlag GmbH & Co KG, see BVA
Bielefelder Verlag GmbH & Co KG

Biermann Verlag GmbH
Otto-Hahn-Str 7, 50997 Cologne
Tel: (02236) 376-0 *Fax:* (02236) 376-999
E-mail: info@biermann.net
Web Site: www.biermann.net
Key Personnel
Publisher: Dr Hans Biermann *E-mail:* bie@
biermann.net
Graphics: Heike Dargel *Tel:* (02236) 376-150
E-mail: hd@biermann.net
Founded: 1989
Subjects: Medicine, Nursing, Dentistry
ISBN Prefix(es): 978-3-924469; 978-3-930505
Parent Company: Biermann Medizin

Bild & Medien Vertriebs GmbH
Muensterstr 17, 33428 Harsewinkel
Tel: (05247) 10 25 9 *Fax:* (05247) 40 87 60
E-mail: info@bild-medien.com
Web Site: www.bild-medien.com
Key Personnel
Mng Dir: Ernst Penner
Subjects: Biblical Studies, Biography, Memoirs,
Inspirational, Spirituality, Poetry
ISBN Prefix(es): 978-3-936605

Bild und Heimat GmbH
Alexanderstr 1, 10178 Berlin
Tel: (030) 20 61 09 0 *Fax:* (030) 20 61 09-75
E-mail: info@bild-und-heimat.de
Web Site: www.bild-und-heimat.de
Key Personnel
Mng Dir: Marko Wuensch
Program & Publishing Dir: Florian Legner
Tel: (030) 20 61 09-72 *E-mail:* florian.legner@
bebug-verlage.de
Founded: 1951
Subjects: Art, Cookery, Criminology, Fiction, His-
tory, Literature, Literary Criticism, Essays, Re-
gional Interests

ISBN Prefix(es): 978-3-7310; 978-3-86789
Parent Company: Eulenspiegel Verlagsgruppe, Neue Gruenstr 18, 10179 Berlin

BW Bildung und Wissen Verlag und Software GmbH+
Suedwestpark 82, 90449 Nuremberg
Mailing Address: Postfach 82 01 50, 90252 Nuremberg
Tel: (0911) 96 76-0 *Fax:* (0911) 96 76 189
E-mail: info@bwverlag.de; presse@bwverlag.de; serviceteam@bwverlag.de
Web Site: www.bwverlag.de
Key Personnel
Mng Dir: Ulrike Sippel
Press: Renate Holley-Rostock *Tel:* (0911) 96 76-151
Marketing & Sales: Rita Rymdjonok
Founded: 1975
Specialist publishers for initial & further training, occupation & employment.
Membership(s): Bavarian Booksellers & Publishers Association; Stock Exchange of German Booksellers.
Subjects: Career Development, Education
ISBN Prefix(es): 978-3-8214
Distribution Center: VuLL-Service GmbH fuer BW Bildung und Wissen, August-Borsig-str 11, 24783 Osterroenfeld *Tel:* (0331) 80 95-780 *Fax:* (0331) 80 95-777 *E-mail:* andreas.dausen@17111.com

Edition bi:libri
Triebstr 3, 80993 Munich
Tel: (089) 80 92 41 34 *Fax:* (089) 92 56 01 28
E-mail: info@edition-bilibri.de
Web Site: www.edition-bilibri.com
Key Personnel
Mng Dir: Dr Kristy Clark Koth *E-mail:* kk@edition-bilibri.de
Press & Marketing: Guel Dilek Schlieker *E-mail:* gs@edition-bilibri.de
Founded: 2004
Specialize in bilingual & multilingual books for preschool age & primary school age children.
ISBN Prefix(es): 978-3-938735
Foreign Rep(s): Edwin Mayr (Austria); Martin E Schnetzer (Switzerland); Juergen Sieberer (Austria)
Distribution Center: VMH Verlagsauslieferung, Max Hueber-Str 4, 85737 Ismaning *Tel:* (089) 9602-9603 *Fax:* (089) 9602-328 *E-mail:* orders@hueber.de

binooki OHG
Koepenickerstr 154a, 10997 Berlin
Tel: (030) 61 65 08 40 *Fax:* (030) 61 64 08 44
E-mail: info@binooki.com
Web Site: binooki.com
Key Personnel
Publisher: Inci Burhaniye; Selma Wels
Founded: 2011
Subjects: Fiction, Literature, Literary Criticism, Essays, Poetry
ISBN Prefix(es): 978-3-943562

Verlag fuer Bioenergetik und Naturheilkunde, see VBN-Verlag Luebeck

Birkhauser, *imprint of* Walter de Gruyter GmbH & Co KG

Birkner GmbH & Co KG
Subsidiary of Dumrath & Fassnacht KG
Winsbergring 38, 22525 Hamburg
Mailing Address: Postfach 54 07 50, 22507 Hamburg
Tel: (040) 800 80 1777 *Fax:* (040) 800 80 1902
E-mail: info@birkner.de
Web Site: www.birkner.de

Key Personnel
Mng Dir: Dr Christoph Dumrath; Olaf H Tonner
Founded: 1903
Subjects: Architecture & Interior Design, Engineering (General), Publishing & Book Trade Reference, Wine & Spirits, Printing, Woodworking
ISBN Prefix(es): 978-3-923543

Verlag Klaus Bittermann, see Edition Tiamat

BKmedia eV
Westheim 42, 93049 Regensburg
Tel: (0941) 3996705 *Fax:* (0941) 3996704
E-mail: info@bkmedia.info
Web Site: www.bkmedia.info
Subjects: Self-Help, Raja Yoga
ISBN Prefix(es): 978-3-939493

Blaetter Verlagsgesellschaft mbH
Torstr 178, 10115 Berlin
Mailing Address: Postfach 540246, 10042 Berlin
Tel: (030) 3088-3644; (030) 3088-3640
   Fax: (030) 3088-3645
E-mail: abo@blaetter.de; info@blaetter.de; redaktion@blaetter.de
Web Site: www.blaetter.de
Key Personnel
Dir: Annett Maengel *Tel:* (030) 3088-3643
   E-mail: annett.maengel@blaetter.de
Marketing & Sales: Daniel Leisegang *Tel:* (030) 3088-3646 *E-mail:* daniel.leisegang@blaetter.de
Subjects: Government, Political Science
ISBN Prefix(es): 978-3-9804925

BuchVertrieb Blank GmbH
Roehrmooser Str 16-20, 85256 Vierkirchen
Tel: (08139) 8 02 91-0 *Fax:* (08139) 8 02 91-20
E-mail: info@buchvertrieb-blank.de
Web Site: www.buchvertrieb-blank.de
Key Personnel
Chief Executive Officer: Ralph M Danna
   E-mail: ralph.danna@buchvertrieb-blank.de
Head, Sales: Oliver Draeger *E-mail:* oliver.draeger@buchvertrieb-blank.de
Subjects: History
ISBN Prefix(es): 978-3-937501

Blank Media, see BuchVertrieb Blank GmbH

Blanvalet, *imprint of* Verlagsgruppe Random House Bertelsmann

Blanvalet Verlag+
Imprint of Verlagsgruppe Random House Bertelsmann
Neumarkter Str 28, 81673 Munich
Tel: (089) 4136-0 *Toll Free Tel:* (0800) 500 33 22
   Fax: (089) 4136-3333
E-mail: kundenservice@randomhouse.de
Web Site: www.randomhouse.de/blanvalet
Key Personnel
Publishing Dir: Nicola Bartels
Foreign Rights Dir: Gesche Wendebourg *Tel:* (089) 4136-3313 *E-mail:* gesche.wendebourg@randomhouse.de
Head, Press & Public Relations: Astrid von Willmann *Tel:* (089) 4136-3318 *Fax:* (089) 4136-3453 *E-mail:* astrid.vonwillmann@randomhouse.de
Founded: 1935
Subjects: Biography, Memoirs, Nonfiction (General), Romance, Science Fiction, Fantasy, Thriller
ISBN Prefix(es): 978-3-7645

Verlag Die Blaue Eule
Annastr 74, 45130 Essen
Tel: (0201) 8 77 69 63 *Fax:* (0201) 8 77 69 64
E-mail: info@die-blaue-eule.de

Web Site: www.die-blaue-eule.de
Key Personnel
Publisher: Dr Werner L Hohmann
Founded: 1983
Specialize in scientific publications.
Membership(s): Boersenvereins des Deutschen Buchhandels eV; Mitglied des Verbandes der Verlage und Buchhandlungen in Nordrhein-Westfalen eV.
Subjects: Art, Education, History, Language Arts, Linguistics, Music, Dance, Philosophy, Psychology, Psychiatry, Science (General), Social Sciences, Sociology, Theology, Humanities
ISBN Prefix(es): 978-3-924368; 978-3-89206; 978-3-89924
Total Titles: 1,000 Print
Distributed by Engros Buchhandlung Dessauer; Freihofer AG Verlagsauslieferung Wissenschaft

Die Blauen Buecher (The Blue Books), *imprint of* Karl Robert Langewiesche Nachfolger Hans Koester Verlagsbuchhandlung KG

Blaukreuz-Verlag und Versandbuchhandel eK+
Sonderfelder Weg 15, 58513 Luedenscheid
Tel: (02351) 4324943 *Fax:* (02351) 4324945
E-mail: info@blaukreuz-verlag.de
Web Site: www.blaukreuz.de
Key Personnel
Mng Dir: Siegmar Lahme
Founded: 1892
Subjects: Health, Nutrition, Human Relations, Literature, Literary Criticism, Essays, Self-Help, Addiction & Assistance
ISBN Prefix(es): 978-3-920106; 978-3-89175
Number of titles published annually: 7 Print
Total Titles: 70 Audio
Distributed by Blaukreuz-Verlag Bern (Switzerland); BMK Wartburg Vertriebsges.mbH (Austria)
Distributor for Nicol-Verlag Kassel
Distribution Center: Chris Media GmbH, Staufenberg

Bleicher Verlag GmbH+
Weilimdorfer Str 76, 70839 Gerlingen
Mailing Address: Postfach 10 01 23, 70826 Gerlingen
Tel: (07156) 43 08-0 *Fax:* (07156) 43 08-27; (07156) 43 08-40
E-mail: info@bleicher-verlag.de
Web Site: www.bleicher-verlag.de
Key Personnel
Mng Dir: Evmarie Bartolitius *Tel:* (07156) 43 08 31 *E-mail:* bartolitius@bleicher-verlag.de
Production: Rainer Abel *Tel:* (07156) 43 08-20
Founded: 1968
Publisher of phone directories.
ISBN Prefix(es): 978-3-88350; 978-3-7953; 978-3-7988; 978-3-921097
Number of titles published annually: 20 Print
Subsidiaries: Hoffmann Verlag GmbH

Blessing, *imprint of* Verlagsgruppe Random House Bertelsmann

Karl Blessing Verlag
Imprint of Verlagsgruppe Random House Bertelsmann
Bayerstr 71-73, 80335 Munich
Tel: (089) 4136-0 *Toll Free Tel:* (0800) 500 33 22
   Fax: (089) 4136-3333
E-mail: kundenservice@randomhouse.de
Web Site: www.randomhouse.de/blessing
Key Personnel
Publisher: Ulrich Genzler
Editor-in-Chief: Holger Kuntze
Foreign Rights Dir: Gesche Wendebourg *Tel:* (089) 4136-3313 *E-mail:* gesche.wendebourg@randomhouse.de

Press: Elisabeth C Bayer *Tel:* (089) 4136-3787 *Fax:* (089) 4136-3730 *E-mail:* elisabeth.bayer@blessing-verlag.de
Founded: 1996
Subjects: Fiction, Nonfiction (General)
ISBN Prefix(es): 978-3-89667

BLISTA, see Deutsche Blinden-Bibliothek

bloomoon, *imprint of* arsEdition GmbH

Eberhard Blottner Verlag GmbH+
Aarstr 254, 65232 Taunusstein
Mailing Address: Postfach 1104, 65219 Taunusstein
Tel: (06128) 2 36 00 *Fax:* (06128) 2 11 80
E-mail: blottner@blottner.de
Web Site: www.blottner.de
Key Personnel
Mng Dir: Britta Blottner
Founded: 1988
Subjects: Architecture & Interior Design, Crafts, Games, Hobbies, Earth Sciences, Environmental Studies, House & Home
ISBN Prefix(es): 978-3-89367
Total Titles: 28 Print
Associate Companies: Blottner Fachverlag GmbH & Co KG
Foreign Rep(s): Othmar Edelmann GmbH (Wolfgang Edelmann & Michael Krizak) (Austria); Axel Kueppers (Germany, Luxembourg)
Distribution Center: Koch, Neff & Oetinger Verlagsauslieferung GmbH, Industriestr 23, 70565 Stuttgart, Contact: Christina Schellenberger *E-mail:* blottner@kno-va.de
Mohr Morawa Buchvertrieb GmbH, Sulzengasse 2, 1230 Vienna, Austria *Tel:* (01) 688 14-0 *Fax:* (01) 688 71 30 *E-mail:* momo@mohrmorawa.at *Web Site:* www.mohrmorawa.at

Blumenbar, *imprint of* Aufbau Verlag GmbH & Co KG

Blumenbar
Imprint of Aufbau Verlag GmbH & Co KG
Prinzenstr 85, 10969 Berlin
Tel: (030) 28394 0 *Fax:* (030) 28394-100
E-mail: info@aufbau-verlag.de
Web Site: www.aufbau-verlag.de
Key Personnel
Publishing Dir: Constanze Neumann
Mng Dir: Matthias Koch
Subjects: Biography, Memoirs, Fiction, Government, Political Science, Humor, Mysteries, Suspense, Nonfiction (General), Social Sciences, Sociology
ISBN Prefix(es): 978-3-936738

BLV Buchverlag GmbH & Co KG+
Albrechtstr 14, 80636 Munich
Tel: (089) 12 02 12-0 *Fax:* (089) 12 02 12-120
E-mail: blv-verlag@blv.de
Web Site: www.blvverlag.de
Key Personnel
Chief Executive Officer: Hans Mueller
Publishing Dir: Antje Wolf *Tel:* (089) 12 02 12-408 *E-mail:* antje.wolf@blv.de
Foreign Rights: Franziska Stockerer *Tel:* (089) 12 02 12-416 *Fax:* (089) 12 02 12-415 *E-mail:* franziska.stockerer@blv.de
Press & Events: Lisa Glassner *Tel:* (089) 12 02 12-420 *E-mail:* lisa.glassner@blv.de
Founded: 1946
Publisher of illustrated reference books.
Subjects: Agriculture, Animals, Pets, Astronomy, Child Care & Development, Cookery, Crafts, Games, Hobbies, Gardening, Plants, Health, Nutrition, Humor, Maritime, Natural History, Outdoor Recreation, Sports, Athletics

ISBN Prefix(es): 978-3-405 (BLV Verlagsgesellschaft mbH); 978-3-331; 978-3-8354 (BLV Buchverlag GmbH & Co KG)
Number of titles published annually: 120 Print
Total Titles: 600 Print
Foreign Rep(s): Michel Guyot (Switzerland); Erich Neuhold (Austria); Harald Rumpold (Austria)
Distribution Center: VVA Vereinigte Verlagsauslieferung, An der Autobahn 100, 33333 Guetersloh *Fax:* (05241) 80-4 03 90
Dr Franz Hain Verlagsauslieferungen GmbH, Dr-Otto-Neurath-Gasse 5, 1220 Vienna, Austria *Tel:* (01) 2 82 65 65-77 *Fax:* (01) 2 82 52 82 *E-mail:* bestell@hain.at
Grafus GmbH, Toni Eber Str Nr 5, 39100 Bozen BZ, Italy *Tel:* (0471) 08 64 44 *Fax:* (0471) 08 64 55 *E-mail:* order@grafus.it *Web Site:* www.athesiabuch.it (South Tyrol)
Schweizer Buchzentrum, Industriestr Ost 10, 4614 Haegendorf, Switzerland *Tel:* (062) 2 09 26 26 *Fax:* (062) 2 09 26 27 *E-mail:* kundendienst@buchzentrum.ch *Web Site:* www.buchzentrum.ch

BLV Verlagsgesellschaft mbH, see BLV Buchverlag GmbH & Co KG

BOCK + HERCHEN Verlag
Rathausplatz 2-4, 53604 Bad Honnef
Mailing Address: Postfach 11 45, 53581 Bad Honnef
Tel: (02224) 57 75 *Fax:* (02224) 7 83 10
E-mail: info@bock-und-herchen.de
Web Site: www.bock-und-herchen.de
Key Personnel
Owner: Andreas Bock
Founded: 1977
Subjects: Library & Information Sciences, Science (General)
ISBN Prefix(es): 978-3-88347

Bocola Verlag GmbH
Ruengsdorfer Str 8, 53173 Bonn
Tel: (0228) 9106174-0 *Fax:* (0228) 9106174-29
E-mail: info@bocola.de
Web Site: www.bocola.de
Key Personnel
Mng Dir: Achim Dressler
Founded: 2006
ISBN Prefix(es): 978-3-939625

Firma Boehlau Verlag GmbH & Cie+
Ursulaplatz 1, 50668 Cologne
Tel: (0221) 91390-0 *Fax:* (0221) 91390-11
E-mail: info@boehlau.de; vertrieb@boehlau.de
Web Site: www.boehlau.de; www.boehlau-verlag.com
Key Personnel
Mng Dir: Dr Peter Rauch *Tel:* (0330) 2427-312 *E-mail:* peter.rauch@boehlau.at
Press & Public Relations: Sabine Rehorst *Tel:* (0221) 91390-16
Founded: 1951
Subjects: Anthropology, Archaeology, Art, Biological Sciences, Education, History, Journalism, Language Arts, Linguistics, Law, Philosophy, Social Sciences, Sociology, Theology, Women's Studies
ISBN Prefix(es): 978-3-412
Number of titles published annually: 180 Print
Total Titles: 1,800 Print
Branch Office(s)
Boehlau Verlag GmbH & Cie, Eisfeld 5, 99423 Weimar *Tel:* (03643) 85 15 70
Boehlau Verlag GmbH, Wiesingerstr 1, 1010 Vienna, Austria *Tel:* (01) 33024270 *Fax:* (01) 3302432 *E-mail:* boehlau@boehlau.at *Web Site:* www.boehlau.at
Foreign Rep(s): Michael Beranek (Western Austria); Dessauer (Claudia Gyr & Stefan Reiss) (Switzerland); Roland Fuerst (Austria); Guenther Lintschinger (Eastern Austria)

Distribution Center: Brockhaus/Commission, Kreidlerstr 9, 70806 Kornwestheim *Tel:* (07154) 1327-75 *Fax:* (07154) 1327-13 *E-mail:* boehlau@brocom.de
Mohr Morawa Buchvertrieb GmbH, Sulzengasse 2, 1230 Vienna, Austria *Tel:* (01) 680 14-0 *Fax:* (01) 680 71 30 *E-mail:* momo@mohrmorawa.at *Web Site:* www.mohrmorawa.at
Buchzentrum AG, Industriestr Ost 10, 4614 Haegendorf, Switzerland *Tel:* (062) 209 26 27
Dessauer, Raffelstr 32, 8045 Zurich, Switzerland *Tel:* (044) 466 96 96 *Fax:* (044) 466 96 69 *E-mail:* dessauer@dessauer.ch *Web Site:* www.dessauer.ch
Orders to: Koch, Neff & Oetinger Verlagsauslieferung GmbH, Industriestr 23, 70565 Stuttgart

Boer Verlag+
Adalmuntstr 17, 82284 Grafrath
Tel: (08144) 998781 *Fax:* (08144) 998782
Web Site: www.boerverlag.de
Key Personnel
Owner: Dr Klaus Boer *E-mail:* klaus.boer@boerverlag.de
Founded: 1984
Subjects: Art, History, Literature, Literary Criticism, Essays, Philosophy
ISBN Prefix(es): 978-3-924963
Orders to: Buchvertrieb Grimmstr, Saalburgstr 3, 12099 Berlin

Boerm Bruckmeier Verlag GmbH
Noerdliche Muenchner Str 28, 82031 Gruenwald
Tel: (089) 697781-0 *Fax:* (089) 697781-28
E-mail: info@media4u.com
Web Site: www.media4u.com/de
Key Personnel
Co-Founder & Mng Dir: Dr Philipp Boerm
Co-Founder: Dr Andreas Bruckmeier
Founded: 1992
Subjects: Medicine, Nursing, Dentistry, Psychology, Psychiatry, Alternative Medicine
ISBN Prefix(es): 978-1-59103; 978-3-929785; 978-3-89862
U.S. Office(s): Boerm Bruckmeier Publishing LLC, 111 1/2 Eucalyptus Dr, El Segundo, CA 90245, United States *Tel:* 310-414-8300 *Fax:* 310-414-8301 *E-mail:* service@media4u.com *Web Site:* www.media4u.com/us

Boersenbuchverlag
Am Eulenhof 14, 95326 Kulmbach
Tel: (09221) 9051-304
E-mail: kontakt@plassen.de; buecher@plassen.de (manuscript submission)
Web Site: www.plassen-buchverlage.de/boersenbuchverlag.htm
Founded: 1989
Subjects: Economics, Finance, Investments, Stock Market
ISBN Prefix(es): 978-3-922669; 978-3-938350; 978-3-941493
Parent Company: Plassen Buchverlage
Ultimate Parent Company: Boersenmedien AG

Edition Boiselle+
Armbruststr 11, 67346 Speyer
Tel: (06232) 100 76-20 *Fax:* (06232) 100 76-29
E-mail: info@editionboiselle.de
Web Site: www.editionboiselle.de
Key Personnel
Mng Dir: Gabriele Boiselle *Tel:* (06232) 100 76-22 *E-mail:* g.boiselle@editionboiselle.de
Founded: 1990
Subjects: Animals, Pets, Equestrian
ISBN Prefix(es): 978-3-927589
Distributed by Buecher Zentrum (Austria); Islandpferdehof Plarenga (Switzerland); Mias Ridsport (Sweden)

Boje Verlag, *imprint of* Bastei Luebbe GmbH & Co KG

Bolanz Verlag
Moettelistr 11, 88045 Friedrichshafen
Tel: (07541) 399069-0 *Fax:* (07541) 399069-99
E-mail: info@bolanz.de
Web Site: www.bolanz.de
Key Personnel
Contact: Bernhard Bolanz
Christian publisher. Specialize in calendars.
Membership(s): Boersenverein des Deutschen
   Buchhandels.
Subjects: Religion - Other
ISBN Prefix(es): 978-3-927744; 978-3-932640;
   978-3-936673; 978-3-86603
Bookshop(s): Ailingerstr 11, 88046
   Friedrichshafen *Tel:* (07541) 27027
   E-mail: buecherecke.fn@bolanz.de
Distribution Center: BMK Wartburg Vertriebs-
   gesellschaft mbH, Trautsongasse 65, 1082 Vi-
   enna, Austria *Tel:* (01) 40 23 946 *Fax:* (01)
   40 89 905 *E-mail:* wartburg@bmk.at *Web
   Site:* www.bmk.at
   L'Evangile Pour Tous, BP 21, 26160 La Be-
   gude de Mazenc, France *Tel:* 06 74 51 50
   55 *Fax:* 04 75 51 54 98 *E-mail:* info@
   evangilepourtous.com *Web Site:* www.
   evangilepourtous.com

CB-Verlag Carl Boldt
Baseler Str 80, 12205 Berlin
Mailing Address: Postfach 45 02 07, 12172
   Berlin
Tel: (030) 833 70 87 *Fax:* (030) 833 91 25
E-mail: mail@cb-verlag.de
Web Site: cb-verlag.de
Key Personnel
Publisher: Peter Gesellius
Founded: 1904
Subjects: Law
ISBN Prefix(es): 978-3-920731

Bonifatius GmbH Druck-Buch-Verlag+
Karl-Schurz Str 26, 33100 Paderborn
Mailing Address: Postfach 12 80, 33042 Pader-
   born
Tel: (05251) 153-0 *Fax:* (05251) 153-104
E-mail: mail@bonifatius.de
Web Site: www.bonifatius.de
Key Personnel
Mng Dir: Eckhard Boelke *Tel:* (05251) 153-300
   E-mail: eckhard.boelke@bonifatius.de; Rolf
   Pitsch *Tel:* (05251) 153-100 *E-mail:* rolf.
   pitsch@bonifatius.de
Sales Manager: Reinhard Kuhn *Tel:* (05251) 153-
   302 *E-mail:* reinhard.kuhn@bonifatius.de
Founded: 1869
Subjects: Art, Environmental Studies, Literature,
   Literary Criticism, Essays, Music, Dance, Reli-
   gion - Catholic, Theology
ISBN Prefix(es): 978-3-87088; 978-3-89710
Imprints: Creator; Kontur

Books on African Studies+
Roemerstr 66, 69115 Heidelberg
Tel: (06221) 41 18 61; (06221) 4 33 22 59
   Fax: (06221) 47 39 46; (06221) 4 34 81 87
Web Site: www.books-on-african-studies.com
Key Personnel
Mng Dir: Jerry Bedu-Addo *E-mail:* jbeduaddo@
   aol.com
Founded: 1982
Also a distributor.
Subjects: Africa
ISBN Prefix(es): 978-3-927198
Associate Companies: Timbuktu
Branch Office(s)
PO Box BT, 328, Tema, Ghana *Tel:* (022) 206135
   Fax: (022) 206134 *E-mail:* beaddo@ghana.com
Book Club(s): African Literature Club, Contact:
   Eva Groppenbaecher *E-mail:* evagroppe@aol.
   com

Bookspot Verlag GmbH
Paul-Gerhardt-Allee 46, 81245 Munich
Tel: (089) 318905-0 *Fax:* (089) 318905-86
E-mail: info@bookspot.de
Web Site: blog.bookspot.de
Key Personnel
Mng Dir: Burkhard P Bierschenck
Founded: 2002
Subjects: Biography, Memoirs, Fiction, Myster-
   ies, Suspense, Poetry, Romance, Crime Thriller,
   Prose
ISBN Prefix(es): 978-3-937357
Imprints: Edition Aglaia; ArtEdition; Buntstein
   Verlag; Edition Carat; DrachenStern Verlag;
   Edition P&L; Edition 211

Richard Boorberg Verlag GmbH & Co KG
Scharrstr 2, 70563 Stuttgart
Tel: (0711) 73 85-0 *Fax:* (0711) 73 85-100
E-mail: mail@boorberg.de
Web Site: www.boorberg.de
Key Personnel
Mng Dir: Dr Berndt Oesterhelt; Markus Ott
Product Development Manager: Hermann Ruck-
   deschel
Customer Service: Sabine Fuchs *Tel:* (0711)
   73 85-343 *Fax:* (0711) 73 85-315 *E-mail:* s.
   fuchs@boorberg.de
Marketing & Sales: Karl-Heinz Schafmeister
Founded: 1927
Subjects: Law
ISBN Prefix(es): 978-3-415
Subsidiaries: Josef Moll Verlag GmbH & Co
Branch Office(s)
Frankfurter Allee 70, 10247 Berlin *Tel:* 0800 73
   85 700 *Fax:* 0800 73 85 800
Martin-Luther-Str 23, 01099 Dresden *Toll Free
   Tel:* 0800 73 85 700 *Toll Free Fax:* 0800 73 85
   800
Kestnerstr 44, 30159 Hannover *Toll Free
   Tel:* 0800 73 85 700 *Toll Free Fax:* 0800 73
   85 800
Levelingstr 6a, 81673 Munich *Tel:* (089) 43 60
   00-0 *Fax:* (089) 43 61 564
Schlachthofstr 8-10, 99423 Weimar *Toll Free
   Tel:* 0800 73 85 700 *Toll Free Fax:* 0800 73
   85 800

Boosey & Hawkes Bote & Bock GmbH+
Luetzowufer 26, 10787 Berlin
Tel: (030) 2500 1300 *Fax:* (030) 2500 1399
E-mail: musikverlag@boosey.com
Web Site: www.boosey.com/publishing
Key Personnel
Mng Dir: Winfried Jacobs *Tel:* (030) 2500 1310
   Fax: (030) 2500 1319 *E-mail:* winfried.
   jacobs@boosey.com
Publishing Dir: Janis Susskind *E-mail:* janis.
   susskind@boosey.com
Head, Rights: Tilman Kannegiesser-Strohmeier
   Tel: (030) 2500 1312 *E-mail:* tilman.
   kannegiesser@boosey.com
Permissions: Birgit Staehle *Tel:* (030) 2500 1333
   E-mail: birgit.staehle@boosey.com
Founded: 1838
Primarily a music store.
Subjects: Music, Dance
ISBN Prefix(es): 978-3-7931; 978-3-87090
Branch Office(s)
Boosey & Hawkes Music Publishers Ltd, Ald-
   wych House, 71-91 Aldwych, London W2CB
   4HN, United Kingdom *Tel:* (020) 7054 7200
   Fax: (020) 7054 7290 *E-mail:* marketing@
   boosey.com
U.S. Office(s): Boosey & Hawkes Inc, 229 W
   28 St, New York, NY 10001-5915, United
   States *Tel:* 212-358-5300 *Fax:* 212-358-5305
   E-mail: info.ny@boosey.com

Born-Verlag+
Leuschnerstr 74, 34134 Kassel

Tel: (0561) 4095-107; (0561) 4095-0 *Fax:* (0561)
   4095-207
E-mail: kontakt@bornverlag.de
Web Site: www.bornverlag.de
Key Personnel
Chair: Hartmut Kaemfer
Mng Dir: Simon Schuh
Publishing Coordinator: Bettina Bohlken
   E-mail: bettina.bohlken@bornverlag.de
Founded: 1898
Subjects: Religion - Catholic, Religion - Protes-
   tant
ISBN Prefix(es): 978-3-87092
Distribution Center: ChrisMedia GmbH,
   Robert-Bosch-Str 10, 35460 Staufenberg
   Tel: (06406) 8346-100 *Fax:* (06406) 8346-110
   E-mail: bestellung@chrismedia24.de
   BMK-Buchauslieferung, Trautsongasse 8, Post-
   fach 65, 1082 Vienna, Austria *Tel:* (01) 405 93
   71 *Fax:* (01) 408 99 05
   Brunnen-Verlag Basel, Wallstr 6, 4002 Basel,
   Switzerland *Tel:* (061) 295 60 00 *Fax:* (061)
   295 60 69

Gustav Bosse GmbH & Co KG+
Division of Baerenreiter Verlag
Heinrich-Schuetz-Allee 35, 34131 Kassel
Tel: (0561) 31 05 0 *Fax:* (0561) 31 05 310;
   (0561) 3105-177 (orders)
E-mail: info@bosse-verlag.de
Web Site: www.bosse-verlag.de
Key Personnel
Mng Dir: Leonhard Scheuch
Manager: Barbara Scheuch-Voetterle
Editor: Berthold Kloss *Tel:* (0561) 31 051-1 41
   E-mail: kloss@bosse-verlag.de
Press: Johannes Mundry *Tel:* (0561) 31 05-1 54
   E-mail: mundry@baerenreiter.com
Founded: 1912
Specialize in music education.
Subjects: Education, Music, Dance
ISBN Prefix(es): 978-3-7649
Subsidiaries: Junior Band; Jekiss; Tina & Tobi;
   Bosse HITs a cappella; Choir News
Distributed by Barenreiter Ltd (UK); Barenreiter
   Verlag Basel AG (Switzerland)

Bouvier Verlag+
c/o Universitaetsbuchhandlung Bouvier Verpach-
   tungs GmbH, Fuerstenstr 3, 53111 Bonn
Tel: (0228) 3 91 82 10 *Fax:* (0228) 3 91 82 21
E-mail: info@bouvier-verlag.de
Web Site: www.bouvier-verlag.de
Key Personnel
Mng Dir: Thomas Grundmann
Founded: 1828
Subjects: Art, Government, Political Science, His-
   tory, Literature, Literary Criticism, Essays,
   Philosophy, Psychology, Psychiatry, Regional
   Interests, Entertainment, Science of Literature
ISBN Prefix(es): 978-3-416
Total Titles: 20 Print
Branch Office(s)
Pferdmengesstr 12, 50968 Cologne

Boyens Buchverlag GmbH & Co KG+
Wulf-Isebrand-Platz 1-3, 25746 Heide
Tel: (0481) 6886-650 *Fax:* (0481) 6886-90650
E-mail: buchverlag@boyens-medien.de
Web Site: buchverlag.boyens-medien.de
Key Personnel
Mng Dir: Inken Boyens; Soenke Boyens
Publishing Manager: Bernd Rachuth *Tel:* (0481)
   6886-651
Sales: Sylvia Scholz *Tel:* (0481) 6886-653
   E-mail: sylvia.scholz@boyens-medien.de
Founded: 1869
Subjects: Art, Cookery, Literature, Literary Crit-
   icism, Essays, Regional Interests, Religion -
   Other
ISBN Prefix(es): 978-3-8042
Subsidiaries: Brunsbuetteler Zeitung GmbH

Branch Office(s)
Albersdorf
Busum
Marne
Meldorf Wesselburen
St Michaelisdorn
Distribution Center: VuLL-Service GmbH,
August-Borsig-Str 11, 24783 Osterroenfeld,
Contact: Andreas Clausen *Tel:* (04331) 80 95-
781 *Fax:* (04331) 80 95-777 *E-mail:* Andreas.
Clausen@17111.com

Bramann-Verlag und Beratung
Alt Erlenbach 17, 60437 Frankfurt
Tel: (06101) 30 78 60 *Fax:* (06101) 30 78 80
E-mail: info@bramann.de
Web Site: www.bramann.de
Key Personnel
Owner: Dr Klaus-Wilhelm Bramann
Founded: 1988
Subjects: Media Industry
ISBN Prefix(es): 978-3-934054

Brandes & Apsel Verlag+
Scheidswaldstr 22, 60385 Frankfurt am Main
Tel: (069) 272 995 17 0 *Fax:* (069) 272 995 17
10
E-mail: info@brandes-apsel.de; presse@brandes-
apsel.de; vertrieb@brandes-apsel.de
Web Site: www.brandes-apsel-verlag.de
Key Personnel
Mng Dir: Roland Apsel; Dr Volkhard Brandes
Founded: 1986
Subjects: Anthropology, Developing Countries,
Drama, Theater, Education, Ethnicity, Fiction,
Government, Political Science, Human Rela-
tions, Literature, Literary Criticism, Essays,
Music, Dance, Nonfiction (General), Poetry,
Psychology, Psychiatry, Social Sciences, So-
ciology, Travel & Tourism, Women's Studies,
Immigration, Jewish Life, Psychoanalysis, Self
Psychology, Sigmund Freud
ISBN Prefix(es): 978-3-925798; 978-3-86099
Number of titles published annually: 40 Print
Total Titles: 300 Print
Foreign Rep(s): Sebastian Graf (Switzerland);
Helga Schuster (Austria)
Distribution Center: Prolit Verlagsauslieferung
GmbH, Siemensstr 16, 35461 Fernwald, Con-
tact: Heike Schenk-Schwarzer *Tel:* (0641) 943
93-203; (0641) 943 93-23 *E-mail:* h.schenk-
schwarzer@prolit.de (Germany & Austria)
Scheidegger & Co AG, c/o AVA Verlagsauslief-
ung AG, Centralweg 16, 8910 Affoltern am
Albis, Switzerland *Tel:* (044) 762 42 50

Oscar Brandstetter Verlag GmbH & Co KG+
Nerotal 66, 65193 Wiesbaden
Tel: (0611) 991200 *Fax:* (0611) 9912019
E-mail: info@brandstetter-verlag.de
Web Site: www.brandstetter-verlag.de
Key Personnel
Mng Dir & Publishing Dir: Guenther H Froehlen
Founded: 1862
Subjects: Chemistry, Chemical Engineering, Com-
munications, Computer Science, Economics,
Electronics, Electrical Engineering, Engineer-
ing (General), Language Arts, Linguistics, Law,
Medicine, Nursing, Dentistry, Physical Sci-
ences, Technology
ISBN Prefix(es): 978-3-87097
Shipping Address: Koch, Neff & Oetinger Ver-
lagsauslieferung GmbH, Industriestr 23, 70565
Stuttgart, Contact: Erika Vogelmann
Warehouse: Koch, Neff & Oetinger & Co, Ver-
lagsauslieferung Smlt, 70551 Stuttgart, Con-
tact: Erika Vogelmann *Tel:* (0711) 78992123
Fax: (0711) 78991010
Orders to: Koch, Neff & Oetinger & Co, Ver-
lagsauslieferung Smlt, 70551 Stuttgart, Con-
tact: Erika Vogelmann *Tel:* (0711) 78992123
Fax: (0711) 78991010

Aspekter der Brasilienkunde, *imprint of*
Brasilienkunde-Verlag

Brasilienkunde-Verlag
Sunderstr 15, 49497 Mettingen
Tel: (05452) 4598 *Fax:* (05452) 4357
E-mail: brasilien@t-online.de
Web Site: www.brasilienkunde.de
Key Personnel
Mng Dir, Rights & Permissions: P Osmar
Gogolok
Founded: 1979
Subjects: Ethnicity, Foreign Countries, Regional
Interests, Religion - Other, Social Sciences, So-
ciology
ISBN Prefix(es): 978-3-88559
Parent Company: Institut fuer Brasilienkunde eV
Imprints: Aspekter der Brasilienkunde; BTB

Edition Braus GmbH
Prinzenstr 85 D, 10969 Berlin
Tel: (030) 28394-234 *Fax:* (030) 28394-100
E-mail: information@editionbraus.de
Web Site: www.editionbraus.de
Key Personnel
Publisher: Jochen Stamm
Subjects: Architecture & Interior Design, Art,
Photography, Berlin, Culture
ISBN Prefix(es): 978-3-89904; 978-3-926318

Breitkopf & Hartel KG+
Walkmuehlstr 52, 65195 Wiesbaden
Mailing Address: Postfach 1707, 65007 Wies-
baden
Tel: (0611) 450080 *Fax:* (0611) 45008 59; (0611)
45008 60; (0611) 45008 61
E-mail: info@breitkopf.com; sales@breitkopf.com
Web Site: www.breitkopf; www.breitkopf.de
Key Personnel
Mng Dir: Nick Pfefferkorn
Editorial: Friedhelm Pramschuefer
International Rights: Vivian Rehman
E-mail: rehman@breitkopf.com
Public Relations: Mr Florian Kleidorfer
Founded: 1719
Music publisher.
Membership(s): BMI; GEMA; MPA.
Subjects: Music, Dance
ISBN Prefix(es): 978-3-7651
Associate Companies: Deutscher Verlag fuer
Musik Leipzig GmbH
Branch Office(s)
Obere Waldstr 30, 65232 Taunusstein
Tel: (06128) 9663 0 *Fax:* (06128) 9663 50;
(06128) 966360
Paris, France, Contact: Mr Farid Aich *Tel:* 01 48
01 01 33 *Fax:* 01 48 01 01 66
48 Great Marlborough St, London W1F 7BB,
United Kingdom, Trade Sales Contact: David
Barker *Tel:* (07778) 574319 *Fax:* (07778)
574319

Breklumer Verlag
Rote Pforte 1, 25813 Husum
Mailing Address: Postfach 1505, 25805 Husum
Tel: (04841) 9041800
E-mail: bv@breklumer.de
Web Site: www.breklumer.de
Key Personnel
Publisher: Hanna Siegel
Founded: 1875
Subjects: Religion - Other
ISBN Prefix(es): 978-3-7793
Associate Companies: Breklumer Print-
Service, Borsbueller Ring 25, 25821 Breklum
Tel: (04671) 91 00 0 *Fax:* (04671) 91 00 30
E-mail: info@breklumer-print-service.com *Web
Site:* www.breklumer-print-service.com

Joh Brendow & Sohn Verlag GmbH+
Gutenbergstr 1, 47443 Moers

Tel: (02841) 809 201; (02841) 809 0
Fax: (02841) 809 210; (02841) 809 291
E-mail: info-verlag@brendow.de; service@
brendow-verlag.de
Web Site: www.brendow.de; www.brendow-verlag.
de
Key Personnel
Mng Dir: Hans-Dieter Holthuis
Marketing: Kai P Treuner
Founded: 1849
Subjects: Fiction, Humor, Nonfiction (General),
Religion - Other
ISBN Prefix(es): 978-3-87067; 978-3-86506
Parent Company: Brendow-Gruppe
Associate Companies: Firma Blank KG, Wein-
garten; Harfe-Printmedien, Bad-Blankenburg

Verlag Das Brennglas GmbH+
Hernsterstr 26, 97892 Kreuzwertheim
Tel: (09391) 50 42 36 *Fax:* (09391) 50 42 37
E-mail: info@brennglas.com
Web Site: www.brennglas.com
Key Personnel
Mng Dir: German Murer
Founded: 2001
Subjects: Animals, Pets, Cookery, Health, Nutri-
tion, Animal Welfare, Vegan Cuisine
ISBN Prefix(es): 978-3-9809855

Brentano-Gesellschaft Frankfurt/M mbh
Grosser Hirschgraben 15, 60311 Frankfurt
Tel: (069) 13377-177 *Fax:* (069) 13377-175
E-mail: info@brentano-gesellschaft.de
Web Site: www.brentano-gesellschaft.de
Key Personnel
Mng Dir: Dr Uwe Frank
Subjects: Poetry
ISBN Prefix(es): 978-3-933800

Brigg Verlag Franz-Josef Buechler KG
Beilingerstr 21, 86316 Friedberg
Tel: (0821) 78 09 46 60 *Fax:* (0821) 78 09 46 61
E-mail: info@brigg-verlag.de
Web Site: www.brigg-verlag.de
Key Personnel
Owner: Franz-Josef Buechler
Founded: 1950
ISBN Prefix(es): 978-3-95660

Brighton Verlag
Strohgasse 8, Gundersheim 67598
Tel: (0152) 531 273 16 *Fax:* (06735) 941 445
E-mail: info@brightonverlag.com
Web Site: www.brightonverlag.com
Founded: 2005
Subjects: Biography, Memoirs, Fiction, Health,
Nutrition, Poetry, Science Fiction, Fantasy, En-
glish Books
ISBN Prefix(es): 978-3-942200

Brinkmann & Bose Verlag
Leuschnerdamm 13, 10999 Berlin
Tel: (030) 615-48-92
E-mail: brinkmann_bose@t-online.de
Web Site: www.brinkmann-bose.de
ISBN Prefix(es): 978-3-922660; 978-3-940048

Verlag Ekkehard & Ulrich Brockhaus KG
Am Wolfshahn 31, 42117 Wuppertal
Tel: (0202) 44 74 74; (0172) 2 55 59 61 (cell)
Fax: (0202) 42 82 82
E-mail: mail@verlag-brockhaus.de
Web Site: www.verlag-brockhaus.de
Key Personnel
Publisher: Ekkehard Brockhaus
Subjects: Genealogy, Cultural History
ISBN Prefix(es): 978-3-930132

Brockhaus Kommissionsgeschaeft GmbH
Kreidlerstr 9, 70806 Kornwestheim
Tel: (07154) 13270 *Fax:* (07154) 132713

E-mail: info@brocom.de
Web Site: www.brocom.de
Key Personnel
Mng Dir: Joachim Bachmann; Matthias Heinrich
Founded: 1827
Subjects: Cookery, Geography, Geology, Nonfiction (General), Self-Help
ISBN Prefix(es): 978-3-87103

Bruckmann Verlag GmbH+
Infanteriestr 11a, 80797 Munich
Tel: (089) 130699-0 *Fax:* (089) 130699-100
E-mail: info@bruckmann.de
Web Site: bruckmann.de
Key Personnel
Mng Dir: Clemens Schuessler *Tel:* (089) 130699-220 *Fax:* (089) 130699-200 *E-mail:* verlagsleitung@verlagshaus.de; Hans-Joachim Hartmann *Tel:* (089) 130699-260 *Fax:* (089) 130699-700 *E-mail:* hans-joachim.hartmann@verlagshaus.de
Book Program Manager: Stefanie Penck *Tel:* (089) 130699-610 *Fax:* (089) 130699-600 *E-mail:* stefanie.penck@verlagshaus.de
Senior Product Manager: Joachim Hellmuth *Tel:* (089) 130699-685 *Fax:* (089) 130699-600 *E-mail:* joachim.hellmuth@bruckmann.de; Ulrich Jahn *Tel:* (089) 130699-674 *Fax:* (089) 130699-600 *E-mail:* ulrich.jahn@bruckmann.de; Dr Gerhard Hirtlreiter *Tel:* (089) 130699-651 *Fax:* (089) 130699-600 *E-mail:* gerhard.hirtlreiter@bruckmann.de
Founded: 1858
Membership(s): TR-Verlagsunion GmbH.
Subjects: Art, Film, Video, Gardening, Plants, History, Humor, Outdoor Recreation, Regional Interests, Science (General), Sports, Athletics, Travel & Tourism, Cycling, Hiking, Skiing
ISBN Prefix(es): 978-3-7654; 978-3-932785
Parent Company: GeraNova Bruckmann Verlagshaus GmbH
Associate Companies: J Berg Verlag; Bucher Verlag; Christian Verlag; Frederking & Thaler; GeraMond Verlag
Distribution Center: Verlegerdienst Muenchen GmbH, Gutenbergstr 1, 82205 Gilching *Tel:* (08105) 388106 *Fax:* (08105) 388187 *E-mail:* verlagshaus@verlegerdienst.de
Mohr Morawa Buchvertrieb GmbH, Sulzengasse 2, 1230 Vienna, Austria *Tel:* (01) 680 14-0 *Fax:* (01) 688 71 30 *E-mail:* momo@mohrmorawa.at *Web Site:* www.mohrmorawa.at
Grafus GmbH SRL Buchauslieferung, Toni-Ebner-Str 5, 39100 Bozen, Italy *Tel:* (047) 86433 *Fax:* (047) 86456 *E-mail:* info@grafus.it (South Tyrol)
Willems Adventure, Honderland 120, 2676 LT Maasdijk, Netherlands *Tel:* (088) 599 0140 *Fax:* (088) 599 0141 *E-mail:* info@willemsadventure.nl
Buchzentrum AG, Industrie Ost, 4614 Haegendorf, Switzerland *Tel:* (062) 209 2701 *Fax:* (062) 209 2788 *E-mail:* kundendienst@buchzentrum.ch

Brunnen Verlag GmbH+
Gottlieb-Daimler-Str 22, 35398 Giessen
Tel: (0641) 6059-0 *Fax:* (0641) 6059-100
E-mail: info@brunnen-verlag.de
Web Site: www.brunnen-verlag.de
Key Personnel
Mng Dir: Detlef Holtgrefe
E-mail: geschaeftsleitung@brunnen-verlag.de
Sales Manager/Marketing: Reinhard Engeln *Tel:* (0641) 6059-120 *E-mail:* reinhard.engeln@brunnen-verlag.de
International Rights: Gabriele Herling *Tel:* (0641) 6059-173 *E-mail:* gabriele.herling@brunnen-verlag.de
Press, Public Relations & International Rights: Ralf Tibusek *Tel:* (0641) 6059-170 *E-mail:* ralf.tibusek@brunnen-verlag.de

Production: Eva Joneleit *Tel:* (0641) 6059-182 *E-mail:* herstellung@brunnen-verlag.de
Founded: 1919
Subjects: Biblical Studies, Biography, Memoirs, Fiction, Inspirational, Spirituality, Music, Dance, Nonfiction (General), Religion - Protestant, Religion - Other, Theology
ISBN Prefix(es): 978-3-7655
Number of titles published annually: 150 Print
Total Titles: 800 Print
Associate Companies: Brunnen Verlag, Basel, Switzerland
Foreign Rights: Claudia Boehme Rights & Literary Agency - Publishing Consultant (worldwide); Bookbank, SL (Alicia Gonzales Sterling) (Spanish); Bruecke Literary Agency (Ms Young Sun Park) (Korea); Brunnen International Rights (worldwide); Eurobuk (Dr Min-Su Lee) (Korea)
Distribution Center: ChrisMedia, Robert-Bosch-Str 10, 35460 Staufenberg *Tel:* (06406) 8346-0 *Fax:* (06406) 8346-125 *E-mail:* info@chrismedia24.de

BTB, *imprint of* Brasilienkunde-Verlag

btb, *imprint of* Verlagsgruppe Random House Bertelsmann

btb Verlag
Imprint of Verlagsgruppe Random House Bertelsmann
Neumarkter Str 28, 81673 Munich
Tel: (089) 4136-0 *Fax:* (089) 4136-3333
E-mail: kundenservice@randomhouse.de
Web Site: www.randomhouse.de/btb
Key Personnel
Publisher: Georg Reuchlein
Publishing Dir: Regina Kammerer
Press: Nina Portheine *Tel:* (089) 4136-3207 *Fax:* (089) 4136-3723 *E-mail:* nina.portheine@btb-verlag.de; Britta Puce *Tel:* (089) 4136-3564 *Fax:* (089) 4136-3723 *E-mail:* britta.puce@btb-verlag.de
Founded: 1996
Subjects: Fiction, Literature, Literary Criticism, Essays, Nonfiction (General), Scandinavian Literature, Women's Literature
ISBN Prefix(es): 978-3-442

Buch- und Kunstverlag Oberpfalz, *imprint of* Battenberg Gietl Verlag GmbH

Buch Verlag Kempen GmbH, see BVK Buch Verlag Kempen GmbH

BUCH&media Gesellschaft fuer Buch- und Medienstleistungen mbH
Merianstr 24, 80637 Munich
Tel: (089) 13 92 90-46 *Fax:* (089) 13 92 90-65
E-mail: info@buchmedia.de; presse@buchmedia.de
Web Site: www.buchmedia.de
Key Personnel
Mng Dir: Alexander Strathern
Press: Kathrin Janke
Subjects: Fiction, Nonfiction (General), Science (General)
ISBN Prefix(es): 978-3-86520; 978-3-935284; 978-3-935877
Subsidiaries: Allitera Verlag

Buchecker Verlag
Frankenstr 52, 91757 Treuchtlingen
Tel: (09142) 975 999 3 *Fax:* (09142) 975 999 4
E-mail: kontakt@buchecker-verlag.de
Web Site: www.buchecker-verlag.de
Key Personnel
Owner: Andreas Drexler
Founded: 2000
ISBN Prefix(es): 978-3-936156

Bucheli Verlag+
Division of Paul Pietsch Verlage GmbH & Co KG
Olgastr 86, 70180 Stuttgart
Tel: (0711) 2 10 80-0 *Fax:* (0711) 2 36 04 15
E-mail: ppv@motorbuch.de
Web Site: www.bucheli-verlag.de
Key Personnel
Publisher: Dr Patricia Scholten *Tel:* (0711) 2 10 80-11
Head, Sales: Christian Pflug *Tel:* (0711) 2 10 80-20 *E-mail:* c.pflug@motorbuch.de
Production: Bernd Leu *Tel:* (0711) 2 10 80-49 *E-mail:* b.leu@motorbuch.de
Rights & Permissions: Patricia Hofmann *Tel:* (0711) 2 10 80-13 *E-mail:* p.hofmann@motorbuch.de
Founded: 1962
Subjects: Automotive
ISBN Prefix(es): 978-3-7168
Distribution Center: Sigloch Distribution, Am Buchberg 8, 74572 Blaufelden *Tel:* (01805) 45 56 00

Bucher Verlag GmbH+
Infanteriestr 11a, 80797 Munich
Tel: (089) 130699-0 *Fax:* (089) 130699-100
E-mail: info@bucher-verlag.de
Web Site: www.bucher-verlag.de
Key Personnel
Mng Dir: Carsten Leininger *E-mail:* carsten.leininger@verlagshaus.de; Clemens Schuessler *Tel:* (089) 130699-220 *Fax:* (089) 130699-200 *E-mail:* verlagsleitung@verlagshaus.de
Sales Manager: Udo Zimmermann *E-mail:* udo.zimmermann@verlagshaus.de
Foreign Rights: Dr Ingeborg Kluge *Tel:* (089) 130699-683 *Fax:* (089) 130699-300 *E-mail:* ingeborg.kluge@verlagshaus.de
Press & Public Relations: Janina Roso *Tel:* (089) 130699-538 *Fax:* (089) 130699-500 *E-mail:* janina.roso@verlagshaus.de
Founded: 1956
Subjects: Art, History, Nonfiction (General), Photography, Travel & Tourism
ISBN Prefix(es): 978-3-7658
Parent Company: GeraNova Bruckmann Verlagshaus GmbH
Associate Companies: J Berg Verlag; Bruckmann Verlag; Christian Verlag; Frederking & Thaler; GeraMond Verlag
Distribution Center: Verlegerdienst Muenchen GmbH, Gutenbergstr 1, 82205 Gilching *Tel:* (08105) 388106 *Fax:* (08105) 388187 *E-mail:* verlagshaus@verlegerdienst.de
Mohr Morawa Buchvertrieb GmbH, Sulzengasse 2, 1230 Vienna, Austria *Tel:* (01) 680 14-0 *Fax:* (01) 688 71 30 *E-mail:* momo@mohrmorawa.at *Web Site:* www.mohrmorawa.at
Grafus GmbH SRL, Toni-Ebner-Str 5, 39100 Bozen BZ, Italy *Tel:* (0471) 086433 *Fax:* (0471) 086456 *E-mail:* info@grafus.it (South Tyrol)
Willems Adventure, Honderland 120, 2676 LT Maasdijk, Netherlands *Tel:* (088) 599 01 40 *Fax:* (088) 599 01 41 *E-mail:* info@willemsadventure.nl
Buchzentrum AG (BZ), Industrie Ost, 4614 Haegendorf, Switzerland *Tel:* (062) 209 2701 *Fax:* (062) 209 2788 *E-mail:* kundendienst@buchzentrum.ch

Buchkinder Leipzig eV
Hans-Poeche-Str 2, 04103 Leipzig
Tel: (0341) 2253742 *Fax:* (0341) 3061777
E-mail: info@buchkinder.de; presse@buchkinder.de
Web Site: www.buchkinder.de
Key Personnel
Press & Public Relations: Susanne Tenzler-Huesler *Tel:* (0341) 2246860
Subjects: Fiction

ISBN Prefix(es): 978-3-938985
Branch Office(s)
Demmeringstr 21, 04177 Leipzig *Tel:* (0341) 2534695

BuchKunst Kleinheinrich+
Oer'scher Hof, Koenigsstr 42, 48143 Muenster
Tel: (0251) 4 84 01 93 *Fax:* (0251) 4 84 01 94
E-mail: kleinheinrich-muenster@t-online.de
Web Site: www.kleinheinrich.de
Key Personnel
International Rights: Dr Josef Kleinheinrich
Founded: 1986
Subjects: Art, Literature, Literary Criticism, Essays
ISBN Prefix(es): 978-3-926608; 978-3-930754

BuchMarkt Verlag K Werner GmbH
Sperberweg 4a, 40668 Meerbusch
Tel: (02150) 9191-0 *Fax:* (02150) 919191
E-mail: redaktion@buchmarkt.de
Web Site: www.buchmarkt.de
Key Personnel
Dir, International Rights: Christian Von Zittwitz *Tel:* (02150) 9191-19 *E-mail:* cvz@buchmarkt.de
Mng Editor: Susanna Wengeler *Tel:* (02150) 9191-15 *E-mail:* susanna.wengeler@buchmarkt.de
Advertising: Kirsten Peters *Tel:* (02150) 9191-27 *E-mail:* kirsten.peters@buchmarkt.de
Sales: Nadine Lettke *Tel:* (02150) 9191-37 *E-mail:* nadine.lettke@buchmarkt.de
Founded: 1966
Publishers of the magazine *BuchMarkt* for the book trade.
Subjects: Publishing & Book Trade Reference
ISBN Prefix(es): 978-3-920518

C C Buchner Verlag GmbH & Co KG
Member of BVG Bamberger VerlagsGruppe
Laubanger 8, 96052 Bamberg
Mailing Address: Postfach 12 69, 96003 Bamberg
Tel: (0951) 16098-200 *Fax:* (0951) 16098-270
E-mail: service@ccbuchner.de
Web Site: www.ccbuchner.de
Key Personnel
Mng Dir: Dr Maren Saiko; Christopher Schell
Founded: 1832
Subjects: Business, Chemistry, Chemical Engineering, Earth Sciences, Economics, Government, Political Science, History, Law, Mathematics, Music, Dance, Philosophy, Physics, Regional Interests, Technology
ISBN Prefix(es): 978-3-7661
Distribution Center: Balmer Buecherdienst AG, Kobiboden, 8840 Einsiedeln, Switzerland

BuchVerlag fuer die Frau GmbH
Gerichtsweg 28, 04103 Leipzig
Tel: (0341) 99 54 371 *Fax:* (0341) 99 54 373
E-mail: info@buchverlag-fuer-die-frau.de; marketing@buchverlag-fuer-die-frau.de; vertrieb@buchverlag-fuer-die-frau.de
Web Site: www.buchverlag-fuer-die-frau.de
Key Personnel
Mng Dir: Christa Winkelmann *Tel:* (0341) 99 54 374 *E-mail:* c.winkelmann@buchverlag-fuer-die-frau.de
Marketing & Press: Susann Jaensch *Tel:* (0341) 99 54 376
Sales: Ulrike Winkelmann *Tel:* (0341) 99 54 378
Founded: 1946
Subjects: Cookery, Crafts, Games, Hobbies, Health, Nutrition
ISBN Prefix(es): 978-3-89798; 978-3-932720
Foreign Rep(s): Verlagsservice AS Hoeller (Alfred Trux) (Austria); Martin E Schnetzer (Switzerland)
Foreign Rights): The Wittmann Agency (Claudia Wittmann)

Distribution Center: Leipziger Kommissions- und Grossbuchhandelsgesellschaft mbH (LKG), An der Suedspitze 1-12, 04571 Roetha *Tel:* (034206) 65-100 *Fax:* (034206) 65-110 *E-mail:* lkg@lkg-service.de *Web Site:* www.lkg-va.de
AS Verlagsservice Hoeller, Schrackgasse 11 a, 8650 Kindberg, Austria *Tel:* (03865) 44 880-11 *Fax:* (03865) 44 880-77
OLF SA, ZI 3 Corminboef, 1701 Fribourg, Switzerland *Tel:* (026) 467 51 11 *Fax:* (026) 467 54 44

Verlag Barbara Budrich
Stauffenbergstr 7, 51379 Leverkusen
Tel: (02171) 344 594 *Fax:* (02171) 344 693
E-mail: info@budrich.eu; info@budrich-verlag.de
Web Site: www.budrich-verlag.de; www.barbara-budrich.net
Key Personnel
Mng Dir: Barbara Budrich-Esser *E-mail:* barbara.budrich@budrich.eu
Head, Sales: Karen Reinfeld *E-mail:* karen.reinfeld@budrich.eu
Public Relations & Marketing: Corinna Hipp *E-mail:* corinna.hipp@budrich.eu
Founded: 2004
Subjects: Government, Political Science, History, Psychology, Psychiatry, Social Sciences, Sociology, Gender Studies, International Relations, Pedagogics
ISBN Prefix(es): 978-3-86649; 978-3-938094
Branch Office(s)
Streustr 42, 13086 Berlin *Tel:* (030) 89 37 65 11 *Fax:* (032) 12 139 08 05 *E-mail:* claudia.kuehne@budrich.de
86 Delma Dr, Toronto, ON M8W 4P6, Canada, Contact: Karen Davey *E-mail:* info@barbara-budrich.net *Web Site:* www.budrich-academic.com
4 Osborne Mews, London E17 6QA, United Kingdom, Contact: Jakob Horstmann *Tel:* (077) 352 518 31 *E-mail:* jakob.horstmann@budrich.eu
Foreign Rep(s): The African Moon Press (Chris Reinders) (South Africa); Apac Publishers Services Pte Ltd (Southeast Asia exc India & Japan); Central Books Ltd (UK); Iberian Book Services (Peter Prout) (Gibraltar, Portugal, Spain); Sara Books Pvt Ltd (Bangladesh, India, Pakistan, Sri Lanka); Scheidegger & Co AG (Ruth Schildknecht) (Switzerland)
Distribution Center: Brockhaus/Commission, Kreidlerstr 9, 70806 Kornwestheim *Tel:* (07154) 13270 *Fax:* (07154) 132713 *E-mail:* info@brocom.de *Web Site:* www.brocom.de
Mohr Morawa Buchvertrieb GmbH, Sulzengasse 2, 1230 Vienna, Austria *Tel:* (01) 680 14-0 *Fax:* (01) 688 71 30 *E-mail:* momo@mohrmorawa.at *Web Site:* www.mohrmorawa.at
Sara Books Pvt Ltd, G-1 Vardaan House, 7/28 Ansari Rd, Darya Ganj, New Delhi 110 002, India *Tel:* (011) 23266107 *Fax:* (011) 23266102 *E-mail:* ravindrasaxena@sarabooksindia.com *Web Site:* www.sarabooksindia.com
Apac Publishers Services Pte Ltd, 8 Lorong Bakar Batu No 05-02, Singapore 348743, Singapore *Tel:* 68447333 *Fax:* 67478916 *E-mail:* service@apacmedia.com.sg *Web Site:* www.apacmedia.com.sg
The African Moon Press, PO Box 1096, Kelvin 2054, South Africa, Contact: Chris Reinders *Tel:* (083) 4633989 (cell); (011) 802 5668 *Fax:* (0865) 167045 *E-mail:* chris@theafricanmoonpress.co.za
Iberian Book Services, Sector Islas, Bloque 12, 1° B, 28760 Tres Cantos, Madrid, Spain, Contact: Peter Prout *Tel:* 918034918 *Fax:* 918035936 *E-mail:* pprout@telefonica.net *Web Site:* www.iberianbookservices.com

AVA Verlagsauslieferung AG, Centralweg 16, 8910 Affoltern am Albis, Switzerland *Tel:* (044) 762 42 50 *Fax:* (044) 762 42 10 *E-mail:* verlagsservice@ava.ch *Web Site:* www.ava.ch
Central Books Ltd, One Heath Park Industrial Estate, Freshwater Rd, Dagenham RM8 1RX, United Kingdom *Tel:* (020) 8525 8800 *Fax:* (020) 8599 2694 *E-mail:* orders@centralbooks.com *Web Site:* www.centralbooks.com
International Specialized Book Services (ISBS), 920 NE 58 Ave, Suite 300, Portland, OR 97213-3786, United States *Fax:* 503-280-8832 *E-mail:* orders@isbs.com *Web Site:* www.isbs.com

Edition Buecherbaer im Arena Verlag, see Arena Verlag GmbH

Edition Buecherbar im Arena Verlag, *imprint of* Arena Verlag GmbH

Edition Buechergilde GmbH
Stuttgarter Str 25-29, 60329 Frankfurt
Tel: (069) 273908-0 *Fax:* (069) 273908-27
E-mail: info@edition-buechergilde.de; service@buechergilde.de
Web Site: www.edition-buechergilde.de; www.buechergilde.de
Key Personnel
Mng Dir: Mario Frueh *Tel:* (069) 273908-20 *E-mail:* frueh@edition-buechergilde.de
Founded: 1924
Subjects: Literature, Literary Criticism, Essays, Mysteries, Suspense, Nonfiction (General), Poetry
ISBN Prefix(es): 978-3-936428
Distribution Center: Germeinsame Verlagsauslieferung Goettingen (GVA), Postfach 2021, 37010 Goettingen, Contact: Jutta Krause *Tel:* (0551) 487177 *Fax:* (0551) 41392 *E-mail:* krause@gva-verlage.de
Mohr Morawa Buchvertrieb GmbH, Sulzengasse 2, 1230 Vienna, Austria *Tel:* (01) 680 14-0 *Fax:* (01) 688 71 30 *E-mail:* momo@mohrmorawa.at *Web Site:* www.mohrmorawa.at
Buch 2000, c/o AVA, Centralweg 16, 8910 Affoltern am Albis, Switzerland *Tel:* (044) 76 24 260 *Fax:* (044) 76 24 210 *E-mail:* buch2000@ava.ch *Web Site:* www.ava.ch

Buchergilde Gutenberg Verlagsgesellschaft mbH
Stuttgarter Str 25-29, 60329 Frankfurt am Main
Mailing Address: Postfach 160165, 60064 Frankfurt am Main
Tel: (069) 27 39 08-0 *Fax:* (069) 27 39 08-26; (069) 27 39 08-25
E-mail: service@buechergilde.de
Web Site: www.buechergilde.de
Key Personnel
Mng Dir: Mario Frueh *Tel:* (069) 27 39 08-20 *Fax:* (069) 27 39 08-76 20 *E-mail:* frueh@buechergilde.de
Founded: 1924
Primarily a Book Club, but also a publisher.
Subjects: Art, Fiction, Government, Political Science, History, Literature, Literary Criticism, Essays, Mysteries, Suspense, Nonfiction (General), Poetry
ISBN Prefix(es): 978-3-7632

Buechse der Pandora Verlags GmbH+
Schulstr 20, 35579 Wetzlar
Tel: (06441) 911312 *Fax:* (06441) 911318
E-mail: buechse.der.pandora.vlg@gmail.com
Founded: 1977
Subjects: Art, Education, Literature, Literary Criticism, Essays, Philosophy
ISBN Prefix(es): 978-3-88178
Orders to: Postfach 2820, 35538 Wetzlar

Bund demokratischer Wissenschaftlerinnen und Wissenschaftler eV, see BdWi-Verlag

Bund fuer deutsche Schrift und Sprache eV
(Association for German Script & Language)
Elchengrund 17, 38723 Seesen
Mailing Address: Postfach 11 45, 38711 Seesen
Tel: (05381) 46355 *Fax:* (05381) 46355
E-mail: verwaltung@bfds.de
Web Site: www.bfds.de; www.deutscheschrift.de
Key Personnel
Mng Dir: Helmut Delbanco
Founded: 1918
ISBN Prefix(es): 978-3-930540

Bund-Verlag GmbH+
Heddernheimer Landstr 144, 60439 Frankfurt am Main
Tel: (069) 79 50 10-0 *Fax:* (069) 79 50 10 11
E-mail: kontakt@bund-verlag.de
Web Site: www.bund-verlag.de
Key Personnel
Mng Dir: Rainer Joede *Tel:* (069) 79 50 10 25
Fax: (069) 79 50 10 16 *E-mail:* rainer.joede@bund-verlag.de
Head, Sales & Marketing: Peter Beuther
Tel: (069) 79 50 10 41 *Fax:* (069) 79 50 10 17
E-mail: peter.beuther@bund-verlag.de
Production: Birgit Fieber *Tel:* (069) 79 50 10 42
Fax: (069) 79 50 10 14 *E-mail:* birgit.fieber@bund-verlag.de
Founded: 1947
Specialize in labor & social security law.
Subjects: Economics, Finance, Government, Political Science, Law, Nonfiction (General), Public Administration
ISBN Prefix(es): 978-3-7663; 978-3-930453

Bundes-Verlag GmbH
Member of Stiftung Christliche Medien
Bodenborn 43, 58452 Witten
Tel: (02302) 930 93 0 *Fax:* (02302) 930 93 689
E-mail: info@bundes-verlag.de
Web Site: bundes-verlag.net
Key Personnel
Publishing Dir: Ulrich Eggers
Mng Dir: Frieder Trommer *E-mail:* trommer@scm-haenssler.de
Head, Marketing & Sales: Marc Brocksieper
Tel: (02302) 930 93 630 *E-mail:* brocksieper@bundes-verlag.de
Founded: 1887
Subjects: Religion - Catholic
ISBN Prefix(es): 978-3-926417; 978-3-933660

Bundesanzeiger Verlag GmbH
Amsterdamer Str 192, 50735 Cologne
Mailing Address: Postfach 10 05 34, 50445 Cologne
Tel: (0221) 9 76 68-0; (0221) 9 76 68-200 (sales)
Toll Free No: 0800 1234339 *Fax:* (0221) 9 76 68-278; (0221) 9 76 68-115 (sales)
E-mail: vertrieb@bundesanzeiger.de; service@bundesanzeiger.de
Web Site: www.bundesanzeiger-verlag.de
Key Personnel
Chief Executive Officer: Dr Matthias Schulenberg
Chairman of the Board: Gerrit Stein
Mng Dir: Fred Schuld
Commercial Marketing & Cooperations: Susanne Naumann *E-mail:* susanne.naumann@bundesanzeiger.de
Founded: 1949
Subjects: Government, Political Science, History, Law, Regional Interests
ISBN Prefix(es): 978-3-88784; 978-3-89817
Subsidiaries: Deutscher Bundesverlag
Branch Office(s)
Kornmarkt 9, 65549 Limburg *Tel:* (06431) 2891-0 *Fax:* (6431) 2891-44 *E-mail:* limburg@bundesanzeiger.de

Bundeszentrale fuer Politische Bildung
Adenauerallee 86, 53113 Bonn
Tel: (0228) 99515-0; (0228) 99515-115 (customer service) *Fax:* (0228) 99515-113
E-mail: info@bpb.de; redaktion@bpb.de
Web Site: www.bpb.de
Key Personnel
Editorial: Juergen Beselt; Pamela Brandt; Martin Hetterich
Subjects: Government, Political Science, History, Current Affairs
ISBN Prefix(es): 978-3-89331; 978-3-921352; 978-3-923423

edition buntehunde GdBR
Kalmuenzergasse 5, 93047 Regensburg
Tel: (0941) 5674510 *Fax:* (0941) 5674511
E-mail: edition.buntehunde@t-online.de
Web Site: www.editionbuntehunde.de
Key Personnel
Publisher: Dr Susanne Geser; Herbert Wittl
ISBN Prefix(es): 978-3-934941

Buntpapierverlag
Wittenbergener Weg 32, 22559 Hamburg
Tel: (040) 81 77 06
E-mail: studio@hamburgerbuntpapier.de
Web Site: www.hamburgerbuntpapier.de
Key Personnel
Owner: Susanne Krause
Subjects: Art, Papermaking
ISBN Prefix(es): 978-3-938423

Buntstein Verlag, *imprint of* Bookspot Verlag GmbH

Aenne Burda Verlag GmbH & Co KG
Hubert Burda Platz 2, 77652 Offenburg
Mailing Address: Arabellastr 23, 81925 Munich
Tel: (089) 9250-0 *Fax:* (089) 9250-2340
E-mail: service@burdastyle.de
Web Site: www.burdastyle.de
Key Personnel
Mng Dir: Henning Ecker
Publishing Dir & Licensing: Pia Hochhut
Founded: 1949
Subjects: Cookery, Crafts, Games, Hobbies, Fashion
ISBN Prefix(es): 978-3-920158; 978-3-88978
Subsidiaries: Burda Patterns Inc; Dipa SA; ZVB Zeitschriften Vertriebs AB

Burg Giebichenstein Kunsthochschule Halle
Neuwerk 7, 06108 Halle
Mailing Address: Postfach 200 252, 06003 Halle
Tel: (0345) 7751-511 *Fax:* (0345) 7751-509
E-mail: rektorat@burg-halle.de; presse@burg-halle.de; presse@burg-halle.de
Web Site: www.burg-halle.de
Key Personnel
Dir, Public Relations: Dr Renate Luckner-Ben
Tel: (0345) 7751-525 *Fax:* (0345) 7755-525
E-mail: rlucknerb@burg-halle.de
Internet Editor: Brigitte Beiling *Tel:* (0345) 7751-527 *Fax:* (0345) 7755-525 *E-mail:* beiling@burg-halle.de
ISBN Prefix(es): 978-3-86019

Burgart Presse
Moerla Nr 45A, 07407 Rudolstadt
Tel: (03672) 41 22 14 *Fax:* (03672) 41 22 14
Web Site: www.burgart-presse.de
Key Personnel
Owner: Jens Henkel *E-mail:* henkel@burgart-presse.de
Subjects: Art, Bibliographies
ISBN Prefix(es): 978-3-910206

Busche Verlagsgesellschaft mbH
Schleefstr 1, 44287 Dortmund
Tel: (0231) 44477-0 *Fax:* (0231) 44477-77

E-mail: info@busche.de
Web Site: www.busche.de
Key Personnel
Management: Johannes Grosspietsch
Founded: 1972
Subjects: Travel & Tourism
ISBN Prefix(es): 978-3-88584; 978-3-921143; 978-3-89764; 978-3-925086

Helmut Buske Verlag GmbH+
Subsidiary of Felix Meiner Verlag GmbH
Richardstr 47, 22081 Hamburg
Tel: (040) 29 99 58-0; (040) 29 99 58-42 (sales)
Fax: (040) 29 99 58-20; (040) 299 36 14
E-mail: info@buske.de
Web Site: www.buske.de
Key Personnel
Publishing Dir: Michael Hechinger
E-mail: hechinger@buske.de
Rights & Marketing: Johannes Kambylis
Tel: (040) 29 99 58-23 *E-mail:* kambylis@buske.de
Sales: Daniela Garbers *E-mail:* garbers@buske.de
Founded: 1959
Membership(s): Boersenverein des Deutschen Buchhandels
Subjects: Asian Studies, Language Arts, Linguistics, Philosophy, Egyptology, Finno-Ugric Studies, German Studies, Indology, Kreolistic, Slavic, Yiddish
ISBN Prefix(es): 978-3-87118; 978-3-87548

Verlag Bussert & Stadeler
Saalbahnhofstr 25a, 07743 Jena
Tel: (03641) 369061 *Fax:* (03641) 369062
E-mail: info@bussert-stadeler.de
Web Site: new.bussert-stadeler.de
Key Personnel
Publisher: Dr Frank Bussert; Helmut Stadeler
Subjects: History, Literature, Literary Criticism, Essays, Regional Interests, Religion - Protestant
ISBN Prefix(es): 978-3-932906; 978-3-9804590

BusseSeewald, see Lifestyle BusseSeewald

Butter & Cream Verlagsgesellschaft Ltd
Postfach 610101, 10921 Berlin
Tel: (030) 61621551
E-mail: butter-and-cream@gmx.de
Web Site: www.butter-and-cream.com
Key Personnel
Dir: Martina Hardten *E-mail:* hardten@gmx.de
Founded: 2006
Subjects: Fiction
ISBN Prefix(es): 978-3-940414
Branch Office(s)
69 Great Hampton St, Birmingham, West Midlands B18 6EW, United Kingdom

Butzon & Bercker GmbH+
Hoogeweg 71, 47623 Kevelaer
Tel: (02832) 929-0 *Fax:* (02832) 929-211
E-mail: service@bube.de
Web Site: www.butzon-bercker.de
Key Personnel
Mng Dir: Dr Edmund Bercker *E-mail:* edmund.bercker@bube.de; Markus Bercker *Tel:* (02832) 929-112 *E-mail:* markus.bercker@bube.de
Press: Dr Jutta Bueckendorf *Tel:* (02832) 929-128 *E-mail:* jutta.bueckendorf@bube.de
Sales: Helga Daniels *Tel:* (02832) 929-297 *E-mail:* helga.daniels@bube.de
Founded: 1870
Subjects: Art, Inspirational, Spirituality, Music, Dance, Nonfiction (General), Regional Interests, Religion - Catholic, Theology
ISBN Prefix(es): 978-3-7666
Distributor for Lahn (Limburg); Styria (Graz/Cologne)

BVA Bielefelder Verlag GmbH & Co KG+
Niederwall 53, 33602 Bielefeld
Tel: (0521) 59 50 *Fax:* (0521) 59 55 18
E-mail: kontakt@bva-bielefeld.de
Web Site: www.bva-bielefeld.de
Key Personnel
Chief Executive Officer: Gerd Franz; Paul von
  Schubert
Publishing Dir: Hans-Joerg Kaiser
Founded: 1947
Publish books & maps for cyclists (travel guides)
  & in Germany bicycle report books.
Membership(s): Borsenverein.
Subjects: How-to, Outdoor Recreation, Travel &
  Tourism
ISBN Prefix(es): 978-3-87073
Total Titles: 170 Print
Parent Company: E Gundlach Grossdruckerei
  GmbH
Distributed by Mairs Geographischer Verlag

BVK Buch Verlag Kempen GmbH
St Huberter Str 67, 47906 Kempen
Tel: (02152) 52976 *Fax:* (02152) 52873
E-mail: info@buchverlagkempen.de; bestellung@
  buchverlagkempen.de
Web Site: www.buchverlagkempen.de
Key Personnel
Publishing Dir: Hildegard van der Gieth
Marketing: Jana Maesmanns; Ines Schaefer
Sales: Valeria Fritzler; Anja Meier; Vanessa
  Schmeinta
Founded: 1996
Specialize in teaching materials for kindergarten
  & elementary schools.
Subjects: Child Care & Development, Education
ISBN Prefix(es): 978-3-932519; 978-3-936577;
  978-3-938458

BWV, see Berliner Wissenschafts-Verlag GmbH
  (BWV)

Caann Verlag, Klaus Wagner
Am Anger 11, 85570 Ottenhofen
Tel: (08121) 7602875
E-mail: info@caann-verlag.de
Web Site: www.caann-verlag.de
Key Personnel
Mng Dir: Klaus Wagner
Founded: 1969
Subjects: Philosophy, Social Sciences, Sociology,
  Theology
ISBN Prefix(es): 978-3-87121
Total Titles: 6 Print; 2 E-Book

Cadmos Verlag GmbH+
Moellner Str 47, 21493 Schwarzenbek
Tel: (04151) 87907-0 *Fax:* (04151) 87907-12
E-mail: info@cadmos.de; rights@cadmos-books.
  com
Web Site: www.cadmos.de
Key Personnel
Publisher & Mng Dir: Hans Joachim Schmidtke
  Fax: (04151) 87907-19
Foreign Rights: Inga Wulf *Tel:* (04151) 87907-17
Founded: 1986
Subjects: Dogs, Equestrian, Horses
ISBN Prefix(es): 978-3-925760; 978-3-86127
Number of titles published annually: 50 Print; 2
  Audio
Total Titles: 150 Print; 8 Audio
Subsidiaries: Cadmos Publishing Ltd (UK)
Foreign Rep(s): Kathrin Heumer (Austria)

Verlag Georg D W Callwey GmbH & Co KG+
Streitfeldstr 35, 81673 Munich
Tel: (089) 436005-0 *Fax:* (089) 436005-113
E-mail: info@callwey.de; buch@callwey.de
  (rights, publicity & sales)
Web Site: www.callwey.de

Key Personnel
Mng Dir: Dominik Baur-Callwey *Tel:* (089)
  436005-159 *E-mail:* d.baur-callwey@callwey.de
Editorial: Dr Marcella Prior-Callwey *Tel:* (089)
  436005-165 *E-mail:* m.prior-callwey@callwey.
  de
Press: Andreas Hagenkord *Tel:* (089) 436005-177
  E-mail: a.hagenkord@callwey.de
Rights & Permissions, Publicity & Sales: Jens-
  Peter Arndt *Tel:* (089) 436005-190 *E-mail:* jp.
  arndt@callwey.de
Founded: 1884
Subjects: Architecture & Interior Design, Crafts,
  Games, Hobbies, Gardening, Plants, House &
  Home, How-to
ISBN Prefix(es): 978-3-7667; 978-3-87467
Returns: KNO Verlagsauslieferung GmbH, Am
  Wallgraben 114, 70565 Stuttgart

Calwer Verlag GmbH+
Loeffelstr 4, 70597 Stuttgart
Tel: (0711) 16722-0 *Fax:* (0711) 16722-77
E-mail: info@calwer.com
Web Site: www.calwer.com
Key Personnel
Dir: Dr Berthold Brohm; Joachim Hinderer
Advertising: Karin Klem *Tel:* (0711) 16722-19
  E-mail: klem@calwer.com
Customer Service: Rita Mast *E-mail:* mast@
  calwer.com
Licensing & Rights: Sieglinde Karpinski
  E-mail: karpinski@calwer.com
Production: Karin Class *E-mail:* class@calwer.
  com
Sales: Beatrice Gerhard *Tel:* (0711) 16722-16
  E-mail: gerhard@calwer.com
Founded: 1836
Subjects: Education, Religion - Other, Theology,
  Learning Materials, Schoolbooks
ISBN Prefix(es): 978-3-7668
Orders to: Brockhaus/Commission, Kreidlerstr
  9, 70806 Kornwestheim *Tel:* (07154) 132737
  Fax: (07154) 132713 *E-mail:* calwer@brocom.
  de

Campus Verlag GmbH+
Kurfuerstenstr 49, 60486 Frankfurt am Main
Tel: (069) 976516-0 *Fax:* (069) 976516-78
E-mail: info@campus.de
Web Site: www.campus.de
Key Personnel
Mng Dir, Publisher & Rights & Permissions:
  Thomas Carl Schwoerer *Tel:* (069) 976 516-43
  E-mail: schwoerer@campus.de
Chief, Program: Dr Annette C Anton
Editor-in-Chief, Science: Adalbert Hepp
  Tel: (069) 976 516-52 *E-mail:* hepp@campus.
  de
Head, Production: Klaus Schoeffner *Tel:* (069)
  976 516-64
Production: Ulrich Begemeier *Tel:* (069) 976 516-
  66
Publicity: Margit Knauer *Tel:* (069) 976 516-20
Rights & Licenses: Annette Prassel *Tel:* (069)
  976 516-815; Gun Roblick *Tel:* (069) 976 516-
  15
Sales & Marketing: Joachim Bischofs *Tel:* (069)
  976 516-14
Founded: 1975
Specialize in cultural studies, German science,
  nonfiction & business.
Subjects: Business, Career Development, Eco-
  nomics, Government, Political Science, History,
  Management, Nonfiction (General), Philoso-
  phy, Psychology, Psychiatry, Self-Help, Social
  Sciences, Sociology, Women's Studies
ISBN Prefix(es): 978-3-593
Number of titles published annually: 240 Print;
  10 Audio
Foreign Rep(s): Michael Orou (Austria); Schei-
  degger & Co AG (Martin Grob, Ruth Schild-
  knecht & Urs Wetli) (Switzerland); Guenter
  Thiel (Austria)

Distribution Center: Sigloch Distribution, Am
  Buchberg 8, 74752 Blaufelde
Mohr Morawa Buchvertrieb GmbH, Sulzengasse 2, 1230 Vienna, Austria *Tel:* (01) 680
  14-0 *Fax:* (01) 688 71 30 *E-mail:* momo@
  mohrmorawa.au *Web Site:* www.mohrmorawa.
  au
AVA Verlagsauslieferung AG, Centralweg
  16, 8910 Affoltern am Albis, Switzerland
  Tel: (044) 76242-50 *Fax:* (044) 76242-10
  E-mail: verlagsservice@ava.ch
Orders to: HGV, Weidestr 122 A, 22083 Hamburg *Tel:* (040) 84000-888 *Fax:* (040) 84000-
  855 *E-mail:* bestellung@hgv-online.de *Web
  Site:* www.webshop.hgv-online.de

Edition Carat, *imprint of* Bookspot Verlag
  GmbH

Carl-Auer Verlag+
Vangerowstr 14, 69115 Heidelberg
Tel: (06221) 64 38 0 *Fax:* (06221) 64 38 22
E-mail: info@carl-auer.de
Web Site: www.carl-auer.de; www.carl-auer.com
Key Personnel
Mng Dir: Dr Fritz B Simon; Beate Ch Ulrich
  Tel: (06221) 64 38 15 *E-mail:* ulrich@carl-
  auer.de; Dr Gunthard Weber
Press & Public Relations: Anja Loesch
  Tel: (06221) 64 38 17 *E-mail:* loesch@carl-
  auer.de
Rights: Klaus W Mueller *Tel:* (06221) 64 38 16
  E-mail: mueller@carl-auer.de
Sales: Mirjam Hegenbarth *Tel:* (06221) 64 38 20
  E-mail: hegenbarth@carl-auer.de
Founded: 1989
Subjects: Child Care & Development, Health,
  Nutrition, Human Relations, Management, Phi-
  losophy, Psychology, Psychiatry, Self-Help
ISBN Prefix(es): 978-3-927809; 978-3-931574;
  978-3-89670
Total Titles: 110 Print; 90 Audio

Fachverlag Hans Carl GmbH+
Andernacher Str 33a, 90411 Nuremberg
Mailing Address: Postfach 99 01 53, 90268
  Nuremberg
Tel: (0911) 95285-0 *Fax:* (0911) 95285-81 60
E-mail: info@hanscarl.com
Web Site: www.hanscarl.com
Key Personnel
Editor-in-Chief: Dr Lydia Winkelmann
  Tel: (0911) 95285-58
Mng Editor: Ulrike Hauffe *Tel:* (0911) 95285-25
Editor: Alexander Hofmann *Tel:* (0911) 95285-24
Management: Michael Schmitt *E-mail:* m.
  schmitt@hanscarl.com
Sales & Marketing Dir: Wolf-Dieter Schoyerer
  Tel: (0911) 95285-44 *Fax:* (0911) 95285-8120
  E-mail: schoyerer@hanscarl.com
Founded: 1861
Subjects: Art, Chemistry, Chemical Engineering,
  Fiction, History, Outdoor Recreation, Philoso-
  phy, Poetry, Regional Interests, Science (Gen-
  eral), Wine & Spirits
ISBN Prefix(es): 978-3-418

Carl Link, *imprint of* Wolters Kluwer
  Deutschland GmbH

Carl Link Kommunalverlag, *imprint of* Wolters
  Kluwer Deutschland GmbH

carl's books, *imprint of* Verlagsgruppe Random
  House Bertelsmann

CARLSEN Verlag GmbH+
Voelckersstr 14-20, 22765 Hamburg
Mailing Address: Postfach 50 03 80, 22703 Ham-
  burg

Tel: (040) 39 804-0; (040) 39 804-271; (040) 39 804-272 *Fax:* (040) 39 804-390
E-mail: info@carlsen.de; presse@carlsen.de
Web Site: www.carlsen.de
Key Personnel
Dir: Renate Herre; Joachim Kaufmann
Head, Rights: Daniela Steiner *Tel:* (040) 39 804 269 *E-mail:* daniela.steiner@carlsen.de
Press Manager: Katrin Hogrebe *Tel:* (040) 39 804-273 *E-mail:* katrin.hogrebe@carlsen.de
Rights Manager: Christiane Bartelsen *Tel:* (040) 39 804 246 *E-mail:* christiane.bartelsen@carlsen.de; Meike Beurer *Tel:* (040) 39 804-157 *Fax:* (040) 39 804-389 *E-mail:* meike.beurer@carlsen.de; Sylvia Schuster *Tel:* (040) 39 804 555 *E-mail:* sylvia.schuster@carlsen.de
Advertising: Marianne Ohmann
Public Relations: Cornelia Berger
Founded: 1953
Specialize in children's books & comics.
Subjects: Fiction, Humor, Comics, Graphic Novels, Manga
ISBN Prefix(es): 978-3-551
Parent Company: Bonnier-Gruppe
Associate Companies: ARS Edition; Piper Verlag; Thienemann Verlag; Ullstein Buchverlage (Germany)
Imprints: Nelson Verlag; Terzio
Foreign Rights: Agentur im Medien- und Verlagswesen (Ivana Beil) (Czechia, Slovakia); Anna Becchi (Italy); Sabina Boerescu (Romania); druckfertig (Hungary); HERCULES Business & Culture GmbH (Hongjun Cai) (China, Taiwan); Ute Koerner Literary Agent SL (Sandra Rodericks) (Spanish & Portuguese); Meike Marx Literary Agency (Japan); Momo Agency (Geenie Han) (Korea); Shinwon Agency (Florian Sommer) (Korea); Eric Yang Agency (Korea)

Carus-Verlag GmbH & Co KG
Sielminger Str 51, 70771 Leinfelden-Echterdingen
Tel: (0711) 797 330-0 *Fax:* (0711) 797 330-29
E-mail: info@carus-verlag.com; sales@carus-verlag.com
Web Site: www.carus-verlag.com
Key Personnel
Management: Dr Johannes Graulich; Waltraud Graulich
Head, Production & Communication: Iris Pfeiffer *Tel:* (0711) 797 330-217 *E-mail:* ipfeiffer@carus-verlag.com
Production: Duck-Ja Shin *Tel:* (0711) 797 330-17 *E-mail:* djshin@carus-verlag.com
Rights & Licenses: Adelheid Duecker *Tel:* (0711) 797 330-26 *E-mail:* aduecker@carus-verlag.com
Founded: 1972
Subjects: Music, Dance, Religion - Other, Christianity
ISBN Prefix(es): 978-3-89948; 978-3-88188; 978-3-923053

Cass Verlag
Im Sundern 16, 32584 Loehne
Tel: (05732) 911496 *Fax:* (05732) 911496
E-mail: info@cass-verlag.de
Web Site: www.cass-verlag.de
Key Personnel
Manager: Dr Katja Cassing
Founded: 2000
Subjects: Fiction, Nonfiction (General), Science (General)
ISBN Prefix(es): 978-3-9809022

Catia Monser Eggcup-Verlag
Werstener Feld 235, 40591 Duesseldorf
Tel: (0211) 215122 *Fax:* (0211) 215122
E-mail: cmonserev@monser.info
Web Site: www.rodobby.de/verlag/index.html
Key Personnel
Contact: Catia Monser

Founded: 1993
Subjects: Disability, Special Needs, Health, Nutrition, Human Relations, Medicine, Nursing, Dentistry, Mysteries, Suspense, Thalidomide (Contergan)
ISBN Prefix(es): 978-3-930004

cbj, *imprint of* Verlagsgruppe Random House Bertelsmann

cbj Verlag
Imprint of Verlagsgruppe Random House Bertelsmann
Neumarkter Str 28, 81673 Munich
Tel: (089) 4136-0 *Fax:* (089) 4136-3333
E-mail: vertrieb.verlagsgruppe@randomhouse.de; kundenservice@randomhouse.de
Web Site: www.randomhouse.de/verlage.rhs
Founded: 2004
Subjects: Humor, Nonfiction (General), Science Fiction, Fantasy, Adventure, Family
ISBN Prefix(es): 978-3-641

cbt Verlag, *imprint of* Verlagsgruppe Random House Bertelsmann

ch. falk-verlag+
Ischl 11, 83370 Seeon
Tel: (08667) 14 13 *Fax:* (08667) 14 17
E-mail: email@chfalk-verlag.de
Web Site: www.chfalk-verlag.de
Key Personnel
Publisher: Christa Falk
Founded: 1982
Specialize in esoteric books.
ISBN Prefix(es): 978-3-924161; 978-3-89568
Number of titles published annually: 10 Print; 4 CD-ROM; 1 Audio
Total Titles: 283 Print; 196 Online; 16 Audio
Foreign Rep(s): AS Hoeller (Austria)

Ch Links Publisher, see Christopher Links Verlag GmbH

Verlag fuer chemische Industrie H Ziolkowsky GmbH
Dorfstr 40, 86470 Thannhausen
Tel: (08281) 79940-0 *Fax:* (08281) 79940-50
E-mail: vci@sofw.com
Web Site: www.sofw.com
Key Personnel
General Manager: Robert Fischer *Tel:* (08281) 79940-30 *E-mail:* robert.fischer@sofw.com
Marketing Manager: Siegfried Fischer *Tel:* (08281) 79940-31 *E-mail:* siegfried.fischer@sofw.com
Subjects: Chemistry, Chemical Engineering, Cosmetics, Pharmacology, Toxicology
ISBN Prefix(es): 978-3-87846
Distribution Center: United Books & Periodicals, 7, Vishwadham, Prabhat Clny Rd No 9, Santacruz (East), 400 055 Mumbai, India, Contact: Rahul M Gavankar *Tel:* (022) 2617 7370; (022) 2611 6909 *Fax:* (022) 2610 5852 *E-mail:* unitedbooks@gmail.com (India, Malaysia & Pakistan)

Chicken House Deutschland
Voelckerstr 14-20, 22765 Hamburg
Mailing Address: Postfach 50 03 80, 22703 Hamburg
Tel: (040) 39 804-0 *Fax:* (040) 39 804-390
E-mail: info@carlsen.de
Web Site: www.carlsen.de/chicken-house
Key Personnel
Mng Dir: Renate Herre; Joachim Kaufman
Press: Hilke Schenck *E-mail:* hilke.schenck@carlsen.de
ISBN Prefix(es): 978-3-551
Parent Company: Carlsen Verlag GmbH

Chiron Verlag+
Riedstr 10, 72070 Tuebingen
Tel: (07071) 8884150 *Fax:* (07071) 8884151
E-mail: info@chironverlag.com
Web Site: www.chiron-verlag.de
Key Personnel
Owner & Publisher: Reinhardt Stiehle
Founded: 1984
Membership(s): Verband der Deutsch Verleger und Buchhaendler.
Subjects: Astrology, Occult
ISBN Prefix(es): 978-3-925100; 978-3-89997

Verlag Chmielorz GmbH+
Member of Verlagsgruppe Chmielorz
Marktplatz 13, 65183 Wiesbaden
Mailing Address: Postfach 2229, 65012 Wiesbaden
Tel: (0611) 3 60 98-0 *Fax:* (0611) 30 13 03
E-mail: info@chmielorz.de
Web Site: www.chmielorz.de
Key Personnel
Mng Dir: Christian Augsburger *E-mail:* christian.augsburger@chmielorz.de; Juergen Biniek *E-mail:* juergen.biniek@chmielorz.de
Founded: 1949
Publish professional magazines (trade press), handbooks, loose-leaf books (law commentaries), CD-ROMs, databases.
Subjects: Business, Civil Engineering, Cookery, Earth Sciences, Economics, Fiction, Geography, Geology, Health, Nutrition, Law, Medicine, Nursing, Dentistry, Public Administration, Publishing & Book Trade Reference, Social Sciences, Sociology, Sports, Athletics, Cinema, Film Industry, Food, International Law, Movies, Sport (Trade, Industry)
ISBN Prefix(es): 978-3-87124; 978-3-87202; 978-3-920570
Branch Office(s)
Druckerei Chmielorz, Ostring 13, 65205 Wiesbaden-Nordenstadt *Tel:* (06122) 7709-01 *Fax:* (06122) 7709-181 *E-mail:* hallo@chmielorz.de
Distributor for EuBuCo-Verlag; mhp-Verlag

Chorus-Verlag fuer Kunst und Wissenschaft
Hinter der Kapelle 54, 55128 Mainz
Tel: (06131) 346 64; (0171) 420 82 80 (cell) *Fax:* (06131) 369 076
E-mail: info@chorus-verlag.de
Web Site: www.chorus-verlag.de
Key Personnel
Mng Dir: Dr Dorothea van der Koelen *E-mail:* dvanderkoelen@chorus-verlag.de
Founded: 1995
Specialize in museum catalogues & catalog raisonnes.
Subjects: Art
ISBN Prefix(es): 978-3-931876; 978-3-926663
Total Titles: 60 Print
Distributed by Arteko Galeria de Arte (Spain); Continent Books (Amsterdam); Hurtado de Ediciones (Spain); Joker Art Diffusion (France)

Chr Belser AG fuer Verlagsgeschaefte & Co KG+
Pfizerstr 5-7, 70184 Stuttgart
Tel: (0711) 2191-0 *Fax:* (0711) 2191-412
E-mail: info@belser.de
Web Site: www.belser-verlag.de
Key Personnel
Publishing Dir: Bernhard Kolb *Tel:* (0711) 2191-400 *E-mail:* b.kolb@belser.de
Editor: Mareen Obst *Tel:* (0711) 2191-256 *E-mail:* m.obst@belser.de
Foreign Rights: Sabine Archilla *Tel:* (0711) 2191-281 *E-mail:* s.archilla@belser.de
Sales: Melanie Ehrlich *Tel:* (0711) 2191-403 *E-mail:* m.ehrlich@belser.de
Founded: 1835

Subjects: Art, History, Music, Dance, Nonfiction (General), Religion - Other, Theology, Travel & Tourism
ISBN Prefix(es): 978-3-7630
Subsidiaries: Amalthea; Bechtle; Mary Hahn; Kronos; LangenMueller; Lentz; Mahnert-Lueg; Meyster; Nymphenburger; Reich; Universitas; USM Soft Media; Wirtschaftsverlag
Foreign Rep(s): B+I Buch und Information AG (Richard Bhend) (Switzerland); Jutta Bussmann (Austria); Jahann Czap (Eastern Austria); Michael Hipp (South Tyrol, Italy, Western Austria)
Distribution Center: Vrvato media GmbH, An der Autobahn 100, 33333 Guetersloh *Tel:* (05241) 806643
Mohr Morawa Buchvertrieb GmbH, Sulzengasse 2, 1230 Vienna, Austria *Tel:* (01) 680 14-0 *Fax:* (01) 688 71 30 *E-mail:* momo@mohrmorawa.au *Web Site:* www.mohrmorawa.au
Buchzentrum AG, Industriestr Ost 10, 4614 Haegendorf, Switzerland *Tel:* (062) 2092626 *Fax:* (062) 2092627

Edition Chrismon, *imprint of* Evangelische Verlagsanstalt GmbH

Edition Chrismon
Imprint of Evangelische Verlagsanstalt GmbH
Blumenstr 76, 04155 Leipzig
Tel: (0341) 71141-15 *Fax:* (0341) 71141-40
Web Site: chrismon.evangelisch.de/ueber-uns/edition-chrismon; www.chrismonshop.de
Key Personnel
Publishing Dir: Sebastian Knoefel *E-mail:* knoefel@eva-leipzig.de
Press: Johannes Popp
Sales & Marketing: Ivonne Dellit
Subjects: Inspirational, Spirituality, Religion - Other
ISBN Prefix(es): 978-3-86921; 978-3-96038
Foreign Rep(s): Balmer Buecherdienst AG (Switzerland)
Distribution Center: Leipziger Kommissions- u Grossbuchhandelsgesellschaft mbH (LKG), An der Suedspitze 1-12, 04571 Roetha, Contact: Christine Falk *Tel:* (034206) 65-129 *Fax:* (034206) 65-1736 *E-mail:* christine.falk@lkg-service.de *Web Site:* www.lkg-va.de

Christian Verlag GmbH+
Infanteriestr 11a, 80797 Munich
Tel: (089) 130699-0 *Fax:* (089) 130699-100
E-mail: info@verlagshaus.de; verlagsleitung@verlagshaus.de
Web Site: www.verlagshaus24.de/christian
Key Personnel
Mng Dir: Clemens Hahn *Tel:* (089) 130699-720 *Fax:* (089) 130699-700
Founded: 1947
Subjects: Architecture & Interior Design, Cookery, Gardening, Plants, Nonfiction (General), Photography, Wine & Spirits
ISBN Prefix(es): 978-3-88472
Parent Company: GeraNova Bruckmann Verlagshaus GmbH
Associate Companies: J Berg Verlag; Bruckmann Verlag; Frederking & Thaler; GeraMond Verlag
Orders to: Postfach 1280, 82197 Gilching *E-mail:* service@verlagshaus.de

Christiana+
Hauptstr 22, 88353 Kisslegg
Tel: (07563) 92006 *Fax:* (07563) 3381
E-mail: info@fe-medien.de
Web Site: www.fe-medien.de
Key Personnel
Mng Dir: Bernhard Mueller
Founded: 1948
Subjects: Biblical Studies, Biological Sciences, Education, History, Literature, Literary Crit-

icism, Essays, Medicine, Nursing, Dentistry, Philosophy, Poetry, Religion - Catholic, Theology, Angeology, Demonology, Hagiographic, Mysticism, Natural Science
ISBN Prefix(es): 978-3-7171
Number of titles published annually: 12 Print
Parent Company: FE-Medienverlags GmbH

Christians Verlag ek+
Raboisen 6, 20095 Hamburg
Tel: (040) 32 90 17 80 *Fax:* (040) 32 90 17 81
E-mail: verlag@christians.de; bestellung@christians.de
Web Site: www.christians.de
Key Personnel
Mng Dir: Susanne Liebelt
Founded: 1740
Subjects: Architecture & Interior Design, Art, Biography, Memoirs, Communications, Cookery, Education, Ethnicity, Gardening, Plants, Geography, Geology, History, Music, Dance, Natural History, Nonfiction (General), Outdoor Recreation, Photography, Regional Interests, Religion - Jewish, Social Sciences, Sociology, Travel & Tourism, Pedagogy
ISBN Prefix(es): 978-3-7672; 978-3-939969
Distributor for CCV; Eylers; Verlag Gronenberg; Land & Meer Verlag; Verlag fuer Medienliteratur; Verlag Robert Wenzel
Warehouse: Vull-Service GmbH, Werftbahnstr 8, 24143 Kiel *Tel:* (0431) 702 82 70 *Fax:* (0431) 702 82 99

Christliche Literatur-Verbreitung eV
Ravensberger Bleiche 6, 33649 Bielefeld
Tel: (0521) 947240 *Fax:* (0521) 9472421
E-mail: info@clv.de
Web Site: www.clv.de
Key Personnel
Mng Dir: Wolfgang Buehne; Peter Lueling
Founded: 1983
Subjects: Biography, Memoirs, Education, Fiction, Nonfiction (General), Self-Help, Christianity, Faith, Family
ISBN Prefix(es): 978-3-86699; 978-3-89397

Christliche Schriftenverbreitung eV Verlag und Versandbuchhandlung
An der Schlossfabrik 30, 42499 Hueckeswagen
Tel: (02192) 9210-0 *Fax:* (02192) 9210-23
E-mail: info@csv-verlag.de
Web Site: www.csv-verlag.de
Key Personnel
Chief Executive Officer: Gerrid Setzer *Tel:* (02192) 9210-14 *E-mail:* setzer@csv-verlag.de
Mng Dir: Hartmut Mohncke *Tel:* (02192) 9210-16 *E-mail:* h.mohncke@csv-verlag.de
Sales: Volkhard Winter *Tel:* (02192) 9210-17 *E-mail:* winter@csv-verlag.de
Marketing & Production: Reinhard Mohncke *Tel:* (02192) 9210-15 *E-mail:* r.mohncke@csv-verlag.de
Subjects: Inspirational, Spirituality, Christianity
ISBN Prefix(es): 978-3-89287

Christliche Verlagsgesellschaft mbH (Christian Publishing Co)+
Molkestr 1, 35683 Dillenburg
Tel: (02771) 83020 *Fax:* (02771) 830230
E-mail: info@cv-dillenburg.de
Web Site: www.cv-dillenburg.de
Key Personnel
Mng Dir: Hartmut Jaeger *E-mail:* h.jaeger@cv-dillenburg.de
Rights & Permissions: Mirko Merten *Tel:* (02771) 830239 *E-mail:* m.merten@cv-dillenburg.de
Founded: 1957
Subjects: Religion - Other
ISBN Prefix(es): 978-3-89436
Subsidiaries: Christliche Buecherstuben GmbH

Distributed by Brunnen Verlag, Basel (Switzerland); CB Medienvertrieb (Germany)
Distributor for CLV; Daniel Verlag; KEB; Leuchtturm Verlag; Media C; Schwengeler; 3L Verlag

Christophorus, *imprint of* Verlag Kreuz GmbH

Christophorus Verlag GmbH & Co KG+
Schnewlinstr 6, 79098 Freiburg
Tel: (0761) 70 578-0 *Fax:* (0761) 70 578-651
E-mail: info@christophorus-verlag.de; buchverlag@c-verlag.de
Web Site: www.christophorus-verlag.de
Key Personnel
Mng Dir: Bernhard Leuz
Head, Foreign Rights: Adelheid Mueller *Tel:* (07623) 964 148 *E-mail:* a.mueller@mg-medweth.de
Marketing: Silke Diedrichs
Sales: Luz-Werner Wissenbach
Founded: 1935
Subjects: Crafts, Games, Hobbies, How-to, Outdoor Recreation
ISBN Prefix(es): 978-3-419; 978-3-86673; 978-3-8388
Imprints: OZ creativ
Branch Office(s)
Toepferstr 14, 65191 Wiesbaden *Tel:* (0611) 942 72-0 *Fax:* (0611) 942 72-40 *E-mail:* info@englisch-verlag.de
Shipping Address: Roemerstr 90, 79618 Rheinfelden *Tel:* (07623) 96 40 *Fax:* (07623) 96 42 00 *E-mail:* info@oz-verlag.de *Web Site:* www.oz-verlag.de
Warehouse: Roemerstr 90, 79618 Rheinfelden *Tel:* (07623) 96 40 *Fax:* (07623) 96 42 00 *E-mail:* info@oz-verlag.de *Web Site:* www.oz-verlag.de
Orders to: Roemerstr 90, 79618 Rheinfelden *Tel:* (07623) 96 40 *Fax:* (07623) 96 42 00 *E-mail:* info@oz-verlag.de *Web Site:* www.oz-verlag.de

Christusbruderschaft Selbitz Buch & Kunstverlag
Wildenberg 23, 95152 Selbitz
Mailing Address: Postfach 1260, 95147 Selbitz
Tel: (09280) 68-134 *Fax:* (09280) 68-68
E-mail: info@verlag-christusbruderschaft.de
Web Site: www.verlag-christusbruderschaft.de
Key Personnel
International Rights: Sr Baerbel Quarg
Founded: 1953
Subjects: Art, Poetry, Religion - Protestant, Theology
ISBN Prefix(es): 978-3-928745

Cicero Presse Verlag & Druckerei & Bibliophiles Antiquariat Timm Zenner eK
Markt 4, 25836 Garding, Schleswig-Holstein
Tel: (0465) 890305
Founded: 1965
Membership(s): International League of Antiquarian Booksellers (ILAB); Verband Deutscher Antiquare (VDA).
ISBN Prefix(es): 978-3-89120
Total Titles: 20 Print

Cisco Press, *imprint of* Pearson Deutschland GmbH

Classicus Verlag GmbH
Heilwigstr 88, 20249 Hamburg
Tel: (040) 41 72 79 *Fax:* (040) 44 61 27
Web Site: www.classicus-verlag.de
Key Personnel
Management: Claudia Ludwig *E-mail:* ludwig@classicus-verlag.de
Subjects: Communications, Education, Management, Nonfiction (General)
ISBN Prefix(es): 978-3-942848

Claudius Verlag+
Birkerstr 22, 80636 Munich
Tel: (089) 12172-0 *Fax:* (089) 12172-138
E-mail: claudius@epv.de
Web Site: www.claudius.de
Key Personnel
Publishing Dir: Dr Martin Scherer *Tel:* (089)
12172-136 *E-mail:* mscherer@epv.de
Mng Dir: Dr Roland Gertz *Tel:* (089) 12172-112
E-mail: rgertz@epv.de
International Rights: Antje Fritsch-Brown
Tel: (089) 12172-132 *E-mail:* afritsch@epv.de
Marketing: Miriam Kurz *Tel:* (089) 12172-127
E-mail: mkurz@epv.de
Press: Barbara Gabor-Pillat *Tel:* (089) 12172-123
E-mail: bgabor@epv.de
Sales: Heide Warkentin *Tel:* (089) 12172-120
E-mail: hwarkentin@epv.de
Founded: 1954
Subjects: Developing Countries, Humor, Psychol-
ogy, Psychiatry, Religion - Protestant, Religion
- Other, Self-Help, Theology
ISBN Prefix(es): 978-3-532
Number of titles published annually: 30 Print
Total Titles: 300 Print
Parent Company: Evangelischer Presseverband
fuer Bayern eV
Foreign Rep(s): Ruth Beuter (Switzerland); Clau-
dia Grueneis-Lambourne (Austria)
Bookshop(s): Claudius Versandbuchhandlung
Tel: (089) 12172-119 *E-mail:* vsb@epv.de
Distribution Center: Umbreit Verlagsaus-
lieferung, Mundelsheimer Str 3, 74321
Bietigheim-Bissingen, Contact: Silke Nadj
Tel: (07142) 596-0 *Fax:* (07142) 596-387
E-mail: verlagsauslieferung@umbreit.de
BMK Buchauslieferung, Trautsongasse 8, 1082
Vienna, Austria *Tel:* (01) 40 59 371 *Fax:* (01)
40 899 056 *E-mail:* bmkbuch@buchhandlung.
co.at
Herder AG Bagel, Muttenzerstr 109, Postfach,
4133 Pratteln 1, Switzerland *Tel:* (061) 827
90 60 *Fax:* (061) 827 90 67 *E-mail:* verkauf@
herder.ch

Cleon Verlag
Eichenweg 35b, 83109 Grokarolinenfeld
Tel: (08031) 9411 654 *Fax:* (08031) 9412 065
E-mail: mail@cleon-verlag.de
Web Site: www.cleon-verlag.de
Key Personnel
Owner: Stefan Seitz
Founded: 2006
Subjects: Science Fiction, Fantasy
ISBN Prefix(es): 978-3-9813171

Cluaran Verlag & Handels OHG
Schillerstr 9, 64683 Einhausen
Fax: (06251) 770 222
E-mail: info@cluaran.de
Web Site: www.cluaran.de
Key Personnel
Chief Executive Officer: Ralf Bernhardt; Hans-
Georg Wuersching
Subjects: Wine & Spirits, Whiskey
ISBN Prefix(es): 978-3-9809344

CoCon Verlag Hanau
In den Tuerkischen Gaerten 13, 63450 Hanau
Tel: (06181) 1 77 00 *Fax:* (06181) 18 13 33
E-mail: cocon-verlag@t-online.de; kontakt@
cocon-verlag.de
Web Site: www.cocon-verlag.de
Key Personnel
Owner: Annette Schulmerich
Founded: 1989
Subjects: Cookery, Regional Interests, Travel &
Tourism
ISBN Prefix(es): 978-3-928100; 978-3-937774

Charles Coleman Verlag GmbH & Co KG
Stolberger Str 84, 50933 Cologne

Mailing Address: Postfach 41 09 49, 50869
Cologne
Tel: (0221) 5497-0 *Fax:* (0221) 5497-326
E-mail: info@coleman-verlag.de; info@rudolf-
mueller.de
Web Site: www.coleman-verlag.de; www.rudolf-
mueller.de
Key Personnel
Mng Dir: Rudolf M Bleser *Tel:* (0221) 5497-214
E-mail: gf@rudolf-mueller.de; Dr Christoph
Mueller *Tel:* (0221) 5497-236 *E-mail:* gl@
rudolf-mueller.de
Founded: 1840
Provide practical technical information in
architecture-related fields.
Subjects: Architecture & Interior Design, Career
Development, Engineering (General), Mechani-
cal Engineering, Real Estate
ISBN Prefix(es): 978-3-87128
Parent Company: Verlagsgesellschaft Rudolf
Mueller GmbH & Co KG

Collection b, *imprint of* Deutsche
Bibelgesellschaft

Compact Verlag GmbH+
Baierbrunner Str 27, 81379 Munich
Tel: (089) 74 51 61-0 *Fax:* (089) 75 60 95
E-mail: info@compactverlag.de
Web Site: www.compactverlag.de
Key Personnel
Chief Executive Officer: Thomas Mohr
Project Manager, Online: Franziska Gornig
Tel: (089) 74 51 61-40 *E-mail:* franziska.
gornig@compactverlag.de
Sales Manager: Anne K Roehr *Tel:* (089) 74 51
61-94 *E-mail:* anne.roehr@compactverlag.de
Foreign Rights: Giancarlo Russo *Tel:* (089) 74 51
61-92 *E-mail:* giancarlo.russo@compactverlag.
de
Founded: 1976
Specialize in nonfiction books.
Subjects: Art, Business, Child Care & Develop-
ment, Cookery, Crafts, Games, Hobbies, Edu-
cation, English as a Second Language, Garden-
ing, Plants, Health, Nutrition, History, House
& Home, How-to, Language Arts, Linguistics,
Nonfiction (General), Real Estate, Self-Help,
Travel & Tourism
ISBN Prefix(es): 978-3-8174
Number of titles published annually: 180 Print
Total Titles: 1,000 Print
Parent Company: Compact Verlagsgruppe
Ultimate Parent Company: European Professional
Publishing Group
Warehouse: CDC GmbH, Rotwandweg 1,
82024 Taufkirchen, Contact: Helga Meier
Tel: (089) 74 51 61-38 *Fax:* (089) 75 60 95
E-mail: info@verlagsauslieferung-cdc.de *Web
Site:* www.verlagsauslieferung-cdc.de

Concordia-BUCHhandlung+
Bahnhofstr 8, 08056 Zwickau
Tel: (0375) 21 28 50 *Fax:* (0375) 29 80 80
E-mail: post@concordiabuch.de
Web Site: www.concordiabuch.de
Key Personnel
Mng Dir: Dr Gottfried Herrmann
Founded: 1990
Publishing house of Evangelisch-Lutherischen
Freikirche.
Subjects: Religion - Other, Theology
ISBN Prefix(es): 978-3-910153

Connection AG+
Hauptstr 5, 84494 Niedertaufkirchen
Tel: (08639) 9834-0 *Fax:* (08639) 1219
E-mail: seminare@connection.de
Web Site: www.connection.de
Key Personnel
Mng Dir: Wolf Schneider *Tel:* (08639) 9834-17
E-mail: schneider@connection.de

Sales & Advertising: Birgit Roeser *Tel:* (08639)
9834-20 *E-mail:* birgit@connection.de
Editor: Christine Hoefig *Tel:* (08639) 9834-22
E-mail: christine.hoefig@connection.de
Sales: Irmi Hauer *Tel:* (08639) 9834-14
E-mail: irmi.hauer@connection.de
Founded: 1985
Subjects: Human Relations, Parapsychology, Reli-
gion - Buddhist, Religion - Other, Self-Help
ISBN Prefix(es): 978-3-928248
Number of titles published annually: 5 Print
Parent Company: Connection Medien GmbH

Conte-Verlag GmbH
Am Rech 14, 66386 Sankt Ingbert
Tel: (06894) 166 41 63 *Fax:* (06894) 166 41 64
E-mail: info@conte-verlag.de
Web Site: www.conte-verlag.de
Key Personnel
Founder: Roland Buhles; Stefan Wirtz
Founded: 2001
Subjects: Fiction, Nonfiction (General)
ISBN Prefix(es): 978-3-936950; 978-3-9808118

Contmedia GmbH
Vogelsanger Weg 91, 40470 Duesseldorf
Tel: (05931) 40 92-40 *Fax:* (05931) 40 92-42
E-mail: info@contmedia.com
Web Site: www.contmedia.com
Key Personnel
Mng Dir: Sebastian Hoogland *E-mail:* sh@
contmedia.com
Membership(s): Boersenverein des Deutschen
Buchhandels eV.
Subjects: Education, Gardening, Plants, Science
(General), Current Affairs
ISBN Prefix(es): 978-3-941497; 978-3-937775
Distribution Center: Brockhaus/Commis-
sion, Kreidlerstr 9, 70806 Kornwestheim
Tel: (07154) 13 27-0 *Fax:* (07154) 13 27-13
E-mail: team1@brocom.de
AS Hoeller GmbH, Schrackgasse 11a, 8650 Kind-
berg, Austria *Tel:* (03865) 44 880 *Fax:* (03865)
44 880-77 *E-mail:* office@ashoeller.com
Herder AG Verlagsauslieferungen, Muttenzer Str
109, 4133 Pratteln, Switzerland *Tel:* (061) 8 27
90 60 *Fax:* (061) 8 27 90 67 *E-mail:* verkauf@
herder.ch

Coppenrath Verlag GmbH & Co KG+
Subsidiary of Wolfgang Hoelker Verlag
Hafenweg 30, 48155 Muenster
Tel: (0251) 41 411-0 *Fax:* (0251) 41 411-20
E-mail: info@coppenrath.de
Web Site: www.coppenrath.de
Key Personnel
Mng Dir: Wolfgang Hoelker
Foreign Rights Dir: Claudia Medin *Tel:* (0251)
41 411-811 *Fax:* (0251) 41 411-800
E-mail: medin@coppenrath.de
Foreign Rights: Nadine Lottes *Tel:* (0251) 41
411-818 *E-mail:* lottes@coppenrath.de
Publicity: Tomas Rensing *E-mail:* rensing@
coppenrath.de
Founded: 1948
Subjects: Architecture & Interior Design, Art,
Nonfiction (General)
ISBN Prefix(es): 978-3-88547; 978-3-8157; 978-
3-920192
Divisions: Edition Spiegelburg
Warehouse: Coppenrath-Hoelker Distribution,
Textilstr 3, 48612 Horstmar *Tel:* (02558) 98818
Fax: (02558) 98819

Copress Sport Verlag, *imprint of* Stiebner Verlag
GmbH

Copress Sport Verlag+
Imprint of Stiebner Verlag GmbH
Nymphenburger Str 86, 80636 Munich
Tel: (089) 1257 414 *Fax:* (089) 1216 2282
E-mail: verlag@stiebner.com

Web Site: www.stiebner.com; www.copress.de
Key Personnel
Manager: Hans-Peter Copony; Dr Joerg D Stiebner
Product Manager: Pierre Sick
Sales Manager: Hannelore Schwingenstein
Tel: (089) 2899 8946-48 *Fax:* (089) 2899 8947-49 *E-mail:* h.schwingenstein@t-online.de
Subjects: Health, Nutrition, History, Outdoor Recreation, Sports, Athletics
ISBN Prefix(es): 978-3-7679; 978-3-8307
Foreign Rep(s): Verlagsvertretung Hoeller (Michael Hoeller & Mario Seiler) (Austria, South Tyrol, Italy); Martin Schnetzer (Switzerland)
Distribution Center: Brockhaus/Commission, Kreidlerstr 9, 70806 Kornwestheim *Tel:* (071) 54 13 27-0 *Fax:* (071) 54 13 27-13 *E-mail:* stiebner@brocom.de
Hillstein Verlag, Rochusgasse 9, Postfach 1, 5017 Salzburg, Austria *Tel:* (0662) 82 7700-0 *Fax:* (0662) 82 7700-33 *E-mail:* info@hillstein.at (Austria & South Tyrol, Italy)
Schweizer Buchzentrum, Industrie Ost, 4601 Olten, Switzerland *Tel:* (062) 209 25 25 *Fax:* (062) 209 26 27

Cora Verlag
Valentinskamp 24, 20354 Hamburg
Mailing Address: Postfach 30 11 61, 20304 Hamburg
Tel: (01805) 63 63 65 (customer service)
Fax: (01805) 18 20 02 (customer service)
E-mail: kundenservice@cora.de (customer service)
Web Site: www.cora.de
Key Personnel
Mng Dir: Thomas Beckmann
Marketing & Advertising: Andrea Luck *Tel:* (040) 60 09 09-380 *Fax:* (040) 60-09 09-469 *E-mail:* andrea.luck@harpercollins.de
Founded: 1976
Subjects: Erotica, Mysteries, Suspense, Romance
ISBN Prefix(es): 978-3-89941; 978-3-934559
Parent Company: Harlequin Enterprises GmbH

Corian-Verlag Heinrich Wimmer
Bernhard-Monath-Str 28, 86405 Meitingen
Mailing Address: Postfach 11 69, 86400 Meitingen
Tel: (08271) 5951 *Fax:* (08271) 6931
Key Personnel
Mng Dir: Heinrich Wimmer
Founded: 1983
Subjects: Erotica, Film, Video, Humor, Science Fiction, Fantasy, Travel & Tourism, Comics
ISBN Prefix(es): 978-3-89048

Cornelsen Schulverlage GmbH+
Mecklenburgische Str 53, 14197 Berlin
Tel: (030) 897 85-0 *Fax:* (030) 897 85-299
E-mail: c-mail@cornelsen.de
Web Site: www.cornelsen.de/international
Key Personnel
Mng Dir: Dr Alexander Bob; Wolf-Ruediger Feldmann; Dr Anja Hagen; Frank Thalhofer; Ulrich Vollmer
International Relations & Foreign Rights: Joachim Larche *E-mail:* joachim.larche@cornelsen.de
Founded: 1946
Textbook publisher in all areas of learning.
Membership(s): European Educational Publishers Group (EEPG); Verband der Deutsch Buchhaendler.
Subjects: Accounting, Advertising, Biological Sciences, Career Development, Chemistry, Chemical Engineering, Communications, Economics, Education, English as a Second Language, Geography, Geology, History, Language Arts, Linguistics, Management, Marketing, Mathematics, Physical Sciences, Physics, Technology
ISBN Prefix(es): 978-3-589; 978-3-464; 978-3-06

Number of titles published annually: 1,000 Print
Total Titles: 20,000 Print
Parent Company: Cornelsen Verlagsholding GmbH & Co
Ultimate Parent Company: Franz Cornelsen Foundation
Associate Companies: AKAD Privat-Hochschulen GmbH, Stuttgart; Bibliographisches Institut AG, Mannheim; Cornelsen Experimenta, Berlin; Cornelsen Verlagskontor GmbH, Bielefeld; Nakladatelstvi Fraus, Plzen, Czech Republic; R Oldenbourg Verlag GmbH, Munich; Sauerlaender Verlage AG, Aarau; VERITAS, Linz, Austria; Verlag an der Ruhr GmbH, Muelheim an der Ruhr
Orders to: CVK Cornelsen Verlagskontor, Kammerratsheide 66, 33609 Bielefeld

Cornelsen Scriptor+
Imprint of Cornelsen Verlag GmbH
Mecklenburgische Str 53, 14197 Berlin
Tel: (030) 897 85-0 *Fax:* (030) 897 85-578
E-mail: service@cornelsen.de
Web Site: www.cornelsen.de
Key Personnel
Mng Dir: Dr Anja Hagen
Founded: 1973
Subjects: Education
ISBN Prefix(es): 978-3-589
Ultimate Parent Company: Franz Cornelsen Bildungsholding GmbH & Co KG
Orders to: Cornelsen Verlagskontor GmbH, Kammerratsheide 66, 33609 Bielefeld *Tel:* (0521) 971 9-0 *Fax:* (0521) 971 9-260 *E-mail:* info@cvk.de *Web Site:* www.cvk.de

Corona Verlag+
Postfach 760 265, 22052 Hamburg
Tel: (040) 642 210 22 *Fax:* (040) 642 210 23
Key Personnel
Publisher: Halina Kamm
Editor: Joachim Stiller
Founded: 1989
Subjects: Astrology, Occult, Inspirational, Spirituality, Music, Dance, Philosophy, Poetry, Psychology, Psychiatry, Self-Help, Esoteric, Meditation, Natural Science
ISBN Prefix(es): 978-3-928084; 978-3-934438
Total Titles: 100 Print; 100 CD-ROM; 100 Audio
Foreign Rep(s): Christian Hirtzy (North Austria); Ernst Sonntag (South Austria); Hugo Weibel (Switzerland)
Distribution Center: Dr Franz Hain, Dr-Otto-Neurath-Gasse 5, 1220 Vienna, Austria *Tel:* (01) 22 65 65 *Fax:* (01) 22 52 82
Schweizer Buchzentrum Verlagsauslieferungen, Industriestr Ost 10, 4614 Haegendorf, Switzerland *Tel:* (062) 209 25 25 *Fax:* (062) 209 26 27

Corso Verlag, *imprint of* Verlagshaus Roemerweg GmbH

Covadonga Verlag
Spindelstr 58, 33604 Bielefeld
Tel: (0521) 5221792 *Fax:* (0521) 5221796
E-mail: info@covadonga.de
Web Site: www.covadonga.de
Key Personnel
Chief Executive Officer: Rainer Sprehe *E-mail:* r.sprehe@covadonga.de
Founded: 2003
Subjects: Sports, Athletics, Cycling
ISBN Prefix(es): 978-3-936973

J Cramer in der Gebrueder Borntraeger Verlagsbuchhandlung, *imprint of* Gebrueder Borntraeger Verlagsbuchhandlung

Creator, *imprint of* Bonifatius GmbH Druck-Buch-Verlag

Cross Cult
Teinacher Str 72, 71634 Ludwigsburg
Tel: (07141) 64 29 22 1 *Fax:* (07141) 64 29 22 3
E-mail: info@cross-cult.de; presse@cross-cult.de
Web Site: www.cross-cult.de
Key Personnel
Mng Dir: Hardy Hellstern; Andreas Mergenthaler
Founded: 2001
Subjects: Criminology, History, Humor, Mysteries, Suspense, Science Fiction, Fantasy, Adventure, Crime, Star Trek, Western
ISBN Prefix(es): 978-3-941248; 978-3-936480; 978-3-942649
Parent Company: Amigo Graphik GbR

Crotona Verlag GmbH
Kammer 11, 83123 Amerang
Tel: (08075) 91 32 74 *Fax:* (08075) 91 32 75
E-mail: kontakt@crotona.de
Web Site: www.crotona.de
Key Personnel
Chief Executive Officer: Annette Wagner
Subjects: Inspirational, Spirituality, Christian Mysticism, Feminine Spirituality, Jewish Mysticism
ISBN Prefix(es): 978-3-86191
Foreign Rep(s): Dessauer-Vertrieb (Claudia Gyr) (Switzerland)
Distribution Center: Brockhaus/Commission, Kreidlerstr 9, 70806 Kornwestheim *Tel:* (07154) 13 27-30 *Fax:* (07154) 13 27-13 *E-mail:* team3@brocom.de
Mohr Morawa Buchvertrieb GmbH, Sulzengasse 2, 1230 Vienna, Austria *Tel:* (01) 680 14 0 *Fax:* (01) 680 141 40 *E-mail:* bestellung@mohrmorawa.at *Web Site:* www.mohrmorawa.at
Schweizer Buchzentrum, Industriestr Ost 10, 4614 Haegendorf, Switzerland *Tel:* (062) 20 926 26 *Fax:* (062) 20 926 27 *E-mail:* losiggio@buchzentrum.ch

CTL-Presse
Borselstr 9-11, 22765 Hamburg
Tel: (040) 3990 2223 *Fax:* (040) 3990 2224
E-mail: mail@ctl-presse.de
Web Site: www.ctl-presse.de
Key Personnel
Dir: Clemens-Tobias Lange
Founded: 1989
Specialize in artist's books & gelatin silver photographic editions.
Subjects: Art, Photography, Poetry
Number of titles published annually: 2 Print
Total Titles: 79 Print

DAAD, see Deutscher Akademischer Austauschdienst eV

DACO Verlag Guenter Blaese+
Siemensstr 52, 70469 Stuttgart
Tel: (0711) 964 210 *Fax:* (0711) 964 2110
E-mail: info@daco-verlag.de
Web Site: www.daco-verlag.de
Key Personnel
Owner: Stephan Goetz
Founded: 1943
Subjects: Art
ISBN Prefix(es): 978-3-87135
Imprints: Hanfstaengl-Verlag; Nadif

Daedalus Verlag+
Oderstr 25, 48145 Muenster
Tel: (0251) 23 13 55 *Fax:* (0251) 23 26 31
E-mail: info@daedalus-verlag.de
Web Site: www.daedalus-verlag.de
Key Personnel
Owner: Joachim Herbst
Founded: 1984
Subjects: Communications, Government, Political Science, Medicine, Nursing, Dentistry, Nonfiction (General), Psychology, Psychiatry, Science

(General), Social Sciences, Sociology, Travel &
Tourism, Women's Studies
ISBN Prefix(es): 978-3-89126
Distribution Center: PROLIT Verlagsausliefer-
ung GmbH, Siemensstr 16, 35463 Fernwald,
Contact: Rita Nitz *Tel:* (0641) 9 43 93-0
Fax: (0641) 9 43 93-89 *E-mail:* r.nitz@prolit.
de (Germany & Austria)

Dagmar Dreves Verlag+
Meisenweg 20, 29229 Celle
Tel: (05086) 987804; (0175) 7229819 (cell)
Fax: (05086) 987806
E-mail: info@dagmar-dreves-verlag.de
Web Site: www.dagmar-dreves-verlag.de
Key Personnel
Publisher: Hans-Juergen Meyer
Founded: 1989
Subjects: Art, Biography, Memoirs, Economics,
Fiction, Government, Political Science, History,
Law, Mysteries, Suspense, Nonfiction (Gen-
eral), Parapsychology, Science (General), Social
Sciences, Sociology, Travel & Tourism
ISBN Prefix(es): 978-3-924532; 978-3-936269

Dana Verlag
Campemoorweg 8, 49565 Bramsche
Tel: (05468) 1813 *Fax:* (05468) 239
E-mail: danaverlag@t-online.de
Web Site: www.dana-verlag.de
Key Personnel
Contact: Gonda Sewald; Wolfgang Sewald
Founded: 1988
Subjects: Science Fiction, Fantasy
ISBN Prefix(es): 978-3-9801976; 978-3-931335

DarCon, see Dareschta Consulting und Handels
GmbH (DarCon)

**Dareschta Consulting und Handels GmbH
(DarCon)+**
Bahnhofstr 41, 26553 Dornum
Tel: (0933) 3389814 *Fax:* (0933) 3389815
Web Site: www.darcon.de; darcon.secu.net
Key Personnel
Mng Dir: Walter Alfred Siebel
Founded: 1999
Membership(s): IHK Wiesbadan; Verband der
Deutsch Verleger und Buchhaendler.
Subjects: Anthropology, Biological Sciences,
Medicine, Nursing, Dentistry, Psychology, Psy-
chiatry, Religion - Catholic, Religion - Protes-
tant, Social Sciences, Sociology, Women's
Studies
ISBN Prefix(es): 978-3-89379; 978-3-9801744

**Das Arsenal Verlag fuer Kultur und Politik
GmbH+**
Tegeler Weg 97, 10589 Berlin
Tel: (030) 3441827; (030) 34651360 *Fax:* (030)
34651362
Key Personnel
Mng Dir: Dr Peter Moses-Krause
Founded: 1977
Membership(s): Stock Exchange of German
Booksellers.
Subjects: Art, Drama, Theater, Fiction, History,
Philosophy, Jewish-German History, Jewish
Studies
ISBN Prefix(es): 978-3-921810; 978-3-931109
Number of titles published annually: 10 Print
Total Titles: 70 Print
Orders to: Runge Verlagsauslieferung GmbH,
Bergstr 2, 33803 Steinhagen, Contact: Team
3 *Tel:* (05204) 998 123 *Fax:* (05204) 998 114
E-mail: msr@rungeva.de *Web Site:* rungeva.de

DATAKONTEXT
Division of Verlagsgruppe Huethig Jehle-Rehm
GmbH
Augustinusstr 9d, 50226 Frechen

Tel: (02234) 98949-30 *Fax:* (02234) 98949-32
E-mail: fachverlag@datakontext.com; tagungen@
datakontext.com; info@datakontext.com
Web Site: www.datakontext.com
Key Personnel
Mng Dir: Karl Ulrich
Corporate Communications: Alexandra Meller
E-mail: meller@datakontext.com
Founded: 1984
Subjects: Computer Science, Human Relations,
Labor, Industrial Relations, Law, Management,
Public Administration, Securities
ISBN Prefix(es): 978-3-89577; 978-3-89209; 978-
3-921899
Orders to: Rhenus Medien Logistik GmbH & Co
KG, Contact: Jutta Mueller *Tel:* (0819) 97000-
641 *E-mail:* aboservice@hjr-verlag.de

dbb Verlag GmbH
Friedrichstr 165, 10117 Berlin
Tel: (030) 726 19 17-0 *Fax:* (030) 726 19 17-40
E-mail: kontakt@dbbverlag.de
Web Site: www.dbbverlag.de
Key Personnel
Mng Dir: Bernhard Nietgen
Subjects: Law, Public Administration
ISBN Prefix(es): 978-3-87863

DBV, *imprint of* Don Bosco Verlag

DCVerlag eK
Auf der Heide 12, 44803 Bochum
Tel: (0234) 94349-0 *Fax:* (0234) 94349-21
E-mail: info@dcverlag.de
Web Site: www.dcverlag.de
Key Personnel
Contact: Daniel Cramer *E-mail:* daniel.cramer@
dcverlag.de
Founded: 1990
Subjects: Health, Nutrition, Hazardous Materials
Management, Health & Safety Law, Occupa-
tional Health & Safety, Risk Assessment
ISBN Prefix(es): 978-3-934966; 978-3-941441

Verlag DeBehr
Kleinwolmsdorfer Str 49, 01454 Radeberg
Tel: (03528) 455955; (0178) 714 1000 (sales)
E-mail: verlag@debehr-verlag.de
Web Site: www.debehr.de
Key Personnel
Contact: Daniela Behr
Membership(s): Boersenverein des Deutschen
Buchhandels.
Subjects: Criminology, Fiction, House & Home,
Humor, Romance, Science Fiction, Fantasy,
Suspenses, Thriller
ISBN Prefix(es): 978-3-9812751; 978-3-941758;
978-3-939241
Orders to: Bichofswerdaer Str 34, 01900 Gross-
roehrsdorf *Tel:* (0178) 714 1000 (sales)
E-mail: debehr-verlag.farys@freenet.de

Dr Kurt Debus GmbH, see Wochenschau Verlag

DEFA-Stiftung
Franz-Mehring-Platz 1, 10243 Berlin
Tel: (030) 29 78 48 10 *Fax:* (030) 29 78 48 11
E-mail: info@defa-stiftung.de
Web Site: www.defa-stiftung.de
Key Personnel
Mng Dir: Dr Ralph Schenk *E-mail:* r.schenk@
defa-stiftung.de
Project Leader: Juliane Haase *E-mail:* j.haase@
defa-stiftung.de
Subjects: Film, Video

Verlag Degener & Co+
Am Bruehl 9, 91610 Insingen
Tel: (09869) 97 82 28-0 *Fax:* (09869) 97 82 28-9
E-mail: degener@degener-verlag.de
Web Site: www.degener-verlag.de

Key Personnel
Publisher: Manfred Dreiss
Editor: Dr Elzbieta Kucharska-Dreiss
Sales: Daniela Hanisch
Founded: 1910
Subjects: Genealogy, History, Military Science,
Regional Interests, Heraldry
ISBN Prefix(es): 978-3-7686
Number of titles published annually: 25 Print; 2
CD-ROM
Total Titles: 1,500 Print; 5 CD-ROM
Associate Companies: Verlag Bauer & Raspe KG;
Verlag Christoph Schmidt; Franz Schubert Ver-
lag
Distributor for Bauer & Raspe; Verlag Christoph
Schmidt; Franz Schubert Verlag

Delius Klasing Verlag GmbH+
Siekerwall 21, 33602 Bielefeld
Tel: (0521) 559-0 *Fax:* (0521) 559 88 114
E-mail: info@delius-klasing.de
Web Site: www.delius-klasing.de
Key Personnel
Mng Dir: Konrad Delius
Head, Communications: Edwin Baaske
Tel: (0521) 559-900 *E-mail:* e.baaske@delius-
klasing.de
Head, Press & Public Relations: Christian
Ludewig *Tel:* (0521) 559-902 *E-mail:* c.
ludewig@delius-klasing.de
Marketing & Sales Manager: Herman Ludewig
Tel: (0521) 559-300 *E-mail:* h.ludewig@delius-
klasing.de
Foreign Rights & Licensing: Verena Schwartz
Tel: (0521) 559-207; Petra Trueltzsch
Tel: (0521) 559-202
Founded: 1911
Subjects: Maritime, Water Sports
ISBN Prefix(es): 978-3-7688; 978-3-87412
Associate Companies: Edition Maritim Hamburg;
Moby Dick Verlag GmbH
Distributed by Ermatingeni; Lechner & Sohn
(Austria); Neptun Verlag; Schweiz

Delp Druck + Medien GmbH
Kegetstr 11, 91438 Bad Windsheim
Tel: (09841) 903-0 *Fax:* (09841) 903-15
E-mail: info@delp-druck.de
Web Site: www.delp-druck.de
Key Personnel
Mng Dir: Johann Delp *E-mail:* johann.delp@
delp-druck.de
Founded: 1961
Subjects: Art, Regional Interests
ISBN Prefix(es): 978-3-7689

Delta, *imprint of* Egmont Ehapa Media GmbH

Demmler Verlag, *imprint of* Verlagsgruppe
gruenes herz

Der Hoerverlag, *imprint of* Verlagsgruppe
Random House Bertelsmann

Der Hoerverlag GmbH (DHV)
Imprint of Verlagsgruppe Random House Bertels-
mann
Lindwurmstr 88, 80337 Munich
Tel: (089) 21 06 940 *Toll Free Tel:* (0800) 500 33
22 *Fax:* (089) 21 06 94 15
E-mail: info@hoerverlag.de; kundenservice@
randomhouse.de
Web Site: www.hoerverlag.de; www.randomhouse.
de/hoerverlag
Key Personnel
Press Dir: Heike Voelker-Sieber *Tel:* (089)
210694-32 *Fax:* (089) 210694-17
E-mail: heike.voelker-sieber@hoerverlag.de
Founded: 1993
ISBN Prefix(es): 978-3-89584; 978-3-89940

Design Pavoni® Verlag
Dinxperloerstr 213a, 46399 Bocholt
Tel: (02871) 2924176; (0172) 2918775 (cell)
Fax: (02871) 43584
E-mail: pavoni1@web.de
Web Site: www.pavoni1.de; www.design-pavoni-verlag.de
Key Personnel
Founder: Nicole J Kueppers
Sales: Renata Kuzu
Founded: 2009
Subjects: Biography, Memoirs, Fiction, Humor, Literature, Literary Criticism, Essays, Poetry, Science Fiction, Fantasy, Young Adult Literature
ISBN Prefix(es): 978-3-942199

Desina Verlag GmbH
Marie-Curie-Str 1, 26129 Oldenburg
Tel: (0441) 30498212 *Fax:* (0441) 30498213
E-mail: redaktion@desinaverlag.de
Web Site: www.desinaverlag.de
Key Personnel
Mng Dir & Publisher: Dr Anna Zeeck
Subjects: Science Fiction, Fantasy, Chinese Culture, Thriller
ISBN Prefix(es): 978-3-940307
Distribution Center: Runge Verlagsauslieferung, Bergstr 2, 33803 Steinhagen *Tel:* (05204) 998-442 *Fax:* (05204) 998-114 *E-mail:* dageroth@rungeva.de

DETAIL, see Institut fuer Internationale Architektur-Dokumentation GmbH & Co KG

Wissenschaftlicher Verlag Harri Deutsch GmbH+
Graefstr 47, 60486 Frankfurt am Main
Tel: (069) 77015860 *Fax:* (069) 77015869
E-mail: verlag@harri-deutsch.de
Web Site: www.harri-deutsch.de/verlag
Key Personnel
Mng Dir & Sales: Martin Kegel
Publicist: Heike Schulze
Electronic Media: Klaus Horn *E-mail:* horn@harri-deutsch.de
Founded: 1961
Subjects: Astronomy, Biological Sciences, Chemistry, Chemical Engineering, Computer Science, Economics, Electronics, Electrical Engineering, Engineering (General), Mathematics, Natural History, Nonfiction (General), Physical Sciences, Physics, Technology, Statistics
ISBN Prefix(es): 978-3-87144; 978-3-8171

Deutsche Bibelgesellschaft (German Bible Society)+
Balinger Str 31, 70567 Stuttgart
Tel: (0711) 7181-0 *Toll Free Tel:* 0800 242 3546
Fax: (0711) 7181-126
E-mail: zentrale@dbg.de
Web Site: www.dbg.de
Key Personnel
Mng Dir: Reinhard Adler *Tel:* (0711) 7181-249
E-mail: adler@dbg.de; Felix Breidenstein
Tel: (0711) 7181-248 *E-mail:* breidenstein@dbg.de; Klaus Sturm *Tel:* (0711) 7181-246
E-mail: sturm@dbg.de
Head, Sales & Advertising: Wolfgang Schweigert
Tel: (0711) 7181-127 *E-mail:* schweigert@dbg.de
Head, Production: Birgit Coconcelli *Tel:* (0711) 7181-233 *E-mail:* coconcelli@dbg.de
Licenses: Beate Schubert *Tel:* (0711) 7181-129
E-mail: schubert@dbg.de
Founded: 1981 (formed by merger of Evangelische Bibelwerk & Deutsche Bibelstiftung)
Subjects: Biblical Studies
ISBN Prefix(es): 978-3-438
Imprints: Collection b

U.S. Office(s): American Bible Society, 1865 Broadway, New York, NY 10023-7505, United States *Fax:* 212-408-1456 *Web Site:* www.americanbible.org

Deutsche Blinden-Bibliothek (German Library for the Blind)+
Am Schlag 8/10, 35037 Marburg
Mailing Address: Postfach 1160, 35001 Marburg
Tel: (06421) 6060 *Fax:* (06421) 606229
E-mail: info@blista.de
Web Site: www.blista.de
Key Personnel
Chairman: Claus Duncker
Commercial Dir: Arno Kraussmann
Founded: 1916
Subjects: Education, Law, Literature, Literary Criticism, Essays, Nonfiction (General)
ISBN Prefix(es): 978-3-89642
Parent Company: Deutsche Blindenstudienanstalt eV (DBSTA)
Divisions: Archiv und Internat Dokumentation zzuum Blinden-und Sehbehindertenwesen; Bibliographic Centre; Deutsche Blindenhoerbuecherei (aufgesprochene Literatur/talking books); Emil-Krueckmann-Bibliothek (Blindenschift/Braille)

Deutsche Gesellschaft fuer Eisenbahngeschichte eV (DGEG)
Kleinsorgenring 14, 59457 Werl
Tel: (02922) 8 49 70 *Fax:* (02922) 8 49 27
E-mail: info@dgeg.de; gst@dgeg.de
Web Site: www.dgeg.de
Key Personnel
President: Guenter Krause
Property Management: Mark Meyer-Eppler
Founded: 1967
Subjects: Transportation
ISBN Prefix(es): 978-3-921700; 978-3-936619

Deutsche Gesellschaft fuer Luft-und Raumfahrt Lilienthal Oberth eV
Godesberger Allee 70, 53175 Bonn
Tel: (0228) 30 80 5-0 *Fax:* (0228) 30 80 5-24
E-mail: info@dglr.de
Web Site: www.dglr.de
Key Personnel
Secretary General: Peter J Brandt *E-mail:* peter.brandt@dglr.de
Subjects: Aeronautics, Aviation, Engineering (General), Science (General), Technology, Aerospace
ISBN Prefix(es): 978-3-922010; 978-3-932182

Deutsche Landwirtschafts-Gesellschaft Verlags GmbH+
Eschborner Landstr 122, 60489 Frankfurt
Tel: (069) 24 788-451 *Fax:* (069) 24 788-484
E-mail: dlg-verlag@dlg.org
Web Site: www.dlg-verlag.de
Key Personnel
Mng Dir: Walter Hoffman *Tel:* (069) 247 88 450
E-mail: w.hoffman@dlg.org
Editorial Dir: Nina Eichberg *Tel:* (069) 247 88 482 *E-mail:* n.eichberg@dlg.org
Dir, Marketing: Vanessa Rickert *Tel:* (069) 247 88-466 *E-mail:* v.rickert@dlg.org
Press & Public Relations: Harms Mentzel *Tel:* (069) 247 88 478 *E-mail:* h.mentzel@dlg.org; Sabine Schilha *E-mail:* s.schilha@dlg.org
Sales: Ralf Bennewitz *Tel:* (069) 247 88-457
E-mail: r.bennewitz@dlg.org
Founded: 1952
Subjects: Agriculture, Health, Nutrition, Travel & Tourism
ISBN Prefix(es): 978-3-7690
Number of titles published annually: 15 Print
Total Titles: 350 Print
Parent Company: DLG eV
Distributed by Verlagsunion Agrar

Distribution Center: Vertriebsunion Meynen GmbH & Co KG, 65431 Eltville *Tel:* (0613) 92 38-263 *Fax:* (0613) 92 38-262 *E-mail:* dlg-verlag@vertriebsunion.de
Medien & Logistik, IZNOE Sued, Str 1 Objekt 34, 2355 Wiener Neudorf, Austria
Tel: (036) 63 535-0 *Fax:* (036) 63 535-243
E-mail: oebz@oebz.co.at
Returns: Vertriebsunion Meynen GmbH & Co KG, 65431 Eltville

Deutsche Lyrik Verlag, *imprint of* Karin Fischer Verlag GmbH

Deutsche Lyrik Verlag
Imprint of Karin Fischer Verlag GmbH
Wallstr 50, 52064 Aachen
Mailing Address: Postfach 10 21 32, 52021 Aachen
Tel: (0241) 960 90 90 *Fax:* (0241) 960 90 99
E-mail: info@deutscher-lyrik-verlag.de; verkauf@karin-fischer-verlag.de (sales); presse@karin-fischer-verlag.de
Web Site: www.deutscher-lyrik-verlag.de
Key Personnel
Mng Dir: Karin Fischer
Publishing Dir: Dr Manfred S Fischer
Subjects: Poetry
ISBN Prefix(es): 978-3-927854; 978-3-89514

Deutsche Nationalbibliothek (German National Library)
Adickesallee 1, 60322 Frankfurt am Main
Tel: (069) 1525-0 *Fax:* (069) 1525-1010
E-mail: info-f@dnb.de; postfach@dnb.de
Web Site: www.dnb.de
Key Personnel
Dir General: Dr Elisabeth Niggemann
Head, Marketing & Communication: Dr Britta Woldering *Tel:* (069) 1525-1541 *E-mail:* b.woldering@dnb.de
Public Relations: Stephan Jockel *Tel:* (069) 1525-1005 *E-mail:* s.jockel@dnb.de
Founded: 1912
Subjects: History, Regional Interests
ISBN Prefix(es): 978-3-922051; 978-3-933641; 978-3-941113

Deutsche Schillergesellschaft eV
Affiliate of Schiller-National Museum & Literatur Archives
Deutsches Literaturarchiv Marbach, Schillerhoehe 8-10, 71672 Marbach am Neckar
Mailing Address: Postfach 1162, 71666 Marbach am Neckar
Tel: (07144) 848-0 *Fax:* (07144) 848-299
E-mail: info@dla-marbach.de; presse@dla-marbach.de
Web Site: www.dla-marbach.de
Key Personnel
President: Dr Peter-Andre Alt
Vice President: Thomas Keller
Mng Dir: Dr Ulrich Raulff *Tel:* (07144) 848-100
Fax: (07144) 848-191 *E-mail:* ulrich.raulff@dla-marbach.de
Press: Alexa Hennemann *Tel:* (07144) 848-173
Fax: (07144) 848-191
Founded: 1955
Subjects: Literature, Literary Criticism, Essays
ISBN Prefix(es): 978-3-928882; 978-3-929146; 978-3-933679; 978-3-937384

Deutsche Verlags-Anstalt (DVA), *imprint of* Verlagsgruppe Random House Bertelsmann

Deutsche Verlags-Anstalt (DVA)+
Imprint of Verlagsgruppe Random House Bertelsmann
Neumarkt Str 28, 81673 Munich
Tel: (089) 4136-0 *Toll Free Tel:* (0800) 500 33 22
Fax: (089) 4136-3333

E-mail: kundenservice@randomhouse.de
Web Site: www.randomhouse.de/dva
Key Personnel
Foreign Rights Dir: Gesche Wendebourg
  Tel: (089) 4136-3313 *E-mail:* gesche.
  wendebourg@randomhouse.de
Dir, Press & Public Relations: Markus Desaga
  Tel: (089) 4136-3702 *Fax:* (089) 4136-3897
  E-mail: markus.desaga@randomhouse.de
Press: Christine Liebl *Tel:* (089) 4136-3703
  Fax: (089) 4136-3897 *E-mail:* christine.liebl@
  dva.de
Founded: 1831
Subjects: Architecture & Interior Design, As-
  tronomy, Biography, Memoirs, Crafts, Games,
  Hobbies, Earth Sciences, Fiction, Gardening,
  Plants, Government, Political Science, History,
  Literature, Literary Criticism, Essays, Music,
  Dance, Philosophy, Poetry, Psychology, Psychi-
  atry, Science (General)
ISBN Prefix(es): 978-3-421
Foreign Rights: ACER Agencia Literaria (Is-
  abel Piedrahita) (Brazil, Portugal, Spain);
  Graal Agencja Literacka (Joanna Maciuk)
  (Poland); Agentur Literatur Hebel & Binder-
  mann GbR (Gudrun Hebel & Guenther Frauen-
  lob) (Scandinavia); Agence Hoffman (Christine
  Scholz) (France); Marianne Schoenbach Liter-
  ary Agency (Belgium, Netherlands)
Warehouse: Verlegerdienst Muenchen, Guten-
  bergstr 1, 82205 Gilching

Deutscher Aerzteverlag GmbH+
Dieselstr 2, 50859 Cologne
Tel: (02234) 7011-0 *Fax:* (02234) 7011-476;
  (02234) 7011-6508
E-mail: service@aerzteverlag.de; bestellung@
  aerzteverlag.de (orders)
Web Site: www.aerzteverlag.de
Key Personnel
Mng Dir & Publisher: Norbert Froitzheim
Mng Dir: Juergen Fuehrer
Dir, Customer Center: Michael Heinrich
  Tel: (02234) 7011-233 *Fax:* (02234) 7011-6233
  E-mail: m.heinrich@aerzteverlag.de
Dir, Product Development, Dental: Manuel Berger
  Tel: (02234) 7011-340 *Fax:* (02234) 7011-6340
  E-mail: berger@aerzteverlag.de
Dir, Product Development, Medicine: Katrin
  Groos *Tel:* (02234) 7011-304 *Fax:* (02234)
  7011-6304 *E-mail:* groos@aerzteverlag.de
Founded: 1949
Subjects: Medicine, Nursing, Dentistry
ISBN Prefix(es): 978-3-7961
Subsidiaries: CEDIP Verlags GmbH; J F
  Lehmanns Med Buchhandlung GmbH;
  Schwarzeck-Verlag GmbH; Otto Spatz GmbH
  & Co KG

Deutscher Akademischer Austauschdienst eV
  (German Academic Exchange Service)
Kennedyallee 50, 53175 Bonn
Mailing Address: Postfach 20 04 04, 53134 Bonn
Tel: (0228) 882-0 *Fax:* (0228) 882-444
E-mail: postmaster@daad.de; presse@daad.de
Web Site: www.daad.de
Key Personnel
President: Dr Margret Wintermantel
Vice President: Dr Joybrato Mukherjee
Head, Press & Public Relations: Francis Hugen-
  roth *Tel:* (0228) 882-454
Subjects: Economics, Education, Government,
  Political Science, Social Sciences, Sociology
ISBN Prefix(es): 978-3-87192

Deutscher Apotheker Verlag Dr Roland
  Schmiedel GmbH & Co (Pharmaceutical Press
  of Germany)+
Birkenwaldstr 44, 70191 Stuttgart
Mailing Address: Postfach 10 10 61, 70009
  Stuttgart
Tel: (0711) 2582-0 *Fax:* (0711) 2582-390

E-mail: service@deutscher-apotheker-verlag.de
Web Site: www.deutscher-apotheker-verlag.de
Key Personnel
Mng Dir: Dr Klaus G Brauer; Dr Christian Rotta
Marketing Dir: Siegmar Bauer *E-mail:* sbauer@
  deutscher-apotheker-verlag.de
International Rights: Sabine Koerner
  E-mail: skoerner@dav-medien.de
Sales: Elisabeth Kerstan *Tel:* (0711) 2582-372
  E-mail: ekerstan@dav-medien.de
Founded: 1861
Subjects: Health, Nutrition, Medicine, Nursing,
  Dentistry, Pharmacy
ISBN Prefix(es): 978-3-7692
Subsidiaries: S Hirzel Verlag GmbH & Co; Med-
  Pharm Polska; MedPharm Scientific Publishers;
  Franz Steiner Verlag GmbH; Wissenschaftliche
  Verlagsgesellschaft mbH
Distributor for American Society of Hospital
  Pharmacists; Pharmaceutical Press (London,
  UK); The Stationery Office (London, UK);
  Thomson Micromedex (USA); United States
  Pharmacopeial Convention Inc (USA)

Deutscher Betriebswirte-Verlag GmbH+
Bleichstr 20-22, 76593 Gernsbach
Tel: (07224) 9397-151 *Fax:* (07224) 9397-905
E-mail: info@betriebswirte-verlag.de
Web Site: www.betriebswirte-verlag.de
Key Personnel
Mng Dir: Christine Katz
Editor, Rights & Permissions, Publicity: Regina
  Meier
Founded: 1926
Subjects: Business, Economics, Public Adminis-
  tration, Logistics, Paper Industry, Purchasing,
  Wood Industry
ISBN Prefix(es): 978-3-921099; 978-3-88640
Distribution Center: Leipziger Kommission-
  und Grossbuchhandelsgellschaft mbH (LKG),
  An der Suedspite 1-12, 04571 Roetha,
  Head, Customer Service: Frank Waldhelm
  Tel: (034206) 6 51 34 *Fax:* (034206) 6 51
  745 *E-mail:* fwaldhelm@lkg-service.de *Web
  Site:* www.lkg-va.de

Deutscher Drucker Verlagsgesellschaft mbH &
  Co KG (German Printer Publishing House)
Riedstr 25, 73760 Ostfildern
Mailing Address: Postfach 4124, 73744 Ostfildern
Tel: (0711) 44817-0 *Fax:* (0711) 442099
E-mail: info@print.de
Web Site: www.print.de
Key Personnel
Mng Dir & Editor-in-Chief: Bernhard Niemela
Information for professionals, dealing with all as-
  pects of digital workflow. Print communication,
  colour publishing & packaging.
ISBN Prefix(es): 978-3-920226
Parent Company: Ebner Verlag
Foreign Rep(s): Babel Marketing (UK); Ebner
  Publishing (USA); Andrew Karning (Scotland)

Deutscher Fachverlag GmbH
Mainzer Landstr 251, 60326 Frankfurt am Main
Tel: (069) 7595-01 *Fax:* (069) 7595-2999
E-mail: info@dfv.de
Web Site: www.dfv.de
Key Personnel
Mng Dir: Peter Kley; Holger Knapp; Soenke
  Reimers; Angela Wisken
Corporate Marketing & Communications: Brita
  Westerholz *Tel:* (069) 7595-2061 *Fax:* (069)
  7595-2055 *E-mail:* presse@dfv.de
Founded: 1946
Membership(s): Verband Deutscher Zeitschriften-
  verleger (VDZ).
Subjects: Advertising, Agriculture, Business,
  Communications, Engineering (General), Fash-
  ion, Law, Marketing, Nonfiction (General),
  Real Estate
ISBN Prefix(es): 978-3-87150

Subsidiaries: B2B Online GmbH; Deutsche
  Fachmedien GmbH; International Business
  Press Publishers GmbH; Matthaes Verlag
  GmbH; Verlag fuer Wirtschaftpraxis GmbH

Deutscher Gemeindeverlag GmbH
Hessbruehlstr 69, 70565 Stuttgart
Tel: (0711) 7863-0; (0711) 7863-7355
  Fax: (0711) 7863-8400
E-mail: dgv@kohlhammer.de; foreign.rights@
  kohlhammer.de; kohlhammerkontakt@
  kohlhammer.de; vertrieb@kohlhammer.de
Web Site: www.kohlhammer.de
Key Personnel
Mng Dir: Dr Juergen Gutbrod; Leopold Freiherr
  von und zu Weiler
Foreign Rights Manager: Henning Gienger
  Tel: (0711) 7863-7207 *Fax:* (0711) 7863-8207
Founded: 1934
Subjects: Education, Government, Political Sci-
  ence, History, Law, Medicine, Nursing, Den-
  tistry, Philosophy, Psychology, Psychiatry, The-
  ology
ISBN Prefix(es): 978-3-555
Parent Company: Verlag W Kohlhammer GmbH
Branch Office(s)
Rudolf-Leonhardstr 28, 01097 Dresden
  Tel: (0351) 5022685 *Fax:* (0351) 5670664
Gustav-Freytag Str 59, 99096 Erfurt *Tel:* (0361)
  3735379 *Fax:* (0361) 3460537
Postfach 1465, 30014 Hannover *Tel:* (0511)
  327029 *Fax:* (0511) 320143
Postfach 1865, 24017 Kiel *Tel:* (0431) 554857
  Fax: (0431) 554944
Schleinufes 14, 39104 Magdeburg *Tel:* (0391)
  597080 *Fax:* (0391) 5970813
Postfach 261134, 55057 Mainz *Tel:* (06131)
  891540 *Fax:* (06131) 891624
Sellostr 19, 14471 Potsdam *Tel:* (0331) 964670
  Fax: (0331) 964672 (German Municipality
  Publishing Company)
Postfach 040204, 19026 Schwerin *Tel:* (0385)
  616105 *Fax:* (0385) 616146

Deutscher Klassiker Verlag GmbH
Subsidiary of Suhrkamp Verlag GmbH & Co KG
Pappelallee 78-79, 10437 Berlin
Tel: (030) 740744-0 *Fax:* (030) 740744-199
E-mail: info@suhrkamp.de
Web Site: www.suhrkamp.de
Key Personnel
Publisher: Ulla Unseld-Berkewicz
Mng Dir: Dr Jonathan Landgrebe
Press: Dr Thomas Sparr *Tel:* (069) 75601-290
  E-mail: sparr@suhrkamp.de
Founded: 1981
Specialize in classic German Literature from the
  Middle Ages to the 20th century.
Subjects: Literature, Literary Criticism, Essays
ISBN Prefix(es): 978-3-618
Associate Companies: Insel Verlag Anton Kip-
  penberg GmbH & Co KG; Juedischer Verlag
  GmbH; Verlag der Weltreligionen

Deutscher Kunstverlag GmbH Berlin
  Muenchen+
Paul-Lincke-Ufer 34, 10999 Berlin
Tel: (030) 279076-0; (030) 279076-51 (sales)
  Fax: (030) 279076-11; (030) 279076-55 (sales)
E-mail: info@deutscherkunstverlag.de; vertrieb@
  deutscherkunstverlag.de
Web Site: www.deutscherkunstverlag.de
Key Personnel
Mng Dir: Stephanie Ecker *E-mail:* ecker@
  deutscherkunstverlag.de
Editorial Dir: Dr Till Meinert *Tel:* (030) 260 05-
  363 *E-mail:* meinert@deutscherkunstverlag.de
Sales & Marketing: Stella Buehler
Founded: 1921
Subjects: Antiques, Architecture & Interior De-
  sign, Art, Biography, Memoirs, English as a

Second Language, Nonfiction (General), Photography, Regional Interests, Science (General)
ISBN Prefix(es): 978-3-422
Number of titles published annually: 100 Print
Total Titles: 600 Print
Branch Office(s)
Schlierseestr 5, 81541 Munich, Publishing Dir:
Rudolf Winterstein *Tel:* (089) 961 60 86-25
Fax: (089) 961 60 86-44 *E-mail:* winterstein@
deutscherkunstverlag.de
Distribution Center: Koch, Neff, Oetinger Verlagsauslieferung GmbH, Industriestr 23, 70565
Stuttgart

Deutscher Psychologen Verlag GmbH (DPV)
Am Koellnischen Park 2, 10179 Berlin
Tel: (030) 209 166-410 *Fax:* (030) 209 166-413
E-mail: verlag@psychologenverlag.de
Web Site: www.psychologenverlag.de; www.bdp-verband.de
Key Personnel
Mng Dir: Ina Jungbluth
Founded: 1984
Subjects: Psychology, Psychiatry
ISBN Prefix(es): 978-3-925559; 978-3-931589
Number of titles published annually: 5 Print
Total Titles: 65 Print
Parent Company: Berufsverband Deutscher Psychologinnen und Psychologen eV
Warehouse: Theodor-Heuss-Str 4, 53177 Bonn
Tel: (0228) 9550210 *Fax:* (0228) 3696210
E-mail: leserservice@psychologenverlag.de

Deutscher Seglers-Verband eV (DSV) (German
Sailing Association eV)
Gruendgens Str 18, 22309 Hamburg
Tel: (040) 632009-0 *Fax:* (040) 632009-28
E-mail: info@dsv.org
Web Site: www.dsv.org
Key Personnel
Mng Dir: Goetz-Ulf Jungmichel
Founded: 1888
Subjects: Aeronautics, Aviation, Maritime, Travel
& Tourism, Pilots
ISBN Prefix(es): 978-3-88412

Deutscher Sparkassen Verlag GmbH
Am Wallgraben 115, 70565 Stuttgart
Tel: (0711) 782-0 *Fax:* (0711) 782-16 35
E-mail: webredaktion@dsv-gruppe.de; presse@
dsv-gruppe.de
Web Site: www.dsv-gruppe.de
Key Personnel
Chairman: Thomas Mang
Mng Dir: Wilhelm Gans; Michael Ilg; Oliver
Lux; Juergen Schneider
Head, Public Relations: Thilo Weinert *Tel:* (0711)
782-2736 *Fax:* (0711) 782-1001 *E-mail:* thilo.
weinert@dsv-gruppe.de
Founded: 1947
Specialize in literature on banking business management.
Membership(s): Boersenverein des Deutschen
Buchhandels; Suedwestdeutsches
Zeitschriftenverleger-Verband; Verband der Verlage und Buchhandlungen.
Subjects: Finance
ISBN Prefix(es): 978-3-09
Parent Company: DSV-Gruppe

Deutscher Studien Verlag+
Subsidiary of Julius Beltz GmbH & Co KG
Werderstr 10, 69469 Weinheim
Tel: (06201) 6007-0 *Fax:* (06201) 6007-310
E-mail: info@beltz.de
Web Site: www.beltz.de
Key Personnel
Publisher & Chief Executive Officer: Marianne
Ruebelmann
Head, Press & Public Relations: Bettina Schaub
Tel: (06201) 6007-443 *Fax:* (06201) 6007-9443
E-mail: b.schaub@beltz.de

Sales Manager: Andrea Foelster *Tel:* (06201)
6007-431 *E-mail:* a.foelster@beltz.de
Marketing & Sales: Andres Horn *Tel:* (06201)
6007-440 *E-mail:* a.horn@beltz.de
Rights: Kerstin Michaelis *Tel:* (06201) 6007-327
Fax: (06201) 6007-338 *E-mail:* k.michaelis@
beltz.de
Subjects: Psychology, Psychiatry, Social Sciences,
Sociology
ISBN Prefix(es): 978-3-89271
Distribution Center: Rhenus Medien Logistik,
Justus-von-Liebig-Str 1, 86899 Landsberg am
Lech *Tel:* (08191) 9 70 00-6 22 *E-mail:* beltz@
de.rhenus.com
Mohr Morawa Buchvertrieb GmbH, Sulzen-gasse 2, 1230 Vienna, Austria *Tel:* (01) 680
14-0 *Fax:* (01) 688 71 30 *E-mail:* momo@
mohrmorawa.at *Web Site:* www.mohrmorawa.at
AVA Verlagsauslieferung AG, Centralweg
16, 8910 Affoltern am Albis, Switzerland
Tel: (044) 762 42 50 *Fax:* (044) 762 42 49
E-mail: verlagsservice@ava.ch *Web Site:* www.
ava.ch

**Deutscher Taschenbuch Verlag GmbH & Co
KG (dtv)+**
Friedrichstr 1a, 80801 Munich
Mailing Address: Postfach 40 04 22, 80704 Munich
Tel: (089) 38167-0 *Fax:* (089) 34 64 28
E-mail: verlag@dtv.de
Web Site: www.dtv.de
Key Personnel
Mng Dir: Wolfgang Balk; Bernard Blum
Head, Press & Public Relations: Petra Buescher
Tel: (089) 38167-115 *Fax:* (089) 38167-315
E-mail: buescher.petra@dtv.de
Foreign Rights Manager: Constanze Chory
Tel: (089) 38167-125 *Fax:* (089) 38167-325
E-mail: chory.constanze@dtv.de; Julia Helfrich
Tel: (089) 38167-127 *Fax:* (089) 38167-327
E-mail: helfrich.julia@dtv.de
Sales: Marietta Frick *E-mail:* frick.marietta@dtv.
de
Founded: 1960
Subjects: Art, Astronomy, Behavioral Sciences,
Biography, Memoirs, Child Care & Development, Education, Fiction, Government, Political
Science, Health, History, Humor, Humor,
Law, Literature, Literary Criticism, Essays,
Music, Dance, Nonfiction (General), Philosophy, Poetry, Psychology, Psychiatry, Religion
- Other, Science (General), Science Fiction,
Fantasy, Self-Help, Social Sciences, Sociology
ISBN Prefix(es): 978-3-423
Foreign Rights: Bardon Chinese Media Agency
(Ms Yu-Shiuan Chen) (Taiwan); Dr Ivana Beil
(Czechia, Slovakia); Dr Giuliana Bernardi
(Italy); Agencja Literacka Graal (Maria Strarz-Kanska) (Poland); Agentur Literatur Gudrun
Hebel (Scandinavia); Hercules Business & Culture (Mainland China); Ute Koerner Literary
Agent (Guenter Rodewald) (Portugal, Spain);
Meike Marx (Japan); Momo Agency (Geenie
Han) (Korea); Marianne Schoenbach Literary
Agency (Netherlands)
Distribution Center: Koch, Neff & Oetinger Verlagsauslieferung GmbH, Industriestr 23, 70565
Stuttgart *E-mail:* dtv@kno-va.de
Mohr Morawa Buchvertrieb GmbH, Sulzen-gasse 2, 1230 Vienna, Austria *Tel:* (01) 680
14-0 *Fax:* (01) 688 71 30 *E-mail:* momo@
mohrmorawa.at *Web Site:* www.mohrmorawa.at
Schweizer Buchzentrum, Industrie Ost, 4614 Hae-gendorf, Switzerland *Tel:* (062) 2 09 26 26
Fax: (062) 2 09 26 27 *E-mail:* kundendienst@
buchzentrum.ch
Orders to: A Stein'sche Buchhandlung GmbH,
Steinerstr 10, 59457 Werl *Tel:* (02922) 95
890 0 *Fax:* (02922) 95 890 95 *E-mail:* info@
buchversand-stein.de

Deutscher Verlag fuer Kunstwissenschaft,
imprint of Dietrich Reimer Verlag GmbH

Deutscher Verlag fuer Kunstwissenschaft+
Imprint of Dietrich Reimer Verlag GmbH
Berliner Str 53, 10713 Berlin
Tel: (030) 700 13 88-0 *Fax:* (030) 700 13 88-11
E-mail: vertrieb-kunstverlage@reimer-verlag.de
Web Site: www.reimer-mann-verlag.de/mann
Key Personnel
Mng Dir: Dr Hans-Robert Cram
Press: Ingrid Schulze *Tel:* (030) 700 13 88-32
E-mail: ischulze@reimer-verlag.de
Founded: 1964
Subjects: Archaeology, Architecture & Interior
Design, Art
ISBN Prefix(es): 978-3-87157
Associate Companies: Gebr Mann Verlag
Returns: Leipziger Kommissions- und Grossbuch-handelsgesellschaft mbH (LKG), An der Sued-spitze 1-12, 04571 Roetha *Tel:* (034206) 65-100 *Fax:* (034206) 65-110 *E-mail:* lkg@lkg-service.de *Web Site:* www.lkg-va.de

Deutscher Wirtschaftsdienst, *imprint of* Wolters
Kluwer Deutschland GmbH

Deutscher Wirtschaftsdienst+
Imprint of Wolters Kluwer Deutschland GmbH
Luxemburger Str 449, 50939 Cologne
Tel: (02631) 801-2211; (0221) 94373-7000
Toll Free Tel: 0800 888-5444 (orders)
Fax: (02631) 801-2223; (0221) 94373-7201
Toll Free Fax: 0800 801-8018 (orders)
E-mail: info@wolterskluwer.de
Web Site: www.dwd-verlag.de
Key Personnel
Mng Dir: Dr Ulrich Hermann
Editorial & Publicity: Michael Rieck
Founded: 1950
Membership(s): The Stock Exchange of German
Publishers.
Subjects: Architecture & Interior Design, Business, Career Development, Communications,
Economics, Energy, Environmental Studies,
Finance, Law, Management, Technology
ISBN Prefix(es): 978-3-87156
Subsidiaries: VWV Verlag fuer Wirtschaft und
Verwaltung GmbH; Weltforum Verlag fuer
Politik und Auslandskunde GmbH; Kontaplan
Werbegesellschaft mbH

Deutscher Wissenschafts-Verlag (DWV)
(German Science Publishing House)
Bobenholzweg 15, 77876 Kappelrodeck/Baden
Mailing Address: Postfach 11 01 35, 76487
Baden-Baden
Tel: (07842) 9959-777; (07842) 9959-805
Fax: (07842) 9959-753
E-mail: geschaeftsfuehrung@dwv-net.de;
herstellung@dwv-net.de; info@dwv-net.de;
lektorat@dwv-net.de; vertrieb@dwv-net.de
Web Site: www.dwverlag.de; www.
UniversityPress.de
Key Personnel
Mng Dir: Dr Werner E Gerabek
Membership(s): Association of German Publishers
& Booksellers.
Subjects: Anthropology, Archaeology, Art, Economics, Education, History, Language Arts,
Linguistics, Law, Literature, Literary Criticism,
Essays, Mathematics, Medicine, Nursing, Dentistry, Music, Dance, Philosophy, Social Sciences, Sociology, Theology, Natural Sciences
ISBN Prefix(es): 978-3-935176; 978-3-9806424
Imprints: German University Press (GUP)
Distribution Center: Runge-Verlagsauslieferung
GmbH, Bergstr 2, 33803 Steinhagen
Tel: (05204) 998 0 *Fax:* (05204) 998 114
E-mail: info@rungeva.de *Web Site:* www.
rungeva.de

Deutsches Filminstitut-DIF eV/Deutsches Filmmuseum
Schaumainkai 41, 60596 Frankfurt am Main
Tel: (069) 96 12 20-0 *Fax:* (069) 96 12 20-999
E-mail: info@deutsches-filminstitut.de
Web Site: www.deutsches-filminstitut.de
Key Personnel
Dir: Claudia Dillman; Dr Nikolaus Hensel
Press & Public Relations: Frauke Hass *Tel:* (069)
96 12 20-307 *E-mail:* hass@deutsches-
filminstitut.de
Founded: 1949
Subjects: Art, Film, Video, Film Archive
ISBN Prefix(es): 978-3-88799

Deutsches Jugendinstitut eV (DJI) (German
Youth Institute)
Nockherstr 2, 81541 Munich
Tel: (089) 62306-0 *Fax:* (089) 62306-162
E-mail: info@dji.de
Web Site: www.dji.de
Key Personnel
Mng Dir: Dr Thomas Rauschenbach
Tel: (089) 62306-280 *Fax:* (089) 62306-269
E-mail: rauschenbach@dji.de
International Relations: Dr Christine Heinke
Tel: (089) 62306-225 *Fax:* (089) 62306-265
E-mail: heinke@dji.de
Media & Public Relations: Andrea Macion
Tel: (089) 62306-218 *Fax:* (089) 62306-265
E-mail: macion@dji.de
Public Relations: Maria Weber *Tel:* (089) 62306-
244 *Fax:* (089) 62306-265 *E-mail:* weber@dji.
de
Sales: Thomas Hummel *Tel:* (089) 62306-241
Fax: (089) 62306-265 *E-mail:* hummel@dji.de
Founded: 1963
Subjects: Education, Social Sciences, Sociology
ISBN Prefix(es): 978-3-87966; 978-3-935701
Branch Office(s)
Franckesche Stiftungen, Franckeplatz 1, Haus
12-13, 06110 Halle *Tel:* (0345) 68178 0
Fax: (0345) 47 68 178

Deutsches Kulturforum oestliches Europa eV
(German Cultural Forum for Eastern Europe)
Berliner Str 135, Haus K1, 14467 Potsdam
Tel: (0331) 200980 *Fax:* (0331) 2009850
E-mail: deutsches@kulturforum.info; presse@
kulturforum.info
Web Site: www.kulturforum.info
Key Personnel
Editorial Manager: Andre Werner *Tel:* (0331)
2009812 *E-mail:* werner@kulturforum.info
Editorial: Susanna Becker *Tel:* (0331) 2009819
E-mail: becker@kulturforum.info
Founded: 2000
Subjects: Film, Video, History, Literature, Liter-
ary Criticism, Essays, Music, Dance, Eastern
Europe History, German Culture
ISBN Prefix(es): 978-3-936168

DGEG, see Deutsche Gesellschaft fuer
Eisenbahngeschichte eV (DGEG)

DGH Verlag, see Der Gute Hirte Verlag

DGVT-Verlag
Hechinger-Str 203, 72072 Tuebingen
Tel: (07071) 792850 *Fax:* (07071) 792851
E-mail: dgvt-verlag@dgvt.de
Web Site: www.dgvt-verlag.de
Key Personnel
Publishing Dir: Otmar Koschar
Editor & Press: Valerie Pogodda *Tel:* (07071)
792852
Production: Iris Beltz
Sales: Thomas Schwerdtfeger; Gina Steidle
Subjects: Behavioral Sciences, Psychology, Psy-
chiatry

ISBN Prefix(es): 978-3-87159; 978-3-922686
Parent Company: Deutsche Gesellschaft fuer Ver-
haltens therapie eV (DGVT)

DHV, see Der Hoerverlag GmbH (DHV)

Edition dia Verlag und Vertrieb GmbH+
Benthaniendamm 61 A, 10999 Berlin
Tel: (030) 623 50 21 *Fax:* (030) 623 50 23
E-mail: mail@editiondia.de
Web Site: www.editiondia.de
Key Personnel
Mng Dir: Helmut Lotz *E-mail:* lotz@editiondia.
de
Mng Dir, International Rights: Kai Precht
E-mail: precht@editiondia.de
Founded: 1984
Subjects: Biography, Memoirs, Cookery, Fiction,
LGBTQ, Nonfiction (General)
ISBN Prefix(es): 978-3-86034

diagonal-Verlag+
Universitaetsstr 55, 35037 Marburg
Mailing Address: Postfach 1248, 35002 Marburg
Tel: (0151) 56060851
E-mail: order@diagonal-verlag.de; post@
diagonal-verlag.de
Web Site: www.diagonal-verlag.de
Key Personnel
Publisher: Steffen Rink *E-mail:* rink@diagonal-
verlag.de; Thomas Schweer *E-mail:* schweer@
diagonal-verlag.de
Founded: 1988
Specialize in science of religion.
Membership(s): Boersenverein des Deutschen
Buchhandels.
Subjects: Literature, Literary Criticism, Essays,
Poetry, Religion - Other, Science (General)
ISBN Prefix(es): 978-3-927165
Total Titles: 35 Print

Diana Verlag, *imprint of* Verlagsgruppe Random
House Bertelsmann

Die Verlag H Schaefer GmbH+
Niederstedter Weg 5, 61348 Bad Homburg
Mailing Address: Postfach 2243, 61292 Bad
Homburg
Tel: (06172) 9583-0 *Fax:* (06172) 9583-21
E-mail: dieverlag@wsth.de
Web Site: www.wsth.de
Key Personnel
Mng Dir: Angelika Vollrath-Kuehne
Founded: 1923
Subjects: Economics, Government, Political Sci-
ence, Law, Management, Radio, TV
ISBN Prefix(es): 978-3-920826
Associate Companies: Menschund Leben Verlags-
gesellschaft

Diederichs Verlag, *imprint of* Verlagsgruppe
Random House Bertelsmann

Verlag Moritz Diesterweg, see Bildungshaus
Schulbuchverlage Westermann Schroedel
Diesterweg Schoeningh Winklers GmbH

Sammlung Dieterich Verlagsgesellschaft mbH
Imprint of Aufbau Verlagsgruppe GmbH & Co
KG
Prinzenstr 85, 10969 Berlin
Tel: (030) 283 94-0 *Fax:* (030) 283 94-100
E-mail: info@aufbau-verlag.de
Web Site: www.aufbau-verlag.de
Key Personnel
Mng Dir: Tom Erben; Matthias Koch; Rene Strien
Founded: 1991
Subjects: Literature, Literary Criticism, Essays,
Philosophy
ISBN Prefix(es): 978-3-7350

Associate Companies: Gustav Kiepenheuer Verlag
GmbH
Foreign Rep(s): Mohr Morawa Buchvertrieb
GmbH (Johann Czap) (Eastern Austria); Mohr
Morawa Buchvertrieb GmbH (Michael Hipp)
(Western Austria); Verlagsauslieferung Schei-
degger & Co AG (Ruedi Amrhein) (Switzer-
land)
Distribution Center: VVA-Vereinigte Verlagsaus-
lieferung, An der Autobahn, 33310 Guetersloh
Tel: (05241) 80 66 959 *E-mail:* VVA-D6F3.
Bestellungen@bertelsmann.de
Mohr Morawa Buchvertrieb GmbH, Sulzen-
gasse 2, 1230 Vienna, Austria *Tel:* (01) 680
14-0 *Fax:* (01) 688 71 30 *E-mail:* momo@
mohrmorawa.at *Web Site:* www.mohrmorawa.at
Buchzentrum AG, Industriestr Ost 10, 4614 Haegendorf, Switzerland *Tel:* (062) 209 26 26
Fax: (062) 209 26 27 *E-mail:* kundendienst@
buchzentrum.ch

Dieterich'sche Verlagsbuchhandlung+
Beuthener Str 17, 55131 Mainz
Tel: (06131) 21 403 79 *Fax:* (06131) 57 10 61
E-mail: dvb-mainz@t-online.de
Web Site: www.dvb-mainz.de
Key Personnel
Publisher: Prof Alfred Klemm, PhD
Founded: 1765
Subjects: Art, Asian Studies, History, Literature,
Literary Criticism, Essays, Philosophy, Poetry,
Religion - Other, Theology
ISBN Prefix(es): 978-3-87162
Number of titles published annually: 3 Print
Distribution Center: GVA Gemeinsame Ver-
lagsauslieferung Goettingen GmbH & Co KG,
Postfach 2021, 37010 Goettingen, Contact:
Klaus Rabe *Tel:* (0551) 48 71 77 *Fax:* (0551)
413 92 *E-mail:* info@gva-verlage.de *Web
Site:* www.gva-verlage.de
Balmer Buecherdienst AG, Kobiboden, 8840 Ein-
siedeln, Switzerland *Tel:* (041) 848 80 820
Fax: (041) 848 840 830

Maximilian Dietrich Verlag+
Weberstr 36, 87700 Memmingen
Tel: (08331) 2853 *Fax:* (08331) 490364
E-mail: dietrich-verlag@freenet.de
Web Site: www.maximilian-dietrich-verlag.
de/index.htm
Key Personnel
Owner: Juergen Schweitzer
Founded: 1946
Subjects: Biography, Memoirs, Human Relations,
Literature, Literary Criticism, Essays, Myster-
ies, Suspense, Regional Interests
ISBN Prefix(es): 978-3-87164
Subsidiaries: Edition Curt Visel

Karl Dietz Verlag Berlin GmbH+
Franz-Mehring-Platz 1, 10243 Berlin
Tel: (030) 44 31 05 33 *Fax:* (030) 44 31 05 97
E-mail: info@dietzberlin.de
Web Site: dietzberlin.de
Key Personnel
Publishing Dir: Martin Beck *Tel:* (030) 44 31 02
41 *E-mail:* beck@dietzberlin.de
Sales: Michael Beck *Tel:* (030) 44 31 05 36
Founded: 1946
Subjects: Biography, Memoirs, Government, Po-
litical Science, History, Social Sciences, Sociol-
ogy
ISBN Prefix(es): 978-3-320
Distribution Center: Sozialistische Verlagsaus-
lieferung GmbH, Philipp-Reis-Str 17, 63477
Maintal *Tel:* (06181) 9 08 80 72 *Fax:* (06181)
9 08 80 73 *E-mail:* sovaffm@t-online.de

Verlag J H W Dietz Nachf GmbH+
Dreizehnmorgenweg 24, 53175 Bonn
Tel: (0228) 18 48 77-0 *Fax:* (0228) 23 41 04
E-mail: info@dietz-verlag.de
Web Site: www.dietz-verlag.de

Key Personnel
Dir & Editor: Dr Alexander Behrens
  E-mail: alexander.behrens@dietz-verlag.de
Manager: Dr Michael Dauderstaedt
Public Relations & Foreign Rights: Mareike
  Malzbender *E-mail:* mareike.malzbender@
  dietz-verlag.de
Founded: 1881
Subjects: Developing Countries, Environmental
  Studies, Government, Political Science, History,
  Labor, Industrial Relations, Nonfiction (Gen-
  eral), Social Sciences, Sociology
ISBN Prefix(es): 978-3-8012; 978-3-87831
Distribution Center: PROLIT Verlagsausliefer-
  ung GmbH, Siemensstr 16, 35463 Fernwald-
  Annerod *Tel:* (0641) 943 93-0 *Fax:* (0641) 943
  93-89
Far Eastern Book Sellers, PO Box 72, Kanda,
  Tokyo, Japan

digital publishing AG
Tumblinger Str 32, 80337 Munich
Tel: (089) 74 74 82 0 *Fax:* (089) 74 79 23 08
E-mail: info@digitalpublishing.de; presse@
  digitalpublishing.de
Web Site: www.digitalpublishing.de; www.speexx.
  com/en
Key Personnel
Founder & Chief Executive Officer: Joerg Kober-
  ling
Founder & Chief Technical Officer: Alfred Ertl
Founder & President: Armin Hopp
Head, Sales, Marketing & Press: Sylvia Tobias
  E-mail: tobias@hueber.de
Founded: 1994
Specialize in online language training. Branch lo-
  cations in Brazil, China, France, Italy, Spain &
  UK.
Subjects: Corporate Language Training
ISBN Prefix(es): 978-3-89747
Total Titles: 130 CD-ROM; 100 Audio
Parent Company: Hueber Verlag GmbH & Co
  KG

Edition Diskord
Schwaerzlocher Str 104B, 72070 Tuebingen
Tel: (07071) 40102 *Fax:* (07071) 44710
Key Personnel
Mng Dir: Gerd Kimmerle
Founded: 1985
Subjects: Biography, Memoirs, History, Philoso-
  phy, Psychology, Psychiatry, Social Sciences,
  Sociology, Women's Studies
ISBN Prefix(es): 978-3-89295

DISTANZ Verlag GmbH
Hallesches Ufer 78, 10963 Berlin
Tel: (030) 240833-200 *Fax:* (030) 240833-250
E-mail: info@distanz.de
Web Site: www.distanz.de
Key Personnel
Mng Dir: Christian Boros; Uta Grosenik
Subjects: Architecture & Interior Design, Art,
  Fashion, Photography
ISBN Prefix(es): 978-3-942405; 978-3-95476

Dittrich Verlag GmbH
Imprint of Velbrueck GmbH
Meckenheimer Str 47, 53919 Weilerswist-
  Metternich
Tel: (02254) 83 603-0 *Fax:* (030) 83 603-33
E-mail: info@dittrich-verlag.de
Web Site: www.dittrich-verlag.de
Key Personnel
Mng Dir: Andreas V Stedman
Founded: 1990
Subjects: Biography, Memoirs, Drama, Theater,
  Fiction, History, Music, Dance
ISBN Prefix(es): 978-3-937717; 978-3-920862
Distribution Center: Prolit Verlagsauslieferung,
  Siemensstr 16, 35463 Fernwald (Annerod),

Contact: Monika Pankratz *Tel:* (0641) 9 43
  93 22 *Fax:* (0641) 9 43 93 93 *E-mail:* m.
  pankratz@prolit.de *Web Site:* www.prolit.de

DIVYANAND Verlags-GmbH+
Saegestr 37, 79737 Herrischried
Tel: (07764) 93 97-0 *Fax:* (07764) 93 97-39
E-mail: info@divyanand.de
Web Site: www.divyanand.de
Key Personnel
Mng Dir: Gerlinde Gloeckner
Founded: 1987
Specialize in spirituality.
Subjects: Inspirational, Spirituality, Parapsychol-
  ogy, Philosophy, Religion - Other, Self-Help
ISBN Prefix(es): 978-3-926696
Number of titles published annually: 2 Print
Total Titles: 23 Print
U.S. Office(s): Creamery Rd, Stanfordville, NY
  12581, United States

DIX Verlag & PR
Am Hinzenbusch 22, 52355 Dueren
Tel: (02421) 501 889
E-mail: post@dix-verlag.de; bestellung@dix-
  verlag.de (orders)
Web Site: www.dix-verlag.eu
Key Personnel
Publisher, Press & Licensing: Dr Elke Fettweis
  E-mail: elke.fettweis@dix-verlag.de
Focus on children's literature.
Subjects: Education, Literature, Literary Criti-
  cism, Essays
ISBN Prefix(es): 978-3-941651
Distribution Center: G Umbreit GmbH & Co
  KG, Mundelsheimer Str 3, 74321 Bietigheim-
  Bissingen, Contact: Jessica Haberlandt
  Tel: (07142) 596-385 *Fax:* (07142) 596-387
  E-mail: jessica.haberlandt@umbreit.de *Web
  Site:* www.umbreit.de (Austria, Switzerland &
  non-German speaking European countries)

DJI, see Deutsches Jugendinstitut eV (DJI)

DK Edition Maritim GmbH+
Raboisen 8, 20095 Hamburg
Tel: (040) 339667-0 *Fax:* (040) 339667-77
E-mail: edmaritim@aol.com
Web Site: www.delius-klasing.de
Key Personnel
Publishing Dir: Dr Nadja Kneissler *Tel:* (040)
  339667-27 *E-mail:* n.kneissler@delius-klasing.
  de
Founded: 1978
Subjects: Crafts, Games, Hobbies, Fiction, Mar-
  itime, Sports, Athletics, Transportation, Travel
  & Tourism
ISBN Prefix(es): 978-3-922117; 978-3-89225
Parent Company: Delius Klasing Verlag, Sieker-
  wall 21, 33602 Bielefeld

DLG-Verlag GmbH, see Deutsche
  Landwirtschafts-Gesellschaft Verlags GmbH

DLV Deutscher Landwirtschaftsverlag GmbH
  (German Agriculture Publishing House)
Kabelkamp 6, 30179 Hannover
Tel: (0511) 67806-0 *Fax:* (0511) 67806-301
E-mail: dlv.hannover@dlv.de
Web Site: www.dlv.de
Key Personnel
Mng Dir: Joern Dwehus; Amos Kotte; Hans
  Mueller
Founded: 2001
Subjects: Agriculture, Animals, Pets, Environmen-
  tal Studies, Gardening, Plants, Music, Dance,
  Beekeeping/Apiculture, Country Life, Farming,
  Folk Music, Forestry, Hunting, Nature
ISBN Prefix(es): 978-3-331
Parent Company: Landbuch-Verlagsgesellschaft
  mbH, Hannover

Branch Office(s)
Berliner Str 112A, 13189 Berlin *Tel:* (030) 29
  39 74-50 *Fax:* (030) 29 39 74-59 *E-mail:* dlv.
  berlin@dlv.de
Lothstr 29, 80797 Munich *Tel:* (089) 12705-1
  Fax: (089) 12705-355 *E-mail:* dlv.muenchen@
  dlv.de

Doelling und Galitz Verlag GmbH+
Schwanthalerstr 79/RG, 80336 Munich
Tel: (089) 23 23 09 66 *Fax:* (089) 23 24 97 03
E-mail: dugherstellung@mac.com
Web Site: www.dugverlag.de
Key Personnel
Mng Dir: Dr Robert Galitz *Tel:* (089) 23 23 09
  85 *E-mail:* robertgalitz@mac.com
Publishing Dir: Sabine Niemann *Tel:* (040) 38 61
  06 20
Founded: 1986
Subjects: Architecture & Interior Design, Art,
  History, Literature, Literary Criticism, Essays,
  Music, Dance, Photography, Religion - Jewish,
  Religion - Other, Nature
ISBN Prefix(es): 978-3-926174; 978-3-930802;
  978-3-933374; 978-3-935549; 978-3-86218;
  978-3-937904
Branch Office(s)
Friedensallee 26, 2 OG, 22765 Hamburg
  Tel: (040) 389 35 15 *Fax:* (040) 389 049 45
  E-mail: dugverlag@mac.com
Warehouse: Siemensstr 16, 35463 Fernwald (An-
  nerod) *Fax:* (0641) 94393-29

Verlag Dohr+
Sindorfer Str 19, 50127 Bergheim
Tel: (02271) 70 72 05; (02271) 70 72 06
  Fax: (02271) 70 72 07
E-mail: info@dohr.de; versand@dohr.de
Web Site: www.dohr.de
Key Personnel
Contact: Christoph Dohr
Founded: 1990
Book, CD & sheetmusic publisher.
Subjects: Music, Dance
ISBN Prefix(es): 978-3-925366; 978-3-936655;
  978-3-86846
Number of titles published annually: 100 Print; 6
  Audio
Total Titles: 1,900 Print; 30 Audio

DoldeMedien Verlag GmbH
Postwiesenstr 5A, 70327 Stuttgart
Tel: (0711) 134 66-50 *Fax:* (0711) 134 66-96
E-mail: info@doldemedien.de
Web Site: www.doldemedien.de
Key Personnel
Mng Dir: Roland Hradek; Kerstin Kuffer
Founded: 1989
Subjects: Automotive, Cookery, Health, Nutrition,
  Outdoor Recreation
ISBN Prefix(es): 978-3-928803

DOM publishers
Caroline-von-Humboldt-Weg 20, 10117 Berlin
Tel: (030) 20 69 69 30 *Fax:* (030) 20 69 69 32
E-mail: info@dom-publishers.com
Web Site: www.dom-publishers.com
Key Personnel
Publisher: Philipp Meuser
Founded: 2005
Subjects: Architecture & Interior Design
ISBN Prefix(es): 978-3-938666

Domino Verlag Guenther Brinek GmbH
Menzinger Str 13, 80638 Munich
Mailing Address: Postfach 190345, 80603 Mu-
  nich
Tel: (089) 17913-0 *Fax:* (089) 17913-211; (089)
  17913-413
E-mail: info@domino-verlag.de; vertrieb@
  domino-verlag.de
Web Site: www.domino-verlag.de

Key Personnel
Mng Dir: Guenther Brinek; Christiane Keller
Founded: 1964
Specialize in educational materials for school.
Subjects: English as a Second Language, Science
(General), Social Sciences, Sociology
ISBN Prefix(es): 978-3-926123

Domowina-Verlag GmbH
Tuchmacherstr 27, 02625 Bautzen
Tel: (03591) 57 70 *Fax:* (03591) 57 72 43
E-mail: geschaeftsfuehrung@domowina-verlag.de;
sales@domowina-verlag.de
Web Site: www.domowina-verlag.de
Key Personnel
Mng Dir: Maria Matschie *Tel:* (03591) 57 72 42
Marketing Manager: Mirana Mieth *Tel:* (03591)
57 72 72 *E-mail:* mieth@domowina-verlag.de
Sales Manager: Manja Bujnowska *Tel:* (03591) 57
72 62
Founded: 1958
Subjects: Ethnicity, Fiction, Nonfiction (General),
Scientific, Technical Literature
ISBN Prefix(es): 978-3-7420
Bookshop(s): Smolerjec kniharnja/Smoler'sche
Verlagsbuchhandlung, Tuchmacherstr 27, 02625
Bautzen, Head: Annett Scholze *Tel:* (03591)
57 72 88 *E-mail:* buchhandlung@domowina-
verlag.de

Don Bosco Verlag+
Sieboldstr 11, 81669 Munich
Tel: (089) 48008-330 *Fax:* (089) 48008-309
E-mail: presse@donbosco-medien.de
Web Site: www.donbosco-medien.de
Key Personnel
Sales & Marketing Manager: Christof Buettgen
Press: Friederike Stoll
Founded: 1948
Subjects: Education, Religion - Other
ISBN Prefix(es): 978-3-7698
Parent Company: Don Bosco Medien GmbH
Imprints: DBV
Distribution Center: Auslieferungszen-
trum Niederrhein (AZN), Hoogeweg 71,
47623 Kevelaer, Contact: Daniela Daniels
Tel: (02832) 9 29-2 93 *Fax:* (02832) 9 29-2
11 *E-mail:* daniela.daniels@azn.de
Mohr Morawa Buchvertrieb GmbH, Sulzen-
gasse 2, 1230 Vienna, Austria *Tel:* (01) 680
14-0 *Fax:* (01) 688 71 30 *E-mail:* momo@
mohrmorawa.at *Web Site:* www.mohrmorawa.at
Balmer Buecherdienst, Kobiboden, 8840 Einsiedeln, Switzerland *Tel:* (0848) 84 08 20
Fax: (0848) 84 08 30 *E-mail:* info@balmer-
bd.ch

Donat Verlag & Antiquariat+
Borgfelder Heerstr 29, 28357 Bremen
Tel: (0421) 274886; (0421) 173 3107 *Fax:* (0421)
275106
E-mail: info@donat-verlag.de
Web Site: www.donat-verlag.de
Key Personnel
Mng Dir: Helmut Donat
Founded: 1988
Membership(s): Boersenverein des Deutschen
Buchhandels.
Subjects: Art, Biography, Memoirs, Economics,
Fiction, Government, Political Science, History,
Literature, Literary Criticism, Essays, Philoso-
phy, Psychology, Psychiatry, Regional Interests,
Religion - Jewish, Social Sciences, Sociology,
Theology, Ecology, Pedagogy
ISBN Prefix(es): 978-3-924444; 978-3-931737;
978-3-934836
Number of titles published annually: 35 Print
Total Titles: 220 Print

Dort-Hagenhausen-Verlag
Platenstr 5, 80336 Munich
Tel: (089) 72 94 96 25 *Fax:* (089) 72 94 96 26

Web Site: www.d-hverlag.de
Key Personnel
Publisher & Rights: Martin Dort *Tel:* (0174) 9 29
88 44 (cell) *E-mail:* martin.dort@d-hverlag.de
Press: Gabriele Becker *Tel:* (089) 15 82 02 06
Fax: (089) 15 82 02 08 *E-mail:* gabriele.
becker@d-hverlag.de
Sales: Michaela Markert-Kaeser *Tel:* (081) 71 48
91 51 *E-mail:* mmk@d-hverlag.de
Specialize in life-style oriented books.
Subjects: Agriculture, Cookery, Crafts, Games,
Hobbies, Environmental Studies, Gardening,
Plants, House & Home, How-to, Nature, Sus-
tainability
ISBN Prefix(es): 978-3-9813104; 978-3-9502896
Distribution Center: Suedost Verlagsser-
vice GmbH, Am Steinfeld 4, 94065 Wald-
kirchen *Tel:* (08581) 96050 *Fax:* (08581) 754
E-mail: service@suedost-verlags-service.de
Web Site: www.suedost-verlags-service.de

DPV, see Deutscher Psychologen Verlag GmbH
(DPV)

Drachen Verlag GmbH
Am See 1, 17440 Klein Jasedow
Tel: (038374) 75224 *Fax:* (038374) 75223
E-mail: mail@drachenverlag.de
Web Site: www.drachenverlag.de
Key Personnel
Publisher: Johannes Heimarth *Tel:* (038374)
75212
Founded: 1991
Subjects: Human Relations, Inspirational, Spiritu-
ality, Philosophy, Alternative
ISBN Prefix(es): 978-3-927369

Der Drachenhaus Verlag
Holgenburg 6, 73728 Esslingen
Tel: (0176) 24001350
E-mail: info@drachenhaus-verlag.com; pr@
drachenhaus-verlag.com
Web Site: www.drachenhaus-verlag.com
Key Personnel
Mng Dir: Nora Frisch
Editorial & Marketing: Dr Sussane Heimburger
E-mail: heimburger@drachenhaus-verlag.com
Press: Mariella Terzo
Founded: 2010
Subjects: Nonfiction (General), China, Chinese
Culture
ISBN Prefix(es): 978-3-943314

DrachenStern Verlag, *imprint of* Bookspot
Verlag GmbH

Draupadi Verlag
Dossenheimer Landstr, 103, 69121 Heidelberg
Tel: (06221) 412 990 *Fax:* (0322) 2372 2343
E-mail: info@draupadi-verlag.de
Web Site: www.draupadi-verlag.de
Mng Dir: Christian Weiss
Founded: 2003
Subjects: Literature, Literary Criticism, Essays,
Nonfiction (General), Indian & South Asian
Literature
ISBN Prefix(es): 978-3-937603

Drei Brunnen Verlag GmbH & Co KG
Heusee 19, 73655 Pluederhausen
Tel: (07181) 8602-0 *Fax:* (07181) 8602-29
E-mail: mail@drei-brunnen-verlag.de
Web Site: www.drei-brunnen-verlag.de
Key Personnel
Mng Dir: Jochen Mueller; Thomas Mueller
Founded: 1951
Specialize in camping, hiking & recreation.
Subjects: Outdoor Recreation, Travel & Tourism
ISBN Prefix(es): 978-3-7956

Number of titles published annually: 10 Print
Total Titles: 60 Print

Drei Eichen Verlag+
Bahnhofstr 36, 97762 Hammelburg
Mailing Address: Postfach 1147, 97754 Hammel-
burg
Tel: (09732) 9142-0 *Fax:* (09732) 9142-20
E-mail: info@dreieichen.de
Web Site: www.dreieichen.com
Key Personnel
Owner: Manuel-Victor Kissener
Founded: 1931
Subjects: Asian Studies, Government, Political
Science, Inspirational, Spirituality, Philosophy,
Science Fiction, Fantasy, Self-Help
ISBN Prefix(es): 978-3-7699
Number of titles published annually: 10 Print
Total Titles: 200 Print
Imprints: Edition Kima; Politik und Spiritualitaet

Drei Hasen in der Abendsonne GmbH
Muehlenstr 10, 91486 Uehlfeld
Tel: (09163) 9999-0 *Fax:* (09163) 9999-5
E-mail: verlag@hasehasehase.de
Web Site: www.hasehasehase.com
Key Personnel
Mng Dir, Products & Public Relations: Johann
Ruettinger
Mng Dir, Products & Sales: Kathi Kappler
Illustrator: Rolf Vogt
ISBN Prefix(es): 978-3-941345

Drei Ulmen Verlag GmbH+
Schleissheimer Str 274, 80809 Munich
Tel: (089) 3087911; (089) 3088343
Founded: 1985
Membership(s): Small Publishers Study Group.
Subjects: Biography, Memoirs, Literature, Liter-
ary Criticism, Essays, Travel & Tourism
ISBN Prefix(es): 978-3-926087
Associate Companies: AVA-GmbH, Seeblickstr
46, 82211 Herrsching

Cecilie Dressler Verlag+
Subsidiary of Verlag Friedrich Oetinger GmbH
Poppenbuetteler Chaussee 53, 22397 Hamburg
Mailing Address: Postfach 65 82 30, 22374 Ham-
burg
Tel: (040) 607909-03 *Fax:* (040) 6072326
E-mail: dressler@verlagsgruppe-oetinger.
de; vertrieb@verlagsgruppe-oetinger.de;
marketing@verlagsgruppe-oetinger.de
Web Site: www.cecilie-dressler.de
Key Personnel
Mng Dir: Jan Weitendorf; Silke Weitendorf
Sales Manager: Susanne Weiss *Tel:* (040) 607909-
777 *Fax:* (040) 607909-550
Marketing Manager: Lars Spicher
International Rights: Renate Reichstein *Tel:* (040)
607909-713 *E-mail:* lizenzen@verlagsgruppe-
oetinger.de
Advertising: Meike Dreyer *E-mail:* werbung@
verlagsgruppe-oetinger.de
Internet Editor: Christine Holk *Tel:* (040)
607909-948 *Fax:* (040) 607909-648
E-mail: internetredaktion@verlagsgruppe-
oetinger.de
Founded: 1928
Subjects: Fiction, Literature, Literary Criticism,
Essays
ISBN Prefix(es): 978-3-7915

Droemer Knaur Verlag, see Verlagsgruppe
Droemer Knaur GmbH & Co KG

**Verlagsgruppe Droemer Knaur GmbH & Co
KG+**
Hilblestr 54, 80636 Munich
Tel: (089) 9271-0 *Fax:* (089) 9271-168

E-mail: info@droemer-knaur.de; presse@droemer-knaur.de
Web Site: www.droemer-knaur.de
Key Personnel
Publisher & Chief Executive Officer: Doris Janhsen
Publisher-at-Large: Dr Hans-Peter Uebleis
Mng Dir, Sales & Marketing: Christian Tesch
Press Dir: Katharina Ilgen *Tel:* (089) 9271-140 *Fax:* (089) 9271-240 *E-mail:* katharina.ilgen@droemer-knaur.de
Sales Manager: Iris Haas *Tel:* (089) 9271-320 *Fax:* (089) 9271-209 *E-mail:* iris.haas@droemer-knaur.de
Editor-at-Large, Knaur: Silvia Kuttny-Walser
Foreign Rights: Elisa Diallo *Tel:* (089) 9271-279 *Fax:* (089) 9271-347 *E-mail:* elisa.diallo@droemer-knaur.de
Founded: 1901
Subjects: Biography, Memoirs, Business, Cookery, Erotica, Fiction, Health, Nutrition, History, How-to, Humor, Mysteries, Suspense, Nonfiction (General), Romance, Science (General), Science Fiction, Fantasy, Self-Help, Wine & Spirits, Anthology, Fairy Tales, Family Saga, Horror, Movie or Television, Thriller
ISBN Prefix(es): 978-3-426
Parent Company: Verlagsgruppe Georg von Holtzbrinck GmbH
Associate Companies: Augustus Verlag; Knaur Taschenbuecher; Midena Verlag; Pattloch Verlag; Schneekluth Verlag GmbH
Imprints: MenSana
Foreign Rep(s): Marcel Gerber (Switzerland)
Foreign Rights: Balla & Sztojkov Agency (Catherine Balla) (Hungary); Giuliana Bernardi (Italy); Il Caduceo SRL (Marinella Magri) (Italy); Editio Dialog Agency (Dr Michael Wenzel) (France); Agencja Literacka Graal (Joanna Maciuk) (Poland); Hercules Business & Culture Development GmbH (Hongjun Cai) (China); Ute Koerner Literary Agent (Guenter G Rodewald) (Latin America, Portugal, Spain); Literary Agency ART Dialog (Daniela Vranovska) (Czechia, Slovakia); Meike Marx Literary Agency (Japan); Nika Literarische Agentur (Vania Kadiyska) (Bulgaria); ONK Agency Ltd (Hatice Gok) (Turkey); Prava i Prevodi International Literary Agency (Milena Lukic) (Croatia, Greece, Montenegro, Romania, Serbia); Marianne Schoenbach Literary Agency (Netherlands)
Distribution Center: Sigloch Distribution Center, Am Buchberg 8, 74572 Blaufelden
Mohr Morawa Buchvertrieb GmbH, Sulzengasse 2, 1230 Vienna, Austria *Tel:* (01) 680 14-0 *Fax:* (01) 688 71 30 *E-mail:* momo@mohrmorawa.at *Web Site:* www.mohrmorawa.at
Buchzentrum AG, Industriestrasse Ost 10, 4614 Haegendorf, Switzerland *Tel:* (062) 2 09 26 26 *Fax:* (062) 2 09 26 27 *E-mail:* kundendienst@buchzentrum.ch
Returns: Sigloch Distribution GmbH Remittende Verlagsgruppe Droemer Knaur, Tor 30-40, Am Buchberg 8, 74572 Blaufelden

Droste Verlag GmbH
Martin-Luther-Platz 26, 40212 Duesseldorf
Mailing Address: Postfach 10 42 51, 40033 Duesseldorf
Tel: (0211) 8 60 52 06 *Fax:* (0211) 3 23 00 98
E-mail: kunst@drosteverlag.de; vertrieb@drosteverlag.de
Web Site: www.droste-verlag.de
Key Personnel
Management: Felix Droste; Dr Manfred Droste
Head, Sales & Marketing: Jochen Papanouscas
E-mail: jochen.papanouscas@drosteverlag.de
Founded: 1711
Subjects: Art, Biography, Memoirs, Economics, Government, Political Science, History, Humor, Nonfiction (General), Social Sciences, Sociology

ISBN Prefix(es): 978-3-7700
Subsidiaries: Wilhelm Knapp Verlag
Warehouse: Xantheuerstr 3a, 41460 Neuss
Distribution Center: Brockhaus/Commission, Kriedlerstr 9, 70806 Kornwestheim *Tel:* (07154) 13 27-37 *Fax:* (07154) 13 27-13
Mohr Morawa Buchvertrieb GmbH, Sulzengasse 2, 1230 Vienna, Austria *Tel:* (01) 680 14-0 *Fax:* (01) 688 71 30 *E-mail:* momo@mohrmorawa.at *Web Site:* www.mohrmorawa.at
Herder AG Basel, Muttenzerstr 109, 4133 Patteln 1, Switzerland *Tel:* (061) 8 27 90 60 *Fax:* (061) 8 27 90 67

Karl Elser Druck GmbH
Kisslingweg 35, 75417 Muehlacker
Tel: (07041) 805-0; (07041) 805-41; (07041) 805-49 *Fax:* (07041) 805-50
E-mail: info@elserdruck.de
Web Site: www.elserdruck.de
Key Personnel
Mng Dir & International Rights: Brigitte Wetzel-Haendle
Mng Dir: Hans-Ulrich Wetzel
Founded: 1890
Also acts as newspaper & printing office.
Subjects: Biography, Memoirs, Fiction, Regional Interests
ISBN Prefix(es): 978-3-7987
Bookshop(s): Buch-Elser, Bahnhofstr 62, 75417 Muehlacker

Gerhard Steidl-Druckerei & Verlag GmbH & Co OHG+
Duestere Str 4, 37073 Goettingen
Tel: (0551) 49 60 60 *Fax:* (0551) 49 60 649
E-mail: mail@steidl.de
Web Site: www.steidl.de
Key Personnel
Mng Dir: Gerhard Steidl
Rights & Licenses: Jan Menkens *Tel:* (0551) 49 60 618 *Fax:* (0551) 49 60 617 *E-mail:* jmenkens@steidl.de
Press & Public Relations: Claudia Glenewinkel *Tel:* (0551) 49 60 650 *Fax:* (0551) 49 60 644 *E-mail:* cglenewinkel@steidl.de
Sales & Marketing: Matthias Wegener *Tel:* (0551) 49 60 616 *E-mail:* mwegener@steidl.de
Founded: 1968
Specialize in quality photography books.
Subjects: Art, Biography, Memoirs, Fiction, History, Literature, Literary Criticism, Essays, Marketing, Nonfiction (General), Philosophy, Photography, Poetry, Psychology, Psychiatry
ISBN Prefix(es): 978-3-88243; 978-3-86521; 978-3-86930
Distributed by DAP Book Distribution Center (USA); Gemeinsame Verlagsauslieferung Goettingen (GVA) (Germany, Switzerland & Austria); Thames & Hudson Ltd; VILO DIFFUSION (France)

Druffel & Vowinckel Verlag+
Talhofstr 32, 82205 Gilching
Tel: (08105) 730560 *Fax:* (08105) 7305629
Web Site: www.druffel-vowinckel.eu
Key Personnel
Publisher: Dr Gert Sudholt *E-mail:* drsudholt@t-online.de
Founded: 1952
Subjects: Government, Political Science, History
ISBN Prefix(es): 978-3-8061; 978-3-86118

DRW-Verlag Weinbrenner GmbH & Co KG+
Fasanenweg 18, 70771 Leinfelden-Echterdingen
Tel: (0711) 7591-0 *Fax:* (0711) 7591-348
E-mail: info@drw-verlag.de
Web Site: www.drw-verlag.de; www.weinbrenner.de
Key Personnel
Publisher: Karl-Heinz Weinbrenner *E-mail:* kh.weinbrenner@weinbrenner.de; Claudia

Weinbrenner-Seibt *E-mail:* c.weinbrenner-seibt@weinbrenner.de
Publishing Dir: Uwe M Schreiner *Tel:* (0711) 7591-240 *E-mail:* uschreiner@drw-verlag.de
Founded: 1874
Subjects: Nonfiction (General), Physical Sciences, Regional Interests
ISBN Prefix(es): 978-3-87181
Parent Company: Weinbrenner GmbH & Co KG
Subsidiaries: bit-Verlag; GKT-Gesellschaft fuer Knowhow-Transfer in Architektur und Bauwesen mbH; Verlagsanstalt Alexander Koch GmbH

Dryas Verlag GbR
Mainzer Landstr 41, 60329 Frankfurt am Main
Tel: (069) 95 925 488 *Fax:* (069) 95 925 489
E-mail: kontakt@dryas.de
Web Site: www.dryas.de
Key Personnel
Owner: Jannis Radeleff
Owner & Press: Sandra Thoms
Founded: 2007
Subjects: Travel & Tourism
ISBN Prefix(es): 978-3-940855
Imprints: Goldfinch Verlag
Distribution Center: Prolit Verlagsauslieferung GmbH, Siemenstr 16, 35463 Fernwald-Annerod *Tel:* (0641) 94393-36 *Fax:* (0641) 94393-29 *E-mail:* areichel@prolit.de
Othmar Edelmann Gesellschaft mbH, Friesenplatz 8-9, 1100 Vienna, Austria *Tel:* (01) 798 10 91 11 *Fax:* (01) 798 63 46 20 *E-mail:* we@edelmann-wien.at
Balmer Buecherdienst AG, Kobiboden, 8840 Einsiedeln, Switzerland, Contact: Martin Schnetzer *Tel:* (026) 475 17 88 *Fax:* (026) 475 47 88 *E-mail:* martin.schnetzer@bluewin.ch

DSI Data Service & Information
Xantener Str 51 A, 47495 Rheinberg
Tel: (049) 2843 3220 *Fax:* (049) 2843 3230
E-mail: dsi@dsidata.com
Web Site: www.dsidata.com; www.statistischedaten.de
Key Personnel
Manager: Dr Wilhelm Hennerkes
Contact: Konrad Wilms *E-mail:* konrad.wilms@dsidata.com
Founded: 1985
Electronic preparation & publishing of national & international statistical information (numerical databases) on CD-ROM & on the Internet.
Subjects: Economics, Social Sciences, Sociology
Distributor for Bernan; Enerdata SA; European Union; International Bank for Reconstruction & Development; Organization for Economic Co-operation & Development (OECD); Smartal Solutions Ltd
Foreign Rep(s): ABE Marketing (Poland); Albertina Data SRO (Czechia, Slovakia); Albertina Incone Praha (Czechia); BH Sistemas de Informacao (Portugal); Diaz de Santos SA (Spain); Edutech (United Arab Emirates); Far Eastern Booksellers (Kyokuto Shoten) (Japan); Greendata (Spain); IBS Buke Sdn Bhd (Malaysia); Info Access & Distribution Pte Ltd (Singapore); Info Technology Supply Ltd (UK); Kaiga Kyozai Center (Japan); Kinokuniya Co Ltd (Japan); Kyobo Book Centre (Korea); Leader Books SA (Greece); Licosa SpA (Italy); Logiser SA (Portugal); LUSODOC (Portugal); Maruzen Co, IRN Import (Books) (Japan); Mundi-Prensa Libros SA (Spain); Paradox Libros (Spain); RoweCom Espana (Spain); Sistemas Documentales SL (Spain)

dtv, see Deutscher Taschenbuch Verlag GmbH & Co KG (dtv)

Duden, *imprint of* Bibliographisches Institut GmbH

Dudenverlag
Imprint of Bibliographisches Institut GmbH
Mecklenburgische Str 53, 14197 Berlin
Tel: (030) 897 85 82-30
E-mail: kundenservice@duden.de; shop@duden.
de
Web Site: www.duden.de
Key Personnel
Mng Dir: Timo Blum; Marion Winkenbach
Children's Books: Katja Franke *Tel:* (0621)
3901-186 *Fax:* (0621) 3901-395 *E-mail:* katja.
franke@duden.de
Subjects: Literature, Literary Criticism, Essays,
Nonfiction (General)
ISBN Prefix(es): 978-3-411; 978-3-89818; 978-3-
8355; 978-3-928707
Ultimate Parent Company: Franz Cornelsen Bil-
dungsholding GmbH & Co KG
Foreign Rights: Beijing Star Media Co Ltd (Wang
Xing) (China, Taiwan); Ivana Beil (Czechia,
Slovakia); The Book Publishers Association
of Israel (Shoshi Grajower) (Israel); Agency
Chang (Heaza Yu) (South Korea); druckfer-
tig (Julia Balogh) (Hungary); Iris Literary
Agency (Catherine Fragou) (Greece); Japan
Uni Agency Inc (Takeshi Oyama & Maiko Fu-
jinaga) (Japan); ONK Agency Ltd (Hatice Gok)
(Turkey)

Duesendruck Verlag
Geschwister-Scholl Str 38, 73207 Plochingen
Tel: (07153) 558 494 *Fax:* (07153) 558 484
E-mail: info@duesendruck.de
Web Site: www.duesendruck.de
Key Personnel
Publisher: Rudi Roedig
Subjects: Aeronautics, Aviation, Humor, Technol-
ogy
ISBN Prefix(es): 978-3-9807174

Dumjahn Verlag
Immenhof 12, 55128 Mainz
Mailing Address: Postfach 1746, 55007 Mainz
Tel: (06131) 330810 *Fax:* (06131) 330811
E-mail: info@dumjahn.de; eisenbahn@dumjahn.
de
Web Site: www.dumjahn.de
Key Personnel
Owner: Horst-Werner Dumjahn
Founded: 1974
Specialize in railway.
Membership(s): Boersenverein des Deutschen
Buchhandels.
Subjects: Publishing & Book Trade Reference,
Transportation, Travel & Tourism
ISBN Prefix(es): 978-3-921426; 978-3-88992
Number of titles published annually: 2 Print; 2 E-
Book
Total Titles: 18 Print
Bookshop(s): Versandbuchhandlung und Antiquar-
iat Horst-Werner Dumjahn

DuMont Buchverlag GmbH & Co KG
Amsterdamer Str 192, 50735 Cologne
Tel: (0221) 224-180 *Fax:* (0221) 224-1973
E-mail: info@dumont-buchverlag.de
Web Site: www.dumont-buchverlag.de
Key Personnel
Mng Dir: Markus Stache
Sales & Marketing Manager: Jochen
Grosse Entrup *Tel:* (0221) 224-1818
E-mail: grossentrup@dumont-buchverlag.de
Foreign Rights: Judith Habermas *Tel:* (0221) 224-
1942 *E-mail:* habermas@dumont-buchverlag.de
International Sales: Claudia Simons *Tel:* (0221)
224-1946 *E-mail:* simons@dumont-buchverlag.
de
Founded: 1956
Subjects: Architecture & Interior Design, Art,
Biography, Memoirs, Government, Political

Science, History, Literature, Literary Criticism,
Essays, Travel & Tourism
ISBN Prefix(es): 978-3-8321

DuMont Reiseverlag GmbH & Co KG+
Marco-Polo-Str 1, 73760 Ostfildern (Kemnat)
Mailing Address: Postfach 3151, 73751 Ostfildern
(Kemnat)
Tel: (0711) 4502-1033 *Fax:* (0711) 4502-411
E-mail: info@dumontreise.de
Web Site: www.dumontreise.de
Key Personnel
Chief Editor: Maria Anna Haelker *E-mail:* m.
haelker@mairdumont.com
Regional Sales Manager: Tahir Balic *Tel:* (0711)
4502-202 *E-mail:* t.balic@mairdumont.com
Sales Manager: Joachim Rau *Tel:* (0711) 4502-
230 *E-mail:* joachim.rau@mairdumont.
com; Barbara Steinert *Tel:* (0711) 4502-330
E-mail: b.steinert@mairdumont.com
Export & Licenses: Monika Abbate *Tel:* (0711)
4502-317 *E-mail:* m.abbate@mairdumont.com
Press: Brigitte Kehl *Tel:* (0711) 4502-245
E-mail: b.kehl@mairdumont.com
Founded: 1968
Subjects: Archaeology, Art, Cookery, Gardening,
Plants, Travel & Tourism
ISBN Prefix(es): 978-3-7701; 978-3-8320; 978-3-
8321

Duncker und Humblot GmbH+
Carl-Heinrich-Becker-Weg 9, 12165 Berlin
Tel: (030) 79 00 06-0 *Fax:* (030) 79 00 06-31
E-mail: info@duncker-humblot.de; rights@
duncker-humblot.de
Web Site: www.duncker-humblot.de
Key Personnel
Publisher: Dr Florian Simon *Tel:* (030) 790006-19
Fax: (030) 790006-43
Head, Marketing: Andreas Reckwerth *Tel:* (030)
790006-25 *E-mail:* reckwerth@duncker-
humblot.de
International Rights: Yasmin Soinegg *Tel:* (030)
790006-46 *Fax:* (030) 790006-746
Founded: 1798
Subjects: Asian Studies, Biography, Memoirs,
Business, Criminology, Developing Countries,
Economics, Environmental Studies, Ethnicity,
Finance, Government, Political Science, His-
tory, Labor, Industrial Relations, Law, Litera-
ture, Literary Criticism, Essays, Management,
Marketing, Military Science, Philosophy, Pub-
lic Administration, Science (General), Social
Sciences, Sociology, Theology, Business Ad-
ministration
ISBN Prefix(es): 978-3-428
Number of titles published annually: 350 Print
Subsidiaries: Berliner Buchdruckerei Union
GmbH; Speyer & Peters GmbH

Verlag duotincta
Theodor-Heuss-Platz 5, 14052 Berlin
Tel: (0157) 85526732
E-mail: kontakt@duotincta.de
Web Site: www.duotincta.de
Founded: 2014
Subjects: Fiction, History, Cultural History
ISBN Prefix(es): 978-3-946086

Dustri-Verlag Dr Karl Feistle GmbH & Co KG
(Dustri-Publishing Dr Karl Feistle)+
Bajuwarenring 4, 82041 Oberhaching-Munich
Mailing Address: Postfach 1351, 82032
Deisenhofen-Munich
Tel: (089) 61 38 61-0 *Fax:* (089) 613 54 12
E-mail: info@dustri.de
Web Site: www.dustri.com
Key Personnel
Dir: Frank Feistle *E-mail:* frank.feistle@dustri.de;
Joerg Feistle *E-mail:* joerg.feistle@dustri.de
Founded: 1947
Subjects: Medicine, Nursing, Dentistry

ISBN Prefix(es): 978-3-87185
U.S. Office(s): Dustri-Verlag Inc, Swiss Point Office Bldg, 2990 S Fiske Blvd, Rockledge, FL,
United States *Tel:* 321-594-4340 *Fax:* 321-414-
0219 *E-mail:* info@dustri.com

DVA, see Deutsche Verlags-Anstalt (DVA)

DVG-Deutsche Verlagsgesellschaft mbH+
Minden Str 34, 32361 Preussisch Oldendorf
Tel: (05742) 930444 *Fax:* (05742) 930455
Founded: 1969
Subjects: Government, Political Science, History,
Military Science
ISBN Prefix(es): 978-3-920722
Associate Companies: Verlag fuer Ausserge-
woehnliche Perspektiven
Orders to: VAP Verlagsauslieferung

DVS Media GmbH+
Subsidiary of Deutscher Verband fuer Schweissen
und verwandte Verfahren eV
Aachenerstr 172, 40223 Duesseldorf
Mailing Address: Postfach 10 19 65, 40010 Dues-
seldorf
Tel: (0211) 1591-0 *Fax:* (0211) 1591-150
E-mail: media@dvs-hg.de
Web Site: www.dvs-media.info; www.dvs-media.
eu
Key Personnel
Manager: Dirk Sieben *E-mail:* dirk.sieben@dvs.
hg.de
Sales Manager: Paul R Hoene *Tel:* (0211) 1591
260 *Fax:* (0211) 1591 250 *E-mail:* paul-robert.
hoene@dvs-hg.de
Founded: 1955
Subjects: Engineering (General), Mechanical En-
gineering, Technology, Welding & Allied Pro-
cesses
ISBN Prefix(es): 978-3-87155
Number of titles published annually: 15 Print; 3
CD-ROM
Total Titles: 419 Print; 10 CD-ROM

E A Seemann Verlag, *imprint of* Seemann
Henschel GmbH & Co KG

E & Z Verlag
Dahlmannstr 22, 47169 Duisburg
Tel: (0203) 93093277 *Fax:* (0203) 9408257
E-mail: euz-verlag@arcor.de
Web Site: www.euz-buchwelt.de
Founded: 2005
ISBN Prefix(es): 978-3-938573
Distribution Center: Marketing- und Ver-
lagsservice des Buchhandels GmbH (MVB),
Braubachstr 16, Postfach 10 04 42, 60004
Frankfurt am Main *Tel:* (069) 1306-550
Fax: (069) 1306-255 *E-mail:* info@mvb-online.
de

earBOOKS
Neumuehlen 17, 22763 Hamburg
Tel: (040) 890 85-0
E-mail: info@edel.com
Web Site: www.earbooks.net; www.edel.de
Key Personnel
General Manager: Jos Bendinelli Negrone
Tel: (040) 890 85-433 *E-mail:* jos.bendinelli.
negrone@edel.com
International Sales Manager: Rene Valjeur
Tel: (040) 890 85-172 *E-mail:* rene.valjeur@
edel.com
Press & Public Relations: Lena Borowski
Tel: (040) 890 85-119 *E-mail:* lena.borowski@
edel.com
Subjects: Art, Pop Culture
ISBN Prefix(es): 978-3-937406
Parent Company: Edel Germany GmbH
Ultimate Parent Company: Edel AG

ebersbach & simon
Corneliusstr 21a, 12247 Berlin
Tel: (030) 7688 64 40 *Fax:* (030) 7688 64 41
E-mail: info@ebersbach-simon.de
Web Site: www.ebersbach-simon.de
Key Personnel
Publisher: Sascha Nicoletta Simon
Advisory Senior Publisher: Brigitte Ebersbach
Subjects: Cookery, Fashion, Travel & Tourism
ISBN Prefix(es): 978-3-938740; 978-3-931782;
978-3-934703; 978-3-86915
Distribution Center: Prolit Verlagsausliefer-
ung, Siemensstr 16, 35463 Fernwald, Con-
tact: Andrea Willenberg *Tel:* (041) 9 43 93 35
Fax: (041) 9 43 93 39 *E-mail:* a.willenberg@
prolit.de
Dr Franz Hain Verlagsauslieferung GmbH, Dr-
Otto-Neurath-Gasse 5, 1220 Vienna, Austria
Tel: (01) 2 82 65 65 *Fax:* (01) 2 82 52 82
E-mail: bestell@hain.at

Th Ebersberg, *imprint of* Eironeia-Verlag

Echo Verlag+
Lotzestr 22a, 37083 Goettingen
Tel: (0551) 79 68 24 *Fax:* (0551) 7 40 35
E-mail: webmaster@echoverlag.de
Web Site: www.echoverlag.de
Key Personnel
Mng Dir: Dr Edmund Haferbeck
Mng Dir, Rights & Permissions: Andrea Clages
Founded: 1985
Membership(s): Land Association Lower Saxony;
The Stock Exchange of German Booksellers.
Subjects: Animals, Pets, Environmental Studies,
Health, Nutrition, Animal Rights, Vegetarian-
ism
ISBN Prefix(es): 978-3-9801216; 978-3-926914

Echter Verlag GmbH+
Dominikanerplatz 8, 97070 Wuerzburg
Tel: (0931) 66068-0 *Fax:* (0931) 66068-23
E-mail: info@echter.de; presse@echter.de;
vertrieb@echter.de
Web Site: www.echter.de
Key Personnel
Publisher: Thomas Haeussner *E-mail:* th.
haeussner@echter.de
Licensing, Advertising & Sales: Marion Eisen-
mann *Tel:* (0931) 66068-60
Production & Press: Sieglinde Bieber *Tel:* (0931)
66068-30
Founded: 1900
Subjects: Art, Biblical Studies, Fiction, History,
Regional Interests, Religion - Catholic, Reli-
gion - Other, Theology, Wine & Spirits
ISBN Prefix(es): 978-3-429
Total Titles: 600 Print

ecomed SICHERHEIT+
Division of Verlagsgruppe Huethig Jehle Rehm
GmbH
Justus-Von-Liebig-Str 1, 86899 Landsberg
Tel: (08191) 125-0 *Fax:* (08191) 125-492
E-mail: info@ecomed.de
Web Site: www.ecomed-storck.de
Key Personnel
Publishing Manager: Udo Graf *Tel:* (08191) 125-
127 *E-mail:* udo.graf@hjr-verlag.de
Marketing Manager: Gerhard Heinzmann
Tel: (08191) 125-399
Press: Gerlinde Stanglmeier *Tel:* (08191) 125-571
E-mail: gerlinde.stanglmeier@hjr-verlag.de
Founded: 1979
Subjects: Chemistry, Chemical Engineering, En-
gineering (General), Environmental Studies,
Labor, Industrial Relations, Medicine, Nursing,
Dentistry, Technology, Transportation, Safety,
Security
ISBN Prefix(es): 978-3-609

Total Titles: 700 Print
Associate Companies: ecomed MEDIZIN; Storck
Verlag Hamburg

Econ, *imprint of* Ullstein Buchverlage GmbH

Econ Verlag+
Imprint of Ullstein Buchverlage GmbH
Friedrichstr 126, 10117 Berlin
Tel: (030) 23456-300 *Fax:* (030) 23456-303
E-mail: info@ullstein-buchverlage.de; zentrale@
ullstein-buchverlage.de
Web Site: www.ullstein-buchverlage.de/verlage/
econ.html
Key Personnel
Head, Media & Communication: Christine Hein-
rich *Tel:* (030) 23456-433 *Fax:* (030) 23456-
445 *E-mail:* christine.heinrich@ullstein-
buchverlage.de
Founded: 1951
Subjects: Biography, Memoirs, Business, Career
Development, Computer Science, Economics,
Fiction, Government, Political Science, Health,
Nutrition, Humor, Maritime, Mysteries, Sus-
pense, Nonfiction (General), Self-Help
ISBN Prefix(es): 978-3-430; 978-3-612; 978-3-
547
Orders to: Distribook, Industriestr 23, 70565
Stuttgart *Tel:* (0800) 66-111-99 *Fax:* (0711)
7899-1010 *E-mail:* service@distribook.de *Web
Site:* www.distribook.de
Mohr Morawa Buchvertrieb GmbH, Sulzengasse
2, 1230 Vienna, Austria *Tel:* (01) 680-14-
0 *Fax:* (01) 688-71-30 *E-mail:* bestellung@
mohrmorawa.at *Web Site:* www.mohrmorawa.at
Buchzentrum AG, Industriestr Ost 10, 4614 Haegendorf, Switzerland *Tel:* (062) 209-25 25
Fax: (062) 209-26 27 *E-mail:* kundienst@
buchzentrum.ch

ECV - Editio Cantor Verlag
Baendelstockweg 20, 88326 Aulendorf
Tel: (07525) 940-0 *Fax:* (07525) 940-180
E-mail: info@ecv.de
Web Site: www.ecv.de
Key Personnel
Mng Dir: Claudius Arndt *Tel:* (07525) 940-159
E-mail: carndt@ecv.de; Andreas Gerth
Tel: (07525) 940-103 *E-mail:* agerth@ecv.de
Subjects: Health, Nutrition, Medicine, Nursing,
Dentistry, Science (General), Cosmetics, Phar-
maceutical Technology, Pharmacy
ISBN Prefix(es): 978-3-87193

Verlag Dr Reiner-Friedemann Edel, see
Oekumenischer Verlag Dr R-F Edel

Edel:Kids
Neumuehlen 17, 22763 Hamburg
Tel: (040) 890 85-0
E-mail: info@edel.com
Web Site: www.edel.com/de/audio/kids
Founded: 1998
ISBN Prefix(es): 978-3-89855
Parent Company: Edel Germany GmbH
Ultimate Parent Company: Edel AG

Eden Books
Rosa-Luxemburg-Str 14, 10178 Berlin
Tel: (030) 208 98 01 60 *Fax:* (030) 208 98 01 80
E-mail: hallo@edenbooks.de
Web Site: www.edel.com/de/buch/eden-books
Key Personnel
Publishing Dir: Jennifer Kroll
Subjects: Biography, Memoirs, Nonfiction (Gen-
eral), Lifestyle, Women's Interest
ISBN Prefix(es): 978-3-959100; 978-3-944296
Parent Company: Edel Germany GmbH
Ultimate Parent Company: Edel AG

Edition & Galerie Volker Huber eK+
Berliner Str 218, 63011 Offenbach
Mailing Address: Postfach 10 11 53, 63011 Of-
fenbach
Tel: (069) 81 45 23 *Fax:* (069) 88 01 55
E-mail: edition-huber@t-online.de
Web Site: www.edition-huber.de
Key Personnel
Mng Dir: Volker Huber
Founded: 1969
Subjects: Art
ISBN Prefix(es): 978-3-921785

Verlag Edition AV
Postfach 12 15, 35420 Lich
Tel: (06404) 6570763 *Fax:* (06404) 668900
E-mail: editionav@gmx.net
Web Site: www.edition-av.de
Key Personnel
Contact: Dr Ansdreas W Hohmann
Founded: 1988
Membership(s): Assoziation Linker Verlage
(aLiVe).
Subjects: Biography, Memoirs, Education, Fiction,
Government, Political Science, History, Poetry,
Satire
ISBN Prefix(es): 978-3-936049; 978-3-9806407;
978-3-86841
Foreign Rep(s): Thomas Ohlsen
Foreign Rights: Agentur Klaus Groener

Egmont Ehapa Media GmbH+
Subsidiary of Egmont Mediengruppe
Alte Jakobstr 83, 10179 Berlin
Tel: (030) 24008-0 *Fax:* (030) 24008-599
E-mail: info@ehapa-service.de; shop@ehapa-
shop.de; pr@ehapa.de
Web Site: www.ehapa.de
Key Personnel
Editorial Dir & Head, New Business: Peter
Hoepfner *Tel:* (030) 24008-400 *E-mail:* p.
hoepfner@ehapa.de
Publishing Dir, Magazines: Joerg Risken
E-mail: j.risken@ehapa.de
Sales Dir: Christian Behr *Tel:* (030) 24008-548
E-mail: c.behr@ehapa.de
Head, Media Sales: Dirk Eggert *Tel:* (030) 24008-
116 *E-mail:* d.eggert@egmont.de
Founded: 1951
Children's magazines.
Subjects: Humor, Comics
ISBN Prefix(es): 978-3-7704; 978-3-89343; 978-
3-928108
Number of titles published annually: 200 Print
Total Titles: 1,000 Print
Imprints: Delta
Subsidiaries: Cultfish Entertainment (teen label)
Divisions: Egmont Manga & Anime Europe
(Manga); OU Character Kids (comic magazine
& juvenile journals); OU Disney Kids (Disney
publication)

Egmont Verlagsgesellschaften mbH+
Gertrudenstr 30-36, 50667 Cologne
Mailing Address: Postfach 10 12 51, 50452
Cologne
Tel: (0221) 20811-0 *Fax:* (0221) 20811-66;
(0221) 20811-67
E-mail: info@vgs.de; info@egmont-vg.de
Web Site: www.vgs.de; www.egmont-vg.de
Key Personnel
Mng Dir: Klaus-Thorsten Firnig *Fax:* (0221)
20811-55
Publishing Dir: Volker Busch
Sales & Marketing Dir: Andrea Rueller
Press Manager: Elisabeth Noss *Tel:* (0221)
20811-49 *Fax:* (0221) 20811-69
Foreign Rights Manager: Gaeelle Toquin
Tel: (0221) 20811-24
Founded: 1970

Market leading TV tie-in publisher in the German speaking territory; popular nonfiction on health subjects, illustrated books.
Subjects: Animals, Pets, Art, Asian Studies, Biography, Memoirs, Cookery, Crafts, Games, Hobbies, Fiction, Film, Video, Foreign Countries, Gardening, Plants, Health, Nutrition, History, House & Home, Music, Dance, Mysteries, Suspense, Natural History, Nonfiction (General), Outdoor Recreation, Radio, TV, Science Fiction, Fantasy, Travel & Tourism
ISBN Prefix(es): 978-3-8025
Number of titles published annually: 120 Print
Total Titles: 500 Print
Parent Company: Egmont Group, Berlin
Foreign Rep(s): Mohr Morawa Buchvertrieb GmbH (Austria); Schweizer Buchzentrum (Switzerland)
Orders to: Cornelsen Verlagskontor Verlagsauslieferung GmbH & Co KG, Kammerratsheide 66, 33609 Bielefeld *Tel:* (0521) 9719140 *Fax:* (0521) 9719291

Egmont Verlagsgesellschaften mbH SchneiderBuch+
Gertrudenstr 30-36, 50667 Cologne
Mailing Address: Postfach 10 12 51, 50452 Cologne
Tel: (0221) 20811-0 *Fax:* (0221) 20811-66
E-mail: info@schneiderbuch.de
Web Site: www.schneiderbuch.de
Key Personnel
Mng Dir: Klaus-Thorstein Firnig
Publishing: Volker Busch
Public Relations: Elisabeth Noss *E-mail:* e.noss@vgs.de
Founded: 1913
Specialize in Disney books, television/film related books.
Subjects: Fiction, Film, Video, History, Nonfiction (General), Science Fiction, Fantasy
ISBN Prefix(es): 978-3-505
Number of titles published annually: 150 Print
Total Titles: 700 Print
Parent Company: Egmont Verlagsgesellschaften mbH

EHP-Verlag Andreas Kohlhage+
Mylinghauser Str 39, 58285 Gevelsberg
Mailing Address: Postfach 1460, 58259 Gevelsberg
Tel: (02332) 666-4207
E-mail: info@ehp-koeln.com
Web Site: www.ehp-koeln.com
Key Personnel
Publisher: Andreas Kohlhage
Founded: 1986
Subjects: Human Relations, Literature, Literary Criticism, Essays, Management, Nonfiction (General), Psychology, Psychiatry, Science (General), Social Sciences, Sociology
ISBN Prefix(es): 978-3-926176; 978-3-9804784; 978-3-89797
Number of titles published annually: 5 Print
Total Titles: 60 Print
Orders to: Brockhaus/Commission, Kreidlerstr 9, 70806 Kornwestheim *Tel:* (07154) 132749 *Fax:* (07154) 132790 *E-mail:* germanbooks@brocom.de *Web Site:* www.brocom.de

Eichborn, *imprint of* Bastei Luebbe GmbH & Co KG

Eichborn+
Imprint of Bastei Luebbe GmbH & Co KG
Schanzenstr 6-20, 51063 Cologne
Tel: (0221) 8200 0
E-mail: webmaster@luebbe.de
Web Site: www.luebbe.de/Eichborn
Founded: 1980

Subjects: Fiction, History, Humor, Literature, Literary Criticism, Essays, Mysteries, Suspense, Nonfiction (General)
ISBN Prefix(es): 978-3-8218; 978-3-8479
Number of titles published annually: 200 Print; 30 Audio

Edition Eichthal
Eichthal 1, 24340 Eckemfoerde
Tel: (04351) 82584 *Fax:* (04351) 476092
Web Site: www.edition-eichthal.de
Key Personnel
Owner: Jens Uwe Jess *E-mail:* jess@edition-eichthal.de
Subjects: Biography, Memoirs, Fiction, Poetry
ISBN Prefix(es): 978-3-9811115

Verlag Eifelkrone-Musik & Buch eK
Layenstr 27, 54570 Neroth
Tel: (06591) 5112 *Fax:* (06591) 985086
E-mail: kontakt@eifelkrone-musik.de
Key Personnel
Publisher: Manfred Ulrich
Founded: 1985
Subjects: Music, Dance, Nonfiction (General), Fairy Tales, Nature
ISBN Prefix(es): 978-3-937640; 978-3-9809028
Foreign Rep(s): Dr Winfried Plattner (Austria)
Distribution Center: Suedost Verlags Service GmbH, Am Steinfeld 4, 94065 Waldkirchen *Tel:* (08581) 9605-0 *Fax:* (08581) 754 *E-mail:* info@suedost-verlag-service.de
Ennsthaler Gesellschaft mbH & Co/Steyr, Stadtplatz 26, 4400 Steyr, Austria *Tel:* (07252) 52 0 53-20 *Fax:* (07252) 52 0 53-22 *E-mail:* auslieferung@ennsthaler.at

ein-FACH-verlag+
Promenade 3-9, 52076 Aachen
Tel: (02408) 5996260
E-mail: kontakt@ein-fach-verlag.de
Web Site: www.ein-fach-verlag.de
Key Personnel
Management: Dr Manfred Dueker; Ursala I Meyer, MA
Founded: 1989
Membership(s): Boersenverein des Deutschen Buchhandels.
Subjects: Language Arts, Linguistics, Philosophy, Religion - Hindu, Science (General), Women's Studies, Feminist Philosophy
ISBN Prefix(es): 978-3-928089
Total Titles: 26 Print
Orders to: GVA - Gemeinsame Verlagsauslieferung, Postfach 20 21, 37010 Gottingen *Tel:* (0551) 487177 *Fax:* (0551) 41392 *E-mail:* rabe@gva-verlage.de

Einhorn-Verlag+Druck GmbH
Sebaldplatz 1, 73525 Schwaebisch Gmuend
Tel: (07171) 92780-0 *Fax:* (07171) 92780-47
E-mail: kontakt@einhornverlag.de; redaktion@einhornverlag.de
Web Site: www.einhornverlag.de
Key Personnel
Mng Dir: Joerg Schumacher *E-mail:* schumacher@einhornverlag.de
Editor: Birgit Markert *Tel:* (07171) 92780-15 *Fax:* (07171) 92780-49; Susanne Roetter *Tel:* (07171) 92780-24 *Fax:* (07171) 92780-49
Founded: 1951
Subjects: Art, Cookery, Criminology, Erotica, Fiction, History, Poetry, Science Fiction, Fantasy
ISBN Prefix(es): 978-3-396373; 978-3-921703; 978-3-927654

Bildungsverlag EINS GmbH+
Hansestr 115, 51149 Cologne
Tel: (02203) 8982-0 *Fax:* (02203) 8982-990
E-mail: info@bv-1.de; kundenservice@bv-1.de
Web Site: www.bildungsverlag1.de

Key Personnel
Mng Dir: Wilmar Diepgrond
Press: Jenny Odenthal *Tel:* (02203) 89 82 813 *Fax:* (02203) 89 82 880 *E-mail:* jenny.odenthal@bv-1.de
Founded: 1953
Specialize in vocational education & training.
Subjects: Education, Language Arts, Linguistics
ISBN Prefix(es): 978-3-427; 978-3-7826; 978-3-8018; 978-3-8181; 978-3-87183; 978-3-87772; 978-3-8237; 978-3-441; 978-3-523; 978-3-8239; 978-3-8242; 978-3-88271; 978-3-89839; 978-3-920213; 978-3-933430

Eironeia-Verlag
Sonnhalde 37, 79194 Gundelfingen
Tel: (0761) 581617
Web Site: www.abschied-vom-absoluten.de
Key Personnel
Mng Dir: Thomas Ebersberg *E-mail:* ebersbergkirch@aol.com
Founded: 1987
Subjects: History, Human Relations, Literature, Literary Criticism, Essays, Philosophy, Photography
ISBN Prefix(es): 978-3-926607
Imprints: Th Ebersberg; K Kirchbaum

Eisenbahn-Kurier Verlag, see EK-Verlag GmbH

EK-Verlag GmbH+
Loerracher Str 16, 79115 Freiburg
Tel: (0761) 70310-0 *Fax:* (0761) 70310-50
E-mail: service@eisenbahn-kurier.de; redaktion@eisenbahn-kurier.de
Web Site: www.eisenbahn-kurier.de; www.ekshop.de
Key Personnel
Management: Dierk Lawrenz
Chief Editor: Thomas Frister
Executive Editor: Joerg Sauter *E-mail:* joerg.sauter@eisenbahn-kurier.de
Advertising Manager: Waltraud Gaenssmantel *Tel:* (0761) 703 10-11 *E-mail:* waltraud.gaenssmantel@eisenbahn-kurier.de
Sales Manager: Roswitha Lickert
Founded: 1966
Subjects: Film, Video, Transportation, Travel & Tourism, Model Railways, Model Train, Model Transport, Traffic History
ISBN Prefix(es): 978-3-88255

Elektor-Verlag GmbH+
Kackertstr 10, 52072 Aachen
Tel: (0241) 955 09-190 *Fax:* (0241) 955 09-013
E-mail: info@elektor.de
Web Site: www.elektor.de
Key Personnel
Mng Dir: Donatus Akkermans
Editor-in-Chief: Jens Nickel
Publisher: Ferdinand te Walvaart
Founded: 1972
Membership(s): German Association of Book Distributors.
Subjects: Computers, Electronics, Electrical Engineering, Engineering (General), Environmental Studies, Nonfiction (General), Physical Sciences, Technology, Travel & Tourism
ISBN Prefix(es): 978-3-921608; 978-3-928051; 978-3-89576
Parent Company: Elektuur BV

Elfenbein Verlag
Gaudystr 7, 10437 Berlin
Tel: (030) 44 32 77 69 *Fax:* (030) 44 32 77 80
E-mail: zentrale@elfenbein-verlag.de
Web Site: www.elfenbein-verlag.de
Key Personnel
Publisher: Ingo Drzecnik; Roman Pliske
Founded: 1996

Subjects: Literature, Literary Criticism, Essays, Music, Dance, Poetry
ISBN Prefix(es): 978-3-932245
Distribution Center: GVA Goettingen, Anna-Vandenhoeck-Ring 36, 37081 Goettingen *Tel:* (0551) 38 42 00 0 *Fax:* (0551) 38 42 00 10 *E-mail:* bestellung@gva-verlage.de
Seth Meyer-Bruhns, Boecklinstr 26/8, 1020 Vienna, Austria *Tel:* (01) 214 73 40 *Fax:* (01) 214 73 40 *E-mail:* meyer_bruhns@yahoo.de

Heinrich Ellermann Verlag+
Subsidiary of Verlag Friedrich Oetinger GmbH
Poppenbuetteler Chaussee 53, 22397 Hamburg
Mailing Address: Postfach 65 82 30, 22374 Hamburg
Tel: (040) 607909-08 *Fax:* (040) 6072326
E-mail: ellermann@verlagsgruppe-oetinger.de; vertrieb@verlagsgruppe-oetinger.de; marketing@verlagsgruppe-oetinger.de
Web Site: www.ellermann.de
Key Personnel
Mng Dir: Jan Weitendorf; Silke Weitendorf
Marketing Manager: Lars Spicher
Sales Manager: Susanne Weiss *Tel:* (040) 607909-777 *Fax:* (040) 607909-550
Advertising: Tina Jacobsen *Tel:* (040) 607909-791 *Fax:* (040) 607909-891 *E-mail:* initiativbewerbung@verlagsgruppe-oetinger.de
Rights & Licensing: Renate Reichstein *Tel:* (040) 607909-713 *E-mail:* lizenzen@verlagsgruppe-oetinger.de
Founded: 1934
ISBN Prefix(es): 978-3-7707

Ellert & Richter Verlag GmbH+
Grosse Brunnenstr 116-120, 22763 Hamburg
Tel: (040) 39 84 77-0 *Fax:* (040) 39 84 77-23
E-mail: info@ellert-richter.de; presse@ellert-richter.de; vertrieb@ellert-richter.de
Web Site: www.ellert-richter.de
Key Personnel
Mng Dir: Gerhard Richter
Press: Nina Golde *Tel:* (040) 39 84 77-15
Sales: Max Hecht *Tel:* (040) 39 84 77-13
Founded: 1979
Subjects: Art, Biography, Memoirs, Criminology, Foreign Countries, Gardening, Plants, History, Humor, Nonfiction (General), Psychology, Psychiatry, Travel & Tourism
ISBN Prefix(es): 978-3-89234; 978-3-8319
Foreign Rep(s): Dr Franz Hain Verlagsauslieferung GmbH (Christian Hirtzy & Ernst Sonntag) (Austria)
Distribution Center: Runge VA GmbH, Bergstr 2, 33803 Steinhagen, Contact: Silke Schoening *Tel:* (05204) 998 123 *Fax:* (05204) 998 116 *E-mail:* ellert-richter@rungeva.de
Dr Franz Hain Verlagsauslieferung GmbH, Dr-Otto-Neurath-Gasse 5, 1220 Vienna, Austria *Tel:* (01) 282 6565 *Fax:* (01) 282 5282 *E-mail:* office@hain.at

Elsengold Verlag
Astemplatz 3, 12203 Berlin
Tel: (030) 64 08 06 88 *Fax:* (030) 65 00 66 85
E-mail: info@elsengold.de
Web Site: www.elsengold.de
Key Personnel
Publisher: Nicola Grabow *E-mail:* grabow@elsengold.de
Sales Dir: Andreas Krauss
Founded: 2013
ISBN Prefix(es): 978-3-944594
Imprints: Palm Verlag

Elsevier GmbH/Urban & Fischer Verlag+
Hackerbruecke 6, 80335 Munich
Mailing Address: Postfach 20 19 30, 80019 Munich
Tel: (089) 5383-0 *Fax:* (089) 5383-939

E-mail: info@elsevier.de; presse@elsevier.de
Web Site: www.elsevier.de
Key Personnel
Mng Dir: Martin Beck; Olaf Lodbrok *Tel:* (089) 5383-600 *Fax:* (089) 5383-609; Dr Thomas Zahn
Rights & Permissions: Elke Reitmayer *Tel:* (089) 5383-770 *E-mail:* e.reitmayer@elsevier.com
Founded: 1866
Subjects: Health, Nutrition, Medicine, Nursing, Dentistry, Science (General)
ISBN Prefix(es): 978-3-437; 978-3-541; 978-3-8243; 978-3-334; 978-3-86126; 978-3-88454; 978-3-921689
Number of titles published annually: 220 Print
Parent Company: Elsevier GmbH
Ultimate Parent Company: RELX Group PLC
Branch Office(s)
Urban & Schwarzenberg GesmbH, Frankgasse 4, 1096 Vienna, Austria
Elsevier Urban & Partner Sp z oo, Focus Plaza, ul Kosciuszki 29, 50-011 Wroclaw, Poland *Tel:* (71) 330 61 61 *Fax:* (71) 330 61 60 *E-mail:* biuro@elsevier.com *Web Site:* www.elsevier.pl
Bookshop(s): Oscar Rothacker Versandbuchhandlung GmbH, Fraunhoferstr 10, 82152 Martinsried
Shipping Address: Servicecenter Fachverlage, Holzwiesenstr 2, 72127 Kusterdingen

Elysion Books
Auenstr 105, 04178 Leipzig
Tel: (0341) 49268297
E-mail: info@elysion-books.com
Web Site: elysion-books.com
Key Personnel
Owner: Jennifer Schreiner
Editor: Tanja Janz
Subjects: Erotica, Romance, Science Fiction, Fantasy
ISBN Prefix(es): 978-3-942602

Emons Verlag Koeln+
Luetticher Str 38, 50674 Cologne
Tel: (0221) 56977-0 *Fax:* (0221) 524937
E-mail: info@emons-verlag.de
Web Site: www.emons-verlag.de
Key Personnel
Mng Dir: Hermann-Josef Emons
Publisher: Hejo Emons *E-mail:* emons@emons-verlag.de
Press: Dr Britta Schmitz *Tel:* (0221) 56977-17 *E-mail:* schmitz@emons-verlag.de
Sales: Ingeborg Simandi *E-mail:* simandi@emons-verlag.de
Founded: 1984
Subjects: Criminology, Film, Video, Mysteries, Suspense, Regional Interests
ISBN Prefix(es): 978-3-924491; 978-3-89705
Total Titles: 120 Print
Foreign Rep(s): Cornelia Frese (Switzerland); Michael Hoeller (Austria)
Distribution Center: VVA Arvato media GmbH, An der Autobahn 100, 33310 Guetersloh
Hillstein-Verlag, Postfach 1, 5017 Salzburg, Austria, Contact: Mrs Bauer *E-mail:* info@hillstein.at
Buchzentrum AG, Industriestr Ost 10, 4614 Haegendorf, Switzerland *E-mail:* kundendienst@buchzentrum.de

Engel & Bengel Verlag+
Haardtweg 3, 67273 Bobenheim
Tel: (06353) 8107 *Fax:* (06353) 507057
Key Personnel
Contact: Erika Neuhaus
Founded: 1990
Subjects: Animals, Pets, Disability, Special Needs, Fiction, How-to, Human Relations
ISBN Prefix(es): 978-3-928129

Orders to: Koch, Neff & Oetinger Verlagsauslieferung GmbH, Industriestr 23, 70565 Stuttgart
Koch, Neff & Volckmar GmbH, Industriestr 23, 70565 Stuttgart

Engelsdorfer Verlag
Schongauer Str 25, 04329 Leipzig
Tel: (0341) 27 11 87-0 *Fax:* (0341) 27 11 87-10
E-mail: info@engelsdorfer-verlag.de
Web Site: www.engelsdorfer-verlag.de
Key Personnel
Publisher & Owner: Tino Hemmann *E-mail:* tino.hemmann@engelsdorfer-verlag.de
Founded: 2001
ISBN Prefix(es): 978-3-937290; 978-3-937930; 978-3-938288; 978-3-938607; 978-3-938873; 978-3-939144; 978-3-9807705; 978-3-9808685
Number of titles published annually: 240 Print; 50 E-Book
Total Titles: 1,680 Print; 290 E-Book

Englisch Verlag+
Toepferstr 14, 65191 Wiesbaden
Tel: (0611) 942 72-0 *Fax:* (0611) 942 72-40
E-mail: info@englisch-verlag.de
Web Site: www.christophorus-verlag.de
Founded: 1973
Membership(s): Boersenverein des Deutschen Buchhandels.
Subjects: Art, Crafts, Games, Hobbies, How-to
ISBN Prefix(es): 978-3-8241; 978-3-88140
Number of titles published annually: 80 Print
Total Titles: 300 Print
Parent Company: Christophorus Verlag GmbH & Co KG, Schnewlinstr 6, 79098 Freiburg
Foreign Rep(s): Dr Franz Hain (Austria); Schweizer Buchzentrum (Switzerland)
Warehouse: VVA Vereinigte Verlagsauslieferung, 33310 Guetersloh *Tel:* (05241) 803893 *Fax:* (05241) 46750
Orders to: VVA Bertelsmann Distribution, Postfach 7777, 33310 Guetersloh

Verlag Peter Engstler
Oberwaldbehrungen, Am Brunnen 6, 97645 Ostheim/Rhoen
Tel: (09774) 858490 *Fax:* (09774) 858491
E-mail: engstler-verlag@t-online.de
Web Site: www.engstler-verlag.de
Key Personnel
Contact: Peter Engstler
Founded: 1988
Subjects: Art, Fiction, Government, Political Science, Literature, Literary Criticism, Essays, Poetry
ISBN Prefix(es): 978-3-929375; 978-3-9801770; 978-3-9802826
Distribution Center: SOVA Sozialistische Verlagsauslieferung, Friesstr 20-24, 60338 Frankfurt am Main *Tel:* (069) 410211 *Fax:* (069) 410280 *E-mail:* sovaffm@t-online.de (Germany & Austria)

Ensslin Verlag im Arena Verlag, *imprint of* Arena Verlag GmbH

EOS Editions Sankt Ottilien+
Erzabtei 14 a, 86941 Sankt Ottilien
Tel: (08193) 71700 *Fax:* (08193) 71709
E-mail: mail@eos-verlag.de
Web Site: www.eos-verlag.de
Key Personnel
Executive Dir: Dr Cyrill Schaefer *Tel:* (08193) 71711 *E-mail:* cyrill@eos-verlag.de
Founded: 1885
Subjects: Art, Fiction, History, Religion - Other, Theology
ISBN Prefix(es): 978-3-88096; 978-3-920289; 978-3-8306

EPLA-Verlag
Am Teich 9, 27777 Ganderkesee-Hoykenkamp
Tel: (04221) 850143 *Fax:* (04221) 850146
E-mail: epla.plachetka@t-online.de
Web Site: www.epla-verlag.de
Key Personnel
Owner & Publisher: Erwin Plachetka
Founded: 1985
Subjects: Biography, Memoirs, Mysteries, Suspense, Nonfiction (General), Poetry, Travel & Tourism
ISBN Prefix(es): 978-3-925580

epodium Verlag
Schraudolphstr 36, 80799 Munich
Tel: (089) 272 723 22 *Fax:* (03212) 104 03 38
Web Site: www.epodium.de
Key Personnel
Management: Dr Andreas Backoefer *E-mail:* a.backoefer@epodium.de
Founded: 2000
Subjects: Art, Fiction, Music, Dance, Poetry
ISBN Prefix(es): 978-3-9807394; 978-3-9808231; 978-3-940388

EPSILON Verlag & Versand
Langer Rehm 29, 25785 Nordhastedt
Tel: (04804) 1866 28 *Fax:* (04804) 1866 31
E-mail: epsilongrafix@web.de
Web Site: www.epsilongrafix.de
Key Personnel
Contact: Mark O Fischer *E-mail:* mofischer@epsilongrafix.de
Comic book publisher.
ISBN Prefix(es): 978-3-932578; 978-3-937898
Distribution Center: PPM Peter Poluda Medienvertrieb, Lortzingstr 5, 32683 Barntrup
Tel: (05263) 95 63 63 *Fax:* (05263) 95 63 62
E-mail: info@ppm-vertrieb.de *Web Site:* www.ppm-vertrieb.de

EPV, see Evangelischer Presseverband fuer Bayern eV (EPV)

Erasmus Grasser-Verlag GmbH
Bachtal 6, 86978 Hohenfurch
Tel: (08861) 9309 742; (08861) 241 900
  Fax: (08861) 8578; (08861) 241 901
E-mail: technik@vogelsgesang.com; info@eg-v.de
Web Site: www.eg-v.de
Key Personnel
Mng Dir: Guntram Vogelsgesang
Founded: 1975
Subjects: Alternative, Health, Nutrition, Inspirational, Spirituality, Regional Interests, Holistic Medicine
ISBN Prefix(es): 978-3-925967
Imprints: edition insole

Edition Erdmann, *imprint of* Verlagshaus Roemerweg GmbH

Eres Edition Musikverlag
Haupstr 35, 28865 Lilienthal
Tel: (04298) 1676 *Fax:* (04298) 5312
E-mail: info@notenpost.de
Web Site: www.notenpost.de
Key Personnel
Mng Dir: Horst Schubert
Founded: 1946
Subjects: Music, Dance
ISBN Prefix(es): 978-3-87204

Ergon Verlag GmbH+
Keesburgstr 11, 97074 Wuerzburg
Tel: (0931) 280084 *Fax:* (0931) 282872
E-mail: service@ergon-verlag.de; orders@ergon-verlag.de; marketing@ergon-verlag.de
Web Site: www.ergon-verlag.de

Key Personnel
Dir: Dr Hans-Juergen Dietrich
  E-mail: verlagsleitung@ergon-verlag.de
Founded: 1989
Membership(s): Boersenverein des Deutschen Buchhandels.
Subjects: Art, Asian Studies, Government, Political Science, History, Library & Information Sciences, Literature, Literary Criticism, Essays, Philosophy, Psychology, Psychiatry, Religion - Other, Social Sciences, Sociology, Theology, Antiquity, Jurisprudence, Pedagogics
ISBN Prefix(es): 978-3-928034; 978-3-932004; 978-3-933563; 978-3-89913; 978-3-935556
Distribution Center: Hora-Verlags-Gesselschaft mbH, Hackhofergasse 8-10, Postfach 24, 1195 Vienna-Nussdorf, Austria *Tel:* (0222) 67 15 80 *Fax:* (0222) 37 63 93
Schweizer Buchzentrum, 4601 Olten 1, Switzerland *Tel:* (062) 209 25 25 *Fax:* (062) 209 26 27

ERICarts - European Institute for Comparative Cultural Research, see ARCult Media GmbH

Erlanger Verlag Fuer Mission und Oekumene
(Erlanger Publishing House for Missions & Ecumerics)+
Hauptstr 2, 91564 Neuendettelsau
Tel: (09874) 9 17 00 *Fax:* (09874) 9 33 70
E-mail: verlagsleitung@erlanger-verlag.de
Web Site: www.erlanger-verlag.de
Key Personnel
Publishing Dir: Martin Backhouse
Founded: 1897
Specialize in Missiological studies.
Subjects: Asian Studies, Developing Countries, Religion - Islamic, Religion - Protestant, Religion - Other, Theology
ISBN Prefix(es): 978-3-87214
Number of titles published annually: 6 Print
Total Titles: 170 Print
Parent Company: Evangelical Lutheran Church in Bavaria
Distribution Center: ChrisMedia GmbH, Robert-Bosch-Str 10, 35460 Staufenberg
Tel: (06406) 83 46 100 *Fax:* (06406) 83 46 110 *E-mail:* erlanger-verlag@chrismedia24.de

Wilhelm Ernst & Sohn, Verlag fuer Architektur und technische Wissenschaften GmbH & Co KG+
Imprint of John Wiley & Sons Inc
Rotherstr 21, 10245 Berlin
Tel: (030) 47031-200 *Fax:* (030) 47031-270
E-mail: info@ernst-und-sohn.de
Web Site: www.ernst-und-sohn.de
Key Personnel
Mng Dir: Sabine Steinbach; Franka Stuermer
  Tel: (030) 47031-385 *E-mail:* franka.stuermer@wiley.com
Founded: 1851
Subjects: Architecture & Interior Design, Civil Engineering, Law, Physics, Technology, Construction Law
ISBN Prefix(es): 978-3-433
Orders to: Wiley-VCH Verlag GmbH & Co KGaA, Boschstr 12, 69469 Weinheim
Tel: (06201) 606-400 *Fax:* (06201) 606-184
E-mail: service@wiley-vch.de *Web Site:* www.wileycustomerhelp.com

Erol Medien GmbH
Koelner Str 256, 51149 Cologne
Tel: (0220) 3369490 *Fax:* (0220) 33694910
E-mail: info@erolmedien.de
Web Site: www.erolmedien.de; www.semerkandonline.de
Key Personnel
Mng Dir: M Siddik Cagil
Founded: 2007

Subjects: Art, History, Literature, Literary Criticism, Essays, Religion - Other, Culture
ISBN Prefix(es): 978-3-95707

Erzaehlen & Zuhoeren Verlag, see E & Z Verlag

Esch-Verlag
Am Weissen See 4, 14469 Potsdam
Tel: (0331) 86 71 92 91
E-mail: kontakt@esch-verlag.de; lektorat@esch-verlag.de
Web Site: www.esch-verlag.de
Key Personnel
Owner: Elisabeth Schulik
Editor: Johanna Padur
Subjects: Fiction, Nonfiction (General)
ISBN Prefix(es): 978-3-943760; 978-3-95555

Verlag am Eschbach+
Im Alten Rathaus, Haupstr 37, 79427 Eschbach
Tel: (07634) 5 05 45-29 *Fax:* (07634) 5 05 45-29
E-mail: vertrieb@verlag-am-eschbach.de
Web Site: www.verlag-am-eschbach.de
Key Personnel
Chief Executive Officer: Ulrich Peters
Chairman: Dr Clemens Stroppel
Public Relations: Andrea Niederstadt *Tel:* (07634) 5 05 45-16
Sales: Guenter Daubenberger *Tel:* (07634) 5 05 45-21
Founded: 1979
Subjects: Art, Religion - Catholic, Religion - Protestant
ISBN Prefix(es): 978-3-88671
Parent Company: Schwabenverlag AG, Senefelderstr 12, 73760 Ostfildern
Foreign Rep(s): Verlagsagentur Erich Neuhold (Austria); Werner Niedermann (Switzerland)
Distribution Center: Mohr Morawa Buchvertrieb GmbH, Sulzengasse 2, 1230 Vienna, Austria *Tel:* (01) 680 14-0 *Fax:* (01) 688 71 30 *E-mail:* momo@mohrmorawa.at *Web Site:* www.mohrmorawa.at
Herder AG Basel Verlagsauslieferungen, Muttenzerstr 109, 4133 Pratteln 1, Switzerland *Tel:* (061) 8 27 90 60 *Fax:* (061) 8 27 90 67
E-mail: verkauf@herder.ch

edition esefeld & traub
Humboldtstr 6, 70178 Stuttgart
Tel: (0711) 645 65 84 *Fax:* (0711) 257 21 25
E-mail: info@edition-et.de; bestellung@edition-et.de (orders)
Web Site: www.edition-et.de
Key Personnel
Publisher: Joerg Esefeld; Johannes Traub
Founded: 2004
Subjects: Archaeology, Architecture & Interior Design, Art, Photography
ISBN Prefix(es): 978-3-9809887
Foreign Rights: Josef Kolar (Eastern Europe)
Distribution Center: Stuttgarter Verlags Kontor SVK GmbH, Rotebuehlstr 77, 70178 Stuttgart, Contact: B Haist *Tel:* (0711) 6672-1426 *Fax:* (0711) 6672-1974 *E-mail:* b.haist@svk.de
Gazelle Book Service Ltd, White Cross Mills Hightown, Lancaster, Lancs LA1 4XS, United Kingdom *Tel:* (01524) 68765 *Fax:* (01524) 63232 *E-mail:* sales@gazellebooks.co.uk (UK, Asia, Middle East, Scandinavia & South Africa)

esogetics GmbH+
Hildastr 8, 76646 Bruchsal
Tel: (07251) 8001-0 *Fax:* (07251) 8001-55
E-mail: info-de@esogetics.com
Web Site: www.esogetics.com
Key Personnel
Mng Dir: Markus Wunderlich

Founded: 1988
Subjects: Health, Nutrition, Medicine, Nursing, Dentistry, Science (General), Holistic Medicine
ISBN Prefix(es): 978-3-925806
Total Titles: 2 Print
Branch Office(s)
Hirschmattstr 16, 6003 Lucerne, Switzerland
Tel: (041) 420 58 36 *Fax:* (041) 420 59 36
E-mail: info-ch@esogetics.com
Foreign Rep(s): Techiche Nuove, Hay (Spain)
Foreign Rights: Techiche Nuove, Hay (Spain)

Verlag Esoterische Philosophie GmbH
Goedekeweg 8, 30419 Hannover
Tel: (0511) 75 53 31 *Fax:* (0511) 75 53 34
E-mail: info@esoterische-philosophie.de
Web Site: www.esoterische-philosophie.de
Key Personnel
Mng Dir: Baerbel Ackermann
Founded: 1984
Subjects: Anthropology, Astrology, Occult, Biography, Memoirs, Inspirational, Spirituality, Parapsychology, Philosophy, Religion - Buddhist, Religion - Other, Science (General), Social Sciences, Sociology, Theology, Cosmology, Esoteric Philosophy
ISBN Prefix(es): 978-3-924849
Distribution Center: Artha Verlagsauslieferung, Gruentenseestr 30c, 87466 Oy-Mittelberg
Tel: (08361) 8031 *Fax:* (08361) 9390
E-mail: va@artha.de *Web Site:* www.artha.de

ESPRESSO Verlag GmbH+
Engeldamm 18, 10179 Berlin
Tel: (030) 275 928 60 *Fax:* (030) 275 928 61
E-mail: info@espresso-verlag.de
Web Site: www.espresso-verlag.de
Key Personnel
Mng Dir: Maruta Schmidt
Founded: 1977
Subjects: Art, Developing Countries, Government, Political Science, History, Humor, Literature, Literary Criticism, Essays, Mysteries, Suspense, Photography, Social Sciences, Sociology, Women's Studies
ISBN Prefix(es): 978-3-88520
Total Titles: 200 Print

Esslinger Verlag J F Schreiber GmbH+
Georg-Christian-von-Kessler-Platz 6, 73728 Esslingen
Mailing Address: Postfach 10 03 25, 73703 Esslingen
Tel: (0711) 310594-6 *Fax:* (0711) 310594-77
E-mail: mail@esslinger-verlag.de
Web Site: www.esslinger-verlag.de
Key Personnel
Mng Dir: Dr Thomas Seng
Foreign Rights Manager: Ivana Bernhard
Tel: (0711) 310594-85 *Fax:* (0711) 310594-95
E-mail: i.bernhard@esslinger-verlag.de
Editorial: Nina Strugholz *E-mail:* n.strugholz@esslinger-verlag.de
Press: Anna-Christina Koehr *Tel:* (0711) 310594-91 *E-mail:* a.koehr@esslinger-verlag.de
Founded: 1831
Children's book publisher.
Specialize in nostalgic children's books, reprints & fairy tales.
ISBN Prefix(es): 978-3-480; 978-3-87286
Parent Company: Klett Gruppe
Foreign Rep(s): Claudia Grueneis-Lamourne (Austria); Wolfgang Panzenboeck (Austria); Verlagsvertretungen GmbH (Andreas Meisel) (Switzerland)
Distribution Center: Koch Neff & Oetinger Verlagsauslieferung GmbH, Schockenriedstr 39, 70565 Stuttgart *Tel:* (0711) 78 99-0 *Fax:* (0711) 78 99-10 10 *E-mail:* essinger-verlag@kno-va.de
Medien Logistik Pichler OEBZ GmbH & Co KG, Postfach 133, 2355 Wiener Neudorf,

Austria *Tel:* (02236) 35-245 *Fax:* (02236) 35-243 *E-mail:* mlo@medien-logistik.at *Web Site:* www.medien-logistik.at
Balmer Buecherdienst AG, Kobiboden, 8840 Einsiedeln, Switzerland *Tel:* (0848) 840 820 *Fax:* (0848) 840 830 *E-mail:* info@balmer-bd.ch

Eudora-Verlag Leipzig
Gerichtsweg 28, 04103 Leipzig
Tel: (0341) 2288 582; (0176) 2261 7202 (cell) *Fax:* (03221) 2369 376
E-mail: info@eudora-verlag.de
Web Site: www.eudora-verlag.de
Key Personnel
Contact: Dr Ralf C Mueller
Subjects: Art, Biography, Memoirs, Ethnicity, History, Music, Dance, Nonfiction (General), Photography, Regional Interests
ISBN Prefix(es): 978-3-938533
Distribution Center: Hora Verlag Wien GmbH, Hackhofergasse 8, 1190 Vienna, Austria, Contact: Dr Winfried Plattner *Tel:* (0676) 7051 974 *Fax:* (02243) 304 94 *E-mail:* plattnerbuch@tmo.at *Web Site:* www.horaverlag-wien.at
International Bookstore Petros Zachariadis, Proxenou Koromila 20, 546 22 Thessaloniki, Greece *Tel:* 2310677634 *Fax:* 2310229936 *E-mail:* info@zbooks.gr *Web Site:* www.zbooks.gr

Eulen Verlag+
Einsteinstr 167, 81677 Munich
Tel: (089) 47 07 77 44 *Fax:* (08581) 91 06 68
E-mail: info@suedost-verlag.de
Web Site: www.suedost-verlag.de
Founded: 1983
Subjects: Mysteries, Suspense, Science Fiction, Fantasy, Mythology
ISBN Prefix(es): 978-3-89102
Total Titles: 125 Print
Parent Company: Verlagshaus Suedost
Distribution Center: Suedost Verlags Service GmbH, Am Steinfeld 4, 94065 Waldkirchen *Tel:* (08581) 9605-0 *Fax:* (08581) 754 *E-mail:* info@suedost-verlags-service.de
Ennsthaler Gesellschaft mbH & Co KG Verlagsauslieferung, Stadtplatz 26, 4400 Steyr, Austria *Tel:* (07252) 52053-20; (07252) 52053-21; (07252) 52053-23 *Fax:* (07252) 52053-22 *E-mail:* auslieferung@ennsthaler.at

Eulenspiegel Verlagsgruppe - Das Neue Berlin Verlagsgesellschaft mbH
Torstr 6, 10119 Berlin
Tel: (030) 23 80 91-0 *Fax:* (030) 23 80 91-23
E-mail: info@eulenspiegelverlag.de
Web Site: www.eulenspiegel-verlag.de
Key Personnel
Publisher: Dr Matthias Oehme
E-mail: geschaeftsleitung@eulenspiegelverlag.de
Mng Dir & Head, Sales/Marketing & Rights/Licenses: Jacquelin Kuehne *Tel:* (030) 23 80 91 22 *E-mail:* kuehne@eulenspiegelverlag.de
Subjects: Biography, Memoirs, Humor, Literature, Literary Criticism, Essays
ISBN Prefix(es): 978-3-359; 978-3-360

Eurailpress-DVV Media Group GmbH
Nordkanalstr 36, 20097 Hamburg
Mailing Address: Postfach 101609, 20010 Hamburg
Tel: (040) 237 14-03 *Fax:* (040) 237 14-259
E-mail: info@eurailpress.de
Web Site: www.eurailpress.de
Key Personnel
Mng Partner: Dr Dieter Flechsenberger
Mng Dir: Martin Weber
Advertising Dir: Silke Haertel *Tel:* (040) 237 14-227 *E-mail:* silke.haertel@dvvmedia.com

Publishing Dir: Detlev K Suchanek *Tel:* (040) 237 14-228 *E-mail:* detlev.suchanek@dvvmedia.com
Head, Editorial Marketing & Product Development: Dr Bettina Guiot *Tel:* (040) 237 14-241 *E-mail:* bettina.guiot@dvvmedia.com
Mng Editor: Jennifer Schykowski *Tel:* (040) 237 14-281 *E-mail:* jennifer.schykowski@dvvmedia.com
Sales Manager: Markus Kukuk *Tel:* (040) 237 14-291 *E-mail:* markus.kukuk@dvvmedia.com
Editor: Ulrike Schuering *Tel:* (040) 237 14-135 *E-mail:* ulrike.schuering@dvvmedia.com
Founded: 1906
Subjects: Transportation, Railway
ISBN Prefix(es): 978-3-87814

euregioverlag
Naumburger Str 40, 34127 Kassel
Tel: (0561) 50049330 *Fax:* (0561) 50049340
E-mail: info@euregioverlag.de
Web Site: www.euregioverlag.de
Key Personnel
Mng Dir: Renate Matthei; Paul Rudert
Founded: 1997
Subjects: Architecture & Interior Design, Art, Crafts, Games, Hobbies, History, Regional Interests, Cultural History, Economy, Kassel & Region, Nature
ISBN Prefix(es): 978-3-933617

Verlag Europa-Lehrmittel Nourney, Vollmer GmbH & Co KG+
Duesselberger Str 23, 42781 Haan-Gruiten
Mailing Address: Postfach 42 04 64, 42404 Haan-Gruiten
Tel: (02104) 6916-0 *Fax:* (02104) 6916-27
E-mail: info@europa-lehrmittel.de; rights@europa-lehrmittel.de
Web Site: www.europa-lehrmittel.de
Key Personnel
General Manager, Rights & Permissions: Joachim Nourney
Mng Dir: Dr Jacob Kloepfer
Rights: Jutta Baxman-Riedel
Sales: Wolfgang Baldauf
Founded: 1948
Subjects: Automotive, Computer Science, Economics, Electronics, Electrical Engineering, Geography, Geology, House & Home, Physics, Publishing & Book Trade Reference
ISBN Prefix(es): 978-3-8085
Associate Companies: Fachbuchverlag Pfanneberg GmbH & Co KG *E-mail:* info@pfanneberg.de
Foreign Rep(s): Bildungsservice Schweiz AG (Switzerland); Fs Fachbuchverlag und Vertriebs GesmbH (Austria)

Europa Verlag GmbH & Co KG
Theresienstr 16, 80333 Munich
Tel: (089) 18 94 733-0 *Fax:* (089) 18 94 733-16
E-mail: info@europa-verlag.com
Web Site: www.europa-verlag.com
Key Personnel
Mng Dir: Christian Strasser
Editorial: Julia Krug-Zickgraf *Tel:* (089) 18 94 733-27 *E-mail:* jk@europa-verlag.com; Franz Leipold *Tel:* (089) 18 94 733-33 *E-mail:* fl@europa-verlag.com
Production & Advertising: Carola Wetzel-Kraxenberger *Tel:* (089) 18 94 733-17 *E-mail:* cwk@europa-verlag.com
Founded: 1933 (originally by Emil Oprecht in Switzerland)
ISBN Prefix(es): 978-3-95890; 978-3-905811; 978-3-906272
Branch Office(s)
Bergstr 67, 10115 Berlin
Foreign Rights: Literarische Agentur Kossack (Lars Schultze-Kossack)
Distribution Center: Prolit Verlagsauslieferung GmbH, Siemensstr 16, 35463 Ferwald, Con-

tact: Alexandra Reichel *Tel:* (0641) 9 43 93-36 *Fax:* (0641) 9 43 93-29 *E-mail:* a.reichel@prolit.de

Mohr Morawa Buchvertrieb GmbH, Sulzengasse 2, 1230 Vienna, Austria *Tel:* (01) 680 14-0 *Fax:* (01) 688 71 30 *E-mail:* bestellung@mohrmorawa.at

Buchzentrum AG, Industriestr Ost 10, 4614 Haegendorf, Switzerland *Tel:* (062) 209 25 25 *Fax:* (062) 209 26 27 *E-mail:* losiggio@buchzentrum.ch

Europaeisches Burgeninstitut (European Castles Institute)
Schlossstr 5, 56338 Braubach
Tel: (02627) 974156 *Fax:* (02627) 970394
E-mail: ebi@deutsche-burgen.org; ebi.sekretariat@deutsche-burgen.org; ebi.leiter@deutsche-burgen.org
Web Site: www.deutsche-burgen.org
Key Personnel
Dir: Dr Reinhard Friedrich
Editorial: Martina Holdorf
Founded: 1899
Subjects: Art, Genealogy, History
ISBN Prefix(es): 978-3-927558
Parent Company: Deutsche Burgenvereinigung eV (DBV)

EVA Europaeische Verlagsanstalt GmbH & Co KG+
Postfach 13 06 13, 20106 Hamburg
Tel: (040) 450194-0 *Fax:* (040) 450194-50
E-mail: info@europaeische-verlagsanstalt.de
Web Site: www.europaeische-verlagsanstalt.de
Key Personnel
Mng Dir: Irmela Ruetters
Founded: 1946
Subjects: Anthropology, Architecture & Interior Design, Art, Biography, Memoirs, Criminology, Government, Political Science, History, Literature, Literary Criticism, Essays, Music, Dance, Philosophy, Science (General), Jewish History
ISBN Prefix(es): 978-3-434; 978-3-88022
Total Titles: 600 Print; 2 CD-ROM
Foreign Rights: Agenzia Letteraria Internazionale SRL (Barbara Griffini) (Italy); Deborah Harris Agency (Efrat Lev) (Israel); Hercules B&C Dev GmbH (China, Taiwan); Internationaal Literatuur Bureau BV (Linda Kohn) (Netherlands); International Editors' Co SA (Henriette Hubacher) (Spain); Meike Marx (Japan); ONK Agency Ltd (Hatice Gok) (Turkey); Rowohlt Verlag GmbH (Michael Toeteberg) (Germany)
Distribution Center: Runge Verlagsauslieferung, Bergstr 2, 33793 Steinhagen *Tel:* (05204) 998-0 *E-mail:* msr@rungeva.de

Evangelische Verlagsanstalt GmbH+
Blumenstr 76, 04155 Leipzig
Mailing Address: Postfach 22 15 61, 04135 Leipzig
Tel: (0341) 711 41 0 *Fax:* (0341) 711 41 50
Web Site: www.eva-leipzig.de
Key Personnel
Mng Dir: Arnd Brummer; Sebastian Knoefel
Publishing Dir: Dr Annette Weidhas *Tel:* (0341) 711 41 14 *Fax:* (0641) 711 41 40
Book Sales: Petra Kretzschmar *Tel:* (0341) 711 41 16
Production: Anne Grabmann *Tel:* (0341) 711 41 37 *Fax:* (0341) 711 41 40
Founded: 1946
Subjects: Biblical Studies, Biography, Memoirs, Fiction, Religion - Protestant, Religion - Other, Theology
ISBN Prefix(es): 978-3-374
Total Titles: 270 Print
Imprints: Edition Chrismon
Distribution Center: Leipziger Kommissions- und Grossbuchhandelsgesellschaft mbH (LKG), An der Suedspitze 1-12, 04571 Roetha, Con-

tact: Christine Falk *Tel:* (034206) 651 29 *Fax:* (034206) 651 736 *E-mail:* cfalk@lkg-service.de *Web Site:* www.lkg-va.de

BMK Wartburg Vertriebsges mbH, Trautsongasse 8, Postfach 65, 1082 Vienna, Austria *Tel:* (01) 4059371 *Fax:* (01) 4089905 *E-mail:* wartburg@bmk.at

Herder AG Basel, Muttenzerstr 109, 4133 Pratteln 1, Switzerland *Tel:* (061) 827 90 60 *Fax:* (061) 827 90 67 *E-mail:* verkauf@herder.ch

Verlag und Buchhandlung der Evangelischen Gesellschaft GmbH+
Augustenstr 124, 70197 Stuttgart
Tel: (0711) 6 01 00-0 *Fax:* (0711) 6 01 00-76
E-mail: info@evanggemeindeblatt.de
Web Site: www.verlag-eva.de
Key Personnel
Mng Dir: Frank Zeithammer *Tel:* (0711) 6 01 00-10 *E-mail:* frank.zeithammer@evanggemeindeblatt.de
Press & Public Relations: Cornelia Fritsch *Tel:* (0711) 6 01 00-27 *E-mail:* cornelia.fritsch@evanggemeindeblatt.de
Founded: 1830
Subjects: Biography, Memoirs, Fiction, History, Philosophy, Religion - Other
ISBN Prefix(es): 978-3-7918
Subsidiaries: Evangelische Gemeindepresse GmbH; Wartburg Verlag GmbH iG
Foreign Rep(s): Claudia Grueneis-Lambourne (Austria); Martin E Schnetzer Verlagsvertretungen GmbH (Switzerland)
Bookshop(s): Buchhandlung der Evangelischen Gesellschaft in Heidenheim, Heilbronn Ludwigsburg, Schaebisch Hall, Stuttgart
Distribution Center: Leipziger Kommissions- und Grossbuchhandelsgesellschaft mbH (LKG), An der Suedspitze 1-12, 04571 Roetha, Contact: Christian Falk *Tel:* (034206) 6 51 29 *Fax:* (034206) 6 51 736 *E-mail:* cfalk@lkg-service.de *Web Site:* www.lkg-va.de
BMK-Warburg Vertriebsgesellschaft mbH, Trautsongasse 8, 1082 Vienna, Austria *Tel:* (01) 4 05 93 71 *Fax:* (01) 4 08 99 05 *E-mail:* warburg@bmk.at
Herder AG Basel Verlagsauslieferung, Muttenzerstr 109, 4133 Pratteln 1, Switzerland *Tel:* (061) 8 27 90 60 *Fax:* (061) 8 27 90 67 *E-mail:* verkauf@herder.ch

Evangelischer Presseverband fuer Bayern eV (EPV)+
Birkerstr 22, 80636 Munich
Tel: (089) 121 72-0 *Fax:* (089) 121 72-138
E-mail: info@epv.de
Web Site: www.epv.de
Key Personnel
Dir & Chief Executive: Dr Roland Gertz *Tel:* (089) 121 72-112 *Fax:* (089) 121 72-307 *E-mail:* rgertz@epv.de
Publisher: Dr Manuel Zelger *Tel:* (089) 121 72-136 *Fax:* (089) 121 72-338 *E-mail:* mzelger@epv.de
Founded: 1932
Bavarian Evangelical Press Union.
Subjects: Religion - Protestant, Theology
ISBN Prefix(es): 978-3-583
Total Titles: 30 Print
Associate Companies: Claudius Verlag

EW Medien und Kongresse GmbH
Kleyerstr 88, 60326 Frankfurt am Main
Tel: (069) 7 10 46 87-0 *Fax:* (069) 7 10 46 87-359
E-mail: info@ew-online.de
Web Site: www.ew-online.de
Key Personnel
Mng Dir: Christina Sternitzke *Tel:* (069) 7 10 46 87-313 *Fax:* (069) 7 10 46 87-9313 *E-mail:* buero.sternitzke@ew-online.de

Specialize in publications for the energy & meter industries.
Subjects: Business, Civil Engineering, Cookery, Energy, Law, Management, Marketing, Nonfiction (General), Technology, Mining
ISBN Prefix(es): 978-3-8022
Branch Office(s)
Reinhardtstr 32, 10117 Berlin *Tel:* (030) 28 44 94-0 *Fax:* (030) 28 44 94-210
Montebruchstr 2, 45219 Essen *Tel:* (02054) 9 24-120 *Fax:* (02054) 9 24-159

Exchange & Dialogue, see Editions AfricAvenir/Exchange & Dialogue

Exil Verlag+
Rheinstr 20, 60325 Frankfurt
Mailing Address: Postfach 17 02 34, 60076 Frankfurt
Tel: (069) 751102
Web Site: www.exilverlagkoch.de
Key Personnel
Publisher: Edita Koch *E-mail:* editakoch@exilverlagkoch.de
Founded: 1981
Publisher of books about German theater in exile 1933-1945 & a journal about literature, arts, theater, film & science of Germans in exile 1933-1945.
ISBN Prefix(es): 978-3-9801652
Total Titles: 36 Print
Distributed by Otto Harrassowitz

expert verlag GmbH+
Wankelstr 13, 71272 Renningen
Tel: (07159) 92 65-0; (07159) 92 65-16 (press & public relations) *Fax:* (07159) 92 65-20
E-mail: expert@expertverlag.de; presse@expertverlag.de; sekretariat@expertverlag.de
Web Site: www.expertverlag.de
Key Personnel
Mng Dir: Elmar Wippler
Editor: Armin Kopp *Tel:* (07159) 92 65-12 *E-mail:* kopp@expertverlag.de
Sales & Advertising: Rainer Paulsen *Tel:* (07159) 92 65-16 *E-mail:* paulsen@expertverlag.de
Founded: 1979
Subjects: Electronics, Electrical Engineering, Energy, Environmental Studies, Management, Mechanical Engineering
ISBN Prefix(es): 978-3-8169; 978-3-88508
Number of titles published annually: 100 Print
Total Titles: 800 Print
Distribution Center: Dessauer Engros Buchhandlung, Raeffelstr 32, 8046 Zurich, Switzerland *Tel:* (044) 466 96-66 *Fax:* (044) 466 96-69 *E-mail:* dessauer@dessauer.ch
AS Hoeller GmbH, Schrackgasse 11a, 8650 Kindberg, Austria *Tel:* (03865) 4 48 80 *Fax:* (03865) 4 48 80-77 *E-mail:* office@ashoeller.com

Extent Verlag und Service+
Pestalozzistr 64, 10627 Berlin-Charlottenburg
Tel: (030) 399 39 447 *Fax:* (030) 399 39 445
E-mail: info@extent-verlag.de
Web Site: www.extent-verlag.de
Key Personnel
Founder & International Rights: Wolfgang Martin Flamm
Founded: 1987
Subjects: Art, Astrology, Occult, Communications, Fashion, Human Relations, Literature, Literary Criticism, Essays, Music, Dance
ISBN Prefix(es): 978-3-926671
Imprints: Pixel Transfer Design Studio

Eyfalia Publishing GmbH
Langenhecke 17, 53902 Bad Muenstereifel
Tel: (02253) 9282290 *Fax:* (02253) 9282299
E-mail: contact@eyfalia.com

Web Site: www.eyfalia.de
Key Personnel
Mng Dir: Dieter Dedeke; Sandra Piepers
Subjects: Mysteries, Suspense, Science Fiction, Fantasy
ISBN Prefix(es): 978-3-939994
Imprints: Spreeside

Fabel Verlag eK+
Raiffeisenstr 29, 85356 Freising-Attaching
Tel: (08161) 872901 *Fax:* (08161) 83424
E-mail: info@fabel-verlag.com
Web Site: www.fabel-verlag.com
Key Personnel
Publisher: Richard Brueckl
Founded: 2001
Subjects: Drama, Theater, Environmental Studies, Literature, Literary Criticism, Essays, Nonfiction (General), Poetry, Fairy Tales
ISBN Prefix(es): 978-3-936776

Fabulus Verlag
Bruckwiesenweg 26, 70734 Fellbach
Tel: (0152) 31098764
E-mail: info@fabulus-verlag.de
Web Site: www.fabulus-verlag.de
Key Personnel
Owner: Tanja Hoefliger
Founded: 2013
Subjects: Fiction
ISBN Prefix(es): 978-3-944788

Fabylon-Verlag+
Guenztalstr 13, 87733 Markt Rettenbach
Tel: (08392) 9347275
E-mail: team@fabylon-verlag.de
Web Site: www.fabylon-verlag.de
Key Personnel
Publisher, Editor, Rights & Permissions: Gerald Jambor
Publisher & Authoress: Uschi Zietsch-Jambor
   E-mail: uschizietsch@fabylon-verlag.de
Founded: 1987
Membership(s): Stock Exchange of German Booksellers.
Subjects: Mysteries, Suspense, Science Fiction, Fantasy
ISBN Prefix(es): 978-3-927071

Fachhochschulverlag der Verlag fuer Angewandte Wissenschaften eK
Kleiststr 10, Bldg 1, 60318 Frankfurt am Main
Tel: (069) 15 33-28 20 *Fax:* (069) 15 33-28 40
E-mail: kontakt@fhverlag.de
Web Site: www.fhverlag.de
Key Personnel
Publishing Dir: Prof Ulrich Stascheit
Accounting & Sales: Jutta Parthe
Editorial & Production: Sarah Kalck
Founded: 1981
Subjects: Economics, Education, Environmental Studies, Health, Nutrition, Language Arts, Linguistics, Law, Nonfiction (General), Women's Studies
ISBN Prefix(es): 978-3-923098; 978-3-931297; 978-3-936065

Fackeltraeger Verlag GmbH+
Subsidiary of VEMAG Verlags- und Medien AG
Emil-Hoffmann-Str 1, 50996 Cologne
Mailing Address: Postfach 50 15 62, 50975 Cologne
Tel: (02236) 39 99 0 *Fax:* (02236) 39 99 97
E-mail: info@fackeltraeger-verlag.de
Web Site: edition.fackeltraeger-verlag.de
Key Personnel
Mng Dir: Juergen Horbach; Dr Holger Schneider
Sales: Doris Zaensdorf *Tel:* (02236) 39 99 111
   E-mail: doris.zaensdorf@fackeltraeger-verlag.de
Founded: 1949

Subjects: Art, Cookery, Education, History, Humor, Nonfiction (General)
ISBN Prefix(es): 978-3-7716
Distribution Center: VVA-Vereinigte Verlagsauslieferung arvato media GmbH, An der Autobahn, Postfach 7777, 33310 Guetersloh *Web Site:* www.vva-online.net
Mohr Morawa Buchvertrieb GmbH, Sulzengasse 2, 1230 Vienna, Austria *Tel:* (01) 680 14-0 *Fax:* (01) 688 71 30 *E-mail:* momo@mohrmorawa.at *Web Site:* www.mohrmorawa.at
Buchzentrum AG, Industriestr Ost 10, 4614 Haegendorf, Switzerland *Tel:* (062) 209 25 25 *Fax:* (062) 209 27 88

Faksimile Verlag
Imprint of inmediaONE] GmbH
Neumarkt Str 18-20, 81673 Munich
Tel: (089) 41 36 83 61 *Fax:* (089) 41 36 54 11
E-mail: info@faksimile.de
Web Site: www.faksimile.de
Key Personnel
Publisher: Armin Sinnwell
Founded: 1974
Subjects: Antiques, Art, Astrology, Occult, Astronomy, Biblical Studies, History, Religion - Other, Prayer
ISBN Prefix(es): 978-3-85672

Christa Falk Verlag, see ch. falk-verlag

Falken, *imprint of* Verlagsgruppe Random House Bertelsmann

familia Verlag
Division of KochDialog eK
Handwerkerhof 9, 04316 Leipzig
Tel: (0341) 231001712 *Fax:* (0341) 231001718
E-mail: info@familia-verlag.de
Web Site: www.familia-verlag.de
Key Personnel
Publishing Dir: Stefanie Steinbrecher
   E-mail: stefanie.steinbrecher@familia-verlag.de
Subjects: Health, Nutrition, Humor, Science Fiction, Fantasy, Leisure
ISBN Prefix(es): 978-3-943987
Imprints: fehu

Family Media GmbH & Co KG
Postfach 5560, 79022 Freiburg
Tel: (0761) 70 578 0 *Fax:* (0761) 70 57 86 51
E-mail: info@familymedia.de
Web Site: www.familymedia.de
Key Personnel
Dir: Marko Petersen *Tel:* (0761) 70578 598
   E-mail: marko.petersen@familymedia.de
Publisher: Thanh Mehrle *Tel:* (0761) 70578 598
   E-mail: thanh.mehrle@familymedia.de
Founded: 2004
Subjects: Child Care & Development, Education
ISBN Prefix(es): 978-3-86613
Imprints: Velber
Orders to: Heuriedweg 19, 88131 Lindau
   Tel: (01805) 00 77 24 *Fax:* (01805) 00 77 25
   E-mail: aboservice@familymedia.de

Edition Faust
Grillparzerstr 53, 60320 Frankfurt am Main
Tel: (069) 56 40 25 *Fax:* (069) 56 43 21
E-mail: verlag@editionfaust.de
Web Site: www.editionfaust.de
Key Personnel
Mng & Publishing Dir: Werner Ost
   E-mail: werner.ost@editionfaust.de
Publishing Dir: Michele Sciurba *E-mail:* michele.sciurba@editionfaust.de
ISBN Prefix(es): 978-3-945400
Distribution Center: Mohr Morawa Buchvertrieb GmbH, Sulzengasse 2, 1230 Vienna, Austria *Tel:* (01) 680 14 0 *Fax:* (01) 680 14

5 *E-mail:* bestellung@mohrmorawa.at *Web Site:* www.mohrmorawa.at (Austria)
Buchzentrum AG, Kundendienst, Industriestr Ost 10, 4614 Haegendorf, Switzerland
Tel: (062) 209 25 25 *Fax:* (062) 209 26 27
E-mail: kundendienst@buchzentrum.ch *Web Site:* www.buchzentrum.ch

Feder&Schwert GmbH
Wasserwerkstr 204, 68309 Mannheim
Tel: (0621) 720 798-0 *Fax:* (0621) 720 798-1
E-mail: verkauf@feder-und-schwert.com; marketing@feder-und-schwert.com
Web Site: www.feder-und-schwert.com
Key Personnel
Dir: Ursula Hoffman
Founded: 1989
Subjects: Fiction, Science Fiction, Fantasy, Crime, Dark Fantasy, Horror, Steampunk, Urban Fantasy
ISBN Prefix(es): 978-3-86762; 978-3-931612; 978-3-933171; 978-3-935282; 978-3-937255

fehu, *imprint of* familia Verlag

Dr Karl Feistle, see Dustri-Verlag Dr Karl Feistle GmbH & Co KG

Feltron-Elektronik Zeissler & Co GmbH
Auf dem Schellerod 22, 53842 Troisdorf
Tel: (02241) 4867-0 *Fax:* (02241) 404241
E-mail: feltron@feltron.de
Web Site: www.feltron-zeissler.de
Key Personnel
Mng Dir: Michael Zeissler
Founded: 1953
Subjects: Communications, Computer Science, Computers, Electronics, Electrical Engineering
ISBN Prefix(es): 978-3-88050

Fenestra-Verlag (Edition Fenestra)
Am Heienberg 4, 65193 Wiesbaden
Mailing Address: Thannhaeuserstr 94, 10318 Berlin
Tel: (0611) 5440693 *Fax:* (0611) 9545911
E-mail: info@fenestra-verlag.de
Web Site: www.fenestra-verlag.de
Key Personnel
Publishing Dir: Dr Karl Martin *Tel:* (030) 20050865 *Fax:* (030) 20050866
Founded: 1955
Subjects: Social Sciences, Sociology, Theology, Social Responsibility
ISBN Prefix(es): 978-3-9805071; 978-3-9809376

Franz Ferzak World & Space Publications+
Am Bachl 1, 93336 Altmannstein
Tel: (09446) 1403
Founded: 1987
Subjects: Astronomy, Electronics, Electrical Engineering, Energy, Engineering (General), Physical Sciences, Physics, Science (General), Technology
ISBN Prefix(es): 978-3-9801465; 978-3-9805835
Number of titles published annually: 2 Print
Total Titles: 11 Print
Orders to: Michaels Verlag, 86971 Peiting *Tel:* (08861) 59018 *E-mail:* mvv@michaelsverlag.de

Festland Verlag GmbH
Basteistr 88, 53173 Bonn
Mailing Address: Postfach 200561, 53135 Bonn
Tel: (0228) 362021; (0228) 362022 (sales)
   Fax: (0228) 351771
E-mail: verlag@oeckl.de
Web Site: www.oeckl.de
Key Personnel
Mng Dir: Joachim Stephan, MA
Founded: 1950

Subjects: Communications, Economics, Education, Government, Political Science, Social Sciences, Sociology
ISBN Prefix(es): 978-3-87224
Number of titles published annually: 2 Print; 2 CD-ROM; 1 Online

Festo Didactic GmbH & Co KG
Rechbergstr 3, 73770 Denkendorf
Tel: (0711) 346 70 *Fax:* (0711) 34 75 48 85 00
E-mail: did@de.festo.com
Web Site: www.festo-didactic.de; www.festo-didactic.com
Key Personnel
Mng Dir: Dr Theodor Niehaus; Dr Wilfried Stoll
Founded: 1980
Membership(s): Association of German Publishing Companies.
Subjects: Career Development, Education, Electronics, Electrical Engineering, Engineering (General)
ISBN Prefix(es): 978-3-8127
U.S. Office(s): Festo Corp, 395 Moreland Rd, PO Box 18023, Hauppauge, NY 11788, United States *Tel:* 631-435-0800 *Fax:* 631-435-8026 *E-mail:* customer.service@us.festo.com *Web Site:* www.festo.com/usa

Edition Ralf Fetzer
Hebelstr 1, 68535 Edingen-Neckarhausen
Tel: (0621) 48179005
E-mail: kontakt@edition-ralf-fetzer.de
Web Site: www.edition-ralf-fetzer.de
Key Personnel
Publisher: Ralf Fetzer
Subjects: Architecture & Interior Design, Art, Biography, Memoirs, History
ISBN Prefix(es): 978-3-940968

Feuervogel-Verlag
Gerhart-Hauptmann-Ring 107-109, 60439 Frankfurt am Main
Tel: (069) 57 42 57 *Fax:* (069) 57 42 57
E-mail: info@feuervogel-verlag.de
Web Site: www.feuervogel-verlag.de
Key Personnel
Owner: Anita Treguboff
Subjects: History, Russian History
ISBN Prefix(es): 978-3-921148

fibre Verlag
Martinistr 37, 49080 Osnabrueck
Tel: (0541) 431838 *Fax:* (0541) 432786
E-mail: info@fibre-verlag.de
Web Site: www.fibre-verlag.de
Key Personnel
Contact: Peter Fischer
Founded: 1993
Subjects: Biography, Memoirs, History, Social Sciences, Sociology
ISBN Prefix(es): 978-3-929759; 978-3-938400

Wolfgang Fietkau Verlag+
Ernst-Thaelmann-Str 152, 14532 Kleinmachnow
Tel: (033203) 711 05 *Fax:* (033203) 711 09
E-mail: post@fietkau.de
Web Site: www.fietkau.de
Key Personnel
Publisher, Rights & Permissions: Wolfgang Fietkau
Founded: 1959
This publisher has indicated that 100% of their product line is author subsidized.
Membership(s): The Stock Exchange of German Booksellers.
Subjects: Poetry
ISBN Prefix(es): 978-3-87352
Number of titles published annually: 2 Print
Total Titles: 50 Print

Barbara Fietz, see ABAKUS Musik Barbara Fietz

FinanzBuch Verlag GmbH
Nymphenburger Str 86, 80636 Munich
Tel: (089) 651285-0 *Fax:* (089) 652096
Web Site: www.m-vg.de/finanzbuchverlag
Key Personnel
Mng Dir: Christian Jund *E-mail:* cjund@finanzbuchverlag.de; Oliver Kuhn
Head, Press & Public Relations: Matthias Setzler *Tel:* (089) 651285-13 *E-mail:* msetzler@finanzbuchverlag.de
Rights Dir/International Affairs: Maria Pinto-Peuckmann *Tel:* (089) 651285-244 *E-mail:* mpinto-peuckmann@finanzbuchverlag.de
Sales & Marketing: Sigrid Klemt *Tel:* (089) 651285-271 *E-mail:* sklemt@finanzbuchverlag.de
Subjects: Finance, Investment, Trading
ISBN Prefix(es): 978-3-89879; 978-3-932114
Parent Company: Muenchner Verlagsgruppe GmbH
Associate Companies: mi-Wirtschaftsbuch; mvg Verlag; Redline Verlag; riva Verlag
Foreign Rep(s): Roland Fuerst (Austria); Giovanni Ravasio (Switzerland)
Distribution Center: Rhenus Medien Logistik GmbH & Co KG, Justus-von-Liebig-Str 1, 86899 Landsberg am Lech *Tel:* (08191) 97000-0 *E-mail:* info.rml@de.rhenus.com
Mohr Morawa Buchvertrieb GmbH, Sulzengasse 2, 1230 Vienna, Austria *Tel:* (01) 680 14-0 *Fax:* (01) 688 71 30 *E-mail:* momo@mohrmorawa.at *Web Site:* www.mohrmorawa.at
AVA Verlagsauslieferung AG, Centralweg 16, 8910 Affoltern am Albis, Switzerland *Tel:* (044) 7624260 *Fax:* (044) 7624210 *E-mail:* verlagsservice@ava.ch

J Fink Verlag GmbH & Co KG+
Zeppelinstr 10, 73760 Ostfildern
Tel: (0711) 280 40 60-0 *Fax:* (0711) 280 40 60-70
E-mail: kontakt@jfink-verlag.de
Web Site: www.jfink-verlag.de
Key Personnel
Chief Executive Officer: Dr Frieder Stein *Tel:* (0711) 280 40 60-20 *E-mail:* f.stein@jfink-verlag.de
Founded: 1935
Firm has developed from an association between the German company J Fink (founded 1894) & the Swiss cartographic company Kuemmerly und Frey (founded 1852). The latter firm also continues as an independent company in Switzerland.
Subjects: Health, Nutrition, Nonfiction (General), Outdoor Recreation, Sports, Athletics
ISBN Prefix(es): 978-3-7718; 978-3-350; 978-3-89142; 978-3-9801113
Parent Company: Kummerly und Frey Verlag, Bern, Switzerland

Kunstverlag Josef Fink
Hauptstr 102 b, 88161 Lindenberg
Tel: (08381) 8 37 21 *Fax:* (08381) 8 37 49
E-mail: info@kunstverlag-fink.de
Web Site: www.kunstverlag-fink.de
Key Personnel
Mng Dir: Josef Fink
Product Manager: Mathias Baumgartner
Founded: 1996
Subjects: Architecture & Interior Design, Art, Religion - Other, Art History, Culture, Historic Monuments
ISBN Prefix(es): 978-3-89870; 978-3-931820; 978-3-933784
Foreign Rep(s): Markus Zimmer (Switzerland)

Verlag Wilhelm Fink GmbH & Co Verlags-KG+
Juehenplatz 1-3, 33098 Paderborn
Mailing Address: Postfach 25 40, 33055 Paderborn
Tel: (05251) 127-5 *Fax:* (05251) 127-860
E-mail: info@fink.de
Web Site: www.fink.de
Key Personnel
Mng Dir: Peter Schaefer; Christiane Vosshans-Schoeningh
Licenses & Press: Dr A Schmidt *Tel:* (05251) 127-790
Production: Heinrich Schniedermann *Tel:* (05251) 127-910
Sales: Ute Schnueckel *Tel:* (05251) 127-640; Ulrike Stutzinger *Tel:* (05251) 127-641
Founded: 1962
Subjects: Art, History, Language Arts, Linguistics, Literature, Literary Criticism, Essays, Music, Dance, Philosophy, Social Sciences, Sociology, Cultural History
ISBN Prefix(es): 978-3-7705
Imprints: Konstanz University Press (KUP)
Foreign Rep(s): Leitner Verlagsvertretungen (Helga Schuster) (Austria); Scheidegger & Co AG (Stephanie Brunner) (Switzerland)
Distribution Center: Brockhaus/Commission, Kreidler Str 9, 70806 Kornwestheim, Contact: Alexandra Hamberger *Tel:* (07154) 13 27 10 *Fax:* (07154) 13 27 13 *E-mail:* schoeningh@brocom.de
Dr Franz Hain Verlagsauslieferungs GmbH, Dr-Otto-Neurath-Gasse 5, 1220 Vienna, Austria *Tel:* (01) 2 82 65 65 *Fax:* (01) 2 82 52 82 *E-mail:* bestell@hain.at
Scheidegger & Co AG, c/o AVA Verlagsauslieferung AG, Centralweg 16, 8910 Affoltern am Albis, Switzerland *Tel:* (044) 7 62 42 50 *Fax:* (044) 762 42 10 *E-mail:* e.bachofner@ava.ch

Finken Junior, *imprint of* Finken Verlag GmbH

Finken Verlag GmbH+
Zimmersmuehlenweg 40, 61440 Oberursel
Mailing Address: Postfach 1456, 61405 Oberursel
Tel: (06171) 6388-0 *Fax:* (06171) 6388-44
E-mail: info@finken.de; kundenservice@finken.de
Web Site: www.finken.de
Key Personnel
Manager: Holger Krick; Manfred Krick
Foreign Rights: Karoline Jockel *Tel:* (06171) 6388-18 *E-mail:* karoline.jockel@finken.de
Public Relations: Hannelore Hartwig *Tel:* (06171) 6388-31 *E-mail:* hannelore.hartwig@finken.de
Founded: 1949
Learning & teaching material for children from 3 to 12 years old at school & at home, LOGICO™ - the new learning system with self-checking; also reading skills & early learning.
Membership(s): Boersenverein des Deutschen Buchhandels Germany; Deutscher Didacta Verband-Germany; VDS-Bildungsmedien.
Subjects: Education, English as a Second Language, Mathematics, Natural History
ISBN Prefix(es): 978-3-8084
Imprints: Finken Junior

Harald Fischer Verlag GmbH+
Theaterplatz 31, 91054 Erlangen
Mailing Address: Postfach 1565, 91005 Erlangen
Tel: (09131) 205620 *Fax:* (09131) 206028
E-mail: info@haraldfischerverlag.de
Web Site: www.haraldfischerverlag.de
Key Personnel
Manager: Dr Harald Fischer; Dr Claudia Schorcht
Founded: 1984
Publish online resources & microfiche collections of primary sources. Also provides digitization services for libraries, archives & publishers.

Membership(s): Boersenverein des Deutschen
Buchhandels.
Subjects: Animals, Pets, Environmental Studies,
Genealogy, History, Language Arts, Linguis-
tics, LGBTQ, Library & Information Sciences,
Medicine, Nursing, Dentistry, Music, Dance,
Philosophy, Publishing & Book Trade Ref-
erence, Religion - Jewish, Science (General),
Women's Studies
ISBN Prefix(es): 978-3-89131
Number of titles published annually: 300 E-Book
Total Titles: 40 Print; 15 CD-ROM; 10 Online;
3,000 E-Book

Verkehrs-Verlag J Fischer GmbH & Co KG
Corneliusstr 49, 40215 Duesseldorf
Mailing Address: Postfach 140265, 40072 Dues-
seldorf
Tel: (0211) 9 91 93-0 *Fax:* (0211) 6 80 15 44;
(0211) 9 91 93 27
E-mail: vvf@verkehrsverlag-fischer.de
Web Site: www.verkehrsverlag-fischer.de
Key Personnel
Publisher: Paul Urban *E-mail:* paul.urban@
verkehrsverlag-fischer.de
Founded: 1904
Subjects: Transportation
ISBN Prefix(es): 978-3-87841

Karin Fischer Verlag GmbH+
Wallstr 50, 52064 Aachen
Mailing Address: Postfach 10 21 32, 52021
Aachen
Tel: (0241) 960 90 90 *Fax:* (0241) 960 90 99
E-mail: info@karin-fischer-verlag.de
Web Site: www.karin-fischer-verlag.de
Key Personnel
Mng Dir: Karin Fischer
Publishing Dir: Dr Manfred S Fischer
Founded: 1989
Subjects: Fiction, Literature, Literary Criticism,
Essays, Nonfiction (General), Philosophy, Po-
etry, Social Sciences, Sociology
ISBN Prefix(es): 978-3-927854; 978-3-89514
Imprints: Deutsche Lyrik Verlag; edition roter
stein; edition serapion

Edition Michael Fischer GmbH
Donnersbergstr 7, 86859 Igling
Tel: (08248) 96 91 67 *Fax:* (08248) 96 91 68
E-mail: info@edition-m-fischer.de
Web Site: www.edition-m-fischer.de
Key Personnel
Mng Dir: Jean-Michel Fischer; Michael Fischer
Founded: 1984
Subjects: Art, Crafts, Games, Hobbies, How-to
ISBN Prefix(es): 978-3-933033; 978-3-924433;
978-3-926651
Branch Office(s)
Warmslerstr 4, 81829 Munich *Tel:* (089) 212 317-
44 *Fax:* (089) 212 317-37
Shipping Address: Rhenus Medien Logistik
GmbH & Co KG, Justus-von-Liebig-Str 1,
86899 Landsberg am Lech *Tel:* (08191) 97000-
720
Orders to: Rhenus Medien Logistik GmbH & Co
KG, Justus-von-Liebig-Str 1, 86899 Landsberg
am Lech *Tel:* (08191) 97000-720
Returns: Rhenus Medien Logistik GmbH & Co
KG, Justus-von-Liebig-Str 1, 86899 Landsberg
am Lech *Tel:* (08191) 97000-720

R G Fischer Verlag GmbH+
Orber Str 30, 60386 Frankfurt am Main
Tel: (069) 941 942-0; (069) 941 942-11 (orders)
Fax: (069) 941 942-98; (069) 941 942-99 (or-
ders)
E-mail: info@rgfischer-verlag.de; bestellung@
rgfischer-verlag.de (orders)
Web Site: www.rgfischer-verlag.de; www.edition-
fischer.com

Key Personnel
Mng Dir: Anike Fischer
Publisher: Rita G Fischer
Founded: 1977
Subjects: Art, Cookery, Economics, Education,
Engineering (General), Erotica, Fiction, Geog-
raphy, Geology, Government, Political Science,
History, How-to, Medicine, Nursing, Dentistry,
Music, Dance, Poetry, Psychology, Psychia-
try, Religion - Other, Science Fiction, Fantasy,
Social Sciences, Sociology, Sports, Athletics
ISBN Prefix(es): 978-3-88323; 978-3-89406; 978-
3-89501; 978-3-8301

S Fischer Verlag GmbH+
Hedderichstr 114, 60596 Frankfurt am Main
Tel: (069) 6062-0 *Fax:* (069) 6062-214 (sales);
(069) 6062-319
Web Site: www.fischerverlage.de
Key Personnel
Chairman: Monika Schoeller
President & Publisher: Joerg Bong
Publishing Dir: Siv Bublitz
Mng Dir: Michael Justus
General Manager, Marketing/Sales: Dr Uwe
Rosenfeld
Founded: 1886
Subjects: Biography, Memoirs, Fiction, Literature,
Literary Criticism, Essays, Mysteries, Suspense,
Nonfiction (General)
ISBN Prefix(es): 978-3-10
Associate Companies: Fischer FJB; Fischer Klas-
sik; Fischer Schatzinsel; Fischer Taschenbuch
Verlag; Krueger Verlag; Scherz Verlag; Theater
& Medien Verlag
Foreign Rights: Anthea Agency (Katalina Sabeva)
(Bulgaria); Berla & Griffini Rights Agency
(Barbara Griffini) (Italy); Kleoniki Douge
Agence Litteratire (France); The Deborah
Harris Agency (Mrs Efrat Lev) (Israel); In-
ternationaal Literatuur Bureau (Linda Kohn)
(Netherlands); International Copyright Agency
(Simona Kessler) (Romania); International Ed-
itors' Co (Nicolas Costa) (Argentina); Interna-
tional Editors' Co (Latin America, Portugal,
Spain); Jia-Xi Books Co Ltd (Becky Lin) (Tai-
wan); Katai & Bolza Literary Agents (Katalin
Katai) (Hungary); Leonhardt & Hoier Litteraert
Agentur (Monica Gram) (Denmark); Dr Alek-
sandra Markiewicz Literary Agency (Poland);
Meike Marx Literary Agent (Japan); ONK
Literary Agency (Hatice Goek) (Turkey); Re-
gal Literary Inc (Markus Hoffmann) (USA);
The Sakai Agency (Mr Tatemi Sakai) (Japan);
Sylvie Zannier-Betts (UK)

Fit fuers Leben Verlag, *imprint of* NaturaViva
Verlags GmbH

Frido Flade, see Verlag Wissen & Literatur Frido
Flade GmbH

Flechsig Verlag+
Imprint of Verlagshaus Wuerzburg GmbH & Co
KG
Beethovenstr 5 B, 97080 Wuerzburg
Tel: (0931) 465 889-11 *Fax:* (0931) 465 889-29
E-mail: info@verlagshaus.com
Web Site: www.verlagshaus.com
Key Personnel
Publishing Dir: Dieter Krause *Tel:* (0931) 465
889-14 *E-mail:* dieter.krause@verlagshaus.com
Dir, Production: Juergen Roth *Tel:* (0931) 465
889-15 *E-mail:* juergen.roth@verlagshaus.com
Sales Dir: Johannes Glesius *Tel:* (0931) 465 889-
13 *E-mail:* johannes.glesius@verlagshaus.com
This publisher has indicated that 80% of their
product line is author subsidized.
Subjects: Military Science, Travel & Tourism
ISBN Prefix(es): 978-3-8035; 978-3-88189

Erich Fleischer Verlag GmbH & Co KG
Clueverstr 20, 28832 Achim
Mailing Address: Postfach 1264, 28818 Achim
Tel: (04202) 517-0 *Fax:* (04202) 517-41
E-mail: info@efv-online.de
Web Site: www.efv-online.de
Key Personnel
Mng Dir: Thomas Holzer; Gerhard Schroeter
Founded: 1954
Subjects: Law
ISBN Prefix(es): 978-3-8168
Number of titles published annually: 10 Print; 2
CD-ROM
Total Titles: 50 Print; 9 CD-ROM

Fleischhauer & Spohn Verlag, *imprint of*
Silberburg-Verlag GmbH

**Fleischhauer & Spohn Verlag GmbH & Co
KG**
Schoenbuchstr 48, 72074 Tuebingen
Tel: (07071) 6885-0 *Fax:* (07071) 6885-20
E-mail: info@silberburg.de
Web Site: www.silberburg.de
Key Personnel
Mng Dir: Titus Haeussermann *Tel:* (07071) 68
85-12; Christel Werner *Tel:* (07071) 68 85-23
Marketing & Advertising: Jutta Silbereisen
Tel: (07071) 68 85-15
Press & Public Relations: Heiko Fischer
Tel: (07071) 68 85-14
Founded: 1830
Subjects: History, Regional Interests, Travel &
Tourism
ISBN Prefix(es): 978-3-87230
Parent Company: Silberburg-Verlag GmbH
Associate Companies: Barsortiment G Umbreit
GmbH & Co (book wholesaler)
Branch Office(s)
Schwarzwaldstr 139, 76532 Baden-Baden
Tel: (07221) 216814 *Fax:* (07221) 216842
E-mail: baden@silberburg.de
Distribution Center: Koch, Neff & Oetinger Ver-
lagsauslieferung GmbH, Industriestr 23, 70565
Stuttgart *E-mail:* silberburg@kno-va.de

Flensburger Hefte Verlag GmbH+
Holm 64, 24937 Flensburg
Tel: (0461) 2 63 63 *Fax:* (0461) 2 69 12
E-mail: info@flensburgerhefte.de
Web Site: www.flensburgerhefte.de
Key Personnel
Mng Dir: Wolfgang Weirauch
Founded: 1987
Subjects: Education, Health, Nutrition, History,
Human Relations, Inspirational, Spirituality,
Philosophy, Religion - Other, Social Sciences,
Sociology, Anthroposophy, Human Wisdom
ISBN Prefix(es): 978-3-926841; 978-3-935679

**FMG Fachverlag fuer Druck und Medien
GmbH**
Friedrichstr 22, 80801 Munich
Tel: (089) 332568 *Fax:* (089) 33036200
Founded: 1955
Subjects: Business
ISBN Prefix(es): 978-3-87218
Imprints: Mitteilungsblatt der Verbandes deds
bayerischen Druckincleestrie eV

**FN-Verlag der Deutschen Reiterlichen
Vereinigung GmbH** (Publishing House of the
German Equestrian Federation)+
Freiherr-von-Langen-Str 13, 48231 Warendorf
Tel: (02581) 63 62-115; (02581) 63 62-154
(sales) *Fax:* (02581) 63 31 46; (02581) 63 62-
212 (sales)
E-mail: vertrieb-fnverlag@fn-dorkr.de; fnverlag@
fn-dorkr.de
Web Site: www.fnverlag.com

Key Personnel
Mng Dir: Siegmund Friedrich *Tel:* (02581) 63
62-153 *E-mail:* sfriedrich@fn-dokr.de; Rainer
Reisloh *Tel:* (02581) 63 62-205
Editorial: Dr Carla Mattis *Tel:* (02581) 63 62-
217 *E-mail:* cmattis@fn-dokr.de; Dr Catharina
Veltjens-Otto-Erley *Tel:* (02581) 63 62-218
E-mail: cveltjens-otto-erley@fn-dokr.de
Licenses: Eva-Maria Seggelmann
E-mail: eseggelmann@fn-dokr.de
Press & Marketing: Viktoria Laufkoetter
Tel: (02581) 63 62-221 *E-mail:* vlaufkoetter@
fn-dokr.de
Production: Beate Winterberg *Tel:* (02581) 63 62-
216 *E-mail:* bwinterberg@fn-dokr.de
Sales: Tanja Katvars *E-mail:* tkatvars@fn-dokr.de;
Tamara Koerner; Cornelia Schaechter
Founded: 1977
Subjects: Animals, Pets, Film, Video
ISBN Prefix(es): 978-3-88542

Fohrmann Verlag+
Gierather Str 177, 51469 Bergisch Gladbach
Tel: (0179) 94 83 939
E-mail: pf@fohrmann-verlag.de
Web Site: www.fohrmann-verlag.de
Key Personnel
Owner: Dr Petra Fohrmann
Founded: 2005
Subjects: Biography, Memoirs
ISBN Prefix(es): 978-3-9810580
Foreign Rights: Giuliana Bernardi (Italy)

Forum Verlag GmbH & Co KG
Zeppelinstr 116, 73730 Esslingen
Tel: (0711) 76727-0 *Fax:* (0711) 76727-28
Founded: 1964
Publisher of the journal *Deutsches Architekten-
blatt*, distributed to members of German Ar-
chitektenkammer.
Subjects: Architecture & Interior Design
ISBN Prefix(es): 978-3-8091

Forum Verlag Herkert GmbH
Mandichostr 18, 86504 Merching
Tel: (08233) 381-123 *Fax:* (08233) 381-222
E-mail: service@forum-verlag.com
Web Site: www.forum-verlag.com
Key Personnel
Mng Dir: Ronald Herkert; Kerstin Kuffer
Founded: 1988
Subjects: Accounting, Business, Child Care &
Development, Education, Electronics, Electrical
Engineering, Human Relations, Management,
Mechanical Engineering, Public Administra-
tion, Real Estate, Transportation, Business Ad-
ministration, Construction, Environmental &
Consumer Protection, Foreign Trade & Logis-
tics, Human Resources, Occupational Safety &
Health
ISBN Prefix(es): 978-3-86586; 978-3-89827; 978-
3-927766; 978-3-932021; 978-3-933803
Parent Company: Forum Media Group GmbH

Forum Verlag Leipzig Buch-Gesellschaft mbH+
Natonekstr 32, 04155 Leipzig
Tel: (0341) 9 80 50 08 *Fax:* (0341) 9 80 50 07
E-mail: info@forumverlagleipzig.de
Web Site: www.forumverlagleipzig.de
Key Personnel
Mng Dir: Helen Jannsen
Founded: 1989
Membership(s): Boersenverein des Deutschen
Buchhandels eV.
Subjects: Biography, Memoirs, History, Humor,
Nonfiction (General), Regional Interests
ISBN Prefix(es): 978-3-931801
Number of titles published annually: 7 Print
Total Titles: 90 Print; 2 CD-ROM; 1 Audio

Forum Wissenschaft Studien, *imprint of*
BdWi-Verlag

Verlag der Francke-Buchhandlung GmbH+
Am Schwanhof 19, 35037 Marburg
Tel: (06421) 1725-11; (06421) 1725-40
Fax: (06421) 1725-29; (06421) 1725-30
E-mail: info@francke-buch.de; francke@francke-
buch.de
Web Site: www.francke-buch.de
Key Personnel
Mng Dir: Dr Klaus Meiss
Publishing Dir: Anne-Ruth Meiss
Marketing: Christian Heinritz *Tel:* (06421) 1725-
15 *E-mail:* heinritz@francke-buch.de
Press & Public Relations: Sven Gerhardt
Tel: (06421) 1725-14
Founded: 1934
Firm is contributor to the Telos series of evangeli-
cal paperbacks.
Subjects: Biography, Memoirs, Fiction, Inspira-
tional, Spirituality, Nonfiction (General), Theol-
ogy
ISBN Prefix(es): 978-3-88224; 978-3-86122; 978-
3-920345
Bookshop(s): Elbingerode; Gunzenhausen; Lemfo-
erde; Neustadt; Oberursel; Velbert

Franckh-Kosmos Verlags-GmbH & Co KG+
Pfizerstr 5-7, 70184 Stuttgart
Tel: (0711) 2191-0 *Fax:* (0711) 2191-422
E-mail: info@kosmos.de
Web Site: www.kosmos.de
Key Personnel
Mng Dir: Michael Fleissner
Foreign Rights Dir: Andrea D Ahlers *Tel:* (0711)
2191-254 *Fax:* (0711) 2191-413 *E-mail:* a.
ahlers@kosmos.de
Publicity: Stephanie Wilhelms *Tel:* (0711)
2191-296 *Fax:* (0711) 2191-122 *E-mail:* s.
wilhelms@kosmos.de
Sales & Marketing Dir: Heiko Windfelder
Tel: (0711) 2191-322 *E-mail:* h.windfelder@
kosmos.de
Founded: 1822
The broad spectrum of the KOSMOS list includes
illustrated guide books & coffee-table books
for adults & nonfiction & fiction books for
children & young adults, videos & DVDs, sci-
ence kits, high quality board games & jigsaw
puzzles.
Subjects: Animals, Pets, Astronomy, Cookery,
Gardening, Plants, Natural History, Nonfiction
(General), Outdoor Recreation, Science Fiction,
Fantasy
ISBN Prefix(es): 978-3-440
Number of titles published annually: 250 Print
Total Titles: 1,500 Print
Imprints: Lentz
Foreign Rep(s): Barbara Haab (Switzerland);
Mohr Morawa Buchvertrieb GmbH (John
Czap) (Eastern Austria); Mohr Morawa
Buchvertrieb GmbH (Michael Hipp) (Western
Austria)
Distribution Center: VVA, An der Autobahn,
33310 Guetersloh *Fax:* (05241) 80 66 43
Mohr Morawa Buchvertrieb GmbH, Sulzen-
gasse 2, 1230 Vienna, Austria *Tel:* (01) 680
14-0 *Fax:* (01) 688 71 30 *E-mail:* momo@
mohrmorawa.at *Web Site:* www.mohrmorawa.at
Buchzentrum AG, Industriestr Ost 10, 4614 Hae-
gendorf, Switzerland *Tel:* (062) 2 09 26 26
Fax: (062) 2 09 26 27

Frank & Timme GmbH
Wittelsbacherstr 27a, 10707 Berlin
Tel: (030) 88 67 79 11 *Fax:* (030) 86 39 87 31
E-mail: info@frank-timme.de; buchbestellung@
frank-timme.de (orders)
Web Site: www.frank-timme.de
Key Personnel
Dir: Dr Karin Timme *E-mail:* k.timme@frank-
timme.de
Founded: 2004
Subjects: Government, Political Science, Social
Sciences, Sociology

ISBN Prefix(es): 978-3-86596; 978-3-7329
Orders to: Leipziger Kommissions- und Grossbuchhandelsgesellschaft mbH (LKG), An der
Suedspitze 1-12, 04571 Roetha, Contact: Nadja
Bellstedt *Tel:* (034206) 65 256 *Fax:* (034206)
65 17 71 *E-mail:* nadja.bellstedt@lkg-service.
de *Web Site:* www.lkg-va.de

Frankfurt School Verlag GmbH
Sonnemannstr 9-11, 60314 Frankfurt am Main
Tel: (069) 154 008-680 *Fax:* (069) 154 008-657
E-mail: info@frankfurt-school-verlag.de
Web Site: www.frankfurt-school-verlag.de
Key Personnel
Management: Christoph Mohr; Dr Udo Steffens
Editorial: Mechthild Eckes *Tel:* (069) 154 008-
684 *E-mail:* eckes@frankfurt-school-verlag.de;
Simone Hoffmann *Tel:* (069) 154 008-685
E-mail: hoffmann@frankfurt-school-verlag.de;
Dr Thomas Lorenz *Tel:* (069) 154 008-659
E-mail: lorenz@frankfurt-school-verlag.de
Founded: 2005
Subjects: Economics, Finance, Management,
Banking
ISBN Prefix(es): 978-3-933165; 978-3-937519;
978-3-940913; 978-3-9802586; 978-3-9805189

Verlag Frankfurter Buecher, *imprint of*
Societaets-Verlag

Frankfurter Literaturverlag GmbH (Frankfurt
Publishing Group)+
Grosser Hirschgraben 15, 60311 Frankfurt am
Main
Tel: (069) 40894-0 *Fax:* (069) 40894-169; (069)
40894-194
E-mail: lektorat@frankfurter-literaturverlag.de
Web Site: www.cgl-verlag.de; www.frankfurter-
literaturverlag.de
Key Personnel
Mng Dir: Dr Uwe Frank
Founded: 1987
Membership(s): AAP; ABA; World Union of
Publishers.
Subjects: Biography, Memoirs, Fiction, Govern-
ment, Political Science, Nonfiction (General),
Poetry, Science (General)
ISBN Prefix(es): 978-3-8267; 978-3-89349
Number of titles published annually: 250 Print
Total Titles: 2,000 Print
Parent Company: Frankfurter Verlagsgruppe
Holding AG
Foreign Rep(s): Fouque London Publishers

Frankfurter Societaets-Medien GmbH, see
Societaets-Verlag

Frankfurter Verlagsanstalt GmbH+
Arndtstr 11, 60325 Frankfurt am Main
Tel: (069) 74 30 55 90 *Fax:* (069) 74 30 55 91
E-mail: info@frankfurter-verlagsanstalt.de;
literatur@frankfurter-verlagsanstalt.de
Web Site: www.frankfurter-verlagsanstalt.de
Key Personnel
Publisher: Dr Joachim Unseld
Foreign Rights: Mareen van Marwyck *Tel:* (069)
74 30 55 97 *E-mail:* marwyck@frankfurter-
verlagsanstalt.de
Press & Public Relations: Anne Michaelis
Tel: (069) 74 30 55 96 *E-mail:* michaelis@
frankfurter-verlagsanstalt.de
Sales & Marketing: Sina Witthoeft
E-mail: witthoeft@frankfurter-verlagsanstalt.de
Founded: 1994
Subjects: Biography, Memoirs, Fiction, Poetry
ISBN Prefix(es): 978-3-627
Parent Company: Unseld
Associate Companies: Sophien Buchhandlung

Foreign Rep(s): Annelies Hohl Solscher (Switzerland); Juergen Sieberer (Eastern Austria); Guenter Thiel (Western Austria)
Distribution Center: Prolit Verlagsauslieferung GmbH, Siemensstr 16, 35463 Fernwald, Contact: Martin Jenne *Tel:* (0641) 94 393 27 *Fax:* (0641) 94 393 29 *E-mail:* m.jenne@prolit. de
Mohr Morawa Buchvertrieb GmbH, Sulzengasse 2, 1230 Vienna, Austria *Tel:* (01) 680 14-0 *Fax:* (01) 688 71 30 *E-mail:* momo@mohrmorawa.at *Web Site:* www.mohrmorawa.at
Buchzentrum AG (BZ), Industriestr Ost 10, 4614 Haendorf, Switzerland, Contact: Regula Aerni *Tel:* (062) 209 25 25 *Fax:* (062) 209 26 27 *E-mail:* aerni@buchzentrum.ch

Franz-Sales-Verlag+
Rosental 1, 85072 Eichstaett
Tel: (08421) 9 34 89-31 *Fax:* (08421) 9 34 89-35
E-mail: info@franz-sales-verlag.de
Web Site: www.franz-sales-verlag.de
Key Personnel
Publishing & Editorial Dir: Pater Herbert Winklehner *E-mail:* herbert.winklehner@franz-sales-verlag.de
Founded: 1931
Disseminate the work of St Francis de Soles (1567-1622) into the modern world.
Membership(s): AKB; Boersenverein des Deutschen Buchhandels; Verband Bayerischer Verlage und Buchhandlungen; VKB.
Subjects: Art, Biography, Memoirs, Religion - Catholic, Theology
ISBN Prefix(es): 978-3-7721
Total Titles: 100 Print

Franzis Verlag GmbH+
Richard-Reizner-Allee 2, 85540 Haar b Munich
Tel: (089) 255 56-1444 *Fax:* (089) 255 56-1696
E-mail: info@franzis.de
Web Site: www.franzis.de
Key Personnel
Mng Dir: Thomas Kaesbohrer; Wolfgang Materna; Werner Muetzel
Foreign Rights: Martin Koschewa *Tel:* (089) 25556-1834 *E-mail:* mkoschewa@franzis.de
Founded: 1924
Subjects: Communications, Computer Science, Electronics, Electrical Engineering
ISBN Prefix(es): 978-3-7723; 978-3-645
Parent Company: WEKA Firmengruppe GmbH & Co KG
Distribution Center: PROLIT Verlagsauslieferung GmbH, Siemensstr 16, 35463 Fernwald-Annerod *Tel:* (0641) 94 393-32 *Fax:* (0641) 94 393-39 (Germany & Austria)
Buchzentrum AG, Industriestr Ost 10, 4614 Haegendorf, Switzerland

Franzius Verlag
Sirius Business Park Geb F+E 1.11, Hermann Ritter Str 106-114, 28197 Bremen
Tel: (0421) 1613 8134
E-mail: info@franzius-verlag.de
Web Site: www.franzius-verlag.de
Key Personnel
Mng Dir: Simone C Franzius
Sales & Finance: Detlev Schultz
Subjects: Mysteries, Suspense, Romance
ISBN Prefix(es): 978-3-945509; 978-3-96050

Fachverlag Dr Fraund GmbH
Weberstr 9, 55130 Mainz
Tel: (06131) 62 05-0 *Fax:* (06131) 62 05-41
E-mail: verlag@fraund.de
Web Site: www.fraund.de
Key Personnel
Mng Dir: Joseph Benner; Henning Seibert; Peter Voss-Fels
Membership(s): Verlags-Karree eV.

Subjects: Agriculture, Wine & Spirits, Equestrian
ISBN Prefix(es): 978-3-921156

Fraunhofer IRB Verlag+
Nobelstr 12, 70569 Stuttgart
Mailing Address: Postfach 800469, 70504 Stuttgart
Tel: (0711) 970-25 00 (enquiries, customer service, orders) *Fax:* (0711) 970-25 08 (customer service, orders)
E-mail: irb@irb.fraunhofer.de
Web Site: www.irb.fraunhofer.de; www. baufachinformation.de (bookshop); www.verlag. fraunhofer.de/bookshop
Key Personnel
Dir: Thomas Morszeck
Mng Dir: Volker Schweizer
Head, Customer Service & International Sales Manager: Sabine Leinweber *Tel:* (0711) 970-25 41
Head, Marketing & Public Relations: Christian Schrodi
Founded: 1947
Specialist publisher for building & planning professionals. Main subjects are building failures, civil & structural engineering, energy efficiency, sustainability, energy saving refurbishments, building physics, planning & preservation of historic buildings & monuments.
Publish science titles written by Fraunhofer employees under the Fraunhofer Verlag imprint.
Membership(s): Borsenverein des Deutschen Buchhandels; European Union Publisher's Forum.
Subjects: Architecture & Interior Design, Chemistry, Chemical Engineering, Civil Engineering, Computer Science, Earth Sciences, Electronics, Electrical Engineering, Engineering (General), Environmental Studies, Geography, Geology, House & Home, Management, Mathematics, Mechanical Engineering, Outdoor Recreation, Physics, Regional Interests, Technology
ISBN Prefix(es): 978-3-8167 (Fraunhofer IRB Verlag-planning & building); 978-3-8396 (Fraunhofer Verlag-science & technology); 978-3-7388 (Fraunhofer IRB Verlag-planning & building)
Number of titles published annually: 100 Print; 100 E-Book
Total Titles: 2,000 Print; 1,500 E-Book
Parent Company: Fraunhofer-Gesellschaft zur Foerderung der angewandten Forschung eV, Hansastr 27c, 80686 Munich
Imprints: Fraunhofer Verlag

Fraunhofer Verlag, *imprint of* **Fraunhofer IRB Verlag**

frechverlag GmbH+
Turbinenstr 7, 70499 Stuttgart
Tel: (0711) 83086-11 *Fax:* (0711) 83086-86
E-mail: kundenservice@frechverlag.de
Web Site: www.topp-kreativ.de
Key Personnel
Mng Dir: Wolfgang Materna; Werner Muetzel; Michael Zirn
Foreign Rights: Franziska Unger
E-mail: franziska.unger@frechverlag.de
Press & Public Relations: Anita Bauer *Tel:* (0711) 83086-66 *E-mail:* anita.bauer@frechverlag.de
Founded: 1955
Specialize in hobby & leisure activities.
Subjects: Crafts, Games, Hobbies, Electronics, Electrical Engineering
ISBN Prefix(es): 978-3-7724
Imprints: Lifestyle BusseSeewald

Edition Fredebold
Schaafenstr 25, 50676 Cologne
Tel: (0221) 650806-00 *Fax:* (0221) 650805-55
E-mail: info@editionfredebold.de; presse@editionfredebold.de

Web Site: www.editionfredebold.de
Key Personnel
Mng Dir: Werner Fredebold
Head, Press & Public Relations: Michaela Fredebold
Subjects: Mysteries, Suspense, Poetry, Crime, Prose
ISBN Prefix(es): 978-3-939674
Parent Company: Fredebold & Partner GmbH

Frederking & Thaler Verlag GmbH+
Infanteriestr 11a, 80797 Munich
Tel: (089) 130699-0 *Fax:* (089) 130699-100
E-mail: info@frederking-thaler.de; info@geramond.de; rights@frederking-thaler.de
Web Site: www.frederking-thaler.de
Key Personnel
Mng Dir: Carsten Leininger; Clemens Schuessler
Sales Manager: Udo Zimmermann *E-mail:* udo.zimmermann@verlagshaus.de
Foreign Rights & Licenses: Ingeborg Kluge *Tel:* (089) 130699-683 *Fax:* (089) 130699-300 *E-mail:* ingeborg.kluge@verlaghaus.de
Founded: 1988
Specialize in high quality illustrated books in the realm of wonders of nature, foreign cultures & their spiritual worlds. Also nonfiction narrative reports (culture, nature & travel).
Subjects: Archaeology, Art, Foreign Countries, Photography, Travel & Tourism, World Religions
ISBN Prefix(es): 978-3-89405
Number of titles published annually: 30 Print
Total Titles: 120 Print; 120 E-Book
Parent Company: GeraNova Bruckmann Verlag GmbH
Associate Companies: J Berg Verlag; Bucher Verlag; Christian Verlag; GeraMond Verlag
Imprints: Sierra; Villa Arceno
Distribution Center: Verlegerdienst Muenchen GmbH, Gutenbergstr 1, 82205 Gilching *Tel:* (08105) 388106 *Fax:* (08105) 388187 *E-mail:* verlagshaus@verlegerdienst.de
Mohr Morawa Buchvertrieb GmbH, Sulzengasse 2, 1230 Vienna, Austria *Tel:* (01) 680 14-0 *Fax:* (01) 688 71 30 *E-mail:* momo@mohrmorawa.at *Web Site:* www.mohrmorawa.at
Grafus GmbH SRL Buchauslieferung, Toni-Ebner-Str 5, 39100 Bozen, Italy *Tel:* (047) 86433 *Fax:* (047) 86456 *E-mail:* info@grafus.it (South Tyrol)
Willems Adventure, Honderland 120, 2676 LT Maasdijk, Netherlands *Tel:* (088) 599 0140 *Fax:* (088) 599 0141 *E-mail:* info@willemsadventure.nl
Buchzentrum AG, Industrie Ost, 4614 Haegendorf, Switzerland *Tel:* (062) 209 2701 *Fax:* (062) 209 2788 *E-mail:* kundendienst@buchzentrum.ch

Verlag Freies Geistesleben+
Division of Verlag Freies Geistesleben und Urachhaus GmbH
Landhausstr 82, 70190 Stuttgart
Mailing Address: Postfach 131122, 70069 Stuttgart
Tel: (0711) 2 85 32-00 *Fax:* (0711) 2 85 32-10
E-mail: info@geistesleben.com
Web Site: www.geistesleben.de
Key Personnel
Mng Dir: Frank Berger; Jean-Claude Lin *Tel:* (0711) 2 85 32 21 *E-mail:* lin@geistesleben.com
Press: Astrid Rueggeberg *Tel:* (0711) 2 85 32-24 *E-mail:* astrid.rueggeberg@geistesleben.com
Sales: Simone Patyna *Tel:* (0711) 2 85 32 32 *E-mail:* simone.patyna@geistesleben.com
Founded: 1947
Specializes in picture books.
Membership(s): Community of Youth Book Publishers.
Subjects: Art, Biography, Memoirs, Education, History, How-to, Inspirational, Spirituality,

Medicine, Nursing, Dentistry, Music, Dance, Philosophy, Psychology, Psychiatry, Religion - Other, Science (General), Social Sciences, Sociology
ISBN Prefix(es): 978-3-7725; 978-3-87838; 978-3-8251
Number of titles published annually: 60 Print
Total Titles: 800 Print
Imprints: Aethera
Distribution Center: Koch, Neff & Oetinger Verlagsauslieferung GmbH, Industriestr 23, 70565 Stuttgart
Dr Franz Hain, Dr-Otto-Neurath-Gasse 5, 1220 Vienna, Austria *Tel:* (01) 2 82 65 65 *Fax:* (01) 2 82 52 82
AVA Verlagsauslieferung AG, Centralweg 16, 8910 Affoltern am Albis, Switzerland *Tel:* (044) 762 42 70 *Fax:* (044) 762 42 10

Freimund-Verlag
Missionsstr 3, 91564 Neuendettelsau
Tel: (09874) 68933-0 *Fax:* (09874) 68933-99
E-mail: kontakt@freimund-verlag.de
Web Site: www.freimund-verlag.de
Key Personnel
Mng Dir: Albrecht I Herzog
Founded: 1933
Subjects: Religion - Other, Theology
ISBN Prefix(es): 978-3-7726
Bookshop(s): Freimund-Buchhandlung, Hauptstr 2, 91564 Neuendettelsau *Tel:* (09874) 6899590 *Fax:* (09874) 6899591 *E-mail:* info@freimund-buchhandlung.de *Web Site:* www.freimund-buchhandlung.de

Paulo Freire Verlag
Unterm Berg 65a, 26123 Oldenburg
Tel: (0441) 381674 *Fax:* (0441) 9330056
E-mail: info@paulo-freire-verlag.de
Web Site: www.paulo-freire-verlag.de
Key Personnel
Owner: Alva Dabisch
Membership(s): Boersenverein des Deutschen Buchhandels.
Subjects: Education, Social Sciences, Sociology
ISBN Prefix(es): 978-3-86585

Margarethe Freudenberger - Selbstverlag fuer Jedermann+
Gartenstr 22, 97906 Faulbach
Tel: (09392) 93306
Founded: 1979
Subjects: Art, Fiction, How-to, Human Relations, Humor, Poetry
ISBN Prefix(es): 978-3-924711

Verlag Walter Frey+
Nestorstr 3, 10711 Berlin
Mailing Address: Postfach 15 04 55, 10666 Berlin
Tel: (030) 883 25 61 *Fax:* (030) 883 25 61
E-mail: tranvia@t-online.de
Web Site: www.tranvia.de
Key Personnel
Mng Dir: Walter Frey
Founded: 1985
Publish literature of & about Spain, Portugal, Latin America & France.
Subjects: Biography, Memoirs, Government, Political Science, History, Literature, Literary Criticism, Essays, Regional Interests, Travel & Tourism, France, Gender Studies, Latin America, Portugal, Spain
ISBN Prefix(es): 978-3-925867; 978-3-938944
Number of titles published annually: 10 Print

Frick Verlag GmbH+
Bernhardstr 40, 75177 Pforzheim
Mailing Address: Postfach 447, 75104 Pforzheim
Tel: (07231) 10 28 42 *Fax:* (07231) 35 77 44
E-mail: info@frickverlag.de

Web Site: www.frickverlag.de
Key Personnel
Mng Dir: Peter D'Orazio
Founded: 1970
Specialize in religion, metaphysics, esoteric.
Membership(s): Deutschief Bosenverlise.
Subjects: Alternative, Inspirational, Spirituality, Religion - Other, Alternative Medicine, Metaphysics, Esoteric
ISBN Prefix(es): 978-3-920780
Number of titles published annually: 3 Print
Total Titles: 3 Print

Friedrich Verlag GmbH
Im Brande 17, 30926 Seelze
Tel: (0511) 4 00 04-0 *Fax:* (0511) 4 00 04-170
E-mail: info@friedrich-verlag.de
Web Site: www.friedrich-verlag.de
Key Personnel
Mng Dir: Michael Conradt; Dr Friedrich Seydel
Founded: 1960
Subjects: Art, Drama, Theater, Education
ISBN Prefix(es): 978-3-617
Imprints: Aulis
Distribution Center: Klett Gruppe

Frieling-Verlag Berlin
Rheinstr 46, 12161 Berlin
Tel: (030) 7 66 99 90 *Fax:* (030) 7 74 41 03
E-mail: lektorat@frieling.de
Web Site: www.frieling.de
Key Personnel
Mng Dir: Dr Johann-Friedrich Huffmann *E-mail:* gf@frieling.de
Founded: 1983
ISBN Prefix(es): 978-3-89009; 978-3-8280
Parent Company: Frieling & Huffmann GmbH & Co KG

From Here to Fame Publishing
Marienburger Str 16 A, 10405 Berlin
Tel: (030) 210 21 86-70 *Fax:* (030) 210 21 86-77
E-mail: info@fhtf.de; orders@fhtf.de; press@fhtf.de
Web Site: www.fromheretofame.com
Key Personnel
Mng Dir: R Karl; A Walta
Founded: 2008
Subjects: Art, Cookery, Music, Dance, Pop Culture, Graffiti & Street Art, Hip Hop, Urban Culture
ISBN Prefix(es): 978-3-937946

Druck- und Verlagshaus FROMM GmbH & Co KG+
Breiter Gang 10-16, 49074 Osnabrueck
Tel: (0541) 310-333 *Fax:* (0541) 310-411
E-mail: druckhaus@fromm-os.de
Web Site: www.druckhaus-fromm.de
Key Personnel
Chief Executive Officer: Georg Landvogt *Tel:* (0541) 310-325 *E-mail:* g.landvogt@fromm-os.de; Laurence Mehl
Head, Sales: Claus Vierkoetter *Tel:* (0541) 310-421 *E-mail:* c.vierkoetter@fromm-os.de
Technical Manager: Joerg Muehlbrodt *E-mail:* j.muehlbrodt@piously-os.de
Founded: 1868
Subjects: Economics, Education, Environmental Studies, Ethnicity, Government, Political Science, History, Science (General), Social Sciences, Sociology
ISBN Prefix(es): 978-3-7729
Associate Companies: Fromm International Publishing Corp, 560 Lexington Ave, New York, NY 10022, United States
Imprints: Osnabrueck
Branch Office(s)
Edition Interfrom AG, Postfach 5005, Zurich, Switzerland *Tel:* (0041) 1 202 0900

frommann-holzboog Verlag eK
(frommann-holzboog Publishers)+
Koenig-Karl-Str 27, 70372 Stuttgart
Mailing Address: Postfach 50 04 60, 70334 Stuttgart
Tel: (0711) 955969-0 *Fax:* (0711) 955969-1
E-mail: info@frommann-holzboog.de
Web Site: www.frommann-holzboog.de
Key Personnel
Mng Dir: Eckhart Holzboog *Tel:* (0711) 955969-54 *E-mail:* eckhart.holzboog@frommann-holzboog.de
Editor & Rights & Permissions: Holger Epp *Tel:* (0711) 955969-4 *E-mail:* lektorat@frommann-holzboog.de
Press & Promotion Manager: Sybille Wittmann *Tel:* (0711) 955969-59 *E-mail:* s.wittmann@frommann-holzboog.de
Production Manager: Margarete Trinks *Tel:* (0711) 955969-51 *E-mail:* herstellung@frommann-holzboog.de
Sales: Ulrike Doerr *Tel:* (0711) 955969-2 *E-mail:* vertrieb@frommann-holzboog.de
Founded: 1727
Specialize in fine editions & textbooks. Independent publisher of arts & humanities. Titles with a focus in philosophy, psychoanalysis & theology.
Subjects: History, Language Arts, Linguistics, Law, Literature, Literary Criticism, Essays, Mathematics, Philosophy, Psychology, Psychiatry, Religion - Protestant, Social Sciences, Sociology, Theology
ISBN Prefix(es): 978-3-7728
Number of titles published annually: 40 Print
Total Titles: 1,300 Print

edition fuenf
Wuermstr 11a, 82166 Graefelfing
Tel: (089) 26018926
E-mail: info@editionfuenf.de; presse@editionfuenf.de
Web Site: www.editionfuenf.de
Key Personnel
Publisher & Founder: Silke Weniger
Editor: Karen Noelle *E-mail:* karen.noelle@editionfuenf.de
Press: Dr Antje Flemming *Tel:* (0163) 2562921
Founded: 2010
ISBN Prefix(es): 978-3-942374
Number of titles published annually: 5 Print

Furore Verlag
Naumburger Str 40, 34127 Kassel
Tel: (0561) 50049311 *Fax:* (0561) 50049320
E-mail: info@furore-verlag.de
Web Site: www.furore-verlag.de
Key Personnel
Publisher: Renate Matthei
Founded: 1986
Print music by & books about women composers.
Subjects: Music, Dance
ISBN Prefix(es): 978-3-927327; 978-3-9801326

FVA, see Frankfurter Verlagsanstalt GmbH

Gabal-Verlag GmbH+
Schumannstr 155, 63069 Offenbach
Tel: (069) 83 00 66-0 *Fax:* (069) 83 00 66-66
E-mail: info@gabal-verlag.de
Web Site: www.gabal-verlag.de
Key Personnel
Mng Dir: Andre Juenger *Tel:* (069) 83 00 66-43 *E-mail:* andre.juenger@gabal-verlag.de
Mng Editor: Ursula Rosengart *Tel:* (069) 83 00 66-46 *E-mail:* ursula.rosengart@gabal-verlag.de
Sales Manager: Kerstin Paulukat *Tel:* (069) 83 00 66-45 *E-mail:* kerstin.paulukat@gabal-verlag.de
Foreign Rights: Kerstin Schlosser *Tel:* (069) 83 00 66-44 *E-mail:* kerstin.schlosser@gabal-verlag.de
Founded: 1979 (Vorlaufer)

Subjects: How-to, Literature, Literary Criticism, Essays, Management
ISBN Prefix(es): 978-3-923984; 978-3-89749; 978-3-930799
Associate Companies: PLS Sprachen, 176 Solothurn, Switzerland

Gabriel Verlag, *imprint of* Thienemann Verlag GmbH

Verlag Galerie Der Spiegel
Richartzstr 10, 50667 Cologne
Tel: (0221) 25 55 52 *Fax:* (0221) 25 55 53
E-mail: info@galerie-der-spiegel.de
Web Site: www.galerie-der-spiegel.de
Key Personnel
Mng Dir: Werner Hillmann
Founded: 1945
Specialize in international art editions & book catalogue portfolios.
Membership(s): Boersenverein des Deutschen Buchhandels; Bundesverband Deutscher Galerien.
Subjects: Art
ISBN Prefix(es): 978-3-87285

Verlag Galerie Design Anita und Klaus Buescher+
Erika-Koeth-Str 56, 67435 Neustadt an der Weinstr
Tel: (06321) 968485 *Fax:* (06321) 968486
Key Personnel
Mng Dir: Anita Buescher
Founded: 1988
ISBN Prefix(es): 978-3-927419

Verlag und Galerie fuer Kunst und Kunsttherapie GmbH
Neckarstr 13, 72622 Nuertingen
Tel: (07022) 5 63 43 *Fax:* (07022) 5 32 86
E-mail: info@verlag-kunst-kunsttherapie.de
Web Site: www.verlag-kunst-kunsttherapie.de
Key Personnel
Mng Dir: Prof Juergen Thies
Founded: 1987
Specialize in art & art history.
Subjects: Art, History
ISBN Prefix(es): 978-3-9801451; 978-3-9806599

Galerie Vevais Verlagsgesellschaft mbH
An der Dombuschmuehle 7, 16269 Bliesdorf
Tel: (0334) 56-15 96-2 *Fax:* (0334) 56-15 96-4
E-mail: info@galerievevais.de
Web Site: galerievevais.de
Key Personnel
Dir: Alexander Scholz
Subjects: Literature, Literary Criticism, Essays, Photography
ISBN Prefix(es): 978-3-936165

Galiani Berlin, *imprint of* Verlag Kiepenheuer & Witsch GmbH & Co KG

G&S Verlag GmbH
Kommerzienrat-Zimmermann-Str 41, 90513 Zirndorf
Mailing Address: Postfach 1274, 90506 Zirndorf
Tel: (0911) 608489; (0911) 208451 (sales)
Fax: (0911) 60046350
E-mail: vertrieb@gus-verlag.de; webmaster@gus-verlag.de
Web Site: www.gus-verlag.de
Key Personnel
Mng Dir: Stefan Staedtler-Ley
Founded: 1985
Subjects: Disability, Special Needs, Education, Science Fiction, Fantasy, Downs Syndrome, Education on Special Needs Care, Fantasy Games, Medieval Times, Mentally Handicapped, Middle Ages
ISBN Prefix(es): 978-3-925698

garant Verlag GmbH
Benzstr 56, 71272 Rennigen
Tel: (07159) 40 687-20 *Fax:* (07159) 40 687-22
E-mail: kontakt@garant-verlag.de
Web Site: www.garant-verlag.de
Key Personnel
Dir: Dirk Halfar
Sales Manager: Peter Boehme *Tel:* (0351) 20 16 779 *Fax:* (0351) 20 01 553 *E-mail:* peter.boehme@garant-verlag.de; Martin Gross *Tel:* (01525) 4554116 (cell) *E-mail:* martin.gross@garant-verlag.de
Subjects: Cookery, Crafts, Games, Hobbies, Fiction, Gardening, Plants, Nonfiction (General), Outdoor Recreation, Romance
ISBN Prefix(es): 978-3-86766
Foreign Rep(s): Verlagsagentur Joachim Klinger (Austria)
Distribution Center: Wiso Buchvertrieb GmbH, Heizwerkstr 8, 1230 Vienna, Austria *Tel:* (01) 616 73 63 *Fax:* (01) 616 74 01
Verlags-Service Imfeld, Bruenigstr 24, 6055 Alpnach, Switzerland *Tel:* (041) 660 34 81; (079) 333 44 03 (cell) *Fax:* (041) 660 32 63

Garbe Verlag+
Kinkelstr 15, 90482 Nuremberg
Tel: (0911) 570 37-20 *Fax:* (0911) 570 37-25
E-mail: verlag@garbeverlag.de
Web Site: www.garbeverlag.de
Key Personnel
Publisher & Author: Ellen Vogt *Tel:* (0911) 570 37-30
Founded: 1994
Subjects: Environmental Studies, Humor, Philosophy, Poetry
ISBN Prefix(es): 978-3-930143

GATZANIS GmbH
Esslinger Str 20, 70182 Stuttgart
Tel: (0711) 964 05 70 *Fax:* (0711) 964 05 72
E-mail: info@gatzanis.de
Web Site: www.gatzanis.de
Key Personnel
Owner: Jolanta Gatzanis *E-mail:* gatzanis@gatzanis.de
Press: Mareile Kurtz *E-mail:* mareile@kurtz-notiert.de
Sales: Nicole Landeck *Tel:* (0176) 24602709 (cell) *E-mail:* landeck@gatzanis.de
Founded: 1995
Subjects: Art, Biography, Memoirs, Child Care & Development, Human Relations, Humor, LGBTQ, Nonfiction (General), Self-Help, Love, Sexuality
ISBN Prefix(es): 978-3-932855; 978-3-9803897
Number of titles published annually: 2 Print
Total Titles: 13 Print
Distribution Center: HEROLD Auslieferung und Service GmbH, Raiffeisenalle 10, 82041 Oberhaching *Tel:* (089) 613871-0 *Fax:* (089) 613871-20 *E-mail:* info@herold-va.de

Gebrueder Borntraeger Verlagsbuchhandlung+
Affiliate of E Schweizerbart'sche Verlagsbuchhandlung
Johannesstr 3 A, 70176 Stuttgart
Tel: (0711) 3514560 *Fax:* (0711) 351456-99
E-mail: mail@schweizerbart.de
Web Site: www.schweizerbart.de
Key Personnel
Mng Dir: Dr Andreas Naegele; Dr Walter Obermiller
Founded: 1790
Subjects: Biological Sciences, Earth Sciences, Environmental Studies, Geography, Geology, Maritime
ISBN Prefix(es): 978-3-443
Imprints: J Cramer in der Gebrueder Borntraeger Verlagsbuchhandlung

DAS GEDICHT, *imprint of* Anton G Leitner Verlag

DAS GEDICHT Chapbook, *imprint of* Anton G Leitner Verlag

Edition DAS GEDICHT, *imprint of* Anton G Leitner Verlag

Geheimsprachen Verlag
Rudolf-von-Langen Str 29, 48147 Muenster
Tel: (0251) 218869-81; (0170) 5469192
Fax: (0251) 289169-82
E-mail: geheimsprachenverlag@gmx.de
Web Site: www.geheimsprachenverlag.de
Key Personnel
Contact: Klaus Siewert
Subjects: Art, Biography, Memoirs, Fiction, History, Language Arts, Linguistics, Photography, Caricature, Culture, Linguistic History (Germany), Minority Languages (Germany)
ISBN Prefix(es): 978-3-9813057
Branch Office(s)
Heinrich-Barth Str 7-9, 20146 Hamburg

Verlag Junge Gemeinde E Schwinghammer GmbH & Co KG+
Max-Eyth-Str 13, 70771 Leinfelden-Echterdingen
Mailing Address: Postfach 100355, 70747 Leinfelden-Echterdingen
Tel: (0711) 99078-0 *Fax:* (0711) 99078-25
E-mail: vertrieb@junge-gemeinde.de
Web Site: www.junge-gemeinde.de
Key Personnel
Mng Dir: Gerd Ulmer
Founded: 1928
Specialize in books for Sunday school.
Membership(s): Boersenverein des Deutschen Buchhandels.
Subjects: Education, Religion - Protestant
ISBN Prefix(es): 978-3-7797

Gemeinde und Schulverlag Bavaria, *imprint of* Kommunal- und Schul-Verlag GmbH & Co KG

Genius Verlag (Genius Publishing House)+
Wilde Rodung 26, 28757 Bremen
Tel: (0421) 17 66 55 86 *Fax:* (0421) 62 67 885
E-mail: info@genius-verlag.de
Web Site: www.genius-verlag.de
Key Personnel
Publisher: Ms Dagmar Neubronner
Founded: 1997
Publication of books & DVDs.
Subjects: Biography, Memoirs, Career Development, Education, Human Relations, Inspirational, Spirituality, Nonfiction (General), Philosophy, Science (General), Self-Help
ISBN Prefix(es): 978-3-9806106; 978-3-934719
Number of titles published annually: 3 Print
Total Titles: 12 Print

Alfons W Gentner Verlag GmbH & Co KG+
Forststr 131, 70193 Stuttgart
Mailing Address: Postfach 10 17 42, 70015 Stuttgart
Tel: (0711) 63 67 2-0 *Fax:* (0711) 63 67 27 47
E-mail: gentner@gentner.de
Web Site: www.gentner.de
Key Personnel
Publisher: Hans Oppermann; Erwin Fidelis Reisch
Founded: 1927
Subjects: Automotive, Business, Career Development, Engineering (General), Environmental Studies, Medicine, Nursing, Dentistry, Air-Conditioning, Electrical & Safety Engineering, Glass, Heating, Plumbing, Refrigeration
ISBN Prefix(es): 978-3-87247
Subsidiaries: B & V Kiado Kft; CNTL spool sra; EUROMEDIA; Gema Strucna Naklada; Insta-

lator Polski zoo; Magyar Mediprint Szakkiado
Kft; Technischer Fachverlag GmbH; Verbatim
Publishers (Pvt) Ltd

Geophon
Friedrichstr 95, 10117 Berlin
Tel: (030) 20 64 49 85
E-mail: info@geophon.de
Web Site: geophon.de
Key Personnel
Mng Dir: Reinhard Kober *E-mail:* kober@
geophon.de; Dr Matthias Morgenroth
E-mail: morgenroth@geophon.de
Founded: 2001
Subjects: Travel & Tourism
ISBN Prefix(es): 978-3-936247
Distribution Center: VVA-Vereinigta Verlagsaus-
lieferung arvato media GmbH, An der Auto-
bahn, Postfach 7777, 33334 Guetersloh, Con-
tact: Gertrud Langkau *Tel:* (05241) 80 93 52
E-mail: gertrude.langkau@bertelsmann.de
Mohr Morawa Buchvertrieb GmbH, Sulzen-
gasse 2, 1230 Vienna, Austria *Tel:* (01) 680
14-0 *Fax:* (01) 688 71 30 *E-mail:* momo@
mohrmorawa.at *Web Site:* www.mohrmorawa.at
Buch- und Medienvertriebs AG, Hochstr 357,
8200 Schaffhausen, Switzerland *Tel:* (052) 643
54 30 *Fax:* (052) 643 54 35 *E-mail:* order@
buch-medien.ch

GeraMond Verlag GmbH
Infanteriestr 11a, 80797 Munich
Tel: (089) 130699-0 *Fax:* (089) 130699-100
E-mail: info@geramond.de
Web Site: www.geramond.de
Key Personnel
Publishing Dir: Clemens Hahn *Tel:* (089) 130699-
720 *Fax:* (089) 130699-700 *E-mail:* c.hahn@
geramond.de
Editorial & Product Manager: Alexandra Wurl
Tel: (089) 130699-758 *Fax:* (089) 130699-700
E-mail: alexandra.wurl@geramond.de
Founded: 1989
Subjects: Aeronautics, Aviation, Art, Automotive,
Cookery, Gardening, Plants, History, Maritime,
Military Science, Travel & Tourism, Military
History
ISBN Prefix(es): 978-3-86245

Musikverlage Hans Gerig KG
Frankenforster Str 21-25, 51427 Bergisch Glad-
bach
Mailing Address: Postfach 100435, 51404 Ber-
gisch Gladbach
Tel: (02204) 2003-0 *Fax:* (02204) 2003-33
E-mail: info@gerig.de; sales@gerig.de
Web Site: gerig.de
Key Personnel
Management: Carsten Ilgner *Tel:* (02204) 2003-26
E-mail: carsten.ilgner@gerig.de; Lutz Ilgner
Tel: (02204) 2003-40 *E-mail:* lutz.ilgner@
gerig.de
Foreign Rights: Anita Bartholemy *Tel:* (02204)
2003-21 *E-mail:* anita.bartholemy@gerig.de
Subjects: Music, Dance
ISBN Prefix(es): 978-3-87252

Gerlach Press+
Division of Gerlach Books
Cicerostr 37, 10709 Berlin
Tel: (030) 323 03 111 *Fax:* (030) 323 5667
E-mail: email@gerlach-press.de; office@gerlach-
press.de; orders@gerlach-books.de
Web Site: www.gerlach-press.de
Key Personnel
Publisher & Mng Dir: Kai-Henning Gerlach
E-mail: gerlach@gerlach-press.de
Founded: 2012
Academic publisher for Middle East & Islamic
studies.
Membership(s): Arbeitskreis Elektronisches Pub-
lizieren; Boersenverein des Deutschen Buch-

handels eV; British Society for Middle East-
ern Studies; Deutsche Arbeitsgemeinschaft
Vorderer Orient eV; Deutsche-Qatarische
Gesellschaft eV; European Association of Mid-
dle East Librarians (MELCom); Gesig eV; In-
ternational Society for Islamic Legal Studies;
Special Libraries Association, Arabian Gulf
Chapter; Vereinigung Oesterreichischer Biblio-
thekarinnen und Bibliothekare.
Subjects: Anthropology, Economics, Law, Liter-
ature, Literary Criticism, Essays, Philosophy,
Religion - Islamic, Social Sciences, Sociology
ISBN Prefix(es): 978-3-940924; 978-3-95994
Number of titles published annually: 50 Print; 50
Online
Total Titles: 20 Print; 20 Online
Foreign Rep(s): Editions de Boccard (France);
China Publishers Services Ltd (China, Hong
Kong, Macau, Taiwan); Dar Kreidieh (Arab
Middle East); International Books & Journal
Services (Vijeh Nashr) (Iran); ISD (Canada,
Mexico, USA); MHM Ltd (Japan)
Distribution Center: Turpin Distribution, Pega-
sus Dr, Biggleswade, Beds SG18 8TQ, United
Kingdom *Tel:* (01767) 604951 *Fax:* (01767)
601640 *E-mail:* custserv@turpin-distribution.
com *Web Site:* ebiz.turpin-distribution.com
(worldwide exc North America)

German University Press (GUP), *imprint of* Deutscher Wissenschafts-Verlag (DWV)

Germanisches Nationalmuseum
Kartaeusergasse 1, 90402 Nuremberg
Mailing Address: Postfach 11 95 80, 90105
Nuremberg
Tel: (0911) 1331 0 *Fax:* (0911) 1331 200
E-mail: info@gnm.de; generaldirektion@gnm.de
Web Site: www.gnm.de
Key Personnel
General Dir: Prof G Ulrich Grossmann
Tel: (0911) 1331 100
Chief, Publishing Dept: Christine Kupper, MA
Tel: (0911) 1331 165 *E-mail:* c.kupper@gnm.
de
Press & Public Relations: Dr Sonja Missfeldt
Tel: (0911) 1331 103 *E-mail:* s.missfeldt@gnm.
de
Founded: 1853
Books & catalogues about artistic & cultural his-
tory from German speaking regions from pre-
historic times to present, related to the mu-
seum's collections.
Subjects: Archaeology, Art, History, Science
(General)
ISBN Prefix(es): 978-3-926982; 978-3-936688
Number of titles published annually: 10 Print
Total Titles: 180 Print; 2 CD-ROM

Gerstenberg Verlag GmbH & Co KG+
Rathausstr 18-20, 31134 Hildesheim
Mailing Address: Postfach 100 555, 31105
Hildesheim
Tel: (05121) 106-0 *Fax:* (05121) 106-499
E-mail: verlag@gerstenberg-verlag.de
Web Site: www.gerstenberg-verlag.de
Key Personnel
General Manager: Daniela Filthaut
Assistant General Manager: Elke Schulz
Tel: (05121) 106-452 *E-mail:* elke.schulz@
gerstenberg-verlag.de
Press & Public Relations Manager: Andrea
Deyerling-Baier *Tel:* (05121) 106-456
E-mail: andrea.deyerling-baier@gerstenberg-
verlag.de
Marketing & Sales Manager/Sales Dir: Hajo
Schwabe *Tel:* (05121) 106-470 *E-mail:* hajo.
schwabe@gerstenberg-verlag.de
Advertising: Maren Albes *Tel:* (05121) 106-474
E-mail: werbung@gerstenberg-verlag.de

Rights & Licenses/Rights Dir: Ulrike Bastong
Tel: (05121) 106-464 *E-mail:* ulrike.bastong@
gerstenberg-verlag.de
Founded: 1792
Subjects: Architecture & Interior Design, Garden-
ing, Plants, Nonfiction (General)
ISBN Prefix(es): 978-3-8369

Gerth Medien, *imprint of* Verlagsgruppe Random House Bertelsmann

Gerth Medien GmbH+
Imprint of Verlagsgruppe Random House Bertels-
mann
Dillerberg 1, 35614 Asslar
Tel: (06443) 68-0 *Fax:* (06443) 68-34
E-mail: info@gerth.de
Web Site: www.gerth.de
Key Personnel
Publishing Dir: Detlef Holtgrefe *Tel:* (06443)
6810 *Fax:* (06443) 6813 *E-mail:* holtgrefe@
gerth.de
Mng Dir: Marco Abrahms *Tel:* (06443) 6811
Fax: (06443) 6813 *E-mail:* abrahms@gerth.de
Founded: 1949
Subjects: Biography, Memoirs, Fiction, Nonfiction
(General), Religion - Other, Self-Help
ISBN Prefix(es): 978-3-89437; 978-3-86591
Number of titles published annually: 90 Print; 5
Audio
Total Titles: 500 Print; 25 Audio
Imprints: adeo

Gerth Medien GmbH Musikverlag+
Dillerberg 1, 35614 Asslar
Tel: (06443) 6843 *Fax:* (06443) 686843
E-mail: info@gerth.de
Web Site: www.gerth.de
Key Personnel
Contact: Anja Christine Seitz *E-mail:* seitz@
gerth.de
Founded: 1949
Subjects: Music, Dance, Religion - Other, Theol-
ogy
ISBN Prefix(es): 978-3-89615; 978-3-922283
Distributor for Ganzteam Music

Verlag fuer Geschichte der Naturwissenschaften und der Technik+
Schlossstr 1, 49356 Diepholz
Tel: (05441) 92 71 29 *Fax:* (05441) 92 71 27
E-mail: info@gnt-verlag.de
Web Site: www.gnt-verlag.de
Key Personnel
Publisher: Reinald Schroeder
Founded: 1990
Specialize in scientific publications.
Subjects: History, History of Science & Technol-
ogy
ISBN Prefix(es): 978-3-928186
Warehouse: Leipziger Kommissions und- Gross-
buchhandelsgesellschaft mbH (LKG), An der
Suedspitze 1-12, 04571 Roetha *Tel:* (034206)
61-100 *Fax:* (034206) 61-110 *E-mail:* lkg@
lkg-service.de *Web Site:* www.lkg-va.de
Orders to: Leipziger Kommissions und- Gross-
buchhandelsgesellschaft mbH (LKG), An der
Suedspitze 1-12, 04571 Roetha *Tel:* (034206)
61-100 *Fax:* (034206) 61-110 *E-mail:* lkg@
lkg-service.de *Web Site:* www.lkg-va.de

Die Gestalten Verlag GmbH & Co KG
Mariannenstr, 9-10, 10999 Berlin
Tel: (030) 726 13 2000 *Fax:* (030) 726 13 22 22
E-mail: verlag@gestalten.com; sales@gestalten.
com
Web Site: news.gestalten.com; usshop.gestalten.
com
Key Personnel
Mng Dir: Robert Klanten; Markus Schneider
Founded: 1995

Subjects: Architecture & Interior Design, Art, Music, Dance, Photography, Pop Culture, Graphic Design, Illustration
ISBN Prefix(es): 978-3-89955; 978-3-931126
Distributor for Hantje Cantz
Foreign Rep(s): Books at Manic (Australia); Buchzentrum AG (BZ) (Denise Lehmann) (Switzerland); Gestalten UK (Emma Ferguson) (UK); Ingram Publisher Services (IPS) (Canada, USA); inter art (Laurence H'Limi) (France); Zaika Design (New Zealand)

Verlag Ernst und Werner Gieseking GmbH
Deckertstr 30, 33617 Bielefeld
Mailing Address: Postfach 130120, 33544 Bielefeld
Tel: (0521) 1 46 74 *Fax:* (0521) 14 37 15
E-mail: kontakt@gieseking-verlag.de
Web Site: www.gieseking-verlag.de
Key Personnel
Mng Dir & Publisher: Dr Klaus Schleicher
Founded: 1937
Subjects: Law
ISBN Prefix(es): 978-3-7694
Orders to: VVA, Guetersloh

Giesel Verlag GmbH
Hans-Boeckler-Allee 9, 30173 Hannover
Mailing Address: Postfach 54 20, 30054 Hannover
Tel: (0511) 7304-0 *Fax:* (0511) 7304-157
E-mail: info@giesel.de
Web Site: www.giesel.de
Key Personnel
Chief Editor: Guenter Koegel *Tel:* (0821) 319880-50 *Fax:* (0821) 319880-80 *E-mail:* g.koegel@giesel.de
Publisher: Joachim Roenisch *Tel:* (0511) 7304-136 *Fax:* (0511) 7304-266 *E-mail:* j.roenisch@giesel.de
Founded: 1965
Subjects: Architecture & Interior Design, Aluminum, Plastics
ISBN Prefix(es): 978-3-87852; 978-3-9802942

Gietl Verlag, *imprint of* Battenberg Gietl Verlag GmbH

Gildebuchverlag GmbH & Co KG+
Foehrster Str 8, 31061 Alfeld (Leine)
Tel: (05181) 80 04-63 *Fax:* (05181) 80 04-90
E-mail: info@gildebuchverlag.de
Web Site: www.gildebuchverlag.de
Key Personnel
Mng Dir: Christian Schlame; Wilhelm Schlame
Founded: 1949
Specialize in gastronomy & crafts.
Subjects: Cookery, Crafts, Games, Hobbies, Health, Nutrition
ISBN Prefix(es): 978-3-7734
Imprints: IWT Magazine Publishing House GmbH

Gilles & Francke Verlag+
Blumenstr 67-69, 47057 Duisburg
Tel: (0203) 36 27 87 *Fax:* (0203) 35 55 20
E-mail: verlag@gilles-francke.de
Web Site: www.gilles-francke.de
Key Personnel
Manager: Barbara Francke
Founded: 1900
Focus on German linguistics & literature, English & nursing science.
Subjects: Fiction, Language Arts, Linguistics, Literature, Literary Criticism, Essays, Nonfiction (General), Poetry, Regional Interests
ISBN Prefix(es): 978-3-921104; 978-3-925348
Number of titles published annually: 4 Print
Total Titles: 183 Print

Gimpel Verlag
Rathenaustr 37, 30853 Langenhagen
Tel: (0511) 96 77 67 59 *Fax:* (0511) 96 77 67 61
E-mail: info@gimpel-verlag.de
Web Site: www.gimpel-verlag.de
Key Personnel
Mng Dir: Luca Emanueli; Adam Opyrchal
Founded: 2006
Subjects: Art
ISBN Prefix(es): 978-3-9811300

Glare Verlag
Postfach 50 07 17, 60395 Frankfurt
Tel: (069) 52 02 83
E-mail: info@glareverlag.de
Web Site: www.glareverlag.de
Subjects: Fiction, Nonfiction (General)
ISBN Prefix(es): 978-3-930761

GLOOR Verlag
Alpspitzstr 1, 82319 Starnberg
Tel: (08151) 5568180 *Fax:* (08151) 5567381
E-mail: info@gloorverlag.de
Web Site: www.gloorverlag.de
Key Personnel
Publisher: Karin Windorfer
Founded: 2004
Subjects: History, Humor, Music, Dance
ISBN Prefix(es): 978-3-938037

Glossabooks, *imprint of* Iris Kater Verlag & Medien GmbH

glotzi Verlag
Jacob-Loehr-Str 18, 64625 Bensheim
Tel: (06251) 705 99 88 *Fax:* (03222) 690 559 3
E-mail: glotzi@glotzi-verlag.de
Web Site: www.glotzi-verlag.de
Key Personnel
Contact: Lothar Glotzbach
ISBN Prefix(es): 978-3-935333

Glueckschuh Verlag
Dammwildsteig 36, 14612 Falkensee
Tel: (03322) 28 68 94 *Fax:* (03322) 240 238
E-mail: info@glueckschuh-verlag.de; vertrieb@glueckschuh-verlag.de
Web Site: www.glueckschuh-verlag.de
Key Personnel
Publisher: Dorothea Flechsig
 E-mail: dorotheaflechsig@glueckschuh-verlag.de
Press, Editorial & Distribution: Jost Pietzcker
ISBN Prefix(es): 978-3-943030

Gmeiner-Verlag GmbH
Im Ehnried 5, 88605 Messkirch
Tel: (07575) 2095-0 *Fax:* (07575) 2095-29
E-mail: info@gmeiner-verlag.de
Web Site: www.gmeiner-verlag.de
Key Personnel
Publisher: Armin Gmeiner *Tel:* (07575) 2095-20 *E-mail:* armin.gmeiner@gmeiner-verlag.de
Foreign Rights: Frank Liebsch *Tel:* (07575) 2095-21 *E-mail:* frank.liebsch@gmeiner-verlag.de
Sales: Diane Kopp *Tel:* (07575) 2095-22 *E-mail:* diane.kopp@gmeiner-verlag.de; Patricia Vogel *Tel:* (07575) 2095-25 *E-mail:* patricia.vogel@gmeiner-verlag.de
Founded: 1986
Subjects: Fiction, Travel & Tourism, Culture, Historical Fiction, Thrillers
ISBN Prefix(es): 978-3-89977; 978-3-926633; 978-3-8392
Foreign Rep(s): Dagmar & Richard Bhend (Switzerland); Erich Neuhold & Wilhelm Platzer (Austria, South Tyrol, Italy)
Distribution Center: Leipziger Kommissions- und Grossbuchhandelsgesellschaft mbH (LKG), An der Suedspitze 1-12, 04571 Roetha, Contact: Ursula Fritzsche *Tel:* (034206) 65-135

Fax: (034206) 65-1739 *E-mail:* ufritzsche@lkg-service.de *Web Site:* www.lkg-va.de
Dr Franz Hain Verlagsauslieferungen GmbH, Dr-Otto-Neurath-Gasse 5, 1220 Vienna, Austria *Tel:* (01) 2826565-52 *Fax:* (01) 2825282 *E-mail:* bestell@hain.at
Buchzentrum AG, Industriestr Ost 10, 4614 Haegendorf, Switzerland *Tel:* (062) 2092626 *Fax:* (062) 2092627 *E-mail:* altermatt@buchzentrum.ch

Gmelin-Verlag GmbH+
Erlinger Hoehe 9, 82346 Andechs
Tel: (08152) 9099762
Key Personnel
Owner, Rights & Permissions: Gerd Erich Gmelin
Founded: 1949
Subjects: Fiction, Health, Nutrition, Literature, Literary Criticism, Essays, Medicine, Nursing, Dentistry, Nonfiction (General), Philosophy, Physical Sciences, Science (General)
ISBN Prefix(es): 978-3-926253

GMP Publishing, see Maas & Peither AG

GNT-Verlag, see Verlag fuer Geschichte der Naturwissenschaften und der Technik

August Von Goethe Literaturverlag
Mainstr 143, 63065 Offenbach
Tel: (069) 40894-0 *Fax:* (069) 40894-194
E-mail: lektorat@august-von-goethe-literaturverlag.de
Web Site: www.august-von-goethe-literaturverlag.de
Subjects: Biography, Memoirs, Cookery, Fiction, Government, Political Science, Nonfiction (General), Philosophy, Poetry, Religion - Other, Travel & Tourism
ISBN Prefix(es): 978-3-8372; 978-3-86548

Cornelia Goethe Literaturverlag (Cornelia Goethe Publishers)+
Grosser Hirschgraben 15, 60311 Frankfurt am Main
Tel: (069) 40894-0 *Fax:* (069) 40894-194
E-mail: lektorat@cornelia-goethe-verlag.de
Web Site: www.cornelia-goethe-verlag.de
Key Personnel
Mng Dir: Dr Uwe Frank
Founded: 1987
Publisher for new authors.
Subjects: Fiction
ISBN Prefix(es): 978-3-8267; 978-3-89349
Number of titles published annually: 200 Print
Total Titles: 1,000 Print
Parent Company: Frankfurter Verlagsgruppe Holding AG August von Goethe
Branch Office(s)
70 Fortune Green Rd, London NW6 1DS, United Kingdom

Goethe-Universitaet Frankfurt am Main, see Johann Wolfgang Goethe-Universitaet Frankfurt am Main

Das Goldene Tor Ltd
Fichtenstr 2, 66583 Spiesen-Elversberg
Tel: (06821) 8690355 *Fax:* (06821) 8690832
E-mail: hallo@das-goldene-tor.de
Web Site: das-goldene-tor.de
Key Personnel
Manager: Rosemarie Gehring; Stefan Sicurella
Founded: 2007
Subjects: Philosophy, Self-Help, Meditation
ISBN Prefix(es): 978-3-940930

Goldfinch Verlag, *imprint of* Dryas Verlag GbR

Goldmann, *imprint of* Verlagsgruppe Random House Bertelsmann

Goldmann Verlag
Imprint of Verlagsgruppe Random House Bertelsmann
Neumarkter Str 28, 81673 Munich
Tel: (089) 4136-0 *Toll Free Tel:* (0800) 500 33 22
  Fax: (089) 4136-3333
E-mail: kundenservice@randomhouse.de
Web Site: www.randomhouse.de/goldmann
Key Personnel
Mng Dir: Andrea Best
Foreign Rights Dir: Gesche Wendebourg
  Tel: (089) 4136-3313 *E-mail:* gesche.
  wendebourg@randomhouse.de
Press Dir: Claudia Hanssen *Tel:* (089) 4136-
  3569 *Fax:* (089) 4136-3723 *E-mail:* claudia.
  hanssen@randomhouse.de
Editorial: Dr Georg Reuchlein
Founded: 1922
Subjects: Art, Astrology, Occult, Biography,
  Memoirs, Criminology, Education, Fiction,
  Film, Video, History, How-to, Law, Medicine,
  Nursing, Dentistry, Psychology, Psychiatry, Sci-
  ence (General), Science Fiction, Fantasy, Social
  Sciences, Sociology
ISBN Prefix(es): 978-3-442

Gondrom Verlag GmbH+
c/o gondolino GmbH, Buehlstr 4, 95463 Bindlach
Tel: (09208) 51-0 *Fax:* (09208) 51-21
E-mail: presse@gondrom-verlag.de
Web Site: www.gondrom-verlag.de
Key Personnel
President: Volker Gondrom
Foreign Rights: Anne Luetkemeyer *Tel:* (09208)
  51-153 *Fax:* (09208) 51 38-153 *E-mail:* a.
  luetkemeyer@gondrom-holding.de
Sales Manager: Birgit Hinkel *Tel:* (09208) 51-
  259 *Fax:* (09208) 51 38-259 *E-mail:* b.hinkel@
  gondolino.de
Founded: 1974
Subjects: Art, History, Literature, Literary Criti-
  cism, Essays, Nonfiction (General)
ISBN Prefix(es): 978-3-8112
Associate Companies: Loewe Verlag
Foreign Rep(s): Dessauer (Claudia Gyr) (Switzer-
  land)
Foreign Rights: Agentur im Medien- und Ver-
  lagswesen (Dr Ivana Beil) (Czechia, Slovakia);
  Editio Dialog Literary Scouting Agency (Dr
  Michael Wenzel) (France); Iris Agency (Cather-
  ine Fragov) (Greece); Kalem Agency (Nermin
  Mollaoglu) (Turkey); Nova Littera Ltd (Sergei
  Cheredov) (Russia)
Distribution Center: Mohr Morawa Buchver-
  trieb GmbH, Sulzengasse 2, 1230 Vienna,
  Austria *Tel:* (01) 680 14-0 *Fax:* (01) 688
  71 30 *E-mail:* momo@mohrmorawa.at *Web
  Site:* www.mohrmorawa.at
  Buchzentrum AG (BZ), Industriestr Ost 10, 4614
  Haegendorf, Switzerland *Tel:* (062) 2092525
  Fax: (062) 2092627

Govi-Verlag Pharmazeutischer Verlag GmbH+
Carl-Mannich-Str 26, 65760 Eschborn
Mailing Address: Postfach 53 60, 65728 Es-
  chborn
Tel: (06196) 928-250 *Fax:* (06196) 928-259;
  (06196) 928-203
E-mail: service@govi.de
Web Site: www.govi.de
Key Personnel
Mng Dir: Harmut Schmitt; Peter Steinke
  Tel: (06196) 928-201 *E-mail:* p.steinke@govi.
  de
Head, Marketing & Sales: Maria Scholz
  Tel: (06196) 928-242 *E-mail:* scholz@govi.de
Marketing & Press: Elke Haus *Tel:* (06196) 928-
  243 *E-mail:* haus@govi.de
Founded: 1949
Specialize in pharmaceuticals & medicine.
Membership(s): Association of German Magazine
  Publishers; Association of German Publishers
  & Booksellers.

Subjects: Biological Sciences, Chemistry, Chem-
  ical Engineering, Fiction, Mathematics,
  Medicine, Nursing, Dentistry, Nonfiction (Gen-
  eral), Physics, Botany
ISBN Prefix(es): 978-3-7741
Total Titles: 140 Print; 20 CD-ROM
Parent Company: ABDA-Bundesvereinigung
  Deutscher Apothekerverbaende, Ginnheimer
  Str 26, 65760 Echborn Tannus
Associate Companies: Marketing-Gesellschaft
  Deutscher Apotheker mbH; Werbe-und Ver-
  triebsgesellschaft Deutscher Apotheker mbH;
  Zentrallaboratorium Deutscher Apotheker
Distributor for WHO World-Health-Organization
Warehouse: Industriestr 1, 65760 Eschborn
Returns: Industriestr 1, 65760 Eschborn

Goya libre, *imprint of* JUMBO Neue Medien &
  Verlag GmbH

Goya LiT, *imprint of* JUMBO Neue Medien &
  Verlag GmbH

Grabert Verlag+
Am Apfelberg 18, 72076 Tuebingen
Tel: (07071) 4070-0 *Fax:* (07071) 4070-26
E-mail: info@grabertverlag.de
Web Site: www.grabert-verlag.de
Key Personnel
Mng Dir: Wigbert Grabert
Founded: 1953
Subjects: Art, Biography, Memoirs, History
ISBN Prefix(es): 978-3-87847
Number of titles published annually: 10 Print
Total Titles: 200 Print
Book Club(s): Deutscher Buchkreis

Graefe und Unzer Verlag GmbH+
Grillparzerstr 12, 81675 Munich
Tel: (089) 4 19 81-0 *Fax:* (089) 4 19 81-250;
  (089) 4 19 81-113
E-mail: info@graefe-und-unzer.de; leserservice@
  graefe-und-unzer.de; rights@graefe-und-unzer.
  de
Web Site: www.graefe-und-unzer.de; www.gu.de
Key Personnel
Mng Dir: Thomas Ganske; Frank H Haeger; Dr
  Christian Kopp; Dorothee Seeliger; Dr Till
  Wahnbaek
Deputy Head, Public Relations: Florian Land-
  graf *Tel:* (089) 4 19 81-333 *E-mail:* florian.
  landgraf@graefe-und-unzer.de
Founded: 1722
Subjects: Animals, Pets, Business, Cookery, Gar-
  dening, Plants, Health, Nutrition, Natural His-
  tory, Self-Help, Travel & Tourism, Wine &
  Spirits
ISBN Prefix(es): 978-3-7742; 978-3-8338
Number of titles published annually: 120 Print
Total Titles: 1,050 Print
Parent Company: Ganske Verlagsgruppe GmbH,
  Harvestehuder Weg 41, 20149 Hamburg
Imprints: GU; Hallwag (Wine); Kuechengoetter
  (Cookery); Teubner Edition (Cookery)
Warehouse: Verlegerdienst Munchen, Guten-
  bergstr 1, 82205 Gilching

Graf Editions
Elisabethstr 29, 80796 Munich
Tel: (089) 2715957 *Fax:* (089) 2715997
E-mail: info@graf-editions.de
Web Site: www.graf-editions.de
Key Personnel
Contact: Dieter Graf
Founded: 1992
Subjects: Language Arts, Linguistics, Travel &
  Tourism, Hiking
ISBN Prefix(es): 978-3-9803130; 978-3-9808802
Total Titles: 12 Print

Grafit Verlag GmbH+
Chemnitzer Str 31, 44139 Dortmund
Tel: (0231) 7214650 *Fax:* (0231) 7214677
E-mail: info@grafit.de
Web Site: www.grafit.de
Key Personnel
Mng Dir: Ulrike Rodi
Foreign Rights: Gudrun Stegemann
  E-mail: gudrun.stegemann@grafit.de
Sales: Alexander Knobbe *Tel:* (0231) 9143308
  E-mail: alexander.knobbe@grafit.de
Founded: 1989
Membership(s): Boersenverein des deutschen
  Buchhandels.
Subjects: Fiction, Mysteries, Suspense, Crime
  Fiction, Modern Detective Stories
ISBN Prefix(es): 978-3-89425
Number of titles published annually: 20 Print
Total Titles: 250 Print
Orders to: CVK Cornelsen, Postfach 100271,
  33502 Bielefeld

Verlag der Stiftung Gralsbotschaft GmbH+
Schuckertstr 8, 71254 Ditzingen
Tel: (07156) 953215 *Fax:* (07156) 18663
E-mail: info@gral.de
Web Site: www.gral.de
Key Personnel
Mng Dir & Editor: Michael Oort
Founded: 1928
Subjects: Health, Nutrition, Human Relations,
  Nonfiction (General), Parapsychology, Philoso-
  phy, Religion - Other, Self-Help
ISBN Prefix(es): 978-3-87860; 978-1-898853
U.S. Office(s): Grail Foundation Press, PO Box
  45, Gambier, OH 43022, United States

Grass-Verlag
Internationales Zentrum Burg Steineck, Simrock-
  str 7, 53619 Rheinbreitbach
Tel: (02224) 7705-0
E-mail: int@burg-steineck.de
Web Site: www.burg-steineck.de/d_verlag.html
Key Personnel
Publisher: Aloys Grass
Founded: 1984
Subjects: Religion - Protestant
ISBN Prefix(es): 978-3-924974

Verlag Graswurzelrevolution eV
Breul 43, 48413 Muenster
Tel: (0251) 48290-57; (02440) 959-250 (sales)
  Fax: (0251) 48290-32; (02440) 959-351 (sales)
E-mail: redaktion@graswurzel.net; buchverlag@
  graswurzel.net
Web Site: www.graswurzel.net
Subjects: Government, Political Science, Social
  Sciences, Sociology, Anarchism, Anti-Fascism,
  Ecology, Nonviolence, Post Colonialism, Spain
ISBN Prefix(es): 978-3-939045; 978-3-9806353

Graue Edition GmbH
Giesserner Str 64, 63128 Dietzenbach
Tel: (06074) 215 49 72 *Fax:* (06074) 48 267 40
E-mail: info@graue-edition-gmbh.de
Web Site: www.die-graue-edition.de
Key Personnel
Manager: Dr Florian Lauermann *E-mail:* florian.
  lauermann@graue-edition-gmbh.de
Editor: Dr Michael Hauskeller *Tel:* (01392)
  7222047 *E-mail:* michael.hauskeller@graue-
  edition-gmbh.de
Subjects: Art, Inspirational, Spirituality, Liter-
  ature, Literary Criticism, Essays, Medicine,
  Nursing, Dentistry, Philosophy, Psychology,
  Psychiatry, Science (General)
ISBN Prefix(es): 978-3-906336
Distribution Center: Brockhaus Kommissions-
  geschaft GmbH, Kreidlerstr 9, 70806 Kornwes-
  theim *E-mail:* bestell@brocom.de

Bernhard Gregor Verlag
Brueckenmuellerstr 4, 36251 Bad Hersfeld

Tel: (06621) 9683720 *Fax:* (06621) 9685308
E-mail: post@gregor-versand.de
Web Site: www.gregor-versand.de
Key Personnel
Mng Dir: Bernhard Gregor
Founded: 1982
Subjects: Biography, Memoirs, Nonfiction (General), Religion - Catholic, Theology
ISBN Prefix(es): 978-3-89150; 978-3-87391; 978-3-922770
Number of titles published annually: 1 Print
Total Titles: 50 Print

Greinus und Wolter GbR, see Verlag Voland & Quist

Greuthof Verlag und Vertrieb GmbH+
Kybfelsenstr 41, 79100 Freiburg
Tel: (0761) 38845996 *Fax:* (0761) 38845997
E-mail: mail@greuthof.de
Web Site: www.greuthof.de
Subjects: Inspirational, Spirituality
ISBN Prefix(es): 978-3-923662

Greven Verlag Koeln GmbH+
Neue Weyerstr 1-3, 50676 Cologne
Mailing Address: Postfach 10 16 44, 50456 Cologne
Tel: (0221) 20 33-161 *Fax:* (0221) 20 33-162
E-mail: greven.verlag@greven.de
Web Site: www.greven-verlag.de
Key Personnel
Chief Executive Officer & Publishing Dir: Dr Damian van Melis
Founded: 1827
Subjects: Art, Regional Interests
ISBN Prefix(es): 978-3-7743
Distribution Center: Sigloch Distribution GmbH & Co KG, Am Buchberg 8, 74572 Blaufelden *Tel:* (07953) 883-757 *Fax:* (07953) 883-700
E-mail: verlagservice@sigloch.de

Grille Verlag
Nechlin 15, 17337 Uckerland
Tel: (039740) 29595 *Fax:* (039740) 29595
E-mail: info@grille-verlag.de
Web Site: www.grille-verlag.de
Key Personnel
Owner: Margarete Bastian *E-mail:* margarete.bastian@t-online.de
Founded: 2010
Subjects: Education, Fiction, Government, Political Science, History, Travel & Tourism
ISBN Prefix(es): 978-3-925914; 978-3-88896

Griot Hoerbuch Verlag GmbH
Furtwaenglerstr 21, 70195 Stuttgart
Tel: (0711) 601 40 32 *Fax:* (0711) 601 40 34
E-mail: info@griot-verlag.de
Web Site: www.griot-verlag.de
Key Personnel
Mng Dir: Elke Bader
Subjects: Biography, Memoirs, History, Literature, Literary Criticism, Essays, Music, Dance, Nonfiction (General), Poetry, Classics of World Literature
ISBN Prefix(es): 978-3-941234
Distribution Center: Verlegerdienst Muenchen GmbH, Gutenbergstr 1, 82205 Gilching, Contact: Cornelia Hass *Tel:* (08105) 388-505 *Fax:* (08105) 388-210 *E-mail:* cornelia.hass@verlegerdienst.de *Web Site:* www.verlegerdienst.de
Dr Franz Hain Verlagsauslieferung GmbH, Dr-Otto-Neurath-Gasse 5, 1220 Vienna, Austria *Tel:* (01) 282 65 65 *Fax:* (01) 282 52 82 *E-mail:* bestell@hain.at
Verlags-Service Imfeld, Bruenigstr 40, 6055 Alpnach, Switzerland, Contact: Ernst Imfeld *Tel:* (041) 660 34 81; (079) 333 44 03

(cell) *Fax:* (041) 660 32 63 *E-mail:* e.imfeld@verlags-service.ch *Web Site:* www.verlags-service.ch

Groessenwahn Verlag Frankfurt am Main
Lenaustr 97, 61318 Frankfurt am Main
Tel: (069) 48 00 29 92 *Fax:* (0171) 28 67 5 49
E-mail: info@groessenwahn-verlag.de
Web Site: www.groessenwahn-verlag.de
Key Personnel
Publisher: Sewastos Sampsounis
Subjects: Biography, Memoirs, Cookery, Literature, Literary Criticism, Essays, Travel & Tourism
ISBN Prefix(es): 978-3-942223
Foreign Rep(s): Tell Schwandt (Berlin, Germany, East Germany)
Distribution Center: SOVA, Friesstr 20-24, 60388 Frankfurt *Tel:* (069) 410211 *Fax:* (069) 410280 *E-mail:* sovaffm@t-online.de *Web Site:* www.sovaffm.de (Germany & Austria)
International Bookstore Zachariadis, Proxenou Koromita Str 20, 54622 Thessaloniki, Greece *Tel:* (02310) 276 334 *Fax:* (02310) 229 936 *E-mail:* info@zbooks.gr *Web Site:* www.zbooks.gr (Greece)

Groh Verlag GmbH
Kleinfeldstr 4, 82110 Germering
Tel: (089) 622 336-0 *Fax:* (089) 622 336-77
E-mail: info@groh.de
Web Site: www.groh.de
Key Personnel
Owner & Mng Dir: Joachim Groh
Founded: 1928
Specilize in gift books & calendars.
ISBN Prefix(es): 978-3-86713

Grubbe Media GmbH
Manzostr 14, 80997 Munich
Tel: (089) 36 89 96 63 *Fax:* (089) 36 89 96 64
E-mail: info@grubbemedia.de
Web Site: www.grubbemedia.de
Key Personnel
Management: Gerhard Grubbe; Bjoern Hoelle
Founded: 2010
Subjects: Photography, Science (General), Travel & Tourism
ISBN Prefix(es): 978-3-942194

Adelheid Gruber Verlag
Danzerweg 12, 85748 Garching
Tel: (089) 320 46 68 *Fax:* (089) 329 29 74
E-mail: adelheidgruberverlag@t-online.de
Web Site: www.gruberverlag.de
Key Personnel
Publisher: Adelheid Gruber
Subjects: Nonfiction (General), Religion - Catholic, Travel & Tourism
ISBN Prefix(es): 978-3-9807241

Verlagsgruppe gruenes herz
Am Hang 27-28, 98693 Ilmenau
Tel: (03677) 46628-0 *Fax:* (03677) 46628-80
E-mail: info@gruenes-herz.de
Web Site: www.vggh.de
Key Personnel
Chief Executive Officer: Lutz Gebhardt
Mng Dir: Christoph Hoffmann
Founded: 1991
Subjects: Art, Biography, Memoirs, Cookery, Fiction, Geography, Geology, History, Nonfiction (General), Regional Interests, Nature
ISBN Prefix(es): 978-3-944102; 978-3-95560
Imprints: Demmler Verlag; RhinoVerlag

Matthias Gruenewald Verlag
Imprint of Schwabenverlag AG
Senefelderstr 12, 73760 Ostfildern
Mailing Address: Postfach 42 80, 73745 Ostfildern

Tel: (0711) 44 06-194 *Fax:* (0711) 44 06-177
E-mail: mail@gruenewaldverlag.de
Web Site: www.gruenewaldverlag.de
Key Personnel
Executive: Ulrich Peters *Tel:* (0711) 44 06-111
Publishing Dir: Gertrud Widmann *Tel:* (0711) 44 06-161 *E-mail:* gertrud.widmann@schwabenverlag.de
Head, Marketing & Sales: Barbara Janssen *Tel:* (0711) 44 06-109 *E-mail:* barbara.janssen@schwabenverlag.de
Foreign Rights Manager: Claudia Stegmann *Tel:* (0711) 44 06-148
Production Manager: Wolfgang Sailer *Tel:* (0711) 44 06-118 *E-mail:* wolfgang.sailer@schwabenverlag.de
Sales Manager: Reiner Morbitzer *Tel:* (0711) 44 06-146
Advertising & Public Relations: Sabrina Reusch *Tel:* (0711) 44 06-168 *E-mail:* sabrina.reusch@schwabenverlag.de
Founded: 1918
Subjects: Biography, Memoirs, Psychology, Psychiatry, Religion - Other, Theology
ISBN Prefix(es): 978-3-7867
Number of titles published annually: 60 Print; 3 Audio
Total Titles: 840 Print; 40 Audio
Foreign Rep(s): Joe Fuchs (Switzerland); Verlagsagentur Erich Neuhold (Austria, South Tyrol, Italy)
Foreign Rights: The Book Publishers Association of Israel (Shoshi Grajower) (Israel); Eulama SRL (Pina von Prellwitz) (Italy, Spanish & Portuguese); Hercules Business & Culture GmbH (Hongjun Cai) (China); jia-xi books co ltd (Becky Lin) (Taiwan); Simona Kessler International Copyright Agency Ltd (Romania); Meike Marx Literary Agency (Japan); ONK Agency Ltd (Hatice Gok) (Turkey)
Distribution Center: Leipziger Kommissions- und Grossbuchhandelsgesellschaft mbH (LKG), An der Suedspitze 1-12, 04571 Roetha, Contact: Robert Winkler *Tel:* (034206) 65 205 *Fax:* (034206) 65 1738 *E-mail:* rwinkler@lkg-service.de *Web Site:* www.lkg-va.de
Mohr Morawa Buchvertrieb GesmbH, Sulzengasse 2, 1230 Vienna, Austria *Tel:* (01) 680 14-0 *Fax:* (01) 688 71 30 *E-mail:* momo@mohrmorawa.at *Web Site:* www.mohrmorawa.at
Herder AG Basel Verlagsauslieferungen, Muttenzer Str 109, 4133 Pratteln 1, Switzerland *Tel:* (061) 8 27 90 60 *Fax:* (061) 8 27 90 67 *E-mail:* verkauf@herder.ch

Verlag Grundlagen und Praxis GmbH & Co+
Bergmannstr 20, 26789 Leer
Tel: (0491) 61 88 6 *Fax:* (0491) 36 34
E-mail: info@grundlagen-praxis.de
Web Site: www.grundlagen-praxis.de
Key Personnel
Mng Dir: Axel Camici
Founded: 1971
Subjects: Alternative, Health, Nutrition, Language Arts, Linguistics, Medicine, Nursing, Dentistry, Alternative Medicine, Homeopathy
ISBN Prefix(es): 978-3-921229

Verlag Gruppenpaedagogischer Literatur+
Rudolf-Diesel-Str 8, 61273 Wehrheim
Mailing Address: Postfach 12 52, 61269 Wehrheim
Tel: (06081) 5 96 38 *Fax:* (06081) 5 74 38
E-mail: info@vglw.de
Web Site: www.vglw.de
Founded: 1976
Subjects: Career Development, Child Care & Development, Crafts, Games, Hobbies, Education, Music, Dance, Outdoor Recreation, Sports, Athletics
ISBN Prefix(es): 978-3-921496; 978-3-89544

De Gruyter Akademie Forschung, *imprint of* Walter de Gruyter GmbH & Co KG

De Gruyter Mouton, *imprint of* Walter de Gruyter GmbH & Co KG

De Gruyter Oldenbourg, *imprint of* Walter de Gruyter GmbH & Co KG

De Gruyter Open, *imprint of* Walter de Gruyter GmbH & Co KG

De Gruyter Saur, *imprint of* Walter de Gruyter GmbH & Co KG

De Gruyter Saur+
Imprint of Walter de Gruyter GmbH & Co KG
Genthiner Str 13, 10785 Berlin
Tel: (030) 260 05-0 *Fax:* (030) 260 05-251
E-mail: service@degruyter.com
Web Site: www.degruyter.com
Key Personnel
Editorial Dir, Library References & History: Dr Alice Keller *Tel:* (089) 769 02-388
   E-mail: alice.keller@degruyter.com
Production Editor, Book: Manfred Link *Tel:* (089) 769 02-355 *E-mail:* manfred.link@degruyter.com
Founded: 1949 (taken over by De Gruyter in 2006)
Subjects: Art, Biography, Memoirs, Communications, History, Library & Information Sciences, Literature, Literary Criticism, Essays, Music, Dance, Philosophy, Publishing & Book Trade Reference, Social Sciences, Sociology
ISBN Prefix(es): 978-3-598; 978-3-11; 978-3-7940; 978-3-907820; 978-3-908255
U.S. Office(s): c/o Walter de Gruyter Inc, 121 High St, 3rd floor, Boston, MA 02110, United States *Tel:* 857-284-7073 ext 118 *Fax:* 857-284-7358

Walter de Gruyter GmbH & Co KG+
Genthiner Str 13, 10785 Berlin
Tel: (030) 260 05-0 *Fax:* (030) 260 05-251
E-mail: orders@degruyter.com; service@degruyter.com
Web Site: www.degruyter.com
Key Personnel
Chief Financial Officer: Carsten Buhr
Mng Dir of the Board & VP Publishing, Humanities & Social Sciences: Anke Beck
Dir, Rights & Licenses: Tiziana Ziesing *Tel:* (089) 76 902-318 *Fax:* (089) 76 902-350 *E-mail:* tiziana.ziesing@degruyter.com
Senior Manager, Marketing Services: Natascha Barrett *Tel:* (030) 260 05-292 *Fax:* (030) 260 05-322 *E-mail:* natascha.barrett@degruyter.com
Founded: 1919
Subjects: Archaeology, Biological Sciences, History, Language Arts, Linguistics, Law, Literature, Literary Criticism, Essays, Management, Marketing, Mathematics, Medicine, Nursing, Dentistry, Philosophy, Physical Sciences, Physics, Science (General), Social Sciences, Sociology, Theology
ISBN Prefix(es): 978-0-202; 978-3-11; 978-3-89949
Total Titles: 8,500 Print
Imprints: Birkhauser; De Gruyter Akademie Forschung; De Gruyter Mouton; De Gruyter Oldenbourg; De Gruyter Open; De Gruyter Saur
Subsidiaries: De Gruyter Mouton
U.S. Office(s): Walter de Gruyter Inc, 121 High St, 3rd floor, Boston, MA 02110, United States, Dir: Michiel Klein Swormink *Tel:* 857-284-7073 *Fax:* 857-284-7358 *E-mail:* usinfo@degruyter.com
Orders to: Rhenus Medien Logistik GmbH & Co KG, Justus-von-Liebig-Str 1, 86899 Landsberg am Lech *Tel:* (08191) 97000-214 (books); (08191) 97000-881 (journals)
   E-mail: degruyter@de.rhenus.com
Books International, PO Box 960, Herndon, VA 20172-0960, United States *Tel:* 703-661-1589 *Fax:* 703-661-1501 *E-mail:* degruytermail@presswarehouse.com (USA, Canada & Mexico)

GU, *imprint of* Graefe und Unzer Verlag GmbH

Gudberg Nerger Publishing
Poolstr 8, 20355 Hamburg
Tel: (040) 8195150 *Fax:* (040) 328 926 729
E-mail: post@gudbergnerger.com
Web Site: publishing.gudbergnerger.com
Key Personnel
Mng Dir: Jan Mueller-Wiefel; Juergen Nerger
Subjects: Art, Photography, Travel & Tourism, Design, Lifestyle
ISBN Prefix(es): 978-3-945772

Guese Verlag GmbH
Am Spitzacker 10, 61184 Karben
Tel: (06039) 48 01-10 *Fax:* (06039) 48 01-48
E-mail: info@guese.de
Web Site: www.guese.de
Key Personnel
Mng Dir: Johannes Guese
Founded: 1954
Subjects: Agriculture, Gardening, Plants
ISBN Prefix(es): 978-3-87278

Guetersloher Verlaghaus+
Imprint of Verlagsgruppe Random House Bertelsmann
Carl-Miele-Str 214, 33311 Guetersloh
Tel: (05241) 7405-0 *Toll Free Tel:* 800 500 33 22 *Fax:* (05241) 7405-48; (089) 4136-3333
E-mail: kundenservice@randomhouse.de
Web Site: www.randomhouse.de/guetersloherverlagshaus
Key Personnel
Publisher: Klaus Altepost *Tel:* (05241) 80-1521 *E-mail:* klaus.altepost@gtvh.de
Head of Public Relations: Justine Pawlas *Tel:* (05241) 80-1554 *E-mail:* justine.pawlas@gtvh.de
Sales Dir: Hans-Joerg Unger *Tel:* (05241) 80-1542 *E-mail:* hans-joerg.unger@gtvh.de
Founded: 1835
Subjects: Religion - Other, Theology
ISBN Prefix(es): 978-3-579; 978-3-7811

Guetersloher Verlagshaus, *imprint of* Verlagsgruppe Random House Bertelsmann

Guggolz Verlag
Gustav-Mueller-Str 46, 10829 Berlin
Tel: (030) 788 91227 *Fax:* (030) 788 91228
E-mail: verlag@guggolz-verlag.de; presse@guggolz-verlag.de
Web Site: www.guggolz-verlag.de
Key Personnel
Publisher & Sales: Sebastian Guggolz
Public Relations: Maren Baier
Founded: 2014
Subjects: Fiction
ISBN Prefix(es): 978-3-945370

Klaus Dieter Guhl
Akazienallee 27a, 14050 Berlin
Tel: (030) 3213062 *Fax:* (030) 30823868
E-mail: kdguhl@t-online.de
Founded: 1974
Subjects: Art, Government, Political Science, Literature, Literary Criticism, Essays
ISBN Prefix(es): 978-3-88220
Subsidiaries: Buchladen Bunter Baer GmbH; Fanel GmbH
Bookshop(s): Bunter Baer-Guhl, Knobelsdorffstr 8, 14059 Berlin

Gustav-Adolf-Werk eV
Pistorisstr 6, 04229 Leipzig
Mailing Address: Postfach 310763, 04211 Leipzig
Tel: (0341) 490 62 0 *Fax:* (0341) 490 62 66; (0341) 490 62 67
E-mail: info@gustav-adolf-werk.de; presse@gustav-adolf-werk.de
Web Site: www.gustav-adolf-werk.de
Key Personnel
Mng Dir: Pfarrer Enno Haaks
Press: Maaja Pauska *Tel:* (0341) 490 62 18
Founded: 1968
Subjects: Developing Countries, Religion - Protestant, Theology
ISBN Prefix(es): 978-3-87593

Der Gute Hirte Verlag
Hochlandstr 27, 01328 Dresden
Tel: (0351) 4109969 *Fax:* (0351) 4109969
Web Site: www.dgh-verlag.de
Key Personnel
Publishing Dir: Gottfried Fischer
Christian publisher.
Subjects: Religion - Other, Theology
ISBN Prefix(es): 978-3-933833

Gutleut Verlag
Kaiserstr 55, 60329 Frankfurt am Main
Tel: (069) 87 87 86 58 *Fax:* (069) 25 32 69
E-mail: mail@gutleut-verlag.com
Web Site: www.gutleut-verlag.com
Key Personnel
Contact: Michael Wagener
Subjects: Art, Poetry
ISBN Prefix(es): 978-3-936826
Distribution Center: GVA Gemeinsame Verlagsauslieferung Goettingen GmbH & Co KG, Postfach 2021, 37010 Goettingen *Tel:* (049) 551 487177 *Fax:* (049) 551 41392 *E-mail:* krause@gva-verlage.de *Web Site:* www.gva-verlage.de

Haag + Herchen Verlag GmbH+
Schwarzwaldstr 23, 63454 Hanan
Tel: (06181) 520670-0 *Fax:* (06181) 520670-40
E-mail: verlag@haagundherchen.de
Web Site: www.haagundherchen.de
Key Personnel
Mng Dir: Doerthe Emig-Herchen
Founded: 1976
Subjects: Biography, Memoirs, Cookery, Engineering (General), Fiction, Government, Political Science, Health, Nutrition, History, How-to, Literature, Literary Criticism, Essays, Medicine, Nursing, Dentistry, Mysteries, Suspense, Nonfiction (General), Poetry, Psychology, Psychiatry, Science (General), Science Fiction, Fantasy, Self-Help, Social Sciences, Sociology, Travel & Tourism, Antologies
ISBN Prefix(es): 978-3-88129; 978-3-86137; 978-3-89228; 978-3-89846
Associate Companies: H-A Herchen Verlag KG; Herchen + Herchen & Co Medien KG

C W Haarfeld, *imprint of* Wolters Kluwer Deutschland GmbH

C W Haarfeld GmbH
Robert-Bosch-Str 6, 50354 Huerth
Toll Free Tel: 0800 88 85 440
Toll Free Fax: 0800 88 85 445
E-mail: online@cw-haarfeld.de; cwh@wolterskluwer.com
Web Site: www.cw-haarfeld.de; www.cwh.de
Key Personnel
Mng Dir: Fr Martina Bruder; Hr Michael Gloss; Hr Juergen Scholl; Hr Adrianus Gerardus Verhoef
Founded: 1867
Trade information & laws in the fields of Social Security.

Subjects: Health, Nutrition, Law
ISBN Prefix(es): 978-3-7747
Parent Company: Wolters Kluwer Deutschland

Wolfgang G Haas - Musikverlag Koeln eK+
Rheinbergstr 92, 51143 Cologne
Mailing Address: Postfach 90 07 48, 51117
Cologne
Tel: (02203) 98 88 3-0 *Fax:* (02203) 98 88 3-50
E-mail: order@haas-koeln.de
Web Site: www.haas-koeln.de
Key Personnel
Contact: Wolfgang G Haas
Founded: 1985
Specialize in wind instrument music.
Membership(s): German Society of Music Publishers; International Trumpet Guild.
Subjects: Music, Dance
ISBN Prefix(es): 978-3-928453

Dr Rudolf Habelt GmbH
Am Buchenhang 1, 53115 Bonn
Mailing Address: Postfach 150104, 53040 Bonn
Tel: (0228) 9 23 83-0; (0228) 9 23 83-55 (antiquarian bookshop) *Fax:* (0228) 9 23 83-6
E-mail: info@habelt.de; verlag@habelt.de
Web Site: www.habelt.de
Key Personnel
Mng Dir: Wolfgang Habelt *Tel:* (0228) 9 23 83-33
Publishing Dir: Dr Susanne Biegert *Tel:* (0228) 9 23 83-22 *Fax:* (0228) 9 23 83-23
Founded: 1954
Subjects: Archaeology, History, Regional Interests
ISBN Prefix(es): 978-3-7749
Number of titles published annually: 30 Print

Hachmeister Verlag + Galerie+
Klosterstr 12, 48143 Muenster
Tel: (0251) 51210 *Fax:* (0251) 57217
Key Personnel
Dir: Dr Heiner Hachmeister
Founded: 1979
Catalogues & books.
Subjects: Art
ISBN Prefix(es): 978-3-88829
Number of titles published annually: 2 Print
Total Titles: 35 Print
Parent Company: Hachmeister Galerie

Walter Haedecke Verlag+
Lukas-Moser-Weg 2, 71263 Weil der Stadt
Tel: (07033) 13 80 80 *Fax:* (07033) 138 08 13
E-mail: info@haedecke-verlag.de
Web Site: www.haedecke-verlag.de
Key Personnel
Owner & Publisher: Joachim Graff *E-mail:* jo.graff@haedecke-verlag.de
Editorial: Monika Graff *Tel:* (07033) 138 08 12
E-mail: mo.graff@haedecke-verlag.de
Production: Simone Graff *E-mail:* simone.graff@haedecke-verlag.de
Press & Sales: Sabine Bruder *E-mail:* sabine.bruder@haedecke-verlag.de
Founded: 1919
Subjects: Cookery, Health, Nutrition, Self-Help, Wine & Spirits
ISBN Prefix(es): 978-3-7750
Number of titles published annually: 16 Print
Total Titles: 112 Print
Distributor for D+R Verlag/Edition A la Carte; Fona Verlag AG; Helmut Metz Verlag; Verlag Ismero; NaturaViva Verlags GmbH
Foreign Rep(s): Christian Hirtzy (Austria); Sebastian Inhauser Vertretung-PR-Marketing fuer Verlage & Buchhandel (Switzerland); Ernst Sonntag (North Austria, South Austria, South Tyrol, Italy)
Distribution Center: Dr Franz Hain Verlagsauslieferungen GmbH, Dr-Otto-Neurath-Gasse

5, 1220 Vienna, Austria *Tel:* (01) 282 65 65
Fax: (01) 282 52 82
Buchzentrum AG, Industriestr Ost 10, 4614 Haegendorf, Switzerland *Tel:* (062) 209 26 26
Fax: (062) 209 26 27

Dr Curt Haefner-Verlag GmbH+
Ernst-Mey-Str 8, 70771 Leinfelden-Echterdingen
Tel: (0711) 7594-0 *Fax:* (0711) 7594-390
Web Site: www.konradin.de
Key Personnel
Mng Dir: Peter Dilger; Katja Kohlhammer *Tel:* (0711) 7594-202 *E-mail:* katja.kohlhammer@konradin.de
Founded: 1958
Subjects: Business, Child Care & Development, Education, Health, Nutrition, Human Relations, Medicine, Nursing, Dentistry, Public Administration, Science (General), Social Sciences, Sociology, Occupational Health & Safety
ISBN Prefix(es): 978-3-87284
Total Titles: 22 Print
Parent Company: Konradin Mediengruppe

Haeusser Media+
Frankfurter Str 64, 64293 Darmstadt
Tel: (06151) 22824 *Fax:* (06151) 26854
E-mail: info@haeusser-media.com
Web Site: www.haeusser-media.com
Key Personnel
Owner: Juergen Haeusser
Founded: 1984
Subjects: Architecture & Interior Design, Art, Literature, Literary Criticism, Essays
ISBN Prefix(es): 978-3-927902; 978-3-89552

Haffmans & Tolkemitt GmbH
Inselstr 12, 10179 Berlin
Tel: (030) 240 472 39 *Fax:* (030) 240 474 15
E-mail: office@haffmans-tolkemitt.de
Web Site: haffmans-tolkemitt.de
Key Personnel
Dir: Till Tolkemitt
Press & Public Relations: Stella Haffmans
E-mail: haffmans@haffmans-tolkemitt.de
Sales & Marketing: Jacob Karsten
E-mail: karsten@haffmans-tolkemitt.de
Subjects: Literature, Literary Criticism, Essays, Nonfiction (General), Outdoor Recreation
ISBN Prefix(es): 978-3-942989

Hagemann & Partner Bildungsmedien Verlagsgesellschaft mbH+
Karlstr 20, 40210 Duesseldorf
Tel: (0211) 17 92 70 0 *Fax:* (0211) 17 92 70 70
E-mail: aktuell@hagemann.de
Web Site: www.hagemann.de
Key Personnel
Mng Dir: Christian Machalet *Tel:* (0211) 179270-33 *E-mail:* machalet@hagemann.de
Dir: Christoph W J Hercher; Roland F O Hercher; Thomas Stark
Founded: 1929
Publisher of educational media to facilitate learning & teaching.
Membership(s): Association of School Book Publishers; German Didactic Associations; VGS (Verlagsgesellschaft mbH & Co KG); Worlddidac.
Subjects: Biological Sciences, Environmental Studies, Health, Nutrition, Physical Sciences
ISBN Prefix(es): 978-3-544
Warehouse: Karlstr 16, 40210 Duesseldorf

Hahner Verlagsgesellschaft mbH+
Heidchenberg 11, 52076 Aachen-Hahn
Tel: (02408) 55 05 *Fax:* (02408) 58081
E-mail: office@hvg.de
Web Site: www.hvg.de
Key Personnel
Mng Dir: Eva Brand; Peter Brand; Dr Winfried Spiegel

Founded: 1986
Subjects: Science (General)
ISBN Prefix(es): 978-3-89294
Parent Company: IZOP-Institut zur Objektivierung von Lern-und Pruefungsverfahren GmbH

Verlag Hahnsche Buchhandlung+
Leinstr 32, 30159 Hannover
Tel: (0511) 80 71 80 40 *Fax:* (0511) 36 36 98
E-mail: info@hahnsche-buchhandlung.de; order@hahnsche-buchhandlung.de
Web Site: www.hahnsche-buchhandlung.de
Key Personnel
Publisher: Elisabeth Freifrau von Schuetz
Founded: 1792
Specialize in German history.
Membership(s): Association of German Magazine Publishers; Stock Exchange of German Booksellers.
Subjects: Archaeology, Education, History, Regional Interests, Classical Languages, Jewish History, Medieval Studies
ISBN Prefix(es): 978-3-7752
Distribution Center: Koch, Neff & Oetinger Verlagsauslieferung GmbH, Industriestr 23, 70565 Stuttgart *E-mail:* hahnsche-buchhandlung@knova.de

Herbert von Halem Verlagsgesellschat mbH & Co KG
Lindenstr 19, 50674 Cologne
Tel: (0221) 9258 29-0 *Fax:* (0221) 9258 29-29
E-mail: info@halem-verlag.de
Web Site: www.halem-verlag.de
Key Personnel
Contact: Herbert von Halem
This publisher has indicated that 40% of their product line is author subsidized.
Subjects: Communications, Government, Political Science, Journalism, Library & Information Sciences, Philosophy, Radio, TV, Social Sciences, Sociology, Sports, Athletics, Cultural Studies, Image Science, Visual Communication
ISBN Prefix(es): 978-3-931606; 978-3-938258; 978-3-86962
Number of titles published annually: 25 Print
Total Titles: 100 Print

Hallwag, *imprint of* Graefe und Unzer Verlag GmbH

Hamburg University Press
Von-Melle-Park 3, 20146 Hamburg
Tel: (040) 42838 71 46 *Fax:* (040) 42838-33 52
E-mail: info.hup@sub.uni-hamburg.de; order.hup@sub.uni-hamburg.de
Web Site: hup.sub.uni-hamburg.de
Key Personnel
Library Dir: Dr Gabriele Beger *Tel:* (040) 42838 22 11 *E-mail:* beger@sub.uni-hamburg.de
Publishing Dir: Isabella Meinecke
E-mail: meinecke@sub.uni-hamburg.de
Publisher of the State & University Library Hamburg Carl von Ossietzky.
Subjects: Science (General)
ISBN Prefix(es): 978-3-937816

Hamburger Edition
Mittelweg 36, 20148 Hamburg
Tel: (040) 414097-0 *Fax:* (040) 414097-11
E-mail: verlag@hamburger-edition.de
Web Site: www.hamburger-edition.de
Founded: 1994
Subjects: Government, Political Science, History, Social Sciences, Sociology
ISBN Prefix(es): 978-3-86854
Parent Company: Hamburger Institut fuer Sozialforschung

Hamburger Lesehefte Verlag Ingwert Paulsen Jr eK
Subsidiary of Husum Druck- und Verlagsge-
sellschaft mbH u Co KG
Nordbahnhofstr 2, 25813 Husum
Mailing Address: Postfach 1480, 25804 Husum
Tel: (04841) 8352-0 *Fax:* (04841) 8352-10
E-mail: info@verlagsgruppe.de
Web Site: www.verlagsgruppe.de
Key Personnel
Mng Dir: Ingwert Paulsen
Founded: 1953
ISBN Prefix(es): 978-3-87291
Associate Companies: Hansa Verlag Ingwert
Paulsen Jr; Verlag der Kunst Dresden Ingwert
Paulsen Jr; Matthiesen Verlag Ingwert Paulsen
Jr; Verlag der Nation Ingwert Paulsen Jr; Turm-
schreiber Verlag Ingwert Paulsen Jr

Liselotte Hamecher
Goethestr 18, 34119 Kassel
Tel: (0561) 775262 *Fax:* (0561) 775262
Key Personnel
Owner: Liselotte Hamecher
Founded: 1947
Subjects: History, Maritime, Military Science
ISBN Prefix(es): 978-3-920307
Shipping Address: Goethestr 74, 34119 Kassel
Warehouse: Goethestr 74, 34119 Kassel

Peter Hammer Verlag GmbH+
Foehrenstr 33-35, 42283 Wuppertal
Mailing Address: Postfach 20 09 63, 42209 Wup-
pertal
Tel: (0202) 505066; (0202) 505067 *Fax:* (0202)
509252
E-mail: info@peter-hammer-verlag.de
Web Site: www.peter-hammer-verlag.de
Key Personnel
Publishing Manager: Monika Bilstein
E-mail: mbilstein@peter-hammer-verlag.de
Advertising & Press: Dr Claudia Putz
E-mail: cputz@peter-hammer-verlag.de
Production: Magdalene Krumbeck
Sales: Moritz Klein *E-mail:* mklein@peter-
hammer-verlag.de
Founded: 1966
Subjects: Developing Countries, Foreign Coun-
tries, Literature, Literary Criticism, Essays,
Nonfiction (General)
ISBN Prefix(es): 978-3-87294; 978-3-7795
Associate Companies: Jugenddienst Verlag,
Foehrenstr 33-35, 42283 Wuppertal
Foreign Rep(s): Beat Eberle (Switzerland); Erich
Neuhold (Austria); Harald Rumpold (Austria)
Distribution Center: Prolit Verlagsauslieferung
GmbH, Postfach 9, 35461 Fernwald-Annerod,
Contact: Rainer Eckert *Tel:* (0641) 94393-33
Fax: (0641) 94393-199 *E-mail:* r.eckert@prolit.
de
Dr Franz Hain GmbH, Dr-Otto-Neurath-Gasse
5, 1220 Vienna, Austria *Tel:* (01) 2826565
Fax: (01) 2825282 *E-mail:* bestell@hain.at
AVA Verlagsauslieferung AG, Centralweg 16,
Postfach 27, 8910 Affoltern am Albis, Switzer-
land *Tel:* (044) 7624260 *Fax:* (044) 7624210
E-mail: verlagsservice@ava.ch

Edition Hamouda
Hermann-Loens-Str 17, 04316 Leipzig
Tel: (0341) 2270370; (0176) 62791221 (cell)
Fax: (0341) 6994260
E-mail: info@hamouda.de
Web Site: www.hamouda.de
Key Personnel
Publisher: Faycal Hamouda
Founded: 2006
Subjects: History, Literature, Literary Criticism,
Essays, Nonfiction (General), Cultural Studies
ISBN Prefix(es): 978-3-940075

Verlagsgruppe Handelsblatt GmbH & Co KG
Kasernenstr 67, 40213 Duesseldorf
Tel: (0211) 8 87 0 *Fax:* (0211) 8 87 29 80
E-mail: info@vhb.de
Web Site: www.vhb.de
Key Personnel
Executive Dir: Marianne Doelz; Joerg Mertens;
Claudia Michalski
Editor-in-Chief: Gabor Steingart
Press: Kerstin Jaumann *Tel:* (0211) 8 87 1015
E-mail: pressestelle@vhb.de
Founded: 1946
Subjects: Business, Finance, Law, Science (Gen-
eral)
ISBN Prefix(es): 978-3-87881; 978-3-7754; 978-
3-923206

Verlag Handwerk und Technik GmbH+
Lademannbogen 135, 22339 Hamburg
Mailing Address: Postfach 63 05 00, 22331 Ham-
burg
Tel: (040) 53808-0; (040) 53808-200 *Fax:* (040)
53808-101
E-mail: info@handwerk-technik.de; vertrieb@
handwerk-technik.de
Web Site: www.handwerk-technik.de
Key Personnel
Mng Dir: Peter Buechner; Ulrich Grunwald
Founded: 1949
Vocational education publisher.
Subjects: Automotive, Career Development, Ed-
ucation, Health, Nutrition, Labor, Industrial
Relations, Technology, Horticulture, Safety &
Security
ISBN Prefix(es): 978-3-582
Showroom(s): Informationsbuero Stuttgart mit
Verlagsausstellung, Feuerseeplatz 2, 70176
Stuttgart *Tel:* (0711) 61439-0 *Fax:* (0711)
61439-22 *E-mail:* verlag@holland-josenhans.de
Orders to: Technischer Fachbuch - Vertrieb AG,
Buerglister 29, 8400 Winterthur, Switzer-
land *Tel:* (052) 224 54 54 *Fax:* (052) 224
54 38 *E-mail:* info@lehrmittelshop.ch *Web
Site:* www.tfv.ch (Switzerland)
Veritas - Verlags und Handelsgessellschaft mbH
& Co OHG, Hafenstr 2 a, 4020 Linz, Aus-
tria *Tel:* (0732) 776451-2280 *Fax:* (0732)
776451-2239 *E-mail:* veritas@veritas.at *Web
Site:* www.veritas.at (Austria)

Verlagsanstalt Handwerk GmbH
Auf'm Tetelberg 7, 40221 Duesseldorf
Mailing Address: Postfach 105162, 40042 Dues-
seldorf
Tel: (0211) 390 98-0 *Fax:* (0211) 390 98-29
E-mail: info@verlagsanstalt-handwerk.de
Web Site: www.verlagsanstalt-handwerk.de
Key Personnel
Mng Dir: Hans Juergen Below
Chairman: Prof Wolfgang Schulhoff
Editorial Dir: Barbara Schnell *Tel:* (0211) 390 98-
12 *E-mail:* schnell@verlagsanstalt-handwerk.de
Sales Manager: Harald Buck *Tel:* (0211) 390 98-
20 *E-mail:* buck@verlagsanstalt-handwerk.de
Book Marketing: Sabine Manning *Tel:* (0211)
390 98-44 *E-mail:* manning@verlagsanstalt-
handwerk.de
Subjects: Architecture & Interior Design, Auto-
motive, Cookery, Electronics, Electrical En-
gineering, Engineering (General), House &
Home, How-to, Mechanical Engineering
ISBN Prefix(es): 978-3-87864

Hanfstaengl-Verlag, *imprint of* DACO Verlag
Guenter Blaese

Edition Hannemann, *imprint of* Verlag Stephanie
Naglschmid

Hansa Verlag Ingwert Paulsen Jr
Subsidiary of Husum Druck- und Verlagsgesellschaft mbH u Co KG

Nordbahnhofstr 2, 25813 Husum
Mailing Address: Postfach 1480, 25804 Husum
Tel: (04841) 8352-0 *Fax:* (04841) 8352-10
E-mail: info@verlagsgruppe.de
Web Site: www.verlagsgruppe.de
Key Personnel
Mng Dir: Ingwert Paulsen
Founded: 1954
Subjects: Literature, Literary Criticism, Essays
ISBN Prefix(es): 978-3-920421; 978-3-941629
Associate Companies: Hamburger Lesehefte Ver-
lag Ingwert Paulsen Jr ek; Verlag der Kunst
Dresden Ingwert Paulsen Jr eK; Matthiesen
Verlag Ingwert Paulsen Jr; Verlag der Nation
Ingwert Paulsen Jr; Turmschreiber Verlag In-
gwert Paulsen Jr; Frank Wagner Verlagsbuch-
handlung Ingwert Paulsen Jr eK

Carl Hanser Verlag GmbH & Co KG+
Kolbergerstr 22, 81679 Munich
Tel: (089) 9 98 30 0 *Fax:* (089) 98 48 09
E-mail: info@hanser.de
Web Site: www.hanser-literaturverlage.de
Key Personnel
Publr: Jo Lendle
Mng Dir & Publisher, Technical & Science:
Wolfgang Beisler *E-mail:* beisler@hanser.de
Mng Dir: Stephan D Joss
Publishing Dir, Professional Books: Dr Hermann
Riedel *E-mail:* riedel@hanser.de
Publishing Dir, Professional Magazines: Michael
Himmelstoss *E-mail:* himmelstoss@hanser.de
Sales Dir, Fiction & Nonfiction: Felici-
tas Feilhauer *Tel:* (089) 9 98 30-508
E-mail: feilhauer@hanser.de
Sales Dir, Technical & Science: Bettina Schubert
E-mail: schubert@hanser.de
Foreign Rights, Fiction & Nonfiction: Friederike
Barakat *E-mail:* barakat@hanser.de
Publicity, Fiction & Nonfiction: Christina Knecht
Tel: (089) 9 98 30-409 *E-mail:* knecht@hanser.
de
Founded: 1928
Subjects: Biography, Memoirs, Business, Com-
puter Science, Computers, Economics, Elec-
tronics, Electrical Engineering, Engineering
(General), Environmental Studies, Fiction,
Government, Political Science, History, Lit-
erature, Literary Criticism, Essays, Manage-
ment, Mathematics, Mechanical Engineering,
Music, Dance, Nonfiction (General), Philoso-
phy, Physics, Poetry, Religion - Other, Social
Sciences, Sociology, Travel & Tourism, Plastics
ISBN Prefix(es): 978-3-446
Subsidiaries: Hanser Berlin; Hanser Kinderbuch;
Hanser Weltgeschehen; Verlag Nagel & Kim-
che AG; Paul Zsolnay Verlag GmbH
U.S. Office(s): Hanser/Gardner Publishers Inc,
6915 Valley Ave, Cincinnati, OH 45244,
United States, Contact: Melissa Kline-Skavlem
Tel: 513-527-8977 *Fax:* 513-527-8950
Foreign Rep(s): Wolfgang Habenschuss (South
Austria, South Tyrol, Italy); Heinz Marti
(Switzerland); Martin Schlieber (Austria, South
Tyrol, Italy); Andrea Spychiger (Switzerland);
Dietmar Vorderwinkler (North Austria)
Foreign Rights: ACER (Spain); Balla & Co Liter-
ary Agents (Hungary); Agencja Literacka Graal
(Poland); The Deborah Harris Agency (Israel);
Hercules Business & Culture GmbH (Mainland
China); Simona Kessler International Copyright
Agency Ltd (Romania); Leonhardt & Hoier
Literary Agency ApS (Scandinavia); LiTrans
(Tino Koehler) (Netherlands); Meike Marx Lit-
erary Agency (Japan); Momo Agency (Korea);
Marco Vigevani (Italy)
Distribution Center: Dr Franz Hain Verlagsaus-
lieferung GmbH, Dr-Otto-Neurath-Gasse 5,
1220 Vienna, Austria *Tel:* (01) 282 65 77
Fax: (01) 282 52 82 *E-mail:* bestell@hain.at
Buchzentrum AG, Industriestr Ost 10, 8840 Hue-
gendorf, Switzerland *Tel:* (062) 209 26 26
Fax: (062) 209 26 27 *E-mail:* kundendiest@
buchzentrum.ch

Happy Science Deutschland eV
Rheinstr 63, 12159 Berlin
Tel: (030) 7895 7477 *Fax:* (030) 7895 7478
E-mail: kontakt@happy-science.de
Web Site: happy-science.de
Founded: 1986
Based on the teachings of Master Ryuho Okawa.
Subjects: Self-Help
ISBN Prefix(es): 978-3-942308

Hardt & Woerner Unternehmensberatung GbR+
Ruedesheimer Str 29, 65197 Wiesbaden
Tel: (0611) 97173902
Web Site: www.hardt-woerner.de
Key Personnel
Mng Dir: Jochen Woerner *E-mail:* j.woerner@hardt-woerner.de
Founded: 1993
Publishers consultants. Specialize in the book market of German speaking countries.
Subjects: Publishing & Book Trade Reference
ISBN Prefix(es): 978-3-930120
Total Titles: 12 Print

Harenberg, *imprint of* Bibliographisches Institut GmbH

Siegfried Haring Literatten-Verlag Ulm+
Weichselstr 21, 89231 Neu-Ulm
Tel: (0731) 9806040 *Fax:* (0731) 9806042
Key Personnel
Mng Dir: Siegfried Haering *E-mail:* siegfried.haering@kabelmail.de
Founded: 1986
Subjects: Drama, Theater
ISBN Prefix(es): 978-3-926217

Harmonie-Verlag (Harmony Publications)
Guenterstalstr 12, 79100 Freiburg im Breisgau
Tel: (0761) 709667
Key Personnel
Dir: Regina Gaus
Subjects: Religion - Other
ISBN Prefix(es): 978-3-929474

HarperCollins Germany GmbH
Valentinskamp 24, 20354 Hamburg
Tel: (040) 6366 420-0 *Fax:* (0711) 7252-399
E-mail: service@harpercollins.de
Web Site: corporate.harpercollins.de
Key Personnel
Mng Dir & Publisher: Ralf Markmeier
Editorial Dir: Claudia Wuttke
Dir, Marketing & Sales: Katrin Jenner
Finance Dir: Eike von Germar
Executive Editor: Heide Kloth
Executive Editor, Children's Books/Young Adult: Carina Mathern
ISBN Prefix(es): 978-3-95967
Foreign Rep(s): Buchzentrum AG (Cornelia Frese) (Switzerland); Mohr Morawa Buchvertrieb GmbH (Austria)
Distribution Center: Sigloch Distribution GmbH & Co KG, Sigloch Service Center, Am Buchberg 8, 74572 Blaufelden
Tel: (07953) 7189-067 *Fax:* (07953) 883-130
E-mail: harpercollins@sigloch.de

Harrassowitz Verlag+
Kreuzberger Ring 7b-d, 65205 Wiesbaden
Tel: (0611) 530-905 *Fax:* (0611) 530-999
E-mail: verlag@harrassowitz.de
Web Site: www.harrassowitz-verlag.de
Key Personnel
Dir: Dr Barbara Krauss *E-mail:* bkrauss@harrassowitz.de
Rights: Andrea Johari *E-mail:* ajohari@harrassowitz.de
Editor: Tamara Kuhn *E-mail:* tkuhn@harrrassowitz.de

Production Manager: Reinhard Friedrich
E-mail: rfriedrich@harrassowitz.de
Sales: Robert Gietz *Tel:* (0611) 530-901
E-mail: rgietz@harrassowitz.de
Order Fulfillment: Gunnar Manz
Founded: 1872
Specialize in Oriental studies, book studies, cultural history, Slavic studies & Eastern European research.
Subjects: Asian Studies, Language Arts, Linguistics, Library & Information Sciences, Civic Studies, Eastern European Research
ISBN Prefix(es): 978-3-447
Number of titles published annually: 180 Print
Total Titles: 3,000 Print
Parent Company: Otto Harrassowitz GmbH & Co KG
Distributor for Herzog August Bibliothek Wolfenbuettel

Haschemi Edition Cologne Kunstverlag fuer Fotografie+
Eupenerstr 124, 50933 Cologne
Tel: (0221) 561007; (0221) 561008 *Fax:* (0221) 529282
E-mail: info@haschemi.de
Web Site: www.haschemi.de; cms.haschemi.de
Key Personnel
International Rights: Baback Haschemi
Founded: 1982
Subjects: Photography, Travel & Tourism
ISBN Prefix(es): 978-3-924169; 978-3-931282; 978-3-936222
Subsidiaries: Haschemi Edition Virginia

Hatje Cantz Verlag GmbH+
Mommsenstr 27, 10629 Berlin
Tel: (030) 3464678-00 *Fax:* (030) 3289042-48
E-mail: contact@hatjecantz.de; berlin@hatjecantz.de; sales@hatjecantz.de; presse@hatjecantz.de
Web Site: www.hatjecantz.de
Key Personnel
Publisher & Program Dir: Dr Cristina Ines Steingraeber
Chief Operating Officer & Head, Operations: Martin Wichert *Tel:* (030) 3646678-43
Mng Dir: Dr Thomas P J Feinen *Tel:* (030) 3464678-04
Marketing Dir: Sascha Perkins *Tel:* (030) 3464678-20
Press Dir: Sara Buschmann *Tel:* (030) 3464678-08 *Fax:* (030) 3289042-62
Production Dir: Nadine Schmidt *Tel:* (030) 3464678-30
Sales Dir: Daniel Engels *Tel:* (030) 3464678-19
Founded: 1945
Publisher of art books, books on architecture, design & photography, exhibition catalogues.
Subjects: Architecture & Interior Design, Art, Photography
ISBN Prefix(es): 978-3-7757
Number of titles published annually: 150 Print
Total Titles: 1,000 Print
Associate Companies: KQ kunstquartal
Branch Office(s)
Postwiesenstr 5a, 70327 Stuttgart *Tel:* (0711) 4405-200 *Fax:* (0711) 4405-220
Distributed by DAP Distributed Art Publishers New York
Foreign Rep(s): Bookport Associates (Alessandro Corno & Joe Portelli) (Southeast Europe, Southern Europe); Elisabeth Harder-Kreimann (Scandinavia); IMA/InterMediaAmericana Ltd (David Williams) (Central America, Mexico, South America); Infinite Book & Art Services (Haruhiko Oguchi) (Japan); Seth Meyer-Bruhns (Austria); Publishers International Marketing Ltd (Chris Ashdown) (East Asia, Russia, Southeast Asia exc Japan); Sara Books Pvt Ltd (Ravindra Saxena) (Bangladesh, India, Pakistan, Sri Lanka); Scheidegger & Co AG (Stephanie Brunner) (Switzerland); Jan Smit

(Netherlands); Ward International Ltd (Richard Ward) (Middle East)
Distribution Center: Koch, Neff & Oetinger Verlagsauslieferung GmbH, Industriestr 23, 70565 Stuttgart, Contact: Antje Grimm *E-mail:* hatjecantz@kno-va.de *Web Site:* www.kno-va.de
booksatmanic distribution, PO Box 8, Carlton North, Victoria 3054, Australia *Tel:* (03) 9380 5337 *Fax:* (03) 9380 5037 *E-mail:* manicex@manic.com.au *Web Site:* www.manic.com.au
Exhibitions International, Kol Begaultlaan 17, 3012 Leuven, Belgium *Tel:* (016) 296900 *Fax:* (016) 296129 *E-mail:* orders@exhibitionsinternational.be *Web Site:* www.exhibitionsinternational.be
Interart, One Rue de l'Est, 75020 Paris, France *Tel:* 01 43 49 36 60 *Fax:* 01 43 49 41 22 *E-mail:* commercial@interart.fr *Web Site:* www.interart.fr
AVA Verlagsauslieferungen AG, Centralweg 16, 8910 Affoltern am Albis, Switzerland *Tel:* (044) 76242-50 *Fax:* (044) 76242-10 *E-mail:* verlagsservice@ava.ch *Web Site:* www.ava.ch
Gestalten UK Ltd, 65 London Wall, London EC2M 5TU, United Kingdom, Contact: Emma Ferguson *Tel:* (020) 7628 4829 *Fax:* (020) 7628 4828 *E-mail:* e.ferguson@gestalten.com *Web Site:* www.gestalten.com
Artbook/DAP, 155 Avenue of the Americas, 2nd floor, New York, NY 10013-1507, United States *Tel:* 212-627-1999 *Fax:* 212-627-9484 *E-mail:* orders@dapinc.com *Web Site:* www.artbook.com

Haufe-Hammonia Corporate Publishing+
Tangstedter Landstr 83, 22415 Hamburg
Tel: (040) 520103-0 *Fax:* (040) 520103-12
E-mail: info@hammonia.de
Web Site: www.hammonia.de
Key Personnel
Dir: Heike Labsch *Tel:* (040) 520103-48 *E-mail:* labsch@haufe-hammonia.de
Contact: Thomas Chiandone *Tel:* (040) 520103-62 *E-mail:* chiandone@haufe-hammonia.de; Birgit Jacobs *Tel:* (040) 520103-61 *E-mail:* jacobs@haufe-hammonia.de
Founded: 1946
Specialize in books, magazines, etc for housing & real estate.
Subjects: Architecture & Interior Design, Civil Engineering, Engineering (General), Real Estate
ISBN Prefix(es): 978-3-87292
Number of titles published annually: 20 Print
Total Titles: 120 Print
Warehouse: VSB-Verlagsservice Braunschweig GmbH, Georg-Westermann-Allee 66, 38104 Braunschweig
Distribution Center: VSB-Verlagsservice Braunschweig GmbH, Georg-Westermann-Allee 66, 38104 Braunschweig

Haufe-Lexware GmbH & Co KG+
Munzinger Str 9, 79111 Freiburg
Tel: (0761) 89 80 *Toll Free Tel:* 0800 50 50 445 *Fax:* (0761) 89 83 900 *Toll Free Fax:* 0800 50 50 446
E-mail: info@haufe.de; service@haufe.de
Web Site: www.haufe.de
Key Personnel
Mng Dir: Markus Reithwiesner
Corporate Communications: Joerg Frey *Tel:* (0761) 898-3184 *Fax:* (0761) 898-993184 *E-mail:* presse@haufe-lexware.com
Editor: Joachim Rotzinger
Founded: 1934
Subjects: Accounting, Business, Career Development, Computer Science, Economics, Finance, Law, Management, Marketing, Real Estate
ISBN Prefix(es): 978-3-448; 978-3-8092

Parent Company: Haufe Gruppe
Orders to: Postfach 1363, 82152 Planegg, Munich
  Tel: (089) 89 51 7245 *Fax:* (089) 89 51 7260
  E-mail: buchhandel@haufe-lexware.com

Dr Ernst Hauswedell & Co KG Verlag+
Haldenstr 30, 70334 Stuttgart
Tel: (0711) 54 99 71-11 *Fax:* (0711) 54 99 71-21
E-mail: verlag@hauswedell.de
Web Site: www.hauswedell.de
Key Personnel
Contact: Gerd Hiersemann
Press: Florian Hiersemann
Founded: 1927
Subjects: Antiques, Art, Library & Information
  Sciences, Publishing & Book Trade Reference,
  Science (General), Theology, Byzantine Stud-
  ies, Central Latin Studies, History of Science,
  Literature, Typography
ISBN Prefix(es): 978-3-7762
Number of titles published annually: 10 Print
Total Titles: 200 Print; 8 CD-ROM
Associate Companies: Anton Hiersemann
  KG Verlag, Haldenstr 30, 70376 Stuttgart
  Tel: (0711) 549971-11 *Fax:* (0711) 549971-21
  E-mail: verlag@hiersemann.de *Web Site:* www.
  hiersemann.de
Distributor for Staats-und Universitaets-Bibliothek
  Hamburg

Hawel Verlag
Haupstr 23, 86757 Wallerstein
Tel: (09081) 27 50 26-5 *Fax:* (09081) 27 50 26-9
E-mail: info@hawelverlag.de
Web Site: www.hawelverlag.de
Key Personnel
Owner & Publisher: Dr Peter Hawel
Subjects: Art, History, Theology
ISBN Prefix(es): 978-3-9810376

Hayit Medien+
Unit of Mundo Marketing GmbH
Vorgebirgstr 59, 50677 Cologne
Tel: (0221) 921635-0 *Fax:* (0221) 921635-24
E-mail: kontakt@hayit.de
Web Site: www.hayit.de
Key Personnel
Mng Dir & Publisher: Ertay Hayit
  E-mail: ertay@hayit.de
Publishing Dir: Cornelia Auschra
  E-mail: auschra@hayit.de
Editorial: Ute Hayit *Tel:* (0221) 921635-11
  E-mail: ute@hayit.de
Founded: 1978
Subjects: How-to, Marketing, Nonfiction (Gen-
  eral), Travel & Tourism
ISBN Prefix(es): 978-3-87322

Haymarket Media GmbH & Co KG+
Member of Horti Media Europe (HME)
Frankfurter Str 3d, 38122 Braunschweig
Tel: (0531) 38 00 4-0 *Fax:* (0531) 38 00 4-25
E-mail: info@haymarket.de
Web Site: www.haymarket.de
Key Personnel
Mng Dir: Dr Nicolas Bogs
Publishing Dir: Uwe Schuett
Founded: 1867
Specialize in technical literature of gardening &
  floral design, newspapers, magazines, technical
  books & reference books.
Membership(s): Boersenverein des Deutschen
  Buchandels; Verband Deutscher Zeitschriften
  Verleger.
Subjects: Agriculture, Gardening, Plants
ISBN Prefix(es): 978-3-87815; 978-3-87170
Number of titles published annually: 10 Print
Total Titles: 80 Print

**Heckner Druck-und Verlagsgesellschaft mbH
  & Co KG**
Harzstr 22, 38300 Wolfenbuettel

Tel: (05331) 80 08-0 *Fax:* (05331) 80 08-16
Founded: 1895
Subjects: Career Development, Economics
ISBN Prefix(es): 978-3-449
Parent Company: Kieser Verlag GmbH, Neusaess
Distributed by Orell Fuessli (Switzerland)

Heel Verlag GmbH+
Pottscheidt 1, 53639 Koenigswinter
Tel: (02223) 9230-0; (02223) 9230-38
  Fax: (02223) 9230-13; (02223) 9230-26
E-mail: info@heel-verlag.de
Web Site: www.heel-verlag.de
Key Personnel
President: Franz-Christoph Heel *Tel:* (02223)
  9230-11 *E-mail:* fc.heel@heel-verlag.de
Foreign Rights Dir: Karin Michelberger
  Tel: (02223) 9230-46 *E-mail:* k.michelberger@
  heel-verlag.de
Founded: 1980
Subjects: Aeronautics, Aviation, Automotive,
  Cookery, Crafts, Games, Hobbies, Fashion,
  Film, Video, Gardening, Plants, Health, Nu-
  trition, Humor, Maritime, Music, Dance, Non-
  fiction (General), Outdoor Recreation, Pho-
  tography, Science Fiction, Fantasy, Technol-
  ogy, Transportation, Travel & Tourism, Wine &
  Spirits
ISBN Prefix(es): 978-3-922858; 978-3-89365;
  978-3-89880
Number of titles published annually: 120 Print
Total Titles: 600 Print
Distributor for Highlights Verlag
Foreign Rights: Copyright Agency of China
  (China, Taiwan); Moseley Road Inc (worldwide
  exc China, Japan, Korea, Spain, Thailand &
  USA); Susanne Theune (Latin America, Span-
  ish & Portuguese)
Warehouse: VSB-Verlagsservice, Helmstetter Str
  99, 38126 Braunschweig *Tel:* (0531) 708650
  Fax: (0531) 708608
Returns: VSB-Verlagsservice, Helmstetter Str
  99, 38126 Braunschweig *Tel:* (0531) 708650
  Fax: (0531) 795939

Edition Elke Heidenreich, *imprint of*
  Verlagsgruppe Random House Bertelsmann

Joh Heider Verlag GmbH
Paffrather Str 102-116, 51465 Bergisch Gladbach
Tel: (02202) 9540-0 *Fax:* (02202) 21531
E-mail: info@heider-medien.de
Web Site: www.heider-verlag.de
Key Personnel
Mng Dir: Hans-Martin Heider; Roberto Heider
Founded: 1889
Subjects: Art, Economics, Law, Social Sciences,
  Sociology
ISBN Prefix(es): 978-3-87314

Verlag Horst Heigl+
Oberhaslach 6, 88633 Heiligenberg
Tel: (07552) 938754 *Fax:* (07552) 938756
E-mail: shop@heigl-verlag.de
Web Site: www.heigl-verlag.de
Key Personnel
Author & Manager: Horst Heigl
Author: Birgitt Heigl
Founded: 1987
Subjects: Art, Asian Studies, Astrology, Occult,
  Biography, Memoirs, Child Care & Develop-
  ment, Fiction, Inspirational, Spirituality, Music,
  Dance, Physical Sciences, Religion - Other,
  Science (General), Self-Help
ISBN Prefix(es): 978-3-89316
Total Titles: 13 Print; 10 Audio

Verlag Otto Heinevetter Lehrmittel GmbH
Papenstr 41, 22089 Hamburg
Tel: (040) 25 90 19 *Fax:* (040) 251 2128
E-mail: info@heinevetter-verlag.de

Web Site: www.heinevetter-verlag.de
Key Personnel
Manager: Werner Klopfer
Founded: 1947
Subjects: Child Care & Development, Education,
  Primary Education
ISBN Prefix(es): 978-3-87474

Heinrich-Boell-Stiftung eV
Schumannstr 8, 10117 Berlin
Tel: (030) 285 34-0 *Fax:* (030) 285 34-109
E-mail: info@boell.de
Web Site: www.boell.de
Key Personnel
Mng Dir: Dr Livia Cotta
Head, Public Relations: Annette Maennel
  E-mail: maennel@boell.de
Germany Public Relations Officer: Vera Lorenz
  Tel: (030) 285 34-217 *E-mail:* lorenz@boell.de
International Public Relations Officer: Michael
  Alvarez Kalverkamp *Tel:* (030) 285 34-202
  E-mail: alvarez@boell.de
Founded: 1997
Subjects: Economics, Education, Government,
  Political Science, Social Sciences, Sociology,
  Culture, Current Affairs, Democracy, Ecology,
  Human Rights, International Politics, Social
  Issues, Sustainability
ISBN Prefix(es): 978-3-86928

Heinrichshofen-Books, see Florian Noetzel
  Verlage GmbH

Heinrichshofen's Verlag GmbH & Co KG+
Liebigstr 16, 26389 Wilhelmshaven
Tel: (04421) 9267-0 *Fax:* (04421) 9267-99
E-mail: info@heinrichshofen.de
Web Site: www.heinrichshofen.de
Key Personnel
Mng Dir: Katharina Kreiner
Sales Manager: Jutta Holtz *Tel:* (04421) 777760
  E-mail: holtz@heinrichshofen.de
Founded: 1797
Instrumental music books for children & adults.
Subjects: Music, Dance
ISBN Prefix(es): 978-3-938202
Number of titles published annually: 25 Print
Total Titles: 5,500 Print; 40 CD-ROM
Associate Companies: Otto Heinrich Noetzel Ver-
  lag; C F Peters Corp, 70-30 80 St, Glendale,
  NY 11385, United States
Distributed by C F Peters Corp (New York); Pe-
  ters Edition (London)

Edition Heitere Poetik, *imprint of* Verlag Beruf
  + Schule

Heitz Librarie, *imprint of* Verlag Valentin
  Koerner GmbH

Helbling Verlag GmbH
Martinstr 42-44, 73728 Esslingen
Mailing Address: Postfach 10 07 54, 73707
  Esslingen
Tel: (0711) 75 87 01-0 *Fax:* (0711) 75 87 01-11
E-mail: service@helbling.com
Web Site: www.helbling-verlag.de
Key Personnel
Chief Executive Officer: Markus Spielmann
Publishing Dir: Alwin Wollinger
Founded: 1946
Specialize in music education, choir, primary edu-
  cation & English language teaching.
Subjects: Education, Language Arts, Linguistics,
  Music, Dance, Choral Music
ISBN Prefix(es): 978-3-85061; 978-3-900590
Distributed by Delta Publishing; Heinle ELT; Hel-
  bling Languages

HelfRecht Verlag und Druck
Markgrafenstr 32, 95680 Bad Alexandersbad

Tel: (09232) 601-0 *Fax:* (09232) 601-280
E-mail: info@helfrecht.de
Web Site: www.helfrecht.de
Key Personnel
Dir: Volkmar Helfrecht *Tel:* (09232) 601-262
   E-mail: v.helfrecht@helfrecht.de
Founded: 1975
Subjects: Career Development, Economics
ISBN Prefix(es): 978-3-920400
Parent Company: HelfRecht Unternehmerische
   Planungsmethoden AG

Heliopolis-Verlag Ewald Katzmann+
Schellingstr 41, 72072 Tuebingen
Tel: (07071) 760444
Key Personnel
Mng Dir: Dr Volker Katzmann
Founded: 1949
ISBN Prefix(es): 978-3-87324
Associate Companies: Katzmann-Verlag KG
Orders to: Postfach 1827, 72072 Tubingen

Hellerau-Verlag Dresden GmbH
Voglerstr 23, 01277 Dresden
Tel: (0351) 803 52 93 *Fax:* (0351) 315 84 30
E-mail: info@hellerau-verlag.de
Web Site: www.hellerau-verlag.de
Key Personnel
Publisher: Dr Lothar Dunsch
Founded: 1990
Subjects: Fiction, History, Regional Interests
ISBN Prefix(es): 978-3-910184

Ulrike Helmer Verlag+
Neugartenstr 36c, 65843 Sulzbach/Taunus
Tel: (06196) 2029977 *Fax:* (06196) 2029976
E-mail: info@ulrike-helmer-verlag.de
Web Site: helmer.txt-web.de; helmer.txt9.de
Key Personnel
Mng Dir: Ulrike Helmer
Founded: 1988
Subjects: Fiction, History, LGBTQ, Literature,
   Literary Criticism, Essays, Nonfiction (Gen-
   eral), Philosophy, Science (General), Social
   Sciences, Sociology, Women's Studies
ISBN Prefix(es): 978-3-927164; 978-3-89741
Foreign Rep(s): Elisabeth Anintach-Hirt (Austria);
   Dagmar Bhend (Switzerland)
Distribution Center: GVA Gemeinsame
   Verlagsauslieferung Goettingen, Anna-
   Vandenhoeck-Ring 36, 37081 Goettingen
   Tel: (0551) 48 71 77 *Fax:* (0551) 4 13 92
   E-mail: bestellung@gva-verlage.de
Medienlogistik Pichler-OEBZ, IZ NOE-Sued Str
   1 Objekt 34, 2355 Wiener Neudorf, Austria
   Tel: (02236) 635 35 290 *Fax:* (02236) 635 35
   243 *E-mail:* bestellen@medien-logistik.at
Scheidegger AG/AVA, Centralweg 16, Af-
   foltern am Albis 8910, Switzerland
   Tel: (01) 762 42 50 *Fax:* (01) 762 42 10
   E-mail: verlagsservice@ava.ch

G Henle Verlag ek
Forstenrieder Allee 122, 81476 Munich
Mailing Address: Postfach 71 04 66, 81454 Mu-
   nich
Tel: (089) 759820 *Fax:* (089) 7598240
E-mail: info@henle.de
Web Site: www.henle.de
Key Personnel
Chief Executive Officer & President: Dr Wolf-
   Dieter Seiffert *E-mail:* seiffert@henle.de
Editor-in-Chief: Dr Norbert Gertsch
   E-mail: gertsch@henle.de
Head, Manufacturing: Gabi Lamprecht
   E-mail: lamprecht@henle.de
Head, Sales & Marketing: Dr Sigrun Jantzen
   E-mail: jantzen@henle.de
Founded: 1948
Subjects: Music, Dance, Complete Editions
   (Brahms, Haydn & Beethoven), Music Books
   & Catalogs, Urtext Editions of Classical Music

ISBN Prefix(es): 978-3-87328
Number of titles published annually: 50 Print
Total Titles: 1,500 Print
Distributed by Hal Leonard (USA)

Henrich Druck + Medien GmbH
Schwanheimer Str 110, 60528 Frankfurt am Main
Tel: (069) 9 67 77-0 *Fax:* (069) 9 67 77-111
E-mail: info@henrich.de
Web Site: www.henrich.de
Key Personnel
Mng Dir: Cristina Calbeto Henrich-Kalveram;
   Ursula Henrich
Founded: 1901
Subjects: Art, Fiction, History, Poetry
ISBN Prefix(es): 978-3-921606; 978-3-943407

Henschel Verlag, *imprint of* Seemann Henschel
   GmbH & Co KG

Hentrich & Hentrich Verlag+
Wilhemstr 118, 10963 Berlin
Tel: (030) 609 23 865 *Fax:* (030) 609 23 866
E-mail: info@hentrichhentrich.de; presse@
   hentrichhentrich.de; vertrieb@hentrichhentrich.
   de
Web Site: www.hentrichhentrich.de
Key Personnel
Owner: Dr Nora Pester
Founded: 1982
Subjects: Art, Biography, Memoirs, Drama, The-
   ater, Government, Political Science, History,
   Nonfiction (General), Religion - Jewish, Social
   Sciences, Sociology, Jewish Life & Culture,
   Nazism
ISBN Prefix(es): 978-3-89468; 978-3-926175;
   978-3-938485; 978-3-942271; 978-3-933471;
   978-3-941450; 978-3-95565
Distribution Center: Runge Verlagsauslieferung
   GmbH, Bergstr 2, 33803 Steinhagen, Contact:
   Team 3 *Tel:* (05204) 998 123 *Fax:* (05204)
   998 114 *E-mail:* msr@rungeva.de *Web
   Site:* rungeva.de

**Edition Hentrich Druck-und Verlag Gebr
   Hentrich und Tank GmbH & Co KG**, see
   Hentrich & Hentrich Verlag

Herausgeber, *imprint of* Johann Wolfgang
   Goethe-Universitaet Frankfurt am Main

F A Herbig Verlagsbuchhandlung GmbH+
Thomas Wimmer Ring 11, 80539 Munich
Tel: (089) 29088-0 *Fax:* (089) 29088-144
E-mail: info@herbig.net
Web Site: www.herbig.net
Key Personnel
Publisher: Brigitte Fleissner-Mikorey
Foreign Rights Dir: Sonja Schmidt *Tel:* (089)
   29088-157 *E-mail:* s.schmidt@herbig.net
Sales Manager: Sissi Klauser *Tel:* (089) 29088-
   129
Press: Anja Volkmer *Tel:* (089) 29088-132
   Fax: (089) 29088-178 *E-mail:* a.volkmer@
   herbig.net
Production: Ina Hesse *Tel:* (089) 29088-128
   Fax: (089) 29088-166 *E-mail:* i.hesse@herbig.
   net
Founded: 1821
Subjects: Art, Astronomy, Biography, Memoirs,
   Cookery, Health, Nutrition, History, Nonfiction
   (General), Physical Sciences, Travel & Tourism
ISBN Prefix(es): 978-3-7766; 978-3-7844; 978-
   3-88010; 978-3-8004; 978-3-485; 978-3-607;
   978-3-922170
Distributed by Amalthea-Verlag
Foreign Rep(s): Johann Czap (Austria); Michael
   Hipp (Austria); Markus Vonarburg (Switzer-
   land)
Orders to: VVA, An der Autobahn, 33310
   Guetersloh

Herder Audio, *imprint of* Verlag Kreuz GmbH

Herder-Institut eV
Gisonenweg 5-7, 35037 Marburg
Tel: (06421) 184-125 *Fax:* (06421) 184-210;
   (06421) 184-194
E-mail: verlag@herder-institut.de
Web Site: www.herder-institut.de
Key Personnel
Head, Publishing Dept: Dr Heidi Hein-Kircher
   Tel: (06421) 184-110 *E-mail:* heidi.hein-
   kircher@herder-institut.de
Manager, Publishing: Ruth Steinebach
   E-mail: ruth.steinebach@herder-institut.de
Specialize in the history & geography of East
   Central Europe.
Subjects: Geography, Geology, History
ISBN Prefix(es): 978-3-87969

Verlag Herder GmbH+
Kunden Service Center, Hermann-Herder-Str 4,
   79104 Freiburg
Tel: (0761) 2717-440; (0761) 2717-0 *Fax:* (0761)
   2717-360; (0761) 2717-520
E-mail: info@herder.de; kundenservice@herder.de
Web Site: www.herder.de
Key Personnel
Publisher & Mng Dir: Manuel Herder
Mng Dir: Olaf Carstens; Roland Grimmelsman
Rights Dir: Stefan Dalmuehle *Tel:* (0761) 2717-
   385 *Fax:* (0761) 2717-540 *E-mail:* dalmuehle@
   herder.de
Foreign Rights: Francesca Bressan
   Tel: (0761) 2717-546 *Fax:* (0761) 2717-540
   E-mail: bressan@herder.de; Polina Kuzavleva
   Tel: (0761) 2717-275 *Fax:* (0761) 2717-540
   E-mail: kuzavleva@herder.de
Founded: 1801
Subjects: Biblical Studies, Education, Govern-
   ment, Political Science, History, Inspirational,
   Spirituality, Nonfiction (General), Psychol-
   ogy, Psychiatry, Religion - Buddhist, Religion -
   Catholic, Religion - Islamic, Religion - Other,
   Self-Help, Theology
ISBN Prefix(es): 978-3-451
Associate Companies: Herder Editorial SL, Calle
   Provenza, 388, 08025 Barcelona, Spain *Tel:* 93
   476 26 26 *Fax:* 93 207 34 48 *E-mail:* herder@
   herdereditorial.com
Imprints: Verlag Karl Alber; Verlag Kerle; Verlag
   Josef Knecht; Verlag Kreuz; Verlag Urbania
Divisions: Spektrum
Foreign Rep(s): Joe A Fuchs (Switzerland); Ver-
   lagsagentur Erich Neuhold (Erich Neuhold)
   (Austria); Harald Rumpold (South Tyrol, Italy,
   Western Austria); Contsaze Wachsmann (Bel-
   gium, Luxembourg)
Book Club(s): Herder Buchgemeinde
Distribution Center: Koch, Neff & Oetinger Ver-
   lagsauslieferung GmbH, Industriestr 23, 70565
   Stuttgart *E-mail:* herder@kno-va.de (Germany
   & Austria)
Herder AG Basel Verlagsauslieferungen, Mut-
   tenzer Str 109, 4133 Pratteln 1, Switzer-
   land *Tel:* (061) 8279060 *Fax:* (061) 8279067
   E-mail: verkauf@herder.ch (Switzerland)

Herold-Verlag Dr Wetzel+
Kirchbachweg 16, 81479 Munich
Tel: (089) 7 91 57 74
E-mail: wetzel@herold-verlag.de
Web Site: www.herold-verlag.de
Key Personnel
Editor: Klaus-Michael Wetzel
Founded: 1871
ISBN Prefix(es): 978-3-7767
Orders to: MVS Meisinger Verlagsservice
   GmbH, Am Steinfeld 4, 94065 Waldkirchen
   Tel: (08581) 9605-0 *Fax:* (08581) 754

Carl Heymanns Verlag, *imprint of* Wolters Kluwer Deutschland GmbH

Carl Heymanns Verlag KG+
Imprint of Wolters Kluwer Deutschland GmbH
Luxemburger Str 449, 50939 Cologne
Tel: (0221) 94373-7000 *Fax:* (0221) 94373-7201
E-mail: info@wolterskluwer.de
Web Site: www.heymanns.com
Key Personnel
Mng Dir: Dr Ulrich Hermann
Chief Publisher: Buckhard Schulz
Founded: 1815
Subjects: Economics, Engineering (General), Government, Political Science, Law, Management, Public Administration
ISBN Prefix(es): 978-3-452
Total Titles: 2,000 Print; 70 CD-ROM
Subsidiaries: Euroliber Verlag- und Vertriebs-GmbH; Gallus Druckerei KG; Albert Nauck & Co
Branch Office(s)
Gutenbergstr 3-4, 12557 Berlin *Tel:* (030) 3914081 *Fax:* (030) 3912861
Steinsdorfstr 10, Postfach 26, 80538 Munich *Tel:* (089) 224811

Heyne, *imprint of* Verlagsgruppe Random House Bertelsmann

Heyne Fliegt, *imprint of* Verlagsgruppe Random House Bertelsmann

Heyne Hardcore, *imprint of* Verlagsgruppe Random House Bertelsmann

Heyne Verlag+
Imprint of Verlagsgruppe Random House Bertelsmann
Neumarkter Str 28, 81673 Munich
Tel: (089) 4136-0 *Toll Free Tel:* (0800) 500 33 22
Fax: (089) 4136-3333
E-mail: kundenservice@randomhouse.de
Web Site: www.randomhouse.de/heyne
Key Personnel
Publisher: Tilo Eckardt
Foreign Rights Dir: Gesche Wendebourg *Tel:* (089) 4136-3313 *E-mail:* gesche. wendebourg@randomhouse.de
Press Dir: Claudia Limmer *Tel:* (089) 4136-3130 *Fax:* (089) 4136-3507 *E-mail:* claudia.limmer@ randomhouse.de
Founded: 1934
Subjects: Astrology, Occult, Biography, Memoirs, Cookery, Fiction, Film, Video, History, How-to, Humor, Mysteries, Suspense, Psychology, Psychiatry, Romance, Science Fiction, Fantasy
ISBN Prefix(es): 978-3-453
Orders to: Schleissheimerstr 106, 85748 Garching-Hochbrueck

Anton Hiersemann KG Verlag+
Haldenstr 30, 70376 Stuttgart
Tel: (0711) 54 99 71-11 *Fax:* (0711) 54 99 71-21
E-mail: verlag@hiersemann.de
Web Site: www.hiersemann.de
Key Personnel
Chairman: Gerd Hiersemann
President & Dir, Rights & Permissions: Florian Hiersemann
Founded: 1884
Also specialize in monographs, publishing & book trade reference.
Subjects: Art, Astronomy, Biography, Memoirs, Drama, Theater, Genealogy, History, Library & Information Sciences, Literature, Literary Criticism, Essays, Religion - Buddhist, Religion - Catholic, Religion - Hindu, Religion - Islamic, Religion - Jewish, Religion - Protestant, Religion - Other, Science (General), Theology, Bookmaking, Medieval History

ISBN Prefix(es): 978-3-7772
Number of titles published annually: 45 Print; 1 Online; 10 E-Book
Total Titles: 1,200 Print; 7 CD-ROM
Associate Companies: Dr Ernst Hauswedell & Co KG Verlag *E-mail:* verlag@hauswedell.de
Subsidiaries: Karl W Hiersemann
Book Club(s): Geschaeftsstelle von: Literarischer Verein in Stuttgart eV

AIG I Hilbinger Verlag GmbH+
Frauensteiner Str 70, 65199 Wiesbaden
Tel: (0611) 181 77 28 *Fax:* (0611) 419 00 88
E-mail: info@aig-hilbinger.de; order@aig-hilbinger.de
Web Site: www.aig-hilbinger.de
Key Personnel
Mng Dir, Rights & Permissions: Immo A Hilbinger
Press: Dr Gabriel de Winter
Founded: 1989
Subjects: Astrology, Occult, Nonfiction (General), Parapsychology, Science (General), Self-Help
ISBN Prefix(es): 978-3-927110
Associate Companies: Agentur fuer Informationsgestaltung, Zum Dornhachtal, 65321 Heidenrod

Himmelstuermer Verlag Hamburg
Kirchenweg 12, 20099 Hamburg
Tel: (040) 64885608 *Fax:* (040) 64885609
E-mail: info@himmelstuermer.de
Web Site: www.himmelstuermer.de
Key Personnel
Mng Dir: Achim Albers
Founded: 1998
Specialize in gay novels & documentaries.
Subjects: LGBTQ
ISBN Prefix(es): 978-3-934825; 978-3-9806249
Number of titles published annually: 20 Print
Total Titles: 206 Print; 663 E-Book

Hinstorff Verlag GmbH+
Lagerstr 7, 18055 Rostock
Tel: (0381) 4 96 90 *Fax:* (0381) 4 96 91 03
E-mail: sekretariat@hinstorff.de; buchbestellung@ hinstorff.de; presse@hinstorff.de
Web Site: www.hinstorff.de
Key Personnel
Mng Dir: Ansgar Heise
Publishing Dir: Eva Maria Buchholz *E-mail:* eva. buchholz@hinstorff.de
Marketing & Press: Conny Ledwig *Tel:* (0381) 4 96 91 30
Sales: Gabriele Schattanek *Tel:* (0381) 4 96 91 40
Founded: 1831
Subjects: Literature, Literary Criticism, Essays
ISBN Prefix(es): 978-3-356
Parent Company: Heise Medien Gruppe GmbH & Co KG, Hannover
Warehouse: VSB Verlagsservice Braunschweig GmbH, Helmstedterstr 99, 38126 Braunschweig
Orders to: VSB Verlagsservice Braunschweig GmbH, Postfach 4738, 38037 Braunschweig
Georg Westermann Allee 66, 38104 Braunschweig

Hippocampus Verlag eK
Bismarckstr 8, 53604 Bad Honnef
Tel: (02224) 919480 *Fax:* (02224) 919482
E-mail: verlag@hippocampus.de
Web Site: www.hippocampus.de
Key Personnel
Mng Dir: Dr B Buelau
Founded: 1997
Subjects: Medicine, Nursing, Dentistry, Psychology, Psychiatry, Science (General), Humanities, Natural Sciences, Neurology
ISBN Prefix(es): 978-3-936817; 978-3-944551

Hirmer Verlag GmbH+
Nymphenburger Str 84, 80636 Munich

Tel: (089) 12 15 16-0 *Fax:* (089) 12 15 16-10; (089) 12 15 16-16 (distribution)
E-mail: vertrieb@hirmerverlag.de; info@ hirmerverlag.de
Web Site: www.hirmerverlag.de
Key Personnel
Chief Executive Officer: Thomas Zuhr *E-mail:* geschaeftsfuehrung@hirmerverlag.de
Mng Dir: Juergen Kleidt *E-mail:* kleidt@ hirmerverlag.de
Editorial Dir: Kerstin Ludolph *E-mail:* ludolph@ hirmerverlag.de
Advertising & Press: Eva-Maria Neuburger *Tel:* (089) 12 15 16-63 *E-mail:* neuburger@ hirmerverlag.de
Sales: Christine Vorhoelzer *Tel:* (089) 12 15 16-61 *E-mail:* vorhoelzer@hirmerverlag.de
Founded: 1948
Subjects: Archaeology, Architecture & Interior Design, Art, History, Photography, Art History, Sculpture
ISBN Prefix(es): 978-3-7774
Foreign Rep(s): Giovanni Ravasio (Switzerland)
Distribution Center: Koch, Neff & Oetinger Verlagsauslieferung GmbH, Industriestr 23, 70565 Stuttgart, Contact: Antje Grimm *E-mail:* hirmer@kno-va.de
Elisabeth Harder-Kreimann, Joachim-Maehl-Str 28, 22459 Hamburg *Tel:* (040) 555 404 46 *Fax:* (040) 555 404 44 *E-mail:* elisabeth@ harder-kreimann.de (Scandinavia)
Dr Franz Hain, Dr-Otto-Neurath-Gasse 5, 1220 Vienna, Austria *Tel:* (01) 28 26 56 50 *Fax:* (01) 282 52 82 *E-mail:* bestell@hain.at
Asia Publishers Services, 17/F Gee Chang Hong Centre, Units B&D, 65 Wong Chuk Hang Rd, Aberdeen, Hong Kong, Contact: Edward Summerson *Tel:* 2553 9289 *Fax:* 2554 2912 *E-mail:* edward_summerson@asiapubs.co.hk (China, Hong Kong, Korea, Philippines & Taiwan)
Marcello SAS Publishers' Representatives, Via Belzoni 12, 35121 Padua, Italy, Contact: Flavio Marcello *Tel:* (049) 8360671 *E-mail:* marcello@marcellosas.it (France, Greece, Italy, Portugal & Spain)
Jan Smit Boeken, Eikbosser Weg 258, 1213 SE Hilversum, Netherlands *Tel:* (035) 621 9 2 67 *Fax:* (035) 62 3 89 05 *E-mail:* jansmitboeken@ xmsnet.nl
buch 2000, c/o AVA Verlagsauslieferung AG, Centralweg 16, 8910 Affoltern am Albis, Switzerland *Tel:* (044) 762 42 60 *Fax:* (044) 762 42 10 *E-mail:* buch2000@ava.ch *Web Site:* www.ava.ch
IMA InterMediaAmericana, PO Box 8734, London SE21 7ZF, United Kingdom, Contact: David Williams *Tel:* (020) 7274 7113 *E-mail:* david@intermediaamericana.com (Caribbean, Central & South America)
Peter Ward Book Exports, One Adams Mews, London SW17 7RD, United Kingdom, Contact: Richard Ward *Tel:* (020) 8672 1171 (Malta, Middle East & Turkey)
Orca Book Services Ltd, Fleets Corner Industrial Estate, Unit A3, Off Nuffield Rd, Fleetsbridge, Poole, Dorset BH17 0HL, United Kingdom *Tel:* (01235) 46 55 00 *E-mail:* tradeorders@ orcabookservices.co.uk (Great Britain & Ireland)
Casemate Academic, PO Box 511, Oakville, CT 06779, United States *Tel:* 860-945-9329 *Fax:* 860-945-9468 *E-mail:* info@ casemateacademic.com (German books-USA & Canada)
The University of Chicago Press, Chicago Distribution Center, 11030 S Langley Ave, Chicago, IL 60628, United States, Contact: Sue Tranchita *Tel:* 773-702-4916 *E-mail:* stranchita@ press.uchicago.edu *Web Site:* www.press. uchicago.edu (English books-USA & Canada)

Antiquariat und Verlag Harro von Hirschheydt
Neue Wiesen 6, 30900 Wedemark-Elze

Tel: (05130) 36758 *Fax:* (05130) 36799
E-mail: kontakt@hirschheydt-online.de
Web Site: www.hirschheydt-online.de
Key Personnel
Owner, Rights & Permissions: Robert von
  Hirschheydt
Founded: 1950
Subjects: Regional Interests
ISBN Prefix(es): 978-3-7777

F Hirthammer Verlag GmbH+
Raiffeisenallee 10, 82041 Oberhaching, Munich
Tel: (089) 3233360 *Fax:* (089) 3241728
E-mail: info@hirthammerverlag.de
Web Site: www.hirthammerverlag.de
Key Personnel
Mng Dir: Wolfgang Fitz
Publishing Dir: Peter Zebold *E-mail:* peter.
  zebold@hirthammerverlag.de
Founded: 1965
Subjects: Education, Environmental Studies, Lit-
  erature, Literary Criticism, Essays, Mechanical
  Engineering, Physical Sciences, Technology,
  Theosophy
ISBN Prefix(es): 978-3-88721; 978-3-921288
Number of titles published annually: 10 Print
Total Titles: 120 Print

S Hirzel Verlag GmbH und Co+
Subsidiary of Deutscher Apotheker Verlag
Birkenwaldstr 44, 70191 Stuttgart
Mailing Address: Postfach 10 10 61, 70009
  Stuttgart
Tel: (0711) 2582 0; (0711) 2582 341 *Fax:* (0711)
  2582 290; (0711) 2582 390
E-mail: service@hirzel.de
Web Site: www.hirzel.de
Key Personnel
Mng Dir: Dr Klaus Brauer *E-mail:* kbrauer@
  hirzel.de; Dr Christian Rotta *E-mail:* crotta@
  hirzel.de
Marketing & Sales Manager: Siegmar Bauer
  E-mail: sbauer@hirzel.de
Rights: Sabine Koerner *Tel:* (0711) 2582 221
  E-mail: skoerner@hirzel.de
Founded: 1853
Subjects: Chemistry, Chemical Engineering, Engi-
  neering (General), Language Arts, Linguistics,
  Natural History, Philosophy, Physics, Psychol-
  ogy, Psychiatry, Regional Interests, Science
  (General)
ISBN Prefix(es): 978-3-7776
Associate Companies: Medpharm Scientific Pub-
  lishers; Franz Steiner Verlag GmbH; Wis-
  senschaftliche Verlagsgesellschaft mbH
Foreign Rights: Sabine Koerner
Returns: Koch, Neff & Oetinger Verlagsaus-
  lieferung GmbH, c/o Verlagsgruppe Deutscher
  Apotheker Verlag, Am Wallgraben 110, 70563
  Stuttgart

HIS Verlagsges-mbh, see Hamburger Edition

Edition Hochfeld
Von Parsevalstr 40, 86159 Augsburg
Tel: (0821) 2431512 *Fax:* (0821) 2431518
E-mail: verlag@edition-hochfeld.de
Web Site: www.edition-hochfeld.de
Key Personnel
Contact: Ulrich Schoenlein
Founded: 2005
ISBN Prefix(es): 978-3-9810268; 978-3-9812820;
  978-3-9814643; 978-3-9816355

Hoefer Verlag
Theodor-Heuss-Ring 46, 63128 Dietzenbach
Tel: (06074) 27550 *Fax:* (06074) 44964
E-mail: info@hoeferverlag.de
Web Site: www.hoeferverlag.de
Key Personnel
Mng Dir: Klaus G Hoefer

Founded: 1985
ISBN Prefix(es): 978-3-931103

Hoelker Verlag+
c/o Coppenrath Verlag GmbH & Co KG, Hafen-
  weg 30, 48155 Muenster
Tel: (0251) 41 411-0 *Fax:* (0251) 41 411-20
E-mail: info@coppenrath.de
Web Site: www.hoelker-verlag.de; www.facebook.
  com/HoelkerVerlag; www.coppenrath.de
Key Personnel
Mng Dir: Wolfgang Hoelker
Foreign Rights Dir: Claudia Medin *Tel:* (0251)
  41 411-811 *Fax:* (0251) 41 411-800
  E-mail: medin@coppenrath.de
Foreign Rights: Rita Davis *Tel:* (0251) 41 411-
  819 *Fax:* (0251) 41 411-800 *E-mail:* davis@
  coppenrath.de; Stefanie Gussmann *Tel:* (0251)
  41 411-813 *Fax:* (0251) 41 411-800
  E-mail: gussmann@coppenrath.de; Nadine
  Lottes *Tel:* (0251) 41 411-818 *Fax:* (0251) 41
  411-800 *E-mail:* lottes@coppenrath.de
Publicity: Tomas Rensing *E-mail:* rensing@
  coppenrath.de
Founded: 1973
Subjects: Cookery
ISBN Prefix(es): 978-3-88117; 978-3-9800058
Parent Company: Coppenrath Verlag GmbH &
  Co KG
Foreign Rep(s): Baumgartner Buecher AG
  (Stefan Baumgartner & Nicole Schliszio)
  (Switzerland); Agentur Buttenhauser (Austria,
  South Tyrol, Italy); Verlagsvertretung Hoeller
  (Michael Hoeller & Mario Seiler) (Austria,
  South Tyrol, Italy)
Distribution Center: Coppenrath Distribution,
  Textilstr 3, 48612 Horstmar *Tel:* (02558) 90
  29 00 *Fax:* (02558) 90 29 01 06 *E-mail:* buero-
  horstmar@coppenrath.de
Verlagsauslieferung Hillstein Verlag, Rochus-
  gasse 9, Postfach 1, 5017 Salzburg, Austria
  Tel: (0662) 82 77 00 0 *Fax:* (0662) 82 77 00
  33 *E-mail:* info@hillstein.at
Baumgartner Beucher AG, c/o AVA Verlagsaus-
  lieferung AG, Centralweg 16, 8910 Affoltern
  am Albis, Switzerland *Tel:* (044) 7 62 42 80
  Fax: (044) 7 62 42 85 *E-mail:* baumgartner@
  ava.ch *Web Site:* www.ava.ch

Hoell Verlag+
Darmstaedter Str 14b, 64397 Modautal
Tel: (06167) 912220 *Fax:* (06167) 912221
E-mail: info@hoellverlag.de
Web Site: www.hoellverlag.de; www.hoellverlag.
  homepage.t-online.de
Key Personnel
Owner: Peter Hoell
Founded: 1987
Subjects: Anthropology, Astrology, Occult, Hu-
  man Relations, Literature, Literary Criticism,
  Essays, Nonfiction (General), Poetry
ISBN Prefix(es): 978-3-9801439; 978-3-928564
Total Titles: 31 Print

Andrea Hoelzel Verlag, see edition ars
  porcellana

Hoerbuch Hamburg HHV GmbH
Paul-Nevermann-Platz 5, 22765 Hamburg
Tel: (040) 897 207 80 *Fax:* (040) 897 207 810
E-mail: info@hoerbuch-hamburg.de
Web Site: www.hoerbuch-hamburg.de
Key Personnel
Mng Dir: Johannes Stricker
Press: Ines Hansla
Sales: Eva Koelle *Tel:* (040) 897 207 8-23
  E-mail: e.koelle@hoerbuch-hamburg.de
Founded: 1999
Subjects: Biography, Memoirs, History, Literature,
  Literary Criticism, Essays, Mysteries, Suspense,
  Poetry, Science Fiction, Fantasy
ISBN Prefix(es): 978-3-89903; 978-3-934120

Associate Companies: Osterwold Audio; Silber-
  fisch
Distribution Center: Koch, Neff & Oetinger Ver-
  lagsauslieferung GmbH, Industriestr 23, 70565
  Stuttgart *E-mail:* ullstein-buchverlage@kno-
  va.de (Germany & Switzerland)
Dr Franz Hain Verlagsauslieferungen GmbH, Dr-
  Otto-Neurath-Gasse 5, 1220 Vienna, Austria
  Tel: (01) 282 65 65-77 *Fax:* (01) 282 52 82
  E-mail: bestell@hain.at

HOERCOMPANY Schaack und Herzog oHG
Schulstr 12, 24376 Rabel
Mailing Address: Jungmannstr 15, 22605 Ham-
  burg
Tel: (040) 8801411; (040) 8892616 *Fax:* (040)
  8892618
E-mail: info@hoercompany.de
Web Site: www.hoercompany.de
Key Personnel
Contact: Angelika Schaack; Andrea Herzog
Founded: 2000
ISBN Prefix(es): 978-3-935036
Branch Office(s)
Friedensallee 26, 22765 Hamburg
Distribution Center: Rhenus Medien Logistik
  GmbH & Co KG, Justus-von-Liebig-Str 1,
  86899 Landsberg am Lech *Tel:* (08191) 9 70
  00-622 *E-mail:* beltz@de.rhenus.com
Mohr Morawa Buchvertrieb GmbH, Sulzen-
  gasse 2, 1230 Vienna, Austria *Tel:* (01) 680
  14-0 *Fax:* (01) 688 71 30 *E-mail:* momo@
  mohrmorawa.at *Web Site:* www.mohrmorawa.at
Verlagsauslieferung Scheidegger & Co AG, c/o
  AVA, Centralweg 16, 8910 Affoltern am Albis,
  Switzerland *Tel:* (044) 762 42 50 *Fax:* (044)
  762 42 49 *E-mail:* scheidegger@ava.ch

Verlag Angelika Hoernig+
Siebenpfeifferstr 18, 67071 Ludwigshafen
Tel: (0621) 65 82 197-0; (0621) 65 82 197-15
  (sales) *Fax:* (0621) 65 82 197-17
E-mail: info@bogenschiessen.de; shop@
  bogenschiessen.de; redaktion@bogenschiessen.
  de
Web Site: www.bogenschiessen.de
Key Personnel
Publisher: Angelika Hoernig *E-mail:* ah@
  bogenschiessen.de
Editor-in-Chief: Volker Alles
Founded: 1996
Publisher of archery books & magazines.
Subjects: Archaeology, History, How-to, Outdoor
  Recreation, Sports, Athletics, Archery, Bow
  Building, History of Bow & Arrow
ISBN Prefix(es): 978-3-9805877; 978-3-9808743;
  978-3-938921
Number of titles published annually: 8 Print; 2 E-
  Book
Total Titles: 120 Print; 8 E-Book

**Christoph Hofbauer, Ilija Trojanow &
  Berthold Klewing+**
Paul-Heyse-Str 31a, 80336 Munich
Tel: (089) 51616151
Key Personnel
Contact: Christoph Hofbauer; Ilija Trojanow
Founded: 1991
Subjects: Anthropology, Business, Economics,
  Literature, Literary Criticism, Essays, Physical
  Sciences
ISBN Prefix(es): 978-3-929115; 978-3-932965
Associate Companies: Marino Verlag, c/o Fred-
  erking & Thaler, Neumarkter Str 18, Munich
Distributor for GBI-Verlag; Faktum

Edgar Hoff Verlag, see Reise Know-How

Edition & Galerie Hoffmann & Co oHG
Goerbelheimer Muehle 1, 61169 Friedberg (Has-
  sen)
Tel: (06031) 2443; (0172) 6602611 (cell)
  Fax: (06031) 62965

E-mail: hoffmann@galeriehoffmann.de
Web Site: www.galeriehoffmann.de
Founded: 1967
Subjects: Architecture & Interior Design, Art
ISBN Prefix(es): 978-3-926026

Hoffmann und Campe Verlag GmbH+
Member of Ganske Verlagsgruppe GmbH
Harvestehuder Weg 42, 20149 Hamburg
Tel: (040) 44188-0 *Fax:* (040) 44188-202
E-mail: email@hoca.de
Web Site: www.hoffmann-und-campe.de
Key Personnel
Mng Dir: Thomas Ganske; Markus Klose; Dr Kai
  Laakmann; Bernd Ziesemer
Foreign Rights: Nadja Mortensen *Tel:* (040)
  44188-281 *Fax:* (040) 44188-319
  E-mail: nadja.mortensen@hoca.de
Press & Public Relations: Julia Strack *Tel:* (040)
  44188-219 *Fax:* (040) 44188-200 *E-mail:* julia.
  strack@hoca.de
Founded: 1781
Subjects: Art, Biography, Memoirs, Fiction, His-
  tory, Music, Dance, Nonfiction (General), Phi-
  losophy, Poetry, Psychology, Psychiatry, Sci-
  ence (General), Social Sciences, Sociology
ISBN Prefix(es): 978-3-455
Foreign Rep(s): Dagmar Bhend (Switzerland);
  Firma Verlagsagentur Kager & Treml (Austria)
Foreign Rights: ACER (Latin America, Portu-
  gal, Spain); Agencja Literacka Graal (Joanna
  Maciuk) (Poland); Agentur Literatur Hebel &
  Bindermann (Susan Bindermann) (Greece);
  Agentur Literatur Hebel & Bindermann (Gu-
  drun Hebel) (Scandinavia); Hercules Business
  & Culture (Hongjun Cai) (China); Internation-
  aal Literatuur Bureau (Linda Kohn) (Nether-
  lands); Simona Kessler International Copy-
  right Agency (Romania); Meike Marx Liter-
  ary Agency (Japan); Daniela Micura Literary
  Services (Italy); Andrew Nurnberg Associates
  Budapest (Judit Hermann) (Croatia, Hungary)

Hofmann-Verlag GmbH & Co KG+
Steinwasenstr 6-8, 73614 Schorndorf
Tel: (07181) 402-0 *Fax:* (07181) 402-111
E-mail: info@hofmann-verlag.de
Web Site: www.hofmann-verlag.de
Key Personnel
Mng Dir: Thomas Hecht
Publishing Manager: Joerg Tochtermann
  Tel: (07181) 402-123 *E-mail:* tochtermann@
  hofmann-verlag.de
Marketing & Licensing: Marita Merkt
  Tel: (07181) 402-124 *E-mail:* merkt@hofmann-
  verlag.de
Founded: 1934
Subjects: Sports, Athletics
ISBN Prefix(es): 978-3-7780

Friedrich Hofmeister Musikverlag+
Buettnerstr 10, 04103 Leipzig
Tel: (0341) 9 60 07 50 *Fax:* (0341) 9 60 30 55
E-mail: info@hofmeister-musikverlag.com
Web Site: www.hofmeister-musikverlag.com
Key Personnel
Owner: Stephanie Clement
Founded: 1807
Subjects: Music, Dance
ISBN Prefix(es): 978-3-7331; 978-3-87350

Hogrefe Verlag GmbH & Co Kg+
Member of Hogrefe Verlagsgruppe
Merkelstr 3, 37085 Goettingen
Tel: (0551) 999 50-0 *Fax:* (0551) 999 50-111
E-mail: verlag@hogrefe.de; press@hogrefe.de
Web Site: www.hogrefe.de
Key Personnel
Chief Executive Officer: Dr G-Juergen Hogrefe
  E-mail: j.hogrefe@hogrefe.de
Mng Dir: Dr Michael Vogtmeier *Tel:* (0551) 999
  50-705 *E-mail:* vogtmeier@hogrefe.de

Press: Nadine Teichert *Tel:* (0551) 999 50-526
Founded: 1949
Subjects: Medicine, Nursing, Dentistry, Psychol-
  ogy, Psychiatry
ISBN Prefix(es): 978-3-456; 978-3-8017; 978-3-
  87844
Subsidiaries: Verlag fuer Angewandte Psychologie
U.S. Office(s): Hogrefe Publishing Corp, 7
  Bulfinch Place, Suite 202, Boston, MA
  02114, United States *Fax:* 617-354-6875
  E-mail: customerservice@hogrefe-publishing.
  com *Web Site:* us.hogrefe.com
Warehouse: Herbert-Quandt-Str 4, 37081 Goet-
  tingen *Tel:* (0551) 999 50-950 *Fax:* (0551) 999
  50-955 *E-mail:* distribution@hogrefe.de
Distribution Center: Brockhaus/Commis-
  sion, Kreidlerstr 9, 70806 Kornwestheim
  Tel: (07154) 1327-0 *Fax:* (07154) 1327-13
  (Germany & Austria)
  Hogrefe AG Verlag Hans Huber, Laenggassstr
  76, 3000 Bern, Switzerland *Tel:* (031) 300
  45 14 *Fax:* (031) 300 45 90 *E-mail:* verlag@
  hanshuber.com
  Marston Book Services Ltd, 160 Eastern
  Ave, Milton Park, Abingdon, Oxon OX14
  4SB, United Kingdom *Tel:* (01235) 465500
  Fax: (01235) 465555 *E-mail:* trade.orders@
  marston.co.uk *Web Site:* www.marston.co.uk
  (English titles)
  Baker & Taylor Publisher Services, 30 Amberwood Pkwy, Ashland, OH 44805, United States
  Tel: 567-215-0030 *E-mail:* info@btpubservices.
  com *Web Site:* www.btpubservices.com (English titles)

Hohenrain Verlag GmbH+
Am Apfelberg 18, 72076 Tuebingen
Tel: (07071) 4070-0 *Fax:* (07071) 4070-26
E-mail: info@hohenrainverlag.de
Web Site: www.hohenrainverlag.de
Key Personnel
Mng Dir: Bernhard Grabert; Wigbert Grabert
Founded: 1985
Subjects: Art, Biography, Memoirs, Fiction, Gov-
  ernment, Political Science, History
ISBN Prefix(es): 978-3-89180
Number of titles published annually: 3 Print
Total Titles: 70 Print

Holos, *imprint of* Holos Wissenschaftlicher Verlag
und Medien

Holos Wissenschaftlicher Verlag und Medien+
Kuedinghovener Str 10, 53227 Bonn
Tel: (0228) 263020
E-mail: info@holos-verlag.de
Web Site: www.holos-verlag.de
Key Personnel
Contact: Wolfgang Guting
Founded: 1987
Specialize in humanities.
Subjects: Anthropology, Archaeology, Fiction,
  Geography, Geology, History, Language Arts,
  Linguistics, LGBTQ, Philosophy, Psychology,
  Psychiatry, Social Sciences, Sociology
ISBN Prefix(es): 978-3-926216; 978-3-86097
Imprints: Holos; Wissenschaftlicher Verlag und
  Medien; Wolfgang Guting

Verlagsgruppe Georg von Holtzbrinck GmbH
Gaensheidestr 26, 70184 Stuttgart
Tel: (0711) 2150-0 *Fax:* (0711) 2150-269
E-mail: info@holtzbrinck.com
Web Site: www.holtzbrinck.com
Key Personnel
Chairman & Partner: Stefan von Holtzbrinck
Chairman & Chief Executive Officer, Holtzbrinck
  Digital: Markus Schunk
Executive Vice President & Manager, Global
  Trade Division: John Sargent
Chief Executive Officer, Holtzbrinck's German
  Trade Publishing Group: Joerg Pfuhl

Partner: Monika Schoeller
Founded: 1971
Subjects: Education, Fiction, Nonfiction (Gen-
  eral), Science (General), Newspapers

Holzmann Medien GmbH & Co KG
Gewerbestr 2, 86825 Bad Woerishofen
Mailing Address: Postfach 13 42, 86816 Bad Wo-
  erishofen
Tel: (08247) 354-01; (08247) 354-333 (bookshop)
  Fax: (08247) 354-170
E-mail: info@holzmann-medien.de; press@
  holzmann-medien.de
Web Site: www.holzmann-medien.de; www.
  holzmann-medienshop.de
Key Personnel
Publisher: Alexander Holzmann
  E-mail: alexander.holzmann@holzmann-
  medien.de
Publishing Dir: Michael Hoelzel *Tel:* (08247)
  354-123 *Fax:* (08247) 354-4123
  E-mail: michael.hoelzel@holzmann-medien.de
Head, Advertising, Sales & Marketing: Jan Peter
  Kruse
Commercial Manager: Werner Forstmaier
Founded: 1936
Subjects: Business, Education, Law, Marketing
ISBN Prefix(es): 978-3-7783; 978-3-920416

Holzmann Verlag GmbH, see Holzmann Medien
GmbH & Co KG

**Verlag Homoeopathie + Symbol Martin
  Bomhardt**
Liebigstr 36, 10247 Berlin
Tel: (030) 857296-74 *Fax:* (030) 857296-75
E-mail: info@homsym.de
Web Site: www.homsym.de
Key Personnel
Owner: Martin Bomhardt
Founded: 1994
Specialize in homoeopathic literature.
Subjects: Alternative, Health, Nutrition, Inspira-
  tional, Spirituality, Medicine, Nursing, Den-
  tistry, Psychology, Psychiatry
ISBN Prefix(es): 978-3-937095; 978-3-9804662

Horlemann Verlag+
Heynstr 28, 13187 Berlin
Tel: (030) 49 30 76 39
E-mail: info@horlemann-verlag.de
Web Site: www.horlemann.info
Key Personnel
Owner: Anja Schwarz
Dir: Michael Adrian
Founded: 1989
Membership(s): The Stock Exchange of German
  Booksellers.
Subjects: Asian Studies, Developing Countries,
  Education, Environmental Studies, Fiction, For-
  eign Countries, Government, Political Science,
  Literature, Literary Criticism, Essays, Nonfic-
  tion (General), Philosophy, Poetry, Religion -
  Islamic, Social Sciences, Sociology
ISBN Prefix(es): 978-3-927905; 978-3-89502
Foreign Rep(s): Elisabeth Hirt (Austria)
Distribution Center: Prolit Verlagsausliefer-
  ung GmbH, Siemensstr 16, 35461 Fernwald,
  Contact: Rainer Eckert *Tel:* (0641) 943 93-
  33 *E-mail:* r.eckert@prolit.de *Web Site:* www.
  prolit.de
  Medianlogistik, Pichler-OEBZ GmbH & Co
  KG, IZ-NOE Sued, Str 1, Objekt 34, 2355
  Wiener Neudorf, Austria *Tel:* (02236) 63 535-
  236 *Fax:* (02236) 63 535-243 *E-mail:* mlo@
  medien-logistik.at *Web Site:* www.medien-
  logistik.at
  Scheidegger & Co AG, c/o AVA Verlagsauslieferung AG, Centralweg 16, 8910 Affoltern am
  Albis, Switzerland *Tel:* (01) 762 425 0

hpsmedia GmbH
An den Hafergaerten 9, 35410 Hungen
Tel: (06402) 809327
E-mail: service@pflege-wissenschaft.info;
  verlag@pflege-wissenschaft.info
Web Site: www.pflege-wissenschaft.info
Key Personnel
Publisher: Wiebke Muench *Tel:* (06402) 7082-666
  Fax: (06402) 7082-669
Mng Dir: Prof Andreas Lauterbach *Tel:* (06402)
  7082-664 *Fax:* (06402) 7082-665
  E-mail: lauterbach@pflege-wissenschaft.info
Editor: Ramona Ruehl *Tel:* (06402) 7082-661
  E-mail: ruehl@geschichte-der-pflege.info
Subjects: Medicine, Nursing, Dentistry
ISBN Prefix(es): 978-3-9814259

HTWK Leipzig, see Hochschule fuer Technik
  Wirtschaft und Kultur Leipzig

Hefei Huang Verlag GmbH
Osterseestr 50a, 82194 Groebenzell
Tel: (08142) 46 58 260 *Fax:* (08142) 44 07 12
E-mail: huang@huang-verlag.de
Web Site: www.huang-verlag.de; www.huang-
  shop.de
Key Personnel
Mng Dir: Hefei Huang
Subjects: Art, Fiction, Language Arts, Linguis-
  tics, Poetry, Science Fiction, Fantasy, Chinese
  Language, East Asia, Japanese Language
ISBN Prefix(es): 978-3-940497

Hueber Verlag GmbH & Co KG+
Baubergerstr 30, 80992 Munich
Mailing Address: Postfach 50 03 90, 80973 Mu-
  nich
Tel: (089) 9602-0 *Fax:* (089) 9602-358
E-mail: kundenservice@hueber.de; orders@
  hueber.de
Web Site: www.hueber.de
Key Personnel
Mng Dir: Wolf Dieter Eggert; Michaela Hueber
International Sales Dir: Sylvia Tobias
  Tel: (089) 9602-226 *Fax:* (089) 9602-354
  E-mail: tobias@hueber.de
International Rights Manager: Rosa Evans
  Fax: (089) 9602-5285 *E-mail:* evans@hueber.
  de
Founded: 1921
Subjects: Education, Language Arts, Linguistics,
  Adult Education in Foreign Languages, Ger-
  man as a Foreign Language
ISBN Prefix(es): 978-3-19
Foreign Rep(s): Ivana Horvatincic (Bosnia and
  Herzegovina, Croatia, Slovenia); Hueber Hellas
  (Christos Karabatos) (Greece); Macmillan (So-
  phie Caesar) (Spain); OLF SA (Gabi Bernet &
  Ivana Perovic Scheck) (Switzerland)
Distribution Center: Mohr Morawa Buchver-
  trieb GmbH, Sulzengasse 2, 1230 Vienna,
  Austria *Tel:* (01) 680 14-0 *Fax:* (01) 688
  71 30 *E-mail:* momo@mohrmorawa.at *Web
  Site:* www.mohrmorawa.at
OLF SA, ZI3, Corminboeuf, CP 1152, 1701
  Fribourg, Switzerland *Tel:* (026) 467 52 50
  Fax: (026) 467 54 66 *Web Site:* www.olf.ch

Felicitas Huebner Verlag GmbH+
Hagenstr 10, 31275 Lehrte
Tel: (05132) 8399-0 *Fax:* (05132) 8399-69
Web Site: www.huebner-books.de/huebner-shop
Key Personnel
Mng Dir: Felicitas Huebner
Founded: 1981
Subjects: Film, Video, Health, Nutrition, Sports,
  Athletics
ISBN Prefix(es): 978-3-927359
Distribution Center: Runge Verlagsausliefer-
  ung GmbH, Bergstr 2, 33803 Steinhagen
  Tel: (05204) 998 0 *Fax:* (05204) 998 111
  E-mail: info@rungeva.de *Web Site:* rungeva.de

Bacopa Handels- & Kulturges mbH, Waidern 42,
  4521 Schiedlberg, Austria *Tel:* (07251) 22235
  Fax: (07251) 22235-16 *E-mail:* versand@
  bacopa.at *Web Site:* www.bacopa.at
Sana Verlag, Via Campagna 13b, 6503
  Bellinzona-Galbisio, Switzerland
  Tel: (091) 835 48 90 *Fax:* (091) 835 48 91
  E-mail: sanaverlag@bluemail.ch

H Hugendubel GmbH & Co KG+
Hilblestr 54, 80636 Munich
Tel: (089) 30 75 75 75
E-mail: service@hugendubel.de
Web Site: www.hugendubel.de
Key Personnel
Executive Partner: Dr Maximilian Hugendubel
Mng Partner: Nina Hugendubel
Management: Dr Stefan Hoellermann; Stephanie
  Lange; Thomas Nitz
Founded: 1893
Subjects: Biography, Memoirs, Cookery, Fiction,
  Humor, Music, Dance, Romance, Science Fic-
  tion, Fantasy, Travel & Tourism
ISBN Prefix(es): 978-3-7205; 978-3-7162; 978-3-
  8267; 978-3-88034
Total Titles: 100 Print

Edition Humanistische Psychologie, see
  EHP-Verlag Andreas Kohlhage

Humanistischer Verband Deutschlands (HVD)
(Humanist Association of Germany)
Wallstr 61-65, 10179 Berlin
Tel: (030) 61 39 04-34 *Fax:* (030) 61 39 04-50
E-mail: hvd@humanismus.de; info@humanismus.
  de
Web Site: www.humanismus.de
Key Personnel
President: Dr Florian Zimmermann
Vice President: Ulrike von Chossy; Jan Gabriel;
  Guido Wiesner
Founded: 1993
Subjects: Humanism
ISBN Prefix(es): 978-3-924041
Number of titles published annually: 4 Print
Total Titles: 55 Print

Humanitas Buchversand GmbH+
Industriepark 3, 56291 Wiebelsheim
Tel: (06766) 903-100 *Fax:* (06766) 903-320
E-mail: service@humanitas-book.de
Web Site: www.humanitas-book.de
Key Personnel
Mng Dir: Gerhard Stahl
Dir: Christel Hanze-Stahl
Founded: 1906
Subjects: Art, Biological Sciences, Education,
  Health, Nutrition, History, Language Arts, Lin-
  guistics, Literature, Literary Criticism, Essays,
  Medicine, Nursing, Dentistry, Music, Dance,
  Philosophy, Psychology, Psychiatry, Religion -
  Other, Social Sciences, Sociology, Sports, Ath-
  letics, Travel & Tourism
ISBN Prefix(es): 978-3-494; 978-3-88988
Associate Companies: AULA-Verlag GmbH,
  Industriepark 3, 56291 Wiebelsheim
  Tel: (06766) 903-141 *Fax:* (06766) 903-
  320 *E-mail:* vertrieb@aula-verlag.de;
  Limpert Verlag GmbH, Industriepark 3,
  56291 Wiebelsheim *Tel:* (06766) 903-160
  Fax: (06766) 903-320 *E-mail:* vertrieb@
  limpert.de; Quelle & Myer Verlag GmbH
  & Co, Industriepark 3, 56291 Wiebelsheim
  Tel: (06766) 903-140 *Fax:* (06766) 903-320
  E-mail: vertrieb@quelle-meyer.de

Ilona Hupe Verlag
Volkartstr 2, 80634 Munich
Tel: (089) 16783783 *Fax:* (089) 1684474
E-mail: info@hupeverlag.de
Web Site: www.hupeverlag.de

Key Personnel
Publisher: Ilona Hupe; Manfred Vachal
Specialize in travel literature on Africa & Aus-
  tralia.
Subjects: Developing Countries, Foreign Coun-
  tries, Travel & Tourism
ISBN Prefix(es): 978-3-932084

HUSS-MEDIEN GmbH+
Am Friedrichsain 22, 10407 Berlin
Tel: (030) 42151-0 *Fax:* (030) 42151-480
E-mail: huss.medien@hussberlin.de
Web Site: www.huss.de
Key Personnel
Mng Dir: Bert Brandenburg; Christoph Huss;
  Rainer Langhammer
Founded: 1946
Subjects: Architecture & Interior Design, Career
  Development, Economics, Education, Electron-
  ics, Electrical Engineering, Engineering (Gen-
  eral), Human Relations, Law, Management,
  Mechanical Engineering, Radio, TV, Technol-
  ogy, Building & Construction, Industrial Law,
  Regulations
ISBN Prefix(es): 978-3-349 (economy); 978-3-
  341 (technology); 978-3-345 (construction)
Number of titles published annually: 28 Print; 3
  CD-ROM
Total Titles: 137 Print; 10 CD-ROM
Parent Company: HUSS-VERLAG GmbH,
  Joseph-Dollinger-Bogen 5, 80807 Munich

HUSS-VERLAG GmbH+
Division of Huss Unternehmensgruppe
Joseph-Dollinger-Bogen 5, 80807 Munich
Mailing Address: Postfach 46 04 80, 80192 Mu-
  nich
Tel: (089) 32391-0; (089) 323 91 317 (sales)
  Fax: (089) 32391-416
E-mail: management@huss-verlag.de
Web Site: www.huss-verlag.de
Key Personnel
President: Wolfgang Huss
Mng Dir: Christoph Huss; Bert Brandenburg;
  Rainer Langhammer
Press & Public Relations: Monica-Ines Oppel
  Tel: (089) 32391-129 *Fax:* (089) 32391-130
  E-mail: ines.oppel@hussverlag.de
Founded: 1975
Subjects: Architecture & Interior Design, Auto-
  motive, Business, Electronics, Electrical Engi-
  neering, Engineering (General), Law, Technol-
  ogy, Transportation, Travel & Tourism
ISBN Prefix(es): 978-3-921455; 978-3-931724;
  978-3-937711
Associate Companies: HUSS-MEDIEN GmbH,
  Am Friedrichshain 22, 10407 Berlin *Fax:* (030)
  42151-0 *E-mail:* huss.medien@hussberlin.de
Subsidiaries: Verlag fuer Bauwesen GmbH; Ver-
  lag Technik GmbH; Verlag Die Wirtschaft
  GmbH
Orders to: HUSS-MEDIEN GmbH, Am
  Friedrichshain 22, 10407 Berlin

Husum Druck- und Verlagsgesellschaft mbH u
Co KG+
Nordbahnhofstr 2, 25813 Husum
Mailing Address: Postfach 1480, 25804 Husum
Tel: (04841) 8352-0 *Fax:* (04841) 8352-10
E-mail: info@verlagsgruppe.de
Web Site: www.verlagsgruppe.de
Key Personnel
Mng Dir: Ingwert Paulsen
Founded: 1973
Subjects: Regional Interests
ISBN Prefix(es): 978-3-88042; 978-3-89876
Subsidiaries: Hamburger Lesehefte Verlag Ingwert
  Paulsen Jr; Hansa Verlag Ingwert Paulsen Jr;
  Verlag der Kunst Dresden Ingwert Paulsen Jr;
  Matthiesen Verlag Ingwert Paulsen Jr; Verlag
  der Nation Ingwert Paulsen Jr; Turmschreiber
  Verlag Ingwert Paulsen Jr

HVD, see Humanistischer Verband Deutschlands (HVD)

IB Verlag Islamische Bibliothek
Ellerstr 148, 40227 Duesseldorf
Tel: (0211) 7952335 *Fax:* (0211) 7952157
E-mail: info@ibverlag.de
Web Site: www.ibverlag.de
Key Personnel
Mng Dir: Abderrahim Khouja
Project Dir: Muhammad Ramdani
    E-mail: ramdani@ibverlag.de
Subjects: Art, Behavioral Sciences, Education, History, Law, Religion - Islamic, Art & Culture, Islamic Law, Qur'an
ISBN Prefix(es): 978-3-94111

ibai-publishing
Fabrikstr 10, 04617 Fockendorf
Tel: (0341) 86 12 274 *Fax:* (0341) 39 19 239
E-mail: info@ibai-publishing.org
Web Site: www.ibai-publishing.org
Key Personnel
Dir: Dr Petra Perner
Subjects: Career Development, Communications, Computer Science
ISBN Prefix(es): 978-3-942952

ibidem-Verlag
Melchiorstr 15, 70439 Stuttgart
Tel: (0711) 9807954 *Fax:* (0711) 8001889
E-mail: ibidem@ibidem-verlag.de
Web Site: www.ibidemverlag.de
Key Personnel
Contact: Jessica Haunschild; Christian Schoen
Subjects: Architecture & Interior Design, Art, Finance, Government, Political Science, Language Arts, Linguistics, Literature, Literary Criticism, Essays, Management, Marketing, Social Sciences, Sociology, Health Care
ISBN Prefix(es): 978-3-932602; 978-3-89821; 978-3-8382
Distributed by Columbia University Press (English language titles exc China & India)

IBM Press, *imprint of* Pearson Deutschland GmbH

ICHverlag Haefner+Haefner
Glockenhofstr 43, 90478 Nuremberg
Tel: (0171) 364 34 51
E-mail: info@brothersinart.de
Web Site: www.ichverlag.com
Key Personnel
Co-Owner: Guido Haefner; Johannes Haefner
Founded: 1991
Subjects: Art, Literature, Literary Criticism, Essays, Science (General)

ID Verlag Tawereit-Fanizadeh GbR+
Gneisenaustr 2a, 10961 Berlin
Tel: (030) 694 77 03 *Fax:* (030) 694 78 08
E-mail: idverlag@t-online.de
Web Site: www.idverlag.com
Key Personnel
Management: Andreas Fanizadeh; Wolfgang Tawereit
Founded: 1988
Subjects: Communications, Developing Countries, Government, Political Science, History, Literature, Literary Criticism, Essays, Publishing & Book Trade Reference
ISBN Prefix(es): 978-3-89408
Orders to: Sova, Philipp-Reis-Str 17, 63477 Maintal *Tel:* (06181) 9088072 *Fax:* (06181) 9088073 *E-mail:* sovaffm@t-online.de *Web Site:* www.sovaffm.de

IDEA Verlag GmbH+
Estingerstr 16, 85232 Palsweis
Mailing Address: Postfach 1361, 82169 Puchheim

Tel: (08142) 4107507 *Fax:* (08142) 4107507
E-mail: info@idea-verlag.de
Web Site: www.idea-verlag.de
Key Personnel
Mng Dir & Rights: Hariet Paschke
Founded: 1980
Subjects: Crafts, Games, Hobbies, Literature, Literary Criticism, Essays, Science (General), Sports, Athletics, Technology
ISBN Prefix(es): 978-3-88793; 978-3-9800371
Distribution Center: HEROLD Verlagsauslieferung & Logistik GmbH, Raiffeisenallee 10, 82041 Oberhachin/Munich *Tel:* (089) 613871-0 *Fax:* (089) 613871-20 *E-mail:* herold@herold-va.de
Orders to: HEROLD Verlagsauslieferung & Logistik GmbH, Raiffeisenallee 10, 82041 Oberhachin/Munich *Tel:* (089) 613871-0 *Fax:* (089) 613871-20 *E-mail:* herold@herold-va.de

IDW Verlag GmbH+
Tersteegenstr 14, 40474 Duesseldorf
Tel: (0211) 4561-280 *Fax:* (0211) 4561-277
E-mail: post@idw-verlag.de
Web Site: www.idw-verlag.de
Key Personnel
Mng Dir: Dr Klaus-Peter Naumann
Editor: Dr Karl-Heinz Armelch
    E-mail: armelch@idw-verlag.de
Marketing: Jochen Kolb *E-mail:* kolb@idw-verlag.de
Founded: 1950
Subjects: Accounting, Business, Finance
ISBN Prefix(es): 978-3-8021
Subsidiaries: IDW Akademic GmbH
Orders to: Rhenus Medien Logistik GmbH & Co KG, Justus-von-Liebig Str 1, 86899 Landsberg am Lech *E-mail:* idw@de.rhenus.com

IFA, see Institut fuer Auslandsbeziehungen eV (IFA)

Igel Verlag
Imprint of Diplomica Verlag GmbH
Hermannstal 119k, 22119 Hamburg
Tel: (040) 65 59 92-29 *Fax:* (040) 65 59 92-22
E-mail: kontakt@igelverlag.de
Web Site: www.igelverlag.com
Key Personnel
Mng Dir: Bjoern Bedey *E-mail:* bedey@igelverlag.com
Editorial: Johanna Seegers
Subjects: Literature, Literary Criticism, Essays, Science (General)
ISBN Prefix(es): 978-3-89621; 978-3-927194; 978-3-86815
Distribution Center: Brockhaus/Commission, Kreidlerstr 9, 70806 Kornwestheim, Contact: Lidija Eisenbarth *Tel:* (07154) 1327-24 *Fax:* (07154) 1327-13 *E-mail:* l.eisenbarth@brocom.de

Ikarus Verlag & Reisen+
Am Heiligenfeld 2, 36041 Fulda
Tel: (0661) 9 01 63 60; (0170) 3 84 49 29 (cell)
E-mail: info@ikarus-verlag.de
Web Site: www.ikarus-verlag.de
Key Personnel
Mng Dir: Dr Wolfgang Hautumm
Founded: 1982
Subjects: Archaeology, History, Literature, Literary Criticism, Essays, Travel & Tourism
ISBN Prefix(es): 978-3-9802064; 978-3-9800471
Number of titles published annually: 2 Print
Total Titles: 25 Print

ikotes eK
Postfach 16 51, 77806 Buehl
Tel: (07223) 8 06 22 66 *Fax:* (07223) 9 12 93 06
E-mail: info@ikotes.de
Web Site: www.ikotes.com

Key Personnel
Contact: Peter Mueller
Founded: 2008
Subjects: Management, Self-Help
ISBN Prefix(es): 978-3-941626

ILS, see Institut fuer Landes- und Stadtentwicklungsforschung GmbH

Michael Imhof Verlag GmbH & Co KG
Stettiner Str 25, 36100 Petersberg
Tel: (0661) 29191660 *Fax:* (0661) 29191669
E-mail: info@imhof-verlag.de
Web Site: www.imhof-verlag.de
Key Personnel
Publisher: Dr Michael Imhof
Mng Dir & Marketing: Thomas Imhof
    E-mail: thomas.imhof@imhof-verlag.de
Editorial & Licenses: Karin Kreuzpaintner
    E-mail: karin.kreuzpaintner@imhof-verlag.de
Press & Public Relations: Dorothee Baganz
    E-mail: dorothee.baganz@imhof-verlag.de
Founded: 1996
Subjects: Animals, Pets, Architecture & Interior Design, Art, Cookery, Crafts, Games, Hobbies, History, Music, Dance, Photography, Regional Interests, Religion - Other, Travel & Tourism, Asia, Conservation, Cultural History, Europe, Germany, Guides, Horses, United States
ISBN Prefix(es): 978-3-86568; 978-3-932526; 978-3-935590; 978-3-937251
Foreign Rep(s): Art Stock Books Ltd & Co KG (Canada, USA); Andeas Meisel Verlagsvertretungen GmbH (Switzerland); Editoriale Umbra SAS (Italy)
Distribution Center: Ennsthaler Gesellschaft mbH & Co KG, Stadtplatz 26, 4400 Steyr, Austria, Publishing Representative: Dr Winfried Plattner *Tel:* (07252) 52053-20; (0676) 7051974 (cell) *Fax:* (07252) 52053-22 *E-mail:* auslieferung@ennsthaler.at
Balmer Buecherdienst AG, Kobiboden, 8840 Einsiedeln, Switzerland *Tel:* (0848) 840 820 *Fax:* (0848) 840 830 *E-mail:* info@balmer-bd.ch
Art Stock Books, c/o Independent Publishers Group, 814 N Franklin St, Chicago, IL, United States *Tel:* 312-337-0747 *Fax:* 312-337-5985 *E-mail:* orders@ipgbook.com (USA & Canada)

ImPrint Verlag
Amelsbuerener Str 203, 48163 Muenster
Tel: (02501) 97 24 496
E-mail: info@imprint-verlag.de
Web Site: www.imprint-verlag.de
Key Personnel
Dir: Joern Essig-Gutschmidt
Founded: 1997
Subjects: Fiction, Nonfiction (General), Poetry
ISBN Prefix(es): 978-3-936536

Impuls-Theater-Verlag+
Postfach 1147, 82141 Planegg
Tel: (089) 8597577 *Fax:* (089) 8593044
E-mail: info@theaterverlag.eu
Web Site: theaterverlag.eu
Key Personnel
Publishing Dir: Florian Laber
Founded: 1932
Specialize in theatre: plays & books.
Subjects: Drama, Theater, Film, Video, Music, Dance
ISBN Prefix(es): 978-3-7660
Distributed by Teaterverlag elgg (Switzerland)
Distributor for Stutz-Velag (Germany & Austria)

Industria-Verlagsbuchhandlung GmbH
Eschstr 22, 44629 Herne
Tel: (02323) 14 10 *Fax:* (02323) 14 11 23
Subjects: Accounting, Law
ISBN Prefix(es): 978-3-87373

Industrieverband Massivumformung eV
(Industry Association of Massive Forming)
Goldene Pforte 1, 58093 Hagen
Tel: (02331) 9588-0 *Fax:* (02331) 51046
E-mail: info@massivumformung.de
Web Site: www.massivumformung.de
Key Personnel
Mng Dir: Tobias Hain *Tel:* (02331) 958813
E-mail: hain@massivumformung.de
Business & Marketing: Holger Ade *Tel:* (02331)
958821 *E-mail:* hade@massivumformung.de
Press & Public Relations: Dorothea Bach-
mann Osenberg *Tel:* (02331) 958830
E-mail: osenberg@massivumformung.de
Strategic Projects: Sabine Widdermann
Tel: (02331) 958833 *E-mail:* swiddermann@
massivumformung.de
Research & Technology: Andreas Kucharzewski
Tel: (02331) 958832 *E-mail:* akucharzewski@
massivumformung.de
Publications of the Forging Industry Association.
Subjects: Engineering (General), Mechanical En-
gineering, Forging
ISBN Prefix(es): 978-3-928726

Informationsstelle Suedliches Afrika eV (ISSA)
(Information Centre on Southern Africa)
Koenigswintererstr 116, 53227 Bonn
Tel: (0228) 464369 *Fax:* (0228) 468177
E-mail: info@issa-bonn.org
Web Site: www.issa-bonn.org
Key Personnel
Mng Dir: Hein Moellers
Founded: 1971
Subjects: Developing Countries, Literature, Liter-
ary Criticism, Essays
ISBN Prefix(es): 978-3-921614

Info3 Verlag
Kirchgartenstr 1, 60439 Frankfurt am Main
Tel: (069) 58 46 47 *Fax:* (069) 58 46 16
E-mail: vertrieb@info3.de
Web Site: www.info3-verlag.de
Key Personnel
Mng Dir: Ramon Bruell *Tel:* (069) 57 00 08 92
E-mail: ramon.bruell@info3.de
Chief Editor: Jens Heisterkamp
Subjects: Art, Biography, Memoirs, Child Care
& Development, Fiction, Health, Nutrition,
History, Inspirational, Spirituality, Medicine,
Nursing, Dentistry, Religion - Other, Science
(General)
ISBN Prefix(es): 978-3-95779

Innenwelt Verlag GmbH
Brabanter Str 15, 50670 Cologne
Tel: (0221) 550 03 29 *Fax:* (0221) 562 62 36
E-mail: info@innenwelt-verlag.de
Web Site: www.innenwelt-verlag.de
Key Personnel
Dir: Martina Jivana Werner
Founded: 2003
Subjects: Astrology, Occult, How-to, Human Re-
lations, Inspirational, Spirituality, Self-Help
ISBN Prefix(es): 978-3-942502; 978-3-936360
Distribution Center: Prolit Verlagsausliefer-
ung GmbH, Siemensstr 16, 35461 Fernwald-
Annerod, Contact: Johanna Gastler *Tel:* (0641)
94 39 32 02 *Fax:* (0641) 94 39 38 9 *E-mail:* j.
gastler@prolit.de
Ennsthaler GmbH & Co KG Verlagsausliefer-
ung, Stadtplatz 26, 4400 Steyr, Austria
Tel: (07252) 520 53 23 *Fax:* (07252) 520 53
22 *E-mail:* distribution@ennsthaler.at
Schweizer Buchzentrum, Industriestr Ost 10, 4614
Haegendorf, Switzerland *Tel:* (062) 209 25 25
Fax: (062) 209 26 27

**Insel Verlag Anton Kippenberg GmbH & Co
KG+**
Subsidiary of Suhrkamp Verlag GmbH & Co KG
Pappelallee 78-79, 10437 Berlin

Tel: (030) 740744-0 *Fax:* (030) 740744-199
E-mail: info@suhrkamp.de
Web Site: www.suhrkamp.de
Key Personnel
Publisher: Ulla Unseld-Berkewicz
Vice President: Dr Thomas Sparr
Mng Dir: Dr Jonathan Landgrebe
Dir, Rights & Foreign Rights Dept: Nora Mercu-
rio
Press: Evelyn Paterson *Tel:* (030) 740744-294
E-mail: paterson@suhrkamp.de
Founded: 1899
Subjects: Art, Ethnicity, History, Literature, Liter-
ary Criticism, Essays, Music, Dance, Poetry
ISBN Prefix(es): 978-3-458
Associate Companies: Deutscher Klassiker Verlag
GmbH; Juedischer Verlag GmbH; Verlag der
Weltreligionen

edition insole, *imprint of* Erasmus Grasser-Verlag
GmbH

Institut fuer Auslandsbeziehungen eV (IFA)
(Institute for Foreign Cultural Relations)
Charlottenplatz 17, 70173 Stuttgart
Mailing Address: Postfach 102463, 70020
Stuttgart
Tel: (0711) 2225-0 *Fax:* (0711) 2264346
E-mail: info@ifa.de
Web Site: www.ifa.de
Key Personnel
Secretary General: Ronald Gratz
Subjects: Architecture & Interior Design, Art,
Film, Video, Photography
ISBN Prefix(es): 978-3-92170

**Institut fuer Baustoffe, Massivbau und
Brandschutz/Bibliothek** (Institute for Building
Materials, Concrete Construction & Fire
Protection Library)
Beethovenstr 52, 38106 Braunschweig
Tel: (0531) 391 5400 *Fax:* (0531) 391 5900
E-mail: info@ibmb.tu-bs.de
Web Site: www.ibmb.tu-bs.de
Key Personnel
Librarian: Oliver Dienelt *E-mail:* o.dienelt@ibmb.
tu-bs.de
Founded: 1963
Publisher of proceedings, reports & theses.
Subjects: Civil Engineering
ISBN Prefix(es): 978-3-89288
Number of titles published annually: 8 Print
Total Titles: 222 Print; 1 CD-ROM

**Institut fuer Internationale
Architektur-Dokumentation GmbH & Co
KG**
Hackerbruecke 6, 80335 Munich
Tel: (089) 38 16 20-0 *Fax:* (089) 38 16 20-77
E-mail: mail@detail.de
Web Site: www.detail-online.com
Key Personnel
Mng Dir: Karin Lang
Editor-in-Chief: Christian Schittich *Tel:* (089) 38
16 20-57
Sales Manager: Claudia Langert *Tel:* (089) 38 16
20-25
Founded: 1961
Specialize in architectural books. Publisher of
DETAIL.
Subjects: Architecture & Interior Design, Engi-
neering (General)
ISBN Prefix(es): 978-3-920034
Distributed by De Gruyter

**Institut fuer Landes- und
Stadtentwicklungsforschung GmbH**
(Research Institute for Regional & Urban
Development GmbH)
Bruederweg 22-24, 44135 Dortmund
Tel: (0231) 9051-0 *Fax:* (0231) 9051-155

E-mail: poststelle@ils-forschung.de
Web Site: www.ils-forschung.de
Key Personnel
Dir: Prof Rainer Danielzyk *Tel:* (0231) 9051-100
Founded: 2008
Subjects: Energy, Environmental Studies, Physi-
cal Sciences, Public Administration, Regional
Interests, Social Sciences, Sociology, Trans-
portation
ISBN Prefix(es): 978-3-8176
Number of titles published annually: 30 Online
Total Titles: 10 Print

Integral, *imprint of* Verlagsgruppe Random
House Bertelsmann

Integral Verlag
Imprint of Verlagsgruppe Random House Bertels-
mann
Bayerstr 71-73, 80335 Munich
Tel: (089) 4136-0 *Toll Free Tel:* 0800 500 33 22
Fax: (089) 4136-3333
E-mail: kundenservice@randomhouse.de
Web Site: www.randomhouse.de/
ansataintegrallotos
Key Personnel
Press: Claudia Grab *Tel:* (089) 4136-3131
Fax: (089) 4136-3507 *E-mail:* claudia.grab@
randomhouse.de
Subjects: Astrology, Occult, Health, Nutrition, In-
spirational, Spirituality, Philosophy, Self-Help,
Esoteric
ISBN Prefix(es): 978-3-7787

Interconnections Medien & Reise eK+
Schillerstr 44, 79102 Freiburg
Tel: (0761) 700 650 *Fax:* (0761) 700 688
E-mail: info@interconnections.de
Web Site: www.interconnections.de
Key Personnel
Owner: Georg Beckmann
Founded: 1984
Membership(s): Boersenverein des Deutschen
Buchhandels.
Subjects: Biography, Memoirs, Fiction, Travel &
Tourism
ISBN Prefix(es): 978-3-924586; 978-3-86040
Orders to: GeoCenter, Schockenriedstr 44, 70565
Stuttgart

**Internationale Gutenberg-Gesellschaft in
Mainz eV**
Liebfrauenplatz 5, 55116 Mainz
Tel: (06131) 22 64 20 *Fax:* (06131) 23 35 30
E-mail: info@gutenberg-gesellschaft.de
Web Site: www.gutenberg-gesellschaft.de
Key Personnel
President: Michael Ebling
Vice President: Guenther Knoedler
Secretary: Dr Stephan Fuessel
Mng Dir: Dr Franz Stephan Pelgen
Founded: 1901
International association dedicated to the history
of printing & of other media based on letters.
Subjects: History, Publishing & Book Trade Ref-
erence
ISBN Prefix(es): 978-3-7755
Number of titles published annually: 1 Print
Distributed by Otto Harrassowitz (yearbook only)

**Edition fuer Internationale Wirtschaft Verlags-
und Kommunikations GmbH**
Kaulbachstr 1, 60594 Frankfurt am Main
Tel: (069) 20515 *Fax:* (069) 289214
E-mail: info@edition-spanien.de
Web Site: www.edition-spanien.de
Key Personnel
Editor: Dr Burckhardt Loeber
Founded: 1975
Subjects: Business, Law
ISBN Prefix(es): 978-3-921326

Foreign Rep(s): Loeber & Lozano Abogados SLP (Spain)
Distribution Center: Verlagsauslieferung W Junior, Lassallestr 15, 34119 Kassel *Tel:* (0700) 33 48 466 *E-mail:* editionspanien@aol.com

Internationales Katholisches Missionswerk eV, see Missio eV

Invertito, *imprint of* Maennerschwarm Verlag GmbH

IRB, see Fraunhofer IRB Verlag

Irisiana, *imprint of* Verlagsgruppe Random House Bertelsmann

Edition Isele+
Heidelstr 9, 79805 Eggingen
Tel: (07746) 91 11-6 *Fax:* (07746) 91 11-7
E-mail: mail@edition-isele.de
Web Site: www.edition-isele.de
Key Personnel
Owner: Klaus Isele
Founded: 1984
Subjects: Art, Fiction, Literature, Literary Criticism, Essays, Nonfiction (General), Poetry, Religion - Buddhist, Travel & Tourism
ISBN Prefix(es): 978-3-925016; 978-3-86142
Number of titles published annually: 18 Print; 6 Audio
Total Titles: 200 Print; 20 Audio

Verlag der Islam+
Genfer Str 11, 60437 Frankfurt am Main
Tel: (069) 50688-651; (069) 50688-653 (sales) *Fax:* (069) 50688-655
Web Site: www.verlagderislam.de
Key Personnel
Contact: Faheem Ahmed
Founded: 1949
Subjects: Nonfiction (General), Religion - Islamic
ISBN Prefix(es): 978-3-921458; 978-3-932244
Number of titles published annually: 5 Print
Total Titles: 110 Print

Verlag Dr Ellen Ismail-Schmidt, see Tabaldi Verlag

ISSA, see Informationsstelle Suedliches Afrika eV (ISSA)

IUDICIUM Verlag GmbH+
Dauthendeystr 2, 81377 Munich
Tel: (089) 718747 *Fax:* (089) 7142039
E-mail: info@iudicium.de
Web Site: www.iudicium.de
Key Personnel
Mng Dir: Kiyoko Kapitza; Elisabeth Schaidhammer
Advertising & Public Relations: Aimee Dornier
Founded: 1983
Subjects: Anthropology, Art, Asian Studies, Biography, Memoirs, Communications, Drama, Theater, Education, Fiction, Foreign Countries, History, Language Arts, Linguistics, Library & Information Sciences, Literature, Literary Criticism, Essays, Music, Dance, Mysteries, Suspense, Philosophy, Poetry, Psychology, Psychiatry, Religion - Catholic, Social Sciences, Sociology, Theology, Women's Studies
ISBN Prefix(es): 978-3-89129
Returns: Hans-Graessel-Weg 13, 81375 Munich

ivi Verlag, *imprint of* Piper Verlag GmbH

Reisebuchverlag Iwanowski GmbH
Salm-Reifferscheidt-Allee 37, 41540 Dormagen
Tel: (02133) 260-311 *Fax:* (02133) 260-333

E-mail: info@iwanowski.de
Web Site: www.iwanowski.de
Key Personnel
Mng Dir: Ursula Iwanowski
Public Relations, Sales & Marketing: Claudia Heinrich *Tel:* (02133) 2603-11
E-mail: cheinrich@iwanowski.de
Founded: 1984
Subjects: Travel & Tourism
ISBN Prefix(es): 978-3-933041; 978-3-923975
Number of titles published annually: 16 Print
Total Titles: 90 Print
Distributed by Agnes Ottensmann; VVA Bertelsmann Distribution

IWT Magazine Publishing House GmbH, *imprint of* Gildebuchverlag GmbH & Co KG

J Ch Mellinger Verlag GmbH+
Burgholzstr 25, 70376 Stuttgart
Tel: (0711) 543787 *Fax:* (0711) 556889
E-mail: info@mellingerverlag.de
Web Site: mellingerverlag.de
Key Personnel
Contact: T Sambo
Founded: 1926
Subjects: Biography, Memoirs, Education, Fiction, Nonfiction (General)
ISBN Prefix(es): 978-3-88069
Orders to: Heidehof-Buchhandlung, Gerokstr 10, 70188 Stuttgart *Tel:* (0711) 246401 *Fax:* (0711) 235314 *E-mail:* info@heidehofbuchhandlung.de
Landi Distributors Ltd, One Cadogan Rd, Ringwood, Hants BH24 1QA, United Kingdom *Tel:* (01425) 485 197 *Fax:* (01425) 485 197 *E-mail:* info@landi-distributors.co.uk *Web Site:* www.landi-distributors.co.uk (UK orders only)

Verlagshaus Jacoby & Stuart GmbH
Strassburger Str 11, 10405 Berlin
Tel: (030) 47 37 47 90 *Fax:* (030) 47 37 47 968
E-mail: verlag@jacobystuart.de
Web Site: www.jacobystuart.de
Key Personnel
Publisher: Edmund Jacoby; Nicola Stuart
Head, Sales & Marketing: Frank Milschewsky *Tel:* (030) 47 37 47 950 *E-mail:* frank. milschewsky@jacobystuart.de
Founded: 2008
Subjects: Cookery, Fiction, Nonfiction (General), Comics, Graphic Novels
ISBN Prefix(es): 978-3-941087

J&D Dagyeli Verlag GmbH
Karl-Marx-Str 24, 12043 Berlin
Tel: (030) 44 308 764
E-mail: info@dagyeli.com
Web Site: www.dagyeli.com
Key Personnel
Mng Dir: Mario Pschera
Founded: 1982
Subjects: Fiction, Poetry
ISBN Prefix(es): 978-3-935597
Distribution Center: Prolit Verlagsauslieferung, Siemensstr 16, 35463 Fernwald/Annerod, Contact: Monika Pankratz *Tel:* (0641) 943 93 22 *Fax:* (0641) 943 93 29 *E-mail:* m.pankratz@prolit.de *Web Site:* www.prolit.de

Verlag & Antiquariat Winfried Jenior
Lassallestr 15, 34119 Kassel
Tel: (0561) 7391621 *Fax:* (0561) 774148
E-mail: jenior@aol.com
Web Site: www.jenior.de
Key Personnel
Mng Dir: Winfried Jenior
Publish book series of Kassel University, travel books on Spain, Spanish cookery books, yearbooks & books on Kassel & region.

Subjects: Cookery, Regional Interests, Travel & Tourism, Nazism
ISBN Prefix(es): 978-3-9801438; 978-3-928172; 978-3-934377
Distributor for Moll Verlag

Jhana Verlag/Buddha-Haus
Uttenbuehl 5, 87466 Oy-Mittelberg
Tel: (08376) 88 38 *Fax:* (08376) 5 92
E-mail: info@jhanaverlag.de
Web Site: buddha-haus-shop.de
Key Personnel
Publishing Dir: Claudia Wildgruber
Founded: 1989
Subjects: Religion - Buddhist
ISBN Prefix(es): 978-3-931274
Branch Office(s)
Duringstr 11, 82299 Tuerkenfeld *Tel:* (08193) 99 72 70 *Fax:* (08193) 997 97 30 *E-mail:* jhana-verlag@buddha-haus.de

JMB Verlag
Rotekreuzstr 25, 30627 Hannover
Tel: (0511) 70033380; (0179) 5176599 *Fax:* (0511) 70033381
E-mail: info@jmb-verlag.de
Web Site: www.jmb-verlag.de
Key Personnel
Publisher: Jens Bolm
Subjects: Literature, Literary Criticism, Essays, Nonfiction (General), Philosophy
ISBN Prefix(es): 978-3-940970; 978-3-944342

Johannes Verlag Einsiedeln+
Lindenmattenstr 29, 79117 Freiburg
Tel: (0761) 64 01 68 *Fax:* (0761) 64 01 69
E-mail: kontakt@johannes-verlag.de
Web Site: www.johannes-verlag.de
Founded: 1947
Christian publisher.
Subjects: Philosophy, Religion - Catholic, Theology
ISBN Prefix(es): 978-3-89411
Number of titles published annually: 10 Print
Total Titles: 340 Print
Orders to: Herder AG Basel, Muttenzerstr 109, 4133 Pratteln 1, Switzerland *E-mail:* verkauf@herder.ch

Jonas Verlag fuer Kunst und Literatur GmbH
Weidenhaeuser Str 88, 35037 Marburg
Tel: (06421) 25132 *Fax:* (06421) 210572
E-mail: jonas@jonas-verlag.de; presse@jonas-verlag.de
Web Site: www.jonas-verlag.de
Key Personnel
Manager & Art History: Dieter Mayer-Guerr *E-mail:* dmg@jonas-verlag.de
Design & Manufacturing: Simone Tavernrath *E-mail:* satz@jonas-verlag.de
Press & Public Relations: Dr Almut Bick
Founded: 1978
Subjects: Architecture & Interior Design, Art, History, Literature, Literary Criticism, Essays, Photography, Regional Interests, Science (General), Architecture History, Art History, Cultural Studies
ISBN Prefix(es): 978-3-89445; 978-3-922561
Foreign Rep(s): Helga Schuster (Austria)
Distribution Center: Prolit Verlagsauslieferung GmbH, Postfach 9, 35461 Fernwald *Tel:* (0641) 94393-25 *Fax:* (0641) 94393-89 *E-mail:* i.peters@prolit.de

Jovis Verlag GmbH+
Kurfuerstenstr 15/16, 10785 Berlin
Tel: (030) 26 36 72-0 *Fax:* (030) 26 36 72-72
E-mail: jovis@jovis.de; info@jovis.de
Web Site: www.jovis.de
Key Personnel
Mng Dir: Jochen Visscher

Sales & Marketing Manager: Jutta Bornholdt-
Cassetti *Tel:* (030) 26 36 72 22
E-mail: bornholdt@jovis.de
Founded: 1995
Subjects: Architecture & Interior Design, Art,
History, Photography
ISBN Prefix(es): 978-3-931321; 978-3-936314;
978-3-939633; 978-3-86859
Number of titles published annually: 45 Print
Total Titles: 195 Print
Foreign Rep(s): Artbook/DAP (North America,
South America, USA); AVA Verlagsausliefer-
ung AG (Switzerland); Jutta Bornholdt-Cassetti
(Austria, Germany, Switzerland); Buchzentrum
AG (Switzerland); China Publishers Market-
ing (Benjamin Pan) (China, Southeast Asia,
Taiwan); Elisabeth Harder-Kreimann (Finland,
Iceland, Norway, Sweden); Flavio Marcello
Publisher's Representative (Southern Europe);
RIBA Enterprises (Ireland, UK); Jan Smit
Boeken (Netherlands)
Distribution Center: LKG, An der Suedspitze 1-
12, 04571 Roetha, Contact: Kathrin Obarski
Tel: (034206) 6 51 06 *Fax:* (034206) 65 1741
E-mail: kathrin.obarski@lkg-service.de

Jowi-Verlag+
Muehlbacher Str 5, 97753 Karlstadt
Tel: (09353) 2921
E-mail: info@jowi-verlag.de
Web Site: www.jowi-verlag.de
Key Personnel
Editor: Johanna Wittstadt
Founded: 1991
ISBN Prefix(es): 978-3-9802897

Joy Verlag GmbH+
Hornweg 11, 87466 Oy-Mittelberg
Tel: (08366) 98 8610 *Fax:* (08366) 98 4192
E-mail: postbox@joy-verlag.de
Web Site: www.joy-verlag.de
Key Personnel
Mng Dir: Thomas Kettenring
Founded: 1987
Subjects: Alternative, Cookery, Health, Nutri-
tion, Religion - Buddhist, Self-Help, Alterna-
tive Medicine, Holistic Healing
ISBN Prefix(es): 978-3-928554; 978-3-9801624
Distribution Center: Brockhaus/Commis-
sion, Kreidlerstr 9, 70806 Kornwestheim
Tel: (07154) 13 27 30; (07154) 13 27 21
Fax: (07154) 13 27 13 *E-mail:* joy@brocom.de
Dr Franz Hain GmbH, Dr-Otto-Neurath-Gasse 5,
1220 Vienna, Austria *Tel:* (01) 2 82 65 65 77
Fax: (01) 2 82 52 82 *E-mail:* vertrieb@hain.at
Dessauer, Raeffelstr 32, 8045 Zurich, Switzer-
land *Tel:* (044) 46696-96 *Fax:* (044) 46696-69
E-mail: dessauer@dessauer.ch

Juedischer Verlag GmbH+
Subsidiary of Suhrkamp Verlag GmbH & Co KG
Pappelallee 78-78, 10437 Berlin
Tel: (030) 740744-291
E-mail: info@suhrkamp.de
Web Site: www.suhrkamp.de
Key Personnel
Publisher: Ulla Unseld-Berkewicz
Mng Dir: Dr Jonathan Landgrebe
Founded: 1902
Subjects: Religion - Jewish, Holocaust
ISBN Prefix(es): 978-3-633
Associate Companies: Deutscher Klassiker Verlag
GmbH; Insel Verlag Anton Kippenberg GmbH
& Co KG; Verlag der Weltreligionen

**Juenger Medien Verlag +
Burckhardthaus-Laetare GmbH+**
Schumannstr 155, 63069 Offenbach
Tel: (069) 83 00 66 43 *Fax:* (069) 83 00 66 33
E-mail: info@juenger.de
Web Site: www.juengermedien.de

Key Personnel
Mng Dir: Andre Juenger *E-mail:* andre.juenger@
juenger.de; Helmut Juenger
Founded: 1950
Subjects: Education, Psychology, Psychiatry, Reli-
gion - Other
ISBN Prefix(es): 978-3-7664

Jugenddienst-Verlag, see Peter Hammer Verlag
GmbH

JUMBO, *imprint of* JUMBO Neue Medien &
Verlag GmbH

JUMBO Neue Medien & Verlag GmbH
Henriettenstr 42a, 20259 Hamburg
Tel: (040) 429 30 40-0 *Fax:* (040) 429 30 40-29
E-mail: info@jumbo-medien.de
Web Site: www.jumboverlag.de
Key Personnel
Dir: Gabriele Swiderski
Founded: 1991
ISBN Prefix(es): 978-3-8337; 978-3-89592; 978-
3-930319; 978-3-9802851
Imprints: Goya libre; Goya LiT; JUMBO

Junfermann Verlag GmbH+
Andreasstr, 1a, 33098 Paderborn
Tel: (05251) 1 34 40 *Fax:* (05251) 13 44 44
E-mail: infoteam@junfermann.de
Web Site: www.junfermann.de
Key Personnel
Mng Dir: Dr Stephan Dietrich *E-mail:* dietrich@
junfermann.de
Customer Service: Christa Guder *Tel:* (05251) 13
44 12 *E-mail:* guder@junfermann.de
Press & Public Relations: Heike Carstensen
Tel: (05251) 13 44 18 *E-mail:* carstensen@
junfermann.de
Sales: Stefanie Linden *Tel:* (05251) 13 44 16
E-mail: linden@junfermann.de
Founded: 1659
Specialize in psychology & psychotherapy.
Subjects: Communications, Management, Psy-
chology, Psychiatry, Self-Help
ISBN Prefix(es): 978-3-87387
Number of titles published annually: 30 Print
Total Titles: 250 Print
Parent Company: Klett-Cotta Verlag, Rotebuehlstr
77, 70178 Stuttgart
Ultimate Parent Company: Ernst Klett Aktienge-
sellschaft, Rotebuehlstr 77, 70178 Stuttgart
Foreign Rights: Susanne Theune (Latin America
exc Brazil, Portugal, Spain)
Distribution Center: Koch, Neff & Oetinger Ver-
lagsauslieferung GmbH, Industriestr 23, 70565
Stuttgart *E-mail:* junfermann@kno-va.de
Returns: Koch, Neff & Oetinger Verlagsauslief-
ung GmbH, Remittendenabteilung, Industriestr
23, 70565 Stuttgart

Junius Verlag GmbH+
Stresemannstr 375, 22761 Hamburg
Tel: (040) 89 25 99 *Fax:* (040) 89 12 24
E-mail: info@junius-verlag.de
Web Site: www.junius-verlag.de
Key Personnel
Mng Dir & Sales: Steffen Herrmann
E-mail: herrmann@junius-verlag.de
Founded: 1979
Subjects: Architecture & Interior Design, Civil
Engineering, Government, Political Science,
Philosophy, Social Sciences, Sociology
ISBN Prefix(es): 978-3-88506
Number of titles published annually: 30 Print
Total Titles: 200 Print
Foreign Rep(s): AVA Verlagsauslieferung AG
(Beat Eberle) (Switzerland); Idea Books (Asia,
Australia, Europe, New Zealand, North Amer-
ica); Mohr Morawa Buchvertrieb GmbH (Aus-
tria)

Distribution Center: Leipziger Kommissions und
Grossbuchhandelsgesellschaft mbH (LKG),
An der Suedspitze 1-12, 04571 Roetha, Con-
tact: Ursula Fritzsche *Tel:* (034206) 65-135
Fax: (034206) 65-102 *E-mail:* ufritzsche@lkg-
service.de *Web Site:* www.lkg-va.de
Mohr Morawa Buchvertrieb GmbH, Sulzen-
gasse 2, 1230 Vienna, Austria *Tel:* (01) 680
14-0 *Fax:* (01) 688 71 30 *E-mail:* momo@
mohrmorawa.at *Web Site:* www.mohrmorawa.at
AVA buch 2000, Centralweg 16, Postfach
27, 8910 Affoltern am Albis, Switzerland
Tel: (01) 7 62 42 60 *Fax:* (01) 7 62 42 10
E-mail: buch2000@ava.ch

Jurion, *imprint of* Wolters Kluwer Deutschland
GmbH

Justus-Liebig-Universitaet Giessen
Ludwigstr 23, 35390 Giessen
Tel: (0641) 99-0; (0641) 99-12041 (press)
Fax: (0641) 99-12259; (0641) 99-12049 (press)
E-mail: pressestelle@uni-giessen.de
Web Site: www.uni-giessen.de
Key Personnel
President: Joybrato Mukherjee
E-mail: praesident@admin.uni-giessen.de
Editorial Manager: Charlotte Brueckner-Ihl
Tel: (0641) 99-12042
Research institution (international economic &
social development & environment).
Subjects: Agriculture, Environmental Studies, Sci-
ence (General), Social Sciences, Sociology
ISBN Prefix(es): 978-3-924840

Jutta Pohl Verlag+
Im Buckeberg 11a, 76307 Karlsbad
Tel: (07202) 2239 *Fax:* (07202) 2239
Subjects: Computer Science, Mathematics
ISBN Prefix(es): 978-3-7911
Total Titles: 60 Print; 2 Audio
Foreign Rep(s): As Bartsch-Holler GmbH (Aus-
tria); Schweizer Buchzentruun (Switzerland);
Uitgeverij de Vraseborch (Netherlands)

Juventa Verlag GmbH+
Subsidiary of Julius Beltz GmbH & Co KG
Ehretstr 3, 69469 Weinheim
Tel: (06201) 9020-0 *Fax:* (06201) 9020-13
E-mail: juventa@beltz.de
Web Site: www.juventa.de
Key Personnel
Publisher & Chief Executive Officer: Marianne
Ruebelmann
Publishing Dir: Frank Engelhardt *Tel:* (06201)
6007-476 *E-mail:* f.engelhardt@beltz.de
Press Officer: Jacob Hochrein *Tel:* (06201) 6007-
389 *E-mail:* j.hochrein@beltz.de
Advertising: Andrea Biernatzki *Tel:* (06201)
6007-470 *E-mail:* a.biernatzki@beltz.de
Founded: 1953
Subjects: Criminology, Education, Health, Nu-
trition, History, Psychology, Psychiatry, Social
Sciences, Sociology
ISBN Prefix(es): 978-3-7799
Number of titles published annually: 70 Print
Total Titles: 800 Print
Ultimate Parent Company: Beltz Ruebelmann
Holding
Foreign Rep(s): Ruedi Amrhein (Switzerland);
Mohr Morawa Buchvertrieb GmbH (Guenther
Raunjak) (Austria)
Distribution Center: Rhenus Medien Logis-
tik GmbH & Co KG, Justus-von-Liebig-Str
1, 86899 Landsberg am Lech *Tel:* (08191)
970 00-622 *Fax:* (08191) 970 00-405
E-mail: bestellung@beltz.de
Mohr Morawa Buchvertrieb GmbH, Sulzen-
gasse 2, 1230 Vienna, Austria *Tel:* (01) 680
14-0 *Fax:* (01) 688 71 30 *E-mail:* momo@
mohrmorawa.at *Web Site:* www.mohrmorawa.at

AVA Verlagsauslieferung AG, Centralweg
16, 8910 Affoltern am Albis, Switzerland
Tel: (044) 762 42 50 *Fax:* (044) 762 42 49
E-mail: verlagsservice@ava.ch

Kulturverlag Kadmos
Waldenserstr 2-4, 10551 Berlin
Tel: (030) 39789394 *Fax:* (030) 39789380
E-mail: vertrieb@kulturverlag-kadmos.de;
bestellung@kulturverlag-kadmos.de
Web Site: www.kulturverlag-kadmos.de
Key Personnel
Publisher: Wolfram Burckhardt *E-mail:* wb@
kulturverlag-kadmos.de
Founded: 1995
Subjects: Fiction, Government, Political Science,
History, Nonfiction (General), Philosophy, Sci-
ence (General), Technology, Arts, Culture, Me-
dia
ISBN Prefix(es): 978-3-86599; 978-3-93165

Kailash, *imprint of* Verlagsgruppe Random House
Bertelsmann

KaJo Verlag+
Imprint of Verlagshaus Wuerzburg GmbH & Co
KG
Beethovenstr 5 B, 97080 Wuerzburg
Tel: (0931) 465 889-11 *Fax:* (0931) 465 889-29
E-mail: info@verlagshaus.com
Web Site: www.verlagshaus.com
Key Personnel
Publishing Dir: Dieter Krause *Tel:* (0931) 465
889-14 *E-mail:* dieter.krause@verlagshaus.com
Dir, Production: Juergen Roth *Tel:* (0931) 465
889-15 *E-mail:* juergen.roth@verlagshaus.com
Sales Dir: Johannes Glesius *Tel:* (0931) 465 889-
13 *E-mail:* johannes.glesius@verlagshaus.com
Founded: 1985
Subjects: Travel & Tourism
ISBN Prefix(es): 978-3-925544; 978-3-8003

Kalam Verlag KG
Rosastr 9, 79098 Freiburg
Tel: (0761) 45002152 *Fax:* (0761) 45002100
E-mail: info@kalam-verlag.de
Web Site: www.kalam-verlag.de
Key Personnel
Mng Dir: Andreas Hodeige
Sales: Heike Spantig
Subjects: Religion - Islamic, Theology
ISBN Prefix(es): 978-3-9815572
Imprints: Salam

Kallmeyer Verlag+
Im Brande 17, 30926 Seelze
Tel: (0511) 40 00 4-175 *Fax:* (0511) 40 00 4-176
E-mail: leserservice@friedrich-verlag.de
Web Site: www.friedrich-verlag.de
Founded: 1986
Specialize in elementary drawings, rhythm &
teaching goods.
Subjects: Career Development, Crafts, Games,
Hobbies, Education, Engineering (General), En-
vironmental Studies, Music, Dance, Nonfiction
(General), Sports, Athletics
ISBN Prefix(es): 978-3-7800
Parent Company: Friedrich Verlag GmbH
Ultimate Parent Company: Klett Gruppe

Verlag und Druckkontor Kamp GmbH
Bergstr 153, 44791 Bochum
Tel: (0234) 51617-0 *Fax:* (0234) 51617-18
E-mail: mail@kamp-verlag.de
Web Site: www.kamp-verlag.de
Key Personnel
Mng Dir: Dr Ferdinand Kamp
Editor & Public Relations: Karoline Kerlin
Tel: (0234) 51617-16 *E-mail:* kerlin@kamp-
verlag.de

Sales: Brigitte Breidenbach *Tel:* (0234) 51617-10
E-mail: breidenbach@kamp-verlag.de
Founded: 1996
Subjects: Education, Fiction, Religion - Other,
Science (General)
ISBN Prefix(es): 978-3-89709

J Kamphausen Verlag+
Imprint of Kamphausen Media GmbH
Goldbach 2, 33615 Bielefeld
Tel: (0521) 5 60 52-0 *Fax:* (0521) 5 60 52-29
E-mail: info@j-kamphausen.de
Key Personnel
Publisher: Joachim Kamphausen
Founded: 1983
Subjects: Business, Health, Nutrition, Inspira-
tional, Spirituality, Management, Philosophy,
Psychology, Psychiatry, Religion - Buddhist,
Religion - Hindu, Religion - Other, Self-Help
ISBN Prefix(es): 978-3-928430; 978-3-89901;
978-3-933496

**edition KAPPA, Verlag fuer Kultur und
Kommunikation GmbH**
Hippmannstr 5, 80639 Munich
Tel: (089) 17 11 82 33 *Fax:* (089) 17 11 82 04
E-mail: info@editionkappa.de
Web Site: www.editionkappa.de
Key Personnel
Management: Dr Bernard Oliver Schmidt; Hanna
Schmidt
Founded: 1994
Subjects: Travel & Tourism
ISBN Prefix(es): 978-3-932000; 978-3-937600

S Karger GmbH+
Wilhelmstr 20A, 79098 Freiburg
Tel: (0761) 45 20 7-0 *Fax:* (0761) 45 20 7-14
E-mail: information@karger.de
Web Site: www.karger.com
Key Personnel
Publishing Dir: Susanne Meister *Tel:* (0761) 45
20 7-18 *E-mail:* s.meister@karger.de
Manager, Publishing: Sibylle Gross *Tel:* (0761)
45 20 7-11 *E-mail:* s.gross@karger.de
Marketing & Advertisement: Ellen Zimmer-
mann *Tel:* (0761) 45 20 7-17 *E-mail:* e.
zimmermann@karger.de
Production: Georg Brunner *Tel:* (0761) 45 20
7-15 *E-mail:* g.brunner@karger.de; Sebas-
tian Zoller *Tel:* (0761) 45 20 7-27 *E-mail:* s.
zoller@karger.de
Founded: 1890
Subjects: Biological Sciences, Health, Nutrition,
Medicine, Nursing, Dentistry, Psychology, Psy-
chiatry, Science (General), Sports, Athletics
ISBN Prefix(es): 978-3-8055
Parent Company: S Karger AG, Allschwilerstr 10,
4055 Basel, Switzerland
U.S. Office(s): S Karger Publishers Inc, 26 W
Avon Rd, PO Box 529, Unionville, CT 06085,
United States *Tel:* 860-675-7834 *Fax:* 860-675-
7302 *E-mail:* karger@snet.net
Bookshop(s): Karger-Buchhandlung Ausstel-
lung und Vertrieb internationale medizinis-
cher Fachliteratur, Loerracher Str 16a, 79115
Freiburg

Karl-May-Verlag GmbH+
Schuetzenstr 30, 96047 Bamberg
Tel: (0951) 9 82 06-0 *Fax:* (0951) 9 82 06-55
E-mail: info@karl-may.de
Web Site: www.karl-may.de
Key Personnel
Mng Dir: Bernhard Schmid
Founded: 1913
Life & works of German writer Karl May.
Subjects: Fiction, Nonfiction (General), Western
Fiction
ISBN Prefix(es): 978-3-7802
Number of titles published annually: 7 Print
Total Titles: 200 Print

Imprints: Edition Ustad
Subsidiaries: Karl May Verwaltungs-und Vertriebs
GmbH

Karren Publishing
Haus Bakenfield, Roxeler Str 392a, 48161 Muen-
ster
Tel: (0151) 120 598 01
Web Site: www.karren-publishing.com
Key Personnel
Publisher: Tom van Endert *E-mail:* tom.
vanendert@karren-publishing.com
Subjects: Automotive, Boats, Car Restoration,
Motorcycles
ISBN Prefix(es): 978-3-947060; 978-3-942153

Kartographischer Verlag Reinhard Ryborsch+
Anzengruberstr 12, 63073 Offenbach am Main
Mailing Address: Postfach 160271, 63034 Offen-
bach am Main
Tel: (069) 85097707 *Fax:* (069) 85097708
Key Personnel
Publisher: Reinhard Ryborsch
Founded: 1987
Membership(s): Boersenverein des Deutschen
Buchhandels; Deutsche Gesellschaft fuer Kar-
tographie.
Subjects: Aeronautics, Aviation, Geography, Geol-
ogy, Travel & Tourism
ISBN Prefix(es): 978-3-920339; 978-3-927549

Kassel University Press GmbH
Diagonale 10, 34127 Kassel
Tel: (0561) 804-2159 *Fax:* (0561) 804-3429
E-mail: info@upress.uni-kassel.de
Web Site: cms.uni-kassel.de/unicms
Key Personnel
Mng Dir: Beate Bergner
E-mail: geschaeftsfuehrung@upress.uni-kassel.
de
Publication Manager: Susanne Schneider
Tel: (0561) 804-2144
Founded: 1997
Subjects: Agriculture, Architecture & Interior De-
sign, Art, Computer Science, Economics, Law,
Medicine, Nursing, Dentistry, Science (Gen-
eral), Social Sciences, Sociology, Ecology, Hu-
manities
ISBN Prefix(es): 978-3-89958; 978-3-933146

Kastell Verlag GmbH+
Giselastr 15, 80802 Munich
Mailing Address: Postfach 440 312, 80752 Mu-
nich
Tel: (089) 33 21 75 *Fax:* (089) 340 11 78
E-mail: info@kastell-verlag.de
Key Personnel
Mng Dir, Rights & Permissions: Christoph Bur-
gauner
Founded: 1984
Subjects: History, Music, Dance
ISBN Prefix(es): 978-3-924592

Iris Kater Verlag & Medien GmbH
Nelsenstr 15, 41748 Viersen
Tel: (02162) 1 02 68 06 *Fax:* (02162) 1 02 68 07
E-mail: info@kater-medien.de
Web Site: www.katercom.de/verlag/; www.
katercom.de
Key Personnel
Mng Dir: Iris Kater
Founded: 2001
Membership(s): Boersenverein des Deutschen
Buchhandels.
Subjects: Fiction, Health, Nutrition, Humor, In-
spirational, Spirituality, Poetry, Science Fiction,
Fantasy, Crime, Thrillers
ISBN Prefix(es): 978-3-940063; 978-3-939061
Imprints: Glossabooks; Katercom; Rotblatt

Katercom, *imprint of* Iris Kater Verlag & Medien
GmbH

Verlag Katholisches Bibelwerk GmbH+

Silberburgstr 121, 70176 Stuttgart
Tel: (0711) 61920-0 *Fax:* (0711) 61920-44
E-mail: info@bibelwerk.de
Web Site: www.bibelwerk.de
Key Personnel
Mng Dir: Winfried Kuhn *E-mail:* w.kuhn@
bibelwerk.de; Daniela-Maria Schilling
E-mail: schilling@bibelwerk.de
Head, Sales & Advertising: Melanie Locker
Tel: (0711) 61920-35 *E-mail:* locker@
bibelwerk.de
Editorial Secretary/Production: Eva Engesser
Tel: (0711) 61920-25 *E-mail:* engesser@
bibelwerk.de
Editorial: Burkhard Menke *Tel:* (0711) 61920-27
E-mail: menke@bibelwerk.de
Founded: 1937
Membership(s): Katholischer Medienverband
(KM).
Subjects: Biblical Studies, Religion - Catholic
ISBN Prefix(es): 978-3-460
Distribution Center: Koch, Neff & Oetinger Ver-
lagsauslieferung GmbH, Industriestr 23, 70565
Stuttgart *E-mail:* bibelwerk@kno-va.de

Verlag Ernst Kaufmann GmbH+

Alleestr 2, 77933 Lahr
Tel: (07821) 9390-0 *Fax:* (07821) 9390-11;
(07821) 9390-30
E-mail: info@kaufmann-verlag.de; bestellung@
kaufmann-verlag.de; lektorat@kaufmann-verlag.
de
Web Site: www.kaufmann-verlag.de
Key Personnel
Mng Dir: Dr Klaus-Christoph Scheffels
Tel: (07821) 9390-22 *E-mail:* k.scheffels@
kaufmann-verlag.de; Thomas Schneble
Tel: (07821) 9390-14 *E-mail:* t.schneble@
kaufmann-verlag.de
Editor: Katia Simon *Tel:* (07821) 9390-20
E-mail: k.simon@kaufmann-verlag.de; Felix
Tolles *Tel:* (07821) 9390-17 *E-mail:* f.tolles@
kaufmann-verlag.de
Foreign Rights: Annette Meier *Tel:* (07821) 9390-
12 *E-mail:* a.meier@kaufmann-verlag.de
Marketing & Sales: Anja Schaile *Tel:* (07821)
9390-19 *E-mail:* a.schaile@kaufmann-verlag.de
Order Processing & Distribution: Ulrike
Schmieder *Tel:* (07821) 9390-10 *E-mail:* u.
schmieder@kaufmann-verlag.de
Production: Annette Aatz *Tel:* (07821) 9390-18
E-mail: a.aatz@kaufmann-verlag.de
Founded: 1816
Membership(s): Arbeitsgemeinschaft von Jugend-
buchverlagen eV (AVJ); ATV; Verlagsring Reli-
gionsunterricht (VRU).
Subjects: Religion - Protestant, Religion - Other
ISBN Prefix(es): 978-3-7806
Foreign Rep(s): B+I Buch und Information AG
(Dagmar Bhend) (Switzerland); Verlagsagen-
tur Erich Neuhold (Erich Neuhold & Wilhelm
Platzer) (Austria); Harald Rumpold (Austria,
South Tyrol, Italy)
Distribution Center: Dr Franz Hain Verlagsaus-
lieferungen, Dr-Otto-Neurath-Gasse 5, 1220
Vienna, Austria *Tel:* (01) 2826565 *Fax:* (01)
2825282 *E-mail:* vertrieb@hain.at
Scheidegger & Co AG, c/o AVA Verlagsausliefer-
ung AG, Centralweg 16, 8910 Affoltern am Al-
bis, Switzerland *Tel:* (044) 7624250 *Fax:* (044)
7624210 *E-mail:* scheidegger@ava.ch

Kawohl Verlag eK

Blumenkamper Weg 16, 46485 Wesel
Tel: (0281) 9 62 99-0 *Fax:* (0281) 9 62 99-1 00
E-mail: verlag@kawohl.de; info@kawohl.de
Web Site: shop.kawohl.de
Key Personnel
Owner: Reinhard Kawohl
Christian picture productions such as picture cal-
endars (with inspirational texts), gift books &
gift items.

Subjects: Inspirational, Spirituality, Religion -
Protestant
ISBN Prefix(es): 978-3-88087
Parent Company: Kawohl Verlagsgruppe

KBV Verlags-und Medien - GmbH+

Augustinerstr 4, 54576 Hillesheim
Tel: (06593) 998960 *Fax:* (06593) 99896-20
E-mail: info@kbv-verlag.de
Web Site: www.kbv-verlag.de
Key Personnel
Mng Dir: Ralf Kramp
Founded: 1989
Subjects: Fiction, Government, Political Sci-
ence, LGBTQ, Mysteries, Suspense, Nonfiction
(General), Adventure, Anthologies, Historical,
Short Stories, Thrillers
ISBN Prefix(es): 978-3-927658
Foreign Rep(s): Martin E Schnetzer (Switzer-
land); Ernst Sonntag & Christian Hirtzy (Aus-
tria)
Distribution Center: Prolit Verlagsausliefer-
ung GmbH, Siemensstr 16, 35463 Fernwald-
Annerod, Contact: Gabriele Lemuth *Tel:* (0641)
94393-201 *Fax:* (0641) 94393-89 *E-mail:* g.
lemuth@prolit.de
Dr Franz Hain Verlagsauslieferung GmbH, Dr-
Otto-Neurath-Gasse 5, 1220 Vienna, Austria
Tel: (01) 282 65 65-77 *Fax:* (01) 282 52 82
E-mail: bestell@hain.at
Herder AG, Muttenzerstr 109, 4133 Pratteln,
Switzerland *Tel:* (061) 827 90 60 *Fax:* (061)
827 90 67 *E-mail:* verkauf@herder.ch

Kehl Verlag

Schillerstr 5, 67580 Hamm am Rhein
Tel: (06246) 9 97 81 *Fax:* (06241) 9 97 82
E-mail: info@kehl-verlag.de; kontakt@kehl-
verlag.de
Web Site: www.kehl-verlag.de
Key Personnel
Contact: Stefan Kehl
Founded: 1998
Subjects: Cookery, Fiction, History, Regional In-
terests, Travel & Tourism
ISBN Prefix(es): 978-3-935651

Kehrer Verlag

Wieblinger Weg 21, 69123 Heidelberg
Tel: (06221) 649 20-10 *Fax:* (06221) 649 20-20
E-mail: contact@kehrerverlag.com
Web Site: www.kehrerverlag.com
Key Personnel
Publisher & Dir: Klaus Kehrer
Deputy Publishing Dir: Ariane Braun
Tel: (06221) 649 20-16 *E-mail:* ariane.braun@
kehrerverlag.com
Production: Alex Kunde *Tel:* (06221) 649 20-24
E-mail: alex.kunde@kehrerdesign.com
Public Relations & Foreign Sales: Barbara Karpf
Tel: (06221) 649 20-18 *E-mail:* barbara.karpf@
kehrerverlag.com
Founded: 1995
Subjects: Art, Photography, Culture, Fine Art
ISBN Prefix(es): 978-3-86828; 978-3-933257;
978-3-9804444; 978-3-936636; 978-3-939583
Foreign Rep(s): Ashton International Market-
ing Services (Julian Ashton) (Far East); Jan
Smit Boeken (Belgium, Luxembourg, Nether-
lands); Bookport Associates Ltd (Joe Portelli)
(Bosnia and Herzegovina, Croatia, Gibraltar,
Greece, Italy, Malta, Portugal, Serbia, Slovenia,
Spain); Consortium Book Sales & Distribution
(Canada, USA); Sebastian Graf (Switzerland);
Elisabeth Harder-Kreimann (Scandinavia);
IMA/Intermediaamericana (David Williams)
(South America); Marcello SAS Publishers'
Representatives (Flavio Marcello) (France);
Alexander Quaynor (South Africa); Turnaround
Publisher Services Ltd (Ireland, UK); Peter
Ward Book Exports (Richard Ward) (Middle
East, North Africa, Turkey)

Distribution Center: Stuttgarter Verlagskontor
SVK GmbH, Rotebuehlstr 77, 70178 Stuttgart
Tel: (0711) 66 72-19 24 *Fax:* (0711) 66 72-19-
74 *E-mail:* h.bauer@svk.de *Web Site:* www.
svk.de (Germany & Austria)
Buch 2000/AVA, Centralweg 16, 8910 Affoltern
am Albis, Switzerland *Tel:* (01) 762 42 60
Fax: (01) 762 42 10 *E-mail:* buch2000@ava.ch
Turnaround Publisher Services Ltd, Unit 3,
Olympia Trading Estate, Coburg Rd, London
N22 6TZ, United Kingdom *Tel:* (020) 8829
3000 *Fax:* (020) 8881 5088 *E-mail:* orders@
turnaround-uk.com (Great Britain & Ireland)
Consortium Book Sales & Distribution, c/o Two
Rivers Distribution, 1094 Flex Dr, Jackson,
TN 38301, United States *E-mail:* orderentry@
perseusbooks.com *Web Site:* www.cbsd.com
(USA & Canada)

Keip & von Delft GmbH+

Holsteinische Str 29, 10717 Berlin
Tel: (030) 401 083 22 *Fax:* (030) 401 083 21
E-mail: info@keip.net; buc@keip.net
Web Site: www.keip.net
Key Personnel
Mng Dir: Ulrich Keip *E-mail:* ulrich@keip.net
Founded: 1967
Also antiquarian bookseller.
Membership(s): International League of Antiquar-
ian Booksellers (ILAB).
Subjects: Economics, History, Law, Social Sci-
ences, Sociology
ISBN Prefix(es): 978-3-8051

Kellner Verlag+

Sankt-Pauli-Deich 3, 28199 Bremen
Tel: (0421) 77 8 66 *Fax:* (0421) 70 40 58
E-mail: info@kellnerverlag.de; buchservice@
kellnerverlag.de
Web Site: www.kellnerverlag.de
Key Personnel
Publisher: Klaus Kellner
Founded: 1988
Also acts as shipping house.
Subjects: Government, Political Science, Labor,
Industrial Relations, Law, Nonfiction (General),
Outdoor Recreation, Public Administration,
Travel & Tourism
ISBN Prefix(es): 978-3-927155
Number of titles published annually: 10 Print
Total Titles: 100 Print

Martin Kelter Verlag GmbH & Co KG

Muehlenstieg 16-22, 22041 Hamburg
Tel: (040) 68 28 95-0 *Fax:* (040) 68 28 95 50
E-mail: info@kelter.de
Web Site: www.kelter.de
Key Personnel
Publisher: Gerhard Melchert
Publishing Dir: Mario Melchert; Oliver Melchert
Management: Rositta Melchert
Sales Manager: Eloff Hoelscher
Editorial: Dr Andreas Schaefer
Founded: 1938
Subjects: Accounting, Finance, Library & Infor-
mation Sciences, Literature, Literary Criticism,
Essays, Marketing, Graphic Design, Informa-
tion Technology, Manufacturing
ISBN Prefix(es): 978-3-88832
Associate Companies: Mero-Druck Otto Melchert
GmbH & Co KG
Shipping Address: Dueneberger Str 130-132,
21502 Geesthacht *Tel:* (04152) 8806-0
Fax: (04152) 8806-30

Kerber Verlag

Windelsbleicher Str 166, 33659 Bielefeld
Tel: (0521) 95 00 810 *Fax:* (0521) 95 00 888
E-mail: info@kerberverlag.com; marketing@
kerberverlag.com
Web Site: www.kerberverlag.com

Key Personnel
Mng Dir: Christof Kerber *E-mail:* christof.
kerber@kerberverlag.com
Project Manager: Katrin Gunther *Tel:* (030) 259
28 280 *Fax:* (030) 259 28 089 *E-mail:* katrin.
gunther@kerberverlag.com
Marketing & Social Media Manager: Michelle
van der Veen *E-mail:* michelle.veen@
kerberverlag.com
Production: Jens Bartnek *Tel:* (0521) 95 00 820
E-mail: jens.bartnek@kerberverlag.com
Founded: 1985
Specialize in paintings & art.
Subjects: Architecture & Interior Design, Art,
History
ISBN Prefix(es): 978-3-924639; 978-3-933040;
978-3-936646; 978-3-938025; 978-3-86678;
978-3-939411
Foreign Rep(s): AVA Verlagsauslieferung AG
(Switzerland); Bookport Associates (Joe
Portelli) (Bosnia and Herzegovina, Croatia,
Gibraltar, Greece, Italy, Malta, Portugal, Ser-
bia, Spain); Coen Sligting Bookimport (Bel-
gium, Netherlands); Cornerhouse Publications
(Eastern Europe, Scandinavia, UK); Critiques
Livres Distribution SAS (France); Distributed
Art Publishers Inc (USA); Infinite Book & Art
Services (Haruhiko Oguchi) (Japan); Michael
Klein (Luxembourg); Seth Meyer-Bruhns (Aus-
tria); Publishers International Marketing (Chris
Ashdown) (China, North Asia, Southeast Asia)
Distribution Center: Umbreit Barsortiment,
Mundelsheimer Str 3, 74321 Bietigheim-
Bissingen *Tel:* (07142) 596-0 *Fax:* (07142)
596-200 *E-mail:* info@umbreit.de
Verlegerdienst Muechen GmbH, Gutenbergstr
1, 82205 Gilching, Contact: Karin Rink
Tel: (08105) 3 88-5 21 *Fax:* (08105) 3 88-2
10 *E-mail:* karin.rink@verlegerdienst.de *Web
Site:* www.verlegerdienst.de
Koenemann GmbH & Co KG, Delsterner Str 134,
58091 Hagen *Tel:* (02331) 789-0 *Fax:* (02331)
75950 *E-mail:* info@koenemann.de
Libri GmbH, Friedensallee 273, 22763 Hamburg
Tel: (040) 85398-0 *Fax:* (040) 85398-7802
E-mail: libri@libri.de
Koch, Neff & Volckmar GmbH, Industriestr 23,
70565 Stuttgart *Web Site:* www.knv.de

Verlag Kerle, *imprint of* Verlag Herder GmbH

Verlag Kerle+
Imprint of Verlag Herder GmbH
Hermann-Herder-Str 4, 79104 Freiburg
Tel: (0761) 2717-300 *Fax:* (0761) 2717-360
E-mail: kundenservice@herder.de
Web Site: www.herder.de/verlag-kerle
Key Personnel
Mng Dir: Roland Grimmelsmann; Manuel Herder
Founded: 1940
ISBN Prefix(es): 978-3-451; 978-3-210; 978-3-
85303
Associate Companies: Herder AG; Verlag A G
Ploetz GmbH & Co KG; Editorial Herder SA,
Spain; Libraria Herder, Spain

Verlag Kern
Bahnhofstr 22, 98693 Ilmenau
Tel: (03677) 4656390 *Fax:* (03677) 4656391
E-mail: kontakt@verlag-kern.de
Web Site: www.verlag-kern.de; www.verlag-kern.
de/zum-bestellshop (bookshop)
Key Personnel
Chief Executive Officer: Ines Rein-Brandenburg
E-mail: rein-brandenburg@verlag-kern.de
Founded: 2006
Membership(s): Boersenverein des Deutschen
Buchhandels eV.
Subjects: Biography, Memoirs, Criminology, Fic-
tion, Literature, Literary Criticism, Essays,
Mysteries, Suspense, Nonfiction (General),

Poetry, Science Fiction, Fantasy, Travel &
Tourism
ISBN Prefix(es): 978-3-95716; 978-3-93947

Ketteler Verlag GmbH
Schlosshof 1, 93449 Waldmuenchen
Tel: (09972) 94 14-51 *Fax:* (09972) 94 14-55
E-mail: kontakt@ketteler-verlag.de
Web Site: www.ketteler-verlag.de
Key Personnel
Mng Dir: Georg Hupfauer
Subjects: Labor, Industrial Relations, Law, Social
Sciences, Sociology
ISBN Prefix(es): 978-3-927494

Thomas Kettler Verlag
Von-Hutten-Str 15, 22761 Hamburg
Tel: (040) 39 10 99 10 *Fax:* (040) 390 68 20
E-mail: mail@thomas-kettler-verlag.de
Web Site: www.thomas-kettler-verlag.de
Key Personnel
Publisher: Thomas Kettler
Press: Carola Hillmann
Publisher of outdoor travel guides.
Subjects: Travel & Tourism
ISBN Prefix(es): 978-3-934014
Foreign Rep(s): Beat Eberle (Switzerland)
Distribution Center: Prolit, Siemensstr 16, 35461
Fernwald *Tel:* (0641) 943 93-24 *Fax:* (0641)
943 93-89 *E-mail:* n.kallweit@prolit.de
Willems Adventure, Honderdland 120, 2676
LT Maasdijk, Netherlands *Tel:* (088) 599
01 40 *Fax:* (088) 599 01 41 *E-mail:* info@
willemsadventure.nl (Benelux)
AVA Verlagsauslieferung AG, Centralweg
16, 8910 Affoltern am Albis, Switzerland
Tel: (044) 762 42 60 *Fax:* (044) 762 42 10
E-mail: verlagsservice@ava.ch

Verlag Kettler
Heinrichstr 21, 44137 Dortmund
Tel: (0231) 223 999-08; (0231) 223 999-09
Fax: (0231) 223 998-69
E-mail: info@verlag-kettler.de
Web Site: www.verlag-kettler.de
Key Personnel
Mng Dir: Gunnar Kettler
Founded: 1980
Subjects: Architecture & Interior Design, Art,
Photography
ISBN Prefix(es): 978-3-86206; 978-3-925608;
978-3-935019; 978-3-937390
Foreign Rep(s): Distributed Art Publishers Inc
(DAP)
Distribution Center: Gemeinsame Ver-
lagsauslieferung Goettingen (GVA)
Tel: (0551) 384200-0 *Fax:* (0551) 384200-10
E-mail: bestellung@gva-verlage.de

Kiehl+
Subsidiary of NWB Verlag GmbH & Co KG
Eschstr 22, 44629 Herne
Tel: (02323) 141-700 *Fax:* (02323) 141-123
E-mail: service@kiehl.de
Web Site: www.kiehl.de
Key Personnel
Mng Dir: Dr Ludger Kleyboldt
Founded: 1932
Subjects: Advertising, Business, Career Devel-
opment, Computer Science, Economics, Ed-
ucation, Finance, Law, Marketing, Medicine,
Nursing, Dentistry
ISBN Prefix(es): 978-3-470
Distributed by Linde Verlag
Distributor for Linde Verlag

Kiener Verlag
Clemensstr 6, 80803 Munich
Tel: (089) 34 12 62 *Fax:* (089) 330 299 13
E-mail: info@kiener-verlag.de
Web Site: www.kiener-verlag.de

Subjects: Fiction, Medicine, Nursing, Dentistry,
Self-Help
ISBN Prefix(es): 978-3-943324

**Verlag Kiepenheuer & Witsch GmbH & Co
KG+**
Bahnhofsvorplatz 1, 50667 Cologne
Tel: (0221) 376 85-0 *Fax:* (0221) 376 85 11
E-mail: verlag@kiwi-verlag.de
Web Site: www.kiwi-verlag.de
Key Personnel
Chief Executive Officer: Helge Malchow
Dir: Peter Roik
Foreign Rights & Permissions: Iris M Brandt
Tel: (0221) 376 85 22 *E-mail:* ibrandt@kiwi-
verlag.de
Founded: 1949
Subjects: Biography, Memoirs, Fiction, History,
Nonfiction (General), Social Sciences, Sociol-
ogy
ISBN Prefix(es): 978-3-462
Parent Company: Verlagsgruppe Georg von
Holtzbrinck
Imprints: Galiani Berlin; Kiwi-Paperback
Foreign Rep(s): Buchkontor (Ulla Harms) (Aus-
tria, South Tyrol, Italy); Giovanni Ravasio
(Switzerland)
Foreign Rights: Carmen Balcells Agencia Liter-
aria SA (Maribel Luque) (Argentina, Portugal,
Spain); Balla & Co Literary Agents (Cather-
ine Balla) (Hungary); Bardon-Chinese Media
Agency (Ms Yu-Shiuan Chen) (China, Tai-
wan); Berla & Griffini Rights Agency (Barbara
Griffini) (Italy); Bestun Korea Literary Agency
(Ms Hyeyoung Lee) (Korea); Karin M Brown
(France); Agencja Literacka Graal (Joanna
Maciuk) (Poland); Tanja Howarth (UK); In-
ternational Literatuur Bureau BV (Linda Kohn)
(Netherlands); JLM Literary Agency (Nelly
Moukakou) (Greece); Simona Kessler Interna-
tional Copyright Agency Ltd (Romania); Leon-
hardt & Hoier Literary Agency aps (Monica
Gram) (Scandinavia); ONK Agency Ltd (Mrs
Hatice Goek) (Turkey); ORION Agency/The
Sakai Agency Inc (Mr Tatemi Sakai) (Japan);
Regal Hoffmann & Associates LLC (Markus
Hoffmann) (USA); Acencia Riff (Laura Riff)
(Brazil)

Kierdorf Verlag+
Im MediaPark 8, 50670 Cologne
Tel: (0221) 55405445 *Fax:* (0221) 5540545
E-mail: kierdorf-verlag@t-online.de; feilen@
westernhorse.de (advertising sales)
Web Site: www.western-horse.de
Key Personnel
Owner & Publisher: Ute Kierdorf
International Rights: Wolfgang Kierdorf
Founded: 1978
Subjects: Equestrian & Feng Shui
ISBN Prefix(es): 978-3-89118

Kilda Verlag+
Muensterstr 71, 48268 Greven
Tel: (02571) 52115 *Fax:* (02571) 953269
E-mail: info@kildaverlag.de
Web Site: www.kildaverlag.de; www.poelking.com
Key Personnel
Mng Dir: Gisela Poelking *E-mail:* gisela.
poelking@kildaverlag.de
Founded: 1969
Subjects: Photography, Nature
ISBN Prefix(es): 978-3-921427; 978-3-88949
Total Titles: 41 Print
Distribution Center: Tecklenborg Verlag,
Siemensstr 4, 48565 Steinfurt *Tel:* (02552) 920
182 *Fax:* (02552) 920 160 *E-mail:* vertrieb@
tecklenborg-verlag.de *Web Site:* www.
tecklenborg-verlag.de

KILLROY media
Wachtelweg 5, 71634 Ludwigsburg

Tel: (07141) 260019 Fax: (07141) 640050
E-mail: jo.schoenauer@t-online.de
Web Site: www.killroy-media.de
Key Personnel
Mng Dir: Michael Schoenauer
Founded: 1995
Subjects: Art, Fiction, Literature, Literary Criticism, Essays, Poetry
ISBN Prefix(es): 978-3-931140

Edition Kima, imprint of Drei Eichen Verlag

Kinderbuchverlag
Lachergarten 7, 86919 Holzhausen
Tel: (08806) 550 Fax: (08806) 923029
E-mail: info@kinderbuchverlag.de
Web Site: www.kinderbuchverlag.de
Key Personnel
Mng Dir: Klaus Wingefeld
Founded: 1880
Subjects: Nonfiction (General)
ISBN Prefix(es): 978-3-358
Parent Company: Verlagsgruppe Beltz

Kindermann Verlag Berlin
Am Lokdepot 12, 10965 Berlin
Tel: (030) 89 757 111 Fax: (030) 89 753 653
Web Site: kindermannverlag.de
Key Personnel
Press & Public Relations: Julia Hoffmann
  E-mail: presse@kindermannverlag.de
Production: Anette Beckmann
  E-mail: anettebeckmann@online.de
Founded: 1994
Subjects: Literature, Literary Criticism, Essays, Poetry
ISBN Prefix(es): 978-3-934029; 978-3-9803778
Foreign Rep(s): Christian Hirtzy (Austria); Giovanni Ravasio (Switzerland); Ernst Sonntag (Austria)
Distribution Center: Prolit Verlagsauslieferung, Siemensstr 16, 35463 Fernwald/Annerod Tel: (0641) 943 93-14 Fax: (0641) 943 93-199 E-mail: service@prolit.de
Dr Franz Hain Verlagsauslieferungen GmbH, Dr-Otto-Neurath-Gasse 5, 1220 Vienna, Austria Tel: (01) 282 65 65 Fax: (01) 282 52 82 E-mail: bestell@hain.at
AVA Verlagsauslieferung AG, Centralweg 16, 8910 Affoltern am Albis, Switzerland Tel: (044) 762 42 60 Fax: (044) 762 42 10 E-mail: verlagsservice@ava.ch

Kindler Verlag, imprint of Rowohlt Verlag GmbH

Kindler Verlag AG GmbH
Hamburger Str, 17, 21465 Reinbek
Tel: (040) 72 72-0 Fax: (040) 72 72-319
E-mail: info@rowohlt.de
Web Site: www.rowohlt.de/verlag/kindler
Key Personnel
Program Dir: Ulrike Beck
Founded: 1945
Subjects: Fiction, Humor, Nonfiction (General)
ISBN Prefix(es): 978-3-463; 978-3-7852
Number of titles published annually: 15 Print
Ultimate Parent Company: Verlagsgruppe Georg von Holtzbrinck GmbH
Imprints: Rowohlt Verlag GmbH

Verlag Donata Kinzelbach
Stolze-Schrey-Str 3, 55124 Mainz
Tel: (06131) 45662; (0171) 2363128 (cell)
  Fax: (06131) 41088
E-mail: kinzelbach@aol.com
Web Site: www.kinzelbach-verlag.de
Founded: 1987
Membership(s): Verlags-Karree eV.
Subjects: Fiction, History, Culture
ISBN Prefix(es): 978-3-927069

K Kirchbaum, imprint of Eironeia-Verlag

P Kirchheim Verlag+
Lindwurmstr 21, 80337 Munich
Mailing Address: Postfach 151102, 80047 Munich
Tel: (089) 267474 Fax: (089) 26949922
E-mail: info@kirchheimverlag.de
Web Site: www.kirchheimverlag.de
Key Personnel
Owner: Peter Kirchheim
Founded: 1977
Publish books & CDs.
Subjects: Foreign Countries, Literature, Literary Criticism, Essays, Poetry, Regional Interests, Science (General), Self-Help, Indology, Iranian Literature
ISBN Prefix(es): 978-3-87410
Number of titles published annually: 5 Print; 1 CD-ROM
Total Titles: 100 Print; 2 CD-ROM
Warehouse: Leipziger Kommissions und- Grossbuchhandelsgesellschaft mbH (LKG), An der Suedspitze 1-12, 04571 Roetha Tel: (034206) 65-100 Fax: (034206) 65-110 E-mail: lkg@lkg-service.de Web Site: www.lkg-va.de
Distribution Center: Leipziger Kommissions und- Grossbuchhandelsgesellschaft mbH (LKG), An der Suedspitze 1-12, 04571 Roetha Tel: (034206) 65-100 Fax: (034206) 65-110 E-mail: lkg@lkg-service.de Web Site: www.lkg-va.de

Kirschbaum Verlag GmbH+
Siegfriedstr 28, 53179 Bonn
Tel: (0228) 95453-0 Fax: (0228) 95453-27
E-mail: info@kirschbaum.de
Web Site: www.kirschbaum.de
Key Personnel
Mng Dir: Bernhard Kirschbaum E-mail: b.kirschbaum@kirschbaum.de
Advertising Manager: Volker Rutkowski
Marketing: Karin Martin Tel: (0228) 95453-29 E-mail: k.martin@kirschbaum.de
Founded: 1948
Subjects: Automotive, Civil Engineering, Geography, Geology, Law, Transportation
ISBN Prefix(es): 978-3-7812
Total Titles: 195 Print

KIT Scientific Publishing
c/o KIT Library, Str am Forum 2, 76131 Karlsruhe
Tel: (0721) 608-43104 Fax: (0721) 608-44886
E-mail: info@ksp.kit.edu
Web Site: www.ksp.kit.edu
Key Personnel
Publishing Dir: Regine Tobias Tel: (0721) 608-47940
Subjects: Architecture & Interior Design, Chemistry, Chemical Engineering, Civil Engineering, Computer Science, Earth Sciences, Economics, Electronics, Electrical Engineering, Environmental Studies, Law, Mathematics, Mechanical Engineering, Physics, Environmental Science, Humanities, Life Sciences, Process Engineering
ISBN Prefix(es): 978-3-86644

Kiwi-Paperback, imprint of Verlag Kiepenheuer & Witsch GmbH & Co KG

Klages-Verlag
Eckermannstr 8, 30625 Hannover
Tel: (0511) 5358936 Fax: (0511) 5358928
Founded: 1917
Membership(s): German Electronic Book Committee.
Subjects: Economics, Law, Public Administration
ISBN Prefix(es): 978-3-7813

Klartext Verlagsgesellschaft mbH+
Hesslerstr 37, 45329 Essen
Tel: (0201) 86 206-0; (0201) 86 206-31
  Fax: (0201) 86 206-22
E-mail: info@klartext-verlag.de
Web Site: www.klartext-verlag.de
Key Personnel
Mng Dir & Publisher: Dr Ludger Classen
  Tel: (0201) 86206-33 E-mail: classen@klartext-verlag.de
Sales Manager: Melanie Brockes Tel: (0201) 86206-29 E-mail: brockes@klartext-verlag.de
Press/Advertising: Kathrin Butt E-mail: butt@klartext-verlag.de
Founded: 1983
Subjects: Architecture & Interior Design, Art, Government, Political Science, History, Nonfiction (General), Regional Interests, Self-Help, Social Sciences, Sociology, Sports, Athletics, Travel & Tourism, Antisemitism
ISBN Prefix(es): 978-3-88474; 978-3-89861; 978-3-8375
Parent Company: WAZ-Mediengruppe
Foreign Rep(s): Helga Schuster (Austria)
Distribution Center: Prolit Verlagsauslieferung GmbH, Siemensstr 16, 35463 Fernwald Tel: (0641) 94 393-22 Fax: (0641) 94 393-29

Klatschmohn Verlag, Druck + Werbung GmbH & Co KG
Am Campus 25, 18182 Bentwisch/Rostock
Tel: (0381) 2066811 Fax: (0381) 2066812
E-mail: info@klatschmohn.de
Web Site: www.klatschmohn.de
Key Personnel
Mng Dir: Angelika Kleinfeldt E-mail: a.kleinfeldt@klatschmohn.de
Sales: Olaf Kreitz
Subjects: Regional Interests, Travel & Tourism
ISBN Prefix(es): 978-3-933574; 978-3-9804800

Klaus Kellner Verlag, see KellnerVerlag

Verlag Reinhard Klein GbR, see McKlein Publishing

Verlag Kleine Schritte (Little Steps Publisher)+
Medardstr 105, 54294 Trier
Tel: (0651) 30 06 98 Fax: (0651) 30 06 99
E-mail: mail@kleine-schritte.de
Web Site: www.kleine-schritte.de
Key Personnel
Mng Dir: Ursula Dahm
Press: Rainer Breuer Tel: (0651) 30 90 10
  Fax: (0651) 30 06 99
Founded: 1980
Membership(s): Verlags-Karree eV.
Subjects: Astrology, Occult, Biography, Memoirs, Fiction, Human Relations, LGBTQ, Nonfiction (General), Poetry, Psychology, Psychiatry, Self-Help, Women's Studies
ISBN Prefix(es): 978-3-88081; 978-3-923261; 978-3-89968

Kleiner Bachmann Verlag+
Hauptstr 279, 51503 Roesrath
Tel: (02205) 904 79 51
E-mail: buch@kleinerbachmann.de
Web Site: www.kleinerbachmann.de
Key Personnel
Owner: Felicitas Jung
Founded: 1997
Specialize in picture books, Scandinavian authors, travel books for children, young authors under 18 years of age. The picture books try to awake sensitivity for environmental issues in a playful & uncomplicated manner.
Membership(s): Arbeitsgemeinschaft von Jugendbuchverlagen eV (AVJ).
Subjects: Environmental Studies, Fiction, Human Relations, Travel & Tourism
ISBN Prefix(es): 978-3-933160

Number of titles published annually: 6 Print
Total Titles: 10 Print; 2 Audio

Klens Verlag GmbH+
Senefelderstr 12, 73760 Ostfildern
Tel: (0711) 44 06-165 *Fax:* (0711) 44 06-177
E-mail: buchverlag@schwabenverlag.de
Web Site: www.schwabenverlag-online.de
Key Personnel
Mng Dir: Ulrich Peters
Licenses: Claudia Stegmann *Tel:* (0711) 44 06-
148
Founded: 1916
Subjects: Education, Religion - Other
ISBN Prefix(es): 978-3-87309
Parent Company: Schwabenverlag AG

Verlag Klett-Cotta+
Rotebuehlstr 77, 70178 Stuttgart
Tel: (0711) 6672-0; (0711) 6672-1225
   Fax: (0711) 6672-2030
E-mail: info@klett-cotta.de
Web Site: www.klett-cotta.de
Key Personnel
Publisher: Michael Klett
Mng Dir: Philipp Haussmann; Tom Kraushaar
   E-mail: t.kraushaar@klett-cotta.de; Michael
   Zoellner *E-mail:* m.zoellner@klett-cotta.de
Press & Public Relations: Katharina Wilts
   Tel: (0711) 6672-1258 *Fax:* (0711) 6672-2032
   E-mail: k.wilts@klett-cotta.de
Rights & Permissions: Roland Knappe
   Tel: (0711) 6672-1257 *Fax:* (0711) 6672-2033
   E-mail: r.knappe@klett-cotta.de
Sales & Advertising: Katja Baeumlis-
   berger *Tel:* (0711) 6672-1801 *E-mail:* k.
   baeumlisberger@klett-cotta.de
Founded: 1659
Subjects: Education, History, Literature, Literary
   Criticism, Essays, Nonfiction (General), Philos-
   ophy, Science Fiction, Fantasy
ISBN Prefix(es): 978-3-7681; 978-3-608
Parent Company: Klett Gruppe
Foreign Rep(s): Heinz-Andrea Spychiger & Heinz
   Marti (Switzerland); Josef Kager & Horst
   Bayer (Austria)
Distribution Center: Koch, Neff & Oetinger Ver-
   lagsauslieferung GmbH, Industriestr 23, 70565
   Stuttgart *E-mail:* klett-cotta@kno-va.de *Web
   Site:* www.kno-va.de
Medienlogishk Pichler-OBZ GmbH & Co KG,
   Postfach 133, 2355 Wiener Neudorf, Austria
   Tel: (02236) 63535-244 *Fax:* (02236) 63535-
   243 *Web Site:* www.oebz.co.at
Buchzentrum AG, Industriestr Ost 10, 4614 Hae-
   gendorf, Switzerland *Tel:* (062) 209 26 26
   Fax: (062) 209 26 27 *E-mail:* kundendienst@
   buchzentrum.at
Orders to: Koch, Neff & Oetinger Verlagsaus-
   lieferung GmbH, Industriestr 23, 70565
   Stuttgart

Ernst Klett Verlag GmbH+
Subsidiary of Ernst Klett AG
Rotebuehlstr 77, 70178 Stuttgart
Mailing Address: Postfach 10 26 45, 70022
   Stuttgart
Tel: (0711) 66 72 13 33 *Fax:* (0711) 98 80 90 00
99
E-mail: kundenservice@klett.de; contact@klett.de
Web Site: www.klett.de
Key Personnel
Publisher: Dr Michael Klett
Mng Dir: Tilo Knoche; Ulrich Pokern; Karl
   Slipek
Founded: 1897
Specialize in language education. Also publishes
   educational software.
Subjects: Education, Geography, Geology, Lan-
   guage Arts, Linguistics
ISBN Prefix(es): 978-3-12; 978-3-7863; 978-3-
   8213; 978-3-88447; 978-3-88448

Klett Kinderbuch Verlag GmbH
Member of Klett Gruppe
Richard-Lehmann-Str 14, 04275 Leipzig
Tel: (0341) 35 05 965 *Fax:* (0341) 96 284 10
E-mail: info@klett-kinderbuch.de; faber@klett-
   kinderbuch.de
Web Site: www.klett-kinderbuch.de
Key Personnel
Mng Dir: Philipp Haussmann; Monika Os-
   berghaus
Press: Hannah Moser *E-mail:* moser@klett-
   kinderbuch.de
Founded: 2008
ISBN Prefix(es): 978-3-941411
Distribution Center: Koch, Neff & Oetinger Ver-
   lagsauslieferung GmbH, Industriestr 23, 70565
   Stuttgart, Contact: Nicole Blum *E-mail:* dtv@
   kno-va.de
Mohr Morawa Buchvertrieb GmbH, Sulzen-
   gasse 2, 1230 Vienna, Austria *Tel:* (01) 680
   14-0 *Fax:* (01) 688 71 30 *E-mail:* momo@
   mohrmorawa.at *Web Site:* www.mohrmorawa.at
Buchzentrum AG, Industriestr Ost 10, 4614 Haegendorf, Switzerland *Tel:* (062) 209 26 26
   Fax: (062) 209 26 27 *E-mail:* kundendienst@
   buchzentrum.ch

Edition Vincent Klink GmbH
Alte Weinsteige 71, 70597 Stuttgart-Degerloch
Tel: (0711) 640 88 48 *Fax:* (0711) 640 94 08
Web Site: www.edition-vincent-klink.de
Key Personnel
Owner: Vincent Klink
Founded: 1988
Subjects: Fiction, Music, Dance, Poetry, Religion
   - Buddhist
ISBN Prefix(es): 978-3-927350

Verlag Julius Klinkhardt KG+
Ramsauer Weg 5, 83670 Bad Heilbrunn
Tel: (08046) 9304 *Fax:* (08046) 9306
E-mail: info@klinkhardt.de
Web Site: www.klinkhardt.de
Key Personnel
Publisher & Editor: Andreas Klinkhardt
Production: Thomas Tilsner
Sales: Margit Schmidl-Klinkhardt
Founded: 1834
Membership(s): Association of School Book Pub-
   lishers; The Stock Exchange of German Book-
   sellers.
Subjects: Education, History, Psychology, Psychi-
   atry, Science (General)
ISBN Prefix(es): 978-3-7815

Von Kloeden KG
Wielandstr 24, 10707 Berlin-Charlottenburg
Tel: (030) 887 125 12 *Fax:* (030) 887 125 19
E-mail: vonkloeden@web.de
Web Site: www.vonkloeden.de
Key Personnel
Mng Dir: Konrad Von Kloeden
Deputy Mng Dir: Charlotte Von Kloeden
Founded: 1967
Subjects: Art, Education, Fiction, History, Non-
   fiction (General), Religion - Other, Science
   (General)
ISBN Prefix(es): 978-3-920564

Kloepfer&Meyer Verlag GmbH & Co KG
Neckarhalde 32, 72070 Tuebingen
Mailing Address: Postfach 1144, 72001 Tuebin-
   gen
Tel: (07071) 7936947 *Fax:* (07071) 793208
E-mail: info@kloepfer-meyer.de
Web Site: www.kloepfer-meyer.de
Key Personnel
Mng Dir: Hubert Kloepfer *Tel:* (07071) 948984
   E-mail: hubert.kloepfer@kloepfer-meyer.de
Press & Public Relations: Annette Maria Rieger
   Tel: (07445) 859086 *Fax:* (07445) 859087
   E-mail: annette-maria.rieger@kloepfer-meyer.de

Rights & Licenses: Petra Waegenbaur
   Tel: (07073) 46 27 *Fax:* (07073) 91 02 28
   E-mail: petra.waegenbaur@kloepfer-meyer.de
Founded: 1991
Subjects: Fiction, Literature, Literary Criticism,
   Essays, Nonfiction (General), Poetry
ISBN Prefix(es): 978-3-86351; 978-3-940086;
   978-3-937667
Foreign Rep(s): Wolfgang Edelmann (Austria);
   Martin E Schnetzer (Switzerland)
Distribution Center: Prolit Verlagsausliefer-
   ung GmbH, Siemensstr 16, 35463 Fernwald-
   Annerod *Tel:* (0641) 94393-0 *Fax:* (0641)
   94393-93
Mohr Morawa Buchvertrieb GmbH, Sulzen-
   gasse 2, 1230 Vienna, Austria *Tel:* (01) 680
   14-0 *Fax:* (01) 688 71 30 *E-mail:* momo@
   mohrmorawa.at *Web Site:* www.mohrmorawa.at
   (Austria & South Tyrol (Italy))
Herder AG Basel, Muttenzerstr 109, 4133
   Pratteln, Switzerland *Tel:* (061) 8279060
   Fax: (061) 8270067 *E-mail:* verkauf@herder.ch

Erika Klopp Verlag+
Subsidiary of Verlag Friedrich Oetinger GmbH
Poppenbuetteler Chaussee 53, 22397 Hamburg
Mailing Address: Postfach 65 82 30, 22374 Ham-
   burg
Tel: (040) 607909 02 *Fax:* (040) 6072326
E-mail: klopp@verlagsgruppe-oetinger.
   de; vertrieb@verlagsgruppe-oetinger.de;
   marketing@verlagsgruppe-oetinger.de
Web Site: www.klopp-buecher.de
Key Personnel
Mng Dir: Jan Weitendorf; Silke Weitendorf; Till
   Weitendorf
Marketing Manager: Lars Spicher
Sales Manager: Susanne Weiss *Tel:* (040) 607909-
   777 *Fax:* (040) 607909-550
Advertising: Meike Dreyer *E-mail:* werbung@
   verlagsgruppe-oetinger.de
Rights & Licensing: Renate Reichstein *Tel:* (040)
   607909-713 *E-mail:* lizenzer@verlagssgruppe-
   oetinger.de
Founded: 1925
Subjects: Literature, Literary Criticism, Essays,
   Children's Literature
ISBN Prefix(es): 978-3-7817
Total Titles: 150 Print
Warehouse: Runge Verlagsauslieferung/Steinhagen
   Tel: (05204) 9181-0 *Fax:* (05204) 9181-93

**Klosterhaus-Verlagsbuchhandlung & Verlag
   Hans Grimm**
Klosterhof 4, 37194 Wahlsburg
Tel: (05572) 73 10 *Fax:* (05572) 99 98 23
E-mail: info@klosterhausbuch.de
Web Site: www.klosterhausbuch.de
Key Personnel
Mng Dir: Margret Nickel
Founded: 1951
Subjects: History
ISBN Prefix(es): 978-3-87418

Vittorio Klostermann GmbH+
Westerbachstr 47, 60489 Frankfurt am Main
Tel: (069) 97 08 16-0 *Fax:* (069) 70 80 38
E-mail: verlag@klostermann.de
Web Site: www.klostermann.de
Key Personnel
Mng Dir & Publisher: Vittorio E Klostermann
International Rights: Anastasia Urban *Tel:* (069)
   97 08 16-17
Marketing: Martin Warny *Tel:* (069) 97 08 16-12
Publicity: Ms Friedrike Haertling *Tel:* (069) 97 08
   16-11
Founded: 1930
Subjects: Genealogy, History, Law, Library &
   Information Sciences, Literature, Literary Crit-
   icism, Essays, Philosophy, Publishing & Book

Trade Reference, Science (General), Chinese
Language
ISBN Prefix(es): 978-3-465

Knabe Verlag Weimar
Trierer Str 65, 99423 Weimar
Tel: (03643) 74 35 72 *Fax:* (03643) 85 27 20
E-mail: info@knabe-verlag.de; verwaltung@
knabe-verlag.de
Web Site: knabe-verlag.de
Key Personnel
Chief Executive Officer: Steffen Knabe
Associate Publisher: Susanne Ramm
E-mail: ramm@knabe-verlag.de
Secretary & Author Support: Regina Doberstein
Founded: 2007
ISBN Prefix(es): 978-3-940442

Fritz Knapp Verlag GmbH+
Aschaffenburger Str 19, 60599 Frankfurt am
Main
Tel: (069) 97 08 33-0 *Fax:* (069) 707 84 00
E-mail: info@kreditwesen.de; verlagsleitung@
kreditwesen.de; redaktion@kreditwesen.de
Web Site: www.kreditwesen.de
Key Personnel
Mng Dir: Uwe Cappel
Publisher: Philipp Otto
Advertising & Marketing: Timo Hartig
Founded: 1949
Subjects: Economics, Finance, Banking
ISBN Prefix(es): 978-3-7819; 978-3-8314
Associate Companies: Verlag fuer Ab-
satzwirtschaft; Kreditwesen Service GmbH;
Helmut Richardi Verlag GmbH
Orders to: Koch, Neff & Oetinger Verlagsaus-
lieferung GmbH, Industriestr 23, 70565
Stuttgart

Knaus, *imprint of* Verlagsgruppe Random House
Bertelsmann

Knaus Verlag+
Imprint of Verlagsgruppe Random House Bertels-
mann
Neumarkter Str 28, 81673 Munich
Tel: (089) 4136-0 *Fax:* (089) 4136-3333 (cus-
tomer service)
E-mail: kundenservice@randomhouse.de
Web Site: www.randomhouse.de/knaus
Key Personnel
Mng Dir: Klaus Eck; Claudia Reitter
Press: Susanne Klein *Tel:* (089) 4136-3800
Fax: (089) 4136-3761 *E-mail:* susanne.klein@
knaus-verlag.de
Founded: 1978
Subjects: Art, Biography, Memoirs, Fiction, His-
tory, Nonfiction (General)
ISBN Prefix(es): 978-3-8135
Orders to: VVA Bertelsmann Distribution, Post-
fach 7777, 33310 Guetersloh

Verlag Josef Knecht, *imprint of* Verlag Herder
GmbH

Verlag Josef Knecht+
c/o Verlag Herder GmbH, Hermann-Herder-Str 4,
79104 Freiburg
Tel: (0761) 27 17-436 *Fax:* (0761) 27 17-212
E-mail: info@knecht-verlag.de
Web Site: www.verlag-josef-knecht.de
Key Personnel
Mng Dir: Olaf Carstens; Roland Grimmelsman;
Manuel Herder
Mng Dir & Rights & Permissions: Dr Lukas Tra-
bert *Tel:* (0761) 27 17-213
Founded: 1946
Specialize in religion, philosophy, social prob-
lems, human sciences, politics & historical Ro-
mans. Special interest: the situation of mankind
in post modern times.

Subjects: Government, Political Science, History,
Mysteries, Suspense, Philosophy, Regional In-
terests, Religion - Other, Social Sciences, So-
ciology, Theology, Travel & Tourism, Cultural
History, Historical Romans
ISBN Prefix(es): 978-3-7820
Total Titles: 15 E-Book
Parent Company: Verlag Karl Alber GmbH

von dem Knesebeck GmbH & Co Verlag KG+
Subsidiary of La Martiniere Groupe
Holzstr 26, 80469 Munich
Tel: (089) 26 40 59 *Fax:* (089) 26 92 58
E-mail: sekretariat@knesebeck-verlag.de; rights@
knesebeck-verlag.de
Web Site: www.knesebeck-verlag.de
Key Personnel
Publisher & International Rights: Dr Rosemarie
von dem Knesebeck *E-mail:* rknesebeck@
knesebeck-verlag.de
Mng Dir: Antonia Buerger
Press Dir: Jule Menig *Tel:* (089) 26 02 35 34
E-mail: jmenig@knesebeck-verlag.de
Sales & Marketing Manager: Birthe Doering
Tel: (089) 23 07 77 69 *E-mail:* bdoering@
knesebeck-verlag.de
Sales/Exhibitions: Sebastian Soler *Tel:* (089) 26
02 35 32 *E-mail:* ssoler@knesebeck-verlag.de
Founded: 1987
Subjects: Architecture & Interior Design, Art,
Biography, Memoirs, Gardening, Plants, Pho-
tography, Travel & Tourism
ISBN Prefix(es): 978-3-926901; 978-3-89660
Number of titles published annually: 20 Print
Total Titles: 70 Print
Foreign Rep(s): Buchzentrum AG (Cornelia
Frese) (Switzerland); Ernst Sonntag (Austria,
South Tyrol, Italy)
Distribution Center: Koch, Neff & Oetinger Ver-
lagsauslieferung GmbH, Industriestr 23, 70565
Stuttgart *E-mail:* knesebeck@kno-va.de
Dr Franz Hain, Dr-Otto-Neurath-Gasse 5, 1220
Vienna, Austria *Tel:* (01) 2 82 65 65 *Fax:* (01)
2 82 52 82 *E-mail:* bestell@hain.at
Buchzentrum AG, Kundendienst, Industriestr Ost
10, 4614 Haegendorf, Switzerland *Tel:* (041)
62 209 25 25 *Fax:* (041) 62 209 26 27
E-mail: kundendienst@buchzentrum.ch

Verlagsanstalt Alexander Koch GmbH (VAK)+
Fasanenweg 18, 70771 Leinfelden-Echterdingen
Tel: (0711) 7591-286 *Fax:* (0711) 7591-410
E-mail: info@ait-online.de
Web Site: www.koch-verlag.de; www.ait-online.de
Key Personnel
Mng Dir: Karl-Heinz Weinbrenner; Claudia
Weinbrenner-Seibt
Publishing Dir & Editor: Dr Dietmar Danner
Tel: (0711) 7591-318 *E-mail:* ddanner@ait-
online.de
Sales Manager: Reiner Pfeifle *Tel:* (0711) 7591-
247 *E-mail:* rpfeifle@ait-online.de
Founded: 1890
Subjects: Architecture & Interior Design
ISBN Prefix(es): 978-3-87422
Parent Company: Weinbrenner GmbH & Co KG
Associate Companies: bit-Verlag Weinbrenner
GmbH & Co KG; GKT-Gesellschaft fuer
Knowhow-Transfer in Architektur und Bauwe-
sen
Foreign Rep(s): Cesare Casiraghi (Italy); Mark-
Oliver Felchner (Austria)

Koehler & Amelang GmbH, *imprint of*
Seemann Henschel GmbH & Co KG

K F Koehler Verlag GmbH
Am Wallgraben 110, 70565 Stuttgart
Tel: (0711) 789 2130 *Fax:* (0711) 789 2132
Key Personnel
Contact: Joachim Herkert; Frank Thurmann
Founded: 1789

Subjects: Biography, Memoirs, Geography, Geology, Government, Political Science, History,
Law, Publishing & Book Trade Reference, Social Sciences, Sociology
ISBN Prefix(es): 978-3-87425

Koehlers Verlagsgesellschaft mbH+
Ballindamm 17, 20095 Hamburg
Tel: (040) 707080-01; (040) 707080-323 (sales)
Fax: (040) 707080-304; (040) 707080-324
(sales)
E-mail: vertrieb@koehler-books.de; vertrieb@
koehler-mittler.de
Web Site: www.koehler-books.de
Key Personnel
Mng Dir: Fritz-Hermann Baete *Tel:* (040)
707080-321 *E-mail:* f-h_baete@koehler-mittler.
de; Thomas Bantle *Tel:* (040) 707080-201
E-mail: t_bantle@koehler-mittler.de
Sales Manager: Susanne Duerr
Founded: 1789
Subjects: Art, Maritime, Nonfiction (General),
Regional Interests, Science (General), Travel &
Tourism
ISBN Prefix(es): 978-3-7822
Total Titles: 20 Print
Parent Company: Maximilian Verlag GmbH &
Co KG
Ultimate Parent Company: TAMM MEDIA
GmbH
Associate Companies: Deutschen Verwal-
tungspraxis; Europlische Sicherheit & Tech-
nik; Marine Forum; Verlag E S Mittler &
Sohn GmbH & Co KG; Mittler Report Verlag
GmbH; Schiff & Zeit

Koelner Universitaetsverlag GmbH (Cologne
University Publishing House)+
Konrad-Adenauer-Ufer 21, 50668 Cologne
Mailing Address: Postfach 101863, 50458
Cologne
Tel: (0221) 4981-421 *Fax:* (0221) 4981-99421
E-mail: iwmedien@iwkoeln.de
Web Site: www.iwmedien.de; www.iwkoeln.de
Key Personnel
Mng Dir: Ulrich Brodersen; Michael Burbach
Subjects: Business, Developing Countries, Eco-
nomics, Education, Government, Political Sci-
ence, Labor, Industrial Relations, Social Sci-
ences, Sociology
ISBN Prefix(es): 978-3-602; 978-3-87427; 978-3-
88054; 978-3-931206
Parent Company: Institut der deutschen
Wirtschaft Koeln Medien GmbH

**Verlag der Buchhandlung Walther Koenig
GmbH & Co KG**
Ehrenstr 4, 50672 Cologne
Tel: (0221) 2059 653; (0221) 2059 60
Fax: (0221) 2059 660; (0221) 2059 640
E-mail: verlag@buchhandlung-walther-koenig.de;
order@buchhandlung-walther-koenig.de
Web Site: www.buchhandlung-walther-koenig.de
Key Personnel
Mng Dir: Franz Koenig; Walther Koenig; Chris-
tian Posthofen
Subjects: Antiques, Architecture & Interior De-
sign, Art, Fashion, Gardening, Plants, Photog-
raphy
ISBN Prefix(es): 978-3-86560; 978-3-88375

Koenigs Abi-Trainer, *imprint of* C Bange Verlag
GmbH

Koenigs Erlaeuterungen, *imprint of* C Bange
Verlag GmbH

Koenigs Kopiervorlagen, *imprint of* C Bange
Verlag GmbH

Koenigs Lernhilfen, *imprint of* C Bange Verlag GmbH

Koenigs Uebersetzungen, *imprint of* C Bange Verlag GmbH

Koenigsdorfer Verlag
Zellwies 11, 82549 Koenigsdorf
Tel: (08179) 1425 *Fax:* (08179) 1425
E-mail: koenigsdorfer-verlag@web.de
Web Site: www.koenigsdorfer-verlag.de
Key Personnel
Owner: Margarete Mueller
Subjects: Inspirational, Spirituality, Philosophy, Religion - Other
ISBN Prefix(es): 978-3-9807847; 978-3-938156

Koenigsfurt-Urania Verlag GmbH+
Koenigsfurt 6, Kl Koenigsfoerde am Nord-Ostsee-Kanal, 24796 Krummwisch
Tel: (04334) 18 22 010 *Fax:* (04334) 18 22 011
E-mail: info@koenigsfurt-urania.com; verleger@
koenigsfurt-urania.com; export@koenigsfurt-urania.com; vertrieb@koenigsfurt-urania.com;
presse@koenigsfurt-urania.com
Web Site: www.koenigsfurt-urania.com; www.
koenigsfurt.com
Key Personnel
Mng Dir: Wilfried Aendekerk; Chris Van
Doorslaer
Mng Dir & Foreign Rights: Johannes Fiebig
E-mail: johannes.fiebig@koenigsfurt-urania.
com
Foreign Rights: Felicia Gaertner *Tel:* (04334) 18
36 061
Press & Public Relations: Evelin Buerger
Tel: (04334) 18 22 007
Sales: Brunhilde Noffke *Tel:* (04334) 18 22 008
Founded: 1989
Also German market leader for Tarot & Co (non-books).
Subjects: Astrology, Occult, Inspirational, Spirituality, Nonfiction (General), Philosophy, Psychology, Psychiatry, Self-Help
ISBN Prefix(es): 978-3-927808; 978-3-933939;
978-3-89875; 978-3-86826
Number of titles published annually: 100 Print
Total Titles: 500 Print
Distribution Center: Prolit Verlagsauslieferung GmbH, Siemensstr 16, 35463 Fernwald, Contact: Gabriele Lemuth *Tel:* (0641) 943 93 201
Fax: (0641) 943 93 89 *E-mail:* g.lemuth@
prolit.de
Dr Franz Hain Verlagsauslieferung GmbH, Dr
Otto Neurath Gasse 5, 1220 Vienna, Austria *Tel:* (01) 28 26 565 *Fax:* (01) 28 25 282
E-mail: bestell@hain.at
Buchzentrum AG, Industriestr Ost 10, 4614 Haegendorf, Switzerland *Tel:* (062) 209 26 26
Fax: (062) 209 26 27
Dessauer, Raeffelstr 32, 8045 Zurich, Switzerland *Tel:* (044) 466 96 96 *Fax:* (044) 466 96
69 *E-mail:* dessauer@dessauer.ch

Verlag Koenigshausen & Neumann GmbH+
Leistenstr 7, 97082 Wuerzburg
Tel: (0931) 329870-0 *Fax:* (0931) 83620
E-mail: info@koenigshausen-neumann.de
Web Site: www.koenigshausen-neumann.de
Key Personnel
Mng Dir: Dr Johannes Koenigshausen; Dr
Thomas Neumann
Founded: 1979
Subjects: Archaeology, Art, Economics, Education, Ethnicity, History, Law, Literature, Literary Criticism, Essays, Mathematics, Medicine, Nursing, Dentistry, Philosophy, Psychology, Psychiatry, Romance, Science (General), Social Sciences, Sociology
ISBN Prefix(es): 978-3-88479; 978-3-8260

Edition Koerber-Stiftung
Kehrwieder 12, 20457 Hamburg
Tel: (040) 80-81-92-0 *Fax:* (040) 80 81 92-304
E-mail: info@koerber-stiftung.de; edition@
koerber-stiftung.de
Web Site: www.koerber-stiftung.de/edition-koerber-stiftung.html
Key Personnel
Mng Dir: Bernd Martin
Editorial & Foreign Rights: Dr Kerstin Schulz
Tel: (040) 80 81 92-190 *E-mail:* schulz@
koerber-stiftung.de
Sales: Ulrike Sonnenschein *Tel:* (040) 80 81 92-
174 *E-mail:* sonnenschein@koerber-stiftung.de
Founded: 1996
Subjects: Biography, Memoirs, Education, Government, Political Science, Literature, Literary Criticism, Essays, Nonfiction (General), Science (General), Social Sciences, Sociology
ISBN Prefix(es): 978-3-89684
Distribution Center: SoVa, Friesstr 20-24, 60388
Frankfurt am Main, Contact: Andreas Jentsch
Tel: (069) 41 02 11 *Fax:* (069) 41 02 80
E-mail: sovaffm@t-online.de

Lucy Koerner Verlag GmbH+
Dieselstr 1a, 70736 Fellbach
Mailing Address: Postfach 1106, 70701 Fellbach
Key Personnel
Mng Dir: Lucy Koerner
Subjects: Fiction
ISBN Prefix(es): 978-3-922028

Verlag Valentin Koerner GmbH
Hermann-Sielcken-Str 36, 76530 Baden-Baden
Mailing Address: Postfach 10 01 64, 76482
Baden-Baden
Tel: (07221) 2 24 23 *Fax:* (07221) 3 86 97
E-mail: info@koernerverlag.de
Web Site: www.koernerverlag.de
Key Personnel
Mng Dir: Tobias Koerner
Founded: 1954
Subjects: Art, History, Music, Dance, Philosophy, Theology
ISBN Prefix(es): 978-3-87320
Number of titles published annually: 20 Print
Total Titles: 500 Print
Imprints: Heitz Librarie

Koesel, *imprint of* Verlagsgruppe Random House Bertelsmann

Koesel-Verlag GmbH & Co+
Imprint of Verlagsgruppe Random House Bertelsmann
Flueggenstr 2, 80639 Munich
Tel: (089) 17801-0 *Fax:* (089) 17801-111
E-mail: leserservice@koesel.de
Web Site: www.randomhouse.de/koesel
Key Personnel
Publishing Dir: Martin Scherer
Mng Dir: Klaus Eck; Claudia Reitter
Advertising: Marion Riedl
Press: Susanne Klumpp *Tel:* (089) 41 36 2654
E-mail: susanne.klumpp@koesel.de
Rights & Permissions: Sabine Stempfle
Tel: (089) 41 36 3225 *Fax:* (089) 41 36 63225
E-mail: sabine.stempfle@randomhouse.de
Sales & Customer Service: Susanne Eckardt
E-mail: eckardt@koesel.de
Founded: 1593
Membership(s): Gesellschafter of Deutscher Taschenbuch Verlag (dtv); TR-Verlagsunion GmbH.
Subjects: Child Care & Development, Education, Philosophy, Psychology, Psychiatry, Religion - Other, Self-Help
ISBN Prefix(es): 978-3-466
Foreign Rights: Balla-Sztojkov Literary Agency (Catherine Balla) (Hungary); BC Agency (Richard Hong) (South Korea); Eliane Benisti

(France); Giuliana Bernardi (Italy); Eurobuk Agency (Dr Min Su Lee) (South Korea); Agencja Literacka Graal (Maria Strarz-Kanska & Joanna Maciuk) (Poland); International Literature Bureau BV (Linda Kohn) (Belgium, Netherlands); Iris Literary Agency (Catherine Fragou) (Greece); Ute Koerner Literary Agents SL (Sandra Rodericks) (Brazil, Latin America, Portugal, South America, Spain); Meike Marx (Japan); Momo Agency (Geenie Han) (South Korea)
Bookshop(s): Koeselsche Buchhandlung, Roncalli-platz 2, 50667 Cologne
Distribution Center: VVA Vereinigte Verlagsaus-lieferung, Abt D6 F5, An der Autobahn, 33310 Guetersloh *Tel:* (05241) 80-88-28-0
Fax: (05241) 46 97 0
Dr Franz Hain Verlagsauslieferungen GmbH, Dr-Otto-Neurath-Gasse 5, 1220 Vienna, Austria
Cornelia Frese, c/o Balmer Buecherdienst, 6301
Zug, Switzerland

Koha Verlag GmbH
St Sebastian 13, 84405 Dorfen
Tel: (08081) 6049844 *Fax:* (08081) 6049845
E-mail: info@koha-verlag.de
Web Site: koha-verlag.de
Key Personnel
Mng Dir: Konrad Halbig; Karin Schnellbach
E-mail: karin@koha-verlag.de
Founded: 1997
Subjects: Health, Nutrition, Inspirational, Spirituality, Psychology, Psychiatry, Holistic Lifestyle
ISBN Prefix(es): 978-3-929512; 978-3-936862;
978-3-86728
Distribution Center: Brockhaus, Kreidlerstr 9,
70806 Kornwestheim *Tel:* (07154) 132721
Fax: (07154) 1327313 *E-mail:* koha@brocom.
de
Dr Franz Hain Verlagsauslieferungen GmbH,
Dr-Otto-Neurath-Gasse 5, 1220 Vienna, Austria *Tel:* (01) 2826565 *Fax:* (01) 2825282
E-mail: bestell@hain.at
Buchzentrum AG, Industriestr Ost 10, 4614
Haegendorf, Switzerland *Tel:* (062) 2092525
Fax: (062) 2092627

Verlag Andreas Kohlhage, see EHP-Verlag
Andreas Kohlhage

W Kohlhammer GmbH
Hessbruehlstr 69, 70565 Stuttgart
Tel: (0711) 7863-0 *Fax:* (0711) 7863-8204
E-mail: kohlhammerkontakt@kohlhammer.de;
foreign.rights@kohlhammer.de
Web Site: www.kohlhammer.de/klv/
Key Personnel
Mng Dir: Dr Juergen Gutbrod; Leopold Freiherr
von und zu Weiler
Sales Dir: Michael Hoersch *Tel:* (0711) 7863-
7270 *Fax:* (0711) 7863-8430 *E-mail:* michael.
hoersch@kohlhammer.de
Rights & Permissions Manager: Henning Gienger
Tel: (0711) 7863-7207 *Fax:* (0711) 7863-8207
Founded: 1866
Subjects: Architecture & Interior Design, Business, Economics, Education, Government, Political Science, History, Language Arts, Linguistics, Law, Management, Marketing, Medicine, Nursing, Dentistry, Philosophy, Psychology, Psychiatry, Public Administration, Religion - Catholic, Religion - Islamic, Religion - Jewish, Religion - Protestant, Religion - Other, Social Sciences, Sociology, Theology
ISBN Prefix(es): 978-3-17
Number of titles published annually: 240 Print
Total Titles: 3,400 Print; 2 CD-ROM
Parent Company: Unternehmensgruppe W
Kohlhammer
Subsidiaries: Data Images Visuelle Kommunikation GmbH; Deutscher Gemeindeverlag GmbH; Dienst am Buch GmbH; Kohlhammer und Wal-

lishauser GmbH; W Kohlhammer Communication GmbH; W Kohlhammer Druckerei GmbH & Co; Media Service; Verlagsvertrieb Stuttgart GmbH
Branch Office(s)
Dresden *Tel:* (0351) 8022685 *Fax:* (0351) 8020664
Gustav-Freytag-Str 59, 99096 Erfurt *Tel:* (0361) 3735379 *Fax:* (0361) 3460537
Alexanderstr 3, 30159 Hannover *Tel:* (0511) 327029 *Fax:* (0511) 320143
Jagersberg 17, 24103 Kiel *Tel:* (0431) 554857 *Fax:* (0431) 554944
Schleinufer 14, 39104 Magdeburg *Tel:* (0391) 597080 *Fax:* (0391) 5970813
Alexander-Diehl-Str 10, 55130 Mainz *Tel:* (06131) 891540 *Fax:* (06131) 891624
Werkstr 209, 19061 Schwerin *Tel:* (0385) 616105 *Fax:* (0385) 616146
Warehouse: Verlagsvertrieb Stuttgart GmbH

Kolibri Verlags GmbH+
Bahrenfelder Steindamm 2, 22761 Hamburg
Tel: (040) 2202258 *Fax:* (040) 2276368
E-mail: kontakt@kolibriversand.de
Web Site: www.kolibriversand.de
Key Personnel
Mng Dir: Mr Foen Tjoeng Lie
Founded: 1990
Subjects: Asian Studies, Health, Nutrition, Nonfiction (General), Philosophy, Religion - Buddhist, Sports, Athletics, Chinese Culture, Daoism, Qigong, Tai Chi, Traditional Chinese Medicine
ISBN Prefix(es): 978-3-928288
Number of titles published annually: 5 Print
Total Titles: 50 Print
Subsidiaries: Kolibri Seminare

Kommunal- und Schul-Verlag GmbH & Co KG
Konrad-Adenauer-Ring 13, 65187 Wiesbaden
Mailing Address: Postfach 36 29, 65026 Wiesbaden
Tel: (0611) 8 80 86-0; (0611) 8 80 86-10 (orders) *Fax:* (0611) 8 80 86-66; (0611) 8 80 86-77 (orders)
E-mail: info@kommunalpraxis.de; presse@kommunalpraxis.de; vertrieb@kommunalpraxis.de
Web Site: www.kommunalpraxis.de
Key Personnel
Publishing Manager: Dr Ulrike Henschel
E-mail: ulrike.henschel@kommunalpraxis.de
Editor: Andrea Lentz *Tel:* (0611) 8 80 86-21 *E-mail:* andrea.lentz@kommunalpraxis.de; Peter Zimmerman *Tel:* (0611) 8 80 86-20 *E-mail:* peter.zimmerman@kommunalpraxis.de
Sales: Detlev Roell *Tel:* (0611) 8 80 86-11 *E-mail:* detlev.roell@kommunalpraxis.de
Subjects: Environmental Studies, Finance, Health, Nutrition, Law, Public Administration, Sports, Athletics, Conservation, Construction, Safety, School & Culture, State & Constitutional Law, Youth
ISBN Prefix(es): 978-3-8293; 978-3-86115; 978-3-86061
Parent Company: Verlagsgruppe C H Beck
Imprints: Gemeinde und Schulverlag Bavaria

Konkret Literatur Verlag (KLV)+
Ehrenbergstr 59, 22767 Hamburg
Tel: (040) 47 52 34 *Fax:* (040) 47 84 15
E-mail: info@konkret-literatur-verlag.de
Web Site: www.konkret-verlage.de
Key Personnel
Mng Dir, Rights & Permissions: Dr Dorothee Gremliza
Founded: 1978
Subjects: Developing Countries, Government, Political Science, Health, Nutrition, History, Medicine, Nursing, Dentistry, Nonfiction

(General), Poetry, Social Sciences, Sociology, Women's Studies
ISBN Prefix(es): 978-3-922144; 978-3-89458
Distributed by B&I (Switzerland); Herder & Co (Austria)
Foreign Rep(s): Richard Bhend/Verena Suery (Switzerland); Seth Meyer-Bruhns (Austria)
Distribution Center: Bertelsmann Distribution/VVA, Postfach 7777, 33310 Guetersloh *Tel:* (05241) 802895 *Fax:* (05241) 809352
Scheidegger & Co AG, c/o AVA Verlagsauslieferung AG, Centralweg 16, 8910 Affoltern am Albis, Switzerland *Tel:* (044) 7624250 *Fax:* (044) 7624210 *E-mail:* scheidegger@ava.ch

konkursbuch Verlag Claudia Gehrke+
Postfach 1621, 72006 Tuebingen
Tel: (07071) 66551; (0701) 78779 (orders) *Fax:* (07071) 63539; (0701) 763780 (orders)
E-mail: office@konkursbuch.com; mailorder@konkursbuch.com (orders)
Web Site: www.konkursbuch.com
Key Personnel
Publisher: Claudia Gehrke *E-mail:* gehrke@konkursbuch.com
Press & Public Relations: Babett Taenzer *Tel:* (030) 609824890 *Fax:* (030) 609824899 *E-mail:* taenzer@konkursbuch.com
Founded: 1978
Subjects: Literature, Literary Criticism, Essays, Travel & Tourism, Women's Studies
ISBN Prefix(es): 978-3-88769

Anton H Konrad Verlag
Schulstr 5, 89264 Weissenhorn
Mailing Address: Postfach 1206, 89259 Weissenhorn
Tel: (07309) 26 57 *Fax:* (07309) 60 69
E-mail: info@konrad-verlag.de; buchhandlung@konrad-verlag.de
Web Site: www.konrad-verlag.de
Key Personnel
Mng Dir, Rights & Permissions: Anton H Konrad
Founded: 1961
Subjects: Art, Biography, Memoirs, Geography, Geology, History, Philosophy, Regional Interests
ISBN Prefix(es): 978-3-87437

Konradin Relations GmbH+
Subsidiary of Konradin Mediengruppe AG
Ernst-Mey-Str 8, 70771 Leinfelden-Echterdingen
Tel: (0711) 7594-340 *Fax:* (0711) 7594-5897
E-mail: relations@konradin.de
Web Site: www.konradin-relations.de
Key Personnel
Publishing Dir: Marei Roeding *Tel:* (0711) 7594-355 *E-mail:* marei.roeding@konradin.de
Mng Dir: Peter Dilger
Founded: 1929
Subjects: Architecture & Interior Design, Chemistry, Chemical Engineering, Computer Science, Electronics, Electrical Engineering, Engineering (General), Technology
ISBN Prefix(es): 978-3-920560

Konstanz University Press (KUP), *imprint of* Verlag Wilhelm Fink GmbH & Co Verlags-KG

Konstanz University Press
Imprint of Verlag Wilhelm Fink GmbH & Co Verlags-KG
Juehenplatz 1-3, 33098 Paderborn
Mailing Address: Postfach 25 40, 33055 Paderborn
Tel: (05251) 127-5 *Fax:* (05251) 127-860
E-mail: info@k-up.de
Web Site: www.k-up.de
Key Personnel
Mng Dir: Peter Schaefer; Dr Raimar Zons

Licenses/Foreign Rights: Alexander Schmitz *Tel:* (07531) 88 4867 *Fax:* (07531) 88 5602 *E-mail:* schmitz@k-up.de
Press: Dr Alexandra Schmidt *Tel:* (05251) 1 27 790 *Fax:* (05251) 1 27 88790 *E-mail:* schmidt@k-up.de
Sales: Ute Schnueckel *Tel:* (05251) 1 27 640 *Fax:* (05251) 1 27 88640 *E-mail:* schnueckel@k-up.de
Subjects: Anthropology, Government, Political Science, History, Language Arts, Linguistics, Literature, Literary Criticism, Essays, Philosophy, Social Sciences, Sociology, Entertainment, Media
ISBN Prefix(es): 978-3-86253
Foreign Rep(s): Scheidegger & Co AG (Stephanie Brunner) (Liechtenstein, Switzerland); Helga Schuster (Austria)
Distribution Center: Brockhaus/Commission, Kreidlerstr 9, 70806 Kornwestheim *Tel:* (07154) 13 27 10 *Fax:* (07154) 13 27 13 *E-mail:* k-up@brocom.de
Dr Franz Hain Verlagsauslieferung GmbH, Dr-Otto-Neurath-Gasse 5, 1220 Vienna, Austria *Tel:* (01) 2 82 65 65 *Fax:* (01) 2 82 52 82 *E-mail:* bestell@hain.at
AVA Verlagsauslieferung AG, Centralweg 16, 8910 Affoltern am Albis, Switzerland *Tel:* (044) 7 62 42 50 *Fax:* (044) 7 62 42 10 *E-mail:* verlagsservice@ava.ch (Switzerland & Liechtenstein)

Kontakte Musikverlag
Windmuellerstr 31, 59557 Lippstadt
Tel: (02941) 14513 *Fax:* (02941) 14654
E-mail: info@kontakte-musikverlag.de
Web Site: www.kontakte-musikverlag.de
Key Personnel
Publishing Dir: Ute Horn
Membership(s): Boersenverein des Deutschen Buchhandels eV; VdS Bildungsmedien eV.
Subjects: Education, Music, Dance, Music Education
ISBN Prefix(es): 978-3-89617
Distribution Center: G Umbreit GmbH & Co KG Verlagsauslieferung, Mundelsheimer Str 3v, 74321 Bietigheim-Bissingen *Tel:* (07142) 596-373 *Fax:* (07142) 596-387 *E-mail:* verlagsauslieferung@umbreit.de
CBZ Christliche Buecherzentrale, Dr Schauer-Str 26, 4600 Wels, Austria *Tel:* (07242) 65745 *Fax:* (07242) 66163
Herder AG Basel, Muttenzerstr 109, 4133 Pratteln, Switzerland *Tel:* (06182) 7906-0 *Fax:* (06182) 7906-7

Kontext Verlag+
Goldschmidtweg 48A, 12307 Berlin
Tel: (030) 94415444
E-mail: service@kontextverlag.de
Web Site: www.kontextverlag.de
Key Personnel
Owner: Torsten Metelka *E-mail:* metelka@kontextverlag.de
Founded: 1990
Subjects: Art, Erotica, Government, Political Science, Literature, Literary Criticism, Essays, Philosophy
ISBN Prefix(es): 978-3-86161; 978-3-931337

Kontrast Verlag
Raiffeisenstr 30, 56291 Pfalzfeld
Tel: (06746) 8502 *Fax:* (06746) 8503
E-mail: webmaster@kontrast-verlag.de; info@kontrast-verlag.de
Web Site: www.kontrast-verlag.de
Key Personnel
Editor: Barbara Jost
Founded: 2001
Membership(s): Boersenverein des Deutschen Buchhandels eV; Verlags-Karree eV.

Subjects: Biography, Memoirs, Fiction, Nonfiction (General), Poetry, Romance, Science Fiction, Fantasy, Crime Fiction, Crime/Thriller, Satire
ISBN Prefix(es): 978-3-941200; 978-3-935286
Distribution Center: Buch-Liefer-Service, Hausbayer Str 14, 56291 Pfalzfeld *Fax:* (06746) 8036552 *E-mail:* buch-liefer-service@t-online.de

Kontur, *imprint of* Bonifatius GmbH Druck-Buch-Verlag

KOOKbooks
Horstweg 34, 14059 Berlin
Tel: (030) 40053974 *Fax:* (030) 40053974
Web Site: www.kookbooks.de
Key Personnel
Publisher: Daniela Seel *E-mail:* daniela.seel@kookbooks.de
Founded: 2003
Subjects: Literature, Literary Criticism, Essays, Poetry
ISBN Prefix(es): 978-3-937445

Verlag der Kooperative Duernau
Im Winkel 11, 88422 Duernau
Tel: (07582) 930093 *Fax:* (07582) 930020
E-mail: verlag@kooperative.de
Web Site: www.kooperative.de
Key Personnel
Owner: Johannes Loriz
Chief Executive Officer: Rolf Reisiger
Founded: 1980
Subjects: Anthropology, Education, Literature, Literary Criticism, Essays, Natural History, Poetry
ISBN Prefix(es): 978-3-88861

kopaed verlagsgmbh
Pfaelzer-Wald-Str 64, 81539 Munich
Tel: (089) 688 900 98 *Fax:* (089) 689 19 12
E-mail: info@kopaed.de
Web Site: www.kopaed.de
Key Personnel
Dir: Dr Ludwig Schlump
Subjects: Art, Communications, Education, Film, Video, Nonfiction (General), Radio, TV, Art Education, Art Therapy, Cultural Education, Media Education, Media Ethics
ISBN Prefix(es): 978-3-935686; 978-3-929061; 978-3-934079; 978-3-938028; 978-3-86736
Number of titles published annually: 40 Print
Total Titles: 300 Print

Bergstadtverlag Wilhelm Gottlieb Korn GmbH Wuerzburg+
Hermann-Herder-Str 4, 79104 Freiburg
Tel: (0761) 27 17 346 *Fax:* (0761) 27 17 265
Web Site: www.bergstadtverlag.de
Key Personnel
Mng Dir: Claus Michaletz
Publishing Dir: Alfred Theisen
Marketing & Sales: Aleksandra Boguth
E-mail: boguth@herder.de
Founded: 1732
Subjects: Art, Biography, Memoirs, History, Literature, Literary Criticism, Essays, Poetry, Regional Interests, Travel & Tourism
ISBN Prefix(es): 978-3-87057
Orders to: Leipziger Kommissions- und Grossbuchhandelsgesellschaft mbH (LKG), An der Suedspitze 1-12, 04571 Roetha, Contact: Baerbel Rosan *Tel:* (034206) 65120 *Fax:* (034206) 651746 *E-mail:* brosan@lkg-service.de *Web Site:* www.lkg-va.de

Verlag Gebrueder Kornmayer GbR
Behringstr 1-3, 63303 Dreieich
Tel: (06074) 4834170 *Fax:* (06074) 4834179
E-mail: info@kornmayer-verlag.de
Web Site: www.kornmayer-verlag.de

Key Personnel
Founder: Christoph Kornmayer; Evert Kornmayer *E-mail:* ek@kornmayer-verlag.de
Marketing & Media: Heike Winter *E-mail:* hw@kornmayer-verlag.de
Founded: 2002
Subjects: Art, Cookery, Fiction, Music, Dance, Nonfiction (General), Poetry, Wine & Spirits, Comics
ISBN Prefix(es): 978-3-938173; 978-3-9808785

A Korsch Verlag GmbH & Co KG
Landsberger Str 77, 82205 Gilching
Mailing Address: Postfach 1130, 86542 Aichach
Tel: (08105) 3763-0 *Fax:* (08105) 3763-44
E-mail: info@korsch-verlag.de; presse@korsch-verlag.de
Web Site: www.korsch-verlag.de
Key Personnel
Mng Dir: Niels Meyne
Press: Alexandra Neumann; Renate Richter
Founded: 1951
Specialize in calendars & gift books.
Subjects: Animals, Pets, Art, Humor, Literature, Literary Criticism, Essays, Maritime
ISBN Prefix(es): 978-3-7827

Kosmos-Verlag, see Franckh-Kosmos Verlags-GmbH & Co KG

Roman Kovar Verlag+
Gartenstr 6, Im Auel 1, 53773 Hennef
Tel: (0176) 62122262 *Fax:* (02242) 9182976
E-mail: roman-kovar@t-online.de
Web Site: www.kovar-verlag.com
Key Personnel
Publisher: Roman Kovar
Founded: 1986
Subjects: Art, Library & Information Sciences, Literature, Literary Criticism, Essays, Poetry, Psychology, Psychiatry, Religion - Jewish
ISBN Prefix(es): 978-3-925845

Karl Kraemer Verlag GmbH + Co KG+
Schulze-Delitzsch-Str 15, 70565 Stuttgart
Tel: (0711) 7 84 96-0 *Fax:* (0711) 7 84 96-20
E-mail: info@kraemerverlag.com
Web Site: www.kraemerverlag.com
Key Personnel
Dir: Gudrun Kraemer *E-mail:* gudrun.kraemer@kraemerverlag.com; Karl H Kraemer *E-mail:* karl.kraemer@kraemerverlag.com
Founded: 1930
Subjects: Architecture & Interior Design, Sports, Athletics
ISBN Prefix(es): 978-3-7828
Total Titles: 170 Print
Bookshop(s): Karl Kraemer Fachbuchhandlung, Rotebuehlstr 42, Postfach 102842, 70178 Stuttgart *Tel:* (0711) 669930 *Fax:* (0711) 628955 *Web Site:* www.karl.kraemer.de
Orders to: Koch, Neff & Oetinger Verlagsauslieferung GmbH, Industriestr 23, 70565 Stuttgart

Reinhold Kraemer Verlag+
Rothenbaumchaussee 103F, 20148 Hamburg
Mailing Address: Postfach 13 05 84, 20105 Hamburg
Tel: (040) 4101429 *Fax:* (040) 41537889
E-mail: info@kraemer-verlag.de; kraemer@kraemer-verlag.de
Web Site: www.kraemer-verlag.de; www.kraemer-verlag.com
Key Personnel
Mng Dir: Dr Reinhold Kraemer
Founded: 1987
Subjects: Education, Environmental Studies, Government, Political Science, History, Science (General), Social Sciences, Sociology, Ecology
ISBN Prefix(es): 978-3-926952; 978-3-89622

Adam Kraft Verlag+
Imprint of Verlagshaus Wuerzburg GmbH & Co KG
Beethovenstr 5 B, 97080 Wuerzburg
Tel: (0931) 465 889-11 *Fax:* (0931) 465 889-29
E-mail: info@verlagshaus.com
Web Site: www.verlagshaus.com
Key Personnel
Publishing Dir: Dieter Krause *Tel:* (0931) 465 889-14 *E-mail:* dieter.krause@verlagshaus.com
Dir, Production: Juergen Roth *Tel:* (0931) 465 889-15 *E-mail:* juergen.roth@verlagshaus.com
Sales Dir: Johannes Glesius *Tel:* (0931) 465 889-13 *E-mail:* johannes.glesius@verlagshaus.com
Founded: 1927
Subjects: Foreign Countries, Regional Interests, Travel & Tourism
ISBN Prefix(es): 978-3-8083

Krafthand Medien GmbH
Formerly Krafthand Verlag Walter Schulz GmbH
Walter-Schulz-Str 1, 86825 Bad Woerishofen
Tel: (08247) 3007-0 *Fax:* (08247) 3007-70; (08247) 3007-85
E-mail: info@krafthand.de
Web Site: www.krafthand.de; www.krafthand-medien.de
Key Personnel
Mng Dir: Andreas Hohenleitner *Tel:* (08247) 3007-42 *E-mail:* andreas.hohenleitner@krafthand.de; Gottfried Karpstein; Steffen Karpstein *Tel:* (08247) 3007-36 *E-mail:* steffen.karpstein@krafthand.de
Marketing Dir: Katja Heid *Tel:* (08247) 3007-184 *Fax:* (08247) 3007-170 *E-mail:* katja.heid@krafthand.de
Editor-in-Chief: Torsten Schmidt *Tel:* (08247) 3007-72 *Fax:* (08247) 3007-73 *E-mail:* torsten.schmidt@krafthand.de
Founded: 1927
Subjects: Civil Engineering
ISBN Prefix(es): 978-3-87441

Krafthand Verlag Walter Schulz GmbH, see Krafthand Medien GmbH

Karin Kramer Verlag+
Niemetzstr 19, 12055 Berlin
Mailing Address: Postfach 440 417, 12004 Berlin
Tel: (030) 684 50 55 *Fax:* (030) 685 85 77
E-mail: info@karin-kramer-verlag.de
Web Site: www.karin-kramer-verlag.de
Key Personnel
Editorial & Publicity: Bernd Kramer
Founded: 1970
Subjects: Alternative, Art, Biography, Memoirs, Fiction, Government, Political Science, History, Literature, Literary Criticism, Essays, Nonfiction (General), Philosophy, Poetry, Science Fiction, Fantasy, Social Sciences, Sociology, Anarchism, Magic & Mysticism
ISBN Prefix(es): 978-3-87956
Foreign Rep(s): Richard Bhend (Switzerland); Judith Heckel & Stefan Pierre-Louis (Germany); Seth Meyer-Bruhns (Austria)
Distribution Center: Sova GmbH, Friesstr 20-24, 60388 Frankfurt am Main *Tel:* (069) 41 02 11 *Fax:* (069) 41 02 80 *E-mail:* sovaffm@t-online.de *Web Site:* www.sovaffm.de (Germany & Austria)
Scheidegger & Co AG, c/o AVA Verlagsauslieferung AG, Centralweg 16, 8910 Affoltern am Albis, Switzerland *Tel:* (01) 762 42 50 *Fax:* (01) 762 42 10 *E-mail:* scheidegger@ava.ch *Web Site:* www.scheidegger-buecher.ch

Waldemar Kramer, *imprint of* Verlagshaus Roemerweg GmbH

Waldemar Kramer+
Imprint of Verlagshaus Roemerweg GmbH

Roemerweg 10, 65187 Wiesbaden
Tel: (0611) 986 98 0 *Fax:* (0611) 986 98 26
E-mail: info@verlagshaus-roemerweg.de
Web Site: www.verlagshaus-roemerweg.de
Key Personnel
Mng Dir: Lothar Wekel *E-mail:* wekel@
  verlagshausroemerweg.de
Founded: 1939
Subjects: Art, Biography, Memoirs, Biological
  Sciences, Education, Environmental Studies,
  Geography, Geology, History, Natural History,
  Nonfiction (General), Regional Interests, Sci-
  ence (General)
ISBN Prefix(es): 978-3-86539; 978-3-7374
Total Titles: 200 Print
Foreign Rep(s): Buchzentrum AG (Switzerland);
  Mohr Morawa Buchvertrieb GmbH (Austria)
Distribution Center: Sigloch Distribution
  GmbH & Co KG, Am Buchberg 8, Tor
  6-10, 74572 Blaufelden *Tel:* (07953)
  718 90 69 *Fax:* (07953) 883 16 0
  E-mail: verlagshausroemerweg@sigloch.de *Web
  Site:* www.sigloch.de

Krankenpflegeforschung, *imprint of* Bibliomed
Medizinische Verlagsgesellschaft mbH

Verlag Hubert Kretschmer+
Tuerkenstr 60/Rgb UG, 80799 Munich
Mailing Address: Postfach 26 01 17, 80058 Mu-
  nich
Tel: (089) 12345 30; (0172) 85 125 88 (cell)
  Fax: (089) 123 86 38
E-mail: mail@verlag-hubert-kretschmer.de;
  mail@archive-artistsbooks.de
Web Site: www.verlag-hubert-kretschmer.de;
  www.artistbooks.de
Key Personnel
Contact: Hubert J Kretschmer *E-mail:* hubert.
  kretschmer@t-online.de
Founded: 1980
Specialize in artist's books, catalogs, new & ab-
  stract photography.
Subjects: Art, Erotica, Photography
ISBN Prefix(es): 978-3-923205
Total Titles: 40 Print

Verlag Kreuz, *imprint of* Verlag Herder GmbH

Verlag Kreuz GmbH
Hermann-Herder-Str 4, 79104 Freiburg
Tel: (0761) 2717-0 *Fax:* (0761) 2717-520
E-mail: kundenservice@herder.de (customer
  service)
Web Site: www.verlag-kreuz.de
Key Personnel
Publisher: Manuel Herder
Mng Dir: Olaf Carstens; Roland Grimmelsmann
Head, Press & Public Relations: Andreas Bern-
  heim *E-mail:* bernheim@herder.de
Founded: 1945
Evangelical publishing house.
Subjects: Inspirational, Spirituality, Psychology,
  Psychiatry, Religion - Other
ISBN Prefix(es): 978-3-7831
Parent Company: Verlag Herder GmbH
Imprints: Christophorus; Herder Audio; Urania

Kriebel Verlag GmbH
Bahnhofallee 14a, 83080 Oberaudorf
Tel: (08033) 3 08 25 55; (0172) 8 50 91 40 (cell)
  Fax: (08033) 3 08 25 56
E-mail: info@kriebelverlag.de
Web Site: www.kriebel-sat.de; www.kriebelverlag.
  de
Key Personnel
Mng Dir: Brigitte Kriebel *E-mail:* brigitte.
  kriebel@kriebelverlag.de
Editor-in-Chief: Henning Kriebel
  E-mail: henning.kriebel@kriebelverlag.de
Founded: 1986

Subjects: Communications
ISBN Prefix(es): 978-3-927617

Alfred Kroener Verlag GmbH & Co KG+
Lenzhalde 20, 70192 Stuttgart
Tel: (0711) 615 53 6-3 *Fax:* (0711) 615 53 6-46
E-mail: kontakt@kroener-verlag.de
Web Site: www.kroener-verlag.de
Key Personnel
Mng Dir: Alfred Klemm
Founded: 1908
Subjects: Art, Drama, Theater, Education, Gov-
  ernment, Political Science, History, Language
  Arts, Linguistics, Literature, Literary Criticism,
  Essays, Music, Dance, Philosophy, Religion -
  Other, Social Sciences, Sociology
ISBN Prefix(es): 978-3-520
Total Titles: 180 Print

Krueger Verlag+
Subsidiary of S Fischer Verlag GmbH
Hedderichstr 114, 60596 Frankfurt am Main
Tel: (069) 6062-0 *Fax:* (069) 6062-319; (069)
  6062-214
Web Site: www.fischerverlage.de/page/krueger
Key Personnel
Chairman: Monika Schoeller
President & Publisher: Dr Joerg Bong
Publishing Dir: Siv Bublitz
Mng Dir: Michael Justus
General Manager, Marketing/Sales: Dr Uwe
  Rosenfeld
Founded: 1934
Subjects: Fiction, Humor, Nonfiction (General),
  Romance
ISBN Prefix(es): 978-3-8105
Associate Companies: Otto Wilhem Barth Ver-
  lag; Fischer Schatzinsel; Fischer Taschenbuch
  Verlag; Scherz Verlag; Theater & Medien

Verlag Krug & Schadenberg+
Hauptstr 8, 10827 Berlin
Tel: (030) 61 62 57 52 *Fax:* (030) 61 62 57 51
E-mail: info@krugschadenberg.de
Web Site: www.krugschadenberg.de
Key Personnel
Editor & International Rights: Andrea Krug
Founded: 1993
Membership(s): Boersenverein des Deutschen
  Buchhandels; Women in Publishing.
Subjects: Fiction, Human Relations, LGBTQ, Lit-
  erature, Literary Criticism, Essays, Self-Help,
  Women's Studies
ISBN Prefix(es): 978-3-930041
Number of titles published annually: 6 Print
Total Titles: 90 Print

Kuebler Verlag GmbH
Gauss-Str 41, 68623 Lampertheim
Tel: (06206) 155694 *Fax:* (06206) 155695
E-mail: info@kueblerverlag.de
Web Site: www.kueblerverlag.de
Key Personnel
Mng Dir: Alena Kuebler; Bernd Kuebler
Subjects: Fiction, History, Science Fiction, Fan-
  tasy
ISBN Prefix(es): 978-3-942270; 978-3-86346

Kuechengoetter, *imprint of* Graefe und Unzer
Verlag GmbH

Verlag Ernst Kuhn (VEK)+
Mendelssohnstr 7, 10405 Berlin
Mailing Address: Postfach 080147, 10001 Berlin
Fax: (030) 44 24 732
Web Site: www.vek.de
Key Personnel
Owner: Ernst Kuhn *E-mail:* kuhn@vek.de
Founded: 1991
Specialize in books on Russian music.

Also online bookshop (books on music, sheet mu-
  sic, scores).
Subjects: Biography, Memoirs, History, Music,
  Dance
ISBN Prefix(es): 978-3-928864; 978-3-936637

Edition Kulapatiim World Teacher Trust eV
Bachstr 20, 42929 Wermelskirchen
Tel: (02196) 971811 *Fax:* (02196) 91166
E-mail: wtt@kulapati.de
Web Site: www.kulapati.de
Subjects: Inspirational, Spirituality
ISBN Prefix(es): 978-3-930637

Kulleraugen-Verlag+
Laaseweg 4, 31174 Schellerten
Tel: (05123) 4330 *Fax:* (05123) 2015
E-mail: kulleraugen-verlag@gmx.de
Web Site: www.kulleraugen-verlag.de
Key Personnel
Contact: Hans-Juergen Tast
Founded: 1977
Subjects: Art, Film, Video, History, Photography
ISBN Prefix(es): 978-3-88842
Number of titles published annually: 5 Print
Total Titles: 70 Print

Kulturbuch-Verlag GmbH (KBV)
Sprosserweg 3, 12351 Berlin-Buckow
Mailing Address: Postfach 47 04 49, 12313
  Berlin
Tel: (030) 661 84 84 *Fax:* (030) 661 78 28
E-mail: kbvinfo@kulturbuch-verlag.de
Web Site: www.kulturbuch-verlag.de
Key Personnel
Mng Dir: Lothar Seikrit
Founded: 1945
Subjects: Art, Environmental Studies, Law, Re-
  gional Interests, Culture, Nature, Preservation
ISBN Prefix(es): 978-3-88961

Kulturstiftung der deutschen Vertriebenen
Kaiserstr 113, 53113 Bonn
Tel: (0228) 91512-0 *Fax:* (0228) 91512-29
E-mail: kulturstiftung@t-online.de
Web Site: kulturportal-west-ost.eu/kulturstiftung
Key Personnel
Contact: Dr Ernst Gierlich *E-mail:* e.gierlich@
  kulturportal-west-ost.eu
Founded: 1974
Subjects: Art, Government, Political Science, His-
  tory, Law, Literature, Literary Criticism, Essays
ISBN Prefix(es): 978-3-88557
Number of titles published annually: 12 Print
Total Titles: 200 Print

**Verlag der Kunst Dresden Ingwert Paulsen Jr
eK**
Subsidiary of Husum Druck -und Verlagsge-
  sellschaft mbH u Co KG
Nordbahnhofstr 2, 25813 Husum
Mailing Address: Postfach 1480, 25804 Husum
Tel: (04841) 8352-0 *Fax:* (04841) 8352-10
E-mail: info@verlagsgruppe.de
Web Site: www.verlagsgruppe.de
Key Personnel
Mng Dir: Ingwert Paulsen
Founded: 1952
Specialize in architecture & fine arts.
Subjects: Architecture & Interior Design, Art,
  Photography, Regional Interests
ISBN Prefix(es): 978-3-364; 978-3-86530
Total Titles: 180 Print
Associate Companies: Hamburger Lesehefte Ver-
  lag Ingwert Paulsen Jr eK; Hansa Verlag In-
  gwert Pausen Jr; Matthiesen Verlag Ingwert
  Paulsen Jr; Verlag der Nation Ingwert Paulsen
  Jr; Turmschreiber Verlag Ingwert Paulsen Jr;
  Frank Wagner Verlagsbuchhandlung Ingwert
  Paulsen Jr eK

Kunstanstifter Verlag e Kfr
Sophienstr 8, 68165 Mannheim
Tel: (0621) 832 61 54 *Fax:* (0621) 832 61 53
E-mail: info@kunstanstifter.de
Web Site: www.kunstanstifter.de
Key Personnel
Publisher & Marketing: Susanne Thierfelder
  E-mail: suse.thierfelder@kunstanstifter.de
Publisher & Sales: Niklas Thierfelder
  E-mail: niklas.thierfelder@kunstanstifter.de
ISBN Prefix(es): 978-3-9812842; 978-3-942795;
  978-3-9811465
Distribution Center: GVA Gemeinsame Ver-
  lagsauslieferung Goettingen GmbH & Co KG,
  Anna-Vandenhoeck-Ring 36, 37081 Goettingen
  Tel: (0551) 488 300 7 *Fax:* (0551) 413 92 *Web
  Site:* www.gva-verlage.de

Verlag Antje Kunstmann GmbH+
Zweigstr 10, Rgb, 80336 Munich
Tel: (089) 12 11 93 0 *Fax:* (089) 12 11 93 20
E-mail: info@kunstmann.de
Web Site: www.kunstmann.de
Key Personnel
Mng Dir, Editorial: Antje Kunstmann *E-mail:* a.
  kunstmann@kunstmann.de
Foreign Rights Manager: Susanne Eversmann
  Tel: (089) 12 11 93-25 *E-mail:* s.eversmann@
  kunstmann.de
Marketing & Sales: Uli Deurer *Tel:* (089) 12 11
  93 23 *E-mail:* u.deurer@kunstmann.de
Press: Andrea Schaefler *Tel:* (089) 12 11 93 24
  E-mail: a.schaefler@kunstmann.de
Founded: 1976
Subjects: Drama, Theater, Education, Fiction,
  Government, Political Science, Humor, Liter-
  ature, Literary Criticism, Essays, Nonfiction
  (General)
ISBN Prefix(es): 978-3-921040; 978-3-88897
Foreign Rep(s): B&I Buch & Information AG
  (Dagmar Bhend) (Switzerland); G Staudinger
  & M Pobegen (Austria)
Distribution Center: Leipziger Kommissions- und
  Grossbuchhandelsgesellschaft mbH (LKG),
  An der Suedspitze 1-12, 04571 Roetha, Con-
  tact: Ursula Fritzsche *Tel:* (034206) 65135
  Fax: (034206) 651739 *E-mail:* ufritzsche@lkg-
  service.de *Web Site:* www.lkg-va.de
Mohr Morawa Buchvertrieb GmbH, Sulzen-
  gasse 2, 1230 Vienna, Austria *Tel:* (01) 680
  14-0 *Fax:* (01) 688 71 30 *E-mail:* momo@
  mohrmorawa.at *Web Site:* www.mohrmorawa.at
AVA Verlagsauslieferung AG, Centralweg
  16, 8910 Affoltern am Albis, Switzerland
  Tel: (044) 762 42 50 *Fax:* (044) 762 42 10
  E-mail: verlagsservice@ava.ch

Kunth Verlag GmbH & Co KG
Koeniginstr 11, 80539 Munich
Tel: (089) 45 80 20-0 *Fax:* (089) 45 80 20-21
E-mail: info@kunth-verlag.de
Web Site: www.kunth-verlag.de
Key Personnel
Publishing Dir: Dr Angela Sendlinger
  E-mail: angela.sendlinger@kunth-verlag.de
Publisher: Calina Kunth *E-mail:* calina.
  kunth@kunth-verlag.de; Wolfgang Kunth
  E-mail: wolfgang.kunth@kunth-verlag.de
International Sales: Markus Pfister *Tel:* (089) 45
  80 20-23 *E-mail:* markus.pfister@kunth-verlag.
  de
Sales & Marketing: Sabine Sommer *Tel:* (089)
  45 80 20-20 *E-mail:* sabine.sommer@kunth-
  verlag.de
Specialize in world atlases, travel books, geog-
  raphy lexicons as well as illustrated books
  covering geographic, ethnological, cultural &
  tourism-related subjects.
Subjects: Foreign Countries, Geography, Geology,
  Travel & Tourism
ISBN Prefix(es): 978-3-933405; 978-3-936368;
  978-3-89944

Associate Companies: GeoGraphic Media GmbH
Foreign Rep(s): Hallwag Kuemmerly+Frey AG
  (Switzerland); KOMPASS-Karten GmbH (Aus-
  tria)

Kurtulus & Friends GmbH
Josef-Wilden-Str 5, 40474 Duesseldorf
Tel: (0211) 26 10 26 00; (0177) 16 33 416 (cell)
E-mail: info@kurtulus-friends.de
Web Site: www.kurtulus-friends.de
Key Personnel
Mng Dir: Guel Kurtulus
Founded: 2007
Subjects: Cookery, Environmental Studies, Envi-
  ronmental Protection
ISBN Prefix(es): 978-3-938631

KV&H Verlag GmbH+
Ottobrunner Str 41, 82008 Unterhaching
Mailing Address: Postfach 1480, 82004 Unter-
  haching
Tel: (089) 693 378-0 *Fax:* (089) 693 378-139
E-mail: info@kvh-verlag.de; medienbuero@kvh-
  verlag.de
Web Site: www.kvh-verlag.de
Key Personnel
Mng Dir: Michael Bork; Ute Edda Hammer; Juer-
  gen Horbach; Christoph Lochner
Licenses: Paulette Lamber *E-mail:* paulette.
  lamber@kvh-verlag.de
Press: Gina Ahrend
Founded: 1962
ISBN Prefix(es): 978-3-88141; 978-3-89400; 978-
  3-8318; 978-3-89529; 978-3-89768
Associate Companies: Heye Top Present Vertrieb
  GmbH
Warehouse: Kapellenstr 13, 85622 Feldkirchen

KVM - Der Medizinverlag
Ifenpfad 2-4, 12107 Berlin
Tel: (030) 761 806 16 *Fax:* (030) 761 806 92
E-mail: info@kvm-verlag.de
Web Site: www.kvm-verlag.de
Key Personnel
Publishing Manager: Dr Bernard C Kolster
  E-mail: b.kolster@kvm-verlag.de
Founded: 1996
Products in the fields of media & services in the
  field of medicine.
Subjects: Medicine, Nursing, Dentistry, Acupunc-
  ture, Physiotherapy
ISBN Prefix(es): 978-3-932119
Parent Company: Quintessenz-Verlagsgruppe

Kynos Verlag Dr Dieter Fleig GmbH+
Konrad-Zuse-Str 3, 54552 Nerdlen/Daun
Tel: (06592) 957389-0 *Fax:* (06592) 957389-20
E-mail: info@kynos-verlag.de; bestellung@kynos-
  verlag.de (orders)
Web Site: www.kynos-verlag.de
Key Personnel
Dir: Gisela Rau *Tel:* (06592) 957389-16
  E-mail: gisela.rau@kynos-verlag.de
Sales & Customer Support: Annika Mohr
  Tel: (06592) 957389-14 *E-mail:* annika.mohr@
  kynos-verlag.de
Production: Nicole Hilgers *Tel:* (06592) 957389-
  15 *E-mail:* nicole.hilgers@kynos-verlag.de
Founded: 1980
Specialize in education about therapy & guide
  dogs.
Subjects: Animals, Pets
ISBN Prefix(es): 978-3-929545; 978-3-924008;
  978-3-933228
Total Titles: 210 Print

Laaber-Verlag GmbH+
Regensburger Str 19, 93164 Laaber
Tel: (09498) 2307 *Fax:* (09498) 2543
E-mail: info@laaber-verlag.de
Web Site: www.laaber-verlag.wslv.de

Key Personnel
Owner & Publishing Dir: Dr Henning Mueller-
  Buscher
Publishing Dir: Matthias Bueckle
Founded: 1977
Subjects: Music, Dance
ISBN Prefix(es): 978-3-89007; 978-3-921518
Total Titles: 1,000 Print

van Laack GmbH
Roermonder Str 312, 52072 Aachen
Tel: (0241) 9319310 *Fax:* (03212) 9319310
E-mail: webmaster@van-laack.de
Web Site: www.vanlaack-buch.de
Key Personnel
Mng Dir: Dr Walter van Laack
Subjects: Philosophy
ISBN Prefix(es): 978-3-936624
Distribution Center: Books on Demand, In de
  Tarpen 42, 22484 Norderstedt *E-mail:* info@
  bod.de *Web Site:* www.bod.de

Labisch & Sundermeier GbR, see Verbrecher
  Verlag

Labyrinth Verlag Amei Helm
Orleanstr 75 E, 31135 Hildesheim
Tel: (05121) 285476
Web Site: www.labyrinth-verlag.de
Key Personnel
General Manager: Amei Helm *E-mail:* amei@
  labyrinth-verlag.de
Founded: 1985
Subjects: Inspirational, Spirituality, Self-Help
ISBN Prefix(es): 978-3-9801010; 978-3-9806542;
  978-3-9807707
Orders to: Verlagsgruppe Neue Erde GmbH, Con-
  tact: Katharina Mueller *Tel:* (0681) 595398-12
  E-mail: katharina@neue-erde.de

Lahn-Verlag GmbH+
Hoogeweg 71, 47623 Kevelaer
Tel: (02832) 929-0 *Fax:* (02832) 929-211
Web Site: www.butzon-bercker.de
Key Personnel
Mng Dir: Dr Edmund Bercker; Markus Bercker
  Tel: (02832) 929-112 *E-mail:* markus.bercker@
  bube.de
Marketing: Silke Loeber *Tel:* (02832) 929-165
  E-mail: silke.loeber@bube.de
Online Sales: Timo Bercker *Tel:* (02832) 929-135
  E-mail: timo.bercker@bube.de
Sales: Helga Daniels *Tel:* (02832) 929-297
  E-mail: helga.daniels@bube.de
Founded: 1991
Subjects: Poetry, Religion - Catholic, Theology
ISBN Prefix(es): 978-3-7840
Total Titles: 200 Print; 50 Audio
Parent Company: Butzon & Bercker GmbH

LAIKA-Verlag GmbH & Co KG
Schulterblatt 25, 20357 Hamburg
Tel: (040) 28416750 *Fax:* (040) 28416751
E-mail: info@laika-verlag.de; presse@laika-
  verlag.de
Web Site: www.laika-verlag.de
Key Personnel
Mng Dir: Willi Baer; Karl-Heinz Dellwo
Press: Carola Ebeling
Founded: 2009
Membership(s): Boersenverein des Deutschen
  Buchhandels.
ISBN Prefix(es): 978-3-942281
Orders to: Sozialistische Verlagsauslieferung
  GmbH, Friesstr 20-24, 60388 Frankfurt am
  Main *Tel:* (069) 410211 *Fax:* (069) 410280
  E-mail: sovaffm@t-online.de

Lambda Edition GmbH+
Grandweg 92a, 22529 Hamburg

Tel: (040) 31 28 36 *Fax:* (040) 319 20 96
E-mail: verlag@lambda-edition.de
Web Site: www.lambda-edition.de
Key Personnel
Publisher: Michael P Hartleben
Founded: 1980
Membership(s): The Stock Exchange of German
Booksellers.
Subjects: Fiction, LGBTQ, Literature, Literary
Criticism, Essays, Nonfiction (General)
ISBN Prefix(es): 978-3-925495

Lambertus Verlag GmbH+
Mitscherlichstr 8, 79108 Freiburg
Tel: (0761) 36825-0 *Fax:* (0761) 36825-33
E-mail: info@lambertus.de
Web Site: www.lambertus.de
Key Personnel
Mng Dir: Dr Thomas Becker *Tel:* (0761) 3 68 25-
23 *E-mail:* becker@lambertus.de; Petra Itschert
Tel: (0761) 3 68 25-18 *E-mail:* itschert@
lambertus.de
Marketing & News Media: Phillipp Zuercher
Tel: (0761) 3 68 25-22 *E-mail:* zuercher@
lambertus.de
Media & Advertising: Klaus Junge *Tel:* (0761) 3
68 25-15 *E-mail:* junge@lambertus.de
Sales: Bernhard Zimmermann *Tel:* (0761) 3 68
25-26 *E-mail:* zimmermann@lambertus.de
Founded: 1897
Subjects: Education, Law, Medicine, Nursing,
Dentistry, Nonfiction (General), Psychology,
Psychiatry, Social Sciences, Sociology, Theol-
ogy, Charity, Social Law, Vocational Training,
Welfare
ISBN Prefix(es): 978-3-7841
Subsidiaries: Freiburge Buchedienst (verlagsbuch-
handlung)
Orders to: Postfach 1026, 79010 Freiburg (Ger-
many & Austria)
Herder AG Basel Verlagsauslieferungen, Mutten-
zerstr 109, Postfach, 4133 Pratteln, Switzer-
land *Tel:* (061) 8279060 *Fax:* (060) 8279067
E-mail: verkauf@herder.ch

Lammers-Koll-Verlag
Auricher Str 10, 71665 Vaihingen an der Enz
Tel: (07042) 815 2405 *Fax:* (07042) 815 2404
E-mail: verlag@lammers-koll-verlag.de
Web Site: www.lammers-koll-verlag.de; www.
yogabuecher.de
Key Personnel
Contact: Hans-Peter Fritsche
Subjects: Biography, Memoirs, Inspirational, Spir-
ituality, Self-Help
ISBN Prefix(es): 978-3-935925

Lamuv Verlag GmbH+
Groner Str 20, 37073 Goettingen
Mailing Address: Postfach 26 05, 37016 Goettin-
gen
Tel: (0551) 44024 *Fax:* (0551) 41392
E-mail: bestsellung@gva-verlage.de
Web Site: www.lamuv.de
Key Personnel
Mng Dir, Editorial: Karl-Klaus Rabe
E-mail: rabe@lamuv.de
Press/Editor: Leonore Frester *E-mail:* frester@
lamuv.de
Founded: 1975
Subjects: Developing Countries, Foreign Coun-
tries, Government, Political Science, History,
Literature, Literary Criticism, Essays, Regional
Interests, Women's Studies
ISBN Prefix(es): 978-3-921521; 978-3-88977
Orders to: Gemeinsame Verlagsauslieferung
Goettingen GmbH & Co KG (GVA), Postfach
2021, 37010 Goettingen *Tel:* (0551) 487177
Fax: (0551) 41392

Landbuch-Verlagsgesellschaft mbH+
Kabelkamp 6, 30179 Hannover

Tel: (0511) 270460 *Fax:* (0511) 27046150
Founded: 1945
Subjects: Agriculture, Animals, Pets, Cookery,
Crafts, Games, Hobbies, House & Home, Hu-
mor, Nonfiction (General), Outdoor Recreation,
Regional Interests, Travel & Tourism, Country
Cooking, Country Life, Guides for Northern
Germany
ISBN Prefix(es): 978-3-7842
Parent Company: Cadmos Verlag GmbH, Moell-
ner Str 47, 21493 Schwarzenbek

Landt Verlag
Wilhelmstr 118, 10963 Berlin
Mailing Address: Postfach 61 03 12, 10925
Berlin
Tel: (030) 23 00 42 51 *Fax:* (030) 23 00 42 52
E-mail: landt@landtverlag.de
Web Site: www.landtverlag.de
Key Personnel
Owner: Andreas Krause Landt
Founded: 2005
Subjects: Economics, Gardening, Plants, Gov-
ernment, Political Science, History, House &
Home, Language Arts, Linguistics, Literature,
Literary Criticism, Essays, Social Sciences, So-
ciology
ISBN Prefix(es): 978-3-938844
Parent Company: Thomas-Hoof-Gruppe

Landwirtschaftsverlag GmbH
Huelsebrockstr 2-8, 48165 Muenster
Tel: (0251) 801-0 *Fax:* (0251) 801204
E-mail: buch@lv.de
Web Site: www.lv.de
Key Personnel
Publisher: Thomas Richter *Tel:* (0251) 8 01 24 59
Fax: (0251) 80 18 51 *E-mail:* thomas.richter@
lv.de
Program Dir: Claudia Rudel *Tel:* (0251) 8 01 37
16 *E-mail:* claudia.rudel@lv.de
Product Management: Elke Foerster *Tel:* (0251) 8
01 33 70 *E-mail:* elke.foerster@lv.de
Founded: 1946
Subjects: Agriculture, Cookery, Crafts, Games,
Hobbies, Gardening, Plants, Mysteries, Sus-
pense, Nature
ISBN Prefix(es): 978-3-7843
Distribution Center: VM-Verlegerdienst Munich,
Gutenbergstr 1, Postfach 1280, 82197 Gilching, Contact: Jana Brose *Tel:* (08105) 38 81
70 *Fax:* (08105) 38 81 87 *E-mail:* lv-buch@
verlegerdienst.de
Mohr Morawa Buchvertrieb GmbH, Sulzengasse 2, 1230 Vienna, Austria *Tel:* (01) 68
01 40 *Fax:* (01) 6 89 68 00 *E-mail:* momo@
mohrmorawa.at *Web Site:* www.mohrmorawa.at
Buchzentrum AG, Industriestr Ost 10, 6414 Haegendorf, Switzerland *Tel:* (062) 2 09 26 26
Fax: (062) 2 09 26 27 *E-mail:* kundendienst@
buchzentrum.ch

**Peter Lang GmbH Internationaler Verlag der
Wissenschaften+**
Eschborner Landstr 42-50, 60489 Frankfurt am
Main
Tel: (069) 78 07 05 0 *Fax:* (069) 78 07 05 50
E-mail: zentrale.frankfurt@peterlang.com
Web Site: www.peterlang.de
Key Personnel
Mng Dir: Dr Joerg Meidenbauer
Sales: Claudia Marcks *E-mail:* c.marcks@
peterlang.com
Founded: 1971
Publisher of academic books, emphasis on law,
economics & social sciences. Presents opportu-
nities for scientists to publish their research.
Subjects: Art, Asian Studies, Business, Commu-
nications, Economics, Education, Environmen-
tal Studies, Ethnicity, Government, Political
Science, History, Language Arts, Linguistics,
Law, Literature, Literary Criticism, Essays, Phi-

losophy, Psychology, Psychiatry, Religion -
Catholic, Religion - Jewish, Religion - Protes-
tant, Science (General), Social Sciences, So-
ciology, Theology, Women's Studies, Natural
Sciences
ISBN Prefix(es): 978-3-8204; 978-3-631
Total Titles: 1,300 Print
Parent Company: Verlag Peter Lang AG,
Hochfeldstr 32, 3012 Bern, Switzerland
Associate Companies: Peter Lang GmbH International Verlag der Wissenschaften, Lenau-
gasse 9/8, 1080 Vienna, Austria, Contact:
Dr Norbert Willenpart *Tel:* (01) 403 58 26
Fax: (01) 406 74 28 *E-mail:* buero.wien@
peterlang.com *Web Site:* www.peterlang.
com; PIE-Peter Lang SA Editions scientifiques internationales, One Ave Maurice,
6e etage, 1050 Brussels, Belgium *Tel:* (02)
347 72 36 *Fax:* (02) 347 72 37 *E-mail:* pie@
peterlang.com; Wydawnictwo Naukowe Peter Lang, Przedstawicielstwo w Polsce, Ul Zi-
morowicza 2 m 11, 02-620 Warsaw, Poland,
Contact: Lukasz Galecki *Tel:* (660) 759467
E-mail: biuro.warszawa@peterlang.com; Peter Lang AG International Academic Publishers, Hochfeldstr 32, 3012 Bern, Switzerland
Tel: (031) 306 17 17 *Fax:* (031) 306 17 27;
Peter Lang Ltd International Academic Pub-
lishers, 52 St Giles, Oxford OX1 3LU, United
Kingdom *Tel:* (01865) 514160 *Fax:* (01865)
604028 *E-mail:* oxford@peterlang.com *Web
Site:* www.peterlang.com; Peter Lang Publish-
ing Inc, 29 Broadway, 18th floor, New York,
NY 10006, United States *Tel:* 212-647-7706
Fax: 212-647-7707 *E-mail:* customerservice@
plang.com *Web Site:* www.peterlang.com
Orders to: Peter Lang International Academic
Publishers, Moosstr 1, Postfach 350, 2542
Pieterlen, Switzerland *Tel:* (032) 376 17 17
Fax: (032) 376 17 27 *E-mail:* info@peterlang.
com

**Buchverlage LangenMueller Herbig
nymphenburger terra magica+**
Thomas Wimmer Ring 11, 80539 Munich
Tel: (089) 29088-0 *Fax:* (089) 29088-144
E-mail: info@herbig.net
Web Site: www.herbig.net
Key Personnel
Publisher: Brigitte Fleissner-Mikorey
Foreign Rights Dir: Sonja Schmidt *Tel:* (089)
29088-157 *E-mail:* s.schmidt@herbig.net
Sales Manager: Sissi Klauser *Tel:* (089) 29088-
129
Press: Anja Volkmer *Tel:* (089) 29088-132
Fax: (089) 29088-178 *E-mail:* a.volkmer@
herbig.net
Production: Ina Hesse *Tel:* (089) 29088-128
Fax: (089) 29088-166 *E-mail:* i.hesse@herbig.
net
Founded: 1893
Subjects: Biography, Memoirs, Cookery, Drama,
Theater, Economics, Fiction, Health, Nutri-
tion, History, Literature, Literary Criticism, Es-
says, Music, Dance, Parapsychology, Self-Help,
Travel & Tourism, Politics, Visual Arts
ISBN Prefix(es): 978-3-87287
Parent Company: F A Herbig Verlagsbuchhand-
lung GmbH
Associate Companies: Franckh-Kosmos Verlags-
GmbH & Co KG, Pfizerstr 5-7, 70184 Stuttgart
Tel: (0711) 2191-0 *Fax:* (0711) 2191-422
E-mail: info@kosmos.de; Amalthea Signum
Verlag GmbH, Am Heumarkt 19, 1030 Vienna,
Austria *Tel:* (01) 7 12 35 60 *Fax:* (01) 7 12 89
95
Subsidiaries: Herbig; LangenMueller; Langen-
Mueller Hoerbuch; nymphenburger; terra mag-
ica

Langenscheidt Fachverlag+
Member of Langenscheidt Verlagsgruppe
Mies-van-der-Rohe-Str 5, 80807 Munich

Tel: (089) 36096-0; (089) 36096-333 (orders)
Fax: (089) 36096-222; (089) 36096-258 (orders)
E-mail: kundenservice@langenscheidt.de;
presse@langenscheidt.de
Web Site: www.langenscheidt.de
Key Personnel
Acting Partner: Andreas Langenscheidt
General Partner: Karl Ernst Tielebier-
Langenscheidt
Head, Customer Service: Angela Reck
E-mail: angela.reck@langenscheidt.de
International Sales & Foreign Rights Man-
ager: Anke Zahlmann *Tel:* (089) 36096-497
Fax: (089) 36096-432 *E-mail:* a.zahlmann@
langenscheidt.de
Sales Manager: Annette Schwartzmanns
Fax: (089) 36096-152 *E-mail:* a.
schwartzmanns@langenscheidt.de
Press & Public Relations: Gabriele Becker
Tel: (089) 15820-206 *Fax:* (089) 15820-208
Founded: 1991
Specialize in print & electronic versions of bilin-
gual & multilingual books.
ISBN Prefix(es): 978-3-86117

Langenscheidt Hachette Verlag+
Member of Langenscheidt Verlagsgruppe
Mies-van-der-Rohe-Str 5, 80807 Munich
Tel: (089) 360960; (089) 36096-333 (orders)
Fax: (089) 36096-222; (089) 36096-258 (or-
ders)
E-mail: kundenservice@langenscheidt.de;
presse@langenscheidt.de
Web Site: www.langenscheidt.de
Key Personnel
Acting Partner: Andreas Langenscheidt
General Partner: Karl Ernst Tielebier-
Langenscheidt
Head, Customer Service: Angela Reck
E-mail: angela.reck@langenscheidt.de
International Sales & Foreign Rights Man-
ager: Anke Zahlmann *Tel:* (089) 36096-497
Fax: (089) 36096-432 *E-mail:* a.zahlmann@
langenscheidt.de
Sales Manager: Annette Schwartzmanns
Fax: (089) 36096-152 *E-mail:* a.
schwartzmanns@langenscheidt.de
Press & Public Relations: Gabriele Becker
Tel: (089) 15820-206 *Fax:* (089) 15820-208
Founded: 1977
Subjects: Education, Language Arts, Linguistics
ISBN Prefix(es): 978-3-595

Langenscheidt KG+
Member of Langenscheidt Verlagsgruppe
Mies-van-der-Rohe-Str 5, 80807 Munich
Tel: (089) 36096-0; (089) 36096-333 (orders)
Fax: (089) 36096-222; (089) 36096-258 (or-
ders)
E-mail: kundenservice@langenscheidt.de;
presse@langenscheidt.de
Web Site: www.langenscheidt.de
Key Personnel
Acting Partner: Andreas Langenscheidt
General Partner: Karl Ernst Tielebier-
Langenscheidt
Head, Customer Service: Angela Reck
E-mail: angela.reck@langenscheidt.de
International Sales & Foreign Rights Man-
ager: Anke Zahlmann *Tel:* (089) 36096-497
Fax: (089) 36096-438 *E-mail:* a.zahlmann@
langenscheidt.de
Sales Manager: Annette Schwartzmanns
Fax: (089) 36096-152 *E-mail:* a.
schwartzmanns@langenscheidt.de
Press & Public Relations: Gabriele Becker
Tel: (089) 15820-206 *Fax:* (089) 15820-208
Founded: 1856
Membership(s): TR-Verlagsunion GmbH.
Subjects: Language Arts, Linguistics, Travel &
Tourism, Cartography
ISBN Prefix(es): 978-3-526

Langenscheidt Verlagsgruppe+
Mies-van-der-Rohe-Str 5, 80807 Munich
Tel: (089) 36096-0; (089) 36096-333 (orders)
Fax: (089) 36096-222; (089) 36096-258 (or-
ders)
E-mail: kundenservice@langenscheidt.de;
presse@langenscheidt.de
Web Site: www.langenscheidt.de
Key Personnel
Acting Partner: Andreas Langenscheidt
General Partner: Karl Ernst Tielebier-
Langenscheidt
Head, Customer Service: Angela Reck
E-mail: angela.reck@langenscheidt.de
International Sales & Foreign Rights Man-
ager: Anke Zahlmann *Tel:* (089) 36096-497
Fax: (089) 36096-432 *E-mail:* a.zahlmann@
langenscheidt.de
Sales Manager: Annette Schwartzmanns
Fax: (089) 36096-152 *E-mail:* a.
schwartzmanns@langenscheidt.de
Press & Public Relations: Gabriele Becker
Tel: (089) 15820-206 *Fax:* (089) 15820-208
Founded: 1856
Subjects: Education, Language Arts, Linguistics,
Travel & Tourism
ISBN Prefix(es): 978-3-468; 978-3-86117; 978-3-
595; 978-3-526; 978-3-493
Distribution Center: Mohr Morawa Buchvertrieb
GmbH, Sulzengasse 2, 1230 Vienna, Austria,
Sales: Peter Kargl *Tel:* (01) 680 14-0 *Fax:* (01)
688 71 30 *E-mail:* momo@mohrmorawa.at *Web
Site:* www.mohrmorawa.at
Langenscheidt Iberica SL, C/ General Arrando,
14 bajo A, 28010 Madrid, Spain, Contact: Vir-
ginia Gil *Tel:* 91 591 42 71 *Fax:* 91 445 98 39
E-mail: langenscheidt@langenscheidt.es *Web
Site:* www.langenscheidt.es
Buchzentrum AG, Industriestr Ost 10, 4614 Hae-
gendorf, Switzerland *Tel:* (062) 2 09 25 25
Fax: (062) 2 09 26 27 *E-mail:* kundendienst@
buchzentrum.ch

**Karl Robert Langewiesche Nachfolger Hans
Koester Verlagsbuchhandlung KG+**
Gruener Weg 6, 61462 Koenigstein
Tel: (06174) 7333 *Fax:* (06174) 933-039
E-mail: info@langewiesche-verlag.de
Web Site: www.langewiesche-verlag.de
Key Personnel
Publisher & Mng Dir, Editorial, Production:
Hans-Curt Koester
Editorial: Gabriele Klempert
Founded: 1902
Specialize in books, journals & calendars.
Membership(s): Boersenverein des Deutschen
Buchhandel eV.
Subjects: Antiques, Archaeology, Architecture &
Interior Design, Art, History, How-to, Photog-
raphy
ISBN Prefix(es): 978-3-7845
Number of titles published annually: 5 Print
Total Titles: 100 Print; 1 Online
Imprints: Die Blauen Buecher (The Blue Books)

Lappan Verlag GmbH+
Subsidiary of Verlag Carl Ueberreuter GmbH
Wuerzburger Str 14, 26121 Oldenburg
Mailing Address: Postfach 3407, 26024 Olden-
burg
Tel: (0441) 980 66-0 *Fax:* (0441) 980 66-34
E-mail: info@lappan.de; presse@lappan.de;
programm@lappan.de
Web Site: www.lappan.de
Key Personnel
Mng Dir: Dieter Schwalm
Press: Ulrike Renneberg *Tel:* (04298) 4190588
Sales: Heike Kroner *E-mail:* h.kroner@lappan.de
Founded: 1983
Publisher of books for children & humor gift
books for adults.
Subjects: Cartoon Books of Uli Stein, Humor
ISBN Prefix(es): 978-3-89082; 978-3-8303

Number of titles published annually: 80 Print
Total Titles: 470 Print
Imprints: Achterbahn
Distributor for Edition C (Switzerland)
Distribution Center: Koepenicker Cartoon
Gesellschaft mbH, Birkenstr 23a, 12559 Berlin
E-mail: kontakt@cartoonkarten.de

**Verlag Michael Lassleben Druckerei und
Buchbinderei** (Michael Lassleben Publishing
House, Printer & Bookbinder)
Lange Gasse 19, 93183 Kallmuenz
Tel: (09473) 20 5 *Fax:* (09473) 83 57
E-mail: druckerei@oberpfalzverlag-lassleben.de
Web Site: www.oberpfalzverlag-lassleben.de
Key Personnel
Owner: Erich Lassleben, Sr
Founded: 1907
Subjects: Archaeology, Geography, Geology, His-
tory
ISBN Prefix(es): 978-3-7847
Number of titles published annually: 20 Print

J Latka Verlag GmbH+
Heilsbachstr 17-19, 53123 Bonn
Tel: (0228) 91932-0 *Fax:* (0228) 9193217
E-mail: info@latka.de
Web Site: www.latka.de
Key Personnel
Dir: Joachim Latka
Mng Editor: Julia A Latka
Founded: 1984
Subjects: History, Travel & Tourism
ISBN Prefix(es): 978-3-925068
Total Titles: 30 Print
Branch Office(s)
Postfach 303126, 10729 Berlin *Tel:* (030)
2887898-0 *Fax:* (030) 288789817
Foreign Rep(s): Sandra Claassen (Angola,
Botswana, Democratic Republic of the Congo,
Lesotho, Madagascar, Malawi, Mauritius,
Mozambique, Namibia, South Africa, Swazi-
land, Tanzania, Zambia, Zimbabwe); Pamela
D'Souza (Middle East, Pakistan); Detlef Fox
(North America); REACH Communications Ltd
(Ms Lim Mey Lian) (Asia); Susanne Schubert
(South Africa)
Orders to: Herold, Raiffeisenallee 10, 82041
Oberhaching *Tel:* (089) 6138710 *Fax:* (089)
61387120

Laumann Druck & Verlag GmbH u Co KG
Viktorstr 18-20, 48249 Duelmen
Mailing Address: Postfach 14 61, 48235 Duelmen
Tel: (02594) 94 34-0 *Fax:* (02594) 94 34 70
E-mail: info@laumann-verlag.de
Web Site: www.laumann-verlag.de
Key Personnel
Chief Executive Officer: Werner Kleine
Founded: 1842
Subjects: Art, Biography, Memoirs, Cookery,
Education, Fiction, History, Humor, Music,
Dance, Philosophy, Regional Interests, Reli-
gion - Catholic, Theology, Travel & Tourism,
Schlesien
ISBN Prefix(es): 978-3-89960

LBO-Dienst, *imprint of* Bauverlag BV GmbH

Lebenshilfe-Verlag+
Raiffeisenstr 18, 35043 Marburg
Tel: (06421) 491-0; (06421) 491-123 (sales)
Fax: (06421) 491-167; (06421) 491-623 (sales)
E-mail: verlag@lebenshilfe.de; vertrieb@
lebenshilfe.de
Web Site: www.lebenshilfe.de
Key Personnel
Dir: Roland Boehm *Tel:* (06421) 491-198
Fax: (06421) 491-698 *E-mail:* roland.boehm@
lebenshilfe.de
Founded: 1958

Subjects: Disability, Special Needs, Health, Nutrition, Law, Medicine, Nursing, Dentistry, Nonfiction (General), Self-Help, Social Sciences, Sociology
ISBN Prefix(es): 978-3-88617

LEDA Verlag
Rathausstr 23, 26789 Leer
Tel: (0491) 91 22 62 86 *Fax:* (0491) 91 22 62 87
E-mail: info@leda-verlag.de
Web Site: www.leda-verlag.de
Key Personnel
Mng Dir: Heike Gerdes *E-mail:* heike.gerdes@leda-verlag.de
Founded: 2000
Membership(s): Boersenverein des Deutschen Buchhandels eV.
Subjects: Fiction, Crime Fiction
ISBN Prefix(es): 978-3-934927; 978-3-939689
Distribution Center: PROLIT Verlagsauslieferung GmbH, Postfach 9, 35461 Fernwald, Contact: Rainer Eckert *Tel:* (0641) 9 43 93 33 *Fax:* (0641) 9 43 93 199 *E-mail:* r.eckert@prolit.de *Web Site:* www.prolit.de

Kochbuchverlag Olli Leeb
Tuttlinger Str 7, 80686 Munich
Tel: (089) 962 936 46
E-mail: rezept@ollileeb.com; anfragen@ollileeb.com; bestellen@ollileeb.com; willkommen@ollileeb.com
Web Site: www.ollileeb.com
Key Personnel
Mng Dir: Olli Leeb
Founded: 1976
Subjects: Cookery
ISBN Prefix(es): 978-3-921799

Legat-Verlag GmbH & Co KG
Lessingweg 26, 72076 Tuebingen
Tel: (07071) 650266 *Fax:* (07071) 650267
E-mail: info@legat-verlag.de
Web Site: www.legat-verlag.de
Key Personnel
Mng Dir: Erhard Gass *E-mail:* erhard.gass@legat-verlag.de
Mng Dir, Editing & Quality: Heike Frank-Ostarhild *Tel:* (07071) 30 24 49 *E-mail:* heike.ostarhild@legat-verlag.de
Mng Dir, Production & Sales: Alexander Frank *E-mail:* alexander.frank@legat-verlag.de
Subjects: Art, Visual Literacy
ISBN Prefix(es): 978-3-932942

Lehmanns Media GmbH
Ottostr 12, 50859 Cologne
Tel: (030) 617911-46 *Fax:* (030) 617911-60
E-mail: info@lehmanns.de
Web Site: www.lehmanns.de
Key Personnel
Publishing Dir: Volker Thurner *Tel:* (030) 617911-22 *E-mail:* thurner@lehmanns.de
Mng Dir: Detlef Buettner *E-mail:* buettner@lehmanns.de
Marketing Dir: Rolf Hammann *Tel:* (02234) 7011-198 *E-mail:* hammann@lehmanns.de
Editorial: Bernhard J Boenisch *Tel:* (030) 617911-30 *E-mail:* boenisch@lehmanns.de
Founded: 1981
Subjects: Art, Computer Science, Crafts, Games, Hobbies, Economics, Government, Political Science, Health, Nutrition, History, Law, Literature, Literary Criticism, Essays, Mathematics, Medicine, Nursing, Dentistry, Nonfiction (General), Psychology, Psychiatry, Science (General), Science Fiction, Fantasy, Social Sciences, Sociology, Technology, Travel & Tourism, Veterinary Science, Comics, Crime & Thrillers, Culture, Graphic Novels, Humanities, Taxes
ISBN Prefix(es): 978-3-86541; 978-3-926998; 978-3-931253; 978-3-936427

Bookshop(s): Kerpener Str 75, 50937 Cologne, Contact: Sabine Schoenfelder *Tel:* (0221) 411075 *Fax:* (0221) 411500 *E-mail:* k-med@lehmanns.de; Friedrichstr 128, 10117 Berlin, Contact: Juergen Seidel *Tel:* (030) 2827079 *Fax:* (030) 2823858 *E-mail:* b-fr@lehmanns.de; Luisenstr 9, 10117 Berlin, Contact: Juergen Seidel *Tel:* (030) 450578037 *Fax:* (030) 450578039 *E-mail:* b-ch@lehmanns.de; Rudower Chaussee 26, 12489 Berlin, Contact: Juergen Seidel *Tel:* (030) 20932028 *Fax:* (030) 20932038 *E-mail:* adlershof@lehmanns.de; Helmholtzstr 2-9, 10587 Berlin, Manager: Eva Schubert *Tel:* (030) 617911-54 *Toll Free Tel:* 0800 749 26 65 *Fax:* (030) 617911-62 *E-mail:* eva.schubert@lehmanns.de; Helmholtzstr 2-9, 10587 Berlin, Contact: Juergen Seidel *Tel:* (030) 617911-25 *Fax:* (030) 619911-60 *E-mail:* info@lehmanns.de (customer service); Hoepfigheimer Str 13, 74321 Bietigheim-Bissingen, Contact: Dirk Skudlarek *Fax:* (07142) 91955-48 *E-mail:* ilc@lehmanns.de; Biasewitzer Str 78, 01307 Dresden, Contact: Martin Haltrich *Tel:* (0351) 4425552 *Fax:* (0351) 4425554 *E-mail:* dd@lehmanns.de; Himmelgeister Str 131, 40225 Duesseldorf, Contact: Sabine Schoenfelder *Tel:* (0211) 347747 *Fax:* (0211) 340940 *E-mail:* dus@lehmanns.de; Universitaetsstr 6, 91054 Erlangen, Contact: Sibylle Peege *Tel:* (09131) 829644 *Fax:* (09131) 829649 *E-mail:* er@lehmanns.de; Robert-Koch-Str 12, 45147 Essen, Contact: Sabine Schoenfelder *Tel:* (0201) 733358 *Fax:* (0201) 737526 *E-mail:* essen@lehmanns.de; Robert-Koch-Str 12, 45147 Essen, Contact: Stefanie Schlichter *Tel:* (0201) 87098574 *Fax:* (0201) 737526 *E-mail:* bibliotheksdienst@lehmanns.de (library service); Frankfurter Str 42, 35392 Giessen, Contact: Thomas Flentge *Tel:* (0641) 975 96-0 *Fax:* (0641) 975 96-20 *E-mail:* gi@lehmanns.de; Universitaetsring 7, 06108 Halle, Contact: Martin Haltrich *Tel:* (0345) 212 15-0 *Fax:* (0345) 212 15-15 *E-mail:* hal@lehmanns.de; Kurze Muehren 6, 20095 Hamburg, Contact: Maike Bialas *Tel:* (040) 336384 *Fax:* (040) 338955 *E-mail:* hamburg@lehmanns.de; Carl-Neuberg-Str 1, 30625 Hannover, Contact: Maike Bialas *Tel:* (0511) 53060-0 *Fax:* (0511) 537334 *E-mail:* hannover@lehmanns.de; Im Neuenheimer Feld 370, 69120 Heidelberg, Contact: Beate Szpakowski *Tel:* (06221) 473040 *Fax:* (06221) 408344 *E-mail:* inf-hd@lehmanns.de; Universitaetsplatz 12, 69117 Heidelberg, Contact: Beate Szpakowski *Tel:* (06221) 90567-0 *Fax:* (06221) 90567-22 *E-mail:* hd-uniplatz@lehmanns.de; Grimmaische Str 10, 04109 Leipzig, Contact: Martina Michels *Tel:* (0341) 3397500-0 *Fax:* (0341) 3397500-199 *E-mail:* leipzig@lehmanns.de; Augustusplatz 5, 55131 Mainz, Contact: Thomas Flentge *Tel:* (06131) 371212 *Fax:* (06131) 373263 *E-mail:* mainz@lehmanns.de; Reitgasse 7/9, 35037 Marburg, Contact: Thomas Flentge *Tel:* (06421) 17090 *Fax:* (06421) 15487 *E-mail:* elwert@lehmanns.de; Pettenkoferstr 18, 80336 Munich, Contact: Sibylle Peege *Tel:* (089) 530294 *Fax:* (089) 534516 *E-mail:* muenchen@lehmanns.de; Ludwig Thoma-Str 43, 93051 Regensburg, Contact: Sibylle Peege *Tel:* (0941) 90830 *Fax:* (0941) 990518 *E-mail:* rgbg@lehmanns.de; Wengengasse 27, 89073 Ulm, Contact: Beate Szpakowski *Tel:* (0731) 63334 *Fax:* (0731) 6022078 *E-mail:* ulm-city@lehmanns.de; Schanzenstr 1 (Im Bubenberghaus), 3008 Bern, Switzerland, Contact: Elke Rehberger *Tel:* (0848) 482482 *Fax:* (0848) 483483 *E-mail:* info@lehmanns.ch

Lehmstedt Verlag
Hainstr 1, Aufgang C, Barthels Hof, 04109 Leipzig

Tel: (0341) 4927366
E-mail: info@lehmstedt.de; vertrieb@lehmstedt.de
Web Site: www.lehmstedt.de
Key Personnel
Owner & Publisher: Dr Mark Lehmstedt
Founded: 2003
Subjects: Biography, Memoirs, History, Journalism, Photography, Travel & Tourism, Cultural History
ISBN Prefix(es): 978-3-937146; 978-3-942473
Distribution Center: Leipziger Kommissions- und Grossbuchhandelsgesellschaft mbH (LKG), An der Suedspitze 1-12, 04571 Roetha, Contact: Martina Koernig *Tel:* (034206) 65 122 *Fax:* (034206) 65 1734 *E-mail:* mkoernig@lkg-service.de *Web Site:* www.lkg-va.de

Verlag fuer Lehrmittel Poessneck GmbH+
Neustaedter Str 63, 07381 Poessneck
Tel: (03647) 425018 *Fax:* (03647) 425020
Key Personnel
Mng Dir; Lothar Stein
Founded: 1947
ISBN Prefix(es): 978-3-7493

Leibniz-Buecherwarte+
Robert-Koch-Str 12, 31848 Bad Muender
Mailing Address: Postfach 1214, 31842 Bad Muender
Tel: (05042) 15 28 *Fax:* (05042) 15 28
E-mail: leibniz-buecherwarte@kabelmail.de
Web Site: www.leibnizbuecherwarte.com
Key Personnel
Contact: Gabrielle Spaeth
Founded: 1985
Specialize in philosophy with children.
Subjects: Literature, Literary Criticism, Essays, Philosophy, Religion - Other
ISBN Prefix(es): 978-3-925237

Leibniz Verlag+
Subsidiary of Reichl Verlag
Ginsterweg 5, 96164 Kemmern
Tel: (09544) 987544 *Fax:* (09544) 987515
Web Site: www.leibniz-verlag.de
Key Personnel
Contact: Philipp Gerst
Founded: 1994
Subjects: Economics, History, Human Relations, Language Arts, Linguistics, Philosophy, Science (General), Social Sciences, Sociology, International Law, Political Science
ISBN Prefix(es): 978-3-931155; 978-3-931239

Leinpfad Verlag
Leinpfad 5, 55218 Ingelheim
Tel: (06132) 83 69 *Fax:* (06132) 89 69 51
E-mail: info@leinpfadverlag.de
Web Site: www.leinpfadverlag.de
Key Personnel
Publishing Dir: Angelika Schulz-Parthu
Marketing: Ulrike Hinck
Press: Carmen Doll
Founded: 1997
Subjects: Regional Interests
ISBN Prefix(es): 978-3-937782; 978-3-9806915; 978-3-9808383; 978-3-9805837; 978-3-9807711; 978-3-9808943

Edition Leipzig, *imprint of* Seemann Henschel GmbH & Co KG

Leipziger Universitaetsverlag GmbH+
Oststr 41, 04317 Leipzig
Tel: (0341) 9900440 *Fax:* (0341) 9900440
E-mail: info@univerlag-leipzig.de
Web Site: www.univerlag-leipzig.de
Key Personnel
Mng Dir: Dr Gerald Diesener
Founded: 1992

Subjects: Communications, History, Law,
Medicine, Nursing, Dentistry, Philosophy, Science (General), Women's Studies
ISBN Prefix(es): 978-3-929031; 978-3-931922;
978-3-933240; 978-3-934565; 978-3-935693;
978-3-936522; 978-3-937209; 978-3-86583

Leipziger Verlagsgesellschaft+
Gerichtsweg 28, 04103 Leipzig
Tel: (0341) 2210229
Founded: 1990
Specialize in high quality catalogs & art books.
Subjects: Art, History, Literature, Literary Criticism, Essays, Regional Interests
ISBN Prefix(es): 978-3-910143

Anton G Leitner Verlag+
Buchenweg 3b, 82234 Wessling
Tel: (08153) 95 25-22
E-mail: service@dasgedicht.de
Web Site: www.aglv.com
Key Personnel
Owner, Publisher & Author: Anton G Leitner
Founded: 1992
Subjects: Literature, Literary Criticism, Essays,
Poetry, Contemporary & International Poetry,
Latin
ISBN Prefix(es): 978-3-929433
Imprints: DAS GEDICHT; DAS GEDICHT
Chapbook; Edition DAS GEDICHT; Lyrik-garten; Poesie 21
Distributor for Initiative Junger Autoren eV

leiv Leipziger Kinderbuchverlag GmbH
Torgauer Platz 1-3, 04315 Leipzig
Fax: (0341) 9 92 78 49
Web Site: www.leiv-verlag.de
Key Personnel
Contact: Steffen Lehmann *Tel:* (0341) 9 92
78 41 *E-mail:* lehmann@leiv-verlag.de;
Marlis Tiepoldt *Tel:* (0341) 9 92 78 40
E-mail: tiepoldt@leiv-verlag.de
Founded: 1991
ISBN Prefix(es): 978-3-89603; 978-3-928885
Foreign Rep(s): Martin E Schnetzer (Switzerland); Alfred Trux (Austria)
Distribution Center: Leipziger Kommissions- und
Grossbuchhandelsgesellschaft mbH (LKG),
An der Suedspitze 1-12, 04571 Roetha, Contact: Robert Winkler *Tel:* (034206) 6 51 28
Fax: (034206) 65 17 38 *E-mail:* r.winkler@lkg-service.de *Web Site:* www.lkg-va.de
AS Hoeller GmbH, Schrackgasse 11a, 8650
Kindberg, Austria *Tel:* (03865) 4 48 80
Fax: (03865) 4 48 80-77 *E-mail:* office@
ashoeller.com
OLF SA, ZI 3 Corminboeuf, 1701 Fribourg,
Switzerland *Tel:* (026) 4 67 51 11 *Fax:* (026)
4 67 54 44

Lemmens Medien GmbH
Matthias-Gruenewald-Str 1-3, 53175 Bonn
Tel: (0228) 42 13 70 *Fax:* (0228) 42 13 7-29
E-mail: info@lemmens.de
Web Site: www.lemmens.de
Key Personnel
Mng Partner: Dr Markus Lemmens *Tel:* (0228) 42
13 7-14 *E-mail:* lemmens@lemmens.de
Founded: 1996
Subjects: Economics, Government, Political Science, Science (General), Research
ISBN Prefix(es): 978-3-932306
Branch Office(s)
Schiffbauerdamm 40, 10117 Berlin *Tel:* (030) 20
62 53-82

Lentz, *imprint of* Franckh-Kosmos Verlags-GmbH
& Co KG

Lentz Verlag+
Imprint of Franckh-Kosmos Verlags-GmbH & Co
KG
Pfizerstr 5-7, 70184 Stuttgart
Tel: (0711) 2191-0 *Fax:* (0711) 2191-422
E-mail: info@kosmos.de
Web Site: www.kosmos.de
Key Personnel
Mng Dir: Michael Fleissner
Founded: 1953
Subjects: Fiction, Nonfiction (General)
ISBN Prefix(es): 978-3-88010
Total Titles: 10 Print
Warehouse: VVA-Bertelsmann Distribution
GmbH, Warenannahme 100, An der Autobahn,
33310 Guetersloh
Orders to: VVA-Vereinigte, Postfach 7600, 33310
Guetersloh, Contact: Mr Borgartz *Tel:* (05241)
805403 *Fax:* (05241) 806643

**LePa-Buecher Gunther Lehmann eK &
Christian Patzner**
Filssstr 3, 99089 Erfurt
Tel: (0361) 6015052 *Fax:* (0361) 6015052
E-mail: mail@lepabuecher.de
Web Site: www.lepa-buecher.de
Key Personnel
Publishing Dir: Gunther Lehmann
Subjects: History, Nonfiction (General), Medieval
Studies
ISBN Prefix(es): 978-3-9808859

Dr Gisela Lermann Verlag+
Am Heiligenhaus 18, 55122 Mainz
Tel: (06131) 31149 *Fax:* (06131) 387945
Web Site: www.lermann-verlag.de
Key Personnel
Owner & Dir: Dr Gisela Lermann *E-mail:* dr-gisela-lermann@lermann-verlag.de
Founded: 1988
Subjects: Biography, Memoirs, Fiction, Government, Political Science, Human Relations, Literature, Literary Criticism, Essays, Mysteries, Suspense, Nonfiction (General), Philosophy, Poetry, Psychology, Psychiatry, Romance, Women's Studies
ISBN Prefix(es): 978-3-927223
Shipping Address: Sigloch Distribution,
Am Buchberg 8, 74572 Blaufelden
Tel: (07953) 883 0 *Fax:* (07953) 883 700
E-mail: verlagservice@sigloch.de *Web
Site:* www.sigloch.de
Warehouse: Sigloch Distribution, Am Buchberg 8, 74572 Blaufelden *Tel:* (07953) 883 0
Fax: (07953) 883 700 *E-mail:* verlagservice@
sigloch.de *Web Site:* www.sigloch.de
Orders to: Sigloch Distribution, Am Buchberg 8, 74572 Blaufelden *Tel:* (07953) 883 0
Fax: (07953) 883 700 *E-mail:* verlagservice@
sigloch.de *Web Site:* www.sigloch.de

Verlag Edition LesArt
Muensterstr 4, 48291 Telgte
Tel: (02504) 88 88 79-0
E-mail: info@edition-lesart.de
Web Site: www.edition-lesart.de
Key Personnel
Owner: Reinhold Schmelter
ISBN Prefix(es): 978-3-9812435
Distribution Center: Gemeinsame Verlagsaus-lieferung Goettingen GmbH & Co KG, Post-fach 2021, 37010 Goettingen *Tel:* (0551) 48 71
77 *Fax:* (0551) 4 13 92 *E-mail:* bestellung@
gva-verlage.de *Web Site:* www.gva-verlage.de

Leu-Verlag+
Kolpingstr 5, 86356 Neusaess
Tel: (0821) 480 430 91 *Fax:* (0821) 480 430 93
E-mail: leuverlag@aol.com
Web Site: www.leu-verlag.de
Key Personnel
Publisher: Wolfgang Leupelt

Founded: 1990
Specialize in music education (play along) books
with CD, sheet music.
Subjects: Education, Music, Dance
ISBN Prefix(es): 978-3-928825; 978-3-89775
Number of titles published annually: 10 Print; 5
Audio
Total Titles: 200 Print; 20 Audio

edition stadt und region im Leue Verlag+
Kanzlerweg 24, 12101 Berlin
Fax: (030) 78 91 38 76
E-mail: vertrieb@leue-verlag.de
Web Site: www.edition-stadt-und-region.de
Founded: 1982
Subjects: How-to, Humor
ISBN Prefix(es): 978-3-923421

LIBERTAS - Europaeisches Institut GmbH
(LIBERTAS - European Institute)
Lindenweg 37, 72414 Rangendingen
Tel: (07471) 984996-0 *Fax:* (07471) 984996-19
E-mail: info@libertas-institut.com
Web Site: www.libertas-institut.com
Key Personnel
Dir: Ms Ute Hirschburger *E-mail:* hirschburger@
libertas-institut.com
Mng Dir: Hans-Juergen Zahorka *Tel:* (07471)
984996-13 *E-mail:* zahorka@libertas-institut.
com
Founded: 1976
Think-tank on European & international economy
& politics with publication division.
Subjects: Asian Studies, Business, Developing
Countries, Economics, Environmental Studies, Finance, Foreign Countries, Government,
Political Science, History, Law, Management,
Nonfiction (General), Philosophy, Regional Interests, Social Sciences, Sociology, Transportation
ISBN Prefix(es): 978-3-921929; 978-3-937642;
978-3-946119
Number of titles published annually: 15 Print; 2
CD-ROM; 20 Online; 20 E-Book
Total Titles: 120 Print; 10 CD-ROM; 90 Online;
98 E-Book

Edition Libri Illustri GmbH
Neissestr 31, 71638 Ludwigsburg
Tel: (07141) 84 72 0 *Fax:* (07141) 87 51 17
E-mail: info@libri-illustri.de
Web Site: www.edition-libri-illustri.de
Key Personnel
Publisher: Peter Teicher
Founded: 1987
Subjects: History, Religion - Other, Aesopus,
Apocalypsis, Nuremberg Chronicle
ISBN Prefix(es): 978-3-927506; 978-3-9806441
Number of titles published annually: 1 Print
Total Titles: 8 Print; 1 Audio
U.S. Office(s): Peter KeLehnert, 510 W Forest Dr,
Houston, TX 77079-6914, United States

Lichtzeichen Verlag GmbH
Elisabethstr 15, 32791 Lage
Tel: (05232) 9601-20 *Fax:* (05232) 9601-21
E-mail: info@lichtzeichen-shop.com
Web Site: www.lichtzeichen-shop.com
Key Personnel
Chief Executive Officer: Walter Baehr
Subjects: Cookery, Fiction, Literature, Literary
Criticism, Essays, Music, Dance, Poetry, Devotionals, Evangelistic, Mennonite Literature
ISBN Prefix(es): 978-3-86954; 978-3-927767;
978-3-933828; 978-3-936850

Edition Lidiarte GmbH
Knesebeckstr 13/14, 10623 Berlin
Tel: (030) 313 74 20 *Fax:* (030) 312 71 17
E-mail: shop@lidiarte.de
Web Site: www.lidiarte.de

Key Personnel
Mng Dir: Dieter Marx
Founded: 1980
Specialize in architectural posters & postcards.
Subjects: Architecture & Interior Design
ISBN Prefix(es): 978-3-9801862
Number of titles published annually: 10 Print
Total Titles: 220 Print

Verlag Liebaug-Dartmann eK+
Johann-Sebastian-Bach-Weg 15, 53340 Mecken-
  heim
Tel: (02225) 90 93 43 *Fax:* (02225) 90 93 45
E-mail: kundenservice@liebaug-dartmann.de
Web Site: www.liebaug-dartmann.de
Key Personnel
Owner: Sarah Klinghammer
Founded: 1982
Membership(s): Boersenverein des Deutschen
  Buchhandels.
Subjects: Education, Language Arts, Linguistics,
  German as a Foreign Language
ISBN Prefix(es): 978-3-922989
Distributed by KNO; KV

**Verlagsbuchhandlung Liebeskind GmbH & Co
KG**
Sendlinger Str 7, 80331 Munich
Tel: (089) 231 138 300 *Fax:* (089) 231 138 310
E-mail: post@liebeskind.de
Web Site: www.liebeskind.de
Key Personnel
Mng Dir: Juergen Christian Kill *Tel:* (089) 231
  138 320 *E-mail:* j.c.kill@liebeskind.de
Press & Public Relations: Susanne Fink
  Tel: (089) 231 138 330 *E-mail:* s.fink@
  liebeskind.de
Founded: 2000
Subjects: Literature, Literary Criticism, Essays,
  Mysteries, Suspense, Contemporary Literature
ISBN Prefix(es): 978-3-935890
Foreign Rep(s): Helga Schuster (Austria); Markus
  Wieser (Switzerland)
Distribution Center: Prolit Verlagsauslieferung,
  Siemensstr 16, 35463 Fernwald-Annerod, Con-
  tact: Gabriele Lemuth *Tel:* (0641) 943 93 201
  Fax: (0641) 943 93 89 *E-mail:* g.lemuth@
  prolit.de *Web Site:* www.prolit.de
Dr Franz Hain, Dr-Otto-Neurath-Gasse 5, 1220
  Vienna, Austria *Tel:* (01) 282 65 65 *Fax:* (01)
  282 52 82 *E-mail:* bestell@hain.at *Web
  Site:* www.hain.at
AVA Verlagsauslieferung, Centralweg 16,
  8910 Affoltern am Albis, Switzerland
  Tel: (044) 762 42 60 *Fax:* (044) 762 42 10
  E-mail: verlagsservice@ava.ch *Web Site:* www.
  ava.ch

Robert Lienau Musikverlag GmbH & Co KG
Strubbergstr 80, 60489 Frankfurt am Main
Tel: (069) 978 286-6 *Fax:* (069) 978 286-79
E-mail: info@musikverlag-lienau.de
Web Site: www.musikverlag-zimmermann.de
Key Personnel
Mng Dir: Cornelia Grossmann
  E-mail: grossmann@zimmermann-frankfurt.
  de; Volker Mandler *Tel:* (069) 978286-71
  E-mail: mandler@zimmermann-frankfurt.de
Rights & Licensing: Saskia Bieber *Tel:* (069) 978
  286-72 *E-mail:* bieber@zimmermann-frankfurt.
  de
Rights & Licensing, Orchestra Library: Bernd
  Schuff *Tel:* (069) 978 286-76 *E-mail:* schuff@
  zimmermann-frankfurt.de
Founded: 1810
Music publisher.
Subjects: Drama, Theater, History, Music, Dance,
  Folk Music, Musical Instuments, Pop Music
ISBN Prefix(es): 978-3-87484
Associate Companies: Allegra Musikverlag
  GmbH & Co KG *E-mail:* info@allegra-

musikverlag.de; Musikverlag Zimmermann
  GmbH & Co KG *E-mail:* info@zimmermann-
  frankfurt.de

Lifestyle BusseSeewald, *imprint of* frechverlag
GmbH

Lifestyle BusseSeewald+
Imprint of frechverlag GmbH
Turbinenstr 7, 70499 Stuttgart
Tel: (0711) 83086-11 *Fax:* (0711) 83086-86
E-mail: kundenservice@frechverlag.de
Web Site: www.busse-seewald.de
Key Personnel
Mng Dir: Wolfgang Materna; Werner Muetzel;
  Michael Zirn
Press: Silke Ross *Tel:* (0711) 83086-81
  E-mail: silke.ross@frechverlag.de
Founded: 1947
Subjects: Architecture & Interior Design, Cook-
  ery, Environmental Studies, Gardening, Plants,
  Maritime, Nonfiction (General), Outdoor Recre-
  ation, Regional Interests, Travel & Tourism,
  Wine & Spirits, Lifestyle
ISBN Prefix(es): 978-3-512; 978-3-87120

Lilienfeld Verlag
Pfalzstr 12, 40477 Duesseldorf
Tel: (0211) 41 60 81 87 *Fax:* (0211) 41 60 72 71
E-mail: elekstropost@lilienfeld-verlag.de;
  presse@lilienfeld-verlag.de
Web Site: www.lilienfeld-verlag.de
Key Personnel
Management: Viola Eckelt; Axel von Ernst
Licensing: Olaf Tschoetschel *Tel:* (0211) 416
  5609 *E-mail:* auftritt@lilienfeld-verlag.de
Press: Britta Bleckman *Tel:* (0177) 273 14 35
Founded: 2006
Subjects: History, Literature, Literary Criticism,
  Essays, Contemporary Literature & History
ISBN Prefix(es): 978-3-940357
Foreign Rep(s): Andreas Meisel Verladsvertretun-
  gen (Switzerland); Seth Meyer-Bruhns (Aus-
  tria)
Distribution Center: Leipziger Kommissions- und
  Grossbuchhandelsgesellschaft mbH (LKG),
  An der Suedspitze 1-12, 04571 Roetha, Con-
  tact: Ursula Fritzsche *Tel:* (034206) 65-135
  Fax: (034206) 65-1739 *E-mail:* ufritzsche@
  lkg-service.de *Web Site:* www.lkg-va.de (Ger-
  many & Austria)
Kaktus Verlagsauslieferung, Langfeldstr 54,
  Postfach 459, 8501 Frauenfeld, Switzer-
  land *Tel:* (052) 7223190 *Fax:* (052) 7221782
  E-mail: auslieferung@kaktus.net *Web
  Site:* www.kaktus.net

Limes, *imprint of* Verlagsgruppe Random House
Bertelsmann

Limes Verlag
Imprint of Verlagsgruppe Random House Bertels-
  mann
Neumarkter Str 28, 81673 Munich
Tel: (089) 4136-0 *Toll Free Tel:* 0800 500 33 22
  Fax: (089) 4136-3333
E-mail: kundenservice@randomhouse.de;
  lizenzen@randomhouse.de
Web Site: www.randomhouse.de/limes
Founded: 2001
Subjects: Criminology, Fiction, Literature, Liter-
  ary Criticism, Essays, Thriller
ISBN Prefix(es): 978-3-8090

Limpert Verlag GmbH+
Industriepark 3, 56291 Wiebelsheim
Tel: (06766) 903-160 *Fax:* (06766) 903-320
E-mail: vertrieb@limpert.de
Web Site: www.verlagsgemeinschaft.com
Key Personnel
Mng Dir: Gerhard Stahl

Marketing & Sales: Ralf Simolka
  E-mail: simolka@quelle-meyer.de
Rights & Permissions: Sigrid Koppenhoefer
  Tel: (06766) 903243 *Fax:* (06766) 903360
  E-mail: koppenhoefer@quelle-meyer.de
Founded: 1921
Specialize in sports & sport science.
Subjects: Sports, Athletics
ISBN Prefix(es): 978-3-7853
Subsidiaries: AULA-Verlag GmbH; Quelle &
  Meyer GmbH & Co
Bookshop(s): Humanitas Buchversand

J Lindauer-Verlag GmbH & Co KG+
Kaufinger Str 16, 80331 Munich
Mailing Address: Postfach 10 08 26, 80082 Mu-
  nich
Tel: (089) 223041 *Fax:* (089) 224315
E-mail: info@lindauer-verlag.de
Web Site: www.lindauer-verlag.de
Key Personnel
Owner, Rights & Permissions: Renate Schaefer
Subjects: Language Arts, Linguistics, Mathemat-
  ics, Physics, Greek, Latin
ISBN Prefix(es): 978-3-87488

H Lindemanns Buchhandlung fuer Fotografie
Tailfingerstr 7, 70576 Stuttgart
Tel: (0711) 71 76 82 *Fax:* (0711) 71 76 82
E-mail: fotobuecher@lindemanns.de
Web Site: www.lindemanns.de
Key Personnel
Owner: Werner Goetze
Photographic literature.
Subjects: Photography
ISBN Prefix(es): 978-3-89506; 978-3-928126

Linden-Verlag GmbH+
Kasseler Str 25, 04155 Leipzig
Tel: (0341) 5902024 *Fax:* (0341) 5904436
Key Personnel
International Rights: Thomas Loest
Founded: 1989
Specialize in books by Buecher von Erich Loest.
ISBN Prefix(es): 978-3-9802139; 978-3-86152
Orders to: LKG (Leipzinger Kommissions-
  und Grossbuchhandelsgesellschaft mbH),
  An der Suedspitze 1-12, 04579 Espenhain
  Tel: (034206) 65-0 *Fax:* (034206) 72361

Helmut Lingen Verlag GmbH & Co KG
Bruegelmannstr 3, 50670 Cologne
Tel: (0221) 33707-0 *Fax:* (0221) 3370744-4
E-mail: info@lingenverlag.de
Web Site: www.lingenverlag.de
Key Personnel
Mng Dir: Helmut Lingen; Werner Schulte
Press & Public Relations: Daniel Hindenberg
  Tel: (0221) 33707154 *E-mail:* presse@lingen-
  koeln.de
Founded: 1950
Subjects: Cookery, Fiction, Health, Nutrition, His-
  tory, Language Arts, Linguistics, Nonfiction
  (General), Travel & Tourism, Contemporary
  History
ISBN Prefix(es): 978-3-941118; 978-3-937490;
  978-3-938323
Imprints: Lingoli

Lingoli, *imprint of* Helmut Lingen Verlag GmbH
& Co KG

Edition Lingua Mundi eK
Petterweilstr 60, 60385 Frankfurt
Tel: (069) 4032 5958; (0177) 3017716 (cell)
  Fax: (069) 1750 9836
E-mail: info@edition-lingua-mundi.com
Web Site: www.edition-lingua-mundi.com
Key Personnel
Mng Dir: Engin Korelli
Focus on multilingual children's books.
ISBN Prefix(es): 978-3-940267

Distribution Center: G Umbreit GmbH & Co
KG, Mundelsheimer Str 3, 74321 Bietigheim
Tel: (07142) 596-385 *Fax:* (07142) 596-387
E-mail: verlagsauslieferung@umbreit.de *Web
Site:* www.umbreit.de

Carl Link Verlag
Imprint of Wolters Kluwer Deutschland GmbH
Luxemburger Str 449, 50939 Cologne
Tel: (0221) 94373-7000 *Fax:* (0221) 94373-7201
E-mail: info@wolterskluwer.de
Web Site: www.carllink.de
Key Personnel
Mng Dir: Dr Ulrich Hermann
Founded: 1884
Subjects: Child Care & Development, Education,
Law, Management
ISBN Prefix(es): 978-3-556
Associate Companies: Bueromarkt, Kronach; Carl
Link Druck GmbH, Kronach
Bookshop(s): Buchdienst, Gueterstr 7, 96317 Kro-
nach
Warehouse: Carl Link Bueromarkt, Gueterstr 7,
96317 Kronach

Christopher Links Verlag GmbH+
Kulturbrauerei / Haus 2, Schoenhauser Allee 36,
10435 Berlin
Tel: (030) 44 02 32-0 *Fax:* (030) 44 02 32-29
E-mail: mail@christoph-links-verlag.de;
vertrieb@linksverlag.de; presse@christoph-
links-verlag.de
Web Site: www.linksverlag.de; www.christoph-
links-verlag.de
Key Personnel
Dir: Dr Christoph Links *E-mail:* verlager@
christoph-links-verlag.de
Foreign Manager: Johanna Links
Sales & Marketing: Benjamin Liehaeuser
Tel: (030) 44 02 32-12
Press: Edda Fensch *Tel:* (030) 44 02 32-10
Founded: 1989
Subjects: Biography, Memoirs, Government, Po-
litical Science, History, Nonfiction (General),
Self-Help
ISBN Prefix(es): 978-3-86153
Number of titles published annually: 30 Print
Total Titles: 330 Print
Orders to: Prolit Verlagsauslieferung, Siemensstr
16, 35463 Fernwald, Contact: Gaby Kraft
Tel: (0641) 94393-21 *Fax:* (0641) 94393-29
E-mail: g.kraft@prolit.de

Siegbert Linnemann Verlag+
Darfeldweg 60, 48161 Muenster
Tel: (0251) 87120288 *Fax:* (0251) 87120299
E-mail: info@linnemann-verlag.com
Web Site: www.linnemann-verlag.com
Key Personnel
Mng Dir: Siegbert Linnemann
Founded: 1986
Specialize in travel picture wall calendars.
Subjects: Geography, Geology, History, Philoso-
phy, Psychology, Psychiatry, Travel & Tourism,
Travel Picture Calendars
ISBN Prefix(es): 978-3-926466; 978-3-89523;
978-3-86292
Number of titles published annually: 60 Print
Total Titles: 10 Audio

List, *imprint of* Ullstein Buchverlage GmbH

List Taschenbuch, *imprint of* Ullstein
Buchverlage GmbH

List Verlag+
Imprint of Ullstein Buchverlag GmbH
Friedrichstr 126, 10117 Berlin
Tel: (030) 23456-300 *Fax:* (030) 23456-303
E-mail: info@ullstein-buchverlage.de
Web Site: www.ullsteinbuchverlage.de/listhc

Key Personnel
Head, Press & Communications: Christine Hein-
rich *Tel:* (030) 23456-433 *Fax:* (030) 23456-
445 *E-mail:* christine.heinrich@ullstein-
buchverlage.de
Founded: 1894
Membership(s): TR-Verlagsunion GmbH.
Subjects: Art, Biography, Memoirs, Business,
Economics, Fiction, Government, Political Sci-
ence, Health, Nutrition, History, Humor, Inspi-
rational, Spirituality, Literature, Literary Criti-
cism, Essays, Maritime, Nonfiction (General),
Philosophy, Psychology, Psychiatry, Religion
- Other, Science (General), Social Sciences,
Sociology, Crime & Thrillers, Mind, Body &
Spirit
ISBN Prefix(es): 978-3-89834
Associate Companies: Allegria; Claassen; Econ;
List Taschenbuch; Propylaeen; Ullstein; Ull-
stein Taschenbuch; Marion von Schroeder

LIT Verlag+
Grevener Str/Fresnostr 2, 48159 Muenster
Tel: (0251) 62032 0; (0251) 62032 22 (sales)
Fax: (0251) 231972
E-mail: lit@lit-verlag.de; vertrieb@lit-verlag.de
(sales)
Web Site: www.lit-verlag.de
Key Personnel
Mng Dir & International Rights: Dr Wilhelm
Hopf
Founded: 1980
Subjects: Anthropology, Art, Asian Studies, Eco-
nomics, Education, Ethnicity, Fashion, Geogra-
phy, Geology, Government, Political Science,
History, Language Arts, Linguistics, Literature,
Literary Criticism, Essays, Psychology, Psychi-
atry, Public Administration, Science (General),
Social Sciences, Sociology, Theology, African
Studies
ISBN Prefix(es): 978-3-88660; 978-3-89473; 978-
3-8258
Subsidiaries:
Branch Office(s)
Schumannstr 18, 10117 Berlin *Tel:* (030) 280 40
880 *Fax:* (030) 280 40 882 *E-mail:* berlin@lit-
verlag.de *Web Site:* www.lit-verlag.de/berlin
Krotenthallergasse 10, 1080 Vienna (Josefstadt),
Austria *Tel:* (01) 4095661 *Fax:* (01) 4095697
E-mail: wien@lit-verlag.at *Web Site:* www.lit-
verlag.at
klosbachstr 107, 8032 Zurich, Switzerland
Tel: (044) 2517505 *Fax:* (044) 2517506
E-mail: zuerich@lit-verlag.ch *Web Site:* www.
lit-verlag.ch
c/o D Styan, 9 Kellet House, Tankerton St,
London WC1H 8HW, United Kingdom
E-mail: london@lit-verlag.de

Henry Litolff's Verlag, *imprint of* Musia
International Musikalien-Handelsgesellschaft
Ehrlich GmbH & Co KG

Little Tiger Verlag GmbH
Gifkendorf 38, 21397 Gifkendorf-Vastorf
Tel: (04137) 7207 *Fax:* (04137) 7948
E-mail: info@little-tiger.de
Web Site: www.little-tiger.de
Key Personnel
Publishing Dir: Andreas J Meyer; Dr Katharina
Eleonore Meyer
Distribution & Press: Andreas Schmitt
Founded: 1987
ISBN Prefix(es): 978-3-931081
Distribution Center: Leipziger Kommissions-
und Grossbuchhandelsgesellschaft mbH
(LKG), An der Suedspitze 1-12, 04571 Roetha
Tel: (034206) 65-100 *Fax:* (034206) 65-110
E-mail: lkg@lkg-service.de *Web Site:* www.
lkg-va.de

LKG Verwaltung KG+
Member of Langenscheidt Verlagsgruppe
Mies-van-der-Rohe-Str 1, 80807 Munich
Tel: (089) 360960 *Fax:* (089) 36096
Founded: 1953
Sales & promotion through Langenscheidt KG.
Subjects: Nonfiction (General), Travel & Tourism
ISBN Prefix(es): 978-3-581
Orders to: Langenscheidt KG, Neusser Str 3,
80807 Munich

Thomas der Loewe Verlag
Schillerstr 7, 76135 Karlsruhe
Tel: (0721) 75 31 53 *Fax:* (0721) 75 31 53
E-mail: info@thomas-der-loewe.de
Web Site: www.thomas-der-loewe.de
Subjects: Fiction, Poetry, Romance
ISBN Prefix(es): 978-3-930231

Loewe Verlag GmbH+
Buehlstr 4, 95463 Bindlach
Mailing Address: Postfach 1101, 95461 Bindlach
Tel: (09208) 51-0 *Fax:* (09208) 51309
E-mail: presse@loewe-verlag.de
Web Site: www.loewe-verlag.de
Key Personnel
Publisher & Mng Dir: Volker Gondrom
Assistant Mng Dir: Christoph Gondrom
Advertising: Verena Fischer *E-mail:* werbung@
loewe-verlag.de
Foreign Rights: Jeannette Hammerschmidt
E-mail: j.hammerschmidt@loewe-verlag.de
Press: Jenny Schwerin *E-mail:* j.schwerin@loewe-
verlag.de
Sales: Lydia Bruennich *E-mail:* vertrieb@loewe-
verlag.de
Founded: 1863
ISBN Prefix(es): 978-3-7855; 978-3-8390
Imprints: Verlag script5

LOGO Verlag
Rosenstr 6, 63785 Obernburg am Main
Tel: (0622) 71988 *Fax:* (0622) 206941
E-mail: info@lvee.de
Web Site: www.lvee.de
Key Personnel
Owner: Eric Erfurth
Founded: 1997
Subjects: Archaeology, Art, Biography, Memoirs,
Criminology, Fiction, History, Literature, Lit-
erary Criticism, Essays, Nonfiction (General),
Religion - Other, Classics, Local Culture, Mod-
ern Art. Modern Literature
ISBN Prefix(es): 978-3-939462; 978-3-9803087

Logophon Verlag und Bildungsreisen GmbH+
Affiliate of Euro-Schulen-Organisation
Alte Gaertnerei 1, 55128 Mainz
Tel: (06131) 7 16 45 *Fax:* (06131) 7 25 96
E-mail: verlag@logophon.de
Web Site: www.logophon.de
Key Personnel
Mng Dir: Jean-Pierre Jouteux; Silvia Semidei
Founded: 1979
Membership(s): Verlags-Karree eV.
Subjects: Business, Education, English as a Sec-
ond Language, Human Relations, Language
Arts, Linguistics, Literature, Literary Criticism,
Essays, Management
ISBN Prefix(es): 978-3-922514; 978-3-936172
Number of titles published annually: 3 Print
Total Titles: 129 Print; 2 CD-ROM

Logos Verlag Berlin GmbH+
Comeniushof, Gubener Str 47, 10243 Berlin
Tel: (030) 42 85 10 90 *Fax:* (030) 42 85 10 92
E-mail: redaktion@logos-verlag.de
Web Site: www.logos-verlag.de
Key Personnel
Mng Dir: Dr Volkhard Buchholtz
Founded: 1995
Specialize in scientific publications.

Subjects: Archaeology, Art, Biological Sciences, Business, Chemistry, Chemical Engineering, Computer Science, Earth Sciences, Economics, Education, Electronics, Electrical Engineering, Energy, Engineering (General), Film, Video, Geography, Geology, History, Language Arts, Linguistics, Law, Library & Information Sciences, Management, Mathematics, Mechanical Engineering, Music, Dance, Philosophy, Physics, Psychology, Psychiatry, Science (General), Social Sciences, Sociology, Theology
ISBN Prefix(es): 978-3-8325; 978-3-89722; 978-3-931216
Number of titles published annually: 300 Print; 100 E-Book
Total Titles: 5,500 Print; 1,200 E-Book
Distribution Center: ISD, 70 Enterprise Dr, Suite 2, Bristol, CT 06010, United States *Tel:* 860-584-6546 *Web Site:* www.isdistribution.com

Logos-Verlag Literatur & Layout GmbH+
Auf der Adt 14, 66130 Saarbruecken
Tel: (06893) 986096
Founded: 1983
Subjects: Biological Sciences, Fiction, Geography, Geology, Literature, Literary Criticism, Essays, Mysteries, Suspense, Nonfiction (General), Poetry, Regional Interests, Science Fiction, Fantasy, Social Sciences, Sociology
ISBN Prefix(es): 978-3-928598; 978-3-9801790

LOK Report, see Lokomotive Fachbuchhandlung GmbH

LOK Report-Verlag GmbH, see Lokomotive Fachbuchhandlung GmbH

Lokomotive Fachbuchhandlung GmbH
Formerly LOK Report-Verlag GmbH
Regensburger Str 25, 10777 Berlin
Tel: (030) 86409263 *Fax:* (030) 86409264
E-mail: redaktion@lok-report.de
Web Site: www.lok-report.de
Key Personnel
Mng Dir: Olaf Bade *Tel:* (030) 86409262
    E-mail: bade@lok-report.de
Editorial: Wolfgang Kieslich
Founded: 1972
Specialize in transport, railways, locomotive, German & Eastern European railways.
Publish monthly railway magazine *LOK Report.*
Subjects: Transportation, Locomotives, Railways
ISBN Prefix(es): 978-3-921980; 978-3-935909
Number of titles published annually: 2 Print
Total Titles: 6 Print

Lokrundschau Verlag GmbH
Postfach 80 01 07, 21001 Hamburg
Tel: (04151) 89 69 13 *Fax:* (04151) 8 28 89
E-mail: verlag@lokrundschau.de
Web Site: www.lokrundschau.de
Key Personnel
Mng Dir: Heike Heitmann; Ulf Heitmann; Dr Britta Obszerninks *E-mail:* britta.obszerninks@lokrundschau.de
Mng Editor: Gerhard Klug *Tel:* (09131) 12 85 34 *Fax:* (09131) 12 85 34 *E-mail:* gerhard.klug@lokrundschau.de
Founded: 1995
Specialize in books about German railway & journals.
Subjects: Civil Engineering, Engineering (General), Mechanical Engineering, Transportation, Locomotive, Railway
ISBN Prefix(es): 978-3-931647

Loon Verlag
Sonnenscheinstr 9, 53175 Bonn
Tel: (0228) 316948
Web Site: www.loon-verlag.de

Key Personnel
Publishing Dir: Dr Rudolf Bachem
    E-mail: rbachem@loon-verlag.de
Founded: 2003
Membership(s): Association of German Publishers & Booksellers.
Subjects: Music, Dance, Poetry
ISBN Prefix(es): 978-3-9808973

Stefan Loose Travel Handbuecher+
Marco-Polo-Str 1, 73760 Ostfildern
Mailing Address: Postfach 3151, 73751 Ostfildern (Kemnat)
Tel: (0711) 4502-1033 *Fax:* (0711) 4502-411
E-mail: info@stefan-loose.de
Web Site: www.stefan-loose.de
Key Personnel
Editor: Renate Loose; Stefan Loose
Founded: 1978
Subjects: Travel & Tourism
ISBN Prefix(es): 978-3-7701
Parent Company: DuMont Reiseverlag GmbH & Co KG

Lorber-Verlag und Turm-Verlag GmbH & Co KG
Hindenburgstr 5, 74321 Bietigheim-Bissingen
Tel: (07142) 94 08 43 *Fax:* (07142) 94 08 44
E-mail: info@lorber-verlag.de; bestellen@lorber-verlag.de; info@turm-verlag.de; bestellen@turm-verlag.de
Web Site: www.lorber-verlag.de; www.turm-verlag.de
Key Personnel
Mng Dir: Manuel Zluhan; Michael Zluhan
Founded: 1952
Subjects: Parapsychology, Religion - Other
ISBN Prefix(es): 978-3-87495; 978-3-7999; 978-3-923193

Lotos, *imprint of* Verlagsgruppe Random House Bertelsmann

Prof Dr Hans Walter Louis Verlag+
Gartenweg 6 B, 38104 Braunschweig
Tel: (0531) 360921 *Fax:* (0531) 363190
Key Personnel
International Rights: Dr Hans Walter Louis
Founded: 1990
Subjects: Environmental Studies, Law
ISBN Prefix(es): 978-3-927942

Luchterhand, *imprint of* Wolters Kluwer Deutschland GmbH

Luchterhand Literaturverlag, *imprint of* Verlagsgruppe Random House Bertelsmann

Luchterhand Literaturverlag GmbH+
Imprint of Verlagsgruppe Random House Bertelsmann
Neumarkter Str 28, 81673 Munich
Tel: (089) 4136-0 *Toll Free Tel:* 0800 500 33 22 *Fax:* (089) 4136-3333
E-mail: kundenservice@randomhouse.de
Web Site: www.randomhouse.de/luchterhand
Key Personnel
Publisher: George Rueuchlein
Publishing Dir: Regina Kammerer
Press & Public Relations: Karsten Roesel
    Tel: (089) 4136-3752 *Fax:* (089) 4136-3723
    E-mail: karsten.roesel@luchterhand-verlag.de
Founded: 1924
Subjects: Fiction, Literature, Literary Criticism, Essays, Nonfiction (General)
ISBN Prefix(es): 978-3-630
Number of titles published annually: 50 Print
Total Titles: 500 Print
Distributor for Gerhard Wolf Janus Press
Orders to: Vereinigte Verlagsauslieferung, An der Autobahn, 33310 Guetersloh

Lucius & Lucius Verlagsgesellschaft mbH+
Gerokstr 51, 70184 Stuttgart
Tel: (0711) 24 20 60 *Fax:* (0711) 24 20 88
E-mail: info@luciusverlag.com
Web Site: www.luciusverlag.com
Key Personnel
Publisher: Prof Wulf D von Lucius
    E-mail: lucius@luciusverlag.com
Founded: 1996
Specialize in academic books & journals in economics, social sciences & sociology; textbooks; research monographs & proceedings; journals.
Privately owned.
Membership(s): Boersenverein des Deutschen Buchhandels.
Subjects: Economics, Social Sciences, Sociology
ISBN Prefix(es): 978-3-8282
Number of titles published annually: 35 Print
Total Titles: 420 Print
Associate Companies: UTB Stuttgart, Industriestr 2, 70565 Stuttgart *Web Site:* www.utb.de
Warehouse: Brockhaus/Commission, Postfach, 70803 Kornwestheim *Tel:* (07154) 13270 *Fax:* (07154) 132713 *E-mail:* lucius@brocom.de
Orders to: Brockhaus/Commission, Postfach, 70803 Kornwestheim *Tel:* (07154) 13270 *Fax:* (07154) 132713 *E-mail:* lucius@brocum.de

Ludowe nakladnistwo Domowina, see Domowina-Verlag GmbH

Ludwig, *imprint of* Verlagsgruppe Random House Bertelsmann

Luebbe Audio, *imprint of* Bastei Luebbe GmbH & Co KG

Bastei Luebbe GmbH & Co KG+
Schanzenstr 6-20, 51063 Cologne
Tel: (0221) 8200-0 *Fax:* (0221) 8200-1900
E-mail: webmaster@luebbe.de
Web Site: www.luebbe.de
Key Personnel
Chief Executive Officer: Carel Halff
Chief Financial Officer: Ulrich Zimmermann
Mng Dir: Klaus Kluge
Head, Foreign Rights: Christian Stuewe
    Tel: (0221) 8200-2700 *Fax:* (0221) 8200-1700
    E-mail: christian.stuewe@luebbe.de
Press & Public Relations: Barbara Fischer
    Tel: (0221) 8200-2850 *Fax:* (0221) 8200-1850
    E-mail: barbara.fischer@luebbe.de
Founded: 1953
Subjects: Archaeology, Biography, Memoirs, Fiction, History, Mysteries, Suspense, Nonfiction (General), Romance, Science Fiction, Fantasy, Crime, Thrillers
ISBN Prefix(es): 978-3-404; 978-3-431; 978-3-7857; 978-3-89185; 978-3-8339 (Baumhaus)
Number of titles published annually: 530 Print; 120 Audio
Imprints: Baumhaus Verlag; Boje Verlag; Eichborn; Luebbe Audio; Bastei Luebbe Taschenbuecher; Luebbe Digital; Luebbe Ehrenwirth; Luebbe Hardcover; Luebbe Paperback; One Verlag; Quadriga
Foreign Rep(s): Gerhard Hirtl (Austria); Katrin Poldervaart (Switzerland)
Foreign Rights: Agence Hoffmann (France); Internationaal Literatuur Bureau (Linda Kohn) (Netherlands); Ute Koerner Literary Agency (Portugal, South America, Spain)

Bastei Luebbe Taschenbuecher, *imprint of* Bastei Luebbe GmbH & Co KG

Luebbe Digital, *imprint of* Bastei Luebbe GmbH & Co KG

Luebbe Ehrenwirth, *imprint of* Bastei Luebbe GmbH & Co KG

Luebbe Hardcover, *imprint of* Bastei Luebbe GmbH & Co KG

Luebbe Paperback, *imprint of* Bastei Luebbe GmbH & Co KG

Lukas Verlag fuer Kunst- und Geistesgeschichte
Kollwitzstr 57, 10405 Berlin
Tel: (030) 44 04 92 20 *Fax:* (030) 442 81 77
E-mail: lukas.verlag@t-online.de; post@
lukasverlag.de
Web Site: www.lukasverlag.com
Key Personnel
Publisher: Dr Frank Boettcher
E-mail: boettcher@lukasverlag.de
Editing & Production: Susan Werner
E-mail: werner@lukasverlag.de
Press & Public Relations, Marketing: Jana Pippel
E-mail: jana.pippel@lukasverlag.de
Founded: 1995
Specialize in art history, cultural studies, musicology, philosophy, Middle Ages, Nazism & resistance against it, German Democratic Republic.
Subjects: Archaeology, Architecture & Interior Design, Art, Government, Political Science, History, Literature, Literary Criticism, Essays, Music, Dance, Philosophy, Social Sciences, Sociology, Historic Preservation
ISBN Prefix(es): 978-3-931836; 978-3-936872; 978-3-86732
Number of titles published annually: 25 Print
Total Titles: 200 Print

Lusatia Verlag-Dr Stuebner & Co KG+
Postplatz 3, 02625 Bautzen
Tel: (03591) 53 24 00 *Fax:* (03591) 53 24 00
E-mail: lusatiaverlag@t-online.de
Web Site: www.lusatiaverlag.de
Key Personnel
Owner: Dr Frank Stuebner
Founded: 1992
Membership(s): Association of German Booksellers.
Subjects: Art, Fiction, Regional Interests, Travel & Tourism
ISBN Prefix(es): 978-3-929091; 978-3-936758
Number of titles published annually: 12 Print
Total Titles: 182 Print
Distributed by Domowina-Verlag
Distributor for Domowina-Verlag

Luther-Verlag GmbH+
Cansteinstr 1, 33647 Bielefeld
Tel: (0521) 9440-0 *Fax:* (0521) 9440-136
E-mail: vertrieb@luther-verlag.de
Web Site: www.lutherverlag.de; www.
evangelische-medien.de/luther-verlag.html
Key Personnel
Mng Dir: Bernd Becker
Marketing: Hille Mrosek *E-mail:* marketing@
luther-verlag.de
Founded: 1911
Subjects: Religion - Protestant
ISBN Prefix(es): 978-3-7858

Lutherische Verlagsgesellschaft mbH
Gartenstr 20, 24103 Kiel
Mailing Address: Postfach 3169, 24030 Kiel
Tel: (0431) 55779-206; (0431) 55779-285 (orders)
Fax: (0431) 55779-292
E-mail: vertrieb@lutherische-verlag.de
Web Site: www.evangelisches-medienwerk.
de/verlage; www.kirchenshop-online.de
Key Personnel
Mng Dir: Bodo Elsner *Tel:* (0431) 55779-260
E-mail: bodo.elsner@epv-nord.de

Head, Publishing: Johannes Keussen *Tel:* (0431) 55779-203 *E-mail:* keussen@epv-nord.de
Founded: 1956
Subjects: Regional Interests, Religion - Other, Theology
ISBN Prefix(es): 978-3-87503
Parent Company: Evangelischer Presseverband Nord eV
Associate Companies: J F Steinkopf Verlag GmbH; Friedrich Wittig Verlag GmbH

Verlag Waldemar Lutz
Basler Str 130, 79540 Loerrach
Tel: (07621) 88812 *Fax:* (07621) 926025
E-mail: wlutz@verlag-lutz.de
Web Site: www.verlag-lutz.de
Key Personnel
Mng Dir, Rights & Permissions: Waldemar Lutz
Founded: 1978
Subjects: Literature, Literary Criticism, Essays, Regional Interests
ISBN Prefix(es): 978-3-922107
Bookshop(s): Lutz-Die Buchhandlung, Tumringer-str 179, 79540 Loerrach

Luxbooks Verlags GmbH
Luxemburgplatz 1, 65185 Wiesbaden
Tel: (0611) 7167891 *Fax:* (0611) 4969013
E-mail: info@luxbooks.de
Web Site: www.luxbooks.de
Key Personnel
Mng Dir: Annette Kuehn; Christian Lux
Subjects: Fiction, Poetry, Culture
ISBN Prefix(es): 978-3-939557; 978-3-945550
Distribution Center: GVA Goettingen *Fax:* (0551) 413 92 *E-mail:* bestellung@gva-verlage.de

Stiftung Lyrik Kabinett
Amalienstr 83a, 80799 Munich
Tel: (089) 34 62 99 *Fax:* (089) 34 53 95
E-mail: info@lyrik-kabinett.de
Web Site: www.lyrik-kabinett.de
Key Personnel
Mng Dir: Dr Holger Pils
Founded: 2003
Subjects: Poetry
ISBN Prefix(es): 978-3-9807150; 978-3-938776

Lyrikgarten, *imprint of* Anton G Leitner Verlag

Maas & Peither AG
Karlstr 2, 79650 Schopfheim
Tel: (07622) 666 86-70 *Fax:* (07622) 666 86-77
E-mail: service@gmp-verlag.de
Web Site: www.gmp-verlag.de
Key Personnel
Chief Executive Officer: Barbara Peither
Tel: (07622) 666 86-76 *E-mail:* barbara.
peither@gmp-verlag.de
Executive Editor: Thomas Peither *Tel:* (07622) 666 86-75 *E-mail:* thomas.peither@gmp-verlag.
de
Marketing: Cynthia Kallmeyer *Tel:* (07622) 666 86-68 *E-mail:* cynthia.kallmeyer@gmp-verlag.
de
Sales & Marketing: Jessica Kroedel *Tel:* (07622) 666 86-85 *E-mail:* jessica.kroedel@gmp-verlag.
de
Founded: 1999
Subjects: Good Manufacturing Practice (GMP)
ISBN Prefix(es): 978-3-934971; 978-3-943267
U.S. Office(s): Maas & Peither America Inc, 1725 "I" St NW, Suite 300, Washington, DC 20006, United States *Tel:* 202-349-3864
E-mail: service@gmp-publishing.com *Web Site:* www.gmp-publishing.com

Mabuse-Verlag GmbH
Kasseler Str 1a (Oekohaus), 60486 Frankfurt am Main
Tel: (069) 70 79 96-0 *Fax:* (069) 70 41 52

E-mail: info@mabuse-verlag.de
Web Site: www.mabuse-verlag.de
Key Personnel
Mng Dir: Hermann Loeffler
Publisher: Alex Feuerherdt *Tel:* (069) 70 79 96-26 *E-mail:* feuerherdt@mabuse-verlag.
de; Tobias Frisch *Tel:* (069) 70 79 96-13
E-mail: tobias.frisch@mabuse-verlag.de
Founded: 1976
Subjects: Health, Nutrition, Medicine, Nursing, Dentistry, Psychology, Psychiatry, Birth, Dementia, Elderly Care, History of Medicine, People with Disability, Pregnancy
ISBN Prefix(es): 978-3-925499; 978-3-929106; 978-3-933050; 978-3-935964; 978-3-938304

Sachbuch-Verlag Karin Mader
Mittelsmoorer Str 80, 28879 Grasberg
Tel: (04208) 556 *Fax:* (04208) 3429
E-mail: info@mader-verlag.de
Web Site: www.mader-verlag.de
Key Personnel
Mng Dir: Karin Mader
Founded: 1978
Publisher of travel books & maps.
Subjects: Regional Interests, Travel & Tourism
ISBN Prefix(es): 978-3-921957
Distribution Center: VAH Jager Verlagsauslieferung, Str der Einheit 142-148, 14612 Falkensee
Tel: (03322) 12869-0 *Fax:* (03322) 12869-98
E-mail: info@vah-jager.de *Web Site:* www.vah-jager.de

Maeander GmbH+
Diepoltsberg 2, 84326 Falkenberg
Tel: (08727) 1657 (orders) *Fax:* (08727) 1569
E-mail: maeanderverlag@aol.com
Web Site: www.maeander-buch-kunst.eu
Key Personnel
Mng Dir, Rights & Permissions: Dr Renate Piel
Founded: 1976
Specialize in monographs & art history in general.
Subjects: Archaeology, Architecture & Interior Design, Art, Philosophy
ISBN Prefix(es): 978-3-88219
Total Titles: 78 Print

Annemarie Maeger Verlag & Hypatia Archiv+
Ebertallee 6, 22607 Hamburg
Tel: (040) 899 24 80 *Fax:* (040) 890 44 75
Web Site: www.a-maeger-verlag.de
Founded: 1993
Subjects: Drama, Theater, History, Literature, Literary Criticism, Essays, Mathematics, Philosophy, Religion - Other, Science (General), Theology, Women's Studies
ISBN Prefix(es): 978-3-929805

Maennerschwarm Verlag GmbH+
Lange Reihe 102, 20099 Hamburg
Tel: (040) 430 26 50; (040) 436 093 (bookshop)
Fax: (040) 430 29 32
E-mail: verlag@maennerschwarm.de
Web Site: www.maennerschwarm.de
Key Personnel
Mng Dir: Joachim Bartholomae
E-mail: bartholomae@maennerschwarm.
de; Detlef Grumbach *E-mail:* grumbach@
maennerschwarm.de
Founded: 1992
Subjects: LGBTQ
ISBN Prefix(es): 978-3-928983; 978-3-935596; 978-3-939542
Number of titles published annually: 15 Print
Total Titles: 200 Print
Imprints: Invertito; Queer Lectures; Edition Waldschloesschen; Bibliothek rosa Winkel
Foreign Rep(s): Andreas Meisel (Switzerland); Seth Meyer-Bruhns (Austria)
Distribution Center: Prolit, Siemensstr 16, 35463 Fernwald *Tel:* (0641) 94393-35 *Fax:* (0641)

94393-39 *E-mail:* a.willenberg@prolit.de (Germany & Austria)

Kaktus Buecher & Comics, Thundorfer Str 15, 8501 Frauenfeld, Switzerland *Tel:* (052) 722 31 90 *Fax:* (052) 722 17 82 *E-mail:* kaktus@solnet.ch

Friedrich Maerker Verlag
Am Vorderen Berg 1, 74855 Hassmersheim
Tel: (06266) 202042 *Fax:* (03212) 2020420
E-mail: info@friedrich-maerker-verlag.de
Web Site: www.friedrich-maerker-verlag.de
Key Personnel
Owner: Christine Schoenfeld
Editor: Matt Schoenfeld
Bilingual books & learning materials for preschool, primary & secondary schools.
Subjects: Language Arts, Linguistics, Culture, Foreign Language Education, Music Education
ISBN Prefix(es): 978-3-941257

MaerkischerVerlag Wilhelmshorst (MVW)
An der Aue 6, 14552 Wilhelmshorst
Tel: (033205) 62211 *Fax:* (033205) 46863
E-mail: post@maerkischerverlag.de
Web Site: www.maerkischerverlag.de
Key Personnel
Chief Executive Officer: Dr Klaus-P Anders
Founded: 1995
Subjects: Biography, Memoirs, Fiction, History, Poetry
ISBN Prefix(es): 978-3-931329

Magdalenen-Verlag C Kopp oHG
Gewerbering 14, 83607 Holzkirchen
Tel: (08024) 47046-0 *Fax:* (08024) 47046-29
E-mail: info@magdalenen-verlag.de
Web Site: www.magdalenen-verlag.de
Key Personnel
Manager: Clemens Kopp
Founded: 1948
Subjects: Religion - Other
ISBN Prefix(es): 978-3-930350; 978-3-9800186; 978-3-936317

Magnus Verlag GmbH+
Im Teelbruch 60-62, 45219 Essen
Tel: (02054) 5080 *Fax:* (02054) 83762
Key Personnel
Mng Dir: Maurice Gervastri-Stender
Subjects: Biography, Memoirs, History, Contemporary History, Cultural History
ISBN Prefix(es): 978-3-88400; 978-3-920617

Theaterverlag Karl Mahnke+
Grosse Str 108, 27283 Verden
Tel: (04231) 30 11 0 *Fax:* (04231) 30 11 11
E-mail: info@mahnke-verlag.de
Web Site: www.mahnke-verlag.de
Key Personnel
Owner: Dierk Mahnke
Publishing Dir & Editor: Alexandra Schlenker
Founded: 1841
Specialize in amateur theater publishing.
Membership(s): Verband Deutscher Buehnen- und Medienverlage eV.
Subjects: Drama, Theater
ISBN Prefix(es): 978-3-920613

Otto Maier Verlag, see Ravensburger Buchverlag Otto Maier GmbH

Druck & Verlagshaus Mainz GmbH+
Suesterfeldstr 83, 52072 Aachen
Tel: (0241) 87 34 34 00 *Fax:* (0241) 87 55 77
E-mail: info@verlag-mainz.de
Web Site: www.verlag-mainz.de
Key Personnel
Mng Dir: Guenter Mainz; Marc-Andre Mainz
E-mail: ma.mainz@verlag.mainz.de; Marcel Mainz *E-mail:* m.mainz@verlag.mainz.de

Founded: 1988
Membership(s): The Stock Exchange of German Booksellers.
Subjects: Biography, Memoirs, Fiction, Nonfiction (General), Poetry, Science (General)
ISBN Prefix(es): 978-3-926987; 978-3-86130; 978-3-8107; 978-3-86073; 978-3-89653; 978-3-925038; 978-3-925714; 978-3-928493; 978-3-930085; 978-3-930911
Subsidiaries: Edition Hathor
Divisions: Belletriotik
Showroom(s): Bundesstr 74, 20140 Hamburg
Warehouse: Bundesstr 74, 20140 Hamburg

Mairdumont GmbH & Co KG
Marco-Polo-Str 1, 73760 Ostfildern
Tel: (0711) 4502-0 *Fax:* (0711) 4502-340
E-mail: info@mairdumont.com
Web Site: www.mairdumont.com
Key Personnel
Mng Dir: Dr Thomas Brinkmann; Dr Frank Mair; Dr Stephanie Mair-Huydts; Uwe Zachmann
Dir, Public Relations: Uta Niederstrasser
Tel: (0711) 4502-434 *E-mail:* u.niederstrasser@mairdumont.com
Founded: 1979
Subjects: Outdoor Recreation, Travel & Tourism
ISBN Prefix(es): 978-3-8279; 978-3-575; 978-3-87504; 978-3-89525; 978-3-8297

mairisch Verlag
Koenigstr 30, 22767 Hamburg
Tel: (040) 43 26 73 83 *Fax:* (040) 22 81 35 099
E-mail: kontakt@mairisch.de; lektorat@mairisch.de
Web Site: www.mairisch.de
Key Personnel
Press & Public Relations: Stefanie Ericke-Keidtel
Tel: (040) 29 04 57 09 *E-mail:* stefanie.ericke@mairisch.de
Program & Communications: Daniel Beskos; Blanka Stolz
Program & Editing: Peter Reichenbach
Founded: 1999
Subjects: Drama, Theater, Fiction, Literature, Literary Criticism, Essays, Music, Dance
ISBN Prefix(es): 978-3-938539
Foreign Rep(s): Indiebook (Nicole Grabert, Judith Heckel & Christiane Kraus)
Distribution Center: GVA Gemeinsame Verlagsauslieferung Goettingen GmbH & Co, Postfach 2021, 37010 Goettingen
Tel: (0551) 384200-0 *Fax:* (0551) 384200-10
E-mail: frester@gva-verlage.de *Web Site:* www.gva-verlage.de

Malik National Geographic, *imprint of* Piper Verlag GmbH

Malik Verlag, *imprint of* Piper Verlag GmbH

MANA-Verlag
Eichhorster Weg 80, 13435 Berlin
Tel: (030) 40 30 3805 *Fax:* (030) 40 37 5995
E-mail: mail@mana-verlag.de; info@mana-verlag.de
Web Site: www.mana-verlag.de
Key Personnel
Owner: Hartmut Jaecksch
Founded: 1998
Subjects: Fiction, Literature, Literary Criticism, Essays, Science (General), Travel & Tourism, Culture
ISBN Prefix(es): 978-3-934031

Manesse, *imprint of* Verlagsgruppe Random House Bertelsmann

Manesse Verlag
Imprint of Verlagsgruppe Random House Bertelsmann

Neumarkter Str 28, 81673 Munich
Tel: (089) 4136-0 *Toll Free Tel:* 0800 500 33 22
Fax: (089) 4136-3333
E-mail: kundenservice@randomhouse.de
Web Site: www.randomhouse.de/manesse
Key Personnel
Press & Public Relations: Markus Desaga
Tel: (089) 4136-3702 *Fax:* (089) 4136-3897
E-mail: markus.desaga@randomhouse.de
Subjects: Literature, Literary Criticism, Essays, Classics
ISBN Prefix(es): 978-3-7175

Manhattan, *imprint of* Verlagsgruppe Random House Bertelsmann

Manhattan Verlag
Imprint of Verlagsgruppe Random House Bertelsmann
Neumarkter Str 28, 81673 Munich
Tel: (089) 4136-0 *Toll Free Tel:* 0800 500 33 22
Fax: (089) 4136-3333
E-mail: kundenservice@randomhouse.de
Web Site: www.randomhouse.de/manhattan
Key Personnel
Events: Manuela Braun *Tel:* (089) 4136-3145
Fax: (089) 4136-3723 *E-mail:* manuela.braun@randomhouse.de
Press: Susanne Gruenbeck *Tel:* (089) 4136-3717
Fax: (089) 4136-3723 *E-mail:* susanne.gruenbeck@randomhouse.de
Founded: 1997
Subjects: Fiction, Humor, Literature, Literary Criticism, Essays, Mysteries, Suspense, Contemporary Literature, Crime, Satire, Women's Literature
ISBN Prefix(es): 978-3-442

Mankau Verlag GmbH
Reschstr 2, 82418 Murnau a Staffelsee
Mailing Address: Postfach 13 22, 82413 Murnau a Staffelsee
Tel: (08841) 627769-0 *Fax:* (08841) 627769-6
E-mail: kontakt@mankau-verlag.de
Web Site: www.mankau-verlag.de
Key Personnel
Owner & Mng Dir: Raphael Mankau
Founded: 2004
Subjects: Health, Nutrition, Medicine, Nursing, Dentistry, Psychology, Psychiatry, Self-Help
ISBN Prefix(es): 978-3-938396; 978-3-9809565; 978-3-86374
Distribution Center: Brockhaus/Commission, Postfach 12 20, 70803 Kornwestheim, Contact: Petra Brandt *Tel:* (07154) 13 27-71
Fax: (07154) 13 27-13 *E-mail:* p.brandt@brocom.de
Dr Franz Hain Verlagsauslieferungen GmbH, Dr-Otto-Neurath-Gasse 5, 1220 Vienna, Austria *Tel:* (01) 282 65 65 *Fax:* (01) 282 52 82
E-mail: bestell@hain.at
Buchzentrum AG, Industriestr Ost 10, 4614 Haegendorf, Switzerland *Tel:* (062) 2 09 25 25
Fax: (062) 2 09 26 27 *E-mail:* kundendiest@buchzentrum.ch

Gebr Mann Verlag, *imprint of* Dietrich Reimer Verlag GmbH

Gebr Mann Verlag+
Imprint of Dietrich Reimer Verlag GmbH
Berliner Str 53, 10713 Berlin
Tel: (030) 700 13 88-0 *Fax:* (030) 700 13 88-11
E-mail: vertrieb-kunstverlage@reimer-verlag.de
Web Site: www.reimer-mann-verlag.de
Key Personnel
Mng Dir: Dr Hans-Robert Cram
Sales & Advertising: Elke Lundt *Tel:* (030) 700 13 88-50 *Fax:* (030) 700 13 88-55
E-mail: elundt@reimer-verlag.de
Press: Ingrid Schulze *Tel:* (030) 700 13 88-32
E-mail: ischulze@reimer-verlag.de

Founded: 1917
Subjects: Archaeology, Architecture & Interior Design, Art, Crafts, Games, Hobbies, History, Sculpture
ISBN Prefix(es): 978-3-496; 978-3-7861
Associate Companies: Deutscher Verlag fuer Kunstwissenschaft
Orders to: Leipziger Kommissions- und Grossbuchhandelsgellschaft mbH (LKG), An der Suedspitze 1-12, 04571 Roetha *Tel:* (034206) 65-100 *Fax:* (034206) 65-110 *E-mail:* lkg@lkg-va.de *Web Site:* www.lkg-va.de

Mantikore-Verlag
Triftstr 9, 60528 Frankfurt
Tel: (0163) 80 58 461 (cell)
E-mail: mantikoreverlag@aol.com
Web Site: mantikore-verlag.de
Key Personnel
Mng Dir: Nicolai Bonczyk
Founded: 2008
Subjects: Science Fiction, Fantasy
ISBN Prefix(es): 978-3-939212; 978-3-9812812

Manutius Verlag Heidelberg+
Eselspfad 2, 69117 Heidelberg
Tel: (06221) 163290 *Fax:* (06221) 167143
E-mail: manutiusverlag@t-online.de
Web Site: www.manutius-verlag.de
Key Personnel
Publisher: Frank Wuerker
Founded: 1985
Subjects: Art, Government, Political Science, History, Human Relations, Law, Literature, Literary Criticism, Essays, Music, Dance, Philosophy, Science (General)
ISBN Prefix(es): 978-3-925678; 978-3-934877
Total Titles: 80 Print

mareverlag GmbH & Co oHG
Sandthorquaihof, Pickhuben 2, 20457 Hamburg
Tel: (040) 36 98 59 0 *Fax:* (040) 36 98 59 90
E-mail: buch@mare.de; leserbrief@mare.de; mare@mare.de
Web Site: www.mare.de
Key Personnel
Mng Dir: Nikolaus Gelpke
Press & Public Relations: Stephanie Haack
   Tel: (040) 36 80 76 22 *Fax:* (040) 36 80 76 76
   E-mail: haack@mare.de
Sales & Marketing: Andrea Kruska *Tel:* (040) 36 80 76 11 *Fax:* (040) 36 98 59 99
   E-mail: kruska@mare.de
Founded: 2002
Subjects: Fiction, Nonfiction (General)
ISBN Prefix(es): 978-3-86648; 978-3-936384; 978-3-936543
Branch Office(s)
mare Redaktion, Oranienstr 10-11, 10997 Berlin
Foreign Rep(s): Piroska Boros (Switzerland); Buchkontor (Ulla Harms & Christiane Eblinger) (Austria)
Foreign Rights: Literarische Agentur Kossak GbR (Lars Schultze-Kossack)
Distribution Center: Leipziger Kommissions- und Grossbuchhandelsgellschaft mbH (LKG), An der Suedspitze 1-12, 04571 Roetha, Contact: Ursula Fritzsche *Tel:* (034206) 65-135 *Fax:* (034206) 65-130 *E-mail:* ufritzsche@lkg-service.de *Web Site:* www.lkg-va.de
Dr Franz Hain Verlagsauslieferungen, Dr-Otto-Neurath-Gasse 5, 1220 Vienna, Austria *Tel:* (01) 282 65 65 0 *Fax:* (01) 282 52 82 *E-mail:* vertrieb@hain.at
Scheidegger & Co AG, Centralweg 16, 8910 Affoltern a Albis, Switzerland, Contact: Barbara Joss *Tel:* (044) 762 42 50 *Fax:* (044) 762 42 10 *E-mail:* scheidegger@ava.ch
Orders to: mare-Service, Postfach 11 10 11, 20410 Hamburg *Tel:* (040) 30 07 35 36 *Fax:* (040) 30 07 85 35 36 *E-mail:* service@abo.mare.de

Margraf Publishers und Morramusik Verlags GmbH
Kanalstr 21, 97990 Weikersheim
Tel: (07934) 30 71 *Fax:* (07934) 81 56
E-mail: info@margraf-verlag.de
Web Site: www.margraf-publishers.eu; shop.margraf-publishers.net
Key Personnel
Chief Executive Officer: Dirk Hangstein
Dir: John Freyer
Founded: 1985
Subjects: Agriculture, Animals, Pets, Biological Sciences, Developing Countries, Economics, Environmental Studies, Geography, Geology, Music, Dance, Science (General), Botany, Entomology, Forestry, Paleontology, Wildlife
ISBN Prefix(es): 978-3-8236; 978-3-924333
Associate Companies: Backhuys Publishers, PO Box 321, 2300 AH Leiden, Netherlands, Contact: Dr W Backhuys *Web Site:* www.backhuys.com
Distributed by DA Books & Journals

Druck- und Verlagsgesellschaft Marienberg mbH
Industriestr 7, 09496 Marienberg
Tel: (03735) 91 64-0 *Fax:* (03735) 23 48-6
E-mail: info@druckerei-marienberg.de
Web Site: www.druckerei-marienberg.de
Key Personnel
Publishing Dir: Manfred Dittrich *E-mail:* m.dittrich@druckerei-marienberg.de
Project Dir: Heike Beckert *Tel:* (03735) 91 64-25 *E-mail:* h.beckert@druckerei-marienberg.de
Production: Denis Neubert *Tel:* (03735) 91 64-33 *E-mail:* d.neubert@druckerei-marienberg.de
Sales & Production: Agnes Mueller *Tel:* (03735) 91 64-25 *E-mail:* a.mueller@druckerei-marienberg.de
Founded: 1992
Subjects: Regional Interests
ISBN Prefix(es): 978-3-931770

Edition Maritim, see DK Edition Maritim GmbH

Marix Verlag
Imprint of Verlagshaus Roemerweg GmbH
Roemerweg 10, 65187 Wiesbaden
Tel: (0611) 986 98 0 *Fax:* (0611) 986 98 26
E-mail: info@verlagshaus-roemerweg.de
Web Site: www.verlagshaus-roemerweg.de/Marix_Verlag.html; www.verlagshaus-roemerweg.de
Key Personnel
Publishing Dir: Lothar Wekel *E-mail:* wekel@verlagshaus-roemerweg.de
Sales & Marketing: Fabian Reinecke *Tel:* (0611) 986 98 15 *E-mail:* reinecke@verlagshaus-roemerweg.de
Founded: 2003
Subjects: Art, History, Literature, Literary Criticism, Essays, Philosophy, Religion - Other, Science (General), Ancient History, Mythology
ISBN Prefix(es): 978-3-86539; 978-3-937715; 978-3-7374
Foreign Rep(s): Buchzentrum AG (Switzerland); Mohr Morawa Buchvertrieb GmbH (Austria)
Distribution Center: Sigloch Distribution GmbH & Co KG, Am Buchberg 8, Tor 6-10, 74572 Blaufelden *Tel:* (07953) 718 90 69 *Fax:* (07953) 883 16 0 *E-mail:* verlagshausroemerweg@sigloch.de *Web Site:* www.sigloch.de

Marixverlag, *imprint of* Verlagshaus Roemerweg GmbH

Markt+Technik, *imprint of* Pearson Deutschland GmbH

MaroVerlag + Druck eK
Zirbelstr 57a, 86154 Augsburg
Tel: (0821) 416034 *Fax:* (0821) 416036
E-mail: info@maroverlag.de
Web Site: www.maroverlag.de
Key Personnel
Proprietor: Benno Kaesmayr
Founded: 1968
Subjects: Fiction, Literature, Literary Criticism, Essays, Poetry, Science (General), American, German & International Literature, Typography
ISBN Prefix(es): 978-3-87512
Number of titles published annually: 5 Print
Total Titles: 120 Print

Masken-Verlag Friedrich Willmann
Eduard-Steinle-Str 13, 70619 Stuttgart
Tel: (0711) 13 27 14 *Fax:* (0711) 13 27 13
E-mail: info@masken-verlag.de
Web Site: www.masken-verlag.de
Key Personnel
Owner: Hans-Frieder Willmann
Subjects: Government, Political Science, History, Nonfiction (General), Religion - Protestant
ISBN Prefix(es): 978-3-939500; 978-3-9800816

MatrixMedia Verlag GmbH
Weender Str 39, 37073 Goettingen
Tel: (0551) 45924 *Fax:* (0551) 487542
E-mail: hh@matrixmedia-verlag.de
Web Site: www.matrixmedia.info
Key Personnel
Mng Dir: Heinrich Prinz von Hannover
Subjects: Art, History, Nonfiction (General), Culture
ISBN Prefix(es): 978-3-932313
Distribution Center: GVA - Gemeinsame Verlagsauslieferung Goettingen, Postfach 2021, 37010 Goettingen *Tel:* (0551) 487177 *Fax:* (0551) 41392

Mattes Verlag GmbH+
Tischbeinstr 62, 69121 Heidelberg
Mailing Address: Steigerweg 69, 69115 Heidelberg
Tel: (06221) 459321 *Fax:* (06221) 459322
E-mail: verlag@mattes.de; bestellung@mattes.de (orders)
Web Site: www.mattes.de
Key Personnel
Mng Dir: Kurt Mattes
Founded: 1990
Subjects: Biography, Memoirs, Literature, Literary Criticism, Essays, Psychology, Psychiatry, Regional Interests, Social Sciences, Sociology, Culture, Group Analysis, Prenatal Psychology, Psychohistory, Psychotherapy
ISBN Prefix(es): 978-3-9802440; 978-3-930978; 978-3-86809
Total Titles: 160 Print; 1 E-Book

Matthaes Verlag GmbH
Subsidiary of Deutscher Fachverlag GmbH
Silberburgstr 122, 70176 Stuttgart
Mailing Address: Postfach 10 31 44, 70027 Stuttgart
Tel: (0711) 21 33-329 *Fax:* (0711) 21 33-320
E-mail: buch@matthaes.de
Web Site: www.matthaes.de
Key Personnel
Mng Dir: Joachim Eckert; Dr Clemens Knoll
Editor & Foreign Rights: Julia Bauer *Tel:* (0711) 21 33-357 *E-mail:* j.bauer@matthaes.de
Marketing & Press: Michela Montesano *Tel:* (0711) 21 33-356 *E-mail:* m.montesano@matthaes.de
Sales: Kornelia Herold *E-mail:* k.herold@matthaes.de
Founded: 1905
Subjects: Cookery
ISBN Prefix(es): 978-3-87515

Branch Office(s)
Frankfurt
Hamburg
Munich

Matthes und Seitz Berlin Verlagsgesellschaft mbH+

Goehrener Str 7, 10437 Berlin
Tel: (030) 44 32 74 01 *Fax:* (030) 44 32 74 02
E-mail: info@matthes-seitz-berlin.de
Web Site: www.matthes-seitz-berlin.de
Key Personnel
Mng Dir: Dr Andreas Rotzer
Dir Foreign Rights: Richard Stoiber
Founded: 1977
Subjects: Art, Biography, Memoirs, Fiction, History, Literature, Literary Criticism, Essays, Music, Dance, Philosophy, Poetry, Theology, Letters
ISBN Prefix(es): 978-3-88221
Foreign Rep(s): Christian Hirtzy (Austria); Scheidegger (Ruth Schildnecht & Urs Wetli) (Switzerland); Ernst Sonntag (Austria)
Distribution Center: Prolit, Siemensstr 16, 35463 Fernwald, Contact: Gabriele Lemuth *Tel:* (0641) 94393201 *Fax:* (0641) 9439389 *E-mail:* g.lemuth@prolit.de
Dr Franz Hain, Dr-Otto-Neurath-Gasse 5, 1220 Vienna, Austria *Tel:* (01) 282 65 65 24 *Fax:* (01) 282 65 65 49 *E-mail:* bestell@hain.at
AVA Verlagsauslieferung AG, Centralweg 16, 8910 Affoltern, Switzerland *Tel:* (01) 762 42 50 *Fax:* (01) 762 42 10 *E-mail:* n.schmid@ava.ch

Matthiesen Verlag Ingwert Paulsen Jr+

Subsidiary of Husum Druck- und Verlagsgesellschaft mbH u Co KG
Nordbahnhofstr 2, 25813 Husum
Mailing Address: Postfach 1480, 25804 Husum
Tel: (04841) 8352-0 *Fax:* (04841) 8352-10
E-mail: info@verlagsgruppe.de
Web Site: www.verlagsgruppe.de
Key Personnel
Mng Dir: Ingwert Paulsen
Founded: 1892
Subjects: Geography, Geology, History, Medicine, Nursing, Dentistry, Science (General)
ISBN Prefix(es): 978-3-7868
Associate Companies: Hamburger Lesehefte Verlag Ingwert Paulsen Jr; Hansa Verlag Ingwert Paulsen Jr; Verlag der Kunst Dresden Ingwert Paulsen Jr; Verlag der Nation Ingwert Paulsen Jr; Turmschreiber Verlag Ingwert Paulsen Jr; Frank Wagner Verlagsbuchhandlung Ingwert Paulsen Jr eK

Hans K Matussek & Sohn oHG+

Marktstr 13, 41334 Nettetal
Tel: (02153) 916430 *Fax:* (02153) 13363
E-mail: buchmatussek@t-online.de
Web Site: www.buchhandlung-matussek.de
Key Personnel
Contact: Hans K Matussek *E-mail:* hans.matussek@t-online.de; Fabian Matussek *E-mail:* fabian.matussek@t-online.de
Founded: 1961
Subjects: Biography, Memoirs, Computer Science, Erotica, Government, Political Science, Nonfiction (General), Poetry, Romance, Science Fiction, Fantasy, Sports, Athletics, Travel & Tourism, Thrillers
ISBN Prefix(es): 978-3-920743

Verlag Hans-Juergen Maurer

Im Trierischen Hof 14, 60311 Frankfurt
Tel: (069) 297 280 31 *Fax:* (069) 297 280 32
E-mail: info@verlaghjmaurer.de
Web Site: www.verlaghjmaurer.de
Key Personnel
Publisher: Hans-Juergen Maurer

Subjects: Inspirational, Spirituality, Literature, Literary Criticism, Essays, Religion - Other
ISBN Prefix(es): 978-3-929345
Foreign Rep(s): Thomas Classen (Switzerland); Dr Winfried Plattner (Austria)
Distribution Center: VAL-Silberschnur, Steinstr 1, 56593 Guellesheim *Tel:* (02687) 929001 *Fax:* (02687) 929524 *E-mail:* info@silberschnur.de
Ennsthaler GmbH, Stadtplatz 26, 4402 Steyr, Austria *Tel:* (07252) 5205320 *Fax:* (07252) 5205322 *E-mail:* auslieferung@ennsthaler.at
Buchzentrum, Industrie-Ost, 4614 Haegendorf, Switzerland *Tel:* (062) 2092525 *Fax:* (062) 2092627

Mayersche Buchhandlung KG

Matthiashofstr 28-30, 52064 Aachen
Tel: (0241) 4777-345 *Fax:* (0241) 4777-475
E-mail: service@mayersche.de
Web Site: www.mayersche.de
Key Personnel
Manager: Dr Hartmut Falter; Helmut Falter; Ullrich Falter
Press & Public Relations: Simone Thelen *E-mail:* s.thelen@mayersche.de
Founded: 1817
Membership(s): AWS-JASV.
Subjects: Art, Business, Cookery, Economics, Erotica, Fiction, Government, Political Science, Management, Medicine, Nursing, Dentistry, Nonfiction (General), Regional Interests, Science Fiction, Fantasy, Travel & Tourism, Culture
ISBN Prefix(es): 978-3-87519
Bookshop(s): Buchkremerstr 1-7, 52062 Aachen *Tel:* (0241) 4777-0 *Fax:* (0241) 4777-167 *E-mail:* info-aachenbk@mayersche.de; Hauptstr 15, 59755 Arnsberg-Neheim *Tel:* (02932) 902861-0 *Fax:* (02932) 902861-1 *E-mail:* info-neheim@mayersche.de; Berliner Platz 2, 46395 Bocholt *Tel:* (02871) 489930-0 *Fax:* (02871) 489930-1 *E-mail:* info-bocholt@mayersche.de; Kortumstr 69-71, 44787 Bochum *Tel:* (0234) 68761-0 *Fax:* (0234) 68761-110 *E-mail:* info-bochum@mayersche.de; Ruhr Park, Am Einkaufszentrum, 44791 Bochum *Tel:* (0234) 68761-161 *Fax:* (0234) 6014356-1 *E-mail:* info-bochum-ruhrpark@mayersche.de; Kornmarkt 4, 46325 Borken *Tel:* (02861) 809477-0 *Fax:* (02861) 809477-1 *E-mail:* info-borken@mayersche.de; Hochstr 31a, 46236 Bottrop *Tel:* (02041) 775975-0 *Fax:* (02041) 775975-1 *E-mail:* info-bottrop@mayersche.de; Muensterstr 5, 44575 Castrop-Rauxel *Tel:* (02305) 929933-0 *Fax:* (02305) 929933-1 *E-mail:* info-castrop-rauxel@mayersche.de; Neumarkt 2, 50667 Cologne *Tel:* (0221) 20307-0 *Fax:* (0221) 20307-27 *E-mail:* info-koeln-gal@mayersche.de; Wiener Platz 1, 51065 Cologne-Muelheim *Tel:* (0221) 6699343-0 *Fax:* (0221) 6699343-1 *E-mail:* info-koeln-muelheim@mayersche.de; Neusser Str 226, 50733 Cologne-Nippes *Tel:* (0221) 669 948-10 *Fax:* (0221) 669 948-11 *E-mail:* info-koeln-nippes@mayersche.de; Suelzburgstr 13, 50937 Cologne-Suelz *Tel:* (0221) 292 73 44-0 *Fax:* (0221) 292 73 44-1 *E-mail:* info-koeln-suelz@mayersche.de; Koelner Str 78, 41539 Dormagen *Tel:* (02133) 778705-0 *Fax:* (02133) 778705-1 *E-mail:* info-dormagen@mayersche.de; Westenhellweg 37-41, 44137 Dortmund *Tel:* (0231) 80905-0 *Fax:* (0231) 80905-10 *E-mail:* info-dortmund@mayersche.de; Harkortstr 61, 44225 Dortmund-Hombruch *Tel:* (0231) 7766663-0 *Fax:* (0231) 7766663-1 *E-mail:* info-hombruch@mayersche.de; Mayersche Droste GmbH & Co KG, Partner der Mayerschen, Koenigsallee 18, 40212 Duesseldorf *Tel:* (0211) 5425690-0 *Fax:* (0211) 5425690-1 *E-mail:* info-duesseldorf-droste-koe@mayersche.de; Friedrichstr 19, 40217 Duesseldorf *Tel:* (0211) 7306048-0 *Fax:* (0211)

7306048-1 *E-mail:* info-duesseldorf-friedrichst@mayersche.de; Nordstr 73, 40477 Duesseldorf *Tel:* (0211) 4163542-0 *Fax:* (0211) 4163542-1 *E-mail:* info-duesseldorf-nord@mayersche.de; Duisburg Forum, Koenigstr 48, 47051 Duisburg *Tel:* (0203) 70 900 4-00 *Fax:* (0203) 70 900 4-01 *E-mail:* info-duisburg@mayersche.de; Marienstr 2, 52249 Eschweiler *Tel:* (02403) 782911-0 *Fax:* (02403) 782911-1 *E-mail:* info-eschweiler@mayersche.de; Markt 5-6, 45127 Essen *Tel:* (0201) 36567-0 *Fax:* (0201) 36567-10 *E-mail:* info-essen@mayersche.de; Ruettenscheider Str 84, 45130 Essen *Tel:* (0201) 890 60 80-0 *Fax:* (0201) 890 60 80-1 *E-mail:* info-essen-ruettenscheid@mayersche.de; Hauptstr 120-122, 50226 Frechen *Tel:* (02234) 21919-80 *Fax:* (02234) 21919-81 *E-mail:* info-frechen@mayersche.de; Bahnhofstr 78-84, 45879 Gelsenkirchen *Tel:* (0209) 92392-3 *Fax:* (0209) 92392-10 *E-mail:* info-gelsenkirchen@mayersche.de; Hochstr 9, 45894 Gelsenkirchen-Buer *Tel:* (0209) 972000-0 *Fax:* (0209) 972000-1 *E-mail:* info-buer@mayersche.de; Hochstr 23, 45964 Gladbeck *Tel:* (02043) 375250-0 *Fax:* (02043) 375250-1 *E-mail:* info-gladbeck@mayersche.de; Koelner Str 23-25, 41515 Grevenbroich *Tel:* (02181) 22848-10 *Fax:* (02181) 22848-11 *E-mail:* info-grevenbroich@mayersche.de; Koenigstr 4, 33330 Guetersloh *Tel:* (05241) 504990-0 *Fax:* (05241) 504990-1 *E-mail:* info-guetersloh@mayersche.de; Kaiserstr 20, 51643 Gummersbach *Tel:* (02261) 92580-20 *Fax:* (02261) 92580-21 *E-mail:* info-gummersbach@mayersche.de; Obermarkt 13a, 45525 Hattingen *Tel:* (02324) 919868-0 *Fax:* (02324) 919868-1 *E-mail:* info-hattingen@mayersche.de; Baeckerstr 24-28, 32052 Herford *Tel:* (05221) 120970-0 *Fax:* (05221) 120970-1 *E-mail:* info-herford@mayersche.de; Bahnhofstr 53, 44623 Herne *Tel:* (02323) 368910-0 *Fax:* (02323) 368910-1 *E-mail:* info-herne@mayersche.de; Weststr 75, 59174 Kamen *Tel:* (02307) 925106-0 *Fax:* (02307) 925106-1 *E-mail:* info-kamen@mayersche.de; Hindenburgstr 115-119, 41061 Moenchengladbach *Tel:* (02161) 81194-0 *Fax:* (02161) 81194-10 *E-mail:* info-moenchengladbach@mayersche.de; Stresemannstr 43, 41236 Moenchengladbach-Rheydt *Tel:* (02166) 94977-0 *Fax:* (02166) 94977-6 *E-mail:* info-rheydt@mayersche.de; Buechel 31, 41460 Neuss *Tel:* (02131) 313764-0 *Fax:* (02131) 313764-1 *E-mail:* info-neuss@mayersche.de; huma Einkaufspark, Rathausallee 16, 53757 Sankt Augustin *Tel:* (02241) 266097-0 *Fax:* (02241) 266097-1 *E-mail:* info-staugustin@mayersche.de; Bahnhofstr 28, 57072 Siegen *Tel:* (0271) 338800-00 *Fax:* (0271) 338800-11 *E-mail:* info-siegen@mayersche.de; Mayersche Interbook KG, Partner der Mayerschen, Kornmarkt 3, 54290 Trier *Tel:* (0651) 9799-0 *Fax:* (0651) 9799-300 *E-mail:* info-trier@mayersche.de; Koelner Str 13, 53840 Troisdorf *Tel:* (02241) 1239930 *Fax:* (02241) 1239931 *E-mail:* info-troisdorf@mayersche.de; Haupstr 12, 41747 Viersen *Tel:* (02162) 946914-0 *Fax:* (02162) 946914-1 *E-mail:* info-viersen@mayersche.de; Hohe Str 20-22, 46483 Wesel *Tel:* (0281) 147931-0 *Fax:* (0281) 147931-11 *E-mail:* info-wesel@mayersche.de; Bahnhofstr 30, 58452 Witten *Tel:* (02302) 28280-0 *Fax:* (02302) 28280-29 *E-mail:* info-witten@mayersche.de; Werth 54, 42275 Wuppertal Barmen *Tel:* (0202) 4304280-0 *Fax:* (0202) 4304280-1 *E-mail:* info-wuppertal-barmen@mayersche.de

McKlein Publishing

In der Rosenau 19, 51143 Cologne
Tel: (02203) 1021561 *Fax:* (02203) 982615
E-mail: klein@mcklein.de

Web Site: www.mcklein-imagedatabase.com/
wordpress/mcklein-publishing
Key Personnel
Founder & Author: Reinhard Klein
Founded: 1979
Publisher of motorsport literature & calendars.
ISBN Prefix(es): 978-3-927458

mdv Mitteldeutscher Verlag GmbH+
Am Steintor 23, 06112 Halle
Tel: (0345) 2 33 22-0 *Fax:* (0345) 2 33 22-66
E-mail: info@mitteldeutscherverlag.de
Web Site: www.mitteldeutscherverlag.de
Key Personnel
Mng Dir: Roman Pliske
Sales: Sigrun Hummel *Tel:* (0345) 2 33 22-16
   E-mail: hummel@mitteldeutscherverlag.de
Founded: 1946
Subjects: Art, Fiction, History, Literature, Literary
   Criticism, Essays, Nonfiction (General), Pho-
   tography, Poetry, Regional Interests, Travel &
   Tourism
ISBN Prefix(es): 978-3-932776; 978-3-89812
Distribution Center: Leipziger Kommissions-
   und Grossbuchhandelsgessellschaft mbH
   (LKG), An der Suedspitze 1-12, 04571 Roetha
   Tel: (034206) 65-100 *Fax:* (034206) 65-110
   E-mail: lkg@lkg-service.de *Web Site:* www.
   lkg-va.de
Mohr Morawa Buchvertrieb GmbH, Sulzen-
   gasse 2, 1230 Vienna, Austria *Tel:* (01) 680
   14-0 *Fax:* (01) 688 71 30 *E-mail:* momo@
   mohrmorawa.at *Web Site:* www.mohrmorawa.at

Media Maria Verlag eK
Nordstr 2, 89257 Illertissen
Tel: (07303) 9523310 *Fax:* (07303) 9523315
E-mail: buch@media-maria.de
Web Site: www.media-maria.de
Key Personnel
Owner: Gisela Geirhos
Founded: 2007
Subjects: Philosophy, Religion - Catholic, Chris-
   tian Literature
ISBN Prefix(es): 978-3-9811452; 978-3-9813003

Median-Verlag von Killisch-Horn GmbH
Im Breitspiel 11 a, 69126 Heidelberg
Tel: (06221) 90 509-0 *Fax:* (06221) 90 509-20
E-mail: info@median-verlag.de
Web Site: www.median-verlag.de
Key Personnel
Mng Dir: Bjoern Kerzmann
Advertising: Lisa Zimmermann *Tel:* (06221) 90
   509-14
Sales: Marion Dallaway *Tel:* (06221) 90 509-15
Founded: 1968
Subjects: Child Care & Development, Education,
   Health, Nutrition, Language Arts, Linguistics,
   Psychology, Psychiatry, Technology, Audiologi-
   cal Acoustics, Audiology
ISBN Prefix(es): 978-3-922766

medico international eV
Burgstr 106, 60389 Frankfurt am Main
Tel: (069) 94438-0 *Fax:* (069) 436002
E-mail: info@medico.de; presse@medico.de
Web Site: www.medico-international.de; www.
   medico.de
Key Personnel
Executive Dir: Thomas Gebauer
Head, Projects: Karin Urschel
Head, Public Relations & Press: Katja Maurer
   Tel: (069) 94438-29
Administration & Finance: Johannes Reinhard
Founded: 1968
Subjects: Developing Countries, Health, Nutri-
   tion, Medicine, Nursing, Dentistry, Alternative
   Medicine, Emergency Relief, Human Rights,
   Preventive Medicine, Psychosocial Work
ISBN Prefix(es): 978-3-923363

Medien-Verlag Bernhard Gregor, see Bernhard
Gregor Verlag

Medienagentur, *imprint of* Rowohlt Verlag
GmbH

**MEDITEG-Gesellschaft fuer Informatik
Technik und Systeme mbH+**
Limesstr 5, 61273 Wehrheim
Tel: (06081) 5171 *Fax:* (06081) 56017
Key Personnel
Manager: Rudolf Putz *E-mail:* putz-wehrheim@t-
online.de
Founded: 1984
Subjects: Medicine, Nursing, Dentistry
ISBN Prefix(es): 978-3-924373

Medium-Buchmarkt GmbH+
Rosenstr 5-6, 48143 Muenster
Tel: (0251) 46000 *Fax:* (0251) 46745
E-mail: info@mediumbooks.com
Web Site: www.medium-books.de
Key Personnel
Chief Executive Officer: Friedrich W Bitzhenner
Subjects: Architecture & Interior Design, Art,
   Computer Science, Cookery, Criminology, Fic-
   tion, Film, Video, Finance, Gardening, Plants,
   History, Literature, Literary Criticism, Essays,
   Music, Dance, Nonfiction (General), Philos-
   ophy, Photography, Psychology, Psychiatry,
   Technology, Travel & Tourism, General Hu-
   manities
ISBN Prefix(es): 978-3-933642

Medpharm Scientific Publishers+
Subsidiary of Deutscher Apotheker Verlag
Birkenwaldstr 44, 70191 Stuttgart
Mailing Address: Postfach 10 10 61, 70009
   Stuttgart
Tel: (0711) 2582-0 *Fax:* (0711) 2582-290
E-mail: service@wissenschaftliche-
   verlagsgesellschaft.de
Web Site: www.wissenschaftliche-
   verlagsgesellschaft.de
Key Personnel
Mng Dir: Dr Klaus G Brauer; Dr Christian Rotta
Marketing & Sales Manager: Siegmar
   Bauer *E-mail:* sbauer@wissenschaftliche-
   verlagsgesellschaft.de
Rights Manager: Sabine Koerner *Tel:* (0711)
   2582-221 *E-mail:* skoerner@dav-medien.de
Founded: 1981
Subjects: Medicine, Nursing, Dentistry, Science
   (General), Pharmacy
ISBN Prefix(es): 978-3-88763
Associate Companies: S Hirzel Verlag GmbH
   & Co; Franz Steiner Verlag GmbH; Wis-
   senschaftliche Verlagsgesellschaft mbH
Returns: Koch, Neff & Oetinger Verlagsaus-
   lieferung GmbH, c/o Verlagsgruppe Deutscher
   Apotheker Verlag, Am Wallgraben 110, 70563
   Stuttgart

MEDU Verlag
Schloss Philippseich, 63303 Dreieich
Tel: (06103) 3 12 54 71 *Fax:* (06103) 3 12 54 75
E-mail: info@medu-verlag.de
Web Site: www.medu-verlag.de
Key Personnel
Owner: Stefan Fassel-Wenz
Founded: 2003
Subjects: Art, Biography, Memoirs, Drama, The-
   ater, Nonfiction (General), Poetry, Romance
ISBN Prefix(es): 978-3-941955; 978-3-944948
Distribution Center: Revilak Service
ver-
   mittlung GmbH, Gutenbergstr 5, 82205
   Gilching *Tel:* (08105) 50 51; (08105) 50
   53 *Fax:* (08105) 54 08 *E-mail:* info@
   revilakservice.de *Web Site:* www.revilakservice.
   de

Mehring Verlag GmbH+
Margaretenstr 12, 45145 Essen
Tel: (0201) 6462106
E-mail: vertrieb@mehring-verlag.de
Web Site: www.mehring-verlag.de
Key Personnel
Contact: Wolfgang Zimmermann
   E-mail: zimmermann@mehring-verlag.de
Founded: 1978
Subjects: Art, Biography, Memoirs, Government,
   Political Science, History, Labor, Industrial Re-
   lations, Social Sciences, Sociology, Capitalism,
   Labor Movement, Socialism
ISBN Prefix(es): 978-3-88634
Number of titles published annually: 4 Print
Total Titles: 32 Print
U.S. Office(s): Mehring Books, PO Box 48377,
   Oak Park, MI 48237, United States *Tel:* 248-
   967-2924 *Fax:* 248-967-3023 *E-mail:* sales@
   mehring.com *Web Site:* www.mehring.com
Distribution Center: Taborstr 28, 1020 Vienna,
   Austria *Tel:* (01) 276 47 36; (06991) 585 16 68
   (cell) *E-mail:* office@literaturbuffet.com
Orders to: DHLOG Auslieferung, 45472 Muel-
   heim an der Ruhr, Postfach 120363, 45439
   Muelheim *Tel:* (0208) 49504-0 *Fax:* (0208)
   49504-95 *E-mail:* mehring@dhlog.de *Web
   Site:* www.dhlog.de

Verlag Meiga GbR
Waldsiedlung 15, 14806 Belzig
Tel: (033841) 30538 *Fax:* (03212) 1048983
E-mail: info@verlag-meiga.org
Web Site: verlag-meiga.org
Key Personnel
Dir: Monika Berghoff; Saskia Breithardt
Subjects: Environmental Studies, Inspirational,
   Spirituality
ISBN Prefix(es): 978-3-927266

Felix Meiner Verlag GmbH+
Richardstr 47, 22081 Hamburg
Tel: (040) 29 87 56-0; (040) 29 87 56-41 (sales)
   Fax: (040) 29 87 56-20; (040) 299 36 14 (or-
   ders)
E-mail: info@meiner.de
Web Site: www.meiner.de
Key Personnel
Publisher: Manfred Meiner *E-mail:* meiner@
   meiner.de
Rights, Marketing: Johannes Kambylis *Tel:* (040)
   29 87 56-23 *E-mail:* kambylis@meiner.de
Sales: Nina Schoen *E-mail:* schoen@meiner.de
Founded: 1951
Membership(s): German Book Trade Association.
Subjects: Philosophy
ISBN Prefix(es): 978-3-7873
Subsidiaries: Helmut Buske Verlag GmbH

Meisenbach Verlag GmbH
Franz-Ludwig-Str 7a, 96047 Bamberg
Tel: (0951) 861-0 *Fax:* (0951) 861-158
E-mail: info@meisenbach.de
Web Site: www.meisenbach.de
Key Personnel
Mng Dir: Ulrich Stetter
Founded: 1922
Subjects: Technology
ISBN Prefix(es): 978-3-87525

Otto Meissners Verlag & Co+
Binger Str 29, 14197 Berlin
Tel: (030) 8249558 *Fax:* (030) 8233338
E-mail: meissners-verlag@hotmail.com
Web Site: www.meissners-verlag.de
Key Personnel
Publisher: Dieter Beuermann
Founded: 1848
Subjects: Art, Biography, Memoirs, Crafts,
   Games, Hobbies, Human Relations, Literature,
   Literary Criticism, Essays, Nonfiction (General)
ISBN Prefix(es): 978-3-87527

Melsunger Medizinische Mitteilungen, *imprint of* Bibliomed Medizinische Verlagsgesellschaft mbH

Idime Verlag Melzer
Kienestr 37/1, 88045 Friedrichshafen
Tel: (07541) 55220 *Fax:* (07541) 55201
Founded: 1983
Subjects: Anthropology, Foreign Countries
ISBN Prefix(es): 978-3-924026; 978-3-933937

memo verlag
Noellenstr 11, 70195 Stuttgart
Tel: (0711) 6979806 *Fax:* (0711) 6979808
E-mail: info@memoverlag.de
Web Site: www.memoverlag.de
Key Personnel
Owner: Hedwig Ladner
Founded: 1991
Subjects: Health, Nutrition, Self-Help, Brain Performance Training, Cognitive Training, Memory Training
ISBN Prefix(es): 978-3-929317

Edition Axel Menges
Esslinger Str 24, 70736 Fellbach
Tel: (0711) 57 47 59 *Fax:* (0711) 57 47 84
E-mail: axelmenges@aol.com
Web Site: www.axelmenges.de
Key Personnel
Mng Dir: Dorothea Duwe *Tel:* (0711) 51 47 53;
Axel Menges *Tel:* (0711) 57 47 53
Founded: 1994
Subjects: Architecture & Interior Design, Art, Film, Video, Photography, Travel & Tourism
ISBN Prefix(es): 978-3-930698; 978-3-932565
Number of titles published annually: 20 Print
Total Titles: 226 Print
Foreign Rep(s): China Publishers Marketing (Benjamin Pan) (China); Graf Verlagsvertretungen GmbH (Sebastian Graf) (Switzerland); Elisabeth Harder-Kreimann (Scandinavia); Michael Klein (Austria); Flavio Marcello (France, Greece, Italy, Portugal, Spain); Maya Publishers Pvt Ltd (Surit Mitra) (India); Robbert J Pleysier (Netherlands); Coen Sligting Bookimport (Belgium); Ralph & Sheila Summers (Bangladesh, Cambodia, Guam, Hong Kong, Indonesia, Korea, Laos, Malaysia, Myanmar, Pakistan, Singapore, Taiwan, Thailand, Vietnam); Peter Ward Book Exports (Richard Ward) (Cyprus, Malta, Middle East); Yasmy International Marketing (Ralph & Sheila Summers) (Japan)
Distribution Center: Brockhaus/Commission Verlagsauslieferung, Kreidlerstr 9, 70806 Kornwestheim *Tel:* (07154) 13270 *Fax:* (07154) 132713 *E-mail:* menges@brocom.de *Web Site:* www.brocom.de
Buchzentrum, Industriestr Ost 10, 4614 Haegendorf, Switzerland *Tel:* (062) 209 25 25 *E-mail:* kundendienst@buchzentrum.ch *Web Site:* www.buchzentrum.ch
Gazelle Book Services Ltd, White Cross Mills, Hightown, Lancaster, Lancs LA1 4XS, United Kingdom *Tel:* (01524) 68765 *Fax:* (01524) 63232 *E-mail:* sales@gazellebooks.co.uk *Web Site:* www.gazellebookservices.co.uk (British Isles, India, South Africa & China)
National Book Network, 4501 Forbes Blvd, Suite 200, Lanham, MD 20706, United States, Contact: Marianne Bohr *Tel:* 301-459-3366 *Fax:* 301-429-5746 *E-mail:* custserv@nbnbooks.com (North America)

MenSana, *imprint of* Verlagsgruppe Droemer Knaur GmbH & Co KG

Menschenkinder Verlag und Vertrieb GmbH+
An der Kleimannbruecke 97, 48157 Muenster
Tel: (0251) 932520 *Fax:* (0251) 9325290

E-mail: info@menschenkinder.de
Web Site: www.menschenkinder.de (orders)
Key Personnel
Mng Dir: Detlev Joecker
Founded: 1987
Subjects: Music, Dance, Religion - Other
ISBN Prefix(es): 978-3-927497; 978-3-89516; 978-3-9801811

mentis Verlag GmbH
Eisenbahnstr 11, 48143 Muenster
Tel: (0251) 981635-10; (0251) 981635-11
Fax: (0251) 981635-14
E-mail: info@mentis.de
Web Site: www.mentis.de
Key Personnel
Contact: Dr Michael Kienecker
E-mail: kienecker@mentis.de
Founded: 1998
Subjects: Language Arts, Linguistics, Literature, Literary Criticism, Essays, Philosophy, Science (General)
ISBN Prefix(es): 978-3-89785; 978-3-95743
Number of titles published annually: 45 Print
Total Titles: 730 Print; 5 CD-ROM
Distribution Center: VSB Verlagsservice Braunschweig, Georg-Westermann-Allee 66, 38104 Braunschweig
Orders to: VSB Verlagsservice Braunschweig, Georg-Westermann-Allee 66, 38104 Braunschweig
Returns: VSB Verlagsservice Braunschweig, Georg-Westermann-Allee 66, 38104 Braunschweig

Mentor Verlag GmbH+
Member of Langenscheidt Verlagsgruppe
Mies-van-der-Rohe-Str 1, 80807 Munich
Tel: (089) 36096-0; (089) 36096-333 (sales)
Fax: (089) 36096-222; (089) 36096-258 (orders)
E-mail: kundenservice@langenscheidt.de; presse@langenscheidt.de
Web Site: www.mentor.de
Key Personnel
Press & Public Relations: Gabriele Becker
Tel: (089) 15820-206 *Fax:* (089) 15820-208
Founded: 1904
Specialize in self-help educational materials for school-age children.
Subjects: Self-Help
ISBN Prefix(es): 978-3-580
Foreign Rep(s): Mohr Morawa Buchvertrieb GmbH (Thomas Lasnik) (Austria); Thomas Rittig (Austria); Schupp Verlagsvertretungen AG (Switzerland)
Distribution Center: Mohr Morawa Buchvertrieb GmbH, Sulzengasse 2, 1230 Vienna, Austria *Tel:* (01) 680 14-0 *Fax:* (01) 688 71 30 *E-mail:* momo@mohrmorawa.at *Web Site:* www.mohrmorawa.at
Buchzentrum AG, Industriestr Ost 10, 4614 Haegendorf, Switzerland *Tel:* (062) 209-2525 *Fax:* (062) 209-2627 *E-mail:* kundendienst@buchzentrum.ch

Mercator-Verlag, *imprint of* Verlagshaus Wohlfarth

Mergus Verlag GmbH Hans A Baensch+
Im Wiele 27, 49328 Melle
Tel: (05422) 3636 *Fax:* (05422) 1404
E-mail: info@mergus.de
Web Site: www.mergus.com
Key Personnel
Mng Dir, Rights & Permissions: Hans A Baensch
Founded: 1977
Subjects: Animals, Pets, Crafts, Games, Hobbies, Natural History, Aquarium, Marine Life
ISBN Prefix(es): 978-3-88244
Total Titles: 50 Print

Distribution Center: VSB Verlagsservice Braunschweig, Georg Westermann Allee 66, 38104 Braunschweig
Pet Pacific Pty Ltd, Lot 8 Leland St, Penrith, NSW 2750, Australia *Fax:* (02) 47323275
Rolf C Hagen Inc, 3225 Sartelon St, Montreal, QC H4R 1E8, Canada *Fax:* 514-335-0165
SAVAC SA, Rue de Commerce ZI Forlen, 67400 Geispoldsheim, France *Fax:* 03 88 67 44 31 (France & Germany)
AcquaPortal Communications SRL, Via GB Morgagni 28, 20129 Milan, Italy *Tel:* (0734) 962589 *E-mail:* marcorosetti@acquaportal.it *Web Site:* www.neogea.it
ICA SA, Apdo de Correos 45, 35220 Linamar, Las Palmas, Spain *Fax:* 928714221
IMAZO AB, Torsgarden, 534 50 Vara, Sweden *Fax:* (0512) 12760
Rolf C Hagen (UK) Ltd, California Dr, Whitewood Industrial Estate, Castleford, W Yorks WF10 5QH, United Kingdom
Steven Simpson Books, 5 Hardingham Rd, Hingham, Norwich, Norfolk NR9 4LX, United Kingdom *Fax:* (01953) 850-471 *Web Site:* www.stevensimpsonbooks.com

Merit, *imprint of* Xenos Verlag

Merlin Verlag+
Gifkendorf 38, 21397 Vastorf
Tel: (04137) 7207 *Fax:* (04137) 7948
E-mail: info@merlin-verlag.de
Web Site: www.merlin-verlag.de
Key Personnel
Publishing Dir & Licenses: Andreas J Meyer
Publishing Dir, Licenses & Editor: Dr Katharina Eleonore Meyer
Media & Marketing: Andreas Schmitt
Founded: 1957
Subjects: Anthropology, Art, Biography, Memoirs, Drama, Theater, Fiction, Government, Political Science, LGBTQ, Literature, Literary Criticism, Essays, Nonfiction (General), Parapsychology, Philosophy, Poetry
ISBN Prefix(es): 978-3-87536; 978-3-926112
Number of titles published annually: 12 Print
Total Titles: 200 Print; 3 Audio
Associate Companies: Little Tiger Verlag GmbH, Poppenbuetteler Chausee 53, 22397 Hamburg
Distribution Center: AS Hoeller GmbH Verlagsservice, Schaldorferstr 16, 8641 St Marein im Muerztal, Austria *Fax:* (03865) 3888
Buch- und Medienvertriebs AG, Hochstr 357, 8200 Schaffhausen, Switzerland *Fax:* (052) 6435435

Verlag Merseburger Berlin GmbH+
Naumburgerstr 40, 34127 Kassel
Tel: (0561) 789809-11 *Fax:* (0561) 789809-16
E-mail: vertrieb@merseburger.de
Web Site: www.merseburger.de
Key Personnel
Dir: Renate Matthei
Founded: 1849
Subjects: Music
ISBN Prefix(es): 978-3-87537

Merve Verlag
Crellestr 22, 10827 Berlin
Tel: (030) 784 8433 *Fax:* (030) 788 1074
E-mail: merve@merve.de
Web Site: www.merve.de
Key Personnel
Chief Executive Officer: Tom Lamberty
Founded: 1970
Subjects: Architecture & Interior Design, Art, Government, Political Science, Literature, Literary Criticism, Essays, Music, Dance, Philosophy
ISBN Prefix(es): 978-3-88396; 978-3-920986

merz&solitude
Teckstr 58, 70190 Stuttgart
Tel: (0711) 26866-0 *Fax:* (0711) 26866-21
E-mail: info@merz-akademie.de; presse@merz-akademie.de
Web Site: www.merz-akademie.de
Key Personnel
Manager: Markus Merz *Tel:* (0711) 26866-20
  E-mail: markus.merz@merz-akademie.de
Project Manager: Birgit Haasen *Tel:* (0711)
  26866-47 *E-mail:* birgit.haasen@merz-akademie.de
Press: Dietmar Bosch *Tel:* (0711) 26866-77
Founded: 1989
Publish literary books, artists' books & catalogs
  by the Akademie Schloss Solitude fellows only.
Subjects: Architecture & Interior Design, Art,
  Communications, Drama, Theater, Fiction, Mu-
  sic, Dance, Nonfiction (General), Philosophy,
  Photography, Fine Arts
ISBN Prefix(es): 978-3-929085; 978-3-937158
Number of titles published annually: 10 Print
Total Titles: 120 Print
Distribution Center: Brockhaus/Commis-
  sion, Kreidlerstr 9, 70806 Kornwestheim
  Tel: (07154) 1327-37 *Fax:* (07154) 1327-13
  E-mail: merzundsolitude@brocom.de *Web
  Site:* www.brocom.de

Verlag fuer Messepublikationen, see Verlag fuer
Messepublikationen Thomas Neureuter GmbH

**Metropolis- Verlag fuer Oekonomie,
Gesellschaft und Politik GmbH**
Am Graben 2B, 35096 Marburg
Tel: (06421) 67377 *Fax:* (06421) 681918
E-mail: info@metropolis-verlag.de
Web Site: www.metropolis-verlag.de
Key Personnel
Chief Operating Officer: Hubert Hoffmann
  E-mail: hoffmann@metropolis-verlag.de
Founded: 1986
Subjects: Business, Economics, Environmental
  Studies, Government, Political Science, Philos-
  ophy, Social Sciences, Sociology
ISBN Prefix(es): 978-3-89518; 978-3-926570

Metropolitan Verlag+
Haus an der Eisemen Bruecke, 93042 Regensburg
Mailing Address: Postfach 10 10 53, 93010 Re-
  gensburg
Tel: (0941) 56 84-0 *Fax:* (0941) 56 84-111
E-mail: walhalla@walhalla.de
Web Site: www.walhalla.de/metropolitan
Key Personnel
Mng Dir: Bernard Roloff
Publishing Dir & Licenses: Eva-Maria Stecken-
  leiter
Founded: 1995
Also specializing in rights.
Subjects: Business, Economics, Law, Manage-
  ment
ISBN Prefix(es): 978-3-8029; 978-3-89623
Total Titles: 100 Print; 1 CD-ROM; 1 Online;
  200 E-Book; 20 Audio
Parent Company: Walhalla & Praetoria Verlag
  GmbH & Co KG

Helmut Metz Verlag
Hermann-Behn-Weg 1, 20146 Hamburg
Tel: (040) 279 32 50 *Fax:* (040) 279 81 14
E-mail: info@metz-verlag.com
Web Site: www.metz-verlag.com
Key Personnel
Editor: Helmut Metz
Press & Public Relations: Susanne Nacke
  E-mail: susanne.nacke@metz-verlag.com
Founded: 1995
Subjects: Social Sciences, Sociology, Travel &
  Tourism
ISBN Prefix(es): 978-3-927655

Peter W Metzler Verlag
Manteuffelstr 20, 47057 Duisburg
Tel: (0203) 2 98 29 25 *Fax:* (0203) 2 98 29 25
E-mail: info@metzler-verlag.de
Web Site: www.metzler-verlag.de
Key Personnel
Publisher: Peter W Metzler
Membership(s): Association of German Publishers
  & Booksellers.
Subjects: Government, Political Science, Chris-
  tianity, Contemporary History, Judaism
ISBN Prefix(es): 978-3-936283

Verlag Gisela Meussling+
Herzbergstr 5-7, 63571 Gelnhausen
Tel: (06196) 2048890 *Fax:* (06196) 2048891
E-mail: info@kollateral-verlag.de
Web Site: www.kollateral-verlag.de
Key Personnel
Mng Dir: Sabine Wegmann
Founded: 1978
Subjects: Anthropology, History, Philosophy,
  Physical Sciences, Women's Studies, Esoter-
  ics/New Age, Ethnology
ISBN Prefix(es): 978-3-922129
Parent Company: Kollateral Verlag UG
Distribution Center: Koch, Neff & Volck-
  mar GmbH, Industriestr 23, 70565 Stuttgart
  E-mail: kontakt@knv.de *Web Site:* www.knv.de
Libri GmbH, Friedensallee 273, 22763 Ham-
  burg *Tel:* (040) 853980 *Fax:* (040) 853987815
  E-mail: libri@libri.de *Web Site:* www.home.
  libri.de
Inter-Info-Buecherdienst, Muehlenstr 1, 4502 St
  Marien, Austria, Contact: Margit Steinwen-
  der *Tel:* (07227) 80188-0 *Fax:* (07227) 80188-
  77 *E-mail:* office@meinbuecherdienst.at *Web
  Site:* www.meinbuecherdienst.at
free energy®, Bahnhofstr 10, 5605 Dottikon,
  Switzerland *Tel:* (056) 616 90 00 *Fax:* (056)
  616 90 09 *E-mail:* info@freeenergy.ch *Web
  Site:* www.freeenergy.ch

Meyer & Meyer Verlag+
Von-Coels-Str 390, 52080 Aachen
Tel: (0241) 95810-0 *Fax:* (0241) 95810-10
E-mail: info@m-m-sports.com
Web Site: www.m-m-sports.com
Key Personnel
Publisher: Martin Meyer *E-mail:* martin.meyer@
  m-m-sports.com
Head, E-Publishing: Gregor Meisen *Tel:* (0241)
  95810-13 *E-mail:* gregor.meisen@m-m-sports.
  com
Head, Editorial: Andreas Mann *Tel:* (0241)
  95810-19 *E-mail:* andreas.mann@m-m-sports.
  com
Head, Sales: Kerstin Meyer *Tel:* (0241) 95810-25
  E-mail: kerstin.meyer@m-m-sports.com
Founded: 1984
Membership(s): World Sport Publishers' Associa-
  tion.
Subjects: Disability, Special Needs, Drama, The-
  ater, Health, Nutrition, Music, Dance, Nonfic-
  tion (General), Psychology, Psychiatry, Sports,
  Athletics, Travel & Tourism
ISBN Prefix(es): 978-3-89124; 978-3-89899; 978-
  3-8403
Number of titles published annually: 120 Print;
  120 E-Book
Total Titles: 1,500 Print; 1,500 E-Book
Foreign Rep(s): Adam Bookshop (Egypt); Car-
  dinal Publisher (Canada, USA); Caspian Book
  Service (Iran); CIEL-Book Distribution Com-
  pany (United Arab Emirates); CIEL-A Book
  Company (Lebanon); Peter Hyde Associates
  Pty Ltd (South Africa); Icon Books & Mul-
  timedia Pte Ltd (Southeast Asia); Magyar
  Sporttudomanyi Tarsasag (Hungary); Meyer
  & Meyer Sport UK (Europe, UK); Woodslane
  Pty Ltd (Australia, New Zealand)
Foreign Rights: John Midgley (worldwide)

Warehouse: Auslieferungszentrum Niederrhein,
  Hoogeweg 71, 47623 Kevelaer *Tel:* (02832)
  929290 *Fax:* (02832) 929211 *E-mail:* helga.
  behr@azn.de *Web Site:* www.azn.de
Distribution Center: Meyer & Meyer Verlag, c/o
  Einhard Verlag, Tempelhofer Str 21, 52068
  Aachen *Tel:* (0241) 16 85-0 *Fax:* (0241) 16
  85-253
Auslieferungszentrum Niederrhein, Hoogeweg
  71, 47623 Kevelaer, Contact: Daniela Daniels
  Tel: (02832) 929-293 *Fax:* (02832) 929-211
  E-mail: daniela.daniels@azn.de
Mohr Morawa Buchvertrieb GmbH, Sulzen-
  gasse 1, 1230 Vienna, Austria *Tel:* (01) 680
  14-0 *Fax:* (01) 688 71 30 *E-mail:* momo@
  mohrmorawa.at *Web Site:* www.mohrmorawa.at
Buchzentrum AG, Industriestr Ost 10, 4614 Hae-
  gendorf, Switzerland *Tel:* (062) 2 09 27 10
  Fax: (062) 2 09 27 88

Peter Meyer Verlag, see pmv Peter Meyer
Verlag

Meyers, *imprint of* Bibliographisches Institut
GmbH

Michaels Verlag & Vertrieb GmbH
Ammergauer Str 80, 86971 Peiting
Tel: (08861) 59018 *Fax:* (08861) 67091
E-mail: info@michaelsverlag.de
Web Site: www.michaelsverlag.de
Key Personnel
Mng Dir: Petra Otto
Subjects: Health, Nutrition, Inspirational, Spiritu-
  ality, Literature, Literary Criticism, Essays
ISBN Prefix(es): 978-3-89539; 978-3-925051
Distribution Center: Dr Franz Hain Verlagsaus-
  lieferung GmbH, Dr-Otto-Neurath-Gasse 5,
  1220 Vienna, Austria *Tel:* (01) 2826565-77
  Fax: (01) 2825282 *E-mail:* bestell@hain.at
Buchzentrum AG, Industriestr Ost 10, 4614
  Haegendorf, Switzerland *Tel:* (062) 2092525
  Fax: (062) 2092627 *E-mail:* kundendienst@
  buchzentrum.ch

Michason & May Verlagsgesellschaft UG
Niddastr 64, 60329 Frankfurt am Main
Tel: (069) 34 87 80 63 *Fax:* (0551) 41 392
E-mail: michason.de; sales@michason.de
Web Site: www.michasonundmay.de
Key Personnel
Chief Executive Officer: Peter Koebel, MA
Founded: 2010
Subjects: Criminology, Fiction, Mysteries, Sus-
  pense, Nonfiction (General), Pop Culture, Ro-
  mance, Anthology
ISBN Prefix(es): 978-3-86286
Distribution Center: GVA Goettingen
  GmbH, Postfach 2021, 37010 Goettin-
  gen *Tel:* (0551) 487177 *Fax:* (0551) 41392
  E-mail: bestellung@gva-verlage.de

MICHEL/Schwaneberger Verlag, see
Schwaneberger Verlag GmbH

Mildenberger Verlag GmbH
Im Lehbuehl 6, 77652 Offenburg
Tel: (0781) 9170-0 *Fax:* (0781) 9170-50
E-mail: info@mildenberger-verlag.de
Web Site: www.mildenberger-verlag.de
Key Personnel
Mng Dir: Frank Mildenberger
Subjects: Art, Music, Dance, Religion - Other,
  Self-Help, Sports, Athletics
ISBN Prefix(es): 978-3-619; 978-3-8140

Militzke Verlag GmbH
Huttenstr 5, 04249 Leipzig
Tel: (0341) 42643-0; (0341) 42643-11 (customer
  service); (0341) 42643-10 (press) *Fax:* (0341)
  42643-99; (0341) 42643-26 (press)

E-mail: info@militzke.de; kundenbetreuung@
militzke.de (customer service); press@militzke.
de
Web Site: www.militzke.de
Key Personnel
Owner: Annetta Militzke
Editorial, Press & Licensing: Julia Loessl
   E-mail: j.loessl@militzke.de
Press & Public Relations: Friederike Grigoleit
Sales: Melitta Siebert *Tel:* (0341) 42643-12
   E-mail: m.siebert@militzke.de
Founded: 1990
Publication of textbooks & special interest hard-
covers.
Membership(s): Association of Publishers &
   Bookshops; German Publishers & Booksellers
   Association.
Subjects: Biography, Memoirs, Government, Po-
   litical Science, Authentic Criminal Cases, De-
   tective Novels, Historical & Political Popular
   Science, Special Interest
ISBN Prefix(es): 978-3-86189
Number of titles published annually: 50 Print; 2
   CD-ROM; 8 Online; 3 E-Book
Total Titles: 700 Print
Foreign Rep(s): Dessaur (Claudia Gyr & Stefan
   Reiss) (Switzerland); Verlagsagentur Neuhold
   (Erich Neuhold & Wilhelm Platzer) (Austria,
   South Tyrol, Italy)
Distribution Center: Leipziger Kommissions- und
   Grossbuchhandelsgesellschaft mbH (LKG),
   An der Suedspitze 1-12, 04571 Roetha, Con-
   tact: Baerbel Jaecklin *Tel:* (034206) 65-120
   Fax: (034206) 65-1758 *E-mail:* bjaecklin@lkg-
   service.de *Web Site:* www.lkg-va.de
Dr Franz Hain Verlagsauslieferungen GmbH, Dr-
   Otto-Neurath-Gasse 5, 1220 Vienna, Austria
   Tel: (01) 2 82 65 65-77 *Fax:* (01) 2 82 52 82
   E-mail: bestell@hain.at
Buchzentrum AG, Industriestr Ost 10, 4614 Hae-
   gendorf, Switzerland *Tel:* (062) 2 09 25 25
   Fax: (062) 2 09 26 27 *E-mail:* boesigera@
   buchzentrum.ch

Minedition, *imprint of* Michael Neugebauer
   Edition GmbH

**Minerva Buch- und Zeitschriftenvertrieb
   Preuss+**
Eisenberger Str 23, Rheinland-Pfalz, 67304
   Kerzenheim
Tel: (06351) 41000 *Fax:* (06351) 41002
E-mail: minerva-kerzenheim@t-online.de
Key Personnel
President: Martin M Preuss
Founded: 1987
STM books on health & psychology.
Subjects: Health, Nutrition, Psychology, Psychia-
   try
ISBN Prefix(es): 978-3-936611
Total Titles: 32 Print; 1 CD-ROM; 3 Audio
Bookshop(s): Akademische Buchhandlung Woet-
   zel *Tel:* (06359) 924726 *Fax:* (06359) 924723

**Edition Minerva Der Kunsthandel Verlag
   GmbH**
Hermannstr 54-56, 63263 Neu-Isenburg
Tel: (06102) 88256-21 *Fax:* (06102) 88256-19
E-mail: info@edminerva.de
Web Site: www.edminerva.de
Key Personnel
Mng Dir: Manfred Moeller
Publishing Dir: Elisabeth Roosens
Specialize in art & cultural history.
Subjects: Architecture & Interior Design, Art,
   Crafts, Games, Hobbies, History
ISBN Prefix(es): 978-3-938832; 978-3-932353

Missio eV+
Goethestr 43, 52064 Aachen
Tel: (0241) 75 07-00 *Fax:* (0241) 75 07-335
E-mail: post@missio.de

Web Site: www.missio.de; www.missio-hilft.de
Key Personnel
President: Dr Klaus Kraemer
Vice President: Dr Gregor von Fuerstenberg
Subjects: Art, Developing Countries, Religion -
   Catholic, Religion - Other
ISBN Prefix(es): 978-3-930556
Bookshop(s): Missio am Dom, Muensterplatz,
   52064 Aachen
Warehouse: Industriestr 12, 52146 Wuerselen

mitp Verlags GmbH & Co KG+
Division of Verlagsgruppe Huethig Jehle Rehm
   GmbH
Augustinusstr 9a, 50226 Frechen
Tel: (02234) 21901-0 *Fax:* (02234) 21901-88
E-mail: info@mitp.de
Web Site: www.mitp.de
Key Personnel
Mng Dir: Steffen Dralle
Founded: 1992
Subjects: Business, Computer Science, Marketing,
   Photography
ISBN Prefix(es): 978-3-8266
Subsidiaries: Datacom; ITP - IWT; Wolframs

**Mitteilungsblatt der Verbandes deds
   bayerischen Druckincleestrie eV,** *imprint of*
   FMG Fachverlag fuer Druck und Medien
   GmbH

Verlag E S Mittler & Sohn GmbH & Co KG+
Georgsplatz 1, 20099 Hamburg
Tel: (040) 707080-01 *Fax:* (040) 707080-304
E-mail: vertrieb@koehler-mittler.de
Web Site: www.koehler-mittler.de
Key Personnel
Mng Dir: Fritz-Hermann Baete *Tel:* (040)
   707080-321 *E-mail:* f-h_baete@koehler-mittler.
   de; Thomas Bantle *Tel:* (040) 707080-201
   E-mail: t_bantle@koehler-mittler.de
Marketing & Sales: Susanne Duerr *Tel:* (040)
   707080-323 *Fax:* (040) 707080-324
Press: Katharina Klockow *Tel:* (040) 707080-320
   E-mail: kk@koehler-mittler.de
Founded: 1789
Subjects: Aeronautics, Aviation, Government,
   Political Science, History, Literature, Literary
   Criticism, Essays, Maritime, Military Science,
   Philosophy, Securities
ISBN Prefix(es): 978-3-87547; 978-3-8132
Associate Companies: Koehler Verlagsgesellschaft
   mbH; Maximilian Verlag GmbH & Co KG

Mittler Report Verlag GmbH
Subsidiary of Maximilian Verlag GmbH & Co
   KG
Hochkreuzallee 1, 53175 Bonn/Bad-Godesburg
Tel: (0228) 30789-0 *Fax:* (0228) 30789-15
E-mail: info@mittler-report.de
Web Site: www.report-verlag.de; www.mittler-
   report.de
Key Personnel
Mng Dir: Fritz-Hermann Baete; Dr Peter Boss-
   dorf
Marketing Dir: Juergen Hensel
Publish materials in the areas of security & de-
   fense policy, armed forces, defense technology
   & national security.
Subjects: Technology, Defense, Security
ISBN Prefix(es): 978-3-932385; 978-3-9802828;
   978-3-9803804

Mixtvision Verlag
Puendterplatz 4, 80803 Munich
Mailing Address: Postfach 44 05 65, 80754 Mu-
   nich
Tel: (089) 383 77 09-0 *Fax:* (089) 383 77 09-20
E-mail: info@mixtvision.de
Web Site: www.mixtvision-verlag.de

Key Personnel
Publisher: Sebastian Zembol
Foreign Rights: Kerstin Kempf *Tel:* (089) 383 77
   09-12 *E-mail:* kk@mixtvision.de
Press: Carolin Brandl *Tel:* (089) 383 77 09-14
   E-mail: cb@mixtvision.de
Founded: 2005
ISBN Prefix(es): 978-3-939435
Foreign Rep(s): Elisabeth Anintah-Hirt (Austria)
Distribution Center: Medien Service Runge
   GmbH (MSR), Bergstr 2, 33803 Steinhagen,
   Contact: Britta Hoehn *Tel:* (05204) 998 445
   E-mail: b.hoehn@rungeva.de
Medienlogistik Pichler OEBZ GmbH & Co
   KG, IZ NOE Sued, Str 1, Objekt 34, 2355
   Wiener Neudor, Austria, Contact: Eva Prinz
   Tel: (02236) 635 352 45 *Fax:* (02236) 635 352
   71 *E-mail:* mlo@medien-logistik.at

ML Verlag+
E-C-Baumann-Str 545, 95326 Kulmbach
Tel: (09221) 949-208 *Fax:* (09221) 949-398
E-mail: vertrieb@mlverlag.de
Web Site: www.ml-buchverlag.de
Key Personnel
Mng Dir & Head, Publishing: Bernd Mueller
   E-mail: b.mueller@mg-oberfranken.de
Mng Dir: Walter Schweinsberg
Sales: Annika Hoffman *Tel:* (09221) 949-204
   Fax: (09221) 949-377 *E-mail:* a.hoffman@
   mg-oberfranken.de; Simone Sesselmann
   Tel: (09221) 949-311 *Fax:* (09221) 949-377
   E-mail: s.sesselmann@mg-oberfranken.de
Founded: 1957
Subjects: Alternative, Cookery, Health, Nutrition,
   Medicine, Nursing, Dentistry, Sports, Athletics
ISBN Prefix(es): 978-3-88136; 978-3-944002
Parent Company: Mediengruppe Oberfranken-
   Fachverlage GmbH & Co KG

Moby Dick Verlag GmbH+
Sickerwall 21, 33602 Bielefeld
Tel: (0521) 55 90 *Fax:* (0521) 55 98 81 14
E-mail: info@delius-klasing.de
Web Site: www.delius-klasing.de
Key Personnel
Publisher: Konrad Delius
Editor: Klaus Bartelt
Foreign Rights: Verena Iding *Tel:* (0521) 559
   207; Anita Keane *Tel:* (0521) 559 206; Petra
   Troeltzsch *Tel:* (0521) 559 202
Subjects: Automotive, Crafts, Games, Hobbies,
   Outdoor Recreation, Sports, Athletics, Technol-
   ogy, Transportation, Travel & Tourism
ISBN Prefix(es): 978-3-7688
Number of titles published annually: 25 Print
Parent Company: Delius Klasing Verlag GmbH

mode...information GmbH
Pilgerstr 20, 51491 Overath
Tel: (02206) 6007-0; (02206) 6007-770 (sales)
   Fax: (02206) 6007-17; (02206) 6007-90 (sales)
E-mail: info@modeinfo.com; service@modeinfo.
   com (sales)
Web Site: www.modeinfo.com
Key Personnel
Mng Dir: Yann Menard *E-mail:* ymenard@
   modeinfo.com; Dr Jens Schumacher
Product Manager: Marcus Berge *Tel:* (02206)
   6007-46 *Fax:* (02206) 6007-71
   E-mail: mberge@modeinfo.com
Sales: Christian Grosse *Tel:* (08223) 961902
   Fax: (08223) 961903 *E-mail:* cgrosse@
   modeinfo.com
Founded: 1957
Specialize in fashion design & trend information.
Subjects: Architecture & Interior Design, Art,
   Fashion, Management, Marketing
Branch Office(s)
mode...information SAS, 52, rue Croix des Petits
   Champs, 75001 Paris, France *Tel:* 01 40 13 81

50 *Fax:* 01 45 08 45 77 *E-mail:* mtorregrossa@
modeinfo.com
mode...information Ltd, Eastgate House, 1st
floor, 16-19 Eastcastle St, London W1W
8DA, United Kingdom *Tel:* (020) 7436 0133
Fax: (020) 7436 0277 *E-mail:* uksales@
modeinfo.com
Shipping Address: Suelztalstr 23, 51491 Overath-
Obersteeg *Tel:* (02206) 6007-141 *Fax:* (02206)
6007-148

Modellsport Verlag GmbH (MSV)+
Schulstr 12, 76532 Baden-Baden
Tel: (07221) 9521-0 *Fax:* (07221) 9521-45
E-mail: info@msv-medien.de
Web Site: www.modellsport.de
Key Personnel
Mng Dir: Hans Rost
Founded: 1977
ISBN Prefix(es): 978-3-923142

Verlag Moderne Industrie GmbH+
Justus-von-Liebig-Str 1, 86899 Landsberg
Tel: (08191) 125-0 *Fax:* (08191) 125-304
E-mail: info@mi-verlag.de
Web Site: www.mi-verlag.de
Key Personnel
Mng Dir: Fabian Mueller
Publishing Manager: Stefan Waldeisen
Founded: 1952
Also publishes loose-leaf editions.
Membership(s): EBP-Network.
Subjects: Advertising, Automotive, Business, Ca-
reer Development, Communications, Computer
Science, Economics, Energy, Management,
Marketing, Technology, Investment, Money,
Success Stories
ISBN Prefix(es): 978-3-478; 978-3-87957; 978-3-
920716; 978-3-87959
Associate Companies: mvg Verlag *Fax:* (089)
548 52-84 21 *E-mail:* info@mvg-verlag.de (ca-
reer development, communications, motivation
& self-help); Verlag Moderne Industrie Buch
AG & Co KG, Koenigswintererstr 418, 53227
Bonn *Tel:* (0228) 97024 41 *Fax:* (0228) 97024
21 *E-mail:* info@vmi-buch.de

Verlag fuer moderne Kunst Nuernberg GmbH
Koenigstr 73, 90402 Nuremberg
Tel: (0911) 23 73 100 0 *Fax:* (0911) 23 73 100
99
E-mail: verlag@moderne-kunst.org
Web Site: www.vfmk.de
Key Personnel
Mng Dir: Dr Karl Gerhard Schmidt
Publishing Dir: Martina Buder *Tel:* (0911) 23 73
100 12
Press: Marion Voigt *Tel:* (0911) 23 73 100 11
E-mail: voigt@moderne-kunst.org
Sales: Johann Zenger *Tel:* (0911) 23 73 100 13
E-mail: zenger@moderne-kunst.org
Subjects: Art, Contemporary Art
ISBN Prefix(es): 978-3-922531; 978-3-928342;
978-3-933096; 978-3-936711; 978-3-938821;
978-3-9800260; 978-3-939738; 978-3-941185;
978-3-940748
Foreign Rep(s): Bookport Associates (Cyprus,
Greece, Italy, Portugal, Spain); Berend Bosch
(Belgium); Josef Kolar (Eastern Europe);
Anselm Robinson (France); Verlagsvertretungen
Stefan Schempp (Austria, Southern Germany);
Markus Wieser (Switzerland)
Distribution Center: Leipziger Kommissions-
und Grossbuchhandelsgesellschaft mbH
(LKG), An der Suedspitze 1-12, 04571 Roetha
Tel: (034206) 65107 *Fax:* (034206) 651732
E-mail: ekaiser@lkg-service.de *Web Site:* www.
lkg-va.de (Europe exc Great Britain & Switzer-
land)
Inspirees International BV, Adama van Schel-
temaplein 86, 2524 PJ Delft, Netherlands

Tel: (015) 8795501 *Fax:* (015) 8795501
E-mail: info@inspirees.com (China)
AVA Verlagsauslieferung AG, Centralweg
16, 8910 Affoltern am Albis, Switzerland
Tel: (044) 7624260 *Fax:* (044) 7624210
E-mail: avainfo@ava.ch
Cornerhouse Publications, 70 Oxford St,
Manchester M15 NH, United Kingdom
Tel: (0161) 2001503 *Fax:* (0161) 2001504
E-mail: publications@cornerhouse.org
Artbook/DAP, 155 Sixth Ave, 2nd floor, New
York, NY 10013, United States *Tel:* 212-627-
1999 *Fax:* 212-627-9484 *E-mail:* eleshowitz@
dapinc.com (worldwide)

**Verlag Modernes Lernen Borgmann GmbH &
Co KG**
Schleefstr 14, 44287 Dortmund
Tel: (0231) 12 80 08; (0180) 534 01 30
Fax: (0231) 12 56 40; (0180) 534 01 20
E-mail: info@verlag-modernes-lernen.de
Web Site: www.verlag-modernes-lernen.de
Key Personnel
Mng Dir: Dieter Borgmann
Focus on early development & child education.
Subjects: Child Care & Development, Psychol-
ogy, Psychiatry
ISBN Prefix(es): 978-3-8080

modo Verlag GmbH
Terlaner Str 8, 79111 Freiburg im Breisgau
Tel: (0761) 44 999 *Fax:* (0761) 44 969
E-mail: info@modoverlag.de
Web Site: www.modoverlag.de
Key Personnel
Mng Dir: Dieter Weber
Founded: 1997
Specialize in artist monographs, exhibition cat-
alogs, reference books on contemporary art,
photography, architecture & design.
Subjects: Architecture & Interior Design, Art,
Literature, Literary Criticism, Essays, Photog-
raphy, Contemporary Art, Late 20th Century
Art
ISBN Prefix(es): 978-3-922675; 978-3-937014;
978-3-86833
Number of titles published annually: 20 Print
Total Titles: 140 Print

Moeck Musikinstrumente + Verlag
Lueckenweg 4, 29227 Celle
Mailing Address: Postfach 3131, 29231 Celle
Tel: (05141) 8853-0 *Fax:* (05141) 8853-42
E-mail: info@moeck.com
Web Site: www.moeck.com
Key Personnel
Owner: Sabine Hasse-Moeck
Founded: 1930
Subjects: Music, Dance
ISBN Prefix(es): 978-3-87549

Karl Heinrich Moeseler Verlag+
Hoffmann-von-Fallersleben-Str 8, 38304 Wolfen-
buettel
Tel: (05331) 9597-0 *Fax:* (05331) 9597-20
E-mail: info@moeseler-verlag.de
Web Site: www.moeseler-verlag.de
Key Personnel
Owner: Jutta Moeseler
Founded: 1949
Subjects: Music, Dance
ISBN Prefix(es): 978-3-7877

Moewig, *imprint of* Pabel-Moewig Verlag GmbH

Mohr Siebeck GmbH & Co KG+
Wilhelmstr 18, 72074 Tuebingen
Mailing Address: Postfach 2040, 72010 Tuebin-
gen
Tel: (07071) 923-0 *Fax:* (07071) 51104
E-mail: info@mohr.de

Web Site: www.mohr.de
Key Personnel
Owner: Georg Siebeck *Tel:* (07071) 923-32
Fax: (07071) 923-67 *E-mail:* siebeck@mohr.de
Mng Dir/Editorial Dir, Law: Dr Franz-Peter Gillig
Tel: (07071) 923-50 *Fax:* (07071) 923-67
E-mail: franz-peter.gillig@mohr.de
Mng Dir/Editorial Dir, Theology: Dr Henning
Ziebritzki *Tel:* (07071) 923-59 *E-mail:* henning.
ziebritzki@mohr.de
Head, Marketing & Sales: Katharina Stich-
ling *Tel:* (07071) 923-56 *E-mail:* katharina.
stichling@mohr.de
Editor, History, Philosophy & Social Sciences: Dr
Stephanie Warnke-De Nobili *Tel:* (07071) 923-
63 *E-mail:* stephanie.warnke@mohr.de
Production: Jana Trispel *Tel:* (07071) 923-34
E-mail: trispel@mohr.de
Rights & Permissions: Elizabeth Wener
Tel: (07071) 923-61 *E-mail:* elizabeth.wener@
mohr.de
Founded: 1801
Academic books & journals, encyclopedias,
historical-critical editions & monographs.
Subjects: Economics, History, Law, Philosophy,
Religion - Protestant, Religion - Other, Social
Sciences, Sociology, Theology, Judaism
ISBN Prefix(es): 978-3-16
Number of titles published annually: 320 Print;
100 E-Book
Total Titles: 4,800 Print; 1 CD-ROM; 600 E-
Book
Warehouse: Christophstr 32, 72072 Tuebingen

Monastica, *imprint of* Beuroner Kunstverlag

Monia Verlag+
Postfach 2120, 66929 Pirmasens
Tel: (06331) 41425 *Fax:* (06331) 41425
Founded: 1971
Novels & bilingual poetry for adults.
Subjects: Biography, Memoirs, Fiction, Literature,
Literary Criticism, Essays, Poetry
ISBN Prefix(es): 978-3-926753; 978-3-9800383

Moritz Verlag GmbH+
Kantstr 12, 60316 Frankfurt am Main
Tel: (069) 430 5084 *Fax:* (069) 430 5083
E-mail: info@moritzverlag.de
Web Site: www.moritzverlag.de
Key Personnel
Mng Dir: Jean Delas; Jean-Luis Fabre
Publishing Dir: Markus Weber
Founded: 1994
Focus on children's books.
ISBN Prefix(es): 978-3-89565
Number of titles published annually: 10 Print
Total Titles: 85 Print
Parent Company: l'ecole des loisirs, Paris, France
Foreign Rep(s): Guenther Raunjak (Austria); Gio-
vanni Ravasio Verlagsvertretungen (Switzer-
land); Guenter Thiel (Austria)
Warehouse: Beltz, Herrmann & Co, Tilsiter Str
17, 69502 Hemsbach
Orders to: Rhenus Medien Logistik GmbH
& Co KG, Justus-von-Liebig-Str 1, 86899
Landsberg am Lech *Tel:* (08191) 9 70 00 622
E-mail: beltz@de.rhenus.com

Morsak Verlag GmbH+
Wittelsbacherstr 2-8, 94481 Grafenau
Tel: (08552) 4200 *Fax:* (08552) 42050
E-mail: info@morsak.de
Web Site: www.morsak.de
Key Personnel
Mng Dir: Stefanie Friedl
Founded: 1884
Membership(s): Boersenverein des Deutschen
Buchhandels eV.
Subjects: Regional Interests
ISBN Prefix(es): 978-3-87553; 978-3-86512

Verlag A Morstadt
Kinzigstr 25, 77694 Kehl am Rhein
Tel: (07851) 2424 *Fax:* (07851) 76494
E-mail: info@morstadt-verlag.de
Web Site: www.morstadt-verlag.de
Key Personnel
Owner: Michael Foshag
Founded: 1858
Subjects: Biography, Memoirs, History, Travel &
   Tourism
ISBN Prefix(es): 978-3-88571

Morus-Verlag GmbH
Chausseestr 128-129, 10115 Berlin
Tel: (030) 2 84 86-0; (030) 2 84 86 111
   Fax: (030) 75 70 81 12
E-mail: bestellung-morusverlag@web.de
Web Site: www.morusverlag.de
Key Personnel
Management: Dr Reimar Witzer
Founded: 1945
Subjects: Religion - Catholic, Religion - Other
ISBN Prefix(es): 978-3-87554

Mosaik, *imprint of* Verlagsgruppe Random House
Bertelsmann

moser verlag GmbH
Widenmayerstr 16, 80538 Munich
Tel: (089) 290015-29 *Fax:* (089) 290015-15
E-mail: info@moser-verlag.com
Web Site: www.moser-verlag.com
Key Personnel
Mng Dir: Ilse Moser
Subjects: Art, Mysteries, Suspense, Photography
ISBN Prefix(es): 978-3-9814177; 978-3-9812344

moses. Verlag GmbH
Arnoldstr 13d, 47906 Kempen
Tel: (02152) 209850 *Fax:* (02152) 209860
E-mail: info@moses-verlag.de
Web Site: www.moses-verlag.de
Key Personnel
Publisher: Gerd Herterich *Tel:* (02152) 209855
   E-mail: herterich@moses-verlag.de
Foreign Rights Manager: Nina Sadler
   Tel: (02152) 2098570 *E-mail:* sadler@moses-
   verlag.de
Sales Manager: Till Zander *Tel:* (02152) 209852
   E-mail: zander@moses-verlag.de
Foreign Rights: Julia Boesing *Tel:* (02152)
   209851 *E-mail:* boesing@moses-verlag.de
Press: Friederike Wehse *Tel:* (02152) 209853
   E-mail: wehse@moses-verlag.de
Subjects: Crafts, Games, Hobbies, Mysteries, Sus-
   pense, Science Fiction, Fantasy
ISBN Prefix(es): 978-3-89777; 978-3-929130
Foreign Rep(s): Claudia Gyr (Switzerland);
   Gertrud Haslwanter (Western Austria); Stefan
   Stoehr (Eastern Austria)
Distribution Center: Leipziger Kommissions- und
   Grossbuchhandelsgesellschaft mbH (LKG),
   An der Suedspitze 1-12, 04571 Roetha, Con-
   tact: Kerstin Hofmann *Tel:* (034206) 65 170
   Fax: (034206) 65 1744 *E-mail:* khofmann@
   lkg-service.de *Web Site:* www.lkg-va.de
Engros Buchhandlung Dessauer, Raeffelstr 32,
   8036 Zurich, Switzerland, Contact: Claudia
   Gyr *Tel:* (01) 4 66 96 66 *Fax:* (01) 4 66 96 69
   E-mail: dessauer@dessauer.ch

Motorbuch-Verlag+
Division of Paul Pietsch Verlage GmbH & Co
   KG
Olgastr 86, 70180 Stuttgart
Tel: (0711) 2 10 80-0 *Fax:* (0711) 2 36 04 15
E-mail: ppv@motorbuch.de
Web Site: www.motorbuch.de
Key Personnel
Publisher: Dr Patricia Scholten *Tel:* (0711) 2 10
   80-11

Head, Sales: Christian Pflug *Tel:* (0711) 2 10 80-
   20 *E-mail:* c.pflug@motorbuch.de
Program Manager: Joachim Kuch *Tel:* (0711) 2
   10 80-18 *E-mail:* j.kuch@motorbuch.de
Press & Public Relations: Clarissa Bayer
   Tel: (0711) 2 10 80-12 *E-mail:* c.bayer@
   motorbuch.de
Production: Bernd Leu *Tel:* (0711) 2 10 80-49
   E-mail: b.leu@motorbuch.de
Rights & Permissions: Patricia Hofmann
   Tel: (0711) 2 10 80-13 *E-mail:* p.hofmann@
   motorbuch.de
Founded: 1962
Subjects: Aeronautics, Aviation, Automotive, His-
   tory, Military Science, Nonfiction (General)
ISBN Prefix(es): 978-3-87943
Orders to: Koch, Neff & Oetinger Verlagsaus-
   lieferung GmbH, Industriestr 23, 70565
   Stuttgart

mox & maritz+
Postfach 101021, 28010 Bremen
Tel: (0421) 7943226 *Fax:* (0421) 7943226
E-mail: info@moxundmaritz.de
Web Site: www.moxundmaritz.de
Key Personnel
Contact: Stefan Ehlert
Founded: 1997
Subjects: Biography, Memoirs, Literature, Liter-
   ary Criticism, Essays
ISBN Prefix(es): 978-3-934790
Number of titles published annually: 2 Print
Total Titles: 6 Print

MSV, see Modellsport Verlag GmbH (MSV)

C F Mueller Verlag+
Division of Verlagsgruppe Huethig Jehle Rehm
   GmbH
Im Weiher 10, 69121 Heidelberg
Mailing Address: Postfach 10 28 69, 69018 Hei-
   delberg
Tel: (06221) 489-0 *Toll Free Tel:* 800-2183-333
   Fax: (06221) 489-279
E-mail: info@hjr-verlag.de
Web Site: www.hjr-verlag.de/marken/c-f-mueller
Founded: 1797
Specialize in legal education, practice & research.
Subjects: Law, Business Law, Criminal Law,
   Family Care Law, Health Care Law, Tax Law
ISBN Prefix(es): 978-3-7880; 978-3-8114
Number of titles published annually: 16 Print

Michael Mueller Verlag GmbH
Gerberei 19, 91054 Erlangen
Mailing Address: Postfach 2609, 91014 Erlangen
Tel: (09131) 81 28 08-0 *Fax:* (09131) 81 28 08-
   60
E-mail: info@michael-mueller-verlag.de
Web Site: www.michael-mueller-verlag.de
Key Personnel
Publisher: Michael Mueller *Tel:* (09131) 81 28
   08-23 *E-mail:* mm@michael-mueller-verlag.de
Subjects: Travel & Tourism
ISBN Prefix(es): 978-3-932410; 978-3-89953
Distributed by Travel House Media GmbH
Distribution Center: Koch, Neff & Oetinger
   Verlagsauslieferung GmbH, Industriestr 23,
   70565 Stuttgart, Contact: Matthias Juergens
   E-mail: travel-house-media@kno-va.de
Freytag & Berndt u Artaria KG, Industriestr 10,
   2120 Wolkersdorf, Austria *Tel:* (01) 869 90 90
   Fax: (01) 88 90 855
Schweizer Buchzentrum AG, Industriestr Ost 10,
   4614 Haegendorf, Switzerland *Tel:* (062) 2 09
   26 26 *Fax:* (062) 2 09 26 27
Verkauf Schweiz, Verenastr 8, 8832 Wollerau,
   Switzerland, Contact: Joe Fuchs *Tel:* (044) 7
   84 79 82 *Fax:* (044) 7 84 53 67 *E-mail:* joe.
   fuchs@mythen.ch

Mueller Rueschlikon Verlags AG+
Division of Paul Pietsch Verlage GmbH & Co
   KG
Olgastr 86, 70180 Stuttgart
Tel: (0711) 2 10 80-0 *Fax:* (0711) 2 36 04 15
E-mail: ppv@motorbuch.de
Web Site: www.mueller-rueschlikon-verlag.de
Key Personnel
Publisher: Dr Patricia Scholten *Tel:* (0711) 2 10
   80-11
Head, Media & Public Relations: Clarissa Bayer
   Tel: (0711) 2 10 80-40 *E-mail:* c.bayer@
   motorbuch.de
Head, Sales: Christian Pflug *Tel:* (0711) 2 10 80-
   20 *E-mail:* c.pflug@motorbuch.de
Program Dir: Claudia Koenig *Tel:* (0711) 2 10
   80-72 *E-mail:* c.koenig@motorbuch.de
Production: Bernd Leu *Tel:* (0711) 2 10 80-49
   E-mail: b.leu@motorbuch.de
Rights & Permissions: Patricia Hofmann
   Tel: (0711) 2 10 80-13 *E-mail:* p.hofmann@
   motorbuch.de
Founded: 1938
Subjects: Animals, Pets, Cookery, Crafts, Games,
   Hobbies, Fiction, How-to, Outdoor Recreation,
   Wine & Spirits, Diving, Dogs, Fishing, Horses
ISBN Prefix(es): 978-3-275

Verlag Mueller und Schindler
Innstr 7 D, 84359 Simbach am Inn
Tel: (08571) 926129 *Fax:* (08571) 8533
E-mail: info@muellerundschindler.de
Web Site: www.muellerundschindler.de
Key Personnel
Owner: Rolf Mueller
Founded: 1965
Subjects: Art, History, Religion - Other
ISBN Prefix(es): 978-3-87560

Verlag Mueller und Steinicke KG
Aidenbachstr 78, 81379 Munich
Tel: (089) 74 99 156 *Fax:* (089) 74 99 157
E-mail: info@mueller-und-steinicke.de
Web Site: www.mueller-und-steinicke.de
Key Personnel
Publisher: Irmgard Gissler
Management: Carol Gissler
Sales: Stefan Mueller Gissler
Founded: 1903
Subjects: Alternative, Medicine, Nursing, Den-
   tistry, Alternative Medicine, Homeopathy,
   Naturopathy, Traditional Chinese Medicine
ISBN Prefix(es): 978-3-87569

Muensterschwarzacher Kleinschriften, *imprint
of* Vier-Tuerme-GmbH-Klosterbetriebe

Muensterschwarzacher Studien, *imprint of*
Vier-Tuerme-GmbH-Klosterbetriebe

Muenzen & Sammeln, *imprint of* Battenberg
Gietl Verlag GmbH

MuenzenRevue, *imprint of* Battenberg Gietl
Verlag GmbH

Mundo Marketing GmbH
Vorgebirgstr 59, 50677 Cologne
Tel: (0221) 92 16 35-0 *Fax:* (0221) 92 16 35-24
E-mail: info@mundo-marketing.de; kontakt@
   mundo-marketing.de
Web Site: www.mundo-marketing.de; www.
   mundo-text.de; www.mundo-akademie.de;
   www.mundo-presse.de
Key Personnel
Mng Dir: Ertay Hayit *E-mail:* ertay.hayit@
   mundo-marketing.de
Editorial: Cornelia Auschra *Tel:* (0221) 921635-
   13 *E-mail:* auschra@mundo-marketing.de;
   Ute Hayit *Tel:* (0221) 921635-11 *E-mail:* ute.
   hayit@mundo-marketing.de
Founded: 1989

Helps business to gain visibility in the media by
providing travel & leisure editorial services.
Subjects: Travel & Tourism
ISBN Prefix(es): 978-3-87322

Munzinger-Archiv GmbH+
Albersfelderstr 34, 88213 Ravensburg
Tel: (0751) 7 69 31-0 *Fax:* (0751) 65 24 24
E-mail: box@munzinger.de
Web Site: www.munzinger.de
Key Personnel
Mng Dir: Ernst Munzinger
Founded: 1913
Subjects: Biography, Memoirs, Economics, Film,
Video, Foreign Countries, Government, Polit-
ical Science, History, Music, Dance, Pop Cul-
ture, Sports, Athletics

Murmann Verlag GmbH
Miramar-Haus, Schopenstehl 15, 20095 Hamburg
Tel: (040) 398 083-0 *Fax:* (040) 398 083-10
E-mail: info@murmann-publishers.de
Web Site: www.murmann-verlag.de
Key Personnel
Mng Dir: Dr Sven Murmann
Press: Maria Reiser *Tel:* (040) 398 083-24
E-mail: reiser@murmann-publishers.de
Subjects: Biography, Memoirs, Economics, Fi-
nance, Government, Political Science, Manage-
ment, Social Sciences, Sociology
ISBN Prefix(es): 978-3-938017
Associate Companies: Osburg Verlag GmbH;
Wachholtz Verlag GmbH
Foreign Rep(s): Buchzentrum AG (Cornelia
Frese) (Switzerland); Michael Orou (Austria);
Guenter Thiel (Austria)
Distribution Center: Leipziger Kommissions- und
Grossbuchhandelsgesellschaft mbH (LKG),
An der Suedspitze 1-12, 04571 Roetha, Con-
tact: Ursula Fritzsche *Tel:* (042) 06-65-135
Fax: (042) 06-65-130 *E-mail:* ufritzsche@lkg-
service.de *Web Site:* www.lkg-va.de
Mohr Morawa Buchvertrieb GmbH, Sulzen-
gasse 2, 1230 Vienna, Austria *Tel:* (01) 680
14-0 *Fax:* (01) 688 71 30 *E-mail:* momo@
mohrmorawa.at *Web Site:* www.mohrmorawa.at
Buchzentrum AG, Industriestr Ost 10, 4614 Haegendorf, Switzerland, Contact: Basil Dembin-
ski *Tel:* (062) 209 27 45 *Fax:* (062) 209 27 88
E-mail: dembinski@buchzentrum.ch

Museum fuer Voelkerkunde Hamburg
Rothenbaumchaussee 64, 20148 Hamburg
Tel: (040) 42 88 79-0 *Fax:* (040) 42 88 79-242
E-mail: info@myhamburg.de; publikationen@
myhamburg.de
Web Site: www.voelkerkundemuseum.com
Subjects: Art, History, Photography
ISBN Prefix(es): 978-3-9812566

Museumslandschaft Hessen Kassel
Schloss Wilhelmshoehe, Schlosspark 1, 34131
Kassel
Mailing Address: Postfach 41 04 20, 34066 Kas-
sel
Tel: (0561) 3 16 80 0 *Fax:* (0561) 3 16 80 111
E-mail: info@museum-kassel.de; presse@
museum-kassel.de
Web Site: www.museum-kassel.de
Key Personnel
Dir: Dr Bernd Kuester
Head, Press & Public Relations: Dr Matthias
Witzmann
Editor: Maike Bartsch
Marketing: Cornelia Ziegler *Tel:* (0561) 3 16 80
119 *E-mail:* c.ziegler@museum-kassel.de
Press: Judith Reitter *Tel:* (0561) 3 16 80 115
Subjects: Antiques, Architecture & Interior De-
sign, Art, History
ISBN Prefix(es): 978-3-931787
Divisions: Museums Bibliothek

Musia International
Musikalien-Handelsgesellschaft Ehrlich
GmbH & Co KG
Hedderichstr 108-110, 60596 Frankfurt am Main
Mailing Address: Postfach 700851, 60558 Frank-
furt am Main
Tel: (069) 63009940 *Fax:* (069) 63009962
E-mail: service@musia.de; info@musia.de;
vertrieb@musia.de
Web Site: www.musia-shop.de
Key Personnel
Mng Dir: Hermann Ecker; Nicholas Riddle
Founded: 1800
Subjects: Music, Dance, Classic Music, Musical
Instruments, Pop Music
ISBN Prefix(es): 978-3-87626; 978-3-920735
Associate Companies: Hinrichsen Edition Ltd,
London, United Kingdom; C F Peters Corp,
NY, United States
Imprints: M P Belaieff; Henry Litolff's Verlag;
Edition Peters GmbH; Edition Schwann

Muster-Schmidt Verlagsgesellschaft mbH+
Schuhstr, 37154 Sudheim
Tel: (05551) 9 08 42-0 *Fax:* (05551) 9 08 42-29
E-mail: muster-schmidt@t-online.de
Web Site: www.muster-schmidt.de
Key Personnel
Mng Dir: Eva Maria Gerhardy
Founded: 1905
Membership(s): Deutsches Farbenzentrum eV
Subjects: Biography, Memoirs, History, Color
ISBN Prefix(es): 978-3-7881
Branch Office(s)
Nansenstr 1, 8050 Zurich, Switzerland
Tel: (044) 251 75 71 *Fax:* (044) 252 44
68 *E-mail:* mail@muster-schmidt.ch *Web
Site:* www.muster-schmidt.ch

MVB Marketing- und Verlagsservice des
Buchhandels GmbH
Subsidiary of Boersenverein des Deutschen Buch-
handels eV
Braubachstr 16, 60311 Frankfurt am Main
Mailing Address: Postfach 10 04 42, 60004
Frankfurt am Main
Tel: (069) 1306-550 (customer service) *Fax:* (069)
1306-255 (customer service)
E-mail: info@mvb-online.de; serviceline@mvb-
online.de
Web Site: www.mvb-online.de
Key Personnel
Management: Ronald Schild
Press & Public Relations Manager: Markus Fer-
tig *Tel:* (069) 1306-374 *Fax:* (069) 1306-295
E-mail: m.fertig@mvb-online.de
Founded: 1947
Subjects: Publishing & Book Trade Reference
ISBN Prefix(es): 978-3-7657
Total Titles: 200 Print; 15 CD-ROM

MVS Medizinverlage Stuttgart GmbH & Co
KG+
Subsidiary of Georg Thieme Verlag KG
Oswald-Hesse-Str 50, 70469 Stuttgart
Tel: (0711) 8931-0 *Fax:* (0711) 8931-298
E-mail: kundenservice@thieme.de
Web Site: www.medizinverlage.de; www.thieme.
de
Key Personnel
Mng Dir: Dr Thomas Scherb
Head, Marketing: Birgit Carlsen *E-mail:* birgit.
carlsen@medizinverlage.de
Founded: 1925
Subjects: Medicine, Nursing, Dentistry
ISBN Prefix(es): 978-3-7773; 978-3-87758; 978-
3-8304
Subsidiaries: Enke Verlag; Karl F Haug Verlag;
Haug Sachbuch; Hippokrates Verlag; Sonntag
Verlag; TRIAS

Shipping Address: Koch, Neff & Oetinger Ver-
lagsauslieferung GmbH, Industriestr 23, 70565
Stuttgart
Warehouse: Koch, Neff & Oetinger Verlagsaus-
lieferung GmbH, Industriestr 23, 70565
Stuttgart
Orders to: Koch, Neff & Oetinger Verlagsaus-
lieferung GmbH, Industriestr 23, 70565
Stuttgart

MZ-Buchverlag, *imprint of* Battenberg Gietl
Verlag GmbH

Nadif, *imprint of* DACO Verlag Guenter Blaese

Verlag Stephanie Naglschmid+
Senefelderstr 10, 70178 Stuttgart
Tel: (0711) 626878 *Fax:* (0711) 612323
E-mail: vertrieb@naglschmid.de
Web Site: www.naglschmid.de
Key Personnel
Owner: Stephanie Naglschmid
Founded: 1984
Also acts as book dealer for diving literature.
Subjects: Biological Sciences, Environmental
Studies, Film, Video, Humor, Natural History,
Outdoor Recreation, Photography, Physical Sci-
ences, Sports, Athletics, Travel & Tourism
ISBN Prefix(es): 978-3-927913; 978-3-89594;
978-3-925342
Associate Companies: JLVA Internationale
Lizenzvewertungs-Agentur; MTI (Medien - und
Touristik Informations Services); Divemaster
(Touchmagatin)
Imprints: Edition Hannemann; Edition Schwab

NARA-Verlag (NARA Publishing)+
Postfach 1241, 85388 Allershausen
Tel: (08166) 8530 *Fax:* (08166) 8530
E-mail: kundenservice@luftfahrt-shop.de
Web Site: www.nara-verlag.de
Key Personnel
Manager, Rights & Permissions: O Krauthaeuser
E-mail: o.krauthaeuser@nara-verlag.de
Founded: 1982
Subjects: Aeronautics, Aviation
ISBN Prefix(es): 978-3-925671

Narayana Verlag GmbH
Blumenplatz 2, 79400 Kandern
Tel: (07626) 974970-0 *Fax:* (07626) 974970-9
E-mail: info@narayana-verlag.de
Web Site: www.narayana-verlag.de
Key Personnel
Mng Dir: Dr Herbert Sigwart; Katrin Sigwart
Subjects: Homeopathy
ISBN Prefix(es): 978-3-921383

Narr Francke Attempto Verlag GmbH & Co
KG+
Dischinger Weg 5, 72070 Tuebingen
Tel: (07071) 9797-0 *Fax:* (07071) 9797-11
E-mail: info@narr.de
Web Site: www.narr.de
Key Personnel
Publisher: Gunter Narr *Tel:* (07071) 9797-45
E-mail: narr@narr.de
Mng Dir: Sonja Narr *Tel:* (07071) 9797-40
E-mail: s.narr@narr.de
Production: Karin Burger *Tel:* (07071) 9797-21
E-mail: burger@narr.de; Barbara Mueller
Tel: (07071) 9797-22 *E-mail:* mueller@narr.de
Foreign Rights: Kathrin Heyng *Tel:* (07071)
9797-32 *E-mail:* heyng@narr.de
Founded: 1831
Subjects: Drama, Theater, Economics, Govern-
ment, Political Science, History, Language
Arts, Linguistics, Literature, Literary Criticism,
Essays, Philosophy, Psychology, Psychiatry,
Social Sciences, Sociology, Theology
ISBN Prefix(es): 978-3-7720

Distribution Center: Brockhaus/Commission, Kreidlerstr 9, 70806 Kornwestheim, Contact: Elisabeth Buehl *Tel:* (07154) 1327-22 *E-mail:* e.buehl@brocom.de

Mohr Morawa Buchvertrieb GmbH, Sulzengasse 2, 1230 Vienna, Austria, Contact: Georg Lukas *Tel:* (01) 680 14-0 *Fax:* (01) 688 71 30 *E-mail:* momo@mohrmorawa.at *Web Site:* www.mohrmorawa.at

Naseweis Verlag
Bergstr 66, 55296 Harxheim
Tel: (06135) 70 76 77 0 *Fax:* (06135) 70 76 77 1
E-mail: info@naseweis-verlag.de
Web Site: www.naseweis-verlag.de
Key Personnel
Owner: Jens Mueller
Founded: 2004
Subjects: How-to, Medicine, Nursing, Dentistry, Emergency Medicine & Services
ISBN Prefix(es): 978-3-937244

National Geographic Deutschland
Am Baumwall 11, 20459 Hamburg
Tel: (040) 3703-0
E-mail: service@nationalgeographic.de
Web Site: www.nationalgeographic.de
Key Personnel
Editor-in-Chief: Florian Gless
ISBN Prefix(es): 978-3-86690; 978-3-95559

Natke Verlag
Ricarda-Huch-Weg 38, 41469 Neuss
Tel: (02137) 92 94 71 *Fax:* (02137) 92 94 72
E-mail: mail@natke-verlag.de
Web Site: www.natke-verlag.de
Key Personnel
Publisher: Dr Ulrich Natke
Specialize in publications on stuttering & its treatment.
Subjects: Health, Nutrition, Medicine, Nursing, Dentistry, Stuttering
ISBN Prefix(es): 978-3-936640

Verlag Natur & Wissenschaft Harro Hieronimus & Dr Juergen Schmidt GbR
(Nature & Science Publisher)+
Dompfaffweg 53, 42659 Solingen
Tel: (0212) 819878 *Fax:* (0212) 816216
E-mail: info@verlagnw.de
Web Site: www.verlagnw.de
Key Personnel
Mng Dir: Harro Hieronimus
Founded: 1990
This publisher has indicated that 20% of its product line is author subsidized.
Subjects: Animals, Pets, Biological Sciences, Earth Sciences, Environmental Studies, Gardening, Plants, Geography, Geology, Natural History
ISBN Prefix(es): 978-3-927889; 978-3-936616
Number of titles published annually: 10 Print; 1 CD-ROM
Total Titles: 150 Print; 2 CD-ROM
Imprints: Bibliothek Natur & Wissenschaft
Distributor for ACS-Verlag

NaturaViva Verlags GmbH+
Lukas-Moser-Weg 2, 71263 Weil der Stadt
Mailing Address: Postfach 1203, 71256 Weil der Stadt
Tel: (07033) 13 80 816 *Fax:* (07033) 13 80 817
Web Site: www.naturavivaverlag.de
Key Personnel
Mng Dir: Simone Graff
Founded: 1999
Membership(s): Borsenverein des Deutschen Buchhandels eV.
Subjects: Health, Nutrition
ISBN Prefix(es): 978-3-89881; 978-3-935407
Number of titles published annually: 6 Print

Total Titles: 80 Print
Imprints: Fit fuers Leben Verlag; Waldthausen Verlag
Distributed by Walter Haedecke Verlag
Foreign Rep(s): Ruth Beutler (Switzerland)
Distribution Center: Dr Franz Hain Verlagsauslieferungen, Dr-Otto-Neurath-Gasse 5, 1220 Vienna, Austria
Auslieferung Scheidegger, c/o AVA Verlagsauslieferung AG, Centralweg 16, 8910 Affoltern am Albis, Switzerland

Albert Nauck & Co
Subsidiary of Carl Heymanns Verlag KG
Luxemburger Str 449, 50939 Cologne
Tel: (0221) 94373-0 *Fax:* (0221) 94373-901
Subjects: History, Religion - Other
ISBN Prefix(es): 978-3-87574

Naumann & Goebel Verlagsgesellschaft mbH (NGV)
Subsidiary of VEMAG Verlags- und Medien AG
Emil-Hoffmann-Str 1, 50996 Cologne
Mailing Address: Postfach 50 18 63, 50978 Cologne
Tel: (02236) 39 99 0 *Fax:* (02236) 39 99 99
E-mail: info@vemag-medien.de
Web Site: www.naumann-goebel.de
Key Personnel
Mng Dir: Stephan Hamann; Dirk Lefherz; Dr Holger Schneider
Founded: 1983
Subjects: Animals, Pets, Art, Biblical Studies, Computer Science, Cookery, Crafts, Games, Hobbies, Education, Fashion, Fiction, Gardening, Plants, Health, Nutrition, History, House & Home, How-to, Human Relations, Mathematics, Medicine, Nursing, Dentistry, Science (General), Travel & Tourism, Family, Foreign Language Study, Nature
ISBN Prefix(es): 978-3-625; 978-3-632; 978-3-8247; 978-3-88703; 978-3-923723
Associate Companies: Daumueller Werbeges mbH; Delphin AG; Delphin Verlag GmbH; Naturalis Verlags- u Vertriebsges mbH; Neuer Pawlak Verlag GmbH; MZ Medien Zentrum GmbH; Verlag Das persoenliche Geburtstagsbuch GmbH; Reichenbach Verlag GmbH; Tigris Verlag GmbH; V & M Verlags & Mediengesellschaft Koeln mbH

Verlag M Naumann, see Naumann Verlag

Naumann Verlag
Formerly Verlag M Naumann
Raiffeisenallee 10, 82041 Oberhaching
Tel: (089) 613 87 1 22 *Fax:* (089) 613 87 1 20
E-mail: info@naumann-verlag.de
Web Site: www.naumann-verlag.de
Key Personnel
Publishing Dir: Andreas Koeglowitz
Publisher: Wolfgang Fitz
Founded: 1984
Subjects: Biography, Memoirs, Cookery, Nonfiction (General), Regional Interests, Comic Books, Crime Stories
ISBN Prefix(es): 978-3-940168
Parent Company: Herold Vertriebs GmbH

Edition Nautilus+
Schuetzenstr 49 a, 22761 Hamburg
Tel: (040) 721 35 36 *Fax:* (040) 721 83 99
E-mail: info@edition-nautilus.de; order@edition-nautilus.de; presse@edition-nautilus.de
Web Site: www.edition-nautilus.de
Key Personnel
Owner: Lutz Schulenburg
Editorial Dir & Rights Manager: Hanna Mittelstaedt *E-mail:* hanna@edition-nautilus.de
Press: Franziska Otto
Production: Klaus Voss

Founded: 1974
Subjects: Art, Biography, Memoirs, Government, Political Science, Literature, Literary Criticism, Essays, Nonfiction (General)
ISBN Prefix(es): 978-3-89401; 978-3-921523
Foreign Rep(s): B+I Buch und Information AG (Richard Bhend) (Switzerland); Michael Orou (Austria); Guenter Thiel (Austria)
Foreign Rights: Agentur Literatur Hebel & Bindermann (Gudrun Hebel) (Greece, Sweden); Tanja Howarth Literary Agency (UK); Ute Koemer Literary Agency (Portugal, Spain); Marianne Schoenbach Literary Agency (Netherlands); Agenzia Servizi Editoriali (Guido Lagomarsino) (Italy)
Distribution Center: Sova GmbH, Friesstr 20-24, 60388 Frankfurt, Contact: Helmut Richter *Tel:* (069) 41 02 11 *Fax:* (069) 41 02 80 *E-mail:* sovaffm@t-online.de
Mohr Morawa Buchvertrieb GmbH, Sulzengasse 2, 1230 Vienna, Austria *Tel:* (01) 680 14-0 *Fax:* (01) 688 71 30 *E-mail:* momo@mohrmorawa.at *Web Site:* www.mohrmorawa.at
AVA Verlagsauslieferung AG, Centralweg 16, 8910 Affoltern am Albis, Switzerland *Tel:* (044) 762 42 70 *Fax:* (044) 762 42 10 *E-mail:* verlagsservice@ava.ch

NDV GmbH & Co KG
Hauptstr 74, 53619 Rheinbreitbach
Mailing Address: Postfach 15 60, 53585 Bad Honnef
Tel: (02224) 3232 *Fax:* (02224) 78639
E-mail: info@ndv.info
Web Site: www.ndv.info; www.politik-kontakte.de
Key Personnel
Publisher & Mng Dir: Andreas Holzapfel *E-mail:* holzapfel@ndv.info
Publisher: Klaus J Holzapfel
Administration & Sales: Sylke Beyer *E-mail:* beyer@ndv.info
Editorial & Databases: Andrea Gertig-Hadaschik *E-mail:* gertig@ndv.info
Editorial, Production & Public Relations: Markus Fleischer *E-mail:* fleischer@ndv.info
Founded: 1949
Subjects: Government, Political Science
ISBN Prefix(es): 978-3-87576
Branch Office(s)
Wittestr 30 K, 13509 Berlin *Tel:* (030) 8557511 *Fax:* (030) 85605332

Nebel Verlag GmbH+
Bahnhofplatz 4, 86919 Utting am Ammersee
Tel: (08806) 92 15-0 *Fax:* (08806) 92 15-22
E-mail: info@nebel-verlag.de
Web Site: www.nebel-verlag.de
Key Personnel
Mng Dir: Pirmin Nebel
Founded: 1989
Membership(s): Verlags-Karree eV.
Subjects: Art, Cookery, Gardening, Plants, History, Literature, Literary Criticism, Essays, Romance, Travel & Tourism
ISBN Prefix(es): 978-3-86862

Neckar-Verlag GmbH+
Klosterring 1, 78008 Villingen-Schwenningen
Mailing Address: Postfach 1820, 78008 Villingen-Schwenningen
Tel: (07721) 8987-0 *Fax:* (07721) 8987-50
E-mail: service@neckar-verlag.de; info@neckar-verlag.de
Web Site: www.webshop.neckar-verlag.de
Key Personnel
Mng Dir: Beate Holtzhauer *E-mail:* b.holtzhauer@neckar-verlag.de; Ruth Holtzhauer *E-mail:* r.holtzhauer@neckar-verlag.de
Head, Sales: Monika Fritschi *Tel:* (07721) 8987-37 *E-mail:* fritschi@neckar-verlag.de
Marketing: Rita Riedmueller *Tel:* (07721) 89 87-44 *E-mail:* riedmueller@neckar-verlag.de
Founded: 1945

Subjects: Aeronautics, Aviation, Literature &
  Plans for RC-Model Aircraft & RC-Model Ship
ISBN Prefix(es): 978-3-7883

Neff, *imprint of* Pabel-Moewig Verlag GmbH

Nelles Verlag GmbH+
Machtlfinger Str 11, 81379 Munich
Tel: (089) 3571940 *Fax:* (089) 35719430
E-mail: info@nelles-verlag.de
Web Site: www.nelles-verlag.de
Key Personnel
Mng Dir: Guenter Nelles; Martin Nelles
Founded: 1975
Subjects: Foreign Countries, Travel & Tourism
ISBN Prefix(es): 978-3-88618; 978-3-920397;
  978-3-922539; 978-3-86574
Orders to: Geocenter/ILH, Postfach 80 08
  30, 70508 Stuttgart *Tel:* (0711) 78194610
  Fax: (0711) 7824375 *E-mail:* vertrieb@
  geocenter.de *Web Site:* www.geocenter.de
Freytag-Berndt/Artaria KG, Brunnestr 69, A-1231
  Vienna, Austria *Tel:* (01) 869909084 *Fax:* (01)
  8698855 *E-mail:* sales@freytagberndt.at *Web
  Site:* www.freytagberndt.at
Scheidegger & Co AG, Centralweg 16,
  8910 Affoltern am Albis, Switzerland
  Tel: (01) 7624250 *Fax:* (01) 7624210
  E-mail: scheidegger@ava.ch *Web Site:* www.
  ava.ch

Nellio Verlag GmbH
Hermann-Fein-Str 9, 70599 Stuttgart
Tel: (0711) 3421 1520 *Fax:* (0711) 3421 1521
E-mail: info@nellio.de
Web Site: www.nellio.de
Key Personnel
Program Management & Licenses: Stefanie
  Koehler *E-mail:* stefanie.koehler@nellio.de
Sales: Nadja Mende *E-mail:* nadja.haussmann@
  nellio.de
Sales & Marketing: Martina Kohnle
  E-mail: martina.kohnle@nellio.de
Founded: 2010
ISBN Prefix(es): 978-3-942394
Foreign Rep(s): Leads! (Stefan Muehlenbein)
  (Austria)
Distribution Center: Brockhaus Kommission-
  sgeschaft GmbH, Kreidlerstr 9, 70806 Ko-
  rnwestheim, Contact: Alexandra Goesch
  Tel: (07154) 13 27 10 *Fax:* (07154) 13 27 13
  E-mail: nellio@brocom.de
AS Hoeller GmbH, Schrackgasse 11a, 8650
  Kindberg, Austria *Tel:* (03865) 44 88 0
  Fax: (03865) 44 88 077 *E-mail:* office@
  ashoeller.com
Dessauer, Raeffelstr 32, 8045 Zurich, Switzer-
  land *Tel:* (044) 466 9600 *Fax:* (044) 466 9669
  E-mail: stefan.reiss@dessauer.ch

Nelson Verlag, *imprint of* CARLSEN Verlag
  GmbH

Nelson Verlag GmbH
Imprint of CARLSEN Verlag GmbH
Voelckersstr 14-20, 22765 Hamburg
Tel: (040) 39 804 400 *Fax:* (040) 39 804 388
E-mail: nelson@carlsen.de
Web Site: www.carlsen.de/nelson
Key Personnel
Mng Dir: Renate Herre; Joachim Kaufmann
Founded: 2003
ISBN Prefix(es): 978-3-86606; 978-3-86885

Neue Darmstaedter Verlagsanstalt, see NDV
  GmbH & Co KG

Neue Erde GmbH+
Cecilienstr 29, 66111 Saarbruecken
Tel: (0681) 595 398 0 *Fax:* (0681) 390 41 02

E-mail: service@neue-erde.de; kontakt@neue-
  erde.de
Web Site: shop.neueerde.de
Key Personnel
Mng Dir: Andreas Lentz
International Rights Manager: Arwen Osmani
  E-mail: arwen.osmani@neue-erde.de
Sales: Katharina Mueller *Tel:* (0681) 595 398 12
  E-mail: katharina.mueller@neue-erde.de
Founded: 1984
Subjects: Astrology, Occult, Environmental Stud-
  ies, Inspirational, Spirituality, Parapsychology,
  Self-Help
ISBN Prefix(es): 978-3-89060
Imprints: Ryvellus
Foreign Rep(s): Claudia Gyr (Switzerland); Dr
  Winfried Plattner (Austria)
Distribution Center: Prolit Verlagsausliefer-
  ung GmbH, Siemensstr 16, 35463 Fernwald-
  Annerod, Contact: Johanna Gastler *Tel:* (0641)
  94 393 202 *Fax:* (0641) 94 393 89
Ennsthaler Gesellschaft mbH & Co KG, Stadt-
  platz 26, 4400 Steyr, Austria *Tel:* (07252)
  52053 0 *Fax:* (07252) 52053 55
Buchzentrum AG, Industriestr Ost 10, 4614 Ha-
  gendorf, Switzerland *Tel:* (041) 62 209 25 25
  Fax: (041) 62 209 26 27

Verlag Neue Kritik+
Kettenhofweg 53, 60325 Frankfurt am Main
Tel: (069) 72 75 76 *Fax:* (069) 72 65 85
E-mail: info@neuekritik.de
Web Site: www.neuekritik.de
Key Personnel
Mng Dir: Dorothea Rein
Founded: 1965
Subjects: Art, Fiction, History, Literature, Literary
  Criticism, Essays, Nonfiction (General), Philos-
  ophy, Poetry, Women's Studies, Eastern Euro-
  pean Literature, Judaica, Holocaust, Nazism
ISBN Prefix(es): 978-3-8015
Foreign Rep(s): Peter Bettelheim (Austria);
  Stroemfeld Verlag (Rudi Deuble) (Germany)
Orders to: Sozialistische Verlagsauslieferung
  GmbH, Franziusstr 20-24, 60388 Frankfurt am
  Main *Tel:* (069) 41 02 11 *Fax:* (069) 41 02 80
  E-mail: sovaffm@t-online.de

Verlag Neue Literatur
Saalbahnhofstr 25a, 07743 Jena
Tel: (03641) 369060 *Fax:* (03641) 369062
E-mail: info@verlag-neue-literatur.com
Web Site: www.vnl.de
Key Personnel
Publishing Dir: Mathias Koebrich *Tel:* (03741)
  550425 *E-mail:* mk@vnl.de; Marko Oettler
  Tel: (03741) 550420 *E-mail:* mo@vnl.de
Marketing: Sabine Moennig *Tel:* (03741) 55040
  E-mail: sm@vnl.de
Founded: 1998
Subjects: Asian Studies, Fiction, Nonfiction (Gen-
  eral), Poetry, South Asia
ISBN Prefix(es): 978-3-940085; 978-3-934141;
  978-3-938157

Verlag Neue Musik GmbH
Grabbeallee 15, 13156 Berlin
Tel: (030) 61 60 81-0 *Fax:* (030) 61 69 81-21
E-mail: vnm@verlag-neue-musik.de
Web Site: www.verlag-neue-musik.de
Key Personnel
Mng Dir: Detlef Kessler
Founded: 1957
Subjects: Music, Dance
ISBN Prefix(es): 978-3-7333
Subsidiaries: Edition Margaux

Verlag Neue Stadt GmbH+
Muenchener Str 2, 85667 Oberpframmern
Tel: (08093) 20 91 *Fax:* (08093) 20 96
E-mail: verlag@neuestadt.com
Web Site: www.neuestadt.com

Key Personnel
Mng Dir: Joachim Schwind
Sales, Publicity & Advertising: Gabriele Hartl
  E-mail: gabriele.hartl@neuestadt.com
Rights: Stefan Liesenfeld
Founded: 1961
Subjects: Biblical Studies, Biography, Memoirs,
  Fiction, How-to, Human Relations, Inspira-
  tional, Spirituality, Music, Dance, Religion -
  Other, Theology, Family
ISBN Prefix(es): 978-3-87996
Parent Company: Citta Nuova Editrice, Italy
Branch Office(s)
Meyrinkgasse 7, 1230 Vienna, Austria *Tel:* (01) 6
  03 81 00 *Fax:* (01) 6 03 81 00 *E-mail:* verlag.
  neuestadt@utanet.at
Verenastr 7, 8038 Zurich, Switzerland
  Tel: (044) 4 82 60 11 *Fax:* (044) 4 82 60 17
  E-mail: verlag@neuestadt.ch
Foreign Rep(s): Handelsvertretung Kager &
  Treml GmbH (Gertrude Haslwanter & Ste-
  fan Stoehr) (Austria); Andreas Meisel Ver-
  lagsvertretungen (Switzerland)
Distribution Center: Mohr Morawa Buchver-
  trieb GmbH, Sulzengasse 2, 1230 Vienna,
  Austria *Tel:* (01) 680 14-0 *Fax:* (01) 688
  71 30 *E-mail:* momo@mohrmorawa.at *Web
  Site:* www.mohrmorawa.at
Balmer Buecherdienst AG, Kobiboden, 8840
  Einsiedeln, Switzerland *Tel:* (055) 418 89
  60; (0848) 840 820 *Fax:* (0848) 840 830
  E-mail: veronica.hagen@balmer-bd.ch

**Verlag Neue Wirtschafts-Briefe GmbH & Co
  KG,** see NWB Verlag GmbH & Co KG

Verlag Neuer Weg GmbH+
Alte Bottroper Str 42, 45356 Essen
Tel: (0201) 2 59 15 *Fax:* (0201) 61 444 62
E-mail: verlag@neuerweg.de
Web Site: www.neuerweg.de
Key Personnel
Mng Dir: Renate Mast
Founded: 1973
Subjects: Biography, Memoirs, Developing Coun-
  tries, Education, Environmental Studies, Gov-
  ernment, Political Science, Health, Nutrition,
  History, Physical Sciences, Travel & Tourism,
  Women's Studies, Capitalism, Critical Science,
  Critique of Capitalism, Labor Movement, So-
  cialism
ISBN Prefix(es): 978-3-88021
Subsidiaries: Druckerei Neur Weg Essen
Bookshop(s): People to People *Tel:* (0209) 177
  65 60 *Fax:* (0209) 177 65 61 *E-mail:* reisen@
  people-to-people.de *Web Site:* www.people-to-
  people.de

Neues Buch Verlag GmbH
Hanauer Str 7b, 61130 Nidderau
Tel: (06187) 2 83 10 *Fax:* (06187) 2 83 07
E-mail: info@neuesbuch.de
Web Site: www.neuesbuch.de
Key Personnel
Mng Partner: Horst Knickel
Subjects: Inspirational, Spirituality, Religion -
  Other
ISBN Prefix(es): 978-3-930180; 978-3-937618

Neues Literaturkontor+
Goldstr 15, 48147 Muenster
Tel: (0251) 45343 *Fax:* (0251) 40565
E-mail: neues-literaturkontor@t-online.de
Web Site: www.neues-literaturkontor.de
Key Personnel
Publishing Dir: Prof Hans D Mummendey
Founded: 1990
Specialize in novels & short stories.
Subjects: Poetry
ISBN Prefix(es): 978-3-920591
Number of titles published annually: 5 Print
Total Titles: 80 Print

Neufeld Verlag
Vdk-Str 21, 92521 Schwarzenfeld
Tel: (09435) 502449 *Fax:* (09435) 502483
E-mail: info@neufeld-verlag.de
Web Site: www.neufeld-verlag.de
Key Personnel
Publisher: David Neufeld
Editor: Lukas Baumann
Founded: 2004
Subjects: Biography, Memoirs, Disability, Special Needs, Inspirational, Spirituality, Theology
ISBN Prefix(es): 978-3-86256; 978-3-937896

Michael Neugebauer Edition GmbH
Kusterstr 3, 18461 Richtenberg
Tel: (038322) 587878 *Fax:* (038322) 587879
E-mail: info@minedition.de
Web Site: www.minedition.com
Key Personnel
Mng Dir: Uwe Achterberg *E-mail:* uwe.
achterberg@minedition.de
ISBN Prefix(es): 978-3-86566
Imprints: Minedition
Distributed by Egmont Publishing Group (Germany)

Neukirchener Theologie+
Andreas-Braem-Str 18/20, 47506 Neukirchen-Vluyn
Mailing Address: Postfach 101265, 47497 Neukirchen-Vluyn
Tel: (02845) 392-234 *Fax:* (02845) 392-250
E-mail: info@neukirchener-verlage.de
Web Site: www.neukirchener-verlage.de
Key Personnel
Publishing Dir: Christoph Siepermann
Tel: (02845) 392-235 *E-mail:* siepermann@neukirchener-verlage.de
Assistant Publishing Dir: Heike Peun *Tel:* (02845) 392-235 *E-mail:* peun@neukirchener-verlage.de
Marketing & Public Relations: Leah Hoffmann-Lohse *Tel:* (02845) 392-210 *Fax:* (02845) 392 19 210 *E-mail:* hoffmann-lohse@neukirchener-verlage.de
Sales: Christina Nitsche *Tel:* (02845) 392-262
E-mail: nitsche@neukirchener-verlage.de
Subjects: Religion - Protestant, Theology
ISBN Prefix(es): 978-3-7887
Parent Company: Neukirchener Verlagsgesellschaft mbH
Associate Companies: Neukirchener Aussaat; Neukirchener Kalenderverlag
Foreign Rep(s): Jessica Haberlandt (Austria); Roland Sigrist (Switzerland)
Distribution Center: G Umbreit GmbH & Co KG Verlagsauslieferung, Mundelsheimer Str 3, 74321 Bietigheim-Bissingen, Austria, Contact: Jessica Haberlandt *Tel:* (07142) 596 385 *Fax:* (07142) 596 387 *E-mail:* jessica.haberlandt@umbreit.de (Germany & Austria)
Brunnen-Verlag Basel, Wallstr 6, 4002 Basel, Switzerland *Tel:* (061) 295 60 01 *Fax:* (061) 295 60 68

Neukirchener Verlagsgesellschaft mbH+
Andreas-Braem-Str 18/20, 47506 Neukirchen-Vluyn
Mailing Address: Postfach 101265, 47497 Neukirchen-Vluyn
Tel: (02845) 392-234 *Fax:* (02845) 392-250
E-mail: info@neukirchener-verlage.de
Web Site: www.neukirchener-verlage.de
Key Personnel
Publishing Dir: Christoph Siepermann
Tel: (02845) 392-235 *E-mail:* siepermann@neukirchener-verlage.de
Assistant Publishing Dir: Heike Peun *Tel:* (02845) 392-235 *E-mail:* peun@neukirchener-verlage.de
Marketing & Public Relations: Leah Hoffmann-Lohse *Tel:* (02845) 392-210 *Fax:* (02845) 392 19 210 *E-mail:* hoffmann-lohse@neukirchener-verlage.de

Sales: Christina Nitsche *Tel:* (02845) 392-262
E-mail: nitsche@neukirchener-verlage.de
Founded: 1891
Subjects: Biblical Studies, Education, Fiction, Religion - Protestant, Religion - Other, Theology
ISBN Prefix(es): 978-3-7615
Number of titles published annually: 50 Print
Total Titles: 400 Print
Parent Company: Neukirchener Verlagsgesellschaft mbH
Associate Companies: Neukirchener Kalenderverlag; Neukirchener Theologie
Foreign Rep(s): Jessica Haberlandt (Austria); Roland Sigrist (Switzerland)
Distribution Center: G Umbreit GmbH & Co KG Verlagsauslieferung, Mundelsheimer Str 3, 74321 Bietigheim-Bissingen, Contact: Jessica Haberlandt *Tel:* (07142) 596 385 *Fax:* (07142) 596 387 *E-mail:* jessica.haberlandt@umbreit.de (Germany & Austria)
Brunnen-Verlag Basel, Wallstr 6, 4002 Basel, Switzerland *Tel:* (061) 295 60 01 *Fax:* (061) 295 60 68

Verlag J Neumann-Neudamm Aktiengesellschaft+
Schwalbenweg 1, 34212 Melsungen
Tel: (05661) 9262-26 *Toll Free Tel:* 800 638 32 66 *Fax:* (05661) 9262-19 *Toll Free Fax:* 800 638 22 66
E-mail: info@neumann-neudamm.de
Web Site: www.neumann-neudamm.de; www.nimrod-verlag.de
Key Personnel
Manager: Heiko Schwartz *E-mail:* heiko.schwartz@neumann-neudamm.de
Sales Manager: Roland Zobel *E-mail:* roland.zobel@neumann-neudamm.de
Founded: 1872
Subjects: Animals, Pets, Cookery, Outdoor Recreation, Science (General), Sports, Athletics, Hunting
ISBN Prefix(es): 978-3-7888
Subsidiaries: JANA Jagd + Natur GmbH
Distribution Center: JANA Jagd + Natur GmbH, Melsungen *Tel:* (05661) 9262-0 *Fax:* (05661) 9262-20 *E-mail:* info@jana-jagd.de *Web Site:* www.jana-jagd.de
MORA Wien, Hackhofergasse 8, 1190 Vienna, Austria, Contact: Dr Winfried Plattner *Tel:* (01) 676 7051974 *Fax:* (01) 2243 30494 *E-mail:* plattnerbuch@tmo.at
Verlags-Service Ernst Imfeld, Brunnmattweg 3, Postfach 1359, 6060 Sarnen, Switzerland *Tel:* (041) 6603481 *Fax:* (041) 6603263 *E-mail:* e.imfeld@verlags-service.ch *Web Site:* www.verlags-service.ch

NeunZehn Verlag
Kreuzstr 21, 13187 Berlin
Tel: (030) 74929797
E-mail: post@neunzehn-verlag.de
Web Site: www.neunzehn-verlag.de
Key Personnel
Owner: Walter Unterweger *E-mail:* walter@wimmelbuchverlag.de
Editorial Dir: Kristina Unterweger
Subjects: Cookery, Vegans
ISBN Prefix(es): 978-3-94249
Associate Companies: Adrian Verlag; Wimmelbuchverlag
Distribution Center: MSR/Runge VA, Bergstr 2, 33803 Steinhagen *Tel:* (05204) 998-123 *Fax:* (05204) 998-116 *E-mail:* msr@rungeva.de

Verlag fuer Messepublikationen Thomas Neureuter GmbH
Frauenstr 7, 80469 Munich
Tel: (089) 99 30 91-0 *Fax:* (089) 93 78 96
E-mail: info@neureuter.de
Web Site: www.neureuter.de

Key Personnel
Chief Executive Officer: Markus Baumann
Tel: (089) 99 3091-20 *E-mail:* baumann@neureuter.de; Peter Schuck *Tel:* (0201) 36547-100 *Fax:* (0201) 36547-125 *E-mail:* schuck@neureuter.de
Publishing Dir: Detlev Bartel *Tel:* (0201) 36547-101 *Fax:* (0201) 36547-225 *E-mail:* bartel@neureuter.de
Founded: 1946
Subjects: Business, Communications, Technology
ISBN Prefix(es): 978-3-921326
Parent Company: NEUREUTER FAIR MEDIA GmbH
Branch Office(s)
Westendstr 1, 45143 Essen *Tel:* (0201) 36547-103 *Fax:* (0201) 36547-325
Messe-Allee 2, 04356 Leipzig *Tel:* (0341) 67827780 *Fax:* (0341) 67827788
Room C2 3/F Po Yip Bldg, 23 Hing Yip Str, Kwun Tong, Kowloon, Hong Kong *Tel:* 2519 3581 *Fax:* 2519 7134 *E-mail:* info@neureuter.com.hk *Web Site:* www.neureuter.com.hk
Centre Point, 7/F, Santacruz West, Mumbai 400 054, India *Tel:* (0222) 6610118 *Fax:* (0222) 66789911 *E-mail:* info@neureuter.in *Web Site:* www.neureuter.in

New Era Publications Deutschland GmbH
Hittfelder Kirschweg 5 A, 21220 Seevetal-Maschen
Tel: (04105) 68330 *Fax:* (04105) 683322
Founded: 1985
Subjects: Religion - Other, Science Fiction, Fantasy, Self-Help
ISBN Prefix(es): 978-3-929284
Parent Company: New Era Publications International ApS, Smedeland 20, 2600 Glostrup, Denmark

NGV, see Naumann & Goebel Verlagsgesellschaft mbH (NGV)

Nicolaische Verlagsbuchhandlung GmbH+
Neue Gruenstrstr 17, 10179 Berlin
Tel: (030) 25 37 38-0 *Fax:* (030) 25 37 38-39
E-mail: info@nicolai-verlag.de
Web Site: www.nicolai-verlag.de
Key Personnel
Mng Dir: Andreas von Stedman
Press & Public Relations: Patrick Davidt
Tel: (030) 253738-16 *E-mail:* patrick.davidt@nicolai-verlag.de
Rights & Licenses: Gaja Busch *Tel:* (030) 253738-60 *E-mail:* gaja.busch@nicolai-verlag.de
Subjects: Architecture & Interior Design, Art, Biography, Memoirs, Photography, Regional Interests
ISBN Prefix(es): 978-3-87584; 978-3-89479; 978-3-9803217
Foreign Rep(s): indiebook (Germany); Phil Richards (UK exc London); Henry Thompson (London)
Distribution Center: VVA Vereinigte Verlagsauslieferung, An der Autobahn, 33310 Guetersloh, Contact: Hildegard Schnitz *Tel:* (05241) 80 89 578 *Fax:* (05241) 80 68 95 78 *E-mail:* hildegard.schnitz@bertelsmann.de
Buchzentrum AG, Industriestr Ost 10, 4614 Haegendorf, Switzerland *Tel:* (062) 20 92 525 *Fax:* (062) 20 92 788

Niederland Verlag
Waldmeisterstr 14, 80935 Munich
Tel: (089) 3541383 *Fax:* (089) 3541383
E-mail: niederlandverlag@aol.com
Web Site: www.niederlandverlag.de
Key Personnel
Publisher: Johannes Liessel
Subjects: History, Regional Interests
ISBN Prefix(es): 978-3-923947

CW Niemeyer Buchverlage GmbH+
Osterstr 19, 31785 Hameln
Mailing Address: Postfach 100752, 31757
  Hameln
Tel: (05151) 200-312 *Fax:* (05151) 200-319
E-mail: info@niemeyer-buch.de
Web Site: www.niemeyer-buch.de
Key Personnel
Mng Dir: Carsten Holzendorff
Sales: Christina Schneider
Founded: 1797
Membership(s):Borsenverein des Deutschen Buch-
  handels.
Subjects: Architecture & Interior Design, Art,
  Fiction, History, Humor, Library & Information
  Sciences, Literature, Literary Criticism, Essays,
  Mysteries, Suspense, Regional Interests
ISBN Prefix(es): 978-3-8271; 978-3-87585
Subsidiaries: Adolf Sponholtz Verlag

Nieswand-Verlag GmbH+
Werftbahnstr 8, 24143 Kiel
Tel: (0431) 7028 163 *Fax:* (0431) 7028 119
E-mail: info@nieswandverlag.de
Web Site: www.nieswandverlag.de
Key Personnel
Manager: Jens Nieswand
Co-Editor: Ingo Wulff
Founded: 1986
Membership(s): The Stock Exchange of German
  Booksellers.
Subjects: Art, Music, Dance, Photography
ISBN Prefix(es): 978-3-926048; 978-3-89567
Distribution Center: Vull-Service GmbH,
  August-Borsig-Str 14, 24783 Osterroenfeld
  Tel: (04331) 8095 777

Hans-Nietsch-Verlag OHG+
Am Himmelreich 7, 79312 Emmendingen
Tel: (07641) 46 88 530 *Fax:* (07641) 46 88 585
E-mail: info@nietsch.de
Web Site: www.nietsch.de
Key Personnel
Management: Hans Nietsch; Ralf Lederer
Founded: 1992
Subjects: Astrology, Occult, Cookery, Environ-
  mental Studies, Health, Nutrition, Inspirational,
  Spirituality, Music, Dance, Religion - Other,
  Self-Help, Occult
ISBN Prefix(es): 978-3-934647; 978-3-929475;
  978-3-939570
Number of titles published annually: 10 Print
Total Titles: 100 Print
Imprints: Edition Sternenprinz
Distributor for Verlag Hans-Juergen Maurer; Edi-
  tion Synthese

Nikol Verlagsgesellschaft mbH & Co KG
Kampstr 7, 20357 Hamburg
Tel: (040) 611 683-0 *Fax:* (040) 611 683-22
E-mail: info@nikol-verlag.de
Web Site: www.nikol-verlag.de
Key Personnel
Mng Dir: Marc Nikol
Founded: 2003
Subjects: Cookery, Crafts, Games, Hobbies,
  Health, Nutrition, History, Language Arts,
  Linguistics, Music, Dance, Religion - Other,
  Science (General), Sports, Athletics, Entertain-
  ment, Nature
ISBN Prefix(es): 978-3-933203; 978-3-86820;
  978-3-937872
Distribution Center: arvato media GmbH, VVA
  Vereinigte Verlagsauslieferung, Verlag 341
  Nikol, An der Autobahn, 33310 Guetersloh,
  Contact: Hildegard Ciolini *Tel:* (05241) 80 50
  73 *Fax:* (05241) 80 60 24

99pages Verlag GmbH
Methfesselstr 46a, 20257 Hamburg
Tel: (040) 35 70 12 40 *Fax:* (040) 35 70 12 28
E-mail: info@99pages.de

Web Site: www.99pages.de
Key Personnel
Mng Dir, Art: Ansgar Pudenz *Tel:* (0172) 7 99 32
  99 *E-mail:* ansgar.pudenz@99pages.de
Mng Dir, Text: Rainer Schillings *Tel:* (0172) 7 99
  31 99 *E-mail:* rainer.schillings@99pages.de
Subjects: Art, Cookery
ISBN Prefix(es): 978-3-942518
Foreign Rights: Collier International (Christo-
  pher Collier) (Asia, Eastern Europe, Italy, UK,
  USA); ST&A (Susanne Theune) (Brazil, Latin
  America, Portugal, Spain)
Distribution Center: Edel Germany GmbH, Neu-
  muehien 17, 22763 Hamburg *Tel:* (040) 89085-
  0 *Fax:* (040) 88085-9970 *E-mail:* buchhandel@
  edel.com

Rainar Nitzsche Verlag+
Gasstr 34, 67655 Kaiserslautern
Tel: (0631) 61305 *Fax:* (0631) 61305
E-mail: info@nitzscheverlag.de
Web Site: www.nitzscheverlag.de
Key Personnel
Contact: Dr Rainar Nitzsche
Founded: 1989
Subjects: Art, Behavioral Sciences, Biological
  Sciences, Fiction, Mysteries, Suspense, Natural
  History, Poetry, Science Fiction, Fantasy
ISBN Prefix(es): 978-3-9802102; 978-3-930304

Nodus Publikationen-Klaus D Dutz
  Wissenschaftlicher Verlag+
Lingener Str 7, 48155 Muenster
Mailing Address: Postfach 5725, 48031 Muenster
Tel: (0251) 65514 *Fax:* (0251) 661692
E-mail: dutz.nodus@t-online.de
Web Site: elverdissen.dyndns.org/~nodus/
Key Personnel
Owner: Angelika Rueter
Contact: Klaus D Dutz
Founded: 1987
Subjects: Film, Video, Language Arts, Linguis-
  tics, Philosophy, Science (General)
ISBN Prefix(es): 978-3-89323
Subsidiaries: Stichting Neerlandistiek VU; Sticht-
  ing Uitgeverij De Keltische Draak

Florian Noetzel Verlage GmbH+
Holtermannstr 32, 26384 Wilhelmshaven
Mailing Address: Postfach 1443, 26354 Wil-
  helmshaven
Tel: (04421) 430 03 *Fax:* (04421) 429 85
E-mail: info@noetzel-verlag.de
Web Site: noetzel-verlag.de
Key Personnel
Contact: Florian Noetzel
Founded: 1986
Subjects: Music, Dance, Theatre
ISBN Prefix(es): 978-3-7959
Number of titles published annually: 30 Print
Total Titles: 650 Print
Warehouse: Luisenstr 1, 26382 Wilhelmshaven

Nomada Verlag GmbH
Ernst-Felger-Weg 9, 72770 Reutlingen
Tel: (07072) 921696 *Fax:* (07072) 60856
Web Site: www.nomada-verlag.de
Key Personnel
Mng Dir: Beate Gohs-Haas *E-mail:* b.gohs-haas@
  nomada-verlag.de
Subjects: Foreign Countries
ISBN Prefix(es): 978-3-938121

Nomen Verlag
Homburger Landstr 105, 60435 Frankfurt
Tel: (069) 95 41 62 13 *Fax:* (069) 95 41 62 14
E-mail: nomen@nomen-verlag.de
Web Site: www.nomen-verlag.de
Key Personnel
Contact: Joachim Schaefer

Subjects: Economics, Government, Political Science, Health, Nutrition, Society
ISBN Prefix(es): 978-3-939816

Nomos Verlagsgesellschaft mbH & Co KG
Waldseestr 3-5, 76530 Baden-Baden
Tel: (07221) 2104-0 *Fax:* (07221) 2104-27
E-mail: nomos@nomos.de
Web Site: www.nomos.de
Key Personnel
Mng Dir: Dr Alfred Hoffmann
Marketing Manager: Axel Klimek
  E-mail: klimek@nomos.de
Founded: 1936
Subjects: Business, Economics, Government, Po-
  litical Science, Health, Nutrition, History, Law,
  Science (General), Social Sciences, Sociology,
  Culture, Research
ISBN Prefix(es): 978-3-7890; 978-3-8329
Parent Company: C H Beck Gruppe
Orders to: International Specialized Book Ser-
  vices (ISBS), 920 NE 58 Ave, Suite 300, Port-
  land, OR 97213-3786, United States *Tel:* 503-
  287-3093 *Fax:* 503-280-8832 *E-mail:* orders@
  isbs.com *Web Site:* www.isbs.com (Canada &
  USA)

Nora Verlagsgemeinschaft
Pettenkoferstr 16-18, 10247 Berlin
Tel: (030) 20454990 *Fax:* (030) 20454991
E-mail: kontakt@nora-verlag.de
Web Site: www.nora-verlag.de
Key Personnel
Mng Partner: Dr Philipp Dyck *E-mail:* dr.philipp.
  dyck@nora-verlag.de; Hans Westerheide
  E-mail: hans.westerheide@nora-verlag.de
Subjects: Fiction, Nonfiction (General)
ISBN Prefix(es): 978-3-86557; 978-3-935445;
  978-3-936735

Novalis Verlag GbR+
Neukirchen 86a, 24972 Steinbergkirche
Tel: (04632) 875482 *Fax:* (04632) 875488
E-mail: info@novalisverlag.de
Web Site: www.novalisverlag.de
Key Personnel
Owner & Chief Editor: Dr Michael Frensch
  E-mail: frensch@novalisverlag.de; Eva Fren-
  sch *E-mail:* evafrensch@novalisverlag.de
Founded: 1944
Membership(s): Boersenverein des Deutschen
  Buchhandels.
Subjects: Art, Biography, Memoirs, Child Care
  & Development, Economics, Education, In-
  spirational, Spirituality, Philosophy, Science
  (General), Anthroposophy, Esoterik
ISBN Prefix(es): 978-3-907160; 978-3-907260;
  978-3-941664
Total Titles: 123 Print
Distribution Center: Herold Fulfillment GmbH,
  Raiffeisenallee 10, 82041 Oberhaching, Con-
  tact: Wolfgang Fitz *Tel:* (089) 613871-0
  Fax: (089) 613871-20 *E-mail:* herold@herold-
  va.de *Web Site:* www.herold-va.de

Nuennerich-Asmus Verlag & Media GmbH
Robert-Koch-Str 8, 55129 Mainz
Tel: (06131) 622 50-91 *Fax:* (06131) 576 57-89
E-mail: verlag@na-verlag.de; vertrieb@na-verlag.
  de
Web Site: www.na-verlag.de
Key Personnel
Publisher: Dr Annette Nuennerich-Asmus
Marketing: Sarah Prause *Tel:* (06131) 622 50-93
Membership(s): Verlags-Karree eV.
Subjects: Archaeology, Art, History, Nonfiction
  (General), Art History
ISBN Prefix(es): 978-3-943904
Distribution Center: Brockhaus Kommission-
  sgeschaeft GmbH, Kreidlerstr 9, 70806
  Kornwestheim, Contact: Klaus Nuebel
  Tel: (07154) 132778 *Fax:* (07154) 132713
E-mail: naverlag@brocom.de

Dr Franz Hain Verlagsauslieferungen GmbH,
Dr-Otto-Neurath-Gasse 5, 1220 Vienna, Austria *Tel:* (01) 2826565 *Fax:* (01) 2822582
E-mail: bestell@hain.at
Buchzentrum AG, Industriestr Ost 10, 4614
Haegendorf, Switzerland, Contact: Markus
Fritz *Tel:* (062) 2092725 *Fax:* (062) 2092788
E-mail: fritz@buchzentrum.ch

NWB Verlag GmbH & Co KG+
Eschstr 22, 44629 Herne
Tel: (02323) 141-900 *Fax:* (02323) 141-123
E-mail: info@nwb.de; service@nwb.de;
bestellung@nwb.de
Web Site: www.nwb.de
Key Personnel
Mng Dir: Dr Ludger Kleyboldt
Press Officer: Nina Voss *Tel:* (02323) 141-151
Fax: (02323) 141-335 *E-mail:* n.voss@nwb.de
Founded: 1947
Specialize in tax & business law.
Subjects: Accounting, Business, Career Development, Law, Management, Business Law, Business Management, Tax Law
ISBN Prefix(es): 978-3-482
Associate Companies: Verlag fuer die Rechts- und
Anwaltspraxis GmbH & Co KG
Subsidiaries: Friedrich Kiehl Verlag GmbH
Shipping Address: Schuechtermannstr 180, 44628
Herne
Warehouse: Schuechtermannstr 180, 44628 Herne

nymphenburger+
Subsidiary of Buchverlage LangenMueller Herbig
nymphenburger terra magica
Thomas Wimmer Ring 11, 80539 Munich
Tel: (089) 29088-0 *Fax:* (089) 29088-144
E-mail: info@herbig.net
Web Site: www.herbig.net; www.herbig.net/
verlage/nymphenburger.html
Key Personnel
Publisher & Mng Dir: Brigitte Fleissner-Mikorey
Foreign Rights Dir: Sonja Schmidt *Tel:* (089)
29088-157 *Fax:* (089) 29088-178 *E-mail:* s.
schmidt@herbig.net
Sales Manager: Sissi Klauser *Tel:* (089) 29088-
129
Press & Public Relations: Anja Volkmer
Tel: (089) 29088-132 *Fax:* (089) 29088-178
E-mail: a.volkmer@herbig.net
Production: Ina Hesse *Tel:* (089) 29088-128
Fax: (089) 29088-166 *E-mail:* i.hesse@herbig.
net
Founded: 1946
Subjects: Art, Biography, Memoirs, Child Care
& Development, Crafts, Games, Hobbies, Fiction, Health, Nutrition, Nonfiction (General),
Outdoor Recreation, Philosophy, Photography,
Religion - Buddhist, Self-Help, Sports, Athletics, True Life Stories
ISBN Prefix(es): 978-3-485
Total Titles: 25 Print
Ultimate Parent Company: F A Herbig Verlagsbuchhandlung GmbH
Associate Companies: Herbig; LangenMueller;
LangenMueller|Hoerbuch; terra magica
Foreign Rep(s): Mohr Morawa Buchvertrieb
GmbH (Johann Czap) (Eastern Austria); Mohr
Morawa Buchvertrieb GmbH (Michael Hipp)
(Western Austria); Markus Vonarburg (Switzerland)

Mediengruppe Oberfranken GmbH & Co KG
Gutenbergstr 1, 96050 Bamberg
Tel: (0951) 188-0 *Fax:* (0951) 188-118
E-mail: info@mg-oberfranken.de;
unternehmenskommunikation@mg-oberfranken.
de
Web Site: www.mediengruppe-oberfranken.de
Key Personnel
Mng Dir: Walter Schweinsberg

Communications: Maren Scholz *Tel:* (0951) 188-
379 *Fax:* (0951) 188-324
Subjects: Career Development, Management,
Self-Help, Wine & Spirits
ISBN Prefix(es): 978-3-944002

Edition Oberkassel
Luetticher Str 15, 40547 Duesseldorf
Tel: (0211) 5595090 *Fax:* (0211) 5595092
E-mail: info@edition-oberkassel.de
Web Site: www.editionoberkassel.de
Key Personnel
Publisher: Detlef Knut
Editor: Barbara Klein *E-mail:* barbarak@edition-
oberkassel.de
Founded: 2010
Subjects: Criminology, Fiction, Mysteries, Suspense, Nonfiction (General)
ISBN Prefix(es): 978-3-943121; 978-3-981305

Oceanum Verlag eK
Thienkamp 93, 26215 Wiefelstede
Tel: (04402) 5 95 56 99 *Fax:* (04402) 5 95 56 98
E-mail: info@oceanum.de
Web Site: www.oceanum.de
Subjects: Maritime, Photography, Regional Interests, Transportation, Travel & Tourism, Shipping, Ships
ISBN Prefix(es): 978-3-86927

Oculum-Verlag GmbH
Spardorfer Str 67, 91054 Erlangen
Tel: (09131) 970694 *Fax:* (09131) 978596
E-mail: info@oculum.de; verlag@oculum.de;
bestellung@oculum.de
Web Site: www.oculum.de
Key Personnel
Mng Dir: Ronald Stoyan
German language publisher for stargazers & amateur astronomers.
Subjects: Astronomy
ISBN Prefix(es): 978-3-938469; 978-3-9807540
Distribution Center: Leipziger Kommissions- und
Grossbuchhandelsgesellschaft mbH (LKG),
An der Suedspitze 1-12, 04571 Roetha, Contact: Christine Falk *Tel:* (034206) 65-129
Fax: (034206) 65-1736 *E-mail:* cfalk@lkg-
service.de *Web Site:* www.lkg-va.de
Mohr Morawa Buchvertrieb GmbH, Sulzengasse 2, 1230 Vienna, Austria *Tel:* (01) 680
14-0 *Fax:* (01) 680 71 30 *E-mail:* momo@
mohrmorawa.at *Web Site:* www.mohrmorawa.at
Alfred Dessauer, Raeffelstr 32, 8045 Zurich,
Switzerland, Contact: Stefan Reiss *Tel:* (044)
46696-96 *Fax:* (044) 46696-69 *E-mail:* stefan.
reiss@dessauer.ch

OEKO-TEST Verlag GmbH
Kassler Str 1a, 60486 Frankfurt am Main
Mailing Address: Postfach 90 07 66, 60447
Frankfurt am Main
Tel: (069) 9 77 77-0 *Fax:* (069) 9 77 77-139
E-mail: verlag@oekotest.de; presse@oekotest.de
Web Site: www.oekotest.de; shop.oekotest.de
Key Personnel
Mng Dir: Patrick Junker *E-mail:* patrick.junker@
oekotest.de
Mng Dir & Editor-in-Chief: Juergen Stellpflug
E-mail: juergen.stellpflug@oekotest.de
Adversting Manager: Peter Staesche *Tel:* (069)
9 77 77-156 *Fax:* (069) 9 77 77-149
E-mail: anzeigen@oekotest.de
Press & Marketing: Edigna Menhard *Tel:* (0821)
450 356-32 *Fax:* (0821) 450 356-78
E-mail: edigna.menhard@oekotest.de
Founded: 1985
Subjects: Child Care & Development, Cookery, Environmental Studies, Fashion, Finance,
Health, Nutrition, House & Home, Technology

ISBN Prefix(es): 978-3-929530
Branch Office(s)
Kobelweg 68a, 86156 Augsburg *Tel:* (0821) 450
356-0

oekobuch Verlag & Versand GmbH+
Gewerbestr 15 a, 79219 Staufen
Mailing Address: Postfach 1126, 79216 Staufen
Tel: (07633) 50613 *Fax:* (07633) 50870
E-mail: verlag@oekobuch.de
Web Site: www.oekobuch.de
Key Personnel
Owner & Mng Dir: Heinz Ladener *E-mail:* heinz.
ladener@oekobuch.de; Claudia Lorenz-Ladener
E-mail: claudia.ladener@oekobuch.de
Founded: 1979
Subjects: Architecture & Interior Design, Civil
Engineering, Crafts, Games, Hobbies, Energy,
Environmental Studies, House & Home
ISBN Prefix(es): 978-3-922964
Total Titles: 42 Print
Distribution Center: Die Werkstatt Verlagsauslieferung, Koenigstr 43, 26180 Rastede
Tel: (04402) 9263-0 *Fax:* (04402) 926-50
E-mail: info@werkstatt-auslieferung.de (Germany & Austria)

oekom verlag GmbH
Waltherstr 29, 80337 Munich
Tel: (089) 54 41 84-0 *Fax:* (089) 54 41 84 49
E-mail: kontakt@oekom.de
Web Site: www.oekom.de
Key Personnel
Chief Executive Officer: Jacob Radloff *Tel:* (089)
54 41 84-0 *E-mail:* radloff@oekom.de
Mng Editor: Dr Ulrike Sehy *Tel:* (043) 311 07-85
E-mail: sehy@oekom.ch
Press & Public Relations: Katharina Nuesslein
Tel: (089) 54 41 84-34 *E-mail:* nuesslein@
oekom.de
Founded: 1989
Specialize in environmental & sustainability issues.
Subjects: Agriculture, Business, Economics, Education, Environmental Studies, Government,
Political Science, Health, Nutrition, Science
(General), Administration, Biodiversity Protection, Climate Change, Ecology, Environmental
Sustainability, Natural Resources
ISBN Prefix(es): 978-3-86581; 978-3-928244;
978-3-936581

Oekotopia Verlag GmbH & Co KG+
Hafenweg 26 a, 48155 Muenster
Tel: (0251) 48198-0 *Fax:* (0251) 48198-29
E-mail: info@oekotopia-verlag.de
Web Site: www.oekotopia-verlag.de
Key Personnel
Mng Dir: Andreas Berg Moser; Stefan Scholz
E-mail: scholz@oekotopia-verlag.de
Sales Manager: Elke Stump *Tel:* (0251) 48198-11
E-mail: elke.stump@oekotopia-verlag.de
Press: Imke Koch *Tel:* (0251) 48198-17
Fax: (0251) 48198-29 *E-mail:* imke.koch@
oekotopia-verlag.de
Founded: 1983
Specialize in environmental/education.
Subjects: Drama, Theater, Education, Environmental Studies, Fiction, History, Human Relations, Humor, Music, Dance, Nonfiction (General), Outdoor Recreation, Psychology, Psychiatry
ISBN Prefix(es): 978-3-925169; 978-3-931902;
978-3-936286
Foreign Rep(s): Jutta Bussmann (Austria); Manfred Fischer-Reingruber (Western Austria);
Guenther Raunjak (Eastern Austria); Scheidegger & Co AG (Angela Kindlimann) (Switzerland)
Foreign Rights: Ute Koerner Literary Agent SL
(Brazil, Latin America, Portugal, Spain); Living (Italy); TRCT MEDIEN GmbH (China,
Taiwan)

Oekumenischer Verlag Dr R-F Edel
Rathmecker Weg 13, 58513 Luedenscheid
Tel: (02351) 51547 *Fax:* (02351) 568908
E-mail: oekverlag@t-online.de
Web Site: www.edel-verlag.de
Key Personnel
Manager: Klaus Busenius
Founded: 1948
Subjects: Art, Biblical Studies, Biography, Memoirs, Ethnicity, History, Language Arts, Linguistics, Nonfiction (General), Philosophy, Religion - Catholic, Theology
ISBN Prefix(es): 978-3-87598

Hayati Oenel Verlag+
Silcherstr 13, 50827 Cologne
Tel: (0221) 58 85 40 *Fax:* (0221) 58 85 48
E-mail: verlag@oenel.de
Web Site: www.oenel.de
Key Personnel
Owner: C Hayati Oenel
Founded: 1982
Subjects: Travel & Tourism
ISBN Prefix(es): 978-3-924542; 978-3-929490; 978-3-933348

Oertel + Spoerer Verlags-GmbH + Co KG+
Beutterstr 10, 72764 Reutlingen
Mailing Address: Postfach 1642, 72706 Reutlingen
Tel: (07121) 302 552 *Fax:* (07121) 302 558
E-mail: info@oertel-spoerer.de
Web Site: www.oertel-spoerer-verlag.de
Key Personnel
Mng Dir: Michael Eyckeler
Founded: 1888
Publishing & printing of books & periodicals.
Subjects: Animals, Pets, Cookery, Crafts, Games, Hobbies, Nonfiction (General)
ISBN Prefix(es): 978-3-921017; 978-3-88627
Total Titles: 140 Print

Verlag Friedrich Oetinger GmbH+
Poppenbuetteler Chaussee 53, 22397 Hamburg
Mailing Address: Postfach 65 82 30, 22374 Hamburg
Tel: (040) 607909-02 *Fax:* (040) 6072326
E-mail: oetinger@verlagsgruppe-oetinger.de
Web Site: www.oetinger.de
Key Personnel
Mng Dir: Silke Weitendorf; Till Weitendorf
Marketing Manager: Lars Spicher
  E-mail: marketing@verlagsgruppe-oetinger.de
Sales Manager: Susanne White *Tel:* (040) 607909-777 *Fax:* (040) 607909-550
  E-mail: vertrieb@verlagsgruppe-oetinger.de
Advertising: Tina Jacobsen *Tel:* (040) 607909-791 *Fax:* (040) 607909-891
  E-mail: initiativbewerbung@verlagsgruppe-oetinger.de
Rights & Licensing: Renate Reichstein *Tel:* (040) 607909-713 *E-mail:* lizenzen@verlagsgruppe-oetinger.de
Founded: 1946
Subjects: Fiction
ISBN Prefix(es): 978-3-7891
Subsidiaries: Cecilie Dressler Verlag; Heinrich Ellermann Verlag; Erika Klopp Verlag; Oetinger Audio; Oetinger Kinderkino; Oetinger34

Dr Oetker Verlag, *imprint of* ZS Verlag GmbH

Dr Oetker Verlag KG+
Imprint of ZS Verlag GmbH
Lutterstr 14, 33617 Bielefeld
Tel: (0521) 155-2862 *Fax:* (0521) 155-2995
E-mail: presse@oetker.de
Web Site: www.oetker-gruppe.de
Founded: 1951

Subjects: Cookery
ISBN Prefix(es): 978-3-7670

Officina Ludi Pressendrucke
Hoisdorfer Landstr 60, 22927 Grosshansdorf
Tel: (04102) 62 521 *Fax:* (04102) 604 800
E-mail: officinaludi@aol.com
Web Site: www.officinaludi.de
Key Personnel
Dir: Dr Claus Lorenzen
Founded: 1989
Subjects: Fiction, Poetry

Offizin-Verlag
Boedekerstr 75, 30161 Hannover
Tel: (0511) 8076194 *Fax:* (0511) 624730
E-mail: info@offizin-verlag.de
Web Site: www.offizin-verlag.de
Key Personnel
Contact: Dr Michael Buckmiller
Specialize in critical literature on politics & society.
Subjects: Government, Political Science
ISBN Prefix(es): 978-3-930345
Distribution Center: SOVA, Friesstr 20-24, 60388 Frankfurt am Main *Tel:* (069) 4102-11 *Fax:* (069) 4102-80 *E-mail:* sovaffm@t-online.de

Oktober Verlag
Am Hawerkamp 31, 48155 Muenster
Tel: (0251) 620 650 814 *Fax:* (0251) 620 650 819
E-mail: mail@oktoberverlag.de
Web Site: www.oktoberverlag.de
Key Personnel
Publishing Dir: Michael Billmann
  E-mail: billmann@oktoberverlag.de; Roland Tauber *E-mail:* tauber@oktoberverlag.de
Founded: 2001
Subjects: Cookery, Criminology, Fiction, Literature, Literary Criticism, Essays, Sports, Athletics
ISBN Prefix(es): 978-3-941895; 978-3-938568

Oldenbourg Schulbuchverlag
Division of Cornelsen Verlag GmbH
Mecklenburgische Str 53, 14197 Berlin
Tel: (030) 897 85-0 *Fax:* (030) 897 85-578
E-mail: service@cornelsen.de; presse@cornelsen.de
Web Site: www.oldenbourg.de/osv
Key Personnel
Mng Dir: Dr Joerg Platiel
Press: Annette Kuenkamp *Tel:* (089) 450 51-245
Founded: 1858
Major publisher of textbooks for public schools.
Subjects: Biological Sciences, Business, Chemistry, Chemical Engineering, English as a Second Language, Environmental Studies, Geography, Geology, History, Literature, Literary Criticism, Essays, Mathematics, Music, Dance, Philosophy, Physics
ISBN Prefix(es): 978-3-7627
Ultimate Parent Company: Franz Cornelsen Bildungsgruppe

Oldenbourg Wissenschaftsverlag+
Genthiner Str 13, 10785 Berlin
Tel: (030) 260 05-0 *Fax:* (030) 260 05-251
E-mail: info@degruyter.com
Web Site: www.degruyter.com
Key Personnel
Senior Editorial Dir, History: Martin Rethmeier *Tel:* (089) 76 902-440 *E-mail:* martin.rethmeier@degruyter.com
Editorial Dir, Business & Economics: Doris Funke *Tel:* (089) 76 902-430 *E-mail:* doris.funke@degruyter.com
Editorial Dir, Engineering: Angelika Sperlich *Tel:* (089) 76 902-420 *E-mail:* angelika.sperlich@degruyter.com

Marketing Dir: Ralf Gruemme *Tel:* (030) 260 05-148 *Fax:* (030) 260 05-322 *E-mail:* ralf.gruemme@degruyter.com
Founded: 1858
Subjects: Economics, Education, Electronics, Electrical Engineering, Engineering (General), History, Language Arts, Linguistics, Philosophy, Psychology, Psychiatry, Science (General), Social Sciences, Sociology, Technology, Natural Sciences
ISBN Prefix(es): 978-3-486
Parent Company: Walter de Gruyter GmbH
Distribution Center: Cornelsen Verlagskontor GmbH, 33598 Bielefeld *Tel:* (0521) 9719-323 *E-mail:* oldenbourg@cvk.de (for shipment to Germany, Austria & Switzerland)

Georg Olms AG - Verlag+
Hagentorwall 7, 31134 Hildesheim
Tel: (05121) 1 50-10 *Fax:* (05121) 1 50-150
E-mail: info@olms.de; rights@olms.de; production@olms.de; public.relations@olms.de
Web Site: www.olms.com
Founded: 1945
Subjects: Architecture & Interior Design, Art, Asian Studies, Biography, Memoirs, Cookery, Drama, Theater, Education, Government, Political Science, History, Language Arts, Linguistics, Library & Information Sciences, Literature, Literary Criticism, Essays, Music, Dance, Philosophy, Religion - Islamic, Religion - Jewish, Religion - Protestant, Romance, Science (General), Social Sciences, Sociology, Sports, Athletics, Theology
ISBN Prefix(es): 978-3-487
Number of titles published annually: 250 Print
Total Titles: 7,000 Print; 350 Online
Parent Company: Georg Olms AG, Zurich, Switzerland
Associate Companies: Weidmannsche Verlagsbuchhandlung
Imprints: Olms New Media; Olms Online (ebook); Olms Presse
Subsidiaries: Edition Olms AG
U.S. Office(s): Georg Olms Verlag, Empire State Bldg, 350 Fifth Ave, 59th floor, New York, NY 10118-0069, United States
Distribution Center: arvato media GmbH - VVA, Abt D6E2, Postfach 1254, 33399 Verl, Contact: Birgit Auberger *Tel:* (05241) 8042221 *Fax:* (05241) 8094123 *E-mail:* birgit.auberger@bertelsmann.de

Olms New Media, *imprint of* Georg Olms AG - Verlag

Olms Online, *imprint of* Georg Olms AG - Verlag

Olms Presse, *imprint of* Georg Olms AG - Verlag

OLZOG Verlag GmbH+
Welserstr 1, 81373 Munich
Tel: (089) 71 04 66 60 *Fax:* (089) 71 04 66 61
E-mail: mailkontakt@olzog.de; service@olzog.de
Web Site: www.olzog.de
Key Personnel
Publisher: Dr Reinhard Moestl
Mng Dir: Klaus Hengster
Marketing & Press: Patricia Fritsch-Lange
Founded: 1949
Membership(s): TR-Verlagsunion GmbH.
Subjects: Economics, Education, Film, Video, Foreign Countries, Government, Political Science, History, Journalism, Management, Marketing, Publishing & Book Trade Reference, Social Sciences, Sociology
ISBN Prefix(es): 978-3-7892
Number of titles published annually: 20 Print
Total Titles: 200 Print
Shipping Address: Rhenus Medien Logistik GmbH & Co KG, Justus-von-Liebig-Str 1, 86899 Landsberg am Lech

Distribution Center: Rhenus Medien Logistik GmbH & Co KG, Justus-von-Liebig-Str 1, 86899 Landsberg am Lech, Contact: Danila Skambracks *Tel:* (08191) 97000-220
Orders to: Rhenus Medien Logistik GmbH & Co KG, Justus-von-Liebig-Str 1, 86899 Landsberg am Lech
Returns: Rhenus Medien Logistik GmbH & Co KG, Justus-von-Liebig-Str 1, 86899 Landsberg am Lech

Omega-Verlag
Imprint of Die Silberschnur Verlag GmbH
Steinstr 1, 56593 Guellesheim
Tel: (02687) 92 90 68; (02687) 92 80 52 (orders) *Fax:* (02687) 92 95 24
E-mail: info@silberschnur.de
Web Site: www.silberschnur.de
Key Personnel
Publisher: Gisela Bongart; Martin Meier
Subjects: Inspirational, Spirituality, Well-being
ISBN Prefix(es): 978-3-930243

One Verlag, *imprint of* Bastei Luebbe GmbH & Co KG

Onkel & Onkel
Gubener Str 47, 10243 Berlin
Tel: (030) 61 07 39 57 *Fax:* (030) 61 07 45 78
E-mail: look@onkelundonkel.com
Web Site: www.onkelundonkel.com
Key Personnel
Publisher: Volker Oppmann
Public Relations: Jana Kuehn *E-mail:* jana-kuehn@gmx.net
Subjects: Art, Humor, Literature, Literary Criticism, Essays, Culture
ISBN Prefix(es): 978-3-940029
Distribution Center: GVA, Postfach 2021, 37010 Goettingen *Tel:* (0551) 48 71 77 *Fax:* (0551) 413 92 *E-mail:* bestellung@gva-verlage.de *Web Site:* www.gva-verlage.de

Open House Verlag
Beethovenstr 31, 04107 Leipzig
Tel: (0341) 222 873 83 *Fax:* (0321) 214 352 35
E-mail: kontakt@openhouse-verlag.de
Web Site: www.openhouse-verlag.de
Key Personnel
Editor: Rainer Hoeltschl *E-mail:* r.hoeltschl@openhouse-verlag.de
Press & Public Relations: Christiane Lang *E-mail:* c.lang@openhouse-verlag.de
Founded: 2011
Subjects: Art, Government, Political Science, History, Literature, Literary Criticism, Essays, Science (General)
ISBN Prefix(es): 978-3-944122

orange-press GmbH
Guenterstalstr 44a, 79100 Freiburg
Tel: (0761) 287 117 *Fax:* (0761) 287 118
E-mail: info@orange-press.com
Web Site: www.orange-press.com
Key Personnel
Manager: Martin Baltes *E-mail:* martin.baltes@orange-press.com
Dir, Publications: Undine Loehfelm *E-mail:* undine.loehfelm@orange-press.com
Subjects: Biological Sciences, Cookery, Fiction, Philosophy
ISBN Prefix(es): 978-3-936086
Foreign Rep(s): Michael Orou (Eastern Austria); Guenter Thiel (Western Austria); Markus Wieser (Switzerland)
Distribution Center: GVA, Postfach 2021, 3710 Goettingen *Tel:* (0551) 487177 *Fax:* (0551) 41392 *E-mail:* blank@gva-verlage.de
Mohr Morawa Buchvertrieb GmbH, Sulzengasse 2, 1230 Vienna, Austria *Tel:* (01) 680

14-0 *Fax:* (01) 688 71 30 *E-mail:* momo@mohrmorawa.at *Web Site:* www.mohrmorawa.at
AVA Verlagsauslieferung AG, Centralweg 16, 8910 Affoltern am Albis, Switzerland *Tel:* (044) 762 42 60 *Fax:* (044) 762 42 10 *E-mail:* verlagsservice@ava.ch

Oreos Verlag eK+
Krottenthal 9, 83666 Waakirchen
Tel: (08021) 86 68 *Fax:* (08021) 17 50
E-mail: oreos@oreos.de
Web Site: www.oreos.de
Key Personnel
Publisher: Walter Lachenmann
Founded: 1982
Subjects: Biography, Memoirs, Music, Dance, Regional Interests
ISBN Prefix(es): 978-3-923657

Edition Orient
Muskauer Str 4, 10997 Berlin
Tel: (030) 61 28 03 61 *Fax:* (030) 61 07 32 91
E-mail: info@edition-orient.de
Web Site: www.edition-orient.de
Key Personnel
Owner & Publisher: Stephan Trudewind
Founded: 1980
Membership(s): Boersenverein des Deutschen Buchhandels eV (Association of German Publishers & Booksellers)
Subjects: Cookery, Drama, Theater, Fiction, Science (General)
ISBN Prefix(es): 978-3-922825
Distribution Center: sozialistische verlagsauslieferung gmbh (sova), Philipp-Reis-Str 17, 63477 Maintal *Tel:* (06181) 9088072 *Fax:* (06181) 9088073 *E-mail:* sovaffm@t-online.de *Web Site:* www.sovaffm.de (Germany & Austria)
ALAM AL KUTUB Arabische Buecher, Postfach 18, 8117 Fallanden, Switzerland, Contact: Rachad Al Kanawati *Tel:* (044) 8254570 *Fax:* (044) 8254570 *E-mail:* info@alam-alkutub.ch *Web Site:* www.alam-alkutub.ch

Orlanda Verlag GmbH+
Furbringerstr 7, 10961 Berlin
Tel: (030) 216 29 60
E-mail: post@orlanda.de; presse@orlanda.de
Web Site: www.orlanda.de
Key Personnel
Management: Anna Mandalka, PhD *E-mail:* mandalka@orlanda.de
Press & Public Relations: Claudia Johann *Tel:* (030) 216 35 66
Founded: 1974
Subjects: Developing Countries, Ethnicity, Health, Nutrition, LGBTQ, Literature, Literary Criticism, Essays, Psychology, Psychiatry, Self-Help, Social Sciences, Sociology
ISBN Prefix(es): 978-3-922166; 978-3-929823; 978-3-936937
Foreign Rep(s): Elisabeth Anintah-Hirt (Austria); AVA Verlagsauslieferung AG (Switzerland)
Distribution Center: Prolit Verlagsauslieferung GmbH, Siemensstr 16, 35463 Fernwald (Annerod), Contact: Nina Kallweit *Tel:* (041) 9 43 93-24 *Fax:* (041) 9 43 93-89 *E-mail:* n.kallweit@prolit.de
Dr Franz Hain Verlagsauslieferung AG, Dr-Otto-Neurath-Gasse 5, 1220 Vienna, Austria *Tel:* (01) 282 65 65 *Fax:* (01) 282 52 82 *E-mail:* bestell@hain.at
Scheidegger & Co AG, c/o AVA Verlagsauslieferung AG, Centralweg 16, 8910 Affoltern, Switzerland *Tel:* (01) 762 42 50 *Fax:* (01) 762 42 10 *E-mail:* scheidegger@ava.ch

Osho Verlag GmbH
Venloer Str 5-7, 50672 Cologne
Tel: (0221) 2780420 *Fax:* (0221) 2780466
E-mail: redaktion@oshotimes.de

Web Site: www.oshotimes.de
Key Personnel
Mng Dir: Robert Doetsch; Susanne Wohlgemuth
Founded: 1988
Also publishes Osho Times (German edition).
Subjects: Behavioral Sciences, Human Relations, Philosophy, Psychology, Psychiatry, Religion - Buddhist, Religion - Catholic, Religion - Hindu, Religion - Islamic, Religion - Jewish, Religion - Protestant, Religion - Other, Self-Help
ISBN Prefix(es): 978-3-925205; 978-3-933556; 978-3-9800883

Osnabrueck, *imprint of* Druck- und Verlagshaus FROMM GmbH & Co KG

Ost-West-Verlag (East West Publications)+
Hauptstr 50, 66333 Voelklingen
Tel: (06802) 994 94 98 *Fax:* (06802) 910 74
E-mail: info@ost-west-verlag.org
Web Site: www.ost-west-verlag.org
Founded: 1978
Subjects: Cookery, Health, Nutrition, Medicine, Nursing, Dentistry, Self-Help, Ecology, Holistic Medicine, Lifestyle
ISBN Prefix(es): 978-3-930564
Number of titles published annually: 40 Print

Ostfalia-Verlag+
Stephanikirchhof 11, 38835 Osterwieck
Tel: (05334) 92 59 02 *Fax:* (05334) 92 59 03
E-mail: info@ostfalia-verlag.de; info@ostfalen-portal.de
Web Site: www.ostfalia-verlag.de; www.ostfalen-portal.de
Key Personnel
Mng Dir: Dr Thomas Dahms *Tel:* (0163) 25 98 456 (cell) *E-mail:* dahms@ostfalen-portal.de
Founded: 1980
Subjects: Fiction, Poetry, Regional Interests
ISBN Prefix(es): 978-3-926560
Total Titles: 32 Print

Ostrecht, *imprint of* Berliner Wissenschafts-Verlag GmbH (BWV)

OZ creativ, *imprint of* Christophorus Verlag GmbH & Co KG

Pabel-Moewig Verlag GmbH+
Karlsruherstr 31, 76437 Rastatt
Tel: (07222) 13 0 *Fax:* (07222) 13 218
E-mail: info@vpm.de
Web Site: www.vpm.de
Key Personnel
Chief Executive Officer: Walter A Fuchs
Publishing Dir, Women's & Children's Magazines: Holger Hinsch
Subjects: Astrology, Occult, Cookery, Crafts, Games, Hobbies, Fashion, Music, Dance, Science Fiction, Fantasy
ISBN Prefix(es): 978-3-8118
Number of titles published annually: 120 Print
Total Titles: 350 Print
Parent Company: Bauer Media Group
Associate Companies: VPM Druck KG
Imprints: Moewig; Neff
Subsidiaries: Hestia Verlag; Paul Neff Verlag

Page & Turner, *imprint of* Verlagsgruppe Random House Bertelsmann

Page & Turner Verlag
Imprint of Verlagsgruppe Random House Bertelsmann
Neumarkter Str 28, 81673 Munich
Tel: (089) 4136-0 *Toll Free Tel:* 0800 500 33 22 *Fax:* (089) 4136-3333
E-mail: kundenservice@randomhouse.de
Web Site: www.randomhouse.de/pageundturner

Key Personnel
Press: Susanne Gruenbeck *Tel:* (089) 4136-3717
Fax: (089) 4136-3723 *E-mail:* susanne.
gruenbeck@randomhouse.de
Founded: 2005
Subjects: Fiction, History, Literature, Literary
Criticism, Essays, Mysteries, Suspense, Sci-
ence Fiction, Fantasy, Crime, Historical Novels,
Women's Novels
ISBN Prefix(es): 978-3-442

PAL Verlagsgesellschaft mbH+
Am Oberen Luisenpark 33, 68165 Mannheim
Tel: (0621) 415741 *Fax:* (0621) 415101
E-mail: info@palverlag.de
Web Site: www.palverlag.de
Key Personnel
Mng Dir: Dr Rolf Merkle
Founded: 1986
Subjects: Biography, Memoirs, Health, Nutrition,
Human Relations, Psychology, Psychiatry, Self-
Help
ISBN Prefix(es): 978-3-923614

Pala-Verlag GmbH+
Rheinstr 35, 64283 Darmstadt
Tel: (06151) 2 30 28 *Fax:* (06151) 29 27 13
E-mail: info@pala-verlag.de
Web Site: www.pala-verlag.de
Key Personnel
Mng Dir: Wolfgang Hertling *E-mail:* w.hertling@
pala-verlag.de
Editorial: Angelika Eckstein *E-mail:* a.eckstein@
pala-verlag.de; Barbara Reis *E-mail:* barbara.
reis@pala-verlag.de
Sales: Katrin Kolb *E-mail:* katrin.kolb@pala-
verlag.de
Founded: 1980
Subjects: Cookery, Environmental Studies, Gar-
dening, Plants, Health, Nutrition, Medicine,
Nursing, Dentistry, Sports, Athletics
ISBN Prefix(es): 978-3-923176; 978-3-89566
Foreign Rep(s): Elisabeth Anintah-Hirt (Austria);
Uta Vonarburg (Switzerland)

Palace Editions
Rheinhohe 33, 53498 Bad Breisig
Tel: (02633) 470110 *Fax:* (02633) 470311
Web Site: www.rusmuseum.ru/eng/editions
Key Personnel
Publisher: Joseph Kiblitsky *E-mail:* kiblitsky@t-
online.de
Subjects: Art
ISBN Prefix(es): 978-3-930775; 978-3-935298;
978-3-938051; 978-3-940761

Palm Verlag, *imprint of* Elsengold Verlag

Palmyra Verlag+
Haupstr 64, 69117 Heidelberg
Tel: (06221) 165409 *Fax:* (06221) 167310
E-mail: palmyra-verlag@t-online.de
Web Site: www.palmyra-verlag.de
Key Personnel
President: Georg Stein
Founded: 1989
Subjects: Anthropology, Foreign Countries, Gov-
ernment, Political Science, Music, Dance, Non-
fiction (General), Religion - Islamic, Middle
East Issues, Muslim
ISBN Prefix(es): 978-3-9802298; 978-3-930378
Foreign Rep(s): Elisabeth Anintah-Hirt (Austria);
Sebastian Graf (Switzerland)
Distribution Center: Leipziger Kommissions- und
Grossbuchhandelsgesellschaft mbH (LKG),
An der Suedspitze 1-12, 04571 Roetha, Con-
tact: Elisabeth Kaiser *Tel:* (034206) 65-106
Fax: (034206) 65-1732 *E-mail:* ekaiser@lkg-
service.de *Web Site:* www.lkg-va.de
Dr Franz Hain Verlagsauslieferung GmbH, Dr-
Otto-Neurath-Gasse 5, 1220 Vienna, Austria

Tel: (01) 282 65 65-77 *Fax:* (01) 282 52 82
E-mail: bestell@hain.at
Scheidegger & Co AG, c/o AVA Verlagsauslieferung AG, Centralweg 16, Postfach 119,
8910 Affoltern am Albis, Switzerland *Tel:* (01)
7624252 *Fax:* (01) 7624210 *E-mail:* b.joss@
ava.ch

Pandion-Verlag+
Gartenstr 10, 55469 Simmern
Tel: (06761) 7142 *Fax:* (06761) 7172
E-mail: info@pandion-verlag.de
Web Site: www.pandion-verlag.de
Key Personnel
Owner & Publisher: Ulrike Schmoll
Founded: 1956
Membership(s): Boersenverein des Deutschen
Buchhandels; Verlags-Karree eV.
Subjects: Art, Fiction, Poetry, Regional Interests,
Religion - Other
ISBN Prefix(es): 978-3-922929

Edition P&L, *imprint of* Bookspot Verlag GmbH

Edition Panorama GmbH
G7, 14, 68159 Mannheim
Tel: (0621) 32 88 69-0 *Fax:* (0621) 32 88 69-20
E-mail: info@editionpanorama.de
Web Site: editionpanorama.com
Key Personnel
Mng Dir: Bernhard Wipfler; Sebastian Wipfler
Subjects: Photography
ISBN Prefix(es): 978-3-89823
Distribution Center: Stuttgarter Verlagskontor
SVK GmbH, Rotebuehlstr 77, 70178 Stuttgart,
Contact: Helga Andler *Tel:* (0711) 66 72-14
39 *Fax:* (0711) 66 72-19 74 *E-mail:* h.andler@
svk.de *Web Site:* www.svk.de
Freytag-Berndt und Artaria KG, Industriestr
10, 2120 Wolkersdorf, Austria *Tel:* (01) 869
90 90 *Fax:* (01) 869 88 55 *E-mail:* sales@
freytagberndt.at *Web Site:* www.freytagberndt.at
Scheidegger & Co AG, c/o AVA Verlagsauslieferung AG, Centralweg 16, 8910 Affoltern
am Albis, Switzerland *Tel:* (044) 7 62 42 50
Fax: (044) 7 62 42 10 *E-mail:* scheidegger@
ava.ch *Web Site:* www.ava.ch

Pantheon, *imprint of* Verlagsgruppe Random
House Bertelsmann

Pantheon Verlag
Imprint of Verlagsgruppe Random House Bertels-
mann
Neumarkter Str 28, 81673 Munich
Tel: (089) 4136-0 *Toll Free Tel:* (0800) 500 33 22
Fax: (089) 4136-3333
E-mail: kundenservice@randomhouse.de
Web Site: www.randomhouse.de/pantheon
Key Personnel
Manager: Thomas Rathnow
Sales Manager: Fiona Arndt *Tel:* (089) 4136-
3035 *Fax:* (089) 4136-63035 *E-mail:* fiona.
arndt@randomhouse.de; Natalie Krieger
Tel: (089) 4136-3852 *Fax:* (089) 4136-63852
E-mail: natalie.krieger@randomhouse.de
Press & Public Relations Lead: Markus Desaga
Tel: (089) 4136-3702 *Fax:* (089) 4136-3897
E-mail: markus.desaga@randomhouse.de
Founded: 2005
Subjects: Biography, Memoirs, Government, Po-
litical Science, History, Nonfiction (General),
Science (General)
ISBN Prefix(es): 978-3-570
Number of titles published annually: 25 Print

PapyRossa Verlags GmbH & Co KG+
Luxemburger Str 202, 50937 Cologne
Tel: (0221) 44 85 45 *Fax:* (0221) 44 43 05
E-mail: mail@papyrossa.de
Web Site: www.papyrossa.de

Key Personnel
Mng Dir: Dr Juergen Harrer
Founded: 1990
Subjects: Developing Countries, Government, Po-
litical Science, History, Human Relations, So-
cial Sciences, Sociology, Women's Studies
ISBN Prefix(es): 978-3-89438
Orders to: SOVA, Friesstr 20-24, 60388 Frank-
furt *Tel:* (069) 41 02 11 *Fax:* (069) 41 02 80
E-mail: sovaffm@t-online.de

**Paranus Verlag der Bruecke Neumuenster
GmbH**
Ehndorfer Str 13-17, 24537 Neumuenster
Mailing Address: Postfach 12 64, 24502 Neu-
muenster
Tel: (04321) 20 04-500 *Fax:* (04321) 20 04-411
E-mail: verlag@paranus.de
Web Site: www.paranus.de
Key Personnel
Founder: Fritz Bremer
Mng Dir: Knud Wieben
Founded: 1989
Publishing project which involves mentally ill
persons in the editing, producing, printing &
distribution of books & periodicals.
Subjects: Art, Literature, Literary Criticism, Es-
says, Psychology, Psychiatry, Science (General)
ISBN Prefix(es): 978-3-926200

Parthas Verlag Berlin
Planufer 92d, 10967 Berlin
Tel: (030) 611 019 10 *Fax:* (030) 611 019 11
E-mail: info@parthasverlag.de; presse@
parthasverlag.de
Web Site: www.parthasverlag.de
Key Personnel
Owner: Gabriel Wachter
Head: Matthias Linnekugel
Foreign Rights: Karin Schneider *Tel:* (030) 61 07
68 28 *E-mail:* k-schneider-literaturagentur@
snafu.de
Press & Public Relations: Barbara Grahlmann
Subjects: Architecture & Interior Design, Art, Bi-
ography, Memoirs, Film, Video, History, Litera-
ture, Literary Criticism, Essays, Music, Dance,
Philosophy, Photography
ISBN Prefix(es): 978-3-86601; 978-3-932529;
978-3-936324
Distribution Center: Berlin Verlag, Berlin
Tel: (030) 44 38 45 36 *Fax:* (030) 44 38 45
46 *E-mail:* vertrieb@berlinverlag.de
Prolit Verlagsauslieferung, Siemensstr 16, 35463
Fernwald, Customer Care: Martin Jenne
Tel: (0641) 9 43 93 27 *Fax:* (0641) 9 43 93
29 *E-mail:* m.jenne@prolit.de
Dr Franz Hain Verlagsauslieferungen GmbH,
Dr-Otto-Neurath-Gasse 5, 1220 Vienna, Aus-
tria *Tel:* (01) 282 65 65 *Fax:* (01) 282 52 82
E-mail: bestell@hain.at
Pegasus Booksellers, Singel 367, 1012 WL Ams-
terdam, Netherlands, Contact: Susan van Oostveen *Tel:* (020) 6 23 11 38 *Fax:* (020) 6 20 34
78 *E-mail:* pegasus@pegasusboek.nl
Buchzentrum AG, Postfach, 4601 Olten, Switzerland *Tel:* (062) 209 25 25 *Fax:* (062) 209 26
27 *E-mail:* kundendienst@buchzentrum.ch

**Parzellers Buchverlag und Werbemittel GmbH
& Co KG+**
Frankfurter Str 8, 36043 Fulda
Tel: (0661) 280363 *Fax:* (0661) 280285
E-mail: bestellungen@parzeller.de
Web Site: www.parzellers.de
Key Personnel
CEO: Rainer Klitsch
Founded: 1873
Subjects: Health, Nutrition, Regional Interests,
Religion - Catholic, Religion - Protestant,
Religion - Other, Social Sciences, Sociology,
Sports, Athletics, Fitness

ISBN Prefix(es): 978-3-7900
Subsidiaries: Parzeller Druck- und Mediendienstleistungen GmbH & Co KG

Passavia Druckservice GmbH & Co KG
(Passavia Printing Service GmbH & Co KG)
Medienstr 5b, 94036 Passau
Tel: (0851) 966 180 0 *Fax:* (0851) 966 180 680
E-mail: info@passavia.de
Web Site: www.passavia.de; www.just-print-it.com
Key Personnel
Senior Manager: Dominik Metzler *Tel:* (0851)
    851 600-24 *Fax:* (0851) 851 600-60
    E-mail: dominik.metzler@passavia.de
Commercial Manager: Karl Maier *Tel:* (0851) 966
    180-349 *Fax:* (0851) 966 180-933 *E-mail:* karl.
    maier@passavia.de
Operations Manager: Peter Oeller *Tel:* (0851)
    966 180-912 *Fax:* (0851) 966 180-931
    E-mail: peter.oeller@passavia.de
Sales Manager: Ernst Schiefersteiner *Tel:* (0851)
    966 180-655 *Fax:* (0851) 966 180-682
    E-mail: ernst.schiefersteiner@passavia.de
Founded: 1888
Specialize in publishing art books, architecture
    books & other fine editions. Also a printer.
Subjects: Fiction, House & Home, Humor, Travel
    & Tourism
ISBN Prefix(es): 978-3-87616
Subsidiaries: Passavia Universitaetsverlag und-
    Druck GmbH

Patmos Verlags+
Imprint of Schwabenverlag AG
Senefelderstr 12, 73760 Ostfildern
Mailing Address: Postfach 42 80, 73745 Ost-
    fildern
Tel: (0711) 44 06-194 *Fax:* (0711) 44 06-177
E-mail: info@patmos.de
Web Site: www.patmos.de
Key Personnel
Executive: Ulrich Peters *Tel:* (0711) 44 06-111
Publishing Dir: Gertrud Widmann *Tel:* (0711)
    44 06-161 *E-mail:* gertrud.widmann@
    schwabenverlag.de
Foreign Rights Manager: Claudia Stegmann
    Tel: (0711) 44 06-148
Production Manager: Wolfgang Sailer *Tel:* (0711)
    44 06-118 *E-mail:* wolfgang.sailer@
    schwabenverlag.de
Advertising & Public Relations: Sabrina Reusch
    Tel: (0711) 44 06-168 *E-mail:* sabrina.reusch@
    schwabenverlag.de
Founded: 1946
Subjects: Antiques, Art, History, Literature, Lit-
    erary Criticism, Essays, Nonfiction (General),
    Religion - Catholic, Religion - Other, Theology
ISBN Prefix(es): 978-3-491; 978-3-8436
Foreign Rep(s): Joe Fuchs (Switzerland); Ver-
    lagsagentur Erich Neuhold (Austria, South Ty-
    rol, Italy)
Foreign Rights: Agenzia Letteraria Internazionale
    (Sibylle Kirchbach) (Italy); The Book Publish-
    ers Association of Israel (Shoshi Grajower)
    (Israel); Hercules Business & Culture GmbH
    (Hongjun Cai) (China); jia-xi books co ltd
    (Becky Lin) (Taiwan); Simona Kessler Interna-
    tional Copyright Agency Ltd (Romania); Meike
    Marx Literary Agency (Japan); ONK Agency
    Ltd (Hatice Gok) (Turkey)
Distribution Center: Leipziger Kommissions- und
    Grossbuchhandelsgesellschaft mbH (LKG),
    An der Suedspitze 1-12, 04571 Roetha, Con-
    tact: Robert Winkler *Tel:* (034206) 65 205
    Fax: (034206) 65 1738 *E-mail:* rwinkler@lkg-
    service.de *Web Site:* www.lkg-va.de
Mohr Morawa Buchvertrieb GmbH, Sulzen-
    gasse 2, 1230 Vienna, Austria *Tel:* (01) 680
    14-0 *Fax:* (01) 688 71-30 *E-mail:* momo@
    mohrmorawa.at *Web Site:* www.mohrmorawa.at

Herder AG Basel Verlagsauslieferungen, Mut-
    tenzer Str 109, 4133 Pratteln 1, Switzerland
    Tel: (061) 8 27 90 60 *Fax:* (061) 8 27 90 67
    E-mail: verkauf@herder.ch

Patris Verlag GmbH
Hoehr Str 109, 56179 Vallendar
Mailing Address: Postfach 1162, 56171 Vallendar
Tel: (0261) 604090 *Fax:* (0261) 671192
E-mail: info@patris-verlag.de; service@patris-
    verlag.de; bestellen@patris-verlag.de
Web Site: www.patris-verlag.de
Key Personnel
Mng Dir: Fr Rudolf Ammann *Tel:* (0261) 60409-
    11 *E-mail:* ammann@patris-verlag.de
Book Production: Anette Kluck
Orders: Sabine Gruenewald *Tel:* (0261) 60409-13
Founded: 1967
Subjects: Biography, Memoirs, Education, In-
    spirational, Spirituality, Literature, Literary
    Criticism, Essays, Psychology, Psychiatry,
    Theology, Educational Literature, Meditation,
    Schoenstatt Movement
ISBN Prefix(es): 978-3-87620
Foreign Rep(s): Martin Hajek Buchhandlung
    GRATIA (Austria)

Pattloch Verlag GmbH & Co KG+
Hilblestr 54, 80636 Munich
Tel: (089) 9271-0 *Fax:* (089) 9271-168
E-mail: vertrieb@droemer-knaur.de; presse@
    droemer-knaur.de
Web Site: www.droemer-knaur.de
Key Personnel
Mng Dir: Josef Roeckl; Christian Tesch; Dr
    Hans-Peter Uebleis
Founded: 1965
Subjects: Nonfiction (General), Religion - Other
ISBN Prefix(es): 978-3-629
Parent Company: Verlagsgruppe Droemer Knaur
    GmbH & Co KG
Distribution Center: Libri de Internet GmbH,
    Friesenweg 1, 22763 Hamburg *Tel:* (040) 4223
    6522 *E-mail:* service@libri.de
Mohr Morawa Buchvertrieb GmbH, Sulzen-
    gasse 2, 1230 Vienna, Austria *Tel:* (01) 680
    14-0 *Fax:* (01) 688 71 30 *E-mail:* momo@
    mohrmorawa.at *Web Site:* www.mohrmorawa.at
Buchzentrum AG, Industriestr Ost 10, 4614 Hae-
    gendorf, Switzerland *Tel:* (062) 2 09 26 26
    Fax: (062) 2 09 26 27 *E-mail:* kundendienst@
    buchzentrum.ch

Paulinus Verlag GmbH+
Max-Planck-Str 14, 54295 Trier
Tel: (0651) 4608-0 *Fax:* (0651) 4608-221; (0651)
    4608-220
E-mail: info@paulinus-verlag.de
Web Site: www.paulinus-verlag.de
Key Personnel
Mng Dir: Annette Peters *Tel:* (0651) 4608-156
Deputy Divisional Manager, Publisher: Adriana
    Walther *Tel:* (0651) 4608-120 *E-mail:* adriana.
    walther@paulinus-verlag.de
Editor: Samuel Hober *Tel:* (0651) 4608-130
    E-mail: samuel.hober@paulinus-verlag.de
Sales & Marketing: Monika Hennen
    E-mail: monika.hennen@paulinus-verlag.de
Founded: 1875
Subjects: Art, History, Regional Interests, Reli-
    gion - Other, Theology
ISBN Prefix(es): 978-3-7902; 978-3-87760

Peachpit/New Riders, *imprint of* Pearson
    Deutschland GmbH

Pearson Business, *imprint of* Pearson
    Deutschland GmbH

Pearson Deutschland GmbH+
Martin-Kollar-Str 10-12, 81829 Munich

Tel: (089) 46003 0 *Fax:* (089) 46003 100
E-mail: info@pearson.de
Web Site: www.pearson.de
Key Personnel
Chief Executive Officer: Dr Detlev Lux
Vice President, Finance & Operations: Helmut
    Schneider
Human Resources Manager: Claudia Marr
    Tel: (089) 46003 122
Product Manager Marketing: Katharina Glueck
    E-mail: katharina.glueck@pearson.com
Production Manager & Marketing: Christine
    Sageder *E-mail:* csageder@pearson.de
Foreign Rights: Angelika Ritthaler *Tel:* (089)
    46003 344 *E-mail:* aritthaler@pearson.de
Founded: 1993
Subjects: Biological Sciences, Business, Chem-
    istry, Chemical Engineering, Computer Science,
    Economics, Electronics, Electrical Engineering,
    Engineering (General), Management, Market-
    ing, Mathematics, Mechanical Engineering,
    Photography, Physics, Psychology, Psychiatry
ISBN Prefix(es): 978-0-7879 (Que); 978-0-672
    (Sams); 978-3-89090; 978-3-87791; 978-3-
    922120; 978-2-7440 (game books); 978-0-
    321 (Peachpit/New Riders/IBM Press/Adobe
    Press); 978-3-8273 (Addison-Wesely); 978-3-
    8272 (Markt+Technik); 978-3-89319; 978-3-
    925118; 978-3-8689 (Pearson Studium); 978-0-
    327 (Prentice Hall); 978-1-58705 (Cisco Press)
Imprints: Addison-Wesley; Adobe Press; Cisco
    Press; IBM Press; Markt+Technik; Peach-
    pit/New Riders; Pearson Business; Pearson
    Studium; Prentice Hall; Que; SAMS

Pearson Studium, *imprint of* Pearson
    Deutschland GmbH

Pelikan Vertriebsgesellschaft mbH & Co KG+
Werftstr 9, 30163 Hannover
Mailing Address: Postfach 11 07 55, 30102 Han-
    nover
Tel: (0511) 6969-0 *Fax:* (0511) 6969-212
E-mail: info@pelikan.com
Web Site: www.pelikan.com
Key Personnel
Mng Dir: Torsten Jahn; Arno Telkaeper
Press & Public Relations: Simone Bahrs
Founded: 1978
Subjects: Fiction
ISBN Prefix(es): 978-3-8144
Parent Company: Pelikan Holding AG, Switzer-
    land
Branch Office(s)
Pelikan PBS-Produktionsgesellschaft mbH &
    Co KG, Pelikanstr 11, 31228 Peine/Voehrum
    Tel: (05171) 299 0 *Fax:* (05171) 299 205
Distributor for Diverse

Pendo Verlag, *imprint of* Piper Verlag GmbH

Pendo Verlag+
Georgenstr 4, 80799 Munich
Tel: (089) 381801-0 *Fax:* (089) 338704
E-mail: info@pendo.de; foreignrights@piper.de
Web Site: www.piper.de
Key Personnel
Publisher: Marcel Hartges
Deputy Sales Manager: Silvio Mohr-Schaaff
    Tel: (089) 381801-44 *Fax:* (089) 381801-68
    E-mail: silvio.mohr-schaaff@piper.de
Foreign Rights: Sven Diedrich *Tel:* (089) 381801-
    26 *Fax:* (089) 381801-120
Press: Eva Brenndoerfer *Tel:* (089) 381801-
    38 *Fax:* (089) 381801-65 *E-mail:* eva.
    brenndoerfer@piper.de
Founded: 1971
Specialize in literature, contemporary history &
    essays.
Subjects: Government, Political Science, History,
    Literature, Literary Criticism, Essays, Nonfic-
    tion (General), Poetry, Religion - Other

ISBN Prefix(es): 978-3-85842
Number of titles published annually: 35 Print
Total Titles: 200 Print
Parent Company: Piper Verlag GmbH
Associate Companies: ivi Verlag; Malik National
Geographic; Malik Verlag; Piper Belletristik;
Piper Fantasy; Piper Gebrauchsanweisungen;
Piper Sachbuch; Piper Taschenbuch; Westend
Imprints: Politics

Pendragon Verlag+
Stapenhorststr 15, 33615 Bielefeld
Tel: (0521) 69689 *Fax:* (0521) 174470
E-mail: kontakt@pendragon.de; presse@
pendragon.de; vertrieb@pendragon.de
Web Site: www.pendragon.de
Key Personnel
Mng Dir, Sales, Rights & Permissions: Guenther
Butkus *E-mail:* guenther.butkus@pendragon.de
Press: Eike Birck
Sales: Jens Gottesleben
Founded: 1981
Subjects: Art, Criminology, Fiction, History, Lit-
erature, Literary Criticism, Essays, Poetry
ISBN Prefix(es): 978-3-923306; 978-3-929096;
978-3-934872; 978-3-86532
Imprints: Edition Bielefelden Kunstverein
Foreign Rep(s): Elisabeth Anintah-Hirt (Austria);
Buch und Medienvertrieb (Markus Vonarburg)
(Switzerland)
Distribution Center: Prolit Verlagsauslieferung
GmbH, Siemensstr 16, 35463 Fern-
wald, Contact: Monika Pankratz *Tel:* (0641)
943930; (0641) 9439322 *Fax:* (0641) 9439329
E-mail: m.pankratz@prolit.de
Dr Franz Hain Verlagsauslieferung, Dr-Otto-
Neurath-Gasse 5, 1220 Vienna, Austria
Tel: (01) 2826565-24 *Fax:* (01) 2825282-70
E-mail: office@hain.at
Buch und Medienvertrieb, Hochstr 357, 8200
Schaffhausen, Switzerland *Tel:* (052) 6435430
Fax: (052) 6435435 *E-mail:* info@buch-
medien.ch

Penhaligon, *imprint of* Verlagsgruppe Random
House Bertelsmann

Penhaligon Verlag
Imprint of Verlagsgruppe Random House Bertels-
mann
Neumarkter Str 28, 81673 Munich
Tel: (089) 4136-0 *Toll Free Tel:* 0800 500 33 22
Fax: (089) 4136-3721; (089) 4136-3333
E-mail: kundenservice@randomhouse.de; vertrieb.
verlagsgruppe@randomhouse.de
Web Site: www.randomhouse.de/penhaligon
Key Personnel
Publisher: Silvia Kuttny-Walser
Program Manager: Urban Holfstetter
Press & Public Relations: Astrid von Willmann
Tel: (089) 4136-3318 *Fax:* (089) 4136-3453
E-mail: astrid.vonwillmann@randomhouse.de
Subjects: Criminology, Humor, Science Fiction,
Fantasy, Satire, Thriller
ISBN Prefix(es): 978-3-7645

Perryman, see Babel Verlag

Persen Verlag GmbH
Bahnhofstr 21-25, 21614 Buxtehude
Mailing Address: Postfach 1656, 21606 Buxte-
hude
Tel: (04161) 7 49 60-40 *Fax:* (04161) 7 49 60-50
E-mail: info@persen.de
Web Site: www.persen.de
Key Personnel
Mng Dir: Christian Glaser
Program Dir: Julia Reinking *E-mail:* j.reinking@
persen.de
Marketing: Ursula Herrmann
Founded: 1976

Provide supportive materials to schools.
Subjects: Biological Sciences, Chemistry, Chemi-
cal Engineering, Computer Science, English as
a Second Language, Geography, Geology, His-
tory, Language Arts, Linguistics, Mathematics,
Music, Dance, Philosophy, Physics, Religion
- Other, Sports, Athletics, Home Economics,
Social Studies
ISBN Prefix(es): 978-3-8344

Persona Verlag
Weberstr 3, 68165 Mannheim
Tel: (0621) 40 96 96 *Fax:* (0621) 401 53 50;
(0621) 69 18 62 (orders)
E-mail: buch@personaverlag.de
Web Site: www.personaverlag.de
Key Personnel
Mng Dir: Lisette Bucholz
Founded: 1983
Subjects: Biography, Memoirs, Government, Po-
litical Science, History, Literature, Literary
Criticism, Essays
ISBN Prefix(es): 978-3-924652
Distribution Center: Sozialistische Verlagsaus-
lieferug SOVA, Friesstr 20-24, 60388 Frankfurt
am Main *Tel:* (069) 41 02 11 *Fax:* (069) 41 02
80

**Verlag J P Peter, Gebr Holstein GmbH & Co
KG**
Erlbacher Str 104, 91541 Rothenburg
Tel: (09861) 4 00-3 81 *Fax:* (09861) 4 00-70
E-mail: peter-verlag@rotabene.de
Web Site: www.peter-verlag.de
Key Personnel
Mng Dir: Wolfgang Schneider
Founded: 1884
Subjects: Poetry, Religion - Other
ISBN Prefix(es): 978-3-87625
Bookshop(s): Evangel Bucherdrenst Rothenburg

C F Peters Musikverlag GmbH & Co KG, see
Musia International
Musikalien-Handelsgesellschaft Ehrlich GmbH
& Co KG

Edition Peters GmbH, *imprint of* Musia
International Musikalien-Handelsgesellschaft
Ehrlich GmbH & Co KG

Jens Peters Publikationen+
Gotenstr 65, 10829 Berlin
Tel: (030) 7847265 *Fax:* (030) 7883127
E-mail: jens.peters@usa.net
Web Site: www.jenspeters.de
Key Personnel
President, Rights & Permissions: Jens Peters
Founded: 1977
Subjects: Travel & Tourism
ISBN Prefix(es): 978-3-923821; 978-3-9800154
Orders to: Osterholzer Dorfstr 45, 28307 Bremen
Tel: (0421) 451743 *Fax:* (0421) 455406

Pfaffenweiler Presse+
Mittlere Str 23, 79292 Pfaffenweiler
Tel: (07664) 8999 *Fax:* (07664) 8999
E-mail: info@pfaffenweiler-presse.de
Web Site: www.pfaffenweiler-presse.de
Key Personnel
Publisher: Herta Flicker *E-mail:* rflicker@
pfaffenweiler-presse.de
Founded: 1974
Subjects: Poetry, Contemporary Literature
ISBN Prefix(es): 978-3-921365; 978-3-927702

Pfalzische Verlagsanstalt GmbH
Industriestr 15, 76829 Landau
Tel: (06341) 06341 *Fax:* (06341) 142-265
Founded: 1892
Subjects: Art, Biography, Memoirs, Fiction, For-
eign Countries, Wine & Spirits

ISBN Prefix(es): 978-3-87629
Orders to: Postfach 1950, 76809 Landau

Fachbuchverlag Pfanneberg GmbH & Co KG
Duesselberger Str 23, 42781 Haan-Gruiten
Mailing Address: Postfach 42 04 64, 42404
Haan-Gruiten
Tel: (02104) 6916-0 *Fax:* (02104) 6916-27
E-mail: info@pfanneberg.de
Web Site: www.europa-lehrmittel.de/c-62/
pfanneberg/
Founded: 1949
Hotel & catering education & training materials.
Subjects: Business, Career Development, Cook-
ery, Health, Nutrition
ISBN Prefix(es): 978-3-8057

**Pfau Verlag Stefan Fricke + Sigrid Konrad
GbR**
Hafenstr 33, 66111 Saarbruecken
Mailing Address: Postfach 102314, 66023 Saar-
bruecken
Tel: (0681) 416 33 94 *Fax:* (0681) 416 33 95
E-mail: info@pfau-verlag.de
Web Site: www.pfau-verlag.de
Key Personnel
Mng Dir: Stefan Fricke; Sigrid Konrad
Founded: 1989
Subjects: Music, Dance
ISBN Prefix(es): 978-3-89727; 978-3-930735

Verlag Dr Friedrich Pfeil
Wolfratshauser Str 27, 81379 Munich
Tel: (089) 742827-0 *Fax:* (089) 7242772
E-mail: info@pfeil-verlag.de
Web Site: www.pfeil-verlag.de
Key Personnel
Editor: Dr Friedrich Pfeil
Founded: 1981
Subjects: Archaeology, Biological Sciences, Ge-
ography, Geology, Philosophy, Ecology, Paleon-
tology
ISBN Prefix(es): 978-3-923871; 978-3-931516;
978-3-89937
Branch Office(s)
Falkweg 37, 81243 Munich

Pferdesport Verlag Ehlers GmbH
Rockwinkeler Landstr 20, 28355 Bremen-
Oberneuland
Mailing Address: Postfach 34 70 95, 28339 Bre-
men
Tel: (0421) 257 55 44 *Fax:* (0421) 257 55 43
E-mail: info@pferdesportverlag.de
Web Site: www.pferdesportverlag.de
Key Personnel
Mng Dir: Marc Oliver Ehlers; Timo Ehlers
Advertising Dir: Maren Arndt
Founded: 1995
Subjects: Sports, Athletics, Equestrian
ISBN Prefix(es): 978-3-934624; 978-3-9804722

Richard Pflaum Verlag GmbH & Co KG+
Lazarettstr 4, 80636 Munich
Mailing Address: Postfach 19 07 37, 80607 Mu-
nich
Tel: (089) 12607-0 *Fax:* (089) 12607-202
E-mail: info@pflaum.de
Web Site: www.pflaum.de
Key Personnel
Publisher: Michael Dietl *E-mail:* dietl@pflaum.de
Mng Dir: Edith Laubner *E-mail:* laubner@
pflaum.de
Sales Manager: Cornelia Kondora *Tel:* (089)
12607-253
Founded: 1919
Subjects: Communications, Electronics, Electri-
cal Engineering, Medicine, Nursing, Dentistry,
Naturopathy, Physiotherapy
ISBN Prefix(es): 978-3-7905

Subsidiaries: Gastgewerbe Verlag GmbH & Co KG; Huethig und Pflaum Verlag GmbH & Co KG Laenderdienst Verlag GmbH
Branch Office(s)
Bad Kissingen
Berlin
Duesseldorf
Heidelberg

Edition Phantasia
Wuenschelstr 18, 76756 Bellheim
Tel: (07272) 8809 *Fax:* (07272) 776081
E-mail: mail@edition-phantasia.de
Web Site: www.edition-phantasia.de
Key Personnel
Publisher & Press: Joachim Koerber
  E-mail: koerber@edition-phantasia.de
Subjects: Literature, Literary Criticism, Essays, Science Fiction, Fantasy
ISBN Prefix(es): 978-3-924959; 978-3-937897

Philipp Reclam jun GmbH & Co KG Stuttgart+
Siemensstr 32, 71254 Ditzingen
Mailing Address: Postfach 1349, 71252 Ditzingen
Tel: (07156) 163 0 *Fax:* (07156) 163 197
E-mail: info@reclam.de
Web Site: www.reclam.de
Key Personnel
Mng Dir: Dr Frank R Max; Franz Schaefer
Marketing & Sales: Dr Karl-Heinz Fallbacher
  Tel: (07156) 163 150 *E-mail:* fallbacher@reclam.de
Press: Claudia Feldtenzer *Tel:* (07156) 163 148
  E-mail: c.feldtenzer@reclam.de
Rights & Permissions: Dr Stephan Koranyi
  Tel: (07156) 163 172 *E-mail:* s.koranyi@reclam.de
Founded: 1828
Subjects: Agriculture, Archaeology, Art, Biography, Memoirs, Drama, Theater, Fiction, Film, Video, History, Literature, Literary Criticism, Essays, Music, Dance, Philosophy, Religion - Other, Jazz
ISBN Prefix(es): 978-3-15

Philippka-Sportverlag eK+
Rektoratsweg 36, 48159 Muenster
Mailing Address: Postfach 150105, 48061 Muenster
Tel: (0251) 23005-0 *Fax:* (0251) 23005-99; (0251) 23005-79
E-mail: info@philippka.de
Web Site: philippka.de/verlag; www.volleyball.de; www.fussballtraining.com
Key Personnel
Publisher: Konrad Honig *Tel:* (0251) 23005-25
  E-mail: honig@philippka.de
Publicity: Peter Moellers *Tel:* (0251) 23005-28
  E-mail: moellers@philippka.de
Founded: 1977
Subjects: Sports, Athletics
ISBN Prefix(es): 978-3-922067; 978-3-89417
Number of titles published annually: 10 Print; 5 CD-ROM
Total Titles: 60 Print; 20 CD-ROM
Associate Companies: Success in Soccer, PO Box 92046, Albuquerque, NM 87109, United States, Contact: Manni Klar *Tel:* 505-889-3680 *Fax:* 505-883-4577 *E-mail:* usorder@successinsoccer.com *Web Site:* www.successinsoccer.com
Foreign Rep(s): Manni Klar (USA)
Foreign Rights: Gudrun Quilling (worldwide)
Warehouse: Albuquerque, NM, United States

Philipps-Universitaet Marburg
Biegenstr 10, 35032 Marburg
Tel: (06421) 28-20 *Fax:* (06421) 28-22500
E-mail: pressestelle@verwaltung.uni-marburg.de
Web Site: www.uni-marburg.de

Key Personnel
President: Prof Dr Katharina Krause *Tel:* (06421) 28-26000 *E-mail:* praesidentin@uni-marburg.de
Head, International Affairs: Petra Kienle
  Tel: (06421) 28-26120 *Fax:* (06421) 28-28998
  E-mail: petra.kienle@verwaltung.uni-marburg.de
Subjects: Anthropology, Archaeology, Biological Sciences, Education, Environmental Studies, History, Language Arts, Linguistics, Library & Information Sciences, Medicine, Nursing, Dentistry, Psychology, Psychiatry, Science (General), Social Sciences, Sociology
ISBN Prefix(es): 978-3-8185

Philo Fine Arts GmbH & Co KG
Wilstorfer Str 71, 21073 Hamburg
Tel: (040) 32083872 *Fax:* (040) 209334879
E-mail: info@philo-fine-arts.de
Web Site: www.philo-fine-arts.de
Key Personnel
Editor: Nicola Torke *E-mail:* torke@philo-fine-arts.de
Sales: Carola Deye *Tel:* (0176) 488 80 394
  E-mail: deye@philo-fine-arts.de
Founded: 1959
Subjects: Art, History, Philosophy
ISBN Prefix(es): 978-3-86572

Philosophia Verlag GmbH+
Gundelindenstr 10, 80805 Munich
Tel: (089) 299975 *Fax:* (089) 30767586
E-mail: info@philosophiaverlag.com
Web Site: www.philosophiaverlag.com; de.philosophiaverlag.com
Key Personnel
Mng Dir & Publisher: Ulrich Staudinger
Editorial Board: Ignacio Angelelli; Hans Burkhardt; Guido Imaguire; Christina Schneider; Barry Smith; Christian Thiel
Sales & Marketing: Frank Kiesebrink
Founded: 1966
Membership(s): Association of Bavarian Publishers & Booksellers; Stock Exchange of German Booksellers
Subjects: Language Arts, Linguistics, Philosophy
ISBN Prefix(es): 978-3-88405
Number of titles published annually: 3 Print
Total Titles: 80 Print
Divisions: Medienbuero Muenchen
Distributed by Vrin (France)

Physica-Verlag+
Imprint of Springer-Verlag GmbH
Tiergartenstr 17, 69121 Heidelberg
Tel: (06221) 487 8345 *Fax:* (06221) 487 8177
Web Site: www.springer.com
Key Personnel
Executive Dir: Dr Werner A Mueller
Founded: 1842
Specialize in economics & management science.
Subjects: Business, Economics, Finance, Management, Mathematics, Regional Interests, Science (General), Econometrics, Information Systems, Statistics
ISBN Prefix(es): 978-3-7908
Number of titles published annually: 100 Print
Total Titles: 500 Print
Orders to: Haberstr 7, 69126 Heidelberg
  Tel: (06221) 345-4301 *Fax:* (06221) 345-4229
  (Germany & Switzerland)
Sachsenplatz 4-6, 1201 Vienna, Austria *Tel:* (01) 330 2415 227 *Fax:* (01) 330 2426 62
  E-mail: books@springer.at

PIAG, see Presse Informations AG (PIAG)

Paul Pietsch Verlage GmbH & Co KG+
Olgastr 86, 70180 Stuttgart
Tel: (0711) 2 10 80-0 *Fax:* (0711) 2 36 04 15
E-mail: ppv@motorbuch.de

Web Site: www.paul-pietsch-verlage.de; www.motorbuch.de
Key Personnel
Publisher: Dr Patricia Scholten *Tel:* (0711) 2 10 80-11
Head, Sales: Christian Pflug *Tel:* (0711) 2 10 80-20 *E-mail:* c.pflug@motorbuch.de
Program Manager: Joachim Kuch *Tel:* (0711) 2 10 80-18 *E-mail:* j.kuch@motorbuch.de
Press & Marketing: Clarissa Bayer *Tel:* (0711) 2 10 80-12 *E-mail:* c.bayer@motorbuch.de
Production: Bernd Leu *Tel:* (0711) 2 10 80-49
  E-mail: b.leu@motorbuch.de
Rights & Permissions: Patricia Hofmann
  Tel: (0711) 2 10 80-13 *E-mail:* p.hofmann@motorbuch.de
Founded: 1962
Subjects: Aeronautics, Aviation, Automotive, How-to, Maritime, Military Science, Travel & Tourism
ISBN Prefix(es): 978-3-87943; 978-3-613; 978-3-344
Divisions: Bucheli Verlag; Motorbuch-Verlag; Mueller Rueschlikon; Pietsch-Verlag; Transpress
Distribution Center: Sigloch Distribution, Am Buchberg 8, 74572 Blaufelden *Tel:* (01805) 45 56 00 *Fax:* (01805) 95 97 29 *E-mail:* ppv@sigloch.de

Piper Belletristik, *imprint of* Piper Verlag GmbH

Piper Fantasy, *imprint of* Piper Verlag GmbH

Piper Gebrauchsanweisungen, *imprint of* Piper Verlag GmbH

Piper Sachbuch, *imprint of* Piper Verlag GmbH

Piper Taschenbuch, *imprint of* Piper Verlag GmbH

Piper Verlag GmbH+
Georgenstr 4, 80799 Munich
Tel: (089) 381801-0 *Fax:* (089) 338704
E-mail: info@piper.de; foreignrights@piper.de
Web Site: www.piper-verlag.de
Key Personnel
Publisher: Felicitas von Lovenberg
Foreign Rights Dir: Sven Diedrich *Tel:* (089) 381801-26 *Fax:* (089) 381801-120
Press Manager: Eva Brenndoerfer *Tel:* (089) 381801-38 *Fax:* (089) 381801-65 *E-mail:* eva.brenndoerfer@piper.de
Sales Manager: Tino Uhlemann *Tel:* (089) 381801-48 *Fax:* (089) 381801-68 *E-mail:* tino.uhlemann@piper.de
Founded: 1904
Specialize in music.
Subjects: Biography, Memoirs, Fiction, History, Music, Dance, Philosophy, Psychology, Psychiatry, Science (General), Theology
ISBN Prefix(es): 978-3-8225; 978-3-89521; 978-3-89029; 978-3-492; 978-3-921909
Number of titles published annually: 300 Print
Parent Company: Bonnier Media Deutschland
Ultimate Parent Company: Bonnier AB
Imprints: ivi Verlag; Malik National Geographic; Malik Verlag; Pendo Verlag; Piper Belletristik; Piper Fantasy; Piper Gebrauchsanweisungen; Piper Sachbuch; Piper Taschenbuch; Westend Verlag
Foreign Rep(s): Buchnetzwerk Verlagsvertretung (Marlene Pobegen & Guenther Staudinger) (Austria, South Tyrol, Italy); Sebastian Inhauser (Switzerland)
Foreign Rights: ACER Agencia Literaria (Isabel Piedrahita) (Portugal, Spanish); Balla-Sztojkov Literary Agency (Catherine Balla) (Hungary); Ivana Beil (Czechia); Berla & Griffini Rights Agency (Barbara Griffini) (Italy); Sabine

Fontaine (France); Markiewicz Litarturagentur (Aleksandra Markiewicz) (Poland); ONK Agency Ltd (Hatice Gok) (Turkey); Marianne Schoenbach Literary Agency (Marianne Schoenbach) (Netherlands)
Distribution Center: Distribook, Schockenriedstr 39, 70565 Stuttgart *Tel:* (0800) 66-111-99 *Fax:* (0711) 7899-1010 *E-mail:* service@distribook.de (Germany & Switzerland)
Dr Franz Hain Verlagsauslieferungen GmbH, Dr-Otto-Neurzth-Gasse 5, 1220 Vienna, Austria *Tel:* (01) 2826565-77 *Fax:* (01) 2825282 *E-mail:* bestell@hain.at

Pixel Transfer Design Studio, *imprint of* Extent Verlag und Service

Planet Girl, *imprint of* Thienemann Verlag GmbH

Planet Girl Verlag
Imprint of Thienemann Verlag GmbH
Blumenstr 36, 70182 Stuttgart
Tel: (0711) 2 10 55-0 *Fax:* (0711) 2 10 55-39
E-mail: info@thienemann.de; planet-girl@thienemann.de
Web Site: cms.thienemann.de
Key Personnel
Mng Dir: Eure Franka
Foreign Rights: Doris Keller-Riehm *Tel:* (0711) 2 10 55 17 *Fax:* (0711) 2 10 55 38
 E-mail: keller-riehm@thienemann.de
Marketing: Sandra Pollex *E-mail:* pollex@thienemann.de
Founded: 2010
Subjects: Literature, Literary Criticism, Essays, Mysteries, Suspense, Science Fiction, Fantasy, Love & Friendship, Thriller, Women's Literature
ISBN Prefix(es): 978-3-522

pmv Peter Meyer Verlag+
Schopenhauer Str 11, 60316 Frankfurt am Main
Tel: (069) 40 56 257-0 *Fax:* (069) 40 56 257-29
E-mail: info@petermeyerverlag.de; vertrieb@petermeyerverlag.de
Web Site: www.petermeyerverlag.de
Key Personnel
Mng Dir & International Rights: Peter Meyer
Mng Dir & Press: Annette Sievers
Founded: 1976
Subjects: Foreign Countries, Language Arts, Linguistics, Outdoor Recreation, Regional Interests, Travel & Tourism
ISBN Prefix(es): 978-3-922057; 978-3-89859
Number of titles published annually: 12 Print
Total Titles: 50 Print
Orders to: Prolit Verlagsauslieferung GmbH, Siemensstr 16, 35463 Fernwald, Contact: Nina Kallweit *Tel:* (0641) 943 93-24 *Fax:* (0641) 943 93-89 *E-mail:* n.kallweit@prolit.de *Web Site:* www.prolit.de

Podszun Buchhandels -und Verlags GmbH+
Elisabethstr 23-25, 59929 Brilon
Tel: (02961) 53213
E-mail: info@podszun-verlag.de
Web Site: www.podszun-verlag.de
Key Personnel
Mng Dir: Walter Podszun
Founded: 1969
Subjects: Automotive, Engineering (General), Transportation
ISBN Prefix(es): 978-3-86133; 978-3-923448
Bookshop(s): Bahnhofstr 9, 59929 Brilon *Tel:* (02961) 2507 *E-mail:* brilon@buecher-podszun.de; Hauptstr 44, 34431 Marsberg *Tel:* (02992) 4505 *E-mail:* marsberg@buecher-podszun.de; Hauptstr 67, 34414 Warburg *Tel:* (05641) 740898 *E-mail:* warburg@buecher-podszun.de

Podzun-Pallas Verlag GmbH+
Juraquelle 26, 91330 Eggolsheim-Bammersdorf
Tel: (09191) 61554-60 *Fax:* (09191) 61554-66
E-mail: info@podzun-pallas-verlag.de
Web Site: www.podzun-pallas.de
Founded: 1979
Subjects: Military Science
ISBN Prefix(es): 978-3-7909

Poesie 21, *imprint of* Anton G Leitner Verlag

Politics, *imprint of* Pendo Verlag

Politik und Spiritualitaet, *imprint of* Drei Eichen Verlag

Polyglott-Verlag+
Harvestehuder Weg 41, 20149 Hamburg
Tel: (040) 44 18 83 36
E-mail: redaktion@polyglott.de
Web Site: www.polyglott.de
Key Personnel
Mng Dir: Thomas Ganske; Frank H Haeger; Peter Notz
Founded: 1902
Sales & promotion through Travelhouse Media.
Subjects: Foreign Countries, Travel & Tourism
ISBN Prefix(es): 978-3-493
Parent Company: GVG Travel Media GmbH (GTM)
Ultimate Parent Company: Ganske Verlagsgruppe
Associate Companies: Polyglott Apa
Distribution Center: Travel House Media GmbH

PONS GmbH
Rotebuehlstr 77, 70178 Stuttgart
Mailing Address: Postfach 10 60 16, 70049 Stuttgart
Tel: (0711) 6672-0; (0711) 6672 1333
 Fax: (0711) 9880 9000 99
E-mail: info@pons.de
Web Site: www.pons.de
Key Personnel
Publisher: Dr Michael Klett
Dir: Gabriele Schmidt
Head, Foreign Rights & Co-Productions: Ulrike Keppler *Tel:* (0711) 6672 5724 *Fax:* (0711) 6672 2004 *E-mail:* u.keppler@pons.de
Press: Anne Pelzer *Tel:* (0711) 6672 5150
 E-mail: a.pelzer@pons.de
Founded: 1897
Dictionaries & language learning materials for students & adults.
Subjects: Business, Education, Language Arts, Linguistics, Language Education, Self-Study
ISBN Prefix(es): 978-3-12
Parent Company: Klett Gruppe
Distribution Center: Balmer Buecherdienst AG, Kobiboden, 8840 Einsiedeln, Switzerland *Tel:* (0848) 8408-20 *Fax:* (0848) 8408-30 *Web Site:* www.balmer-bd.ch

Pop Verlag
Stuttgarterstr 98, 71638 Ludwigsburg
Tel: (07141) 920-317 *Fax:* (07141) 970-284
E-mail: pop-verlag@gmx.de
Web Site: www.pop-verlag.com
Key Personnel
Mng Dir: Traian Pop
Founded: 2003
Subjects: Literature, Literary Criticism, Essays, Poetry
ISBN Prefix(es): 978-3-937139; 978-3-86356

Portikus
Alte Bruecke 2 Maininsel, 60594 Frankfurt am Main
Tel: (069) 962 44 54-0 *Fax:* (069) 962 44 54-24
E-mail: info@portikus.de
Web Site: www.portikus.de

Key Personnel
Dir: Nikolaus Hirsch
Curator: Sophie von Olfers
Founded: 1987
Specialize in exhibition catalogues.
Subjects: Art, Contemporary Art
ISBN Prefix(es): 978-3-928071
Number of titles published annually: 8 Print
Total Titles: 90 Print
Parent Company: Staedelschule

Possev-Verlag GmbH+
Flurscheideweg 15, 65936 Frankfurt
Tel: (069) 34-12-65 *Fax:* (069) 34-38-41
E-mail: possev-ffm@t-online.de
Web Site: www.posev.de
Founded: 1945
Publishes works by Russian dissidents. Also runs a translation agency.
ISBN Prefix(es): 978-3-7912

Praesenz Medien & Verlag+
Am Amthof 7, 65520 Bad Camberg
Tel: (06434) 9085225 *Fax:* (06434) 9085226
E-mail: info@praesenz-verlag.com
Web Site: www.praesenz-kunst-und-buch.de
Founded: 1962
Membership(s): Evangelischen Medienverband Deutschland; Katholischen Medienverband.
Subjects: Art, Inspirational, Spirituality, Literature, Literary Criticism, Essays, Poetry, Religion - Other, Self-Help
ISBN Prefix(es): 978-3-87630

Premop Verlag GmbH+
Joergstr 86, 80689 Munich
Tel: (089) 562257 *Fax:* (089) 5803214
Founded: 1988
Subjects: Music, Dance
ISBN Prefix(es): 978-3-927724
Subsidiaries: Edition Premop

Prentice Hall, *imprint of* Pearson Deutschland GmbH

Presse Informations AG (PIAG)+
Rathausplatz 7, 76532 Baden-Baden
Tel: (07221) 30175-60 *Fax:* (07221) 30175-70
E-mail: office@piag.de
Web Site: www.piag.de
Key Personnel
Publisher & Mng Dir: Dieter Brinzer
Editor: Dieter Franzen
Founded: 1963
Publisher of specialized books & magazines for the trade of published photography.
Subjects: Advertising, Film, Video, Law, Photography, Photo Law, Photo Prices in Europe
ISBN Prefix(es): 978-3-921864; 978-3-922725

Presse Verlagsgesellschaft mbH+
Ludwigstr 33-37, 60327 Frankfurt am Main
Tel: (069) 97460-0 *Fax:* (069) 97460-400
E-mail: marketing@mmg.de
Web Site: www.mmg.de; www.journal-frankfurt.de
Key Personnel
Mng Dir: Dr Jan-Peter Eichorn; Gerhardt Krauss; Stefan Wolff
Marketing Head: Michelle Weise *Tel:* (069) 97460-332
Founded: 1980
Subjects: Regional Interests, Homeopathy
ISBN Prefix(es): 978-3-928789
Number of titles published annually: 2 Print
Total Titles: 7 Print
Parent Company: MMG - Medien & Marketing Gruppe GmbH
Associate Companies: Content & Community Systems GmbH; EC Partner Unternehmensberater; Genussakademie; k/c/e Marketing3

GmbH; Konzept Verlagsgesellschaft mbH; MultiMediaManufaktur GmbH; Rhein-Main Net GmbH

Prestel, *imprint of* Verlagsgruppe Random House Bertelsmann

Prestel Verlag+
Imprint of Verlagsgruppe Random House Bertelsmann
Neumarkter Str 28, 81673 Munich
Tel: (089) 4136-0 *Toll Free Tel:* (0800) 500 33 22 *Fax:* (089) 4136-3333
E-mail: sales@prestel.de; rights@prestel.de
Web Site: www.randomhouse.de/prestel
Key Personnel
Mng Dir: Christian Rieker
Press & Publicity Dir: Pia Werner *Tel:* (089) 4136-2355 *Fax:* (089) 4136-2335
E-mail: werner@prestel.de
Sales Manager: Fiona Arndt *Tel:* (089) 4136-3035 *Fax:* (089) 4136-63035 *E-mail:* fiona.arndt@randomhouse.de
Foreign Rights: Kai-Ting Pan *Tel:* (089) 4136-3106
Founded: 1924
Subjects: Architecture & Interior Design, Art, Photography
ISBN Prefix(es): 978-3-7913
Branch Office(s)
Prestel Publishing Ltd, 4 Bloomsbury Pl, London WC1A 2QA, United Kingdom, Marketing & Publicity Executive: Florence Andrew *Tel:* (020) 7323 5004 *Fax:* (020) 7636 8004 *E-mail:* sales@prestel-uk.co.uk
U.S. Office(s): Prestel Publishing, 900 Broadway, Suite 603, New York, NY 10003, United States, Publicity: Samantha Waller *Tel:* 212-995-2720 *Fax:* 212-995-2733 *E-mail:* sales@prestel-usa.com *Web Site:* www.prestel.com

Preussische Koepfe, *imprint of* Stapp Verlag

Helmut Preussler Verlag+
Dagmarstr 8, 90482 Nuremberg
Tel: (0911) 95478-0 *Fax:* (0911) 542486
E-mail: preussler-verlag@t-online.de
Web Site: www.preussler-verlag.de
Key Personnel
Mng Dir, Editorial, Production & Rights & Permissions: Achim Raak
Founded: 1973
ISBN Prefix(es): 978-3-921332; 978-3-925362; 978-3-934679
Associate Companies: Preussler Druck & Versand GmbH & Co KG
Subsidiaries: Versandbuchhandlung Gebhart
Bookshop(s): Ernst Gebhard, Dagmarstr 8, 90482 Nuremberg

Prignitz-pur Verlag
Birkenweg 16, 16945 Meyenburg
Mailing Address: Jahnstr 64, 66740 Saarlouis
Tel: (06831) 966 45 00 *Fax:* (06831) 966 45 01
Key Personnel
Founder & Owner: Elke Knoblauch
Founded: 2005
Subjects: Geography, Geology, History, Photography, Local History

Primus Verlag GmbH
Imprint of WBG (Wissenschaftlichen Buchgesellschaft)
Riedeselstr 57A, 64283 Darmstadt
Mailing Address: Postfach 10 11 53, 64211 Darmstadt
Tel: (06151) 31 80 47 *Fax:* (06151) 3 30 82 08
Web Site: www.wbg-verlage.de
Key Personnel
Mng Dir: Wolfgang Hornstein
E-mail: hornstein@wbg-wissenverbindet.de

Advertising & Production: Gabriele Sauer
E-mail: sauer@wbg-wissenverbindet.de
Distribution & Sales: Beate Gemuenden
E-mail: gemuenden@wbg-wissenverbindet.de
Press & Public Relations: Christina Herborg
E-mail: herborg@wbg-wissenverbindet.de
Distribution & Sales: Esther Herzhauser
E-mail: herzhauser@wbg-wissenverbindet.de
Founded: 1996
Subjects: Antiques, Archaeology, Art, Government, Political Science, Literature, Literary Criticism, Essays, Philosophy, Psychology, Psychiatry, Theology
ISBN Prefix(es): 978-3-89678
Imprints: Reprint Verlag-Leipzig
Foreign Rep(s): Dagmar Bhend (Switzerland); Christian Hirtzy (Austria); Ernst Sonntag (Austria)
Distribution Center: Koch Neff & Oetinger Verlagsauslieferung GmbH, Schockenriedstr 39, 70565 Stuttgart *Tel:* (0711) 78 99 20 51 *Fax:* (0711) 78 99 10 10
E-mail: primusverlag@kno-va.de
Dr Franz Hain Verlagsauslieferungen, Dr-Otto-Neurath-Gasse 5, 1220 Vienna, Austria *Tel:* (01) 282 65 65 *Fax:* (01) 282 52 82 *E-mail:* bestell@hain.at
Scheidegger & Co AG, c/o AVA Verlagsauslieferung, Centralweg 16, Postfach 119, 8910 Affoltern am Albis, Switzerland *Tel:* (044) 760 42 50 *Fax:* (044) 760 42 10 *E-mail:* scheidegger@ava.ch

Principal Verlag
Diekbree 8, 48157 Muenster
Tel: (02571) 589645 *Fax:* (02571) 589639
E-mail: principal.verlag@t-online.de; verlag@principal.de
Web Site: www.principal.de
Key Personnel
Mng Dir: Dr Horst Schwenk
Subjects: Animals, Pets, Biography, Memoirs, Criminology, Fiction, Mysteries, Suspense, Nonfiction (General), Poetry, Psychology, Psychiatry, Science (General), Science Fiction, Fantasy, Travel & Tourism, Adventure, Lifestyle, Sexuality
ISBN Prefix(es): 978-3-89969

Pro Natur-Verlag Andreas Probst+
Schafweide 19, 88364 Wolfegg
Tel: (07527) 91 59 14 *Fax:* (07527) 91 59 42
E-mail: info@pro-natur-verlag.de
Web Site: www.pro-natur-verlag.de
Founded: 1979
Subjects: Environmental Studies
ISBN Prefix(es): 978-3-88582
Parent Company: Pro Natur Gesellschaft zur Foerderung des Umweltschutzes mbH

Projekte-Verlag Cornelius GmbH (Projects Publisher Cornelius Inc)+
Thueringer Str 30, 06112 Halle (Saale)
Tel: (0345) 6 86 56 65 *Fax:* (0345) 1 20 22 38
E-mail: info@projekte-verlag.de
Web Site: www.projekte-verlag.de
Key Personnel
Mng Dir: Reinhardt O Cornelius-Hahn
Founded: 1990
Also printer.
This publisher has indicated that 80% of their product line is author subsidized.
Subjects: Agriculture, Animals, Pets, Astronomy, Biography, Memoirs, Earth Sciences, Economics, Environmental Studies, Fiction, History, Literature, Literary Criticism, Essays, Medicine, Nursing, Dentistry, Nonfiction (General), Philosophy, Poetry, Science Fiction, Fantasy, Travel & Tourism
ISBN Prefix(es): 978-3-86634; 978-3-931950; 978-3-937027; 978-3-938227

Number of titles published annually: 200 Print
Total Titles: 900 Print; 160 E-Book

Propylaen, *imprint of* Ullstein Buchverlage GmbH

Propylaen Verlag+
Imprint of Ullstein Buchverlage
Friedrichstr 126, 10117 Berlin
Tel: (030) 23456-300 *Fax:* (030) 23456-303
E-mail: info@propylaeen-verlag.de
Web Site: www.ullsteinbuchverlage.de/propylaen
Key Personnel
Head, Media & Communications: Christine Heinrich *E-mail:* christine.heinrich@ullstein-buchverlage.de
Founded: 1903
Subjects: Architecture & Interior Design, Art, Biography, Memoirs, Business, Economics, Education, Ethnicity, Fiction, Film, Video, Geography, Geology, Government, Political Science, Health, Nutrition, History, How-to, Humor, Literature, Literary Criticism, Essays, Maritime, Military Science, Music, Dance, Mysteries, Suspense, Nonfiction (General), Poetry, Romance, Science (General), Social Sciences, Sociology, Travel & Tourism
ISBN Prefix(es): 978-3-549
Associate Companies: Allegria Verlag; Claassen Verlag; Econ Verlag; List Verlag; List Taschenbuch Verlag; Marion von Schroeder Verlag; Ullstein Verlag; Ullstein Taschenbuch Verlag

Psychiatrie-Verlag GmbH+
Ursula Platz 1, 50668 Cologne
Tel: (0221) 167 989-0 *Fax:* (0221) 167 989-20
E-mail: verlag@psychiatrie.de
Web Site: www.psychiatrie-verlag.de
Key Personnel
Mng Dir: York Bieger *E-mail:* bieger@psychiatrie.de; Jan Haaf
Founded: 1978
Subjects: Film, Video, Health, Nutrition, Psychology, Psychiatry, Self-Help
ISBN Prefix(es): 978-3-88414
Number of titles published annually: 15 Print; 10 E-Book
Total Titles: 170 Print; 30 E-Book; 1 Audio
Imprints: BALANCE buch + medien verlag
Orders to: PROLIT Verlagsauslieferung, Siemensstr 16, 35463 Femwald-Annerod *Tel:* (0641) 9439389

Psychologie Verlags Union GmbH+
Subsidiary of Julius Beltz GmbH & Co KG
Werderstr 10, 69469 Weinheim
Tel: (06201) 6007-0 *Fax:* (06201) 6007-310
E-mail: info@beltz.de
Web Site: www.beltz.de
Key Personnel
Publisher & Chief Executive Officer: Marianne Ruebelmann
Publishing Dir: Dr Svenja Wahl *Tel:* (06201) 60 07-363 *E-mail:* s.wahl@beltz.de
Head, Press & Public Relations: Bettina Schaub *Tel:* (06201) 6007-443 *Fax:* (06201) 6007-9443 *E-mail:* b.schaub@beltz.de
Sales Manager: Andrea Foelster *Tel:* (06201) 6007-431 *E-mail:* a.foelster@beltz.de
Marketing & Sales: Andreas Horn *Tel:* (06201) 6007-440 *E-mail:* a.horn@beltz.de
Rights: Kerstin Michaelis *Tel:* (06201) 6007-327 *Fax:* (06201) 6007-338 *E-mail:* k.michaelis@beltz.de
Founded: 1986
Subjects: Behavioral Sciences, Biological Sciences, Business, Child Care & Development, Communications, Education, Environmental Studies, Psychology, Psychiatry, Social Sciences, Sociology
ISBN Prefix(es): 978-3-407; 978-3-621
Ultimate Parent Company: Beltz Ruebelmann Holding

Distribution Center: Rhenus Medien Logistik GmbH & Co KG, Justus-von-Liebig-Str 1, 86899 Landsberg am Lech *Tel:* (01891) 9 70 00-6 22 *E-mail:* beltz@de.rhenus.com
Mohr Morawa Buchvertrieb GmbH, Sulzengasse 2, 1230 Vienna, Austria *Tel:* (01) 680 14-0 *Fax:* (01) 688 71 30 *E-mail:* momo@mohrmorawa.at *Web Site:* www.mohrmorawa.at
AVA Verlagsauslieferung AG, Centralweg 16, 8910 Affoltern am Albis, Switzerland *Tel:* (044) 762 42 50 *Fax:* (044) 762 42 49 *E-mail:* verlagsservice@ava.ch *Web Site:* www.ava.ch

Psychosozial-Verlag+
Walltorstr 10, 35390 Giessen
Tel: (0641) 96 99 78 0 *Fax:* (0641) 96 99 78 19
E-mail: info@psychosozial-verlag.de; vertrieb@ psychosozial-verlag.de
Web Site: www.psychosozial-verlag.de
Key Personnel
Publisher: Dr Hans-Juergen Wirth *Tel:* (0641) 96 99 78-23 *E-mail:* hjw@psychosozial-verlag.de; Trin Haland-Wirth *E-mail:* trin.haland-wirth@ psychosozial-verlag.de
Press & Advertising: Melanie Fehr *Tel:* (0641) 96 99 78-14 *E-mail:* melanie.fehr@psychosozial-verlag.de
Production & Editorial: Grit Suendermann *Tel:* (0641) 96 99 78-29 *E-mail:* grit. suendermann@psychosozial-verlag.de
Rights: Christian Flierl *Tel:* (0641) 96 99 78-28 *E-mail:* christian.flierl@psychosozial-verlag.de
Sales: Jeanette Klaft *Tel:* (0641) 96 99 78-26
Founded: 1991
Specialize in psychological & social issues.
Subjects: History, Psychology, Psychiatry, Social Sciences, Sociology
ISBN Prefix(es): 978-3-932133; 978-3-930096; 978-3-89806
Number of titles published annually: 60 Print
Total Titles: 1,400 Print

Publik-Forum Verlagsgesellschaft mbH
Krebsmuehle, 61440 Oberursel
Mailing Address: Postfach 2010, 61410 Oberursel
Tel: (06171) 7003-0 *Fax:* (06171) 7003-40
E-mail: redaktion@publik-forum.de; verlag@ publik-forum.de
Web Site: www.publik-forum.de
Key Personnel
Mng Dir: Richard Baehr
Editor-in-Chief: Dr Wolfgang Kessler
Subjects: Art, Government, Political Science, Inspirational, Spirituality, Religion - Other, Self-Help, Theology
ISBN Prefix(es): 978-3-88095; 978-3-921807

Pulp Master Frank Nowatzki Verlag GbR+
Samariterstr 6, 10247 Berlin
Tel: (030) 686 8292
E-mail: hq@pulpmaster.de
Web Site: www.pulpmaster.de
Key Personnel
Mng Dir, Rights & Permissions: Frank Nowatzki
Subjects: Fiction, Mysteries, Suspense
ISBN Prefix(es): 978-3-927734
Number of titles published annually: 4 Print
Orders to: Prolit Verlagsauslieferung GmbH, Siemensstr 16, 35461 Fernwald, Contact: G Lemuth *Tel:* (0641) 94393-201 *Fax:* (0641) 94393-89 *E-mail:* g.lemuth@prolit.de *Web Site:* www.prolit.de

Verlag Friedrich Pustet+
Gutenbergstr 8, 93051 Regensburg
Tel: (0941) 92022-0 *Toll Free Tel:* 0800 0787838
Fax: (0941) 92022-330
E-mail: verlag@pustet.de; buecher@pustet.de; presse-werbung@pustet.de
Web Site: www.verlag-pustet.de

Key Personnel
Mng Dir & Editorial: Fritz Pustet *Tel:* (0941) 92022-317 *E-mail:* fpustet@pustet.de
Foreign Rights: Susanne Voelkl *Tel:* (0941) 92022-313
Order & Distribution: Angilika Rauscher *Tel:* (0941) 92022-321 *E-mail:* rauscher@ pustet.de
Press: Marina Werkmeister *Tel:* (0941) 92022-319
Sales & Marketing: Sabine Karlstetter *Tel:* (0941) 92022-318 *E-mail:* karlstetter@pustet.de
Founded: 1826
Specialize in theological & historical literature.
Subjects: Archaeology, Biblical Studies, Biography, Memoirs, Foreign Countries, History, Music, Dance, Nonfiction (General), Regional Interests, Religion - Catholic, Theology
ISBN Prefix(es): 978-3-7917
Number of titles published annually: 50 Print; 3 CD-ROM; 1 Online
Total Titles: 550 Print; 10 CD-ROM; 1 Online
Foreign Rep(s): Verlagsagentur Claudia Grueneis-Lambourne (Austria, South Tyrol, Italy); Andreas Meisel (Switzerland)
Bookshop(s): Gesandtenstr 6-8, 93047 Regensburg, Branch Manager: Susanne Borst *Tel:* (0941) 5697-0 *Fax:* (0941) 5697-36 *E-mail:* regensburg@pustet.de; Universitaetsstr 31, 93053 Regensburg, Branch Manager: Karen Nielsen *Tel:* (0941) 91069790 *Fax:* (0941) 9455629 *E-mail:* uni@pustet.de; Weichser Weg 5, 93059 Regensburg, Branch Manager: Christine Lehner *Tel:* (0941) 46686-0 *Fax:* (0941) 46686-66 *E-mail:* dez@pustet. de; Bruecken-Center, Residenzstr 2-6, 91522 Ansbach, Branch Manager: Bettina Wasser *Tel:* (0981) 48886-0 *Fax:* (0981) 48886-66 *E-mail:* ansbach@pustet.de; Karolinenstr 12, 86150 Augsburg, Branch Manager: Anja Voellger *Tel:* (0821) 50224-0 *Fax:* (0821) 50224-59 *E-mail:* augsburg@pustet.de; Pfleggasse 1, 94469 Deggendorf, Branch Manager: Barbara Bergmueller *Tel:* (0991) 250344-0 *Fax:* (0991) 250344-20 *E-mail:* deggendorf@pustet.de; Obere Hauptstr 45, 85354 Freising, Branch Manager: Jutta Ederer *Tel:* (08161) 5377-30 *Fax:* (08161) 5377-50 *E-mail:* freising@pustet. de; Altstadt 28, 84028 Landshut, Branch Manager: Franziska Schaefer *Tel:* (0871) 965855-0 *Fax:* (0871) 965855-20 *E-mail:* landshut@ pustet.de; Nibelungenplatz 1, 94032 Passau, Branch Manager: Michael Henkel *Tel:* (0851) 56089-0 *Fax:* (0851) 56089-50 *E-mail:* passau@pustet.de; Theresienplatz 51, 94315 Straubing, Branch Manager: Axel Wegener *Tel:* (09421) 9622-30 *Fax:* (09421) 9622-33 *E-mail:* straubing@pustet.de
Distribution Center: Mohr Morawa Buchvertrieb GmbH, Sulzengasse 2, 1230 Vienna, Austria *Tel:* (01) 680 14-0 *Fax:* (01) 688 71 30 *E-mail:* momo@mohrmorawa.at *Web Site:* www.mohrmorawa.at
AVA Verlagsauslieferung AG, Centralweg 16, 8910 Affoltern am Albis, Switzerland *Tel:* (044) 7624200 *Fax:* (044) 7624210 *E-mail:* verlagsservice@ava.ch *Web Site:* www.ava.ch

pVS - pro Verlag und Service GmbH & Co KG
Member of Mediengruppe Heilbronner Stimme
Stauffenbergstr 18, 74523 Schwaebisch Hall
Tel: (0791) 95061-0 *Fax:* (0791) 95061-41
E-mail: info@pro-vs.de
Web Site: www.pro-vs.de
Key Personnel
Mng Dir: Tilmann Distelbarth; Bernd Herzberger
Publishing Dir: Marcus Baumann
Founded: 1970
Subjects: Business, Career Development, Developing Countries, Economics, Foreign Coun-

tries, Management, Regional Interests, Technology
ISBN Prefix(es): 978-3-87176

Quadriga, *imprint of* Bastei Luebbe GmbH & Co KG

Que, *imprint of* Pearson Deutschland GmbH

Queer Lectures, *imprint of* Maennerschwarm Verlag GmbH

Quelle & Meyer Verlag GmbH & Co+
Industriepark 3, 56291 Wiebelsheim
Tel: (06766) 903-140 *Fax:* (06766) 903-320
E-mail: fossilien@quelle-meyer.de; sales@quelle-meyer.de; vertrieb@quelle-meyer.de
Web Site: www.verlagsgemeinschaft.com/cms/ quelle.php; www.fossilien-journal.de
Key Personnel
Mng Dir: Gerhard Stahl
Publisher & Editor: Dr Michael Maisch *E-mail:* maisch@uni-tuebingen.de; Dr Guenter Schweigert *E-mail:* guenter.schweigert@smns-bw.de
Founded: 1984
Specialize in paleontology.
Subjects: Geography, Geology, Paleontology
ISBN Prefix(es): 978-3-494; 978-3-88988
Number of titles published annually: 2 Print

Querverlag GmbH
Akazienstr 25, 10823 Berlin
Tel: (030) 78 70 23 39 *Fax:* (030) 788 49 50
E-mail: mail@querverlag.de
Web Site: www.querverlag.de
Key Personnel
Founder & Mng Dir: Jim Baker
Founder: Ilona Bubeck
Founded: 1995
Gay & lesbian book publisher.
Membership(s): Boersenverein des Deutschen Buchhandels.
Subjects: Fiction, LGBTQ, Nonfiction (General), Gay & Lesbian Fiction & Nonfiction, Homosexuality, Queer Studies
ISBN Prefix(es): 978-3-89656
Shipping Address: Prolit Verlagsauslieferung, Siemensstr 16, 35463 Fernwald, Contact: Andrea Willenberg *Tel:* (0641) 9439-335 *Fax:* (0641) 9439-339 *E-mail:* a.willenberg@ prolit.de *Web Site:* www.prolit.de

Quintessenz Verlags-GmbH+
Imprint of Quintessence Publishing Co
Ifenpfad 2-4, 12107 Berlin
Mailing Address: Postfach 420452, 12064 Berlin
Tel: (030) 7 61 80-5 *Fax:* (030) 7 61 80-692
E-mail: info@quintessenz.de
Web Site: www.quintessenz.de
Key Personnel
Publisher: Horst-Wolfgang Haase
Mng Dir: Alexander Ammann *E-mail:* ammann@ quintessenz.de; Christian Haase *E-mail:* cwhaase@quintessenz.de
Publishing Dir: Johannes Wolters *E-mail:* wolters@quintessenz.de
Sales Manager: Leo Korff *E-mail:* korff@ quintessenz.de
Founded: 1949
Subjects: Biography, Memoirs, Career Development, Communications, Fiction, Film, Video, Health, Nutrition, Literature, Literary Criticism, Essays, Management, Medicine, Nursing, Dentistry, Mysteries, Suspense
ISBN Prefix(es): 978-3-86124; 978-3-928024; 978-3-8148; 978-3-87652; 978-3-9801163; 978-3-938947
Branch Office(s)
Quintessence Editora Ltda, Rua Joaquim Tavora, 112, Viela Mariana, 04015-010 Sao Paulo-

SP, Brazil, Contact: Rui M Santos *Tel:* (011) 55741200 *Fax:* (011) 55393183 *E-mail:* yara@ quintessenceditora.com.br
Chang Chun Qiao Lu No 5, New Start Garden Bldg 12, Room 1707, Haidian District Beijing 100089, China, Contact: Shanshan Peng *Tel:* (010) 82 56 31 45 *Fax:* (010) 82 56 31 46 *E-mail:* chinabranch2003@yahoo.com.cn
Nakaladatelstvi Quintessenz sro, J Plachty 2, 150 00 Prague 5, Czech Republic, Contact: Dr Josef Rakovec *Tel:* 257 328 723 *Fax:* 257 328 723 *E-mail:* info@quintessenz.cz *Web Site:* www.quintessenz.cz
Quintessence International Sarl, 18 Ave Winston Churchill, 94220 Charenton-le-Pont, France, Contact: Dr Christian Knellesen *Tel:* 01 43 78 40 50 *Fax:* 01 43 78 78 85 *E-mail:* quintess@ wanadoo.fr *Web Site:* www.quintessence-international.fr
Quintessence Science Communications Pvt Ltd, 303-304, Virat Bhawan, Commercial Complex, 110 009 Delhi, India, Contact: Sarvesh Passi *Tel:* (011) 2765 2341; (011) 2765 2369 *Fax:* (011) 2765 2658 *E-mail:* passip@ndb. vsnl.net.in *Web Site:* www.quintasia.com
Quintessenza Edizioni SRL, via C Menotti 65, 20017 Passirana di Rho MI, Italy, Contact: Lauro Dusetti *Tel:* (02) 931 82 264 *Fax:* (02) 931 86 159 *E-mail:* info@quintessenzaedizioni. it *Web Site:* www.quintessenzaedizioni.it
Quintessence Publishing Co Ltd, Quint House Bldg 3-2-6, Hongo, Bunkyo-ku, Tokyo 113-0033, Japan, Contact: Ikko Sasaki *Tel:* (03) 5482 2271 *Fax:* (03) 5800 7598 *E-mail:* info@ quint-j-co.jp *Web Site:* www.quint-j-co.jp
Wydawnictwo Kwintesencja Sp zoo, ul Rozana75, 02-569 Warsaw, Poland, Contact: Ireneusz Czyzewski *Tel:* (22) 845 69 70 *Fax:* (22) 845 05 53 *E-mail:* wydawnictwo@kwintesencja. com.pl *Web Site:* www.kwintesencja.com.pl
Quintessence Moscow, Usacheva St, 62, Bldg 1, Business Center, Off 14, 119048 Moscow, Russia, Contact: Alexander Ostrovsky *Tel:* (495) 245-5270 *Fax:* (495) 245-5279 *E-mail:* sash@ quintessence.ru *Web Site:* www.quintessence.ru
Quintessence International Group (S) Pte Ltd, 10 Ubi Crescent, No 06-97 Ubi Techpark Lobby E, Singapore 408564, Singapore, Contact: Jeffrey Chia *Tel:* 6848-9238 *Fax:* 6848-9138 *E-mail:* jeffrey@quintessence-singapore.com *Web Site:* www.quintessence-singapore.com
Quintessence, Room 1003, Sangji B/D, No 326, Euljiro-3GA, Choong-gu, Seoul, South Korea *Tel:* (02) 2264-4231; (02) 2264-4233 *Fax:* (02) 2264-4234
Editorial Quintessence SL, Torres Trade (Torre Sur), Gran Via Carlos III, 84, 08028 Barcelona, Spain, Contact: Javier Teixido *Tel:* 934912300; 639363229 *Fax:* 934091360 *E-mail:* javier@ quintessence.es *Web Site:* www.quintessence.es
Quintessence Yayincilik Tanitim, Buyukdere Caddesi, Sakarya Apartment No 8/7, 34360 Sisli-Istanbul, Turkey, Contact: Dr Ertugrul Cetinkaya *Tel:* (0212) 343 05 99 *Fax:* (0212) 230 34 19 *E-mail:* bilgi@quintessence.com.tr *Web Site:* www.quintessence.com.tr
Quintessence Publishing Co Ltd, Grafton Rd, New Malden, Surrey KT3 3AB, United Kingdom, Contact: Susan Newbury *Tel:* (020) 8949 6087 *Fax:* (020) 8336 1484 *E-mail:* info@ quintpub.co.uk *Web Site:* www.quintpub.co.uk
U.S. Office(s): Quintessence Publishing Co Inc, 4350 Chandler Dr, Hanover Park, IL 60133, United States, Contact: William Hartmann *Tel:* 630-736-3600 *Fax:* 630-736-3632 *E-mail:* contact@quintbook.com *Web Site:* www.quintpub.com

Dr Josef Raabe-Verlags GmbH

Rotebuehlstr 77, 70178 Stuttgart
Mailing Address: Postfach 10 39 22, 70034 Stuttgart
Tel: (0711) 629 00-45 *Fax:* (0711) 629 00-99

E-mail: info@raabe.de; kundenservice@raabe.de
Web Site: www.raabe.de
Key Personnel
Mng Dir: Anneliese Gruezinger
Founded: 1985
Specialize in loose leaf editions, universities, school management.
Subjects: Education, Environmental Studies, Health, Nutrition, Management, Public Administration, Science (General), Social Sciences, Sociology
ISBN Prefix(es): 978-3-88649; 978-3-8183
Parent Company: RAABE Gruppe
Ultimate Parent Company: Klett Gruppe
Subsidiaries: RAABE Bulgarien; Dr Josef Raabe Spolka Wydawnicza; RAABE Fachverlag fuer Bildungsmanagement; RAABE Fachverlag fuer die Schule; RAABE Fachverlag fuer Oeffentliche Verwaltung Duesseldorf; RAABE Fachverlag fuer Wissenschaftsinformation; RAABE Koenyvkiado; RAABE Nakladatelstvi
Warehouse: BDK Buecherdienst Koeln, Koelner Str 248, 51149 Cologne

Radius-Verlag GmbH+

Alexanderstr 162, 70180 Stuttgart
Tel: (0711) 607 66 66 *Fax:* (0711) 607 55 55
E-mail: info@radius-verlag.de
Web Site: www.radius-verlag.de
Key Personnel
Mng Dir: Wolfgang Erk
Editor-in-Chief: Pierangelo Maset
Editor: Martin Scharpe
Founded: 1962
Subjects: Fiction, Government, Political Science, Literature, Literary Criticism, Essays, Music, Dance, Philosophy, Psychology, Psychiatry, Religion - Other, Theology
ISBN Prefix(es): 978-3-87173

Edition RainRuhr

Kiek ut 20, 45359 Essen
Tel: (0201) 68 96 62 *Fax:* (03221) 110 44 30
E-mail: info@edition-rainruhr.de
Web Site: www.edition-rainruhr.de
Key Personnel
Publisher: Rainer Henselowsky
Subjects: History, Regional Interests, Culture
ISBN Prefix(es): 978-3-941676

Rake Verlag Rau und Keune GbR+

Koenigsweg 20, 24103 Kiel
Tel: (0431) 6611515 (sales)
Key Personnel
Publisher: Michael Rau
Sales: Peter Keune
Founded: 1994
Specialize in contemporary German authors.
Subjects: Fiction, Humor, Self-Help
ISBN Prefix(es): 978-3-931476
Number of titles published annually: 20 Print
Total Titles: 35 Print; 1 Audio
Distribution Center: PNV Vertriebs Service, Werftbahnstr 8, 24143 Kiel *Tel:* (0431) 730060 *Fax:* (0431) 7300674

Random House Audio, *imprint of* Verlagsgruppe Random House Bertelsmann

Verlagsgruppe Random House Bertelsmann

Neumarkter Str 28, 81673 Munich
Tel: (089) 4136-0 (customer service); (089) 4136-3733 (rights) *Toll Free Tel:* 0800 500 33 22 (customer service) *Fax:* (089) 4136-3333 (customer service)
E-mail: kundenservice@randomhouse.de
Web Site: www.randomhouse.de
Founded: 1835
ISBN Prefix(es): 978-3-8135; 978-3-570; 978-3-7645; 978-3-8068; 978-3-8094; 978-3-630; 978-3-8090; 978-3-576; 978-3-572; 978-3-517;

978-3-88680; 978-3-353; 978-3-7787; 978-3-442; 978-3-8275; 978-3-453; 978-3-89480; 978-3-635; 978-3-86604; 978-3-89830; 978-3-8371
Imprints: adeo; Ansata; Ariston; Arkana; Bassermann; C Bertelsmann; cbt Verlag; Blanvalet; Blessing; btb; carl's books; cbj; Der Hoerverlag; Deutsche Verlags-Anstalt (DVA); Diana Verlag; Diederichs Verlag; Falken; Gerth Medien; Goldmann; Guetersloher Verlagshaus; Edition Elke Heidenreich; Heyne; Heyne Fliegt; Heyne Hardcore; Integral; Irisiana; Kailash; Knaus; Koesel; Limes; Lotos; Luchterhand Literaturverlag; Ludwig; Manesse; Manhattan; Mosaik; Page & Turner; Pantheon; Penhaligon; Prestel; Random House Audio; Random House Entertainment; Riemann; Siedler; Sphinx; Suedwest; Tag & Nacht
Foreign Rights: ACER Agencia Literaria (Isabel Piedrahita) (Brazil, Portugal, Spain); Agencja Literacka Graal (Maria Strarz-Kanska & Joanna Maciuk) (Poland); Balla & Sztojkov Literary Agency (Catherine Balla) (Hungary); Eliane Benisti Literary Agency (France); Berla & Griffini Rights Agency (Barbara Griffini) (Italy); Book Publishers Association of Israel (Beverly Levit) (Israel); BookCosmos Agency (Richard Hong) (South Korea); EUROBUK Agency (Ms Min-Su Lee) (South Korea); Agentur Literatur Gudrun Hebel (Scandinavia); International Copyright Agency Ltd (Simona Kessler) (Moldova, Romania); International Editors SA (Portugal, Spain); Iris Literary Agency (Catherine Fragou) (Greece); Ute Koerner Literary Agent SL (Sandra Rodericks) (Brazil, Latin America, Portugal, South America, Spain); Meike Marx (Japan); Momo Agency (Geenie Han) (South Korea); Andrew Nurnberg Associates International Ltd (Ms Jackie Huang) (China); Andrew Nurnberg Associates Taiwan (Whitney Hsu) (Taiwan); ONK Agency Ltd (Ms Nazli Cokdu Ulas) (Turkey); Prava i prevodi (Milena Kaplarevic) (Albania, Baltic States, Bosnia and Herzegovina, Bulgaria, Croatia, Greece, Kosovo, Macedonia, Montenegro, Romania, Russia, Serbia, Slovenia, Turkey); Marianne Schoenbach Literary Agency (Marianne Schoenbach) (Belgium, Netherlands)

Random House Entertainment, *imprint of* Verlagsgruppe Random House Bertelsmann

R&W Fachmedien Recht und Wirtschaft+

Subsidiary of Deutscher Fachverlag GmbH
Mainzer Landstr 251, 60326 Frankfurt am Main
Tel: (069) 7595-01 *Fax:* (069) 7595-2999
Web Site: www.ruw.de
Key Personnel
Mng Dir: Peter Kley *Tel:* (069) 7595-1141 *Fax:* (069) 7595-2700 *E-mail:* peter.kley@dfv. de
Publishing Dir: Claudia Peschke *Tel:* (069) 7595-2721 *Fax:* (069) 7595-2780 *E-mail:* claudia. peschke@dfv.de
Marketing & Press: Sarah Bauer *Tel:* (069) 7595-2723 *Fax:* (069) 7595-2780 *E-mail:* sarah. bauer@dfv.de
Founded: 1946
Subjects: Business, Economics, Law, Public Administration, Social Sciences, Sociology
ISBN Prefix(es): 978-3-8005
Subsidiaries: I H Sauer Verlag GmbH

ratio-books

Danziger Str 30, 53797 Lohmar
Tel: (02246) 94 92 61 *Fax:* (02246) 94 92 24
E-mail: info@ratio-books.de
Web Site: www.ratio-books.de
Key Personnel
Mng Dir: Franz Koenig *E-mail:* f.koenig@ratio-books.de
Subjects: History, Local History

ISBN Prefix(es): 978-3-939829
Distribution Center: Sigloch Distribution GmbH
& Co KG *Tel:* (07953) 883-757 *Fax:* (07953)
883-700 *E-mail:* verlagservice@sigloch.de

Werner Rau Verlag+
Feldbergstr 54, 70569 Stuttgart
Tel: (0711) 687 21 43 *Fax:* (0711) 687 22 47
E-mail: info@rau-verlag.de
Web Site: www.rau-verlag.de
Key Personnel
Owner: Werner Rau
Founded: 1986
Subjects: Travel & Tourism
ISBN Prefix(es): 978-3-926145
Distribution Center: GeoCenter Touristik Medi-
enservice GmbH, Schockenriedstr 44, 70565
Stuttgart *Tel:* (0711) 78 19 46 10 *Fax:* (0711)
782 43 75
Koch, Neff & Oetinger Verlagsauslieferung
GmbH, Industriestr 23, 70565 Stuttgart
Freytag-Berndt und Artaria KG, Brunner Str
69, 1231 Vienna, Austria *Tel:* (01) 869 90 90
Fax: (01) 869 88 55
Schweizer Buchzentrum, Postfach, 4601 Olten,
Switzerland *Tel:* (062) 47 61 61 *Fax:* (062) 46
41 12

Karl Rauch Verlag GmbH & Co KG
Grafenberger Allee 82, 40237 Duesseldorf
Tel: (0211) 96 82 219 *Fax:* (0211) 96 82 11 219
E-mail: info@karl-rauch-verlag.de
Web Site: www.karl-rauch-verlag.de
Key Personnel
Manager: Tullio Aurelio *E-mail:* aurelio@karl-
rauch-verlag.de
Founded: 1923
Subjects: Fiction, Nonfiction (General)
ISBN Prefix(es): 978-3-7920
Parent Company: Bagel Gruppe
Distribution Center: Koch, Neff & Oetinger Ver-
lagsauslieferung GmbH, Industriestr 23, 70565
Stuttgart, Contact: Nicole Blum *E-mail:* dtv@
kno-va.de
Mohr Morawa Buchvertrieb GmbH, Sulzen-
gasse 2, 1230 Vienna, Austria *Tel:* (01) 680
14-0 *Fax:* (01) 688 71-30 *E-mail:* momo@
mohrmorawa.at *Web Site:* www.mohrmorawa.at
Buchzentrum AG, Industriestr Ost 10, 4614 Hae-
gendorf, Switzerland *Tel:* (062) 2 09 26 26
Fax: (062) 2 09 26 27 *E-mail:* kundendienst@
buchzentrum.ch

Rautenberg Verlag
Imprint of Verlagshaus Wuerzburg GmbH & Co
KG
Beethovenstr 5 B, 97080 Wuerzburg
Tel: (0931) 465 889-11 *Fax:* (0931) 465 889-29
E-mail: info@verlagshaus.com
Web Site: www.verlagshaus.com
Key Personnel
Publishing Dir: Dieter Krause *Tel:* (0931) 465
889-14 *E-mail:* dieter.krause@verlagshaus.com
Dir, Production: Juergen Roth *Tel:* (0931) 465
889-15 *E-mail:* juergen.roth@verlagshaus.com
Sales Dir: Johannes Glesius *Tel:* (0931) 465 889-
13 *E-mail:* johannes.glesius@verlagshaus.com
Founded: 1825
Subjects: Drama, Theater, Fiction, Humor, Re-
gional Interests
ISBN Prefix(es): 978-3-7921; 978-3-8003
Bookshop(s): Rautenberg Buchhandlung in der
Verlagshaus Wuerzburg GmbH & Co KG
Tel: (0931) 465 889-12

Ravensburger Buchverlag Otto Maier GmbH+
Robert-Bosch-Str 1, 88214 Ravensburg
Tel: (0751) 86 0 *Fax:* (0751) 86 13 11
E-mail: info@ravensburger.de; buchverlag@
ravensburger.de
Web Site: www.ravensburger.de

Key Personnel
Mng Dir: Johannes Hauenstein
Founded: 1883
Subjects: Art, Crafts, Games, Hobbies, Education,
Fiction, Nonfiction (General)
ISBN Prefix(es): 978-3-473
Parent Company: Ravensburger AG
Associate Companies: Ravensburger GesmbH,
Ricoweg 24, 2351 Wiener Neudorf, Austria
Tel: (02236) 72 055 0 *Fax:* (02236) 72 059
Web Site: www.ravensburger.at; Ravensburger
SA/NV, International Trade Mart, Atomium-
square/Bologna 274-275, 1020 Brussels, Bel-
gium *Tel:* (02) 4784975 *Fax:* (02) 4785440
Web Site: www.ravensburger.be; Jeux Ravens-
burger, 21 rue de Dornach, 68120 Pfastatt,
France *Tel:* 03 89 50 65 00 *Fax:* 03 89 50 65
09 *Web Site:* www.ravensburger.fr; Ravens-
burger SpA, Via Enrico Fermi, 20090 Assago MI, Italy *Tel:* (02) 45 77 131 *Fax:* (02)
45 71 34 00 *Web Site:* www.ravensburger.it;
Ravensburger BV, Spaceshuttle 50, 3824 ML
Amersfoort, Netherlands *Tel:* (033) 46 11
445 *Fax:* (033) 46 18 145 *Web Site:* www.
ravensburger.nl; Ravensburger Iberica SLU,
C/ Pesquera nº 18, 28850 Torrejon de Ardoz
(Madrid), Spain *Tel:* 917 219 526 *Fax:* 913
885 560 *Web Site:* www.ravensburger.es;
Carlit + Ravensburger AG, Grundstr 9,
5436 Wuerenlos, Switzerland *Tel:* (056)
4368484 *Fax:* (056) 4368485 *Web Site:* www.
ravensburger.ch; Ravensburger Ltd, Avonbury
Business Park, Unit 1, Howes Lane, Bicester OX26 2UB, United Kingdom *Tel:* (01869)
363830 *Fax:* (01869) 363835 *Web Site:* www.
ravensburger.co.uk
Divisions: Ravensburger Digital GmbH; Ravens-
burger Freizeit & Promotion Service GmbH;
Ravensburger International; Ravensburger
SpieleVerlag GmbH
U.S. Office(s): Ravensburger USA Inc, One Puzzle Lane, Newton, NH 03858, United States
Tel: 603-257-1500 *Fax:* 603-257-1599 *Web
Site:* www.ravensburger.us

Verlag Razamba Martin Ebbertz
Carl-Goerdeler-Str 19, 60320 Frankfurt am Main
Tel: (069) 95015642 *Fax:* (069) 95015644
E-mail: info@razamba.de
Web Site: www.razamba.de
Key Personnel
Publisher: Martin Ebbertz
ISBN Prefix(es): 978-3-941725
Orders to: Runge Verlagsauslieferung, Bergstr
2, 33803 Steinhagen *Tel:* (05204) 998123
Fax: (05204) 998114 *E-mail:* msr@rungeva.de

**Reader's Digest Deutschland: Verlag Das Beste
GmbH** (Reader's Digest Germany)+
Vordernbergstr 6, 70191 Stuttgart
Mailing Address: Postfach 10 60 20, 70049
Stuttgart
Tel: (0711) 66 02-0 *Fax:* (0711) 66 02-547
E-mail: verlag@readersdigest.de
Web Site: www.readersdigest.de
Key Personnel
Mng Dir: Werner Neunzig
Public Relations: Uwe Horn *Fax:* (0711) 66 02-
160
Founded: 1948
Also publishes journals, audiobooks, music &
video editions.
Subjects: Gardening, Plants, Geography, Geol-
ogy, Health, Nutrition, History, Law, Medicine,
Nursing, Dentistry, Music, Dance, Science
(General), Travel & Tourism
ISBN Prefix(es): 978-3-89915
Parent Company: Trusted Media Brands Inc, 750
Third Ave, 3rd floor, New York, NY 10017,
United States
Branch Office(s)
Ernst-Gnoss-Str 24, 40219 Duesseldorf

Singerstr 2, 1010 Vienna, Austria
Raeffelstr 11, Gallushof, 8045 Zurich, Switzerland

Verlag Thomas Reche
Schweninger Str 6, 92318 Neumarkt
Tel: (09181) 408 99 55 *Fax:* (09181) 408 99 55
E-mail: thomas-reche@web.de
Web Site: www.verlag-thomas-reche.de
Key Personnel
Owner: Thomas Reche
Subjects: Literature, Literary Criticism, Essays,
Philosophy
ISBN Prefix(es): 978-3-929566; 978-3-9801759

Recom, *imprint of* RECOM GmbH & Co KG

RECOM GmbH & Co KG
Gartenstr 9, 34125 Kassel
Tel: (0561) 87 08 97-0 *Fax:* (0561) 87 08 97-18
E-mail: info@recom.eu
Web Site: www.recom-verlag.de
Key Personnel
Mng Dir: Joerg Gohl
Founded: 1988
Publications & consulting service for the health
care sector.
Subjects: Medicine, Nursing, Dentistry
ISBN Prefix(es): 978-3-7245; 978-3-497
Imprints: Recom

Redaktion & Gestaltung, *imprint of* Johann
Wolfgang Goethe-Universitaet Frankfurt am
Main

Redline Verlag+
Nymphenburger Str 86, 80636 Munich
Tel: (089) 65 12 85-0 *Fax:* (089) 65 20 96
E-mail: info@redline-verlag.de
Web Site: www.m-vg.de/redline
Key Personnel
Mng Dir: Christian Jund *E-mail:* cjund@redline-
verlag.de
Publishing Dir: Matthias Setzler *Tel:* (089) 65 12
85-13 *E-mail:* msetzler@redline-verlag.de
Foreign Rights: Maria Pinto-Peuckmann
Tel: (089) 65 12 85-244 *E-mail:* mpinto-
peuckmann@redline-verlag.de
Press & Public Relations: Verena Schoerner
Tel: (089) 65 12 85-226 *E-mail:* vschoerner@
redline-verlag.de
Sales: Sigrid Klemt *Tel:* (089) 65 12 85-271
E-mail: sklemt@redline-verlag.de
Founded: 1988
Subjects: Accounting, Business, Economics, Gov-
ernment, Political Science, Law, Management
ISBN Prefix(es): 978-3-86881
Parent Company: Muenchner Verlagsgruppe
GmbH
Foreign Rep(s): Roland Fuerst (Austria); Giovanni
Ravasio (Switzerland)
Distribution Center: Rhenus Medien Logistik
GmbH & Co KG, Justus-von-Liebig-Str 1,
86899 Landsberg am Lech *Tel:* (08191) 97000-
0 *E-mail:* info.rml@de.rhenus.com
Mohr Morawa Buchvertrieb GmbH, Sulzen-
gasse 2, 1230 Vienna, Austria *Tel:* (01) 680
14-0 *Fax:* (01) 688 71 30 *E-mail:* momo@
mohrmorawa.at *Web Site:* www.mohrmorawa.at
AVA Verlagsauslieferung AG, Centralweg
16, 8910 Affoltern am Albis, Switzerland
Tel: (044) 7624260 *Fax:* (044) 7624210
E-mail: verlagsservice@ava.ch

Verlag fuer Regionalgeschichte+
Windelsbleicher Str 13, 33335 Guetersloh
Mailing Address: Postfach 120423, 33653 Biele-
feld
Tel: (05209) 6714; (05209) 980266 *Fax:* (05209)
6519; (05209) 980277
E-mail: regionalgeschichte@t-online.de

Web Site: www.regionalgeschichte.de
Key Personnel
Publisher: Olaf Eimer
Founded: 1987
Subjects: Art, History, Regional Interests, Social Sciences, Sociology
ISBN Prefix(es): 978-3-927085; 978-3-89534
Number of titles published annually: 40 Print
Total Titles: 500 Print
Distribution Center: Runge Verlagsauslieferung, Bergstr 2, 33803 Steinhagen *Tel:* (05204) 998-441 *Fax:* (05204) 998-114 *E-mail:* msr@rungeva.de *Web Site:* www.rungeva.de

regiospectra Verlag
Strassmannstr 10, 10249 Berlin
Tel: (030) 67962863 *Fax:* (030) 484987479
E-mail: kontakt@regiospectra.de
Web Site: www.regiospectra.de
Subjects: Asian Studies, Nonfiction (General), Science (General), African Studies
ISBN Prefix(es): 978-3-940132

regura verlag
Reza Haidari Kahkesh, Bockelstr 79, 70619 Stuttgart
Tel: (0711) 4790218 *Fax:* (0711) 34215873
E-mail: haidari@regura.de
Web Site: www.regura.de
Founded: 1997
Digital publications, Internet solutions & services for publishers.
International cultural exchange, priority: Orient, Persia & Germany.
Subjects: Art, Cookery, Fiction
ISBN Prefix(es): 978-3-932814

Dr Ludwig Reichert Verlag+
Tauernstr 11, 65199 Wiesbaden
Tel: (0611) 461851; (0611) 946 59 11 (orders) *Fax:* (0611) 468613
E-mail: info@reichert-verlag.de
Web Site: www.reichert-verlag.de
Key Personnel
Publisher: Ursula Reichert
Founded: 1969
Worldwide distribution.
Subjects: Archaeology, Art, Asian Studies, Geography, Geology, History, Language Arts, Linguistics, Library & Information Sciences, Music, Dance, Religion - Jewish, Science (General)
ISBN Prefix(es): 978-3-920153; 978-3-88226; 978-3-89500
Number of titles published annually: 60 Print
Warehouse: Brockhaus/Commission, Kreidlerstr 9, 70806 Kornwestheim *Tel:* (07154) 132726 *Fax:* (07154) 132713 *E-mail:* reichert@brocom.de
Distribution Center: Brockhaus/Commission, Kreidlerstr 9, 70806 Kornwestheim *Tel:* (07154) 132726 *Fax:* (07154) 132713 *E-mail:* reichert@brocom.de
Orders to: Brockhaus/Commission, Kreidlerstr 9, 70806 Kornwestheim *Tel:* (07154) 132726 *Fax:* (07154) 132713 *E-mail:* reichert@brocom.de
Returns: Brockhaus/Commission, Kreidlerstr 9, 70806 Kornwestheim *Tel:* (07154) 132726 *Fax:* (07154) 132713 *E-mail:* reichert@brocom.de

Reichl Verlag+
Auf dem Haehnchen 32, 56329 St Goar
Tel: (06741) 1720 *Fax:* (06741) 1749
Web Site: www.reichl-verlag.de
Key Personnel
Mng Dir: Matthias Draeger *E-mail:* draeger5@hotmail.com
Founded: 1909

Subjects: Astrology, Occult, Medicine, Nursing, Dentistry, Parapsychology, Religion - Other, Self-Help
ISBN Prefix(es): 978-3-87667
Subsidiaries: Leibniz Verlag
Divisions: Edition Asklepios

Reihe Hochschule, *imprint of* BdWi-Verlag

Dietrich Reimer Verlag GmbH+
Berliner Str 53, 10713 Berlin
Tel: (030) 700 13 88-0 *Fax:* (030) 700 13 88-11
E-mail: vertrieb-kunstverlage@reimer-verlag.de
Web Site: www.reimer-mann-verlag.de
Key Personnel
Mng Dir: Dr Hans-Robert Cram
Publishing Manager: Beate Behrens *Tel:* (030) 700 13 88-73 *E-mail:* behrens@reimer-verlag.de
Sales & Advertising: Elke Lundt *Tel:* (030) 700 13 88-50 *Fax:* (030) 700 13 88-55 *E-mail:* elundt@reimer-verlag.de
Press: Ingrid Schulze *Tel:* (030) 700 13 88-32 *E-mail:* ischulze@reimer-verlag.de
Founded: 1845
Subjects: Anthropology, Art, Drama, Theater, Ethnicity, Music, Dance, Cartography, Customs & Traditions, Television
ISBN Prefix(es): 978-3-496; 978-3-7861
Imprints: Deutscher Verlag fuer Kunstwissenschaft; Gebr Mann Verlag
Orders to: Leipziger Kommissions- und Grossbuchhandelsgesellschaft mbH (LKG), An der Suedspitze 1-12, 04571 Roetha *Tel:* (034206) 65-100 *Fax:* (034206) 65-110 *E-mail:* lkg@lkg-service.de *Web Site:* www.lkg-va.de

Ernst Reinhardt Verlag GmbH & Co KG+
Kemnatenstr 46, 80639 Munich
Mailing Address: Postfach 20 07 65, 80007 Munich
Tel: (089) 17 80 16-0 *Fax:* (089) 17 80 16-30
E-mail: info@reinhardt-verlag.de; webmaster@reinhardt-verlag.de; foreignrights@reinhardt-verlag.de
Web Site: www.reinhardt-verlag.de
Key Personnel
Mng Dir: Hildegard Wehler *E-mail:* wehler@reinhardt-verlag.de
Finance: Monika Enter *Tel:* (089) 17 80 16-17 *E-mail:* enter@reinhardt-verlag.de
Foreign Rights: Bettina Hoelzl *Tel:* (089) 178 016-12 *Fax:* (089) 178 016-30
Production: Anna Strommer *Tel:* (089) 17 80 16-20 *E-mail:* strommer@reinhardt-verlag.de
Sales: Daniela Postleb *Tel:* (089) 17 80 16-22 *E-mail:* postleb@reinhardt-verlag.de
Founded: 1899
Subjects: Child Care & Development, Education, Management, Medicine, Nursing, Dentistry, Music, Dance, Philosophy, Psychology, Psychiatry, Religion - Other, Science (General), Social Sciences, Sociology, ADHD, Autism, Dyscalculia, Early Intervention, Pedagogy, Psychotherapy, Special Education, Speech Therapy
ISBN Prefix(es): 978-3-497
Foreign Rep(s): Mohr Morawa Buchvertrieb GmbH (Roland Fuerst) (Austria); Scheidegger & Co AG (Ruth Schildknecht) (Switzerland); Uta Vonarburg (Switzerland)
Distribution Center: Brockhaus/Commission, Postfach 12 20, 70806 Kornwestheim *Tel:* (07154) 13 27-0 *Fax:* (07154) 13 27-13 *E-mail:* reinhardt@brocom.de
Rhenus Medien Logistik GmbH & Co KG, Justus-von-Liebig-Str 1, 86899 Landsberg am Lech *Tel:* (08191) 97 000-640
Mohr Morawa Buchvertrieb GmbH, Sulzengasse 2, 1230 Vienna, Austria *Tel:* (01) 680 14-0 *Fax:* (01) 688 71 30 *E-mail:* momo@mohrmorawa.at *Web Site:* www.mohrmorawa.at

Scheidegger & Co AG, AVA Verlagsauslieferung AG, Centralweg 16, 8910 Affoltern am Albis, Switzerland *Tel:* (044) 762 42-50 *Fax:* (044) 762 42-10 *E-mail:* e.bachofner@ava.ch

E Reinhold Verlag (E Reinhold Publishing)
Division of Verlagsgruppe Kamprad
Theo-Neubauer-Str 7, 04600 Altenburg
Tel: (03447) 375610 *Fax:* (03447) 892850
E-mail: verlag@vkjk.de
Web Site: vkjk.de; querstand.de
Key Personnel
Publisher: Klaus-Juergen Kamprad *E-mail:* klaus.kamprad@vkjk.de
Founded: 1990
Books about East Germany (Saxony, Saxony-Anhalt & Thuringia).
Membership(s): Boersenverein des Deutschen Buchhandels - Landesverband Sachsen/Sachsen-Anhalt/Thueringen.
Subjects: Biography, Memoirs, History, Photography, Regional Interests, Travel & Tourism, East Germany
ISBN Prefix(es): 978-3-910166; 978-3-937940; 978-3-930550
Number of titles published annually: 10 Print
Total Titles: 160 Print

Reise Know-How+
Member of Verlagsgruppe Reise Know-How
Zwalbacher Str 3, 66709 Rappweiler
Tel: (06872) 91737 *Fax:* (06872) 91738
E-mail: info@reise-know-how.de
Web Site: www.reise-know-how.com
Key Personnel
Mng Dir: Myriam Bohr; Edgar P Hoff
Founded: 1981
Publisher of travel guides.
Subjects: Travel & Tourism, Travel Guides
ISBN Prefix(es): 978-3-923716
Number of titles published annually: 2 Print
Total Titles: 13 Print
Subsidiaries: Backpacker Information Service

Reise Know-How Verlag Dr Hans-R Grundmann GmbH
Member of Verlagsgruppe Reise Know-How
Koenigsberger Str 11, 23701 Eutin
Tel: (04521) 78457 *Fax:* (04521) 7761934
E-mail: info@reise-know-how.de; info@reisebuch.de
Web Site: www.reise-know-how.de; reisebuch.de
Key Personnel
Contact: Hartmut Ihnenfeldt *E-mail:* ihnenfeldt@reisebuch.de
Founded: 1988
Specialize in North America travel publications.
Subjects: Travel & Tourism
ISBN Prefix(es): 978-3-927554; 978-3-9800151
Orders to: Germinal GmbH, Postfach 70, 35461 Fernwald *Tel:* (0641) 41700 *Fax:* (0641) 943251 *E-mail:* bestellservice@germinal.de

Reise Know-How Verlag Helmut Hermann
Member of Verlagsgruppe Reise Know-How
Untere Muehle, 71706 Markgroeningen
Tel: (07145) 82 78 *Fax:* (07145) 2 67 36
E-mail: rkhhermann@aol.com
Web Site: www.reise-know-how.de
Key Personnel
Mng Dir: Peter Rump
Contact: H Hermann
Founded: 1985
Subjects: Language Arts, Linguistics, Music, Dance, Photography, Sports, Athletics, Travel & Tourism
ISBN Prefix(es): 978-3-929920; 978-3-9800975
Distribution Center: Germinal GmbH Verlags- und Medienhandlung, Postfach 70, 35461 Fernwald *Tel:* (0641) 41700 *Fax:* (0641) 943251 *E-mail:* bestellservice@germinal.de

Mohr Morawa Buchvertrieb GmbH, Sulzengasse 2, 1230 Vienna, Austria *Tel:* (01) 680
14-0 *Fax:* (01) 688 71 30 *E-mail:* momo@
mohrmorawa.at *Web Site:* www.mohrmorawa.at
KIWI Svet map a pruvodcu, Jungmannova 23,
110 00 Prague 1, Czech Republic *Tel:* 224 948
455 *Fax:* 296 245 555 *E-mail:* mapy@kiwick.
cz *Web Site:* www.kiwick.cz
Librairie Ulysse, 26, rue St Louis en l'Ile, 75004
Paris, France *Tel:* 01 43 25 17 35 *Fax:* 01
43 29 52 10 *E-mail:* ulysse@ulysse.fr *Web
Site:* www.ulysse.fr
Les librairies voyageurs du monde, 55 rue Ste-
Anne, 75002 Paris, France *Tel:* 01 42 86 17 37
Web Site: www.vdm.com
Steinhart Katzir Publishers Ltd, Sappir Indus-
trial Park, 19 Yad Harutzim St, PO Box 8333,
42505 Netanya, Israel *Tel:* (09) 885 4770
Fax: (09) 885 4771 *E-mail:* info@haolam.co.il
Web Site: www.haolam.co.il
Centro Cartografico Del Riccio, Via E Pistelli, 46,
50135 Florence FI, Italy *Tel:* (055) 6120323
Fax: (055) 6120324 *E-mail:* ricciocc@tin.it
Willems Adventure, Honderdland 120, 2676
LT Maasdijk, Netherlands *Tel:* (088) 599
01 40 *Fax:* (088) 599 01 41 *E-mail:* info@
willemsadventure.nl *Web Site:* www.
willemsadventure.nl
Sklep Podroznika, ul Grojecka 46/50, 02-320
Warsaw, Poland *Tel:* (22) 822 44 56 *Fax:* (22)
822 44 56 *E-mail:* sklep@traveler.com.pl *Web
Site:* www.sp.com.pl
mapiberia f&b, Parque Empresarial El Pinar,
Nave A2, C/ Rio Cea, Poligono Industrial Las
Hervencias, 05004 Avila, Spain *Tel:* 920 03 01
06 *Fax:* 920 03 01 08 *E-mail:* info@mapiberia.
com *Web Site:* www.mapiberia.com
Kartbutiken, Kungsgatan 74, 111 22 Stockholm,
Sweden *Tel:* (08) 202 303 *Fax:* (08) 202 711
Web Site: www.kartbutiken.se
Kartcentrum, Vasagatan 16, 111 20 Stockholm,
Sweden *Tel:* (08) 411 16 97; (08) 411 16 99
Fax: (08) 21 32 95 *E-mail:* info@kartcentrum.
se *Web Site:* www.kartcentrum.se
buch2000, Centralweg 16, 8910 Affoltern,
Switzerland *Tel:* (044) 762 42 60 *Fax:* (044)
762 42 10 *E-mail:* info@scheidegger-buecher.
ch
Stanfords, 12-14 Long Acre, London WC2E
9LP, United Kingdom *Tel:* (020) 7836 1321
Fax: (020) 7836 0189 *E-mail:* sales@stanfords.
co.uk *Web Site:* www.stanfords.co.uk
The Map Shop, 15 High St, Upton upon Severn, Worcs WR8 0HJ, United Kingdom
Tel: (01684) 593146 *Toll Free:* 0800 085
40 80 (UK only) *Web Site:* www.themapshop.
co.uk
Omni Resources, 1004 South Mebane St, Burlington, NC 27215, United States *Tel:* 336-227-
8300 *Fax:* 336-227-3748 *E-mail:* inquiries@
omnimap.com *Web Site:* www.omnimap.com

Reise Know-How Verlag Peter Rump GmbH+
Member of Verlagsgruppe Reise Know-How
Osnabruecker Str 79, 33649 Bielefeld
Tel: (0521) 94649-0 *Fax:* (0521) 441047
E-mail: info@reise-know-how.de
Web Site: www.reise-know-how.de
Key Personnel
Mng Dir: Peter Rump
Founded: 1981
Subjects: Foreign Countries, Geography, Geology,
Health, Nutrition, Language Arts, Linguistics,
Outdoor Recreation, Religion - Other, Travel &
Tourism, Culture, Outdoor & Nature
ISBN Prefix(es): 978-3-922376; 978-3-89416;
978-3-8317
Distribution Center: Germinal GmbH Verlags-
und Medienhandlung, Siemensstr 16,
35463 Fernwald *Fax:* (0641) 943251
E-mail: bestellservice@germinal.de
Mohr Morawa Buchvertrieb GmbH, Sulzen-
gasse 2, 1230 Vienna, Austria *Tel:* (01) 680

14-0 *Fax:* (01) 688 71 30 *E-mail:* momo@
mohrmorawa.at *Web Site:* www.mohrmorawa.at
Versandbuchhandlung buch2000, c/o Scheideg-
ger & Co AG, Obere Bahnhofstr 10A, 8910
Affoltern, Switzerland *Fax:* (044) 7624249
E-mail: info@scheidegger-buecher.ch

Reise Know-How Verlag Tondok
Member of Verlagsgruppe Reise Know-How
Nadistr 18, 80809 Munich
Tel: (089) 351 4857 *Fax:* (089) 351 8485
E-mail: info@tondok-verlag.de
Web Site: www.tondok-verlag.de; www.reise-
know-how.de
Key Personnel
Contact: Wil Tondok
Founded: 1980
Subjects: Foreign Countries, Travel & Tourism
ISBN Prefix(es): 978-3-921838
Associate Companies: Reise Know-How Verlag
Brigitte Blume; Reise Know-How Verlag Dr
Hans Grundmann GmbH; Reise Know-How
Verlag Helmut Hermann; Reise Know-How
Verlag Peter Rump GmbH
Distribution Center: Germinal GmbH Verlags-
und Medienhandlung, Postfach 70, 35461 Fern-
wald *Tel:* (0641) 41700 *Fax:* (0641) 943251
E-mail: bestellservice@germinal.de

Verlag Norman Rentrop+
Ruengsdorfer Str 2e, 53173 Bonn
Tel: (0228) 36 88 40 *Fax:* (0228) 36 58 75
Web Site: www.normanrentrop.de
Key Personnel
Mng Dir: Norman Rentrop *E-mail:* nr@rentrop.
com
Founded: 1975
Specialize in looseleaf services.
Subjects: Business, Finance, Public Administra-
tion, Real Estate
Branch Office(s)
Arenbergstr 33, 5020 Salzburg, Austria
One Place du Lycee, 68005 Colmar, France
Sagestr 14, 5600 Lenzburg/Zurich, Switzerland
27A Old Gloucester St, London WC1N 3XX,
United Kingdom
U.S. Office(s): Georgetown Publishing House,
1101 30 St NW, Washington, DC 20007,
United States *Tel:* 202-337-5960 *Fax:* 202-337-
1512
117 W Harrison, Suite R-246, Chicago, IL 60605,
United States

Reprint Verlag-Leipzig, *imprint of* Primus
Verlag GmbH

Reprodukt
Gottschedstr 4, Aufgang 1, 13357 Berlin
Tel: (030) 469 064 38 *Fax:* (030) 466 088 69
E-mail: info@reprodukt.com
Web Site: www.reprodukt.com
Key Personnel
Editor: Michael Groenewald *E-mail:* michael.
groenewald@reprodukt.com; Christian Maiwald
E-mail: christian.maiwald@reprodukt.com
Foreign Rights: Sebastian Oehler *Tel:* (030) 466
076 88 *E-mail:* sebastian.oehler@reprodukt.
com
Marketing & Sales: Marion Jaiser *Tel:* (030) 469
064 45 *E-mail:* marion.jaiser@reprodukt.com
Subjects: Fiction, Humor
ISBN Prefix(es): 978-3-943143
Distribution Center: Leipziger Kommissions- und
Grossbuchhandelsgesellschaft mbH (LKG),
An der Suedspitze 1-12, 04571 Roetha, Con-
tact: Elisabeth Kaiser *Tel:* (034206) 65 107
Fax: (034206) 65 1732 *E-mail:* ekaiser@lkg-
service.de *Web Site:* www.lkg-va.de
Pictopia Verlagsauslieferung, Liechtensteinstr 64/
4, 1090 Vienna, Austria *Tel:* (0676) 93 00 789
Fax: (01) 922 37 38 *E-mail:* office@pictopia.at
Web Site: www.pictopia.at

kaktus verlagsauslieferung, Langfeldstr 54,
Postfach 459, 8501 Frauenfeld, Switzerland
Tel: (052) 722 31 90 *Fax:* (052) 722 17 82
E-mail: kaktus@solnet.ch *Web Site:* www.
kaktus.net

Resch Verlag
Maria-Eich-Str 77, 82166 Graefelfing
Tel: (089) 8 54 65-0 *Fax:* (089) 8 54 65-11
E-mail: info@resch-verlag.com
Web Site: www.resch-verlag.com
Key Personnel
Publishing Dir: Michaela Grosser
Mng Dir: Dr Ingo Resch
Founded: 1955
Subjects: Economics, Energy, Engineering (Gen-
eral), Government, Political Science, Health,
Nutrition, Law, Religion - Islamic, Religion -
Other, Social Sciences, Sociology, Automation,
Biotechnology, Industrial Engineering, Safety
ISBN Prefix(es): 978-3-935197; 978-3-930039

Respublica-Verlag, see Verlag Franz Schmitt

Retap Verlag GmbH
Clausthal-Zellerfelder-Str 69, 40595 Duesseldorf
Tel: (0211) 73779348 *Fax:* (0211) 77058840
E-mail: verwaltung@retap-verlag.de
Web Site: www.retap-verlag.de
Key Personnel
Founder: Siegfried Pater
Mng Dir: Eva Roethel
Subjects: Social Sciences, Sociology, Foreign Aid
Development, Foreign Trade
ISBN Prefix(es): 978-3-931988

RETORIKA GmbH
Emil-von-Behring-Allee 16, 14624 Dallgow-
Doeheritz
Tel: (03322) 837363
E-mail: info@retorika.de
Web Site: www.retorika.de
Key Personnel
Founder: Dr Victoria Viererbe; Aleksej Zuckov
Subjects: Education, Fiction, Literature, Liter-
ary Criticism, Essays, German & Russian Lan-
guages
ISBN Prefix(es): 978-3-944172

Edition Reuss GmbH
Postfach 100142, 63701 Aschaffenburg
Tel: (06021) 5839175 *Fax:* (06021) 5839176
E-mail: photobooks@edition-reuss.de
Web Site: www.editionreuss.de
Key Personnel
Mng Dir: Matthias Reuss
Founded: 1996
Membership(s): Bayerischen Verlegerverbands;
Boersenverein des Deutschen Buchhandels.
Subjects: Animals, Pets, Art, Erotica, Nature,
Nude Photography, Tattoo
ISBN Prefix(es): 978-3-934020

Revolver Publishing
Immanuelkirchstr 12, 10405 Berlin
Tel: (030) 616 092 36 *Fax:* (030) 616 092 38
E-mail: info@revolver-publishing.com
Web Site: www.revolver-publishing.com; www.
revolver-books.de (orders)
Key Personnel
Manager: Heike Salchli; Melte Nisch
Founded: 2008
Subjects: Architecture & Interior Design, Art,
Biography, Memoirs, Computer Science, Gar-
dening, Plants, Government, Political Science,
History, Artists, Culture, Textbooks
ISBN Prefix(es): 978-3-86895; 978-3-95763
Number of titles published annually: 13 Print
Total Titles: 193 Print
Distribution Center: Vice Versa Distribution
GmbH, Immanuelkirchstr 12, 10405 Berlin
Tel: (030) 616 092 36 *Fax:* (030) 616 092 38

E-mail: info@vice-versa-distribution.com Web Site: www.vice-versa-distribution.com (Germany, Austria & Switzerland)
Idea Books, Nieuwe Herengracht 11, 1011 RK Amsterdam, Netherlands Tel: (020) 6226164 Fax: (020) 6209299 Web Site: www.ideabooks. nl (worldwide)
art data, 12 Bell Industrial Estate, 50 Cunnington St, London W4 5HB, United Kingdom Tel: (020) 8747 1061 Fax: (020) 8742 2319 E-mail: orders@artdata.co.uk Web Site: www. artdata.co.uk

Rhein-Mosel-Verlag GmbH
Bradenburg 17, 56856 Zell/Mosel
Tel: (06542) 5151 Fax: (06542) 61158
E-mail: info@rmv-web.de; rhein-mosel-verlag@t-online.de
Web Site: www.rmv-web.de; www.r-m-v.de
Key Personnel
Owner: Arne Houben
Founded: 1991
Membership(s): Verlags-Karree eV.
Subjects: Fiction, History, Nonfiction (General), Contemporary History, Crime
ISBN Prefix(es): 978-3-89801; 978-3-929745; 978-3-9802610

Rheinland-Verlag-und Betriebsgesellschaft des Landschaftsverbandes Rheinland mbH+
Abtei Brauweiler, Ehrenfriedstr 1, 50259 Pulheim
Tel: (02234) 98 54-263 Fax: (02234) 98 54-219
Key Personnel
Mng Dir: Christian Buegel
Founded: 1958
Subjects: Archaeology, History, Regional Interests
ISBN Prefix(es): 978-3-7927
Subsidiaries: Rhein Eifel Mosel Verlag
Shipping Address: Dr Rudolf Habelt Verlag, Am Buchenhang 2, 53315 Bonn

Rhema - Verlag und Herstellung
Eisenbahnstr 11, 48143 Muenster
Tel: (0251) 44088 Fax: (0251) 44089
E-mail: info@rhema-verlag.de
Web Site: www.rhema-verlag.de
Key Personnel
Owner: Tim Doherty
Subjects: Art, History
ISBN Prefix(es): 978-3-930454

RhinoVerlag, imprint of Verlagsgruppe gruenes herz

Helmut Richardi Verlag GmbH+
Aschaffenburger Str 19, 60599 Frankfurt am Main
Tel: (069) 97 08 33-0 Fax: (069) 707 84 00
E-mail: info@kreditwesen.de; vertrieb@kreditwesen.de (sales)
Web Site: www.kreditwesen.de
Key Personnel
Publisher: Philipp Otto Tel: (069) 97 08 33-48
Mng Dir: Uwe Cappel E-mail: verlagsleitung@kreditwesen.de
Sales & Press: Stefanie Mitsch Tel: (069) 97 08 33-24 E-mail: s.mitsch@kreditwesen.de
Sales: Brigitte Woellner Tel: (069) 97 08 33-21
Founded: 1949
Subjects: Finance, Real Estate, Banking, Investment
ISBN Prefix(es): 978-3-921722
Associate Companies: Verlag fuer Absatzwirtschaft; Friz Knapp Verlag

Richter-Verlag
Paul-Schroeder-Str 18, 24229 Daenischenhagen
Tel: (04349) 1725 Fax: (04349) 571
E-mail: richter-verlag@t-online.de
Web Site: www.richter-verlag.de

Key Personnel
Chief Executive Officer: Hans-Peter Richter
Deputy Mng Dir: Christiane Gierke
Founded: 1984
Subjects: Law, Civil Law, Criminal Law, Public Law
ISBN Prefix(es): 978-3-935150

Richter Verlag GmbH
Am Rittersberg 18, 40595 Duesseldorf
Tel: (0211) 370202 Fax: (0211) 377099
E-mail: office@richterverlag.com
Web Site: www.richterverlag.com
Founded: 2008
Subjects: Art, Photography, Art History
ISBN Prefix(es): 978-3-941459
Foreign Rep(s): Cornerhouse Publications (UK); DAP Distributed Art Publishers (North America); Elisabeth Harder-Kreimann (Scandinavia); Verlagsvertretungen Stefan Schempp (Austria); Coen Sligting Bookimport (Belgium, Luxembourg, Netherlands); Vilo Groupe (France)

Susanna Rieder Verlag
Offenbachstr 46a, 81245 Munich
Tel: (089) 82 08 67 65 Fax: (089) 12 71 09 96
E-mail: info@riederbuch.de; presse@riederbuch. de; vertrieb@riederbuch.de
Web Site: www.riederbuch.de
Key Personnel
Owner: Susanna Rieder
ISBN Prefix(es): 978-3-941172
Foreign Rep(s): Elisabeth Anintah-Hirt (Austria); Andreas Meisel (Switzerland)
Distribution Center: MSR/Runge VA, Bergstr 2, 33803 Steinhagen Tel: (05204) 99 81 23 Fax: (05204) 99 81 14 E-mail: msr@rungeva. de Web Site: www.rungeva.de
Medienlogistik Pichler-OEBZ GmbH, IZ NOE Sued, Str 1, Objekt 34, 2355 Wiener Neudorf, Austria, Contact: Eva-Maria Prinz Tel: (02236) 63 53 52 45 Fax: (02236) 63 53 52 71 E-mail: eva.prinz@medien-logistik.at
Herder AG Basel, Muttenzerstr 109, Postfach, 4133 Pratteln 1, Switzerland Tel: (061) 8279060 Fax: (061) 8279067 E-mail: verkauf@herder.ch

Riemann, imprint of Verlagsgruppe Random House Bertelsmann

Riemann Verlag
Imprint of Verlagsgruppe Random House Bertelsmann
Neumarkter Str 28, 81673 Munich
Tel: (089) 4136-0 Toll Free Tel: 0800 500 33 22 Fax: (089) 4136-3333
E-mail: kundenservice@randomhouse.de
Web Site: www.randomhouse.de/riemann
Key Personnel
Press: Claudia Hanssen Tel: (089) 4136-3723 E-mail: claudia.hanssen@randomhouse.de
Subjects: Economics, Government, Political Science, Nonfiction (General), Ecology, Environmental
ISBN Prefix(es): 978-3-570

Edition Riesenrad, imprint of Xenos Verlag

Rigodon-Verlag Norbert Wehr+
Nieberdingstr 18, 45147 Essen
Tel: (0201) 77 81 11 Fax: (0201) 77 51 74
E-mail: schreibheft@netcologne.de
Web Site: www.schreibheft.de
Key Personnel
Manager: Norbert Wehr
Founded: 1977
Subjects: Literature, Literary Criticism, Essays
ISBN Prefix(es): 978-3-924071

Rimbaud Verlagsgesellschaft mbH+
Oppenhoffallee 20, 52066 Aachen
Mailing Address: Postfach 10 01 44, 52001 Aachen
Tel: (0241) 54 25 32 Fax: (0241) 51 41 17
E-mail: info@rimbaud.de
Web Site: www.rimbaud.de
Key Personnel
Mng Dir: Bernard Albers; Walter Hoerner
Founded: 1983
Subjects: Literature, Literary Criticism, Essays, Music, Dance, Photography, Poetry
ISBN Prefix(es): 978-3-89086
Distributed by Hora-Verlag (Austria); Pegasus Verlagsauslieferung (Switzerland)

Ritterbach Verlag GmbH
Rudolf-Diesel-Str 5-7, 50226 Frechen
Mailing Address: Postfach 1820, 50208 Frechen
Tel: (02234) 18 66-0 Fax: (02234) 18 66-90; (02234) 18 66 13
E-mail: verlag@ritterbach.de; service@ritterbach. de
Web Site: www.ritterbach.de; www.kunstwelt-online.de; www.kunsthandwerk-design.de
Key Personnel
Mng Dir: Markus Ritterbach
Founded: 1987
Subjects: Architecture & Interior Design, Art, Career Development, Crafts, Games, Hobbies, Education
ISBN Prefix(es): 978-3-89314

riva Verlag
Nymphenburger Str 86, 80636 Munich
Tel: (089) 65 12 85-0 Fax: (089) 65 20 96
E-mail: info@rivaverlag.de
Web Site: www.m-vg.de/riva
Key Personnel
Publisher: Christian Jund E-mail: cjund@m-vg.de
Publishing Dir: Matthias Setzler E-mail: msetzler@m-vg.de
Mng Dir: Oliver Kuhn
Rights Dir & International Affairs: Maria Pinto-Peuckmann Tel: (089) 65 12 85-244 E-mail: mpinto-peuckmann@m-vg.de
Founded: 2004
Subjects: Biography, Memoirs, Humor, Mysteries, Suspense, Nonfiction (General), Sports, Athletics, Beauty, Fitness
ISBN Prefix(es): 978-3-936994; 978-3-86883
Parent Company: Muencher Verlagsgruppe GmbH
Associate Companies: FinanzBuch Verlag; mi-Wirtschaftsbuch; mvg Verlag; Redline Verlag
Foreign Rep(s): Mohr Morawa Buchvertrieb GmbH (Thomas Lasnik & Michael Hipp) (Austria); Giovanni Ravasio (Switzerland)
Distribution Center: Rhenus Medien Logistik GmbH & Co KG, Justus-von-Liebig-Str 1, 86899 Landsberg am Lech Tel: (08191) 97000-0 E-mail: info.rml@de.rhenus.com
Mohr Morawa Buchvertrieb GmbH, Sulzengasse 2, 1230 Vienna, Austria Tel: (01) 680 14-0 Fax: (01) 688 71 30 E-mail: momo@mohrmorawa.at Web Site: www.mohrmorawa.at
AVA Verlagsauslieferung AG, Centralweg 16, 8910 Affoltern am Albis, Switzerland Tel: (044) 7624260 Fax: (044) 7624210 E-mail: verlagsservice@ava.ch

Rockbuch Verlag
Neumuehlen 17, 22763 Hamburg
Tel: (040) 890 85 0 Fax: (040) 890 85 9320
E-mail: rockbuch@edel.com
Web Site: www.rockbuch.de
Key Personnel
Dir: Michael Haentjes
Press: Michaela Guhl Tel: (040) 890 85 290 E-mail: michaela.guhl@edel.com
Subjects: Biography, Memoirs, Music, Dance, Nonfiction (General), Pop Culture
ISBN Prefix(es): 978-3-927638
Parent Company: Edel Germany GmbH

Verlag Rockstuhl
Lange Bruedergasse 12, 99947 Bad Langensalza
Tel: (03603) 812246 *Fax:* (03603) 812247
E-mail: verlag-rockstuhl@web.de
Web Site: www.verlag-rockstuhl.de
Key Personnel
Publisher: Harald Rockstuhl
Sales & Marketing: Annekathrin Rockstuhl
Founded: 1990
Membership(s): Boersenverein des Deutschen
Buchhandels eV.
Subjects: Aeronautics, Aviation, Cookery, Fiction,
History, Military Science, Nonfiction (General),
Philosophy, Hiking
ISBN Prefix(es): 978-3-86777; 978-3-929000;
978-3-932554; 978-3-936030; 978-3-934748;
978-3-938997; 978-3-937135
Total Titles: 1,010 Print

Roehrig Universitaets Verlag GmbH
Eichendorffstr 37, 66386 Sankt Ingbert
Mailing Address: Postfach 1806, 66386 Sankt
Ingbert
Tel: (06894) 87 957 *Fax:* (06894) 87 0330
E-mail: info@roehrig-verlag.de
Web Site: www.roehrig-verlag.de
Key Personnel
Publisher: Werner J Roehrig; Andreas Schorr
Founded: 1984
Membership(s): Boersenverein des Deutschen
Buchhandels; National Federation of Book-
sellers & Publishers; Provincial Federation of
Booksellers & Publishers
Subjects: Government, Political Science, History,
Language Arts, Linguistics, Literature, Literary
Criticism, Essays, Science (General)
ISBN Prefix(es): 978-3-924555; 978-3-86110
Number of titles published annually: 25 Print
Total Titles: 560 Print

J H Roell Verlag GmbH
Wuerzburger Str 16, 97337 Dettelbach
Mailing Address: Postfach 1109, 97335 Dettel-
bach
Tel: (09324) 99770 *Fax:* (09324) 99771
E-mail: info@roell-verlag.de
Web Site: www.roell-verlag.de
Key Personnel
Mng Dir: Dr Joseph H Roell
Subjects: Archaeology, Art, Education, Geogra-
phy, Geology, History, Language Arts, Lin-
guistics, Literature, Literary Criticism, Essays,
Medicine, Nursing, Dentistry, Philosophy, Po-
etry, Regional Interests, Religion - Other, Sci-
ence (General), Social Sciences, Sociology,
Technology, Egyptology
ISBN Prefix(es): 978-3-89754; 978-3-927522

Verlagshaus Roemerweg GmbH
Roemerweg 10, 65187 Wiesbaden
Tel: (0611) 986 98 0 *Fax:* (0611) 986 98 26
E-mail: info@verlagshaus-roemerweg.de
Web Site: www.verlagshaus-roemerweg.de
Key Personnel
Publishing Dir: Lothar Wekel *E-mail:* wekel@
verlagshaus-roemerweg.de
Press: Rona Sommer *Tel:* (0611) 986 98 70
E-mail: sommer@verlagshaus-roemerweg.de
Sales & Marketing: Fabien Reinecke *Tel:* (0611)
986 98 15 *Fax:* (0611) 986 98 78 15
E-mail: reinecke@verlagshaus-roemerweg.de
ISBN Prefix(es): 978-3-86539; 978-3-937715;
978-3-940432; 978-3-86280; 978-3-7374
Imprints: Berlin University Press; Corso Verlag;
Edition Erdmann; Waldemar Kramer; Marixver-
lag; Weimarer Verlagsgesselschaft
Foreign Rep(s): Buchzentrum AG (Switzerland);
Mohr Morawa Buchvertrieb GmbH (Austria)
Distribution Center: Sigloch Distribution
GmbH & Co KG, Am Buchberg 8, Tor
6-10, 74572 Blaufelden *Tel:* (07953)

718 906 9 *Fax:* (07953) 883 700
E-mail: verlagshausroemerweg@sigloch.de *Web
Site:* www.sigloch.de

Rombach Verlag KG+
Unterwerkstr 5, 79115 Freiburg
Tel: (0761) 4500-2135 *Fax:* (0761) 4500-2125
E-mail: info@buchverlag.rombach.de
Web Site: www.rombach-verlag.de
Key Personnel
Mng Dir: Andreas Hodeige
Publishing Dir: Dr Torang Sinaga *Tel:* (0761)
4500-2134 *E-mail:* sinaga@rombach.de
Sales/Marketing: Melanie Panzer
E-mail: panzer@rombach.de
Founded: 1936
Subjects: Art, Government, Political Science, His-
tory, Literature, Literary Criticism, Essays, Re-
gional Interests, Social Sciences, Sociology
ISBN Prefix(es): 978-3-7930
Associate Companies: Rombach Druckhaus KG,
Bertoldstr 10, 79098 Freiburg; Rombach Han-
delshaus KG, Bertoldstr 10, 79098 Freiburg;
Rombach Medienhaus KG, Bertoldstr 10,
79098 Freiburg
Bookshop(s): Rombach Buchhandlung, Bertold-
str 10, 79098 Freiburg *Tel:* (0761) 45002400
E-mail: service@buchhandlung-rombach.de

Romiosini Verlag+
Venloestr 30, 50672 Cologne
Tel: (0221) 510 12 88 *Fax:* (0221) 510 12 88
E-mail: edition.romiosini@cemog.fu-berlin.de
Web Site: bibliothek.edition-romiosini.de
Key Personnel
Publisher: Niki Eideneier
Founded: 1982
Specialize in Greek literature in German transla-
tion.
Subjects: Cookery, Fiction, History, Literature,
Literary Criticism, Essays, Music, Dance, Po-
etry, Travel & Tourism
ISBN Prefix(es): 978-3-923728; 978-3-929889
Distributed by Athener Buchhandlung AG
(Greece); Griechische Buecher Eliki (Switzer-
land); MAM (Cypress)
Distribution Center: UNISOLO Buchvertrieb,
Gaussstr 7, 38106 Braunschweig *Tel:* (0531)
12161-20 *Fax:* (0531) 12161-29
Orders to: Unisolo/Despina Kazantzidou, Nor-
dohr 11, 38106 Braunschweig *Tel:* (0531)
336050 *Fax:* (0531) 336049 *E-mail:* despina.
kazantzidou@unisolo.de *Web Site:* www.
unisolo.de/romiosini.htm

rororo, *imprint of* Rowohlt Verlag GmbH

rororo rotfuchs, *imprint of* Rowohlt Verlag
GmbH

Rosenheimer Verlagshaus GmbH & Co KG+
Am Stocket 12, 83022 Rosenheim
Tel: (08031) 28 38 0 *Fax:* (08031) 28 38 44
E-mail: info@rosenheimer.com; presse1@
rosenheimer.com; vertrieb1@rosenheimer.com
Web Site: www.rosenheimer.com
Key Personnel
Mng Dir: Klaus G Foerg *Tel:* (08031) 28 38 14
Editorial Off: Elisabeth Grohsmann *Tel:* (08031)
28 38 41
Press & Public Relations: Katharina Angne
Tel: (08031) 28 38 67
Press Off: Siriporn Nathibal *Tel:* (08031) 28 38
64
Founded: 1949
Subjects: Crafts, Games, Hobbies, Fiction, His-
tory, Regional Interests, Romance
ISBN Prefix(es): 978-3-475
Total Titles: 200 Print; 30 Audio

Rossipaul Kommunikation GmbH+
Menzinger Str 37, 80638 Munich
Mailing Address: Postfach 20 16 55, 80016 Mu-
nich
Tel: (089) 17 91 06-0 *Fax:* (089) 17 91 06-22
E-mail: info@rossipaul.de
Web Site: www.rossipaul.de
Key Personnel
Mng Dir, Rights & Permissions: Rainer Rossipaul
Marketing & Sales Management: Ingo Neubert
Tel: (089) 17 91 06-27 *E-mail:* ineubert@
rossipaul.de
Advertising & Product Management: Ur-
sula Rossipaul *Tel:* (089) 17 91 06-24
E-mail: urossipaul@rossipaul.de
Founded: 1953
Subjects: Advertising, Career Development, Com-
puter Science, Finance, Health, Nutrition, Lan-
guage Arts, Linguistics, Law, Management,
Nonfiction (General), Outdoor Recreation
ISBN Prefix(es): 978-3-87686

Rotblatt, *imprint of* Iris Kater Verlag & Medien
GmbH

Rotbuch Verlag
Alexanderstr 1, 10178 Berlin
Tel: (030) 20 61 09-0 *Fax:* (030) 20 61 09-75
E-mail: info@rotbuch.de; rights@rotbuch.de
Web Site: www.rotbuch.de
Key Personnel
Mng Dir: Marko Wuensch
Head, Sales: Jacqueline Kuehne *Tel:* (030) 23 80
91-22 *E-mail:* kuehne@rotbuch.de
Sales Manager: Sabine Asshoff *Tel:* (030) 23 80
91-105 *E-mail:* asshoff@rotbuch.de
Foreign Rights: Maria Oehlschlegel *Tel:* (030) 20
61 09-71
Founded: 1973
Subjects: Biography, Memoirs, Drama, Theater,
Fiction, Government, Political Science, Liter-
ature, Literary Criticism, Essays, Mysteries,
Suspense, Nonfiction (General), Crime
ISBN Prefix(es): 978-3-86789
Parent Company: Eulenspiegel Verlagsgruppe
Distribution Center: Leipziger Kommissions- und
Grossbuchhandelsgesellschaft mbH (LKG),
An der Suedspitze 1-12, 04571 Roetha, Con-
tact: Martina Koernig *Tel:* (034206) 651 22
Fax: (034206) 65 17 34 *E-mail:* mkoernig@
lkg-service.de *Web Site:* www.lkg-va.de
Mohr Morawa Buchvertrieb GmbH, Sulzengasse
2, 1230 Vienna, Austria, Contact: Ulrich Wal-
lenschewski *Tel:* (01) 680 14-13 *Fax:* (01) 680
14-140 *E-mail:* momo@mohrmorawa.at *Web
Site:* www.mohrmorawa.at
Buchzentrum AG (BZ), Industriestr Ost 10, 4614
Haegendorf, Switzerland, Contact: Nicole
Geissbuehler *Tel:* (062) 209 26 44 *Fax:* (062)
209 27 88 *E-mail:* geissbuehler@buchzentrum.
ch

Roter Fleck Verlag
Herderstr 19, 64285 Darmstadt
Tel: (06151) 9516885 *Fax:* (06151) 3968460
E-mail: info@roter-fleck-verlag.de
Web Site: www.roter-fleck-verlag.de
Key Personnel
Publisher: Dr Katinka Pantz *Tel:* (0172) 3127 491
(cell) *E-mail:* katinka.pantz@roter-fleck-verlag.
de
Founded: 2006
Subjects: Science (General)
ISBN Prefix(es): 978-3-940082

edition roter stein, *imprint of* Karin Fischer
Verlag GmbH

Rowohlt Berlin Verlag GmbH, *imprint of*
Rowohlt Verlag GmbH

Rowohlt-Berlin Verlag GmbH+
Imprint of Rowohlt Verlag GmbH
Kreuzbergstr 30, 10965 Berlin
Tel: (030) 28 53 84-11 *Fax:* (030) 28 53 84-22
E-mail: info@rowohlt.de
Web Site: www.rowohlt.de
Key Personnel
Mng Dir: Dr Helmut Daehne
Publishing Dir: Gunnar Schmidt
Foreign Rights Dir: Carolin Kettmann
    Tel: (040) 72 72 257 *Fax:* (040) 72 72 319
    E-mail: carolin.kettmann@rowohlt.de
Marketing Manager: Lutz Kettmann
Rights & Permissions: Kristina Krombholz
Founded: 1990
Specialize in fiction from East & Central Europe;
    political nonfiction.
Subjects: Fiction, Government, Political Science,
    Nonfiction (General)
ISBN Prefix(es): 978-3-87134
Number of titles published annually: 30 Print
Total Titles: 160 Print

Rowohlt Polaris, *imprint of* Rowohlt Verlag
GmbH

Rowohlt Verlag, *imprint of* Rowohlt Verlag
GmbH

Rowohlt Verlag GmbH, *imprint of* Kindler
Verlag AG GmbH

Rowohlt Verlag GmbH+
Hamburger Str 17, 21465 Reinbek
Tel: (040) 72 72 0 *Fax:* (040) 72 72 319
E-mail: info@rowohlt.de
Web Site: www.rowohlt.de
Key Personnel
Publishing Dir: Alexander Fest
Commercial Dir: Peter Kraus vom Cleff
Foreign Rights: Carolin Mungard *Tel:* (040) 72 72
    257 *E-mail:* carolin.mungard@rowohlt.de
Marketing Manager: Lutz Kettmann
Founded: 1910
Subjects: Fiction, Nonfiction (General)
ISBN Prefix(es): 978-3-498; 978-3-499; 978-3-
    8052
Parent Company: Verlagsgruppe Georg von
    Holtzbrinck GmbH
Imprints: Kindler Verlag; Medienagentur; rororo;
    rororo rotfuchs; Rowohlt Berlin Verlag GmbH;
    Rowohlt Polaris; Rowohlt Verlag; Theater Ver-
    lag; Wunderlich Verlag
Foreign Rep(s): Josef Birsak (Austria); Buchzen-
    trum AG (Michael Guyot) (Switzerland)
Foreign Rights: Balla & Co (Catherine Balla)
    (Hungary); Bardon-Chinese Media Agency
    (Yu-Shiuan Chen) (Taiwan); Berla & Griffini
    Rights Agency (Barbara Griffini) (Italy);
    Agence Hoffman (Christine Scholz) (France);
    Internationaal Literatuur Bureau (Linda Kohn)
    (Netherlands); Leonhardt & Hoier Literary
    Agency A/S (Monica Gram) (Scandinavia);
    Meike Marx (Japan); Ilidio da Fonseca Matos
    (Portugal); Andrew Nurnberg Baltic (Tatjana
    Zoldnere) (Baltic States, Ukraine); Andrew
    Nurnberg Prague (Jitka Nemeckova) (Czechia,
    Slovakia, Slovenia); Andrew Nurnberg Sofia
    (Anna Droumeva) (Albania, Bulgaria, Mace-
    donia, Serbia); Karin Schindler (Brazil); Julio
    F Yanez Agencia Literaria (Montse F Yanez)
    (Spain)
Distribution Center: Libri de Internet GmbH,
    Friesenweg 1, 22763 Hamburg *Tel:* (040) 4223
    6522 *E-mail:* service@libri.de (ebooks)

Dieter Rueggeberg+
Siegesstr 166, 42287 Wuppertal
Mailing Address: Postfach 13 08 44, 42035 Wup-
    pertal
Tel: (0202) 59 28 11 *Fax:* (0202) 59 28 11

E-mail: vrggeberg@aol.com
Web Site: www.verlag-dr.de
Key Personnel
Mng Dir, Rights & Permissions: Dieter Ruegge-
    berg
Founded: 1968
Subjects: Astrology, Occult, Government, Political
    Science, History, Mysteries, Suspense, Psychol-
    ogy, Psychiatry, Religion - Other, Self-Help,
    Kabbalah, Scientific Magic, Spiritual Science
ISBN Prefix(es): 978-3-921338

Ruetten & Loening Verlag+
Lindenstr 20-25, 10969 Berlin
Tel: (030) 283 94 0 *Fax:* (030) 283 94 100
E-mail: info@aufbau-verlag.de; presse@aufbau-
    verlag.de
Web Site: www.aufbau-verlag.de
Key Personnel
Dir: Rene Strien
Marketing Dir: Tom Erben
Press & Public Relations: Andrea Doberenz
Founded: 1844
Subjects: Biography, Memoirs, Environmental
    Studies, Fiction, Government, Political Science,
    History, Humor, Literature, Literary Criticism,
    Essays, Mysteries, Suspense, Poetry, Romance,
    Science Fiction, Fantasy, Society
ISBN Prefix(es): 978-3-352
Number of titles published annually: 30 Print
Total Titles: 100 Print
Parent Company: Aufbau Verlag GmbH & Co
    KG
Foreign Rep(s): Mohr Morawa Buchvertrieb
    GmbH (Johann Czap) (Eastern Austria); Mohr
    Morawa Buchvertrieb GmbH (Michael Hipp)
    (Western Austria); Verlagsauslieferung Schnei-
    degger & Co AG (Ruedi Amrhein) (Switzer-
    land)
Distribution Center: VVA-Vereinigte Verlagsaus-
    lieferung Betreuung Aufbau Verlag, An der
    Autobahn, 33310 Guetersloh *Tel:* (05241) 80
    88 077 *Fax:* (05241) 80 66 959 *E-mail:* vva-
    d6f3.bestellugen@bertelsmann.de
Mohr Morawa Buchvertrieb GmbH, Sulzen-
    gasse 2, 1230 Vienna, Austria *Tel:* (01) 680
    14-0 *Fax:* (01) 688 71 30 *E-mail:* momo@
    mohrmorawa.at *Web Site:* www.mohrmorawa.at
Buchzentrum AG, Industriestr Ost 10, 4614 Ha-
    gendorf, Switzerland *Tel:* (062) 209 26 26
    Fax: (062) 209 26 27 *E-mail:* kundendienst@
    buchzentrum.ch

Verlag an der Ruhr GmbH+
Wilhelmstr 20, 45468 Muelheim an der Ruhr
Mailing Address: Postfach 102251, 45422 Muel-
    heim an der Ruhr
Tel: (0208) 439 54 50 *Fax:* (0208) 439 54 239
E-mail: info@verlagruhr.de; rights@verlagruhr.de
Web Site: www.verlagruhr.de
Key Personnel
Mng Dir: Hartmuth Brill; Wolf-Ruediger Feld-
    mann; Dorothea Kieler; Annika Renker
Foreign Rights: Kathrin Schuetzdeller *Tel:* (0208)
    439 54 540
Press: Katrin Neuhaeuser *Tel:* (0208) 439 54 402
    E-mail: katrin.neuhaeuser@verlagruhr.de
Founded: 1981
Books & worksheets for pedagogical & educa-
    tional work in school & extracurricular work.
    Unconventional methods, innovative content &
    topical themes.
Membership(s): German Booksellers Association.
Subjects: Art, Communications, Developing
    Countries, Education, English as a Second Lan-
    guage, Environmental Studies, Geography, Geo-
    logy, History, Human Relations, Literature,
    Literary Criticism, Essays, Mathematics, Phi-
    losophy, Physical Sciences, Religion - Other
ISBN Prefix(es): 978-3-86072; 978-3-927279;
    978-3-924884; 978-3-8346
Number of titles published annually: 100 Print
Total Titles: 717 Print

Parent Company: Cornelsen Verlagsholding
    GmbH & Co
Distributed by Schulverlag blmv AG; Veritas
Orders to: Paedexpress GmbH & Co KG
    Tel: (0208) 495040 *Fax:* (0208) 4950495
    E-mail: info@paedexpress.de

Edition Ruprecht eK
Postfach 1716, 37007 Goettingen
Tel: (0551) 488 3751 *Fax:* (0551) 488 3753
E-mail: info@edition-ruprecht.de
Web Site: www.edition-ruprecht.de
Key Personnel
Owner: Dr Reinhilde Ruprecht
Subjects: Economics, Education, Government, Po-
    litical Science, History, Philosophy, Religion -
    Other, Science (General), Social Sciences, So-
    ciology, Theology, Classical Studies, Ethics,
    Modern Philology, Natural Science
ISBN Prefix(es): 978-3-7675; 978-3-89725

RVBG, see Rheinland-Verlag-und
    Betriebsgesellschaft des Landschaftsverbandes
    Rheinland mbH

RWS Verlag Kommunikationsforum GmbH
Aachener Str 222, 50931 Cologne
Tel: (0221) 400 88-0 *Fax:* (0221) 400 88-28
E-mail: internet@rws-verlag.de; lektorat@rws-
    verlag.de
Web Site: www.rws-verlag.de
Key Personnel
Mng Dir: Dr Felix Hey; Dr Bruno M Kuebler
Publishing Dir: Katja Schwind *Tel:* (0221) 400
    88-99 *Fax:* (0221) 400 88-33
Deputy Publishing Dir: Markus J Sauerwald
Founded: 1976
Subjects: Accounting, Law, Accounting & Tax
    Law, Banking Law, Business Law, Construc-
    tion Law, Contract Law, Corporate & Commer-
    cial Law, Employment, Insolvency Law, Land
    Rights, Right of the New Federal States
ISBN Prefix(es): 978-3-8145
Orders to: Postfach 51 10 26, 50946 Cologne
    Tel: (0221) 93738-01 *Fax:* (0221) 93738-943

Reinhard Ryborsch, see Kartographischer Verlag
    Reinhard Ryborsch

Ryvellus, *imprint of* Neue Erde GmbH

Ryvellus+
Imprint of Neue Erde GmbH
Cecilienstr 29, 66111 Saarbruecken
Tel: (0681) 595 398 0 *Fax:* (0681) 390 41 02
E-mail: service@neue-erde.de
Web Site: www.neue-erde.de; www.neueerde.de
Key Personnel
Mng Dir: Andreas Lentz
International Rights Manager: Nadine Fritz
    E-mail: nadine.fritz@neue-erde.de
Sales: Katharina Mueller *Tel:* (0681) 595 398 12
    E-mail: katharina.mueller@neue-erde.de
Founded: 1989
Subjects: Environmental Studies, Health, Nutri-
    tion, Nonfiction (General), Psychology, Psychi-
    atry, Body, Mind & Spirit, Esoterics/New Age,
    Popular
ISBN Prefix(es): 978-3-89453

SachBuchService, see KellnerVerlag

Verlag W Sachon GmbH + Co KG
Schloss Mindelburg, 87714 Mindelheim
Tel: (08261) 999-0 *Fax:* (08261) 999-391
E-mail: info@sachon.de
Web Site: www.sachon.de; www.industriedaten.de
Key Personnel
Owner: Ernestine Sachon
Publishing Dir: Wolfgang Burkart
    E-mail: burkart@sachon.de

Founded: 1945
Subjects: Engineering (General), Health, Nutrition, Management, Marketing, Mechanical Engineering, Wine & Spirits
ISBN Prefix(es): 978-3-920819; 978-3-929032

Sachsenbuch Verlagsgesellschaft mbH
Franzosenallee 14g, 04289 Leipzig
Tel: (0341) 230 55 75; (0341) 8608462 (bookshop) *Fax:* (0341) 230 55 75; (0341) 8608538 (bookshop)
E-mail: kontakt@sachsenbuecher.de
Web Site: www.sachsenbuecher.de
Key Personnel
Manager: Gudrun Zastrutzki; Wolf-Diethelm Zastrutzki *Tel:* (0341) 4620051 *Fax:* (0341) 4620053 *E-mail:* zastrutzki@sachsenbuecher.de
Founded: 1990
Specialize in literature on Saxon history & culture.
Membership(s): Stock Exchange of German Booksellers.
Subjects: Art, History, Regional Interests
ISBN Prefix(es): 978-3-910148; 978-3-89664
Branch Office(s)
Neuer Sachsenverlag Leipzig, Coppistr 36, 04157 Leipzig
Orders to: Leipziger Kommissions- und Grossbuchhandelgesellschaft mbH (LKG), An der Suedspitze 1-12, 04571 Roetha, Contact: Veronika Reumann *Tel:* (034206) 65 126 *Fax:* (034206) 65 1735 *E-mail:* lkg@lkg-service.de *Web Site:* www.lkg-va.de

St Benno-Verlag GmbH
Stammerstr 11, 04159 Leipzig
Tel: (0341) 46777-0; (0341) 46777-21 (orders)
    Fax: (0341) 46777-40
E-mail: service@st-benno.de; presse@st-benno.de
Web Site: www.st-benno.de
Key Personnel
Mng Dir: Michael Birkner; Christiane Voelkel
Publishing Dir: Ingrid Dlugos *E-mail:* i.dlugos@st-benno.de
Program Dir: Volker Bauch *E-mail:* v.bauch@st-benno.de
Licenses: Willi Krug *E-mail:* w.krug@st-benno.de
Press: Annemarie Block *Tel:* (0341) 46777-7
Founded: 1951
Subjects: Inspirational, Spirituality, Religion - Other
ISBN Prefix(es): 978-3-7462

Salam, *imprint of* Kalam Verlag KG

Salleck Publications, see Eckart Schott Verlag

Salon Verlag & Edition
Etrium Haus, Am Wassermann 36, 58029 Cologne
Mailing Address: PO Box 301270, 50782 Cologne
Tel: (0221) 499 58 22
E-mail: mail@salon-verlag.de
Web Site: www.salon-verlag.de
Key Personnel
Dir: Gerhard Theewen
Founded: 1995
Subjects: Art, History, Literature, Literary Criticism, Essays, Philosophy, Physics, Travel & Tourism
ISBN Prefix(es): 978-3-932189; 978-3-89770

SAMS, *imprint of* Pearson Deutschland GmbH

Elisabeth Sandmann Verlag GmbH
Theresienstr 40, 80333 Munich
Tel: (089) 550 59 80-0 *Fax:* (089) 550 59 80-29
E-mail: es@esverlag.de
Web Site: www.esverlag.de

Key Personnel
Mng Dir: Dr Elisabeth Sandmann-Knoll
Founded: 2004
Subjects: Art, History, Photography, Cultural History, Society
ISBN Prefix(es): 978-3-938045
Distributed by Suhrkamp Verlag
Foreign Rep(s): Buchzentrum AG (Switzerland); Mohr Morawa Buchvertrieb GmbH (Austria)
Distribution Center: Koch, Neff & Oetinger Verlagsauslieferung GmbH, Industriestr 23, 70565 Stuttgart

Sandstein Kommunikation GmbH
Goetheallee 6, 01309 Dresden
Tel: (0351) 44078-0 *Fax:* (0351) 44078-12
E-mail: verlag@sandstein.de
Web Site: sandstein-verlag.de
Key Personnel
Mng Dir: Rainer Lutz Stellmacher *Tel:* (0351) 44078-14 *E-mail:* stellmacher@sandstein.de
Publishing Dir: Meike Griese-Storck
Marketing & Press: Christine Jaeger *Tel:* (0351) 44078-36 *E-mail:* jaeger@sandstein.de
Production: Katrin Hoyer *Tel:* (0351) 44078-11 *E-mail:* hoyer@sandstein.de
Founded: 1990
Subjects: Architecture & Interior Design, Art, History, Music, Dance, Art & Music History, Historic Preservation
ISBN Prefix(es): 978-3-937602; 978-3-942422; 978-3-940319; 978-3-930382

Sankt Michaelsbund
Herzog-Wilhelm-Str 5, 80331 Munich
Tel: (089) 23225-0 *Fax:* (089) 23225-162
E-mail: info@st-michaelsbund.de
Web Site: www.st-michaelsbund.de
Key Personnel
Mng Dir: S Ess *Tel:* (089) 23225-500 *E-mail:* s.ess@st-michaelsbund.de
Dir, Media Services: Christine Schmehrer *E-mail:* c.schmehrer@st-michaelsbund.de
Founded: 1908
Subjects: Art, Theology, Current Events, Faith
ISBN Prefix(es): 978-3-920821; 978-3-939905

Sankt Ulrich Verlag GmbH
Henisiusstr 1, 86152 Augsburg
Mailing Address: Postfach 11 19 20, 86044 Augsburg
Tel: (0821) 50242-0 *Fax:* (0821) 50242-41
E-mail: buch@suv.de; vertrieb@sankt-ulrich-verlag.de
Web Site: www.sankt-ulrich-verlag.de; www.suv.de
Key Personnel
Publisher: Dr Peter Bornhausen *Tel:* (0821) 50242-17 *Fax:* (0821) 50242-46 *E-mail:* bornhausen@suv.de
Mng Dir: Johann Buchart *Tel:* (0821) 50242-40 *E-mail:* buchart@suv.de
Editorial: Johannes Mueller *Tel:* (0821) 50242-60 *Fax:* (0821) 50242-81 *E-mail:* mueller@suv.de
Sales: Karola Ritter *Tel:* (0821) 50242-12 *Fax:* (0821) 50242-80 *E-mail:* ritter@suv.de
Subjects: Biography, Memoirs, Inspirational, Spirituality, Nonfiction (General), Religion - Catholic, Self-Help
ISBN Prefix(es): 978-3-87904; 978-3-929246; 978-3-936484; 978-3-86744
Parent Company: Mediengruppe Sankt Ulrich Verlag GmbH
Distribution Center: Brockhaus/Commission, Kreidlerstr 9, 70806 Kornwestheim, Contact: Martina Patzner *Tel:* (07154) 13 27 21 *Fax:* (07154) 13 27 13 *E-mail:* suv@brocom.de
Mohr Morawa Buchvertrieb GmbH, Sulzengasse 2, 1230 Vienna, Austria *Tel:* (01) 680 14-0 *Fax:* (01) 688 71 30 *E-mail:* momo@mohrmorawa.at *Web Site:* www.mohrmorawa.at

Herder AG Basel, Muttenzerstr 109, 4133 Pratteln 1, Switzerland *Tel:* (061) 8 27 90 60 *Fax:* (061) 8 27 90 67 *E-mail:* verkauf@herder.ch

Sassafras Verlag
Dreikoenigenstr 146, 47798 Krefeld
Tel: (02151) 787770 *Fax:* (02151) 771302
Founded: 1975
Subjects: Literature, Literary Criticism, Essays, Poetry
ISBN Prefix(es): 978-3-922690

Sathya Sai Vereinigung eV
Grenzstr 43, 63128 Dietzenbach
Tel: (06074) 3901 *Fax:* (06074) 309785
E-mail: buchzentrum@sathya-sai.de
Web Site: www.sathyasai-buchzentrum.de
Key Personnel
Contact: Werner Herzog; Benno Wesener
Founded: 1965
Subjects: Inspirational, Spirituality, Literature, Literary Criticism, Essays, Music, Dance
ISBN Prefix(es): 978-3-924739; 978-3-932957; 978-3-900790

I H Sauer Verlag GmbH+
Subsidiary of R&W Fachmedien Recht und Wirtschaft
Postfach 10 59 60, 69049 Heidelberg
Tel: (06221) 9060 *Fax:* (06221) 906 259
Founded: 1964
Subjects: Career Development, Communications, Economics, Labor, Industrial Relations, Management, Marketing, Psychology, Psychiatry
ISBN Prefix(es): 978-3-7938
Ultimate Parent Company: Verlagsgruppe Deutscher Fachverlag

Sauerlaender, *imprint of* Bibliographisches Institut GmbH

Sauerlaender Audio, *imprint of* Bibliographisches Institut GmbH

J D Sauerlaender's Verlag+
Berliner Str 46, 63619 Bad Orb
Tel: (06052) 3094667; (0173) 6972970 (cell) *Fax:* (06052) 3094668
Web Site: www.sauerlaender-verlag.com
Key Personnel
Publisher: Stephanie Aulbach-Stankovic *E-mail:* aulbach@sauerlaender-verlag.com
Founded: 1816
Specialize in forest genetics.
Subjects: Agriculture, Language Arts, Linguistics, Philosophy, Forestry
ISBN Prefix(es): 978-3-7939
Number of titles published annually: 6 Print

Saur, see De Gruyter Saur

Sax-Verlag
Eibenweg 62, 04416 Markkleeberg
Tel: (0341) 3 50 21 17 *Fax:* (0341) 3 50 21 16
E-mail: info@sax-verlag.de
Web Site: www.sax-verlag.de
Key Personnel
Owner: Birgit Roehling
Founded: 1992
Subjects: Biography, Memoirs, Education, History, Nonfiction (General), Regional Interests, Science (General), Social Sciences, Sociology, Art History, Culture
ISBN Prefix(es): 978-3-930076; 978-3-934544; 978-3-9802997
Number of titles published annually: 15 Print
Total Titles: 100 Print
Branch Office(s)
An der Halde 12, 04824 Beucha, Contact: Erika Heydick *Tel:* (034292) 7 52 10 *Fax:* (034292) 7 52 20 *E-mail:* heydick@sax-verlag.de

Distribution Center: Mueller Buchbinderei GmbH Leipzig, Ringstr 8, 04827 Gerichshain *Tel:* (034292) 6 19-70 *Fax:* (034292) 6 19-75 *E-mail:* buchversand@bubi-mueller.de

scaneg Verlag eK
Haderunstr 31a, 81375 Munich
Mailing Address: Postfach 70 16 06, 81316 Munich
Tel: (089) 759 33 36 *Fax:* (089) 759 39 14
E-mail: verlag@scaneg.de
Web Site: www.scaneg.de
Key Personnel
Dir: Matthias Klein
Founded: 1983
Subjects: Art, History, Literature, Literary Criticism, Essays, Poetry, Art History
ISBN Prefix(es): 978-3-89235; 978-3-9800671
Distribution Center: GVA Gemeinsame Verlagsauslieferung Goettingen GmbH & Co KG
Tel: (0551) 4883007 *Fax:* (0551) 41392 (Germany & Austria)

Schachversand Ullrich+
Zur Wallfahrtskirche 5, 97483 Eltmann, Limbach
Tel: (09522) 30 45 80 *Fax:* (09522) 30 45 90
E-mail: info@schachversand-ullrich.de
Web Site: www.schachversand-ullrich.de
Key Personnel
Owner: Robert Ullrich
Founded: 1972
Specialize in chess literature.
Subjects: Crafts, Games, Hobbies, Chess
ISBN Prefix(es): 978-3-88805; 978-3-921202; 978-3-86958

Verlag Th Schaefer
Division of Vincentz Network GmbH & Co KG
Plathnerstr 4c, 30175 Hannover
Mailing Address: Postfach 6247, 30062 Hannover
Tel: (0511) 99 10-304 *Fax:* (0511) 99 10-339
E-mail: th.schaefer@vincentz.de
Web Site: www.verlag-th-schaefer.de
Key Personnel
Mng Dir: Jonas Vincentz
Program & Marketing Dir: Dirk Hennies
Marketing Officer: Renate Rossmann
Founded: 1980
Specialize in reprints of professional books.
Subjects: Architecture & Interior Design, Art, Crafts, Games, Hobbies, House & Home
ISBN Prefix(es): 978-3-88746

Schaeffer-Poeschel Verlag fuer Wirtschaft Steuern Recht GmbH+
Reinsburgstr 27, 70178 Stuttgart
Mailing Address: Postfach 15 03 35, 70076 Stuttgart
Tel: (0711) 2194-0 *Fax:* (0711) 2194-111
E-mail: info@schaeffer-poeschel.de
Web Site: www.schaeffer-poeschel.de
Key Personnel
Mng Dir: Volker Dabelstein *E-mail:* dabelstein@schaeffer-poeschel.de; Stephanie Walter *E-mail:* walter@schaeffer-poeschel.de
Head, Rights: Andrea Rupp *E-mail:* rupp@schaeffer-poeschel.de
Marketing: Sabine Zobeley
Founded: 1902
Subjects: Accounting, Business, Economics, Finance, Management, Marketing
ISBN Prefix(es): 978-3-7910; 978-3-8202; 978-3-7992
Number of titles published annually: 200 Print
Total Titles: 800 Print
Parent Company: Haufe Gruppe

Schaltzeit GmbH
Sorauer Str 3, 10997 Berlin
Tel: (030) 61 62 69 63 *Fax:* (030) 61 28 96 35
E-mail: info@schaltzeitverlag.de
Web Site: www.schaltzeitverlag.de
Key Personnel
Mng Dir: Andre Winzer
Subjects: Education, Humor
ISBN Prefix(es): 978-3-941362

M & H Schaper GmbH+
Hans-Boeckler-Allee 7, 30173 Hannover
Tel: (0511) 8550-2412 *Fax:* (0511) 8550-2404
E-mail: info@schaper-verlag.de
Web Site: www.schaper-verlag.de
Key Personnel
Mng Dir: Lutz Bandte
Founded: 1897
Subjects: Agriculture, Animals, Pets, Crafts, Games, Hobbies, Veterinary Science, Forestry
ISBN Prefix(es): 978-3-7944

Schardt Verlag eK
Uhlhornsweg 99A, 26129 Oldenburg
Tel: (0441) 21779287 *Fax:* (0441) 21779286
E-mail: kontakt@schardtverlag.de
Web Site: www.schardt-verlag.de
Key Personnel
Publisher: Renee Repotente *Tel:* (0441) 2176054 *E-mail:* repotente@schardtverlag.de
Founded: 1998
Subjects: Animals, Pets, Biography, Memoirs, Criminology, Nonfiction (General), Poetry, Travel & Tourism
ISBN Prefix(es): 978-3-89841; 978-3-933584

Schattauer GmbH Verlag fuer Medizin und Naturwissenschaften+
Hoelderlinstr 3, 70174 Stuttgart
Mailing Address: Postfach 104543, 70040 Stuttgart
Tel: (0711) 22987-0 *Fax:* (0711) 22987-50
E-mail: info@schattauer.de
Web Site: www.schattauer.de
Key Personnel
Owner, Chief Executive Officer & Publisher: Dieter Bergemann
Executive Dir: Wulf Bertram
Mng Dir: Jan Haaf
Seminar & Conference Manager: Cornelia Di Martino *Tel:* (0711) 22987-46 *E-mail:* cornelia.dimartino@schattauer.de
International Rights: Marion Ullrich *Tel:* (0711) 22987-80 *E-mail:* marion.ullrich@schattauer.de
Marketing & Sales: Christine Reich *Tel:* (0711) 22987-24 *Fax:* (0711) 22987-85 *E-mail:* christine.reich@schattauer.de
Public Relations: Stefanie Albert *Tel:* (0711) 22987-20 *Fax:* (0711) 22987-85 *E-mail:* stefanie.albert@schattauer.de
Founded: 1949
Publishing house for medicine & natural sciences.
Subjects: Medicine, Nursing, Dentistry, Science (General)
ISBN Prefix(es): 978-3-7945
Foreign Rep(s): Ajamin Brothers International Publishers/Representatives (Middle East, North Africa); APAC Publishers Services (Lorong Bakar Batu) (China, Hong Kong, Indonesia, Korea, Malaysia, Myanmar, Philippines, Singapore, Taiwan, Thailand, Vietnam)
Distribution Center: Koch, Neff & Oetinger Verlagsauslieferung GmbH, Industriestr 23, 70565 Stuttgart *E-mail:* schattauer@kno-va.de *Web Site:* www.kno-va.de
D A Book Depot Pty Ltd, 648 Whitehorse Rd, Mitcham, Victoria 3132, Australia *Tel:* (03) 92 10 77 77 *Fax:* (03) 92 10 77 88 *E-mail:* service@dadirect.com.au (Australia & New Zealand)
Mohr Morawa Buchvertrieb GmbH, Sulzengasse 2, 1230 Vienna, Austria *Tel:* (01) 680 14-0 *Fax:* (01) 688 71 30 *E-mail:* momo@mohrmorawa.at *Web Site:* www.mohrmorawa.at
MEDCOR Europe Medical Publishing & Production, U Landronky 17/1341, Brevnov, 169 00 Prague 6, Czech Republic *Tel:* 2 2051 0750 *Fax:* 2 2051 0750 *E-mail:* medeurop@pha.pvtnet.cz (Czech Republic & Slovakia)
Allied Publishers Pvt Ltd, 17 Chittaranjan Ave, Kolkata 700 072, India *Tel:* (033) 27 70 23; (033) 27 45 14 *Fax:* (033) 26 11 58
ABE Marketing, ul Grzybowska 37A, 00-855 Warsaw, Poland *Tel:* (22) 654 06 75 *Fax:* (22) 652 07 67 *E-mail:* info@abe.com.pl

SchauHoer-Verlag
Orrer Str 29, 50259 Pulheim
Tel: (02238) 474826; (02238) 455 99-04 *Fax:* (02238) 474827
E-mail: info@schauhoer-verlag.de; presse@schauhoer-verlag.de
Web Site: www.schauhoer-verlag.de
Key Personnel
Owner: Patricia Hahn-Wolter
Founded: 2006
ISBN Prefix(es): 978-3-940106

Verlag Heinrich Scheffler, *imprint of* Societaets-Verlag

Verlag Lothar Scheffler+
Goethestr 26, 58313 Herdecke
Tel: (02330) 1743 *Fax:* (02330) 1743
Key Personnel
President: Lothar Scheffler
Vice President: Barbel Scheffler
Founded: 1989
ISBN Prefix(es): 978-3-89704; 978-3-9802922; 978-3-9803249; 978-3-929885
Total Titles: 15 Print

Schenk Verlag GmbH
Martin-Seitz-Str 9, 94036 Passau
Tel: (0851) 49095271 *Fax:* (0851) 49095273
E-mail: info@schenkbuchverlag.de
Web Site: www.schenkbuchverlag.de
Key Personnel
Mng Dir & Licenses: Dr Susanne Bazing *E-mail:* bazing@schenkbuchverlag.de
Mng Dir: Richard Schenk
Mng Dir, Editing & Production: Janos Schenk *E-mail:* j.schenk@schenkbuchverlag.de
Founded: 2005
Membership(s): Boersenverein des Deutschen Buchhandels
Subjects: Economics, Fiction, History, Law, Medicine, Nursing, Dentistry, Mysteries, Suspense, Nonfiction (General), Science (General), Science Fiction, Fantasy, Sports, Athletics, Crime, Medical Science, Sports Science, Vampires
ISBN Prefix(es): 978-3-939337

Scherz Verlag+
Subsidiary of S Fischer Verlag GmbH
Hedderichstr 114, 60596 Frankfurt am Main
Tel: (069) 6062-0 *Fax:* (069) 6062-214; (069) 6062-319
Web Site: www.fischerverlage.de/page/scherz
Key Personnel
Chairman: Monika Schoeller
President & Publisher: Dr Joerg Bong
Publishing Dir: Siv Bublitz
Mng Dir: Michael Justus
General Manager, Marketing/Sales: Dr Uwe Rosenfeld
Founded: 1938
Specialize in hardcover fiction & nonfiction.
Subjects: Biography, Memoirs, Fiction, History, Humor, Mysteries, Suspense, Nonfiction (General), Parapsychology, Philosophy, Psychology, Psychiatry
ISBN Prefix(es): 978-3-502; 978-3-89304
Total Titles: 1,200 Print
Associate Companies: Otto Wilhelm Barth Verlag; Fischer Schatzinsel; Fischer Taschenbuch Verlag; Krueger Verlag; Theater & Medien

Fachverlag Schiele & Schoen GmbH+
Markgrafenstr 11, 10969 Berlin
Tel: (030) 25 37 52-0 *Fax:* (030) 25 37 52-99
E-mail: service@schiele-schoen.de
Web Site: www.schiele-schoen.de
Key Personnel
Mng Dir: Karl-Michael Mehnert; Harald Rauh
Advertising Manager: Stefan Nepita *Tel:* (030) 25 37 52-41 *E-mail:* nepita@schiele-schoen.de
Founded: 1946
Technical & scientific publications.
Subjects: Architecture & Interior Design, Business, Communications, Crafts, Games, Hobbies, Engineering (General), Film, Video, Literature, Literary Criticism, Essays, Music, Dance, Radio, TV, Technology
ISBN Prefix(es): 978-3-7949

Schiffahrts-Verlag Hansa GmbH & Co KG
Ballindamm 17, 20095 Hamburg
Tel: (040) 70 70 80-01 *Fax:* (040) 70 70 80-208
Web Site: www.hansa-online.de
Key Personnel
Editor-in-Chief: Krischan Foerster *Fax:* (040) 70 70 80-206 *E-mail:* k_foerster@hansa-online.de
Editor: Michael Meyer *Tel:* (040) 70 70 80-212 *Fax:* (040) 70 70 80-214 *E-mail:* m_meyer@hansa-online.de; Thomas Waegener *Tel:* (040) 70 70 80-209 *Fax:* (040) 70 70 80-214 *E-mail:* t_waegener@hansa-online.de
Sales & Advertising Manager: Dana Gottschalk *Tel:* (040) 70 70 80-312 *E-mail:* d_gottschalk@hansa-online.de
Founded: 1864
Specialize in shipbuilding, ship technology & shipping.
Subjects: Maritime
ISBN Prefix(es): 978-3-87700
Number of titles published annually: 2 Print
Total Titles: 20 Print

Verlag Hans Schiler+
Fidicinstr 29, 10965 Berlin
Tel: (030) 3228523 *Fax:* (030) 3225183
E-mail: info@schiler.de; berlin@schiler.de
Web Site: www.schiler.de
Key Personnel
Mng Dir: Hans Schiler
Specialize in political & social sciences, exile, migration & Arabic literature.
Subjects: Architecture & Interior Design, Art, Asian Studies, Developing Countries, Economics, Fiction, Foreign Countries, Geography, Geology, Government, Political Science, History, Literature, Literary Criticism, Essays, Nonfiction (General), Poetry, Religion - Islamic, Social Sciences, Sociology, Politics & Society
ISBN Prefix(es): 978-3-89930
Number of titles published annually: 12 Print; 10 E-Book
Total Titles: 250 Print; 10 E-Book
Branch Office(s)
Franzoesische Allee 20, 72072 Tuebingen
 Tel: (07071) 9798390 *E-mail:* tuebingen@schiler.de
Distributor for Al-Kamel Verlag; Klaus Schwarz

Schillinger Verlag GmbH+
Wallstr 14, 79098 Freiburg
Mailing Address: Postfach 1502, 79098 Freiburg
Tel: (0761) 33233 *Fax:* (0762) 39055
E-mail: schillingerverlag@online.de
Web Site: www.schillingerverlag.de
Key Personnel
Mng Dir: Wolfgang Schillinger
Founded: 1984
Membership(s): Association of German Publishers & Booksellers.
Subjects: Art, Asian Studies, Environmental Studies, Fiction, Foreign Countries, History, Nonfiction (General), Regional Interests, Travel & Tourism
ISBN Prefix(es): 978-3-89155
Number of titles published annually: 15 Print
Total Titles: 214 Print

Schirmer/Mosel Verlag GmbH+
Widenmayerstr 16, 80538 Munich
Mailing Address: Postfach 221641, 80506 Munich
Tel: (089) 21 26 70 0 *Fax:* (089) 33 86 95
E-mail: mail@schirmer-mosel.com
Web Site: www.schirmer-mosel.com
Key Personnel
General Manager: Lothar Schirmer
Founded: 1974
Specialize in collector's editions & photography.
Subjects: Archaeology, Art, Drama, Theater, Erotica, Fiction, Film, Video, Geography, Geology, Music, Dance, Photography, Pop Culture, Art History, Art Theory
ISBN Prefix(es): 978-3-88814; 978-3-8296; 978-3-921375; 978-3-86555
Showroom(s): In den Hofgartenarkaden, Galeriestr 2, 80539 Munich *Tel:* (089) 29 16 16 01 *Fax:* (089) 29 16 16 02 *E-mail:* showroom@schirmer-mosel.com
Orders to: German Art Books, Hofbrunnstr 11B, 81479 Munich, Executive Dir: Monika Gnad *Tel:* (089) 74 91 14 70 *Fax:* (089) 74 91 14 71 *E-mail:* monika@germanartbooks.com

Schirner Kunstverlag, *imprint of* Schirner Verlag GmbH & Co KG

Schirner Verlag GmbH & Co KG
Member of Aurora Group
Elisabethenstr 20-22, 64283 Darmstadt
Tel: (06151) 39183-103 *Fax:* (06151) 39183-101
E-mail: verlag@schirner.com
Web Site: www.schirner.com
Key Personnel
Chief Executive Officer: Markus Schirner *Tel:* (06151) 39183-114 *E-mail:* markus.schirner@schirner.com
Sales Manager: Manfred Hoefler *Tel:* (06151) 39183-123 *E-mail:* manfred.hoefler@schirner.com
Licensing: Tamara Kuhn *Tel:* (06151) 398183-104 *E-mail:* tamara.kuhn@schirner.com
Press: Christin Milosevic *Tel:* (06151) 39183-150 *E-mail:* christin.milosevic@schirner.com
Founded: 1994
Subjects: Alternative, Astrology, Occult, Ethnicity, Fiction, Health, Nutrition, Human Relations, Nonfiction (General), Parapsychology, Philosophy, Psychology, Psychiatry, Religion - Buddhist, Religion - Other, Self-Help
ISBN Prefix(es): 978-3-930944; 978-3-89767
Number of titles published annually: 80 Print; 30 CD-ROM; 1 Audio
Total Titles: 500 Print; 80 CD-ROM; 2 Audio
Imprints: Schirner Kunstverlag (calendars, postcards, posters); Stb (mass market pocket book)
Foreign Rep(s): Michael Beranek (Western Austria); Dessauer (Switzerland); Guenther Lintschinger (Eastern Austria)
Foreign Rights: Daniele Doglioli (Italy); Peter Schmidt Media Service International (France, Spain)

H L Schlapp Buch- und Antiquariatshandlung GmbH & Co KG
Heidelberger Landstr 190, 64297 Darmstadt
Tel: (06151) 593833
E-mail: darmstadt@schlapp.de
Web Site: schlapp.shop-asp.de
Founded: 1836
Subjects: Regional Interests
ISBN Prefix(es): 978-3-87704

Schluetersche Verlagsgesellschaft mbH & Co KG
Hans-Boeckler-Allee 7, 30173 Hannover
Tel: (0511) 8550-0 *Fax:* (0511) 8550-1100
E-mail: info@schluetersche.de
Web Site: schluetersche.de
Key Personnel
Mng Dir: Lutz Bandte; Stefan Schnieder
Subjects: Cookery, Health, Nutrition, Nonfiction (General), Veterinary Science, Health Professions, Veterinary Medicine
ISBN Prefix(es): 978-3-87706; 978-3-89993

Schmetterling Verlag GmbH+
Lindenspuerstr 38 B, 70176 Stuttgart
Tel: (0711) 62 67 79 (orders); (0711) 6 36 96 98 (sales) *Fax:* (0711) 62 69 92
E-mail: info@schmetterling-verlag.de
Web Site: www.schmetterling-verlag.de
Key Personnel
Mng Dir: Joerg Hunger; Paul Sandner
Subjects: Government, Political Science, Culture
ISBN Prefix(es): 978-3-926369; 978-3-89657

Schmid Verlag GmbH
Hedwigstr 13 b, 93049 Regensburg
Tel: (0941) 21519 *Fax:* (0941) 28766
E-mail: info@schmid-verlag.de
Web Site: www.schmid-verlag.de
Key Personnel
Owner & Manager: Roland Schmid
Founded: 1947
Subjects: Travel & Tourism
ISBN Prefix(es): 978-3-930572; 978-3-921657
Branch Office(s)
Karl-Wurmbstr 3, 5020 Salzburg, Austria

Verlag Dr Otto Schmidt KG+
Gustav-Heinemann-Ufer 58, 50968 Cologne
Mailing Address: Postfach 51 10 26, 50946 Cologne
Tel: (0221) 93738-01 *Fax:* (0221) 93738-900
E-mail: info@otto-schmidt.de; vertrieb@otto-schmidt.de
Web Site: www.otto-schmidt.de
Key Personnel
Mng Partner: Prof Hey Felix
Head, Marketing: Christian Kamradt *E-mail:* kamradt@otto-schmidt.de
Head, Sales: Sylvia Kern *Tel:* (0221) 93738-456 *Fax:* (0221) 93738-943
Founded: 1905
Subjects: Business, Finance, Law
ISBN Prefix(es): 978-3-504
Associate Companies: Centrale fuer GmbH Dr Otto Schmidt, Gustav-Heinemann-Ufer 58 *Tel:* (0221) 93738-571 *Fax:* (0221) 93738-954 *E-mail:* centrale@otto-schmidt.de *Web Site:* www.centrale.de
Subsidiaries: Anwalt-Suchservice GmbH; Centrale fuer Verbaende und Vereine Verlag Dr Otto Schmidt GmbH
Branch Office(s)
Haus Bayenthalguertel, Bayenthalguertel 13, 50968 Cologne (Marienburg)
Buerocenter Bonnerstr 484-486, 50968 Cologne (Marienburg)
Bookshop(s): Am Yustizzentrum 3, 50939 Cologne 47; Friedrich-Verlegerstr 7, 33602 Bielefeld; Struppe u Winckler, Postfach 10 24 91, 33527 Bielefeld; Buchhandlung Hermann Sack, Klosterstr 22, 40211 Duesseldorf; Buchhandlung Hermann Sack, Guenthersburgallee 1, 60316 Frankfurt am Main; Harkortstr 7, 04107 Leipzig
Distribution Center: Kirschbaumweg 18a, 50996 Cologne (Rodenkirchen)

Erich Schmidt Verlag GmbH & Co KG
Genthiner Str 30 G, 10785 Berlin - Tiergarten
Tel: (030) 25 00 85-0 *Fax:* (030) 25 00 85-305
E-mail: esv@esvmedien.de

Web Site: www.esv.info
Key Personnel
Mng Dir: Dr Joachim Schmidt *Tel:* (030) 25 00 85-555 *Fax:* (030) 25 00 85-503 *E-mail:* j. schmidt@esvmedien.de
Manager, Corporate Communications: Christine Freer *Tel:* (030) 25 00 85-855 *Fax:* (030) 25 00 85-870 *E-mail:* c.freer@esvmedien.de
Sales Manager: Sibylle Boehler *Tel:* (030) 25 00 85-220 *Fax:* (030) 25 00 85-275 *E-mail:* s. boehler@esvmedian.de
Founded: 1924
Membership(s): Boersenverein des Deutschen Buchhandels eV.
Subjects: Accounting, Business, Finance, Law, Philological Topics
ISBN Prefix(es): 978-3-503; 978-3-89161
Number of titles published annually: 220 Print

Verlag Hermann Schmidt GmbH & Co KG+
Robert Koch-Str 8, 55129 Mainz
Tel: (06131) 50 60 30 *Fax:* (06131) 50 60 80
E-mail: info@typografie.de
Web Site: www.typografie.de
Key Personnel
Mng Dir: Karin Schmidt-Friderichs *Tel:* (06131) 50 60 29 *E-mail:* ksf@typografie.de; Bertram Schmidt-Friderichs *Tel:* (06131) 50 60 15 *E-mail:* bsf@typografie.de
Foreign Rights & Licensing: Brigitte Raab *Tel:* (06131) 50 60 15 *E-mail:* b.raab@ typografie.de
Marketing & Public Relations: Jutta Schober *Tel:* (06131) 50 60 30 *E-mail:* j.schober@ typografie.de
Sales: Jonas Leis *Tel:* (06131) 50 60 32 *E-mail:* j. leis@typografie.de; Birgit Severin *Tel:* (06131) 50 60 34 *E-mail:* b.severin@typografie.de
Founded: 1992
Specialize in typography & design.
Subjects: Art
ISBN Prefix(es): 978-3-87439
Orders to: Luisenstr 6, 55124 Mainz

Schmidt Periodicals GmbH
Dettendorf Roemerring 12, 83075 Bad Feilnbach
Tel: (08064) 221 *Fax:* (08064) 557
E-mail: schmidt@periodicals.com
Web Site: www.periodicals.com
Founded: 1962
Specialize in back sets, volumes & issues of periodicals, serials & reference works in all subjects & languages.
Subjects: Art, Asian Studies, Astronomy, Biblical Studies, Biological Sciences, Business, Chemistry, Chemical Engineering, Child Care & Development, Civil Engineering, Communications, Computer Science, Criminology, Drama, Theater, Earth Sciences, Economics, Education, Electronics, Electrical Engineering, Engineering (General), Environmental Studies, Film, Video, Finance, Geography, Geology, Government, Political Science, Health, Nutrition, History, Journalism, Language Arts, Linguistics, Law, Library & Information Sciences, Literature, Literary Criticism, Essays, Management, Mathematics, Mechanical Engineering, Medicine, Nursing, Dentistry, Military Science, Music, Dance, Native American Studies, Natural History, Philosophy, Photography, Physical Sciences, Physics, Poetry, Psychology, Psychiatry, Public Administration, Religion - Buddhist, Religion - Catholic, Religion - Hindu, Religion - Islamic, Religion - Jewish, Religion - Protestant, Religion - Other, Science (General), Social Sciences, Sociology, Sports, Athletics, Technology, Theology, Travel & Tourism, Veterinary Science, Wine & Spirits, Women's Studies
Total Titles: 34,782 Print

U.S. Office(s): Periodicals Service Co, 351 Fairview Ave, Suite 300, Hudson, NY 12534, United States *Tel:* 518-822-9300 *Fax:* 518-822-9305 *E-mail:* psc@periodicals.com

Max Schmidt-Roemhild KG+
Mengstr 16, 23552 Luebeck
Tel: (0451) 70 31-01 *Fax:* (0451) 70 31-253
E-mail: info@schmidt-roemhild.de
Web Site: www.schmidt-roemhild.de
Key Personnel
Publisher: Norbert Beleke
Founded: 1579
Subjects: Criminology, History, Law, Medicine, Nursing, Dentistry, Regional Interests, Social Sciences, Sociology, Sports, Athletics
ISBN Prefix(es): 978-3-7950; 978-3-8016
Parent Company: Verlagsgruppe Beleke
Subsidiaries: Hansisches Verlags Kontor
Branch Office(s)
Wihelmsaue 12A, 10715 Berlin, Contact: Mrs Vielitz *Tel:* (030) 8 53 38-02 *Fax:* (030) 8 53 91-95 *E-mail:* berlin@gewusst-wo.de
Schmidt-Roemhild Verlagsgesellschaft mbH Leipzig, Coppistr 2, 04129 Leipzig, Contact: Mrs C Konjetzky *Tel:* (0341) 90 48 50 *Fax:* (0341) 90 48-520 *E-mail:* leipzig@ schmidt-roemhild.de
Schmidt-Roemhild Verlagsgesellschaft mbH Schwerin, Graf-Schack-Allee 6, 19053 Schwerin *Tel:* (0385) 5 91 88-0 *Fax:* (0385) 5 91 88-10 *E-mail:* schwerin@schmidt-roemhild.de

Verlag Franz Schmitt
Kaiserstr 99, 53721 Siegburg
Tel: (02241) 62925 *Fax:* (02241) 53891
E-mail: info@verlagfranzschmitt.de
Web Site: www.verlagfranzschmitt.de
Key Personnel
President, International Rights: Franz Schmitt
Founded: 1932
Subjects: Music, Dance, Regional Interests
ISBN Prefix(es): 978-3-87710

Martin Schmitz Verlag
Dresdener Str 31, 10179 Berlin
Tel: (030) 262 00 73 *Fax:* (030) 23 00 45 61
E-mail: hallo@martin-schmitz.de
Web Site: www.martin-schmitz-verlag.de
Subjects: Architecture & Interior Design, Art, Film, Video, Literature, Literary Criticism, Essays, Music, Dance, Philosophy, Photography
ISBN Prefix(es): 978-3-927795
Distribution Center: Gemeinsame Verlagsauslieferung Goettingen GmbH & Co KG, Postfach 2021, 37010 Goettingen *Tel:* (0551) 487177 *Fax:* (0551) 41392 *E-mail:* info@gva-verlage.de

Lambert Schneider Verlag, *imprint of* WBG (Wissenschaftliche Buchgesellschaft)

Musikantiquariat und Verlag Prof Dr Hans Schneider OHG+
Bahnhofstr 9-15, 82327 Tutzing
Tel: (08158) 30 50; (08158) 69 67 *Fax:* (08158) 76 36
E-mail: musikbuch@aol.com
Web Site: www.schneider-musikbuch.de
Key Personnel
Manager: Dr Hans Schneider
Founded: 1949
Subjects: Antiques, Biography, Memoirs, History, Music, Dance, Science (General)
ISBN Prefix(es): 978-3-7952

SchneiderBuch, see Egmont Verlagsgesellschaften mbH SchneiderBuch

Verlag Schnell und Steiner GmbH+
Leibnizstr 13, 93055 Regensburg

Mailing Address: Postfach 20 04 29, 93063 Regensburg
Tel: (0941) 7 87 85-0 *Fax:* (0941) 7 87 85-16
E-mail: info@schnell-und-steiner.de; post@ schnell-und-steiner.de
Web Site: www.schnell-und-steiner.de
Key Personnel
Publisher & Mng Dir: Dr Albrecht Weiland *E-mail:* a.weiland@schnell-und-steiner.de
Marketing & Press: Niclas Martens *E-mail:* n. martens@schnell-und-steiner.de
Founded: 1933
Subjects: Archaeology, Art, Biblical Studies, Biography, Memoirs, History, Music, Dance, Religion - Catholic, Religion - Protestant, Theology, Travel & Tourism
ISBN Prefix(es): 978-3-7954
Number of titles published annually: 45 Print
Total Titles: 3,500 Print
Imprints: Zodiaque
Distributed by Rex Verlag (Switzerland)
Foreign Rep(s): Christian Hirtzy (Austria); Independent Publishers Group (Canada, USA); Giovanni Ravasio (Switzerland); Ernst Sonntag (Austria, South Tyrol, Italy)
Distribution Center: Dr Franz Hain Verlagsauslieferungen GmbH, Dr-Otto-Neurath-Gasse 5, 1220 Vienna, Austria *Tel:* (01) 282 65 65-77 *Fax:* (01) 282 52 82 *E-mail:* bestell@hain.at
Critiques Livres SAS, 24 rue Malmaison, BP 93, 93172 Bagnolet Cedex, France *Tel:* 01 43 60 39 10 *Fax:* 01 48 97 37 06 *E-mail:* contact@ critiqueslivres.fr
Balmer Buecherdienst AG, Kobiboden, 8840 Einsiedeln, Switzerland *Tel:* (0848) 840 820 *Fax:* (0848) 840 830

Schnitzer GmbH & Co KG+
Marlener Str 9, 77656 Offenburg
Tel: (0781) 504-7500 *Fax:* (0781) 504-7509
E-mail: info@schnitzer.eu
Web Site: www.schnitzer.eu
Key Personnel
Mng Dir: Matthias Niemann
Founded: 1966
Subjects: Cookery, Health, Nutrition
ISBN Prefix(es): 978-3-922894; 978-3-921123

Schoeffling & Co+
Kaiserstr 79, 60329 Frankfurt am Main
Tel: (069) 92 07 87-0 *Fax:* (069) 92 07 87-20
E-mail: info@schoeffling.de
Web Site: www.schoeffling.de
Key Personnel
Publisher: Klaus Schoeffling
Press: Ida Schoeffling *Tel:* (069) 92 07 87-11 *E-mail:* ida.schoeffling@schoeffling.de
Rights & Permissions, International Rights & Foreign Acquisitions: Kathrin Scheel *Tel:* (069) 92 07 87-16 *E-mail:* kathrin.scheel@schoeffling.de
Founded: 1993
Subjects: Biography, Memoirs, Fiction, Literature, Literary Criticism, Essays, Travel & Tourism
ISBN Prefix(es): 978-3-89561
Number of titles published annually: 30 Print

Verlag Hans Schoener GmbH+
Walther-Rathenaustr 13, 75203 Koenigsbach-Stein
Mailing Address: Postfach 69, 75197 Koenigsbach-Stein
Tel: (07232) 4007-0 *Fax:* (07232) 4007-99
E-mail: info@verlag-schoener.de
Web Site: www.verlag-schoener.de
Key Personnel
Mng Dir & Editor-in-Chief: Elke Schoener *Tel:* (07232) 4007-20
Founded: 1972
Subjects: Fashion, Music, Dance, Photography
ISBN Prefix(es): 978-3-923765

Verlag Ferdinand Schoeningh GmbH & Co KG
Juehenplatz 1-3, 33098 Paderborn
Mailing Address: Postfach 25 40, 33055 Paderborn
Tel: (05251) 127-5 *Fax:* (05251) 127-860
E-mail: info@schoeningh.de; bestellung@schoeningh.de
Web Site: www.schoeningh.de
Key Personnel
Management: Peter Schaefer; Christiane Vosshans-Schoeningh
Licensing & Foreign Rights: Angelika Bentfeld *Tel:* (05251) 127-753 *Fax:* (05251) 127-88753 *E-mail:* bentfeld@schoeningh.de
Press & Foreign Rights: Dr Christiane Bacher *Tel:* (05251) 127-790 *Fax:* (05251) 127-88790 *E-mail:* bacher@schoeningh.de
Founded: 1847
Subjects: Art, Education, History, Literature, Literary Criticism, Essays, Music, Dance, Philosophy, Social Sciences, Sociology, Theology
ISBN Prefix(es): 978-3-506

Eckart Schott Verlag
Carlsberger Str 19, 67319 Wattenheim
Tel: (06356) 91062 *Fax:* (06356) 919 302
E-mail: eschott@aol.com; bestellung@salleckpublications.de
Web Site: www.salleck-publications.de; salleckpublications.de
Key Personnel
Publisher: Eckart Schott *E-mail:* e.schott@salleckpublications.de
Comic book publisher.
Subjects: History, Humor, Science Fiction, Fantasy
ISBN Prefix(es): 978-3-89908
Distribution Center: Peter Poluda Medienvertrieb, Lortzingstr 5, 32683 Barntrup *Tel:* (05263) 95 63 63 *Fax:* (05263) 95 63 62 *Web Site:* www.ppm-vertrieb.de (Germany & Austria)
Kaktus Buecher & Comics, Langfeldstr 54, 8501 Frauenfeld, Switzerland *Tel:* (052) 722 31 90 *Fax:* (052) 722 17 82 *Web Site:* www.kaktus.net

Schott Music GmbH & Co KG+
KG Weihergarten 5, 55116 Mainz
Tel: (06131) 246-0; (020) 7534 0740 (press) *Fax:* (06131) 246-211
E-mail: info@schott-music.com; press@schott-music.com; foreign-rights@schott-music.com
Web Site: de.schott-music.com; en.schott-music.com (English)
Key Personnel
Chairman & Mng Dir: Dr Peter Hanser-Strecker
Chief Operating Officer & Mng Dir: Michael Petry
Head, Legal Dept: Jens Bernlughaus
Foreign Rights Manager: Monika Snitch
Public Relations Manager: Dr Christiane Krautscheid
Financial: Wolfgang Emmerich
Marketing: Susanne Hain
Press: Konstantinos Zafiriadis *Tel:* (06131) 246-814 *Fax:* (06131) 246-75814
Founded: 1770
Subjects: Biography, Memoirs, Education, Music, Dance
ISBN Prefix(es): 978-3-7957
Associate Companies: Wiener Urtext Edition-Musikverlag GmbH & Co KG, Australia (jointly owned with Universal Edition AG, Austria)
Subsidiaries: Ars-Viva-Verlag GmbH; Atlantis Musikbuch-Verlag AG; Cranz GmbH; Eulenburg AG; Ernst Eulenburg & Co GmbH; Fuerstner Musikverlag GmbH; Hohner-Verlag; Music Factory GmbH; Musikverlag Kompositor International GmbH; Panton International GmbH; Arnold Schoenberg Gesamtausgabe GmbH; Schotta Wergo Music Media GmbH;

SMD Schott Music Distribution GmbH; Wega Verlag GmbH
Branch Office(s)
Schott Music GmbH & Co KG, Book Division, Zimmerstr 11, 10969 Berlin *Tel:* (030) 25 93 70 90 *E-mail:* buch@schott-music.com
Schott Music Publishers (Canada) Ltd, 28, Tarlton Rd, Toronto, ON M5P 2M4, Canada, Contact: Dr Peter Hanser-Strecker *Tel:* 416-489-4155 *Fax:* 416-489-8474 *E-mail:* matejan@sympatico.ca
Schott Music Panton sro, Radlicka 99/2487, 150 00 Prague 5, Czech Republic *Tel:* 251 553 952; 251 554 511 *Fax:* 251 554 511 *E-mail:* panton@panton.cz
Schott Music SA, 175, rue Saint-Honore, 75040 Paris Cedex 1, France *Tel:* 08 05 63 98 13 *Fax:* 08 05 63 98 14 *E-mail:* paris@schott-music.com
Schott Music China, Hong Kong, Hong Kong, Contact: Feili Tang *E-mail:* feili.tang@schott-music.com
Schott Music Co Ltd, Kasuga Bldg, 2-9-3 Iidabashi, Chiyoda-ku, Toyko 102-0072, Japan *Tel:* (03) 3263-6530 *Fax:* (03) 3263-6672 *E-mail:* info@schottjapan.com *Web Site:* www.schottjapan.com
Schott Music SL, Alcala 70, 28009 Madrid, Spain *Tel:* 915770751 *Fax:* 915757645 *E-mail:* seemsa@seemsa.com
Schott Music Ltd, 48 Great Marlborough St, London W1F 7BB, United Kingdom *Tel:* (020) 7534 0700 *Fax:* (020) 7534 0719
U.S. Office(s): Schott Music Corp, 254 W 31 St, 15th floor, New York, NY 10001, United States *Tel:* 212-461-6940 *Fax:* 212-810-4565 *E-mail:* ny@schott-music.com
European American Music Distributors Corp, Valley Forge, PA, United States
Bookshop(s): Mainzer Musikalienzentrum, KG Weihergarten 9, Mainz
Orders to: SMD Schott Music Distribution GmbH, Postfach 3640, 55026 Mainz *Tel:* (06131) 5050 *Fax:* (06131) 505115

Verlag Schreiber & Leser
Grosse Bergstr 252, 22767 Hamburg
Tel: (040) 4018 9454
E-mail: verlag@schreiberundleser.de
Web Site: www.schreiberundleser.de
Key Personnel
Mng Dir: Philipp Schreiber
Subjects: Fiction
ISBN Prefix(es): 978-3-937102; 978-3-929497; 978-3-933187; 978-3-941239

Verlag Silke Schreiber+
Agnesstr 12, 80798 Munich
Tel: (089) 2710180 *Fax:* (089) 2716957
Web Site: www.verlag-silke-schreiber.de
Key Personnel
Manager, Rights & Permissions: Dr Luise Metzel *E-mail:* metzel@verlag-silke-schreiber.de
Founded: 1982
Subjects: Art, History, Art History, Modern Art
ISBN Prefix(es): 978-3-88960
Foreign Rep(s): Seth Meyer-Bruhns (Austria); Giovanni Ravasio (Switzerland)
Distribution Center: Koch, Neff & Oetinger Verlagsauslieferung GmbH, Industriestr 23, 70565 Stuttgart
Marcello SAS, Via Belzoni, 12, 35121 Padua, Italy *Tel:* (049) 836 06 71 *Fax:* (049) 878 67 59 *E-mail:* marcello@marcellosas.it (France, Greece, Italy, Portugal & Spain)
Jan Smit Boeken, Eikbosser Weg 258, 1213 SE Hilversum, Netherlands *Tel:* (035) 621 92 67 *Fax:* (035) 623 89 05 *E-mail:* jansmitboeken@xmsnet.nl
AVA Verlagsauslieferung AG, Centralweg 16, 8910 Affoltern am Albis, Switzerland
Thomas Heneage Art Books, 42 Duke St St James's, London SW1Y 6DJ, United Kingdom

Tel: (0171) 930 92 23 *Fax:* (0171) 839 92 23 (Great Britain)
Art Stock Books, Independent Publishers Group, 814 N Franklin St, Chicago, IL 60610, United States *Fax:* 312-337-5985 *E-mail:* frontdesk@ipgbook.com *Web Site:* www.ipgbook.com (USA & Canada)
Orders to: Vice Versa Vertrieb, Immanuelkirchstr 123, 10405 Berlin, Contact: Kurt Salchli *Tel:* (030) 61609236 *Fax:* (030) 61609238 *E-mail:* info@vice-versa-vertrieb.de

Schrenk-Verlag
Alramweg 3, 91187 Roettenbach
Tel: (0151) 424 603 68 *Fax:* (09831) 880 98 99
E-mail: schrenk@buchhausschrenk.de
Web Site: www.buchhausschrenk.de
Key Personnel
Owner: Dr Johann Schrenk
Founded: 1982
Membership(s): Verband Bayerischer Verlage und Buchhandlungen.
Subjects: Literature, Literary Criticism, Essays, German Literature, Regional Literature
ISBN Prefix(es): 978-3-924270

Schriften zur Kontemplation, *imprint of* Vier-Tuerme-GmbH-Klosterbetriebe

Schroedel Schulbuchverlag, see Bildungshaus Schulbuchverlage Westermann Schroedel Diesterweg Schoeningh Winklers GmbH

Marion von Schroeder, *imprint of* Ullstein Buchverlage GmbH

CH SCHROER GmbH
Postfach 1245, 51780 Lindlar
Tel: (02266) 478950 *Fax:* (02266) 4789525
E-mail: info@chsbooks.de
Web Site: www.chsbooks.de
Key Personnel
Publisher: Christopher Schroer
Founded: 2009
Subjects: Art, Fiction, Literature, Literary Criticism, Essays, Photography
ISBN Prefix(es): 978-3-95445; 978-3-942139

Carl Ed Schuenemann KG
Zweite Schlachtpforte 7, 28195 Bremen
Mailing Address: Postfach 10 60 67, 28060 Bremen
Tel: (0421) 3 69 03-0 *Fax:* (0421) 3 69 03-39
E-mail: kontakt@schuenemann-verlag.de
Web Site: www.schuenemann-verlag.de
Key Personnel
Mng Dir: Hermann Schuenemann
Founded: 1810
Subjects: Art, Literature, Literary Criticism, Essays, Regional Interests
ISBN Prefix(es): 978-3-7961

Schueren Verlag GmbH+
Universitaetsstr 55, 35037 Marburg
Tel: (06421) 6 30 84 *Fax:* (06421) 68 11 90
E-mail: info@schueren-verlag.de; presse@schueren-verlag.de
Web Site: www.schueren-verlag.de
Key Personnel
Manager: Dr Annette Schueren *E-mail:* schueren@schueren-verlag.de
Press: Nadine Schrey *E-mail:* schrey@schueren-verlag.de
Production: Erik Schuessler *E-mail:* schuessler@schueren-verlag.de
Sales & Marketing: Katrin Ahnemann *E-mail:* ahnemann@schueren-verlag.de
Founded: 1985
Membership(s): Boersenverein des Deutschen Buchhandels.

Subjects: Biography, Memoirs, Communications, Economics, Film, Video, Government, Political Science, Labor, Industrial Relations, Nonfiction (General), Photography, Radio, TV, Regional Interests, Science (General), Social Sciences, Sociology
ISBN Prefix(es): 978-3-89472
Number of titles published annually: 30 Print
Total Titles: 200 Print
Foreign Rep(s): Sebastian Graf (Switzerland); Seth Meyer-Bruhns (Austria, South Tyrol, Italy)
Distribution Center: Prolit Verlagsauslieferung, Siemensstr 16, 35463 Fernwald, Contact: Rita Nitz *Tel:* (0641) 94393-0 *Fax:* (0641) 94393-89 *E-mail:* r.nitz@prolit.de *Web Site:* www.prolit. de (Germany & Austria)
Verlagsauslieferung Scheidegger & Co AG, c/o AVA, Centralweg 16, Affoltern am Albis, Switzerland *Tel:* (044) 762 42 50 *Fax:* (044) 762 42 10 *E-mail:* scheidegger@ava.ch *Web Site:* www.ava.ch

Schulbuchverlag Anadolu GmbH
Postfach 13 07, 48125 Hueckelhoven
Tel: (02433) 4091 *Fax:* (02433) 41608
E-mail: info@anadolu-verlag.de; office@anadolu-verlag.de
Web Site: www.anadolu-verlag.de
Key Personnel
Mng Dir: Ahmet Celik; Zeliha Celik
Customer Service: Heike Lorenz
Sales: Tolga Celik *E-mail:* tc@anadolu-verlag.de
Specialize in children's books & educational materials.
Subjects: Education, Literature, Literary Criticism, Essays
ISBN Prefix(es): 978-3-86121; 978-3-923143
Foreign Rep(s): Insegna Booksellers (Australia); Verlag Jugend & Volk GmbH (Austria); Tuerk-Alman Kitabevi (Turkey)

Verlag Lutz Schulenburg, see Edition Nautilus

Schulz-Kirchner Verlag GmbH+
Mollweg 2, 65510 Idstein
Mailing Address: Postfach 12 75, 65502 Idstein
Tel: (06126) 93 20 0; (06126) 9320-13
Fax: (06126) 93 20 50
E-mail: info@schulz-kirchner.de; vertrieb@schulz-kirchner.de
Web Site: www.schulz-kirchner.de
Key Personnel
Mng Dir: Dr Ullich Schulz-Kirchner
E-mail: usk@schulz-kirchner.de
Production: Petra Jeck *Tel:* (06216) 93 20 17 *E-mail:* pjeck@schulz-kirchner.de; Susanne Koch *Tel:* (06126) 93 20 24 *E-mail:* skoch@schulz-kirchner.de; Ina Richter *Tel:* (06126) 93 20 16 *E-mail:* irichter@schulz-kirchner.de
Rights & Licenses: Margit Croenlein *Tel:* (06126) 93 20 31 *E-mail:* mcroenlein@schulz-kirchner.de
Sales: Christel Conradi *Tel:* (06126) 93 20 13 *E-mail:* cconradi@schulz-kirchner.de
Founded: 1984
Subjects: Business, Economics, Energy, Finance, Health, Nutrition, History, Labor, Industrial Relations, Language Arts, Linguistics, Marketing, Medicine, Nursing, Dentistry, Philosophy, Science (General), Social Sciences, Sociology, Ergotherapy, Foster Children Care, Occupational Therapy, Physiotherapy, Speech Therapy
ISBN Prefix(es): 978-3-8248; 978-3-925196

Verlag R S Schulz GmbH+
Division of Wolters Kluwer Deutschland GmbH
Sitz der Gesellschaft, Luxemburger Str 449, 50939 Cologne
Tel: (0221) 94373-7000 *Fax:* (0221) 94373-7201
E-mail: info@wolterskluwer.de; info-wkd@wolterskluwer.com; wkd@wolterskluwer.com
Web Site: www.wolterskluwer.de

Subjects: Architecture & Interior Design, Fiction, Health, Nutrition, Law, Social Sciences, Sociology, Veterinary Science
ISBN Prefix(es): 978-3-7962

H O Schulze KG
Marktplatz 15, 96215 Lichtenfels
Tel: (09571) 7 80 18 *Fax:* (09571) 7 80 57
E-mail: verkauf@schulze-kg.de
Web Site: www.schulze-kg.de
Key Personnel
Contact: Peter Steiner *E-mail:* peter.steiner@schulze-kg.de
Founded: 1865
Subjects: Art, Fiction, Geography, Geology, History, Nonfiction (General), Travel & Tourism
ISBN Prefix(es): 978-3-87735
Distributed by Colloquium Historicum Wirsbergense; Verlag des Historischen Vereins Bamberg

Buchdruckerei und Verlag SchumacherGebler KG
Goethestr 21, 80336 Munich
Tel: (089) 5 99 49-0 *Fax:* (089) 5 99 49-149
E-mail: info@schumachergebler.com
Web Site: www.schumachergebler.com; www.bibliothek-sg.de
Key Personnel
Mng Dir: Eckehart SchumacherGebler
Founded: 1829
Subjects: Literature, Literary Criticism, Essays
ISBN Prefix(es): 978-3-920856

Verlag Schuster Leer
Muehlenstr 15/17, 26789 Leer
Tel: (0491) 92 590 0 *Fax:* (0491) 92 590 59
E-mail: buchhandlung-schuster@t-online.de
Web Site: www.verlag-schuster.de
Key Personnel
Owner: Ingrid Schuster
Subjects: Fiction, Humor, Nonfiction (General), Poetry
ISBN Prefix(es): 978-3-7963
Number of titles published annually: 5 Print; 1 CD-ROM; 2 Audio

Edition Schwab, *imprint of* Verlag Stephanie Naglschmid

Heinrich Schwab Verlag GmbH & Co KG+
Eglofstal 42, 88260 Argenbuehl
Mailing Address: Gschwend 77, 6932 Langen bei Bregenz, Austria
Tel: (05575) 20101 *Fax:* (05575) 4745
E-mail: office@heinrichschwabverlag.de
Web Site: www.heinrichschwabverlag.de
Founded: 1926
Subjects: Inspirational, Spirituality, Medicine, Nursing, Dentistry, Parapsychology, Philosophy, Psychology, Psychiatry, Religion - Other, Alternative Medicine, Biological Horticulture, Breathe Therapies, Border Sciences, Esoteric Works & Meditation, Life Assistance, Life-Wise, Mental Healing, Naturopathy, Positive Thinking, Religion Science, Yoga
ISBN Prefix(es): 978-3-7964
Total Titles: 130 Print; 5 CD-ROM; 10 Audio

Schwabenverlag+
Imprint of Schwabenverlag AG
Senefelderstr 12, 73760 Ostfildern
Mailing Address: Postfach 42 80, 73745 Ostfildern
Tel: (0711) 44 06-162 *Fax:* (0711) 44 06-177
E-mail: buchverlag@schwabenverlag.de
Web Site: www.schwabenverlag-online.de
Key Personnel
Executive: Ulrich Peters *Tel:* (0711) 44 06-111 *Fax:* (0711) 44 06-101 *E-mail:* ulrich.peters@schwabenverlag.de

Publishing Dir: Gertrud Widmann *Tel:* (0711) 44 06-161 *E-mail:* gertrud.widmann@schwabenverlag.de
Head, Marketing & Sales: Barbara Janssen *Tel:* (0711) 44 06-109 *E-mail:* barbara.janssen@schwabenverlag.de
Foreign Rights Manager: Claudia Stegmann *Tel:* (0711) 44 06-148
Production Manager: Wolfgang Sailer *Tel:* (0711) 44 06-118 *Fax:* (0711) 44 06-198 *E-mail:* wolfgang.sailer@schwabenverlag.de
Advertising & Public Relations: Sabrina Reusch *Tel:* (0711) 44 06-168 *E-mail:* sabrina.reusch@schwabenverlag.de
Founded: 1848
Subjects: Art, Regional Interests, Religion - Catholic, Religion - Other, Theology
ISBN Prefix(es): 978-3-7966
Foreign Rep(s): Joe Fuchs (Switzerland); Verlagsagentur Erich Neuhold (Austria, South Tyrol, Italy)
Foreign Rights: Agenzia Letteraria Internazionale (Sibylle Kirchbach) (Italy); The Book Publishers Association of Israel (Shoshi Grajower) (Israel); Hercules Business & Culture GmbH (Hongjun Cai) (China); jia-xi books co ltd (Becky Lin) (Taiwan); Simona Kessler International Copyright Agency Ltd (Romania); Meike Marx Literary Agency (Japan); ONK Agency Ltd (Hatice Gok) (Turkey)
Distribution Center: Leipziger Kommissions- und Grossbuchhandelsgesellschaft mbH (LKG), An der Suedspitze 1-12, 04571 Roetha, Contact: Robert Winkler *Tel:* (034206) 65 205 *Fax:* (034206) 65 1738 *E-mail:* rwinkler@lkg-service.de *Web Site:* www.lkg-va.de
Mohr Morawa Buchvertrieb GmbH, Sulzengasse 2, 1230 Vienna, Austria *Tel:* (01) 680 14-0 *Fax:* (01) 688 71 30 *E-mail:* momo@mohrmorawa.at *Web Site:* www.mohrmorawa.at
Herder AG Basel Verlagsauslieferungen, Muttenzer Str 109, 4133 Pratteln 1, Switzerland *Tel:* (061) 8 27 90 60 *Fax:* (061) 8 27 90 67 *E-mail:* verkauf@herder.ch

Schwaneberger Verlag GmbH
Ohmstr 1, 85716 Unterschleissheim
Tel: (089) 323 93-02 *Fax:* (089) 323 93-248
E-mail: info@michel.de; presse@michel.de; vertrieb@michel.de (sales); vertriebsleitung@michel.de
Web Site: www.michel.de; www.briefmarken.de
Key Personnel
Mng Dir, Rights & Permissions: Hans Hohenester
Editor-in-Chief: Oscar Klan *E-mail:* cr@michel.de
Sales Manager: Susanne Ueze
Press: Anett Schulze
Founded: 1910
Subjects: Crafts, Games, Hobbies
ISBN Prefix(es): 978-3-87858; 978-3-86524
Associate Companies: Carl Gerber Verlag GmbH
Distribution Center: Sigloch Distribution GmbH & Co KG, Am Buchberg 8, 74572 Blaufelden *Tel:* (07953) 883 192 *Fax:* (07953) 883 380 *E-mail:* distribution@sigloch.de *Web Site:* www.sigloch-distribution.de

Edition Schwann, *imprint of* Musia International Musikalien-Handelsgesellschaft Ehrlich GmbH & Co KG

Fachbuchhandlung Otto Schwartz+
Willi-Eichler-Str 11, 37079 Goettingen
Tel: (0551) 31051 *Fax:* (0551) 372812
E-mail: fachbuchhandlung-schwartz@t-online.de
Web Site: schwartzbuch.homepage.t-online.de
Founded: 1871
Subjects: Ethnicity, Law, Public Administration, Science (General), Social Sciences, Sociology, Economy, Taxes
ISBN Prefix(es): 978-3-509

Parent Company: Buchhandlung Decius GmbH, Markstr 52, 30159 Hannover
Bookshop(s): Barfuesserstr 13, 37073 Goettingen *Tel:* (0551) 5085978 *Fax:* (0551) 5085983 *E-mail:* schwartz.stadt@t-online.de

Schwarzkopf & Schwarzkopf Verlag GmbH
Kastanienallee 32, 10435 Berlin
Tel: (030) 44 33 63 00 *Fax:* (030) 44 33 63 044
E-mail: info@schwarzkopf-schwarzkopf.de
Web Site: www.schwarzkopf-schwarzkopf.de
Key Personnel
Mng Dir: Oliver Schwarzkopf
Subjects: Biography, Memoirs, Erotica, Fiction, Film, Video, Humor, Nonfiction (General), Sports, Athletics, Travel & Tourism
ISBN Prefix(es): 978-3-89602

Verlag Schweers + Wall GmbH+
Eupener Str 150, 50933 Cologne
Tel: (0221) 290 27 72 *Fax:* (0221) 290 27 73
E-mail: mail@schweers-wall.de
Web Site: www.schweers-wall.de
Key Personnel
Mng Dir: Henning Wall
Founded: 1986
Subjects: Transportation, Travel & Tourism
ISBN Prefix(es): 978-3-921679; 978-3-89494

E Schweizerbart'sche Verlagsbuchhandlung (Naegele und Obermiller)+
Affiliate of Gebrueder Borntraeger Verlagsbuchhandlung
Johannesstr 3A, 70176 Stuttgart
Tel: (0711) 351456-0 *Fax:* (0711) 351456-99
E-mail: mail@schweizerbart.de
Web Site: www.schweizerbart.de
Key Personnel
Exhibition Manager: Martina Ihringer
Founded: 1826
Subjects: Anthropology, Archaeology, Biological Sciences, Earth Sciences, Environmental Studies, Geography, Geology, Maritime, Science (General)
ISBN Prefix(es): 978-3-510 (Schweizerbart); 978-3-443 (Borntraeger)
Distributor for Bundesanstalt fuer Geowissenschaften und Rohstoffe; Senckenberg Gesellschaft fuer Naturforschung
Distribution Center: Balogh International Inc, 1911 N Duncan Rd, Champaign, IL 61822, United States, Contact: Pamela Burns-Balogh *Tel:* 217-355-9331 *Fax:* 217-355-9413 *E-mail:* balogh@balogh.com *Web Site:* www.balogh.com

SCM Collection im SCM-Verlag GmbH & Co KG+
Member of Stiftung Christliche Medien
Bodenborn 43, 58452 Witten
Tel: (02302) 930 93-800 *Fax:* (02302) 930 93-801
E-mail: info@scm-collection.de
Web Site: www.scm-collection.de
Key Personnel
Mng Dir: Frieder Trommer *Tel:* (02302) 930 93-611 *Fax:* (02302) 930 93-619 *E-mail:* frieder.trommer@icmedienhaus.de
Customer Service: Christiane Rahrbach *Tel:* (02302) 930 93-721 *E-mail:* rahrbach@scm-brockhaus.de
Press & Public Relations: Juergen Asshoff *Tel:* (02302) 930 93-781 *E-mail:* asshoff@scm-brockhaus.de
Rights & Licenses: Volker Halfmann *Tel:* (02302) 930 93-736 *E-mail:* halfmann@scm-brockhaus.de
Founded: 1828
Subjects: Fiction, Religion - Other
ISBN Prefix(es): 978-3-7893

Associate Companies: SCM R Brockhaus im SCM-Verlag GmbH & Co KG
Distributed by BMU (Austria); Brunnen (Switzerland)

SCM ERF-Verlag im SCM-Verlag GmbH und Co KG+
Member of Stiftung Christliche Medien
Bodenborn 43, 58452 Witten
Tel: (02302) 930 93-782 *Fax:* (02302) 930 93-801
E-mail: info@scm-erf-verlag.de
Web Site: www.scm-erf-verlag.de
Key Personnel
Mng Dir: Frieder Trommer *Tel:* (02302) 930 93-611 *Fax:* (02302) 930 93-619 *E-mail:* frieder.trommer@icmedienhaus.de
Press & Public Relations: Juergen Asshoff *Tel:* (02302) 930 93-781 *E-mail:* asshoff@scm-brockhaus.de
Rights & Permissions: Sigrun Helbig *Tel:* (02302) 930 93-736 *E-mail:* helbig@scm-brockhaus.de
Founded: 1978
Specialize in audio & video.
Subjects: Music, Dance, Religion - Other
ISBN Prefix(es): 978-3-89562

SCM Haenssler im SCM-Verlag GmbH & Co KG+
Member of Stiftung Christliche Medien
Max-Eyth-Str 41, 71088 Holzgerlingen
Tel: (07031) 7414-0 *Fax:* (07031) 7414-119
E-mail: info@scm-haenssler.de
Web Site: www.scm-haenssler.de
Key Personnel
Publisher & Mng Dir: Frieder Trommer
Publishing Dir: Hans-Werner Durau *E-mail:* durau@scm-haenssler.de
Head, Sales: Winfried Kuhn *E-mail:* kuhn@scm-haenssler.de
Founded: 1919
Christian music publisher. Also publishes all of the American Institute of Musicology publications.
Membership(s): The Telos Group.
Subjects: Art, Fiction, Film, Video, Literature, Literary Criticism, Essays, Music, Dance, Religion - Other
ISBN Prefix(es): 978-3-7751
Number of titles published annually: 100 Print; 10 CD-ROM; 10 Online
Total Titles: 10 E-Book
Associate Companies: Edition Johannis; SCM Bundes-Verlag; SCM Collection; SCM ERF-Verlag; SCM R Brockhaus

SCM R Brockhaus im SCM-Verlag GmbH & Co KG+
Member of Stiftung Christliche Medien
Bodenborn 43, 58452 Witten
Tel: (02302) 930 93-800 *Fax:* (02302) 930 93-801
E-mail: info@scm-brockhaus.de
Web Site: www.scm-brockhaus.de
Key Personnel
Mng Dir: Frieder Trommer *Tel:* (02302) 930 93-611 *Fax:* (02302) 930 93-619 *E-mail:* frieder.trommer@icmedienhaus.de
Advertising: Heiko Wetzel *Tel:* (02302) 930 93-761 *E-mail:* wetzel@scm-brockhaus.de
Editor: Katja Lieschke *Tel:* (02302) 930 93-737 *E-mail:* lieschke@scm-brockhaus.de
Press & Public Relations: Juergen Asshoff *Tel:* (02302) 930 93-781 *E-mail:* asshoff@scm-brockhaus.de
Rights & Permissions, Abroad: Sigrun Helbig *Tel:* (02302) 930 93-736 *E-mail:* helbig@scm-brockhaus.de
Rights & Permissions, Domestic: Christina Schneider *Tel:* (02302) 930 93-745
Founded: 1853
Subjects: Biography, Memoirs, Fiction, Music, Dance, Philosophy, Psychology, Psychiatry, Religion - Other, Self-Help, Theology

ISBN Prefix(es): 978-3-417
Associate Companies: Oncken Verlag KG
Subsidiaries: SCM Collection im SCM-Verlag GmbH & Co KG

Scorpio Verlag GmbH & Co KG
Theresienstr 16, 80333 Munich
Tel: (089) 18 94 733-0 *Fax:* (089) 18 94 733-16
E-mail: info@scorpio-verlag.de
Web Site: www.scorpio-verlag.de
Key Personnel
Mng Dir: Christian Strasser
Publishing Dir: Dagmar Olzog *Tel:* (089) 18 94 733-23 *E-mail:* do@scorpio-verlag.de
Press & Advertising: Sabine Koska *Tel:* (089) 18 94 733-22 *E-mail:* sk@scorpio-verlag.de
Production: Carola Wetzel-Kraxenberger *Tel:* (089) 18 94 733-17 *E-mail:* cwk@scorpio-verlag.de
Subjects: Inspirational, Spirituality, Alternative Science, Holistic Living
ISBN Prefix(es): 978-3-942166; 978-3-9812442
Distribution Center: Alexander Herrmann Sales & Consulting, Eversbuschstr 40a, 80999 Munich *Tel:* (089) 38 38 06 90 *Fax:* (089) 38 38 06 91-0 *E-mail:* a.herrmann@vertriebundberatung.de *Web Site:* www.vertriebundberatung.de

Scribo Verlagsgesellschaft
Goethestr 10, 71144 Steinenbronn
Tel: (07157) 52 77 59 *Fax:* (07157) 52 77 60
E-mail: info@scriboverlag.de
Web Site: www.scriboverlag.de
Key Personnel
Publisher: Goetz Gussmann
Founded: 2003
Subjects: Art, Cookery, Fiction, Photography, Poetry
ISBN Prefix(es): 978-3-937310

Verlag script5, *imprint of* Loewe Verlag GmbH

Verlag script5
Imprint of Loewe Verlag GmbH
Buehlstr 4, 95463 Bindlach
Tel: (09208) 51-0 *Fax:* (09208) 51-309
E-mail: info@script5.de; vertrieb@loewe-verlag.de
Web Site: www.script5.de
Key Personnel
Mng Dir: Volker Gondrom
Sales: Lydia Bruennich
Founded: 2009
Subjects: Fiction
ISBN Prefix(es): 978-3-8390
Distribution Center: Mohr Morawa Buchvertrieb GmbH, Sulzengasse 2, 1230 Vienna, Austria *Tel:* (01) 680 14-0 *E-mail:* momo@mohrmorawa.at *Web Site:* www.mohrmorawa.at
Buchzentrum AG, Industriestr Ost 10, 4614 Haegendorf, Switzerland *Tel:* (062) 2092626 *E-mail:* kundendienst@buchzentrum.ch

SecuMedia Verlags GmbH
Lise-Meitner-Str 4, 55435 Gau-Algesheim
Mailing Address: Postfach 1234, 55205 Ingelheim
Tel: (06725) 9304-0 *Fax:* (06725) 5994
E-mail: info@secumedia.de
Web Site: www.secumedia.com; buchshop.secumedia.de
Key Personnel
Mng Dir: Peter Hohl; Veronika Laufersweiler; Nina Malchus
Founded: 1980
Subjects: Literature, Literary Criticism, Essays, Corporate Security, IT Security
ISBN Prefix(es): 978-3-922746

Edition SEE-IGEL
Strandbadstr 8, 78345 Iznang

Mailing Address: Aaraustr 61, 72762 Reutlingen
Tel: (07121) 24526 *Fax:* (07121) 25269
E-mail: post@see-igel.de
Web Site: www.see-igel.de
Key Personnel
Contact: Ute Kleeberg
Subjects: Music, Dance, Classical Music
ISBN Prefix(es): 978-3-935261; 978-3-9804507
Distribution Center: Prolit, Siemensstr 16, 35463
Fernwald

Seehamer Verlag GmbH
Seestr 2, 83629 Weyarn-Orsteil Grossseeham
Mailing Address: Postfach 61, 83629 Weyarn-
Orsteil Grossseeham
Tel: (08020) 90760 *Fax:* (08020) 907620
E-mail: info@seehamer.de
Web Site: www.seehamer.de
Key Personnel
Mng Dir: Peter Karg-Cordes *E-mail:* karg@
seehamer.de
Subjects: Cookery, Health, Nutrition, Science
(General), Technology
ISBN Prefix(es): 978-3-929626; 978-3-932131;
978-3-934058
Distribution Center: VVA-Vereinigte Ver-
lagsauslieferung, Abt D6 E2, Postfach 1222,
33399 Verl, Contact: Hildegard Ciolini
Tel: (05241) 80 50 73 *Fax:* (05241) 80 60 24
E-mail: hildegard.ciolini@bertelsmann.de
Dr Franz Hain Verlagsauslieferungen GmbH,
Dr-Otto-Neurath-Gasse 5, 1220 Vienna, Aus-
tria *Tel:* (01) 282 65 65 *Fax:* (01) 282 52 82
E-mail: vertrieb@hain.at

Seemann Henschel GmbH & Co KG+
Gerichtsweg 28, 04103 Leipzig
Tel: (0341) 98 210 10 *Fax:* (0341) 98 210 19
E-mail: info@seemann-henschel.de
Web Site: www.seemann-henschel.de
Key Personnel
Management: Dr Juergen A Bach; Bernd Kolf
Founded: 1925
Subjects: Architecture & Interior Design, Art, Bi-
ography, Memoirs, History, Regional Interests
ISBN Prefix(es): 978-3-361; 978-3-89487; 978-3-
7338; 978-3-86502
Imprints: Henschel Verlag; Koehler & Amelang
GmbH; Edition Leipzig; E A Seemann Verlag
Foreign Rep(s): B+I Buch und Information AG
(Richard Bhend) (Switzerland); Verlagsagen-
tur Erich Neuhold (Eastern Austria); Harald
Rumpold (Western Austria)
Distribution Center: Leipziger Kommissions-
und Grossbuchhandelsgesellschaft mbH
(LKG), An de Suedspitze 1-12, 04571 Roetha
Tel: (034206) 65 127 *Fax:* (034206) 65
255 *E-mail:* kzborala@lkg-service.de *Web
Site:* www.lkg-va.de
Dr Franz Hain Verlagsauslieferungen, Dr-
Otto-Neurath-Gasse 5, 1220 Vienna, Austria
Tel: (01) 2 82 65 65 *Fax:* (01) 2 82 65 65 70
Continent Books, Van Oldenbarneveldstr 77, 1052
JW Amsterdam, Netherlands *Tel:* (020) 6 76
82 86 *Fax:* (020) 6 88 08 00 *E-mail:* continent.
books@12move.nl (Netherlands & Belgium)
Scheidegger & Co AG, c/o AVA Verlagsaus-
lieferung AG, Centralweg 16, 8910 Affoltern
am Albis, Switzerland *Tel:* (044) 7 62 42 70
Fax: (044) 7 62 42 10
Art Stock, 213 W Main St, Barrington, IL 60010,
United States *E-mail:* info@artstockbooks.com
(USA & Canada)

Michael Seipp, Kartographie & Verlag+
Schoenberger Weg 17, 60488 Frankfurt am Main
Tel: (069) 74309806 *Fax:* (069) 74309852
E-mail: info@hildebrands.de
Web Site: www.hildebrands.de
Key Personnel
Mng Dir & Owner: Michael Seipp
Founded: 1980

Subjects: Travel & Tourism
ISBN Prefix(es): 978-3-88989
Total Titles: 100 Print
Distributed by Cartotheque EGG (France); Geo-
Center ILH (Germany); Libridis NV (Belgium,
Luxembourg & Netherlands); Cartografica del
Riccio (Italy); Stanford Ltd (UK)

Sellier/de Gruyter, see Dr Arthur L Sellier & Co
KG-Walter de Gruyter GmbH & Co KG OHG

**Dr Arthur L Sellier & Co KG-Walter de
Gruyter GmbH & Co KG OHG+**
Geibelstr 8, 81679 Munich
Tel: (089) 45 10 84 58-0 *Fax:* (089) 45 10 84 58-
9
E-mail: info@sellier.de
Web Site: www.sellier.de
Key Personnel
Publishing Dir: Andreas Pittrich
E-mail: pittrich@sellier.de
Mng Dir: Dr Felix Hey
Production: Karina Hack *E-mail:* hack@sellier.de
Sales & Marketing: Anja Urbanek
E-mail: urbanek@sellier.de
Founded: 1990
Subjects: Law, Commentary to the German Civil
Code
ISBN Prefix(es): 978-3-8059

**seltmann+soehne Kunst- und Fotobuchverlag
GbR**
Wefelshohler Str 31, 58511 Luedenscheid
Tel: (02351) 94 87 0
E-mail: info@seltmannundsoehne.de
Web Site: www.seltmannundsoehne.de
Key Personnel
Editorial: Oliver Seltmann *E-mail:* oliver@
seltmann.de
Production & Sales: Arno Seltmann
E-mail: arno@seltmann.de; Frank Seltmann
Founded: 2004
Subjects: Art, Literature, Literary Criticism, Es-
says, Photography, Icelandic Literature
ISBN Prefix(es): 978-3-934687; 978-3-9804960
Branch Office(s)
Prinzenstr 85D/Aufbau Haus, 10969 Berlin-
Kreuzberg, Contact: Oliver Seltmann *Tel:* (030)
91 52 68 91

Semikolon-Verlag
Zeppelinstr 29, 12459 Berlin
Tel: (030) 53 79 00 75
Key Personnel
Publishing Dir: Olaf Kannenberg
Subjects: Meditation
ISBN Prefix(es): 978-3-934955; 978-3-940129

Sensei Verlag Kernen
Cannstatterstr 13, 71394 Kernen
Tel: (07151) 910222 *Fax:* (07151) 46553
E-mail: info@sensei.de
Web Site: www.sensei.de
Key Personnel
Mng Dir: Lothar Hirneise
Subjects: Health, Nutrition, Inspirational, Spiri-
tuality, Medicine, Nursing, Dentistry, Sports,
Athletics, Holistic Medicine, Oncology/Cancer,
Personal Development
ISBN Prefix(es): 978-3-932576

edition serapion, *imprint of* Karin Fischer Verlag
GmbH

Shaker Verlag GmbH
Kaiserstr 100, 52134 Herzogenrath
Tel: (02407) 9596-0 *Fax:* (02407) 9596-9
E-mail: info@shaker.de
Web Site: www.shaker.de
Key Personnel
Mng Dir: Dr C Shaker

Sales: Marcel Triebel *Tel:* (02407) 9596-36
E-mail: marcel.triebel@shaker.de
Membership(s): Boersenverein des Deutschen
Buchandels; EU Verleger Forum; Koninklijke
Vereniging van het Boekenvak; VG Wort.
Subjects: Science (General)
ISBN Prefix(es): 978-3-8265; 978-3-8322; 978-3-
86111; 978-3-8440
Branch Office(s)
Shaker Publishing BV, St Maartenslaan 26, 6221
AX Maastricht, Netherlands

Siebenberg Verlag+
Hagenstr 10, 31275 Lehrte
Tel: (05132) 8399-0 *Fax:* (05132) 8399-69
Web Site: www.huebner-books.de/huebner-shop
Key Personnel
Owner: Felicitas Huebner
Founded: 1936
Subjects: Art, Asian Studies, Poetry
ISBN Prefix(es): 978-3-87747
Parent Company: Felicitas Huebner Verlag GmbH
Distribution Center: BACOPA Handels- & Kultur
GesmbH, Waidern 42, 4521 Schiedlberg, Aus-
tria *Tel:* (0751) 22235 *Fax:* (0751) 22235-16
E-mail: versand@bacopa.at *Web Site:* www.
bacopa.at
Sana Verlag, Via Campagna 13b, 6503
Bellinzona-Galbisio, Switzerland
Tel: (091) 835 48 90 *Fax:* (091) 835 48 91
E-mail: sanaverlag@bluemail.ch

Siedler, *imprint of* Verlagsgruppe Random House
Bertelsmann

Siedler Verlag+
Imprint of Verlagsgruppe Random House Bertels-
mann
Neumarkter Str 28, 81673 Munich
Tel: (089) 4136-0 *Toll Free Tel:* 0800 500 33 22
Fax: (089) 4136-3333
E-mail: kundenservice@randomhouse.de
Web Site: www.randomhouse.de/siedler
Key Personnel
Press: Markus Desaga *Tel:* (089) 4136-702
Fax: (089) 4136-897 *E-mail:* markus.desaga@
randomhouse.de
Founded: 1980
Subjects: Biography, Memoirs, Government, Po-
litical Science, History, Journalism, Nonfiction
(General), Science (General)
ISBN Prefix(es): 978-3-88680; 978-3-8275

Siegler & Co Verlag fuer Zeitarchive GmbH+
Hauptstr 354, 53639 Koenigswinter
Tel: (02223) 900036 *Fax:* (02223) 900038
Key Personnel
Contact: Joachim Hack
Founded: 1931
Subjects: Government, Political Science, History
ISBN Prefix(es): 978-3-87748

Georg Siemens Verlag GmbH & Co KG
Boothstr 11, 12207 Berlin
Mailing Address: Postfach 450169, 12171 Berlin
Tel: (030) 769904-0 *Fax:* (030) 769904-18
E-mail: service@zevrail.de
Web Site: www.zevrail.de
Key Personnel
Contact: Andre Plambeck
Founded: 1882
Subjects: Transportation, Railways
ISBN Prefix(es): 978-3-87749

Sierra, *imprint of* Frederking & Thaler Verlag
GmbH

Sigloch Edition KG+
Am Buchberg 8, 74572 Blaufelden
Tel: (07953) 883-0; (01805) 004 172
Fax: (07953) 883-320

E-mail: edition@sigloch.de; info@sigloch.de
Web Site: www.sigloch.de
Key Personnel
President & Mng Dir: Helmut Sigloch
Founded: 1972
Subjects: Cookery, Technology, Nature
ISBN Prefix(es): 978-3-89393
Parent Company: Sigloch Gruppe
Warehouse: Sigloch Distribution GmbH
& Co KG *Fax:* (07953) 883-380
E-mail: distribution@sigloch.de *Web
Site:* www.sigloch-distribution.de

Edition Sigma eKfm
Leuschnerdamm 13, 10999 Berlin
Tel: (030) 623 23 63 *Fax:* (030) 623 93 93
E-mail: verlag@edition-sigma.de
Web Site: www.edition-sigma.de
Key Personnel
Contact: Mr R Bohn
Founded: 1984
This publisher has indicated that 50% of their
product line is author subsidized.
Subjects: Social Sciences, Sociology
ISBN Prefix(es): 978-3-924859; 978-3-89404;
978-3-8360
Number of titles published annually: 35 Print; 5
E-Book
Total Titles: 500 Print; 20 E-Book
Distribution Center: Suedost Verlags Service, Am
Steinfeld 4, 94065 Waldkirchen *Tel:* (08581)
96050 *Fax:* (08581) 754 *E-mail:* service@
suedost-verlags-service.de

Silberburg-Verlag GmbH
Schoenbuchstr 48, 72074 Tuebingen-Bebenhausen
Tel: (07071) 6885-0 *Fax:* (07071) 6885-20
E-mail: info@silberburg.de
Web Site: www.silberburg.de
Key Personnel
Publisher: Titus Haeussermann *E-mail:* titus.
haeussermann@silberburg.de
Business Manager: Christel Werner
Founded: 1985
Specialize in books, CDs, calendars & other
media on the German region of Baden-
Wuerttemberg.
Membership(s): Boersenverein des Deutschen
Buchhandels.
Subjects: Regional Interests
ISBN Prefix(es): 978-3-925344; 978-3-87407;
978-3-8425
Number of titles published annually: 70 Print; 30
E-Book; 3 Audio
Total Titles: 600 Print; 100 E-Book; 30 Audio
Imprints: Fleischhauer & Spohn Verlag
Distributed by Maeule & Gosch Tontraegerver-
trieb
Distributor for Der Loewe lacht - Verlag und Ver-
trieb; Maeule & Gosch Tontragervertrieb; Pe-
ter Nagel; Heiner Reiff Musik; Schmidmusic;
Schwoissfuass GmbH; Christoph Sonntag; in-
akustik
Warehouse: c/o Koch, Neff & Oetinger Ver-
lagsauslieferung GmbH, Industriestr 23, 70565
Stuttgart *E-mail:* silberburg@kno-va.de *Web
Site:* www.kno-va.de

Die Silberschnur Verlag GmbH+
Steinstr 1, 56593 Guellesheim
Tel: (02687) 929068; (02687) 929001 (sales)
Fax: (02687) 929524
E-mail: info@silberschnur.de; bestellung@
silberschnur.de
Web Site: www.silberschnur.de
Key Personnel
Mng Dir: Stefan Huber *E-mail:* stefan.huber@
silberschnur.de
Editor: Isabelle Wolf *E-mail:* i.wolf@silberschnur.
de
Foreign Rights: Peter Schmidt *E-mail:* p.
schmidt@silberschnur.de

Founded: 1982
Subjects: Alternative, Astrology, Occult, Health,
Nutrition, Inspirational, Spirituality, Literature,
Literary Criticism, Essays, Parapsychology,
Philosophy, Science (General), Self-Help, Al-
ternative Healing, Esoteric Teachings, Life Af-
ter Death
ISBN Prefix(es): 978-3-923781; 978-3-931652;
978-3-89845
Number of titles published annually: 20 Print
Total Titles: 300 Print
Distributor for Adama; Adwaita; Arun;
Bergkristall; Coudris; Devas Edition; Dude;
EVT; Grasmuck; Heindel; ICH; Kamasha;
Kopp; 1 zu 1; Medicum Keg; Mirzadeh; Mym;
Nietsch; NLS; Omega; Ostergaard; PAN;
Quadropol; Reichel; Rocke; Silberschnur;
Simeunovic; Subtilis; Julia White; WuWei;
Yantra

Edition Sirius im Aisthesis Verlag+
c/o Aisthesis Verlag GmbH & Co KG, Oberntor-
wall 21 (Eingang Mauerstr), 33602 Bielefeld
Tel: (0521) 17 26 04 *Fax:* (0521) 17 28 12
E-mail: info@edition-sirius.de
Web Site: www.edition-sirius.de
Key Personnel
Representative: Hans Haessig; Dr Detlev Kopp;
Dr Michael Vogt
Founded: 2004
Subjects: Art, Biography, Memoirs, Education,
Fiction, Health, Nutrition, History, Inspira-
tional, Spirituality, Language Arts, Linguistics,
Literature, Literary Criticism, Essays, Music,
Dance, Philosophy, Poetry, Psychology, Psy-
chiatry, Self-Help, Social Sciences, Sociology,
Travel & Tourism, Chinese Medicine, Fitness,
Psychotherapy
ISBN Prefix(es): 978-3-925670; 978-3-89528
Branch Office(s)
Blaesiring 136, 4057 Basel, Switzerland, Contact:
Hans Haessig *Tel:* (061) 683 16 18

Slavica Verlag+
Elisabethstr 22, 80796 Munich
Tel: (089) 272 56 12 *Fax:* (089) 271 65 94
Web Site: www.slavica-kovac.com
Key Personnel
Owner: Anton Kovac *E-mail:* anton.kovac@t-
online.de
Founded: 1987
Specialize in scientific publishing.
Membership(s): Boersenvereins des Deutschen
Buchhandels.
Subjects: Anthropology, Ethnicity, Fiction, For-
eign Countries, Government, Political Science,
History, Language Arts, Linguistics, Literature,
Literary Criticism, Essays, Philosophy, Poetry,
Religion - Other
ISBN Prefix(es): 978-3-927077
Bookshop(s): Balkan & Southeast European Pub-
lications Suedosteuopa Versandbuchhandel

Smaragd Verlag GmbH
Neuwieder Str 2, 56269 Dierdorf
Tel: (02689) 922 59 10 *Fax:* (02689) 922 59 20
E-mail: info@smaragd-verlag.de
Web Site: smaragd-verlag.de
Key Personnel
Publishing Dir: Mara Ordemann
Head, Marketing/Editorial: Gaby Heuchemer
E-mail: g.heuchemer@smaragd-verlag.de
Founded: 1989
Subjects: Inspirational, Spirituality, Self-Help,
Spiritual Healing
ISBN Prefix(es): 978-3-938489; 978-3-934254;
978-3-941363; 978-3-926374

Rudolf G Smend+
Mainzer Str 31, 50678 Cologne
Tel: (0221) 312 0 47 *Fax:* (0221) 932 0718
E-mail: smend@smend.de

Web Site: www.smend.de
Key Personnel
Owner: Rudolf G Smend *E-mail:* rudolf@smend.
de
Founded: 1973
Art gallery & publisher of catalogues.
Subjects: Art, Asian Studies, Indonesian Art, Tex-
tile Art
ISBN Prefix(es): 978-3-926779
Number of titles published annually: 1 Print
Total Titles: 10 Print

Snoeck Verlagsgesellschaft mbH
Nievenheimer Str 18, 50739 Cologne
Mailing Address: Postfach 130217, 50496
Cologne
Tel: (0221) 5104386 *Fax:* (0221) 5108753
E-mail: mail@snoeck.de
Web Site: www.snoeck.de
ISBN Prefix(es): 978-3-936859; 978-3-940953;
978-3-9811606; 978-94-6161; 978-3-86442
Foreign Rep(s): Berend Bosch (Belgium, Hol-
land); Stefan Schempp (Austria, Germany);
Markus Wieser (Switzerland)
Distribution Center: Leipziger Kommissions-
und Grossbuchhandelsgesellschaft mbH
(LKG), An der Suedspitze 1-12, 04579 Es-
penhain *Tel:* (034206) 65122 *Fax:* (034206)
651734 *E-mail:* mkoernig@lkg-service.de *Web
Site:* www.lkg-va.de (Austria, Benelux & Ger-
many)
Pollen Diffusion, 81 rue Romain Rolland, 93260
Les Lilas, France *Tel:* 01 43 62 08 07 *Fax:* 01
72 71 84 51 *E-mail:* commande@pollen-
diffusion.com
AVA Verlagsauslieferung AG, Centralweg
16, 8910 Affoltern am Albis, Switzerland
Tel: (044) 7624200 *Fax:* (044) 7624210
E-mail: verlagsservice@ava.ch
Marston Book Services Ltd, PO Box 269, Abing-
don, Oxon OX14 4YN, United Kingdom
Tel: (01235) 465500 *Fax:* (01235) 465555
E-mail: trade.orders@marston.co.uk *Web
Site:* www.marston.co.uk (Eastern Europe,
Great Britain, Scandinavia & South Europe)
ram publications + distributions inc, 2525 Michi-
gan Ave, Bldg 2A, Santa Monica, CA 90404,
United States *Tel:* 310-453-0043 *E-mail:* info@
rampub.com *Web Site:* www.rampub.com

Societaets-Verlag+
Frankenallee 71-81, 60327 Frankfurt am Main
Tel: (069) 75 01-0 *Fax:* (069) 75 11 01-45
E-mail: vertrieb-sv@fs-medien.de
Web Site: www.societaets-verlag.de
Key Personnel
Mng Dir: Hans Homrighausen
Publishing & Program Dir: Dr Rene Heinen
Production Manager: Cordula Tippkoetter
Sales Manager: Gabriele Karcher *Tel:* (069) 75
01-42 97
Founded: 1921
Subjects: Art, Business, Economics, Government,
Political Science, History, Literature, Literary
Criticism, Essays, Regional Interests, Sports,
Athletics
ISBN Prefix(es): 978-3-7973; 978-3-87235
Imprints: Verlag Frankfurter Buecher; Verlag
Heinrich Scheffler

Sokrates Verlag GmbH
Seeshaupter Str 2, 82393 Iffeldorf
Tel: (08856) 9107892 *Fax:* (08856) 9360788
E-mail: info@sokrates-verlag.de
Web Site: www.sokrates-verlag.de
Key Personnel
Mng Dir: Volker Wendel
ISBN Prefix(es): 978-3-9812912; 978-3-9810031

Sonnentanz-Druck+
Piccardstr 10, 86159 Augsburg
Tel: (0821) 311070 *Fax:* (0821) 158979

Key Personnel
Contact: Roland Kron
Founded: 1988
Specialize in rock literature & rock biographies.
Subjects: Biography, Memoirs, Music, Dance
ISBN Prefix(es): 978-3-926794

Sonntag Verlag+
Subsidiary of MVS Medizinverlage Stuttgart
    GmbH & Co KG
Ruedigerstr 14, 70469 Stuttgart
Mailing Address: Postfach 30 11 20, 70451
    Stuttgart
Tel: (0711) 8931-0; (0711) 8931-900 (customer
    service) *Fax:* (0711) 8931-298; (0711) 8931-
    901 (customer service)
E-mail: kundenservice@thieme.de
Web Site: www.thieme.de
Key Personnel
Mng Dir: Dr Wolfgang Knueppe
General Partner: Dr Albercht Hauff
Founded: 1920
Specialize in books, magazines, medicine, com-
    plementary medicine.
Subjects: Holistic Veterinary Medicine, Homeopa-
    thy, Naturopathy
ISBN Prefix(es): 978-3-87758
Number of titles published annually: 25 Print
Total Titles: 150 Print
Ultimate Parent Company: Georg Thieme Verlag
    KG
Associate Companies: Enke Verlag; Haug Verlag;
    Hippokrates Verlag; TRIAS Verlag

Spektrum Akademischer Verlag
Tiegartenstr 17, 69121 Heidelberg
Tel: (06221) 487 0
E-mail: customerservice@springernature.com
Web Site: www.springer.com
Key Personnel
Mng Dir: Martin Mos; Dr Heinrich Weinheimer
Founded: 1991
Subjects: Nonfiction (General), Science (General)
ISBN Prefix(es): 978-3-8274
Parent Company: Springer-Verlag GmbH
Ultimate Parent Company: Springer Sci-
    ence+Business Media Deutschland GmbH

**Spektrum der Wissenschaft Verlagsgesellschaft
    mbH**
Slevogtstr 3-5, 69126 Heidelberg
Mailing Address: Postfach 10 48 40, 69038 Hei-
    delberg
Tel: (06221) 9126-600 *Fax:* (06221) 9126-751
E-mail: service@spektrum.de
Web Site: www.spektrum.de
Key Personnel
Mng Dir: Thomas Bleck; Markus Bossle
Contact: Karin Schmidt *E-mail:* schmidt@
    spektrum.de
Founded: 1978
Subjects: Science (General), Technology
ISBN Prefix(es): 978-3-936278; 978-3-938639
Parent Company: Scientific American Inc, 75
    Varick St, 9th floor, New York, NY 10013-
    1917, United States

Verlagshaus Speyer GmbH
Beethovenstr 4, 67346 Speyer
Tel: (06232) 2 49 26 *Fax:* (06232) 13 23-44
E-mail: info@verlagshaus-speyer.de
Web Site: www.presseverlag-pfalz.de; www.
    verlagshaus-speyer.de
Key Personnel
Mng Dir: Hartmut Metzger
Subjects: Art, Biblical Studies, Biography, Mem-
    oirs, History, Music, Dance, Religion - Protes-
    tant, Travel & Tourism
ISBN Prefix(es): 978-3-925536

Sphinx, *imprint of* Verlagsgruppe Random House
    Bertelsmann

**SPIEGEL-Verlag Rudolf Augstein GmbH &
    Co KG+**
Ericusspitze 1, 20457 Hamburg
Tel: (040) 3007-0 *Fax:* (040) 3007-2246; (040)
    3007-2247
E-mail: spiegel@spiegel.de
Web Site: www.spiegelgruppe.de
Key Personnel
Chief Executive Officer: Ove Saffe
Publishing Dir: Matthias Schmolz; Rolf-Dieter
    Schulz
Sales Dir: Thomas Hass
Founded: 1946
ISBN Prefix(es): 978-3-87763
Subsidiaries: a+i art & information GmbH &
    Co KG; manager magazine ONLINE GmbH;
    manager magazine Verlagsgesellschaft mbH;
    Quality Channel GmbH; SPIEGEL ONLINE
    GmbH; Spiegel TV GmbH; SPIEGELnet
    GmbH
Orders to: Postfach 105840, 20039 Hamburg

Spieth Verlag+
Postfach 60 13 20, 14413 Potsdam
Tel: (0331) 2000309 *Fax:* (03212) 107 07 29
E-mail: info@spiethverlag.de
Web Site: www.spiethverlag.de
Key Personnel
Owner: Rudolf Arnold Spieth
Founded: 1969
Specialize in esoteric astrology.
Subjects: Anthropology, Astrology, Occult, Para-
    psychology, Philosophy, Psychology, Psychia-
    try, Religion - Other, Self-Help
ISBN Prefix(es): 978-3-88093
Subsidiaries: Bund der Runenforscher Deutsch-
    lands (BRD)/Internationaler Zentralverband
    Germanischer Runenforscher (IZGR)

Spiridon-Verlags GmbH+
Dorfstr 18A, 40699 Erkrath
Mailing Address: Postfach 10 45 27, 40036 Dues-
    seldorf
Tel: (0211) 3618 4937 *Fax:* (0211) 3618 4935
E-mail: spiridon@gmx.com
Web Site: www.laufmagazin-spiridon.de
Key Personnel
Publisher: Manfred Steffny; Dr Ernst van Aaken
Founded: 1974
Subjects: Health, Nutrition, Sports, Athletics,
    Marathon Running
ISBN Prefix(es): 978-3-922011
Bookshop(s): Steffnys Laufladen, Linienstr 12,
    40227 Duesseldorf

Adolf Sponholtz Verlag+
Subsidiary of C W Niemeyer Buchverlage GmbH
Osterstr 19, 31785 Hameln
Mailing Address: Postfach 100752, 31757
    Hameln
Tel: (05151) 200-312 *Fax:* (05151) 200-319
E-mail: info@niemeyer-buch.de
Web Site: www.niemeyer-buch.de
Key Personnel
Mng Dir: Carsten Holzendorff
Sales: Christina Schneider
Founded: 1894
Subjects: Animals, Pets, Energy, Environmental
    Studies, Fiction, History, Literature, Literary
    Criticism, Essays, Nonfiction (General), Out-
    door Recreation
ISBN Prefix(es): 978-3-87766

Spreeside, *imprint of* Eyfalia Publishing GmbH

Axel Springer Verlag AG
Axel-Springer-Str 65, 10888 Berlin
Tel: (030) 2591 0
E-mail: information@axelspringer.de
Web Site: www.axelspringer.de

Key Personnel
Head, Corporate Communications: Edda Fels
    Tel: (030) 2591 77600 *Fax:* (030) 2591 77603
    E-mail: edda.fels@axelspringer.de
Information & Public Relations: Lars Schewe
Founded: 1946
Subjects: Automotive, Business, Fashion, Music,
    Dance, Regional Interests, Sports, Athletics,
    Travel & Tourism
ISBN Prefix(es): 978-3-921305
Branch Office(s)
Axel-Springer-Platz 1, 20350 Hamburg *Tel:* (040)
    34700

Springer Gabler+
Imprint of Springer DE
Abraham-Lincoln-Str 46, 65189 Wiesbaden
Tel: (0611) 7878-0 *Fax:* (0611) 7878-400
Web Site: www.springer-gabler.de
Key Personnel
Public Relations Manager: Karen Ehrhardt
    Tel: (0611) 7878-394 *Fax:* (0611) 7878-451
    E-mail: karen.ehrhardt@springer.com
Founded: 1929
Professional information for managers, personal
    assistants; textbooks for students, encyclope-
    dias.
Subjects: Accounting, Business, Economics, Fi-
    nance, Management, Marketing
ISBN Prefix(es): 978-3-409; 978-3-8349
Total Titles: 1,500 Print
Ultimate Parent Company: Springer Sci-
    ence+Business Media

**Springer Science+Business Media Deutschland
    GmbH+**
Heidelberger Platz 3, 14197 Berlin
Tel: (030) 82787-0 *Fax:* (030) 8214091
Web Site: www.springer.com
Founded: 1842
Publisher of scientific & specialist literature. In
    addition to scientific literature, competent in-
    formation service for the B2B (business-to-
    business) market provided.
Subjects: Architecture & Interior Design, Com-
    puter Science, Economics, Engineering (Gen-
    eral), Mathematics, Medicine, Nursing, Den-
    tistry, Physics, Science (General), Social Sci-
    ences, Sociology, Technology, Transportation,
    Construction, Life Sciences, Statistics
Number of titles published annually: 5,000 Print
Total Titles: 40,000 Print

Springer-Verlag GmbH+
Tiegartenstr 17, 69121 Heidelberg
Mailing Address: Postfach 105280, 69042 Heidel-
    berg
Tel: (06221) 487-0 *Fax:* (06221) 487-8366
E-mail: sdc-bookorder@springer.com;
    permissions.dordrecht@springer.com
Web Site: www.springer-sbm.de
Key Personnel
Chief Executive Officer: Daniel Ropers
Head, Rights: Berendina van Straalen
    Fax: (06221) 487 8223
Customer Service: Eric Schmitt *Tel:* (06221) 345-
    148 *E-mail:* eric.schmitt@springer.com
Marketing: Juliane Ritt *Tel:* (06221) 487-8159
    E-mail: juliane.ritt@springer.com
Founded: 1991
Membership(s): TR-Verlagsunion GmbH.
Subjects: Agriculture, Anthropology, Architec-
    ture & Interior Design, Astronomy, Automo-
    tive, Behavioral Sciences, Biological Sciences,
    Business, Chemistry, Chemical Engineering,
    Child Care & Development, Civil Engineering,
    Computer Science, Earth Sciences, Economics,
    Education, Energy, Engineering (General), En-
    vironmental Studies, Finance, Geography, Ge-
    ology, Government, Political Science, Health,
    Nutrition, Law, Management, Marketing, Math-
    ematics, Mechanical Engineering, Medicine,
    Nursing, Dentistry, Physics, Psychology, Psy-

chiatry, Science (General), Social Sciences, Sociology, Technology, Transportation, Human Sciences
ISBN Prefix(es): 978-3-540
Parent Company: Springer Science+Business Media GmbH, Heidelberger Platz 3, 14197 Berlin
Associate Companies: Springer-VDI-Verlag GmbH & Co KG, VDI-Haus, VDI-Platz 1, 40468 Duesseldorf *Tel:* (0211) 6103-0 *Fax:* (0211) 6103-300 *Web Site:* www.technikwissen.de; Urban & Vogel GmbH, Aschauer Str 30, 81549 Munich *Tel:* (089) 20 30 43 1300 *Fax:* (089) 4372 1370; Sachsenpl 4-6, 1201 Vienna, Austria *Tel:* (01) 3302415552 *Fax:* (01) 330242665 *Web Site:* www.springer.at; Springer France Sarl, 22, rue de Palestro, 75002 Paris, France, Contact: Sylvie Kamara *Tel:* 01 53 00 98 60 *Fax:* 01 53 00 98 61 *E-mail:* sylvie.kamara@springer.com *Web Site:* www.springer.com; Springer Asia Ltd, Unit 1706-1707 Exchange Tower, 33 Wang Chiu Rd, Kowloon Bay, Hong Kong *Tel:* 2723 9698 *Fax:* 2724 2366 *Web Site:* www.springer.com; Springer (India) Pvt Ltd, 7/F Vijaya Bldg, 17 Barakhamba Rd, New Delhi 110 001, India *Tel:* (011) 4575 5888 *Fax:* (011) 4575 5889 *Web Site:* www.springer.com; Springer Healthcare Italia SRL, Via Lanino, 20144 Milan MI, Italy *Tel:* (02) 4234562 *Fax:* (02) 4221200 *Web Site:* www.springerhealthcare.com; Springer Japan KK, First Bldg E, 3-8-1 Nishi-kanda, Chiyoda-ku, Tokyo 101-0065, Japan *Tel:* (03) 68317000 *Fax:* (03) 68317001 *Web Site:* www.springer.jp; Springer-Verlag London Ltd, 236 6/F Gray's Inn Rd, London WC1X 8HB, United Kingdom *Tel:* (020) 3192 2000 *Web Site:* www.springer.com; Springer Healthcare LLC, 233 Spring St, New York, NY 10013-1578, United States, Contact: Rick Werdann *Tel:* 212-460-1500 *Fax:* 212-460-1575 *Web Site:* www.springer.com
Distributor for AIP Press (American Institute of Physics)
Foreign Rep(s): Springer China Beijing (China); Springer Dordrecht (Netherlands); Springer Moscow (Russia)
Warehouse: Springer Distribution Center GmbH, Haberstr 7, 69126 Heidelberg *Tel:* (06221) 345-112 *Fax:* (06221) 345-182 *E-mail:* orders@springer.com

Springer Vieweg+
Imprint of Springer DE
Abraham-Lincoln-Str 46, 65189 Wiesbaden
Tel: (0611) 7878-0 *Fax:* (0611) 7878-400
Web Site: www.springer-vieweg.de
Key Personnel
Dir, Technology: Dr Axel Garbers *Tel:* (0611) 7878 330 *Fax:* (0611) 7878 78330
  E-mail: axel.garbers@springer.com
Deputy Dir, Technology: Ewald Schmitt
  Tel: (0611) 7878 387 *Fax:* (0611) 7878 78387
  E-mail: ewald.schmitt@springer.com
Founded: 2012
Professional information for engineers & technicians; textbooks for students in technology & mathematics.
Subjects: Automotive, Civil Engineering, Computer Science, Electronics, Electrical Engineering, Mathematics, Mechanical Engineering, Technology, Automotive Engineering, Natural Sciences
ISBN Prefix(es): 978-3-8348
Number of titles published annually: 5 CD-ROM
Total Titles: 1,500 Print; 25 CD-ROM
Ultimate Parent Company: Springer Science+Business Media
Branch Office(s)
Heidelberger Platz 3, 14197 Berlin
Tiergartenstr 17, 69121 Heidelberg

Springer VS+
Imprint of Springer DE

Abraham-Lincoln-Str 46, 65189 Wiesbaden
Tel: (0611) 7878-0 *Fax:* (0611) 7878-400
Web Site: www.springer-spektrum.de
Key Personnel
Dir, Social Science & Research Publications: Dr Reinald Klockenbusch *Tel:* (0611) 7878-368 *Fax:* (0611) 7878-453 *E-mail:* reinald.klockenbusch@springer.com
Public Relations Manager: Karen Ehrhardt
  Tel: (0611) 7878-394 *Fax:* (0611) 7878-451
  E-mail: karen.ehrhardt@springer.com
Founded: 1947
Books & periodicals which cover all important topics in the social sciences.
Subjects: Communications, Education, Government, Political Science, Psychology, Psychiatry, Social Sciences, Sociology, Media
ISBN Prefix(es): 978-3-8100; 978-3-531
Total Titles: 2,000 Print
Ultimate Parent Company: Springer Science+Business Media
Foreign Rights: Springer Science+Business Media

Spurbuchverlag
Am Eichenhuegel 4, 96148 Baunach
Tel: (09544) 1561 *Fax:* (09544) 809
E-mail: info@spurbuch.de
Web Site: www.spurbuch.de
Key Personnel
Mng Dir: Paul-Thomas Hinkel
Founded: 1982
Subjects: Architecture & Interior Design, Art, Health, Nutrition, History, Mysteries, Suspense, Travel & Tourism, Design
ISBN Prefix(es): 978-3-88778

L Staackmann Verlag KG+
Lochener Str 6, 83623 Linden-Dietramszell
Tel: (08027) 337 *Fax:* (08027) 816
E-mail: info@staackmann.de
Web Site: www.staackmann.de
Key Personnel
Mng Dir: Dr Friedrich Vogel
Founded: 1869
Subjects: Fiction
ISBN Prefix(es): 978-3-920897; 978-3-88675

Staatsbibliothek zu Berlin - Preussischer Kulturbesitz (Berlin State Library - Prussian Cultural Heritage)
Unter den Linden 8, 10117 Berlin
Mailing Address: Potsdamer Str 33, 10785 Berlin
Tel: (030) 266-0 *Fax:* (030) 266-2814
E-mail: info@sbb.spk-berlin.de
Web Site: staatsbibliothek-berlin.de
Key Personnel
Dir General: Barbara Schneider-Kempf
  E-mail: barbara.schneider-kempf@sbb.spk-berlin.de
Founded: 1661
Subjects: Library & Information Sciences
ISBN Prefix(es): 978-3-88053; 978-3-7361

Stadler Verlagsgesellschaft mbH+
Max-Stromeyer-Str 172, 78467 Konstanz
Tel: (07531) 898-0 *Fax:* (07531) 898-101
E-mail: info@verlag-stadler.de
Web Site: www.verlag-stadler.de
Key Personnel
Mng Dir: Christian Stadler *Tel:* (07531) 898-116
  E-mail: c.stadler@verlag-stadler.de; Michael Stadler
Sales: Monika Schmittel *Tel:* (07531) 898-162
  E-mail: schmittel@verlag-stadler.de
Founded: 1815
Membership(s): Boersenverein des Deutschen Buchhandels eV.
Subjects: Art, Geography, Geology, History, Maritime, Music, Dance, Nonfiction (General), Outdoor Recreation, Regional Interests
ISBN Prefix(es): 978-3-7977

Distribution Center: Merkur Logistics GmbH, Roemerstr 49, 33758 Scholss Holte-Stukenbrock, Contact: Simone Alice Berkenmeyer *Tel:* (05207) 95778-25 *Fax:* (05207) 95778-29 *E-mail:* berkenmeyer@merku-psy.de
Orders to: Runge Verlagsauslieferung, Bergstr 2, 33803 Steinhagen, Contact: Jutta Hartmann *Tel:* (05204) 9181-85 *Fax:* (05204) 9181-95 *E-mail:* stadler@rungeva.de
Returns: Merkur Logistics GmbH, Roemerstr 49, 33758 Scholss Holte-Stukenbrock, Contact: Simone Alice Berkenmeyer *Tel:* (05207) 95778-25 *Fax:* (05207) 95778-29 *E-mail:* berkenmeyer@merkur-psg.de *Web Site:* www.merkur-psg.de

Stadt Duisburg, Stabsstelle fuer Wahlen, Europaangelegenheiten und Informationslogistik
Bismarckplatz 1, 47198 Duisburg
Tel: (0203) 283 3274 *Fax:* (0203) 283 4404
E-mail: stabsstellei-03@stadt-duisburg.de
Web Site: www.duisburg.de/vv/I-03/index.php
Key Personnel
Dir: Burkhard Beyersdorff
Administrator: Anita Rauser *E-mail:* a.rauser@stadt-duisburg.de
Specialize in public administration-abstracting, statistics & bibliographies. Periodicals & irregulars.
This publisher has indicated that 100% of their product line is author subsidized.
Subjects: Public Administration
ISBN Prefix(es): 978-3-89279
Total Titles: 15 Print

Staedte-Verlag E v Wagner & J Mitterhuber GmbH+
Steinbeisstr 9, 70736 Fellbach
Tel: (0711) 576201 *Fax:* (0711) 5762199
E-mail: info@staedte-verlag.de
Web Site: www.staedte-verlag.de
Key Personnel
Mng Dir: Meinhard Mitterhuber; Michael Mitterhuber; Peter Zwierzynski
Founded: 1951
Publisher of cartographic programs & advertising.
Subjects: Geography, Geology, Outdoor Recreation, Cartography
ISBN Prefix(es): 978-3-8164
Number of titles published annually: 500 Print
Subsidiaries: CartoStadt (Hungary); CB Fotosatz (Germany); Geoplan (Poland); Geoplana (Germany); Geoplan Srl (Italy); Magyar Terkephaz Kft (Hungary); Miplan AG (Switzerland); Novoprint Inc (USA); Staedte-Verlag (Austria)

Verlag Stahleisen GmbH+
Sohnstr 65, 40237 Duesseldorf
Mailing Address: Postfach 10 51 64, 40042 Duesseldorf
Tel: (0211) 6707-0 *Fax:* (0211) 6707-517
E-mail: stahleisen@stahleisen.de; verlagsleitung@stahleisen.de
Web Site: www.stahleisen.de
Key Personnel
Mng Dir & Rights: Juergen Beckers
Founded: 1908
Specialize in steel, casting practice.
Subjects: Chemistry, Chemical Engineering, Civil Engineering, Engineering (General), Mechanical Engineering, Technology
ISBN Prefix(es): 978-3-514
Associate Companies: Giesserei-Verlag GmbH, Postfach 102532, 40016 Duesseldorf *E-mail:* giesserei@stahleisen.de *Web Site:* www.giesserei-verlag.de
Subsidiaries: Montan- und Wirtschaftsverlag GmbH

Verlag fuer Standesamtswesen GmbH
Hanauer Landstr 197, 60314 Frankfurt am Main

Tel: (069) 40 58 94 0; (069) 40 58 94 555 (sales)
  Fax: (069) 40 58 94 900; (069) 40 58 94 550
  (sales)
E-mail: info@vfst.de
Web Site: www.vfst.de
Key Personnel
Manager: Dr Guenther Metzner; Klaudia Metzner;
  Anna Metzner
Founded: 1929
Subjects: Law, Family Law, Personal Law, Private
  International Law
ISBN Prefix(es): 978-3-8019
Branch Office(s)
Wilmersdofer Str 99, 10629 Berlin *Tel:* (030) 23
  08 14 0 *Fax:* (030) 23 08 14 901

Stapp Verlag+
Luisenstr 11a, 12209 Berlin (Lichterfelde)
Tel: (030) 262 20 97 *Fax:* (030) 262 19 90
E-mail: info@stapp-verlag.de
Web Site: www.stapp-verlag.de
Key Personnel
Owner & Mng Dir: Wolfgang Stapp
Founded: 1953
Subjects: Biography, Memoirs, Geography, Ge-
  ology, History, Literature, Literary Criticism,
  Essays, Music, Dance, Natural History, Nonfic-
  tion (General), Outdoor Recreation, Regional
  Interests, Travel & Tourism
ISBN Prefix(es): 978-3-87776
Imprints: Preussische Koepfe
Distributed by Neue Buecher (Switzerland)

C A Starke Verlag+
Frankfurter Str 51-53, 65549 Limburg an der
  Lahn
Tel: (06431) 9615-0 *Fax:* (06431) 9615-15
E-mail: starkeverlag@t-online.de
Web Site: www.starkeverlag.de
Founded: 1847
Subjects: Biography, Memoirs, Genealogy, His-
  tory, Nonfiction (General), Heraldry, Family
ISBN Prefix(es): 978-3-7980

Stauffenburg Verlag GmbH+
August Bebel-Str 17, 72072 Tuebingen
Mailing Address: Postfach 2525, 72015 Tuebin-
  gen
Tel: (07071) 97 30 0 *Fax:* (07071) 97 30 30
E-mail: info@stauffenburg.de
Web Site: www.stauffenburg.de
Key Personnel
Mng Dir & Publisher: Brigitte Narr
Founded: 1982
Subjects: Communications, English as a Second
  Language, Language Arts, Linguistics, Litera-
  ture, Literary Criticism, Essays, Women's Stud-
  ies
ISBN Prefix(es): 978-3-923721; 978-3-86057
Number of titles published annually: 70 Print
Total Titles: 2,000 Print
Associate Companies: Julius Groos Verlag
Distribution Center: Sigloch Distribution GmbH
  & Co KG, Postfach 11 60, 74568 Blaufelden
  Tel: (07953) 718 9015 *Fax:* (07953) 883 130
  E-mail: stauffenburg@sigloch.de

Stb, *imprint of* Schirner Verlag GmbH & Co KG

Conrad Stein Verlag GmbH+
Kiefernstr 6, 59514 Welver
Mailing Address: Postfach 1233, 59512 Welver
Tel: (02384) 963912 *Fax:* (02384) 963913
E-mail: info@conrad-stein-verlag.de
Web Site: www.conrad-stein-verlag.de
Key Personnel
Manager: Marie-Luise Grosselohmann
Founded: 1980
Subjects: Outdoor Recreation, Travel & Tourism,
  Electronic Books

ISBN Prefix(es): 978-3-922965; 978-3-89392;
  978-3-86686
Number of titles published annually: 30 Print; 50
  E-Book
Total Titles: 250 Print
Foreign Rep(s): Beat Eberle (Switzerland)
Distribution Center: Prolit, Siemensstr 16, 35461
  Fernwald *Tel:* (0641) 94393-0 *Fax:* (0641)
  94393-93 *E-mail:* n.kallweit@prolit.de *Web
  Site:* www.prolit.de
Freytag & Berndt und Artaria KG Aus-
  lieferung und Bestellannahme, Industriestr
  10, 2110 Wolkersdorf, Austria *Tel:* (01)
  8699090 *Fax:* (01) 8698855 *E-mail:* sales@
  freytagberndt.at *Web Site:* www.freytagberndt.at
Leimgruber A Co OHG/snc, Handwekerzone
  31, 39050 Kaltern, Italy *Tel:* (04171) 965473
  Fax: (04171) 965472 *E-mail:* info@leimgruber.
  it
Willems Adventure, Honderland 120, 2676 LT
  Maasdijk, Netherlands *Tel:* (088) 5990140
  Fax: (088) 5990141 (Benelux)
Mapiberia f&b, Parque Empresarial EL Pinar,
  Nave A2 C/Rio Casa Pol Ind Las Herven-
  cias, 05004 Avila, Spain *Tel:* 920030106
  Fax: 920030108 *E-mail:* mapiberia@gmail.com
AVA Verlagsauslieferung AG, Centralweg 16,
  Postfach 27, 8910 Affoltern, Switzerland
  Tel: (044) 7624200 *Fax:* (044) 7624110
  E-mail: avainfo@ava.ch *Web Site:* www.ava.ch

Franz Steiner Verlag GmbH (Franz Steiner
  Publishing)+
Subsidiary of Deutscher Apotheker Verlag
Birkenwaldstr 44, 70191 Stuttgart
Mailing Address: Postfach 101061, 70009
  Stuttgart
Tel: (0711) 2582 0 *Fax:* (0711) 2582 390
E-mail: service@steiner-verlag.de
Web Site: www.steiner-verlag.de
Key Personnel
Publishing Dir: Dr Thomas Schaber *Tel:* (0711)
  2582-309 *E-mail:* tschaber@steiner-verlag.de
Mng Dir: Dr Klaus Brauer *Tel:* (0711) 2582
  228 *E-mail:* kbrauer@steiner-verlag.de;
  Dr Christian Rotta *Tel:* (0711) 2582 230
  E-mail: crotta@steiner-verlag.de
Distribution: Siegmar Bauer *Tel:* (0711) 2582 270
  E-mail: sbauer@steiner-verlag.de
Publicity: Susanne Szoradi *Tel:* (0711) 2582 321
  E-mail: sszoradi@steiner-verlag.de
Rights & Permissions: Constanze Steinecke
  Tel: (0711) 2582-310 *E-mail:* csteinecke@
  steiner-verlag.de
Founded: 1949
Membership(s): Boersenverein des Deutschen
  Buchhandels.
Subjects: African American Studies, Archaeol-
  ogy, Art, Asian Studies, Developing Countries,
  Earth Sciences, Education, Foreign Countries,
  Geography, Geology, History, Language Arts,
  Linguistics, Law, Music, Dance, Philosophy,
  Religion - Buddhist, Religion - Hindu, Religion
  - Islamic, Classical Studies, History of Science
ISBN Prefix(es): 978-3-515
Number of titles published annually: 180 Print
Total Titles: 4,000 Print; 1 CD-ROM
Associate Companies: Behr's Verlag; Deutscher
  Apotheker Verlag; S Hirzel Verlag GmbH &
  Co *E-mail:* service@hirzel.de *Web Site:* www.
  hirzel.de; Medpharm Polska; Medpharm
  Scientific Publishers; Verlag Oesterre-
  ich; Wissenschaftliche Verlagsgesellschaft
  mbH *E-mail:* service@wissenschaftliche-
  verlagsgesellschaft.de *Web Site:* www.
  wissenschaftliche-verlagsgesellschaft.de
Distribution Center: Brockhaus/Kommissions-
  geschaeft GmbH, Kreidlerstr 9, 70806 Kornwestheim *Tel:* (07154) 1327-0 *Fax:* (07154)
  132713 *E-mail:* bestell@brocom.de

Rudolf Steiner Ausgaben eK
Formerly Archiati Verlag eK

Burghaldenweg 37, 75378 Bad Liebenzell
Tel: (07052) 935284 *Fax:* (07052) 934809
E-mail: anfrage@rudolfsteinerausgaben.com
Web Site: www.rudolfsteinerausgaben.com
Key Personnel
Publisher: Rudolf Steiner
Contact: Monika Grimm
Subjects: Biography, Memoirs, Philosophy, Self-
  Help
ISBN Prefix(es): 978-3-937078; 978-3-938650;
  978-3-86772
Distribution Center: Sigloch Distribution GmbH
  & Co KG, Am Buchberg 8, 74572 Blaufelden
  Tel: (07953) 7189 016 *Fax:* (07953) 7189
  081 *E-mail:* rudolfsteiner@sigloch.de *Web
  Site:* www.sigloch.de

J F Steinkopf Verlag GmbH+
Gartenstr 20, 24103 Kiel
Mailing Address: Postfach 3169, 24030 Kiel
Tel: (0431) 55779-206; (0431) 55779-285 (orders)
  Fax: (0431) 55779-292
E-mail: vertrieb@steinkopf-verlag.de
Web Site: www.evangelisches-medienwerk.
  de/verlage; www.kirchenshop-online.de
Key Personnel
Mng Dir: Bodo Elsner *Tel:* (0431) 55779-260
  E-mail: bodo.elsner@epv-nord.de
Head, Publishing: Johannes Keussen *Tel:* (0431)
  55779-203 *E-mail:* keussen@epv-nord.de
Founded: 1792
Subjects: Art, Biblical Studies, History, How-to,
  Literature, Literary Criticism, Essays, Religion
  - Other, Social Sciences, Sociology
ISBN Prefix(es): 978-3-7984
Parent Company: Evangelischer Presseverband
  Nord eV
Associate Companies: Lutherische Verlagsge-
  sellschaft mbH; Friedrich Wittig Verlag GmbH

edition steinrich
Arndtstr 34, 10965 Berlin
Tel: (030) 600 311 20 *Fax:* (030) 600 311 22
E-mail: info@edition-steinrich.de
Web Site: www.edition-steinrich.de
Key Personnel
Management: Ursula Richard
Marketing: Traudel Reiss
Founded: 2009
Subjects: Art, Inspirational, Spirituality, Poetry,
  Religion - Buddhist, Self-Help
ISBN Prefix(es): 978-3-942085

Steintor Verlag GmbH
Bahnhofstr 6a, 59519 Moehnesee
Tel: (02924) 391; (02924) 2097 *Fax:* (0294)
  878699
E-mail: klaus.juedes@t-online.de
Web Site: www.kunsthaus-moehnesee.de
Key Personnel
Owner: Rudolf Juedes
Founded: 1969
Subjects: Art
ISBN Prefix(es): 978-3-9801506
Parent Company: Kunsthaus Moehnesee
Bookshop(s): Gallerie Meiborssen, 37647 Mei-
  borssen *Tel:* (05535) 8851

Verlag Stendel+
Mozartstr 42, 70734 Fellbach
Mailing Address: Postfach 1713, 71307 Waiblin-
  gen
Tel: (0711) 57700888 *Fax:* (0711) 57700888
E-mail: info@stendel-verlag.de; verlagstendel@
  aol.com
Web Site: www.stendel-verlag.de
Key Personnel
Manager: Dagmar Kuebler *E-mail:* dagmar.
  stendel-kuebler@stendel-verlag.de
Editor: Roland Kuebler *E-mail:* roland-kuebler@
  stendel-verlag.de
Founded: 1987

Subjects: Fiction, Literature, Literary Criticism, Essays, Psychology, Psychiatry, Science Fiction, Fantasy
ISBN Prefix(es): 978-3-926789

Edition Sternenprinz, *imprint of* Hans-Nietsch-Verlag OHG

Sternenstaub-Verlag
Am Birkicht 12a, 81827 Munich
Tel: (089) 430 15 15 *Fax:* (089) 431 13 59
Web Site: www.sternenstaub-verlag.de
Key Personnel
Owner: Gabriele Schab *E-mail:* schab@ sternenstaub-verlag.de

Steyler Verlag+
Arnold-Janssen-Str 28, 53757 Sankt Augustin
Tel: (02241) 92 48 16 *Fax:* (02241) 92 48 17
E-mail: verlag@steyler.de
Web Site: www.steyler.eu/svd/de/median/steyler-verlag.php
Key Personnel
Press: Tamara Haeussler-Eisenmann
Founded: 1927
Subjects: Anthropology, Biography, Memoirs, Developing Countries, Language Arts, Linguistics, Religion - Catholic, Science (General)
ISBN Prefix(es): 978-3-87787; 978-3-8050
Parent Company: Steyler Missionare eV, Bahnhofstr 9, 41334 Nettetal
Bookshop(s): Steyler Buchhandlung Sankt Wendel, Missionshausstr 50, 66606 Sankt Wendel *Tel:* (06851) 805-320 *Fax:* (06851) 805-321

Stiebner Verlag GmbH+
Nymphenburger Str 86, 80636 Munich
Tel: (089) 1257 414 *Fax:* (089) 1216 2282
E-mail: verlag@stiebner.com
Web Site: www.stiebner.com
Key Personnel
Mng Dir: Hans-Peter Copony; Dr Joerg D Stiebner
Sales Manager: Pierre Sick
Founded: 1998
Subjects: Architecture & Interior Design, Art, Fashion, Film, Video, Sports, Athletics, Animation, Cartoon, Graphic Design
ISBN Prefix(es): 978-3-7679; 978-3-8307
Imprints: Copress Sport Verlag
Foreign Rep(s): Verlagsvertretung Hoeller (Michael Hoeller & Mario Seiler) (Austria, South Tyrol, Italy); Martin Schnetzer (Switzerland)
Distribution Center: Brockhaus/Commission, Kreidlerstr 9, 70806 Kornwestheim *Tel:* (07154) 13 27-0 *Fax:* (07154) 13 27-13 *E-mail:* stiebner@brocom.de
Hillstein Verlag, Postfach 1, 5017 Salzburg, Austria *Tel:* (0662) 82 7700-0 *Fax:* (0662) 82 7700-33 *E-mail:* info@hillstein.at
Schweizer Buchzentrum, Industrie Ost, 4601 Olten, Switzerland *Tel:* (062) 2 09 25 25 *Fax:* (062) 2 09 26 27

Stiefel Eurocart GmbH+
Felix-Wankel-Ring 13a, 85101 Lenting
Tel: (08456) 92 41 00 *Fax:* (08456) 92 41 34
E-mail: eurocart@stiefel-online.de
Web Site: www.stiefel-online.de
Key Personnel
Mng Dir: Heinrich Stiefel
Press & Public Relations: Oliver Flade *Tel:* (08456) 92 43 47 *E-mail:* o.flade@stiefel-online.de
Founded: 1982
Membership(s): Didacta Verband.
Subjects: Biological Sciences, English as a Second Language, Environmental Studies, Geography, Geology, History, Language Arts, Linguistics, Mathematics, Religion - Other, French

ISBN Prefix(es): 978-3-929627
Parent Company: Stiefel Group Europe
Branch Office(s)
Stiefel Verlag, Annaburg 7, 8630 Mariazell, Austria *Tel:* (03882) 3065 *Fax:* (03882) 30654 *E-mail:* stiefel.verlag@aon.at
Stiefel Eurocart KG/SAS, Giottostr 8, 39100 Bozen, Italy *Tel:* (0471) 930191 *Fax:* (0471) 506991 *E-mail:* stiefel.eurocart@rolmail.net

Stiftung Buchkunst (Book Art Foundation)
Adickesallee 1, 60322 Frankfurt am Main
Tel: (069) 1525-1800 *Fax:* (069) 1525-1805
E-mail: info@stiftung-buchkunst.de
Web Site: www.stiftung-buchkunst.de
Key Personnel
Chairman: Karin Schmidt-Friderichs
Mng Dir: Alexandra Sender
Founded: 1966
Subjects: Law, Civil Law
Branch Office(s)
Gerichtsweg 28, 04103 Leipzig *Tel:* (0341) 9954-210 *Fax:* (0341) 9954-211 *E-mail:* regina.ruesse@web.de

Stiftung Warentest
Luetzowplatz 11-13, 10785 Berlin
Mailing Address: Postfach 30 41 41, 10724 Berlin
Tel: (030) 26 31-0 *Fax:* (030) 26 31-27 27
E-mail: email@stiftung-warentest.de; pressestelle@stiftung-warentest.de
Web Site: www.test.de
Key Personnel
Chief Editor: Andreas Gebauer *E-mail:* a.gebauer@stiftung-warentest.de
Mng Editor: Lutz Wilde
Head, Press & Public Relations: Heike van Laak
Founded: 1964
Subjects: Finance, Gardening, Plants, Health, Nutrition, House & Home, Law
ISBN Prefix(es): 978-3-86851

Stollfuss Medien GmbH & Co KG+
Dechenstr 7, 53115 Bonn
Tel: (0228) 72 40 *Fax:* (0228) 72 49 11 81
E-mail: info@stollfuss.de
Web Site: www.stollfuss.de
Key Personnel
Mng Dir: Michael Stollfuss; Wolfgang Stollfuss
Founded: 1913
Specialize in tax & fiscal law.
Subjects: Accounting, Economics, Finance, Law, Public Administration
ISBN Prefix(es): 978-3-08
Distributor for Schriften des BMF und BMA
Warehouse: Justus-von Liebig Str 6, 53121 Bonn

Stories & Friends Verlag eK
Am alten Schulhaus 9, 74251 Lehrensteinsfeld
Tel: (07134) 912902 *Fax:* (07134) 912901
E-mail: info@stories-and-friends.com
Web Site: www.stories-and-friends.de
Key Personnel
Mng Dir: Karen Grol-Langner
Founded: 2006
Subjects: Cookery, Humor, Mathematics, Music, Dance, Wine & Spirits, Chocolate, Coffee, Herbs & Spices, Orient, Perfume
ISBN Prefix(es): 978-3-9811560; 978-3-942181

Straelener Manuskripte Verlag+
Venloer Str 45, 47638 Straelen
Mailing Address: Postfach 1324, 47630 Straelen
Tel: (02834) 6588 *Fax:* (02834) 6588
Web Site: www.straelener-manuskripte.de
Key Personnel
Manager: Dr Renate Birkenhauer *E-mail:* r.birkenhauer@straelener-manuskripte.de
Founded: 1984

Subjects: Literature, Literary Criticism, Essays, Poetry
ISBN Prefix(es): 978-3-89107
Number of titles published annually: 2 Print
Total Titles: 33 Print
Distribution Center: GVA Gemeinsame Verlagsauslieferung, Postfach 2021, 37010 Goettingen *Tel:* (0551) 48 71 77 *Fax:* (0551) 4 13 92 *E-mail:* info@gva-verlage.de *Web Site:* www.gva-verlage.de

Stroemfeld/Nexus, *imprint of* Stroemfeld Verlag GmbH

Stroemfeld/Roter Stern, *imprint of* Stroemfeld Verlag GmbH

Stroemfeld Verlag GmbH+
Holzhausenstr 4, 60322 Frankfurt
Tel: (069) 955 226-0; (069) 955 226-22 (sales) *Fax:* (069) 955 226-24
E-mail: info@stroemfeld.de
Web Site: www.stroemfeld.de
Key Personnel
Publisher & Mng Dir: Karl D Wolff *E-mail:* kdwolff@stroemfeld.de
Production & Editing: Doris Kern *E-mail:* doriskern@stroemfeld.de
Founded: 1981 (Nexus)
Subjects: Literature, Literary Criticism, Essays, Psychology, Psychiatry
ISBN Prefix(es): 978-3-87877; 978-3-86109 (Nexus); 978-3-86600
Parent Company: Stroemfeld Verlag AG, Altkircherstr 17, 4054 Basel, Switzerland
Imprints: Stroemfeld/Nexus; Stroemfeld/Roter Stern
Orders to: Sova, Philipp Reis Str 17, 63477 Maintal

Stuenings Medien GmbH
Diessemer Bruch 167, 47805 Krefeld
Mailing Address: Postfach 10 21 55, 47721 Krefeld
Tel: (02151) 51 00-0 *Fax:* (02151) 51 00-105
E-mail: medien@stuenings.de
Web Site: www.stuenings.de
Key Personnel
Mng Dir: Petra Neumann; Volker Neumann
Publishing Dir: Joerg Montag *Tel:* (02151) 51 00-175 *E-mail:* joerg.montag@stuenings.de
Subjects: Architecture & Interior Design, Business, Regional Interests, Transportation, Travel & Tourism, Construction
ISBN Prefix(es): 978-3-9811654

Leitfadenverlag Sudholt eK+
Grondlegasse 8, 82541 Muensing
Tel: (08177) 204725 *Fax:* (08177) 204726
E-mail: info@leitfadenverlag.de
Web Site: www.leitfadenverlag.de
Key Personnel
Owner: Joseph Thoma
Founded: 1957
Subjects: Business, Economics, Law
ISBN Prefix(es): 978-3-543
Associate Companies: Leitfadenverlag Gesellschaft mbH, Innsbruck, Austria

Sueddeutsche Verlagsgesellschaft mbH+
Nicolaus-Otto-Str 14, 89079 Ulm
Mailing Address: Postfach 3660, 89026 Ulm
Tel: (0731) 94 57-0 *Fax:* (0731) 94 57-224
E-mail: info@suedvg.de
Web Site: www.suedvg.de
Key Personnel
Publisher: Angelika Grundgeir *Tel:* (0731) 94 57-202
Mng Dir: Ulrich Peters
Manager: Udo Vogt *Tel:* (0731) 94 57-200

Production Manager: Manfred Liebler *Tel:* (0731) 94 57-222

Sales Manager: Lothar Inger *Tel:* (0731) 94 57-219

Editorial: Gudrun von Wasielewski *Tel:* (0731) 94 57-201

Founded: 1898

Subjects: Art, History, Nonfiction (General), Regional Interests, Religion - Catholic

ISBN Prefix(es): 978-3-88294; 978-3-920921

Parent Company: Schwabenverlag AG, Senefelderstr 12, 73760 Ostfildern

SuedOst Verlag

Imprint of Battenberg Gietl Verlag GmbH

Pfaelzer Str 11, 93128 Regenstauf

Mailing Address: Postfach 166, 93122 Regenstauf

Tel: (09402) 93 37-0 *Fax:* (09402) 93 37-24

E-mail: info@gietl-verlag.de

Web Site: www.suedost-verlag.de

Key Personnel

Mng Dir & Publishing Dir: Josef Roidl

Press & Public Relations: Verena Roesch *Tel:* (09402) 93 37-20 *E-mail:* verena.roesch@gietl-verlag.de

Sales & Marketing: Andrea Krampfl *Tel:* (09402) 93 37-11 *E-mail:* andrea.krampfl@gietl-verlag.de

Subjects: Literature, Literary Criticism, Essays, Regional Literature

ISBN Prefix(es): 978-3-89682

SuedOst-Verlag, *imprint of* Battenberg Gietl Verlag GmbH

Suedverlag GmbH+

Schuetzenstr 24, 78462 Konstanz

Mailing Address: Postfach 10 20 51, 78420 Konstanz

Tel: (07531) 90 53-0 *Fax:* (07531) 90 53-98

E-mail: willkommen@suedverlag.de; willkommen@uvk.de

Web Site: www.suedverlag.de

Key Personnel

Mng Dir: Walter Engstle *E-mail:* walter.engstle@suedverlag.de; Dr Brigitte Weyl *E-mail:* brigitte.weyl@uvk.de

Licenses: Ines Ende *Tel:* (07531) 90 53-14 *E-mail:* ines.ende@uvk.de

Founded: 1945

Subjects: Biography, Memoirs, Humor, Regional Interests

ISBN Prefix(es): 978-3-87800

Associate Companies: UVK Verlagsgesellschaft mbH

Foreign Rep(s): Thomas Bielohaubek (North Austria, South Austria); Erich Neuhold (Eastern Austria); Martin Schnetzer (Switzerland); Guenther Staudinger (South Tyrol, Italy, Western Austria)

Distribution Center: VVA-Vereinigte Verlagsauslieferung, An der Autobahn, 33310 Guetersloh *Tel:* (05241) 80 40 39 6 *Fax:* (05241) 80 66 95 9 *E-mail:* vva-d6f3.bestellungen@bertelsmann.de

OEBZ-Buchauslieferung GmbH, Industriezentrum Noe-Sued, Str I/Objekt 34, 2355 Wiener Neudorf, Austria *Tel:* (02236) 6 35 35 290 *Fax:* (02236) 6 35 35 243

Schweizer Buchzentrum Haegendorf, Postfach 522, 4601 Olten, Switzerland *Tel:* (062) 20 92 525 *Fax:* (062) 20 92 627

Orders to: Lappan Verlag GmbH, Wuerzburger Str 14, 26121 Oldenburg *Tel:* (0441) 9 80 66 0 *Fax:* (0441) 9 80 66 22; (0441) 9 80 66 34

Web Site: www.lappan.de

Suedwest, *imprint of* Verlagsgruppe Random House Bertelsmann

Suedwest Verlag GmbH & Co KG+

Imprint of Verlagsgruppe Random House Bertelsmann

Bayerstr 71-73, 80335 Munich

Tel: (089) 4136-0 *Toll Free Tel:* 0800 500 33 22 *Fax:* (089) 4136-3333

E-mail: kundenservice@randomhouse.de

Web Site: www.suedwest-verlag.de; www.randomhouse.de/suedwest

Key Personnel

Press & Public Relations: Claudia Limmer *Tel:* (089) 4136-3130 *Fax:* (089) 4136-3507 *E-mail:* claudia.limmer@randomhouse.de

Founded: 1949

Subjects: Cookery, Health, Nutrition, Nonfiction (General), Sports, Athletics, Travel & Tourism, Fitness, Mind, Body & Spirit, Recreation

Suhrkamp Verlag GmbH & Co KG+

Pappelalle 78-79, 10437 Berlin

Tel: (030) 740744-0 *Fax:* (030) 740744-199

E-mail: geschaeftsleitung@suhrkamp.de; sales@suhrkamp.de

Web Site: www.suhrkamp.de

Key Personnel

Publisher: Ulla Unseld-Berkewicz

Vice President: Dr Thomas Sparr

Mng Dir: Dr Jonathan Landgrebe

Dir, Rights & Foreign Rights Dept: Nora Mercurio

Foreign Rights: Petra Hardt *Tel:* (030) 740744-230 *E-mail:* hardt@suhrkamp.de

Press: Dr Tanja Postpischil *Tel:* (030) 740744-290 *E-mail:* postpischil@suhrkamp.de

Founded: 1950

Subjects: Biography, Memoirs, Drama, Theater, Fiction, Literature, Literary Criticism, Essays, Philosophy, Poetry, Psychology, Psychiatry, Science (General), Social Sciences, Sociology

ISBN Prefix(es): 978-3-518

Subsidiaries: Deutscher Klassiker Verlag GmbH; Insel Verlag Anton Kippernberg GmbH & Co KG; Juedischer Verlag GmbH; Verlag der Weltreligionen

Sujet Verlag UG

Breitenweg 57, 28195 Bremen

Tel: (0421) 703737

E-mail: kontakt@sujet-verlag.de

Web Site: www.sujet-verlag.de

Key Personnel

Mng Dir: Madjid Mohit

Editing & Public Relations: Ulrike Gies

Founded: 1996

Subjects: Fiction, Nonfiction (General), Poetry

ISBN Prefix(es): 978-3-933995; 978-3-944201

Sulamith Wulfing Edition, *imprint of* Aquamarin Verlag GmbH

Sulamith Wulfing Verlag, *imprint of* Aquamarin Verlag GmbH

Swiridoff Verlag GmbH & Co KG

Subsidiary of Wuerth Group

Goethestr 14, 74653 Kuenzelsau

Tel: (07940) 15-1762 *Fax:* (07940) 15-4610

E-mail: info@swiridoff.de

Web Site: www.swiridoff.de

Key Personnel

Publisher: Ludger Kruthoff

Management: C Sylvia Weber

Founded: 1999

Subjects: Economics, Regional Interests, Social Sciences, Sociology, Technology

ISBN Prefix(es): 978-3-934350; 978-3-89929

SYBEX+

Boschstr 12, 69469 Weinheim

Tel: (06201) 606-400 *Fax:* (06201) 606-184; (06201) 606-100 (sales); (06201) 606-615 (press & marketing)

E-mail: service@wiley-vch.de

Web Site: www.wiley-vch.de/books/info/sybex

Key Personnel

Marketing: Friedhelm Linke *Tel:* (06201) 606-247 *E-mail:* flinke@wiley.com; Kal Zoellig *Tel:* (06201) 606-486 *E-mail:* kzoellig@wiley.com

Sales: Anette Martine *Tel:* (06201) 606-407 *E-mail:* amartine@wiley.com; Sibylle Martine *Tel:* (06201) 606-405 *E-mail:* smartine@wiley.com; Claudia Mittnacht *Tel:* (06201) 606-406 *E-mail:* cmittnacht@wiley.com

Press: Sabine Dabergott *Tel:* (06201) 606-294 *E-mail:* presse@wiley.com

Founded: 1981

Subjects: Computer Science

ISBN Prefix(es): 978-3-88745; 978-3-8155; 978-3-527; 978-1-118

Parent Company: Wiley-VCH Verlag

Ultimate Parent Company: John Wiley & Sons Inc

Foreign Rep(s): Michael Beranek (Western Austria); Freitag Verlagsvertretungen (Urs Freitag) (Switzerland); Guenther Lintschinger (Eastern Austria)

Synthesis Verlag+

Graffweg 53, 45276 Essen

Mailing Address: Postfach 14 32 06, 45262 Essen

Tel: (0201) 510188 *Fax:* (0201) 511049

E-mail: info@synthesis-verlag.com; presse.synthesis@online.ms

Web Site: www.synthesis-verlag.com; www.synthesisverlag.de

Key Personnel

Publisher: Siegmar Gerken, PhD

Founded: 1978

Subjects: Alternative, Health, Nutrition, Inspirational, Spirituality, Philosophy, Science (General), Self-Help, Alternative Medicine, Healing, Holistic Thinking, Therapy

ISBN Prefix(es): 978-3-922026; 978-3-936503

Orders to: VSB-Verlagsservice Braunschweig GmbH, Georg-Westermann-Allee 66, 38104 Braunschweig *Tel:* (0531) 70 80 *Fax:* (0531) 70 89 62 *E-mail:* info@vsb-service.de *Web Site:* www.vsb-service.de

systemed GmbH

Kastanienstr 10, 44534 Luenen

Tel: (02306) 6 39 34 *Fax:* (02306) 6 14 60

E-mail: faltin@systemed.de; info@systemed.de

Web Site: www.systemed.de

Key Personnel

Mng Dir: Sabine Schmieder

Subjects: Cookery, Health, Nutrition, Medicine, Nursing, Dentistry, Science (General), Sports, Athletics, Allergy, Cancer, Diabetes, Homeopathy, Stress Management, Yoga

ISBN Prefix(es): 978-3-927372

Foreign Rep(s): Christian Hirtzy (Austria); Ernst Sonntag (Austria); Alfred Trux (Austria)

Tabaldi Verlag

Formerly Verlag Dr Ellen Ismail-Schmidt

Archternkamp 8, 21227 Bendestorf

Tel: (04183) 6936 *Fax:* (04183) 6936

E-mail: tabaldi@ellen-ismail.de

Web Site: www.ellen-ismail.de

Key Personnel

Owner & Publisher: Dr Ellen Ismail-Schmidt

Subjects: Regional Interests, Social Sciences, Sociology, Women's Studies, Sudanese Women

ISBN Prefix(es): 978-3-9801259

Tag & Nacht, *imprint of* Verlagsgruppe Random House Bertelsmann

Talheimer Verlag Medienberatung und Consulting GmbH
Rietsweg 2, 72116 Moessingen-Talheim
Tel: (07473) 2701111 *Fax:* (07473) 24166
Web Site: www.talheimer.de
Key Personnel
Mng Dir: Irene Scherer *E-mail:* scherer@talheimer.de; Welf Schroeter
E-mail: schroeter@talheimer.de
Subjects: Biography, Memoirs, Education, Philosophy, Technology, Theology, Women's Studies, Employment
ISBN Prefix(es): 978-3-89376

TALISA Kinderbuch-Verlag
Konrad-Adenauer-Str 74, 30853 Langenhagen
Tel: (0511) 89 79 768 *Fax:* (0511) 89 79 769
E-mail: info@talisa-verlag.de
Web Site: www.talisa-verlag.de
Key Personnel
Chief Executive Officer: Aylin Keller
Founded: 2005
ISBN Prefix(es): 978-3-939619

TAOASIS Verlag+
Dahlbrede 3, 32758 Detmold
Tel: (05321) 45 989 0 *Fax:* (05321) 45 989 22
E-mail: info@taoasis.de
Web Site: www.taoasis.com
Key Personnel
Chief Executive Officer & Mng Dir: Axel Meyer
Marketing: Ira Hollmann *E-mail:* ih@taoasis.de
Subjects: Cookery, Health, Nutrition
ISBN Prefix(es): 978-3-926014

TASCHEN GmbH
Hohenzollernring 53, 50672 Cologne
Tel: (0221) 20 180-0 *Fax:* (0221) 20180 800
E-mail: contact@taschen.com
Web Site: www.taschen.com
Key Personnel
Mng Dir: Benedikt Taschen
Founded: 1980
Subjects: Architecture & Interior Design, Art, Erotica, Photography
ISBN Prefix(es): 978-3-8228
Subsidiaries: TASCHEN America; TASCHEN Deutschland; TASCHEN Espana; TASCHEN France; TASCHEN Hong Kong; TASCHEN UK
Bookshop(s): Hohenzollernring 28, 50672 Cologne *Tel:* (0221) 2573304 *E-mail:* store-koeln@taschen.com; Bleichenbruecke 1-7, 20354 Hamburg *Tel:* (040) 80793302 *Fax:* (040) 80793303 *E-mail:* store-hamburg@taschen.com; Grand Sablon/Grote Zavel, Rue Lebeaustr 18, 1000 Brussels, Belgium *Tel:* (02) 513 80 23 *E-mail:* store-brussels@taschen.com; Ostergade 2A, 1100 Copenhagen, Denmark *Tel:* 33363437 *Fax:* 33365837 *E-mail:* store-copenhagen@taschen.com; 2 rue de Buci, 75006 Paris, France *Tel:* 01 40 51 79 22 *E-mail:* store-paris@taschen.com; P C Hooftstr 44, 1071 BZ Amsterdam, Netherlands *Tel:* (020) 6627820 *Fax:* (020) 6701367 *E-mail:* store-amsterdam@taschen.com; 12 Duke of York Sq, London SW3 4LY, United Kingdom *Tel:* (020) 7881 0795 *Fax:* (020) 7881 0795 *E-mail:* store-london@taschen.com; 354 N Beverly Dr, Beverly Hills, CA 90210, United States *Tel:* 310-274-4300 *Fax:* 310-274-4040 *E-mail:* store-beverly@taschen.com; Farmers Market, 6333 W Third St, CT-10, Los Angeles, CA 90036, United States *Tel:* 323-931-1168 *Fax:* 323-931-1149 *E-mail:* store-hollywood@taschen.com; 1111 Lincoln Rd, Miami Beach, FL 33139, United States *Tel:* 305-538-6185 *Fax:* 305-538-6186 *E-mail:* store-miami@taschen.com; 107 Greene St, New York, NY 10012, United States *Tel:* 212-226-2212 *Fax:* 212-226-2218 *E-mail:* store-ny@taschen.com

Hochschule fuer Technik Wirtschaft und Kultur Leipzig (College of Engineering, Economics & Culture in Leipzig)
Karl-Liebknecht-Str 132, 04277 Leipzig
Mailing Address: Postfach 301166, 04251 Leipzig
Tel: (0341) 3076-6624 *Fax:* (0341) 3076-6456
E-mail: marketing@htwk-leipzig.de
Web Site: www.htwk-leipzig.de/de/presse/publikationen
Key Personnel
Marketing: Stefan Schmeisser *E-mail:* stefan.schmeisser@htwk-leipzig.de
Founded: 1992
Subjects: Economics, Science (General), Technology

Tecklenborg Verlag
Siemensstr 4, 48565 Steinfurt
Tel: (02552) 920-02 *Fax:* (02552) 920-160
E-mail: info@tecklenborg-verlag.de
Web Site: www.tecklenborg-verlag.de
Key Personnel
Publishing Dir: Hubert Tecklenborg; Stefanie Tecklenborg *E-mail:* tecklenborg@tecklenborg-verlag.de
Subjects: Animals, Pets, Cookery, Photography, Regional Interests, Travel & Tourism
ISBN Prefix(es): 978-3-924044; 978-3-934427; 978-3-939172

Tectum Wissenschaftsverlag Marburg
Lahn Center, Biegenstr 4, 35037 Marburg
Tel: (06421) 481523 *Fax:* (06421) 43 470
E-mail: email@tectum-verlag.de
Web Site: www.tectum-verlag.de
Key Personnel
Publishing Dir & Editor: Dr Heinz-Werner Kubitza *E-mail:* heinz-werner-kubitza@tectum-verlag.de
Sales Manager, USA: Deborah Levine
Editor: Dr Guido Gerstgarbe *E-mail:* guido-gerstgarbe@tectum-verlag.de; Dr Thomas Sukopp *E-mail:* thomas-sukopp@tectum-verlag.de
Press & Public Relations: Christina Sieg *E-mail:* christina-sieg@tectum-verlag.de
Sales & Distribution: Stefanie Hoyer *E-mail:* stefanie-hoyer@tectum-verlag.de
Founded: 1992
Scientific books with a focus on humanities, social sciences & economics.
Subjects: Architecture & Interior Design, Drama, Theater, Economics, Education, English as a Second Language, History, Human Relations, Language Arts, Linguistics, Law, Medicine, Nursing, Dentistry, Music, Dance, Psychology, Psychiatry, Religion - Other, Romance, Social Sciences, Sociology, Sports, Athletics, Technology, Ethnology, Humanities, Musicology, Nature, Sports Science
ISBN Prefix(es): 978-3-8288; 978-3-89608; 978-3-929019

Otto Teich Verlag+
Hilpertstr 9, 64295 Darmstadt
Mailing Address: Postfach 200 144, 64300 Darmstadt
Tel: (06151) 824120 *Fax:* (06151) 895656
E-mail: mail@teich-verlag.de
Web Site: www.teich-verlag.de
Key Personnel
Mng Dir & International Rights: Christine Otto
Founded: 1888
Specialize in humorous performances.
Subjects: Drama, Theater, Humor
ISBN Prefix(es): 978-3-8069
Associate Companies: Bergwald Verlag, Hilpertstr 9, 64295 Darmstadt; Eduard Bloch Verlag, Hilpertstr 9, 64295 Darmstadt
Imprints: Baerenreiter-Spieltexte

Edition Temmen+
Hohenlohestr 21, 28209 Bremen
Tel: (0421) 34 843-0 *Fax:* (0421) 34 80 94
E-mail: info@edition-temmen.de
Web Site: www.edition-temmen.de
Key Personnel
Owner & Dir: Horst Temmen
Founded: 1983
Subjects: Government, Political Science, History, Literature, Literary Criticism, Essays, Maritime, Military Science, Nonfiction (General), Social Sciences, Sociology, Travel & Tourism
ISBN Prefix(es): 978-3-926958; 978-3-86108; 978-3-8378
Number of titles published annually: 70 Print; 5 CD-ROM
Total Titles: 1,100 Print
Distribution Center: Mohr Morawa Buchvertrieb GmbH, Sulzengasse 2, 1230 Vienna, Austria *Tel:* (01) 680 14-0 *Fax:* (01) 688 71 30 *E-mail:* momo@mohrmorawa.at *Web Site:* www.mohrmorawa.at

teNeues Verlag GmbH + Co KG+
Am Selder 37, 47906 Kempen
Tel: (02152) 916-0 *Fax:* (02152) 916-111
E-mail: verlag@teneues.de
Web Site: www.teneues.com
Key Personnel
Publisher & Mng Dir: Hendrik teNeues; Sebastian teNeues
Founded: 1958
International publishing group with offices in Duesseldorf, New York, London, Paris & Madrid; worldwide distribution in over 60 countries.
Calendars, art merchandise & Internet reference guides.
Subjects: Architecture & Interior Design, Art, Computers, Fashion, Photography, Travel & Tourism
ISBN Prefix(es): 978-3-8238; 978-3-570; 978-3-87580; 978-3-8327; 978-3-89865; 978-3-929278; 978-1-933427; 978-1-60160; 978-1-62325
Total Titles: 20 E-Book
Parent Company: teNeues Publishing Group
Associate Companies: teNeues Digital Media, Kohlfurter Str 41-43, 10999 Berlin *Tel:* (030) 70077650 *E-mail:* mail@tndm.de *Web Site:* www.teneues-dm.com; teNeues France Sarl, 39 rue du Bill, 18250 Henrichemont, France *Tel:* 02 48 26 93 48 *Fax:* 01 70 72 34 82 *E-mail:* fjouannel@teneues.fr; teNeues Publishing UK Ltd, 21 Marlowe Court, Lymer Ave, London SE19 1LP, United Kingdom, Sales Manager: Bridget Clark *Tel:* (020) 8670 7522 *Fax:* (020) 8670 7523 *E-mail:* bclark@teneues.co.uk (calendars & stationery)
U.S. Office(s): teNeues Publishing Company, 7 W 18 St, New York, NY 10010, United States *Tel:* 212-627-9090 *Fax:* 212-627-9511 *E-mail:* tnp@teneues-usa.com

Teo Ferrer de Mesquita Verlag-Vertrieb-Versandbuchhandlung
Grosse Seestr 47, 60486 Frankfurt am Main
Mailing Address: Postfach 10 08 39, 60008 Frankfurt am Main
Tel: (069) 282647 *Fax:* (069) 287363
E-mail: info@tfmonline.de
Web Site: www.tfmonline.de
Founded: 1980
Literature & music for Portuguese speaking countries.
Subjects: Architecture & Interior Design, Astrology, Occult, Biological Sciences, Criminology, Erotica, Film, Video, Geography, Geology, Government, Political Science, Humor, Philosophy, Poetry, Psychology, Psychiatry, Science Fiction, Fantasy, Sports, Athletics, Culture, Ethnology, Esoteric, Grammar, Soccer
ISBN Prefix(es): 978-3-925203

Terzio, *imprint of* CARLSEN Verlag GmbH

Terzio
Imprint of CARLSEN Verlag GmbH
Voelckersstr 14-20, 22765 Hamburg
Mailing Address: Postfach 50 03 80, 22703 Hamburg
Tel: (040) 39 804-0 *Fax:* (040) 39 804-390; (040) 39 804-398 (sales)
E-mail: info@carlsen.de
Web Site: www.carlsen.de/terzio
Key Personnel
Chief Financial Officer: Iris Bellinghausen
Mng Dir: Ralph Moellers
Founded: 1997
Subjects: Fiction, History, Humor, Mysteries, Suspense, Nonfiction (General), Romance, Science Fiction, Fantasy
ISBN Prefix(es): 978-3-551
Ultimate Parent Company: Bonnier-Gruppe
Distribution Center: Distribook, Schockenriedstr 39, 70565 Stuttgart *Toll Free Tel:* 0800 66 111 99 *Fax:* (0711) 78 99 10 10 *E-mail:* service@distribook.de (Germany & Switzerland)
Dr Franz Hain Verlagsauslieferungen GmbH, Dr-Otto-Neurath-Gasse 5, 1220 Vienna, Austria, Contact: Brigitte Perrotta *Tel:* (01) 282 65 65 77 *Fax:* (01) 282 52 82 *E-mail:* bestell@hain.at

Tessloff Verlag Ragnar Tessloff GmbH & Co KG
Burgschmietstr 2-4, 90419 Nuremberg
Tel: (0911) 399 06-0 *Fax:* (0911) 399 06-28
E-mail: info@tessloff.com
Web Site: www.tessloff.com
Key Personnel
General Manager: Dr Thomas Seng
Manager: Anja Saemann-Ischenko; Bernd Seliger; Eberhard Tackenberg
Foreign Rights Manager: Claudia Hartwig *E-mail:* hartwig@tessloff.com
Press & Public Relations: Nicole Hummel *E-mail:* hummel@tessloff.de
Founded: 1956
Subjects: Nonfiction (General)
ISBN Prefix(es): 978-3-7886

Tetra Verlag GmbH+
Am Markt 5, 16727 Berlin-Velten
Tel: (03304) 20 22-0 *Fax:* (03304) 20 22-20
E-mail: info@tetra-verlag.de
Web Site: www.tetra-verlag.de
Key Personnel
Owner: Dr Hans-Joachim Herrmann
Founded: 1972
Membership(s): Boersenverein des Deutsche Buchhandels.
Subjects: Animals, Pets, Maritime, Popular Scientific & Lobbyist Literature
ISBN Prefix(es): 978-3-89745
Number of titles published annually: 8 Print
Total Titles: 93 Print

Teubner Edition, *imprint of* Graefe und Unzer Verlag GmbH

edition text & kritik im Richard Boorberg Verlag GmbH & Co KG+
Levelingstr 6a, 81673 Munich
Mailing Address: Postfach 800529, 81605 Munich
Tel: (089) 43 60 00 12 *Fax:* (089) 43 60 00 19
E-mail: info@etk-muenchen.de
Web Site: www.etk-muenchen.de
Key Personnel
Mng Dir: Dr Berndt Oesterhelt; Markus Ott
International Rights: Melanie Heusel *E-mail:* m.heusel@etk-muenchen.de
Sales: Nadine Henoeckl *Tel:* (089) 436 000 15 *Fax:* (089) 436 15 45 *E-mail:* n.henoeckl@etk-muenchen.de

Founded: 1975
Subjects: Film, Video, Literature, Literary Criticism, Essays, Music, Dance
ISBN Prefix(es): 978-3-921402; 978-3-88377
Divisions: Auslieferung von Verlag der Autoren
Distribution Center: AVA Verlagsauslieferung AG, Centralweg 16, 8910 Affoltern am Albis, Switzerland, Contact: Beat Eberle
Tel: (044) 762 4260 *Fax:* (044) 762 4210
E-mail: avainfo@ava.ch

Theater Verlag, *imprint of* Rowohlt Verlag GmbH

Konrad Theiss Verlag, *imprint of* WBG (Wissenschaftliche Buchgesellschaft)

Konrad Theiss Verlag+
Imprint of WBG (Wissenschaftliche Buchgesellschaft)
Hindenburgstr 40, 64295 Darmstadt
Tel: (06151) 3308-292 *Fax:* (06151) 3308-208
E-mail: service@wbg-verlag.de; buchhandel@wbg-wissenverbindet.de
Web Site: www.wbg-verlag.de/theiss
Key Personnel
Sales & Advertising Manager: Wolfgang Hornstein *E-mail:* hornstein@wbg-wissenverbindet.de
Advertising: Gabriele Sauer *E-mail:* sauer@wbg-wissenverbindet.de
Press & Public Relations: Christina Herborg *E-mail:* herborg@wbg-wissenverbindet.de
Sales: Beate Gemuenden *E-mail:* gemuenden@wbg-wissenverbindet.de
Founded: 1997
Subjects: Archaeology, Art, Astronomy, Biography, Memoirs, Foreign Countries, Geography, Geology, History, Maritime, Military Science, Natural History, Nonfiction (General)
ISBN Prefix(es): 978-3-8062
Total Titles: 2 CD-ROM
Distributed by Wissenschiftliche Buchgesellschaft
Foreign Rights: Agenzia Servizi Editoriali (Guido Lagomarsino) (Italy); Collier International (Christopher Collier) (UK, USA); Ilustrata Iniciativas Empresariales SL (Angela Reynolds) (Portugal, Spain, Spanish Latin America); MAF Servicos Literarios (Peter-Michael Faustle) (Brazil); Marianne Schoenbach Literary Agency (Belgium, Netherlands); Wagner Literary Agency (Ulf Wagner) (Scandinavia); Eric Yang Agency (Jerome Lee) (Korea)
Distribution Center: Koch, Neff & Oetinger Verlagsauslieferung GmbH, Industriestr 23, 70565 Stuttgart *E-mail:* theiss@kno-va.de
Dr Franz Hain Verlagsauslieferungen GmbH, Dr-Otto-Neurath-Gasse 5, 1220 Vienna, Austria *Tel:* (01) 282-656577 *Fax:* (01) 282-5282 *E-mail:* bestell@hain.at
AVA Verlagsauslieferung AG, Centralweg 16, 8910 Affoltern am Albis, Switzerland
Tel: (044) 76242-50 *Fax:* (044) 76242-10
E-mail: verlagsservice@ava.ch

Thekla Verlag GbR
Bahnhofstr 83, 64823 Gross-Umstadt
Tel: (06078) 9679131 *Fax:* (06078) 967154
E-mail: info@thekla-verlag.de
Web Site: www.thekla-verlag.de
Key Personnel
Mng Partner: Heike Walther; Silke Wessner
ISBN Prefix(es): 978-3-945711

Theseus Verlag GmbH
Holstenring 2, 22763 Hamburg
Tel: (040) 67 95 09 00 *Fax:* (040) 28 46 30 00
Web Site: verlag.weltinnenraum.de
Key Personnel
Program Dir: Susanne Klein *E-mail:* susanne.klein@j-kamphausen.de

Subjects: Inspirational, Spirituality, Religion - Buddhist, Esoteric, Yoga
ISBN Prefix(es): 978-3-85936; 978-3-89620; 978-3-89901
Parent Company: J Kamphausen Mediengruppe, Goldbach 2, 33615 Bielefeld
Associate Companies: Aurum; Lebensbaum Verlag; Luechow; TAO Cinemathek
Foreign Rep(s): Claudia Gyr (Switzerland); Alfred Trux (Austria)
Distribution Center: Prolit Verlagsauslieferung GmbH, Siemensstr 16, 35463 Fernwald-Annerod, Representative: Gabriele Lemuth *Tel:* (0641) 94393-0 *Fax:* (0641) 94393-93 *E-mail:* service@prolit.de *Web Site:* www.prolit.de
AS Hoeller GmbH, Schrackgasse 11a, 8650 Kindberg, Austria *Tel:* (03865) 44880 *Fax:* (03865) 44880-77 *E-mail:* office@ashoeller.com
Engros Buchhandlung Dessauer, Raeffelstr 32, 8045 Zurich, Switzerland *Tel:* (044) 4 66 96 96 *Fax:* (044) 4 66 96 69 *E-mail:* dessauer@dessauer.ch

Thiekoetter Druck GmbH & Co KG
An der Kleimannbruecke 32, 48157 Muenster
Tel: (0251) 14 14 60 *Fax:* (0251) 14 14 666
E-mail: info@thiekoetter-druck.de
Web Site: www.thiekoetter-druck.de
Subjects: Art, History, Photography, Culture
ISBN Prefix(es): 978-3-939838

Druck-und Verlagshaus Thiele & Schwarz GmbH+
Werner-Heisenberg-Str 7, 34123 Kassel
Tel: (0561) 9 59 25-0 *Fax:* (0561) 9 59 25-68
E-mail: info@thiele-schwarz.de
Web Site: www.thiele-schwarz.de
Key Personnel
Mng Dir: Andreas Schwarz *Tel:* (0561) 9 59 25-11 *Fax:* (0561) 9 59 25-67 *E-mail:* andreas.schwarz@thiele-schwarz.de; Rolf Schwarz *Tel:* (0561) 9 59 25-13 *Fax:* (0561) 9 59 25-67 *E-mail:* schwarz@thiele-schwarz.de
Founded: 1879
ISBN Prefix(es): 978-3-87816
Associate Companies: Verlag Schule und Elternhaus
Bookshop(s): Buch und Musik Center Wilhelmshoehe, Wilhelmshoeheer Allee 256, 34119 Kassel; Buchhandlung Am Markt, Marktstr 10, 99310 Armkstadt

Thiele Verlag
Member of Thiele & Brandstaetter Verlag GmbH
Neureutherstr 31, 80798 Munich
Tel: (089) 27 370-997 *Fax:* (089) 27 370-998
E-mail: info@thiele-verlag.com
Web Site: www.thiele-verlag.com
Key Personnel
Publisher: Daniela Thiele; Johannes Thiele *E-mail:* j.thiele@thiele-verlag.com
Mng Dir: Heinrich Kratochwill *Tel:* (01) 512 15 43-253 *E-mail:* h.kratochwill@thiele-verlag.com
Subjects: Literature, Literary Criticism, Essays
ISBN Prefix(es): 978-3-85179

Georg Thieme Verlag KG+
Ruedigerstr 14, 70469 Stuttgart
Mailing Address: Postfach 30 11 20, 70451 Stuttgart
Tel: (0711) 8931-0; (0711) 8931-421 *Fax:* (0711) 8931-298; (0711) 8931 410 (sales)
E-mail: info@thieme.de; customerservice@thieme.de; kunden.service@thieme.de; permissions@thieme.com; tips@thieme.de (sales)
Web Site: www.thieme.de; www.thieme.com
Key Personnel
Publisher: Albrecht Hauff
Mng Dir: Dr Wolfgang Knueppe

Vice President, International Business Develop-
ment: Malik Lechelt *Tel:* (011) 2326 3522
E-mail: malik.lechelt@thieme.com
Vice President, International Marketing & Sales:
Cornelia Schulze *Tel:* (0711) 8931-162
E-mail: corneila.schulze@thieme.de
International Sales Manager: Alastair Paul
Tel: (0711) 8931-458 *E-mail:* alastair.paul@
thieme.de
International Rights Manager: Heike Schwaben-
than *Tel:* (0711) 8931-184 *Fax:* (0711) 8931-
143 *E-mail:* heike.schwabenthan@thieme.com
Marketing Manager, Journals & Events:
Christiane Sherman *Tel:* (0711) 8931-401
E-mail: christiane.sherman@thieme.de
Customer Service Manager: Birgid Haertel
Tel: (0711) 8931-421 *E-mail:* birgid.haertel@
thieme.de
Press & Public Relations: Anne-Katrin Doebler
Tel: (0711) 8931-115 *Fax:* (0711) 8931-566
E-mail: anne.doebler@thieme.de
Founded: 1886
Membership(s): Association of American Publish-
ers; Independent Book Publishers Association.
Subjects: Biological Sciences, Chemistry, Chemi-
cal Engineering, Health, Nutrition, Medicine,
Nursing, Dentistry, Psychology, Psychiatry,
Physiotherapy
ISBN Prefix(es): 978-3-13; 978-3-8304; 978-1-
58890
Number of titles published annually: 600 Print;
20 CD-ROM; 10 Audio
Total Titles: 5,100 Print; 100 CD-ROM; 50 Audio
Associate Companies: AnyCare GmbH,
Oswald-Hesse-Str 50, 70469 Stuttgart
E-mail: kontakt@anycare.de (disease man-
agement); Centrum fuer Reisemedizin GmbH
(CRM), Hansaallee 321, 40549 Duesseldorf
E-mail: info@crm.de (travel medicine)
Subsidiaries: MVS Medizinverlage Stuttgart
GmbH & Co KG
Divisions: Thieme South Asia Development Of-
fice
U.S. Office(s): Thieme Medical Publishers, 333
Seventh Ave, 5th floor, New York, NY 10001,
United States *Tel:* 212-760-0888 *Fax:* 212-947-
1112 *E-mail:* info@thieme.com
Distributor for AANS; Martin Dunitz
Foreign Rep(s): Academic Marketing Services
(Pty) Ltd (Michael Brightmore) (Botswana,
Namibia, South Africa); Aiko Hosoya (Japan);
IDC ASIA Inc (iGoup Korea) (Korea); Inter-
national Publishers Representatives (David N
Atiyah) (Middle East, North Africa); Jacek
Lewinson (Central Europe, Eastern Europe);
Lidel-Edicoes Tecnicas Lda (Angola, Cape
Verde, Guinea-Bissau, Mozambique, Por-
tugal, Sao Tome and Principe); Mare Nos-
trum Consultants (David Pickering) (Bel-
gium, France, Italy, Netherlands); Taiwan Pub-
lishers Marketing Services Ltd (George Liu)
(Taiwan); Thieme Medical & Scientific Pub-
lishers Pvt Ltd (Bangladesh, Bhutan, India,
Nepal, Pakistan, Sri Lanka); Thieme New York
(Caribbean, Central America, Mexico, South
America, USA); David Towle International
(Baltic States, Scandinavia); Trinidad Lopez
Gonzalez (Korea); Woodslane Pty Ltd (Derek
Hall) (Australia, New Zealand)
Bookshop(s): Frohberg Buchhandlung fuer Medi-
zin, Tempelhofer Weg 11-12, 10829 Berlin
Tel: (030) 8390030
Warehouse: Koch, Neff & Oetinger & Co,
Verlagsauslieferung, Industriestr 23, 70565
Stuttgart

Thienemann Verlag GmbH+
Blumenstr 36, 70182 Stuttgart
Tel: (0711) 21055-0 *Fax:* (0711) 21055 39
E-mail: info@thienemann.de; kontakt@
thienemann.de
Web Site: www.thienemann.de

Key Personnel
Mng Dir: Klaus Willberg
Foreign & Domestic Rights: Doris Keller-Riehm
Tel: (0711) 210 55-17 *Fax:* (0711) 210 55-38
E-mail: keller-riehm@thienemann.de
Marketing: Sandra Pollex *E-mail:* pollex@
thienemann.de
Press: Svea Unbehaun *Tel:* (0711) 210 55-29
E-mail: unbehaun@thienemann.de
Founded: 1849
Subjects: Fiction
ISBN Prefix(es): 978-3-522
Number of titles published annually: 100 Print
Total Titles: 800 Print
Imprints: Gabriel Verlag (religious children's
books); Planet Girl
Distribution Center: Koch, Neff & Oetinger
Verlagsauslieferung GmbH, Industriestr 23,
Stuttgart 70565

Verlag Theodor Thoben
Langestr 77-79, 49610 Quakenbrueck
Tel: (05431) 3486 *Fax:* (05431) 3584
E-mail: info@buecher-thoben.de
Web Site: www.buecher-thoben.de
Key Personnel
Publisher: Theodor Thoben
Founded: 1903
Subjects: Regional Interests
ISBN Prefix(es): 978-3-921176

Jan Thorbecke Verlag+
Senefelderstr 12, 73760 Ostfildern
Mailing Address: Postfach 4201, 73745 Ostfildern
Tel: (0711) 44 06-195; (0711) 44 06-0
Fax: (0711) 44 06-199
E-mail: online@thorbecke.de
Web Site: www.thorbecke.de
Key Personnel
Executive: Ulrich Peters
Board: Dr Clemens Stroppel
Publishing Dir: Juergen Weis *Tel:* (0711) 44 06-
191 *E-mail:* juergen.weis@thorbecke.de
Foreign Rights Manager: Claudia Stegmann
Tel: (0711) 44 06-148 *Fax:* (0711) 44 06-177
Advertising & Public Relations: Sabrina Reusch
Tel: (0711) 44 06-168
Sales: Sabine Warth *Tel:* (0711) 44 06-167
Fax: (0711) 44 06-177 *E-mail:* sabine.warth@
schwabenverlag.de
Founded: 1946
Subjects: Archaeology, Art, Foreign Countries,
History, Literature, Literary Criticism, Essays,
Regional Interests, Theology, Travel & Tourism
ISBN Prefix(es): 978-3-7995
Parent Company: Schwabenverlag AG
Foreign Rep(s): B+M Buch- und Medienvertriebs
AG (Markus & UTA Vonarburg) (Switzerland);
Verlagsvertretung KEG (Guenter Lorenzoni)
(Austria)
Distribution Center: Leipziger Kommissions- und
Grossbuchhandelsgesellschaft mbH (LKG),
An der Suedspitze 1-12, 04571 Roetha, Con-
tact: Robert Winkler *Tel:* (034206) 65 205
Fax: (034206) 65 1738 *E-mail:* rwinkler@lkg-
service.de *Web Site:* www.lkg-va.de
Mohr Morawa Buchvertrieb GmbH, Sulzen-
gasse 2, 1230 Vienna, Austria *Tel:* (01) 680
14-0 *Fax:* (01) 688 71 30 *E-mail:* momo@
mohrmorawa.at *Web Site:* www.mohrmorawa.at
Editions A et J Picard, 82, Rue Bonaparte, 75006
Paris, France *Tel:* 01 43 26 96 73 *Fax:* 01 43
26 42 64 *E-mail:* info@editions-picard.fr

Edition Tiamat
Grimmstr 26, 10967 Berlin
Tel: (030) 6937734 *Fax:* (030) 6944687
E-mail: mail@edition-tiamat.de
Web Site: www.edition-tiamat.de
Key Personnel
Publisher & Mng Dir: Klaus Bittermann

Subjects: History, Literature, Literary Criticism,
Essays, Music, Dance, Social Sciences, Sociol-
ogy
ISBN Prefix(es): 978-3-89320; 978-3-923118
Foreign Rep(s): Beat Eberle (Switzerland); Seth
Meyer-Bruhns (Austria)
Distribution Center: Sova, Friesstr 20-24, 60388
Frankfurt *Tel:* (069) 41 02 11 *Fax:* (069) 41 02
80 (Germany & Austria)
AVA Buch 2000, Centralweg 16, 8910 Affoltern
am Albis, Switzerland *Tel:* (044) 762 42 60
Fax: (044) 762 42 10

Tibethaus Deutschland eV Frankfurt
Kaufunger Str 4, 60486 Frankfurt
Tel: (069) 7191 3595 *Fax:* (069) 7191 3596
E-mail: info@tibethaus.com
Web Site: www.tibethaus.com
Key Personnel
Contact: Elke Hessel *E-mail:* hessel@
tibethaus.com; Gerd Storm *E-mail:* storm@
tibethaus.com; Puntsok Tsering Duechung
E-mail: tsering@tibethaus.com
Subjects: Art, Inspirational, Spirituality, Medicine,
Nursing, Dentistry, Religion - Buddhist, Sci-
ence (General), Culture, Prayer
ISBN Prefix(es): 978-3-931442

Tibetisches Zentrum eV+
Hermann-Balk-Str 106, 22147 Hamburg
Tel: (040) 644 35 85 *Fax:* (040) 644 35 15
E-mail: tz@tibet.de; presse@tibet.de
Web Site: www.tibet.de
Key Personnel
Mng Dir: Christof Spitz *Tel:* (040) 644 92 653
E-mail: cs@tibet.de
Press & Public Relations: Judith Kaulbars
Tel: (040) 180 57 746
Founded: 1977
Subjects: Inspirational, Spirituality, Religion -
Buddhist
ISBN Prefix(es): 978-3-927862
Bookshop(s): Fachbuchhandlung Tsongkang

TibiaPress Verlag GmbH
Abigstr 11, 88662 Ueberlingen
Tel: (07551) 30 92 72 *Fax:* (07551) 30 92 73
E-mail: info@tibiapress.de
Web Site: www.tibiapress.de
Key Personnel
Publisher: Wilfried Stascheit *E-mail:* wstascheit@
tibiapress.de
Marketing & Sales: Annelie Loeber-Stascheit
E-mail: a.stascheit@tibiapress.de
Subjects: Computers, Education, History, Litera-
ture, Literary Criticism, Essays
ISBN Prefix(es): 978-3-935254
Distribution Center: Die Werkstatt Verlagsaus-
lieferung, Koenigstr 43, D, 26180 Rastede
Tel: (04402) 92 6320 *Fax:* (04402) 92 6350
E-mail: bestellung@werkstatt-auslieferung.de
Dr Franz Hain Verlagsauslieferung GmbH, Dr-
Otto-Neurath-Gasse 5, 1220 Vienna, Aus-
tria *Tel:* (01) 2826656-77 (orders) *Fax:* (01)
2825282 *E-mail:* office@hain.at

Edition Tintenfass
Neckarsteinacher Str 7, 69239 Neckarsteinach
Tel: (06229) 2322 *Fax:* (06229) 2322
E-mail: info@verlag-tintenfass.de
Web Site: www.verlag-tintenfass.de
Key Personnel
Owner & Publishing Dir: Dr Walter Sauer
Mng Dir: Alison Sauer; Philipp Sauer
Founded: 2001
Specialize in foreign language literature.
Subjects: Language Arts, Linguistics, Literature,
Literary Criticism, Essays, Regional Interests
ISBN Prefix(es): 978-3-937467; 978-3-9808205
Number of titles published annually: 10 Print
Total Titles: 80 Print

Distribution Center: Herold Verlagsausliefer-
ung, Raiffeisenallee 10, 82041 Oberhaching
Tel: (089) 6138710 *Fax:* (089) 6138720
E-mail: herold@herold-va.de

TintenTrinker Verlag
Alteburger Str 39, 50678 Cologne
Tel: (0221) 27239198
E-mail: contact@tintentrinker.de
Web Site: www.tintentrinker.de
Key Personnel
Contact: Julie Cazier
ISBN Prefix(es): 978-3-9816323
Associate Companies: Le Buveur D'encre
Foreign Rep(s): AVA Verlagsauslieferung AG
(Switzerland); Dr Franz Hain Verlagsausliefer-
ungen GmbH (Austria)
Distribution Center: MSR Runge Verlagsaus-
lieferung GmbH, Bergstr 2, 33803 Steinhagen
Tel: (05204) 998-123 *Fax:* (05204) 998-111
E-mail: msr@rungeva.de

Tipp Creative, *imprint of* Xenos Verlag

Tipress Deutschland GmbH, see Tipress
Dienstleistungen fuer das Verlagswesen GmbH

**Tipress Dienstleistungen fuer das Verlagswesen
GmbH+**
Obertalstr 20a, 79295 Sulzburg
Tel: (07634) 591193 *Fax:* (07634) 591192
E-mail: tipress@tipress.com
Web Site: www.tipress.com
Key Personnel
President: Roberto Toso
Founded: 1980
Also a literary agency & provider of services for
publishers in 4 languages; projects of series of
books, realization of books & consultants.
Subjects: Art, Cookery, Crafts, Games, Hobbies,
Fiction, Film, Video, Health, Nutrition, Nonfic-
tion (General)
Number of titles published annually: 30 Print; 20
E-Book
Total Titles: 30 Print; 20 E-Book

Titania Verlag+
Industriestr 19, 64407 Fraenkisch-Crumbach
Tel: (06164) 50 41-0 *Fax:* (06164) 50 41-41;
(06164) 50 41-42 (sales)
E-mail: info@xxl-medien-service.de
Web Site: www.xxl-medien-service.de
Founded: 1949
Subjects: Fiction
ISBN Prefix(es): 978-3-7996
Parent Company: XXL Medien Service GmbH

S Toeche-Mittler Verlagsbuchhandlung GmbH
Hindenburgstr 33, 64295 Darmstadt
Tel: (06151) 33665; (06151) 311551 *Fax:* (06151)
314048
E-mail: info@net-library.de; stmv@net-library.de;
orders@net-library.de
Web Site: www.net-library.de
Key Personnel
Mng Dir: Jens Toeche-Mittler *E-mail:* toeche-
mittler@net-library.de
Sales Manager: Albrecht Lueft *E-mail:* triops@
net-library.de
Founded: 1789
Subjects: Economics, Law, Nonfiction (General),
Sports, Athletics
ISBN Prefix(es): 978-3-87820
Divisions: TRIOPS, Tropical Scientific Books

TOKYOPOP GmbH
Holstenplatz 20, 22765 Hamburg
Tel: (040) 89 06 34-0; (040) 89 06 34-60 (sales)
Fax: (040) 89 06 34-72
E-mail: info@tokyopop.de; vertrieb@tokyopop.de
Web Site: www.tokyopop.de

Key Personnel
Mng Dir: Stuart Joel Levy *E-mail:* stu@
tokyopop.de
Editor: Aranka Schindler *E-mail:* arankas@
tokyopop.de
International Licensing: Arika Yanaka
E-mail: arika@tokyopop.com
Marketing & Public Relations: Kristin Eckstein
E-mail: kristine@tokyopop.de
Production: Sonja Lesch *E-mail:* sonjal@
tokyopop.de
Founded: 2004
Subjects: Romance, Science Fiction, Fantasy,
Comics, Manga
ISBN Prefix(es): 978-3-8420; 978-3-86580; 978-
3-86719

Tomus Verlag GmbH+
Industriestr 19, 64407 Fraenkisch-Crumbach
Tel: (06164) 50 41-0 *Fax:* (06164) 50 41-41;
(06164) 50 41-42 (sales)
E-mail: info@xxl-medien-service.de
Web Site: www.xxl-medien-service.de
Founded: 1962
Subjects: Animals, Pets, Cookery, Crafts, Games,
Hobbies, Humor, Science (General), Travel &
Tourism, Cartoons
ISBN Prefix(es): 978-3-8231; 978-3-920954
Parent Company: XXL Medien Service GmbH

Edition Tonger GmbH
Haid-und-Neu-Str 18, 76131 Karlsruhe
Tel: (07243) 94 56 770
E-mail: info@tonger.de
Web Site: www.tonger.de
Key Personnel
Mng Dir: Boris Bjoern Bagger; Matthias Ham-
merschmitt; Valdo Preema
Sales: Eva Baader
Founded: 1822
Specializes in sheet music books.
Subjects: Music, Dance
ISBN Prefix(es): 978-3-920950
Associate Companies: edition 49; Vogt & Fritz
Subsidiaries: Carl Engels Musikverlag; Musikver-
lage Gerhard Rabe; Fritz Spies GmbH

Trademark Publishing
Westendstr 87, 60325 Frankfurt am Main
Tel: (069) 430 578 47; (0160) 9630 2406 (cell)
Fax: (069) 944 324-50
E-mail: info@trademarkpublishing.de
Web Site: www.trademarkpublishing.de
Key Personnel
Publisher: Karl W Henschel
Mng Dir: Armin J Noll
Management: Christa Henschel
Subjects: Architecture & Interior Design, Art,
Fashion, Fiction, Photography, Pop Culture
ISBN Prefix(es): 978-3-9812294; 978-3-9813228

Transcript Verlag
Hermannstr 26, 33602 Bielefeld
Tel: (0521) 39 37 97-0 *Fax:* (05121) 39 37 97-34
E-mail: live@transcript-verlag.de
Web Site: www.transcript-verlag.de
Key Personnel
Editorial: Kai Reinhardt
Press: Daniela Pixa *E-mail:* pixa@transcript-
verlag.de
Production: Oliver Schoenebaeumer
E-mail: schoenebaeumer@transcript-verlag.de
Sales & Marketing: Vivian Eikenberg
E-mail: eikenberg@transcript-verlag.de
Subjects: Architecture & Interior Design, Art,
Drama, Theater, Education, Government, Po-
litical Science, History, Literature, Literary
Criticism, Essays, Music, Dance, Philosophy,
Psychology, Psychiatry, Social Sciences, Soci-
ology, Cultural Studies, Media Studies, Movies,
Museum & Cultural Management, Visual Sci-
ence

ISBN Prefix(es): 978-3-933127; 978-3-89942;
978-3-8376
Distribution Center: Otto Harrassowitz KG,
Kruezberger Ring 7b-d, 65205 Wies-
baden *Tel:* (0611) 530-0 *Fax:* (0611) 530
560 *E-mail:* service@harrassowitz.de *Web
Site:* www.harrassowitz.de (international)
Prolit Verlagsauslieferung GmbH, Siemensstr 16,
35643 Fernwald, Contact: Ingeborg Peters-
Meyer *Tel:* (0641) 943 93 25 *Fax:* (0641) 943
93 89 *E-mail:* i.peters@prolit.de (Great Britain)
AVA/Scheidegger & Co AG, Obere Bahnhofstr
10A, 8910 Affoltern am Albis, Switzerland,
Contact: Nicole Schmid *Tel:* (044) 762 42 50
Fax: (044) 762 42 10 *E-mail:* scheidegger@
ava.ch *Web Site:* www.ava.ch

Transit Buchverlag GmbH
Brueckenstr 6, 95126 Schwarzenbach OT Foerbau
Mailing Address: Postfach 12 11 11, 10605
Berlin
Tel: (030) 69 40 18-11 *Fax:* (030) 69 40 18-12
E-mail: transit@transit-verlag.de
Web Site: www.transit-verlag.de
Key Personnel
Mng Dir: Gudrun Froeba; Dr Rainer Nitsche
Founded: 1981
Subjects: Architecture & Interior Design, Biogra-
phy, Memoirs, Criminology, History, Literature,
Literary Criticism, Essays, Music, Dance, So-
cial Sciences, Sociology, Travel & Tourism
ISBN Prefix(es): 978-3-88747

Transpress+
Division of Paul Pietsch Verlage GmbH & Co
KG
Olgastr 86, 70180 Stuttgart
Tel: (0711) 2 10 80-0 *Fax:* (0711) 2 36 04 15
E-mail: ppv@motorbuch.de
Web Site: www.transpress.de; www.paul-pietsch-
verlag.de
Key Personnel
Publisher: Dr Patricia Scholten *Tel:* (0711) 2 10
80-11
Head, Sales: Christian Pflug *Tel:* (0711) 2 10 80-
20 *E-mail:* c.pflug@motorbuch.de
Program Manager: Joachim Kuch *Tel:* (0711) 2
10 80-18 *E-mail:* j.kuch@motorbuch.de
Press & Public Relations: Clarissa Bayer
Tel: (0711) 2 10 80-40 *E-mail:* c.bayer@
motorbuch.de
Production: Bernd Leu *Tel:* (0711) 2 10 80-49
E-mail: b.leu@motorbuch.de
Rights & Permissions: Patricia Hofmann
Tel: (0711) 2 10 80-13 *E-mail:* p.hofmann@
motorbuch.de
Founded: 1990
Subjects: Automotive, Transportation
Bookshop(s): Transpress Buchhandlung, Haupt-
bahnhof, Mittelbau-Ladenstr, 04103 Leipzig
Distribution Center: Sigloch Distribution, Am
Buchberg 8, 74572 Blaufelden *Tel:* (01805) 45
56 00 *Fax:* (01805) 95 97 29 *E-mail:* ppv@
sigloch.de

Edition Tranvia, see Verlag Walter Frey

**TraumFaenger Verlag GmbH & Co
Buchhandel KG**
Dorfener Weg 14, 83104 Hohenthann-Schoenau
Tel: (080) 65 17 92 *Fax:* (080) 65 10 93
E-mail: info@traumfaenger-verlag.de
Web Site: www.traumfaenger-verlag.de
Key Personnel
Mng Dir: Bruno Schmaeling
Marketing: Miriam Schmaeling
Subjects: Native American Studies
ISBN Prefix(es): 978-3-941485

Traumsalon GbR
Brunschweiger Str 71, 12055 Berlin
Tel: (030) 60031349 *Fax:* (030) 62736398

E-mail: info@traum-salon.de
Web Site: www.traum-salon.de
Key Personnel
Mng Dir: Rolf Barth
Marketing & Communications: Stephanie Miester
Sales: Kathleen Roth
Founded: 2006
ISBN Prefix(es): 978-3-938625

TRAVEL HOUSE MEDIA GmbH
Member of Ganske Verlags Gruppe GmbH
Grillparzerstr 12, 81675 Munich
Tel: (089) 450009-900 *Fax:* (089) 450009-901
E-mail: info@travel-house-media.de
Web Site: www.travel-house-media.de
Key Personnel
Mng Dir: Gerhard Denndorf; Thomas Ganske;
   Frank-H Haeger; Dr Stefan Riess
Sales: Veronica Reisenegger *Tel:* (089) 4500
   09-912 *E-mail:* veronica.reisenegger@travel-
   house-media.de
Team Marketing Manager: Paulina Gessl
   E-mail: paulina.gessl@travel-house-media.de
Press & Public Relations: Heike Mueller
   Tel: (089) 450009-926 *E-mail:* heike.mueller@
   travel-house-media.de
Founded: 2004
Specialize in travel guide publishing.
Subjects: Travel & Tourism
ISBN Prefix(es): 978-3-89905; 978-3-86207
Associate Companies: Hoffmann und Campe Ver-
   lag GmbH; Graefe und Unzer Verlag GmbH
Distributor for Adac Verlag GmbH; Bergver-
   lag Rother; Der Feinschmecker Guide und
   Bookazines; Merian; Michelin; Michael
   Mueller Verlag; Polyglott-Verlag; White Star
   Verlag
Orders to: Koch, Neff & Oetinger Ver-
   lagsauslieferung GmbH, Industriestr 23,
   70565 Stuttgart, Contact: Donna Hempfer
   E-mail: travel-house-media@kno-va.de
Mohr Morawa Buchvertrieb GmbH, Sulzengasse 2, 1230 Vienna, Austria *Tel:* (01) 680
   14-0 *Fax:* (01) 688 71 30 *E-mail:* momo@
   mohrmorawa.at *Web Site:* www.mohrmorawa.at
Schweizer Buchzentrum AG, Industriestr Ost 10,
   4614 Haegendorf, Switzerland *Tel:* (062) 2 09
   26 26 *Fax:* (062) 2 09 26 27

traveldiary.de Reiseliteratur-Verlag
Stuehmtwiete 3 D, 22175 Hamburg
Tel: (040) 5343 0022 *Fax:* (040) 5343 0023
E-mail: verlag@traveldiary.de
Web Site: www.traveldiary.de
Key Personnel
Publisher: Jens Freyler
Founded: 2001
Subjects: Travel & Tourism
ISBN Prefix(es): 978-3-937274; 978-3-9807655

Tre Torri Verlag GmbH
Sonnenberger Str 43, 65191 Wiesbaden
Tel: (0611) 505 58 40 *Fax:* (0611) 505 58 42
E-mail: info@tretorri.de
Web Site: www.tretorri.de; tretorri-shop.de
Key Personnel
Mng Dir: Ralf Frenzel
Press & Events: Silvia Boeving *Tel:* (0611) 57 99
   272 *Fax:* (0611) 57 99 222 *E-mail:* presse@
   tretorri.de
Sales: Christine Schloetterer *E-mail:* c.
   schloetterer@tretorri.de
Subjects: Cookery, Wine & Spirits
ISBN Prefix(es): 978-3-937963
Distribution Center: Koch, Neff & Oetinger
   Verlagsauslieferung GmbH, Industriestr 23,
   70565 Stuttgart *E-mail:* tretorri@kno-va.de *Web
   Site:* www.kno-va.de
Buchzentrum AG (BZ), Industriestr Ost 10, 4614
   Haegendorf, Switzerland *Tel:* (062) 2 09 25
   25 *Fax:* (062) 2 09 26 27 *E-mail:* losiggio@
   buchzentrum.ch

tredition GmbH
Grindelallee 188, 20144 Hamburg
Tel: (040) 41 42 778 00 *Fax:* (040) 41 42 778 01
E-mail: info@tredition.de; verlag@tredition.de
Web Site: www.tredition.de
Key Personnel
Mng Dir: Sandra Latusseck; Soenke Schulz
Founded: 2006
Membership(s): Boersenverein des Deutschen
   Buchhandels eV.
Subjects: Business, Fiction, How-to, Nonfiction
   (General), Pop Culture
ISBN Prefix(es): 978-3-940921; 978-3-86850
Distribution Center: Brockhaus Kommis-
   siongeschaeft GmbH *Tel:* (07154) 13 27-0
   Fax: (07154) 13 27-13

Trescher Verlag GmbH
Reinhardtstr 9, 10117 Berlin
Tel: (030) 2 83 24 96 *Fax:* (030) 2 81 59 94
E-mail: post@trescher-verlag.de; presse@trescher-
   verlag.de
Web Site: www.trescherverlag.de
Key Personnel
Dir: Detlev Von Oppeln
Sales: Bernd Schwenkros
Founded: 1992
Primarily publish travel guides to Eastern Europe,
   Russia, the CIS countries & to Central & East
   Asia.
Subjects: Film, Video, Nonfiction (General), Out-
   door Recreation, Travel & Tourism
ISBN Prefix(es): 978-3-928409; 978-3-89794

Editions Treves+
Postfach 1550, 54205 Trier
Tel: (0651) 30 90 10 *Fax:* (0651) 30 06 99
E-mail: mail@treves.de
Web Site: www.treves.de
Key Personnel
Mng Dir: Rainer Breuer
Founded: 1974
Club for the promotion of artistic work.
Membership(s): Verlags-Karree eV.
Subjects: Art, Erotica, Fiction, Health, Nutrition,
   History, Literature, Literary Criticism, Essays,
   Music, Dance, Mysteries, Nonfiction
   (General), Poetry, Travel & Tourism
ISBN Prefix(es): 978-3-88081

TRIAS Verlag+
Subsidiary of MVS Medizinverlage Stuttgart
   GmbH & Co KG
Ruedigerstr 14, 70469 Stuttgart
Mailing Address: Postfach 30 11 20, 70451
   Stuttgart
Tel: (0711) 8931-0; (0711) 8931-900 (customer
   service) *Fax:* (0711) 8931-298; (0711) 8931-
   901 (customer service)
E-mail: kundenservice@thieme.de
Web Site: www.thieme.de/de/trias-77.htm
Key Personnel
Mng Dir: Dr Wolfgang Knueppe
General Partner: Dr Albercht Hauff
Founded: 1989
Subjects: Health, Nutrition, Nonfiction (General),
   Psychology, Psychiatry, Veterinary Medicine
ISBN Prefix(es): 978-3-8304
Ultimate Parent Company: Georg Thieme Verlag
   KG
Associate Companies: Enke Verlag; Haug Verlag;
   Hippokrates Verlag; Sonntag Verlag

Troetsch Verlag eK
Am Moellenberg 25-28, 15713 Koenigs Wuster-
   hausen
Tel: (03375) 217 62-25 *Fax:* (03375) 217 62-50
E-mail: vertrieb@troetsch.de
Web Site: troetsch-verlag.de
Key Personnel
Owner: Andreas Troetsch
ISBN Prefix(es): 978-3-86848; 978-3-938558

Trotzdem Verlagsgenossenschaft eG+
Mainzer Landstr 107, 60329 Frankfurt
Tel: (069) 238 028 73 *Fax:* (069) 238 028 74
E-mail: info.trotzdem@freenet.de
Web Site: www.trotzdem-verlag.de
Key Personnel
Mng Dir: Juergen Malcher; Dieter Schmidt
Founded: 1978
Publishing of books & magazines from a libertar-
   ian viewpoint.
Subjects: Alternative, Biography, Memoirs,
   Drama, Theater, Education, Government, Po-
   litical Science, History, Photography, Social
   Sciences, Sociology, Global Political Issues,
   Libertarian Movement
ISBN Prefix(es): 978-3-922209; 978-3-931786
Divisions: Redaktion Schwarzer Faden
Distributor for Anares; Anarchijtische Buchhand-
   lung

Mario Truant Verlag+
Frauenlobstr 95, 55118 Mainz
Tel: (06131) 961660
Web Site: www.truant.de
Key Personnel
Publisher: Mario Truant *E-mail:* mario@truant.de
Founded: 1990
Subjects: Crafts, Games, Hobbies, Fiction, Para-
   psychology, Science Fiction, Fantasy
ISBN Prefix(es): 978-3-926801; 978-3-934282

Tuebinger Vereinigung fuer Volkskunde eV
   (TVV)
Schloss, 72070 Tuebingen
Tel: (07071) 29-72374 *Fax:* (07071) 29-5330
E-mail: info@tvv-verlag.de
Web Site: www.tvv-verlag.de
Key Personnel
Mng Dir: Dr Thomas Thiemeyer
Treasurer: Dr Gesa Ingendahl
Founded: 1963
Subjects: Ethnicity, Film, Video, History, Lan-
   guage Arts, Linguistics, Regional Interests, So-
   cial Sciences, Sociology, Women's Studies,
   Folklore Studies
ISBN Prefix(es): 978-3-925340; 978-3-932512

TUEV Media GmbH
Am Grauen Stein, 51105 Cologne
Tel: (0221) 806-3535 *Fax:* (0221) 806-3510
E-mail: tuev-media@de.tuv.com
Web Site: www.tuev-media.de; www.tuv.com
Key Personnel
Mng Dir: Gabriele Landes *Tel:* (0221) 806 3501
   E-mail: gabriele.landes@de.tuv.com
Publishing Dir: Joerg Fischer *Tel:* (0221) 806
   3508 *E-mail:* joerg.fischer@de.tuv.com
Head, Marketing: Markus Pieper *Tel:* (0221) 806
   3530 *E-mail:* markus.pieper@de.tuv.com
Founded: 1971
Subjects: Energy, Environmental Studies, Re-
   gional Interests, Technology, Transportation
ISBN Prefix(es): 978-3-8249; 978-3-88585
Parent Company: TUEV Rheinland Group

Tulipan Verlag
Albestr 16, 12159 Berlin
Tel: (030) 809 22 49 30 *Fax:* (030) 809 22 49 31
E-mail: info@tulipan-verlag.de
Web Site: www.tulipan-verlag.de
Key Personnel
Founder: Simone Klussmann
   E-mail: klussmann@tulipan-verlag.de; Mascha
   Schwarz *E-mail:* schwarz@tulipan-verlag.de
Management: Sascha Nicoletta Simon
Press & Public Relations: Constance Margraf
   E-mail: margraf@tulipan-verlag.de
Founded: 2006

Membership(s): Arbeitsgemeinschaft von Jugend-
buchverlagen eV; Boersenverein des Deutschen
Buchhandels.
Subjects: Fiction
ISBN Prefix(es): 978-3-939944
Foreign Rep(s): Buchkontor (Ulla Harms &
Christiane Eblinger) (Austria); Annelies Hohl
(Switzerland)
Distribution Center: Prolit Verlagsauslieferung
GmbH, Siemensstr 16, 35463 Fernwald, Con-
tact: Johanna Gastler *Tel:* (0641) 943 93 25
Fax: (0641) 943 93 89 *E-mail:* j.gastler@prolit.
de
Mohr Morawa Buchvertrieb GmbH, Sulzen-
gasse 2, 1230 Vienna, Austria *Tel:* (01) 680
14-0 *Fax:* (01) 688 71 30 *E-mail:* momo@
mohrmorawa.at *Web Site:* www.mohrmorawa.at
Buchzentrum AG, Industriestr Ost 10, 4614 Hae-
gendorf, Switzerland *Tel:* (062) 209 25 25
Fax: (062) 209 26 27 *E-mail:* kundendienst@
buchzentrum.ch

Turm-Verlag, see Lorber-Verlag und Turm-Verlag
GmbH & Co KG

tus-verlag
Yorckstr 20, 79110 Freiburg
Tel: (0761) 1207086 *Fax:* (0761) 5958350
E-mail: info@tus-verlag.de
Web Site: www.tus-verlag.de
ISBN Prefix(es): 978-3-941672

Tushita Verlag GmbH
Meidericher Str 6-8, 47058 Duisburg
Tel: (0203) 80097-0 *Fax:* (0203) 80097-15
E-mail: tushita@tushita.com; service@tushita.com
Web Site: www.tushita.com; www.tushita.de
Key Personnel
Mng Dir: Michael Hellbach
Founded: 1980
Publisher of ethic & spiritual editions with em-
phasis on Tibet & Buddhism.
Subjects: Ethnicity, Inspirational, Spirituality, Re-
ligion - Buddhist
ISBN Prefix(es): 978-3-928555; 978-3-932531;
978-3-89789; 978-3-86765; 978-3-86547
Branch Office(s)
Tushita France, 13 Villa Curial, 75019 Paris,
France *Tel:* (06) 17 30 35 60 *E-mail:* france@
tushita.com
Tushita GB, Andoversford Industrial Estate,
Units 19 A&B Coln Park, Andoversford, Chel-
tenham, Glos GL54 4H, United Kingdom
U.S. Office(s): Tushita Inc, 456 Penn St, Yeadon,
PA 19050, United States *Tel:* 610-626-7770
Fax: 610-626-2778

Edition 211, *imprint of* Bookspot Verlag GmbH

Uccello
Utermarkt 19, 82418 Murnau am Staffelsee
Tel: (08841) 4055188; (08152) 993085 (press)
Fax: (08841) 4053655; (08152) 794196 (press)
E-mail: info@uccello.de
Web Site: www.uccello.de
Key Personnel
Publisher: Martina Muehlbauer
Press: Martina Deppe-Spinelli *E-mail:* spinelli@
uccello.de; Katharina Krimmer
ISBN Prefix(es): 978-3-937337
Foreign Rep(s): Alfred Trux (Austria)
Distribution Center: Prolit GmbH, Siemensstr 16,
35463 Fernwald-Annerod *Tel:* (0641) 94393-14
Fax: (0641) 94393-29 *E-mail:* h.birk@prolit.de

UEM, see Vereinte Evangelische Mission

Verlag Dr Alfons Uhl+
Mittlere Gerbergasse 1, 86720 Noerdlingen
Tel: (09081) 87248 *Fax:* (09081) 23710

Key Personnel
Dir, Rights & Permissions: Dr Alfons Uhl
Subjects: Architecture & Interior Design, Art, Ge-
ography, Geology, Art Theory, Horticulture
ISBN Prefix(es): 978-3-921503

h f ullmann publishing GmbH
Member of Ullmann Medien GmbH
Birkenstr 10, 14469 Potsdam
Tel: (0331) 23 624-0 *Fax:* (0331) 23 624-200
E-mail: info@ullmannmedien.com
Web Site: www.ullmannmedien.com/hfullmann
Key Personnel
Mng Dir: Florian Ullmann
Head, Editorial Dept: Lars Pietzchmann
Head, International Sales: Pierre Toromanoff
E-mail: p.toromanoff@ullmann-publishing.com
ISBN Prefix(es): 978-3-8480
Foreign Rep(s): Consortium Book Sales & Distri-
bution (USA); Nationwide Book Distributors
(New Zealand); Peribo Pty Ltd (Australia);
Roundhouse Group (UK); SG Distributors
(Giulietta Campanelli) (South Africa); Words
& Visuals Press Pte Ltd (William Tay) (Far
East, Southeast Asia)

Ullstein, *imprint of* Ullstein Buchverlage GmbH

Ullstein Buchverlage GmbH+
Friedrichstr 126, 10117 Berlin
Tel: (030) 23456-300 *Fax:* (030) 23456-303
E-mail: info@ullstein-buchverlage.de
Web Site: www.ullstein-buchverlage.de
Key Personnel
Mng Dir: Christian Schumacher-Gebler
Sales Dir: Stephanie Martin *Tel:* (030) 23456-
333 *Fax:* (030) 23456-355 *E-mail:* stephanie.
martin@ullstein-buchverlag.de
Foreign Rights: Pia Goetz *Tel:* (030) 23456-450
Fax: (030) 23456-515 *E-mail:* pia.goetz@
ullstein-buchverlag.de
Press & Public Relations: Christine Heinrich
Tel: (030) 23456-433 *Fax:* (030) 23456-445
E-mail: christine.heinrich@ullstein-buchverlag.
de
Subjects: Biography, Memoirs, Business, Eco-
nomics, Fiction, History, How-to, Humor, Man-
agement, Maritime, Mysteries, Suspense, Non-
fiction (General), Romance, Science (General),
Crime & Thrillers
ISBN Prefix(es): 978-3-430; 978-3-612; 978-3-
547
Imprints: Allegria; Econ; List; List Taschenbuch;
Propylaeen; Marion von Schroeder; Ullstein;
Ullstein Extra; Ullstein Taschenbuch
Distributor for Hoerbuch Hamburg (audiobook
publisher)
Distribution Center: Distribook, Schockenriedstr
39, 70565 Stuttgart *Toll Free Tel:* 0800 66-111-
99 *Fax:* (0711) 7899-1010 *E-mail:* service@
distribook.de (Germany & Switzerland)
Dr Franz Hain Verlagsauslieferung GmbH, Dr-
Otto-Neurath-Gasse 5, 1220 Vienna, Austria
Tel: (01) 282 65 65-77 *Fax:* (01) 282 52 82
E-mail: bestell@hain.at

Ullstein Extra, *imprint of* Ullstein Buchverlage
GmbH

Ullstein Taschenbuch, *imprint of* Ullstein
Buchverlage GmbH

Verlag Eugen Ulmer KG (Eugen Ulmer
Publishers)+
Wollgrasweg 41, 70599 Stuttgart
Mailing Address: Postfach 700561, 70574
Stuttgart
Tel: (0711) 4507-0 *Fax:* (0711) 4507-120
E-mail: info@ulmer.de
Web Site: www.ulmer.de

Key Personnel
Mng Dir: Matthias Ulmer *E-mail:* mulmer@
ulmer.de
Program Dir: Susanne Boettcher
E-mail: sboettcher@ulmer.de
Sales Dir: Michael Kurzer
Rights Manager: Andrea Keller *E-mail:* akeller@
ulmer.de; Sigrun Wagner *E-mail:* swagner@
ulmer.de
Production: Juergen Sprenzel *E-mail:* jsprenzel@
ulmer.de
Founded: 1868
Membership(s): UTB.
Subjects: Agriculture, Animals, Pets, Biological
Sciences, Cookery, Crafts, Games, Hobbies,
Earth Sciences, Environmental Studies, Garden-
ing, Plants, Geography, Geology, Health, Nutri-
tion, History, House & Home, How-to, Natural
History, Outdoor Recreation, Physical Sciences,
Science (General), Veterinary Science, Wine &
Spirits
ISBN Prefix(es): 978-3-8001
Number of titles published annually: 180 Print; 2
CD-ROM; 120 E-Book
Total Titles: 1,500 Print; 40 CD-ROM; 700 E-
Book
Imprints: Bede Verlag
Subsidiaries: Editions Ulmer (France)

Guenter Albert Ulmer Verlag
Hauptstr 16, 78609 Tuningen
Tel: (07464) 98740 *Fax:* (07464) 3054
E-mail: info@ulmertuningen.de
Web Site: www.ulmertuningen.de
Key Personnel
Mng Dir: Guenter Albert Ulmer
Founded: 1983
Subjects: Earth Sciences, Environmental Studies,
Gardening, Plants, Health, Nutrition, Human
Relations, Natural History, Nonfiction (Gen-
eral), Poetry, Regional Interests, Religion -
Protestant, Theology, Meditation
ISBN Prefix(es): 978-3-924191; 978-3-932346

Neuer Umschau Buchverlag GmbH+
Subsidiary of Unternehmensgruppe Niederberger
Molkestr 14, 67433 Neustadt/Weinstr
Tel: (06321) 877-855 *Fax:* (06321) 877-859
E-mail: info@umschau-buchverlag.de
Web Site: www.umschau-buchverlag.de
Key Personnel
Mng Dir: Guenther Matheis
Publisher: Angela Thomaschik *Tel:* (06321)
877-853 *E-mail:* a.thomaschik@umschau-
buchverlag.de
Sales Manager: Uwe Marsen *Tel:* (06171) 69 99
83 *Fax:* (06171) 69 47 87 *E-mail:* u.marsen@
umschau-buchverlag.de
Foreign Rights: Stefanie Simon *Tel:* (06321) 877-
861 *E-mail:* s.simon@umschau-buchverlag.de
Founded: 1850
Also acts as distributor.
Membership(s): Boersenverein des Deutschen
Buchhandels.
Subjects: Cookery, Health, Nutrition, Nonfiction
(General), Science (General)
ISBN Prefix(es): 978-3-524; 978-3-8295
Foreign Rep(s): Mohr Morawa Buchvertrieb
GmbH (Juergen Sieberer) (Eastern Austria);
Mohr Morawa Buchvertrieb GmbH (Edwin
Mayr) (South Tyrol, Italy, Western Austria);
Mohr Morawa Buchvertrieb GmbH (Jutta Buss-
mann) (Austria); Hugo Weibel (Switzerland)
Distribution Center: Koch, Neff & Oetinger Ver-
lagsauslieferung GmbH, Industriestr 23, 70565
Stuttgart *E-mail:* umschau@kno-va.de
Mohr Morawa Buchvertrieb GmbH, Sulzen-
gasse 2, 1230 Vienna, Austria *Tel:* (01) 680
14-0 *Fax:* (01) 688 71 30 *E-mail:* momo@
mohrmorawa.at *Web Site:* www.mohrmorawa.at

Buchzentrum AG, Industriestr Ost 10, 4614 Haegendorf, Switzerland *Tel:* (062) 2 09 26 26 *Fax:* (062) 2 09 26 27 *E-mail:* kundendienst@ buchzentrum.ch

Unikum Verlag UG
Marktplatz 4, 88131 Lindau am Bodensee
E-mail: mail@unikum-verlag.de
Web Site: unikum-verlag.de
Key Personnel
Publisher: Dietmar Hofer; Marion Hofer
Founded: 2015
Subjects: Architecture & Interior Design, Art, Biography, Memoirs, History, Nature
ISBN Prefix(es): 978-3-8457
Branch Office(s)
Schregenbergstr 22, 6800 Feldkirch, Austria
Tel: (0664) 4648013

UniScripta Verlag
Burkhardweg 9, 65817 Eppstein
Tel: (06198) 8767 *Fax:* (06198) 8766
E-mail: info@uniscripta.de
Web Site: www.uniscripta.de
Key Personnel
Manager: Christa Semke-Boehm *Tel:* (06103) 985385 *E-mail:* semke-boehm@uniscripta.de; Wolfgang Ullrich *E-mail:* ullrich@uniscripta.de
Marketing & Public Relations: Peter Luyendyk *Tel:* (0176) 70 53 95 96 *E-mail:* luyendyk@ uniscripta.de
Founded: 2010
Subjects: Fiction, History, Poetry, Crime, Thrillers
ISBN Prefix(es): 978-3-942728

Universitaetsverlag der TU Berlin
Fasanenstr 88, 10623 Berlin
Tel: (030) 314-76131; (030) 314-76132
Fax: (030) 314-76133
E-mail: publikationen@ub.tu-berlin.de
Web Site: www.ub.tu-berlin.de/publizieren/ universitaetsverlag/
Key Personnel
Manager: Dagmar Schobert *Tel:* (030) 314-76127
Membership(s): Arbeitsgemeinschaft der Universitaetsverlage (Association of University Publishers).
Subjects: Architecture & Interior Design, Economics, Engineering (General), Environmental Studies, Geography, Geology, Science (General), Humanities
ISBN Prefix(es): 978-3-7983

Universitaetsverlag Ilmenau
Langewiesener Str 37, 98693 Ilmenau
Mailing Address: Postfach 10 05 65, 98684 Ilmenau
Tel: (03677) 69-4701 *Fax:* (03677) 69-4700
E-mail: verlag.ub@tu-ilmenau.de
Web Site: www.tu-ilmenau.de/ilmedia/ universitaetsverlag
Key Personnel
Contact: Johannes Wilken *Tel:* (03677) 69-4594
Founded: 2006
Subjects: Computer Science, Economics, Engineering (General), Law, Mathematics
ISBN Prefix(es): 978-3-939473; 978-3-86360
Distributed by Verlaghaus Monsenstein und Vannerdat OHG

Universitaetsverlag Regensburg GmbH
Leibnizstr 13, 93055 Regensburg
Tel: (0941) 7 87 85-0 *Fax:* (0941) 7 87 85-16
E-mail: info@univerlag-regensburg.de
Web Site: www.universitaetsverlag-regensburg.de
Key Personnel
Mng Dir: Dr Albrecht Weiland *E-mail:* a. weiland@univerlag-regensburg.de
Founded: 1992
Subjects: Archaeology, Architecture & Interior Design, Art, Economics, History, Law, Physics, Science (General), Banking

ISBN Prefix(es): 978-3-930480; 978-3-9803470
Distribution Center: Verlag Schnell und Steiner GmbH, Postfach 20 04 29, 93063 Regensburg
Tel: (0941) 7 87 85-26 *Fax:* (0941) 7 87 85-16
E-mail: bestellung@univerlag-regensburg.de

Universitaetsverlag Winter GmbH+
Dossenheimer Landstr 13, 69121 Heidelberg
Mailing Address: Postfach 10 61 40, 69051 Heidelberg
Tel: (06221) 7702-60 *Fax:* (06221) 7702-69
E-mail: info@winter-verlag.de
Web Site: www.winter-verlag.de
Key Personnel
Publishing Dir & Editor: Dr Andreas Barth *Tel:* (06221) 7702-63 *E-mail:* a.barth@winter-verlag.de
Mng Dir: Theo Schuster
Marketing & Sales: Dagmar Konetzka *Tel:* (06221) 7702-65 *E-mail:* d.konetzka@ winter-verlag.de
Production: Ralf Stemper *Tel:* (06221) 7702-67 *E-mail:* r.stemper@winter-verlag.de
Founded: 2002
Academic publisher.
Membership(s): Boersenverein des Deutschen Buchhandels.
Subjects: African American Studies, Language Arts, Linguistics, Literature, Literary Criticism, Essays, Philosophy, Religion - Islamic, Religion - Jewish, Religion - Other
ISBN Prefix(es): 978-3-8253
Number of titles published annually: 120 Print
Total Titles: 2,600 Print
Associate Companies: Heidelberger Verlagsanstalt (HVA) & Edition S
Distribution Center: Sigloch Distribution GmbH & Co KG, Am Buchberg 8, 74572 Blaufelden, Contact: Christine Buscher *Tel:* (07953) 883-0 *Fax:* (07953) 883-380 (Germany & other countries)
Buchzentrum AG, Industriestr Ost 10, 4614 Haegendorf, Switzerland *Tel:* (062) 209 26 25 *Fax:* (062) 209 26 27 *E-mail:* kundendienst@ buchzentrum.ch *Web Site:* www.buchzentrum.ch

Universum Verlag GmbH
Taunusstr 54, 65183 Wiesbaden
Tel: (0611) 90 30 0 *Fax:* (0611) 90 30 183
E-mail: uv@universum.de
Web Site: www.universum.de
Key Personnel
Mng Dir: Frank-Ivo Lube *Tel:* (0611) 9030-120 *E-mail:* flube@universum.de; Siegried Pabst *Tel:* (0611) 9030-150 *E-mail:* spabst@ universum.de
Editorial: Angela Krueger *Tel:* (0611) 9030-383 *E-mail:* akrueger@universum.de
Marketing: Susan Dauber *Tel:* (0611) 9030-121 *E-mail:* susan.dauber@universum.de
Founded: 1930
Subjects: Career Development, Disability, Special Needs, Environmental Studies, Health, Nutrition, Transportation
ISBN Prefix(es): 978-3-89869

UNO-Verlag, Vertriebs-und Verlagsgessellschaft GmbH
Postfach 72 81, 53072 Bonn
Tel: (0228) 94 90 2-0 *Fax:* (0228) 94 90 2-22
Web Site: www.uno-verlag.de
Key Personnel
Mng Dir: Dr Beate Wagner
Publisher: Joachim Krause
Founded: 1982
Subjects: Aeronautics, Aviation, Agriculture, Developing Countries, Economics, Education, Energy, Environmental Studies, Finance, Government, Political Science, Health, Nutrition, Labor, Industrial Relations, Social Sciences, Sociology
ISBN Prefix(es): 978-3-923904

Distributor for Asian Development Bank (ADB); Council of Europe; Food & Agricultural Organization (FAO); International Atomic Energy Agency (IAEA); International Civil Aviation Organization (ICAO); International Maritime Organization (IMO); International Monetary Fund (IMF); Nordic Council; Organization for Economic Cooperation & Develpment (OECD); The United Nations University (UNU); United Nations Association of Germany (DGVN); United Nations Educational, Scientific & Cultural Organization (UNESCO); United Nations Environment Programme (UNEP); United Nations Publications; World Health Organization (WHO); World Bank Group; World Intellectual Property Organization (WIPO); World Meteorological Organization (WMO); World Tourism Organization (UNWTO); World Trade Organization (WTO)

Unrast eV+
Hafenweg 31, 48155 Muenster
Mailing Address: Postfach 8020, 48043 Muenster
Tel: (0251) 66 62 93 *Fax:* (0251) 66 61 20
E-mail: kontakt@unrast-verlag.de; presse@unrast-verlag.de
Web Site: www.unrast-verlag.de
Key Personnel
Contact: Joern Essig-Gutschmidt; Martin Schuering
Founded: 1989
Subjects: Developing Countries, Fiction, Government, Political Science, Women's Studies
ISBN Prefix(es): 978-3-89771; 978-3-928300
Foreign Rep(s): Seth Meyer-Bruhns
Distribution Center: aLiVe-Gemeinschaftsauslieferung, Schmetterling-Verlag, Lindenspuerstr 38 B, 70176 Stuttgart *Tel:* (0711) 6369698 *Fax:* (0711) 626992 *E-mail:* auslieferung@schmetterling-verlag.de *Web Site:* www.alive-auslieferung.de (Germany & Austria)
Herder AG Basel, Muttenzerstr 109, 4133 Pratteln 1, Switzerland *Tel:* (061) 82790960 *Fax:* (061) 8279067 *E-mail:* disposition@herder.ch

Unsichtbar Verlag
Wellenburger Str 1, 86420 Diedorf
Tel: (0821) 22 848 61
E-mail: info@unsichtbar-verlag.de
Web Site: www.unsichtbar-verlag.de
Key Personnel
Publisher: Andreas Koeglowitz
Public Relations: Frank Oberpichler
Founded: 2011
ISBN Prefix(es): 978-3-942920

Unterwegs Verlag+
Werner-von-Siemens-Str 22, 78224 Singen
Tel: (07731) 838-0 *Fax:* (07731) 83819
E-mail: info@unterwegs.de
Web Site: www.reisefuehrer.com
Key Personnel
Publisher: Manfred Klemann
Publishing Dir: Pablo Klemann
Founded: 1983
ISBN Prefix(es): 978-3-924334; 978-3-86112
Subsidiaries: Hohentwiel-Verlag & Internet GmbH
Warehouse: VVA-Bertelsmann Distribution GmbH, An der Autonbahn, 33310 Guetersloh

Verlag Urachhaus
Division of Verlag Freies Geistesleben und Urachhaus GmbH
Landhausstr 82, 70191 Stuttgart
Tel: (0711) 285 3200 *Fax:* (0711) 285 3210
E-mail: info@urachhaus.com
Web Site: www.urachhaus.de
Key Personnel
Mng Dir: Michael Stehle *Tel:* (0711) 285 3238 *E-mail:* michael.stehle@urachhaus.com

Subjects: Literature, Literary Criticism, Essays, Religion - Other, Christianity
ISBN Prefix(es): 978-3-8251

Urania, *imprint of* Verlag Kreuz GmbH

Urania Verlag+
Imprint of Verlag Kreuz GmbH
Hermann-Herder-Str 4, 79104 Freiburg
Tel: (0761) 2717-0 *Fax:* (0761) 2717-520
E-mail: service@urania-verlag.de; presse@herder.de
Web Site: www.urania-verlag.de
Key Personnel
Mng Dir & Publisher: Manuel Herder
Mng Dir: Olaf Carstens; Roland Grimmelsmann
Head, Press & Public Relations: Andreas Bernheim
Rights: Francesca Bressan *Tel:* (0761) 2717-546
Fax: (0761) 2717-540 *E-mail:* bressan@herder.de
Founded: 1924
Subjects: Biological Sciences, Career Development, Child Care & Development, Education, Health, Nutrition, Nonfiction (General)
ISBN Prefix(es): 978-3-332
Ultimate Parent Company: Herder Verlag GmbH
Shipping Address: Leipziger Kommissions- und Grosbuchhandelsgesellschaft mbH (LKG), An der Suedspitze 1-12, 04571 Roetha
Tel: (034206) 65-100 *Fax:* (034206) 65-110
E-mail: lkg@lkg-service.de *Web Site:* www.lkg-va.de
Orders to: Leipziger Kommissions- und Grosbuchhandelsgesellschaft mbH (LKG), An der Suedspitze 1-12, 04571 Roetha *Tel:* (034206) 65-100 *Fax:* (034206) 65-110 *E-mail:* lkg@lkg-service.de *Web Site:* www.lkg-va.de

Urban & Vogel GmbH
Aschauer Str 30, 81549 Munich
Tel: (089) 20 30 43 1300
Web Site: www.springerfachmedien-medizin.de
Founded: 1972
Subjects: Medicine, Nursing, Dentistry
ISBN Prefix(es): 978-3-8208
Parent Company: Springer Medizin
Ultimate Parent Company: Springer Science+Business Media
Distributed by Vleweg Verlag (Germany)

Verlag Urbania, *imprint of* Verlag Herder GmbH

Edition Ustad, *imprint of* Karl-May-Verlag GmbH

UTB GmbH
Industriestr 2, 70565 Stuttgart
Tel: (0711) 7 82 95 55-0 *Fax:* (0711) 7 80 13 76
E-mail: utb@utb.de
Web Site: www.utb.de
Key Personnel
Mng Dir: Dr Joerg Platiel
Sales: Andrea Euchner *Tel:* (0711) 7289 555 13
E-mail: euchner@utb.de
Press: Susanne Ziegler *Tel:* (0711) 7289 555 12
E-mail: ziegler@utb.de
Founded: 1970
The company represents a group of 13 publishers (shareholders) producing paperbacks of a general academic/technical/scientific nature.
Membership(s): forum independent GmbH.
Subjects: Agriculture, Biological Sciences, Business, Chemistry, Chemical Engineering, Computer Science, Economics, Electronics, Electrical Engineering, Engineering (General), Government, Political Science, Health, Nutrition, History, Language Arts, Linguistics, Law, Library & Information Sciences, Literature, Literary Criticism, Essays, Medicine, Nursing, Dentistry, Philosophy, Physics, Psychology,

Psychiatry, Religion - Other, Science (General), Social Sciences, Sociology, Veterinary Science
ISBN Prefix(es): 978-3-8252; 978-3-920971
Foreign Rep(s): Mohr Morawa Buchvertrieb GmbH (Roland Fuerst) (Austria); Scheidegger & Co AG (Stephanie Brunner) (Switzerland)
Distribution Center: Brockhaus/Commission, Postfach 1220, 70803 Kornwestheim
Tel: (07154) 13 27-25 *Fax:* (07154) 13 27-13
E-mail: bestell@brocom.de
Mohr Morawa Buchvertrieb GmbH, Sulzengasse 2, 1230 Vienna, Austria *Tel:* (01) 680 14-0 *Fax:* (01) 688 7130 *E-mail:* momo@mohrmorawa.at *Web Site:* www.mohrmorawa.at
Scheidegger & Co AG c/o AVA Verlagsauslieferung AG, Centralweg 16, 8910 Affoltern am Albis, Switzerland *Tel:* (044) 76242 50 *Fax:* (044) 76242 10 *E-mail:* e.bachofner@ava.ch *Web Site:* www.scheidegger-buecher.ch

Herbert Utz Verlag GmbH+
Adalbertstr 57, 80799 Munich
Tel: (089) 27 77 91-00 *Fax:* (089) 27 77 91-01
E-mail: info@utzverlag.de
Web Site: www.utzverlag.de
Key Personnel
Mng Dir: Dipl Ing Herbert Utz
Founded: 1994
Subjects: Art, Biography, Memoirs, Communications, Computer Science, Economics, Ethnicity, Government, Political Science, History, Language Arts, Linguistics, Law, Literature, Literary Criticism, Essays, Medicine, Nursing, Dentistry, Philosophy, Science (General), Social Sciences, Sociology, Technology, Theology
ISBN Prefix(es): 978-3-8316; 978-3-89675; 978-3-931327; 978-3-9803925
Number of titles published annually: 170 Print
Total Titles: 3,150 Print

UVIS Verlag eK
Burgstr 6, 88483 Burgrieden
Tel: (07392) 1 03 72 *Fax:* (07392) 1 05 97
E-mail: info@uvis-verlag.de
Web Site: www.uvis-verlag.de
Key Personnel
Mng Dir: Juergen Arnold
Founded: 2005
Membership(s): Boersenverein des Deutschen Buchhandels.
Subjects: Business, Health, Nutrition, Wellness
ISBN Prefix(es): 978-3-938684

UVK Universitatsverlag GmbH+
Schuetzenstr 24, 78462 Konstanz
Mailing Address: Postfach 10 20 51, 78420 Konstanz
Tel: (07531) 9053-0 *Fax:* (07531) 9053-98
E-mail: willkommen@uvk.de
Web Site: www.uvk.de
Key Personnel
Mng Dir: Dr Brigitte Weyl *E-mail:* brigitte.weyl@uvk.de
Publishing Manager & International Rights Contact: Walter Engstle *E-mail:* walter.engstle@uvk.de
Foreign Rights & Licenses: Ines Ende *Tel:* (07531) 9053-14 *E-mail:* ines.ende@uvk.de
Marketing Assistant: Felix Kaus *Tel:* (07531) 9053-31 *E-mail:* felix.kaus@uvk.de
Founded: 1963
Subjects: Archaeology, Communications, Economics, History, Literature, Literary Criticism, Essays, Philosophy, Science (General), Social Sciences, Sociology
ISBN Prefix(es): 978-3-87940
Number of titles published annually: 10 Print
Total Titles: 400 Print
Associate Companies: Suedverlag GmbH/uvk Verlagsgesellschaft mbH
Orders to: Brockhaus/Commission, Kreidlerstr 9, 70806 Kornwestheim

UVK Verlagsgesellschaft mbH+
Schuetzenstr 24, 78462 Konstanz
Mailing Address: Postfach 10 20 51, 78420 Konstanz
Tel: (07531) 9053-0 *Fax:* (07531) 9053-98
E-mail: willkommen@uvk.de
Web Site: www.uvk.de
Key Personnel
Publishing Manager & International Rights: Walter Engstle *E-mail:* walter.engstle@uvk.de
Founded: 1995
Subjects: Communications, Film, Video, History, Journalism, Radio, TV, Social Sciences, Sociology
ISBN Prefix(es): 978-3-89669; 978-3-86764
Number of titles published annually: 80 Print
Total Titles: 1,000 Print
Orders to: Brockhaus/Commission Verlagsauslieferung, Kreidlerstr 9, 70806 Kornwestheim bei Stuttgart

Verlag Franz Vahlen GmbH+
Subsidiary of C H Beck oHG
Wilhelmstr 9, 80801 Munich
Tel: (089) 38189-381; (089) 38189-0 *Fax:* (089) 38189-477; (089) 38189-402
E-mail: info@vahlen.de
Web Site: www.vahlen.de
Key Personnel
Mng Dir: Dr Hans Dieter Beck
Press Dir: Mathias Bruchmann *Tel:* (089) 38189-266 *Fax:* (089) 38189-480 *E-mail:* mathias.bruchmann@beck.de
Press: Karen Geerke *Tel:* (089) 38189-512 *Fax:* (089) 38189-480 *E-mail:* karen.geerke@beck.de
Founded: 1870
Subjects: Economics, Finance, Law, Management, Marketing
ISBN Prefix(es): 978-3-8006
Associate Companies: Verlag C H Beck (oHG) *Tel:* (089) 381 89-0 *Fax:* (089) 381 89-358 *E-mail:* info@beck.de *Web Site:* www.beck.de
Distribution Center: Dr Franz Hain, Dr-Otto-Neurath-Gasse 5, 1220 Vienna, Austria *Tel:* (01) 282 65 65 77 *Fax:* (01) 282 52 82
Schweizer Buchzentrum Haegendorf, Postfach, 4601 Olten 1, Switzerland *Tel:* (062) 2092525

VAK, see Verlagsanstalt Alexander Koch GmbH (VAK)

VAK Verlags GmbH
Eschbachstr 5, 79199 Kirchzarten
Tel: (07661) 98 71 50 *Fax:* (07661) 98 71 99
E-mail: info@vakverlag.de; marketing@vakverlag.de
Web Site: www.vakverlag.de
Key Personnel
Manager: Helga Petres; Alfred Schatz; Beate Walter
Press: Sophia Doerrbeck *Tel:* (07661) 98 71 53
E-mail: presse@vakverlag.de
Founded: 1983
Subjects: Education, Energy, Health, Nutrition, Music, Dance, Psychology, Psychiatry, Self-Help, Sports, Athletics, Alternative, Colloidal Silver, Kinesiology
ISBN Prefix(es): 978-3-86731
Foreign Rep(s): Dessauer (Claudia Gyr) (Switzerland); Mohr Morawa Buchvertrieb GmbH (Michael Hipp) (North Austria, Western Austria); Mohr Morawa Buchvertrieb GmbH (Thomas Lasnik) (Eastern Austria)

van Laack GmbH, see van Laack GmbH

Vandenhoeck & Ruprecht GmbH & Co KG+
Theaterstr 13, 37073 Goettingen
Tel: (0551) 5084-40 *Fax:* (0551) 5084-422

E-mail: info@v-r.de; order@v-r.de; rights@v-r.de
Web Site: www.v-r.de
Key Personnel
Mng Dir: Carola Mueller *E-mail:* c.mueller@v-r.
de
Rights Manager: Christa Bommart *Tel:* (0551) 50
84-445
Sales: Claudia Smolski *Tel:* (0551) 50 84-459
E-mail: c.smolski@v-r.de
Founded: 1735
Publisher of scientific literature.
Subjects: Archaeology, Education, History, Language Arts, Linguistics, Management, Philosophy, Psychology, Psychiatry, Religion - Other, Social Sciences, Sociology, Theology
ISBN Prefix(es): 978-3-525
Subsidiaries: Druckerei Hubert & Company; V&R unipress GmbH
U.S. Office(s): Vandenhoeck & Ruprecht LLC, 70 Enterprise Dr, Bristol, CT 06010, United States *Tel:* 860-584-8476 *E-mail:* v-r.us@v-r.de
Distributed by Oxford University Press LLC
Distributor for V&R unipress GmbH
Distribution Center: BMK Wartburg mbH, Trautsongasse 8, PO Box 65, 1082 Vienna, Austria *Tel:* (01) 4 05 93 71 *Fax:* (01) 4 08 99 05 *E-mail:* info@bmk.at
AVA Verlagsauslieferung AG, Centralweg 16, 8910 Affoltern am Albis, Switzerland *Tel:* (044) 762 42 00 *Fax:* (044) 762 42 10 *E-mail:* avainfo@ava.ch
ISD, 70 Enterprise Dr, Bristol, CT 06010, United States *Tel:* 860-584-6546 *Fax:* 860-516-4873 *E-mail:* info@isdistribution.com
Orders to: Brockhaus/Commission, Kreidlerstr 9, 70806 Kornwestheim, Contact: Sonja Woessner *Tel:* (07154) 13 27-0; (07154) 13 27-9216 *Fax:* (07154) 13 27-13 *E-mail:* vr@brocom.de (books)
HGV Hanseatische Society Publishing GmbH, Holzwiesenstr 2, 72127 Kusterdingen *Tel:* (07071) 9353-16 *Fax:* (07071) 9353-93 *E-mail:* vr-journals@hgv-online.de (magazines)

V&R unipress GmbH
Subsidiary of Vandenhoeck & Ruprecht GmbH & Co KG
Robert-Bosch-Breite 6, 37079 Goettingen
Tel: (0551) 50 84-301 *Fax:* (0551) 50 84-333
E-mail: info@vr-unipress.de
Web Site: www.v-r.de
Key Personnel
Publishing Dir: Susanne Franzkeit *Tel:* (0551) 50 84-303 *E-mail:* s.franzkeit@v-r.de
Project Manager & Public Relations: Ruth Vacheck
Founded: 2003
Subjects: Art, History, Language Arts, Linguistics, Law, Literature, Literary Criticism, Essays, Medicine, Nursing, Dentistry, Music, Dance, Philosophy, Psychology, Psychiatry, Social Sciences, Sociology, Theology, Natural Science
ISBN Prefix(es): 978-3-89971

Vantage Point World-Verlag
Theodor-Heuss-Str 15, 64732 Bad Koenig
Tel: (06063) 9517977 *Fax:* (06063) 9517977
E-mail: info@vantagepointworld-verlag.com
Web Site: www.vantagepointworld-verlag.com
Key Personnel
Contact: Georg Stauth
Founded: 2012
Subjects: Art, Travel & Tourism, Culture
ISBN Prefix(es): 978-3-981009

VAS Verlag fuer Akademische Schriften (VAS Publisher Academic Journals)+
Altkonigstr 32, 61350 Bad Homburg
Tel: (06172) 6811-656 *Fax:* (06172) 6811-657
E-mail: info@vas-verlag.de
Web Site: www.vas-verlag.de

Key Personnel
Publisher: Karl-Heinz Balon
Founded: 1982
Subjects: Art, Economics, Education, Environmental Studies, Fiction, Government, Political Science, History, Human Relations, Language Arts, Linguistics, Nonfiction (General), Philosophy, Psychology, Psychiatry, Social Sciences, Sociology, Women's Studies, Ecology, Public Health
ISBN Prefix(es): 978-3-88864

VBN-Verlag Luebeck
Kuecknitzer Hauptstr 53, 23569 Luebeck
Tel: (0451) 38 46 48 96 *Fax:* (0451) 38 46 48 95
E-mail: info@vbn-verlag.de
Web Site: www.vbn-verlag.de
Key Personnel
Mng Dir: Peter-Hansen Volkmann
Specialize in bioenergetics, naturopathy & holistic health topics.
Subjects: Alternative, Health, Nutrition, Medicine, Nursing, Dentistry
ISBN Prefix(es): 978-3-9806850; 978-3-9806274

VDE-Verlag GmbH+
Bismarckstr 33, 10625 Berlin
Mailing Address: Postfach 12 01 43, 10591 Berlin
Tel: (030) 34 80 01 0; (030) 34 80 01-222 (orders) *Fax:* (030) 34 80 01-9088
E-mail: kundenservice@vde-verlag.de
Web Site: www.vde-verlag.de
Key Personnel
Management: Dr Stefan Schlegel; Margaret Schneider
Subjects: Architecture & Interior Design, Communications, Electronics, Electrical Engineering
ISBN Prefix(es): 978-3-87907 (Wichmann-Verlag); 978-3-8007
Imprints: Wichmann-Verlag (geodesy)
Branch Office(s)
Goethering 58, 63067 Offenbach *Tel:* (069) 84 00 06-0 *Fax:* (069) 84 00 06-1399

VDG Verlag und Datenbank fuer Geisteswissenschaften
Eselsweg 17, 99441 Kromsdorf/Weimar
Tel: (03643) 83030 *Fax:* (03643) 830313
E-mail: info@vdg-weimar.de; herstellung@vdg-weimar.de; presse@vdg-weimar.de
Web Site: www.vdg-weimar.de
Key Personnel
Publisher: Dr Bettina Preiss *E-mail:* bettina. preiss@vdg-weimar.de
Production: Lydia Krueger
Sales & Press: Cathrin Rollberg
Founded: 1992
Specialize in humanities literature.
Membership(s): Boersenverein des Deutschen Buchhandels.
Subjects: Architecture & Interior Design, Art, Civil Engineering, Fiction, History, Literature, Literary Criticism, Essays, Nonfiction (General), Philosophy, Science (General), Social Sciences, Sociology
ISBN Prefix(es): 978-3-89739; 978-3-929742; 978-3-932124; 978-3-9803234
Distribution Center: Die Werkstatt Verlagsauslieferung, Koenigsstr 43, 26180 Rastede, Contact: Manon Clausen *Tel:* (04402) 92 63 0 *Fax:* (04402) 92 63 50 *E-mail:* info@werkstatt-auslieferung.de

VDI Verlag GmbH+
Subsidiary of VDI GmbH
VDI-Platz 1, 40468 Duesseldorf
Mailing Address: Postfach 10 10 54, 40001 Duesseldorf
Tel: (0211) 6188-0 *Fax:* (0211) 6188-112
E-mail: info@vdi-nachrichten.com

Web Site: www.vdi-verlag.de; www.vdi-nachrichten.com
Key Personnel
Mng Dir: Ken Fouhy
E-mail: geschaeftsfuehrung@vdi-nachrichten. com
Founded: 1923
Subjects: Engineering (General), Science (General), Technology
ISBN Prefix(es): 978-3-18

VEK, see Verlag Ernst Kuhn (VEK)

Velber, *imprint of* Family Media GmbH & Co KG

Velbrueck Wissenschaft
Meckenheimer Str 47, 53919 Weilerswist-Metternich
Tel: (02554) 83 603-0 *Fax:* (02554) 83 603-33
E-mail: info@velbrueck-wissenschaft.de
Web Site: www.velbrueck-wissenschaft.de
Key Personnel
Dir: Marietta Thien *E-mail:* m.thien@velbrueck. de
Founded: 1999
Subjects: Art, Law, Literature, Literary Criticism, Essays, Philosophy, Psychology, Psychiatry, Social Sciences, Sociology, Humanities
ISBN Prefix(es): 978-3-938808; 978-3-934730; 978-3-95832

VEM, see Vereinte Evangelische Mission

Ventil Verlag KG
Boppstr 25, 55118 Mainz
Tel: (06131) 22 60 78 *Fax:* (06131) 22 60 79
E-mail: mail@ventil-verlag.de; presse@ventil-verlag.de
Web Site: www.ventil-verlag.de
Key Personnel
Mng Dir: Theo Bender
Graphic: Oliver Schmitt
Press & Marketing: Ingo Ruediger
Sales: Jens Neumann
Founded: 1999
Subjects: Biography, Memoirs, Cookery, Fiction, Pop Culture
ISBN Prefix(es): 978-3-930559; 978-3-931555
Foreign Rep(s): Andrea Meisel (Switzerland); Seth Meyer-Bruhns (Austria)
Distribution Center: Sova, Friesstr 20-24, 60388 Frankfurt *Tel:* (069) 41 02 11 *Fax:* (069) 41 02 80 (Germany & Austria)
Kaktus Verlagsauslieferung, Thundorferstr 15, 8501 Frauenfeld, Switzerland *Tel:* (052) 722 31 90 *Fax:* (052) 722 17 82

Verbrecher Verlag
Gneisenaustr 2a, 10961 Berlin
Tel: (030) 28 38 59 54 *Fax:* (030) 28 38 59 55
E-mail: info@verbrecherei.de
Web Site: www.verbrecherei.de
Key Personnel
Publisher: Joerg Sundermeier
Press: Heike Joswig
Founded: 1995
Subjects: Art, Biography, Memoirs, Fiction, Film, Video, Government, Political Science, History, Literature, Literary Criticism, Essays, Nonfiction (General), Social Sciences, Sociology
ISBN Prefix(es): 978-3-935843; 978-3-9804471
Distribution Center: Leipziger Kommissions- und Grossbuchhandelsgesellschaft mbH (LKG), An der Suedspitze 1-12, 04571 Roetha, Contact: Baerbel Jaecklin *Tel:* (034206) 65120 *Fax:* (034206) 651758 *E-mail:* bjaecklin@lkg-service.de *Web Site:* www.lkg-va.de (Germany & Austria)

Kaktus Verlagsauslieferung, Langfeldstr 54, 8501 Frauenfeld, Switzerland *Tel:* (052) 722 31 90 *Fax:* (052) 722 17 82 *E-mail:* auslieferung@ kaktus.net

Vereinigte Fachverlage GmbH
Lise-Meitner-Str 2, 55129 Mainz
Mailing Address: Postfach 100465, 55135 Mainz
Tel: (06131) 992-0 *Fax:* (06131) 992-100
E-mail: info@vfmz.de
Web Site: www.vereinigte-fachverlage.info; www. cahensly-medien.de
Key Personnel
Manager: Dr Olaf Theisen
Publishing Dir: Dr Michael Werner *Tel:* (06131) 992-401 *E-mail:* m.werner@vfmz.de
Sales & Advertising: Beatrice Thomas-Meyer *Tel:* (06131) 992-265 *Fax:* (06131) 992-255 *E-mail:* b.thomas-meyer@vfmz.de
Founded: 1937
Subjects: Automotive, Civil Engineering, Engineering (General), Environmental Studies, Mechanical Engineering, Technology
ISBN Prefix(es): 978-3-7830
Parent Company: PP Cahensly GmbH
Subsidiaries: VF Verlagsgesellschaft GmbH
Foreign Rep(s): Automobilista Sp zoo (Dr Miroslaw Bugajski) (Poland); Rob Brewer (Ireland, UK); Heinz-Joachim Greiner (Austria); Intern Media Press & Marketing (Marc Jouanny) (France); Jordi Publipress GmbH (Hermann Jordi) (Italy, Switzerland); Malte Mezger (Scandinavia); Ksenia Mikhajlowa (Kazakhstan, Russia, Ukraine); Trade Media International Corp (Corrie de Groot) (Canada, USA)

Vereinte Evangelische Mission (United Evangelical Mission)
Rudolfstr 137, 42285 Wuppertal
Tel: (0202) 8 90 04-0 *Fax:* (0202) 8 90 04-179
E-mail: info@vemission.org
Web Site: www.vemission.org
Key Personnel
Editor: Brunhild von Local *E-mail:* local-b@ vemission.org
Founded: 1828
Communion of churches in 3 continents.
Subjects: Theology
ISBN Prefix(es): 978-3-87855; 978-3-921900
Total Titles: 2 Print

Verlag Bau+Technik GmbH
Steinhof 39, 40699 Erkrath
Mailing Address: Postfach 12 01 10, 40601 Duesseldorf
Tel: (0211) 9 24 99-0 *Fax:* (0211) 9 24 99-55
E-mail: info@verlagbt.de
Web Site: www.verlagbt.de
Key Personnel
Mng Dir: Rainer Buechel *Tel:* (0211) 9 24 99-32 *E-mail:* buechel@verlagbt.de
Editorial: Dr Stefan Deckers *Tel:* (0211) 9 24 99-51 *E-mail:* deckers@verlagbt.de
Marketing & Sales: Michael Fiolka *Tel:* (0211) 9 24 99-21 *E-mail:* fiolka@verlagbt.de
Production: Michael Spielmann *Tel:* (0211) 9 24 99-40 *E-mail:* spielmann@verlagbt.de
Subjects: Architecture & Interior Design, Engineering (General), Concrete & Cement Industry
ISBN Prefix(es): 978-3-7640

Verlag fuer Wissenschaft und Bildung, see VWB-Verlag fuer Wissenschaft und Bildung

Verlagsgruppe Huethig Jehle-Rehm GmbH
Im Weiher 10, 69121 Heidelberg
Mailing Address: Postfach 10 28 69, 69018 Heidelberg
Tel: (06221) 489-0 *Toll Free Tel:* 800-2183-333
Fax: (06221) 489-279

E-mail: info@hjr-verlag.de; vertrieb-handel@hjr-verlag.de
Web Site: www.jehle-rehm.de
Key Personnel
Mng Dir: Dr Karl Ulrich
Press: Christiane Koeken *Tel:* (06221) 489-327 *E-mail:* christiane.koeken@hjr-verlag.de
Sales & Marketing: Stefan Jaitner *Tel:* (06221) 489-555 *Fax:* (06221) 489-410
Founded: 1988
Subjects: Business, Computer Science, Economics, Health, Nutrition, Law, Management, Medicine, Nursing, Dentistry, Public Administration, Transportation, Security, Taxes
ISBN Prefix(es): 978-3-8073; 978-3-7825; 978-3-87253; 978-3-7719
Parent Company: Sueddeutscher Verlag Huethig Fachinformationen, Munich
Divisions: BHV; DATAKONTEXT; ecomed Medizin; ecomed Sicherheit; Forkel; Jehle; Kriminalistik; mitp & bhv-Buch; C F Mueller; Rehm; R v Decker; Storck
Branch Office(s)
Augustinusstr 9d, Postfach 4057, 50216 Frechen *Tel:* (02234) 98949-0 *Fax:* (02234) 98949-88
Striepenweg 31, 21147 Hamburg *Tel:* (040) 79713-01 *Fax:* (040) 797130-101 *E-mail:* info@storck-verlag.de
Justus-von-Liebig-Str 1, 86899 Landsberg *Tel:* (08191) 125-0 *Fax:* (08191) 125-492
Hultschiner Str 8, 81677 Munich *Tel:* (089) 2183-7222 *Fax:* (089) 2183-7620

Vervuert Verlagsgesellschaft
Elisabethenstr 3-9, 60594 Frankfurt
Tel: (069) 597 4617 *Fax:* (069) 597 8743
E-mail: info@iberoamericanalibros.com
Web Site: www.ibero-americana.net
Key Personnel
Mng Dir: Klaus Dieter Vervuert
Founded: 1975
Focus on academic books about Latin America & Spain. Also bookshop & library supplier.
Subjects: Art, Developing Countries, Drama, Theater, Ethnicity, Foreign Countries, Government, Political Science, History, Language Arts, Linguistics, Literature, Literary Criticism, Essays, Social Sciences, Sociology
ISBN Prefix(es): 978-3-89354; 978-3-921600; 978-3-86527; 978-84-8489; 978-84-95107
Associate Companies: Iberoamericana Editorial Vervuert SL, C/Amor de Dios, 1, 28014 Madrid, Spain *Tel:* 91 429 35 22 *Fax:* 91 429 53 97
Bookshop(s): Libreria Iberoamericana, c/Huertas, 40, 28014 Madrid, Spain *Tel:* 91 360 12 29 *Fax:* 91 429 53 97 *E-mail:* libreria@ iberoamericanalibros.com; Libreria Iberoamerican en CCHS, Albasanz, 26-28, 28037 Madrid, Spain *Tel:* 91 754 15 03 *E-mail:* libreria_cchs@ibero-americana.net
Distribution Center: Silvermine International Books LLC, 25 Perry Ave, Suite 11, Norwalk, CT 06850, United States *Tel:* 203-451-2396 *E-mail:* info@jawilsons.com *Web Site:* jawilsons.com/pages/who-we-are

VGE Verlag GmbH+
Montebruchstr 20, 45219 Essen
Mailing Address: Postfach 18 56 20, 45206 Essen
Tel: (02054) 924-0 *Fax:* (02054) 924-149 (sales)
E-mail: info@vge.de
Web Site: www.vge.de
Key Personnel
Mng Dir: Christina Sternitzke
Editorial: Ines Henning *E-mail:* ih@vge.de
Founded: 1918
Membership(s): Austrian Society for Geomechanics (OEGG); German Society for Geotechnical Engineering (DGGT).
Subjects: Earth Sciences, Energy, Engineering (General), Environmental Studies, Technology

ISBN Prefix(es): 978-3-7739
Branch Office(s)
Kleyerstr 88, 60326 Frankfurt am Main *Tel:* (069) 7104687-0

vhw-Dienstleistung GmbH+
Hinter Hoben 149, 53129 Bonn
Tel: (0228) 7 25 99-30 *Fax:* (0228) 7 25 99-19
E-mail: verlag@vhw.de
Web Site: www.vhw.de
Key Personnel
Mng Dir: Peter Rohland *E-mail:* prohland@vhw. de
Founded: 1982
Subjects: House & Home, Law
ISBN Prefix(es): 978-3-87941

Verlag Via Nova Werner Vogel und Martin Buettner GmbH
Alte Landstr 12, 36100 Petersberg
Tel: (0661) 62973 *Fax:* (0661) 9679560
E-mail: info@verlag-vianova.de
Web Site: www.verlag-vianova.de
Key Personnel
Mng Dir: Martin Buettner; Werner Vogel
Subjects: Health, Nutrition, Psychology, Psychiatry
ISBN Prefix(es): 978-3-86616; 978-3-928632; 978-3-936486; 978-3-9801787

ViaTerra Verlag
Steinweg 21, 65326 Aarbergen
Tel: (06120) 1497; (0163) 8809894
Web Site: www.viaterra-verlag.de
Key Personnel
Publisher: Mechthild D Zimmermann *E-mail:* mechthild.zimmermann@viaterra-verlag.de
Subjects: Mysteries, Suspense, Romance, Crime
ISBN Prefix(es): 978-3-941970

Vice Versa Verlag+
Planufer 92d, 10967 Berlin
Tel: (030) 611 019 010 *Fax:* (030) 611 019 011
E-mail: info@parthasverlag.de
Web Site: www.viceversaverlag.de
Key Personnel
Mng Dir: Gabriela Wachter
Founded: 1992
Subjects: Architecture & Interior Design, Art, Photography
ISBN Prefix(es): 978-3-9803212; 978-3-932809
Parent Company: Parthas Verlag GmbH
Associate Companies: Vice Versa Vertrieb

Vielflieger Verlag
Eppenhainer Str 3, 60326 Frankfurt am Main
Tel: (069) 74731099
E-mail: kontakt@vielflieger-verlag.com
Web Site: www.vielflieger-verlag.com
Key Personnel
Publisher: Felix Busse *E-mail:* felix.busse@ vielflieger-verlag.com
Founded: 2008
ISBN Prefix(es): 978-3-943223

Vier-Tuerme-GmbH-Klosterbetriebe (Four Towers Ltd, Publishing Division)+
Schweinfurter Str 40, 97359 Muensterschwarzach
Tel: (09324) 20 292 *Fax:* (09324) 20 495
E-mail: info@vier-tuerme.de
Web Site: www.vier-tuerme-verlag.de
Key Personnel
Publisher: Dr Mauritius Wilde
Mng Dir: P Christoph Gerhard
Foreign Rights Manager: Hilde Wilbs *Tel:* (09324) 20 473 *Fax:* (09324) 20 668 473 *E-mail:* h.wilbs@vier-tuerme.de
Founded: 1955
Subjects: How-to, Religion - Catholic, Theology
ISBN Prefix(es): 978-3-87868; 978-3-89680

Number of titles published annually: 15 Print; 10
Audio
Total Titles: 35 Audio
Imprints: Muensterschwarzacher Kleinschriften;
Muensterschwarzacher Studien; Schriften zur
Kontemplation

Villa Arceno, *imprint of* Frederking & Thaler
Verlag GmbH

Vincentz Network GmbH & Co KG+
Plathnerstr 4C, 30175 Hannover
Mailing Address: Postfach 6247, 30062 Hannover
Tel: (0511) 9910000 *Fax:* (0511) 9910099
E-mail: info@vincentz.de
Web Site: www.vincentz.de
Key Personnel
Mng Dir: Jonas Vincentz
Commercial Dir: Helmut Fitting
Sales: Dirk Goedeke
Founded: 1893
Subjects: Chemistry, Chemical Engineering,
Medicine, Nursing, Dentistry
ISBN Prefix(es): 978-3-87870; 978-3-86630
Divisions: Verlag Th Schaefer
Warehouse: Emil-Meyer-Str 18a, 30165 Hannover

Edition Curt Visel+
Subsidiary of Maximilian Dietrich Verlag
Weberstr 36, 87700 Memmingen
Tel: (08331) 2853 *Fax:* (08331) 490364
E-mail: info@edition-curt-visel.de
Web Site: www.edition-curt-visel.de
Key Personnel
Owner: Juergen Schweitzer
Founded: 1963
Subjects: Art, Biography, Memoirs
ISBN Prefix(es): 978-3-922406; 978-3-87164

Vista Point Verlag GmbH+
Haendelstr 25-29, 50674 Cologne
Mailing Address: Postfach 27 05 72, 50511
Cologne
Tel: (0221) 92 16 13-0 *Fax:* (0221) 92 16 13-14
E-mail: info@vistapoint.de
Web Site: www.vistapoint.de
Key Personnel
Mng Dir: Andreas Schulz
Publishing Dir: Dr Andrea Herfurth-Schindler
Sales: Claudia Polywka
Founded: 1977
Subjects: Travel & Tourism
ISBN Prefix(es): 978-3-88973

ars vivendi verlag GmbH & Co KG+
Bauhof 1, 90556 Cadolzburg
Tel: (09103) 71929-0; (09103) 71929-10
Fax: (09103) 71929-19
E-mail: info@arsvivendi.com
Web Site: www.arsvivendi.com
Key Personnel
Owner: Norbert Treuheit *E-mail:* n.treuheit@
arsvivendiverlag.de
Press & Public Relations: Anna Philipp
Tel: (09103) 71929-53 *E-mail:* a.philipp@
arsvivendiverlag.de
Founded: 1988
Subjects: Cookery, Drama, Theater, Literature,
Literary Criticism, Essays, Nonfiction (General), Poetry, Travel & Tourism
ISBN Prefix(es): 978-3-927482; 978-3-931043;
978-3-89716
Distribution Center: Leipziger Kommissions- und
Grossbuchhandelsgesellschaft mbH (LKG),
An der Suedspitze 1-12, 04571 Roetha, Contact: Kathrin Obarski *Tel:* (034206) 65-106
Fax: (034206) 65-130 *E-mail:* kobarski@lkg-
service.de *Web Site:* www.lkg-va.de
Mohr Morawa Buchvertrieb GmbH, Sulzen-
gasse 2, 1230 Vienna, Austria *Tel:* (01) 680

14-0 *Fax:* (01) 688 71 30 *E-mail:* momo@
mohrmorawa.at *Web Site:* www.mohrmorawa.at
AVA Verlagsausl AG, Centralweg 16, 8910 Affoltern am Albis, Switzerland, Contact: Beat
Eberle *Tel:* (044) 7 62 42 00 *Fax:* (044) 7 62
42 10 *E-mail:* verlagsservice@ava.ch

VJK, see Verlag Josef Knecht

VNR Verlag fuer die Deutsche Wirtschaft AG
Theodor-Heuss-Str 2-4, 53177 Bonn
Tel: (0228) 82 05 0 *Fax:* (0228) 36 96 480
E-mail: info@vnr.de
Web Site: www.vnrag.de
Key Personnel
Publishing Dir: Helmut Graf
Public Affairs: Mechthild Alves
Subjects: Business, Management
ISBN Prefix(es): 978-3-8125

VNW, see Verlag Neuer Weg GmbH

Vogel Business Media GmbH & Co KG+
Max-Planck-Str 7/9, 97082 Wuerzburg
Tel: (0931) 418-0 *Fax:* (0931) 418-2100
E-mail: info@vogel.de
Web Site: www.vogel.de
Key Personnel
Mng Dir: Florian Fischer; Stefan Ruehling;
Guenter Schuerger
Head, Communications & Corporate Market-
ing: Dr Gunther Schunk *Tel:* (0931) 418-
2590 *Fax:* (0931) 418-2860 *E-mail:* gunther.
schunk@vogel.de
Founded: 1891
Subjects: Automotive, Business, Chemistry,
Chemical Engineering, Civil Engineering,
Communications, Computer Science, Elec-
tronics, Electrical Engineering, Environmental
Studies, Law, Management, Mechanical En-
gineering, Medicine, Nursing, Dentistry, Con-
struction, Information Technology
ISBN Prefix(es): 978-3-8023
U.S. Office(s): Vogel Europublishing, 632 Sunflower Court, San Ramon, CA 94583, United
States, Contact: Mark Hauser *Tel:* 510-648-
1170 *Fax:* 510-648-1171

Voggenreiter Verlag GmbH+
Viktoriastr 25, 53173 Bonn
Tel: (0228) 935750 *Fax:* (0228) 9357575
E-mail: sales@voggenreiter.de
Web Site: www.voggenreiter.de
Key Personnel
Proprietor: Charles Voggenreiter; Ralph Voggen-
reiter
Founded: 1919
Rock, pop & folk music publisher. Specialize in
full tutorials, method & reference books, sheet
music, videos & instrumental sets.
Membership(s): DMV; NAMM; Retail Print Mu-
sic Dealers Association.
Subjects: Education, How-to, Literature, Literary
Criticism, Essays, Music, Dance, Self-Help
ISBN Prefix(es): 978-3-8024
Total Titles: 300 Print; 200 Audio
Distribution Center: Voggenreiter Logistikzen-
trum, Wittfelder Stich 1, 53343 Wachtberg-
Villip *Tel:* (0228) 34 10 43 *Fax:* (0228) 95 16
334

Vogt Multimedia Verlag
Erlenweg 18, 64354 Reinheim
Tel: (06162) 911 252 *Fax:* (06162) 911 253
E-mail: vogt.webdesign@t-online.de
Web Site: www.vogt-multimedia-verlag.de
Key Personnel
Publisher: Dr Hans-Peter Vogt
Subjects: Mysteries, Suspense, Science Fiction,
Fantasy, Travel & Tourism
ISBN Prefix(es): 978-3-942652

Verlag Voland & Quist
Glacisstr 22, 01099 Dresden
Mailing Address: Postfach 10 05 52, 01075 Dres-
den
Tel: (0351) 79 54 771 *Fax:* (0351) 79 54 769
E-mail: vertrieb@voland-quist.de; presse@voland-
quist.de; info@voland-quist.de
Web Site: www.voland-quist.de
Key Personnel
Owner: Sebastian Wolter *Tel:* (0341) 225 34 18
Fax: (0341) 225 34 18; Leif Greinus
Founded: 2004
Subjects: Literature, Literary Criticism, Essays,
Poetry
ISBN Prefix(es): 978-3-938424
Foreign Rep(s): Andreas Meisel (Switzerland);
Seth Meyer-Bruhns (Austria)

Volk Verlag
Streitfeldstr 19, 81673 Munich
Tel: (089) 420 79 69 80 *Fax:* (089) 420 79 69 86
E-mail: info@volkverlag.de
Web Site: www.volkverlag.de
Key Personnel
Publisher: Michael Volk *E-mail:* volk@
volkverlag.de
Public Relations: Katja Sebald *E-mail:* sebald@
volkverlag.de
Subjects: Architecture & Interior Design, Art,
Biography, Memoirs, History, Art History,
Comics, Customs
ISBN Prefix(es): 978-3-86222

Verlag Vopelius Jena
August-Bebel-Str 10, 07743 Jena
Tel: (03641) 219860 *Fax:* (03641) 561770
E-mail: verlagvopelius@email.de
Web Site: www.verlagvopelius.de
Key Personnel
Publisher: Bernd Rolle
Founded: 1891
Subjects: History, Culture
ISBN Prefix(es): 978-3-939718

Vorwaerts Buch Verlagsgesellschaft mbH
Stresemannstr 30, 10963 Berlin
Mailing Address: Paul-Singer-Haus, Postfach 61
03 22, 10925 Berlin
Tel: (030) 255 94 520 *Fax:* (030) 255 94 190;
(030) 255 94 192
E-mail: info@vorwaerts-buch.de
Web Site: www.vorwaerts-buch.de
Key Personnel
Mng Dir: Guido Schmitz
Editor: Jens Kreibaum *Tel:* (030) 2 55 94-5 21
E-mail: kreibaum@vorwaerts-buch.de
Distribution: Reglind Doerner *E-mail:* doerner@
vorwaerts-buch.de
Subjects: Government, Political Science, History,
Social Sciences, Sociology
ISBN Prefix(es): 978-3-86602

Verlag Vorwerk 8
Grossgoerschenstr 5, 10827 Berlin
Tel: (030) 784 61 01 *Fax:* (030) 784 06 104
E-mail: verlag@vorwerk8.de
Web Site: www.vorwerk8.de
Key Personnel
Publishing Manager: Reinald Gussman
Subjects: Film, Video, Literature, Literary Crit-
icism, Essays, Music, Dance, Philosophy, Po-
etry, Culture
ISBN Prefix(es): 978-3-930916
Distribution Center: Runge Verlagsauslieferung
GmbH, Bergstr 2, 33803 Steinhagen, Contact:
Team 3 *Tel:* (05204) 998 123 *Fax:* (05204)
998 114 *E-mail:* msr@rungeva.de *Web
Site:* rungeva.de

VS-BOOKS Torsten Verhuelsdonk+
Grenzweg 41, 44623 Herne

Mailing Address: Postfach 20 05 40, 44635
Herne
Tel: (02323) 946 252 0 *Fax:* (02323) 946 252 9
E-mail: vertrieb@vs-books.de (orders); info@vs-
books.de
Web Site: www.vs-books.de
Key Personnel
Manager: Torsten Verhuelsdonk *E-mail:* torsten@
vs-books.de
Founded: 1998
Subjects: History, Technology, Costume Design,
Military History, Weapon Technology
ISBN Prefix(es): 978-3-932077

VSA: Verlag Hamburg GmbH
St Georgs Kirchhof 6, 20099 Hamburg
Mailing Address: Postfach 10 61 27, 20042 Ham-
burg
Tel: (040) 28 09 52 77-0 *Fax:* (040) 28 09 52 77-
50
E-mail: info@vsa-verlag.de
Web Site: www.vsa-verlag.de
Key Personnel
Manager: Bernhard Mueller *Tel:* (040) 28 09 52
77-40 *E-mail:* bernhard.mueller@vsa-verlag.
de; Gerd Siebecke *Tel:* (040) 28 09 52 77-30
E-mail: gerd.siebecke@vsa-verlag.de
Sales: Christoph Lieber *Tel:* (040) 28 09 52 77-11
E-mail: christoph.lieber@vsa-verlag.de
Distribution: Johannes Tesfai *Tel:* (040) 28 09 52
77-20 *E-mail:* johannes.tesfai@vsa-verlag.de
Subjects: Government, Political Science, Social
Sciences, Sociology, Capitalism, Global Crisis,
International Law, Socialism
ISBN Prefix(es): 978-3-87975; 978-3-89965

VSRW-Verlag Dr Hagen Pruehs GmbH
Rolandstr 48, 53179 Bonn
Tel: (0228) 95124-0 *Fax:* (0228) 95124-90
E-mail: vsrw@vsrw.de
Web Site: www.vsrw.de
Key Personnel
Mng Dir: Dr Hagen Pruehs
Founded: 1977
Subjects: Economics, Law, Taxation
ISBN Prefix(es): 978-3-923763; 978-3-936623

VUD Medien GmbH
Wallstr 7, 72250 Freudenstadt
Mailing Address: Postfach 420, 72234 Freuden-
stadt
Tel: (07441) 91030 *Fax:* (07441) 910333
E-mail: info@vud.com
Web Site: www.vud.com
Key Personnel
Founder & Mng Partner: Juergen Walther
E-mail: j.walther@vud.com
Deputy Mng Dir: Saskia Klima *E-mail:* s.klima@
vud.com
Founded: 1982
Membership(s): Deutscher Tourismusverband eV.
Subjects: Travel & Tourism
ISBN Prefix(es): 978-3-923719

Vulkan-Verlag GmbH+
Subsidiary of Oldenbourg Industrieverlag GmbH
Huyssenallee 52-56, 45128 Essen
Tel: (0201) 82002-14 *Fax:* (0201) 82002-40
E-mail: info@oiv.de
Web Site: www.oldenbourg-industrieverlag.de
Key Personnel
General Manager: Hans-Jochim Jauch
E-mail: hjjauch@oldenbourg.de
Marketing Manager: Thomas Steinbach
Tel: (0201) 82002-11 *E-mail:* t.steinbach@
vulkan-verlag.de
Sales: Silvia Spies *E-mail:* s.spies@vulkan-verlag.
de
Founded: 1928
Provide professional technical literature & digital
media for engineers & technicians.

Subjects: Chemistry, Chemical Engineering, Civil
Engineering, Electronics, Electrical Engineering, Energy, Engineering (General), Environmental Studies, Mechanical Engineering, Technology, Manufacturing Engineering
ISBN Prefix(es): 978-3-8027; 978-3-8356

VWB-Verlag fuer Wissenschaft und Bildung
Urbanstr 71, 10967 Berlin
Mailing Address: Postfach 11 03 68, 10833
Berlin
Tel: (030) 251 04 15 *Fax:* (030) 251 11 36
E-mail: info@vwb-verlag.com
Web Site: www.vwb-verlag.com
Key Personnel
Owner: Amand Aglaster
Founded: 1988
Subjects: Anthropology, Art, Biological Sciences,
Education, Ethnicity, Geography, Geology,
Medicine, Nursing, Dentistry, Music, Dance,
Psychology, Psychiatry, Science (General), So-
cial Sciences, Sociology, Women's Studies
ISBN Prefix(es): 978-3-927408; 978-3-86135

Wachholtz Verlag GmbH
Rungestr 4, 24537 Neumuenster
Tel: (04321) 25093-0 *Fax:* (04321) 250930-15
E-mail: info@wachholtz-verlag.de
Web Site: www.wachholtz.de
Key Personnel
Mng Dir: Dr Sven Murmann
Mng Dir & Permissions: Gabriele Wachholtz
Tel: (04321) 25093-10
Mng Dir: Henner Wachholtz *Tel:* (04321)
25093-93 *Fax:* (04321) 25093-94 *E-mail:* h.
wachholtz@wachholtz.de
Production: Renate Braus *Tel:* (04321) 25093-13
Fax: (04321) 25093-33 *E-mail:* r.braus@
wachholtz.de
Founded: 1871
Membership(s): Boersenverein des Deutschen
Buchhandels.
Subjects: Archaeology, Art, Biography, Mem-
oirs, Environmental Studies, History, Language
Arts, Linguistics, Literature, Literary Criticism,
Essays, Regional Interests, Social Sciences, So-
ciology
ISBN Prefix(es): 978-3-529

Verlag Klaus Wagenbach
Emser Str 40/41, 10719 Berlin
Tel: (030) 23 51 51-0 *Fax:* (030) 211 61 40
E-mail: mail@wagenbach.de; presse@wagenbach.
de
Web Site: www.wagenbach.de
Key Personnel
Mng Dir: Susanne Schuessler
Press: Annette Wasserman
Sales & Marketing: Jorg Englbrecht *Tel:* (030) 23
51 51 51 *E-mail:* j.englbrecht@wagenbach.de
Sales: Nina Wagenbach *Tel:* (030) 23 51 51 52
E-mail: n.wagenbach@wagenbach.de
Founded: 1964
Subjects: Art, Government, Political Science,
History, Literature, Literary Criticism, Essays,
Nonfiction (General), Cultural History
ISBN Prefix(es): 978-3-8031
Distribution Center: Koch, Neff & Oetinger
Verlagsauslieferung GmbH, Industriestr 23,
70565 Stuttgart, Contact: Baldur Schmoeller
E-mail: wagenbach@kno-va.de
Mohr Morawa Buchvertrieb GmbH, Sulzengasse
2, 1230 Vienna, Austria, Contact: Gabriele
Samek *Tel:* (01) 680 14-0 *Fax:* (01) 688
71 30 *E-mail:* momo@mohrmorawa.at *Web
Site:* www.mohrmorawa.at
Book Centre Ltd, Industriestr Ost 10, 4614
Haegendorf, Switzerland, Contact: Regula
Aerni *Tel:* (02) 09 27 04 *Fax:* (02) 09 27 60
E-mail: kundendienst@buchzentrum.ch

Orders to: Shakespeare & Co, Ludwigkirchstr 9a,
10719 Berlin-Wilmersdorf *Tel:* (030) 74 76 01
71 *Fax:* (030) 74 76 01 72 *E-mail:* webshop@
wagenbach.de

**Friedenauer Presse Katharina
Wagenbach-Wolff+**
Carmerstr 10, 10623 Berlin
Tel: (030) 3 12 99 23 *Fax:* (030) 3 12 99 02
E-mail: frpresse@t-online.de
Web Site: www.friedenauer-presse.de
Key Personnel
Mng Dir & International Rights: Katharina
Wagenbach-Wolff
Founded: 1963
Subjects: Literature, Literary Criticism, Essays
ISBN Prefix(es): 978-3-921592; 978-3-932109

Wagner Verlag GmbH
Langgass 2, 63571 Gelnhausen
Tel: (06051) 9779900; (06051) 88381-0
Fax: (06051) 9779901; (06051) 88381-29
E-mail: info@wagner-verlag.de; buch@wagner-
verlag.de
Web Site: www.wagner-verlag.de
Key Personnel
Mng Dir: Hauke Joachim Wagner *E-mail:* hmw@
wagner-verlag.de
Founded: 2000
Subjects: Animals, Pets, Biography, Memoirs,
Drama, Theater, History, Inspirational, Spiritu-
ality, Nonfiction (General), Philosophy, Photog-
raphy, Poetry, Science Fiction, Fantasy, Travel
& Tourism, Crime Fiction, Drug Prevention,
Narrative, New Age, Roman, Self-Awareness,
Sexual Abuse, Violence
ISBN Prefix(es): 978-3-86683
Branch Office(s)
Hamilton House, Mabledon Pl, Bloomsbury, Lon-
don WC1H 9BB, United Kingdom
U.S. Office(s): Seafirst Fifth Ave Plaza, 800 Fifth
Ave, Suite 4100, Seattle, WA 98104, United
States

Waldhardt Verlag
Unterhauser Str 10, 35085 Ebsdorfergrund
Tel: (06424) 30928901 *Fax:* (06424) 30928909
Web Site: waldhardt.com
Key Personnel
Founder: Melanie Waldhardt *E-mail:* melanie@
waldhardt-verlag.de
Subjects: Romance, Science Fiction, Fantasy
ISBN Prefix(es): 978-3-945746

Edition Waldschloesschen, *imprint of*
Maennerschwarm Verlag GmbH

Waldthausen Verlag, *imprint of* NaturaViva
Verlags GmbH

Walhalla Fachverlag+
Haus an der Eisernen Bruecke, 93042 Regensburg
Mailing Address: Postfach 10 10 53, 93010 Re-
gensburg
Tel: (0941) 56 84-0 *Fax:* (0941) 56 84-111
E-mail: walhalla@walhalla.de
Web Site: www.walhalla.de
Key Personnel
Mng Dir: Bernhard Roloff
Publishing Dir & Licenses: Eva-Maria Stecken-
leiter
Founded: 1949
Subjects: Business, Career Development, Law,
Public Administration
ISBN Prefix(es): 978-3-8029
Parent Company: Walhalla & Praetoria Verlag
GmbH & Co KG

Wallstein Verlag GmbH
Geiststr 11, 37073 Goettingen
Tel: (0551) 548 98-0 *Fax:* (0551) 548 98-33

E-mail: info@wallstein-verlag.de
Web Site: www.wallstein-verlag.de
Key Personnel
Publisher & Mng Dir: Thedel von Wallmoden
Sales: Claudia Hillebrand
Foreign Rights: Hajo Gevers *Tel:* (0551) 548 98-22 *E-mail:* hgevers@wallstein-verlag.de
Founded: 1986
Subjects: Fiction, History, Literature, Literary Criticism, Essays, Philosophy, Religion - Jewish
ISBN Prefix(es): 978-3-8353; 978-3-86621; 978-3-89244
Foreign Rights: Agence Hoffman (Christine Scholz) (France); Berla & Griffini (Barbara Griffini) (Italy); Sophia Georgopoulou (Greece); Sebastian Graf (Switzerland); Ute Koerner Literary Agent SL (Guenter G Rodewald) (Brazil, Latin America, Portugal, Spain); Helga Schuster Verlagsvertretungen (Austria)

Uwe Warnke Verlag Entwerter/Oder+
Sonntagstr 22, 10245 Berlin
Tel: (030) 29049903
Key Personnel
Publisher/Author: Uwe Warnke
Founded: 1982
Subjects: Art, Literature, Literary Criticism, Essays, Photography, Poetry
ISBN Prefix(es): 978-3-910165
Total Titles: 100 Print; 1 CD-ROM

Wartberg Verlag GmbH & Co
Im Wiesental 1, 34281 Gudensberg
Tel: (05603) 93 05-0 *Fax:* (05603) 93 05-28
E-mail: info@wartberg-verlag.de
Web Site: www.wartberg-verlag.de
Key Personnel
Publisher & Chief Executive Officer: Jannis Wieden
Founded: 1984
Subjects: Cookery, Mysteries, Suspense
ISBN Prefix(es): 978-3-8313; 978-3-86134; 978-3-925277

Wartburg Verlag GmbH+
Lisztstr 2 A, 99423 Weimar
Tel: (03643) 246144 *Fax:* (03643) 246118
E-mail: buch@wartburgverlag.de
Web Site: www.wartburgverlag.de
Key Personnel
Mng Dir: Torsten Bolduan; Barbara Harnisch
Founded: 1990
Subjects: Art, Fiction, Literature, Literary Criticism, Essays, Music, Dance, Regional Interests, Religion - Protestant
ISBN Prefix(es): 978-3-86160
Number of titles published annually: 12 Print
Total Titles: 90 Print

Ernst Wasmuth Verlag GmbH & Co
Fuerststr 133, 72072 Tuebingen
Mailing Address: Postfach 27 28, 72017 Tuebingen
Tel: (07071) 97 55 00 *Fax:* (07071) 97 55 013
E-mail: info@wasmuth-verlag.de
Web Site: www.wasmuth-verlag.de
Key Personnel
Mng Dir: Ernst-Juergen Wasmuth
Editorial Dir: Dr Sigrid Hauser
Sales & Public Relations: Markus Baumgart
Founded: 1872
A majority of titles are published by contract with organizations or universities.
Subjects: Archaeology, Architecture & Interior Design, Art
ISBN Prefix(es): 978-3-8030
Number of titles published annually: 30 Print
Total Titles: 250 Print
Distributor for L'Arcaedizioni
Foreign Rep(s): Jan Smit Boeken (Netherlands); Marcello SAS Publishers' Representatives

(Flavio Marcello) (France, Gibraltar, Greece, Italy, Portugal, Spain); Ernst Sonntag (North Austria, South Austria, South Tyrol, Italy)
Bookshop(s): Wasmuth Buchhandlung & Antiquariat GmbH & Co, Pfalzburgerstr 43-44, 10717 Berlin *Tel:* (030) 8 63 09 90 *Fax:* (030) 86 30 99 99 *E-mail:* info@wasmuth.de *Web Site:* www.wasmuth.de
Distribution Center: Brockhaus/Commission Verlagsauslieferung, Kreidlerstr 9, 70806 Kornwestheim *Tel:* (07154) 1327 0 *Fax:* (07154) 1327 13 *E-mail:* wasmuth@brocom.de
Dr Franz Hain Verlagsauslieferungen GmbH, Dr-Otto-Neurath-Gasse 5, 1220 Vienna, Austria *Tel:* (01) 2 82 65 65 77 *Fax:* (01) 2 82 65 65 49 *E-mail:* bestell@hain.at
RIBA Bookshops Distribution, 15 Bonhill St, London EC2P 2EA, United Kingdom *Tel:* (020) 7256 7222 *Fax:* (020) 7374 2737 *E-mail:* sales@ribabookshops.com
DAP Distributed Art Publishers, 155 Avenue of the Americas, 2nd floor, New York, NY, United States *Tel:* 212-627-1999 *Fax:* 212-627-9484 *E-mail:* orders@dapinc.com

Dr Watson Books GbR
Koellestr 12, 70193 Stuttgart
Tel: (0711) 955 969-30 *Fax:* (0711) 955 969-39
E-mail: watson@food-detektiv.de; interessenten@food-detektiv.de
Web Site: www.food-detektiv.de
Key Personnel
Mng Dir: Dr Hans-Ulrich Grimm
Founded: 2005
Subjects: Health, Nutrition, Diet, Food
ISBN Prefix(es): 978-3-9810915

Waxmann Verlag GmbH
Steinfurterstr 555, 48159 Muenster
Tel: (0251) 26504-0 *Fax:* (0251) 26504-26
E-mail: info@waxmann.com
Web Site: www.waxmann.com
Key Personnel
Mng Dir: Dr Ursula Heckel *Tel:* (0251) 26504-12 *E-mail:* heckel@waxmann.com
Editorial: Werner Hecker
Contact: Beate Plugge *Tel:* (0251) 26504-14 *E-mail:* plugge@waxmann.com
Founded: 1987
Subjects: Education, Ethnicity, History, Literature, Literary Criticism, Essays, Psychology, Psychiatry, Science (General), Social Sciences, Sociology, Theology, Women's Studies
ISBN Prefix(es): 978-3-89325; 978-3-8309
Number of titles published annually: 150 Print
Total Titles: 1,800 Print
Branch Office(s)
Garnisonkirchplatz 2, 10178 Berlin
Maria-Einsiedel-Str 22, 81379 Munich
U.S. Office(s): Waxmann Publishing Co, PO Box 1318, New York, NY 10028, United States

WBG (Wissenschaftliche Buchgesellschaft)
(Scientific Book Society)+
Hindenburgstr 40, 64295 Darmstadt
Tel: (06151) 33 08-0 *Fax:* (06151) 31 41 28
E-mail: service@wbg-wissenverbindet.de
Web Site: www.wbg-wissenverbindet.de
Key Personnel
Mng Dir: Andreas Auth *Tel:* (06151) 33 08-140 *E-mail:* auth@wbg-wissenverbindet.de
Head, Marketing: Holger Wochnowski *E-mail:* wochnowski@wbg-wissenverbindet.de
Program Dir: Dr Beate Varnhorn *Tel:* (06151) 33 08-162 *E-mail:* varnhorn@wbg-wissenverbindet.de
Foreign Rights: Britta Henning *Tel:* (06151) 33 08-159 *Fax:* (06151) 33 08-212 *E-mail:* henning@wbg-wissenverbindet.de
Press: Christina Herborg *Tel:* (06151) 33 08-161 *Fax:* (06151) 33 08-208 *E-mail:* herborg@wbg-wissenverbindet.de

Founded: 1949
Subjects: Archaeology, Art, Economics, Education, History, Language Arts, Linguistics, Law, Literature, Literary Criticism, Essays, Mathematics, Medicine, Nursing, Dentistry, Music, Dance, Philosophy, Psychology, Psychiatry, Religion - Other, Science (General), Social Sciences, Sociology
ISBN Prefix(es): 978-3-534
Imprints: Lambert Schneider Verlag; Konrad Theiss Verlag; Phillipp von Zabern Verlag
Book Club(s): Wissenschaftliche Buchgesellschaft
Distribution Center: AVA Verlagsauslieferung AG (Switzerland)
Dr Franz Hain Verlagsausliefering (Austria)

wdv Gesellschaft fuer Medien und Kommunikation mbH & Co OHG+
Siemensstr 6, 61352 Bad Homburg vdH
Tel: (06172) 670 0 *Fax:* (06172) 670 144
E-mail: info@wdv.de
Web Site: www.wdv.de
Key Personnel
Mng Dir: Thomas Kuhn; Klaus Tonello
Founded: 1948
Subjects: Health, Nutrition, Travel & Tourism
ISBN Prefix(es): 978-3-926181; 978-3-938790
Parent Company: Zeitschriften VVG Verlags- und Verwaltungsgesellschaft mbH & Co KG
Subsidiaries: Analyse & Concept Kommunikationsberatung GmbH; Montan-Wirtschaftsverlag GmbH
Warehouse: Hertzweg 4, 63071 Offenbach am Main

Weidle Verlag
Beethovenplatz 4, 53115 Bonn
Tel: (0228) 632954 *Fax:* (0228) 697842
E-mail: rpd@weidle-verlag.de
Web Site: www.weidle-verlag.de
Key Personnel
Mng Dir: Stefan Weidle *E-mail:* sw@weidle-verlag.de
Subjects: Art, Biography, Memoirs, History, Nonfiction (General)
ISBN Prefix(es): 978-3-931135; 978-3-938803
Foreign Rep(s): Helga Schuster Verlagsvertretungen (Austria)
Distribution Center: GVA Goettingen, Postfach 2021, 37010 Goettingen, Contact: Leonore Frester *Tel:* (0551) 48 71 77 *Fax:* (0551) 4 13 92 *E-mail:* frester@gva-verlage.de *Web Site:* www.gva-verlage.de (Germany, Austria & Switzerland)

Weidler Buchverlag Berlin GbR+
Luebecker Str 8, 10559 Berlin
Mailing Address: Postfach 21 03 15, 10503 Berlin
Tel: (030) 394 86 68 *Fax:* (030) 394 86 98
E-mail: weidler_verlag@yahoo.de
Web Site: www.weidler-verlag.de
Key Personnel
Mng Dir: Joachim Weidler
Founded: 1985
Membership(s): Boersenverein des Deutschen Buchhandels.
Subjects: Communications, Disability, Special Needs, Drama, Theater, Economics, Education, History, Language Arts, Linguistics, Literature, Literary Criticism, Essays, Music, Dance, Nonfiction (General), Philosophy, Psychology, Psychiatry, Romance, Science (General), Social Sciences, Sociology, Cultural
ISBN Prefix(es): 978-3-925191; 978-3-89693
Number of titles published annually: 35 Print
Total Titles: 430 Print

Weidlich Verlag+
Imprint of Verlagshaus Wuerzburg GmbH & Co KG
Beethovenstr 5 B, 97080 Wuerzburg
Tel: (0931) 465 889-11 *Fax:* (0931) 465 889-29

E-mail: info@verlagshaus.com
Web Site: www.verlagshaus.com
Key Personnel
Publishing Dir: Dieter Krause *Tel:* (0931) 465
889-14 *E-mail:* dieter.krause@verlagshaus.com
Dir, Production: Juergen Roth *Tel:* (0931) 465
889-15 *E-mail:* juergen.roth@verlagshaus.com
Sales Dir: Johannes Glesius *Tel:* (0931) 465 889-
13 *E-mail:* johannes.glesius@verlagshaus.com
Subjects: Foreign Countries, Travel & Tourism
ISBN Prefix(es): 978-3-8035

Weidmannsche Verlagsbuchhandlung GmbH+
Hagentorwall 7, 31134 Hildesheim
Tel: (05121) 150 10 *Fax:* (05121) 150 150
E-mail: info@olms.de
Web Site: www.olms.de
Key Personnel
Mng Dir: Dr W Georg Olms
Program Dir/Marketing: Dietrich Olms, MA
Editor: Dr Peter Guyot; Dr Doris Wendt, MA;
Danielle Winter
Licenses/Rights: Christiane Busch, MA
Production: Andreas Maybaum
Public Relations: Agnes Kuehlechner, MA
Sales: Gabriele Sorg; Sigrun Stark
Founded: 1680
Subjects: Antiques, History, Language Arts, Lin-
guistics, Philosophy, Romance, Classical Stud-
ies, Medieval Studies
ISBN Prefix(es): 978-3-615; 978-3-296
Number of titles published annually: 20 Print
Total Titles: 450 Print
Parent Company: Georg Olms Verlag
U.S. Office(s): Empire State Bldg, 350 Fifth Ave,
Suite 3304, New York, NY 10118-0069, United
States
Warehouse: VVA, Postfach 1254, 33399 Verl,
Contact: Laura Baljak *Tel:* (05241) 803844
Fax: (05241) 8094123 *E-mail:* laura.baljak@
bertelsmann.de

Weimarer Verlagsgesselschaft, *imprint of*
Verlagshaus Roemerweg GmbH

Verlag W Weinmann+
Beckerstr 7, 12157 Berlin
Tel: (030) 855 4895 *Fax:* (030) 855 9464
E-mail: info@weinmann-verlag.de
Web Site: www.weinmann-verlag.de
Key Personnel
Publisher: Wolfgang Weinmann
Founded: 1961
Membership(s): Boersenverein des Deutschen
Buchhandels.
Subjects: Crafts, Games, Hobbies, Humor, Sports,
Athletics, Martial Arts
ISBN Prefix(es): 978-3-87892
Total Titles: 80 Print
Foreign Rep(s): Dessauer CH; Ennsthaler A

Weissbooks GmbH
Englischer Hof, 2 Etage, Am Hauptbahnhof, 10,
60329 Frankfurt am Main
Tel: (069) 25 781 29-0 *Fax:* (069) 25 781 29-29
E-mail: info@weissbooks.com
Web Site: www.weissbooks.com
Key Personnel
Mng Dir: Anya Schutzbach; Dr Rainer Weiss
Founded: 2008
Subjects: Fiction, Nonfiction (General)
ISBN Prefix(es): 978-3-940888
Distribution Center: Prolit Verlagsausliefer-
ung GmbH, Siemensstr 16, 35463 Fernwald-
Annerod, Contact: Thomas Blortz *Tel:* (0641)
94393 21 *Fax:* (0641) 94393 29 *E-mail:* t.
blortz@prolit.de (Germany & Austria)
Buchzentrum AG, Industriestr Ost 10, 4614 Hae-
gendorf, Switzerland, Contact: Nicole Grueter
Tel: (062) 209 26 26 *Fax:* (062) 209 26 27
E-mail: kundendienst@buchzentrum.ch

Weisser Ring Verlags-GmbH
Weberstr 16, 55130 Mainz
Tel: (06131) 83 03 0 *Fax:* (06131) 83 03 45
E-mail: info@weisser-ring.de; presse@weisser-
ring.de
Web Site: www.weisser-ring.de
Key Personnel
Press: Helmut K Ruester *Tel:* (0631) 83 03 38
Fax: (0631) 83 03 60
Founded: 1989
Specializing in the production of books (Mainzer
Schriften) relating to issues concerning victims
of crime.
Subjects: Criminology, Law, Psychology, Psychi-
atry, Crime Prevention, Sexual Offense, Victi-
mology, Victims of Crime
ISBN Prefix(es): 978-3-9802412; 978-3-9803526;
978-3-9806463; 978-3-9807624
Total Titles: 40 Print
Parent Company: Weisser Ring eV

WEKA Firmengruppe GmbH & Co KG+
Division of WEKA Holding GmbH & Co KG
Roemerstr 4, 86438 Kissing
Mailing Address: Postfach 13 31, 86438 Kissing
Tel: (08233) 23-0 *Fax:* (08233) 23-195
E-mail: info@weka-holding.de
Web Site: www.weka-holding.de/firmengruppe.php
Key Personnel
Owner & Mng Dir: Werner Muetzel
Mng Dir: Wolfgang Materna
Publishing Dir: Dr Eberhard Opl *Tel:* (08233)
23-431 *Fax:* (02833) 23-195 *E-mail:* eberhard.
opl@weka.de
Founded: 1973
Subjects: Architecture & Interior Design, Behav-
ioral Sciences, Business, Career Development,
Civil Engineering, Communications, Electron-
ics, Electrical Engineering, Energy, Engineer-
ing (General), Environmental Studies, How-to,
Law, Management, Mechanical Engineering,
Medicine, Nursing, Dentistry, Outdoor Recre-
ation, Real Estate, Technology
ISBN Prefix(es): 978-3-8111; 978-3-8245; 978-3-
8276; 978-3-8277; 978-3-928663
Subsidiaries: Uitgeverij BV; Demeter Verlag
GmbH & Co KG, Batinger; DMV Daten-
und Medien-Verlag GmbH & Co KG; ECPA;
Franzis-Verlag GmbH & Co KG; Interest-
Verlag GmbH; Nidderau und Busborn; Ver-
lag Recht & Praxis GmbH; Spitta Verlag
GmbH; Turnus GmbH; Verwaltungs-Verlag
GmbH; WAGO-Curadata Steuerberatungs-
Systeme GmbH; WEKA Baufach-Software
GmbH; WEKA Baufachverlage GmbH; Edi-
tions WEKA Sarl; Editions WEKA SA; Edi-
zioni WEKA SpA; WEKA Fachverlag fuer Be-
hoerden und Institutionen; WEKA Fachverlag
fuer technische Fuhrungskrafte GmbH; WEKA
Handels-GmbH; WEKA Informationsschriften-
und Werbefachverlage GmbH; WEKA Man-
agement Fachverlag GmbH; WEKA Publishing
Inc; WEKA-Verlag AG; WEKA Verlag Ges
mbH; WEKA Verlagsgesellschaft fuer aktuelle
Publikationen mbH; WEKA Verlagsservice
GmbH

Wellhoefer Verlag
Weinbergstr 26, 68259 Mannheim
Tel: (0621) 7188167 *Fax:* (0621) 7188168
E-mail: info@wellhoefer-verlag.de
Web Site: www.wellhoefer-verlag.de
Key Personnel
Publisher: Ulrich Wellhoefer
Subjects: Art, Biography, Memoirs, History, Mys-
teries, Suspense, Poetry
ISBN Prefix(es): 978-3-939540; 978-3-95428

Weltbild GmbH & Co KG+
Werner-von-Siemenstr 1, 86159 Augsburg
Tel: (0180) 6354360; (0180) 6444888 (orders)
E-mail: info@weltbild.de

Web Site: www.weltbild.de; www.weltbild.com
Key Personnel
Chief Executive Officer: Christian Sailer
Mng Dir: Angela Schuenemann
Founded: 1948
Subjects: Animals, Pets, Art, Cookery, Crafts,
Games, Hobbies, Environmental Studies, Eth-
nicity, Fashion, Fiction, Gardening, Plants,
Health, Nutrition, History, Nonfiction (Gen-
eral), Philosophy
ISBN Prefix(es): 978-3-8289; 978-3-89350; 978-
3-927117; 978-3-89897; 978-3-86047
Bookshop(s): KIDOH Shop, Steinerne Furt 67,
86167 Augsburg *Tel:* (0821) 70 04 82 02

WELTBUCH Verlag GmbH
Enderstr 59 (im Seidnitz-Center), 01277 Dresden
Tel: (0351) 4794244 *Fax:* (0351) 4794245
E-mail: weltbuch@mac.com; weltbuch@gmx.com
Web Site: www.weltbuch.com
Key Personnel
Mng Dir: Dirk Kohl
Membership(s): Boersenverein des Deutschen
Buchhandels; DJV-Deutscher Journalisten
Verband; Italien-Zentrum der TU Dresden;
Marketing-Club Dresden; Presseclub Dres-
den; Wirtschaftsbeirat Bayern; Wirtschaftsrat
Deutschland.
Subjects: Economics, History, Literature, Literary
Criticism, Essays
ISBN Prefix(es): 978-3-938706
Distribution Center: Runge VA *Tel:* (05204)
998-123 *Fax:* (05204) 998-116 *E-mail:* info@
rungeva.de *Web Site:* www.rungeva.de (Ger-
many, Austria & Switzerland)

Weltforum Verlag GmbH+
Amselweg 8, 53604 Bad Honnef
Tel: (0228) 3682430 *Fax:* (0228) 3682439
Key Personnel
Dir: Peter John von Freyend
Founded: 1963
Subjects: Developing Countries
ISBN Prefix(es): 978-3-8039

Wenz Verlag
Schloss Philippseich, 63303 Dreieich
Tel: (06103) 3 12 54 70 *Fax:* (06103) 3 12 54 75
E-mail: info@wenz-verlag.de; lektorat@wenz-
verlag.de (editorial)
Web Site: www.wenz-verlag.de
Key Personnel
Publisher: Stefan Fassel-Wenz
Subjects: Automotive, Biological Sciences, Lit-
erature, Literary Criticism, Essays, Nonfiction
(General), Poetry
ISBN Prefix(es): 978-3-937791

Wer liefert was? GmbH (Who Supplies What?)
ABC-Str 21, 20354 Hamburg
Mailing Address: Postfach 100549, 20004 Ham-
burg
Tel: (040) 25440-0 *Fax:* (040) 25440-100
E-mail: info@wlw.de
Web Site: www.wer-liefert-was.de
Key Personnel
Chief Executive Officer: Peter F Schmid
Founded: 1948
Supplier search engine for all branches in B2B
(business-to-business).
Membership(s): Europaeischer Verband der
Adressbuch- und Datenbankverleger; Infor-
mationsgemeinschaft zur Feststellung der
Verbreitung von Werbetraegern eV; Verband
Deutscher Auskunfts- und Verzeichnismedien
eV.
Subjects: Business, Marketing
ISBN Prefix(es): 978-3-923878
Total Titles: 1 Online
Branch Office(s)
Mariahilfer Str 34, 1070 Vienna, Austria
Tel: (017431) 528 *Fax:* (017431) 527

E-mail: info@wlw.at *Web Site:* www.wer-liefert-was.at

Wer liefert was? doo, Fallerovo setaliste 22, 10000 Zagreb, Croatia *Tel:* (01) 3030500 *Fax:* (01) 3030501 *E-mail:* info@wlw.hr *Web Site:* www.wlw.hr

Wer liefert was? spol sro, Siemensova 2717/4, 155 80 Prague 13, Czech Republic *Tel:* 274 000 200 *E-mail:* info@wlw.cz *Web Site:* www. wlw.cz

Lindenstr 16, 6340 Baar, Switzerland *Tel:* (041) 766 33 88 *Fax:* (041) 766 33 89 *E-mail:* info@wlw.ch *Web Site:* www.wer-liefert-was.ch

Verlag Die Werkstatt GmbH
Lotzestr 22a, 37083 Goettingen
Tel: (0551) 789 651-0 *Fax:* (0551) 789 651-25
E-mail: info@werkstatt-verlag.de
Web Site: www.werkstatt-verlag.de
Key Personnel
Mng Dir: Bernd-M Beyer *E-mail:* b.beyer@ werkstatt-verlag.de
Head, Production: Erich Schuenemann *E-mail:* e.schuenemann@werkstatt-verlag.de
Head, Sales & Marketing: Bernd Weidmann *E-mail:* bernd.weidmann@werkstatt-auslieferung.de
Founded: 1981
Subjects: Biography, Memoirs, Cookery, Environmental Studies, Nonfiction (General), Sports, Athletics
ISBN Prefix(es): 978-3-89533; 978-3-923478
Foreign Rep(s): Elisabeth Anintah-Hirt (Austria)
Distribution Center: Koenigsstr 43, 26180 Rastede *Tel:* (04402) 92630 *Fax:* (04402) 926350 *E-mail:* info@werkstatt-auslieferung.de *Web Site:* www.werkstatt-auslieferung.de

Werner Verlag, *imprint of* Wolters Kluwer Deutschland GmbH

Werner Verlag+
Imprint of Wolters Kluwer Deutschland GmbH
Luxemburger Str 449, 50939 Cologne
Tel: (02631) 801 2222 *Toll Free Tel:* 0800 888 5444 *Fax:* (02631) 801 2223
Toll Free Fax: 0800 801 8018
E-mail: info@wolterskluwer.de
Web Site: www.werner-verlag.de
Subjects: Economics, Engineering (General), Law
ISBN Prefix(es): 978-3-8041

Westdeutscher Universitaets Verlag
Querenburger Hoehe 281, 44801 Bochum
Mailing Address: Universitaets Str 150, 44801 Bochum
Tel: (0234) 32-11993 *Fax:* (0234) 32-14993
Web Site: www.universitaetsverlag.com
Key Personnel
Publisher & Dir: Martin Woesler *E-mail:* martin.woesler@rub.de
Founded: 1999
ISBN Prefix(es): 978-3-89966

Westend Verlag, *imprint of* Piper Verlag GmbH

Westend Verlag GmbH
Neue Kraeme 28, 60311 Frankfurt
Tel: (069) 24750 18-0 *Fax:* (069) 24750 18-20
E-mail: info@westendverlag.de
Web Site: www.westendverlag.de
Key Personnel
Foreign Rights Dir: Ruediger Gruenhagen *Tel:* (069) 24750 18-10 *E-mail:* gruenhagen@ westendverlag.de
ISBN Prefix(es): 978-3-938060
Distribution Center: Koch, Neff & Oetinger Verlagsauslieferung GmbH, Industriestr 23, 70565 Stuttgart, Contact: Simone Spermann *E-mail:* piper@kno-va.de

Dr Franz Hain Verlagsauslieferungen GmbH, Dr-Otto-Neurath-Gasse 5, 1220 Vienna, Austria *Tel:* (01) 2 82 65 65-77 *Fax:* (01) 2 82 52 82 *E-mail:* bestell@hain.at

Buchzentrum AG, Industriestr Ost 10, 4614 Haegendorf, Switzerland *Tel:* (062) 2 09 26 26 *Fax:* (062) 2 09 26 27 *E-mail:* kundendienst@ buchzentrum.ch

Georg Westermann Verlag, see Bildungshaus Schulbuchverlage Westermann Schroedel Diesterweg Schoeningh Winklers GmbH

Westermann Lernspielverlage GmbH
Georg-Westermann-Allee 66, 38104 Braunschweig
Tel: (0531) 708 85 71 *Fax:* (0531) 708 84 90
E-mail: service@schubi.de
Web Site: www.schubi.de
Key Personnel
Mng Dir: Hartmuth Brill
Press: Dr Regine Meyer-Arlt *E-mail:* regine.meyer-arlt@westermann.de
Subjects: Education, Language Arts, Linguistics, Mathematics, Music, Dance, Creative Design, English Language, French Language, German Language, Therapy
ISBN Prefix(es): 978-3-86723; 978-3-89891

Bildungshaus Schulbuchverlage Westermann Schroedel Diesterweg Schoeningh Winklers GmbH
Georg-Westermann-Allee 66, 38104 Braunschweig
Tel: (0531) 708-0 *Fax:* (0531) 708-664
Web Site: www.westermann.de; www.schroedel.de; www.diesterweg.de; www.winklers.de
Key Personnel
Mng Dir: Ulrike Juergens; Thomas Michael; Dr Peter Schell
Subjects: Art, Chemistry, Chemical Engineering, English as a Second Language, Mathematics, Music, Dance, Religion - Other
ISBN Prefix(es): 978-3-07 (Georg Westermann); 978-3-425 (Diesterweg); 978-3-14 (Winklers); 978-3-8045 (Winklers); 978-3-507 (Schroedel)

Westermann Schulbuchverlag, see Bildungshaus Schulbuchverlage Westermann Schroedel Diesterweg Schoeningh Winklers GmbH

Verlag Westfaelisches Dampfboot+
Hafenweg 26a, 48155 Muenster
Tel: (0251) 39 00 48 0 *Fax:* (0251) 39 00 48 50
E-mail: info@dampfboot-verlag.de
Web Site: www.dampfboot-verlag.de
Key Personnel
Publishing Dir & Mng Dir: Prof Hans Guenter Thien *E-mail:* thien@dampfboot-verlag.de
Mng Dir: Prof Hanns Wienold
Press: Henning Scheer *E-mail:* scheer@ dampfboot-verlag.de
Production: Susanne Paul-Menn *E-mail:* paul-menn@dampfboot-verlag.de
Founded: 1984
Subjects: Labor, Industrial Relations, Law, Social Sciences, Sociology, Women's Studies, Gender Studies
ISBN Prefix(es): 978-3-924550; 978-3-929586; 978-3-89691
Foreign Rep(s): Elisabeth Anintah-Hirt (Austria); Sebastian Graf (Switzerland)
Distribution Center: Prolit Verlagsauslieferung, Siemensstr 16, 35463 Fernwald *Tel:* (0641) 943 93 33 *Fax:* (0641) 943 93 199 *E-mail:* r.eckert@prolit.de (Germany & Austria)
Herder AG Basel, Muttenzerstr 109, 4133 Pratteln, Switzerland *Tel:* (061) 827 90 64 *Fax:* (061) 827 90 67 *E-mail:* verkauf@herder.ch

Orders to: Germinal Versandbuchhandlung, Siemensstr 16, 35463 Fernwald *E-mail:* service@germinal.de *Web Site:* www.germinal.de

Verlag und Medienagentur Michael Weyand GmbH
Friedlandstr 4, 54293 Trier
Tel: (0651) 9960140 *Fax:* (0651) 9960141
E-mail: verlag@weyand.de
Web Site: www.weyand.de
Key Personnel
Mng Dir: Michael Weyand *E-mail:* m.weyand@ weyand.de
Advertising & Sales: Elvi Zimmermann *E-mail:* e.zimmermann@weyand.de
Subjects: Travel & Tourism
ISBN Prefix(es): 978-3-924631; 978-3-935281

Wichern-Verlag GmbH+
Georgenkirchstr 69-70, 10249 Berlin
Tel: (030) 28 87 48 10 *Fax:* (030) 28 87 48 12
E-mail: info@wichern.de; vertrieb@wichern.de
Web Site: www.wichern.de
Key Personnel
Publisher: Dr Elke Rutzenhoefer
Marketing: Christian Peetz
Sales: Sabine Hoffmann
Founded: 1920
Membership(s): The Association of Publishers & Bookstores in Berlin-Brandenburg; The Stock Exchange of German Booksellers
Subjects: Biography, Memoirs, History, Religion - Other, Theology
ISBN Prefix(es): 978-3-88981; 978-3-7674; 978-3-87906
Divisions: CZV-Verlag
Distributed by BMK Buchauslieferung (Austria); Evangelische Verlagsauslieferung (Switzerland)
Warehouse: Mehringdamm 32-34, 10961 Berlin

Wichmann-Verlag, *imprint of* VDE-Verlag GmbH

Wichmann Verlag+
Imprint of VDE-Verlag GmbH
Postfach 120143, 10591 Berlin
Tel: (030) 34 80 01-0 *Fax:* (030) 34 80 01-9088
Web Site: www.vde-verlag.de; www.facebook.com/wichmannverlag
Key Personnel
Manager: Dr Stefan Schlegel; Margret Schneider
Founded: 1933
Subjects: Aeronautics, Aviation, Communications, Earth Sciences, Geography, Geology, Geodesy, Geoinformatics, Photogrammetry, Transport Planning
ISBN Prefix(es): 978-3-87907
Number of titles published annually: 11 Print

Wiechmann Verlag GmbH
Deggenhauser Str 8, 88693 Deggenhausertal
Tel: (0700) 08000035 *Fax:* (0700) 08000036
Founded: 1893
Subjects: Art, History
ISBN Prefix(es): 978-3-87908

Wieland Verlag GmbH
Rosenheimer Str 22, 83043 Bad Aibling
Tel: (08061) 38 998-0 *Fax:* (08061) 38 998-20
E-mail: info@wieland-verlag.de
Web Site: wieland-verlag.com
Key Personnel
Mng Dir: Hans Joachim Wieland *Tel:* (08061) 38 998-40 *E-mail:* h.wieland@wieland-verlag.com
Subjects: Automotive, Outdoor Recreation, Biking, Forging, Knives, Swords, Weaponry
ISBN Prefix(es): 978-3-613; 978-3-938711

Wienand Verlag GmbH
Weyertal 59, 50937 Cologne

Mailing Address: Postfach 410948, 50869 Cologne
Tel: (0221) 47 22-0 *Fax:* (0221) 44 89 11
E-mail: info@wienand-verlag.de
Web Site: www.wienand-verlag.de
Key Personnel
Mng Dir & Publisher: Michael Wienand
Tel: (0221) 47 22-100
Subjects: Art, History
ISBN Prefix(es): 978-3-87909; 978-3-86832
Foreign Rep(s): Art Stock Books/Independent Publishers Group (Canada, USA); Bookport Associates (Gibraltar, Greece, Italy, Malta, Portugal, Spain); China Publishers Marketing (Benjamin Pan) (China, Hong Kong, Taiwan); Elisabeth Harder-Kreimann (Scandinavia); Georg Kroemer (Luxembourg); Seth Meyer-Bruhns (Austria); SAVECA - Art & Paper (France); Scheidegger & Co AG (Urs Wetli) (Switzerland); Jan Smit Boeken (Jan Smit) (Netherlands)
Distribution Center: Sigloch Verlagservice, Am Buchberg 8, 74572 Blaufelden
Tel: (07953) 88 37 57 *Fax:* (07953) 88 37 00
E-mail: wienand@sigloch.de

Wiley-VCH Verlag GmbH & Co KGaA+
Boschstr 12, 69469 Weinheim
Mailing Address: Postfach 10 11 61, 69451 Weinheim
Tel: (06201) 606-0 *Fax:* (06201) 606-328
E-mail: info@wiley-vch.de; service@wiley-vch.de (customer service)
Web Site: www.wiley-vch.de
Key Personnel
Mng Dir & Head, Publishing: Guido Herrmann
Vice President, Executive Dir, Chemistry Journals: Dr Eva-E Wille *E-mail:* ewille@wiley-vch.de
Publisher, Books & References: Dr Gudrun Walter *E-mail:* gwalter@wiley-vch.de
Publishing Dir, Global Materials Science Journals & Global Physics Journals/Books: Dr Peter Gregory *E-mail:* pgregory@wiley-vch.de
Publishing Dir, Life Sciences Journals & Books: Dr Carol Bacchus *E-mail:* cbacchus@wiley-vch.de
Publishing Dir, Professional & Trade Books: Hartmut Gante *E-mail:* hgante@wiley-vch.de
Customer Service: Nils Schoepe
Electronic Media Production: Peter Fischer *E-mail:* pfischer@wiley-vch.de
Sales: Paul Kwiatkowskyj *E-mail:* pkwiatkowskyj@wiley-vch.de
Founded: 1921
Subjects: Biological Sciences, Business, Chemistry, Chemical Engineering, Law, Physical Sciences, Physics, Science (General)
ISBN Prefix(es): 978-0-471; 978-3-527
Total Titles: 1,580 Print
Parent Company: John Wiley & Sons Inc, 111 River St, Hoboken, NJ 07030, United States
Subsidiaries: Chemical Concepts; Wilhelm Ernst & Sohn Verlag fuer Architektur und technische Wissenschaft; Verlag Helvetica Chimica Acta; Verlagsservice Suedwest

Windmuehle Verlag GmbH+
Bei der Neuen Muenze 4a, 22145 Hamburg
Mailing Address: Postfach 73 02 40, 22122 Hamburg
Tel: (040) 679430-0 *Fax:* (040) 67943030
E-mail: info@windmuehle-verlag.de
Web Site: www.windmuehle-verlag.de
Key Personnel
Mng Dir: Dietrich Asmus; Hendrik Asmus
Founded: 1981
Specialize in furthering education in organization & management.
Subjects: Career Development, Education, Human Relations, Management

ISBN Prefix(es): 978-3-922789; 978-3-937444; 978-3-86451
Parent Company: FELDHAUS Gruppe

Windpferd Verlagsgesellschaft mbH+
Wasachstr 34a, 87561 Oberstdorf
Tel: (08322) 987-1149 *Fax:* (08322) 987-1489
E-mail: info@windpferd.de
Web Site: www.windpferd.de
Key Personnel
Manager: Monika Juenemann
Foreign Rights: Cristina Perlea
Founded: 1987
Subjects: Psychology, Psychiatry, Religion - Buddhist, Self-Help
ISBN Prefix(es): 978-3-89385
Distribution Center: arvato media GmbH, VVA, Postfach 77 77, 33310 Guetersloh *Tel:* (05241) 80-8 93 42 *Fax:* (05241) 80-93 52
Dr Franz Hain Verlagsauslieferungen GmbH, Dr-Otto-Neurath-Gasse 5, 1220 Vienna, Austria *Tel:* (01282) 65 65 65 *Fax:* (01282) 65 65 49
Dessauer, Raeffelstr 32, 8045 Zurich, Switzerland *Tel:* (04) 66 96 96 *Fax:* (04) 66 96 69

Bibliothek rosa Winkel, *imprint of* Maennerschwarm Verlag GmbH

Verlag Dr Dieter Winkler+
Katharinastr 37, 44793 Bochum
Mailing Address: Postfach 102665, 44726 Bochum
Tel: (0234) 9650200 *Fax:* (0234) 9650201
E-mail: order@winklerverlag.com
Web Site: www.winklerverlag.com
Key Personnel
Owner: Dr Dieter Winkler
Founded: 1984
Membership(s): Boersenverein des Deutschen Buchhandels.
Subjects: Education, History, Nonfiction (General), Regional Interests, Science (General), Social Sciences, Sociology
ISBN Prefix(es): 978-3-924517; 978-3-930083; 978-3-89911
Number of titles published annually: 10 Print
Total Titles: 145 Print

Winklers Verlag, see Bildungshaus Schulbuchverlage Westermann Schroedel Diesterweg Schoeningh Winklers GmbH

Carl Winter Universitaetsverlag, see Universitaetsverlag Winter GmbH

Verlag fuer Wirtschaft und Verwaltung Hubert Wingen GmbH & Co KG+
Alfredistr 32, 45127 Essen
Tel: (0201) 22 25 41 *Fax:* (0201) 22 96 60
E-mail: wingenverlag@t-online.de
Web Site: www.wingenverlag.de
Key Personnel
Manager: Martha Wingen; Rainer Wingen
Founded: 1955
Subjects: Architecture & Interior Design, Civil Engineering, Education, Law, Nonfiction (General), Public Administration, Real Estate, Religion - Catholic, Canon Law, Construction Law, Education Law
ISBN Prefix(es): 978-3-8028

Wirtschaftsverlag NW-Verlag fuer neue Wissenschaft GmbH, see Carl Ed Schuenemann KG

Verlag Wissen & Literatur Frido Flade GmbH+
Elisabethstr 34, 80796 Munich
Tel: (089) 278 134 17 *Fax:* (089) 273 128 91
E-mail: info@vmw-flade.de

Web Site: www.vmw-flade.de; vmw-flade.jimdo.com
Key Personnel
Publisher: Frido Flade *E-mail:* frido.flade@vmw-flade.de
Founded: 1979
Membership(s): Boersenverein des Deutschen Buchhandels.
Subjects: Economics, Energy
ISBN Prefix(es): 978-3-922804
Subsidiaries: Edition Wissen & Literatur
Warehouse: Revilak Verlags-Service, Gutenbergstr 5, 82205 Gilching

Verlag Wissen-Kompakt GmbH
Postfach 60 07 74, 60337 Frankfurt am Main
Tel: (069) 9819-1682 *Fax:* (069) 9819-1681
E-mail: info@wissen-kompakt.eu
Web Site: www.wissen-kompakt.eu
Founded: 2011
Subjects: Economics, Education, Health, Nutrition, Law, Nature
ISBN Prefix(es): 978-3-943082

Wissenschaftliche Buchgesellschaft, see WBG (Wissenschaftliche Buchgesellschaft)

Wissenschaftliche Verlagsgesellschaft mbH+
Subsidiary of Deutscher Apotheker Verlag
Birkenwaldstr 44, 70191 Stuttgart
Mailing Address: Postfach 10 10 61, 70009 Stuttgart
Tel: (0711) 2582 0; (0711) 2582 341 *Fax:* (0711) 2582 290; (0711) 2582 390
E-mail: service@wissenschaftliche-verlagsgesellschaft.de
Web Site: www.wissenschaftliche-verlagsgesellschaft.de
Key Personnel
Mng Dir: Dr Klaus G Brauer; Dr Christian Rotta
Marketing Dir: Siegmar Bauer *E-mail:* sbauer@wissenschaftliche-verlagsgesellschaft.de
Founded: 1921
Subjects: Biological Sciences, Health, Nutrition, Law, Medicine, Nursing, Dentistry, Physics, Science (General), Pharmacy
ISBN Prefix(es): 978-3-8047
Associate Companies: Firma DAN Netzwerk Deutscher Apotheker; S Hirzel Verlag GmbH & Co; Medpharm Polska; Medpharm Scientific Publishers; Franz Steiner Verlag GmbH

Wissenschaftlicher Autorenverlag KG, see Verlag Grundlagen und Praxis GmbH & Co

Wissenschaftlicher Verlag und Medien, *imprint of* Holos Wissenschaftlicher Verlag und Medien

Wissenschaftsrat
Brohler Str 11, 50968 Cologne
Tel: (0221) 37 76-0 *Fax:* (0221) 38 84 40
E-mail: post@wissenschaftsrat.de
Web Site: www.wissenschaftsrat.de
Key Personnel
Chairman: Prof Wolfgang Marquardt
Secretary General: Thomas May
Contact: Dr Christiane Kling-Mathey *Tel:* (0221) 37 76-243 *E-mail:* kling-mathey@wissenschaftsrat.de
Founded: 1957
Subjects: Science (General), Technology, Research, Scientific Training, University Accreditation
ISBN Prefix(es): 978-3-923203; 978-3-935353

Wittgenstein Verlag
Schlossplatz 3, 86685 Huisheim
Tel: (09092) 911570 *Fax:* (09092) 911572
E-mail: info@wittgenstein-verlag.de
Web Site: www.wittgenstein-verlag.de
ISBN Prefix(es): 978-3-944354

Friedrich Wittig Verlag GmbH+
Gartenstr 20, 24103 Kiel
Mailing Address: Postfach 3169, 24030 Kiel
Tel: (0431) 55779-206; (0431) 55779-285 (orders)
  Fax: (0431) 55779-292
E-mail: vertrieb@lutherische-verlag.de
Web Site: www.evangelisches-medienwerk.
  de/verlage; www.kirchenshop-online.de
Key Personnel
Mng Dir: Bodo Elsner *Tel:* (0431) 55779-260
  E-mail: bodo.elsner@epv-nord.de
Head, Publishing: Johannes Keussen *Tel:* (0431)
  55779-203 *E-mail:* keussen@epv-nord.de
Founded: 1946
Subjects: Art, Biblical Studies, History, Religion -
  Other
ISBN Prefix(es): 978-3-8048
Parent Company: Evangelischer Presseverband
  Nord eV
Associate Companies: Lutherische Verlagsge-
  sellschaft mbH; J F Steinkopf Verlag GmbH

Konrad Wittwer GmbH+
Koenigstr 30, 70173 Stuttgart
Tel: (0711) 25 07 0 *Fax:* (0711) 25 07 145
E-mail: info@wittwer.de
Web Site: www.wittwer.de
Key Personnel
Mng Dir: Dr Konrad M Wittwer; Michael Wit-
  twer
Founded: 1867
Subjects: Earth Sciences, Mathematics, Nonfiction
  (General), Science (General)
ISBN Prefix(es): 978-3-87919
Bookshop(s): Breuninger Stuttgart Buchhandlung
  Wittwer, Marktstr 1-3, Stuttgart *Tel:* (0711)
  2507-373; (0711) 2507-374; (0711) 2507-
  375 *Fax:* (0711) 2507-380; Uni-Buch Hohen-
  heim, Fruwirthstr 24, Stuttgart *Tel:* (0711)
  4586265 *Fax:* (0711) 4570664; Uni-Buch
  Pfaffenwald, Pfaffenwaldring 45, Stuttgart
  Tel: (0711) 682709 *Fax:* (0711) 6875278; Bre-
  uninger Ludwigsburg Buchhandlung Wittwer,
  Heinkeistr 1-11, Ludwigsburg *Tel:* (07141)
  22177-12; (07141) 22177-13; (07141) 22177-
  14 *Fax:* (07141) 22177-20; Breuningerland
  Sindelfingen Buchhandlung Wittwer, Tilsiter
  Str 15, Sindelfingen *Tel:* (07031) 410 34-72
  Fax: (07031) 410 34-80

WLW, see Wer liefert was? GmbH

Wochenschau Verlag+
Adolf-Damaschke-Str 10, 65824 Schwalbach-
  Taunus
Tel: (06196) 860-65 *Fax:* (06196) 860-60
E-mail: info@wochenschau-verlag.de
Web Site: www.wochenschau-verlag.de
Key Personnel
Chief Executive Officer: Silke Schneider
Publishing Dir: Bernward Debus
Editor-in-Chief: Tessa Debus *E-mail:* tessa.
  debus@wochenschau-verlag.de
Founded: 1949
Subjects: Education, Geography, Geology, Gov-
  ernment, Political Science, History
ISBN Prefix(es): 978-3-87920; 978-3-89974
Number of titles published annually: 120 Print
Total Titles: 120 Print
Imprints: bd-edition (adult nonfiction)

Gert Wohlfarth GmbH, see Verlagshaus
  Wohlfarth

Verlagshaus Wohlfarth+
Stresemannstr 20-22, 47051 Duisburg
Tel: (0203) 3 0527 0 *Fax:* (0203) 3 0527 820
E-mail: info@wohlfarth.de
Web Site: www.wohlfarth.de
Key Personnel
Mng Dir, Publishing: Frank Wohlfarth *E-mail:* f.
  wohlfarth@wohlfarth.de

Mng Dir, Editorial: Uwe Hennig
Book Sales Manager: Lothar Koopmann
  E-mail: l.koopmann@wohlfarth.de
Founded: 1953
Membership(s): Borsenverein des Deutschen
  Buchhandels.
Subjects: Architecture & Interior Design, Cook-
  ery, Crafts, Games, Hobbies, Gardening, Plants,
  House & Home, Regional Interests
ISBN Prefix(es): 978-3-87463
Total Titles: 5 Print
Imprints: Verlagsbereich Bau; Mercator-Verlag

Kinderbuchverlag Wolff
Heddernheimer Landstr 1, 60439 Frankfurt
Tel: (069) 50 68 21 34
E-mail: info@kinderbuchverlagwolff.de
Web Site: www.kinderbuchverlagwolff.de
Key Personnel
Chief Executive Officer: Thomas Wolff
Founded: 2005
Subjects: Fiction, Nonfiction (General)
ISBN Prefix(es): 978-3-938766
Foreign Rep(s): Claudia Gyr (Switzerland); Al-
  fred Trux (Austria)
Distribution Center: PROLIT Verlagsausliefer-
  ung GmbH, Siemensstr 16, 35463 Femwald-
  Annerod, Contact: Monica Pankratz *Tel:* (0641)
  9439322 *Fax:* (0641) 9439329

Wolff Verlag R Eberhardt
Unter den Linden 40, 10117 Berlin
Tel: (0162) 2877301
E-mail: kontakt@wolffverlag.de
Web Site: www.wolffverlag.de; www.
  roberteberhardt.com
Key Personnel
Publisher: Robert Eberhardt
Founded: 2008
Subjects: Art, History, Literature, Literary Criti-
  cism, Essays
ISBN Prefix(es): 978-3-941461

Wolfgang Guting, *imprint of* Holos
  Wissenschaftlicher Verlag und Medien

**Johann Wolfgang Goethe-Universitaet
  Frankfurt am Main**
Senckenberganlage 31, 60325 Frankfurt am Main
Tel: (069) 798-0 *Fax:* (069) 798-28383
E-mail: praesident@uni-frankfurt.de
Web Site: www.rz.uni-frankfurt.de; www.uni-
  frankfurt.de
Key Personnel
President: Dr Werner Mueller-Esterl
Founded: 1983
Subjects: Education, Management, Science (Gen-
  eral)
ISBN Prefix(es): 978-3-923184
Imprints: Anzeigenverwaltung & Herstellung;
  Bezugsbedingungen; Herausgeber; Redaktion
  & Gestaltung

Wolke Verlags GmbH+
Wickerer Weg 19, 65719 Hofheim am Taunus
Tel: (06192) 72 43 *Fax:* (06192) 95 29 39
E-mail: info@wolke-verlag.de
Web Site: www.wolke-verlag.de
Key Personnel
Mng Dir: Peter Mischung
Founded: 1980
Subjects: Music, Dance
ISBN Prefix(es): 978-3-923997; 978-3-936000
Distribution Center: Runge Verlagsauslieferung
  GmbH, Bergstr 2, 33803 Steinhagen, Contact:
  Team 3 *Tel:* (05204) 998 123 *Fax:* (05204)
  998 114 *E-mail:* msr@rungeva.de *Web
  Site:* rungeva.de

Wolters Kluwer Deutschland GmbH
Luxemburger Str 449, 50939 Cologne

Tel: (0221) 94373-7000 *Fax:* (0221) 94373-7201
E-mail: info@wolterskluwer.de
Web Site: www.wolterskluwer.de
Key Personnel
Chief Executive Officer: Martina Bruder
Chief Financial Officer: Adriaan Verhoef
Founded: 1924
Subjects: Business, Education, Law, Management
ISBN Prefix(es): 978-3-472
Parent Company: Wolters Kluwer NV, Nether-
  lands
Imprints: ADDISON; Akademische Arbeitsge-
  meinschaft Verlag; AnNo Text; Carl Link;
  Deutscher Wirtschftsdienst; Carl Heymanns Verlag; Carl Link Kommu-
  nalverlag; Jurion; Luchterhand; Werner Verlag
Divisions: Verlag R S Schulz GmbH
Branch Office(s)
Annastr 32-36, 45130 Essen *Tel:* (0201) 7 20 95-
  5500 *Fax:* (0201) 7 20 95-33
Adolf-Kolping-Str 10, 96317 Kronach
  Tel: (09261) 969-4100 *Fax:* (09261) 969-4111
Janderstr 10, 68199 Mannheim *Tel:* (0621) 8 62
  62 62 *Fax:* (0621) 8 62 62 63
Heddesdorfer Str 31, 56564 Neuwied *Tel:* (02631)
  801-0 *Fax:* (02631) 801-2204
Freisinger Str 3, 85716 Unterschleissheim
  Tel: (089) 36007-0 *Fax:* (089) 36007-3310

Worms Verlag
Von-Steuben-Str 5, 67549 Worms
Tel: (06241) 2000314 *Fax:* (06241) 2000399
E-mail: info@kvg-worms.de
Web Site: wormsverlag.de
Key Personnel
Contact: Berthold Roeth
Founded: 2003
Subjects: Art, History, Religion - Jewish, Ju-
  daism, Local History
ISBN Prefix(es): 978-3-936118

Verlag DAS WORT GmbH (The Word
  Publishing House)
Max-Braun-Str 2, 97828 Marktheidenfeld-Altfeld
Tel: (09391) 504135 *Fax:* (09391) 504133
E-mail: info@das-wort.com; info@gabriele-
  verlag.de
Web Site: www.universal-spirit.cc; www.gabriele-
  verlag.de
Key Personnel
Mng Dir: Elena Dell Eva; Christine Schulte
Membership(s): Borsenverein des Deutschen
  Buchhandels.
Subjects: Health, Nutrition, Human Relations,
  Philosophy, Religion - Other, Self-Help
ISBN Prefix(es): 978-3-89201
Total Titles: 68 Print
Orders to: Postfach 90, 1127 Vienna, Austria
  Tel: (01) 8029852
PO Box 55133, Toronto, ON M25 5A0, Canada
Verlag Vita Vera, Oberebene 67, 5620 Brem-
  garten, Switzerland
Universelles Leben, Fellenbergstr 272, 8047
  Zurich, Switzerland *Tel:* (01) 4925426
PO Box 3459A, Woodbridge, CT 06525, United
  States *Fax:* 203-457-9693

WortArt
Lindenstr 22, 50674 Cologne
Tel: (0221) 99 22 77 90 *Fax:* (0221) 99 22 77
  920
E-mail: info@wortart.de
Web Site: wortart.de
Founded: 1994 (book publisher since 2009)
Subjects: Humor
ISBN Prefix(es): 978-3-942454

Verlag Das Wunderhorn GmbH
Rohrbacherstr 18, 69115 Heidelberg
Tel: (06221) 40 24 28 *Fax:* (06221) 40 24 83
E-mail: info@wunderhorn.de; wunderhorn.
  verlag@t-online.de

Web Site: www.wunderhorn.de
Key Personnel
Publisher: Angelika Andruchowicz; Manfred Metzner *E-mail:* metzner@wunderhorn.de
Press: Kai Hammer
Founded: 1978
Subjects: Art, Biography, Memoirs, Fiction, Film, Video, History, Literature, Literary Criticism, Essays, Nonfiction (General), Photography, Poetry, Regional Interests, Science (General), Women's Studies
ISBN Prefix(es): 978-3-88423
Number of titles published annually: 16 Print
Total Titles: 230 Print
Foreign Rep(s): Rudi Deuble (Germany); Sebastian Graf (Switzerland); Helga Schuster (Austria)
Distribution Center: Prolit Buchvertrieb GmbH, Postfach 9, 35461 Fernwald, Contact: Monika Pankratz *Tel:* (0641) 9439322 *Fax:* (0641) 94393199 *E-mail:* m.pankratz@prolit.de (Germany & Austria)
AVA Verlagsauslieferung AG, Centralweg 16, 8910 Affoltern am Albis, Switzerland *Tel:* (01) 762 42 50 *Fax:* (01) 762 42 10 *E-mail:* verlagsservice@ava.ch

Wunderlich Verlag, *imprint of* Rowohlt Verlag GmbH

Wunderlich Verlag+
Imprint of Rowohlt Verlag GmbH
Hamburger Str 17, 21465 Reinbek
Tel: (040) 72 72 0 *Fax:* (040) 72 72 319
E-mail: info@rowohlt.de
Web Site: www.rowohlt.de/verlag/wunderlich
Key Personnel
Program Dir: Kathrin Blum
Founded: 1926
Subjects: Biography, Memoirs, Fiction, History, Nonfiction (General), Thriller
Ultimate Parent Company: Verlagsgruppe Georg von Holtzbrinck GmbH

Xenos Verlag+
Imprint of Nelson Verlag GmbH
Voelckersstr 14-20, 22765 Hamburg
Mailing Address: Postfach 50 03 80, 22703 Hamburg
Tel: (040) 39 804 400 *Fax:* (040) 39 804 390; (040) 39 804 388 (sales)
E-mail: nelson@carlsen.de
Web Site: www.carlsen.de/xenos/
Key Personnel
Publishing Dir: Torben Thies
Mng Dir: Renate Herre; Joachim Kaufmann
Founded: 1975
Children's book publishers specializing in wall charts, colony & activity books, atlases.
Also acts as book packager.
Membership(s): Membership(s): Borsenverein des Deutschen Buchhandels.
Subjects: Nonfiction (General)
ISBN Prefix(es): 978-3-8212; 978-3-933697; 978-3-935746
Number of titles published annually: 180 Print
Ultimate Parent Company: CARLSEN Verlag GmbH
Imprints: Merit; Edition Riesenrad; Tipp Creative
Foreign Rep(s): Heinz Widmer (Switzerland)
Distribution Center: Distribook, Schockenriedstr 39, 70565 Stuttgart *Toll Free Tel:* 800 66 111 99 *Fax:* (0711) 78 99 10 10 *E-mail:* service@distribook.de (Germany & Switzerland)
Dr Franz Hain Verlagsauslieferungen GmbH, Dr-Otto-Neurath-Gasse 5, 1220 Vienna, Austria, Contact: Brigitte Perrotta *Tel:* (01) 282 65 65 77 *Fax:* (01) 282 52 82 *E-mail:* bestell@hain.at

Edition XXL GmbH
Industriestr 19, 64407 Fraenkisch-Crumbach

Tel: (06164) 50 41-0 *Fax:* (06164) 50 41-41; (06164) 50 41-42 (sales)
E-mail: info@xxl-medien-service.de
Web Site: www.xxl-medien-service.de
Key Personnel
Mng Dir: Ingrid Sammueller
International Sales Dir: Sonja Sammueller *E-mail:* sonja.sammueller@xxl-medien-service.de
Founded: 1997
Subjects: Cookery, How-to, Nonfiction (General), Wine & Spirits
ISBN Prefix(es): 978-3-89736
Parent Company: XXL Medien Service GmbH

YinYang Media Verlag
Im Tal 1, 65779 Kelkheim
Tel: (06195) 9000 10; (06195) 9000 08 *Fax:* (06195) 9000 10; (06195) 9000 08
E-mail: info@yinyang-verlag.de
Web Site: www.yinyang-verlag.de
Key Personnel
Publisher: Regina Berlinghof *E-mail:* regina.berlinghof@yinyang-verlag.de
Subjects: Inspirational, Spirituality, Literature, Literary Criticism, Essays
ISBN Prefix(es): 978-3-935727; 978-3-9806799

Verlag Philipp von Zabern GmbH
Imprint of WBG (Wissenschaftlichen Buchgesellschaft)
Riedeselstr 57, 64283 Darmstadt
Tel: (06151) 3308-127 *Fax:* (06151) 3308-208
E-mail: buchhandel@wbg-verlage.de
Web Site: www.wbg-verlage.de/zabern
Key Personnel
Mng Dir: Dr Juergen Kron
Sales Manager: Wolfgang Hornstein *E-mail:* hornstein@wbg-verlage.de
Press & Public Relations: Christina Herborg *Tel:* (06151) 3308-161 *E-mail:* herborg@wbg-verlage.de
Founded: 1802
Subjects: Archaeology, Art, History, Regional Interests
ISBN Prefix(es): 978-3-8053
Number of titles published annually: 100 Print
Distribution Center: Koch, Neff & Oetinger Verlagsauslieferung GmbH, Industriestr 23, 70565 Stuttgart *E-mail:* zabern@kno-va.de
Dr Franz Hain Verlagsauslieferungen GmbH, Dr-Otto-Neurath-Gasse 5, 1220 Vienna, Austria *Tel:* (01) 282-656577 *Fax:* (01) 282-5282 *E-mail:* bestell@hain.at
Pegasus, PO Box 11470, 1001 GL Amsterdam, Netherlands, Contact: Susan van Oostveen *Tel:* (020) 62 31 11 38 *Fax:* (020) 62 31 11 78 *E-mail:* import@pegasusboek.nl
AVA Verlagsauslieferung AG, Centralweg 16, 8910 Affoltern am Albis, Switzerland *Tel:* (044) 76242-50 *Fax:* (044) 76242-10 *E-mail:* verlagsservice@ava.ch

Phillipp von Zabern Verlag, *imprint of* WBG (Wissenschaftliche Buchgesellschaft)

Zambon Verlag & Vertrieb+
Leipziger Str 24, 60487 Frankfurt am Main
Tel: (069) 779223 *Fax:* (069) 773054
E-mail: zambon@zambon.net
Web Site: www.zambonverlag.de; www.zambon.net
Key Personnel
Publisher: Dr Giuseppe Zambon
Founded: 1974
Subjects: Cookery, Developing Countries, Government, Political Science, History, Library & Information Sciences, Literature, Literary Criticism, Essays, Mysteries, Suspense, Nonfiction (General), Poetry, Regional Interests, Travel & Tourism

ISBN Prefix(es): 978-3-88975
Bookshop(s): Internationale Buchhandlung, Kaiserstr 55, 60239 Frankfurt *Tel:* (069) 25 29 14 *Fax:* (069) 23 02 77

ZAP Verlag GmbH+
Rochusstr 2-4, 53123 Bonn
Tel: (0228) 9191122 *Fax:* (0228) 9191166
E-mail: info@zap-verlag.de; service@zap-verlag.de (customer service)
Web Site: www.zap-verlag.de
Key Personnel
Manager: Uwe Hagemann *Tel:* (0228) 9191190
Publishing Dir: Jutta Weil *Tel:* (0228) 9191114 *E-mail:* weil@zap-verlag.de
Product Manager: Maria Teresa Feldkirchner *Tel:* (0228) 9191165 *E-mail:* feldkirchner@zap-verlag.de; Dennis Flohr *Tel:* (0228) 9191163 *E-mail:* flohr@zap-verlag.de; Eva Marie Marzinkowski *Tel:* (0228) 9191164 *E-mail:* marzinkowski@zap-verlag.de
Head of Marketing & Sales: Thorsten Thierbach *Tel:* (0228) 9191172
Marketing: Karen Schwettmann *Tel:* (0228) 9191141
Customer Service: Astrid Eickhoff *Tel:* (0228) 919110
Founded: 1989
Subjects: Law
ISBN Prefix(es): 978-3-89655
Total Titles: 120 Print
Parent Company: Deutscher AnwaltVerlag

ZEIT Kunstverlag GmbH & Co KG+
Buceriusstr, Eingang Speersort 1, 20095 Hamburg
Tel: (040) 3280-0
E-mail: info@weltkunst.de; kundenservice@weltkunst.de
Web Site: www.weltkunst.de
Key Personnel
Mng Dir: Stefanie Hauer *E-mail:* stefanie.hauer@zeit.de; Nathalie Senden *E-mail:* nathalie.senden@zeit.de
Press & Public Relations: Sandra Friedrich *Tel:* (040) 3280-424 *E-mail:* sandra.friedrich@zeit.de
Sales & Marketing: Michael Menzer *Tel:* (040) 3280-3463 *E-mail:* michael.menzer@zeit.de
Founded: 1930
Subjects: Art, Antiques
ISBN Prefix(es): 978-3-921669
Subsidiaries: Antiquitaeten-Zeitung Verlag

Zeitgeist Media GmbH Verlag und Neue Medien+
Niederkasseler Str 2, 40547 Duesseldorf
Tel: (0211) 556255 *Fax:* (0211) 575167
E-mail: info@zeitgeistmedia.de
Web Site: www.zeitgeistmedia.de
Key Personnel
Mng Dir: Hubert Buecken *E-mail:* hb@zeitgeistmedia.de
Founded: 1989
Subjects: Cookery, Human Relations, Humor, Nonfiction (General), Outdoor Recreation, Travel & Tourism, Formula One (Motorsports)
ISBN Prefix(es): 978-3-926224; 978-3-934046
Branch Office(s)
Franzoesische Str 24, 10117 Berlin *Tel:* (030) 27 57 21 50

Zeitgut Verlag GmbH+
Klausenpasse 14, 12107 Berlin
Tel: (030) 70 20 93 0 *Fax:* (030) 70 20 93 22
E-mail: info@zeitgut.com
Web Site: www.zeitgut.com
Key Personnel
Mng Dir: Juergen Kleindienst *Tel:* (030) 70 20 93 27 *E-mail:* j.kleindienst@zeitgut.com
Sales Manager: Volker Mathieu *Tel:* (030) 70 20 93 12 *E-mail:* v.mathieu@zeitgut.com

Public Relations: Lydia Beier *Tel:* (030) 70 20 93
  14 *E-mail:* lydia.beier@zeitgut.com
Membership(s): Boersenverein des Deutschen
  Buchhandels.
Subjects: Biography, Memoirs, History
ISBN Prefix(es): 978-3-933336; 978-3-86614
Distribution Center: Stuttgarter Verlagskon-
  tor SVK, Rotebuehlstr 77, 70178 Stuttgart
  Tel: (0711) 66 72 14 83 *Fax:* (0711) 66 72 19
  74 *E-mail:* j.schuldt@svk.de

ZfKf-Zentrum fuer Kulturforschung, see
  ARCult Media GmbH

Verlag im Ziegelhaus+
Pflasteraeckerstr 20, 70186 Stuttgart
Tel: (0711) 46 63 63 *Fax:* (0711) 46 13 41
Web Site: www.verlag-im-ziegelhaus.de
Key Personnel
Owner: Ulrich Gohl *E-mail:* u.gohl@verlag-im-
  ziegelhaus.de
Founded: 1985
Subjects: History
ISBN Prefix(es): 978-3-925440
Number of titles published annually: 3 Print

Ziethen-Panorama Verlag GmbH (ZVP)+
Flurweg 15, 53902 Bad Muenstereifel
Tel: (02) 253-6047 *Fax:* (02) 253-6756
E-mail: mail@ziethen-panoramaverlag.de
Web Site: www.ziethen-panoramaverlag.de
Key Personnel
Mng Dir: Horst Ziethen
Founded: 1992
Publisher for picture landscape books.
Subjects: Foreign Countries, Photography, Re-
  gional Interests, Travel & Tourism
ISBN Prefix(es): 978-3-921268; 978-3-929932;
  978-3-934328
Parent Company: Ziethen-Medien GmbH & Co
  KG

Musikverlag Zimmermann GmbH & Co KG+
Strubbergstr 80, 60489 Frankfurt am Main
Tel: (069) 978286-6 *Fax:* (069) 978286-79
E-mail: info@zimmermann-frankfurt.de;
  vertrieb@zimmermann-frankfurt.de
Web Site: www.zimmermann-frankfurt.de
Key Personnel
Mng Dir: Cornelia Grossmann
  E-mail: grossmann@zimmermann-frankfurt.
  de; Volker Mandler *Tel:* (069) 978286-71
  E-mail: mandler@zimmermann-frankfurt.de
Rights & Licensing: Saskia Bieber *Tel:* (069)
  978286-72 *E-mail:* bieber@zimmermann-
  frankfurt.de
Rights & Licensing, Orchestra Library: Bernd
  Schuff *Tel:* (069) 978286-76 *E-mail:* schuff@
  zimmermann-frankfurt.de
Founded: 1876
Subjects: Music, Dance
ISBN Prefix(es): 978-3-921729
Associate Companies: Allegra Musikverlag
  GmbH & Co KG; Robert Lienau Musikverlag
  GmbH & Co KG
Distributed by C F Peters, New York (USA &
  Canada)

Zodiaque, *imprint of* Verlag Schnell und Steiner
  GmbH

ZS Verlag GmbH+
Tuerkenstr 9, 80333 Munich
Tel: (089) 548 25 15-0 *Fax:* (089) 548 25 15-222
E-mail: contact@zsverlag.de; rights@zsverlag.de;
  vertrieb@zsverlag.de
Web Site: www.zs-verlag.com
Key Personnel
Mng Dir: Michael Haentjes; Friedrich-Karl Sand-
  mann

Head, Marketing: Nina Vogel *Tel:* (089) 548 25
  15-168 *E-mail:* vogel@zsverlag.de
Sales Manager: Matthias Zehnder *Tel:* (089) 548
  25 15-291 *E-mail:* zehnder@zsverlag.de
Press & Public Relations: Friederike Koch-
  Buettner *Tel:* (089) 548 25 15-289 *Fax:* (089)
  550 1891 *E-mail:* koch-buettner@zsverlag.de
Production: Karin Mayer *Tel:* (089) 548 25 15-
  286 *E-mail:* mayer@zsverlag.de
Rights & Licenses: Katrin Pilars de Pilar
  Tel: (089) 548 25 15-225 *Fax:* (089) 548 25
  15-221 *E-mail:* pilars-de-pilar@zsverlag.de
Founded: 1984
Subjects: Cookery, Health, Nutrition, Wine &
  Spirits
ISBN Prefix(es): 978-3-924678; 978-3-932023;
  978-3-89883
Parent Company: Edel AG
Associate Companies: Elisabeth Sandmann Verlag
Imprints: Dr Oetker Verlag
Foreign Rep(s): Wolfgang Edelmann & Har-
  ald Rumpold (Austria); Martin E Schnetzer
  (Switzerland)
Distribution Center: VM Verlegerdienst Munich,
  Gutenbergstr 1, 82205 Gilching, Contact: Flo-
  rian Bartl *Tel:* (08105) 388-120 *Fax:* (08105)
  388-187 *E-mail:* zsverlag@verlegerdienst.de
Mohr Morawa Buchvertrieb GmbH, Sulzen-
  gasse 2, 1230 Vienna, Austria *Tel:* (01) 680
  14-0 *Fax:* (01) 688 71 30 *E-mail:* momo@
  mohrmorawa.at *Web Site:* www.mohrmorawa.at
Buchzentrum AG, Industriestr Ost 10, 4614 Haegendorf, Switzerland *Tel:* (062) 209 26 26
  Fax: (062) 209 26 27

**Dietrich zu Klampen Verlag & Dr Rolf
  Johannes GbR+**
Hermannshof Voelksen Roese 21, 31832 Springe
Tel: (05041) 801133 *Fax:* (05041) 801336
E-mail: info@zuklampen.de
Web Site: www.zuklampen.de
Key Personnel
Owner: Dietrich zu Klampen *E-mail:* dietrich.zu.
  klampen@zuklampen.de
Publisher: Dr Rolf Johannes *E-mail:* rolf.
  johannes@zuklampen.de
Press: Gert Deppe *E-mail:* gert.deppe@
  zuklampen.de
Founded: 1983
Subjects: Government, Political Science, Philos-
  ophy, Poetry, Psychology, Psychiatry, Science
  (General), Social Sciences, Sociology
ISBN Prefix(es): 978-3-924245; 978-3-933156;
  978-3-934920; 978-3-86674

**W Zuckschwerdt Verlag GmbH fuer Medizin
  und Naturwissenschaften**
Industriestr 1, 82110 Germering bei Munich
Tel: (089) 894349-0 *Fax:* (089) 89434950
E-mail: post@zuckschwerdtverlag.de; info@
  zuckschwerdtverlag.de
Web Site: www.zuckschwerdtverlag.de
Key Personnel
Mng Dir: Dr Annemarie Goeggler; Werner
  Zuckschwerdt
Medical & science books.
Subjects: Health, Nutrition, Medicine, Nursing,
  Dentistry, Anesthesiology, Biochemistry, Gy-
  necology, Hematology, Immunology, Intensive
  Care, Internal Medicine, Neurology, Oncology,
  Orthopedics, Pediatrics, Pharmacology, Radiol-
  ogy, Surgery, Urology
ISBN Prefix(es): 978-3-88603

ZVP, see Ziethen-Panorama Verlag GmbH (ZVP)

edition zweihorn GmbH & Co KG+
Riedelsbach 46, 94089 Neureichenau
Tel: (08583) 2454 *Fax:* (08583) 91435
E-mail: edition-zweihorn@web.de
Web Site: www.edition-zweihorn.de

Key Personnel
Contact: Gerhard Kaelberer
Subjects: Art, Education, Fiction, Humor, Nonfic-
  tion (General), Poetry, Science Fiction, Fantasy,
  Comics
ISBN Prefix(es): 978-3-935265; 978-3-943199
Number of titles published annually: 8 Print; 8 E-
  Book
Total Titles: 110 Print; 35 E-Book

Zweitausendeins Versand-Dienst GmbH
Karl-Tauchnitz-Str 6, 04107 Leipzig
Tel: (0341) 21 339 0 (editorial); (0341) 21 339
  339 (orders) *Fax:* (0341) 21 339 179
E-mail: info@zweitausendeins.de; service@
  zweitausendeins.de
Web Site: www.zweitausendeins.de
Key Personnel
Mng Dir: Peter Deisinger; Nicolas Koelmel
Founded: 1969
Subjects: Humor, Literature, Literary Criticism,
  Essays, Music, Dance, Mysteries, Suspense,
  Nonfiction (General), Poetry, Science (General)
ISBN Prefix(es): 978-3-86150

Ghana

General Information

Capital: Accra
Language: English
Religion: About 42% Christian, remainder follow
  traditional beliefs
Population: 16.2 million
Bank Hours: 0830-1400 Monday-Thursday; 0830-
  1500 Friday
Shop Hours: 0830-1230, 1330-1730 Monday,
  Tuesday, Thursday, Friday; 0830-1330 Wednes-
  day & Saturday
Currency: 100 pesawas = 1 new cedi
Export/Import Information: No tariffs on books;
  advertising matter over 1 kg gross weight 50%.
  Import license required, but single copies of
  books under Open General License. Levy
  charged on import licenses required. Credit
  terms not permitted.
Copyright: UCC, Berne, Florence (see Copyright
  Conventions, pg viii)

Adaex Educational Publications Ltd+
Gicel, H18 Rooms 160-163, Weija
Mailing Address: PO Box Ao 252, Accra
Tel: (030) 285 4188 *Fax:* (030) 285 4189
E-mail: info@adaexpub.com
Web Site: www.adaexpub.com
Key Personnel
President, Dir & Chief Publishing Officer: Asare
  Konadu Yamoah
Founded: 1995
Also acts as printer, book & literary agent.
Membership(s): Ghana Book Publishers Associa-
  tion (GBPA)
Subjects: Cookery, Fiction, Health, Nutrition, His-
  tory, How-to
ISBN Prefix(es): 978-9988-573
Number of titles published annually: 5 Print
Total Titles: 37 Print

Advent Press+
Adjacent Labadi Veterinary Services, La Rd, Ac-
  cra
Tel: (030) 2777861; (030) 2769301; (030)
  2764687
E-mail: advent_press@yahoo.com
Key Personnel
General Manager: Kingsley Osei
Founded: 1937
Subjects: Religion - Other
ISBN Prefix(es): 978-9964-962

Adwinsa Publications Ghana Ltd+
Agbogba Off Haatso Rd, North Legon, Accra
Mailing Address: PO Box 92, Legon, Accra
Tel: (021) 501515 (marketing); (021) 503636
 Fax: (021) 501515
E-mail: adwinsa@yahoo.com
Web Site: www.adwinsa.net
Key Personnel
General Manager: Mr Kwabena Oppong Ampon-
sah
Founded: 1977
Membership(s): Ghana Book Publishers Associa-
tion (GBPA).
ISBN Prefix(es): 978-9964-955; 978-9964-975
Branch Office(s)
Adwinsa Bookstand (Eredec Hotel), PO Box 845,
 Koforidua
Bookshop(s): Adwinsa Distribution Agency Ltd,
 Adwinsa House (North Legon), PO Box 92,
 Legon

Afram Publications, *imprint of* Afram
 Publications Ltd

Afram Publications Ltd+
C/184/22 Midway Lane, Abofu, Achimota, Accra
Mailing Address: PO Box M18, Accra
Tel: (024) 4314 103; (028) 9554 446
E-mail: info@aframpubghana.com
Web Site: www.aframpubghana.com
Key Personnel
Mng Dir: Harriet Tagoe
Chief Manager: Bennett Honutse
Sales & Marketing Manager: Richard Atobrah
Founded: 1974
Membership(s): Afro-Asian Book Council; Ghana
 Book Publishers Association (GBPA).
Subjects: Fiction, Nonfiction (General)
ISBN Prefix(es): 978-9964-70
Imprints: Afram Publications
Branch Office(s)
M45 Mbrom Link, Behind St Louis Training Col-
lege, PO Box KS13259, Kumasi *Tel:* (028)
9554 255; (032) 2047524; (032) 2047525
 E-mail: kumasi@aframpubghana.com
Distributed by African Books Collective

Allgoodbooks Ltd+
Kwame Nkrumah Ave, Adabraka
Mailing Address: PO Box AN 10416, Accra
Tel: (030) 2246729; (024) 3430430 (cell)
E-mail: allgoodbooks@hotmail.com;
 allgoodbooksgh@yahoo.com
Founded: 1992
ISBN Prefix(es): 978-9964-88
Bookshop(s): D803/4 Granville Ave, Okaishie,
 Accra

Asempa Publishers+
Subsidiary of Christian Council of Ghana (CCG)
No 8 13 St Close, Atomic Gate, Haatso, Accra
Mailing Address: PO Box GP 919, Accra
Tel: (028) 967 2514
Web Site: www.asempapublishers.com
Founded: 1970
Membership(s): Ghana Book Publishers Associa-
tion (GBPA).
Subjects: Biblical Studies, Biography, Memoirs,
 Fiction, Music, Dance, Nonfiction (General),
 Poetry, Religion - Protestant, Religion - Other,
 Social Sciences, Sociology, Theology
ISBN Prefix(es): 978-9964-78; 978-9964-91
Number of titles published annually: 20 Print
Total Titles: 112 Print
Imprints: IBRA (Ghana)

Assembly Press, see Ghana Publishing Co Ltd

Blackmask Ltd+
Near Mothers Inn, Bubuashie, Accra
Tel: (030) 2222204; (030) 8199532 (cell)

E-mail: bmask4u@yahoo.com
Founded: 1979
Membership(s): African Books Collective.
Subjects: Cookery, Drama, Theater, Economics,
 Education, Social Sciences, Sociology
ISBN Prefix(es): 978-9964-960

BRRI, see Building & Road Research Institute
 (BRRI)

Building & Road Research Institute (BRRI)
PO Box 40, Kumasi
Tel: (032) 2060064; (032) 2060065 *Fax:* (032)
 2060080
E-mail: admin@brri.csir.org.gh; brriadmin@
 gmail.com
Web Site: www.brri.org
Founded: 1952
Subjects: Architecture & Interior Design, Civil
 Engineering, Computer Science, Earth Sci-
 ences, Real Estate, Technology, Transportation
ISBN Prefix(es): 978-9964-86; 978-9964-977
Parent Company: Council for Scientific & Indus-
 trial Research (CSIR), PO Box M 32, Accra

Bureau of Ghana Languages
Division of National Commission on Culture
PO Box 1851, Accra
Tel: (021) 760551; (021) 772151
E-mail: info@ghanaculture.gov.gh
Web Site: www.ghanaculture.gov.gh
Founded: 1958
Specialize in publications in Ghanaian languages.
Also acts as a translation agency/association.
Membership(s): Ghana Book Publishers Associa-
tion (GBPA).
Subjects: Biography, Memoirs, Drama, Theater,
 Fiction, Poetry, Pop Culture, Science (General)
ISBN Prefix(es): 978-9964-2
Total Titles: 493 Print
Branch Office(s)
PO Box 177, Educational Ridge, Tamale, North-
 ern Region, Deputy Dir: Paul Agangba
 Tel: (071) 22872; 0248196332 (cell)

EPP Books Services+
La Education Centre, Behind Ghana Trade Fair
 Centre, No 7 Lagoon St, Off Giffard Rd, Accra
Mailing Address: PO Box TF 490, Accra
Tel: (030) 2784849 *Fax:* (030) 2779099
E-mail: info@eppbookservices.com
Web Site: www.eppbookservices.com
Key Personnel
Executive Dir: Gibrine Adam *E-mail:* gibrine.
 adam@eppbookservices.com
Founded: 1991
Also acts as bookseller & stationery distributor.
Subjects: Accounting, Mathematics, Social Sci-
 ences, Sociology
ISBN Prefix(es): 978-9964-997
Associate Companies: Excellent Publishing &
 Printing, Accra, Contact: Wendy Linda Wordie
 Tel: (0247) 685456 *E-mail:* wendylinus@
 yahoo.com; Staples Systems Ghana Ltd, Ac-
 cra Central, Contact: Kenneth Mills *Tel:* (0244)
 361664 *Fax:* (0302) 688795
Distributor for Elsevier; McGraw; John Wiley
Foreign Rep(s): Epp Books Services (Nigeria)
Foreign Rights: Sterling Publishers Pvt (India)

Frank Publishing Ltd+
A-Lang Yard, Adabraka-Official Town, Accra
Tel: (021) 240711; (020) 8186747 (cell)
Founded: 1976
Specialize in school textbooks & typesetting for
 other publishing houses.
Membership(s): Ghana Association of Book Edi-
 tors; Ghana Publishers Association.
Subjects: Economics, English as a Second Lan-
 guage, Government, Political Science, Religion

- Catholic, Religion - Protestant, Religion -
Other
ISBN Prefix(es): 978-9964-959

Ghana Academy of Arts & Sciences+
PO Box M32, Accra
Tel: (021) 77 20 02 *Fax:* (021) 77 20 32
Key Personnel
President: Francis K A Allotey
 E-mail: fkallotey@gmail.com
Founded: 1959
Subjects: Art, Literature, Literary Criticism, Es-
 says, Music, Dance, Science (General)
ISBN Prefix(es): 978-9964-90; 978-9964-969;
 978-9964-950

**Ghana Institute of Linguistics Literacy &
 Bible Translation (GILLBT)**
Affiliate of University of Ghana
PO Box OS-3063, Osu, Accra
Tel: (030) 5240 281
Web Site: www.gillbt.org
Key Personnel
Chairman: Thomas Sayibu Imoro
Deputy Chairperson: Prof Akosua Adomako Am-
 pofo
Founded: 1962
Membership(s): Wycliffe Bible Translators Inter-
 national (WBTI).
Subjects: Anthropology, Biblical Studies, English
 as a Second Language, Environmental Studies,
 Health, Nutrition, Language Arts, Linguistics,
 Religion - Protestant, Women's Studies
ISBN Prefix(es): 978-9964-92; 978-9988-7525
Branch Office(s)
New Karaga Rd, Kanvilli, Near School of Hy-
 giene, PO Box TL-378, Tamale *Tel:* (037) 2023
 175; (037) 2023 179 *E-mail:* press@gillbt.org

Ghana Publishing Co Ltd
PO Box GP 124, Accra
Tel: (027) 7802 324 (cell); (0302) 664 3389 (ext
 130); (0302) 664 3389 (ext 128)
E-mail: info@ghpublishingcompany.com
Web Site: ghpublishingcompany.com
Founded: 1965
Subjects: Biography, Memoirs, Ethnicity, Fiction,
 History, Language Arts, Linguistics, Nonfiction
 (General), Poetry, Science (General), Social
 Sciences, Sociology, Technology
ISBN Prefix(es): 978-9964-1

Ghana Standards Authority
PO Box MB 245, Accra
Tel: (030) 2500231; (030) 2500065; (030)
 2500066; (030) 2506992-6 *Fax:* (030)
 2500092; (030) 2500231
E-mail: info@gsa.gov.gh
Web Site: www.gsa.gov.gh
Key Personnel
Executive Dir: Dr George Ben Crentsil *Tel:* (030)
 2501495
Founded: 1967
Standards promulgation, quality assurance,
 metrology, conformity assessment.
Membership(s): International Organization for
 Standardization.
Subjects: Chemistry, Chemical Engineering, Civil
 Engineering, Computer Science, Developing
 Countries, Disability, Special Needs, Electron-
 ics, Electrical Engineering, Energy, Engineering
 (General), Environmental Studies, Library &
 Information Sciences, Management, Physical
 Sciences, Physics, Science (General)
ISBN Prefix(es): 978-9964-990
Branch Office(s)
PO Box 634, Ho *Tel:* (036) 2026485
 E-mail: gsbho@gsa.gov.gh (Volta region)
PO Box KF 117, Koforidua *Tel:* (034) 2022786
 Fax: (034) 20227865 *E-mail:* gsbkoforidua@
 gsa.gov.gh (Eastern region)

PO Box KS 1201, Kumasi *Tel:* (032) 2025344
  Fax: (032) 20253442 *E-mail:* gsbkumasi@gsa.
  gov.gh (Ashanti & Brong Ahafo regions)
PO Box TD 676, Takoradi *Tel:* (031) 20221363
  E-mail: gsbtakoradi@gsa.gov.gh (Western &
  Central regions)
PO Box TL 1150, Tamale *Tel:* (037) 20223724
  E-mail: gsbtamale@gsa.gov.gh (Northern, Up-
  per East & Upper West regions)

Ghana Universities Press (GUP)+
North End of Volta Rd, University of Ghana, Ac-
  cra
Tel: (030) 2513401; (020) 8178076 (cell)
Founded: 1962
Membership(s): African Books Collective; Ghana
  Book Publishers Association (GBPA); Interna-
  tional Association of Scholarly Publishers.
Subjects: Agriculture, Biological Sciences, Com-
  munications, Government, Political Science,
  History, Language Arts, Linguistics, Medicine,
  Nursing, Dentistry, Social Sciences, Sociology
ISBN Prefix(es): 978-9964-3

GILLBT, see Ghana Institute of Linguistics
  Literacy & Bible Translation (GILLBT)

GUP, see Ghana Universities Press (GUP)

IBRA (Ghana), *imprint of* Asempa Publishers

Sedco, *imprint of* Sedco Publishing Ltd

Sedco-Longman, see Sedco Publishing Ltd

Sedco Publishing Ltd+
Sedco House, 5 Tabon St, North Ridge, Accra
Mailing Address: PO Box 2051, Accra
Tel: (030) 2221332 *Fax:* (030) 2220107
E-mail: sedco@africaonline.com.gh
Web Site: www.sedco-longman.com
Key Personnel
Contact: Julian M Segbawu *E-mail:* jmsjms190@
  yahoo.com
Founded: 1975
Educational materials for all levels.
Subjects: Agriculture, Biological Sciences, Chem-
  istry, Chemical Engineering, Cookery, Drama,
  Theater, Education, English as a Second Lan-
  guage, Fiction, Geography, Geology, History,
  Law, Mathematics, Physics, Science (General)
ISBN Prefix(es): 978-9964-72
Number of titles published annually: 5 Print
Total Titles: 520 Print
Imprints: Sedco
Subsidiaries: Sedco Enterprise
Distributed by African Books Collective Ltd
Orders to: Kings Meadow, Ferry Hinksey Rd,
  Unit 13, Oxford OX2 0DP, United Kingdom

Sub-Saharan Publishers+
No 9 Goodwill Rd, PO Box 358, Legon-Accra
Tel: (021) 23 33 71 *Fax:* (021) 23 42 51
E-mail: saharanp@africaonline.com.gh
Key Personnel
Mng Dir: Akoss Ofori-Mensah
Founded: 1992
Membership(s): African Books Collective; Ghana
  Book Publishers Association (GBPA).
Subjects: Education, Environmental Studies,
  African Literature
ISBN Prefix(es): 978-9988-550; 978-9988-647
Total Titles: 30 Print
Orders to: PO Box 1176, Cantonments, Accra

SWL Books, *imprint of* Sam Woode Ltd,
  Educational Publishers

Unimax Macmillan Ltd
42 Ring Rd South, Industrial Area, Accra North
Mailing Address: PO Box 10722, Accra North
Tel: (021) 227 443 *Fax:* (021) 225 215
Key Personnel
Publisher: Edward Addo
Sales & Marketing Manager: Sampson Gyampoh
Founded: 1985
International education division of Macmillan
  Publishers Ltd.
Subjects: Agriculture, Environmental Studies,
  Mathematics, Science (General)
ISBN Prefix(es): 978-9988-553; 978-9988-0; 978-
  9988-601
Parent Company: Macmillan Publishers Ltd
Showroom(s): Unicorn House, Prempah 11 St,
  PO Box KS 16659, Adum, Kumasi, Manager:
  Edward Udzu *Tel:* (051) 39284; (051) 39286
  Fax: (051) 39285
Warehouse: Unicorn House, Prempah 11 St, PO
  Box KS 16659, Adum, Kumasi, Manager:
  Edward Udzu *Tel:* (051) 39284; (051) 39286
  Fax: (051) 39285

Waterville Publishing House+
101 Miamona Close, South Industrial Area, Accra
Tel: (0302) 689971; (0302) 689972; (0277)
  539103
Founded: 1963
Subjects: Agriculture, Biography, Memoirs, Eth-
  nicity, Fiction, History, Inspirational, Spiritu-
  ality, Medicine, Nursing, Dentistry, Nonfiction
  (General), Poetry, Religion - Protestant, Re-
  ligion - Other, Science (General), Social Sci-
  ences, Sociology
ISBN Prefix(es): 978-9964-5
Parent Company: A-riis Co Ltd
Divisions: Presbyterian Press

Woeli Publishing Services
PO Box NT 601, Accra-New Town
Fax: (021) 777098; (021) 229294
E-mail: info@woelipublishing.com
Key Personnel
Publisher: Mr Woeli Dekutsey
Founded: 1984
This publisher has indicated that 60% of their
  product line is author subsidized.
Membership(s): Ghana Association of Book Edi-
  tors; Ghana Book Publishers Association.
Subjects: Drama, Theater, Fiction, Poetry,
  Women's Studies
ISBN Prefix(es): 978-9964-90; 978-9964-970;
  978-9964-978
Number of titles published annually: 8 Print; 5 E-
  Book
Total Titles: 203 Print; 20 E-Book
Orders to: African Books Collective, Unit 13,
  Kings Meadow, Ferry Hinksey Rd, Oxford
  OX2 0DP, United Kingdom *Tel:* (01865)
  726686

Sam Woode Ltd, Educational Publishers+
No One Adole Abla Link, Opposite St Augustine
  Anglican Church, Sahara-Dansoman, Accra
Mailing Address: PO Box AN 12719, Accra-
  North
Tel: (030) 2305287 *Fax:* (030) 2310482
E-mail: info@samwoode.com
Web Site: www.samwoode.com
Key Personnel
Chairman: Kwesi Sam-Woode
Mng Dir: Kenneth Kofi Asamoah
Publishing Manager: Michael Ayensu Mensah
Founded: 1984
Membership(s): Ghana Book Publishers Associa-
  tion (GBPA).
Subjects: Agriculture, Career Development, En-
  glish as a Second Language, Mathematics,
  Physical Sciences, Science (General)
ISBN Prefix(es): 978-9964-979; 978-9988-609

Imprints: SWL Books
Distributed by West African Book Publishers Ltd
  (Nigeria)

Greece

General Information

Capital: Athens
Language: Greek (official), English, French
Religion: Predominantly Greek Orthodox
Population: 10.6 million
Bank Hours: 0800-1400 Monday-Friday
Shop Hours: Vary. Generally 0800-1500 Monday,
  Wednesday, Saturday; 0800-1400, 1730-2030
  Tuesday, Thursday, Friday
Currency: 100 Eurocents = 1 Euro
Export/Import Information: Member of the Eu-
  ropean Union. No tariff on non-Greek books
  except children's picture books (free from EU).
  Foreign language advertising catalogues &
  other advertising matter free from EU. Chil-
  dren's picture books & advertising matter subject to stamp duty, and books & advertising
  subject to small additional taxes, University
  Tax & Bank Fee, Contribution for Farmer's Social Assistance. Only books printed in Greek
  need import license; all advertising matter other
  than price lists require license. No special exchange controls. 4% VAT on books.
Copyright: UCC, Berne, Florence (see Copyright
  Conventions, pg viii)

Agra Publications
99 Zoodochou Pighis, 114 73 Athens
Tel: 2107011461 *Fax:* 2107018649
E-mail: info@agra.gr; orders@agra.gr
Web Site: www.agra.gr
Key Personnel
Editor & Publisher: Stavros Petsopoulos
Communications Manager: Dimitra Pipili
Founded: 1979
Subjects: Architecture & Interior Design, Art,
  Drama, Theater, Fiction, Literature, Literary
  Criticism, Essays, Photography, Poetry, Ancient
  Greek, Roman & Byzantine Literature, Crime
  Fiction, Foreign Fiction, Paintings
ISBN Prefix(es): 978-960-325
Distribution Center: Center for the Book, Las-
  sani 3, 546 22 Thessaloniki *Tel:* 2310237463
  Fax: 2310285857 *E-mail:* puluktsi@otenet.gr
  (Thessaloniki & Northern Greece)

Aiora Press
11 Mavromichali St, 106 79 Athens
Tel: 2103839000 *Fax:* 2103839039
E-mail: info@aiora.gr
Web Site: aiora.gr
Founded: 1997
Subjects: Biography, Memoirs, Drama, Theater,
  Environmental Studies, Government, Political
  Science, Health, Nutrition, Language Arts, Lin-
  guistics, Literature, Literary Criticism, Essays,
  Philosophy, Social Sciences, Sociology
ISBN Prefix(es): 978-960-7872; 978-618-5048

Alamo Ellas+
6 Sarantaporou, 111 44 Athens
Tel: 2102280027 *Fax:* 2102280027
Subjects: Biblical Studies, Cookery, English as
  a Second Language, Gardening, Plants, Law,
  Philosophy, Religion - Catholic, Religion - Is-
  lamic, Religion - Jewish, Religion - Protestant,
  Theology, Travel & Tourism
ISBN Prefix(es): 978-960-7639
Associate Companies: Alpha Delta

Vefa Alexiadou Editions+
PO Box 520 24, 144 10 Metamorfosis
Tel: 2102846984 *Fax:* 2102840734
Key Personnel
Mng Dir: Vefa Alexiadou
Founded: 1979
Membership(s): IACP.
Subjects: Cookery
ISBN Prefix(es): 978-960-85018; 978-960-8125;
   978-960-90137; 978-960-91230
Associate Companies: Alba Editions
Distributed by Howell Press (USA & Canada);
   Tower Books (Australia)
Distributor for Sterling Editions (USA)
Bookshop(s): One Kresnas St, 141 23 Ly Kovrisi,
   Athens

Apostoliki Diakonia tis Ekklisias tis Ellados
   (Apostolic Diakonia of the Church of Greece)+
One Iasiou St, 115 21 Athens
Tel: 2107272381 *Fax:* 2107272380
E-mail: editions@apostoliki-diakonia.gr;
   sellsbooks@apostoliki-diakonia.gr
Web Site: www.apostoliki-diakonia.gr
Key Personnel
Supervisor: Evangelos Karakovounis
   Tel: 2107272331
Head, Book Distribution: Leonidas G Psarianos
   Tel: 2108161544
Founded: 1936
Subjects: Biblical Studies, Film, Video, History,
   Music, Dance, Religion - Other, Social Sci-
   ences, Sociology, Theology
ISBN Prefix(es): 978-960-315
Bookshop(s): 2 Dragatsaniou Str, Klafthmonos
   Sq. 105 59 Athens, Contact: Andreas Poret-
   sanos *Tel:* 2103310977 *Fax:* 2103228637; 143
   Riga Ferreou & 24 Filopimenos Str, 262 21 Pa-
   tra, Contact: Panagiotis Pettas *Tel:* 2610223110
   Fax: 2610223110; 9a Ethnikis Aminis Str, 546
   21 Thessaloniki, Contact: Maria Kyrmeli-Skeva
   Tel: 2310275126 *Fax:* 2310278559

Aik Arsenidou & Co, see Ekdoseis Arsenidi

Ekdotike Athenon SA+
13 Ippokratous Str, 106 79 Athens
Tel: 2103608911 *Fax:* 2103608914
E-mail: info@ekdotikeathenon.gr
Web Site: www.ekdotikeathenon.gr
Founded: 1962
Specialize in books on Greek history & culture.
Subjects: Archaeology, Art, Cookery, History, Lit-
   erature, Literary Criticism, Essays, Religion -
   Other, Science (General), Travel & Tourism,
   Mythology
ISBN Prefix(es): 978-960-213
Associate Companies: Ekdotike Hellados SA,
   Philadelphias 8, Athens (printer)
Distribution Center: Oxbow Books Ltd

Editions Axiotellis+
78 Trikoupi Charilaou St, Exarchia, 106 80
   Athens
Tel: 2103618247
E-mail: info@axiotelis.gr
Founded: 1974
Membership(s): European Educational Publishers
   Group.
Subjects: Education, Government, Political Sci-
   ence
ISBN Prefix(es): 978-960-7053; 978-960-7807

Bell, *imprint of* Harlenic Hellas Publishing SA

Benaki Mouseio (Benaki Museum)
One Koumbari St & Vas Sofias Ave, 106 74
   Athens
Tel: 2103671000 *Fax:* 2103671063
E-mail: benaki@benaki.gr
Web Site: www.benaki.gr

Key Personnel
Publications Dept: Dimitris Arvanitakis; Maria
   Diamanti; Vassiliki Karagelou
Founded: 1974
Subjects: Architecture & Interior Design, Art,
   History, Literature, Literary Criticism, Essays,
   Music, Dance
ISBN Prefix(es): 978-960-7671; 978-960-85160;
   978-960-8347; 978-960-8452

Beta Medical Publishers Ltd+
Andrianeiou 3, 115 25 Athens
Tel: 2106714371; 2106714340 *Fax:* 2106715015
E-mail: betamedarts@otenet.gr
Web Site: www.betamedarts.gr
Founded: 1976
Subjects: Medicine, Nursing, Dentistry, Veterinary
   Science
ISBN Prefix(es): 978-960-7308; 978-960-8071
Total Titles: 106 Print

Boukoumanis Editions+
Mavromichali 1, 106 79 Athens
Tel: 2103618502; 2103637426 *Fax:* 2103630669
Key Personnel
Mng Dir: Marita Boukoumani
Founded: 1969
Subjects: Education, Environmental Studies, Gov-
   ernment, Political Science, History, Philosophy,
   Psychology, Psychiatry, Social Sciences, Soci-
   ology
ISBN Prefix(es): 978-960-7458

Chrissi Penna - Golden Pen Books+
16, Zoodohou Pigis Str, 106 81 Athens
Tel: 2103805672 *Fax:* 2103825205
E-mail: info@chrissipenna.com; xpenna@acci.gr
Web Site: www.chrissipenna.com
Key Personnel
Mng Dir: K Papachrysanthou
Founded: 1964
Specializes in cookbooks, paperback books & ref-
   erence.
Subjects: Animals, Pets, Astrology, Occult, Child
   Care & Development, Cookery, Education, Fic-
   tion, Health, Nutrition, Nonfiction (General),
   Technology
ISBN Prefix(es): 978-960-245
Number of titles published annually: 18 Print
Total Titles: 135 Print
Warehouse: H Trikoupi Str 157, 114 72 Athens

DARK MOON, *imprint of* Harlenic Hellas
   Publishing SA

Diachronikes Ekdoseis SA+
77 Vas Sofias, 115 21 Athens
Tel: 2107213225; 2107213387 *Fax:* 2107246180
ISBN Prefix(es): 978-960-85630; 978-960-86959
Parent Company: ASCENT Ltd, Athens

Diavlos SA+
72-74 Mavromichali Str, 106 80 Athens
Tel: 2103631169 *Fax:* 2103617473
E-mail: info@diavlos-books.gr
Web Site: www.diavlos-books.com
Key Personnel
Mng Dir: Emmanuel Deligiannakis
Founded: 1988
Subjects: Astronomy, Computer Science, How-
   to, Humor, Mathematics, Nonfiction (General),
   Physical Sciences, Physics, Science (General),
   Science Fiction, Fantasy
ISBN Prefix(es): 978-960-7140; 978-960-531

Dioptra Ekdoseis
Agias Paraskevis 40, 121 32 Peristeri
Tel: 2103805228 *Fax:* 2103300439
Web Site: www.dioptra.gr
Founded: 1985

Specialize in alternative therapies, metaphysics &
   esotericism.
Subjects: Literature, Literary Criticism, Essays,
   Psychology, Psychiatry
ISBN Prefix(es): 978-960-364
Total Titles: 100 Print
Branch Office(s)
Pesmazoglou 5, 105 64 Athens *Tel:* 2103300774

Ekdoseis Dodoni
Themistocles & Gravias 15, 106 78 Athens
Tel: 2130232404 *Fax:* 2130232404
E-mail: info@dodonipublications.gr
Web Site: www.dodonipublications.gr
Founded: 1962
Subjects: Drama, Theater, Fiction, Government,
   Political Science, History, Literature, Literary
   Criticism, Essays, Music, Dance, Nonfiction
   (General), Philosophy, Poetry, Religion - Other,
   Folklore, Mythology
ISBN Prefix(es): 978-960-248; 978-960-385

Dorikos A I Klados & Co+
29 Zood Pigis Str, 106 81 Athens
Tel: 2103303609 *Fax:* 2103301866
Founded: 1958
Subjects: Biography, Memoirs, Crafts, Games,
   Hobbies, Drama, Theater, Fiction, Government,
   Political Science, History, Literature, Literary
   Criticism, Essays, Philosophy, Poetry, Psychol-
   ogy, Psychiatry
ISBN Prefix(es): 978-960-279
Associate Companies: Aposperitis Editions, Eres-
   sou 9, 106 80 Athens *Tel:* 2103604161

Ecole Francaise d'Athenes+
6, rue Didotou, 106 80 Athens
Tel: 2103679900 *Fax:* 2103632101
Web Site: www.efa.gr
Key Personnel
Dir: Dominique Mulliez
Founded: 1846
Subjects: Archaeology, History
ISBN Prefix(es): 978-2-86958
Number of titles published annually: 6 Print
Total Titles: 200 Print; 2 CD-ROM
Distributed by De Boccard Edition-Diffusion
Orders to: De Boccard Edition-Diffusion, 11, rue
   de Medicis, 75006 Paris, France, Contact: Mr J
   B Chaulet *Tel:* 01 43 26 00 37 *Fax:* 01 43 54
   85 83 *E-mail:* deboccard@deboccard.com *Web
   Site:* www.deboccard.com

Ekdoseis Arsenidi (Arsenides Publishers)+
57, Akadimias Str, 106 79 Athens
Tel: 2103633923; 2103629538 *Fax:* 2103633923
Subjects: Anthropology, Biography, Memoirs,
   History, Literature, Literary Criticism, Essays,
   Philosophy, Psychology, Psychiatry, Social Sci-
   ences, Sociology
ISBN Prefix(es): 978-960-253

G C Eleftheroudakis SA
15 Panepistimiou, 105 64 Athens
Tel: 2103258440 *Fax:* 2103239821
E-mail: internet@books.gr
Web Site: books.gr
Key Personnel
Owner & Chief Executive Officer: Sofika Elefth-
   eroudaki
Founded: 1915
Subjects: Fiction, Nonfiction (General)
ISBN Prefix(es): 978-960-200

Ekdoseis Epikairotita+
42 Mavromichali, 106 80 Athens
Tel: 2103607382 *Fax:* 2103636083
E-mail: epikero@yahoo.gr; info@epikerotita.com
Web Site: www.epikerotita.com.gr
Key Personnel
Contact: Michalis Bakirtzis
Founded: 1970

Subjects: Art, Computer Science, History, Literature, Literary Criticism, Essays
ISBN Prefix(es): 978-960-205

Etaireia Spoudon Neoellinikou Politismou Kai Genikis Paideias (Society for Studies of Modern Greek Culture & General Education)+
Agiou Dimitriou & Papanastasiou Sts, 154 52 Athens
Tel: 2106795000 *Fax:* 2106795090
E-mail: admin@moraitis.edu.gr
Web Site: www.moraitis.edu.gr; www.moraitis-school.com
Key Personnel
Mng Dir: Chrysanthi Moraiti-Kartali
Founded: 1972
Subjects: Art, Drama, Theater, Education, History, Literature, Literary Criticism, Essays, Poetry, Social Sciences, Sociology
ISBN Prefix(es): 978-960-259

Eurodimension Publication Advertising
49 Kallifrona, 113 64 Athens
Tel: 2108611303 *Fax:* 2108611303
Founded: 1992
Folios with collection of engravings & texts. Ideal for libraries, museums, universities, schools & collections.
Subjects: Archaeology, Art, History, Travel & Tourism
ISBN Prefix(es): 978-960-85724; 978-960-86262; 978-960-8212

Exandas Publishers
Didotou 57, 106 81 Athens
Tel: 2103822064; 2103084885 *Fax:* 2103813065
Key Personnel
President: Magda N Kotzia
Founded: 1974
Membership(s): International Alliance of Independent Publishers.
Subjects: Art, Cookery, Economics, Environmental Studies, Erotica, Fiction, Government, Political Science, History, Literature, Literary Criticism, Essays, Mysteries, Suspense, Philosophy, Psychology, Psychiatry, Public Administration, Romance, Science Fiction, Fantasy, Social Sciences, Sociology, Fairy Tales, Horror
ISBN Prefix(es): 978-960-256

Ekdoseis ton Filon (Friends' Publications)
Pentagon L Villa 1, St Anargyos, 135 61 Athens
Tel: 2108547723
E-mail: gelbesi@hol.gr
Founded: 1961
Book publishing house & sole distributor of *Eythini* magazine & Eythini publications (book & art).
Subjects: Art, Drama, Theater, Literature, Literary Criticism, Essays, Nonfiction (General), Philosophy, Poetry
ISBN Prefix(es): 978-960-289 (Filon); 978-960-7033 (Eythini); 978-960-8150 (Eythini)
Number of titles published annually: 10 Print
Total Titles: 580 Print; 1 Audio
Parent Company: Eythini

Fotolio & Typicon, *imprint of* Ekdoseis Stochastis

Foundation for Mediterranean Cooperation+
130, Solonos Str, 106 81 Athens
Tel: 2103810465 *Fax:* 2103805113
Subjects: Art, Biography, Memoirs, Economics, Government, Political Science, History, Literature, Literary Criticism, Essays, Philosophy, Poetry, Psychology, Psychiatry, Social Sciences, Sociology
ISBN Prefix(es): 978-960-86302

Fytraki Publications SA
G Papageorgiou & 20 K Katara Str, 136 78 Athens
Tel: 2102400722 *Fax:* 2102400720
Founded: 1934
Subjects: Cookery, Health, Nutrition, Literature, Literary Criticism, Essays, Music, Dance, Recreation, Social Issues
ISBN Prefix(es): 978-960-246; 978-960-535; 978-960-7038
Bookshop(s): 67 Ippokratous Str & Arahovis, 106 80 Athens *Tel:* 2106842110 *Fax:* 2106818561 *E-mail:* store@fytraki.gr

Ekdoseis Gartaganis
Kon Melenikou 3, 546 35 Thessaloniki
Tel: 2310201210 *Fax:* 2310209680
E-mail: gartaganisbooks@gmail.com
Web Site: www.gartaganisbooks.gr
Founded: 1934
Subjects: Agriculture, Veterinary Science, Food Technology
ISBN Prefix(es): 978-960-7013; 978-960-6859; 978-960-88706

Giourdas Moschos+
70-74 Zoodohou Pigis & Kallidromiou, 106 81 Athens
Tel: 2103630219; 2103303145 *Fax:* 2103303126
E-mail: info@mgiurdas.gr
Web Site: www.mgiurdas.gr
Founded: 1958
Translations from USA & German titles.
Subjects: Architecture & Interior Design, Computer Science, Engineering (General)
ISBN Prefix(es): 978-960-512
Total Titles: 500 Print; 18 Online; 25 E-Book

Govostis Publishing SA+
Zoodohou Pigis 73, 106 81 Athens
Tel: 2103815433; 2103822251 *Fax:* 2103816661
E-mail: cotsos@govostis.gr
Web Site: www.govostis.gr
Key Personnel
President: Costas Govostis
Mng Dir: Francis Govostis
Founded: 1926
Subjects: Art, Astrology, Occult, Biography, Memoirs, Child Care & Development, Computer Science, Drama, Theater, Fiction, Government, Political Science, History, Nonfiction (General), Physics, Poetry
ISBN Prefix(es): 978-960-270
Warehouse: 58-60 Laskareos, 114 72 Athens

Harlenic Hellas Publishing SA
Feidiou 18, 106 78 Athens
Tel: 2103609438; 2103629723 *Fax:* 2103614846
E-mail: info@harlenic.gr
Web Site: www.harlenic.gr; www.bell.gr
Key Personnel
Mng Dir: Constantine N Ordolis *E-mail:* c.n. ordolis@harlenic.gr
Editorial Manager: Marina Kouloumoundra
Marketing Manager: Eleftheria Mavroidi *E-mail:* el.mavroidi@harlenic.gr
Founded: 1979
Subjects: Fiction, Literature, Literary Criticism, Essays, Romance
ISBN Prefix(es): 978-960-450; 978-960-620
Total Titles: 450 Print; 180 Online; 100 E-Book
Parent Company: Harlequin Enterprises Ltd, 225 Duncan Mill Rd, Don Mills, ON M3B 3K9, Canada
Associate Companies: Cora Verlag; Forlaget Harlequin AB; Harlequin Holland; Harlequin Iberica SA; Harlequin Japan; Harlequin Mills & Boon; Harlequin Mondadori; Harlequin SA
Imprints: Bell; DARK MOON; Harlequin; Silk

Harlequin, *imprint of* Harlenic Hellas Publishing SA

Denise Harvey (Publisher)+
Katounia, 340 05 Limni, Evia
Tel: 2227031154 *Fax:* 2227031154
E-mail: dhp@dharveypublisher.gr
Web Site: www.deniseharveypublisher.gr
Key Personnel
Mng Dir: Denise Harvey *E-mail:* denise@deniseharveypublisher.gr
Founded: 1972
Independent publisher of books mainly, but not exclusively, concerned with post-Byzantine Greek culture.
Subjects: Biography, Memoirs, Ethnicity, Literature, Literary Criticism, Essays, Nonfiction (General), Philosophy, Poetry, Theology
ISBN Prefix(es): 978-960-7120
Number of titles published annually: 3 Print
Total Titles: 50 Print
Imprints: Romiosyni (series)
Distributed by Cosmos Publishing Co Inc (USA)

Hestia Publishers & Booksellers+
84 Evripidou St, 105 53 Athens
Tel: 2103213907; 2103213704 *Fax:* 2103214610
E-mail: info@hestia.gr
Web Site: www.hestia.gr
Key Personnel
President: Marina Karaitidi
Founded: 1885
Subjects: Animals, Pets, Anthropology, Archaeology, Architecture & Interior Design, Art, Astrology, Occult, Behavioral Sciences, Biblical Studies, Biography, Memoirs, Business, Career Development, Child Care & Development, Communications, Drama, Theater, Education, Energy, Fiction, Geography, Geology, History, Human Relations, Journalism, Language Arts, Linguistics, Law, Library & Information Sciences, Literature, Literary Criticism, Essays, Management, Music, Dance, Mysteries, Suspense, Natural History, Philosophy, Photography, Poetry, Psychology, Psychiatry, Public Administration, Romance, Science Fiction, Fantasy, Social Sciences, Sociology, Travel & Tourism, Veterinary Science, Women's Studies
ISBN Prefix(es): 978-960-05
Branch Office(s)
Thessaloniki *Tel:* 2310220821 *Fax:* 2310220821
Bookshop(s): 60 Solonas St, 106 72 Athens *Tel:* 2103633780; 2103615077 *Fax:* 2103606759

Hillside Press
13 Doiranis St, 113 62 Kypseli
Tel: 2108829041 *Fax:* 2108827677
E-mail: info@elthillside.com
Web Site: www.elthillside.com
Materials for teaching English to speakers of other languages.
Subjects: Art, English as a Second Language, Poetry, Grammar
ISBN Prefix(es): 978-960-424
Branch Office(s)
18 Thisseos St, 712 01 Crete *Tel:* (02810) 301357 *Fax:* (02810) 301358
20 Asklipiou St & Kouma, 412 22 Larissa *Tel:* (02410) 539880 *Fax:* (02410) 539881
84 Patreos St, 262 21 Patra *Tel:* (02610) 625467 *Fax:* (02610) 625469
43 Tsimiski St, 546 23 Thessaloniki *Tel:* (02310) 273711; (02310) 273799; (02310) 273268 *Fax:* (02310) 273938
12-14 Archermou St, Polikatoikia Penteli, 1045 Nicosia, Cyprus *Tel:* 22 459635; 22 459636 *Fax:* 22 34 88 40
202 Coppergate House, 16 Brune St, London E1 7NJ, United Kingdom

Ianos SA+
Aristotelous 7, 546 24 Thessaloniki
Tel: 2310277004 *Fax:* 2310284832
E-mail: customerservice@ianos.gr

Web Site: www.ianos.gr
Founded: 1984
Membership(s): Thessaloniki's Booksellers Association.
Subjects: Biography, Memoirs, Ethnicity, History, Literature, Literary Criticism, Essays, Philosophy
ISBN Prefix(es): 978-960-7771; 978-960-7827
Subsidiaries: Gallery Ianos

Idryma Meleton Chersonisou tou Aimou
(Institute for Balkan Studies)
31A Meg Alexandrou Ave, 546 41 Thessaloniki
Mailing Address: PO Box 50932, 540 14 Thessaloniki
Tel: 2310832143 *Fax:* 2310831429
E-mail: imxa@imxa.gr
Web Site: www.imxa.gr
Key Personnel
President: Ioannis Tsekouras
Vice President: Ioannis Mourelos
Contact: Eleni Chaidia
Founded: 1953
Subjects: Art, Economics, Education, Ethnicity, History, Social Sciences, Sociology, Balkan Area from Ancient Times to Present Day
ISBN Prefix(es): 978-960-7387
Number of titles published annually: 6 Print; 250 E-Book
Total Titles: 279 Print; 26,000 E-Book
Distribution Center: Pournaras Panagiotis, 12 Kastritsiou Str, 546 23 Thessaloniki
E-mail: pournarasbooks@the.forthnet.gr

Ikaros Ekdotiki (Ikaros Publications)
4 Voulis St, 105 62 Athens
Tel: 2103225152 *Fax:* 2103235262
E-mail: info@ikarosbooks.gr
Web Site: ikarosbooks.gr
Founded: 1943
Specialize in Greek poetry.
Subjects: Literature, Literary Criticism, Essays, Poetry
ISBN Prefix(es): 978-960-7233; 978-960-7721; 978-960-8399

IMXA, see Idryma Meleton Chersonisou tou Aimou

Institute of Modern Greek Studies (Manolis Triandaphyllidis Foundation)+
Aristotle University of Thessaloniki, School of Philosophy (New Bldg), 4th floor, Room 418, 541 24 Thessaloniki
Tel: 2310997128 *Fax:* 2310997122
E-mail: ins@phil.auth.gr
Web Site: ins.web.auth.gr
Key Personnel
Dir: Dr George Papanastassiou
Founded: 1959
Subjects: Art, Education, Language Arts, Linguistics, Law, Literature, Literary Criticism, Essays, Philosophy
ISBN Prefix(es): 978-960-231
Orders to: S Patakis, Panagi Tsaldari 38, 104 37 Athens *Tel:* 2103650000 *Fax:* 2103650069
E-mail: export@patakis.gr *Web Site:* www.patakis.gr

Kalendis Editions+
70 Vouliagmenis Ave, 167 77 Elliniko
Tel: 2109638790; 2103601551 *Fax:* 2109638791
E-mail: info@kalendis.gr
Web Site: kalendis.gr
Founded: 1980
Subjects: Biological Sciences, Child Care & Development, Cookery, Erotica, Fiction, Health, Nutrition, History, Medicine, Nursing, Dentistry, Philosophy, Poetry, Psychology, Psychiatry
ISBN Prefix(es): 978-960-219

Number of titles published annually: 40 Print; 10 CD-ROM; 10 Online
Total Titles: 822 Print; 32 CD-ROM; 32 Online
Distributor for Delithanasis Publications; Ereynites Publications; Kirki Publicatitons; Malliaris Publications

Kapon Editions
23-27 Makriyianni Str, 117 42 Athens
Tel: 2109235098 *Fax:* 2109214089
E-mail: info@kaponeditions.gr
Web Site: www.kaponeditions.gr
Key Personnel
Contact: Moses Kapon; Rachel Kapon
Founded: 1980
Subjects: Archaeology, Architecture & Interior Design, Art, Drama, Theater, Environmental Studies, History, Literature, Literary Criticism, Essays, Medicine, Nursing, Dentistry, Science (General), Nature
ISBN Prefix(es): 978-960-7037; 978-960-7254

Kardamitsa Publications+
8 Hippocratous Str, 106 79 Athens
Tel: 2103615156
E-mail: info@kardamitsa.gr
Web Site: www.kardamitsa.gr
Founded: 1970
Subjects: Archaeology, History, Literature, Literary Criticism, Essays, Philosophy
ISBN Prefix(es): 978-960-7262; 978-960-354
Number of titles published annually: 10 Print
Total Titles: 270 Print
Parent Company: Institut du Livre

Karydaki Publishing
Strofiliou 55, 145 64 Kifissa, Athens
Tel: 2102717140
E-mail: info@karydaki-publishing.gr
Web Site: www.karydaki-publishing.gr
Founded: 2001
ISBN Prefix(es): 978-960-98963

Kastaniotis Editions SA+
Themistokleous 104, 106 81 Athens
Tel: 2103301208 *Fax:* 2103822530
E-mail: info@kastaniotis.com
Web Site: www.kastaniotis.com
Key Personnel
Mng Dir, Editorial: Athanasios Kastaniotis
Foreign Rights: Anteos Chrysostomidis
Publicity, Rights & Permissions: Sophie Catris
Founded: 1968
Membership(s): Association of Publishers & Booksellers of Athens.
Subjects: Anthropology, Architecture & Interior Design, Art, Astrology, Occult, Biography, Memoirs, Business, Child Care & Development, Computer Science, Cookery, Crafts, Games, Hobbies, Drama, Theater, Economics, Education, Fiction, Film, Video, Government, Political Science, Health, Nutrition, History, Humor, Literature, Literary Criticism, Essays, Philosophy, Poetry, Psychology, Psychiatry, Travel & Tourism, Astrology, Beauty, Cartoons & Comics, Esoterics & New Age
ISBN Prefix(es): 978-960-03
Total Titles: 3,000 Print
Bookshop(s): 11 Zalogou St, 106 78 Athens
Tel: 2103816310 *Fax:* 2103301331

Katoptro Publications
8, Korizi Str, 117 43 Athens
Tel: 2109244827; 2109244852 *Fax:* 2109244756
E-mail: info@katoptro.gr; vivliopolio@katoptro.gr
Web Site: www.katoptro.gr
Founded: 1987
Specialize in sciences.
Subjects: Astronomy, Biological Sciences, Computer Science, Education, History, Mathematics, Medicine, Nursing, Dentistry, Nonfiction (Gen-

eral), Philosophy, Physics, Science (General), Social Sciences, Sociology
ISBN Prefix(es): 978-960-7023; 978-960-7778
Number of titles published annually: 15 Print
Total Titles: 250 Print
Bookshop(s): 5 Pesmazoglou St, 105 64 Athens
Tel: 2103247785

Ekdoseis Kazantzaki (Kazantzakis Publications)+
Charilaou Trikoupi 116, 114 72 Athens
Tel: 2103642829 *Fax:* 2103642830
E-mail: contact@kazantzakispublications.org
Web Site: www.kazantzakispublications.org
Key Personnel
Owner & Publisher: Patroclos Stavrou
Publish only works by Nikos Kazantzakis & his wife Helen, both reprints & new titles.
Subjects: Drama, Theater, Fiction, Literature, Literary Criticism, Essays, Philosophy, Poetry, Travel & Tourism
ISBN Prefix(es): 978-960-7948
Number of titles published annually: 9 Print
Total Titles: 39 Print; 39 E-Book

Kedros Publishers+
3, G Gennadiou St, 106 78 Athens
Tel: 2103802007; 2103809712 *Fax:* 2103302655; 2103821981 (orders)
E-mail: books@kedros.gr
Web Site: www.kedros.gr
Key Personnel
Publisher: Katya Lembessi; Evangelos Papathanassopoulos
Sales Manager: John Pahidis *E-mail:* pahidis@kedros.gr
Advertising: Maria Zampara *E-mail:* zampara@kedros.gr
Foreign Rights, Adult Books: Lefteris Kalospyros *E-mail:* lefteris@kedros.gr
Foreign Rights, Children's Books: Angeliki Portokaloglou *E-mail:* angeliki@kedros.gr
Founded: 1954
Subjects: Biography, Memoirs, Child Care & Development, Drama, Theater, Education, Fiction, Health, Nutrition, History, Humor, Literature, Literary Criticism, Essays, Philosophy, Poetry, Psychology, Psychiatry, Romance, Science (General), Self-Help, Social Sciences, Sociology, Travel & Tourism
ISBN Prefix(es): 978-960-04
Number of titles published annually: 250 Print
Total Titles: 2,000 Print
Distributed by Cosmos Publishing Co (USA)

Kentro Byzantinon Erevnon, see Pournaras Panagiotis

Ekdoseis Klidarithmos+
Stournara 27b, 106 82 Athens
Tel: 2103832044 *Fax:* 2103817950
E-mail: info@klidarithmos.gr
Web Site: www.klidarithmos.gr
Founded: 1985
Subjects: Architecture & Interior Design, Automotive, Civil Engineering, Computer Science, Computers, Economics, Education, Electronics, Electrical Engineering, Management, Marketing, Mechanical Engineering
ISBN Prefix(es): 978-960-209; 978-960-461
Bookshop(s): 5 Pesmazoglou St, 105 64 Athens
Tel: 2103300104 *E-mail:* shop@klidarithmos.gr
Warehouse: 4 Domokou St, 104 40 Athens
Tel: 2105237635 *Fax:* 2105237677
E-mail: sales@klidarithmos.gr

Kritiki Publishing SA+
4 Papadiamantopoulou, 115 28 Athens
Tel: 2108211811; 2106842110 (sales); 2108212266 (marketing) *Fax:* 2106818561 (sales)
E-mail: biblia@kritiki.gr; sales@kritiki.gr; marketing@kritiki.gr

Web Site: kritiki.gr
Founded: 1987
Specialize in social sciences.
Subjects: Anthropology, Business, Economics, Environmental Studies, Fiction, Finance, Geography, Geology, Government, Political Science, Health, Nutrition, History, Language Arts, Linguistics, Law, Literature, Literary Criticism, Essays, Management, Marketing, Mathematics, Nonfiction (General), Philosophy, Psychology, Psychiatry, Self-Help, Social Sciences, Sociology, Travel & Tourism, Humanities, Minority Issues, Parenting, Political Theory, World Affairs
ISBN Prefix(es): 978-960-218
Number of titles published annually: 60 Print
Total Titles: 530 Print

Kyriakidis Brothers Publishing House SA+
5 Konstantinou Melenikou, 546 35 Thessaloniki
Tel: 2310208540 *Fax:* 2310245541
E-mail: info@kyriakidis.gr
Web Site: www.kyriakidis.gr
Key Personnel
President: Anastasios I Kyriakidis
Vice President: Anastasios D Kyriakidis
Founded: 1993
Subjects: Accounting, Chemistry, Chemical Engineering, Economics, History, Mathematics, Theology
ISBN Prefix(es): 978-960-343

Kyriakidis Editions
Panagias Dexias 7, 54635 Thessaloniki
Tel: 2310200376
E-mail: info@kyriakidiseditions.gr
Web Site: www.kyriakidiseditions.gr
Founded: 2013
Subjects: Art, Biography, Memoirs, Health, Nutrition, History, Literature, Literary Criticism, Essays, Poetry, Psychology, Psychiatry, Religion - Other
ISBN Prefix(es): 978-960-328; 978-960-6775

Leon, *imprint of* Spanos

A G Leventis Foundation
9, Fragoklissias St, 151 25 Maroussi-Athens
Tel: 2106165232 *Fax:* 2106165233
E-mail: foundation@leventis.net
Web Site: www.leventisfoundation.org
Founded: 1979
Subjects: Archaeology, Art, History
ISBN Prefix(es): 978-9963-560
Branch Office(s)
40 Gladstonos St, PO Box 2543, 1095 Nicosia, Cyprus *Tel:* 22 667706 *Fax:* 22 675002
    E-mail: leventcy@zenon.logos.cy.net
Iddo House, PO Box 159, Lagos, Nigeria
    E-mail: foundation@leventis-overseas.com
Todistr 44, PO Box 1527, 8027 Zurich, Switzerland *E-mail:* foundation@leventis-overseas.com

Libro AE
Glykonos 10-12, 106 75 Athens
Tel: 2107228647 *Fax:* 2107228648
E-mail: info@libro.gr
Web Site: www.libro.gr
Key Personnel
Contact: Peter Panteleskou
Founded: 1979
Subjects: Architecture & Interior Design, Art, Biography, Memoirs, Government, Political Science, Literature, Literary Criticism, Essays, Poetry
ISBN Prefix(es): 978-960-7009; 978-960-490
Bookshop(s): Patriarchou Ioakim 8, 106 74 Athens *Tel:* 2107247116 *Fax:* 2107232066

Livani Publishing SA+
Solonos 98, 106 80 Athens

Tel: 2103661200 *Fax:* 2103617791
E-mail: info@livanis.gr
Web Site: www.livanis.gr
Key Personnel
Selling Rights: Natasa Kalomiri *E-mail:* natasa@livanis.gr
Founded: 1972
Subjects: Art, Biography, Memoirs, Cookery, Economics, Education, Fiction, Government, Political Science, History, Inspirational, Spirituality, Journalism, Literature, Literary Criticism, Essays, Mysteries, Suspense, Nonfiction (General), Philosophy, Poetry, Psychology, Psychiatry, Religion - Other, Romance, Science (General), Science Fiction, Fantasy, Self-Help, Social Sciences, Sociology
ISBN Prefix(es): 978-960-236; 978-960-14
Total Titles: 200 Print

Lycabettus Press
PO Box 65101, 154 01 Athens
Tel: 2106741788 *Fax:* 2106710666
E-mail: sales@lycabettus.com; info@lycabettus.com
Web Site: www.lycabettus.com
Key Personnel
Editor: John Chapple *E-mail:* j.chapple@lycabettus.com
Founded: 1968
Text in English about Greece.
Subjects: Cookery, History, Travel & Tourism
ISBN Prefix(es): 978-960-7269

Mamouth Comix EPE+
128 Solonos, 106 81 Athens
Tel: 2103825055 *Fax:* 2103825054
E-mail: info@mamouthcomix.gr
Web Site: www.mamouthcomix.gr
Founded: 1982
Comic book publisher.
Subjects: Humor
ISBN Prefix(es): 978-960-321
Distributed by Ehapa Verlag (Germany)

Manolis Triandaphyllidis Foundation, see Institute of Modern Greek Studies (Manolis Triandaphyllidis Foundation)

Medousa/Selas Ekdotiki+
26 Didotou, 106 80 Athens
Tel: 2103648323; 2103648324 *Fax:* 2103648321
E-mail: medusa@otenet.gr
Founded: 1994
Subjects: Art, Fiction, Film, Video, Health, Nutrition, Music, Dance, Nonfiction (General), Science Fiction, Fantasy, Comics & Cartoons, Humor
ISBN Prefix(es): 978-960-7246; 978-960-85004
Imprints: Topos
Bookshop(s): Synergasia Andrea Metaxa 4, Athens
Warehouse: 63 Eressou Str, 106 83 Athens

Melissa Publishing House+
58 Skoufa St, 106 80 Athens
Tel: 2103611692 *Fax:* 2103600865
E-mail: info@melissabooks.com; webmaster@melissabooks.com
Web Site: www.melissabooks.com
Founded: 1954
Specialize in illustrated books on art, architecture, history & culture.
Subjects: Archaeology, Architecture & Interior Design, Art, History, Maritime, Greek Civilization
ISBN Prefix(es): 978-960-204
Distributed by Harry N Abrams Inc

Metaixmio
118 Ippokratous St, 114 72 Athens
Mailing Address: PO Box 21001, 114 10 Athens

Tel: 211 300 3500 *Fax:* 211 300 3562
E-mail: eshop@metaixmio.gr
Web Site: www.metaixmio.gr
Key Personnel
Commercial Dir: Eugenia Sourlantzi *Tel:* 211 300 3500 ext 570 *E-mail:* e.sourlantzi@metaixmio.gr
Sales Manager: Manos Kapetanakis *Tel:* 211 300 3500 ext 571 *E-mail:* m.kapetanakis@metaixmio.gr
Subjects: Art, Education, Health, Nutrition, Literature, Literary Criticism, Essays, Science (General)
ISBN Prefix(es): 978-960-375; 978-960-7399; 978-960-7976

MIET, see Morfotiko Idryma Ethnikis Trapezas-MIET

Minoas SA+
Korinthou 34, 144 51 Metamorfosi, Athens
Mailing Address: PO Box 50488, 144 51 Metamorfosi, Athens
Tel: 2102711222 *Fax:* 2102711056
E-mail: info@minoas.gr
Web Site: www.minoas.gr
Key Personnel
Mng Dir: Yannis Konstantaropoulos
Founded: 1952
Subjects: Art, Biography, Memoirs, Fiction, History, Music, Dance, Nonfiction (General), Self-Help, Classic & Modern Greek Literature
ISBN Prefix(es): 978-960-240; 978-960-542; 978-960-699; 978-960-893
Number of titles published annually: 80 Print
Total Titles: 800 Print

Modern Times SA
One George Papandreou St, 166 73 Voula, Athens
Tel: 2109659904 *Fax:* 2108992101
Founded: 1996
Subjects: Biography, Memoirs, Health, Nutrition, History, Literature, Literary Criticism, Essays, Mysteries, Suspense, Psychology, Psychiatry, Gastronomy
ISBN Prefix(es): 978-960-691

Morfotiko Idryma Ethnikis Trapezas-MIET
(National Bank of Greece Cultural Foundation)+
Publications Dept, 13 Thoukydidou St, 105 58 Athens
Tel: 2103230841 *Fax:* 2103227057
E-mail: mietekd@otenet.gr; sales@greekbooks.gr
Web Site: www.miet.gr
Key Personnel
President: George Zanias
Head, Publications: Antigone Philippopoulou
Founded: 1966
Subjects: Archaeology, History, Language Arts, Linguistics, Literature, Literary Criticism, Essays, Nonfiction (General), Philosophy, Science (General)
ISBN Prefix(es): 978-960-250
Bookshop(s): 5 Pesmazoglou St (Book Arcade), 105 64 Athens *Tel:* 2103215606 *Fax:* 2103214052; 108 Vasilissis Olgas St, 546 43 Thessaloniki *Tel:* 2310295171 *Fax:* 2310295276

Philippos Nakas SA+
19 km Lavriou Ave, 190 02 Peania
Tel: 2106686232 *Fax:* 2106686230
E-mail: books@nakas.gr
Web Site: www.nakas.gr
Key Personnel
President & Mng Dir: Konstantinos F Nakas
Vice President & Mng Dir: George Nakas
General Manager: Apostolia Gerogianni
    Tel: 2106686137 *E-mail:* lia@nakas.gr
Publications: Anna Fanourgaki *Tel:* 2106686255
    E-mail: anna-f@nakas.gr

Public Relations: Despina Nakas *Tel:* 2106686151
    E-mail: dnakas@nakas.gr
Founded: 1937
Subjects: Music, Dance
ISBN Prefix(es): 978-960-290
Distributor for Boosey & Hawkes; Henley Verlag;
    Ricordi

Narcissus Publishing
41, Ekataiou Str, 117 43 Athens
Tel: 2109247056; 2109211749 *Fax:* 2109211749
E-mail: info@narcissusbooks.gr
Web Site: www.narcissusbooks.gr
Key Personnel
Publisher: Philip Pyknis
Founded: 2001
Subjects: Animals, Pets, Biography, Memoirs,
    Cookery, Government, Political Science, His-
    tory, Literature, Literary Criticism, Essays,
    Poetry, Social Sciences, Sociology, Theology,
    Travel & Tourism
ISBN Prefix(es): 978-960-8239
Number of titles published annually: 14 Print
Total Titles: 90 Print

Ekdoseis Nea Akropoli+
29 Agiu Meletiu, 113 61 Athens
Tel: 2108231301 *Fax:* 2108847639
E-mail: info@nea-acropoli.gr; ena@nea-acropoli.
    gr; shop@nea-acropoli.gr
Web Site: www.nea-acropoli.gr
Key Personnel
President: Maria Jimenez
Founded: 1981
Subjects: Anthropology, Archaeology, Drama,
    Theater, History, Music, Dance, Mysteries, Sus-
    pense, Parapsychology, Philosophy, Culture
ISBN Prefix(es): 978-960-8407

Nikas Publications
120 Solonos St, 106 81 Athens
Tel: 2103307079 *Fax:* 2103834078
E-mail: info@nikasbooks.gr; rights@nikasbooks.
    gr
Web Site: www.nikasbooks.gr
Founded: 1948
Subjects: History, Language Arts, Linguistics, Lit-
    erature, Literary Criticism, Essays, Philosophy
ISBN Prefix(es): 978-960-296
Associate Companies: E Nikas Inc; Editions Hell-
    niki Paedia SA

S Nikolopoulos
Omirou 32, 106 72 Kolonaki
Tel: 2103645779 *Fax:* 2103645779
E-mail: bkyriakid@otenet.gr; libreria@otenet.gr
Web Site: www.bkyriakidis.gr
Key Personnel
Publisher: Sotiris Nikolopoulos
Founded: 1994
Publish books for Greek language as a foreign
    language.
Membership(s): Book Publishers Association.
Subjects: History, Literature, Literary Criticism,
    Essays, Psychology, Psychiatry, Social Sci-
    ences, Sociology, Ancient Greek History &
    Literature, Byzantine, European, Global, Gram-
    mar, Orthography, Vocabulary
ISBN Prefix(es): 978-960-7634
Total Titles: 100 Print

Nomiki Bibliothiki+
Mavromichali 23, 106 80 Athens
Tel: 2103678800 *Fax:* 2103678922
E-mail: info@nb.org
Web Site: www.nb.org
Key Personnel
Mng Dir & International Rights Contact: Adonis
    Karatzas *E-mail:* adonik@nb.org
Founded: 1977

Financial & legal services, professional training
    courses & seminars also provided.
Subjects: Economics, Finance, Law, Management,
    Marketing
ISBN Prefix(es): 978-960-272
Number of titles published annually: 100 Print;
    20 CD-ROM; 1 Online
Branch Office(s)
Mavromichali 2, 106 80 Athens *Tel:* 2103607521
    Fax: 2103603975 *E-mail:* m2bookstr@nb.org
Kanari 28-30, 262 22 Patras *Tel:* 2610361600
    Fax: 2610361515 *E-mail:* nbpatra@nb.org
Philo 107-109, 185 36 Piraeus *Tel:* 2104184212;
    2104184286 *Fax:* 2104524851
    E-mail: nbpetkar@otenet.gr
Franks 1, 546 26 Thessaloniki *Tel:* 2310532134;
    2310545618 *Fax:* 2310551530
    E-mail: nbthess@nb.org

Notos
Omirou 15, 106 72 Athens
Tel: 2103629746; 2103636577 *Fax:* 2103636737
E-mail: info@notosbooks.gr
Web Site: www.notosbooks.gr
Founded: 1977
Subjects: Archaeology, Education, Health, Nu-
    trition, Language Arts, Linguistics, Literature,
    Literary Criticism, Essays, Teaching & Learn-
    ing German as a Foreign Language
ISBN Prefix(es): 978-960-8491

Oceanida Publications SA+
38 Dervenion Str, 106 81 Athens
Tel: 2103806137 *Fax:* 2103805531
E-mail: info@oceanida.gr; sales@oceanida.gr
Web Site: oceanida.internet.gr; www.oceanida.gr
Founded: 1986
Subjects: Art, Biography, Memoirs, Cookery, His-
    tory, Literature, Literary Criticism, Essays
ISBN Prefix(es): 978-960-7213; 978-960-410
Number of titles published annually: 30 Print
Total Titles: 250 Print
Branch Office(s)
17 Platonos Str, 546 31 Thessaloniki
    Tel: 2310231800 *Fax:* 2310231036
Distributor for Erevnites
Distribution Center: 25 Solomou Str, 106 82
    Athens *Tel:* 2103827341 *Fax:* 2103304169

Ekdoseis Odysseas+
3 Andrea Moraiti St, 114 71 Athens
Tel: 2103624326; 2103625575 *Fax:* 2103648030
E-mail: info@odisseas.gr
Web Site: www.odisseas.gr
Founded: 1973
Subjects: Biography, Memoirs, Child Care & De-
    velopment, History, Human Relations, Phi-
    losophy, Psychology, Psychiatry, Romance,
    Women's Studies
ISBN Prefix(es): 978-960-210
Bookshop(s): Pesmazoglou 5, 105 64 Athens
    Tel: 2103212111

Omakoio Trikalon & Thessalonikis
21 Kefallinias St, 421 00 Trikala
Tel: 2431075505; 6974580768 (cell)
    Fax: 2431075505
E-mail: omakoio@omakoio.gr; omakoio@aias.gr
Web Site: www.omakoio.gr
Key Personnel
Contact: Ilias L Katsiampas
Founded: 1992
Specialize in the writings of Nikolas A Margioris
    (1913-1993).
Subjects: Archaeology, Astrology, Occult, Philos-
    ophy, Theology, Esoteric-Metaphysical, Mysti-
    cism, Yoga
Total Titles: 145 Print

Opera Ekdoseis, Georges Miressiotis
23a, Koletti, 106 77 Athens

Tel: 2103304546 *Fax:* 2103303634
E-mail: info@operabooks.gr
Web Site: www.operabooks.gr
Key Personnel
Contact & Opera Editions: Georges Miressiotis
Founded: 1989
Literary books & translations.
Private book publishing house specializing in Eu-
    ropean & Latin American authors.
ISBN Prefix(es): 978-960-7073; 978-960-8397
Total Titles: 90 Print

Ekdoseis Ouvas (Ouvas Publications)
Ipeirou 60, 104 39 Athens
Tel: 2108822075; 2108822063 *Fax:* 2108824960
Web Site: www.oyba.gr
Founded: 1979
Subjects: Fiction, History, Language Arts, Lin-
    guistics, Nonfiction (General)
ISBN Prefix(es): 978-960-87184

Pagoulatos Bros+
Panepistimiou 56, 106 78 Athens
Tel: 2103818780; 2103801485 *Fax:* 2103838028
E-mail: pagoulatos_publ@ath.forthnet.gr
Key Personnel
Contact: Anthony Pagoulatos
Founded: 1965
Subjects: Biography, Memoirs, English as a Sec-
    ond Language, Mathematics
ISBN Prefix(es): 978-960-7208

Theofilos Palevratzis SA+
25, 3 Septemvriou Str, Vathis Sq, 104 32 Athens
Tel: 2105230382 *Fax:* 2105233574
Founded: 1980
Subjects: English as a Second Language
ISBN Prefix(es): 978-960-7166; 978-960-8341

Panepistimio Ioanninon (University of
    Ioanninon)
PO Box 1186, 451 10 Ioannina
Tel: 2651007288; 2651007439 *Fax:* 2651007087
E-mail: webmaster@uoi.gr
Web Site: www.uoi.gr
Key Personnel
General Dir, Administration & Academic Affairs:
    Erminia Varotsi
Head, Dept of Publications: Kon Efthymiades
    E-mail: keythymi@cc.uoi.gr
Subjects: Anthropology, Archaeology, Chemistry,
    Chemical Engineering, Education, History,
    Physics, Psychology, Psychiatry, Social Sci-
    ences, Sociology
ISBN Prefix(es): 978-960-233

Dim N Papadimas Ekdoseis+
8 Ippokratous, 106 79 Athens
Tel: 2103627318; 2103642692 *Fax:* 2103610271
E-mail: info@papadimasbooks.gr; sales@
    papadimasbooks.gr; papadimas@atp.gr
Web Site: www.papadimasbooks.gr
Founded: 1960
Subjects: Antiques, Archaeology, Geography, Ge-
    ology, History, Regional Interests, Theology
ISBN Prefix(es): 978-960-206

Papadopoulos Publishing+
Kapodistriou 9, 144 52 Metamorfosi, Athens
Tel: 2102816134 *Fax:* 2102817127
E-mail: info@picturebooks.gr
Web Site: www.picturebooks.gr
Key Personnel
Publisher: John Papadopoulos *E-mail:* publisher@
    picturebooks.gr
Marketing Manager: Natassa Mela
    E-mail: nmela@picturebooks.gr
Production Manager: Stavroula Tzourtzioti
    E-mail: production@picturebooks.gr
Public Relations Manager: Frantzeska Alex-
    opoulou *E-mail:* fran@picturebooks.gr

Sales Manager: George Papadakis *E-mail:* sales@
picturebooks.gr
Editor: Eleni Katsama *E-mail:* editor@
picturebooks.gr
Foreign Rights: Palaki Sofia
Founded: 1953
Subjects: Animals, Pets, Fiction, History, Literature, Literary Criticism, Essays, Nonfiction
(General), Adventure, Classics, Social Situations
ISBN Prefix(es): 978-960-261; 978-960-412
Number of titles published annually: 100 Print
Total Titles: 600 Print
Bookshop(s): Massalias 14 & Solonos St, 106 80
Athens *Tel:* 2103615334

Papazissis Publishers SA
2 Nikitara, 106 78 Athens
Tel: 2103838020; 2103822496 *Fax:* 2103809150;
2103816476
E-mail: papazisi@otenet.gr; sales@papazisi.gr
Web Site: www.papazisi.gr
Key Personnel
Production: Jenny Palmou
Sales: Alexopoulos Panagiotis
E-mail: alexopoulospanagiotis@yahoo.gr
University Textbooks: Rania Karamasi
E-mail: raniakaramasi@papazisi.gr
Founded: 1929
Subjects: Economics, Education, Environmental
Studies, Government, Political Science, History,
Law, Philosophy, Regional Interests, Social Sciences, Sociology
ISBN Prefix(es): 978-960-02
Branch Office(s)
Siatistis 7, 54631 Thessaloniki *Tel:* 2310227416
E-mail: natasapelagidou@papazisi.gr

Ekdoseis Paraskino-Marinis Spyridon & Co
76, Solonos St, 106 80 Athens
Tel: 2103648170; 2103648197 *Fax:* 2103648033
Founded: 1990
Subjects: Government, Political Science, History
ISBN Prefix(es): 978-960-7107; 978-960-8342

Patakis Publishers+
38, Panagi Tsaldari St, 104 37 Athens
Tel: 2103650000; 2105205600 *Fax:* 2103650069
E-mail: info@patakis.gr; sales@patakis.gr;
foreignrights@patakis.gr
Web Site: www.patakis.gr
Key Personnel
Founder & Chairman: Stefanos Patakis
Sales Dir: Peter Lazaridis *Tel:* 2103650082
Fax: 2103650089 *E-mail:* plasarid@patakis.gr
Foreign Rights, Literature: George Pantsios
Tel: 2105205651 *Fax:* 2105205651
Founded: 1974
Also acts as retailer, wholesaler & distributor.
Membership(s): European Educational Publishers
Group (EEPG).
Subjects: Animals, Pets, Anthropology, Archaeology, Art, Biography, Memoirs, Business, Child
Care & Development, Cookery, Crafts, Games,
Hobbies, Disability, Special Needs, Drama,
Theater, Economics, Education, English as a
Second Language, Environmental Studies, Fiction, Geography, Geology, Government, Political Science, Health, Nutrition, History, Humor,
Language Arts, Linguistics, Literature, Literary
Criticism, Essays, Management, Mathematics,
Music, Dance, Mysteries, Suspense, Natural
History, Nonfiction (General), Philosophy, Poetry, Psychology, Psychiatry, Science Fiction,
Fantasy, Self-Help, Social Sciences, Sociology,
Sports, Athletics, Travel & Tourism
ISBN Prefix(es): 978-960-293; 978-960-360; 978-
960-600; 978-960-378; 978-960-16
Number of titles published annually: 500 Print
Total Titles: 3,000 Print
Branch Office(s)
Thessaloniki, Contact: John Tasiopou-

los *Tel:* 2310706354; 2310706715
Fax: 2310706355 *E-mail:* thess@patakis.gr
Distributor for Centre for Greek Language; Editions of New Technologies; Educational Institute of the National Bank of Greece; Nakas
Editions; Photochoros; Playful; Triantafyllidis
Institute
Bookshop(s): 65, Akadimias St, 106 78
Athens *Tel:* 2103811740; 2103811850
Fax: 2103811940 *E-mail:* bookstore@patakis.gr
Warehouse: Tzaverdela Area, 193 00 Aspropyrgos, Contact: Georgia Kandila *Tel:* 2105590953
Fax: 2105590954 *E-mail:* stck@patakis.gr

Pearson Hellas
21 Amfitheas Ave, 175 64 P Faliro, Athens
Tel: 2109373170 *Fax:* 2109373199
E-mail: info.elt@pearson.com
Web Site: www.longman.gr; www.pearsonelt.gr
Founded: 1985
ELT supplementary titles.
Number of titles published annually: 10 Print
Total Titles: 20 Print
Parent Company: Pearson Education
Ultimate Parent Company: Pearson Plc

Pergamini, *imprint of* Spanos

Polaris Ekdoseis (Polaris Publishers)
17 Navarinou St, 106 81 Athens
Tel: 2103836482 *Fax:* 2103807608
E-mail: info@polarisekdoseis.gr
Web Site: www.polarisekdoseis.gr
Founded: 1996
ISBN Prefix(es): 978-960-6829

Pournaras Panagiotis
Panagias Dexias 7, 546 35 Thessaloniki
Tel: 2310270941 *Fax:* 2310228922
E-mail: info@kyriakidiseditions.gr
Web Site: www.pournarasbooks.gr
Founded: 1960
Subjects: Theology
ISBN Prefix(es): 978-960-242

I Prooptiki Ekdoseis+
3 Septemvriou 152, 112 51 Athens
Tel: 2108226254 *Fax:* 2108226254
Key Personnel
Contact: Polychronis Papacristou
Founded: 1991
Specialize in educational books & editions.
Subjects: Education, Language Arts, Linguistics,
Medicine, Nursing, Dentistry, Psychology, Psychiatry
ISBN Prefix(es): 978-960-7331
Total Titles: 8 Print

Psichogios Publications SA+
121 Tatoiou Ave, 144 52 Metamorfossi Attiki
Tel: 2102804800 *Toll Free Tel:* 80011646464
Fax: 2102819550
E-mail: info@psichogios.gr
Web Site: www.psichogios.gr
Key Personnel
Mng Dir: Thanos Psichogios
Marketing Dir: Mrs Klio Zachariadi
E-mail: klio@psichogios.gr
Editorial, Rights & Permissions: Angela Sotiriou
E-mail: angela.sotiriou@psichogios.gr
Public Relations: Mrs Popi Galatoula
E-mail: popi@psichogios.gr
Founded: 1979
Subjects: Fiction, Philosophy, Human Science,
Lifestyle
ISBN Prefix(es): 978-960-7020; 978-960-274;
978-960-7021; 978-960-453
Number of titles published annually: 180 Print

Total Titles: 1,000 Print
Branch Office(s)
32 Vassileos Irakleiou, 546 24 Thessaloniki
Tel: 2310251373 *Fax:* 2310251373

Romiosyni, *imprint of* Denise Harvey (Publisher)

Ekdoseis H Rossi+
8 Lycoudi Str, 111 41 Athens
Tel: 2102020126 *Fax:* 2102020131
E-mail: info@rossi.com.gr
Web Site: www.rossi.com.gr
Key Personnel
Contact: Helen Rossi-Petsiou
Founded: 1895
Subjects: Education, Student's Aid
ISBN Prefix(es): 978-960-225

P N Sakkoulas
49, Panepistimiou & Arsaki Str, 105 64 Athens
Tel: 2103256000 *Fax:* 2103312710
E-mail: mail@sakkoulas.com
Web Site: www.sakkoulas.com
Key Personnel
Mng Dir: Panos N Sakkoulas
Subjects: Economics, Finance, Law
ISBN Prefix(es): 978-960-420

Sakkoulas Publications SA+
23, Ippokratous Str, 106 79 Athens
Tel: 2103387500 *Fax:* 2103390075
E-mail: info@sakkoulas.gr
Web Site: www.sakkoulas.gr; sakkoulas.tessera.gr
Founded: 1958
Subjects: Business, Economics, Labor, Industrial
Relations, Law, Management, Maritime, Public
Administration, Social Sciences, Sociology
ISBN Prefix(es): 978-960-301; 978-960-445
Number of titles published annually: 100 Print
Total Titles: 900 Print
Distributor for Nomos Verlagsgesellschaft; Verlag
Recht und Wirtschaft mbH
Foreign Rep(s): Yushodo Co Ltd (Japan)
Bookshop(s): 42, Ethnikis Amynis Str,
546 21 Thessaloniki *Tel:* 2310244228;
2310244229 *Fax:* 2310244230; One Fragon
Str, 546 26 Thessaloniki *Tel:* 2310535381
Fax: 2310546812

Ekdoseis I Sideris
115 Alexandreias St, Akadimia Platonos, 104 41
Athens
Tel: 2105140627
E-mail: contact@isideris.gr
Web Site: www.isideris.gr
Founded: 1897
Subjects: Language Arts, Linguistics, Literature,
Literary Criticism, Essays, Science (General),
Academics, Political Science
ISBN Prefix(es): 978-960-08
Bookshop(s): 116 Solonos St, 106 81 Athens
Tel: 2103833434 *Fax:* 2103832294
Distribution Center: 116 Solonos St, 106 81
Athens *Tel:* 2103833434 *Fax:* 2103832294

Sideris Publications SA+
28 A Metaxa, Themistokleous, 106 81 Athens
Tel: 2103301161; 2103301162; 2103301163
Fax: 2103301164
E-mail: info@siderisbooks.gr
Web Site: www.siderisbooks.gr
Founded: 1978
Subjects: Business, Cookery, Drama, Theater,
Earth Sciences, Economics, Education, Energy, English as a Second Language, Fiction,
Finance, History, Humor, Management, Marketing, Mathematics, Music, Dance, Nonfiction
(General), Physics, Poetry, Pop Culture, Regional Interests, Religion - Other, Romance,
Science Fiction, Fantasy, Theology, Travel &
Tourism, Wine & Spirits

ISBN Prefix(es): 978-960-7012; 978-960-6604;
978-960-468
Number of titles published annually: 10 Print
Total Titles: 194 Print

Sigma Publications+
30, Lekanidi Str, Ag Dimitrios, 173 43 Athens
Tel: 2103607667 *Fax:* 2103638941
Web Site: www.sigmabooks.gr
Key Personnel
Contact: Dimitris M Stephanides
Founded: 1973
Subjects: Art, Fiction, Folk Tales, Mythology
ISBN Prefix(es): 978-960-425
Total Titles: 95 Print
Distributed by Cosmos Publishing Co Inc (USA)
Foreign Rep(s): Cosmos Publishing Co Inc
(Canada, USA)
Foreign Rights: Shin Won Agency Co (China,
Japan, Korea)
Bookshop(s): One Pandrosou St, Mitropoleos
Sq, Athens *Tel:* 2103245405; Elefther-
oudakis Bookstores, 15 Panepistimiou, Athens
Tel: 2103258440 *E-mail:* internet@books.gr
Web Site: books.gr; Eleftheroudakis Book-
stores, 20, Nikis St, Syntagma, Athens
Tel: 2103231401 *E-mail:* internet@books.
gr *Web Site:* books.gr; Eleftheroudakis
Bookstores, 39, Mitropoleos St, Inside
Starbucks Cafe, Athens *Tel:* 2103226580
E-mail: internet@books.gr *Web Site:* books.gr;
Eleftheroudakis Bookstores, Newstand 43,
Panepistimiou St, Athens *Tel:* 2103317018
E-mail: internet@books.gr *Web Site:* books.
gr; Infognomon Bookstores, 14, Filelinon St,
Sintagma, Athens *Tel:* 2103316036; Kyri-
akidis Bookstores, 62, Mitropoleos St, Athens
Tel: 2103227830; Tsigaridas Bookstore, 10-
12, Ippocratous St, Athens *Tel:* 2103626028;
Tritaios Ioannis, 52, Acadimias St, 4th floor,
Athens *Tel:* 2103636632; Gallerie Orphee, An-
cient Olympia *Tel:* 2624023463; Grivas Book-
store, Ithaca *Tel:* 2674032223
Distribution Center: Hellenic Distribution Agency
Ltd

Silk, *imprint of* Harlenic Hellas Publishing SA

Siokis Medical Publications+
Tetrapoleos 10-12, 115 27 Ambelokipi
Tel: 2107470255; 2107470253 *Fax:* 2107713187
E-mail: siokis@medbooks.gr
Web Site: www.siokis.gr
Key Personnel
Publisher: Dimitrios Siokis
Founded: 1957
Subjects: Medicine, Nursing, Dentistry
ISBN Prefix(es): 978-960-7461
Number of titles published annually: 10 Print

Spanos
7 Mavromichali Str, 106 79 Athens
Tel: 2103614332; 2103623917 *Fax:* 2108953076
E-mail: biblioph@otenet.gr
Web Site: www.spanosrarebooks.gr
Key Personnel
Mng Dir, Editorial: Costas Spanos
Founded: 1929
Subjects: Regional Interests
ISBN Prefix(es): 978-960-262
Imprints: Leon; Pergamini

F & D Stephanides OE, see Sigma Publications

Ekdoseis Stochastis (Stochastis Editions)+
Mavromichali 39, 106 80 Athens
Tel: 2103601956 *Fax:* 2103610445
E-mail: info@stochastis.gr
Web Site: www.stochastis.gr
Key Personnel
Publisher: Daphne Papaspiliopoulos

Communications Officer: Christina Andreou
E-mail: xixina.a@gmail.com
Founded: 1969
Subjects: Ethnicity, History, Literature, Literary
Criticism, Essays, Philosophy, Social Sciences,
Sociology, Travel & Tourism
ISBN Prefix(es): 978-960-303
Number of titles published annually: 10 Print
Total Titles: 300 Print
Imprints: Fotolio & Typicon
Distributor for Epistimoniki Eteria Meletis Feron-
Velestinou-Riga; Evrialos
Book Club(s): Cosmos Book Club; The Friends
of Book Book Club; Mos Book Club

Technical Chamber of Greece (TEE-TCG)
Victory 4, 105 63 Athens
Tel: 2103291615; 2103291258 *Fax:* 2103226035
E-mail: ekdoseis@central.tee.gr; tee@central.tee.
gr
Web Site: portal.tee.gr/portal/page/portal/
PUBLICATIONS
Founded: 1923
Corporate body, under public law, supervised by
the Ministry of Public Works.
Subjects: Science (General), Technology
ISBN Prefix(es): 978-960-7018; 978-960-8369

Thymari Publications+
24 Har Trikoupi Str, 106 79 Athens
Tel: 2103634901; 2103643015 *Fax:* 2103636591
E-mail: thymari@thymari.gr
Web Site: thymari.gr
Key Personnel
Foreign Rights: Lina Kalamida
Founded: 1979
Subjects: Behavioral Sciences, Education, Hu-
man Relations, Psychology, Psychiatry, Social
Sciences, Sociology
ISBN Prefix(es): 978-960-7161; 978-960-349
Warehouse: Sarantaporou 98, 155 61 Ho-
largos *Tel:* 2106512216; 2106540811
Fax: 2106549207

To Rodakio+
35 Apollonos St, 105 56 Athens
Tel: 2103221700; 2103221742; 2103839355
Fax: 2103221700
E-mail: rodakio@otenet.gr
Founded: 1992
Subjects: Art, Drama, Theater, Fiction, Literature,
Literary Criticism, Essays, Poetry
ISBN Prefix(es): 978-960-7360; 978-960-8372
Number of titles published annually: 10 Print
Total Titles: 110 Print
Foreign Rights: Kleoniki Douqe (France)

Topos, *imprint of* Medousa/Selas Ekdotiki

Topos Books
2 Plapouta & Kallidromiou St, 114 73 Athens
Tel: 2108222835; 2103221580 (bookshop)
Fax: 2108222684; 2103211246 (bookshop)
E-mail: info@motibo.com; bookstore@motibo.
com
Web Site: www.toposbooks.gr
Key Personnel
Chief Executive Officer: Vangelis Georgakakis
E-mail: vgeorgakakis@motibo.com
Publications Dir: Aris Margkopoulos
E-mail: amaragkopoulos@motibo.com
Rights & Acquisitons Dir: Vicky Christophoridou
E-mail: vchristophoridou@motibo.com
Editor: Artemis Loi *E-mail:* aloi@motibo.com
Academic Publications: Sevasti Boubalou
E-mail: sboubalou@motibo.com
Focus is mainly on Greek & foreign literary fic-
tion & nonfiction about current affairs issues
as well as academic books with emphasis on
human sciences.

Subjects: Art, Fiction, Literature, Literary Crit-
icism, Essays, Nonfiction (General), Current
Affairs, Human Sciences
ISBN Prefix(es): 978-960-6863; 978-960-6760
Parent Company: Motibo SA

Michalis Toubis SA
Nisise Karela, Koropi, 194 00 Athens
Tel: 2106029974 *Fax:* 2106646856; 2106640205
E-mail: info@toubis.gr
Web Site: www.toubis.gr
Founded: 1965
Development, production & distribution of high
quality tourist publications.
ISBN Prefix(es): 978-960-540; 978-960-7504

Ekdoseis Tropos Zois+
One Solomou Str, 152 32 Chalandri, Athens
Tel: 2106840156; 2106858878
E-mail: info@tropos-zois.gr
Web Site: www.tropos-zois.gr
Key Personnel
Owner: Anastasia vas Anastasopoulou
Tel: 2106841773 *E-mail:* a-anast@otenet.gr
Subjects: Art, Cookery, Foreign Countries,
Health, Nutrition, Inspirational, Spirituality,
Medicine, Nursing, Dentistry, Music, Dance,
Religion - Other, Travel & Tourism, Women's
Studies, Alternative Medicine, Aromatherapy,
Homeopathic Medicine, Natural Eating & Liv-
ing, Orthodox Christianity, Yoga
ISBN Prefix(es): 978-960-7118
Number of titles published annually: 6 Print; 1
CD-ROM
Total Titles: 10 Print; 2 CD-ROM; 50 Audio
Distribution Center: dance-library.com
greekbooks-cds.gr

Ulysses, see Ekdoseis Odysseas

Vivliotechnica Hellas
Metaxa Andrea 2, 106 81 Athens
Tel: 2103831146 *Fax:* 2109564354
Key Personnel
Mng Dir: Dimitrios Vardikos
Founded: 1978
Subjects: Aeronautics, Aviation
ISBN Prefix(es): 978-960-7810
Branch Office(s)
Davaki 34, Kallithea, Athens
Bookshop(s): Inter-Attica, Davaki 34, Kallithea,
Athens

G Vlassi Afoi OE+
Solonos 116 & 2-4 Lontou, 106 81 Athens
Tel: 2103812900 *Fax:* 2103827557
E-mail: info@vlassi.gr
Web Site: www.vlassi.gr
Key Personnel
General Manager: John H Vlassi
Publisher, Marketing Manager & International
Rights Contact: Anna-Marie Vlassis-Galerou
Founded: 1964
Publisher of hardcover & paperback books.
Subjects: Biography, Memoirs, Fiction, Literature,
Literary Criticism, Essays
ISBN Prefix(es): 978-960-302
Total Titles: 600 Print

Nikos Votsis Publications
Emm Benaki 16, 106 78 Athens
Tel: 2103820646; 2103835503 *Fax:* 2103820646
Key Personnel
Executive: Michael Dimitrios-Votsis; Ersi Ange-
liki Votsis
Founded: 1957
Subjects: Art, History, Humor, Language Arts,
Linguistics, Music, Dance
ISBN Prefix(es): 978-960-7444

S I Zacharopoulos Publishing House SA+
Stadiou 5, 105 62 Athens

Tel: 2103231525; 2103225011; 2108142611
   Fax: 2103243814
E-mail: info@sizacharopoulos.gr
Web Site: www.sizacharopoulos.gr
Key Personnel
President, Publicity, Rights & Permissions:
   Stavros Zacharopoulos
Editorial: Stefanos Zacharopoulos
Production: Loucas Zacharopoulos
Sales: George Zacharopoulos
Founded: 1959
Subjects: Drama, Theater, History, Poetry, Science
   (General)
ISBN Prefix(es): 978-960-208
Bookshop(s): Praxitelous 141, 185 35 Piraeus

Greenland

General Information

Capital: Nuuk
Language: Greenlandic (East Inuit), Danish and
   English
Religion: Evangelical Lutheran
Population: 56,344
Currency: 100 ore = 1 krone

Ilinniusiorfik Undervisningsmiddelforlag+
H J Rinksvej 35, 1 sal, Postboks 1610, 3900
   Nuuk
Tel: 34 98 89 *Fax:* 32 62 36
E-mail: ilinniusiorfik@ilinniusiorfik.gl;
   inerisaavik@inerisaavik.gl (Greenland orders)
Web Site: www.ilinniusiorfik.gl
Key Personnel
Publishing Dir: Carla Rosing Olsen *Tel:* 34 61 50
   E-mail: crol@nanoq.gl
Editor: Angunnguaq Karlsen *Tel:* 38 58 13
   E-mail: ank@inerisaavik.gl; Mette Rasmussen
   Larsen *Tel:* 38 58 12 *E-mail:* mrl@inerisaavik.
   gl; Laila Vivian Petersen *Tel:* 38 58 14
   E-mail: lvp@inerisaavik.gl
Founded: 1956
Also acts as educational book publisher, public
   relations.
Subjects: Art, Education, Fiction, Nonfiction
   (General)
ISBN Prefix(es): 978-87-558; 978-87-7975
Number of titles published annually: 35 Print

Guadeloupe

General Information

Capital: Basse-Terre
Language: French, Creole patois
Religion: Roman Catholic
Population: 400,000
Bank Hours: 0800-1200, 1400-1600 Monday-
   Friday
Shop Hours: 0900-1300, 1500-1800 Monday-
   Friday
Currency: 100 Eurocents = 1 Euro

Editions Jasor
46 rue Schoelcher, 97110 Pointe-a-Pitre
Tel: 0590911848
E-mail: editionsjasor@wanadoo.fr
Web Site: www.editionsjasor.com
Founded: 1989
Subjects: Architecture & Interior Design, Biogra-
   phy, Memoirs, Government, Political Science,
   History, Language Arts, Linguistics, Literature,

Literary Criticism, Essays, Music, Dance, Photography, Heritage, Painting
ISBN Prefix(es): 978-2-912594

Guatemala

General Information

Capital: Guatemala City
Language: Spanish
Religion: Roman Catholic
Population: 10 million
Bank Hours: 0900-1500 Monday-Friday
Shop Hours: 0900-1300, 1500-1900 Monday-
   Friday; 0900-1300 Saturday
Currency: 100 centavos = 1 quetzal
Export/Import Information: Member of the Cen-
   tral American Common Market. Duty on cat-
   alogues is Q 0.03 per gross kilo. No import
   licenses, no exchange control.
Copyright: UCC, Buenos Aires, Florence (see
   Copyright Conventions, pg viii)

Grupo Amanuense
3ra Ave Tronco 2, section A, Lote 5, Colonia san
   Antonio, El Encinal, Zona 7 de Mixco
Tel: 24347831; 24318243
E-mail: info@grupo-amanuense.com
Web Site: www.grupo-amanuense.com
Subjects: Anthropology, Education, Poetry, Folk-
   lore
ISBN Prefix(es): 978-99922-959

Editorial Cultura
6ta Calle y 6ta Ave Palacio Nacional de la Cul-
   tura, Tercel nivel of 5 del patio de la Cultura,
   01001 Guatemala
Tel: 22395000 (ext 3592)
E-mail: editorialcultura@mcd.gob.gt
Web Site: www.mcd.gob.gt/arte/editorial-cultura
Key Personnel
Editorial Dir: Francisco Morales Santos
   E-mail: fmoralessantos@gmail.com
Subjects: Anthropology, Art, History, Literature,
   Literary Criticism, Essays, Philosophy, Poetry,
   Regional Interests, Social Sciences, Sociology,
   Sports, Athletics
ISBN Prefix(es): 978-99922-0

F&G Editores
31 Ave "C" 5-54, Zona 7, Col Centroamerica,
   01007 Guatemala
Tel: 2439 8358; 5406 0909 *Fax:* 2439 8358
E-mail: informacion@fygeditores.com
Web Site: www.fygeditores.com
Key Personnel
Publisher & Chief Editor: Raul Figueroa Sarti
Subjects: Biography, Memoirs, Fiction, Geog-
   raphy, Geology, History, Literature, Literary
   Criticism, Essays, Social Sciences, Sociology
ISBN Prefix(es): 978-84-89876; 978-84-921356;
   978-99922-61; 978-9929-552

Editorial Palo de Hormigo SRL+
0 Calle 16-40 B, Zona 15, colonia El Maestro,
   Guatemala
Tel: 23693089 *Fax:* 23698858
E-mail: palodehormigo@hotmail.com
Founded: 1990
Promotes Guatemalan culture through the support
   of its writers.
Membership(s): Camara de Industria de
   Guatemala; Gremial de Editores de Guatemala.
Subjects: Archaeology, Fiction, History, Litera-
   ture, Literary Criticism, Essays, Military Sci-
   ence, Philosophy, Poetry, Science Fiction, Fan-
   tasy, Social Sciences, Sociology

ISBN Prefix(es): 978-99922-710; 978-99922-720;
   978-99939-62
Number of titles published annually: 10 Print
Total Titles: 150 Print

Piedra Santa Editorial & Librerias
37 Ave, 1-26, Zona 7, 01007 Guatemala City
SAN: 002-6204
Tel: 2422-7676
E-mail: info@piedrasanta.com
Web Site: www.piedrasanta.com; www.facebook.
   com/editorialpiedrasanta/
Key Personnel
Dir: Irene Piedra Santa
Founded: 1947
Subjects: Art, Biography, Memoirs, Communi-
   cations, Inspirational, Spirituality, Language
   Arts, Linguistics, Literature, Literary Criticism,
   Essays, Philosophy, Social Sciences, Sociology
ISBN Prefix(es): 978-84-8377; 978-99922-1; 978-
   99922-58
Branch Office(s)
11° Calle 6-50, Zona 1, Guatemala City
   Tel: 2204-6600 *E-mail:* 11calle@piedrasanta.
   com
5a calle 7-55 zona 1, Guatemala City *Tel:* 2204-
   6601 *E-mail:* 5acalle@piedrasanta.com
12 calle, 1-25 zona 10, Edificio Geminis, piso 2,
   locales 202 y 203, Guatemala City *Tel:* 2204-
   6602 *E-mail:* geminis@piedrasanta.com
Km 5 Carretera al Atlantico zona 17, CC
   Metronorte, local 251, Guatemala City
   Tel: 2204-6603 *E-mail:* metronorte@
   piedrasanta.com
Bookshop(s): Axis SA de CV, Condominio Residencial Normandia, 1era Calle Poniente 47
   ave N, Local 6C, San Salvador, El Salvador
   Tel: 2260-4809

Guyana

General Information

Capital: Georgetown
Language: English & Amerindian dialects
Religion: Christian, Hindu, Islamic
Population: 739,000
Shop Hours: 0800-1130, 1300-1600 Monday-
   Friday; 0800-1130 Saturday
Currency: 100 cents = 1 Guyana dollar
Export/Import Information: No tariff on books.
   Only advertising of commercial value, subject
   to duty. There are numerous businesses that im-
   port books. Import license required. Nominal
   exchange controls.
Copyright: Berne (see Copyright Conventions, pg
   viii)

Caribbean Community (CARICOM)
Secretariat
Turkeyen, PO Box 10827, Greater Georgetown
Tel: (02) 22-0001-75 *Fax:* (02) 22-0171
E-mail: registry@caricom.org
Web Site: www.caricom.org
Key Personnel
Chairman: Dean Oliver Barrow
Secretary General: Irwin LaRocque
Deputy Programme Manager: Maureen Newton
   E-mail: doccentre@caricom.org
Founded: 1973
Regional integration movement whose ultimate
   goal is the improvement of the standard of liv-
   ing of all peoples in the community. At present
   the community has 14 member states. The sec-
   retariat is the administrative arm of the com-
   munity.
Subjects: Accounting, Economics, English as a
   Second Language, Language Arts, Linguistics,

Mathematics, Regional Interests, Social Sciences, Sociology
ISBN Prefix(es): 978-976-600
Total Titles: 24 Print; 1 CD-ROM

CARICOM, see Caribbean Community
(CARICOM) Secretariat

New Guyana Co Ltd
8 Industrial Estate, Ruimveldt, Georgetown
Tel: 226-2471
Printers of Mirror Newspaper.
Subjects: Regional Interests
ISBN Prefix(es): 978-976-8000

Roraima Publishers
77 Robb St, Lacytown, Georgetown
Mailing Address: PO Box 10322, Georgetown
Tel: 227-3551; 227-3553
Founded: 1994
Subjects: Fiction, Nonfiction (General), Guyanese Works
ISBN Prefix(es): 978-976-8147
Associate Companies: Roraima Distributors

Walter Roth Museum of Anthropology+
61 Main St, Georgetown
Tel: 225-8486
E-mail: walterrothmuseum1974@gmail.com
Web Site: www.mcys.gov.gy/walter_roth_museum.
html
Key Personnel
Contact: Jennifer Wishart
E-mail: jenniferwishart@yahoo.com
Founded: 1996
Subjects: Anthropology, Archaeology
ISBN Prefix(es): 978-976-8152

Holy See (Vatican City)

General Information

Language: Italian, Latin, French
Religion: Roman Catholic
Population: 802
Currency: 100 Eurocents = 1 Euro
Copyright: UCC, Berne (see Copyright Conventions, pg viii)

Archivio Segreto Vaticano (Vatican Secret Archives)
Cortile del Belvedere, 00120 Citta del Vaticano
Tel: (06) 698-83314; (06) 698-83211 *Fax:* (06) 698-83150; (06) 698-85574
E-mail: economato@asv.va; asv@asv.va
Web Site: www.archiviosegretovaticano.va
Key Personnel
Secretary General: Luca Carboni
Archivist: Jean-Louis Brugues
Subjects: Religion - Catholic
ISBN Prefix(es): 978-88-85042

Biblioteca Apostolica Vaticana (Vatican Apostolic Library)
Cortile del Belvedere, 00120 Vatican City
Tel: (06) 698 79512; (06) 698 79450 *Fax:* (06) 698 84795
Web Site: www.vaticanlibrary.va
Subjects: Art, History, Language Arts, Linguistics, Law, Philosophy, Theology
ISBN Prefix(es): 978-88-210
Number of titles published annually: 12 Print
Total Titles: 800 Print

LEV, *imprint of* Libreria Editrice Vaticana

Pontificia Academia Scientiarum (The Pontifical Academy of Sciences)
Casina Pio IV, 00120 Citta del Vaticano
Tel: (06) 69883451 *Fax:* (06) 69885218
E-mail: pas@pas.va
Web Site: www.casinapioiv.va
Key Personnel
President: Prof Werner Arber
Chancellor: Marcelo Sanchez Sorondo
Founded: 1847
To promote the progress of the mathematical, physical & natural sciences & the study of epistemological problems relating thereto.
Subjects: Biological Sciences, Chemistry, Chemical Engineering, Earth Sciences, Environmental Studies, Mathematics, Medicine, Nursing, Dentistry, Physics, Science (General)
ISBN Prefix(es): 978-88-7761
Number of titles published annually: 3 Print
Total Titles: 110 Print

Scuola Vaticana di Paleografia, Diplomatica e Archivistica
Cortile del Belvedere, 00120 Citta del Vaticano
Tel: (06) 69883595 *Fax:* (06) 69881377
E-mail: scuolavaticana@asv.va
Web Site: www.scuolavaticanapaleografia.va
Key Personnel
Dir: Rev Sergio B Pagano
Founded: 1884
Subjects: Human Relations, Language Arts, Linguistics, Library & Information Sciences
ISBN Prefix(es): 978-88-85054

Libreria Editrice Vaticana+
Via della Posta s/n, 00120 Citta del Vaticano
Tel: (06) 698 83849 *Fax:* (06) 698 84716
Web Site: www.libreriaeditricevaticana.va
Key Personnel
Dir: Don Guiseppe Costa *Tel:* (06) 698 84039
Founded: 1926
The publishing activity of the acts & documents of the Pope & the Holy See, also publications relating to doctrine, liturgy & Catholic culture.
Subjects: Art, History, Literature, Literary Criticism, Essays, Philosophy, Religion - Catholic, Theology
ISBN Prefix(es): 978-88-2090
Imprints: LEV
Bookshop(s): Libreria Internazionale Giovanni Paolo II, Piazza San Pietro, Citta del Vaticano *Tel:* (06) 698 83345 *Fax:* (06) 698 85326; Libreria Internazionale Paolo VI, Via di Propaganda 4, Rome, Italy *Tel:* (06) 698 80141 *Fax:* (06) 698 80141

Musei Vaticani (Vatican Museums)
Viale Vaticano, 00165 Rome
Tel: (06) 69881398 *Fax:* (06) 69882163
E-mail: infoshop.musei@scv.va
Web Site: mv.vatican.va
Key Personnel
Dir: Antonio Paolucci
Subjects: Art, History, Religion - Catholic
ISBN Prefix(es): 978-88-8117; 978-88-8271; 978-88-86921

Honduras

General Information

Capital: Tegucigalpa
Language: Spanish (English on northern coast)
Religion: Predominantly Roman Catholic
Population: 5.0 million

Bank Hours: 0900-1200, 1400-1630 Monday-Friday
Shop Hours: Tegucigalpa: 0800-1800, 1330-1800 Monday-Friday; 0800-1200 Saturday; San Pedro Sula: 0700-1200, 1400-1900 Monday-Friday; 0800-1200 Saturday
Currency: 100 centavos = 1 lempira
Export/Import Information: Member of the Central American Common Market but has applied tariffs to imports from other CACM countries since December 1970. No tariff on books. Duty on catalogues is per kilo. No import licenses. No exchange controls.
Copyright: Berne, Buenos Aires (see Copyright Conventions, pg viii)

Editorial Guaymuras+
Barrio La Leona Ave, Zaragoza, Apdo 1843, FM1100 Tegucigalpa
Tel: 2237-5433; 2237-4931; 2238-3401
E-mail: info@guaymuras.hn
Web Site: www.guaymuras.hn
Key Personnel
Dir: Isolda Arita Melzer
Founded: 1980
Also acts as printer, bookseller & distributor.
Membership(s): Camara Hondurena del Libro; Grupo Libros de Centroamerica.
Subjects: Anthropology, Art, Biography, Memoirs, Drama, Theater, Education, Environmental Studies, Ethnicity, Government, Political Science, Health, Nutrition, History, Language Arts, Linguistics, Poetry, Social Sciences, Sociology, Folklore
ISBN Prefix(es): 978-99926-15
Number of titles published annually: 54 Print
Total Titles: 320 Print
Distributed by Abya-Yala de Ecuador; Arco Iris de El Salvador; Libros sin Fronteras (USA); Piedra Santa de Guatemala
Distributor for Centro Editorial; ENLACE y Nuevos Libros de Nicaragua; Roxsil; UCA de El Salvador; Libreria de la UNAH
Bookshop(s): Libreria Guaymuras, Ave Cervantes No 1055, FM1100 Tegucigalpa *Tel:* 2263-0579; 2222-4140

Hong Kong

General Information

Language: English and Chinese (Cantonese Chinese community)
Religion: Predominantly Buddhist, also some Confucianism, Islamic, Hinduism & Daoism
Population: 5.8 million
Bank Hours: 0900-1640 Monday-Friday; 0900-1200 Saturday
Shop Hours: 1000-2000 Monday-Saturday
Currency: 100 cents = 1 Hong Kong dollar
Export/Import Information: No tariffs on books and advertising. No import licenses required. No exchange controls.
Copyright: Berne, UCC (see Copyright Conventions, pg viii)

American Chamber of Commerce in Hong Kong
1904 Bank of America Tower, 12 Harcourt Rd, Hong Kong
Tel: 2530 6900 *Fax:* 2810 1289
E-mail: amcham@amcham.org.hk
Web Site: www.amcham.org.hk
Key Personnel
Editor-in-Chief: Daniel Kwan *Tel:* 2530 6943
Advertising Sales Manager: Regina Leung
Tel: 2530 6942
Assistant Editor & Listing Sales: Kenny Lau
Tel: 2530 6940

Subjects: Business
ISBN Prefix(es): 978-962-7422

Asia Private Equity Review, see Centre for Asia
Private Equity Research Ltd

B & I Publication Co Ltd+
Bold Win Industrial Bldg, Flat C 1, 15/F, 16-18
Wah Sing St, Kwai Chung, New Territories
Tel: 2785 6622 *Fax:* 2866 7732
Key Personnel
Manager: Mr Cyrus Tang
Founded: 1974
Subjects: Mechanical Engineering, Technology
ISBN Prefix(es): 978-962-7701
Associate Companies: Business & Industrial
Trade Fairs Ltd

Blacksmith Books+
Unit 26, 19/F, Block B, Wah Lok Industrial Centre, 37-41 Shan Mei St, Fo Tan, New Territories
Tel: 2877 7899
E-mail: mail@blacksmithbooks.com
(submissions)
Web Site: www.blacksmithbooks.com; www.
facebook.com/BlacksmithBooks
Key Personnel
Publisher: Pete Spurrier
Founded: 2003
Publisher of English-language China-related
books.
Subjects: Biography, Memoirs, Business, Cookery, Fiction, History, Literature, Literary Criticism, Essays, Nonfiction (General), Photography, Travel & Tourism, Culture, Current Affairs, True Crime
ISBN Prefix(es): 978-962-86732; 978-988-17742;
978-988-19003; 978-988-16139; 978-988-13765; 978-988-99799; 978-988-77927; 978-988-77928; 978-988-16138; 978-988-13764;
978-988-19002
Number of titles published annually: 11 Print
Total Titles: 80 Print
Foreign Rep(s): Alpa Books Pty Ltd (Australia,
New Zealand); Far East Media Ltd (Hong
Kong); Gazelle Book Services (Europe, Ireland,
Middle East, UK); National Book Network
(NBN) (Canada, USA); Select Books (Singapore)

Book One, *imprint of* SCMP Book Publishing
Ltd

Book Vision, *imprint of* SCMP Book Publishing
Ltd

Breakthrough Ltd - Breakthrough Publishers+
Breakthrough Youth Village, 33 A Kung Kok
Shan Rd, Sha Tin, New Territories
Tel: 2632 0000; 2632 0257 *Fax:* 2632 0388
E-mail: breakthrough@breakthrough.org.hk;
marketing@breakthrough.org.hk; pub@
breakthrough.org.hk
Web Site: www.breakthrough.org.hk; www.
btproduct.com
Key Personnel
General Secretary: Dr Leung Wing Tai
Founded: 1973
Membership(s): Hong Kong Article Numbering
Association; Hong Kong Book & Magazine
Trade Association Ltd.
Subjects: Fiction, How-to, Human Relations, Humor, Inspirational, Spirituality, Literature, Literary Criticism, Essays, Poetry
ISBN Prefix(es): 978-962-264; 978-962-8791;
978-962-8913; 978-962-8996; 978-988-8073
Warehouse: Flats A, S-V, 14/F, Haribest Industrial
Bldg, Shatin Town Lot 173, Fo Tan, Sha Tin

Centre for Asia Private Equity Research Ltd
27/F, Fook Lee Commercial Centre, 33 Lockhart
Rd, Wan Chai
Tel: 2861 0102 *Fax:* 2529 6816
E-mail: info@asiape.com
Web Site: www.asiape.com
Key Personnel
Mng Dir: Kathleen Ng
Founded: 1991
Focus on the Asian private equity investment industry. Produces publications, customized research reports, educational programs & events.
Subjects: Finance, Asian Private Equity, Venture
Capital
ISBN Prefix(es): 978-962-85096
Subsidiaries: Institute of Asian Private Equity Investment

Chinese Christian Literature Council Ltd+
14/F, 140-142 Austin Rd, Kowloon
Tel: 2367 8031 *Fax:* 2739 6030
E-mail: info@cclc.org.hk
Web Site: www.cclc.org.hk
Key Personnel
Publisher: Rev Yung Chuen-Hung
Administration Secretary: Amy Tang
Founded: 1951
An interdenominational publishing house-mainly
in the Chinese language. Also a nonprofit organization.
Subjects: Literature, Literary Criticism, Essays,
Music, Dance, Religion - Protestant, Theology
ISBN Prefix(es): 978-962-294
Number of titles published annually: 24 Print
Total Titles: 1,000 Print
Bookshop(s): G/F, 10 Tung Fong St,
Kowloon *Tel:* 2385 5880 *Fax:* 2782 5845
E-mail: bookroom@cclc.org.hk
Warehouse: 702 Yan Hing Centre, 9-13, Wong
Chuk Yeung St, Shatin, New Territories
Tel: 2697 0304; 2697 0286 *Fax:* 2697 7760
E-mail: warehouse@cclc.org.hk

The Chinese University Press+
The Chinese University of Hong Kong, Shatin,
New Territories
Tel: 3943 9800 (general office) *Fax:* 2603 7355
E-mail: cup@cuhk.edu.hk
Web Site: www.chineseupress.com
Key Personnel
Dir: Qi Gan *Tel:* 3943 9818 *E-mail:* ganqi@cuhk.
edu.hk
Mng Editor: Dr Ying Lin, PhD *Tel:* 3943 9811
E-mail: linying@cuhk.edu.hk
Acquisition Editor: Dr Minlei Ye, PhD *Tel:* 3943
9812 *E-mail:* minleiye@eservices.cuhk.edu.hk
Business Manager: Angelina Wong *Tel:* 3943
9822 *E-mail:* laifunwong@cuhk.edu.hk
Production Manager: Kingsley Ma *Tel:* 3943
9808 *E-mail:* kwaihungma@cuhk.edu.hk
Founded: 1977
Membership(s): Association for Asian Studies;
Association of University Presses (AUPresses);
International Association of Scholarly Publishers; Society of Scholarly Publishing.
Subjects: Anthropology, Archaeology, Art, Asian
Studies, Biography, Memoirs, Business, Child
Care & Development, Education, Finance, Geography, Geology, Government, Political Science, History, Journalism, Language Arts, Linguistics, Law, Literature, Literary Criticism,
Essays, Management, Philosophy, Psychology,
Psychiatry, Science (General), Social Sciences,
Sociology
ISBN Prefix(es): 978-962-201; 978-962-996
Number of titles published annually: 70 Print; 30
E-Book
Total Titles: 1,000 Print; 210 E-Book
Parent Company: The Chinese University of Hong
Kong
Distributed by Columbia University Press (Australia & North America); Eurospan Group

(Continental Europe & UK); San Min Book
Co Ltd (Taiwan)
Distributor for The Chinese University of Hong
Kong
Foreign Rep(s): Columbia University Press
(Australia, North America); Eurospan Group
(Africa, Central Asia, Europe, Middle East);
San Min Book Co Ltd (Taiwan)

Chopsticks Cooking Centre+
8A Soares Ave, Ground floor, Kowloon
Tel: 2336 8433 *Fax:* 2338 1462
E-mail: chopsticks1971@netvigator.com
Key Personnel
Mng Dir: Cecilia J Au-Yeung *E-mail:* cauyeung@
netvigator.com
Founded: 1971
Specialize in Oriental cuisine.
Membership(s): International Association of Culinary Professionals (IACP).
Subjects: Cookery, Dim Sum, Health Cookery,
Oriental Cuisine
ISBN Prefix(es): 978-962-7018
Associate Companies: Cherrytree Press Ltd
Distribution Center: Gazelle Book Services
Ltd, White Cross Mills, Hightown, Lancaster,
Lancs LA1 4XS, United Kingdom *Tel:* (01524)
528500 *Fax:* (01524) 528510 *E-mail:* sales@
gazellebookservices.co.uk *Web Site:* www.
gazellebookservices.co.uk

Christian Communications Ltd
19/F, King Palace Plaza, 52A Sha Tsui Rd, Tsuen
Wan, New Territories
Tel: 2725 8558 *Fax:* 2386 1804
E-mail: hkccl@ccl.org.hk
Web Site: www.ccl.org.hk
Key Personnel
General Secretary: Thomas Tang
Founded: 1971
Also acts as bookseller & printing service.
Subjects: Biblical Studies, Electronics, Electrical
Engineering, Religion - Protestant
ISBN Prefix(es): 978-962-202; 978-962-8740;
978-962-8810; 978-962-8891
U.S. Office(s): Christian Communications Inc,
9600 Bellaire Blvd, Suite 111, Houston, TX
77036-4534, United States, Executive Dir: Lillian Chen *Tel:* 713-778-1144; 713-778-1155
Fax: 713-778-1180 *E-mail:* cciusalm@cc-us.
org *Web Site:* www.cc-us.org

Chung Hwa Book Co (HK) Ltd+
Eastern Centre, Room 1306, 1065 King's Rd,
Quarry Bay
Tel: 2525 0120 *Fax:* 2713 8202
E-mail: info@chunghwabook.com.hk
Web Site: www.chunghwabook.com.hk
Key Personnel
Dir & General Manager: Tung-Hiu Chiu
Founded: 1927
Membership(s): Hong Kong Publishing Federation Ltd; Hong Kong Publishing Professionals
Society Ltd.
Subjects: Antiques, Art, Asian Studies, Business,
Career Development, Computer Science, English as a Second Language, History, Language
Arts, Linguistics, Literature, Literary Criticism,
Essays, Management, Marketing, Philosophy,
Religion - Buddhist, Self-Help, Social Sciences, Sociology, Chinese History & Culture
ISBN Prefix(es): 978-962-231; 978-962-8820;
978-962-8885
Parent Company: Sino United Publishing (Holdings) Ltd
Distributor for Longman Asia Ltd; Open Learning Univeristy of Hong Kong (Macau & Hong
Kong); Oxford University Press (Hong Kong);
Publications (Holding) Ltd; University of H K
Press
Bookshop(s): Metro City Plaza II, No 2066,
Tseung Kwan O, Kowloon *Tel:* 2394

0397 *Fax:* 2391 3377 *E-mail:* chtko@
chunghwabook.com.hk; 450 Nathan Rd, Yau
Ma Tei, Kowloon *Tel:* 2385 6588 *Fax:* 2782
3525 *E-mail:* chym@chunghwabook.com.hk; Pa
St, Tsuen Wan Plaza, No 435-438, Tsuen Wan,
New Territories *Tel:* 2492 2224 *Fax:* 2405
1783 *E-mail:* chtw@chunghwabook.com.hk

The Commercial Press (HK) Ltd+
Subsidiary of Sino United Publishing (Holdings)
Ltd
8/F, Eastern Central Plaza, 3 Yiu Hing Rd, Shau
Kei Wan
Tel: 2565 1371 *Fax:* 2565 1113
E-mail: corpcomm@commercialpress.com.hk;
editorial@commercialpress.com.hk
Web Site: www.commercialpress.com.hk; www.
cp1897.com.hk (orders)
Key Personnel
Mng Dir & Editor-in-Chief: Man Hung Chan
Founded: 1897
Also distributor & retailer.
Subjects: Art, Education, Ethnicity, How-to, Lan-
guage Arts, Linguistics, Medicine, Nursing,
Dentistry
ISBN Prefix(es): 978-962-07
Subsidiaries: Hong Kong Educational Publishing
Co
Branch Office(s)
Commercial Press Ltd, Singapore, Singapore
Bookshop(s): Aberdeen Branch, Shop H 1/F, Ab-
erdeen Centre (Site 5), 6-12 Nam Ning St, Ab-
erdeen *Tel:* 2552 3621 *Fax:* 2552 3639; Cause-
way Bay Book Centre, 9 Yee Wo St, Causeway
Bay *Tel:* 2890 8028 *Fax:* 2895 1027; Causeway
Bay Branch Annex, Basement, 68 Yee Wo St,
Causeway Bay *Tel:* 2972 2038 *Fax:* 2972 0035;
University Bookstore, Hong Kong University of
Science & Technology, G015, Entrance Piazza,
Hong Kong University of Science & Technol-
ogy, Clear Water Bay, Kowloon *Tel:* 2358 6400
Fax: 2332 6413; University Bookstore, City
University of Hong Kong, 3/F, Academic 1,
City University of Hong Kong, Tat Chee Ave,
Kowloon *Tel:* 3442 2290 *Fax:* 2776 4897; West
Rail Mei Foo Station 106, Kowloon *Tel:* 2741
1030 *Fax:* 2741 1023; Telford Book Plaza,
Shop 301A, Level 3, Telford Plaza II, 33 Wai
Yip St, Kowloon Bay, Kowloon *Tel:* 2305
0877 *Fax:* 2305 0322; Mongkok Branch, 608
Nathan Rd, Mongkok, Kowloon *Tel:* 2384
8228 *Fax:* 2770 3861; North Point Branch,
395 King's Rd, North Point *Tel:* 2562 0266
Fax: 2565 6763; Kornhill Branch, Shop S39,
2/F, Kornhill Plaza, One Kornhill Rd, Quarry
Bay *Tel:* 2560 0238 *Fax:* 2567 9801; The Chi-
nese University of Hong Kong, Hong Kong
Chinese University of Health of the Interna-
tional Academic Park, Room 101, Shatin, New
Territories *Tel:* 2603 6308 *Fax:* 2603 6399;
Sha Tin Book Plaza, Sha Tin New Town Plaza
III, 1st floor, Shop A197, Shatin, New Territo-
ries *Tel:* 2693 1933 *Fax:* 2691 2064; Sheung
Shui Branch, 22 Lung Sum Rd, Sheung Shui,
New Territories *Tel:* 2672 0774 *Fax:* 2639
9907; Tai Po Branch, Shop 308-312, Level
3, Oi Wo Hse, Tai Wo Plaza, Tai Po, New
Territories *Tel:* 2650 2628 *Fax:* 2651 5177;
MTR Station, 4-5 (B export), Tai Wai, New
Territories *Tel:* 2602 1008 *Fax:* 2602 1102;
Tin Shui Wai Branch, Shop 220, Chung Fu
Plaza, Phase Two, Tin Shui Wai, New Terri-
tories *Tel:* 2616 0366 *Fax:* 2616 9166; Tse-
ung Kwan O Branch, G02-04, G/F, PopCorn, 9
Tong Yin St, Tseung Kwan O *Tel:* 2628 6966
Fax: 2628 7798; Tsimshatsui Book Centre,
Shops B1007-1010, B1/F, Miramar Shop-
ping Centre, 132 Nathan Rd, Tsimshatsui,
Kowloon *Tel:* 2904 1988 *Fax:* 2562 5978;
Tuen Mun Branch, Shop 21-22, Level 2, South
Wing, Trend Plaza, Tuen Mun, New Territories
Tel: 2458 9332 *Fax:* 2459 1925; Mei Tung St,
Tung Chung, Crescent 11-12, G (MTR Tung

Chung Station Exit B), Tung Chung, Lan-
tau Island, New Territories *Tel:* 3147 4012
Fax: 3147 4016; Olympian City Branch, Shop
115, 1/F, Olympian City, 1,11 Hoi Fai Rd,
West Kowloon *Tel:* 2625 0311 *Fax:* 2625 0667;
Jordan Book Plaza, G/F, New Lucky House,
13 Jordan Rd, Yaumatei, Kowloon *Tel:* 2770
8881 *Fax:* 2782 1031; Macau Branch Library,
Luo Constitution New St, No 280, Rua do
Campo, 2-2B, Macau, Macau *Tel:* 28353391
Fax: 28353359

Design Media Publishing Co Ltd
Subsidiary of Liaoning Science & Technology
Publishing House
18th floor, Manulife Tower, 169 Electric Rd,
North Point
Tel: 6950 0355 *Fax:* 2505 0311
E-mail: dsdesignmedia@gmail.com
Founded: 2010
Subjects: Architecture & Interior Design, Graphic
Design, Landscape
ISBN Prefix(es): 978-988-19508; 978-988-19740;
978-988-15069; 978-988-15070; 978-988-
15071; 978-988-19738; 978-988-15452
Branch Office(s)
YY International Co Ltd, Room 2210, Guidu
Bldg, 52-56, Chunfeng Rd, Shenzhen 518002,
China

Educational Publishing House Ltd
14/F, Tsuen Wan Industrial Centre, 220-248 Tex-
aco Rd, Tsuen Wan, New Territories
Tel: 2942 9338 *Fax:* 2408 0174
Web Site: www.ephhk.com
Key Personnel
Senior Sales Manager: May Kwok
Founded: 1960
Educational products & services - retail & distri-
bution, publishing & e-learning.
Subjects: Education, English as a Second Lan-
guage, Mathematics, Medicine, Nursing, Den-
tistry, Music, Dance, Religion - Other, Chinese
Learning, General Studies, English Learning
ISBN Prefix(es): 978-962-12
Parent Company: Popular Holdings Ltd
Associate Companies: Fook Hing Offset Print-
ing Co Ltd; Harris Book Co Ltd; Hong Kong
Housing Projects Corp Ltd; Kam Pui Enter-
prises Ltd; Pan-Lloyds (HK) Ltd; The Seashore
Publishing Co; The World Publishing Co
Branch Office(s)
Alameda Dr Carlos D'Assumpcao, nºs 411 e 417,
Edificio Dynasty Plaza 4º, Andar I, Macau,
Macau *Tel:* 2872 5523 *Fax:* 2872 5521

Electronic Technology Publishing Co Ltd+
Room 1, 9/F, 15-17 Shing Yip St, Kwun Tong,
Kowloon
Mailing Address: PO Box 73205, Kowloon Cen-
tral Post Office, Kowloon
Tel: 2342 8298 (customer service); 2342 8299
(advertising); 2342 9845 *Fax:* 2341 4247
E-mail: info@electronictechnology.com
Web Site: www.electronictechnology.com
Key Personnel
Manager: Ming-Kee Luk
Founded: 1969
Subjects: Electronics, Electrical Engineering,
Marketing, Technology
ISBN Prefix(es): 978-962-7007
Subsidiaries: Modern Electronic & Computing
Publishing Co Ltd

Enrich Professional Publishing Ltd
Member of Enrich Culture Group Ltd
11/F, Benson Tower, 74 Hung To Rd, Kwun
Tong, Kowloon
Tel: 2793 5678 *Fax:* 2793 5030
E-mail: epp.info@enrichculture.com
Web Site: www.enrichprofessional.com

Key Personnel
Chief Executive Officer & Founder: Derek Lee
E-mail: derek@enrichculture.com
Mng Dir: Stephen Wong *E-mail:* stephen@
enrichculture.com
Senior Manager, Marketing & Sales: Chris Che-
ung *E-mail:* chris.cheung@enrichculture.com
Subjects: Business, Economics, Finance, Gov-
ernment, Political Science, Law, Banking, Re-
gional Studies, Tax
ISBN Prefix(es): 978-981-4298
Imprints: Silkroad Press
Branch Office(s)
Enrich Professional Publishing (S) Pvt Ltd, 16L,
Enterprise Rd, Singapore 627660, Singapore
Tel: 9363 7838 *Fax:* 6472 5977 *E-mail:* pc.
tham@enrichculture.com
U.S. Office(s): Enrich Professional Publishing
Inc, 20221 E Euclid Lane, Aurora, CO 80016,
United States, Business Development Man-
ager: Maureen Shelburn *Tel:* 703-517-2156
E-mail: maureen.shelburn@enrichculture.com

FormAsia Books Ltd+
706 Yu Yuet Lai Bldg, 45 Wyndham St, Central
Hong Kong
Tel: 2525 8572 *Fax:* 2522 4234
E-mail: needinfo@formasiabooks.com
Web Site: www.formasiabooks.com
Key Personnel
Mng Dir: Frank Fischbeck
Hong Kong Marketing: Anna Hui
Overseas Marketing: N Poomesh
Founded: 1975
Subjects: Art, History, Chinese Colonial Arts,
Culture & History
ISBN Prefix(es): 978-962-7283; 978-988-98270
Distributed by Weatherhill

Friends of the Earth (HK) Charity Ltd
Unit 1301-1302, 13F, Block A, Sea View Estate,
Nº 2 Watson Rd, Hong Kong
Tel: 2528 5588 *Fax:* 2529 2777
E-mail: foehk@foe.org.hk
Web Site: www.foe.org.hk
Key Personnel
Executive Dir: Chen Mei-Ling
Associate Dir: Edwin Lau
Founded: 1983
Major local environmental groups aimed at edu-
cating & arousing environmental awareness.
Subjects: Agriculture, Energy, Environmental
Studies, Government, Political Science, Health,
Nutrition, Environmental Protection
ISBN Prefix(es): 978-962-8119

Geocarto International Centre Ltd
Wah Ming Centre, Rooms 15-17, 2/F, 421
Queen's Rd West, Hong Kong
Tel: 2546 4262 *Fax:* 2559 3419
E-mail: geocarto@geocarto.com
Web Site: www.geocarto.com
Key Personnel
Dir: K N Au
Founded: 1985
Subjects: Earth Sciences, Geography, Geology,
Remote Sensing
ISBN Prefix(es): 978-962-8226

Hong Kong China Tourism Press
24/F Westlands Centre, 20 Westlands Rd, Quarry
Bay
Tel: 2561 8001 *Fax:* 2586 8196
E-mail: hotline@hkctp.com.hk
Web Site: www.hkctp.com.hk
Key Personnel
General Manager: James Jiang
Founded: 1980
Subjects: Travel & Tourism
ISBN Prefix(es): 978-962-7799; 978-962-7166;
978-962-8746
Subsidiaries: HK China Tourism Company Ltd

Hong Kong University Press+

The University of Hong Kong, Pokfulam Rd, Hong Kong
E-mail: hkupress@hku.hk
Web Site: www.hkupress.org
Key Personnel
Publisher: Malcolm Litchfield
Mng Editor: Clara Ho *E-mail:* cscho@hku.hk
Founded: 1956
Specialize in academic publishing in Chinese & English.
This publisher has indicated that 30% of their product line is author subsidized.
Subjects: Anthropology, Art, Asian Studies, Behavioral Sciences, Biography, Memoirs, Biological Sciences, Child Care & Development, Communications, Criminology, Disability, Special Needs, Education, English as a Second Language, Environmental Studies, Film, Video, Geography, Geology, Government, Political Science, History, Labor, Industrial Relations, Language Arts, Linguistics, Law, Library & Information Sciences, Medicine, Nursing, Dentistry, Natural History, Philosophy, Public Administration, Real Estate, Religion - Buddhist, Social Sciences, Sociology, Women's Studies
ISBN Prefix(es): 978-962-209
Number of titles published annually: 50 Print
Total Titles: 1,000 Print; 600 E-Book
Bookshop(s): HKUP Bookshop, Run Run Heritage House, Pokfulam Rd, Hong Kong
E-mail: uporders@hku.hk

Joint Publishing (HK) Co Ltd

3/F, Commercial Printing Bldg 36, Ting Lai Rd,, Tai Po, New Territories
Tel: 2868 6704 *Fax:* 2868 2471
E-mail: jpchk@jointpublishing.com; publish@jointpublishing.com; retail@jointpublishing.com
Web Site: www.jointpublishing.com
Key Personnel
General Manager: Fan Xian
Editor-in-Chief: Li Xin
Founded: 1948
Subjects: Architecture & Interior Design, Art, Asian Studies, Business, Environmental Studies, Film, Video, Finance, Health, Nutrition, History, Language Arts, Linguistics, Law, Literature, Literary Criticism, Essays, Management, Marketing, Medicine, Nursing, Dentistry, Philosophy, Social Sciences, Sociology
ISBN Prefix(es): 978-962-04
Parent Company: Sino United Publishing (Holdings) Ltd
Subsidiaries: JPC Collection Ltd (Flags & Gifts); JPC Data Chu Ltd
Bookshop(s): 9 Queen Victoria St, Central Hong Kong *Tel:* 2868 6844 *Fax:* 2525 8355; 282-283, Level 2, Plaza Hollywood, Lung Poon St, Diamond Hill *Tel:* 2955 5986 *Fax:* 2955 5910; Shop 107, 1/F Literte, 833 Lai Chi Kok Rd, Kowloon *Tel:* 2310 8048; Shop 3153D, 3/F Lok Fu Plaza, Wang Tau Hom, Kowloon *Tel:* 2338 4438 *Fax:* 2338 4881; S54-58, 2/F, Amoy Plaza 1, Kowloon Bay *Tel:* 2243 3123 *Fax:* 2243 3566; Shop 89, L15, Kwai Chung Plaza, 7-11 Kwai Food Rd, Kwai Fong *Tel:* 2420 3103 *Fax:* 2420 3126; Shop L6-5, Level 6, apm, Millennium City 5, 418 Kwun Tong Rd, Kwun Tong *Tel:* 3148 1089 *Fax:* 3148 1109; 232B, L2, Kai Tin Shopping Center, Lam Tin *Tel:* 2346 5220 *Fax:* 2379 6079; 3065, L3, Sunshine City Plaza, Ma On Shan *Tel:* 2631 6182 *Fax:* 2633 7827; 188, L1, Grand Century Pl, Mongkok *Tel:* 2264 3108 *Fax:* 2264 3103; Shop 111, Level 1, The Westwood, 8 Belcher's St, Sai Wan *Tel:* 2258 9320 *Fax:* 2258 9391; Shop 213, 2/F, Choi Ming Shopping Center, Choi Ming Court, Tseng Kwan O *Tel:* 3143 9009 *Fax:* 3143 9100; Shop 209, Maritime Sq, 33 Tsing King Rd, Tsing Yi *Tel:* 2495 8780 *Fax:* 2495 8485; Shop A, 3/F Fou Wah Center, 210 Castle Peak Rd, Tsuen

Wan *Tel:* 2412 3696 *Fax:* 2412 3799; 512-515, 5/F, Tsz Wan Shan Shopping Center, 23 Yuk Wah St, Tsz Wan Shan *Tel:* 2322 5309 *Fax:* 2322 5310; 141 Johnston Rd, Wan Chai *Tel:* 2838 2081 *Fax:* 2838 2482; 328-332, 3/F, Yuen Long Plaza, Castle Peak Rd, Yuen Long *Tel:* 2475 6587 *Fax:* 2475 8736; Shop 201-203, 2/F Citimall, Kau Yuk Rd, Yuen Long *Tel:* 2470 5228 *Fax:* 2473 9032

LexisNexis Hong Kong

3901, 39/F Hopewell Center, 183 Queen's Rd East, Hong Kong
Tel: 2179 7888; 2965 1400 *Fax:* 2976 0840
E-mail: asia.pacific@lexisnexis.com; help.hk@lexisnexis.com; sales.hk@lexisnexis.com
Web Site: www.lexisnexis.com.hk
Key Personnel
Mng Dir: Tyson Wienker
Subjects: Law
Parent Company: LexisNexis Group
Ultimate Parent Company: Reed Elsevier

Ling Kee Publishing Group+

14/F, Zung Fu Industrial Bldg, 1067 King's Rd, Quarry Bay
Tel: 2561 6151 *Fax:* 2811 1980
E-mail: admin@lingkee.com
Web Site: www.lingkee.com
Key Personnel
Founder-Owner, Chairman & Chief Executive: Bak Ling Au
Founded: 1943
Membership(s): Hong Kong Educational Publishers Association.
Subjects: Antiques, Education, English as a Second Language, History, How-to, Nonfiction (General)
ISBN Prefix(es): 978-962-605; 978-962-608; 978-962-609; 978-962-610
Subsidiaries: BLA Publishing Ltd; Ling Kee Book Store Ltd; Ling Kee Publishing Co Ltd; Unicorn Books Ltd; Ward Lock Educational Co Ltd
Distributor for Encyclopedia of China Publishing House (Beijing, China)
Showroom(s): G/F Hop Xing Commercial Center, 755 Nathan Rd, Mong Kok, Kowloon *Tel:* 2545 1490 *E-mail:* lkbs@lingkee.com
Bookshop(s): Ling Kee Bookstore Ltd, 127-131 Des Voeux Rd, Central Hong Kong *Tel:* 2545 1540; 2545 1490 *Fax:* 2541 1383 *E-mail:* lkbs@lingkee.com; Ling Kee Bookstore Ltd, 733 Nathan Rd, Mong Kok, Kowloon *Tel:* 2394 3486; 2394 1800 *Fax:* 2393 3288 *E-mail:* lkbs@lingkee.com

Macmillan Publishers (China) Ltd

Subsidiary of Macmillan Publishers Ltd
Suite 811, 8/F, Exchange Tower, 33 Wang Chiu Rd, Kowloon Bay, Kowloon
Tel: 2811 8781 *Fax:* 2811 0743
E-mail: china.publishing@macmillan.com.hk
Web Site: www.macmillan.com.hk; www.macmillanchinapublishing.com
Key Personnel
Editorial Manager: Mary-Jane Newton
Senior Sales Executive: Emilie Chan
E-mail: emilie.chan@macmillan.com.hk
Founded: 1970
Subjects: Foreign Countries, Language Arts, Linguistics, Science (General), English & Chinese Language Teaching
ISBN Prefix(es): 978-962-03

MCCM Creations+

Room 5A Sing Kui Commercial Press, 27 Des Voeux Rd West, Sheung Wan
Tel: 3106 4010 *Fax:* 2110 0858
E-mail: info@mccmcreations.com
Web Site: www.mccmcreations.com
Founded: 2001

Publisher of books on city & visual culture.
Subjects: Architecture & Interior Design, Art, Literature, Literary Criticism, Essays, Photography, Poetry, Adventure, Customs & Culture, Design, Performing Arts, Urbanism, Visual Art
ISBN Prefix(es): 978-962-86132; 978-962-86816; 978-988-99842; 978-988-18583; 978-988-99843; 978-988-99266; 978-988-97610; 978-988-18584; 978-988-98653; 978-988-15217
Total Titles: 80 Print
Foreign Rep(s): Book Manic (Australia); China Publishers Services (Mainland China); Consortium Book Sales & Distribution (USA); English Books.jp (Japan); Idea Books (Europe); Select Books Pte Ltd (Singapore)

Ming Pao Publications Ltd+

Subsidiary of Media Chinese International Ltd
15/F, Block A, Ming Pao Industrial Centre, 18 Ka Yip St, Chai Wan, Hong Kong
Tel: 2595 3111; 2515 5111 *Fax:* 2898 2691
E-mail: mpp@mingpao.com; pyso@mingpao.com (ordering)
Web Site: www.mediachinesegroup.com; books.mingpao.com
Key Personnel
Group Chief Executive Officer: Tiong Kiew Chiong
General Manager & Chief Editor: Mr Poon Yiu Ming
Founded: 1986
Subjects: Biography, Memoirs, Business, Child Care & Development, Cookery, Economics, Fiction, Government, Political Science, Health, Nutrition, History, Management, Nonfiction (General), Philosophy, Psychology, Psychiatry, Regional Interests, Religion - Other, Travel & Tourism, Investment
ISBN Prefix(es): 978-962-357; 978-962-973; 978-962-8871; 978-962-8872; 978-962-8917; 978-962-8918
Associate Companies: Ming Pao Magazines Ltd *Tel:* 3605 3705 *Fax:* 2898 2590 *Web Site:* www.mingpaoweekly.com; Ming Pao Newspapers Ltd; Yazhou Zhoukan Ltd *Tel:* 2515 5358 *Fax:* 2505 9662 *E-mail:* y22k@mingpao.com *Web Site:* www.yzzk.com
Book Club(s): Ming Pao Book Club

NTK Publishing Ltd

Subsidiary of NTK Academic Group
7F Lee Garden Five, 18 Hysan Ave, Causeway Bay, Hong Kong
Tel: 2577 7844 *Fax:* 2881 6708
E-mail: enquiry@ntk.edu.hk
Web Site: www.ntk.edu.hk
ISBN Prefix(es): 978-988-98831

Peace Book Co Ltd+

17/F, Paramount Bldg, 12 Ka Yip St, Chai Wan, Hong Kong
Tel: 2804 6687 *Fax:* 2804 6238; 2804 6409
E-mail: info@peacebook.com.hk; publish@peacebook.com.hk; intl@peacebook.com.hk (orders)
Web Site: www.peacebook.com.hk
Key Personnel
President: Gang Xie
Founded: 1958
Subjects: Asian Studies, Health, Nutrition, Chinese Culture
ISBN Prefix(es): 978-962-7176; 978-962-238

Pearson Education Asia Ltd

18th floor, Cornwall House, Taikoo Pl, 979 King's Rd, Quarry Bay
Tel: 3181 0123 *Fax:* 2516 6860
E-mail: hkcs@pearson.com
Web Site: www.pearson.com.hk
Key Personnel
Senior Education Solutions Manager, Primary Education: Franky Chong *Tel:* 3181 0393

Senior Education Solutions Manager, Secondary Education: Fanny Yip *Tel:* 3181 0429
Education Solutions Manager, Pre-school: Janet Ma *Tel:* 3181 0323
Senior Marketing Manager: Yvonne Lee
Founded: 1958
Subjects: Business, Computer Science, Economics, Geography, Geology, Mathematics, Music, Dance, Physics, Science (General), Social Sciences, Sociology, Technology, Chinese Language
ISBN Prefix(es): 978-962-359; 978-962-00; 978-962-01; 978-962-999
Parent Company: Pearson Asia Pacific
Showroom(s): Ave Praia Grande, Ed China Plaza, 762-804, 14 Andar F, Macau *Tel:* 2837 1156 *Fax:* 2837 1152 *E-mail:* macauoffice@pearson.com

Pearson Hong Kong, see Pearson Education Asia Ltd

PPP Co Ltd
Unit 713, Level 7, Core E, Cyberport 3, 100 Cyberport Rd, Central Hong Kong
Tel: 2201 9716 *Fax:* 2869 4554
E-mail: inquiries@ppp.com.hk
Web Site: www.ppp.com.hk
Key Personnel
Chief Executive Officer & Publisher: David Tait
Chief Operating Officer: Raja Kanthan
Dir, Publications & Rights Dir: Jo Allum
  E-mail: jo.allum@ppp.com.hk
Dir, Translation Services: Yin Dalu
Associate Publisher, Contract & Financial Publishing: Rose Torrance
Associate Publisher, Primary Mandarin: Helen Terrington
Head, Business Development: Amberly Walker
Public Relations & Marketing Manager: Audrey Reisdorffer *Tel:* 2201 9725 *E-mail:* audrey@ppp.com.hk
Subjects: Education, Fiction, Finance, Language Arts, Linguistics, Lifestyle, Mandarin Language
ISBN Prefix(es): 978-988-99795

Professional Publishing People, see PPP Co Ltd

P3, see PPP Co Ltd

Red Banana Books, *imprint of* Visionary World Ltd

Research Centre for Translation+
Institute of Chinese Studies, Chinese University of Hong Kong, Sha Tin, New Territories
Tel: 3943 7399 *Fax:* 2603 5110
E-mail: rct@cuhk.edu.hk
Web Site: www.cuhk.edu.hk/rct
Key Personnel
Dir: Lawrence Wang-chi Wong *Tel:* 3943 1501
  E-mail: lwcwong@cuhk.edu.hk
Chief Editor: Theodore Huters *Tel:* 3943 7415
Project Officer: Olivia Lui Wui Sze *Tel:* 3943 7385 *E-mail:* wslui@cuhk.edu.hk
Production Assistant: Cecilia Ip *Tel:* 3943 7407
  E-mail: ceci@cuhk.edu.hk
Founded: 1971
Specialize in English translations of Chinese literature.
Subjects: Asian Studies, Fiction, Literature, Literary Criticism, Essays, Poetry
ISBN Prefix(es): 978-962-7255
Distributed by China Books (Australia); Chinese University Press (worldwide)

SCMP Book Publishing Ltd+
G/F-3/F, One Leighton Rd, Causeway Bay
Tel: 2565 2222
E-mail: communications@scmp.com
Web Site: www.scmpgroup.com

Key Personnel
Chief Executive Officer: Robin Hu
Chief Operating Officer: Elsie Cheung Hoi Sze
Chief Financial Officer: Alex Kam Kwong Fai
Editor-in-Chief: Wang Xiang Wei
Corporate Communications: Anne Wong
  Tel: 2680 8163
Founded: 1981
Subjects: Accounting, Advertising, Animals, Pets, Antiques, Astrology, Occult, Business, Career Development, Child Care & Development, Cookery, Crafts, Games, Hobbies, Fiction, Finance, Gardening, Plants, Health, Nutrition, How-to, Management, Marketing, Mysteries, Suspense, Nonfiction (General), Psychology, Psychiatry, Travel & Tourism
ISBN Prefix(es): 978-962-17
Parent Company: SCMP Group Ltd
Associate Companies: Audio-Visual Travel Ltd; CV Idayus; Highlight Tours Ltd; Retail Corp Ltd; TV Week Ltd
Imprints: Book One; Book Vision; SCMP Books

SCMP Books, *imprint of* SCMP Book Publishing Ltd

Sesame Publication Co Ltd+
Room 505, Winner House, 4/F, 310 King's Rd, North Point, Hong Kong
Tel: 2508 9920 *Fax:* 2806 3267
E-mail: info@sesame.com.hk
Web Site: www.sesame.com.hk
Founded: 1988
Specialize in children's books & printing services.
Subjects: Animals, Pets, Child Care & Development, English as a Second Language, Fiction
ISBN Prefix(es): 978-962-347; 978-962-8795; 978-962-983; 978-962-8811; 978-962-8818
Warehouse: Blk B, 23/F, Jing Ho Industrial Bldg, 78 Wang Lung St, Tsuen Wan, New Territories
Tel: 2408 7685 *Fax:* 2407 2565

Shanghai Book Co Ltd
Flat A, 5/F, 179-180 Connaught Rd West, Sai Ying Pun, Hong Kong
Tel: 25489765 *Fax:* 25486160
Key Personnel
Mng Dir: Lap Shan Wong
Founded: 1946
Subjects: Music, Dance
ISBN Prefix(es): 978-962-239
Associate Companies: China Cultural Corp
Imprints: The Won Yit Book Co
Distributor for People's Music Publishing House

Silkroad Press, *imprint of* Enrich Professional Publishing Ltd

Sinminchu Publishing Co Ltd
Member of Sino United Publishing (Holdings) Ltd
Hunghom Commercial Centre, Room 1015, 39 Ma Tau Wai Rd, Tower A, Hunghom, Kowloon
Tel: 2334 9327 *Fax:* 2765 8471
Web Site: www.sup.com.hk/sinminchu
Founded: 1946
ISBN Prefix(es): 978-962-336

South China Morning Post Publishers Ltd, see SCMP Book Publishing Ltd

Springer Asia Ltd
Unit 1706-1707, Exchange Tower, 33 Wang Chiu Rd, Kowloon Bay
Tel: 2723 9698 *Fax:* 2724 2366
Web Site: www.springer.com
Key Personnel
Mng Dir: Maurice Kwong *E-mail:* maurice.kwong@springer.com
Founded: 1986

Subjects: Astronomy, Behavioral Sciences, Business, Chemistry, Chemical Engineering, Computer Science, Earth Sciences, Economics, Education, Energy, Engineering (General), Environmental Studies, Geography, Geology, Health, Nutrition, Language Arts, Linguistics, Law, Management, Mathematics, Medicine, Nursing, Dentistry, Philosophy, Physics, Social Sciences, Sociology
ISBN Prefix(es): 978-962-430
Parent Company: Springer-Verlag GmbH, Tiergartenstr 17, 69121 Heidelberg, Germany

Sun Mui Press
PO Box 24286, Aberdeen Post Office
Tel: 9219 5150
E-mail: pioneerhk2003@yahoo.com.hk
Web Site: www.xinmiao.com.hk
Subjects: Economics, Government, Political Science, History
ISBN Prefix(es): 978-962-7529

Sun Ya Publications (HK) Ltd+
Subsidiary of Sino United Publishing (Holdings) Ltd
18/F, Industrial Bldg, 499 King's Rd, North Point
Tel: 2562 0161 (sales); 2138 7998 (customer service) *Fax:* 2565 9951 (sales); 2597 4003 (customer service)
E-mail: marketing@sunya.com.hk
Web Site: www.sunya.com.hk
Key Personnel
Mng Dir: Irene Yim
Founded: 1961
Subjects: Fiction, Nonfiction (General)
ISBN Prefix(es): 978-962-08
Subsidiaries: Sunbeam Publications (HK) Ltd

Ta Kung Pao (HK) Ltd
3/F Kodak House II, 39 Healthy St East, North Point
Tel: 2575 7181
E-mail: marketing@takung.cn
Web Site: www.takungpao.com
Key Personnel
Contact: Guo-Hua Wang
Subjects: China
ISBN Prefix(es): 978-962-582

Tai Yip Co+
No 9, 4/F, Cochrane St, Central Hong Kong
Tel: 2524 5963 *Fax:* 2845 3296; 2312 1208 (orders)
E-mail: tybook@taiyipart.com.hk
Web Site: www.taiyipart.com.hk
Founded: 1975
Specialize in Chinese art books.
Subjects: Archaeology, Art, Literature, Literary Criticism, Essays, Chinese Culture
ISBN Prefix(es): 978-962-7239
Bookshop(s): Tai Yip Art Book Centre, 1/F, Hong Kong Museum of Art, 10 Salisbury Rd, Tsim Sha Tsui, Kowloon *Tel:* 2732 2088; 2732 2089 *Fax:* 2312 1208; Tai Yip Art Book Centre, 1/F, Hong Kong Museum of History, 100 Chatham Rd South, TSTE, Kowloon *Tel:* 2191 9188 *Fax:* 2191 9083

Thomson Reuters Financial
City Plaza, 10th floor, Taikoo Shing, Hong Kong
Tel: 2520 3688
Web Site: www.thomsonreuters.com
Subjects: Finance

Times Publishing (Hong Kong) Ltd+
Subsidiary of Times Publishing Group
10/F, Block C, Seaview Estate, 2-8 Watson Rd, North Point, Hong Kong
Tel: 3965 7800 *Fax:* 2979 4528
E-mail: enquiries@tplhk.com.hk
Web Site: www.tplhk.com.hk
Founded: 1959

Membership(s): Educational Booksellers Association; Hong Kong Educational Publishers Association.
Subjects: Biblical Studies, Biological Sciences, Computer Science, Education, Geography, Geology, Health, Nutrition, Mathematics, Religion - Protestant, Science (General)
ISBN Prefix(es): 978-962-302; 978-962-8781; 978-962-8834; 978-988-208

Timezone 8 Ltd
28/F, 3 Lockhart Rd, Hong Kong
Tel: 2887 4222 *Fax:* 2234 5620
E-mail: timezone8@163.com
Web Site: www.timezone8.com
Key Personnel
Contact: Robert Bernell
Founded: 2002
Subjects: Architecture & Interior Design, Art, Photography, Artists, Contemporary Art, Design, Street Culture, Urban Planning
ISBN Prefix(es): 978-988-99265; 978-988-97262; 978-988-98086; 978-988-98680; 978-988-18816; 978-988-19912
Branch Office(s)
No 4 Jiu Xian Qiao Rd, PO Box 8503, Beijing 100 015, China *Tel:* (010) 5978 9072 *Fax:* (010) 5978 9074
Foreign Rep(s): Asia Publishing Services Ltd (Hong Kong, Taiwan); China Publishers Marketing (Cambodia, China, Indonesia, Malaysia, Singapore, Thailand, Vietnam); Coen Sligting Bookimport (Belgium, Netherlands); Distributed Art Publishers Inc (Australia, Japan, Korea, New Zealand, North America, South America); Visual Books Sales Agency (Austria, Germany, Switzerland)

Unicorn Books Ltd+
14/F, Zung Fu Industrial Bldg, 1067 King's Rd, Quarry Bay, Hong Kong
Tel: 2561 6151 (ext 25) *Fax:* 2811 1980
E-mail: unicorn@lingkee.com
Web Site: www.lingkee.com/ubl
Subjects: Antiques, Child Care & Development, Crafts, Games, Hobbies, Gardening, Plants, History, How-to, Language Arts, Linguistics, Self-Help, Chinese Language, Hong Kong History
ISBN Prefix(es): 978-962-232
Parent Company: Ling Kee Publishing Group
Distributed by Encyclopedia Publishing House of China (Beijing, China)

The University of Hong Kong, Department of Philosophy
Run Run Shaw Tower, Room 10-13, 10/F, Centennial Campus, Pokfulam Rd, Hong Kong
Tel: 3917 2796 *Fax:* 2559 8452
E-mail: philosophy@hku.hk
Web Site: www.philosophy.hku.hk
Key Personnel
Chairperson: Dr Joe Lau
Subjects: Computer Science, Philosophy
ISBN Prefix(es): 978-962-375

Vision Publishing Co Ltd+
Flat 33, 5/F, Tower B, Cambridge Plaza, Sheung Shui, New Territories
Tel: 2679 8119 *Fax:* 2679 4478
E-mail: mail@visionhk.com.hk; pe@visionhk.com.hk
Web Site: www.visionhk.com.hk
Key Personnel
Manager: Kai-man Pang
Founded: 1987
Membership(s): Hong Kong Educational Publishers Association Ltd.
Subjects: Economics, Mathematics, Technology, Physical Education
ISBN Prefix(es): 978-962-407

Visionary World Ltd
Liberty Mansion, 11th floor, Flat D, 26E Jordan Rd, Yau Ma Tei, Kowloon
Tel: 2723 1376 *Fax:* 2723 6653
E-mail: info@visionary-world.com
Web Site: www.visionary-world.com
Subjects: Art, Asia
ISBN Prefix(es): 978-962-85637; 978-988-16556; 978-988-16557
Imprints: Red Banana Books

Witman Publishing Co (HK) Ltd+
G/F, 9-11 Tsat Tsz Mui Rd, North Point, Hong Kong
Tel: 2562 6279 *Fax:* 2565 5482
E-mail: info@witmanhk.com; sales@witmanhk.com
Web Site: www.witmanhk.com
Key Personnel
Dir: Yau Suk Ching
Founded: 1979
Specialize in the production of materials for learning & mastering of the English language & printing.
Membership(s): The Hong Kong Association of Professional Publishing Ltd (HKAPEPL).
Subjects: Fiction, Language Arts, Linguistics
ISBN Prefix(es): 978-962-7044; 978-962-304

The Won Yit Book Co, *imprint of* Shanghai Book Co Ltd

Yazhou Zhoukan Ltd
Subsidiary of Media Chinese International Ltd
15/F, Blk A, Ming Pao Industrial Centre, 18 Ka Yip St, Chai Wan
Tel: 2515 5358 *Fax:* 2505 9662
E-mail: yzzk@mingpao.com; yzad@mingpao.com
Web Site: www.yzzk.com
Key Personnel
Deputy General Manager: Terry Chan *Tel:* 2515 5486 *Fax:* 2595 0497 *E-mail:* yochan@mingpao.com
Founded: 1987
Subjects: Asian Studies, Business, Economics, Finance, Regional Interests
ISBN Prefix(es): 978-962-85434

Hungary

General Information

Capital: Budapest
Language: Hungarian (German widely known)
Religion: Predominantly Roman Catholic, also Hungarian Reformed, Lutheran & Hungarian Orthodox
Population: 10.3 million
Bank Hours: 0800-1630 Monday-Friday
Shop Hours: 1000-1800 Monday-Friday; 1000-1500 Saturday
Currency: 100 filler = 1 forint
Export/Import Information: Any companies should be registered at the Registry Court. 12% VAT on books.
Copyright: UCC, Berne (see Copyright Conventions, pg viii)

Agape Kft
Szeksosi ut 16, Szeged 6791
Tel: (062) 444 002 *Fax:* (062) 442 592
E-mail: office@agape.hu; agape123@invitel.hu
Web Site: www.agape.hu
Key Personnel
Dir: Karoly Harmath
Founded: 1991

Subjects: Religion - Catholic
ISBN Prefix(es): 978-963-458; 978-963-8112

Agrargazdasagi Kutato Intezet (Agricultural Economics Research Institute)
Zsil u 3-5, Budapest 1093
Mailing Address: Pf 944, Budapest 1463
Tel: (01) 217 1011 *Fax:* (01) 217 7037
E-mail: akii@akii.hu
Web Site: www.akii.hu
Key Personnel
General Dir: Istvan Kapronczai *Tel:* (01) 476-3063 *Fax:* (01) 217-4469 *E-mail:* foigazgato@aki.gov.hu
Founded: 1954
Centre of agricultural economics research, collects & analyzes information, performs research & distributes the results obtained through its publications.
Subjects: Agriculture, Economics
ISBN Prefix(es): 978-963-491

Akademiai Kiado+
Prielle Korneila u 21-35, Budapest 1117
Mailing Address: Pf 245, Budapest 1519
Tel: (01) 464 8282 *Fax:* (01) 464 8201 (customer service); (01) 464 8251
E-mail: info@akkrt.hu
Web Site: www.akkrt.hu
Key Personnel
President & Mng Dir: Zsolt Bucsi Szabo
Founded: 1828
Publishing House of the Hungarian Academy of Sciences & Wolters Kluwer.
Subjects: Antiques, Archaeology, Art, Biological Sciences, Earth Sciences, Economics, Education, Engineering (General), Government, Political Science, History, Language Arts, Linguistics, Law, Literature, Literary Criticism, Essays, Medicine, Nursing, Dentistry, Music, Dance, Philosophy, Science (General), Social Sciences, Sociology, Technology, Veterinary Science, Cultural Studies, Ethnography, Oriental Studies
ISBN Prefix(es): 978-963-05

Alexandra Kiado
Uszogi-kiserdo u 1, Pecs 7630
Tel: (072) 777 122
E-mail: kiado@alexandra.hu
Web Site: www.alexandrakiado.hu
Founded: 1993
Subjects: Architecture & Interior Design, Art, Business, Computers, Cookery, Crafts, Games, Hobbies, Drama, Theater, Economics, Education, Fiction, Finance, Health, Nutrition, Literature, Literary Criticism, Essays, Music, Dance, Photography, Religion - Buddhist, Religion - Jewish, Religion - Other, Social Sciences, Sociology, Sports, Athletics, Travel & Tourism, Entertainment
ISBN Prefix(es): 978-963-367; 978-963-368; 978-963-369; 978-963-8086; 978-963-8409; 978-963-85111

Atlantisz Kiado+
Gerloczy u 4, Budapest 1052
Tel: (01) 266 3870 *Fax:* (01) 266 3870
E-mail: atlantis@budapest.hu
Web Site: www.atlantiszkiado.hu
Key Personnel
Publisher: Dr Tamas Miklos
Founded: 1990
Also international bookshop.
Subjects: History, Philosophy, Religion - Other, Social Sciences, Sociology, Theology, Humanities
ISBN Prefix(es): 978-963-7978; 978-963-9165
Bookshop(s): Atlantisz Koenyvsziget, Anker koez 1-3, Budapest 1061 *Fax:* (01) 267 6258
E-mail: atlbook@t-online.hu

Balassi Kiado Kft+
Hollan Erno u 33 IV em 5, Budapest 1136
Tel: (01) 483 07 50; (01) 483 07 49; (01) 235 02
04 *Fax:* (01) 266 83 43
E-mail: balassi@balassikiado.hu
Web Site: www.balassikiado.hu
Key Personnel
Dir: Andrea Sooky
Deputy Dir: Agnes Gilicze
Scientific Dir: Dr Peter Koeszeghy
Editor-in-Chief: Zsuzsanna Tamas
Founded: 1991
Membership(s): Hungarian Publishers & Book-
sellers Association.
Subjects: Archaeology, Art, Education, Electron-
ics, Electrical Engineering, History, Language
Arts, Linguistics, Library & Information Sci-
ences, Literature, Literary Criticism, Essays,
Music, Dance, Nonfiction (General), Philoso-
phy, Social Sciences, Sociology
ISBN Prefix(es): 978-963-506; 978-963-7873
Total Titles: 533 Print; 1 CD-ROM
Distributed by Harrassowitz; Polis (Romania)
Distributor for Cambridge UP; Kaligram (Roma-
nia, Slovakia); Polis (Romania)
Bookshop(s): Katona Jozsef u 9-11, Budapest
1137 *Tel:* (01) 335 28 85 *Fax:* (01) 212 02 14
E-mail: balassikonyvesbolt@t-online.hu
Distribution Center: Libro-Trade Ltd, Pesti
ut, Budapest 1173 *Tel:* (01) 254 0254
E-mail: librotrade@librotrade.hu

Boook Kiado Kft
Raday u, 11-13, Budapest 1092
Tel: (020) 3490897
E-mail: info@boook.hu
Web Site: www.boook.hu
Founded: 2009
Subjects: Cookery
ISBN Prefix(es): 978-963-88942

**Budapesti Muszaki es Gazdasagtudomanyi
Egyetem** (Budapest University of Technology
& Economics)
Muegyetem rkp 3-9, Budapest 1111
Tel: (01) 463-1111 *Fax:* (01) 463-1110
E-mail: info@bme.hu
Web Site: www.bme.hu
Subjects: Business, Economics, Engineering
(General), Social Sciences, Sociology, Tech-
nology
ISBN Prefix(es): 978-963-420; 978-963-421

Cartaphilus Kiado
Bem u 13, Kistarcsa 2143
Tel: (0628) 506-135 *Fax:* (0628) 506-136
E-mail: cartaphilus@cartaphilus.hu
Web Site: www.cartaphilus.hu
Key Personnel
Head, Publishing: Zsolt Szasz
Editor: Jozsef Takacs *E-mail:* joseph@cartaphilus.
hu
Founded: 1993
Subjects: Biography, Memoirs, Film, Video, Gov-
ernment, Political Science, History, Literature,
Literary Criticism, Essays, Music, Dance, Phi-
losophy, Poetry, Religion - Other
ISBN Prefix(es): 978-963-7448; 978-963-85486;
978-963-85882; 978-963-9303; 978-963-266

Cartographia Kft+
Nyugati Sq 1, Budapest 1066
Mailing Address: Pf 80, Budapest 1590
Tel: (01) 222 6726 *Fax:* (01) 222 6726
E-mail: exp_imp@cartographia.hu
Web Site: www.cartographiaonline.com; www.
cartographia.hu
Key Personnel
Publishing & Export Manager: Szigeti Borbala
E-mail: bszigeti@cartographia.hu
Sales Assistant: Utasi Tunde
E-mail: utasi_tunde@cartographia.hu

Founded: 1954
Specialize in publishing & distributing maps &
atlases for travel.
Membership(s): International Map Industry Asso-
ciation (IMIA).
Subjects: Geography, Geology, Outdoor Recre-
ation, Travel & Tourism, Cartography
ISBN Prefix(es): 978-963-350; 978-963-351; 978-
963-353; 978-963-352
Bookshop(s): Cartographia Globe & Map Shop,
Bajcsy-Zsilinszky u 37, Budapest 1065
Tel: (01) 312-6001 *E-mail:* terkepbolt@mail.
datanet.hu

Central European University Press+
Imprint of Central European University LLC
Oktober 6, u 14, Budapest 1051
Tel: (01) 327-3000 *Fax:* (01) 327-3183
E-mail: ceupress@ceu.hu
Web Site: www.ceupress.com
Key Personnel
Dir & Editor: Kristina Kos *Tel:* (01) 327-3844
E-mail: kosk@ceu.hu
Deputy Dir: Peter Inkei *Tel:* (01) 327-3181
E-mail: inkeip@ceu.hu
Marketing Manager: Agnes Barla-Szabo *Tel:* (01)
327-3138 *E-mail:* barla-szaboa@ceu.hu
Editor: Linda Kunos *Tel:* (01) 327-3136
E-mail: kunosl@ceu.hu
Founded: 1993
Dedicated to broadening the range of literature
available in English or topics concerning the
past & present history & culture of people liv-
ing in the countries of Central & Eastern Eu-
rope.
Subjects: Economics, Government, Political Sci-
ence, History, Literature, Literary Criticism,
Essays, Social Sciences, Sociology, Cultural
Studies, Medieval History
ISBN Prefix(es): 978-963-9116; 978-963-9241;
978-963-7326; 978-963-9776; 978-615-5053;
978-615-5225; 978-963-386
Total Titles: 98 Print; 1 Online
U.S. Office(s): Central European University
Press, 400 W 59 St, New York, NY 10019,
United States, Sales Manager: Martin Green-
wald *Tel:* 212-547-6932 *Fax:* 646-557-2416
E-mail: mgreenwald@sorosny.org
Orders to: Books International, PO Box
605, Herndon, VA 20172, United States
Tel: 703-661-1500 *Fax:* 703-661-1501
E-mail: mgreenwald@sorosny.org
NBN International, 10 Thornbury Rd, Ply-
mouth PL6 7PP, United Kingdom *Tel:* (01752)
202301 *Fax:* (01752) 202333 *E-mail:* orders@
nbninternational.com *Web Site:* www.
nbninternational.com (Europe & Asia)
c/o University of Toronto Press Inc, 5201
Dufferin St, Toronto, Ontario M3H 5T8,
Canada *Tel:* 800-565-9523 *Fax:* 800-221-9985
E-mail: utpbooks@utpress.utoronto.ca

Complex Kiado Kft+
Prielle Kornelia u 21-35, Budapest 1117
Tel: (01) 464-565; (01) 464-5656 *Fax:* (01) 464-
5657
E-mail: info@complex.hu
Web Site: www.complex.hu
Founded: 1986
Subjects: Accounting, Business, Cookery, Eco-
nomics, Finance, How-to, Law, Management,
Marketing, Public Administration, Real Estate,
Taxation
ISBN Prefix(es): 978-963-485
Parent Company: Wolters Kluwer

Corvina Kiado Kft+
Danko u 4-8, Budapest 1086
Tel: (01) 411-2410 *Fax:* (01) 318-4410
E-mail: corvina@lira.hu
Web Site: www.corvinakiado.hu

Key Personnel
General Manager: Laszlo Kunos
Founded: 1955
Subjects: Art, Cookery, History, Language Arts,
Linguistics, Social Sciences, Sociology
ISBN Prefix(es): 978-963-13

Europa Konyvkiado Kft+
Lajos u 74-76, Budapest 1036
Mailing Address: Pf 65, Budapest 1363
Tel: (01) 331-2700 *Fax:* (01) 331-4162
E-mail: info@europakiado.hu
Web Site: www.europakiado.hu
Key Personnel
Publisher: Imre Barna
Editor: Klara Takacs
Founded: 1946
Subjects: Biography, Memoirs, Fiction, Literature,
Literary Criticism, Essays, Philosophy, Poetry
ISBN Prefix(es): 978-963-07
Number of titles published annually: 200 Print

Gondolat Kiado
Szentkiralyi u 16, Budapest 1088
Tel: (01) 486-1527 *Fax:* (01) 486-1527
E-mail: info@gondolatkiado.hu
Web Site: www.gondolatkiado.hu
Key Personnel
Dir: Bacskai Istvan *E-mail:* bacskai.istvan@
gondolatkiado.hu
Editor-in-Chief: Berenyi Gabor *E-mail:* berenyi.
gabor@gondolatkiado.hu
Subjects: Fiction, Nonfiction (General)
ISBN Prefix(es): 978-963-280; 978-963-281; 978-
963-282

HarperCollins Hungary
Division of HarperCollins Publishers
Varosmajor u 11, Budapest 1122
Tel: (01) 488-5569
E-mail: harpercollins@harpercollins.hu
Web Site: www.harpercollins.hu
Key Personnel
Publisher: Dr Jozsef Bayer
Editor-in-Chief: Beatrix Vasko
Subjects: Romance
ISBN Prefix(es): 978-963-448

Hatter Kiado es Kereskedelmi Kft+
Szent Istvan Krt 18, Budapest 1137
Mailing Address: Pf 97, Budapest 1525
Tel: (01) 452 1768 *Fax:* (01) 452 1751
E-mail: hatterkiado@hatterkiado.hu; marketing@
hatterkiado.hu
Web Site: www.hatterkiado.hu
Key Personnel
Head, Publishing: David Klopfer *E-mail:* klopfer.
david@hatterkiado.hu
Mng Dir: Diana Kali *E-mail:* kali.diana@
hatterkiado.hu
Distribution: Kata Vjhazy *E-mail:* terjesztes@
hatterkiado.hu
Founded: 1987
Subjects: Art, Literature, Literary Criticism, Es-
says, Psychology, Psychiatry, Science (Gen-
eral), Transportation
ISBN Prefix(es): 978-963-7403; 978-963-7455;
978-963-8128; 978-963-9365

Helikon Kiado Kft+
Nyugati ter 1, Budapest 1066
Tel: (01) 423-0080 *Fax:* (01) 423-0087
E-mail: helikon@helikon.hu
Web Site: www.helikon.hu
Key Personnel
Mng Dir: Adam Halmos
Founded: 1982
Subjects: Art, History, Literature, Literary Criti-
cism, Essays
ISBN Prefix(es): 978-963-207; 978-963-208; 978-
963-227
Bookshop(s): Helikon Bookshop, Bajcsy-
Zsilinszky ut 35, Budapest 1065, Shop

Manager: Loczi Zoltan *Tel:* (01) 331-2329
Fax: (01) 302-6479 *E-mail:* konyveshaz@
helikon.hu

Holnap Kiado kft
Zenta u 5, Budapest 1111
Tel: (01) 466 69 28 *Fax:* (01) 466 69 28
E-mail: holnapkiado@holnapkiado.hu
Web Site: www.holnapkiado.hu
Founded: 1989
Subjects: Architecture & Interior Design, Cook-
ery, History, Language Arts, Linguistics, Litera-
ture, Literary Criticism, Essays, Music, Dance,
Philosophy
ISBN Prefix(es): 978-963-345; 978-963-346; 978-
963-3466; 978-963-3490
Bookshop(s): Budai Tan-Tars Konyvesbolt, At-
tila u 133, Budapest 1012 *Tel:* (01) 225 81
51 *E-mail:* budaitantars@tantars.hu; Olva-
sok Boltja, Pesti Barnabas u4, Budapest
1052 *Tel:* (01) 266 00 18 *E-mail:* info@
olvasokboltja.hu

HVG Kiado Zrt (HVG Publishing Ltd)
Montevideo u 14, Budapest 1037
Tel: (01) 436-2000; (01) 436-2045 (customer ser-
vice) *Fax:* (01) 436-2012
E-mail: ugyfelszolgalat@hvg.hu; hvgkonyvek@
hvg.hu (editorial)
Web Site: www.hvgkonyvek.hu
Key Personnel
Head, Publishing: Arpad Budahazy *E-mail:* a.
budahazy@hvg.hu
Foreign Rights Manager: Kata Kormos *E-mail:* k.
kormos@hvg.hu
Marketing & Public Relations: Adrienne Darvas
Tel: (01) 436-2066 *E-mail:* a.darvas@hvg.hu
Subjects: Biography, Memoirs, Business, Career
Development, Management, Psychology, Psy-
chiatry, Science (General)
ISBN Prefix(es): 978-963-9686; 978-963-304

Jelenkor Kiado+
Munkacsy Mihaly u 30/A, Pecs 7621
Tel: (072) 314-782; (072) 335-767 *Fax:* (072)
532-047
Web Site: jelenkor.libricsoport.hu
Key Personnel
Dir: Dr Gabor Csordas
Sales Manager: Ildiko Andrasi
Editor: Kata Csordas
Marketing: Gabriella Koszta
Founded: 1993
Promote contemporary Hungarian poetry, fiction
& philosophy.
Subjects: Art, Drama, Theater, Fiction, Film,
Video, History, Literature, Literary Criticism,
Essays, Philosophy, Poetry
ISBN Prefix(es): 978-963-676; 978-963-7770
Branch Office(s)
Rakoczi ut 59 II/9, Budapest 1081 *Tel:* (01)
3133804 *Fax:* (01) 3230376

Joszoveg Muhely Kiado+
O u 11, Budapest 1066
Mailing Address: Pf 826, Budapest 1244
Tel: (01) 302-16-08 *Fax:* (01) 226-59-35
Key Personnel
Publications Manager: Dr Peter Foti
Founded: 1997
Specialize in social sciences, general information,
books, fiction.
Subjects: Cookery, Government, Political Science,
Health, Nutrition, How-to, Literature, Literary
Criticism, Essays, Philosophy, Psychology, Psy-
chiatry, Social Sciences, Sociology
ISBN Prefix(es): 978-963-7052; 978-963-9134
Number of titles published annually: 20 Print
Total Titles: 140 Print

Kijarat Kiado
Veder u 20, Budapest 1035

Tel: (01) 388-6312 *Fax:* (01) 388-6312
E-mail: kijarat@enternet.hu
Key Personnel
Manager: Gyorgy Palinkas
Founded: 1995
Three book series: Hungarian architecture, philo-
sophical essays & youngest generation of Hun-
garian literature.
Limited Partnership.
Membership(s): Magyar Konyvkiadok es
Konyvterjesztok Egyesulese (MKKE).
Subjects: Architecture & Interior Design, Litera-
ture, Literary Criticism, Essays, Philosophy
ISBN Prefix(es): 978-963-85415; 978-963-85696;
978-963-9136; 978-963-9529
Total Titles: 69 Print
Foreign Rights: Agency Balla & Co (Hungary)

Kossuth Kiado RT (Kossuth Publishing)+
Bocskai u 26, Budapest 1043
Mailing Address: Pf 55, Budapest 1327
Tel: (01) 888-9100 *Fax:* (01) 888-9102
E-mail: info@kossuth.hu
Web Site: www.kossuth.hu
Key Personnel
President & Chief Executive Officer: Mr Andras
Sandor Kocsis *Tel:* (01) 370-0600
Publishing Dir: Mrs Jolanta Szabone Szuba
Tel: (01) 370-0603
Chief Editor: Attila Nadori
Multimedia Manager: Mr Laszlo Foldes *Tel:* (01)
370-0608 *E-mail:* it@kossuth.hu
International Relations Manager: Rita Tanner
Marketing Manager: Juhasz Lajos
E-mail: marketing@kossuth.hu
Founded: 1944
Subjects: Art, Business, Child Care & Develop-
ment, Communications, Education, Finance,
Geography, Geology, Health, Nutrition, Litera-
ture, Literary Criticism, Essays, Management,
Natural History, Philosophy, Psychology, Psy-
chiatry, Religion - Catholic, Sports, Athletics,
Travel & Tourism, Wine & Spirits
ISBN Prefix(es): 978-963-09
Number of titles published annually: 80 Print; 12
CD-ROM
Total Titles: 80 Print; 45 CD-ROM

Libri Kiado
Nyugati ter 1, Budapest 1066
Tel: (01) 789 5158
E-mail: info@libri-kiado.hu
Web Site: www.libri-kiado.hu
Key Personnel
Publisher: Halmos Adam; Sarkozy Bence
Public Relations & Marketing: Szabados Balazs
Tel: (0630) 353 6363 *E-mail:* szabados.
balazs@libri-kiado.hu
Founded: 2011
Subjects: Anthropology, Biography, Memoirs,
Economics, Environmental Studies, History,
Literature, Literary Criticism, Essays, Psychol-
ogy, Psychiatry, Comics, Entertainment, Peda-
gogy
ISBN Prefix(es): 978-963-310

Magveto Konyvkiado es Kereskedelmi Kft+
Danko u 4-8, Budapest 1086
Mailing Address: Pf 205, Budapest 1403
Tel: (01) 235-5020; (01) 484-7040 *Fax:* (01) 318-
4107
E-mail: magveto.kiado@lira.hu
Web Site: kiadok.lira.hu/kiado/magveto
Key Personnel
Dir: Anna David
Public Relations & Marketing: Judit Arvai
Tel: (01) 235-5027 *E-mail:* arvai.judit@lira.hu
Trade Representative: Rozalia Janos *Tel:* (01)
235-5034 *E-mail:* janos.lia@lira.hu
Founded: 1955
Rights & Permissions: Artisjus (under Literary
Agents).

Membership(s): Magyar Konyvkiadok es
Konyvterjesztok Egyesulese (MKKE).
Subjects: Art, Fiction, Film, Video, History, Mu-
sic, Dance, Philosophy, Poetry
ISBN Prefix(es): 978-963-14; 978-963-270; 978-
963-271
Parent Company: Lira Konyv Zrt
Bookshop(s): Magvetoe Koenyvesbolt, Szent Ist-
van Koerut 26, Budapest 1137
Warehouse: Vaci ut 19, Budapest 1134

Magyar Kemikusok Egyesulete (MKE)
(Hungarian Chemical Society)
Hattye u 16, Budapest 1015
Tel: (01) 201-6883; (01) 225-8777; (01) 201-2535
Fax: (01) 201-8056
E-mail: mail@mke.org.hu; mke@mke.org.hu
Web Site: www.mke.org.hu
Key Personnel
President: Dr Livia Simonne Sarkadi
E-mail: sarkadi@mail.bme.hu
Vice President: Tamas Kiss *E-mail:* tkiss@chem.
u-szeged.hu; Gyorgy Liptay *E-mail:* liptay.g@
mail.bme.hu
Secretary-General: Attila Kovacs *E-mail:* a.j.
kovacs@t-online.hu
Deputy Secretary-General: Janos Bognar
E-mail: jbognar@festekkutato.hu; Peter Szalay
E-mail: szalay@chem.elte.hu
Founded: 1907
Subjects: Chemistry, Chemical Engineering
ISBN Prefix(es): 978-963-8191

**Magyar Konyvkiadok es Konyvterjesztok
Egyesulese (MKKE)** (Hungarian Publishers' &
Booksellers' Association)
Kertesz u 41 I/4, Budapest 1073
Mailing Address: Pf 130, Budapest 1367
Tel: (01) 343-2540 *Fax:* (01) 343-2541
E-mail: mkke@mkke.hu
Web Site: www.mkke.hu
Key Personnel
President, Independent Publishing Dept: Gabor
Csordas
Dir: Kereszatury Tibor
Founded: 1795
Subjects: Biography, Memoirs, History, Literature,
Literary Criticism, Essays
ISBN Prefix(es): 978-963-7002; 978-963-7409

Magyar Szabvanykiado Testulet (Hungarian
Standards Institution)+
Horvath Mihaly ter 1, Budapest 1082
Tel: (01) 456-6800 *Fax:* (01) 456-6809
E-mail: kiado@mszt.hu; isoline@mszt.hu
Web Site: www.mszt.hu
Key Personnel
President: Dr Janos Ginsztler *E-mail:* ginsztler@
mszt.hu
Vice President: Peter Simon *E-mail:* p.simon@
mszt.hu
Mng Dir: Gyorgy Ponyai *E-mail:* gy.ponyai@
mszt.hu
Customer Service: Sandorne Pali *E-mail:* s.pali@
mszt.hu
Founded: 1921
Subjects: Law, Management, Nonfiction (Gen-
eral), Public Administration, Civil Code, Qual-
ity Management
ISBN Prefix(es): 978-963-402

Medicina Konyvkiado Zrt+
Rakoczi ut 16 ll emelet, Budapest 1072
Tel: (01) 312-2650 *Fax:* (01) 312-2450
E-mail: medkiad@euroweb.hu
Web Site: www.medicina-kiado.hu
Key Personnel
Chief Executive Officer: Frigyesne Farkasvolgyi
Tel: (01) 331-0781
Editor: Dr Judit Banki; Katalin Benjamin; Erika
Biro; Dr Agnes Cornides; Dr Katalin Nagy;
Agnes Pobozsnyi; Andrea Valovics
Founded: 1957

Publishing house of medical literature.
Membership(s): Hungarian Magyar Konyvkiadok es Konyvterjesztok Egyesulese (MKKE).
Subjects: Medicine, Nursing, Dentistry, Sports, Athletics, Travel & Tourism
ISBN Prefix(es): 978-963-240; 978-963-242; 978-963-241
Bookshop(s): Baross u 21, Budapest 1088, Contact: Katalin Bontovics *Tel:* (01) 317-0931 *E-mail:* medicina@mail.datanet.hu; Petnehazy u 34-36, Budapest 1139 *Tel:* (01) 302-6293; (01) 302-6288 *E-mail:* kerosztaly@medicinazrt.hu; Medicina Olvasoszalon, Ulloi ut 89/C, Budapest 1091 *Tel:* (01) 216-0596; Medicina Konyvesbolt, Ulloi ut 91/A, Budapest 1091, Contact: Dr Andrasne Melly *Tel:* (01) 215-3786; (01) 215-9618 *E-mail:* medicinakonyvesboltbp@medicinazrt.hu; Medicina Konyvesbolt, Nagyerdei krt 98, Debrecen 4032, Contact: Barta Laszlo *Tel:* (052) 423-855 *E-mail:* medicinadebrecen@gportal.hu; Ferencesek u 7, Pecs 7621 *Tel:* (072) 242-634; Szigeti ut 12, Pecs 7624, Contact: Czigany Istvanne *Tel:* (072) 536-001; (072) 536-1720; Tisza L krt 48, Szeged 6720, Contact: Maria Lagzi *Tel:* (062) 420-418 *E-mail:* bolt@medicinaszeged.t-online.hu

Mezogazda Kiado (Agricultural Publishing Co)
Lajos u 48-66/B II, Budapest 1036
Tel: (01) 489-8891 *Fax:* (01) 430-1536
E-mail: info@mezogazdakiado.hu
Web Site: www.mezogazdakiado.hu
Key Personnel
Dir: Lelkes Lajos; Dr M Bodi Adel
Sales: Gaborne Peto *Tel:* (01) 407-1020
    E-mail: kereskedelem@mezogazdakiado.hu
Founded: 1992
Specialize in agricultural publishing.
Subjects: Agriculture, Animals, Pets, Economics, Engineering (General), Environmental Studies, Gardening, Plants, Health, Nutrition, Science (General), Veterinary Science, Wine & Spirits, Food Safety, Nature Conservation
ISBN Prefix(es): 978-963-7362; 978-963-8160; 978-963-8439; 978-963-9121; 978-963-9239; 978-963-9358; 978-963-286
Number of titles published annually: 50 Print
Total Titles: 150 Print
Branch Office(s)
Ecseri ut 14-16, Budapest 1097 *Tel:* (01) 407 1020 *E-mail:* kereskedelem@mezogazdakiado.hu

MKE, see Magyar Kemikusok Egyesulete (MKE)

Mora Konyvkiado Zrt+
Vaci ut 19, Budapest 1134
Tel: (01) 320-4740 *Fax:* (01) 320-5382
E-mail: mora@mora.hu; shop@mora.hu
Web Site: www.mora.hu
Key Personnel
President: Janos Janikovsky
Chief Financial Officer: Edit Fulop *E-mail:* fulop.edit@mora.hu
Editor-in-Chief: Agnes Merenyi *E-mail:* merenyi.agnes@mora.hu
Deputy Editor-in-Chief: Viktoria Dian *E-mail:* dian.viktoria@mora.hu
Editor: Peter Doka *E-mail:* doka.peter@mora.hu
Marketing & Public Relations Manager: Sylvia Halmai *E-mail:* halmai.sylvia@mora.hu
Foreign Relations: Csilla Szabo *E-mail:* szabo.csilla@mora.hu
Founded: 1950
Intellectual workshop of the Hungarian literature for children & the young by bringing out quality new books.
Subjects: Child Care & Development, Education, Science Fiction, Fantasy
ISBN Prefix(es): 978-963-11

Bookshop(s): BabyPlanet Babaaruhaz, Daroci ut 1-3, Budapest 1113 *Tel:* (01) 209 1488; Millennium Konyveshaz, Terez Krt 22, Budapest 1066 *Tel:* (01) 354 15 02 *Fax:* (01) 354 15 03
Book Club(s): Mora Koenyvklub (Mora Bucklub)-Kinderbuecher

Mozaik Kiado Kft
Debreceni u 3/B, Szeged 6723
Tel: (062) 554-660; (062) 470-101 (orders)
    Fax: (062) 554-666
E-mail: kiado@mozaik.info.hu; rendeles@mozaik.info.hu (orders)
Web Site: www.mozaik.info.hu
Key Personnel
Science Chief Editor: Katalin Toth
    E-mail: katalin.toth@mozaik.info.hu
Literary Editor: Ildiko Arokszallasi
    E-mail: ildiko.arokszallasi@mozaik.info.hu
Sales Dir: Imre Gargyan *E-mail:* imre.gargyan@mozaik.info.hu
Publisher of textbooks for public education.
Subjects: Art, Biological Sciences, Chemistry, Chemical Engineering, Geography, Geology, History, Language Arts, Linguistics, Literature, Literary Criticism, Essays, Mathematics, Music, Dance, Physics, Science (General)
ISBN Prefix(es): 978-963-697
Bookshop(s): VIII Ker, Ulloi ut 70, Budapest 1082 *Tel:* (01) 31-42-612

Mult es Jovo Kiado+
Keleti Karoly u 16 II/3, Budapest 1024
Tel: (01) 316-70-19 *Fax:* (01) 316-70-19
E-mail: info@multesjovo.hu
Web Site: www.multesjovo.hu
Key Personnel
Editor-in-Chief: Janos Kobanyai
General Manager: Agnes Fenyo
Founded: 1989
Subjects: History, Literature, Literary Criticism, Essays, Social Sciences, Sociology, Jewish Literature, History & Culture
ISBN Prefix(es): 978-963-85295; 978-963-85697; 978-963-85817; 978-963-9171; 978-963-9512
Foreign Rep(s): Liepman AG Literary Agency

Editio Musica Budapest+
Victor Hugo u 11-15, Budapest 1132
Mailing Address: Pf 322, Budapest 1370
Tel: (01) 2361 106; (01) 2361-104 (sales)
    Fax: (01) 2361 101
E-mail: info@emb.hu
Web Site: www.emb.hu
Key Personnel
Mng Dir: Antal Boronkay *Tel:* (01) 2361-102
    E-mail: boronkay@emb.hu
Publishing Dir: Szilvia Tisler *Tel:* (01) 2361-103
    E-mail: szilvia.tisler@emb.hu
Editor-in-Chief: Marton Kerekfy *Tel:* (01) 2361-111 *E-mail:* kerekfy@emb.hu
Marketing Manager: Mr Tekla Uszkay *Tel:* (01) 2361-126 *E-mail:* uszkay@emb.hu
Sales Manager: Bea Baracsi *Tel:* (01) 2361-104
    E-mail: baracsi@emb.hu
Founded: 1950
Subjects: Biography, Memoirs, Music, Dance
ISBN Prefix(es): 978-963-330
Parent Company: Universal Music Publishing Group
Foreign Rep(s): Albersen Verhuur BV (Holland); Boosey & Hawkes Inc (Canada, USA); Boosey & Hawkes Ltd (Ireland, UK); Edicije DSS (Slovenia); Editions Durand Salabert Esching (Belgium, France); Hrvatsko Drustvo Skladatelja ZAMP-Hire Dept (Bosnia and Herzegovina, Croatia); Intermusica (Portugal); Israel Music Associates (Israel); Hal Leonard Australia Pty Ltd (Australia, New Zealand); LM Edition AB Sweden (Denmark, Estonia, Finland, Latvia, Lithuania, Norway, Sweden); Monge y Bocata Asociados Musicales

SL (Spain); Music Forum vos (Slovakia); G Ricordi und Co Buehnen- und Musikverlag GmbH Germany (Czechia, Germany, Poland, Switzerland); Universal Edition AG (Austria); Universal Music Publishing Ricordi SRL (Italy); Yamaha Music Media Corp International Division (Japan)
Bookshop(s): Andrassy ut 45, Budapest 1061 *Tel:* (01) 322-4091 *Fax:* (01) 322-4091

Muszaki Konyvkiado Kft (Technical Publishing Ltd)+
Topol u 3, Piliscsev 2519
Tel: (033) 473-473 *Fax:* (033) 473-473
E-mail: info@mkkonyvkiado.hu
Web Site: www.muszakikiado.hu
Key Personnel
Mng Dir: Simon Istvan
Marketing Officer: Barfi Adrienn *E-mail:* barfi.adrienn@mkkonyvkiado.hu
Customer Service: Horvath Sandorne
Founded: 1955
Subjects: Architecture & Interior Design, Career Development, Chemistry, Chemical Engineering, Computer Science, Electronics, Electrical Engineering, Management, Mathematics, Physics, Science (General), Technology
ISBN Prefix(es): 978-963-10; 978-963-16
Book Club(s): Kozos Tobbszoros Klub; Pedagogusklub

Nemzetkozi Szinhazi Intezet Magyar Kozpontja (Hungarian Centre of the International Theatre Institute)
Krisztina Krt 57, Budapest 1013
Tel: (01) 212-5247; (01) 225-0874 *Fax:* (01) 225-5247
E-mail: mail@itihun.hu
Web Site: www.itihun.hu
Key Personnel
President: Anna Lakos
Subjects: Drama, Theater, Literature, Literary Criticism, Essays
ISBN Prefix(es): 978-963-691

OKKER Zrt
Cinka Panna u 8, Budapest 1145
Tel: (01) 320-2474 *Fax:* (01) 320-2474
E-mail: titkarsag@okker.hu
Web Site: www.okker.hu
Key Personnel
Chief Executive Officer: Keresztes Tibor
Senior Project Manager: Gelanyine Kosa Iren *E-mail:* kosa.iren@okker.hu
Specialize in education, teachers training & school management.
Subjects: Education, Co-education, Continuing Education, Disadvantaged Children, Inclusive Education, Intercultural Education, Pedagogy, School Management, Teachers Training
ISBN Prefix(es): 978-963-7315; 978-963-85136; 978-963-85351; 978-963-85206; 978-963-9228

Osiris Kiado (Osiris Publishing)+
Egyetem ter 5, Budapest 1053
Tel: (01) 266-6560 *Fax:* (01) 267-0935
E-mail: kiado@osirismail.hu
Web Site: www.osiriskiado.hu
Key Personnel
Dir & Editor: Janos Gyurgyak
Editor: Zsejke Nagy *Tel:* (01) 266-6560 ext 102 *E-mail:* nagy.zsejke@osirismail.hu
Founded: 1994
Subjects: Anthropology, Communications, Economics, Film, Video, Government, Political Science, History, Language Arts, Linguistics, Law, Library & Information Sciences, Literature, Literary Criticism, Essays, Philosophy, Psychology, Psychiatry, Religion - Catholic, Religion - Protestant, Social Sciences, Sociology, Theology
ISBN Prefix(es): 978-963-276
Number of titles published annually: 200 Print

Bookshop(s): Kepiro utca 8, Budapest 1053
Tel: (01) 266-65-60
Distribution Center: Vaci ut 100, Budapest 1133

Panem Konyvkiado+
Ov u 146, Budapest 1147
Tel: (01) 460-0272 *Fax:* (01) 460-0274
E-mail: info@panem.hu; webbolt@panem.hu
Web Site: www.panem.hu
Founded: 1990
Subjects: Computer Science, Economics, Education, Engineering (General), Language Arts, Linguistics, Science (General)
ISBN Prefix(es): 978-963-545; 978-963-7628
Branch Office(s)
Delceg u 45, Budapest 1162

Pannon-Literatura Ltd, see Szalay Konyvkiado es Kereskedohaz Kft

Park Kiado Kft+
Pf 539, Budapest 1538
Tel: (01) 346-0560; (01) 346-0570 *Fax:* (01) 346-0561
E-mail: info@parkkiado.hu
Web Site: www.parkkiado.hu
Key Personnel
Chief Operating Officer: Zuleika Kuha *Tel:* (01) 346-0563 *E-mail:* kuha.zuleika@parkkiado.hu
Mng Dir: Andras Rochlitz
Commercial Dir: Attila Nagyivan *Tel:* (01) 346-0572 *Fax:* (01) 346-0572 *E-mail:* nagyivan.attila@parkkiado.hu
Marketing Manager: Harmat Eszter *Tel:* (01) 346-0567 *E-mail:* harmat.eszter@parkkiado.hu
Founded: 1989
Subjects: Art, Business, Child Care & Development, Cookery, Education, Gardening, Plants, Health, Nutrition, History, House & Home, Literature, Literary Criticism, Essays, Management, Nonfiction (General), Psychology, Psychiatry, Self-Help
ISBN Prefix(es): 978-963-530; 978-963-7737; 978-963-7970; 978-963-8227
Total Titles: 110 Print

Pecsi Tudomanyegyetem
Vasvari Pal u 4, Pecs 7622
Tel: (072) 501-500 *Fax:* (072) 501-500
E-mail: info@pte.hu; univpecs@pte.hu
Web Site: www.pte.hu; www.univpecs.pte.hu
Key Personnel
Mng Dir: Eva Harka *E-mail:* harka.eva@pte.hu
Advertising: Eszter Csizmadia
Sales: Dusan Filakovity *Tel:* (070) 209-3353
Founded: 1991
Subjects: Earth Sciences, History, Law, Management, Marketing, Philosophy, Physical Sciences, Social Sciences, Sociology
ISBN Prefix(es): 978-963-641; 978-963-642

Polgart Konyvkiado Kft+
Szent Laszlo ut 150, Budapest 1131
Tel: (01) 450-0193 *Fax:* (01) 450-0194
Founded: 1994
Provides values & guidance for the slowly developing Hungarian middle classes.
Subjects: Literature, Literary Criticism, Essays, Science (General)
ISBN Prefix(es): 978-963-9306; 978-963-85943; 978-963-86014
Subsidiaries: Polgar Video Ltd

Saldo Penzugyi Tanacsado es Informatikai Zrt+
Mor u 2-4, Budapest 1135
Mailing Address: Pf 397, 1394 Budapest 62
Tel: (01) 237-9800 *Fax:* (01) 237-9811
E-mail: inform@saldo.hu
Web Site: www.saldo.hu

Key Personnel
Chief Executive Officer: Dr Pal Bokor *Tel:* (01) 237-9810
Founded: 1959
Subjects: Accounting, Economics, Finance, Law, Public Administration
ISBN Prefix(es): 978-963-621; 978-963-638
Bookshop(s): Paulay E u 13, Budapest 1061
Tel: (01) 268-1058

Szalay Konyvkiado es Kereskedohaz Kft
Deak Ferenc ut 87, Kisujzallas 5310
Tel: (059) 322-555 *Fax:* (059) 321-444
E-mail: kiado@szalaykonyvek.hu; rendeles@szalaykonyvek.hu (orders); szalay@szalaykonyvek.hu
Web Site: www.szalaykonyvek.hu
Key Personnel
Mng Dir: Peter Szalay
Publishing Dir: Zsolt Szabo
Sales Dir: Istvan Deme
Publishing Manager: Zoltan Geczi
Rights Manager: Veronica Toth
Subjects: Cookery, Education, Gardening, Plants, How-to, Language Arts, Linguistics, Literature, Literary Criticism, Essays, Travel & Tourism
ISBN Prefix(es): 978-963-237; 978-963-85627; 978-963-9080; 978-963-9178

Szarvas Andras Cartographic Agency+
Repasy u 2 IV 27, Budapest 1149
Tel: (01) 363 0672 *Fax:* (01) 363 0672
Web Site: www.map.hu
Key Personnel
Owner: Andras Szarvas *E-mail:* szarvas.andras@map.hu
Founded: 1991
Map publishing & distribution.
Subjects: Earth Sciences, Geography, Geology, Regional Interests, Transportation, Travel & Tourism, Cartography
ISBN Prefix(es): 978-963-9251
Number of titles published annually: 10 Print
Total Titles: 25 Print

Szazadveg Politikai Iskola Adapitavany
Hidegkuti Nandor u 8-10, Budapest 1037
Tel: (01) 479-5280; (01) 479-5298 *Fax:* (01) 479-5290
E-mail: kiado@szazadveg.hu (publishing)
Web Site: www.szazadveg.hu
Key Personnel
Dir: Barthel-Ruzsa Zsolt *E-mail:* barthel-ruzsa@szazadveg.hu
Deputy Dir: Julia Varga *E-mail:* vargaj@szazadveg.hu
Chief Editor: G Fodor Gabor
Publishing Coordinator: Toth Krisztian *E-mail:* toth@szazadveg.hu
Founded: 1990
Nonpartisan, nonprofit organization financed by the contributions of its supporters & the sale of its publications & services.
Subjects: Economics, Government, Political Science, History, Law, Philosophy, Social Sciences, Sociology, Foreign policy
ISBN Prefix(es): 978-963-85619; 978-963-9211; 978-963-7340

Magyar Eszperanto Szovetseg
Thokoly u 58-60, II/209, Budapest 1146
Tel: (070) 932-74-64; (070) 953-51-79
E-mail: hungario@gmail.com
Web Site: esperantohea.hu
Key Personnel
President: Szabo Imre *E-mail:* saluton.imre@gmail.com
Subjects: Biography, Memoirs, Fiction
ISBN Prefix(es): 978-963-571

Tajak-Korok-Muzeumok Egyesuelete (TKME)
XI Kerulet, Etele ut 59-61, Budapest 1119

Tel: (020) 946-4659
E-mail: tkme@tkme.hu
Web Site: www.tkme.hu
Key Personnel
Executive Chairman: Gabor Haraszti
President: Jeno Zamola *Tel:* (030) 656-3667
Vice President: Marianna Mocsnik Korompaine *Tel:* (030) 228-1634; Janos Peczka *Tel:* (020) 538-7572
Founded: 1977
Organizes the movements which play a significant role in popularizing Hungary's natural resources, monuments & exhibitions.
Subjects: Archaeology, Architecture & Interior Design, Art, History, Natural History
ISBN Prefix(es): 978-963-554; 978-963-555

TKME, see Tajak-Korok-Muzeumok Egyesuelete (TKME)

Typotex Elektronikus Kiado Kft (Typotex Electronic Publishing Ltd)+
Retek u 33-35, Budapest 1024
Tel: (01) 315-0256 *Fax:* (01) 316-3759
E-mail: info@typotex.hu; marketing@typotex.hu
Web Site: www.typotex.hu
Key Personnel
Mng Dir: Zsuzsa Votisky *Tel:* (01) 316-2473; (030) 357-8274 (cell) *E-mail:* votisky.zsuzsa@typotex.hu
Editor-in-Chief: Balazs Horvath *Tel:* (01) 315-0498 *E-mail:* balazs@typotex.hu
Editor: Sosity Beata *Tel:* (01) 315-0256 *E-mail:* bea@typotex.hu
Sales Manager: Adam Fekete *Tel:* (070) 513-3450 (cell) *E-mail:* fekete.adam@typotex.hu
Marketing: Hajabacs Eniko *Tel:* (01) 316-3759 *E-mail:* eniko@typotex.hu
Founded: 1989
Subjects: Mathematics, Philosophy, Physics
ISBN Prefix(es): 978-963-7546; 978-963-9132; 978-963-9326
Total Titles: 100 Print
Subsidiaries: Index Buchladen
Bookshop(s): Millennium Center uzletkozpont, vaci 19-21, illetve a Pesti Barnabas u 4 felol, Budapest, Contact: Viktor Palvolgyi *Tel:* (01) 266-0018; XI Kerulet, Pazmany Peter Setany 1/a, Budapest *Tel:* (030) 308-7384

Uj Ember Kiado
Papnovelde u 7, Budapest 1053
Mailing Address: Pf 111, Budapest 1364
Tel: (01) 317-3933 *Fax:* (01) 317-3471
E-mail: ujember@ujember.hu
Web Site: www.ujember.hu
Key Personnel
Publisher & Editor: Ratkai Balazs
Mng Dir: David Ferenc
Founded: 1992
Subjects: Education, Human Relations, Religion - Catholic, Theology
ISBN Prefix(es): 978-963-7947; 978-963-9011; 978-963-9435; 978-963-7688; 978-963-9527

Magyar Tudomanyos Akademia Kozgazdasag-es Regionalis Tudomanyi Kutatokozpont Vilaggazdasagi Kutatointezet (The Institute of World Economics of the Research Centre for Economic & Regional Studies of the Hungarian Academy of Sciences)
Budaorsi u 45, Budapest 1112
Tel: (01) 309-2643 *Fax:* (01) 309-2643; (01) 319-3136
E-mail: vki@vki.hu; vki@krtk.mta.hu
Web Site: www.vki.hu
Key Personnel
Dir: Karoly Fazekas *Tel:* (01) 309-2652 *Fax:* (01) 309-2650 *E-mail:* fazekas.karoly@krtk.mta.hu
Mng Dir: Eva Nagy *E-mail:* nagyeva@vki.hu
Founded: 1973

Subjects: Economics
ISBN Prefix(es): 978-963-301

Vince Kiado Kft (Vince Books)+
Margit krt 64/b, Budapest 1027
Tel: (01) 375 7288 *Fax:* (01) 202 7145
E-mail: info@vincekiado.hu
Web Site: www.vincekiado.hu
Key Personnel
Executive Dir: Katalin Gal
Dir: Gyorgy Vince
Editor-in-Chief: Katalin Kren
Public Relations Manager: Julia Takacs Emrine
Trade Coordinator: Andrea Aranykovi
International Relations: Eszter Vince
Founded: 1991
Membership(s): Museum Store Association.
Subjects: Architecture & Interior Design, Art,
Cookery, Education, Health, Nutrition, How-
to, Law, Literature, Literary Criticism, Essays,
Music, Dance, Photography, Physical Sciences,
Psychology, Psychiatry, Travel & Tourism
ISBN Prefix(es): 978-963-7826; 978-963-9069;
978-963-9192; 978-963-9323; 978-963-9552
Distributor for Konemann; Taschen International
Bookshop(s): Szilagyi Erzsebet fasor 121, Budapest 1026 *Tel:* (01) 275-0839; (01) 275-
0310 *E-mail:* budagyongye@vincekiado.
hu; Klauzal ter 13, Budapest 1072 *Tel:* (01)
413-0731 *E-mail:* k13info@gmail.com;
Krisztina krt 34, Budapest 1013 *Tel:* (01) 375-
7682 *E-mail:* krisztinabolt@vincekiado.hu;
Jaszberenyi u 55, Budapest 1106 *Tel:* (01)
321-4133 *Fax:* (01) 321-4133 *E-mail:* raktar@
vincekiado.hu; Komor Marcell u 1, Budapest 1095 *Tel:* (01) 555-3380 *Fax:* (01)
555-3379 *E-mail:* vince@mupa.hu; Topark
u 1/a, Torokbalint 2045 *Tel:* (023) 532-667
E-mail: maxcity.vince@gmail.com

Zrinyi Kiado
Kerepesi u 29/b, Budapest 1087
Tel: (01) 459 5327 *Fax:* (01) 459 5382
Web Site: www.hmzrinyi.hu
Key Personnel
Contact: Cynthia Bartha *Tel:* (030) 633 0619
E-mail: cinti@armedia.hu; Edina Gyor
Tel: (030) 578 1048 *E-mail:* gyoredina@
armedia.hu
Publishing House of the Hungarian Army.
Subjects: Military Science, Science (General)
ISBN Prefix(es): 978-963-327; 978-963-326

Iceland

General Information

Capital: Reykjavik
Language: Icelandic (widespread knowledge of
English)
Religion: Lutheran
Population: 259,000
Bank Hours: 0915-1600 Monday-Friday (winter);
0800-1600 (summer); some open 1700-1800
Thursday
Shop Hours: 0900-1800 Monday-Thursday; 0900-
1700/1900 Friday; most open 0900-1600 Satur-
day (winter)
Currency: 100 aurar = 1 krona
Export/Import Information: Member of the Eu-
ropean Economic Area. 14% VAT on books.
Sales Tax. No import licenses required. No ex-
change controls on books but they may not be
imported on credit.
Copyright: UCC, Berne, Florence (see Copyright
Conventions, pg viii)

Bokautgafan Aeskan
Faxafeni 5, 108 Reykjavik

Tel: 530-5402 *Fax:* 530-5401
Web Site: www.aeskanbok.is
Key Personnel
Owner: Karl Helgason *E-mail:* karl@aeskanbok.is
Founded: 1930
ISBN Prefix(es): 978-9979-808; 978-9979-9395;
978-9979-9411; 978-9979-9416; 978-9979-767;
978-9979-9443; 978-9979-9472

Bjartur & Verold
Braedraborgarstig 9, 101 Reykjavik
Tel: 414 14 50
E-mail: bjartur@bjartur.is
Web Site: www.bjartur.is
Key Personnel
Publisher: Petur Mar Olafsson *E-mail:* pmo@
bjartur.is
Publishing Dir & Foreign Rights: Gudrin Vil-
mundardottir *E-mail:* gv@bjartur.is
Founded: 1990
Publish translations of world literature & contem-
porary Icelandic works.
Subjects: Biography, Memoirs, Fiction, Literature,
Literary Criticism, Essays, Nonfiction (Gen-
eral), Poetry
ISBN Prefix(es): 978-9979-865; 978-9979-9046
Associate Companies: Verold Bokaforlag

Crymogea ehf
Baronsstigur 27, 101 Reykjavik
Tel: 511 0910
E-mail: crymogea@crymogea.is
Web Site: www.crymogea.is
Key Personnel
Owner & Publishing Dir: Kristjan B Jonasson
Tel: 899 7839 (cell) *E-mail:* kbj@crymogea.is
Owner: Snaebjorn Arngrimsson
Editor: Margret Askelsdottir *Tel:* 773 6766 (cell)
E-mail: margret@crymogea.is
Founded: 2007
Subjects: Art, Photography
ISBN Prefix(es): 978-9979-9856

Forlagid+
Braedraborgarstig 7, 101 Reykjavik
Tel: 575-5600 *Fax:* 575-5601
E-mail: forlagid@forlagid.is
Web Site: www.forlagid.is
Key Personnel
Dir: Egill Orn Johannsson *E-mail:* egill@forlagid.
is
Rights Dir: Ua Matthiasdottir *E-mail:* ua@
forlagid.is
Sales Manager: Anna Gudrun *E-mail:* anna@
forlagid.is
Marketing: Solrun Samundsen *E-mail:* solrun@
forlagid.is
Founded: 1984
Subjects: Photography, Travel & Tourism
ISBN Prefix(es): 978-9979-53; 978-9979-3
Imprints: Idunn; JPV Utgafa; Mal og Menning;
Vaka Helgafell

Haskolautgafan - University of Iceland Press
Dunhagi 18, 107 Reykjavik
Tel: 525-4003
E-mail: hu@hi.is
Web Site: www.haskolautgafan.hi.is
Key Personnel
Dir: Jorundur Gudmundsson, MA *E-mail:* jorig@
hi.is
Editor: Egill Arnarson *Tel:* 525-5215
E-mail: egillarn@hi.is; Sigridur Hardardottir
Tel: 525-5420 *E-mail:* sigriduh@hi.is
Founded: 1988
Publishes English & Icelandic titles on Norse
studies.
Subjects: Computer Science, Criminology, Devel-
oping Countries, Earth Sciences, Economics,
Education, Environmental Studies, Government,
Political Science, History, Philosophy, Poetry,
Science (General)

ISBN Prefix(es): 978-9979-54
Foreign Rep(s): Casemate Academic (Canada,
USA); Oxbow Books (Europe)

Hid Islenzka Bokmenntafelag (Icelandic
Literary Society)+
Skeifan 3b, 128 Reykjavik
Tel: 588 90 60 *Fax:* 581 40 88
E-mail: hib@hib.is
Web Site: hib.is
Key Personnel
President: Sigurdur Lindal *E-mail:* lindal@hi.is
Dir: Sverrir Kristinsson
Mng Dir: Gunnar H Ingimundarsson
E-mail: bokmenntafelag@isl.is
Founded: 1816
Subjects: Art, Government, Political Science, His-
tory, Language Arts, Linguistics, Literature,
Literary Criticism, Essays, Natural History,
Psychology, Psychiatry, Social Sciences, Soci-
ology, Icelandic Art, Literature, Philosophy &
Saga
ISBN Prefix(es): 978-9979-804; 978-9979-66

Iceland Review+
Borgartun 23, 105 Reykjavik
Tel: 512-7575 *Fax:* 561-8646
E-mail: icelandreview@icelandreview.com
Web Site: www.icelandreview.com
Key Personnel
Chairman of the Board: Haraldur J Hamar
Editor: Bjarni Brynjolfsson *E-mail:* bjarni@
icelandreview.com
Founded: 1963
Subjects: Art, Literature, Literary Criticism, Es-
says, Regional Interests
ISBN Prefix(es): 978-9979-51

IDNU Bokautgafa
Brautarholti 8, 105 Reykjavik
Tel: 517 7210; 517 7200 *Fax:* 562 3497; 552
6793
E-mail: idnu@idnu.is
Web Site: www.idnu.is
Key Personnel
Dir: Disa Palsdottir *E-mail:* disa@idnu.is
Manager: Heidar Ingi Svansson *E-mail:* heidar@
idnu.is
Sales Manager: Heida Bjork Porbergsdottir
E-mail: heida@idnu.is
Editor: Volundur Oskarsson *E-mail:* volundur@
idnu.is
Founded: 1999
Publish & distribute materials for industrial, tech-
nical & vocational schools.
Subjects: Accounting, Biological Sciences, Chem-
istry, Chemical Engineering, Computer Science,
Education, Electronics, Electrical Engineering,
Fashion, Geography, Geology, Mathematics,
Physics, Social Sciences, Sociology, Sports,
Athletics, Beauty, Construction, Fitness, For-
eign Language
ISBN Prefix(es): 978-9979-67; 978-9979-806;
978-9979-830

Idunn, *imprint of* Forlagid

Idunn+
Imprint of Forlagid
Braedraborgarstig 7, 101 Reykjavik
Tel: 575 5600 *Fax:* 575 5601
E-mail: forlagid@forlagid.is
Web Site: www.forlagid.is
Founded: 1945
Subjects: Biography, Memoirs, Fiction, History,
Nonfiction (General), Poetry
ISBN Prefix(es): 978-9979-1

JPV Utgafa, *imprint of* Forlagid

Stofnun Arna Magnussonar i islenskum fraedum (Arni Magnusson Institute for Icelandic Studies)
Unit of University of Iceland
Arnagardi v/Sudurgotu, 101 Reykjavik
Tel: 525-4010 *Fax:* 525-4035
E-mail: arnastofnun@hi.is
Web Site: www.arnastofnun.is
Key Personnel
Dir: Dr Gudrun Nordal *Tel:* 525 4011
   E-mail: gnordal@hi.is
Founded: 1972
Specialize in research & publication of Icelandic manuscripts & folklore.
Subjects: History, Language Arts, Linguistics, Literature, Literary Criticism, Essays, Music, Dance, Poetry, Regional Interests
ISBN Prefix(es): 978-9979-819
Number of titles published annually: 4 Print
Total Titles: 75 Print; 2 CD-ROM
Distributed by University of Iceland Press

Mal og Menning, *imprint of* Forlagid

Mal og Menning (Language & Culture)+
Imprint of Forlagid
Braedraborgarstigor 7, 101 Reykjavik
Tel: 575 5600 *Fax:* 575 5601
E-mail: forlagid@forlagid.is
Web Site: www.forlagid.is
Key Personnel
Publisher: Johann Pall Valdimarsson
   E-mail: johann@forlagid.is
Dir: Egill Orn Johannson *E-mail:* egill@forlagid.is
Sales Manager: Anna Gudrun Gudnadottir
   E-mail: anna@forlagid.is
Foreign Rights: Ua Matthiasdottir *E-mail:* ua@forlagid.is
Founded: 1937
Subjects: Education, Fiction, Literature, Literary Criticism, Essays, Nonfiction (General), Poetry, Travel & Tourism
ISBN Prefix(es): 978-9979-3
Associate Companies: Vaka-Helgafell
Imprints: Uglan Paperback Bookclub
Subsidiaries: Heimskringla
Book Club(s): Uglan

Namsgagnastofnun (National Centre for Educational Materials)
Vikurhvarf 3, 203 Kopavogur
Mailing Address: PO Box 5020, 125 Reykjavik
Tel: 535 0400 *Fax:* 535 0401
E-mail: postur@mms.is
Web Site: www.mms.is
Key Personnel
Chief Executive Officer: Arnor Gudmundsson
   E-mail: arnor.gudmundsson@mms.is
Dir: Ingibjorg Asgeirsdottir
Editor: Tryggvi Jakobsson
Rights & Permissions: Eirikur Grimsson
Sales: Gudrun Sigudardottir
Founded: 1937
National Centre for Educational Materials is a nonprofit publishing house run by the Icelandic government.
Membership(s): International Council for Educational Media (ICEM); International Group of Educational Publishers (IGEP).
Subjects: Disability, Special Needs, Education
ISBN Prefix(es): 978-9979-0

Opna Publishing
Skipholti 50 B, 105 Reykjavik
Tel: 578 9080
E-mail: opna@opna.is
Web Site: opna.is
Key Personnel
Publisher: Sigurdur Svavarsson *Tel:* 578 9081
   E-mail: sigurdur@opna.is

Manager: Gudrun Magnusdottir *E-mail:* gudrun@opna.is
Founded: 2008
Subjects: Art, Biography, Memoirs, Literature, Literary Criticism, Essays, Social Sciences, Sociology, Travel & Tourism, Humanities
ISBN Prefix(es): 978-9935-10

Ormstunga+
Ranargotu 20, 101 Reykjavik
Tel: 561 0055
E-mail: books@ormstunga.is
Web Site: www.ormstunga.is
Key Personnel
Mng Dir: Gisli Mar Gislason
Founded: 1992
Subjects: Biography, Memoirs, Fiction, History, Literature, Literary Criticism, Essays, Nonfiction (General)
ISBN Prefix(es): 978-9979-63; 978-9979-9048

Setberg
Akralind 2, 203 Kopavogur
Tel: 551 7667
E-mail: setberg@setberg.is
Web Site: www.setberg.is
Key Personnel
Dir: Arnbjoern Kristinsson
Founded: 1952
Subjects: Cookery, Education, Fiction, Nonfiction (General)
ISBN Prefix(es): 978-9979-52

Skjaldborg Ltd+
Morkin 1, 108 Reykjavik
Tel: 588 2400 *Fax:* 588 8994
Key Personnel
Dir: Bjorn Eiriksson
Subjects: Animals, Pets, Astrology, Occult, Biography, Memoirs, Crafts, Games, Hobbies, Fiction, Gardening, Plants, How-to, Humor, Nonfiction (General)
ISBN Prefix(es): 978-9979-57
Subsidiaries: Lestrarhesturinn
Book Club(s): Lestrarhesturinn

Skrudda+
Eyjarslod 9, 101 Reykjavik
Tel: 552 8866 *Fax:* 552 8870
E-mail: skrudda@skrudda.is
Web Site: www.skrudda.is
ISBN Prefix(es): 978-9979-655; 978-9979-9184; 978-9979-9303; 978-9979-9333; 978-9979-9353; 978-9979-9399; 978-9979-9438; 978-9979-772

Bokautgafan Tindur (Tindur Publishing)
Lerkilundur 32, 600 Akureyri
Tel: 773 7300
E-mail: tindur@tindur.is
Web Site: www.tindur.is
Founded: 1989
Subjects: Biography, Memoirs, Fiction, Music, Dance, Nonfiction (General), Poetry, Science (General)
ISBN Prefix(es): 978-9979-653
Distribution Center: Fiskislod 75, 101 Reykjavik

Uglan Paperback Bookclub, *imprint of* Mal og Menning

Vaka Helgafell, *imprint of* Forlagid

India

General Information

Capital: New Delhi
Language: Hindi & English are used for official purposes. Seventeen regional languages are accorded recognition by the constitution. Generally each administrative state includes speakers of a particular major language. In all, over 1500 languages & dialects are spoken
Religion: Predominantly Hindu, some Muslims (about 11%)
Population: 886.4 million
Bank Hours: 1000-1400 (1100-1500 Mumbai) Monday-Friday; 1000-1200 (1100-1300 Mumbai) Saturday
Shop Hours: Delhi: 0930-1930; Kolkata & Mumbai: 1000-1830; Chennai: 0900-1930. All effective Monday-Saturday, some open Sunday. Many close 2 hours for lunch
Currency: 100 paise = 1 Indian rupee
Export/Import Information: No tariff on books but advertising matter is dutied. Import licenses required. Educational books may be imported by booksellers under open general license. Exchange transactions restricted.
Copyright: UCC, Berne, Buenos Aires (see Copyright Conventions, pg viii)

Aadarsh Pvt Ltd
Shikhar Varta 4, Press Complex, MP Nagar, Zone 1, Bhopal 462 011
Tel: (0755) 2555442; (0755) 4270555 *Fax:* (0755) 2555449
E-mail: info@aadarsh.com; info@purpleturtle.com
Web Site: aadarsh.com; www.purpleturtle.com
Founded: 1989
ISBN Prefix(es): 978-93-81070; 978-93-81592
Imprints: Purple Turtle

Aarti Books, *imprint of* Spectrum Publications

Abhinav Publications+
E-37 Hauz Khas, New Delhi 110 016
Tel: (011) 26566387; (011) 26524658 *Fax:* (011) 26857009
E-mail: info@abhinavexports.com
Web Site: www.abhinavexports.com; www.abhinavpublications.net
Key Personnel
Contact: Abhinav Malik *E-mail:* abhinav@abhinavexports.com; Ateev Malik
   E-mail: ateev@abhinavexports.com
Founded: 1972
Subjects: Anthropology, Archaeology, Architecture & Interior Design, Art, Criminology, Drama, Theater, Economics, Ethnicity, Government, Political Science, History, Human Relations, Literature, Literary Criticism, Essays, Music, Dance, Philosophy, Religion - Other, Social Sciences, Sociology
ISBN Prefix(es): 978-81-7017
Number of titles published annually: 18 Print; 13 E-Book
Total Titles: 480 Print; 13 E-Book
Distribution Center: A1 Books, 35 Love Lane, Netcong, NJ 07857, United States (USA)

Abhishek Publications
SCO 57-59, Sector 17-C, Chandigarh 160 017
Tel: (0172) 5003768 *Fax:* (0172) 2707562
E-mail: contact@abhishekpublications.com; editorial@abhishekpublications.com (publishing); sales@abhishekpublications.com (sales)
Web Site: www.abhishekpublications.com
Key Personnel
Publisher & Dir: Bharat Bhushan

E-mail: bharatbhushan@abhishekpublications.
com
Manager: Vaibhav Mehndiratta *E-mail:* vaibhav@
abhishekpublications.com
Founded: 1977
Subjects: Architecture & Interior Design, Govern-
ment, Political Science, History, Management,
Philosophy
ISBN Prefix(es): 978-81-85733; 978-81-8247;
978-81-88988; 978-81-89916
Associate Companies: Nirjhar Prakashan, 3625
Sector 23-D, Chandigarh 160 023
Branch Office(s)
7/10, Ansari Rd, Darya Ganj, New Delhi

Academic Foundation
4772-73/23 Bharat Ram Rd, Darya Ganj, New
Delhi 110 002
Tel: (011) 23245001 *Fax:* (011) 23245005
E-mail: books@academicfoundation.com
Web Site: www.academicfoundation.com
Subjects: Anthropology, Economics, Education,
Environmental Studies, Fiction, Finance, Gov-
ernment, Political Science, History, Language
Arts, Linguistics, Literature, Literary Criticism,
Essays, Banking, Indian Economy
ISBN Prefix(es): 978-81-7188

Academic India Publishers
Unit of Angel Publishing House
508 Rattan Jyoti Bldg, 18, Rajendra Pl, New
Delhi 110 008
Tel: (011) 25742171; (011) 25812181 *Fax:* (011)
25722671
E-mail: academic@airtelmail.in
Web Site: www.academicindiapublishers.com
Subjects: Art, Crafts, Games, Hobbies, Education,
Literature, Literary Criticism, Essays, Science
(General), Self-Help, Foreign Language, Gram-
mer
ISBN Prefix(es): 978-81-85185; 978-81-88385

The Academic Press+
887/5, St No 6, Patel Nagar, Gurgaon, Haryana
122 001
Tel: (0124) 2324782 *Fax:* (0124) 2324782
E-mail: indocu@gmail.com
Key Personnel
Dir: Ankur Jain *E-mail:* pancuj@gmail.com
Editorial: Pankaj Jain
Sales, Rights & Permissions: Gautam Jain
Founded: 1968
Subjects: History, Human Relations, Philosophy,
Religion - Other, Social Sciences, Sociology
ISBN Prefix(es): 978-81-85260
Total Titles: 40 Print

Academic Publishers
5A Bhawani Dutta Lane, Kolkata 700 073
Tel: (033) 2257-1071
E-mail: info@acabooks.net; sales@acabooks.net
Web Site: www.acabooks.net
Founded: 1958
Subjects: Accounting, Biological Sciences, Busi-
ness, Chemistry, Chemical Engineering, Eco-
nomics, Management, Mathematics, Medicine,
Nursing, Dentistry, Physics
ISBN Prefix(es): 978-81-86358; 978-81-85086;
978-81-87504
Distributed by UBS Publishers' Distributors Pvt
Ltd (outside Kolkata)

Advaita Ashrama
5 Dehi Entally Rd, Kolkata 700 014
Tel: (033) 22840210; (033) 22866483; (033)
22890898; (033) 22866450
E-mail: mail@advaitaashrama.org
Web Site: www.advaitaashrama.org; www.
advaitaonline.com
Key Personnel
Manager: Swami Vibhatmananda

Founded: 1899
Publication department of Ramakrishina Math &
Ramakrishna Mission.
Subjects: Art, Inspirational, Spirituality, Philos-
ophy, Religion - Hindu, Bhagavad Gita, Com-
parative Religion, Hindu Scriptures, Human
Development, Mimamsa, Patanjali Yoga Su-
tras, Personality Development, Upanishads &
Vedanta
ISBN Prefix(es): 978-81-85301; 978-81-7505
Number of titles published annually: 20 Print; 2
CD-ROM; 50 E-Book
Total Titles: 450 Print; 15 CD-ROM; 100 E-Book
Parent Company: Ramakrishna Math, PO Belur
Math, Howrah 711 202
Distributed by Ramakrishna Vedanta Cen-
tre (UK); Vedanta Press & Catalog (USA);
Vedanta Society of Southern California (USA);
Vivekananda Vedanta Society (USA)

Affiliated East-West Press Pvt Ltd+
G-116, Ansari Rd, Darya Ganj, New Delhi 110
002
Tel: (011) 23264180; (011) 23279113 *Fax:* (011)
23260538
E-mail: aewp.pub@gmail.com
Web Site: www.aewpress.com
Key Personnel
Owner: Sunny Malik
Founded: 1962
Membership(s): Delhi State Booksellers' & Pub-
lishers' Association; Federation of Indian Pub-
lishers; Federation of Publishers' & Book-
sellers' Associations of India (FPBAI).
Subjects: Aeronautics, Aviation, Agriculture, An-
thropology, Biological Sciences, Chemistry,
Chemical Engineering, Civil Engineering,
Computer Science, Computers, Economics,
Electronics, Electrical Engineering, Environ-
mental Studies, Geography, Geology, Manage-
ment, Mathematics, Mechanical Engineering,
Physical Sciences, Physics, Poetry, Psychol-
ogy, Psychiatry, Science (General), Veterinary
Science, Women's Studies
ISBN Prefix(es): 978-81-85095; 978-81-85336;
978-81-85938; 978-81-7671
Imprints: EWP
Distributor for American Association of
Petroleum Geologists; American Ceramic So-
ciety; American Society for Photogrammetry
& Remote Sensing; Conveyor Equipment Man-
ufacturers Association; Coxmoor Publishing;
Geological Society Publishing House; Horwood
Publishing; Society for Mining, Metallurgy &
Exploration; Society of Manufacturing Engi-
neers; TAPPI Press; Technomic Publishing

Agam Kala Prakashan
34 Central Market, Ashok Vihar, New Delhi 110
052
Tel: (011) 27212195; (011) 65688806-07
Fax: (011) 27212195
E-mail: agambooks@gmail.com
Web Site: www.agamkala.com
Founded: 1977
Membership(s): Intach.
Subjects: Anthropology, Antiques, Archaeology,
Art, Asian Studies, Earth Sciences, History,
Language Arts, Linguistics
ISBN Prefix(es): 978-81-85415; 978-81-7186;
978-81-7320
Associate Companies: Agam Prakashan; Rahul
Publishing House; Swati Publication
Distributed by Munshiram Manoharlal Pvt Ltd;
UBS Publishers' Distributors Pvt Ltd
Distributor for Rahul Publishing House; Swati
Publications

Ahuja Book Co Pvt Ltd
4348-C Madan Mohan St, Ansari Rd, Darya
Ganj, New Delhi 110 002

Tel: (011) 23245859; (011) 23276564; (011)
23289999 *Fax:* (011) 23281514
Web Site: www.ahujabooks.com
Founded: 1982
Also distributor.
Subjects: Agriculture, Architecture & Interior De-
sign, Chemistry, Chemical Engineering, Civil
Engineering, Computer Science, Electronics,
Electrical Engineering, Environmental Stud-
ies, Geography, Geology, Management, Math-
ematics, Mechanical Engineering, Medicine,
Nursing, Dentistry, Social Sciences, Sociology,
Sports, Athletics, Veterinary Science, Agricul-
tural Science, Biomechanics, Environmental
Science, Histology
ISBN Prefix(es): 978-81-901769; 978-81-89443;
978-81-7619
Branch Office(s)
616, 4th Main, Pipeline, Srinagar, Bangalore 560
050 *Tel:* (080) 26670322; (080) 26670323
Fax: (080) 26670321 *E-mail:* blr@ahujabooks.
com
No 41/2897, First floor, St Vincent Rd, Er-
nakulam 682 018 *Tel:* (0484) 4031078
E-mail: kochi@ahujabooks.com

AITBS Publishers
J-5/6, Krishan Nagar, Delhi 110 051
Tel: (011) 22009084; (011) 22009096 *Fax:* (011)
22009074
E-mail: aitbs@bol.net.in; aitbsindia@gmail.com
Web Site: www.aitbspublishersindia.com
Founded: 1983
Subjects: Economics, Engineering (General), Lit-
erature, Literary Criticism, Essays, Manage-
ment, Mathematics, Medicine, Nursing, Den-
tistry, English Literature
ISBN Prefix(es): 978-81-7473; 978-81-85386

Ajanta Publications+
S-417, Greater Kailash-I, New Delhi 110 048
Tel: (011) 23234749; (011) 32545527; (011)
43081977; 9811185527 (cell) *Fax:* (011)
23221114
E-mail: enquiry@ajantapublications.com
Web Site: www.ajantapublications.com
Key Personnel
Chief Executive: Harsh Arora
E-mail: harsharora@ajantapublications.com
Founded: 1980
Also acts as academic/general/literary agent &
printer.
Membership(s): Federation of Indian Publishers
(FIP).
Subjects: Anthropology, Archaeology, Art, Eth-
nicity, Government, Political Science, Language
Arts, Linguistics, Literature, Literary Criticism,
Essays, Management, Philosophy, Public Ad-
ministration, Religion - Other, Social Sciences,
Sociology
ISBN Prefix(es): 978-81-202
Parent Company: Ajanta Books International,
One UB Jawahar Nagar, Bangalow Rd, New
Delhi 110 007

Aleph Book Co
161, B-4, Ground floor, Gulmohar House, Yusuf
Sarai Community Centre, New Delhi 110 049
E-mail: info@alephbookcompany.com; sales@
alephbookcompany.com
Web Site: www.alephbookcompany.com
Key Personnel
Publisher & Co-Founder: David Davidar
Founded: 2011
Subjects: Biography, Memoirs, Business, Envi-
ronmental Studies, Fiction, History, Nonfiction
(General), Philosophy, Pop Culture, Travel &
Tourism, Current Events, Nature Studies, Popu-
lar Science
ISBN Prefix(es): 978-93-83064; 978-93-82277

Allied Publishers Pvt Ltd+
1/13-14 Asaf Ali Rd, New Delhi 110 002
Tel: (011) 2323 9001; (011) 2323 3002
E-mail: editorials@alliedpublishers.com;
printdiv@alliedpublishers.com
Web Site: www.alliedpublishers.com
Key Personnel
Dir: Mr R N Purwar *Tel:* 9810114020 (cell)
E-mail: rnpurwar@alliedpublishers.com
Mng Dir: Mr Sunil Sachdev *Tel:* (011) 2323 5967
Dir, Allied Printing Division: Mr Ravi Sachdev
Tel: (011) 2811 3682
Sales Dir: Mr Amit Sachdev
E-mail: amitsachdev@alliedpublishers.com
Publishing Mgr: Ms Tripti Singh *Tel:* (011) 4184
5190 *Fax:* (011) 2811 6584
Export Manager: Satish Kumar
Founded: 1934
Subjects: Agriculture, Behavioral Sciences, Computer Science, Economics, Education, Electronics, Electrical Engineering, Energy, Engineering (General), Government, Political Science, Health, Nutrition, Management, Marketing, Mechanical Engineering, Medicine, Nursing, Dentistry, Physical Sciences
ISBN Prefix(es): 978-81-7023; 978-81-7764
Parent Company: Allied Publishers Group
Associate Companies: Allied Chambers (India) Ltd; Allied Publishers Subscription Agency, Contact: Mr Rajinder K Kanjhlia
Tel: (0120) 252 5916 *Fax:* (0120) 251 6099
E-mail: kanjhlia@alliedpublishers.com *Web Site:* www.apsaonline.net
Branch Office(s)
F/1, Sun House, 1st floor, CG Rd, Ahmedabad 380 006, Sales Manager: Mr D C Khopker
Tel: (079) 2646 5916 *E-mail:* ahmbd.books@alliedpublishers.com
The Hebbar Sreevaishnava Sabha, Sudarshan Complex-2, No 22, Seshadri Rd, Bangalore 560 009, Branch Manager: Mr P Chandrashekar *Tel:* (080) 2226 2081 *E-mail:* bngl.books@alliedpublishers.com
751, Anna Salai, Chennai 600 002, Branch Manager: Mr S Ramdos *Tel:* (044) 2852 3938
E-mail: chennai.books@alliedpublishers.com
3-2-844/6 & 7, Kachiguda Station Rd, Hyderabad 500 027, Branch Manager: Mr L Vasanthakrishnan *Tel:* (040) 2461 9079 *E-mail:* hyd.books@alliedpublishers.com
17, Chittaranjan Ave, Kolkata 700 072, Branch Manager: Mr Jatinder Sachdev *Tel:* (033) 2212 9618 *E-mail:* cal.books@alliedpublishers.com
87/4, Chander Nagar, Alambagh, Lucknow 226 005, Manager: Mr Atul Srivastava *Tel:* (0522) 4012850 *E-mail:* appltdlko9@gmail.com
15, JN Heredia Marg, Dubash House, Ballard Estate, Mumbai 400 001, Branch Manager: Mr A George *Tel:* (022) 4212 6969 *E-mail:* mumbai.books@alliedpublishers.com
Shiv Sundar Apartments, Ground floor, 60 Bajaj Nagar, Central Bazar Rd, Nagpur 440 010, Branch Manager: Mr Pradeep Parashar
Tel: (0712) 2234210 *E-mail:* ngp.books@alliedpublishers.com

Ambar Prakashan+
888 East Park Rd, Karol Bagh, New Delhi 110 005
Tel: (011) 7770067; (011) 522997; (011) 7525528
Fax: (011) 7776058
Founded: 1977
Subjects: Education, English as a Second Language, Mathematics, Science (General)
ISBN Prefix(es): 978-81-7289
Total Titles: 100 Print
Parent Company: Pitambar Publishing Co Pvt Ltd
Distributed by Pitambar Publishing Co Pvt Ltd

Ameya Prakashan+
207, Business Guild, Law College Rd, Pune 411 004
Tel: (020) 25457571

E-mail: ameyaprakashan@gmail.com
Web Site: www.ameyainspiringbooks.com
Key Personnel
Publisher: Ulhas Latkar *E-mail:* latkarulhas@gmail.com
Founded: 1993
Membership(s): Federation of Indian Publishers.
Subjects: Biography, Memoirs, How-to, Social Sciences, Sociology, Travel & Tourism
ISBN Prefix(es): 978-81-86172
Number of titles published annually: 24 Print
Total Titles: 128 Print

Ananda Publishers Pvt Ltd+
45, Beniatola Lane, Kolkata 700 009
Tel: (033) 22414352; (033) 22413417 *Fax:* (033) 22193856
E-mail: ananda@cal3.vsnl.net.in;
anandapublishers@gmail.com
Founded: 1957
Subjects: Anthropology, Art, Biography, Memoirs, Cookery, Drama, Theater, Economics, Fiction, Finance, Gardening, Plants, History, Music, Dance, Mysteries, Suspense, Philosophy, Photography, Poetry, Psychology, Psychiatry, Science (General), Science Fiction, Fantasy, Social Sciences, Sociology, Sports, Athletics
ISBN Prefix(es): 978-81-7215; 978-81-7066; 978-81-7756
Orders to: Ruposhi Bangla Ltd, 220, Tooting Hight St, London SW17 OSG, United Kingdom *Tel:* (020) 8672 7843 *Fax:* (020) 8672 9214 *E-mail:* ruposhi@freenetname.co.uk

Ane Books Pvt Ltd
4821 Parwana Bhawan, 24 Ansari Rd, Darya Ganj, New Delhi 110 002
Tel: (011) 23276843; (011) 23276844 *Fax:* (011) 23276863
Web Site: www.anebooks.com
Key Personnel
Chief Executive Officer: Jai Raj Kapoor
E-mail: kapoor@anebooks.com
Dir: Sunil Saxena
General Manager, South: A Rathinam
Regional Manager, West: T M Mathew
Founded: 1997
Subjects: Architecture & Interior Design, Biological Sciences, Economics, Engineering (General), Finance, Human Relations, Management, Medicine, Nursing, Dentistry, Physical Sciences, Social Sciences, Sociology, Training
ISBN Prefix(es): 978-81-8052
Branch Office(s)
Avantika Niwas, 19, Doraiswamy Rd, 1st floor, T Nagar, Chennai, Tamil Nadu 600 017 *Tel:* (044) 28141554; (044) 42127568
E-mail: anebookschennai@gmail.com
138, Chandan Chambers, 1st floor, Off No 3, Modi St Fort, Mumbai, Maharashtra 400 001 *Tel:* (022) 22622440; (022) 22622441
E-mail: anebooksmum@gmail.com

Ankur Publishing Co
C-1, Anandvan, Anandpark, Thane, Maharashtra, Mumbai 400 601
Tel: (022) 25369907; (022) 25432817 *Fax:* (022) 543 2817
Key Personnel
Contact: Chandrashekhar Salvi
Founded: 1990
Subjects: Government, Political Science, Literature, Literary Criticism, Essays, Science (General)
ISBN Prefix(es): 978-81-85043
Associate Companies: Sanjay Composers & Printers, Uphar Cinema Bldg, Green Park Ext, New Delhi 110 016

Anmol Publications Pvt Ltd+
4360/4, Ansari Rd, Darya Ganj, New Delhi 110 002

Tel: (011) 23255577; (011) 23261597; (011) 23278000 *Fax:* (011) 23280289
E-mail: info@anmolpublications.com;
anmolpub@gmail.com
Web Site: www.anmolpublications.com
Key Personnel
Mng Dir: J L Kumar
Dir of Sales & Production: Ashish Kumar
Founded: 1984
Subjects: Education, Environmental Studies, Geography, Geology, Library & Information Sciences, Management, Science (General), Social Sciences, Sociology, Women's Studies
ISBN Prefix(es): 978-81-7041; 978-81-7488; 978-81-261
Number of titles published annually: 500 Print
Branch Office(s)
No 1015, First Main Rd, BSK 3rd Stage, 3rd Phase, 3rd Block, Bangalore 560 085 *Tel:* (080) 41723429; 9845518763 (cell) *Fax:* (080) 26723604
E-mail: anmolpublicationsbangalore@gmail.com

APH Publishing Corp, see Ashish Publishing House

Arihant Publishers+
Kalindi Colony, Transport Nagar, Meerut, Uttar Pradesh 250 002
Tel: (0121) 4004199; (0121) 2401479
E-mail: info@arihantbooks.com
Web Site: www.arihantbooks.com
Key Personnel
Chairman: Mr Yogesh C Jain
Founded: 1997
Subjects: Biological Sciences, Education, Human Relations, Social Sciences, Sociology
ISBN Prefix(es): 978-81-7230
Subsidiaries: Arihant Edu Web Pvt Ltd; Arihant Media Promoters; Arihant Prakashan; Arihant Print Solution; Arihant Publications (India) Ltd
Branch Office(s)
8/195, New Engineering's Colony, Kaushalpur, Agra 282 005 *Tel:* (0562) 4045596
E-mail: agra.arihant@gmail.com
Door No 362, 1st floor, 10 Main, 2 Cross, Basveshbwara, Bangalore 560 079 *Tel:* (080) 42060560 *E-mail:* arihant_bangalore@yahoo.co.in
14, Sahid Nagar, Bhubaneswar 751 007
Tel: 09938211103; (064) 2503050
E-mail: bbsrarihant7@gmail.com
21 Motilal Nehru Rd, Guwahati 781 001 *Tel:* (088) 11908717
E-mail: arihant_guwahati@yahoo.co.in
Raja Enterprises, Varun Complex, Rampur Rd, Haldwani 263 139 *Tel:* (05946) 235456
E-mail: arihant_kashipur@yahoo.co.in
R R & Sons Complex, Silver Sand-1, H No 2-3-, 692/1/8/1/A, Durga Nagar, Main Rd, Amberpet, Hyderabad 500 013 *Tel:* (040) 65347774
E-mail: hyd.arihant@gmail.com
C-8, Link Rd, Jalupura, MI Rd, Near Hotel, Apporva, Jaipur 302 001 *Tel:* (0141) 4033077
E-mail: arihant.jaipurbranch@gmail.com
5 Princep Lane, Kolkata 700 072 *Tel:* (033) 65400560
5-J-18, Talwandi, Kota 324 009 *Tel:* (0744) 2406760 *E-mail:* arihant_kota@yahoo.co.in
C-22, Vijay Laxmi Transport Bldg, Transport Nagar, Kanpur Rd, Lucknow 226 012
Tel: (0522) 6459009 *Fax:* (0522) 4028575
E-mail: arihant_lko@yahoo.com
Plot No 27, Nathu Ji Pise Complex, New Gate, Great Nag Rd, Nagpur 440 003 *Tel:* (0712) 6464499 *E-mail:* arihant_nagpur1@yahoo.co.in
Basement, 4577/15, Ramchhaya, Agarwal Rd, Darya Ganj, New Delhi 110 002 *Tel:* (011) 47630600 *E-mail:* arihant.delhi1@gmail.com
Gangotri Complex, U/465, Lohia Nagar, Kankarbagh, Patna 800 020 *Tel:* (0612)

2360623 *E-mail:* arihant.patnabranch@gmail. com
6/2, 1st floor, Balwant Bldg, Hamal Panchayat, Bhawani Peth, Pune 411 002 *Tel:* (020) 32399292 *E-mail:* arihantpublication.pune@ gmail.com

Arya (Medi) Publishing House Pvt Ltd
4805/24 Bharat Ram Rd, Darya Ganj, New Delhi 110 002
Tel: (011) 23274004; (011) 23277444; (011) 30124004; 7838456224 (cell)
E-mail: mail@aryamedipublishing.com; aryamedi@bol.net.in
Web Site: aryamedipublishing.com
Key Personnel
Publisher: Mr Sudhir Kumar Arya
Founded: 1980
Subjects: Medicine, Nursing, Dentistry
ISBN Prefix(es): 978-81-7063; 978-81-7064; 978-81-86809

Ashish Publishing House+
5 Ansari Rd, Darya Ganj, New Delhi 110 002
Tel: (011) 23285807; (011) 23274050 *Fax:* (011) 23274050
E-mail: aphbooks@vsnl.net
Founded: 1974
Also acts as distributor.
Membership(s): Federation of Indian Publishers.
Subjects: Accounting, Agriculture, Archaeology, Architecture & Interior Design, Biography, Memoirs, Chemistry, Chemical Engineering, Criminology, Economics, Education, Energy, Environmental Studies, Ethnicity, Fiction, Geography, Geology, Government, Political Science, Health, Nutrition, History, Labor, Industrial Relations, Law, Library & Information Sciences, Management, Marketing, Natural History, Philosophy, Public Administration, Religion - Hindu, Religion - Islamic, Religion - Other, Science (General), Social Sciences, Sociology, Travel & Tourism, Women's Studies
ISBN Prefix(es): 978-81-7024; 978-81-7648
Number of titles published annually: 100 Print
Total Titles: 1,200 Print
Branch Office(s)
8/81, Punjabi Bagh, New Delhi 110 026
Distributed by UBS Publishers' Distributors Pvt Ltd

Asia Pacific Business Press Inc+
c/o National Institute of Industrial Research, 106-E, Kamla Nagar, New Delhi 110 007
Tel: (011) 23843955; (011) 23845886; (011) 23845654 *Fax:* (011) 23841561
E-mail: npcs.india@gmail.com; apbp.books@ gmail.com; info@apbp-techbooks.com
Web Site: www.niir.org
Key Personnel
Chief Executive Officer & President: Mr Ajay Kr Gupta
Founded: 2000
Subjects: Business, Chemistry, Chemical Engineering, Science (General), Technology
ISBN Prefix(es): 978-81-7833
Number of titles published annually: 50 Print
Distributed by National Institute of Industrial Research

Asian Educational Services+
RZ 256, St No 19, Tughalakabad Ext, New Delhi 110 019
Tel: (011) 29992586; (011) 29994059 *Fax:* (011) 29994946
E-mail: aes@aes.ind.in
Web Site: www.aes.ind.in
Key Personnel
Publisher: Mr Gautam Jetley *E-mail:* gautam@ aes.ind.in
Chief Financial Officer: Mr Gaurav Jetley
Publicity, Rights & Permissions: Mrs Saroj Jetley

Founded: 1973
Specialize in limited edition antiquarian reprints of books first published between the 17th & early 20th centuries.
Membership(s): Federation of Indian Publishers.
Subjects: Anthropology, Archaeology, Asian Studies, Astrology, Occult, Biography, Memoirs, Ethnicity, History, Language Arts, Linguistics, Military Science, Music, Dance, Natural History, Philosophy, Religion - Buddhist, Religion - Hindu, Religion - Islamic, Religion - Other, Social Sciences, Sociology, Theology, Travel & Tourism
ISBN Prefix(es): 978-81-206
Number of titles published annually: 39 Print
Total Titles: 1,100 Print
Branch Office(s)
19, (New No 40), First St, Balaji Nagar, Royapettah, Chennai 600 014, Branch Manager: Mr Walajapet Jagannathan Surresh *Tel:* (044) 28133040; 9382293487 (cell) *Fax:* (044) 28131391 *E-mail:* asianeds@md3.vsnl.net.in
Showroom(s): 2/15, 2nd floor, Ansari Rd, Darya Ganj, New Delhi 110 002, Contact: Mr Binu Prabhakaran *Tel:* (011) 23262044 *E-mail:* aesdg@aes.ind.in

Asian Trading Corp+
No 58, Second Cross, Da Costa Layout, St Mary's Town, Bangalore 560 084
Mailing Address: PO Box 8444, Bangalore 560 084
Tel: (080) 25487444 *Fax:* (080) 25479444
E-mail: info@atcbooks.in; atcbooks@gmail.com
Web Site: www.atcbooks.in
Founded: 1946
Also bookseller, exporter & importer.
Subjects: Communications, Philosophy, Religion - Other, Social Sciences, Sociology, Theology
ISBN Prefix(es): 978-81-7086
Number of titles published annually: 40 Print
Total Titles: 750 Print
Branch Office(s)
DVK Central Library, Hosur Rd, Bangalore 560 029 *Tel:* (080) 41116354
St Anthony's Friary Church, Madiwala, Bangalore 560 095, Contact: Arvind Frank
Paalanaa Bhavana, Pastoral Centre, Archbishop's House, Bangalore, Contact: Justin Mario Raj
Distributor for Abingdon; ATF Press (Australia); Augsburg Fortress; Eerdmans; Liturgical Press; Orbis Books

Atma Ram & Sons
1376 Kashmere Gate, New Delhi 110 006
Tel: (011) 23973082; (011) 23946466
Key Personnel
Sales: Ashutosh Pury
Contact: Sudhir Puri
Founded: 1909
Subjects: Art, Education, Engineering (General), History, How-to, Medicine, Nursing, Dentistry, Philosophy, Science (General), Social Sciences, Sociology, Technology
ISBN Prefix(es): 978-81-7043
Branch Office(s)
17 Ashok Marg, Lucknow

Authorspress
E-35, Jawahar Park, Laxmi Nagar, New Delhi 110 092
Tel: 9818049852 (cell)
E-mail: authorspress@rediffmail.com; authorspress@hotmail.com
Web Site: www.authorspressbooks.com
This publisher has indicated that 50% of their product line is author subsidized.
Subjects: Asian Studies, Computer Science, Economics, Education, Finance, History, Journalism, Library & Information Sciences, Philosophy, Religion - Islamic, Social Sciences, Sociology, Technology, Women's Studies

ISBN Prefix(es): 978-81-7273
Number of titles published annually: 100 Print
Total Titles: 1,200 Print

K P Bagchi & Co+
286 BB, Ganguli St, Bow Bazaar, Kolkata 700 012
Tel: (033) 22367474; (033) 22369496 *Fax:* (033) 22369496
E-mail: kpbagchi@hotmail.com
Key Personnel
Co-Owner & Founder: Parimal Kumar Bagchi
Editorial, Sales, Production: K K Bagchi
Founded: 1972
Subjects: Anthropology, Economics, Government, Political Science, History, Language Arts, Linguistics, Literature, Literary Criticism, Essays, Social Sciences, Sociology
ISBN Prefix(es): 978-81-7074
Number of titles published annually: 15 Print
Total Titles: 250 Print

Baha'i Publishing Trust of India+
F-3/6, Okhla Industrial Area, Phase-I, New Delhi 110 020
Tel: (011) 40523382
Web Site: www.bahaipublishingtrust.in
Key Personnel
General Manager: Arun Sinha
Founded: 1954
Subjects: Education, Religion - Other, Social Sciences, Sociology
ISBN Prefix(es): 978-81-85091; 978-81-7896; 978-81-86953
Parent Company: National Spiritual Assembly of the Baha'is of India, 6-Shrimant Madhavrao Scindia Marg, New Delhi 110 001
U.S. Office(s): Baha'i Publishing Trust, 401 Greenleaf Ave, Wilmette, IL 60091, United States

The Bangalore Press, see The Bangalore Printing & Publishing Co Ltd

The Bangalore Printing & Publishing Co Ltd+
88, Mysore Rd, Bangalore 560 018
Tel: (080) 26709638; (080) 26709027
E-mail: bangalorepress@gmail.com
Web Site: www.bangalorepress.com
Key Personnel
Mng Dir: H R Ananth
Founded: 1916
Membership(s): Federation of Indian Publishers.
Subjects: Agriculture, Biography, Memoirs, Fiction, Health, Nutrition, Philosophy, Psychology, Psychiatry, Religion - Other, Social Sciences, Sociology
ISBN Prefix(es): 978-81-87145
Distributed by UBS Publishers' Distributors Pvt Ltd (India)

Bani Mandir+
917/36, Panbazar, Guwahati 781 001
Tel: (0361) 520241; (0361) 513886
Key Personnel
Founder & Chief Executive: Chandra Kanta Hazarika
Editorial, Rights & Permissions: Surjya Kanta Hazarika
Publicity: Utpal Kumar Hazarika
Sales: Ujjal Kumar Hazarika
Founded: 1949
Also booksellers & educational suppliers.
Membership(s): Federation of Indian Booksellers & Publishers Association; Federation of Indian Publishers.
Subjects: Anthropology, Biological Sciences, Chemistry, Chemical Engineering, Cookery, Economics, Education, Environmental Studies, Ethnicity
ISBN Prefix(es): 978-81-7206
Subsidiaries: Chandra Kanta Press Pvt Ltd

BBA, see Bharat Books & Arts

Bharat Books & Arts
Subsidiary of Purple Peacock Books & Arts Pvt Ltd
119, Lake Terrace, 3rd floor, Kolkata 700 029
Tel: (033) 2466 2309 *Fax:* (033) 3292 1756
E-mail: purplepeacockbooks@gmail.com
Web Site: www.bharatbooks.com
Key Personnel
Contact: Ketaki Dutt-Paul
Founded: 2000
Publisher, bookseller & art seller.
Subjects: Asian Studies, History, Inspirational, Spirituality, Language Arts, Linguistics, English Language Training (ELT)
ISBN Prefix(es): 978-81-88908
Number of titles published annually: 6 Print
Total Titles: 13 Print

Bharat Law House Pvt Ltd+
T-1/95, Mangolpuri Industrial Area, Phase 1, New Delhi 110 083
Tel: (011) 27910001; (011) 27910002; (011) 27910003
Web Site: www.bharatlaws.com
Founded: 1957
Subjects: Law
ISBN Prefix(es): 978-81-85224; 978-81-7737; 978-81-7733
Branch Office(s)
Shop 6, 1st floor, Amar Towers 1, First Cross, Gandhinagar, Bangalore 560 009 *Tel:* (080) 2263434
Showroom(s): 4779/23 Ansari Rd, Darya Ganj, New Delhi 110 002 *Tel:* (011) 3275884; (011) 3278282

Bharat Publishing House+
123 Durga Chambers, Desh Bandhu Gupta Rd, Anand Parbat, New Delhi 110 005
Tel: (011) 2875081
Membership(s): Federation of Indian Publishers.
Subjects: Geography, Geology, Language Arts, Linguistics, Mathematics, Physics, Science (General)
ISBN Prefix(es): 978-81-86378; 978-81-7692
Foreign Rep(s): S Rattan (Middle East)

Bharatiya Vidya Bhavan
Munshi Sadan, Bharatiya Vidya Bhavan Chowk, Kulapati K M Munshi Marg, 4th floor, Mumbai 400 007
Tel: (022) 23631261; (022) 23630265; (022) 23634462; (022) 23634463; (022) 23634464
Fax: (022) 23630058
E-mail: bhavan@bhavans.info
Web Site: www.bhavans.info
Key Personnel
President: Surendralal Mehta
Vice President: Murli S Deora; B N Srikrishna
Executive Secretary & Dir General: H N Dastur
Founded: 1938
Subjects: Art, Biography, Memoirs, Ethnicity, Fiction, History, Literature, Literary Criticism, Essays, Philosophy, Religion - Other, Social Sciences, Sociology
ISBN Prefix(es): 978-81-7276
U.S. Office(s): 305 Seventh Ave, 17th floor, New York, NY 10001, United States *Tel:* 212-989-8383; 212-989-5764 *Fax:* 212-989-6482
E-mail: bhavanus@hotmail.com
Bookshop(s): Agartala; Allahabad; Bangalore; Bhopal; Bhubaneswar; Chandigarh; Chennai; Chhattisgarh; Gujarat; Hyderabad; Jaipur; Kochi; Kolkata; New Delhi; 4-A Castletown Rd, London W14 9HQ, United Kingdom *Tel:* (020) 7381 3086; (020) 7381 4608 *Fax:* (020) 7381 8758 *E-mail:* info@bhavan.net

BHGA, see Bihar Hindi Granth Academy (BHGA)

Bi Publications Pvt Ltd+
Member of Bi Group
Link House, 3, Bhadhur Shah Zafar Marg, New Delhi 110 002
Tel: (011) 46209999 *Fax:* (011) 23323138
E-mail: contactus@bipgroup.com
Web Site: www.bipgroup.com
Key Personnel
Chairman: Shashank Bhagat *E-mail:* sb@bipgroup.com
Dir: Dr Reshma Khattar Bhagat
Founded: 1959
Subjects: Health, Nutrition, Medicine, Nursing, Dentistry
ISBN Prefix(es): 978-81-7225
Associate Companies: British Institute of Engineering & Technology (India) Pvt Ltd
Branch Office(s)
Darya Ganj, New Delhi 110 002, Regional Manager: Y K Handa *Tel:* (011) 3274443; (011) 23255118; (011) 23259352; (011) 46208888 *Fax:* (011) 3261290 *E-mail:* delhi@bipgroup.com
5 Mill, Officers Colony, La Gajjar Chambers, Ashram Rd, Ahmedabad 380 009, Regional Manager: Sarang Khadkikar *Tel:* (079) 26578147; (079) 26578112 *Fax:* (079) 26401303 *E-mail:* ahmedabad@bipgroup.com
147, Infantry Rd, Bangalore 560 001, Regional Manager: J Ullas Kumar *Tel:* (080) 22204652; (080) 22205696; (080) 22260542 *Fax:* (080) 22205696 *E-mail:* bangalore@bipgroup.com
9/10, Agurchand Mansion, 1st floor, 150, Mount Rd, Chennai 600 002, Regional Manager: Isen V Abraham *Tel:* (044) 28461287; (044) 28461289 *Fax:* (044) 28460361 *E-mail:* chennai@bipgroup.com
37/116, Opposite V B Classic Apartment, Lisie Hospital Rd, Ernakulam-North, Cochin 682 018, Assistant Manager: K V Vinod *Tel:* (0484) 2401080; (0484) 4023454 *E-mail:* cochin@bipgroup.com
4-4-1, Dilshad Plaza, Sultan Bazar, Hyderabad, Andhra Pradesh 500 095, Regional Manager: E Satish Kumar *Tel:* (040) 66465252; (040) 66465262 *Fax:* (040) 66465262 *E-mail:* hyderabad@bipgroup.com
13/1 A Government Pl E, Kolkata 700 069, Contact: A K Banerjee *Tel:* (033) 22488742; (033) 22201351; (033) 22488417 *Fax:* (033) 22488743 *E-mail:* kolkata@bipgroup.com
Heritage Bldg, Madhav Nagar, Manipal 576 104, In Charge: Harish Kumar *Tel:* (0820) 2925224; (0820) 429173; (0820) 2922065 *E-mail:* manipal@bipgroup.com
Lansdowne House, 18, Mahakavi Bhushan Marg, Behind Regal Cinema, Colaba, Mumbai 400 039, Regional Manager: Bhaskar B Malgair *Tel:* (022) 22021766; (022) 22022396; (022) 22876136 *Fax:* (020) 22046778 *E-mail:* mumbai@bipgroup.com
28/2776, Geethanjali, Chettikulangara, Thiruvananthapuram 695 001, Regional Manager: B Vaidheeswaran *Tel:* (0471) 2472013; (0471) 2467058 *Fax:* (0471) 2472073 *E-mail:* tvm@bipgroup.com
Distributor for ASM International; Elsevier Science; Macmillan Group; McGraw-Hill; Roskill; Routledge Chapman & Hall

Biblia Impex Pvt Ltd
2/18, Ansari Rd, New Delhi 110 002
Tel: (011) 2327 8034 *Fax:* (011) 2328 2047
E-mail: contact@bibliaimpex.com
Web Site: www.bibliaimpex.com
Founded: 1963
Also export Indian publications.
Subjects: Alternative, Anthropology, Archaeology, Art, Astrology, Occult, Astronomy, Biography, Memoirs, Business, Drama, Theater, Economics, Education, Environmental Studies, Geography, Geology, Government, Political Science, History, Language Arts, Linguistics, Law,

Literature, Literary Criticism, Essays, Management, Mathematics, Music, Dance, Philosophy, Religion - Buddhist, Religion - Hindu, Religion - Other, Science (General), Social Sciences, Sociology, Technology, Women's Studies
ISBN Prefix(es): 978-81-85012

Bihar Hindi Granth Academy (BHGA)
Premchand Marg, Rajender Nagar, Patna 800 016
Tel: (0612) 2924136 *Fax:* (0612) 2660811
E-mail: biharhindi@gmail.com
Web Site: www.bhga.co.in
Subjects: Archaeology, Art, Chemistry, Chemical Engineering, Economics, History, Human Relations, Mathematics, Medicine, Nursing, Dentistry, Physics, Psychology, Psychiatry, Science (General), Social Sciences, Sociology, Botany
ISBN Prefix(es): 978-81-7351

Bishen Singh Mahendra Pal Singh+
23-A Connaught Pl 3, Dehradun 248 001
Mailing Address: PO Box 137, Dehradun 248 001
Tel: (0135) 655748; (0135) 2715748 *Fax:* (0135) 650107; (0135) 2715107
Key Personnel
Owner: Abhimanyu Gahlot
Founded: 1957
Subjects: Agriculture, Biological Sciences, Earth Sciences, Environmental Studies, Geography, Geology, Natural History
ISBN Prefix(es): 978-81-211
Distributed by Koeltz Scientific Books (Germany)

Bloomsbury Publishing India Pvt Ltd
DDA Complex, LSC Bldg No 4, 2nd floor, Pocket C-6&7, Vasant Kunj, New Delhi 110 070
Web Site: www.bloomsbury.com/bloomsbury-india
Key Personnel
Publisher, Special Projects: Paul Kumar *E-mail:* paul.kumar@bloomsbury.com
Founded: 2012
Subjects: Business, Career Development, Economics, Education, Fiction, Nonfiction (General), Outdoor Recreation, Sports, Athletics
ISBN Prefix(es): 978-93-82563

Book Circle+
Ground floor, Ravindra Mansion, 19-A, Ansari Rd, Darya Ganj, New Delhi 110 002
Tel: (011) 23266633; (011) 23264444 (orders & returns) *Fax:* (011) 23263050
Key Personnel
Proprietor: Himanshu Chawla
Specialize in medical & technical books.
Subjects: Agriculture, Architecture & Interior Design, Asian Studies, Criminology, Engineering (General), Mathematics, Mechanical Engineering, Medicine, Nursing, Dentistry, Philosophy, Religion - Buddhist, Social Sciences, Sociology, Veterinary Science, Women's Studies
Parent Company: Heritage Publishers
Associate Companies: Heritage Impex Worldwide, Ground floor, Rajendra Mansion, 19-A, Ansari Rd, Darya Ganj, New Delhi 110 002, Contact: Baldev Raj Chawla *Tel:* (011) 23266258 *Fax:* (011) 23263050 *E-mail:* heritage@nda.vsnl.net.in
Subsidiaries: Book Circle Monthly Magazine

Book Faith India+
416, Express Tower, Azadpur Commercial Complex, Azadpur, New Delhi 110 033
Tel: (011) 27132459
Founded: 1990
Subjects: Asian Studies, Religion - Buddhist, Religion - Hindu
ISBN Prefix(es): 978-81-7303

Associate Companies: Pilgrims Book House, B-27/98 A-8 Durgakund, Habasganj, Varanasi *E-mail:* pilgrim@rw1.vsnl.net.in
Distributed by Moving Books; Pilgrims Book House (Nepal)
Orders to: Pilgrims Book House, PO Box 3872, Kathmandu, Nepal

Booklinks Corp
3-4-423/5, Narayanguda Himayath Nagar, Gaganmahal, Hyderabad, Andhra Pradesh 500 029
Tel: (040) 7567068; (040) 7611582
Key Personnel
Chief Executive, Editorial: K B Satyanarayana
Sales, Production, Publicity: K Ramakrishna
Founded: 1965
Publish educational books.
Subjects: Alternative, Education, Self-Help, Social Sciences, Sociology, Humanities, New Age
ISBN Prefix(es): 978-81-85194

Books & Books+
Shop No 10 Near Madumal School, Sadar Bazar, Gurgaon, Haryana 122 001
Tel: (0124) 4066922
Founded: 1980
Specializes in Archaeology & Art.
Membership(s): Federation of Indian Publishers.
Subjects: Anthropology, Archaeology, Architecture & Interior Design, Art, History, Philosophy, Religion - Buddhist, Religion - Hindu, Religion - Islamic
ISBN Prefix(es): 978-81-85016

BPB Publications+
Munish Plaza, 20, Ansari Rd, Darya Ganj, New Delhi 110 002
Tel: (011) 23254990; (011) 23254991; (011) 23272329; (011) 23250318 *Fax:* (011) 23266427
E-mail: orders@bpbonline.com; sales@bpbonline.com
Web Site: www.bpbonline.com
Key Personnel
President: Manish Jain
Founded: 1958
Subjects: Computer Science, Electronics, Electrical Engineering
ISBN Prefix(es): 978-81-7029; 978-81-7656; 978-81-8333
Showroom(s): B-14, Connaught Pl, Next to Bata, Inner Circle, New Delhi 110 001 *Tel:* (011) 23325162; (011) 41513681 *Fax:* (011) 41513682; Infotech, G-2, Sidhartha Bldg, 96 Nehu Pl, New Delhi 110 019 *Tel:* (011) 26438245; (011) 41808059; Infotech, Shop No 2, F-38, South Ext-1, New Delhi 110 049 *Tel:* (011) 24691288; Micro Book Centre, 2, City Centre, CG Rd, Near Swastik Char Rasta, Ahmedabad 380 009 *Tel:* (079) 26421611; Computer Book Centre, 12, Shrungar Shopping Centre, 80/1, M G Rd, Bangalore 560 001 *Tel:* (080) 25587923; (080) 25584641; Surendra Department Store, Dhobi Baza, Bhatinda 151 005 *Tel:* (0164) 2237387; Universal Book Store, SCO 68, Sector 17-D, Chandigarh 160 017 *Tel:* (0172) 2702558; Business Promotion Bureau, 8/1 Ritchie St, Mount Rd, Chennai 600 002 *Tel:* (044) 28410796; (044) 28550491; Cyber Books, Indu Town Hall Rd, Ernakulam-North, Cochin 682 018 *Tel:* (0484) 2366101; Books Gallery, Shop No 4 (Lower Ground floor), Capri Trade Centre, Connaught Pl, Dehradun 248 001 *Tel:* 9358100177 (cell); BPB Book Centre, 376 Old Lajpat Rai Market, Next to Bata, Inner Circle, Delhi 110 006 *Tel:* (011) 23861747; New Age Books, c/o Moti Lal Banarasi Dass, 40, UA, Bunglow Rd, Z, Near Delhi University, Delhi 110 007 *Tel:* (011) 23922151; Deccan Agencies, 4-3-329, Bank St, Hyderabad 500 195 *Tel:* (040) 24756967; (040)

24756400 *Fax:* (040) 24756969; Micro Books, Shanti Niketan Bldg, 8, Camac St, Kolkata 700 017 *Tel:* (033) 22826518; (033) 22826519 *E-mail:* bpb_kol@vsnl.net; News & Literature House, 44-45 Kalawati Paliwal Gumanpura, Kota 324 007 *Tel:* (0744) 2364155; (0744) 2451339; (0744) 2330779 *Fax:* (0744) 2392079; Compu Shoppe, 82, Hazratganj, Lucknow 226 001 *Tel:* (0522) 2625894; (0522) 2618547 *Fax:* (0522) 2618547; Micro Media, Shop No 5, Mahendra Chambers, 150 DN Rd, Next to Capital Cinema, VT (CST) Station, Mumbai 400 001 *Tel:* (022) 22078296; (022) 22078297 *Fax:* (022) 22002731 *E-mail:* bpb@bom4.vsnl.net.in; Lotia Infotech, Station Rd, Near Deshbandhu, English Medium School, Raipur 492 009 *Tel:* (0771) 2524068; (0771) 2529261; Tonic Choice, Simis Complex, President Bazar, Kuruppam Rd, Trichur (Kerala) 680 001 *Tel:* (0487) 2427629; Ask Infotech, 2 & 3, Konark Complex, B/h Kalyan Cafe, Fatehgunj, Vadodara, Gujarat 390 002 *Tel:* (0265) 3019067; (0265) 6625467 *E-mail:* askinfotech@yahoo.com

BR Publishing Corp+
4737-A/23, Main Ansari Rd, Opposite Bank of India, Darya Ganj, New Delhi 110 002
Tel: (011) 23259196; 9810441875 (cell)
E-mail: brpc@vsnl.com
Key Personnel
Chief Executive, Editorial, Production & Publicity: Praveen Mittal
Founded: 1974
Subjects: Agriculture, Anthropology, Archaeology, Art, Economics, Government, Political Science, Health, Nutrition, History, Literature, Literary Criticism, Essays, Social Sciences, Sociology
ISBN Prefix(es): 978-81-7018; 978-81-7646; 978-81-7343; 978-81-921028
Parent Company: BRPC (India) Ltd
Associate Companies: Books for All; Low Price Publications
U.S. Office(s): South Asia Books, PO Box 502, Columbia, MO 65205-0502, United States
Orders to: D K Publisher's Distributors Pvt Ltd

Brijbasi Printers Pvt Ltd+
E-46/11, Okhla Industrial Area, Phase II, New Delhi 110 020
Tel: (011) 26841897; (011) 26314115; (011) 26314119
Key Personnel
Dir: M L Garg
Founded: 1980
Subjects: Art, Cookery, Natural History, Religion - Hindu, Travel & Tourism
ISBN Prefix(es): 978-81-7107
Associate Companies: S S Brijbasi & Sons

BS Publications+
Imprint of BSP Books Pvt Ltd
4-4-309/316, Giriraj Lane, Sultan Bazar, Hyderabad 500 095
Tel: (040) 23445600; (040) 23445688; (040) 23445605 *Fax:* (040) 23445611
Web Site: www.bspbooks.net
Key Personnel
Dir, Marketing: Mr Anil Kumar Shah
Tel: 9849021905 (cell) *E-mail:* anilshah@bspbooks.net
Founded: 1999
Publisher of science, technology & management text & reference books.
Membership(s): Federation of Publishers' & Booksellers' Associations in India (FPBAI).
Subjects: Aeronautics, Aviation, Agriculture, Automotive, Biological Sciences, Business, Career Development, Chemistry, Chemical Engineering, Civil Engineering, Communications, Computer Science, Computers, Earth Sciences,

Economics, Electronics, Electrical Engineering, Energy, Engineering (General), Environmental Studies, Finance, Geography, Geology, Health, Nutrition, Human Relations, Management, Marketing, Mathematics, Mechanical Engineering, Medicine, Nursing, Dentistry, Physical Sciences, Physics, Technology, Transportation, Veterinary Science
ISBN Prefix(es): 978-93-81075
Number of titles published annually: 50 Print
Total Titles: 300 Print

BSMPS, see Bishen Singh Mahendra Pal Singh

BSP, see BS Publications

Campfire India
Imprint of Kalyani Navyug Media Pvt Ltd
101 C Shiv House, Hari Nagar Ashram, New Delhi 110 014
Tel: (011) 26348225; (011) 42828379
E-mail: info@campfire.co.in
Web Site: www.campfire.co.in
Founded: 2008
Subjects: Biography, Memoirs, Literature, Literary Criticism, Essays, Mythology
ISBN Prefix(es): 978-93-800280; 978-81-906963; 978-81-907326; 978-81-907829

CBS Publishers & Distributors Pvt Ltd+
CBS Plaza, 4819/XI, Prahlad St, 24 Ansari Rd, Darya Ganj, New Delhi 110 002
Tel: (011) 23266861; (011) 23289259; (011) 23266867 *Fax:* (011) 23243014
E-mail: delhi@cbspd.com; cbspubs@airtelmail.in
Web Site: www.cbspd.com
Key Personnel
Head: Mr Satish Kumar Jain
Founded: 1972
Also distributor & exporter.
Subjects: Agriculture, Engineering (General), Management, Medicine, Nursing, Dentistry, Science (General), Social Sciences, Sociology
ISBN Prefix(es): 978-81-239
Total Titles: 2,000 Print
Associate Companies: Scientific International (P) Ltd, 4850, 24 Prahlad St, Darya Ganj, New Delhi 110 002 *Tel:* (011) 23287580; (011) 23287584 *Fax:* (011) 23286096 *E-mail:* sipldelhi@vsnl.net; Varun Exports, 204, F I E, Patparganj, New Delhi 110 002 *Tel:* (011) 43012064; (011) 22141751; (011) 22141748 *E-mail:* varunex@vsnl.net
Branch Office(s)
204 Patparganj, Industrial Area, New Delhi 110 092 *Tel:* (011) 49344934 *Fax:* (011) 49344935 *E-mail:* admin@cbspd.com
Seema House, 2975, 17th Cross, K R Rd, Bansankari 2nd Stage, Bangalore 560 070 *Tel:* (080) 26771678; (080) 26771679 *Fax:* (080) 26771680 *E-mail:* bangalore@cbspd.com
No 7, Subbaraya St, Shenoy Nagar, Chennai 600 030 *Tel:* (044) 26680620; (044) 26681266 *E-mail:* chennai@cbspd.com
Ashana House, No 39/1904, AM Thomas Rd, Valanjambalam, Ernakulam, Kochi 682 016 *Tel:* (0484) 4059061; (0484) 4059067 *E-mail:* kochi@cbspd.com
Rameswar Shaw Rd, No 6/B, Ground floor, Kolkata 700 014 *Tel:* (033) 22891126; (033) 22891128 *E-mail:* kolkata@cbspd.com
83-C, 1st floor, Dr E Moses Rd, Worli, Mumbai 400 018 *Tel:* (022) 24902340; (022) 24902341 *E-mail:* mumbai@cbspd.com

Cedar Books, *imprint of* Pustak Mahal Publishers

S Chand & Co Ltd+
7361, Ram Nagar, Qutub Rd, New Delhi 110 055
Tel: (011) 23672080; (011) 23672081; (011) 23672082 *Fax:* (011) 23677446

E-mail: info@schandpublishing.com; info@ schandgroup.com
Web Site: www.schandgroup.com
Key Personnel
Chairman & Mng Dir: Ravindra Kumar Gupta
General Administration & Export: B N Chatterjee
Sales & Marketing: R K Sahni
Sales: Prakash Chandra; Amit Goel; Bishan Goel; Madan Singh
Founded: 1937
Subjects: Art, Business, Economics, Government, Political Science, Medicine, Nursing, Dentistry, Philosophy, Science (General), Social Sciences, Sociology, Technology
ISBN Prefix(es): 978-81-219
Associate Companies: Rajendra Ravindra Printers Pvt Ltd, New Delhi; Shyam Lal Charitable Trust, New Delhi (publications)
Subsidiaries: Eurasia Publishing House Pvt Ltd
Divisions: S Chand Education Worldwide (direct sales for Encyclopaedia Britannica products)
Branch Office(s)
S Chand International, 7361, Ram Nagar, Qutab Rd, New Delhi 110 055, Contact: L K Kathuria *Tel:* (011) 23672080; (011) 23672081; (011) 23672082 *Fax:* (011) 3677446 *E-mail:* info@ schandgroup.com
Heritage, 1st floor, Ashram Rd, Near Gujarat Vidhyapeeth, Ahmedabad 380 014, Contact: Deepak Chaturvedi *Tel:* (079) 27542369; (079) 27541965 *Fax:* (079) 27541965 *E-mail:* ahmedabad@schandgroup.com
No 6, Ahuja Chambers, 1st Cross, Kumara Krupa Rd, Bangalore 560 001, Contact: Murlidhar Rao *Tel:* (080) 22268048; (080) 22354008 *Fax:* (080) 22268048 *E-mail:* bangalore@ schandgroup.com
Bajaj Tower, Plot No 2&3, Lala Lajpat Rai Colony, Raisen Rd, Bhopal 462 011, Contact: A R Bhonsale *Tel:* (0755) 4274723; (0755) 4209587 *Fax:* (0755) 4274723 *E-mail:* bhopal@schandgroup.com
SCO-2419-20, 1st floor, Sector-22C, Chandigarh 160 022, Contact: Surindar Singh *Tel:* (0712) 2725443; (0712) 2725446 *E-mail:* chandigarh@schandgroup.com
One, Whites Rd, Opposite Express Ave, Royapettah, Chennai 600 014, Contact: P Rajalingam *Tel:* (044) 28410027; (044) 28410058 *Fax:* (044) 28460026 *E-mail:* chennai@ schandgroup.com
Kochi Kachapally Sq, Mullassery Canal Rd, Cochin 682 011, Contact: Mohandas Menon *Tel:* (0484) 237807; (0484) 2378208; (0484) 2378740 *Fax:* (0484) 2378207 *E-mail:* cochin@schandgroup.com
1790, Trichy Rd, LGB Colony, Ramanathapuram, Coimbatore 641 045, Contact: Mr G Shivakumar *Tel:* 9444228242 (cell); (0422) 2323620; (0422) 4217136 *E-mail:* coimbatore@ schandgroup.com
Bharitia Tower, 1st floor, Badambadi, Cuttack 753 009, Contact: A R Das *Tel:* (0671) 2332580; (0671) 2332581 *Fax:* (0671) 2332581 *E-mail:* cuttack@schandgroup.com
1st floor, 20, New Rd, Near Dwarka Store, Dehradun 248 001, Contact: Bachman Singh *Tel:* (0135) 2711101; (0135) 2710861 *Fax:* (0135) 2711101 *E-mail:* dehradun@ schandgroup.com
Dilip Commercial, 1st floor, M N Rd, Pan Bazaar, Guwahati 780 001, Contact: P Chaudhary *Tel:* (0361) 2738811; (0361) 2735640 *Fax:* (0361) 2738811 *E-mail:* guwahati@ schandgroup.com
3-4-630, Opposite Ratna College, Narayanguda, Hyderabad 500 029, Contact: N S Bisht *Tel:* (040) 27550194; (040) 27550195 *Fax:* (040) 27550194; (040) 27550195 *E-mail:* hyderabad@schandgroup.com
1st floor, Nand Plaza, Hawa Sarak, Ajmer Rd, Jaipur 302 006, Contact: Gyanendra Sharma *Tel:* 9784210045 (cell) *E-mail:* jaipur@ schandgroup.com

Mai Hiran Gate, Jalandhar 144 008, Contact: P J Singh *Tel:* (0181) 2401630; (0181) 5000630 *Fax:* (0181) 2401630 *E-mail:* jalandhar@ schandgroup.com
285/J, Bipin Bihari, Ganguli St, Kolkata 700 012, Contact: Mr S K Bagal *Tel:* (033) 22367459; (033) 22373914 *Fax:* (033) 22373914 *E-mail:* kolkata@schandgroup.com
Mahabeer Market, 25 Gwynne Rd, Aminabad, Lucknow 226 018, Contact: Sanjay Joshi *Tel:* (0522) 4076971; (0522) 4026791; (0522) 406546; (0522) 4027188 *Fax:* (0522) 4077681 *E-mail:* lucknow@schandgroup.com
Blackie House, 2nd floor, 103/5 Walchand Hirachand Marg, Opposite GPO, Mumbai 400 001, Contact: D R Parab *Tel:* (022) 22690881; (022) 65102804 *Fax:* (022) 22610885 *E-mail:* mumbai@schandgroup.com
Karnal Bagh, Near Model Mill Chowk, Nagpur 440 032, Contact: Vijay Shribas *Tel:* (0712) 2720523; (0712) 2777666 *Fax:* (0712) 2723091 *E-mail:* nagpur@schandgroup.com
S Chand Technologies Pvt Ltd, D-5, Lower Ground floor, Sector-10, Noida 201 301 *Tel:* (095120) 4254864; (095120) 4254865; (095120) 4254869 *Fax:* (095130) 4254853 *E-mail:* info@sctpl.com *Web Site:* www.sctpl. com
104, Citicentre Ashok, Mahima Palace, Govind Mitra Rd, Patna 800 004, Contact: R C Bhatt *Tel:* (0612) 2302100; (0612) 2300489 *Fax:* (0612) 2300489 *E-mail:* patna@ schandgroup.com
291, Flat No 16, Ganesh Gayatri Complex, 2nd floor, Somwarpeth, Near Jain Mandir, Pune 411 011, Contact: Niranjan Baghel *Tel:* (020) 64017298 *Fax:* (020) 26055375 *E-mail:* pune@ schandgroup.com
Kailash Residency, Plot No 4B, Bollte House Rd, Shankar Nagar, Raipur, Chhattisgarh, Contact: Shyam Ughade *Tel:* 9381200834 (cell); (0771) 2443142 *E-mail:* raipur@schandgroup.com
104, Shri Draupadi Smriti Apartment, Near Jaipal Singh Stadium, Neelratan St, Upper Bazaar, Ranchi 834 001, Contact: Mr R N Singh *Tel:* 2208761 *E-mail:* ranchi@schandgroup.com
122, Raja Ram Mohan Roy Rd, East Visakanandapally, PO Siliguri, District Jalpaiguri, Contact: Debasis Ghosh *Tel:* (0353) 2520750 *E-mail:* siliguri@schandgroup.com
No 49-54-15/53/8, Plot No 7, 1st floor, Opposite Radhakrishna Towers, Seethammadhara N Ext, Visakhapatnam, Andhra Pradesh 530 013, Contact: Raj Kiran *Tel:* (0891) 2782609 *E-mail:* visakhapatnam@schandgroup.com
Distributor for Britannica (India)
Orders to: Nirja Construction & Development Co (P) Ltd, Publishers, Ram Nagar, New Delhi 110 055

S Chand International
7361, Ram Nagar, Qutub Rd, New Delhi 110 055
Tel: (011) 23672080; (011) 23672081; (011) 23672082 *Fax:* (011) 23677446
E-mail: info@schandgroup.com; schand@vsnl. com; info@schandpublishing.com
Web Site: www.schandgroup.com; www. schandpublishing.com
Founded: 1993
Subjects: Education, Engineering (General), Management, Psychology, Psychiatry, Science (General), Social Sciences, Sociology, Commerce
ISBN Prefix(es): 978-81-219
Parent Company: S Chand & Co Ltd

Paul Chapman Publishing, *imprint of* SAGE Publications India Pvt Ltd

Charkha Audiobooks, *imprint of* Karadi Tales Co Pvt Ltd

Charotar Publishing House Pvt Ltd+
Old Civil Court Rd, Opposite Amul Dairy, Post Box 65, Anand, Gujarat 388 001
Tel: (02692) 256237 *Fax:* (02692) 240089
E-mail: charotar@cphbooks.com
Web Site: www.cphbooks.in
Key Personnel
Dir: Mr Parth Pradipkumar Patel *Tel:* 9825862223 (cell) *E-mail:* parth20p3@gmail.com
Contact: Pradipkumar R Patel
Founded: 1944
Publisher of engineering textbooks.
Subjects: Civil Engineering, Education, Electronics, Electrical Engineering, Engineering (General), Environmental Studies, Publishing & Book Trade Reference, Technology
ISBN Prefix(es): 978-81-85594; 978-93-80358
Number of titles published annually: 5 Print
Total Titles: 53 Print
Bookshop(s): Charotar Book Stall, Near Post Office, Vallabh Vidyanagar, Anand, Gujarat 388 120

Chetana Pvt Ltd Publishers & International Booksellers
34 K Dubash Marg, Kala Ghoda, Mumbai 400 023
Tel: (022) 2288 1159
E-mail: orders@chetana.com; chetana1946@ chetana.com
Web Site: www.chetana.com
Key Personnel
Chairperson & Mng Dir: Chhaya Arya
Founded: 1946
Subjects: Philosophy, Religion - Other
ISBN Prefix(es): 978-81-85300; 978-0-85655
Total Titles: 35 Print
Distributed by Acorn Press (USA & Canada)

Children's Book Trust+
Nehru House 4, Bahadur Shah Zafar Marg, New Delhi 110 002
Tel: (011) 23316974; (011) 23316970 *Fax:* (011) 23721090
E-mail: cbtnd@cbtnd.com
Web Site: www.childrensbooktrust.com
Founded: 1957
ISBN Prefix(es): 978-81-7011
Branch Office(s)
18-B, Rayala Towers, Anna Salai, Chennai 600 002, Contact: V Badrinarynan *Tel:* (044) 30221850
G-14, Kamalalaya Centre, 156-A, Lenin Sarani, Kolkata 700 013, Contact: Bimal Datta *Tel:* (033) 22155094

Chitra, *imprint of* Karadi Tales Co Pvt Ltd

Choice International+
484 Double Storey, New Rajinder Nagar, New Delhi 110 060
Tel: (011) 64163037; 9212013637 (cell)
E-mail: narkambooks@gmail.com; narkambooks@yahoo.com; narkambooks@ ibibo.com
Key Personnel
Proprietor: Naresh Kumar Chowdhry
Representative: Dr Kamal Chowdhry
Author: Rajat Chowdhry *Tel:* 9136684584 (cell)
Founded: 1999
Subjects: Accounting, Agriculture, Anthropology, Art, Biography, Memoirs, Business, Chemistry, Chemical Engineering, Civil Engineering, Computer Science, Computers, Cookery, Economics, Education, Electronics, Electrical Engineering, Geography, Geology, History, Law, Literature, Literary Criticism, Essays, Mathematics, Mechanical Engineering, Medicine, Nursing, Dentistry, Physics, Psychology, Psychiatry, Publishing & Book Trade Reference, Science (General), Political Science
ISBN Prefix(es): 978-81-87659

Total Titles: 264 Print
Associate Companies: Dream Palace Book Distributors; Narkam Books

Chowkhamba Sanskrit Series Office
K-37/99 Gopal Lane, Near Golghar (Maidagin), Uttar Pradesh, Varanasi 221 001
Mailing Address: PO Box 1008, Uttar Pradesh, Varanasi 221 001
Tel: (0542) 2333458; (0542) 2334032; (0542) 2335020
E-mail: cssoffice01@gmail.com
Web Site: www.chowkhambasanskritseries.com
Founded: 1892
Printing & selling Ayurvedic books & books on Indology.
Memberbership(s): Association of Indian Publishers & Booksellers.
Subjects: Anthropology, Archaeology, Architecture & Interior Design, Art, Asian Studies, Astrology, Occult, Astronomy, Biography, Memoirs, Economics, Geography, Geology, Health, Nutrition, History, Music, Dance, Philosophy, Physical Sciences, Poetry, Religion - Other, Indology
ISBN Prefix(es): 978-81-7080
Number of titles published annually: 20 Print
Total Titles: 475 Print
Associate Companies: Chowkhamba Krishnadas Academy, K No 7/118 Gopal Mandir Lane, PO Box 1118, Uttar Pradesh, Varanasi 221 001 *Tel:* (0542) 2335020

The Christian Literature Society+
No 68, Evening Bazaar Rd, Park Town, Chennai 600 003
Tel: (044) 25354296 *Fax:* (044) 25354297
Key Personnel
General Secretary: Dr T Dayanandan Francis
Founded: 1858
Subjects: Asian Studies, Biblical Studies, Biography, Memoirs, Philosophy, Religion - Protestant, Technology, Women's Studies
ISBN Prefix(es): 978-81-85884
Distributed by ISPCK: Indian Society for Promoting Christian Knowledge
Bookshop(s): CLS Bookshop, The Estate, Ground floor, Rear Block, 121, Dickenson Rd, Bangalore 560 042 *Tel:* (080) 25582729; CLS Bookshop, PO Box 501, Park Town, Chennai 600 003; CLS Bookshop, M G Rd, Cochin 682 011 *Tel:* (0484) 2381677; CLS Bookshop, 775, Avanashi Rd, Coimbatore 641 018 *Tel:* (0422) 2301609; CLS Bookshop, Nampally Station Rd, Hyderabad 500 001 *Tel:* (040) 23202046; CLS Bookshop, 15-D, W Veli St, Madurai 625 001 *Tel:* (0452) 2342405; CLS Bookshop, M G Rd, Pulimood, Trivandrum 695 001 *Tel:* (0471) 478115

Chugh Publications
2 Strachey Rd, Civil Lines, Allahabad 211 001
Tel: (0532) 623063
Founded: 1973
Subjects: Human Relations, Social Sciences, Sociology
ISBN Prefix(es): 978-81-85076; 978-81-85613
Associate Companies: R S Publishing House, 20 Mahatma Gandhi Marg, Allahabad
Bookshop(s): Universal Book Shop

CICC Book House
Press Club Rd, Ernakulam, Kochi 682 011
Tel: (0484) 2353557; 9847165324 (cell)
Key Personnel
Contact: T Jayachandran
Founded: 1962
Subjects: Drama, Theater, Fiction, Literature, Literary Criticism, Essays
ISBN Prefix(es): 978-81-7174
Book Club(s): Crime Book Club

Clarion Books, *imprint of* Hind Pocket Books

Classical Publishing Co
28 Shopping Centre, Karampura, New Delhi 110 015
Tel: (011) 25465978; 9015777018 (cell)
Key Personnel
Mng Dir, Editorial: Bal Krishan Taneja
Contact: Rajat Taneja
Founded: 1976
Subjects: Economics, Government, Political Science, History, Management, Music, Dance, Philosophy, Religion - Other, Social Sciences, Sociology, Commerce, English, Hindi, Patrakarita, Sanskrit
ISBN Prefix(es): 978-81-7054

Concept Publishing Co Pvt Ltd+
A/15-16, Commercial Block, Mohan Garden, New Delhi 110 059
Tel: (011) 2535 1460; (011) 2535 1794
Fax: (011) 2535 7109
E-mail: publishing@conceptpub.com
Web Site: www.conceptpub.com
Key Personnel
Dir: Nitin Mittal
Founded: 1974
Academic publishing specializing in humanities & social sciences.
Subjects: Alternative, Anthropology, Asian Studies, Behavioral Sciences, Communications, Earth Sciences, Economics, Education, Energy, Environmental Studies, Ethnicity, Geography, Geology, History, Journalism, Library & Information Sciences, Management, Philosophy, Psychology, Psychiatry, Public Administration, Self-Help, Social Sciences, Sociology, Women's Studies
ISBN Prefix(es): 978-81-7022; 978-81-8069
Number of titles published annually: 90 Print
Total Titles: 2,400 Print
Parent Company: D K Agencies (P) Ltd
Subsidiaries: Logos Press
Showroom(s): Bldg No 4788-90, 23 Ansari Rd, Darya Ganj, New Delhi 110 002 *Tel:* (011) 23272187

Corwin Press, *imprint of* SAGE Publications India Pvt Ltd

Cosmo Publications+
4820/24-B Ansari Rd, Darya Ganj, New Delhi 110 002
Tel: (011) 23278779; (011) 23280455 *Fax:* (011) 23271200; (011) 23241200 (orders)
E-mail: genesis@ndb.vsnl.net.in; igeindia@gmail.com
Key Personnel
Chairman & Mng Dir: Mrs Rani Kapoor
Chief Editor: Mr Subodh Kapoor
  E-mail: subaryan@gmail.com
Dir, Foreign Sales, Rights & Permissions: Mr Sunil Kapoor
Dir, Sales & Marketing: Mr Kaartikeya K Kapoor
  Tel: 9560192388 (cell)
Founded: 1972
One of the leading Indian publishers of scholarly books & reference works. Well known for specialization in Indology & Sanskrit studies.
Membership(s): Chemicals & Allied Export Promotions Council; Federation of Indian Publishers; Federation of Publishers' & Booksellers' Associations in India (FPBAI).
Subjects: Agriculture, Alternative, Anthropology, Archaeology, Art, Asian Studies, Astrology, Occult, Behavioral Sciences, Biography, Memoirs, Biological Sciences, Business, Child Care & Development, Criminology, Developing Countries, Drama, Theater, Economics, Education, Ethnicity, Geography, Geology, Government, Political Science, Health, Nutrition, History, Inspirational, Spirituality, Journal-

ism, Language Arts, Linguistics, Law, Library & Information Sciences, Literature, Literary Criticism, Essays, Music, Dance, Mysteries, Suspense, Natural History, Nonfiction (General), Parapsychology, Philosophy, Psychology, Psychiatry, Regional Interests, Religion - Buddhist, Religion - Hindu, Religion - Islamic, Religion - Other, Science (General), Self-Help, Social Sciences, Sociology, Theology, Travel & Tourism, Veterinary Science, Women's Studies, Alternative Healing, Ancient Indian Sciences, Central Asian Studies, Cultural Studies, Ethics & Logic, Everest Himalayas, Family, Marriage & Kinship, Feminism, Gazetteers & Manuals, Herbal Science, Hindu Scriptures & Sacred Books, Hypnosis, Indian Philosophy, Indology, Jainism, Jurisprudence, Kashmir, Numerology, Occult & Esoteric, Other World, Palmistry, Parapsychology, Sanskrit Literature, Research Methodology, Sexuality, Sikkim, Social Work & Social Survey, Study Guides & Skills, Tantra & Indian Mysticism, Tibet, Tribal Studies, Yoga & Meditation
ISBN Prefix(es): 978-81-7020; 978-81-7755; 978-81-307; 978-81-292 (Indigo Books)
Number of titles published annually: 200 Print
Total Titles: 3,000 Print
Parent Company: Genesis Publishing Pvt Ltd
Imprints: Indigo Books; Siddhi Books
Subsidiaries: Cosmopolitan Book House
Divisions: Cosmo Dictionaries; Falcon Books
U.S. Office(s): Cosmo Global US LLC, 10 Sugarvale Way, Lutherville, MD 21093, United States
Distributor for Impact Global Publishing Inc (exclusive world distribution rights)
Warehouse: 4/16 West Patel Nagar, New Delhi 110 008

CSIR-National Institute of Science Communication & Information Resources (CSIR-NISCAIR)+
Dr K S Krishanan Marg, Pusa Campus, New Delhi 110 012
Tel: (011) 25846301; (011) 25846304; (011) 25846305; (011) 25846306; (011) 25846307
Fax: (011) 25847062
E-mail: sales@niscair.res.in
Web Site: www.niscair.res.in
Key Personnel
Dir & Editor-in-Chief: Dr Manoj Kumar Patairiya
  Tel: (011) 25847062
Sales & Distribution Officer: Mr A K Srivastava
  Tel: (011) 25843359
Founded: 1942
Subjects: Biological Sciences, Chemistry, Chemical Engineering, Physics, Science (General), Technology
ISBN Prefix(es): 978-81-7236; 978-81-85038
Parent Company: Council of Scientific & Industrial Research (CSIR)
Branch Office(s)
14 Satsang Vihar Marg, Spl Institutional Area, New Delhi 110 067 *Tel:* (011) 26560141
Fax: (011) 26862228

Current Books
Good Shepherd St, Kottayam, Kerala 686 001
Tel: (0481) 2563114; (0481) 2301614
E-mail: info@dcbooks.com
Web Site: www.dcbooks.com; www.currentbooks.com
Key Personnel
Chief Executive: D C Kizhakemuri Edam
Founded: 1952
Subjects: Fiction, Nonfiction (General), Religion - Other, Science (General), Self-Help, Children's Literature
ISBN Prefix(es): 978-81-226
Associate Companies: DC Books; Kairali Children's Book Trust; Kairali Mudralayam

Branch Office(s)
Pichu Iyer Junction, Alappuzha *Tel:* (0477)
2261197 *E-mail:* dcb029@dcbookshop.in
Convent Junction, Market Rd, Ernakulam
Tel: (0484) 2351590; (0484) 3231590
E-mail: dcb008@dcbookshop.in
Nakkara Complex Oasis, Irinjalakkuda
Tel: (0480) 2820667 *E-mail:* dcb032@
dcbookshop.in
VNR Bldg, Near SBT, Main Rd, Kalpetta
Tel: (0493) 6203766 *E-mail:* dcb013@
dcbookshop.in
Main Rd, Kanhangadu *Tel:* (0467) 2209818
E-mail: dcb023@dcbookshop.in
YMCA Bldgs, Chinnakada, Kollam *Tel:* (0474)
2749055 *E-mail:* dcb034@dcbookshop.in
K K Rd, Kottayam *Tel:* (0481) 2560342
E-mail: dcb041@dcbookshop.in
Noor Complex, Mavoor Rd, Kozhikode
Tel: (0495) 2727299 *E-mail:* dcb001@
dcbookshop.in
City Plaza, Central Bazar, Manjery *Tel:* (0483)
2762039 *E-mail:* dcb025@dcbookshop.in
Rubin Plaza, M G Rd, Thalassery *Tel:* (0490)
2320668 *E-mail:* dcb030@dcbookshop.in
Releesh Towers, M C Rd, Thiruvalla *Tel:* (0469)
2631596 *E-mail:* dcb033@dcbookshop.in
Pallimukkil Chambers, Thodupuzha *Tel:* (04862)
223915 *E-mail:* dcb035@dcbookshop.in
Karimpanal Statue Ave, Trivandrum *Tel:* (0471)
2477693 *E-mail:* dcb018@dcbookshop.in
Book Club(s): VIP Book Club

Dastane Ramchandra & Co+
830, Sadashiv Peth, nr Chitrashala Chowk, Pune,
Maharashtra 411 030
Tel: (020) 24478193
E-mail: drcopune@gmail.com
Key Personnel
Mng Dir, Editorial, Production: Vishwas Dastane
Founded: 1960
Specialize in social sciences, career development
& help books.
Membership(s): Marathi Publishers' Association;
Poona Press Owners Association Ltd.
Subjects: Career Development, Economics, His-
tory, Library & Information Sciences, Lit-
erature, Literary Criticism, Essays, Science
(General), Science Fiction, Fantasy, Self-Help,
Social Sciences, Sociology, Sports, Athletics,
Women's Studies
ISBN Prefix(es): 978-81-85080
Associate Companies: Abhang Stores, Printers &
Stationers; Anuja Prakashan Publishers, 13A,
Abhang Poona-Bombay Rd, Pune, Maharashtra;
Sports Publications
Bookshop(s): 456 Raviwar Peth, Pune, Maharash-
tra 411002

Daya Publishing House+
4760-61/63, Ansari Rd, New Delhi 110 002
Tel: (011) 23244987; (011) 23245578 *Fax:* (011)
23260116
Web Site: www.dayabooks.com
Key Personnel
Contact: Anil Mittal; Sunil Mittal
Founded: 1986
Subjects: Agriculture, Architecture & Interior De-
sign, Biological Sciences, Earth Sciences, Eco-
nomics, Education, Engineering (General), En-
vironmental Studies, Geography, Geology, Gov-
ernment, Political Science, History, Language
Arts, Linguistics, Law, Library & Information
Sciences, Literature, Literary Criticism, Essays,
Natural History, Philosophy, Religion - Other,
Social Sciences, Sociology, Veterinary Sci-
ence, Anthropology, Botany, Fisheries, Forestry
Horticulture, Medicinal Plants, Oceanography,
Public Administration, Rural Development,
Wildlife, Women & Children, Zoology
ISBN Prefix(es): 978-81-7035
Number of titles published annually: 50 Print

DC Books+
DC Kizhakemuri Edam, Good Shepherd St, Kot-
tayam, Kerala 686 001
Tel: (0481) 2563114; (0481) 2301614
E-mail: info@dcbooks.com; publish@dcbooks.
com; marketing@dcbooks.com; sales@dcbooks.
com
Web Site: www.dcbooks.com
Founded: 1974
Subjects: Biography, Memoirs, Fiction, Litera-
ture, Literary Criticism, Essays, Management,
Poetry, Self-Help, Yoga
ISBN Prefix(es): 978-81-7130; 978-81-264
Associate Companies: Current Books; Kairali
Children's Book Trust; Kairali Mudralayam
Book Club(s): Classics Club; DC Book Club

DC Press, *imprint of* Kairali Children's Book
Trust

Diamond Comics (P) Ltd+
257, Dariba Kalan, Chandni Chowk, New Delhi
110 006
Tel: (0120) 4238008; (0120) 4238009 *Fax:* (0120)
4238010
E-mail: diamondcomicsindia@gmail.com;
diamondcomicsindia@yahoo.com
Key Personnel
Chairman/Mng Dir: Gulshan Rai *Tel:* 9810003062
(cell)
Founded: 1948
Publish fiction, nonfiction, comic books & maga-
zines.
Membership(s): Federation of Indian Publishers &
Distributors.
Subjects: Cookery, Fiction, Health, Nutrition,
Nonfiction (General), Religion - Hindu, Comic
ISBN Prefix(es): 978-81-7184
Number of titles published annually: 504 Print;
120 Online
Total Titles: 280 E-Book
Parent Company: Diamond Comics Group of
Publications
Ultimate Parent Company: Punjabi Pustak Bhan-
dar, 257, Dariba Kalan, New Delhi 110 006
Associate Companies: DC Magazines
Subsidiaries: Diamond Magazines

Discovery Publishing House Pvt Ltd
4383/4 A, Ansari Rd, Darya Ganj, New Delhi
110 002
Tel: (011) 23279245; (011) 43596064; (011)
43596065 *Fax:* (011) 23253475
E-mail: sales@discoverypublishinggroup.com;
editorial@discoverypublishinggroup.com;
export@discoverypublishinggroup.com
Web Site: www.discoverypublishinggroup.com
Key Personnel
Mng Dir: T R Wasan
International Inquiries: Mr Parul Wasan
E-mail: parul.wasan@gmail.com
Founded: 1983
Subjects: Education, Science (General), Islam
ISBN Prefix(es): 978-81-7141; 978-81-8356

Disha Prakashan
B-32, Shivalik, Malviya Nagar, New Delhi 110
017
Tel: (011) 27108832 *Fax:* (011) 27196746
Web Site: www.dishapublication.com
Founded: 1973
Specializing in exam books.
Subjects: Biography, Memoirs, Economics, His-
tory, Language Arts, Linguistics, Literature,
Literary Criticism, Essays, Philosophy, Religion
- Other, Social Sciences, Sociology
ISBN Prefix(es): 978-81-85045; 978-81-88081
Parent Company: Heritage Publishers
Associate Companies: Intellectuals' Rendezvous,
Aggarwal Bhawa, 4C Ansari Rd, New Delhi
110 002; Pankaj Publications International
Subsidiaries: Book Circle

DK Printworld (P) Ltd+
F-395, Sudarshan Park, Near ESI Hospital, New
Delhi 110 015
Tel: (011) 254 53975; (011) 254 66019
Fax: (011) 254 65926
E-mail: indology@dkprintworld.com
Web Site: www.dkprintworld.com
Key Personnel
Dir: Susheel K Mittal
Founded: 1992
Specialize in books on Indology.
Subjects: Archaeology, Art, Asian Studies, As-
trology, Occult, Drama, Theater, Economics,
Education, History, Language Arts, Linguis-
tics, Law, Music, Dance, Philosophy, Religion -
Buddhist, Religion - Hindu, Religion - Islamic,
Science (General), Social Sciences, Sociology,
Ecology
ISBN Prefix(es): 978-81-246; 978-81-869
Total Titles: 300 Print

Doaba House
1688 Nai Sarak, New Delhi 110 006
Tel: (011) 23274669; (011) 65363037 *Fax:* (011)
23247322
Web Site: doabahouse.com
Founded: 1924
Subjects: Education, English as a Second Lan-
guage, Literature, Literary Criticism, Essays
ISBN Prefix(es): 978-81-85173; 978-81-87764

Dreaming Fingers, *imprint of* Karadi Tales Co
Pvt Ltd

Dreamland Publications+
J-128, Kirti Nagar, New Delhi 110 015
Tel: (011) 25106050; (011) 25435657; (011)
25455657 *Fax:* (011) 25438283
E-mail: info@dreamlandpublications.com;
dreamland@vsnl.com
Web Site: www.dreamlandpublications.com
Key Personnel
Sales Dir: Aman Chawla
Production: Anuj Chawla *E-mail:* anuj@
dreamlandpublications.com
Founded: 1986
Educational charts.
ISBN Prefix(es): 978-81-7301
Parent Company: Indian Book Depot

Dreamtech Press
19-A, Ansari Rd, Darya Ganj, New Delhi 110
002
Tel: (011) 4355180
E-mail: editorial@dreamtechpress.com;
marketing@dreamtechpress.com
Web Site: www.dreamtechpress.com
Key Personnel
Senior Publishing Manager: Anita Jalan
Manager, Marketing & Digital Solutions: Deepak
Bohra
Subjects: Business, Career Development, Com-
puter Science, Engineering (General), Finance,
Management, Marketing, Self-Help, Human
Resources, Information Technology
ISBN Prefix(es): 978-81-7722
Distribution Center: Wiley India Pvt Ltd, 4435-
36/7, Ansari Rd, Darya Ganj, New Delhi
110 002 *Tel:* (011) 4363 0000 *Fax:* (011)
2327 5895 *E-mail:* csupport@wiley.com *Web
Site:* www.wileyindia.com

Dutta Baruah Publishing Co Pvt Ltd+
College Hostel Rd, Panbazar, Guwahati-1, Assam
781 001
Tel: (0361) 2543995
Founded: 1938
Also act as distributors.
Membership(s): Federation of Indian Publishers.

Subjects: Art, Cookery, Language Arts, Linguistics, Literature, Literary Criticism, Essays, Poetry, Religion - Hindu, Religion - Other, Sports, Athletics
ISBN Prefix(es): 978-81-7373
Number of titles published annually: 150 Print
Total Titles: 1,600 Print
Subsidiaries: Parbati Prakashan
U.S. Office(s): 1738 Red Bud Lane, Rayne, LA 70578, United States, Contact: Pallvi D Simon
Tel: 337-783-8454

Dynamic Books, *imprint of* Krishna Prakashan Media (P) Ltd

Eastern Book Co
34 Lalbagh, Lucknow 226 001
Tel: (0522) 4033608; (0522) 4033619; (0522) 4033620 *Toll Free Tel:* 1800-1800-6666 *Fax:* (0522) 4033633
E-mail: sales@ebc.co.in
Web Site: www.ebc.co.in
Key Personnel
Mng Dir: Mr Vijay Malik, MD *Tel:* (0522) 4033666
Editorial: Mr Surendra Malik *E-mail:* editor@ ebc-india.com
Founded: 1942
Specialize in law books & law reports in print media & electronic media (CD-ROM). Sales offices located in New Delhi, Bangalore & Mumbai.
This publisher has indicated that 50% of their product line is author subsidized.
Membership(s): Avadh Chamber of Commerce & Industry; Chemicals & Allied Products Export Promotion Council; Federation of Indian Publishers; Federation of Publishers' & Booksellers' Associations in India (FPBAI); Indian Industries Association; Lalbagh Vyapar Mandal; Lucknow Management Association.
Subjects: Law
ISBN Prefix(es): 978-93-5145
Number of titles published annually: 100 Print; 2 CD-ROM; 2 Online; 100 E-Book
Total Titles: 1,200 Print; 250 E-Book
Parent Company: EBC Group of Companies
Associate Companies: EBC Publishing Pvt Ltd, 28 B, Sringarnagar, Alambagh, Lucknow 226 005, Contact: Mr Sumeet Malik *Tel:* (0522) 4050630; (0522) 4059680 *E-mail:* ps1.director4@ebc-india.com
Divisions: EBC Africa
Branch Office(s)
G-F, 07-Shop, Satyamev Complex-1, S-G Highway Rd, SOLA, Ahmedabad 380 060 *Tel:* (0922) 80125539 *E-mail:* sales.ahmd@ ebc.co.in
Manav Law House, Opposite Dr Chandra's Eye Clinic, Elgin Rd, Civil Lines, Allahabad 211 001 *Tel:* (0532) 2560710; (0532) 2422023 *Fax:* (0532) 2623584
25/1, Anand Nivas, 3rd Cross, 6th Main, Gandhi Nagar, Bangalore 560 009 *Tel:* (080) 41225368 *E-mail:* sales.bglr@ebc.co.in
Eastern Book Co Pvt Ltd, G-17, Brigade Plaza, 71/1, SC Rd, Ananda Rao Circle, Bangalore 560 009 *Tel:* (080) 4149 6522
Eastern Book Co Pvt Ltd, SCO-19, 2nd floor, Sector-17E, Chandigarh 160 017 *Tel:* (0172) 467 0766
1267, Kashmere gate, Delhi 110 006, Branch Manager: Mr Bhakt Raj Singh *Tel:* (011) 23917616 *Fax:* (011) 23921656 *E-mail:* sales. kg@ebc-india.com
Eastern Book Co Pvt Ltd, 301, 3rd floor, Erucshaw Bldg, 249, Dr D N Rd, Fort, Mumbai 440 001 *Tel:* (022) 22630300 *Fax:* (022) 22630400 *E-mail:* sales@scconline.com
F-9, Girish Heights, 1st floor, LIC Sq, Kamptee Rd, Nagpur 440 001 *Tel:* (0712) 6607650 *E-mail:* sales.ngpr@ebc.co.in

Eastern Book Co Pvt Ltd, 5-B, Atma Ram House, 5th floor, One Tolstoy Marg, Connaught Pl, New Delhi 110 001, Executive Dir: Mr Sumain Malik *Tel:* (011) 45752323 *Fax:* (011) 41504440 *E-mail:* sales@scconline.com *Web Site:* www.scconline.com
Distributed by Anupam Gyan Bhandar (Bangladesh); Bhrikuti Pustak Tatha Maslanda Bhandar (Nepal); Booknet Co Ltd (Thailand); Dar es Salaam Printers Pvt Ltd (Tanzania); Enche Sdn Bhd (Malaysia); Namdhari Trading Co Ltd (Tanzania); Pakistan Law House (Pakistan); Mr Tony Poh (Singapore); Profes Book Co (Sri Lanka); Sehweitzer Sortiment (Germany); State Mutual Book & Periodical Services Ltd (USA); Wildy & Sons Ltd (UK)
Foreign Rep(s): Steve Adegbola (Nigeria)

Eastern Law House Pvt Ltd
54 Ganesh Chunder Ave, Kolkata 700 013
Tel: (033) 2215-1989; (033) 2215-2301 *Fax:* (033) 2215-0491
E-mail: elh@cal.vsnl.net.in; elh.cal@gmail.com
Web Site: www.easternlawhouse.com
Key Personnel
Dir: Asok De
Founded: 1918
Membership(s): Federation of Publishers' & Booksellers' Associations in India (FPBAI); Publishers & Booksellers Guild.
Subjects: Accounting, Fiction, Government, Political Science, Law, Management, Maritime, Marketing, Social Sciences, Sociology
ISBN Prefix(es): 978-81-7177
Number of titles published annually: 20 Print; 1 CD-ROM
Total Titles: 1,000 Print
Branch Office(s)
36 Netaji Subhash Marg, Darya Ganj, New Delhi 110 002 *Tel:* (011) 2327-9982 *Fax:* (011) 2325-3844
Foreign Rights: William S Hein & Co (USA); Oceana Publications Inc (USA)

EastWest, *imprint of* Westland Ltd

The Energy & Resources Institute (TERI)
Darbari Seth Block, IHC Complex, Lodi Rd, New Delhi 100 003
Tel: (011) 2468 2100; (011) 4150 4900 *Fax:* (011) 2468 2144; (011) 2468 2145
E-mail: mailbox@teri.res.in; teripress@teri.res.in
Web Site: www.teriin.org
Key Personnel
Executive Dir: Dr Leena Srivastava
General Manager: Dr R K Pachauri
Publications Manager: Ms Anupama Jauhry *E-mail:* anupama.jauhry@teri.res.in
Subjects: Energy, Environmental Studies, Technology, Development Studies
ISBN Prefix(es): 978-81-85419; 978-81-7993

Ess Ess Publications+
4831/24, Ansari Rd, Darya Ganj, New Delhi 110 002
Tel: (011) 23260807; (011) 41563444 *Fax:* (011) 41563334
E-mail: info@essessreference.com
Web Site: www.essessreference.com
Key Personnel
Mng Dir: Sumit Sethi *E-mail:* sumit.sethi@ essessreference.com
Founded: 1974
Specialize in all Indian books on library & information science. Publishing rights arrangement with major USA/UK publishers of library & information science titles.
Subjects: Economics, History, Human Relations, Library & Information Sciences, Management, Philosophy, Religion - Hindu, Social Sciences, Sociology
ISBN Prefix(es): 978-81-7000

Imprints: Reference Press
Subsidiaries: Sumit Publications
Distribution Center: International Specialized Book Services, 920 NE 58 Ave, Suite 300, Portland, OR 97213, United States, Marketing Manager: Tamma Green *Tel:* 503-287-3093 *Fax:* 503-280-8832 *E-mail:* tamma@isbs.com *Web Site:* www.isbs.com

EWP, *imprint of* Affiliated East-West Press Pvt Ltd

EWP, see Affiliated East-West Press Pvt Ltd

Firewall Media, *imprint of* Laxmi Publications Pvt Ltd

Firma KLM Pvt Ltd+
257B, B B Ganguly St, Near Bowbazar Post Office, Kolkata 700 012
Mailing Address: PO Box 7818, Kolkata 700 012
Tel: (033) 2221 7294; (033) 2237 4391
E-mail: firmaklm@yahoo.com
Key Personnel
Mng Dir, Rights & Permissions: Mrs Swati Mukherjee, MD *Tel:* (094) 3301 6943
Editorial & Production: Mr Swarup Mitra *Tel:* (094) 3242 4186
Founded: 1952
Subjects: Alternative, History, Human Relations, Philosophy, Social Sciences, Sociology, Humanities, Indology
ISBN Prefix(es): 978-81-7102
Distributed by Blue Dove Press (USA); Malshow Co Ltd (Japan); South Asia Books (USA)
Distributor for Asiatic Society: K P Bagchi; Burdwan University; D K Publishers & Distributors; Manorlal; Monahar Book Services; Motilal Banarsidass; Munshiram; Punti Pustak; Sanskrit College (Kolkata); Spectrum

Focus, *imprint of* Popular Prakashan Pvt Ltd

4Hour Press, *imprint of* India Research Press/TARA Press

Frank Brothers & Co (Publishers) Ltd+
4675-A, Ansari Rd, 21, Darya Ganj, New Delhi 110 002
Tel: (011) 23263393 *Fax:* (011) 23269032
Founded: 1930
Subjects: Accounting, Art, Biological Sciences, Business, Computer Science, Cookery, Economics, Education, English as a Second Language, Environmental Studies, Fiction, Geography, Geology, Government, Political Science, Health, Nutrition, History, Management, Mathematics, Nonfiction (General), Physics, Science (General), Social Sciences, Sociology, Commerce
ISBN Prefix(es): 978-81-7170; 978-81-8409
Number of titles published annually: 50 Print
Total Titles: 1,000 Print
Branch Office(s)
300, Shankaran Complex, Langford Rd, Bangalore 560 025 *Tel:* (080) 22278047; 9845204543 (cell)
Jr MIG 31, E-3, Arera Colony, Madhya Pradesh, Bhopal 462 016
136, Motilal Nehru Rd, Pan Bazar, Guwahati 781 001 *Tel:* (0361) 2630150
302 K, Kamalalaya Centre, Lenin Sarani, Kolkata 700 013 *Tel:* (033) 22158779
375/377, Babu Bldg, Room 24, 2nd floor, Lamington Rd, Mumbai 400 007 *Tel:* (022) 23880678; 9892883588 (cell)
Showroom(s): IV/85, Chandni Chowk, Opposite Central Baptist Church, New Delhi 110 006 *Tel:* (011) 23276791; (011) 23268884

Frog Books
Imprint of Leadstart Publishing Pvt Ltd

Regus Business Centre, Level 1, Trade Center, Bandra Kurla Complex, Bandra (East), Mumbai 400 051
Tel: (022) 40700804 *Fax:* (022) 40700800
E-mail: info@leadstartcorp.com
Web Site: www.leadstartcorp.com
Key Personnel
Chairman & Chief Executive Officer: Swarup Nanda
Executive Dir: Chandralekha Maitra
Founded: 1994
Subjects: Biography, Memoirs, Business, Cookery, Government, Political Science, Health, Nutrition, History, Philosophy, Religion - Other, Self-Help, Sports, Athletics, Travel & Tourism, Fitness
ISBN Prefix(es): 978-81-88811; 978-81-90577
U.S. Office(s): Axis Corp, 7845 E Oakbrook Circle, Madison, WI 53717, United States
Warehouse: Leadstart Publishing Pvt Ltd, Unit 122, Bldg B/2, Near Wadale RTO, Wadala, Mumbai 400 037 *Tel:* (022) 24046887

Full Circle, *imprint of* Hind Pocket Books

Full Circle Publishing Pvt Ltd+
Imprint of Hind Pocket Books (P) Ltd
J-40, Jorbagh Lane, New Delhi 110 003
Tel: (011) 24620063; (011) 24621011
E-mail: editorial@fullcirclebooks.in
Web Site: fullcirclebooks.in
Key Personnel
Owner & Editor: Priyanka Malhotra
Contact: Sheela Thomas
Founded: 1958
Membership(s): Federation of Indian Publishers.
Subjects: Archaeology, Asian Studies, Astrology, Occult, Child Care & Development, Cookery, Economics, Gardening, Plants, Health, Nutrition, How-to, Humor, Inspirational, Spirituality, Language Arts, Linguistics, Law, Management, Marketing, Nonfiction (General), Philosophy, Poetry, Religion - Other, Self-Help, Arts of India, Indology, Mind/Body/Spirit
ISBN Prefix(es): 978-81-7621
Associate Companies: Clarion Books; Global Business Press; Mainstreet Books; Saraswati Vihar
Distributor for Embassy Books; Manjul Publications; Pentagon Press; Wilco
Bookshop(s): Shop No 23, 1st & 2nd floor, Middle Lane, Khan Market, New Delhi 110 003 *Tel:* (011) 24655641; (011) 24655643; (011) 24655642 *E-mail:* km@fullcirclebooks.in; N-16, Basement & 3rd floor, New Delhi 110 048 *Tel:* (011) 29245641; (011) 24655642; (011) 24655643; No 8, Nizamuddin East Market, New Delhi 110 003 *Tel:* (011) 41826124
Warehouse: 173, Neb Sarai, New Delhi 110 068, Contact: Sales Manager *Tel:* (011) 29532140

Galgotia Publications Pvt Ltd+
5 Ansari Rd, Darya Ganj, New Delhi 110 002
Mailing Address: PO Box 7221, New Delhi 110 002
Tel: (011) 23288134 *Fax:* (011) 23281909
Key Personnel
Mng Dir: Suneel Galgotia
Sales: Vinod Behl
Founded: 1933
Distributor of childrens, technical & management books in India.
Subjects: Computer Science, Engineering (General), Management, Medicine, Nursing, Dentistry
ISBN Prefix(es): 978-81-7515; 978-81-85623; 978-81-86011; 978-81-86340
Branch Office(s)
Galgotia Towers, G-64, Manas Sarover Business Complex Sector 18, Noida 201 301

Showroom(s): 17B Conn Pl, New Delhi 110 001
Tel: (011) 23713227 *Fax:* (011) 23713228
Bookshop(s): E D Galgotia & Sons

Ganesh & Co+
38, Thanikachalam Rd T Nagar, Chennai 600 017
Tel: (044) 24344519 *Fax:* (044) 24342009
Key Personnel
Dir: K Srinivasamurthy
Founded: 1910
Subjects: Inspirational, Spirituality, Music, Dance, Philosophy, Religion - Other, Acupuncture, Tantra, Yoga
ISBN Prefix(es): 978-81-85988
Parent Company: Productivity & Quality Publishing Pvt Ltd

GBD Books, see General Book Depot

Geeta Prakashan
4-2-771, Ramkoti X Rd, Hyderabad 500 001
Tel: (040) 24751344
E-mail: geetaprakashan7@gmail.com
Web Site: geetaprakashan.yolasite.com/
Key Personnel
General Manager: Raj Kumar Tandon
Tel: 9346462551 (cell)
Founded: 1984
Membership(s): Hyd Book Fair Society.
Subjects: Biography, Memoirs, History, Literature, Literary Criticism, Essays, Philosophy, Poetry, Religion - Other, Science (General), Social Sciences, Sociology
ISBN Prefix(es): 978-81-900754; 978-81-89035

General Book Depot+
I-2/16, Ansari Rd, 1st floor, Opposite Saraswati School, Darya Ganj, New Delhi 110 002
Tel: (011) 2326 0022
E-mail: contact@goyalbookshop.com; generalbookdepot@yahoo.com
Web Site: www.pigeonbooks.in
Key Personnel
Partner: Arjun Goyal *Tel:* 9871225151 (cell) *E-mail:* gbd.arjun@gmail.com; Kaushal Goyal *Tel:* 9810229648 (cell) *E-mail:* kaushalgoyal@yahoo.com
Founded: 1933
Specialize in English & German language reprints & French language books.
Subjects: Business, Career Development, English as a Second Language, How-to, Language Arts, Linguistics, Nonfiction (General), Self-Help, Travel & Tourism
ISBN Prefix(es): 978-81-85288
Total Titles: 300 Print
Imprints: W R Goyal Publisher & Distributors; GOYLSaaB
Distributor for Oscar Brandstetter Verlag (Indian Sub-continent)
Showroom(s): 1691, Nai Sarak, PO Box 1220, New Delhi 110 006 *Tel:* (011) 2326 3695; (011) 2325 0635

General Printers & Publishers+
263, Rajaram Mohan Roy Rd, Girgaon, Mumbai 400 004
Tel: (022) 2387 3113; (022) 2382 6854
Key Personnel
Executive Dir: Vijay P Thakker *E-mail:* thakker@gpp.ind.in
Founded: 1952
Membership(s): Afro-Asian Book Council; Federation of Educational Publishers in India; Federation of Indian Publishers.
Subjects: Education, Test Papers, Workbooks
ISBN Prefix(es): 978-81-85619
Number of titles published annually: 20 Print
Total Titles: 100 Print

Global Business Press, *imprint of* Hind Pocket Books

Goel Publishing House, *imprint of* Krishna Prakashan Media (P) Ltd

Golden Bells, *imprint of* Laxmi Publications Pvt Ltd

Good Times Books Pvt Ltd+
H-13, Bali Nagar, New Delhi 110 015
Tel: (011) 259 133 01; (011) 450 690 86 *Fax:* (011) 450 690 86
E-mail: info@goodtimesbooks.com
Web Site: www.goodtimesbooks.com
Key Personnel
Publisher: Devashish Mittal
Founded: 2009
Independent publisher of fiction & nonfiction in English & Indian regional languages.
Subjects: Business, Career Development, Child Care & Development, Crafts, Games, Hobbies, Fiction, Health, Nutrition, How-to, Humor, Inspirational, Spirituality, Management, Marketing, Nonfiction (General), Poetry, Religion - Buddhist, Religion - Hindu, Romance, Self-Help
ISBN Prefix(es): 978-81-909396; 978-81-909595; 978-93-80619
Number of titles published annually: 50 Print
Associate Companies: Concept Publishing Co Pvt Ltd
Branch Office(s)
A/15-16, Commercial Block, Mohan Garden, New Delhi 110 059

Goodwill Publishing House
Unit of Chowdhry Export House
G-1A, Rattan Jyoti Bldg, 18 Rajendra Pl, New Delhi 110 008
Tel: (011) 25750801; (011) 25755519; (011) 25820556 *Fax:* (011) 25763428; (011) 25764396
E-mail: contact@goodwillpublishinghouse.com; info@goodwillpublishinghouse.com
Web Site: www.goodwillpublishinghouse.com
Key Personnel
President: Rajneesh Chowdhry
Founded: 1965
Subjects: Crafts, Games, Hobbies, Health, Nutrition, Humor, Science (General), Chess, Fitness, Jokes & Riddles, Numerology, Palmistry, Puzzles, Writing
ISBN Prefix(es): 978-81-7245
Associate Companies: Goodwill Books International
Imprints: Young Learner Publications

Goodword Books
One, Nizamuddin West Market, New Delhi 110 013
Tel: (011) 4652 1511; (011) 4182 7083; (011) 2435 5454; (011) 2435 6666 *Fax:* (011) 4565 1771
E-mail: info@goodwordbooks.com
Web Site: www.goodwordbooks.com; www.goodword.net
Key Personnel
Founder: Saniyasnain Khan
Subjects: Crafts, Games, Hobbies, Education, History
ISBN Prefix(es): 978-81-85063; 978-81-87570; 978-81-7898

W R Goyal Publisher & Distributors, *imprint of* General Book Depot

GOYLSaaB, *imprint of* General Book Depot

Green Books Pvt Ltd
Ayyanthole, Thrissur, Kerala 680 003
Tel: (0487) 2361038; (0487) 2364439
E-mail: info@greenbooksindia.com
Web Site: www.greenbooksindia.com
Key Personnel
Mng Dir: Valsan Krishnadas *Tel:* 9447161778
   (cell)
Dir, Operations & Sales: Prasad Ek
   Tel: 9446764925 (cell)
Deputy Manager, Publications: Snehalatha Tb
   Tel: 9567123724 (cell)
Customer Relations: Swapna Dilip
   Tel: 9745239868 (cell)
Founded: 2002
Subjects: Biography, Memoirs, Fiction, Poetry,
   Self-Help
ISBN Prefix(es): 978-81-8423
Branch Office(s)
Green Books, Joby's Mall, 2nd floor, GB Rd,
   Palakkad 678 001 *Tel:* (0491) 2546162
   E-mail: palakkad@greenbooksindia.com
Bookshop(s): Brahmaswam Madam Bldg, MG
   Rd, Thrissur 680 001 *Tel:* (0487) 2422515
   E-mail: thrissur@greenbooksindia.com

GTB, see Good Times Books Pvt Ltd

Gyan Bharati, *imprint of* National Publishing
House

Gyan Books Pvt Ltd+
Gyan Kunj, 23 Main Ansari Rd, Darya Ganj,
   New Delhi 110 002
Tel: (011) 23261060; (011) 23282060 *Fax:* (011)
   23285914
E-mail: editor@gyanbooks.com (for authors);
   order@gyanbooks.com; data@gyanbooks.com
   (for publishers)
Web Site: www.gyanbooks.com
Key Personnel
Owner & Dir, Publications: Amit Garg
Founded: 1984
Specialize in humanities & social science books.
Membership(s): Delhi State Booksellers' & Pub-
   lishers' Association; Federation of Indian Pub-
   lishers; Federation of Indian Publishers &
   Booksellers Association.
Subjects: Agriculture, Anthropology, Archaeol-
   ogy, Art, Asian Studies, Astrology, Occult,
   Astronomy, Biography, Memoirs, Career De-
   velopment, Child Care & Development, Com-
   munications, Cookery, Crafts, Games, Hobbies,
   Developing Countries, Drama, Theater, Earth
   Sciences, Economics, Education, Environmen-
   tal Studies, Geography, Geology, Government,
   Political Science, History, Human Relations,
   Journalism, Language Arts, Linguistics, Law,
   Library & Information Sciences, Management,
   Music, Dance, Natural History, Philosophy,
   Psychology, Psychiatry, Public Administration,
   Religion - Buddhist, Religion - Hindu, Reli-
   gion - Islamic, Self-Help, Social Sciences, So-
   ciology, Sports, Athletics, Travel & Tourism,
   Women's Studies
ISBN Prefix(es): 978-81-212
Number of titles published annually: 150 Print
Total Titles: 2,500 Print
Associate Companies: Gyan Books (P) Ltd; Gyan
   Exports
Warehouse: 30-C, Satyawati Colony, Ashok
   Vihar, Phase III, New Delhi 110 052
   E-mail: gyanbook@vsnl.com

Hachette Book Publishing India Pvt Ltd
Division of Hachette UK
Corporate Centre, 4th/5th floors, Plot no 94, Sec-
   tor 44, Gurgaon 122 003
Tel: (0124) 4195000 *Fax:* (0124) 4148900
E-mail: sales@hachetteindia.com; rights@
   hachetteindia.com; publicity@hachetteindia.
   com

Web Site: www.hachetteindia.com
Key Personnel
Publisher & Editorial Dir: Poulomi Chatterjee
Founded: 2008
Subjects: Biography, Memoirs, Business, Fiction,
   History, Nonfiction (General), Pop Culture,
   Self-Help, Sports, Athletics, Travel & Tourism
ISBN Prefix(es): 978-93-80143

Hans Prakashan
18 Nyaya Marg, Allahabad, Uttar Pradesh 211
   001
Tel: (0532) 623077
Founded: 1950
Subjects: Fiction
ISBN Prefix(es): 978-81-85954

HarperCollins Publishers India Ltd
Subsidiary of HarperCollins Publishers
A 53, Sector 57, Noida 201 301
Tel: (0120) 4044800
Web Site: www.harpercollins.co.in
Key Personnel
Chief Executive Officer: Ananth Padmanabhan
Mng Dir: Krisha Naroor
Finance Dir: Amit Abrol
Marketing: Neha Punj *E-mail:* neha.punj@
   harpercollins-india.com
Sales: Manisha Bhatia *E-mail:* manisha.bhatia@
   harpercollins-india.com
ISBN Prefix(es): 978-93-5029
Ultimate Parent Company: News Corp
Distributor for Lonely Planet India Pvt Ltd

Health-Harmony, *imprint of* B Jain Publishers
Pvt Ltd

Arnold Heineman Publishers (India) Pvt Ltd
24, Vaniampathy St, R A Puram, Chennai 600
   028
Tel: (044) 24936255
Founded: 1969
Subjects: Art, Engineering (General), Fiction,
   Government, Political Science, Literature, Lit-
   erary Criticism, Essays, Medicine, Nursing,
   Dentistry, Philosophy, Poetry, Religion - Other,
   Social Sciences, Sociology
ISBN Prefix(es): 978-81-7031
Associate Companies: Edward Arnold (Publish-
   ers) Ltd, United Kingdom
Imprints: Mayfair Paperbacks; Sanskriti; Zebra
   Books for Children

Heritage Publishers+
19 A Ansari Rd (Near Fire Station), Darya Ganj,
   New Delhi 110 002
Tel: (011) 23266633; (011) 23264444; (011)
   23266258 *Fax:* (011) 23263050
E-mail: online@heritagepublishers.in; sales@
   heritagepublishers.in
Web Site: www.heritagepublishers.in
Key Personnel
Proprietor: Baldev Rai Chawla
Founded: 1973
Subjects: Aeronautics, Aviation, Agriculture, Ar-
   chitecture & Interior Design, Art, Astronomy,
   Automotive, Biography, Memoirs, Chemistry,
   Chemical Engineering, Civil Engineering,
   Computer Science, Crafts, Games, Hobbies,
   Disability, Special Needs, Economics, Educa-
   tion, Electronics, Electrical Engineering, Engi-
   neering (General), Geography, Geology, Health,
   Nutrition, History, Language Arts, Linguistics,
   Literature, Literary Criticism, Essays, Manage-
   ment, Medicine, Nursing, Dentistry, Military
   Science, Philosophy, Physics, Religion - Other,
   Science (General), Social Sciences, Sociology,
   Technology, Commerce
ISBN Prefix(es): 978-81-7026
Number of titles published annually: 10 Print
Total Titles: 250 Print

Associate Companies: Heritage Impex Worldwide
Subsidiaries: Book Circle; Intellectuals' Ren-
   dezvous
Branch Office(s)
3-4-215 E, 1st floor, Kanchi Guda, Main Rd,
   Hydrabad 500 027 *Tel:* (040) 27552322
   Fax: (040) 27552448 *E-mail:* heritbooks@vsnl.
   com
Distributor for Blackwell; CRC Press; Pluto
   Press; Routledge; Taschen; Taylor & Francis;
   Thames & Hudson; John Wiley & Sons
Showroom(s): Book Circle, Rajendra Man-
   sion, Ground floor, 19 A Ansari Rd, Darya
   Ganj, New Delhi 110 002, Contact: Himanshu
   Chawla *Tel:* (011) 23264444
Bookshop(s): Book Circle, Rajendra Mansion,
   Ground floor, 19 A Ansari Rd, Darya Ganj,
   New Delhi 110 002, Contact: Himanshu
   Chawla *Tel:* (011) 23264444

Himalaya Publishing House Pvt Ltd
Ramdoot, Dr Bhalerao Marg, Girgaon, Mumbai
   400 004
Tel: (022) 23863863; (022) 23860170 *Fax:* (022)
   23877178
E-mail: himpub@vsnl.com
Web Site: www.himpub.com
Key Personnel
Sales Manager: S K Srivastava
   E-mail: srivastavask@himpub.com
Sales & Rights: Niraj Pandey
Strategy & New Product Development: Anuj
   Pandey
Administration: K N Pandey
Founded: 1938
Subjects: Accounting, Art, Business, Economics,
   History, Law, Management, Psychology, Psy-
   chiatry, Science (General), Social Sciences,
   Sociology, Commerce, Humanities, Information
   Technology
ISBN Prefix(es): 978-81-7040
Branch Office(s)
No 114, Shail, 1st floor, Opposite Madhu Sudan
   House, C G Rd, Navrang Pura, Ahmedabad
   380 009 *Tel:* (079) 26560126
16/1 Madhavar Nagar, 1st floor, Race Course Rd,
   Bangalore 560 001, Regional Manager: Vijay
   Pandey *Tel:* (080) 22281541; (080) 22385461
   Fax: (080) 22286611 *E-mail:* hphbir@vsnl.com
No 8/2 Ground floor Madley 2nd St, T Na-
   gar, Chennai 600 017, Regional Manager:
   Rajesh Naidu *Tel:* 9345345055 (cell)
   E-mail: chennai@himpub.com
39/176 (New No 60/251) 1st floor, Karikkamuri
   Rd, Emakulam, Cochin 682 011, Regional
   Manager: K Sivadasan *Tel:* (0484) 2378012;
   (0484) 2378016 *E-mail:* emakulam@himpub.
   com
House No 15, Behind Pragjyotish College, Near
   Sharma Printing Press PO Bharalumukh,
   Guwahati 781 009
No 3-4-184, Lingampally, Besides Raghaven-
   dra Swamy Matham, Kachiguda, Hyderabad
   500 027, Regional Manager: Krishna Poo-
   jari *Tel:* (040) 27550139; (040) 65501745
   E-mail: hphhyd@hotmail.com
Kesardeep Ave Ext, 73 Narayan Bagh, Flat No
   302, 3rd floor, Near Humpty Dumpty School,
   Narayan Bagh, Indore 452 007, Sales Man-
   ager: S K Srivastava *Tel:* 9301386468 (cell)
   E-mail: srivastavask@himpub.com
108/4, Beliaghata Main Rd, Near ID Hospital,
   Opposite SBI Bank, Kolkata 700 010, Regional
   Manager: N K Mitra *Tel:* (033) 32449649
   E-mail: kolkata@himpub.com
House No 731, Sekhupuram Colony, Near B D
   Convent School, Lucknow 226 024 *Tel:* (0522)
   2339329; (0522) 4068914 *E-mail:* lucknow@
   himpub.cm
Kudanlal Chandak Industrial Estate, Ghat Rd,
   Nagpur 440 018, Dir: G N Pandey *Tel:* (0712)
   2738731; (0712) 3296733 *Fax:* (0712) 2721215
   E-mail: nagpur@himpub.com

Pooja Apartments, 4-B Murari Lal St, Ansari Rd, Darya Ganj, New Delhi 110 002, Dir: Sudhir Joshi *Tel:* (011) 23270392; (011) 23278631 *E-mail:* hphdel@yahoo.co.in
5 Station Sq, Bhubaneshwar, Orissa 751 001, Regional Manager: Bijoy Ojha *Tel:* (0674) 2532129; 9338746007 (cell) *E-mail:* bijoyojha@himpub.com
Laksh Apartment, 1st floor, No 527, Mehunpura, Shaniwarpeth (Near Prabhat Theatre), Pune 411 030, Regional Manager: K Surendra *Tel:* (020) 24496323 *Fax:* (020) 24496333 *E-mail:* surendra@himpub.com

Himalayan Books+
17-L, Connaught Circus, New Delhi 110 001
Tel: (011) 2341-7936; (011) 2341-7126; (011) 2341-5031 *Fax:* (011) 2341-7731
Founded: 1986
Specializes in aviation, Indian art & culture, travel, religion & philosophy.
Subjects: Aeronautics, Aviation, Architecture & Interior Design, Art, Military Science, Music, Dance, Philosophy, Regional Interests, Religion - Other, Travel & Tourism
ISBN Prefix(es): 978-81-7002
Number of titles published annually: 12 Print
Total Titles: 200 Print
Associate Companies: English Book Store

Hind Pocket Books+
J-40 Jor Bagh Lane, New Delhi 110 003
Tel: (011) 24620063; (011) 24621011
E-mail: sales@hindpocketbooks.in
Founded: 1957
Membership(s): Federation of Indian Publishers.
Subjects: Biography, Memoirs, Fiction, How-to, Nonfiction (General), Self-Help
ISBN Prefix(es): 978-81-216
Parent Company: Penguin Random House
Imprints: Clarion Books; Full Circle; Global Business Press; Mainstreet Books; Saraswati Vihar
Book Club(s): Clarion Book Club; Gharelu Library Yojna

Hindi Pracharak Sansthan+
E-21/30, Pishach Mochan, Main Rd, A G Palace, Varanasi, Uttar Pradesh 221 001
Tel: (0542) 2356850; (0542) 2421741
Subjects: Fiction
ISBN Prefix(es): 978-81-7337
Associate Companies: Hindi Pracharak Publications Pvt Ltd; HPS Publications Pvt Ltd; Sahitya Bharati Publications Pvt Ltd
Subsidiaries: Kashi Offset Printers Pvt Ltd
Branch Office(s)
Cal Sahitya Bharati Publications Pvt Ltd, 211/1, Bidhan Sarin

Hindoology Books, *imprint of* Pustak Mahal Publishers

I K International Publishing House Pvt Ltd+
Imprint of I K International Pvt Ltd
4435-36/7, Ansari Rd, Darya Ganj, New Delhi 110 002
Tel: (011) 43205400
E-mail: info@ikinternational.com
Web Site: www.ikbooks.com
Key Personnel
Mng Dir: Krishan Makhijani *E-mail:* k.makhijani@ikinternational.com
Founded: 2005
International education & professional STM publisher. Have championed developments in the industry & played an integral role in the evolution of the STM textbooks, monographs, edited books & journals in the areas of life, earth & environmental sciences, chemistry, physics, mathematics, engineering & technology, man-

agement, economics, finance & medicine for students, researchers & practitioners.
Membership(s): International Association of STM Publishers.
Subjects: Accounting, Aeronautics, Aviation, Agriculture, Animals, Pets, Architecture & Interior Design, Behavioral Sciences, Biological Sciences, Business, Chemistry, Chemical Engineering, Civil Engineering, Communications, Computer Science, Computers, Earth Sciences, Economics, Electronics, Electrical Engineering, Energy, Engineering (General), English as a Second Language, Environmental Studies, Finance, Gardening, Plants, Geography, Geology, Health, Nutrition, Human Relations, Library & Information Sciences, Management, Marketing, Mathematics, Mechanical Engineering, Medicine, Nursing, Dentistry, Physical Sciences, Physics, Public Administrion, Publishing & Book Trade Reference, Religion - Hindu, Science (General), Technology, Transportation, Veterinary Science
ISBN Prefix(es): 978-81-88237; 978-81-89866; 978-81-906566; 978-81-906757; 978-81-906942; 978-81-907462; 978-81-907770; 978-93-80026; 978-93-80578; 978-93-81141; 978-93-82332
Number of titles published annually: 250 Print
Total Titles: 700 Print; 500 E-Book
Distribution Center: Eurospan Group, 3 Henrietta St, Covent Garden, London WC2E 8LU, United Kingdom, Contact: Michael Geelan *Tel:* (020) 7845 0802 *E-mail:* michael.geelan@eurospangroup.com

ICAR, see Indian Council of Agricultural Research

ICSSR, see Indian Council of Social Science Research (ICSSR)

Idara Isha'at-E-Diniyat (P) Ltd
168/2 Jha House, Hazrat Nizamuddin, New Delhi 110 013
Tel: (011) 26956832; (011) 26956834 *Fax:* (011) 26942787; (011) 66173545
E-mail: sales@idara.com
Web Site: www.idara.com
Key Personnel
Dir, Exports: Mohammad Yunus
Founded: 1950
Specialize in Holy Qur'an & Islamic religious books. Cover Urdu, Arabic, English, French, Hindi & Gujrati languages.
Subjects: Religion - Islamic, Religion - Other
ISBN Prefix(es): 978-81-7101
Returns: D/80 Abul Fazal Enclave-I, Jamia Nagar, New Delhi 110 025

IIAS, see Indian Institute of Advanced Study

Impact, *imprint of* B Jain Publishers Pvt Ltd

India Book House Pvt Ltd+
3rd floor, Forum Bldg, Raghuvanshi Mills, Lower Parel, Mumbai 400 013
Tel: (022) 66296999 *Fax:* (022) 66296900
E-mail: contact@ibhworld.com
Web Site: www.ibhworld.com
Key Personnel
Publisher & Executive Dir: Padmini Mirchandani *E-mail:* padmini@ibhworld.com
Mng Dir: Deepak Mirchandani
Founded: 1952
Distripress.
Subjects: Architecture & Interior Design, Art
ISBN Prefix(es): 978-81-7508; 978-81-85028
Parent Company: Mirchandani & Co Pvt Ltd
Associate Companies: IBH Subscription Agency, Fleet Fasteners Bldg, MV Rd, Marol Naka, Andheri (East), Mumbai 400 059, Con-

tact: Moti Wadhwani *Tel:* (022) 2850-2316 *Fax:* (022) 2850-0645 *E-mail:* journals@ibhworld.com
Branch Office(s)
IBH Magazine Services
IBH Publishing Services, Fleet Bldg, M V Rd, Marol Naka, Andheri East, Mumbai 400 059 *Tel:* (022) 2852-7619 *Fax:* (022) 2852-9473 *E-mail:* info@ibhsolves.com
501, Mahalaxmi Chambers, 22 Bhulabhai Desai Rd, Mumbai 400 026 *Tel:* (022) 2352-3827 *Fax:* (022) 2353-8406 *E-mail:* publishing@ibhworld.com
Distributed by Art Books International
Distributor for HarperCollins (USA); Hodder & Stoughton Ltd (UK); Littlehampton Publishers (UK); Random House Inc (USA); Simon & Schuster (UK & USA); Transworld Publishers Ltd (UK)

India Research Press, *imprint of* India Research Press/TARA Press

India Research Press/TARA Press+
Flat 6, Khan Market, New Delhi 110 003
Tel: (011) 41757124
E-mail: contact@indiaresearchpress.com
Web Site: indiaresearchpress.com
Key Personnel
Publisher & CEO: Anuj Bahri
Chief Editor: Sharvani Pandit
Editor: Aanchal Malhotra
Founded: 2002
Promoting high quality books in the genres of fiction, narrative nonfiction & illustrated histories.
Membership(s): Delhi State Books & Publishers Association (DSBPA).
Subjects: Alternative, Biography, Memoirs, Cookery, Economics, Fiction, Government, Political Science, History, Management, Nonfiction (General), Regional Interests, Romance, Social Sciences, Sociology, Travel & Tourism, Development, Healing, Meditation, Mind, Naturopathy, New Age, Yoga
ISBN Prefix(es): 978-81-8386
Number of titles published annually: 30 Print; 30 Online
Total Titles: 140 Print; 140 Online
Parent Company: Bahrisons Booksellers
Imprints: 4Hour Press (commercial list); India Research Press (academic list); TARA Press (trade list)
Distributed by Prakash Books India Pvt Ltd

The Indian Anthropological Society, see Indian Museum, Kolkata

Indian Book Depot (Map House)+
2937, Bahadurgarh Rd, Near Sadar Bazar, New Delhi 110 006
Tel: (011) 23673927; (011) 23523635 *Fax:* (011) 23552096
E-mail: info@ibdmaphouse.com; ibdmaphouse@gmail.com
Web Site: www.ibdmaphouse.com
Key Personnel
Proprietor: Harish Chawla
Administrative Manager: Mr Karan Chawla *Tel:* 9899100170 (cell)
Founded: 1936
Subjects: Agriculture, Animals, Pets, Automotive, Chemistry, Chemical Engineering, Computer Science, Environmental Studies, Fiction, History, Nonfiction (General), Religion - Hindu, Transportation, Travel & Tourism
ISBN Prefix(es): 978-81-87172
Total Titles: 464 Print

Indian Council for Cultural Relations
Azad Bhavan, Indraprastha Estate, New Delhi 110 002
Tel: (011) 23379309; (011) 23379310 *Fax:* (011) 23378639

Web Site: www.iccr.gov.in
Key Personnel
President: Prof Lokesh Chandra *Tel:* (011)
23378616 *Fax:* (011) 23370702
E-mail: president.iccr@nic.in
Dir General: Satish C Mehta *Tel:* (011) 23378103
Fax: (011) 23378647 *E-mail:* dg.iccr@nic.in
Publications (Hindi): D S Rawat *Tel:* (011)
23379930 ext 3399 *E-mail:* pdpub.iccr@nic.in
Founded: 1950
Subjects: Art, Drama, Theater, Ethnicity, Litera-
ture, Literary Criticism, Essays, Music, Dance,
Philosophy, Indian Culture
ISBN Prefix(es): 978-81-85434
Branch Office(s)
3 Sanidhya Bungalows, Opposite Hotel
Landmark, Ambli Rd, Ahmedabad 380
058, Regional Officer: Makrand Shukla
Tel: (079) 26921263 *Fax:* (079) 26921594
E-mail: iccrgujarat@gmail.com
No 7/2, 1st floor, 2nd Main, Palace Cross Rd,
Bangalore 560 052, Regional Dir: Sarla
Unnikrishnan *Tel:* (080) 23466175; (080)
23462714; (080) 23462715; (080) 28436906
Fax: (080) 23566917 *E-mail:* iccrbengaluru@
gmail.com
Ustad Alauddin Khan Sangeet, Evam Kala
Akadami Bldg, Tagore Marg, Banganga,
Bhopal 462 003, Regional Officer: Nityanand
Shrivastava *Tel:* (0755) 2770420 *Fax:* (0755)
2770429 *E-mail:* robpl@iccrindia.net
House No 1210, Sector 34-C, Chandigarh
160 022, Regional Officer: Nalini Singhal
Tel: (0172) 2663908 *Fax:* (0172) 2601762
E-mail: iccr_chd@yahoo.com
7/4, First Cross Rd, Karpagam Garden, Adyar,
Chennai 600 020, Regional Dir: S Manoran-
jitham *Tel:* (044) 24460766; (044) 24460767
Fax: (044) 24460768 *E-mail:* iccrchennai@
bsnl.in
Ravenshaw University Campus, Cuttack 753
003, Regional Dir: Ms Minakshi Mishra
Tel: (0671) 2527111 *Fax:* (0671) 2525111
E-mail: minakshimishra@gmail.com
Annexure Pavilion, Shilpgram, Panjabari Rd,
Guwahati 781 037, Regional Dir: SP Katoti
Bora *Tel:* (0361) 2335358 *Fax:* (0361) 2335359
E-mail: icccrro.guwahati@gmail.com
Kala Bhavan, 2nd floor, Ravindra Bharati Com-
plex, Saifabad, Hyderabad 500 004, Re-
gional Officer: G Laxmi *Tel:* (040) 23236398;
(040) 23298638 *Fax:* (040) 23240035
E-mail: iccr38_hyd@dataone.in
Jawahar Kala Kendra, Opposite Commerce Col-
lege, Jawahar Lal Nehru Marg, Jaipur 302
004, Regional Dir: Anil Pawar *Tel:* (0141)
2701201; (0141) 2712213 *Fax:* (0141) 2701468
E-mail: iccrjpr@gmail.com
46 Garden Ave, Behind Circuit House, Talab
Tillo, Jammu 180 002, Regional Dir: Balwant Thakur *Tel:* (0191) 2555736 *Fax:* (0191)
2505736 *E-mail:* iccrjammu@gmail.com
Rabindranath Tagore Centre, 9A, Ho Chi Minh
Sarani, Kolkata 700 071, Regional Dir: Dr
Reba Som *Tel:* (033) 22872680; (033) 2284890
Fax: (033) 22870028 *E-mail:* iccrcal@
giasc101.vsnl.net.in
3A Gulmohar Colony, Gokhale Marg, Luc-
know 226 001, Regional Officer: Kavita
Pande *Tel:* (0522) 2209592; (0522) 2209594
Fax: (0522) 2209587 *E-mail:* iccrluck@gmail.
com
One, Hemprabha, 68, Netaji Subhash Marg,
Mumbai 400 020, Regional Dir: Manjistha
Mukherjee Bhatt *Tel:* (022) 22814581;
(022) 22813302 *Fax:* (022) 22811964
E-mail: iccrmum@mtnl.net.in
67-68/40 Officer's Flats, Bailey Rd, Patna 800
001, Regional Officer: Vinay Kumar
Survey No 163/2, Plot No 31, Deo-Phadke
Bungalow, Kotbagi Lane, Off D P Rd,
Aundh, Pune 411 067, Regional Officer: R
Parthiban *Tel:* (020) 25884194; (020) 25885464

Fax: (020) 25884140 *E-mail:* iccrpune@gmail.
com
ICCR (Goa), Ground floor, Francis Luis Gomes
District Library, Behind Rosary Church, Nave-
lim, Salcette 403 729, Regional Dir: Rajan Sa-
tardekar *Tel:* (0832) 2757091; (0832) 2757092
Fax: (0832) 2463444 *E-mail:* iccrgoa@gmail.
com
Rabindra Art Gallery, New Assembly Compound,
Brookside, Rilbong, Shilong 793 004
H No 18 Kralsangri Brein Nishat, Srinagar 191
121, Regional Dir: Dr Ayaz Rasool Nazki
Tel: (0194) 2461330 *E-mail:* iccrkralsangri@
gmail.com
Rohini, TC-16/131, Eswaravilasom Rd, Vazhutha-
caud, Thiruvananthapuram 695 014, Regional
Officer: M R Krishnamoorthy *Tel:* (0471)
2326712; (0471) 2320825 *Fax:* (0471) 2332479
E-mail: iccrtvm08@bsnl.in
C-3/3, Tagore House, Banaras Hindu Univer-
sity, Varanasi 221 005, Regional Officer:
Anurag Singh *Tel:* (0542) 2368631 *Fax:* (0542)
2368632 *E-mail:* iccrbhu@gmail.com

Indian Council of Agricultural Research
Krishi Bhavan, Dr Rajendra Prasad Rd, New
Delhi 110 001
Tel: (011) 2388991 *Fax:* (011) 2387293
Web Site: www.icar.org.in
Key Personnel
Project Dir: Dr Rameshwar Singh *Tel:* (011)
25842787 *Fax:* (011) 25843285
E-mail: pddkma@icar.org.in
Business Manager: S K Joshi *Tel:* (011)
25843657 *Fax:* (011) 25841282
E-mail: bmicar@icar.org.in
Public Relations: Anil K Sharma *Tel:* (011)
25843301 *E-mail:* anil.cpro@gmail.com
Subjects: Agriculture, Animals, Pets
ISBN Prefix(es): 978-81-7164

Indian Council of Social Science Research (ICSSR)
JNU Institutional Area, Aruna Asaf Ali Marg,
New Delhi 110 067
Tel: (011) 26179849; (011) 26179850; (011)
26179851 *Fax:* (011) 26179836
Web Site: www.icssr.org
Key Personnel
Chairman: Dr Braj Bihari Kumar *Tel:* (011)
26741679 *E-mail:* chairman@iccsr.org
Dir, Publication & Research Surveys: Ajay
Kumar Gupta *Tel:* (011) 26742149
E-mail: ajaygupta@icssr.org
Founded: 1969
Promote, sponsor & support social science re-
search & social science information activities
in India by providing financial assistance in the
form of fellowship, sponsorship, study grants
& grants-in-aid to individuals as well as institu-
tions.
Subjects: Anthropology, Behavioral Sciences,
Business, Child Care & Development, Crim-
inology, Economics, Education, Government,
Political Science, History, Human Relations,
Law, Library & Information Sciences, Man-
agement, Marketing, Psychology, Psychiatry,
Public Administration, Social Sciences, Sociology, Women's Studies
ISBN Prefix(es): 978-81-85008
Total Titles: 500 Print

Indian Documentation Service+
887/5 Patel Nagar St, No 6, Gurgaon, Haryana
122 001
Tel: (0124) 2324782 *Fax:* (0124) 2324782
E-mail: indocu@gmail.com
Key Personnel
Dir: Pankaj Jain
Sales & Publicity: Pankaj Kumar
Founded: 1971

Subjects: Anthropology, Art, Asian Studies, As-
trology, Occult, Astronomy, Biblical Studies,
Developing Countries, Drama, Theater, En-
glish as a Second Language, Erotica, Fashion,
History, Music, Dance, Philosophy, Psychol-
ogy, Psychiatry, Religion - Buddhist, Religion -
Catholic, Religion - Hindu, Religion - Islamic,
Religion - Jewish, Religion - Protestant, Reli-
gion - Other, Self-Help, Social Sciences, Soci-
ology, Theology, Travel & Tourism, Women's
Studies
ISBN Prefix(es): 978-81-85258
Total Titles: 100 Print

Indian Institute of Advanced Study
Rashtrapati Nivas, Shimla 171 005
Tel: (0177) 2832930; (0177) 2831376
E-mail: spro@iias.ac.in
Web Site: iias.ac.in; books.iias.org (orders)
Key Personnel
Dir: Prof Chetan Singh *E-mail:* director@iias.ac.
in
Sales & Public Relations Officer: Bhajan Dass
Kaith
Founded: 1965
Subjects: Social Sciences, Sociology
ISBN Prefix(es): 978-81-85952; 978-81-7986
Number of titles published annually: 10 Print
Total Titles: 118 Print

Indian Museum, Kolkata
27, Jawaharlal Nehru Rd, Kolkata 700 016
Tel: (033) 2286-1702; (033) 2286-1699
Fax: (033) 2286-1696
Web Site: www.indianmuseumkolkata.org
Key Personnel
Dir: Dr Anup K Matilal
Education Officer: Sayan Bhattacharya *Tel:* (91)
9230001451 *E-mail:* educationofficerim@
gmail.com
Founded: 1814
Subjects: Anthropology, Archaeology, Art, Geog-
raphy, Geology, Science (General)
ISBN Prefix(es): 978-81-85525

Indian Society for Promoting Christian Knowledge (ISPCK)+
1654, Madarsa Rd, Kashmere Gate, New Delhi
110 006
Mailing Address: PO Box 1585, New Delhi 100
006
Tel: (011) 23866323 *Fax:* (011) 23865490
E-mail: mail@ispck.org.in
Web Site: www.ispck.org.in
Key Personnel
General Secretary/Dir: Dr Ashish Amos
E-mail: ashish@ispck.org.in
Senior Executive Officer: Simon Kingston
Founded: 1957 (as autonomous body 1958)
Membership(s): Association of Christian Publish-
ers & Booksellers in India; Board of Theolog-
ical Education (BTE); Delhi State Booksellers
Association of India; Inter-Anglican Publish-
ing Network; National Association of Christian
Communication (NACC); National Council of
Churches in India (NCCI); SPCK Worldwide;
World Association for Christian Communica-
tion (WACC).
Subjects: Biblical Studies, Biography, Mem-
oirs, Government, Political Science, Religion
- Other, Social Sciences, Sociology, Theology
ISBN Prefix(es): 978-81-7214
Subsidiaries: Navdin Prakashan Kendra
Branch Office(s)
Andhra Christian Theological College, Lower
Tank Bund Rd, Gandhi Nagar (PO), Andhra
Pradesh, Hyderabad 500 080 *Tel:* (033)
22421804 *E-mail:* sales@ispck.org.in
The Church of South India, CSI Center, No 5,
White Rd, Royapettah, Chennai, Tamil Nadu
600 014

Christian Book Depot, Diocese of Eastern Himilaya CNI, Diocesan Centre, Gandhi Rd, Darjeeling, Bengla *Tel:* (03) 54256389 *Fax:* (011) 3865490 *E-mail:* ispck@nde.vsnl.net.in
Leonard Theological College, Post Box 36, Civil Lines, Jabalpur, Madhya Pradesh 482001
Bookshop(s): Jabalpur Diocesan Bookshop, Mission Boys Hostel, Jarbhata, Bilashpur, Madhya Pradesh 495001; 51, Chowringhee Rd, Kolkata, Bengla 700071 *Tel:* (033) 22821804 *E-mail:* sales@ispck.org.in; Opposite Liberty Cinema, Residency Rd, Sadar, Nagpur, Maharastra 400 001 *Tel:* (0712) 2543425 *E-mail:* sales@ispck.org.in; Chotanagpur Diocesan Bookshop, PO Church Rd, Ranchi, Bihar 834001

IndianInk, *imprint of* Roli Books Pvt Ltd

Indigo Books, *imprint of* Cosmo Publications

Indus Publishing Co+
E-241, Tagore Garden, New Delhi 110 027
Tel: (011) 2545 9969; (011) 6516 4040
E-mail: induspubco@gmail.com
Web Site: www.indus-publishing.com
Key Personnel
Mng Dir: M L Gidwani
Dir Sales & Product Development: Lokesh Gidwani
Founded: 1987
Publisher, bookseller & exporter. Specialize in Himalayan studies, forestry, environment, mountaineering & trekking.
Membership(s): Delhi State Booksellers' & Publishers' Association.
Subjects: Agriculture, Archaeology, Art, Economics, Environmental Studies, Gardening, Plants, Government, Political Science, History, Natural History, Philosophy, Religion - Buddhist, Religion - Hindu, Social Sciences, Sociology, Travel & Tourism, Botany, Culture, Forestry, Himalayan Studies, Horticulture, Trekking & Climbing, Wildlife
ISBN Prefix(es): 978-81-85182; 978-81-7387
Number of titles published annually: 25 Print
Total Titles: 250 Print
Associate Companies: Indus International, 5-A (MIG), Rajouri Garden, New Delhi 110 027 (exporters of Indian books & journals; worldwide delivery)
Distributed by Duggal Publishers & Distributors (Kalka); India Book House (Hyderabad); Paramount Book Agency (Ahmedabad); United Publishers (Guwahati)
Book Club(s): Indus Club (special discount for members)

Infinity Science Press LLC (USA), *imprint of* Laxmi Publications Pvt Ltd

Institute of Book Publishing, *imprint of* Sterling Publishers Pvt Ltd

Inter-India Publications+
D-17, Raja Garden, New Delhi 110 015
Tel: (011) 25441120; (011) 25467082 *Fax:* (011) 25467082
E-mail: inter_india@yahoo.co.in
Key Personnel
Chief Executive, Editorial, Rights & Permissions: M C Mittal
Founded: 1975
Specialize in tribes, women & forests.
Membership(s): Federation of Indian Publishers.
Subjects: Agriculture, Anthropology, Archaeology, Art, Asian Studies, Crafts, Games, Hobbies, Economics, Ethnicity, Geography, Geology, Government, Political Science, History,

Philosophy, Religion - Other, Social Sciences, Sociology, Transportation, Women's Studies
ISBN Prefix(es): 978-81-210

IPH, see Islamic Publishing House

Islamic Publishing House+
Division of Islamic Service Trust, Kerala
Rajaji Rd, Fourland Bldg, Kozhikode 4, Kerala 673 004
Tel: (0495) 2720072; (0495) 2724618
E-mail: iphdir@gmail.com; iphcalicut@gmail.com
Web Site: www.iphkerala.com
Key Personnel
Dir, International Rights: T K Farooque
Founded: 1945
Publish & distribute books in Malayalam language on various topics of Islam.
Subjects: Biography, Memoirs, Government, Political Science, Health, Nutrition, History, Human Relations, Law, Philosophy, Religion - Islamic, Travel & Tourism
ISBN Prefix(es): 978-81-7204; 978-81-8271
Number of titles published annually: 150 Print
Distributor for Markazi Maktaba Islami (India)
Book Club(s): IPH Book Club

ISPCK, see Indian Society for Promoting Christian Knowledge (ISPCK)

Jaico Publishing House
A-2, Jash Chambers, 7-A Sir Phirozshah Mehta Rd, Mumbai 400 001
Tel: (022) 4030 67 67 *Fax:* (022) 4030 67 42
E-mail: jaicopub@jaicobooks.com
Web Site: www.jaicobooks.com
Key Personnel
Mng Dir: Ashwin J Shah
Executive Dir: S C Sethi
Assistant General Manager: D M Patel
Chief Editor: Rayasam H Sharma
Founded: 1946
Subjects: Astrology, Occult, Behavioral Sciences, Biography, Memoirs, Cookery, Criminology, Economics, Engineering (General), Ethnicity, Government, Political Science, Health, Nutrition, History, Humor, Language Arts, Linguistics, Law, Management, Philosophy, Psychology, Psychiatry, Religion - Other, Self-Help
ISBN Prefix(es): 978-81-7224; 978-81-7992
Number of titles published annually: 200 Print
Subsidiaries: Jaico Press Pvt Ltd
Branch Office(s)
Shop No C-149, 1st floor, Sumel Business Park-6, Opposite Hanumanpura Brts, Dudheshwar Rd, Shahibaug, Ahmedabad 380 004, Branch Manager: Mr Sujesh Kumar *Tel:* (079) 2560 59 05; (079) 2560 59 22 *E-mail:* sujesh.kumar@jaicobooks.com
14/1, First Main Rd, 6th Cross, Gandhi Nagar, Bangalore 560 009, Branch Manager: Mr S Sreevatsa *Tel:* (080) 2226 70 16; (080) 2225 70 83 *E-mail:* bangalore.sales@jaicobooks.com
42-A Ground floor, VYAS Complex, Zone-II, M P Nagar, Bhopal 462 011, Branch Manager: Mr K S Mishra *Tel:* (0755) 422 92 45 *E-mail:* bhopal.sales@jaicobooks.com
Plot No 661/3404, Ground floor, Jayadurga Nagar, Backside of New Kalika Hotel, Bhubaneswar, Odisha 751 006, Branch Manager: Mr Shubomoy Sengupta *Tel:* (0674) 257 18 02 *E-mail:* bhubaneswar.sales@jaicobooks.com
No 48, Arya Gowder Rd, West Mambalam, Chennai 600 033, Branch Manager: Mr A R Sivaraman *Tel:* (044) 2480 30 91; (044) 2480 30 92; (011) 2480 30 93; (011) 2480 30 94 *E-mail:* chennai.sales@jaicobooks.com
3-4-512/75, (35/4RT), Opposite Lane to Raghvendra Swamy Mutt, Barkatpura, Hyderabad 500 027, Branch Manager: Mr B N Rao *Tel:* (040)

2755 19 92; (040) 2755 56 99; (040) 2755 13 29 *E-mail:* hyderabad.sales@jaicobooks.com
302, Acharya Prafulla Chandra Roy Rd, Kolkata 700 009, Branch Manager: Mr Sujit Kumar Guha *Tel:* (033) 2360 05 42; (033) 2360 05 43; (033) 2360 80 27 *E-mail:* kolkata.sales@jaicobooks.com
Hotel D/D International (Basement), 196, Gautam Budh Marg Bans Mandi Crossing, Lucknow 226 018, Branch Manager: Mr Rajnish Sinha *Tel:* (0522) 407 16 13 *E-mail:* lucknow.sales@jaicobooks.com
4736/23, G/F, Plot No 1, Ansari Rd, Darya Ganj, New Delhi 110 002, Branch Manager: Mr D K Kapoor *Tel:* (011) 4937 21 50 *E-mail:* delhi.sales@jaicobooks.com
Bookshop(s): Jaicos

B Jain Publishers Pvt Ltd+
Member of B Jain Publishing Group
D-157, Sector-63, Noida, Uttar Predesh 201 307
Tel: (0120) 4933333
E-mail: info@bjain.com
Web Site: www.bjain.com
Key Personnel
Dir: Nitin Jain *E-mail:* nitin@bjain.com
Editor-in-Chief: Dr Geeta Rani Arora *E-mail:* hb@bjain.com
Production Dir: Manish Jain *E-mail:* manish@bjain.com
Business Development: Nishant Jain *E-mail:* nishant@bjain.com
Founded: 1966
Subjects: Alternative, Business, Health, Nutrition, Inspirational, Spirituality, Medicine, Nursing, Dentistry, Self-Help, Fashion Designing, Homeopathy
ISBN Prefix(es): 978-81-7021; 978-81-8056; 978-81-319
Number of titles published annually: 150 Print
Total Titles: 1,400 Print
Imprints: Health-Harmony; Impact; Leads Press; Pegasus

Jaipur Publishing House (JPH)
Lalji Sand Ka Rasta, Chaura Rasta, Jaipur 302 004
Tel: (0141) 2319198; (0141) 2319094
Founded: 1960
Publisher of text & competitive books.
Subjects: Biological Sciences, Chemistry, Chemical Engineering, Economics, History, Mathematics, Physics
ISBN Prefix(es): 978-81-8047

Jaypee Brothers Medical Publishers (P) Ltd+
4838/24 Ansari Rd, Darya Ganj, New Delhi 110 002
Tel: (011) 43574357 *Fax:* (011) 43574314
E-mail: jaypee@jaypeebrothers.com
Web Site: www.jaypeebrothers.com
Key Personnel
Chairman & Chief Executive Officer: Jitendar P Vij
Dir: Tarun Vij
Dir, Sales: P G Bandhu
General Manager, Publishing: Tarun Duneja
Founded: 1969
Subjects: Medicine, Nursing, Dentistry
ISBN Prefix(es): 978-81-7179; 978-81-8061; 978-93-80704; 978-93-5025; 978-81-8448
Total Titles: 1,500 Print
Subsidiaries: AJR Medi Solutions; Jaypee Digital; Jaypee-Highlights Medical Publishers; Jaypee Journals; Jaypee Pharma Customized Imprints (P) Ltd; JP Medical Ltd
Branch Office(s)
2/8 Akruti Society, Jodhpur Gam Rd Satellite, Ahmedabad 380 015 *Tel:* (079) 26926233; (079) 32988717 *Fax:* (079) 26927094 *E-mail:* ahmedabad@jaypeebrothers.com

202 Batavia Chambers, 8 Kumara Kruppa Rd, Kumara Park East, Bangalore 560 001 *Tel:* (080) 22285971; (080) 22382956; (080) 32714073 *Fax:* (080) 22281761 *E-mail:* bangalore@jaypeebrothers.com
282, 3rd floor, Khaleel Shirazi Estate, Fountain Plaza, Pantheon Rd, Chennai 600 008 *Tel:* (044) 28193265; (044) 28194897; (044) 32972089 *Fax:* (044) 28193231 *E-mail:* chennai@jaypeebrothers.com
4-2-1067/1-3, 1st floor, Balaji Bldg, Ramkote Cross Rd, Hyderabad 500 095 *Tel:* (040) 66610020; (040) 24758498; (040) 32940929 *Fax:* (040) 24758499 *E-mail:* hyderabad@ jaypeebrothers.com
20 No 41/3098, B & B1, Kuruvi Bldg, St Vincent Rd, Kochi, Kerala 682 018 *Tel:* (0484) 4036109 *E-mail:* kochi@jaypeebrothers.com
1A India Mirror St, Wellington Sq, Kolkata 700 013 *Tel:* (033) 22651926; (033) 22276404; (033) 32901926 *Fax:* (033) 22656075 *E-mail:* kolkata@jaypeebrothers.com
292/31, 1st floor Shama, Afroze Complex, Tulsi Das Marg, Lucknow 226 003 *Tel:* (0522) 3293848; (0522) 3293847; (0522) 4108504 *E-mail:* lucknow@jaypeebrothers.com
106 Amit Industrial Estate, 61 Dr SS Rao Rd, Near MGM Hospital, Parel, Mumbai 400 012 *Tel:* (022) 24124863; (022) 24104532 *Fax:* (022) 24160828 *E-mail:* mumbai@ jaypeebrothers.com
Kamalpushpa 38 Reshimbaj, Opposite Mohata Science College, Umred Rd, Nagpur 440 009 *Tel:* (0712) 3245220 *Fax:* (0712) 2704275 *E-mail:* nagpur@jaypeebrothers.com
U.S. Office(s): Jaypee Medical Inc, The Bourse, III South Independence Mall East, Suite 835, Philadelphia, PA 19106, United States *Tel:* 267-519-9789 *E-mail:* jpmed.us@gmail.com
Distributed by Anshan Ltd (UK); Arnold Publishing (UK); Blackwell Publishing (UK); McGraw-Hill (USA)
Distributor for American Psychiatric Press Inc; Edward Arnold (UK); Blackwell Science Ltd (UK); BMJ (UK); Butterworths (UK); F A Davis Co (USA); Highlights of Ophthalmology (USA); ISIS Medical Media (UK); Lippincott Williams & Wilkins (USA); Martin-Dunitz (UK); Mosby Year Book (UK & USA); Munksgard (Denmark); Parthenon Publishing Group (UK); W B Saunders (UK & USA); SLACK Inc (USA); Springer Verlag, Heidelberg (Germany); Georg Thieme Verlag, Stuttgart (Germany)
Foreign Rep(s): F & J De Jesus Inc (Philippines); Ho-Chi Book Publishing Co (Taiwan); Jahan Adib Publishing (Iran); Masuro The Book Sellers Ltd (Nigeria); McGraw-Hill (USA); Nobel Tip Kitabevleri Ltd (Turkey); Panmum Book Col Ltd (South Korea); Paramount Books (Pvt) Ltd (Pakistan)

JPH, see Jaipur Publishing House (JPH)

Kairali Children's Book Trust
c/o DC Books, DC Kizhakemuri Edam, Good Shepherd St, Kottayam, Kerala 686 001 *Tel:* (0481) 2563114; (0481) 2301614 *E-mail:* info@dcbooks.com; publish@dcbooks. com
Web Site: www.dcbooks.com/children.asp
Founded: 1982
Subjects: Biography, Memoirs, Fiction, Foreign Countries
ISBN Prefix(es): 978-81-7152
Associate Companies: Current Books; DC Books; Kairali Mudralayam
Imprints: DC Press
Book Club(s): Kairali Club
Orders to: Current Books, VIII/493 Railway Station Rd, Kottayam 686 001

Kairali Mudralayam
c/o DC Books, DC Kizhakemuri Edam, Good Shepherd St, Kottayam 686 001
Tel: (0481) 2563114; (0481) 2301614 *Fax:* (0481) 2564758
E-mail: info@dcbooks.com; sales@dcbooks.com; marketing@dcbooks.com; rights@dcbooks.com
Web Site: www.dcbooks.com/kairali.asp
Founded: 1978
Subjects: Biography, Memoirs, Fiction, Humor
ISBN Prefix(es): 978-81-85226
Number of titles published annually: 500 Print
Associate Companies: Current Books; DC Books; Kairali Children's Book Trust

Kali For Women, see Zubaan

Kalyani Publishers+
B-1, Rajinder Ngr, Ludhiana 141 008
Tel: (0161) 2760031 *Fax:* (0161) 2745872
E-mail: kalyanibooks@yahoo.co.in
Key Personnel
Mng Dir: Raj Kumar
Founded: 1935
Educational & other research publications.
Subjects: Science (General), Humanities
ISBN Prefix(es): 978-81-272; 978-81-7663
Number of titles published annually: 200 Print
Total Titles: 2,000 Print
Branch Office(s)
No 10/2B, Ramnathy Mazumdar St, Kolkata 700 09 *Tel:* (033) 22416024
No 1, Lakshmi St, T Nagar, Chennai 600 017 *Tel:* (044) 24344684
110/111 Bharatia Towers, Badambadi, Cuttack 753 001 *Tel:* (0671) 2311391
3-5-1103 Narayanguda, Hyderabad 500 002 *Tel:* (040) 24750368
4863-2B Bharat Ram Rd, 24 Darya Ganj, New Delhi 110 002 *Tel:* (011) 23274393; (011) 23271469
B16, Sector 8, Noida *Tel:* (0120) 2424492
Bookshop(s): Lyall Book Depot, Chaura Bazar, Ludhiana *Tel:* (0161) 2760031; (0161) 2745872

Karadi Tales Co Pvt Ltd
3A Dev Regency, 11, First Main Rd, Gandhinagar, Adyar, Chennai 600 020
Tel: (044) 2442 1775; (044) 4205 4243 *Fax:* (044) 2440 3728
E-mail: contact@karaditales.com
Web Site: www.karaditales.com
Founded: 1996
ISBN Prefix(es): 978-81-8190
Imprints: Charkha Audiobooks; Chitra; Dreaming Fingers
Foreign Rep(s): Consortium Book Sales & Distribution (USA)

S K Kataria & Sons
4885/109, Prakash Mahal, Dr Subhash Bhargav Lane, Near Gurudwara, Darya Ganj, New Delhi 110 002
Tel: (011) 3243489; (011) 23269324
E-mail: katariabooks@yahoo.com; katson_sanjeev@yahoo.co.in; katariabook@ gmail.com
Web Site: www.skkatariaandsons.com
Founded: 1969
Subjects: Computer Science, Engineering (General), Technology, Applied Science
ISBN Prefix(es): 978-81-85749; 978-81-88458; 978-81-906919; 978-81-907386; 978-81-89757; 978-93-5014

Katson Books, see S K Kataria & Sons

Khanna Publishers+
2-B Nath Market, Nai Sarak, New Delhi 110 006
Tel: (011) 2912380; (011) 7224179
E-mail: khannapublishers@yahoo.in

Web Site: www.khannapublishers.in
Key Personnel
Dir: R C Khanna
Founded: 1959
Subjects: Civil Engineering, Communications, Computer Science, Electronics, Electrical Engineering, Energy, Engineering (General), Environmental Studies, Management, Mathematics, Mechanical Engineering, Technology
ISBN Prefix(es): 978-81-7409
Branch Office(s)
11 Community Centre, Ashok Vihar, Phase II, New Delhi 110 052 *Tel:* (011) 7224179

Kitab Ghar
4855/24 Ansari Rd, Darya Ganj, New Delhi 110 002
Tel: (011) 23281244; (011) 32932084; (011) 23266207
E-mail: kitab_ghar@hotmail.com; kitabghar-prk@ yahoo.com
Key Personnel
Chief Executive, Rights & Permissions: Satya Brat Sharma
Editorial & Production: Jagat Ram Sharma
Sales & Publicity: Dev Datt
Founded: 1970
Subjects: Biography, Memoirs, Drama, Theater, Fiction, Poetry, Science (General), Social Sciences, Sociology
ISBN Prefix(es): 978-81-7016; 978-81-7891

Konark Publishers Pvt Ltd+
206, 1st floor, Peacock Lane, Shakarpur Jat, New Delhi 110 049
Tel: (011) 41055065; (011) 65254972
E-mail: india@konarkpublishers.com
Web Site: www.konarkpublishers.com/ konark_india; www.konarkpublishers.com
Key Personnel
Founder & Mng Dir: K P R Nair
Vice President: Latha Ramachandran
Founded: 1986
Subjects: Government, Political Science, Human Relations, Labor, Industrial Relations, Social Sciences, Sociology
ISBN Prefix(es): 978-81-220; 978-81-85650
Number of titles published annually: 40 Print
Total Titles: 750 Print

Kosi Books, *imprint of* Vidyarthi Mithram Press & Book Depot

Krishna Prakashan Media (P) Ltd+
Krishna House, 11 Shivaji Rd, Meerut, Uttar Pradesh 250 001
Tel: (0121) 4026111; (0121) 4026112; (0121) 2644766; (0121) 2642946 *Fax:* (0121) 2645855
E-mail: support@krishnaprakashan.com
Web Site: www.krishnaprakashan.com
Key Personnel
Executive Dir: Mr Sugam Rastogi *E-mail:* sugam. rastogi@krishnaprakashan.com
Mng Dir: Mr Satyendra Kumar Rastogi
Founded: 1942
Educational publisher.
Membership(s): Federation of Educational Publishers in India (FEPI); Federation of Indian Publishers.
Subjects: Accounting, Architecture & Interior Design, Art, Astrology, Occult, Astronomy, Career Development, Chemistry, Chemical Engineering, Child Care & Development, Civil Engineering, Computer Science, Economics, Electronics, Electrical Engineering, Engineering (General), Environmental Studies, Government, Political Science, Humor, Inspirational, Spirituality, Management, Mathematics, Mechanical Engineering, Nonfiction (General), Physics, Science (General)
ISBN Prefix(es): 978-81-8283
Total Titles: 800 Print; 400 Online

Associate Companies: gMasteRg Educorp
  E-mail: gmasterg@krishnaprakashan.com (e-commerce & export partner)
Imprints: Dynamic Books; Goel Publishing House

Lalit Kala Akademi (National Academy of Art)
Rabindra Bhavan, 35 Ferozeshah Rd, New Delhi 110 001
Tel: (011) 23009200 *Fax:* (011) 23009292
E-mail: lka@lalitkala.gov.in
Web Site: www.lalitkala.gov.in
Key Personnel
Chairman: Mr K K Mittal *E-mail:* chairman@lalitkala.gov.in
Secretary: Dr Sudhakar Sharma
  E-mail: secretary@lalitkala.gov.in
Founded: 1954
Promote study & research in the field of creative arts such as painting, sculpture, graphics & other such forms.
Subjects: Art, Ethnicity
ISBN Prefix(es): 978-81-87507
Branch Office(s)
Regional Centre, Garhi, Artist Studio, Near East of Kailash, Kalka Devi Marg, New Delhi 110 065, Contact: N M Nawani *Tel:* (011) 26431849; (011) 26432225 *Fax:* (011) 26217764 *E-mail:* rcgarhi@lalitkala.gov.in
Lalit Kala Kendra, 111/4, Kharvela Nagar, Unit 3, 750 001 Bhubaneswar, Regional Secretary: Mr Ramakrishma Vedala *Tel:* (0674) 2391884 *Fax:* (0674) 2391369 *E-mail:* rcbbsr@lalitkala.gov.in
Regional Centre, 4 Greams Rd, Chennai 600 006, Contact: R M Palaniappan *Tel:* (044) 28291692 *Fax:* (044) 28290804 *E-mail:* rccchennai@lalitkala.gov.in
Rashtriya Lalit Kala Kendra, 361, Keyatala Lane, Kolkata 700 029, Regional Secretary: Siddhartha Ghosh *Tel:* (033) 24641719 *Fax:* (033) 24641719 *E-mail:* rckolkata@lalitkala.gov.in
Rashtriya Lalit Kala Kendra, One Ekta Vihar, Sector E, Aliganj, Lucknow 226 024, Regional Officer: Vinod Kumar Aggarwal *Tel:* (0522) 2324067; (0522) 2329183 *Fax:* (0522) 2324067 *E-mail:* rclucknow@lalitkala.gov.in

Law Publishers (India) Pvt Ltd+
18, A Sardar Patel Marg, PO Box 1077, Civil Lines, Allahabad 211 001
Tel: (0532) 262374; (0532) 2623735; (0532) 2420733 *Fax:* (0532) 622781; (0532) 2622276
E-mail: sai@lawpublisherindia.com; virandra@sanchar.net.in
Web Site: www.lawpublisherindia.com
Key Personnel
Chief Executive: Naresh Sagar
Founded: 1961
Export of law & non-law journals & subscription service on back sets.
Subjects: Agriculture, Business, Criminology, Economics, Engineering (General), Environmental Studies, Government, Political Science, History, Law, Library & Information Sciences, Management, Mechanical Engineering, Physical Sciences, Psychology, Psychiatry, Religion - Buddhist, Religion - Hindu, Religion - Islamic, Science (General), Technology, Women's Studies
ISBN Prefix(es): 978-81-7111
Foreign Rep(s): Shekhar Srivastava (Brunei, Malaysia, Singapore, Southeast Asia, Sri Lanka)
Distribution Center: Kumar Law Publications Ltd, Shop No 1, Civil Wing, Tis Hazari Courts, Delhi 110 006 *Tel:* (011) 2397 3794

Laxmi Publications Pvt Ltd+
113, Golden House, Darya Ganj, New Delhi 110 002
Tel: (011) 4353 2500; (011) 4353 2501
Fax: (011) 2325 2572; (011) 4353 2528

E-mail: info@laxmipublications.com; order@laxmipublications.com
Web Site: www.laxmipublications.com
Key Personnel
Chairman: Mr R K Gupta
Mng Dir: Mr Saurabh Gupta
Founded: 1974
Specialize in computer books, engineering, college & school textbooks.
Membership(s): Federation of Indian Publishers.
Subjects: Civil Engineering, Computer Science, Electronics, Electrical Engineering, Mathematics, Mechanical Engineering
ISBN Prefix(es): 978-81-7008; 978-81-900524; 978-81-318; 978-81-908563; 978-93-80856; 978-93-81159
Number of titles published annually: 50 Print
Total Titles: 900 Print
Imprints: Firewall Media; Golden Bells; Infinity Science Press LLC (USA); New Age International
Branch Office(s)
No 37/22, 8 Cross, Chamrajpet, Bangalore 560 018 *Tel:* (080) 26756930 *Fax:* (080) 26756930 *E-mail:* bangalore@laxmipublications.com
26, Damodaran St, T Nagar, Chennai 600 017 *Tel:* (044) 24344726; (044) 24359507 *E-mail:* chennai@laxmipublications.com
CC-39/1016, Carrier Station Rd, Near Jomer Avalon Flats, Ernakulam S, Cochin 682 016 *Tel:* (0484) 4051303; (0484) 2377004 *Fax:* (0484) 2377004 *E-mail:* cochin@laxmipublications.com
Hemsen Complex, Near Star Line Hotel, Md Shah Rd, Palton Bazar, Guwahati 781 008 *Tel:* (0361) 2543669; (0361) 2513881 *Fax:* (0361) 2543669 *E-mail:* guwahati@laxmipublications.com
No 104, 1st floor, Madhiray Kaveri Tower, 3-2-19, Azam Jahi Rd, Nimboliadda, Hyderabad 500 027 *Tel:* (040) 24652333 *E-mail:* hyderabad@laxmipublications.com
ND-365, Adda Tanda Chowk, Jalandhar City 144 008 *Tel:* (0181) 2221272 *E-mail:* jalandhar@laxmipublications.com
RDB Chambers, 106/A, 1st floor, SN Banerjee Rd, Kolkata 700 014 *Tel:* (033) 22274384 *Fax:* (033) 22275247 *E-mail:* kolkata@laxmipublications.com
16-A, Jopling Rd, Lucknow 226 001 *Tel:* (0522) 2209916 *Fax:* (0522) 2204098 *E-mail:* lucknow@laxmipublications.com
142-C, Victor House, Ground floor, NM Joshi Marg, Lower Parel (W), Mumbai 400 013 *Tel:* (022) 24915415; (022) 24927869 *E-mail:* mumbai@laxmipublications.com
Laxmi Narayan Complex, Near Telephone Exchange, Ranchi 834 001 *Tel:* (0651) 2214764; (0651) 2204464 *Fax:* (0651) 2214764 *E-mail:* ranchi@laxmipublications.com

Leads Press, *imprint of* B Jain Publishers Pvt Ltd

Learners+
A-59, Okhla Industrial Area, Phase II, New Delhi 110 020
Tel: (011) 2638 6165; (011) 2638 7070
  Fax: (011) 2638 3788
E-mail: mail@sterlingpublishers.com
Web Site: www.sterlingpublishers.com
Key Personnel
Publisher: Mr S K Ghai
Founded: 1991
Membership(s): Federation of Indian Publishers.
ISBN Prefix(es): 978-81-7181
Parent Company: Sterling Publishers Pvt Ltd

LexisNexis Butterworths Wadhwa Nagpur
Division of RELX Group India
14th floor, Tower B, Bldg 10, DLF Cyber City, Phase II, Gurgaon 122 002
Tel: (0124) 4774444 *Fax:* (0124) 4774100

E-mail: info.in@lexisnexis.com
Web Site: www.lexisnexis.co.in; www.lexisnexis.in
Key Personnel
Chief Executive Officer, Asia: Shawn Clark
Publishers of law, taxation & business books.
Subjects: Business, Law, Taxation
ISBN Prefix(es): 978-81-8038
Associate Companies: LexisNexis China, Unit 1-6, 7/F Tower W1, Oriental Pl, No 1, E Chang An Ave, Dong Cheng District, Beijing 100738, China *Tel:* (010) 8518 5801 *Fax:* (010) 8518 9287 *E-mail:* asia.pacific@lexisnexis.com *Web Site:* www.lexisnexis.ch; LexisNexis China, 1201, Westgate Mall, 1038 Nanjing Rd W, Shanghai, China *Tel:* (021) 52286122 *Fax:* (021) 52286133 *Web Site:* www.lexisnexis.com.cn; LexisNexis Hong Kong, 39/F Hopewell Centre, 183 Queen's Rd E, Hong Kong, Hong Kong *Tel:* 2965 1400 *Fax:* 2976 0840 *E-mail:* asia.pacific@lexisnexis.com *Web Site:* www.lexisnexis.com.hk; LexisNexis Japan, 4-1-1 Taishido, Setagaya-ku, Tokyo 154-004, Japan *Tel:* (03) 5787-3511 *Fax:* (03) 5787-3512 *E-mail:* asia.pacific@lexisnexis.com *Web Site:* www.lexisnexis.jp; LexisNexis Malaysia Sdn Bhd, T1-6, Jaya 33, 3, Jl Semangat Seksyen 13, 46100 Petaling Jaya, Selangor Darul Ehsan, Malaysia *Tel:* (03) 7882 3551 (sales) *Toll Free Tel:* 800-88-8856; LexisNexis NZ Ltd, 181 Wakefield St, PO Box 472, Wellington 6140, New Zealand *Tel:* (04) 385 1479 *Fax:* (04) 385 1598 *E-mail:* customer.service@lexisnexis.co.nz *Web Site:* www.lexisnexis.co.nz; Level 2, Bldg H, UP-Ayala Technohub, Commonwealth Ave, Quezon City, Metro Manila, Philippines *Toll Free Tel:* 800-227-9597; LexisNexis Singapore, 3 Killiney Rd, 08-08 Winsland House 1, Singapore 239519, Singapore, Regional Publishing Dir: Conita Leung *Tel:* 6733 1380 *Fax:* 6733 1175 *E-mail:* asia.pacific@lexisnexis.com *Web Site:* www.lexisnexis.com.sg; LexisNexis Korea, Chunwoo Bldg, 4th floor, 534 Itaewon-dong, Yongsan-gu, Seoul 140-861, South Korea *Tel:* (02) 6714-3111 *Fax:* (02) 725-4388 *E-mail:* korea.sales@lexisnexis.com *Web Site:* www.lexisnexis.kr; LexisNexis Taiwan, 4F-1, No 51, Fujian St, Lingya Chiu, Kaohsiung 802, Taiwan *Tel:* (07) 333-7702 *Fax:* (07) 3333-9348 *E-mail:* asia.pacific@lexisnexis.com *Web Site:* www.lexisnexis.com.tw; LexisNexis Taiwan, 10Fl-1, No 166, Jianyi Rd, Chung Ho City, Taipei Hsien 235, Taiwan *Tel:* (02) 8226-3132 *Fax:* (02) 8226-3172 *E-mail:* asia.pacific@lexisnexis.com *Web Site:* www.lexisnexis.com.tw
Branch Office(s)
No 1961-B Vijaya Complex, 3rd floor, Asiad Colony, Anna Negar Western Ext, Chennai 600 101 *Tel:* (044) 43459999; (044) 43459923 *E-mail:* chennai@lexisnexis.com
309, Apeejay House, 130, Mumbai Samachar Marg, Fort, Mumbai 400 023 *Tel:* (022) 22029595 *E-mail:* mumbai@lexisnexis.com

Little Pearl Books (LPB)
C-74, Okhla, Phase I, New Delhi 110 020
E-mail: sales@littlepearlbooks.com
Web Site: www.littlepearlbooks.com
Associate Companies: Nutech Print Services

Lok Vangmaya Griha Pvt Ltd
Bhupesh Gupta Bhavan, 85 Sayani Rd, Prabhadevi, Mumbai 400 025
Tel: (022) 4362474 *Fax:* (022) 4313220
Key Personnel
Partner/Dir: Manohar Madhao Deshkar; Madhavrao Bayaji Gaikwad; Laxmar Sadashiv Karkhanis; Ardhendu Bhushan Hemendra Kumar Bardhan; Govind Pandharinath Pansare
Founded: 1973

Subjects: Human Relations, Social Sciences, Sociology
ISBN Prefix(es): 978-81-86995; 978-81-88284
Bookshop(s): 5-22-32 Tilak Path, Aurangabad 431 001; People's Book House, Meher House, 15, Cawasji Patel St, Ballard Estate, Fort Mumbai 400 001; Red Flag Bldg, Bindu Chowk, Kolhapur 416 002; 562 Sadashiv Peth, Chirtashala Prakalp, Pune 411 030

Lonely Planet India Pvt Ltd
302, DLF City Court, Sikanderpur, Gurgaon 122 004
Tel: (0124) 423 1645
E-mail: contact@lonelyplanet.co.in
Web Site: www.lonelyplanet.in
Key Personnel
Dir & General Manager: Sesh Seshadri
    E-mail: sesh.s@lonelyplanet.co.in
National Marketing Manager: Ekta Kapoor
    E-mail: ekta.kapoor@lonelyplanet.co.in
Subjects: Travel & Tourism
ISBN Prefix(es): 978-1-74360; 978-1-74321
Distributed by HarperCollins Publishers India Ltd

Lotus, *imprint of* Roli Books Pvt Ltd

Lustre Press, *imprint of* Roli Books Pvt Ltd

Lustre Press Pvt Ltd, see Roli Books Pvt Ltd

Macaw Books
204, Mohan Complex, H-block Market Ashok Vihar, Phase I, Delhi 110 052
Tel: (011) 47091409; (011) 47091472 *Fax:* (011) 47091473
E-mail: info@macawbooks.com; sales@macawbooks.com
Web Site: www.macawbooks.com
Subjects: Animals, Pets, Art, Crafts, Games, Hobbies, Fiction, Science (General)
ISBN Prefix(es): 978-1-60346

Mahajan Publishers Pvt Ltd+
Super Market Basement, Near Natraj Cinema, Ashram Rd, Ahmedabad 380 009
Tel: (079) 26588537; (079) 26878157; (079) 26583159
Key Personnel
Owner & Mng Dir: Mr Dinker Mahajan
Founded: 1953
Specialize in textiles.
ISBN Prefix(es): 978-81-85401
Associate Companies: Mahajan Book Distributors

Mainstreet Books, *imprint of* Hind Pocket Books

Manjul Publishing House Pvt Ltd
2nd floor, Usha Preet Complex, 42, Malviya Nagar, Bhopal 462 003
Tel: (0755) 4240 340 *Fax:* (0755) 4055 791
E-mail: manjul@manjulindia.com
Web Site: www.manjulindia.com
Founded: 1999
Subjects: Architecture & Interior Design, Art, Biography, Memoirs, Cookery, Fiction, Finance, Health, Nutrition, History, Inspirational, Spirituality, Management, Marketing, Nonfiction (General), Self-Help, Personal Finance
ISBN Prefix(es): 978-81-8322

Manohar Publishers & Distributors+
4753/23 Ansari Rd, Darya Ganj, New Delhi 110 002
Tel: (011) 23289100; (011) 23262796; (011) 23284848; (011) 23260774 *Fax:* (011) 23265162
E-mail: manbooks@vsnl.com; sales@manoharbooks.com
Web Site: www.manoharbooks.com

Key Personnel
Mng Dir, Rights & Permissions, Publicity: Ajay Jain
Founded: 1969
Also acts as bookseller.
Subjects: Anthropology, Archaeology, Architecture & Interior Design, Art, Economics, Education, Ethnicity, Government, Political Science, History, Literature, Literary Criticism, Essays, Philosophy, Religion - Other, Science (General), Social Sciences, Sociology, Politics
ISBN Prefix(es): 978-81-85054; 978-81-85425; 978-81-7304; 978-81-7099; 978-81-8324
Number of titles published annually: 45 Print
Distributed by South Asia Books

Manosabdam Books, *imprint of* Vidyarthi Mithram Press & Book Depot

Mapin Publishing Pvt Ltd+
706 Kaivana, Near Panchvati, Ellisbridge, Ahmedabad 380 006
Tel: (079) 40228228 *Fax:* (079) 40228201
E-mail: mapin@mapinpub.com
Web Site: www.mapinpub.com
Key Personnel
Publisher & Mng Dir: Bipin Shah
Founded: 1984
Specialize in books on art, crafts, architecture, culture of India, heritage & archaeology.
Membership(s): Federation of Indian Publishers.
Subjects: Archaeology, Architecture & Interior Design, Art, Asian Studies, Crafts, Games, Hobbies, Literature, Literary Criticism, Essays, Photography, Religion - Hindu, Religion - Islamic
ISBN Prefix(es): 978-81-85822; 978-81-88204
Number of titles published annually: 15 Print; 2 CD-ROM
Total Titles: 70 Print; 2 CD-ROM
Imprints: MapinLit
Foreign Rep(s): Antique Collectors' Club (North America); Gazelle Book Services (Europe, UK); Paragon Asia Co Ltd (Southeast Asia); Periloo Pty Ltd (Australia, New Zealand); Visual Books (Austria, Germany, Netherlands, Switzerland)
Orders to: MapinLit *E-mail:* mapin@icenet.net

MapinLit, *imprint of* Mapin Publishing Pvt Ltd

Marg Foundation
Army & Navy Bldg, 3rd floor, 148 Mahatma Gandhi Rd, Mumbai 400 001
Tel: (022) 22821151; (022) 22045947; (022) 22842520 *Fax:* (022) 22047102
E-mail: margfound@vsnl.net
Web Site: marg-art.org
Key Personnel
Publisher & General Manager: Radhika Sabavala
Administrative Consultant: Asha Shiralikar
Designer: Naju Hirani
Founded: 1946
Marg meaning pathway leads the reader through the cultural heritage of India & its neighboring countries.
Subjects: Architecture & Interior Design, Music, Dance, The Arts, Built Heritage, Cultural Heritage, Natural Heritage
ISBN Prefix(es): 978-81-85026; 978-93-80581; 978-81-921106

Sri Ramakrishna Math
31, Sri Ramakrishna Math Rd, Mylapore, Chennai 600 004
Tel: (044) 24621110 *Fax:* (044) 24934589
E-mail: mail@chennaimath.org
Web Site: www.chennaimath.org
Founded: 1897
Subjects: Biography, Memoirs, Philosophy, Religion - Hindu, Self-Help

ISBN Prefix(es): 978-81-7120; 978-81-7823; 978-81-86465
Distributor for Advaita Ashrama (Kolkata)
Showroom(s): 99, Pondy Bazaar, T Nagar, Chennai 600 017; Chennai Central Railway Station, Chennai 600 004
Bookshop(s): 16, Ramakrishna Math Rd, Mylapore, Chennai 600 004; No 26, S Mada St, Mylapore, Chennai 600 004

Maya Publishers Pvt Ltd+
4821, Parwana Bhawan, 3rd floor, 24 Ansari Rd, Darya Ganj, New Delhi 110 002
Tel: (011) 43549145; (011) 64712521 *Fax:* (011) 23243829
E-mail: surit@airtelmail.in
Key Personnel
Dir: Surit Mitra *E-mail:* suritmaya@gmail.com
Freelance representation for overseas publishers & original publishing, reprinting under license.
Membership(s): Delhi State Booksellers' & Publishers' Association.
Subjects: Management
ISBN Prefix(es): 978-81-86268

Mayfair Paperbacks, *imprint of* Arnold Heineman Publishers (India) Pvt Ltd

Mayoor Paperbacks, *imprint of* National Publishing House

McGraw-Hill Education India
B-4, Sector 63, Noida, Uttar Pradesh 201 301
Tel: (0120) 4383400 *Fax:* (0120) 4383401; (0120) 4383402; (0120) 4383403
Founded: 1970
66.5% owned by McGraw-Hill Book Co & 33.5% owned by Tatas.
Subjects: Business, Computer Science, Engineering (General), Finance, Management, Science (General), Social Sciences, Sociology, Technology, Computing
ISBN Prefix(es): 978-0-07
Number of titles published annually: 500 Print; 3 CD-ROM; 2 Audio
Total Titles: 3,500 Print; 25 CD-ROM; 10 Audio
Parent Company: McGraw-Hill Global Education Holdings LLC

Mehta Publishing House+
1941, Sadashiv Peth, Madiwale Colony, Pune - Maharashtra 411 030
Tel: (020) 24476924; (020) 24463048
E-mail: info@mehtapublishinghouse.com; production@mehtapublishinghouse.com
Web Site: www.mehtapublishinghouse.com
Key Personnel
Proprietor: Sunil Mehta *E-mail:* sm@mehtapublishinghouse.com
Founded: 1976
Membership(s): CAPEXIL; Federation of Indian Publishers.
ISBN Prefix(es): 978-81-7161; 978-81-7766; 978-81-8498; 978-81-907574; 978-81-907791
Number of titles published annually: 200 Print
Total Titles: 4,000 Print
Subsidiaries: Mehta Book Sellers
Book Club(s): T Book Club

Ministry of Information & Broadcasting Publications Division (Prakashan Vibhag)+
Soochna Bhawan, CGO Complex, Lodhi Rd, New Delhi 110 003
Tel: (011) 24362958; (011) 26100207 *Fax:* (011) 26175516
E-mail: dpd@sb.nic.in; dpd@mail.nic.in
Web Site: publicationsdivision.nic.in
Key Personnel
Dir General: Ms Ira Joshi *Fax:* (011) 24366671
Dir: Anurag Misra *Tel:* (011) 26193316
    Fax: (011) 26105875 *E-mail:* director.employmentnews@gmail.com

Dir, Publication Division: Ms Nidhi Pandey
Tel: (011) 24366672 *Fax:* (011) 24366670
E-mail: nidhidpd@gmail.com
Subjects: Agriculture, Animals, Pets, Anthropology, Archaeology, Architecture & Interior Design, Art, Asian Studies, Astronomy, Biography, Memoirs, Biological Sciences, Child Care & Development, Communications, Developing Countries, Earth Sciences, Economics, Education, Environmental Studies, Ethnicity, Gardening, Plants, Geography, Geology, Government, Political Science, Health, Nutrition, History, Inspirational, Spirituality, Journalism, Labor, Industrial Relations, Language Arts, Linguistics, Law, Maritime, Music, Dance, Nonfiction (General), Public Administration, Radio, TV, Religion - Buddhist, Religion - Catholic, Religion - Hindu, Religion - Islamic, Science (General), Social Sciences, Sociology, Sports, Athletics, Women's Studies
ISBN Prefix(es): 978-81-230
Number of titles published annually: 100 Print; 1 CD-ROM
Total Titles: 7,500 Print; 8 CD-ROM; 1 Audio
Branch Office(s)
Sales Emporium, Hall No 196, Old Secretariat, New Delhi *Tel:* (011) 23890205
Sales Emporium, A Wing, Rajaji Bhavan, Besant Nagar, Chennai, Contact: Business Manager *Tel:* (044) 24917673
Sales Emporium, Block 4, 1st floor, Gruhakalpa Complex, M J Rd, Nampally, Hyderabad 500 001, Contact: Business Manager *Tel:* (040) 24605383
Sales Emporium, 8 Esplanade East, Kolkata, Contact: Business Manager *Tel:* (033) 22488030
Sales Emporium, Hall No 1, 2nd floor, Kendriya Bhawan, Sector-H, Aliganj, Lucknow 226 024, Contact: Business Manager *Tel:* (0522) 2325455
Commerce House, Currimhoy Rd, Ballard Pier, Mumbai 400 038, Contact: Business Manager *Tel:* (022) 27570686
Sales Emporium, Bihar State Co-operative Bank Bldg, Ashoka Rajpath, Patna 800 004, Contact: Business Manager *Tel:* (0612) 2683407
Sales Emporium, Press Rd, Near Government Press, Thiruvananthapuram 695 001, Contact: Business Manager *Tel:* (0471) 2330650
Distributor for Archaeological Survey of India; Council of Scientific & Industrial Research (CSIR); Indian Council of Agricultural Research (ICAR); Lok Sabha Secretariat; National Institute of Science Communication & Information Resource (NISCAIR); National Museum

Mittal Publications
4594/9, Darya Ganj, New Delhi 110 002
Tel: (011) 23250398
E-mail: info@mittalbooks.com
Web Site: www.mittalbooks.com
Key Personnel
Contact: K M Mittal
Founded: 1979
Membership(s): Federation of Publishers' & Booksellers' Associations in India (FPBAI).
Subjects: Agriculture, Art, Biography, Memoirs, Child Care & Development, Communications, Criminology, Drama, Theater, Education, Geography, Geology, History, Library & Information Sciences, Music, Dance, Philosophy, Religion - Buddhist, Religion - Protestant, Religion - Other, Science (General), Social Sciences, Sociology, Technology, Women's Studies, Culture
ISBN Prefix(es): 978-81-7099
Orders to: A-110 Mohan Garden, New Delhi 110 059

MLBD, see Motilal Banarsidass Publishers Pvt Ltd

Motilal Banarsidass Publishers Pvt Ltd+
A-44, Naraina Industrial Area, Phase I, New Delhi 110 028
Tel: (011) 25795180; (011) 25792734; (011) 25793423; (011) 25895218 (warehouse) *Fax:* (011) 23850689; (011) 25797221
E-mail: web@mlbd.com; warehouse@mlbd.com
Web Site: www.mlbd.com
Key Personnel
Chairperson: Leela Jain
Mng Dir & Editor-in-Chief: Narendra Prakash Jain
Customer Service: Abhishek Jain
Domestic Sales: Varun Jain
Printing, Domestic Sales: Jainendra Prakash Jain
Publicity: Rajendra Prakash Jain
Founded: 1903
Asian religion.
Subjects: Archaeology, Architecture & Interior Design, Astrology, Occult, Astronomy, History, Language Arts, Linguistics, Literature, Literary Criticism, Essays, Medicine, Nursing, Dentistry, Music, Dance, Philosophy, Religion - Other, Asian Religion, Culture Arts, Mysticism, Tantra, Yoga
ISBN Prefix(es): 978-81-208; 978-81-782
Branch Office(s)
236, Ninth Main III Block, Jayanagar, Bangalore 560 011, Contact: Mr Anil Mukhi *Tel:* (080) 26542591; (080) 32711690
E-mail: bangalore@mlbd.com
203 Royapettah High Rd, Mylapore, Chennai 600 004, Contact: Mr V R Ravi *Tel:* (044) 24982315; (044) 43535417 *E-mail:* chennai@mlbd.com
8 Camac St, Kolkata 700 017, Contact: Mr Tapan Chatterjee *Tel:* (033) 22824872; (033) 32967029 *E-mail:* kolkata@mlbd.com
8 Mahalakshmi Chambers, Mahalaxmi Temple Lane, 22 Bhulabhai Desai Rd, Mumbai 400 026, Contact: Mr Cowsie Amra *Tel:* (022) 23516583; (022) 32922105 *E-mail:* mumbai@mlbd.com
Ashok Rajpath, Patna 800 004, Contact: Mr S N Yagnik *Tel:* (0612) 2671442; (0612) 3296812
E-mail: patna@mlbd.com
Chowk, Varanasi 221 001, Contact: Mr G P Pandey *Tel:* (0542) 2412331; (0542) 3295108
E-mail: varanasi@mlbd.com
Showroom(s): 41 UA Bungalow Rd, Jawahar Nagar, Delhi 110 007, Contact: Mr R P Jain *Tel:* (011) 23858335; (011) 23851985; (011) 23852747; (011) 23854826 *Fax:* (011) 23850689

Mudrak Publishers & Distributors+
W-152, Greater Kailash I, New Delhi 110 048
Tel: (011) 6416317
Books of academic interest on subjects of humanities.
ISBN Prefix(es): 978-81-87161
Total Titles: 5 Print

A Mukherjee & Co Pvt Ltd
No 2, Bankim Chatterjee St, Kolkata 700 073
Tel: (033) 22417406; (033) 22418199
Key Personnel
Contact: Ranjan Sengupta
Founded: 1940
Subjects: Education, Government, Political Science, Nonfiction (General), Religion - Other, Travel & Tourism
ISBN Prefix(es): 978-81-7610

Munshiram Manoharlal Publishers Pvt Ltd+
54 Rani Jhansi Rd, New Delhi 110 055
Mailing Address: PO Box 5715, New Delhi 110 055
Tel: (011) 23671668; (011) 23673650; (011) 23636097; (011) 23638992 *Fax:* (011) 23612745

E-mail: info@mrmlonline.com; editorial@mrmlonline.com; rightsandpermissions@mrmlonline.com; marketing@mrmlonline.com; orders@mrmlonline.com; production@mrmlonline.com; sales@mrmlonline.com
Web Site: www.mrmlonline.com
Key Personnel
Owner & Mng Dir: Ashok Jain
General Editor: D P Chattopadhyaya
Founded: 1952
Also major book dealer.
Subjects: Anthropology, Archaeology, Architecture & Interior Design, Art, Asian Studies, Astrology, Occult, Drama, Theater, History, Language Arts, Linguistics, Music, Dance, Philosophy, Religion - Buddhist, Religion - Hindu, Religion - Islamic, Religion - Other, Social Sciences, Sociology, Indology
ISBN Prefix(es): 978-81-215; 978-81-87586
Number of titles published annually: 80 Print
Total Titles: 1,500 Print
Imprints: Sanctum Books
Showroom(s): Sanctum Books, 68 Medical Association Rd, Darya Ganj, New Delhi 110 002
Bookshop(s): 4416 Nai Sarak, New Delhi 110 006 (Amir Chand Marg)

Narosa Publishing House Pvt Ltd+
22 Delhi Medical Association Rd, Darya Ganj, New Delhi 110 002
Tel: (011) 23243415; (011) 23243417 *Fax:* (011) 23243225; (011) 23258934
E-mail: info@narosa.com; editorial@narosa.com
Web Site: www.narosa.com
Key Personnel
Owner: S Mehra
Mng Dir: N K Mehra
Founded: 1977
Publish & distribute scientific, technical & medical books.
Subjects: Biological Sciences, Chemistry, Chemical Engineering, Computer Science, Earth Sciences, Engineering (General), Environmental Studies, Mathematics, Medicine, Nursing, Dentistry, Physics
ISBN Prefix(es): 978-81-85015; 978-81-85198; 978-81-7319; 978-81-8487
Number of titles published annually: 100 Print
Associate Companies: Narosa Book Distributors Pvt Ltd; Narosa Information Services
Branch Office(s)
35-36 Greams Rd, Thousand Lights, Chennai 600 006 *Tel:* (044) 28295362; (044) 28294592 *Fax:* (044) 28290377 *E-mail:* narosamds@vsnl.net
2F-2G Shivam Chambers, 53 Syed Amir Ali Ave, Kolkata 700 019 *Tel:* (033) 22814834; (033) 22902891 *Fax:* (033) 22902892
E-mail: narosakol@narosa.com
306 Shiv Centre, D B C Sector 17 KU Bazar PO, Mumbai 400 705 *Tel:* (022) 27890977; (022) 27896907; (022) 27892210 *Fax:* (022) 27891930 *E-mail:* narosamum@narosa.com

National Academy of Letters, see Sahitya Akademi

National Book Trust India (NBT)+
5, Institutional Area, Nehru Bhawan, Vasant Kunj, Phase-II, New Delhi 110 070
Tel: (011) 26707700 *Fax:* (011) 26121883
E-mail: office.nbt@nic.in
Web Site: www.nbtindia.gov.in
Key Personnel
Chairman: Mr A Sethumadhavan *Tel:* (011) 26707732
Dir: Mr M A Sikandar *Tel:* (011) 26707738 *E-mail:* director@nbtindia.com
Joint Dir, Production: Satish Kumar *Tel:* (011) 26707810 *E-mail:* satish.nbt@nic.in

Manager, Sales & Marketing: Syed Haider M Rizvi *Tel:* (011) 26707714 *E-mail:* shmrizvi. nbt@nic.in

Chief Editor: Dr Baldev Singh *Tel:* (011) 26707755 *E-mail:* baldevsingh.nbt@nic.in

Founded: 1957

Publisher & promoter of reading material.

Subjects: Agriculture, Anthropology, Archaeology, Architecture & Interior Design, Behavioral Sciences, Child Care & Development, Developing Countries, Economics, Education, Environmental Studies, Geography, Geology, Government, Political Science, History, Human Relations, Labor, Industrial Relations, Law, Management, Military Science, Religion - Other, Social Sciences, Sociology, Women's Studies

ISBN Prefix(es): 978-81-85135; 978-81-237; 978-81-87521

Number of titles published annually: 250 Print

Total Titles: 17,000 Print

Branch Office(s)

BDA Shopping Complex, Hall No 1, Banashankari II Stage, Bangalore, Karnataka 560 070 *Tel:* (080) 26711994 *Fax:* (080) 26711994 *E-mail:* sro@nbtindia.org.in

61, Mahatma Gandhi Rd, Kolkata, Bengla 700 009 *Tel:* (033) 22413899 *Fax:* (033) 22413899 *E-mail:* ero@nbtindia.org.in

Municipal Urdu Primary School, Babula Tank Cross Lane, Opposite J J Hospital, Mumbai, Maharashtra 400 009 *Tel:* (022) 23720442 *Fax:* (022) 23720442 *E-mail:* wro@nbtindia. org.in

Distributed by UBS Publishers' Distributors Pvt Ltd

Bookshop(s): Municipal Flat No 18, Bungalos Rd, New Delhi 110 007

National Council of Applied Economic Research, Publications Division

Parisila Bhawan, 11, Indraprastha Estate, New Delhi 110 002

Tel: (011) 23379861; (011) 23379862; (011) 23379863; (011) 23379865; (011) 23379866; (011) 23379868; (011) 23379857 *Fax:* (011) 23370164

E-mail: info@ncaer.org; publ@ncaer.org

Web Site: www.ncaer.org

Key Personnel

Dir General: Dr Shekhar Shah

Senior Executive, Publications: Jagbir Singh Punia *E-mail:* jspunia@ncaer.org

Founded: 1956

Subjects: Agriculture, Behavioral Sciences, Business, Economics, Health, Nutrition

ISBN Prefix(es): 978-81-85877

National Council of Educational Research & Training, Publication Department

Sri Aurobindo Marg, New Delhi 110 016

Tel: (011) 26560620; (011) 26864811 *Fax:* (011) 26868419

E-mail: cbm.ncert@nic.in

Web Site: www.ncert.nic.in

Key Personnel

Dir: Prof A K Srivastava *Tel:* (011) 26852261 *E-mail:* pd.ncert@nic.in

Chief Editor: Naresh Yadav *Tel:* 9717738654 (cell) *E-mail:* ce.ncert@nic.in

Chief Business Manager: Gautam Ganguly *Tel:* (011) 26852261

Chief Production Officer: Shiv Kumar *Tel:* (011) 26562085 *E-mail:* cpo.ncert@nic.in

Founded: 1963

Specializes in school textbooks, research monographs, supplementary readers.

Membership(s): Afro-Asian Book Council.

Subjects: Education

ISBN Prefix(es): 978-81-7450

Distribution Center: Navjivan Trust Bldg, PO Navjivan, Ahmedabad 380 014 *Tel:* (079) 7541446 *E-mail:* bm-ahd.ncert@nic.in

108, Hoskerehalli Ext, 100 Feet Rd, Banashankari 3rd Stage, Bangalore 560 085 *Tel:* (080) 6725740 *E-mail:* bm-bang.ncert@nic.in

CWC Campus, 1st floor, Kishori Mohan Banerjee Rd, Opposite Dhankal Bus Stop, PO Panihati, Kolkata 700 114 *Tel:* (033) 25530454 *E-mail:* bm-kol.ncert@nic.in

CWC Godown Maligaon, Guwahati 781 021 *Tel:* (0361) 2570521 *E-mail:* bm-guw.ncert@ nic.in

National Institute of Industrial Research (NIIR), see NIIR Project Consultancy Services (NPCS)

National Institute of Science Communication & Information Resources, see CSIR-National Institute of Science Communication & Information Resources (CSIR-NISCAIR)

National Museum

Janpath, New Delhi 110 011

Tel: (011) 23792249; (011) 23011901; (011) 23792775 *Fax:* (011) 23012988

E-mail: nationalmuseumoutreach@gmail.com

Web Site: www.nationalmuseumindia.gov.in

Key Personnel

Dir General: Dr B R Mani

E-mail: dgnationalmuseum11@gmail.com

Subjects: Antiques, Archaeology, Art, Ethnicity, Indian Art & Culture

ISBN Prefix(es): 978-81-85832

National Publishing House

2/35 Ansari Rd, Darya Ganj, New Delhi 110 002

Tel: (011) 23275267 *Fax:* (011) 23254407

Key Personnel

Mng Dir: K L Malik

Editorial, Production, Rights & Permissions: S K Malik

Sales: M K Malik

Founded: 1945

Subjects: Ethnicity, Human Relations, Social Sciences, Sociology

ISBN Prefix(es): 978-81-214

Parent Company: K L Malik & Sons Pvt Ltd

Imprints: Gyan Bharati; Mayoor Paperbacks

Branch Office(s)

Malik & Co, Chaura Rasta, Jaipur 302 003 *Tel:* (0141) 2575258

Showroom(s): K L Malik & Sons Pvt Ltd, 23, Darya Ganj, New Delhi 110 022 *Tel:* (011) 23274161; (011) 23242257

Navajivan Trust+

Ahmedabad, Gujarat 380 014

Tel: (079) 27541329; (079) 27542634; (079) 27540635

E-mail: ashok_bhatt23@hotmail.com; ashok_bhatt@yahoo.com; jitnavjivan10@gmail. com

Web Site: www.navajivantrust.org

Key Personnel

Chairman: Biharibhai P Shah

Manager, Sales & Permissions: Kapil Rawal

Founded: 1929

Printing, publishing & distribution of Gandhian literature.

Subjects: Biography, Memoirs, History, Philosophy, Religion - Other

ISBN Prefix(es): 978-81-7229

Branch Office(s)

130 Princess St, Mumbai 400 002

Navayana Publishing Pvt Ltd

155 Shahpur Jat, 2nd floor, New Delhi 110 049

Tel: (011) 26494795

E-mail: anand@navayana.org

Web Site: www.navayana.org

Subjects: Social Sciences, Sociology

ISBN Prefix(es): 978-81-89059

Navneet Education Limited+

Navneet Bhavan, Bhavani Shankar Rd, Dadar (W), Mumbai 400 028

Tel: (022) 6662 6565 *Fax:* (022) 6662 6470

E-mail: inquiry@navneet.com

Web Site: www.navneet.com

Key Personnel

Mng Dir: Amarchand R Gala

Dir, Marketing: Jitendra L Gala

Dir, Sales & Distribution: Harakhchand R Gala

Founded: 1959

Educational & children's book publishing. Scholastic paper stationery & non-paper stationery products.

Subjects: Art, Computer Science, Cookery, Crafts, Games, Hobbies, Health, Nutrition, Regional Interests

ISBN Prefix(es): 978-81-243

Total Titles: 3,000 Print

Branch Office(s)

Navneet House, Gurukul Rd, Memnagar, Ahmedabad 380 052

Foreign Rep(s): Mitesh Dharod (USA); Dilip Lilani (Latin America); Jessica Rebello (Far East); Vikrant Srivastava (Europe); Rinu John Thomas (Africa)

Navyug Publishers

K-24, Hauz Khas Enclave, Hauz Khas, New Delhi 110 016

Tel: (011) 26518248

Web Site: www.facebook.com/Navyug.88/

Founded: 1949

Subjects: Ethnicity

ISBN Prefix(es): 978-81-7599; 978-81-85267; 978-81-86216

Naya Prokash+

206 Bidhan Sarani, Kolkata 700 006

Tel: (033) 22414709 *Fax:* (033) 5382897

Founded: 1960

Subjects: Agriculture, Environmental Studies, Gardening, Plants, Government, Political Science, History, Language Arts, Linguistics, Management, Military Science, Science (General), Social Sciences, Sociology

ISBN Prefix(es): 978-81-85109; 978-81-85421

Parent Company: Darbari Offset Pvt Ltd

Associate Companies: Mitrata Offset Print; Prokash Pvt Ltd

Subsidiaries: NP Sales Pvt Ltd

NBT, see National Book Trust India (NBT)

NCAER, see National Council of Applied Economic Research, Publications Division

NCERT, see National Council of Educational Research & Training, Publication Department

Neeta Prakashan+

A-4 Ring Rd, South Ext Part-I, New Delhi 110 049

Tel: (011) 24636010; (011) 24636022; (011) 24636030 *Fax:* (011) 24636011

E-mail: info@neetaprakashan.com; neetabooks@ vsnl.com

Web Site: www.neetaprakashan.com

Key Personnel

Chief Executive Officer: Rajesh Gupta

Mng Proprietor: Shanti Devi

Founded: 1959

Subjects: Art, Crafts, Games, Hobbies, Education, Inspirational, Spirituality, Language Arts, Linguistics, Philosophy, Religion - Other, Science (General), Social Sciences, Sociology

ISBN Prefix(es): 978-81-7202

Parent Company: Children's Book House

Neha Mini Katha, *imprint of* Spectrum Publications

Nem Chand & Brothers+
22, Civil Lines, Roorkee, UK 247 667
Tel: (01332) 272258; (01332) 272752; (01332)
264343 *Fax:* (01332) 273258
E-mail: info@nemchandbros.com; ncb_rke@
rediffmail.com
Web Site: www.nemchandbros.com
Key Personnel
Owner: Anil K Jain *Tel:* 9412071555 (cell)
E-mail: akj@nemchandbros.com
Mng Dir, Rights & Permissions: Mr N C
Jain *Tel:* 9760099779 (cell) *E-mail:* ncj@
nemchandbros.com
Editorial Dir: Dr Ashok K Jain
Production Dir: Shanil Jain *E-mail:* shanil.dude@
gmail.com
Publicity, Advertising Dir: Mr Shaleen Jain
Tel: 9897998990 (cell) *E-mail:* shaleen.jss@
live.co.uk
Founded: 1951
Also book packager.
Membership(s): Chemical & Allied Products Ex-
port Promotion Council (books division).
Subjects: Accounting, Agriculture, Architecture
& Interior Design, Astrology, Occult, Auto-
motive, Business, Career Development, Child
Care & Development, Civil Engineering, Com-
munications, Computer Science, Computers,
Cookery, Crafts, Games, Hobbies, Disability,
Special Needs, Earth Sciences, Economics,
Electronics, Electrical Engineering, Energy,
Engineering (General), Environmental Studies,
Fashion, Fiction, Finance, Gardening, Plants,
Geography, Geology, Health, Nutrition, House
& Home, Law, Literature, Literary Criticism,
Essays, Management, Marketing, Mathematics,
Mechanical Engineering, Nonfiction (General),
Physical Sciences, Physics, Science (General),
Self-Help, Technology, Transportation, Travel
& Tourism, Women's Studies
ISBN Prefix(es): 978-81-85240
Subsidiaries: Roorkee Press

New Age International, *imprint of* Laxmi
Publications Pvt Ltd

New Age International (P) Ltd Publishers
Imprint of Laxmi Publications Pvt Ltd
7/30 A, Darya Ganj, New Delhi 110 002
Tel: (011) 23276802; (011) 23258865; (011)
23253771; (011) 23253472 *Fax:* (011)
23267437
E-mail: info@newagepublishers.com;
rights@newagepublishers.com; orders@
newagepublishers.com; sales@
newagepublishers.com
Web Site: newagepublishers.com
Key Personnel
Chairman: R K Gupta
Mng Dir: Saumya Gupta *E-mail:* sgupta@
newagepublishers.com
Founded: 1966
Specialize in pure & applied sciences, engineer-
ing, technology & humanities. Publish mostly
university & college-level standard textbooks
used in institutions in India & the developing
countries.
Subjects: Biological Sciences, Chemistry, Chemi-
cal Engineering, Economics, Engineering (Gen-
eral), Management, Mathematics, Medicine,
Nursing, Dentistry, Physics, Science (General),
Technology, Commerce
ISBN Prefix(es): 978-81-224
Total Titles: 1,500 Print
Branch Office(s)
No 37/10, 8th Cross (Near Hanuman Temple), Bangalore 560 018 *Tel:* (080) 26756823
Fax: (080) 26756820 *E-mail:* bangalore@
newagepublishers.com
26, Damodaran St, T Nagar, Chennai 600
017 *Tel:* (044) 24353401; (044) 24351463
Fax: (044) 24354463 *E-mail:* chennai@
newagepublishers.com

CC-39/1016, 1st floor, Carrier Station Rd, Near
Paulson Park Hotel, Ernakulam South, Cochin
682 016 *Tel:* (0484) 4051303 *Fax:* (0484)
4051303 *E-mail:* cochin@newagepublishers.
com
Hemsen Complex, Mohd Shah Rd, Paltan
Bazar, Near Starline Hotel, Guwahati 781
008 *Tel:* (0361) 2513881 *Fax:* (0361) 2543669
E-mail: guwahati@newagepublishers.com
No 105, 1st floor, Madhiray Kaveri Tower,
3-2-19, Azam Jahi Rd, Nimboliadda, Hyderabad 500 027 *Tel:* (040) 24652456
Fax: (040) 24652457 *E-mail:* hyderabad@
newagepublishers.com
c/o Laxmi Publications (P) Ltd, Adda Tanda
Chowk, Jalandhar City 144 001 *Tel:* (0181)
2221272
RDB Chambers (formerly Lotus Cinema), 106A,
1st floor, S N Banerjee Rd, Kolkata 700 014
Tel: (033) 22273773 *Fax:* (033) 22275247
E-mail: kolkata@newagepublishers.com
16-A, Jopling Rd, Lucknow 226 001 *Tel:* (0522)
2209578; (0522) 4045297 *Fax:* (0522) 2204098
E-mail: lucknow@newagepublishers.com
142C, Victor House, Ground floor, N M
Joshi Marg, Lower Parel, Mumbai 400 013
Tel: (022) 24927869 *Fax:* (022) 24915415
E-mail: mumbai@newagepublishers.com
c/o Laxmi Publications (P) Ltd, Radha Govind
St, Tharpagma, Ranchi 834 001 *Tel:* (0651)
2307764 *E-mail:* ranchi@laxmipublications.
com

New Light Publishers+
B-8, Rattan Jyoti Blvd, 18 Rajendra Pl, New
Delhi 110 008
Tel: (011) 25737448
E-mail: newlightpublishers@gmail.com
Founded: 1963
Membership(s): Delhi State Booksellers' & Pub-
lishers' Association (DSBPA); The Federation
of Publishers' & Booksellers' Associations in
India (FPBAI).
Subjects: Language Arts, Linguistics, Self-Help
ISBN Prefix(es): 978-81-85018; 978-81-86332

New Saraswati House (India) Pvt Ltd
MGM Tower, 2nd floor, Ansari Rd, Plot No 19,
Darya Ganj, New Delhi 110 002
Tel: (011) 43556600; (011) 23281022 *Fax:* (011)
43556688
E-mail: delhi@saraswatihouse.com
Web Site: www.saraswatihouse.com
Key Personnel
Dir: Atul Gupta
Founded: 1950
Subjects: Child Care & Development, Education
ISBN Prefix(es): 978-81-7335; 978-93-5041
Total Titles: 1,000 Print
Parent Company: Saraswati Group
Branch Office(s)
264-265, 2nd floor, Austlaxmi Complex, Near
Vasant Cinema, O/S Dariyapur Gate, Bar-
dolpura, Ahmedabad 380 004 *Tel:* 9727787282
(cell)
48, V Main Rd,, Chamrajpet, Bangalore 560
018 *Tel:* (080) 26619880; (080) 26672813
Fax: (080) 26619880 *E-mail:* bengaluru@
saraswatihouse.com
SCO 31, Sector 31-D, Chandigarh 160 030
Tel: (0172) 2624882 *Fax:* (0172) 5086882
E-mail: chandigarh@saraswatihouse.com
10/34, Mahalakshmi St, T Nagar, Chennai 600
017 *Tel:* (044) 24343740; (044) 24346531;
(044) 24333508 *Fax:* (044) 24333508
E-mail: chennai@saraswatihouse.com
1A, Archon Arcade, 1st floor, Dr B Baruah Rd,
Ulubari, Near Stadium Flyover, Guwahati 781
007
3-5-170/1/8/2, Ground floor, Ashish Orchids,
Near Shanti Theater, YMCA, Narayanguda,
Hyderabad, Andhra Pradesh 500 029

1 & 2, UGF, Parijat Palace, Sector 12, Behind Post Office, Indra Nagar, Lucknow 226
016 *Tel:* (0522) 4062517 *E-mail:* lucknow@
saraswatihouse.com
Crown Sq, Off No 505, Gandhi Path, Vaishali
Nagar, Jaipur 302 019 *Tel:* 9672987282 (cell)
E-mail: jaipur@saraswatihouse.com
39/741, Sudarshanam, Karikkamuri Cross Rd,
Ernakulam S, Kochi 682 011 *Tel:* (0484)
3925288; (0484) 3062576 *E-mail:* kochi@
saraswatihouse.com
27/1A, 1st floor, Rameshwar Shah Rd, Opposite
to CIT Rd Ladies Park, Kolkata 700 014
347, (Sasonvilla), Gautam Nagar, Opposite Allahabad Bank, Near Chetak Bridge, Bhopal,
Madhya Pradesh
32 Corporate Ave, 2D, 2nd floor, Off Mahakali
Caves Rd, Near Paper Box, Andheri (E), Mumbai 400 093 *Tel:* (022) 28343022
4, Sitayan Apartments, Vivekanand Marg, North
S K Puri, Patna 800 013 *Tel:* (0612) 2570403
E-mail: patna@saraswatihouse.com
Plot No 1495, New Ward No 17, Radha Govind
St, Tharapkhana, Ranchi 834 401 *Tel:* (0651)
2210300

NIIR Project Consultancy Services (NPCS)
Affiliate of NIIR Project Exports India (P) Ltd
106-E Kamla Nagar, New Delhi 110 007
Tel: (011) 23843955; (011) 23845654; (011)
23845886 *Fax:* (011) 23841561
E-mail: npcs.india@gmail.com
Web Site: www.niir.org
Key Personnel
President & Chief Executive Officer: Mr Ajay
Kumar Gupta
Founded: 1994
Publishers of process technology books &
databases.
Subjects: Business, Chemistry, Chemical Engi-
neering, Science (General), Technology
ISBN Prefix(es): 978-81-86623; 978-81-7833
Number of titles published annually: 20 Print
Total Titles: 70 Print

NISCAIR, see CSIR-National Institute of Science
Communication & Information Resources
(CSIR-NISCAIR)

Niyogi Books
D-78, Okhla Industrial Area, Phase 1, New Delhi
110 020
Tel: (011) 26816301; (011) 49327000 *Fax:* (011)
26810483; (011) 26813830
E-mail: niyogibooks@gmail.com; pr@
niyogibooksindia.com
Web Site: www.niyogibooksindia.com
Key Personnel
Publisher & Mng Dir: Bikash D Niyogi
Tel: 9810645410 (cell) *E-mail:* bikashniyogi@
niyogibooksindia.com
Publisher: Tultul Niyogi *E-mail:* tultulniyogi@
niyogibooksindia.com
Public Relations: Ashinish V Adhikari
Tel: 9810121806 (cell)
Founded: 2004
Subjects: Art, Asian Studies, Cookery, Fiction,
History, Religion - Buddhist, Religion - Hindu,
Self-Help, Culture, South Asia
ISBN Prefix(es): 978-81-89738; 978-93-81523
Total Titles: 200 Print

Om Books International
A-12, Sector 64, Noida, Uttar Pradesh 201 301
Tel: (0120) 477 4100 *Fax:* (0120) 422 9356
E-mail: editorial@ombooks.com
Web Site: www.ombooksinternational.com
Subjects: Biography, Memoirs, Cookery, Drama,
Theater, Fashion, Fiction, Film, Video
ISBN Prefix(es): 978-81-87108; 978-93-80069
Imprints: OmKidz

OmKidz, *imprint of* Om Books International

Omsons Publications+
4379/4, Prakash House, Ansari Rd, Darya Ganj, New Delhi 110 002
Tel: (011) 23289353; (011) 23246448 *Fax:* (011) 23289353
Key Personnel
Contact: Rahul Virmani; Ramesh Kumar Virmani
Founded: 1990
Subjects: Agriculture, Anthropology, Behavioral Sciences, Biography, Memoirs, Business, Career Development, Drama, Theater, Economics, Education, Environmental Studies, Fiction, Foreign Countries, Geography, Geology, Government, Political Science, History, Humor, Library & Information Sciences, Literature, Literary Criticism, Essays, Management, Marketing, Philosophy, Psychology, Psychiatry, Social Sciences, Sociology, Travel & Tourism, Veterinary Science, Women's Studies
ISBN Prefix(es): 978-81-7117
Parent Company: Western Book Depot, 4675/21 Ganpati Bhawan, Ansari Rd, Darya Ganj, New Delhi 110 002
Branch Office(s)
Jasomanta Rd, Panbazar, Guwahati 781 001
Bookshop(s): Western Book Depot, Pan Bazar, Guwahati 781 001

Orient Paperbacks, *imprint of* Vision Books Pvt Ltd

Orient Paperbacks+
Imprint of Vision Books Pvt Ltd
5 A/8 Ansari Rd, 1st floor, Darya Ganj, New Delhi 110 002
Tel: (011) 2327 8877 *Fax:* (011) 2327 8879
E-mail: info@orientpaperbacks.com
Web Site: www.orientpaperbacks.com
Founded: 1975
Specialize in fitness.
Subjects: Astrology, Occult, Business, Career Development, Cookery, Crafts, Games, Hobbies, Drama, Theater, Fiction, Health, Nutrition, How-to, Humor, Nonfiction (General), Poetry, Self-Help, Sports, Athletics, Fitness
ISBN Prefix(es): 978-81-222
Number of titles published annually: 50 Print
Total Titles: 700 Print
Associate Companies: Rajpal & Sons; Ravindra Printing Press; Shiksha Bharati; Shiksha Bharati Press
Imprints: Orient Publishing
Branch Office(s)
3-6-280/A/5 Himayatnagar, Hyderabad *Tel:* (040) 2322 3252
Vasant, Ground floor, 3-B Pedder Rd, Mumbai 400 026 *Tel:* (022) 2351 0343 *Fax:* (022) 2351 0229
Book Club(s): Orient Book Club

Orient Publishing, *imprint of* Orient Paperbacks

Oxford & IBH Publishing Co Pvt Ltd+
113-B Shahpur Jat, 2nd floor, Behind JP House, New Delhi 110 049
Tel: (011) 41745490; (011) 41745356; (011) 41745358 *Fax:* (011) 41517559
E-mail: oxford@oxford-ibh.in
Web Site: oxford-ibh.in
Key Personnel
Dir: Mohan Primlani
Founded: 1962
Subjects: Agriculture, Asian Studies, Biological Sciences, Civil Engineering, Earth Sciences, Engineering (General), Mechanical Engineering, Natural History, Psychology, Psychiatry, Science (General)
ISBN Prefix(es): 978-81-204
Subsidiaries: Science Publishers Inc

Oxford University Press+
YMCA Library Bldg, 1st floor, One Jai Singh Rd, New Delhi 110 001
Mailing Address: PO Box 43, New Delhi 110 001
Tel: (011) 43600300 *Fax:* (011) 23360897
E-mail: customerservice.in@oup.com
Web Site: www.oup.co.in
Founded: 1912
Subjects: Biography, Memoirs, Business, Developing Countries, Earth Sciences, Economics, Government, Political Science, History, Literature, Literary Criticism, Essays, Medicine, Nursing, Dentistry, Natural History, Philosophy, Religion - Hindu, Science (General), Social Sciences, Sociology, Culture Studies, Gender Studies
ISBN Prefix(es): 978-81-7025; 978-0-19
Parent Company: Oxford University Press, United Kingdom
Branch Office(s)
289 Anna Salai, Chennai, Tamil Nadi 600 006
Tel: (044) 2811 2107 *Fax:* (044) 2811 0962
E-mail: chennai.in@oup.com
Plot No A1-5, Block GP, Sector V, Salt Lake Electronics Complex, Kolkata 700 091
Tel: (033) 235 73739; (033) 2357 3740; (033) 23573741 *Fax:* (033) 2357 3738
E-mail: kolkata.in@oup.com
Off Nos 4B-30-33, Phoenix Paragon Pl, LBS. Marg, Kurla (West), Mumbai 400 070
Tel: (022) 61801491; (022) 61801492; (022) 61801493; (022) 61801494; (022) 61801495 *Fax:* (022) 26521133 *E-mail:* westcare.in@oup.com
Showroom(s): 2/11 Ansari Rd, PO Box 7035, Darya Ganj, New Delhi 110 002 *Tel:* (011) 2327 3841; (011) 2327 3842 *Fax:* (011) 2327 7812 *E-mail:* csdel.in@oup.com; Lilavati Chambers, Ground floor, Behind Handloom House, Ashram Rd, Ahmedabad 380 009 *Tel:* (079) 2657 4291; (079) 2657 5137 *Fax:* (079) 2657 5291 *E-mail:* oupahd@oup.com; 167, Sreekara, 4th Cross, Dollar's Colony, 4th Phase, J P Nagar, Bangalore 560 078 *Tel:* (080) 26492022; (080) 26492033 *Fax:* (080) 26492044 *E-mail:* bangalore.in@oup.com; Plot No 2B & 2C, Unit 3, Kharavela Nagar, Behind Ram Mandir, Bhubaneswar 751 001 *Tel:* (0674) 2530116; (0674) 3262888 *Fax:* (0674) 2530117 *E-mail:* oupbbsr@bsnl.in; SCO 60 & 61, 1st floor, Sector 34 A, Chandigarh 160 034 *Tel:* (0172) 2601794 *Fax:* (0172) 2601617 *E-mail:* oup_chd@dataone.in; 28/71-B, G 66, Elders Forum Rd, Panampalli Nagar, Ernakulam, Kerala 682 036 *Tel:* (0484) 2322 425 *Fax:* (0484) 2322 428 *E-mail:* ernakulam.in@oup.com; Pragjyotish Apartments, 1st floor, M Tayabullah Rd, Dighali Pukhuri (East), Guwahati 781 001 *Tel:* (0361) 2131349; (0361) 2543050 *Fax:* (0361) 2513310 *E-mail:* oxfordguw@dataone.in; H No 8-2-577, 1st floor, Rd No 7, Banjara Hills, Hyderabad 500 034 *Tel:* (040) 23350129; (040) 23350139 *Fax:* (040) 23356424 *E-mail:* hyderabad.in@oup.com; A-19, Main Sahakar Path, Near Nehru Sahakar Bhavan, Jaipur 302 001 *Tel:* (0141) 5124989; (0141) 2743 816 *E-mail:* oupjaipur@yahoo.co.uk; B-7/18, Sector K, Aliganj, Lucknow 226 024 *Tel:* (0522) 4024120 *Fax:* (0522) 2745994 *E-mail:* lucknow.in@oup.com; Emarat-Al-Harmain, Near Panjab National Bank, Maidan Bank Rd, Patna 800 001 *Tel:* (0612) 2230971 *Fax:* (0612) 2200845 *E-mail:* oup_patna@sify.com; 3, Vitthal Rao Shivarkar Rd, Natraj Enclave Society, Parma Nagar, Wanwadi, Pune 411 040 *Tel:* (020) 41206871; (020) 41206872; (020) 41206873 *Fax:* (020) 41206874 *E-mail:* ouppune.in@oup.com
Warehouse: C-3 & C-38, Block C, Sector-59, District Gautam Budh Nagar, Noida

Tel: (0120) 2587738; (0120) 2587742; (0120) 2587743; (0120) 2587745 *Fax:* (0120) 2587741
E-mail: customerservice.in@oup.com

Pan Macmillan India
707, 7th floor, Kailash Bldg, 26, K G Marg, New Delhi 110 001
Tel: (011) 23320837
E-mail: customer.service@macmillan.co.in; pansales@macmillan.co.in; paneditorial@macmillan.co.in
Web Site: www.panmacmillan.co.in
Key Personnel
Publisher: Diya Kar Hazra
National Sales Head: Vijay Sharma
  Tel: 9810444501 (cell) *E-mail:* v.sharma@macmillan.co.in
Customer Care: Amit Pratap Singh
  Tel: 8826130385 (cell) *E-mail:* amit.singh@macmillan.co.in
Subjects: Fiction, Nonfiction (General)
ISBN Prefix(es): 978-93-82616
Parent Company: Macmillan Group
Distributor for Frances Lincoln Children's Books; Walker Books

Panchsheel Prakashan
Film Colony, Jaipur, Rajasthan 302 003
Tel: (0141) 2315072
Key Personnel
Editorial: Moolchand Gupta
Founded: 1968
Subjects: Art, Astrology, Occult, Biography, Memoirs, Computer Science, Crafts, Games, Hobbies, Drama, Theater, Economics, Education, Environmental Studies, Fiction, Gardening, Plants, Geography, Geology, Government, Political Science, History, Mathematics, Music, Dance, Philosophy, Science (General), Social Sciences, Sociology, Consumer Rights
ISBN Prefix(es): 978-81-7056

Pankaj Publications+
47/17, Old Rajinder Nagar, New Delhi 110 060
Tel: (011) 23363395; 9810015008 (cell)
E-mail: contact@pankajmusic.com
Web Site: www.pankajmusic.com
Key Personnel
Owner: Vikas Bajaj *E-mail:* bajajvikas@hotmail.com
Founded: 1972
Subjects: Animals, Pets, Astrology, Occult, Cookery, Crafts, Games, Hobbies, Ethnicity, Health, Nutrition, Human Relations, Language Arts, Linguistics, Literature, Literary Criticism, Essays, Music, Dance, Self-Help, Sports, Athletics
ISBN Prefix(es): 978-81-87155
Number of titles published annually: 20 Print
Total Titles: 150 Print
Foreign Rep(s): M/s Aafreen International
Bookshop(s): Cambridge Book Depot, 3, Regal Bldg, Connaught Circus, New Delhi 110 001, Contact: Mr Ranjana Bajaj
E-mail: cambridgebooks@hotmail.com

Parimal Prakashan+
17 MIG, Bhagambari Avas Yojana, Allapur, Allahabad 211 006
Tel: (0532) 661771
Founded: 1974
Subjects: Archaeology, Astrology, Occult, Career Development, Education, Ethnicity, Human Relations, Literature, Literary Criticism, Essays, Medicine, Nursing, Dentistry, Social Sciences, Sociology
ISBN Prefix(es): 978-81-7088; 978-81-86298
Number of titles published annually: 10 Print; 10 Online
Total Titles: 2,200 Print; 2,200 Online

Distributed by D K Publishers & Distributors
Distributor for Classical Publishing; Gyan Publication

Pegasus, *imprint of* B Jain Publishers Pvt Ltd

Penguin India
Infinity Tower C, 7th floor, DLF Cyber City, Gurgaon 122 002
Tel: (0124) 478-5600
E-mail: prh_publicity@penguinrandomhouse.in;
prh_rights@penguinrandomhouse.in
Web Site: penguin.co.in
Founded: 1985
ISBN Prefix(es): 978-0-14; 978-0-670
Number of titles published annually: 250 Print
Total Titles: 3,000 Print
Parent Company: Penguin Random House India
Ultimate Parent Company: Penguin Random House Inc
Distributor for A&C Black; Atlantic Books; Faber & Faber; Granta; Hay House; Icon; Kyle Cathie; Marshall Cavendish; Mira; Penguin Group; Quercus; Sterling Publishing; Zubaan
Distribution Center: Trafalgar Square Publishing (USA)

Penguin Random House India
Subsidiary of Penguin Random House Inc
Windsor IT Park, 7th floor, Tower B, A-1, Sector 125, Noida 201 301
Tel: (0120) 4607500 *Fax:* (0120) 4607518
E-mail: prh_business@penguinrandomhouse.in (sales); prh_publicity@penguinrandomhouse.in; prh_rights@penguinrandomhouse.in
Web Site: penguin.co.in
Key Personnel
Chief Executive Officer: Gaurav Shrinagesh
Chief Operating Officer: Sanjiv Gupta
SVP, Mktg & Publr, Children's Books: Hemali Sodhi
Vice President, Product & Sales: Nandan Jha
Publisher: Chiki Sarkar
Publishing Dir: Milee Ashwarya; Meru Gokhale
Founded: 2005
Subjects: Biography, Memoirs, Business, Cookery, Economics, Fiction, Government, Political Science, History, Humor, Nonfiction (General), Philosophy, Poetry, Psychology, Psychiatry, Romance, Science (General), Science Fiction, Fantasy, Self-Help, Travel & Tourism
ISBN Prefix(es): 978-81-8400
Distributor for Pushkin Press
Distribution Center: Trafalgar Square Publishing (USA)

Pentagon Earth, *imprint of* Pentagon Press

Pentagon Energy Press, *imprint of* Pentagon Press

Pentagon Press
206, Peacock Lane, Shahpur Jat, New Delhi 110 049
Tel: (011) 26491568 *Fax:* (011) 26490600
E-mail: rajan@pentagonpress.in
Web Site: www.pentagonpress.in
Founded: 1999
Subjects: Archaeology, Architecture & Interior Design, Art, Business, Economics, Education, Government, Political Science, Law, Management, Religion - Buddhist, Religion - Hindu, Religion - Other, Science (General)
ISBN Prefix(es): 978-81-86830; 978-81-8274
Imprints: Pentagon Earth; Pentagon Energy Press; Pentagon Tech Press; Pentagon Security International; Pentagon World of Learning; Third Eye

Pentagon Security International, *imprint of* Pentagon Press

Pentagon Tech Press, *imprint of* Pentagon Press

Pentagon World of Learning, *imprint of* Pentagon Press

People's Publishing House Ltd
5-E Rani Jhansi Rd, New Delhi 110 055
Tel: (011) 23523349; (011) 23529823
E-mail: mail@peoplespublishinghouse.in
Web Site: www.peoplespublishinghouse.in
Key Personnel
Contact: Shamim Faizee
Founded: 1948
Subjects: Biography, Memoirs, Engineering (General), History, Philosophy, Poetry, Social Sciences, Sociology
ISBN Prefix(es): 978-81-7007
Bookshop(s): 18A Marina Arcade, G Block, Outer Circle, Connaught Place, New Delhi 110 001, Contact: Rishabh Kumar *Tel:* (011) 23324064; (011) 23523349 *E-mail:* 5e@bol.net.in

Pharma Med Press+
Imprint of Pharma Book Syndicate
4-4-309 & 316, Giriraj Lane, Sultan Bazar, Koti, Hyderabad 500 095
Tel: (040) 23445688 *Fax:* (040) 23445611
E-mail: info@pharmamedpress.com
Web Site: www.bspublications.net
Founded: 1995
Publisher of pharmaceutical science, biotechnology & allied science.
Subjects: Biological Sciences, Medicine, Nursing, Dentistry, Physical Sciences, Biochemistry, Medicinal Chemistry, Pharmaceuticals, Pharmacognosy, Pharmacology, Pharmacy
ISBN Prefix(es): 978-81-91019
Number of titles published annually: 20 Print
Total Titles: 90 Print
Ultimate Parent Company: BSP Books Pvt Ltd

PHI Learning Ltd
Imprint of Eastern Economy Editions
M-97, Connaught Circus, New Delhi 110 001
Tel: (011) 23411779; (011) 23418078; (011) 23415326 *Fax:* (011) 23417179
E-mail: phi@phindia.com; customerservice@phindia.com
Web Site: www.phindia.com
Key Personnel
Chairman & Mng Dir: Asoke Ghosh
Sales & Marketing: V Balamurugan
E-mail: balamurugan@phindia.com
Founded: 1963
Subjects: Computer Science, Management, Science (General), Social Sciences, Sociology, English, Humanities, Information Technology
ISBN Prefix(es): 978-81-203
Branch Office(s)
Rimjhim House, 111, Patparganj Industrial Estate, Delhi 110 092 *Tel:* (011) 43031100 *Fax:* (011) 43031144

Pine Forge Press, *imprint of* SAGE Publications India Pvt Ltd

Pitambar Publishing Co (P) Ltd+
888 E Park Rd, Karol Bagh, New Delhi 110 005
Tel: (011) 23625528 *Fax:* (011) 23676058
Key Personnel
Mng Dir, Publicity: Anand Bhushan
Sales: Manish Aggarwal
Founded: 1938
Membership(s): Akhil Bhartia Hindi Prakashak Sangh; Delhi State Booksellers' & Publishers' Association; Federation of Indian Publishers.
Subjects: Accounting, Chemistry, Chemical Engineering, Computer Science, Computers, Economics, Electronics, Electrical Engineering,

Fiction, History, Mathematics, Religion - Buddhist, Religion - Hindu
ISBN Prefix(es): 978-81-209
Number of titles published annually: 100 Print
Total Titles: 2,000 Print
Associate Companies: Ambar Prakashan, 888 E Park Rd, Karol Bagh, New Delhi 110 005, Contact: Ved Bhushan *Tel:* (011) 23522997; Bharat Publishing House, 123 Durga Chambers, Desh Bandhu Gupta Rd, New Delhi 110 005, Contact: Anand Bhushan *Tel:* (011) 28757081; Computel Systems & Services, 10, Community Centre, Mayapuri, Phase-I, New Delhi 110 064, Contact: Dr V B Aggarwal *Tel:* (011) 28116652; (011) 28115683 *Fax:* (011) 28117683; Piyush Printers Publishers Pvt Ltd, 435/1/3, Village Mundka, New Delhi 110 041, Contact: Jaideep Aggarwal; Reliant Microsystem Pvt Ltd, 10, Community Centre, Mayapuri, Phase-I, New Delhi 110 064, Contact: Prof V B Aggarwal *Tel:* (011) 28113560
Branch Office(s)
Pitambar Publishing Co Pvt Ltd, No 30, KG1-119/1, HBR, 2nd Stage, AC Post, Bangalore 560 045 *Tel:* 9448836776 (cell)

Pointer Publishers+
No 807, Vyas Bldg, SMS Highway, Chaura Rasta, Jaipur 302 003
Tel: (0141) 2578159 *Fax:* (0141) 2578159
E-mail: info@pointerpublishers.com;
pointerpub@hotmail.com
Web Site: www.pointerpublishers.com
Key Personnel
Manager: Vipin Jain
Founded: 1986
Publish reference & general books in agriculture, humanities arts, science & commerce.
Subjects: Accounting, Agriculture, Art, Biological Sciences, Child Care & Development, Economics, Education, Environmental Studies, Gardening, Plants, Geography, Geology, Government, Political Science, History, Journalism, Law, Library & Information Sciences, Literature, Literary Criticism, Essays, Management, Military Science, Philosophy, Psychology, Psychiatry, Science (General), Social Sciences, Sociology, Travel & Tourism, Women's Studies, Botany, Commerce, Humanities, Indian Culture, Physiology, Zoology
ISBN Prefix(es): 978-81-7132
Total Titles: 450 Print

Popular Prakashan Pvt Ltd+
301, Mahalaxmi Chambers, 22, Bhulabhai Desai Rd, Mumbai, Maharashtra 400 026
Tel: (022) 23530303
E-mail: info@popularprakashan.com
Web Site: www.popularprakashan.com
Key Personnel
Founder & Mng Dir: Ramdas Ganesh Bhatkal
Publisher: Harsha Bhatkal
Founded: 1924
Subjects: Anthropology, Art, Biography, Memoirs, Computer Science, Cookery, Crafts, Games, Hobbies, Economics, Fiction, Government, Political Science, Health, Nutrition, History, Literature, Literary Criticism, Essays, Management, Medicine, Nursing, Dentistry, Music, Dance, Philosophy, Social Sciences, Sociology, Women's Studies
ISBN Prefix(es): 978-81-7154; 978-81-7185; 978-81-7991
Parent Company: Popular Book Depot
Associate Companies: Bhatkal & Sen; Indiancookery.com Pvt Ltd, 501, Damini, Plot No 889, Juhu Tara Rd, Juhu, Mumbai 400 049 *Tel:* (022) 26171070 *Fax:* (022) 26132416
Imprints: Focus
Branch Office(s)
S-217, South Block, Manipal Centre, 42, Dickenson Rd, Bangalore, Karnataka 560 042

Tel: 9845541268 (cell) *E-mail:* murugeshk@
popularprakashan.com
4648/1, Ansari Rd, 21, Darya Ganj, New Delhi
110 002 *Tel:* (011) 2326 5245; (011) 2328
0068 *Fax:* (011) 2328 7588 *E-mail:* brajeshk@
popularprakashan.com
16 Southern Ave, Kolkata, Bengla 700 026
Tel: 9830600468 (cell) *E-mail:* najims@
popularprakashan.com

Prabhat Prakashan+
4/19 Asaf Ali Rd, Darya Ganj, New Delhi 110
002
Tel: (011) 2328 9555
E-mail: prabhatbooks@gmail.com
Web Site: www.prabhatbooks.com
Key Personnel
Chairman: Shyam Sunder
Founded: 1932
Subjects: Art, Biography, Memoirs, Cookery, Fiction, Humor, Library & Information Sciences,
Nonfiction (General), Poetry
ISBN Prefix(es): 978-81-7315
Divisions: Ocean Books

Pratibha Pratishthan+
1661 Dakhni Rai St, Netaji Subhash Marg, New
Delhi 110 002
Tel: (011) 3289555 *Fax:* (011) 3289555
E-mail: pratibhapbooks@gmail.com
Key Personnel
President: Prabhat Kumar
Founded: 1981
Subjects: Art, Biography, Memoirs, Cookery, Fiction, History, Humor, Library & Information
Sciences, Nonfiction (General), Poetry, Science
(General), Culture
ISBN Prefix(es): 978-81-85827; 978-81-88266

Promilla & Co Publishers
C-127, Sarvodaya Enclave, New Delhi 110 017
Tel: (011) 65284748; (011) 26864124 *Fax:* (011)
41829791
E-mail: books@biblioasia.com
Web Site: www.biblioasia.com
Key Personnel
Chief Executive Officer: Ashok Butani
Tel: 9899192862 (cell) *E-mail:* ashok@
ashokbutani.com
Founded: 1970
Subjects: Art, Biography, Memoirs, Economics,
Government, Political Science, History, Religion - Other, Social Sciences, Sociology,
Women's Studies
ISBN Prefix(es): 978-81-85002
Distribution Center: Motilal (UK) Books of Asia,
367, High St, London Colony, St Albans, Herts
AL2 1EA, United Kingdom, Contact: Ray
McLennan *Tel:* (01727) 761677 *Fax:* (01727)
761677 *E-mail:* info@mlbduk.com (Europe)
South Asia Books, PO Box 502, Columbia, MO
65205, United States, Contact: Matt Luccione *Tel:* 573-474-0116 *Fax:* 573-474-8124
E-mail: sabooks@juno.com (North & South
America)

Publication Bureau
E-162, Shastri Nagar, New Delhi 110 052
Tel: (011) 23656503; (011) 23656950 *Fax:* (011)
23656950
E-mail: mail@publicationbureau.com;
info@publicationbureau.com; sales@
publicationbureau.com
Web Site: www.publicationbureau.com
Key Personnel
Contact: Mr Vivek Sehgal
Founded: 1992
Membership(s): Federation of Indian Publishers.
Subjects: Biography, Memoirs, History, Philosophy, Poetry, Religion - Other, Social Sciences,
Sociology
ISBN Prefix(es): 978-81-85822; 978-81-7380

Purple Turtle, *imprint of* Aadarsh Pvt Ltd

Pustak Mahal Publishers+
J3/16, Ansari Rd, Darya Ganj, New Delhi 110
002
Tel: (011) 23272783; (011) 23272784; (011)
23276539 *Fax:* (011) 23260518
E-mail: pustak@pustakmahal.com
Web Site: www.pustakmahal.com
Key Personnel
Chairman: Ram Avtar Gupta
Mng Dir: Dr Ashok Gupta
Dir, Overseas: Rohit Gupta
Dir, Production: Vinod Gupta
Dir, Sales: Ramesh Gupta
Founded: 1974
Specialize in supplementary educational literature for children & informative books of mass
appeal. Publishes in 12 languages.
Membership(s): Delhi State Booksellers Association; Federation of Educational Publishers of
India; Federation of Indian Publishers; Federation of Publishers' & Booksellers' Associations
in India (FPBAI); Publishers of South India.
Subjects: Architecture & Interior Design, Astrology, Occult, Biography, Memoirs, Computer
Science, Cookery, Crafts, Games, Hobbies,
Health, Nutrition, History, House & Home,
Humor, Language Arts, Linguistics, Medicine,
Nursing, Dentistry, Music, Dance, Parapsychology, Religion - Other, Romance, Science (General), Career Guidance, Comedy, Fun, Hygiene,
Mythology
ISBN Prefix(es): 978-81-223
Total Titles: 500 Print
Imprints: Cedar Books; Hindoology Books; Rapidex
Subsidiaries: M/S Hind Pustak Bhandar
Branch Office(s)
8 1st floor, Second Cross, First Main Rd, Sudama Nagar, Bangalore 560 027 *Tel:* (080)
2234025 *Fax:* (080) 2240209 *E-mail:* pustak@
sancharnet.in
5-1-707/1 Brij Bhawan, Bank St, Koti, 500 095
Hyderabad *Tel:* (040) 24737530 *Fax:* (040)
24737290 *E-mail:* pustakmahalhyd@yahoo.co.
in
23-25 Zaoba Wadi, Thakurdwar, Mumbai 400
002 *Tel:* (022) 22010941 *Fax:* (022) 22053387
E-mail: rapidex@bom5.vsnl.net.in
Khemka House, 1st floor, Ashok Rajpath,
Patna 800 004 *Fax:* (0612) 2673644
E-mail: rapidexptn@rediffmail.com
Book Club(s): Comdex Book Club

Quixot Multimedia Pvt Ltd
Khasra No 1208, Hall No 1, Near Bagga Link,
Village & Post, Rithala, Delhi 110 085
Tel: (011) 27042565; (011) 27042564
E-mail: sales@quixotmultimedia.com;
customercare@quixotmultimedia.com
Web Site: quixotkid.com
Founded: 2005
ISBN Prefix(es): 978-93-82269

Radiant Publishing House+
4-5-64 Beside Andhra Bank, Book Basement,
Koti, Hyderabad, Andhra Pradesh 500 001
Tel: (040) 24754430; (040) 66360677
E-mail: rph_pph@yahoo.co.in
Founded: 1973
Subjects: Economics, Education, Environmental Studies, Government, Political Science,
Religion - Other, Social Sciences, Sociology,
Women's Studies
ISBN Prefix(es): 978-81-7027
Number of titles published annually: 10 Print
Total Titles: 200 Print

Rahul Publishing House
34, Central Market, Ashok Vihar, New Delhi 110
052

Tel: (011) 27212195
Founded: 1993
Subjects: Anthropology, Antiques, Archaeology,
Art, Asian Studies, Earth Sciences, History,
Language Arts, Linguistics, Regional Interests
ISBN Prefix(es): 978-81-7388; 978-81-88791
Associate Companies: Agam Kala Prakashan;
Agam Prakashan; Swati Publication

Rajasthan Hindi Granth Academy+
Plot No 1, Jhalana Institutional Area, Jaipur, Rajasthan 302 004
Tel: (0141) 511129
E-mail: rajhindigranth@gmail.com
Founded: 1969
Subjects: Agriculture, Art, Chemistry, Chemical
Engineering, Economics, Education, Human
Relations, Language Arts, Linguistics, Law, Library & Information Sciences, Medicine, Nursing, Dentistry, Philosophy, Physics, Science
(General), Social Sciences, Sociology
ISBN Prefix(es): 978-81-7137

Rajesh Publications+
4226-A/1, Ansari Rd, Darya Ganj, New Delhi
110 002
Tel: (011) 23274550; 9212752511 (cell)
E-mail: rajeshpublications@gmail.com
Web Site: www.rajeshpublications.com
Key Personnel
Mng Dir: Mohan Lal Gupta
Contact: Sanjay Gupta
Founded: 1970
Subjects: Economics, Education, Geography, Geology, Government, Political Science, History,
Literature, Literary Criticism, Essays, Management, Philosophy, Regional Interests, Religion
- Other, India History & Culture, Life Science,
Northeast India
ISBN Prefix(es): 978-81-85891
Distributed by Janki Prakashan
Distributor for Seema Publications

Rajkamal Prakashan Pvt Ltd
One-B, Netaji Subhash Marg, Darya Ganj, New
Delhi 110 002
Tel: (011) 23288769; (011) 23274463 *Fax:* (011)
23278144
E-mail: info@rajkamalprakashan.com
Web Site: www.rajkamalprakashan.com
Key Personnel
Mng Dir: Ashok Maheshwari
Dir: Amod Maheshwari
Editorial: Chetan Kranti
Sales: Ashok Tyagi *Tel:* 9310984842 (cell)
Subjects: Education
ISBN Prefix(es): 978-81-7178; 978-81-267
Branch Office(s)
Darbari Bldg, Mahatma Gandhi Marg, Allahabad,
Uttar Pradesh 211 001 *Tel:* (0532) 2427274;
(0532) 3293838 *Fax:* (0532) 2427274
Ashok Rajpath, Opposite Science College, Patna,
Bihar 800 006 *Tel:* (0612) 2672280

Rajpal & Sons+
1590 Madarsa Rd, Kashmere Gate, New Delhi
110 006
Tel: (011) 23869812; (011) 23865483 *Fax:* (011)
23867791
E-mail: pranav@rajpalpublishing.com (sales)
Web Site: www.rajpalpublishing.com/index.asp
Key Personnel
Editorial: Meera Johri *E-mail:* meera@
rajpalpublishing.com
Founded: 1912
Subjects: Biography, Memoirs, Cookery, Drama,
Theater, Economics, Fiction, Health, Nutrition,
History, Human Relations, Inspirational, Spirituality, Literature, Literary Criticism, Essays,
Management, Philosophy, Poetry, Psychology,

Psychiatry, Religion - Other, Science (General), Culture, Novels
ISBN Prefix(es): 978-81-7028
Associate Companies: Orient Paperbacks, 5-A/8 Ansari Rd, Darya Ganj, New Delhi 110 002 *Tel:* (011) 2327 8877 *Web Site:* www. orientpaperbacks.com; Shiksha Bharati; Vision Books Pvt Ltd, 24, Feroze Gandhi Rd, Lajpat Nagar 111, New Delhi 110 024 *Tel:* (011) 2386 2201; (011) 2386 2935 *Fax:* (011) 2983 6490 *Web Site:* www.visionbooksindia.com
Branch Office(s)
3-6-280/A5, Himayat Nagar, Hyderabad 500 029 *Tel:* (040) 2322 3252 *Fax:* (040) 2322 3252
3B Peddar Rd, Mumbai 400 026 *Tel:* (022) 4929343
Bookshop(s): Lothian Rd, Kashmere Gate, New Delhi 110 006 *Tel:* (011) 2516602

Random House India, see Penguin Random House India

Rapidex, *imprint of* Pustak Mahal Publishers

Rastogi Publications+
Shivaji Rd, Meerut 250 002
Tel: (0121) 2510688; (0121) 2516080; (0121) 2515142 *Fax:* (0121) 2521545
E-mail: info@rastogipublications.com
Web Site: www.rastogipublications.com
Key Personnel
Sales, Publicity: Vivek Rastogi
Founded: 1966
Subjects: Agriculture, Animals, Pets, Biological Sciences, Earth Sciences, Education, Government, Political Science, Science (General), Biotechnology, Botany, Cell Biology, Environmental Science, Zoology
ISBN Prefix(es): 978-81-7133; 978-81-85711
Subsidiaries: Pioneer Printers

Reference Press, *imprint of* Ess Ess Publications

Regency Publications+
1123/74, Deva Ram Park, Tri Nagar, New Delhi 110 035
Tel: (011) 27383999 *Fax:* (011) 23244987
E-mail: info@regencybooks.com
Web Site: www.regencybooks.com
Key Personnel
Owner: Anil Mittal
Founded: 1993
Membership(s): Delhi State Publishers & Booksellers Association.
Subjects: Agriculture, Anthropology, Archaeology, Art, Biological Sciences, Education, Environmental Studies, Ethnicity, Fiction, Geography, Geology, Government, Political Science, History, Language Arts, Linguistics, Law, Philosophy, Regional Interests, Religion - Other, Social Sciences, Sociology, Sports, Athletics, Women's Studies
ISBN Prefix(es): 978-81-86030; 978-81-87498; 978-81-89233
Number of titles published annually: 20 Print
Total Titles: 200 Print
Parent Company: DAYA Publishing House
Distributed by DK Agencies; M K Book Distributors (UK); UBS Publishers' Distributors
Showroom(s): 4760-61/23, Ansari Rd, New Delhi 110 002 *Tel:* (011) 23245578; (011) 23244987

Rekha Prakashan+
16 Darya Ganj, New Delhi 110 002
Tel: (011) 23279907; (011) 23279904 *Fax:* (011) 2321783
E-mail: rekha.prakashan16@gmail.com
Web Site: www.museumoffolkandtribalart.in/publications.htm

Key Personnel
Chief Executive, Rights & Permissions: K C Aryan
Head, Sales: B N Aryan
Publicity Dir: G D Aryan
Editorial: S Aryan
Founded: 1973
Publisher of books on art & Indology.
Membership(s): Delhi State Booksellers' & Publishers' Association.
Subjects: Art, Regional Interests, History of Art (India); Indian Folk & Tribal Art
ISBN Prefix(es): 978-81-900002; 978-81-900003; 978-81-904394
Number of titles published annually: 3 Print
Total Titles: 27 Print

Reliance Publishing House+
3026/7H, S Patel Nagar, New Delhi 110 008
Tel: (011) 25847377 *Fax:* (011) 25842605
Web Site: www.facebook.com/Reliance-Publishing-House-224753730896673/
Key Personnel
Manager: Manish Batia
Founded: 1985
Publishers of reference books & trade directories on the Indian book industry, humanities & social sciences.
Membership(s): Delhi State Booksellers' & Publishers' Association.
Subjects: Accounting, Advertising, Agriculture, Anthropology, Archaeology, Architecture & Interior Design, Art, Asian Studies, Astrology, Occult, Astronomy, Behavioral Sciences, Biography, Memoirs, Biological Sciences, Business, Career Development, Child Care & Development, Communications, Criminology, Developing Countries, Disability, Special Needs, Drama, Theater, Earth Sciences, Economics, Education, Energy, Environmental Studies, Ethnicity, Fiction, Finance, Geography, Geology, Government, Political Science, History, Human Relations, Humor, Journalism, Labor, Industrial Relations, Library & Information Sciences, Literature, Literary Criticism, Essays, Management, Marketing, Medicine, Nursing, Dentistry, Military Science, Music, Dance, Mysteries, Suspense, Nonfiction (General), Philosophy, Poetry, Psychology, Psychiatry, Public Administration, Publishing & Book Trade Reference, Regional Interests, Religion - Buddhist, Religion - Hindu, Science Fiction, Fantasy, Social Sciences, Sociology, Sports, Athletics, Technology, Travel & Tourism, Women's Studies, Mythology
ISBN Prefix(es): 978-81-85047; 978-81-85972; 978-81-7510
Total Titles: 525 Print; 4 Online; 4 E-Book
Associate Companies: Geeta Enterprises, J436, Baljit Nagar, New Delhi 110 008; Geeta Graphics, J436, Baljit Nagar, New Delhi 110 008, Contact: Manish K Bhatia
Distributed by DK Publishers' Distributors; UBS Publishers Distributors Pvt Ltd
Warehouse: J-436, Baljit Nagar, New Delhi 110 008 *Tel:* (011) 25845330 *Fax:* (011) 25846769; (011) 25842748 *E-mail:* reliance@indiatimes.com
Distribution Center: 3026/7H, Shiv Chowk, S Patel Nagar (Ranjit Nagar), New Delhi 110 008 *Tel:* (011) 5852605 *Fax:* (011) 5786769

Research Signpost
Division of Transworld Research Network
TC 37/661(2), Fort PO, Trivandrum, Kerala 695 023
Tel: (0471) 2452918; (0471) 2468850 *Fax:* (0471) 2573051
E-mail: admin@rsflash.com; signpost99@gmail.com
Web Site: www.ressign.com
Key Personnel
Mng Editor: Dr S G Pandalai

Publications Manager: Anandavalli Gayathri
Founded: 1995
Publishers of scientific, technical, medical & agricultural books & journals. Also produces CD-ROMs.
Subjects: Agriculture, Medicine, Nursing, Dentistry, Science (General)
ISBN Prefix(es): 978-81-86481
Number of titles published annually: 150 Print
Total Titles: 1,500 Print
Distribution Center: 4 Big Red Ave, Scarborough, Ontario M1V 1N7, Canada

Researchco Books & Periodicals Pvt Ltd+
4735/22, Prakash Deep Bldg, 2nd floor, Near Delhi Medical Association, Ansari Rd, Darya Ganj, New Delhi 110 002
Tel: (011) 4324 0200 *Fax:* (011) 4324 0215
E-mail: akj@researchco.net; researchco@researchco.net
Key Personnel
Owner: Anil Jain
Contact: Arvind Jain
Founded: 1970
Specialize in stocking & supplying of books & back volume journals.
Subjects: Science (General), Social Sciences, Sociology, Technology, Medical Science
ISBN Prefix(es): 978-81-901785
Total Titles: 10 Print
Branch Office(s)
9-A, 1st floor, Chunchappa Block Rd, BDA - Auction Sites, Near New Puja Bakery, Matada Halli, R-T - Nagar, Karnataka, Bangalore 560 032, Contact: Mr Abdul Basheer *Tel:* 9880992690 (cell) *E-mail:* researchco.bangalore@gmail.com
c/o Mr P Pattnaik, 1st floor, MDL-7, Shanti Vihar, Barmuda, Orissa, Bhubaneswar, Contact: Mr Santosh Sahoo *Tel:* 9337443095 (cell) *E-mail:* sksresearchco@gmail.com
Plot No 71-72, Flat No B2, Vanamaali Apartment, Ganesh Nagar Main Rd, Selaiyur, Chennai 600 073, Contact: Mr Sivarama Krishnan *Tel:* 9444021992 (cell) *E-mail:* sivaramakrishnan.a@gmail.com
Nisha Mansion, 1st floor, Fatasil Ambari, Assam, Guwahati 781 025, Contact: Mr Sanjay Jain *Tel:* 9435110839 (cell) *E-mail:* skyinfoghy@yahoo.co.in
11-4-321, Nityananda Nilayam, Near Wesley Church, Chilakalaguda, Secunderabad, Hyderabad 500 061, Contact: Mr K Satyanandam *Tel:* 9390169044 (cell) *E-mail:* k_satya05@yahoo.co.in
c/o Mr K K Dwivedi, Hig-36, Madhavpuram, Gooba Garden, IIT Employee Housing Society, Kanpur 208 016, Contact: Mr Anjani Kumar Dwivedi *Tel:* 9450351433 (cell)
Mahavir Varsha Co-op Housing Society Ltd, Plot No 8/9/10, Sector-6, Flat No-B-208, Ghansoli, Maharashtra, Navi Mumbai 400 701, Contact: Mr D K Sinha *Tel:* (098) 67000877 (cell) *E-mail:* mumbai@researchco.net
308, Radha Bldg, Shree Krishnanagar (Near Bank of Maharashtra), NDA-Pashan Rd, Bavdhan, Pune 411 021, Contact: Mr Alok Jha *Tel:* 9325516817 (cell) *Fax:* (020) 22953859 *E-mail:* researchcopune@gmail.com
Ram Nagar, Tarapur, Assam, Silchar 788 008, Contact: Mr P K Singh *Tel:* 9864441081 (cell) *E-mail:* silchar@researchco.net
Distributor for Cabi; Cambridge University Press; Cengage Learning; Elsevier; Jones & Bartlett Publishers; Lippincott Williams & Wilkins; McGraw-Hill; Oxford University Press; Palgrave Macmillan; Pearson Education; RSC; Sage; Springer Science+Business Media; Studium Press; Taylor & Francis Group; Wageningen Academic Publishers; Wiley; Woodhead Publishing; World Scientific

Response Books, *imprint of* SAGE Publications India Pvt Ltd

Roli Books Pvt Ltd+
M-75, Greater Kailash 2 Market, New Delhi 110 048
Tel: (011) 4068 2000 *Fax:* (011) 29217185
E-mail: info@rolibooks.com; sales@rolibooks.com; editorial@rolibooks.com
Web Site: rolibooks.com
Key Personnel
Founder: Pramod Kapoor
Contact: Mr Shammi Kapoor *E-mail:* delhisales@rolibooks.com
Founded: 1978
Publishing house & distributor for foreign publishers. Sells titles to other houses under their logo. Specializes in plain text & coffee table books, destinations & monuments & politics.
Subjects: Art, Business, Cookery, Erotica, Fiction, Government, Political Science, History, Management, Music, Dance, Religion - Buddhist, Religion - Hindu, Religion - Islamic, Religion - Jewish, Travel & Tourism
ISBN Prefix(es): 978-81-7437; 978-81-7436
Total Titles: 122 Print; 122 Online; 4 Audio
Parent Company: Roli Books
Imprints: IndianInk; Lotus; Lustre Press; Showcase

Roorkee Press, see Nem Chand & Brothers

Rupa Paperbacks, *imprint of* Rupa Publications India

Rupa Publications India+
161-B/4, Ground floor Gulmohar House, Yusuf Sarai Commmunity Centre, New Delhi 110 049
Tel: (011) 49226666
E-mail: info@rupapublications.com; rupa@rupapublications.com; sales@rupapublications.com
Web Site: rupapublications.co.in
Key Personnel
Owner: Kapish G Mehra
Productions & International Rights: R K Mehra
Founded: 1936
Subjects: Art, Crafts, Games, Hobbies, Education, Fiction, History, Literature, Literary Criticism, Essays, Philosophy, Religion - Other, Sports, Athletics
ISBN Prefix(es): 978-81-7167; 978-81-291
Associate Companies: HarperCollins Publishers India
Imprints: Rupa Paperbacks
Distributor for Affiliated East-West (India); Elbs titles (UK); Faber & Faber (UK); Hamlyn (UK); Ladybird (UK); Macmillan (UK); McGraw-Hill Kogakusha (Singapore); Penguin (UK); Prentice-Hall (India); Tata McGraw-Hill (India); Unwin Hyman (UK); Wiley Eastern (India)

SABDA+
Unit of Sri Aurobindo Ashram Trust
No 17, Rue de la Marine, Pondicherry 605 002
Tel: (0413) 2233656; (0413) 2223328 *Fax:* (0413) 2223328
E-mail: mail@sabda.in
Web Site: www.sabda.in
Key Personnel
Manager: Mira Gupta; Jay Raichura
International Rights & Permissions: Manoj Das Gupta
Founded: 1952
Specialize in works by or on the philosopher Sri Aurobindo & his spiritual collaborator known as "the Mother," the spiritual teachings & system of "Integral Yoga" of Sri Aurobindo.
Membership(s): CAPEXIL (Export Promotion Council).

Subjects: Asian Studies, Education, Government, Political Science, Literature, Literary Criticism, Essays, Philosophy, Poetry, Psychology, Psychiatry, Religion - Hindu, Religion - Other, Social Sciences, Sociology
ISBN Prefix(es): 978-81-7058; 978-81-7060; 978-81-86413; 978-93-5210
Total Titles: 1,700 Print
Distributed by Auromere (USA only); East-West Cultural Center (USA only); Lotus Press (USA only); Matagiri (USA only)
Distributor for Sri Aurobindo Ashram; Sri Aurobindo Society; Sri Mira Trust
Showroom(s): 13 Rue de la Marine, Pondicherry 605 002 *Tel:* (0413) 2233657
Bookshop(s): Sri Aurobindo Society, 11 Sahakar, B Rd, Churchgate, Mumbai 400 020 *Tel:* (022) 22043076 *E-mail:* sasbombay@mtnl.net.in; Matri Store, Sri Aurobindo Marg, New Delhi 110 016 *Tel:* (011) 65684153 *Fax:* (011) 26857449 *E-mail:* contact@aurobindoonline.in

Ratna Sagar Ltd+
Virat Bhavan, Mukherjee Nagar Commercial Complex, New Delhi 110 009
Tel: (011) 47038000 *Toll Free Tel:* 1800-102-0201 *Fax:* (011) 47038099; (011) 27650787
E-mail: rsagar@ratnasagar.com
Web Site: www.ratnasagar.com
Key Personnel
Mng Dir: Dhanesh Jain
Founded: 1982
Subjects: Economics, Education, Language Arts, Linguistics, Medicine, Nursing, Dentistry, Science (General), Social Sciences, Sociology
ISBN Prefix(es): 978-81-7070; 978-81-8332; 978-93-5036
Branch Office(s)
B-577 Kamla Nagar, Agra *Tel:* (0562) 4040945 *Fax:* (0562) 4040945 *E-mail:* rsagar.agra@ratnasagar.com
1st floor, Bungalow No 12, Ambika Society, Opposite Usmanpura Municipal Garden, Usmanpura, Ahmedabad 380 013 *Tel:* (079) 27553627 *E-mail:* rsagar.ahm@ratnasagar.com
No 116, 1st floor, 1st Main Rd, MLA Layout, RT Nagar, Bangalore 560 032 *Tel:* (080) 23637479 *Fax:* (080) 23637479 *E-mail:* rsagar.blr@ratnasagar.com
No 1 Gugan St, Puliyurpuram, Kodambakkam, Chennai 600 024 *Tel:* (044) 42208000 *Fax:* (044) 42322050 *E-mail:* rsagar.chn@ratnasagar.com
1790 B LGB Colony, OLYMPUS, Ramanathapuram, Coimbatore 641 045 *Tel:* (0422) 6554130 *E-mail:* rsagar.cbe@ratnasagar.com
11, Hem Kunj, Vijay Park, Opposite IMA Blood Bank, Dehradun 248 001 *Tel:* (0135) 3245795; (0135) 2530435 *E-mail:* rsagar.ddn@ratnasagar.com
59, FC Rd, Uzan Bazar, Guwahati 781 001 *Tel:* (0361) 2731762; (0361) 2735610 *Fax:* (0361) 2731762 *E-mail:* rsagar.guw@ratnasagar.com
1-1-287/31/1, Bapu Nagar, Municipal Market Rd, Chikkadpally, Hyderabad 500 020 *Tel:* (040) 66611100; (040) 27662275; (040) 64592220 *Fax:* (040) 27662275 *E-mail:* rsagar.hyd@ratnasagar.com
C-35, Raghu Marg, Gom Defence Colony, Hanuman Nagar, Vaishali Nagar, Jaipur 302 021 *Tel:* (0141) 4138000 *Fax:* (0141) 4138029 *E-mail:* rsagar.jaipur@ratnasagar.com
128/41, Block-D, Kidwai Nagar, Kanpur 208 011 *Tel:* (0512) 3022144; (0512) 3046495 *E-mail:* rsagar.kanpur@ratnasagar.com
50/935 E, Bank Junction, Edappally, Kochi 682 024 *Tel:* (0484) 6577993 *Fax:* (0484) 4055972 *E-mail:* rsagar.kochi@ratnasagar.com
60, 1st floor, Dr Sundari Mohan Ave, Kolkata 700 014 *Tel:* (033) 40238000 *Fax:* (033) 40238099 *E-mail:* rsagar.kol@ratnasagar.com

A-1539, Indira Nagar, Lucknow 226 016 *Tel:* (0522) 4058000 *Fax:* (0522) 4058099 *E-mail:* rsagar.lko@ratnasagar.com
Ground floor (Eastern Side), 29/1, Chandragandhi Nagar, Bypass Rd, Madurai 625 010 *Tel:* (0452) 6462888 *Fax:* (0452) 4354231 *E-mail:* rsagar.madurai@ratnasagar.com
Plot No 3, Asha Nagar, 1st floor, Agarwal Bhawan, Opposite Shopper's Stop, Chembur, Mumbai 400 089 *Tel:* (022) 25226025 *E-mail:* rsagar.mumbai@ratnasagar.com
110, Gandhi Path, Nehru Nagar, North S K Puri, Patna 800 013 *Tel:* (0612) 2574273 *Fax:* (0612) 2574273 *E-mail:* rsagar.patna@ratnasagar.com
10A, Purulia Rd, Kantatoli, Ranchi 834 001 *Tel:* (0651) 6570417 *E-mail:* rsagar.ranchi@ratnasagar.com
Showroom(s): 4808/24, Bharat Ram Rd, Darya Ganj, New Delhi 110 002 *Tel:* (011) 43028000 *Fax:* (011) 45166099

SAGE Publications India Pvt Ltd+
B-1/I-1, Mohan Cooperative Area, Mathura Rd, New Delhi 110 044
Tel: (011) 4053 9222 *Fax:* (011) 4053 9234
E-mail: customerservicebooks@sagepub.in; editors@sagepub.in; info@sagepub.in; marketing@sagepub.in
Web Site: www.sagepub.in
Key Personnel
Mng Dir & Chief Executive Officer: Vivek Mehra
Customer Service: Saroj K Sahoo
Marketing: Sunanda Ghosh *E-mail:* sunanda.ghosh@sagepub.in
Founded: 1981
An independent international publisher of books, journals & electronic media.
Subjects: Anthropology, Asian Studies, Behavioral Sciences, Business, Communications, Developing Countries, Economics, Environmental Studies, Government, Political Science, Management, Psychology, Psychiatry, Public Administration, Social Sciences, Sociology, Women's Studies
ISBN Prefix(es): 978-81-7036; 978-81-7829; 978-81-3210
Total Titles: 900 Print
Associate Companies: SAGE Publications Asia-Pacific Pte Ltd, 3 Church St, No 10-04, Samsung Hub, Singapore 049483, Singapore, Executive Dir, Consortia/Library Sales & Marketing: Rosalia da Garcia *Tel:* 6220 1800 *Fax:* 6438 1008 *Web Site:* www.sagepublications.com; SAGE Publications Ltd, One Oliver's Yard, 55 City Rd, London EC1Y 1SP, United Kingdom *Tel:* (020) 7324 8500 *Fax:* (020) 7324 8600 *E-mail:* market@sagepub.co.uk *Web Site:* uk.sagepub.com; SAGE Publications Inc, 2455 Teller Rd, Thousand Oaks, CA 91320-2218, United States *Tel:* 805-499-9774 *Fax:* 805-499-0871 *E-mail:* order@sagepub.com *Web Site:* us.sagepub.com
Imprints: Paul Chapman Publishing; Corwin Press; Pine Forge Press; Response Books; Sage Science Press; Scolari; Vistaar Publications
Branch Office(s)
E-1 Karthik Apartments, New No 16 (old 6), Vijayaraghava Rd, T Nagar, Chennai 600 017 *Tel:* (044) 2815 8405; (044) 2815 8406; (044) 2815 8407 *E-mail:* chennai@sagepub.in
H No: 5- 9-1037/2, Next to Madina Medical Centre, Basheerbagh King Koti Rd, Hyderaguda, PO Box 1031, Hyderabad 500 029 *Tel:* (040) 2323 1447; (040) 2323 0674 *E-mail:* hyderabad@sagepub.in
59/5 Prince Baktiar Shah Rd, Ground floor, Tollygunge, Kolkata 700 033 *Tel:* (033) 2417 2642; (033) 2422 0611 *E-mail:* kolkata@sagepub.in
3E, 2nd floor, Apeejay House, 5, Dinshaw Vachha Rd, Churchgate, Mumbai 400 020 *Tel:* (022) 6636 4344 *Fax:* (022) 2202 9967 *E-mail:* anand.vithalkar@sagepub.in

Sage Science Press, *imprint of* SAGE Publications India Pvt Ltd

Sahitya Akademi (National Academy of Letters)
Rabindra Bhavan, 35, Ferozeshah Rd, New Delhi 110 001
Tel: (011) 23386626; (011) 23386627; (011) 23386628; (011) 23735297 (sales); (011) 23364207 (sales) *Fax:* (011) 23382428; (011) 23364207 (sales)
E-mail: secy@ndb.vsnl.net.in; sahityaakademisale@yahoo.com (sales)
Web Site: www.sahitya-akademi.gov.in
Key Personnel
President: Dr Vishwanath Prasad Tiwari
  Tel: (011) 23386623 *Fax:* (011) 23074168
  E-mail: vptiwari378@hotmail.com
Vice President: Dr Chandrashekhar Kambar
  Tel: (011) 23386623 *Fax:* (011) 23074168
Sales: Dr Khurshid Alam *Tel:* (011) 23745295
Founded: 1954
Subjects: Literature, Literary Criticism, Essays
ISBN Prefix(es): 978-81-7201; 978-81-260
Branch Office(s)
Central College Campus, University Library Bldg, Bangalore 560 001, Contact: Dr B R Ambedkar Veedhi *Tel:* (080) 22245152 *Fax:* (080) 22121932 *E-mail:* sa.bengaluru@gmail.com
Guna Bldgs, 2nd floor, No 443(304), Anna Salai, Teynampet, Chennai 600 018 *Tel:* (044) 24311741 *E-mail:* sahityaakademichennai@gmail.com
4DL Khan Rd, Kolkata 700 025 *Tel:* (033) 24787405; (033) 24781806 *Fax:* (033) 24789375 *E-mail:* regsecy@vsnl.net
Sharada Cinema Bldg, 172, Mumbai Marathi Granth, Sangrahalaya Marg, Dadar (East), Mumbai 400 014 *Tel:* (022) 24135744; (022) 24131948 *Fax:* (022) 24147650 *E-mail:* sahityakademimumbai@gmail.com

Sai Early Learners (P) Ltd, *imprint of* Sterling Publishers Pvt Ltd

Samya, *imprint of* Stree-Samya

Sanctum Books, *imprint of* Munshiram Manoharlal Publishers Pvt Ltd

Sanskriti, *imprint of* Arnold Heineman Publishers (India) Pvt Ltd

Saraswati Vihar, *imprint of* Hind Pocket Books

M C Sarkar & Sons (P) Ltd+
14 Bankim Chatterjee St, Kolkata 700 073
Tel: (033) 2241-7490; (033) 2464-0763
E-mail: mcsarkar@gmail.com
Key Personnel
Dir: Samit Sarkar
Founded: 1910
Publication of books & magazines.
Subjects: Fiction, Nonfiction (General)
ISBN Prefix(es): 978-81-7157
Number of titles published annually: 30 Print
Total Titles: 500 Print

Sasta Sahitya Mandal+
N-77 Connaught Circus, New Delhi 110 001
Tel: (011) 23310505; (011) 41523565 *Fax:* (011) 23310505
E-mail: info@sastasahityamandal.org; sales@sastasahityamandal.org
Web Site: www.sastasahityamandal.org
Key Personnel
President: P N Bhagwati
Vice President: Sudarshan Birla
Secretary: Prof Krishna Dutt Paliwal
Founded: 1925

Subjects: Agriculture, Animals, Pets, Biography, Memoirs, Economics, Education, Ethnicity, Government, Political Science, History, Literature, Literary Criticism, Essays, Philosophy, Religion - Hindu
ISBN Prefix(es): 978-81-7309
Total Titles: 2,000 Print
Branch Office(s)
126, Zero Rd, Allahabad 211 003
  Tel: (0532) 2400034 *E-mail:* allahabad@sastasahityamandal.org

Sat Sahitya Prakashan Trust+
16, Vipul Bldg, 28, B G Kher Marg, Malabar Hills, Mumbai 400 006
Tel: (022) 2368 2055
Web Site: www.satsahitya.com
Founded: 1970
Subjects: Art, Biography, Memoirs, Cookery, Fiction, Humor, Library & Information Sciences, Nonfiction (General), Poetry
ISBN Prefix(es): 978-81-7721; 978-81-85830
Branch Office(s)
Sat Sahitya Prakashan Trust - Shri Akhandanand Pustakalaya Library, Anand Kutir, Swami Shri Akhandanand Marg, Moti Jheel, Vrindavan (Mathura District), UP 281 124 *Tel:* (0565) 254 0487 (Ashram office)

Satyam Books
2/13 Ansar Rd, Darya Ganj, New Delhi 110 002
Tel: (011) 23242686; (011) 23245698 *Fax:* (011) 23267131; (011) 22459334
E-mail: customercare@satyambooks.net; satyambooks@hotmail.com
Web Site: www.satyambooks.net
Key Personnel
Proprietor: Mr Satish Upadhyay *Tel:* 9811132241 (cell)
Founded: 1996
Subjects: Architecture & Interior Design, Law, Management, Medicine, Nursing, Dentistry, Science (General), Technology
ISBN Prefix(es): 978-81-921204; 978-93-828223; 978-81-902883; 978-81-905852

Sawan Kirpal Publications Spiritual Society
Kirpal Ashram, Sant Kirpal Singh Marg, Viyay Nagar, New Delhi 110 009
Tel: (011) 27117100 *Fax:* (011) 27214040
Web Site: sos.org
Key Personnel
Mng Dir: Sant Rajinder Singh Ji Maharaj
Founded: 1977
Subjects: Inspirational, Spirituality, Religion - Other, Meditation, Vegetarian
ISBN Prefix(es): 978-81-85380
U.S. Office(s): SK Publications, 4S175 Naperville Rd, Naperville, IL 60563, United States
  Tel: 630-955-1200 *Fax:* 630-955-1205
  E-mail: napervillecenter@sos.org

Scientific Publishers India+
5A, New Pali Rd, Jodhpur 342 001
Mailing Address: PO Box 91, Jodhpur 342 001
Tel: (0291) 2433323; (0291) 2624154 *Fax:* (0291) 2613449
E-mail: info@scientificpub.com
Web Site: www.scientificpub.com
Key Personnel
Mng Dir: Mr Tanay Sharma *E-mail:* tanay@scientificpub.com
Sales: Mr Rajendra Choudhary
  E-mail: rajendrac@scientificpub.com
Founded: 1976
Also acts as bookseller, subscription agent, exporter & importer.
Subjects: Agriculture, Animals, Pets, Biological Sciences, Chemistry, Chemical Engineering, Earth Sciences, Engineering (General), Geography, Geology, History, Mathematics, Natural History, Social Sciences, Sociology

ISBN Prefix(es): 978-81-7233
Total Titles: 800 Print
Parent Company: United Book Traders
Branch Office(s)
4806/24, Ansari Rd, Darya Ganj, New Delhi 110 002 *Tel:* (011) 4151 1055 *E-mail:* delhi@scientificpub.com

Scolari, *imprint of* SAGE Publications India Pvt Ltd

Seagull Books Pvt Ltd
31A, S P Mukherjee Rd, Kolkata 700 025
Tel: (033) 24765869; (033) 24765865
E-mail: books@seagullindia.com
Web Site: www.seagullbooks.org; www.seagullindia.com/books
Subjects: Drama, Theater, Fiction, Government, Political Science, Literature, Literary Criticism, Essays, Philosophy, Pop Culture, Cinema, Contemporary Politics, Cultural Studies, French Literature, German Literature
ISBN Prefix(es): 978-1-906497; 978-81-7046
Branch Office(s)
Seagull Books London Ltd, 1276/1278 Greenford Rd, Greenford, Middx UB6 0HH, United Kingdom

Selina Publishers
4725/21A Daya Nand Marg, Darya Ganj, New Delhi 110 002
Tel: (011) 23280711; (011) 23947699; 9313542601 (cell)
E-mail: selinapublishers@gmail.com
Key Personnel
Mng Dir, Publicity, Rights & Permissions: H L Gupta
Founded: 1975
Membership(s): Delhi State Booksellers' & Publishers' Association.
Subjects: Education
ISBN Prefix(es): 978-81-85612
Associate Companies: Granth Bharati (printing press)
Subsidiaries: Mudra Prakashan
Book Club(s): Sanket Library Yojna

Shaibya Prakashan Bibhag+
86/1 Mahatma Gandhi Rd, Kolkata 700 009
Tel: (033) 2241 1748
Key Personnel
Owner: Somnath Bal
Founded: 1984
Subjects: Biography, Memoirs, Computer Science, Electronics, Electrical Engineering, English as a Second Language, Publishing & Book Trade Reference, Religion - Hindu, Science (General), Science Fiction, Fantasy
ISBN Prefix(es): 978-81-87051

Sharda Prakashan
F-3/16, Gay House, Ansari Rd, Darya Ganj, New Delhi 110 002
Tel: (011) 23280234; (011) 45652462 *Fax:* (011) 23280234
E-mail: shardaprakashan@gmail.com; info@shardaprakashan.co.in
Web Site: www.shardaprakashan.co.in
Key Personnel
Proprietor & Chief Executive, Production, Rights & Permissions: Mr Ruder Dev Jhari
  Tel: 9811175171 (cell) *E-mail:* ruderjhari@yahoo.com
Editorial, Publicity & Finance: Mr Deepanshu Jhari *Tel:* 9899882010 (cell)
  E-mail: deepanshujhari@gmail.com
Sales: Mr Rajpal Singh Rathi
Founded: 1971
Membership(s): Delhi State Booksellers' & Publishers' Association.
Subjects: Biography, Memoirs, Career Development, Drama, Theater, Education, Fiction, Health, Nutrition, Humor, Language Arts, Lin-

guistics, Literature, Literary Criticism, Essays, Nonfiction (General), Religion - Hindu, Science (General), Sports, Athletics
ISBN Prefix(es): 978-81-85023
Associate Companies: Bal Sahitya Prakashan, 29/502 East End Apartments, Mayur Vihar Ext, Phase-1, New Delhi 110 096 *Tel:* (011) 22742291; Shalimar Books, A-740, Prem Nagar, Paharganj, New Delhi 110 055
Tel: 9310144101 (cell)
Subsidiaries: Books India; Nalanda Prakashan; Sahyog Prakashan

R R Sheth & Co Pvt Ltd+
110-112 Princess St, Keshav Baug, Mumbai 400 002
Tel: (022) 2201 34 41 *Fax:* (022) 2205 82 93
Web Site: rrsheth.com
Key Personnel
Proprietor: Bhagatbhai Bhuralal Sheth
Founded: 1926
Publisher & bookseller for Gujarati language.
Membership(s): Federation of Indian Publishers.
Subjects: Biography, Memoirs, Career Development, Child Care & Development, Cookery, Drama, Theater, Fiction, Health, Nutrition, History, How-to, Human Relations, Humor, Journalism, Language Arts, Linguistics, Literature, Literary Criticism, Essays, Mysteries, Suspense, Philosophy, Poetry, Public Administration, Regional Interests, Religion - Hindu, Romance, Science (General), Self-Help, Travel & Tourism, Western Fiction
ISBN Prefix(es): 978-81-89919
Number of titles published annually: 100 Print
Total Titles: 4,500 Print
Associate Companies: R R Sheth Publishers & Distributors
Branch Office(s)
Dwarkesh, near Royal Apartment, Nehru Bridge Corner, Khanpur, Ahmedabad 380 001
Tel: (079) 2550 65 73 *Fax:* (079) 2550 17 32
Showroom(s): Ghandi Rd, Opposite Jumma Masjid, Ahmedabad 380 001, Contact: Mr Ratnaraj B Sheth *Tel:* (079) 2550 65 73
Orders to: Dwarkesh, near Royal Apartment, Nehru Bridge Corner, Khanpur, Ahmedabad 380 001, Contact: Mr Ratnaraj B Sheth
Tel: (079) 2550 65 73

Shiksha Bharti+
Madarsa Rd, Kashmers Gate, New Delhi 110 006
Tel: (011) 2965483; (011) 2969812 *Fax:* (011) 2967791
Founded: 1959
Subjects: Biography, Memoirs, Education, Science (General)
ISBN Prefix(es): 978-81-7483
Associate Companies: Orient Paperbacks; Rajpal & Sons; Vision Books Pvt Ltd
Subsidiaries: Shiksha Bharati Press
Bookshop(s): Lothian Rd, Kashmere Gate, New Delhi 110 006 *Tel:* (011) 23867791

Showcase, *imprint of* Roli Books Pvt Ltd

Shree Book Centre
No 8, S Keer Marg, LJ Rd, Kakad Industrial Estate, Matunga West, Mumbai, Maharashtra 400 016
Tel: (022) 24377516
Web Site: www.shreebookcentre.com; www.facebook.com/pages/Shree-Book-Centre/593052314056168?ref=hl
Subjects: Education, Fiction
ISBN Prefix(es): 978-81-7963

Siddhi Books, *imprint of* Cosmo Publications

Simon & Schuster India
Division of Simon & Schuster, Inc

163, Tower A, The Corenthum, A -41, Sector -62, Noida 201 301
Tel: (0120) 4089 389 *Fax:* (0120) 4089 301
E-mail: enquiries@simonandschuster.co.in; cservice@simonandschuster.co.in
Web Site: www.simonandschuster.co.in
Key Personnel
Manager, Publicity & Marketing: Bharti Taneja *Tel:* (0120) 4089 306 *E-mail:* bharti.taneja@simonandschuster.co.in
Mng Dir: Mr Rahul Srivastava *E-mail:* rahul.srivastava@simonandschuster.co.in
Editorial Dir: Mrs Dharini Bhaskar *Tel:* (0120) 4089 307 *E-mail:* dharini.bhaskar@simonandschuster.co.in
Senior Accountant: Mr Sagar Tanwar *Tel:* (0120) 4089 302 *E-mail:* sagar.tanwar@simonandschuster.co.in
Manager, Digital Sales: Mr Richie Maheshwary *Tel:* (0120) 4089 304 *E-mail:* richie.maheshwary@simonandschuster.co.in
Subjects: Biography, Memoirs, Business, Fiction, Health, Nutrition, Literature, Literary Criticism, Essays, Management, Nonfiction (General), Self-Help, Social Sciences, Sociology, Sports, Athletics, Travel & Tourism
Number of titles published annually: 18 Print; 18 E-Book
Total Titles: 6 Print; 6 E-Book
Ultimate Parent Company: CBS Corporation, 51 W 52 St, New York, NY 10019-6188, United States

Sita Books & Periodicals Pvt Ltd+
213/B, Arjun Centre, Govandi Station Rd, Govandi East, Mumbai 400 088
Tel: (022) 25555589; (022) 67973281; (022) 67973282; (022) 67973283; (022) 42156327 *Fax:* (022) 67973284
E-mail: info@sitabooks.com; enquiry@sitainfobytes.com
Web Site: www.sitabooks.com
Founded: 1987
Importers of international books & journals. Publishers of textbooks, general & technical books.
Membership(s): Federation of Indian Publishers; Federation of Publishers' & Booksellers' Association in India (FPBAI); Indian Association of Special Libraries & Information Centres (ISALIC).
Subjects: Accounting, Advertising, Aeronautics, Aviation, Agriculture, Architecture & Interior Design, Automotive, Biological Sciences, Business, Chemistry, Chemical Engineering, Child Care & Development, Civil Engineering, Computer Science, Computers, Economics, Education, Electronics, Electrical Engineering, Energy, Engineering (General), Environmental Studies, Fashion, Finance, Labor, Industrial Relations, Library & Information Sciences, Literature, Literary Criticism, Essays, Management, Maritime, Marketing, Mathematics, Mechanical Engineering, Physics, Psychology, Psychiatry, Publishing & Book Trade Reference, Technology
ISBN Prefix(es): 978-81-86052
Divisions: Sita BPO; Sita InfoBytes
Distributor for Blackwell; Euromoney; Gower Press; Morgan Kaufmann; PalGrave Publishers; Technip; John Wiley
Bookshop(s): Herikripa, 3 Krishna, Govandi East, Mumbai 400 088

Somaiya Publications Pvt Ltd+
Fazalbhoy Bldg, 45/47, Mahatma Gandhi Rd, Fort, Mumbai 400 001
Tel: (022) 2048272 *Fax:* (022) 2047297
Web Site: www.somaiya.com
Founded: 1967
Membership(s): Federation of Indian Publishers.
Subjects: Agriculture, Anthropology, Archaeology, Asian Studies, Astrology, Occult, Behavioral Sciences, Business, Communications, Dis-

ability, Special Needs, Economics, Education, Engineering (General), English as a Second Language, Fiction, Government, Political Science, Health, Nutrition, History, Journalism, Labor, Industrial Relations, Language Arts, Linguistics, Management, Marketing, Mechanical Engineering, Music, Dance, Nonfiction (General), Parapsychology, Philosophy, Psychology, Psychiatry, Religion - Buddhist, Religion - Hindu, Social Sciences, Sociology, Technology, Women's Studies
ISBN Prefix(es): 978-81-7039
Total Titles: 300 Print
Parent Company: The Godavari Sugar Mills Ltd
Associate Companies: The Book Centre Ltd, Ranade Rd, Dadar, Mumbai 400 028 (book sales division); The Book Centre Ltd, Plot No 103, Sixth Rd, Sion, Mumbai, Contact: S S Sathe *Tel:* (022) 4076812; (022) 4077416 (printing press division)

South Asia Publications+
29, Central Market, Ashok Vihar, New Delhi 110 052
Tel: (011) 7241865
Founded: 1986
Subjects: Advertising, Agriculture, Anthropology, Art, Business, Economics, Finance, History, Management, Religion - Other
ISBN Prefix(es): 978-81-7433
Associate Companies: SanPark Press Pvt Ltd

South Asian Publishers Pvt Ltd+
50 Sidharth Enclave, PO Jangpura 110 014
Tel: (011) 6925315; (011) 6835713
Specialize in international relations.
Subjects: Anthropology, Asian Studies, Biological Sciences, Chemistry, Chemical Engineering, Civil Engineering, Developing Countries, Electronics, Electrical Engineering, Engineering (General), Environmental Studies, Government, Political Science, Labor, Industrial Relations, Mathematics, Physics, Religion - Buddhist, Religion - Hindu, Science (General), Social Sciences, Sociology, Technology
ISBN Prefix(es): 978-81-7003

Spectrum Publications+
Panbazar Main Rd, Guwahati 781 001
Mailing Address: PO Box 45, Guwahati 781 001
Tel: (0361) 2638434; (0361) 2638435
Key Personnel
Publisher: Krishan Kumar
Editorial: Ms Aarti Kumar
Publicity: Ms Neha Kumar
Sales: Ms Anita Kumar
Founded: 1976
Membership(s): Federation of Indian Publishers.
Subjects: Anthropology, Asian Studies, Social Sciences, Sociology, Travel & Tourism
ISBN Prefix(es): 978-81-85319; 978-81-87502; 978-81-900396; 978-81-900750
Imprints: Aarti Books; Neha Mini Katha; Sunny Classics
Branch Office(s)
298-B Tagore Park Ext, Model Town 1, New Delhi 110 009 *Tel:* (011) 27241674 *Fax:* (011) 23241471 *E-mail:* dli@spectrumpublications.in
G S Rd, Shillong 793 001 *Tel:* (0364) 223476
Distributor for Abilac; DIPR Arunachal Pradesh; Law Research Institute; Nehu Publications
Showroom(s): 4754-57 Darya Ganj, 23 Ansari Rd, New Delhi 110 002
Orders to: United Publishers, Panbazar, PO Box 82, Guwahati 781 001

Sri Rama Publishers
15-1-513, Siddiamber Bazar, Afzalgunj, Hyderabad
Tel: (040) 2474 3514; (040) 6516 2212
Key Personnel
Contact: P Bhaskar Rao
Founded: 1916

Subjects: Theology
ISBN Prefix(es): 978-81-7275
Associate Companies: Popular Book House; Secunderabad; Sree Sita Rama Book Depot
Bookshop(s): Sree Rama Book Depot, Gunfoundry, Hyderabad 500 001; Sree Rama Book Depot, Siddiamber Bazaar, Hyderabad
Orders to: 113 Sarojinin Devi Rd, Secunderabad 500 003

Sri Satguru Publications+
24/4 (Basement) Shakti Nagar, New Delhi 110 007
Tel: (011) 23844930 *Fax:* (011) 23847336
Founded: 1976
Subjects: Asian Studies, Music, Dance, Regional Interests, Religion - Buddhist
ISBN Prefix(es): 978-81-7030
Number of titles published annually: 80 Print
Total Titles: 1,000 Print
Parent Company: Indian Books Centre
Associate Companies: Bibliotheca Indo-Buddhica Series; Sri Garib Dass Oriental Series

STAR Publications Pvt Ltd+
4/5 B Asaf Ali Rd, New Delhi 110 002
Tel: (011) 2325 7220; (011) 2327 4874; (011) 2326 1696; (011) 2328 6757 *Fax:* (011) 2327 3335
E-mail: info@hindibook.com
Web Site: www.starpublic.com
Key Personnel
Chairman: Mr Amar Varma
Chief Executive: Anil K Varma *Tel:* (011) 3258993
Dir: Sunil Varma *Tel:* (011) 6468427
Production, Publicity: Sanjay Varma *Tel:* (011) 3274874
Founded: 1957
Publisher & distributor of English & Indian language books.
Membership(s): Federation of Booksellers & Publishers.
Subjects: English as a Second Language, Government, Political Science, History, Language Arts, Linguistics, Literature, Literary Criticism, Essays, Religion - Hindu, Religion - Islamic, Religion - Other, Religion - Jain, Religion - Sikh
ISBN Prefix(es): 978-81-85243
Total Titles: 600 Print; 50 Audio
Subsidiaries: Publications India; Hindi Book Centre; Star Publishers Distributors
Branch Office(s)
Wembley Point, Suite 4b, floor 15, One Harrow Rd, Wembley Middx, London HA9 6DE, United Kingdom *Tel:* (020) 8900 2640; (020) 8900 2840 *Fax:* (020) 8900 2840
E-mail: order@foreignlanguagebooks.co.uk
Showroom(s): Hindi Book Centre
Bookshop(s): Hindi Book Centre
Shipping Address: D-92/3 Okhla Industrial Area I, New Delhi 110 020

Sterling Press (P) Ltd, *imprint of* Sterling Publishers Pvt Ltd

Sterling Publishers Pvt Ltd+
A-59, Okhla Industrial Area, Phase II, New Delhi 110 020
Tel: (011) 2638 6165; (011) 2638 7070
Fax: (011) 2638 3788
E-mail: info@sterlingpublishers.com; mail@sterlingpublishers.com; sterlingpublishers@airtelmail.in
Web Site: www.sterlingpublishers.com; ebooks.sterlingpublishers.com
Key Personnel
Chairman & Mng Dir: S K Ghai
Dir: Mr Gaurav K Ghai
Contact: Mr Balram Shukla
Export: Bhupender Sharma

Sales: Vikas Ghai
Founded: 1965
Specialize in children's books, trade paperbacks (nonfiction) & academic books in humanities & social science.
Membership(s): Afro Asian Book Council; Asian Association of Scholarly Publishers; Federation of Indian Publishers.
Subjects: Agriculture, Art, Asian Studies, Astrology, Occult, Biography, Memoirs, Communications, Developing Countries, Economics, Education, English as a Second Language, Fiction, Gardening, Plants, Government, Political Science, History, Journalism, Library & Information Sciences, Literature, Literary Criticism, Essays, Management, Medicine, Nursing, Dentistry, Philosophy, Public Administration, Religion - Hindu, Religion - Islamic, Religion - Other, Science (General), Social Sciences, Sociology, Technology, Women's Studies, Humanities
ISBN Prefix(es): 978-81-207; 978-81-7359
Number of titles published annually: 100 Print; 2 CD-ROM
Total Titles: 500 Print; 5 CD-ROM
Associate Companies: Learners Press (P) Ltd, Sterling House, New Delhi
Imprints: Institute of Book Publishing; Sai Early Learners (P) Ltd; Sterling Press (P) Ltd
Branch Office(s)
Sterling Publishers UK Ltd, 2 Tintern Close, Chalvey Slough, Berkshire SL1 2TB, United Kingdom *Tel:* (01753) 820091 *E-mail:* sterling.uk@sterlingpublishers.com

Stree-Samya (Women-Equality)+
Imprint of Bhatkal & Sen
16 Southern Ave, Kolkata 700 026
Tel: (033) 2466-0812 *Fax:* (033) 2464-4614; (033) 2464-4614
E-mail: streesamya@gmail.com
Web Site: www.stree-samyabooks.com
Key Personnel
Dir: Mandira Sen *Tel:* (033) 6519-5737
   E-mail: streesamya.manager@gmail.com
Founded: 1990 (as Stree, name changed in 1996)
Publish women's studies in English & Bengali, also culture & dissent & dalit literature (under Samya imprint).
One of the 8 partners of the distribution group Independent Publishers Distribution Alternatives (IPDA), Delhi.
Subjects: Anthropology, Asian Studies, Biography, Memoirs, Fiction, Government, Political Science, History, Nonfiction (General), Psychology, Psychiatry, Social Sciences, Sociology, Women's Studies
ISBN Prefix(es): 978-81-85604; 978-81-906760; 978-93-81345
Total Titles: 80 Print
Imprints: Samya
Foreign Rep(s): Gazelle Book Services (Europe, UK)

Sultan Chand & Sons (P) Ltd+
4859/24 Darya Ganj, New Delhi 110 002
Tel: (011) 43546000; (011) 23243939
Web Site: www.sultan-chand.com
Key Personnel
Mng Dir: Mr Satish Agarwal; Vivek Aggarwal
Founded: 1950
Membership(s): Delhi State Booksellers' & Publishers' Association (DSBPA); Federation of Educational Publishers in India; Federation of Publishers' & Booksellers' Associations in India (FPBAI).
Subjects: Accounting, Behavioral Sciences, Biological Sciences, Business, Career Development, Chemistry, Chemical Engineering, Computer Science, Economics, Education, Electronics, Electrical Engineering, Engineering (General), English as a Second Language, Finance, Geography, Geology, Government, Political

Science, Health, Nutrition, History, How-to, Human Relations, Labor, Industrial Relations, Law, Management, Marketing, Mathematics, Physics, Public Administration, Self-Help, Social Sciences, Sociology, Technology
ISBN Prefix(es): 978-81-86819; 978-81-8350
Subsidiaries: Prakash Sons (India)
Distributed by Prakash Sons (India)

Suman Prakashan Pvt Ltd+
24 B/9, Desh Bandhu Gupta Rd, Dev Nagar, New Delhi 110 005
Tel: (011) 28711759
Founded: 1970
Specialize in children's textbooks.
Membership(s): FICCI; PHDCCI.
Subjects: Art, History, Mathematics, Science (General)
ISBN Prefix(es): 978-81-85869; 978-81-7795
Associate Companies: Pearl (India) Publishing House (P) Ltd
Branch Office(s)
408, Lingapur Bldg, Amrutha Estate, Himayat Nagar, Hyderabad 500 029 *Tel:* (040) 23224078
2, Bankim Chatterjee St, 2nd floor, Kolkata 700 073 *Tel:* (033) 22347042 *Fax:* (033) 22348762
1st floor, Shiv Vindhaya Complex, Sector-22, Near Amrapali Bazaar, Indira Nagar, Lucknow 226 016 *Tel:* (0522) 2347798
10, Kitab Bhavan Rd, North Shri Krishnapura, Patna 800 013 *Tel:* (0612) 2572210
103, Satyam Plaza, 3rd Lane, Dwarakangar, Vishakapatnam 530 016 *Tel:* (0891) 2748623

Sunny Classics, *imprint of* Spectrum Publications

Surjeet Publications+
7-K Kolhapur Rd, Kamla Nagar, New Delhi 110 007
Tel: (011) 23852395; (011) 23854746 *Fax:* (011) 23858475
E-mail: surpub@gmail.com
Key Personnel
Owner: Surjeet Singh Chhabra
Contact: Manpreet Singh
Founded: 1976
Also acts as bookseller, distributor & remainder dealer.
Subjects: Literature, Literary Criticism, Essays, Social Sciences, Sociology
ISBN Prefix(es): 978-81-229

Tara India Research Press, see India Research Press/TARA Press

TARA Press, *imprint of* India Research Press/TARA Press

Tara Books Pvt Ltd+
Plot No 9, CGE Colony, Off Kuppan Beach Rd, Thiruvanmiyur, Chennai 600 041
Tel: (044) 42601033
E-mail: mail@tarabooks.com; promotions@tarabooks.com (Europe); sales@tarabooks.com
Web Site: www.tarabooks.com
Key Personnel
Publisher: Gita Wolf
Editorial Dir: V Geetha
Editorial Dir & Rights Manager: Sirish Rao
Press: Jennifer Abel *E-mail:* jennifer.abel@tarabooks.com
Founded: 1994
Independent publishing house.
Subjects: Art, Asian Studies, Crafts, Games, Hobbies, Education, Fiction, History, How-to, Religion - Buddhist, Religion - Hindu
ISBN Prefix(es): 978-81-86211; 978-81-906756
Number of titles published annually: 15 Print
Total Titles: 50 Print
Foreign Rep(s): Frances Lincoln (Europe, Ireland, UK)

Foreign Rights: Autoren- und Projektagentur (Germany); Motovun (Japan); Sea of Stories (France, Spain); Servizi Editoriali (Italy); Sigma (Korea)
Distribution Center: Rupa & Co, 7/16 Ansari Rd, Darya Ganj, New Delhi 110 002 *Tel:* (011) 2327-8586; (011) 2327-2161 *Fax:* (011) 2327-7294 *E-mail:* info@rupabooks.com (India, Bangladesh, Bhutan, Maldives, Nepal, Pakistan & Sri Lanka)
Publishers Group Canada/Raincoast Books, 559 College St, Suite 402, Toronto, ON M6G 1A9, Canada *Tel:* 416-934-9900 *Fax:* 416-934-1410 *E-mail:* info@pgcbooks.ca *Web Site:* www.pgcbooks.ca
Frances Lincoln, Torriano Ave, London NW5 2RZ, United Kingdom *Tel:* (020) 7284 4009 *Fax:* (020) 7485 0490 *E-mail:* sales@franceslincoln.com *Web Site:* www.franceslincoln.com (Europe, Ireland & UK)
Publishers Group West, 1700 Fourth St, Berkeley, CA 94710, United States *Tel:* 510-809-3700 *Fax:* 510-809-3777 *E-mail:* info@pgw.com *Web Site:* www.pgw.com

TERI, see The Energy & Resources Institute (TERI)

Theosophical Publishing House+
Division of The Theosophical Society
Besant Gardens, Besant Avenue Rd, Adyar, Chennai 600 020
Tel: (044) 24911338; (044) 24466613 *Fax:* (044) 24901399
E-mail: tphindia@gmail.com
Web Site: www.ts-adyar.org; www.adyarbooks.com
Key Personnel
General Manager: Ramu S Ramu
Accounts Officer: M Kannan
Founded: 1913
Publishers of books & journals on subjects such as thoesophy, religion, philosophy, spirituality, yoga, occultism, music, science, meditation, mysticism, etc.
Subjects: Inspirational, Spirituality, Philosophy, Meditation, Mysticism, Theosophy, Yoga
ISBN Prefix(es): 978-81-7059
Number of titles published annually: 50 Print
Total Titles: 500 Print; 1 Online
Bookshop(s): Besant Bookshop, The Brisbane Theosophical Society, 315 Wickham Terrace, Brisbane, Qld 4600, Australia *Tel:* (07) 3839 1453 *Fax:* (07) 3859 3692; Adyar Bookshop, 230 Clarence St, Corner Druitt St, Sydney, NSW 2000, Australia *Tel:* (02) 9267-8509 *Fax:* (02) 9267-4719 *E-mail:* inquiry@adyar.com.au *Web Site:* www.adyar.com; Theosophical Society in West Africa, PO Box 720, Accra, Ghana *Tel:* (0233) 21 771249 *E-mail:* boulders@ghana.com; Theosophical Society in East & Central Africa, PO Box 45928, Nairobi 00100, Kenya *Tel:* (020) 745174 *Fax:* (020) 745655 *E-mail:* telesales@insightkenya.com; Theosofische Vereniging in Nederland, Tolstr 154, 1074 VM Amsterdam, Netherlands *Tel:* (020) 676 5672 *Fax:* (020) 675 7657 *E-mail:* info@theosofie.nl *Web Site:* www.theosofie.nl; Theosophical Society in New Zealand Inc, 18 Belvedere St, Epsom, Auckland 1051, New Zealand *Tel:* (09) 523 1797 *Fax:* (09) 523 1797 *E-mail:* hq@theosophy.org.nz *Web Site:* www.theosophy.org.nz; One, Iba St, Quezon City, Metro Manila, Philippines *Tel:* (02) 741-5740 *Fax:* (02) 740-3751 *E-mail:* tspeace@info.com.ph *Web Site:* www.theosophy.ph; The Theosophical Society in Southern Africa, 22, Buffels Rd, Rietondale, Pretoria 0084, South Africa *Tel:* (012) 329 3082 *E-mail:* thosdavis@icon.co.za *Web Site:* panafrican-theos.org; The Theosophical Book Ltd, 50 Gloucester Pl, London WIH 4EA, United Kingdom *Tel:* (0171) 935-9261

Fax: (0171) 935-9543 *E-mail:* theosophical@freenetname.co.uk *Web Site:* www.theosophical-society.org.uk; The Theosophical Publishing House (Quest Books), 306 W Geneva Rd, PO Box 270, Wheaton, IL 60189-0270, United States *Tel:* 630-665-0130 *Fax:* 630-665-8791 *E-mail:* questorders@theosmail.org *Web Site:* www.questbooks.com

Think Big, *imprint of* S Viswanathan (Printers & Publishers) Pvt Ltd

Third Eye, *imprint of* Pentagon Press

Today & Tomorrow Printers & Publishers+
4436/7 Ansari Rd, Darya Ganj, New Delhi 100 002
Tel: (011) 2324 1021; (011) 2324 2621 *Fax:* (011) 2324 2621
E-mail: info@ttpp.in
Web Site: www.ttpp.in
Key Personnel
Owner: Magan Jain
Founded: 1954
Membership(s): Federation of Publishers' & Booksellers' Associations in India (FPBAI).
Subjects: Agriculture, Natural History, Science (General)
ISBN Prefix(es): 978-81-7019
Distributed by Scholarly Publications (USA)
Distributor for ABD; Blackwell; Cabi; Cambridge University Press; Elsevier Science; Johns & Barllet; McGraw-Hill; Oxford University Press; Sage Publication; Springer Verlag; Taylor & Francis; John Wiley & Sons

Tranquebar Press, *imprint of* Westland Ltd

Transworld Research Network
TC 37/661(2), Fort PO, Trivandrum, Kerala 695 023
Tel: (0471) 2452918 *Fax:* (0471) 2573051
E-mail: ggcom@vsnl.com; admin@rsflash.com; signpost99@gmail.com
Web Site: www.trnres.com
Key Personnel
Mng Editor: Dr S G Pandalai
Publications Manager: Anandavalli Gayathri
Founded: 1996
Publishes review books in all areas of science, agriculture, medicine, pure science & technology. Also does CD-ROM production & software development.
Subjects: Agriculture, Biological Sciences, Electronics, Electrical Engineering, Medicine, Nursing, Dentistry, Science (General), Technology
ISBN Prefix(es): 978-81-86846; 978-81-7895
Divisions: Research Signpost
Foreign Rep(s): APAC Publishing Services Pte Ltd (Singapore); IHS ATP (UK); Old City Publishing Inc (USA); Research Publishing Services (Southeast Asia); Sci Resources Lab Inc (Japan)

Tulika Publishers
24/1 Ganapathy Colony Third St, Teynampet, Chennai 600 018
Tel: (044) 2433 1639; (044) 2433 1117; (044) 2433 1118
E-mail: tulikabooks@vsnl.com
Web Site: www.tulikabooks.com
ISBN Prefix(es): 978-81-8146
Foreign Rep(s): Jade Group International Pte Ltd (Singapore); Madhu Bhasha Kendra/Parrots Books (USA); Kiran Shah (Australia); Tulika Books USA (Gauri Bhalakia) (USA)

UBS Publishers' Distributors Pvt Ltd
5, Ansari Rd, Darya Ganj, New Delhi 110 002
Tel: (011) 23273601; (011) 23273604 *Fax:* (011) 23276593

E-mail: ubspd@ubspd.com
Web Site: www.ubspd.com
Key Personnel
Dir, Information Systems: Abhay Nagar
Founded: 1963
Also acts as distributor.
Subjects: Art, Astrology, Occult, Biography, Memoirs, Career Development, Cookery, Economics, Fiction, Finance, Government, Political Science, Health, Nutrition, Literature, Literary Criticism, Essays, Management, Religion - Other, Self-Help, Sports, Athletics, Beauty, Current Affairs, English Literature, Self Improvement
ISBN Prefix(es): 978-81-7476; 978-81-85273; 978-81-85674; 978-81-85944; 978-81-86112
Branch Office(s)
1st floor, Shop No 133-134, Aust Laxmi, Apparel Park, Outside Dariyapur Gate, Ahmedabad 380 016 *Tel:* (079) 22160371; (079) 22160373; (079) 29092241; (079) 29092248; (079) 29092258 *E-mail:* mukesh.brahmbhatt@ubspd.com
Crescent No 148, 1st floor, Mysore Rd, Bangalore 560 026 *Tel:* (080) 26756377; (080) 26756362 *Fax:* (080) 26756462 *E-mail:* balram.sadhwani@ubspd.com
Z-18, MP Nagar, Zone-I, Bhopal 462 011 *Tel:* (0755) 4203183; (0755)55203193; (0755) 2555228 *Fax:* (0755) 2555285 *E-mail:* sanjay.sharma@ubspd.com
1st floor, Plot No 145, Cuttack Rd, Bhubaneshwar 751 006 *Tel:* (0674) 2314446; (0674) 2314447 *Fax:* (0674) 2314448 *E-mail:* v.radhakrishnan@ubspd.com
60, Nelson Manickam Rd, Aminjikarai, Chennai 600 029 *Tel:* (044) 23746222; (044) 23746351; (044) 23746352 *Fax:* (044) 23745074 *E-mail:* s.viswanathan@ubspd.com
2nd & 3rd floors, Sri Guru Towers, No 1-7 Sathy Rd, Cross III, Gandhipuram, Coimbatore 641 012 *Tel:* (0422) 2499916; (0422) 2499917 *Fax:* (0422) 2499914 *E-mail:* ak.sukumaran@ubspd.com
No 40/8199A, 1st floor, Public Library Bldg, Convent Rd, Ernakulam 682 035 *Tel:* (0484) 2353901; (0484) 2363905 *Fax:* (0484) 2365511 *E-mail:* vj.abraham@ubspd.com
Alekhya Jagadish Chambers, 3rd & 4th floors, H No 4-1-1058, Boggukunta, Tilak Rd, Hyderabad 500 001 *Tel:* (040) 24754473; (040) 24754474 *Fax:* (040) 24754472 *E-mail:* vinaay.kumar@ubspd.com
8/1-B Chowringhee Lane, Kolkata 700 016 *Tel:* (033) 22529473; (033) 22521821; (033) 22522910 *Fax:* (033) 22523027 *E-mail:* desh.nagpal@ubspd.com
9, Ashok Nagar, Near Pratibha Press, Gautam Buddha Marg, Latouche Rd, Lucknow 226 018 *Tel:* (0522) 4025124; (0522) 4025134 *Fax:* (0522) 4025144 *E-mail:* rk.sethi@ubspd.com
Apeejay Chambers, 2nd floor, 5 Wallace St, Fort, Mumbai 400 001 *Tel:* (022) 66376922; (022) 66376923 *Fax:* (022) 66376921 *E-mail:* manoj.salvi@ubspd.com
2nd floor, Shree Renuka Plaza, Tilak Rd, Mahal, Nagpur 440 002 *Tel:* (0712) 6457909; (0712) 2736010 *Fax:* (0712) 2736011 *E-mail:* ps.chaoji@ubspd.com
Annapurna Complex, Ground floor, Naya Tola, Patna 800 004 *Tel:* (0612) 2672856; (0612) 2673973; (0612) 2686170 *Fax:* (0612) 2686169 *E-mail:* b.ganguly@ubspd.com
680 Budhwar Peth, 2nd floor, Near Appa Balwant Chowk, Pune 411 002 *Tel:* (020) 24461653 *Fax:* (020) 24433976 *E-mail:* pravin.indalkar@ubspd.com
Distributor for BPB; CBS; Cengage Learning; Kaplan Publishing; Macmillan; McGraw-Hill International; New Age; Oxford University Press; Pearson Education; PHI Learning; Tata McGraw-Hill; Vikas Publishing House; John Wiley

UBSPD, see UBS Publishers' Distributors Pvt Ltd

University of Kerala Department of Publications
Thiruvananthapuram, Kerala 695 034
Tel: (0471) 2305994 *Fax:* (0471) 2307158
E-mail: ku.release@gmail.com
Web Site: www.keralauniversity.ac.in/publication-information.html
Key Personnel
Dir: Dr K S Prakash *Tel:* (0471) 303995
  E-mail: dr.ksprakash@gmail.com
Founded: 1937
ISBN Prefix(es): 978-81-86397; 978-81-87590

Vadehra Art Gallery (VAG)+
D-40, Defence Colony, New Delhi 110 024
Tel: (011) 24615368; (011) 24622545
E-mail: art@vadehraart.com
Web Site: www.vadehraart.com
Founded: 1987
Subjects: Art, Fiction
ISBN Prefix(es): 978-81-87737
Number of titles published annually: 5 Print
Total Titles: 13 Print
Parent Company: Vadehra Builders Pvt Ltd, D-178 Okhla Industrial Area, Phase 1, New Delhi 110 020

VAG, see Vadehra Art Gallery (VAG)

Vakils Feffer & Simons Pvt Ltd+
A Mahtre Marg, Industry Manor, 2nd floor, Prabhadevi, Mumbai 400 025
Tel: (022) 2430 6780 *Fax:* (022) 2422 5111
E-mail: sales@vakilsonline.com; info@vakilsonline.com
Web Site: www.vakilsonline.com
Key Personnel
Chairman & Mng Dir: Arun Mehta
Chief Executive Officer: Bimal Mehta
  E-mail: bimal@vakilspremedia.com
Chief Financial Officer: R B Desai
Vice President: Rishi Anand
Executive Dir: Sangeeta Bhansali
Dir: Raj Mehta
Founded: 1946
Subjects: Art, Cookery, Gardening, Plants, Management, Religion - Hindu, Religion - Islamic, Religion - Other, Travel & Tourism
ISBN Prefix(es): 978-81-87111; 978-81-8462
Associate Companies: Bowne & Co Inc; Heywood Innovation; Softype Inc
U.S. Office(s): Vakils LLC, 1008 Sheringham Court, Kingsport, TN 37660-4725, United States *Tel:* 484-571-1835 *E-mail:* brenda@vakilspremedia.com
Showroom(s): Vakil & Sons Ltd, Vakils House, 18 Ballard Estate, Mumbai 400 001
Bookshop(s): Vakil & Sons Ltd, Vakils House, 18 Ballard Estate, Mumbia 400 001

Vani Prakashan+
21-A Ansari Rd, Darya Ganj, New Delhi 110 002
Tel: (011) 23273167; (01) 65456829 *Fax:* (011) 23275710
E-mail: sales@vaniprakashan.in; marketing@vaniprakashan.in
Web Site: www.vaniprakashan.in
Key Personnel
Chief Executive, Editorial, Production, Publicity & Sales: Arun Kumar Maheshwari
Founded: 1968
Subjects: Ethnicity, Fiction, History, Literature, Literary Criticism, Essays, Poetry, Hindi (with various subjects)
ISBN Prefix(es): 978-81-7055; 978-81-8143
Associate Companies: Navodaya Sales, 35, A, DDA Flat, Mansarovar Park, Shadhara, New

Delhi 32; Swarn Jyanti, 1/5971, Kabool Nagar, Shadhara, New Delhi 32
Branch Office(s)
Book Corner, Sri Ram Center, Safdar Hashni Marg, New Delhi 110 001
Book Club(s): Jan Sulakh Pathak Manch

Vidhi Sahitya Prakashan
Connaught Pl, Delhi 110 001
Tel: (011) 23389001
Founded: 1975
Specialize in publications of the Acts in diglot form.
Subjects: Law
ISBN Prefix(es): 978-81-85956

Vidyapuri+
Balubazar, Cuttack, Odisha 753 002
Tel: (0671) 2308237; (0671) 6545557
E-mail: contact@vidyapuri.com
Web Site: www.vidyapuri.com
Founded: 1961
Subjects: Accounting, Animals, Pets, Biography, Memoirs, Biological Sciences, Business, Chemistry, Chemical Engineering, Computer Science, History, Literature, Literary Criticism, Essays, Travel & Tourism
ISBN Prefix(es): 978-81-7411

Vidyarthi Mithram Press & Book Depot+
Baker Rd, Kottayam, Kerala 686 001
Tel: (0481) 2563281; (0481) 2563282; (0481) 2561713 *Fax:* (0481) 2563281; (0481) 2563282
Web Site: vidyarthimithram.com
Founded: 1928
Subjects: Biography, Memoirs, Biological Sciences, Chemistry, Chemical Engineering, Child Care & Development, Computer Science, Cookery, Drama, Theater, Economics, Poetry, Sports, Athletics
Associate Companies: Auroville Publishers, Kottayam
Imprints: Kosi Books; Manosabdam Books
Branch Office(s)
Municipal Bldg, Chinnakkada, Kollam *Tel:* (0474) 2747365
Hospital Rd, Kozhikkode *Tel:* (0495) 2720871
Robinson Rd, Palakkad *Tel:* (0491) 2522873
Marthomasabha Bldg, M C Rd, Thiruvalla *Tel:* (0469) 2702997
Rincy Bldg, Opposite RBI Bakery Junction, Thiruvananthapuram *Tel:* (0471) 2331684; (0471) 2334926
Thatha Shopping Complex, M G Rd, Thrissur *Tel:* (0487) 2384065
Book Club(s): Vidyarthi Mithram Novel Club

Vikas Publishing House Pvt Ltd+
E-28, Sector-8, Noida, Uttar Pradesh 201 301
Tel: (0120) 4078900 *Fax:* (0120) 4078999
E-mail: helpline@vikaspublishing.com
Web Site: www.vikaspublishing.com
Key Personnel
Dir: Sharda Chawla
Founded: 1969
Vikas focuses on textbooks & professional books on management, computers, engineering & technology. Madhubun, the children's book imprint, offers a range from preschool upwards.
Subjects: Chemistry, Chemical Engineering, Computer Science, Economics, Education, Engineering (General), Management, Mathematics, Physics, Science (General), Technology
ISBN Prefix(es): 978-81-259
Number of titles published annually: 200 Print
Total Titles: 2,000 Print
Associate Companies: Madhubun Educational Books; Vikas Higher Education Books
Branch Office(s)
A-308, Neelkanth Palace 100 ft Symal Rd, Opposite Godrej Showroom, Satellite, Ahmedabad 380 051 *Tel:* (079) 65254204

1st floor, NS Bhawan, 4th Cross, 4th Main, Gandhi Nagar, Bangalore 560 009 *Tel:* (080) 22281254 *Fax:* (080) 22204639
E-12, Nelson Chambers, 115 Nelson Manickam Rd, Aminjikarai, Chennai 600 029 *Tel:* (044) 23744547; (044) 23746090
P 51/1, CIT Rd, SCHEME - 52, Kolkata 700 014 *Tel:* (033) 2286 6995; (033) 2286 6996
Aditya Industrial Estate, Chincholi Bunder, Malad (West), Mumbai 400 064 *Tel:* (022) 2876 8301; (022) 2877 2545
Flat No 204, Temple Tower, Sabjibagh, Birla Mandir Rd, Patna 800 004 *Tel:* 9431015579 (cell)

Vishv Books Private Ltd, see Vishv Vijay Pte Ltd

Vishv Vijay Pte Ltd
36-A, Site-Iv, Sahibabad Industrial Area, Ghaziabad
Tel: (0120) 4698888; (0120) 4129946; 9899888203 (cell) *Fax:* (0120) 4111522
Web Site: www.vishvbook.com
Founded: 1939
ISBN Prefix(es): 978-81-7987; 978-81-85679; 978-81-87164
Number of titles published annually: 300 Print
Associate Companies: Delhi Press Patra

Vision Books Pvt Ltd+
24 Feroze Gandhi Rd, Lajpat Nagar-III, New Delhi 110 024
Tel: (011) 23862201; (011) 23862935 *Fax:* (011) 29836490
E-mail: editor@visionbooksindia.com; publicity@visionbooksindia.com; rights@visionbooksindia.com; sales@visionbooksindia.com; service@visionbooksindia.com
Web Site: www.visionbooksindia.com
Key Personnel
Owner & Publishing Dir: Kapil Malhotra
Mng Dir: Mrs Pervin Malhotra; Mr Subodh Yadav
Founded: 1975
Membership(s): Delhi State Booksellers & Publishers Association; Federation of Indian Publishers.
Subjects: Anthropology, Cookery, Education, Fiction, Health, Nutrition, History, How-to, Humor, Management, Medicine, Nursing, Dentistry, Military Science, Nonfiction (General), Religion - Other, Science (General), Sports, Athletics, Travel & Tourism, Career Guides, Fitness, Puzzle Books
ISBN Prefix(es): 978-81-7094
Total Titles: 700 Print
Associate Companies: Orient Publishing; Rajpal & Sons; Ravindra Printing Press
Imprints: Orient Paperbacks
Branch Office(s)
5A/8 Ansari Rd, Darya Ganj, New Delhi 110 002 *Tel:* (011) 23278877; (011) 23278878 *Fax:* (011) 23278879
  E-mail: orientpaperbacks@gmail.com
3-6-280/A/5 Himayatnagar, Hyderabad 500 029 *Tel:* (040) 23223252
3-B Peddar Rd, Vasant Ground floor, Mumbai 400 007 *Tel:* (022) 4929343 *Fax:* (022) 4960229
Book Club(s): Orient Book Club

Vistaar Publications, *imprint of* SAGE Publications India Pvt Ltd

S Viswanathan (Printers & Publishers) Pvt Ltd+
Acton Lodge, No 38, McNichols Rd, Chetpet, Chennai 600 031
Tel: (044) 2836 2723; (044) 2836 3633
Fax: (044) 2836 3002

Founded: 1949
Subjects: Biological Sciences, Chemistry, Chemical Engineering, Computer Science, English as a Second Language, History, Mathematics, Medicine, Nursing, Dentistry, Physics, Religion - Hindu, Science (General)
ISBN Prefix(es): 978-81-87156
Associate Companies: Beta Photo-Comps Pvt Ltd
Imprints: Think Big
Bookshop(s): Ananda Book Depot, 38, McNichols Rd, Chetpet, Chennai 600 031

Viva Books Pvt Ltd+
4737/23 Ansari Rd, Darya Ganj, New Delhi 110 002
Tel: (011) 42242200 *Fax:* (011) 42242240
E-mail: viva@vivagroupindia.net
Web Site: www.vivagroupindia.com
Key Personnel
Mng Dir: Vinod Vasishtha *Tel:* (011) 42242222
    E-mail: vinod@vivagroupindia.net
Vice President, Marketing: Pradeep Kumar
    E-mail: pradeep@vivagroupindia.net
Sales Dir: Sujit Dey *Tel:* (011) 42242244
    E-mail: sujit@vivagroupindia.net
Subjects: Advertising, Business, Career Development, Chemistry, Chemical Engineering, Child Care & Development, Civil Engineering, Communications, Crafts, Games, Hobbies, Earth Sciences, Economics, Education, Electronics, Electrical Engineering, Energy, Engineering (General), English as a Second Language, Environmental Studies, Geography, Geology, Health, Nutrition, Library & Information Sciences, Management, Marketing, Mechanical Engineering, Medicine, Nursing, Dentistry, Military Science, Philosophy, Physical Sciences, Psychology, Psychiatry, Public Administration, Science (General), Self-Help, Social Sciences, Sociology, Technology, Travel & Tourism, Women's Studies
ISBN Prefix(es): 978-81-7649; 978-81-85617; 978-81-3090; 978-81-3191; 978-81-8327 (Viva Education); 978-81-7554 (Kogan Page India)
Number of titles published annually: 500 Print
Total Titles: 5,000 Print
Branch Office(s)
7 Sovereign Park Apartments, 56-58 K R Rd, Basavanagudi, Bangalore 560 004, General Manager: Rajesh Devrajan *Tel:* (080) 26607409 *Fax:* (080) 26607410 *E-mail:* rajesh@vivagroupindia.net
Old No 307, New No 165, Poonamalle High Rd, Chennai 600 095, Branch Manager: R Manoharan *Tel:* (044) 23780991; (044) 23780992;(044) 23780994 *Fax:* (044) 23780995 *E-mail:* manoharan@vivagroupindia.net
232 GNB Rd, Beside UCO Bank, Silpukhuri, Guwahati 781 003, Sales Officer: Jayanta Pal *Tel:* (0361) 2666386 *E-mail:* jayanta@vivagroupindia.net
101-102 Mughal Marc Apartments, 3-4-637 to 641 Narayanguda, Hyderabad 500 029, Branch Executive: Alice Pinto *Tel:* (040) 27564481; (040) 27564482 *E-mail:* alice@vivagroupindia.net
Beevi Towers, 1st floor, SRM Rd, Kaloor, Kochi 18, Branch Manager: K V Vinod *Tel:* (0484) 2403055; (0484) 2403056 *E-mail:* kvvinod@vivagroupindia.net
B-103, Jindal Towers, 21/1A/3 Darga Rd, Kolkata 700 017, General Manager (East): M Rahman *Tel:* (033) 22816713; (033) 22836381
    E-mail: rahman@vivagroupindia.net
76 Service Industries, Shirvane, Sector 1, Nerul, Navi Mumbai 400 706, Assistant General Manager: Mukesh Srivastava *Tel:* (022) 27721273; (022) 27721274 *E-mail:* mukesh@vivagroupindia.net

Vivek Prakashan
Dhamani Market, Chaura Rasta, Jaipur 302 003

Tel: (0141) 2310111; 9829523905 (cell)
E-mail: vivekprakashan@yahoo.com
Web Site: vivekprakashan.com
Founded: 1974
Subjects: Economics, Fiction, Literature, Literary Criticism, Essays, Social Sciences, Sociology
ISBN Prefix(es): 978-81-7004

VK Global Publications Pvt Ltd+
4323/3, Ansari Rd, Darya Ganj, New Delhi 110 002
Tel: (011) 23250105; (011) 23250106 *Fax:* (011) 23250141
E-mail: mail@vkpublications.com; sales@vkpublications.com
Web Site: www.vkpublications.com
Founded: 1979
Subjects: Accounting, Astronomy, Biography, Memoirs, Career Development, Child Care & Development, Computer Science, Cookery, Crafts, Games, Hobbies, Economics, Education, Electronics, Electrical Engineering, Engineering (General), Fashion, Finance, Gardening, Plants, Health, Nutrition, House & Home, Journalism, Law, Literature, Literary Criticism, Essays, Management, Marketing, Mathematics, Mechanical Engineering, Medicine, Nursing, Dentistry, Music, Dance, Photography, Physics, Psychology, Psychiatry, Religion - Hindu, Religion - Islamic, Sports, Athletics, Travel & Tourism
Associate Companies: Economica; Future Kids Publications (P) Ltd
Branch Office(s)
Bazar Radha Kishan, Ambala City 134 002
    Tel: (0171) 2519130; (0171) 2519448
383, Ground floor, 65th Cross, 5th Block, Rajaji Nagar, Bangalore, Kamataka *Tel:* (080) 23145345
No 33/62, Valluvar St, Arumbakkam, Chennai, Tamilnadu 600 106 *Tel:* (044) 24751202
83, Marudhar Nagar, PO Hirapur, DCM Ajmer Rd, Jaipur *Tel:* (0141) 9829155441
A-228 P C Colony, 1st floor, Tiwari Bechar Lane, Kankarbagh, Patna, Bihar *Tel:* (0612) 2355242
LS/21, Harmu Housing Colony, Near High Court Colony, Harmu, Ranchi, Jharkhand *Tel:* (0651) 2242137

Westland, *imprint of* Westland Ltd

Westland Ltd
No 61, Silverline, Alapakkam Main Rd, Maduravoyal, Chennai 600 095
E-mail: contact@westland-tata.com
Web Site: westlandbooks.in
Key Personnel
Publisher: V K Karthika
Branch offices in Bangalore, New Delhi, Hyderabad & Mumbai.
Subjects: Art, Biography, Memoirs, Business, Cookery, Economics, Fiction, Government, Political Science, History, Mysteries, Suspense, Nonfiction (General), Religion - Other, Romance, Self-Help, Travel & Tourism
ISBN Prefix(es): 978-93-85152
Parent Company: Amazon
Imprints: EastWest (South India heritage & academic crossover books); Tranquebar Press (literary fiction & nonfiction); Westland (fiction & nonfiction trade books)

Wisdom Tree
4779/23, Ansari Rd, 110 002 Darya Ganj, New Delhi
Tel: (011) 23247966; (011) 23247967; (011) 23247968
E-mail: frontoffice@wisdomtreeindia.com; editor@wisdomtreeindia.com; sales@wisdomtreeindia.com
Web Site: www.wisdomtreeindia.com

Key Personnel
Publisher: Shobit Arya *E-mail:* shobit.arya@wisdomtreeindia.com
Subjects: Art, Cookery, Fiction, Health, Nutrition, Humor, Inspirational, Spirituality, Management, Nonfiction (General), Self-Help, Culture, Hindi, Parenting, Yoga
ISBN Prefix(es): 978-81-86685; 978-81-8328

XACT Books
2, Modi Complex, Commercial Complex, Ashok Vihar, Phase II, Delhi 110 052
Tel: 9810563212 (cell)
E-mail: mohinder.xact@gmail.com
Web Site: www.xactbook.com
Key Personnel
Chief Executive Officer & Dir: Rahul Singhal
    E-mail: rahul.xact@gmail.com
Parent Company: XACT Group
Associate Companies: XACT Studio International

Yoda Press
Flat No 268, Sector A, Pocket C, Vasant Kunj, New Delhi 110 070
Tel: (011) 41787201
E-mail: yodapress@yodakin.com
Web Site: www.yodapress.in; yodapress.tumblr.com
Key Personnel
Publisher: Arpita Das *E-mail:* arpitadasribeiro@gmail.com
Senior Editor & Rights Manager: Nishtha Vadehra *E-mail:* nishtha.yodapress@gmail.com
Subjects: Government, Political Science, History, Nonfiction (General), Pop Culture, Social Sciences, Sociology
ISBN Prefix(es): 978-81-902272
Distribution Center: Soma Books, 38 Kennington Lane, London SE11 4LS, United Kingdom (UK & Europe)

Young Angels International
70-A, Rama Rd, Opposite Kirti Nagar Metro Station, New Delhi 110 015
Tel: (011) 45733876; (011) 45733751
E-mail: contact@youngangelsinternational.com; youngangels01@gmail.com
Web Site: www.youngangelsinternational.com
Subjects: Education, Fiction, Science (General)

Young Learner Publications, *imprint of* Goodwill Publishing House

Young Zubaan, *imprint of* Zubaan

Zebra Books for Children, *imprint of* Arnold Heineman Publishers (India) Pvt Ltd

Zubaan+
Imprint of Kali for Women
128B Shahpur Jat, 1st floor, New Delhi 110 049
Tel: (011) 26494617; (011) 26494618; (011) 26494613
E-mail: contact@zubaanbooks.com
Web Site: www.zubaanbooks.com
Key Personnel
Dir: Urvashi Butalia
Senior Editor: Preeti Gill
Commissioning Editor, Young Zubaan: Anita Roy
Founded: 1984
Subjects: Art, Biography, Memoirs, Drama, Theater, Environmental Studies, Fiction, Health, Nutrition, History, Law, Nonfiction (General), Social Sciences, Sociology, Women's Studies
ISBN Prefix(es): 978-81-85107; 978-81-86706
Imprints: Young Zubaan
Distributed by Diversion Books

Indonesia

General Information

Capital: Jakarta
Language: Bahasa Indonesia (a form of Malay)
is official language. English is common second
language. About 25 local languages & over 250
dialects are spoken
Religion: About 87% Islamic, 10% Christian &
some Hindu & Buddhist
Population: 195 million
Bank Hours: Generally 0800-1400 Monday-
Thursday; 0800-1500 Friday; 0800-1300 Saturday
Currency: Rupiah
Export/Import Information: Books subject to
import tax & VAT tax. No exchange control.
Books & printed matter using Indonesian languages prohibited. Importers require no license
but are categorized into four groups for credit
arrangement controls.
Copyright: No copyright conventions signed but
Indonesia has recently enacted tougher domes-
tic copyright laws

Alumni Penerbit PT
Jl Bukit Pakar Timur II/109, Bandung, Jawa Barat
40135
Tel: (022) 2501251; (022) 2503039; (022)
2503038 *Fax:* (022) 2503044
Founded: 1968
Subjects: Economics, Law, Medicine, Nursing,
Dentistry, Psychology, Psychiatry, Social Sci-
ences, Sociology
ISBN Prefix(es): 978-979-414
Branch Office(s)
Jl Jend A Yani 206E, Banjarmasin
Wisma Sawah Besar, 8th floor, Jl Sukarjo Wiry-
opranoto 30, Jakarta *Tel:* (021) 372730 (Telex:
46810 Alumni Ia)
Putri Hijaubaru 37, Medan *Tel:* (061) 510615
Jl Kartini 22B, Tanjungkarang *Tel:* (0721) 53135
Bookshop(s): H Juanda St 54, Bandung, Jawa
Barat *Tel:* (022) 58290

AndiPublisher+
Jl Beo No 38-40, Demangan, Yogyakarta 55281
Tel: (0274) 561881 *Fax:* (0274) 588282
Web Site: www.andipublisher.com
Key Personnel
Dir: J H Gondowijoyo
Founded: 1980
Membership(s): Indonesian Publishers Association
(IKAPI).
Subjects: Accounting, Chemistry, Chemical Engi-
neering, Computer Science, Economics, Elec-
tronics, Electrical Engineering, Management,
Marketing, Mathematics, Science (General),
Technology
ISBN Prefix(es): 978-979-533
Branch Office(s)
Jl Ganetri III/2 Denpasar, Bali *Tel:* (0361) 221346
E-mail: bali@andipublisher.com
Jl Flamboyan I No 29, Kel Enggal Tanjung
Karang Pusat, Bandar Lampung 35118
Tel: (0721) 262584 *Fax:* (0721) 262584
Jl Srimahi Baru No 18, Bandung, Jawa Barat
Tel: (022) 5200290 *Fax:* (022) 5204135
E-mail: bdg@andipublisher.com
Jl Raya Ceger No 42 Rt 10 RW 02, Kel Ceger,
Kec Cipayung, Jakarta Timur *Tel:* (021) 8459
0064 *Fax:* (021) 8459 0064
Jl Danau Tanjung Bunga No 101, Makas-
sar, Sulawesi Selatan *Tel:* (0411) 856465
E-mail: mks@andipublisher.com
Jl Stadion Klabat Barat No 43, Manado, Sulawesi
Utara *Tel:* (0431) 822887 *Fax:* (0431) 822887
E-mail: man@andipublisher.com
Komplek Perumahan Setiabudi Indah I, Blok
vv No 5 Tanjung Rejo, Medan *Tel:* (061)

8217623 *Fax:* (061) 8217623 *E-mail:* mdn@
andipublisher.com
Villa Bangun Indah B-1, Jl Sukabangun I KM 6,
Palembang *Tel:* (0711) 412624 *E-mail:* plb@
andipublisher.com
Jl Kuantan II, Gang Jawa No 5, Kec Lima Puluh,
Pikan Baru *Tel:* (0761) 38966 *E-mail:* riau@
andipublisher.com
Komplek Batu Alam Permai, Jl Anggrek Merpati
VIII No 39, Samarinda *Tel:* (0541) 7773562
E-mail: smd@andipublisher.com
Perum Semarang Indah Blok C-IX No 20, Se-
marang 50144 *Tel:* (024) 7605523 *Fax:* (024)
7605523
Jl Raya Tenggilis R-17, Surabaya *Tel:* (031)
8436604; (031) 8473115 *Fax:* (031) 8410731
E-mail: sby@andipublisher.com
Jl Raden Saleh No 68, Karang Tengah, Cile-
dug, Tangerang *Tel:* (021) 70601240; (021)
70601241 *E-mail:* jkt@andipublisher.com
Distributor for Prenhallindo

Angkasa Group+
Jl Ibrahim Adji No 437, Kiaracondong, Bandung
40284
Tel: (022) 7320373; (022) 7320383; (022)
7310984 *Fax:* (022) 7320373
E-mail: pemasaran_angkasa@yahoo.co.
id; pemasaran_titianilmu@yahoo.co.id;
pemasaran@angkasagroup.co.id
Web Site: www.angkasagroup.co.id
Key Personnel
Chief Executive: Dr Fachri Said
Editorial Manager, Rights & Permissions: R Dja-
joesman
Production Manager: Tom Gunadi
Founded: 1966
Subjects: Fiction, Nonfiction (General), Religion -
Other
ISBN Prefix(es): 978-979-404; 978-979-547; 978-
979-665
Associate Companies: PT Mutiara Sumber Widya
Bookshop(s): Balai Buku Angkasa, Jl Merdeka,
No 6, Jawa Barat, Bandung

Badan Penerbit Kristen Gunung Mulia
(Gunung Mulia Christian Publishing House Ltd
Co)+
Jl Kwitang No 22-23, Jakarta 10420
Tel: (021) 3901208 *Fax:* (021) 3901633
E-mail: marketing@bpkgm.com; promosi@
bpkgm.com; publishing@bpkgm.com
Web Site: www.bpkgm.com
Founded: 1951
Membership(s): CBA.
Subjects: Christian, Theological General Litera-
ture
ISBN Prefix(es): 978-979-415; 978-979-9290
Number of titles published annually: 100 Print
Total Titles: 900 Print

Badan Pusat Statistik (Bureau of Statistical
Information System)
Jl dr Sutomo No 6-8, Jakarta 10710
Tel: (021) 384-1195; (021) 384-2508; (021) 385-
7046; (021) 350-7057; (021) 381-0291 (ext
3230) *Fax:* (021) 385-7046
E-mail: bpshq@bps.go.id
Web Site: www.bps.go.id
Key Personnel
Contact: Mrs Bana Bodri *E-mail:* bana@bps.go.id
Subjects: Agriculture, Communications, Eco-
nomics, Education, Energy, Finance, Geogra-
phy, Geology, Government, Political Science,
Health, Nutrition, Travel & Tourism
ISBN Prefix(es): 978-979-724
Bookshop(s): BPS Book Gallery, Jl Dr Sutomo
No 6-8, Jakarta 10710 *Tel:* (021) 381-0291 ext
7445 *E-mail:* bookstore@bps.go.id

Balai Pustaka+
Jl Rawa Gatel, No 17, Kawasan Industri Pulo-
gadung, Jakarta 10710
Tel: (021) 3451616 *Fax:* (021) 3855740
E-mail: bp_online@yahoo.com
Web Site: www.balaipustakaonline.com
Founded: 1997
Subjects: Education, Ethnicity
ISBN Prefix(es): 978-979-407
Branch Office(s)
Jl Pulogadung Kav Jl5, Pulogadung, Jakarta
Timur
Book Club(s): KPI (Klub Perpustakaan Indonesia)

BPS, see Badan Pusat Statistik

Bulan Bintang+
Jl Kramat Kwitang I/8, Kwitang, Senen, Jakarta
10420
Tel: (021) 3901651; (021) 3107027 *Fax:* (021)
3901652
Key Personnel
Mng Dir: Mr Fauzi Amelz
Founded: 1954
Subjects: Art, Business, Economics, Education,
Engineering (General), Fiction, Finance, Gov-
ernment, Political Science, History, Law, Lit-
erature, Literary Criticism, Essays, Nonfiction
(General), Philosophy, Psychology, Psychiatry,
Religion - Islamic, Science (General), Social
Sciences, Sociology, Sports, Athletics, Technol-
ogy
ISBN Prefix(es): 978-979-418

Bumi Aksara Group (Earth Aksara Group)+
Jl Sawo Raya No 18, Rawamangun, Jakarta
13220
Tel: (021) 4700988
E-mail: info@bumiaksara.com; info@
bumiaksaraonline.com
Web Site: bumiaksara.com; bumiaksaraonline.com
(orders)
Key Personnel
Supervisor: Zuherman Usmsn
Contact: Alamat Kantor Pusat
Founded: 1990
Membership(s): Indonesian Publishers Association
(IKAPI).
Subjects: Accounting, Agriculture, Business, Eco-
nomics, Law, Management, Marketing, Reli-
gion - Islamic
ISBN Prefix(es): 978-979-526

PT Dian Rakyat+
Kawasan Industri Pulogadung, Jl Rawa Gelam I/
4, Jakarta Timur 13930
Tel: (021) 4604444 *Fax:* (021) 4609115
Key Personnel
Mng Editor: Nining Suryadi
Founded: 1963
Subjects: Cookery, Economics, Literature, Lit-
erary Criticism, Essays, Medicine, Nursing,
Dentistry
ISBN Prefix(es): 978-979-523

Dinastindo Adiperkasa Internasional PT+
Jl Kemiri Raya 68 RT 004/04, Pondok Cabe Hilir,
Ciputat, Jakarta 15418
Tel: (021) 7496733 *Fax:* (021) 7407078
E-mail: dinastindo@yahoo.com
Founded: 1984
Membership(s): Apkomindo; ASP; Indonesian
Publishers Association (IKAPI).
Subjects: Business, Career Development, Com-
puter Science, Management, Self-Help
ISBN Prefix(es): 978-979-552
Branch Office(s)
Surabaya & Bandung
Distributor for Abdi Tandu Publisher; Der Die
Das; Pisi 2 Ribu Software; Solid Pro Publisher

Dioma, Kanisius, Obor, *imprint of* Nusa Indah

Penerbit Diponegoro+
Jl Mohammad Toha 44-46, Bandung 40252
Tel: (022) 520 1215; (022) 520 1801 *Fax:* (022)
　520 1215; (022) 520 1801
E-mail: dpnegoro@indosat.net.id
Web Site: www.penerbitdiponegoro.com
Key Personnel
Mng Dir: H A Dahlan
Founded: 1963
Membership(s): Indonesian Publishers Association
　(IKAPI).
Subjects: Religion - Other
ISBN Prefix(es): 978-979-8155

Djambatan
Jl Prapanca Raya 16B, Jakarta 10440
E-mail: pustakadjambatan@gmail.com
Web Site: penerbitdjambatan.wordpress.com
Founded: 1958
Subjects: Art, Literature, Literary Criticism, Es-
　says, Philosophy, Religion - Other, Social Sci-
　ences, Sociology
ISBN Prefix(es): 978-979-428

Dunia Pustaka Jaya PT
Jl Kramat Raya 5-K, Kramat, Senen, Jakarta
　10450
Tel: (021) 31900629; (021) 3909284 *Fax:* (021)
　3909320
Web Site: www.twitter.com/PUSTAKA_JAYA
Founded: 1971
Subjects: Art, Drama, Theater, Ethnicity, Fiction,
　Literature, Literary Criticism, Essays, Philoso-
　phy, Poetry
ISBN Prefix(es): 978-979-419

Erlangga for Kids, *imprint of* Penerbit Erlangga

Penerbit Erlangga
Jl H Baping Raya No 100, Ciracas, Jakarta 13740
Tel: (021) 8717006 *Fax:* (021) 87794609
Web Site: www.erlangga.co.id
Key Personnel
Rights Editor: Fikri Somyadewi *E-mail:* fikri.
　somyadewi@erlangga.co.id; Maya Yulianty
　E-mail: maya.yulianty@erlangga.co.id
Founded: 1952
Subjects: Education, Fiction, Nonfiction (General)
ISBN Prefix(es): 978-602-241
Imprints: Erlangga for Kids; Esis; Essensi; Phi-
　beta

Esis, *imprint of* Penerbit Erlangga

Essensi, *imprint of* Penerbit Erlangga

PT Gramedia Pustaka Utama+
Gedung Kompas Gramedia lantai 6, Jl Palmerah
　Barat 29-37, Jakarta 10270
Tel: (021) 35880760; (021) 53650110; (021)
　53650111 (ext 87627)
E-mail: customercare@gramedia.com
Web Site: www.gramedia.com
Key Personnel
President: Jakob Oetama
Founded: 1985
Publisher, software house, multimedia.
Specialize in educational software & comics.
Subjects: Accounting, Animals, Pets, Antiques,
　Child Care & Development, Computer Science,
　Computers, Cookery, Crafts, Games, Hobbies,
　Electronics, Electrical Engineering, Fiction,
　Gardening, Plants, How-to, Management, Mys-
　teries, Suspense, Technology
ISBN Prefix(es): 978-979-511; 978-979-403; 978-
　979-605; 978-979-655; 978-979-686
Parent Company: Kompas-Gramedia Group

Indonesia Publishing House (Percetakan Advent
　Indonesia)
Jl Raya Cimindi 72, Bandung 40184
Mailing Address: PO Box 1188, Bandung 40011
Tel: (022) 603-0392; (022) 604-2006 *Fax:* (022)
　602-7784
E-mail: iph@bdg.centrin.net.id
Web Site: www.ssd.org/territories/wium/iph/index.
　html
Key Personnel
President: Emilkam Tambunan *Tel:* (0819) 251-
　5412 *E-mail:* emiltambunan@gmail.com
Treasurer: Agustinus Ricky *Tel:* (0852) 5002-
　7507 *E-mail:* agustricky@gmail.com
Publishing Dir: J B Banjarnahor
Marketing Manager: Djinan Sinaga *Tel:* (0812)
　247-3990 *E-mail:* djinan@gmail.com
Editorial: Elisha Gultom
Production: Elisha Onsoe
Founded: 1954
Subjects: Child Care & Development, Health, Nu-
　trition, Human Relations, Religion - Protestant,
　Religion - Other
ISBN Prefix(es): 978-979-504
Parent Company: Seventh-Day Adventist, West
　Indonesia Union Mission
Ultimate Parent Company: Seventh-Day Adventist
　Church, Southern Asia-Pacific Division

Institut Teknologi Bandung, see Penerbit ITB

Penerbit ITB (ITB Press)+
Jl Ganesa 10, Bandung 40132
Tel: (022) 2504257 *Fax:* (022) 2534155
E-mail: itbpress@penerbit.itb.ac.id
Web Site: www.penerbit.itb.ac.id
Key Personnel
Head: Dr Ir Yahdi Zaim
Publishing: Tuti Sarah
Production & Marketing: Gungun Waldi Gumilar
Founded: 1971
Subjects: Chemistry, Chemical Engineering, Ed-
　ucation, Electronics, Electrical Engineering,
　Engineering (General), Health, Nutrition, Math-
　ematics, Science (General), Technology
ISBN Prefix(es): 978-979-8001; 978-979-8591;
　978-979-9299; 978-979-3507; 978-979-1344

Kaifa, *imprint of* Mizan Publika

Karunia CV
Jl Peneleh No 18, Surabaya, Jawa Timur 60274
Tel: (031) 5344120; (031) 5342551
Web Site: karuniasby.wordpress.com
Subjects: Religion - Other
ISBN Prefix(es): 978-979-9039

Karya Anda CV+
Jl Praban No 55, Surabaya, Jawa Timur 60275
Tel: (031) 5322580; (031) 5344215 *Fax:* (031)
　5310594
Subjects: Agriculture, Anthropology, Automotive,
　Behavioral Sciences, Education, Environmental
　Studies, Fiction, Humor
ISBN Prefix(es): 978-979-8002

Katalis / Bina Mitra Plaosan
Jl Asem V/10, Cipete Selatan (Alamat Baru),
　Jakarta 12410
Tel: (021) 7501477 *Fax:* (021) 7697869
E-mail: katalis@cbn.net.id
Founded: 1986
Subjects: Career Development, How-to, Liter-
　ature, Literary Criticism, Essays, Nonfiction
　(General), Science (General)
ISBN Prefix(es): 978-979-8060
Imprints: Siemens-Penuntun Berencana

Kesaint Blanc Publishng+
Mega Grosir Cempaka Mas Blok G2 & G3, Jl
　Letjen Suprapto, Jakarta Pusat 10640

Tel: (021) 4290 6862; (021) 4288 6726
　Fax: (021) 4288 6725
E-mail: editorial@kesaintblanc.co.id; info@
　kesaintblanc.co.id; marketing@kesaintblanc.
　co.id
Web Site: www.kesaintblanc.co.id
Founded: 1979
Foreign languages.
Subjects: Education, Language Arts, Linguistics
ISBN Prefix(es): 978-979-8295; 978-979-593
Total Titles: 200 Print
Associate Companies: Kesaint Krakatau; Kesaint
　Sibayak; Mitra Utama
Imprints: Megapoin; Oriental; Renaisans; Tamtan
　Gabara; Visipro
Branch Office(s)
Jl Sandang Sari I, Gg Anggrek Sari No 4, Anta-
　pani, Bandung *Tel:* (022) 723 0636 *Fax:* (022)
　723 0636 *E-mail:* bandung@kesaintblanc.co.id
Jl Lentong No 9 Narogong Raya Km 6.8,
　Rawalumbu, Bekasi Timur 17116 *Tel:* (021)
　820 7554; (021) 820 7555 *Fax:* (021) 820 7557
　E-mail: banjarmasin@kesaintblanc.co.id
Jl Raya Sesetan, Gg Marlin No 3, Den-
　pasar *Tel:* (0361) 3666381 *E-mail:* bali@
　kesaintblanc.co.id
Jl Kutilang No 2 Sei Sikambing B, Medan
　Tel: (0812) 6061 0220 *E-mail:* medan@
　kesaintblanc.co.id
Jl Siwalankerto Timur I No 76, Surabaya
　Tel: (08786) 3258307; (08983) 962559
　E-mail: surabaya@kesaintblanc.co.id
Jl Sidika Gg Radjiman No 527B, Umbulharjo V
　Jogjakarta *Tel:* (0274) 6509422 *Fax:* (0274)
　372795 *E-mail:* jogja@kesaintblanc.co.id

Kurnia Esa CV
Jl Kramat II 33, Jakarta 10420
Tel: (021) 3104948
Subjects: Biography, Memoirs
ISBN Prefix(es): 978-979-446

**Lembaga Demografi Fakultas Ekonomi
　Universitas Indonesia** (Demographic Institute,
　Faculty of Economics, University of Indonesia)
Gedung A, Lantai 2 dan 3, Kampus FEBUI, De-
　pok 16424
Tel: (021) 787 2911 *Fax:* (021) 787 2909
E-mail: info@ldfebui.org
Web Site: ldfebui.org
Key Personnel
Chief Editor: Omas Bulan Samosir
Founded: 1964
Subjects: Child Care & Development, Developing
　Countries, Economics, Education, Environmen-
　tal Studies, Ethnicity, Health, Nutrition, Labor,
　Industrial Relations, Library & Information
　Sciences, Social Sciences, Sociology, Women's
　Studies
ISBN Prefix(es): 978-979-525
Parent Company: Faculty of Economics Univer-
　sity of Indonesia

Little-K, *imprint of* Mizan Publika

Megapoin, *imprint of* Kesaint Blanc Publishng

Mizan: Khazanah, *imprint of* Mizan Publika

Mizan Publika+
Jl Jagakarsa 1 No 12 Rt 04/02, Jakarta 12620
Tel: (021) 7865767 *Fax:* (021) 7863283
E-mail: info@mizan.com; marketing.olmizan@
　mizan.com
Web Site: www.mizan.com
Key Personnel
Chairman: Abdillah Toha
President & Dir: Haidar Bagir
Mng Dir: Putut Widjanarko
Founded: 1983

Membership(s): Indonesian Publishers Association (IKAPI).
Subjects: Asian Studies, Religion - Islamic
ISBN Prefix(es): 978-979-433
Number of titles published annually: 600 Print
Imprints: Kaifa (how-to, self-improvement & learning books); Little-K (children's books); Mizania (Islamic how-to books); Mizan: Khazanah (Islamic thoughts, philosophy); Mizan Pustaka: Kronik Indonesia Baru (general nonfiction); Qanita (fiction & hobbies)
Branch Office(s)
Jl Cinambo No 135, Ujungberung, Bandung 40294 *Tel:* (022) 7834310

Mizan Pustaka: Kronik Indonesia Baru, *imprint of* Mizan Publika

Mizania, *imprint of* Mizan Publika

Mutiara Sumber Widya+
Gedung Maya Indah, Jl Kramat Raya No 5C, Jakarta Pusat 10450
Tel: (021) 3909864 *Fax:* (021) 3160313
Subjects: Economics, Education, Mathematics, Music, Dance, Physics, Religion - Other
ISBN Prefix(es): 978-979-8011; 978-979-9331
Associate Companies: CV Angkasa (publishers)
Subsidiaries: CV Mutiara Bhakti; Mutiara Permata Widya

Nusa Indah+
Jl El Tari, Ende Flores-NTT 86318
Tel: (0381) 21502 *Fax:* (0381) 21645; (0381) 22373
Founded: 1970
Membership(s): Indonesian Christian Publishers' Association (PLKI); Indonesian Publishers Association (IKAPI).
Subjects: Biblical Studies, Human Relations, Language Arts, Linguistics, Literature, Literary Criticism, Essays, Poetry, Religion - Catholic, Theology
ISBN Prefix(es): 978-979-429
Total Titles: 350 Print
Parent Company: PT ANI
Imprints: Dioma, Kanisius, Obor (East Indonesia)
Branch Office(s)
Perwakilan Nusa Indah, Jl Matraman Raya 125, Jakarta *Tel:* (021) 8582447 *Fax:* (021) 8502403
Gudang Buku Nusa Indah, Jl Polisi Istimewa 9, Surabaya 60265 *Tel:* (031) 5617746 *Fax:* (031) 5684307
Distributed by Dioma (East Java); Gramedia (all Gramedia bookshops in Jakarta, Surabaya, Kalimantan, Timor Timur, etc.); Kanisius (Central Java); Obor (Jakarta)
Showroom(s): Jl Matraman Raya 125, Jakarta 13012; Jl Polisi Istimewa 9, Surabaya 60265
Book Club(s): Kanisius Reading Community

Oriental, *imprint of* Kesaint Blanc Publishng

Phibeta, *imprint of* Penerbit Erlangga

PT Indira Ltd+
Jl Borobudur 20, Jakarta, Pusat 10320
Tel: (021) 3904290; (021) 3148868; (021) 3147468; (021) 3904288
Founded: 1950
Subjects: Automotive, Business, Career Development, Computer Science, Crafts, Games, Hobbies, Energy, English as a Second Language, Film, Video
ISBN Prefix(es): 978-979-8063
Parent Company: Grolier Inc, United States
Associate Companies: PT Widyadara
Subsidiaries: PT Radio Prambors-Commercial Radio Broadcasting

Pustaka LP3ES Indonesia
Jl Letjen S Parman Kavling 81, Jakarta 11420
Tel: (021) 567-4211
Founded: 1971
Membership(s): Indonesian Publishers Association (IKAPI).
Subjects: Economics, Education, Environmental Studies, Finance, Government, Political Science, History, Management, Public Administration, Science (General), Social Sciences, Sociology
ISBN Prefix(es): 978-979-8015
Parent Company: LP3ES

Pustaka Utama Grafiti PT+
Jl Utan Kayu No 68 E-F-G, Jakarta 13120
Tel: (021) 8567502 *Fax:* (021) 8582430
Founded: 1986
Membership(s): Indonesian Publishers Association (IKAPI).
Subjects: Anthropology, Art, Biography, Memoirs, Business, Economics, Government, Political Science, History, Humor, Literature, Literary Criticism, Essays, Philosophy, Religion - Other, Social Sciences, Sociology
ISBN Prefix(es): 978-979-444
Parent Company: Grafiti Pers
Bookshop(s): Ancol, Pasar Seni, Jakarta Utara; Pertokoan Italiano, Jl Margonda Raya No 166, Depok; Slipi Jaya Plaza, Basement, Jl S Parman Kav 17-18, Jakarta 11410; Jl Sumatera 31 Block G-H, Surabaya
Warehouse: Jl Cipinang Kebembem I No 3 A, Jakarta Timur

Qanita, *imprint of* Mizan Publika

Remaja Rosdakarya CV
Jl Mother Inggit Garnasih, No 40, Bandung 40252
Tel: (022) 5200287 *Fax:* (022) 5202529
E-mail: rosdakarya@rosda.c.id; pemasaran@rosda.co.id (publishing)
Web Site: www.rosda.co.id
Key Personnel
President & Dir: H Rozali Usman
Vice President & Dir: Ir Hj Rosidayati Rozaline
Printing Dir: Dr Aan Soenendar
Publishing Dir: H Zamzami
Founded: 1961
Membership(s): Indonesian Publishers Association (IKAPI).
Subjects: Education, Engineering (General), Language Arts, Linguistics, Education, Engineering, Language
ISBN Prefix(es): 978-979-514; 978-979-425; 978-979-692
Associate Companies: Jl Raya Cimahi Padalarang No 93, Bandung, Jawa Barat 40553 *Tel:* (022) 6654007 *Fax:* (022) 6654017 *E-mail:* percetakan@rosda.co.id

Renaisans, *imprint of* Kesaint Blanc Publishng

Republika Penerbit
Subsidiary of Mahaka Media
Jl Kavling Polri Blok I No 65, Jagakarsa, Jakarta Selatan 12260
Tel: (021) 781 9127 *Fax:* (021) 781 912
E-mail: redaksipab@republikapenerbit.com
Web Site: bukurepublika.id
Key Personnel
Dir: Arys Hilman Nugraha
General Manager, Marketing: Awod Said
General Manager, Promotions & Editorial: Syahruddin El-Fikri
Founded: 2002
Subjects: Fiction, Religion - Islamic
ISBN Prefix(es): 978-602-0822; 978-602-8997; 978-602-9474

Siemens-Penuntun Berencana, *imprint of* Katalis / Bina Mitra Plaosan

Sumatera Utara University Press
Jl Universitas No 9, Gedung F, Kampus USU, Medan 20155
Tel: (061) 8213737 *Fax:* (061) 8213737
E-mail: usupress@usu.ac.id
Web Site: www2.usu.ac.id
Founded: 1982
Subjects: Library & Information Sciences
ISBN Prefix(es): 978-979-458

Tamtan Gabara, *imprint of* Kesaint Blanc Publishng

Tinta Mas Indonesia+
Jl Raya Kramat 60, Kwitang, Senen, Jakarta 10420
Tel: (021) 3911459; (021) 3927679; (021) 3143481 *Fax:* (021) 31900842
Key Personnel
Dir: Marhamah Djambek
Founded: 1947
Membership(s): Indonesian Publishers Association (IKAPI).
Subjects: Biography, Memoirs, History, Law, Philosophy, Religion - Other
ISBN Prefix(es): 978-979-590

UGM Press
Jl Grafika No 1, Kampus Universitas Gadjah Mada, Bulaksumur, Yogyakarta 55281
Tel: (0274) 561 037 (ext 17) *Fax:* (0274) 561 037
E-mail: ugmpress@ugm.ac.id
Web Site: www.gmup.ugm.ac.id
Founded: 1971
Subjects: Education, Science (General), Technology
ISBN Prefix(es): 978-979-420
Total Titles: 2,000 Print

Universitas Sebelas Maret
Jl Ir Sutami 36 A, Surakarta 57126
Tel: (0271) 646994 *Fax:* (0271) 646655
Web Site: www.uns.ac.id
Founded: 1986
Subjects: Art, Economics, Education, Health, Nutrition, Philosophy, Religion - Other, Science (General), Social Sciences, Sociology, Technology
ISBN Prefix(es): 978-979-498

Visipro, *imprint of* Kesaint Blanc Publishng

Yayasan Lontar (Lontar Foundation)+
Jl Danau Laut Tawar No 53, Pejompongan, Jakarta 10210
Tel: (021) 574-6880 *Fax:* (021) 572-0353
E-mail: contact@lontar.org
Web Site: www.lontar.org
Key Personnel
Chairman: Rohmad Hadiwijoyo
Executive Dir: Kestity Pringgohardjono
Secretary: Ilia Afiyanti
Treasurer: Tuti Zairati
Publication Division: Wikan Satriati
Founded: 1987
Subjects: Art, Ethnicity, Literature, Literary Criticism, Essays
ISBN Prefix(es): 978-979-8083

Yayasan Obor Indonesia+
Jl Plaju No 10, Jakarta 10230
Tel: (021) 31920114; (021) 31926978 *Fax:* (021) 31924488
E-mail: yayasan_obor@cbn.net.id
Web Site: www.obor.or.id
Key Personnel
Chairperson: Kartini Nurdin *Tel:* (08) 128066511 (cell) *E-mail:* kartininurdin@yrci.or.id

Marketing Manager: Widodo Pamuji
Editor: Andreas Haryono; Nur Kusumawardani
Founded: 1978
Subjects: Environmental Studies, Government,
Political Science, History, Literature, Literary
Criticism, Essays, Nonfiction (General), Pub-
lishing & Book Trade Reference, Social Sci-
ences, Sociology, Global Issues, Human Rights
ISBN Prefix(es): 978-979-461
Number of titles published annually: 100 Print;
200 Online; 50 E-Book
Total Titles: 1,200 Print; 400 E-Book
Branch Office(s)
Perum Jombor Baru, Jl Pajajaran Blok 2 No 21,
Sleman, Yogyakarta 55282 *Tel:* (0274) 865557
E-mail: oborjogja@yahoo.com

Zikrul Hakim-Bestari
Jl Sodong Raya No 16, Rawamangun, Jakarta
Timur 13220
Tel: 0813 2090 0052 (cell) *Fax:* (021) 4754429
E-mail: zikrulbestari@gmail.com
Web Site: www.penerbitbestari.com
ISBN Prefix(es): 978-979-9140; 978-979-3802

Iran

General Information

Capital: Tehran
Language: Persian (Farsi), Turkish and Armenian
in Northwest, Arabic in Southwest, Kurdish in
Kurdistan (English or French also)
Religion: Islamic (Shi'a sect and some Sunni
sect)
Population: 61.2 million
Bank Hours: Generally Winter: 0800-1300
Saturday-Thursday; 1600-1800 Saturday-
Wednesday; Summer: 0730-1300, 1700-1900
Saturday-Wednesday, 0730-1130 Thursday
Shop Hours: Generally Winter: 0800-2000
Saturday-Thursday; 0800-1200 Friday; Sum-
mer: 0800-1300, 1700-2100 Saturday-Thursday,
0800-1200 Friday
Currency: 100 dinars = 1 Iranian rial
Export/Import Information: No tariff on books
and advertising but catalogs subject to VAT.
Import licenses required. Publications offend-
ing public order, official religion or morality
prohibited. Exchange controls, with new regu-
lations issued each March.
Copyright: No copyright conventions signed

Caravan Books Publishing House+
18 Salehi St, Sartip Fakouri Ave, Northern Kare-
gar Ave, Tehran 14136
Mailing Address: PO Box 186, Tehran 14145
Tel: (021) 88007421 *Fax:* (021) 88029486
E-mail: info@caravan.ir
Web Site: www.caravan.ir
Key Personnel
Publisher: Arash Hejazi *E-mail:* ahejazi@caravan.
ir
Founded: 1997
Membership(s): Tehran's Union of Publishers &
Booksellers.
Subjects: Biography, Memoirs, Business, Fiction,
Literature, Literary Criticism, Essays, Nonfic-
tion (General), Philosophy, Poetry, Religion -
Other, Women's Studies
ISBN Prefix(es): 978-964-7033; 978-964-8497;
978-964-91607
Number of titles published annually: 100 Print; 2
Online
Total Titles: 250 Print; 5 Online

Elmi Farhangi Publishing Co (Scientific &
Cultural Publishing Co)
25 Kaman Alley, Haghghani Junction, Africa
Highway, Tehran 1518736313
Tel: (021) 88774569; (021) 88774570 *Fax:* (021)
88797604; (021) 88797605
E-mail: info@elmifarhangi.ir; office@
elmifarhangi.ir; sales@elmifarhangi.ir
Web Site: elmifarhangi.ir
Subjects: Religion - Islamic, Iran
ISBN Prefix(es): 978-964-445

**KANOON, Institute for the Intellectual
Development of Children & Young Adults**
(KANOON, Den Iranske Institusjonen for
Utvikling av Barne- og Ungdomskultur)
Fatemi Ave, Hejab St, Tehran 14156
Mailing Address: PO Box 14145136, Tehran
11369
Tel: (021) 88967392 *Fax:* (021) 88821121
E-mail: kanoon@jamejam.net
Web Site: www.kanoonparvaresh.com;
kanoonnord.com; www.kanoonintl.com; www.
kids.kanoonparvaresh.com
Key Personnel
Chief Executive Officer: Mr Hussain Kirmani
Manager: Seyyed Sadegh Rezaei
Contact: Leili Hayeri Yazdi
Founded: 1966
Subjects: Art, Literature, Literary Criticism, Es-
says
ISBN Prefix(es): 978-964-432; 978-964-391

Nazar Publication
No 2 Sharif Ave S Iranshahr, Tehran 1581614815
Tel: (021) 88 82 89 03
E-mail: info@nazarpub.com
Web Site: www.nazarpub.com
Subjects: Architecture & Interior Design, Art,
Philosophy, Photography, Art Theory, Contem-
porary Iranian Art, Painting, World Art
ISBN Prefix(es): 978-964-6994; 978-964-91847

Shabaviz Publishing Co
No 2-4, Nouri Alley, Jomhouri Eslami Ave,
between Golshan St & Bastan St, Tehran
1318645163
Tel: (021) 66423995; (021) 66427539 *Fax:* (021)
66427858
E-mail: shabaviz_publication@yahoo.com
Web Site: www.shabaviz.com
Key Personnel
Chairman & Mng Dir: Farideh Khalatbaree
ISBN Prefix(es): 978-964-505; 978-964-5511;
978-964-5555

University of Tehran Press
Tehran front carpet (XVI) Shahid Farshi Moqad-
dam St, N Karegar St, PO Box 14155-6464,
Tehran 1439814451
Tel: (021) 88026412; (021) 88012080 *Fax:* (021)
88012077
E-mail: press@ut.ac.ir
Web Site: press.ut.ac.ir
Founded: 1946
Subjects: Architecture & Interior Design, Art, En-
gineering (General), Medicine, Nursing, Den-
tistry, Science (General), Social Sciences, Soci-
ology
ISBN Prefix(es): 978-964-03
Bookshop(s): Enqelab Ave, Tehran

**University of Tehran Printing & Publishing
Institute,** see University of Tehran Press

Ireland

General Information

Capital: Dublin
Language: English & Irish (Gaelic)
Religion: Predominantly Roman Catholic, some
Church of Ireland
Population: 3.8 million
Bank Hours: 1000-1230, 1330-1500 Monday-
Friday. Open until 1700 one night a week
Shop Hours: 0900 or 0930-1730 Monday-
Saturday
Currency: 100 Eurocents = 1 Euro
Export/Import Information: Member of the Euro-
pean Union. BH & VMcK No tariff on books
except on prayer & similar books from non-UK
& children's picture books from non-EU. Pam-
phlets duties from non-EU. VAT is charged.
No import licenses. Exchange controls.
Copyright: UCC, Berne (see Copyright Conven-
tions, pg viii)

A&A Farmar+
Beech House, 78 Ranelagh Village, Dublin 6
Tel: (01) 496 3625
Key Personnel
International Rights & Editorial Dir: Anna Farmar
Production Dir: Tony Farmar
Founded: 1992
Specialize in nonfiction books of Irish interest,
including history, travel, biography, business &
food & drink.
Subjects: Biography, Memoirs, Business, Child
Care & Development, Cookery, History, Lit-
erature, Literary Criticism, Essays, Travel &
Tourism, Wine & Spirits
ISBN Prefix(es): 978-1-899047; 978-0-9509295;
978-1-906353
Number of titles published annually: 12 Print
Total Titles: 50 Print
Distribution Center: Gill Distribution, Hume Ave,
Park West, Dublin D12 YV96 *Tel:* (01) 500
9500 *Web Site:* www.gilldistribution.ie
Central Books Ltd, One Heath Park Indus-
trial Estate, Freshwater Rd, Dagenham RM8
1RX, United Kingdom *Tel:* (020) 8525 8800
Fax: (020) 8599 2694 *E-mail:* orders@
centralbooks.com *Web Site:* www.centralbooks.
com
Orders to: Brookside Publishing Services, 2
Brookside, Dundrum Rd, Dublin 14 *Tel:* (01)
298 9937 *E-mail:* sales@brookside.ie

An Gum+
24-27 Frederick St North, Dublin D01 R7R9
Tel: (01) 8892800 *Fax:* (01) 8731140
E-mail: angum@forasnagaeilge.ie
Web Site: www.gaeilge.ie/angum
Key Personnel
Editorial: Seosamh O Murchu
Production: John Dixon
Publicity: Paul Williams
Founded: 1926
Subjects: Art, Cookery, Education, Geography,
Geology, Mathematics, Science (General)
ISBN Prefix(es): 978-1-85791
Parent Company: Foras na Gaeilge, Dublin 2
Warehouse: Johnston Logistics, Blackchurch,
Rathcoole, Co Dublin
Orders to: An Ais, 31 Sr na bhFinini, Dublin
2, Manager: Breandan Mac Craith *Tel:* (01)
6616522 *Fax:* (01) 6616378 *E-mail:* ais@
forasnagaeilge.ie *Web Site:* www.gaeilge.ie

Anvil Books, *imprint of* Mercier Press Ltd

Atrium, *imprint of* Cork University Press

Attic Press, *imprint of* Cork University Press

Attic Press+

Imprint of Cork University Press (CUP)
c/o Cork University Press, Youngline Industrial
Estate, Pouladuff Rd, Cork
Tel: (021) 490 2980 *Fax:* (021) 431 5329
E-mail: corkuniversitypress@ucc.ie
Web Site: www.corkuniversitypress.com
Key Personnel
Publications Dir: Mike Collins *E-mail:* mike.
collins@ucc.ie
Editor: Maria O'Donovan *E-mail:* maria.
odonovan@ucc.ie
Founded: 1984
Subjects: Biography, Memoirs, Cookery, Gov-
ernment, Political Science, Health, Nutrition,
History, Humor, Literature, Literary Criticism,
Essays, Social Sciences, Sociology, Women's
Studies
ISBN Prefix(es): 978-0-946211; 978-1-85594
Distribution Center: Gill Distribution, Hume Ave,
Park West, Dublin D12 YV96 *Tel:* (01) 500
9500 *Web Site:* www.gilldistribution.com
Orders to: Gill Distribution, Hume Ave, Park
West, Dublin D12 YV96 *Tel:* (01) 500 9500
Web Site: www.gilldistribution.com
Marston Book Services Ltd, 160 Eastern
Ave, Milton Park, Abingdon, Oxon OX14
4SB, United Kingdom *Tel:* (01235) 465500
Fax: (01235) 465555 *E-mail:* trade.orders@
marston.co.uk *Web Site:* www.marston.co.uk
Dufour Editions Inc, Buyers Rd, PO Box 7,
Chester Springs, PA 19425-0007, United States
Tel: 610-458-5005 *Fax:* 610-458-7103 *Web
Site:* www.dufoureditions.com

Ballinakella Press+

Whitegate, Co Clare V94 T956
Tel: (061) 927030
E-mail: ballinakella@hotmail.com
Web Site: www.ballinakellapress.com
Founded: 1984
Specialize in Irish historical, topographical, ge-
nealogical & biographical books.
Subjects: Architecture & Interior Design, Biogra-
phy, Memoirs, Genealogy, Geography, Geology,
History, Regional Interests, Travel & Tourism
ISBN Prefix(es): 978-0-946538
Number of titles published annually: 2 Print
Total Titles: 39 Print
Parent Company: Weir Publishing
Imprints: Weir's Guides

Belser Wissenschaftlicher Dienst

Ballinlough, Co Roscommon F45 K062
Web Site: www.belser.com
Key Personnel
Executive Dir: Dr Rolf D Schmid, PhD
Founded: 1989
Specialize in conversion medieval manuscripts,
rare books, pamphlets, paintings & drawings of
the 16th - early 20th centuries into microfiche,
ebooks or CD-ROMs with various electronic
access options.
Subjects: Art, Behavioral Sciences, Biblical Stud-
ies, Drama, Theater, Fiction, History, Labor,
Industrial Relations, Library & Information
Sciences, Literature, Literary Criticism, Essays,
Philosophy, Poetry, Psychology, Psychiatry, Re-
ligion - Catholic, Social Sciences, Sociology,
Theology, Women's Studies, English, French &
German Literature, Fine Art, Mysticism, Poli-
tics, Psychoanalysis
ISBN Prefix(es): 978-3-628
Total Titles: 24,500 CD-ROM; 35,000 E-Book

Blackhall Publishing

Lonsdale House, Avoca Ave, Blackrock, Co
Dublin
Tel: (01) 278 5090
E-mail: info@blackhallpublishing.com
Web Site: www.blackhallpublishing.com
Founded: 1997

Subjects: Law, Nonfiction (General)
ISBN Prefix(es): 978-1-901657; 978-1-84218
Associate Companies: Lonsdale Law Publishing
E-mail: info@lonsdalelawpublishing.com *Web
Site:* www.lonsdalelawpublishing.com
Distribution Center: Gill Distribution, Hume Ave,
Park West, Dublin D12 YV96 *Tel:* (01) 500
9500 *Web Site:* www.gilldistribution.ie

Blackwater Press, *imprint of* Folens Publishers

Blue Flag, *imprint of* The O'Brien Press Ltd

Bord na Gaeilge

Library Bldg, Room L508, University College
Dublin, Belfield 4
Tel: (01) 716 7387
E-mail: oifigeach.gaeilge@ucd.ie
Web Site: www.ucd.ie/bnag
Key Personnel
Chairman: Prof Michael Doherty *E-mail:* michael.
doherty@ucd.ie
Irish Language Officer: Clar Ni Bhuachallo
Founded: 1997
Subjects: Language Arts, Linguistics, Irish Lan-
guage
ISBN Prefix(es): 978-0-946339

Brandon, *imprint of* The O'Brien Press Ltd

Brandon+

Imprint of O'Brien Press
12 Terenure Rd E, Dublin D06 HD27
Tel: (01) 4923333 *Fax:* (01) 4922777
E-mail: books@obrien.ie; sales@obrien.ie
Web Site: www.obrien.ie/brandon
Key Personnel
Mng Dir: Ivan O'Brien *E-mail:* ivan@obrien.ie
Publisher: Michael O'Brien *E-mail:* michael@
obrien.ie
Founded: 1982
Subjects: Biography, Memoirs, Fiction, Literature,
Literary Criticism, Essays, Nonfiction (General)
ISBN Prefix(es): 978-0-86322; 978-1-84717; 978-
1-78849
Total Titles: 60 Print; 40 E-Book
Foreign Rep(s): JB Booksales (UK)
Distribution Center: Gill Distribution, Hume
Ave, Park West, Dublin D12 YV96 *Tel:* (01)
5009555 *Fax:* (01) 5009599 *E-mail:* sales@gill.
ie *Web Site:* www.gilldistribution.ie

Edmund Burke Publisher+

Cloonagashel, 27 Priory Dr, Blackrock, Co
Dublin
Tel: (01) 288 2159 *Fax:* (01) 283 4080
E-mail: deburca@indigo.ie
Web Site: www.deburcararebooks.com/publish.htm
Key Personnel
Contact: Eamonn de Burca
Founded: 1980
Historical, topographical & genealogical works on
Ireland.
Subjects: Biography, Memoirs, History, Aca-
demic, Bibliography
ISBN Prefix(es): 978-0-946130
Branch Office(s)
51a Dawson St, Dublin 2 *Tel:* (01) 671 9609
Fax: (01) 283 4080

Children's Poolbeg, *imprint of* Poolbeg Press Ltd

The Children's Press, *imprint of* Mercier Press Ltd

Clo Iar-Chonnachta Teo+

Sailearna Business Park, Indreabhan, Conamara,
Galway, Co Galway
Tel: (091) 593 307 *Fax:* (091) 593 362
E-mail: info@cic.ie; cic@iol.ie

Web Site: www.cic.ie
Key Personnel
Mng Dir: Michael O'Conghaile *E-mail:* moccic@
eircom.net
Literary Editor: Lochlainn O'Tuairisg
General Manager: Deirdre Thuathail
Sales Manager: Lisa McDonagh *E-mail:* lisa@cic.
ie
Marketing Executive: Bridget Bhreathnach
E-mail: poibliocht@cic.ie
Founded: 1985
Most publications are in the Irish language.
Subjects: Drama, Theater, Fiction, History, Music,
Dance, Poetry, Regional Interests
ISBN Prefix(es): 978-1-874700; 978-1-900693;
978-1-902420; 978-1-905560
Number of titles published annually: 15 Print; 2
Audio
Total Titles: 360 Print; 25 Audio
Distributed by Dufour Editions
Foreign Rep(s): Dufour Editions (Canada, USA)
Foreign Rights: Toner Quinn

Clodhanna Teoranta

6 Sraid Fhearchair, Dublin 2
Tel: (01) 475 7401 *Fax:* (01) 475 7844
E-mail: eolas@cnag.ie
Web Site: cnag.ie
Key Personnel
President: Donnchadh O Laodha
General Secretary: Julian de Spainn
Publications Officer: Daragh O'Tuama
Founded: 1893
Subjects: Biography, Memoirs, Drama, The-
ater, History, Music, Dance, Poetry, Religion
- Other, Travel & Tourism
ISBN Prefix(es): 978-0-905027; 978-0-9501264
Parent Company: Conradh na Gaeilge

The Collins Press+

Unit 8, West Link Park, Doughcloyne, Wilton, Co
Cork
Tel: (021) 4347717 *Fax:* (021) 4347720
E-mail: enquiries@collinspress.ie
Web Site: www.collinspress.ie
Key Personnel
Contact: Con Collins *E-mail:* con.collins@
collinspress.ie
Founded: 1989
Membership(s): Publishing Ireland.
Subjects: Archaeology, Biography, Memoirs, His-
tory, Human Relations, Natural History, Pho-
tography, Drama, Mind, Body & Spirit
ISBN Prefix(es): 978-0-9516036; 978-1-895256;
978-1-903464; 978-1-84889; 978-1-905172
Number of titles published annually: 17 Print
Total Titles: 91 Print
Foreign Rep(s): Compass DSA Ltd (Europe, UK);
Compass Ireland Independent Books Sales (Ire-
land)
Foreign Rights: AMV Agencia Literaria SL;
Gundhild Lenz-Mulligan
Distribution Center: Gill Distribution, Hume Ave,
Park West, Dublin D12 YV96 *Tel:* (01) 500
9500 *Web Site:* www.gilldistribution.com (Ire-
land, Britain & Europe)
Orders to: Gill Distribution, Hume Ave, Park
West, Dublin D12 YV96 *Tel:* (01) 500 9500
Web Site: www.gilldistribution.com (Ireland,
Britain & Europe)
Dufour Editions, PO Box 7, Chester Springs,
PA 19425-0007, United States *Tel:* 610-
458-5005 *Fax:* 610-458-7103 *E-mail:* info@
dufoureditions.com *Web Site:* www.
dufoureditions.com (North America)

The Columba Press+

Imprint of The Columba Bookservice Ltd
Stillorgan Industrial Park, 55A Spruce Ave,
Blackrock, Dublin
Tel: (01) 294 2556 *Fax:* (01) 294 2564
E-mail: info@columba.ie
Web Site: www.columba.ie

Key Personnel
Mng Dir: Garry O'Sullivan *E-mail:* garry@
columba.ie
Mng Editor: Mags Gargan *E-mail:* mags@
columba.ie
Marketing & Sales Executive: Nelson Valenzuela
E-mail: nelson@columba.ie
Junior Marketing & Sales Executive: Anais
Tomas *E-mail:* anais@columba.ie
Editorial Assistant: Emilie Condron
E-mail: emilie@columba.ie
Founded: 1985
Specialize in Christian pastoral resources.
Membership(s): Publishing Ireland.
Subjects: Art, History, Religion - Catholic, Reli-
gion - Protestant, Self-Help, Theology
ISBN Prefix(es): 978-0-948183; 978-1-85607
Total Titles: 450 Print
Imprints: Currach Press
Distribution Center: Irish Book Distribu-
tion, Unit 12 North Park, North Rd, Finglas
Dublin 11 *Tel:* (01) 8239580 *E-mail:* sales@
irishbookdistribution.ie
Gill Distribution, Hume Ave, Park West, Dublin
D12 YV96 *Tel:* (01) 500 9500 *Web Site:* www.
gilldistribution.ie

Connolly Books
43 E Essex St, Temple Bar, Dublin D02 XH96
Tel: (01) 6708707
E-mail: connollybooks@eircom.net
Web Site: www.connollybooks.org
Subjects: Economics, Government, Political Sci-
ence, History, Philosophy
ISBN Prefix(es): 978-0-902912

Cork University Press+
Youngline Industrial Estate, Pouladuff Rd, Cork
Tel: (021) 490 2980
E-mail: corkuniversitypress@ucc.ie
Web Site: www.corkuniversitypress.com
Key Personnel
Publications Dir: Mike Collins *E-mail:* mike.
collins@ucc.ie
Editor: Maria O'Donovan *E-mail:* maria.
odonovan@ucc.ie
Founded: 1925
Specialize in Irish studies, history, literature, cul-
tural studies & politics.
Membership(s): Publishing Ireland.
Subjects: Archaeology, Geography, Geology, Gov-
ernment, Political Science, History, Social Sci-
ences, Sociology, Women's Studies
ISBN Prefix(es): 978-0-902561; 978-1-85918;
978-0-9502440
Number of titles published annually: 15 Print; 10
E-Book
Total Titles: 150 Print; 40 E-Book
Imprints: Atrium; Attic Press
Foreign Rep(s): Gill (Ireland); Marston Book Ser-
vices Ltd (UK); Peter Prout (Portugal, Spain);
Stylus (USA)
Distribution Center: Gill Distribution, Hume Ave,
Park West, Dublin D12 YV96 *Tel:* (01) 500
9500 *Web Site:* www.gilldistribution.ie
Longleaf Services, 116 S Boundary St,
Chapel Hill, NC 27514-3808, United States
E-mail: customerservice@longleafservices.org

Currach Press, *imprint of* The Columba Press

Dee-Jay Publications+
3 Meadows Lane, Arklow, Co Wicklow
Tel: (0402) 39125 *Fax:* (0402) 39064
E-mail: mail@dee-jay.ie
Web Site: www.dee-jay.ie
Key Personnel
Contact: Dorothy Rees; Jim Rees *E-mail:* jrees@
eircom.net
Founded: 1992
Subjects: Archaeology, Biography, Memoirs, Ge-
nealogy, History, Maritime, Nonfiction (Gen-

eral), Regional Interests, Travel & Tourism,
Folklore
ISBN Prefix(es): 978-0-9519239

Dominican Publications
42 Parnell Sq, Dublin 1
Tel: (01) 872-1611 *Fax:* (01) 873-1760
E-mail: sales@dominicanpublications.com
Web Site: www.dominicanpublications.com
Key Personnel
Mng Editor: Bernard Treacy
Founded: 1897
Specialize in books & periodicals on theology.
Subjects: Biography, Memoirs, History, Religion -
Catholic, Theology
ISBN Prefix(es): 978-0-9504797; 978-0-907271;
978-1-871552; 978-1-905604
Total Titles: 20 Print; 2 CD-ROM
Distributed by Columba
Book Club(s): Doctrine & Life Book Club; Re-
ligious Life Review Book Club; Scripture in
Church Book Club

Dublin Institute for Advanced Studies
10 Burlington Rd, Dublin 4
Tel: (01) 6140100 *Fax:* (01) 6680561; (01)
6140160
Web Site: www.dias.ie
Key Personnel
Dir: Liam Breatnach *Tel:* (01) 6140165
E-mail: lbreatnach@celtic.dias.ie; Padraig A
Breatnach *E-mail:* pbreatnach@celtic.dias.ie
Administrative Officer: Mary Burke *Tel:* (01)
6140188
Registrar: Cecil Keaveney *Tel:* (01) 6140121
Founded: 1940
Specialize in research & advanced study in Celtic
studies & physics.
Subjects: Ethnicity, Physics
ISBN Prefix(es): 978-0-901282; 978-1-85500

The Economic & Social Research Institute
Whitaker Sq, Sir John Rogerson's Quay, Dublin 2
Tel: (01) 8632000 *Fax:* (01) 8632100
E-mail: admin@esri.ie
Web Site: www.esri.ie
Key Personnel
Dir: Prof Alan Barrett *E-mail:* director@esri.ie
Assistant Dir & Secretary: Gillian Davidson
E-mail: gillian.davidson@esri.ie
Founded: 1960
Subjects: Economics, Education, Environmental
Studies, Finance, Health, Nutrition, Labor, In-
dustrial Relations, Social Sciences, Sociology,
Transportation
ISBN Prefix(es): 978-0-7070; 978-0-901809
Total Titles: 300 Print

Edco, see The Educational Company of Ireland

The Educational Company of Ireland+
Member of Smurfit Kappa Group PLC
Ballymount Rd, Walkinstown, Dublin 12
Tel: (01) 4500611 *Fax:* (01) 4500993
E-mail: info@edco.ie
Web Site: www.edco.ie
Key Personnel
Chief Executive: Martina Harford
Publisher: Emer Ryan
Commercial Dir: Julie Glennon
Founded: 1910
Subjects: Accounting, Agriculture, Art, Biolog-
ical Sciences, Business, Career Development,
Chemistry, Chemical Engineering, Computer
Science, Cookery, Earth Sciences, Economics,
Engineering (General), Geography, Geology,
History, Language Arts, Linguistics, Litera-
ture, Literary Criticism, Essays, Mathematics,
Physics, Religion - Other, Science (General)
ISBN Prefix(es): 978-0-901802; 978-0-904916;
978-0-86167; 978-1-84536

Enodare Ltd
Dublin Rd, Athlone, Co Westmeath
E-mail: info@enodare.com
Web Site: enodare.com
Subjects: Business, Finance, Law
ISBN Prefix(es): 978-1-906144
U.S. Office(s): 4747 36 St, Suite 75091, Long Is-
land City, NY 11101, United States
Foreign Rep(s): International Publishers Market-
ing Inc (IPM) (USA)

ESRI, see The Economic & Social Research
Institute

Estragon Press Ltd+
Ballycommane, Durrus, Bantry, Co Cork
Tel: (027) 61186
E-mail: estragon@eircom.net
Web Site: www.bestofbridgestone.com
Key Personnel
Dir, Publisher & Author: John McKenna; Sally
McKenna
Press: Grainne Byrne *Tel:* (087) 245 9463
E-mail: grainne@gbc-pr.com
Founded: 1991
Subjects: Cookery, Travel & Tourism, Wine &
Spirits
ISBN Prefix(es): 978-1-874076
Distribution Center: Gill Distribution, Hume Ave,
Park West, Dublin D12 YV96 *Tel:* (01) 500
9500 *Web Site:* www.gilldistribution.ie
Portfolio, Perivale Industrial Park, Unit 5,
Perivale, Middx UB6 7RL, United King-
dom *E-mail:* sales@portfoliobooks.com *Web
Site:* www.portfoliobooks.com
Irish Books & Media, 1433 Franklin Ave
E, Minneapolis, MN 55404-2135, United
States *Tel:* 612-871-3505 *Fax:* 612-871-3358
E-mail: irishbook@aol.com *Web Site:* www.
irishbook.com

**European Foundation for the Improvement of
Living & Working Conditions**
Wyattville Rd, Loughlinstown, Dublin 18
Tel: (01) 2043100 *Fax:* (01) 2826456; (01)
2824209
E-mail: information@eurofound.europa.eu
Web Site: www.eurofound.europa.eu
Key Personnel
Dir: Juan Menendez-Valdes
Deputy Dir: Erika Mezger *E-mail:* eme@
eurofound.europa.eu
Head, Administration: Markus Grimmeisen
E-mail: mgr@eurofound.europa.eu
Head, Information & Communication: Mary Mc-
Caughey *E-mail:* mcu@eurofound.europa.eu
Founded: 1975
Subjects: EU Social Policy
ISBN Prefix(es): 978-92-897
Branch Office(s)
Ave d'Auderghem 20, 1040 Brussels, Bel-
gium, Contact: Sylvie Jacquet *Tel:* (02) 280
64 76; (02) 230 51 61 *Fax:* (02) 280 64 79
E-mail: eurofound.brussels.office@eurofound.
europa.eu

C J Fallon Ltd
Block B, Ground floor, Liffey Valley Office Cam-
pus, Dublin 22
Tel: (01) 6166400; (01) 6166490 (sales) *Fax:* (01)
6166499
E-mail: sales@cjfallon.ie; editorial@cjfallon.ie;
info@cjfallon.ie
Web Site: www.cjfallon.ie
Key Personnel
Chief Executive: Brian Gilsenan
Project Manager: Barry Meade
Founded: 1927
Subjects: Geography, Geology, History, Mathe-
matics, Science (General)
ISBN Prefix(es): 978-0-7144

Flyers, *imprint of* The O'Brien Press Ltd

Flyleaf Press+
4 Spencer Villas, Glenageary, Co Dublin
Tel: (01) 2854658
E-mail: books@flyleaf.ie
Web Site: www.flyleaf.ie
Key Personnel
Mng Editor: James Ryan *E-mail:* jim.ryan@circa.
ie
Founded: 1987
Specialist publisher of family history & geneal-
ogy titles.
Membership(s): Publishing Ireland.
Subjects: Genealogy, Natural History, Family His-
tory
ISBN Prefix(es): 978-0-9508466; 978-0-9539974;
978-1-907990
Number of titles published annually: 2 Print; 1
CD-ROM
Total Titles: 14 Print; 1 CD-ROM

Folens Publishers+
Hibernian Industrial Estate, Greenhills Rd, Tal-
laght, Dublin 24
Tel: (01) 4137200 *Fax:* (01) 4137282
E-mail: info@folens.ie; orders@folens.ie
Web Site: www.folens.ie
Key Personnel
Mng Dir: John Cadell
Mng Dir, Blackwater Press: John O'Connor
Publishing Manager: Margaret Burns
E-mail: margaret.burns@folens.ie
Founded: 1958
Subjects: Education
ISBN Prefix(es): 978-0-86121; 978-0-902592;
978-1-84131
Associate Companies: Folens Limited, United
Kingdom; JUKA-91 Spzoo, Poland
Imprints: Blackwater Press

Four Courts Press Ltd+
7 Malpas St, Dublin 8
Tel: (01) 453-4668 *Fax:* (01) 453-4672
E-mail: info@fourcourtspress.ie
Web Site: www.fourcourtspress.ie
Key Personnel
Publisher: Martin Healy
Editorial Dir: Martin Fanning
Editor: Dr Michael Patterton
Sales & Marketing Manager: Anthony Tierney
Founded: 1970
Academic book publishers.
Subjects: Archaeology, Art, Film, Video, History,
Law, Literature, Literary Criticism, Essays,
Music, Dance, Philosophy, Religion - Catholic,
Theology, Celtic & Medieval Studies
ISBN Prefix(es): 978-0-906127; 978-1-85182;
978-1-84682; 978-1-84862
Number of titles published annually: 50 Print
Total Titles: 650 Print
Imprints: Open Air
Warehouse: Gill Distribution, Hume Ave, Park
West, Dublin D12 YV96 *Tel:* (01) 500 9500
Web Site: www.gilldistribution.ie
Distribution Center: Gill Distribution, Hume Ave,
Park West, Dublin D12 YV96 *Tel:* (01) 500
9500 *Web Site:* www.gilldistribution.ie
ISBS (International Specialized Book Services),
920 NE 58 Ave, Suite 300, Portland, OR
97213, United States *Fax:* 503-280-8832
E-mail: fcp@isbs.com *Web Site:* www.isbs.com
(North America)
Orders to: Gill Distribution, Hume Ave, Park
West, Dublin D12 YV96 *Tel:* (01) 500 9500
Web Site: www.gilldistribution.ie

Futa Fata+
An Spideal, Spideal, Co Galway
Tel: (091) 504 612
E-mail: info@futafata.ie; foreignrights@futafata.
com

Web Site: www.futafata.ie
Key Personnel
Dir: Tadhg Mac Dhonnagain *E-mail:* tadhg@
futafata.ie
This publisher has indicated that 50% of their
product line is author subsidized.
Subjects: Gaelic Literature
ISBN Prefix(es): 978-0-9550983; 978-1-906907
Number of titles published annually: 10 Print
Total Titles: 65 Print; 6 CD-ROM; 65 Online
Distributed by CIC
Distribution Center: AIS *Tel:* (01) 6616522
Fax: (01) 6612378 *E-mail:* ais@forasnagaeilge.
ie
Argosy Books, Unit 12, North Park, North Rd,
Finglas, Dublin 11 *Tel:* (01) 8239500 *Fax:* (01)
8239599 *E-mail:* info@argosybooks.ie
Gill Distribution, Hume Ave, Park West, Dublin
D12 YV96 *Tel:* (01) 500 9500 *Web Site:* www.
gilldistribution.ie

The Gallery Press+
Loughcrew, Oldcastle, Co Meath
Tel: (049) 8541779 *Fax:* (049) 8541779
E-mail: contactus@gallerypress.com
Web Site: www.gallerypress.com
Key Personnel
Editor & Publisher: Peter Fallon
Administrator & Rights & Permissions: Jean
Barry
Founded: 1970
Specialize in contemporary Irish poetry.
Subjects: Drama, Theater, Poetry
ISBN Prefix(es): 978-0-902996; 978-0-904011;
978-1-85235

Gandon Editions+
Oysterhaven, Kinsale, Co Cork
Tel: (021) 4770830 *Fax:* (021) 4770755
E-mail: gandon@eircom.net
Web Site: www.gandon-editions.com
Founded: 1983
Specialize in art & architecture books.
Subjects: Archaeology, Architecture & Interior
Design, Art, Environmental Studies, History,
Nonfiction (General)
ISBN Prefix(es): 978-0-946641; 978-0-946846;
978-0-948037
Number of titles published annually: 20 Print
Total Titles: 320 Print

Geography Publications
24 Kennington Rd, Templeogue, Dublin 6W
Tel: (01) 4566085 *Fax:* (01) 4566085
E-mail: info@geographypublications.com
Web Site: www.geographypublications.com
Key Personnel
Contact: Dr William Nolan
Founded: 1974
Subjects: Archaeology, Biography, Memoirs, Ge-
nealogy, Geography, Geology, History
ISBN Prefix(es): 978-0-906602
Number of titles published annually: 2 Print
Total Titles: 35 Print
Foreign Rep(s): The Genealogical Society of Vic-
toria (Australia)

Gill
10 Hume Ave, Park West, Dublin 12
Tel: (01) 500 9500; (01) 500 9555 (orders)
Fax: (01) 500 9596 (orders)
E-mail: info@gill.ie; sales@gill.ie
Web Site: www.gill.ie
Key Personnel
Mng Dir: Dermot O'Dwyer *E-mail:* dodwyer@
gill.ie
Dir, Education: Ruth Gill *E-mail:* rgill@gill.ie
Dir, Trade: Nicki Howard *E-mail:* nhoward@gill.
ie
Distribution Dir: John Manning
E-mail: jmanning@gill.ie

Finance & Operations Dir: Brian Curtin
E-mail: bcurtin@gill.ie
Publishing Dir, Education: Margaret Burns
E-mail: mburns@gill.ie
Public Relations: Teresa Daly *E-mail:* tdaly@gill.
ie
Founded: 1968
Subjects: Biography, Memoirs, Business, Child
Care & Development, Cookery, Economics,
Education, Government, Political Science,
Health, Nutrition, History, Law, Literature, Lit-
erary Criticism, Essays, Nonfiction (General),
Regional Interests
ISBN Prefix(es): 978-0-7171
Number of titles published annually: 75 Print; 75
Online
Total Titles: 900 Print; 400 Online
Imprints: Gill Books; Gill Education
Foreign Rep(s): Bounce! Sales & Marketing
Ltd (Robert Snuggs) (UK); Dufour Editions
(Canada, USA); Macmillan Caribbean (Dan
Wilson) (Caribbean); Macmillan Education
Australia (Peter Huntley) (Australia); Macmil-
lan South Africa (Belinda Germeshuizen)
(South Africa)
Foreign Rights: Maria White (worldwide)

Gill Books, *imprint of* Gill

Gill Education, *imprint of* Gill

Government Publications Ireland, see
Stationery Office Dublin

IAP, *imprint of* Irish Academic Press

Institute of Public Administration
57-61 Landsdowne Rd, Ballsbridge, Dublin 4
Tel: (01) 240 3600 *Fax:* (01) 668 9135
E-mail: information@ipa.ie
Web Site: www.ipa.ie
Key Personnel
Dir General: Dr Brian Cawley *E-mail:* bcawley@
ipa.ie
Assistant Dir General & Registrar: Michael Mul-
reany *E-mail:* mmulreany@ipa.ie
Head, Research, Publishing & Corporate Rela-
tions: Dr Richard Boyle *E-mail:* rboyle@ipa.ie
Advertising: Carolyn Gormley
E-mail: cgormley@ipa.ie
Editor: Joanna O'Riordan *E-mail:* editor@ipa.ie
Founded: 1957
Specialize in public service administration &
management.
Subjects: Economics, Education, Environmental
Studies, Government, Political Science, Health,
Nutrition, History, Law, Management, Public
Administration, Social Sciences, Sociology,
Administration, International Affairs, Public
Affairs
ISBN Prefix(es): 978-0-902173; 978-0-906980;
978-1-872002; 978-1-902448; 978-1-90451

Irish Academic Press+
8 Chapel Lane, Sallins, Kildare 4
Tel: (045) 89 55 62 *Fax:* (045) 89 55 63
E-mail: info@iap.ie
Web Site: www.iap.ie; www.irishacademicusa.com
Key Personnel
Publisher & Mng Dir: Conor Graham
Marketing Manager: Myles McCionnaith
E-mail: myles.mccionnaith@iap.ie
Editor: Lisa Hyde *E-mail:* lisa.hyde@iap.ie
Founded: 1974
Subjects: Architecture & Interior Design, Art,
Biography, Memoirs, Criminology, Drama,
Theater, Education, Genealogy, Government,
Political Science, History, Law, Literature, Lit-
erary Criticism, Essays, Military Science, Mu-
sic, Dance, Religion - Other, Women's Studies,
Social History

ISBN Prefix(es): 978-0-7165
Imprints: IAP; Irish University Press
Distribution Center: Gill Distribution, Hume Ave,
Park West, Dublin D12 YV96 *Tel:* (01) 500
9500 *Web Site:* www.gilldistribution.ie
ALI Agenzia Libraria International srl, Via Scar-
latti, 12, 20090 Trezzano sul Naviglio MI,
Italy *Tel:* (02) 48400501; (02) 48400505; (02)
48400507 *Fax:* (02) 48400512 *E-mail:* alisrl@
tin.it
Orders to: Gill Distribution, Hume Ave, Park
West, Dublin D12 YV96 *Tel:* (01) 500 9500
Web Site: www.gilldistribution.ie

Irish Management Institute+
Sandyford Rd, Dublin 16
Tel: (01) 207 8400 *Fax:* (01) 295 5147
E-mail: info@imi.ie
Web Site: www.imi.ie
Founded: 1952
The Institute is concerned with management, ed-
ucation, training & development. Publishing &
bookselling are complementary activities.
Membership(s): Publishing Ireland.
Subjects: Accounting, Business, Communications,
Economics, Finance, Labor, Industrial Rela-
tions, Management
ISBN Prefix(es): 978-0-903352; 978-0-9500327;
978-1-902664

Irish Texts Society
ITS, Elsemere, Tibradden Rd, Rockbrook, Dublin
16
Web Site: www.irishtextssociety.org
Key Personnel
President: Prof Maire Herbert
Honorary Treasurer: Michael J Burns
E-mail: hon.treasurer@irishtextssociety.org
Founded: 1898
Specialize in educational charity publishing Irish
language texts with translations & a subsidiary
series of supporting commentaries, studies, in-
dexes, etc; organization of annual seminar in
conjunction with the combined departments of
Irish, University College, Cork, Ireland; publi-
cation of catalogue & newsletter.
Subjects: Anthropology, History, Poetry
ISBN Prefix(es): 978-1-870166

Irish University Press, *imprint of* Irish Academic
Press

Irish YouthWork Press
Youth Work Ireland, 20 Dominick St Lower,
Dublin 1
Tel: (01) 8584500 *Fax:* (01) 8724183
E-mail: info@youthworkireland.ie
Web Site: www.youthworkireland.ie
Key Personnel
Chief Executive Officer: Patrick Burke *Tel:* (01)
8584505 *E-mail:* pburke@youthworkireland.ie
Assistant Chief Executive Officer: Paul Gralton
E-mail: pgralton@youthworkireland.ie
Head, Advocacy & Communication: Michael
McLoughlin *E-mail:* mmcloughlin@
youthworkireland.ie
Founded: 1962
Specialize in youth work publications.
Subjects: Child Care & Development, Education,
Social Sciences, Sociology
ISBN Prefix(es): 978-0-9522207; 978-1-900416
Total Titles: 17 Print

Kells Publishing Co Ltd
John St, Kells, Co Meath
Tel: (046) 40117 *Fax:* (046) 41522
Subjects: Fiction, Regional Interests
ISBN Prefix(es): 978-1-872490

Albertine Kennedy Publishing
5 Henrietta St, Dublin 1

Web Site: albertinekennedy.com
Key Personnel
Editor: Tom Kennedy
Subjects: Animals, Pets, Geography, Geology, Re-
gional Interests, Science (General)
ISBN Prefix(es): 978-0-906002

Liberties Press+
140 Terenure Rd North, Terenure, Dublin 6W
Tel: (01) 405 5703
E-mail: info@libertiespress.com; editorial@
libertiespress.com; publicity@libertiespress.
com; rights@libertiespress.com
Web Site: www.libertiespress.com
Key Personnel
Publisher: Sean O'Keeffe
Mng Editor: Daniel Bolger
Rights Assistant: Caelen Dwane
Founded: 2003
Subjects: Biography, Memoirs, Cookery, Fiction,
Film, Video, Government, Political Science,
Health, Nutrition, History, How-to, Literature,
Literary Criticism, Essays, Music, Dance, Non-
fiction (General), Sports, Athletics
ISBN Prefix(es): 978-0-9545335; 978-1-905483
Number of titles published annually: 10 Print
Total Titles: 20 Print
Distributed by Dufour Editions Inc (USA)
Distribution Center: International Publishers Mar-
keting (IPM) (USA)
Turnaround Publisher Services (UK)
Gill Distribution, Hume Ave, Park West, Dublin
D12 YV96 *Tel:* (01) 500 9500 *Web Site:* www.
gilldistribution.ie

The Liffey Press
Raheny Shopping Center, 2nd floor, Raheny,
Dublin 5
Tel: (01) 851 1458
E-mail: theliffeypress@gmail.com; sales@
theliffeypress.com
Web Site: www.theliffeypress.com
Key Personnel
Publisher: David Givens
Founded: 2001
Subjects: Nonfiction (General), Irish Interest
ISBN Prefix(es): 978-1-904148; 978-1-905785;
978-1-908308
Number of titles published annually: 15 Print
Total Titles: 175 Print
Distributed by Dufour Editions (North America)
Distribution Center: Gill Distribution, Hume Ave,
Park West, Dublin D12 YV96 *Tel:* (01) 500
9500 *Web Site:* www.gilldistribution.ie

The Lilliput Press+
62-63 Sitric Rd, Arbour Hill, Dublin 7
Tel: (01) 671 16 47 *Fax:* (01) 671 12 33
E-mail: info@lilliputpress.ie; publicity@
lilliputpress.ie
Web Site: www.lilliputpress.ie
Key Personnel
Publisher: Antony Farrell
Founded: 1984
Membership(s): Publishing Ireland.
Subjects: Architecture & Interior Design, Biogra-
phy, Memoirs, Cookery, Fiction, Government,
Political Science, History, Literature, Literary
Criticism, Essays, Music, Dance, Natural His-
tory, Philosophy, Photography, Poetry, Regional
Interests, Sports, Athletics, Travel & Tourism,
Ecology
ISBN Prefix(es): 978-0-946640; 978-1-874675;
978-1-901866; 978-1-84351
Distribution Center: Gill Distribution, Hume Ave,
Park West, Dublin D12 YV96 *Tel:* (01) 500
9500 *Web Site:* www.gilldistribution.ie

Little Island
7 Kenilworth Park, Dublin 6W
Tel: (01) 2283060
E-mail: info@littleisland.ie

Web Site: www.littleisland.ie
Key Personnel
Publisher & Commissioning Editor: Siobhan
Parkinson
Publishing Manager & Art Dir: Grainne Clear
E-mail: grainne.clear@littleisland.ie
Sales: Conor Hackett; Flynn Hackett
Founded: 2008
ISBN Prefix(es): 978-1-84840; 978-1-908195
Distributed by Trafalgar Square Publishing

Management Briefs Ltd
30 The Palms, Clonskeagh, Dublin 14
Tel: (01) 2788980
E-mail: info@managementbriefs.com
Web Site: www.managementbriefs.com
Key Personnel
Mng Dir: Frank Scott-Lemon
Marketing Executive: Sallyann Hynes
Dir & Design Coordinator: Claire Scott-Lemon
Administration Manager: Deborah Mason
Founded: 2008
Subjects: Management
ISBN Prefix(es): 978-0-9519738; 978-1-906946
Foreign Rep(s): Argosy Books (Ireland); Book-
Masters (USA); Durnell Marketing (Europe);
Easons Wholesale (Ireland); Juta Books (South
Africa)
Distribution Center: Broomfield Book Sales (UK)
Orca Book Distributors (UK)
Gill Distribution, Hume Ave, Park West, Dublin
D12 YV96 *Tel:* (01) 500 9500 *Web Site:* www.
gilldistribution.ie

Marino Books, *imprint of* Mercier Press Ltd

Maverick House Publishers
Dunboyne Business Park, Off 19, Dunboyne, Co
Meath
Tel: (01) 825 5717 *Fax:* (01) 686 5036
E-mail: info@maverickhouse.com; sales@
maverickhouse.com; editorial@maverickhouse.
com; rights@maverickhouse.com; publicity@
maverickhouse.com
Web Site: www.maverickhouse.com
Subjects: Biography, Memoirs, Nonfiction (Gen-
eral), Current Affairs, True Crime
ISBN Prefix(es): 978-0-9542945; 978-1-905379;
978-0-9548707
Branch Office(s)
Maverick House Publishers Asia, Level 43,
United Centre, 323 Silom Rd, Bangrak,
Bangkok 10500, Thailand *Tel:* (02) 231 1590;
(08) 9448 4047 *E-mail:* asia@maverickhouse.
com
Foreign Rep(s): Ashton International Market-
ing Services (Julian Ashton) (Cambodia,
China, Hong Kong, Indonesia, Japan, Myan-
mar, Philippines, South Korea, Taiwan, Viet-
nam); Nationwide Book Distributors Ltd (New
Zealand); Paperclip Pte Ltd (Roger Karl)
(Malaysia, Singapore); Quartet Sales & Mar-
keting (South Africa); Tower Books (Australia);
Turnaround Publisher Services Ltd (UK)
Distribution Center: Gill Distribution, Hume Ave,
Park West, Dublin D12 YV96 *Tel:* (01) 500
9500 *Web Site:* www.gilldistribution.ie

Mentor Books+
Sandyford Industrial Estate, 43 Furze Rd, Dublin
18
Tel: (01) 2952112 *Fax:* (01) 2952114
E-mail: admin@mentorbooks.ie
Web Site: www.mentorbooks.ie
Key Personnel
Mng Dir: Daniel McCarthy
Mng Editor: Treasa O'Mahony
Sales: Daniel Healy
Founded: 1979
Subjects: Criminology, Education, Fiction, Gov-
ernment, Political Science, History, Nonfiction
(General), Photography, Sports, Athletics

ISBN Prefix(es): 978-0-947548; 978-1-84210;
978-1-902586
Total Titles: 329 Print

Mercier, *imprint of* Mercier Press Ltd

Mercier Press Ltd+
Unit 3b, Oak House, Bessboro Rd, Blackrock, Co
Cork
Tel: (021) 4614700 *Fax:* (021) 4614802
E-mail: info@mercierpress.ie
Web Site: www.mercierpress.ie
Key Personnel
Mng Dir: Mary Feehan *E-mail:* publishing@
mercierpress.ie
General Manager: Sharon O'Donovan
E-mail: business@mercierpress.ie
Marketing & Public Relations: Deirdre Roberts
E-mail: deirdre.roberts@mercierpress.ie
Sales Executive: Niamh Hatton *E-mail:* sales@
mercierpress.ie
Founded: 1944
Subjects: Archaeology, Art, Biography, Memoirs,
Business, Cookery, Crafts, Games, Hobbies,
Drama, Theater, Fiction, Government, Politi-
cal Science, Health, Nutrition, History, Humor,
Inspirational, Spirituality, Literature, Literary
Criticism, Essays, Nonfiction (General), Poetry,
Psychology, Psychiatry, Regional Interests, Re-
ligion - Catholic, Self-Help, Women's Studies,
Folklore
ISBN Prefix(es): 978-0-85342; 978-1-85635; 978-
1-86023
Number of titles published annually: 30 Print
Total Titles: 380 Print
Imprints: Anvil Books; The Children's Press;
Marino Books; Mercier
Foreign Rights: Amer-Asia (Asia); Lora Fountain
(France); Agence Hoffman (Germany); Natoli
Stefan Oliva (Italy); Andrew Nurnberg Asso-
ciates (Croatia, Hungary); Julio F Yanez (Latin
America, Spain)
Distribution Center: Gill Distribution, Hume Ave,
Park West, Dublin D12 YV96 *Tel:* (01) 500
9500 *Web Site:* www.gilldistribution.ie
Dufour Editions, PO Box 7, Chester Springs,
PA 19425, United States *E-mail:* info@
dufoureditions.com (USA-Trade)

Messenger Publications+
37 Lower Leeson St, Dublin D02 W938
Tel: (01) 676 7491 *Fax:* (01) 676 7493
E-mail: sales@messenger.ie
Web Site: www.messenger.ie
Key Personnel
Publisher: Cecilia West *Tel:* (01) 775 8577
E-mail: c.west@messenger.ie
Dir: Fr Donal Neary *E-mail:* dneary@messenger.
ie
Commissioning Editor: Fr Paddy Carberry
E-mail: p.carberry@messenger.ie
Founded: 1888
Religious book & magazine publisher. Publishers
of The Father Browne Collection. An Aposto-
late of the Irish Jesuits.
Subjects: Biblical Studies, Inspirational, Spiritual-
ity, Photography, Religion - Catholic, Theology,
Ignatian Spirituality, Jesuit
ISBN Prefix(es): 978-0-901335; 978-1-872245;
978-1-910248
Number of titles published annually: 20 Print
Total Titles: 60 Print
Foreign Rep(s): Dufour Editions (USA)
Distribution Center: Gill Distribution, Hume Ave,
Park West, Dublin D12 YV96 *E-mail:* sales@
gill.ie

Morrigan Book Co+
Gore St, Killala, Co Mayo
Tel: (096) 32555 *Fax:* (096) 32555
E-mail: morriganbooks@gmail.com
Web Site: www.conankennedy.com/MBC.html

Key Personnel
Publisher: Gerald Conan Kennedy
Founded: 1980
Subjects: Archaeology, Fiction, Nonfiction (Gen-
eral), Folklore, Mythology & General Irish In-
terest
ISBN Prefix(es): 978-0-907677

The National Library of Ireland
Kildare St, Dublin 2
Tel: (01) 603 0200 *Fax:* (01) 661 2523
E-mail: info@nli.ie
Web Site: www.nli.ie
Key Personnel
Dir: Dr Sandra Collins *Tel:* (01) 603 0244
E-mail: scollins@nli.ie
Founded: 1877
Subjects: Genealogy, History, Literature, Literary
Criticism, Essays, Photography
ISBN Prefix(es): 978-0-907328; 978-0-9511585

New Island+
16 Priory Off Park, Stillorgan, Co Dublin
Tel: (01) 278 4225
Web Site: www.newisland.ie
Key Personnel
Publisher: Edwin Higel *E-mail:* edwin.higel@
newisland.ie
Editorial Manager: Justin Corfield *E-mail:* justin.
corfield@newisland.ie
Accounts Manager: Aisling Glynn
E-mail: aisling.glynn@newisland.ie
Commissioning Editor: Daniel Bolger
E-mail: dan.bolger@newisland.ie
Sales & Marketing: Hannah Shorten
E-mail: hannah.shorten@newisland.ie
Founded: 1992
Subjects: Biography, Memoirs, Drama, Theater,
English as a Second Language, History, Liter-
ature, Literary Criticism, Essays, Poetry, Ro-
mance
ISBN Prefix(es): 978-1-904301; 978-1-84840
Total Titles: 130 Print
Foreign Rep(s): Dufour Editions (USA); Gill Dis-
tribution (worldwide exc North America); In-
ternational Specialized Book Services (North
America)
Foreign Rights: Maria White (worldwide)
Distribution Center: Gill Distribution, Hume Ave,
Park West, Dublin D12 YV96 *Tel:* (01) 500
9500 *Web Site:* www.gilldistribution.com

NuBooks
Division of Oak Tree Press
33 Rochestown Rise, Rochestown, Cork, Co Cork
T12 EVT0
Tel: (086) 244 1633
E-mail: info@oaktreepress.com
Web Site: oaktreepress.eu
Key Personnel
Mng Dir: Brian O'Kane *E-mail:* brian.okane@
oaktreepress.com
Founded: 2010
Publish short, focused, relevant ebooks for busy
entrepreneurs & managers.
Ebook downloads available at
www.SuccessStore.com.
Membership(s): Publishing Ireland.
Subjects: Accounting, Business, Career Develop-
ment, Economics, Finance, Labor, Industrial
Relations, Law, Management, Marketing
ISBN Prefix(es): 978-1-84621
Number of titles published annually: 10 E-Book
Total Titles: 50 E-Book
Ultimate Parent Company: Cork Publishing Ltd
Distribution Center: Vearsa, National Software
Centre, Mahon, Cork, Co Cork *Tel:* (021) 730
4650 *E-mail:* info@vearsa.com

Oak Tree Press
33 Rochestown Rise, Rochestown, Cork, Co Cork
T12 EVT0

Tel: (086) 2441633 (cell)
E-mail: info@oaktreepress.com
Web Site: oaktreepress.eu; www.successstore.com
(e-commerce)
Key Personnel
Mng Dir: Brian O'Kane *E-mail:* brian.okane@
oaktreepress.com
Founded: 1991
Business book publishers & developers of enter-
prise training & support materials.
Subjects: Accounting, Business, Career Develop-
ment, Economics, Finance, Labor, Industrial
Relations, Law, Management, Marketing
ISBN Prefix(es): 978-1-872853; 978-1-86076;
978-1-904887; 978-1-78119
Number of titles published annually: 14 Print; 10
E-Book
Total Titles: 90 Print; 50 E-Book
Parent Company: Cork Publishing Ltd
Divisions: NuBooks (short, focused ebooks on
business topics)
Distribution Center: Gill Distribution, Hume Ave,
Park West, Dublin D12 YV96, Distribution
Manager: John Manning *Tel:* (01) 500 9500
Web Site: www.gilldistribution.ie

O'Brien Press, *imprint of* The O'Brien Press Ltd

The O'Brien Press Ltd+
12 Terenure Rd East, Rathgar, Dublin 6
Tel: (01) 4923333 *Fax:* (01) 4922777
E-mail: books@obrien.ie; sales@obrien.ie;
rights@obrien.ie; marketing@obrien.ie;
publicity@obrien.ie
Web Site: www.obrien.ie
Key Personnel
Mng Dir: Ivan O'Brien *E-mail:* ivan@obrien.ie
Publisher: Michael O'Brien *E-mail:* michael@
obrien.ie
Founded: 1974
Independent publisher of books for adults & chil-
dren.
Membership(s): Independent Publisher's Guild;
Publishing Ireland.
Subjects: Architecture & Interior Design, Art,
Biography, Memoirs, Business, Cookery, Crim-
inology, Fiction, Government, Political Sci-
ence, History, Humor, Music, Dance, Nonfic-
tion (General), Photography, Self-Help, Sports,
Athletics, Travel & Tourism, Wine & Spirits,
Women's Studies
ISBN Prefix(es): 978-0-86322 (Brandon); 978-0-
905140; 978-0-86278; 978-0-9502046; 978-1-
84717
Number of titles published annually: 40 Print; 30
E-Book
Total Titles: 720 Print; 250 E-Book; 4 Audio
Imprints: Blue Flag; Brandon; Flyers; O'Brien
Press; Pandas; Red Flag; Solos
Foreign Rep(s): Dufour Editions (Canada, USA);
Peter Newsom (Asia, Europe exc Ireland &
UK, Middle East); Turnaround (UK exc Ire-
land)
Foreign Rights: Agenzia Letteraria Internazionale
SRL (Italy); Author Rights Agency (Rus-
sia); L'Autre Agence (France); Big Apple
Agency Inc (China); The English Agency
(Japan) Ltd (Japan); Ersilia Literary Agency
(Greece); Agencja Literacka Graal (Poland);
The Deborah Harris Agency (Israel); Ilus-
trata SL (children's books) (Catalonia, Por-
tugal, South America exc Brazil, Spain); In-
ternational Literatuur Bureau (Netherlands);
Yu Ri Jang Agency (Korea); Kalem Agency
(Turkey); Katai & Bolza (Hungary); Antonia
Kerrigan Literary Agency (general books) (Cat-
alonia, Portugal, South America exc Brazil,
Spain); Simona Kessler International Copy-
right Agency Ltd (Romania); Liepman AG
(Germany); Harold Ober Associates (general) (Canada, USA); Kristin Olson Literary
Agency SRO (Czechia); Rights People (children's books) (Canada, USA); Villas-Boas &

Moss Literary Agency (Brazil); Silke Weniger Literary Agency (Brandon, crime only) (Germany)
Distribution Center: Gill Distribution, Hume Ave, Park West, Dublin D12 YV96 *Tel:* (01) 500 9500 *Web Site:* www.gilldistribution.ie (Ireland & worldwide exc Britain, Canada & USA)
Turnaround Publisher Services, Unit 2/3, Olympia Trading Estate, Coburg Rd, London N22 6TZ, United Kingdom *Tel:* (020) 8829 3000 *Fax:* (020) 8881 5088 *Web Site:* www. turnaround-uk.com (Britain, Brandon titles only)
Dufour Editions, PO Box 7, Chester Springs, PA 19425-0007, United States, Contact: Christopher May *Tel:* 610-458-5005 *Fax:* 610-458-7103 *E-mail:* info@dufoureditions.com *Web Site:* www.dufoureditions.com (USA & Canada)
Orders to: Gill Distribution, Hume Ave, Park West, Dublin D12 YV96 *Tel:* (01) 500 9500 *Web Site:* www.gilldistribution.ie (Ireland & worldwide exc Britain, Canada & USA)

Onstream Publications Ltd+
Cloghroe, Blarney, Co Cork
Tel: (021) 4385798
E-mail: info@onstream.ie
Web Site: www.onstream.ie
Key Personnel
Mng Dir & Editor: Roz Crowley
Founded: 1992
Subjects: Agriculture, Behavioral Sciences, Biography, Memoirs, Cookery, Developing Countries, Health, Nutrition, History, How-to, Medicine, Nursing, Dentistry, Nonfiction (General), Travel & Tourism, Wine & Spirits
ISBN Prefix(es): 978-1-897685; 978-0-9510018
Number of titles published annually: 3 Print
Total Titles: 13 Print

Open Air, *imprint of* Four Courts Press Ltd

Orpen Press
Lonsdale House, Avoca Ave, Blackrock, Co Dublin
Tel: (01) 278 5090
E-mail: info@orpenpress.com
Web Site: www.orpenpress.com
Subjects: Health, Nutrition, Sports, Athletics, Culture, Current Affairs, Personal Development
ISBN Prefix(es): 978-1-871305
Associate Companies: Blackhall Publishing
Distribution Center: Gill Distribution, Hume Ave, Park West, Dublin D12 YV96 *Tel:* (01) 500 9500 *Web Site:* www.gilldistribution.ie

Pandas, *imprint of* The O'Brien Press Ltd

Penguin Random House Ireland
Morrison Chambers, Suites 47-51, 32 Nassau St, Dublin D02 YH68
Tel: (01) 5314150 *Fax:* (01) 5314150
E-mail: info@penguin.ie
Web Site: www.penguin.ie
Key Personnel
Publicity Dir: Cliona Lewis *E-mail:* clewis@penguinrandomhouse.ie
Publicity & Editorial Officer: Patricia McVeigh *E-mail:* pmcveigh@penguinrandomhouse.ie
Subjects: Fiction, Nonfiction (General)
ISBN Prefix(es): 978-1-84488

Poolbeg Press Ltd+
123 Grange Hill, Baldoyle Industrial Estate, Baldoyle, Dublin 13
Tel: (01) 832 1477
E-mail: info@poolbeg.com
Web Site: www.poolbeg.com

Key Personnel
Publishing Dir & Marketing Manager: Paula Campbell
Founded: 1976
Subjects: Cookery, Fiction, Gardening, Plants, History, Nonfiction (General)
ISBN Prefix(es): 978-1-85371; 978-0-905169; 978-1-84223; 978-0-907085
Imprints: Children's Poolbeg

Prim-Ed Publishing Ltd
Bosheen, New Ross, Co Wexford
Tel: (01890) 92 99 59; (051) 440075
E-mail: sales@prim-ed.com
Web Site: www.prim-ed.com
Founded: 1996
Publisher & supplier of educational & teacher resources for use in primary & secondary schools.
Subjects: Education, Geography, Geology, History, Language Arts, Linguistics, Mathematics, Religion - Other, Science (General), English, Grammar, Writing
ISBN Prefix(es): 978-1-86400; 978-1-920962; 978-1-84654
Total Titles: 850 Print

Prism, *imprint of* Royal Irish Academy

RDS Library, see Royal Dublin Society (RDS)

Real Ireland Design-Picture Press Ltd
Picture House, 16/17 Bullford Business Park, Kilcoole, Co Wicklow
Tel: (01) 2812422 *Fax:* (01) 2812466
E-mail: info@realireland.ie; info@picturepress.ie
Web Site: www.realireland.ie; www.picturepress.ie
Founded: 1979
Subjects: Photography, Travel & Tourism, Calendars
ISBN Prefix(es): 978-0-946887

Red Flag, *imprint of* The O'Brien Press Ltd

Relay Books
Tyone, Nenagh, Co Tipperary
Tel: (067) 31734 *Fax:* (067) 31734
E-mail: relaybooks@eircom.net
Key Personnel
Founder, Dir & Editor: Donal A Murphy
Founder: Nancy Murphy *E-mail:* nancy@tipperarynorthlocalhistory.com
Founded: 1980
Membership(s): Publishing Ireland.
Subjects: History, Regional Interests
ISBN Prefix(es): 978-0-946327
Distributed by Seeves (USA)

Roads Publishing
19-22 Dame St, Dublin 2
Tel: (01) 675 5278
E-mail: publishing@roads.co
Web Site: roads.co/books
Key Personnel
Owner: Danielle Ryan
Sales: Sophie Smyth *E-mail:* sophie.smyth@roads.co
Subjects: Art, Photography, Culture
ISBN Prefix(es): 978-1-909399
Foreign Rep(s): ACC (USA); Roundhouse Group (UK)
Distribution Center: Gill Distribution, Hume Ave, Park West, Dublin D12 YV96 *Tel:* (01) 500 9500 *Web Site:* www.gilldistribution.ie

Round Hall+
43 Fitzwilliam Pl, Dublin 2
Tel: (01) 662 5301 *Fax:* (01) 662 5302
E-mail: info@roundhall.ie
Web Site: www.roundhall.ie

Key Personnel
Dir: C Dolan
Editorial Manager: Martin McCann
 E-mail: martin.mccann@thomsonreuters.com
Marketing Manager: Maura Smyth
 E-mail: maura.smyth@thomsonreuters.com
Production Manager: Terri McDonnell
 E-mail: terri.mcdonnell@thomsonreuters.com
Direct Sales: Pauline Ward *E-mail:* pauline.ward@thomsonreuters.com
Founded: 1980
Subjects: Criminology, Finance, Labor, Industrial Relations, Law
ISBN Prefix(es): 978-0-947686; 978-1-899738; 978-0-9508725; 978-1-85800
Total Titles: 200 Print
Parent Company: The Thomson Corp

Royal Dublin Society (RDS)
Anglesa Rd, Ballsbridge, Dublin 4
Tel: (01) 668 0866 *Fax:* (01) 660 4014
E-mail: info@rds.ie; sales@rds.ie
Web Site: www.rds.ie
Key Personnel
Chief Executive: Michael Duffy
Commercial Dir: Michele Griffin *Tel:* (01) 240 7223
Foundation Dir: Joanna Quinn *Tel:* (01) 240 7299 *Fax:* (01) 240 7293 *E-mail:* members@rds.ie
Foundation & Membership Development Manager: Dr Claire Mulhall *Tel:* (01) 240 7217 *E-mail:* claire.mulhall@rds.ie
Founded: 1731
Subjects: Biological Sciences, Geography, Geology, Physical Sciences, Science (General)
ISBN Prefix(es): 978-0-86027

Royal Irish Academy
19 Dawson St, Dublin 2
Tel: (01) 6762570 *Fax:* (01) 6762346
E-mail: publications@ria.ie
Web Site: www.ria.ie
Key Personnel
Administrator: Dr Valeria Cavalli *Tel:* (01) 6090650 *E-mail:* v.cavalli@ria.ie
Mng Editor: Ruth Hegarty *E-mail:* r.hegarty@ria.ie
Senior Editor: Helena King *Tel:* (01) 6090638 *E-mail:* h.king@ria.ie
Senior Publications Assistant: Trevor Mullins *E-mail:* t.mullins@ria.ie
Assistant Editor: Jonathan Dykes *E-mail:* j.dykes@ria.ie
Founded: 1785 (academic publisher since 1787)
Academy for the sciences, humanities & social sciences for Ireland, which promotes excellence in scholarship, recognizes achievements in learning, directs research programs & undertakes research projects, particularly in areas relating to Ireland & its heritage.
Subjects: Archaeology, Art, Astronomy, Biological Sciences, Chemistry, Chemical Engineering, Earth Sciences, Education, Environmental Studies, Ethnicity, Geography, Geology, Government, Political Science, History, Language Arts, Linguistics, Literature, Literary Criticism, Essays, Mathematics, Physical Sciences, Physics, Science (General), Social Sciences, Sociology, Humanities
ISBN Prefix(es): 978-0-901714; 978-1-874045; 978-0-9543855; 978-1-904890
Number of titles published annually: 6 Print; 3 Online
Total Titles: 200 Print; 3 Online
Imprints: Prism
Distributor for Environmental Institute; University College Dublin
Foreign Rep(s): ISBS (North America)

Salmon Poetry+
Knockeven, Cliffs of Moher, Co Clare
Tel: (065) 7081941 *Fax:* (065) 7081941

E-mail: info@salmonpoetry.com; bookshop@
    salmonpoetry.com
Web Site: www.salmonpoetry.com
Key Personnel
Editor: Jessie Lendennie *E-mail:* jessie@
    salmonpoetry.com
Founded: 1981
Subjects: Poetry
ISBN Prefix(es): 978-1-897648; 978-0-948339;
    978-1-903392
U.S. Office(s): Dufour Editions Inc, PO Box
    7, Chester Springs, PA 19425, United States
    Fax: 610-458-7103
Foreign Rep(s): Inpress (Australia, Europe, UK)
Distribution Center: Irish Book Distribution, c/o
    Argosy Books, Unit 12, North Park, North Rd,
    Finglas, Dublin 11 *Tel:* (01) 8239500 *Fax:* (01)
    8239599
Central Books Ltd, One Heath Park Indus-
    trial Estate, Freshwater Rd, Dagenham RM8
    1RX, United Kingdom *Tel:* (020) 8525 8800
    Fax: (020) 8599 2694 *E-mail:* orders@
    centralbooks.com *Web Site:* www.centralbooks.
    com

Solos, *imprint of* The O'Brien Press Ltd

Stationery Office Dublin
Division of Government Supplies Agency
52 St Stephen's Green, Dublin 2
Tel: (01) 6476843 *Fax:* (01) 6476843
E-mail: info@opw.ie; publications@opw.ie
Web Site: www.opw.ie
Founded: 1922
Heritage books, Irish language books, government
    reports, daily & senate debates.
Subjects: Government, Political Science
ISBN Prefix(es): 978-0-7076; 978-0-7557
Ultimate Parent Company: Office of Public
    Works
Bookshop(s): Government Publications Sales
    Office, Sun Alliance House, Molesworth St,
    Dublin 2
Warehouse: Mount Shannon Rd, Rialto, Dublin 8

Stinging Fly Press
PO Box 6016, Dublin 1
E-mail: stingingfly@gmail.com
Web Site: www.stingingfly.org
Key Personnel
Publisher & Founding Editor: Declan Meade
Editor: Thomas Morris
Poetry Editor: Eabhan Ni Shuileabhain
Founded: 2005
Subjects: Fiction, Irish Literary Fiction
ISBN Prefix(es): 978-0-9550152; 978-1-906539

Tir Eolas (Knowledge of the Land)
Newtownlynch, Doorus, Kinvara, Co Galway
Tel: (091) 637452 *Fax:* (091) 637452
E-mail: info@tireolas.com
Web Site: www.tireolas.com
Key Personnel
Dir: Anne Korff
Founded: 1985
Membership(s): Publishing Ireland.
Subjects: Anthropology, Archaeology, Biography,
    Memoirs, Environmental Studies, History, Nat-
    ural History, Outdoor Recreation
ISBN Prefix(es): 978-1-873821
Total Titles: 14 Print
Distributed by Colin Smythe Ltd (England)

Transport Infrastructure Ireland
Parkgate Business Centre, Parkgate St, Dublin 8
Tel: (01) 6463600
E-mail: infopubs@tii.ie
Web Site: www.tiipublications.ie
Founded: 2015
Standards & technical publications related to na-
    tional road & light rail networks in Ireland.

Subjects: Transportation
ISBN Prefix(es): 978-0-9932315

University College Dublin Press
Newman House, 86 St Stephen's Green, Dublin 2
Tel: (01) 477 9812 *Fax:* (01) 477 9821
E-mail: ucdpress@ucd.ie
Web Site: www.ucdpress.ie
Key Personnel
Executive Editor: Barbara Mennell
    E-mail: barbara.mennell@ucd.ie
Founded: 1995
Academic publisher.
Subjects: Environmental Studies, Government,
    Political Science, History, Language Arts, Lin-
    guistics, Literature, Literary Criticism, Essays,
    Music, Dance, Science (General), Social Sci-
    ences, Sociology, Diaries, Letters
ISBN Prefix(es): 978-1-900621; 978-1-904558;
    978-1-906359
Number of titles published annually: 25 Print
Total Titles: 210 Print
Distributed by Dufour Editions (North America)
Foreign Rep(s): Eleanor Brasch Enterprises (Aus-
    tralia, New Zealand); Dufour Edtions (North
    America); Iberian Book Services (Portugal,
    Spain); SHS Publishers' Consultants & Repre-
    sentatives (Austria, Germany, Switzerland); Van
    de Bilt Sales & Marketing (Belgium, Luxem-
    bourg, Netherlands, UK)
Distribution Center: Irish Book Distribution, Unit
    12 North Park, North Rd, Finglas, Dublin
    11 *Tel:* (01) 8239580 *Fax:* (01) 8239599
    E-mail: sales@irishbookdistribution.ie
Central Books Ltd, One Heath Park Indus-
    trial Estate, Freshwater Rd, Dagenham RM8
    1RX, United Kingdom *Tel:* (020) 8525 8800
    Fax: (020) 8599 2694 *E-mail:* orders@
    centralbooks.com *Web Site:* www.centralbooks.
    com

Veritas Co Ltd+
Veritas House, 7-8 Lower Abbey St, Dublin 1
Tel: (01) 878 8177 *Fax:* (01) 878 6507; (01) 874
    4913
E-mail: sales@veritas.ie; veritas2@veritas.ie
Web Site: www.veritasbooksonline.com
Key Personnel
Dir: Aidan Chester
Mng Editor: Daragh Reddin *E-mail:* daragh.
    reddin@veritas.ie
Editor: Brendan O'Reilly
Commissioning Editor: Donna Doherty
    E-mail: donna.doherty@veritas.ie
Founded: 1969
Veritas Publications is the publishing division of
    the Catholic Communications Institute of Ire-
    land Inc.
Subjects: Biblical Studies, Biography, Memoirs,
    Child Care & Development, Developing Coun-
    tries, Disability, Special Needs, Education, En-
    vironmental Studies, Inspirational, Spiritual-
    ity, Nonfiction (General), Philosophy, Religion
    - Catholic, Religion - Protestant, Religion -
    Other, Theology, Catechetical, Parenting
ISBN Prefix(es): 978-0-905092; 978-0-86217;
    978-0-901810; 978-1-85390; 978-1-84730
Number of titles published annually: 40 Print; 1
    CD-ROM; 2 Audio
Parent Company: The Catholic Communications
    Institute of Ireland
Imprints: Veritas Publications
Branch Office(s)
Blanchardstown Centre, Unit 309,
    Dublin 15, Manager: Jeff Stills
    Tel: (01) 886 4030 *Fax:* (01) 886 4031
    E-mail: blanchardstownshop@veritas.ie
Carey's Lane, Cork T12 AW26, Manager: Vicky
    Leng *Tel:* (021) 425 1255 *Fax:* (021) 427 9165
    E-mail: corkshop@veritas.ie
20 Shipquay St, Derry BT48 6DW, Manager:
    Lucy Gillespie *Tel:* (028) 7126 6888 *Fax:* (028)
    7136 5120 *E-mail:* derryshop@veritas.ie

83 O'Connell St, Ennis, Co Clare V95 KD34,
    Manager: Geraldine Considine *Tel:* (065) 682
    8696 *Fax:* (065) 682 0176 *E-mail:* ennisshop@
    veritas.ie
13 Lower Main St, Letterkenny, Co Done-
    gal F92 N4C8, Manager: Sheila McMacken
    Tel: (074) 912 4814 *Fax:* (074) 912 2716
    E-mail: letterkennyshop@veritas.ie
16-18 Park St, Monaghan, Manager: Mary Kelly
    Flynn *Tel:* (047) 84077 *Fax:* (047) 84019
    E-mail: monaghanshop@veritas.ie
Sallins Rd, Naas, Co Kildare W91 E3YN,
    Manager: Helen Murray *Tel:* (045) 856 882
    Fax: (045) 856 871 *E-mail:* naasshop@veritas.
    ie
40-41 The Mall, Newry, Co Down BT34 1AN,
    Manager: Eugene McAlinden *Tel:* (028)
    30250321 *E-mail:* newryshop@veritas.ie
Adelaide St, Sligo F91 AP28, Manager: Ann
    O'Neill *Tel:* (071) 916 1800 *Fax:* (071) 916
    0121 *E-mail:* sligoshop@veritas.ie
13 Rue Du Bourg, 65100 Lourdes, France,
    Manager: David Mann *Tel:* (0562) 422 794
    E-mail: lourdesshop@veritas.ie
Distributed by Dufour Editions Inc (USA); John
    Garratt Publishers (Australia); Ignatius Press
    (USA)
Distributor for Abbey Press; Abingdon Press;
    ACTA; Augsburg Press; Ave Maria Press;
    Bantam Press; Baronius Press; Candle Books;
    Catholic Word; Catholic Truth Society; Cross-
    road Publishing; Darton, Longman & Todd;
    Doubleday; Eerdman; HarperCollins; Harper-
    One (USA); Ignatius Press; Liturgy Training
    Publications; Orbis Books; Our Sunday Visi-
    tor; Oxford University Press; Piatkus; Sheldon
    Press; SPCK
Foreign Rep(s): Tony Biviano (Australia); Ann
    O'Neill (UK)
Warehouse: 14 Rosemount Business Park, Bal-
    lycoolin, Dublin 11, Manager: Stephen Kear-
    ney *Tel:* (0926) 451 730 *Fax:* (0926) 451 733
    E-mail: warehouse@veritas.ie (Ireland & UK)

Veritas Publications, *imprint of* Veritas Co Ltd

Weir's Guides, *imprint of* Ballinakella Press

Wolfhound Press Ltd+
18 Fitzwilliam Pl, Dublin 2
Founded: 1974
Membership(s): Irish Publishers Association.
Subjects: Biography, Memoirs, Fiction, Photogra-
    phy
ISBN Prefix(es): 978-0-9503454; 978-0-905473;
    978-0-86327
Total Titles: 300 Print
Associate Companies: Wolfhound Music
Distribution Center: Gill Distribution, Hume Ave,
    Park West, Dublin D12 YV96 *Tel:* (01) 500
    9500 *Web Site:* www.gilldistribution.ie

The Woodfield Press+
17 Jamestown Sq, Dublin DO8 KN24
Tel: (01) 454 7991
E-mail: woodfield-press@mail.com
Web Site: www.woodfield-press.com
Key Personnel
Founder & Publisher: Terri McDonnell
Founded: 1995
Subjects: Biography, Memoirs, History, Women's
    Studies, Local History
ISBN Prefix(es): 978-0-9528453; 978-0-9534293;
    978-1-905094
Number of titles published annually: 2 Print
Total Titles: 22 Print

Israel

General Information

Capital: Jerusalem
Language: Hebrew and Arabic (English and German widely known)
Religion: Predominantly Jewish (about 82%) and Muslim (about 14%)
Population: 4.7 million
Bank Hours: 0830-1230 Sunday-Thursday; also 1600-1700 Sunday-Tuesday & Thursday
Shop Hours: Usually Sunday 0900-1300, 1600-1800; weekdays 0900-1300, 1600-1900; many close Friday afternoon
Currency: 100 agorot = 1 new sheqel
Export/Import Information: Books (except for children's picture books) and advertising duty-free. 17% VAT on books. No import license required for books but must apply for importing number; exchange granted automatically. Import restrictions on Hebrew books.
Copyright: UCC, Berne, Florence (see Copyright Conventions, pg viii)

Academy of the Hebrew Language
Giv'at Ram Campus, 9190401 Jerusalem
Tel: (02) 6493555 *Fax:* (02) 5617065
Web Site: hebrew-academy.org.il
Key Personnel
President: Prof Moshe Bar-Asher
Publishing Coordinator: Liza Mohar
  E-mail: lizamohar@hebrew-academy.org.il
Founded: 1953
Specialize in research & development of the Hebrew language.
This publisher has indicated that 100% of their product line is author subsidized.
Subjects: Language Arts, Linguistics, Hebrew Language & Linguistics
ISBN Prefix(es): 978-965-481
Number of titles published annually: 12 Print

Ach Publishing House Ltd+
PO Box 170, 27001 Kiryat Bialik
Tel: (04) 8727227; (04) 8722096 *Fax:* (04) 8417839
E-mail: ach@netvision.net.il
Web Site: www.achbooks.co.il
Founded: 1967
Subjects: Art, Behavioral Sciences, Child Care & Development, Criminology, Education, Health, Nutrition, Psychology, Psychiatry, Social Sciences, Sociology, Early Childhood, Parenthood
ISBN Prefix(es): 978-965-267

Achiasaf Publishing House Ltd
PO Box 8414, 42504 Netanya
Tel: (09) 8851390 *Fax:* (09) 8851391
E-mail: info@achiasaf.co.il
Web Site: www.achiasaf.co.il
Key Personnel
Mng Dir: Matan Achiasaf; Shiri Achiasaf
Founded: 1937
Subjects: Crafts, Games, Hobbies, Fiction, History, Nonfiction (General), Science (General)

Am Oved Publishers Ltd (Working Nation Publishers Ltd)
22 Mazeh St, 65213 Tel Aviv
Mailing Address: PO Box 470, 61003 Tel Aviv
Tel: (03) 6288524 *Fax:* (03) 6298911
E-mail: info@am-oved.co.il
Web Site: www.am-oved.co.il
Key Personnel
Mng Dir: Hanital Swisa *E-mail:* hanital@am-oved.co.il
Marketing Manager: Iris Ben-Haim *E-mail:* iris@am-oved.co.il
Publicity Manager: Irit Elkabetz *E-mail:* irit@am-oved.co.il

Editorial Coordinator: Batia Mishor
  E-mail: batia@am-oved.co.il
Founded: 1942
Subjects: Biography, Memoirs, Fiction, History, Philosophy, Poetry, Psychology, Psychiatry, Science Fiction, Fantasy, Social Sciences, Sociology
ISBN Prefix(es): 978-965-13
Orders to: Distributor's Centre for Israeli Books Ltd, 22 Nachmani St, PO Box 2811, Tel Aviv

Amichai Publishing House Ltd
19 Yad Harotzim St, 42505 Netanyah
Mailing Address: PO Box 8448, 42505 Netanyah
Tel: (09) 8859099 *Fax:* (09) 8853464
E-mail: ami1000@bezeqint.net
Key Personnel
Chief Executive Officer: Dr Itzhak Oron
Founded: 1948
Subjects: Fiction, Language Arts, Linguistics, Science (General)

Astrolog Publishing House+
PO Box 1123, 45111 Hod-Hasharon
Tel: (09) 9 19 09 57 *Fax:* (09) 9 19 09 58
Founded: 1994
A general publisher in the Hebrew language, New Age & alternative medicine in English & other languages. Also specializing in mysticism, prediction of the future, awareness & various religions.
Membership(s): The Book Publishers' Association of Israel.
Subjects: Astrology, Occult, Nonfiction (General), Religion - Other, Alternative Medicine, New Age
ISBN Prefix(es): 978-965-494
Number of titles published annually: 260 Print
Total Titles: 600 Print
Distributed by Independent Publishers Group (IPG) (United States)

Bar-Ilan University Press
Bar-Ilan University, 52900 Ramat Gan
Tel: (03) 5318575 *Fax:* (03) 7384064
E-mail: press@mail.biu.ac.il; info.press@mail.biu.ac.il
Web Site: www.biupress.co.il
Key Personnel
Dir: Margalit Avisar
Chairman, Book Committee: Prof Yossi Katz
Founded: 1966
Membership(s): The Book Publishers' Association of Israel.
Subjects: Archaeology, Art, Behavioral Sciences, Biblical Studies, Economics, Education, Geography, Geology, Government, Political Science, History, Language Arts, Linguistics, Law, Literature, Literary Criticism, Essays, Music, Dance, Philosophy, Psychology, Psychiatry, Religion - Jewish, Social Sciences, Sociology
ISBN Prefix(es): 978-965-226
Number of titles published annually: 25 Print
Total Titles: 700 Print

Beit Hatfutsot
PO Box 39359, 61392 Tel Aviv
Tel: (03) 6408000; (03) 7457800 *Fax:* (03) 6405727
Web Site: www.bh.org.il
Key Personnel
Dir, Public Relations & Publications: Asia Reuben *Tel:* (03) 7457883 *E-mail:* asia@bh.org.il
Marketing Dir: Moria Zelltser Volstin *Tel:* (03) 7457870 *E-mail:* moriav@bh.org.il
Founded: 1978
Subjects: Genealogy, History, Inspirational, Spirituality, Religion - Jewish
ISBN Prefix(es): 978-965-425

Ben-Zvi Institute+
12 Abarbanel St, 91076 Jerusalem
Mailing Address: PO Box 7660, 91076 Jerusalem
Tel: (02) 539 8888; (02) 539 8844 *Fax:* (02) 563 8310; (02) 561 2329
E-mail: bzi@ybz.org.il; mbz@ybz.org.il
Web Site: www.ybz.org.il
Key Personnel
Head: Prof Yom Tov
Deputy Head: Dr Menash Anzi
  E-mail: menashe@ybz.org.il
Academic Secretary: Michael Glatzer
Founded: 1947
Specialize in Sephardi & Eastern Jewry.
Subjects: Economics, Ethnicity, Foreign Countries, History, Language Arts, Linguistics, Literature, Literary Criticism, Essays, Poetry, Regional Interests, Religion - Jewish
ISBN Prefix(es): 978-965-235
Total Titles: 150 Print
Parent Company: Yad Izhak Ben-Zvi & The Hebrew University of Jerusalem

Bezalel Academy of Art & Design
Mount Scopus, PO Box 24046, 91240 Jerusalem
Tel: (02) 5893333 *Fax:* (02) 5823094
E-mail: mail@bezalel.ac.il
Web Site: www.bezalel.ac.il
Key Personnel
President: Prof Eva Illouz
Founded: 1906
Subjects: Architecture & Interior Design, Art, Photography
ISBN Prefix(es): 978-965-324

The Bialik Institute+
PO Box 53290, 91531 Jerusalem
Tel: (02) 6797942; (02) 6783554 *Fax:* (02) 6783706
E-mail: bialik@actcom.co.il; sales@bialik-publishing.co.il
Web Site: www.bialik-publishing.com
Key Personnel
Mng Dir: Amos Yovel
Founded: 1935
Subjects: Archaeology, Art, Biblical Studies, Economics, History, Law, Literature, Literary Criticism, Essays, Medicine, Nursing, Dentistry, Music, Dance, Philosophy, Poetry, Psychology, Psychiatry, Religion - Jewish, Social Sciences, Sociology, Gender Studies, Holocaust, Judaism
ISBN Prefix(es): 978-965-481; 978-965-342
Number of titles published annually: 46 Print
Distributor for Ben Gurion University of the Neger Press; Moreshet (Holocaust publications); The Zionist Library

Books in the Attic+
5 Emden St, 62741 Tel Aviv
Tel: (03) 6029010 *Fax:* (03) 6040013
E-mail: info@booksintheattic.co.il
Web Site: www.booksintheattic.co.il
Key Personnel
Owner & Editor-in-Chief: Dr Yehuda Melzer
  E-mail: yuda@actcom.co.il
Editor: Hanan Elstein *E-mail:* hanan@booksintheattic.co.il
Public Relations: Shirley Itzhaki *Tel:* (054) 7206348 (cell) *E-mail:* sir@actcom.co.il
Founded: 1988
Subjects: Biography, Memoirs, Biological Sciences, Business, Economics, Fiction, Health, Nutrition, History, Mathematics, Medicine, Nursing, Dentistry, Nonfiction (General), Philosophy, Poetry, Psychology, Psychiatry, Religion - Jewish, Science (General), Sports, Athletics
ISBN Prefix(es): 978-965-419

Breslov Research Institute+
PO Box 5370, 91053 Jerusalem
Tel: (02) 582-4641 *Fax:* (02) 582-5542
E-mail: sales@breslov.org

Web Site: www.breslov.org
Key Personnel
Executive Dir: Rabbi Chaim Kramer
  E-mail: chaimk@breslov.org
Founded: 1979
Specialize in writings in English, French, Spanish, Russian & Hebrew.
This publisher has indicated that 100% of their product line is author subsidized.
Subjects: Biblical Studies, Biography, Memoirs, Education, Health, Nutrition, History, Literature, Literary Criticism, Essays, Nonfiction (General), Philosophy, Psychology, Psychiatry, Religion - Jewish, Self-Help, Theology
ISBN Prefix(es): 978-0-930213; 978-1-928822; 978-1-944731
Number of titles published annually: 5 Print
Total Titles: 158 Print
U.S. Office(s): 44 St Nicholas Ave, Lakewood, NJ 08701, United States, Administration: Mr Yossi Katz *Tel:* 732-534-7263 *Fax:* 732-608-8461 *E-mail:* yossik@breslov.org
Distributed by Feldheim Publishers
Showroom(s): 44 St Nicholas Ave, Lakewood, NJ 08701, United States, Administration: Mr Yossi Katz *Tel:* 732-534-7263 *E-mail:* yossik@breslov.org
Distribution Center: Feldheim Publishers, 208 Airport Executive Park, Nanuet, NY 10954, United States, Contact: Moe Grossman *Tel:* 845-356-2282 *E-mail:* moshe@feldheim.com *Web Site:* www.feldheim.com
Orders to: 44 St Nicholas Ave, Lakewood, NJ 08701, United States, Administration: Mr Yossi Katz *Tel:* 732-534-7263 *E-mail:* yossik@breslov.org

Carta, The Israel Map & Publishing Co Ltd+
18 Ha'uman St, 91024 Jerusalem
Mailing Address: PO Box 2500, 91024 Jerusalem
Tel: (02) 678 3355 *Fax:* (02) 678 2373
E-mail: carta@carta.co.il
Web Site: www.holyland-jerusalem.com
Key Personnel
Chairman: Emanuel Hausman
President & Chief Executive Officer: Shay Hausman
Editorial: Barbara Ball *E-mail:* barbara.ball@carta.co.il; Pirchia Cohen; Lorraine Kessel
Founded: 1958
Cartographic & foreign language publisher - English, German, Russian & Hebrew.
Subjects: Archaeology, Education, Health, Nutrition, History
ISBN Prefix(es): 978-965-220
Number of titles published annually: 30 Print; 1 CD-ROM
Total Titles: 300 Print; 3 CD-ROM
Imprints: Nitzanim
Subsidiaries: Cana Publishing House; W Van Leer Publishing Ltd
Warehouse: Lonnie Kahn Ltd, 20, Eliahu Eitan, 58851 Rishon Le Zion, Contact: Aaron Segal *Tel:* (03) 9520158; (03) 9518408 *Fax:* (03) 9520251; (03) 9518415; (03) 9518416
Orders to: Eisenbrauns Inc, PO Box 275, Winona Lake, IN 46590-0275, United States *Tel:* 574-269-2011 *E-mail:* orders@eisenbrauns.com *Web Site:* www.eisenbrauns.com (Canada & USA)

Center for Research & Study of Sephardi & Oriental Jewish Heritage, see Misgav Yerushalayim

The Centre for Educational Technology (CET)
16 Klausner St, 61394 Tel Aviv
Mailing Address: PO Box 39513, 61394 Tel Aviv
Tel: (03) 6460160 *Fax:* (03) 6422679
Web Site: www.cet.ac.il; www.cet.org.il
Key Personnel
Chief Executive Officer: Ms Gila Ben Har

Founded: 1971
Subjects: History, Mathematics, Science (General), Technology
ISBN Prefix(es): 978-965-354

CET, see The Centre for Educational Technology (CET)

Classikaletet+
34 Ha'hofer St, 58858 Holon
Tel: (03) 5582080
Key Personnel
Owner: Mark Amos
Head, Content: Motti Aviram
Founded: 1987
Subjects: Child Care & Development, Cookery, House & Home, How-to, Humor, Music, Dance, Nonfiction (General), Psychology, Psychiatry, Travel & Tourism
ISBN Prefix(es): 978-965-01; 978-965-286; 978-965-03; 978-965-509; 978-965-517

DAT Publications
PO Box 27019, 6127001 Jaffa
Tel: (03) 5071239 *Fax:* (03) 5070458
E-mail: dat@y-dat.co.il
Web Site: www.y-dat.co.il
Key Personnel
Publisher & General Dir: Yigal Miller
Vice President: Nizah Miller *Tel:* (03) 5072149
  E-mail: nizahmiller@gmail.com
Founded: 1969
Publishers of fiction & nonfiction in Hebrew & English. Occasionally publish some gift titles & music CDs performed by Rivka Zohar. Publisher & international literary agent of Shlomo Kalo's works (sold in 17 countries).
Privately owned.
Subjects: Biography, Memoirs, Fiction, History, Humor, Literature, Literary Criticism, Essays, Mysteries, Suspense, Nonfiction (General), Philosophy, Poetry, Religion - Other, Self-Help
ISBN Prefix(es): 978-965-7028
Total Titles: 77 Print; 3 CD-ROM; 8 E-Book
Showroom(s): 22 Dov mi-Mezerich, 6804542 Tel Aviv (contact prior to visiting)
Warehouse: 22 Dov mi-Mezerich, 6804542 Tel Aviv (contact prior to visiting)

Dekel Academic Press, *imprint of* Dekel Publishing House

Dekel Publishing House+
PO Box 45094, 6145002 Tel Aviv
Tel: (03) 5063235 *Fax:* (03) 5067332
E-mail: dekelpbl@netvision.net.il
Web Site: www.dekelpublishing.com
Key Personnel
President: Ms Dusia Morik
Mng Dir: Mr Zvi Morik *Fax:* (03) 6044627
  E-mail: zvimor@dekelpublishing.com
Founded: 1975
Membership(s): IBPA, the Independent Book Publishers Association.
Subjects: Animals, Pets, Archaeology, Art, Biography, Memoirs, Child Care & Development, Cookery, Crafts, Games, Hobbies, Drama, Theater, Education, Energy, English as a Second Language, Fiction, History, How-to, Literature, Literary Criticism, Essays, Mathematics, Medicine, Nursing, Dentistry, Military Science, Mysteries, Suspense, Nonfiction (General), Physics, Poetry, Romance, Securities, Self-Help, Sports, Athletics, Technology, Travel & Tourism, Krav Maga Self-Defense
ISBN Prefix(es): 978-965-7178
Imprints: Dekel Academic Press; Duvdevan; Tamai Books
Distributed by Frog Co Ltd; North Atlantic Books

Distribution Center: Gazelle Book Services Ltd, White Cross Mills, Hightown, Lancaster, Lancs LA1 4XS, United Kingdom *E-mail:* sales@gazellebookservices.co.uk

Doko Media Ltd
10 Ha'Amal St, 60371 Or Yehuda
Mailing Address: PO Box 611, 60371 Or Yehuda
Tel: (03) 634-4776 *Toll Free Tel:* 888-470-6739 (USA only) *Fax:* (03) 634-4690
E-mail: bible@biblelandshop.net; dokosite@yahoo.com (customer service); info@dokomedia.com
Web Site: www.dokomedia.com
Key Personnel
Mng Dir: Reuven Dorot
Sales & Operations Dir: Avi Mohalem
Founded: 1980
Subjects: Music, Dance, Religion - Other
ISBN Prefix(es): 978-965-478

Domino, *imprint of* Keter Books

Duvdevan, *imprint of* Dekel Publishing House

Encyclopaedia Judaica, *imprint of* Keter Books

Eretz Hemdah Institute for Advanced Jewish Studies
2 Bruriya St, Corner of Rav Chiya St, 91080 Jerusalem
Mailing Address: PO Box 8178, 91080 Jerusalem
Tel: (02) 537-1485 *Fax:* (02) 537-9626
E-mail: info@eretzhemdah.org
Web Site: www.eretzhemdah.org
Key Personnel
President: Harav Shaul Israeli
Founded: 1987
Subjects: Law, Religion - Jewish
ISBN Prefix(es): 978-965-436

ESH (English for Speakers of Hebrew), *imprint of* University Publishing Projects Ltd

Focus Publishing+
PO Box 863, 52108 Ramat-Gan
Fax: (03) 5746513
E-mail: shaul@focus.co.il
Web Site: www.focus.co.il
Key Personnel
Chief Executive Officer: Dr Shaul Tal
Founded: 1993
Subjects: Alternative, Child Care & Development, Health, Nutrition, Medicine, Nursing, Dentistry, Self-Help, Alternative Medicine, Exercises, Parenthood, Personal Growth, Veganism, Vegetarianism
Number of titles published annually: 25 Print
Total Titles: 500 Print

Freund Publishing House Ltd+
7 Ravnitzki St, 67210 Tel Aviv
Tel: (03) 562-8540 *Fax:* (03) 562-8538
Founded: 1972
Subjects: Aeronautics, Aviation, Behavioral Sciences, Biography, Memoirs, Chemistry, Chemical Engineering, Engineering (General), Environmental Studies, Mathematics, Mechanical Engineering, Medicine, Nursing, Dentistry, Science (General), Social Sciences, Sociology
ISBN Prefix(es): 978-965-294
Branch Office(s)
Suite 500, Chesham House, 150 Regent St, London W1R 5FA, United Kingdom

Gefen, *imprint of* Gefen Publishing House Ltd

Gefen Publishing House Ltd+
6 Hatzvi St, 94386 Jerusalem

Tel: (02) 538-0247 *Fax:* (02) 538-8423
E-mail: gefenny@gefenpublishing.com
Web Site: www.gefenpublishing.com
Key Personnel
Chief Executive, Publicity: Murray S Greenfield
Publisher: Ilan Greenfield
Founded: 1981
Distributor of books published by many Israeli publishers, in Hebrew, English & other languages.
Subjects: Archaeology, Art, Biblical Studies, Biography, Memoirs, Cookery, English as a Second Language, Fiction, Government, Political Science, Health, Nutrition, History, How-to, Humor, Language Arts, Linguistics, Law, Literature, Literary Criticism, Essays, Medicine, Nursing, Dentistry, Military Science, Music, Dance, Nonfiction (General), Photography, Poetry, Psychology, Psychiatry, Religion - Jewish, Self-Help, Theology, Travel & Tourism, Wine & Spirits, Holocaust
ISBN Prefix(es): 978-965-229
Imprints: Gefen
Subsidiaries: Israbook Purchasing Service
U.S. Office(s): Gefen Books, 86 Cedarhurst Ave, Suite 134, Cedarhurst, NY 11516, United States *Tel:* 516-593-1234 *Fax:* 516-295-2739
Distributor for The Hebrew University Magnes Press Ltd; Israel Museum Products; Matan Arts; Modan Publishing Ltd; Palphot; Schocken; Yad Vashem

Habermann Institute for Literary Research+
20 David Ha'melech Blvd, Lod
Mailing Address: PO Box 166, 71101 Lod
Tel: (08) 9234008 *Fax:* (08) 9234008
Key Personnel
Dir: Dr Michal Saraf
Founded: 1982
Also publishes Mahut - Journal of Jewish Literature & Art.
Subjects: Ethnicity, Literature, Literary Criticism, Essays, Poetry, Religion - Jewish
ISBN Prefix(es): 978-965-351
Number of titles published annually: 15 Print
Total Titles: 100 Print

Haifa University Press
Mount Carmel, 31905 Haifa
Tel: (04) 8240601; (04) 8240781 *Fax:* (04) 8249158
E-mail: haifaup@univ.haifa.ac.il
Web Site: www.haifa.ac.il; press2.haifa.ac.il
Key Personnel
Chief Editor: Prof Dafna Erdinast-Vulcan
Dir, Publishing: Sharon Hanuka Ben-Chimol
E-mail: shanuka@univ.haifa.ac.il
Publishing Coordinator: Marsha Bar
Secretary: Ms Shoshi Leber *E-mail:* sleber@univ.haifa.ac.il
Subjects: Archaeology, Biblical Studies, Education, History, Language Arts, Linguistics, Literature, Literary Criticism, Essays, Philosophy, Public Administration
ISBN Prefix(es): 978-965-311
Distributed by University Press of New England (outside of Israel)

Hakibbutz Hameuchad-Sifriat Poalim Publishing Group
Hayarkon 23, 51114 Bnei Brak
Mailing Address: PO Box 1432, 51114 Bnei Brak
Tel: (03) 5785810 *Fax:* (03) 5785811
E-mail: info@kibutz-poalim.co.il
Web Site: www.kibutz-poalim.co.il
Key Personnel
Dir General: Uzi Shavit *E-mail:* uzi@kibutz-poalim.co.il
Assistant Dir General, Editorial & Foreign Rights: Avram Kantor *E-mail:* avram@kibutz-poalim.co.il

Assistant Dir General, Financial: Nachman Gil
E-mail: nachman@kibutz-poalim.co.il
Public Relations: Sigal Zalait *E-mail:* sigal@kibutz-poalim.co.il; Michal Bachar
E-mail: michal@kibutz-poalim.co.il
Founded: 1939
Membership(s): The Book Publishers' Association of Israel.
Subjects: Agriculture, Archaeology, Art, Biblical Studies, Biography, Memoirs, Biological Sciences, Drama, Theater, Economics, Education, Fiction, Foreign Countries, Geography, Geology, Government, Political Science, Health, Nutrition, History, Human Relations, Literature, Literary Criticism, Essays, Music, Dance, Natural History, Nonfiction (General), Philosophy, Poetry, Psychology, Psychiatry, Regional Interests, Religion - Jewish, Science (General), Social Sciences, Sociology, Theology, Travel & Tourism, Women's Studies
ISBN Prefix(es): 978-965-02
Number of titles published annually: 160 Print
Total Titles: 8,000 Print

Hod-Ami Publishing Ltd+
Imprint of Bookchamp, USA
PO Box 6108, 46160 Herzliya
Tel: (09) 9564716 *Fax:* (09) 9571582
E-mail: info@hod-ami.co.il
Web Site: www.hod-ami.co.il
Key Personnel
Chief Executive Officer: Itzhak Amihud
Finance & Production: Sara Amihud
Founded: 1968
Specialize in computer & information technology.
Subjects: Computer Science, Management, Technology
ISBN Prefix(es): 978-965-361
Total Titles: 150 Print
Warehouse: Independent Publishers Group (IPG), 814 N Franklin St, Chicago, IL 60610, United States *Tel:* 312-337-0747 *Web Site:* www.ipgbook.com

Even Hoshen Pvt Press Ltd
42b Hameyasdim St, 43217 Ra'anana
Tel: (09) 7433543 *Fax:* (09) 7425753
E-mail: sales@evenhoshen.co.il; shvo@evenhoshen.co.il
Web Site: www.evenhoshen.co.il
Key Personnel
Publisher: Uzi Agassi *E-mail:* uagassi1@netvision.net.il
Founded: 1994
Subjects: Art, Inspirational, Spirituality, Poetry, Religion - Jewish, Judaism, Prose, Short Stories, Visual Art
ISBN Prefix(es): 978-965-7270; 978-965-90205

IIOSH, see Israel Institute for Occupational Safety & Hygiene (IIOSH)

IMI, see Israel Music Institute (IMI)

The Institute for the Translation of Hebrew Literature (ITHL)
23 Baruch Hirsch St, 5120217 Bnei Brak
Tel: (03) 579 6830 *Fax:* (03) 579 6832
E-mail: litscene@ithl.org.il
Web Site: www.ithl.org.il
Key Personnel
Dir: Nilli Cohen
Founded: 1962
Promotion of translated Hebrew literature & children's literature; literary agency services; supporting anthologies of Hebrew literature; international literary meetings & conferences.
Subjects: Literature, Literary Criticism, Essays, Poetry
ISBN Prefix(es): 978-965-255

The Israel Academy of Sciences and Humanities+
Publications Dept, PO Box 4040, 9104001 Jerusalem
Tel: (02) 5676233 *Fax:* (02) 5666059
Web Site: www.academy.ac.il
Key Personnel
Executive Dir: Dr Meir Zadok *Tel:* (02) 5676204
E-mail: meir@academy.ac.il
Dir & Editor-in-Chief: Tali Amir *Tel:* (02) 5676208 *E-mail:* tali@academy.ac.il
Distribution & Copyrights: Rita Sapozhnikov
E-mail: rita@academy.ac.il
Founded: 1959
Subjects: Antiques, Archaeology, Asian Studies, Biblical Studies, Biological Sciences, Earth Sciences, Environmental Studies, Geography, Geology, History, Language Arts, Linguistics, Literature, Literary Criticism, Essays, Natural History, Philosophy, Religion - Catholic, Religion - Islamic, Religion - Jewish, Science (General), Theology
ISBN Prefix(es): 978-965-208

Israel Antiquities Authority
Rockefeller Museum Bldg, PO Box 586, 91004 Jerusalem
Tel: (02) 6204611 *Fax:* (02) 6260460
Web Site: www.antiquities.org.il
Key Personnel
Publications Dir: Judith Ben-Michael *Tel:* (02) 5638421 ext 102
Editorial Coordinator: Aviva Schwartzfeld *Tel:* (02) 5638421 ext 101
Production Coordinator: Lori Lender *Tel:* (02) 5638421 ext 105
Founded: 1990 (formerly a dept of the Israel Ministry of Education)
Designated by the government of Israel to administer the Law of Antiquities, responsible for all archeological matters, custodianship of all archeological sites, conducts excavations & surveys, issues excavation permits, curatorship, documentation & storage of all finds. Also, lends finds to museums, conservation & restoration of antiquities sites & antiquities, documentation, publication & education. Publications include excavation reports, surveys, bibliographies, monographs, guide books & video cassettes.
Subjects: Archaeology, Archaeology of Israel (the Holy Land)
ISBN Prefix(es): 978-965-406
Number of titles published annually: 6 Print; 1 Online
Total Titles: 78 Print; 1 CD-ROM; 1 Online
Orders to: Eisenbrauns Inc, PO Box 275, Winona Lake, IN 46590-0275, United States *Web Site:* www.eisenbrauns.com (Canada & USA)
Oxbow Books Ltd, Park End Pl, Oxford OX1 1HN, United Kingdom *Web Site:* www.oxbowbooks.com

Israel Brass Woodwind Publications, see OR-TAV Music Publications

Israel Exploration Society+
PO Box 7041, 91070 Jerusalem
Tel: (02) 6257991 *Fax:* (02) 6247772
E-mail: ies@vms.huji.ac.il
Web Site: israelexplorationsociety.huji.ac.il
Founded: 1914
Subjects: Archaeology, Biblical Studies, Geography, Geology, History
ISBN Prefix(es): 978-965-221

Israel Institute for Occupational Safety & Hygiene (IIOSH)
22 Maze St, Tel Aviv
Mailing Address: PO Box 1122, 61010 Tel Aviv
Tel: (03) 5266444 *Fax:* (03) 5266457
E-mail: info@osh.org.il; publish@osh.org.il
Web Site: www.osh.org.il

Key Personnel

General Dir: Daniel Hadad *Tel:* (03) 5266430
Fax: (03) 5266448 *E-mail:* danielhadad@osh.
org.il
Deputy Dir: Mr Israel Shreibman *Tel:* (03)
5266432 *Fax:* (03) 5266448 *E-mail:* israel@
osh.org.il
Head, Publishing: Mr Andrei Matias *Tel:* (03)
5266476 *Fax:* (03) 6208232 *E-mail:* andre@
osh.org.il
Specialize in books about occupational safety &
hygiene in the work place.
Subjects: Health, Nutrition, Labor, Industrial Relations, Management, Transportation
ISBN Prefix(es): 978-965-490

The Israel Museum

PO Box 71117, 91710 Jerusalem
Tel: (02) 6708811 *Fax:* (02) 6771332
E-mail: info@imj.org.il
Web Site: www.imj.org.il
Key Personnel
Head, Publications: Nirit Zur *Tel:* (02) 6708979
E-mail: niritzu@imj.org.il
Marketing Dir: Ran Lior *Tel:* (01) 6771323
E-mail: ranli@imj.org.il
Senior Editor, Hebrew Publications: Tami
Michaeli *Tel:* (02) 6708979 *E-mail:* tamim@
imj.org.il
Senior Editor, English Publications: Anna Barber
Tel: (02) 6708981 *E-mail:* anna_b@imj.org.il
Founded: 1965
Subjects: Archaeology, Architecture & Interior
Design, Art, History
ISBN Prefix(es): 978-965-278

Israel Music Institute (IMI)

55 Menachem Begin Rd, 67138 Tel Aviv
Mailing Address: PO Box 51197, 6713813 Tel
Aviv
Tel: (03) 624 70 95 *Fax:* (03) 561 28 26
E-mail: musicinst@bezeqint.net
Web Site: www.imi.org.il
Key Personnel
Chairman: Daniela Rabinowitz
Dir & Editor-in-Chief: Paul Landau
Founded: 1961
Membership(s): International Association of Mu-
sic Information Centres; International Federa-
tion of Serious Music Publishers.
Subjects: Music, Dance
ISBN Prefix(es): 978-965-90565
Total Titles: 2,300 Print
Distributed by AB Nordiska Musikfoerlaget
(Sweden); Albersen & Co BV (Netherlands);
Cesky Hudebni Fond (Czech Republic, Hun-
gary & Slovak Republik); Danmusik ApS
(Denmark); Harald Lyche & Co AS (Nor-
way); Intermusica (Spain & Portugal); Peer
Musikverlag GmbH (Austria, Germany &
Switzerland); Ricordi Americana SAEC (Ar-
gentina); Theodore Presser Co (Canada, Mex-
ico & USA)
Distributor for Theodore Presser Co

Israel Program for Scientific Translations, see
Keter Books

ITHL, see The Institute for the Translation of
Hebrew Literature (ITHL)

Jabotinsky Institute in Israel

38 King George St, 1st floor, Tel Aviv
Mailing Address: PO Box 23110, 6123002 Tel
Aviv
Tel: (03) 5287320 *Fax:* (03) 5285587
E-mail: office@jabotinsky.org
Web Site: www.jabotinsky.org
Key Personnel
Chairman: Mordechai Sarig
Dir General: Yossi Ahimeir

Founded: 1937
Subjects: Government, Political Science, History
ISBN Prefix(es): 978-965-416

JCPA, see Jerusalem Center for Public Affairs

Jerusalem Center for Public Affairs

Beit Milken, 13 Tel Hai St, 92107 Jerusalem
Tel: (02) 561-9281 *Fax:* (02) 561-9112
E-mail: info@jcpa.org
Web Site: www.jcpa.org
Key Personnel
President: Dr Dore Gold
Dir, Publications: Mark Ami-El
Founded: 1976
Specialize in Israel, Jewish communities, Jewish
political tradition, Israeli security, diplomacy &
war on terror.
Subjects: Foreign Countries, Government, Politi-
cal Science, Law, Regional Interests
ISBN Prefix(es): 978-965-218
Total Titles: 60 Print

K Dictionaries, *imprint of* K Dictionaries Ltd

K Dictionaries Ltd+

8 Nahum St, 63503 Tel Aviv
Tel: (03) 5468102 *Fax:* (03) 5468103
E-mail: kdl@kdictionaries.com
Web Site: kdictionaries.com
Key Personnel
Chief Executive Officer: Ilan Kernerman
Administration & Projects: Ms Yifat Ben Moshe
Founded: 1993
Creates lexicographic content that serves to de-
velop monolingual, bilingual & multilingual
dictionaries, for over 40 languages, in all types
of digital media, for language learning, transla-
tion & integration with NLP applications.
Cooperates with publishing houses, ICT firms,
professional associations & the academe world-
wide.
Subjects: English as a Second Language, Lan-
guage Arts, Linguistics, Cross-Language Learn-
ing, Mapping, Translation
ISBN Prefix(es): 978-965-90207
Imprints: K Dictionaries; Kernerman Semi-
Bilingual Dictionaries; Passport Dictionary
Distributed by Abbyy (Russia); Alma Littera
(Lithuania); Assimil (France); Bookman Books
(Taiwan); Cambridge University Press (UK);
CBS (India); Colibri (Bulgaria); Compass (Ko-
rea); Cornelsen (Germany); Daolsoft (Korea);
Edusoft (Israel); ELI (Italy); Encyclopaedia
Britannica (Brazil); Erlangga (Indonesia);
Forlagid (Iceland); 4n Media (France); iFin-
ger (Norway, UK); Inkilap (Turkey); Kesaint
Blanc (Indonesia); Kielikone (Finland); Mar-
tins Fontes Editora (Brazil); MV-Nordic (Den-
mark, Sweden); Niculescu (Romania); Ord-
bogen (Denmark); Paragon (Germany); The
Popular Group (USA); Publifolha (Brazil);
Reverso (France); Rokus (Slovenia); Seiko
(Japan); Shanghai Lexicographical Publishing
House (China); Grupo SM (Spain); Uitgeverij
Unieboek|Het Spectrum BV; SPN - Mlada Leta
(Slovak Republic); TEA (Estonia); TheFreeD-
ictionary.com (USA); Vega Forlag (Norway);
woorden.org (Netherlands); YBM Si-sa-yong-o-
sa (Korea); Zvaigzne ABC Publishers (Latvia)

Kernerman Semi-Bilingual Dictionaries, *imprint
of* K Dictionaries Ltd

Keter, *imprint of* Keter Books

Keter Books+

Industrial Zone 16, Givat Shaul, 91071 Jerusalem
Mailing Address: PO Box 7145, 91071 Jerusalem
Tel: (02) 6557822 *Fax:* (02) 6510339
E-mail: info@keter-books.co.il

Web Site: www.keter-books.co.il
Key Personnel
Editor-in-Chief: Einat Niv
Production Manager: Adi Segal *E-mail:* adi-s@
keter-books.co.il
Sales & Marketing Manager: Dan Vinokur
E-mail: dan@keter-books.co.il
Founded: 1958
Subjects: Art, Cookery, Crafts, Games, Hobbies,
Fiction, Health, Nutrition, How-to, Nonfiction
(General), Philosophy, Poetry, Psychology, Psy-
chiatry, Science Fiction, Fantasy, Social Sci-
ences, Sociology, Judaica
ISBN Prefix(es): 978-0-7065; 978-965-07
Parent Company: Modan Publishing
Imprints: Domino; Encyclopaedia Judaica; Keter
Subsidiaries: Domino Press; Encyclopaedia Ju-
daica; Israel Program for Scientific Translations

Koren Publishers Jerusalem

PO Box 4044, Jerusalem 91040
Tel: (02) 633-0536
Web Site: www.korenpub.com
Key Personnel
Sales Dir: Shlomo Peterseil *E-mail:* shlomop@
korenpub.com
Founded: 1961
Jewish religious texts & general interest books in
Hebrew, English & other languages.
Subjects: Religion - Jewish
ISBN Prefix(es): 978-965-301
Imprints: Maggid Books
U.S. Office(s): PO Box 8531, Milford, CT
06776-8531, United States *Tel:* 203-830-8508
Fax: 203-830-8512 *E-mail:* orders@korenpub.
com
Distribution Center: Kuperard, 59 Hutton Grove,
London N12 8DS, United Kingdom *Tel:* (020)
8446-2440 *E-mail:* office@kuperard.co.uk

Maaliyot-Institute for Research Publications

Mitzpeh Nevo 21, 98410 Ma'aleh Adumim
Tel: (02) 5353655 *Fax:* (02) 5353947
E-mail: maaliyotstore@ybm.org.il
Subjects: Religion - Jewish
ISBN Prefix(es): 978-965-417

Ma'alot Publishing Co Ltd

29 Carlebach St, 67132 Tel Aviv
Tel: (03) 5614121 *Fax:* (03) 5611996
E-mail: maalot@tbpai.co.il
Web Site: www.maalot-sfarim.co.il
Key Personnel
Mng Dir: Amnon Ben-Shmuel
Founded: 1969
Established by The Book Publishers' Association
of Israel as a jointly-owned publishing house in
which most of the members of the Association
are shareholders.
Parent Company: The Book Publishers' Associa-
tion of Israel

Maarachot, *imprint of* Ministry of Defence
Publishing House

Machbarot Lesifrut

Imprint of Kinneret Zmora-Bitan Dvir
10 Hataasiya St, 60212 Or Yehuda
Tel: (03) 6344977 *Fax:* (03) 6340953
Web Site: www.kinbooks.co.il
Founded: 1939
Subjects: Fiction, Government, Political Science,
History, Language Arts, Linguistics, Literature,
Literary Criticism, Essays
Number of titles published annually: 20 Print
Total Titles: 250 Print
Associate Companies: Zmora Bitan-Publishers
(ZBM)

Maggid Books, *imprint of* Koren Publishers
Jerusalem

The Magnes Press+
The Hebrew University, Sherman Bldg for Research Management, Edmund J Safra Campus, Givaat-Ram, 9139002 Jerusalem
Mailing Address: PO Box 39099, 9139002 Jerusalem
Tel: (02) 6585882 *Fax:* (02) 5633370; (02) 5660341
E-mail: info@magnespress.co.il; marketing@magnespress.co.il; production@magnespress.co.il; sales@magnespress.co.il
Web Site: www.magnes-press.com
Key Personnel
Dir: Jonathan Nadav *E-mail:* jonathan@magnespress.co.il
Marketing & Public Relations Manager, Israel Market: Tami Edri *E-mail:* tami@magnespress.co.il
Production Manager: Ram Goldberg
Coordinating Editor: Benny Mer
Secretary: Ruhama Halevi
Founded: 1929
This publisher has indicated that 30% of their product line is author subsidized.
Subjects: Agriculture, Archaeology, Art, Asian Studies, Biography, Memoirs, Economics, Education, Geography, Geology, History, Language Arts, Linguistics, Law, Literature, Literary Criticism, Essays, Music, Dance, Philosophy, Poetry, Psychology, Psychiatry, Religion - Islamic, Religion - Jewish, Religion - Other, Science (General), Social Sciences, Sociology, Folklore, Hebrew, Holocaust, Jewish Languages, Jewish Studies, Middle East Studies, Musicology Education
ISBN Prefix(es): 978-965-13; 978-965-223; 978-965-493
Number of titles published annually: 50 Print
Total Titles: 3,000 Print
Parent Company: The Hebrew University of Jerusalem
Imprints: Mount Scopus Press

MAPA-Mapping & Publishing Ltd
17 Tchernikhovski St, 61560 Tel Aviv
Mailing Address: PO Box 56024, 61560 Tel Aviv
Tel: (03) 6210500 *Fax:* (03) 5257725
E-mail: info@mapa.co.il
Web Site: www.mapa.co.il; www.books.mapa.co.il
Key Personnel
Mng Dir: Dani Tracz
Editor-in-Chief: Mulli Meltzer
Founded: 1985
Membership(s): Science Navigation Group
Subjects: History, Nonfiction (General), Travel & Tourism
ISBN Prefix(es): 978-965-7009; 978-965-7184; 978-965-521
Number of titles published annually: 25 Print
Total Titles: 200 Print
Imprints: Tel Aviv Books

Rubin Mass Ltd
7 Ha-ayin-Het St, 91009 Jerusalem
Mailing Address: PO Box 990, 91009 Jerusalem
Tel: (02) 627-7863 *Fax:* (02) 627-7864
E-mail: rmass@barak.net.il
Web Site: rubinmass.net
Key Personnel
Manager: Oren Mass
Founded: 1927
Also acts as exporters of all Israeli publications & periodicals.
This publisher has indicated that 50% of their product line is author subsidized.
Subjects: Biblical Studies, Biography, Memoirs, Education, Government, Political Science, Medicine, Nursing, Dentistry, Philosophy, Psychology, Psychiatry, Publishing & Book Trade Reference, Religion - Jewish, Religion - Other
ISBN Prefix(es): 978-965-09
Total Titles: 2,100 Print; 3 CD-ROM

Matar Publishing House
24 Levontin St, 65112 Tel Aviv
Tel: (03) 7105105 *Fax:* (03) 5660488
E-mail: info@matar.biz
Web Site: www.matarbooks.co.il
Key Personnel
Owner: Moshe Triwaks
Mng Dir: Benjamin Triwaks; Itzhak Triwaks
Founded: 1985
Subjects: Crafts, Games, Hobbies, Health, Nutrition, Management, Marketing, Medicine, Nursing, Dentistry, Nonfiction (General)
Subsidiaries: Triwaks Books Ltd

Ministry of Defence Publishing House+
Haqirya, 61909 Tel Aviv
Mailing Address: PO Box 916, 55108 Qiryat Omo
Tel: (03) 7380-701; (03) 7380-709 *Fax:* (03) 7380-635; (03) 7380-636
Web Site: www.mod.gov.il; mfa.gov.il
Founded: 1939
Also publishes albums & picture books.
Subjects: Foreign Countries, Geography, Geology, History, Military Science, History of the Land of Israel; Holocaust
ISBN Prefix(es): 978-965-05
Total Titles: 1,800 Print
Imprints: Maarachot; MOD: Broadcast University; To Live (Holocaust)

Mirkam Publishers
PO Box 10209, 12000 Rosh Pina
Tel: (04) 6922967
E-mail: 6mirkam@gmail.com
Web Site: www.mirkam.org
Key Personnel
Owner, Chief Editor & General Manager: Yafa Shoham
Founded: 1993
Mostly translations of material to acquaint the Israeli reader with current metaphysical understanding & information.
Privately owned enterprise.
Subjects: Channeling; Spiritual Growth
Total Titles: 35 Print

Misgav Yerushalayim
Unit of Faculty of Humanities, Hebrew University of Jerusalem
Faculty of Humanities, Hebrew University, Mount Scopus, 91905 Jerusalem
Tel: (02) 5883962 *Fax:* (02) 5815460
E-mail: hmisgav@mail.huji.ac.il
Founded: 1972
University research center specializing in academic teaching & research on Shephardi & Oriental Jewry (multi-disciplinary).
Subjects: Art, Ethnicity, History, Language Arts, Linguistics, Literature, Literary Criticism, Essays, Philosophy, Religion - Jewish
ISBN Prefix(es): 978-965-296; 978-965-493
Total Titles: 1 Print

Miskal Publishing & Distribution Ltd+
10 Kehilat Venezia St, 69400 Tel Aviv-Yafo
Tel: (03) 7683333 *Fax:* (03) 7683300
Key Personnel
President: Dov Eichenwald
Mng Dir: Haim Eichenwald
Founded: 1984
Subjects: Religion - Jewish
ISBN Prefix(es): 978-965-448; 978-965-511
Parent Company: Yedioth Ahronot
Warehouse: 19 Merkava St, Holon

MOD: Broadcast University, *imprint of* Ministry of Defence Publishing House

Modan Publishing House
Meshek 33, 73115 Moshav Ben-Shemen
Tel: (08) 9180000; (08) 9180002; (08) 9180003 *Fax:* (08) 9221299
E-mail: abigail@modan1.co.il
Web Site: www.modan.co.il
Key Personnel
Chairman: Oded Modan *E-mail:* modan@modan.co.il
Publisher & Dir: Roni Modan *E-mail:* roni@modan.co.il
Founded: 1970
Subjects: Cookery, Religion - Jewish, Classics
ISBN Prefix(es): 978-965-341; 978-965-7141

Mosad Harav Kook, see Rav Kook Institute

The Moshe Dayan Center for Middle Eastern & African Studies
Tel Aviv University, Ramat Aviv, 69978 Tel Aviv
Tel: (03) 6409646; (03) 6409100 *Fax:* (03) 6415802
E-mail: dayancen@post.tau.ac.il
Web Site: www.dayan.org
Key Personnel
Dir: Prof Uzi Rabi *E-mail:* urabi@post.tau.ac.il
Founded: 1959
Research center devoted to the study of the modern history & current affairs of the Middle East & Africa.
Subjects: History, Modern Middle East
ISBN Prefix(es): 978-965-224
Parent Company: Tel Aviv University
Distributed by Frank Cass; Oxford University Press; Syracuse University Press; Westview Press

Mount Scopus Press, *imprint of* The Magnes Press

The Myers-JDC-Brookdale Institute
JDC Hill, PO Box 3886, 91037 Jerusalem
Tel: (02) 6557400 *Fax:* (02) 5635851
E-mail: brook@jdc.org.il
Web Site: www.jdc.org.il/brookdale/
Key Personnel
Dir: Jack Habib
Dir, Publications: Jenny Rosenfeld
Dir, Human Resources & Administration: Kobi Wirtzer
Founded: 1974
Subjects: Health, Nutrition, Social Sciences, Sociology, Aging, Autism, Disabilities, Disadvantaged Children & Youth, Employment, Immigrants, Minorities, Poverty, Quality of Care
ISBN Prefix(es): 978-965-353

Younes & Soraya Nazarian Library, University of Haifa, see University of Haifa, The Library

Nehora Press
3, Kiriat Sara, 13410 Safed
Mailing Address: PO Box 2586, 13410 Safed
Tel: (04) 6923254 *Fax:* (04) 6970255
E-mail: yedidah@nehorapress.com
Web Site: www.nehorapress.com; www.nehoraschool.com (podcast)
Key Personnel
Publisher: Amanda Cohen *E-mail:* yedidah@nehorapress.com
Founded: 2003
Publish authentic translations of Kabbalah from Hebrew into English.
Membership(s): Publishers Marketing Association.
Subjects: Philosophy, Religion - Jewish
ISBN Prefix(es): 978-965-7222
Number of titles published annually: 3 Print
Distribution Center: Independent Publishers Group (IPG), 814 N Franklin St, Chicago, IL 60610, United States *Tel:* 312-337-0747 *Fax:* 312-337-5985 *E-mail:* orders@ipgbook.com *Web Site:* www.ipgbook.com

Orders to: Independent Publishers Group (IPG),
814 N Franklin St, Chicago, IL 60610, United
States *Tel:* 312-337-0747 *Fax:* 312-337-5985
E-mail: orders@ipgbook.com *Web Site:* www.
ipgbook.com

Nitzanim, *imprint of* Carta, The Israel Map &
Publishing Co Ltd

Open University of Israel+
The Dorothy de Rothschild Campus, One Univer-
sity Rd, 43107 Raanana
Mailing Address: PO Box 808, 43107 Raanana
Tel: (09) 7782222 *Fax:* (09) 7780664
E-mail: infodesk@openu.ac.il
Web Site: www.openu.ac.il
Key Personnel
Dir General: Amit Streit
Dir, Publishing: Yona Leshed
Manager, Rights & Permissions: Nava Segal
Tel: (09) 7781811 *E-mail:* navase@openu.ac.il
Founded: 1974
Occasionally engages in joint publications with
Yale University Press & Boston University.
Specialize in academic publications & textbooks
in Hebrew.
Subjects: Accounting, Biblical Studies, Biologi-
cal Sciences, Chemistry, Chemical Engineer-
ing, Computer Science, Economics, Education,
Government, Political Science, History, Jour-
nalism, Literature, Literary Criticism, Essays,
Management, Mathematics, Physics, Psychol-
ogy, Psychiatry, Religion - Jewish, Social Sci-
ences, Sociology
ISBN Prefix(es): 978-965-302; 978-965-06
U.S. Office(s): American Friends of the Open
Univeristy of Israel, 180 W 80 St, New York,
NY 10024, United States *Tel:* 212-712-1800
Fax: 212-496-3296

Opus Press Ltd+
61a Derech Shlomo St, 66089 Tel Aviv
Mailing Address: PO Box 65101, 61650 Tel Aviv
Tel: (03) 6814231 *Fax:* (03) 6814230
E-mail: info@opus.co.il; dorit@opus.co.il
(marketing & sales)
Web Site: www.opus.co.il
Key Personnel
Chief Executive Officer: Gil Tagar *E-mail:* gil@
opus.co.il
Founded: 1989
Also distributor.
Subjects: Alternative, Behavioral Sciences, Com-
puter Science, Economics, Fiction, How-to,
Literature, Literary Criticism, Essays, Manage-
ment, Marketing, Nonfiction (General), Science
Fiction, Fantasy, Self-Help, Travel & Tourism,
New Age
Number of titles published annually: 50 Print
Total Titles: 600 Print
Distributor for Asia; Fridman; Rotem-Rozmanim;
Shalgi

OR-TAV Music Publications
Gruzenberg Str 20, 6581123 Tel Aviv
Tel: (03) 566-1599 *Fax:* (03) 566-1688
E-mail: info@ortav.com
Web Site: www.ortav.com
Key Personnel
Owner: Yosef Zucker
Founded: 1967
Publisher of sheet music & books on music. Im-
porter & dealer of music scores & books.
Membership(s): Association of Composers, Au-
thors & Publishers of Music in Israel (ACUM).
Subjects: Music, Dance
ISBN Prefix(es): 978-965-505
Number of titles published annually: 10 Print
Total Titles: 300 Print
Foreign Rep(s): Musica Viva (Switzerland); MusT
(Music Trading Co Ltd) (worldwide exc Israel,
North America & Switzerland)

Passport Dictionary, *imprint of* K Dictionaries
Ltd

Prolog Publishing House Ltd
PO Box 300, 48101 Rosh Ha'ayin
Tel: (03) 9022904; (03) 9022905 *Fax:* (03)
9022906
E-mail: info@prolog.co.il
Web Site: www.prolog.co.il; www.prologhebrew.
us
Key Personnel
Dir: Oded Ahiasaf *E-mail:* oded@prolog.co.il
Founded: 1988
Specialize in language teaching audio-video cas-
sette courses, how-to books.
Subjects: How-to, Language Arts, Linguistics

Rav Kook Institute+
Shchunat Maimon St, 91006 Jerusalem
Mailing Address: PO Box 642, 9100601
Jerusalem
Tel: (02) 6526231 *Fax:* (02) 6526968
Web Site: www.mosadharavkook.com
Key Personnel
Chairman: Yehuda Leib Rafael
Executive Dir: Yosef Elyahu Movshowitz; Natan
David Shapira
Founded: 1937
Nonprofit public corporation supported by the
Jewish Agency, Ministry of Education & Cul-
ture & Ministry of Religious Affairs. Also pro-
vides financial support for works in subject
below.
Subjects: Religion - Jewish
ISBN Prefix(es): 978-965-7265
Number of titles published annually: 18 Print
Total Titles: 600 Print
U.S. Office(s): 702 Ocean Parkway, Suite 1A,
Brooklyn, NY 11230, United States *Tel:* 718-
215-1197 *E-mail:* office@mosadharavkookusa.
com

Sa'ar Publishing House
7 Kaplan St, 62744 Tel Aviv
Mailing Address: PO Box 26243, 62744 Tel Aviv
Tel: (03) 5445292 *Fax:* (03) 5445293
Web Site: www.h-saar.co.il
Key Personnel
Publisher: Enoch Sa'ar
Founded: 1979
Specialize in the publication of original & trans-
lated poetry.
Subjects: Fiction, Humor, Poetry, Travel &
Tourism

**The Dr Falk Schlesinger Institute for Medical
Halachic Research**
Shaare Zedek Medical Center, PO Box 3235,
91031 Jerusalem
Tel: (02) 655 5266 *Fax:* (02) 652 3295
E-mail: info@medethics.org.il
Web Site: www.medethics.org.il
Key Personnel
Dir: Dr Mordechai Halperin, MD *Tel:* (052) 260
2349 *E-mail:* halperin@medethics.org.il
Subjects: Law, Medicine, Nursing, Dentistry, Re-
ligion - Jewish, Jewish Medical Ethics & Ha-
lacha (Jewish Law)
Number of titles published annually: 8 Print; 2
CD-ROM; 100 Online; 2 Audio
Total Titles: 70 Print; 8 CD-ROM; 2,000 Online;
8 Audio

Schocken Publishing House+
24 Nathan Yelin Mor, 61022 Tel Aviv
Mailing Address: PO Box 57 188, 61022 Tel
Aviv
Tel: (03) 5610130 *Fax:* (03) 5622668
Web Site: www.schocken.co.il
Key Personnel
Publisher: Racheli Edelman

General Manager: Yael Hadass *E-mail:* yael_h@
haaretz.co.il
Rights & Permissions: Liat Karat *E-mail:* liat_k@
haaretz.co.il
Sales: Eti Harel *E-mail:* eti_h@haaretz.co.il
Founded: 1938
Membership(s): The Book Publishers' Association
of Israel.
Subjects: Anthropology, Behavioral Sciences, Bi-
ography, Memoirs, Child Care & Development,
Criminology, Drama, Theater, Economics, Edu-
cation, Fiction, Health, Nutrition, History, Law,
Literature, Literary Criticism, Essays, Nonfic-
tion (General), Philosophy, Poetry, Psychology,
Psychiatry, Religion - Jewish, Science Fiction,
Fantasy, Social Sciences, Sociology, Travel &
Tourism, Women's Studies
ISBN Prefix(es): 978-965-19
Imprints: Schocken Publishing House for Chil-
dren; Shin, Shin, Shin
Warehouse: 19 Lilienblum St, Tel Aviv

Schocken Publishing House for Children,
imprint of Schocken Publishing House

Shalem Press
13 Yehoshua Bin-Nun St, 93102 Jerusalem
Tel: (02) 560-5555 *Fax:* (02) 560-5556
E-mail: shalempress@shalem.org.il
Web Site: www.shalem.org.il; www.shalempress.
co.il
Key Personnel
Contact: Ayala Brendel *Tel:* (02) 560-5577
E-mail: ayalab@shalem.org.il
Founded: 1995
Publish original books in Hebrew & English.
Translate books into Hebrew.
Subjects: Economics, Government, Political Sci-
ence, History, Philosophy, Cultural Issues
ISBN Prefix(es): 978-965-7052
Total Titles: 3 Print
Parent Company: The Shalem Center
U.S. Office(s): The Shalem Center, 1140 Con-
necticut Ave NW, Suite 801, Washington,
DC 20036, United States *Tel:* 202-887-1270
Fax: 202-887-1277
Distributed by Armony Ltd

Shin, Shin, Shin, *imprint of* Schocken Publishing
House

Sifri, *imprint of* Steimatzky's Agency Ltd

Sinai Publishing Co
Rambam 24, 65812 Tel Aviv
Tel: (03) 5163672; (03) 5176783; (03) 5100994
Fax: (03) 5163672
E-mail: sinaipub@zahav.net.il
Web Site: www.sinaibooks.com
Founded: 1853
Subjects: Religion - Jewish
Subsidiaries: Sinai Export Co Ltd
Bookshop(s): Sinai Bookstore

R Sirkis Publishers Ltd+
30 Gutman St, 6139001 Tel Aviv
Mailing Address: PO Box 39035, 6139001 Tel
Aviv
Tel: (03) 6428865 *Fax:* (03) 6413963
E-mail: info@sirkis.co.il
Web Site: www.sirkis.co.il
Key Personnel
Chairman of the Board: Rafael Sirkis
E-mail: rafael@sirkis.co.il
President & Chief Editor: Ruth Sirkis
E-mail: ruth@sirkis.co.il
Founded: 1983
Specialize in the publishing of cookbooks, chil-
dren's books, sex education, do-it-yourself &
self-help books.

Subjects: Archaeology, Art, Child Care & Development, Cookery, Crafts, Games, Hobbies, Fashion, Gardening, Plants, Health, Nutrition, How-to, Psychology, Psychiatry, Self-Help, Travel & Tourism
ISBN Prefix(es): 978-965-387
Distributed by Larousse (France); Scholastic (USA)
Distribution Center: Gefen Publishing, 600 Broadway, Lynbrook, NY 11563, United States
Tel: 516-593-1234 *Fax:* 516-295-2739

Steimatzky, *imprint of* Steimatzky's Agency Ltd

Steimatzky's Agency Ltd+
Jabotinsky St 61, 49517 Petach Tikva
Tel: (03) 577-5760 *Toll Free Tel:* 1-700-70-66-00
  Fax: (03) 579-6833
E-mail: service@steimatzky.co.il
Web Site: www.steimatzky-publishing.co.il; www.steimatzky.co.il
Key Personnel
Chief Executive Officer: Iris Barel
Founded: 1925
130 bookshops around the country. Also wholesaler, distributor, publisher, book club & mail order.
Subjects: Art, Biography, Memoirs, Cookery, Fiction, Health, Nutrition, Nonfiction (General), Psychology, Psychiatry, Religion - Jewish, Science Fiction, Fantasy, Travel & Tourism
ISBN Prefix(es): 978-965-236
Parent Company: Arledan Investments Ltd
Associate Companies: SIFRI Ltd
Imprints: Sifri; Steimatzky
U.S. Office(s): Steimatzky USA, 17612 Ventura Blvd, Encino, CA 91316, United States
  E-mail: sales@stmus.com *Web Site:* www.stmus.com

Steinhart Katzir Publishers Ltd+
19 Yad Haruzim St, Sappir Industrial Area, 42505 Netanya
Mailing Address: PO Box 8333, 42505 Netanya
Tel: (09) 8854770 *Fax:* (09) 8854771
E-mail: mail@haolam.co.il
Web Site: www.haolam.co.il
Key Personnel
Chief Executive Officer: Ohad Sharav
Founded: 1991
Subjects: Travel & Tourism
ISBN Prefix(es): 978-965-420
Number of titles published annually: 20 Print
Total Titles: 100 Print
Distributor for Berndtson & Berndtson; Freytag & Berndt; ITM; Karto Alatier; National Geographic

Talmudic Encyclopedia Institute
Yad Harav Herzog, 30 Shmuel Hanagid, 91710 Jerusalem
Mailing Address: PO Box 71111, 91710 Jerusalem
Tel: (02) 642-3242 *Fax:* (02) 642-3821
E-mail: office@e-tal.org
Web Site: www.yadharavherzog.org; yadharavherzog.org/en
Key Personnel
President: Yisrael Meir Lau
Editor-in-Chief: Zalman Mechemia Goldberg; Prof Avraham Steinberg
Founded: 1942
Subjects: Religion - Jewish
ISBN Prefix(es): 978-965-445

Tamai Books, *imprint of* Dekel Publishing House

Tel Aviv Books, *imprint of* MAPA-Mapping & Publishing Ltd

Tel Aviv University+
PO Box 39040, 69978 Tel Aviv
Tel: (03) 640-8111 *Fax:* (03) 642-2404
E-mail: tauinfo@post.tau.ac.il
Web Site: www.tau.ac.il
Key Personnel
President: Prof Joseph Klafter
Vice President: Prof Raanan Rein
  E-mail: raanan@post.tau.ac.il
Founded: 1977
Subjects: Foreign Countries, Government, Political Science, History, Military Science, Regional Interests, Social Sciences, Sociology
ISBN Prefix(es): 978-965-459; 978-965-245
U.S. Office(s): Westview Press, 5500 Central Ave, Boulder, CO 80301, United States
Distributed by Jerusalem Post (Israel); Westview Press

To Live (Holocaust), *imprint of* Ministry of Defence Publishing House

University of Haifa, The Library
Abba Khoushy Blvd 199, Mount Carmel, 3498838 Haifa
Tel: (04) 8240264
E-mail: libmaster@univ.haifa.ac.il
Web Site: lib.haifa.ac.il
Key Personnel
Library Dir: Pnina Erez *E-mail:* epnina@univ.haifa.ac.il
Deputy Dir: Naomi Greidinger *E-mail:* naomig@univ.haifa.ac.il
Head of Administration: Ms Humi Rekem
  E-mail: hrekem@univ.haifa.ac.il
Academic Dir: Joseph Ziegler *E-mail:* jziegler@univ.haifa.ac.il
Founded: 1963
Subjects: Library & Information Sciences

University Publishing Projects Ltd+
8 Zarhin St, 43104 Raanana
Mailing Address: PO Box 393, 43104 Raanana
Tel: (09) 7459955 *Fax:* (09) 7459966
E-mail: upp@upp.co.il
Web Site: www.upp.co.il
Key Personnel
Mng Dir: Mr Uzi Eden
Dir: Nathan Eden
Founded: 1970
This publisher has indicated that 25% of its product line is author subsidized.
Subjects: English as a Second Language, Religion - Jewish
ISBN Prefix(es): 978-965-372
Number of titles published annually: 16 Print
Total Titles: 481 Print
Imprints: ESH (English for Speakers of Hebrew)

Urim Publications+
PO Box 52287, 9152102 Jerusalem
Tel: (02) 679-7633 *Fax:* (02) 679-7634
E-mail: urimpublisher@gmail.com
Web Site: www.urimpublications.com
Key Personnel
Publisher: Tzvi Mauer
Founded: 1997
Also worldwide distributor of new & classic books with Jewish content.
Subjects: Biblical Studies, Biography, Memoirs, Cookery, Ethnicity, Fiction, History, Human Relations, Law, Literature, Literary Criticism, Essays, Religion - Jewish, Women's Studies
ISBN Prefix(es): 978-965-7108; 978-965-524
Number of titles published annually: 8 Print
Total Titles: 22 Print; 1 CD-ROM
Distribution Center: 527 Empire Blvd, Brooklyn, NY 11225, United States *Tel:* 718-972-5449
  Fax: 718-972-6307 *E-mail:* mh@ejudaica.com

The Van Leer Jerusalem Institute
43 Jabotinsky St, 91040 Jerusalem

Mailing Address: PO Box 4070, 91040 Jerusalem
Tel: (02) 5605222 *Fax:* (02) 5619293
E-mail: vanleer@vanleer.org.il
Web Site: www.vanleer.org.il
Key Personnel
Editor-in-Chief & Head, Publications: Dr Tal Kohavi *E-mail:* talk@vanleer.org.il
Founded: 1959
Subjects: Economics, Foreign Countries, Government, Political Science, Psychology, Psychiatry, Religion - Jewish, Science (General), Social Sciences, Sociology, Jewish Culture
ISBN Prefix(es): 978-965-271; 978-965-346

Yachdav United Publishers Co Ltd
Subsidiary of The Book Publishers' Association of Israel
29 Carlebach St, 67132 Tel Aviv
Mailing Address: PO Box 20123, 61201 Tel Aviv
Tel: (03) 5614121 *Fax:* (03) 5611996
E-mail: info@tbpai.co.il; hamol@tbpai.co.il
Web Site: www.tbpai.co.il
Key Personnel
Chief Executive Officer: Amnon Ben-Shmuel
Founded: 1939
Specialize in Academic books.
Subjects: Philosophy, Poetry, Psychology, Psychiatry, Public Administration, Social Sciences, Sociology, Religion-Hebrew

Yad Ben-Zvi Press
c/o Yad Izhak Ben-Zvi, 14 Ibn Gabirol St, 91076 Jerusalem
Mailing Address: PO Box 7660, 91076 Jerusalem
Tel: (02) 5398888 *Fax:* (02) 5638310
E-mail: ybz@ybz.org.il
Web Site: ybz.org.il
Key Personnel
Dir: Jacob Yaniv *E-mail:* yaniv@ybz.org.il
English Publications Coordinator: Yohai Goell
  Tel: (02) 5398824
Founded: 1966
Specialize in the history of Palestine/Israel & the Oriental Jewish communities.
Subjects: Geography, Geology, History, Regional Interests, Religion - Jewish
ISBN Prefix(es): 978-965-235; 978-965-217
Number of titles published annually: 40 Print
Total Titles: 540 Print
Distributed by Eisenbrauns Inc (some titles, North America only)

Yad Tabenkin-The Research & Document Center of the Kibbutz Movement
One Hayasmin St, 52960 Ramat Efal
Tel: (03) 5344458 *Fax:* (03) 5346376
E-mail: yadtabmaz@bezeqint.net
Web Site: www.yadtabenkin.org.il
Key Personnel
Archive Dir: Aharon Azati
Founded: 1976 (as a research institute)
Subjects: Biography, Memoirs, Economics, History, Social Sciences, Sociology
ISBN Prefix(es): 978-965-282
Number of titles published annually: 4 Print

Yad Vashem - The Holocaust Martyrs' & Heroes' Remembrance Authority+
PO Box 3477, 91034 Jerusalem
Tel: (02) 6443768 *Fax:* (02) 6443509
E-mail: publications.marketing@yadvashem.org.il
Web Site: www.yadvashem.org
Key Personnel
Chairman & Dir: Avner Shalev
Founded: 1953
Subjects: Biography, Memoirs, Education, History, Nonfiction (General), Holocaust Research
ISBN Prefix(es): 978-965-308
Branch Office(s)
Heychal Wolyn, 10 Korazin St, PO Box 803, Givatayim
U.S. Office(s): American Society for Yad Vashem, 500 Fifth Ave, 42nd floor, New York, NY

10110, United States, Executive Dir: Ron B
Meier, PhD *Tel:* 212-220-4304 *Fax:* 212-220-
4308 *E-mail:* meier@yadvashemusa.org *Web
Site:* www.yadvashemusa.org
Distributed by Rubin Mass Ltd, Publishers &
Booksellers

Yavneh Publishing House Ltd+
Mazeh 4, 65213 Tel Aviv
Tel: (03) 6297856 *Fax:* (03) 6293638
E-mail: publishing@yavneh.co.il
Founded: 1932
Subjects: Fiction, Music, Dance, Religion - Jew-
ish, Religion - Other, Science (General)
ISBN Prefix(es): 978-965-7305

Yediot Aharonot Books+
Book Dept, 10 Kehilat Venezia, 61534 Tel Aviv
Tel: (03) 7683333 *Fax:* (03) 7683300
Web Site: www.ybook.co.il
Key Personnel
Chief Executive Officer: Dov Eichenwald
 E-mail: dov@yedbooks.co.il
Vice President, Marketing: Eyal Dadush
 E-mail: eyalda@yedbooks.co.il
Editor-in-Chief: Netta Gurevich *E-mail:* netta-g@
 yedbooks.co.il
Production: Natasha Knovic *E-mail:* natashat@
 yedbooks.co.il
Founded: 1952
Subjects: Art, Biography, Memoirs, Cookery, Fic-
tion, Government, Political Science, Health,
Nutrition, How-to, Medicine, Nursing, Den-
tistry, Music, Dance, Nonfiction (General), Re-
ligion - Jewish
ISBN Prefix(es): 978-965-482
Number of titles published annually: 300 Print
Total Titles: 1,500 Print
Parent Company: Yedioth Ahronoth (The Evening
 Newspaper of Israel)
Associate Companies: Books in the Attic, Amdan
 5, Tel Aviv, Editor-in-Chief: Yehuda Melzer
 Tel: (03) 602-9010 *E-mail:* ilai@actcom.co.il
Subsidiaries: Miskal
Distributor for Babel; Astrolog
Warehouse: Yedioth Books, 6 Hahortim St, Holon

**The Zalman Shazar Center for Jewish
 History+**
2 Beitar St, 91041 Jerusalem
Tel: (02) 5650444; (02) 5650445 *Fax:* (02)
 6712388
E-mail: shazar@shazar.org.il
Web Site: www.shazar.org.il
Key Personnel
Chief Executive Officer: Michal Nakar
 E-mail: michal@shazar.org.il
Publications Manager: Talia Yakir *Tel:* (02)
 5650449
Academic Secretary: Maayan Avineri-Rebhun
 Tel: (02) 5650433 *E-mail:* maayan@shazar.org.
 il
Founded: 1973
Specialize in Jewish history. Collected essays,
 historical novels for youth, monographs, picto-
 rial albums & textbooks.
Membership(s): The Historical Society of Israel.
Subjects: Biography, Memoirs, History, Literature,
 Literary Criticism, Essays, Religion - Jewish
ISBN Prefix(es): 978-965-227
Total Titles: 250 Print

Italy

General Information

Capital: Rome
Language: Italian. Various others according to
 region

Religion: Predominantly Roman Catholic
Population: 57.6 million
Bank Hours: 0830-1330, 1500-1600 Monday-
 Friday
Shop Hours: 0830 or 0900-1300, 1500 or 1600-
 1930 or 2000 Monday-Saturday; many close
 Monday morning
Currency: 100 Eurocents = 1 Euro
Export/Import Information: Member of the Eu-
 ropean Union. 4% VAT on books; advertising
 matter other than single copies is dutied. No
 import license required.
Copyright: UCC, Berne, Florence (see Copyright
 Conventions, pg viii)

Editrice Abitare Segesta
Via Ventura, 5, 20134 Milan MI
Tel: (02) 210581 *Fax:* (02) 21058271
E-mail: redazione@abitare.rcs.it; shop@abitare.
 rcs.it
Web Site: www.abitare.it
Key Personnel
Publisher: Renato Minetto
Founded: 1976
Subjects: Architecture & Interior Design, Art
ISBN Prefix(es): 978-88-86116

Abracadabra, *imprint of* DeA Planeta Libri SRL

Accademia editoriale, see Instituti Editoriali e
 Poligrafici Internazionali

Acco Editore-Acero Edizioni
Corso Marconi, 77, 28883 Gravellona, Toce VB
Tel: (0323) 34 10 79 *Fax:* (0322) 34 10 79
E-mail: info@accoeditore.com
Subjects: Fiction, Nonfiction (General)
ISBN Prefix(es): 978-88-95902

AdArte SRL
Via Manara 6g, 10133 Turin TO
Tel: (011) 197 152 89 *Fax:* (011) 197 152 89
E-mail: info@adartepublishing.com
Web Site: www.adartepublishing.com
Founded: 2003
Subjects: Archaeology, Architecture & Interior
 Design, Art, Photography, Applied Arts, Egyp-
 tology, Painting, Sculpture
ISBN Prefix(es): 978-88-89082

Mario Adda Editore SNC
Via Tanzi, 59, 70121 Bari BA
Tel: (080) 5539502 *Fax:* (080) 5539502
E-mail: info@addaeditore.it; redazione@
 addaeditore.it
Web Site: www.addaeditore.it
Key Personnel
Dir: Giacoma Adda
Founded: 1963
Subjects: Archaeology, Architecture & Interior
 Design, Art, Crafts, Games, Hobbies, Drama,
 Theater, Environmental Studies, Fiction, His-
 tory, Literature, Literary Criticism, Essays, Mu-
 sic, Dance, Philosophy, Photography, Poetry,
 Regional Interests, Social Sciences, Sociology,
 Sports, Athletics, Travel & Tourism, Nature
ISBN Prefix(es): 978-88-8082

Adea Books, *imprint of* Adea Edizioni

Adea Edizioni+
via don L Milani, 37, 26028 Sesto ed Uniti CR
Tel: (0372) 710 999
E-mail: info@adeaedizioni.it; ordini@
 adeaedizioni.it; redazione@adeaedizioni.it
Web Site: www.adeaedizioni.it
Founded: 1992
Subjects: Astrology, Occult, Biography, Memoirs,
 Human Relations, Literature, Literary Criti-

cism, Essays, Philosophy, Physical Sciences,
 Religion - Buddhist, Theology
ISBN Prefix(es): 978-88-86274
Imprints: Adea Books
Subsidiaries: Adea Education; Adea Incense;
 Adea Music; Adea SRL
Distribution Center: Consorzio Distributori As-
 sociati, Via Mario Alicata, 2F, 40050 Monte
 San Pietro BO *Tel:* (051) 969316 *Fax:* (051)
 969320 *E-mail:* info@cdanet.it

Adelphi Edizioni SpA+
Via San Giovanni sul Muro 14, 20121 Milan MI
Tel: (02) 725731 *Fax:* (02) 89010337
E-mail: info@adelphi.it; rights.dept@adelphi.it;
 redazione@adelphi.it
Web Site: www.adelphi.it
Key Personnel
Mng Dir, Editorial Dir & Chairman: Roberto
 Calasso
Founded: 1962
Subjects: Anthropology, Biography, Memoirs,
 Fiction, History, Literature, Literary Criticism,
 Essays, Mathematics, Mysteries, Suspense, Phi-
 losophy, Physics, Poetry, Religion - Buddhist,
 Religion - Hindu, Science (General)
ISBN Prefix(es): 978-88-459
Foreign Rights: Ute Koerner Literary Agency
 (Spain); Nouvelle Agence (France)
Bookshop(s): Via Brentano 2, 20121 Milan MI
Warehouse: Via Mecenate 87/4, 20138 Milan MI
Orders to: Servizio Vendita Libri c/o RCS Libri
 & Grandi Opere SpA, Via Mecenate 91, 20138
 Milan MI *Tel:* (02) 50951

AdP, *imprint of* Segretariato Nazionale
 Apostolato della Preghiera

Aesthetica Edizioni Palermo
Via Giusti 25, 90144 Palermo PA
Tel: (091) 308290 *Fax:* (091) 308290
E-mail: estetica@unipa.it
Web Site: www.unipa.it/~estetica/editrice.html
Key Personnel
Editorial Dir: Luigi Russo
Founded: 1985
Subjects: Art, Philosophy
ISBN Prefix(es): 978-88-7726
Parent Company: University of Palermo, Interna-
 tional Center Studies of Aesthetic

Edizioni della Fondazione Giovanni Agnelli
 (Giovanni Agnelli Foundation Publishing)+
Via Nizza 250, 10126 Turin TO
Tel: (011) 6500500 *Fax:* (011) 6500012
E-mail: segreteria@fga.it
Web Site: www.fga.it
Key Personnel
President: Maria Sole
Dir: Andrea Gavosto *E-mail:* andrea.gavosto@fga.
 it
Administration: Franco Picollo *E-mail:* fpicollo@
 fga.it
Founded: 1966
Subjects: Economics, Geography, Geology, Gov-
 ernment, Political Science, Social Sciences,
 Sociology
ISBN Prefix(es): 978-88-7860
Number of titles published annually: 8 Print

De Agostini Scuola
Via Montefeltro, 6/B, 20156 Milan MI
Tel: (02) 380861 *Fax:* (02) 38086851
E-mail: scrivi@scuola.com
Web Site: www.deagostiniscuola.it; www.scuola.
 com
Subjects: Education, Geography, Geology, His-
 tory, Science (General)
ISBN Prefix(es): 978-88-402

AIB, Associazione Italiana Bibliotheche (Italian
Library Association)+
c/o Biblioteca nazionale centrale, Viale Castro
Pretorio 105, 00185 Rome RM
Tel: (06) 4463532 *Fax:* (06) 4441139
E-mail: aib@aib.it; segreteria@aib.it; servizi@aib.
it
Web Site: www.aib.it
Key Personnel
Chairman: Stefano Parise *E-mail:* parise@aib.it
Vice President: Enrica Manenti *E-mail:* manenti@
aib.it
Secretary: Giovanna Frigimelica
E-mail: frigimelica@aib.it
Founded: 1930
The Italian association of professional librarians
& information specialists.
Membership(s): The European Bureau of Library,
Information & Documentation Associations
(EBLIDA); The International Association of
School Librarianship (IASL); The International
Federation of Library Associations & Institu-
tions (IFLA).
Subjects: Library & Information Sciences
ISBN Prefix(es): 978-88-7812
Number of titles published annually: 13 Print; 1
CD-ROM; 2 Online
Total Titles: 148 Print; 1 CD-ROM; 2 Online

L'Airone Editrice, *imprint of* Gremese Editore

L'Airone Editrice+
Imprint of Gremese Editore
Via Virginia Agnelli, 88, 00151 Rome RM
Tel: (06) 65740507 *Fax:* (06) 65740509
E-mail: gremese@gremese.com; rights@gremese.
com; ufficiostampa@gremese.com
Web Site: www.gremese.com
Key Personnel
Publisher & Executive Manager: Alberto Gremese
Founded: 1977
Subjects: Art, Astrology, Occult, Crafts, Games,
Hobbies, Drama, Theater, Humor, Literature,
Literary Criticism, Essays, Music, Dance, Mys-
teries, Suspense, Nonfiction (General), Para-
psychology, Photography, Science (General),
Sports, Athletics, Travel & Tourism, Perform-
ing Arts
ISBN Prefix(es): 978-88-7605; 978-88-7742; 978-
88-7944; 978-88-7301; 978-88-8440
Distribution Center: Messaggerie Libri SpA *Web
Site:* www.messaggerielibri.it

AISM, see Associazione Italiana Sclerosi
Multipla (AISM)

Alaya, *imprint of* Gruppo Editoriale Macro

Alaya+
Imprint of Gruppo Editoriale Macro
Via Bachelet, 65, 47522 Cesena FC
Tel: (0547) 1900103 *Fax:* (0547) 1900127
E-mail: info@macroedizioni.it
Web Site: www.macroedizioni.it
Key Personnel
President & Editor: Giorgio Gustavo Rosso
Founded: 2004
Membership(s): Associazione Italiana Editori
(AIE).
Subjects: Alternative, Archaeology, Biblical Stud-
ies, Cookery, Education, Environmental Stud-
ies, Health, Nutrition, House & Home, How-to,
Philosophy, Psychology, Psychiatry, Religion -
Other, Science (General)
ISBN Prefix(es): 978-88-7616
Number of titles published annually: 5 Print
Total Titles: 20 Print
Ultimate Parent Company: Macro Societa Coop-
erativa
Distributor for Amici di Dirk; Archiati Verlag;
Bonomi; NLP Italy; Lo Scarabeo

Showroom(s): Salone del Libro, Turin
Book Club(s): Il Giardino dei Libri, Via del
Lavoro 40, 47814 Bellaria RN *Tel:* (0541)
340567 *E-mail:* ordini@ilgiardinodeilibri.it *Web
Site:* www.ilgiardinodeilibri.it; Macro Librarsi,
Via Savona 70, 47023 Diegaro di Cesena FC
Tel: (0547) 346290; (0547) 346312 *Fax:* (0547)
345091 *E-mail:* ordini@macrolibrarsi.it *Web
Site:* www.macrolibrarsi.it

Gruppo Albatros Il Filo
Via Sistina, 121, 00187 Rome RM
Tel: (07) 611763012 *Fax:* (07) 611763022
Web Site: www.gruppoalbatros.eu
Key Personnel
Dir General: Giuseppe Lastaria
Subjects: Literature, Literary Criticism, Essays
ISBN Prefix(es): 978-88-7842; 978-88-88797

Libreria Alfani Editrice SRL
via degli Alfani 84/86 R, 50121 Florence FI
Tel: (055) 2398800 *Fax:* (055) 218251
E-mail: info@librerialfani.it
Web Site: www.librerialfani.it; www.librerialfani.
com
Key Personnel
Chief Executive: Umberto Panerai
Founded: 1967
Subjects: Anthropology, Archaeology, Architec-
ture & Interior Design, Art, Drama, Theater,
Economics, Environmental Studies, Fiction,
History, Language Arts, Linguistics, Literature,
Literary Criticism, Essays, Mathematics, Music,
Dance, Philosophy, Poetry, Psychology, Psychi-
atry, Social Sciences, Sociology
ISBN Prefix(es): 978-88-88288
Total Titles: 40 Print
Bookshop(s): Libreria Alfani, Via Alfani 84/86R,
50121 Florence FI

Compagnia Editoriale Aliberti SRLS
Formerly Aliberti Editore
Vicolo Scaletta, 1, 42121 Regio Emilia RE
Tel: 392 9667175; 331 7053692
E-mail: info@cealiberti.it; ordini@cealiberti.it
Web Site: www.aliberticompagnieditoriale.it
Key Personnel
Publisher: Francesco Aliberti
Editorial Dir: Alessandro Di Nuzzo
Founded: 2001
Subjects: Fiction, Literature, Literary Criticism,
Essays
ISBN Prefix(es): 978-88-7424

Aliberti Editore, see Compagnia Editoriale
Aliberti SRLS

Edizioni Alice
via dello Spiraglio, 5, 40139 Bologna BO
Tel: (051) 534286 *Fax:* (051) 534286
E-mail: alice.edizioni@tiscali.it
Web Site: www.edizionialice.it
Subjects: Fiction, Geography, Geology, Philoso-
phy, Sports, Athletics, English, Italian, Latin
ISBN Prefix(es): 978-88-88513
Distribution Center: Editrice La Scuola, Via An-
tonio Gramsci, 26, 25121 Brescia BS

Alinari
Largo Fratelli Alinari, 15, 50123 Florence FI
Tel: (055) 23951 *Fax:* (055) 2382857
E-mail: casaeditrice@alinari.it
Web Site: www.alinari.it
Founded: 1885
Subjects: Art, History, Photography, Landscape,
Social Traditions
ISBN Prefix(es): 978-88-7292; 978-88-6302; 978-
88-95849
Branch Office(s)
Alinari Roma, Via Alibert, 16/A, 00187 Rome
RM *Tel:* (06) 6792923 *Fax:* (06) 69941998

All'Insegna del Giglio
via del Termine 36, 50019 Sesto Fiorentino FI
Tel: (055) 84 50 216 *Fax:* (055) 84 53 188
E-mail: info@edigiglio.it; ordini@edigiglio.it
(orders); redazione@edigiglio.it (editorial)
Web Site: www.insegnadelgiglio.it/
Founded: 1976
Subjects: Archaeology, History
ISBN Prefix(es): 978-88-7814

Umberto Allemandi & C SpA+
Via Mancini 8, 10131 Turin
Tel: (011) 8199111 *Fax:* (011) 8193090
E-mail: allemandi@allemandi.com
Web Site: www.allemandi.com
Key Personnel
President: Umberto Allemandi
Dir General: Antonella Romagnolo
E-mail: antonella.romagnolo@allemandi.com
Communications: Alessandro Allemandi
Press & Communications: Cristina Casoli
E-mail: cristina.casoli@allemandi.com
Sales: Antonio Marra
Founded: 1983
Subjects: Antiques, Archaeology, Architecture
& Interior Design, Art, Biography, Memoirs,
Gardening, Plants, History, House & Home,
Photography, Science (General)
ISBN Prefix(es): 978-88-422

Alma Edizioni SRL
Viale dei Cadorna, 44, 50129 Florence FI
Tel: (055) 476644 *Fax:* (055) 473531
E-mail: alma@almaedizioni.it
Web Site: www.almaedizioni.it
Key Personnel
Marketing Manager: Giacomo Pierini *Tel:* (335)
8108276 (cell) *E-mail:* gpierini@almaedizioni.
it
Founded: 1994
Subjects: Italian Language
ISBN Prefix(es): 978-88-86440

ALP, *imprint of* Vivalda Editori SRL

Alpha Test - Sironi Editore
via Mercalli 14, 20122 Milan
Tel: (02) 5845981 *Fax:* (02) 58459896
E-mail: rights@alphatest.it
Web Site: rights.alphatest.it
Key Personnel
Foreign Rights: Doriana Rodino
Founded: 1993
Subjects: Biography, Memoirs, Fiction, History,
Music, Dance, Nonfiction (General), Philoso-
phy, Science (General), Popular Science
ISBN Prefix(es): 978-88-483
Foreign Rights: Tempi Irregolari (Stefano Bisac-
chi) (Albania, Bulgaria, Croatia, Macedonia,
Romania, Serbia, Slovenia)

Altralinea Edizioni SRL
Via Pietro Carnesecchi 39, 50131 Florence FI
Tel: (055) 333428
E-mail: info@altralinea.it
Web Site: altralineaedizioni.it
Founded: 2013
Subjects: Architecture & Interior Design, Urban
Planning, Visual Arts
ISBN Prefix(es): 978-88-98743

Edizioni Amrita SRL+
Via San Quintino, 36, 10121 Turin TO
Mailing Address: CP 1, 10094 Giaveno TO
Tel: (011) 9340579; (011) 9363018 (orders)
Fax: (011) 9349128; (011) 9363114 (orders)
E-mail: ciao@amrita-edizioni.com; ordini@
amrita-edizioni.com
Web Site: www.amrita-edizioni.com
Founded: 1986

Subjects: Art, Astrology, Occult, Health, Nutrition, How-to, Parapsychology, Philosophy, Religion - Other
ISBN Prefix(es): 978-88-96865

AMZ, *imprint of* DeA Planeta Libri SRL

Editorial Anagrama, *imprint of* Giangiacomo
Feltrinelli Editore SRL

AnankeLab
via Lodi, 27/c, 10152 Turin
Tel: (011) 020 5368
E-mail: info@anankelab.com
Web Site: www.anankelab.com
Founded: 1995
Subjects: Anthropology, Art, Drama, Theater, Fic-
tion, History, Medicine, Nursing, Dentistry,
Music, Dance, Philosophy, Poetry, Psychology,
Psychiatry, Religion - Islamic, Science (Gen-
eral), Egyptology
ISBN Prefix(es): 978-88-7325; 978-88-86626

Ancora Editrice+
Via GB Niccolini, 8, 20154 Milan
Tel: (02) 3456081 *Fax:* (02) 34560866
E-mail: commerciale@ancoralibri.it; editrice@
ancoralibri.it; foreign.rights@ancoralibri.it;
redazione@ancoralibri.it; ufficio.stampa@
ancoralibri.it (press)
Web Site: www.ancoralibri.it
Key Personnel
Mng Dir: Gilberto Zini
Press: Andrea Bertino
Founded: 1934
Subjects: Religion - Other, Social Sciences, Soci-
ology
ISBN Prefix(es): 978-88-7610; 978-88-514
Bookshop(s): via Larga, 7, 20122 Milan *Tel:* (02)
58307006 *Fax:* (02) 58312449 *E-mail:* libreria.
larga@ancoralibri.it; via Tosio, 1, 25121
Brescia *Tel:* (030) 40433 *Fax:* (030) 40433
E-mail: libreria.brescia@ancoralibri.it; via
Pavoni, 1, 20052 Monza *Tel:* (039) 324745
Fax: (039) 2301379 *E-mail:* libreria.monza@
ancoralibri.it; via della Conciliazione, 63,
00193 Rome *Tel:* (06) 6868820 *Fax:* (06)
6833050 *E-mail:* libreria.roma@ancoralibri.it;
via Santa Croce, 35, 38100 Trento *Tel:* (0461)
274444 *Fax:* (0461) 983630 *E-mail:* libreria.
trento@ancoralibri.it

Anteprima, *imprint of* Edizioni Lindau

Editrice Antroposofica SRL
Via Sangallo 34, 20133 Milan
Tel: (02) 7491197
E-mail: info@editrice-antroposofica.it
Web Site: www.editriceantroposofica.com
Key Personnel
Mng Dir: Dr Maurizio Lieti
Founded: 1959
Subjects: Agriculture, Anthropology, Art, As-
trology, Occult, Earth Sciences, Economics,
Education, Medicine, Nursing, Dentistry, Phi-
losophy, Anthroposophy
ISBN Prefix(es): 978-88-7787
Number of titles published annually: 20 Print
Total Titles: 308 Print
Distributor for Edizioni Arcobaleno; Filadelfia
Editore; Fior di Pesco Edizioni; Fondazione Le
Madri; Libreria Editrice Psiche

Apogeo, *imprint of* Giangiacomo Feltrinelli
Editore SRL

Apogeo SRL - Editrice di Informatica
Member of Gruppo Giangiacomo Feltrinelli Edi-
tore
Via Natale Battaglia, 12, 20127 Milan

Tel: (02) 289981 *Fax:* (02) 26116334
Web Site: www.apogeonline.com; www.
apogeoeditore.com
Key Personnel
Founder: Ivo Quartiroli
Editor: Fabio Brivio *E-mail:* fabio.brivio@
apogeonline.com
Marketing & Communications: Federica Dardi
E-mail: federica.dardi@apogeonline.com
Founded: 1989
Software manuals.
Subjects: Computer Science, Information Science
ISBN Prefix(es): 978-88-85146; 978-88-7303;
978-88-503

Apogeo Sushi, *imprint of* Giangiacomo Feltrinelli
Editore SRL

Apostolato della Preghiera+
Segretariato Nazionale Apostolato della Preghiera,
Via Degli Astalli, 16, 00186 Rome
Tel: (06) 697 607 1 *Fax:* (06) 678 10 63
E-mail: edizioniadp@adp.it (AdP Editions);
redazione@adp.it (editorial); ufficiostampa@
adp.it (press)
Web Site: www.adp.it
Founded: 1844 (in France, 1861 in Italy)
Publisher of Bibles, books & leaflets.
Subjects: Psychology, Psychiatry, Religion -
Other, Pastoral Activities, Prayer, Spirituality
ISBN Prefix(es): 978-88-7357
Total Titles: 344 Print; 344 Online
Parent Company: ADP International
Bookshop(s): Via Degli Astalli, 17, 00186 Rome
Tel: (06) 697 607 201 *E-mail:* libreria@adp.it
Distribution Center: Messaggero Distribution
SRL, Via Orto Botanico 11, 35123 Padova,
Contact: Marcello Volpato *Tel:* 049 658288
Fax: 049 8754359 *E-mail:* messdis@mbox.vol.
it

Nino Aragno Editore
via S Francesco d'Assisi 22/bis, 10121 Turin TO
Tel: (011) 7221085
E-mail: info@ninoaragnoeditore.it
Web Site: www.ninoaragnoeditore.it
Founded: 1999
Subjects: Art, History, Literature, Literary Criti-
cism, Essays, Philosophy
ISBN Prefix(es): 978-88-8419
Distribution Center: Proliber SRL, Via Leonardo
da Vinci, 8/10, 00015 Monterotondo RM
Tel: (06) 66166173 *Fax:* (06) 66167503

Archimede Edizioni
Imprint of Pearson Italia SpA
Via Archimede 10, 23 e 51, 20129 Milan
Tel: (02) 748231 *Fax:* (02) 74823278; (02)
74823312; (02) 74823362
Web Site: pearson.it/archimede_edizioni.com
Key Personnel
Mng Dir: Roberto Gulli
Editorial Dir & International Rights: Emilio
Zanette
Head, Press & Communications: Elena Grossi
Tel: (02) 74823384 *E-mail:* elena.grossi@
pearson.it
Founded: 1990
Educational publisher.
Subjects: Biological Sciences, Earth Sciences,
Education, English as a Second Language, Fic-
tion, History, Mathematics
ISBN Prefix(es): 978-88-7952
Ultimate Parent Company: Pearson plc

Rosellina Archinto Editore+
Division of RCS Libri SpA
Via Santa Valeria 3, 20123 Milan
Tel: (02) 86460237 *Fax:* (02) 86451955
E-mail: info@archinto.it
Web Site: archinto.rcslibri.corriere.it

Key Personnel
President: Rosellina Archinto
Founded: 1986
Subjects: Biography, Memoirs, Literature, Lit-
erary Criticism, Essays, Nonfiction (General),
Poetry
ISBN Prefix(es): 978-88-7768
Number of titles published annually: 25 Print
Shipping Address: RCS Libri SpA, Via Mecenate,
91, 20138 Milan
Distribution Center: RCS Libri SpA, Via Mece-
nate, 91, 20138 Milan, Contact: Francesco
Nani *Tel:* (02) 50952484 *Fax:* (02) 50952969
Orders to: RCS Libri SpA, Via Mecenate, 91,
20138 Milan

Archivio Guido Izzi SRL
Via Lazzarini, 19, 00136 Rome
Tel: (06) 39734433
Founded: 1984
Subjects: Art, History, Literature, Literary Criti-
cism, Essays
ISBN Prefix(es): 978-88-85760; 978-88-88846

Edizioni L'Archivolto+
Via Marsala 3, 20121 Milan
Tel: (02) 29010424; (02) 29010444 *Fax:* (02)
29001942
E-mail: editions@archivolto.com; archivolto@
archivolto.com
Web Site: www.archivolto.com
Key Personnel
Founder: Silvio San Pietro *E-mail:* silvio.
sanpietro@archivolto.com
Founded: 1986
Specialize in architecture & interior design.
Subjects: Architecture & Interior Design, Art,
Gardening, Plants, Photography
ISBN Prefix(es): 978-88-7685
Number of titles published annually: 5 Print
Total Titles: 100 Print
Distributed by Edizioni L'Archivolto; Hoepli Edi-
tore SpA
Foreign Rep(s): ACC Distribution (all other ter-
ritories, Canada, Europe, UK, USA); Ionnis
N Petrotos (Greece); Librairie Stephan Sal
(Lebanon); Sanart Yayincilik (Turkey)
Bookshop(s): Via Marsala 2, 20121 Mi-
lan *Tel:* (02) 6590842 *Fax:* (02) 6595552
E-mail: bookshop@archivolto.com

Edizioni l'Arcipelago Edizioni+
Via Arnolfo 58, 50100 Florence FI
Tel: (055) 0516384 *Fax:* (055) 0516384
E-mail: info@edizionilarcipelago.it
Web Site: www.edizionilarcipelago.it
Founded: 1971
Subjects: Advertising, English as a Second Lan-
guage, Film, Video, Language Arts, Linguis-
tics, Literature, Literary Criticism, Essays,
Management, Marketing, Social Sciences, Soci-
ology, Italian as a Second Language
ISBN Prefix(es): 978-88-7695
Number of titles published annually: 30 Print; 1
CD-ROM; 1 Audio
Total Titles: 1 CD-ROM; 1 Audio
Bookshop(s): Via Marsala 2, 20121 Milan

Edizioni ARES+
Via Stradivari 7, 20131 Milan
Tel: (02) 29514202 *Fax:* (02) 29520163
E-mail: info@ares.mi.it
Web Site: www.ares.mi.it
Key Personnel
Dir: Dr Cesare Cavalleri *E-mail:* cesare.
cavalleri@ares.mi.it
Deputy Dir Editorial: Andrea Beolchi
E-mail: andrea.beolchi@ares.mi.it
Sales Manager: Paolo Graziano *E-mail:* paolo.
graziano@ares.mi.it
Editor: Alessandro Rivali *E-mail:* alessandro.
rivali@ares.mi.it

Press: Riccardo Caniato *E-mail:* riccardo.
caniato@ares.mi.it
Founded: 1956
Subjects: Architecture & Interior Design, Philoso-
phy, Psychology, Psychiatry, Theology
ISBN Prefix(es): 978-88-8155

Argalia Editore Urbino
Via della Stazione, 41, 61029 Urbino PU
Tel: (0722) 328733 *Fax:* (0722) 328756
E-mail: marketing@ageurbino.it
Web Site: www.ageurbino.it
Key Personnel
Commercial: Silvia Argalia
Founded: 1942
Also book packager.
Subjects: Drama, Theater, Economics, Education,
Fiction, History, Literature, Literary Criticism,
Essays, Philosophy, Poetry, Science (General)
ISBN Prefix(es): 978-88-89731

Arianna Editrice, *imprint of* Gruppo Editoriale
Macro

Arianna Editrice+
Imprint of Gruppo Editoriale Macro
Viale Carducci, 24, 40125 Bologna BO
Tel: (051) 8554602; (335) 5846937 (cell)
   Fax: (051) 8554602
E-mail: redazione@ariannaeditrice.it
Web Site: www.ariannaeditrice.it
Founded: 1998
Subjects: Alternative, Archaeology, Biblical Stud-
ies, Cookery, Education, Environmental Stud-
ies, Health, Nutrition, History, House & Home,
How-to, Philosophy, Psychology, Psychiatry,
Religion - Other, Science (General)
ISBN Prefix(es): 978-88-87307
Number of titles published annually: 10 Print
Total Titles: 40 Print
Ultimate Parent Company: Macro Societa Coop-
erativa
Showroom(s): Salone del Libro, Turin
Book Club(s): Il Giardino dei Libri, Via del
   Lavoro 40, 47814 Bellaria RN *Tel:* (0541)
   340567 *E-mail:* ordini@ilgiardinodeilibri.it *Web
   Site:* www.ilgiardinodeilibri.it; Macro Librarsi,
   Via Savona 70, 47023 Diegaro di Cesena FC
   Tel: (0547) 346290; (0547) 346312 *Fax:* (0547)
   345091 *E-mail:* ordini@macrolibrarsi.it *Web
   Site:* www.macrolibrarsi.it

edizioni ARKA+
Via Raffaello Sanzio 7, 20149 Milan
Tel: (02) 4818230 *Fax:* (02) 4816752
E-mail: arka@arkaedizioni.it
Web Site: www.arkaedizioni.it
Key Personnel
Mng Dir: Ginevra Viscardi
Founded: 1985
Subjects: Animals, Pets, Art
ISBN Prefix(es): 978-88-8072; 978-88-85762
Number of titles published annually: 20 Print

Arkivia Books
Via Provinciale, 68, 24022 Alzano Lombardo BG
Tel: (035) 515851 *Fax:* (035) 515851
E-mail: info@arkiviabooks.com; info@
   vincenzosguera.com
Web Site: www.arkiviabooks.com; www.
   vincenzosguera.com
Key Personnel
Contact: Vincenzo Sguera
Founded: 2002
Subjects: Art, Graphic Design
ISBN Prefix(es): 978-88-88766
Foreign Rep(s): European Publishers Representa-
tion (EPR) (Europe); Windsor Books Interna-
tional (worldwide exc Europe)
Distribution Center: Librimport, Via Biondelli 9,
   20141 Milan MI *Tel:* (02) 89501422 *Fax:* (02)
   89502811 *E-mail:* librimport@libero.it

Edizioni Arktos
Via Valobra F, 128, 10022 Carmagnola TO
Tel: (011) 9773941 *Fax:* (011) 9715340
E-mail: arktos@cometacom.it; edizioniarktos@
   yahoo.it
Founded: 1976
Subjects: Astrology, Occult, Philosophy, Religion
- Islamic
ISBN Prefix(es): 978-88-7049

Armando Editore SRL+
Viale di Trastevere, 236, 00153 Rome RM
Tel: (06) 58 94 525; (06) 58 17 245; (06) 58 10
840 *Fax:* (06) 58 18 564
E-mail: info@armando.it; segreteria@armando.it;
   redazione@armando.it; press@armando.it
Web Site: www.armando.it
Key Personnel
Chief Executive Officer: Enrico Iacometti
   E-mail: enrico.iacometti@armando.it
Editorial Dir: Bianca Spadolini *E-mail:* b.
   spadolini@armando.it
Sales Manager: Andrea Iacometti *E-mail:* andrea.
   iacometti1@tin.it
International Rights: Annalisa Esposito
Founded: 1963
Subjects: Anthropology, Behavioral Sciences,
Child Care & Development, Communications,
Disability, Special Needs, Education, Health,
Nutrition, Journalism, Language Arts, Linguis-
tics, Medicine, Nursing, Dentistry, Philosophy,
Psychology, Psychiatry, Radio, TV, Self-Help,
Social Sciences, Sociology, Comparative Edu-
cation
ISBN Prefix(es): 978-88-7144; 978-88-8358
Number of titles published annually: 150 Print; 4
CD-ROM
Total Titles: 4 CD-ROM
Bookshop(s): Via Vincenzo Brunacci, 55, 00146
   Rome *Tel:* (06) 5587850 *Fax:* (06) 5580723
Distribution Center: Dehoniana Libri SpA,
   Rampa delle Mura Aurelie, 8/11, 00165
   Rome, Contact: Rosa Saltarini *Tel:* (06) 638
   26 07 *Fax:* (06) 639 04 02 *E-mail:* dlroma@
   dehoniane.it *Web Site:* www.dehonianalibri.it
Dehoniana Libri SpA, Via delle Industrie, 31/b,
   35020 Albignasego PD, Contact: Marco
   Simionato *Tel:* (049) 880 53 13 *Fax:* (049)
   68 61 68 *E-mail:* dlpadova@dehoniane.it *Web
   Site:* www.dehonianalibri.it
Dehoniana Libri SpA, via Scipione dal Ferro,
   4, 40138 Bologna BO, Contact: Alessan-
   dro Mazzoni *Tel:* (051) 4290451 *Fax:* (051)
   4290491 *E-mail:* dlbologna@dehoniana.it *Web
   Site:* www.dehonianalibri.it
Dehoniana Libri SpA, Via Andolfato, 3, 20126
   Milan, Contact: Renato Nitri *Tel:* (02) 27 00 13
   09 *Fax:* (02) 27 00 10 21 *E-mail:* dlmilano@
   dehoniane.it *Web Site:* www.dehonianalibri.it
Dehoniana Libri SpA, Via Campana 205/B,
   80078 Pozzuoli NA, Contact: Bruno Tubelli
   Tel: (081) 5261866 *Fax:* (081) 5266401
   E-mail: dlnapoli@dehoniane.it *Web Site:* www.
   dehonianalibri.it

Armenia SRL+
Via Milano 73/75, 20010 Cornaredo MI
Tel: (02) 99762433 *Fax:* (02) 99762445
E-mail: info@armenia.it
Web Site: www.armenia.it
Founded: 1972
Specialize in New Age, positive thinking & fan-
tasy.
Subjects: Alternative, Animals, Pets, Archaeology,
Asian Studies, Astrology, Occult, Astronomy,
Business, Career Development, Erotica, Fiction,
Health, Nutrition, Humor, Inspirational, Spir-
ituality, Parapsychology, Religion - Buddhist,
Science Fiction, Fantasy, Self-Help, New Age
ISBN Prefix(es): 978-88-344; 978-88-7216
Number of titles published annually: 80 Print
Total Titles: 715 Print; 2 CD-ROM

Distribution Center: Agenzia Libraria Inter-
national SRL, Contact: Moreno Arrighi
Tel: (02) 99762430 *Fax:* (02) 36548188
E-mail: infoali@alilibri.it

Arsenale Editrice+
Via Monte Comun 40, 37057 San Giovanni Lupa-
toto VR
Tel: (045) 545166 *Fax:* (045) 545057
Web Site: www.arsenale.it
Key Personnel
Editor: Andrea Darra *E-mail:* andrea.darra@
   arsenale.it
Administrator: Elisabetta Bortolazzi
   E-mail: elisabetta.bortolazzi@arsenale.it
Foreign Sales Dir: Jonathan Bortolazzi
   E-mail: jonathanbortolazzi@ebs-bortolazzi.com
Founded: 1984
Subjects: Archaeology, Architecture & Interior
Design, Art, Cookery
ISBN Prefix(es): 978-88-7743
Parent Company: Editoriale Bortolazzi - Stei SRL
Branch Office(s)
San Polo 1789, 37125 Venice *Tel:* (041) 5240610
   Fax: (041) 5240685

Artioli Editore
Division of Poligrafico Artioli SpA
Via Emilia Ovest, 669, 41123 Modena
Tel: (059) 827181 *Fax:* (059) 826819
E-mail: artioli@artioli.it
Web Site: www.artioli.it
Key Personnel
Commercial Dir: Dr Angela Artioli
   E-mail: angela@artioli.it
Administrative Dir: Dr Antonella Artioli
   E-mail: anto@artioli.it
Acquisitions: Dr Alessandra Artioli
   E-mail: alessandra@artioli.it
Editorial: Dr Augusto Artioli
Founded: 1899
Subjects: Antiques, Architecture & Interior De-
sign, Art, Drama, Theater, Photography, Re-
gional Interests
ISBN Prefix(es): 978-88-7792

L'Artistica Editrice
Via Torino 197, 12038 Savigliano CN
Tel: (0172) 726622 *Fax:* (0172) 375904
E-mail: editrice@lartisavi.it
Web Site: www.edarpi.com; www.lartisavi.it
Founded: 1969
Subjects: Architecture & Interior Design, Art,
History, Language Arts, Linguistics, Nonfic-
tion (General), Photography, Poetry, Travel &
Tourism, Wine & Spirits
ISBN Prefix(es): 978-88-7320
Parent Company: L'Artistica Savigliano Gruppo
Grafico

l'asino d'oro edizioni SRL
Via Saturnia 14, 00184 Rome RM
Tel: (06) 90286555 *Fax:* (06) 48906391
E-mail: info@lasinodoroedizioni.it
Web Site: www.lasinodoroedizioni.it
Key Personnel
Press: Giovanni Senatore *Tel:* (338) 3965779
   (cell) *E-mail:* giovanni.senatore@
   lasinodoroedizioni.it
Specialize in books by Massimo Fagioli.
Subjects: Biography, Memoirs, Psychology, Psy-
chiatry, Science (General)
ISBN Prefix(es): 978-88-6443
Distribution Center: Messaggerie Libri SpA

Edizioni Associate+
Via Affile, 30, 00132 Rome RM
Tel: (06) 876 799 38 *Fax:* (06) 876 799 49
Key Personnel
Chairman, Editorial Board: Giorgio Cortellessa
General Manager: Claudio Capotosti

Press: Dr Simonetta Stefanini
Founded: 1991
Subjects: Government, Political Science, History, Literature, Literary Criticism, Essays, Psychology, Psychiatry, Science (General), Social Sciences, Sociology
ISBN Prefix(es): 978-88-267
Number of titles published annually: 13 Print; 13 Online
Total Titles: 450 Print; 5 CD-ROM; 450 Online
Warehouse: RDE, Via H Spencer 16, 00177 Rome RM *Tel:* (06) 2154010 *Fax:* (06) 2153549

Associazione Culturale Ilios Editore
via Argiro 7, 70122 Bari BA
Tel: (080) 5243926; (0338) 6327989
E-mail: info@ilioseditore.it
Web Site: www.iliosbooks.com
Subjects: Architecture & Interior Design, Urban Design
ISBN Prefix(es): 978-88-908024; 978-88-903456; 978-88-941483

Associazione Internazionale di Archeologia Classica (International Association for Classical Archaeology)
Via degli Astalli, 4, 00186 Rome RM
Mailing Address: Piazza San Marco, 49, 00186 Rome RM
Tel: (06) 67 98 798 *Fax:* (06) 67 98 798
E-mail: info@aiac.org
Web Site: www.aiac.org
Key Personnel
President: Dr Elizabeth Fentress
  E-mail: elizabeth.fentress@gmail.com
Vice President: Dr Olof Brandt
  E-mail: ollebrandt@gmail.com
Secretary General: Dr Maria Teresa d' Alessio
  E-mail: tessa@inwind.it
Founded: 1945
Associated with the National Committee of Research & The Jean Berard Centre in Naples.
Membership(s): International Association of Classical Archeology; International Association of Research Institutes in the History of Art (RIHA); International Union of the Institutes of Archeology, History & History of Art in Rome; The National Institute of Studies of the Renaissance.
Subjects: Archaeology, Art
ISBN Prefix(es): 978-88-7275

Associazione Italiana Sclerosi Multipla (AISM)
Via Operai 40, 16149 Genoa
Tel: (010) 27131 *Toll Free Tel:* (0800) 803028 *Fax:* (010) 2713205
E-mail: aism@aism.it
Web Site: www.aism.it
Key Personnel
Chief Executive: Antonella Moretti
President: Franco Giacomazzi
Founded: 1967
Subjects: Disability, Special Needs, Multiple Sclerosis
ISBN Prefix(es): 978-88-7148

Atanor+
Via Avezzano, 16, 00182 Rome
Tel: (06) 7024595 *Fax:* (06) 7014422
E-mail: atanor.editrice@libero.it
Web Site: www.atanoreditrice.it
Founded: 1912
Subjects: Asian Studies, Astrology, Occult, Science (General), Esotericism
ISBN Prefix(es): 978-88-7169

Edizioni dell'Ateneo, see Instituti Editoriali e Poligrafici Internazionali

Athesia Buchverlag, see Athesia-Tappeiner Verlag

Athesia-Tappeiner Verlag+
Member of Athesia Unternehmensgruppe
Avogadrostr 6, 39100 Bozen BZ
Tel: (0471) 081081 *Fax:* (0471) 081079
E-mail: buchverlag@athesia.it
Web Site: www.athesia-tappeiner.com
Key Personnel
Publishing Dir: Dr Ingrid Marmsoler *Tel:* (0471) 081073 *E-mail:* ingrid.marmsoler@athesia.it
Subjects: Art, Cookery, Fiction, Gardening, Plants, Geography, Geology, History, House & Home, How-to, Humor, Law, Literature, Literary Criticism, Essays, Military Science, Nonfiction (General), Outdoor Recreation, Poetry, Religion - Catholic, Travel & Tourism
ISBN Prefix(es): 978-88-7083; 978-88-7014; 978-88-8266; 978-88-6839
Associate Companies: Athesia Druck GmbH; Athesia Medien
Distribution Center: Grafus GmbH, Sir-Isaac-Newton-Str 1, 39100 Bozen BZ *Tel:* (0471) 086444 *Fax:* (0471) 086555 *E-mail:* order@grafus.it *Web Site:* www.grafus.it
Mohr Morawa Buchvertrieb GmbH, Postfach 260, 1230 Vienna, Austria *Tel:* (01) 68014-0 *Fax:* (01) 6896800 *E-mail:* bestellung@mohrmorawa.at *Web Site:* www.mohrmorawa.at
Herold Fulfillment GmbH, Raiffeisenallee 10, 82041 Oberhaching, Germany, Contact: Francesca Mohr *Tel:* (089) 61387116 *Fax:* (089) 61387120 *E-mail:* f.mohr@herold-va.de *Web Site:* www.herold-va.de

Atlantyca Entertainment SpA
Via Leopardi 8, 20123 Milan
Tel: (02) 43 00 10 32 *Fax:* (02) 43 00 10 20
E-mail: foreignrights@atlantyca.it
Web Site: www.atlantyca.com
Key Personnel
Founder: Pietro Marietti
Founded: 2006

Atlas, see Istituto Italiano Edizioni Atlas SpA

ATS Italia Editrice SRL
Via di Brava 41/43, 00163 Rome
Tel: (06) 66415961 *Fax:* (06) 66512461
E-mail: atsitalia@atsitalia.it
Web Site: www.atsitalia.it
Founded: 1988
Subjects: Art, Cookery, Travel & Tourism, Cuisine, Monographs, Sacred Texts
ISBN Prefix(es): 978-88-7571; 978-88-86542; 978-88-87654; 978-88-88536
Branch Office(s)
Largo M Liverani, 12/3, 50141 Florence
  Tel: (055) 4220577 *Fax:* (055) 4220649
  E-mail: atsitalia.firenze@atsitalia.it

Babalibri
Via Brisa, 3, 20123 Milan MI
Tel: (02) 86460237 *Fax:* (02) 36598241
E-mail: info@babalibri.it
Web Site: www.babalibri.it
Key Personnel
Press: Motta Max *E-mail:* motta.max@gmail.com
Founded: 1999
Specialize in Italian/French preschool picture books.
ISBN Prefix(es): 978-88-8362

Edizioni del Baldo SRL
Via Maria Gaetana Agnesi, 49/51, 37014 Castelnuovo del Gardo VR
Tel: (045) 8960275
E-mail: commerciale@pizzighella.com
Web Site: www.edizionidelbaldo.it
ISBN Prefix(es): 978-88-6363; 978-88-6721

Bancaria Editrice SpA
Subsidiary of ABI Italian Banking Association
Via delle Botteghe Oscure, 54, 00186 Rome
Tel: (06) 6767561
E-mail: editoriale@bancariaeditrice.it
Web Site: www.bancariaeditrice.it
Key Personnel
Publishing & Editorial: Fernanda Silvi
Founded: 1974
Subjects: Business, Economics, Finance, Law, Management, Marketing
ISBN Prefix(es): 978-88-449; 978-88-86373
Branch Office(s)
Via Olona 2, 20123 Milan

Bastogi Editrice Italiana SRL
Via Zara, 47, 71100 Foggia FG
Tel: (0881) 725070 *Fax:* (0881) 728119
E-mail: bastogi@tiscali.it
Web Site: www.bastogi.it
Founded: 1987
Subjects: History, Literature, Literary Criticism, Essays, Music, Dance, Religion - Other
ISBN Prefix(es): 978-88-86452; 978-88-8185; 978-88-6273

Il Battello a Vapore, *imprint of* Edizioni Piemme SpA

BC News, *imprint of* Edizioni del Centro Camuno di Studi Preistorici

BCSP, *imprint of* Edizioni del Centro Camuno di Studi Preistorici

BE-MA editrice
Via Teocrito 47, 20128 Milan
Tel: (02) 252071 *Fax:* (02) 27000692
E-mail: amministrazione@bema.it; segreteria@bema.it
Web Site: www.bema.it
Key Personnel
Publisher: Fiorella Baserga; Gisella Bertini Malgarini
Founded: 1975
Subjects: Antiques, Architecture & Interior Design, Earth Sciences, Engineering (General), English as a Second Language, Environmental Studies, Geography, Geology, Technology
ISBN Prefix(es): 978-88-7143
Imprints: Visual Itineraries

Beisler Editore
Via del Forte Bravetta 100, 00164 Rome RM
Tel: (06) 95227473 *Fax:* (06) 95227476
E-mail: info@beisler.it; amministrazione@beisler.it; ufficiostampa@beisler.it; u.beisler@beisler.it
Web Site: www.beislereditore.com
ISBN Prefix(es): 978-88-7459
Distribution Center: PDE SpA, Via Forlanini, 36, 50019 Osmannoro-Sesto F no FI *Tel:* (05) 5301371; (05) 5315373; (05) 5318332 *Fax:* (05) 5301372 *Web Site:* www.pde.it/partners.php
L S Distribuzione Editoriale, Via Badini 17, 40050 Quarto Inferiore, Bologna *Tel:* (051) 768165; (051) 6061167 *Fax:* (051) 6058752 *Web Site:* www.lsc.it (for libraries)

BEL srl, *imprint of* Salomone Belforte & C SRL

Salomone Belforte & C SRL+
Via Roma 43, 57126 Livorno
Tel: (0586) 808730 *Fax:* (0586) 808730
E-mail: info@salomonebelforte.com
Web Site: www.libreriabelforte.it; www.libreriabelforte.com
Key Personnel
Dir: Pasquale Di Paolo
Contact: Silvia Guastalla
Founded: 1834

Subjects: Antiques, Art, Behavioral Sciences, Biography, Memoirs, Child Care & Development, Education, Fiction, Human Relations, Library & Information Sciences, Literature, Literary Criticism, Essays, Nonfiction (General), Philosophy, Poetry, Psychology, Psychiatry, Regional Interests, Religion - Jewish, Wine & Spirits, Women's Studies
ISBN Prefix(es): 978-88-7997
Imprints: BEL srl
Subsidiaries: Librinformatica SRL

Biancoenero Edizioni SRL
via dei Barbieri 6, 00186 Rome RM
Tel: (06) 6874091 *Fax:* (06) 6874091
E-mail: info@biancoeneroedizioni.com
Web Site: www.biancoeneroedizioni.com
Key Personnel
Editorial Dir: Irene D'Intino *E-mail:* i.dintino@biancoeneroedizioni.com
Communications: Barbara Ruiz *E-mail:* b.ruiz@biancoeneroedizioni.com
Founded: 2005
Subjects: Art, Fiction
ISBN Prefix(es): 978-88-89921

Editrice Bibliografica SRL
Via F De Sanctis 33/35, 20141 Milan MI
Tel: (02) 49581707 *Fax:* (02) 49581712
E-mail: bibliografica@bibliografica.it; redazione.bibliografica@bibliografica.it
Web Site: www.editricebibliografica.it
Key Personnel
Mng Dir: Michele Costa
Founded: 1974
Membership(s): Associazione Italiana Editori; Associazione Italiana per la difesa della reprografia delle opere.
Subjects: Library & Information Sciences
ISBN Prefix(es): 978-88-7075
Number of titles published annually: 20 Print
Total Titles: 100 Print; 1 CD-ROM

Bibliopolis, Edizioni di Filosofia e Scienze SRL
Via Arangio Ruiz 83, 80122 Naples
Tel: (081) 664606 *Fax:* (081) 7616273
E-mail: info@bibliopolis.it
Web Site: www.bibliopolis.it
Key Personnel
Owner & Dir: Dr Francesco del Franco
Founded: 1976
Subjects: Archaeology, Literature, Literary Criticism, Essays, Mathematics, Philosophy, Physical Sciences, Physics, Science (General)
ISBN Prefix(es): 978-88-7088
Total Titles: 374 Print
Distributed by Maruzen Co
Distribution Center: ALI Agenzia Libraria Internationale SRL, Via Milano 73/75, 20010 Cornaredo MI *Tel:* (02) 99762430 *Fax:* (02) 36548188 *E-mail:* infoali@alilibri.it *Web Site:* www.alilibri.it
Librairie J Vrin, 6, Place de la Sorbonne, 75005 Paris, France
Maruzen Co Ltd, PO Box 5050, Tokyo International, Tokyo 100-31, Japan

Edizioni Biblioteca Francescana+
Piazza Sant'Angelo, 2, 20121 Milan MI
Tel: (02) 29 00 27 36 *Fax:* (02) 29 00 27 36
E-mail: info@bibliotecafrancescana.it
Web Site: www.bibliotecafrancescana.it
Founded: 1977
Specialize in Francescanesimo.
Subjects: History, Religion - Catholic, Theology
ISBN Prefix(es): 978-88-7962
Number of titles published annually: 10 Print
Total Titles: 201 Print
Imprints: EBF
Distributed by Messaggero Distribuzione

Biblos SRL+
Via delle Pezze, 23, 35013 Cittadella PD
Tel: (049) 5975236 *Fax:* (049) 5972841
E-mail: info@biblos.it
Web Site: www.biblos.it
Key Personnel
Mng Dir: Lanfranco Lionello *E-mail:* lion@biblos.it
Founded: 1992
Subjects: Architecture & Interior Design, Art, Cookery, Literature, Literary Criticism, Essays, Photography, Poetry
ISBN Prefix(es): 978-88-86214; 978-88-88064

BIS Edizioni, *imprint of* Gruppo Editoriale Macro

BIS Edizioni+
Imprint of Gruppo Editoriale Macro
Via Bachelet, 65, 47522 Diegaro di Cesena FC
E-mail: ordini@gruppomacro.com (orders)
Web Site: www.gruppomacro.com/editori/bis-edizioni
Founded: 2007
Subjects: Cookery, Health, Nutrition, Philosophy, Psychology, Psychiatry, Religion - Other, Self-Help, Gastronomy, Holistic Medicine, Mind, Body, Spirit, Mind Science
ISBN Prefix(es): 978-88-6228
Number of titles published annually: 30 Print
Total Titles: 60 Print
Ultimate Parent Company: Macro Societa Cooperativa
Warehouse: Golden Books SRL, Via Savona 70, 47023 Diegaro di Cesena FC *Tel:* (0547) 346317 *Fax:* (0547) 345091 *E-mail:* ordini@macrolibrarsi.it *Web Site:* www.macrolibrarsi.it

Black Cat, *imprint of* Cideb Editrice SRL

Blu Edizioni SRL
Via Po 20, 10123 Turin
Tel: (011) 74616 *Fax:* (011) 8127634
E-mail: info@bluedizioni.it
Web Site: www.bluedizioni.it
Key Personnel
Press: Silvia Ferrero *E-mail:* ferrero@bluedizioni.it
Founded: 1995
Subjects: Cookery, Environmental Studies, History, Sports, Athletics, Travel & Tourism, Mountains, Nature
ISBN Prefix(es): 978-88-7904; 978-88-87417
Foreign Rights: Nabu International Literary & Film Agency (Silvia Brunelli)
Distribution Center: ALI Agenzia Libraria Internationale SRL, Via Milano 73/75, 20010 Cornaredo MI *Tel:* (02) 99 76 24 30 *Fax:* (02) 36 54 81 88 *E-mail:* infoali@alilibri.it *Web Site:* www.alilibri.it

Edizioni Blues Brothers, *imprint of* Kaos Edizioni SRL

Universita Bocconi Editore (UBE), *imprint of* EGEA SpA (Edizioni Giuridiche Economiche Aziendali)

Bolis Edizioni
Via Emilia, 25, 24052 Azzano San Paolo BG
Tel: (035) 330474 *Fax:* (035) 316462
E-mail: info@bolisedizioni.it
Web Site: www.bolisedizioni.it
Founded: 1833
Subjects: Architecture & Interior Design, Art, Cookery, Health, Nutrition, History, Photography, Sports, Athletics, Travel & Tourism, Bicycling, Culture
ISBN Prefix(es): 978-88-7827

Bollati Boringhieri Editore+
Corso Vittorio Emanuele II 86, 10121 Turin
Tel: (011) 5591711 *Fax:* (011) 543024
E-mail: info@bollatiboringhieri.it
Web Site: www.bollatiboringhieri.it
Key Personnel
President: Romilda Bollati di Saint Pierre
Vice President: Stefano Mauri
Editorial Dir: Renzo Guidieri
Rights: Flavia Abbinante *E-mail:* flavia.abbinante@bollatiboringhieri.it
Founded: 1957
Subjects: Economics, History, Literature, Literary Criticism, Essays, Philosophy, Science (General), Social Sciences, Sociology
ISBN Prefix(es): 978-88-339
Parent Company: Gruppo Editoriale Mauri Spagnol SpA

Bompiani-RCS Libri
Division of RCS Libri SpA
Via Mecenate, 91, 20138 Milan MI
Web Site: www.rcslibri.it; www.bompiani.rcslibri.it
Key Personnel
Foreign Rights & Acquisitions Manager: Anna Falavena *E-mail:* anna.falavena@rcs.it
Corporate Communications: Valentina Ciolfi *Tel:* (02) 2584 4164 *E-mail:* valentina.ciolfi@rcs.it
Founded: 1929
Subjects: Art, Drama, Theater, Fiction, Literature, Literary Criticism, Essays, Nonfiction (General), Philosophy, Science (General)
ISBN Prefix(es): 978-88-451; 978-88-452; 978-88-450
Number of titles published annually: 175 Print

Bonacci Editore SRL+
Via degli Olmetti, 38, 00060 Formello RM
Tel: (06) 90 75 091 *Fax:* (06) 90 60 03 26
E-mail: info@bonacci.it
Web Site: www.bonacci.it
Key Personnel
Mng Dir: Alessandra Bonacci; Giorgio Bonacci
Founded: 1941
Specialize in the production of material for the teaching of Italian as a foreign language.
Subjects: Education, Italian as a Foreign Language
ISBN Prefix(es): 978-88-7573
Total Titles: 4 Print; 1 Audio

Bonania University Press SpA
Via Farini 37, 40124 Bologna BO
Tel: (051) 232882 *Fax:* (051) 221019
E-mail: info@buponline.com
Web Site: www.buponline.com
Key Personnel
Dir: Maria Rita Sperotti
Editor: Milena Aguzzoli; Marco Manzi; Mattia Righi
Founded: 1998
Subjects: Art, Law, Literature, Literary Criticism, Essays, Medicine, Nursing, Dentistry, Photography, Social Sciences, Sociology
ISBN Prefix(es): 978-88-7395
Number of titles published annually: 90 Print

Bonanno Editore+
Via Veneto, 28, 95024 Acireale, Catania
Tel: (095) 7648675
Key Personnel
Press: Alfio Grasso
Founded: 1966
Subjects: Anthropology, Archaeology, Architecture & Interior Design, Art, Behavioral Sciences, Communications, Cookery, Criminology, Drama, Theater, Economics, Education, Engineering (General), Environmental Studies, Fiction, Film, Video, Foreign Countries, Geography, Geology, Government, Political Science, History, Language Arts, Linguistics, Law, Lit-

erature, Literary Criticism, Essays, Medicine, Nursing, Dentistry, Music, Dance, Philosophy, Photography, Poetry, Psychology, Psychiatry, Religion - Other, Social Sciences, Sociology, Sports, Athletics, Travel & Tourism, Comics, Gastronomy, Methodology, Pedagogy, Social Policies
ISBN Prefix(es): 978-88-7796
Number of titles published annually: 30 Print
Total Titles: 250 Print
Divisions: AEB Editrice
Branch Office(s)
Bonanno Editore Roita, Via Torino 150, Rome
Bookshop(s): Libreria Bonanno
Warehouse: Via Cozzale, 36, 95024 Acireale, Catania

Bonsignori Editore SRL+
Via Leonardo Fibonacci 112, 00166 Rome
Tel: (06) 99709447 *Fax:* (06) 99709447
E-mail: redazione@bonsignori.it
Web Site: www.bonsignori.it
Key Personnel
Chief Executive: Simona Bonsignori
 E-mail: bons@bonsignori.it
Founded: 1992
Specializes in archeology, architecture & the history of art.
Subjects: Archaeology, Architecture & Interior Design, Art, History
ISBN Prefix(es): 978-88-7597
Number of titles published annually: 20 Print

Book Editore
Via Ca' Pompa, 4/a, 44030 Ro Ferrarese FE
Tel: (0532) 874814 *Fax:* (0532) 874814
E-mail: info@bookeditore.it
Web Site: www.bookeditore.it
Key Personnel
Dir: Massimo Scrignoli *E-mail:* m.scrignoli@bookeditore.it
Sales Dir: Annalisa Piva *E-mail:* a.piva@bookeditore.it
Founded: 1987
Subjects: Language Arts, Linguistics, Literature, Literary Criticism, Essays, Philosophy, Poetry
ISBN Prefix(es): 978-88-7232
Bookshop(s): Diest, Via Cavalcanti, 11, 10132 Turin *Tel:* (011) 89 81 164 *Fax:* (011) 89 81 164

Book Service SAS+
Via Bardonecchia 174/D, 10141 Turin
Tel: (011) 77 24 391 *Fax:* (011) 77 24 495
E-mail: info@bookservice.it
Web Site: www.bookservice.it
Founded: 1990
Subjects: History, Literature, Literary Criticism, Essays, Philosophy, Poetry, Social Sciences, Sociology
ISBN Prefix(es): 978-88-87106

Bookme, *imprint of* DeA Planeta Libri SRL

Edizioni del Borgo, *imprint of* Giunti Editore SpA

Edizioni Borla SRL+
Via delle Fornaci, 50, 00165 Rome
Tel: (06) 39375379; (06) 39377294 *Fax:* (06) 39376620
E-mail: borla@edizioni-borla.it
Web Site: www.edizioni-borla.it
Key Personnel
Mng Dir: Dr Vincenzo D'Agostino
Founded: 1853
Subjects: Anthropology, Education, Government, Political Science, History, Inspirational, Spirituality, Philosophy, Psychology, Psychiatry, Religion - Other, Social Sciences, Sociology
ISBN Prefix(es): 978-88-263

Boroli Editore, see Il Castello SRL

Italo Bovolenta Editore
Subsidiary of Zanichelli Editore SpA
Via della Ginestra, 227/1, 44100 Ferrara
Tel: (0532) 259386 *Fax:* (0532) 259387
E-mail: bovolenta@bovolentaeditore.it; bovolenta@iol.it
Web Site: multimedia.bovolentaeditore.com
Founded: 1975
Subjects: Art, Biological Sciences, Chemistry, Chemical Engineering, Communications, Earth Sciences, Genealogy, History, Literature, Literary Criticism, Essays, Philosophy, Physics, Natural Sciences
ISBN Prefix(es): 978-88-369

Bozen-Bolzano University Press
Universitaetsplatz 1-piazza Universita, 1, 39100 Bozen-Bolzano
Tel: (0471) 012300 *Fax:* (0471) 012309
E-mail: universitypress@unibz.it; info@unibz.it
Web Site: bupress.unibz.it; www.unibz.it
Key Personnel
Dir: Gerda Winkler *Tel:* (0471) 012310
 E-mail: gerda.winkler@unibz.it
Contact: Dr Astrid Parteli *Tel:* (0471) 012312
 E-mail: astrid.parteli@unibz.it
Founded: 2005
Subjects: Art, Economics, Education, Engineering (General), Language Arts, Linguistics, Music, Dance, Science (General), Social Sciences, Sociology, Technology, Design, Language Teaching
ISBN Prefix(es): 978-88-6046

Bradipolibri Editore SRL
Via Dora Baltea, 16, 10015 Ivrea TO
Mailing Address: CP 7, 10015 Ivrea TO
Tel: (0125) 639428 *Fax:* (0125) 639428
E-mail: edizioni@bradipolibri.it
Web Site: www.bradipolibri.it
Founded: 1999
Subjects: Fiction, History, Nonfiction (General), Sports, Athletics, Current Events, Narrative
ISBN Prefix(es): 978-88-96184

Brenner Editore+
Via Adige, 41, 87100 Cosenza CS
Tel: (0984) 74537 *Fax:* (0984) 74537
Web Site: brennereditore.com
Key Personnel
Publisher: Walter Brenner
Founded: 1956
Subjects: Biography, Memoirs, Ethnicity, History, Medicine, Nursing, Dentistry, Philosophy, Poetry, Regional Interests, Culture, Esotericism

Giorgio Bretschneider Editore
Via Crescenzio, 43, 00193 Rome
Tel: (06) 6879361 *Fax:* (06) 6864543
E-mail: info@bretschneider.it; orders@bretschneider.it
Web Site: www.bretschneider.it
Key Personnel
Mng Dir: Boris Bretschneider
Founded: 1973
Subjects: Archaeology, History, Ancient History, Greek & Roman Antiquities, Greek & Roman Archaeology
ISBN Prefix(es): 978-88-85007; 978-88-7689
Number of titles published annually: 20 Print
Total Titles: 400 Print
Distributor for Italiana Di Atene; Scuola Archaeologica; Universita di Macerata; Universita di Messina

The British School at Rome
via Antonio Gramsci 61, 00197 Rome
Tel: (06) 326 4939 *Fax:* (06) 322 1201
E-mail: info@bsrome.it

Web Site: www.bsr.ac.uk
Key Personnel
Dir: Christopher Smith *E-mail:* director@bsrome.it
Subjects: Architecture & Interior Design, Art, Social Sciences, Sociology
ISBN Prefix(es): 978-0-904152
Branch Office(s)
BSR London Office, The BSR at the British Academy, 10 Carlton House Terrace, London SW1Y 5AH, United Kingdom *Tel:* (020) 79695202 *Fax:* (020) 79695401

Le Brumaie Editore
Via Roma 70/10, 10600 Cantalupa TO
Tel: (0121) 354428 *Fax:* (0121) 354428
E-mail: direct@lebrumaieeditore.it
Web Site: www.lebrumaieeditore.it
Founded: 2005
Subjects: Cookery, Fairy Tales, Novels
ISBN Prefix(es): 978-88-902599; 978-88-96570

Edizioni Lina Brun
Via Cardinal Maurizio, 12, 10131 Turin TO
Tel: (011) 8198145
E-mail: linabrun@edizionilinabrun.it
Web Site: edizionilinabrun.it
Founded: 1999
Subjects: Fiction, Literature, Literary Criticism, Essays, Travel & Tourism
ISBN Prefix(es): 978-88-87846

Edizioni Bucalo SNC
CP 51, 04100 Latina
Tel: (0773) 602451 *Fax:* (0773) 602451
E-mail: info@bucalo.it
Web Site: www.bucalo.it
Key Personnel
Chief Executive: Andrea Bucalo
Founded: 1965
Subjects: Law
ISBN Prefix(es): 978-88-7456
Parent Company: C Sopra

Gruppo Buffetti SpA
Via Antolisei 10, 00173 Rome
Tel: (06) 2319150
Web Site: www.buffetti.it
Founded: 1973
Subjects: Economics, Law, Management
ISBN Prefix(es): 978-88-19
Parent Company: Dylog Italia SpA

Bulzoni Editore SRL (Le Edizioni Universitarie d'Italia')+
via dei Liburni, 14, 00185 Rome
Tel: (06) 4455207 *Fax:* (06) 4450355
E-mail: administrazione@bulzoni.it; bulzoni@bulzoni.it
Web Site: www.bulzoni.it
Key Personnel
Mng Dir, Editorial: Anna Bulzoni
Founded: 1967
Subjects: Art, Drama, Theater, Engineering (General), Fiction, Film, Video, Language Arts, Linguistics, Law, Literature, Literary Criticism, Essays, Philosophy, Science (General), Social Sciences, Sociology
ISBN Prefix(es): 978-88-7119; 978-88-8319
Bookshop(s): Libreria Ricerche, Via Liburni 10/12, 00185 Rome *Tel:* (06) 491851

Bur
Via Mondadori, 1, 20090 Segrate MI
E-mail: info@rizzolilibri.it; ufficiostampa.rizzoli@rizzolilibri.it; rizzoli.rights@rizzolilibri.it
Web Site: www.bur.eu; www.rizzolilibri.it
Founded: 1949
Subjects: Art, Biography, Memoirs, Cookery, Economics, Fashion, Fiction, Government, Po-

litical Science, History, Humor, Inspirational, Spirituality, Literature, Literary Criticism, Essays, Music, Dance, Mysteries, Suspense, Philosophy, Poetry, Psychology, Psychiatry, Religion - Other, Romance, Science (General), Science Fiction, Fantasy, Sports, Athletics, Adventure, Cinema & TV, Current Affairs, Entertainment, Leisure, Lifestyle
ISBN Prefix(es): 978-88-6126
Parent Company: Rizzoli Libri SpA

Cacucci Editore+
Via Nicolai, 39, 70122 Bari
Tel: (080) 5214220 *Fax:* (080) 5234777
E-mail: info@cacucci.it; ordini@cacucci.it (orders)
Web Site: www.cacucci.it
Key Personnel
Mng Dir: Dr Nicola Cacucci
Editorial: Michele de Serio *E-mail:* mdeserio@cacucci.it
Founded: 1929
Subjects: Economics, Geography, Geology, History, Law, Mathematics, Philosophy, Public Administration, Science (General)
ISBN Prefix(es): 978-88-8422
Bookshop(s): Via B Cairoli 140, 70122 Bari, Contact: Vito Lobuono *Tel:* (080) 521550 *Fax:* (080) 5219471 *E-mail:* libreriasede@cacucci.it; Via S Matarrese, 2/d, 70124 Bari, Contact: Michele Lobuono *Tel:* (080) 5617175 *Fax:* (080) 5617175 *E-mail:* libreriafiliale@cacucci.it

CADR, see Centro Ambrosiano di Dialogo con le Religioni (CADR)

CADSR, *imprint of* Centro Ambrosiano di Dialogo con le Religioni (CADR)

Calzetti & Mariucci Editori
Via del Sottopasso, 7, 06089 Torgiano PG
Tel: (075) 599 73 10 *Fax:* (075) 599 73 10
E-mail: dir@calzetti-mariucci.it
Web Site: www.calzetti-mariucci.it
Founded: 1993
Subjects: Medicine, Nursing, Dentistry, Psychology, Psychiatry, Sports, Athletics, Fitness, Rehabilitation, Sport Physiology & Anatomy, Sport Psychology
ISBN Prefix(es): 978-88-6028; 978-88-80042
Orders to: Via della Valtiera 229, 06087 Ponte San Giovanni PG *Tel:* (075) 599 73 10; (075) 599 00 17 *E-mail:* ordini@calzetti-mariucci.it

Camelozampa
Via Main 8, 35043 Monselice PD
Tel: (0429) 767247
E-mail: info@camelozampa.com
Web Site: www.camelozampa.com
Key Personnel
Foreign Rights: Sara Saorin *E-mail:* sara@camelozampa.com; Francesca Segato *E-mail:* francesca@camelozampa.com
Founded: 2011
ISBN Prefix(es): 978-88-96323

Camera dei Deputati+
via del Seminario 76, 00186 Rome
Tel: (06) 67603476 *Fax:* (06) 6786886
E-mail: bib_segreteria@camera.it
Web Site: www.camera.it
Key Personnel
Dir: Giovanni Rizzoni
Founded: 1848
Specialize in bibliographies, books, pamphlets, proceedings, reference works.
Subjects: Economics, History, Law
Number of titles published annually: 20 Print

Total Titles: 250 Print
Bookshop(s): Libreria della Camera dei Deputati, Via Uffici del Vicario 17, Rome *Tel:* (06) 67603715 *E-mail:* sg-pi_libreria@camera.it

Campanotto Editore+
Via Marano 46, 33037 Pasian di Prato UD
Tel: (0432) 699390; (0432) 690155 *Fax:* (0432) 644728
E-mail: edizioni@campanottoeditore.it; campanottoed@libero.it
Web Site: www.campanottoeditore.it
Key Personnel
President: Franca Campanotto
Publishing Dir: Carlo Marcello Conti
Marketing Manager: Conti Ezra
Press: Inga Conti
Founded: 1977
Subjects: Archaeology, Art, Fiction, History, Literature, Literary Criticism, Essays, Music, Dance, Philosophy, Photography, Poetry, Radio, TV, Religion - Catholic, Religion - Other
ISBN Prefix(es): 978-88-456
Subsidiaries: Grafiche Piratello
Distribution Center: Distribook Srl di Vincenzo Nagari, Via M F Quintiliano, 20, 20138 Milan *Tel:* (02) 58012329 *Fax:* (02) 58012329
Book Service sas, Via Bardonecchia, 174/D, 10141 Turin *Tel:* (011) 7724369 *Fax:* (011) 7724495

Canova Edizioni
Viale Giacomelli, 16, 31100 Treviso
Tel: (0422) 262397; (0422) 298163 *Fax:* (0422) 433673
E-mail: info@canovaedizioni.eu
Web Site: www.canovaedizioni.eu
Founded: 1853
Subjects: Art, History
ISBN Prefix(es): 978-88-85066; 978-88-86177; 978-88-87061; 978-88-8409
Bookshop(s): Libreria Canova, Via Cavour 6/b, 31015 Conegliano *Tel:* (0438) 22680 *E-mail:* libreria.con@canovaedizioni.it; Libreria Canova, Piazzetta Lombardi, 1, 31100 Treviso *Tel:* (0422) 546253 *E-mail:* libreria.tv@canovaedizioni.it

Edizioni Cantagalli SRL+
Str Massetana Romana, 12, 53100 Siena
Mailing Address: CP 155, 53100 Siena
Tel: (0577) 42102 *Fax:* (0577) 45363
E-mail: cantagalli@edizionicantagalli.com; foreignrights@edizionicantagalli.com
Web Site: www.edizionicantagalli.com
Founded: 1925
Subjects: Biblical Studies, Disability, Special Needs, History, Music, Dance, Nonfiction (General), Philosophy, Regional Interests, Religion - Catholic, Science (General), Theology
ISBN Prefix(es): 978-88-8272

Franco Cantini Editore, see Octavo-Franco Cantini Editore

Octavo-Franco Cantini Editore+
CP 1490, 50122 Florence
Tel: (055) 861341
Web Site: www.francocantini.it
Key Personnel
Mng Dir: Franco Cantini
Founded: 1993
Specialize in art.
Subjects: Antiques, Archaeology, Architecture & Interior Design, Art, Cookery, Education, Fashion, Fiction, Health, Nutrition, History, Photography, Travel & Tourism
ISBN Prefix(es): 978-88-8030

Capone Editore SRL+
Via Prov le Lecce-Cavallino, Km 1,250, 73100 Lecce
Tel: (0832) 611877 *Fax:* (0832) 611877
E-mail: info@caponeeditore.it
Web Site: www.caponeeditore.it
Key Personnel
Editorial: Lorenzo Capone
Founded: 1980
Subjects: Art, Communications, Ethnicity, History, Literature, Literary Criticism, Essays, Philosophy, Regional Interests
ISBN Prefix(es): 978-88-8349

Edizioni del Capricorno
Imprint of Centro Scientifico Arte SRL
Corso Montecucco, 73, 10141 Turin
Tel: (011) 385 36 56 *Fax:* (011) 385 32 44
E-mail: info@edizionidelcapricorno.com
Web Site: www.edizionidelcapricorno.com
Key Personnel
Editor: Dr Walter Martiny
Subjects: Cookery, Health, Nutrition, History, Outdoor Recreation, Photography, Wine & Spirits, Food, Hiking
ISBN Prefix(es): 978-88-7707

Edizioni Carmelitane (Carmelite Press)+
Via Sforza Pallavicini, 10, 00193 Rome
Tel: (06) 46201807 *Fax:* (06) 46201808
E-mail: edizioni@ocarm.org
Web Site: www.ocarm.org/edizioni
Founded: 1954
Publishing house of the Carmelite Order.
Subjects: Biblical Studies, History, Religion - Catholic, Theology
ISBN Prefix(es): 978-88-7288
Number of titles published annually: 5 Print
Total Titles: 1,000 Print
Distributed by Camelite Media (USA & Canada)

Carocci Editore SpA
Via Sardegna, 50, 00187 Rome
Tel: (06) 42818417 *Fax:* (06) 42747931
E-mail: stampa@carocci.it
Web Site: www.carocci.it
Founded: 1980
Subjects: Archaeology, Architecture & Interior Design, Art, Communications, Economics, Education, Engineering (General), History, Literature, Literary Criticism, Essays, Philosophy, Psychology, Psychiatry, Social Sciences, Sociology, Contemporary Art, Humanities, Statistics
ISBN Prefix(es): 978-88-430
Distribution Center: Messaggerie Libri SpA *Web Site:* www.messaggerielibri.it

Carthusia Edizioni SRL
Via Caradosso, 10, 20123 Milan MI
Tel: (02) 4981750 *Fax:* (02) 4987106
E-mail: info@carthusiaedizioni.it
Web Site: www.carthusiaedizioni.it
Founded: 1987
ISBN Prefix(es): 978-88-87212

Edizioni Cartografiche Milanesi SRL (ECM)+
Via Reali, 3/5-SP 44 ex SS 35 dei Giovi Comasina, 20037 Paderno Dugnano MI
Tel: (02) 9101649 *Fax:* (02) 9101118
E-mail: info@ortelio-ecm.it
Web Site: www.ortelio-ecm.it
Key Personnel
President: Vitale Franciosi
Founded: 1961
Subjects: Geography, Geology
ISBN Prefix(es): 978-88-8151
Number of titles published annually: 40 Print
Total Titles: 70 Print
Imprints: Ortelio

Cartoonseries, *imprint of* Stampa Alternativa - Nuovi Equilibri

Casa Editrice ALBA
Via Borgo Punta, 187, 44100 Ferrara FE
Tel: (0532) 75 44 61; (329) 4753136 (cell)
    Fax: (0532) 75 44 61
Key Personnel
Dir: Roberto Puviani
Founded: 1972
Subjects: Art, Literature, Literary Criticism, Essays, Poetry

Casa Editrice Ambrosiana
Viale Romagna, 5, 20089 Rozzano MI
Tel: (02) 52202250 *Fax:* (02) 52202260
E-mail: direzione@ceaedizioni.it
Web Site: www.ceaedizioni.it
Founded: 1940
Subjects: Biological Sciences, Chemistry, Chemical Engineering, Engineering (General), Mathematics, Medicine, Nursing, Dentistry, Physics, Psychology, Psychiatry, Science (General), Veterinary Science, Complementary Medicine
ISBN Prefix(es): 978-88-08

Casa Editrice Astrolabio-Ubaldini Editore+
Via Guido D'Arezzo 16, 00198 Rome
Tel: (06) 855 21 31 *Fax:* (06) 855 27 56
E-mail: astrolabio@astrolabio-ubaldini.
    com; redazione@astrolabio-ubaldini.com
    (editorial); rights@astrolabio-ubaldini.com;
    ufficiostampa@astrolabio-ubaldini.com
Web Site: www.astrolabio-ubaldini.com
Key Personnel
Chief Executive: Francesco Gana
Founded: 1944
Subjects: Philosophy, Psychology, Psychiatry, Social Sciences, Sociology, Oriental Studies
ISBN Prefix(es): 978-88-340
Number of titles published annually: 35 Print
Total Titles: 1,050 Print
Distribution Center: Messaggerie Libri SpA,
    Via Verdi, 8, 20090 Assago MI *Tel:* (02)
    457741 *Fax:* (02) 45701032 *Web Site:* www.
    messaggerielibri.it
Eredi Venturini Sas, Via Mose Bianchi, 95,
    20149 Milan MI *Tel:* (02) 4989391 *Fax:* (02)
    48006862 *E-mail:* eredi.venturini@tiscalinet.it
    (Lombardia & Italian-speaking Switzerland)
Agenzia Libraria Fozzi Sas, Viale Elmas, 154,
    09122 Cagliari CA *Tel:* (070) 2128011
    Fax: (070) 241288 *E-mail:* agfozzi@tiscali.it
    Web Site: www.agenziafozzi.it (Sardinia)

Casa Editrice Baha'i
Via Stoppani, 10, 00197 Rome
Tel: (06) 9334334
E-mail: ceb@bahai.it
Web Site: www.editricebahai.com
Founded: 1969
Subjects: Biography, Memoirs, Economics, Education, Religion - Other, Social Sciences, Sociology
ISBN Prefix(es): 978-88-7214

Casa Editrice Bonechi SRL+
Via Cairoli 18/b, 50131 Florence
Tel: (055) 576841 *Fax:* (055) 5000766
E-mail: info@bonechibooks.it
Web Site: www.bonechi.it; www.bonechi.com
Key Personnel
Owner: Monica Bonechi
    E-mail: monicabonechi@bonechibooks.it
Founded: 1973
Subjects: Art, Cookery, Travel & Tourism, Nature
ISBN Prefix(es): 978-88-7204; 978-88-7009; 978-88-8029; 978-88-8182; 978-88-476
Imprints: CEB

Casa Editrice Corbaccio SRL+
Via Giuseppe Parini 14, 20121 Milan
Tel: (02) 00623201 *Fax:* (02) 00623310
E-mail: info@corbaccio.it; ufficiostampa@
    corbaccio.it
Web Site: www.corbaccio.it
Key Personnel
President: Luigi Spagnol
Mng Dir: Stefano Mauri
Editorial Dir: Cecilia Perucci
Rights & Acquisitions Dir: Cristina Foschini
Founded: 1992
Subjects: Fiction, Health, Nutrition, Inspirational, Spirituality, Nonfiction (General), Romance, Self-Help
ISBN Prefix(es): 978-88-7972
Parent Company: Gruppo Editoriale Mauri Spagnol SpA
Warehouse: Messaggerie Italiane SpA, Maggazzino Editoriale, Via Bereguardina, 20080 Casarile MI
Orders to: Pro Libro, Via Gherardini 10, 20145
    Milan *Tel:* (02) 34597630 *Fax:* (02) 34597220
    E-mail: prolibro@prolibro.it

Casa editrice d'arte FMR (FMR Fine Art Publishing House)+
via della Tecnica 75, 40068 San Lazzaro di Savena BO
Tel: (051) 6008911 *Fax:* (051) 6008950
E-mail: fmr@fmrarte.it; ufficiostampa@fmrarte.it
Web Site: www.fmronline.com; www.fmrarte.it
Key Personnel
Founder: Davide Bolognesi; Fabio Lazzari
Communications Dir: Roberta Cardinali *E-mail:* r.
    cardinali@fmrarte.it
Founded: 1992
Subjects: Art
ISBN Prefix(es): 978-88-216
Number of titles published annually: 20 Print
Total Titles: 1,000 Print
Parent Company: Gruppo Marilena Ferrari-FMR
Branch Office(s)
Fortuny 7-3°, 28010 Madrid, Spain *Tel:* (034)
    915488550 *Fax:* (034) 915488552
    E-mail: fmrarte@fmrarte.es
Foreign Rep(s): Hipproj (Portugal)

Casa Editrice Dr A Milani, see CEDAM SpA

Casa Editrice Dott Eugenio Jovene SRL
Via Mezzocannone, 109, 80134 Naples
Tel: (081) 552 10 19; (081) 552 12 74; (081) 552
    34 71 *Fax:* (081) 552 06 87
E-mail: info@jovene.it
Web Site: www.jovene.it
Key Personnel
Mng Dir: Dr Alessandro Rossi
Founded: 1854
Subjects: Economics, Law
ISBN Prefix(es): 978-88-243
Foreign Rep(s): ABE Marcheting (Poland); Almedina Libr (Portugal); Andaluza Libr (Spain); Libreria Bibliografica Miro Romano (Switzerland); Biblios Service (Greece); Blackwell B H Libr Ltd (England); J Ontiveros Blanco Libr (Spain); Bookimpex Libr (Netherlands); Librairie du Boulevard (Switzerland); Buchholz Libr (Portugal); Liberia Centrale (Switzerland); Centro Importador Libro Italiano (Spain); Coimbra Editora (Portugal); F Del Blanco International Books (Germany); Deuticke Franz Universitatbuch (Austria); Diaz De Santos Libr (Spain); Didaskalia Editora Porto (Portugal); Diffusion de Boccard (France); Dos Advogados Editora Ltda (Brazil); EBSCO (USA); La Librairie Europeenne SA (Belgium); Ex Libris (Germany); Faxon F W Company Inc (USA); Ferin Lda Libr (Portugal); Trenkle K G Gerhard (Germany); Golf Verlag - Universitatbuchhandlung (Austria); Buchvertrieb Golfverlog (Austria); Grant & Cutler at Foyles

(England); Rohr Hans Libr (Switzerland); Harrassowitz Booksellers (Germany); Heffer & Sons Ltd (England); Behrendt Hermann Libr (Germany); International Literature and Information Center (Hungary); Italia Shobo Co Ltd (Japan); Libreria Italiana (Spain); Kinikuniya Company Ltd (Japan); Kokusai Shobo Ltd (Japan); L & S (Lange & Springer) (Germany); Franz Led & Company KG Libr (Austria); Louisiana State University Law Library (USA); Hantzschel Dott Ludwig (Germany); Minerva Wissenschaftliche Buchhandlung GmbH (Austria); Miura Shoten Booksellers Ltd (Japan); Mundi-Prensa Libr SA (Spain); Martinus Nijhoff (Netherlands); Oniense Libr (Spain); Gothier Paul Libr (Belgium); Editions Pedone (France); Philobiblos Book Mart (USA); Marcial Pons Libr (Spain); Portico SA Libr (Spain); Portugal Dias & Andrade Lda Libr (Portugal); Presses Universitaires Libr (Belgium); Fred B Rothman & Co (USA); Rowecom France (France); Otto Schneid Libr (Austria); Stern-Verlag Janssen & Co (Germany); Stockmann Libr (Finland); Librairie de l'Universite (France); Santo Vanasia Libr (Argentina, Spain)

Casa Editrice Giuseppe Principato SpA+
Via GB Fauche 10, 20154 Milan
Tel: (02) 312025; (02) 3315309 *Fax:* (02) 33104295
E-mail: info@principato.it
Web Site: www.principato.it
Key Personnel
Editorial Dir: Franco Menin
Founded: 1926
Subjects: Chemistry, Chemical Engineering, Earth Sciences, English as a Second Language, Geography, Geology, History, Literature, Literary Criticism, Essays, Mathematics, Physics
ISBN Prefix(es): 978-88-416
Number of titles published annually: 20 Print
Total Titles: 500 Print

Casa Editrice Herbita+
Via Vincenzo Errante, 44, 90127 Palermo
Tel: (091) 616 77 32 *Fax:* (091) 616 77 16
E-mail: mail@herbitaeditrice.it
Web Site: www.herbitaeditrice.it
Key Personnel
Chief Executive: Leonardo Palermo
Founded: 1973
Subjects: Archaeology, Art, Computer Science, Economics, Geography, Geology, Government, Political Science, Law, Literature, Literary Criticism, Essays, Mathematics, Philosophy, Religion - Catholic
ISBN Prefix(es): 978-88-7994

Casa Editrice Le Lettere
Via Duca di Calabria 1/1, 50125 Florence
Tel: (055) 2342710; (055) 2466911 *Fax:* (055) 2346010
E-mail: staff@lelettere.it
Web Site: www.lelettere.it
Key Personnel
Editorial Dir: Nicoletta Gentile Pescarolo
    E-mail: n.pescarolo@lelettere.it
Mng Editor: Tiziana Battisti *E-mail:* redazione@
    lelettere.it
Founded: 1976
Subjects: History, Language Arts, Linguistics, Literature, Literary Criticism, Essays, Philosophy
ISBN Prefix(es): 978-88-7166
Warehouse: Via Francesco Gioli 5-11, 50018 Scandicci

Casa Editrice Libraria Ulrico Hoepli+
Via Hoepli 5, 20121 Milan
Tel: (02) 864871 *Fax:* (02) 8052886; (02) 864322
E-mail: hoepli@hoepli.it; info@hoepli.it; press@
    hoepli.it
Web Site: www.hoepli.it

Key Personnel
President: Dr Ulrico Carlo Hoepli
Mng Dir: Gianni Hoepli
Founded: 1870
Subjects: Art, Engineering (General), How-to, Law, Science (General), Social Sciences, Sociology, Technology
ISBN Prefix(es): 978-88-203
Bookshop(s): Libreria Internazionale Hoepli, Milan Tel: (02) 864871 Fax: (02) 864322 E-mail: libreria@hoepli.it
Shipping Address: Via Mameli 13, 20129 Milan Tel: (02) 733142; (02) 70126381 Fax: (02) 7382084; (02) 7380382 E-mail: orders@hoepli.it

Casa Editrice Longanesi SpA+
Via Gherardini 10, 20145 Milan
Tel: (02) 34597620 Fax: (02) 34597212
E-mail: info@longanesi.it
Web Site: www.longanesi.it
Key Personnel
Mng Dir: Stefano Mauri
Publishing Dir, Gruppo Editorial: Luigi Brioschi
Editorial Dir: Giuseppe Strazzeri
Rights & Acquisitions Dir, Gruppo Editorial: Cristina Foschini
Founded: 1946
Subjects: Archaeology, Art, Biography, Memoirs, Fiction, History, How-to, Medicine, Nursing, Dentistry, Music, Dance, Mysteries, Suspense, Nonfiction (General), Philosophy, Psychology, Psychiatry, Religion - Other, Science (General), Social Sciences, Sociology
ISBN Prefix(es): 978-88-304
Number of titles published annually: 100 Print
Total Titles: 1,000 Print
Parent Company: Gruppo Editoriale Mauri Spagnol SpA
Orders to: Pro Libro

Casa Editrice Luigi Battei
Borgo Santa Brigida, 1, 43100 Parma PR
Tel: (0521) 231291; (0521) 207529 Fax: (0521) 231291; (0521) 207529
E-mail: casaeditrice@battei.it; administrazione@battei.it; redazione@battei.it
Web Site: www.battei.it
Key Personnel
Chief Executive: Antonio Battei
Founded: 1872
Subjects: Architecture & Interior Design, Literature, Literary Criticism, Essays, Regional Interests
ISBN Prefix(es): 978-88-7883
Bookshop(s): Strada Cavour, 5/c, Parma PR Tel: (0521) 233733 E-mail: libreriabattei@battei.it

Casa Editrice Luigi Trevisini SRL
via Tito Livio 12, 20137 Milan
Tel: (02) 54 50 704 Fax: (02) 55 19 57 82
E-mail: trevisini@trevisini.it
Web Site: www.trevisini.it
Key Personnel
Chief Executive: Luigi Trevisini
Founded: 1859
ISBN Prefix(es): 978-88-292

Casa Editrice Marietti SpA+
Via Donizetti 41, 20122 Milan
Tel: (02) 77889911 Fax: (02) 76003491
E-mail: mariettieditore@mariettieditore.it
Web Site: www.mariettieditore.it
Key Personnel
President: Flavio Repetto
Foreign Rights: Beatrice Costa
Founded: 1820
Subjects: Biblical Studies, History, Literature, Literary Criticism, Essays, Philosophy, Religion - Catholic, Religion - Islamic, Religion - Jewish, Theology

ISBN Prefix(es): 978-88-211
Number of titles published annually: 30 Print
Total Titles: 600 Print

Casa Editrice Menna+
Via Scandone, 16, 83100 Avellino
Founded: 1976
Subjects: Drama, Theater, History, Law, Literature, Literary Criticism, Essays, Poetry
ISBN Prefix(es): 978-88-89588
Imprints: Verso il Futuro

Casa Editrice RIREA+
Via delle Isole, 30, 00198 Rome RM
Tel: (06) 8417690 Fax: (06) 8845732
E-mail: rivista@rirea.it
Web Site: www.rirea.it
Key Personnel
Dir: Dr Giovanna Nobile
Editorial: Prof Mario Mari
Founded: 1901
Subjects: Economics
ISBN Prefix(es): 978-88-96004
Number of titles published annually: 20 Print

Casa Musicale Edizioni Carrara SRL
Via A da Calepio, 4, 24125 Bergamo
Tel: (035) 243618 Fax: (035) 270298
E-mail: info@edizionicarrara.it
Web Site: www.edizionicarrara.it
Key Personnel
Dir: Vittorio Carrara, Jr
Curator: Vinicio Carrara
Founded: 1912
Subjects: Music, Dance, Religion - Catholic

Casagrande Fidia Sapiens - Editori Associati SRL (Casagrande Fidia Sapiens - Associated Publishers)+
Via Sant'Ampelio 5, 20141 Milan
Tel: (02) 895 462 86
E-mail: info@cfs-editore.com
Web Site: cfs-editore.ch
Founded: 1982
Subjects: Architecture & Interior Design, Art, Business, Cookery, Education, Foreign Countries, Government, Political Science, History, Journalism, Literature, Literary Criticism, Essays, Nonfiction (General), Photography, Swiss Culture, Swiss Society
ISBN Prefix(es): 978-88-7269 (Fidia Edizioni d'Arte); 978-88-7795 (Giampiero Casagrande editore (gC)); 978-88-8380 (Sapiens edizioni)
Imprints: Giampiero Casagrande editore (gC); Fidia Edizioni d'Arte; Gottardo Edizioni Verlag; Sapiens edizioni
Branch Office(s)
Via Marconi 4, 6901 Lugano, Switzerland Tel: (091) 923 567 7 Fax: (091) 922 017 1 E-mail: g.casagrande@cfs-editore.com
Distribution Center: Libreria Pecorini, Foro Buonaparte, 48, 20121 Milan Tel: (02) 864 606 60 Fax: (02) 720 014 62 E-mail: commerciale@pecorini.it

Casalini Libri SpA
Via Benedetto da Maiano, 3, 50014 Fiesole FI
Mailing Address: CP 12, 50014 Fiesole FI
Tel: (055) 50 18 1 Fax: (055) 50 18 201
E-mail: orders@casalini.it
Web Site: www.casalini.it
Key Personnel
President: Barbara Casalini E-mail: barbara@casalini.it
Mng Dir: Michele Casalini E-mail: michele@casalini.it
Head, Customer Services: Manuela Classen E-mail: manuela.classen@casalini.it
Head, Sales: Patricia O'Loughlin E-mail: patricia.oloughlin@casalini.it
Founded: 1958

Company also functions as book exporter, bibliographic agent & library supplier.
ISBN Prefix(es): 978-88-85297
Associate Companies: CADMO

Casi Ricordi+
Via Benigno Crespi, 19, 20159 Milan
Tel: (02) 80282 811 Fax: (02) 80282 882
E-mail: promozione.ricordi.italy@umusic.com
Web Site: www.ricordi.com
Founded: 1808
Music publisher.
Subjects: Art, Drama, Theater, Music, Dance
ISBN Prefix(es): 978-88-7592; 978-88-8192; 978-88-492; 978-88-87018
Parent Company: Universal Music Group
Associate Companies: Ricordi Americana SAEC, Argentina; Ricordi Brasileira S/A, Sao Paulo, Brazil; Ricordi Canada, Canada; Ricordi Parigi, France; G Ricordi & Co, Paseo de la Reforma 481-A, 06500 Mexico, DF, Mexico; Ricordi Monaco, Monaco; Ricordi Londra, United Kingdom
Subsidiaries: Arti Grafiche Ricordi SpA; Dischi Ricordi SpA; Gruppo Editoriale Musica Leggera Ricordi
Distributor for Aebersold; Bosworth; Chester Music; Ciriaco; Clarius Audi Didactic; Editio Musica Budapest; Fentone Music; Hal Leonard; Hal Leonard Europe; Music Sales; Novello; Philarmonia; Pwm; Ricordi Americana; Ricordi Londra; Ricordi Monaco; Union Musical Espanola; Universal Edition; Wiener Urtext
Foreign Rep(s): Broekmans & Van Poppel BV (Netherlands); Consortium Musical Distribution (France); Daihan Music Co Ltd (Korea); Europa Music (France); ID Music SA (France); Josquin Bvba Sprl (Belgium); Hal Leonard Australia Pty Ltd (Australia, New Zealand); Hal Leonard Publishing Co (Canada, USA); MDS UK (UK); Editio Musica Budapest (Hungary); Musica Viva AG (Switzerland); Ricordi & Co (Austria, Germany); United Music Publishers Ltd (UK); The University of Chicago Press (Canada, USA); Yamaha Music Media Corp (Japan)
Warehouse: Via Salomone, 77, 20138 Milan

Castalia Edizioni SAS+
Via Palmieri 14, 10143 Turin
Tel: (011) 437 41 76 Fax: (011) 437 41 76
Key Personnel
Editor: Maria Miglietti
Founded: 1984
Publisher of children's books.
Subjects: Fiction
ISBN Prefix(es): 978-88-7701
Number of titles published annually: 10 Print
Total Titles: 140 Print
Imprints: Maria Miglietti

Il Castello SRL+
via Milano 73/75, 20010 Cornaredo MI
Tel: (02) 99762433 Fax: (02) 99762445
E-mail: info@ilcastelloeditore.it
Web Site: www.ilcastelloeditore.it
Key Personnel
Administration: Daisy Zonato E-mail: daisy.zonato@ilcastelloeditore.it
Acquisitions Manager: Laura Chiappella E-mail: laura.chiappella@ilcastelloeditore.it
Founded: 1955
Subjects: Art, Astronomy, Cookery, Crafts, Games, Hobbies, Gardening, Plants, Outdoor Recreation, Photography, Sports, Athletics, Fitness
ISBN Prefix(es): 978-88-8039; 978-88-88112
Number of titles published annually: 60 Print
Total Titles: 300 Print

Alberto Castelvecchi Editore SRL
Via Isonzo, 34, 00198 Rome
Tel: (06) 8412007 Fax: (06) 85865742

E-mail: info@castelvecchieditore.com; rights@
castelvecchieditore.com
Web Site: www.castelvecchieditore.com
Key Personnel
Editorial Dir: Pietro D'Amore
Editor-in-Chief: Elisa Passacantilli
Production Manager: Maria Chiara De Silvestri
Sales Manager: Frederico Pancaldi
Rights: Miriam Capaldo
Founded: 1993
Subjects: Anthropology, Fiction, Government, Po-
litical Science, Literature, Literary Criticism,
Essays, Nonfiction (General), Philosophy, Cy-
berculture, International Politics, New Trends,
Youth Culture
ISBN Prefix(es): 978-88-7615

Editrice Il Castoro SRL+
viale Andrea Dora, 7, 20124 Milan
Tel: (02) 29513529 *Fax:* (02) 29529896
E-mail: info@castoro-on-line.it; redazione@
castoro-on-line.it
Web Site: www.castoro-on-line.it
Key Personnel
Editorial Dir: Renata Gorgani
Mng Editor: Alessandro Zontini
Foreign Rights: Pico Floridi *E-mail:* floridi.
castoro@fastwebnet.it
Administration Manager: Giovanna Corigliano
E-mail: corigliano@castoro-on-line.it
Founded: 1993
Subjects: Biography, Memoirs, Fiction, Film,
Video, Philosophy
ISBN Prefix(es): 978-88-8033
Distribution Center: Messaggerie Libri Spa, Via
G verdi, 8, 20900 Assago MI *Tel:* (02) 457741
Fax: (02) 45701032

CCSP, *imprint of* Edizioni del Centro Camuno di
Studi Preistorici

CEB, *imprint of* Casa Editrice Bonechi SRL

CEDAM SpA
Imprint of Wolters Kluwer Italia
Via Jappelli 5/6, 35121 Padua PD
Tel: (049) 8239111; (02) 82476707 *Fax:* (049)
8239120; (02) 82476403
E-mail: info.commerciali@cedam.it;
servizioclienti.cedam@wki.it
Web Site: www.cedam.com
Founded: 1903
Subjects: Biological Sciences, Criminology, Eco-
nomics, Finance, Government, Political Sci-
ence, Law, Management, Marketing, Mathemat-
ics, Medicine, Nursing, Dentistry, Philosophy,
Psychology, Psychiatry, Public Administration,
Social Sciences, Sociology
ISBN Prefix(es): 978-88-13
Warehouse: Via Uruguay n 14, 35127 Camin PD

Edizioni CELI, *imprint of* Gruppo Editorial
Faenza Editrice SpA

CELID
Via Enrico Cialdini, 26, 10138 Turin TO
Tel: (011) 447 47 74 *Fax:* (011) 447 47 59
E-mail: edizioni@celid.it; info@celid.it
Web Site: www.celid.it
Founded: 1974
Subjects: Architecture & Interior Design, Art,
Engineering (General), History, Psychology,
Psychiatry, Social Sciences, Sociology
ISBN Prefix(es): 978-88-7661
Bookshop(s): Castello del valentino, Viale Matti-
oli, 39, 10125 Turin TO *Tel:* (011) 650 89 64
E-mail: architettura@celid.it; Corso Duca degli
Abruzzi, 24, 10129 Turin TO *Tel:* (011) 54 08
75 *Fax:* (011) 564 79 22 *E-mail:* ingegneria@
celid.it; Corso Unione Sovietica 218 bis, 10134
Turin TO *Tel:* (011) 670 61 76 *Fax:* (011) 670

61 76 *E-mail:* economia@celid.it; Via Bog-
gio, 71/A, 10129 Turin TO *Tel:* (011) 564 79
11 *Fax:* (011) 564 79 11 *E-mail:* viaboggio@
celid.it; Via S Ottavio, 20, 10124 Turin TO
Tel: (011) 83 51 14 *E-mail:* palazzonuovo@
celid.it

Celtic Publishing, *imprint of* Raffaello Editrice
SRL

Celuc Libri SRL
Via Santa Valeria, 5, 20123 Milan MI
Tel: (02) 86450776 *Fax:* (02) 86451424
E-mail: celuclibri@libero.it
Web Site: www.celuclibri.it
Key Personnel
Mng Dir: Rita Barbatiello *E-mail:* celuclibri-
rita@live.it
Founded: 1969 (as Celuc), 1974 (as Celuc Libri)
Subjects: Economics, Government, Political Sci-
ence, History, Law, Literature, Literary Crit-
icism, Essays, Mathematics, Philosophy, Re-
ligion - Other, Science (General), Social Sci-
ences, Sociology

**Centro Ambrosiano di Dialogo con le Religioni
(CADR)**
Corso di Porta Ticinese, 33, 20123 Milan
Tel: (02) 8375476 *Fax:* (02) 8375476
E-mail: cadr@cadr.it
Web Site: www.cadr.it
Key Personnel
President: Don Augusto Casolo
Vice President: Don Giampiero Alberti
E-mail: giampieroalberti@tiscali.it
Secretary: Maria Caffarati; Lia Santi
Founded: 1972
Subjects: History, Religion - Buddhist, Religion
- Hindu, Religion - Islamic, Religion - Jewish,
Religion - Other
ISBN Prefix(es): 978-88-7098
Imprints: CADSR

Centro Ambrosiano IPL
Via Antonio da Recanate 1, 20124 Milan
Tel: (02) 6713161 *Fax:* (02) 66984388
E-mail: itlbook@tin.it
Key Personnel
Dir: Giovanni Cappelletto *E-mail:* gianni.
cappelletto@chiesadimilano.it
Founded: 1947
Subjects: Education, Government, Political Sci-
ence, Inspirational, Spirituality, Religion -
Catholic, Travel & Tourism
ISBN Prefix(es): 978-88-8025

Edizioni Centro Biblico
Via Masseria Vecchia 112, 80014 Giugliano NA
Tel: (081) 3340532 *Toll Free Tel:* 800 13 46 28
Fax: (081) 3340877
Founded: 1947
Subjects: Biblical Studies, Religion - Protestant,
Theology
ISBN Prefix(es): 978-88-7054

**Edizioni del Centro Camuno di Studi
Preistorici+**
Via Marconi, 7, 25044 Capo di Ponte BS
Tel: (0364) 42091 *Fax:* (0364) 42572
E-mail: info@ccsp.it
Web Site: www.ccsp.it
Key Personnel
Scientific Dir: Prof Emmanuel Anati
Founded: 1964
Publishing division of a research institution.
This publisher has indicated that 25% of their
product line is author subsidized.
Subjects: Anthropology, Antiques, Archaeology,
Art, Biblical Studies, Ethnicity, History, Reli-
gion - Other
ISBN Prefix(es): 978-88-86621

Number of titles published annually: 3 Print
Total Titles: 90 Print
Associate Companies: Arts & Crafts International;
IDAPEE (Institut des Arts Prehistoriques et
Ethnologique), Paris, France
Imprints: BCSP; BC News; CCSP
Subsidiaries: WARA: World Archives of Rock
Art

Edizioni Centro Di
Lungarno Serristori, 35, 50125 Florence
Tel: (055) 2342666 *Fax:* (055) 2342667
E-mail: edizioni@centrodi.it
Web Site: www.centrodi.it
Key Personnel
Publisher: Alessandra Marchi Pandolfini
Editor: Ginevra Marchi
Journals & Press: Silvia Cangioli *E-mail:* silvia@
centrodi.it
Founded: 1968
Subjects: Antiques, Architecture & Interior De-
sign, Art, Fashion, Decorative Arts
ISBN Prefix(es): 978-88-7038
Distributed by Antique Collectors Club
Distribution Center: Libro Co Italia SRL, 50026
San Casciano in Val di Pesa FI *Tel:* (055) 822
94 14; (055) 822 84 61 *Fax:* (055) 829 46 03;
(055) 822 84 62 *E-mail:* libroco@libroco.it
Web Site: www.libroco.it
Antique Collectors Club Ltd, Sandy Lane,
Old Martlesham, Woodbridge, Suffolk IP12
4SD, United Kingdom *Tel:* (01394) 389950
Fax: (01394) 389999 *E-mail:* sales@antique-
acc.com *Web Site:* www.accdistribution.com/uk
Antique Collectors Club Inc, 6 W 18 St,
Suite 4B, New York, NY 10011, United
States *E-mail:* sales@antique-acc.com *Web
Site:* www.accdistribution.com/us

Centro Editoriale Valtortiano SRL+
Viale Piscicelli 89/91, 03036 Isola del Liri FR
Tel: (0776) 807032 *Fax:* (0776) 809789
E-mail: info@mariavaltorta.com
Web Site: www.mariavaltorta.com
Key Personnel
Editor: Emilio Pisani
Founded: 1985
Publish the works of Maria Valtorta.
Subjects: Religion - Catholic, Theology
ISBN Prefix(es): 978-88-7987
Number of titles published annually: 6 Print
Total Titles: 124 Print

Centro Italiano Studi Sull'alto Medioevo
Piazza della Liberta, 12, Palace Ancaiani, 06049
Spoleto PG
Tel: (0743) 225630 *Fax:* (0743) 49902
E-mail: cisam@cisam.org
Web Site: www.cisam.org
Key Personnel
Chairman: Prof Enrico Menesto
Editorial: Roberto Arelli *E-mail:* roberto.arelli@
cisam.org
Sales: Andrea Trabalza *E-mail:* trabalza@cisam.
org
Founded: 1952
To promote meetings & scientific publications on
the High Middle Ages.
Subjects: Art, History, Literature, Literary Criti-
cism, Essays, Philosophy
ISBN Prefix(es): 978-88-7988
Number of titles published annually: 24 Print
Total Titles: 500 Print
Imprints: CISAM

Centro Psicologia Clinica Pescara+
Via Renato Paolini, 102, 65121 Pescara
Tel: (085) 4211986 *Fax:* (085) 4211986
E-mail: centro.psicologia@tin.it
Web Site: www.centro-psicologia.it
Key Personnel
President: Dr Carlo Di Berardino
Dir: Dr Spiridione Masaraki

Founded: 1982
Subjects: Psychology, Psychiatry

Il Cerchio Iniziative Editoriali+
Via di Mezzo 6/A, 47900 Rimini
Tel: (0541) 775977 *Fax:* (0541) 799173
E-mail: info@ilcerchio.it; amministrazione@ ilcerchio.it; ordini@ilcerchio.it
Web Site: www.ilcerchio.it
Key Personnel
Mng Dir, Production, Rights & Permissions: Dr Adolfo Morganti
Editorial & Desktop Publishing: Davide Pezzi
Sales & Customer Service: Gabriella Di Maggio
Founded: 1978
Subjects: Anthropology, Art, Economics, Government, Political Science, History, Literature, Literary Criticism, Essays, Nonfiction (General), Philosophy, Religion - Islamic, Religion - Other, Science (General), Social Sciences, Sociology, Mythology
ISBN Prefix(es): 978-88-86583; 978-88-8474

CG Ediz Medico-Scientifiche SRL+
Via Candido Viberti, 7, 10141 Turin
Mailing Address: CP 3232, Via Marsigli, 10141 Turin
Tel: (011) 338 507; (011) 37 57 38 *Fax:* (011) 38 52 750
E-mail: cgems.clienti@cgems.it
Web Site: www.cgems.it; www.cgemsformazione. it
Founded: 1958
Specialize in medical books.
Subjects: Biological Sciences, Medicine, Nursing, Dentistry, Veterinary Science
ISBN Prefix(es): 978-88-7110
Distribution Center: Messaggerie Libri SpA

Chiarelettere editore SRL
Via Guerrazzi, 9, 20145 Milan MI
Tel: (02) 34597436
E-mail: info@chiarelettere.it
Web Site: www.chiarelettere.it
Key Personnel
Editorial Dir: Lorenzo Fazio
Founded: 2007
Subjects: Economics, Government, Political Science, History, Society
ISBN Prefix(es): 978-88-6190

CIC Edizioni Internazionali+
Corso Trieste, 42, 00198 Rome
Tel: (06) 84 12 673 *Fax:* (06) 84 12 688
E-mail: info@gruppocic.it; editoriale@gruppocic. it; ordini@gruppocic.it
Web Site: www.gruppocic.it
Key Personnel
President & Marketing Manager: Dr Raffaele Salvati *E-mail:* r.salvati@gruppocic.it
Mng Editor: Prof Andrea Salvati *E-mail:* a. salvati@gruppocic.it
Advertising: Patrizia Arcangioli *E-mail:* arcangioli@gruppocic.it
Foreign Rights Dept: Marilena Cefa *E-mail:* cefa@gruppocic.it
Marketing: Carlo Bianchini *E-mail:* bianchini@ gruppocic.it
Founded: 1974
Membership(s): AIE; ANES; USPI.
Subjects: Health, Nutrition, Medicine, Nursing, Dentistry, Psychology, Psychiatry
ISBN Prefix(es): 978-88-7141
Number of titles published annually: 150 Print; 10 CD-ROM; 15 Audio
Total Titles: 600 Print; 10 CD-ROM; 30 Audio
Subsidiaries: Centro Italiano Congressi; Librerie CIC Edizioni Internazionali; Kairos
Branch Office(s)
Centro Italiano Congressi, CIC Sud, Via Escriva 28, 70124 Bari, Contact: Olimpia Cassano

Tel: (080) 50 43 737 *Fax:* (080) 50 43 736
E-mail: info@cicsud.it
Via Matteotti 52/a, 21012 Cassano Magnago VA
Tel: (0331) 28 23 59 *Fax:* (0331) 28 74 89
Distributor for George Thieme Verlag (Italian territory)
Warehouse: Via della Fontana 18, 00198 Rome
Tel: (06) 44 25 1281 *Fax:* (06) 44 26 2189
E-mail: ordini@gruppocic.it

Cideb Editrice SRL+
Subsidiary of De Agostini Edizioni Scolastiche SpA
Piazza Garibaldi, 11/2, 16035 Rapallo GE
Tel: (0185) 55803; (0185) 55804 *Fax:* (0185) 67150
E-mail: info@blackcat-cideb.com
Web Site: www.blackcat-cideb.com
Founded: 1973
Subjects: Literature, Literary Criticism, Essays
ISBN Prefix(es): 978-88-7754; 978-88-530
Imprints: Black Cat
Distribution Center: Vico del Pozzo, 12, 16035 Rapallo GE *Tel:* (0185) 1874100 *Fax:* (0185) 1874105
Returns: REAR, Strada del Portone 179, 10095 Grugliasco, Turin *E-mail:* info@black-cideb. com

Il Cigno Galileo Galilei, see Il Cigno GG Edizioni

Il Cigno GG Edizioni
Piazza San Salvatore in Lauro 15, 00186 Rome
Tel: (06) 6865493 *Fax:* (06) 6892109
E-mail: info@ilcigno.org; redazione@ilcigno.org
Web Site: www.ilcigno.org
Key Personnel
Editor & Event Organizer: Sonia Vazzano
Founded: 1968
Also specialize in printing graphic works. Publish catalogues & art volumes.
Subjects: Art, Computer Science, Law, Mathematics, Science (General)
ISBN Prefix(es): 978-88-7831
Number of titles published annually: 40 Print; 4 CD-ROM
Total Titles: 385 Print; 4 CD-ROM
Showroom(s): Archivi Greco, Museo Mastroianni & Il Cigno Galileo Galilei La Stamperia
Distribution Center: Gaetano Amodio, Via Francesco Battiato 24, 95039 Catania
Tel: (03095) 321328 (South Italy)
Pecorini Sas, Foro Buonaparte 48, 20121 Milan
Tel: (02) 86460660 *Fax:* (02) 72001462 (North Italy)

Edizioni Il Ciliegio
Via A Diaz 14E, 22040 Lurago D'erba CO
Tel: (031) 696284 *Fax:* (031) 8120257
E-mail: info@edizioniilciliegio.com
Web Site: www.edizioniilciliegio.com
Key Personnel
Head: Giovanna Mancini
Editorial Dir: Maurizio Marsi *E-mail:* m.marsi@ edizioniilciliegio.com
Founded: 2003
Subjects: Fiction, Literature, Literary Criticism, Essays
ISBN Prefix(es): 978-88-88996

Edizioni Cinque SRL
Imprint of Tipografia Litografia A Scotti SRL
Via E Berlinguer 6, 20872 Cornate d'Adda MB
Tel: (0346) 98 37 211 *Fax:* (039) 69 27 071
E-mail: contabalita@edizionicinque.it; info@ edizionicinque.it
Web Site: www.edizionicinque.it
Key Personnel
Dir: Mario Vittone *E-mail:* mvittone@ edizionicinque.it

Founded: 1988
Subjects: Animals, Pets, Dogs, Kennel
ISBN Prefix(es): 978-88-87072

Cisalpino, *imprint of* Monduzzi Editoriale

Cisalpino
Via B Eustachi, 12, 20129 Milan
Tel: (02) 2040 4031; (0521) 1711449 (orders)
Fax: (02) 2040 4044; (0521) 1711445 (orders)
E-mail: cisalpino@monduzzieditore.it; ordinilibrerie@monduzzieditore.it
Web Site: www.monduzzieditore.it/cisalpino
Founded: 1946
Subjects: Economics, History, Language Arts, Linguistics, Law, Literature, Literary Criticism, Essays, Management, Science (General)
ISBN Prefix(es): 978-88-205; 978-88-323
Parent Company: Monduzzi Editore SpA, Via Roberto Longhi 14/a, 40128 Bologna

CISAM, *imprint of* Centro Italiano Studi Sull'alto Medioevo

Citta Nuova Editrice+
Via Pieve Torina, 55, 00156 Rome
Tel: (06) 32 16 212; (06) 96 522 200 *Fax:* (06) 32 07 185
E-mail: info@cittanuova.it
Web Site: editrice.cittanuova.it
Key Personnel
Literary Dir: Lucia Velardi
Editorial Dir: Luca Gentile
Head, Marketing: Franco Fortuna
Sales Manager: Paolo Friso
Press: Elena Cardinali
Founded: 1959
Subjects: Biblical Studies, Education, Philosophy, Psychology, Psychiatry, Religion - Other, Social Sciences, Sociology, Theology
ISBN Prefix(es): 978-88-311
Subsidiaries: Cidade Nova (Portugal); Cidade Nova Editora (Brazil); Cita Nuova (Switzerland); Ciudad Nueva (Argentina, Spain & Venezuela); Enad Varld (Sweden); Verlag Neue Stadt GmbH (Germany); New City (Philippines & UK); New City Press (United States); Nieuwe Stad (Belgium & Netherlands); Nouvelle Cite (France); Uj Varos (Hungary)
Distribution Center: Messaggero Distribuzione SRL, Via Orto Botanico, 11, 35123 Padova
Web Site: www.mesdis.it

Cittadella Editrice+
Imprint of Pro Civitate Christiana
Via Ancaini 3, 06081 Assisi
Tel: (075) 813595 *Fax:* (075) 813719
E-mail: amministrazione@cittadellaeditrice.com
Web Site: www.cittadellaeditrice.com
Founded: 1939
Subjects: Biblical Studies, Biography, Memoirs, Inspirational, Spirituality, Philosophy, Psychology, Psychiatry, Religion - Catholic, Religion - Other, Social Sciences, Sociology, Theology
ISBN Prefix(es): 978-88-308
Number of titles published annually: 21 Print
Total Titles: 501 Print
Bookshop(s): Libreria Cittadella

Claudiana Editrice+
Via S Pio V, 15, 10125 Turin
Tel: (011) 668 98 04 *Fax:* (011) 65 75 42
E-mail: info@claudiana.it
Web Site: www.claudiana.it
Key Personnel
Dir: Manuel Kromer *E-mail:* kromer@claudiana.it
Editorial: Laura Pellegrin *E-mail:* l.pellegrin@ claudiana.it
Press: Bianca Piazzese *E-mail:* biancapiazzese@ claudiana.it
Production: Andrea Vinti *E-mail:* vinti@ claudiana.it

Sales: Costanza Armillotta *E-mail:* c.armillotta@
claudiana.it
Founded: 1855
Membership(s): Associazione Italiana Editori
(AIE).
Subjects: Biblical Studies, Biography, Memoirs,
Fiction, History, Literature, Literary Criticism,
Essays, Religion - Protestant, Theology
ISBN Prefix(es): 978-88-7016
Distributor for Edizioni GBU (Rome)
Bookshop(s): Via Principe Tommaso 1, 10125
Turin *Tel:* (011) 669 24 58 *Fax:* (011) 669 24
58 *E-mail:* libreria.torino@claudiana.it; Borgo
Ognissanti, 14/R, Florence *Tel:* (055) 28 28 96
Fax: (055) 28 28 96 *E-mail:* libreria.firenze@
claudiana.it; Via Francesco Sforza, 12a, 20122
Milan *Tel:* (02) 76 02 15 18 *Fax:* (02) 76 02
15 18 *E-mail:* libreria.milano@claudiana.it; Pi-
azza Cavour, 32, 00193 Rome *Tel:* (06) 322 54
93 *Fax:* (06) 322 54 93 *E-mail:* libreria.roma@
claudiana.it; Piazza Liberta, 10066 Torre Pel-
lice TO *Tel:* (0121) 91 422 *Fax:* (0121) 91 422
E-mail: libreria.torrepellice@claudiana.it

**CLEUP (Cooperativa Libraria Editrice
Universita di Padova)+**
Via G Belzoni, 118/3, 35121 Padua PD
Tel: (049) 8753496 *Fax:* (049) 650261
E-mail: redazione@cleup.it; info@cleup.it
Web Site: www2.cleup.it
Key Personnel
President: Ambrogio Fassina
Vice President: Luigi Fabbris
Dir: Valentina D'Urso
Founded: 1962
Also book packager.
Subjects: Engineering (General), Government,
Political Science, Language Arts, Linguistics,
Mathematics, Medicine, Nursing, Dentistry,
Psychology, Psychiatry, Science (General)
ISBN Prefix(es): 978-88-7178
Bookshop(s): Via G Gradenigo, 2, Padua PD
Tel: (049) 8071998 *E-mail:* libreria@cleup.it

CLUEB, see Casa Editrice Clueb SRL

Casa Editrice Clueb SRL+
Via Marsala 31, 40126 Bologna
Tel: (051) 220736 *Fax:* (051) 237758
E-mail: clueb@clueb.com; info@clueb.com
Web Site: www.clueb.com
Key Personnel
Mng Dir: Luigi Guardigli *E-mail:* gua@clueb.
com
Founded: 1959
Subjects: Accounting, Agriculture, Architecture
& Interior Design, Art, Business, Drama, The-
ater, Economics, Education, History, Human
Relations, Language Arts, Linguistics, Litera-
ture, Literary Criticism, Essays, Music, Dance,
Philosophy, Psychology, Psychiatry, Science
(General)
ISBN Prefix(es): 978-88-8091; 978-88-491
Number of titles published annually: 150 Print; 3
CD-ROM
Total Titles: 15 Print; 1 CD-ROM
Subsidiaries: Clueb DPE
U.S. Office(s): Paul & Company Publishers Con-
sortium, PO Box 442, Concord, MA 01742,
United States
Distributor for Universita di Trento
Bookshop(s): Libreria Clueb, Bologna

CLUT Editrice+
Corso Duca degli Abruzzi, 24, 10129 Turin TO
Tel: (011) 0907980; (011) 542192 *Fax:* (011)
542192
E-mail: clut@inrete.it
Web Site: www.clut.it
Key Personnel
Mng Dir: Michele Ruffino
Founded: 1960

Subjects: Aeronautics, Aviation, Architecture &
Interior Design, Art, Chemistry, Chemical En-
gineering, Computer Science, Economics, Elec-
tronics, Electrical Engineering, Engineering
(General), Human Relations, Law, Mathemat-
ics, Physics, Science (General), Technology,
Electronics
ISBN Prefix(es): 978-88-7992
Parent Company: Cooperativa Libraria Universi-
taria Torinese Scrl
Distribution Center: Del Porto SpA, Via Meucci
17, 43015 Noceto PR *Tel:* (0521) 620544
Fax: (0521) 627977

CNR Edizioni
Piazzale Aldo Moro, 7, 00185 Rome
Tel: (06) 4993 2287; (06) 4993 3542 (sales); (06)
4993 3428 (sales); (06) 4993 2538 (sales)
Fax: (06) 4461954
E-mail: bookshop@cnr.it
Web Site: www.edizioni.cnr.it
Key Personnel
Mng Dir: Sara Di Marcello *E-mail:* sara.
dimarcello@cnr.it
Editorial Board: Francesco Antinucci
E-mail: francesco.antinucci@istc.cnr.it
Subjects: Environmental Studies, Medicine, Nurs-
ing, Dentistry, Science (General)
ISBN Prefix(es): 978-88-8080; 978-88-906859
Parent Company: CNR Consiglio Nazionale delle
Ricerche

La Coccinella SRL
Via Belfiore 5, 20145 Milan
Tel: (02) 4381161 *Fax:* (02) 436923
E-mail: trade@coccinella.com; segreteria@
coccinella.com
Web Site: www.coccinella.com
Key Personnel
Editorial Dir: Domenico Caputo
Sales, Rights & Permissions: Giuliana Crespi
Founded: 1977
Subjects: Crafts, Games, Hobbies, Education
ISBN Prefix(es): 978-88-7703; 978-88-7548
Parent Company: Gruppo Editoriale Mauri Spag-
nol
Distribution Center: Messaggerie Libri SpA, Via
Giuseppe Verdi 8, 20090 Assago MI *Tel:* (02)
457741 *Fax:* (02) 45701032 *Web Site:* www.
messaggerielibri.it

Edizioni Coccole e Caccole
Via Antonio Pepe, 20, 87021 Belvedere Marit-
timo CS
Tel: (0985) 887823 *Fax:* (0985) 887823; (0985)
250456
E-mail: edizioni@coccolebooks.com; editor@
coccoleecaccole.it
Web Site: www.coccoleecaccole.it
Key Personnel
Editorial Dir: Daniela Valente
Editor: Hilary Giuliano
Founded: 2004
ISBN Prefix(es): 978-88-89532

Codice Edizioni SRL
via San Francesco de Paola, 37, 10123 Turin
Tel: (011) 19700579; (011) 19700580 *Fax:* (011)
19700582
E-mail: info@codiceedizioni.it; press@
codiceedizioni.it
Web Site: www.codiceedizioni.it
Key Personnel
President: Vittorio Bo
Dir: Marco Bo
Foreign Rights: Daiana Galigani *E-mail:* d.
galigani@codiceedizioni.it
Founded: 2003
Subjects: Art, Biography, Memoirs, Chemistry,
Chemical Engineering, Economics, Energy, En-
vironmental Studies, Government, Political Sci-
ence, Health, Nutrition, History, Mathematics,

Philosophy, Physics, Psychology, Psychiatry,
Technology, Astrophysics, Complexity Science,
Democracy, Design, Evolution, Genetics, Me-
dia, Neuroscience, Power, Science Communica-
tion
ISBN Prefix(es): 978-88-7578
Distribution Center: Messaggerie Libri *Toll
Free Tel:* 800 804 900 *Fax:* (02) 84406056
E-mail: assistenza.ordini@meli.it *Web
Site:* www.messaggerielibri.it

Gaetano Colonnese Editore SAS+
Via San Pietro a Majella, 7, 80138 Naples NA
Tel: (081) 293900; (081) 459858 (orders)
Fax: (081) 455420
E-mail: editore@colonnese.it; ordini@colonnese.it
(orders); stampa@colonnese.it
Web Site: www.colonnese.it
Key Personnel
Dir, Publishing & Sales: Edgar Colonnese
Administration & Customer Relations: Vladimiro
Colonnese *E-mail:* vladimiro@colonnese.it
Founded: 1965
Subjects: Archaeology, Drama, Theater, Fiction,
History, Humor, Language Arts, Linguistics,
Literature, Literary Criticism, Essays, Photogra-
phy, Poetry, Women's Studies
ISBN Prefix(es): 978-88-87501
Number of titles published annually: 12 Print
Total Titles: 400 Print
Distributed by Zambon Verlag & Vertrieb (Ger-
many)
Foreign Rights: Agenzia Servizi Editoriali (Italy)
Bookshop(s): Libreria Colonnese SAS, Via San
Pietro a Majella, 32/33, 80138 Naples NA
Tel: (081) 459858 *E-mail:* libreria@colonnese.
it
Distribution Center: PDE SRL, Via Tevere 54-
Loc Osmannoro, 50019 Sesto Fiorentino
FI *Tel:* (055) 301371 *Fax:* (055) 301372
E-mail: info@pde.it
Orders to: Colonnese, Via San Pietro a Majella,
32/33, 80138 Naples NA *Tel:* (081) 459858

Le Comete, *imprint of* Passigli Editori SRL

Edizioni di Comunita SpA+
Via G Zanardelli 34, 00186 Rome
Tel: (0347) 6393002 *Fax:* (06) 68696193
E-mail: info@edizionidicomunita.it; ordini@
edizionidicomunita.it
Web Site: www.edizionidicomunita.it
Key Personnel
Editorial Dir: Beniamino de' Liguori Carino
Founded: 1946
Subjects: Architecture & Interior Design, Art,
Computer Science, Economics, Government,
Political Science, History, Law, Science (Gen-
eral), Social Sciences, Sociology
ISBN Prefix(es): 978-88-245
Total Titles: 70 Print

Consiglio Nazionale delle Ricerche, see CNR
Edizioni

Conte Editore+
Via Luigi Carluccio 3, 73100 Lecce
Tel: (0832) 228827 *Fax:* (0832) 220280
E-mail: casaeditrice@conteditore.it
Web Site: www.conteditore.it
Key Personnel
Editor: Gabriel Conte
Founded: 1967
Subjects: Agriculture, Architecture & Interior De-
sign, Art, Environmental Studies, Fiction, His-
tory, Music, Dance, Philosophy, Poetry, Travel
& Tourism, Culture & Tradition
ISBN Prefix(es): 978-88-87143; 978-88-85979

Contrasto SRL
Via delgi Scialoja, 3, 00196 Rome RM
Tel: (06) 328281 *Fax:* (06) 32828240

E-mail: customer@contrastobooks.com
Web Site: www.contrastobooks.com; www.
  contrasto.it
Key Personnel
Editorial Dir: Alessandra Mauro
Foreign Rights: Barbara Barattolo
  E-mail: bbarattolo@contrasto.it
Marketing: Isabella Dothel *E-mail:* isabella.
  dothel@gmail.com
Founded: 1995
Publish photography books.
Subjects: Photography
ISBN Prefix(es): 978-88-89032; 978-88-86982;
  978-88-6965
Branch Office(s)
Via Cardinale Ascanio, Storza 29, 20136 Milan
  MI *Tel:* (02) 6553101 *Fax:* (02) 65531055
Distribution Center: Messaggerei Libri, Via
  Verdi, 8, 20090 Assago MI *Tel:* (02) 45774200
  Web Site: www.messaggerielibri.it
Thames & Hudson, 181A High Holborn, London
  WC1V 7QX, United Kingdom *Tel:* (020) 7845
  5000 *Fax:* (020) 7845 5050 *Web Site:* www.
  thamesandhudson.com (worldwide exc Italy &
  North America)
Consortium Book Sales & Distribution, c/o Two
  Rivers Distribution, 1094 Flex Dr, Jackson,
  TN 38301-5070, United States *Web Site:* www.
  cbsd.com (North America)

**Cooperativa Editrice Libraria di Informazione
Democratica**, see CELID

**Cooperativa Libraria Editrice Universita di
Padova**, see CLEUP (Cooperativa Libraria
Editrice Universita di Padova)

Cooperativa Libraria Universitaria Torinese,
see CLUT Editrice

**Cooperativa Universitaria Editrice
Cagliaritana**, see CUEC Editrice (Cooperativa
Universitaria Editrice Cagliaritana)

Corraini Edizioni
Via Ippolito Nievo 7a, 46100 Mantova MN
Tel: (0376) 322753 *Fax:* (0376) 365566
E-mail: sito@corraini.com
Web Site: www.corraini.com
Key Personnel
Dir: Pietro Corraini
Subjects: Art
ISBN Prefix(es): 978-88-7570; 978-88-86250;
  978-88-87942

Edizioni Corsare
Via Ambrosi, 15, 06125 Perugia PG
Tel: (075) 58 47 055 *Fax:* (075) 58 47 055
E-mail: edizionicorsare@gmail.com
Web Site: www.edizionicorsare.it
Subjects: Art, Drama, Theater, Music, Dance
ISBN Prefix(es): 978-88-87938

Corso Bacchilega Editore
Via Emilia 25, 40026 Imola BO
Tel: (0542) 31208 *Fax:* (0542) 31240
E-mail: info@bacchilegaeditore.it
Web Site: www.bacchilegaeditore.it
Key Personnel
President: Davide Tronconi
Vice President: Paolo Bernardi
Founded: 1992
Subjects: Fiction, History, Poetry, Sports, Athletics, Culture, Nature
ISBN Prefix(es): 978-88-88775; 978-88-96328

Libreria Cortina Editrice SRL+
Via Alberto Mario, 10, 37121 Verona
Tel: (045) 59 41 77 *Fax:* (045) 59 75 51

E-mail: info@libreriacortina.it; libreriacortina@
  tin.it
Web Site: www.libreriacortina.it
Founded: 1971
Also book packager.
Subjects: Medicine, Nursing, Dentistry, Science
  (General), Alternative Medicine
ISBN Prefix(es): 978-88-85037; 978-88-7749
Branch Office(s)
Piazzale Ludovico Antonio Scuro 10, 37134
  Verona *Tel:* (045) 505270 *Fax:* (045) 584594
Via dell'Artigliere, 3, 37129 Verona
  Tel: (045) 2226596 *Fax:* (045) 2226597
  E-mail: cortinaunivr@libreriacortina.it
Bookshop(s): Palazzetto d'Ingresso, Policlin-
  ico Borgo Roma - Ple L Scuro, 10, 37134
  Verona *Tel:* (045) 505270 *Fax:* (045) 584594
  E-mail: infob@libreriacortina.it

Raffaello Cortina Editore
via Rossini 4, 20122 Milan MI
Tel: (02) 781544 *Fax:* (02) 76021315
E-mail: info@raffaellocortina.it; ufficiostampa@
  raffaellocortina.it
Web Site: www.raffaellocortina.it
Key Personnel
Foreign Rights: Laura Maccagni
  E-mail: maccagni@raffaellocortina.it
Press: Elisa Montanucci *Tel:* (02) 781544 ext 21
Subjects: Anthropology, Philosophy, Psychology,
  Psychiatry, Social Sciences, Sociology
ISBN Prefix(es): 978-88-6030

Edizioni Crisalide+
Via Campodivivo, 43, 04020 Spigno Saturnia LT
Tel: (0771) 64463 *Fax:* (0771) 639121
E-mail: crisalide@crisalide.com
Web Site: www.crisalide.com
Key Personnel
President & Owner: Raffaele Iandolo
Founded: 1988
This publisher has indicated that 70% of their
  product line is author subsidized.
Subjects: Astrology, Occult, Parapsychology, Psy-
  chology, Psychiatry, Religion - Buddhist
ISBN Prefix(es): 978-88-7183
Number of titles published annually: 20 Print
Total Titles: 200 Print
Foreign Rep(s): DG Diffusion (France); Neue
  Erde (Germany)

**CUEC Editrice (Cooperativa Universitaria
Editrice Cagliaritana)**
Via Basilicata n 57/59, 09127 Cagliari CA
Tel: 070271573 *Fax:* 070271573
E-mail: info@cuec.eu
Web Site: www.cuec.eu
Founded: 1974
Subjects: Literature, Literary Criticism, Essays,
  Science (General), Culture
ISBN Prefix(es): 978-88-8467; 978-88-85998;
  978-88-87088
Bookshop(s): Libreria CUEC, Via Is Mir-
  rionis 1, 09123 Cagliari *Tel:* 070291201
  Fax: 070291201 *E-mail:* cuec74@tiscali.it; Li-
  breria Fahrenheit 451 *E-mail:* fahrenheit_451@
  tiscali.it

Edizioni Culturali Internazionali Genova, see
ECIG - Edizioni Culturali Internazionali
Genova

Edizioni Curci SRL+
Galleria del Corso, 4, 20122 Milan
Tel: (02) 760361 *Fax:* (02) 76014504
E-mail: info@edizionicurci.it
Web Site: www.edizionicurci.it
Key Personnel
Chief Executive Officer & Mng Dir: Alfredo
  Ricci Gramitto
General Manager: Claudia Mescoli

Administrative & Financial Dir: Claudio Sedini
  E-mail: contabilita@edizionicurci.it
Editorial Dir: Laura Moro *E-mail:* laura.moro@
  edizionicurci.it
Chief Sales Officer: Lina Manfra *E-mail:* lina.
  manfra@edizionicurci.it
Editor: Francesca Centuori *E-mail:* francesca.
  centuori@edizionicurci.it; Samuel Pellizari
  E-mail: samuel.pellizari@edizionicurci.it
Press: Bertolini Curci *E-mail:* bertolini.curci@
  yahoo.com
Founded: 1860
Subjects: Music, Dance
ISBN Prefix(es): 978-88-485
Associate Companies: Edizioni Accordo SRL
Warehouse: Via Ripamonti, 129, 20141 Milan
  Tel: (02) 57410561 *Fax:* (02) 5390043

Damanhur
Via Pramarzo, 3, 10080 Baldissero Canavese TO
Tel: (0124) 512236 *Fax:* (0124) 512371
E-mail: welcome@damanhur.it; university@
  damanhur.it
Web Site: www.damanhur.org
Founded: 1975
Membership(s): Casa Edittice Della Comunita Di
  Damanhur.
Subjects: Astrology, Occult, Earth Sciences, Mys-
  teries, Suspense, Social Sciences, Sociology
ISBN Prefix(es): 978-88-7012; 978-88-901438

Dami Editore, *imprint of* Giunti Editore SpA

Dami International+
c/o Giunti International Division, Str 1, Palazzo
  F/9, 20090 Milanofiori, Assago MI
Tel: (02) 575471 *Fax:* (02) 57547503
Web Site: www.dami-int.com
Key Personnel
Owner: Piero Dami
Editorial Dir: Andrea Dami
Foreign Rights Manager: LeeAnn Bortolussi
  E-mail: l.bortolussi@giunti.it
Export Manager: Ilaria Nasini *E-mail:* export@
  giunti.it
Founded: 1972
Subjects: Animals, Pets, Fiction
ISBN Prefix(es): 978-88-89902
Parent Company: Giunti Group
Ultimate Parent Company: Giunti International
  Division
Branch Office(s)
c/o Villa la Loggia, Via Bolognese 165, 50139
  Florence
U.S. Office(s): 4607 Lakeview Canyon, Rd 115,
  Westlake Village, CA 91361, United States

Damiani Editore
Via Zanardi, 376, 40131 Bologna
Tel: (051) 6356811 *Fax:* (051) 6347188
E-mail: info@damianieditore.com; press@
  damianieditore.com
Web Site: www.damianieditore.it
Founded: 2004
Subjects: Architecture & Interior Design, Art,
  Fashion, Music, Dance, Photography, Pop Cul-
  ture, Sports, Athletics, Contemporary Art, De-
  sign, Lifestyle, Urban Art, Watch Collecting
ISBN Prefix(es): 978-88-901304; 978-88-89431;
  978-88-6208
Foreign Rep(s): Distributed Art Publishers Inc
  (Elisa Leshowitz) (Central America, North
  America, South America); Publishers Inter-
  national Marketing (Ray Potts) (Middle East,
  Turkey); Publishers International Marketing Ltd
  (Chris Ashdown) (China, Far East, Hong Kong,
  Indonesia, Japan, Korea, Malaysia, Philippines,
  Singapore, Taiwan, Thailand)
Distribution Center: Messaggeri Libri, Via
  Bergonzoli Y5, 20127 Milan MI *Tel:* (02)
  45774355; (02) 45774348; (02) 45774350
  Fax: (02) 45774377 *E-mail:* ufficio.
  promozione.meli@meli.it

G D'Anna Casa Editrice SpA+
Via Mannelli 3/5, 50136 Florence
Tel: (055) 93 36 600 *Fax:* (055) 93 36 650
E-mail: scrivo@danna.it; proposte.editorial@
danna.it; curriculum@danna.it (sales);
editoriale@danna.it
Web Site: www.danna.it
Key Personnel
Chief Executive Officer: Mark Griffa
President & Mng Editor: Gabriele D'Anna
Founded: 1926
Subjects: Art, Chemistry, Chemical Engineering,
Education, History, Literature, Literary Criti-
cism, Essays
ISBN Prefix(es): 978-88-8104; 978-88-8321
Imprints: Editoriale Paradigma; G D'Anna-Sintesi
Warehouse: Loescher Editore, Via Vajont 93,
Cascine Vica Rivoli, Turin
Orders to: Loescher Editore, Via V Amedeo II,
18, 10121 Turin *E-mail:* mail@loescher.it *Web
Site:* www.loescher.it

G D'Anna-Sintesi, *imprint of* G D'Anna Casa
Editrice SpA

Datanews Editrice SRL+
Via Orazio, 31, 00193 Rome RM
Tel: (06) 44202211 *Fax:* (06) 44117029
E-mail: info@datanews.it; ufficiostampa@
datanews.it
Web Site: www.datanews.it
Founded: 1985
Subjects: Economics, Environmental Studies, Eth-
nicity, Government, Political Science, History,
Religion - Islamic
ISBN Prefix(es): 978-88-7981
Parent Company: Gruppo Eurispes
Distribution Center: PDE SpA, Via Forlanini, 36,
50019 Sesto Fiorentino FI *Tel:* (055) 301371
Fax: (055) 301372 *E-mail:* info@pde.it

M D'Auria Editore SAS+
Palazzo Pignatelli, Calata Trinita Maggiore 52-53,
80134 Naples
Tel: (081) 5518963 *Fax:* (081) 19577695
E-mail: info@dauria.it
Web Site: www.dauria.it
Key Personnel
Dir: Dr Gianni Macchiavelli
Publicity: Paola Raeli
Founded: 1837
Also acts as sales agent.
Subjects: Antiques, Archaeology, Art, History,
Law, Literature, Literary Criticism, Essays, Phi-
losophy, Religion - Other, Theology, Philology
ISBN Prefix(es): 978-88-7092
Number of titles published annually: 20 Print
Total Titles: 45 Print
Distributor for Instituto Universitario Orientale;
Edizioni Di Storia E Letteratura SRL
Bookshop(s): Libreria Internazionale-International
Book Center M d'Auria

De Agostini, *imprint of* DeA Planeta Libri SRL

De Luca Editori d'Arte
Via di Novella 22, 00199 Rome
Tel: (06) 32650712 *Fax:* (06) 32650715
E-mail: libreria@delucaeditori.com
Web Site: www.delucaeditori.com
Key Personnel
Mng Dir: Stefano De Luca
Founded: 1935
Subjects: Archaeology, Art, Fashion, History, Lit-
erature, Literary Criticism, Essays, Photography
ISBN Prefix(es): 978-88-8016
Distribution Center: Messaggerie Libri SpA, Via
G Verdi 8, 20090 Assago MI *Tel:* (02) 457741
Fax: (02) 45701032 *E-mail:* meli.dirgen@meli.
it *Web Site:* www.messaggerielibri.it

DeA, *imprint of* DeA Planeta Libri SRL

DeA Planeta Libri SRL
Via Inverigo, 2, 20151 Milan MI
Tel: (02) 380861
E-mail: ufficiostampa.deaplanetalibri@deagostini.
it
Web Site: www.deaplanetalibri.it
Key Personnel
Foreign Rights Manager: Maria Luisa Borsarelli
E-mail: mluisa.borsarelli@deagostini.it
Press & Communications: Riccardo Barbagallo
Subjects: Fiction, Nonfiction (General)
ISBN Prefix(es): 978-88-511
Parent Company: De Agostini Libri SpA & Edi-
torial Planeta Sau
Ultimate Parent Company: Grupo Planeta
Imprints: Abracadabra; AMZ; Bookme; De Agos-
tini; DeA; UTET
Subsidiaries: Libromania SRL

Edizioni Dedalo SRL+
Viale Luigi Jacobini, 5, 70123 Bari
Mailing Address: CP BA/19, 70123 Bari
Tel: (080) 531 14 13; (080) 531 14 00; (080) 531
14 01 *Fax:* (080) 531 14 14
E-mail: info@edizionidedalo.it; redazione@
edizionidedalo.it
Web Site: www.edizionidedalo.it
Key Personnel
President: Raimondo Coga
Mng Dir & Mng Editor: Claudia Coga
E-mail: claudiacoga@edizionidedalo.it
Production Manager: Sergio Coga
Editorial & Press Office: Luciana Bellini
Founded: 1965
Also acts as printing house.
Subjects: Anthropology, Architecture & Interior
Design, Art, Film, Video, Government, Politi-
cal Science, History, Philosophy, Physical Sci-
ences, Physics, Psychology, Psychiatry, Science
(General), Social Sciences, Sociology
ISBN Prefix(es): 978-88-300; 978-88-220
Number of titles published annually: 30 Print
Total Titles: 1,100 Print
Parent Company: Dedalo Litostampa

Edizioni Dehoniane Bologna (EDB)+
Via Scipione dal Ferro, 4, 40138 Bologna BO
Tel: (051) 3941511 *Fax:* (051) 3941499
E-mail: edb.redazione@dehoniane.it
Web Site: www.dehoniane.it
Key Personnel
Editorial Dir: Pierluigi Cabri
Dir Emeritus: Alfio Filippi
Chief Editor: Dr Roberto Allessandrini
Editorial Secretary: Maria Costanza Mazzoni
Rights & Permissions: Vanda Persiani
Founded: 1965
Subjects: Art, Biblical Studies, Economics, Edu-
cation, History, Inspirational, Spirituality, Psy-
chology, Psychiatry, Religion - Catholic, Reli-
gion - Other, Theology
ISBN Prefix(es): 978-88-10
Associate Companies: Data Service Center
Imprints: EDB
Distributed by Dehoniana Libri SpA
Bookshop(s): Dehoniana Libri, Bologna
Shipping Address: Via Scipione dal Ferro,
4, 40138 Bologna BO *Tel:* (051) 4290011
Fax: (051) 4290099

DEI Tipographia del Genio Civile
Via Nomentana 16/20, 00161 Rome
Tel: (06) 44 163 71; (06) 44 163 751 *Fax:* (06)
44 03 307
E-mail: dei@build.it
Web Site: www.build.it
Key Personnel
Chief Executive: Antonella Buttelli
Dir: Giuseppe Rufo
Founded: 1869

Subjects: Architecture & Interior Design, Civil
Engineering, Electronics, Electrical Engineer-
ing, Law, Technology
ISBN Prefix(es): 978-88-7722; 978-88-496
Warehouse: Via Mesula 12, 00161 Rome

Edizioni del Delfino, *imprint of* Adriano Gallina
Editore SAS

Edizioni Della Torre+
Viale Elmas, 154, 09122 Cagliari
Tel: (070) 2110346 *Fax:* (070) 2111165
E-mail: dellatorre@tiscali.it; info@
edizionidellatorre.it
Web Site: www.edizionidellatorre.it
Key Personnel
Chief Executive: Salvatore Fozzi
Founded: 1974
Subjects: Archaeology, Art, Biography, Memoirs,
Geography, Geology, History, Language Arts,
Linguistics, Natural History, Photography, Po-
etry, Regional Interests
ISBN Prefix(es): 978-88-7343
Total Titles: 225 Print
Associate Companies: Scuola Domani, via
Toscana 82, 09124 Cagliari
Subsidiaries: Agenzia Libraria Fozzi & C
Bookshop(s): Libreria Fozzi, Via Dante 72, 09100
Cagliari

Edizioni dell'Orso SRL+
Via Urbano Rattazzi, 47, 15121 Alessandria
Tel: (0131) 252349 *Fax:* (0131) 257567
E-mail: info@ediorso.it
Web Site: www.ediorso.it
Founded: 1979
Subjects: Art, Fiction, Geography, Geology, His-
tory, Language Arts, Linguistics, Literature,
Literary Criticism, Essays, Philosophy, Poetry,
Regional Interests
ISBN Prefix(es): 978-88-7694

Demetra, *imprint of* Giunti Editore SpA

Di Baio Editore SpA+
Via Settembrini 11, 20124 Milan
Tel: (02) 67495299 *Fax:* (02) 67495228
Web Site: www.dibaio.com
Key Personnel
Dir: Giuseppe Maria Jonghi-Lavarini
Editorial Dir: Gjlla Giani
Marketing & Communications: Giulia Belcamino
Publicity: Maria Luigia Canel
Founded: 1972
Subjects: Architecture & Interior Design, Cook-
ery, Crafts, Games, Hobbies, Gardening, Plants,
House & Home, Technology
ISBN Prefix(es): 978-88-7080; 978-88-7499

I Diamanti, *imprint of* HarperCollins Italia SpA

Direzione Generale per gli Archivi (General
Directorate for Archives)
Via Gaeta 8a, 00185 Rome
Tel: (06) 492251 *Fax:* (06) 49225266
E-mail: dg-a.valorizzazione@beniculturali.it
Web Site: www.archivi.beniculturali.it
Key Personnel
Dir General: Rossana Rummo *Tel:* (06) 4469928
Fax: (06) 4882358 *E-mail:* dg-a@beniculturali.
it
Founded: 1975
Publishing branch of the Italian State Archives
Administration.
Subjects: History, Law, Library & Information
Sciences, Public Administration, Archival Sci-
ence
ISBN Prefix(es): 978-88-7125
Number of titles published annually: 20 Print
Total Titles: 540 Print

Parent Company: Ministero per i Beni e le Attivita Culturali
Orders to: l'Agenzia dell' Istituto poligrafico e Zecca dello stato, Piazza Verdi, 10, 00198 Rome *Tel:* (06) 85082147 *Fax:* (06) 85084117
Libreria dello Stato, Via Salaria, 691, 00138 Rome *Tel:* (06) 85082530 *Fax:* (06) 85084117

Editrice Domenicana Italiana SRL+
Via Giuseppe Marotta, 12, 80133 Naples
Tel: (081) 5526670 *Fax:* (081) 4109563
E-mail: info@edi.na.it; diredi@edi.na.it
Web Site: www.edi.na.it
Key Personnel
Editorial Dir: G Piccinno
Membership(s): Societas Editorum Dominicanorum.
Subjects: History, Inspirational, Spirituality, Philosophy, Religion - Catholic, Theology
ISBN Prefix(es): 978-88-89094
Number of titles published annually: 10 Print
Total Titles: 101 Print
Distribution Center: Messaggero Distribuzione SRL, Via Orto Botanico 11, 35123 Padua PD *Tel:* (049) 658288 *Fax:* (049) 8754359 *Web Site:* www.mesdis.it

Domus Academy
Via C Darwin 20, 20143 Milan
Tel: (02) 42414001
E-mail: info@domusacademy.it; press@ domusacademy.it
Web Site: www.domusacademy.com
Key Personnel
Founder: Maria Grazia Mazzocchi
Founded: 1983
Subjects: Architecture & Interior Design, Business, Fashion, Landscape & Urban Design
ISBN Prefix(es): 978-88-7184; 978-88-85187

Editoriale Domus SpA+
Via Gianni Mazzocchi 1/3, 20089 Rozzano MI
Tel: (02) 82472 1
E-mail: editorialedomus@edidomus.it; press@ edidomus.it
Web Site: www.edidomus.it
Key Personnel
Advertising Marketing Manager: Stefania Cappellini *E-mail:* direzionepubblicita@edidomus.it
Founded: 1929
Subjects: Aeronautics, Aviation, Architecture & Interior Design, Art, Automotive, Cookery, Transportation, Travel & Tourism
ISBN Prefix(es): 978-88-7212

Donzelli Editore SRL
Via Mentana, 2b, 00185 Rome
Tel: (06) 4440600 *Fax:* (06) 4440607
E-mail: editore@donzelli.it
Web Site: www.donzelli.it
Key Personnel
Chief Executive Officer: Carmine Donzelli
Foreign Rights: Marta Donzelli *E-mail:* m. donzelli@donzelli.it
Press: Antonella Sarandrea *E-mail:* a.sarandrea@ donzelli.it
Founded: 1993
Subjects: Fiction, History, Literature, Literary Criticism, Essays, Philosophy, Social Sciences, Sociology
ISBN Prefix(es): 978-88-7989; 978-88-6036
Distribution Center: Pde SpA, Borgo Albizi 10, 50122 Florence

Editions du Dromadaire
Castello 6656 - Barbaria de le Tole, 30122 Venice VE
Tel: (041) 2412268; (041) 5299014 *Fax:* (041) 2412268
E-mail: info@dromadaire.it
Web Site: www.dromadaire.it

Founded: 2000
ISBN Prefix(es): 978-88-88973

e-Harmony, *imprint of* Arnoldo Mondadori Editore SpA

E/O Edizioni SRL+
Via Gabriele Camozzi, 1, 00195 Rome
Tel: (06) 3722829 *Fax:* (06) 37351096
E-mail: info@edizionieo.it; ufficiostampa@ edizionieo.it
Web Site: www.edizionieo.it
Key Personnel
Mng Dir, Rights & Permissions: Sandro Ferri
International Rights Manager: Emanuela Anechoum
Editorial: Sandra Ozzola Ferri
Foreign Rights: Karin Wessel
E-mail: karinwessel@edizionieo.it
Press: Ester Hueting
Founded: 1979
Subjects: Fiction
ISBN Prefix(es): 978-88-7641
Subsidiaries: Europa Editions (USA)
Foreign Rights: Clementina Liuzzi Literary Agency; Ella Sher Literary Agency

Edizioni EBE
Via Alighieri Dante, 39, 01016 Tarquinia VT
Tel: (0766) 858878
Founded: 1973
Subjects: Government, Political Science, History
ISBN Prefix(es): 978-88-7977
Orders to: Via FS Nitti 12, 00191 Rome *Tel:* (06) 3272972

EBF, *imprint of* Edizioni Biblioteca Francescana

ECIG - Edizioni Culturali Internazionali Genova+
Via Brignole De Ferrari 9, 16125 Genoa
Tel: (010) 2512399 *Fax:* (010) 2512398
E-mail: amministrazione@ecig.it
Web Site: www.ecig.it
Founded: 1971
Specialize in sapiential essays.
Subjects: Anthropology, Architecture & Interior Design, Biological Sciences, Chemistry, Chemical Engineering, Economics, Engineering (General), Fiction, Geography, Geology, History, Library & Information Sciences, Literature, Literary Criticism, Essays, Mathematics, Medicine, Nursing, Dentistry, Philosophy, Physics, Psychology, Psychiatry, Travel & Tourism, Botany, Informatics, Pedagogy, Veterinary Medicine
ISBN Prefix(es): 978-88-7545; 978-88-7544
Bookshop(s): Piazza della Nunziata 27r, Genoa *Tel:* (010) 2465806 *Fax:* (010) 2465823 *E-mail:* genova.fontane@clu.it; Sal Inf della Noce, 8r, Genoa *Tel:* (010) 510355 *Fax:* (010) 5185308 *E-mail:* genova.noce@clu.it; V le Fra Ignazio, 54a, Cagliari *Tel:* (070) 658776 *E-mail:* cagliari.ignazio@clu.it; Via Forlanini, 8r/b, Florence *Tel:* (055) 4362089 *Fax:* (055) 429154 *E-mail:* firenze.forlanini@clu.it; Via San Gallo, 21r, Florence *Tel:* (055) 2381693 *Fax:* (055) 2728383 *E-mail:* firenze.sangallo@ clu.it; Via De Amicis, 40-42, Naples *Tel:* (081) 5468963 *Fax:* (081) 5469304 *E-mail:* napoli. deamicis@clu.it; Via Roma, 28, Pisa *Tel:* (050) 501426 *Fax:* (050) 41588 *E-mail:* pisa.roma@ clu.it; Via Ormea, 83c, Turin *Tel:* (011) 6508445 *Fax:* (011) 6687695 *E-mail:* torino. ormea@clu.it
Distribution Center: Via Brignole De Ferrari 11/1, 16125 Genoa *Tel:* (010) 2512380 *E-mail:* clucomm@clu.it

ECM, see Edizioni Cartografiche Milanesi SRL (ECM)

Ecole Francaise de Rome+
Piazza Navona 62, 00186 Rome
Tel: (06) 68 60 13 33 *Fax:* (06) 687 48 34; (06) 68 42 95 50
E-mail: publ@efrome.it
Web Site: www.ecole-francaise.it; www.efrome.it; www.publications.efrome.it
Key Personnel
Dir, Publications: Richard Figuier *Tel:* (06) 68 42 95 20 *E-mail:* richard.figuier@efrome.it
Editorial: Franco Bruni *Tel:* (06) 68 42 95 12; Bertrand Grandsagne *Tel:* (06) 68 42 95 11 *E-mail:* bertrand.grandsagne@efrome.it
Founded: 1875
Subjects: Archaeology, Art, History, Law
ISBN Prefix(es): 978-2-7283
Number of titles published annually: 30 Print
Total Titles: 400 Print
Distributed by De Boccard (France); Casalini Libri (Italy); L'Erma di Bretschneider (Italy); Libreria gia Nardecchia Srl (Italy); Portico librerias S A (Spain); Viella Libreria Editrice (Italy)

Edagricole - Edizioni Agricole+
Via Goito n 13, 40126 Bologna
Tel: (051) 65751 *Fax:* (051) 6575800
E-mail: servizioclienti.periodici@ newbusinessmedia.it
Web Site: www.edagricole.it
Key Personnel
Chief Executive Officer: Antonio Greco, Jr
President: Eraldo Minella
Founded: 1937
Subjects: Agriculture, Animals, Pets, Biological Sciences, Gardening, Plants, Health, Nutrition, Science (General), Veterinary Science
ISBN Prefix(es): 978-88-206
Total Titles: 2,000 Print
Parent Company: New Business Media SRL
Associate Companies: Edizioni Calderini; Calderini Industrie Grafiche ed Editoriali SRL; Edagricole Periodici SpA
Bookshop(s): Via Zamboni 18, Bologna; Via Bronzino 14, Milan; Via Boncompagni 73, Rome

EDAS
Via San Giovanni Bosco, 17, 98122 Messina
Tel: (090) 675653 *Fax:* (090) 675653
E-mail: info@edas.it
Web Site: www.edas.it
Founded: 1970
Subjects: History, Science (General)
ISBN Prefix(es): 978-88-7820
Number of titles published annually: 10 Print
Total Titles: 100 Print

EDB, *imprint of* Edizioni Dehoniane Bologna (EDB)

EDB, see Edizioni Dehoniane Bologna (EDB)

Edi.Artes SRL+
Viale Enrico Forlanini, 65, 20134 Milan
Tel: (02) 7021121 *Fax:* (02) 70211283
E-mail: ediartes@eenet.it
Web Site: www.ediartes.it
Key Personnel
Mng Dir: Raffaele Grandi
Founded: 1985
Subjects: Art, Engraving
ISBN Prefix(es): 978-88-7724
Associate Companies: Edi.Ermes SRL

Edi.Ermes SRL+
Viale Enrico Forlanini, 65, 20134 Milan
Tel: (02) 7021121 *Fax:* (02) 70211283
E-mail: eeinfo@eenet.it
Web Site: www.eenet.it; www.eenet.eu; www. ediermes.it

Key Personnel
Chief Executive Officer: Raffaele Grandi
Founded: 1973
Specialize in medical & scientific publications.
Subjects: Art, Biological Sciences, Economics, Medicine, Nursing, Dentistry, Science (General), Sports, Athletics, Veterinary Science
ISBN Prefix(es): 978-88-85019; 978-88-7051
Associate Companies: Edi.Artes SRL
Imprints: EE

Ediart Editrice
Loc Montelupino, 82/13, 06059 Todi PG
Tel: (075) 8942411 *Fax:* (075) 8942411
E-mail: ediart@ediart.it; info@ediart.it
Web Site: www.ediart.it
Key Personnel
Publisher: Leonilde Dominici *E-mail:* leonilde. dominici@gmail.com
Editorial Dir: Marcello Castrichini *E-mail:* m. castrichini@gmail.com
Founded: 1983
Specialize in the history of art & architecture.
Subjects: Architecture & Interior Design, Art
ISBN Prefix(es): 978-88-85311
Number of titles published annually: 4 Print
Total Titles: 70 Print

Edicart
Via Jucker, 28, 20025 Legnano, Milan
Tel: (0331) 74 291 *Fax:* (0331) 74 292
E-mail: info@edicart.it
Web Site: www.edicart.it
Key Personnel
Founder & President: Ezio Cagnola
Founded: 1986
ISBN Prefix(es): 978-88-474; 978-88-7774
Parent Company: Gruppo Edicart Srl

Ediciclo Editore SRL+
Via Cesar Beccaria, 13/15, 30026 Portogruaro (Venice)
Tel: (0421) 74475 *Fax:* (0421) 280065
E-mail: posta@ediciclo.it; marketing@ediciclo.it
Web Site: www.ediciclo.it
Key Personnel
Administrative Dir: Vittorio Anastasia
Founded: 1987
Subjects: Economics, Environmental Studies, History, Outdoor Recreation, Science (General), Social Sciences, Sociology, Sports, Athletics, Travel & Tourism, Cycling
ISBN Prefix(es): 978-88-85327; 978-88-85318; 978-88-88829; 978-88-89100
Imprints: Nuova Dimensione

Edifir - Edizioni Firenze+
Via Fiume, 8, 50123 Florence
Tel: (055) 289639 *Fax:* (055) 289478
E-mail: edizioni-firenze@edifir.it
Web Site: www.edifir.it
Key Personnel
Dir: Francesca Pacini *Tel:* (055) 289506 *E-mail:* fpacini@edifir.it
Administration, Advertising & Orders: Paola Acquarelli *Tel:* (055) 289506 *E-mail:* pacquarelli@edifir.it
Administration & Orders: Susanna Pierotti *Tel:* (055) 289506 *E-mail:* spierotti@edifir.it
Editorial: Silvia Frassi *Tel:* (055) 2675721 *E-mail:* sfrassi@edifir.it; Elena Mariotti *Tel:* (055) 2675721 *E-mail:* emariotti@edifir.it
Marketing: Simone Gismondi *Tel:* (055) 2679661 *E-mail:* sgismondi@edifir.it
Founded: 1985
Subjects: Architecture & Interior Design, Art, Environmental Studies, History
ISBN Prefix(es): 978-88-7970

Edizioni Edilingua
Via Alberico 11 n4-212, 00192 Rome

Tel: (06) 967 27 307 *Fax:* (06) 944 43 13
E-mail: info@edilingua.it; info4@edilingua.it; redazione@edilingua.it
Web Site: www.edilingua.it
Key Personnel
Dir & Editor-in-Chief: T Marin
Financial Dir: Gianfranco Pinto
Import Export Manager: Emanuele Romagnoli
Editorial: Antonio Bidetti
Marketing: Tania Sanna
Founded: 1996
Subjects: Language Arts, Linguistics, Italian Language
ISBN Prefix(es): 978-960-6632; 978-88-98433

Edipuglia
Via Dalmazia 22/b, 70127 Santo Spirito BA
Tel: (080) 5333056 *Fax:* (080) 5333057
E-mail: info@edipuglia.it
Web Site: www.edipuglia.it
Key Personnel
Administrator: Ceglie Oronzo
Founded: 1979
Subjects: Antiques, Archaeology, Biblical Studies, History
ISBN Prefix(es): 978-88-7228
Number of titles published annually: 15 Print
Total Titles: 700 Print

Edisco Editrice+
Via Pastrengo 28, 10128 Turin
Tel: (011) 54 78 80 *Fax:* (011) 51 75 396
E-mail: info@edisco.it
Web Site: www.edisco.it
Key Personnel
General Manager: Corrado Jaria
Founded: 1952
Subjects: Chemistry, Chemical Engineering, Education, Electronics, Electrical Engineering, English as a Second Language, Literature, Literary Criticism, Essays, Mechanical Engineering, Physics, Science (General)
ISBN Prefix(es): 978-88-441
Number of titles published annually: 25 Print
Total Titles: 300 Print
Shipping Address: Via Barletta 124, 10136 Turin
Warehouse: Via Barletta 124, 10136 Turin

Edisport Editoriale SpA
Via Don Sturzo, 7, 20016 Pero MI
Tel: (02) 380851 *Fax:* (02) 38010393
E-mail: edisport@edisport.it; comedi@edisport.it
Web Site: www.edisport.it
Key Personnel
Editor-in-Chief: Massimo Vallini
Editor: Paolo Tognoni
Events Manager: Paola Bacchetti
Founded: 1914
Subjects: Automotive, Outdoor Recreation, Sports, Athletics, Boating, Cycling, Hunting, Motoring, Motorcycling, Running, Shooting, Tennis
ISBN Prefix(es): 978-88-88593
Branch Office(s)
Via Durazzo, 12, 00195 Rome *Tel:* (06) 5917462 *Fax:* (06) 5915082 *E-mail:* comediroma@ edisport.it

Edistudio+
Via U Forti 30/9, Montacchiello, 56100 Pisa
Mailing Address: CP 213, 56100 Pisa
Tel: (050) 982955; (050) 9656359 *Fax:* (050) 9656235
Web Site: www.edistudio.it
Founded: 1977
Also specialize in local culture & local magazines.
Subjects: Drama, Theater, Education, Fiction, Geography, Geology, Language Arts, Linguistics, Literature, Literary Criticism, Essays, Music, Dance, Poetry, Science (General), Sports, Athletics, Anthology, Comics

ISBN Prefix(es): 978-88-7036
Total Titles: 70 Print
Subsidiaries: Composit (phototypesetting, graphics, processing)

Editalia SpA
Gruppo Istituto Poligrafico e Zecca dello Stato, Viale Gottardo 146, 00141 Rome
Toll Free Tel: 800 01 4858
E-mail: info@editalia.it
Web Site: www.editalia.it
Founded: 1952
Subjects: Art, Ethnicity, History
ISBN Prefix(es): 978-88-7060

Editrice Ciranna AED Selino's SRL
Via G Besio, 143, 90145 Palermo
Tel: (091) 224499 *Fax:* (091) 311064
E-mail: info@ciranna.it; selinos@alice.it
Web Site: www.ciranna.it
Key Personnel
Dir: Francesco Pomara
Editorial Dir: Luca Pomara
Sales: Giovanna Bua
Founded: 1950
Subjects: Art, Business, Education, Geography, Geology, History, Language Arts, Linguistics, Law, Literature, Literary Criticism, Essays, Mathematics, Philosophy, Psychology, Psychiatry, Public Administration, Science (General), Technology
ISBN Prefix(es): 978-88-8322
Orders to: Via Capograssa 1115

Edizioni Giuridiche Economiche Aziendali, see EGEA SpA (Edizioni Giuridiche Economiche Aziendali)

Macro Edizioni, see Gruppo Editoriale Macro

Edizioni di Storia e Letteratura
Via delle Fornaci, 24, 00165 Rome
Tel: (06) 39 67 03 07 *Fax:* (06) 39 67 12 50
E-mail: info@storiaeletteratura.it; clienti@ storiaeletteratura.it (sales); editoriale@ storiaeletteratura.it; redazione@ storiaeletteratura.it
Web Site: www.storiaeletteratura.it
Key Personnel
Chief Executive: Lodovico Steidl
Editorial: Sebastiano Bisson
Press: Valentina Saraceni
Sales: Fabiana Amadei
Founded: 1943
Subjects: History, Literature, Literary Criticism, Essays, Philosophy
ISBN Prefix(es): 978-88-900138; 978-88-87114; 978-88-8498
Number of titles published annually: 120 Print; 10 Online
Total Titles: 1,000 Print; 10 Online
Distributor for Dehoniana Libri Srl; Licosa SpA

Edizioni Universitarie di Lettere Economia Diritto, see LED Edizioni Universitarie di Lettere Economia Diritto

Edra SpA
Via Spadolini, 7, 20141 Milan
Tel: (02) 881841 *Fax:* (02) 88184304
Web Site: www.edizioniedra.it
Subjects: Medicine, Nursing, Dentistry, Psychology, Psychiatry
ISBN Prefix(es): 978-88-86457; 978-88-6895
Parent Company: LSWR Group

EDT SRL+
Via Pianezza, 17, 10149 Turin TO
Tel: (011) 5591 811 *Fax:* (011) 2307 034
E-mail: edt@edt.it
Web Site: www.edt.it

Key Personnel
Commercial & Marketing Dir: Angelo Pittro
Press Officer: Antonella D'Antoni *E-mail:* a.
dantoni@edt.it; Carla Primo *E-mail:* c.primo@
edt.it
Founded: 1976
Subjects: Music, Dance, Travel & Tourism
ISBN Prefix(es): 978-88-7063
Distributor for Instituto di Studi Verdiani; Lonely
Planet Inc

EE, *imprint of* Edi.Ermes SRL

Effata Editrice+
Via Tre Denti 1, 10060 Cantalupa, Turin
Tel: (0121) 35 34 52 *Fax:* (0121) 35 38 39
E-mail: info@effata.it
Web Site: www.effata.it
Key Personnel
Dir: Paolo Pellegrino *E-mail:* paolo.pellegrino@
effata.it
Publishing Dir: Gabriella Segarelli
E-mail: gabriella.segarelli@effata.it
Editor: Alberto Rezzi *E-mail:* alberto.rezzi@
effata.it
Press & External Relations: Roberto Falciola
E-mail: roberto.falciola@effata.it
Founded: 1995
Specialize in books about inner development,
with main themes of education, family life &
Christian spirituality.
Subjects: Education, Fiction, Human Relations,
Inspirational, Spirituality, Psychology, Psychia-
try, Religion - Catholic, Self-Help
ISBN Prefix(es): 978-88-86617; 978-88-7402
Number of titles published annually: 100 Print
Total Titles: 600 Print
Orders to: Messaggero Distribuzione, Via Orto
Botanico, 11, 35123 Padua *Tel:* (049) 8603123
Fax: (049) 8077121 *E-mail:* info@mesdis.it
Web Site: www.mesdis.it

EGA Editore+
Corso Trapani, 91/b, 10141 Turin
Tel: (011) 3841011; (011) 3841066 *Fax:* (011)
3841031
E-mail: u.comunicazione@gruppoabele.org;
edizioni@gruppoabele.org
Web Site: www.gruppoabele.org
Founded: 1983
Subjects: Child Care & Development, Commu-
nications, Education, Environmental Studies,
Ethnicity, Health, Nutrition, Human Relations,
Military Science
ISBN Prefix(es): 978-88-7670
Parent Company: Gruppo Abele
Warehouse: Via Bologne 164, Turin

egbooks, *imprint of* Edizioni Goliardiche SRL

EGEA SpA (Edizioni Giuridiche Economiche Aziendali)+
Via Sarfatti, 25, 20136 Milan MI
Tel: (02) 58365751 *Fax:* (02) 58365753
E-mail: editoriale@egeaonline.it
Web Site: www.egeaonline.it
Key Personnel
Press: Susanna Dellavedova *Tel:* (02) 58362325
E-mail: susanna.dellavedova@unibocconi.it
Founded: 1988
Subjects: Advertising, Business, Career Devel-
opment, Economics, Finance, Government,
Political Science, History, Law, Management,
Marketing, Philosophy, Public Administration,
Social Sciences, Sociology
ISBN Prefix(es): 978-88-238
Number of titles published annually: 90 Print
Total Titles: 600 Print
Parent Company: Universita Bocconi
Associate Companies: Giuffre Editore SpA, Via
Busto Arsizio 40, 20151 Milan

Imprints: Universita Bocconi Editore (UBE)
Bookshop(s): Via Bocconi 8, 20136 Milan
Tel: (02) 58362181 *Fax:* (02) 58362037
Orders to: Messaggerie Libri SpA, Via G Car-
cano 32, 20141 Milan

EGGM, *imprint of* Euro GeoGrafiche Mencattini
SRL (EGM)

Giulio Einaudi Editore SpA+
Subsidiary of Arnoldo Mondadori Editore SpA
Via Biancamano, 2, 10121 Turin TO
Tel: (011) 56561 *Fax:* (011) 542903
E-mail: eirights@einaudi.it; einaudi@einaudi.it
(editorial)
Web Site: www.einaudi.it
Key Personnel
President: Roberto Cerati
Editorial Dir: Ernesto Franco
Founded: 1933
Subjects: Art, Fiction, History, Music, Dance,
Philosophy, Poetry, Psychology, Psychiatry, So-
cial Sciences, Sociology
ISBN Prefix(es): 978-88-06; 978-88-446
Associate Companies: Elemond SpA/ Edizioni E
Elle SpA
Bookshop(s): Libreria Einaudi, Via Manzoni 40,
20121 Milan MI
Warehouse: Arnoldo Mondadori, Via Montelun,
37131 Verona VR

Einaudi Scuola, *imprint of* Mondadori Education

EL, *imprint of* Edizioni Lavoro SRL

Edizioni EL
Via J Ressel, 5, 34018 San Dorligo della Valle TS
Tel: (040) 3880311 *Fax:* (040) 3880330
E-mail: edizioniel@edizioniel.it
Web Site: www.edizioniel.com
Key Personnel
Sales: Monica Groves *E-mail:* boschetti@
edizioniel.it
Founded: 1973
ISBN Prefix(es): 978-88-477; 978-88-7068; 978-
88-85012

Electa, *imprint of* Mondadori Electa SpA

Electa Scuola, *imprint of* Mondadori Education

ELI Edizioni
Via Brecce snc, 60025 Loreta AN
Mailing Address: CP 6, 62019 Recanati MC
Tel: (071) 750701 *Fax:* (071) 977851
E-mail: commerciale@elionline.com; editorial@
elionline.com; info@elionline.com;
international@elionline.com (foreign sales);
marketing@elionline.com; service@elionline.
com
Web Site: www.elionline.com
Founded: 1977
Subjects: Language Arts, Linguistics
ISBN Prefix(es): 978-88-536; 978-88-8148; 978-
88-85148
Branch Office(s)
ELI Edizioni/La Spiga - Modern Languages, Via
Soperga 2, 20124 Milan
Eli Publishing Ltd, Windsor House, Bayshill Rd,
Cheltenham GL50 3AT, United Kingdom
Foreign Rep(s): ABIMO (Belgium); AEL Publi-
cations (Israel); AH2 International (Norway); T
P Albatros (Macedonia); Algoritam doo (Croa-
tia); Allecto (Estonia); Alnur for Pedagogy (Is-
rael); Alresalah Imports of Books & Interna-
tional Publications Ltd (Libya); Las Americas
Bookstore (Canada); Anvar Book Distribution
(Iran); Applause Learning Resources (USA);
Arif Books Distribution LLC (United Arab
Emirates); Attica - La Librairie des Langues

(France); Bessler Englisch Lernen (Germany);
Beta Pedagog AB (Sweden); BLS Costa Rica
SA (Costa Rica); Book Stars (Egypt); Calliope
- La Librairie des Langues (Morocco); Casa
Delle Lingue EU (Austria); Caves Book Ltd
(Taiwan); Centercom Ltd (Russia); Centrul
de Carte Straina (Romania); Editions du Col-
lege (France); Continental Book Co (USA);
CTC-Cairo Trade Center (Egypt); M Kemal
Deniz (Turkey); Didaktis (Slovakia); Disal S/A
(Brazil); Ebooks SA (Chile); Educational Cen-
tre (Moldova, Montenegro); Edugate Publish-
ing & Distribution (Egypt); ELI SRL (Italy);
ELI SRL International Department (all other
territories); EMC/Paradigm Publishing Cus-
tomer Care Center (USA); The English Book
Center (Ecuador); English Books jp (Japan);
English Bookshop (Austria); Enrichment Service Ltd Bookmark (Malta); Ernst Ingold +
Co AG (Liechtenstein, Luxembourg, Switzerland); Esperanza Querol Opciones en Educacion (Uruguay); Euroknyga (Lithuania); Eu-
romatex SAC (Peru); Europa Books (USA);
The European Bookshop (Ireland, UK); European Schoolbooks Ltd (Ireland, UK); FHU Et
Toi - Atelier Et Toi (Poland); Librairie Franco-
Egyptienne (Egypt); GES Global ELT Solu-
tions (Lebanon); Global Publishing & Distribu-
tion Co (Egypt); Globuss (Latvia); GM Publi-
cations (Cyprus, Greece); Goyal Publishers &
Distributions Pvt Ltd (India); Grapounge Ltd
(Armenia); Libreria Guayaquil (Ecuador); Das
Haus Des Buches (Argentina); Libreria Hemy-
books (Mexico); Hub Editorial Ltda (Brazil);
Iber dis Ticaret Ltd STI (Turkey); Libreria Im-
pacto (USA); INFOA (Czechia); INFOA sro
(Slovakia); Instrumentao Cultural Pro Sapi-
ens (Brazil); International Journals (Southern
Africa); INTEXT Book Co (Australia); Libreria
Italiana de Puebla (Mexico); Italicus (Poland);
Jarir Distribution Book Store Sarl (Iraq, Jor-
dan, Oman); Jarir Distribution Bookshop LLC
(Bahrain, Oman, Qatar, Saudi Arabia, United
Arab Emirates); Jarir Publishing House (Syria);
Ernst Klett Sprachen GmbH (Germany); Klett
Kiado Kft (Hungary); Korinor Skoleavdelingen
AVD (Norway); Ksiegarnia Edukator (Poland);
Langenscheidt KG (Germany); LCL Interna-
tional Booksellers Ltd (UK); Wydawilictwo
Lektorklett sp z oo (Poland); Lenguas Mod-
ernas Editores (Colombia); Lettera Publish-
ers (Bulgaria); Libra Books Kft (Hungary);
Libro Trade Kft (Hungary); Litterula UAB
(Lithuania); Forlaget Lkke A/S (Denmark, Ice-
land); Master Books Co Ltd (Thailand); Mega-
books CZ (Czechia); Merlijn Educatieve Media
(Netherlands); Midwest European Publications
Inc (USA); Mladinska Knjiga Trgovina (Slove-
nia); Libreria Morgana (Mexico); Al Mutan-
abbi Bookshop (United Arab Emirates); Norli
Gruppen AS (Norway); Nuevas Tecnicas Ed-
ucativas SAC-NUTESA (Peru); Octopus Kids
(Australia); OEBV Buchhandlung (Austria);
Oksinia Educational Centre (Bulgaria); Oxford
Bookshop (Slovakia); Libreria Hernandez Paez
OEG (Austria); Pearson Australia (Australia);
Planeta Asistencioni Servis (Serbia); PM As-
sociates (Malaysia, Thailand); Power (Poland);
Prior Books Distributors (Romania); Editorial
Progreso (Mexico); Promoculture (Tunisia);
Editora Replicacao Lda (Portugal); The Re-
source Centre (Canada); Resource Room (New
Zealand); SBS (Brazil, Peru); SBS Distribu-
tion Centre (Argentina); Schoenhof's Foreign
Books (USA); Schoolstoreng Ltd (Nigeria);
Sierra Book Distributors (Malta); Editions du
Soleil (Canada); Spiga Skolservice (Norway);
Editorial Stanley (Spain); Stockmann (Finland);
Sun Young Books Co (Hong Kong); Sunny
Publishing Co (Taiwan); Ian Taylor & Asso-
ciates (China); Teacher's Discovery (USA);
Transglobal Publishers Service (Hong Kong);
Uab Rotas (Lithuania); VBZ doo (Croatia); Ul-

rich Weyel GmbH & Co (Germany); World of Foreign Languages International Bookshop (Albania); World of Reading (USA); Xunhasaba (Vietnam); YBM si-sa (Korea); Zambon Verlag und Vertrieb (Germany)

Eliseo, *imprint of* Loescher Editore SRL

eLit, *imprint of* HarperCollins Italia SpA

Editrice Elledici
Corso Francia, 333/3, 10142 Turin TO
Tel: (011) 95 52 111 *Fax:* (011) 95 74 048
E-mail: info@elledici.org; vendite@elledici.org (sales); ufficiostampa@elledici.org
Web Site: www.elledici.org
Key Personnel
Press: Alessandro Mormile *Tel:* (011) 95 52 162
Founded: 1941
Subjects: Biblical Studies, Child Care & Development, Education, Music, Dance, Religion - Catholic, Theology
ISBN Prefix(es): 978-88-01
Bookshop(s): Via Maria Ausiliatrice 10/A, 10152 Turin *Tel:* (011) 5216159 *Fax:* (011) 4390485 *E-mail:* torino@elledici.org; Corso Carlo Alberto, 77, 60127 Ancona *Tel:* (071) 2810306 *Fax:* (071) 2812783 *E-mail:* ancona@elledici.org; Via Sant'Alo 2/A, 40129 Bologna *Tel:* (051) 234 915 *Fax:* (051) 227 668 *E-mail:* libreria.s.alo@dehoniane.it; Viale Mario Rapisardi, 22, 95124 Catania *Tel:* (095) 441 379 *Fax:* (095) 44 22 97 *E-mail:* catania@elledici.org; Via Gioberti 37/A, 50121 Florence *Tel:* (055) 66 94 02 *Fax:* (055) 66 76 67 *E-mail:* firenze@elledici.org; Via Carlo Rolando 61/r, 16151 Genoa *Tel:* (010) 64 59 306 *Fax:* (010) 41 50 48 *E-mail:* genova@elledici.org; Via S Giovanni Bosco 33, 98122 Messina *Tel:* (090) 718 874 *Fax:* (090) 64 12 942 *E-mail:* messina@elledici.org; Via Melchiorre Gioia, 62, 20124 Milan *Tel:* (02) 67 072 085 *Fax:* (02) 67 071 776 *E-mail:* milano@elledici.org; Via Donnaregina 7, 80138 Naples *Tel:* (081) 449 167 *Fax:* (081) 291 862 *E-mail:* napoli@elledici.org; Via G Jappelli, 6, 35121 Padua *Tel:* (049) 87 51 386 *Fax:* (049) 87 51 386 *E-mail:* padova@elledici.org; Corso Francia 137/B, 10098 Rivoli TO *Tel:* (011) 95 52 333 *Fax:* (011) 95 52 383 *E-mail:* rivoli@elledici.org; Via della Conciliazione 26/28, 00193 Rome *Tel:* (06) 68 806 735 *Fax:* (06) 68 74 559 *E-mail:* roma1@elledici.org; Via Marsala 44, 00185 Rome *Tel:* (06) 491 400 *Fax:* (06) 44 50 370 *E-mail:* roma2@elledici.org; Via Battisti 6, 21100 Varese *Tel:* (0332) 24 16 09 *Fax:* (0332) 23 29 85 *E-mail:* varese@elledici.org

Elliot Edizioni SRL
Via Isonzo 34, 00198 Rome
Tel: (06) 8844749 *Fax:* (06) 84085336
E-mail: info@elliotedizioni.it; rights@elliotedizioni.it
Web Site: www.elliotedizioni.com
Key Personnel
Dir: Loretta Santini
Editor: Simone Caltabellota
Foreign Rights: Irene Pepiciello
Press: Patrizia Renzi *E-mail:* patriziarenzi@elliotedizioni.it
Founded: 2007
Subjects: Drama, Theater, Fiction, Nonfiction (General)
ISBN Prefix(es): 978-88-6192
Number of titles published annually: 35 Print

Ellissi, *imprint of* Gruppo Editoriale Esselibri Simone

ELS, *imprint of* Edizioni Librarie Siciliane

EM Publishers SRL, see EncycloMedia Publishers SRL

EMI, see Editrice Missionaria Italiana (EMI)

EMP, see Edizioni Messaggero Padova

EncycloMedia Publishers SRL
Via C B Castiglioni 7, 20156 Milan
Tel: (02) 300 76 1 *Fax:* (02) 380 10 437
E-mail: info@encyclomedia.it
Web Site: www.encyclomedia.it
Key Personnel
Press: Elena Dal Pra *E-mail:* elena.dalpra@encyclomedia.it
Subjects: Art, Literature, Literary Criticism, Essays, Music, Dance, Philosophy, Science (General), Customs
ISBN Prefix(es): 978-88-905082

EQ, *imprint of* Edizioni Quasar di Severino Tognon SRL

Equilibri
Via San Giovanni Bosco 32, 41100 Modena MO
Tel: (059) 365327 *Fax:* (059) 365327
E-mail: info@equilibri-libri.it
Web Site: www.equilibri-libri.it
Key Personnel
President: Vera Sighinolfi
Vice President: Alfonso Noviello
Founded: 1999
ISBN Prefix(es): 978-88-900518
Distribution Center: Distribook, Via M F Quintiliano 20, 20138 Milan *Tel:* (02) 58012329 *Fax:* (02) 58012329 *E-mail:* distribook@gmail.com

ER, *imprint of* Editori Riuniti

Edizioni Era Nuova SRL
Corso Garibaldi 26, 06123 Perugia PG
E-mail: info@edizionieranuova.it
Web Site: www.edizionieranuova.it
Key Personnel
Editorial Dir: Paolo Alessandro Lombardi
Subjects: Art, History, Literature, Literary Criticism, Essays, Nonfiction (General), Art History, Cultural History, Regional Art
ISBN Prefix(es): 978-88-85411; 978-88-85412; 978-88-89233

ERGA Edizioni+
Via Imperiale 41, Palazzina Casa Pavoni, 16143 Genoa
Tel: (010) 8328441 *Fax:* (010) 8328799
E-mail: edizioni@erga.it
Web Site: www.erga.it/edizioni
Key Personnel
Chief Executive: Marcello Merli
Sales Dir: Marco Merli *E-mail:* marco.merli@erga.it
Founded: 1964
Subjects: Art, Cookery, Drama, Theater, Ethnicity, Fiction, History, Law, Literature, Literary Criticism, Essays, Music, Dance, Poetry, Regional Interests, Religion - Other, Romance, Science (General), Self-Help, Sports, Athletics, Martial Arts
ISBN Prefix(es): 978-88-8163
Total Titles: 700 Print
Subsidiaries: Erga Direct; Erga Multimedia

Edizioni Centro Studi Erickson SRL+
Via del Pioppeto 24, 38121 Fraz Gardolo TN
Tel: (0461) 950690 *Fax:* (0461) 950698
E-mail: info@erickson.it
Web Site: www.erickson.it
Key Personnel
Dir: Dario Ianes; Fabio Folgheraiter

Editor: Carmen Calovi *E-mail:* calovi@erickson.it; Francesca Cretti *E-mail:* cretti@erickson.it
Foreign Rights: Valeria Agliuzzo *E-mail:* valeria.agliuzzo@erickson.it; Riccardo Mazzeo *E-mail:* riccardo.mazzeo@erickson.it
Founded: 1984
Subjects: Behavioral Sciences, Child Care & Development, Education, Nonfiction (General), Psychology, Psychiatry, Self-Help, Social Sciences, Sociology
ISBN Prefix(es): 978-88-7946; 978-88-85857
Number of titles published annually: 30 Print; 8 CD-ROM
Total Titles: 250 Print; 8 CD-ROM

L'Erma di Bretschneider SRL+
Via Cassiodoro, 11, 00193 Rome
Mailing Address: CP 6192, 00193 Rome
Tel: (06) 68 74 127 *Fax:* (06) 68 74 129
E-mail: lerma@lerma.it; edizioni@lerma.it
Web Site: www.lerma.it
Key Personnel
Chairman: Dr Roberto Marcucci *E-mail:* roberto.marcucci@lerma.it
Mng Dir: Elena Montani *E-mail:* elena.montani@lerma.it
Sales Manager: Erik Pender *E-mail:* erik.pender@lerma.it
Founded: 1945
Subjects: Archaeology, Architecture & Interior Design, Art, History, Language Arts, Linguistics, Law, Religion - Other, Classical studies, Epigraphy, Iconography, Mythology, Restoration/Conservation
ISBN Prefix(es): 978-88-7062; 978-88-8265
Number of titles published annually: 65 Print
Total Titles: 2,000 Print
Distributor for Accademia Danese; Istituto Italiano di Preistoria; Istituto Orientale di Napoli; Musei Vaticani; Universita della Tuscia
Bookshop(s): Via R Montecuccoli, 34, 00176 Rome, Sales & Bookshop Manager: Valentina Barroc *Tel:* (06) 96040214; (06) 96040248 *Fax:* (06) 96038796

ES, *imprint of* Editoriale Scienza srl

ESI SpA, see Edizioni Scientifiche Italiane

Edizioni Essegi+
Via Villanova 58, 48010 Villanova di Ravenna RA
Tel: (0544) 499 066 *Fax:* (0544) 499 122
E-mail: info@edizioniessegi.it
Web Site: www.edizioniessegi.it
Key Personnel
President: Dal Re Patrizia
Founded: 1982
Specialize in contemporary art.
Subjects: Anthropology, Antiques, Archaeology, Architecture & Interior Design, Art, Astronomy, Drama, Theater, Fashion, History, Language Arts, Linguistics, Literature, Literary Criticism, Essays, Photography
ISBN Prefix(es): 978-88-7189
Divisions: Spazio Espositivo Essegi
Showroom(s): Spazio Espositivo Essegi

Gruppo Editoriale Esselibri Simone+
Via F Russo, 33, 80123 Naples
Tel: (081) 575 72 55; (081) 575 72 93 *Fax:* (081) 575 79 44
Web Site: www.esselibri.it
Founded: 1989
Publish academic, legal, technical & professional books.
Subjects: Architecture & Interior Design, Business, Communications, Computer Science, Economics, Government, Political Science, Labor, Industrial Relations, Law, Psychology, Psychia-

try, Public Administration, Securities, Technology
ISBN Prefix(es): 978-88-244; 978-88-378; 978-88-85016
Number of titles published annually: 450 Print
Imprints: Ellissi; Finanze & Lavoro; Libri & Professioni; Nissolino; Sigma; Edizioni Simone; Edizioni Giuridiche Simone; Simone per la Scuola; Sistemi Editoriali; Villa Angelina
Branch Office(s)
Via Stradella 13, 20129 Milan MI *Tel:* (02) 706 02 671 *Fax:* (02) 706 02 831
Via Montenuovo Licola Patria, 131/c, 80078 Pozzuoli *Tel:* (081) 804 39 20 *Fax:* (081) 804 39 18

Essere Felici, *imprint of* Gruppo Editoriale Macro

Essere Felici+
Imprint of Gruppo Editoriale Macro
Via Bachelet, 65, 47522 Cesena FC
Tel: (0547) 1900103 *Fax:* (0547) 1900127
E-mail: info@macroedizioni.it
Web Site: www.macroedizioni.it
Key Personnel
President & Editor: Giorgio Gustavo Rosso
Founded: 2002
Subjects: Alternative, Archaeology, Biblical Studies, Cookery, Education, Environmental Studies, Health, Nutrition, House & Home, How-to, Philosophy, Psychology, Psychiatry, Religion - Other, Science (General)
ISBN Prefix(es): 978-88-95531; 978-88-86493
Number of titles published annually: 22 Print
Total Titles: 40 Print
Ultimate Parent Company: Macro Societa Cooperativa
Showroom(s): Salone del Libro, Turin
Book Club(s): Il Giardino dei Libri, Via del Lavoro 40, 47814 Bellaria RN *Tel:* (0541) 340567 *E-mail:* ordini@ilgiardinodeilibri.it *Web Site:* www.ilgiardinodeilibri.it; Macro Librarsi, Via Savona 70, 47023 Diegaro di Cesena FC *Tel:* (0547) 346290; (0547) 346312 *Fax:* (0547) 345091 *E-mail:* ordini@macrolibrarsi.it *Web Site:* www.macrolibrarsi.it

Edizioni L'Eta dell'Acquario, *imprint of* Edizioni Lindau

Edizioni L'Eta dell'Acquario+
Imprint of Edizioni Lindau
Corso Re Umberto 37, 10128 Turin
Tel: (011) 517 53 24 *Fax:* (011) 669 39 29
E-mail: etadellacquario@etadellacquario.it
Web Site: www.etadellacquario.it
Key Personnel
Editorial Manager: Gabriele Giuliano
    E-mail: gabriele@lindau.it
Sales Manager: Andrea Maria Allolio
    E-mail: andrea@lindau.it
Foreign Rights: Alberto Sorassi *E-mail:* sorassi@lindau.it
Press Office: Federica Sassi
    E-mail: ufficiostampa@etadellacquario.it
Founded: 1971
Subjects: Nonfiction (General), Parapsychology, Religion - Other, Esotericism, Health & Fitness, Historical Crime Mystery Novels, New Age, Spirituality
ISBN Prefix(es): 978-88-7136

Etas Libri+
Division of RCS Libri SpA
Via Rizzoli 8, 20132 Milan
Tel: (02) 2584 2368 *Fax:* (02) 2584 2218
E-mail: etaslab@rcs.it
Web Site: etaslab.corriere.it
Founded: 1963
Subjects: Business, Economics, Engineering (General), Management, Mathematics

ISBN Prefix(es): 978-88-451; 978-88-452; 978-88-453
Total Titles: 500 Print
Ultimate Parent Company: Gruppo Editoriale RCS MediaGroup

ETR (Editrice Trasporti su Rotaie) (Rail Transport Publishing)+
Piazza Vittorio Emanuele II, 42, 25087 Salo BS
Tel: (03) 6541092 *Fax:* (03) 6541092
E-mail: etr@etreditrice.eu; direzione@etreditrice.eu
Web Site: www.etreditrice.eu
Key Personnel
President: Mariangela Scarpini
Founded: 1980
Publish the monthly illustrative magazine *iTreni*.
Membership(s): FerPress (International Railway Press Association).
Subjects: Crafts, Games, Hobbies, Transportation, Travel & Tourism
ISBN Prefix(es): 978-88-85068
Number of titles published annually: 2 Print

ETS, see Edizioni Terra Santa (ETS)

EUR, see Edizioni Universitarie Romane

Euro GeoGrafiche Mencattini SRL (EGM)+
Via Po, 45, 52100 Arezzo
Tel: (0575) 900010 *Fax:* (0575) 911161
E-mail: info@egm.it
Web Site: www.egm.it
Key Personnel
President: Dr Silvano Mencattini
Founded: 1974
Specialize in tourist guides & cartography.
Membership(s): AIPE; Associazione Italiana Editori (AIE); USPI.
Subjects: Geography, Geology, Health, Nutrition, Poetry, Travel & Tourism
ISBN Prefix(es): 978-88-86263
Imprints: EGGM

European Language Institute, see ELI Edizioni

Fabbri Editori
Via Mondadori, 1, 20090 Segrate MI
E-mail: info@rizzolilibri.it; ufficiostampa.rizzoli@rizzolilibri.it; rizzoli.rights@rizzolilibri.it
Web Site: www.fabbrieditori.eu; www.rizzolilibri.it
Founded: 1947
Subjects: Art, Biography, Memoirs, Cookery, Fiction, Government, Political Science, Health, Nutrition, History, Humor, Inspirational, Spirituality, Music, Dance, Mysteries, Suspense, Psychology, Psychiatry, Religion - Other, Romance, Science Fiction, Fantasy, Sports, Athletics, Adventure, Current Affairs, Entertainment, Leisure, Lifestyle
ISBN Prefix(es): 978-88-451; 978-88-450; 978-88-7854; 978-88-915
Parent Company: Rizzoli Libri SpA

Gruppo Editorial Faenza Editrice SpA+
Via Crescenzi Pietro 44, 48018 Faenza RA
Tel: (0546) 670411 *Fax:* (0546) 660440
Key Personnel
Mng Dir: Franco Rossi
Sales: Luisa Teston
Founded: 1966
Magazines & books specializing in ceramic, architecture, electronic, medicine & building field.
Subjects: Architecture & Interior Design, Art, Chemistry, Chemical Engineering, Crafts, Games, Hobbies, Electronics, Electrical Engineering, Engineering (General), Medicine, Nursing, Dentistry, Science (General)

ISBN Prefix(es): 978-88-8138
Number of titles published annually: 98 Print
Parent Company: Il Sole 24 ORE Business Media SRL
Imprints: Edizioni CELI
Branch Office(s)
Faenza Editrice Do Brasil Ltda, Av Visconde do Rio Claro, 1082, Scala 1, Centro, 13500 Rio Claro-SP, Brazil *Tel:* (019) 35335047 *Fax:* (019) 35335047 *E-mail:* faenzabr@claretianas.com.br
Faenza Editrice Iberica SLU, Poligono Comercial Parque Sur Calle Higueras, nave U-2, 12006 Castellon de la Plana, Spain *Tel:* 964 216570 *Fax:* 964 241010 *E-mail:* info@faenza.es *Web Site:* www.faenza.es

Fanucci Editore SRL
Via delle Fornaci, 66, 00165 Rome
Tel: (06) 39366384 *Fax:* (06) 6382998
E-mail: info@fanucci.it; foreign.rights@fanucci.it; info.ordini@fanucci.it; comunicazione@fanucci.it
Web Site: www.fanucci.it
Key Personnel
Publisher: Sergio Fanucci
Founded: 1971
Subjects: Science Fiction, Fantasy, Horror
ISBN Prefix(es): 978-88-347
Imprints: FE
Distribution Center: Messaggerie Libri SpA

Fatatrac, *imprint of* Giunti Editore SpA

Fatatrac SRL+
Imprint of Edizioni Del Borgo SRL
Via Caduti di Reggio Emilia 15, 40033 Casalecchio di Reno BO
Tel: (051) 753358 *Fax:* (051) 752637
E-mail: info@fatatrac.com
Web Site: www.fatatrac.com; www.edizionidelborgo.it
Key Personnel
Mng Dir: Stefano Cassanelli *E-mail:* cassanelli@edizionidelborgo.it
Founded: 1981
Publisher of children's books.
Subjects: Animals, Pets, Art, Child Care & Development, Developing Countries, Education, Literature, Literary Criticism, Essays, Photography, Science Fiction, Fantasy
ISBN Prefix(es): 978-88-85089; 978-88-86228; 978-88-8222
Number of titles published annually: 18 Print
Distribution Center: Giunti Editore SpA, Via Bolognese 165, 50139 Florence *Tel:* (055) 5062382 *Fax:* (055) 5062319 *E-mail:* commva@giunti.it *Web Site:* www.giunti.it

Fazi Editore
Via Isonzo 42/c, 00198 Rome
Tel: (06) 96 03 14 00 *Fax:* (06) 85 57 532
E-mail: info@fazieditore.it
Web Site: www.fazieditore.it
Key Personnel
Founder: Elido Fazi
Press Coordinator: Ambretta Senes
Founded: 1994
Subjects: Fiction
ISBN Prefix(es): 978-88-8112
Parent Company: Gruppo Editoriale Mauri Spagnol

Maria Pacini Fazzi Editore
Via dell'Angelo Custode, 33, 55100 Lucca
Mailing Address: CP 210, 55100 Lucca
Tel: (0583) 440188 *Fax:* (0583) 464656
E-mail: mpf@pacinifazzi.it
Web Site: www.pacinifazzi.it
Key Personnel
President: Maria Pacini Fazzi

Editorial Dir: Francesca Fazzi
Founded: 1966
Subjects: Architecture & Interior Design, Art,
Cookery, Drama, Theater, History, Literature,
Literary Criticism, Essays, Music, Dance, Philosophy, Photography, Social Sciences, Sociology
ISBN Prefix(es): 978-88-7246; 978-88-6550

FE, *imprint of* Fanucci Editore SRL

Federighi Editori
Via Torino 18, 50052 Certaldo FI
Tel: (0571) 664016 *Fax:* (0571) 663568
E-mail: info@federighieditori.it
Web Site: www.federighieditori.it
Key Personnel
Chief Editor: Gloria Pampaloni
Founded: 1929
Subjects: Art, Photography
ISBN Prefix(es): 978-88-89159; 978-88-900705

Feguagiskia' Studios+
Via Crosa di Vergagni, 3 R, 16124 Genoa GE
Tel: (010) 2510829 *Fax:* (010) 2510838
Key Personnel
Mng Editor: Barbara Schiaffino *E-mail:* barbara.
schiaffino@andersen.it
Founded: 1982
Subjects: Child Care & Development, Literature,
Literary Criticism, Essays

Feltrinelli, *imprint of* Giangiacomo Feltrinelli
Editore SRL

Giangiacomo Feltrinelli Editore SRL
Via Andegari, 6, 20121 Milan
Tel: (02) 725721 *Fax:* (02) 72572500; (02)
72001064 (press)
E-mail: commerciale@feltrinelli.it; ufficio.
stampa@feltrinelli.it
Web Site: www.feltrinellieditore.it; www.
feltrinelli.it
Founded: 1954
Subjects: Art, Economics, Education, Fiction,
Government, Political Science, History, Law,
Literature, Literary Criticism, Essays, Nonfiction (General), Philosophy, Poetry, Science
(General), Social Sciences, Sociology, Technology, Travel & Tourism, Foreign Literature,
Italian Literature
ISBN Prefix(es): 978-88-07
Parent Company: Gruppo Feltrinelli SpA
Imprints: Editorial Anagrama; Apogeo; Apogeo Sushi; Feltrinelli; Feltrinelli Kids; Feltrinelli Zoom; FoxCrime; Gribaudo; Kowalski;
Ragazzi; RoughGuides; Universale Economica
Feltrinelli; Urra

Feltrinelli Kids, *imprint of* Giangiacomo
Feltrinelli Editore SRL

Feltrinelli Zoom, *imprint of* Giangiacomo
Feltrinelli Editore SRL

Fermoeditore
Via Cairoli, 15, 43121 Parma PR
Tel: (0521) 977384 *Fax:* (0521) 4463726
E-mail: info@fermoeditore.it
Web Site: www.fermoeditore.it
Key Personnel
Owner: Fermo Tanzi
Founded: 2009
Subjects: Fiction, Photography
ISBN Prefix(es): 978-88-6317

Festina Lente+
Via della Condotta 18, 50122 Florence
Tel: (055) 292612

Key Personnel
Contact: Paolo Gori Savellini
Founded: 1989
Subjects: Architecture & Interior Design, Art,
History, Literature, Literary Criticism, Essays,
Medicine, Nursing, Dentistry, Psychology, Psychiatry
ISBN Prefix(es): 978-88-85171

Fiabesca, *imprint of* Stampa Alternativa - Nuovi
Equilibri

FIDIA, *imprint of* Fidia Edizioni d'Arte

Fidia Edizioni d'Arte, *imprint of* Casagrande
Fidia Sapiens - Editori Associati SRL

Fidia Edizioni d'Arte+
Via Pezzotti 8, 20141, Milan
Tel: (02) 895 462 86 *Fax:* (02) 843 941 1
E-mail: info@cfs-editore.com
Web Site: www.cfs-editore.com
Founded: 1990
Subjects: Archaeology, Architecture & Interior
Design, Art, Photography
ISBN Prefix(es): 978-88-7269; 978-88-7795; 978-88-8380; 978-88-7155
Associate Companies: Giampiero Casagrande Editore; Sapiens Edizioni
Imprints: FIDIA
Branch Office(s)
Via Marconi 4, 6901 Lugano, Switzerland
Tel: (091) 923 567 7 *Fax:* (091) 922 017 1
E-mail: g.casagrande@cfs-editore.com
Distribution Center: Libreria Pecorini,
Foro Buonaparte, 48, 20121 Milan
Tel: (02) 864 606 60 *Fax:* (02) 720 014 62
E-mail: commerciale@pecorini.it

Finanze & Lavoro, *imprint of* Gruppo Editoriale
Esselibri Simone

Libreria Editrice Fiorentina (Florentine
Publishing Library)+
Via De Pucci 4, 50122 Florence FI
Tel: (055) 2399342 *Fax:* (055) 2399342
E-mail: editrice@lef.firenze.it
Web Site: www.lef.firenze.it
Key Personnel
Owner & Editor: Giannozzo Pucci
Founded: 1902
Subjects: Agriculture, Alternative, Animals, Pets,
Architecture & Interior Design, Biblical Studies, Biography, Memoirs, Cookery, Crafts,
Games, Hobbies, Economics, Education, Energy, Environmental Studies, Gardening, Plants,
Health, Nutrition, Regional Interests, Religion
- Catholic, Religion - Other, Social Sciences,
Sociology, Theology
ISBN Prefix(es): 978-88-89542
Number of titles published annually: 10 Print
Total Titles: 300 Print
Warehouse: Via Giambologna, 5, 50132 Florence FI *Tel:* (055) 579921 *Fax:* (055) 3905997
E-mail: ordini@lef.firenze.it
Distribution Center: Via Giambologna, 5, 50132
Florence FI *Tel:* (055) 579921 *Fax:* (055)
3905997 *E-mail:* ordini@lef.firenze.it

Edizioni Firenze, see Edifir - Edizioni Firenze

Firenze Libri
Imprint of Maremmi Editore Firenze (MEF)
Via dei Cadolingi 6, 50018 Scandicci
Tel: (055) 5357250 *Fax:* (055) 5609191
E-mail: info@firenzelibri.it
Web Site: www.firenzelibri.net
Founded: 1958

Subjects: Art, Fiction, Nonfiction (General), Poetry
ISBN Prefix(es): 978-88-7256

5 Continents Editions SRL+
Piazza Caiazzo, 1, 20124 Milan
Tel: (02) 33 60 32 76 *Fax:* (02) 92 87 14 57
E-mail: info@fivecontinentseditions.com
Web Site: www.fivecontinentseditions.com
Key Personnel
Founder: Eric Ghysels
Founded: 2002
Art books.
This publisher has indicated that 50% of their
product line is author subsidized.
Subjects: African American Studies, Archaeology, Architecture & Interior Design, Art, Asian
Studies, Ethnicity, Geography, Geology, History, Literature, Literary Criticism, Essays, Natural History, Photography
ISBN Prefix(es): 978-88-7439
Number of titles published annually: 30 Print
Distribution Center: Les Belles Lettres, 25 rue
du General Leclerc, 94270 Le Kremlin Bicetre, France, Contact: Marion Letoublon *Tel:* 01
45 15 19 70 *Fax:* 01 45 15 19 80 *E-mail:* m.
letoublon@lesbelleslettres.com *Web Site:* www.
lesbelleslettres.com (France & French-speaking
countries)
Yale University Press, 47 Bedford Sq, London
WC1B 3DP, United Kingdom, Contact: Rosie
Parnham *Tel:* (020) 7079 4900 *Fax:* (020) 7079
4901 *E-mail:* rosie.parnham@yaleup.co.uk
Web Site: www.yalebooks.co.uk/pid/page/
representation (worldwide exc Canada, France,
French-speaking countries, Italy & USA)
Abrams, 195 Broadway, 9th floor, New York, NY
10007, United States, Contact: Ms Marti Malovany *Tel:* 212-206-7715 *Fax:* 212-645-8437
E-mail: mmalovany@abramsbooks.com *Web
Site:* www.abramsbooks.com (USA & Canada)

Dario Flaccovio Editore SRL+
Via Croce Rossa, 28, 90144 Palermo
Tel: (091) 6700686 *Fax:* (091) 525738
E-mail: editore@darioflaccovio.it; direzione@
darioflaccovio.it
Web Site: www.darioflaccovio.com
Key Personnel
Owner & Dir: Dario Flaccovio
Founded: 1980
Membership(s): Federazione Italiana Editori Indipendenti.
Subjects: Architecture & Interior Design, Art,
Cookery, Economics, Environmental Studies,
Fiction, Geography, Geology, Law, Management, Mysteries, Suspense, Science Fiction,
Fantasy, Environment, Urban Planning
ISBN Prefix(es): 978-88-7758
Bookshop(s): Via Ausonia, 70-90144 Palermo

Flaccovio Editore
Via Ruggero Settimo, 37, 90139 Palermo
Tel: (091) 589442 *Fax:* (091) 331992
E-mail: editore@flaccovio.com;
viaruggerosettimo@flaccovio.com
Web Site: www.flaccovio.com
Key Personnel
Dir: Francesco Flaccovio; Sergio Flaccovio
Founded: 1939
Membership(s): Associazione Italiana Editori
(AIE).
Subjects: Archaeology, Architecture & Interior
Design, Art, Energy, History, Regional Interests, Science (General), Urban Planning
ISBN Prefix(es): 978-88-7804
Parent Company: S F Flaccovio sas
Bookshop(s): Libreria Dante, Via Maqueda, 172,
Palermo *Tel:* (091) 585927 *Fax:* (091) 323103
E-mail: libreriadante@flaccovio.com; Libroasi
Flaccovio, Aeroporto Falcone Borsellino, Punta

Raisi *Fax:* (091) 6525052; Libreria SF Flaccovio, Forum Palermo, Localita Roccella via Pecoraino, 90100 Palerno

Fogola Editore+
Piazza Carlo Felice, 19, 10123 Turin
Tel: (011) 53 58 97 *Fax:* (011) 53 03 05
E-mail: info@fogola.it
Web Site: www.fogola.it
Founded: 1965
Subjects: Fiction, History, Literature, Literary Criticism, Essays
ISBN Prefix(es): 978-88-7406
Total Titles: 115 Print
Showroom(s): Paztecipozione al Salone Del Libro Ditorino
Bookshop(s): Liberia Dante Alighieri, Piazza Carlo Felice 15, 10123 Turin

Editoriale Fernando Folini+
Imprint of Fernando Folini Productions
c/o Studio Lamberti, via San Marziano 33, 15057 Tortona AL
Tel: (0131) 1826301 *Fax:* (0131) 1826301
E-mail: folini@edifolini.com
Web Site: www.edifolini.com
Key Personnel
President: Dr Fernando Folini
Founded: 1986
Subjects: Biological Sciences, Cookery, Environmental Studies, Health, Nutrition, Medicine, Nursing, Dentistry, Self-Help
ISBN Prefix(es): 978-88-7266

Fondazione Museo Storico del Trentino+
Via Torre d'Augusto, 41, 38122 Trento
Tel: (0461) 230482 *Fax:* (0461) 237418
E-mail: info@museostorico.tn.it
Web Site: www.museostorico.tn.it
Key Personnel
Editorial Coordinator: Rodolfo Taiani *Tel:* (0461) 264660 *E-mail:* rtaiani@museostorico.tn.it
Founded: 1923
Subjects: History, Literature, Literary Criticism, Essays, Social Sciences, Sociology
ISBN Prefix(es): 978-88-7197
Number of titles published annually: 8 Print
Total Titles: 160 Print

Arnaldo Forni Editore SRL
Via Stelloni 3/A, 40010 Sala Bolognese (Bologna)
Tel: (051) 6814142; (051) 6814198 *Fax:* (051) 6814672
E-mail: info@fornieditore.com
Web Site: www.fornieditore.com
Key Personnel
Mng Dir: Aurelia Forni
Founded: 1973
Subjects: Antiques, Archaeology, Architecture & Interior Design, Art, Astrology, Occult, Astronomy, Biography, Memoirs, Cookery, Drama, Theater, Earth Sciences, Economics, Gardening, Plants, Genealogy, Geography, Geology, Government, Political Science, History, Language Arts, Linguistics, Law, Literature, Literary Criticism, Essays, Medicine, Nursing, Dentistry, Music, Dance, Philosophy, Psychology, Psychiatry, Regional Interests, Religion - Catholic, Religion - Other, Social Sciences, Sociology, Folklore, Religious Studies
ISBN Prefix(es): 978-88-271
Number of titles published annually: 20 Print
Total Titles: 3,200 Print

FoxCrime, *imprint of* Giangiacomo Feltrinelli Editore SRL

Edizioni FrancoAngeli SRL+
Viale Monza 106, 20127 Milan
Tel: (02) 2837141 *Fax:* (02) 2613268
E-mail: redazioni@francoangeli.it
Web Site: www.francoangeli.it
Key Personnel
Sales: Dr Stefano Angeli
Founded: 1955
Subjects: Anthropology, Business, Economics, History, How-to, Management, Marketing, Psychology, Psychiatry, Social Sciences, Sociology
ISBN Prefix(es): 978-88-204; 978-88-464
Number of titles published annually: 600 Print
Total Titles: 9,000 Print
Branch Office(s)
Via Savoia 80, 00198 Rome *Tel:* (06) 8543430 *Fax:* (06) 8542389

Edizioni Frassinelli SRL, *imprint of* Sperling & Kupfer Editori SpA

Edizioni Frassinelli SRL+
Imprint of Sperling & Kupfer Editori SpA
Corso Como, 15, 20152 Milan
Tel: (02) 217211 *Fax:* (02) 21721377
E-mail: info@sperling.it
Web Site: www.sperling.it
Key Personnel
Chairman: Marina Berlusconi
Chief Executive: Ernesto Mauri
Head, Press & Events: Paola Caviggioli
Communications & Media Relations: Federico Angrisano
Foreign Rights: Francesca Villa *E-mail:* fvilla@sperling.it
Founded: 1932
Subjects: Art, Biography, Memoirs, Fiction, Nonfiction (General)
ISBN Prefix(es): 978-88-7684; 978-88-7824; 978-88-8274; 978-88-88320
Ultimate Parent Company: Arnoldo Mondadori Editore SpA

Frati Editori di Quaracchi
Via Vecchia per Marino, 28-30, 00046 Grottaferrata RM
Tel: (06) 94551259 *Fax:* (06) 94551267
E-mail: quaracchi@ofm.org
Web Site: www.fratiquaracchi.it
Founded: 1877
Subjects: History, Religion - Other, Theology
ISBN Prefix(es): 978-88-7013
Parent Company: Fondazione Collegio San Bonaventura Grottaferrata

Fusta Editore
Via Colombaro dei Rossi, 2b, 12037 Saluzzo CN
Tel: (0175) 211955 *Fax:* (0175) 211955
E-mail: info@fustaeditore.it
Web Site: www.fustaeditore.it
Founded: 2002
Subjects: Cookery, Fiction, History, Nonfiction (General), Photography, Poetry, Science (General), Sports, Athletics, Travel & Tourism
ISBN Prefix(es): 978-88-95163

Adriana Gallina Editore, *imprint of* Adriano Gallina Editore SAS

Adriano Gallina Editore SAS+
Salita Tarsia, 142, 80135 Naples NA
Tel: (081) 5448747
E-mail: agallinaeditore@libero.it
Key Personnel
Mng Dir: Rossana Gallina
Founded: 1969
Subjects: Archaeology, Art, Cookery, Ethnicity, Music, Dance, Poetry, Regional Interests, Travel & Tourism
ISBN Prefix(es): 978-88-87350
Imprints: Edizioni del Delfino; Adriana Gallina Editore
Divisions: Edizioni del Delfino

Carlo Gallucci Editore SRL
Via Liberiana, 17, 00185 Rome
Tel: (06) 8413033; (06) 84130332 (orders) *Fax:* (06) 85832005
E-mail: info@galluccieditore.com; biz@galluccieditore.com; media@galluccieditore.com
Web Site: www.galluccieditore.com
Key Personnel
Press: Chiara Di Fonzo *Tel:* 3929280792
ISBN Prefix(es): 978-88-6145
Distribution Center: Messaggerie Libri SpA *Tel:* (02) 84406039 *Toll Free Tel:* 800 804 900 *E-mail:* customer.service@meli.it

Galzerano Editore+
Via Vigne 51, 84040 Casalvelino Scalo
Tel: (0974) 62028 *Fax:* (0974) 62028
Web Site: galzeranoeditore.blogspot.com/
Key Personnel
Chief Executive: Giuseppe Galzerano
E-mail: giuseppe.galzerano@tiscalinet.it
Founded: 1975
Subjects: Biography, Memoirs, Ethnicity, Fiction, Government, Political Science, History, Poetry
ISBN Prefix(es): 978-88-95637
Number of titles published annually: 10 Print
Total Titles: 250 Print

Gamberetti Editrice SRL+
Via Del Casaletto 186, 00151 Rome
Tel: (06) 535469
Founded: 1991
Specializes in the conflicts of the "New World Order," Middle East, former Yugoslavia, Ireland, Italy, Latin America, Armenia, Polisario & North-South relationship.
Subjects: Fiction, Literature, Literary Criticism, Essays
ISBN Prefix(es): 978-88-7990
Total Titles: 32 Print
Distribution Center: PDE Distribuzione, Via Teubre 54, Osmannoro, 50079 Sesto Florentino *Tel:* (0551) 301371 *Fax:* (0551) 301372 (Florence)

Gammalibri-Rock Books, *imprint of* Kaos Edizioni SRL

Gangemi Editore SpA+
Via Giulia, 142, 00186 Rome RM
Tel: (06) 6872774; (06) 68806404; (06) 99921020 *Fax:* (06) 68806189
E-mail: info@gangemieditore.it
Web Site: www.gangemieditore.com
Key Personnel
Chief Executive: Giuseppe Gangemi
Founded: 1962
Subjects: Agriculture, Anthropology, Archaeology, Architecture & Interior Design, Art, Disability, Special Needs, History, Literature, Literary Criticism, Essays, Medicine, Nursing, Dentistry, Philosophy, Romance, Social Sciences, Sociology
ISBN Prefix(es): 978-88-492; 978-88-7448
Number of titles published annually: 100 Print
Total Titles: 3,000 Print
Branch Office(s)
Via Giacomo Peroni 130-150, 00131 Rome RM
Distributed by Iter Mundi; Licosa; Messaggerie Libri; Parrini & C SpA; Sies SRL

Garamond Editoria e Formazione
Via Tevere, 21, 00198 Rome RM
Tel: (06) 97270514 *Fax:* (06) 97625760
Key Personnel
Founder, Dir & Chief Executive Officer: Agostino Quadrino
Founded: 1989
Specialize in school materials.

Subjects: Education, Music, Dance, Technology, Multimedia
ISBN Prefix(es): 978-88-86180

Libreria Universitaria Editrice Garigliano SRL+
Via Abate Aligerno, 91-93, 03043 Cassino FR
Tel: (0776) 21869 *Fax:* (0776) 21869
E-mail: info@libreriagarigliano.it; ordini@
libreriagarigliano.it (orders)
Web Site: www.libreriagarigliano.it
Founded: 1973
Subjects: Art, Education, Literature, Literary Criticism, Essays, Philosophy, Psychology, Psychiatry, Classics
ISBN Prefix(es): 978-88-7103

Archivio Federico Garolla
Via Pinamonte da Vimercate 6, 20121 Milan
Tel: (02) 6554548
Web Site: www.garolla.net
Key Personnel
Contact: Isabella Garolla *Tel:* (0333) 3777047
E-mail: isabella.garolla@garolla.net
Subjects: Archaeology, Art, Fashion, Photography, Culture, Photojournalism
ISBN Prefix(es): 978-88-7682

Garzanti Libri SRL+
Via Giuseppe Parini, 14, 20121 Milan
Tel: (02) 00623-201
E-mail: info@garzantilibri.it; redazione@
garzantilibri.it; ufficiostampa@garzantilibri.it
Web Site: www.garzantilibri.it
Key Personnel
President: Gherardo Colombo
Editorial Dir: Paolo Zaninoni
Mng Dir: Stefano Mauri
Dir, Italian Fiction: Elisabetta Migliavada
Head, Communications: Chiara Moscardelli
Founded: 1939
Trade Publisher.
Subjects: Art, Biography, Memoirs, Fiction, Government, Political Science, History, Literature, Literary Criticism, Essays, Nonfiction (General), Poetry
ISBN Prefix(es): 978-88-11
Number of titles published annually: 150 Print
Total Titles: 2,500 Print
Parent Company: Gruppo Editoriale Mauri Spagnol SpA, Via Gherardini, 10, 20145 Milan

Geo Mondadori, *imprint of* Arnoldo Mondadori Editore SpA

Gereria Cortina Editrice SRL, see Libreria Cortina Editrice SRL

Bruno Ghigi Editore+
Via Pleiadi, 6, 47900 Rimini RN
Tel: (0541) 775179 *Fax:* (0541) 775179
Key Personnel
Contact: Bruno Ghigi
Founded: 1955
Subjects: Geography, Geology, History
ISBN Prefix(es): 978-88-85640

Ghisetti e Corvi
Via Montefeltro 6/b, 20156 Milan
Tel: (02) 38086341 *Fax:* (02) 38086448
E-mail: commerciale_mi@deagostiniscuola.it
Web Site: www.ghisetticorvi.it
Founded: 1936
Publisher of textbooks & materials for schools.
Subjects: Art, Literature, Literary Criticism, Essays, Mathematics, Physics, Science (General)
ISBN Prefix(es): 978-88-8013
Parent Company: De Agostini Scuola
Ultimate Parent Company: De Agostini Editore

Giampiero Casagrande editore (gC), *imprint of* Casagrande Fidia Sapiens - Editori Associati SRL

G Giappichelli Editore SRL+
Via Po, 21, 10124 Turin TO
Tel: (011) 81-53-511 *Fax:* (011) 81-25-180
E-mail: editorale@giappichelli.it
Web Site: www.giappichelli.it
Key Personnel
Sales & Marketing Dir: Francesca Leva *Tel:* (011) 81 53 535 *Fax:* (011) 81 25 100 *E-mail:* leva@giappichelli.it
Sales: Marco Regruto *Tel:* (011) 81 53 114
E-mail: regruto@giappichelli.it
Founded: 1921
Subjects: Business, Economics, Government, Political Science, Law, Management, Philosophy, Social Sciences, Sociology
ISBN Prefix(es): 978-88-348; 978-88-7524
Bookshop(s): Libreria Editrice Scientifica di G Giappichelli, Via Vasco 2, 1-10124 Turin TO

Giardini Editori e Stampatori, see Instituti Editoriali e Poligrafici Internazionali

Il gioco di leggere Edizioni SRL
Piazza Santissima Trinita, 9, 20154 Milan
Tel: (02) 36 55 53 58 *Fax:* (02) 99 98 07 54
E-mail: edizioni@ilgiocodileggere.it
Web Site: www.ilgiocodileggere.it
Key Personnel
Editor: Mr Gabriele Cacciatori *E-mail:* g.cacciatori@ilgiocodileggere.it
Foreign Rights Manager: Valentina Lenko
E-mail: valentina.lenko@ilgiocodileggere.it
Marketing & Communication: Angela Langone
E-mail: angela.langone@ilgiocodileggere.it
Founded: 2006
ISBN Prefix(es): 978-88-6103
Distribution Center: ALI Agenzia Libraria International SRL, Via Milano 73/75, 20010 Cornaredo MI, Contact: Moreno Arrighi
Tel: (02) 99 76 24 30 *Fax:* (02) 36 54 81 88
E-mail: infoali@alilibri.it

Edizioni del Girasole SRL
Via Giuseppe Pasolini 45, 48121 Ravenna
Tel: (0544) 212830; (0544) 418986
E-mail: edizionigirasole@libero.it; ufficiostampa.girasole@virgilio.it
Key Personnel
President: Ivan Simonini
Founded: 1964
Subjects: Archaeology, Art, Drama, Theater, History, Language Arts, Linguistics, Photography, Poetry, Romance, Folklore
ISBN Prefix(es): 978-88-7567

Girotondo SNC
Via Pomaretto, 4C, 10135 Turin
Tel: (011) 320 30 94 *Fax:* (011) 47 85 115
E-mail: info@girotondoedizioni.it
Web Site: www.girotondoedizioni.it
Key Personnel
Art Dir: Silvia Forzani *E-mail:* silviaforzani@
girotondoedizioni.it
Founded: 2006
ISBN Prefix(es): 978-88-902576
Distribution Center: Nda, Via Pascoli 32, 47853 Cerasolo di Coriano RN *Tel:* (05421) 68 21 86
Fax: (05421) 68 35 56 *E-mail:* info@ndanet.it

Dott A Giuffre' Editore SpA+
Via Busto Arsizio, 40, 20151 Milan
Tel: (02) 380891; (02) 38089311 *Fax:* (02) 38009582; (02) 38089432
E-mail: service@giuffre.it; editoriale@giuffre.it
Web Site: www.giuffre.it
Key Personnel
President: Giuseppe Giuffre

Dir General: Antonio Giuffre
Founded: 1931
Membership(s): Law Publishers in Europe.
Subjects: Economics, Government, Political Science, History, Law, Social Sciences, Sociology
ISBN Prefix(es): 978-88-14
Branch Office(s)
Via V Colonna 40, 00193 Rome *Tel:* (06) 659938; (06) 6569792

Giunti, *imprint of* Giunti Editore SpA

Giunti Editore SpA+
Via Bolognese, 165, 50139 Florence
Tel: (055) 5062 1; (02) 5754 71 (rights)
Fax: (055) 5062 298; (02) 5754 7503 (rights)
E-mail: info@giunti.it; ufficiostampa@giunti.it
Web Site: www.giunti.it
Key Personnel
Chief Executive Officer: Martino Montanarini
President: Sergio Giunti
Vice President: Bruno Mari
Dir General: Daniele Tinelli
Editorial Dir: Beatrice Fini
Communication & Press Office: Laura Guidi
E-mail: l.guidi@giunti.it
Foreign Rights: Valentina Mazza *E-mail:* v.mazza@giunti.it
Foreign Rights, Co-editions: Brunella Tiso
E-mail: b.tiso@giunti.it
Strategy & Development: Jose Grade
Founded: 1841
Subjects: Art, Chemistry, Chemical Engineering, Cookery, Education, Fiction, Health, Nutrition, History, How-to, Language Arts, Linguistics, Literature, Literary Criticism, Essays, Mathematics, Nonfiction (General), Psychology, Psychiatry, Science (General), Travel & Tourism
ISBN Prefix(es): 978-88-89902; 978-88-440; 978-88-507; 978-88-09
Imprints: Edizioni del Borgo; Dami Editore; Demetra; Fatatrac; Giunti; Giunti Junior; Giunti Kids; Giunti Scuola; Motta Junior; Giorgio Nada Editore; Editoriale Scienza srl; Slow Food Editore; Touring Editore; Touring Junior; De Vecchi Editore
Branch Office(s)
Ancona
Bari
Cagliari
Catania
Genoa
Lamezia Terme
Milan
Naples
Padua
Palermo
Rome

Giunti Junior, *imprint of* Giunti Editore SpA

Giunti Kids, *imprint of* Giunti Editore SpA

Giunti Scuola, *imprint of* Giunti Editore SpA

Editrice la Giuntina
Via Mannelli 29 rosso, 50136 Florence FI
Tel: (055) 2476781 *Fax:* (055) 2009800; (055) 2349067
E-mail: info@giuntina.it
Web Site: www.giuntina.it
Key Personnel
Founder: Daniel Vogelmann
Foreign Rights: Shulim Vogelmann
E-mail: shulim@giuntina.it
Founded: 1980
Specialize in European Jewish culture.
Subjects: Religion - Jewish
ISBN Prefix(es): 978-88-85943; 978-88-8057
Total Titles: 240 Print

Gius Laterza e Figli SpA+
Piazza Umberto I, 54, 70121 Bari BA
Tel: (080) 528 12 11 *Fax:* (080) 524 34 61
E-mail: commerciale@laterza.it (sales);
    foreignrights@laterza.it
Web Site: www.laterza.it
Key Personnel
Editorial Dir, Rome: Alessandro Laterza;
    Giuseppe Laterza *E-mail:* glaterza@laterza.it
Founded: 1885
Subjects: Archaeology, Architecture & Interior
    Design, Art, Biography, Memoirs, Economics,
    History, Philosophy, Psychology, Psychiatry,
    Religion - Other, Science (General), Social Sci-
    ences, Sociology
ISBN Prefix(es): 978-88-420
Branch Office(s)
Via di Villa Sacchetti, 17, 00197 Rome RM
Tel: (06) 45 46 5311 *Fax:* (06) 322 3853
    E-mail: attadio@laterza.it
Bookshop(s): Libreria Laterza, Via Sparano 136,
    70121 Bari BA *Tel:* (080) 5211714 *Fax:* (080)
    5211780 *E-mail:* libreria@laterza.it *Web
    Site:* www.librerialaterza.it

GLF, see Gius Laterza e Figli SpA

Glossa Editrice SRL+
Piazza Paolo VI, 6, 20121 Milan MI
Tel: (02) 877609 *Fax:* (02) 72003162
E-mail: informazioni@glossaeditrice.it
Web Site: www.glossaeditrice.it
Founded: 1987
Book production & sales.
Subjects: Theology
ISBN Prefix(es): 978-88-7105
Number of titles published annually: 12 Print
Total Titles: 262 Print
Distribution Center: Dehoniana Libri SpA, Via
    Scipione dal Ferro 4, 40138 Bologna BO, Con-
    tact: Mr Lenzi *Tel:* (051) 4290452 *Fax:* (051)
    4290431

Goliardica Editrice, *imprint of* Edizioni
    Goliardiche SRL

La Goliardica Pavese SRL+
Via Camillo Golgi, 2, 27100 Pavia PV
Tel: (0382) 529570 *Fax:* (0382) 423140
Key Personnel
Chief Executive: Dario De Bona
Founded: 1977
Subjects: Biological Sciences, Chemistry, Chem-
    ical Engineering, Law, Medicine, Nursing,
    Dentistry, Physical Sciences, Physics, Science
    (General)
ISBN Prefix(es): 978-88-7830
Bookshop(s): Via Lombroso, 21, 27100 Pavia
    Tel: (0382) 525709; Viale Taramelli, 18, 27100
    Pavia *Tel:* (0382) 526220

Edizioni Goliardiche SRL
Via Aquileia, 64a, 33050 Bagnaria Arsa UD
Tel: (0432) 996332 *Fax:* (040) 566278
E-mail: info@edizionigoliardiche.it
Web Site: www.edizionigoliardiche.it
Founded: 1994
Subjects: Architecture & Interior Design, Biologi-
    cal Sciences, Chemistry, Chemical Engineering,
    Communications, Drama, Theater, Economics,
    Education, Fiction, Government, Political Sci-
    ence, History, Language Arts, Linguistics, Law,
    Mathematics, Medicine, Nursing, Dentistry,
    Nonfiction (General), Philosophy, Physics, Po-
    etry, Psychology, Psychiatry, Science (General),
    Social Sciences, Sociology, Technology, Na-
    ture, Physical Education
ISBN Prefix(es): 978-88-86573; 978-88-88171
Imprints: egbooks; Goliardica Editrice; l'informa
    professional

Gottardo Edizioni Verlag, *imprint of* Casagrande
    Fidia Sapiens - Editori Associati SRL

Gozzini, see Libreria Gozzini di Pietro e
    Francesco Chellini (SNC)

Grafica & Arte SRL+
Via Francesco Coghetti, 108, 24128 Bergamo
Tel: (035) 255014 *Fax:* (035) 250164
E-mail: info@graficaearte.it; ordini@graficaearte.
    it (orders)
Web Site: www.graficaearte.it
Founded: 1975
Subjects: Architecture & Interior Design, Art,
    Ethnicity, History, Photography
ISBN Prefix(es): 978-88-7201
Number of titles published annually: 10 Print
Total Titles: 268 Print
Distributed by Dehoniana Libri SpA Bologna
Showroom(s): Via Francesco Coghetti, 90, 24128
    Bergamo

Grafiche Calosci+
Loc Vallone 35/L, 52044 Camucia-Cortona AR
Tel: (0575) 67 82 82 *Fax:* (0575) 67 82 82
E-mail: info@calosci.com
Web Site: www.calosci.com
Key Personnel
Contact: Giuseppe Calosci
Founded: 1963
Subjects: Archaeology, Architecture & Interior
    Design, Art, Drama, Theater, Fiction, His-
    tory, Literature, Literary Criticism, Essays,
    Medicine, Nursing, Dentistry, Music, Dance,
    Nonfiction (General), Philosophy, Regional In-
    terests, Transportation, Travel & Tourism
ISBN Prefix(es): 978-88-7785
Distributed by The Courier srl

Grafo
Division of IGB Group
via Alessandro Volta, 21/A, 25010 San Zeno
    Naviglio BS
Tel: (030) 3542997
E-mail: libreria@grafo.it; info@grafo.it
Web Site: www.grafo.it
Founded: 1973
Subjects: Anthropology, Archaeology, Art, Eth-
    nicity, History, Regional Interests
ISBN Prefix(es): 978-88-7385

Graphot Editrice
Lungo Dora Colletta 113/10 bis, 10153 Turin TO
Tel: (011) 2386281 *Fax:* (011) 2358882
E-mail: graphot@graphot.com
Web Site: www.graphot.com
Founded: 1984
Subjects: Cookery, Fiction, History, Literature,
    Literary Criticism, Essays, Mysteries, Suspense,
    Nonfiction (General), Photography, Sports, Ath-
    letics
ISBN Prefix(es): 978-88-86906; 978-88-89509
Imprints: Spoon River

Gremese Editore
Via Virginia Agnelli, 88, 00151 Rome
Tel: (06) 65740507 *Fax:* (06) 65740509
E-mail: gremese@gremese.com; rights@gremese.
    com; ufficiostampa@gremese.com
Web Site: www.gremese.com
Key Personnel
Mng Dir: Alberto Gremese
Founded: 1977
Subjects: Animals, Pets, Architecture & Inte-
    rior Design, Art, Astrology, Occult, Cookery,
    Crafts, Games, Hobbies, Drama, Theater, Eco-
    nomics, Erotica, Fashion, Fiction, Film, Video,
    Gardening, Plants, Health, Nutrition, House
    & Home, How-to, Humor, Literature, Liter-
    ary Criticism, Essays, Management, Medicine,
    Nursing, Dentistry, Music, Dance, Photography,

Radio, TV, Religion - Other, Science (General),
    Sports, Athletics, Travel & Tourism, Wine &
    Spirits, Mythology
ISBN Prefix(es): 978-88-7605; 978-88-7742; 978-
    88-7944; 978-88-8440; 978-88-7301
Number of titles published annually: 80 Print
Total Titles: 1,000 Print
Imprints: L'Airone Editrice; Gremese France
Bookshop(s): Gremese Libreria, Via Belsiana, 22,
    00187 Rome *Web Site:* www.libreriagremese.it
Distribution Center: Messaggerie Libri SpA *Web
    Site:* www.messaggerielibri.it

Gremese France, *imprint of* Gremese Editore

Gremese International, see Gremese Editore

Gribaudi Editore
Via C Baroni, 190, 20142 Milan
Tel: (02) 89302244; (02) 89304648 *Fax:* (02)
    89302376
E-mail: info@gribaudi.it
Web Site: www.gribaudi.it; www.gribaudi.biz
    (bookshop)
Key Personnel
Publisher: Maurizio Sola
Foreign Rights: Sandra Zerilli
Founded: 1966
Subjects: Behavioral Sciences, Biblical Studies,
    Biography, Memoirs, Education, Human Rela-
    tions, Humor, Religion - Catholic, Religion -
    Jewish, Self-Help, Theology
ISBN Prefix(es): 978-88-7152; 978-88-6366
Number of titles published annually: 50 Print
Total Titles: 800 Print
Imprints: PGE

Gribaudo, *imprint of* Giangiacomo Feltrinelli
    Editore SRL

Edizioni Gribaudo SRL
Via Natale Battaglia 12, 20127 Milan MI
Web Site: www.edizionigribaudo.it
Founded: 2001
Subjects: Architecture & Interior Design, Art, Bi-
    ography, Memoirs, Cookery, Crafts, Games,
    Hobbies, Fashion, Film, Video, Music, Dance,
    Photography
ISBN Prefix(es): 978-88-7906

Gruppo Editoriale Internazionale, see Instituti
    Editoriali e Poligrafici Internazionali

Ugo Guanda Editore SpA+
Via Gherardini 10, 20145 Milan
Tel: (02) 34597628 *Fax:* (02) 34597214
E-mail: info@guanda.it
Web Site: www.guanda.it
Key Personnel
President & Editorial Dir: Luigi Brioschi
Founded: 1932
Subjects: Art, Fiction, Nonfiction (General), Po-
    etry
ISBN Prefix(es): 978-88-7746; 978-88-235; 978-
    88-8246; 978-88-6088
Parent Company: Gruppo Editoriale Mauri Spag-
    nol SpA
U.S. Office(s): Del Commune Enterprises, 285 W
    Broadway, Suite 310, New York, NY 10013,
    United States
Distribution Center: Messaggerie Italiane SpA
Orders to: Pro Libro

Edizioni Angelo Guerini e Associati SpA+
Viale Filippetti 28, 20122 Milan
Tel: (02) 582980 *Fax:* (02) 58298030
E-mail: info@guerini.it
Web Site: www.guerini.it
Key Personnel
President: Angelo Guerini

Foreign Rights Manager: Brunella Salvaderi
Tel: (02) 58298016 *E-mail:* salvaderi@guerini.
it
Founded: 1987
Essays, books & reviews.
Subjects: Anthropology, Architecture & Interior
Design, Art, Economics, Gardening, Plants,
History, Literature, Literary Criticism, Essays,
Management, Medicine, Nursing, Dentistry,
Music, Dance, Philosophy, Psychology, Psychi-
atry, Social Sciences, Sociology, Media Studies
& Geopolitics
ISBN Prefix(es): 978-88-7802; 978-88-8107
(Guerini Scientifica); 978-88-8335; 978-88-
8195 (Cantiere Italia); 978-88-6250
Total Titles: 1,000 Print
Foreign Rights: Servizi Editoriali
Bookshop(s): Libreria Guerini, Piazza Soldini
5, 21053 Castellanza *Tel:* (0331) 508918
Fax: (0331) 508972 *E-mail:* libreria@liuc.it
Shipping Address: TNT Logistics Italia SpA, Str
Provinciale, 13, 20064 Gorgonzola MI
Distribution Center: Via Verdi, 8, 20090 Assago
MI *Tel:* (02) 45 774 1 *Fax:* (02) 45701032
E-mail: meli.dirgen@meli.it

Guerra Edizioni GURU SRL
Via Aldo Manna, 25/27, 06132 Perugia
Tel: (075) 5289090 *Fax:* (075) 5288244
E-mail: info@guerraedizioni.com
Web Site: www.guerra-edizioni.com
Key Personnel
Chief Executive Officer: Sara Maria Chellini
Dir: Patrizia Bellavita; Mirelle Leonesi; Alfa
Petrolati
Founded: 1883
Books & materials for learning Italian as a for-
eign language.
Subjects: Education, Language Arts, Linguistics
ISBN Prefix(es): 978-88-7715

Guide del Cuore, *imprint of* Passigli Editori SRL

Guide del Sole, *imprint of* Passigli Editori SRL

Harmony, *imprint of* HarperCollins Italia SpA

HarperCollins Italia SpA
Division of HarperCollins Publishers
Viale Monte Nero, 84, 20135 Milan
E-mail: ufficiostampa@harpercollins.it
Web Site: www.harpercollins.it
Key Personnel
Mng Dir & Publisher: Laura Donnini
Editorial Dir: Sabrina Annoni
Commercial Dir: Giovanni Dutto
Subjects: Romance
ISBN Prefix(es): 978-88-6905
Imprints: eLit; Harmony; hc; I Diamanti

hc, *imprint of* HarperCollins Italia SpA

Edizioni Hermes SRL+
Subsidiary of Edizioni Mediterranee SRL
Via Flaminia 109, 00196 Rome
Tel: (06) 3235433 *Fax:* (06) 3236277
E-mail: info@edizionimediterranee.net; press@
edizionimediterranee.net
Web Site: www.edizionimediterranee.it
Key Personnel
General Manager: Giovanni Canonico
Editorial: Paola Maria Canonico
Contact: Eleasa Canonico
Founded: 1979
Subjects: Anthropology, Health, Nutrition, How-
to, Medicine, Nursing, Dentistry, Parapsy-
chology, Psychology, Psychiatry, Religion -
Buddhist, Religion - Hindu, Religion - Other,
Sports, Athletics
ISBN Prefix(es): 978-88-7938
Total Titles: 300 Print

Institutum Historicum Societatis Iesu (Jesuit
Historical Institute)
Borgo Santo Spirito, 4, 00193 Rome RM
Tel: (06) 68977536 *Fax:* (06) 68977461
E-mail: arsi-seg@sjcuria.org
Web Site: www.sjweb.info
Key Personnel
Manager: Raul Gonzalez *E-mail:* arsi-gonzalez@
sjcuria.org
Publication Editor: Norman Tanner *E-mail:* arsi-
pubb@sjcuria.org
Founded: 1932
Subjects: History, Philosophy, Religion - Other
ISBN Prefix(es): 978-88-7041
Total Titles: 50 Print

Hopefulmonster Editore
Via Santa Chiara, 30/F, 10122 Turin
Tel: (011) 4367197 *Fax:* (011) 4369025
E-mail: info@hopefulmonster.net
Web Site: www.hopefulmonster.net
Key Personnel
Dir: Beatrice Merz *E-mail:* beatricemerz@
hopefulmonster.net
Press: Cristina Cioppa *E-mail:* cristinacioppa@
hopefulmonster.net
Editorial: Luisa Borio *E-mail:* luisaborio@
hopefulmonster.net
Founded: 1986
Specialize in art books & catalogues concerning
contemporary art.
Subjects: Art, History, Philosophy, Photography,
Science (General), Travel & Tourism
ISBN Prefix(es): 978-88-7757
Number of titles published annually: 15 Print
Foreign Rep(s): Art Books International (Asia,
Ireland, UK); Bitacora Arte y Humanidades
(Portugal, Spain); Distributed Art Publisher
Inc (Canada, USA); Garzon Diffusion Interna-
tionale (Belgium, Europe, France, South Amer-
ica); Visual Books Sales Agency (Austria, Ger-
many, Netherlands, Switzerland)
Distribution Center: Vivalibri SpA, via Isonzo,
34, 00198 Rome *Tel:* (06) 84242153 *Fax:* (06)
8413252 *E-mail:* vendite.dirette@vivalibri.it

Ibis+
Via Crispi 8, 22100 Como CO
Tel: (031) 3371367 *Fax:* (031) 306829
E-mail: info@ibisedizioni.it
Web Site: www.ibisedizioni.it
Key Personnel
President: Giulio Veronesi
Editorial Dir: Paolo M Veronesi
Founded: 1989
Subjects: Anthropology, Biological Sciences, Fic-
tion, History, Literature, Literary Criticism,
Essays, Philosophy, Social Sciences, Sociology,
Travel & Tourism
ISBN Prefix(es): 978-88-7164
Number of titles published annually: 30 Print
Total Titles: 500 Print

Ibiskos - di A Ulivieri
Via Lavagnini 40, 50053 Empoli FI
Tel: (0571) 79807 *Fax:* (0571) 700633
E-mail: info@ibiskosulivieri.it
Web Site: www.ibiskosulivieri.it
Subjects: Literature, Literary Criticism, Essays,
Nonfiction (General), Poetry, Children's Litera-
ture
ISBN Prefix(es): 978-88-7841
Distribution Center: EdiQ Distribuzione, CP
56, 21040 Gerenzano-Varese VA *Tel:* (02)
9689323; (347) 4140016 (cell) *Fax:* (02)
9689323

ICCU, see Istituto Centrale per il Catalogo Unico
delle Biblioteche Italiane e per le Informazioni
Bibliografiche

Idea Books+
Via Regia, 53, 55049 Viareggio LU
Tel: (0584) 425410 *Fax:* (178) 609 8685
E-mail: info@ideabooks.com
Web Site: www.ideabooks.com
Founded: 1980
Subjects: Architecture & Interior Design, Art,
Fashion, Photography
ISBN Prefix(es): 978-88-7017; 978-88-88033
Number of titles published annually: 8 Print

Idelson-Gnocchi Edizioni Scientifiche
Via Michele Pietravalle, 85, 80131 Naples
Tel: (081) 5453443 *Fax:* (081) 5464991
E-mail: ordini@idelsongnocchi.it; info@
idelsongnocchi.it
Web Site: www.idelsongnocchi.it
Key Personnel
Contact: Guido Gnocchi
Founded: 1908
Subjects: Medicine, Nursing, Dentistry
ISBN Prefix(es): 978-88-7069; 978-88-7947
U.S. Office(s): Idelson Gnocchi Scientific Pub-
lications, 1316 King's Bay Dr, Crystal River,
FL 34429, United States *Tel:* 352-794-6234
Fax: 352-794-6234 *E-mail:* candotti@att.net

IHSI, see Institutum Historicum Societatis Iesu

IHT Gruppo Editoriale SRL
Via Monte Napoleone, 9, 20121 Milan
Tel: (02) 794181 *Fax:* (02) 784021
Key Personnel
Founder, President & Publisher: Lisa Massimil-
iano
Founded: 1985
Subjects: Art, Computers, Film, Video, Military
Science, Science (General), Technology
ISBN Prefix(es): 978-88-7803
Imprints: IHT Video
Distributed by Messaggerie Periodic

IHT Video, *imprint of* IHT Gruppo Editoriale
SRL

IIM, see Istituto Idrografico della Marina (IIM)

Il Filo Edizioni, see Gruppo Albatros Il Filo

Il Mulino a Vento, *imprint of* Raffaello Editrice
SRL

In Dialogo+
Imprint of Impresa Tecnoeditoriale Lombarda
SRL
Via A de Recanate, 1, 20142 Milan MI
Tel: (02) 67131639; (02) 67131645 (administra-
tion) *Fax:* (02) 66984388
E-mail: libri@chiesadimilano.it;
amministrazione@chiesadimilano.it
Web Site: www.itl-libri.com
Founded: 1979
Subjects: Biblical Studies, Child Care & Devel-
opment, Communications, Education, Gov-
ernment, Political Science, Human Relations,
Religion - Catholic, Theology
ISBN Prefix(es): 978-88-8123; 978-88-85985
Distribution Center: Dehoniana Libri-
Distribuzione Commerciale, Via Scipione Dal
Ferro, 4, 40138 Bologna *Tel:* (051) 4290451
E-mail: distribuzionedl@dehoniane.it

l'informa professional, *imprint of* Edizioni
Goliardiche SRL

Iniziative Culturali SRL, see Servitium Editrice

Editrice Innocenti SNC+
Via Zara 36/40, 38100 Trento
Tel: (0461) 236521 *Fax:* (0461) 230115
Key Personnel
Publicity: Silvia Nones *E-mail:* silvianones@
 hotmail.com
Founded: 1972
Subjects: Language Arts, Linguistics
Associate Companies: Casa Editrice Bulgar-
 ini, Via Ettore Petrolini 8/10, 50137 Florence
 Tel: (055) 6161 1 *Fax:* (055) 6161 230; Casa
 Editrice Principato, Via Fauche, 20154 Milan
 Tel: (023) 12025 *Fax:* (023) 3104295

Instar Libri SRL
Via Mazzini 41, 10123 Turin
Tel: (011) 885630 *Fax:* (011) 885630
E-mail: info@instarlibri.it
Web Site: www.instarlibri.it
Key Personnel
Press: Silvia Ferrero *E-mail:* ferrero@bluedizioni.
 it
Founded: 1991
Subjects: Fiction, Nonfiction (General)
ISBN Prefix(es): 978-88-461
Parent Company: Blu Edizioni srl
Foreign Rights: Nabu-International Literary &
 Film Agency (Silvia Brunelli) (worldwide exc
 Austria, Germany, Netherlands & German-
 speaking Switzerland); Schwermann Literary
 Agency (Michaela Schwermann) (Austria,
 Germany, Netherlands, Switzerland (German-
 speaking))

Instituti Editoriali e Poligrafici Internazionali+
Imprint of Fabrizio Serra Editore
Via Santa Bibbina 28, 56127 Pisa
Mailing Address: CP N 1, Succursale 8, 56123
 Pisa
Tel: (050) 542332 *Fax:* (050) 574888
E-mail: fse@libraweb.net
Web Site: www.libraweb.net
Key Personnel
Editorial Dir: Fabrizio Serra
Editor: Dr Alberto Pizzigati *E-mail:* alberto.
 pizzigati@libraweb.net
Founded: 1994
Specialize in philosophy, archaeology, history,
 sociology, anthropology & Italian.
Subjects: Anthropology, Archaeology, History,
 Language Arts, Linguistics, Philosophy, Social
 Sciences, Sociology, Transportation
ISBN Prefix(es): 978-88-8147
Branch Office(s)
Via Carlo Emanuelei 48, 00185 Rome *Tel:* (06)
 70493456 *Fax:* (06) 70476605 *E-mail:* fse.
 roma@libraweb.net
Warehouse: Via delle Sorgenti 87, 56010 Agnano
 Pisano (Pisa) *Tel:* (050) 939160

Interlinea Edizioni SRL
via Enrico Mattei 21, 28100 Novara
Tel: (0321) 612571 *Fax:* (0321) 612636
E-mail: edizioni@interlinea.com; ufficiostampa@
 interlinea.com
Web Site: www.interlinea.com
Key Personnel
Founder & Editor: Roberto Cicala; Carlo Robiglio
Subjects: Fiction, Literature, Literary Criticism,
 Essays, Culture, Italian Literature
ISBN Prefix(es): 978-88-8212; 978-88-86121
Distribution Center: Messaggerie Libri SpA, via
 Giuseppe Verdi 8, 20090 Assago MI *Tel:* (02)
 457741

Iperborea SRL
Via Palestro, 20, 20121 Milan
Tel: (02) 87398098; (02) 87398099 *Fax:* (02)
 798919
E-mail: ufficio.stampa@iperborea.com
Web Site: www.iperborea.com

Key Personnel
Publisher: Emilia Lodigiani
Publishing Dir: Pietro Biancardi
Administration: Paola Terzoli
Copy Editor: Christina Marasti
Editor & Press Office: Cristina Gerosa
Production: Anna Basile
Sales: Simona Cattaneo
Founded: 1987
Subjects: Literature, Literary Criticism, Essays
ISBN Prefix(es): 978-88-7091

**ISAL (Istituto per la Storia dell'Arte
 Lombarda)**
Palazzo Arese Jacini, Piazza Arese, 12, 20031
 Cesano Maderno MI
Tel: (0362) 528118 *Fax:* (0362) 659417
E-mail: info@istitutoartelombarda.org
Web Site: www.istitutoartelombarda.org
Key Personnel
President: Diego Meroni
Vice President: Edoardo Bregani
Science Dir: Prof Maria Antonietta Crippa
Founded: 1967
Subjects: Archaeology, Art
ISBN Prefix(es): 978-88-85153
Number of titles published annually: 3 Print

IsIAO, see Istituto Italiano per l'Africa e
 l'Oriente (IsIAO)

ISPER SRL+
Corso Dante 122, 10126 Turin
Tel: (011) 66 47 803 *Fax:* (011) 66 70 829
E-mail: isper@isper.org; fondazione@fondazione-
 isper.edu
Web Site: www.isper.org
Key Personnel
Chief Executive Officer: Marco Actis Grosso
 E-mail: marco.actisgrosso@isper.org
Dir of Development: Laura Actis Grosso
 Tel: (011) 66 47 803 ext 201 *E-mail:* laura.
 actisgrosso@isper.org
Dir of Research & Documentation: Anna
 Manavella *Tel:* (011) 66 47 803 ext 210
 E-mail: anna.manavella@isper.org
Communications & Relations: Lorena Don-
 adonibus *Tel:* (011) 66 47 803 ext 231
 E-mail: lorena.donadonibus@isper.org
Founded: 1965
Subjects: Business, Management
Number of titles published annually: 15 E-Book
Total Titles: 83 E-Book
Branch Office(s)
Via Paisiello, 29, 00198 Rome *Tel:* (06)
 85303054 *Fax:* (06) 853050156
 E-mail: fondazione.roma@f-isper.eu
Book Club(s): Isper Club

**Istituto Centrale per il Catalogo Unico delle
 Biblioteche Italiane e per le Informazioni
 Bibliografiche** (Central Institute for the Union
 Catalog of Italian Libraries & Bibliographic
 Information)
Viale Castro Pretorio, 105, 00185 Rome RM
Tel: (06) 49210425; (06) 4989424 *Fax:* (06)
 4959302
E-mail: venditapubbl@iccu.sbn.it; ic-cu@
 beniculturali.it
Web Site: www.iccu.sbn.it
Key Personnel
Dir: Simonetta Butto *E-mail:* simonetta.butto@
 beniculturali.it
Secretary: Susanne Cesaroni *E-mail:* susanne.
 cesaroni@beniculturali.it
Publications Sales: Roberta Rizzoni
 Fax: rizzoni@iccu.sbn.it
Subjects: Library & Information Sciences
ISBN Prefix(es): 978-88-7107

Istituto della Enciclopedia Italiana+
Piazza della Enciclopedia Italiana, 4, 00186 Rome

Tel: (06) 68981; (06) 68982347 *Fax:* (06)
 68982266; (06) 68982156
E-mail: infotreccani@treccani.it; ufficiostampa@
 treccani.it; servizioclienti@treccani.it;
 redazione@treccani.it
Web Site: www.treccani.it
Key Personnel
President: Giuliano Amato
Dir: Francesco Tato
Editorial Dir: Bray Massimo
Head, Press: Mariella Di Donna *Tel:* (06)
 68982231 *Fax:* (06) 68982266
Event: Ornella Gila *Tel:* (06) 68982244 *Fax:* (06)
 68982170 *E-mail:* att.culturali@treccani.it
Founded: 1925
Subjects: Art
ISBN Prefix(es): 978-88-12
Foreign Rep(s): Longueville Books (Australia,
 China, New Zealand); Silvermine (USA); Slovo
 Publishing (Russia); Yushodo Group (Japan,
 Korea, Taiwan)

Istituto Geografico de Agostini SpA
cso della Vittoria, 91, 28100 Novara
Tel: (0321) 4241
E-mail: info@deagostini.it
Web Site: www.deagostini.it
Key Personnel
Contact: Chiara Boroli
Founded: 1901
Subjects: Art, Cookery, Gardening, Plants, Geog-
 raphy, Geology, History, Language Arts, Lin-
 guistics, Literature, Literary Criticism, Essays,
 Regional Interests, Religion - Other
ISBN Prefix(es): 978-88-402; 978-88-415; 978-
 88-410; 978-88-418; 978-88-406
Parent Company: De Agostini Editore SpA
Ultimate Parent Company: Gruppo de Agostini
Branch Office(s)
Uffici di Milano, Via Montefeltro 6/B, 20156 Mi-
 lan *Tel:* (02) 380861 *Fax:* (02) 38086324

Istituto Idrografico della Marina (IIM)
Passo dell'Osservatorio 4, 16134 Genoa
Tel: (010) 24431 *Fax:* (010) 261400
E-mail: iim.sre@marina.difesa.it
Web Site: www.marina.difesa.it
Key Personnel
Mng Dir: Antonio Cosentino *E-mail:* antonio.
 cosentino@marina.difesa.it
Editorial Dir: Michele Carosella
Founded: 1872
Specialize in official nautical documentation.
Subjects: Maritime

Istituto Italiano Edizioni Atlas SpA+
Via G Crescenzi, 88, 24123 Bergamo
Tel: (035) 249711
E-mail: edizioniatlas@edatlas.it
Web Site: www.edatlas.it
Key Personnel
Dir General: Dr Marco Carreri
Founded: 1949
Subjects: Art, Biography, Memoirs, Biological
 Sciences, Chemistry, Chemical Engineering,
 Computer Science, Fiction, History, Mathemat-
 ics, Philosophy, Science (General), Technology
ISBN Prefix(es): 978-88-268

**Istituto Italiano per l'Africa e l'Oriente
 (IsIAO)** (Italian Institute for Africa & the East)
Via Ulisse Aldrovandi, 16, 00197 Rome
Tel: (06) 32855223 *Fax:* (06) 32855217
Key Personnel
Dir: Francesco D'Arelli *E-mail:* biblio.dir@isiao.
 it
Founded: 1933
Subjects: Archaeology, Asian Studies, History,
 Language Arts, Linguistics, Religion - Other,
 Africa, Philology

Istituto Nazionale di Studi Romani
Piazza dei Cavalieri di Malta, 2, 00153 Rome
RM
Tel: (06) 574 34 42; (06) 574 34 45 *Fax:* (06)
574 34 47
E-mail: studiromani@studiromani.it; segreteria@
studiromani.it
Web Site: www.studiromani.it
Key Personnel
President: Prof Paolo Sommella
E-mail: presidente@studiromani.it
Dir: Letizia Lanzetta *E-mail:* lanzetta@
studiromani.it
Associate Dir, Publishing: Massimiliano Ghilardi
E-mail: ghilardi@studiromani.it
Founded: 1925
Subjects: Architecture & Interior Design, Art,
History, Literature, Literary Criticism, Essays
ISBN Prefix(es): 978-88-7311
Number of titles published annually: 7 Print
Total Titles: 848 Print

Istituto per la Storia dell'Arte Lombarda, see
ISAL (Istituto per la Storia dell'Arte
Lombarda)

Istituto Poligrafico e Zecca dello Stato SpA
(Government Printing Office & Mint SpA)+
Piazza Giuseppe Verdi, 1, 00198 Rome
Toll Free Tel: 800 864035 *Fax:* (06) 85084117
E-mail: editoriale@ipzs.it; informazioni@ipzs.it
Web Site: www.editoria.ipzs.it
Key Personnel
Chief Executive Officer: Dr Ferruccio Ferranti
Dir, Communications: Manuela Bravi
Founded: 1928
State Publishing House & Italian State Stationery
Office.
Subjects: Art, Government, Political Science,
Language Arts, Linguistics, Law, Literature,
Literary Criticism, Essays
ISBN Prefix(es): 978-88-240
Subsidiaries: Editalia SpA

**Istituto Storico Italiano per l'Eta Moderna e
Contemporanea** (Italian Historical Institute for
Modern & Contemporary Age)
Via Michelangelo Caetani, 32, 00186 Rome
Tel: (06) 68806922 *Fax:* (06) 6875127
E-mail: segreteria@iststor.it
Key Personnel
Mng Dir: Prof Luigi Lotti
Founded: 1934
Subjects: History

Editoriale Itaca+
Piazza Ernesto De Angeli, 1, 20146 Milan
Tel: (02) 48009484
Founded: 1989
Specialize in total quality management.
Subjects: Business, Communications, Manage-
ment, Marketing
ISBN Prefix(es): 978-88-7206

Editoriale Jaca Book SpA+
Via G Frua 11, 20146 Milan
Tel: (02) 4856151; (02) 48561520-29 (customer
service) *Fax:* (02) 48193361
E-mail: jacabook@pec.netorange.it;
ufficiostampa@jacabook.it (press)
Web Site: www.jacabook.it
Key Personnel
President & Publisher: Sante Bagnoli
E-mail: direzione@jacabook.it
Vice President & Publisher: Vera Minazzi
E-mail: vera.minazzi@jacabook.it
Chief Financial Officer: Roberto Tagliabue
E-mail: roberto.tagliabue@jacabook.it
International Rights Sales Manager: Marie Jeanne
Schutz *Tel:* (02) 48561528 *E-mail:* marie.
schutz@jacabook.it

Rights Manager: Giulia Mercanti *Tel:* (02)
48561527 *E-mail:* giulia.mercanti@jacabook.it
Founded: 1966
Human sciences publisher of essays & academic
texts in the fields of anthropology, philosophy,
history, prehistory, medieval culture, religions,
Christianity, economic & social sciences, ecology, current affairs & literary criticism. Currently developing a new department of foreign
fiction. Existing department of art, archaeology,
architecture & music with a list of high quality
illustrated volumes as well as children's book
department also for international co-editions.
Subjects: African American Studies, Anthropology, Archaeology, Architecture & Interior Design, Art, Asian Studies, Earth Sciences, Eco-
nomics, Environmental Studies, Fiction, Gov-
ernment, Political Science, History, Literature,
Literary Criticism, Essays, Native American
Studies, Natural History, Nonfiction (General),
Philosophy, Photography, Poetry, Religion -
Catholic, Religion - Other, Science (General),
Social Sciences, Sociology, Theology
ISBN Prefix(es): 978-88-16
Number of titles published annually: 100 Print
Total Titles: 5,000 Print
Distribution Center: Messaggerie Libri SpA, Via
G Verdi 8, 20090 Assago MI *Tel:* (02) 457741
Web Site: www.messaggerielibri.it

Jandi Sapi Editori
Via Crescenzio, 62, 00193 Rome
Tel: (06) 68805515; (06) 6876054 *Fax:* (06)
6832612
Founded: 1941
Subjects: Art, Law, Literature, Literary Criticism,
Essays
ISBN Prefix(es): 978-88-7142
Imprints: JSE
Divisions: Archivi Arte Antica
Bookshop(s): Libreria Forense, Via Marianna
Dionigi, 26, 00193 Rome RM *Tel:* (06)
3204698 *Fax:* (06) 3207696; L E G Libreria
economico giuridica, Via di S Maria Mag-
giore, 121, 00185 Rome RM *Tel:* (06) 4883331
Fax: (06) 4745964; Libreria Medichini, P
le Clodio, 26, 00195 Rome RM *Tel:* (06)
3613059; Libreria De Miranda, VI Giulio Ce-
sare, 51/E, 00192 Rome RM *Tel:* (06) 3213303
Fax: (06) 3216695

Japadre Editori+
Via Montorio al Vomano 2, 67100 l'Aquila AQ
Tel: (0862) 26025 *Fax:* (0862) 25587
E-mail: japadre.editore@virgilio.it
Key Personnel
Mng Dir: Leandro Ugo Japadre
Founded: 1966
Subjects: Art, Economics, Ethnicity, Fiction, His-
tory, Language Arts, Linguistics, Literature,
Literary Criticism, Essays, Philosophy, Poetry,
Psychology, Psychiatry, Religion - Other, Sci-
ence (General), Social Sciences, Sociology,
Technology
ISBN Prefix(es): 978-88-7006
Branch Office(s)
Via G Boni 20, 00162 Rome *Tel:* (06) 44291182
Distributor for DASP (Deputazione Abruzzese Di
Storia Patria)
Warehouse: Contrada Cappelli
Pal Prosperini

Jazz People, *imprint of* Stampa Alternativa -
Nuovi Equilibri

Edizioni Joker
Via Crosa della Maccarina, 28/B, 15067 Novi
Ligure AL
Tel: (0143) 322383 *Fax:* (0143) 322383
E-mail: info@edizionijoker.com
Web Site: www.edizionijoker.com

Key Personnel
Editorial Dir: Sandro Montalto
Technical Dir: Monica Liberatore
Sales Manager: Gennaro Fusco
Founded: 1993
Subjects: Fiction, Nonfiction (General), Poetry
ISBN Prefix(es): 978-88-7536
Distribution Center: EdiQ Distribuzione, CP
56, 21040 Gerenzano-Varese VA *Tel:* (02)
9689323; (347) 4140016 (cell) *Fax:* (02)
9689323 *E-mail:* commerciale@ediq.eu
Libro Co Italia, CP 23, 50026 S Casciano VP
FI *Tel:* (055) 8228461 *Fax:* (055) 8228462
E-mail: libroco@libroco.it *Web Site:* www.
libroco.it
Interno 30 Servizi editoriali, Via Agostino Monti,
3, 17100 Savona SV *Tel:* (0333) 7994253
Fax: (0348) 8233602 *E-mail:* interno30@gmail.
com
Melisa SA, via Industrie, 6930 Bedano, Switzerland *Tel:* (091) 936 61 61 *Fax:* (091) 936 61
60 *E-mail:* melisa@melisa.ch *Web Site:* www.
melisa.ch

Jouvence Societa Editoriale+
Via Cassia, 1081, 00189 Rome
Tel: (06) 30207115 *Fax:* (06) 45472048
E-mail: info@jouvence.it
Web Site: www.jouvence.it
Key Personnel
Press: Luca Cardin
Founded: 1979
Subjects: Archaeology, Asian Studies, History,
Literature, Literary Criticism, Essays, Philoso-
phy, Religion - Islamic
ISBN Prefix(es): 978-88-7801

JSE, *imprint of* Jandi Sapi Editori

Juvenilia Scuola, *imprint of* Mondadori
Education

Kalandraka Italia
Paizzale Donatello 29, 50132 Florence FI
Tel: (055) 38 40 340
E-mail: info@kalandraka.it
Web Site: www.kalandraka.it; www.kalandraka.
com/it
ISBN Prefix(es): 978-88-95933
Parent Company: Kalandraka Editora

Kaos Edizioni SRL+
Via Catone, 3, 20161 Milan
Tel: (02) 39310296 *Fax:* (02) 39325749
E-mail: kaosedizioni@kaosedizioni.com
Web Site: www.kaosedizioni.com
Founded: 1985
Subjects: Art, Biography, Memoirs, Business,
Drama, Theater, Film, Video, Government, Po-
litical Science, History, Music, Dance, Nonfic-
tion (General), Social Sciences, Sociology
ISBN Prefix(es): 978-88-7953
Imprints: Edizioni Blues Brothers; Gammalibri-
Rock Books

Kellermann Editore
Piazza S Michele, 29, 31029 Vittorio Veneto TV
Tel: (0438) 940903 *Fax:* (0438) 947653
E-mail: info@kellermanneditore.it;
ufficiostampa@kellermanneditore.it
Web Site: www.kellermanneditore.it
Founded: 1991
Subjects: Literature, Literary Criticism, Essays,
Poetry
ISBN Prefix(es): 978-88-86089

Casa Editrice Kimerik
Piazza Gramsci, 1/3, 98066 Patti ME
Mailing Address: Via S Pietro Tommaso, 28,
98066 Patti ME
Tel: (0941) 21503 *Fax:* (0941) 243561

E-mail: redazione@kimerik.it
Web Site: www.kimerik.it
Founded: 2003
Subjects: Fiction, Poetry, Religion - Other
ISBN Prefix(es): 978-88-6884; 978-88-6096

Kite Edizioni SRL
Via Nizza 40, 35016 Piazzola sul Brenta PD
Tel: (049) 9600022; (049) 9601667 *Fax:* (049)
   9600782
E-mail: kite@kiteedizioni.it; rights@kiteedizioni.
   it
Web Site: www.kiteedizioni.it
Key Personnel
Dir: Caterina Arcaro
Administration: Francesca Passerini
   E-mail: francesca.passerini@kiteedizioni.it
Foreign Rights: Susanna Filipozzi
Founded: 2006
ISBN Prefix(es): 978-88-96023; 978-88-95799;
   978-88-67450

Kowalski, *imprint of* Giangiacomo Feltrinelli
   Editore SRL

La Nave di Teseo Editore
Via Stefano Jacini 6, 20121 Milan MI
E-mail: info@lanavediteseo.eu
Web Site: www.lanavediteseo.eu
Key Personnel
President: Mario Andreose
Editorial Dir: Elisabetta Sgarbi
Editor-in-Chief: Eugenio Lio
Head, Press: Laura Valetti
Head, Rights: Silvia Zamperini
Marketing Dir: Paola Sala
Editor: Oliviero Toscani
Subjects: Biography, Memoirs, Fiction, Mysteries,
   Suspense, Nonfiction (General), Poetry
ISBN Prefix(es): 978-88-9344

LAC - Litografia Artistica Cartografica SRL
Via del Romito, 11/13 R, 50134 Florence
Tel: (055) 483 557 *Fax:* (055) 483 690
Key Personnel
Owner: Andrea Bonomo
Founded: 1949
Subjects: Geography, Geology, Travel & Tourism
ISBN Prefix(es): 978-88-7914

Lalli Editore SRL+
Via Fiume, 60, 53036 Poggibonsi SI
Tel: (0577) 933305; (339) 7887154 (cell)
   Fax: (0577) 983308
E-mail: lalli@lallieditore.it
Web Site: www.lallieditore.it
Key Personnel
Chief Executive: Antonio Lalli
Editorial: Fioranna Casamenti
Founded: 1966
Subjects: Art, Biography, Memoirs, Drama, The-
   ater, Education, Ethnicity, Fiction, Film, Video,
   Government, Political Science, Humor, Phi-
   losophy, Poetry, Regional Interests, Religion -
   Other, Science (General), Social Sciences, So-
   ciology
ISBN Prefix(es): 978-88-95798
Warehouse: Via Modena 12, 53036 Poggibonsi SI

Lanfranchi Editore
Via Madonnina, 10, 20121 Milan
Tel: (02) 86465210 *Fax:* (02) 8056083
E-mail: info@lanfranchieditore.com
Web Site: www.lanfranchieditore.com
Founded: 1980
Subjects: Drama, Theater, Fiction, Nonfiction
   (General), Poetry, Contemporary Art, Current
   Affairs
ISBN Prefix(es): 978-88-363

Edizioni Lapis
via Francesco Ferrara 50, 00191 Rome RM
Tel: (06) 3295 935 *Fax:* (03) 3630 7062
E-mail: lapis@edizionilapis.it
Web Site: www.edizionilapis.it
Key Personnel
Contact: Francesca Barra
Founded: 1996
ISBN Prefix(es): 978-88-7874

Laruffa Editore SRL+
Via Dei 3 Mulini, 14 (Citta Universitaria), 89124
   Reggio, Calabria
Tel: (0965) 814954 *Fax:* (0965) 027185
E-mail: segreteria@laruffaeditore.it
Web Site: www.laruffaeditore.it
Key Personnel
Publisher: Dr Roberto Laruffa
Founded: 1980
Subjects: Agriculture, Archaeology, Architecture
   & Interior Design, Education, History, Religion
   - Catholic, Social Sciences, Sociology, Travel
   & Tourism
ISBN Prefix(es): 978-88-7221

Editrice LAS+
Piazza dell'Ateneo Salesiano, 1, 00139 Rome RM
Tel: (06) 87290626; (06) 87290445 *Fax:* (06)
   87290629
E-mail: las@unisal.it
Web Site: www.las.unisal.it
Founded: 1974
Subjects: Biblical Studies, Education, Philosophy,
   Psychology, Psychiatry, Religion - Catholic,
   Social Sciences, Sociology, Theology
ISBN Prefix(es): 978-88-213
Number of titles published annually: 30 Print
Total Titles: 400 Print; 2 CD-ROM

Editori Laterza+
Via di Villa Sacchetti 17, 00197 Rome
Tel: (06) 454 65 311 *Fax:* (06) 322 38 53
E-mail: glaterza@laterza.it; foreignrights@laterza.
   it
Web Site: www.laterza.it
Key Personnel
Publisher: Alessandro Laterza; Dr Giuseppe Lat-
   erza
Publishing Proposals: Teresa Ferrara
   E-mail: tferrara@laterza.it
Founded: 1901
Subjects: Anthropology, Archaeology, Commu-
   nications, History, Law, Philosophy, Religion -
   Other
ISBN Prefix(es): 978-88-420
Number of titles published annually: 120 Print
Branch Office(s)
piazza Umberto I 54, 70121 Bari *Tel:* (080) 528
   12 11 *Fax:* (080) 524 34 61
Foreign Rep(s): Alice Chambers; Eulama Literary
   Agency

Edizioni Giuseppe Laterza SRL+
Via Suppa 14, 70122 Bari
Tel: (080) 5237936 *Fax:* (080) 5237360
E-mail: info@edizionigiuseppelaterza.it
Web Site: www.edizionigiuseppelaterza.it
Key Personnel
Founder: Caterina Laterza
Founded: 2011
Subjects: Computer Science, Electronics, Electri-
   cal Engineering, Government, Political Science,
   Law, Literature, Literary Criticism, Essays, Po-
   etry, Psychology, Psychiatry, Veterinary Science
ISBN Prefix(es): 978-88-86243; 978-88-8231

Lavieri Edizioni
Via Canala, 55, 85050 Villa D'agri PZ
Tel: (0975) 352680 *Fax:* (0823) 1760173
E-mail: info@lavieri.it; ordini@lavieri.it; rights@
   lavieri.it; uff.stampa@lavieri.it

Web Site: www.lavieri.it
Key Personnel
Founder: Marcello Lavieri; Rosa Lavieri
Founded: 2004
Subjects: Humor, Literature, Literary Criticism,
   Essays
ISBN Prefix(es): 978-88-89312
Branch Office(s)
via IV Novembre, 19, 81020 S Angelo in Formis
   CE
Distribution Center: Dehoniana Libri

Il Lavoro Editoriale+
Division of Progetti Editoriali SRL
Redazione via Cialdini 76, 60122 Ancona AN
Mailing Address: CP 297, 60100 Ancona AN
Tel: (071) 2072210 *Fax:* (071) 2083058
E-mail: redazione@lavoroeditoriale.com;
   ordini@lavoroeditoriale.com; info@
   anconauniversitypress.it
Web Site: www.illavoroeditoriale.com
Key Personnel
Dir: Giorgio Mangani
Founded: 1980
Subjects: Architecture & Interior Design, Art, En-
   vironmental Studies, History, Human Relations,
   Literature, Literary Criticism, Essays, Regional
   Interests, Science (General), Travel & Tourism,
   Marche Region, Italy
ISBN Prefix(es): 978-88-7663
Number of titles published annually: 15 Print
Orders to: Libro.co Italia, PO Box 23, 50026 San
   Casciano Valdi Pesa VP *Tel:* (055) 8229414
   Fax: (055) 8294603 *E-mail:* libroco@libroco.it
   Web Site: www.libroco.it
Casalini Libri SpA, Via Benedetto de Ma-
   jano 3, 50014 Fiesole FI *Tel:* (055) 50181
   E-mail: orders@casalini.it

Edizioni Lavoro SRL+
Via G M Lancisi, 25, 00161 Rome
Tel: (06) 44251174 *Fax:* (06) 44251177
E-mail: info@edizionilavoro.it; amministrazione@
   edizionilavoro.it; marketing@edizionilavoro.it
Web Site: www.edizionilavoro.it
Key Personnel
President: Antonio Lombardi
Marketing: Alessandra Belardelli *E-mail:* a.
   belardelli@edizionilavoro.it
Founded: 1982
Subjects: Economics, Fiction, Government, Po-
   litical Science, History, Labor, Industrial Re-
   lations, Law, Philosophy, Religion - Islamic,
   Romance, Social Sciences, Sociology
ISBN Prefix(es): 978-88-7910; 978-88-7313
Number of titles published annually: 40 Print
Imprints: EL
Foreign Rights: Eulama Literary Agency (world-
   wide)

Lecce Spazio Vivo SRL, see Edizioni Milella
   Lecce

**LED Edizioni Universitarie di Lettere
   Economia Diritto**
Via Cervignano 4, 20137 Milan
Tel: (02) 59902055 *Fax:* (02) 55193636
E-mail: led@lededizioni.com
Web Site: www.lededizioni.com
Key Personnel
Mng Dir: Valeria Passerini
Founded: 1991
Subjects: Archaeology, Architecture & Interior
   Design, Business, Child Care & Development,
   Communications, Criminology, Developing
   Countries, Economics, Education, English as
   a Second Language, History, Language Arts,
   Linguistics, Law, Literature, Literary Criticism,
   Essays, Management, Mathematics, Medicine,
   Nursing, Dentistry, Philosophy, Psychology,
   Psychiatry, Public Administration, Social Sci-
   ences, Sociology
ISBN Prefix(es): 978-88-7916

Number of titles published annually: 30 Print; 1
CD-ROM; 10 Online; 5 E-Book
Total Titles: 450 Print; 2 CD-ROM; 30 Online;
20 E-Book
Distributor for Istituto Lombardo Accademia di
Scienze e Lettere

LEF, see Libreria Editrice Fiorentina

Leonardo, *imprint of* Raffaello Editrice SRL

Leone Editore SRL
Via M Gioia 121, 20125 Milan MI
Mailing Address: Corso Milano 19, 20900 Monza
MB
Tel: (039) 23 04 442 *Fax:* (039) 23 04 342
E-mail: redazione@leoneeditore.it
Web Site: www.leoneeditore.it
Founded: 2009
Subjects: Art, Economics, Fiction, History, Po-
etry, Science Fiction, Fantasy, Mythology
ISBN Prefix(es): 978-88-6303; 978-88-6393

Il Leone Verde Edizioni
Via della Consolata, 7, 10122 Turin TO
Tel: (011) 5211790 *Fax:* (011) 09652658
E-mail: leoneverde@leoneverde.it
Web Site: www.leoneverde.it
Key Personnel
Foreign Rights: Anna Spadolini
E-mail: annaspadolini@gmail.com
Founded: 1997
Subjects: Cookery, Fiction, Religion - Other, Par-
enting
ISBN Prefix(es): 978-88-87139; 978-88-95177

LER, see Libreria Editrice Rogate (LER)

L'eta D'oro Dell Illustrazione, *imprint of*
Stampa Alternativa - Nuovi Equilibri

Levante Editori+
Via Napoli 35, 70123 Bari
Tel: (080) 521 37 78 *Fax:* (080) 521 37 78
E-mail: levanted@levantebari.it
Web Site: www.levantebari.com
Key Personnel
Contact: Sara Cavalli
Founded: 1967
Subjects: Criminology, Drama, Theater, History,
Literature, Literary Criticism, Essays, Myster-
ies, Suspense, Philosophy, Psychology, Psychia-
try, Travel & Tourism, Greek Literature
ISBN Prefix(es): 978-88-7949
Number of titles published annually: 20 Print

**Levrotto & Bella Libreria Editrice
Universitaria SAS+**
Cso Luigi Einaudi 57/c, 10129 Turin
Tel: (011) 4275423 *Fax:* (011) 4275425
E-mail: ammin@levrotto-bella.net
Web Site: www.levrotto-bella.net
Founded: 1942
Also book packager.
Subjects: Aeronautics, Aviation, Agriculture, Ar-
chitecture & Interior Design, Art, Astronomy,
Biological Sciences, Chemistry, Chemical En-
gineering, Computers, Economics, Electronics,
Electrical Engineering, Engineering (General),
Fiction, Geography, Geology, History, Lan-
guage Arts, Linguistics, Law, Management,
Marketing, Mathematics, Mechanical Engineer-
ing, Medicine, Nursing, Dentistry, Photography,
Physics, Psychology, Psychiatry, Real Estate,
Science (General), Sports, Athletics, Technol-
ogy, Travel & Tourism, Veterinary Science,
Mineralogy, Natural World, Safety, Training
ISBN Prefix(es): 978-88-8218; 978-88-8184

Alberti Libraio Editore
Corso Garibaldi, 74, 28921 Verbania
Tel: (0323) 402534 *Fax:* (0323) 401074
E-mail: info@albertilibraio.it
Web Site: www.albertilibraio.it
Founded: 1954
Subjects: History, Natural History, Regional Inter-
ests, Textbooks
ISBN Prefix(es): 978-88-7245; 978-88-85004
Number of titles published annually: 5 Print; 1
CD-ROM
Total Titles: 200 Print; 1 CD-ROM

Libri & Professioni, *imprint of* Gruppo
Editoriale Esselibri Simone

Liguori Editore SRL
Via Posillipo 394, 80123 Naples
Tel: (081) 5751272 *Fax:* (081) 5751231
E-mail: info@liguori.it; foreignrights@liguori.it;
stampa@liguori.it (press)
Web Site: www.liguori.it
Key Personnel
Chief Executive Officer: Franco Liguori
Publicity & Press: Maria Liguori
Sales: Dario Liguori
Founded: 1949
Subjects: Anthropology, Biological Sciences,
Business, Civil Engineering, Economics, Ed-
ucation, Film, Video, History, Language Arts,
Linguistics, Law, Literature, Literary Criticism,
Essays, Mathematics, Medicine, Nursing, Den-
tistry, Philosophy, Science (General), Social
Sciences, Sociology
ISBN Prefix(es): 978-88-207
Number of titles published annually: 150 Print; 4
Online; 140 E-Book
Total Titles: 4,000 Print; 10 CD-ROM; 11 Online;
190 E-Book
Bookshop(s): Libreria Commissionaria Liguori
SRL, Via Mezzocannone 21-23, 80134 Naples
Tel: (081) 5526279
Warehouse: Via Ciccarelli 164, 80167 Naples

LIM, *imprint of* LIM Editrice SRL

LIM Editrice SRL+
Via di Arsina 296F, 55100 Lucca
Tel: (0583) 394464 *Fax:* (0583) 394469
E-mail: lim@lim.it
Web Site: www.lim.it
Key Personnel
Contact: Ugo Giani *Tel:* (0348) 6019847
E-mail: ugo.giani@lim.it; Silvio Malgarini
Tel: (0348) 6019846 *E-mail:* silvio.malgarini@
lim.it
Founded: 1988
Membership(s): Associazione Italiana Editori
(AIE).
Subjects: Music, Dance
ISBN Prefix(es): 978-88-7096
Associate Companies: Akademos, Una Cosa Rara
Imprints: LIM
Distributor for Fondazione Locatelli; Edition
Minkoff

L'immaginazion, *imprint of* Piero Manni SRL

Edizioni Lindau+
Corso Re Umberto 37, 10128 Turin
Tel: (011) 517 53 24 *Fax:* (011) 669 39 29
E-mail: lindau@lindau.it; amministrazione@
lindau.it
Web Site: www.lindau.it
Key Personnel
Editorial Dir: Ezio Quarantelli
E-mail: quarantelli@lindau.it
Mng Editor: Gabriele Giuliano *E-mail:* gabriele@
lindau.it
Sales Manager: Andrea Maria Allolio
E-mail: andrea@lindau.it

Foreign Rights Contact: Alberto Sorassi
E-mail: sorassi@lindau.it
Administration: Carla Baldo
Press: Silvja Manzi *E-mail:* silvja@lindau.it;
Francesca Ponzetto *E-mail:* francesca@lindau.it
Founded: 1989
Subjects: Biography, Memoirs, Fiction, Film,
Video, Government, Political Science, History,
Mysteries, Suspense, Nonfiction (General), Re-
ligion - Other, Current Events
ISBN Prefix(es): 978-88-7180
Number of titles published annually: 60 Print
Total Titles: 600 Print
Imprints: Anteprima; Edizioni L'Eta
dell'Acquario

Linea d'Ombra Libri (Linea D'Ombra Books)
Str di Sant'Artemio 6/8, 31100 Treviso TV
Tel: (0422) 3095 *Fax:* (0422) 309777
E-mail: info@lineadombra.it; libri@lineadombra.
it
Web Site: www.lineadombra.it
Key Personnel
Mng Dir: Ida Bortoluzzi
Dir General: Marco Goldin
Deputy Dir: David Martinelli
Editorial: Silvia Zancanella
Founded: 1996
Publisher of art books & exhibition catalogues.
Subjects: Art, Photography, Poetry
ISBN Prefix(es): 978-88-89902; 978-88-87582
Number of titles published annually: 20 Print
Parent Company: Linea D'Ombra

Lineadaria Editore
Via Schiapparelli 10, 13900 Biella BI
Tel: (015) 402304 *Fax:* (015) 402304
E-mail: lineadariaeditore@gmail.com
Web Site: www.lineadaria.it
Key Personnel
Publisher: Vincenzo Lerro
Founded: 2005
Children's book publisher.
ISBN Prefix(es): 978-88-97867

Lint Editoriale SRL
Via Udine n 59/a, 34135 Trieste TS
Tel: (040) 41 43 94; (040) 45 29 378 *Fax:* (040)
41 53 78
E-mail: info@linteditoriale.com; segreteria@
linteditoriale.com; redazione@linteditoriale.com
Web Site: www.linteditoriale.com
Key Personnel
Head: Giancarlo Stavro Santarosa
Founded: 1962
Subjects: Art, Science (General)
ISBN Prefix(es): 978-88-86179; 978-88-85083;
978-88-8190
Parent Company: Editorial Associates Ltd

Litografia Artistica Cartografia SRL, see LAC
- Litografia Artistica Cartografica SRL

Vincenzo Lo Faro Editore
Via di San Giovanni in Laterano, 276, 00184
Rome RM
Tel: (06) 70451187
Founded: 1967
Subjects: Art, Drama, Theater, Education, En-
vironmental Studies, Fiction, Law, Medicine,
Nursing, Dentistry, Philosophy, Poetry, Religion
- Other, Social Sciences, Sociology
ISBN Prefix(es): 978-88-87428

Loescher Editore SRL+
Via Vittorio Amedeo II, 18, 10121 Turin
Tel: (011) 56 54 111 *Fax:* (011) 56 25 822; (011)
56 54 200
E-mail: mail@loescher.it
Web Site: www.loescher.it

Key Personnel
President: Lorenzo Enriques Zanichelli
Commercial Dir: Giorgio Sacco
Founded: 1861
Subjects: Chemistry, Chemical Engineering, English as a Second Language, Geography, Geology, History, Language Arts, Linguistics, Literature, Literary Criticism, Essays, Philosophy
ISBN Prefix(es): 978-88-201; 978-88-7608; 978-88-8094; 978-88-7159; 978-88-8433; 978-88-8244
Parent Company: Zanichelli Editore SpA
Imprints: Eliseo; Thema
Distributed by Alfa Edizioni SRL (Italy); Cambridge University Press (Italy); Cle International (Italy); G D'Anna Casa Editrice SpA (Italy); enClave-ELE (Italy); Helbing Languages (Italy); Klett International (Italy)

Loffredo Editore SpA
Via Kerbaker 19, 80121 Naples NA
Tel: (081) 2508 511 *Fax:* (081) 5785 313
E-mail: info@loffredo.it
Web Site: www.loffredo.it
Key Personnel
President: Alfredo Loffredo
Mng Dir: Luigi Loffredo
Founded: 1880
Subjects: History, Language Arts, Linguistics, Literature, Literary Criticism, Essays, Philosophy, Religion - Other, Science (General)
ISBN Prefix(es): 978-88-8096; 978-88-7564
Warehouse: Via Pisciarelli 92/a, Pozzuoli
Tel: (081) 619 0257 *Fax:* (081) 610 0168

Logos Edizioni
Via Curtatona 5/2, 41126 Modena MO
Tel: (059) 412648; (059) 412573 (press)
E-mail: commerciale@logos.info
Web Site: www.logosedizioni.it; www.libri.it
Subjects: Architecture & Interior Design, Art, Cookery, Fashion, Health, Nutrition, History, Language Arts, Linguistics, Music, Dance, Photography, Sports, Athletics
ISBN Prefix(es): 978-88-7940; 978-88-576
Number of titles published annually: 20 Print
Parent Company: Inter Logos SRL
Distributor for Taschen GmbH

Angelo Longo Editore+
Via P Costa 33, 48121 Ravenna
Tel: (0544) 217 026 *Fax:* (0544) 217 554
E-mail: longo@longo-editore.it
Web Site: www.longo-editore.it
Key Personnel
General Manager: Alfio Longo
Founded: 1965
Subjects: Archaeology, Art, Drama, Theater, Fiction, Film, Video, History, Language Arts, Linguistics, Literature, Literary Criticism, Essays, Music, Dance, Philosophy, Photography, Poetry, Women's Studies
ISBN Prefix(es): 978-88-8063
Number of titles published annually: 60 Print; 30 Online
Total Titles: 1,230 Print; 128 Online
Bookshop(s): Libreria Dante di Longo, Via A Diaz 39, 48121 Ravenna RA, Contact: Roberta Plazzi *Tel:* (0544) 33500

Lorenzo Editore+
Via Monza, 6, 10152 Turin
Mailing Address: CP 23, 10100 Turin
Tel: (011) 2485387 *Fax:* (011) 2485387
E-mail: info@loredi.it
Web Site: www.loredi.it
Key Personnel
Dir: Lorenzo Masetta
Founded: 1991
Specialize in poetry.

Subjects: Biography, Memoirs, Drama, Theater, Fiction, Literature, Literary Criticism, Essays, Poetry, Science Fiction, Fantasy
ISBN Prefix(es): 978-88-85199; 978-88-87362
Subsidiaries: Associazione Culturale Talento (ACTA) (current events periodical)

LPE, *imprint of* Luigi Pellegrini Editore

Lubrina Editore SRL+
via Cesare Correnti, n 50, 24124 Bergamo
Tel: 3470139396 *Fax:* 035241547
E-mail: editorelubrina@lubrina.it
Web Site: www.lubrina.it
Key Personnel
Chief Executive Officer: Ornella Bramani Mastropietro *E-mail:* obramas@lubrina.it
Founded: 1995
Membership(s): EQ Consorzio di Editor di Qualita.
Subjects: Biblical Studies, Biography, Memoirs, Literature, Literary Criticism, Essays, Philosophy, Psychology, Psychiatry
ISBN Prefix(es): 978-88-7766

Edizioni La Luna
Via A Di Giovanni 14, 90144 Palermo
Tel: (091) 344403 *Fax:* (091) 301650
E-mail: lalunaedizioni@gmail.com
Founded: 1986
Membership(s): Arcidonna.
Subjects: Anthropology, Art, Fiction, Journalism, Literature, Literary Criticism, Essays, Nonfiction (General), Romance, Women's Studies
ISBN Prefix(es): 978-88-7823
Total Titles: 60 Print
Distributed by PDE

Edizioni Lybra Immagine+
Via Giovanni Lulli 5, 20131 Milan
Tel: (02) 48000818 *Fax:* (02) 48012748
Key Personnel
Editor: Mario Mastropietro
Founded: 1984
Subjects: Architecture & Interior Design, Fashion, Marketing, Photography
ISBN Prefix(es): 978-88-8223

Macro Edizioni, *imprint of* Gruppo Editoriale Macro

Gruppo Editoriale Macro (Macro Publishing Group)+
Via Bachelet, 65, 47522 Cesena FC
Tel: (0547) 1900103 *Fax:* (0547) 1900127
E-mail: info@macroedizioni.it; copyright@gruppomacro.net
Web Site: www.macroedizioni.it; www.gruppomacro.com
Key Personnel
President & Editor: Giorgio Gustavo Rosso
Foreign Rights, English: Isabella Monti *E-mail:* isabella.monti@gruppomarco.net
Foreign Rights, French: Chiara Naccarato *Tel:* (0547) 1900121 *E-mail:* chiara.naccarato@gruppomacro.net
Foreign Rights, German & Spanish: Simona Empoli *E-mail:* simona.empoli@gruppomacro.net
Founded: 1987
Subjects: Alternative, Archaeology, Biblical Studies, Cookery, Education, Environmental Studies, Health, Nutrition, House & Home, How-to, Philosophy, Psychology, Psychiatry, Religion - Other, Science (General)
ISBN Prefix(es): 978-88-7507
Number of titles published annually: 80 Print; 10 Online; 20 E-Book
Total Titles: 800 Print; 10 Online; 20 E-Book
Parent Company: Macro Societa Cooperativa
Imprints: Alaya; Arianna Editrice; BIS Edizioni; Essere Felici; Macro Edizioni

Distributor for Amici di Dirk; Archiati Verlag; Bonomi; NLP Italy
Book Club(s): Il Giardino dei Libri, Via del Lavoro 40, 47814 Bellaria RN *Tel:* (0541) 340567 *E-mail:* ordini@ilgiardinodeilibri.it *Web Site:* www.ilgiardinodeilibri.it; Macro Librarsi, Via Savona 70, 47023 Diegaro di Cesena FC *Tel:* (0547) 346290; (0547) 346312 *Fax:* (0547) 345091 *E-mail:* ordini@macrolibrarsi.it *Web Site:* www.macrolibrarsi.it

Magnus Edizioni SRL+
Via dei Fabrizio, 57, 33034 Fagagna UD
Tel: (0432) 800081 *Fax:* (0432) 810071
E-mail: info@magnusedizioni.it
Web Site: www.magnusedizioni.it
Key Personnel
Publisher & Editorial Manager: Antonio Stella
Administration Manager: Claudio Navari
Foreign Rights Manager: Sabrino Gitto
Founded: 1977
Subjects: Archaeology, Architecture & Interior Design, Art, History, Photography, Travel & Tourism
ISBN Prefix(es): 978-88-7057
Subsidiaries: Grafiche Lema SpA

Giuseppe Maimone Editore+
Via A di Sangiuliano, 278, 95124 Catania
Tel: (095) 310315 *Fax:* (095) 310315; (095) 312240 (sales)
E-mail: maimone@maimone.it
Web Site: www.maimone.it
Founded: 1985
Subjects: Archaeology, Architecture & Interior Design, Art, Biography, Memoirs, Fiction, Film, Video, Geography, Geology, History, Literature, Literary Criticism, Essays, Music, Dance, Photography, Poetry, Regional Interests, Travel & Tourism
ISBN Prefix(es): 978-88-7751
Subsidiaries: Maimone & Associati; SAS di Maimone Giuseppe
Showroom(s): Mostra Parole Nel Tempo, 25-26 Settembre, c/o Castello Di Belgioioso, via Garibaldi 1, Belgioioso PV; Il Libro, Salone Della Editoria Siciliana, 24 27 Marzo, c/o Ente Autonomo Fiera Di Messina Campionaria Internazionale, Viale Della Liberta, 98121 Messina; Salone Del Libro Torino, 19-24 Maggio, c/o Palazzo Lingotto, 10152 Turin TO

Mandragora SRL
Piazza del Duomo 9, 50122 Florence
Tel: (055) 2654384 *Fax:* (055) 2655120
E-mail: info@mandragora.it; redazione@mandragora.it
Web Site: www.mandragora.it
Key Personnel
Founder & Chief Executive Officer: Maria Curia *E-mail:* m.curia@mandragora.it
Mng Dir: Sandra Rosi *E-mail:* s.rosi@mandragora.it
General Manager: Franco Cesati *E-mail:* direzione@mandragora.it
Editor: Michele Fantoli *E-mail:* m.fantoli@mandragora.it; Marco Salucci
Administration: Chiara Rosadoni *E-mail:* c.rosadoni@mandragora.it
Design Dept: Paola Vannucchi *E-mail:* p.vannucchi@mandragora.it
Marketing & Sales: Matteo Mariotti *E-mail:* m.mariotti@mandragora.it
Founded: 1985
Subjects: Architecture & Interior Design, Art, Photography, Regional Interests, Florence, History of Art, Tuscany
ISBN Prefix(es): 978-88-7461; 978-88-85957
Foreign Rep(s): Antique Collector's Club (UK, USA); Paulsen Buchimport (Germany)

Manifesto Libri SRL+
Via Bargoni 8, 00153 Rome
Tel: (06) 99709447 *Fax:* (06) 99709447
E-mail: redazione@manifestolibri.it; book@
manifestolibri.it (orders); ufficiostampa@
manifestolibri.it
Web Site: www.manifestolibri.it
Key Personnel
Chief Editor: Marco Bascetta
General Manager: Simona Bonsignori
Founded: 1991
Publishing house in the group of "il Manifesto"
daily newspaper. Carries books, online services,
audio & CD-ROMs.
Subjects: Anthropology, Government, Political
Science, History, Philosophy, Social Sciences,
Sociology, Socio-Economic Issues & Affairs
ISBN Prefix(es): 978-88-7285
Number of titles published annually: 40 Print
Total Titles: 400 Print; 2 CD-ROM; 10 Audio
Branch Office(s)
Via Maragliario 31a, Florence *Tel:* (055) 363263
Fax: (055) 354634
Via Pindemonte 2, 20129 Milan *Tel:* (02) 77396-1
Vico San Pietro a Maiella, 6, Naples *Tel:* (081)
4420782
Distribution Center: Messaggerie Libri SpA

Manni/Lupetti, *imprint of* Piero Manni SRL

Piero Manni SRL+
Via Umberto I, 47/51, 73016 S Cesario di Lecce
Tel: (0832) 205577 *Fax:* (0832) 200373
E-mail: info@mannieditori.it
Web Site: www.mannieditori.it
Key Personnel
Dir: Grazia Manni *E-mail:* gmanni@mannieditori.
it
Editorial Dir & Press: Anna Grazia D'Oria
E-mail: agdoria@mannieditori.it
Sales Manager: Piero Manni
E-mail: commerciale@mannieditori.it
Project Manager: Giancarlo Greco
E-mail: promozione@mannieditori.it
Editor: Agnese Manni *E-mail:* agnesemanni@
mannieditori.it
Founded: 1984
Membership(s): Italian Publishers Association.
Subjects: Anthropology, Drama, Theater, Eco-
nomics, Fiction, Film, Video, History, Human
Relations, Law, Literature, Literary Criticism,
Essays, Philosophy, Poetry, Social Sciences,
Sociology
ISBN Prefix(es): 978-88-8176
Imprints: Manni/Lupetti; L'immaginazion

Edizioni Angolo Manzoni SRL
Via Cibrario 28, 10144 Turin
Tel: (011) 47 30 775 *Fax:* (011) 48 94 52
E-mail: info@angolomanzoni.it
Web Site: www.angolomanzoni.it
Founded: 1988
Subjects: Fiction, History, Photography, Poetry
ISBN Prefix(es): 978-88-6204
Distribution Center: Casalini Libri, Via Benedetto
da Maiano, 3, 50014 Fiesole FI *Tel:* (055)
50181 *Fax:* (055) 5018201
Promozione e Distribuzione RCS Libri, via Mece-
nate 91, 20138 Milan MI *Tel:* (02) 50951

Marcianum Press SRL
Dorsoduro, 1, 30123 Venice
Tel: (041) 29 60 608; (041) 29 60 287 *Fax:* (041)
24 19 658
E-mail: marcianumpress@marcianum.it
Web Site: www.marcianumpress.it
Key Personnel
Editorial Dir: Roberto Donadoni *Tel:* (041) 52 20
353 *E-mail:* direttoremp@marcianum.it
Editorial Manager: Giuseppe Antonio Valletta
Head, Administration: Gabriella Perini *Tel:* (041)
27 43 942 *E-mail:* perini@marcianum.it

Administration: Cristiano Rigoni *Tel:* (041) 27 43
922 *E-mail:* rigoni@marcianum.it
Sales Dir: Giorgio Famengo
Promotion & Sales: Giorgia Dalle Ore
Special Projects: Massimilliano Vianello
Founded: 2005
Subjects: Art, Economics, History, Inspirational,
Spirituality, Poetry, Religion - Other, Romance,
Theology, Literary Nonficion
ISBN Prefix(es): 978-88-89736

Marcovalerio Edizioni
Imprint of Associazione Culturale Centro Studi
Silvio Pellico
Via Vittorio Emanuele 29, 10060 Cercenasco TO
E-mail: marcovalerio@marcovalerio.com
Web Site: www.marcovalerio.com
Founded: 2000
Subjects: Poetry, Italian Narrative
ISBN Prefix(es): 978-88-7547
Distribution Center: FAG Edizioni, Via G
Garibaldi 5, 20090 Assago MI *Tel:* (02)
4885241 *Fax:* (02) 48841936; (02) 45701657
(Lombardia)
Euroservizi, Via Agucchi 84/86, 40133 Bologna
BO *Tel:* (051) 31 40 183 *Fax:* (051) 31 51
26 (Emilia-Romagna, Province of Mantua &
Marche)
Macrocampania, Via Toraldo 33/A, 82030 Lima-
tola BN *Tel:* (0823) 95 65 27 *Fax:* (0823) 95
65 27 (Campania & Puglia)
Cierrevecchi SRL, Via Breda 26, 35010 Limena
PD *Tel:* (049) 88 40 299 *Fax:* (049) 88 40 277
(Friuli-Venezia Giulia, Trentino & Veneto)
Medialibri Diffusione SRL, Via Baldo degli
Ubaldi, 144, 00167 Rome RM *Tel:* (06)
6627304 *E-mail:* ordini@medialibridiffusione.
it *Web Site:* www.medialibridiffusione.com
(Abruzzo & Lazio)
Libro Co Italia, Via Borromeo 48, 50026 San
Casciano FI *Tel:* (055) 822 84 61 *Fax:* (055)
822 84 62 (Tuscany & Umbria)
Bookservice, via Bardonecchia 174/D, 10141
Turin TO *Tel:* (011) 772 43 69 *Fax:* (011) 772
44 95 (Liguria, Piedmont & Valle d'Aosta)

Marietti Scuola
Via Montefeltro 6/b, 20156 Milan
Tel: (02) 380861
E-mail: scrivi@scuola.com
Web Site: www.mariettiscuola.it
Subjects: Accounting, Agriculture, Art, Computer
Science, Economics, Electronics, Electrical En-
gineering, Geography, Geology, History, Law,
Mathematics, Music, Dance, Philosophy, Re-
ligion - Other, Civics, Classics, Geometry,
Grammar, Humanities, Italian, Road Safety
Education, Sport Sciences, Statistics, Telecom-
munications
ISBN Prefix(es): 978-88-393
Parent Company: De Agostini Scuola SpA

Casa Editrice Marna, *imprint of* Editrice Velar

Marotta & Cafiero Editori+
Disc Posillipo 213, 80123 Naples NA
Tel: (081) 5758060 *Fax:* (081) 5758060
Founded: 1979
Subjects: Art, Biography, Memoirs, Fiction, His-
tory, Music, Dance, Poetry, Regional Interests
ISBN Prefix(es): 978-88-88234
Distribution Center: Pde Napoli Srl, Via E
Scarfoglio, 28/b, 80078 Agnano Pozzuoli
NA *Tel:* (081) 2428301 *Fax:* (081) 5700413
E-mail: pdenapoli@pde.it

Marsilio Editori SpA+
Marittima - Fabbricato 205, 30135 Venice
Tel: (041) 2406511 *Fax:* (041) 5238352
E-mail: info@marsilioeditori.it
Web Site: www.marsilioeditori.it

Key Personnel
President: Prof Cesare De Michelis
Editorial Dir: Emanuela Bassetti
Founded: 1961
Subjects: Art, Computer Science, Fiction, Film,
Video, Literature, Literary Criticism, Essays,
Nonfiction (General), Psychology, Psychiatry,
Social Sciences, Sociology
ISBN Prefix(es): 978-88-317; 978-88-7693
U.S. Office(s): Marsilio Publishers, 853 Broad-
way, Suite 1509, New York, NY 10003, United
States *Tel:* 212-473-5300 *Fax:* 212-473-7865
Distributor for Giovanni Tranchida Editore

Editrice Massimo di Crespi Cesare & C SAS+
Viale Bacchiglione 20, 20139 Milan
Tel: (02) 55211315
Founded: 1951
Subjects: Astronomy, Biblical Studies, Biography,
Memoirs, Drama, Theater, Fiction, History, Lit-
erature, Literary Criticism, Essays, Philosophy,
Psychology, Psychiatry, Religion - Catholic,
Religion - Other, Romance, Science (General),
Social Sciences, Sociology, Theology
ISBN Prefix(es): 978-88-7030
Total Titles: 400 Print
Bookshop(s): Agenzia Mescat, Milan

The McGraw-Hill Companies SRL
Via Ripamonti 89, 20139 Milan
Tel: (02) 5357181 *Fax:* (02) 5397633
E-mail: servizio.clienti@mheducation.com
Web Site: www.mcgraw-hill.it
Key Personnel
Rights Manager: Cinzia Fabiani
Founded: 1986
Subjects: Architecture & Interior Design, Biolog-
ical Sciences, Business, Chemistry, Chemical
Engineering, Computer Science, Economics,
Engineering (General), Mathematics, Medicine,
Nursing, Dentistry, Physical Sciences, Psychol-
ogy, Psychiatry, Social Sciences, Sociology,
Humanities, Information Science
ISBN Prefix(es): 978-88-386; 978-88-7700
Parent Company: The McGraw-Hill Companies,
1221 Avenue of the Americas, New York, NY
10020, United States
Associate Companies: McGraw-Hill Book Co Eu-
rope
Warehouse: McGraw-Hill Magazzine Editoriale,
Via Milano 6/2, 20068 Peschiera Borroreo, Mi-
lan

Edizioni Medicea SRL
Via della Villa Lorenzi 8, 50139 Florence
Tel: (055) 416048 *Fax:* (055) 416048
E-mail: info@edizionimediceafirenze.it
Web Site: www.edizionimediceafirenze.it
Founded: 1974
Subjects: Architecture & Interior Design, Art,
Engineering (General), Fiction, Government,
Political Science, History, Radio, TV, Science
(General), Social Sciences, Sociology
ISBN Prefix(es): 978-88-900171

L'Officina di Studi Medievali
via del Parlamento, 32, 90133 Palermo PA
Tel: (091) 586314 *Fax:* (091) 333121
E-mail: info@officinastudimedievali.it
Web Site: www.officinastudimedievali.it
Key Personnel
President: Alessandro Musco
Dir: Diego Ciccarelli
Editorial: Giuseppe Allegro
Founded: 1980
Subjects: Science (General), Culture, Medieval
Studies
ISBN Prefix(es): 978-88-88615

Mediserve+
Via G Quagliariello, 35/E, 80131 Naples
Tel: (081) 5452717 *Fax:* (081) 5462026
E-mail: contact@mediserve.it

Web Site: www.mediserve.it
Key Personnel
Mng Dir, Editorial: Luigi Martinucci
Founded: 1978
Subjects: Medicine, Nursing, Dentistry, Science
   (General)
ISBN Prefix(es): 978-88-8204
Branch Office(s)
Via San Fermo della Battaglia, 1, 20121 Milan
   Tel: (02) 6572366
Bookshop(s): Libreria Scienze Mediche Martin-
   ucci, Via T de Amicis 60, 80145 Naples

Edizioni Mediterranee SRL+
Via Flaminia, 109, 00196 Rome
Tel: (06) 3235433 *Fax:* (06) 3236277
E-mail: info@edizionimediterranee.net;
   ordinipv@edizionimediterranee.net; press@
   edizionimediterranee.net
Web Site: www.edizionimediterranee.net
Key Personnel
Chairman: Pietro Canonico
General Manager: Giovanni Canonico *Tel:* (06)
   3222797
Editorial: Paola Maria Canonico
Marketing: Eleasa Canonico
Press: Mara Morini
Founded: 1953
Subjects: Alternative, Archaeology, Art, Astrol-
   ogy, Occult, Biography, Memoirs, Gardening,
   Plants, Health, Nutrition, How-to, Medicine,
   Nursing, Dentistry, Military Science, Parapsy-
   chology, Philosophy, Psychology, Psychiatry,
   Religion - Other, Sports, Athletics, Alchemy,
   Esotherism, Magic, Martial Arts, Meditation,
   New Age, UFO, Yoga
ISBN Prefix(es): 978-88-272
Total Titles: 1,500 Print
Subsidiaries: Edizioni Arkeios; Hermes Edizioni
   SRL; Edizioni Studio Tesi SRL

Melino Nerella Edizioni Solarino SRL
Via Bissolati 18, 96010 Solarino SR
Mailing Address: CP 8, 96010 Solarino SR
Tel: (0931) 922491 *Fax:* (0931) 922491
Key Personnel
President & Chief Executive Officer: Silvia Aparo
Administration: Amalia Calafiore
Editorial Dir: Salvo Zappulla
Founded: 2009
Subjects: Fiction, Historical Novels, Thriller
ISBN Prefix(es): 978-88-904115

Meltemi Editore SRL
Via Labicana, 24, 00185 Rome
Tel: (06) 97619551 *Fax:* (06) 97619551
Web Site: www.meltemieditore.it
Key Personnel
Dir: Manolo Morlacci *E-mail:* manolo@
   meltemieditore.it
Founded: 1994
Subjects: Anthropology, History, Social Sciences,
   Sociology
ISBN Prefix(es): 978-88-8353; 978-88-86479;
   978-88-7881
Distribution Center: Messaggerie Libri
   SpA, Via G Verdi, 8, 20090 Assago MI
   E-mail: meli.dirgen@meli.it *Web Site:* www.
   messaggerielibri.it

Edizioni La Meridiana
Via G Di Vittorio 7, 70056 Molfetta BA
Tel: (080) 9722786; (080) 3340399; (080)
   3971945; (080) 3346971 *Fax:* (080) 3340399
E-mail: info@lameridiana.it; redazione@
   lameridiana.it; media@lameridiana.it; diritti@
   lameridiana.it
Web Site: www.lameridiana.it
Key Personnel
Dir: Guglielmo Minervini
General Manager: Elvira Zaccagnino
Rights Office: Marilena Sallustio

Founded: 1987
Subjects: Child Care & Development, Education
ISBN Prefix(es): 978-88-6153; 978-88-85221;
   978-88-87507; 978-88-89197

Edizioni Messaggero Padova+
Via Orto Botanico 11, 35123 Padua
Tel: (049) 8225 777; (049) 8225 926
   Toll Free Tel: (800) 508036 *Fax:* (049) 8225
   650; (049) 8225 688
E-mail: emp@santantonio.org; ufficiostampa@
   santantonio.org
Web Site: www.edizionimessaggero.it; www.
   messaggerosantantonio.it; www.santantonio.org
Key Personnel
Publishing Dir: Luigi Dal Lago
Subjects: Biography, Memoirs, History, Journal-
   ism, Religion - Other, Theology
ISBN Prefix(es): 978-88-7026; 978-88-250
Parent Company: Messaggero di Sant'Antonio
   Editrice
Bookshop(s): Libreria Messaggero, Piazza del
   Santo 17, 35123 Padua

Midgard Editrice
Via Cortonese 27, Interno 708, 06124 Perugia
Tel: (075) 9662764
E-mail: info@midgard.it
Web Site: www.midgard.it
Founded: 2004
Subjects: Fiction, Nonfiction (General), Poetry
ISBN Prefix(es): 978-88-95708

Maria Miglietti, *imprint of* Castalia Edizioni
SAS

Nicola Milano Editore+
Via Antonio Gramsci, 26, 25121 Brescia BS
Tel: (030) 2993 1 *Fax:* (030) 2993 299
E-mail: servizioclienti@lascuola.it
Web Site: nuovo.lascuola.it; www.lascuoladigitale.
   it; www.education.lascuola.it
Founded: 1969
ISBN Prefix(es): 978-88-419
Parent Company: Editrice La Scuola

Edizioni Milella Lecce+
Via Palmieri 30, 73100 Lecce
Tel: (0832) 241131 *Fax:* (0832) 241131
E-mail: leccespaziovivo@tiscali.it
Web Site: www.milellalecce.it
Key Personnel
Founder: Gaetano Quarta
Dir: Augusto Ponzio
Founded: 1952
Subjects: Disability, Special Needs, Education,
   English as a Second Language, History, Hu-
   man Relations, Literature, Literary Criticism,
   Essays, Philosophy, Psychology, Psychiatry,
   Social Sciences, Sociology
ISBN Prefix(es): 978-88-7048
Bookshop(s): Via M DePietro, Via Palmieri
   30, 73100 Lecce; Via G Palmieri, Viale
   dell'UniVersite, 1, 30-73100 Lecce *Tel:* (0832)
   308885 *Fax:* (0832) 308885
Warehouse: Via M DePietro, Via Palmieri, 30, 9-
   73100 Leece *Tel:* (0832) 308885
Orders to: Via M DePietro, Viale dell'UniVersite,
   1, 9-73100 Lecce *Tel:* (0832) 308885

Editrice Minerva Assisi
Vicolo degli Archi, 06081 Assisi PG
Tel: (075) 812381 *Fax:* (075) 816564
E-mail: info@minervassisi.com
Web Site: www.minervassisi.com
Founded: 1991
Subjects: Archaeology, Art, History, Literature,
   Literary Criticism, Essays, Poetry, Religion -
   Other, Travel & Tourism
ISBN Prefix(es): 978-88-98110; 978-88-87021

Edizioni Minerva Medica SpA
Corso Bramante 83-85, 10126 Turin
Tel: (011) 678282 *Fax:* (011) 674502
E-mail: minervamedica@minervamedica.it; book.
   dept@minervamedica.it
Web Site: www.minervamedica.it
Key Personnel
Mng Editor: Dr Alberto Oliaro
Chief Editor: Roberto Gambari
Founded: 1909
Specialize in scientific literature for the medical
   field.
Subjects: Medicine, Nursing, Dentistry
ISBN Prefix(es): 978-88-7711
Branch Office(s)
Via Spallanzani 9, 00161 Rome *Tel:* (06)
   44251210 *Fax:* (06) 44291500
   E-mail: minmed.rome@minervamedica.it

Minerva Scuola, *imprint of* Mondadori Education

Minimum Fax Ltd
Via Giuseppe Pisanelli, 2, 00196 Rome
Tel: (06) 333-65-45; (06) 333-65-53
E-mail: info@minimumfax.com
Web Site: www.minimumfax.com
Key Personnel
Editorial Dir: Giorgio Gianotto
Publisher: Marco Cassini; Daniele di Gennaro
Head of Press: Alessandro Grazioli
Founded: 1993
Subjects: Fiction, Literature, Literary Criticism,
   Essays, Poetry, Contemporary Classics, Italian
   Literature
ISBN Prefix(es): 978-88-7521; 978-88-86568;
   978-88-87765
Distribution Center: Messaggerie Libri SpA,
   Via Verdi 8, 20090 Assago MI *Tel:* (02)
   457741 *Fax:* (02) 45701032 *Web Site:* www.
   messaggerielibri.it

Il Minotauro Editore+
Monteverde 11/A & 12/A, 00152 Rome
Tel: (06) 5374060
E-mail: info@ilminotauro.com
Web Site: www.ilminotauro.com
Founded: 1993
Subjects: Art, Fiction, Government, Political Sci-
   ence, History, Literature, Literary Criticism, Es-
   says, Medicine, Nursing, Dentistry, Philosophy,
   Social Sciences, Sociology, Sports, Athletics,
   Travel & Tourism
ISBN Prefix(es): 978-88-8073
Distributed by PDE Milano

Editrice Missionaria Italiana (EMI) (Italian
Missionary Publishing)+
Via di Corticella 179/4, 40128 Bologna
Tel: (051) 326027 *Fax:* (051) 327552
E-mail: info@emi.it; ordini@emi.it; sermis@emi.
   it; stampa@emi.it (press)
Web Site: www.emi.it
Key Personnel
Dir & Rights Dept Manager: Giovanni Munari
Administrator: Lorenzo Fazzini
Press: Francesco Saldi
Founded: 1977
Subjects: Anthropology, Education, Environmen-
   tal Studies, Fiction, Inspirational, Spirituality,
   Religion - Other, Social Sciences, Sociology,
   Africa, Human Rights
ISBN Prefix(es): 978-88-307
Bookshop(s): Libreria Comboniana, Galleria
   Mazzini, 37121 Verona

Momento Medico SRL
Via Terre Risaie 13 Zona Industriale le Fuorni,
   84131 Salerno SA
Tel: (089) 3055 611 *Fax:* (089) 3018 09
Web Site: www.mmrights.it

Key Personnel
Head, Foreign Rights: Daniela de Feo
E-mail: defeo@momentomedico.it
Founded: 1986
Subjects: Health, Nutrition, Medicine, Nursing,
Dentistry, Psychology, Psychiatry, Dermatol-
ogy, Gynecology, Oncology, Pediatrics, Sports
Medicine
ISBN Prefix(es): 978-88-8160
Distributor for Alter; Coformed; EuroMultiMedia;
MB&Care; MMIbero; OGM

A Mondadori Scuola, *imprint of* Mondadori
Education

Arnoldo Mondadori Editore SpA+
via Privata Mondadori 1, 20090 Segrate MI
Tel: (02) 75421 *Fax:* (02) 75422302
Web Site: www.mondadori.it
Key Personnel
Chairman of the Board & Chief Executive Offi-
cer: Ernesto Mauri
Chief Financial Officer: Carlo Maria Vismara
Dir, Communications & Media Relations: Fed-
erico Angrisano
Associate Publisher, Edizioni Mondadori: Antonio
Riccardi
Mng Dir, Mondadori Trade: Enrico Selva Codde
Mng Dir, Education: Antonio Porro
Senior Editor, Foreign Imprint Authors &
Women's Fiction, Edizioni Mondadori: Joy
Terekiev
Senior Editor, Paperback Dept Oscar Imprint,
Edizioni Mondadori: Luigi Sponzilli
Editor, Foreign Entertainment Fiction, Fantasy,
Crossover & New Adult, Edizioni Mondadori:
Marta Treves
Editor, Foreign Literary & General Fiction, Edi-
zioni Mondadori: Federica Manzon
Editor, Popular Nonfiction Dept, Edizioni Mon-
dadori: Chiara Scaglioni
Media Relations: Carmen Mugione
E-mail: carmen.mugione@mondadori.it
Founded: 1907
Subjects: Art, Biography, Memoirs, Education,
Fiction, History, How-to, Medicine, Nursing,
Dentistry, Music, Dance, Mysteries, Suspense,
Philosophy, Poetry, Psychology, Psychiatry, Re-
ligion - Other, Romance, Science (General)
ISBN Prefix(es): 978-88-04; 978-88-356; 978-88-
86372; 978-88-520; 978-88-521
Imprints: e-Harmony; Mondadori Boys; Geo
Mondadori; Mondadori Education; Mondadori
Informatica
Subsidiaries: Giulio Einaudi Editore SpA;
Harlequin Mondadori SpA; Edizioni Mon-
dadori; Mondadori Education; Mondadori
Electa SpA; Edizioni Piemme SpA; Penguin
Random House Grupo Editorial; Sperling &
Kupfer Editori SpA
Branch Office(s)
Via Sicilia 136, 00187 Rome *Tel:* (06) 474971
Fax: (06) 47497301
Via Mondadori 15, 37100 Verona *Tel:* (045)
934111 *Fax:* (045) 934618
Foreign Rights: AME Publishing Ltd (USA);
Continental Printing Ltd (UK); E-M Livres
(France); Mondadori (Spain); Arnoldo Mon-
dadori Deutschland GmbH (Germany); Mono-
graph (France); Tuttle Mori Agency Inc (Japan)
Bookshop(s): Via Vittorio Emanuele 36, 22100
Como *Tel:* (031) 273424 *Fax:* (031) 273314;
Via XX Settembre 210/R, 16121 Genoa
Tel: (010) 585743 *Fax:* (010) 5704810; Largo
Corsia de Servi 11, 20122 Milan *Tel:* (02)
76005832 *Fax:* (02) 76014902; Piazza Cola Di
Rienzo 81/83, 00192 Rome *Tel:* (06) 3220188
Fax: (06) 3210323; Via Appia Vuova 51,
00183 Rome *Tel:* (06) 7003690 *Fax:* (06)
7003450

Mondadori Boys, *imprint of* Arnoldo Mondadori
Editore SpA

Bruno Mondadori+
Imprint of Pearson Italia SpA
Corso Trapani 16, 10139 Turin
Tel: (011) 75021 11 *Fax:* (011) 75021 510
Web Site: www.brunomondadori.com; www.
pearson.it/bruno_mondadori
Key Personnel
Press Officer: Elena Grossi
Founded: 1995
Membership(s): Associazione Italiana Editori
(AIE).
Subjects: Anthropology, Architecture & Interior
Design, Biological Sciences, Communications,
Earth Sciences, Economics, Education, English
as a Second Language, Fashion, Film, Video,
Geography, Geology, History, Law, Literature,
Literary Criticism, Essays, Mathematics, Music,
Dance, Philosophy, Photography, Psychology,
Psychiatry, Social Sciences, Sociology, Travel
& Tourism
ISBN Prefix(es): 978-88-424
Number of titles published annually: 300 Print;
50 CD-ROM
Total Titles: 3,500 Print; 200 CD-ROM
Ultimate Parent Company: Pearson plc

Mondadori Education, *imprint of* Arnoldo
Mondadori Editore SpA

Mondadori Education+
Subsidiary of Arnoldo Mondadori Editore SpA
Via Durazzo 4, 20134 Milan MI
Tel: (02) 212131 *Toll Free Tel:* 800 12 39 31
Fax: (02) 21213697
E-mail: servizioclienti.edu@mondadorieducation.
it
Web Site: www.mondadorieducation.it
Key Personnel
Head, Communications: Monica Brognoli
Tel: (02) 21563456 *E-mail:* brognoli@
mondadori.it
Press: Manuela Sollai *Tel:* (02) 21213643
Subjects: Biography, Memoirs, Education, His-
tory, Language Arts, Linguistics, Philosophy,
Religion - Catholic
ISBN Prefix(es): 978-88-00; 978-88-7249 (Ju-
venilia Scuola); 978-88-425 (Mursia Scuola);
978-88-298 (Minerva Scuola); 978-88-8332
(Mursia Scuola); 978-88-434 (C Signorelli
Scuola); 978-88-247 (Mondadori Scuola); 978-
88-286 (Einaudi Scuola); 978-88-7485 (Juve-
nilia Scuola)
Imprints: Einaudi Scuola; Electa Scuola; Juve-
nilia Scuola; Minerva Scuola; Mondadori for
English; A Mondadori Scuola; Le Monnier
Scuola; Mursia Scuola; Piemme Scuola; Posei-
donia Scuola; Scuola & Azienda; C Signorelli
Scuola
Branch Office(s)
Via Fanti 53, 50137 Florence FI
Distributor for Burlington Books; Hueber;
Macmillan

Mondadori Electa SpA
Subsidiary of Arnoldo Mondadori Editore SpA
Via Battistotti Sassi 11/A, 20133 Milan
Tel: (02) 21563363; (02) 710461; (02) 21563419
Fax: (02) 21563246
E-mail: electaweb@gmail.com
Web Site: www.electaweb.it
Key Personnel
Press: Carlo Pirovano
Founded: 1945
Subjects: Archaeology, Architecture & Interior
Design, Art, Fashion, Film, Video, Music,
Dance, Photography, Industrial Design
ISBN Prefix(es): 978-88-435; 978-88-370
Total Titles: 1,200 Print
Imprints: Electa
Subsidiaries: Alfieri Edizioni d'Arte; Electa Ed-
itori Umbri Associati; Electa Firenze; Electa
Moniteu; Fantonigrafica

Branch Office(s)
Via dei Mille 16, 80121 Naples *Tel:* (081)
4297421
Via Sicilia 154, 00187 Rome *Tel:* (06) 42029200

Mondadori for English, *imprint of* Mondadori
Education

Editoriale Giorgio Mondadori+
Corso Magenta, 55, 20123 Milan
Tel: (02) 433131 *Fax:* (02) 43313550
E-mail: infolibri@cairoeditore.it
Web Site: www.cairoeditore.it
Key Personnel
President: Urbano Cairo
General Manager: Giuseppe Ferrauto
Deputy General Manager: Marco Garavaglia
Head, Sales & Marketing: Virginia Rosetti
Press: Carolina Tinicolo
Founded: 1978
Subjects: Antiques, Architecture & Interior De-
sign, Art, Foreign Countries, Gardening, Plants,
House & Home
ISBN Prefix(es): 978-88-374; 978-88-6052
Parent Company: Cairo Publishing SRL
Distribution Center: Messaggerie Libri, Via G
Verdi 8, 20090 Assago MI *Tel:* (02) 457741
Fax: (02) 45703342

Mondadori Informatica, *imprint of* Arnoldo
Mondadori Editore SpA

Monduzzi Editoriale
Via B Eustachi, 12, 20129 Milan
Tel: (02) 20404031 *Fax:* (02) 20404044
E-mail: info@monduzzieditore.it; redazione@
monduzzieditore.it
Web Site: www.monduzzieditore.it
Key Personnel
President: Dr Gianni Monduzzi
Mng Dir: Dr Mauro Bettocchi
Founded: 1978
Subjects: Art, Biological Sciences, Chemistry,
Chemical Engineering, Economics, Engineer-
ing (General), Government, Political Science,
Law, Literature, Literary Criticism, Essays,
Medicine, Nursing, Dentistry, Physics, Psy-
chology, Psychiatry, Social Sciences, Sociology
ISBN Prefix(es): 978-88-323; 978-88-475
Imprints: Cisalpino
Divisions: International Proceedings Division

Le Monnier Scuola, *imprint of* Mondadori
Education

Editrice Morcelliana SpA+
Via Gabriele Rosa 71, 25121 Brescia
Tel: (030) 46451 *Fax:* (030) 2400605
E-mail: redazione@morcelliana.it;
ufficiostampa@morcelliana.it
Web Site: www.morcelliana.it
Key Personnel
Mng Editor: Dr Ilario Bertoletti
Editor-in-Chief: Dr Sara Bignotti
Founded: 1925
Subjects: History, Literature, Literary Criticism,
Essays, Philosophy, Religion - Other, Social
Sciences, Sociology, Theology, Humanities,
Judaism
ISBN Prefix(es): 978-88-372
Distribution Center: Dehoniana Libri SpA,
Via Scipione dal Farro, 4, 40138 Bologna
Tel: (051) 4290451 *Fax:* (051) 4290491
E-mail: dbologna@dehoniane.it

Elena Morea Editore
Via Lugaro, 38, 10126 Turin
Tel: (347) 7904 921 (cell)
Key Personnel
Owner: Elena Morea

Founded: 1998
Subjects: Biography, Memoirs, Fiction, Poetry
ISBN Prefix(es): 978-88-95395

Moretti & Vitali Editori SRL+
Via Segantini 6a, 24128 Bergamo
Tel: (035) 251300 *Fax:* (035) 4329409
E-mail: info@morettievitali.it; ordini@
morettievitali.it (orders); redazione@
morettievitali.it
Web Site: www.morettievitali.it
Key Personnel
President & Editorial Dir: Enrico Moretti
E-mail: direzione@morettievitali.it
Editorial Dir: Carla Stroppa
Press & External Relations: Angela Melgriti
Founded: 1989
Subjects: Architecture & Interior Design, Art,
Biography, Memoirs, Human Relations, Liter-
ature, Literary Criticism, Essays, Philosophy,
Poetry, Psychology, Psychiatry, Mythology
ISBN Prefix(es): 978-88-7186

Morlacchi Editore
Via Guardabassi 9, 06123 Perugia
Tel: (075) 9660291 *Fax:* (075) 9006528
E-mail: editore@morlacchilibri.com; radazione@
morlacchilibri.com; ufficiostampa@
morlacchilibri.com (press office)
Web Site: www.morlacchilibri.com/
universitypress/
Subjects: Anthropology, Archaeology, Architec-
ture & Interior Design, Art, Chemistry, Chem-
ical Engineering, Computer Science, Drama,
Theater, Economics, Engineering (General),
Geography, Geology, Government, Political
Science, Health, Nutrition, History, Language
Arts, Linguistics, Law, Library & Information
Sciences, Literature, Literary Criticism, Essays,
Mathematics, Medicine, Nursing, Dentistry,
Music, Dance, Philosophy, Physics, Psychol-
ogy, Psychiatry, Radio, TV, Religion - Other,
Sports, Athletics
ISBN Prefix(es): 978-88-6074

Federico Motta Editore SpA+
Via Branda Castiglioni, 7, 20156 Milan
Tel: (02) 300761 *Fax:* (02) 38010046
E-mail: info@mottaeditore.it
Web Site: www.mottaeditore.it
Key Personnel
President: Achilles Gerli
Chief Executive Officer & Publisher: Federico
Motta
Assistant Dir: Massimo Fumagalli
Founded: 1929
Subjects: Architecture & Interior Design, Art,
Photography
ISBN Prefix(es): 978-88-7179; 978-88-6413

Motta Junior, *imprint of* Giunti Editore SpA

Enrico Mucchi Editore SRL
via Emilia est, 1527, 41122 Modena
Tel: (059) 37 40 94 *Fax:* (059) 28 26 28
E-mail: info@mucchieditore.it; ufficiostampa@
mucchieditore.it
Web Site: www.mucchieditore.it
Key Personnel
Contact: Enrico Mucchi; Marco Mucchi
Founded: 1646
Subjects: Crafts, Games, Hobbies, Education, His-
tory, Language Arts, Linguistics, Law, Litera-
ture, Literary Criticism, Essays, Philosophy,
Science (General)
ISBN Prefix(es): 978-88-7000

Mursia Scuola, *imprint of* Mondadori Education

Ugo Mursia Editore+
Via Melchiorre Gioia 45, 20124 Milan

Tel: (02) 67378500; (02) 67378518 (sales)
Fax: (02) 67378605
E-mail: venditeonline@mursia.com; press@
mursia.com; commerciale@mursia.com (sales)
Web Site: www.mursia.com
Key Personnel
Chief Executive Officer & President: Fiorenza
Mursia
Dir, Communications: Lorenza Sala
Press: Martina Fornasaro
Founded: 1955
Subjects: Animals, Pets, Art, Biography, Mem-
oirs, Cookery, Drama, Theater, Education, Fic-
tion, Government, Political Science, History,
Literature, Literary Criticism, Essays, Maritime,
Music, Dance, Philosophy, Poetry, Religion -
Other, Science (General), Social Sciences, So-
ciology, Sports, Athletics
ISBN Prefix(es): 978-88-425
Bookshop(s): Libraries Mursia, Via Galvani, 24,
Milan *Tel:* (02) 67378530 *Fax:* (02) 67378603
E-mail: libreria@mursia.com
Warehouse: Via Cassanese antica, 20060 Vignate,
Milan

Libreria Musicale Italiana, see LIM Editrice
SRL

Musumeci Editore+
Loc Amerique, 99, 11020 Quart, Valle d'Aosta
AO
Tel: (0165) 1825572 *Fax:* (0165) 1825574
E-mail: info@musumecieditore.it
Web Site: www.musumecieditore.it
Key Personnel
Editorial Dir: Alessandra Norat
Founded: 1837
Subjects: History, Travel & Tourism, Culture
ISBN Prefix(es): 978-88-7032

Franco Muzzio Editore+
Via di Fioranello, 56, 00134 Rome RM
Tel: (06) 79781367 *Fax:* (06) 79349574
E-mail: info@editorefrancomuzzio.it
Web Site: www.librigei.com; www.
editorefrancomuzzio.it
Founded: 1974
Subjects: Computer Science, Cookery, Electron-
ics, Electrical Engineering, Energy, Gardening,
Plants, Literature, Literary Criticism, Essays,
Music, Dance, Nonfiction (General), Science
(General)
ISBN Prefix(es): 978-88-7021; 978-88-7413
Parent Company: Gruppo Editoriale Italiano SRL
Associate Companies: Edizioni per La Decrescita
Felice; Editori Riuniti
Warehouse: Via Torino, 64, 10060 Airasca TO

Giorgio Nada Editore, *imprint of* Giunti Editore
SpA

Giorgio Nada Editore SRL
Imprint of Giunti Editore SpA
Via Claudio Treves 15/17, 20090 Vimodrone MI
Tel: (02) 27301126 *Fax:* (02) 27301454
E-mail: info@giorgionadaeditore.it; ordini@
giorgionadaeditore.it; ufficiostampa@
giorgionadaeditore.it
Web Site: www.giorgionadaeditore.it
Key Personnel
Editorial Dir: Leonardo Acerbi *E-mail:* leonardo.
acerbi@giorgionadaeditore.it
Sales & Marketing Dir: Stefano Nada
E-mail: stefano.nada@giorgionadaeditore.com
Administration: Mary Baracco
E-mail: amministrazione@giorgionadaeditore.it
Founded: 1987
Specialize in books on history of Italian cars &
motorcycles (Ferrari, Ducati, etc).
Subjects: Automotive, History, Transportation
ISBN Prefix(es): 978-88-7911

Number of titles published annually: 20 Print
Total Titles: 200 Print
Subsidiaries: Libreria dell'Automobile
Distributed by Giunti Editore SpA
Bookshop(s): Libreria dell'Automobile,
Corso Venezia, 45, 20121 Milan *Tel:* (02)
76006624 *Fax:* (02) 76006624 *E-mail:* info@
libreriadellautomobile.it *Web Site:* www.
libreriadellautomobile.it
Distribution Center: Orca Book Services,
Fleets Corner, Unit A3, Poole, Dorset BH17
0HL, United Kingdom *Tel:* (01202) 665432
Fax: (01202) 666219 *E-mail:* orders@
orcabookservices.co.uk (Europe & UK)
Star Book Sales, PO Box 20, Whimple,
Exeter EX5 2WY, United Kingdom
Tel: (0845) 156 7082 *Fax:* (01404) 823820
E-mail: dennisbuckingham@starbooksales.com
(Europe & UK)
Motorbooks, 400 First Ave North, Suite 400,
Minneapolis, MN 55401, United States
Tel: 612-344-8100 *Fax:* 612-344-8691 *Web
Site:* www.quartoknows.com/Motorbooks
(North America)

Accademia Nazionale dei Lincei
Palazzo Corsini, Via della Lungara, 10, 00165
Rome
Tel: (06) 680271 *Fax:* (06) 6893616
E-mail: segreteria@lincei.it; stampa@lincei.it;
redazione@lincei.it
Web Site: www.lincei.it
Key Personnel
Dir General: Dr Ada Baccari *Tel:* (06) 6868223
E-mail: baccari@lincei.it
Founded: 1847
Subjects: Archaeology, Art, Biological Sciences,
Economics, History, Management, Mathematics
ISBN Prefix(es): 978-88-218; 978-88-7052
Orders to: Scienze e Lettere, Casa Editrice
e Commissionaria, Via Piave, 7, 00187
Rome *Tel:* (06) 4817656 *Fax:* (06) 48912574
E-mail: info@scienzeelettere.com *Web
Site:* www.scienzeelettere.com

Edizioni Nemapress
Via Manzoni 67, 07041 Alghero SS
Tel: (079) 981621
Web Site: www.nemapress.com
Key Personnel
Mng Dir & Editorial Dir: Neria De Giovanni
Founded: 1989
Subjects: Art, Fiction, Literature, Literary Criti-
cism, Essays, Poetry
ISBN Prefix(es): 978-88-7629

Neos Edizioni SRL
Via Genova 57, 10090 Cascine Vica-Rivoli TO
Tel: (011) 9576450 *Fax:* (011) 9576450
E-mail: info@neosedizioni.it
Web Site: www.neosedizioni.it
Key Personnel
President: Silvia Ramasso
Founded: 1996
Membership(s): Federazione Italiana degli Editori
Indipendenti.
Subjects: Fiction, Nonfiction (General), Historical
Art, Historical Fiction & Biography, Regional
Traditions, Social & Political History, Women's
Interest
ISBN Prefix(es): 978-88-95899
Distribution Center: EdiQ Distribuzione, CP
56, 21040 Gerenzano-Varese VA *Tel:* (02)
9689323; (347) 4140016 (cell) *Fax:* (02)
9689323 *E-mail:* commerciale@ediq.eu
Interlibri, via S Giovanni Bosco, 73, Turin
TO *Tel:* (011) 4379152 *Fax:* (011) 4734678
E-mail: interlibri@libero.it

New Magazine Edizioni+
Via dei Mille 69, 38100 Trento
Tel: (335) 6597487 (cell)
E-mail: info@newmagazine.it

Web Site: www.newmagazine.it; www.
  rivistamedica.it/new_magazine.htm
Key Personnel
Mng Dir: Bruno Zanotti *E-mail:* bruno.zanotti@
  rivistamedica.com
Editorial Dir: Angela Verlicchi
  E-mail: redazione@rivistamedica.it
Founded: 1982
Specialize in medicine.
Subjects: Civil Engineering, Literature, Literary
  Criticism, Essays, Medicine, Nursing, Dentistry
ISBN Prefix(es): 978-88-8041
Distributed by Del Porto SpA (worldwide)

Newton Compton Editori
Via Panama 22, 00198 Rome RM
Tel: (06) 65002553; (06) 65002908 *Fax:* (06)
  65002892
E-mail: info@newtoncompton.com
Web Site: www.newtoncompton.com
Key Personnel
Chief Executive Officer: Raffaello Avanzini
President: Vittorio Avanzini
Founded: 1969
Subjects: Anthropology, Archaeology, Art, Biog-
  raphy, Memoirs, Fiction, Government, Political
  Science, History, How-to, Language Arts, Lin-
  guistics, Literature, Literary Criticism, Essays,
  Mathematics, Medicine, Nursing, Dentistry,
  Philosophy, Poetry, Psychology, Psychiatry,
  Science (General), Social Sciences, Sociology,
  Classics
ISBN Prefix(es): 978-88-7983; 978-88-8183; 978-
  88-8289
Distribution Center: Messaggerie Libri SpA, Via
  Giuseppe Verdi, 8, 20094 Assago MI *Tel:* (02)
  457741 *Fax:* (02) 457010 32 *Web Site:* www.
  messaggerielibri.it

NIE, *imprint of* La Nuova Italia

Nissolino, *imprint of* Gruppo Editoriale Esselibri
Simone

Nistri-Lischi Editori+
Lungarno Pacinotti 43/44, 56123 Pisa PI
Tel: (050) 563371 *Fax:* (050) 562726
E-mail: lischi.press@unipi.it
Web Site: www.nistri-lischi.it
Key Personnel
Mng Dir: Luciano Lischi
Sales: Lucia Lischi
Founded: 1780
Subjects: Literature, Literary Criticism, Essays
ISBN Prefix(es): 978-88-8381
Warehouse: Via Carducci, La Fontina, Pisa
Distribution Center: Promozione e Distribuzione
  Editoriale, Via Natale Battaglia, 12, 20127 Mi-
  lan *Tel:* (02) 2611 1870 *Fax:* (02) 2611 6254
  Web Site: www.epde.it

NodoLibri+
via Volta, 38, 22100 Como
Tel: (031) 243113 *Fax:* (031) 273163
E-mail: info@nodolibri.it
Web Site: www.nodolibri.it
Key Personnel
Dir: Fabio Cani *E-mail:* f.cani@nodolibri.it; Ger-
  ardo Monizza *E-mail:* g.monizza@nodolibri.it
Founded: 1989
Subjects: Art, History, Photography, Regional In-
  terests
ISBN Prefix(es): 978-88-7185
Number of titles published annually: 10 Print
Total Titles: 150 Print

Nomos Edizioni SRL
Via Piave, 15, 21052 Busto Arsizio VA
Tel: (0331) 382339 *Fax:* (0331) 367429
E-mail: info@nomosedizioni.it; editor@
  nomosedizioni.it; press@nomosedizioni.it

Web Site: www.nomosedizioni.it
Founded: 1997
Subjects: Art, History, Literature, Literary Criti-
  cism, Essays, Music, Dance, Nonfiction (Gen-
  eral), Poetry, Culture, Local History
ISBN Prefix(es): 978-88-88145
Foreign Rep(s): Libro Co Italia srl
Foreign Rights: Factotum Agency

Nord, *imprint of* Editrice Nord Srl

Editrice Nord Srl+
Via Gherardini, 10, 20145 Milan
Tel: (02) 34597631 *Fax:* (02) 34597216
Web Site: www.editricenord.it; www.facebook.
  com/CasaEditriceNord
Key Personnel
Chief Executive Officer & President: Stefano
  Mauri
Mng Dir: Marco Taro
Rights & Acquisitions Dir: Cristina Foschini
Editorial Dir: Cristina Prasso
Press: Barbara Trianni
Founded: 1970
Subjects: Fiction, Mysteries, Suspense, Science
  Fiction, Fantasy, Thrillers
ISBN Prefix(es): 978-88-429
Parent Company: Gruppo Editoriale Mauri Spag-
  nol SpA, via Gherardini, 10, 20145 Milan
Imprints: Nord

Nottetempo SRL
Via Zanardelli, 34, 00186 Rome RM
Tel: (06) 683 08 320 *Fax:* (06) 681 391 07
E-mail: nottetempo@edizioninottetempo.it;
  ufficiostampa@edizioninottetempo.it
Web Site: www.edizioninottetempo.it
Key Personnel
Foreign Rights: Maria Leonardi *E-mail:* maria.
  leonardi@edizioninottetempo.it
Founded: 2002
Subjects: Fiction
ISBN Prefix(es): 978-88-7452
Distribution Center: Messaggerie Libri SpA

Novecento Editrice SRL+
Via Agrigento, 57, 90141 Palermo
Tel: (091) 6257147
Key Personnel
Dir: Domitilla Alessi
Editorial: Priscilla Alessi Wanstall
Distribution: Nicola Salvia
Founded: 1980
Subjects: Art, Literature, Literary Criticism, Es-
  says, Photography
ISBN Prefix(es): 978-88-373
Bookshop(s): Libreria Novelento, via Siracusa 7/
  A, 90141 Palermo *Tel:* (091) 6256814
Warehouse: Via Agrigento 15, 90141 Palermo

Nuages
Via del Lauro, 10, 20121 Milan MI
Tel: (02) 72004482
E-mail: nuages@nuages.net
Web Site: www.nuages.net
Subjects: Art, Comics
ISBN Prefix(es): 978-88-86178
Distribution Center: Messaggerie Libra SpA, Via
  G Verdi 8, 20090 Assago MI *Tel:* (02) 45774

Nuova Editoriale Bios+
Via G De Rada, 10, 87100 Cosenza CS
Mailing Address: CP 191, 87100 Cosenza
Tel: (0984) 458692 *Fax:* (0984) 25606
E-mail: info@edibios.it
Web Site: www.edibios.it
Founded: 1980
Subjects: Engineering (General), Medicine, Nurs-
  ing, Dentistry
ISBN Prefix(es): 978-88-7740

Nuova Dimensione, *imprint of* Ediciclo Editore
SRL

La Nuova Frontiera
Via Pietro Giannone, 10, 00195 Rome RM
Tel: (06) 39751129 *Fax:* (06) 39726296
E-mail: info@lanuovafrontiera.it
Web Site: www.lanuovafrontiera.it
Subjects: Literature, Literary Criticism, Essays,
  Portuguese Language, Spanish Language
ISBN Prefix(es): 978-88-8373
Distribution Center: PDE Distribuzione, Via For-
  lanini, 36, 50019 Sesto Fiorentino FI *Tel:* (055)
  301371 *Fax:* (055) 301372

Nuova Ipsa Editore SRL
Via Giuseppe Crispi, 50, 90145 Palermo PA
Tel: (091) 6819025 *Fax:* (091) 6816399
E-mail: info@nuovaipsa.it; amministrazione@
  nuovaipsa.it; nuovaipsa@nuovaipsa.it
Web Site: www.nuovaipsa.it
Key Personnel
Publisher: Claudio Mazza
Dir: Antonella Liberto
Public Relations: Alessio Mazza *E-mail:* alex@
  nuovaipsa.it
Founded: 1981
Subjects: Alternative, Health, Nutrition, Medicine,
  Nursing, Dentistry
ISBN Prefix(es): 978-88-7676

La Nuova Italia
Via Angelo Rizzoli, 8, 20132 Milan MI
Tel: (02) 25841
Web Site: www.lanuovaitalia.it; www.
  rcsmediagroup.it
Key Personnel
Corporate Communications: Valentina Ciolfi
  Tel: (02) 2584 4164 *E-mail:* valentina.ciolfi@
  rcs.it
Founded: 1926
Subjects: Art, Biography, Memoirs, History, Phi-
  losophy, Psychology, Psychiatry, Social Sci-
  ences, Sociology
ISBN Prefix(es): 978-88-221
Parent Company: RCS Libri
Ultimate Parent Company: RCS Media Group
Imprints: NIE

Nuove Edizioni Romane SRL
Piazza Santa Cecilia, 18, 00153 Rome RM
Tel: (06) 5881064 *Fax:* (06) 5818091
E-mail: ner@mclink.it
Web Site: www.nuoveedizioniromane.it
Key Personnel
Publisher: Gabriella Armando; Claudio Saba
Founded: 1977
Subjects: Architecture & Interior Design, Drama,
  Theater, Fiction, History, Mysteries, Suspense,
  Poetry
ISBN Prefix(es): 978-88-7457; 978-88-85890;
  978-88-85990
Distribution Center: Dehoniana Libri SpA,
  Via Scipione dal Ferro, 4, 40138 Bologna
  Tel: (051) 4290451 *Fax:* (051) 4290491

Le Nuove Muse SRL
Via Galliari, 5, 10125 Turin
Tel: (011) 650 43 31
E-mail: info@lenuovemuse.it
Web Site: www.lenuovemuse.it
Key Personnel
Vice President & Editorial Dir: Egi Volterrani
Editor: Irene Stelli
International Relations: Andrea Dosio
Subjects: Literature, Literary Criticism, Essays
ISBN Prefix(es): 978-88-95364

Il Nuovo Melangolo SRL+
Via di Porta Soprana, 3, 16123 Genoa
Tel: (010) 2514002 *Fax:* (010) 2514037
E-mail: info@ilmelangolo.com

Web Site: www.ilmelangolo.com
Key Personnel
President & Chief Executive Officer: Francangelo Scapolla
Dir General: Marco Fidora *E-mail:* m.fidora@ilmelangolo.com
Editorial Dir: Simone Regazzoni *E-mail:* s.regazzoni@ilmelangolo.com
Editor: Francesco Chiossone *E-mail:* f.chiossone@ilmelangolo.com
External Relations: Magiu Viardo *E-mail:* m.viardo@ilmelangolo.com
Press: Francesca Romana Gallerani *E-mail:* f.gallerani@ilmelangolo.com
Founded: 1976
Subjects: Anthropology, Fiction, Literature, Literary Criticism, Essays, Nonfiction (General), Philosophy, Poetry, Religion - Buddhist, Religion - Catholic, Religion - Jewish, Religion - Other, Theology
ISBN Prefix(es): 978-88-7018

Nutrimenti SRL
via Marco Aurelio, 44, 00184 Rome
Tel: (06) 70492976 *Fax:* (06) 77591872
E-mail: nutrimenti@nutrimenti.net; ufficiostampa@nutrimenti.net; rights@nutrimenti.net
Web Site: www.nutrimenti.net
Key Personnel
Dir: Ada Carpi de Resmini
Editorial Dir: Andrea Palombi
Head, Press: Luigi Scaffidi
Editorial Coordinator: Riccardo Trani
Founded: 2001
Subjects: Biography, Memoirs, Fiction, Nonfiction (General), Outdoor Recreation, Travel & Tourism, Ocean, Sailing
ISBN Prefix(es): 978-88-88389; 978-88-95842

Edizioni OCD
Via Vitellia 14, 00152 Rome RM
Tel: (06) 5812385 *Fax:* (06) 79890840
E-mail: info@edizioniocd.com; info@ocd.it (orders)
Web Site: www.edizioniocd.it
Key Personnel
Dir: P Roberto Fornara *Fax:* (06) 79890842
    E-mail: roberto.fornara@ocd.it
Editorial: Michela Rotondo *Fax:* (06) 79890843
    E-mail: michela.rotondo@ocd.it; Serena Pico
    Fax: (06) 79890843 *E-mail:* serena.pico@ocd.it
Press & Marketing: Marco Vranicich
    E-mail: marco.vranicich@ocd.it
Customer Service: Teresa Alpini *Fax:* (06) 79890841 *E-mail:* teresa.alpini@ocd.it
Founded: 1979
Subjects: Anthropology, Inspirational, Spirituality, Nonfiction (General), Religion - Other, Theology
ISBN Prefix(es): 978-88-7229

Editoriale Olimpia SpA+
Via Enrico Fermi, 24, 50019 Sesto Fiorentino, Florence FI
Tel: (055) 30321 *Fax:* (055) 3032280
Key Personnel
Chairman & Chief Executive Officer: Rodolfo Mostardi
Chief Executive Officer: Pasquale Cacciapuoti
President: Marcello Cacciapuoti
Founded: 1939
Specializes in publications on hunting, fishing, dogs, scuba diving, weapons, boats, tourism, digital photography, etc.
Subjects: Aeronautics, Aviation, Animals, Pets, Biological Sciences, Mysteries, Suspense, Outdoor Recreation, Photography, Sports, Athletics, Technology, Travel & Tourism
ISBN Prefix(es): 978-88-253

Number of titles published annually: 220 Print; 20 CD-ROM; 20 Online
Subsidiaries: Editoriale Olimpia

Edizioni Olivares
Via Borgogna, 7, 20122 Milan
Tel: (02) 76003602 *Fax:* (02) 76018474
E-mail: olivares@edizioniolivares.com
Web Site: www.edizioniolivares.com
Founded: 1986
Membership(s): Associazione Italiana Editori (AIE); Associazione Italiana Piccoli Editori (AIPE).
Subjects: Business, Management, Women's Studies
ISBN Prefix(es): 978-88-85982
Parent Company: Redifin SpA, Via P Mascagni, 7, 20122 Milan
Showroom(s): Parole In Tasca-Salone del libro tascabile, c/o Castello di Belgioso, Via Garibaldi 1, 27011 Belgioso (Paira)

Leo S Olschki
Viuzzo del Pozzetto, 8, 50126 Florence
Tel: (055) 6530684 *Fax:* (055) 6530214
E-mail: orders@olschki.it; pressoffice@olschki.it
Web Site: www.olschki.it
Key Personnel
Editorial Manager: Daniele Olschki
    E-mail: daniele@olschki.it
Administrative Manager: Stefano Manetti
    E-mail: s.manetti@olschki.it
Marketing: Georgia Corbo *E-mail:* g.corbo@olschki.it
Press Off: Serena Ruffilli
Public Relations: Costanza Olschki
    E-mail: costanza@olschki.it
Founded: 1886
Subjects: Anthropology, Archaeology, Architecture & Interior Design, Art, Astronomy, Biblical Studies, Geography, Geology, Government, Political Science, History, Language Arts, Linguistics, Library & Information Sciences, Literature, Literary Criticism, Essays, Music, Dance, Natural History, Philosophy, Physical Sciences, Religion - Catholic, Religion - Jewish, Science (General), Social Sciences, Sociology, Theology
ISBN Prefix(es): 978-88-222
Number of titles published annually: 150 Print
Total Titles: 3,000 Print

OL3 SRL
Via delle Caravelle 21, 06127 Perugia PG
Tel: (075) 5011993 *Fax:* (075) 5016791
E-mail: info@ol3online.it
Web Site: www.ol3online.it
Founded: 2012

Ontopsicologia Editrice+
Via San Sebastiano 130, 00065 Fiano Romano RM
Tel: (0765) 45 53 47 *Fax:* (0765) 20 71 31
E-mail: books@psicoedit.com
Web Site: www.psicoedit.com
Key Personnel
Contact: Antonio Meneghetti
Subjects: Art, Economics, Education, Philosophy, Psychology, Psychiatry, Science (General), Women's Studies, Ontopsychology
ISBN Prefix(es): 978-88-86766; 978-88-89391
Number of titles published annually: 5 Print
Total Titles: 60 Print
Branch Office(s)
Viale delle Medaglie d'Oro, 428, 00136 Rome
    Tel: (06) 35 45 35 58 *Fax:* (06) 35 34 14 66
    E-mail: info@ontopsicologia.org
Bookshop(s): Bookshop Atlantide, Via Mazzini 93, 40024 Castel San Pietro Terme BO
    Tel: (051) 6951180 *Fax:* (051) 6951180;
    Bookshop Mailtrade Srl, Via Liano 3720, 40024 Castel San Pietro Terme BO *Tel:* (051)

6951382 *Fax:* (051) 942784; Bookshop La Fenice, Via Battisti 6, 34125 Galleria Fenice TS; Bookshop Italo Svevo, Corso Italia 9, 34122 Galleria Rosono TS; Bookshop Mebs Srl, Via N D'Apulia 11, 20127 Milan *Tel:* (02) 26149008; Bookshop La Meridiana, Via Beccarla 1, 12084 Mondovi CN; Bookshop Becco Giallo, Corso Umberto 1, 31046 Oderzo TV; Bookshop Anglo American Book Co srl, Via della Vite, 102, 00187 Rome *Tel:* (06) 6797636; (06) 6795222 *Fax:* (06) 6783890 *Web Site:* www.aab.it; Bookshop Caffe Barumba, Piazza delle Vaschette 15, 00193 Rome; Bookshop Dea SpA, Via Salaria 28, 00136 Rome; Bookshop Kappa, V Salaria 121/E, 00136 Rome *Tel:* (06) 85357042; Bookshop Caffe Punto, Via Belvedere Principe di Piemonte 52, 90018 Termini Imerese PA *Tel:* (091) 8113571 *Fax:* (091) 8113571; Bookshop in der Tat, Via Diaz 22, 34123 Trieste

orecchio acerbo editore
viale Aurelio Saffi 54, 00152 Rome RM
Tel: (06) 5811861; (06) 58364814 *Fax:* (06) 5811861
E-mail: ufficiostampa.orecchioacerbo@gmail.com; ordini.orecchioacerbo@gmail.com
Web Site: www.orecchioacerbo.com
Key Personnel
Editorial Dir: Fausta Orecchio
Commercial Dir: Simone Tonucci
Foreign Rights: Valeria Genovese
Press: Paolo Cesari
Founded: 2001
ISBN Prefix(es): 978-88-96806; 978-88-89025

Edizioni Orientalia Christiana, see Pontificio Istituto Orientale

Ortelio, *imprint of* Edizioni Cartografiche Milanesi SRL (ECM)

Osanna Edizioni SRL+
Via Appia, 3/a, 85029 Venosa PZ
Tel: (0972) 35 952 *Fax:* (0972) 35 723
E-mail: osanna@osannaedizioni.it
Web Site: www.osannaedizioni.it
Key Personnel
Editorial Dir: Antonio Vaccaro
Founded: 1982
Subjects: Archaeology, History, Literature, Literary Criticism, Essays
ISBN Prefix(es): 978-88-8167

Mauro Pagliai Editore, *imprint of* Edizioni Polistampa

Paideia Editrice Brescia+
Via Manzoni 20, 25020 Flero BS
Tel: (030) 3582434 *Fax:* (030) 3582691
E-mail: info@paideiaeditrice.it
Web Site: www.paideiaeditrice.it
Key Personnel
Editorial: Dr Marco Scarpat
Founded: 1945
Subjects: Art, Asian Studies, Biblical Studies, Music, Dance, Philosophy, Poetry, Religion - Catholic, Religion - Jewish, Religion - Protestant, Religion - Other
ISBN Prefix(es): 978-88-394

Palombi Editori
Via Gregorio VII, 224, 00165 Rome
Tel: (06) 63 69 70 *Fax:* (06) 63 57 46
E-mail: info@palombieditori.it
Web Site: www.palombieditori.it
Key Personnel
Dir: Alessandro Palombi; Francesco Palombi
Founded: 1914
Subjects: Art, History, Regional Interests
ISBN Prefix(es): 978-88-7621; 978-88-6060

Subsidiaries: Organizzazione Rab (sales)
Distribution Center: PDE, Via Edison 81 A, 20090 Assage MI *Tel:* (02) 457192676 *Fax:* (02) 45717016

G B Palumbo & C Editore SpA+
Via B Ricasoli 59, 90139 Palermo
Tel: (091) 588850; (091) 334961 *Fax:* (091) 6111848
E-mail: redazione@palumboeditore.
   it; promozione@palumboeditore.it;
   amministrazione@palumboeditore.it
Web Site: www.palumboeditore.it
Key Personnel
President: Giorgio Palumbo
Editorial Dir: Italo Rosato
Dir, Promotions & Public Relations: Michele Badagliacca
Administration: Fabio Di Martino
Editorial: Salvo Grassi
Founded: 1939
Subjects: Language Arts, Linguistics, Literature, Literary Criticism, Essays
ISBN Prefix(es): 978-88-8020
Branch Office(s)
Viale Alessandro Volta 78/80, 50131 Florence, Editorial: Federica Giovannini
   Tel: (055) 0517238 *Fax:* (055) 0946384
   E-mail: redazione.firenze@palumboeditore.it
Warehouse: Via Maggiore G Galliano 17, Palermo

Franco Cosimo Panini Editore SpA
Via Giardini 474/D Direzionale 70, 41124 Modena
Tel: (059) 291 7311; (059) 291 7330 *Fax:* (059) 291 7381
E-mail: info@fcp.it; ufficiostampa@fcp.it
Web Site: grandiopere.fcp.it
Key Personnel
President: Laura Panini
Press: Silvia Stagi
Founded: 1960 (1st book published in 1978)
Subjects: Archaeology, Architecture & Interior Design, Art, Crafts, Games, Hobbies, Education, History, Literature, Literary Criticism, Essays, Poetry, Regional Interests, Sports, Athletics
ISBN Prefix(es): 978-88-7686; 978-88-248; 978-88-8290
Divisions: Divisione Ragazzi

Paoline Editoriale Libri
Via Francesco Albani 21, 20149 Milan
Tel: (02) 43 85 11 *Fax:* (02) 43 85 12 42
E-mail: fsp@paoline.it; edlibri.mi@paoline.it; marketing@paoline.it; rights.mi@paoline.it
Web Site: www.paoline.it
Key Personnel
Foreign Rights: Nora Tavelli
Subjects: Inspirational, Spirituality, Literature, Literary Criticism, Essays, Psychology, Psychiatry, Religion - Other, Theology, Biblical Literature, Liturgy
ISBN Prefix(es): 978-88-315

Editoriale Paradigma, *imprint of* G D'Anna Casa Editrice SpA

Edizioni Parnaso
Via Coroneo 5, 34133 Trieste TS
Tel: (040) 370200 *Fax:* (040) 3728970
Founded: 1922
Subjects: Literature, Literary Criticism, Essays, Philosophy
ISBN Prefix(es): 978-88-86474
Number of titles published annually: 10 Print
Total Titles: 116 Print

Passigli Editori SRL+
Via Chiantigiana, 62, 50012 Bagno a Ripoli FI

Tel: (055) 640265 *Fax:* (055) 644627
E-mail: info@passiglieditori.it
Web Site: www.passiglieditori.it
Key Personnel
Mng Dir: Prof Stefano Passigli
Marketing & Production Manager: Dr Luca Merlini
Editor: Dr Fabrizio Dall'Aglio
Assistant Editor: Vittoria Schweizer
Press: Annalisa Passigli
   E-mail: annalisapassigli@gmail.com
Founded: 1981
Subjects: Biography, Memoirs, History, Literature, Literary Criticism, Essays, Music, Dance, Poetry, Travel & Tourism
ISBN Prefix(es): 978-88-368; 978-88-86161
Number of titles published annually: 50 Print
Total Titles: 1,500 Print
Imprints: Le Comete; Guide del Cuore; Guide del Sole
Distribution Center: Messaggerie Books, Via G Verdi 8, 20090 Assago MI *Web Site:* www.messaggerielibri.it

Institutum Patristicum Augustinianum
via Paolo VI, 25, 00193 Rome
Tel: (06) 6800 69 *Fax:* (06) 6800 6298
E-mail: segreteria@patristicum.org
Web Site: www.patristicum.org
Key Personnel
Secretary General: Amado Llorente Abanzas
Founded: 1969
Subjects: Antiques, Literature, Literary Criticism, Essays, Religion - Catholic
ISBN Prefix(es): 978-88-7961
Imprints: SEA

Patron Editore SRL+
via Badini 12, Quarto Inferiore, 40057 Granarolo dell'Emilia BO
Tel: (051) 767003 *Fax:* (051) 768252
E-mail: info@patroneditore.com
Web Site: www.patroneditore.com
Founded: 1925
Subjects: Agriculture, Art, Engineering (General), History, Language Arts, Linguistics, Law, Literature, Literary Criticism, Essays, Medicine, Nursing, Dentistry, Philosophy, Psychology, Psychiatry, Social Sciences, Sociology
ISBN Prefix(es): 978-88-555
Bookshop(s): Libreria Internazionale Patron, Via Zamboni 26, 40121 Bologna

Pearson Education Italia
via Archimede 10, 23 e 51, 20129 Milan
Tel: (02) 74823 1 *Fax:* (02) 74823278; (02) 74823312; (02) 74823362
Web Site: www.pearsoned.it
Key Personnel
Head, Press: Elena Grossi *Tel:* (02) 74823384
   E-mail: elena.grossi@pearson.it
Founded: 2007
Subjects: English as a Second Language, History, Language Arts, Linguistics, Literature, Literary Criticism, Essays, Mathematics, Physics, Science (General), Technology
ISBN Prefix(es): 978-88-8339; 978-88-7192
Branch Office(s)
Corso Trapani 16, 10139 Turin *Tel:* (011) 7502111 *Fax:* (011) 75021510

Peliti Associati
Viale Beata Vergine del Carmelo, 12, 00144 Rome RM
Tel: (06) 5295548 *Fax:* (06) 5292351
E-mail: peliti@peliti.it
Web Site: www.pelitiassociati.eu
Key Personnel
Mng Dir: Francesca Peliti
Founded: 1986

Membership(s): Associazione Agenzie di Relazioni Pubbliche a Servizio Completo (ASSOREL); Associazione Italiana Editori (AIE).
Subjects: Photography
ISBN Prefix(es): 978-88-85121; 978-88-89412
Branch Office(s)
Via Giovanni Battista Pergolesi, 23, 20124 Milan MI *Tel:* (02) 66982357 *Fax:* (02) 67199937
   E-mail: infopeliti@peliti.it
Distribution Center: Messaggerie Libri SpA, Via Giuseppe Verdi, 8, 20090 Assago MI *Web Site:* www.messaggerielibri.it

Luigi Pellegrini Editore+
Via de Rada, 67/c, 87100 Cosenza CS
Tel: (0984) 795065 *Fax:* (0984) 792672
E-mail: info@pellegrinieditore.it
Web Site: www.pellegrinieditore.com
Key Personnel
Chief Executive, Rights & Permissions: Luigi Pellegrini
Editorial & Sales: Walter Pellegrini
Press: Antoinette Cozza *Tel:* (0984) 795065 ext 4
   E-mail: acozza@pellegrinieditore.it
Public Relations: Marta Pellegrini *Tel:* (0984) 795065 ext 4 *E-mail:* marta.pellegrini@pellegrinieditore.it
Founded: 1952
Subjects: Drama, Theater, Education, Fiction, History, Law, Literature, Literary Criticism, Essays, Poetry, Religion - Other, Social Sciences, Sociology, Travel & Tourism
ISBN Prefix(es): 978-88-8101
Imprints: LPE
Branch Office(s)
Via Rendano, 25, 87040 Castrolibero

Il Pensiero Scientifico Editore SRL+
Via San Giovanni Valdarno, 8, 00138 Rome
Tel: (06) 86282 1 *Fax:* (06) 86282 250
Toll Free Fax: 800-259620
E-mail: pensiero@pensiero.it
Web Site: www.pensiero.it
Key Personnel
Dir General: Luca De Fiore *Tel:* (06) 86282 328
   E-mail: luca.defiore@pensiero.it
General Executive Manager: Francesco De Fiore *Tel:* (06) 86282 327 *E-mail:* francesco.defiore@pensiero.it
External Relations: Luciano De Fiore *Tel:* (06) 86282 346 *E-mail:* luciano.defiore@pensiero.it
Foreign Rights: Andrea De Fiore *Tel:* (06) 86282 324 *E-mail:* andrea.defiore@pensiero.it
Press: Erica Sorelli *Tel:* (06) 86282 347
   E-mail: e.sorelli@pensiero.it
Founded: 1946
The publishing mission is the statement of the human values as the basis of medical research & the development of all evidence based clinical practice.
Subjects: Education, Health, Nutrition, Medicine, Nursing, Dentistry, Psychology, Psychiatry, Oncology
ISBN Prefix(es): 978-88-7002
Number of titles published annually: 50 Print

Petruzzi SRL
Via Venturelli, 7/b, Zona Industriale Regnano, 06012 Citta di Castello
Tel: (075) 85 11 345 *Fax:* (075) 85 18 038
E-mail: info@petruzzistampa.it
Web Site: www.petruzzieditore.it; www.petruzzistampa.it
Key Personnel
Publisher: Corrado Petruzzi
Subjects: Art, Fiction, History, Nonfiction (General), Social Sciences, Sociology, Travel & Tourism
ISBN Prefix(es): 978-88-89797; 978-88-900915

PGE, *imprint of* Gribaudi Editore

PIAC, *imprint of* Pontificio Istituto di Archeologia Cristiana

Daniela Piazza Editore+
Via Polonghera 34, 10138 Turin
Tel: (011) 434 27 06 *Fax:* (011) 434 24 71
E-mail: info@danielapiazzaeditore.com
Web Site: www.danielapiazzaeditore.com
Key Personnel
Publisher: Daniela Piazza
Founded: 1972
Subjects: Art, Biography, Memoirs, Cookery, Fiction, History, Poetry, Regional Interests, Travel & Tourism
ISBN Prefix(es): 978-88-7889

Piccin Nuova Libraria SpA+
Via Altinate 107, 35121 Padua
Tel: (049) 655566 *Fax:* (049) 8750693
E-mail: info@piccinonline.com
Web Site: www.piccinonline.com
Key Personnel
Foreign Rights Manager: Dr Nicola Piccin
   E-mail: n.piccin@piccinonline.com
Editorial & Sales: Dr Antonella Noventa
   E-mail: a.noventa@piccinonline.com
Founded: 1980
Subjects: Biological Sciences, Law, Literature, Literary Criticism, Essays, Medicine, Nursing, Dentistry, Science (General)
ISBN Prefix(es): 978-88-299

Piemme Freeway, *imprint of* Edizioni Piemme SpA

Piemme Scuola, *imprint of* Mondadori Education

Edizioni Piemme SpA+
Subsidiary of Arnoldo Mondadori Editore SpA
Corso Como, 15, 20154 Milan
Tel: (02) 430051 *Fax:* (02) 43005299
E-mail: info@edizpiemme.it
Web Site: www.edizpiemme.it
Key Personnel
Chief Editor: Francesca Cristoffanini
Head, Publicity: Elena Cassarotto
Press Officer: Valerie Caprioglio
Founded: 1982
Subjects: Biblical Studies, Biography, Memoirs, Cookery, Fiction, Gardening, Plants, History, Nonfiction (General), Religion - Catholic, Romance, Self-Help, Theology, Thrillers, Women
ISBN Prefix(es): 978-88-384; 978-88-566; 978-88-585
Imprints: Il Battello a Vapore; Piemme Freeway
Distribution Center: Via Telesio, 25, 20145 Milan
   Tel: (02) 49961242 *Fax:* (02) 48518381

Piero Lacaita Editore+
Vico degli Albanesi, 4, 74024 Manduria TA
Tel: (099) 971 11 24 *Fax:* (099) 971 11 24
E-mail: info@lacaita.com
Web Site: www.lacaita.com
Key Personnel
Editorial Dir: Piero Lacaita
Founded: 1987
Subjects: History, Literature, Literary Criticism, Essays
ISBN Prefix(es): 978-88-87280; 978-88-88546

Libreria Gozzini di Pietro e Francesco Chellini (SNC)
Via Ricasoli 49-103r, 50122 Florence FI
Tel: (055) 212433 *Fax:* (055) 211105
E-mail: info@gozzini.it; info@gozzini.com; order@gozzini.it
Web Site: www.gozzini.com
Founded: 1850
Membership(s): ALAI-ILAB.
Subjects: Architecture & Interior Design, Art, Geography, Geology, History, Literature, Literary

Criticism, Essays, Music, Dance, Poetry, Science (General)
Total Titles: 200 E-Book

Pitagora Editrice SRL+
Via del Legatore 3, 40138 Bologna BO
Tel: (051) 530003 *Fax:* (051) 535301
E-mail: pited@pitagoragroup.it
Web Site: www.pitagoragroup.it
Key Personnel
Administration: Adolfo Francioni
Founded: 1958
Subjects: Architecture & Interior Design, Economics, Engineering (General), Environmental Studies, Geography, Geology, Health, Nutrition, Language Arts, Linguistics, Literature, Literary Criticism, Essays, Mathematics, Medicine, Nursing, Dentistry, Psychology, Psychiatry, Science (General), Social Sciences, Sociology, Technology
ISBN Prefix(es): 978-88-371
Number of titles published annually: 60 Print
Total Titles: 1,200 Print
Associate Companies: Tecnoprint S N C
   Tel: (051) 531159 *E-mail:* tecnoprint@pitagoragroup.it
Bookshop(s): Via Saragozza 112, 40135 Bologna
   Tel: (051) 6446460; Via Zamboni 57, 40126
   Bologna *Tel:* (051) 243360

Plurigraf SpA
Via Cairoli, 18a, 50131 Florence
Tel: (055) 571028 *Fax:* (055) 5000766
E-mail: info@bonechibooks.it
Web Site: www.bonechi.com
Founded: 1972
Subjects: Travel & Tourism
ISBN Prefix(es): 978-88-7280; 978-88-7551
Parent Company: Bonechi Publishing Group

Edizioni Il Polifilo
Via Donizetti 37, 20122 Milan
Tel: (0335) 6030255 *Fax:* (02) 91390232
E-mail: ordini@ilpolifilo.it (orders)
Web Site: www.ilpolifilo.it
Key Personnel
Dir: Paolo Vigevani
Founded: 1959
Subjects: Architecture & Interior Design, Art, Drama, Theater, Gardening, Plants, History, Literature, Literary Criticism, Essays, Regional Interests, Travel & Tourism, Bibliology, History of Technology, Milan & Lombardy, Renaissance, Views
ISBN Prefix(es): 978-88-7050
Number of titles published annually: 4 Print
Total Titles: 200 Print

Il Poligrafo Casa Editrice
Via Carlo Cassan, 34, 35121 Padua PD
Tel: (049) 8360887 *Fax:* (049) 8360864
E-mail: casaeditrice@poligrafo.it
Web Site: www.poligrafo.it
Key Personnel
Editorial Dir: Romano Tonin
Editor: Chiara Finesso
Founded: 1988
Subjects: Architecture & Interior Design, Art, History, Literature, Literary Criticism, Essays, Philosophy, Psychology, Psychiatry, Regional Interests, Science (General), Social Sciences, Sociology
ISBN Prefix(es): 978-88-7115

Edizioni Polistampa
Via Livorno 8/32, 50142 Florence FI
Tel: (055) 7378730 *Fax:* (055) 7378760
E-mail: contab@polistampa.com
Web Site: www.polistampa.com
Founded: 1966

Subjects: Art, History, Literature, Literary Criticism, Essays, Science (General)
ISBN Prefix(es): 978-88-596; 978-88-8304; 978-88-85977
Total Titles: 3,200 Print
Imprints: Mauro Pagliai Editore; Sarnus
Distribution Center: Casemate | academic, 1950 Lawrence Rd, Havertown, PA 19083, United States *Tel:* 610-853-9131 *Fax:* 610-853-9146
   E-mail: info@casemateacademic.com *Web Site:* www.oxbowbooks.com/dbbc/ (North America)
Erudist-Distribution & diffusion d'erudition, 69-71, rue du Chevaleret, 75013 Paris, France
   Tel: 01 49 26 07 26 *Fax:* 01 73 79 02 12
   E-mail: info@erudist.net

Giancarlo Politi Editore SRL
Via Carlo Farini, 68, 20159 Milan MI
Tel: (02) 6887341 *Fax:* (02) 66801290
E-mail: info@flashartonline.com
Web Site: www.flashartonline.com
Key Personnel
Mng Editor: Umberta Genta *E-mail:* umberta@flashartonline.com
Editor: Helena Kontova *E-mail:* helena@flashartonline.com; Giancarlo Politi
   E-mail: giancarlo.politi@tin.it
Subjects: Art
ISBN Prefix(es): 978-88-7816
U.S. Office(s): 799 Broadway, Room 224, New York, NY 10003, United States, Contact: Isabel Halley *Tel:* 212-477-4905 *Fax:* 212-477-5016
   E-mail: isabel@flashartonline.com

Adelmo Polla Editore+
Via Prato, 2, 67044 Cerchio AQ
Tel: (0863) 78522; (339) 4948611 (cell)
   Fax: (0863) 78522
E-mail: pollaeditore@gmail.com
Web Site: www.pollaeditore.com
Key Personnel
Mng Dir: Adelmo Polla
Founded: 1974
Subjects: Archaeology, History, Language Arts, Linguistics, Literature, Literary Criticism, Essays, Travel & Tourism
ISBN Prefix(es): 978-88-7407
Number of titles published annually: 15 Print
Total Titles: 220 Print

Il Pomerio
Via Della Costa, 4, 26900 Lodi
Tel: (0371) 420381 *Fax:* (0371) 422080
E-mail: info@ilpomerio.com
Web Site: www.ilpomerio.com
Founded: 1995
Subjects: Architecture & Interior Design, Art, Cookery, Education, Environmental Studies, History, Literature, Literary Criticism, Essays, Poetry, Pop Culture, Sports, Athletics, Travel & Tourism, Folklore
ISBN Prefix(es): 978-88-7121

Ponte alle Grazie
Via Gherardini 10, 20145 Milan MI
Tel: (02) 34597626 *Fax:* (02) 34597206
E-mail: info@ponteallegrazie.it
Web Site: www.ponteallegrazie.it
Key Personnel
President & Chief Executive Officer: Stefano Mauri
Chief Executive Officer & Editorial Dir: Luigi Spagnol
Press: Matteo Columbo *Tel:* (02) 34597632
   E-mail: matteo.columbo@ponteallegrazie.it
Founded: 1993
Subjects: Biography, Memoirs, Cookery, Economics, Environmental Studies, Fiction, Government, Political Science, Humor, Literature, Literary Criticism, Essays, Poetry, Psychology, Psychiatry, Travel & Tourism
ISBN Prefix(es): 978-88-7928; 978-88-6220

Parent Company: Gruppo Editoriale Mauri-Spagnol
Distribution Center: Messaggerie Libri *Toll Free Tel:* 800-804-900 *Fax:* (02) 84406056
E-mail: assistenza.ordini@meli.it *Web Site:* www.messaggerielibri.it

Pontificio Istituto di Archeologia Cristiana
Via Napoleone III, 1, 00185 Rome
Tel: (06) 4465574 *Fax:* (06) 4469197
E-mail: piac@piac.it
Web Site: www.piac.it
Key Personnel
Rector: Prof Vincenzo Fiocchi Nicolai
  E-mail: piac.rettore@piac.it
Library Dir: Dr Giorgio Nestori *E-mail:* piac.biblio@piac.it
Sales & Distribution: Claudio Ermacora
  E-mail: piac.editrice@pica.it
Founded: 1925
Specialize in Christianity in the areas of the last Roman painting, sculpture & mosaics.
Subjects: Archaeology, History, Religion - Other, Christianity, Epigraphy
ISBN Prefix(es): 978-88-85991
Imprints: PIAC

Pontificio Istituto Orientale (Pontifical Oriental Institute)+
Piazza S Maria Maggiore, 7, 00185 Rome
Tel: (06) 447417104 *Fax:* (06) 4465576
E-mail: edizioni@orientaliachristiana.it
Web Site: www.orientaliachristiana.it
Key Personnel
Mng Editor: Jaroslaw Dziewicki
Founded: 1917
Subjects: Antiques, Archaeology, Art, Asian Studies, Biblical Studies, Religion - Catholic, Religion - Other
ISBN Prefix(es): 978-88-7210

Poseidonia Scuola, *imprint of* Mondadori Education

Postcart Edizioni
Via Prenestina 435, 00177 Rome RM
Tel: (06) 25 91 030 *Fax:* (06) 25 91 030
E-mail: postcartedizioni@pec.postcart.com; ordini@postcart.com
Web Site: www.postcart.com
Subjects: Photography
ISBN Prefix(es): 978-88-86795
Distribution Center: Consortium Book Sales & Distribution, The Keg House, 34 13 Ave NE, Minneapolis, MN 55413-1007, United States *Tel:* 612-746-2600 *Fax:* 612-746-2606 *E-mail:* info@cbsd.com

Neri Pozza Editore SpA+
Via Fatebenefratelli, 4, 20121 Milan
Tel: (02) 869 987 26 *Fax:* (02) 869 199 43
Web Site: www.neripozza.it
Key Personnel
Chief Executive Officer: Alessandro Zelger
President: Laura Della Vecchia
Editorial Dir: Giuseppe Russo
Founded: 1946
Subjects: Art, History, Literature, Literary Criticism, Essays
ISBN Prefix(es): 978-88-7305; 978-88-545
Parent Company: Longanesi & C
Subsidiaries: Athesis, Longanesi, GdP
Warehouse: Magazzino Editoriale Medi srl, Milano Oltre Due - via Londra, 35, 20090 Segrate MI *Tel:* (02) 269 29 329 *Fax:* (02) 269 29 338
Distribution Center: Messaggerie Libri SpA, Via Giuseppe Verdi, 8, 20094 Assago MI *Tel:* (02) 457 741 *Fax:* (02) 457 010 32 *Web Site:* www.meli.it

Edizioni Luigi Pozzi SRL+
Via Panama, 68, 00198 Rome RM
Tel: (06) 8553548 *Fax:* (06) 8554105
Web Site: www.edizioniluigipozzi.it
Founded: 1893
Subjects: Medicine, Nursing, Dentistry
ISBN Prefix(es): 978-88-7025
Number of titles published annually: 15 Print

Prismi Editrice Politecnica
Via Giovanni Capurro 1, 80123 Naples
Tel: (081) 5752524 *Fax:* (081) 5983196
E-mail: info@arte-m.net
Web Site: www.arte-m.net
Key Personnel
Dir: Maria Battimiello *E-mail:* battimiello@arte-m.net
Editorial Dir: Guido Savarese *E-mail:* savarese@arte-m.net
Press & Events: Margherita de Foe
  E-mail: defoe@arte-m.net
Founded: 1980
Subjects: Art, History, Regional Interests
ISBN Prefix(es): 978-88-7065
Distributed by PDE SpA
Distribution Center: Messaggerie Libri

Priuli e Verlucca editori+
Via Masero 55, 10010 Scarmagno TO
Tel: (0125) 71 22 66 *Fax:* (0125) 71 28 07
E-mail: info@priulieverlucca.it
Web Site: www.priulieverlucca.it
Key Personnel
Founder & Co-Owner: Gherardo Priuli
Founded: 1971
Subjects: Anthropology, Antiques, Art, Cookery, Environmental Studies, Ethnicity, Photography, Regional Interests, Travel & Tourism
ISBN Prefix(es): 978-88-8068
Distribution Center: PDE SpA, Via Forlanini 36, 50019 Osmannoro FI *Tel:* (055) 301371 *Fax:* (055) 301372 *E-mail:* info@pde.it

Edizioni Il Punto d'Incontro SAS+
Via Zamenhof, 685, 36100 Vicenza
Tel: (0444) 239189 *Fax:* (0444) 239266
E-mail: info@edizionilpuntodincontro.it; rights@edizionilpuntodincontro.it
Web Site: www.edizionilpuntodincontro.it
Key Personnel
International Rights: Cristina Levi; Patrizia Saterini
Founded: 1987
Specialize in books intended to sustain life's deepest foundations.
Subjects: Alternative, Astrology, Occult, Fiction, Health, Nutrition, Inspirational, Spirituality, Philosophy, Psychology, Psychiatry, Religion - Buddhist, Religion - Hindu, Self-Help
ISBN Prefix(es): 978-88-8093
Distribution Center: Messaggerie Libri, Via Verdi 8, 20090 Assago MI *Tel:* (02) 457741 *Fax:* (02) 45701032

Edizioni Qiqajon+
Comunita monastica di Bose, 13887 Magnano (Biella)
Tel: (015) 679 264 *Fax:* (015) 679 290
E-mail: edizioni@qiqajon.it
Web Site: www.qiqajon.it
Key Personnel
Chief Executive Officer: Guido Dotti
President: Enzo Bianchi
Founded: 1983
Subjects: Inspirational, Spirituality, Poetry, Religion - Catholic, Religion - Jewish, Religion - Protestant, Religion - Other, Theology
ISBN Prefix(es): 978-88-85227; 978-88-8227
Number of titles published annually: 25 Print
Total Titles: 320 Print

Edizioni Quasar di Severino Tognon SRL+
Via Ajaccio 41/43, 00198 Rome RM
Tel: (06) 85358444 *Fax:* (06) 85833591
E-mail: promozione@edizioniquasar.it
Web Site: www.edizioniquasar.it
Founded: 1972
Subjects: Archaeology, Art, History, Poetry
ISBN Prefix(es): 978-88-7097; 978-88-7140; 978-88-85086
Imprints: EQ
Bookshop(s): Libreria Quasar SRL

Edizioni QuattroVenti SRL+
Piazza Rinascimento, 4, 61029 Urbino PU
Mailing Address: CP 156, 61029 Urbino PU
Tel: (0722) 2588 *Fax:* (0722) 320998
E-mail: info@edizioniquattroventi.it
Web Site: www.edizioniquattroventi.it
Founded: 1981
Subjects: Archaeology, Art, History, Language Arts, Linguistics, Literature, Literary Criticism, Essays, Philosophy, Religion - Other, Sports, Athletics, Philology
ISBN Prefix(es): 978-88-392
Bookshop(s): Libreria La Goliardica
Distribution Center: PDE, Via Tevere, 54, 50019 Sesto Fiorentino FI *Tel:* (055) 301371 *Fax:* (055) 301372 *E-mail:* info@pde.it *Web Site:* www.pde.it

Editrice Queriniana+
Via Ferri, 75, 25123 Brescia
Tel: (030) 2306925 *Fax:* (030) 2306932
E-mail: direzione@queriniana.it; redazione@queriniana.it; info@queriniana.it
Web Site: www.queriniana.it
Key Personnel
Mng Dir: Dr Rosino Gibellini
Founded: 1965
Subjects: Biblical Studies, Philosophy, Religion - Catholic, Religion - Other, Theology
ISBN Prefix(es): 978-88-399

Edition Raetia+
Via Grappoli 23, 39100 Bolzano BZ
Tel: (0471) 976904 *Fax:* (0471) 976908
E-mail: info@raetia.com
Web Site: www.raetia.com
Key Personnel
Publishing Dir: Dr Gottfried Solderer *Tel:* (335) 1303404 (cell) *E-mail:* gottfried.solderer@raetia.com
Editorial Dir & Public Relations: Dr Thomas Kager *Tel:* (333) 6460073 (cell) *E-mail:* thomas.kager@raetia.com
Founded: 1991
Subjects: Architecture & Interior Design, Art, Government, Political Science, History, Humor, Literature, Literary Criticism, Essays, Photography, Regional Interests
ISBN Prefix(es): 978-88-7283

Raffaello Editrice SRL
Via dell' Industria, 21, 60037 Monte San Vito AN
Tel: (071) 749851 *Fax:* (071) 7498520
E-mail: info@gruppuraffaello.it
Web Site: www.raffaelloeditrice.it
Key Personnel
President: Renzo Boccadoro
Dir: Cav Franco Bastianelli
Subjects: Child Care & Development, Education
ISBN Prefix(es): 978-88-472
Parent Company: Gruppo Editoriale Raffaello
Imprints: Celtic Publishing; Il Mulino a Vento; Leonardo; Raphael Digitale; Raphael Ragazzi; Raphaello Editrice
Branch Office(s)
Via G Brodolini, 18, 60037 Monte San Vito AN
Via G Brodolini (ZIPA), 60035 Jesi AN

Ragazzi, *imprint of* Giangiacomo Feltrinelli Editore SRL

RAI-ERI+
Imprint of RAI Radiotelevisione Italiana
Viale Mazzini 14, 00195 Rome
Tel: (06) 36865241 *Fax:* (06) 36822071
E-mail: rai-eri@rai.it
Web Site: www.eri.rai.it
Key Personnel
Mng Dir: Francesco Devescovi
Founded: 1949
Membership(s): AIE-FEIG.
Subjects: Art, Communications, Drama, Theater, Fiction, Film, Video, Journalism, Music, Dance, Nonfiction (General), Photography, Radio, TV, Social Sciences, Sociology
ISBN Prefix(es): 978-88-397
Associate Companies: Raitrade, Via U Novaro 18, 00195 Rome; Sipra, Via Bertola 34, Turin; Telespazio, Via Alberto Bergamini 50, Rome
Distributed by Arnoldo Mondadori Editore (Italy)

Edizioni RAI Radiotelevisione Italiano SpA,
see RAI-ERI

Raphael Digitale, *imprint of* Raffaello Editrice SRL

Raphael Ragazzi, *imprint of* Raffaello Editrice SRL

Raphaello Editrice, *imprint of* Raffaello Editrice SRL

RCS Libri SpA+
Subsidiary of RCS MediaGroup SpA
Via Angelo Rizzoli, 8, 20132 Milan MI
Tel: (02) 50951; (02) 25841 *Fax:* (02) 50952647 (rights)
Web Site: www.rcsmediagroup.it
Key Personnel
President: Paolo Mieli
Vice President: Teresa Cremisi
Rights Dir: Giovanna Canton *E-mail:* giovanna.canton@rcs.it
Media Relations: Annamaria Guadagni *Tel:* (02) 8448 4337 *E-mail:* ufficiostampa.rizzoli@rcs.it
Founded: 1945
Other members of the RCS MediaGroup are Rizzoli, Bompiani, Fabbri, Sonzogno, Adelphi & Marsilio.
Subjects: Art, Business, Crafts, Games, Hobbies, History, Medicine, Nursing, Dentistry, Music, Dance, Outdoor Recreation, Science (General)
ISBN Prefix(es): 978-88-17 (Rizzoli); 978-88-451 (Fabbri); 978-88-452 (Fabbri); 978-88-454 (Fabbri); 978-88-486 (Rizzoli); 978-88-450 (Fabbri)

RE, *imprint of* Rugginenti Editore

Edizioni red!+
Imprint of Il Castello Group
Via Milano 73/75, 20010 Cornaredo MI
Tel: (01275) 851075 *Fax:* (01275) 851075
E-mail: ilcastello@123media.co.uk; info@ilcastelloeditore.it
Web Site: www.rededizioni.it; www.ilcastelloeditore.it
Key Personnel
Foreign Rights: Cristina Galimberti
Founded: 1977
Subjects: Agriculture, Child Care & Development, Earth Sciences, Environmental Studies, Health, Nutrition, Medicine, Nursing, Dentistry, Music, Dance, Psychology, Psychiatry, Technology, Fitness
ISBN Prefix(es): 978-88-573; 978-88-7447

Edizioni Rinnovamento nello Spirito Santo (RnS)
Via del Grano, 49, 00172 Rome RM

Tel: (06) 2310577 *Fax:* (06) 2305014
E-mail: segreteria@edizionirns.it
Web Site: www.edizionirns.it
Subjects: Inspirational, Spirituality, Music, Dance, Religion - Other, Christian Life, Family
ISBN Prefix(es): 978-88-7878
Parent Company: Odos Servizi SCPL

Edizioni Ripostes+
Via Cavour n 48, 84091 Battipaglia SA
Tel: (0828) 303621 *Fax:* (0828) 303621
E-mail: info@libreriamistral.it
Web Site: www.ripostesedizioni.it
Key Personnel
Owner: Anna Carelli
Founded: 1981
Subjects: Architecture & Interior Design, Art, Biography, Memoirs, Drama, Theater, Economics, Engineering (General), History, Literature, Literary Criticism, Essays, Music, Dance, Philosophy, Photography, Poetry, Psychology, Psychiatry, Science (General), Science Fiction, Fantasy, Theology, Comics
ISBN Prefix(es): 978-88-86819

Editori Riuniti+
Via di Fioranello, 56, 00134 Rome RM
E-mail: info@editoririuniti.it
Web Site: www.editoririuniti.it
Founded: 1953
Subjects: Art, Economics, Education, Fiction, Government, Political Science, History, Language Arts, Linguistics, Law, Literature, Literary Criticism, Essays, Philosophy, Psychology, Psychiatry, Science (General), Social Sciences, Sociology
ISBN Prefix(es): 978-88-359
Parent Company: Gruppo Editoriale Italiano SRL
Imprints: ER; Editori Riuniti University Press

Editori Riuniti University Press, *imprint of*
Editori Riuniti

Rivista Italiana di Ragioneria e di Economia Aziendale, see Casa Editrice RIREA

Edizioni Riza SpA+
via Luigi Anelli, 1, 20122 Milan MI
Tel: (02) 5845961 *Fax:* (02) 58318162
E-mail: info@riza.it
Web Site: www.riza.it
Subjects: Health, Nutrition, Psychology, Psychiatry, Natural Remedies
ISBN Prefix(es): 978-88-7071
Number of titles published annually: 100 Print

Rizzoli
Via Mondadori, 1, 20090 Segrate MI
E-mail: info@rizzolilibri.it; ufficiostampa.rizzoli@rizzolilibri.it; rizzoli.rights@rizzolilibri.it
Web Site: www.rizzoli.eu; www.rizzolilibri.it
Founded: 1927
Subjects: Art, Biography, Memoirs, Cookery, Economics, Fashion, Fiction, Government, Political Science, Health, Nutrition, History, Humor, Inspirational, Spirituality, Literature, Literary Criticism, Essays, Music, Dance, Mysteries, Suspense, Philosophy, Psychology, Psychiatry, Religion - Other, Romance, Science (General), Science Fiction, Fantasy, Sports, Athletics, Technology, Adventure, Cinema & TV, Current Affairs, Entertainment, Leisure, Lifestyle
ISBN Prefix(es): 978-0-8478; 978-88-318; 978-88-17; 978-0-9713268; 978-88-7423; 978-962-85274; 978-99928-39
Parent Company: Rizzoli Libri SpA

RnS, see Edizioni Rinnovamento nello Spirito Santo (RnS)

Laurus Robuffo Edizioni
Via della Macchiarella, 146, 00119 Rome
Tel: (06) 565 1492 *Fax:* (06) 565 1233
E-mail: laurus@laurus.tv; redazione@laurusrobuffo.it
Web Site: www.laurusrobuffo.it
Key Personnel
Chief Executive: Mario Robuffo
Founded: 1973
Subjects: Law
ISBN Prefix(es): 978-88-8087
Bookshop(s): Distributrice Libraria Laziale Srl, Via di Tor Fiorenza, 27, 00199 Rome *Tel:* (06) 86211556 *Fax:* (06) 86210227 *E-mail:* gpanimo@consorzioegaf.it; Libri & Libri Srl, Via Guido Rossa, 4, Baraccola Ovest, 60020 Ancona *Tel:* (071) 2866668 *Fax:* (071) 2866912 *E-mail:* fornasiero@librielibri.191.it; Edizioni Fag Srl, Via Garibaldi 5, 20090 Assago MI *Tel:* (02) 48841920 *Fax:* (02) 48841936 *E-mail:* fag@fag.it; Nuova Distribuzione Meridionale Srl, Via Conte Giusso, 4/c, 70125 Bari *Tel:* (080) 5461219 *Fax:* (080) 5461398 *E-mail:* beppe@barisera.it; Epidromo Srl, Via Zanardi 106/6, 40131 Bologna *Tel:* (051) 6346798 *Fax:* (051) 6344412 *E-mail:* edipromo@edipromo.it; Dielleci Srl, Via Capri, 67, 80026 Casoria NA *Tel:* (081) 7598899 *Fax:* (081) 7592198 *E-mail:* dlc.perrella@alice.it; DLB Srl, Via Romairone, 42R N° 2.19, 16163 Genoa *Tel:* (010) 710794 *Fax:* (010) 7260395 *E-mail:* dlbgenova@yahoo.it; Alfe Libri Srl, Via Stefano Breda 26/b, 35010 Limena PD *Tel:* (049) 8840333 *Fax:* (049) 8840444 *E-mail:* info@alfe.it; Libraria Distribuzioni di Loi Emanuele, Via Cucca, 9, 08100 Nuoro *Tel:* (0784) 204050 *Fax:* (0784) 204080 *E-mail:* emaloi@tin.it; MM Distribuzione Libraria Srl, Via Beato Angelico, 13/23, 90145 Palermo *Tel:* (091) 552172 *Fax:* (091) 552172 *E-mail:* mmdislib@libero.it; Tecnolibri Distribuzione Srl, Via del Pratignone, 13/4, 50019 Sesto Fiorentino FI *Tel:* (055) 8826698 *Fax:* (055) 8825822 *E-mail:* info@tecnolibri.it; Egaf Srl, Via Tibaldi 22/22a, 10151 Turin *Tel:* (011) 4530537 *Fax:* (011) 4552619 *E-mail:* amministrazione@egafsrl.191.it

Libreria Editrice Rogate (LER)+
Via dei Rogazionisti, 8, 00182 Rome
Tel: (06) 7023430 *Fax:* (06) 7020767
E-mail: info@editricerogate.it
Web Site: www.editricerogate.it
Key Personnel
Editorial: Vito Magno
Founded: 1970
Subjects: Religion - Other, Theology
ISBN Prefix(es): 978-88-8075

Edizioni Universitarie Romane
Via Michelangelo Poggioli 2,3, 00161 Rome
Tel: (06) 44 36 13 77; (06) 49 40 658; (06) 49 15 03 *Fax:* (06) 44 53 438
Web Site: www.eurom.it
Key Personnel
Owner: Gian Luca Pallai
Founded: 1974
Subjects: Biological Sciences, Business, Chemistry, Chemical Engineering, Fiction, Human Relations, Mathematics, Medicine, Nursing, Dentistry, Nonfiction (General), Psychology, Psychiatry, Science (General), Social Sciences, Sociology
ISBN Prefix(es): 978-88-7730

Edizioni Gino Rossato+
Via Bella Venezia, 13/C, 36078 Novale di Valdagno VI
Tel: (0455) 411000 *Fax:* (0455) 411550
E-mail: info@edizionirossato.it

Web Site: www.edizionirossato.it
Membership(s): Associazione Italiana Editori
(AIE).
Subjects: History, Military Science, Travel &
Tourism
ISBN Prefix(es): 978-88-8130

RoughGuides, *imprint of* Giangiacomo Feltrinelli
Editore SRL

Rubbettino Editore+
Viale Rosario Rubbettino, 10, 88049 Soveria
Mannelli CZ
Tel: (0968) 6664201 *Fax:* (0968) 662035
E-mail: rubbettinoeditore@pec.it; editore@
rubbettino.it
Web Site: www.rubbettinoeditore.it
Key Personnel
Publisher: Florindo Rubbettino
Commercial Dir: Giuseppe Paletta *Tel:* (0968)
6664275 *E-mail:* giuseppe.paletta@rubbettino.it
Editorial Dir: Luigi Franco *Tel:* (0968) 6664204
E-mail: luigi.franco@rubbettino.it
Administration: Bernardo Talarico *Tel:* (0968)
6664221 *E-mail:* bernardo.talarico@rubbettino.
it
Editorial: Giuseppe D'Arro *Tel:* (0968) 6664222
E-mail: giuseppe.darro@rubbettino.it;
Gabriella Grandinetti *Tel:* (0968) 6664223
E-mail: gabriella.grandinetti@rubbettino.it
Foreign Rights: Amalia Nicolazzo *Tel:* (0968)
6664255 *E-mail:* amalia.nicolazzo@rubbettino.
it
Press: Antonio Cavallaro *Tel:* (0968) 6664210
E-mail: antonio.cavallaro@rubbettino.it; Maria
Rizzo *Tel:* (0968) 6664210 *E-mail:* maria.
rizzo@rubbettino.it
Sales: Antonio Colosimo *Tel:* (0968) 6664208
E-mail: antonio.colosimo@rubbettino.it
Founded: 1972
Subjects: Anthropology, Art, Drama, Theater,
Economics, Government, Political Science,
History, Law, Literature, Literary Criticism, Es-
says, Philosophy, Poetry, Public Administration,
Religion - Other, Romance, Social Sciences,
Sociology, Theology, Women's Studies
ISBN Prefix(es): 978-88-7284; 978-88-498; 978-
88-88948 (Citta Calabria)
Parent Company: Rubbettino Industrie Grafiche
ed Editoriali
Associate Companies: Calabria Letteraria Editrice
E-mail: cle@rubbettino.it
Distribution Center: PDE Promozione Dis-
tribuzione Editoriale, Via Tevere 54 Loc Os-
mannoro, 50019 Sesto Fiorentino FI *Tel:* (055)
301371 *Fax:* (055) 301372

Rugginenti Editore+
Via Giuseppe Scalarini, 8, 20139 Milan
Tel: (02) 36693990 *Fax:* (02) 36693991
E-mail: info@rugginenti.it
Web Site: www.rugginenti.it
Key Personnel
General Manager: Gianni Rugginenti
E-mail: gianni@rugginenti.it
Deputy Dir: Maurizio Rugginenti
E-mail: maurizio@rugginenti.it
Founded: 1968
Specialize in music education for professionals,
students & enthusiasts.
Subjects: Music, Dance
ISBN Prefix(es): 978-88-7665
Total Titles: 40 Audio
Imprints: RE

Rusconi Libri SpA+
Via dell'Industria, 36, 47822 Santarcangelo di
Romagna RN
Tel: (0541) 326306 *Fax:* (0541) 329344
E-mail: info@rusconilibri.it
Web Site: www.rusconilibri.it

Key Personnel
Production Manager: Manuela Guaccio
E-mail: manuela@marketpioneer.net
Rights Manager: Luca Carpigiani *E-mail:* luca@
marketpioneer.net
Founded: 1969
Subjects: Animals, Pets, Art, Cookery, Crafts,
Games, Hobbies, Environmental Studies, Fic-
tion, Geography, Geology, History, How-to,
Religion - Other, Science (General), Nature
ISBN Prefix(es): 978-88-18
Parent Company: RL Gruppo Editoriale
Associate Companies: Eurolibri
U.S. Office(s): Rusconi Inc, 375 Park Ave, Suite
3307, New York, NY 10152, United States
Warehouse: Via Pacinotti, 16-20092 Cinisello
Balsamo

Sagep Editori SRL
Via Corsica 21/5, 16128 Genoa
Tel: (010) 5959539 *Fax:* (010) 8686209
E-mail: info@sagep.it
Web Site: www.sagep.it
Founded: 1965
Subjects: Architecture & Interior Design, Art,
Economics, Ethnicity, Fiction, History, Nonfic-
tion (General), Photography, Science (General),
Travel & Tourism
ISBN Prefix(es): 978-88-7058

il Saggiatore+
Via Melzo 9, 20129 Milan
Tel: (02) 202301
E-mail: stampa@ilsaggiatore.com
Web Site: www.ilsaggiatore.com
Key Personnel
Editor & President: Luca Formenton
Vice President: Mattia Formenton
Editorial Dir: Andrea Gentile
Sales Dir: Eleonora Col
Rights Dir & Acquistions Editor: Andrea Morsta-
bilini *E-mail:* morstabilini@ilsaggiatore.com
Founded: 1958
Subjects: Anthropology, Art, Asian Studies, Eco-
nomics, Fiction, Film, Video, History, Litera-
ture, Literary Criticism, Essays, Mathematics,
Music, Dance, Nonfiction (General), Philoso-
phy, Poetry, Romance, Science (General), So-
cial Sciences, Sociology, Nature
ISBN Prefix(es): 978-88-428; 978-88-515
Associate Companies: Marco Tropea Editore;
Nuova Practiche Editrice

Adriano Salani Editore SpA+
Via Gherardini 10, 20145 Milan
Tel: (02) 34597624 *Fax:* (02) 34597206
E-mail: info@salani.it
Web Site: www.salani.it
Key Personnel
President: Luigi Spagnol
Vice President: Guglielmo Tognetti
General Manager: Gianluca Mazzitelli
Publishing Dir: Mariagrazia Mazzitelli
Rights & Acquisitions Dir: Cristina Foschini
Press: Simona Scandellari *Tel:* (02) 34597632
E-mail: simona.scandellari@salani.it
Founded: 1862
Subjects: Fiction, Literature, Literary Criticism,
Essays, Nonfiction (General), Poetry
ISBN Prefix(es): 978-88-7782; 978-88-8451
Parent Company: Gruppo Editoriale Mauri Spag-
nol SpA
U.S. Office(s): Del Commune Enterprises, 285 W
Broadway, Suite 310, New York, NY 10013,
United States
Warehouse: Messaggerie Italiane, Magazzino Edi-
toriale, Via Bereguardina, 20080 Casarile MI
Orders to: ProLibro

Salerno Editrice SRL+
Via Valadier 52, 00193 Rome
Tel: (06) 3608 201 *Fax:* (06) 3223 132

E-mail: info@salernoeditrice.it;
ufficiomarketing@salernoeditrice.it
Web Site: www.salernoeditrice.it
Key Personnel
President & Dir, Publishing: Enrico Malato
E-mail: e.malato@salernoeditrice.it
Sales Manager: Luigi Cavo *E-mail:* luigi.cavo@
salernoeditrice.it
External Relations & Press: Debora Pisano
E-mail: d.pisano@salernoeditrice.it
Marketing: Annalisa Capparelli
Rights: Cetty Spadaro *E-mail:* c.spadaro@
salernoeditrice.it
Founded: 1972
Subjects: Art, Biography, Memoirs, Drama, The-
ater, Fiction, History, Language Arts, Linguis-
tics, Literature, Literary Criticism, Essays, Mu-
sic, Dance, Social Sciences, Sociology, Historic
Studies, Italian Literature
ISBN Prefix(es): 978-88-85026; 978-88-8402
Number of titles published annually: 40 Print
Warehouse: Viale dei Colli Portuensi, 591, Rome
00151 *Tel:* (06) 55266684

Edizioni San Lorenzo
Via Mohandas Karamchand Gandhi 18, 42123
Reggio Emilia RE
Tel: (0522) 323140 *Fax:* (0522) 323140
Founded: 1985
Subjects: Inspirational, Spirituality, Religion -
Catholic, Theology
ISBN Prefix(es): 978-88-8071

Edizioni San Paolo+
Piazza Soncino 5, 20092 Cinisello Balsamo MI
Tel: (02) 660751 *Fax:* (02) 66075211
E-mail: sanpaoloedizioni@stpauls.it; disp.
segreteria@stpauls.it
Web Site: www.edizionisanpaolo.it
Key Personnel
Editorial Dir: Giacomo Perego
Founded: 1914
Subjects: Art, Biography, Memoirs, Fiction, His-
tory, How-to, Medicine, Nursing, Dentistry,
Music, Dance, Philosophy, Psychology, Psy-
chiatry, Religion - Catholic, Science (General),
Theology
ISBN Prefix(es): 978-88-215
Parent Company: Societa San Paolo, Rome
Subsidiaries: DISP SRL; Multimedia San Paolo
SRL; Periodici San Paolo SRL; SAIE Editrice
SRL
Warehouse: DISP SRL, Piazza San Paolo 14, I-
12051 Alba *Tel:* (0173) 361040 (Cuneo)

Sapere 2000 SRL
Piazza Manfredo Fanti 42, 00185 Rome
Tel: (06) 4465363 *Fax:* (06) 4465363
Web Site: www.sapere2000.it
Founded: 1976
Subjects: Architecture & Interior Design, Ethnic-
ity, Government, Political Science, Religion -
Other, Social Sciences, Sociology
ISBN Prefix(es): 978-88-7673

Sapiens edizioni, *imprint of* Casagrande Fidia
Sapiens - Editori Associati SRL

Sardini Editrice SRL+
Via della Pace, 73, 25046 Bornato in Franciacorta
BS
Tel: (030) 7750430 *Fax:* (030) 7254348
E-mail: sardini@sardini.it
Web Site: www.sardini.it
Key Personnel
Chief Executive & Editorial: Davide Sardini
Founded: 1969
Subjects: Agriculture, Anthropology, Archaeol-
ogy, Art, Biblical Studies, Fiction, History,
Inspirational, Spirituality, Literature, Literary
Criticism, Essays, Medicine, Nursing, Den-
tistry, Nonfiction (General), Poetry, Regional

Interests, Religion - Catholic, Science (General), Theology, Travel & Tourism
ISBN Prefix(es): 978-88-7506
Subsidiaries: Bibbia e Oriente; Intelligenza e Informatica SRL

Sarnus, *imprint of* Edizioni Polistampa

Sassi Editore SRL
Viale Roma 122/b, 36015 Schio VI
Tel: (0445) 523772
E-mail: info@sassieditore.it
Web Site: www.sassieditore.it
Key Personnel
Dir: Luca Sassi
Commercial Dir: Massimo Comin
  E-mail: massimo@sassieditore.it
Founded: 2005
Also publishes coffee table books.
Subjects: Architecture & Interior Design, Art, Gardening, Plants, Photography, Travel & Tourism, Fine Arts, Lifestyle, Nature
ISBN Prefix(es): 978-88-96045
Distribution Center: Messaggerie Libri SpA, Via Verdi 8, 20090 Assago MI *Tel:* (02) 45 774 200; (02) 45 774 210 *Web Site:* www. messaggerielibri.it

Edizioni la Scala
Abbazia Madonna Della Scala, Zona B58, 70015 Noci (Bari)
Tel: (080) 4975838 *Fax:* (080) 4975839
E-mail: edizionilascala@gmail.com
Web Site: www.abbazialascala.it
Key Personnel
Chief Executive, Editorial: Padre Giuseppe Quirino Poggi
Founded: 1947
Subjects: Biography, Memoirs, Music, Dance, Philosophy, Religion - Catholic
Number of titles published annually: 3 Print
Total Titles: 3 Print

Scala Group SpA+
Via Chiantigiana 62/I, 50012 Bagno a Repoli FI
Tel: (055) 6233200; (055) 6233257; (055) 6233210 *Fax:* (055) 641124
E-mail: firenze@scalarchives.it
Web Site: www.scalarchives.it
Key Personnel
President: Prof Stefano Passigli *Tel:* (055) 6233333 *E-mail:* s.passigli@scalagroup.com
Vice President: Alvise Passigli *Fax:* (055) 6233280 *E-mail:* a.passigli@scalagroup.com
Mng Dir: Gianni Mancassola *Tel:* (055) 6233211
Founded: 1953
Publisher of museum & art guides. Also book packager & broadband files.
Subjects: Archaeology, Art, Education, Film, Video, Photography, Travel & Tourism
ISBN Prefix(es): 978-88-8117; 978-88-87090
Number of titles published annually: 100 Print; 20 CD-ROM; 5 Online
Total Titles: 500 Print; 200 CD-ROM; 10 Online
Subsidiaries: E-ducation.it
Distributed by Hazan (Francophone countries); Riverside (Canada & USA); Slovo (Russia)
Foreign Rights: Art Resource (USA); Scala/Art Resource (London)

Scalpendi Editore SRL
Piazza Antonio Gramsci, 9, 20154 Milan
Tel: (02) 8055266 *Fax:* (02) 8055266
E-mail: info@scalpendieditore.eu; redazione@scalpendieditore.eu
Web Site: www.scalpendieditore.eu
Key Personnel
Editor: Simone Amerigo *E-mail:* s.amerigo@scalpendieditore.eu; Manuela Beretta *E-mail:* m.beretta@scalpendieditore.eu; Carla

Bombari *E-mail:* c.bombari@scalpendieditore.eu
Founded: 1996
Subjects: Art, Fiction, History, Photography, Religion - Other
ISBN Prefix(es): 978-88-89546

Lo Scarabeo+
Via Cigna, 110, 10155 Turin
Tel: (011) 283793 *Fax:* (011) 280756
E-mail: info@loscarabeo.com
Web Site: www.loscarabeo.com
Key Personnel
Chief Executive Officer: Mario Pignatiello
Art Dir: Pietro Alligo
Founded: 1987
Specialize in tarot publishing.
Subjects: Art, Comics, Tarot
ISBN Prefix(es): 978-88-86131; 978-88-6527; 978-88-8395

Schena Editore SRL+
Via dell' Agricoltura 63/65-Zona Industriale, 72015 Fasano BR
Tel: (080) 4426690 *Fax:* (080) 4426690
E-mail: info@schenaeditore.it
Web Site: www.schenaeditore.it
Key Personnel
Editor: Angela Schena
Founded: 1972
Subjects: Archaeology, Architecture & Interior Design, Art, Fiction, Geography, Geology, History, Language Arts, Linguistics, Literature, Literary Criticism, Essays, Medicine, Nursing, Dentistry, Philosophy, Poetry, Psychology, Psychiatry, Religion - Other, Travel & Tourism, Cinema
ISBN Prefix(es): 978-88-7514; 978-88-8229

Salvatore Sciascia Editore
Corso Umberto I, 111, 93100 Caltanissetta
Tel: (0934) 21946; (0934) 551509 *Fax:* (0934) 551336
E-mail: sciasciaeditore@virgilio.it
Key Personnel
Mng Dir: Giuseppe Sciascia
Founded: 1946
Subjects: Art, History, Literature, Literary Criticism, Essays, Poetry
ISBN Prefix(es): 978-88-8241
Warehouse: Via Pietro Leone SN, 93100 Caltanissetta

Libreria Scientifica Cortina, see Libreria Cortina Editrice SRL

Edizioni Scientifiche Italiane+
Via Chiatamone, 7, 80121 Naples
Tel: (081) 7645443 *Fax:* (081) 7646477
E-mail: info@edizioniesi.it; amministrazione@edizioniesi.it; redazione@edizioniesi.it (editorial); ufficiovendite@edizioniesi.it (sales)
Web Site: www.edizioniesi.it
Key Personnel
President: Pietro Perlingieri
Founded: 1945
Subjects: Architecture & Interior Design, Art, Cookery, Drama, Theater, Economics, Engineering (General), Geography, Geology, History, Law, Literature, Literary Criticism, Essays, Medicine, Nursing, Dentistry, Music, Dance, Philosophy, Psychology, Psychiatry, Science (General), Social Sciences, Sociology, Technology
ISBN Prefix(es): 978-88-7104; 978-88-8114; 978-88-495
Branch Office(s)
Via dei Taurini, 27, 00185 Rome *Tel:* (06) 4462664 *Fax:* (06) 4461308 *E-mail:* roma@edizioniesi.it

Editoriale Scienza srl, *imprint of* Giunti Editore SpA

Editoriale Scienza srl (Science Publishing)+
Imprint of Giunti Editore SpA
Via Beccaria, 6, 34133 Trieste TS
Tel: (040) 364810 *Fax:* (040) 364909
E-mail: info@editorialescienza.it
Web Site: www.editorialescienza.it
Key Personnel
Editorial Dir & Publisher: Helene Stavro
  E-mail: redazione@editorialescienza.it
Editor: Federica Frederich *E-mail:* segreteria@editorialescienza.it
Administration: Federica Carisi
  E-mail: amministrazione@editorialescienza.it
Sales: Sabina Stavro *E-mail:* commerciale@editorialescienza.it
Press: Marilisa Cons *E-mail:* ufficiostampa@editorialescienza.it
Founded: 1993
Specialize in science books for children.
Membership(s): Associazione Italiana Editori (AIE).
Subjects: Animals, Pets, Astronomy, Biological Sciences, Computer Science, Crafts, Games, Hobbies, Earth Sciences, Geography, Geology, Health, Nutrition, Mathematics, Nonfiction (General), Physical Sciences, Science (General), Science Fiction, Fantasy, Technology
ISBN Prefix(es): 978-88-7307
Number of titles published annually: 20 Print
Imprints: ES
Distributed by Messaggerie Libri

Scienze e Lettere
Via Piave 7, 00817 Rome
Tel: (06) 4817656 *Fax:* (06) 48912574
E-mail: info@scienzeelettere.com
Web Site: www.scienzeelettere.it
Key Personnel
Mng Editor & Press: Dr Helga Di Giuseppe
  E-mail: helgadigiuseppe@scienzeelettere.com
Mng Editor: Dr Laurentino Garcia y Garcia
Founded: 1919
Specialize in Oriental studies, scientific books, subscription & mail order books.
Subjects: Antiques, Archaeology, Architecture & Interior Design, Fiction, History, Language Arts, Linguistics, Music, Dance, Science (General), Oriental Studies
ISBN Prefix(es): 978-88-85699; 978-88-88620
Total Titles: 100 Print
Bookshop(s): Palazzo Corsini, Via della Lungara, 10, Piano Terra, Rome, Contact: Bruno Chillemi *Tel:* (06) 68027211 *Fax:* (06) 4817656 *E-mail:* bookshopscienzeelettere@gmail.com

Scripta Maneant SRL
Via Yuri Gagarin, 33/4, 42123 Reggio Emilia RE
Tel: (051) 223535 *Toll Free Tel:* 0800 144 944
E-mail: segreteria@scriptamaneant.it; ufficio.stampa@scriptamaneant.it (press)
Web Site: www.scriptamaneant.it
Key Personnel
Chief Executive Officer: Giorgio Armaroli
  E-mail: g.armaroli@scriptamaneant.it
President: Raffaele Martena *E-mail:* r.martena@scriptamaneant.it
Editorial Dir: Federico Ferrari *E-mail:* f.ferrari@scriptamaneant.it
Press: Silvia Gnoni *E-mail:* s.gnoni@scriptamaneant.it
Subjects: Architecture & Interior Design, Art, History
ISBN Prefix(es): 978-88-95847

Scuola & Azienda, *imprint of* Mondadori Education

Editrice la Scuola SpA+
Via Antonio Gramsci, 26, 25121 Brescia

Tel: (030) 2993 1 *Fax:* (030) 2993 299
E-mail: servizioclienti@lascuola.it
Web Site: www.lascuola.it
Key Personnel
President: Dr Ing Luciano Silveri
Marketing Manager: Valentina Rinaldi *Tel:* (030) 2993 290 *E-mail:* pubblicita@lascuola.it
Founded: 1904
Subjects: Education, Philosophy, Psychology, Psychiatry, Religion - Other
ISBN Prefix(es): 978-88-350
Associate Companies: Editrice Morcelliana SpA
Branch Office(s)
via G Petroni 21 a/e, 70124 Bari *Tel:* (080) 5573841 *E-mail:* bari@lascuola.it
via Bligny, 7, 20136 Milan *Tel:* (02) 58301579 *E-mail:* milano@lascuola.it
Salita S Elia ai Miracoli, 19/21, 80137 Naples *Tel:* (081) 441200 *E-mail:* napoli@lascuola.it
via della Croce Rossa, 116, 35129 Padua *Tel:* (049) 8076775 *E-mail:* padova@lascuola.it
via Donatello, 7/11, 65124 Pescara *Tel:* (085) 74792 *E-mail:* pescara@lascuola.it
via Crescenzio, 23, 00193 Rome *Tel:* (06) 68803989 *E-mail:* roma@lascuola.it

SEA, *imprint of* Institutum Patristicum Augustinianum

Edizioni SEB27
via Accademia Albertina, 21, 10123 Turin
Tel: (011) 19504203 *Fax:* (011) 0207676
Web Site: www.seb27.it
Founded: 1992
Subjects: Drama, Theater, History, Literature, Literary Criticism, Essays, Social Sciences, Sociology, Women's Studies, World History
ISBN Prefix(es): 978-88-86618
Distribution Center: DIEST, V Cognetti de Martiis 39, 10149 Turin *Tel:* (011) 898 11 64 *Fax:* (011) 898 11 64 *E-mail:* posta@diestlibri.it
Messaggerie Libri SpA, Via G Verdi 8, 20090 Assago MI *Tel:* (02) 45774 1 *Fax:* (02) 45701032 *E-mail:* meli.dirgen@meli.it *Web Site:* www.messaggerielibri.it

SEEd SRL
Via Vittorio Alfieri, 17, 10121 Turin
Tel: (011) 566 02 58
E-mail: info@edizioniseed.it
Web Site: www.edizioniseed.it
Subjects: Medicine, Nursing, Dentistry, Science (General), Diagnostic
ISBN Prefix(es): 978-88-8968

Edizioni Segno SAS+
Via E Fermi, 80/1, 33010 Tavagnacco UD
Tel: (0432) 575179 *Fax:* (0432) 575589
E-mail: info@edizionisegno.it; ordini@edizionisegno.it; redazione@edizionisegno.it
Web Site: www.edizionisegno.it
Key Personnel
Dir: Pietro Mantero
Founded: 1988
Subjects: Biblical Studies, Fiction, Inspirational, Spirituality, Mysteries, Suspense, Nonfiction (General), Poetry, Religion - Catholic, Theology, Private Revelations, Signs of the Times Based on a Catholic Background, Supernatural
ISBN Prefix(es): 978-88-7282; 978-88-6138
Number of titles published annually: 70 Print
Total Titles: 400 Print

Segretariato Nazionale Apostolato della Preghiera+
Via degli Astalli, 16, 00186 Rome
Tel: (06) 697 607 207 *Fax:* (06) 678 10 63
E-mail: adp@adp.it
Web Site: www.adp.it

Key Personnel
Dir: Rev Tommaso Guadagno *Tel:* (06) 697 607 203 *E-mail:* tg@adp.it
Founded: 1844
Subjects: Religion - Catholic
ISBN Prefix(es): 978-88-7357
Imprints: AdP

SEI, see Societa Editrice Internazionale (SEI)

Sellerio Editore SRL
Via Siracusa, 50, 90141 Palermo PA
Tel: (091) 6254194 *Fax:* (091) 9255737
E-mail: info@sellerio.it; commerciale@sellerio.it (sales)
Web Site: www.sellerio.it
Founded: 1969
Subjects: Anthropology, Archaeology, Art, History, Literature, Literary Criticism, Essays, Photography, Social Sciences, Sociology
ISBN Prefix(es): 978-88-7681
Distribution Center: Messaggerie Libri SpA, Via Verdi, 8, 20090 Assago MI *Tel:* (02) 457741 *Fax:* (02) 45701032 *Web Site:* www.messaggerielibri.it/irj/portal

Servitium Editrice
Priorato S Egidio, 24039 Sotto il Monte BG
E-mail: ordini@servitium.it
Web Site: www.servitium.it
Founded: 1964
Subjects: Anthropology, Religion - Catholic, Romance, Theology, Spiritual
ISBN Prefix(es): 978-88-8166
Distributed by Dehoniana Libri SpA (Italy only)

Servizio Italiano Pubblicazioni Internazionali SRL, see SIPI (Servizio Italiano Pubblicazioni Internazionali) SRL

Edizioni Dr Antonino Sfameni, see EDAS

Sicania+
Imprint of Gem SRL
Via Catania 62, 98124 Messina ME
Tel: (090) 2936373 *Fax:* (090) 2932461
E-mail: info@gem.me.it; redazione@sicania.me.it
Web Site: www.sicania.me.it; www.gem.me.it
Key Personnel
Publisher: Ugo Magno
Dir: Francesco Alibrandi
Editor: Anita Magno
Public Relations: Melania Crisafi
Founded: 1886
Subjects: Archaeology, Philosophy
ISBN Prefix(es): 978-88-7268
Subsidiaries: Edizioni GBM

Edizioni Librarie Siciliane+
Contrada Rebuttone Ciaramella, 90030 Santa Cristina Gela PA
Tel: (091) 8570221
Founded: 1978
Subjects: Anthropology, Antiques, Archaeology, Architecture & Interior Design, Art, History, Human Relations, Natural History, Philosophy
Imprints: ELS

Sigma, *imprint of* Gruppo Editoriale Esselibri Simone

C Signorelli Scuola, *imprint of* Mondadori Education

Sillabe SRL
Scali d'Azeglio 22-24, 57123 Livorno
Tel: (0586) 839784; (0586) 829931 *Fax:* (0586) 208826

E-mail: info@sillabe.it; commerciale@sillabe.it (sales)
Web Site: www.sillabe.it
Key Personnel
Dir: Elisabetta Tedeschi *E-mail:* tedeschi@sillabe.it
Editorial Dir: Maddalena Paola Winspeare
Press: Ethel Santacroce *E-mail:* santacroce@sillabe.it
Sales: Sandra Bernardi
Founded: 1998
Subjects: Architecture & Interior Design, Art, Drama, Theater, Music, Dance, Nonfiction (General)
ISBN Prefix(es): 978-88-8347; 978-88-86392

Silva Editore SRL
Via Pelacani, 8, 43123 Parma PR
Tel: (0521) 804106 *Fax:* (0521) 804406
E-mail: info@silvaeditore.it
Web Site: www.silvaeditore.it
Founded: 1993
ISBN Prefix(es): 978-88-7765

Silvana Editoriale D'Arte+
Via Margherita de Vizzi 86, 20092 Cinisello Balsamo, Milan MI
Tel: (02) 61836 1 *Fax:* (02) 6172464
E-mail: direzione@silvanaeditoriale.it; silvanaeditoriale@silvanaeditoriale.it; press@silvanaeditoriale.it
Web Site: www.silvanaeditoriale.it
Key Personnel
Chief Executive Officer & Editorial Dir: Dario Cimorelli *Tel:* (02) 61836357
Library Mng Dir: Laura Varisco *Tel:* (02) 61836395 *E-mail:* laura.varisco@silvanaeditoriale.it
Press: Lidia Masolini *Tel:* (02) 61836287 *Fax:* (02) 61836392
Founded: 1948
Subjects: Architecture & Interior Design, Art, Photography
ISBN Prefix(es): 978-88-366; 978-88-8215
Parent Company: Amilcare Pizzi SpA
Foreign Rep(s): Garzon Diffusion Internationale (Europe); John Rules Sales & Marketing (Denmark, Faroe Islands, Finland, Greenland, Iceland, Ireland, Norway, Sweden, UK); United Publishers Services Ltd (Japan); Vilo groupe (France)
Distribution Center: Messaggerie Libri SpA, Via Giuseppe Verdi, 8, 20090 Assago MI *Tel:* (02) 45774200 *Fax:* (02) 45774230

SIME Books
Via Italia 34/E, 31020 San Vendemiano TV
Tel: (0438) 402 581 *Fax:* (0438) 408 630
E-mail: info@simebooks.com
Web Site: www.simebooks.com
Subjects: Cookery, Travel & Tourism
ISBN Prefix(es): 978-88-95218

Edizioni Simone, *imprint of* Gruppo Editoriale Esselibri Simone

Edizioni Giuridiche Simone, *imprint of* Gruppo Editoriale Esselibri Simone

Simone per la Scuola, *imprint of* Gruppo Editoriale Esselibri Simone

Sinnos
Via dei Foscari 18, 00162 Rome RM
Tel: (06) 44240603; (06) 44119098 *Fax:* (06) 62276832
E-mail: info@sinnos.org
Web Site: www.sinnos.org
Key Personnel
President: Della Passarelli
E-mail: dellapassarelli@sinnos.org

Vice President: Elisa Battaglia
    E-mail: elisabattaglia@sinnos.org
Dir: Rossella Donato *E-mail:* rosselladonato@
    sinnos.org
Editor: Elia Crivelli *E-mail:* eliacrivelli@sinnos.
    org
ISBN Prefix(es): 978-88-7609; 978-88-86061

SIPI, *imprint of* SIPI (Servizio Italiano
Pubblicazioni Internazionali) SRL

**SIPI (Servizio Italiano Pubblicazioni
Internazionali) SRL**
Viale Pasteur, 6, 00100 Rome
Tel: (06) 5918856; (06) 5920509; (06) 5924819
E-mail: sipi@confindustria.it
Key Personnel
President: Daniel Kraus
Mng Dir: Luigi Paparoni
Founded: 1952
Offers insight into & up-to-date information on
    the Italian economic situation, taking into ac-
    count current developments & the increasingly
    competitive environment in Italian industry.
Subjects: Economics, Government, Political Sci-
    ence, Labor, Industrial Relations, Regional In-
    terests
ISBN Prefix(es): 978-88-7153
Imprints: SIPI

Sironi Editore, see Alpha Test - Sironi Editore

Sistemi Editorali, *imprint of* Gruppo Editoriale
Esselibri Simone

66thand2nd
Via Marcello Malpighi, 12 A, 00161 Rome RM
Tel: (06) 44254467
E-mail: info@66thand2nd.com
Web Site: www.66thand2nd.com
Founded: 2008
Subjects: Biography, Memoirs, Criminology, Fic-
    tion, Mysteries, Suspense, Sports, Athletics,
    Travel & Tourism
ISBN Prefix(es): 978-88-96538; 978-88-98970

Skira Editore
Palazzo Casati Stampa, Via Torino, 61, 20123
    Milan
Tel: (02) 724441 *Fax:* (02) 72444211
E-mail: bookstore@skira.net; international@skira.
    net
Web Site: www.skira.net
Key Personnel
International Marketing & Sales Manager: Silvia
    Riboldi
Marketing & Sales Dir: Fabio Abate
Founded: 1928
Subjects: Archaeology, Architecture & Interior
    Design, Art, Education, Fashion, Fiction, Liter-
    ature, Literary Criticism, Essays, Music, Dance,
    Photography, Poetry, Applied Arts, Art History,
    Entertainment, Modern Art, Visual Arts
ISBN Prefix(es): 978-2-605 (Skira Geneve); 978-
    88-7624; 978-88-8118; 978-88-8491; 978-88-
    85215; 978-88-6130; 978-88-572
Distributed by Random House (Canada, Central
    & South America, USA)
Foreign Rep(s): Bas van der Zee (Belgium, Lux-
    embourg, Netherlands); Bookcity Co (Iran);
    Per Burell (Baltic States, Russia, Scandinavia);
    Peter Hyde Associates (Botswana, Lesotho,
    Namibia, South Africa, Swaziland, Zimbabwe);
    Interart Sarl (France); Levant Distributors
    (Lebanon); Thames & Hudson (Australia) Pty
    Ltd (Australia, New Zealand, Pacific Islands,
    Papua New Guinea); Thames & Hudson China
    Ltd (China, Hong Kong, Macau); Thames &
    Hudson Ltd (Scipio Stringer) (India, Japan,
    Pakistan, Sri Lanka); Thames & Hudson Ltd
    (Sara Ticci) (Germany, Switzerland); Thames

& Hudson Ltd (Stephen Embrey) (Eastern Eu-
rope, Eastern Mediterranean, Egypt, Middle
East); Thames & Hudson Ltd (Ian Bartley)
(Africa exc South Africa); Thames & Hudson
Ltd (Natasha French) (Italy, Portugal, Spain);
Thames & Hudson Pty Ltd (Malaysia); Thames
& Hudson Singapore (Singapore, Southeast
Asia); Vertreterbuero Wuerburg (Michael Klein)
(Austria, Germany exc South Germany); Karin
White (Ireland); Zeenat Book Supply Ltd
(Bangladesh)
Distribution Center: Littlehampton Book Ser-
vices Ltd, Faraday Close, Durrington, Wort-
ing, West Sussex BN13 3RB, United Kingdom
Tel: (01903) 828500; (01903) 828501 (cus-
tomer service) *Web Site:* lbsltd.wp.hachette.co.
uk

Slow Food Editore, *imprint of* Giunti Editore
SpA

Societa editrice il Mulino Spa+
Str Maggiore 37, 40125 Bologna
Tel: (051) 256011 *Fax:* (051) 256034
E-mail: info@mulino.it; diffusione@mulino.it
    (sales); stampa@mulino.it (press)
Web Site: www.mulino.it
Key Personnel
Mng Dir: Giuliano Bassani
Editorial Dir: Andrea Angiolini
Sales Dir: Barbara Puccini
Foreign Rights Manager: Paola Pecchioli
    E-mail: paola.pecchioli@mulino.it
Press Office: Cristina Ricotti
Founded: 1954
Academic publisher. Specialize in humanities &
    social sciences.
This publisher has indicated that 25% of their
    product line is author subsidized.
Membership(s): Associazione Italiana Editori
    (AIE).
Subjects: Economics, Government, Political Sci-
    ence, History, Language Arts, Linguistics, Law,
    Philosophy, Psychology, Psychiatry, Social Sci-
    ences, Sociology, Humanities
ISBN Prefix(es): 978-88-15

Societa Editrice Internazionale (SEI)+
Corso Regina Margherita, 176, 10152 Turin
Tel: (011) 5227 1 *Fax:* (011) 5211 320
E-mail: editoriale@seieditrice.com
Web Site: www.seieditrice.com
Founded: 1908
Subjects: Architecture & Interior Design, Art, Bi-
    ography, Memoirs, Biological Sciences, Chem-
    istry, Chemical Engineering, Civil Engineer-
    ing, Education, Fiction, Geography, Geology,
    History, Literature, Literary Criticism, Essays,
    Mathematics, Philosophy, Physics, Psychology,
    Psychiatry, Religion - Catholic, Science (Gen-
    eral), Sports, Athletics, Construction, Physical
    Education
ISBN Prefix(es): 978-88-05

Societa Napoletana di Storia Patria Napoli
Via Vittorio Emanuelle III, Castelnuovo, 80133
    Naples
Tel: (081) 551 03 53 *Fax:* (081) 551 03 53
E-mail: info@storiapatrianapoli.it
Web Site: www.storiapatrianapoli.it
Key Personnel
President: Prof Renata De Lorenzo
    E-mail: deloren@unina.it
Vice President: Prof Aurelio Musi *E-mail:* musi@
    unina.it
Treasurer: Prof Nichola De Blasi
    E-mail: deblasi@unina.it
Founded: 1861
Subjects: History, Art History, Diplomatics,
    Monographies
ISBN Prefix(es): 978-88-8044

Societa Stampa Sportiva SRL+
Viale di Villa Pamphili n 33/F, 00152 Rome
Tel: (06) 5817311; (06) 5882314 *Fax:* (06)
    5806526
Key Personnel
President: Francesco Paolo Palumbo
Founded: 1967
Subjects: Physical Sciences, Sports, Athletics
ISBN Prefix(es): 978-88-8313
Number of titles published annually: 20 Print
Total Titles: 532 Print

Societa Storica Catanese
Via Etnea, 248, 95131 Catania CT
Tel: (095) 311124
E-mail: societastoricacatanese@gmail.com
Founded: 2012
Subjects: History, Law, Literature, Literary Criti-
    cism, Essays, Poetry, Regional Interests, Social
    Sciences, Sociology
Imprints: SSC

Il Sole 24 Ore Pirola
Via Monte Rosa, 91, 20149 Milan
Tel: (02) 3022-1 *Fax:* (02) 30225400
E-mail: servizioclienti.libri@ilsole24ore.com
Web Site: www.ilsole24ore.com
Founded: 1781
Subjects: Architecture & Interior Design, Busi-
    ness, Economics, Engineering (General), Law,
    Management, Social Sciences, Sociology
ISBN Prefix(es): 978-88-7187; 978-88-324; 978-
    88-8363
Parent Company: Gruppo24Ore

Edizioni Sonda+
Corso Indipendenza 63, 15033 Casale Monferrato
    AL
Tel: (0142) 461516 *Fax:* (0142) 461523
E-mail: sonda@sonda.it
Web Site: www.sonda.it
Key Personnel
Editor: Antonio Monaco
Foreign Rights: Alice Assandri *E-mail:* alice.
    assandri@sonda.it
Founded: 1988
Subjects: Animals, Pets, Education, Health, Nutri-
    tion, Humor
ISBN Prefix(es): 978-88-7106
Associate Companies: Consorzio "Leonardo";
    Consorzio "Omniatech"; Il Tappeto Volante srl

Sonzogno Editori SpA
Division of RCS Libri SpA
Marittima-Fabbricato 205, 30135 Venice
Tel: (041) 2406511 *Fax:* (041) 5238352
E-mail: redazione@sonzognoeditori.it;
    ufficiostampa@sonzognoeditori.it
Web Site: www.sonzognoeditori.it
Founded: 1818
Subjects: Fiction, Mysteries, Suspense, Nonfiction
    (General)
ISBN Prefix(es): 978-88-451; 978-88-452; 978-
    88-454
Ultimate Parent Company: RCS MediaGroup
    SpA

Edizioni Sorbona+
Via Michele Pietravalle, 85, 80131 Naples
Tel: (081) 5453443 *Fax:* (081) 5464991
E-mail: info@igmultimedia.it
Web Site: www.idelsongnocchi.it
Founded: 1981
Subjects: Chemistry, Chemical Engineering,
    Medicine, Nursing, Dentistry, Physics, Science
    (General)
ISBN Prefix(es): 978-88-7150
Parent Company: Idelson Gnocchi
U.S. Office(s): 1316 Kings Bay Dr, Crystal River,
    FL 34429, United States *Tel:* 352-794-6234
    Fax: 352-794-6234 *E-mail:* candotti@att.net

Sovera Edizioni SRL
Via Vicenzo Brunacci, 55-55A, 00146 Rome
Tel: (06) 5585265; (06) 5562429 *Fax:* (06)
5580723
E-mail: info@soveraedizioni.it
Web Site: www.soveraedizioni.it
Key Personnel
Editorial Dir: Salvatore Merra
Sales Dir: Andrea Lacometti
Press: Lucia Pasquini
Founded: 1982
Subjects: Biography, Memoirs, Drama, Theater,
Fiction, Poetry, Psychology, Psychiatry, Sci-
ence Fiction, Fantasy, Cinema, Esoterism, Psy-
chotherapy
ISBN Prefix(es): 978-88-8124; 978-88-85119

Sperling & Kupfer, *imprint of* Sperling &
Kupfer Editori SpA

Sperling & Kupfer Editori SpA+
Subsidiary of Arnoldo Mondadori Editore SpA
Corso Como, 15, 20154 Milan
Tel: (02) 217211 *Fax:* (02) 21721377
E-mail: info@sperling.it
Web Site: www.sperling.it
Key Personnel
Chief Executive Officer: Giuseppe Baroffio
Head, Press & Events: Paola Caviggioli
Foreign Rights: Agnese Fabbri *E-mail:* skrights@
sperling.it
Rights & Permissions & Contract: Stefania Klein
De Pasquale
Founded: 1899
Subjects: Biography, Memoirs, Economics, Fic-
tion, Health, Nutrition, How-to, Management,
Nonfiction (General), Science (General)
ISBN Prefix(es): 978-88-7684; 978-88-200; 978-
88-86845; 978-88-87592; 978-88-7339; 978-
88-7824; 978-88-8274; 978-88-88320; 978-88-
6061; 978-88-6114
Total Titles: 350 Print
Imprints: Edizioni Frassinelli SRL; Sperling &
Kupfer
U.S. Office(s): 38 E 57 St, 7th floor, New York,
NY 10022, United States (scout office)
Foreign Rep(s): Franklin & Siegal Associates
(Kalah McCaffrey)

Spirali Edizioni+
Via Gabrio Serbelloni 5, 20122 Milan
Tel: (02) 8054417; (02) 8053602 *Fax:* (02)
8692631
E-mail: press.spirali.mi@gmail.com
Web Site: www.spirali.it
Key Personnel
President: Cristina Frua De Angeli
Founded: 1973
Subjects: Architecture & Interior Design, Art, Bi-
ography, Memoirs, Business, Drama, Theater,
Economics, Environmental Studies, Fiction,
History, Language Arts, Linguistics, Law, Lit-
erature, Literary Criticism, Essays, Medicine,
Nursing, Dentistry, Music, Dance, Philosophy,
Poetry, Psychology, Psychiatry
ISBN Prefix(es): 978-88-7770
Number of titles published annually: 10 Print

Spoon River, *imprint of* Graphot Editrice

SSC, *imprint of* Societa Storica Catanese

Stampa Alternativa - Nuovi Equilibri+
Str Tuscanese Km 4, 800, 01100 Viterbo
Tel: (0761) 35 22 77; (0761) 35 34 85
Fax: (0761) 35 27 51
E-mail: redazione@stampalternativa.it
Web Site: www.stampalternativa.it
Key Personnel
Mng Dir, Editorial: Marcello Baraghini
Sales: Angelo Leone

Founded: 1971
Subjects: Art, Health, Nutrition, Literature, Lit-
erary Criticism, Essays, Medicine, Nursing,
Dentistry, Music, Dance
ISBN Prefix(es): 978-88-7226
Imprints: Cartoonseries; Fiabesca; Jazz People;
L'eta D'oro Dell Illustrazione
Orders to: Nuovi Equilibri, PO Box 97, 01100
Viterbo *Tel:* (0761) 352277 *Fax:* (0761) 352751
E-mail: ordini@stampalternativa.it

Edizioni Studio Domenicano+
Via Dell'Osservanza, 72, 40136 Bologna BO
Tel: (051) 582034 *Fax:* (051) 331583
Web Site: www.esd-domenicani.it
Key Personnel
Dir: Giorgio Carbone
Sales Manager: Domenico Gamarro
Press: Roberto Viglino
Founded: 1985
Subjects: Philosophy, Religion - Catholic, Social
Sciences, Sociology, Theology, Ancient Au-
thors (Armenian, Greek, Latin, Siriac), Works
of St Thomas Aquinas (Italian & Latin)
ISBN Prefix(es): 978-88-7094
Number of titles published annually: 45 Print; 1
CD-ROM
Total Titles: 750 Print
Distribution Center: Messaggero Distribuzione
SRL, Via Orto Botanico, 11, 35123 Padua

Edizioni Studio Tesi SRL
Subsidiary of Edizioni Mediterranee SRL
Via Flaminia, 109, 00196 Rome
Tel: (06) 3235433 *Fax:* (06) 3236277
E-mail: info@edizionimediterranee.net
Web Site: www.edizionimediterranee.net
Key Personnel
Chief Executive & Editorial: Giovanni Canonico
Founded: 1977
Subjects: Economics, Fiction, History, Literature,
Literary Criticism, Essays, Music, Dance, Sci-
ence (General)
ISBN Prefix(es): 978-88-7692
Subsidiaries: Edizioni dello Zibaldone

Edizioni Studium SRL+
Via Crescenzio, 25, 00193 Rome
Tel: (06) 6865846; (06) 6875456 *Fax:* (06)
6875456
E-mail: info@edizionistudium.it
Web Site: www.edizionistudium.it
Key Personnel
President: Vincenzo Cappelletti
Vice President: Giuseppe Camadini
Founded: 1927
Periodicals.
Subjects: History, Literature, Literary Criticism,
Essays, Philosophy, Religion - Catholic, Re-
ligion - Other, Science (General), Social Sci-
ences, Sociology
ISBN Prefix(es): 978-88-382
Number of titles published annually: 30 Print
Total Titles: 600 Print
Distributed by Editrice La Scuola

Sugarco Edizioni SRL
Via don Gnocchi, 4, 20148 Milan
Tel: (02) 4078370 *Fax:* (02) 4078493
E-mail: info@sugarcoedizioni.it
Web Site: www.sugarcoedizioni.it
Founded: 1957
Subjects: Biography, Memoirs, Fiction, History,
How-to, Philosophy, Poetry
ISBN Prefix(es): 978-88-7198

Tappeiner GmbH
Industriezone 6, 39011 Lana BZ
Tel: (0473) 56 36 66 *Fax:* (0473) 56 36 89
E-mail: info@tappeiner.it
Web Site: www.tappeiner.it

Subjects: Archaeology, Architecture & Interior
Design, Art, Cookery, Geography, Geology,
History, Outdoor Recreation
ISBN Prefix(es): 978-88-7073
Distribution Center: Grafus GmbH, Sir-Isaac-
Newton-Str, 39100 Bozen *Tel:* (0471) 08 64 44
Fax: (0471) 08 65 55 *E-mail:* order@grafus.it
(South Tyrol)
Mohr Morawa Buchvertrieb GmbH, Postfach
260, 1101 Vienna, Austria, Contact: Florian
Buechler *Tel:* (01) 680 14-0 *Fax:* (01) 680
14-140 *E-mail:* momo@mohrmorawa.at *Web
Site:* www.mohrmorawa.at
Herold Auslieferung & Service GmbH, Raiffeise-
nallee 10, 82041 Oberhaching, Germany, Con-
tact: Tina Ledebuhr *Tel:* (089) 61 38 71 16
Fax: (089) 61 38 71 55 16 *E-mail:* t.ledebuhr@
herold-va.de *Web Site:* www.herlod-va.de

Tascabili degli Editori Associati SpA, see TEA
(Tascabili degli Editori Associati SpA)

Tassotti Editore
Via S F Lazzaro, 103, 36061 Bassano del Grappa
VI
Tel: (0424) 882882 *Fax:* (0424) 566205
E-mail: info@tassotti.it
Web Site: www.tassotti.it
Founded: 1984
Subjects: Art, History, Travel & Tourism
ISBN Prefix(es): 978-88-7691
Divisions: Grafiche Tassotti SRL
Showroom(s): Via Ferracina, 16/18, 36061
Bassano del Grappa VI *Tel:* (0424) 523013
Fax: (0424) 523013 *E-mail:* carteriabassano@
tassotti.it; Via dei Servi, 9/11r, 50122 Flo-
rence *Tel:* (055) 2645477 *Fax:* (055) 2645477
E-mail: carteriafirenze@tassotti.it; Corso
Garibaldi, 54, 20121 Milan *Tel:* (02) 29011282
Fax: (02) 29011282 *E-mail:* carteriamilano@
tassotti.it

TEA (Tascabili degli Editori Associati SpA)+
Via Gherardini 10, 20145 Milan
Tel: (02) 34597625 *Fax:* (02) 34597204
E-mail: info@tealibri.it
Web Site: www.tealibri.it
Key Personnel
Chairman: Stefano Mauri
Mng Dir: Marco Taro
Editorial Dir: Stefano Res
Rights & Acquisitions Dir: Christina Foschini
Founded: 1987
Subjects: Art, Cookery, Fiction, Health, Nutrition,
History, How-to, Humor, Nonfiction (General),
Philosophy, Poetry, Psychology, Psychiatry,
Science Fiction, Fantasy, Self-Help
ISBN Prefix(es): 978-88-7818; 978-88-502; 978-
88-7819
Number of titles published annually: 200 Print
Total Titles: 1,600 Print
Parent Company: Gruppo Editoriale Mauri Spag-
nol SpA

Tecniche Nuove SpA+
Via Eritrea, 21, 20157 Milan
Tel: (02) 39090440 *Fax:* (02) 39090373; (02)
39090335 (subscriptions)
E-mail: info@tecnichenuove.com
Web Site: www.tecnichenuove.com
Key Personnel
Editorial: Antonio Ratti *Tel:* (02) 39090330
E-mail: antonio.ratti@tecnichenuove.com
Founded: 1960
Subjects: Agriculture, Architecture & Interior De-
sign, Biological Sciences, Business, Chem-
istry, Chemical Engineering, Computer Science,
Electronics, Electrical Engineering, Energy,
Health, Nutrition, Medicine, Nursing, Dentistry,
Music, Dance, Psychology, Psychiatry, Tech-
nology, Travel & Tourism, Veterinary Science,
Foreign Languages, Leisure

ISBN Prefix(es): 978-88-7081; 978-88-85009; 978-88-481
Number of titles published annually: 150 Print; 15 CD-ROM; 20 E-Book
Total Titles: 700 Print; 30 CD-ROM; 30 E-Book
Subsidiaries: Grafica Quadrifoglio
U.S. Office(s): Tecniche Nuove USA, 844 Gage Dr, San Diego, CA 92106, United States
Warehouse: Via Castel Morrone 15

Edizioni del Teresianum
Piazza San Pancrazio, 5/A, 00152 Rome
Tel: (06) 58540248 *Fax:* (06) 58540243
E-mail: segreteria.teresianum@gmail.com
Web Site: www.teresianum.org
Founded: 1966
Subjects: Biblical Studies, Biography, Memoirs, History, Religion - Catholic, Theology
ISBN Prefix(es): 978-88-85317
Parent Company: Edizioni dei Padri Carmelitani Scalzi, Corso d'Italia 38, 00198 Rome

Edizioni Terra Santa (ETS)
via Gherardini 5, 20145 Milan MI
Tel: (02) 34592679 *Fax:* (02) 31801980
E-mail: info@edizioniterrasanta.it
Web Site: www.edizioniterrasanta.it
Key Personnel
Foreign Rights: Elena Bolognesi
  E-mail: bolognesi@edizioniterrasanta.it; Roberto Orlandi *E-mail:* orlandi@edizioniterrasanta.it
Founded: 2005
Subjects: Archaeology, Religion - Islamic, Religion - Jewish, Religion - Other, Christianity, Judaism
ISBN Prefix(es): 978-88-6240
Distributor for Franciscan Printing Press (FPP)

Sandro Teti Editore
Viale Manzoni, 39, 00185 Rome
Tel: (06) 58179056; (06) 58334070 *Fax:* (06) 233236789
E-mail: info@sandrotetieditore.it; stampa@sandrotetieditore.it; redazione@sandrotetieditore.it
Web Site: www.sandrotetieditore.it
Key Personnel
Founder: Sandro Teti
Founded: 2002
Membership(s): Associazione Italiana Editori (AIE); Osservatorio Degli Editori Independenti (ODEI).
Subjects: Art, Drama, Theater, Fiction, Government, Political Science, History, Literature, Literary Criticism, Essays, Music, Dance, Photography, Poetry
ISBN Prefix(es): 978-88-88249

Thema, *imprint of* Loescher Editore SRL

Edizioni Thyrus SRL+
Via della Rinascita, 12, 05031 Arrone TR
Tel: (0744) 389496 *Fax:* (0744) 388700
E-mail: thyrusedizioni@libero.it; redazionethyrus@tiscali.it (press)
Web Site: www.edizionithyrus.it
Key Personnel
Mng Dir, Production, Rights & Permissions: Dr Osvaldo Panfili
Sales: Nobili Nevia
Founded: 1956
Subjects: Art, Education, Fiction, History, Literature, Literary Criticism, Essays, Nonfiction (General), Poetry, Psychology, Psychiatry, Regional Interests, Social Sciences, Sociology, Theology
ISBN Prefix(es): 978-88-87675
Book Club(s): Circolo Astrolabio

Tilgher-Genova SAS
Via Assarotti 31/15, 16122 Genoa GE
Tel: (010) 8391140 *Fax:* (010) 870653
Key Personnel
Chief Executive: Lucio Bozzi
Founded: 1972
Subjects: Biological Sciences, Literature, Literary Criticism, Essays, Philosophy
ISBN Prefix(es): 978-88-7903

Tomo Edizioni SRL+
Via Pienza, 255, 00138 Rome
Tel: (06) 8100920 *Fax:* (06) 8100920
Founded: 1989
Subjects: Art, Photography
ISBN Prefix(es): 978-88-7151

Topipittori
Viale Isonzo, 16, 20135 Milan MI
Tel: (02) 54107384 *Fax:* (02) 54107384
E-mail: redazione@topipittori.it
Web Site: www.topipittori.it
Key Personnel
Publisher: Giovanna Zoboli *E-mail:* giovanna@topipittori.it
Founded: 2004
ISBN Prefix(es): 978-88-89210

Edizioni di Torino, see EDT SRL

Touring Editore, *imprint of* Giunti Editore SpA

Touring Editore SRL
Str 1, Palazzo F/9, Milanofiori, 20090 Assago MI
Tel: (02) 5754 71 *Fax:* (02) 5754 7503
Web Site: internationaldivision.giunti.it
Key Personnel
Rights Manager: LeeAnn Bortolussi *E-mail:* l.bortolussi@giunti.it
Foreign Rights: Valentina Mazza *E-mail:* v.mazza@giunti.it
Founded: 1841
Subjects: Art, Cookery, Gardening, Plants, Health, Nutrition, History, Inspirational, Spirituality, Language Arts, Linguistics, Science (General), Travel & Tourism, Design, Nature
ISBN Prefix(es): 978-88-447; 978-88-7815; 978-88-365
Total Titles: 700 Print
Parent Company: Giunti Editore SpA

Touring Junior, *imprint of* Giunti Editore SpA

Giovanni Tranchida Editore+
Via Giuseppe Frua, 18, 20146 Milan
Tel: (02) 66 80 22 70 *Fax:* (02) 66 80 22 70
E-mail: info@tranchida.it
Web Site: www.tranchida.it
Key Personnel
Mng Dir: Giovanni Tranchida *E-mail:* tranchida@infinito.it
Founded: 1983
Membership(s): Associazione Italiana Editori (AIE).
Subjects: Architecture & Interior Design, Art, Fiction, History, Literature, Literary Criticism, Essays, Philosophy, Photography, Psychology, Psychiatry
ISBN Prefix(es): 978-88-8003; 978-88-85685
Distributor for Messaggerie Libri SpA

Editrice Trasporti su Rotaie, see ETR (Editrice Trasporti su Rotaie)

24 ORE Cultura SRL
Subsidiary of Gruppo 24 ORE
Via Monte Rosa 91, 20149 Milan
Tel: (02) 3022 1 *Fax:* (02) 3022 3776
E-mail: info@24orecultura.com; ufficiostampa@24orecultura.com

Web Site: www.24orecultura.com
Founded: 2011
Subjects: Architecture & Interior Design, Art, Fashion, Photography
ISBN Prefix(es): 978-88-6648

22publishing SRL
Via Morozzo della Rocca 9, 20123 Milan
Tel: (02) 8738 9383; (02) 8738 9384 *Fax:* (02) 8738 9945
E-mail: info@22publishing.it; press@22publishing.it; bookshop@22publishing.com
Web Site: www.22publishing.it
Key Personnel
Editorial Dir & Associate Editor: Francesca Tatarella *E-mail:* mf.tatarella@22publishing.it
Administrative Dir & Associate Editor: Marco Tatarella *E-mail:* m.tatarella@22publishing.it
Subjects: Architecture & Interior Design, Art, Contemporary Art, Landscape
ISBN Prefix(es): 978-88-95185
Distribution Center: Messaggerie Libri

Edizioni Ubulibri SAS+
Via Ramazzini, 8, 20129 Milan
Tel: (02) 20241604; (02) 45491573 *Fax:* (02) 36514067
E-mail: segreteria@ubulibri.it
Web Site: www.ubulibri.it
Key Personnel
Co-Owner: Lorenzo Quadri
Coordinator: Francesco Gajani
Founded: 1979
Subjects: Drama, Theater, Film, Video, Music, Dance
ISBN Prefix(es): 978-88-7748
Number of titles published annually: 12 Print
Total Titles: 160 Print
Warehouse: Messaggerie Libri SpA, Via Verdi 8, 20090 Assago *Tel:* (02) 457741

Editoriale Umbra SAS
Via Pignattara, 34, 06034 Foligno PG
Tel: (0742) 357541 *Fax:* (0742) 351156
E-mail: editumbra@libero.it; info@editorialeumbra.it
Web Site: www.editorialeumbra.it
Key Personnel
Mng Dir, Editorial, Rights & Permissions, Sales: Giovanni Carnevali
Founded: 1982
Subjects: Art, History, Literature, Literary Criticism, Essays, Regional Interests
ISBN Prefix(es): 978-88-85659; 978-88-88802

Edizioni Unicopli SRL+
Via Don Giuseppe Andreoli 20, 20158 Milan
Tel: (02) 42299666; (02) 4221067; (02) 48951687 *Fax:* (02) 58439561
E-mail: info@edizioniunicopli.it
Web Site: www.edizioniunicopli.it
Key Personnel
Chief Editor: Marzio Zanantoni
Editorial, Psychology, Psychiatry: Stefano Nutini
Founded: 1985
Subjects: Economics, Geography, Geology, Language Arts, Linguistics, Literature, Literary Criticism, Essays, Music, Dance, Philosophy
ISBN Prefix(es): 978-88-7061; 978-88-400; 978-88-7090
Warehouse: Via Velleia 4, 20900 Monza MB
  Tel: (039) 6056568 *Fax:* (039) 9462256
  E-mail: commerciale@edizioniunicopli.it

Unione Tipografico-Editrice Torinese, see UTET

Unipress Editrice+
Via Venezia 4/a, 35131 Padua
Tel: (049) 8075886
E-mail: info@unipress.it

Web Site: www.unipress.it
Founded: 1987
Subjects: Agriculture, Biological Sciences, Chemistry, Chemical Engineering, Language Arts, Linguistics, Literature, Literary Criticism, Essays, Philosophy, Psychology, Psychiatry
ISBN Prefix(es): 978-88-8098

Universale Economica Feltrinelli, *imprint of* Giangiacomo Feltrinelli Editore SRL

Editrice Uomini Nuovi SRL
Via G Mazzini 73, 21030 Marchirolo VA
Tel: (0332) 723007 *Fax:* (0332) 998080
E-mail: eunitaly@eun.ch (English matters)
Web Site: www.eun.ch
Key Personnel
President & Chief Executive, Editorial: Anna Laiso Rossinelli
Founded: 1964
Publish Christian books in Italian.
Subjects: Biblical Studies, Biography, Memoirs, Human Relations, Psychology, Psychiatry, Religion - Other, Self-Help
ISBN Prefix(es): 978-88-8077

Uovonero Edizioni SNC
via Marazzi 7, 26013 Crema CR
Tel: (0373) 500 622; (349) 3772839 (cell)
Fax: (0373) 09 08 88
E-mail: libri@uovonero.com
Web Site: www.uovonero.com
Key Personnel
Dir & Editor: Enza Crivelli *E-mail:* enza@uovonero.com
Editorial Dir & Foreign Rights: Sante Bandirali *E-mail:* sante@uovonero.com
Sales Dir & Editor: Lorenza Pozzi *E-mail:* lorenza@uovonero.com
Founded: 2010
ISBN Prefix(es): 978-88-96918

Urbaniana University Press (UUP)+
Division of Pontificia Universitas Urbaniana
Via Urbano VIII, 16, 00165 Rome RM
Tel: (06) 6988 9688 *Fax:* (06) 6988 2182
E-mail: redazioneuup@urbaniana.edu
Web Site: www.urbaniana.edu/uup
Key Personnel
Dir: Prof Leonardo Sileo *E-mail:* uupdir@urbaniana.edu
Editorial: Sandro Scalabrin *Tel:* (06) 6988 9651 *E-mail:* sscalabrin@urbaniana.edu
Founded: 1968
Specialize in periodicals & essays.
Membership(s): Unione Editori e Librai Cattolici Italiani (UELCI); University Press Italiane (UPI).
Subjects: Anthropology, Biblical Studies, Law, Philosophy, Psychology, Psychiatry, Religion - Catholic, Theology, Missiology
ISBN Prefix(es): 978-88-401
Number of titles published annually: 15 Print
Total Titles: 500 Print
Imprints: UUP
Distribution Center: Messaggerie Libri SpA, Via G Verdi 8, 20090 Assago MI *Tel:* (02) 45774 1 *Fax:* (02) 45701032 *E-mail:* info@meli.it *Web Site:* www.messaggerielibri.it

Urra, *imprint of* Giangiacomo Feltrinelli Editore SRL

UT Orpheus Edizioni SRL+
Piazza di Porta Ravegnana 1, 40126 Bologna
Tel: (051) 226468 *Fax:* (051) 263720
E-mail: info@utorpheus.com; sales@utorpheus.com
Web Site: www.utorpheus.com
Key Personnel
Chairman: Roberto De Caro

Business Administration & Public Relations: Valeria Tarsetti
Editorial Dept: Andrea Schiavina
Sales & Marketing: Elisabetta Pistolozzi
Founded: 1994
Italian publisher specializing in the publication of books on different music subjects, classical music.
Subjects: Music, Dance, Classical Music Editions
ISBN Prefix(es): 978-88-8109
Number of titles published annually: 100 Print
Total Titles: 1,400 Print
Associate Companies: Ut Orpheus Libreria Musicale, Via Marsala 31/E, 40126 Bologna, Dir: Antonello Lombardi *Tel:* (051) 239295 *Fax:* (051) 239295 *E-mail:* alombardi@utorpheus.com
Foreign Rep(s): MKT (Italy)
Bookshop(s): Ut Orpheus Libreria Musicale, Via Marsala 31/E, 40126 Bologna *Tel:* (051) 239295 *Fax:* (051) 239295 *E-mail:* bookshop@utorpheus.com
Warehouse: Via Aldina 26/A, Calderara Di Reno *Tel:* (051) 726138

UTET, *imprint of* DeA Planeta Libri SRL

UTET+
Lungo Dora Colletta, 67, 10153 Turin
Tel: (011) 2099111 *Fax:* (011) 2099394
E-mail: info@utetlibri.it; ufficiostampa@utet.it
Web Site: www.utetlibri.it
Founded: 1791
Subjects: Art, History, Medicine, Nursing, Dentistry, Music, Dance, Philosophy, Psychology, Psychiatry, Religion - Other, Science (General), Social Sciences, Sociology, Veterinary Science
ISBN Prefix(es): 978-88-02
Parent Company: De Agostini Editore SpA

UUP, *imprint of* Urbaniana University Press (UUP)

Vaccari SRL
Via M Buonarroti 46, 41058 Vignola MO
Tel: (059) 764106; (059) 771251 *Fax:* (059) 760157
E-mail: info@vaccari.it; pressoffice@vaccari.it
Web Site: www.vaccari.it; www.vaccarinews.it
Key Personnel
President: Paolo Vaccari
Dir: Fabio Bonacina
Chief Editor: Valeria Vaccari
Administration: Silvia Vaccari
Editorial, Media Relations: Claudia Zanetti
Founded: 1989
Subjects: Crafts, Games, Hobbies, Collecting, Philately, Postal History
ISBN Prefix(es): 978-88-85335; 978-88-96381
Number of titles published annually: 10 Print; 10 Online
Total Titles: 125 Print; 105 Online

Antonio Vallardi Editore
Via Belfiore 5, 20145 Milan
Tel: (02) 43811650; (02) 34597655 (sales) *Fax:* (02) 436923
E-mail: info@vallardi.it
Web Site: www.vallardi.it
Key Personnel
Contact: Antonio Vallardi
Press: Silvia Pilloni
Founded: 1750
Publisher of *Rough Guides.*
Subjects: Language Arts, Linguistics, Travel & Tourism, Foreign Languages Education
ISBN Prefix(es): 978-88-11; 978-88-8211; 978-88-8062; 978-88-7887
Parent Company: Gruppo Editoriale Mauri Spagnol SpA

Distribution Center: Messaggerie Libri SpA-Emmelibri SRL, Via G Verdi 8, 20090 Assago MI *Tel:* (02) 457741 *E-mail:* info@emmelibri.it
Web Site: www.messaggerie.it

Vallardi Industrie Grafiche SRL+
Viale Montello, 16, 20154 Milan MI
Tel: (02) 34537609
E-mail: info@vallardi.com
Web Site: www.vallardi.com
Key Personnel
Publisher: Giuseppe Vallardi
Founded: 1969
ISBN Prefix(es): 978-88-7696
Distribution Center: ALI Agenzia Libraria International srl, Via Milano 73/75, 20010 Cornaredo MI *Tel:* (02) 99 76 24 30; (02) 99 76 24 31; (02) 99 76 24 32 *Fax:* (02) 36 54 81 88 *E-mail:* infoali@alilibri.it

Roberto Vallardi editore
Via Borromeo, 1, 20871 Oreno di Vimercate MB
Tel: (039) 9080276 *Fax:* (039) 9080275
E-mail: segreteria@vallardieditore.com
Web Site: www.editvallardi.com
Key Personnel
Publisher: Roberto Vallardi
Subjects: Sports, Athletics
ISBN Prefix(es): 978-88-95684

Vallecchi SpA
via Maragliano, 31, 50144 Florence FI
Tel: (055) 324761 *Fax:* (055) 3215387
E-mail: info@vallecchi.it
Web Site: www.vallecchi.it
Key Personnel
Editor: Patrizia Vallario *E-mail:* vallario@vallecchi.it
Subjects: Art, Biography, Memoirs, Fiction, Health, Nutrition, Religion - Other, Travel & Tourism
ISBN Prefix(es): 978-88-252; 978-88-8252

Valmartina Editore SRL+
Via Montefeltro 6/b, 20156 Milan
Tel: (02) 380861
E-mail: scrivi@scuola.com
Web Site: www.valmartina.it
Founded: 1951
Subjects: Language Arts, Linguistics, Travel & Tourism
ISBN Prefix(es): 978-88-494
Parent Company: De Agostini Scuola SpA

Vannini Editrice SRL+
Via Mandolossa, 117/A, 25064 Gussago
Tel: (030) 313374 *Fax:* (030) 314078
E-mail: gea@vanninieditrice.it; info@vanninieditrice.it
Web Site: www.vanninieditrice.it
Key Personnel
Dir: Umberto Mezzana
Founded: 1905
Publisher & printer.
Subjects: Disability, Special Needs, Education, Psychology, Psychiatry, Special Eductation
ISBN Prefix(es): 978-88-86430; 978-88-7436; 978-88-6446
Number of titles published annually: 20 Print; 4 CD-ROM
Total Titles: 80 Print; 7 CD-ROM

De Vecchi Editore, *imprint of* Giunti Editore SpA

Las Vegas edizioni SAS
Via Genovo, 208, 10127 Turin
Tel: (011) 6962663
E-mail: info@lasvegasedizioni.com; ordini@lasvegasedizioni.com
Web Site: www.lasvegasedizioni.com

Key Personnel
Editorial Dir: Andrea Malabaila
Press: Carlotta Borasio *E-mail:* carlottaborasio@
    lasvegasedizioni.com
Founded: 2007
Subjects: Fiction
ISBN Prefix(es): 978-88-95744
Distribution Center: PDE SpA, Via Forlanini, 36,
    50019 Osmannoro-Sesto FI *Tel:* (055) 301371;
    (055) 315373; (055) 318332 *Fax:* (055) 301372
    E-mail: info@pde.it
LS Distribuzione Editoriale, Via Badini, 17,
    40050 Quarto Inferiore BO *Tel:* (051)
    768165; (051) 6061167 *Fax:* (051) 6058752
    E-mail: info@lsc.it

Editrice Velar
Via Torquato Tasso, 10, 24020 Gorle BG
Tel: (035) 6592811 *Fax:* (035) 6592888
E-mail: velar@velar.it
Web Site: www.velar.it
Founded: 1969
Subjects: Art, Biography, Memoirs, Health, Nu-
    trition, Inspirational, Spirituality, Literature,
    Literary Criticism, Essays, Poetry, Religion -
    Other, Culture
ISBN Prefix(es): 978-88-7135
Total Titles: 1,000 Print
Imprints: Casa Editrice Marna

Verso il Futuro, *imprint of* Casa Editrice Menna

Villa Angelina, *imprint of* Gruppo Editoriale
Esselibri Simone

Vinciana Editrice SAS+
Via V Foppa, 14, 20144 Milan
Tel: (02) 4982306 *Fax:* (02) 48003275
E-mail: info@vinciana.com
Web Site: www.vinciana.com
Founded: 1976
Specialize in fine art.
Subjects: Art, Crafts, Games, Hobbies, How-to
ISBN Prefix(es): 978-88-86256; 978-88-8172
Total Titles: 42 Print

Vision SRL
Via Livorno, 20, 00162 Rome
Tel: (06) 44292688 *Fax:* (06) 44292688
E-mail: sales@visionpubl.com; ufficiostampa@
    visionpubl.com
Web Site: www.visionpubl.com
Founded: 1959
Subjects: Archaeology
ISBN Prefix(es): 978-88-8162

Visual Itineraries, *imprint of* BE-MA editrice

Vita e Pensiero+
Largo A Gemelli, 1, 20123 Milan
Tel: (02) 72342335 *Fax:* (02) 72342260
E-mail: editrice.vp@unicatt.it; libreria.vp@
    unicatt.it; ufficiostampa.vp@unicatt.it
Web Site: www.vitaepensiero.it
Key Personnel
Dir: Aurelio Mottola *E-mail:* aurelio.mottola@
    unicatt.it
Editorial: Marina Malabarba *Tel:* (02) 72342368
    E-mail: marina.malabarba@unicatt.it
Press: Velania La Mendola *Tel:* (02) 72342259
    E-mail: velania.lamendola@unicatt.it
Founded: 1918
Membership(s): Associazione Italiana Editori;
    Associazione Librai Italiani; Unione Editori
    Cattolici Italiani.
Subjects: Communications, Education, History,
    Law, Literature, Literary Criticism, Essays,
    Nonfiction (General), Philosophy, Psychology,
    Psychiatry, Religion - Catholic
ISBN Prefix(es): 978-88-343
Number of titles published annually: 100 Print

Total Titles: 1,000 Print
Parent Company: Universita Cattolica di Milano

Edizioni La Vita Felice+
via Lazzaro Palazzi 15, 20124 Milan
Tel: (02) 20520585 *Fax:* (02) 20520585
E-mail: info@lavitafelice.it
Web Site: www.lavitafelice.it
Key Personnel
Publishing Dir: Gerardo Mastrullo
Founded: 1992
Subjects: Fiction, Literature, Literary Criticism,
    Essays, Poetry
ISBN Prefix(es): 978-88-86314; 978-88-7799;
    978-88-9346
Number of titles published annually: 30 Print; 10
    E-Book; 2 Audio
Total Titles: 600 Print; 10 E-Book; 4 Audio

Vivalda Editori SRL+
Via Invorio 24/a, 10146 Turin
Tel: (011) 7720444 *Fax:* (011) 7732170
E-mail: info@vivaldaeditori.it; ordini@
    vivaldaeditori.it
Web Site: www.vivaldaeditori.it
Key Personnel
Administrator: Giorgio Vivalda *E-mail:* giorgio.
    vivalda@vivaldaeditori.it
Founded: 1972
Subjects: Sports, Athletics, Travel & Tourism
ISBN Prefix(es): 978-88-7808
Imprints: ALP
Divisions: CDA

Edizioni VivereIn
Contrada Piangevino, 224a, 70043 Monopoli BA
Tel: (080) 6907030 *Fax:* (080) 6907026
E-mail: edizioniviverein@tin.it
Web Site: www.edizioniviverein.it
Founded: 1978
Subjects: Biblical Studies, Biography, Memoirs,
    Literature, Literary Criticism, Essays, Philos-
    ophy, Poetry, Regional Interests, Religion -
    Catholic, Social Sciences, Sociology, Theology
ISBN Prefix(es): 978-88-7263
Number of titles published annually: 15 Print
Total Titles: 440 Print
Branch Office(s)
Via A Solario 91, 00142 Rome *Tel:* (06)
    69640096 *Fax:* (06) 59640096
Distribution Center: Distrimedia SRL
Messaggero Distribuzione

Viviani Editore SRL+
Piazza della Maddalena, 6, 00186 Rome
Tel: (06) 6872855 *Fax:* (06) 6872856
E-mail: viviani@vivianieditore.com;
    vivianieditore@tin.it
Web Site: www.vivianieditore.net
Key Personnel
Dir & Editorial Dir: Lia Viviani Cursi
Founded: 1992
Membership(s): Associazione Italiana Editori
    (AIE).
Subjects: Art, Biography, Memoirs, Drama, The-
    ater, History, Literature, Literary Criticism, Es-
    says
ISBN Prefix(es): 978-88-7993
Bookshop(s): Bookshop Chiostro del Bra-
    mante, Arco della Pace, 5, 00186 Rome
    Tel: (06) 68809035 *Fax:* (06) 68809036
    E-mail: direzione@chiostrodelbramante.it;
    Libreria Montecitorio, Piazza Montecitorio,
    59, 00186 Rome *Tel:* (06) 6781103 *Fax:* (06)
    6781103 *E-mail:* montecitorio@arion-dpe.
    it; Libro Co Italia Srl, Via Borromeo, 48,
    50026 Florence *Tel:* (055) 8228461 *Fax:* (055)
    8228462 *E-mail:* libroco@libroco.it

Voland SRL
Via Napoleone III, 12, 00185 Rome

Tel: (06) 4461946
E-mail: redazione@voland.it; ufficiostampa@
    voland.it
Web Site: www.voland.it
Key Personnel
Publisher: Daniela Di Sora
Press: Marina Fanasca
Rights: Valentina Parlato *E-mail:* diritti@voland.it
Founded: 1995
Subjects: Fiction, History, Literature, Literary
    Criticism, Essays, Nonfiction (General)
ISBN Prefix(es): 978-88-88700; 978-88-86586

Volumnia Editrice
Palazzo Bonucci, Via Baldeschi, 2, 06123 Perugia
    PG
Tel: (075) 5724950; (075) 5733187 *Fax:* (075)
    5724950
E-mail: volumnia@volumnia.it;
    volumniaeditrice@gmail.com
Web Site: www.volumnia.it
Founded: 1968
Subjects: Art, History, Literature, Literary Criti-
    cism, Essays, Poetry
ISBN Prefix(es): 978-88-85330; 978-88-89024
Distribution Center: Editoriale Umbra SAS,
    Via Pignattara, 34, 06034 Foligno PG
    Tel: (0742) 357541 *Fax:* (0742) 351156
    E-mail: info@editorialeumbra.it *Web
    Site:* www.editorialeumbra.it

Edizioni White Star SRL
c/o De Agostini Libri SpA, Via G da Verrazano
    15, 28100 Novara
Tel: (0321) 4241 *Fax:* (0321) 424176
E-mail: whitestar@whitestar.it; ordini@whitestar.
    it
Web Site: www.whitestar.it
Founded: 1984
Subjects: Archaeology, Art, Music, Dance, Pho-
    tography, Technology, Cinema, Ethnology,
    Haute Cuisine, Marine Biology, Mountaineer-
    ing, Nature, Social Customs
ISBN Prefix(es): 978-88-544; 978-88-540; 978-
    88-7844; 978-88-8095
Branch Office(s)
Editions White Star, France *Tel:* 01 78 09 74 41
    Fax: 01 78 09 75 23
White Star Verlag GmbH, Friedrichstr 8, 65185
    Wiesbaden, Germany *Tel:* (0611) 95 000-0
    Fax: (0611) 95 000-20 *E-mail:* info@whitestar-
    verlag.de *Web Site:* www.whitestar-verlag.de
White Star Publishers SA, 13, Rue Bertholet,
    1233 Luxembourg, Luxembourg
White Star Publishers SA, Immeuble Laver-
    dure, 3963 Crans sur Sierre, Switzerland
    Tel: (027) 4842580 *Fax:* (027) 4842585
    E-mail: wssuisse@whitestar.it
Foreign Rep(s): Bookwise International Pty Ltd
    (Australia, New Zealand); European Publish-
    ers Representation (Cyprus, Europe exc Ireland
    & UK); Intermedia Africa Ltd (Africa); Inter-
    media Americana (Caribbean, Central Amer-
    ica, South America); Koch, Neff & Oetinger
    Verlagsauslieferung GmbH (Germany); Maya
    Publishers Pvt Ltd (India); Miller Distribu-
    tors Ltd (Malta); Mohr Morawa Buchvertrieb
    GmbH (Austria); PMS Publishers Marketing
    Services Pte Ltd (Brunei, Malaysia, Singa-
    pore); Publishers Group UK (Ireland, UK);
    Random House Distribution Services (Canada,
    North America); Rizzoli International Publica-
    tions (Canada, North America); Janis Roze Ltd
    (Latvia); Schweizer Buchzentrum AG (Switzer-
    land); Steimatzky Group Ltd (Israel); Ralph &
    Sheila Summers (Cambodia, Indonesia, Korea,
    Philippines, Taiwan, Thailand, Vietnam); Trin-
    ity Books CC (South Africa); United Century
    Books Services Ltd (China, Hong Kong); Pe-
    ter Ward Book Exports (Middle East, North
    Africa); Yasmy International Marketing (Japan)

Who's Who In Italy SRL
Via E De Amicis, 2, 20091 Bresso MI
Tel: (02) 6101627 *Fax:* (02) 6105587
Web Site: www.whoswho.eu
Key Personnel
Mng Editor: Enrica Vigato
Founded: 1957
Specialize in reference books, International publishers of Who's Who titles in 6 different nations in the English language & of particular interest to the world of business, politics, culture, art, science, education, etc, with cross-references between biographies & profiles of companies & institutions.
Membership(s): Associazione Italiana Editori (Italian Publishers' Association).
Subjects: Biography, Memoirs, Business, Economics, Finance, Management
ISBN Prefix(es): 978-88-85246
Number of titles published annually: 3 Print; 3 Online
Parent Company: Who's Who Strategic Area AG, Seestr 357, 8038 Zurich, Switzerland
Subsidiaries: Who's Who in China; Who's Who in Russia; Who's Who in Spain; Who's Who Strategic Area
Branch Office(s)
Viale Aldo Moro, 52, 62019 Recanati MC
Tel: (071) 7572081 *Fax:* (071) 7572081
E-mail: liala.scanavini@fastwebnet.it
Via Marcantonio Odescalchi 4, 00152 Rome
Tel: (06) 58201976 *Fax:* (06) 5346026
E-mail: cappucci.annamarie@libero.it
Via Lomellina, 45, 10132 Turin *Tel:* (011) 5682181 *Fax:* (011) 591765 *E-mail:* rosangela. arcuri@alice.it
Distributed by The Eurospan Group (Canada, Great Britain, Japan, Northern Europe & USA); Independent Publishers Group (Canada & USA); United Publishers Services Ltd (Japan)

XY.IT Editore SRL
Via Roma, 42, 28041 Arona NO
Tel: (0322) 019200 *Fax:* (0322) 019209
E-mail: info@editorexy.it
Web Site: www.editorexy.com
Key Personnel
Dir: Gaetano Oliva
Founded: 2006
Subjects: Drama, Theater, Education, History, Literature, Literary Criticism, Essays, Nonfiction (General), Philosophy, Psychology, Psychiatry, Science (General), Social Sciences, Sociology

Silvio Zamorani editore
Courso San Maurizio 25, 10124 Turin TO
Tel: (011) 8125700 *Fax:* (011) 8126144
E-mail: info@zamorani.com
Web Site: www.zamorani.com
Founded: 1984
Subjects: Fiction, Literature, Literary Criticism, Essays, Philosophy
ISBN Prefix(es): 978-88-7158

Zanichelli Editore SpA+
via Irnerio, 34, 40126 Bologna BO
Tel: (051) 293 111; (051) 245 024 *Fax:* (051) 249 782; (051) 293 224
E-mail: zanichelli@zanichelli.com; vendite@ zanichelli.com (sales)
Web Site: www.zanichelli.it
Key Personnel
Chairman: Lorenzo Enriques
Dir General & Vice President: Federico Enriques
Founded: 1859
Subjects: Anthropology, Architecture & Interior Design, Art, Biological Sciences, Chemistry, Chemical Engineering, Computer Science, Drama, Theater, Earth Sciences, Economics, Education, Electronics, Electrical Engineering, Engineering (General), English as a Second Language, Environmental Studies, Film, Video, Gardening, Plants, Geography, Geology, Health, Nutrition, History, Language Arts, Linguistics, Law, Literature, Literary Criticism, Essays, Mechanical Engineering, Medicine, Nursing, Dentistry, Philosophy, Photography, Physics, Psychology, Psychiatry, Science (General), Social Sciences, Sociology, Sports, Athletics
ISBN Prefix(es): 978-88-08
Subsidiaries: Italo Bovolenta Italo Editore srl; CEA Casa Editrice Ambrosiana srl; G D'Anna Casa Editrice; Il Foro Italiano; Loescher Editore srl
Distributor for Italo Bovolenta Italo Editore srl; Clitt Edizioni; Edizioni Cremonese; Decibel Edizioni; ESAC; Grasso Editore; Franco Lucisano Editore; Masson Editore
Warehouse: Via Del Lavoro 15, 40057 Quarto Inferiore, Bologna BO *Tel:* (051) 293 254 *Fax:* (051) 60 60 549
E-mail: magazzino_quarto@zanichelli.it

Giancarlo Zedde Editore
Via Duchessa Iolanda 12, 10138 Turin TO
Tel: (011) 4331241 *Fax:* (011) 19790468; (011) 4343202
Web Site: www.zedde.com
Key Personnel
Publisher: Giancarlo Zedde
Editorial Dir: Francesco Rodolfo Russo
E-mail: russo@zedde.com
Founded: 1997
Subjects: Fiction, Music, Dance, Poetry
ISBN Prefix(es): 978-88-88849

ZOOlibri
via Carlo Piaggia 5, 42122 Reggio Emilia RE
Tel: (0522) 330566 *Fax:* (0522) 330566
E-mail: info@zoolibri.com; press@zoolibri.com; rights@zoolibri.com
Web Site: www.zoolibri.com
Key Personnel
Founder: Corrado Rabitti
Foreign Rights: Sara Bompani; Isabella Fanfarillo
Press: Erika Rondoni
Founded: 2001
ISBN Prefix(es): 978-88-88254
Bookshop(s): Via Gozzano 2/1, 42100 Reggio Emilia RE
Distribution Center: Agenzia Libraria International SRL, Via Milano 73/75, 20010 Cornarado MI *Tel:* (02) 99762430 *Fax:* (02) 36548188 *E-mail:* infoali@alilibri.it *Web Site:* www.alilibri.it

Jamaica

General Information

Capital: Kingston
Language: English
Religion: Predominantly Protestant
Population: 2.5 million
Bank Hours: 0900-1400 Monday-Thursday; 0900-1200, 1430-1700 Friday
Shop Hours: Downtown Kingston: 0900-1600 Monday and Tuesday, Thursday-Saturday; 0900-1200 Wednesday. Other areas: 0900-1700, with early closing Thursday
Currency: 100 cents = 1 Jamaican dollar
Export/Import Information: No tariff on books, but advertising matter dutied. No import license required for books; no obscene literature permitted. No exchange restrictions.
Copyright: Berne (see Copyright Conventions, pg viii)

ADA, see Association of Development Agencies

AMCHAMS, see The American Chamber of Commerce of Jamaica

The American Chamber of Commerce of Jamaica+
The Jamaica Pegasus, 81 Knutsford Blvd, Suite 106, Kingston 5
Tel: (876) 929-7866 *Fax:* (876) 929-8597
E-mail: amcham@cwjamaica.com
Web Site: www.amchamjamaica.org
Key Personnel
President: Derrick Nembhard
Executive Dir: Becky Stockhausen
General Manager: Kim Mair
Founded: 1986
Membership(s): Chamber of Commerce of the United States of America.
Subjects: Environmental Studies, Management, Marketing
ISBN Prefix(es): 978-976-8113
Parent Company: Chamber of Commerce of the United States of America
Divisions: Association of American Chamber of Commerce of Latin America (AACCLA)

Arawak Publications+
26 Victory Dr, Kingston 19
Mailing Address: PO Box 1743, Kingston 8
Tel: (876) 620-8572
Web Site: www.arawakpublications.com
Key Personnel
Publisher: Pansy Benn *E-mail:* bpancmj@aol.com
Founded: 2000
Independent publisher & publishing consultancy. This publisher has indicated that 50% of their product line is author subsidized.
Subjects: Biography, Memoirs, Criminology, Disability, Special Needs, Economics, Education, Fiction, History, Language Arts, Linguistics, Law, Management, Philosophy, Social Sciences, Sociology, Travel & Tourism, Humanities
ISBN Prefix(es): 978-976-8189
Number of titles published annually: 7 Print; 2 CD-ROM; 5 Online
Total Titles: 90 Print; 2 CD-ROM; 60 Online; 1 E-Book
Distributor for Zed Books
Shipping Address: Edwards Brothers Malloy, 5411 Jackson Rd, Ann Arbor, MI 48103, United States *Tel:* 734-665-6113 *E-mail:* fulfillment@edwardsbrothersmalloy.com *Web Site:* www.edwardsbrothersmalloy.com
Warehouse: Edwards Brothers Malloy, 5411 Jackson Rd, Ann Arbor, MI 48103, United States *Tel:* 734-665-6113 *E-mail:* fulfillment@edwardsbrothersmalloy.com *Web Site:* www.edwardsbrothersmalloy.com
Distribution Center: Novelty Trading Co Ltd, 53 Hanover St, PO Box 80, Kingston, Executive Assistant: Gillian Morgan *Tel:* (876) 922-5663 *Fax:* (876) 922-4743 *E-mail:* novtra@cwjamaica.com
The Blue Edition, 32 St Vincent St, Tunapuna, Trinidad and Tobago, Contact: Pat Gibbons *Tel:* (868) 645-8384 *E-mail:* sales@theblueedition.com (Eastern Caribbean)
Orders to: Edwards Brothers Malloy, 5411 Jackson Rd, Ann Arbor, MI 48103, United States *Tel:* 734-665-6113 *E-mail:* fulfillment@edwardsbrothersmalloy.com *Web Site:* www.edwardsbrothersmalloy.com
Returns: Edwards Brothers Malloy, 5411 Jackson Rd, Ann Arbor, MI 48103, United States *E-mail:* fulfillment@edwardsbrothersmalloy.com *Web Site:* www.edwardsbrothersmalloy.com

Association of Development Agencies
12 Easton Ave, Kingston 5
Tel: (876) 927-8568 *Fax:* (876) 927-4580

E-mail: asdevgen@cwjamaica.com;
ada9274580@yahoo.com
Key Personnel
Chairperson: Ms Amsale Maryam
Founded: 1985
Forum for collective analysis, discussion, planning & collaboration.
Subjects: Communications, Developing Countries, House & Home, Regional Interests, Self-Help, Women's Studies
ISBN Prefix(es): 978-976-8112

Bureau of Standards Jamaica
6 Winchester Rd, Kingston 10
Mailing Address: PO Box 113, Kingston 10
Tel: (876) 926-3140; (876) 632-4275; (876) 619-1131 *Fax:* (876) 929-4736
E-mail: info@jbs.org.jm
Web Site: www.jbs.org.jm
Key Personnel
Executive Dir: Yvonne Hall *Tel:* (876) 926-3140, ext 3303 *E-mail:* yhall@bsj.org.jm
Founded: 1968
Formulate, promote & implement standards for products, processes & practices.
Membership(s): The International Organization for Standardization.
ISBN Prefix(es): 978-976-604
Bookshop(s): Shop 16, Caledonia Plaza Annex, 71/2 Caledonia Rd, Mandeville *Tel:* (876) 962-7102 *E-mail:* mandeville@jbs.org.jm; The UGI Bldg, 1st floor, 30-34 Market St, Montego Bay *Tel:* (876) 952-7119 *E-mail:* mobay@jbs.org.jm; WG Walters Bldg, 103 Main St, Ocho Rios *Tel:* (876) 795-1965 *E-mail:* ochorios@jbs.org.jm; Shop 15, 62 Great Georges St, Savanna-La-Mar *Tel:* (876) 918-1652 *E-mail:* savlamar@jbs.org.jm

Caribbean Law Publishing Co, *imprint of* Ian Randle Publishers Ltd

Carlong Publishers (Caribbean) Ltd+
17 Ruthven Rd, Bldg 3, Kingston 10
Tel: (876) 960-9364; (876) 960-9365; (876) 960-9366 *Fax:* (876) 968-1353
E-mail: publishing@carlongpublishers.com; marketing@carlongpublishers.com
Web Site: www.carlongpublishers.com
Key Personnel
Mng Dir: Shirley Carby
Publisher: Jenni Anderson
Publishing Services Executive (Rights & Permissions): Julie-Ann Ewart
Marketing Manager: Vinton Samms
Publishing Manager: Dorothy Noel
Sales & Distribution Manager: Lorna Allen
Development Editor: Benedicta Nakawuki
Editor: Fiona Edwards; Rose Lewis-Stone
Educational Technologist: Sonia Bennett Cunningham
Founded: 1990
Subjects: Business, Drama, Theater, Foreign Countries, Geography, Geology, History, Human Relations, Language Arts, Linguistics, Literature, Literary Criticism, Essays, Mathematics, Science (General), Social Sciences, Sociology
ISBN Prefix(es): 978-976-8010; 978-976-638
Total Titles: 105 Print
Branch Office(s)
37 Second St, Newport West, Kingston 13
Tel: (876) 923-6505; (876) 923-7019
Fax: (876) 923-7003 *E-mail:* sales.distrib@carlongpublishers.com (sales)
Distributor for Pearson/Longman Books
Foreign Rights: Ken Jaikaransingh (Trinidad and Tobago)
Distribution Center: 38 First St, Newport West, Kingston 13 *Tel:* (876) 923-6505-7; (876) 923-7008; (876) 923-7019 *Fax:* (876) 923-7003
E-mail: sales.distrib@carlongpublishers.com

Gleaner Co Ltd
7 North St, Kingston
Mailing Address: PO Box 40, Kingston
Tel: (876) 922-3400 *Toll Free Tel:* 888-453-2637 (Jamaica only); 800-233-9540 (USA & Canada) *Fax:* (876) 922-6223
E-mail: feedback@jamaica-gleaner.com
Web Site: www.jamaica-gleaner.com
Key Personnel
Editor-in-Chief: Garfield Grandison
Founded: 1834
Subjects: Art, Business, Cookery, Health, Nutrition, Regional Interests, Sports, Athletics
ISBN Prefix(es): 978-976-612
Branch Office(s)
The Gleaner Co (Canada) Inc, 1390 Eglinton Ave W, Toronto, ON, Canada *Tel:* (416) 784-3002 *Fax:* (416) 784-5719 *E-mail:* gleanercan@gleanerna.com *Web Site:* www.gleanerextra.com
The Weekly Gleaner UK, c/o GV Media Group Ltd, Northern & Shell Towers, 6th floor, 4 Selsdon Way, London E14 9GL, United Kingdom *Tel:* (020) 7510 0340 *Fax:* (020) 7274 8994 *E-mail:* letters@gvmedia.co.uk *Web Site:* www.voice-online.co.uk
U.S. Office(s): The Gleaner Company USA Ltd, 172-06 Jamaica Ave, Jamaica, NY 11433, United States *Tel:* 718-687-0788 *Fax:* 718-657-0857

Jamaica Information Service (JIS)
58a Half Way Tree Rd, Kingston 10
Tel: (876) 926-3740; (876) 926-3590 *Fax:* (876) 926-6715
E-mail: jis@jis.gov.jm; research@jis.gov.jm
Web Site: www.jis.gov.jm
Subjects: Cookery, History, Jamaican Culture
ISBN Prefix(es): 978-976-633
Branch Office(s)
NHT Bldg, 2nd floor, 42 B-C Union St, Montego Bay *Tel:* (876) 952-6604 *Fax:* (876) 952-0544 *E-mail:* jismobay@jis.gov.jm

Jamaica Publishing House Ltd+
Subsidiary of Jamaica Teachers' Association
97B Church St, Kingston
Tel: (876) 922-1385; (876) 922-1387 *Fax:* (876) 922-3257
E-mail: jph@cwjamaica.com
Key Personnel
President: Clayton Hall
Founded: 1969
Subjects: Biography, Memoirs, Education, Geography, Geology, History, House & Home, Language Arts, Linguistics, Literature, Literary Criticism, Essays, Mathematics, Psychology, Psychiatry, Social Sciences, Sociology
ISBN Prefix(es): 978-976-606
Distributor for A&C Black Publishers Ltd; Schofield & Sims

JIS, see Jamaica Information Service (JIS)

LMH Publishing Ltd
Sagicor Industrial Complex, 7 Norman Rd, Suite 10-11, Kingston CSO
Mailing Address: PO Box 8296, Kingston CSO
Tel: (876) 938-0005 *Fax:* (876) 759-8752
E-mail: lmhbookpublishing@cwjamaica.com; weborders@lmhpublishing.com; sales@lmhpublishing.com
Web Site: www.lmhpublishing.com
Key Personnel
Mng Dir: Dawn Chambers-Henry
Mng Editor: Kevin Harris
Subjects: Art, Cookery, Education, Fiction, History, Nonfiction (General), Romance, Travel & Tourism, Culture
Imprints: RGD Sea Press
U.S. Office(s): Zebra International, Empire State Bldg, 350 Fifth Ave, Suite 2611, New York,

NY 10118, United States *Tel:* 212-244-8194 *Fax:* 212-244-8160
Distributed by Africa World Press
Foreign Rep(s): Island Merchants Ltd (The Bahamas); Turnaround Publisher Services Ltd (Europe, UK)
Shipping Address: Antilles Freight Corp, 11206 NW 36 Ave, Miami, FL 33167, United States *Tel:* 305-688-5488 *Fax:* 305-688-9651 *E-mail:* ggarcia@antillesfreight.com

Ian Randle Publishers Ltd+
11 Cunningham Ave, Kingston 6
Mailing Address: PO Box 686, Kingston 6
Tel: (876) 978-0739; (876) 978-0745 *Toll Free Tel:* 866-330-5469 (orders, USA); 800-744-1114 (Caribbean) *Fax:* (876) 978-1156
Web Site: www.ianrandlepublishers.com
Key Personnel
President & Publisher: Ian Randle *Tel:* (876) 978-3587 *E-mail:* ian@ianrandlepublishers.com
Mng Dir: Christine Randle *E-mail:* clp@ianrandlepublishers.com
Business Manager: Carlene Randle
Founded: 1991
Specializes in Caribbean Studies including Law, as well as trade & general books.
Membership(s): Caribbean Publishers Network; Caribbean Studies Association; Society for Caribbean Studies (UK).
Subjects: Architecture & Interior Design, Art, Biography, Memoirs, Cookery, Drama, Theater, History, Law, Literature, Literary Criticism, Essays, Music, Dance, Poetry, Religion - Other, Social Sciences, Sociology, Sports, Athletics, Women's Studies, Gender Studies
ISBN Prefix(es): 978-976-8100; 978-976-8123; 978-976-8167 (Caribbean Law Publishing); 978-976-637
Number of titles published annually: 50 Print
Total Titles: 250 Print
Imprints: Caribbean Law Publishing Co (law books & journals)
Foreign Rep(s): Global Book Marketing (Europe, UK)
Distribution Center: Global Book Marketing, 99B Wallis Rd, London E9 5LN, United Kingdom *Tel:* (020) 8533 5800 *E-mail:* tz@globalbookmarketing.co.uk
Caribbean Book Distributors, 11206 NW 36 Ave, Miami, FL 33167, United States *Tel:* 305-953-9332 *E-mail:* caribbooks@gmail.com (Canada, USA)

RGD Sea Press, *imprint of* LMH Publishing Ltd

Scientific Research Council (SRC)
Hope Gardens, Kingston 6
Mailing Address: PO Box 350, Kingston 6
Tel: (876) 927-1771; (876) 977-1110 *Fax:* (876) 927-1990
E-mail: prinfo@src-jamaica.org; srchead@src-jamaica.org
Web Site: www.src.gov.jm
Key Personnel
Administrative Manager: Eleanor Leiba
Information Services: Hawthorne Watson
Founded: 1960
The national center for the transformation, acquisition, conversion & application of knowledge to run the engine of growth & development.
Subjects: Agriculture, Energy, Environmental Studies, Science (General), Technology
ISBN Prefix(es): 978-976-8126
Subsidiaries: Marketech Ltd
Branch Office(s)
Montego Bay Outpost, 34 Market St, Montego Bay *Tel:* (876) 971-9891 *E-mail:* outpost-mobay@src-jamaica.org

Twin Guinep Publishers Ltd+
Seymour Park, Suite 21, 2 Seymour Ave, Kingston 10

Tel: (876) 944-4324 (administration) *Fax:* (876) 944-4324
E-mail: info@twinguinep.com; sales@twinguinep.com
Web Site: www.twinguinep.com
Key Personnel
International Rights: Dennis Ranston; Jacqueline Ranston
Founded: 1974
Subjects: Child Care & Development, Education, History
ISBN Prefix(es): 978-976-8007
Foreign Rights: Jacqueline Twyman (UK); University of Toronto Press (Canada, USA)

University of the West Indies Press+
7A Gibraltar Hall Rd, Mona, Kingston 7
Tel: (876) 977-2659; (876) 702-4081 *Fax:* (876) 977-2660
E-mail: cuserv@cwjamaica.com (customer service & orders); uwipress_marketing@cwjamaica.com
Web Site: www.uwipress.com
Key Personnel
Dir: Dr Joseph B Powell *E-mail:* joseph.powell@uwimona.edu.jm
Finance Manager: Nadine Buckland
  E-mail: nadine.buckland@uwimona.edu.jm
Marketing & Sales Manager: Donna Muirhead
  E-mail: donna.muirhead@uwimona.edu.jm
Founded: 1992
Academic book publisher.
Subjects: Anthropology, Environmental Studies, Ethnicity, History, Literature, Literary Criticism, Essays, Natural History, Social Sciences, Sociology, Women's Studies
ISBN Prefix(es): 978-976-8125; 978-976-640; 978-976-41
Number of titles published annually: 25 Print
Total Titles: 235 Print
Foreign Rep(s): Eurospan (Africa, Middle East, UK & the continent)
Distribution Center: Eurospan Group, 3 Henrietta St, London WC2E 8LU, United Kingdom *Tel:* (01767) 604972 *Fax:* (01767) 601640 *E-mail:* eurospan@turpin-distribution.com *Web Site:* www.eurospanbookstore.com
Orders to: Kingston Bookshop Ltd, 74 King St, Kingston, Contact: Denroy Mullings *Tel:* (876) 922-7016 *Fax:* (876) 922-0127 *E-mail:* denroy.mullings@kingstonbookshop.com *Web Site:* www.kingstonbookshopjm.com
Longleaf Services Inc, PO Box 8895, Chapel Hill, NC 27515-8895, United States *E-mail:* customerservice@longleafservices.org *Web Site:* www.longleafservices.org
Scholarly Book Services Inc, 289 Bridgeland Ave, Unit 105, Toronto M6A 1Z6, ON, Canada *E-mail:* orders@sbookscan.com *Web Site:* www.sbookscan.com

UWI Press, see University of the West Indies Press

Japan

General Information

Capital: Tokyo
Language: Japanese
Religion: Shinto and Buddhism
Population: 125 million
Bank Hours: 0900-1500 Monday-Friday; 0900-1200 Saturday
Shop Hours: Same as bank hours
Currency: 100 yen = 1 dollar

Export/Import Information: 3% consumption; tax on books.
Copyright: UCC, Berne, Florence, Rome (see Copyright Conventions, pg viii)

ACCJ, *imprint of* The American Chamber of Commerce in Japan

ADA Edita Tokyo Co Ltd
3-12-14 Sendagaya, Shibuya-ku, Tokyo 151-0051
Tel: (03) 3403-1461
E-mail: info@ga-ada.co.jp; sales@ga-tbc.co.jp
Web Site: www.ga-ada.co.jp
Founded: 1972
Subjects: Architecture & Interior Design
ISBN Prefix(es): 978-4-87140

Akane Shobo Co Ltd+
3-2-1 Nishikanda, Chiyoda-ku, Tokyo 101-0065
Tel: (03) 3263-0641 *Fax:* (03) 3263-5440
E-mail: info@akaneshobo.co.jp; order@akaneshobo.co.jp; eigyo@akaneshobo.co.jp
Web Site: www.akaneshobo.co.jp
Key Personnel
President: Masaharu Okamoto
Foreign Rights & Trade: Mitsuharu Okamoto
  E-mail: mitsuharu02@akaneshobo.co.jp
Founded: 1949
Membership(s): Japan Book Publishers Association.
Subjects: Fiction, Literature, Literary Criticism, Essays, Nonfiction (General), Science (General)
ISBN Prefix(es): 978-4-251
Branch Office(s)
1-21-1-402 Showa, Abeno-ku, Osaka 545-0011
Distribution Center: 32 Sanjo-cho, Nishi-ku, Saitama 331-0056

Akita Shoten Publishing Co Ltd
2-10-8 Iidabashi, Chiyoda-ku, Tokyo 102-8101
Tel: (03) 3264-7011 *Fax:* (03) 3265-5906
E-mail: media@akitashoten.co.jp
Web Site: www.akitashoten.co.jp
Key Personnel
President: Sadami Akita
Foreign Rights & Trade: Hirokazu Takahashi
Founded: 1948
Membership(s): Japan Book Publishers Association.
Subjects: Fiction, History, Humor, Literature, Literary Criticism, Essays, Social Sciences, Sociology, Comics
ISBN Prefix(es): 978-4-253
Branch Office(s)
2-3-6 Lidabashi, Chiyoda-ku, Tokyo 102-8101
2-10-6 Lidabashi, Chiyoda-ku, Tokyo 102-8101
Distribution Center: 970 Mukoda Bijogi, Toda, Saitama 335-0031 *Tel:* (048) 422-0220

Alice-Kan+
5-5-5 Koishikawa, Bunkyo-ku, Tokyo 112-0002
Tel: (03) 5976-7013; (03) 5976-7011 (sales)
  Fax: (03) 3944-1228
E-mail: info@alicekan.com
Web Site: www.alicekan.com
Key Personnel
Editor-in-Chief: Ikuko Yamaguti
Founded: 1981
Subjects: Art, Child Care & Development
ISBN Prefix(es): 978-4-7520
Parent Company: Rodojunposh

The American Chamber of Commerce in Japan+
Masonic 39 MT Bldg 10F, 2-4-5 Azabudai, Minato-ku, Tokyo 106-0041
Tel: (03) 3433-5381 *Fax:* (03) 3433-8454
E-mail: info@accj.or.jp
Web Site: www.accj.or.jp
Key Personnel
President: Thomas W Whitson

Founded: 1948
Organiztion that helps US business expand in Japan.
Membership(s): Chamber of Commerce of the United States of America.
Subjects: Business, Foreign Countries, Marketing, Travel & Tourism
ISBN Prefix(es): 978-4-915682
Parent Company: Chamber of Commerce of the United States of America
Imprints: ACCJ
Distributed by Charles E Tuttle Co (Japan & USA)

Aoki Shoten Co Ltd
1-60, Kanda-Jimbocho, Chiyoda-ku, Tokyo 101-0051
Tel: (03) 3219 2341 *Fax:* (03) 3219 2585
E-mail: eigyo@aokishoten.co.jp
Web Site: www.aokishoten.co.jp
Key Personnel
President, Foreign Rights & Trade: Masato Aoki
Founded: 1948
Membership(s): Japan Book Publishers Association.
Subjects: Economics, Education, History, Philosophy, Social Sciences, Sociology
ISBN Prefix(es): 978-4-250
Orders to: 8-12-12 Akatsuka, Itabashi-ku, Tokyo 175-0092

Asahiya Shuppan (Asahiya Publishing Co Ltd)
8F Capital-Akasaka Bldg, 1-7-19 Akasaka, Minato-ku, Toyko 107-0052
Tel: (03) 3560-9065 *Fax:* (03) 3560-9071
E-mail: mail-asahiyashuppan@asahiya-jp.com
Web Site: www.asahiya-jp.com
Key Personnel
President: Shigeru Hayashima
Contact: Masato Nagase
Founded: 1968
Membership(s): Japan Book Publishers Association.
Subjects: Cookery
ISBN Prefix(es): 978-4-7511

Asakura Publishing Co Ltd+
6-29 Shin-Ogawamachi, Shinjuku-ku, Tokyo 162-8707
Tel: (03) 3260 0141 *Fax:* (03) 3260 0180
E-mail: edit@asakura.co.jp; info@asakura.co.jp; e-shop@asakura.co.jp (orders)
Web Site: www.asakura.co.jp
Key Personnel
President: Kunizo Asakura
Foreign Rights: Makoto Morikawa
  E-mail: morikawa@asakura.co.jp
Founded: 1929
Membership(s): Japan Book Publishers Association.
Subjects: Agriculture, Engineering (General), Geography, Geology, History, Medicine, Nursing, Dentistry, Social Sciences, Sociology, Medical Science, Natural Science
ISBN Prefix(es): 978-4-254

Aspect+
Kinsan Bldg, 3-18-3, Kanda, Nishiki-cho, Chiyoda-ku, Tokyo 101-0054
Tel: (03) 5281-2550 *Fax:* (03) 5281-2552
Web Site: www.aspect.co.jp
Key Personnel
President & Publisher: Kosei Takahira
  E-mail: takahira@aspect.co.jp
Founded: 1985
Specialize in publishing of US & European titles in Japanese.
Subjects: Art, Business, Economics, Fiction, Health, Nutrition, History, Management, Marketing, Mysteries, Suspense, Nonfiction (General), Photography, Pop Culture, Psychology,

Psychiatry, Science (General), Science Fiction, Fantasy, Self-Help, Movie & Corporate Tie-ins
ISBN Prefix(es): 978-4-7572; 978-4-89366
Number of titles published annually: 150 Print
Total Titles: 3,000 Print; 100 Online; 100 E-Book
Parent Company: Aspect Corp
Subsidiaries: Aspect Digital Media Corp
Foreign Rep(s): David Russell (UK & Commonwealth, USA)
Bookshop(s): Aspect Digital Media *Web Site:* www.aspect.co.jp/ebook/index.do (online book & ebook store)

Babel Press+
2-23-1 Akasaka, Ark Hills Front Tower, Minato-ku, Tokyo 107-0052
Tel: (03) 6229-2441
E-mail: press@babel.co.jp
Web Site: www.babel.edu; www.babel.co.jp
Key Personnel
President: Miyoko Yuasa
Founded: 1977
ISBN Prefix(es): 978-4-931049; 978-4-89449
Parent Company: Babel K K
U.S. Office(s): 1720 Ala Moana Blvd, Honolulu, HI 96815, United States

Baifukan Co Ltd
4-3-12 Kudanminami, Chyoda-ku, Tokyo 102-8260
Tel: (03) 3262-5256 *Fax:* (03) 3262-5276
E-mail: bfkeigyo@mx7.mesh.ne.jp
Web Site: www.baifukan.co.jp
Key Personnel
President & Foreign Rights & Trade: Itaru Yamamoto
Founded: 1924
Subjects: Biological Sciences, Chemistry, Chemical Engineering, Computer Science, Engineering (General), Mathematics, Physics, Psychology, Psychiatry, Social Sciences, Sociology
ISBN Prefix(es): 978-4-563

Baseball Magazine-Sha Co Ltd+
3-10-10 Misakicho, Chiyoda-ku, Tokyo 101-8381
Tel: (03) 3238-0081; (025) 780-1231 (order)
Fax: (03) 3238-0107
E-mail: bbm-order@bbm-japan.com
Web Site: www.bbm-japan.com
Key Personnel
President: Tetsuo Ikeda
Founded: 1946
Membership(s): Japan Book Publishers Association.
Subjects: History, Psychology, Psychiatry, Sports, Athletics, Travel & Tourism, Baseball, Softball
ISBN Prefix(es): 978-4-583
Subsidiaries: Kobunsha Co Ltd
Branch Office(s)
486-24 Minamiuonama Kiniti Ara, Niigata 949-7235 *Tel:* (025) 780-1234
Doujma TSS Bldg, 6F 2-5-3 Sonezaki-Shinchi, Kita-ku, Osaka-shi, Osaka 530-0002 *Tel:* (06) 6341-8850

Bijutsu Shuppan-sha Co Ltd
11-1 Saragaku-cho, Shibuya-ku, Tokyo 150-0033
Tel: (03) 6809-0259
Web Site: www.bijutsu.press
Key Personnel
Chairman & President: Tomoharu Inoue
Dir: Kazuo Nakanishi
Founded: 2015 (originally 1944 as Art Publishers Inc)
Membership(s): Japan Book Publishers Association.
Subjects: Architecture & Interior Design, Art, Crafts, Games, Hobbies, How-to, Self-Help, Wine & Spirits
ISBN Prefix(es): 978-4-568; 978-4-7630

BL Publishing Co Ltd
2-2-20 Dezaike-cho, Hyogo-ku, Kobe 652-0846
Tel: (078) 681-3111 *Fax:* (078) 681-3155
E-mail: blpnew@blg.co.jp
Web Site: www.blg.co.jp/blp
Key Personnel
President: Naoya Ochiai
Founded: 1974
Membership(s): Japan Book Publishers Association; Japanese Association of Children's Book Publishers; Osaka Publishers Association.
ISBN Prefix(es): 978-4-7764; 978-4-89238

BNN Inc
21 Arai Bldg, 1-20-6, Ebisu-Minami, Shibuya-ku, Tokyo 150-0022
Fax: (03) 5725-1511
E-mail: world_info@bnn.co.jp
Web Site: www.bnn.co.jp
Founded: 1985
Subjects: Art, Computer Science, Fashion, Anime & Manga, Computer Graphics, Culture, Design, Graphic Design, Printing Technique
ISBN Prefix(es): 978-4-86100; 978-4-89369
Number of titles published annually: 60 Print
Parent Company: AZ Group
Distributed by Kyobo Book Centre; Sendpoints Books
Foreign Rep(s): art data (Europe); Asia Books (Thailand); B J Sungood Trading Co Ltd (Taiwan); Basheer Graphic Books (Hong Kong, Indonesia, Malaysia, Singapore); books@manic distribution (Australia, New Zealand); Eslite Bookstore (Taiwan); Kyobo Book Centre (Korea); ram publications + distributions inc (USA); Sendpoints Books (China)

Bronze Publishing Inc
Mansion 31-3B, 6-31-15 Jingumae, Shibuya-ku, Tokyo 150-0001
Tel: (03) 3498-3272 *Fax:* (03) 3498-5966
E-mail: editorial@bronze.co.jp; foreignrights@bronze.co.jp
Web Site: www.bronze.co.jp
Key Personnel
President: Machiko Wakatsuki
Dir, Foreign Rights: Naoko Takano
Founded: 1983
ISBN Prefix(es): 978-4-89309

Bun-ichi Sogo Shuppan
Kawakami Bldg, 2-5 Nishi-Gokencho, Shinjuku-ku, Tokyo 162-0812
Tel: (03) 3235-7341 (sales); (03) 3235-7342
Fax: (03) 3269-1402
E-mail: bunichi@bun-ichi.co.jp
Web Site: www.bun-ichi.co.jp
Key Personnel
President: Hiroshi Saito
Foreign Rights & Trade: Chihiro Kikuchi
Founded: 1959
Membership(s): Japan Book Publishers Association.
Subjects: Biological Sciences, Electronics, Electrical Engineering, Engineering (General), Environmental Studies, Natural History, Photography, Science (General), Bird Watching, Ecology
ISBN Prefix(es): 978-4-8299

Bunkasha Publishing Co Ltd+
Affiliate of Kaiohsha Co Ltd
29-6, Ichibancho, Chiyoda-ku, Tokyo 102-8405
Tel: (03) 3222-5111 *Fax:* (03) 3222-3672
E-mail: general-info@bunkasha.co.jp
Web Site: www.bunkasha.co.jp
Key Personnel
Chief Executice Officer: Kenichi Kai
Founded: 1948
Membership(s): Japan Book Publishers Association; Japan Magazine Fair Trade Council for the Promotion of Book Reading; Japan Magazine Publishers Association; Japan Publishers Club; National Council to Promote Ethics of Mass Media; Publishers Association for Cultural Exchange.
Subjects: Fashion, Fiction, Film, Video, History, Humor, Literature, Literary Criticism, Essays, Social Sciences, Sociology, Sports, Athletics
ISBN Prefix(es): 978-4-8211

Bunkashobo-Hakubun-Sha
1-9-9 Mejirodai, Bunkyo-ku, Tokyo 112-0015
Tel: (03) 3947-2034 *Fax:* (03) 3947-4976
E-mail: bunka@mvg.biglobe.ne.jp
Web Site: user.net-web.ne.jp/bunka
Key Personnel
President: Sadayoshi Suzuki
Foreign Rights & Trade: Yoshio Amano
Founded: 1957
Subjects: Art, Education, Health, Nutrition, History, Literature, Literary Criticism, Essays, Social Sciences, Sociology, Physical Education
ISBN Prefix(es): 978-4-8301

Cengage Learning K K+
5/F, Daini Funato Bldg, 1-11-11 Kudankita, Chiyoda-ku, Tokyo 102-0073
Tel: (03) 3511 4390 *Fax:* (03) 3511 4391
E-mail: asia.infojapan@cengage.com
Web Site: www.cengage.jp; www.gale.cengage.jp
Key Personnel
President: Tatsuo Matsumura
Product Manager: Masaki Morisawa
E-mail: masaki.morisawa@cengage.com
Founded: 1989
Publisher for ELT & academic texts.
Subjects: Communications, English as a Second Language, Language Arts, Linguistics
Parent Company: Cengage Learning, Stamford, CT, United States

Chijin Shokan Co Ltd+
15, Nakamachi, Shinjuku-ku, Tokyo 162-0835
Tel: (03) 3235-4422 *Fax:* (03) 3235-8984
E-mail: chijinshokan@nifty.com
Web Site: www.chijinshokan.co.jp
Key Personnel
President: Osamu Kamijo
Foreign Rights & Trade: Yukio Nagayama
Founded: 1930
Membership(s): Japan Book Publishers Association.
Subjects: Architecture & Interior Design, Astronomy, Engineering (General), Medicine, Nursing, Dentistry, Physical Sciences, Science (General), Technology
ISBN Prefix(es): 978-4-8052
Total Titles: 450 Print
Foreign Rep(s): Asano Agency (worldwide); English Agency (Japan); Japan Uni Agency (Japan); Orion Press (worldwide); Tuttle-Mori Agency (Japan)

Chikuma Shobo Publishing Co Ltd+
2-5-3 Kuramae, Taito-ku, Tokyo 111-8755
Tel: (03) 5687-2671; (03) 5687-2693 *Fax:* (03) 5687-1585
E-mail: henshuinfo@chikumashobo.co.jp
Web Site: www.chikumashobo.co.jp
Key Personnel
Chairman: Akio Kikuchi
President: Toshiyuki Kumazawa
Foreign Rights & Trade: Kana Miyachi
Founded: 1940
Membership(s): Japan Book Publishers Association.
Subjects: Art, Biography, Memoirs, Communications, Economics, Education, Fiction, History, Human Relations, Nonfiction (General), Philosophy, Religion - Buddhist, Social Sciences, Sociology, Women's Studies
ISBN Prefix(es): 978-4-480

Chikura Shobo Co Ltd
2-4-12 Kyobashi, Chuo-ku, Tokyo 104-0031
Tel: (03) 3273-3931 *Fax:* (03) 3273-7668
E-mail: sales@chikura.co.jp
Web Site: www.chikura.co.jp
Key Personnel
President: Seiji Chikura
Founded: 1929
Membership(s): Japan Book Publishers Association.
Subjects: Business, Economics, Law, Social Sciences, Sociology
ISBN Prefix(es): 978-4-8051
Number of titles published annually: 20 Print
Total Titles: 2,200 Print

Chikyu-sha Co Ltd
4-3-5 Akasaka, Minato-ku, Tokyo 107-0052
Tel: (03) 3585-0087 *Fax:* (03) 3589-2902
Founded: 1946
Subjects: Agriculture, Civil Engineering, Education, Forestry, Home Economics
ISBN Prefix(es): 978-4-8049

Chuokoron-Shinsha Inc
2-8-7 Kyobashi, Yomiuri-Chuko Bldg, Chuo-ku, Tokyo 104-8320
Tel: (03) 3563-1261; (03) 3563-1431 (sales); (03) 3563-3666 (editorial) *Fax:* (03) 3561-5920
E-mail: chosaku@chuko.co.jp; hanbai@chuko.co.jp
Web Site: www.chuko.co.jp
Key Personnel
Chairman: Akira Toriyama
President: Keiwa Kobayashi
Sales Dir: Osamu Yoshimura
Founded: 1886
Membership(s): Japan Book Publishers Association.
Subjects: Art, Economics, Government, Political Science, History, Literature, Literary Criticism, Essays, Philosophy, Religion - Other, Science (General), Social Sciences, Sociology
ISBN Prefix(es): 978-4-12

ChuoTosho Co Ltd+
40-1 Kamitoba-Minaminawashiro-chou, Minami-ku, Kyoto 601-8113
Tel: (075) 662-0222 *Fax:* (075) 662-1222
Key Personnel
President: Tsuneo Takeuchi
Founded: 1950
Subjects: Education
ISBN Prefix(es): 978-4-482

CMC Publishing Co Ltd+
Teshimaya Bldg 4F, 1-13-1 Uchi-Kanda, Chiyoda-ku, Tokyo 101-0047
Tel: (03) 3293-2061 *Fax:* (03) 3293-2069
E-mail: info@cmcbooks.co.jp
Web Site: www.cmcbooks.co.jp
Key Personnel
President & Chief Executive Officer: Kenji Tsuji
Foreign Rights/Trade: Kazunobu Mishima
    E-mail: mishima@cmcbooks.co.jp
Founded: 1961
Membership(s): Institute of Natural Sciences Book Association; Japan Book Publishers Association.
Subjects: Biological Sciences, Business, Chemistry, Chemical Engineering, Electronics, Electrical Engineering, Science (General), Technology
ISBN Prefix(es): 978-4-88231
Branch Office(s)
Otemae aj Dinasuti Bldg 4F, 1-3-12 Uchihirano, Chuo-ku, Osaka 540-0037 *Tel:* (06) 4794-8234
Fax: (06) 4794-8235

Corona Publishing Co Ltd
4-46-10 Sengoku, Bunkyo-ku, Tokyo 112-0011
Tel: (03) 3941-3131; (03) 3941-3134 (editing)
    Fax: (03) 3941-3137
E-mail: gyomu@coronasha.co.jp; henshu-1@coronasha.co.jp
Web Site: www.coronasha.co.jp
Key Personnel
Chairman: Gorai Tatsumi
President: Shinya Gorai
Founded: 1927
Subjects: Civil Engineering, Computer Science, Electronics, Electrical Engineering, Mechanical Engineering, Science (General), Technology, Metallurgy
ISBN Prefix(es): 978-4-339

Daiichi Shuppan Co Ltd
1-39, Kanda-Jimbocho, Chiyoda-ku, Tokyo 101-0051
Tel: (03) 3291-4576; (03) 3291-4577 *Fax:* (03) 3291-4579; (03) 3291-4415
E-mail: daiichi-eigyo@my.email.ne.jp
Web Site: www.daiichi-shuppan.co.jp
Key Personnel
President & Chief Executive Officer: Akira Kato
Dir: Shigeru Kurita; Kiyoshi H Sawa
Founded: 1944
Membership(s): Institute of Natural Sciences Book Society; Japan Book Publishers Association.
Subjects: Economics, Health, Nutrition, House & Home, Medicine, Nursing, Dentistry
ISBN Prefix(es): 978-4-8041
Number of titles published annually: 10 Print; 1 CD-ROM
Total Titles: 150 Print; 5 CD-ROM

Dainippon Tosho Publishing Co Ltd+
3-11-6, Otsuka, Bunkyo-ku, Tokyo 112-0112
Tel: (03) 5940-8670 (administration); (03) 5940-8675 *Fax:* (03) 5940-8682 (administration); (03) 5940-8688
Web Site: www.dainippon-tosho.co.jp
Key Personnel
President: Takeshi Hatano
Foreign Rights/Trade: Masumi Tohda *E-mail:* m-tohda@dainippon-tosho.co.jp
Founded: 1890
Membership(s): Japan Book Publishers Association.
Subjects: Chemistry, Chemical Engineering, Education, Fiction, Psychology, Psychiatry, Science (General)
ISBN Prefix(es): 978-4-477
Branch Office(s)
2-4-21 Wakababiru, Chuo Ku, Kyushu 810-0062
    Tel: (092) 721-5340 *Fax:* (092) 716-9090
    E-mail: kyushu@dainippon-tosho.co.jp
1-14-19 Takashima Bldg, Nagoya 464-0075
    Tel: (052) 733-6662 *Fax:* (052) 733-6827
2-9-4 Chiyoda Bldg, Osaka 530-0044
    Tel: (06) 6354-7315 *Fax:* (06) 6354-7316
    E-mail: osaka@dainippon-tosho.co.jp

Diamond Inc+
Diamond Bldg, 6-12-17 Jingumae, Shibuya-ku, Tokyo 150-8409
Tel: (03) 5778-7200 *Fax:* (03) 5778-6612
E-mail: info@diamond.co.jp
Web Site: www.diamond.co.jp
Key Personnel
President: Fumiaki Shikatani
Foreign Rights/Trade: Eiji Mitachi
    E-mail: rights@diamond.co.jp
Founded: 1913
Membership(s): Japan Book Publishers Association.
Subjects: Business, Career Development, Economics, Environmental Studies, Management, Marketing, Nonfiction (General), Psychology, Psychiatry, Science (General), Self-Help, Forecasting, Industrial, Research & Development
ISBN Prefix(es): 978-4-478

Subsidiaries: Diamond Agency; Diamond Big; Diamond Fund; Diamond Graphics; Diamond Service
Branch Office(s)
1-4-19 Dojimahama, Kita-ku, Osaka *Tel:* (06) 6342-0570

Discover 21 Inc
2-16-1 Hirakawa-cho, Chiyoda-ku, Tokyo 102-0093
Tel: (03) 3237-8392
E-mail: global@d21.co.jp
Web Site: en.d21.co.jp
Key Personnel
President: Yumiko Hoshiba
Founded: 1985
Subjects: Business, Education, Health, Nutrition, Management, Marketing, Science (General), Life Style, Popular Science
ISBN Prefix(es): 978-4-7993; 978-4-88759

Dobunshoin Publishers Co
5-24-3 Koishikawa, Bunkyo-ku, Tokyo 112-0002
Tel: (03) 3812-7903; (03) 3812-5157 (editorial); (03) 3812-5151 (editorial); (03) 3812-7777 (sales) *Fax:* (03) 3812-7792; (03) 3812-8456
Web Site: www.dobun.co.jp
Key Personnel
President: Fumihiro Uno
Foreign Rights/Trade: Tomokatsu Fujiyama
Founded: 1929
Membership(s): Japan Book Publishers Association.
Subjects: Business, Computer Science, Computers, Education, How-to, Medicine, Nursing, Dentistry, Nonfiction (General), Science (General), Social Sciences, Sociology, Sports, Athletics
ISBN Prefix(es): 978-4-8103

Dogakusha Verlag AG
1-10-7 Suido, Bunkyo-ku, Tokyo 112-0005
Tel: (03) 3816-7011 *Fax:* (03) 3816-7044 (sales)
E-mail: eigyoubu@dogakusha.co.jp
Web Site: www.dogakusha.co.jp
Key Personnel
President: Takao Kondo
Founded: 1950
All publications in German.
Membership(s): Japan Book Publishers Association.
Subjects: Education, Language Arts, Linguistics
ISBN Prefix(es): 978-4-8102

Doshinsha Publishing Co Ltd
4-6-6 Sengoku, Bunkyo-ku, Tokyo 112-0011
Tel: (03) 5976-4181; (03) 5976-4402 (editorial) *Fax:* (03) 5978-1078; (03) 5978-1079 (editorial)
Web Site: www.doshinsha.co.jp
Key Personnel
Chief Executive Officer & President: Masami Tanaka
Founded: 1957
ISBN Prefix(es): 978-4-494

Dou Shuppan
14-17-103 Matsugae-cho, Sagamihara-shi, Kanagawa 252-0313
Tel: (042) 748-1240; (042) 748-2423 (sales) *Fax:* (042) 748-2421
Web Site: www.dou-shuppan.com
Key Personnel
Editor-in-Chief: Ikuko Kimura
Founded: 1988
Membership(s): COSMEP.
Subjects: Philosophy, Sports, Athletics, Karate, Martial Arts
ISBN Prefix(es): 978-4-900586

The Eihosha Ltd
2-7-7, Iwamotocho, Chiyoda-ku, Tokyo 101-0032

Tel: (03) 5833-5870; (03) 5833-5871 *Fax:* (03) 5833-5872
E-mail: e@eihosha.co.jp; text@eihosha.co.jp
Web Site: www.eihosha.co.jp
Key Personnel
President: Hajime Sasaki
Founded: 1949
Membership(s): Japan Book Publishers Association.
Subjects: Language Arts, Linguistics, Literature, Literary Criticism, Essays, English as a Second Language
ISBN Prefix(es): 978-4-269

Elsevier Japan KK
1-9-15 Higashi Azabu, One Chome Bldg, 4th floor, Minato-ku, Tokyo 106-0044
Tel: (03) 5561-5033; (03) 5561-1051
Toll Free Tel: (0120) 383608 (within Japan)
Fax: (03) 5561-5047
E-mail: jp.stbooks@elsevier.com
Web Site: japan.elsevier.com; www.elsevier.com
Founded: 1880
Sales & editorial services office of Elsevier Science BV, Netherlands.
Subjects: Accounting, Agriculture, Art, Astronomy, Business, Chemistry, Chemical Engineering, Computer Science, Earth Sciences, Economics, Energy, Engineering (General), Environmental Studies, Finance, Management, Mathematics, Medicine, Nursing, Dentistry, Physics, Psychology, Psychiatry, Social Sciences, Sociology, Technology, Veterinary Science
ISBN Prefix(es): 978-4-86034
Parent Company: Elsevier Science BV, Netherlands

Filmart-Sha Co Ltd
21 Arai Bldg, 1-20-6 Ebisu-minami, Shibuya-ku, Tokyo 150-0022
Tel: (03) 5725-2001 *Fax:* (03) 5725-2626
E-mail: info@filmart.co.jp
Web Site: www.filmart.co.jp
Founded: 1968
Subjects: Japanese Art & Dance
ISBN Prefix(es): 978-4-8459

Froebel-kan Co Ltd+
6-14-9 Honkomagome, Bunkyo-ku, Tokyo 113-8611
Tel: (03) 5395-6600; (03) 5395-6641 *Fax:* (03) 5395-6642
Web Site: www.froebel-kan.co.jp
Key Personnel
President: Hideo Muto
Founded: 1907
Membership(s): Japan Book Publishers Association.
Subjects: Animals, Pets, Education, Anpanman
ISBN Prefix(es): 978-4-577
Number of titles published annually: 120 Print
Total Titles: 1,000 Print; 1 CD-ROM
Parent Company: Toppan Printing Co Ltd

Fuji Keizai Co Ltd
Kodenma-cho YS Bldg, 12-5 Nihonbashi Kodenma-cho, Chou-ku, Tokyo 103-0001
Tel: (03) 3664-5821 *Fax:* (03) 3661-9514
E-mail: info@fk-m.co.jp
Web Site: www.fuji-keizai.co.jp; www.group.fuji-keizai.co.jp
Key Personnel
President: Sakai Abe
Founded: 1962
Subjects: Electronics, Electrical Engineering
ISBN Prefix(es): 978-4-89225; 978-4-8349
Parent Company: Fuji-Keizai Group
Associate Companies: Fuji Chimera Research Institute Inc; Fuji-Keizai Zhonglian Consulting Co Ltd

U.S. Office(s): Fuji-Keizai USA Inc, 141 E 55 St, Suite 3F, New York, NY 10022, United States, Contact: S Abe *Tel:* 212-371-4773 *Fax:* 212-758-9040 *E-mail:* sabe@fuji-keizai.com

Fukuinkan Shoten Publishers Inc+
6-6-3, Honkomagome, Bunkyo-ku, Tokyo 113-8686
Tel: (03) 3942-2151 (administration); (03) 3942-0032 (international dept) *Fax:* (03) 3942-1401 (international dept)
E-mail: international-rights@fukuinkan.co.jp (international dept)
Web Site: www.fukuinkan.com; www.fukuinkan.co.jp
Key Personnel
President & Chief Executive Officer: Noboru Ogura
Manager, International Dept: Nobuhiro Takai
Founded: 1952
Specialize in children's books, including illustrated books.
Membership(s): Japan Book Publishers Association.
Subjects: Fiction, Literature, Literary Criticism, Essays, Nonfiction (General), Science (General), Science Fiction, Fantasy
ISBN Prefix(es): 978-4-8340
Number of titles published annually: 230 Print
Total Titles: 2,000 Print

Fukumura Shuppan Inc+
2-14-11 Yushima, Bunkyo-ku, Tokyo 113-0034
Tel: (03) 5812-9702 *Fax:* (03) 5812-9705
Web Site: www.fukumura.co.jp
Key Personnel
President: Akio Ishii
Foreign Rights: Motoyuki Miyashita
   E-mail: mmiyashita@fukumura.co.jp
Founded: 1939
Membership(s): Japan Book Publishers Association; Press Association Azusa.
Subjects: Education, Government, Political Science, History, Philosophy, Psychology, Psychiatry, Social Sciences, Sociology, Politics
ISBN Prefix(es): 978-4-571

Fumaido Publishing Co Ltd+
2-14-9 Otsuka, Bunkyo-ku, Tokyo 112-0012
Tel: (03) 3946-2345 *Fax:* (03) 3947-0110
E-mail: fumaido@tkd.att.ne.jp
Founded: 1960
Subjects: Education, Health, Nutrition, Sports, Athletics, Physical Education, Recreation
ISBN Prefix(es): 978-4-8293

Fuzambo International+
1-3, Kanda-Jimbocho, Chiyoda-ku, Tokyo 101-0051
Tel: (03) 3291-2577; (03) 3291-2578 (orders); (03) 5210-1331 (editorial) *Fax:* (03) 3219-4866; (03) 5210-1332 (editorial)
E-mail: info@fuzambo-intl.com; fuzambo-intl-hensyu@bridge.ocn.ne.jp (editing)
Web Site: www.fuzambo-intl.com
Key Personnel
President: Kiichi Sakamoto
Founded: 1886
Membership(s): Japan Book Publishers Association.
Subjects: Art, Geography, Geology, History, Language Arts, Linguistics, Law, Literature, Literary Criticism, Essays, Philosophy, Religion - Other, Social Sciences, Sociology
ISBN Prefix(es): 978-4-572
Branch Office(s)
13 Kisshoin'ikedaminami, Minami-ku, Kyoto 601-8346 *Tel:* (075) 671-7306 *Fax:* (075) 671-7309
Tatsumi Bldg D, Room 3, 607 Higashishiokoji, Nishinotoin, Shimogyo, Kyoto 600-8216

Tel: (075) 361-5766 *Fax:* (075) 361-5755
E-mail: k-eigyou@fuzambo-intl.com
Bookshop(s): 3-24-22 Sakurajosui, Setagaya-ku, Tokyo 156-0045 *Tel:* (03) 5374-8610 *Fax:* (03) 5374-8610 *E-mail:* sakura@fuzambo-intl.com; 3-25-40 Sakurajosui, Setagaya-ku, Tokyo 156-8550 *Tel:* (03) 5374-8376 *Fax:* (03) 5374-6814

Gakken Holdings Co Ltd+
2-11-8 Nishigotanda, Shinagawa-ku, Tokyo 141-8510
Tel: (03) 6431-1001 *Fax:* (03) 6431-1660
Web Site: www.gakken.co.jp
Key Personnel
President: Hiroaki Miyahara
Mng Dir: Michinori Kimura; Satoru Nakamori
Founded: 1947
Subjects: Art, Astrology, Occult, Automotive, Business, Child Care & Development, Computer Science, Education, Electronics, Electrical Engineering, Environmental Studies, Gardening, Plants, House & Home, Nonfiction (General), Outdoor Recreation, Radio, TV, Comic Books
ISBN Prefix(es): 978-4-05

Gakuseisha Publishing Co Ltd
3-27-14 Shikahama, Adachi-ku, Tokyo 123-0864
Tel: (03) 3857-3031 *Fax:* (03) 3857-3037
E-mail: info@gakusei.co.jp
Web Site: www.gakusei.co.jp
Key Personnel
President: Ichiro Tsuruoka
Founded: 1952
Subjects: Archaeology, Business, Geography, Geology, History, Language Arts, Linguistics, Law, Literature, Literary Criticism, Essays, Philosophy, Religion - Other, Social Sciences, Sociology
ISBN Prefix(es): 978-4-311

Genkosha
4-1-5 Iidabashi, Chiyoda-ku, Tokyo 102-8716
Tel: (03) 3263-3511; (03) 3263-3515 (sales) *Fax:* (03) 3263-3830; (03) 3263-3045 (sales)
E-mail: gks@genkosha.co.jp
Web Site: www.genkosha.co.jp
Key Personnel
President: Hiroshi Kitahara
Foreign Rights/Trade: Toshimitsu Katsuyama
Founded: 1931
Membership(s): Japan Book Publishers Association.
Subjects: Art, Film, Video, How-to, Photography
ISBN Prefix(es): 978-4-7683
Subsidiaries: Salon Agency Co Ltd (advertising agency)
Warehouse: Ono Poking Co Ltd, Inari Souka City *Tel:* (0489) 32 2911 *Fax:* (0489) 36 5333
Orders to: Nippan Shuppan Hanabai Inc International Division, 4-3 Kandasurugadai, Chiyoda-ku, Tokyo 101-8710 *Tel:* (03) 3233-4083 *Fax:* (03) 3233-4106 *E-mail:* nakamura_s@ nippan.co.jp *Web Site:* www.nippan.co.jp

Gyosei Corp
1-18-11, Shinkiba, Koto-ku, Tokyo 136-8575
Tel: (03) 6892-6342; (03) 6892-6589 *Fax:* (03) 6892-6932; (03) 6892-6925
E-mail: business@gyosei.co.jp
Web Site: www.gyosei.co.jp
Key Personnel
President: Yujiro Sawado
Foreign Rights/Trade: Osamu Yamashita
Founded: 1893
Membership(s): Japan Book Publishers Association.
Subjects: Business, Education, Law, Management
ISBN Prefix(es): 978-4-324

Hakubunkan-Shinsha Publishers Ltd
Hakubunkan Bldg, 5-9-7 Arakawa, Arakawa-ku,
Tokyo 116-0002
Tel: (03) 6458-3838 *Fax:* (03) 5604-3391
Web Site: www.hakubunkan.co.jp
Key Personnel
President: Kazuhiro Ohashi
Foreign Rights/Trade: Tomoe Ohashi *E-mail:* t-
ohashi@hakubunkan.co.jp
Founded: 1950
Membership(s): Japan Book Publishers Associa-
tion.
Subjects: Agriculture, Art, Poetry
ISBN Prefix(es): 978-4-89177; 978-4-86115
Parent Company: Hakuyusha Publishing Co Ltd

Hakusuisha Publishing Co Ltd
3-24, Kanda-Ogawa-cho, Chiyoda-ku, Tokyo 101-
0052
Tel: (03) 3291-7816 (general affairs); (03) 3291-
7821 (editorial); (03) 3291-7811 (sales)
Fax: (03) 3291-8448 (sales)
E-mail: hpmaster@hakusuisha.co.jp; hporder@
hakusuisha.co.jp
Web Site: www.hakusuisha.co.jp
Key Personnel
Chairman: Masayuki Kawamura
President: Naoshi Oikawa
Foreign Rights/Trade: Hiroshi Shibayama
Founded: 1915
Membership(s): Japan Book Publishers Associa-
tion.
Subjects: Art, Drama, Theater, Fiction, History,
Language Arts, Linguistics, Literature, Literary
Criticism, Essays, Music, Dance, Nonfiction
(General), Philosophy
ISBN Prefix(es): 978-4-560

Hakuteisha+
2-65-1, Ikebukuro, Toshima-ku, Tokyo 171-0014
Tel: (03) 3986-3271 *Fax:* (03) 3986-3272 (sales);
(03) 3986-8892 (editorial)
E-mail: info@hakuteisha.co.jp
Web Site: www.hakuteisha.co.jp
Key Personnel
President: Yasuo Sato
Founded: 1977
Membership(s): Japan Book Publishers Associa-
tion.
Subjects: Health, Nutrition, Language Arts, Lin-
guistics, Literature, Literary Criticism, Essays,
Religion - Buddhist, Sports, Athletics
ISBN Prefix(es): 978-4-89174

Hakuyo-Sha Publishing Co Ltd
1-7-7 Kanda-Surugadai, Chiyoda-ku, Tokyo 101-
0062
Tel: (03) 5281-9772 *Fax:* (03) 5281-9886
E-mail: info@hakuyo-sha.co.jp; hakuyo@mars.
dti.ne.jp
Web Site: www.hakuyo-sha.co.jp
Key Personnel
President: Hiroshi Nakamura
Foreign Rights/Trade: Kazuhiko Takao
Founded: 1916
Membership(s): Japan Book Publishers Associa-
tion.
Subjects: Animals, Pets, Nonfiction (General),
Psychology, Psychiatry, Science (General)
ISBN Prefix(es): 978-4-8269

Hakuyu-Sha
5-9-7, Arakawa, Arakawa-ku, Tokyo 116-0002
Tel: (03) 6458-3838 *Fax:* (03) 5604-3391
Web Site: www.hakubunkan.co.jp
Key Personnel
President: Kazuhiro Ohashi
Founded: 1950
Membership(s): Japan Book Publishers Associa-
tion.

Subjects: Agriculture, Labor, Industrial Relations,
Science (General), Haiku
ISBN Prefix(es): 978-4-8268

Hankyu Communications Co Ltd
1-24-12 Meguro, Meguro-ku, Tokyo 153-8541
Tel: (03) 5436-5701; (03) 5436-5712 *Fax:* (03)
5436-5746
Key Personnel
President: Takeshi Ioi
Founded: 1969
Membership(s): Japan Book Publishers Associa-
tion.
Subjects: Art, Literature, Literary Criticism, Es-
says, Social Sciences, Sociology
ISBN Prefix(es): 978-4-484

Hara Shobo
2-3 Kanda Jimbocho, Chiyoda-ku, Tokyo 101-
0051
Tel: (03) 5212 7801 *Fax:* (03) 3230 1158
E-mail: toshi@harashobo.com; sales@harashobo.
com
Web Site: www.harashobo.com
Handle wide variety of ukiyo-e prints, paintings,
illustrated books from 17th century to 20th
century & shin-hanga (modern prints) as well
as reproductions, catalogues & reference books.
Membership(s): International Ukiyo-e Society;
Japan Print & Arts Auction (JPAA); Ukiyo-e
Dealers Association of Japan; Ukiyo-e Society
of America.
Subjects: Art
ISBN Prefix(es): 978-4-562

HarperCollins Japan
Division of HarperCollins Publishers
Tokyo Akihabara Sanwa Toyo Bldg 3-16-8,
Kotobuki-ku, Tokyo 101-0021
Tel: (03) 5295-8090 *Fax:* (03) 5295-8091 (sales)
Web Site: corporate.harpercollins.co.jp; www.
harlequin.co.jp
Key Personnel
Chief Executive Officer: Suzuki Yukitsuki
President: Frank Foley
Publishing Dir: Shigenori Hamaguchi
Marketing Dir: Matthew Pride
Founded: 1988
Subjects: Business, Economics, Management,
Mysteries, Suspense, Nonfiction (General), Sci-
ence Fiction, Fantasy
ISBN Prefix(es): 978-0-596

Hayakawa Publishing Inc
2-2 Kanda-Tacho, Chiyoda-ku, Tokyo 101-0046
Tel: (03) 3252-3111 *Fax:* (03) 3254-1550
E-mail: customer@hayakawa-online.co.jp
Web Site: www.hayakawa-online.co.jp
Key Personnel
President: Hiroshi Hayakawa
Executive Vice President: Atsushi Hayakawa
Founded: 1945
Membership(s): Japan Book Publishers Associa-
tion (JBPA).
Subjects: Art, Astrology, Occult, Astronomy, Be-
havioral Sciences, Biography, Memoirs, Biolog-
ical Sciences, Business, Drama, Theater, Earth
Sciences, Economics, Fiction, Government,
Political Science, History, Literature, Literary
Criticism, Essays, Management, Mathemat-
ics, Mysteries, Suspense, Nonfiction (General),
Philosophy, Photography, Physics, Psychol-
ogy, Psychiatry, Publishing & Book Trade Ref-
erence, Religion - Other, Romance, Science
(General), Science Fiction, Fantasy, Self-Help,
Social Sciences, Sociology, Sports, Athletics,
Travel & Tourism, Western Fiction, Wine &
Spirits
ISBN Prefix(es): 978-4-15
Bookshop(s): 10-2 Itakura-machi, Ora-gun,
Gunma 374-0131 *Tel:* (0276) 82-2000

Heibonsha Ltd Publishers+
3-29 Kanda-jimbocho, Chiyoda-ku, Tokyo 101-
0051
Tel: (03) 3230-6570; (03) 3230-6572 (sales)
Fax: (03) 3230-6586
E-mail: webmaster@heibonsha.co.jp; shop@
heibonsha.co.jp; hanbai@heibonsha.co.jp
(books)
Web Site: www.heibonsha.co.jp
Founded: 1914
Subjects: Art, Education, History, Nonfiction
(General), Philosophy, Science (General), So-
cial Sciences, Sociology
ISBN Prefix(es): 978-4-582; 978-4-256
Number of titles published annually: 250 Print

Hikarinokuni Ltd
3-2-14 Uehonmachi, Tennoji-ku, Osaka 543-0001
Tel: (06) 6768-1151 *Fax:* (06) 6768-6970
E-mail: honsya-somu@hikarinokuni.co.jp
Web Site: www.hikarinokuni.co.jp
Key Personnel
President: Takeshi Okamoto
Founded: 1946
Specialize in early childhood education.
Membership(s): Japan Book Publishers Associa-
tion (JBPA).
Subjects: Crafts, Games, Hobbies, Economics,
Education, House & Home, Medicine, Nursing,
Dentistry
ISBN Prefix(es): 978-4-564
Branch Office(s)
6-1-1 Takashimadaira, Itabasi-ku, Tokyo 175-0082
Tel: (03) 379-3111

Hinoki Shoten Co Ltd
2-1 Kanda-Ogawamachi, Chiyoda-ku, Tokyo 101-
0052
Tel: (03) 3291-2488 *Fax:* (03) 3295-3554
E-mail: info@hinoki-shoten.co.jp; sales@hinoki-
shoten.co.jp
Web Site: www.hinoki-shoten.co.jp
Key Personnel
President & Foreign Rights/Trade: Tsunemasa
Hinoki *E-mail:* hinoki@hinoki-shoten.co.jp
Founded: 1659
Publisher of Noh & Kyogen Books.
Membership(s): Japan Book Publishers Associa-
tion (JBPA).
Subjects: Drama, Theater, Kyogen, Noh
ISBN Prefix(es): 978-4-8279
Bookshop(s): Kanze Noh Theater Shops, 1-16-4
Shoto, Shibuya-ku, Tokyo 150-0052 *Tel:* (03)
3469-5241; Nijo Kikuyachou, Nakagyo-ku, Ky-
oto 604-0821 *Tel:* (075) 231-1990 *Fax:* (075)
231-2508; 44 Enshoji-cho, Sakyo-ku, Kyoto
606-8344 *Tel:* (075) 771-6114

Hirokawa Publishing Co+
3-27-14 Hongo, Bunkyo-ku, Tokyo 113-0033
Tel: (03) 3815-3651 *Fax:* (03) 5684-7030
Key Personnel
President: Setsuo Hirokawa
Foreign Rights: Haruo Hirokawa
Founded: 1925
Subjects: Biological Sciences, Chemistry, Chemi-
cal Engineering, Mathematics, Medicine, Nurs-
ing, Dentistry, Science (General), Pharmaceuti-
cal Sciences
ISBN Prefix(es): 978-4-567
Total Titles: 50 Print

Hituzi Shobo Publishing Ltd
Yamato Bldg 2F, Sengoku 2-1-2, Bunkyo-ku,
Tokyo 112-0011
Tel: (03) 5319-4916 *Fax:* (03) 5319-4917
E-mail: toiawase@hituzi.co.jp
Web Site: www.hituzi.co.jp
Key Personnel
President: Isao Matsumoto
Manager: Kumiko Matsumoto
Founded: 1990

Membership(s): Japan Book Publishers Association.
Subjects: Anthropology, Asian Studies, Behavioral Sciences, Civil Engineering, Communications, Education, English as a Second Language, Human Relations, Language Arts, Linguistics, Library & Information Sciences, Social Sciences, Sociology, Wine & Spirits
ISBN Prefix(es): 978-4-89476; 978-4-938669
Number of titles published annually: 60 Print; 5 CD-ROM
Total Titles: 380 Print; 20 CD-ROM

Hokkaido University Press
N9, W8 Kita-ku, Sapporo 060-0809
Tel: (011) 747-2308 *Fax:* (011) 736-8605
E-mail: hupress_1@hup.gr.jp
Web Site: www.hup.gr.jp
Key Personnel
President: Dr Hiroshi Saeki
Foreign Rights & Trade: Kauzuo Narita
Founded: 1970
Membership(s): Japan Book Publishers Association.
Subjects: Science (General), Social Sciences, Sociology, Technology, Humanities, Natural Science
ISBN Prefix(es): 978-4-8329

Hokuryukan & New Science Co Ltd+
3-8-14 Takanawa, Minato-ku, Tokyo 108-0074
Tel: (03) 5449-4591 *Fax:* (03) 5449-4950
E-mail: hk-ns2@hokuryukan-ns.co.jp
Web Site: www.hokuryukan-ns.co.jp
Key Personnel
President: Hisako Fukuda
Foreign Rights & Trade: Hiroyuki Kadoya
Founded: 1891
Membership(s): Japan Book Publishers Association (JBPA).
Subjects: Agriculture, Archaeology, Biological Sciences, Education, Medicine, Nursing, Dentistry, Science (General)
ISBN Prefix(es): 978-4-8326; 978-4-8216
Subsidiaries: New Science Publishing Co

Holp Shuppan Publishing
3-8-5 Misakicho, Chiyoda-ku, Tokyo 101-0061
Tel: (03) 3556-3991 *Fax:* (03) 3556-3992
E-mail: holp@holp-pub.co.jp
Web Site: www.holp-pub.co.jp
Key Personnel
President: Nobuyuki Takahashi
Dir: Kunihiko Oka
ISBN Prefix(es): 978-4-593

Child Honsha Co Ltd+
5-24-21 Koishikawa, Bunkyo-ku, Tokyo 112-8512
Tel: (03) 3813-3785; (03) 3813-2141 (sales)
   Fax: (03) 3818-3765
Web Site: www.childbook.co.jp
Key Personnel
President & Chief Executive Officer: Asaka Shunji
Foreign Rights & Trade: Satoshi Ito
Founded: 1944
Specialize in child care & early childhood education.
Subjects: Child Care & Development, Education
ISBN Prefix(es): 978-4-8054
Associate Companies: Kyodo Printing Co Ltd
Subsidiaries: Basic Inc; Hisakata Child Co Ltd

Horitsu Bunka Sha
71 Kamigamo-Iwagakakiuchi-machi, Kita-ku, Kyoto 603-8053
Tel: (075) 791-7131 *Fax:* (075) 721-8400
E-mail: eigyo@hou-bun.co.jp
Web Site: www.hou-bun.com
Key Personnel
President: Junko Tanabiki

Founded: 1946
Subjects: Economics, Law, Philosophy, Public Administration, Social Sciences, Sociology, Politics
ISBN Prefix(es): 978-4-589

Hyoronsha Publishing Co Ltd
2-21 Tsukudo Hachimancho, Shinjuku-ku, Tokyo 162-0815
Tel: (03) 3260-9403; (03) 3260-9409 (sales)
   Fax: (03) 3260-9408
Web Site: www.hyoronsha.co.jp
Key Personnel
President: Harunobu Takeshita *Tel:* (03) 3260-9401
Founded: 1948
Membership(s): Japan Book Publishers Association.
Subjects: Education, History, Language Arts, Linguistics, Law, Philosophy, Religion - Buddhist, Religion - Other, Social Sciences, Sociology
ISBN Prefix(es): 978-4-566

IBC Publishing Inc+
Ryoshu Kagurazaka Bldg, 9F, 29-3 Nakazato-cho, Shinjuku-ku, Tokyo 162-0804
Tel: (03) 3513-4511 *Fax:* (03) 3513-4512
Web Site: www.ibcpub.co.jp
Key Personnel
Chief Executive Officer & President: Kuniaki Ura
Founded: 2003
Subjects: Art, Asian Studies, English as a Second Language, Language Arts, Linguistics
ISBN Prefix(es): 978-4-89684; 978-4-925080; 978-4-7946
Parent Company: Yohan Inc
Associate Companies: Heian International

Ie-No-Hikari Association+
11, Funagawara-cho, Shinjuku-ku, Tokyo 162-8448
Tel: (03) 3266-9000; (03) 3266-9038 (sales)
   Fax: (03) 3266-9337 (sales)
Web Site: www.ienohikari.net
Key Personnel
President: Toshihiro Sonoda
Foreign Rights & Trade: Takayuki Kawachi
Founded: 1925
Membership(s): Japan Book Publishers Association (JBPA).
Subjects: Agriculture, Economics, House & Home, Social Sciences, Sociology, Cooperatives
ISBN Prefix(es): 978-4-259

Igaku-Shoin Ltd+
1-28-23 Hongo, Bunkyo-ku, Tokyo 113-8719
Tel: (03) 38175600 *Fax:* (03) 38157791
E-mail: info@igaku-shoin.co.jp
Web Site: www.igaku-shoin.co.jp
Key Personnel
CEO & President: Yu Kanehara
Vice President & Editor, Medical Publications: Minoru Sakamoto
Vice President & Editor, Nursing Publications: Kiyoshi Nanao
Vice President, Production & Electronic Publishing: Shun Kanehara
Vice President, Publishing & System Administration: Kazuaki Hayasaka
Vice President, Sales & Marketing: Akihiro Takahashi
Mng Dir & Chief Editor: Nanao Qing
Founded: 1944
Subjects: Medicine, Nursing, Dentistry
ISBN Prefix(es): 978-4-260
Number of titles published annually: 250 Print; 6 CD-ROM; 37 Online
Total Titles: 1,800 Print; 6 CD-ROM; 37 Online
Subsidiaries: Medical Sciences International Ltd

Intercultural Book Co, see IBC Publishing Inc

Ishihara Publishing Co Ltd
Kandabashi Bldg, 20-2, Shinshouin-chou, Kagoshima-shi, Kagoshima 890-0016
Tel: (099) 239-1200 *Fax:* (099) 239-1202
E-mail: info@isihara-kk.co.jp
Web Site: www.isihara-kk.co.jp
Key Personnel
President: Mitsuko Ishihara
Foreign Rights/Trade: Tetsu Nakahata
Founded: 1990
Membership(s): Japan Book Publishers Association (JBPA).
ISBN Prefix(es): 978-4-900611
Imprints: Ishihara's Decade Diary

Ishihara's Decade Diary, *imprint of* Ishihara Publishing Co Ltd

Ishiyaku Publishers Inc
1-7-10, Honkomagome, Bunkyo-ku, Tokyo 113-8612
Tel: (03) 5395-7600; (03) 5395-7605 (sales)
   Fax: (03) 5395-7614
E-mail: wdomaster@ishiyaku.co.jp; copyright@ishiyaku.co.jp (publications affairs dept)
Web Site: www.ishiyaku.co.jp
Key Personnel
President: Hideho Ohata
Publisher, Dental Division: Hiroshi Gojobori
Publisher, Medical Division: Seiji Nuruki
Foreign Rights/Trade: Yasuke Iwamoto
Founded: 1921
Subjects: Health, Nutrition, Medicine, Nursing, Dentistry, Veterinary Science, Natural Science, Oriental Medicine
ISBN Prefix(es): 978-4-260; 978-4-263; 978-4-281
Orders to: Tokyo Mail Service Co Ltd, 1-30-6 Sugamo, Toshimaku, Tokyo 170-8640 *Tel:* (03) 5976-0631 *Fax:* (03) 5976-0630 *E-mail:* tokyo-ms@d1.dion.ne.jp

Italia Shobo Ltd
2-23, Kanda-Jimbocho, Chiyoda-ku, Tokyo 101-0051
Tel: (03) 3262-1656 *Fax:* (03) 3234-6469
E-mail: info@italiashobo.co.jp
Web Site: italiashobo.com
Key Personnel
President & Foreign Rights/Trade: Doichi Ito
Founded: 1958
Specialize in Italian, Spanish & Portuguese imported books.
Membership(s): Japan Association of International Publications (JAIP).
Subjects: Architecture & Interior Design, Art, Cookery, Language Arts, Linguistics
ISBN Prefix(es): 978-4-900143
Branch Office(s)
Casa dei Libri Giaponesi, Viale Petrarca, 42/R, 50124 Florence FI, Italy *Tel:* (055) 223619 *Fax:* (055) 223619 *E-mail:* firenze@italiashobo.co.jp

Iwanami Shoten, Publishers+
2-5-5, Hitotsubashi, Chiyoda-ku, Tokyo 101-8002
Tel: (03) 5210-4000 *Fax:* (03) 5210-4039
E-mail: rights@iwanami.co.jp
Web Site: www.iwanami.co.jp
Key Personnel
President: Akio Yamaguchi
Foreign Rights: Rika Ito *E-mail:* rika-ito@iwanami.co.jp
Founded: 1913
Subjects: Art, Biography, Memoirs, Economics, Electronics, Electrical Engineering, History, Literature, Literary Criticism, Essays, Philosophy, Photography, Psychology, Psychiatry, Science (General), Social Sciences, Sociology
ISBN Prefix(es): 978-4-00

Number of titles published annually: 700 Print; 10 CD-ROM
Total Titles: 5,000 Print; 30 CD-ROM; 10 Audio
Orders to: Japan Publications Trading Co Ltd, 1-2-1 Sarugakucho, Chiyoda-ku, Tokyo 101-0064
Tel: (03) 3292-3751 *Fax:* (03) 3292-0410

Iwasaki Shoten Co Ltd
1-9-2 Suido, Bunkyo-ku, Tokyo 112-0005
Tel: (03) 3812-9131 *Fax:* (03) 3816-6033
E-mail: info@iwasakishoten.co.jp
Web Site: www.iwasakishoten.co.jp
Key Personnel
President: Hiroaki Iwasaki
Foreign Rights: Miyuki Yamalita
Founded: 1934
Membership(s): Japan Children's Books Association.
Subjects: Art, Fiction
ISBN Prefix(es): 978-4-265
Number of titles published annually: 170 Print
Associate Companies: Iwasaki Gakujitsu Publishing Co
Subsidiaries: Iwasaki Art Publishing Co
Branch Office(s)
Hoei Bldg, Room 101, 3-62, Tamachi, Kita-Ku, Nagoyu 462-0813 *Tel:* (052) 916-2002 *Fax:* (052) 916-2006
2-12 Ryutsudanchi, Koshigaya (Saitama) 343-0824 *Tel:* (048) 989-2321 *Fax:* (048) 989-2322
Yuai Bldg, Room 703, 3-1-15 Kyutaromachi, Chuo-Ku, Osaka 541-0056 *Tel:* (06) 6241 1005 *Fax:* (06) 6241 1115

Japan Bible Society
5-1, Ginza 4-chome, Chuo-ku, Tokyo 104-0061
Tel: (03) 3567-0385 *Fax:* (03) 3567-4451
E-mail: info@bible.or.jp
Web Site: www.bible.or.jp
Key Personnel
President: Hiroshi Omiya
General Secretary: Rev Makoto Watabe
  E-mail: makoto-w@bible.or.jp
Founded: 1875
Specialize in Bible translation.
Membership(s): Japan Book Publisher Association; United Bible Societies.
ISBN Prefix(es): 978-4-8202

Japan Broadcast Publishing Co Ltd+
41-1, Udagawa-cho, Shibuya-ku, Tokyo 150-8081
Tel: (03) 3464-7311 *Fax:* (03) 3780-3353
Web Site: www.nhk-book.co.jp
Key Personnel
President: Akihide Mizoguchi
Foreign Rights/Trade: Naoki Momohara
  E-mail: momohara-n@nhk-book.co.jp
Founded: 1931
Membership(s): Japan Book Publishers Association.
Subjects: Art, Crafts, Games, Hobbies, Drama, Theater, Education, Fiction, Geography, Geology, History, How-to, Language Arts, Linguistics, Literature, Literary Criticism, Essays, Nonfiction (General), Science (General), Social Sciences, Sociology
ISBN Prefix(es): 978-4-14

Japan Educational Publishing Co Ltd, see
Nihon-Bunkyo Shuppan (Japan Educational Publishing Co Ltd)

The Japan Foundation
4-4-1 Yotsuya, Shinjuku-ku, Tokyo 160-0004
Tel: (03) 5369-6064 *Fax:* (03) 5369-6038
E-mail: jf-toiawase@jpf.go.jp
Web Site: www.jpf.go.jp
Key Personnel
President: Hiroyasu Ando
Subjects: Art, Education, Film, Video, Language Arts, Linguistics, Culture
ISBN Prefix(es): 978-4-87540

Japan Industrial Publishing Co Ltd+
6-3-26 Honkomagome, Bunkyo-ku, Tokyo 113-8610
Tel: (03) 3944-1181; (03) 3944-8001 (sales)
  Fax: (03) 3944-6826; (03) 3944-0389 (sales)
E-mail: info@nikko-pb.co.jp; sale@nikko-pb.co.jp
Web Site: www.nikko-pb.co.jp
Founded: 1953
Subjects: Construction Machinery & Equipment, Hydraulics & Pneumatics
ISBN Prefix(es): 978-4-88045
Subsidiaries: Nikko Techno Research Co Ltd
Branch Office(s)
1-6-8 Hirano-cho, Chuo-ku, Osaka 541-0046
  Tel: (06) 6202-8218 *Fax:* (06) 6202-8287
  E-mail: info-o@nikko-pb.co.jp

Japan Publications Inc+
5-2-2 Hongo, Bunkyo-ku, Tokyo 113-0033
Tel: (03) 5805-3303 *Fax:* (03) 5805-3307
E-mail: jpub@nichibou.co.jp
Web Site: www.nichibou.co.jp
Key Personnel
Chairman: Mizuno Atsumi *E-mail:* mizuno@nichibou.co.jp
Founded: 1966
Subjects: Agriculture, Asian Studies, Child Care & Development, Cookery, Crafts, Games, Hobbies, Health, Nutrition
ISBN Prefix(es): 978-4-8170
Parent Company: Japan Publications Trading Co Ltd, 1-2-1 Sarugaku-cho, Chiyoda-ku, Tokyo 101-0064 (import & export)
Orders to: Oxford University Press, 198 Madison Ave, New York, NY 10016, United States

The Japan Times Ltd
4-5-4 Shibaura, Minato-ku, Tokyo 108-0014
Tel: (03) 3453-5312 *Fax:* (03) 3452-0659
E-mail: jtsales@japantimes.co.jp
Web Site: www.japantimes.co.jp
Key Personnel
Chairman & Publisher: Toshiaki Ogasawara
Foreign Rights/Trade: Takatoshi Michimata
  E-mail: michimata@japantimes.co.jp
Founded: 1897
Specialize in Japanese language learning books & materials.
Membership(s): Japan Book Publishers Association (JBPA).
Subjects: Asian Studies, Nonfiction (General)
ISBN Prefix(es): 978-4-7890
Book Club(s): The Japan Times Bookclub *Web Site:* bookclub.japantimes.co.jp

Japan Travel Bureau, see JTB Publishing Inc

Jiho Inc
1-5-15 Sarugakucho, Chiyoda-ku, Tokyo 101-8421
Tel: (03) 3233-6381; (03) 3233-6333 (sales); (03) 3233-6361 (publications) *Fax:* (03) 3233-6389; (03) 3233-6338 (sales); (03) 3233-6369 (publications)
Web Site: www.jiho.co.jp
Key Personnel
President: Shoichiro Takeda
Specialize in pharmaceutical industry & regulation & pharmaceutical sciences.
Subjects: Medicine, Nursing, Dentistry
ISBN Prefix(es): 978-4-8407
Branch Office(s)
2-1-1 Fushimi-cho, Chuo-ku, Osaka 541-0044
  Tel: (06) 6231-7061 *Fax:* (06) 6227-5404

JTB Publishing Inc
25-5 Haraikatacho, Shinjuku-ku, Tokyo 162-8446
Tel: (03) 6888-7821 *Fax:* (03) 6888-7829
E-mail: jtbpublishing@rurubu.ne.jp
Web Site: www.jtbpublishing.com

Key Personnel
President & Chief Executive Officer: Yuji Yokoyama
Founded: 2004
Subjects: Geography, Geology, History, Language Arts, Linguistics, Travel & Tourism, Fine Arts
ISBN Prefix(es): 978-4-533
Parent Company: JTB Corp
Subsidiaries: Densan Process Co; Kotsu Print Co; Kotsu Seihon Co; Toyo Books Co

JUSE Press Ltd, see Nikkagiren Shuppan-Sha (JUSE Press Ltd)

Kadokawa Group Publishing Co Ltd
2-13-3 Fujimi, Chiyoda-ku, Tokyo 102-8177
Tel: (03) 3238-8521; (03) 3238-8530 (sales)
  Fax: (03) 3262-7734 (sales)
E-mail: k-master@kadokawa.co.jp; customer@kadokawa.co.jp
Web Site: www.kadokawa.co.jp
Key Personnel
Chief Executive Officer & President: Tatsuo Sato
Executive Dir: Koichi Sekiya
Founded: 1945
Membership(s): Japan Book Publishers Association (JBPA).
Subjects: Art, Fiction, History, Literature, Literary Criticism, Essays, Religion - Other, Comics
ISBN Prefix(es): 978-4-04
Bookshop(s): 1-8-19 Fujimi, Chiyoda-ku, Tokyo 102-8024

Kadokawa S S Communications Inc
Kinsan Bldg, 3-18-3, Kanda-nishikicho, Chiyoda-ku, Tokyo 101-0054
Tel: (03) 52830220 *Fax:* (03) 52830229
Founded: 1983
Subjects: Fiction, Nonfiction (General)
ISBN Prefix(es): 978-4-8275
Parent Company: Kadokawa Group Publishing Co Ltd

Kagaku-Dojin Publishing Co Inc+
Yanaginobanba-nishiiru, Bukkoji-dori, Shimogyo-ku, Kyoto 600-8074
Tel: (075) 352-3373 (sales); (075) 352-3711 (editorial) *Fax:* (075) 351-8301
Web Site: www.kagakudojin.co.jp
Key Personnel
President: Ryosuke Sone
Editor & Foreign Rights & Trade: Takahiro Kato
  E-mail: tkato@kagakudojin.co.jp
Founded: 1954
Membership(s): Japan Book Publishers Association.
Subjects: Biological Sciences, Chemistry, Chemical Engineering, Environmental Studies, Health, Nutrition, Physical Sciences, Science (General)
ISBN Prefix(es): 978-4-7598

Kaibundo Publishing Co Ltd
2-5-4 Suido, Bunkyo-ku, Tokyo 112-0005
Tel: (03) 3815-3291 (editorial) *Fax:* (03) 3815-3953
E-mail: henshu@kaibundo.jp (editorial); hanbai@kaibundo.jp (sales)
Web Site: www.kaibundo.jp
Key Personnel
President: Setsuo Okada
Editorial Dir & Foreign Rights/Trade: Toshio Iwamoto *E-mail:* soumu@kaibundo.jp
Founded: 1914
Membership(s): Japan Book Publishers Association (JBPA).
Subjects: Business, Computers, Engineering (General), Maritime, Technology, Navigation, Shipbuilding
ISBN Prefix(es): 978-4-303

Kaisei-Sha Publishing Co Ltd+
3-5 Ichigaya Sadohara-cho, Shinjuku-ku, Tokyo
162-8450
Tel: (03) 3260-3229 *Fax:* (03) 3260-3540
E-mail: foreign@kaiseisha.co.jp
Web Site: www.kaiseisha.co.jp; www.kaiseisha.net
Key Personnel
President: Masaki Imamura
Foreign Rights: Yuko Nonaka
Founded: 1936
Membership(s): Japan Book Publishers Association (JBPA).
Subjects: Animals, Pets, Art, Astronomy, Biography, Memoirs, Cookery, Crafts, Games, Hobbies, Disability, Special Needs, Earth Sciences, Environmental Studies, Fiction, Foreign Countries, Health, Nutrition, History, Nonfiction (General), Science (General), Science Fiction, Fantasy
ISBN Prefix(es): 978-4-03
Number of titles published annually: 150 Print
Total Titles: 4,000 Print

Kaitakusha Publishing Co Ltd+
1-5-2, Mukogaoka, Bunkyo-ku, Tokyo 113-0023
Tel: (03) 5842-8900 *Fax:* (03) 5842-5560
E-mail: info@kaitakusha.co.jp
Web Site: www.kaitakusha.co.jp
Founded: 1927
Subjects: Education, English as a Second Language, Language Arts, Linguistics, Literature, Literary Criticism, Essays
ISBN Prefix(es): 978-4-7589
Number of titles published annually: 30 Print; 3 CD-ROM; 3 Audio
Total Titles: 300 Print; 10 CD-ROM; 50 Audio
Distribution Center: Japan Publications Trading Co Ltd, 1-2-1 Sarugaku-cho, Chiyoda-ku, Tokyo 101-0064 *Tel:* (03) 3292-3751 *Fax:* (03) 3292-0410 *E-mail:* jpt@jptco.co.jp

Kajima Institute Publishing Co Ltd
6-2-8, Akasaka, Minato-ku, Tokyo 107-0052
Tel: (03) 6202 5200 *Fax:* (03) 6202 5204
E-mail: info@kajima-publishing.co.jp
Web Site: www.kajima-publishing.co.jp
Key Personnel
President: Koichi Kashima
Founded: 1963
Subjects: Architecture & Interior Design, Civil Engineering, Engineering (General), Social Sciences, Sociology, Fine Arts, Urban Problems
ISBN Prefix(es): 978-4-306
Bookshop(s): Shinjuku Mitsui Bldg Bookstore, 2-5-14, Yaesu, Chuo-ku, Tokyo 104-0028; Shibuya Tohoseimei Bldg Bookstore, 2-15 Shibuya, Shibuya-ku, Tokyo

Kanehara & Co Ltd
2-31-14 Yushima, Bunkyo-ku, Tokyo 113-8687
Tel: (03) 3811-7185; (03) 3811-7184 (sales)
Fax: (03) 3813-0288
E-mail: sales@kanehara-shuppan.co.jp
Web Site: www.kanehara-shuppan.co.jp
Key Personnel
President: Sumio Furuya
Foreign Rights: Toshiyuki Otera
Founded: 1875
Membership(s): Japan Book Publishers Association (JBPA).
Subjects: Medicine, Nursing, Dentistry
ISBN Prefix(es): 978-4-307; 978-4-907751

Kawade Shobo Shinsha Publishers
2-32-2 Sendagaya, Shibuya-ku, Tokyo 151-0051
Tel: (03) 3404-1201; (03) 3478-3251; (03) 3404-8611 (editorial) *Fax:* (03) 3404-6386
E-mail: info@kawade.co.jp; rights@kawade.co.jp
Web Site: www.kawade.co.jp
Key Personnel
President: Masaru Onodera
Foreign Rights/Trade: Toshio Motegi

Founded: 1886
Membership(s): Japan Book Publishers Association.
Subjects: Art, Fiction, History, Nonfiction (General), Philosophy, Science (General), Social Sciences, Sociology
ISBN Prefix(es): 978-4-309
Number of titles published annually: 500 Print

Kazamashobo Co Ltd+
1-34 Kanda Jimbocho, Chiyoda-ku, Tokyo 101-0051
Tel: (03) 3291-5729 *Fax:* (03) 3291-5757
E-mail: pub@kazamashobo.co.jp
Web Site: www.kazamashobo.co.jp
Key Personnel
President: Keiko Kazama
Founded: 1933
Membership(s): Japan Book Publishers Association (JBPA).
Subjects: Education, History, Language Arts, Linguistics, Literature, Literary Criticism, Essays, Medicine, Nursing, Dentistry, Philosophy, Psychology, Psychiatry, Social Sciences, Sociology
ISBN Prefix(es): 978-4-7599

Keisuisha Co Ltd+
1-4 Komachi, Naka-ku, Hiroshima 730-0041
Tel: (082) 246-7909 *Fax:* (082) 246-7876
E-mail: info@keisui.co.jp
Web Site: www.keisui.co.jp
Key Personnel
President: Kimura Itsushi *E-mail:* kimura@keisui.co.jp
Founded: 1975
Membership(s): Japan Book Publishers Association (JBPA).
Subjects: Asian Studies, Economics, Education, Geography, Geology, History, Language Arts, Linguistics, Literature, Literary Criticism, Essays, Philosophy, Psychology, Psychiatry, Religion - Other, Social Sciences, Sociology
ISBN Prefix(es): 978-4-87440; 978-4-86327
Number of titles published annually: 40 Print
Total Titles: 950 Print

Kenkyusha Co Ltd
2-11-3, Fujimi, Chiyoda-ku, Tokyo 102-8152
Tel: (03) 3288-7777; (03) 3288-7811 *Fax:* (03) 3288-7799; (03) 3288-7813
E-mail: eigyo-bu@kenkyusha.co.jp; publishing@kenkyusha.co.jp; editors@kenkyusha.co.jp
Web Site: www.kenkyusha.co.jp
Key Personnel
President & Foreign Rights/Trade: Yusuke Kosakai
Founded: 1907
Membership(s): Japan Book Publishers Association (JBPA).
Subjects: Language Arts, Linguistics, English as a second language
ISBN Prefix(es): 978-4-327; 978-4-7674

Kin-No-Hoshi Sha Co Ltd
1-4-3 Kojima, Taito-ku, Tokyo 111-0056
Tel: (03) 3861-1861 *Fax:* (03) 3861-1507
E-mail: usagi1@kinnohoshi.co.jp
Web Site: www.kinnohoshi.co.jp
Key Personnel
President: Kenji Saito
Foreign Rights/Trade: Masumi Ikeda
Founded: 1919
Subjects: Education
ISBN Prefix(es): 978-4-323
Warehouse: 1997-1 Hizaore 3-chome, Asaka-City, Saitama

Kindai Kagaku Sha Co Ltd+
2-7-15 Ichigaya-Tamachi, Shinjuku-ku, Tokyo 162-0843
Tel: (03) 3260-6161 *Fax:* (03) 3260-6059

E-mail: web-info@kindaikagaku.co.jp
Web Site: www.kindaikagaku.co.jp
Founded: 1959
Membership(s): Japan Book Publishers Association (JBPA).
Subjects: Computer Science, Electronics, Electrical Engineering, Mathematics, Physics, Information Technology
ISBN Prefix(es): 978-4-7649
Parent Company: Impress Holdings Inc, 20 Sanbancho, Chiyoda-ku, Tokyo 102-0075

Kinokuniya Co Ltd (Publishing Dept)+
3-7-10 Shimomeguro, Meguro-ku, Tokyo 153-8504
Tel: (03) 6910-0508 *Fax:* (03) 6420-1354
E-mail: publish@kinokuniya.co.jp; info@kinokuniya.co.jp
Web Site: www.kinokuniya.co.jp
Key Personnel
President: Masashi Takai
General Manager: Takao Hashimoto
Founded: 1927
Subjects: Art, Biography, Memoirs, History, Literature, Literary Criticism, Essays, Philosophy, Psychology, Psychiatry, Science (General), Social Sciences, Sociology
ISBN Prefix(es): 978-4-314
Associate Companies: Kinokuniya Publications Service of London Co Ltd, Carrington House, 2nd floor, 126-130 Regent St, London W1B 5SE, United Kingdom *Tel:* (020) 7734 3074; Kinokuniya Bookstores of America Co Ltd, 1581 Webster St, San Francisco, CA 94115, United States *Tel:* 415-567-7625; Kinokuniya Publications Service of New York Co Ltd, 1073 Avenue of the Americas, New York, NY 10018, United States *Tel:* 212-869-1700

Kinpodo Inc
34, Nishi-Teramaecho, Shishigatani, Sakyo-ku, Kyoto 606-8425
Tel: (075) 751-1111 *Fax:* (075) 751-6858
E-mail: eigyo@kinpodo-pub.co.jp
Web Site: www.kinpodo-pub.co.jp
Key Personnel
President: Terukazu Ichii
Foreign Rights/Trade: Yasufumi Uyama *E-mail:* uyama@kinpodo-pub.co.jp
Founded: 1948
Membership(s): Japan Book Publishers Association (JBPA).
Subjects: Medicine, Nursing, Dentistry
ISBN Prefix(es): 978-4-7653

KINZAI Institute for Financial Affairs Inc+
19 Minamimotomachi, Shinjuku-ku, Tokyo 160-8519
Tel: (03) 3358-1161
Web Site: www.kinzai.or.jp
Key Personnel
President: Hiroshi Tomikawa
Foreign Rights/Trade: Tetsuya Furuhashi *E-mail:* t.furuhashi@kinzai.or.jp
Founded: 1950
Membership(s): Japan Book Publishers Association (JBPA).
Subjects: Finance, Banking, Security Business
ISBN Prefix(es): 978-4-322
Branch Office(s)
Fukuoka Cities
Nagoya
Osaka
U.S. Office(s): 600 Third Ave, 23rd floor, New York, NY 10016, United States *Tel:* 212-687-8316 *Fax:* 212-687-8317

Kirihara Shoten
4-15-3, Nishishinjuku, Shinjuku-ku, Tokyo 160-0023
Tel: (03) 5302-7020 *Fax:* (03) 5302-7031
E-mail: publisher.jp@kirihara.co.jp
Web Site: www.kirihara.co.jp

Subjects: Language Arts, Linguistics, Literature, Literary Criticism, Essays, Mathematics
ISBN Prefix(es): 978-4-342

Kodansha Ltd+
2-12-21 Otowa, Bunkyo-ku, Tokyo 112-8001
Tel: (03) 3945-1111; (03) 5395-3574 (foreign rights) *Fax:* (03) 3944-9915 (foreign rights)
E-mail: g-info@kodansha.co.jp; release@ kodansha.co.jp
Web Site: www.kodansha.co.jp; kc.kodansha.co.jp
Key Personnel
President: Yoshinobu Noma
Foreign Rights: Yoshio Irie
Founded: 1909
Membership(s): Japan Book Publishers Association (JBPA).
Subjects: Art, Economics, Education, Fiction, Geography, Geology, History, House & Home, Humor, Language Arts, Linguistics, Literature, Literary Criticism, Essays, Medicine, Nursing, Dentistry, Nonfiction (General), Philosophy, Photography, Religion - Other, Social Sciences, Sociology, Comics, Manga
ISBN Prefix(es): 978-4-06
Associate Companies: King Records Co Ltd; Kobunsha Co Ltd; Kodansha Editorial Co Ltd; Kodansha Famous Schools Co Ltd; Kodansha International Ltd; Kodansha-pal Co Ltd; Kodansha Scientific Ltd; Kodansha USA Inc; Kodansha USA Publishing LLC
Branch Office(s)
Osaka
U.S. Office(s): Kodansha America LLC, 451 Park Ave S, New York, NY 10016, United States *Tel:* 917-322-6200 *Fax:* 212-935-6929 *E-mail:* info@kodanshaamerica.com
Book Club(s): Kodansha Disney Children's Book Club

Kokudo-Sha Co Ltd
1-16-7, Kamiochiai, Shinjuku-ku, Tokyo 161-8510
Tel: (03) 5348-3710 *Fax:* (03) 5348-3765
Web Site: www.kokudosha.co.jp
Key Personnel
President: Kensei Nomura
Foreign Rights/Trade: Jirow Uchida
E-mail: uchida@kokudosha.co.jp
Founded: 1948
Also printer.
Subjects: Biography, Memoirs, Child Care & Development, Education, Literature, Literary Criticism, Essays, Psychology, Psychiatry, Social Sciences, Sociology
ISBN Prefix(es): 978-4-337
Branch Office(s)
1560 Matoba Kawagoe, Saitama 350-1101
Tel: (049) 233-0111 *Fax:* (049) 233-0114

Kokushokankokai Corp Ltd
1-13-15 Shimura, Itabashi-ku, Tokyo 174-0056
Tel: (03) 5970-7421; (03) 5970-7426 (editorial) *Fax:* (03) 5970-7427; (03) 5970-7428 (editorial)
E-mail: sales@kokusho.co.jp
Web Site: www.kokusho.co.jp
Key Personnel
President: Kesao Sato
Founded: 1971
Subjects: Asian Studies, Education, Fiction, History, Language Arts, Linguistics, Literature, Literary Criticism, Essays, Military Science, Mysteries, Suspense, Religion - Buddhist, Western Fiction
ISBN Prefix(es): 978-4-336
Associate Companies: Kokusho Japanese Language School
Warehouse: 3-11-26 Vchiya, Vrawa-sh, Saitama Prefecture 336
Distribution Center: 1-8-10 Shingashi, Itabashi-ku, Tokyo 175-0081 *Tel:* (03) 5922-7163 *Fax:* (03) 5922-7163

Komine Shoten Co Ltd
4-15, Ichigaya-Daimachi, Shinjuku-ku, Tokyo 162-0066
Tel: (03) 3357-3521 *Fax:* (03) 3357-1027
Web Site: www.komineshoten.co.jp
Key Personnel
President: Norio Komine
Foreign Rights/Trade: Tsuyoshi Yamagishi
Founded: 1947
Membership(s): Japan Book Publishers Association (JBPA).
Subjects: Education, Science (General)
ISBN Prefix(es): 978-4-338

Kosei Publishing Co
Affiliate of Rissho Kosei-kai
2-7-1 Wada, Suginami-ku, Tokyo 166-8535
Tel: (03) 5385-2319 *Fax:* (03) 5385-2331
E-mail: kspub@kosei-shuppan.co.jp; dharmaworld@kosei-shuppan.co.jp
Web Site: www.kosei-shuppan.co.jp/english
Key Personnel
President & Chief Executive Officer: Moriyasu Okabe
Foreign Rights/Trade: Kazumasa Osaka
Founded: 1966
Specialize in Buddhist doctrine & practice focusing on the Lotus Sutra.
Membership(s): Japan Book Publishers Association (JBPA).
Subjects: Art, Child Care & Development, Education, History, Human Relations, Literature, Literary Criticism, Essays, Music, Dance, Nonfiction (General), Philosophy, Psychology, Psychiatry, Religion - Buddhist, Self-Help, Travel & Tourism
ISBN Prefix(es): 978-4-333
Number of titles published annually: 83 Print; 7 Audio
Total Titles: 1,140 Print; 1 CD-ROM; 142 Audio
Distributed by Charles E Tuttle Co Inc
Foreign Rights: Evergreen Buddhist Culture Service Pte Ltd (Singapore); Tuttle Publishing (Canada, Latin America, USA)

Kouseisha Kouseikaku Co Ltd
8, San'eicho, Shinjuku-ku, Tokyo 160-0008
Tel: (03) 3359-7371 *Fax:* (03) 3359-7375
E-mail: info@kouseisha.com; sales@kouseisha.com
Web Site: www.kouseisha.com
Key Personnel
President: Kazunari Kataoka
Founded: 1922
Membership(s): Japan Book Publishers Association (JBPA).
Subjects: Astrology, Occult, Astronomy, Education, Labor, Industrial Relations, Philosophy, Science (General), Social Sciences, Sociology, Technology, Fishery
ISBN Prefix(es): 978-4-7699

Koyo Shobo+
7 Kita-Yakakecho, Saiin, Ukyo-ku, Kyoto 615-0026
Tel: (075) 312-0788 *Fax:* (075) 312-7447
E-mail: mail@koyoshobo.co.jp
Web Site: www.koyoshobo.co.jp
Key Personnel
President: Yoshiki Ueda
Foreign Rights/Trade: Toshiki Takasago
Founded: 1960
Membership(s): Japan Book Publishers Association (JBPA).
Subjects: Archaeology, Art, Business, Developing Countries, Drama, Theater, Economics, Education, Environmental Studies, Ethnicity, Geography, Geology, Government, Political Science, History, Language Arts, Linguistics, Law, Literature, Literary Criticism, Essays, Management, Marketing, Philosophy, Psychology, Psychiatry,

Religion - Other, Social Sciences, Sociology, Industrial Engineering, Natural Science
ISBN Prefix(es): 978-4-7710

Kumon Publishing Co Ltd
Keikyu Dai-ichi Bldg 13F, 4-10-18 Takanawa, Minato-ku, Tokyo 108-8617
Tel: (03) 6836-0307 *Fax:* (03) 5421-1615
E-mail: info@kumonshuppan.com; international@kumonshuppan.com
Web Site: www.kumonshuppan.com
Key Personnel
President: Naoto Shimura
Founded: 1988
ISBN Prefix(es): 978-4-7743; 978-4-87576
U.S. Office(s): 300 Frank W Burr Blvd, Suite 6, Teaneck, NJ 07666, United States *Tel:* 201-836-2105 *Fax:* 201-836-1559 *E-mail:* books@kumon.com *Web Site:* www.kumonbooks.com

Kyodo-Isho Shuppan Co Ltd+
3-21-10 Hongo, Bunkyo-ku, Tokyo 113-0033
Tel: (03) 3818-2361; (03) 3818-2846 (sales) *Fax:* (03) 3818-2368; (03) 3818-2847 (sales)
E-mail: kyodo-ed@fd5.so-net.ne.jp; kyodo-se@fd5.so-net.ne (sales)
Web Site: www.kyodo-isho.co.jp
Key Personnel
President & Foreign Rights/Trade: Setsu Kinoshita
Founded: 1946
Membership(s): Japan Book Publishers Association (JBPA); Japan Medical Publishers Association (JMPA).
Subjects: Medicine, Nursing, Dentistry
ISBN Prefix(es): 978-4-7639

Kyoiku-Kaikan-Bekkan (Kansai University Press)
3-3-35, Yamate-cho, Suita-Shi, Osaka 564-8680
Tel: (06) 6368-0238; (06) 6368-1121 *Fax:* (06) 6389-5162
E-mail: shuppan@ml.kandai.jp
Web Site: www.kansai-u.ac.jp/Syppan/index.php
Key Personnel
Chairman, Board of Trustees: Yoin Uehara
Founded: 1947
Membership(s): Japan Book Publishers Association (JBPA).
Subjects: History, Language Arts, Linguistics, Literature, Literary Criticism, Essays, Philosophy, Psychology, Psychiatry, Social Sciences, Sociology, Natural Science
ISBN Prefix(es): 978-4-87354

Kyoritsu Shuppan Co Ltd
4-6-19, Kohinata, Bunkyo-ku, Tokyo 112-8700
Tel: (03) 3947-2511; (03) 3947-2513 (sales) *Fax:* (03) 3947-2539
E-mail: general@kyoritsu-pub.co.jp; sales@kyoritsu-pub.co.jp; rights@kyoritsu-pub.co.jp
Web Site: www.kyoritsu-pub.co.jp
Key Personnel
President, Editorial Dir & Foreign Rights/Trade: Mitsuaki Nanjo *E-mail:* nanjo@kyoritsu-pub.co.jp
Founded: 1926
Membership(s): Japan Book Publishers Association (JBPA).
Subjects: Biological Sciences, Chemistry, Chemical Engineering, Computer Science, Engineering (General), Mathematics, Medicine, Nursing, Dentistry, Natural History, Physics, Technology, Information Science, Natural Science
ISBN Prefix(es): 978-4-320

Library & Information Science, *imprint of* Riso-Sha

M-ON! Entertainment Inc+
Aoba Roppongi Bldg 5F, 3-16-33 Roppongi,
Minato-ku, Tokyo 106-8531
Tel: (03) 5549-7500 *Fax:* (03) 5549-7507
Web Site: magazine.m-on-ent.jp; www.sme.co.jp/
sme/corporate/moe.html; www.m-on-ent.jp
Key Personnel
President: Yasuhiro Sato
Founded: 1972
Subjects: Literature, Literary Criticism, Essays,
Music, Dance
ISBN Prefix(es): 978-4-7897
Parent Company: Sony Music Entertainment
(Japan) Inc
Ultimate Parent Company: Sony Corp

Maruzen Publishing Co Ltd
Kanda Jimbo-cho Bldg 6F, Kanda Jimbo-cho 2-
17, Chiyoda-ku, Tokyo 101-0051
Tel: (03) 3512-3256 *Fax:* (03) 3512-3270
Web Site: pub.maruzen.co.jp
Key Personnel
President: Kazuhiro Ikeda
Founded: 2011
Publishes books, videos, CD-ROMs & ebooks in
various academic fields.
Subjects: Architecture & Interior Design, Art, Bi-
ological Sciences, Business, Chemistry, Chem-
ical Engineering, Civil Engineering, Educa-
tion, Electronics, Electrical Engineering, Man-
agement, Mechanical Engineering, Medicine,
Nursing, Dentistry, Physics, Psychology, Psy-
chiatry, Science (General), Technology, Phar-
macognosy, Physical Education, Rudimentary
Medicine, Welfare
ISBN Prefix(es): 978-4-621

Medical Sciences International Ltd+
Subsidiary of Igaku-Shoin Ltd
1-28-36 Hongo, Bunkyo-ku, Tokyo 113-0033
Tel: (03) 5804-6050; (03) 5804-6056 (sales)
Fax: (03) 5804-6055; (03) 5804-6055 (sales)
E-mail: info@medsi.co.jp
Web Site: www.medsi.co.jp
Key Personnel
Chief Executive Officer: Hiroshi Wakamatsu
Dir: Yu Kanehara; Oing Nanao
Foreign Rights: Akane Shozui
Editing & Production: Kazuyuki Kurahashi
Founded: 1979
Medical Book Publisher.
Subjects: Medicine, Nursing, Dentistry, Psy-
chology, Psychiatry, Anatomy, Anesthesiol-
ogy, Emergency Medicine, Internal Medicine,
Molecular Biology, Radiology
ISBN Prefix(es): 978-4-89592; 978-4-943921
Number of titles published annually: 40 Print
Total Titles: 300 Print

MEDSi, see Medical Sciences International Ltd

Meijishoin Co Ltd
1-1-7 Okubo Takagi Bldg 2F, Shinjuku-ku, Tokyo
169-0072
Tel: (03) 5292-0117; (03) 5292-0172 (orders)
Fax: (03) 5292-6182; (03) 5292-6183 (orders)
E-mail: info@meijishoin.co.jp
Web Site: www.meijishoin.co.jp
Key Personnel
President: Satoshi Miki
Foreign Rights/Trade: Katsumi Takada
Founded: 1896
Membership(s): Japan Book Publishers Associa-
tion.
Subjects: History, Literature, Literary Criticism,
Essays, Philosophy, Poetry, Chinese Philosophy
& Literature, Haiku & Tanka Poetry, Japanese
& Chinese Classic Literature, Japanese & Kanji
Dictionaries, Japanese Textbooks
ISBN Prefix(es): 978-4-625

Branch Office(s)
Fukuoka
Osaka

Mejikarufurendo-sha (Medical Friend Co Ltd)+
3-2-4 Kudan Kita, Chiyoda-ku, Tokyo 102-0073
Tel: (03) 3264-6611; (03) 3263-7666 (sales); (03)
3264-6615 (editorial) *Fax:* (03) 3264-6639;
(03) 3261-6602 (sales); (03) 3264-0704 (edito-
rial)
Web Site: www.medical-friend.co.jp
Key Personnel
President & Chief Executice Officer: Yoshihiro
Ogura
Executive Dir: Hiroshi Ogura
Founded: 1947
Subjects: Art, Health, Nutrition, Medicine, Nurs-
ing, Dentistry
ISBN Prefix(es): 978-4-8392
Associate Companies: The International Nursing
Foundation of Japan (INFJ)
Warehouse: 36-1 Hiraoka-cho, Hachioji, Tokyo
192

Minerva Shobo Co Ltd+
One Tsutsumidani-cho, Hinooka, Yamashina-ku,
Kyoto 607-8494
Tel: (075) 581-5191; (075) 581-0296 (sales);
(075) 581-0661 (editorial) *Fax:* (075) 581-
8379; (075) 581-0296 (sales); (075) 581-8379
(editorial)
E-mail: info@minervashobo.co.jp
Web Site: www.minervashobo.co.jp
Key Personnel
President & Foreign Rights: Keizo Sugita
Founded: 1948
Membership(s): Japan Book Publishers Associa-
tion.
Subjects: Biography, Memoirs, Child Care &
Development, Disability, Special Needs, Eco-
nomics, Education, Government, Political Sci-
ence, History, Law, Medicine, Nursing, Den-
tistry, Philosophy, Psychology, Psychiatry, So-
cial Sciences, Sociology, Gerontology
ISBN Prefix(es): 978-4-623
Total Titles: 4,000 Print
Imprints: Tohan-Nippan
Branch Office(s)
2-4-17 Ogawa-machi, Omiga 1F Bldg, Kanda,
Chiyoda-ku, Tokyo 101-0034 *Tel:* (03) 8296-
1615 *Fax:* (03) 3396-1620
Distributed by Nihon Shuppan Hanbai Co
Foreign Rights: The Asano Agency Inc

Mirai-Sha Publishers
3-7-2, Koisikawa, Bunkyo-ku, Tokyo 112-0002
Tel: (03) 3814-5521 *Fax:* (03) 3814-8600; (03)
3814-5596
E-mail: info@miraisha.co.jp
Web Site: www.miraisha.co.jp
Key Personnel
President & Foreign Rights/Trade: Yoshihide
Nishitani
Founded: 1951
Membership(s): Japan Book Publishers Associa-
tion.
Subjects: History, Human Relations, Literature,
Literary Criticism, Essays, Philosophy, Religion
- Other, Social Sciences, Sociology, Politics,
Theatre
ISBN Prefix(es): 978-4-624

Misuzu Shobo Ltd+
5-32-21 Hongo, Bunkyo-ku, Tokyo 113-0033
Tel: (03) 3815-9181; (03) 3814-0131 (sales)
Fax: (03) 3818-8497; (03) 3818-6435 (sales)
Web Site: www.msz.co.jp
Key Personnel
President: Hisao Mochitani
Foreign Rights: Shogo Morita; Ms Misako Naka-
gawa *E-mail:* nakagawa@msz.co.jp
Founded: 1946

Membership(s): Japan Book Publishers Associa-
tion.
Subjects: Art, Education, History, Human Rela-
tions, Literature, Literary Criticism, Essays,
Philosophy, Psychology, Psychiatry, Religion
- Other, Science (General), Social Sciences,
Sociology
ISBN Prefix(es): 978-4-622
Branch Office(s)
2752-1 Yamazaki, Noda, Chiba 277-0022
Tel: (04) 7123-7243 *Fax:* (04) 7123-7244

Morikita Publishing Co Ltd
1-4-11 Fujimi, Chiyoda-ku, Tokyo 102-0071
Tel: (03) 3265-8341; (03) 3265-8342 (sales)
Fax: (03) 3264-8709
E-mail: info@morikita.co.jp; editor@morikita.co.
jp; eigyo@morikita.co.jp
Web Site: www.morikita.co.jp
Key Personnel
President & Foreign Rights: Hiroshi Morikita
Sales Manager: Satosi Nakamura
Founded: 1950
Subjects: Civil Engineering, Earth Sciences, Elec-
tronics, Electrical Engineering, Engineering
(General), Geography, Geology, Mathemat-
ics, Mechanical Engineering, Physics, Science
(General), Technology, Botany, Natural Sci-
ence, Zoology
ISBN Prefix(es): 978-4-627

Myrtos Inc+
Kudan-sakura Bldg 2F, 1-10-5 Kudankita,
Chiyoda-ku, Tokyo 102-0073
Tel: (03) 3288-2200 *Fax:* (03) 3288-2225
Web Site: www.myrtos.co.jp
Key Personnel
President: Mitsuru Kawai
Founded: 1985
Specialize in Jewish culture.
Subjects: Archaeology, Education, History, Liter-
ature, Literary Criticism, Essays, Philosophy,
Religion - Jewish, Religion - Protestant
ISBN Prefix(es): 978-4-89586
Branch Office(s)
Jerusalem, Israel

Nagai Shoten Co Ltd
8-21-15, Fukushima, Fukushima-ku, Osaka 553-
0003
Tel: (06) 6452-1881 *Fax:* (06) 6452-1882
E-mail: info@nagaishoten.co.jp; daihyo@
nagaishoten.co.jp
Web Site: www.nagaishoten.co.jp
Key Personnel
President: Mitsuo Matsuura
Foreign Rights/Trade: Michihiro Sasatani
Founded: 1946
Membership(s): Japan Book Publishers Associa-
tion.
Subjects: Medicine, Nursing, Dentistry
ISBN Prefix(es): 978-4-8159
Branch Office(s)
2-10-6 Kanda Suruga, Chiyoda-ku, Toyko 101-
0062 *Tel:* (03) 3291-9717 *Fax:* (03) 3291-9710

Nagaoka Shoten Co Ltd+
1-7-14, Toyotama-Kami, Nerima-ku, Tokyo 176-
8518
Tel: (03) 3992-5155; (03) 3948-7191 (editorial)
Fax: (03) 3948-3021
E-mail: info@nagaokashoten.co.jp
Web Site: www.nagaokashoten.co.jp
Key Personnel
President: Shuichi Nagaoka
Foreign Rights/Trade: Yoji Tamaki
Founded: 1963
Membership(s): Japan Book Publishers Associa-
tion.
Subjects: Animals, Pets, Cookery, Crafts, Games,
Hobbies, Gardening, Plants, Health, Nutrition,

House & Home, How-to, Law, Sports, Athletics, Travel & Tourism
ISBN Prefix(es): 978-4-522
Subsidiaries: Lesson Co Ltd; Okaichi Co Ltd

Nakayama Shoten Co Ltd+
1-25-14 Hakusan, Bunkyo-ku, Tokyo 113-8666
Tel: (03) 3813-1100 *Toll Free Tel:* 0120-377-883
Fax: (03) 3816-1015 *Toll Free Fax:* 0120-381-306
E-mail: eigyo@nakayamashoten.co.jp
Web Site: www.nakayamashoten.co.jp
Key Personnel
President: Tadashi Hirata
Foreign Rights/Trade: Makoto Kojima
 E-mail: kojima@nakayamashoten.co.jp
Founded: 1948
Membership(s): Japan Book Publishers Association; Japan Medical Publishers Association.
Subjects: Biological Sciences, Medicine, Nursing, Dentistry, Science (General)
ISBN Prefix(es): 978-4-521
Number of titles published annually: 70 Print; 5 CD-ROM
Total Titles: 3,850 Print; 5 CD-ROM
Distributor for American Heart Association

Nankodo Co Ltd+
3-42-6 Hongo, Bunkyo-ku, Tokyo 113-8410
Tel: (03) 3811-7140; (03) 3811-9957 (sales); (03) 3811-7239 (sales) *Fax:* (03) 3811-7265; (03) 3811-5031 (sales)
E-mail: nkdyosho@nankodo.co.jp
Web Site: www.nankodo.co.jp
Key Personnel
President: Kanehiko Kodachi
Foreign Rights/Trade: Mikio Aoyagi
Founded: 1879
Membership(s): Japan Book Publishers Association.
Subjects: Biological Sciences, Chemistry, Chemical Engineering, Health, Nutrition, Language Arts, Linguistics, Medicine, Nursing, Dentistry, Science (General), Technology, Pharmacology
ISBN Prefix(es): 978-4-524
Branch Office(s)
Oike-minami Teramachi dori, Nakakyo-ku, Kyoto 604

Nan'un-Do Co Ltd+
361, Yamabukicho, Shinjuku-ku, Tokyo 162-0801
Tel: (03) 3268-2311 *Fax:* (03) 3269-2486
E-mail: nanundo@post.email.ne.jp
Web Site: www.nanun-do.co.jp
Key Personnel
President: Kazunori Nagumo
Foreign Rights/Trade: Goro Saso
Founded: 1950
Membership(s): Japan Book Publishers Association.
Subjects: Education, Language Arts, Linguistics, Literature, Literary Criticism, Essays
ISBN Prefix(es): 978-4-523
Subsidiaries: Nan'un-Do Phoenix Co Ltd

Nanzando Co Ltd
4-1-11 Yushima, Bunkyo-ku, Tokyo 113-0034
Tel: (03) 5689-7868; (03) 5689-7855 (sales) *Fax:* (03) 5689-7869; (03) 5689-7857 (sales)
E-mail: information@nanzando.com
Web Site: www.nanzando.com
Key Personnel
President: Hajime Suzuki
Founded: 1901
Subjects: Medicine, Nursing, Dentistry, Pharmaceutical
ISBN Prefix(es): 978-4-525

Nenshosha
3-5, Kitayama Cho, Tennoji-ku, Osaka 543-0035
Tel: (06) 6771-9223 *Fax:* (06) 6771-9424

E-mail: fujinami@nenshosha.co.jp
Web Site: www.nenshosha.co.jp
Key Personnel
President: Masaru Fujinami
Founded: 1934
Membership(s): Japan Book Publishers Association.
Subjects: History, Literature, Literary Criticism, Essays, Science (General), Technology, Entertainment, Secretarial Science
ISBN Prefix(es): 978-4-88978

NHK Publishing, see Japan Broadcast Publishing Co Ltd

Nigensha Publishing Co Ltd+
6-2-1, Honkomagome, Bunkyo-ku, Tokyo 113-0021
Tel: (03) 5395-2041; (03) 5395-0511 (sales) *Fax:* (03) 5395-2045; (03) 5395-0515 (sales)
E-mail: info@nigensha.jp
Web Site: www.nigensha.co.jp
Key Personnel
Chairman & President: Mr Takao Watanabe
Founded: 1955
Membership(s): Azusakai Publishers Association; Japan Book Publishers Association.
Subjects: Art, Automotive, History, Art Reproduction, Calligraphy, Watch
ISBN Prefix(es): 978-4-544

Nihon Bunka Kagakusha Co Ltd
6-15-17 Honkomagome, Bunkyo-ku, Tokyo 113-0021
Tel: (03) 39463131 *Fax:* (03) 39463592; (03) 39463567 (sales)
Web Site: www.nichibun.co.jp
Key Personnel
President: Hideyuki Motegi
Founded: 1948
Subjects: Disability, Special Needs, Education, Medicine, Nursing, Dentistry, Psychology, Psychiatry, Social Sciences, Sociology
ISBN Prefix(es): 978-4-8210
Branch Office(s)
1-2-26 Motogo, Kawaguchi, Saitama 332-0011

Nihon-Bunkyo Shuppan (Japan Educational Publishing Co Ltd)
4-7-5, Minami-Sumiyoshi, Sumiyoshi-ku, Osaka 558-0041
Tel: (06) 6692-1261 *Fax:* (06) 6606-5171
Key Personnel
President: Hideki Sasaki
Founded: 1951
Membership(s): Japan Book Publishers Association.
Subjects: Art, Education, English as a Second Language, Social Sciences, Sociology, Sports, Athletics
ISBN Prefix(es): 978-4-536; 978-4-8212
Subsidiaries: Kiroku Eigasha Production Co Ltd; Shugakusha Co Ltd

Nihon Rodo Kenkyu Kiko (The Japan Institute for Labour Policy & Training)
4-8-23, Kami Shakujii, Nerima-ku, Tokyo 177-8502
Tel: (03) 5903-6111 *Fax:* (03) 3594-1113
E-mail: book@jil.go.jp
Web Site: www.jil.go.jp
Key Personnel
President: Kazuo Kanno
Dir: Nomura Kotaro; Kasuno Takahiko
Subjects: Labor, Industrial Relations
ISBN Prefix(es): 978-4-538

Nihon Tosho Center Co Ltd
3-8-2 Otsuka, Bunkyo-ku, Tokyo 112-0012
Tel: (03) 3947-9387 *Fax:* (03) 3947-1774
E-mail: info@nihontosho.co.jp

Web Site: www.nihontosho.co.jp
Key Personnel
President: Yoshio Takano
Founded: 1975
Subjects: Biography, Memoirs, Education, History, Literature, Literary Criticism, Essays, Social Sciences, Sociology, Social Welfare
ISBN Prefix(es): 978-4-8205; 978-4-284
Branch Office(s)
Osaka

Nihon Vogue Co Ltd+
3-23 Ichigaya-Honmura-cho, Shinjuku-ku, Tokyo 162-8705
Tel: (03) 5261-5082 *Fax:* (03) 3269-8760
E-mail: n-koukoku@tezukuritown.com
Web Site: www.tezukuritown.com; www.nihonvogue.co.jp
Key Personnel
President: Nobuaki Seto
Foreign Rights/Trade: Takuya Wada
 E-mail: wada-t@tezukuritown.com
Founded: 1954
Specialize in publication of handicrafts books.
Membership(s): Japan Book Publishers Association.
Subjects: Crafts, Games, Hobbies, Beading, Crochet, Decorative Painting, Embroidery, Knit, Paper Craft, Pressed Flowers, Quilting, Sewing
ISBN Prefix(es): 978-4-529
Subsidiaries: NV Planing Co Ltd

Nikkagiren Shuppan-Sha (JUSE Press Ltd)
5-4-2, Sendagaya, Shibuya-ku, Tokyo 151-0051
Tel: (03) 5379-1240 *Fax:* (03) 3356-3419
E-mail: sales@juse-p.co.jp
Web Site: www.juse-p.co.jp
Key Personnel
President: Takeshi Tanaka
Foreign Rights/Trade: Takafumi Toba *E-mail:* t.toba@juse-p.com
Founded: 1955
Membership(s): Japan Book Publishers Association.
Subjects: Business, Computer Science, Education, Finance, Human Relations, Library & Information Sciences, Management, Mathematics, Science (General), Self-Help, Technology
ISBN Prefix(es): 978-4-8171

The Nikkan Kogyo Shimbun Ltd
14-1 Nihombashi Koami-cho, Chuo-ku, Tokyo 103-8548
Tel: (03) 5644-7000 *Fax:* (03) 5644-7100
E-mail: info@media.nikkan.co.jp
Web Site: www.nikkan.co.jp
Key Personnel
President: Haruhiro Imizu
Foreign Rights/Trade: Toru Suzuki
Founded: 1915
Membership(s): Japan Book Publishers Association.
Subjects: Business, Education, Engineering (General), Science (General), Technology, Information Management, Manufacturing Industry
ISBN Prefix(es): 978-4-526
Associate Companies: Nikkan Kogyo Advertising Inc; Nikkan Kogyo Development Center Inc; Nikkan Kogyo Kansai Advertising Inc; Nikkan Kogyo Publication Inc; Nikkan Kogyo Service Center Inc; Nikkan Kogyo Shimbun Information Center Inc
Branch Office(s)
2-16 Kitahama-higashi, Chuo-ku, Osaka 540 0031
 Tel: (06) 6946-3321 *Fax:* (06) 6946-3329
1-1 Furumonndo-Cho, Hakata-ku, Fukuoka
 Tel: (092) 271-5711 *Fax:* (092) 271-5751
2-21-28 Izumi, Higashi-ku, Nagoya 461-001
 Tel: (052) 931-6151 *Fax:* (052) 931-6200
No 44 Ludgate House, 107/111 Fleet St, London EC4, United Kingdom

U.S. Office(s): 611 W Sixth St, No 3201, Los Angeles, CA 90017, United States
60 E 42 St, No 1411, New York, NY 10165, United States

Nikkei Business Publications Inc
1-17-3 Shirokane, Minato-ku, Tokyo 108-8646
Tel: (03) 6811-8311 *Fax:* (03) 5421-9804
Web Site: www.nikkeibp.com
Subjects: Business, Management, Technology
ISBN Prefix(es): 978-4-8222; 978-4-8227
Subsidiaries: BP Advertising (Shanghai) Co Ltd (China); Nikkei Business Publications Asia Ltd (Hong Kong & Taiwan); Nikkei Business Publications Europe Ltd (UK); Nikkei-Mutlu Dergi Grubu AS (Turkey)

Nippon Jitsugyo Publishing Co Ltd+
3-2-12, Hongo, Bunkyo-ku, Tokyo 113-0033
Tel: (03) 3814-5161; (03) 3818-9481 (sales)
　　Fax: (03) 3818-2723; (03) 3818-1881 (sales)
E-mail: koukoku@njg.co.jp
Web Site: www.njg.co.jp
Key Personnel
President: Junichi Sugimoto; Keiji Yoshida
Foreign Rights/Trade: Jun Yasumura
　　E-mail: yasumura@njg.co.jp
Mng Dir: Tanigawa Yoshihiko
Founded: 1950
Membership(s): Japan Book Publishers Association.
Subjects: Accounting, Business, Computer Science, Economics, Finance, Management, Marketing, Psychology, Psychiatry, Science (General)
ISBN Prefix(es): 978-4-534
Associate Companies: Four U (Publishing) Co Ltd
Branch Office(s)
6-1-8 Nishitenma, Kita-ku, Osaki 530-0047
　　Tel: (06) 6362-6141

Nishimura Co Ltd+
1-754-39, Asahimachi-dori, Chuo-ku, Niigat-shi, Niigata 951-8122
Tel: (025) 223-2388 *Fax:* (025) 224-7165
E-mail: office@nishimurashoten.co.jp; order@nishimurashoten.co.jp; tokyo@nishimurashoten.co.jp
Web Site: www.nishimurashoten.co.jp
Key Personnel
President: Masanori Nishimura
Foreign Rights/Trade: Azumi Nishimura
Founded: 1916
Membership(s): Japan Book Publishers Association.
Subjects: Art, Medicine, Nursing, Dentistry, Veterinary Science
ISBN Prefix(es): 978-4-89013
Branch Office(s)
2-4-6 Fujimi, Chiyoda-ku, Toyko 102-0071
　　Tel: (03) 3239-7671 *Fax:* (03) 3239-7622
Bookshop(s): 68-2 Aza-Hasunuma, Hiroomote, Akita-shi 010-0041

Nosan Gyoson Bunka Kyokai (Rural Culture Association)
7-6-1 Akasaka, Minato-ku, Tokyo 107-8668
Tel: (03) 3585-1141 *Fax:* (03) 3589-1387
E-mail: lib@mail.ruralnet.or.jp
Web Site: www.ruralnet.or.jp
Key Personnel
President: Yoshihiro Hamaguchi
Foreign Rights/Trade: Takashi Endo
Founded: 1940
Membership(s): Japan Book Publishers Association.
Subjects: Agriculture, Education, Environmental Studies, Health, Nutrition, Medicine, Nursing, Dentistry

ISBN Prefix(es): 978-4-540
Bookshop(s): Nobunkyo Otemachi Branch, JA Bldg, Basement floor, 1-8-3 Otemachi, Chiyoda-ku, Tokyo 100

Obunsha Co Ltd
55, Yokoderacho, Shinjuku-ku, Tokyo 162-8680
Tel: (03) 3266-6429 *Fax:* (03) 3266-6412
E-mail: info@obunsha.co.jp
Web Site: www.obunsha.co.jp
Key Personnel
Chief Executive Officer & President: Fumio Akao
Foreign Rights/Trade: Masao Takahashi
　　E-mail: masao.takahashi@obunsha.co.jp
Founded: 1931
Membership(s): Japan Book Publishers Association.
Subjects: Computer Science, Education, History, Language Arts, Linguistics, Science (General), Sports, Athletics
ISBN Prefix(es): 978-4-01
Associate Companies: The Asahi National Broadcasting Co Ltd, 1-1-1 Roppong, Minato-ku, Toyko 106; English Educational Foundation of Japan, 55 Yokodera-cho, Shinjuku-ku, Toyko 162; Japan LL Education Center, Tokyo; Nippon Cultural Broadcasting Inc, 1-5 Wakabacho, Shinjuku-ku, Toyko 160; The Society for Testing English Proficiency, 1 Yarai-cho, Shinjuku-ku, Tokyo 162
Branch Office(s)
Fukuoka
Hiroshima
Nagoya
Osaka
Sapporo
Sendai

Ohmsha Ltd+
3-1 Kanda-Nishiki-cho, Chiyoda-ku, Tokyo 101-8460
Tel: (03) 3233-0641; (03) 3233-2425; (03) 3233-0536 (sales) *Fax:* (03) 3233-2426; (03) 3233-3440 (sales)
E-mail: kaigaika@ohmsha.co.jp
Web Site: www.ohmsha.co.jp
Key Personnel
Mng Dir: Kazuo Murakami
President & Senior, Foreign Rights & International Business: Osami Takeo
Founded: 1914
Publisher of science & engineering books.
Subjects: Engineering (General), Science (General)
ISBN Prefix(es): 978-4-274
Number of titles published annually: 250 Print
Total Titles: 3,000 Print
Distributed by Akademische Velagsgesellschaff Aka GmbH (Germany); Beijing Oriental Kelong Typesetting & Productions Co Ltd (China); IOS Press BV (Netherlands); IOS Press Inc (USA); Science Press (China); Springer GmbH (Germany); Springer Japan KK (Japan); Sung An Dang Publishing Co (Korea)
Distributor for IOS Press BV (Netherlands); O'Reily & Associates Inc; O'Reily Japan Inc

Ongakuno Tomo Sha Corp (Friend of Music)+
6-30, Kagurazaka, Shinjuku-ku, Tokyo 162-8716
Tel: (03) 3235-2111; (03) 3235-2116 *Fax:* (03) 3235-2110
Web Site: www.ongakunotomo.co.jp
Key Personnel
President: Kumio Horiuchi
Copyright Dept & Foreign Rights/Trade: Kuibong Han
Founded: 1941
Also publishes magazines for music & musical education, folios for classical music & books about music.
Membership(s): Japan Association of Music Publishing; JASRAC.

Subjects: Education, Music, Dance
ISBN Prefix(es): 978-4-276
Number of titles published annually: 100 Print
Total Titles: 2,800 Print; 4 CD-ROM
Subsidiaries: Suiseisha Music Publishers
Distributed by Music Sales Co
Foreign Rights: Music Sales Co

The Oriental Economist, see Toyo Keizai Inc

Otsuki Shoten Publishers+
2-11-9, Hongo, Bunkyo-ku, Tokyo 113-0033
Tel: (03) 3813-4651 *Fax:* (03) 3813-4656
E-mail: info@otsukishoten.co.jp
Web Site: www.otsukishoten.co.jp
Key Personnel
President: Susumu Nakagawa
Foreign Rights/Trade: Shinobu Matsubara
Founded: 1946
Membership(s): Japan Book Publishers Association.
Subjects: Economics, History, Literature, Literary Criticism, Essays, Philosophy, Social Sciences, Sociology, Politics
ISBN Prefix(es): 978-4-272

Oxford University Press KK
3F Sotetsu Tamachi Bldg, 4-17-5 Shiba, Minato-ku, Tokyo 108-8386
Tel: (03) 5444-5454 *Fax:* (03) 3454-2221
E-mail: elt.japan@oup.com
Web Site: www.oupjapan.co.jp
Key Personnel
Mng Dir: Mr Kiyokazu Nakamura
Subjects: Art, Computer Science, Geography, Geology, History, Literature, Literary Criticism, Essays, Mathematics, Philosophy, Psychology, Psychiatry, Religion - Other, Science (General), Social Sciences, Sociology, Technology
ISBN Prefix(es): 978-4-7552
Parent Company: Oxford University Press, United Kingdom

Pearson Education Japan+
Shinjuku Oak Tower 23F, 6-8-1 Nishi-Shinjuku, Shinju-ku, Tokyo 163-6023
Tel: (03) 5339-8550 *Fax:* (03) 5339-8555
Web Site: www.pearsoned.co.jp
Key Personnel
President: Brendan Delahanty
Founded: 1967
Subjects: Business, Computer Science, Computers, Economics, English as a Second Language, Medicine, Nursing, Dentistry
ISBN Prefix(es): 978-4-89471
Number of titles published annually: 100 Print
Total Titles: 400 Print
Parent Company: Pearson Education, 225 River St, Hoboken, NJ 07030-4772, United States
Ultimate Parent Company: Pearson plc
Branch Office(s)
1-13-19 Sekiguchi, Bunkyo-ku, Tokyo 112-0014
　　Tel: (03) 3266 0404 *Fax:* (03) 3266 0326
Distributed by Hachette (France); SGEL (Spain)
Distributor for Chambers Harrap (UK); Hachette (France); SGEL (Spain)
Foreign Rights: Fumi Nishijima

PHP Institute Inc
11 Nishikujo-Kitanouchicho, Minami-ku, Kyoto City, Kyoto 601-8411
Tel: (075) 681-4431
E-mail: book@php.co.jp
Web Site: www.php.co.jp
Key Personnel
Chairman of the Board & President: Takatoshi Shimizu
Foreign Rights/Trade: Shinji Toyomaki *E-mail:* s-toyomaki@php.co.jp
Founded: 1946

Membership(s): Japan Book Publishers Association.
Subjects: Business, Social Sciences, Sociology
ISBN Prefix(es): 978-4-569
Parent Company: PHP Group
Associate Companies: PHP Editors Group Inc; PHP Publishing Inc
Subsidiaries: PHP Editors Group Inc; PHP Institute of America Inc; PHP International (Singapore) Pte Ltd
Branch Office(s)
5-6-52 NBF-toyosu-Canal Front, Koto-ku, Tokyo 135-8137 *Tel:* (03) 3520-9611

PIE International
2-32-4 Minami-Otsuka, Toshima-ku, Tokyo 170-0005
Tel: (03) 5395-4820 *Fax:* (03) 5395-4821
E-mail: editor@piebooks.com; tsuhan@pie.co.jp
Web Site: pie.co.jp
Founded: 1971
Subjects: Advertising, Art, Crafts, Games, Hobbies, Photography, Comic/Manga/Anime Art, Graphic Design, Japanese Culture
ISBN Prefix(es): 978-4-89444; 978-4-938586; 978-4-7562
Foreign Rep(s): Artland Book Co Ltd (Taiwan); Asia Books Co Ltd (Thailand); Basheer Graphic Books (Singapore); Dongnam Books Inc (Korea); Keng Seng Trading & Co Ltd (Hong Kong); Long Sea International Book Co Ltd (Taiwan); Nippon International Publication Service (HK) Co Ltd (Hong Kong); Page One The Bookshop Pte Ltd (Singapore); Ryh Sheng (Taiwan); Tongjin Chulpan Muyeok Co Ltd (Korea)
Distribution Center: Ingram Publisher Services, 14 Ingram Blvd, La Vergne, TN 37086, United States *E-mail:* ips@ingramcontent.com (USA & Canada)

Poplar Publishing Co Ltd+
22-1 Daikyo Cho, Shinjuku-ku, Tokyo 160-8565
Tel: (03) 3357-2215 *Fax:* (03) 3357-2308
E-mail: info@poplar.co.jp
Web Site: www.poplar.co.jp
Key Personnel
President: Hiroyuki Sakai
Foreign Rights/Trade: Junko Saegusa
E-mail: saegusa@poplar.co.jp
Founded: 1948
Membership(s): Japan Book Publishers Association.
Subjects: Biography, Memoirs, Fiction, Geography, Geology, History, Science (General)
ISBN Prefix(es): 978-4-591
Subsidiaries: Beijing Poplar Culture Project Co Ltd; Japan Poplar Culture Project Co Ltd; JIVE Co Ltd; Soensha Co Ltd
Branch Office(s)
27-1 Kandamachi, Chigusa-ku, Nagoya-shi, Aichi 464-0077
3-3-26 Yakuin, Chuo-ku, Fukuoka-shi, Fukuoka 810-0022
2-1 Nagatsuka, Hiroshima-shi, Hiroshima 731-0135
14-6-1 Kita 33 Jo Higashi, Sapporo-shi, Hokkaido 065-0033
3-2-53 Hara, Miyagino-ku, Sendai-shi, Miyagi 983-0841
2-13-49 Terauchi, Toyonaka-shi, Osaka 561-0872
Warehouse: Iruma Logistic Center, 11-13, Kasumino, Sayamagahara, Iruma-shi, Saitama

President Inc+
Hirakawacho Mori Tower 13F, 2-16-1 Hirakawa-cho, Chiyoda-ku, Tokyo 102-8641
Tel: (03) 3237-3731; (03) 3237-3711 *Fax:* (03) 3237-3746
Web Site: www.president.co.jp/englindex.html; www.president.co.jp/pre/english.html

Key Personnel
President: Yoshiaki Nagasaka
Sales: Akihiro Fujiware
Founded: 1963
Subjects: Business, Cookery, Economics, Finance, Government, Political Science, Management, Marketing, Philosophy
ISBN Prefix(es): 978-4-8334
Parent Company: Time Warner Publishing BV
Branch Office(s)
2-3-18 Nakanoshima, Kita-ku, Osaka
Orders to: 2-1-2 Ryutsudanchi, Koshigaya, Saitama 343-0824 *Tel:* (048) 989-6500 *Fax:* (048) 989-6533

Reimei-Shobo Co Ltd+
EBS-Bldg 8 F, 3-6-27 Marunouchi, Naka-ku, Nagoya 460-0002
Tel: (052) 962-3045 *Fax:* (052) 951-9065
E-mail: eigyo@reimei-shobo.com
Web Site: www.reimei-shobo.com
Key Personnel
Chief Executive Officer: Kuni Hiro Takema
President: Kunihiro Buma
Foreign Rights: Hiromasa Ito *E-mail:* ito@reimei-shobo.com
Founded: 1947
Membership(s): Japan Book Publishers Association.
Subjects: Child Care & Development, Disability, Special Needs, Education, Psychology, Psychiatry
ISBN Prefix(es): 978-4-654
Number of titles published annually: 50 Print
Total Titles: 1,700 Print
Warehouse: 374 Sangen-cho, Kita-ku, Nagoya 462-0004

Rinsen Book Co+
No 8, Tanaka-Shimoyanagi-Cho, Sakyo-ku, Kyoto 606-8204
Tel: (075) 721-7111 *Fax:* (075) 781-6168
E-mail: kyoto@rinsen.com
Web Site: www.rinsen.com
Key Personnel
President & Foreign Rights: Atushi Kataoka
Founded: 1932
Publisher & Antiquarian Bookseller.
Membership(s): Antiquarian Booksellers' Association of Japan; International League of Antiquarian Booksellers.
Subjects: Archaeology, Asian Studies, History, Literature, Literary Criticism, Essays, Religion - Buddhist, Fine Arts, Japanology, Orientalism
ISBN Prefix(es): 978-4-653
Branch Office(s)
Saikachizaka Bldg, 2-11-16 Kanda-Surugadai, Chiyoda-ku, Tokyo 101-0062, Contact: Atushi Kataoka *Tel:* (03) 3293-5021 *Fax:* (03) 3293-5023 *E-mail:* tokyo@rinsen.com

Riso-Sha
2-58-2, Minoridai, Matsudo-shi, Chiba 270-2231
Tel: (047) 366-8003 *Fax:* (047) 360-7301
E-mail: risosha@risosha.co.jp
Key Personnel
President: Sumio Miyamoto
Founded: 1927
Membership(s): Japan Book Publishers Association.
Subjects: Education, Library & Information Sciences, Philosophy, Psychology, Psychiatry, Religion - Buddhist, Religion - Catholic, Social Sciences, Sociology
ISBN Prefix(es): 978-4-650
Parent Company: Iwao-Syobou
Imprints: Library & Information Science

Saela Shobo (Librairie Ca et La)+
3-1, Ichigaya-Sadohara-cho, Shinjuku-ku, Tokyo 162-0842

Tel: (03) 3268-4261 *Fax:* (03) 3268-4264; (03) 3268-4262
E-mail: info@saela.co.jp
Web Site: www.saela.co.jp
Key Personnel
President: Toshiichi Uraki
Founded: 1948
Specialize in children's books.
Membership(s): Japan Book Publishers Association; Japanese Association of Children's Book Publishers.
Subjects: Education, Fiction, Language Arts, Linguistics, Mathematics, Science (General), Technology
ISBN Prefix(es): 978-4-378
Number of titles published annually: 24 Print
Total Titles: 450 Print
Imprints: Toshiichi Uraki

Sagano Shoin Corp
39, Minaminokuchicho, Ushigase, Nishikyo-ku, Kyoto 615-8045
Tel: (075) 391-7686 *Fax:* (075) 391-7321
E-mail: sagano@mbox.kyoto-inet.or.jp
Web Site: www.saganoshoin.co.jp
Key Personnel
President: Tadayoshi Nakamura
Founded: 1968
Membership(s): Japan Book Publishers Association.
Subjects: Business, Computer Science, Economics, Education, Ethnicity, Law, Literature, Literary Criticism, Essays, Marketing, Philosophy, Social Sciences, Sociology, Sports, Athletics, Women's Studies
ISBN Prefix(es): 978-4-7823

Saiensu-Sha Co Ltd
1-3-25 Sendagaya, Shibuya-ku, Tokyo 151-0051
Tel: (03) 5474-8500 *Fax:* (03) 5474-8900
E-mail: rikei@saiensu.co.jp; sales@saiensu.co.jp
Web Site: www.saiensu.co.jp
Key Personnel
President: Toshitaka Kinoshita
Foreign Rights/Trade: Nobuhiko Tajima
Founded: 1969
Membership(s): Japan Book Publishers Association.
Subjects: Biological Sciences, Chemistry, Chemical Engineering, Computer Science, Economics, Engineering (General), Finance, Mathematics, Physics, Psychology, Psychiatry, Social Sciences, Sociology, Computers
ISBN Prefix(es): 978-4-7819
Subsidiaries: Shinsei-sha Co Ltd; Suurikougaku-sha Co Ltd

The Sailor Publishing Co Ltd
7-20-16-404 Nishi-Shinjuku, Shinjuku-ku, Tokyo 160-0023
Tel: (03) 6908-6424 *Fax:* (03) 6908-6425
Key Personnel
Contact: Keisuke Takahashi
Founded: 1985
Membership(s): Japan Book Publishers Association.
ISBN Prefix(es): 978-4-88330; 978-4-915632
Parent Company: The Sailor Fountain Pen Co Ltd

Salesian Press/Don Bosco Sha+
1-9-7 Yotsuya, Shinjuku-ku, Tokyo 160-0004
Tel: (03) 3351-7041 *Fax:* (03) 3351-5430
E-mail: order@donboscosha.com
Web Site: www.donboscosha.com
Founded: 1930
Subjects: Religion - Catholic
ISBN Prefix(es): 978-4-88626
Warehouse: 1-22-12 Wakaba Cho, Shinjuku-ku, Tokyo

Sangyo-Tosho Publishing Co Ltd
2-11-3, Iidabashi, Chiyoda-ku, Tokyo 102-0072

Tel: (03) 3261-7821 *Fax:* (03) 3239-2178
E-mail: info@san-to.co.jp
Web Site: www.san-to.co.jp
Key Personnel
President & Foreign Rights/Trade: Naohiko Iizuka
Founded: 1924
Membership(s): Japan Book Publishers Association.
Subjects: Biological Sciences, Chemistry, Chemical Engineering, Computer Science, Electronics, Electrical Engineering, Engineering (General), Mathematics, Mechanical Engineering, Philosophy, Physical Sciences, Physics, Psychology, Psychiatry, Religion - Other, Science (General), Technology, Industry, Natural Science
ISBN Prefix(es): 978-4-7828
Total Titles: 500 Print

Sankyo Publishing Co Ltd
3-2, Kanda-Jimbocho, Chiyoda-ku, Tokyo 101-0051
Tel: (03) 3264-5711 *Fax:* (03) 3264-5713 (editorial); (03) 3264-5149 (sales)
E-mail: hanbai@sankyoshuppan.co.jp
Web Site: www.sankyoshuppan.co.jp
Key Personnel
President & Foreign Rights: Isao Hideshima
Founded: 1947
Membership(s): Japan Book Publishers Association.
Subjects: Chemistry, Chemical Engineering, Economics, Engineering (General), Health, Nutrition, House & Home, Physics, Science (General), Environmental Science, Life Sciences
ISBN Prefix(es): 978-4-7827

Sanseido Co Ltd
2-22-14, Misaki Cho, Chiyoda-ku, Tokyo 101-8371
Tel: (03) 3230-9412; (03) 3230-9411
Toll Free Tel: 0120-399-264 (orders) *Fax:* (03) 3230-9569; (03) 3230-9547
E-mail: ssd-s@sanseido-publ.co.jp
Web Site: www.sanseido-publ.co.jp
Key Personnel
President: Katsuhiko Kitaguchi
Foreign Rights/Trade: Hiroki Tabo
Founded: 1881
Subjects: Earth Sciences, Education, History, Language Arts, Linguistics, Law, Literature, Literary Criticism, Essays, Science (General), Social Sciences, Sociology
ISBN Prefix(es): 978-4-385
Parent Company: Sanseido Group
Associate Companies: Sanseido Bookstore Ltd; Sanseido Printing Co

Sanshusha Publishing Co Ltd+
Aoyamakumanojinja Bldg, 2-2-22, Jingu-mae, Shibuya-ku, Tokyo 150-0001
Tel: (03) 3405-4511 (sales) *Fax:* (03) 3551-4522 (sales)
E-mail: eigyo@sanshusha.co.jp (sales)
Web Site: www.sanshusha.co.jp
Key Personnel
President: Toshihide Maeda
Founded: 1938
Specialize in electronic publishing.
Membership(s): Asian Pacific Publishers Association (APPA); Japan Book Publishers Association (JBPA); Multimedia & Electronic Book International Committee (MEBIC).
Subjects: Education, English as a Second Language, Language Arts, Linguistics, Literature, Literary Criticism, Essays, Philosophy, Religion - Buddhist, Science (General), Social Sciences, Sociology, Travel & Tourism
ISBN Prefix(es): 978-4-384

Seibido Publishing Co Ltd+
3-22, Kanda Ogawamachi, Chiyoda-ku, Tokyo 101-0052
Tel: (03) 3291-2261 *Fax:* (03) 3291-5490
E-mail: seibido@seibido.co.jp
Web Site: www.seibido.co.jp/english/index.html
Key Personnel
President: Eiichiro Sano
Founded: 1955
Publisher of ESL textbooks for the university market.
Membership(s): Japan Book Publishers Association.
Subjects: English as a Second Language, Language Arts, Linguistics, Literature, Literary Criticism, Essays
ISBN Prefix(es): 978-4-7919
Number of titles published annually: 20 Print

Seibido Shuppan Co Ltd
1-7 Shinogawamachi, Shiniuku-ku, Tokyo 162-8445
Tel: (03) 5206-8151 *Fax:* (03) 5206-8159
Web Site: www.seibidoshuppan.co.jp
Key Personnel
President & Mng Dir: Kenji Kazahaya
Foreign Rights/Trade: Etsuji Fukami
Founded: 1966
Membership(s): Japan Book Publishers Association.
Subjects: Animals, Pets, Astrology, Occult, Automotive, Business, Career Development, Child Care & Development, Computer Science, Cookery, Crafts, Games, Hobbies, Gardening, Plants, Geography, Geology, Health, Nutrition, History, House & Home, How-to, Medicine, Nursing, Dentistry, Music, Dance, Outdoor Recreation, Photography, Sports, Athletics, Travel & Tourism, Women's Studies
ISBN Prefix(es): 978-4-415
Number of titles published annually: 300 Print; 5 CD-ROM; 10 Audio
Total Titles: 1,400 Print; 20 CD-ROM; 30 Audio

Seibundo Publishing Co Ltd+
2-8-5, Shimanouchi, Chuo-ku, Osaka 542-0082
Tel: (06) 6211-6265 *Fax:* (06) 6211-6492
E-mail: seibundo@triton.ocn.ne.jp; order@seibundo-pb.co.jp
Web Site: www.seibundo-pb.co.jp
Key Personnel
President & Foreign Rights/Trade: Hiroo Maeda
Founded: 1877
Membership(s): Japan Book Publishers Association.
Subjects: History, Language Arts, Linguistics, Literature, Literary Criticism, Essays, Regional Interests
ISBN Prefix(es): 978-4-7924
Distributed by Japan Publication Trading Co Ltd
Distributor for Tohan Co Ltd

Seibundo Shinkosha Publishing Co Ltd
3-3-11, Honogo, Bunkyo-ku, Tokyo 113-0033
Tel: (03) 5800-5780 *Fax:* (03) 5800-5781
E-mail: inquiry@seibundo.com; cs@seibundo.com
Web Site: www.seibundo-shinkosha.net
Key Personnel
President: Yuichi Ogawa
Operation Dir: Satoshi Shimizu
Foreign Rights/Trade: Kiyoshi Motoki
Founded: 1912
Membership(s): Japan Book Publishers Association.
Subjects: Astronomy, Business, Crafts, Games, Hobbies, Electronics, Electrical Engineering, Gardening, Plants, Management, Science (General), Technology, Graphic Design
ISBN Prefix(es): 978-4-416

Seibundoh
514, Waseda-Tsurumakicho, Shinjuku-ku, Tokyo 162-0041
Tel: (03) 3203-9201; (03) 3203-4806 (sales) *Fax:* (03) 3203-9206; (03) 3203-2038 (sales)
E-mail: eigyobu@seibundoh.co.jp; hanbaibu@seibundoh.co.jp (sales); henshubu@seibundoh.co.jp
Web Site: www.seibundoh.co.jp
Key Personnel
President: Koichi Abe
Founded: 1947
Membership(s): Japan Book Publishers Association.
Subjects: Business, Economics, Law, Social Sciences, Sociology, Politics
ISBN Prefix(es): 978-4-7923

Seiryu Publishing Co Ltd+
New Kanda Bldg, 3-7-1, Kanda-Jimbocho, Chiyoda-ku, Tokyo 101-0051
Tel: (03) 3288-5405 *Fax:* (03) 3288-5340
E-mail: seiryu1@seiryupub.co.jp
Web Site: www.seiryupub.co.jp
Key Personnel
President: Kentaro Fujiki
Foreign Rights/Trade: Toshiko Matsubara
Founded: 1994
Membership(s): Japan Book Publishers Association.
Subjects: Art, Education, Health, Nutrition, Literature, Literary Criticism, Essays, Music, Dance, Psychology, Psychiatry, Social Sciences, Sociology, Natural Sciences
ISBN Prefix(es): 978-4-86029; 978-4-916028
Foreign Rep(s): Katsuyoshi Saito (worldwide)
Foreign Rights: Katsuyoshi Saito (worldwide)

Seishin Shobo
3-20-6, Otsuka, Bunkyo-ku, Tokyo 112-0012
Tel: (03) 3946-5666 *Fax:* (03) 3945-8880
E-mail: sei@seishinshobo.co.jp
Web Site: www.seishinshobo.co.jp
Key Personnel
President: Toshiki Shibata
Foreign Rights/Trade: Yuriko Matsuyama
E-mail: matsu@seishinshobo.co.jp
Founded: 1955
Membership(s): Japan Book Publishers Association.
Subjects: Psychology, Psychiatry, Social Sciences, Sociology, Psychoanalysis, Social Work & Welfare, Zen
ISBN Prefix(es): 978-4-414

Seiun-sha+
3-21-10 Otsuka, Bunkyo-ku, Toyko 112-0012
Tel: (03) 3947-1021 *Fax:* (03) 3947-1617
Founded: 1982
Publicize Christian Truth.
Subjects: Christian
ISBN Prefix(es): 978-4-7952; 978-4-434
Total Titles: 1,000 Print
Parent Company: The Zion Press Corp

Seiwa Shoten Co Ltd
1-2-5 Kamitakaido, Suginami-ku, Tokyo 168-0074
Tel: (03) 3329-0031; (03) 3329-0033 (editorial) *Fax:* (03) 5374-7186; (03) 5374-7185 (editorial)
Web Site: www.seiwa-pb.co.jp
Key Personnel
President: Youji Ishizawa
Founded: 1976
Subjects: Language Arts, Linguistics, Medicine, Nursing, Dentistry, Psychology, Psychiatry
ISBN Prefix(es): 978-4-7911
Bookshop(s): 1-11 Kamitakaido, 1-chome, Suginami-ku, Tokyo 168-0074
Book Club(s): Bookclub Psyche

Seizando-Shoten Publishing Co Ltd
4-51, Minami-Motomachi, Shinjuku-ku, Tokyo
160-0012
Tel: (03) 3357-5861 *Fax:* (03) 3357-5867
E-mail: publisher@seizando.co.jp; order@
seizando.co.jp
Web Site: www.seizando.co.jp
Key Personnel
President: Noriko Ogawa
Foreign Rights/Trade: Yosuke Itagaki
Founded: 1954
Specialize in maritime transportation books.
Membership(s): Japan Book Publishers Associa-
tion.
Subjects: Economics, Law, Maritime, Technology,
Transportation, Aviation, Fishery
ISBN Prefix(es): 978-4-425

Sekai Bunka Publishing Inc
4-2-29, Kudan-Kita, Chiyoda-ku, Tokyo 102-8187
Tel: (03) 3262-5111 *Fax:* (03) 3262-5750
E-mail: bookcenter@sekaibunka.co.jp
Web Site: www.sekaibunka.com
Key Personnel
President & Chief Executive Officer: Minako
Suzuki
Founded: 1954
Membership(s): Japan Book Publishers Associa-
tion.
Subjects: Art, Cookery, Crafts, Games, Hobbies,
Education, Geography, Geology, Health, Nutri-
tion, History, How-to, Culture & Traditions
ISBN Prefix(es): 978-4-418
U.S. Office(s): 501 Fifth Ave, Suite 2102, New
York, NY 10017, United States

Shibundo Publishing
1-18-11 Shin-Kiba, Koto-ku, Tokyo 136-8575
Tel: (03) 6892-6961 *Fax:* (03) 6892-6962
Web Site: www.shibundo.net
Founded: 1915
Subjects: Art, Asian Studies, History, Literature,
Literary Criticism, Essays, Philosophy, Re-
gional Interests
ISBN Prefix(es): 978-4-7843

Shiko-Sha Co Ltd+
10-12 Hiroo 2-chome, Shibuya-ku, Tokyo 150-
0012
Tel: (03) 3400-7151 *Fax:* (03) 3400-7294
E-mail: shikosha@gol.com
Web Site: www.ehon-artbook.com
Founded: 1949
Subjects: Religion - Catholic, Religion - Protes-
tant
ISBN Prefix(es): 978-4-7834
Number of titles published annually: 10 Print

Shimizu-Shoin Co Ltd
3-11-6, Iidabashi, Chiyoda-ku, Tokyo 102-0072
Tel: (03) 5213-7151 *Fax:* (03) 5213-7160
Web Site: www.shimizushoin.co.jp
Key Personnel
President: Tetsuji Watanabe
Foreign Rights/Trade: Sakae Nakaoki
E-mail: nakaoki@shimizushoin.co.jp
Founded: 1946
Specialize in school aids & textbooks.
Membership(s): Japan Book Publishers Associa-
tion.
Subjects: Biography, Memoirs, Education, His-
tory, Nonfiction (General), Philosophy
ISBN Prefix(es): 978-4-389
Branch Office(s)
10-19-203 Hukushima, Fukushima-ku, Osaka
553-0003 *Tel:* (06) 6131-6226 *Fax:* (06) 6131-
6227
4-114 Kawakita, Hokkaido Ishikari 061-3214
Tel: (013) 374-4174 *Fax:* (013) 374-2115

Shinchosha Publishing Co Ltd+
71 Yaraicho, Shinjuku-ku, Tokyo 162-8711

Tel: (03) 3266-5411 *Toll Free Tel:* 0120-468-465
Fax: (03) 3266-5432 *Toll Free Fax:* 0120-493-
746
Web Site: www.shinchosha.co.jp
Key Personnel
President: Takanobu Sato
Foreign Rights/Trade: Yoji Takimoto
E-mail: takimoto@shinchosha.co.jp
Founded: 1896
Membership(s): Japan Book Publishers Associa-
tion.
Subjects: Biography, Memoirs, Business, Fic-
tion, Film, Video, Literature, Literary Criticism,
Essays, Mysteries, Suspense, Nonfiction (Gen-
eral), Photography, Romance, Science (Gen-
eral), Science Fiction, Fantasy
ISBN Prefix(es): 978-4-10

Shingakusha Co Ltd+
11-39 Naka-Inoue-cho, Higashino, Yamashina-ku,
Kyoto 607-8501
Tel: (075) 581-6111; (075) 501-0510 *Fax:* (075)
501-0514; (075) 501-5321
E-mail: info@sing.co.jp
Web Site: www.sing.co.jp
Key Personnel
President & Chief Executive Officer: Nakagawa
Eiji
Foreign Rights/Trade: Hiroshi Sengan
Founded: 1957
Membership(s): Japan Book Publishers Associa-
tion.
Subjects: Education
ISBN Prefix(es): 978-4-7868
Branch Office(s)
Fukuoka
Sapporo
1-15 Nakashimada, Tokushima *Tel:* (088) 631-
5699
14-1 Haraikata, Shinjuku-ku, Tokyo *Tel:* (03)
5225-6011; (03) 5225-6107 *Fax:* (03) 5225-
6945; (03) 5225-6117

Shinkenchiku-Sha Co Ltd+
3-2-5 Kasumigaseki, Chiyoda-ku, Tokyo 100-
6017
Tel: (03) 6205-4380 *Fax:* (03) 6205-4386
E-mail: ja-business@japan-architect.co.jp;
editor@japlusu.com
Web Site: www.japan-architect.co.jp; www.
japlusu.com (English)
Key Personnel
President: Nobuyuki Yoshida
Founded: 1925
Subjects: Architecture & Interior Design
ISBN Prefix(es): 978-4-7869
Associate Companies: A+U Publishing Pte Ltd;
Shinkenchiku-sha, Germany
Distribution Center: Idea Books, Nieuwe Heren-
gracht 11, 1011 RK Amsterdam, Nether-
lands *Tel:* (020) 6226154 *Fax:* (020) 6209299
E-mail: idea@ideabooks.nl
Basheer Graphic Books, 231 Bain St, 04-19
Bras Basah Complex, Singapore 180231, Sin-
gapore *Tel:* 06336 0810 *Fax:* 06334 1950
E-mail: enquiry@basheergraphic.com
Publicaciones de Arquitectura y Arte SL, Gen-
eral Rodrigo, 1, 28003 Madrid, Spain *Tel:* 91
5546106 *Fax:* 91 5532444 *E-mail:* publiarq@
publiarq.com
Prosper International Book Co Ltd, 3F, No
163, An-Mei St, Nei-Hu, 114, Taipei, Taiwan *Tel:* (02) 2792 1633 *Fax:* (02) 2791 3431
E-mail: prosperb@ms12.hinet.net

Shobunsha Publications Inc+
3-1, Kojimachi, Chiyoda-ku, Tokyo 102-8238
Tel: (03) 3556-8153; (03) 3556-8155 *Fax:* (03)
3556-8161; (03) 3556-8881
Web Site: www.mapple.co.jp
Key Personnel
President: Shigeo Kuroda

Foreign Rights/Trade: Shinya Ono
Founded: 1960
Membership(s): Japan Book Publishers Associ-
ation; Japan Digital Road Map Association;
Mapping Enterprises Association of Japan.
Subjects: Travel & Tourism
ISBN Prefix(es): 978-4-398
Total Titles: 300 Print
Branch Office(s)
6-11-23 Nisinaka, Yodogawa-ku, Osaka 532-0011
Tel: (06) 6303-5721 *Fax:* (06) 6838-1182

Shogakukan Inc+
2-3-1 Hitotsubashi, Chiyoda-ku, Tokyo 101-8001
Tel: (03) 3230-5211 *Toll Free Tel:* 0120-494-656
Fax: (03) 5281-1650
E-mail: info@shogakukan.co.jp
Web Site: www.shogakukan.co.jp
Key Personnel
President: Masahiro Oga
Foreign Rights/Trade: Bunsho Kajiya
E-mail: bunsho88@mail.shogakukan.co.jp
Founded: 1922
Also publishes comic books & magazines.
Membership(s): Japan Book Publishers Associa-
tion.
Subjects: Art, Earth Sciences, Economics, Educa-
tion, Gardening, Plants, Geography, Geology,
History, Literature, Literary Criticism, Essays,
Medicine, Nursing, Dentistry, Photography,
Comics, Folklore, Japanese Manga
ISBN Prefix(es): 978-4-09
Associate Companies: Shanghai Viz Communi-
cation Inc; Shogakukan Production Co Ltd
(ShoPro); Viz Media, San Francisco, CA,
United States

Mitsumura Suiko Shoin Publishing Co Ltd+
Sagaru, Sanjo, Horikawa-dori, 217-2 Hashiura-
cho, Nakagyo-ku, Kyoto 604-8257
Tel: (075) 251-2888 *Fax:* (075) 251-2881
E-mail: info@mitsumura-suiko.co.jp; hanbai@
mitsumura-suiko.co.jp (orders)
Web Site: www.mitsumura-suiko.co.jp
Key Personnel
President: Yasuhiro Asano
Foreign Rights/Trade: Yusaku Goda
Founded: 1958
Membership(s): Japan Book Publishers Associa-
tion.
Subjects: Architecture & Interior Design, Art,
Philosophy, Religion - Buddhist
ISBN Prefix(es): 978-4-8381

Shokabo Publishing Co Ltd
8-1, Yombancho, Chiyoda-ku, Tokyo 102-0081
Tel: (03) 3262-9166 *Fax:* (03) 3262-9130
E-mail: info@shokabo.co.jp; c-right@shokabo.co.
jp
Web Site: www.shokabo.co.jp
Key Personnel
President: Kazuhiro Yoshino
Founded: 1716
Membership(s): Institute of Natural Sciences
Book Society; Japan Book Publishers Asso-
ciation; Publishers Association for Cultural Ex-
change (PACE).
Subjects: Biological Sciences, Chemistry, Chemi-
cal Engineering, Mathematics, Physics, Science
(General), Technology, Natural Sciences
ISBN Prefix(es): 978-4-7853

Shokokusha Publishing Co Ltd
T & T Bldg, 8-21 Tomihisacho, Shinjuku-ku,
Tokyo 162-0067
Tel: (03) 3359-3231; (03) 3359-3232 (sales); (03)
3353-5391 (editorial) *Fax:* (03) 3353-5391;
(03) 3357-3961 (sales)
E-mail: eigyo@shokokusha.co.jp
Web Site: www.shokokusha.co.jp
Key Personnel
Chairman: Takeshi Goto
Founded: 1932

Membership(s): Japan Book Publishers Association.

Subjects: Architecture & Interior Design, Art, Education, Engineering (General), Science (General), Technical

ISBN Prefix(es): 978-4-395

Shorin-Sha Co ltd+
Kasuga-Shogaku Bldg, 2-3-23 Koishikawa, Bunkyo-ku, Tokyo 112-0002
Tel: (03) 3815-4921 (editorial); (03) 5689-7377 (sales) *Fax:* (03) 5689-7577 (sales)
Web Site: www.shorinsha.co.jp
Key Personnel
President: Shuichi Takahashi
Founded: 1984
Membership(s): Japan Book Publishers Association.
Subjects: Medicine, Nursing, Dentistry
ISBN Prefix(es): 978-4-7965

Shueisha Publishing Co Ltd
2-5-10 Hitotsubashi, Chiyoda-ku, Tokyo 101-8050
Tel: (03) 3230-6314
Web Site: www.shueisha.co.jp
Key Personnel
President: Marue Horiuchi
Foreign Rights/Trade: Ryosuke Mori
  E-mail: mori@shueisha.co.jp; Makoto Oyoshi
  E-mail: oyoshi@shueisha.co.jp
Founded: 1926
Specialize in comics, magazines & smaller-sized paperbacks.
Membership(s): Japan Book Publishers Association.
Subjects: Art, Fiction, Language Arts, Linguistics, Literature, Literary Criticism, Essays, Nonfiction (General), Comics
ISBN Prefix(es): 978-4-08
Associate Companies: Shogakukan Inc

Shufu-to-Seikatsu Sha Co Ltd
3-5-7, Kyobashi, Chuo-ku, Tokyo 104-8357
Tel: (03) 3563-5120 *Fax:* (03) 3563-2073
Web Site: www.shufu.co.jp
Key Personnel
President: Katsuhisa Takanou
Foreign Rights/Trade: Keusuke Mimura
  E-mail: houmu@mb.shufu.co.jp
Founded: 1935
Also publishes comic books.
Membership(s): Japan Book Publishers Association.
Subjects: Art, Cookery, Crafts, Games, Hobbies, Economics, Fashion, Fiction, History, House & Home, Literature, Literary Criticism, Essays, Medicine, Nursing, Dentistry, Philosophy, Religion - Other, Technology, Fishing, Interior, Recreation
ISBN Prefix(es): 978-4-391

Shufunotomo Co Ltd+
2-9 Kanda-Surugadai, Chiyoda-ku, Tokyo 101-8911
Tel: (03) 5280-7500; (03) 5280-7551 (sales); (049) 259-1122 (orders) *Fax:* (03) 5280-7587; (049) 259-1188 (orders)
Web Site: www.shufunotomo.co.jp
Key Personnel
President: Yoshiyuki Ogino
Foreign Rights/Trade: Kazuhiro Ohashi
  E-mail: kohashi@shufunotomo.co.jp
Founded: 1916
Membership(s): Japan Book Publishers Association.
Subjects: Architecture & Interior Design, Career Development, Child Care & Development, Cookery, Crafts, Games, Hobbies, Education, Fashion, Fiction, Gardening, Plants, Health, Nutrition, House & Home, How-to, Medicine, Nursing, Dentistry, Nonfiction (General), Photography, Religion - Buddhist, Travel & Tourism
ISBN Prefix(es): 978-4-07
Total Titles: 1,200 Print; 10 CD-ROM; 3 E-Book

Shunjusha Publishing Co
2-18-6, Soto-Kanda, Chiyoda-ku, Tokyo 101-0021
Tel: (03) 3255-9610; (03) 3255-9614 (editorial); (03) 3255-9611 (sales) *Fax:* (03) 3255-5418; (03) 3255-9370 (editorial); (03) 3253-1384 (sales)
E-mail: main@shunjusha.co.jp
Web Site: www.shunjusha.co.jp
Key Personnel
President: Akira Kanda
Founded: 1918
Membership(s): Japan Book Publishers Association.
Subjects: Economics, Health, Nutrition, History, Literature, Literary Criticism, Essays, Music, Dance, Philosophy, Psychology, Psychiatry, Religion - Other, Social Sciences, Sociology
ISBN Prefix(es): 978-4-393
Warehouse: 5-4-8 Nishimizue, Edogawa-ku, Tokyo 134-0015

Shuppan News Co Ltd
2-40-7 Kanda-Jinbo-cho, Chiyoda-ku, Tokyo 101-0051
Tel: (03) 3262-2076 *Fax:* (03) 3261-6817
E-mail: snews@snews.net
Web Site: www.snews.net
Key Personnel
President: Yosiaki Kiyota
Founded: 1949
Subjects: Publishing & Book Trade Reference
ISBN Prefix(es): 978-4-7852

Sobunsha Publishing Co
2-6-7 Kojimachi, Chiyoda-ku, Tokyo 102-0083
Tel: (03) 3263-7101; (03) 3263-6725 (editorial) *Fax:* (03) 3263-6789
E-mail: info@sobunsha.co.jp; sales@sobunsha.co.jp
Web Site: www.sobunsha.co.jp
Key Personnel
President: Hirotoshi Kuboi
Founded: 1951
Academic Publishers.
Membership(s): Japan Book Publishers Association.
Subjects: Asian Studies, Biblical Studies, Business, Developing Countries, Economics, Education, Ethnicity, Finance, Foreign Countries, History, Law, Philosophy, Religion - Other, Humanities
ISBN Prefix(es): 978-4-423; 978-4-915475

Sogensha Inc+
4-3-6, Awaji-machi, Chuo-ku, Osaka City, Osaka 541-0047
Tel: (06) 6231-9010 *Fax:* (06) 6233-3111
E-mail: sgse@sogensha.com; shuppan@sogensha.com
Web Site: www.sogensha.co.jp
Key Personnel
President: Mr Keiichi Yabe
Dir of Editorial Dept: Ms Akemi Watanabe
  Tel: (06) 6231-9011 *Fax:* (06) 6233-3112
  E-mail: a.watanabe@sogensha.com
Founded: 1892
Subjects: Archaeology, Art, Business, Education, History, Human Relations, Medicine, Nursing, Dentistry, Natural History, Nonfiction (General), Philosophy, Psychology, Psychiatry, Religion - Other, Science (General), Self-Help
ISBN Prefix(es): 978-4-422

Soryusha
1-5-7 Hongo, Housiyou Heights 203, Bunkyo-ku, Tokyo 113-0033
Tel: (03) 3818-2271 *Fax:* (03) 3818-2273
Web Site: www.soryusha.com
Key Personnel
President: Noriyuki Kurozuka
Founded: 1986
Subjects: How-to, Mathematics
ISBN Prefix(es): 978-4-88176
Parent Company: Tokyo Hyoujun
Associate Companies: Kougakusha; Tokyo Souken

Soshisha Publishing Co Ltd+
5-3-15 Shinjuku, Shinjuku, Tokyo 160-0022
Tel: (03) 4580-7676 (sales); (03) 4580-7680 (editorial) *Fax:* (03) 4580-7677 (sales); (03) 4580-7681 (editorial)
Web Site: www.soshisha.com
Key Personnel
President: Huruuti Toshiaki
Foreign Rights/Trade: Hiroshi Fujita
  E-mail: fujita@soshisha.com
Founded: 1968
Membership(s): Japan Book Publishers Association.
Subjects: Literature, Literary Criticism, Essays, Nonfiction (General), Science (General)
ISBN Prefix(es): 978-4-7942

Springer Japan KK+
Chiyoda First Bldg East, 3-8-1 Nishi-kanda, Chiyoda-ku, Tokyo 101-0065
Tel: (03) 6831-7000; (03) 6831-7007 (editorial) *Fax:* (03) 6831-7001; (03) 6831-7010 (editorial)
E-mail: info@springer.jp; market@springer.jp; puboperations@springer.jp (editorial)
Web Site: www.springer.jp
Key Personnel
President & Mng Dir: Koji Yamashita
Founded: 2006 (merger of Springer Tokyo & Eastern Book Service)
Membership(s): Japan Book Publishers Association.
Subjects: Computer Science, Engineering (General), Mathematics, Medicine, Nursing, Dentistry, Physical Sciences, Physics, Science (General), Biomedicine, Clinical Medicine, Life Sciences, Statistics
ISBN Prefix(es): 978-4-431
Total Titles: 300 Print; 15 CD-ROM
Parent Company: Springer Science+Business Media Deutschland GmbH, Heidelberger Platz 3, 14197 Berlin, Germany

Sunmark Publishing Inc+
2-16-11 5F, Takadanobaba, Shinjuku-ku, Tokyo 169-0075
Tel: (03) 5272-3166 *Fax:* (03) 5272-3167
E-mail: rights@sunmark.co.jp
Web Site: www.sunmark.co.jp/eng
Key Personnel
President: Nobutaka Ueki
Foreign Rights & Trade: Ichiro Takeda
Founded: 1971
Membership(s): Japan Book Publishers Association.
ISBN Prefix(es): 978-4-7631
Number of titles published annually: 80 Print
Total Titles: 3,000 Print; 300 E-Book

Surugadai-Shuppansha
3-7 Kanda-Surugadai, Chiyoda-ku, Tokyo 101-0062
Tel: (03) 3291-1676 *Fax:* (03) 3291-1675
E-mail: info@e-surugadai.com; s.henshu@e-surugadai.com
Web Site: www.e-surugadai.com
Key Personnel
President: Yoji Ida
Foreign Rights/Trade: Naoko Ueno
Founded: 1954
Membership(s): Japan Book Publishers Association.

Subjects: Economics, Language Arts, Linguistics, Law, Literature, Literary Criticism, Essays, Philosophy
ISBN Prefix(es): 978-4-411

Suzuki Publishing Co Ltd (Suzuki Shuppan)
6-4-21 Honkomagome, Bunkyo-ku, Tokyo 113-021
Tel: (03) 3947-5161 *Fax:* (03) 3947-5144
E-mail: trans-info@suzuki-syuppan.co.jp
Web Site: www.suzuki-syuppan.co.jp
Key Personnel
Chief Executive Officer & President: Yuzen Suzuki
Founded: 1954
ISBN Prefix(es): 978-4-7902

Takahashi Shoten Co Ltd
1-26-1, Otowa, Bunkyo-ku, Tokyo 112-0013
Tel: (03) 3943-4525; (03) 3943-4045 *Fax:* (03) 3943-4288
E-mail: ta_saiyou@takahashishoten.co.jp
Web Site: www.takahashishoten.co.jp
Key Personnel
President: Hideo Takahashi
Foreign Rights & Trade: Yoshiko Takahashi
   E-mail: ta_contact@takahashishoten.co.jp
Founded: 1952 (as Kowado Co Ltd)
Guidebooks, juvenile, picture books.
Membership(s): Japan Book Publishers Association.
Subjects: Education, Language Arts, Linguistics, Law, Medicine, Nursing, Dentistry, Technology
ISBN Prefix(es): 978-4-471

Tamagawa University Press+
Division of Tamagawa Gakuen
6-1-1, Tamagawa-Gakuen, Machida-shi, Tokyo 194-8610
Tel: (042) 739-8935 *Fax:* (042) 739-8940
E-mail: tup@tamagawa.ac.jp
Web Site: www.tamagawa.jp/introduction/press/
Key Personnel
President: Yoshiaki Obara
Foreign Rights & Trade: Takashi Mori
Founded: 1929
Publisher has indicated that 40% of its product line is author subsidized.
Membership(s): The Association of Japanese University Press (AJUP); International Association of Scholarly Publishers (IASP).
Subjects: Art, Biological Sciences, Business, Drama, Theater, Education, English as a Second Language, Gardening, Plants, Music, Dance, Philosophy, Photography, Religion - Other, Social Sciences, Sociology, Sports, Athletics, Travel & Tourism
ISBN Prefix(es): 978-4-472
Number of titles published annually: 35 Print
Total Titles: 500 Print

Tankosha Publishing Co Ltd
Horikawa Kuramaguchi, Kita-ku, Kyoto 603-8588
Tel: (075) 432 5151 *Fax:* (075) 432 5152
E-mail: eigyo_kyoto@tankosha.co.jp; sec@tankosha.co.jp (foreign rights)
Web Site: www.tankosha.co.jp
Key Personnel
President & Chief Executive Officer: Yoshito Naya
Vice President: Tomohiko Hattori
Founded: 1949
Membership(s): Japan Book Publishers Association.
Subjects: Antiques, Architecture & Interior Design, Art, Cookery, Crafts, Games, Hobbies, Ethnicity, Gardening, Plants, History, Philosophy, Photography, Religion - Other, Tea Ceremony
ISBN Prefix(es): 978-4-473
Total Titles: 4,000 Print

Branch Office(s)
Sugaya Bldg, 39-1 Ichigaya Yanagi-cho, Shinjuku-ku, Tokyo 162-0061 *Tel:* (03) 5269-7941 *Fax:* (03) 5269-7949

TBS-Britannica Co Ltd, see Hankyu Communications Co Ltd

Teikoku-Shoin Co Ltd
3-29 Kanda jinbo-cho, Chiyoda-ku, Tokyo 101-0051
Tel: (03) 3262-0834 *Fax:* (03) 3262-7770
Web Site: www.teikokushoin.co.jp
Key Personnel
President & Dir: Masayoshi Saito
Representative Dir: Hiroyuki Sugiyama
Founded: 1926
Specialize in textbooks & atlases for students.
Subjects: Geography, Geology, Government, Political Science, History
ISBN Prefix(es): 978-4-8071

3A Corp
Trusty Kojimachi Bldg 2F, 3-4, Kojimachi, Chiyoda-ku, Tokyo 102-0083
Tel: (03) 5275-2721 *Fax:* (03) 5275-2729
E-mail: sales@3anet.co.jp; mcneill@3anet.co.jp (English enquiries)
Web Site: www.3anet.co.jp
Key Personnel
President: Takuji Kobayashi
Foreign Rights: Kyoko Horiuchi
Founded: 1973
Subjects: Education, Language Arts, Linguistics, Management
ISBN Prefix(es): 978-4-88319; 978-4-906224
Distributed by Chapman & Hall, London (exc Japan & USA); Quality Resources, New York (USA)

Tohan-Nippan, *imprint of* Minerva Shobo Co Ltd

Toho Shoten+
1-3 Kanda-Jinbo-cho, Chiyoda-ku, Tokyo 101-0051
Tel: (03) 3233-1001 *Fax:* (03) 3294-1003
E-mail: info@toho-shoten.co.jp
Web Site: www.toho-shoten.co.jp
Key Personnel
President: Yamada Masashi
Founded: 1951
Specialize in China.
Subjects: Archaeology, Art, Asian Studies, Crafts, Games, Hobbies, Economics, Geography, Geology, History, Language Arts, Linguistics, Literature, Literary Criticism, Essays, Medicine, Nursing, Dentistry, Nonfiction (General), Philosophy, Regional Interests, Religion - Other
ISBN Prefix(es): 978-4-497
Branch Office(s)
2-6-1 Esake-cho, Suita, Osaka 564-0063
Tel: (06) 6337-4760 *Fax:* (06) 6337-4762
   E-mail: kansai@toho-shoten.co.jp
Bookshop(s): 1-10-2 Takashimadaira, Itabashi-ku, Tokyo 175-0082 *Tel:* (03) 3937-0300 *Fax:* (03) 3937-0955
Warehouse: 1-10-2 Takashimadaira, Itabashi-ku, Tokyo 175-0082
Orders to: 1-10-2 Takashimadaira, Itabashi-ku, Tokyo 175-0082 *Tel:* (03) 3937-0300 *Fax:* (03) 3937-0955

Toho Shuppan+
2-3-2 Ohsaka, Tennoji-ku, Osaka 543-0062
Tel: (06) 6779-9571 *Fax:* (06) 6779-9573
E-mail: info@tohoshuppan.co.jp
Web Site: www.tohoshuppan.co.jp
Key Personnel
President: Shigeto Imahigashi
Founded: 1978

Membership(s): Japan Book Publishers Association.
Subjects: Art, Asian Studies, Crafts, Games, Hobbies, History, Philosophy, Photography, Religion - Buddhist
ISBN Prefix(es): 978-4-88591

Tokai University Press
Affiliate of Tokai University Educational System (TES)
Tokai University Alumni Hall, 3-10-35 Miramiyana, Hadano-shi, Kanagawa 257-0003
Tel: (0463) 79-3921 (sales & administration); (0463) 79-3941 (editorial) *Fax:* (0463) 69-5087
E-mail: webmaster@press.tokai.ac.jp; tupsalesdpt@press.tokai.ac.jp
Web Site: www.press.tokai.ac.jp
Key Personnel
President: Dr Tatsuro Matsumae
Dir: Tamotsu Otsuka
Editor-in-Chief, Foreign Rights & Trade: Yoshihiro Miura
Founded: 1962
Subjects: Art, Biological Sciences, Earth Sciences, History, Language Arts, Linguistics, Literature, Literary Criticism, Essays, Philosophy, Religion - Other, Social Sciences, Sociology, Technology
ISBN Prefix(es): 978-4-486

Tokuma Shoten Publishing Co Ltd+
2-2-1 Shiba-daimon, Minato-ku, Tokyo 105-8055
Tel: (03) 5403-4300 *Fax:* (03) 5403-4375
Web Site: www.tokuma.jp
Key Personnel
President: Toru Iwabuchi
Foreign Rights/Trade: Kyoko Aoyama
Founded: 1954
Specialize in classics.
Membership(s): Japan Book Publishers Association.
Subjects: Art, Crafts, Games, Hobbies, Economics, Fiction, History, House & Home, How-to, Literature, Literary Criticism, Essays, Nonfiction (General), Social Sciences, Sociology, Sports, Athletics
ISBN Prefix(es): 978-4-19

Tokyo Kagaku Dojin Co Ltd+
3-36-7, Sengoku, Bunkyo-ku, Tokyo 112-0011
Tel: (03) 3946-5311 *Fax:* (03) 3946-5316; (03) 3946-5317 (sales)
E-mail: info@tkd-pbl.com
Web Site: www.tkd-pbl.com
Key Personnel
President: Minako Ozawa
Foreign Rights/Trade: Mutsure Sumita
   E-mail: msumita@tkd-pbl.com
Founded: 1961
Membership(s): Japan Book Publishers Association.
Subjects: Biological Sciences, Chemistry, Chemical Engineering, Medicine, Nursing, Dentistry, Science (General)
ISBN Prefix(es): 978-4-8079
Number of titles published annually: 40 Print
Total Titles: 1,100 Print

Tokyo Shoseki Co Ltd+
2-17-1 Horifune, Kita-ku, Tokyo 114-8524
Tel: (03) 5390-7200 *Fax:* (03) 5390-7220
Web Site: www.tokyo-shoseki.co.jp
Key Personnel
President: Yasunori Kawabata
Manager, Foreign Rights & Trade: Shigeki Oyama
Founded: 1909
Membership(s): Japan Book Publishers Association.
Subjects: Art, Disability, Special Needs, Education, English as a Second Language, Fiction,

History, Mathematics, Religion - Buddhist, Science (General), Travel & Tourism
ISBN Prefix(es): 978-4-487
Total Titles: 1,000 Print; 100 CD-ROM
Associate Companies: Toppan International Group
Subsidiaries: Astro Publishing Co Ltd; Froebel-Kan Co Ltd
Branch Office(s)
Chikusa Sumitomo Seimei Bldg 19F, 3-15-31 Ai, Higashi-ku, Nagaya 461-0004 *Tel:* (052) 939-2722 *Fax:* (052) 939-2720
1-53-3 Danbaraminami, Minami-ku, Hiroshima 732-0814 *Tel:* (082) 568-2577 *Fax:* (082) 568-2580
6-1 Kanazawa, Minami-ku, Hiroshima 920-0919 *Tel:* (076) 222-7581 *Fax:* (076) 232-2719
14-1-5 Sapporo, Chuo-ku, Hokkaido 064-0806 *Tel:* (011) 562-5721 *Fax:* (011) 562-5492
1-17-28 Yakuin chuo, Chuo-ku, Kyushu 810-0022 *Tel:* (092) 771-1536 *Fax:* (092) 714-3519
1-2-1 Tsubogawa, Naha 900-0025 *Tel:* (098) 834-8084 *Fax:* (098) 834-8095
3-7-22 Tsutsujigaoka, Sendai, Miyagino-ku, Miyagi 983-0852 *Tel:* (022) 297-2666 *Fax:* (022) 297-6040
1-4-10 Nishimiyahara, Yodogawa-ku, Osaka 532-0004 *Tel:* (06) 6397-1350 *Fax:* (06) 6397-1358

Tokyo Sogensha Co Ltd
1-5, Shin-Ogawamachi, Shinjuku-ku, Tokyo 162-0814
Tel: (03) 3268-8201; (03) 3268-8231 *Fax:* (03) 3268-8230
E-mail: tss@tsogen.co.jp
Web Site: www.tsogen.co.jp
Key Personnel
Chief Executive Officer: Shinichi Hasegawa
Foreign Rights/Trade: Mari Igaki
Founded: 1954
Membership(s): Japan Book Publishers Association.
Subjects: Art, Criminology, History, Literature, Literary Criticism, Essays, Music, Dance, Mysteries, Suspense, Philosophy, Science Fiction, Fantasy, Social Sciences, Sociology
ISBN Prefix(es): 978-4-488
Associate Companies: Sogensha Publishing Co Ltd

Tokyo Tosho Co Ltd
3-11-9, Iidabashi, Chiyoda-ku, Tokyo 102-0072
Tel: (03) 3288-9461 *Fax:* (03) 3288-9470
Web Site: www.tokyo-tosho.co.jp
Key Personnel
President: Tooru Katayama
Foreign Rights/Trade: Naoki Norimatsu
Founded: 1954
Membership(s): Japan Book Publishers Association.
Subjects: Biography, Memoirs, Mathematics, Physics, Science (General), Technical
ISBN Prefix(es): 978-4-489

Tosui Shobo Publishers & Co Ltd
2-4-1, Nishi-Kanda, Chiyoda-ku, Tokyo 101-0065
Tel: (03) 3261-6190 *Fax:* (03) 3261-2234
E-mail: tousuishobou@nifty.com
Web Site: www.tousuishobou.com
Key Personnel
President: Michiya Kuwabara
Foreign Rights/Trade: Fumie Nakamura
Founded: 1978
Membership(s): Japan Book Publishers Association.
Subjects: Anthropology, Archaeology, History, Folklore
ISBN Prefix(es): 978-4-88708

Toyo Keizai Inc+
1-2-1 Nihombashi-Hongokucho, Chuo-ku, Tokyo 103-8345
Tel: (03) 3246-5551 *Fax:* (03) 3270-0332

E-mail: info@toyokeizai.co.jp
Web Site: www.toyokeizai.net
Key Personnel
President: Yuichiro Yamagata
Foreign Rights/Trade: Keiko Takanezawa
Founded: 1895
Membership(s): Japan Book Publishers Association.
Subjects: Business, Economics, Finance, Labor, Industrial Relations, Nonfiction (General), Social Sciences, Sociology
ISBN Prefix(es): 978-4-492
Branch Office(s)
Dojima Avanza 5F, 1-6-20 Dojima, Kita-ku, Osaka 530-0003
Sakae RICCO 6F, 3-14-7 Sakae, Naka-ku, Nagoya 460-0008

Tsukiji Shokan Publishing Co
7-4-4-201, Tsukiji, Chuo-ku, Tokyo 104-0045
Tel: (03) 3542-3731 *Fax:* (03) 3541-5799
E-mail: eigyo@tsukiji-shokan.co.jp
Web Site: www.tsukiji-shokan.co.jp
Key Personnel
President & Foreign Rights/Trade: Jiro Doi
E-mail: doi@tsukiji-shokan.co.jp
Founded: 1953
Membership(s): Japan Book Publishers Association.
Subjects: Anthropology, Archaeology, Biological Sciences, Child Care & Development, Earth Sciences, Environmental Studies, Social Sciences, Sociology, Sports, Athletics
ISBN Prefix(es): 978-4-8067

The University of Nagoya Press
One Furo-cho, Chikusa-ku, Nagoya 464-0814
Tel: (052) 781-5027; (052) 781-5353 (sales) *Fax:* (052) 781-0697
E-mail: info@unp.nagoya-u.ac.jp
Web Site: www.unp.or.jp
Key Personnel
Chairman: Mitsuki Ishii
Sales Manager: Hachiro Ito
Foreign Rights/Trade: Sogo Tachibana
E-mail: sogo@unp.nagoya-u.ac.jp
Founded: 1982
Membership(s): Japan Book Publishers Association.
Subjects: Economics, Education, Government, Political Science, History, Language Arts, Linguistics, Law, Literature, Literary Criticism, Essays, Medicine, Nursing, Dentistry, Philosophy, Social Sciences, Sociology, Natural Sciences
ISBN Prefix(es): 978-4-8158; 978-4-930689
Orders to: Japan Publications Trading Co Ltd, 1-2-1 Sarugaku-cho 1-chome, PO Box 5030, Chiyoda-ku, Tokyo 101-0064 *Tel:* (03) 3292-3751 *Fax:* (03) 3292-0410

University of Tokyo Press+
Tokyo University, 7-3-1 Hongo, Bunkyo-ku, Tokyo 113-8654
Tel: (03) 3811-8814; (03) 3812-6862 (sales) *Fax:* (03) 3812-6958
E-mail: info@utp.or.jp; order@utp.or.jp
Web Site: www.utp.or.jp
Key Personnel
Foreign Rights/Trade: Mitsuo Takayanagi
Founded: 1951
Membership(s): AJUP; Association of University Presses (AUPresses); International Association of STM Publishers; Japan Book Publishers Association.
Subjects: Engineering (General), History, Medicine, Nursing, Dentistry, Philosophy, Psychology, Psychiatry, Religion - Other, Science (General), Social Sciences, Sociology
ISBN Prefix(es): 978-4-13

Toshiichi Uraki, *imprint of* Saela Shobo (Librairie Ca et La)

Waseda University Press
1-1-7 Nishiwaseda, Shinjuku-ku, Tokyo 169-0051
Tel: (03) 3203-1551 *Fax:* (03) 3207-0406
Web Site: www.waseda-up.co.jp
Key Personnel
President: Yoichi Shimada
Foreign Rights/Trade: Yutaka Sasaki
E-mail: shuppanbu@list.waseda.jp
Founded: 1886
Membership(s): Japan Book Publishers Association.
Subjects: Anthropology, Archaeology, Economics, Education, Film, Video, Finance, Government, Political Science, History, Law, Literature, Literary Criticism, Essays, Philosophy, Psychology, Psychiatry, Social Sciences, Sociology, Sports, Athletics
ISBN Prefix(es): 978-4-657
Number of titles published annually: 35 Print
Total Titles: 550 Print

Yakuji Nippo Ltd
1-11 Kanda Izumi Cho, Chiyoda-ku, Tokyo 101-8648
Tel: (03) 3862-2141 *Fax:* (03) 3866-8408
E-mail: shuppan@yakuji.co.jp
Web Site: www.yakuji.co.jp
Key Personnel
President: Norio Kayama
Foreign Rights & Trade: Daisuke Koyama
Founded: 1948
Subjects: Medicine, Nursing, Dentistry, Cosmetics, Medical Devices, Pharmacy
ISBN Prefix(es): 978-4-8408
Branch Office(s)
2-1-10 Doshomachi Chuno Ku Rd, Chuno-ku, Osaka 541-0045 *Tel:* (06) 6203-4191 *Fax:* (06) 6233-3681

Yama-Kei Publishers Co Ltd+
Kudan Bldg Annex 8F, 3-2-11 Kudan-kita, Chiyoda-ku, Tokyo 102-0073
Tel: (03) 6744-1900
E-mail: info@yamakei.co.jp; eigyo@yamakei.co.jp (sales)
Web Site: www.yamakei.co.jp
Key Personnel
President & Chief Executive Officer: Akira Sekimoto
Vice President: Miyuki Kawasaki; Junichi Saitou
Founded: 1930
Subjects: Earth Sciences, Geography, Geology, Sports, Athletics, Travel & Tourism
ISBN Prefix(es): 978-4-635
Branch Office(s)
20 Sanbancho, Chiyoda-ku, Tokyo 102-0075

Yamaguchi-Shoten+
72, Ichijoji-Tsukudacho, Sakyo-ku, Kyoto 606-8175
Tel: (075) 781-6121 *Fax:* (075) 705-2003
Web Site: www.yamaguchi-shoten.co.jp
Key Personnel
President: Kanya Yamaguchi
Founded: 1949
Membership(s): Japan Book Publishers Association.
Subjects: Education, English as a Second Language, Language Arts, Linguistics, Literature, Literary Criticism, Essays
ISBN Prefix(es): 978-4-8411
Branch Office(s)
Fukuoka
Hiroshima
Nagoya

Yokendo Co Ltd
5-30-15 Hongo, Bunkyo-ku, Tokyo 113-0033
Tel: (03) 3814-0911 *Fax:* (03) 3812-2615
E-mail: info@yokendo.co.jp
Web Site: www.yokendo.com

Key Personnel
President: Kiyoshi Oikawa
Foreign Rights/Trade: Nobuyuki Miura
　E-mail: m-kogakul@yokendo.co.jp
Founded: 1914
Subjects: Agriculture, Engineering (General),
　Physical Sciences, Science (General)
ISBN Prefix(es): 978-4-8425

Yoshioka Shoten
87, Tanaka-Monzencho, Sakyo Ku, Kyoto 606-
8225
Tel: (075) 781-4747 *Fax:* (075) 701-9075
E-mail: book-y@chive.ocn.ne.jp
Web Site: www3.ocn.ne.jp/~yoshioka
Key Personnel
President: Makoto Yoshioka
Founded: 1964
Membership(s): Japan Book Publishers Associa-
tion.
Subjects: Science (General), Technical
ISBN Prefix(es): 978-4-8427

Yuhikaku Publishing Co Ltd
2-17, Kanda Jimbo-cho, Chiyoda-ku, Tokyo 101-
0051
Tel: (03) 3264-1312 *Fax:* (03) 3264-5030
Web Site: www.yuhikaku.co.jp
Key Personnel
President: Sadaharu Egusa
Foreign Rights Dir: Mr Yasuki Nishino
　E-mail: henshusomu@yuhikaku.co.jp
Founded: 1877
Publishes works aimed at particularly university
　students, members of the legal profession &
　various business people in general.
Subjects: Economics, Education, History, Law,
　Management, Psychology, Psychiatry, Social
　Sciences, Sociology, Humanities
ISBN Prefix(es): 978-4-641
Associate Companies: Yuhikaku Academic Co
　Ltd; Yuhikaku Gakujutsu Center Co Ltd (YGC);
Subsidiaries: Yuhikaku Service Center Co Ltd
　(YSC)

Yuki Shobo Co Ltd
3-7-9 Kudan-minami, Chiyoda-ku, Tokyo 102-
0074
Tel: (03) 5275-8088 *Fax:* (03) 5275-8099
Key Personnel
President: Masao Okajima
Foreign Rights/Trade: Takeshi Nanri
Founded: 1957
Membership(s): Japan Book Publishers Associa-
tion.
Subjects: Social Sciences, Sociology, Sports, Ath-
letics, Home Economics, Recreation
ISBN Prefix(es): 978-4-638
Branch Office(s)
39-12, Sekiguchi 1-chome, Bunkyo-ku, Tokyo
　112-0014 *Tel:* (03) 3203-0151 *Fax:* (03) 3203-
　0157

Zeikei Insatsu, *imprint of* Zeimukeiri-Kyokai Co
Ltd

Zeimukeiri-Kyokai Co Ltd+
2-5-13 Shimo-Ochiai, Shinjuku-ku, Toyko 161-
0033
Tel: (03) 3953 3301; (03) 3953-3325 (sales)
　Fax: (03) 3565 3391
E-mail: zaiko@zeikei.co.jp; postmaster@zeikei.
co.jp
Web Site: www.zeikei.co.jp
Key Personnel
President: Yosiharu Otsubo
Foreign Rights/Trade: Katsuyuki Otsubo
Founded: 1945
Membership(s): Japan Book Publishers Associa-
tion.

Subjects: Accounting, Behavioral Sciences, Busi-
ness, Economics, Human Relations, Law, Man-
agement, Marketing
ISBN Prefix(es): 978-4-419
Number of titles published annually: 100 Print
Total Titles: 1,500 Print
Parent Company: Zeikei Group
Imprints: Zeikei Insatsu
Subsidiaries: Senbundo (Japan)

Zenkoku Kyoudou Publishing Co Ltd
1-10-32, Wakaba, Shinjuku-ku, Tokyo 160-0011
Tel: (03) 3359-4811 (sales); (03) 3359-4815 (edi-
torial) *Fax:* (03) 3358-6174 (sales); (03) 3341-
3919 (editorial)
Web Site: www.zenkyou.com
Key Personnel
President: Takao Onaka
Founded: 1946
Subjects: Agriculture, Economics, Law, Manage-
ment, Social Sciences, Sociology, Co-operatives
ISBN Prefix(es): 978-4-7934

Zoshindo JukenKenkyusha Publishing Co Ltd
2-19-15, Shinmachi, Nishi-ku, Osaka 550-0013
Tel: (06) 6532-1581 *Fax:* (06) 6532-1588
Web Site: www.zoshindo.co.jp
Key Personnel
President: Akitaka Okamoto
Foreign Rights/Trade: Yasuhara Okamoto
　E-mail: y.okamoto@zoshindo.co.jp
Founded: 1890
Membership(s): Japan Book Publishers Associa-
tion.
Subjects: Education, Bookkeeping
ISBN Prefix(es): 978-4-424

Jordan

General Information

Capital: Amman
Language: Arabic. English widely used by busi-
ness people
Religion: Predominantly Sunni Muslim
Population: 3.6 million
Bank Hours: 0830-1230 Saturday-Thursday
Shop Hours: 0900-1300, 1500-1900 Saturday-
Thursday
Currency: 1000 fils = 1 dinar; 10 fils is known as
　a piastre
Export/Import Information: No tariffs on books
　and advertising matter, but tax applies. Import
　licenses required but granted freely. Air freight
　must be by Jordanian national airline. Trans-
　portation insurance must be arranged in Jordan.
Copyright: No copyright conventions signed

Al Salwa Publishing House
PO Box 925826, Amman 11190
Tel: (079) 7661331 *Fax:* (06) 4641132
E-mail: info@alsalwabooks.com
Web Site: www.alsalwabooks.com
Key Personnel
Founder: Taghreed A Najjar
Founded: 1996
ISBN Prefix(es): 978-9957-04

Arab Foundation for Studies & Publishing
c/o Amman, Shmeisani-Abdul-Hameed, Shoman
St, Amman 11191
Mailing Address: PO Box 9157, Amman 11191
Tel: (06) 5605431 9626 *Fax:* (06) 5685501 9626
E-mail: info@airpbooks.com
Web Site: www.airpbooks.com
Founded: 1969
Subjects: Architecture & Interior Design, Art,
　Astronomy, Biography, Memoirs, Business,

Communications, Economics, Education, Gov-
ernment, Political Science, Health, Nutrition,
History, Language Arts, Linguistics, Literature,
Literary Criticism, Essays, Medicine, Nurs-
ing, Dentistry, Military Science, Music, Dance,
Philosophy, Poetry, Psychology, Psychiatry, Re-
ligion - Other, Science (General), Technology,
Media, Mythology

JBC, *imprint of* Jordan Book Centre

Jordan Book Centre+
152 Queen Rania Al Abdallah St, Amman 11941
Mailing Address: PO Box 301, Al-Jubeiha, Am-
man 11941
Tel: (06) 5151882 *Fax:* (06) 5152016
E-mail: info@jbc.com.jo; cs@jbc.com.jo
　(customer service)
Web Site: www.jbc.com.jo/web
Founded: 1982
Subjects: Agriculture, Business, Computer Sci-
ence, Cookery, Crafts, Games, Hobbies, Eco-
nomics, Education, Engineering (General), Fic-
tion, Law, Mathematics, Medicine, Nursing,
Dentistry, Nonfiction (General), Science (Gen-
eral), Travel & Tourism, Veterinary Science,
Humanities
ISBN Prefix(es): 978-9957-406
Imprints: JBC

Majdalawi Masterpieces
Subsidiary of Majdalawi Educational Institute
39 Issam Ajlouni St, Shmaisani, Amman 11118
Mailing Address: PO Box 1819, Amman 11118
Tel: 65676363 *Fax:* 65651900
E-mail: info@majdalawi.jo
Web Site: www.majdalawi.jo
Founded: 1992
ISBN Prefix(es): 978-9957-03

Kazakhstan

General Information

Capital: Almaty
Language: Kazakh
Religion: Islamic (mostly Sunni Muslim)
Population: 17.1 million
Bank Hours: Generally open for short hours be-
tween 0930-1230 Monday-Friday
Shop Hours: Generally 0900-1800 Monday-
Friday; often open weekends
Currency: 100 kopeks = 1 rubl
Export/Import Information: According to
　Ukrainian quotas and customs duties, com-
　panies engaged in trade should register with
　the Ukraine Ministry of Foreign Relations. Li-
　censes for export and import are also required
　for trade with Russia.
Copyright: UCC (see Copyright Conventions, pg
viii)

Al-Farabi Kazakh National University+
Al-Farabi Ave, 71, Almaty 050038
Tel: (8727) 377-33-33 *Fax:* (8727) 377-33-44
E-mail: info@kaznu.kz
Web Site: www.kaznu.kz
Founded: 1934
Subjects: Archaeology, Asian Studies, Biologi-
cal Sciences, Business, Chemistry, Chemical
Engineering, Computer Science, Criminology,
Economics, Environmental Studies, Foreign
Countries, Geography, Geology, Government,
Political Science, History, Journalism, Law,
Management, Mathematics, Mechanical En-
gineering, Philosophy, Physics, Psychology,
Psychiatry, Social Sciences, Sociology

Almatykitap Baspasy
ul Zhambyl, 111, Almaty 050012
Tel: (8727) 250 29 58; (8727) 292 92 23; (8727) 292 57 20 *Fax:* (8727) 292 81 10
E-mail: alkitap@intelsoft.kz; info@almatykitap.kz
Web Site: www.almatykitap.kz
Founded: 1993
Subjects: Art, Education, Fiction, Mathematics, Religion - Other, Science (General), Humanities
ISBN Prefix(es): 978-601-01
Warehouse: Angarsk, 95 "A", Almaty 050012
Tel: (8727) 290 49 66 *Fax:* (8727) 290 49 67

Daik Press
143, Abai Ave, Off 200, Almaty 050009
Tel: (8727) 394-40-45 *Fax:* (8727) 394-42-32
E-mail: daikpress@mail.ru; daikpress@inbox.ru
Web Site: www.daik-press.com
Founded: 1993
Subjects: Art, Fiction, Government, Political Science, History, Military Science, Music, Dance, Nonfiction (General), Culture, Music Notes & Hieroglyphs
ISBN Prefix(es): 978-9965-441; 978-9965-699; 978-601-7170

Foliant Publishing House
Shaken Aimanov St 13, Astana 010000
Tel: (8727) 2395459 *Fax:* (8727) 2397249
E-mail: foliant@foliant.kz
Web Site: www.foliant.kz
Key Personnel
Editor: Zangar Karimkhan
Founded: 1996
Subjects: Education, Fiction, Law, Literature, Literary Criticism, Essays, Science (General)
ISBN Prefix(es): 978-601-292; 978-601-271

Kenya

General Information

Capital: Nairobi
Language: Kiswahili (officially); English, Kikuyu & Luo also spoken
Religion: Most follow traditional beliefs; some Christian and Muslim also
Population: 26.2 million
Bank Hours: 0900-1400 Monday-Friday; 0900-1100 first and last Saturday of each month (except on coast, where banks open and close half an hour earlier)
Shop Hours: 0830-1230, 1400-1630 Monday-Friday; 0830-1200 or 1230 Saturday
Currency: 100 cents = 1 Kenya shilling
Export/Import Information: No tariff on books or advertising matter. Import licenses and exchange controls.
Copyright: UCC, Berne (see Copyright Conventions, pg viii)

Action Publishers+
PO Box 74419, Nairobi GPO 00200
Tel: (0722) 753-227 (cell)
E-mail: info@acton.co.ke
Web Site: www.acton.co.ke
Key Personnel
Founder, Publisher & General Editor: Prof J N K Mugambi
Founded: 1992
Publish books by African scholars.
Subjects: Career Development, Developing Countries, Education, How-to, Music, Dance, Philosophy, Religion - Other, Self-Help, Theology
ISBN Prefix(es): 978-9966-888

ACTS, see African Centre for Technology Studies (ACTS)

African Centre for Technology Studies (ACTS)+
Girigi Court No 49, off United Nations Crescent, Nairobi
Mailing Address: PO Box 45917, Nairobi 00100
Tel: (0710) 607210 (cell); (0737) 916566 (cell)
E-mail: info@acts-net.org
Web Site: www.acts-net.org
Key Personnel
Executive Dir: Cosmas Milton Obate Ochieng
Founded: 1988
Conducts policy research for sustainable development, publication of research findings.
Subjects: Agriculture, Developing Countries, Environmental Studies, Health, Nutrition, Science (General), Technology
ISBN Prefix(es): 978-9966-41
Divisions: Acts Press, Policy Outreach
Distributed by Zed Books (UK)

Bookman Consultants Ltd+
Kijabe St, Barot House, Nairobi
Mailing Address: PO Box 31191, Nairobi GPO 00600
Tel: (020) 245146 *Fax:* (020) 245314
Key Personnel
Owner: Stanley Irura
Founded: 1988
Also acts as publishing consultant & publisher of the Kenya Bookseller.
Membership(s): Kenya Publishers Association.
Subjects: Publishing & Book Trade Reference
ISBN Prefix(es): 978-9966-867

British Institute in Eastern Africa (BIEA)
Laikipia Rd, Kileleshwa, Nairobi
Mailing Address: PO Box 30710, Nairobi GPO 00100
Tel: (020) 434 3190; (020) 434 7195 *Fax:* (020) 434 3365
E-mail: office@biea.ac.uk
Web Site: www.biea.ac.uk; www.facebook.com/BIEA.Nairobi
Key Personnel
Dir: Dr Joost Fontein *E-mail:* joost.fontein@biea.ac.uk
Head Librarian: Innocent Gathungu *E-mail:* innocent.mwangi@biea.ac.uk
Founded: 1962
Subjects: Archaeology, Ethnicity, History, Language Arts, Linguistics
ISBN Prefix(es): 978-1-872566
Number of titles published annually: 1 Print
Branch Office(s)
British Institute in Eastern Africa, 10 Carlton House Terrace, London SW1Y 5AH, United Kingdom, Secretary: Jane Gillespie
Tel: (020) 7969 5201 *Fax:* (020) 7969-5401
E-mail: biea@britac.ac.uk
Distributed by Oxbow Books (UK & USA)

Camerapix Publishers International Ltd+
ABC Pl, 3rd floor, Waiyaki Way, Nairobi GPO 00100
Mailing Address: PO Box 45048, Nairobi GPO 00100
Tel: (020) 4448923; (020) 4448924; (020) 4448925 *Fax:* (020) 4448818
E-mail: info@camerapix.com; camerapix@iconnet.co.ke; customercare@camerapix.co.ke
Web Site: www.camerapixmagazines.com
Key Personnel
Chief Executive Officer, Operations & Business Development Dir: Salim Amin *E-mail:* salim.amin@camerapix.com
Mng Dir: Rukhsana Haq
Founded: 1963
Specialize in travel-related publications & photography.

Subjects: Art, Regional Interests, Travel & Tourism, Culture, Landscape, Wildlife
ISBN Prefix(es): 978-1-874041
Imprints: CPI
Branch Office(s)
6 Alston Rd, Barnet, Herts EN5 4ET, United Kingdom *Tel:* (020) 8449 5503 *Fax:* (020) 8449 8120 *E-mail:* camerapixuk@btinternet.com
No 3, Mzima Springs Rd, Lavington, PO Box 45048, 00100 Nairobi *Tel:* (020) 434 9274; (020) 434 9275; (020) 434 9543 *Fax:* (020) 434 9186

CPI, *imprint of* Camerapix Publishers International Ltd

Dhillon Publishers Ltd+
Factory St, Industrial Area, Nairobi
Mailing Address: PO Box 32197, Nairobi 00600
Tel: (020) 6537553; (020) 3567102; (020) 537553; (020) 552566 *Fax:* (020) 537553
Founded: 1992
Subjects: English as a Second Language, Mathematics, Science (General), Social Sciences, Sociology
ISBN Prefix(es): 978-9966-890

East African Educational Publishers Ltd+
PO Box 45314, Nairobi 00100
Tel: (020) 4445260; (020) 4445261
E-mail: marketing@eastafricanpublishers.com
Web Site: www.eastafricanpublishers.com
Key Personnel
Chairman & Mng Dir: Dr Henry Chakava
Mng Dir: Mr S Ngigi
Founded: 1965 (under the name Heinemann-Cassell Publishers. In 1992 it became a fully Kenyan company under the name EAEP)
Co-publishers with James Currey, Africa Books Collective Publishers (UK), Ohio University Press (USA), African Publishing Network (APNET) (Zimbabwe). Partners with Uchuuzi E-market, online book sale partners.
Membership(s): Kenya Publishers Association.
Subjects: Accounting, Agriculture, Anthropology, Art, Automotive, Behavioral Sciences, Biography, Memoirs, Biological Sciences, Business, Chemistry, Chemical Engineering, Child Care & Development, Computer Science, Cookery, Crafts, Games, Hobbies, Developing Countries, Drama, Theater, Economics, Education, Environmental Studies, Ethnicity, Fashion, Fiction, Finance, Gardening, Plants, Geography, Geology, Government, Political Science, Health, Nutrition, History, House & Home, Humor, Language Arts, Linguistics, Law, Literature, Literary Criticism, Essays, Management, Marketing, Mathematics, Music, Dance, Mysteries, Suspense, Nonfiction (General), Philosophy, Photography, Physical Sciences, Physics, Poetry, Public Administration, Publishing & Book Trade Reference, Religion - Other, Science Fiction, Fantasy, Social Sciences, Sociology, Theology, African Literature, Comics
ISBN Prefix(es): 978-9966-46; 978-9966-9953
Number of titles published annually: 2,000 Online
Total Titles: 2,500 Print; 2,000 Online
Associate Companies: Gustro Ltd, PO Box 9997 Kla, Madhvani Bldg, Jinja Rd, Plot No 16/4, Kampala, Uganda *Tel:* (0414) 251467 *Fax:* (0414) 251468 *E-mail:* gus@utonline.co.ug
Imprints: Kenway Publications (Handles publication of lifestyle & general recreational books)
Subsidiaries: Ujuzi Books Ltd (Tanzania)
Distributor for James Currey Publishers (UK); Heinemann International (UK)
Distribution Center: Uchuuzi E-market, Hospital Rd, Upper Hill, Nairobi, Team Leader, Online Partners: Zachary Njuguna *E-mail:* zack@uchuuzi.com *Web Site:* www.uchuuzi.com

Orders to: African Books Collective, PO Box 721, Oxford OX1 9EN, United Kingdom *Tel:* (01869) 349110 *Fax:* (01869) 349110 *E-mail:* orders@africanbookscollective.com (outside Africa exc North America)
Michigan State University Press, 25 Manly Miles Bldg, East Lansing, MI 48823-5245, United States *Tel:* 517-355-9543 *Fax:* 517-432-2611 *E-mail:* msup@msu.edu *Web Site:* www. msupress.msu.edu (North America)

Egerton University
PO Box 536, Egerton 20115
Tel: (051) 2217891; (051) 2217781
E-mail: info@egerton.ac.ke
Web Site: www.egerton.ac.ke
Subjects: Agriculture, Art, Education, Engineering (General), Environmental Studies, Law, Science (General), Social Sciences, Sociology, Technology, Veterinary Science, Women's Studies
ISBN Prefix(es): 978-9966-838

Evangel Publishing House, Nairobi+
Private Bag 28963, Nairobi City Square 00200
Tel: (020) 8560839; (020) 856204 *Fax:* (020) 8562050
E-mail: info@evangelpublishing.org; editorial@evangelpublishing.org; accounts@ evangelpublishing.org
Web Site: www.evangelpublishing.org
Key Personnel
Mng Editor: Wilson Macharia
Business Development & Marketing Manager: Esther W Nyaga *Tel:* (020) 2320565
Finance & Administration: Lucy N Ndungu
Founded: 1952
Christian publishing.
This publisher has indicated that 50% of their product line is author subsidized.
Subjects: Business, Child Care & Development, Management, Religion - Protestant, Religion - Other, Theology
ISBN Prefix(es): 978-9966-850; 978-9966-20
Number of titles published annually: 20 Print; 3 CD-ROM
Total Titles: 320 Print
Distributed by Church Strengthening Ministry (Philippines)
Distributor for Broadman & Holman (Bibles & other literature); Simon & Schuster Ltd (motivational books)
Foreign Rep(s): Apostolic Faith Mission Bookshop (Zimbabwe); FreshVine (Uganda); Soma Biblia - Dar es Salaam (Tanzania)
Distribution Center: Keswick Books & Gifts, Bruce House, Opposite City Hall, Nairobi, General Manager: Ephantus Gitonga *Tel:* (0713) 621938 (cell) *E-mail:* keswick@ swiftkenya.com (main distributors in Nairobi)
Cana Publishing (UK) Ltd, 13 Walnut Close, NN17 3EE Weldon, Corby, United Kingdom, Chief Executive Officer: Harry Brice *Tel:* (01536) 443502 *Fax:* (01536) 443502 *E-mail:* harry@brice4676.fsnet.co.uk *Web Site:* www.canapublishinguk.com

Focus Publishers Ltd+
Howse & McGeorge Centre, Factory St, Off Bunyala Rd, 00200 Nairobi
Mailing Address: PO Box 28176, Nairobi GPO 00200
Tel: (020) 559296; (020) 559315; (0722) 835649 (cell)
E-mail: focus@africaonline.co.ke
Web Site: www.focuspublishers.co.ke
Founded: 1991
Subjects: Accounting, Business, Economics, Education, English as a Second Language, Fiction, Finance, Geography, Geology, Law, Literature, Literary Criticism, Essays, Mathematics, Philosophy, Religion - Catholic, Catechism
ISBN Prefix(es): 978-9966-882

Number of titles published annually: 20 Print
Total Titles: 120 Print
Distributor for Scepter Ltd (UK); Sinag-Tala (Philippines)

Gaba Publications, AMECEA Pastoral Institute+
PO Box 4002, Eldoret 30100
Tel: (053) 2061218 *Fax:* (053) 2062570
E-mail: gabapubs@africaonline.co.ke; publicationsgaba@cuea.edu
Founded: 1958
Subjects: Anthropology, Biblical Studies, Religion - Catholic, Religion - Other, Theology
ISBN Prefix(es): 978-9966-836

The Government Printer, Nairobi
PO Box 30128, Nairobi 00100
Tel: (020) 317840; (020) 317841
Key Personnel
Contact: S N Migwi
Subjects: Law, Regional Interests
ISBN Prefix(es): 978-9966-26

Jacaranda Designs Ltd+
80 Muthithi Rd, Off Museum Hill, Westlands, Nairobi 00606
Mailing Address: PO Box 1202, Nairobi 00606
Tel: (020) 260-4433
E-mail: info@jacaranda-africa.com
Web Site: www.jacaranda-africa.com; www. youngafricanexpress.net
Key Personnel
Mng Dir & International Rights: Susan Scull-Carvalho
Editor: Bridget King
Founded: 1991
Membership(s): Association of International Schools in Africa (AISA); Kenya Publishers Association; Multi-Cultural Publishers Exchange Association.
Subjects: Education, Fiction, Nonfiction (General)
ISBN Prefix(es): 978-9966-884
U.S. Office(s): Jacaranda Designs Ltd USA, PO Box 7936, Boulder, CO 80306, United States
Distributed by Southern Book Publishers (South Africa)

JKF, *imprint of* The Jomo Kenyatta Foundation

JKF, see The Jomo Kenyatta Foundation

KEMRI, see Kenya Medical Research Institute (KEMRI)

KENGO, see Kenya Energy & Environment Organisation (KENGO)

Kenway Publications, *imprint of* East African Educational Publishers Ltd

Kenway Publications Ltd+
Subsidiary of East African Educational Publishers Ltd
Brick Court, Mpaka Rd, Woodvale Grove, Westlands, Nairobi 00100
Mailing Address: PO Box 45314, Nairobi 00100
Tel: (020) 4444700; (020) 2324762 *Fax:* (020) 4448753
E-mail: info@eastafricanpublishers.com; sales@ eastafricanpublishers.com; marketing@ eastafricanpublishers.com; publishing@ eastafricanpublishers.com
Web Site: www.eastafricanpublishers.com
Key Personnel
Chairman & Chief Executive Officer: Dr H Chakava
Mng Dir: Mr S Ngigi
Founded: 1981
Specialize in tourism books, city maps.

Membership(s): African Publishing Network; Kenya Publishers Association.
Subjects: Accounting, Agriculture, Animals, Pets, Anthropology, Biblical Studies, Biography, Memoirs, Biological Sciences, Business, Career Development, Chemistry, Chemical Engineering, Child Care & Development, Communications, Computer Science, Computers, Cookery, Crafts, Games, Hobbies, Developing Countries, Disability, Special Needs, Drama, Theater, Earth Sciences, Economics, Education, Electronics, Electrical Engineering, Environmental Studies, Ethnicity, Fiction, Finance, Foreign Countries, Geography, Geology, Government, Political Science, Health, Nutrition, History, How-to, Human Relations, Humor, Inspirational, Spirituality, Journalism, Labor, Industrial Relations, Language Arts, Linguistics, Law, Library & Information Sciences, Literature, Literary Criticism, Essays, Management, Marketing, Mathematics, Medicine, Nursing, Dentistry, Music, Dance, Natural History, Nonfiction (General), Philosophy, Physical Sciences, Physics, Poetry, Psychology, Psychiatry, Public Administration, Publishing & Book Trade Reference, Regional Interests, Science (General), Science Fiction, Fantasy, Social Sciences, Sociology, Sports, Athletics, Technology, Travel & Tourism, Veterinary Science, Women's Studies, Comics
ISBN Prefix(es): 978-9966-46; 978-9966-848; 978-9966-25
Number of titles published annually: 4 Print
Total Titles: 58 Print
Associate Companies: Transmedia Uganda, Plot 51/53, Nkrumah Rd, PO Box 28104, Kampala, Uganda, Contact: Ignatius Tumwesigye *Tel:* (041) 235860 *Fax:* (041) 347235 *E-mail:* transmed@swiftuganda.com
Distributed by African Books Collective (UK)
Foreign Rep(s): African Books Collective (Europe, UK)

Kenya Energy & Environment Organisation (KENGO)
PO Box 48197, Nairobi 00100
Tel: (020) 748281 *Fax:* (020) 749382
Founded: 1981
Subjects: Agriculture, Energy, Environmental Studies
ISBN Prefix(es): 978-9966-841

Kenya Literature Bureau (KLB)+
South C, Popo Rd Bellevue Area, off Mombasa Rd, Nairobi 00100
Mailing Address: PO Box 30022, Nairobi 00100
Tel: (020) 3541196; (020) 3541197 *Fax:* (020) 6001474
E-mail: info@klb.co.ke
Web Site: www.kenyaliteraturebureau.com; www. klb.co.ke
Key Personnel
Mng Dir: Eve A Obara
Production Manager: Joseph A Emojong
Publishing Manager: Mary N Khasiani
Sales & Marketing Manager: Bernard O Obura
Publishes, prints & distributes affordable books & other reading materials. Also encourages Kenyan authors through financial incentives, advice on how to write, etc.
Subjects: Agriculture, Animals, Pets, Business, Chemistry, Chemical Engineering, Child Care & Development, Education, Finance, Geography, Geology, Health, Nutrition, House & Home, Law, Literature, Literary Criticism, Essays, Management, Marketing, Mathematics, Medicine, Nursing, Dentistry, Nonfiction (General), Poetry, Science (General), Science Fiction, Fantasy, Social Sciences, Sociology, Veterinary Science
ISBN Prefix(es): 978-9966-44
Total Titles: 700 Print

Kenya Medical Research Institute (KEMRI)
Mbagathi Rd, Nairobi
Mailing Address: PO Box 54840, Nairobi 00200
Tel: (020) 722541; (020) 2713349
E-mail: webmaster@kemri.org
Web Site: www.kemri.org
Key Personnel
Chairperson: Prof Ruth Nduati
Dir: Solomon Mpoke
Founded: 1979
Subjects: Biological Sciences, Environmental
  Studies, Health, Nutrition, Medicine, Nursing,
  Dentistry
ISBN Prefix(es): 978-9966-869

The Jomo Kenyatta Foundation+
Enterprise Rd, Industrial Area, Nairobi GPO
  00100
Tel: (020) 2329987; (020) 2330002; (0723)
  286993 (cell); (020) 2330003 *Fax:* (020)
  6531966
E-mail: info@jkf.co.ke
Web Site: www.jkf.co.ke
Key Personnel
Mng Dir: Nancy N Karimi
Founded: 1966
Membership(s): Kenya Publishers Association.
Subjects: Education
ISBN Prefix(es): 978-9966-22
Parent Company: Ministry of Education, PO Box
  30040-00100, Nairobi GPO 00100
Imprints: JKF
Warehouse: Kijabe St, PO Box 30533, Nairobi
  GPO 00100 *Tel:* (020) 2224499 *Fax:* (020)
  8074604 *E-mail:* kijabe@jkf.co.ke

KLB, see Kenya Literature Bureau (KLB)

Kwani Trust
PO Box 2895, Nairobi 00100
Tel: (020) 4441801 *Fax:* (020) 4441802
E-mail: info@kwani.org; sales@kwani.org
Web Site: www.kwani.org
Key Personnel
General Manager: Velma Kiome
Executive Dir: Angela Wachuka
Mng Editor: Billy Kahora
Sales & Marketing: Mike Mburu
Subjects: Literature, Literary Criticism, Essays
ISBN Prefix(es): 978-9966-9836

Lake Publishers & Printers Enterprises Ltd+
PO Box 1743, Kisumu 40100
Tel: (057) 2021715
Founded: 1982
Book publishing & printing.
Membership(s): African Publishing Network (AP-
  NET); Kenya Booksellers Association; Kenya
  Publishers Association.
Subjects: How-to, Journalism, Labor, Industrial
  Relations, Language Arts, Linguistics, Litera-
  ture, Literary Criticism, Essays, Management,
  Marketing, Music, Dance, Nonfiction (General),
  Philosophy, Public Administration, Religion -
  Catholic, Religion - Protestant, Romance, Sci-
  ence (General), Science Fiction, Fantasy, Social
  Sciences, Sociology, Sports, Athletics, Theol-
  ogy, Women's Studies
ISBN Prefix(es): 978-9966-847
Total Titles: 80 Print
Associate Companies: Thu Tinda Book Distribu-
  tion Ltd; Thu Tinda Bookshop
Subsidiaries: Innervision Communication
Distributor for ABC (outside Africa)
Showroom(s): Kenya Industrial Estate, Airport
  Rd, Kisumu

LCA, see Life Challenge Africa (LCA)

Life Challenge Africa (LCA)
PO Box 50770, Nairobi GPO 00200

Tel: (020) 3870 824; (020) 272 4622; (020) 272
  5133 *Fax:* (020) 3871 829
E-mail: info@lifechallenge.de
Web Site: www.lifechallenge.de
Key Personnel
Contact: Walter Eric *Tel:* (0734) 231 239 (cell);
  Jared Oginga *Tel:* (0733) 870 336 (cell)
Subjects: Religion - Protestant
ISBN Prefix(es): 978-9966-895
Branch Office(s)
PO Box 9958-KIA, Accra, Ghana
  E-mail: ghana@christian-literature.net
PMB 2008, Jos, Plateau State, Nigeria
  Tel: (08053) 468 634 *E-mail:* lcanig@gmail.
  com
LCA West, BP 17553, Dakar-Liberte, Senegal
  Tel: 77 371 6468 (cell) *E-mail:* lca-west@
  bigfoot.com
CCM Services, PO Box 12322, Edleen, Kemp-
  ton Park 1625, South Africa *E-mail:* services@
  ccm.org.za

Moran (EA) Publishers Ltd+
Judda Complex, Forest Rd, Nairobi 00100
Mailing Address: PO Box 30797, Nairobi 00100
Tel: (020) 2013580 *Fax:* (020) 2013583
E-mail: info@moranpublishers.co.ke
Web Site: www.moranpublishers.co.ke
Founded: 1970
ISBN Prefix(es): 978-9966-885; 978-9966-945

Phoenix Publishers Ltd+
22 Kijabe St, Nairobi GPO 00500
Mailing Address: PO Box 18650, Nairobi GPO
  00500
Tel: (020) 223262; (020) 222309
Web Site: www.phoenixpublishers.co.ke
Founded: 1987
Membership(s): Kenya Publishers Association.
Subjects: Education, Environmental Studies, Ge-
  ography, Geology, History, Mathematics, Phys-
  ical Sciences, Poetry, Social Sciences, Sociol-
  ogy, Women's Studies
ISBN Prefix(es): 978-9966-47
Distributed by MK Publishers (Uganda); Taasisi
  ya Uchunguzi wa Kiswahili (TUKI) (Tanzania)
Distributor for MK Publishers (Uganda); Taasisi
  ya Uchunguzi wa Kiswahili (TUKI) (Tanzania)
Foreign Rep(s): MK Publishers (Uganda)
Foreign Rights: Taasisi ya Uchunguzi wa
  Kiswahili (TUKI) (Tanzania)

Sasa Sema Publications Ltd+
Imprint of Longhorn Publishers
Funzi Rd, Industrial Area, PO Box 18033,
  Nairobi 00500
Tel: (020) 6532579; (020) 6532580; (020)
  6532581 *Fax:* (020) 6558551
E-mail: enquiries@longhornpublishers.com
Web Site: www.longhornpublishers.com
Founded: 1996
Publisher of Kenyan children's books, especially
  comic books (graphic novels; bandes dessinees)
  in Swahili & English; children's biographies of
  great African women & men in English; short
  literature in English & Swahili. Also publishes
  editorial cartoons, study guides & preschool
  activity books.
Membership(s): Kenya Publishers Association.
Subjects: African American Studies, Biography,
  Memoirs, Developing Countries, Education,
  Fiction, Foreign Countries, History, Humor, Po-
  etry, Religion - Islamic, Religion - Protestant,
  Science Fiction, Fantasy
ISBN Prefix(es): 978-9966-36
Number of titles published annually: 6 Print
Total Titles: 35 Print
Branch Office(s)
Longhorn Tanzania Ltd, New Bagamoyo/Gar-
  den Rd, Mikocheni B, Plot No MKC/MCB/
  81, PO Box 1237, Dar es Salaam, Tanza-

nia *Tel:* (022) 2760637 *Fax:* (022) 2774599
  E-mail: longhorntz@longhornpublishers.com
Longhorn Uganda Publishers Ltd, Kanjokya
  St, Plot 74, PO Box 24745, Kampala,
  Uganda *Tel:* (041) 286093 *Fax:* (041) 286397
  E-mail: ug@longhornpublishers.com

Sudan Literature Centre
Karen, Ndege Rd 70, PO Box 21033, Nairobi
  00505
Tel: (020) 3869685; (020) 3869688; (0722)
  923203 (cell) *Fax:* (020) 3864141
E-mail: slc.across@gmail.com
Key Personnel
Media Manager: Walter Duku *Tel:* (097) 712
  2206 (cell) *E-mail:* dukwal@across-sudan.org
Founded: 1988
Producer of church & other books for South Su-
  dan & Sudan.
Subjects: Biography, Memoirs, English as a Sec-
  ond Language, Health, Nutrition, Regional In-
  terests, Religion - Protestant, Culture, Literacy
ISBN Prefix(es): 978-9966-876; 978-9966-32
Number of titles published annually: 20 Print
Total Titles: 1,500 Print
Parent Company: Across, Old Mission Rd, Yei,
  Sudan

Transafrica Press
Kenwood House, Kimathi St, 2nd floor, PO Box
  48239, Nairobi 00100
Tel: (020) 2244235; (020) 2217897 *Fax:* (020)
  2217891; (020) 2344328
Founded: 1976
Subjects: Biography, Memoirs, Education, Fiction,
  History, How-to, Nonfiction (General), Poetry,
  Regional Interests, Religion - Other, Social Sci-
  ences, Sociology
ISBN Prefix(es): 978-9966-940

UN-Habitat
Gigiri Ave, Block 4-South Wing Top Level,
  Nairobi GPO 00100
Mailing Address: PO Box 30030, Nairobi GPO
  00100
Tel: (020) 7621234; (020) 7623120 (information
  services); (020) 762 5518 (press) *Fax:* (020)
  7624266
E-mail: infohabitat@unhabitat.org; habitat.press@
  unhabitat.org
Web Site: mirror.unhabitat.org; www.unhabitat.org
Key Personnel
Executive Dir: Dr Joan Clos
Deputy Executive Dir: Ms Aisa Kirabo Kacyira
Subjects: Environmental Studies, Social Sciences,
  Sociology, Disaster Management, Housing,
  Risk Management, Urban Development
ISBN Prefix(es): 978-92-113

United Nations Human Settlements
Programme, see UN-Habitat

University of Nairobi Press (UONP)+
3rd floor, Jomo Kenyatta Memorial Library Bldg,
  University of Nairobi, University Way, Nairobi
  00100
Mailing Address: PO Box 30197, Nairobi 00100
Tel: (020) 318262
E-mail: nup@uonbi.ac.ke
Web Site: www.uonbi.ac.ke/press
Founded: 1984
Subjects: Accounting, African American Stud-
  ies, Behavioral Sciences, Developing Coun-
  tries, Engineering (General), Environmental
  Studies, Geography, Geology, Government,
  Political Science, Health, Nutrition, History,
  Language Arts, Linguistics, Law, Library & In-
  formation Sciences, Mathematics, Philosophy,
  Physical Sciences, Physics, Real Estate, Reli-
  gion - Protestant, Social Sciences, Sociology,
  Veterinary Science
ISBN Prefix(es): 978-9966-846

Number of titles published annually: 10 Print
Distributed by African Books Collective (Europe,
USA)

UONP, see University of Nairobi Press (UONP)

Uzima Publishing House+
Imani House, 2nd floor, St John's Gate, Nairobi
GPO 00100
Mailing Address: PO Box 48127, Nairobi GPO
00100
Tel: (020) 2216836; (020) 220239; (0722) 461670
E-mail: uzima@wananchi.com
Web Site: www.ackenya.org/institutions/
uzima_publishing.html
Key Personnel
Chairman: Rev Joseph Wasonga
General Manager: Clement Ouko
Editorial Manager: Amos Omollo
Sales & Marketing Manager: Joel Kichwen
Founded: 1974
Specialize in Christian books.
Membership(s): Christian Booksellers Association
(CBA); Christian Trade International; Kenya
Publishers Association (KPA).
Subjects: Biblical Studies, Biography, Memoirs,
Career Development, Fiction, Management,
Nonfiction (General), Religion - Protestant,
Self-Help, Women's Studies
ISBN Prefix(es): 978-9966-855
Parent Company: Anglican Church of Kenya
Foreign Rep(s): Harry Brice (Canada, Europe,
UK, USA)
Foreign Rights: Annie D'Villiers (South Africa,
Southern Africa)

WordAlive Publishers Ltd
Unit 5 Korosho Rd/Hendred Ave, Valley Arcade,
Nairobi 00100
Mailing Address: PO Box 4547, Nairobi 00100
Tel: (020) 357 2380 *Fax:* (020) 357 2382
E-mail: info@wordalivepublishers.com; sales@
wordalivepublishers.com
Web Site: www.wordalivepublishers.com
Key Personnel
Chief Executive Officer: David Waweru
Founded: 2001
Membership(s): Kenya Publishers Association.
Subjects: Biblical Studies, Biography, Memoirs,
History, Religion - Other, Theology, Christian
Living, Leadership, Personal Growth
ISBN Prefix(es): 978-9966-805

World Agroforestry Centre
United Nations Ave, Gigiri, Nairobi GPO 00100
Mailing Address: PO Box 30677, Nairobi GPO
00100
Tel: (020) 722 4000 *Fax:* (020) 722 4001
E-mail: worldagroforestry@cgiar.org
Web Site: www.worldagroforestry.org
Key Personnel
Dir General: Tony Simons
Deputy Dir General: Laksiri Abeysekera
Head, Communications: Paul Stapleton
Founded: 1977
International not-for-profit organization.
Subjects: Agriculture, Environmental Studies
ISBN Prefix(es): 978-92-9059
Branch Office(s)
PO Box 2389, Kisumu 40100 *Tel:* (057) 2021234;
(057) 2021456 *E-mail:* g.aertssen@cgiar.org
c/o Bangbandhu Sheikh Mujibur Rehman
Agricultural University, Gazipur 1706,
Bangladesh, Liaison Scientist: Dr Giashuddin
Miah *Tel:* (02) 9205310 *Fax:* (02) 9205330
E-mail: g.miah@cgiar.org
Instituto Iniciativa Amazonica-IIA/ICRAF, Em-
brapa Amazonia Oriental, Travessa Dr Eneas
Pinheiro s/n, 66095-100 Marco-Belem-PA,
Brazil *Tel:* (091) 3204 1108; (091) 3276 2902
E-mail: icraf_brazil@cgiar.org

PO Box 16317, Yaounde, Cameroon
Tel: 222215084 *Fax:* 222215089 *E-mail:* icraf-
aht@cgiar.org
No 12 Zhongguancun Nan Da Jie, CAAS
Mailbox 195, Beijing 100081, China
Tel: (010) 8210 5693 *Fax:* (010) 8210 5694
E-mail: cmes-icraf@mail.kib.ac.cn
Centre for Mountain Ecosystem Studies, c/o Kun-
ming Institute of Botany, 3/F North Research
Bldg, Heilongtan, Kunming 650201, China
Tel: (0871) 5223014 *Fax:* (0871) 5223377
E-mail: cmes@mail.kib.ac.cn
c/o INERA, Ave des cliniques No 13, Gombe,
Kinshasa, Democratic Republic of the Congo
Tel: 817762807; 993373922 *E-mail:* a.biloso@
cgiar.org
3 km Carretera a Siquirres, Turrialba,
Cartago 30501, Costa Rica *Tel:* 2558 2611
E-mail: icraf_cr@cgiar.org
Cocody Mermoz, Ave 9, BP 2823, Abidjan 08,
Cote d'Ivoire *Tel:* 22446774 *E-mail:* icraf.cdi@
cgiar.org
c/o ILRI Campus, Gura Shola, PO Box 5689,
Addis Ababa, Ethiopia *Tel:* (011) 617 2491
Fax: (011) 617 2001 *E-mail:* k.hadgu@cgiar.
org
NASC Complex, 1st floor, Block C, Dev
Prakash Shastri Marg, Pusa Campus, New
Delhi 110 012, India *Tel:* (011) 25609800;
(011) 25847885; (011) 25847886 *Fax:* (011)
25847884 *E-mail:* v.p.singh@cgiar.org
JL, CIFOR, Situ Gede, Sindang Barang, PO
Box 161, Bogor 16001, Indonesia *Tel:* (0251)
8625415 *Fax:* (0251) 8625416 *E-mail:* u.
pradhan@cgiar.org
Chitedze Research Station, off Mchinji Rd, PO
Box 30798, Liongwe 3, Malawi *Tel:* 01 707
332; 01 707 319 *Fax:* 01 707 319 *E-mail:* s.
weldesemayat@cgiar.org
BP E5118, Bamako, Mali *Tel:* 2070 9220; 4490
1806 *Fax:* 4490 1807 *E-mail:* icraf-wca@cgiar.
org
Av das FPLM, CP 1884, 3698 Mavalane, Maputo,
Mozambique *Tel:* (021) 461775 *E-mail:* arnela.
mausse@yahoo.com
Edo ADP Premises, Ogba Rd, Oko, PMB 1698,
Benin City, Edo State, Nigeria *Tel:* (052) 894
750 *E-mail:* icraf-nigeria@cgiar.org
Av La Molina 1895, PO Box 1558, Lima 12,
Peru *Tel:* (01) 349 6017 *Fax:* (01) 317 5326
E-mail: icraf_brazil@cgiar.org
INIA, Carretera Federico Basadre Km 4.2, Pu-
callpa, Peru *Tel:* (061) 579078
Khush Hall Bldg, 2nd floor, International Rice
Research Institute, Los Banos, PO Box
35024, UPLB College, 4031 Laguna, Philippines *Tel:* (02) 5805600 *Fax:* (049) 5392925
E-mail: icrafphi@cgiar.org
c/o IRST Campus, Huye, Rwanda *Tel:* (025)
2531350 *E-mail:* mukuratha@yahoo.com
No 5 Presidential Lodge Rd, Makeno Northern Province, Sierra Leone *Tel:* (079) 274500
E-mail: icraf-sl@cgiar.org
c/o Faculty of Agriculture, University of Peradeniya, Peradeniya 20400, Sri Lanka
Tel: (081) 239 5110 *Fax:* (081) 239 5110;
(081) 238 8041 *E-mail:* ngpkumara@pdn.ac.lk
c/o Mari-Mikocheni, Coca Cola Rd, PO Box
6226, Dar es Salaam, Tanzania *Tel:* (022)
2700660 *E-mail:* a.kimaro@cgiar.org
Faculty of Social Sciences, 5th floor Chiang Mai
University, PO Box 267, CMU Post Office,
Chiang Mai 50202, Thailand *Tel:* (066) 5335
7906; (066) 5335 7907 *Fax:* (066) 5335 7908
E-mail: icraf@cgiar-cm.org
c/o NaFORRI, Kifu, Mukono, PO Box 26416,
Kampala, Uganda *Tel:* (041) 4220601
Fax: (041) 4220611 *E-mail:* c.okia@cgiar.org
No 8, Lot 13A, Trung Yen Hoa St, Yen Hoa
Ward, Cau Giay District, Cau Giay District,
Hanoi, Vietnam *Tel:* (04) 3783 4645 *Fax:* (04)
3783 4644 *E-mail:* d.c.catacutan@cgiar.org
c/o Provincial Agriculture Office (East-
ern Province), Msekera Agriculture Re-

search, PO Box 510046, Chipata, Zambia
Tel: (021) 6221404 *Fax:* (021) 6221725
E-mail: drsmartlungu@yahoo.com

Kuwait

General Information

Capital: Kuwait
Language: Arabic. English also used commercially
Religion: Muslim
Population: 1.58 million
Bank Hours: 0800-1200 (0830-1230 during Ramadan) Saturday-Thursday
Shop Hours: 0800-1200 or 1230, 1530 or 16-
2030 Saturday-Thursday; 0800-1200 Friday
(markets and shopping centers also open 1530-
2030); during Ramadan: 0830 or 0900-1230,
1930-1030 or 0200 Saturday-Thursday. Some
shopping centers open 1600-2100 Friday
Export/Import Information: No tariffs on books or
advertising in reasonable quantity; all immoral
and seditious publications prohibited. Import
license required. No exchange permit required.
Copyright: No copyright conventions signed

Kuwait Publishing House Co
PO Box 1446, 13015 Safat, Kuwait City
Tel: 22449686; 22455171 *Fax:* 22436956
Subjects: Regional Interests, Travel & Tourism

Ministry of Information
PO Box 193, 13002 Safat, Kuwait City
Tel: 24847312 (publications); 24814883 (publica-
tions); 22327196 (press); 22327447
E-mail: admin@media.gov.kw; pressoffice@
media.gov.kw
Web Site: www.media.gov.kw
Subjects: Art, Education, Geography, Geology,
History, Language Arts, Linguistics, Litera-
ture, Literary Criticism, Essays, Mathematics,
Physics, Social Sciences, Sociology

Latvia

General Information

Capital: Riga
Language: Latvian (Lettish)
Religion: Predominantly Christian (mostly
Lutheran)
Population: 2.7 million
Bank Hours: Generally open for short hours be-
tween 0930-1230 Monday-Friday
Shop Hours: Generally 0900-1800 Monday-
Friday; often open weekends
Currency: 100 Eurocents = 1 Euro
Copyright: Berne (see Copyright Conventions, pg
viii)

Izdevnieciba AGB
Brivibas gatve 202, Riga LV-1039
Tel: 67280464; 29239977
E-mail: info@izdevnieciba.com
Web Site: www.izdevnieciba.com
Founded: 1994
Subjects: Education, History, Travel & Tourism,
Culture
ISBN Prefix(es): 978-9984-663; 978-9984-777;
978-9984-9169; 978-9984-9288

Izdevnieciba Avots+
Puskina iela 1a, Riga LV-1050

Tel: 67212612 *Fax:* 67212612
E-mail: avots@apollo.lv
Web Site: www.avotsabc.lv
Key Personnel
Mng Dir: Janis Leja
Founded: 1980
Membership(s): Latvian Publishers' Association (LPA).
Subjects: English as a Second Language, Gardening, Plants, House & Home, How-to, Language Arts, Linguistics, Nonfiction (General)
ISBN Prefix(es): 978-9984-757

Bibliography Institute of the National Library of Latvia
Anglikanu 5, 2nd floor, Riga LV-1423
Tel: 67365250; 67287620; 67806135
Fax: 67280851
E-mail: lnb@lnb.lv; konstultants@lnb.lv
Web Site: www.lnb.lv/en/structure/bibliography-institute
Key Personnel
Dir: Anita Goldberga *Tel:* 67559975
E-mail: anita.goldberga@lnb.lv
Deputy Dir: Ilona Dukure *Tel:* 67559974
E-mail: ilona.dukure@lnb.lv
Founded: 1940
Statistical information & analysis of publishing activities & national bibliography.
Membership(s): Latvian Publishers' Association (LPA).
Subjects: Publishing & Book Trade Reference, Publishing/reference library & information sciences
ISBN Prefix(es): 978-9984-607; 978-9984-9006; 978-9984-9007
Number of titles published annually: 3 Print; 1 CD-ROM; 4 Online
Total Titles: 3 Print; 1 CD-ROM; 4 Online
Parent Company: The National Library of Latvia (NLL)

Egmont Latvija SIA+
Bikernieku iela 1, Riga LV-1039
Tel: 6718 5783; 6718 5784; 6718 5785 *Fax:* 6718 5786
Web Site: www.egmont.lv
Key Personnel
Chairman of the Board: Romans Filipovs
E-mail: roma@egmont.lv
Production Manager: Tatjana Vitze
E-mail: tatjana@egmont.lv
Editor-in-Chief: Antra Jansone *E-mail:* antra@egmont.lv
Book Editor: Ilze Collenkopfa *E-mail:* ilze@egmont.lv
Sales: Olga Zaharova *E-mail:* olga@egmont.lv
Founded: 1991
Subjects: Advertising, Fiction, Film, Video, Nonfiction (General), Sports, Athletics, Western Fiction, Cartoons, Comics
Parent Company: Egmont International Holding A/S, Vognmagergade 11, 1148 Copenhagen K, Denmark
Warehouse: Elijas St 17, 1st floor, Riga LV-1050 *Tel:* 67210120 *Fax:* 67210078
E-mail: noliktava@egmont.lv

Karsu Izdevnieciba Jana Seta (Jana Seta Map Publishers)
Krasta iela 105A, Riga LV-1019
Tel: 67317540; 67290669; 07290806
Fax: 67317541
E-mail: kartes@kartes.lv
Web Site: www.kartes.lv
ISBN Prefix(es): 978-9984-508; 978-9984-07

Jumava Apgads
Dzirnavu 73-1, Riga LV-1011
Tel: 67288104; 67280314
E-mail: redakcija@jumava.lv
Web Site: www.jumava.lv

Key Personnel
Editor: Renata Reiman *Tel:* 67280215
Production: Sarma Matveka *Tel:* 67280319
E-mail: sarma.matveka@jumava.lv
Office Manager: Zane Vitols *E-mail:* zane@jumava.lv
ISBN Prefix(es): 978-9984-05; 978-9984-506

Latvijas Ekologiskas Izglitibas Apgads, see Vieda SIA

Latvijas Universitates Akademiska Biblioteka (Academic Library of the University of Latvia)
Rupniecibas iela 10, Riga LV-1235
Tel: 67033951; 26373599
E-mail: acadlib@lib.acadlib.lv
Web Site: www.acadlib.lv
Key Personnel
Dir: Venta Kocere *Tel:* 67033955 *E-mail:* venta.kocere@lu.lv
Deputy Dir: Ineta Kivle *Tel:* 22021550
E-mail: ineta.kivle@lu.lv
Founded: 1524
Publisher of bibliographic indexes.
Subjects: Chemistry, Chemical Engineering, Library & Information Sciences, Science (General), Information Technology, Latvian Culture, Library Technology
ISBN Prefix(es): 978-9984-538; 978-9984-9008

Liels un Mazs
Terbatas 49/51-12, Riga LV-1011
Tel: 67282133
E-mail: pasts@lielsmazs.lv
Web Site: www.lielsmazs.lv
Key Personnel
Dir: Alise Zirne *E-mail:* limze@lielsmazs.lv
Founded: 2004
ISBN Prefix(es): 978-9984-9801

Izdevnieciba Lielvards+
Skolas iela 5, Lielvarde LV-5070
Tel: 67801787 *Fax:* 67556592
E-mail: info@lielvards.lv
Web Site: www.lielvards.lv
Key Personnel
Executive Dir: Andris Gribuste *Tel:* 26399012
Founded: 1992
Subjects: Biological Sciences, Chemistry, Chemical Engineering, Computer Science, Education, Geography, Geology, Health, Nutrition, History, Language Arts, Linguistics, Mathematics, Physics, Science (General), Social Sciences, Sociology
ISBN Prefix(es): 978-9984-11; 978-9984-513
Showroom(s): Bikernieku 15, Riga LV-1039, Manager: Vita Skele *Tel:* 67801787; 67801788
Fax: 67556592 *E-mail:* realriga@lielvards.lv

Madris SIA+
Tallinas 36a, Riga LV-1001
Tel: 67374020; 29906392 *Fax:* 67374005
E-mail: madris@madris.lv; madris@latnet.lv
Web Site: www.madris.lv
Key Personnel
General Manager: Skaidrite Naumova
Founded: 1996
Subjects: Fiction, Literature, Literary Criticism, Essays, Poetry, Science (General), Travel & Tourism
ISBN Prefix(es): 978-9984-592; 978-9984-31
Number of titles published annually: 20 Print

Neputns
Terbatas St 49/51-8, Riga LV-1011
Tel: 67222647
E-mail: neputns@neputns.lv
Web Site: neputns.lv
Key Personnel
Dir: Elgita Bertina
Editor-in-Chief: Laima Slava

Founded: 1997
Subjects: Architecture & Interior Design, Art, Music, Dance, Photography, Poetry, Cinema
ISBN Prefix(es): 978-9984-729; 978-9934-512; 978-9984-807

Patmos
Baznicas iela 12a, Riga LV-1010
Tel: 67289674
Founded: 1995
Subjects: Biblical Studies, Health, Nutrition, Religion - Protestant, Theology
ISBN Prefix(es): 978-9984-514

Izdevnieciba Petergailis SIA
Stabu iela 54, Riga LV-1011
Tel: 67272220; 67843062 (orders)
Fax: 67871762; 67871761 (orders)
E-mail: info@petergailis.lv
Web Site: www.petergailis.lv
Founded: 1990
Subjects: Fiction, Health, Nutrition, History, Literature, Literary Criticism, Essays, Poetry, Science (General), Children's Literature, Cultural History, Popular Science, Prose
ISBN Prefix(es): 978-9984-673; 978-9984-33; 978-9984-504

Vaidelote SIA+
Stacijas iela 34-37, Olaine, Olaines nov, Rigas Rajons LV-2114
Tel: 29552391
Founded: 1993
Subjects: Animals, Pets, Fiction
ISBN Prefix(es): 978-9984-507

Valters un Rapa
Aspazijas bulv, 24, Riga LV-1050
Tel: 29375009; 67222422
E-mail: info@valtersunrapa.lv; gramatunams@valtersunrapa.lv
Web Site: www.valtersunrapa.lv
Key Personnel
Human Resources & Marketing: Iveta Ozola
Tel: 67224630 *E-mail:* iveta@valtersunrapa.lv
Founded: 1912
Subjects: Architecture & Interior Design, Art, Crafts, Games, Hobbies, Fiction, History, Language Arts, Linguistics, Literature, Literary Criticism, Essays, Music, Dance, Philosophy, Poetry, Travel & Tourism
ISBN Prefix(es): 978-9984-595; 978-9984-768; 978-9958-9673

Vieda SIA+
Lubanas 6-4, Riga LV-1019
Tel: 67140680
E-mail: smart.info@gmail.com
Web Site: www.vieda.lv
Key Personnel
Chairman of the Board: Aivars Garda
Founded: 1989
Subjects: Astrology, Occult, History, Parapsychology, Philosophy
ISBN Prefix(es): 978-5-85745; 978-9984-701

Apgads Zinatne SIA
Akademijas laukums 1, Riga LV-1050
Tel: 67212797; 67225767 (bookstore)
Fax: 67227825
E-mail: zinatne@zinatne.com.lv
Web Site: www.zinatnesgramatas.lv
Key Personnel
Chairwoman: Ingrida Seglina
Project Manager: Ieva Jansone
Founded: 1951
Subjects: Art, Economics, Fiction, History, Language Arts, Linguistics, Literature, Literary Criticism, Essays, Medicine, Nursing, Dentistry, Philosophy, Theology, Folklore, Latvian History
ISBN Prefix(es): 978-9984-808; 978-5-7966

Zvaigzne ABC+
K Valdemara iela 6, Riga LV-1010
Tel: 67324518
E-mail: reklama@zvaigzne.lv
Web Site: www.zvaigzne.lv
Key Personnel
President: Vija Kilbloku
Founded: 1966
Specialize in textbooks, reference, children's literature & fiction.
Subjects: Animals, Pets, Astrology, Occult, Child Care & Development, Education, English as a Second Language, Fiction, Literature, Literary Criticism, Essays, Nonfiction (General), Psychology, Psychiatry, Romance, Science Fiction, Fantasy, Travel & Tourism, Adventure, Classics, Estoerics/New Age, Fairy Tales
ISBN Prefix(es): 978-5-405; 978-9984-04; 978-9984-17; 978-9984-560; 978-9984-22; 978-9984-36
Total Titles: 1,400 Print
Bookshop(s): Bikernieku iela 19, Riga LV-1039 *Tel:* 67801979 *E-mail:* gramatu.nams@zvaigzne.lv; Dzirnavu iela 84, Riga *Tel:* 67288404 *E-mail:* bergs@zvaigzne.lv; K Barona iela 24/26, Riga *Tel:* 67212557 *E-mail:* barona24@zvaigzne.lv; K Valdemara 6, Riga *Tel:* 67334603 *E-mail:* gramatnica@zvaigzne.lv; Marupes iela 3, Riga *Tel:* 67618504 *E-mail:* agenskalns@zvaigzne.lv; Mukusalas iela 71, Riga *Tel:* 22368589 *E-mail:* plaza@zvaigzne.lv; Rezeknes iela 3, Riga *Tel:* 67138200 *E-mail:* cenuklubs@zvaigzne.lv; Terbatas iela 39, Riga *Tel:* 67224921 *E-mail:* terbata@zvaigzne.lv; Valnu iela 19-1C, Riga *Tel:* 67212207 *E-mail:* valnu@zvaigzne.lv; Rigas gatve 5, t/c Apelsins, Adazi *Tel:* 67996175 *E-mail:* adazi@zvaigzne.lv; Spidolas iela 11, Aizkraukle *Tel:* 65120310 *E-mail:* aizkraukle@zvaigzne.lv; Atmodas iela 13, Aizpute *Tel:* 63448102 *E-mail:* aizpute@zvaigzne.lv; Liela Ezera iela 2, Aluksne *Tel:* 64321468 *E-mail:* aluksne@zvaigzne.lv; Brivibas iela 57, t/c 2 stava, Balvi *Tel:* 64520292 *E-mail:* balvi@zvaigzne.lv; Darza iela 14A, Bauska *Tel:* 63927243 *E-mail:* bauska@zvaigzne.lv; Rigas iela 2, Cesis *Tel:* 64122243 *E-mail:* cesis@zvaigzne.lv; Abelu iela 17 b, Gulbene *Tel:* 64471495 *E-mail:* gulbene@zvaigzne.lv; Rigas iela 175, Jekabpils *Tel:* 65221432 *E-mail:* jekabpils@zvaigzne.lv; Liela iela 13, Jelgava *Tel:* 63023636 *E-mail:* jelgava@zvaigzne.lv; Liepajas iela 46, Kuldiga *Tel:* 63325110 *E-mail:* kuldiga@zvaigzne.lv; Mucenieku iela 33, Kuldiga *Tel:* 63324088 *E-mail:* kuldiga@zvaigzne.lv; Ganibu iela 53/55, Liepaja *Tel:* 63425750 *E-mail:* liepaja@zvaigzne.lv; Liela iela 13, Tirdzniecibas centrs "kurzeme", 3 stavs, Liepaja *Tel:* 63428825 *E-mail:* liepaja@zvaigzne.lv; Rigas iela 7, Limbazi *Tel:* 64021053 *E-mail:* limbazi@zvaigzne.lv; Rigas iela 118, Livani *Tel:* 65341200 *E-mail:* livani@zvaigzne.lv; K Barona iela 43A, Ludza *Tel:* 65725015 *E-mail:* ludza@zvaigzne.lv; Poruka iela 3a, Madona *Tel:* 64822402 *E-mail:* madona@zvaigzne.lv; Brivibas iela 2, Ogre *Tel:* 65023909 *E-mail:* ogre@zvaigzne.lv; Atbrivosanas aleja 119, Rezekne *Tel:* 64605659 *E-mail:* rezekne@zvaigne.lv; Tirgus laukums 4, Preili *Tel:* 65322148 *E-mail:* preili@zvaigzne.lv; Rigas iela 11, Saldus *Tel:* 63822415 *E-mail:* saldus@zvaigzne.lv; Strclnieku iela 2, t/c Sokolade, Sigulda *Tel:* 67970108 *E-mail:* sigulda@zvaigzne.lv; Raina iela 1, Talsi *Tel:* 63223099 *E-mail:* talsi@zvaigzne.lv; Brivibas laukums 13, Tukums *Tel:* 63124027 *E-mail:* tukums@zvaigzne.lv; Rigas iela 20, Valmiera *Tel:* 64223500 *E-mail:* valmiera@zvaigzne.lv

Lebanon

General Information

Capital: Beirut
Language: Arabic (French widely used)
Religion: 43% Christian (mostly Roman Catholic, predominantly Maronite), 57% Muslim (mostly Sunni & Shiite)
Population: 3.4 million
Bank Hours: 0830-1230 Monday-Friday; 0830-1200 Saturday
Shop Hours: Vary. Generally 0900-1900 in winter, 0800-1500 in summer
Currency: 100 piastres = 1 Lebanese pound
Copyright: UCC, Berne (see Copyright Conventions, pg viii)

Editions Africaines, *imprint of* World Book Publishing

Al Khayyat Al Saghir Sarl
Verdun, Rachid Karami St, Beirut
Mailing Address: PO Box 114-5077, Beirut
E-mail: khayyatsaghir@gmail.com
Key Personnel
Owner: Rania Zaghir
Founded: 2007
Specialize in Arabic picture books.

All Prints Distributors & Publishers sal
Hamra, Jeanne D'Arc St Al, Wehad Bldg, Beirut 2034-4013
Tel: (01) 75 08 72; (01) 35 07 72 (sales); (01) 35 07 22 (marketing) *Fax:* (01) 34 19 07; (01) 75 25 47 (sales)
E-mail: tradebooks@all-prints.com; copyrights@all-prints.com; allprints@allprints.ae; marketing@all-prints.com
Web Site: www.all-prints.com
Founded: 1969
Subjects: Art, Cookery, Economics, Education, Government, Political Science, History, Language Arts, Linguistics, Law, Literature, Literary Criticism, Essays, Medicine, Nursing, Dentistry, Alternative Medicine, Humanitarian Science, Islamic Studies, Macrobiotic Foods, Work
ISBN Prefix(es): 978-9953-88

Arab Scientific Publishers Inc+
Reem Bldg, Tawfig Khalid Str, Ain El-Teneh, Chouran, Beirut 1102 2050
Mailing Address: PO Box 13-5574, Chouran, Beirut 1102 2050
Tel: (01) 785107; (01) 785108 *Fax:* (01) 786230
E-mail: asp@asp.com.lb
Web Site: www.asp.com.lb
Key Personnel
President: Bassam Chebaro *E-mail:* bchebaro@asp.com.lb
Founded: 1986
Membership(s): Publishers Association in Lebanon; Union of Arab Publishers Association.
Subjects: Agriculture, Automotive, Biological Sciences, Computer Science, Cookery, Crafts, Games, Hobbies, Geography, Geology, History, Literature, Literary Criticism, Essays, Medicine, Nursing, Dentistry, Military Science, Philosophy, Psychology, Psychiatry, Religion - Other, Science (General), Social Sciences, Sociology, Sports, Athletics, Travel & Tourism
ISBN Prefix(es): 978-9953-29; 978-614-0122
Number of titles published annually: 300 Print; 10 CD-ROM; 15 E-Book
Associate Companies: Abjad Graphics; Mediterranean Press, Arabization & Software Center

Editions Arabes, *imprint of* Naufal Group

Asala Publishers
Kreidieh Bldg, Zeidanieh, Midhat Bacha St, Beirut
Mailing Address: PO Box 113434, Beirut
Tel: (01) 736093; (01) 743166; (01) 743167 *Fax:* (01) 736071; (01) 735295
E-mail: infos@asala-publishers.com
Web Site: www.asala-publishers.com
Founded: 1998
Specialize in children's books in Arabic.
ISBN Prefix(es): 978-9953-445

Center for Arab Unity Studies
Beit Al-Nahda Bldg, Basra St, Hamra, Beirut 2034 2407
Mailing Address: PO Box 113-6001, Hamra, Beirut
Tel: (01) 750084; (01) 750085; (01) 750086; (01) 750087 *Fax:* (01) 750088
E-mail: info@caus.org.lb
Web Site: www.caus.org.lb; www.causlb.org
Founded: 1975
Subjects: Government, Political Science, Arab Culture & Politics
ISBN Prefix(es): 978-9953-82

Dar Al-Farabi
PO Box 11/3181, Beirut 1107 2130
Tel: (01) 301461; (01) 301138 *Fax:* (01) 307775
E-mail: info@dar-alfarabi.com; sales@dar-alfarabi.com; contact@dar-alfarabi.com
Web Site: www.dar-alfarabi.com
Founded: 1956
Subjects: Government, Political Science, Literature, Literary Criticism, Essays, Philosophy, Poetry, Science (General), Arabic Novels, Culture, Islamic Studies
ISBN Prefix(es): 978-9953-71; 978-9953-24; 978-9953-411; 978-9953-438

Dar Al Hadaek (Al-Hadaek Group)
Hwaylan Bldg, 3rd floor, Above Khoury Home, Beirut
Mailing Address: PO Box 25/216, Beirut
Tel: (01) 840389 *Fax:* (01) 840390
E-mail: alhadaek@alhadaekgroup.com
Web Site: www.alhadaekgroup.com
Founded: 1987
Membership(s): Arab Children's Book Publishers Forum; Arab Publishers' Association; Lebanese Board on Books for Young People (LBBY); Syndicate of Lebanese Publishers.
Subjects: Literature, Literary Criticism, Essays
ISBN Prefix(es): 978-9953-496
Number of titles published annually: 12 Print
Total Titles: 400 Print

Dar Al Kitab Al-Alami, *imprint of* World Book Publishing

Dar Al-Kitab Al-Lubnani
Madam Kuri St Verdin, in front of Beirut Hotel, Beirut 8330
Tel: (01) 735731 *Fax:* (01) 351433
E-mail: info@daralkitabalmasri.com
Web Site: www.daralkitabalmasri.com
Founded: 1929
Specialize in educational publications & textbooks for many countries worldwide.
Associate Companies: Dar Al-Kitab Al-Masri, 33 Kasr El Nile St, Ataba, Cairo 11511, Egypt *Tel:* (02) 3924614
Branch Office(s)
Paris, France
Casablanca, Morocco
Madrid, Spain
Geneva, Switzerland

Dar Al-Maaref
Korniche El Mazraa, Iskandarani Bldg, 2nd floor,
Beirut
Mailing Address: PO Box 11/1761, Beirut
Tel: (01) 653852 *Fax:* (01) 653857
E-mail: info@daralmaaref.com; al_maaref@
hotmail.com
Web Site: www.daralmaaref.com
Key Personnel
Partner & Mng Dir: Mazen Mehio
Founded: 1948
Subjects: Education, Fiction, How-to, Humor,
Nonfiction (General), Philosophy, Religion -
Other, Adventure
ISBN Prefix(es): 978-9973-16

Dar Al Majani Sal, *imprint of* Librairie Orientale
Sal

Dar Al Moualef Publishing House
Beer Hassan, Embassy st al Amira Bldg, Beirut
1102 206
Mailing Address: PO Box 13-5687, Beirut 1102
206
Tel: (01) 824203 *Fax:* (01) 825815
E-mail: info@daralmoualef.com
Web Site: www.daralmoualef.com
Founded: 1991
Membership(s): Arab Publishers Association;
Children's Book Publishers Association; Syndi-
cate of Publishers Union in Lebanon.
Subjects: Cookery, Education, Fiction, Health,
Nutrition, Management, Medicine, Nursing,
Dentistry, Poetry
ISBN Prefix(es): 978-9953-76

Editions Dar An-Nahar
An-Nahar Bldg, Banque du Liban Str, Beirut
Tel: (01) 747 620 *Fax:* (01) 747 623
E-mail: darannahar@darannahar.com; info@
darannahar.com
Web Site: www.darannahar.com; www.annahar.
com
Key Personnel
President: Ali Hamade *E-mail:* ali.hamade@
annahar.com.lb
Founded: 1967
Subjects: Archaeology, Art, Biography, Memoirs,
Business, Economics, Government, Political
Science, History, Literature, Literary Criticism,
Essays, Photography, Social Sciences, Sociol-
ogy
ISBN Prefix(es): 978-2-84289; 978-9953-10

Dar El Ilm Lilmalayin
Tallet 1/c khayat, Mar-Elias St, Medco Center,
2nd floor, Beirut
Mailing Address: PO Box 1085, Beirut 2045
8402
Tel: (01) 306666 *Fax:* (01) 701657
E-mail: info@malayin.com
Web Site: www.malayin.com
Founded: 1945
Also distributor.
Subjects: Business, Cookery, Education, Liter-
ature, Literary Criticism, Essays, Medicine,
Nursing, Dentistry, Philosophy, Religion -
Other, Science (General)
ISBN Prefix(es): 978-9953-63
Associate Companies: Bookland; Dar-Shahrazad;
Future Publishing Co; Lebanese Book Shop
Co; Lebanese Educational Publishing Co;
Lebanese Publishing Co; Secondary Publish-
ing Co

Dar Onboz
PO Box 11-8007, Beirut
Tel: (01) 380 533 *Fax:* (01) 380 533
Key Personnel
Contact: Nadine R L Touma
ISBN Prefix(es): 978-9953-465

Dar-El-Machreq+
PO Box 166778, Ashrafieh, Beirut 2150 1100
Tel: (01) 202423 *Fax:* (01) 202424
E-mail: info@darelmachreq.com;
communication@darelmachreq.com
Web Site: www.darelmachreq.com
Founded: 1848
Subjects: Biblical Studies, History, Language
Arts, Linguistics, Literature, Literary Criticism,
Essays, Philosophy, Religion - Catholic, Reli-
gion - Islamic, Theology
ISBN Prefix(es): 978-2-7214
Number of titles published annually: 25 Print
Total Titles: 600 Print
Distribution Center: Librairie Orientale SAL, PO
Box 55206, Beirut *Tel:* (01) 485793 *Fax:* (01)
485796 *E-mail:* libor@cyberia.net.lb *Web
Site:* www.librairieorientale.com.lb

GEOprojects Sarl
Hamra, 13 Jeanne D'arc Str, Barakat Bldg, Beirut
Mailing Address: PO Box 113, Beirut 5294
Tel: (01) 342 110 *Fax:* (01) 342 217
E-mail: info@geo-publishers.com
Web Site: www.geo-publishers.com; www.geo-
cartographers.com
Key Personnel
Head, Production & Editorial Dept: Samira Dar-
wish
Founded: 1978
Subjects: Regional Interests, Travel & Tourism,
Cartographic Design
Branch Office(s)
Ainkawa, Yazdan Dokht, 8 Karez Str, Erbil, Iraq
Tel: (066) 256 9202
PO Box 2911, 13030 Safat, Kuwait *Tel:* 2440 889
Fax: 2411 688
PO Box 857, Abu Dhabi, United Arab Emirates
Tel: (02) 6336999 *Fax:* (02) 6320844
GEOprojects (UK) Ltd, 8 Southern Court, South
St, Reading RG1 4QS, United Kingdom
Tel: (0118) 939 3567 *Fax:* (0118) 959 7356
E-mail: enquiries@geoprojects.net

Habib Publishers
PO Box 458, Zouk Mikael
Tel: (09) 224090 *Fax:* (09) 210037
E-mail: info@habibpublishers.com
Web Site: www.habibpublishers.com
Founded: 1970
Subjects: Fiction, Geography, Geology, History,
Language Arts, Linguistics, Physics, Science
(General)
ISBN Prefix(es): 978-9953-522

Institute for Palestine Studies (IPS) (Muassasat
al-Dirasat al-Filastiniyah)
Anis Nsouli St Verdun, Beirut 1107 2230
Mailing Address: PO Box 11-7164, Beirut 1107
2230
Tel: (01) 868387; (01) 814175; (01) 804959
Fax: (01) 814193; (01) 868387
E-mail: ipsbeirut@palestine-studies.org; sales@
palestine-studies.org; ipsdc@palestine-studies.
org
Web Site: www.palestine-studies.org
Founded: 1963
Independent nonprofit research & publication cen-
ter, not affiliated with any political organization
or government.
Subjects: Art, Economics, Education, Energy,
Law, Library & Information Sciences, Litera-
ture, Literary Criticism, Essays, Publishing
& Book Trade Reference, Technology, Arab-
Israeli Conflict, Palestinian Affairs
ISBN Prefix(es): 978-2-905448
Branch Office(s)
Institut des Etudes Palestiniennes, France, Con-
tact: Farouk Mardam Bey *Tel:* 01 55 42 63
04 *Fax:* 01 46 34 02 08 *E-mail:* fmarbey@
hotmail.fr

Institute for Palestine Studies-Jerusalem Office,
Al-Amin Bldg, 3rd & 4th floors, Tal al-Zaatar
St, Ramallah, PO Box 487, Ramallah, Israel,
Dir: Khaled Farraj *Tel:* (02) 2989108 *Fax:* (02)
2950767 *E-mail:* ipsquds@palestine-studies.org
U.S. Office(s): Institute for Palestine Studies
(USA) Inc, 3501 "M" St NW, Washington,
DC 20007, United States, Dir: Michele Es-
posito *Tel:* 202-342-3990 *Fax:* 202-342-3927
E-mail: ipsdc@palestine-studies.org
Orders to: IPS Marketing Dept, 3501 "M"
St NW, Washington, DC 20007, United
States *Tel:* 202-342-3990 *Fax:* 202-342-3927
E-mail: ipsdc@palestine-studies.org

IPS, see Institute for Palestine Studies (IPS)

Jarrous Press
Jamil Adra Str, Bacel Center, Tripoli
Mailing Address: PO Box 189, Tripoli
Tel: (06) 44 35 42 *Fax:* (06) 44 35 42
E-mail: info@jarrouspress.com
Web Site: www.jarrouspress.com
Founded: 1982
Subjects: Art, Education, Government, Political
Science, Health, Nutrition, History, Language
Arts, Linguistics, Literature, Literary Criticism,
Essays, Medicine, Nursing, Dentistry, Psychol-
ogy, Psychiatry, Religion - Other, Social Sci-
ences, Sociology
ISBN Prefix(es): 978-9953-468

Librairie du Liban Publishers SAL+
PO Box 11-9232, Beirut
Tel: (09) 217 944; (09) 217 945; (09) 217 946
Fax: (09) 217 734
E-mail: info@ldlp.com; sales@ldlp.com; orders@
ldlp.com
Web Site: www.ldlp-dictionary.com
Key Personnel
Mng Dir: Habib Sayegh *E-mail:* habib.sayegh@
ldlp.com; Pierre Sayegh *E-mail:* pierre.
sayegh@ldlp.com
Founded: 1944
Also a distributor.
Subjects: Animals, Pets, Astronomy, Child Care
& Development, Computer Science, Cookery,
Education, Fiction, Health, Nutrition, Language
Arts, Linguistics, Literature, Literary Criticism,
Essays, Mysteries, Suspense, Physics, Science
(General), Science Fiction, Fantasy, Technol-
ogy, Travel & Tourism, Adventure, Nature,
Thriller
Branch Office(s)
Esseily Bldg, Riad El Solh Sq, Beirut *Tel:* (01)
972515; (01) 966170
Lazarieh Bldg, Al Amir Bashir St, Beirut
Tel: (01) 970602; (01) 970603
Rubeiz Bldg, Hamra St, Beirut *Tel:* (01) 344 070
42, Bliss St, Ras Beirut, Beirut *Tel:* (01) 373 204
Sayegh Bldg Baabdat, Al Metn *Tel:* (04)
820 804; (04) 820 728 *Fax:* (04) 977 435
E-mail: ksayegh@ldlp.com
Distribution Center: Sayegh Bldg, Zokak el Blat,
PO Box 11-945, Beirut *Tel:* (01) 376 821; (01)
376 822; (01) 376 823 *Fax:* (01) 376 818

Macdonald, *imprint of* Naufal Group

Naufal, *imprint of* Naufal Group

Naufal Group+
PO Box 11/2161, Beirut
Tel: (01) 354898 *Fax:* (01) 354394
Founded: 1970
Subjects: Fiction, History, Law, Literature, Liter-
ary Criticism, Essays
ISBN Prefix(es): 978-9953-26
Imprints: Editions Arabes; Macdonald; Naufal
Subsidiaries: Les Editions Arabes SA; Macdonald
Middle East Sarl

Bookshop(s): Librairies Antoine, Hamra, PO
 Box 656, Beirut, Chairman & Chief Executive Officer: Sami Naufal *E-mail:* contact@
 antoineonline.com *Web Site:* www.
 antoineonline.com (five shops)

Librairie Orientale Sal+
Jisr el-Wati, Sin El-Fil (Metn), Beirut
Mailing Address: PO Box 55206, Beirut
Tel: (01) 485793 *Fax:* (01) 485796
E-mail: admin@librairieorientale.com.lb
Web Site: www.librairieorientale.com.lb
Key Personnel
Chief Executive Officer: M Maroun Nehme
Founded: 1946
Specialize in dictionaries, research, philosophy,
 literature, children books & textbooks in Ara-
 bic, French & English.
Membership(s): Syndicate of Publishers Union in
 Lebanon.
Subjects: Accounting, Animals, Pets, Archae-
 ology, Child Care & Development, Cookery,
 Education, English as a Second Language, His-
 tory, How-to, Language Arts, Linguistics, Lit-
 erature, Literary Criticism, Essays, Nonfiction
 (General), Philosophy, Regional Interests, Reli-
 gion - Catholic, Theology
ISBN Prefix(es): 978-9953-17
Number of titles published annually: 200 Print
Total Titles: 1,500 Print
Imprints: Dar Al Majani Sal
Branch Office(s)
Ashrafieh-Park Bldg, Beirut
Distributor for Dar el-Majani; Dar el-Mashreq
Foreign Rep(s): Aladdin Books UK (Middle
 East, North Africa); DTV Germany (Middle
 East, North Africa); Edicart-Italy (Middle East,
 North Africa)

Editions de la Revue d'Etudes Palestiniennes,
 see Institute for Palestine Studies (IPS)

Samir Editeur sal (Samir Publisher)+
Rue Camille Chamoun, Jisr al-Waty Sin al-Fil,
 Beirut
Mailing Address: BP 55542, Beirut
Tel: (01) 489 464 *Fax:* (01) 482 541
E-mail: contact@samirediteur.com
Web Site: www.samirediteur.com
Key Personnel
Publishing Dir: Marwan Abdo-Hanna
Founded: 1947
Specialize in children's books in Arabic, French
 & English.
Subjects: Education, Fiction, Nonfiction (General)
ISBN Prefix(es): 978-9953-31
Number of titles published annually: 20 Print
Total Titles: 300 Print
Branch Office(s)
Librairie Samir, Rue Gouraud, Gemmayze, BP
 175 132, Beirut *Tel:* (01) 448 181
Distributor for Oxford University Press

Librairie Stephan
BP 50165, Beirut
Tel: (01) 283333
Web Site: www.librairiestephan.com
ISBN Prefix(es): 978-9953-523
Branch Office(s)
Rue Achrafieh, Beirut *Tel:* (01) 335503

World Book Publishing+
Al Khansa St, Rifai Bldg, Beirut
Mailing Address: PO Box 11-3176, Beirut
Tel: (01) 659894 *Fax:* (01) 659894
E-mail: info@wbpbooks.com; marketing@
 wbpbooks.com; rights@wbpbooks.com;
 editor@wbpbooks.com
Web Site: www.wbpbooks.com; www.arabook.
 com
Founded: 1926

Subjects: Art, Business, Education, Geogra-
 phy, Geology, Government, Political Science,
 Health, Nutrition, History, Literature, Literary
 Criticism, Essays, Philosophy, Poetry, Religion
 - Islamic, Religion - Other, Science (General),
 Social Sciences, Sociology, Entertainment
ISBN Prefix(es): 978-9953-14
Total Titles: 3,000 Print; 1,000 Online
Imprints: Editions Africaines; Dar Al Kitab Al-
 Alami
Subsidiaries: Librairie de L'Ecole
Divisions: Livre Scolaire
Showroom(s): Hawd Al-Wilaga, Basta, Beirut
Bookshop(s): Librairie de l'Ecole, Rue Emile
 Edde, Beirut

Yuki Press Publishers
HMG Offices, Gefinor Center, Block B, 16th
 floor, Clemenceau, Beirut
Tel: (01) 756633; (01) 741677 *Fax:* (01) 756644
E-mail: yuki@yukipress.com
Web Site: www.yukipress.com
Key Personnel
Founder: Hadia Debs Ghandour
Founded: 2004
Subjects: Education, Medicine, Nursing, Den-
 tistry, Social Sciences, Sociology, Arabic, En-
 glish & French Books for Children, Civic Edu-
 cation, Culture
ISBN Prefix(es): 978-9953-478

Lesotho

General Information

Capital: Maseru
Language: English, Sesotho (a Bantu language)
Religion: Roman Catholic, Lesotho, Evangelical
 and Anglican
Population: 1.8 million
Bank Hours: 0830-1300 Monday-Friday; 0830-
 1100 Saturday
Shop Hours: Winter: 0830-1630 Monday-Friday;
 0830-1300 Saturday; Summer: 0800-1630
 Monday-Friday; 0800-1300 Saturday. Usually
 closed weekdays 1300-1400
Currency: 100 lisente = 1 loti. South African currency is also legal tender
Export/Import Information: No tariffs on books or
 advertising matter. No import license required;
 no obscene literature permitted. Exchange controls being relaxed.
Copyright: Berne (see Copyright Conventions, pg
 viii)

Government Printer
Lioli St, Industrial Area, Maseru
Mailing Address: PO Box 268, Maseru 100
Tel: 22313023 *Fax:* 22310452
E-mail: gpsec@printer.gov.ls
Subjects: Government, Political Science

Libya

General Information

Capital: Tripoli
Language: Arabic (official), also English and Ital-
 ian
Religion: Muslim
Population: 4.5 million
Bank Hours: Generally Winter: 0830-1230; Sum-
 mer: 0800-1200 Saturday-Thursday

Shop Hours: Vary greatly. Friday is weekly holiday but some Christian shops closed Sunday. Many are open 0830-1230, 1500-1730
 Saturday-Thursday (slightly earlier hours in
 summer months)
Currency: 1,000 dirhams = 1 Libyan dinar
Export/Import Information: No tariff on books;
 advertising dutied. Charity Tax and Municipal
 Tax levied on dutiable goods. Open General
 License for books. Exchange permit, liberally granted, is required. Import and export
 of books is handled by the General Company
 for Publishing, Advertising and Distribution,
 Tripoli.
Copyright: Berne (see Copyright Conventions, pg
 viii)

University of Tripoli
PO Box 00218, Tripoli
Tel: (021) 8214627910 *Fax:* (021) 8214628839
E-mail: president@uot.edu.ly
Web Site: www.uot.edu.ly
Founded: 1957
ISBN Prefix(es): 978-9959-816
Bookshop(s): University Bookshop, PO Box
 13113, Tripoli

Liechtenstein

General Information

Capital: Vaduz
Language: German
Religion: Predominantly Roman Catholic
Population: 28,642
Bank Hours: 0800-1200, 1330-1630 Monday-
 Friday
Shop Hours: 0800-1200, 1330-1830 Monday-
 Friday; 0800-1600 Saturday
Currency: 100 rapen = 1 francen (swiss franc)
Export/Import Information: 2% VAT on books.
 Most books exempt from Turnover Tax. Ad-
 vertising matter usually dutiable, some ex-
 empt from Turnover Tax. No import licenses
 required. No exchange controls. Swiss regula-
 tions to a Customs Treaty.
Copyright: UCC, Berne, Florence (see Copyright
 Conventions, pg viii)

Bonafides Verlags-Anstalt
Auring 52, 9490 Vaduz
Tel: 265 46 80 *Fax:* 390 05 94
E-mail: bva-fl@adon.li
Founded: 1991
Subjects: Accounting, Finance, Government, Po-
 litical Science, Nonfiction (General)
ISBN Prefix(es): 978-3-905193

Botanisch-Zoologische Gesellschaft,
 Liechtenstein-Sarganserland-Werdenberg eV
Im Bretscha 22, 9494 Schaan
Tel: 232 48 19 *Fax:* 233 28 19
E-mail: bzg@bzg.li
Web Site: www.bzg.li
Founded: 1970
Subjects: Animals, Pets, Earth Sciences, Garden-
 ing, Plants, Physical Sciences, Natural Science
ISBN Prefix(es): 978-3-905195

A R Gantner Verlag KG
Industriestr 6, 9491 Ruggell
Mailing Address: Postfach 131, 9491 Ruggell
Tel: 377 1808 *Fax:* 377 1802
E-mail: bgc@adon.li
Subjects: Animals, Pets, Gardening, Plants, Re-
 gional Interests, Botany, Zoology
ISBN Prefix(es): 978-3-7182

Associate Companies: Koeltz Scientific Books
Foreign Rep(s): Koeltz Scientific Books (Germany)

Das Gute Buch Verlagsanstalt
Meierhofstr 18, 9495 Triesen
Tel: 390 09 03 *Fax:* 390 09 02
E-mail: dasgutebuch@verlag.li
Web Site: www.verlag.li; www.dasgutebuch.net
Key Personnel
Mng Dir: Gertraud Wohlwend
Founded: 1983
Subjects: Inspirational, Spirituality, Exoteric, New Age
ISBN Prefix(es): 978-3-9521219

Historischer Verein fuer das Fuerstentum Liechtenstein (Historical Society of the Principality of Liechtenstein)
Plankner Str 39, 9494 Schaan
Tel: 392 17 47
E-mail: info@historischerverein.li
Web Site: www.historischerverein.li/
Key Personnel
Mng Dir: Marco Schaedler
Yearbook Editor: Klaus Biedermann
Founded: 1901
Historical research.
Subjects: Archaeology, History, Culture, Folklore
ISBN Prefix(es): 978-3-906393
Number of titles published annually: 1 Print

Kunstmuseum Liechtenstein
Staedtle 32, 9490 Vaduz
Tel: 235 03 00; 232 63 00 *Fax:* 235 03 29
E-mail: mail@kunstmuseum.li
Web Site: www.kunstmuseum.li
Key Personnel
Marketing & Communications: Franziska Hilbe
Tel: 235 03 17 *E-mail:* franziska.hilbe@kunstmuseum.li
Specialize in modern & contemporary art.
Subjects: Architecture & Interior Design, Art, Education
ISBN Prefix(es): 978-3-906790
Number of titles published annually: 5 Print
Total Titles: 40 Print

Liechtenstein Verlag AG+
Landstr 30, 9494 Schaan, Fuerstentum
Tel: 239 60 10 *Fax:* 239 60 19
E-mail: books@liechtensteinverlag.com
Web Site: www.liechtensteinverlag.com
Founded: 1946
Also acts as literary agent.
Subjects: Finance, Government, Political Science, History, Law
ISBN Prefix(es): 978-3-85789

Verlag der Liechtensteinischen Akademischen Gesellschaft
In der Fina 26, 9494 Schaan
Mailing Address: Postfach 829, 9494 Schaan
Tel: 232 30 28 *Fax:* 233 14 49
E-mail: info@verlag-lag.li
Web Site: www.verlag-lag.li
Key Personnel
Dir: Norbert Jansen
Founded: 1972
Subjects: Economics, Government, Political Science, Law
ISBN Prefix(es): 978-3-7211
Number of titles published annually: 3 Print
Total Titles: 110 Print
Bookshop(s): Buchzentrum Liechtenstein, Feldkircherstr 13, 9494 Schaan *Tel:* 239 50 40
E-mail: office@buchzentrum.li *Web Site:* www.buchzentrum.li

Saendig Reprint Verlag
Am Schraegen Weg 12, 9490 Vaduz

Tel: 232 36 27 *Fax:* 232 36 49
E-mail: saendig@adon.li
Web Site: www.saendig.com
Key Personnel
Manager: Christian Wohlwend
Founded: 1981
Subjects: Art, History, Language Arts, Linguistics, Mathematics, Music, Dance, Physical Sciences, Religion - Other, Science (General)
ISBN Prefix(es): 978-3-253

Topos Verlag AG
Industriestr 26, 9491 Ruggell
Tel: 377 11 11 *Fax:* 377 11 19
E-mail: topos@topos.li
Web Site: www.topos.li
Key Personnel
Mng Dir: Graham A P Smith
Founded: 1977
Subjects: Economics, Education, Law, Social Sciences, Sociology
ISBN Prefix(es): 978-3-289

Frank P van Eck Verlagsanstalt+
Haldenweg 8, 9495 Triesen
Tel: 392 30 00 *Fax:* 392 22 77
E-mail: info@vaneckverlag.li
Web Site: www.vaneckverlag.li
Key Personnel
Founder & Editor: Frank P van Eck
Founded: 1982
Subjects: Art, Regional Interests, Sports, Athletics, Golf
ISBN Prefix(es): 978-3-905501
Associate Companies: Saentis Verlag
Subsidiaries: Edition Fuchs & Hase
Shipping Address: Schweizer Buchzertrum, Industrie Ost, 4614 Magendorf
Warehouse: Schweizer Buchzertrum, Industrie Ost, 4614 Magendorf
Orders to: Schweizer Buchzertrum, Industrie Ost, 4614 Magendorf

Wanger Advokaturbuero+
Aeulestr 45, 9490 Vaduz
Tel: 237 52 52 *Fax:* 237 52 53
E-mail: office@wanger.net
Web Site: www.wanger.net
Key Personnel
Founder & Mng Dir: Dr Markus H Wanger
Founded: 1987
Subjects: Art, Business, Economics, Law
ISBN Prefix(es): 978-3-9520331; 978-3-909331

Lithuania

General Information

Capital: Vilnius
Language: Lithuanian
Religion: Predominantly Roman Catholic
Population: 3.8 million
Bank Hours: 0900-1200/1300 Monday-Friday
Shop Hours: 0900-1300 and 1400-1800 Monday-Friday
Currency: 100 Eurocents = 1 Euro
Export/Import Information: Member of the European Union. There are no customs duties and very few export restrictions.
Copyright: Berne (see Copyright Conventions, pg viii)

Leidykla Algarve (Algarve Publishers)+
Algirdo g 37, LT-03217 Vilnius
Tel: (05) 272 5910 *Fax:* (05) 272 1462
E-mail: algarve@takas.lt
Web Site: www.algarve.lt
Founded: 1996

Joint stock company.
Subjects: Business, Fiction, Health, Nutrition, Psychology, Psychiatry, Science (General), Applied Health Education Literature, Esoteric
ISBN Prefix(es): 978-9986-856; 978-9955-87
Total Titles: 40 Print

Leidykla Alma Littera+
Ulonu g 2, LT-08245 Vilnius
Tel: (05) 263 88 77 *Fax:* (05) 272 80 26
E-mail: post@almalittera.lt
Web Site: www.almalittera.lt
Key Personnel
Dir: Danguole Viliuniene
Public Relations Project Manager: Audrone Mockiene *Tel:* (0613) 82160 *E-mail:* a.mockiene@almalittera.lt
Founded: 1990
Membership(s): European Educational Publishers Group (EEPG); Lithuanian Publishers Association.
Subjects: Education, English as a Second Language, Fiction, Nonfiction (General), Comics
ISBN Prefix(es): 978-9986-02; 978-9955-08; 978-9955-38
Number of titles published annually: 260 Print; 2 CD-ROM
Total Titles: 3,000 Print; 8 Audio
Associate Companies: Leidykla Sviesa

Andrena+
Pasilaiciu g 8/13, LT-06116 Vilnius
Tel: (05) 270 3834
E-mail: leidykla.andrena@gmail.com
Key Personnel
Dir: Nijole Petrosiene
Founded: 1995
Subjects: Biography, Memoirs, Geography, Geology, Poetry, Psychology, Psychiatry, Religion - Catholic, Romance
ISBN Prefix(es): 978-9986-37
Total Titles: 64 Print; 1 CD-ROM

AS Narbuto Leidykla (AS Narbutas' Publishers)+
Zemaiciu 31, LT-84160 Joniskis
Key Personnel
Contact: Amalijus S Narbutas *E-mail:* amalijus@gmail.com
Founded: 1990
Subjects: Art, Astrology, Occult, Humor, Language Arts, Linguistics, Literature, Literary Criticism, Essays, Medicine, Nursing, Dentistry, Parapsychology, Philosophy, Psychology, Psychiatry
ISBN Prefix(es): 978-9986-552

Baltos Lankos Leidykla (Baltos Lankos Publishing House)+
Gedimino pr 28, LT-01104 Vilnius
Tel: (05) 240 79 06 *Fax:* (05) 240 74 46
E-mail: leidykla@baltoslankos.lt
Web Site: www.baltoslankos.lt
Key Personnel
Owner: Saulius Zukas
Dir: Kotryna Zukaite *E-mail:* kotryna@baltoslankos.lt
Editor-in-Chief: Saulius Repecka *E-mail:* saulius.repecka@baltoslankos.lt
Head, Sales: Kasparas Cibulskas *Tel:* (05) 203 25 58 *E-mail:* kasparas@baltoslankos.lt
Founded: 1992
A humanities & social sciences publisher.
Subjects: Art, Biography, Memoirs, Cookery, Education, Fiction, History, Language Arts, Linguistics, Literature, Literary Criticism, Essays, Mysteries, Suspense, Nonfiction (General), Philosophy, Photography, Poetry, Psychology, Psychiatry, Romance, Science (General), Social Sciences, Sociology, Travel & Tourism, Classics
ISBN Prefix(es): 978-9986-403; 978-9986-813; 978-9986-861; 978-9955-23

U.S. Office(s): 2016 W Huron, No 2F, Chicago, IL, United States, Contact: Jura Avizienis
Tel: 312-243-0799
Bookshop(s): Palanga, Str 4, LT-01402 Vilnius *Tel:* (05) 203 25 59 *E-mail:* knygynas@baltoslankos.lt

Centre of Legal Information
Zirmunu g 68A, LT-09124 Vilnius
Tel: (05) 261 7529; (05) 261 1065 (bookshop)
Toll Free Tel: 800 22 088 *Fax:* (05) 262 1523
E-mail: tminfo@tm.lt
Web Site: www.teisingumas.lt
Founded: 1997
Subjects: Law
ISBN Prefix(es): 978-9986-452

Dargenis UAB+
Gedimino g 10, LT-44318 Kaunas
Tel: (037) 205241 *Fax:* (037) 205241
Key Personnel
Dir: Dalia Celiesiute
Founded: 1997
Subjects: Child Care & Development, English as a Second Language, Human Relations, Psychology, Psychiatry, Self-Help
ISBN Prefix(es): 978-9986-9196; 978-9955-403

UAB Egmont Lietuva+
Algirdo g 51A, LT-03609 Vilnius
Tel: (05) 213 12 65 *Fax:* (05) 213 12 69
E-mail: donaldas@egmont.lt (editorial)
Web Site: egmont.lt
Founded: 1993
Subjects: Fiction, Nonfiction (General), Cartoons & Comics
ISBN Prefix(es): 978-9986-22
Parent Company: Egmont International Holding A/S, Vognmagergade 11, 1148 Copenhagen K, Denmark

Leidykla Eugrimas+
Kalvariju g 98-42, LT-08211 Vilnius
Tel: (05) 273 3955; (05) 275 4754 *Fax:* (05) 273 3955; (05) 275 4754
E-mail: info@eugrimas.lt
Web Site: www.eugrimas.lt
Key Personnel
Owner & Mng Dir: Saulius Petrulis
E-mail: saulius.petrulis@eugrimas.lt
Founded: 1995
Specialize in publishing law, European Union, politics, philosophy, economics & education in Lithuania.
Subjects: Criminology, Economics, Education, Government, Political Science, History, Law, Management, Philosophy, Ethics
ISBN Prefix(es): 978-9986-752
Total Titles: 150 Print

Flintas Publishing House
V Putvinskio str 34-1, LT-44211 Kaunas
Mailing Address: PO Box 2392, LT-44015 Kaunas
Tel: (061) 007 362 *Fax:* (037) 224 489
E-mail: info@flintaspublishing.com
Web Site: www.flintaspublishing.com
Key Personnel
Chief Executive Officer: Sikstas Ridzevicius
Commercial Dir: Giedrius Blockis
Export Operations Manager: Andrius Mazrimus
E-mail: andrius@flintaspublishing.com
Founded: 1996
ISBN Prefix(es): 978-609-419; 978-9955-874

Leidykla Kataliku Pasaulio Leidiniai
Pylimo g 27/14, LT-01309 Vilnius
Tel: (05) 212 2422 *Fax:* (05) 262 6462
E-mail: referente@katalikuleidiniai.lt; leidykla@katalikuleidiniai.lt; redakcija@katalikuleidiniai.lt

Web Site: www.katalikuleidiniai.lt
Key Personnel
Dir: Birute Bartasunaite
Publishing Manager: Ruta Bronusiene
Subjects: Religion - Catholic
ISBN Prefix(es): 978-9955-619
Bookshop(s): Pranciskonu g 3/6, LT-01133 Vilnius *Tel:* (05) 262 0572 *E-mail:* knygynas@katalikuleidiniai.lt; Sventaragio g 4, LT-01122 Vilnius *Tel:* (05) 212 4057
E-mail: katalikupasaulis@katalikuleidiniai.lt

Klaipedos Universiteto Leidykla (Klaipeda University Press)
Herkaus Manto g 84, LT-92294 Klaipeda
Tel: (046) 39 88 91; (046) 39 89 08 *Fax:* (046) 39 89 99
E-mail: leidykla@ku.lt
Web Site: www.ku.lt/leidykla
Key Personnel
Dir: Lolita Zemliene
Deputy Dir: Alfonsas Jankantas *Tel:* (046) 39 88 92 *E-mail:* alfonsas.jankantas@ku.lt
Designer: Ingrid Sirvydaite *Tel:* (046) 39 88 96 *E-mail:* ingrida.sirvydaite@ku.lt; Danguole Stepukoniene *Tel:* (046) 39 88 93 *E-mail:* danguole.stepukoniene@ku.lt
Editor: Roma Nikzentaitiene *Tel:* (046) 39 88 94 *E-mail:* romualda.nikzentaitiene@ku.lt; Brigita Praneviciute *Tel:* (046) 39 88 97 *E-mail:* brigita.praneviciute@ku.lt; Vilma Urbonaviciute *Tel:* (046) 39 88 95 *E-mail:* vilma.urbonaviciute@ku.lt
Founded: 1992
Membership(s): Lithuanian Association of Academic Publishers.
Subjects: Agriculture, Archaeology, Art, Biological Sciences, Chemistry, Chemical Engineering, Computer Science, Drama, Theater, Economics, Education, Geography, Geology, History, Library & Information Sciences, Literature, Literary Criticism, Essays, Management, Maritime, Marketing, Mathematics, Mechanical Engineering, Music, Dance, Philosophy, Physical Sciences, Poetry, Psychology, Psychiatry, Public Administration, Religion - Catholic, Religion - Protestant, Science (General), Social Sciences, Sociology, Technology, Theology
ISBN Prefix(es): 978-9955-18
Number of titles published annually: 130 Print
Total Titles: 1,850 Print

Lietuviu Kalbos Institutas (Institute of the Lithuanian Language)
P Vileisio g 5, LT-10308 Vilnius
Tel: (05) 263 80 55; (05) 234 64 72 *Fax:* (05) 234 72 00
E-mail: lki@lki.lt
Web Site: www.lki.lt
Key Personnel
Dir: Dr Jolanta Zabarskaite *E-mail:* jolanta.zabarskaite@lki.lt
Marketing Manager: Elida Drapiene
E-mail: elida.drapiene@lki.lt
Membership(s): Association INFOBALT; Association of Lithuanian Academic Publishers (LALA); Lithuanian Publishers Association.
Subjects: Language Arts, Linguistics
ISBN Prefix(es): 978-9986-668

Lietuviu Literaturos ir Tautosakos Institutas (Institute of Lithuanian Literature & Folklore)
Antakalnio g 6, LT-10308 Vilnius
Tel: (05) 212 5332; (05) 262 1943 *Fax:* (05) 261 6254
E-mail: knyga@llti.lt; direk@llti.lt
Web Site: www.llti.lt
Key Personnel
Dir: Mindaugas Kvietkauskas
E-mail: kvietkauskas@llti.lt
Head of Publishing: Gytis Vaskelis
E-mail: gytis@llti.lt

Subjects: Literature, Literary Criticism, Essays, Culture, Folklore
ISBN Prefix(es): 978-9986-513

Lietuvos gyventoju genocido ir rezistencijos tyrimo centras (Genocide & Resistance Research Centre of Lithuania)
Didzioji Str 17/1, LT-01128 Vilnius
Tel: (05) 231 41 39 *Fax:* (05) 279 10 33
E-mail: leidyba@genocid.lt
Web Site: genocid.lt
Key Personnel
Head, Publishing Dept: Birute Anaitiene
Membership(s): Lithuanian Publishers Association.
Subjects: Crimes, Genocide, War Crimes
ISBN Prefix(es): 978-9986-757

Lietuvos Leideju Asociacija (Lithuanian Publishers Association)
Lukiskiu g 5-317, LT-01108 Vilnius
Tel: (05) 261 77 40 *Fax:* (05) 261 77 40
E-mail: info@lla.lt
Web Site: www.lla.lt
Key Personnel
President: Remigilus Jokubauskas
Founded: 1993
Membership(s): Federation of European Publishers; International Publishers Association.
Subjects: Art, Fiction, History, Language Arts, Linguistics, Literature, Literary Criticism, Essays
ISBN Prefix(es): 978-9955-9464; 978-9955-9557

Lietuvos Mokslu Akademijos Leidykla (Lithuanian Academy of Sciences Publishers)
Gedimino pr 3, LT-01103 Vilnius
Tel: (05) 2626851; (05) 2613620
E-mail: leidyba@lma.lt
Web Site: www.lmaleidykla.lt
Key Personnel
Head: Zina Turcinskiene
Founded: 1999
Subjects: Agriculture, Art, Biological Sciences, Chemistry, Chemical Engineering, Energy, Geography, Geology, Language Arts, Linguistics, Medicine, Nursing, Dentistry, Philosophy, Physical Sciences, Physics, Social Sciences, Sociology, Ecology
ISBN Prefix(es): 978-9986-08

Lietuvos Nacionaline Martyno Mazvydo biblioteka (Martynas Mazvydas National Library of Lithuania)+
Gedimino pr 51, LT-01504 Vilnius
Tel: (05) 249 7028; (05) 249 7028 *Fax:* (05) 249 6129
E-mail: biblio@lnb.lt
Web Site: www.lnb.lt
Key Personnel
Dir General: Renaldas Gudauskas *E-mail:* r.gudauskas@lnb.lt
Head, Publishing Dept: Jurate Bickauskiene
Tel: (05) 239 8687 *Fax:* (05) 263 9111
E-mail: leidyba@lnb.lt
Founded: 1919
Subjects: Biography, Memoirs, Computer Science, Library & Information Sciences
ISBN Prefix(es): 978-9986-530

Lietuvos Rasytoju Sajungos Leidykla (Lithuanian Writers' Union Publishers)+
K Sirvydo g 6, LT-01101 Vilnius
Tel: (05) 262 89 45 *Fax:* (05) 262 89 45
E-mail: info@rsleidykla.lt
Web Site: www.rsleidykla.lt
Key Personnel
Dir: Giedre Soriene *E-mail:* vadovas@rsleidykla.lt
Editor-in-Chief: Valentinas Sventickas *Tel:* (05) 212 48 66
Editor: Janina Riskute *E-mail:* redaktore@rsleidykla.lt
Founded: 1990

Membership(s): Lithuanian Publishers Association.
Subjects: Fiction, Literature, Literary Criticism, Essays, Poetry
ISBN Prefix(es): 978-9986-39; 978-9986-413
Number of titles published annually: 60 Print
Bookshop(s): Atzalynas, Antakalnio g 97, LT-10218 Vilnius *Tel:* (05) 276 88 37

Lietvous Nacionalinis Muziejus (Lithuanian National Museum Publishing House)
Division of National Museum of Lithuania
Arsenalo g 1, LT-01143 Vilnius
Tel: (05) 212 34 98; (05) 262 77 74; (05) 262 94 26 *Fax:* (05) 261 10 23
E-mail: leidyba@lnm.lt
Web Site: www.lnm.lt
Key Personnel
Dir: Birute Kulnyte *E-mail:* birute.kulnyte@lnm.lt
Deputy Dir: Zygintas Bucys *Tel:* (05) 212 42 86
    E-mail: zygintas.bucys@lnm.lt
Subjects: Archaeology, History, Photography, Ethnography, Iconography, Numismatics
ISBN Prefix(es): 978-9955-415
Number of titles published annually: 10 Print
Total Titles: 105 Print

Lithuanian Publishers Association, see Lietuvos Leideju Asociacija

Leidykla Mintis (Mintis Publishing House)
Z Sierakausko g 15, LT-03105 Vilnius
Tel: (05) 233 2943; (05) 233 0519 (editorial); (05) 233 3444 (bookstore) *Fax:* (05) 216 3157
E-mail: info@mintis.org; redakcija@mintis.org; mintis@mintis.org
Web Site: www.mintis.org
Key Personnel
Dir: Leonardas Armonas
Founded: 1945
Also distributor.
Membership(s): Lithuanian Publishers Associaton.
Subjects: Biography, Memoirs, Biological Sciences, Fiction, Government, Political Science, History, Philosophy, Culture, Current Events, Mythology, Nature
ISBN Prefix(es): 978-5-417

Mokslo ir enciklopediju leidybos centras
    (Science & Encyclopedia Publishing Centre)+
L Asanaviciutes g 23, LT-04315 Vilnius
Tel: (05) 243 13 34; (05) 245 85 26; (05) 245 77 20 (warehouse) *Fax:* (05) 245 85 37
E-mail: melc@melc.lt; knygnas@melc.lt (bookshop); knygynas@melc.lt (warehouse)
Web Site: www.melc.lt
Key Personnel
Dir: Rimantas Kareckas *E-mail:* rimantas.kareckas@melc.lt
Founded: 1992
Publisher of the *Universal Lithuanian Encyclopaedia*, dictionaries, monographs, other academic literature.
Membership(s): Lithuanian Publishers Association.
Subjects: Agriculture, Architecture & Interior Design, Biological Sciences, Chemistry, Chemical Engineering, Foreign Countries, Geography, Geology, Government, Political Science, History, Language Arts, Linguistics, Literature, Literary Criticism, Essays, Mathematics, Medicine, Nursing, Dentistry, Philosophy, Physics, Regional Interests, Science (General), Technology
ISBN Prefix(es): 978-5-420
Parent Company: Ministry of Education & Science

Nieko rimto
Dumu g 3a, LT-11119 Vilnius
Tel: (05) 212 2061 *Fax:* (05) 212 2061

E-mail: info@niekorimto.lt
Web Site: www.niekorimto.lt
Key Personnel
Dir: Arvydas Vereckis *E-mail:* arvydas@niekorimto.lt
Marketing: Milda Bazaraite
Founded: 2001
ISBN Prefix(es): 978-9955-9543

Leidykla Presvika
Kauno g 28, LT-03202 Vilnius
Tel: (05) 2623182; (05) 2104208 (sales) *Fax:* (05) 2333894
E-mail: presvika@presvika.lt
Web Site: www.presvika.lt
Founded: 1996
Subjects: Cookery, Crafts, Games, Hobbies, Education, Fiction, Health, Nutrition, Language Arts, Linguistics, Literature, Literary Criticism, Essays, Psychology, Psychiatry
ISBN Prefix(es): 978-9955-424; 978-9986-805

Margi Rastai Leidykla (Margi Rastai Publishers)+
Laisves pr 60, LT-05120 Vilnius
Fax: (05) 278 45 28
E-mail: redaktorius@margirastai.lt
Web Site: www.margirastai.lt
Key Personnel
Dir: Sigitas Ladukas *Tel:* (05) 242 70 04
Editor-in-Chief: Antanas Rybelrs *Tel:* 614 54949 (cell)
Subjects: Agriculture, Economics, Fiction, Government, Political Science, History, Literature, Literary Criticism, Essays, Philosophy
ISBN Prefix(es): 978-9986-09
Total Titles: 400 Print

Rosma LT
Fabijonisku g 24A, LT-07100 Vilnius
Tel: (05) 262 35 98; (06) 154 39 66 *Fax:* (05) 261 19 97
E-mail: prekyba@rosmos.leidyklos.lt
Web Site: rosmos.leidyklos.lt
Founded: 1992
Subjects: Animals, Pets, Architecture & Interior Design, Education, Fiction, Gardening, Plants, Health, Nutrition, Esoteric
ISBN Prefix(es): 978-9955-06; 978-9986-958

Rotas
Pylimo g 42, LT-01137 Vilnius
Tel: (05) 212 47 60 *Fax:* (05) 261 54 87
E-mail: knygnas@rotas.lt; info@rotas.lt
Web Site: www.rotas.lt
Founded: 1991
Specialize in foreign language instructional materials.
Subjects: Art, Cookery, Economics, Education, Fiction, Health, Nutrition, History, Language Arts, Linguistics, Literature, Literary Criticism, Essays, Management, Philosophy, Psychology, Psychiatry
ISBN Prefix(es): 978-9986-661
Parent Company: Macmillan Education
Ultimate Parent Company: Macmillan Publishers Ltd
Bookshop(s): Kestucio g 15, LT-44320 Kaunas *Tel:* (06) 867 48 38 48 *E-mail:* kaunas@rotas.lt; I Simonaitytes vieoji biblioteka, H Manto g 25, LT-92234 Klaipeda *Tel:* (06) 867 47 18 83 *E-mail:* klaipeda@rotas.lt; Vytauto g 20, LT-68298 Marijampole *Tel:* (06) 867 47 16 26 *E-mail:* marijampole@rotas.lt; Basanaviciaus g 3, LT-35182 Panevezys *Tel:* (06) 865 28 28 85 *E-mail:* panevezys@rotas.lt

Leidykla Sviesa (Sviesa Publishers)+
E Ozeskienes g 10, LT-44252 Kaunas
Tel: (037) 40 91 26 *Fax:* (037) 34 20 32

E-mail: mail@sviesa.lt; info@knyguklubas.lt (book club)
Web Site: www.sviesa.lt; www.knyguklubas.lt (book club)
Key Personnel
Dir: Jurgita Naceviciene
Founded: 1945
Membership(s): Lithuanian Publishers Association.
Subjects: Career Development, Chemistry, Chemical Engineering, Child Care & Development, Crafts, Games, Hobbies, Education, English as a Second Language, Geography, Geology, History, House & Home, Mathematics, Physics, Psychology, Psychiatry, Sports, Athletics, Travel & Tourism, Natural Science
ISBN Prefix(es): 978-5-430
Number of titles published annually: 400 Print
Associate Companies: Alma Littera Leidykla

Teisines Informacijos Centras, see Centre of Legal Information

TEV Leidykla+
Mokslininku g 2a, LT-08412 Vilnius
Tel: (05) 272 9318 *Fax:* (05) 272 9804
E-mail: tev@tev.lt; pardavimai@tev.lt (sales)
Web Site: www.tev.lt
Key Personnel
Mng Dir: Elmundas Zalys
Senior Sales Manager: Rasa Vaskeliene *Tel:* (05) 272 9020
Founded: 1989
Subjects: Computer Science, Education, Engineering (General), Mathematics, Physics, Science (General)
ISBN Prefix(es): 978-9986-546
Distributed by VSP International Publications; Zeist
Distributor for VSP International Publications; Zeist

Tyto alba Publishers+
J Jasinskio g 10, LT-01112 Vilnius
Tel: (05) 249 74 53; (05) 249 75 95 (sales); (05) 249 75 98 *Fax:* (05) 249 75 95
E-mail: info@tytoalba.lt; sigitas@tytoalba.lt
Web Site: www.tytoalba.lt
Key Personnel
Dir: Lolita Varanaviciene
Deputy Dir: Jadwiga Barciene
Rights Manager: Jurgita Ludaviciene
Founded: 1993 (joint-stock company)
Subjects: Art, Biography, Memoirs, Business, Education, Fiction, How-to, Human Relations, Literature, Literary Criticism, Essays, Nonfiction (General), Philosophy, Poetry, Science (General), Self-Help
ISBN Prefix(es): 978-9986-16
Number of titles published annually: 90 Print
Total Titles: 300 Print

Leidykla VAGA (VAGA Publishers Ltd)+
Gedimino pr 50, LT-01110 Vilnius
Tel: (05) 249 8121; (05) 249 8393 *Fax:* (05) 249 8122
E-mail: info@vaga.lt
Web Site: www.vaga.lt
Key Personnel
Dir General: Vytas V Petrosius *E-mail:* centras@vaga.lt
Editor-in-Chief: Agne Puzauskatie *Tel:* (05) 249 8118 *E-mail:* agne.puzauskatie@vaga.lt
Founded: 1945
Subjects: Art, Biography, Memoirs, Ethnicity, Fiction, Government, Political Science, Literature, Literary Criticism, Essays, Nonfiction (General), Philosophy, Photography, Poetry, Religion - Catholic, Religion - Jewish, Self-Help, Social Sciences, Sociology, Theology
ISBN Prefix(es): 978-5-415
Parent Company: VAGOS Grupe

Associate Companies: UAB VAGOS Prekyba;
UAB VAGOS Knygu Centras
Bookshop(s): Gedimino pr 2, Vilnius, Head:
Kristina Sokolove *Tel:* (05) 268 5080
E-mail: draugyste.knygynas@vaga.lt;
Didzioji g 27, Vilnius *Tel:* (05) 262 6410
E-mail: versme@knygunamai.lt; Ateities g
20, Vilnius *Tel:* (05) 267 5383 *E-mail:* mru@
knygunamai.lt; Gedimino pr 9, Vilnius,
Head: Vilija Aukstuoliene *Tel:* (05) 245
8511 *E-mail:* gedimino9.knygynas@vaga.
lt; Ukmerges g 369, Vilnius, Head: Dale
Lieguviene *Tel:* (05) 243 0083 *E-mail:* big.
knygynas@vaga.lt; Ozo g 18, Vilnius,
Head: Olga Aniciene *Tel:* (05) 260 9073
E-mail: ozas.knygynas@vaga.lt; Pilies g 22,
Vilnius, Head: Izabele Vilkanciene *Tel:* (05)
261 1467 *E-mail:* pilies.knygynas@vaga.
lt; Priegliaus g 1, Vilnius, Head: Vera Ce-
chovskaja *Tel:* (05) 265 3506 *E-mail:* pupa.
knygynas@vaga.lt; Savanoriu pr 43, Vilnius, Head: Jekaterina Slyckova *Tel:* (05) 213
2992 *E-mail:* savanoriaivln.knygynas@vaga.lt;
Ateities g 91, Vilnius, Head: Lijana Katilevi-
ciute *Tel:* (05) 279 3681 *E-mail:* mandarinas.
knygynas@vaga.lt; Mindaugo g 11, Vilnius,
Head: Jurgita Bindoryte *Tel:* (05) 265 1119
E-mail: mindaugomax.knygynas@vaga.lt; Kon-
stitucijos pr 7A, Vilnius, Head: Erika Nau-
reckaite *Tel:* (05) 248 7061 *E-mail:* europa.
knygynas@vaga.lt; Zirmuenu g 2, Vilnius,
Head: Violeta Jukneviciute *Tel:* (05) 275
4868 *E-mail:* zirmunai.knygynas@vaga.lt;
Gariunu g 70, Vilnius *Tel:* (05) 250 5839
E-mail: gariunai.knygynas@vaga.lt; Gedimino pr 13, Vilnius *Tel:* (05) 2621609
E-mail: centrinisvln.knygynas@vaga.lt;
Parko g 7, N Vilnia, Vilnius *Tel:* (05) 267
4903 *E-mail:* n.vilnia@knygunamai.lt; M K
Ciurlionio g 50, Druskininkuose *Tel:* (0313)
58 076 *E-mail:* aidas@knygunamai.lt; Run-
gos g 4, Elektenai, Elektrenuose *Tel:* (0652)
89442 *E-mail:* p.elektrenai@knygunamai.
lt; Livonijos g 3, Joniskyje *Tel:* (0426) 51
354 *E-mail:* joniskis@knygunamai.lt; Is-
landijos pl 32, Kaune, Head: Vilma Nagule-
viciene *Tel:* (037) 239 024 *E-mail:* mega.
knygynas@vaga.lt; Savanoriu pr 346, Kaune,
Head: Jurate Anusauskiene *Tel:* (037) 730
893 *E-mail:* savas.knygynas@vaga.lt; Kovo
11-osios g 22, Kaune *Tel:* (037) 457 172
E-mail: girstupis@knygunamai.lt; Savanoriu
pr 255, Kaune, Head: Gintare Dabkeviciene
Tel: (037) 330 602 *E-mail:* savanoriaikn.
knygynas@vaga.lt; Smilgos g 2, Kedainiu-
ose *Tel:* (0347) 52 661 *E-mail:* kedainiai@
knygunamai.lt; H Manto g 84, Klaipedoje,
Head: Anzelika Petrauskiene *Tel:* (046)
410 664 *E-mail:* studlendas.knygynas@
vaga.lt; H Manto g 9, Klaipedoje, Head:
Joana Narmontiene *Tel:* (046) 402 912
E-mail: mantas.knygynas@vaga.lt; Bazny-
cios g 38, Marijampoleje *Tel:* (0343) 50 816
E-mail: marijampole@knygunamai.lt; Vytauto g 48A, Marijampoleje *Tel:* (0655) 78033
E-mail: suduva@knygunamai.lt; Zemaiti-
jos g 51/Sedo g 18, Mazeikiuose *Tel:* (0655)
76921 *E-mail:* p.mazeikiai@knygunamai.lt;
Klaipedos 143 a, Panevezyje, Head: Jurgita Ne-
maniene *Tel:* (045) 508 010 *E-mail:* babilonas.
knygynas@vaga.lt; Gedimino g 31B,
Radviliskyje *Tel:* (0652) 08742 *E-mail:* p.
radviliskis@knygunamai.lt; Tilzes g 109,
Siauliuose, Head: Violeta Murziene *Tel:* (041)
421 648 *E-mail:* saulesmiestas.knygynas@vaga.
lt; Vytauto g 71, Taurageje *Tel:* (0446) 54 862;
Vlenuolyno g 5, Ukmergeje *Tel:* (0340) 60 051
E-mail: ukmerge@knygunamai.lt; Tauragnu g
2, Utenoje *Tel:* (0389) 62 280 *E-mail:* utena@
knygunamai.lt

Vilnius Academy of Arts Publishing House
Dominikonu St 15/1, Bldg 1, Vilnius

Tel: (05) 2791 015 *Fax:* (05) 2105 444
E-mail: leidykla@vda.lt
Web Site: www.vda.lt
Key Personnel
Dir: Marius Irsenas *E-mail:* marius.irsenas@vda.lt
Chief Editor: Terese M Valiuviene *Tel:* (05) 2105
475
Art Dir: Sigute Chlebinskaite
Head, Book Distribution & Advertising Dept:
Egle Telyceniene *Tel:* (05) 2105 459
E-mail: egletel@yahoo.com
Subjects: Art

Magazyn Wilenski
Laisves pr 60, LT-05120 Vilnius
Tel: (05) 242 77 18 *Fax:* (05) 242 77 18
E-mail: magazyn@magwil.lt
Web Site: www.magwil.lt
Key Personnel
Dir: Slawomir Subotowicz
Editor: Helena Ostrowska *E-mail:* ostrowska@
magwil.lt
Subjects: Regional Interests
ISBN Prefix(es): 978-9986-542

Luxembourg

General Information

Capital: Luxembourg
Language: Luxembourgian, German, French, English
Religion: Predominantly Roman Catholic (about
97%)
Population: 437,389
Bank Hours: Vary. Generally 0830-1200, 1330-
1630 Monday-Friday
Shop Hours: 0830-1200, 1330-1800 Monday-
Saturday. Most close Monday morning. Some
have late night shopping until 2000
Currency: 100 Eurocents = 1 Euro
Export/Import Information: Member of the European Union. In economic and monetary union
with Belgium and Netherlands. No Tariff on
books except children's picture books from
non-EU; advertising other than single copied
dutied. VAT on books and advertising. No import license required. No exchange controls.
Copyright: UCC, Berne, Florence (see Copyright
Conventions, pg viii)

Editions APESS ASBL
389, route d'Arlon, 8011 Strassen
Tel: 31 76 05
E-mail: apess@education.lu
Web Site: www.apess.lu
Key Personnel
President: Daniel Reding *Tel:* 691 273770 (cell)
Secretary General: Eric Bruch
Founded: 1982
Subjects: Art, Education, History, Literature, Lit-
erary Criticism, Essays, Philosophy, Poetry,
Science (General)
ISBN Prefix(es): 978-2-87979
Total Titles: 35 Print

**Association des Professeurs de l'Enseignement
Secondaire et Superieur du Grand-Duche de
Luxembourg ASBL**, see Editions APESS
ASBL

Editions Paul Bauler Sarl
3, rue Glesener, 1631 Luxembourg
Tel: 48 88 93 *Fax:* 40 46 22
E-mail: libuf@pt.lu
Web Site: www.libuf.lu
Founded: 1996

Subjects: Law, Science (General)
ISBN Prefix(es): 978-2-919885
Parent Company: Librairie um Fieldgen

Editions Guy Binsfeld+
14, Place du Parc, 2313 Luxembourg
Mailing Address: BP 2773, 1027 Luxembourg
Tel: 49 68 68-1 *Fax:* 40 76 09
E-mail: editions@binsfeld.lu
Web Site: www.editionsguybinsfeld.lu
Key Personnel
Publisher: Guy Binsfeld
Dir: Marc Binsfeld *E-mail:* mbinsfeld@binsfeld.
lu
Editorial Dir: Thomas Schoos *E-mail:* tschoos@
binsfeld.lu
Chief Editor: Rob Kieffer *E-mail:* rkieffer@
binsfeld.lu
Founded: 1979
Membership(s): Federation Luxembourgeoise de
Editeurs de Livres (FLEL).
Subjects: Biography, Memoirs, Cookery, Fiction,
Gardening, Plants, How-to, Law, Nonfiction
(General), Photography, Travel & Tourism
ISBN Prefix(es): 978-3-88957; 978-2-87954
Total Titles: 250 Print
Divisions: Binsfeld-Conseils Communications
Agency
Distributed by Fausto Gardini (USA); Mes-
sageries du Livre (Luxembourg); Editions Ser-
penoise (France); Weyrich Edition & Com-
munication (Belgium); Willems Adventure
(Netherlands)

Cahiers Luxembourgeois
67, rue Roger Barthel, 7212 Bereldange
Tel: 338885 *Fax:* 336513
Founded: 1993
Subjects: Biography, Memoirs, History, Literature,
Literary Criticism, Essays, Poetry, Regional
Interests
ISBN Prefix(es): 978-2-919976; 978-2-919939
Divisions: Edition Raymon Mehlen

Centre Culturel Differdange
69, rue Prinzenberg, 4650 Differdange
Tel: 587045 *Fax:* 580295
Key Personnel
President & Editor: Cornel Meder *E-mail:* cornel.
meder@ci.culture.lu
Founded: 1982
Subjects: Ethnicity, History, Literature, Literary
Criticism, Essays
ISBN Prefix(es): 978-2-87991

**Centre des Technologies de l'Information de
l'Etat**, see CTIE-Division Imprimes et
Fournitures de Bureau

Centre national de litterature (CNL) (National
Center for Literature)
2, rue Emmanuel Servais, 7565 Mersch
Tel: 326955 1 *Fax:* 327090
E-mail: info@cnl.public.lu
Web Site: www.cnl.public.lu
Key Personnel
Dir: Claude D Conter *Tel:* 326955 315
E-mail: claude.conter@cnl.etat.lu
Honorary Dir: Germaine Goetzinger
E-mail: germaine.goetzinger@cnl.etat.lu
Subjects: Literature, Literary Criticism, Essays
ISBN Prefix(es): 978-2-919903

Chambre des Salaries
18, rue Auguste Lumiere, 1950 Luxembourg
Tel: 27 494 200 *Fax:* 27 494 250
E-mail: csl@csl.lu
Web Site: www.csl.lu
Key Personnel
President: Jean-Claude Reding
Dir: Norbert Tremuth

Subjects: Government, Political Science, Labor, Industrial Relations, Law, Public Administration, Social Sciences, Sociology
ISBN Prefix(es): 978-2-919888
Distribution Center: Librairie Um Fieldgen, 3, rue Glesener, 1631 Luxembourg *Tel:* 48 88 93 *Fax:* 40 46 22 *E-mail:* libuf@pt.lu *Web Site:* www.libuf.lu

CTIE-Division Imprimes et Fournitures de Bureau
22, rue des Bruyeres, 1274 Howald
Mailing Address: BP 1302, 1013 Howald
Tel: 247-73000 *Fax:* 40 08 81
E-mail: hotline-ifb@ctie.etat.lu
Web Site: www.ctie-ifb.etat.lu
Key Personnel
Contact: Cynthia Schwickerath *Tel:* 247-73010
E-mail: cynthia.schwickerath@ctie.etat.lu
Founded: 1969
Specialize in textbooks.
Subjects: Archaeology, Art, Education, Language Arts, Linguistics, Law, Natural History, Public Administration
ISBN Prefix(es): 978-2-495
Number of titles published annually: 70 Print
Total Titles: 1,023 Print
Branch Office(s)
One, rue Mercier, 2144 Luxembourg
Tel: 247-81800 *Fax:* 247-81822
E-mail: machinesdebureau@ctie.etat.lu

Editpress Luxembourg SA
44 rue du Canal, 4050 Esch-Sur-Alzette
Tel: 54 71 31 *Fax:* 54 17 61
Key Personnel
General Manager: Daniele Fonck
Founded: 1913
Subjects: Automotive, Business, Economics, Government, Political Science, Regional Interests, Sports, Athletics, Culture, Entertainment
ISBN Prefix(es): 978-2-87964

Grande Loge de Luxembourg
5, rue de la Loge, Luxembourg
Mailing Address: BP 851, 2018 Luxembourg
Tel: 22 94 51 *Fax:* 26 86 49 77
E-mail: info@grande-loge.lu
Web Site: www.grande-loge.lu
Subjects: Religion - Other, Freemasonry
ISBN Prefix(es): 978-2-9599875

Institut National de la Statistique et des Etudes Economiques du Grand-Duche du Luxembourg
Les bureaux du Statec se trouvent a Luxembourg-Kirchberg, Centre Administratif Pierre Werner, 13, rue Erasme, 1468 Luxembourg-Kirchberg
Mailing Address: BP 304, 2013 Luxembourg
Tel: 46 42 89 *Fax:* 247-84219
E-mail: info@statistiques.public.lu
Web Site: www.statistiques.public.lu
Founded: 1962
National Statistical Institute of Luxembourg, under the authority of the Ministry of Economy.
Subjects: Agriculture, Business, Economics, Finance, Labor, Industrial Relations, Library & Information Sciences, Public Administration, Social Sciences, Sociology
ISBN Prefix(es): 978-2-87988
Number of titles published annually: 100 Print; 2 CD-ROM; 150 Online

Ministere de la Culture
4, blvd F-D Roosevelt, 2450 Luxembourg
Tel: 247-86600
E-mail: info@mc.public.lu
Web Site: www.mc.public.lu
Subjects: Culture
ISBN Prefix(es): 978-2-87984

L'Office des publications de l'Union europeenne (Publications Office of the European Union)
2, rue Mercier, 2985 Luxembourg
Tel: 29291 *Fax:* 2929-42758
E-mail: info@publications.europa.eu; bookshop@publications.europa.eu; op-info-copyright@publications.europa.eu
Web Site: publications.europa.eu; publications.europa.eu/en/web/general-publications/publications (online bookshop)
Key Personnel
Dir General: Rudolph Strohmeier
Publications Dir: H Celms *Tel:* 2929-44969 *Fax:* 2929-42758 *E-mail:* harolds.celms@publications.europa.eu
Founded: 1969
Subjects: Economics, Law, European Affairs
ISBN Prefix(es): 978-92-894; 978-92-79; 978-92-825; 978-92-826; 978-92-828; 978-92-827
Branch Office(s)
135, rue Adolphe Fischer, 1521 Luxembourg

Op der Lay+
25, rue d'Eschdorf, 9650 Esch-sur-Sure
Tel: 839742 *Fax:* 899350
E-mail: opderlay@pt.lu
Web Site: www.opderlay.lu; www.opderlay.com (online store)
Key Personnel
Contact: Doris Bintner; Robert Gollo Steffen *E-mail:* robert.gollo.steffen@opderlay.lu
Founded: 1987
Specialize in literature & music from Luxembourg.
Subjects: Drama, Theater, Fiction, History, Literature, Literary Criticism, Essays, Music, Dance, Poetry, Pop Culture, Science Fiction, Fantasy
ISBN Prefix(es): 978-2-87967
Total Titles: 200 Print; 33 E-Book; 15 Audio

Passerelle Editions, *imprint of* Editions Promoculture

Editions Phi SA+
51 rue Emile Nork, 4620 Diffendange
Tel: 44 44 33
E-mail: commandes@editionsphi.lu
Web Site: www.phi.lu
Founded: 1980
Subjects: Art, Drama, Theater, Literature, Literary Criticism, Essays
ISBN Prefix(es): 978-2-87962
Number of titles published annually: 20 Print
Total Titles: 380 Print

Editions Promoculture+
14, rue Andre Duchscher, 1424 Luxembourg-Gare
Tel: 48 06 91 *Fax:* 40 09 50
E-mail: info@promoculture.lu
Web Site: www.promoculture.lu
Key Personnel
Dir: Maggy Fantier
Sales: Anais Matholet
Founded: 1989
Law & fiscal publisher.
Also major book dealer.
Subjects: Accounting, Architecture & Interior Design, Computers, Economics, Finance, Law, Management, Marketing, Medicine, Nursing, Dentistry, Tax Law
ISBN Prefix(es): 978-2-87974
Number of titles published annually: 12 Print; 1 CD-ROM; 2 E-Book
Total Titles: 140 Print; 2 CD-ROM; 2 E-Book
Parent Company: Groupe Larcier
Imprints: Passerelle Editions
Warehouse: One rue Duscher, 1424 Luxembourg

Editions Saint-Paul+
2, rue Christophe Plantin, 2339 Luxembourg

Tel: 4993 275 *Fax:* 4993 580
E-mail: editions@editions.lu
Web Site: www.editions.lu
Founded: 1886
Subjects: Biography, Memoirs, History, Law, Literature, Literary Criticism, Essays, Religion - Other, Sports, Athletics, Theology, Travel & Tourism
ISBN Prefix(es): 978-2-87963
Parent Company: Groupe Saint-Paul Luxembourg
Bookshop(s): Librairie Beaumont, 24 rue Beaumont, 1249 Luxembourg; Librairie Bourbon, rue du Fort Bourbon, 1249 Luxembourg; Librairie Daman, 4 rue de Brabant, 9213 Diekirch; Librairie du Sud, 74 rue de l'Alzette, 4010 Eschlalzette

Editions Schortgen
108, rue de l'Alzette, 4010 Esch-sur-Alzette
Mailing Address: BP 367, 4004 Esch-sur-Alzette
Tel: 54 64 87 *Fax:* 53 05 34
E-mail: editions@schortgen.lu
Web Site: www.editions-schortgen.lu
Subjects: Biography, Memoirs, Cookery, History, Literature, Literary Criticism, Essays, Poetry
ISBN Prefix(es): 978-2-87953

STATEC, see Institut National de la Statistique et des Etudes Economiques du Grand-Duche du Luxembourg

Verlag Synaisthesis
70, rue de l'Horizon, 5960 Itzig
Tel: 6914 6915 1
E-mail: verlag@synaisthesis.com
Web Site: www.synaisthesis.com
Subjects: Art, Music, Dance, Fine Arts, Life & Identity, Synaesthesia
ISBN Prefix(es): 978-99959-622

Editions Ultimomondo
35 rue de Dondelange, 8391 Nospelt
Tel: 30 87 01
E-mail: info@umo.lu
Web Site: www.umo.lu
Key Personnel
Founder & Manager: Guy Rewenig *E-mail:* guyrewenig6@gmail.com
Founder: Michel Dimmer; Roger Manderscheid; Micheline Scheuren; Paul Thiltges
Founded: 2000
ISBN Prefix(es): 978-2-919933
Number of titles published annually: 6 Print

Macau

General Information

Capital: Macau
Language: Portuguese and Chinese (Cantonese dialect) both official. English also widely spoken
Religion: Roman Catholic, Chinese Buddhist, Daoism & Confucianism
Population: 373,904
Bank Hours: 0930-1700 Monday-Friday; 0930-1200 Saturday
Shop Hours: 0900-1730 Monday-Saturday
Currency: 100 avos = 1 pataca. Hong Kong currency is also widely used but there is no fixed exchange rate.
Export/Import Information: Macau is a free port.
Copyright: Berne (see Copyright Conventions, pg viii)

Instituto Portugues do Oriente (IPOR)
Rua Pedro Nolasco da Silva, nº 45-1º, Macau
Tel: 2853 0227 *Fax:* 2853 0277

E-mail: info.macau@ipor.org.mo; info.clp@ipor.
   org.mo
Web Site: ipor.mo
Key Personnel
Dir: Dr Joao Laurentino Neves
Founded: 1989
Subjects: Asian Studies, Business, Economics,
   History, Language Arts, Linguistics, Literature,
   Literary Criticism, Essays, Portuguese Culture
   & Language
ISBN Prefix(es): 978-972-8013
Branch Office(s)
Instituto Camoes, Rua Rodrigues Sampaio, 113,
   1150-279 Lisbon, Portugal *Tel:* 213109100
   Fax: 213109183
Bookshop(s): Livraria Portuguesa, Rua de S
   Domingos, 18-20, Macau, Contact: Manuel
   Almeida *Tel:* 2856 6442 *Fax:* 2837 8014
   E-mail: livraria@ipor.org.mo

IPOR, see Instituto Portugues do Oriente (IPOR)

Livros Do Oriente+
Ave da Amizade n° 876, Edificio Marina Gardens,
   15 E, Macau
Tel: 2870 0320 *Fax:* 2870 0423
Key Personnel
Founder & Executive Manager: Cecilia Jorge
Founder & General Manager: Rogerio Beltrao
   Coelho
Founded: 1990
Subjects: Anthropology, Biography, Memoirs,
   Fiction, History, Photography, Poetry, Ro-
   mance, Social Sciences, Sociology, Travel &
   Tourism, Local Interest
ISBN Prefix(es): 978-972-9418; 978-99937-658

Museu Maritimo (Maritime Museum)
Largo do Pagode da Barra, no 1, Macau
Tel: 2859 5481 *Fax:* 2851 2160
E-mail: museumaritimo@marine.gov.mo
Web Site: www.museumaritimo.gov.mo
Subjects: Asian Studies, History, Maritime, Tech-
   nology, Transportation
ISBN Prefix(es): 978-972-96755; 978-972-97714
Number of titles published annually: 3 Print
Total Titles: 58 Print

Universidade de Macau, Centro de Publicacoes
   (University of Macau, Publications Centre)
Unit A, Lower Ground floor, Block 1, Av Padre
   Tomas Pereira, Taipa
Tel: 8397 8189 *Fax:* 8397 8198
E-mail: pub.enquiry@umac.mo
Web Site: www.umac.mo/pub/
Key Personnel
Head: Dr Raymond Wong *E-mail:* raymondw@
   umac.mo
Founded: 1995
Subjects: Art, Economics, Education, Govern-
   ment, Political Science, History, Language
   Arts, Linguistics, Law, Literature, Literary Crit-
   icism, Essays, Management, Medicine, Nurs-
   ing, Dentistry, Public Administration, Religion
   - Buddhist, Religion - Catholic, Science (Gen-
   eral), Social Sciences, Sociology, Population
ISBN Prefix(es): 978-972-97631; 978-972-96791;
   978-972-97050; 978-972-97834; 978-99937-26
Number of titles published annually: 10 Print; 3
   CD-ROM
Total Titles: 250 Print; 8 CD-ROM

Macedonia

General Information

Capital: Skopje
Language: Macedonian

Religion: Predominantly Eastern Orthodox, some
   Muslim
Population: 2.1 million
Copyright: UCC, Berne (see Copyright Conven-
   tions, pg viii)

Furkan ISM
II Makedonska Brigada, lokal 22, 1000 Skopje
Tel: (02) 2622 360 *Fax:* (02) 2622 393
E-mail: furkan@furkan.com.mk; kontakt@furkan.
   com.mk
Web Site: www.furkan.com.mk
Key Personnel
Dir: Muhamed Murtezi
Founded: 1993
Subjects: Government, Political Science, History,
   Religion - Other
ISBN Prefix(es): 978-9989-869

Narodna i univerzitetska biblioteka, see St
   Klement of Ohrid National & University
   Library

Prosvetno Delo AD
Dimitie Cupovski 15, 1000 Skopje
Tel: (02) 3117 255 *Fax:* (02) 3220 373
E-mail: prodelo@mt.net.mk
Web Site: prosvetnodelo.com.mk; prosvetnodelo-
   com-mk.webcentar.biz
Key Personnel
General Manager: Pavle Petrov *Tel:* (02) 3129
   402
Editor-in-Chief: Eli Makazlieva *E-mail:* eli.
   makazlieva@mt.net.mk
Dir, Marketing: Vesna Dukoski
Founded: 1945
Specialize in school textbooks, pedagogical mate-
   rials & teaching aids.
Subjects: Education, Literature, Literary Criti-
   cism, Essays
ISBN Prefix(es): 978-86-351; 978-9989-0
Number of titles published annually: 400 Print
Total Titles: 8,000 Print
Warehouse: Aco Sopov, 6 91000 Skopje

Prosvetno Delo Redakcija Detska Radost+
Dimitrie Cupovski 15, 1000 Skopje
Tel: (02) 3117 255 *Fax:* (02) 3220 373
Web Site: prosvetnodelo.com.mk
Key Personnel
Dir General: Paul Petrov
Dir, Marketing: Vesna Dukoski
Founded: 1945
Specialize in children's books.
Subjects: Fiction, Literature, Literary Criticism,
   Essays, Nonfiction (General), Poetry, Science
   Fiction, Fantasy
ISBN Prefix(es): 978-9989-30

**St Klement of Ohrid National & University
   Library+**
Bul Goce Delcev 6, PO Box 566, 1000 Skopje
Tel: (02) 3115 177; (02) 3226 846 *Fax:* (02) 3226
   846
E-mail: kliment@nubsk.edu.mk
Web Site: nubsk.edu.mk
Key Personnel
Dir: Dr Ivan K Zarov
Secretary General: Arsena Gligorova
   E-mail: gligorovaarsena@yahoo.com
Founded: 1944
Scholarly & scientific works collections, includ-
   ing monograph titles, periodicals, newspa-
   pers & other printed materials (patents, stan-
   dards, etc). Specialized collections include: old
   Slavonic manuscripts, printed & rare books &
   periodicals, oriental manuscripts, archive copies
   of Macedonia publications (1944 to present),
   prints & drawings, cartographic items, microfilms, doctoral dissertations, Master's theses,
   scientific & scholarly research projects.

Subjects: Education, Library & Information Sciences
ISBN Prefix(es): 978-9989-652
Membership(s): International Federation of Library Associations & Institutions

Seizmoloska Opservatorija (Seismological
   Observatory)+
PO Box 422, 1000 Skopje
Tel: (02) 2733001 *Fax:* (02) 2700713
E-mail: webmaster@seismobsko.pmf.ukim.edu.
   mk
Web Site: seismobsko.pmf.ukim.edu.mk
Key Personnel
Head: Dr Lazo Pekevski *E-mail:* lpekevski@
   seismobsko.pmf.ukim.edu.mk
Editor & International Rights: Vera Cejkovska
   E-mail: vcejkovska@seismobsko.pmf.ukim.
   edu.mk; Dragana Cernih-Anastasovska
   E-mail: dcernih@seismobsko.pmf.ukim.edu.mk
Membership(s): International Association of Seis-
   mology & Physics of the Earth's Interior -
   (IASPEI); International Union of Geodesy &
   Geophysics (IUGG)
Subjects: Computer Science, Earth Sciences,
   Electronics, Electrical Engineering, Geography,
   Geology
ISBN Prefix(es): 978-9989-631

STRK+
ul Jurij Gagarin 17/2/17, 1000 Skopje
Tel: (02) 3080430
Founded: 1992
Also acts as importer/exporter of office supplies
   & paper; wholesale & retail.
Subjects: Astrology, Occult, Behavioral Sciences,
   Biography, Memoirs, Economics, History, Lit-
   erature, Literary Criticism, Essays, Poetry, Ro-
   mance
ISBN Prefix(es): 978-9989-662

Madagascar

General Information

Capital: Antananarivo
Language: French and Malagasy
Religion: Most follow traditional beliefs, about
   43% Christian and some Islamic
Population: 12.6 million
Bank Hours: 0800-1100, 1400-1600 Monday-
   Friday. Closed afternoon preceding a holiday
Shop Hours: 0800-1200, 1400-1800 Monday-
   Saturday
Currency: 100 centimes = 1 franc malgache
   (Malagasy franc)
Export/Import Information: For books and adver-
   tising matter, customs and import duties, also
   unique tax. Import license required.
Copyright: Berne, Florence (see Copyright Con-
   ventions, pg viii)

Imprimerie Nationale de Madagascar
27-29, rue Refotaka, Ambatomena, 101 Antana-
   narivo
Tel: 22 236 75 *Fax:* 22 226 29
E-mail: dinm101@gmail.com
Web Site: www.mfb.gov.mg/imprimerie-nationale
Subjects: Government, Political Science, Regional
   Interests

Editions Jeunes Malgaches
Imprint of Press Edition et Diffusion
51 rue Tsiombikibo Ambatovinaky, 101 Antana-
   narivo
Tel: 22 566 58
E-mail: prediff@prediff.mg
Web Site: www.prediff.mg

Key Personnel
Manager: Marie Michele Razafintsalama
Founded: 2004
ISBN Prefix(es): 978-2-916362

Librairie Mixte Sarl
Analakely 17 Ave d'Andrianampoinimerina, pres
Terminus Bus 134, 101 Antananarivo
Tel: 34 04 902 23 (cell)
Founded: 1940
Foreign Rep(s): M Tahina Razakasoa (Europe)

TPFLM, see Trano Printy Fiangonana Loterana
Malagasy (TPFLM)

**Trano Printy Fiangonana Loterana Malagasy
(TPFLM)**
Imprint of Fiangonana Loterana Malagasy
9, rue General Gabriel Ramanantsoa, 101 Antana-
narivo
Tel: 22 245 69 *Fax:* 22 626 43
Founded: 1877
More than 80% of titles are published in native
language of Malagasy & more than 15% are
published in second language of French.
Membership(s): F L M; Union Professionnelle
Des Imprimeurs De Madagascar (UNPRIMM).
Subjects: Accounting, Animals, Pets, Biblical
Studies, Cookery, Education, History, Math-
ematics, Music, Dance, Poetry, Religion -
Catholic, Religion - Protestant, Romance, En-
glish as a Third Language
Number of titles published annually: 250 Print; 1
Online
Bookshop(s): Analakely & Antsahamanitra
Distribution Center: BP 533, 101 Antananarivo

Malawi

General Information

Capital: Lilongwe
Language: English and Chichewa
Religion: About 50% Christian (Roman Catholic
and Presbyterian), some Islamic and Hindu,
remainder traditional beliefs
Population: 9.6 million
Bank Hours: 0800-1300 Monday-Friday; Saturday
closed
Shop Hours: 0730 or 0800-1600 or 1700
Monday-Friday (with some closing for lunch);
until midday Saturday
Currency: 100 tambala = 1 Malawi kwacha
Export/Import Information: No tariff on books;
some advertising matter subject to duty. Import
license required on certain category of goods.
Exchange controls.
Copyright: UCC, Berne (see Copyright Conven-
tions, pg viii)

Central Africana Ltd+
PO Box 631, Blantyre
Tel: 01876110
E-mail: centralafricana@africa-online.net
Web Site: www.centralafricana.com
Key Personnel
Chairman & Publisher: Frank M I Johnston
Tel: 01821316
Founded: 1989
New & reissued titles covering primarily the his-
tory & development of Malawi as well as its
tourism appeals.
Subjects: History, Regional Interests, Travel &
Tourism
ISBN Prefix(es): 978-99908-14
Number of titles published annually: 3 Print
Total Titles: 15 Print

Branch Office(s)
A231 St Martini Gardens, Queen Victo-
ria St, Cape Town 8000, South Africa
Tel: (021) 4243595 *Fax:* (021) 4243595
E-mail: africana@iafrica.com
Foreign Rep(s): Struik & Southern Book Publish-
ers (South Africa)

Christian Literature Association in Malawi, see
CLAIM Mabuku

CLAIM Mabuku
PO Box 503, Blantyre
Tel: 01 833 714 *Fax:* 01 824 894
E-mail: info@claimmabuku.org
Web Site: www.claimmabuku.org
Key Personnel
General Manager: Andrew Chisamba
Founded: 1968
Subjects: Biography, Memoirs, Fiction, History,
Poetry, Regional Interests, Religion - Other
ISBN Prefix(es): 978-99908-16

Dzuka Publishing Ltd
Ginnery Corner, Scott Rd, Private Bag 39, Blan-
tyre
Tel: 0888 453 185 (sales)
E-mail: martinyewo@gmail.com
Web Site: www.facebook.com/dzukapublishing;
www.times.mw/dzuka-publishing
Key Personnel
Editor: Chalo Jawadu
Sales Executive: Martin Yewo Phiri
Founded: 1975
Publisher of educational & other materials.
Subjects: Agriculture, Biography, Memoirs, Busi-
ness, Education, Fiction, Geography, Geology,
History, Mathematics
ISBN Prefix(es): 978-99908-17
Total Titles: 150 Print
Parent Company: Blantyre Printing & Publishing
Co Ltd

Government Printer (Imprimerie Nationale)
PO Box 37, Zomba
Subjects: Government, Political Science, Regional
Interests
ISBN Prefix(es): 978-99908-85

Malaysia

General Information

Capital: Kuala Lumpur
Language: Bahasa Malaysia (based on Malay)
is official language; English widely used; Chinese, Tamil and Iban also spoken
Religion: Islam predomininates, there is a large
Buddhist group among the Chinese, Hindu
among the Indians
Population: 18.4 million
Bank Hours: West Malaysia (some states observe
Muslim weekly holiday): 1000-1500 Monday-
Friday; 0930-1130 Saturday. Sabah: 0800-1200,
1400-1500 Monday-Friday; 0900-1100 Sat-
urday. Sarawak: 1000-1500 Monday-Friday;
0930-1130 Saturday
Shop Hours: West Malaysia varies; average
0830-1830 Monday-Saturday. Sabah: 0800-
1830 Monday-Saturday. Sarawak: 0900-1800
Monday-Friday; 0900-1300 Saturday
Currency: 100 sen = 1 ringgit or Malaysian dollar
Export/Import Information: No tariff on books.
Advertising matter dutied per lb, subject to CIF
surtax. No obscene literature allowed. Import
licenses required only in Sabah, for books not

having the name, printer and publisher on first
or last printed page. No exchange controls.
Copyright: Berne (see Copyright Conventions, pg
viii)

AED, see Associated Educational Distributors
(M) Sdn Bhd

Al-Ameen Serve Holdings Sdn Bhd
2-1, Tingkat 1, Jl 9/23A, Medan Makmur Off Jl
Usahawan, Setapak, 53200 Kuala Lumpur
Tel: (03) 4143 4343 *Fax:* (03) 4149 1414
E-mail: ameenbooks@alameenserve.com
Web Site: ameenbooks.com.my
Founded: 1996
Subjects: Child Care & Development, Economics,
Education, Health, Nutrition, Literature, Liter-
ary Criticism, Essays, Management, Self-Help,
Self-Improvement
ISBN Prefix(es): 978-983-2334; 978-967-5391;
978-967-362; 978-983-3991
Warehouse: Lot 41, KK SME Bank, Jl SBC 8,
Taman Sri Bt Caves, 6810 Bt Caves, Selangor
Tel: (03) 6186 8440 *Fax:* (03) 6186 8441

Arah Pendidikan Sdn Bhd
No 29, Jl 10/91, Taman Shamelin Perkasa, 56100
Cheras, Kuala Lumpur
Tel: (03) 92814309 *Fax:* (03) 92828684
E-mail: enquiry@arahbooks.com; enquiry@
arahpendidikan.com.my
Web Site: www.arahbooks.com; www.facebook.
com/arahpendidikan; www.arahpublishing.
weebly.com
Key Personnel
Publishing Dir: Hasri Hasan
Dir: Faridah Shamsudin *Tel:* (019) 2201776
E-mail: faridah@arahpendidikan.com.my
General Manager: Rahanah Mohd Shoib
E-mail: rahanah@arahpendidikan.com.my
Marketing Manager: Mohd Nikmat Musa
E-mail: nik@arahpendidikan.com.my
Founded: 2005
ISBN Prefix(es): 978-983-3718; 978-983-3716

Aras Mega (M) Sdn Bhd
No 18, Jl Damai 2, Taman Desa Damai Sg
Merab, 43000 Kajang, Selangor Darul Ehsan
Tel: (03) 89258975 *Fax:* (03) 89258985
E-mail: amsb@arasmega.com
Web Site: www.arasmega.com
Founded: 1987
Subjects: Education
ISBN Prefix(es): 978-983-99794

Asean Academic Press Ltd, *imprint of* Pelanduk
Publications (M) Sdn Bhd

**Associated Educational Distributors (M) Sdn
Bhd+**
550 Taman Melaka Raya, 75000 Melaka
Tel: (06) 284 4786 *Fax:* (06) 284 4697
Key Personnel
Dir: Steven KH Lee
Founded: 1975
Specialize in preschool books & supplier of
school library books throughout Malaysia.
Subjects: Fiction
ISBN Prefix(es): 978-967-948

August Publishing Sdn Bhd
3A-10, IOI Business Park, One Persiaran Pu-
chong Jaya Selatan, Bandar Puchong Jaya,
47170 Puchong, Selangor
Tel: (03) 8075 9168 *Fax:* (03) 8076 3142
E-mail: renee.see@augustpub.com
Subjects: Accounting, Business, Communications,
Film, Video, Finance, Language Arts, Linguis-
tics, Marketing, Medicine, Nursing, Dentistry,
ELT, Financial Planning, Media
ISBN Prefix(es): 978-983-3317

Awan Metro (M) Sdn Bhd

3A, Jl 1/5, Seksyen 1, Bandar Teknologi Kajang,
43500 Semenyih, Selangor Darul Ehsan
Tel: (03) 8723 5769 *Fax:* (03) 8724 5189
E-mail: md.awanmetro@yahoo.com.my
Web Site: awanmetro.blogspot.com
Key Personnel
Contact: Abdul Rahman Muhammad Zarihi
ISBN Prefix(es): 978-983-9302

Berita Publishing Sdn Bhd

16-20, Jl 4/109E, Desa Business Park, Taman
Desa, Off Jl Klang Lama, 58100 Kuala
Lumpur
Tel: (03) 7620 8111 *Fax:* (03) 7620 8018
Key Personnel
Executive Dir: Juhaidi Yean Abdullah
Senior Manager, Corporate Services: Zuraini Ka-
maruzzaman
Editorial: Sarimah Husin *E-mail:* ema@
beritapublishing.com.my
Founded: 1973
Subjects: Business, Cookery, Education, Fiction
ISBN Prefix(es): 978-967-969; 978-983-99124
Subsidiaries: Berita Book Centre Sdn Bhd; Berita
Distributors Sdn Bhd

Karya Bestari Sdn Bhd

Imprint of Grup Buku Karangkraf
Lot 26, Jl Renggam 1515, Seksyen 15, 40200
Shah Alam, Selangor
Tel: (03) 51013785 *Fax:* (03) 51013685
Web Site: karyabestari.karangkraf.com
Founded: 1978
Subjects: Religion - Other
ISBN Prefix(es): 978-967-86
Ultimate Parent Company: Kumpulan Media
Karangkraf Sdn Bhd

Butterworths, *imprint of* LexisNexis Malaysia
Sdn Bhd

Cerdik Publications Sdn Bhd

39, Jl Nilam 1/2, Subang Sq, Subang Hi-Tech In-
dustrial Park, Batu Tiga, 40000 Shah Alam,
Selangor
Tel: (03) 5637 9044 *Fax:* (03) 5637 9043
E-mail: inquiry@cerdik.com.my
Web Site: www.cerdik.com.my
Key Personnel
General Manager: Rozida Binti Ismail
Senior Manager, Operations: Esrifitri Bin Subohi
Senior Manager, Publishing: Zuriana Binti Dzulk-
ifli
Founded: 1988 (as Mahih Publications)
ISBN Prefix(es): 978-983-3316

Dewan Bahasa dan Pustaka (Institute of

Language & Literature)+
Jl Dewan Bahasa, 50460 Kuala Lumpur
Tel: (03) 2147 9000 *Fax:* (03) 2147 9619
E-mail: knbsa@dbp.gov.my
Web Site: www.dbp.gov.my
Key Personnel
Dir, Publications: Haji Abd Khalik Bin Sulaiman
Tel: (03) 2148 1085 *E-mail:* khalik@dbp.gov.
my
Founded: 1956
Specialize in Malay language & linguistics, litera-
ture & culture.
Subjects: Language Arts, Linguistics, Literature,
Literary Criticism, Essays
ISBN Prefix(es): 978-983-62
Number of titles published annually: 300 Print
Branch Office(s)
Dewan Bahasa dan Pustaka Cawangan Sabah,
Beg Berkunci 149, 88999 Kota Kinabalu,
Sabah *Tel:* (088) 439 314 *Fax:* (088) 439 732
Dewan Bahasa dan Pustaka Cawangan Sarawak,
Peti Surat 1390, 93728 Kuching, Sarawak
Tel: (082) 444 711 *Fax:* (082) 444 707

Dewan Bahasa dan Pustaka Wilayah Selatan, No
1 & 3, Jl Susur Dato' Muhd Said Sulaiman,
Larkin Perdana, 80350 Johor Bharu, Johor
Tel: (07) 2365 588 *Fax:* (07) 2358 686
Dewan Bahasa dan Pustaka Wilayah Timur, Lot
107-109, Seksyen 26, Jl Abdul Kadir Adabi,
15200 Kota Bharu, Kelantan *Tel:* (09) 7475
656 *Fax:* (09) 7475 252
Dewan Bahasa dan Pustaka Wilayah Utara, No
31, Lorong Perda Selatan 2, Bandar Perda,
14000 Bukit Mertajam, Pulau Pinang *Tel:* (04)
5377 241 *Fax:* (04) 5377 245

Dewan Pustaka Islam+

10-2, 1st floor, Jl 14/22, Seksyen 14, 46100 Petal-
ing Jaya, Selangor
Tel: (03) 7955 7225
Founded: 1971
Membership(s): Book Contractor Association of
Malaysia.
Subjects: Religion - Islamic
ISBN Prefix(es): 978-983-66
Associate Companies: Blue-T Sdn Bhd
Subsidiaries: Budaya Ilmu Sdn Bhd; Tradisi Ilmu
Sdn Bhd
Distributed by Cekap Edar; Hizbi
Distributor for Institut Kajan Dasar; Institute of
Strategic & International Studies (ISIS); Juta &
Co (South Africa); Universiti Malaya Publica-
tion
Bookshop(s): Tradisi Ilmu Sdn Bhd, 10-2 Corner
Jl 14/22, 46100 Petaling Jaya, Selangor Darul
Ehsan
Warehouse: Lot 1032, Jl Cempaka, Kg Sg Kayu
Ara, 47400 Damansara Utama

Eliteguh Industries Sdn Bhd

20-1, Wisma Blue, Jl Manis 1, Taman Segar,
56100 Cheras, Kuala Lumpur
Tel: (03) 9130 8931
Founded: 1998
Membership(s): Malaysian Book Publishers Asso-
ciation (MABOPA).
Subjects: Mathematics, Science (General)
ISBN Prefix(es): 978-983-2458

Fairy Tales, *imprint of* Mecron Sdn Bhd

GBC, see Golden Books Centre Sdn Bhd (GBC)

Geetha Sdn Bhd

13A Jl Kovil Hilir, 51100 Kuala Lumpur
Tel: (03) 40417073 *Fax:* (03) 40417073
Subjects: Education, History, How-to, Publishing
& Book Trade Reference
ISBN Prefix(es): 978-983-9594

Golden Books Centre Sdn Bhd (GBC)+

Wisma ILBS, No 10 Jl PJU 8/5G, Perdana Busi-
ness Centre, Bandar Damansara Perdana, 47820
Petaling Jaya, Selangor
Tel: (03) 7727 3890; (03) 7728 3890; (03) 7727
4121; (03) 7727 4122 *Fax:* (03) 7727 3884
E-mail: gbc@pc.jaring.my
Web Site: www.goldenbookscentre.com
Founded: 1981
Also publisher's representative & distributor.
Does project publishing for government agen-
cies, institutions & corporations & packaging
for publishing companies.
Membership(s): Kuala Lumpur & Indian Cham-
ber of Commerce & Industry; Malaysian Book
Publishers Association (MABOPA); Malaysian
External Trade Development Corp.
Subjects: Automotive, Behavioral Sciences, Bi-
ography, Memoirs, Business, Career Devel-
opment, Communications, Computer Science,
How-to, Inspirational, Spirituality, Language
Arts, Linguistics, Literature, Literary Criticism,
Essays, Management, Marketing, Medicine,

Nursing, Dentistry, Nonfiction (General), Self-
Help, Technology
ISBN Prefix(es): 978-983-72; 978-967-9959
Number of titles published annually: 45 Print
Total Titles: 950 Print
Associate Companies: International Law Book
Services (ILBS)

H I Holdings Sdn Bhd

No 9 & 11, Jl Wawasan 4/6 Bandar Baru Am-
pang, 68000 Ampang, Selangor
Tel: (03) 4270 1340 *Fax:* (03) 4270 1344
ISBN Prefix(es): 978-983-411507; 978-983-9399

Hardy Books, *imprint of* Mecron Sdn Bhd

Horror & Adventure Stories, *imprint of* Mecron
Sdn Bhd

IBS Buku Sdn Bhd

B3-06, P J Industrial Park, Jl Kemajuan, 46200
Petaling Jaya, Selangor Darul Ehsan
Tel: (03) 79579282; (03) 79579470 *Fax:* (03)
79576026
E-mail: ibsbuku@ibsbuku.com; hibs@tm.net.my
Web Site: www.ibsbuku.com
Founded: 1972
Subjects: Anthropology, Biography, Memoirs,
Business, Career Development, Child Care &
Development, Health, Nutrition, Law, Manage-
ment
ISBN Prefix(es): 978-967-950
Subsidiaries: Pelanduk Publications (M) Sdn Bhd
U.S. Office(s): 8152 Misty Shore Dr, West
Chester, OH 45069, United States *Tel:* 513-
275-4669 *Fax:* 513-942-3308 *E-mail:* masinc@
gmail.com
Distributed by Badan Warisan; Cambridge Sci-
entific Abstracts; Discovery Publishing House;
Malita Jaya; MBRAS; Pelanduk Publications;
Putrajaya Holdings; Read Resources Sdn Bhd;
Total IT Solution

ILBS, see International Law Book Services
(ILBS)

Institut Terjemahan & Buku Malaysia (ITBM)

Wisma ITBM, No 2, Jl 2/27E, Seksyen 10,
Wangsa Maju, 53300 Kuala Lumpur
Tel: (03) 4145 1800 *Fax:* (03) 4149 1535
E-mail: info@itbm.com.my
Web Site: www.itbm.com.my
Key Personnel
Chief Executive Officer & Mng Dir: Mohd Khair
Ngadiron *E-mail:* mkhair@itbm.com.my
General Manager: Sakri Abdullah *E-mail:* sakri@
itbm.com.my
Head, Communications, Sales & Marketing:
Mohd Khairulanuar Anshor *E-mail:* anuar@
itbm.com.my
Head, Dept of Translation & Training: Siti Rafiah
Sulaiman *E-mail:* s.rafiah@itbm.com.my
Subjects: Art, Biography, Memoirs, Education,
Government, Political Science, Language Arts,
Linguistics, Literature, Literary Criticism, Es-
says, Poetry, Science (General), Sports, Athlet-
ics
ISBN Prefix(es): 978-983-068

International Book Service, see IBS Buku Sdn
Bhd

International Law Book Services (ILBS)+

Wisma ILBS, No 10 Jl PJU 8/5G, Damansara
Perdana, 47820 Petaling Jaya
Tel: (03) 7727 4121; (03) 7727 4122; (03) 7727
3890; (03) 7728-3890 *Fax:* (03) 7727 3884
E-mail: ilbslaw@gmail.com
Web Site: www.malaysialawbooks.com
Key Personnel
Sole Proprietor: Dr Syed Ibrahim
Founded: 1981

Publishes the *Malaysian Law Statutes* & other
general titles pertaining to law.
This publisher has indicated that 25% of their
product line is author subsidized.
Membership(s): Malaysian Book Publishers Association (MABOPA).
Subjects: Law
ISBN Prefix(es): 978-967-89
Number of titles published annually: 75 Print
Total Titles: 1,550 Print; 2 CD-ROM
Associate Companies: Golden Books Centre Sdn
Bhd
Distributed by Golden Books Centre Sdn Bhd

ITBM, see Institut Terjemahan & Buku Malaysia
(ITBM)

Penerbitan Jaya Bakti Sdn Bhd+
30, Wisma Jaya Bakti, Kamal, Jl Cenderuh 2,
Batu 4, Jl Ipoh, 51200 Kuala Lumpur
Tel: (03) 6250977213 *Fax:* (03) 62509890
E-mail: jayabakthi@gmail.com
Web Site: jayabakti.com
Key Personnel
Mng Dir: Dr K Silvaraju Datuk
Founded: 1980
Membership(s): Malaysian Book Publishers Association (MABOPA).
Subjects: Fiction, Inspirational, Spirituality, Language Arts, Linguistics, Mathematics, Science
(General)
ISBN Prefix(es): 978-967-900

K Publishing Sdn Bhd+
No 53, Jl Nilam 1/2, Subang Hi-Tech Industrial
Park, Batu Tiga, 40000 Shah Alam, Selangor
Tel: (03) 5637 6775 *Fax:* (03) 5637 4775
E-mail: info@k-publishing.com.my
Web Site: www.k-publishing.com.my
Founded: 1985
Subjects: Fiction
ISBN Prefix(es): 978-967-9906; 978-983-852
Shipping Address: Master Agencies Sdn Bhd, 110
Jl 27, Kawasan 16, Sungei Rasa, 41300 Kelang
Warehouse: 28, Jl SS26/13 Taman Mayang Jaya,
47301 Petaling Jaya, Selangor

Key Words Readers, *imprint of* Mecron Sdn Bhd

Key Words Series, *imprint of* Mecron Sdn Bhd

**Kohwai & Young Publications (Malaysia) Sdn
Bhd**
15 Jl Seri Sentosa 3A, Taman Seri Sentosa, 6.5
Mile Jl Klang Lama, 58000 Kuala Lumpur
Tel: (03) 7785 1191 *Fax:* (03) 7785 1192
E-mail: enquiry@kohwaiyoung.com; padirector@
kohwaiyoung.com (foreign rights)
Web Site: www.kohwaiyoung.com
Key Personnel
Founder & President: Tam Koh Wai
Chief Executive Officer: Chin Yee Tee
Co-Founder & Chief Operating Officer: Young
Poh Loon
Founded: 1992
Publisher & packager of children's books.
Subjects: Fiction
ISBN Prefix(es): 978-983-148

Kreatif Kembara Sdn Bhd
C-516 Kelana Sq, SS7/26, Kelana Jaya, 47301
Petaling Jaya, Selangor
Tel: (03) 7494 0212
Web Site: www.facebook.com/Kreatif-Kembara-
404921192896401
Founded: 1995
Subjects: Management, Technology
ISBN Prefix(es): 978-983-9278

Lamina Picture Books, *imprint of* Mecron Sdn
Bhd

Language Skills Series, *imprint of* Mecron Sdn
Bhd

LexisNexis Malaysia Sdn Bhd
Division of RELX Group PLC
T1-6, Jaya 33, 3, Jl Semangat, Seksyen 13, 46100
Petaling Jaya, Selangor Darul Ehsan
Tel: (03) 7882-3500 *Toll Free Tel:* 1800-88-8856
Fax: (03) 7882-3501
E-mail: help.my@lexisnexis.com; my.marketing@
lexisnexis.com
Web Site: www.lexisnexis.com.my
Key Personnel
Chief Executive Officer, Asia: Shawn Clark
Mng Dir, Southeast Asia: Ella Wang
Founded: 1932
Subjects: Accounting, Business, Law
ISBN Prefix(es): 978-967-962
Imprints: Butterworths; MLJ
Shipping Address: No 3, Jl PJS 11/20, Bandar Sunway, 46150 Petaling Jaya, Selangor
Tel: (03) 733 1893 *Fax:* (03) 733 1823
Warehouse: No 4, Lot 752, Jl Subang 3, Taman
Perindustrian Subang, 47610 Subang Jaya,
Selangor Darul Ehsan, Warehouse Manager:
Patrick Lee *Tel:* (03) 5636 1740
Orders to: No 3, Jl PJS 11/20, Bandar Sunway,
46150 Petaling Jaya, Selangor *Tel:* (03) 733
1893 *Fax:* (03) 733 1823

Little Board Books, *imprint of* Mecron Sdn Bhd

SA Majeed & Co Sdn Bhd+
7, Jl Bangsar Utama 3, 59000 Bangsar Kuala
Lumpur
Tel: (03) 2283 2230 *Fax:* (03) 2282 5670
E-mail: sambooks.my@gmail.com
Web Site: www.sambooks.com.my
Key Personnel
Management: Mr Mohd Kasim
Founded: 1952
Subjects: Asian Studies, Child Care & Development, Cookery, English as a Second Language,
Health, Nutrition, Management, Marketing, Religion - Islamic, Travel & Tourism
ISBN Prefix(es): 978-983-9629; 978-983-9550;
978-983-136; 978-983-899
Imprints: Malaysia Heritage Series
Branch Office(s)
35, Jl Sekerat off Tranofer Rd, 10050 Pinang
Showroom(s): 107c, Jl Rajalaut, 50350 Kuala
Lumpur

The Malaya Press Sdn Bhd
No 1, Jl TSB 10, Taman Perindustrian Sungai
Buloh, 47000 Sungai Buloh, Selangor
Tel: (03) 61573158 *Fax:* (03) 61573957 (sales
& administration); (03) 61567053 (editorial &
production)
E-mail: tmp@tmpsb.com (sales &
administration); editorial@tmpsb.com (editorial
& production)
Web Site: www.malayapress.com.my
Founded: 1959
Subjects: Education
ISBN Prefix(es): 978-967-934
Associate Companies: Hong Kong Cultural Press
Ltd, 9 College Rd, Kowloon, Hong Kong; Singapore Press (Pte) Ltd, 303 North Bridge Rd,
Singapore 7, Singapore

Malaysia Heritage Series, *imprint of* SA Majeed
& Co Sdn Bhd

Malaysian Palm Oil Board (MPOB)
6, Persiaran Institusi, Bandar Baru Bangi, 43000
Kajang, Selangor

Mailing Address: PO Box 10620, 50720 Kuala
Lumpur
Tel: (03) 8769 4400; (03) 8925 6332 *Fax:* (03)
8925 9446
E-mail: pub@mpob.gov.my; general@mpob.gov.
my
Web Site: www.mpob.gov.my; jopr.mpob.gov.my
Key Personnel
Dir General: Yuen May Choo
Subjects: Agriculture, Chemistry, Chemical Engineering, Economics, Health, Nutrition, Marketing, Technology
ISBN Prefix(es): 978-967-961

Marshall Cavendish (Malaysia) Sdn Bhd+
Times Subang, Bangunan Times Publishing, Lot
46, Subang Hi-Tech Industrial Park, Batu Tiga,
40000 Shah Alam, Selangor Darul Ehsan
Tel: (03) 5628 6888; (03) 5635 2191 *Fax:* (03)
5635 2706
E-mail: bizinfo@my.marshallcavendish.com
Web Site: www.marshallcavendish.com
Founded: 1957
Subjects: Astronomy, Career Development, Child
Care & Development, Computer Science, Education, English as a Second Language, Gardening, Plants, Mathematics, Science (General),
Self-Help, Sports, Athletics
ISBN Prefix(es): 978-983-384
Total Titles: 500 Print
Parent Company: Marshall Cavendish Business
Information
Ultimate Parent Company: Times Publishing
Group
Associate Companies: Direct Educational Technologies India Pvt Ltd; Educational Technologies Ltd (Taiwan); Marshall Cavendish International (Singapore) Pvt Ltd; Marshall Cavendish
International (Thailand) Co Ltd; Times Publishing (Hong Kong) Ltd
U.S. Office(s): Marshall Cavendish International Corp, 99 White Plains Rd, Tarrytown, NY 10591, United States *Tel:* 914-
332-8888 *Fax:* 914-332-8882 *E-mail:* mcc@
marshallcavendish.com

MDC Publishers Sdn Bhd
MDC Bldg, 2717 & 2718, Jl Permata Empat,
Taman Permata, Hulu Kelang, 53300 Kuala
Lumpur
Tel: (03) 4108 6600 *Fax:* (03) 4108 1506
E-mail: ecommerce@mdcp.com.my; fb@mdcp.
com.my
Web Site: www.mdcpublishers.com
Founded: 1978
Publisher, distributor & printer of professional
books.
Membership(s): Malaysian Book Importers Association; Malaysian Book Publishers Association
(MABOPA); Malaysian Booksellers Association.
Subjects: Agriculture, Architecture & Interior Design, Business, Communications, Economics,
Education, Environmental Studies, Finance,
Government, Political Science, Health, Nutrition, Law, Management, Maritime, Medicine,
Nursing, Dentistry, Science (General), Social
Sciences, Sociology, Technology, Transportation, Travel & Tourism, Women's Studies, Employment & Human Resources, Islamic Books,
Security & Defence, Statistics, Trade & Investment, Women & Gender
ISBN Prefix(es): 978-967-70
Associate Companies: MDC Book Distributors
Sdn Bhd; MDC Printers & Book Binders Sdn
Bhd
Branch Office(s)
Lot L3-04, 3rd floor, Shaw Parade, Changkat
Thambi Dollah, 55100 Kuala Lumpur *Tel:* (03)
2145 7745
Distributor for Asian Development Bank; The
Emirates Centre for Strategic Studies & Research; Food & Agriculture Organization

(FAO); International Atomic Energy Agency (IAEA); International Chamber of Commerce (ICC); International Labour Organization; International Maritime Organization (IMO); International Monetary Fund (IMF); Islamic Development Bank; United Nations; United Nations Educational, Scientific & Cultural Organization (UNESCO); United Nations Industrial Development Organization (UNIDO); World Bank; World Health Organization (WHO); World Intellectual Property Organization (WIPO); World Tourism Organization (WTO)

Mecron Sdn Bhd+
No B5-5 Binova Industrial Center, No 1 Jl 2/57 B Segambut Bawah, 51200 Kuala Lumpur
Tel: (016) 2808772 *Fax:* (03) 6251 9869
E-mail: nmansoor@tm.net.my
Web Site: www.mecronbooks.com
Founded: 1984
Specialize in children's educational books.
ISBN Prefix(es): 978-983-9072; 978-983-9556; 978-983-9387
Imprints: Fairy Tales; Hardy Books; Horror & Adventure Stories; Key Words Readers; Key Words Series; Lamina Picture Books; Language Skills Series; Little Board Books; See & Read Series; Well Loved Tales

Minerva Publications
51, Jl SG 3/1, Taman Sri Gombak, 68100 Batu Caves Selangor
Tel: (03) 61882876 *Fax:* (03) 61883876
Web Site: minervaebooks.com
Founded: 1940
Subjects: Business, Career Development, English as a Second Language, Religion - Islamic, Self-Help
ISBN Prefix(es): 978-983-68
Branch Office(s)
No 6, 1st floor, Pycrofts Rd, Triplicane, Chennai 600 005, India *Tel:* (044) 28445674
E-mail: info@minervaebooks.com

MLJ, *imprint of* LexisNexis Malaysia Sdn Bhd

MPOB, see Malaysian Palm Oil Board (MPOB)

Multi Media Synergy Corp Sdn Bhd
80-4, Jl Tasik Utama 5, Medan Niaga Tasik Damai, 57100 Kuala Lumpur
Tel: (03) 8948 9900 *Fax:* (03) 8945 8128
E-mail: info@mmsc.com.my; mmsc@mmsc.com.my
Web Site: www.mmsc.com.my
Key Personnel
Chief Financial Officer: Johari Kamarudin
E-mail: johari@mmsc.com.my
Mng Dir: Dr Adbul Rahman *Tel:* (03) 8948 5200
E-mail: ara@mmsc.com.my
Publication Manager: Rosmah Talib
E-mail: rosmah@mmsc.com.my
Founded: 1997
ISBN Prefix(es): 978-983-41491

Odonata Publishing Sdn Bhd
Alam Damai Industrial Park, 2, Jl Damai Puspa 2, 56000 Cheras, Kuala Lumpur
Tel: (03) 9101 1179 *Fax:* (03) 9101 7991
E-mail: online@odonatabooks.com; info@odonatabooks.com
Web Site: www.odonatabooks.com; www.odonata.com.my
ISBN Prefix(es): 978-983-3738

Oscar Book International+
37A Jl 20/16 Paramount Garden, 46300 Petaling Jaya, Selangor
Tel: (03) 78753515 *Fax:* (03) 78762797
Founded: 1980
Specialize in English & Malay.

Subjects: Language Arts, Linguistics
ISBN Prefix(es): 978-967-941
Total Titles: 120 Print

Oxford Fajar Sdn Bhd+
Subsidiary of Oxford University Press (OUP)
No 4 Jl Pemaju U1/15, Section U1, Hicom-Glenmarie Industial Park, 40150 Shah Alam, Selangor Darul Ehsan
Tel: (03) 5629 4000 *Fax:* (03) 5629 4006
E-mail: dcs@oxfordfajar.com.my
Web Site: www.oxfordfajar.com.my
Key Personnel
Marketing Dir: Angeline M David
Founded: 1957
ISBN Prefix(es): 978-967-65; 978-967-933

Pearson Malaysia Sdn Bhd+
Level 1, Tower 2A, Ave 5, Bangsar South, No 8, Jl Kerinchi, 59200 Kuala Lumpur
Tel: (03) 2289 7000 *Fax:* (03) 2289 7199
Founded: 1961
Subjects: Education, English as a Second Language, Literature, Literary Criticism, Essays, Mathematics, Physics, Science (General)
ISBN Prefix(es): 978-983-3927
Number of titles published annually: 300 Print
Total Titles: 2,000 Print
Parent Company: Pearson Education
Ultimate Parent Company: Pearson PLC
Branch Office(s)
11-1-2, 1st floor, Jl Gottieb, Pulau Tikus, 10350 Penang *Tel:* (04) 227 5140 *Fax:* (04) 227 4937

Pelanduk Publications (M) Sdn Bhd+
Subang Jaya Industrial Estate, 12, Jl SS 13/3E, 47500 Subang Jaya, Selangor Darul Ehsan
Tel: (03) 56386573; (03) 56386885 *Fax:* (03) 56386577; (03) 56386575
E-mail: pelandukpub@gmail.com
Web Site: www.pelanduk.com
Founded: 1984
Publisher of English language books on Malaysia & Asia.
Subjects: Anthropology, Architecture & Interior Design, Biography, Memoirs, Business, Economics, Fiction, Government, Political Science, Health, Nutrition, Language Arts, Linguistics, Law, Management, Medicine, Nursing, Dentistry, Religion - Islamic, Science (General), Social Sciences, Sociology, Chinese Language Education
ISBN Prefix(es): 978-967-978; 978-1-901919 (Asean Academic Press Ltd)
Imprints: Asean Academic Press Ltd

Penerbitan Pelangi Sdn Bhd (PPSB) (Pelangi Publishing Pte Ltd)+
66, Jl Pingai, Taman Pelangi, 80400 Johor Bahru, Johor Darul Takzim
Tel: (07) 3316288 *Fax:* (07) 3329201
E-mail: info@pelangibooks.com; pelangi@pelangibooks.com
Web Site: www.pelangibooks.com
Key Personnel
Chief Executive Officer & Mng Dir: Mr Sum Kown Cheek
Founded: 1979
Also publish teaching aids.
Subjects: Art, Business, English as a Second Language, Language Arts, Linguistics, Management, Nonfiction (General), Photography, Chinese Language Teaching (CLT)
ISBN Prefix(es): 978-967-951; 978-983-50; 978-983-878
Number of titles published annually: 500 Print; 300 Online
Total Titles: 8,000 Print

PPSB, see Penerbitan Pelangi Sdn Bhd (PPSB)

Preston Corp Sdn Bhd
18, Jl 19/3, 46300 Petaling Jaya, Selangor
Tel: (03) 79563734 *Fax:* (03) 79573607
Key Personnel
Contact: Foong Chui Ling
Subjects: Education
ISBN Prefix(es): 978-967-917; 978-983-158
Associate Companies: Times Educational Co Sdn Bhd; Vista Productions Ltd, Westland Centre, No 6, 9th floor, 20 Westland Rd, Quarry Bay, Hong Kong *Tel:* 2563 2492; 2562 3496 *Fax:* 2565 5803; Preston Corp Pte Ltd, 30 Shaw Rd, No 05 - 01/02/03, Singapore 367957, Singapore

Penerbit Prisma Sdn Bhd+
No 10, Jl PJS 7/17, Bandar Sunway, 46150 Petaling Jaya, Selangor
Tel: (03) 56380541 *Fax:* (03) 56347256
Key Personnel
Mng Dir: Wong Peng Khuen
Founded: 1988
ISBN Prefix(es): 978-983-9665; 978-983-99556; 978-983-823; 978-983-877

PTS Media Group Sdn Bhd
No 12, Jl DBP, Dolomite Business Park, 68100 Batu Caves, Selangor
Tel: (03) 6188 0316 *Fax:* (03) 6189 0316
E-mail: sales@pts.com.my; editorial@pts.com.my; marketing@pts.com.my
Web Site: pts.com.my
Key Personnel
Chairman: Ms Ainon Mohd
Mng Dir: Arief Hakim Sani Rahmat
General Sales Manager: Mohn Nazrul Shamizan B Mohd Samsudin
Publications Manager: Mohd Ikram Mohamad Nor Wazir
Marketing Manager: Muhammad Izzat Amir bin Mohammad Jamal
ISBN Prefix(es): 978-983-2311; 978-983-3654; 978-983-3892

Pustaka Aman Press Sdn Bhd
4200-A Simpang Tiga Telipot, Jl Sultan Yahya Petra, 15150 Kota Bharu
Tel: (09) 7481849; (09) 7443681 *Fax:* (09) 7487064
E-mail: marketing@pap.com.my
Web Site: www.pap.com.my
Key Personnel
Mng Dir: Aman Bin Haji Hassan
Founded: 1960
Subjects: Computers, Education, Religion - Islamic
ISBN Prefix(es): 978-983-867

Pustaka Antara Sdn Bhd
Lot UG 7 & 9, Upper Ground floor, Kompleks Wilayah, No 2 Jl Munsyik Abdullah, 50100 Kuala Lumpur
Tel: (03) 26980044 *Fax:* (03) 26917997
ISBN Prefix(es): 978-967-937

Pustaka Cipta Sdn Bhd+
32-3 Jl USJ 9/5Q, Subang Jaya, 47620 Selangor
Tel: (03) 80236303 *Fax:* (03) 80236306
Web Site: ciptatrainings.weebly.com
Key Personnel
Publication Dir: Rosihan Juara Baharuddin
E-mail: rjuara@gmail.com
Founded: 1985
Membership(s): IKATAN; Malaysian Bumiputera Book Publishers & Distributors Association.
Subjects: Art, Biography, Memoirs, Communications, Computer Science, Education, English as a Second Language, Fiction, Journalism, Literature, Literary Criticism, Essays, Nonfiction (General), Poetry, Publishing & Book Trade Reference, Religion - Islamic, Science (Gen-

eral), Science Fiction, Fantasy, Technology, Travel & Tourism, Women's Studies
ISBN Prefix(es): 978-967-9974; 978-967-99962; 978-983-101
Associate Companies: Essential Mark (M) Sdn Bhd; Puncak Indah Sdn Bhd
Subsidiaries: Dasar Buku Sdn Bhd; Dasar Cetak Sdn Bhd; Dasar Padu Sdn Bhd

Pustaka Sistem Pelajaran Sdn Bhd+
Lot 17-22, Jl Satu, Bersatu Industrial Park, Cheras Jaya, 43200 Kuala Lumpur
Tel: (03) 90747558 *Fax:* (03) 90747573
Key Personnel
Mng Dir: Song Khoon Heng
Founded: 1973
Subjects: Education
ISBN Prefix(es): 978-967-902
Parent Company: BHS Industries Berhad
Bookshop(s): The Bintang Store, 251 Jl Tun Sambanthan, 50470 Kuala Lumpur

Sasbadi Sdn Bhd
No 12, Jl Teknologi 3/4, Taman Sains Selangor 1, Kota Damansara, 47810 Petaling Jaya, Selangor Darul Ehsan
Tel: (03) 6145 1188 *Fax:* (03) 6145 1199
E-mail: enquiry@sasbadi.com
Web Site: www.sasbadi.com
Key Personnel
Marketing Dir: Lee Eng Sang *E-mail:* eslee@sasbadi.com
Sales Dir: Y C Chen *E-mail:* ycchen@sasbadi.com
Founded: 1985
ISBN Prefix(es): 978-983-029; 978-983-59

SBT Professional Publications Sdn Bhd
33-35, 7th floor, Bangunan Systematic, Jln Hang LeKiu, 50100 Kuala Lumpur
Tel: (03) 20789828
Founded: 1985
Subjects: Accounting
ISBN Prefix(es): 978-967-9924

See & Read Series, *imprint of* Mecron Sdn Bhd

Syarikat Cultural Supplies Sdn Bhd+
No 1, Jl TSB 10, Taman Perindustrian Sungai Buloh, 47000 Selangor
Tel: (03) 61573158 *Fax:* (03) 61573957
Key Personnel
Dir: Kow Ching Chuan
Founded: 1973
Subjects: Education
ISBN Prefix(es): 978-967-9917

Times Educational Co Sdn Bhd
22 Jl 19/3, Seksyen 19, 46300 Petaling Jaya, Selangor
Tel: (03) 79571766; (03) 79563734 *Fax:* (03) 79573607
E-mail: presco18@yahoo.com
Web Site: www.timeseducational.com.my
Subjects: Cookery
ISBN Prefix(es): 978-967-919
Parent Company: Times Educational Co Ltd, Hong Kong
Associate Companies: Preston Corp Sdn Bhd; Preston Corp Pte Ltd, Singapore
Orders to: Preston Corp Sdn Bhd, 18 Jl 19/3, Petaling Jaya, Selangor

Tintarona Publications Sdn Bhd, *imprint of* Utusan Publications & Distributors Sdn Bhd

Tropical Press Sdn Bhd+
No 56-1 & 2, Jl Maarof, Bangsar Baru, 59100 Kuala Lumpur
Tel: (03) 22825138 *Fax:* (03) 22823526

Key Personnel
Mng Dir: Winston Ee Soon Kee
E-mail: win898ee@well.com
Founded: 1975
Membership(s): Malaysian Book Publishers Association (MABOPA).
Subjects: Child Care & Development, Cookery, Mathematics, Natural History, Physical Sciences, Science (General), Technology, Cuisine, Food
ISBN Prefix(es): 978-967-73
Associate Companies: Art Printing Works Sdn Bhd

UiTM Press+
Universiti Teknologi MARA, Block 9, 4th floor, INTEKMA Resort & Convention Centre, Persiaran Raja Muda, Section 7, 40000 Shah Alam, Selangor Darul Ehsan
Tel: (03) 55225402 *Fax:* (03) 55225403
E-mail: penerbit@salam.uitm.edu.my
Web Site: penerbit.uitm.edu.my
Key Personnel
Dir: Dr Hajibah Osman *E-mail:* dhajibah@salam.uitm.edu.my
Founded: 1981
Subjects: Accounting, Mathematics, Medicine, Nursing, Dentistry, Science (General), Technology
ISBN Prefix(es): 978-967-958; 978-967-305; 978-967-363; 978-983-3644

Penerbit Universiti Sains Malaysia+
Universiti Sains Malaysia, 11800 Pulau Pinang
Tel: (04) 6533888; (04) 6534421; (04) 6534420
Fax: (04) 6575714
E-mail: penerbit@usm.my
Web Site: www.penerbit.usm.my
Key Personnel
Dir: Mr Akhiar Salleh *Tel:* (04) 6534422
Founded: 1972
Subjects: Biological Sciences, Chemistry, Chemical Engineering, Computer Science, Education, Electronics, Electrical Engineering, Management, Mathematics, Social Sciences, Sociology
ISBN Prefix(es): 978-983-861

Penerbit Universiti Teknologi Malaysia
(Universiti Teknologi Malaysia Press)+
Universiti Teknoligi Malaysia, 81310 UTM Johor Bahru
Tel: (07) 5536336; (07) 5535826 *Fax:* (07) 5536337
E-mail: sitisahrina@utm.my; galeribuku@utm.my
Web Site: www.penerbit.utm.my
Key Personnel
Marketing & Sales: Yosman Mohd Bain *Tel:* (07) 5535754 *E-mail:* yosman@utm.my
Founded: 1986
Subjects: Aeronautics, Aviation, Behavioral Sciences, Chemistry, Chemical Engineering, Civil Engineering, Computer Science, Education, Electronics, Electrical Engineering, Engineering (General), Mathematics, Mechanical Engineering, Physical Sciences, Physics, Regional Interests, Religion - Islamic, Science (General), Social Sciences, Sociology, Technology
ISBN Prefix(es): 978-983-52
Number of titles published annually: 30 Print
Total Titles: 316 Print

University of Malaya Press (Penerbit Universiti Malaya)+
Pantai Valley, 50603 Kuala Lumpur
Tel: (03) 7957 4361; (03) 7967 5941 *Fax:* (03) 7957 4473
E-mail: terbit@um.edu.my
Web Site: umpress.um.edu.my
Key Personnel
Dir: Adam Wong Abdullah *E-mail:* adamwong@um.edu.my

Editor: Shaaban Mustapa *Tel:* (03) 7967 5998 *E-mail:* shaaban@um.edu.my; Devaraj P Thangaraju *Tel:* (03) 7967 5809 *E-mail:* devarajt@um.edu.my
Founded: 1954
Subjects: Anthropology, Architecture & Interior Design, Asian Studies, Biography, Memoirs, Business, Child Care & Development, Disability, Special Needs, Economics, Education, Foreign Countries, Government, Political Science, Health, Nutrition, History, Language Arts, Linguistics, Library & Information Sciences, Management, Medicine, Nursing, Dentistry, Nonfiction (General), Poetry, Psychology, Psychiatry, Public Administration, Regional Interests, Science (General), Social Sciences, Sociology, Technology, Theology
ISBN Prefix(es): 978-967-9940; 978-983-9705; 978-983-100
Number of titles published annually: 50 Print; 12 E-Book
Total Titles: 550 Print; 60 E-Book

Penerbit USM, see Penerbit Universiti Sains Malaysia

UTM Press, see Penerbit Universiti Teknologi Malaysia

Utusan Publications & Distributors Sdn Bhd+
No 1 & 3, Jl 3/91A, Taman Shamelin Perkasa Cheras, 56100 Kuala Lumpur
Tel: (03) 9285 6577; (03) 9285 2645 *Fax:* (03) 9284 6554
E-mail: corporate@utusan.com.my
Web Site: www.utusangroup.com.my
Key Personnel
Chief Executive Officer: Zin Mahmud
Founded: 1976
Publishes educational books, children's story books, novels, dictionaries, encyclopedia, business/management, motivation & women's titles. Distributes local & imported books to institutions of higher education, libraries & government agencies.
Subjects: Business, Career Development, Cookery, Crafts, Games, Hobbies, Economics, Education, Fashion, Fiction, Government, Political Science, Health, Nutrition, Management, Religion - Islamic, Technology
ISBN Prefix(es): 978-967-61
Number of titles published annually: 130 Print
Parent Company: Utusan Melayu (Malaysia) Bhd, 46M, Jl Lima Melalui, Jl Chan Sow Lin, 55200 Kuala Lumpur
Imprints: Tintarona Publications Sdn Bhd
Distributor for McGraw-Hill; Pearson; Oxford University Press; Taylor & Francis; John Wiley

Well Loved Tales, *imprint of* Mecron Sdn Bhd

Maldives

General Information

Capital: Male
Language: Dhivehi (Maldivian)
Religion: Islam is the state religion (most Sunni Muslim)
Population: 226,000
Currency: 100 laari (larees) = 1 rufiyaa (maldivian rupee)

Novelty Printers & Publishers Pvt Ltd+
M Utility, Male 20340
Tel: 3318844 *Fax:* 3327039
Web Site: www.novelty.com.mv; printers.novelty.com.mv

Key Personnel
Chairman: Ali Hussain
Founded: 1965
Subjects: Animals, Pets, Foreign Countries, Regional Interests, Travel & Tourism
ISBN Prefix(es): 978-99915-3
Parent Company: Novelty Group
Subsidiaries: Novelty Overseas (Pte) Ltd
Bookshop(s): Henveiru Novelty Bookshop, Soasan Magu, Male *Tel:* 3322334 *Fax:* 3322335
E-mail: henveiru@bookshop.novelty.com.mv; Novelty Maafannu Bookshop, M Pinkrose, Fareedhee Magu, Male, General Manager: Mr Ahmed Nasheed *Tel:* 3311334 *Fax:* 3311335
E-mail: maafannu@bookshop.novelty.com.mv
Web Site: bookshop.novelty.com.mv

Mali

General Information

Capital: Bamako
Language: French
Religion: Predominantly Islamic
Population: 10 million
Currency: 100 centimes = 1 CFA franc
Export/Import Information: Member of the West African Economic Community. No tariff on books but subject to VAT at varying rates. Advertising matter (more than single copy) subject to tariff, import tax and VAT. All goods subject to local tax of percentage of customs value. Import license required. Importation is either by private importers or state enterprises. Exchange controls for non-franc zone.
Copyright: Berne (see Copyright Conventions, pg viii)

Editions Donniya+
Cite du Niger, BP 1273, Bamako
Tel: 20 21 46 46; 20 21 45 99; 20 21 58 54
  Fax: 20 21 90 31
E-mail: imprimcolor@orangemali.net
Web Site: www.editionsdonniya.com
Founded: 1996
Specialize in books for children & young adults.
Subjects: African American Studies, Archaeology, Art, Government, Political Science, History, Literature, Literary Criticism, Essays, Poetry, Religion - Islamic, Science (General), Social Sciences, Sociology, Technology
ISBN Prefix(es): 978-2-911741; 978-2-35071
Number of titles published annually: 6 Print
Total Titles: 52 Print
Distribution Center: Servedit, 15, rue Victor Cousin, 75005 Paris, France *Tel:* 01 44 41 49 35 *Fax:* 01 43 25 77 41 *E-mail:* servedit@ wanadoo.fr

EDIM+
Ave Kasse Keita, Bamako
Mailing Address: BP 21, Bamako
Tel: 20 22 44 57; 20 29 30 00 *Fax:* 20 29 30 01
E-mail: edim@groupe-tomota.com
Web Site: www.groupe-tomota.net
Key Personnel
Mng Dir: Aliou Tomota
Founded: 1972
Membership(s): Malian Organisation of Book Publishers (OMEL).
Subjects: Biography, Memoirs, Education, Fiction, History, Nonfiction (General), Poetry, Religion - Other, Social Sciences, Sociology
ISBN Prefix(es): 978-2-913213
Parent Company: Groupe Tomota

Editions Imprimeries Du Mali, see EDIM

Malta

General Information

Capital: Valletta
Language: Maltese and English (official), Italian widely spoken
Religion: Predominantly Roman Catholic
Population: 365,000
Bank Hours: 0830-1230 Monday-Thursday; 0830-1230, 1700-1900 Friday; 0830-1200 Saturday
Shop Hours: 0900-1300, 1530-1900 Monday-Saturday
Currency: 100 Eurocents = 1 Euro
Export/Import Information: Member of the European Union. No tariff on books or advertising. No import license required. Exchange control by Central Bank. All Malta made goods that enter the European Union are duty and quota free. Different rates of duty apply for imports with special preference for European Union countries.
Copyright: Berne, UCC (see Copyright Conventions, pg viii)

Fondazzjoni Patrimonju Malti (Maltese Heritage Foundation)
63 Old Mint St, Valletta VLT 1518
Tel: 21231515
E-mail: info@patrimonju.org
Web Site: www.patrimonju.org
Key Personnel
Administrative Secretary: Angela Ghirxi
Founded: 1992
Specialize in catalogues raisonne, collections of essays, art quality of Maltese history & cultural heritage subjects (known collectively as "Melitensia").
Subjects: Antiques, Archaeology, Art, Biography, Memoirs, History
ISBN Prefix(es): 978-99932-10; 978-99909-959; 978-99932-7
Number of titles published annually: 3 Print
Total Titles: 72 Print; 1 CD-ROM

Merlin Library Ltd
Mountbatten St, Blata 1-Bajda HMR 1574
Tel: 2123 4438
E-mail: mail@merlinlibrary.com
Web Site: www.merlinlibrary.com
Founded: 1964
Subjects: Education, Fiction, Literature, Literary Criticism, Essays, Nonfiction (General)
ISBN Prefix(es): 978-99909-1

RTK Ltd+
National Rd, Blata I-Bajda HMR 1460
Tel: 2569 9100; 2569 9000 *Fax:* 2569 9160
Web Site: www.rtk.org.mt
Key Personnel
Chairperson: John Avellino *Tel:* 2569 9154
  E-mail: john.avellino@rtk.org.mt
Manager, Programs: Tonio Bonello *Tel:* 2569 9158 *E-mail:* toniobonello@rtk.org.mt
Manager, Sales & Marketing: Mario J Micallef *Tel:* 2569 9116 *E-mail:* mjmicallef@rtk.org.mt
Founded: 1980
Subjects: Biblical Studies, Communications, Education, Religion - Catholic, Social Sciences, Sociology
ISBN Prefix(es): 978-99909-2
Book Club(s): Klaab Qari Nisrani (Maltese language publications)

University of Malta Library
Msida MSD 2080
Tel: 21 310239 *Fax:* 21 314306
Web Site: www.um.edu.mt/library
Founded: 1954

Subjects: Ethnicity, Language Arts, Linguistics, Law, Natural History, Regional Interests
ISBN Prefix(es): 978-99909-46

Martinique

General Information

Capital: Fort-de-France
Language: French and Creole
Religion: Predominantly Roman Catholic
Population: 359,579
Currency: 100 Eurocents = 1 Euro
Export/Import Information: Tariff same as France. Overseas tax and reduced VAT on books. Small quantity of advertising free. No import licenses required. Exchange restrictions as in France.
Copyright: Berne (see Copyright Conventions, pg viii)

Editions-Lafontaine (Lafontaine Publishing)
Bat 12 - Maniba, 97222 Case Pilote
Tel: 05 96 78 87 98 *Fax:* 05 96 78 87 98; 05 96 93 99 02
Key Personnel
Dir General: Jeannine Lafontaine
Founded: 1994
Publish adult & children's books. Specialize in romance, coloring, essay, school & educational books.
Subjects: Education, Romance
ISBN Prefix(es): 978-2-912006; 978-2-9505357
Number of titles published annually: 5 Print
Total Titles: 90 Print; 1 CD-ROM

Mauritius

General Information

Capital: Port Louis
Language: English (official) and Creole
Religion: Hindu, Christian and Muslim
Population: 1.1 million
Bank Hours: 1000-1400 Monday-Friday, 0930-1130 Saturday
Shop Hours: 0800-1600 or later Monday-Saturday
Currency: 100 cents = 1 Mauritian rupee
Export/Import Information: No tariff on books and advertising but there is a special levy. No import license required.
Copyright: UCC, Berne (see Copyright Conventions, pg viii)

ELP, see Editions Le Printemps Ltee (ELP)

EOI Ltd, see Editions de l'Ocean Indien Ltd

Nelson Mandela Centre for African Culture
La Tour Koenig, Pointe aux Sables
Tel: 234 1416; 234 1421 *Fax:* 234 1417
E-mail: nelmac@intnet.mu; nelson.mandela. centre@gmail.com
Web Site: mandelacentre.govmu.org
Key Personnel
Chairperson: Philippe Fanchette
Officer-in-Charge: Chettandeo Bhugun
Head, Research & Documentation: Stephen Jerome Karghoo
Founded: 1986
Subjects: Economics, Genealogy, History, Literature, Literary Criticism, Essays, Philosophy, Religion - Other, Social Sciences, Sociology
ISBN Prefix(es): 978-99903-904

Editions de l'Ocean Indien Ltd+
22B, Rue Marcel Cabon, Stanley, Rose Hill
Tel: 464 6761 *Fax:* 464 3445
E-mail: eoimarketing@intnet.mu
Founded: 1977
Subjects: Accounting, Agriculture, Art, Biography, Memoirs, Business, Career Development, Computer Science, Cookery, Economics, Education, Fiction, Geography, Geology, Health, Nutrition, Literature, Literary Criticism, Essays, Management, Marketing, Philosophy, Poetry, Science (General), Travel & Tourism
ISBN Prefix(es): 978-99903-0; 978-99949-0
Number of titles published annually: 140 Print
Total Titles: 820 Print
Branch Office(s)
Ground floor, Manhattan Complex, Curepipe
  Tel: 6749065
Charles de Gaulle St, Flacq *Tel:* 4131138
Ground floor, Seeneevassen Bldg, (ex NPF), Jules Koening St, Port Louis *Tel:* 2111310
Kung Hing Mall Bldg, 30, Joseph Riviere St, Port Louis *Tel:* 2423738
Bookshop(s): Le Bookstore, Royal Rd, Belle Rose *Tel:* 464 6391, 464 3959
  E-mail: eoibookstore@intnet.mu

Editions Le Printemps Ltee (ELP)+
4 Club Rd, Vacoas
Tel: 696 1017 *Fax:* 686 7302
E-mail: elp@intnet.mu; elp.editorial@intnet.mu; munsoor.sales@elpmauritius.com; marketing@elpmauritius.com
Web Site: elpmauritius.com
Founded: 1968
Subjects: Biography, Memoirs, Fiction
ISBN Prefix(es): 978-99903-23; 978-99903-70; 978-99903-87
Subsidiaries: AIS Marketing

Editions Vizavi+
3, Rue Nahaboo Solim, Port Louis
Tel: 211 24 35 *Fax:* 211 30 47
E-mail: vizavi@orange.mu
Web Site: www.tikoulou.com
Key Personnel
Dir: Pascale Siew
Founded: 1993
Membership(s): Association of Mauritian Publishers.
Subjects: Biography, Memoirs, Cookery, Government, Political Science, History, Literature, Literary Criticism, Essays, Nonfiction (General)
ISBN Prefix(es): 978-99903-37
Number of titles published annually: 3 Print

Mexico

General Information

Capital: Mexico City
Language: Spanish
Religion: Predominantly Roman Catholic
Population: 92.4 million
Bank Hours: 0900-1330 Monday-Friday
Shop Hours: 1000-1900 Monday, Tuesday, Thursday, Friday; 1100-2000 Wednesday and Saturday
Currency: 100 centavos = 1 Mexican peso
Export/Import Information: Member of the Latin American Free Trade Association. Foreign language books and textbooks generally dutied per kg legal weight, children's picture books ad valorem or per kg, whichever greater, and require import license. Three copies of non-Spanish advertising catalogs free but all others require license and dutied ad valorem. Customs request from Bank of Mexico all necessary information to decide cases of tariff.
Copyright: UCC, Berne, Buenos Aires (see Copyright Conventions, pg viii)

Addison Wesley, *imprint of* Pearson Educacion de Mexico SA de CV

AGT Editor SA
Av Progreso No 202, Colonia Escandon, Delegacion Miguel Hidalgo, 11800 Mexico, CDMX
Tel: (0155) 5515 2922; (0155) 5515 4964; (0155) 5516 4261 *Fax:* (0155) 5277 1696
Founded: 1978
Subjects: Agriculture, Biological Sciences, Veterinary Science
ISBN Prefix(es): 978-968-463; 978-607-7551
Associate Companies: RGS Libros SA de CV

Alamah, *imprint of* Editorial Santillana SA de CV

Alfaomega Grupo Editor SA de CV+
Pitagoras No 1139, Colonia Del Valle-Delegacion Benito Juarez, 03100 Mexico, DF
Tel: (0155) 5575-5022 *Toll Free Tel:* 800-020-4396 *Fax:* (0155) 5575-2420; (0155) 5575-2490
E-mail: universitaria@alfaomega.com.mx; atencionalcliente@alfaomega.com.mx
Web Site: www.alfaomega.com.mx; libroweb.alfaomega.com.mx
Founded: 1965
Subjects: Computer Science, Computers, Electronics, Electrical Engineering, Engineering (General), Management, Technology, Administration
ISBN Prefix(es): 978-968-6223; 978-970-12; 978-970-15
Associate Companies: Publicaciones Marcombo SA

Editorial Alfil SA de CV
Insurgentes Centro 51-Loc A, Colonia San Rafael, 06470 Mexico, CDMX
Tel: (0155) 5566-9676; (0155) 5705-4845; (0155) 5546-9357 *Fax:* (0155) 5705-4845
E-mail: alfil@editalfil.com
Web Site: www.editalfil.com
Key Personnel
Dir General: Jose Paiz Tejada *Tel:* (0155) 5705-4845 ext 107 *E-mail:* jose.paiz@editalfil.com
Sales Dir: Eduardo Obregon Leal *Tel:* (0155) 5705-4845 ext 103 *E-mail:* eduardo.obregon@editalfil.com
Editorial: Norma Berenice Flores Lopez *Tel:* (0155) 5705-4845 ext 105 *E-mail:* berenice@editalfil.com
Production: Luz del Carmen Granados Lince *Tel:* (0155) 5705-4845 ext 106 *E-mail:* cgranados@editalfil.com
Founded: 1995
Subjects: Anthropology, Medicine, Nursing, Dentistry, Science (General), Acupuncture, Dermatology, Pediatrics, Toxicology, Trauma
ISBN Prefix(es): 978-968-7620

Alianza Editorial Mexicana SA de CV
Renacimiento No 180, San Juan Tlihuaca, Azcapotzalco, 02400 Mexico, CDMX
Tel: (0155) 53 54 31 00
Web Site: www.alianzaeditorial.es
Subjects: Art, Biography, Memoirs, Cookery, Drama, Theater, Fiction, Film, Video, Geography, Geology, Government, Political Science, History, Literature, Literary Criticism, Essays, Music, Dance, Nonfiction (General), Philosophy, Poetry, Science Fiction, Fantasy, Social Sciences, Sociology, Sports, Athletics

ISBN Prefix(es): 978-968-6001; 978-968-6354; 978-968-6423; 978-970-664
Associate Companies: Alianza Editorial SA, Spain

Allyn & Bacon, *imprint of* Pearson Educacion de Mexico SA de CV

Editorial Almadia SC
Av Independencia No 1001 Centro, 68000 Oaxaca, OAX
Tel: (01951) 5 16 21 33; (01951) 5144854; (01951) 51600489
E-mail: informacion@almadia.com.mx
Web Site: www.almadia.com.mx
Key Personnel
Dir General: Guillermo Quijas Corzo-Lopez *E-mail:* guillermoquijas@almadia.com.mx
Editorial Dir: Martin Solares *E-mail:* martinsolares@almadia.com.mx
Sales Dir: Gerardo Carrera Madero *E-mail:* gerardocarrera@almadia.com.mx
Public Relations & Press: Ariana Gonzales Santos *E-mail:* ariana@almadia.com.mx
Founded: 2005
Subjects: Fiction, Literature, Literary Criticism, Essays, Poetry, Short Stories
ISBN Prefix(es): 978-607-411
Distribution Center: Fondo de Cultura Economica de Espana, Via de los Poblados, 17-4° 15, 28033 Madrid, Spain *Tel:* 917632800; 917635044 *Fax:* 917635133

AM Editores SA de CV
Paseo de Tamarindos 400B, Suite 109, Bosques de las Lomas, 05120 Mexico, DF
Tel: (0155) 52580279
E-mail: ame@ameditores.com
Web Site: www.ameditores.com
Key Personnel
Dir General/General Manager: Carlos Herver *E-mail:* cherver@ameditores.com
Corporate Sales: Claudia Jardon Yarza *E-mail:* cjardon@ameditores.com
Founded: 1997
Specialize in architecture, interior design & art books.
Subjects: Architecture & Interior Design, Art
ISBN Prefix(es): 978-968-5336; 978-970-97260; 978-970-97269; 978-607-437

Arbol Editorial SA de CV+
Ave Cuauhtemoc 1430, Colonia Santa Cruz Atoyac, 03310 Mexico, CDMX
Tel: (0155) 5605-7677 *Fax:* (0155) 5605-7600
Web Site: www.arboleditorial.com.mx
Key Personnel
Owner: Sebastian Pezoa Di Domenico
Founded: 1979
Subjects: Drama, Theater, Education, Environmental Studies, Health, Nutrition, Religion - Other
ISBN Prefix(es): 978-968-461

Ariel, *imprint of* Editorial Paidos Mexicana

Ediciones Arlequin
Morelos 1742, Colonia Americana, 44160 Guadalajara, JAL
Tel: (0133) 36573786; (0133) 36575045
E-mail: arlequin@arlequin.mx
Web Site: www.arlequin.mx
Key Personnel
Dir General: Felipe Ponce *E-mail:* felipeponce@arlequin.mx
Editorial Process Manager: Monica Millan *E-mail:* monicamillan@arlequin.mx
Sales Manager: Elizabeth Alvarado *E-mail:* elizabethalvarado@arlequin.mx
Founded: 1994

Subjects: Drama, Theater, Education, Literature, Literary Criticism, Essays, Poetry
ISBN Prefix(es): 978-968-7463

Arquine
Culiacan 123, Colonia Hipodromo Condesa, 06170 Mexico, DF
Tel: (0155) 52082289
E-mail: administracion@arquine.com; publicidad@arquine.com
Web Site: www.arquine.com
Key Personnel
Dir: Miquel Adria
Administration: Carlos Coca *Tel:* (0155) 52082289 ext 108
Editor: Juan Jose Kochen
Publicity: Maui Cittadini
Founded: 1997
Subjects: Architecture & Interior Design
ISBN Prefix(es): 978-968-5616

Artes de Mexico+
Cordoba No 69, Colonia Roma, Mexico, DF 06700
Tel: (0155) 5525-5905; (0155) 5525-4036; (0155) 5208-3684
E-mail: direccion@artesdemexico.com
Web Site: www.artesdemexico.com
Key Personnel
Editor-in-Chief: Alberto Ruy Sanchez
Founded: 1953
Subjects: Antiques, Archaeology, Architecture & Interior Design, Art, Biography, Memoirs, Ethnicity, History, Literature, Literary Criticism, Essays, Photography, Poetry, Women's Studies, Mexican Culture
ISBN Prefix(es): 978-970-683; 978-968-6533; 978-607-461
Number of titles published annually: 20 Print
Total Titles: 174 Print
Distributed by The Bilingual Publications Co (USA); Brodart Co (USA); Chulainn Publishing Corp (USA); Howard Karno Books Inc (USA); Latin American Book Source (USA); Libro America, S de RL de CV (USA); Libros sin Fronteras c/o Baker & Taylor (USA)

Editorial Avante SA de CV
Luis Gonzalez Obregon No 9 bis, Colonia Centro, 06020 Mexico, CDMX
Tel: (0155) 9140-6500
E-mail: didactips@editorialavante.com.mx
Web Site: www.editorialavante.com.mx
Key Personnel
Commercial Dir: Jose Castro Hernandez
E-mail: jcastro@editorialavante.com.mx
Sales Management: Julio Morin *E-mail:* jmorin@editorialavante.com.mx
Founded: 1947
Subjects: Biography, Memoirs, Drama, Theater, Education, Language Arts, Linguistics, Poetry, Science (General), Social Sciences, Sociology
ISBN Prefix(es): 978-968-6006; 978-968-6986
Imprints: Impresora Galve SA; Heidel Impresos SA de CV; Impresora Multiple SA

Grupo Azabache Sa de CV+
Lord Byron 706, Colonia Bosques de Chapultepec, 11580 Mexico, CDMX
Tel: (0155) 5280-7241
Founded: 1987
Membership(s): National Association of the Publishing Industry.
Subjects: Archaeology, Architecture & Interior Design, Art, Cookery, History, Journalism, Photography, Painting
ISBN Prefix(es): 978-968-6084; 978-968-6963; 978-970-678

Ediciones B Mexico SA de CV
Imprint of Penguin Random House Grupo Editorial

Bradley 52, esquina Gutemberg, Delegacion Miguel Hidalgo Colonial Anzures, 11590 Mexico, CDMX
Tel: (0155) 525 51 50 *Fax:* (0155) 525 64 54
Web Site: www.edicionesb-mexico.com
Subjects: Geography, Geology, History, Literature, Literary Criticism, Essays, Science (General)
ISBN Prefix(es): 978-970-710; 978-607-480; 978-607-529; 978-607-530; 978-968-453
Branch Office(s)
Paseo Colon 221, 6° piso 1399, C1063AAC Buenos Aires, Argentina *Tel:* (011) 4343 7510
Web Site: www.edicionesb-argentina.com
Av Las Torres 1375- A Huechuraba, Santiago, Chile *Tel:* (02) 27295400 *Fax:* (02) 27295430
Carrera 15 No 52 A-33, Bogota DC, Colombia *Tel:* (01) 212 40 12 *Fax:* (01) 248 02 64 *Web Site:* www.edicionesb.com.co
Consell de Cent, 425-427, 08009 Barcelona, Spain *Tel:* 93 484 66 00 *Fax:* 93 232 46 60
C/ Orduna, 3, 28034 Madrid, Spain *Tel:* 91 586 33 00; 91 586 33 02 *Fax:* 91 586 34 11
Constituyente, 2032, 11200 Montevideo, Uruguay *Tel:* 2419 86 03 *Fax:* 2418 90 05 *Web Site:* www.edicionesb.com.uy
Av Romulo Gallegos, c/c Rep Dominicana, Edif Vista, Mezzanina, Boleita Norte, 1050, A Caracas, Venezuela *Tel:* (0212) 235 31 34 *Fax:* (0212) 235 58 55 *E-mail:* brozados@edicionesb.com.ve

Libreria y Ediciones Botas SA de CV
Justo Sierra No 52, 06020 Mexico, DF
Tel: (0155) 57023083 *Fax:* (0155) 57025403
Key Personnel
Owner: Gabriela Botas Hernandez
Dir: Laura Botas Hernandez
Founded: 1910
Subjects: Art, Economics, Fiction, History, Law, Medicine, Nursing, Dentistry, Philosophy, Science (General)
ISBN Prefix(es): 978-968-6334

Casa Juan Pablos Centro Cultural
Malintzin 199, Colonia del Carmen, 04100 Mexico, CDMX
Tel: (0155) 56590252; (0155) 55541056 *Fax:* (0155) 56594480
Founded: 1971
Subjects: Fiction, Geography, Geology, History, Literature, Literary Criticism, Essays, Philosophy, Social Sciences, Sociology
ISBN Prefix(es): 978-968-5422

Ediciones Castillo SA de CV
Imprint of Editorial Macmillan de Mexico SA de CV
Insurgentes Sur 1886, Colonia Florida, 01030 Mexico, CDMX
Tel: (0155) 54822200 *Toll Free Tel:* 01800 5361777; 01800 0064100 *Fax:* (0155) 54822200
Web Site: www.edicionescastillo.com; macmillan.com.mx
Key Personnel
Dir General: Patricia Lopez
Founded: 1977
Subjects: Biography, Memoirs, Education, Fiction, Nonfiction (General)
ISBN Prefix(es): 978-968-6635; 978-968-7415; 978-970-20

CEMCA, see Centro de Estudios Mexicanos y Centroamericanos

CEMLA, see Centro de Estudios Monetarios Latinoamericanos (CEMLA)

Cengage Learning Latin America
Cengage Learning Mexico, Av Santa Fe 505 piso 12, Colonia Cruz Manca Santa Fe, Cuajimalpa, 05349 Mexico, CDMX
Tel: (0155) 1500 6000
E-mail: clientes.mexicoca@cengage.com
Web Site: www.cengage.com
Subjects: Education, English as a Second Language, Mathematics, Science (General)
ISBN Prefix(es): 978-968-7529; 978-970-686; 978-970-830
Parent Company: Gale Cengage Learning
Branch Office(s)
Cengage Learning Argentina, Rojas 2128, C1416CPX Buenos Aires, Argentina
Tel: (011) 4582 0601 *Fax:* (011) 4582 0087
E-mail: clientes.conosur@cengage.com
Cengage Learning Edicoes Ltda, Av das Nacoes Unidas 21.476, 04795-000 Sao Paulo-SP, Brazil *Tel:* (011) 3665-9900 *E-mail:* sac.brasil@cengage.com
Cengage Learning Chile, Carlos Antunez 2719, Providencia, Santiago, Chile *Tel:* (02) 231-7974 *E-mail:* clientes.conosur@cengage.com
Cengage Learning SA Colombia, Carrera 7 No 74-21 Bldg, 8th floor, Aurora Insurance, Bogota, Colombia *Tel:* (01) 2 12 33 40 *Fax:* (01) 2 11 39 95 *E-mail:* clientes.pactoandino@cengage.com
Cengage Learning Peru, Av Javier Prado Este 3502, San Borja 41, Lima, Peru *Tel:* (01) 250-1876 *E-mail:* clientes.conosur@cengage.com
Cengage Learning Puerto Rico, Metro Office Park 3, Suite 520, San Juan 00968, Puerto Rico *Tel:* 787-641-1112 *Fax:* 787-641-1119 *E-mail:* clientes.caribe@cengage.com

Centro de Estudios Mexicanos y Centroamericanos+
Sierra Leona 330, Lomas de Chapultepec, Miguel Hidalgo, 11000 Mexico, DF
Tel: (0155) 55405921; (0155) 55405922; (0155) 55405923 *Fax:* (0155) 52027794
E-mail: difusion@cemca.org.mx; publicaciones@cemca.org.mx
Web Site: www.cemca.org.mx
Key Personnel
Dir: Francoise Lestage
Founded: 1982
Subjects: Anthropology, Archaeology, Biological Sciences, Earth Sciences, Economics, Environmental Studies, Ethnicity, Foreign Countries, Government, Political Science, History, Music, Dance, Science (General), Social Sciences, Sociology
ISBN Prefix(es): 978-968-6029; 978-970-758
Subsidiaries: Ministere des Affaires Etrangeres
Branch Office(s)
5 av 8-59 zona 14, Sede Embajada de Francia, 1er Nivel, Guatemala 01014, Guatemala
E-mail: info@cemca-ac.org *Web Site:* www.cemca-ac.org
Distributed by INAH

Centro de Informacion y Desarrollo de la Comunicacion y la Literatura Infantiles, see CIDCLI SC

Centro de Investigacion y Docencia Economicas (CIDE)
Carretera Mexico-Toluca 3655, Colonia Lomas de Santa Fe, Delegacion Alvaro Obregon, 01210 Mexico, CDMX
Tel: (0155) 57279800 *Toll Free Tel:* (800) 021 2433
Web Site: www.cide.edu
Key Personnel
Dir General: Enrique Cabrero Mendoza
E-mail: enrique.cabrero@cide.edu
Editorial Dir: Natalia Cervantes *Tel:* (0155) 57279800 ext 6090 *E-mail:* natalia.cervantes@cide.edu

Publication: Leticia Hernandez *Tel:* (0155) 57279800 ext 2410 *E-mail:* leticia.hernandez@cide.edu
Founded: 1974
Subjects: Geography, Geology, History, Literature, Literary Criticism, Essays, Social Sciences, Sociology
ISBN Prefix(es): 978-968-7420

CIDCLI SC
Av Mexico 145-601, Colonia Coyoacan, 04100 Mexico, CDMX
Tel: (0155) 5659 7524 *Fax:* (0155) 5659 3186
Web Site: www.cidcli.com.mx
Key Personnel
Rights: Elisa Castellanos *E-mail:* elisa@cidcli.com
Sales: Miguel Angel Colin *E-mail:* miguel@cidcli.com
Founded: 1980
ISBN Prefix(es): 978-968-494; 978-607-7749

CIDE, see Centro de Investigacion y Docenia Economicas (CIDE)

Editora Cientifica Medica Latinoamericana SA de CV
Av Constituyentes 357, 11830 Mexico, DF
Tel: (0155) 52020929 *Fax:* (0155) 56766400
Founded: 1986
Subjects: Computer Science, Medicine, Nursing, Dentistry
ISBN Prefix(es): 978-968-6166

Circe, *imprint of* Editorial Oceano de Mexico SA de CV

El Colegio de Jalisco
Calle 5 de Mayo No 321, Colonia Centro, 45100 Zapopan, JAL
Tel: (0133) 3633 2616
E-mail: publicaciones@coljal.edu.mx
Web Site: coljal.edu.mx
Key Personnel
President: Jose Luis Leal Sanabria *Tel:* (0133) 3833 0209 *E-mail:* presidencia@coljal.edu.mx
Mng Dir: Jose Fernandez Aceves *Tel:* (0133) 3833 4905 *E-mail:* jfa@coljal.edu.mx
Publication: Iliana Avalos Gonzalez *Tel:* (0133) 3836 0391
Founded: 1982
Subjects: Anthropology, Art, Economics, Government, Political Science, History, Social Sciences, Sociology
ISBN Prefix(es): 978-968-6142; 978-968-6255

El Colegio de la Frontera Norte (Colef)
Km 18.5, Carretera Escenica Tijuana-Ensenada, Colonia San Antonia del Mar, 22560 Tijuana, BC
Tel: (01664) 631-6300
E-mail: informes@colef.mx; publica@colef.mx; libros@colef.mx
Web Site: www.colef.mx
Key Personnel
President: Tonatiuh Guillen Lopez *Tel:* (01664) 631-6300 ext 1444 *E-mail:* tguillen@colef.mx
Coordinator, Publications: Erika Moreno Paez *Tel:* (01664) 631-6300 ext 1101
Founded: 1982
Subjects: Geography, Geology, History, Social Sciences, Sociology
ISBN Prefix(es): 978-968-7947; 978-607-479

El Colegio de la Frontera Sur (ECOSUR)
Carretera Panamericana y Periferico Sur s/n, Barrio Maria Auxiliadora, 29290 San Cristobal de Las Casas
Tel: (01967) 674-9000 *Fax:* (01976) 674-9021
E-mail: contacto@ecosur.mx
Web Site: www.ecosur.mx

Key Personnel
Dir General: Dr Mario Gonzalez Espinosa *E-mail:* dg@ecosur.mx
Sales Manager: Adriana Cisternas *Tel:* (01967) 674-9000 ext 1780 *E-mail:* acistern@ecosur.mx
Publications: Laura Lopez Argoytia *Tel:* (01967) 674-9000 ext 1784 *E-mail:* llopez@ecosur.mx
Founded: 1973
ISBN Prefix(es): 978-970-9712

El Colegio de Mexico AC (COLMEX)
Camino al Ajusco No 20, Colonia Pedregal de Santa Teresa, 10740 Mexico, CDMX
Tel: (0155) 5449 3000 *Fax:* (0155) 5449 3000 (ext 3157)
Web Site: publicaciones.colmex.mx; www.colmex.mx
Key Personnel
Publications Dir: Francisco Gomez Ruiz *Tel:* (0155) 5449 3000 ext 3080 *E-mail:* fgomez@colmex.mx
Production Coordinator: Gabriela Said Reyes *Tel:* (0155) 5449 3000 ext 3081 *E-mail:* gsaid@colmex.mx
Founded: 1940
Subjects: Anthropology, Asian Studies, Business, Economics, Environmental Studies, Government, Political Science, History, Language Arts, Linguistics, Library & Information Sciences, Literature, Literary Criticism, Essays, Nonfiction (General), Philosophy, Science (General), Social Sciences, Sociology, Women's Studies
ISBN Prefix(es): 978-607-462

El Colegio de Michoacan AC
Affiliate of ANUIES
Martinez de Navarete 505, Colonia Las Fuentes, 59699 Zamora, MICH
Tel: (0351) 5157100 *Fax:* (0351) 5157100
E-mail: publica@colmich.edu.mx
Web Site: www.colmich.edu.mx/index.php/publicaciones; www.libreriacolmich.com
Key Personnel
Head, Publications: Patricia Delgado Gonzalez *E-mail:* pdelgado@colmich.edu.mx
Founded: 1979
Centro Publico de Investigacion.
Subjects: Americana, Regional, Anthropology, Archaeology, Behavioral Sciences, Developing Countries, Education, Environmental Studies, Government, Political Science, History, Language Arts, Linguistics, Native American Studies, Philosophy, Religion - Catholic, Social Sciences, Sociology, Theology, Research Results
ISBN Prefix(es): 978-968-6959; 978-968-7230; 978-970-679
Number of titles published annually: 35 Print; 2 CD-ROM; 4 Online
Total Titles: 510 Print; 6 CD-ROM; 40 Online
Distributed by Ebsco; Sweets

Colegio de Postgraduados en Ciencias Agricolas
Km 36.5 Carretera Mexico-Texcoco, 56230 Texcoco
Tel: (01595) 58046800
E-mail: contacto@colpos.mx
Web Site: www.colpos.mx
Key Personnel
Dir: Sergio S Gonzalez Munoz
Editor General: Said Infante Gil
Founded: 1959
Membership(s): Mexican National Association of Publishers.
Subjects: Agriculture, Biological Sciences, Economics, Education, Mathematics, Science (General), Social Sciences, Sociology, Technology, Veterinary Science
ISBN Prefix(es): 978-968-839

El Colegio de San Luis
Parque de Macul No 155, Colonia Colinas del Praque, 78299 San Luis Potosi, SLP
Tel: (01444) 8110101 (ext 3045)
E-mail: publicaciones@colsan.edu.mx; difusioncolsan@gmail.com; ventaslibros@colsan.edu.mx
Web Site: www.colsan.edu.mx
Key Personnel
Dir General: Maria Isabel Monroy Castillo *Tel:* (01444) 8110101 ext 3010 *E-mail:* imonroy@colsan.edu.mx
Publications: Ernesto Alberto Zavaleta Erana *Tel:* (01444) 8110101 ext 8333 *E-mail:* ezavaleta@colsan.edu.mx
Founded: 1997
Subjects: Literature, Literary Criticism, Essays, Social Sciences, Sociology
ISBN Prefix(es): 978-968-7727; 978-970-94161

El Colegio de Sonora
Av Obregon No 54, Colonia Centro, 83000 Hermosillo, SON
Tel: (01662) 259-5300 *Fax:* (01662) 212-5021
Web Site: www.colson.edu.mx
Key Personnel
President: Gabriela Grijalva Monteverde *Tel:* (01662) 259-5300 ext 2252
Head, Cultural Dept: Ines Martinez de Castro Navarrete *Tel:* (01662) 259-5300 ext 2258
Head, Dept of Documentation & Library: Estanislao Arauz Mela
Founded: 1982
Subjects: Social Sciences, Sociology
ISBN Prefix(es): 978-968-6755

El Colegio Mexiquense AC
Ex-Hacienda Santa Cruz de los Patos, 51350 Zinacantepec
Tel: (01722) 2799908; (01722) 2180100 *Fax:* (01722) 2799908 (ext 200)
E-mail: public@cmq.edu.mx
Web Site: www.cmq.edu.mx
Founded: 1986
Subjects: Social Sciences, Sociology
ISBN Prefix(es): 978-968-6341; 978-970-669

COLMEX, see El Colegio de Mexico AC (COLMEX)

Comision Nacional Forestal
Periferico Poniente 5360, San Juan de Ocotan, 45019 Zapopan, JAL
Tel: (0133) 3777 7000 *Toll Free Tel:* 01 800 7370 00 (within Mexico)
E-mail: conafor@conafor.gob.mx
Web Site: www.conafor.gob.mx
Key Personnel
Dir General: Juan Manuel Torres Rojo *Tel:* (0133) 3777 7077 *Fax:* (0133) 3777 7012 *E-mail:* directorgeneral@conafor.gob.mx
Subjects: Government, Political Science, History, Medicine, Nursing, Dentistry, Social Sciences, Sociology, Forestry Development
ISBN Prefix(es): 978-968-6021

Compania General de Ediciones SA de CV, see Selector SA de CV

CONAFOR, see Comision Nacional Forestal

CONARTE, see Consejo para la Cultura y las Artes de Nuevo Leon (CONARTE)

Editorial Conexion Grafica SA de CV
Victoriano Agueros No 2198, Colonia Barreda, 44150 Guadalajara, JAL
Tel: (0133) 3615-7424
E-mail: conexiongrafica@conexiongrafica.mx
Web Site: www.conexiongrafica.mx
ISBN Prefix(es): 978-968-6295

Consejo para la Cultura y las Artes de Nuevo Leon (CONARTE) (The Council for Culture and the Arts of Nuevo Leon)
Torre administrativa, piso 32, Washington 2000 Ote, Colonia Obrera, 64000 Monterrey, NL
Tel: (0181) 2033 8450
E-mail: contacto@conarte.org.mx
Web Site: www.conarte.org.mx
Key Personnel
President: Katzir Meza Medina
  E-mail: presidencia@conarte.org.mx
Founded: 1995
Subjects: Art, Fiction, Outdoor Recreation
ISBN Prefix(es): 978-968-5724

Ediciones Corunda SA de CV+
Calle Tlaxcala 17, Barrio San Francisco, 10500 Mexico, CDMX
Tel: (0155) 5568-4741
Key Personnel
Dir: Silvana Cervera
Founded: 1988
Subjects: Literature, Literary Criticism, Essays, Science Fiction, Fantasy
ISBN Prefix(es): 978-968-6044; 978-968-7444

Critica, *imprint of* Editorial Paidos Mexicana

Ediciones Culturales Internacionales SA de CV (ECISA)+
Lago Mask 393, Colonia Granada, Delegacion Miguel Hidalgo, 11520 Mexico, CDMX
Tel: (0155) 5250-8099 *Toll Free Tel:* 01 800 024 90 86 *Fax:* (0155) 5531-5176
E-mail: atencionaclientes@ediciones.com.mx
Web Site: www.ediciones.com.mx
Key Personnel
General Dir: Mireya Cuentas Montejo
Head, Editorial Dept: Claudia Canela Obrego
Founded: 1983
Subjects: Art, Child Care & Development, Ethnicity, Language Arts, Linguistics
ISBN Prefix(es): 978-968-418

Ediciones Dabar SA de CV+
Mirador 42, Colonia El Mirador, 04950 Mexico, CDMX
Tel: (0155) 5594-0143; (0155) 5603-3630; (0155) 5673-8855 *Fax:* (0155) 5603-3674
E-mail: ventas@dabar.com.mx
Web Site: www.dabar.com.mx
Founded: 1992
Also distributors of religious books in Spanish; theological, Bibles, spiritual & catechisms.
Subjects: Religion - Other
ISBN Prefix(es): 978-968-6768; 978-968-7506; 978-970-652

Del Verbo Emprender SA de CV+
Fuente de Piramides 20 PB Local B, Tecamachalco, 53950 Edo de Mexico
Tel: (0155) 5294 8407; (0155) 5294 8633
  Fax: (0155) 5294 8633
Web Site: www.delverboemprender.com.mx
Key Personnel
Founder & Chief Executive Officer: Salo Grabinsky *E-mail:* gzsalo@gmail.com
Founded: 1989
Subjects: Business, Child Care & Development, Human Relations, Management, Self-Help, Entrepreneurship
ISBN Prefix(es): 978-968-6427

DGP, see Direccion General de Publicaciones de Secretaria de Cultura

Editorial Diana SA de CV+
Av Presidente Masarik No 111, 2do Piso, Colonia Chapultepec Morales, Delegacion Miguel Hidalgo, 11570 Mexico, CDMX
Tel: (0155) 3000-6200 *Fax:* (0155) 3000-6257

E-mail: info@planeta.com.mx
Web Site: www.diana.com.mx
Founded: 1946
Membership(s): National Association of the Mexican Publishing Industry.
Subjects: Advertising, Animals, Pets, Archaeology, Astrology, Occult, Biography, Memoirs, Career Development, Child Care & Development, Cookery, Economics, Education, Fiction, Health, Nutrition, History, Human Relations, Journalism, Literature, Literary Criticism, Essays, Management, Nonfiction (General), Parapsychology, Philosophy, Religion - Catholic, Self-Help, Sports, Athletics
ISBN Prefix(es): 978-968-13
Parent Company: Editorial Planeta Mexicana SA de CV
Ultimate Parent Company: Grupo Planeta
Shipping Address: Roberto Cayol 1323, Colonia del Valle, 03100 Mexico, CDMX

Direccion General de Publicaciones de Secretaria de Cultura
Av Paseo de la Reforma 175 piso 1, Colonia Cuauhtemoc, 06500 Mexico, CDMX
Tel: (0155) 4155 0200
E-mail: dgp01@conaculta.gob.mx
Web Site: programanacionalsalasdelectura.cultura. gob.mx
Key Personnel
Dir: Marina Nunez Bespalova
  E-mail: marinanunez@conaculta.gob.mx
Subjects: Biography, Memoirs, Fiction, History, Mexican Culture
ISBN Prefix(es): 978-968-29; 978-970-18; 978-970-35

Directorio, *imprint of* Medios y Medios SA de CV

Ediciones ECA SA de CV+
Los Juarez No 3, Colonia Insurgentes, 03920 Mexico, CDMX
Tel: (0155) 5615-4162; (0155) 5615-4187; (0155) 5615-4088; (0155) 5615-4289
Web Site: edicioneseca.com
Founded: 1950
Subjects: Accounting, Business, Technology
ISBN Prefix(es): 978-968-14

ECISA, see Ediciones Culturales Internacionales SA de CV (ECISA)

ECOSUR, see El Colegio de la Frontera Sur (ECOSUR)

Edebe Ediciones Internacionales SA de CV
Ignacio Mariscal, No 8, Colonia Tabacalera, 06030 Mexico, CDMX
Tel: (0155) 5535-7557; (0155) 5535-5729
  Fax: (0155) 5592-1306
Web Site: www.edebe.com.mx
Founded: 1997
Subjects: Literature, Literary Criticism, Essays, Religion - Other, Social Sciences, Sociology
ISBN Prefix(es): 978-968-7964; 978-968-7957

Editorial Edicol SA
Murcia 2, Colonia Mixcoac Insurgentes, 03920 Mexico, CDMX
Tel: (0155) 5563-6966
Founded: 1970
Subjects: Architecture & Interior Design, Communications, Education, History, Language Arts, Linguistics, Social Sciences, Sociology
ISBN Prefix(es): 978-968-408

Edilar SA de CV
Blvd Manuel Avila Camacho, No 1994-103, Colonia San Lucas Tepetlacalco, 54055 Tlalnepantla, MEX
Toll Free Tel: 1800-31-222-00
E-mail: info@edilar.com
Web Site: www.edilar.com
Key Personnel
Dir General: Ignacio Uribe Ferrari
Subjects: Art, Geography, Geology, History, Language Arts, Linguistics, Literature, Literary Criticism, Essays
ISBN Prefix(es): 978-968-5418

EMU, see Editores Mexicanos Unidos SA de CV (EMU)

Ediciones Era SA de CV+
Calle del Trabajo, 31, Colonia La Fama, Tlalpan, 14269 Mexico, CDMX
Tel: (0155) 5528 1221 *Fax:* (0155) 5606 2904
E-mail: info@edicionesera.com.mx; erapedidos@edicionesera.com.mx; editorial@edicionesera.com.mx
Web Site: www.edicionesera.com.mx
Founded: 1960
Subjects: Art, Economics, Fiction, Government, Political Science, History, Literature, Literary Criticism, Essays, Social Sciences, Sociology
ISBN Prefix(es): 978-968-411
Number of titles published annually: 25 Print
Total Titles: 300 Print

Ediciones del Ermitano
Division of Solar, Servicios Editoriales SA de CV
Calle 2, No 21, Colonia San Pedro de los Pinos, Del Benito Juarez, 03800 Mexico, DF
Tel: (0155) 5515-1657
E-mail: minimalia@edicionesdelermitano.com
Web Site: www.edicionesdelermitano.com
Key Personnel
Dir General: Alejandro Zenker
Project Manager: Rasheny Lazcano *Tel:* (0155) 5515-1657 ext 232
Founded: 1984
Subjects: Fiction, Poetry
ISBN Prefix(es): 978-968-879

Revista Mensual Escuela, *imprint of* Fernandez Editores SA de CV

Editorial Esfinge SA de CV
Member of Grupo Cultural Esfinge SA de CV
Calle Esfuerzo 18-A, Colonia Industrial Atoto, 53519 Naucalpan de Juarez, MEX
Tel: (0155) 5359 1111 *Fax:* (0155) 5576 1343
E-mail: contacto@esfinge.com.mx
Web Site: esfinge.mx/home
Founded: 1957
Specialize in textbooks.
Membership(s): National Chamber of the Industrial Editorial.
Subjects: Accounting, Chemistry, Chemical Engineering, Education, Geography, Geology, History, Law, Literature, Literary Criticism, Essays, Mathematics, Physics
ISBN Prefix(es): 978-968-412; 978-970-647
Associate Companies: Altadir SA de CV; Distr Imagen Esfinge SA de CV; Inmobiliaria Acribia SA de CV
Distributor for Addison-Wesley Iberoamericana Mexico

Espasa Calpe Mexicana, *imprint of* Editorial Planeta Mexicana SA de CV

Centro de Estudios Monetarios Latinoamericanos (CEMLA)+
Durango 54, Colonia Roma Norte, Delegacion Cuauhtemoc, 06700 Mexico, CDMX
Tel: (0155) 5061-6680 *Fax:* (0155) 5061-6695

E-mail: sibaja@cemla.org
Web Site: www.cemla.org/publicaciones.html
Founded: 1952
Subjects: Computer Science, Economics, Finance
ISBN Prefix(es): 978-968-6154; 978-968-5696

ETM, see Editores de Textos Mexicanos (ETM)

Ediciones Exclusivas SA+
Balboa 514, Benito Juarez, 03300 Mexico, DF
Tel: (0155) 5672-1816
Founded: 1973
Subjects: Health, Nutrition, Human Relations, Medicine, Nursing, Dentistry, Psychology, Psychiatry
ISBN Prefix(es): 978-968-7039

Facultad Latinoamericana de Ciencias Sociales (FLACSO)
Carretera al Ajusco 377, Colonia Heroes de Padierna, Delegacion Tlalpan, 14200 Mexico, CDMX
Tel: (0155) 30000200; (0155) 30000251; (0155) 30000224; (0155) 30000244 *Fax:* (0155) 30000284
E-mail: public@flacso.edu.mx
Web Site: www.flacso.edu.mx/publicacions/novedades
Key Personnel
Dir General: Francisco Valdes Ugalde *Tel:* (0155) 30000200 ext 203 *E-mail:* direccion@flacso.edu.mx
Editorial Dir: Gisela Gonzalez Guerra *Tel:* (0155) 30000200 ext 255 *E-mail:* ggonzalez@flacso.edu.mx
Founded: 1975
Subjects: Social Sciences, Sociology
ISBN Prefix(es): 978-968-6728

Editorial Fata Morgana SA de CV+
Virgilio No 7 Desp 12, Polanco, 11560 Mexico, DF
Tel: (0155) 5280-0829
E-mail: editorial@fatamorgana.com.mx
Web Site: www.fatamorgana.com.mx
Key Personnel
Dir: Maria Abac Klemm
Founded: 1990
Subjects: Psychology, Psychiatry
ISBN Prefix(es): 978-968-6757
Number of titles published annually: 1 Print
Total Titles: 8 Print

Ediciones Felou
Amsterdam 124, Despacho 403 Condesa, 06170 Mexico, DF
Tel: (0155) 525 60 561 *Fax:* (0155) 525 62 168
E-mail: ventas@felou.com
Web Site: www.felou.com
Subjects: Art, Fiction, Photography, Poetry
ISBN Prefix(es): 978-970-49; 978-607-7757

Fernandez Editores SA de CV+
Eje 1 Pte Mexico-Coyoacan No 321, Colonia Xoco, 03330 Mexico, CDMX
Tel: (0155) 5090 7700 *Toll Free Tel:* 01 800 712 49 99; 01 800 021 50 16
E-mail: tecnologia.fesa@gmail.com
Web Site: www.tareasya.com.mx
Founded: 1943
Manufacturer of game tables & materials.
Membership(s): Camara Editorial of Mexico.
Subjects: Animals, Pets, Child Care & Development, Education, Environmental Studies, History, Literature, Literary Criticism, Essays, Mathematics, Nonfiction (General), Physics, Religion - Catholic, Science (General), Science Fiction, Fantasy, Social Sciences, Sociology
ISBN Prefix(es): 978-970-03; 978-968-416
Parent Company: Grupo Qumma
Imprints: Revista Mensual Escuela

FLACSO Mexico, see Facultad Latinoamericana de Ciencias Sociales (FLACSO)

Flauta De Pan, *imprint of* Editorial Lectorum SA de CV

Fondo de Cultura Economica
Carretera Picacho-Ajusco 227, Colonia Bosques del Pedregal, Tlalpan, 14738 Mexico, CDMX
Tel: (0155) 5227-4672 *Fax:* (0155) 5227-4694
E-mail: foreign.rights@fondodeculturaeconomica.com
Web Site: www.fondodeculturaeconomica.com
Key Personnel
Chief Executive Officer: Jose Carreno Carlon *Tel:* (0155) 5227-4601 *E-mail:* direccion.general@fondodeculturaeconomica.com
Mng Editor: Tomas Granados Salinas *Tel:* (0155) 5227-4633 *Fax:* (0155) 5227-4640 *E-mail:* gerente.editorial@fondodeculturaeconomica.com
Sales Manager: Martha Cantu *Tel:* (0155) 5227-4652 *E-mail:* gerente.comercial@fondodeculturaeconomica.com
General Coordinator of International Affairs: Susana Lopez *Tel:* (0155) 5449-1874 *Fax:* (0155) 5227-4698 *E-mail:* coordinadora.internacional@fondodeculturaeconomica.com
Founded: 1934
Also bookseller.
Membership(s): Camara Nacional de la Industria Editorial Mexicana.
Subjects: Anthropology, Archaeology, Architecture & Interior Design, Art, Behavioral Sciences, Biography, Memoirs, Biological Sciences, Communications, Developing Countries, Drama, Theater, Earth Sciences, Economics, Education, Energy, Ethnicity, Fiction, Government, Political Science, History, Language Arts, Linguistics, Literature, Literary Criticism, Essays, Music, Dance, Philosophy, Photography, Poetry, Psychology, Psychiatry, Public Administration, Publishing & Book Trade Reference, Science (General), Social Sciences, Sociology, Women's Studies
ISBN Prefix(es): 978-968-16; 978-607-16
Number of titles published annually: 700 Print; 2 Online; 250 E-Book; 2 Audio
Total Titles: 9,500 Print; 30 Audio
Branch Office(s)
Fondo de Cultura Economica de Argentina SA, El Salvador 5665, C1414BQE Buenos Aires, Argentina, General Manager: Alejandro Archain *Tel:* (011) 4771-8977 *Fax:* (011) 4771-4788 *E-mail:* info@fce.com.ar *Web Site:* www.fce.com.ar
Fondo de Cultura Economica de Brasil Ltda, Rua Bartira 351, Perdizes, 05009-000 Sao Paulo-SP, Brazil, Manager: Susana Ema Acosta *Tel:* (011) 3875-3835; (011) 3672-3397 *Fax:* (011) 3864-1496 *E-mail:* aztecafondo@uol.com.br
Fondo de Cultura Economica Chile SA, Paseo Bulnes 152, Santiago, Chile, General Manager: Julio Sau *Tel:* (02) 594-4100 *Fax:* (02) 594-4101 *E-mail:* julio.sau@fcechile.cl *Web Site:* www.fcechile.cl
Fondo de Cultura Economica Ltda, Calle de la Ensenanza 11 No 5-60 La Candelaria, Bogota, Colombia, General Manager: Juan Camilo Sierra Restrepo *Tel:* (01) 283-2200 *Fax:* (01) 337-4289 *E-mail:* jsierra@fce.com.co *Web Site:* www.fce.com.co
Fondo de Cultura Economica Centroamerica y el Caribe, 6a Ave 8-65, Zona 9, Guatemala, Guatemala, General Manager: Cesar Medina *Tel:* 2334-1635 *Fax:* 2332-4216 *E-mail:* cmedina@fondodeculturaeconomica.com *Web Site:* www.fceguatemala.com
Fondo de Cultura Economica de Peru SA, Jiron Berlin 238, Miraflores, Lima 18, Peru, General Manager: Carmen Gloria Chavez *Tel:* (01) 447-2848 *Fax:* (01) 447-0760 *Web Site:* www.fceperu.com.pe

Fondo de Cultura Economica de Espana SL, Via de los Poblados 17, Edificio Indubuilding-Goico 4-15, 28033 Madrid, Spain, General Manager: Marcelo Diaz Alessi *Tel:* 91 763-2800; 91 763-5044 *Fax:* 91 763-5133 *E-mail:* marcelo.diaz@fondodeculturaeconomica.es *Web Site:* www.fondodeculturaeconomica.es
Fondo de Cultura Economica de Venezuela SA, Edificio Torre Polar, PB Local E, Plaza Venezuela, Caracas, Venezuela, General Manager: Pedro Juan Tucat Zunino *Tel:* (0212) 574-4753 *Fax:* (0212) 574-7442 *E-mail:* fceven@gmail.com *Web Site:* www.fcevenezuela.com
U.S. Office(s): Fondo de Cultura Economica de USA Inc, 2293 Verus St, San Diego, CA 92154, United States, Contact: Dorina Maciel Razo Miranda *Tel:* 619-429-0455 *Fax:* 619-651-9684 *E-mail:* drazo@fceusa.com *Web Site:* www.fceusa.com
Bookshop(s): Libreria Juan Jose Arreola, Eje Central Lazaro Cardenas 24, esquina Venustiano Carranza, Colonia Centro Historico, Delegacion Cuauhtemoc, 06300 Mexico, CDMX, Contact: Roman Castaneda Contreras *Tel:* (0155) 5518 3225; (0155) 5518 3231; (0155) 5518 3236 *Fax:* (0155) 5518 3242 *E-mail:* libreria.juanjose.arreola@fondodeculturaeconomica.com; Libreria Rosario Castellanos, Tamaulipas 202, esquina Benjamin Hill, Colonia Hipodromo de la Condesa, Delegacion Cuauhtemoc, 06170 Mexico, CDMX, Contact: Luz Elena Silva Guerrero *Tel:* (0155) 5276 7110; (0155) 5276 7139 *E-mail:* libreria.rosario.castellanos@fondodeculturaeconomica.com; Libreria Ali Chumacero, Aeropuerto Internacional de la Ciudad de Mexico Benito Juarez, Av Capitan Carlos Leon Gonzalez s/n, locales 38 y 39 Colonia Penon de los Banos Terminal 2 Ambulatorio de Llegadas, Delegacion Venustiano Carranza, 15620 Mexico, CDMX, Contact: Elizabeth Tovar Gaytan *Tel:* (0155) 2598 3441 *E-mail:* libreria.ali@fondodeculturaeconomica.com; Libreria Daniel Cosio Villegas, Av Universidad 985, Colonia del Valle, Delegacion Benito Juarez, 03100 Mexico, CDMX, Contact: Juan Manuel Magarino Guzman *Tel:* (0155) 5524 8933; (0155) 5524 1261 *E-mail:* libreria.daniel.cosio@fondodeculturaeconomica.com; Libreria Salvador Elizondo, Aeropuerto Internacional de la Ciudad de Mexico Benito Juarez, Av Capitan Carlos Leon Gonzalez s/n, local A95, sala D, Colonia Penon de los Banos, Terminal 1, Delegacion Venustiano Carranza, 15620 Mexico, CDMX, Contact: Elizabeth Tovar Gaytan *Tel:* (0155) 2599 0911; (0155) 2599 0912 *E-mail:* elizabeth.tovar@fondodeculturaeconomica.com; Libreria Elsa Cecilia Frost, Calle Allende s/n, entre Juarez y Madero, Colonia Tlalpan Centro, Delegacion Tlalpan, 14000 Mexico, CDMX, Contact: Jose Maria Diaz Bimbela *Tel:* (0155) 54 85 84 32; (0155) 56 55 29 97; Libreria en el IPN, Av IPN s/n, esquina Wilfrido Massieu, instalaciones del IPN Zacatenco, Colonia Lindavista, Delegacion Gustavo A Madero, 07738 Mexico, CDMX, Contact: Laura Gonzalez *Tel:* (0155) 5119 2829; (0155) 5119 1192 *E-mail:* libreria.ipn@fondodeculturaeconomica.com; Libreria Trinidad Martinez Tarrago, Dento del Centro de Investigacion y Docencia Economicas, Carretera Mexico-Toluca Km, 16 1/2, 3655, Colonia Lomas de Santa Fe, Delegacion Alvaro Obregon, 01210 Mexico, CDMX, Contact: Michel Alavez *Tel:* (0155) 57 27 98 00 ext 2906; (0155) 57 27 98 00 ext 2910 *Fax:* (0155) 57 27 29 10 *E-mail:* libreria.cide@fondodeculturaeconomica.com; Libreria Un Paseo por los Libros, Pasaje Zocalo-Pino Suarez del Metro local 4, Colonia Centro Historico, Delegacion Cuauhtemoc, 06060 Mexico, CDMX, Contact: Marcelo

Tolentino Moroto *Tel:* (0155) 5522 3078; (0155) 5522 3016 *E-mail:* libreriaunpaseo@ fondodeculturaeconomica.com; Libreria Octavio Paz, Av Miguel Angel de Quevedo 115, Colonia Chimalistac, Delegacion Alvaro Obregon, 01070 Mexico, CDMX, Contact: Mauro Gutierrez Gonzalez *Tel:* (0155) 5480 1801; (0155) 5480 1803; (0155) 5480 1805; (0155) 5480 1806 *Fax:* (0155) 5480 1804 *E-mail:* libreria.octavio.paz@ fondodeculturaeconomica.com; Libreria Alfonso Reyes, Carretera Picacho-Ajusco 227, Colonia Bosques del Pedregal, Delegacion Tlalpan, 14738 Mexico, CDMX, Contact: Martin Herrera Velasco *Tel:* (0155) 5227 4681; (0155) 5227 4682 *Fax:* (0155) 5227 4682 *E-mail:* libreria.alfonso.reyes@ fondodeculturaeconomica.com; Libreria Victor L Urquidi, Camino al Ajusco 20, Colonia Pedregal de Santa Teresa, Delegacion Tlalpan, 10740 Mexico, CDMX, Contact: Julio Eduardo Legorreta *Tel:* (0155) 5449 3000 ext 1001 *E-mail:* jlegorreta@fondodeculturaeconomica. com; Libreria Isauro Martinez, Matamoros 240 Poniente, Colonia Centro, 27000 Torreon, COAH, Contact: Adriana Hermosillo Morales *Tel:* (01871) 716 62 61; (01871) 712 71 99 ext 112 *Fax:* (01871) 716 82 38; Libreria Efrain Huerta, Farallon 416, esquina Blvd, Campestre Fraccionamiento Jardines del Moral, 37160 Leon, GTO, Contact: Raul Ivan Garcia Martinez *Tel:* (01477) 779 24 39; Libreria Jose Luis Martinez, Av Chapultepec Sur 198, Colonia Americana, 44310 Guadalajara, JAL, Contact: Enedina Reyes Banicio *Tel:* (0133) 36 15 12 14; Libreria Elena Poniatowska Amor, Av Chimalhuacan s/n esquina Clavelero, Colonia Benito Juarez, 57000 Nezahualcoyotl, MEX, Contact: Rosa Jimenez Espinosa *Tel:* (0155) 57 16 90 70 ext 1724; Libreria Luis Gonzalez y Gonzalez, Francisco l Madero Oriente 369, Colonia Centro, 58000 Morelia, MICH, Contact: Maria Mercedes Sanchez *Tel:* (01443) 3133-992; Libreria Fray Servando Teresa de Mier, Calz San Pedro 222 Norte, Colonia Miravalle, 64660 Monterrey, NL, Contact: Juan Raymundo Cruz Leon *Tel:* (0181) 83 35 03 19; (0181) 83 35 03 71 *Fax:* (0181) 83 35 08 69; Libreria Ricardo Pozas, Calle Prospero C Vega 1 y 3 esquina, Av 16 de Septiembre, Colonia Centro, 76000 Santiago de Queretaro, QRO, Contact: Francisco Garcia Munoz *Tel:* (01442) 214 46 98; Libreria Huytlale, Av Juarez 7, Colonia Centro Historico, 90000 Tlaxcala, TLAX, Contact: Oswaldo Garcia Marquez *Tel:* (01246) 462 09 62
Shipping Address: Jose Maria Joaristi 205, Paraje San Juan, San Lorenzo, Iztapalapa, 09830 Mexico, CDMX

Impresora Galve SA, *imprint of* Editorial Avante SA de CV

Gil Editores
2 sur 6114, Colonia Bugambilias, 72580 Puebla, PUE
Tel: (01222) 2642980 *Fax:* (01222) 2640919
E-mail: info@gileditores.com
Web Site: www.gileditores.com
Key Personnel
Commercial Dir: Elier Lopez Gil
Subjects: Education, Pedagogy
ISBN Prefix(es): 978-968-7936

Editorial Gustavo Gili de Mexico SA
Valle de Bravo 21, Colonia El Mirador, 53050 Naucalpan de Juarez, MEX
Tel: (0155) 5560-6011 *Fax:* (0155) 5360-1453
E-mail: info@ggili.com.mx; ventas@ggili.com. mx; servicliente@ggili.com.mx
Web Site: ggili.com.mx

Subjects: Architecture & Interior Design, Art, Fashion, Photography
ISBN Prefix(es): 978-968-887; 978-968-6085
Associate Companies: Editorial Gustavo Gili Lda, Praceta Noticias da amadora 4-B, 2700-606 Amadora, Portugal *Tel:* 21 491 09 36 *Fax:* 21 491 09 37 *E-mail:* ggili@mail.telepac.pt *Web Site:* www.ggili.pt; Editorial Gustavo Gili SL, Rossello, 87-89, 08029 Barcelona, Spain *Tel:* 93 322 81 61 *Fax:* 93 322 92 05 *Web Site:* www.ggili.com
Distributor for Quarto Iberoamericana

Gomez Gomez Hermanos Editores S de RL+
Calzada San Lorenzo 37, Colonia Los Angeles, Iztapalapa, 09830 Mexico, CDMX
Tel: (0155) 56743548; (0155) 56727625; (0155) 55225903
Subjects: Education, Literature, Literary Criticism, Essays
ISBN Prefix(es): 978-968-7030
Subsidiaries: El Mejor Regalo un Libro SRL

Heidel Impresos SA de CV, *imprint of* Editorial Avante SA de CV

Ibcon SA+
Gutenberg 224, Colonia Anzures, 11590 Mexico, CDMX
Tel: (0155) 5255-4577
E-mail: ibcon@ibcon.com.mx
Web Site: www.ibcon.com.mx
Founded: 1954
Specialized directories (print, CD, online).
Subjects: Business, Computers, Government, Political Science, Health, Nutrition, Law, Library & Information Sciences, Marketing, Women's Studies
ISBN Prefix(es): 978-968-5097; 978-970-760
Number of titles published annually: 18 Print; 2 CD-ROM; 1 Online
Total Titles: 21 Print; 2 CD-ROM; 1 Online
Foreign Rep(s): Netlibrary (USA)

III, see Instituto Indigenista Interamericano (III)

INACIPE, see Instituto Nacional de Ciencias Penales (INACIPE)

INEGI, see Instituto Nacional de Estadistica, Geographia e Informatica

Instituto de Ecologia AC (INECOL)
Km 2.5 Carretera Antigua a Coatepec No 351, Congregacion El Haya, 91070 Xalapa, VER
Tel: (0228) 842 18 00 *Fax:* (0228) 818 78 09
E-mail: vadamb@ecologia.edu.mx
Web Site: www.inecol.edu.mx
Key Personnel
Dir General: Martin Ramon Aluja Schuneman Hofer *Tel:* (0228) 8186609 *E-mail:* martin. aluja@inecol.mx
Subjects: Biological Sciences, Biodiversity, Conservation, Ecology
ISBN Prefix(es): 978-970-709; 978-968-7863; 978-968-7213

Instituto de Investigaciones Dr Jose Maria Luis Mora
Plaza Valentin Gomez Farias No 12, Colonia San Juan Mixcoac, 03730 Mexico, CDMX
Tel: (0155) 5598-3777 *Fax:* (0155) 5563-7162
Web Site: www.mora.edu.mx
Key Personnel
Dir General: Dr Luis Jauregui *Tel:* (0155) 5598-3777 ext 1136 *E-mail:* ljauregui@mora.edu.mx
Subjects: Economics, Government, Political Science, History, Social Sciences, Sociology
ISBN Prefix(es): 978-968-6173; 978-968-6382; 978-968-6914; 978-970-684

Instituto Indigenista Interamericano (III)
(Inter-American Indian Institute)
Av de las Fuentes 106, Colonia Jardines del Pedregal, Delegacion Alvaro Obregon, 01900 Mexico, CDMX
Tel: (0155) 5595 8404
Founded: 1940
Specialize in the development of the Pueblo Indian in America.
Membership(s): OEA.
Subjects: Anthropology, History
ISBN Prefix(es): 978-968-6020
Number of titles published annually: 600 Print

Instituto Nacional de Antropologia e Historia (INAH) (National Institute of Anthropology & History)+
Insurgentes Sur No 421, Colonia Hipodromo, 06100 Mexico, CDMX
Tel: (0155) 4040-4624; (0155) 4040-4300
Web Site: www.inah.gob.mx
Key Personnel
Dir General: Maria Teresa Franco *Tel:* (0155) 4040-5001 *E-mail:* direccion.dgeneral@inah. gob.mx
Founded: 1822
Governmental institution devoted to the preservation, research & promotion of Mexican historical heritage.
Subjects: Americana, Regional, Anthropology, Antiques, Archaeology, Art, History, Language Arts, Linguistics, Music, Dance, Native American Studies, Photography, Social Sciences, Sociology, Conservation, Ethnography, Paleontology
ISBN Prefix(es): 978-968-6038; 978-968-6068; 978-968-6487
Number of titles published annually: 50 Print
Distributed by Educal Libros y Arte
Orders to: Coordinacion de Bienes y Servicios, Nautla 131-B, Colonia San Nicolas Tolentino, 09850 Mexico, CDMX, Contact: Rosa Laura Hernandez *Tel:* (0155) 5612-9861; (0155) 5612-7200 *Fax:* (0155) 5612-9861; (0155) 5612-7200 *E-mail:* lhernandez.cncpbs@inah. gob.mx *Web Site:* www.tiendadelmuseo.com.mx

Instituto Nacional de Ciencias Penales (INACIPE) (National Institute of Criminal Science)
Magisterio Nacional 113, Colonia Tlalpan Centro, Delegacion Tlalpan, 14000 Mexico, CDMX
Tel: (0155) 5487-1500
E-mail: publicaciones@inacipe.gob.mx; inacipe@ inacipe.gob.mx
Web Site: www.inacipe.gob.mx
Subjects: Criminology, Public Safety
ISBN Prefix(es): 978-968-5074; 978-968-6679

Instituto Nacional de Estadistica, Geographia e Informatica (National Institute of Statistics, Geography & Informatics)
Av Heroe de Nacozari Sur No 2301, Fracc Jardines del Parque, 20276 Aguascalientes, AGS
Tel: (01449) 910 53-00 (ext 5201)
Toll Free Tel: 800 111 4634
E-mail: atencion.usuarios@inegi.org.mx
Web Site: www.inegi.gob.mx
Key Personnel
Contact: Fabiola Morones *E-mail:* fabiola. morones@inegi.org.mx
Founded: 1983
Subjects: Developing Countries, Earth Sciences, Economics, Geography, Geology, Social Sciences, Sociology
ISBN Prefix(es): 978-970-13; 978-968-892

Instituto Nacional de Salud Publica
Communicacion Cientifica y Publicaciones, Universidad No 655, Colonia Santa Maria Ahuacatitlan, Cerrada Los Pinos y Caminera, 62100 Cuernavaca, MOR
Tel: (01777) 329 3000

E-mail: spm@insp.mx
Web Site: www.insp.mx/produccion-editorial.html
Key Personnel
Deputy Dir: Carlos Oropeza
Subjects: Health, Nutrition, Medicine, Nursing, Dentistry
ISBN Prefix(es): 978-607-511; 978-970-9874; 978-970-9097

Instituto Panamericano de Geografia e Historia (IPGH) (Pan American Institute of Geography & History)
Ex-Arzobispado 29, Colonia Observatorio, 11860 Mexico, CDMX
Mailing Address: Apdo 18879, 11870 Mexico, CDMX
Tel: (0155) 5277-5888; (0155) 5277-5791; (0155) 5515-1910
E-mail: publicaciones@ipgh.org; info@ipgh.org; secretariageneral@ipgh.org
Web Site: www.ipgh.org
Key Personnel
Secretary General: Dr Rodrigo Barriga Vargas
Publications: Prof Julieta Garcia
Founded: 1928
Specialized organization of the Organization of American States.
Subjects: Anthropology, Archaeology, Ethnicity, Geography, Geology, History, Regional Interests
ISBN Prefix(es): 978-968-6384; 978-84-8420

Instituto Politecnico Nacional
Revillagigedo 83, Colonia Centro, Delegacion Cuauhtemoc, 06070 Mexico, CDMX
Tel: (0155) 5729-6000; (0155) 5729-6000 ext 66538 (publications) *Fax:* (0155) 66515
E-mail: promocioneditorial@ipn.mx (publications)
Web Site: www.publicaciones.ipn.mx
Key Personnel
Dir: Adan Cruz Bencomo *Tel:* (0155) 5729-6000 ext 66508 *E-mail:* abenecomo@ipn.mx
ISBN Prefix(es): 978-970-36

Intersistemas SA de CV+
Aguiar y Seijas num 75, Lomas de Chapultepec, Delegacion Miguel Hidalgo, 11000 Mexico, CDMX
Tel: (0155) 55202073
E-mail: intersistemas@intersistemas.com.mx
Web Site: www.intersistemas.com.mx
Key Personnel
Mng Dir: Pedro Vera-Cervera
Founded: 1970
Subjects: Medicine, Nursing, Dentistry
ISBN Prefix(es): 978-970-655; 978-968-6116
Branch Office(s)
Guachipelin de Escazu Del BAC San Jose de Guachipelin, 900 metros oeste, Condominio Villa Toscana No 5, San Jose, Costa Rica
Tel: 2228 4487

El Inversionista Mexicano SA de CV
Colonia Valle del Campestre 330, San Pedro Garza Garcia, 66265 Monterrey, NL
E-mail: cuentas@elinversionista.com.mx; cservice@elinversionista.com.mx
Web Site: www.elinversionista.com.mx
Founded: 1969
Subjects: Finance

IPGH, see Instituto Panamericano de Geografia e Historia (IPGH)

IPN - Direccion de Publicaciones, see Instituto Politecnico Nacional

Ediciones Fiscales ISEF SA
Av del Taller 82, Colonia Transito, 06820 Mexico, CDMX

Tel: (0155) 5096 5100
E-mail: editorial@grupoisef.com.mx
Web Site: www.libreriaisef.com.mx
Key Personnel
Dir General: Efrain Lechuga Santillan
Founded: 1920
Subjects: Accounting, Business, Finance, Taxes
ISBN Prefix(es): 978-968-6193; 978-968-7427; 978-970-676

Editorial Itaca
Calle Pirana 16, Colonia Del Mar, Delegacion Tlahuac, 13270 Mexico, CDMX
Tel: (0155) 5840-5452
E-mail: itaca00@hotmail.com; itaca.editorial@gmail.com
Web Site: editorialitaca.com.mx
Key Personnel
Dir General: David Moreno Soto
Founded: 1983
Subjects: Art, Fiction, Geography, Geology, History, Literature, Literary Criticism, Essays, Philosophy
ISBN Prefix(es): 978-968-6250

Editorial Iztaccihuatl SA de CV+
Miguel E Schultz 21, San Rafael, 06470 Mexico, DF
Tel: (0155) 57051063
E-mail: iztaventas@editorializtaccihuatl.com.mx
Founded: 1946
Subjects: Cookery, Literature, Literary Criticism, Essays, Wine & Spirits
ISBN Prefix(es): 978-968-421

Janibi Editores SA de CV
Martires De Rio Blanco 239, Xochimilco, Jardines Del Sur, 16050 Mexico, DF
Tel: (0155) 5675-5350
Founded: 1975
Subjects: Fashion, Music, Dance

Editorial Joaquin Mortiz SA de CV+
Member of Grupo Planeta
Av Presidente Masaryk, 111, 2º Piso, Colonia Chapultepec Morales, Delegacion Migul Hidalgo, 11570 Mexico, CDMX
Tel: (0155) 3000-6200 *Fax:* (0155) 3000-6257
E-mail: info@planeta.com.mx
Web Site: www.editorialplaneta.com.mx
Founded: 1962
Subjects: Fiction, History, Literature, Literary Criticism, Essays, Nonfiction (General), Philosophy, Poetry, Psychology, Psychiatry, Social Sciences, Sociology
ISBN Prefix(es): 978-968-27
Associate Companies: Editorial Planeta SA, Spain
Warehouse: Ave Gavilan 3, Bodega 1 & 2, Colonia Guadalupe del Mora, Delegacion Iztapalapa, 09360 Mexico, CDMX
Orders to: Editorial Planeta Mexicana

Jorale Editores SA de CV
Aniceto Ortega-D 817, Colonia del Valle, 03100 Mexico, CDMX
Tel: (0155) 5555-8776; (0155) 5555-8777 *Fax:* (0155) 5641-1223
E-mail: info@jorale-editores.com.mx; info@joraleeditores.com
Web Site: www.jorale-editores.com.mx; joraleeditores.com
Key Personnel
Dir General: Jorge Cleto Ruiz
   E-mail: jorgecleto@jorale-editores.com.mx
Editorial Dir: Guadalupe Ortiz Elguea
   E-mail: editorial@jorale-editores.com.mx
Founded: 1992
Subjects: Government, Political Science, History, Technology
ISBN Prefix(es): 978-968-5863

Editorial Jus SA de CV+
Donceles 66, Colonia Centro Mexico, 06010 Mexico, CDMX
Tel: (0155) 12 03 37 81
E-mail: ventas@jus.com.mx; contacto@jus.com.mx
Web Site: jus.com.mx
Founded: 1942
Subjects: Biblical Studies, Economics, Education, Fiction, Government, Political Science, History, Law, Literature, Literary Criticism, Essays, Philosophy, Religion - Catholic, Self-Help, Social Sciences, Sociology, Theology
ISBN Prefix(es): 978-968-423
Subsidiaries: Distribuidora Editorial Jus SA

Ediciones Larousse SA de CV+
Renacimiento 180, Colonia San Juan Tlihuaca, Delegacion Azcapotzalco, 02400 Mexico, CDMX
Tel: (0155) 1102 1300
E-mail: larousse@larousse.com.mx
Web Site: www.larousse.com.mx
Founded: 1965
Subjects: Education, English as a Second Language
ISBN Prefix(es): 978-970-607; 978-968-6042; 978-968-6147; 978-968-6347; 978-970-22
Parent Company: Grupo Havas
Warehouse: Acalotenco 94-1, Mexico, CDMX

Lasser Press Mexicana SA de CV
Praga 56 P H, Colonia Juarez, 06600 Mexico, CDMX
Tel: (0155) 55112312 *Fax:* (0155) 55112576
Key Personnel
Dir: Guillermo Menendez Castro
Founded: 1972
Subjects: Biography, Memoirs, Literature, Literary Criticism, Essays, Nonfiction (General)
ISBN Prefix(es): 978-968-458; 978-968-7063

Lectorum Coediciones, *imprint of* Editorial Lectorum SA de CV

Editorial Lectorum SA de CV
Centeno No 79-A, Colonia Granjas Esmeralda, 09810 Mexico, CDMX
Tel: (0155) 5581-3202 *Fax:* (0155) 5646-6892
E-mail: ventas@lectorum.com.mx
Web Site: www.lectorum.com.mx
Key Personnel
Dir General: Porfirio Romo Lizarraga
Founded: 1993
Subjects: Art, Fiction, Geography, Geology, History, Literature, Literary Criticism, Essays, Religion - Other, Science (General), Sports, Athletics
ISBN Prefix(es): 978-968-5270; 978-968-7748; 978-970-732
Imprints: Flauta De Pan; Lectorum Coediciones; Lectorum Marea Alta; Otras Inquisiciones; Sin Limites
Distributed by Ediciones Alpe; Ediciones El Ateneo; Ediciones Atlantida; Audiolibros; Ediciones Biblos; Budo Internacional (DVDs); Editorial Cenzontle; Editorial Cidcli; Ediciones Clarentiana; Ediciones La Cruz; Cuatro Camino Ediciones; Ediciones Distal; Ediciones Edico; Equipo Difusor; Ediciones La Flor; Fundalectura; Gilavil Y/O Bienes La Conica; Ediciones Gran Aldea; Hara Press; Intercomputo; Ediciones Keller; Ediciones Lanai; LD Books; Editorial Llewellyn; Longseller; Mexram Ediciones; MTM Ediciones; Porcia Ediciones; Publicaciones Cruz O; Self-Realization; Libreria Sigal; Taller Del Exito; Ediciones Teohua; Editorial Tyndale; Ediciones Ugerman

Lectorum Marea Alta, *imprint of* Editorial Lectorum SA de CV

Editorial Libra SA de CV+
Member of Grupo Editorial Scorpio
Calle Melesio Morales No 16, Colonia Guadalupe
Inn, 01020 Mexico, CDMX
Tel: (0155) 5664-1454 *Fax:* (0155) 5660-5561
Founded: 1984
Subjects: Astrology, Occult, Child Care & Devel-
opment, Cookery, Education, How-to, Humor,
Language Arts, Linguistics, LGBTQ, Nonfic-
tion (General), Self-Help, Women's Studies
ISBN Prefix(es): 978-970-606; 978-968-6636

Libraria
Pitagoras 1143-E, Colonia del Valle, 03100 Mex-
ico, CDMX
Tel: (0155) 5335 1213 *Fax:* (0155) 5335 1214
Key Personnel
Dir General: Tomas Granados Salinas
Subjects: History, Mathematics
ISBN Prefix(es): 978-968-5374

Limusa, *imprint of* Editorial Limusa

Editorial Limusa+
Balderas No 95, Colonia Centro, 06040 Mexico,
CDMX
Tel: (0155) 51300700 *Toll Free Tel:* 800 706 91
00 (Mexico only); 800 703 75 00 (Mexico
only) *Fax:* (0155) 55122903; (0155) 55109415
E-mail: limusa@noriegaeditores.com
Web Site: www.noriega.com.mx
Key Personnel
Chairman of the Board: Carlos Noriega Milera
Chairman & Chief Executive Officer: Carlos Nor-
iega Arias
Vice President & Editorial Dir: Miguel Noriega
Arias
Founded: 1954
Edit, publish & distribute scholarly, technical, sci-
entific & educational books.
Subjects: Accounting, Agriculture, Art, Astron-
omy, Automotive, Behavioral Sciences, Bio-
logical Sciences, Business, Career Develop-
ment, Chemistry, Chemical Engineering, Child
Care & Development, Civil Engineering, Com-
munications, Computer Science, Computers,
Cookery, Crafts, Games, Hobbies, Criminology,
Disability, Special Needs, Earth Sciences, Eco-
nomics, Education, Electronics, Electrical Engineering, Energy, Engineering (General), En-
vironmental Studies, Fashion, Finance, Geog-
raphy, Geology, Government, Political Science,
Health, Nutrition, How-to, Human Relations,
Labor, Industrial Relations, Law, Management,
Marketing, Mathematics, Mechanical Engineer-
ing, Medicine, Nursing, Dentistry, Philosophy,
Physical Sciences, Physics, Psychology, Psy-
chiatry, Public Administration, Real Estate,
Science (General), Social Sciences, Sociology,
Sports, Athletics, Technology, Transportation,
Travel & Tourism, Veterinary Science
ISBN Prefix(es): 978-968-18; 978-607-05
Number of titles published annually: 180 Print;
10 E-Book
Total Titles: 2,100 Print; 50 E-Book
Imprints: Limusa (technical & scientific textbooks
for all educational levels); Limusa-Wiley (col-
lege textbooks); Nori (preschool & primary
education); Noriega Editores (illustrated books)
Subsidiaries: Noriega Editores de Colombia; Nor-
iega Editores de Guatemala; Noriega Editores
de Venezuela
Branch Office(s)
E Robles Gil No 437, Colonia Americana SJ,
44290 Guadalajara, JAL
Plaza Comercial Tecnologico, Av del Estado 120
L 7, Col Tecnologico, 64700 Monterrey, NL

Limusa-Wiley, *imprint of* Editorial Limusa

Longman, *imprint of* Pearson Educacion de
Mexico SA de CV

Macmillan Publishers SA de CV
Subsidiary of Macmillan Publishers Ltd
Insurgentes Sur 1886, Colonia Florida, Delega-
cion Alvaro Obregon, 01030 Mexico, CDMX
Tel: (0155) 5482 2200 *Toll Free Tel:* 1800 00 64
100
E-mail: elt@grupomacmillan.com
Web Site: www.macmillan.com.mx; www.
grupomacmillan.com
Founded: 1982
English language teaching publishers.
Subjects: English Language Teaching
ISBN Prefix(es): 978-968-6589; 978-968-7188;
978-968-7380; 978-970-650; 978-970-662
Ultimate Parent Company: Verlagsgruppe Georg
Von Holtzbrinck

Mantis Editores
Rio Atotonilco 1038 uno, Coto Residencial Ato-
tonilco, Colonia Atlas, 44870 Guadalajara, JAL
Tel: (033) 3657-7864
E-mail: mantiseditores@gmail.com
Web Site: www.mantiseditores.com
Key Personnel
Editorial Dir: Luis Armenta Malpica
General Coordination: Juan Castaneda Arciniega
Editorial Coordination: Elias Carlo Salazar
Specialize in poetry.
Subjects: Literature, Literary Criticism, Essays,
Poetry
ISBN Prefix(es): 978-968-7859

Editorial El Manual Moderno SA de CV+
Av Sonora 206, Colonia Hipodromo, 06100 Mex-
ico, CDMX
Tel: (0155) 5265 1100 *Fax:* (0155) 5265 1135
E-mail: info@manualmoderno.com
Web Site: www.manualmoderno.com
Key Personnel
General Dir: Norma Guevara *Tel:* (0155) 5265
1147 *E-mail:* norma.guevara@manualmoderno.
com
Editorial Dir: Rosario Garcia *Tel:* (0155) 5265
1102 *E-mail:* rosario.garcia@manualmoderno.
com
Business Manager: Adriana Romero *Tel:* (0155)
5265 1125 *E-mail:* adriana.romero@
manualmoderno.com
Customer Service Manager: Lina Roa *Tel:* (0155)
5265 1132 *E-mail:* lina.roa@manualmoderno.
com
Founded: 1958
Membership(s): International Association of STM
Publishers.
Subjects: Biological Sciences, Health, Nutrition,
Medicine, Nursing, Dentistry, Psychology, Psy-
chiatry, Self-Help, Veterinary Science
ISBN Prefix(es): 978-968-426; 978-970-729
Branch Office(s)
Manual Moderno Colombia Ltda, Carrera 12-
A No 79-03/05, Bogota, Colombia *Tel:* (01)
2110519 *Fax:* (01) 2126127
Distributed by Editorial Atlante Argentina SRL
(Argentina); Ediciones Nueva Vision CA
(Venezuela); Ediciones Tecnicas Paraguayas
(Paraguay); Ediciones Trecho (Uruguay)
Distributor for Appleton & Lange (Mexico); At-
lante Argenti (Mexico); Celsus (Mexico); Edi-
ciones Diaz de Santos, Medicina (Latin Amer-
ica); Harcourt Brace/Mosby-Doyma Libros
(Mexico); Springer Verlag Iberica (Latin Amer-
ica)

Mass + Medios, *imprint of* Medios y Medios SA
de CV

**McGraw-Hill Interamericana Editores SA de
CV+**
Prol Paseo de la Reforma 1015 torre A piso 17,
Colonia Santa Fe, 01376 Mexico, CDMX
Tel: (0155) 1500 5010 (customer service)
Toll Free Tel: 1800 228 4300 (customer ser-

vice) *Fax:* (0155) 1500 5050; (0155) 1500
5051 (customer service)
E-mail: mx_universidades@mcgraw-hill.com;
mxcsalud@mcgraw-hill.com; ebooks-la@
mcgraw-hill.com; mx_escolar@mcgraw-hill.
com; mx_elt@mcgraw-hill.com
Web Site: www.mcgraw-hill.com.mx
Key Personnel
Mng Dir: Carlos Rios
Founded: 1966
Subjects: Business, Engineering (General), Mathe-
matics, Public Administration, Social Sciences,
Sociology
ISBN Prefix(es): 978-968-25; 978-968-451; 978-
968-422; 978-968-6046; 978-970-10

Medios Publicitarios Mexicanos SA de CV
Av Eugenia No 811, Colonia Del Valle, 03100
Mexico, CDMX
Tel: (0155) 55-23-33-42; (0155) 55-23-33-46
Fax: (0155) 55-23-33-79
E-mail: suscripciones@mpm.com.mx;
administracion@mpm.com.mx
Web Site: www.mpm.com.mx
Key Personnel
General Manager: Fernando Villamil Avila
E-mail: fernando.villamil@mpm.com.mx
Editorial Manager: Sonia Villamil Avila
E-mail: sonia.villamil@mpm.com.mx
Founded: 1958
Publish directories with rates & data of advertis-
ing media.
Subjects: Advertising, Marketing
Total Titles: 12 Print
Associate Companies: SRDS LP, 1700 Higgins
Rd, Des Plaines, IL 60018, United States

Medios y Medios SA de CV
Universidad 783-4, Colonia Del Valle, Delegacion
Benito Juarez, 03100 Mexico, CDMX
Tel: (0155) 56-01-85-13
Founded: 1993
Subjects: Advertising, Radio, TV
Imprints: Directorio; Mass + Medios

Mercametrica Ediciones SA
Av Universidad 1621, piso 3, Colonia Hacienda
de Guadalupe Chimalistac, 01050 Mexico,
CDMX
Tel: (0155) 56-61-62-93; (0155) 56-61-92-86
Web Site: www.mercametrica.com
Key Personnel
President: Ignacio Gomez
Founded: 1976
Subjects: Economics, Management, Marketing
ISBN Prefix(es): 978-968-7267
Branch Office(s)
Santa Rosa 5010, Colonia Santa Isabel, 67184
Guadalupe, NL, Contact: Sr Raul Resendez
Tel: (081) 83-60-12-35

Editores Mexicanos Unidos SA de CV (EMU)
Luis Gonzalez Obregon, No 5, Colonia Centro,
06020 Mexico, DF
E-mail: atencionaclientes@editmusa.com.mx
Web Site: www.grupoamatl.com
Key Personnel
Contact: Lidia Hernandez
Founded: 1954
Subjects: Art, Astrology, Occult, Communica-
tions, Cookery, English as a Second Language,
Fiction, Health, Nutrition, Literature, Liter-
ary Criticism, Essays, Music, Dance, Myster-
ies, Suspense, Nonfiction (General), Poetry,
Religion - Other, Self-Help, Sports, Athletics,
Mythology, Nature, New Age
ISBN Prefix(es): 978-968-15
Parent Company: Grupo Amatl

MPM-Directorios Publicitarios, see Medios Publicitarios Mexicanos SA de CV

Impresora Multiple SA, *imprint of* Editorial Avante SA de CV

El Naranjo Ediciones
Cerrada Nicolas Bravo 21-1, Colonia San Jeronimo Lidice, 10200 Mexico, CDMX
Tel: (0155) 5652-1974 *Fax:* (0155) 5652-1974
E-mail: elnaranjo@edicioneselnaranjo.com.mx
Web Site: www.edicioneselnaranjo.com.mx
Subjects: Literature, Literary Criticism, Essays
ISBN Prefix(es): 978-968-5389

Naves Internacional de Ediciones SA+
Pestalozzi No 810, Del Valle, 03100 Mexico, DF
Tel: (0155) 5523 4179; (0155) 5543 2848
Fax: (0155) 5682 2506
Key Personnel
Dir: Pablo Llaca
Founded: 1981
Subjects: Advertising, Architecture & Interior Design, Art, Cookery, Photography
Associate Companies: Ramon Llaca y Cia SA
Distributor for Celeste; Folio; Idea Books; Juventud; Naturart; Tursen
Book Club(s): Club de Editores, AC

Nori, *imprint of* Editorial Limusa

Noriega Editores, *imprint of* Editorial Limusa

Nostra Ediciones SA de CV
Imprint of Grupo Editorial Nostra
Av Revolucion 1181, 7 mo p, Colonia Merced Gomez, 03930 Mexico, CDMX
Tel: (0155) 5554-7030
E-mail: contacto@nostraediciones.com
Web Site: www.nostraediciones.com
Key Personnel
Dir General: Mauricio Volpi Corona
Mng Editor: Sandra Ferrer Alarcon
Commercial Manager: Antonio Marron
Subjects: Economics, Education, Environmental Studies, Fiction, Geography, Geology, Government, Political Science, Health, Nutrition, History, Law, Literature, Literary Criticism, Essays, Poetry, Social Sciences, Sociology, Ecology, Entertainment, Statistics
ISBN Prefix(es): 978-968-5447; 978-607-8237
Branch Office(s)
Nostra Ediciones SL, Plaza de America, 2-8° E, 36211 Vigo, Pontevedra, Spain, Contact: Sonia Formoso Aldir *E-mail:* sonia@nostraediciones.com

Editorial Nova SA de CV+
Luis Kuhne 55-B, Colonia Las Aguilas, 01710 Mexico, CDMX
Tel: (0155) 5337-2200; (0155) 5680-2150
Toll Free Tel: 1 800 823 4844 *Fax:* (0155) 5337-2222
E-mail: ventas@boletinindustrial.com
Web Site: www.boletinindustrial.com
Key Personnel
President: Humberto Valades Diaz
Founded: 1983
Industry B2B publications & directories in Mexico.
Subjects: Advertising, Industrial Advertising & Directories
Foreign Rep(s): Jose Valades (Canada, USA)

Editorial Nueva Palabra Sa de CV
Lago Chalco No 184, Colonia Anahuac, 11320 Mexico, CDMX
Tel: (0155) 52602275; (0155) 52606542
Fax: (0155) 52602275; (0155) 52606542
Web Site: www.palabraediciones.com

Founded: 1981
Subjects: Religion - Catholic
ISBN Prefix(es): 978-968-6460; 978-968-7515
Associate Companies: Cosmos Libros SRL, Av Callao 737, 1023 Buenos Aires, Argentina

Oceano Ambar, *imprint of* Editorial Oceano de Mexico SA de CV

Editorial Oceano de Mexico SA de CV
Blvd Manuel Avila Camacho, No 76, Piso 10, Colonia Lomas de Chapultepec, 11000 Mexico, CDMX
Tel: (0155) 91785100
E-mail: info@oceano.com.mx
Web Site: www.oceano.mx
Subjects: Biography, Memoirs, Drama, Theater, Education, History, Literature, Literary Criticism, Essays, Poetry, Religion - Other, Science (General)
ISBN Prefix(es): 978-968-6321; 978-970-651
Imprints: Circe; Oceano Ambar; Oceano El lado oscuro; Oceano Expres; Oceano Gran Travesia; Oceano Idiomas; Oceano Travesia
Distributor for El Aleph; Arkano Books; Cahiers du cinema; Corimbo; Dojo Ediciones; Dolmen Editorial; Dolmen expres; Dvomo Ediciones; La Factoria de ideas; La Factoria de Ideas expres; Gaia Ediciones; Global Rhythm; El grano de mostaza; Gulaab; La Gunilla Editores; Jaguar; Karma 7; Kraken; Peace of God Eu; Peninsula; Phaidon; Phaidon Espanol; Rigden Institut Gestalt; Salamandra; Salamandra Graphic; Salsa Books; Serieve; Sitesa; SRF; Taller del exito; Taller del exito expres; Turner; Usborne; Viceversa
Foreign Rep(s): Baker & Taylor Publisher Services (Puerto Rico, USA)

Oceano El lado oscuro, *imprint of* Editorial Oceano de Mexico SA de CV

Oceano Expres, *imprint of* Editorial Oceano de Mexico SA de CV

Oceano Gran Travesia, *imprint of* Editorial Oceano de Mexico SA de CV

Oceano Idiomas, *imprint of* Editorial Oceano de Mexico SA de CV

Oceano Travesia, *imprint of* Editorial Oceano de Mexico SA de CV

Oniro, *imprint of* Editorial Paidos Mexicana

Organizacion Cultural LP SA de CV+
Ozumba No 50, Colonia El Conde, 53500 Naucalpan de Juarez, MEX
Tel: (0155) 53584721; (0155) 53584761; (0155) 53570279
Subjects: Accounting, Astronomy, Biological Sciences, Child Care & Development, Computer Science, Cookery, Management, Sports, Athletics
ISBN Prefix(es): 978-968-6007; 978-970-01

Otras Inquisiciones, *imprint of* Editorial Lectorum SA de CV

Oxford University Press Mexico Sa de CV
Division of Oxford University Press
Antonio Caso, 142, Colonia San Rafael, Delegacion Cuauhtemoc, 06470 Mexico, CDMX
Tel: (0155) 5592 4277; (0155) 5592 5600
Fax: (0155) 5705 3738; (0155) 5535 6820
E-mail: atencionaclientes@oup.com
Web Site: global.oup.com/mexico
Founded: 1994

Subjects: Business, Law, Psychology, Psychiatry
ISBN Prefix(es): 978-968-6199; 978-968-6356; 978-970-613
Branch Office(s)
Calderon de la Barca 76, Arcos Vallarta, Guadalajara, JAL *Tel:* (0133) 3826 2095

Editorial Paidos Mexicana
Av Presidente Masarik 111, piso 2, Colonia Chapultepec Morales, Delegacion Miguel Hidalgo, 11570 Mexico, CDMX
Tel: (0155) 3000-6200; (0155) 3000-6202 (sales); (0155) 3000-6203 (sales); (0155) 3000-6204 (sales)
E-mail: ventaspaidos@paidos.com.mx
Web Site: www.paidos.com.mx
Founded: 1945
Subjects: Anthropology, Communications, Education, Film, Video, Philosophy, Psychology, Psychiatry, Social Sciences, Sociology, Humanities
ISBN Prefix(es): 978-968-853
Imprints: Ariel; Critica; Oniro
Warehouse: Carr Mexico-Queretaro km 34.5 Nave 5, Colonia Ejido, 54730 Tultitlan, MEX
Tel: (0155) 22 39 50 24 *Fax:* (0155) 22 39 50 25

Panorama Editorial SA de CV+
Imprint of Grupo Editorial Nostra
Av Revolucion 1181, 7 mo p, Colonia Merced Gomez, 06470 Mexico, CDMX
Tel: (0155) 5554 7030
E-mail: contacto@nostraediciones.com
Web Site: www.nostraediciones.com/nostra
Key Personnel
Dir General: Mauricio Volpi Corona
Mng Editor: Sandra Ferrer Alarcon
Commercial Manager: Antonio Marron
Founded: 1979
Subjects: Business, Health, Nutrition, History, Human Relations, Humor, Inspirational, Spirituality, Management, Medicine, Nursing, Dentistry, Regional Interests, Self-Help, Travel & Tourism, Entertainment, Gastronomy
ISBN Prefix(es): 978-968-38; 978-607-452; 978-607-8237
Number of titles published annually: 100 Print
Total Titles: 700 Print

Libreria Parroquial de Claveria SA de CV+
Floresta No 79, Colonia Calveria, Azcapotzalco, 02080 Mexico, DF
Tel: (0155) 5399-5716; (0155) 5386-1719; (0155) 5399-4975; (0155) 5386-0443 *Toll Free Tel:* 01 800 536 9536
Web Site: www.parroquial.com.mx
Founded: 1964
Subjects: Religion - Catholic
ISBN Prefix(es): 978-968-442

Editorial Patria SA de CV+
Renacimiento 180, Colonia San Juan Tlihuaca, Azcapotzalco, 02400 Mexico, CDMX
Tel: (0155) 5354 9100 *Fax:* (0155) 5354 9109
E-mail: info@editorialpatria.com.mx
Web Site: www.editorialpatria.com.mx
Key Personnel
Mng Dir: Miguel Cruz
Founded: 1933
Subjects: Biography, Memoirs, History, How-to, Literature, Literary Criticism, Essays, Philosophy
ISBN Prefix(es): 978-968-6054; 978-968-39
Parent Company: Grupo Editorial Patria
Associate Companies: CECSA; Publicaciones Cultural; Nueva Imagen; Promexa

Grupo Editorial Patria
Renacimiento 180, Colonia San Juan Tlihuaca, Azcapotzalco, 02400 Mexico, CDMX
Tel: (0155) 5354 9100 *Fax:* (0155) 5354 9109

E-mail: info@editorialpatria.com.mx
Web Site: www.editorialpatria.com.mx
Founded: 1933
Subjects: Economics, Education, Engineering
(General), Management, Science (General)
ISBN Prefix(es): 978-970-817; 978-607-438
Number of titles published annually: 210 Print
Parent Company: Hachette Livre

Editorial Pax Mexico SA+
Member of Grupo Editorial Pax
Av Cuauhtemoc 1430, Colonia Santa Cruz
Atoyac, 03310 Mexico, CDMX
Tel: (0155) 56 05 76 77 *Fax:* (0155) 56 05 76 00
E-mail: editorialpax@editorialpax.com
Web Site: www.editorialpax.com
Key Personnel
Publisher: Gerardo Gally
Editorial Dir: Maria de Lourdes Arellano Bolio
Commercial Dir: Francisco Martinez Silva
Foreign Trade Manager: Virginia Santiago Torres
Founded: 1930
Subjects: Architecture & Interior Design, Busi-
ness, Career Development, Cookery, Drama,
Theater, Education, Health, Nutrition, How-to,
Psychology, Psychiatry, Religion - Other, Alter-
native Medicine, Parenting, Sexuality
ISBN Prefix(es): 978-968-461; 978-968-860
Subsidiaries: Arbol Editorial SA

Pearson Educacion de Mexico SA de CV
Calle Antonio Dovali Jaime No 70, piso 6, Torre
B, Sante Fe, Edificio Corporativo Samara, Del-
egacion Alvaro Obregon, 01210 Mexico, DF
Tel: (0155) 5387-0700
E-mail: soporte@pearson.com
Web Site: www.pearsoneducacion.net; www.
mypearsonshop.com.mx
Founded: 1984
Subjects: Art, Biological Sciences, Business,
Chemistry, Chemical Engineering, Computer
Science, Computers, Economics, Education,
History, Language Arts, Linguistics, Manage-
ment, Mathematics, Physics, Psychology, Psy-
chiatry, Science (General), Securities, Sports,
Athletics, Technology
ISBN Prefix(es): 978-968-444; 978-968-880; 978-
970-17
Total Titles: 700 Print
Parent Company: Pearson PLC
Imprints: Addison Wesley; Allyn & Bacon; Long-
man; Penguin Readers; Prentice Hall His-
panoamericana; Scott Foresman; Silver Bur-
dette Ginn
Branch Office(s)
Av Ricardo Margain N, 575, Colonia Santa En-
gracia, 66267 San Pedro Garza Garcia, Nuevo
Leon *Tel:* (0181) 8676-2680
Av Patria N° 2085, Fraccionamiento Puerta de
Hierro, Piso 1, Andares Corporativo Patria,
45116 Zapopan, Jalisco *Tel:* (0133) 3122-4096
Foreign Rep(s): Baker & Taylor Publisher Ser-
vices (Canada, USA)
Warehouse: Calle Negra Modelo No 12 & 12B,
Fracc Industrial Alce Blanco, 53770 Naucal-
pan de Juarez *Tel:* (05) 363 0842 *Fax:* (05) 363
4579

Penguin Random House Grupo Editorial
Blvd Miguel de Cervantes Saavedra No 301,
Colonia Granada, 11520 Mexico, CDMX
Tel: (0155) 3067-8400
Web Site: www.megustaleer.com.mx
Key Personnel
Marketing Dir: Pilar Gordoa
Subjects: Business, Fiction, Government, Political
Science, History, Literature, Literary Criticism,
Essays, Mysteries, Suspense, Religion - Other,
Romance, Self-Help, Sports, Athletics
ISBN Prefix(es): 978-968-5958
Parent Company: Penguin Random House

Penguin Readers, *imprint of* Pearson Educacion
de Mexico SA de CV

Ediciones Pentagrama SA de CV
Coahuila 49, Colonia Roma, Delegacion Cuauhte-
moc, 06700 Mexico, CDMX
Tel: (0155) 5564-3877; (0155) 5564-3894; (0155)
5564-3618
E-mail: ediciones@pentagrama.com.mx
Web Site: www.pentagrama.com.mx
Key Personnel
Dir: Modesto Lopez
Founded: 1981
Subjects: Music, Dance
ISBN Prefix(es): 978-968-5044

Petra Ediciones SA de CV
El Carmen 268-2, Colonia Camino Real, 45040
Zapopan, JAL
Tel: (033) 3629 0832 *Fax:* (033) 3629 3376
E-mail: petra@petraediciones.com; ventas@
petraediciones.com
Web Site: www.petraediciones.com
Key Personnel
Dir General: Peggy Espinosa
Subjects: Art, Drama, Theater, Literature, Literary
Criticism, Essays, Photography
ISBN Prefix(es): 978-968-6445; 978-607-7646

Editorial Planeta Mexicana SA de CV
Member of Grupo Planeta
Av Presidente Masarik No 111, 2 do, Piso, Colo-
nia Chapultepec Morales, Delegacion Miguel
Hidalgo, 11570 Mexico, CDMX
Tel: (0155) 3000-6200 *Fax:* (0155) 3000-6257
E-mail: info@planeta.com.mx
Web Site: www.editorialplaneta.com.mx
Founded: 1977
Subjects: Fiction, History, Nonfiction (General),
Psychology, Psychiatry, Social Sciences, Soci-
ology
ISBN Prefix(es): 978-968-6640; 978-970-9031
Imprints: Espasa Calpe Mexicana

Plaza y Valdes Editores+
Manuel Maria Contreras, 73, Colonia San Rafael,
06470 Mexico, CDMX
Tel: (0155) 50972070 *Fax:* (0155) 50972070
E-mail: informacion@plazayvaldes.com
Web Site: www.plazayvaldes.com
Founded: 1987
This publisher has indicated that 50% of their
product line is author subsidized.
Membership(s): Mexican Publishing Association.
Subjects: Agriculture, Anthropology, Archaeol-
ogy, Communications, Public Administration,
Religion - Buddhist, Science (General), Science
Fiction, Fantasy, Social Sciences, Sociology,
Humanities
ISBN Prefix(es): 978-968-856; 978-970-722; 978-
607-402
Total Titles: 3,000 Print
U.S. Office(s): Libros Sin Fronteras, PO Box
2085, Olympia, WA 98507-2085, United States
Tel: 206-357-4332 *Fax:* 206-357-4332
Foreign Rep(s): Baker & Taylor (USA); The
Bilingual Publications Co (USA); Libreria El
Campus-Grupo Hengar SA (Panama); Interna-
cional libros Miguel Concha SA (Chile); Di-
fusora Cultural Mexico-Libreria Mexico (Hon-
duras); EnRed-Arte, Libros en la Web (Mex-
ico); Latin American Book Store (USA); Li-
breria Lehmann SA (Costa Rica); Livraria do
Maneco (Brazil); Libreria Mascara (Argentina);
Libreria Mateca (Dominican Republic); Nuevos
Libros (Nicaragua); La Odisea Distribucion e
importacion de libros (El Salvador); Plaza y
Janes Editores Colombia SA (Colombia); Distribuidora Venezolana del Libro (Venezuela);
Libreria Yachaywasi (Bolivia)
Bookshop(s): Insurgentes sur 32, Colonia Juarez,
06600 Mexico, CDMX

Distribution Center: EnRed-Arte, Libros en
la Web, Av 602 92, 07970 Mexico, CDMX
Tel: (0155) 68290789 *E-mail:* ventas@enred-
arte.com *Web Site:* enred-arte.com

Editorial Porrua SA de CV
Av Republica de Argentina No 17, Colonia Cen-
tro, 06020 Mexico, CDMX
Tel: (0155) 5704 7506; (0155) 58 04 35 35
Toll Free Tel: 01 800 019 23 00
E-mail: atencion_a_clientesp3@porrua.com
Web Site: www.porrua.mx
Founded: 1900
Subjects: Computer Science, Cookery, Earth Sci-
ences, Engineering (General), History, Liter-
ature, Literary Criticism, Essays, Medicine,
Nursing, Dentistry, Religion - Other, Science
(General), Sports, Athletics, Travel & Tourism
ISBN Prefix(es): 978-968-432; 978-968-452; 978-
970-07
Orders to: Libreria de Porrua Hnos y Cia SA,
Apdo M-7990, Colonia Central, Argentina,
Mexico, CDMX

Editorial Miguel Angel Porrua
Chihuahua No 34, Tizapan, San Angel, Del Al-
varo Obregon, 01000 Mexico, DF
Tel: (0155) 5550 4225; (0155) 5550 4194
Web Site: www.maporrua.com.mx
Key Personnel
Dir General: Miguel Angel Porrua
Editorial Coordinator: Gabriela Pardo Avila
E-mail: gabrielapardo@maporrua.com.mx
Founded: 1978
Subjects: Anthropology, Architecture & Interior
Design, Biological Sciences, Economics, Ed-
ucation, Geography, Geology, Government,
Political Science, History, Literature, Literary
Criticism, Essays, Medicine, Nursing, Den-
tistry, Science (General), Social Sciences, Soci-
ology, Technology
ISBN Prefix(es): 978-970-701; 978-968-842
Bookshop(s): Amargura 4, San Angel, Del Alvaro
Obregon, 01000 Mexico, DF *Tel:* (0155) 5616
2705; (0155) 5616 0071 *Fax:* (0155) 5550
2555

**Ediciones Cientificas La Prensa Medica
Mexicana SA de CV+**
Paseo de las Facultades 29, Colonia Copilco Uni-
versidad Coyoacan, 04360 Mexico, CDMX
Tel: (0155) 56589155; (0155) 56589892
Founded: 1945
Membership(s): National Chamber of the Mexi-
can Editorial Industry.
Subjects: Biological Sciences, Education,
Medicine, Nursing, Dentistry, Social Sciences,
Sociology, Veterinary Science
ISBN Prefix(es): 978-968-435

Prentice Hall Hispanoamericana, *imprint of*
Pearson Educacion de Mexico SA de CV

Progreso Editorial+
Sabino No 275, Colonia Santa Maria la Rib-
era, Delegacion Cuauhtemoc, 06400 Mexico,
CDMX
Tel: (0155) 1946-0620 *Toll Free Tel:* 01-800-777-
0077 *Fax:* (0155) 1946-0625
E-mail: editorial@editorialprogreso.com.mx;
servicioalcliente@editorialprogreso.com.mx;
pedidos@editorialprogreso.com.mx
Web Site: www.editorialprogreso.com.mx
Founded: 1952
Subjects: Education, Mathematics, Religion -
Catholic, Science Fiction, Fantasy, Self-Help
ISBN Prefix(es): 978-968-436; 978-970-641
Number of titles published annually: 100 Print; 8
CD-ROM

Total Titles: 300 Print; 12 CD-ROM; 300 Online
Bookshop(s): Naranjo No 248, Colonia Santa
  Maria la Ribera, Delegacion Cuauhtemoc,
  06400 Mexico, CDMX

Ediciones Promesa SA de CV+
Justo Sierra, 53-A, 53100 Naucalpan
Tel: (0155) 5623174; (0155) 3938707
Key Personnel
President: Luis Jesus Sanchez Gil
Founded: 1979
Subjects: Anthropology, Architecture & Inte-
  rior Design, Biography, Memoirs, Child Care
  & Development, Education, Fashion, Fiction,
  Film, Video, Human Relations, Language Arts,
  Linguistics, Music, Dance, Philosophy, Poetry,
  Psychology, Psychiatry, Religion - Catholic,
  Theology, Women's Studies
ISBN Prefix(es): 978-968-7224

Publicaciones Turisticas CU SA de CV
Londres No 22, Colonia Juarez, 06600 Mexico,
  CDMX
Tel: (0155) 55925022
Web Site: www.travelersguidemexico.com; www.
  boletinturistico.com
Specialize in publishing & editing. Publishes a
  guide book to Mexico.
Subjects: Travel & Tourism
ISBN Prefix(es): 978-968-7367
Total Titles: 3 Print
Parent Company: Grupo BT

Editorial Quehacer Politico SA de CV
Calle General Juan Cano 78, Colonia San Miguel
  Chapultepec, 11850 Mexico, DF
Subjects: Economics, Government, Political Sci-
  ence, Social Sciences, Sociology
ISBN Prefix(es): 978-968-6553; 978-968-7320

Editorial Raices SA de CV
Rodolfo Gaona 86, Colonia Lomas de Sotelo,
  Delegacion Miguel Hidalgo, 11200 Mexico,
  CDMX
Tel: (0155) 5557 5004 *Fax:* (0155) 5557 5078
Key Personnel
President: Sergio Autrey Maza
Dir General: Maria Nieves Noriega de Autrey
  E-mail: dirgral@arqueomex.com
Sales: Gerardo Ramirez
Founded: 1992
Subjects: Archaeology
ISBN Prefix(es): 978-968-7744

Random House Mondadori, see Penguin
  Random House Grupo Editorial

Editorial RM SA de CV
Rio Panuco 141, Colonia Cuauhtemoc, 06500
  Mexico, CDMX
Tel: (0155) 5533 5658 *Fax:* (0155) 5514 6799
E-mail: info@editorialrm.com
Web Site: www.editorialrm.com
Key Personnel
General Manager: Ramon Reverte
Subjects: Architecture & Interior Design, Art, Lit-
  erature, Literary Criticism, Essays, Poetry
ISBN Prefix(es): 978-968-5208

Editorial Santillana SA de CV
Division of Grupo Santillana Mexico
Av Rio Mixcoac numero 274, Colonia Acacias,
  03240 Mexico, DF
Tel: (0155) 5420-7530 *Toll Free Tel:* 01 800 0081
  900 *Fax:* (0155) 5604-2304
Web Site: www.santillana.com.mx; www.
  santillana.com
Key Personnel
Chairman: Ignacio Santillana
Chief Executive Officer: Miguel Angel Cayuela
Founded: 1960

Subjects: Education
ISBN Prefix(es): 978-968-430; 978-970-642; 978-
  970-29
Imprints: Alamah

Grupo Santillana Mexico
Av Rio Mixcoac numero 274, Colonia Acacias,
  03240 Mexico, DF
Tel: (0155) 5420-7530 *Toll Free Tel:* 01 800 008
  1900 *Fax:* (0155) 5604-2304
Web Site: www.santillana.com; www.santillana.
  com.mx
Key Personnel
Editorial Dir: Antonio Moreno
Communication: Darragh O'Grady
Founded: 1960
Subjects: Fiction, Nonfiction (General)
ISBN Prefix(es): 978-968-430; 978-970-642; 978-
  970-29
Parent Company: Grupo PRISA
Divisions: Editorial Nuevo Mexico SA de CV;
  Punta de Lectura SA de CV; Richmond Pub-
  lishing SA de CV; Santillana Ediciones Gen-
  erales SA de CV; Editorial Santillana SA de
  CV

Scott Foresman, *imprint of* Pearson Educacion
  de Mexico SA de CV

Secretaria de Relaciones Exteriores (SRE)
  (Ministry of Foreign Affairs)
Plaza Juarez 20, Colonia Centro, Cuauhtemoc,
  06010 Mexico, CDMX
Tel: (0155) 3686-5100 *Fax:* (0155) 3686-5028
E-mail: uenlace@sre.gob.mx
Web Site: www.sre.gob.mx
Subjects: Geography, Geology, History, Social
  Sciences, Sociology
ISBN Prefix(es): 978-968-810; 978-607-446
Bookshop(s): Libreria Ignacio L Vallarta,
  Plaza Juarez No 20, PB, Colonia Centro,
  Delegacion Cuauhtemoc, 06010 Mexico,
  CDMX *Tel:* (0155) 3686-5100 ext 6156
  E-mail: libreriavallarta@sre.gob.mx

Ediciones Selectas Diamante SA de CV
Mariano Escobedo No 62, Colonia Centro, Tlal-
  nepantla, 54000 Mexico, CDMX
Tel: (0155) 55650333; (0155) 55656120
  Toll Free Tel: (800) 888-9300
E-mail: ventas@editorialdiamante.com
Web Site: www.editorialdiamante.com
Founded: 1992
Subjects: Education, How-to, Philosophy, Family
  Development
ISBN Prefix(es): 978-968-7277; 978-607-7627
Foreign Rep(s): Libreria Artemis Edinter SA
  (Guatemala); Brodart Co (Pennsylvania); Car-
  vajal Educacion SA (Panama); Chulainn Pub-
  lishing Corp (Colorado); Desarrollos Culturales
  Costarricenses SA (Costa Rica); Libreria Es-
  panola (Ecuador); Distribuidora Fuente de Vida
  (California, Florida, Texas); Ediciones Gaviota
  Cia Ltda (Colombia); Libreria Hispanoameri-
  cana SA (Nicaragua); Honeycomb Distribution
  (California); Ibero A&G SAC (Peru); Jose Li-
  bros y mas (Dominican Republic); Editorial
  Planeta Chilena (Chile)

Selector SA de CV+
Dr Erazo 120, Colonia Doctores Del Cuauhtemoc,
  06720 Mexico, CDMX
Tel: (0155) 51 34 05 70 *Toll Free Tel:* 01800
  821-7280 *Fax:* (0155) 51 34 05 91
E-mail: info@selector.com.mx
Web Site: www.selector.com.mx
Key Personnel
Distribution: Daniel Araico *E-mail:* daniel.
  araico@selector.com.mx
Founded: 1949

Subjects: Child Care & Development, Crafts,
  Games, Hobbies, English as a Second Lan-
  guage, Health, Nutrition, Human Relations,
  Humor, Nonfiction (General), Science Fiction,
  Fantasy, Self-Help
ISBN Prefix(es): 978-968-403; 978-970-643
Number of titles published annually: 77 Print
Branch Office(s)
Prisciliano Sanchez 579, Colonia Centro, 44100
  Guadalajara, JAL
Washington 112 B, Altos, Colonia Centro,
  Monterrey, NL, Contact: Francisco Mendoza
  Salazar *Tel:* (08) 340 3260
Foreign Rep(s): Almacen y libreria regional
  (Panama); Almacenes Siman SA (El Salvador);
  Artemis Edinter (Guatemala); Carlos Federspiel
  y Co SA (Costa Rica); Central de Libros C
  Por A (Dominican Republic); Grupo Editorial
  Circulo (Puerto Rico); Editorial Diana Colom-
  biana Ltda (Colombia); Giron Spanish Book
  Distributors Inc (USA); Lectorum Publications
  Inc (USA); Distribuidora Lewis SA (Panama);
  Ediciones Oceano Argentina SA (Argentina);
  Editorial Oceano de Venezuela SA (Venezuela);
  Editorial Oceano Ecuatoriana SA (Ecuador);
  Editorial Oceano Peruana SA (Peru); Random
  House Inc (Carlos Azula) (USA); Spanish Lan-
  guage Book Services (USA); Libreria Yachay-
  wasi (Bolivia)
Bookshop(s): Pasaje Zocalo-Pino Suarez, Local
  21, Colonia Centro, 06040 Mexico, CDMX
  Tel: (0155) 5522 3486; (0155) 5522 3578
Warehouse: Oriente 217 No 194-A local C, Colo-
  nia Agricola Oriental, 08500 Mexico, CDMX
  Tel: (0155) 5700 3055; (0155) 5716 0009
  Fax: (0155) 5558 0856

Editorial Serpentina SA de CV
Santa Margarita 430, Colonia del Valle, Delega-
  cion Benito Juarez, 03100 Mexico, CDMX
Tel: (0155) 5559-8338; (0155) 5559-8267
E-mail: editorial@editorialserpentina.com
Web Site: editorialserpentina.com
Key Personnel
Founder: Adriana Canales; Alejandra Canales;
  Claudia Canales
Founded: 2004
Subjects: Education, Language Arts, Linguistics,
  Literature, Literary Criticism, Essays
ISBN Prefix(es): 978-968-5950

Editorial Sexto Piso Mexico
Paris 35A, Colonial del Carmen, 04100 Mexico,
  DF
Tel: (0155) 5689 6381 *Fax:* (0155) 5336 4972
E-mail: informes@sextopiso.com
Web Site: www.sextopiso.com
Key Personnel
Foreign Rights Dir: Eduardo Rabasa *Tel:* (0155)
  5659 4331 *E-mail:* erabasa@sextopiso.com
Editorial: Diana Gutierrez *E-mail:* dgutierrez@
  sextopiso.com
Sales: Alfonso Martin *E-mail:* alfonso@sextopiso.
  com
Founded: 2002
Subjects: Fiction, Literature, Literary Criticism,
  Essays
ISBN Prefix(es): 978-968-5679

Siglo XXI Editores SA de CV+
Cerro del Agua 248, Colonia Romero de Terreros,
  Delegacion Coyoacan, 04310 Mexico, CDMX
Tel: (0155) 5658 7999 *Fax:* (0155) 5658 7599
E-mail: ventas@sigloxxieditores.com.mx
Web Site: www.sigloxxieditores.com.mx
Key Personnel
Mng Dir, Editorial: Jaime Labastida
  E-mail: direcciongeneral@sigloxxieditores.com.
  mx
General Manager: Jose Maria Castro Mussot
  E-mail: gerenciageneral@sigloxxieditores.com.
  mx

Production Manager: Maria Oscos
  E-mail: maria_oscos@sigloxxieditores.com.mx
Sales Manager: Policarpo Bastida Fabila
Founded: 1966
Subjects: Anthropology, Architecture & Interior
  Design, Art, Criminology, Economics, Educa-
  tion, Government, Political Science, Health,
  Nutrition, History, Language Arts, Linguis-
  tics, Law, Literature, Literary Criticism, Essays,
  Philosophy, Psychology, Psychiatry, Regional
  Interests, Science (General), Social Sciences,
  Sociology, Technology
ISBN Prefix(es): 978-968-23
Branch Office(s)
Enrique Diaz de Leon 150, esquina Lopez
  Cotilla, Colonia Americas, 44100 Guadalajara,
  JAL, Coordinator: German Ildefonso Garcia
  Tel: (0133) 3827 0289 *E-mail:* guadalajara@
  sigloxxieditores.com.mx
Guatemala, 4824, C1425BUP Buenos Aires, Ar-
  gentina, Editorial Dir: Carlos E Diaz *Tel:* (011)
  4770 9090 *E-mail:* info@sigloxxieditores.com.
  ar *Web Site:* www.sigloxxieditores.com.ar
Foreign Rep(s): Ediciones Akal SA (Spain);
  Alianza Distribuidora Ecuatoriana C Ltda
  (Ecuador); Baker & Taylor Inc (USA); Casalini
  Libri SpA (Italy); La Familia Distribuidora
  de Libros SA (Peru); Inversiones Codice CA
  (Venezuela); Ediciones Mil Hojas (Chile); Ediciones Trecho SA (Uruguay)

Silver Burdette Ginn, *imprint of* Pearson
Educacion de Mexico SA de CV

Sin Limites, *imprint of* Editorial Lectorum SA de
CV

Sistemas Tecnicos de Edicion SA de CV+
San Marcos No 102, Colonia Tlalpan, 14000
  Mexico, CDMX
Tel: (0155) 56559144 *Fax:* (0155) 55739412
Founded: 1985
Subjects: Animals, Pets, Behavioral Sciences, Bi-
  ological Sciences, Cookery, Earth Sciences,
  History, Language Arts, Linguistics, Manage-
  ment, Mathematics, Self-Help
ISBN Prefix(es): 978-968-6579; 978-970-629;
  978-968-6048; 978-968-6394; 978-968-6135

Sistemas Universales SA+
Chiapas No 207, 1 Er piso Roma, 06700 Mexico,
  DF
Tel: (0155) 5574-4895 *Fax:* (0155) 5574-4938
Key Personnel
Contact: Lidia Orihuela de Juarez
Founded: 1970
Specialize in post secondary technical books for
  distance education.
Subjects: Accounting, Automotive, Computers,
  Electronics, Electrical Engineering, English as
  a Second Language
ISBN Prefix(es): 978-968-6064
Total Titles: 290 Print

SM Ediciones SA de CV
Magdalena No 211, Colonia del Valle, 03100
  Mexico, CDMX
Tel: (0155) 1087-8400 *Fax:* (0155) 1087-8484
Web Site: www.ediciones-sm.com.mx
Key Personnel
Sales Executive: Luis Rafael Solis
  E-mail: rsolis@ediciones-sm.com.mx
Subjects: Geography, Geology, History, Literature,
  Literary Criticism, Essays, Mathematics, Music,
  Dance, Science (General)
ISBN Prefix(es): 978-968-7791; 978-970-688

Ediciones Suromex SA+
Av Mexico No 57, Colonia Agricola Pantitlan,
  Delegacion Iztacalco, 08100 Mexico, CDMX

Tel: (0155) 2235-7948; (0155) 2235-7949; (0155)
  2235-7423 *Fax:* (0155) 5763-3669
E-mail: suromex@gmail.com
Web Site: edicionesuromex.com
Founded: 1982
Subjects: Animals, Pets, Art, Astrology, Occult,
  Astronomy, Biography, Memoirs, Cookery,
  Earth Sciences, Education, Gardening, Plants,
  House & Home, Humor, Religion - Other, Sci-
  ence (General), Self-Help, Sports, Athletics
ISBN Prefix(es): 978-968-855
Number of titles published annually: 70 Print
Total Titles: 350 Print
Parent Company: Susaeta Ediciones SA

Ediciones Tecolote SA de CV
Jose Ceballos 10, Colonia San Miguel Chapulte-
  pec, 11850 Mexico, CDMX
Tel: (0155) 5272 8085; (0155) 5272 8139
E-mail: tecolote@edicionestecolote.com
Web Site: www.edicionestecolote.com
Founded: 1993
Subjects: Art, Biography, Memoirs, Biological
  Sciences, Fiction, Geography, Geology, History
ISBN Prefix(es): 978-968-7381

TEPJF, see Tribunal Electoral del Poder Judicial
de la Federacion (TEPJF)

Editores de Textos Mexicanos (ETM)
Manuel M Ponce No 74, Colonia Guadalupe Inn,
  01020 Mexico, CDMX
Tel: (0155) 56 61 33 30 *Fax:* (0155) 56 61 30 07
Key Personnel
Dir General: Rafael Sainz Gutierrez
Subjects: Communications, Economics, Engineer-
  ing (General), Management, Medicine, Nurs-
  ing, Dentistry, Science (General), Occupational
  Health
ISBN Prefix(es): 978-968-5610

Grupo Editorial Tomo SA de CV
Nicolas San Juan No 1043, Colonia Del Valle,
  03100 Mexico, CDMX
Tel: (0155) 5575-6615; (0155) 5575-8701; (0155)
  5575-1716; (0155) 5575-0186 *Fax:* (0155)
  5575-6695
E-mail: info@grupotomo.com.mx
Web Site: www.grupotomo.com.mx
Key Personnel
Projects: Marco A Garibay *E-mail:* tatogaribay@
  grupotomo.com.mx
Rights: Silvia Morales *E-mail:* moralesvi@
  grupotomo.com.mx
Sales: Ana Lilia Torres *E-mail:* altorres@
  grupotomo.com.mx
Subjects: Art, Biography, Memoirs, Fiction,
  Health, Nutrition, Literature, Literary Criticism,
  Essays, Poetry, Metaphysics, Natural Health
ISBN Prefix(es): 978-970-666; 978-607-415

Travelers Guide to Mexico, see Publicaciones
Turisticas CU SA de CV

**Tribunal Electoral del Poder Judicial de la
Federacion (TEPJF)**
Av Carlota Armero 5000, Colonia CTM Culhua-
  can, 04480 Mexico, CDMX
Tel: (0155) 5728-2300; (0155) 5484-5410
E-mail: contactoweb@te.gob.mx
Web Site: www.trife.gob.mx; te.gob.mx
Key Personnel
President: Jose Alejandro Luna Ramos
Subjects: Government, Political Science, Law,
  Electoral Issues
ISBN Prefix(es): 978-970-671

Trilce Ediciones SA de CV
Carlos B Zetina No 61, Escandon Miguel Hi-
  dalgo, 11800 Mexico City
Tel: (0155) 5255 5804

E-mail: trilce@trilce.com.mx
Web Site: www.trilce.com.mx
ISBN Prefix(es): 978-607-7663; 978-968-6842

Editorial Trillas SA de CV+
Av Rio Churubusco 385, Colonia General Pedro
  Maria Anaya, 03340 Mexico, CDMX
Tel: (0155) 56 88 40 07; (0155) 56 88 42 33;
  (0155) 56 88 83 88 *Fax:* (0155) 56 04 13 64
E-mail: atencion.clientes@trillas.mx
Web Site: www.etrillas.com.mx
Key Personnel
Editorial Dir: Carlos Trillas
Logistics Manager: Jesus Galera
Publicity Manager: Sergio Shinji
Founded: 1953
Subjects: Architecture & Interior Design, Busi-
  ness, Child Care & Development, Crafts,
  Games, Hobbies, Education, English as a Sec-
  ond Language, House & Home, Law, Math-
  ematics, Medicine, Nursing, Dentistry, Psy-
  chology, Psychiatry, Science (General), Social
  Sciences, Sociology, Veterinary Science
ISBN Prefix(es): 978-968-24
Associate Companies: Editorial Trillas de Colom-
  bia Ltda, Carrera 15 No 33A-35, Teusaquillo,
  Bogota, Colombia, Manager: Alfonso Lopez
  Fernandez *Tel:* (01) 285 71 87; (01) 232
  83 05; (01) 232 83 36 *Fax:* (01) 285 89 05
  E-mail: trillas@etb.net.com; Limex Venezolana
  AC, Ave Lima Quinta Lourdes, Los Caobos,
  Caracas, Venezuela *Tel:* (0212) 238 77 39
  Fax: (0212) 239 12 62 *E-mail:* limex@cantv.
  net
U.S. Office(s): Trillas-Daamars International, 2704
  E Griffin Parkway, Mission, TX 78572, United
  States *Tel:* 956-664-9350 *Fax:* 956-630-1007
Orders to: Calzada de la Viga 1132, Colonia Ap-
  atlaco, Delegacion Iztapalapa, 09439 Mexico,
  CDMX *Tel:* (0155) 56 33 06 12 *Fax:* (0155) 56
  33 08 70

Editorial Turner de Mexico
Alberto Zamora, 64, Coyoacan, Mexico, DF
Tel: (0155) 47566066
E-mail: turner@turnerlibros.com
Web Site: www.turnerlibros.com
Founded: 2003
General nonfiction in the fields of history, literary
  criticism, art philosophy, music & bullfighting.
Subjects: Art, Business, Economics, Finance, His-
  tory, Literature, Literary Criticism, Essays, Mu-
  sic, Dance, Nonfiction (General), Philosophy,
  Photography, Bullfighting
Number of titles published annually: 120 Print
Total Titles: 400 Print
Parent Company: Turner Publicaciones, Rafael
  Calvo, 42, 2° esc izda, 28010 Madrid, Spain
Distributed by Art Data (UK); Distributed Art
  Publishers Inc (DAP) (USA & Canada); Ide-
  abooks (Europe); Editorial Oceano SA de CV
  (Latin America)

Publicaciones UACM, see Universidad
Autonoma de la Ciudad de Mexico

UJAT, see Universidad Juarez Autonoma de
Tabasco (UJAT)

Umbral Editorial SA de CV
Eje Central, Lazaro Cardenas No 1201, Colonia
  Nueva Industrial Vallejo, Delegacion Custavo A
  Madero, 07700 Mexico, CDMX
Tel: (0155) 5119 2341; (0155) 2062 0022
E-mail: castillo.fuentes@umbral.com.mx
Web Site: www.umbral.com.mx
Key Personnel
President: Juan Jose Comparan Rizo
Founded: 1995
Specialize in high school educational materials.
Subjects: Fiction, Geography, Geology, History,
  Literature, Literary Criticism, Essays
ISBN Prefix(es): 978-968-5115

Branch Office(s)
Priv Porfirio Diaz, Parque Industrial del Bosque,
45609 Tlaquepaque, JAL *Tel:* (0133) 3133
3053; (0133) 3133 3059 *E-mail:* direccion@
umbral.com.mx

Libros UNAM, see Universidad Nacional
Autonoma de Mexico (UNAM)

Universidad Autonoma Chapingo
Direccion General de Difusion Cultural y Servi-
cio, Km 38.5 Carretera Mexico-Texcoco, Colo-
nia Chapingo, 56230 Mexico, CDMX
Tel: (0155) 5952 1500
E-mail: centrodeatencion@chapingo.mx;
libroschapingo@gmail.com
Web Site: www.chapingo.mx/cultura/publicaciones
Key Personnel
Dir General: Martin Soto Escobar
  E-mail: msotoes2006@yahoo.com.mx
Publications Dept: Alfonso Castillo Beltran
  Tel: (0155) 5952 1500 ext 5142
Subjects: Literature, Literary Criticism, Essays,
  Science (General)
ISBN Prefix(es): 978-968-884

Universidad Autonoma de Aguascalientes
Av Universidad 940, Ciudad Universitaria, 20131
  Aguascalientes, AGS
Tel: (0449) 9107400; (0449) 9107402 (publica-
  tions)
E-mail: libreria@correo.uaa.mx
Web Site: www.uaa.mx
Key Personnel
Dir, Broadcasting: Maria de Lourdes Chiquito
  Diaz de Leon
Editorial Dir: Martha Esparza Ramirez
  E-mail: mespar@correo.uaa.mx
Subjects: Geography, Geology, History, Literature,
  Literary Criticism, Essays, Science (General),
  Social Sciences, Sociology
ISBN Prefix(es): 978-968-6259; 978-968-5073;
  978-970-728

**Universidad Autonoma de la Ciudad de
Mexico**
Dr Garcia Diego 170, Colonia Doctores, Delega-
  cion Cuauhtemoc, 06720 Mexico, CDMX
Tel: (0155) 1107-0280
E-mail: publicaciones@uacm.edu.mx
Web Site: publicaciones.uacm.edu.mx; portal.
  uacm.edu.mx
Key Personnel
Head, Publications: Carlos H Lopez Bar-
  rios *Tel:* (0155) 1107-0280 ext 16218
  E-mail: carlos.lopez@uacm.edu.mx
Founded: 2001
Subjects: Literature, Literary Criticism, Essays,
  Philosophy, Science (General), Social Sciences,
  Sociology
ISBN Prefix(es): 978-968-5720

Universidad Autonoma del Estado de Morelos
Av Universidad 1001, Colonia Chamilpa, 62209
  Cuernavaca, MOR
Tel: (0777) 3297000; (0777) 3297063 (editorial);
  (0777) 3297009 (editorial)
E-mail: web@uaem.mx
Web Site: www.uaem.mx/editorial
Key Personnel
Editorial Dir: Lydia Guadalupe Elizalde Valdes
Subjects: Art, History, Literature, Literary Criti-
  cism, Essays, Philosophy, Social Sciences, So-
  ciology
ISBN Prefix(es): 978-968-878

Universidad Autonoma del Estudo de Mexico
Av Instituto Literario 100 ote, Colonia Centro,
  50000 Toluca, MEX
Tel: (0722) 2262300
E-mail: rectoria@uaemex.mx

Web Site: www.uaemex.mx
Subjects: Art, Fiction, Geography, Geology, His-
  tory, Language Arts, Linguistics, Literature,
  Literary Criticism, Essays, Philosophy, Science
  (General)
ISBN Prefix(es): 978-968-835; 978-970-757

Universidad de Colima
Direccion General de Publicaciones, Av Universi-
  dad 333, Colonia Las Viboras, 28040 Colima,
  COL
Tel: (0312) 31 61 039
E-mail: publicac@ucol.mx
Web Site: www.ucol.mx
Key Personnel
Dir General: Miguel Angel Aguayo Lopez
Editorial Dir: Gloria Guillermina Araiza Torres
Subjects: Education, Engineering (General), Ge-
  ography, Geology, History, Literature, Literary
  Criticism, Essays, Science (General), Social
  Sciences, Sociology, Technology, Humanities
ISBN Prefix(es): 978-968-6190; 978-970-692

Universidad del Claustro de Sor Juana
Izazaga 92, Colonia Centro Historico, 06080
  Mexico, CDMX
Tel: (0155) 51303300
E-mail: promocion@elclaustro.edu.mx
Web Site: elclaustro.edu.mx
Key Personnel
President: Carmen Beatriz Lopez-Portillo
  Tel: (0155) 51303300 ext 3300
  E-mail: rectoria@elclaustro.edu.mx
Vice President: Sandra Lorenzano Schifrin
  Tel: (0155) 51303300 ext 3311
  E-mail: slorenzano@elclaustro.edu.mx
ISBN Prefix(es): 978-968-7631

**Universidad Iberoamericana, Ciudad de
Mexico**
Prolongacion Paseo de Reforma 880, Colonia Lo-
  mas de Santa Fe, 01219 Mexico, CDMX
Tel: (0155) 5950-4000; (0155) 9177-4400 (ext
  4919); (0155) 9177-4400 (ext 7330); (0155)
  9177-4400 (ext 7600) *Toll Free Tel:* (01800)
  627-7615 *Fax:* (0155) 5950-4331
E-mail: publica@uia.mx
Web Site: www.uia.mx
Key Personnel
President: Dr Jose Morales Oroaco SJ
Dir General: Araceli Tellez Trejo *E-mail:* araceli.
  tellez@uia.mx
Subjects: Art, Biography, Memoirs, Geography,
  Geology, History, Literature, Literary Criticism,
  Essays, Philosophy, Religion - Other, Science
  (General), Social Sciences, Sociology
ISBN Prefix(es): 978-968-859

**Universidad Juarez Autonoma de Tabasco
(UJAT)**
Av Universidad s/n, Zona de la Cultura, Colonia
  Magisterial, 86040 Villahermosa, TAB
Tel: (0993) 358 1500
E-mail: direccion.drp@ujat.mx
Web Site: www.publicaciones.ujat.mx/
  publicaciones
Key Personnel
Dir, Public Relations: Erasmo Marin Villegas
Subjects: Geography, Geology, History, Literature,
  Literary Criticism, Essays, Science (General),
  Social Sciences, Sociology, Sports, Athletics
ISBN Prefix(es): 978-968-5748; 978-968-7991;
  978-968-9024

**Universidad Nacional Autonoma de Mexico
(UNAM)+**
Av del Iman numero 5, Ciudad Universitaria,
  04510 Mexico, DF
Tel: (0155) 5622-6189 *Toll Free Tel:* 1800-50-10-
  400

E-mail: contacto@libros.unam.mx; htrujano@
  libros.unam.mx
Web Site: www.libros.unam.mx
Key Personnel
Dir General of Publications & Development:
  Javier Martinez Ramirez *Tel:* (0155) 5622 2653
  E-mail: javier.martinez@libros.unam.mx
Assistant Dir: Elsa Concepcion Botello Lopez
  Tel: (0155) 5665 1262 *E-mail:* botello@libros.
  unam.mx
Assistant Dir, Marketing: Miguel Angel
  Avalos Gutierrez *Tel:* (0155) 5622 6573
  E-mail: mavalos@libros.unam.mx
Coordinator of Communication & Public Rela-
  tions: Omar Cruz Garcia *Tel:* (0155) 5622 6755
  E-mail: ocruzg@libros.unam.mx
Founded: 1935
Subjects: Anthropology, Archaeology, Architec-
  ture & Interior Design, Chemistry, Chemical
  Engineering, Drama, Theater, Economics, Edu-
  cation, Engineering (General), Ethnicity, Geog-
  raphy, Geology, History, Journalism, Language
  Arts, Linguistics, Law, Literature, Literary Crit-
  icism, Essays, Mathematics, Medicine, Nursing,
  Dentistry, Music, Dance, Philosophy, Physics,
  Psychology, Psychiatry, Science (General), So-
  cial Sciences, Sociology, Technology, Veterinary Science
ISBN Prefix(es): 978-968-36; 978-968-837; 978-
  970-32; 978-970-701
U.S. Office(s): Hemisfair Plaza, PO Box 830426,
  San Antonio, TX 78283-0426, United States
Bookshop(s): Casa de las Humanidades, Presidente Carranza 162, Col Del Carmen, Coyoacan, 04000 Mexico, DF *Tel:* (0155) 5554 8513;
  (0155) 5554 5579 *E-mail:* lib_coyoacan@
  libros.unam.mx; Henrique Gonzalez Casanova,
  Corredor de Zona Comercial, Ciudad Universitaria, 04510 Mexico, DF *Tel:* (0155) 5622
  0271 *Fax:* (0155) 5622 0276 *E-mail:* lib_hgc@
  libros.unam.mx; Casa Universitaria del Libro,
  Orizaba y Puebla, Col Roma, 06710 Mexico,
  DF *Tel:* (0155) 5207 1787 *E-mail:* lib_casul@
  libros.unam.mx; Libreria del Palacio de Mine-
  ria, Tacuba 5, 06000 Mexico, DF *Tel:* (0155)
  5518 1315 *E-mail:* lib_mineria@libros.unam.
  mx; Jamie Garcia Terres, Av Universidad
  3000, 04510 Mexico, DF *Tel:* (0155) 5616
  1286 *E-mail:* lib_jgt@libros.unam.mx; Libreria
  Julio Torri, Zona Cultura, Ciudad Universitaria,
  04510 Mexico, DF; Un Paseo por los Libros,
  Pasaje Zocalo-Pino Suarez, local 28, Col Centro, 06000 Mexico, DC *Tel:* (0155) 5542 2548
  E-mail: lib_zocalo@libros.unam.mx

**Universidad Veracruzana Direccion General
Editorial y de Publicaciones+**
Hidalgo No 9, Colonia Centro, 91000 Xalapa,
  VER
Tel: (01228) 8181388; (01228) 8185980; (01228)
  8184843
E-mail: direccioneditorial@uv.mx
Web Site: www.uv.mx/editorial
Key Personnel
Dir: Edgar Garcia Valencia *E-mail:* edggarcia@
  uv.mx
Coordinator, Communications & Promotion: Ger-
  man Martinez Aceves *E-mail:* gemartinez@uv.
  mx
Founded: 1957
This publisher has indicated that 60% of their
  product line is author subsidized.
Subjects: Anthropology, Art, Drama, Theater, Ed-
  ucation, Fiction, History, Music, Dance, Philos-
  ophy, Psychology, Psychiatry, Social Sciences,
  Sociology
ISBN Prefix(es): 978-968-834
Number of titles published annually: 70 Print;
  100 Online; 25 E-Book
Total Titles: 2,000 Print; 180 Online; 180 E-Book
Parent Company: Universidad Veracruzana
Foreign Rights: Viclit (worldwide)
Distribution Center: Libreria Bonilla y Asocia-
  dos, Miguel Angel de Quevedo No 477, Colo-

nia Romero de Terreros, Coyoacan, 04310
Mexico, CDMX *Tel:* (0155) 5554 94 02 *Web
Site:* www.libreriabonilla.com.mx

**Editorial Universitaria-Universidad de
Guadalajara**
Jose Bonifacio Andrada 2679, Colonia Lomas de
Guevara, 44657 Guadalajara, JAL
Tel: (033) 3640 6326; (033) 3640 4594
Web Site: www.editorial.udg.mx
Key Personnel
Manager: Edgardo F Lopez Martinez
E-mail: edgardo.lopez@editorial.udg.mx
Head, Marketing: Eric Fabricio Tirado Fuentes
E-mail: eric.tirado@editorial.udg.mx
Editorial Coordinator: Sayri Karp Mitastein
E-mail: sayri.karp@editorial.udg.mx
Subjects: Art, Biography, Memoirs, Geography,
Geology, History, Language Arts, Linguistics,
Literature, Literary Criticism, Essays, Philoso-
phy, Science (General), Social Sciences, Soci-
ology
ISBN Prefix(es): 978-968-895

Editorial UV, see Universidad Veracruzana
Direccion General Editorial y de Publicaciones

Vaso Roto Ediciones S de RL de CV
Gruta Azul 147, Colonia Valle de San Angel,
66290 San Pedro Garza Garcia, NL
Tel: (0181) 8303 4247
E-mail: vasoroto@vasoroto.com
Web Site: www.vasoroto.com
Founded: 2003
Subjects: Art, Drama, Theater, Literature, Literary
Criticism, Essays, Poetry
ISBN Prefix(es): 978-607-95580
Branch Office(s)
c/ Alcala 85, 7° izda, 28009 Madrid, Spain
Tel: 915 779 152
Distribution Center: IPG Spanish Books, 814 N
Franklin St, Chicago, IL 60610, United States

Javier Vergara Editor SA de CV
Kansas 161, Benito Juarez, 03810 Mexico, DF
Tel: (0155) 5543 4802; (0155) 5682 8194
Fax: (0155) 5682 9511
Founded: 1978
Subjects: Biography, Memoirs, Business, Fiction,
History, Music, Dance, Nonfiction (General),
Psychology, Psychiatry, Self-Help
ISBN Prefix(es): 978-968-497
Parent Company: Javier Vergara Editor Argentina

Editorial Vuelta SA de CV+
Chilaque No 9, Colonia San Diego Churubusco,
04120 Mexico, CDMX
Tel: (0155) 9183 7800 *Fax:* (0155) 9183 7836
E-mail: cartas@letraslibres.com
Web Site: www.letraslibres.com
Key Personnel
Dir: Enrique Krauze
Executive Editor: Cynthia Ramirez
Mng Editor: Patricia Nieto
Deputy Editor: Ramon Gonzalez Ferriz
Subjects: Art, Drama, Theater, Economics, Gov-
ernment, Political Science, History, Literature,
Literary Criticism, Essays
ISBN Prefix(es): 978-968-6229; 978-968-7656

Moldova

General Information

Capital: Kishinev
Language: Romanian

Religion: Predominantly Christian (mostly Eastern
Orthodox)
Population: 4.5 million
Bank Hours: Generally open for short hours be-
tween 0930-1230 Monday-Friday
Shop Hours: Generally 0900-1800 Monday-
Friday; often open weekends
Currency: 100 kopeks = 1 rubl
Export/Import Information: According to
Ukrainian quotas & customs duties, compa-
nies engaged in trade should register with the
Ukraine Ministry of Foreign Economic Rela-
tions. Licenses for export & import are also
required for trade with Russia.
Copyright: UCC (see Copyright Conventions, pg
viii)

Editura Arc
Str G Meniuc, nr 3, 2009 Chisinau
Tel: (022) 735329; (022) 733619 *Fax:* (022)
733623
E-mail: info.edituraarc@gmail.com
Web Site: www.edituraarc.md; www.facebook.
com/Editura-Arc-138047819542467
Founded: 1994
Subjects: Accounting, Economics, Education, His-
tory, Language Arts, Linguistics, Law, Manage-
ment, Music, Dance, Psychology, Psychiatry
ISBN Prefix(es): 978-9975-61
Foreign Rep(s): Allas Trading SRL (Romania)

Editura Cartier SRL
Str Bucuresti nr 68, 2012 Chisinau
Tel: (0322) 203491; (0322) 240587 *Fax:* (0322)
240587
E-mail: cartier@cartier.md
Web Site: www.cartier.md
Key Personnel
Editorial Dir: Emilian Galaicu-Paun
Founded: 1995
Subjects: Biography, Memoirs, Economics, Edu-
cation, Fiction, Law, Philosophy, Psychology,
Psychiatry, Travel & Tourism, Culture
ISBN Prefix(es): 978-9975-79; 978-9975-949
Number of titles published annually: 90 Print
Total Titles: 160 Print

Intreprinderea Editorial-Poligrafica Stiinta
Str Academiei, nr 3, 2028 Chisinau
Tel: (022) 73-96-16; (022) 73-97-44; (022) 73-99-
30 *Fax:* (022) 73-96-27
Web Site: www.stiinta.asm.md
Key Personnel
Dir: Gheorghe Prini *E-mail:* prini@stiinta.asm.md
Editor-in-Chief: Mircea V Ciobanu
Founded: 1959
Subjects: Art, History, Literature, Literary Criti-
cism, Essays, Management, Marketing, Science
(General), Social Sciences, Sociology, Ecology
ISBN Prefix(es): 978-5-376; 978-9975-67

Editura Lumina
bd Stefan cel Mare, 180, 2004 Chisinau
Tel: (022) 29-58-64; (022) 29-58-68 *Fax:* (022)
29-58-64; (022) 29-58-68
E-mail: luminamd@mail.ru
Web Site: www.edituralumina.md
Key Personnel
Dir: Elena Popovschi
Founded: 1966
Specialize in textbooks, University presses &
scholarly books.
Subjects: Biological Sciences, Chemistry, Chem-
ical Engineering, Child Care & Development,
Geography, Geology, History, Language Arts,
Linguistics, Literature, Literary Criticism, Es-
says, Mathematics, Medicine, Nursing, Den-
tistry, Physics, Psychology, Psychiatry, Training
Manuals & Literature
ISBN Prefix(es): 978-5-372; 978-9975-65

Monaco

General Information

Capital: Monaco
Language: French. Monegasque, Italian and En-
glish also spoken
Religion: Roman Catholic
Population: 29,712
Bank Hours: 0830-1730 Monday-Friday
Shop Hours: 0830-1300, 1600-1930 Monday-
Friday
Currency: 100 Eurocents = 1 Euro
Copyright: Berne, UCC (see Copyright Conven-
tions, pg viii)

Alpen Editions
9, Ave Albert II, 98000 Monaco
Tel: 97 77 62 10
E-mail: contact@alpen.mc; editionalpen@gmail.
com
Web Site: www.alpen.mc
Subjects: Health, Nutrition, Psychology, Psychia-
try, Beauty, Children, Fitness, Parenting
ISBN Prefix(es): 978-2-35934; 978-2-914923;
978-2-916784

Publications des Archives du Palais de Princier
BP 518, 98015 Monaco Cedex
Tel: 93 25 18 31
E-mail: archives@palais.mc
Web Site: www.palais.mc
Subjects: Biography, Memoirs, History
ISBN Prefix(es): 978-2-903147

Editions du Rocher+
Subsidiary of Groupe Artege
28, rue Comte Felix Gastaldi, 98015 Monaco
Mailing Address: BP 521, 98015 Monaco, Cedex
Tel: 99 99 67 17 *Fax:* 93 50 73 71
E-mail: contact@editionsdurocher.fr
Web Site: www.editionsdurocher.fr
Founded: 1943
Subjects: Antiques, Astrology, Occult, Biogra-
phy, Memoirs, Crafts, Games, Hobbies, Drama,
Theater, Fiction, Health, Nutrition, History,
How-to, Humor, Literature, Literary Criticism,
Essays, Military Science, Mysteries, Suspense,
Philosophy, Psychology, Psychiatry, Religion
- Other, Romance, Science Fiction, Fantasy,
Self-Help, Sports, Athletics, Western Fiction
ISBN Prefix(es): 978-2-268
Branch Office(s)
10, rue Mercoeur, 75011 Paris, France
Tel: 01 40 46 54 00 *Fax:* 01 58 51 10 48
E-mail: contact@editionsddb.fr
Distribution Center: Sodis, 128 Ave du Marechal
de Lattre de Tassigny, 77400 Lagny-sur-Marne,
France *Tel:* 01 60 07 82 00 *Toll Free Fax:* por-
tail@sodis.fr

Montenegro

General Information

Capital: Podgorica
Language: Montenegrin (official). Serbian,
Bosnian, Albanian and Croatian also spoken
Religion: Orthodox, Muslim and Roman Catholic
Population: 678,177
Currency: 100 Eurocents = 1 Euro

Izdavacko Preduzece Obod Drustvo SA
Ul Njegoseva br 3, 81250 Cetinje
Founded: 1946

Subjects: Education, Fiction, Language Arts, Linguistics, Nonfiction (General), Poetry, Science (General)
ISBN Prefix(es): 978-86-305; 978-86-7420
Number of titles published annually: 30 Print
Branch Office(s)
Dobracina 32, 11000 Belgrade, Serbia
Bookshop(s): Njegoseva 11, 11000 Belgrade, Serbia

Morocco

General Information

Capital: Rabat
Language: Arabic (official), Berber, French, Spanish (northern regions)
Religion: Islamic
Population: 27 million
Bank Hours: Summer: 0830-1130, 1500-1700 Monday-Friday; rest of year: 0815-1130, 1415-1630 Monday-Friday
Shop Hours: Tangiers: 0900-1200, 1600-2000; rest: 0900-1200, 1500-1800 or 1900
Currency: 100 centimes = 1 Moroccan dirham
Export/Import Information: No tariff on books; most advertising dutiable. Special Tax, and Stamp Duty of percentage of import duty. No import licenses required. Exchange controls but permission liberally granted.
Copyright: UCC, Berne (see Copyright Conventions, pg viii)

Editions La Croisee des Chemins
Immeuble Oued Dahab, 1er etage gauche, Rue Essanaani, Bourgogne, 20050 Casablanca
Tel: 0522 279 987 *Fax:* 0565 795 454
E-mail: editionslacroiseedeschemins@gmail.com
Web Site: www.lacroiseedeschemins.ma
Founded: 1993
Subjects: Architecture & Interior Design, Art, Fiction, History, Literature, Literary Criticism, Essays, Moroccan Culture & History
ISBN Prefix(es): 978-9954-1

Dar Nachr Al Maarifa+
10, Ave Al Fadila, Quartier Industriel CYM, 10130 Rabat
Tel: 05 37 79 79 63; 05 37 79 57 02; 05 37 79 79 64; 05 37 79 69 38; 05 37 79 69 14 *Fax:* 05 37 79 03 43
Web Site: www.facebook.com/darnachralmaarifa
Key Personnel
Manager: Mr Zhiri Samir
Founded: 1988
Also acts as printer & distributor.
Membership(s): International Publishers Association; Moroccan Association of Publishers.
Subjects: Economics, Education, History, Law, Literature, Literary Criticism, Essays, Mathematics, Medicine, Nursing, Dentistry, Philosophy, Religion - Other, Science (General), Social Sciences, Sociology
ISBN Prefix(es): 978-9981-808
Number of titles published annually: 10 Print
Total Titles: 3 Print
Distributor for APREJ
Bookshop(s): Librairie Al Maarif, rue Bab Chellah, BP 239, Rabat, Manager: Mr Mohamed Moubtassim *Tel:* 05 37 72 65 24; 05 37 73 07 01 *Fax:* 05 37 20 01 37 *E-mail:* info.impmaarif@groupeelmaarif.com

Editions Le Fennec+
91 Blvd d'Anfa, 14e etage, Casablanca
Tel: 05 22 20 93 14; 05 22 20 92 68 *Fax:* 05 22 27 77 02
E-mail: info@lefennec.com
Web Site: www.lefennec.com

Key Personnel
Dir: Layla B Chaouni *E-mail:* laylachaouni@lefennec.com
Editor: Annie Azzou *E-mail:* anazzou@lefennec.com
Founded: 1987
Subjects: Drama, Theater, Economics, Fiction, Health, Nutrition, Language Arts, Linguistics, Literature, Literary Criticism, Essays, Mysteries, Suspense, Poetry, Psychology, Psychiatry, Religion - Islamic, Social Sciences, Sociology, Women's Studies
ISBN Prefix(es): 978-9981-838; 978-9954-415; 978-9954-1
Distributed by Vilo-Diffusion-Paris (Europe & Canada)

Government Printer (Imprimerie Officielle)
Ave Yacoub El Mansour, 10000 Rabat
Tel: 05 37 76 50 24 *Fax:* 05 37 76 51 79
Subjects: Government, Political Science, Regional Interests

Editions Okad+
4, ave Hassan II, Quatier Industeriel, Vita, Route de Casablanca, 10050 Rabat
Tel: 05 37 79 69 70; 05 37 79 69 71 *Fax:* 05 37 79 85 56
Founded: 1981
Subjects: Economics, History, Language Arts, Linguistics, Poetry
ISBN Prefix(es): 978-9981-806

Editions La Porte+
281 Ave Mohammed V, Rabat
Mailing Address: BP 331, Rabat
Tel: 05 37 70 99 58 *Fax:* 05 37 70 64 76
Subjects: Economics, Government, Political Science, Language Arts, Linguistics, Law, Religion - Islamic, Religion - Other, Travel & Tourism
ISBN Prefix(es): 978-9981-889
Subsidiaries: Librairie aux Belles Images (bookshop)

Mozambique

General Information

Capital: Maputo
Language: Portuguese
Religion: Catholic, Protestant & Islamic
Population: 16.6 million
Bank Hours: 0800-1200 Monday - Friday
Shop Hours: 0800-1230, 1400-1700 Monday-Saturday
Export/Import Information: Children's picture books dutied per kg net weight, otherwise books and advertising matter duty-free. No additional taxes apply. Import licenses and strict exchange controls; authorities have classified books and advertising as List 3 in priorities.

CEA, see Centro de Estudos Africanos (CEA)

Centro de Estudos Africanos (CEA)+
Universidade Eduardo Mondlane, Av Julius Nyerere nº 1993, Maputo
Tel: (021) 49 34 71 *Fax:* (021) 49 08 28
E-mail: cea@uem.mz
Web Site: www.uem.mz
Key Personnel
Dir: Prof Armindo Ngunga
Founded: 1976

Specialize in social science.
Subjects: Economics, Foreign Countries, Government, Political Science, History, Regional Interests

Plural Editores Lda
Ave Patrice Lumumba 765, Maputo
Tel: 21 36 09 00 *Fax:* 21 30 88 68
E-mail: plural@pluraleditores.co.mz
Web Site: www.pluraleditores.co.mz
Publish educational & technical books.
Subjects: Biological Sciences, Crafts, Games, Hobbies, Education, Health, Nutrition, History, Law, Mathematics, Music, Dance, Philosophy, Physics, Science (General), Social Sciences, Sociology, Technology, Travel & Tourism
ISBN Prefix(es): 978-989-611
Parent Company: Grupo Porto Editora

Myanmar

General Information

Capital: Yangon
Language: Burmese (English used for foreign correspondence)
Religion: Buddhism
Population: 42.6 million
Bank Hours: 1000-1400 Monday-Friday; 1000-1200 Saturday
Shop Hours: Generally 0800-1700 Monday-Saturday
Currency: 100 pyas = 1 kyat
Export/Import Information: Myanmar has own complex tariff system, but duties are paid by State Trading Corporation No 9, 550-552 Merchant St, Rangoon, and Printing and Publishing Corporation, 228 Theinbyu St, Rangoon, principally. No tariffs on advertising. Books exempt from sales tax. Import license required. Exchange controls; priorities apply.
Copyright: No copyright conventions signed

Knowledge Press & Bookhouse
130, Bokyoke Aung San St, Pazundaung
Tel: (01) 290927
Subjects: Art, Education, Government, Political Science, Religion - Other, Social Sciences, Sociology
Bookshop(s): Knowledge Book House

Namibia

General Information

Capital: Windhoek
Language: English (official), Afrikaans and German widely used
Religion: Predominantly Christian
Population: 1.6 million
Bank Hours: 0900-1530 Monday-Friday
Shop Hours: 0830-1700 Monday-Friday, 0800-1300 Saturday
Currency: 100 cents = 1 Namibian dollar
Export/Import Information: Part of the Southern African Customs Union (SACU). Import licenses required. Payment of hard currency or any other currency for trade transactions strictly against documentation. Strict foreign exchange controls and regulations. No exchange control applicable to non-residents. Gradual easing exchange control of residents.
Copyright: Berne (see Copyright Conventions, pg viii)

Bible Society of Namibia
Independence Ave 428, Windhoek
Mailing Address: Private Bag 13294, Windhoek
9000
Tel: (061) 235-090; (061) 224-878 *Fax:* (088)
616-726
E-mail: bibleshop@nambible.org.na; pa@
nambible.org.na
Web Site: www.nambible.org.na
Key Personnel
General Secretary: Barnie van der Walt
Programs Manager: Schalk Botha
Financial & Business Manager: Alda Smuts
Founded: 1979
Subjects: Biblical Studies
ISBN Prefix(es): 978-99916-713; 978-99916-766;
978-99916-841; 978-99916-866
Branch Office(s)
Shop 28, Maroela Mall, Ndemufayo St, Ongwe-
diva 9000 *Tel:* (065) 231-308 *Fax:* (088) 616-
728 *E-mail:* bibleshop.north@nambible.org.na

Desert Research Foundation of Namibia (DRFN)
7 Rossini St, Windhoek West
Mailing Address: PO Box 20232, Windhoek
Tel: (061) 377 500 *Fax:* (061) 230 172
E-mail: drfn@drfn.org.na
Web Site: drfn.org.na
Key Personnel
Dir: Viviane Kinyaga
Founded: 1963
A nongovernmental organization that strives to-
wards enhancing capacity for sustainable devel-
opment on all levels of society.
Subjects: Agriculture, Animals, Pets, Behavioral
Sciences, Biological Sciences, Developing
Countries, Earth Sciences, Education, Energy,
Environmental Studies, Gardening, Plants, Ge-
ography, Geology, Natural History, Physical
Sciences, Regional Interests, Science (General),
Botany, Zoology, Desertification Issues, Envi-
ronmental Training, Water Management
ISBN Prefix(es): 978-99916-709
U.S. Office(s): Friends of Gobabeb, c/o Prof C
S Crawford, Dept of Biology, University of
New Mexico, Albuquerque, NM 87131, United
States

DRFN, see Desert Research Foundation of
Namibia (DRFN)

ELCIN Printing Press
Private Bag 2018, Ondangwa
Tel: (065) 240241; (065) 240242 *Fax:* (065)
240472
E-mail: gen.sec@elcin.org.na
Web Site: www.elcin.org.na
Publishes books, booklets, a newpaper & mag-
azines in local languages for parish & church
use, as well as various printed articles for
schools & businesses purposes.
Subjects: Religion - Other
ISBN Prefix(es): 978-99916-33

Evangelical Lutheran Church in Namibia, see
ELCIN Printing Press

Kuiseb-Verlag (Kuiseb Publishers)
PO Box 67, Windhoek
Tel: (061) 225372 *Fax:* (061) 226846
E-mail: nwg@iway.na
Web Site: www.kuiseb-verlag.com
Founded: 1925
Publishing books on Namibia, reference library -
Namibiana.
Subjects: Agriculture, Animals, Pets, Archaeol-
ogy, Art, Astronomy, Biological Sciences, En-
vironmental Studies, History, Natural History,
Science (General), Travel & Tourism
ISBN Prefix(es): 978-99916-703

Number of titles published annually: 2 Print
Total Titles: 2 Print
Foreign Rep(s): Namibiana Buchdepot (Germany)

Media Institute of Southern Africa (MISA)
21 Johann Albrecht St, Windhoek
Tel: (061) 232975 *Fax:* (061) 248016
E-mail: info@misa.org
Web Site: www.misa.org
Key Personnel
National Dir, Namibia Chapter: Natasha
Tibinyane
Regional Dir: Zoe Titus
Founded: 1992
Promotes media diversity, pluralism, self-
sufficiency & independence.
Subjects: Film, Video, Journalism, Radio, TV, So-
cial Sciences, Sociology, Media Law, Media
Directory, Media Freedom
ISBN Prefix(es): 978-99916-62; 978-99916-728
Number of titles published annually: 4 Print
Total Titles: 10 Print; 6 E-Book

MISA, see Media Institute of Southern Africa
(MISA)

Multidisciplinary Research Centre
340 Mandume Ndemufayo Ave, Pionierspark,
Windhoek
Mailing Address: Private Bag 13301, Windhoek
9000
Tel: (061) 2063052 *Fax:* (061) 2063050
E-mail: tgases@unam.na; apick@unam.na
Web Site: www.unam.edu.na/multidisciplinary-
research-centre
Key Personnel
Dir: Ms Nelago Indon, PhD
Deputy Dir: Davis Mumbengegwi
Founded: 1994
Subjects: Agriculture, Developing Countries, Eco-
nomics, Environmental Studies, Geography,
Geology, Government, Political Science, Sci-
ence (General), Social Sciences, Sociology,
Gender Issues, Life Sciences
ISBN Prefix(es): 978-99916-53; 978-99916-701
Parent Company: University of Namibia
Divisions: Life Sciences Division; Science Tech-
nology & Innovation Division; Social Sciences
Division
U.S. Office(s): J Diescho, University of Namibia
Office, Africa/American Institute, 833 United
Nations Plaza, New York, NY 10017, United
States

Namibia Publishing House
19 Faraday St, Windhoek
Mailing Address: PO Box 22830, Windhoek
Tel: (061) 232165 *Fax:* (061) 233538
E-mail: info@nph.com.na
Web Site: www.nph.com.na
Key Personnel
Sales Administrator: Dency Tjiroze
    E-mail: tjirozed@nph.com.na
Founded: 1977
Subjects: Agriculture, Biography, Memoirs, Bio-
logical Sciences, Business, Chemistry, Chem-
ical Engineering, Computers, Crafts, Games,
Hobbies, Education, Fiction, Geography, Ge-
ology, History, Literature, Literary Criticism,
Essays, Natural History, Physical Sciences, Po-
etry, Religion - Islamic, Religion - Jewish
ISBN Prefix(es): 978-0-86848; 978-99916-0; 978-
99916-2; 978-99916-37

Nepal

General Information

Capital: Kathmandu
Language: Nepali (official), also Maithali & sev-
eral other languages
Religion: Predominantly Hindu, also some Bud-
dhist and Muslim
Population: 20.1 million
Bank Hours: 1000-1430 Sunday-Thursday; 1000-
1230 Friday
Shop Hours: 1000-2000 Sunday-Friday
Currency: 100 paisa = 1 Nepalese rupee
Export/Import Information: No tariff on books
and advertising. Import licenses required. Ex-
change controls.

Nepal Academy
Kamaladi, Kathmandu 44600
Tel: (01) 4221242 *Fax:* (01) 4221175
E-mail: info.nepalacademy@gmail.com
Web Site: www.nepalacademy.org.np
Key Personnel
Chancellor/Chairperson: Mr Bairagi Kainla
Vice Chancellor/Vice Chairperson: Mr Ganga
Prasad Uprety
Founded: 1957
Subjects: Art, History, Literature, Literary Crit-
icism, Essays, Philosophy, Poetry, Science
(General), Social Sciences, Sociology
ISBN Prefix(es): 978-9937-589

Ratna Pustak Bhandar
Bank Rd, 71 Ga, Bagbazar, Kathmandu
Mailing Address: GPO Box No 98, Kathmandu
Tel: (01) 4223026; (01) 4242077; (01) 4221818
(bookshop) *Fax:* (01) 4248421
E-mail: rpb@wlink.com.np; ratnapustak@gmail.
com
Web Site: www.ratnabooks.com
Founded: 1939 (as Ram Das & Sons)
ISBN Prefix(es): 978-99933-0

Sajha Prakashan+
Pulchock, Lalitpur, Kathmandu
Tel: (01) 5521118; (01) 5521023 *Fax:* (01)
5544236
Web Site: www.sajha.org.np
Founded: 1966
Printing, publication & distribution.
Subjects: Accounting, Agriculture, Archaeology,
Architecture & Interior Design, Art, Asian
Studies, Biography, Memoirs, Economics, En-
glish as a Second Language, Environmental
Studies, Foreign Countries, Geography, Ge-
ology, Government, Political Science, Health,
Nutrition, History, Language Arts, Linguis-
tics, Law, Literature, Literary Criticism, Essays,
Music, Dance, Physical Sciences, Psychology,
Psychiatry, Publishing & Book Trade Refer-
ence, Religion - Other
ISBN Prefix(es): 978-99933-2; 978-99933-30;
978-99933-32; 978-99933-50
Number of titles published annually: 35 Print
Total Titles: 1,357 Print

Netherlands

General Information

Capital: Amsterdam
Language: Dutch; Frisian in Friesland (though all
speakers of Frisian also speak Dutch). English
is common second language
Religion: Mainly Roman Catholic and Protestant

Population: 15.9 million
Bank Hours: 0900-1600 Monday-Friday; some open Saturday morning and on late night shopping evenings
Shop Hours: 0900-1730 or 1800 Monday-Saturday. Many close Monday morning
Currency: 100 Eurocents = 1 Euro
Export/Import Information: Member of the European Union. No tariff on books except children's picture books from non-EU; advertising other than single copies is dutied; 6% VAT on books. Import licenses required for certain countries (not USA or UK).
Copyright: UCC, Berne, Florence (see Copyright Conventions, pg viii)

Academic Publishers Associated, see APA (Academic Publishers Associated)

Adveniat Geloofseducatie+
Amalialaan 126-G, 3743 KJ Baarn
Mailing Address: Postbus 44, 3740 AA Baarn
Tel: (088) 23 83 600 *Fax:* (088) 23 83 609
E-mail: info@adveniat.nl
Web Site: www.adveniat.nl
Founded: 1961
Subjects: Biblical Studies, Inspirational, Spirituality, Religion - Catholic, Theology, Judaism
ISBN Prefix(es): 978-90-6173
Number of titles published annually: 20 Print; 2 CD-ROM; 1 Online; 1 Audio
Total Titles: 100 Print; 2 CD-ROM; 1 Online; 1 Audio

Agon, *imprint of* Uitgeverij de Arbeiderspers

Uitgeversmaatschappij Agon BV+
Herengracht 370-372, 1016 CH Amsterdam
Tel: (020) 524 75 00 *Fax:* (020) 622 49 37
Founded: 1987
Subjects: History, Regional Interests, Travel & Tourism
ISBN Prefix(es): 978-90-5157

Aksan, *imprint of* Amsterdam University Press BV (AUP)

Altamira, *imprint of* Gottmer Uitgevers Groep

Altamira+
Imprint of Gottmer Uitgevers Groep
Zijlweg 308, 2015 CN Haarlem
Mailing Address: Postbus 317, 2000 AH Haarlem
Tel: (023) 54 111 90 *Fax:* (023) 52 744 04
E-mail: info@gottmer.nl
Web Site: www.gottmer.nl/spiritueleboeken
Key Personnel
Publisher: Gonnie Mulder
Foreign Rights Manager: Ingrid van der Mooren *Tel:* (023) 54 116 09 *E-mail:* ivdm@gottmer.nl
Foreign Rights: Renee Ferment *E-mail:* rf@gottmer.nl
Founded: 1985
Specialize in mind, body & spirit publications.
Subjects: Inspirational, Spirituality
ISBN Prefix(es): 978-90-77478; 978-94-013

Ambo|Anthos Uitgevers+
Subsidiary of Veen Bosch & Keuning Uitgeversgroep BV
Herengracht 499, 1017 BT Amsterdam
Tel: (020) 524 54 11 *Fax:* (020) 420 04 22
E-mail: info@amboanthos.nl
Web Site: www.amboanthos.nl
Key Personnel
Marketing Manager: Maartje de Jong *Tel:* (020) 524 54 26 *E-mail:* mdejong@amboanthos.nl
Sales Manager: Vanessa van Hofwegen *Tel:* (020) 524 54 52
Founded: 1996

Specialize in literary thrillers.
Subjects: Biography, Memoirs, Fiction, Mysteries, Suspense, Philosophy, Psychology, Psychiatry, Science (General), Social Sciences, Sociology
ISBN Prefix(es): 978-90-263; 978-90-6074; 978-90-414; 978-90-76341; 978-90-8549

Amsterdam University Press BV (AUP)
Herengracht 221, 1016 BG Amsterdam
Tel: (020) 420 00 50 *Fax:* (020) 420 32 14
E-mail: info@aup.nl; marketing@aup.nl
Web Site: www.aup.nl
Key Personnel
Head, Desk Editing & Production: Chantal Nicolaes *E-mail:* c.nicolaes@aup.nl
Head, International Sales: Magdalena Hernas *E-mail:* m.hernas@aup.nl
Marketing & Sales: Michiel van der Drift *E-mail:* m.vander.drift@aup.nl
Founded: 1992
Subjects: Archaeology, Art, Asian Studies, Film, Video, Government, Political Science, Language Arts, Linguistics, Social Sciences, Sociology, Art History, Cultural History, Film & Media Studies, Humanities, Language & Literature, Policy Sciences
ISBN Prefix(es): 978-90-5356
Imprints: Aksan; Leiden University Press (LUP); Pallas Publications; Salome; Vossiupers UvA

Uitgeverij AnkhHermes BV+
Subsidiary of Veen Bosch & Keuning Uitgeversgroep BV
Herculesplein 96, 3584 AA Utrecht
Mailing Address: Postbus 13288, 3507 LG Utrecht
Tel: (088) 700 2700
E-mail: info@ankh-hermes.nl
Web Site: www.ankh-hermes.nl
Key Personnel
Publisher: Pieter de Boer *E-mail:* pdeboer@vbkmedia.nl
Founded: 1923 (as part of N Kluwer, became independent in 1973)
Specialize in spirituality & esotericism.
Subjects: Astrology, Occult, Education, Gardening, Plants, Health, Nutrition, Inspirational, Spirituality, Management, Parapsychology, Philosophy, Religion - Buddhist, Religion - Protestant, Esotericism
ISBN Prefix(es): 978-90-202
Number of titles published annually: 60 Print
Total Titles: 120 Print

APA (Academic Publishers Associated) (APA Uitgevers Associatie)
Archangelkade 2-A, 1013 BE Amsterdam
Tel: (068) 1472742 (cell)
E-mail: info@apa-publishers.com; orders@apa-publishers.com; apantiqua@apa-publishers.com (bookshop)
Web Site: www.apa-publishers.com
Key Personnel
Mng Dir: G van Heusden
Founded: 1966
Subjects: Art, Asian Studies, Biblical Studies, History, Human Relations, Language Arts, Linguistics, Law, Library & Information Sciences, Philosophy, Religion - Other, Science (General), Social Sciences, Sociology, Theology, European Studies, History of Religions, Orientalia
ISBN Prefix(es): 978-90-6037; 978-90-6023; 978-90-302; 978-90-6039; 978-90-6022; 978-90-6024; 978-90-6025; 978-90-6042
Total Titles: 500 Print
Subsidiaries: Apantiqua (antiquarian, old & new scholarly booksellers); Fontes Pers (nautical books, shipbuilding); Gerard Th van Heusden (bibliographies, books about books, typography); Hissink & Co (graphic arts, history of art); Holland University Press BV (European

studies, history, cultural history, law, social studies); Oriental Press (Orientalia, oriental history, languages, religions, text editions); Philo Press CV (Orientalia, oriental history, languages, religions, text editions, early Christianity)
Distributor for Apantiqua; Fontes Pers; Gerard Th van Heusden; G W Hissink & Co; Holland University Press; Oriental Press; Philo Press

Uitgeverij de Arbeiderspers+
Spui 10, 1012 WZ Amsterdam
Tel: (020) 76 07 210
E-mail: info@arbeiderspers.nl
Web Site: www.singeluitgeverijen.nl/de-arbeiderspers
Key Personnel
Sales & Marketing Manager: Nathalie Doruijter
Subjects: Biography, Memoirs, Criminology, Fiction, History, Literature, Literary Criticism, Essays, Nonfiction (General), Philosophy, Poetry, Romance, Travel & Tourism
ISBN Prefix(es): 978-90-295
Parent Company: Singel Uitgeverijen
Imprints: Agon

Architectura & Natura
Leliegracht 22, 1015 DG Amsterdam
Tel: (020) 6236186 *Fax:* (020) 6382303
E-mail: info@architectura.nl
Web Site: www.architectura.nl
Founded: 1939
Specialize in architecture & landscape architecture.
Subjects: Architecture & Interior Design, Gardening, Plants, Photography
ISBN Prefix(es): 978-90-71570; 978-90-76863
Number of titles published annually: 6 Print
Total Titles: 96 Print
Imprints: Goose Press
Subsidiaries: Goose Press

Ark Media+
Donauweg 4, 1043 AJ Amsterdam
Tel: (020) 480 29 99 *Fax:* (020) 611 48 64
E-mail: info@arkmedia.nl
Web Site: www.arkmedia.nl
Key Personnel
Publisher: Paul Abspoel
Editor: Marieke Slagter
Founded: 1913
Ark Boeken Publishing House combines the activities of Vereniging tot Verspreiding der Heilige Schrift (Association for Distribution of the Holy Scripture) & Bijbel Kiosk Vereniging (Bible Kiosk Society).
Subjects: Poetry, Religion - Protestant
ISBN Prefix(es): 978-90-338; 978-90-427
Total Titles: 500 Print; 1 Audio
Bookshop(s): Dorpsster 51, 3881 BB Putten *Tel:* (0341) 740 085 *E-mail:* info@arkboekhandel.nl *Web Site:* www.kameel.nl

Uitgeverij Jan van Arkel+
Grifthoek 151, 3514 JK Utrecht
Tel: (030) 2731 840
E-mail: info@janvanarkel.nl; bestel@janvanarkel.nl
Web Site: www.janvanarkel.nl; www.clubgroen.nl
Key Personnel
Publishing Dir: Jan van Arkel
Founded: 1974
Specialize in books on the environment & development, in books in the Dutch & English languages.
Subjects: Economics, Environmental Studies, Geography, Geology, Government, Political Science, Social Sciences, Sociology, Women's Studies, Migrant Issues, Women's Issues
ISBN Prefix(es): 978-90-6224; 978-90-5727; 978-90-76308; 978-90-77024
Total Titles: 150 Print
Imprints: International Books

Foreign Rep(s): Global Book Marketing Ltd
(UK); Independent Publishers Group (North
America); John Reed Book Distribution (Aus-
tralia)

Ars Scribendi Uitgeverij BV+
Leerlooierstr 6, 4871 EN Etten-Leur
Mailing Address: Postbus 628, 4870 AP Etten-
Leur
Tel: (076) 5041810 *Fax:* (084) 7381509
E-mail: info@arsscribendi.com; redactie@
arsscribendi.com; bestelling@arsscribendi.com
Web Site: www.arsscribendi.com
Founded: 1988
Membership(s): KVB.
Subjects: Education, Environmental Studies, His-
tory
ISBN Prefix(es): 978-90-72718; 978-90-5495;
978-90-74777; 978-90-5566
Number of titles published annually: 120 Print
Total Titles: 1,500 Print
Imprints: Corona; Fantom; Flash; Magnum
Subsidiaries: Handelsonderneming Dykhof BV;
De Laude Scriptorum BV
Distributed by Agora bvba (Belgium)
Distribution Center: Uitgeverij het Davidsfonds,
Blijde-Inkomstr 79-81, 3000 Leuven, Bel-
gium *Tel:* (016) 310600 *E-mail:* uitgeverij@
davidsfonds.be

Uitgeverij Asoka
Imprint of Milinda Uitgevers
Mathenesserlaan 326, 3021 HX Rotterdam
Mailing Address: Postbus 61220, 3002 HE Rot-
terdam
Tel: (010) 4113867 *Fax:* (010) 4113932
E-mail: info@milinda.nl
Web Site: www.milinda-uitgevers.nl
Key Personnel
Publisher: Gerolf T'Hooft
Subjects: Inspirational, Spirituality, Religion -
Buddhist, Meditation, Tibet
ISBN Prefix(es): 978-90-567

Uitgeverij Athenaeum-Polak & Van Gennep
Spui 10, 1012 WZ Amsterdam
Tel: (020) 76 07 210
E-mail: info@uitgeverijathenaeum.nl
Web Site: www.singeluitgeverijen.nl/athenaeum
Founded: 1962
Subjects: Art, Fiction, Nonfiction (General), Po-
etry, Religion - Other
ISBN Prefix(es): 978-90-253
Parent Company: Singel Uitgeverijen

Uitgeverij Atlas Contact
Subsidiary of Veen Bosch & Keuning Uitgevers-
groep BV
Prinsengracht 911-915, 1017 KD Amsterdam
Mailing Address: Postbus 13, 1000 AA Amster-
dam
Tel: (020) 524 98 00
Web Site: www.atlascontact.nl
Key Personnel
Publishing Dir: Chris Herschdorfer
E-mail: cherschdorfer@atlascontact.nl
Publisher: Nelleke Geel
Head, Marketing & Sales: Rianne Blaakmeer
E-mail: rblaakmeer@atlascontact.nl
Editor: Huguette Hornstra
Founded: 1887
Subjects: Fiction, Literature, Literary Criticism,
Essays, Nonfiction (General)
ISBN Prefix(es): 978-90-254
Branch Office(s)
Katwilgweg 2, 2050 Antwerp, Belgium *Tel:* (03)
355 2842

AUP, see Amsterdam University Press BV (AUP)

Backhuys Publishers BV
Slikweg 6, 4321 SV Kerkwerve
Tel: (0111) 672975
E-mail: info@backhuys.com; sales@backhuys.
com
Web Site: www.euronet.nl/users/backhuys
Key Personnel
President: Dr W Backhuys
Founded: 1989
Publish & distribute scholarly books in the natu-
ral sciences (botany, zoology, geology).
Also acts as distributor of museum publications,
University Presses & sells antiquarian books in
the same subjects.
Subjects: Biological Sciences, Earth Sciences,
Geography, Geology, Natural History
ISBN Prefix(es): 978-90-73348; 978-90-73239;
978-90-220; 978-90-327; 978-90-5103; 978-2-
85653; 978-90-5782; 978-2-86515
Number of titles published annually: 2 Print
Total Titles: 400 Print
Subsidiaries: Seashell Treasure Books

Uitgeverij Balans+
Subsidiary of WPG Uitgevers
Van Mierevaldstr 1, 1071 DW Amsterdam
Mailing Address: Postbus 75184, 1070 AD Ams-
terdam
Tel: (020) 305 9810 *Fax:* (020) 305 9824
E-mail: balans@uitgeverijbalans.nl;
klantenservice@uitgeverijbalans.nl
Web Site: www.uitgeverijbalans.nl
Key Personnel
Publisher: Plien van Albada
Founded: 1986
Subjects: Biography, Memoirs, Fiction, Govern-
ment, Political Science, Health, Nutrition, His-
tory, Journalism, Law, Literature, Literary Criti-
cism, Essays, Nonfiction (General), Psychology,
Psychiatry, Regional Interests, Religion - Other
ISBN Prefix(es): 978-90-5018; 978-94-6003
Total Titles: 40 Print
Orders to: Centraal Boekhuis, Postbus 100, 4100
BA Culemborg *Tel:* (0345) 475896

Balkema, see CRC Press/Balkema

BBNC Uitgevers BV+
Bergstr 11, 3811 NE Amersfoort
Tel: (033) 4600339
E-mail: info@bbnc.nl; bestellen@bbnc.nl
Web Site: www.bbnc.nl
Key Personnel
Dir: Arend Meijboom *E-mail:* arend@bbnc.nl
Commercial Manager: Karel Waerts
Marketing: Myrthe van Dongen *E-mail:* myrth@
bbnc.nl
Founded: 1970
Subjects: Animals, Pets, Astrology, Occult, Biog-
raphy, Memoirs, Child Care & Development,
Cookery, Fiction, Finance, Health, Nutrition,
History, Humor, Literature, Literary Criticism,
Essays, Management, Music, Dance, Mysteries,
Suspense, Nonfiction (General), Philosophy,
Real Estate, Religion - Buddhist, Religion -
Hindu, Religion - Jewish, Romance, Self-Help,
Sports, Athletics, Travel & Tourism, Women's
Studies
ISBN Prefix(es): 978-90-453
Number of titles published annually: 130 Print
Parent Company: Progresso Media Groep

Becht, *imprint of* Gottmer Uitgevers Groep

Becht
Imprint of Gottmer Uitgevers Groep
Zijlweg 308, 2015 CN Haarlem
Mailing Address: Postbus 317, 2000 AH Haarlem
Tel: (023) 54 111 90 *Fax:* (023) 52 744 04
E-mail: info@gottmer.nl
Web Site: www.gottmer.nl/lifestyleboeken

Key Personnel
Publisher: Gonnie Mulder
Foreign Rights Manager: Ingrid van der Mooren
Tel: (023) 54 116 09 *E-mail:* ivdm@gottmer.nl
Subjects: Cookery, Crafts, Games, Hobbies,
Health, Nutrition, Sports, Athletics, Etiquette
ISBN Prefix(es): 978-90-230

Bekking & Blitz Uitgevers BV
Textielweg 22, 3812 RV Amersfoort
Mailing Address: Postbus 286, 3800 AG Amers-
foort
Tel: (033) 4613718 *Fax:* (033) 4653156
E-mail: info@bekkingblitz.com
Web Site: www.bekkingblitz.com
Founded: 1929
Subjects: Art, History, Photography, Travel &
Tourism, Culture
ISBN Prefix(es): 978-90-6109
Branch Office(s)
Koninqin Asrtidlaan 22, 8200 Brugge, Belgium
Tel: (050) 394410
Konrad-Wolf-Str 29, 13055 Berlin, Germany

Benjamin & Partners Art Books, *imprint of*
Boekwerk & Partners

John Benjamins Publishing Co+
Klaprozenweg 756, 1033 NN Amsterdam
Mailing Address: PO Box 36224, 1020 ME Ams-
terdam
Tel: (020) 6304747 *Fax:* (020) 6739773
Web Site: www.benjamins.com
Key Personnel
Dir, Publishing: Jan Reijer Groesbeek *E-mail:* jr.
groesbeek@benjamins.nl
General Manager: Seline Benjamins
Editorial: Isja Conen *E-mail:* isja.conen@
benjamins.nl; Anke de Looper *E-mail:* anke.
delooper@benjamins.nl; Kees Vaes
E-mail: kees.vaes@benjamins.nl
Marketing & Customer Service: Karin Plijnaar
E-mail: customer.services@benjamins.nl
Production: Peter Lamers *E-mail:* pieter.lamers@
benjamins.nl
Founded: 1964
Subjects: Art, Education, Language Arts, Lin-
guistics, Literature, Literary Criticism, Essays,
Philosophy, Psychology, Psychiatry, Social Sci-
ences, Sociology, Applied Linguistics, Cogni-
tive Science, Historical Linguistics, Pragamat-
ics, Translation Cognition
ISBN Prefix(es): 978-90-272
Number of titles published annually: 150 Print
Total Titles: 3,000 Print
Imprints: B R Gruener Publishing Co
Branch Office(s)
John Benjamins North America Inc, PO Box
27519, Philadelphia, PA 19118-0519, United
States, Contact: Paul Peranteau *Tel:* 215-836-
1200 *Fax:* 215-836-1204 *E-mail:* service@
benjamins.com
Foreign Rep(s): Asia Information Services ltd
(China); Bournemouth English Book Centre
(UK); Capital Books (India); CEPIEC (China);
CNPIEC (China); Co Info Pty Ltd (Australia);
Disvan Enterprises (India); Information & Cul-
ture Korea (South Korea)
Distribution Center: Ta Dong Book Co Ltd,
162-44 Hsin Yi Rd, Sec 3, Taipei 106, Tai-
wan *Tel:* (02) 2701 5677 *Fax:* (02) 2701 8033
E-mail: tatong@tatong.com.tw
Orders to: John Benjamins Publishing Co, PO
Box 960, Herndon, VA 20172-0960, United
States *E-mail:* benjamins@presswarehouse.com

Bertram + de Leeuw Uitgevers
Jacob van Lennepkade 307, 1054 ZW Amsterdam
Tel: (020) 7762552
E-mail: info@bertramendeleeuw.nl
Web Site: www.bertramendeleeuw.nl
Key Personnel
General Manager, Acquisition & Public-

ity: Marij Bertram *Tel:* (06) 461 757 00
E-mail: mbertram@bertramendeleeuw.nl
Financial Dir & Sales: Hendrik de Leeuw
Tel: (06) 461 756 00 *E-mail:* hdeleeuw@
bertramendeleeuw.nl
Editorial & Publicity: Anna Noorda *Tel:* (06) 430
408 62 *E-mail:* anoorda@bertramendeleeuw.nl
Subjects: Fiction, Nonfiction (General)
ISBN Prefix(es): 978-94-6156

Uitgeverij De Bezige Bij BV
Subsidiary of WPG Uitgevers
Van Miereveldstr 1, 1071 DW Amsterdam
Mailing Address: Postbus 75184, 1070 AD Amsterdam
Tel: (020) 305 98 10 *Fax:* (020) 305 98 24; (020) 305 98 39 (sales)
E-mail: info@debezigebij.nl
Web Site: www.debezigebij.nl
Key Personnel
Dir & Publisher: Henk Propper
Founded: 1944
Subjects: Fiction, Literature, Literary Criticism, Essays, Nonfiction (General), Poetry
ISBN Prefix(es): 978-90-234; 978-90-76682
Imprints: Cargo; Ludion; Oog en Blik; Thomas Rap; Slaughterhouse Books; Zoem
Distribution Center: WPG Uitgevers Belgium nv, Nassaustr 37-41, 2000 Antwerp, Belgium *Tel:* (03) 285 7200 *Fax:* (03) 233 9569 *E-mail:* boeken@wpg.be (Belgium)

Uitgeverij Big Balloon BV+
Herenweg 29a III, 2105 MB Heemstede
Mailing Address: Postbus 136, 2100 AC Heemstede
Tel: (023) 517 66 20 *Fax:* (023) 517 66 40
E-mail: info@bigballoon.nl
Web Site: www.bigballoon.nl
Key Personnel
Dir: Kees Kooijman *E-mail:* kooijman@
bigballoon.nl
Editorial Manager: Corinne van Roozendaal
E-mail: vanroozendaal@bigballoon.nl
Editorial: Anette Ebbing *E-mail:* ebbing@
bigballoon.nl; Marieke Hoeber
E-mail: hoeber@bigballoon.nl
Marketing: Gwendolyn Westerwoudt
E-mail: westerwoudt@bigballoon.nl; Karin
Witte *E-mail:* witte@bigballoon.nl
Founded: 1990
ISBN Prefix(es): 978-90-320; 978-90-5425

Boekencentrum Bijbel, Lied & Muziek, *imprint of* Boekencentrum Uitgevers BV

Erven J Bijleveld+
Janskerkhof 7, 3512 BK Utrecht
Tel: (030) 2317008; (030) 2310800 (bookshop)
Fax: (030) 2368675; (030) 2311774 (bookshop)
E-mail: bijleveld.publishers@wxs.nl
Web Site: www.bijleveldbooks.nl
Founded: 1865
Subjects: Art, Child Care & Development, Computer Science, Computers, History, Literature, Literary Criticism, Essays, Nonfiction (General), Philosophy, Psychology, Psychiatry, Religion - Jewish, Religion - Other, Social Sciences, Sociology, Theology
ISBN Prefix(es): 978-90-72019; 978-90-5548; 978-90-6131
Imprints: Bijleveld Press

Bijleveld Press, *imprint of* Erven J Bijleveld

BIS Publishers
Het Sieraad, Postjesweg 1, 1057 DT Amsterdam
Tel: (020) 515 02 30 *Fax:* (020) 515 02 39
E-mail: bis@bispublishers.nl
Web Site: www.bispublishers.nl

Key Personnel
Mng Dir: Bionda Dias
Founded: 1986
Subjects: Architecture & Interior Design, Communications, Crafts, Games, Hobbies, Fashion
ISBN Prefix(es): 978-90-72007; 978-90-6369
Parent Company: Laurence King Publishing
Foreign Rep(s): Basheer Graphic Books (Singapore); Books Import Srl (Italy); buchArt Verlagsvertretungen (Northern Germany); Consortium Book Sales & Distribution (USA); Critique Livres Distribution SAS (France); Evrensel Yayincilik (Turkey); Exhibitions International (Belgium); Index Book SL (Spain); Kahkeshan Book Shop (Iran); Levant Distributors Sarl (Lebanon); Librimport SAS (Italy); Long Sea International Book Co Ltd (Taiwan); Modern Journal (Australia); Page One Pte Ltd (Singapore); Stephan Phillips (Pty) Ltd (South America); Publishers Group UK (UK); Vertreterbuero Wuerzburg (Michael Klein) (Austria, Southern Germany)
Distribution Center: Runge Verlagsauslieferung GmbH, Bergstr 2, 33803 Steinhagen, Germany, Contact: Team 3 *Tel:* (05204) 998 123 *Fax:* (05204) 998 114 *E-mail:* msr@rungeva.de
Web Site: rungeva.de

Blossom Books, *imprint of* Uitgeverij Kluitman Alkmaar BV

Boekencentrum Uitgevers BV+
Goudstr 50, 2718 RC Zoetermeer
Mailing Address: Postbus 29, 2700 AA Zoetermeer
Tel: (079) 361 54 81; (079) 362 82 82 (sales) *Fax:* (079) 361 54 89
E-mail: info@boekencentrum.nl; verkoop@boekencentrum.nl
Web Site: www.boekencentrum.nl
Key Personnel
General Dir: Nico de Waal
Founded: 1948
Subjects: Education, Religion - Protestant, Theology
ISBN Prefix(es): 978-90-239; 978-90-211
Imprints: Boekencentrum Bijbel, Lied & Muziek; Dienstboek; Uitgeverij Jes!; Uitgeverij Klement; Uitgeverij Meinema; Uitgeverij Mozaiek; Boekencentrum Tijdschriften

Boekwerk & Partners+
Emmastr 31-2, 9722 EW Groningen
Tel: (06) 51285050
Founded: 1988
Subjects: Art, Business, Computer Science, Computers, Management, Marketing
ISBN Prefix(es): 978-90-5402; 978-90-71677
Imprints: Benjamin & Partners Art Books

Bohn Scheltema & Holkema, see Uitgeverij Bohn Stafleu Van Loghum BV

Uitgeverij Bohn Stafleu Van Loghum BV
Het Spoor 2, 3994 AK Houten
Mailing Address: Postbus 246, 3990 GA Houten
Tel: (030) 638 3838; (030) 638 3736; (030) 638 5250 *Fax:* (030) 638 3839
E-mail: klantenservice@bsl.nl
Web Site: www.bsl.nl
Key Personnel
Senior Editor: Linda Boer *Tel:* (030) 638 3782 *E-mail:* linda.boer@bsl.nl
Founded: 1752
Specialize in health care.
Subjects: Biography, Memoirs, Health, Nutrition, Human Relations, Medicine, Nursing, Dentistry, Social Sciences, Sociology
ISBN Prefix(es): 978-90-313; 978-90-368; 978-90-6016; 978-90-6065; 978-90-311; 978-90-

6001; 978-90-6014; 978-90-6051; 978-90-6060; 978-90-6502
Parent Company: Spring Media BV

Boom Lemma Uitgevers+
Paleisstr 9, 2514 JA Den Haag
Mailing Address: Postbus 85576, 2508 CG Den Haag
Tel: (070) 330 70 94; (070) 330 70 33; (0522) 237 555 (orders) *Fax:* (070) 330 70 30
E-mail: infodesk@lemma.nl; budh@boomdistributiecentrum.pl (orders); verkoop@budh.nl
Web Site: www.boomlemma.nl
Key Personnel
Dir: Dr Wirt Soetenhorst *Tel:* (070) 330 70 31 *E-mail:* w.soetenhorst@budh.nl
Founded: 1988
Independent educational & scientific publishing company.
Subjects: Business, Communications, Economics, Education, Health, Nutrition, Labor, Industrial Relations, Law, Management, Marketing, Physical Sciences, Psychology, Psychiatry, Social Sciences, Sociology, Technology, Industrial Design
ISBN Prefix(es): 978-90-5189
Total Titles: 400 Print
Parent Company: Boom Uitgevers Den Haag

Uitgeverij Boom Nelissen
Prinsengracht 747-751, 1017 JX Amsterdam
Mailing Address: Postbus 15970, 1001 NL Amsterdam
Tel: (020) 5218 933; (0522) 237 555 *Fax:* (020) 6253 327
E-mail: service@boomnelissen.nl
Web Site: www.boomnelissen.nl
Key Personnel
Publisher: Eline Crijns *E-mail:* e.crijns@boomnelissen.nl
Domestic Sales: Claudia Seppen *E-mail:* c.seppen@boomnelissen.nl
Marketing: Martine Siemons *E-mail:* m.siemons@boomnelissen.nl
Founded: 1922
Specialize in management & coaching literature.
Subjects: Business, Communications, Economics, Education, Government, Political Science, Labor, Industrial Relations, Management, Philosophy, Psychology, Psychiatry, Religion - Other, Social Sciences, Sociology
ISBN Prefix(es): 978-90-244
Parent Company: Boom Uitgevers Amsterdam
Distribution Center: Centraal Boekhuis, Postbus 125, 4100 AC Culemborg *Tel:* (0345) 47 59 11 *Fax:* (0345) 47 53 43 *E-mail:* info@cb-logistics.nl *Web Site:* www.cb-logistics.nl
Boom Distributiecentrum, Postbus 400, 7940 AK Meppel *Tel:* (0522) 23 75 55 *Fax:* (0522) 25 38 64 *E-mail:* info@boomdistributiecentrum.nl
CB Vlaanderen *Tel:* (052) 45 69 40 *Fax:* (052) 45 69 50 *E-mail:* info@cb-logistics.be

Borre Educatief BV
Stephensonstr 10-C, 2723 RN Zoetermeer
Mailing Address: Postbus 583, 2700 AN Zoetermeer
Tel: (079) 343-1427 *Fax:* (079) 341-0286
E-mail: mail@borre.nl
Web Site: www.borre.nl
Key Personnel
Rights Manager: Mark Tijs
Subjects: Fiction
ISBN Prefix(es): 978-90-8922

Brandaan, *imprint of* Uitgeverij Vuurbaak

Brill+
Plantijnstr 2, 2321 JC Leiden
Mailing Address: Postbus 9000, 2300 PA Leiden

Tel: (071) 53 53 500 *Fax:* (071) 53 17 532
E-mail: marketing@brill.com; sales-nl@brill.com
Web Site: www.brill.com
Key Personnel
Chief Executive Officer: Herman Pabbruwe
Executive Vice President, Finance & Operations:
Olivier de Vlam
Executive Vice President, Sales & Marketing: Peter Coebergh
Publishing Dir: Joed Elich *E-mail:* elich@brill.com
Marketing Manager: Stijn Van der Heide
E-mail: heide@brill.com
Founded: 1683
Academic publisher in humanities & social sciences.
Subjects: Archaeology, Asian Studies, Behavioral Sciences, Biblical Studies, Biological Sciences, History, Language Arts, Linguistics, Law, Philosophy, Religion - Islamic, Religion - Jewish, Religion - Other, Science (General), Social Sciences, Sociology, Theology, Humanities
ISBN Prefix(es): 978-0-391; 978-0-916846; 978-90-04; 978-90-420 (Brill Rodopi); 978-90-74822; 978-1-901903; 978-1-905246; 978-1-906876; 978-90-474; 978-90-6764
Total Titles: 2,700 Print
Imprints: Brill/Hes & De Graaf; Brill/Nijhoff; Brill/Rodopi; Global Oriental; Hotei Publishing
U.S. Office(s): 2 Liberty Sq, 11th floor, Boston, MA 02109, United States *Tel:* 617-263-2323 *Fax:* 617-263-2324 *E-mail:* sales-us@brill.com
Distribution Center: c/o Turpin Distribution, Stratton Business Park, Pegasus Dr, Biggleswade, Beds SG18 8TQ, United Kingdom *Tel:* (01767) 604-954 *Fax:* (01767) 601-640 *E-mail:* brill@turpin-distribution.com (outside North America)
c/o Turpin Distribution, 143 West St, New Milford, CT 06776, United States *Tel:* 860-350-0041 *Fax:* 860-350-0039 *E-mail:* brillna@turpin-distribution.com (North America)

Brill/Hes & De Graaf, *imprint of* Brill

Brill/Nijhoff, *imprint of* Brill

Brill/Rodopi, *imprint of* Brill

De Brink, *imprint of* Uitgeverij Ploegsma BV

A W Bruna Uitgevers BV+
Subsidiary of WPG Uitgevers
Johannes Vermeerstr 24, 1071 OK Amsterdam
Mailing Address: Postbus 51077, 1007 EB Amsterdam
Tel: (020) 218 1600; (030) 247 0468 (foreign rights) *Fax:* (030) 241 0018 (foreign rights)
E-mail: info@awbruna.nl
Web Site: www.awbruna.nl
Key Personnel
Associate Publisher, Fiction & Publisher, Signatuur: Juliette van Wersch
Mng Dir: Marieke Niezen
Head, Sales: Edo Dietvorst *E-mail:* edo.dietvorst@awbruna.nl
Publicity: Saskia Hausel *E-mail:* saskia.hausel@awbruna.nl
Founded: 1868
Subjects: Computer Science, Fiction, History, Literature, Literary Criticism, Essays, Mysteries, Suspense, Nonfiction (General), Philosophy, Psychology, Psychiatry, Science (General), Social Sciences, Sociology
ISBN Prefix(es): 978-90-229; 978-90-449; 978-90-5672
Imprints: Gloriae; Happinez; LeV (nonfiction); Signatuur; VIP; Voetbal International

Dick Bruna, *imprint of* Mercis Publishing BV

BSL, see Uitgeverij Bohn Stafleu Van Loghum BV

Buijten & Schipperheijn BV+
Paasheuvelweg 44, 1105 BJ Amsterdam
Mailing Address: Postbus 22708, 1100 DE Amsterdam
Tel: (020) 524 10 10 *Fax:* (020) 524 10 11
E-mail: info@buijten.nl
Web Site: www.buijten.nl
Key Personnel
Mng Dir: Guido Sneep *E-mail:* sneep@buijten.nl
Founded: 1902
Subjects: Biblical Studies, Human Relations, Philosophy, Poetry, Psychology, Psychiatry, Religion - Other, Theology, Travel & Tourism
ISBN Prefix(es): 978-90-6064; 978-90-5881
Imprints: Buijten en Schipperheijn Motief; Buijten en Schipperheijn Recreatief

Buijten en Schipperheijn Motief, *imprint of* Buijten & Schipperheijn BV

Buijten en Schipperheijn Recreatief, *imprint of* Buijten & Schipperheijn BV

Uitgeverij De Buitenspelers, see Voetbal International Boeken

Uitgeverij Business Contact+
Subsidiary of Veen Bosch & Keuning Uitgeversgroep BV
Prinsengracht 915, 1017 KD Amsterdam
Mailing Address: Postbus 13, 1000 AA Amsterdam
Tel: (020) 524 98 00
E-mail: start@businesscontact.nl; verkoop@atlascontact.nl (sales)
Web Site: www.businesscontact.nl; www.boekenwereld.com
Key Personnel
Publisher: John Numan
Editorial: Merel Poldervaart; Cecilia Schouten; Pim van Tol; Sandra Wouters
Marketing & Publicity: Femke Bilderbeek
Tel: (020) 524 98 34 *E-mail:* fbilderbeek@atlascontact.nl
Sales: Ingrid Kee *E-mail:* ikee@atlascontact.nl
Subjects: Accounting, Business, Career Development, Economics, Finance, How-to, Management, Marketing, Psychology, Psychiatry
ISBN Prefix(es): 978-90-254
Number of titles published annually: 30 Print
Total Titles: 400 Print
Foreign Rights: Shared Stories (Hayo Deijnum)

Callenbach, *imprint of* Uitgeverij Kok

Callenbach+
Imprint of Uitgeefmaatschappij Kok ten Have BV
Herculesplein 96, 3584 AA Utrecht
Mailing Address: Postbus 13288, 3507 LG Utrecht
Tel: (088) 700 2600 *Fax:* (088) 700 2999
E-mail: promotie@kok.nl
Web Site: www.kok.nl
Key Personnel
Promotion: Frances Driessen *Tel:* (088) 700 2652 *E-mail:* fdriessen@vbkmedia.nl
Founded: 1854
Membership(s): Combo Group, Netherlands.
Subjects: Animals, Pets, Biblical Studies, Fiction, History, Mysteries, Suspense, Poetry, Religion - Protestant, Religion - Other, Theology
ISBN Prefix(es): 978-90-266
Ultimate Parent Company: Veen Bosch & Keuning Uitgeversgroep BV
Foreign Rep(s): Rene Slotboom (Netherlands); Julien Stessens (Belgium)

Caplan BV
Van Oldenbarneveldtstr 92-1, 6827 AN Arnhem
Tel: (026) 751 88 51
E-mail: info@caplan.nl
Web Site: www.caplan.nl
Subjects: Cookery, Health, Nutrition, Wine & Spirits
ISBN Prefix(es): 978-90-8724; 978-90-76218; 978-90-79383

Cargo, *imprint of* Uitgeverij De Bezige Bij BV

Uitgeverij Carrera, *imprint of* Overamstel Uitgevers

Uitgeverij Carrera
Imprint of Overamstel Uitgevers
Paul van Vlissingenstr 18, 1096 BK Amsterdam
Mailing Address: Postbus 3626, 1001 AK Amsterdam
Tel: (020) 4624 300
Web Site: www.uitgeverijcarrera.nl
Key Personnel
Dir: Martijn Griffioen
Publisher: Arjan Weenink *E-mail:* arjan@uitgeverijcarrera.nl; Harold de Croon
Editor: Marieke Dijkman *E-mail:* marieke@uitgeverijcarrera.nl
Marketing: Meike Wensink *E-mail:* meike.wensink@overamstel.com
Publicity & Domestic Sales: Martin Griffioen
Sales: Willem Verduijn *E-mail:* willem@overamstel.com
Subjects: Government, Political Science, Literature, Literary Criticism, Essays, Music, Dance, Sports, Athletics, Entertainment, Media, Politics
ISBN Prefix(es): 978-90-488
Number of titles published annually: 30 Print

Castrum Peregrini Presse+
Herengracht 401, 1017 BP Amsterdam
Mailing Address: Postbus 645, 1000 AP Amsterdam
Tel: (020) 623 52 87
E-mail: mail@castrumperegrini.nl
Web Site: castrumperegrini.org
Key Personnel
Executive Dir: Michael Defuster *E-mail:* m.defuster@castrumperegrini.nl
Communication & Marketing Manager: Frans Damman *E-mail:* f.damman@castrumperegrini.nl
Program Manager: Lars Ebert *E-mail:* l.ebert@castrumperegrini.nl
Founded: 1951
Subjects: Antiques, Biography, Memoirs, Literature, Literary Criticism, Essays, Poetry
ISBN Prefix(es): 978-90-6034
Total Titles: 100 Print
Orders to: Hermannstr 61, 53225 Bonn, Germany

CED Rotterdam
Dwerggras 30, 3068 PC Rotterdam
Mailing Address: Postbus 8639, 3009 AP Rotterdam
Tel: (010) 4071 599 *Fax:* (010) 4202 227
E-mail: info@cedgroep.nl
Web Site: www.cedgroep.nl
Key Personnel
Chief Executive Officer & Mng Dir: Theo Magito *Tel:* (010) 4071 565 *E-mail:* t.magito@cedgroep.nl
Dir, Finance: Wim Wellens
Manager, Sales, Marketing & Communication: Marijke Erades *Tel:* (010) 4071 726 *E-mail:* m.erades@cedgroep.nl
Dir, Regional Market: Hans Piederiet *Tel:* (010) 4071 527 *E-mail:* h.piederiet@cedgroep.nl
Dir, Research & Development: Margeke Hoogenkamp *Tel:* (010) 4071 518 *E-mail:* m.hoogenkamp@cedgroep.nl

Founded: 1992
Specialize in training for professionals in child education.
Subjects: Education
ISBN Prefix(es): 978-90-5819; 978-90-75074
Total Titles: 104 Print; 11 Audio
Parent Company: CED Groep
Branch Office(s)
Tolakkerweg 153, 3738 JL Maartensdijk
  Tel: (0346) 219777

Uitgeverij Christofoor
Steniaweg 32, 3702 AG Zeist
Mailing Address: Postbus 234, 3700 AE Zeist
Tel: (030) 6923974 *Fax:* (030) 6914834
E-mail: info@christofoor.nl
Web Site: www.christofoor.nl
Key Personnel
Publisher: Femke de Wolff
Founded: 1975
Subjects: Animals, Pets, Biblical Studies, Biography, Memoirs, Child Care & Development, Cookery, Crafts, Games, Hobbies, Education, Fiction, History, How-to, Philosophy, Psychology, Psychiatry, Science Fiction, Fantasy
ISBN Prefix(es): 978-90-6238; 978-90-6038

Citerreeks, *imprint of* Uitgeverij Kok

Uitgeverij Conserve+
Tureluur 12, 1873 JW Groet Schoorl
Mailing Address: Postbus 74, 1870 AB Schoorl
Tel: (072) 509 3693 *Fax:* (072) 509 4370
E-mail: info@conserve.nl
Web Site: www.conserve.nl
Key Personnel
Publisher: Kees De Bakker
Founded: 1983
Subjects: Biography, Memoirs, Fiction, History, Literature, Literary Criticism, Essays, Mysteries, Suspense, Caribbean, Surinam, World War II
ISBN Prefix(es): 978-90-71380; 978-90-5429
Total Titles: 250 Print

Corona, *imprint of* Ars Scribendi Uitgeverij BV

Uitgeverij Cossee
Kerkstr 361, 1071 HW Amsterdam
Tel: (020) 528 99 11 *Fax:* (020) 528 99 12
E-mail: info@cossee.com
Web Site: www.cossee.com
Key Personnel
Publisher: Christoph Buchwald
  E-mail: buchwald@cossee.com; Eva Cossee
Editor: Irwan Droog *E-mail:* droog@cossee.com
Founded: 2001
Subjects: Fiction, Nonfiction (General), Poetry
ISBN Prefix(es): 978-90-5936

Uitgeverij Coutinho BV (Coutinho Publishing)+
Slochterenlaan 7, 1400 AH Bussum
Mailing Address: Postbus 333, 1400 AH Bussum
Tel: (035) 6949991 *Fax:* (035) 6947165
E-mail: info@coutinho.nl
Web Site: www.coutinho.nl
Key Personnel
Dir: Dick Coutinho *E-mail:* coutinho@coutinho.nl
Publishing Dir: NynKe Coutinho *E-mail:* nynke.coutinho@coutinho.nl
Marketing: Carlijn Leijen *E-mail:* leijen@coutinho.nl
Founded: 1976
Membership(s): NUV.
Subjects: Communications, Economics, Education, English as a Second Language, History, Human Relations, Language Arts, Linguistics, Literature, Literary Criticism, Essays, Philosophy, Science (General)
ISBN Prefix(es): 978-90-6283
Distributed by EPO (Belgium)

Otto Cramwinckel Uitgever
Charlotte Pallandtlaan 18, 2272 TR Voorburg
Tel: (020) 627 66 09 *Fax:* (020) 638 38 17
E-mail: info@cram.nl
Web Site: www.cram.nl
Key Personnel
Publisher: Otto Cramwinckel *E-mail:* otto@cramwinckel.nl
Founded: 1985
Membership(s): Nederlands Uitgeversverbond (Dutch Publishers Association).
Subjects: Communications, Radio, TV
ISBN Prefix(es): 978-90-71894; 978-90-75727

CRC Press/Balkema+
Member of Taylor & Francis Group, an Informa Business
Schipholweg 107C, 2316 XC Leiden
Mailing Address: PO Box 11320, 2301 EH Leiden
Tel: (071) 524 30 80
E-mail: pub.nl@taylorandfrancis.com
Web Site: www.balkema.nl; www.crcpress.com
Key Personnel
Senior Publisher: Janjaap Blom *E-mail:* janjaap.blom@taylorandfrancis.com
Founded: 1972
Specialize in engineering, Earth sciences & water sciences.
Subjects: Archaeology, Biological Sciences, Civil Engineering, Earth Sciences, Engineering (General), Environmental Studies, Geography, Geology, Mechanical Engineering, Natural History, Physics
ISBN Prefix(es): 978-0-415; 978-90-6191; 978-90-5410; 978-90-265; 978-90-5809; 978-0-86961
Number of titles published annually: 80 Print; 80 E-Book
Total Titles: 1,000 Print; 10 CD-ROM
Ultimate Parent Company: Informa Ltd UK
Branch Office(s)
CRC Press/Chapman & Hall, Albert House, 4th floor, 1-4 Singer St, London EC2A 4BQ, United Kingdom *Tel:* (020) 7017 6331 *Fax:* (020) 7017 6747 *E-mail:* orders@taylorandfrancis.com
U.S. Office(s): CRC Press/Taylor & Francis Group, 6000 Broken Sound Blvd NW, Suite 300, Boca Raton, FL 33487, United States *Tel:* 561-994-0555 *Fax:* 561-989-9732 *E-mail:* orders@taylorandfrancis.com
Foreign Rep(s): Taylor & Francis Group
Foreign Rights: Taylor & Francis Group
Distribution Center: Bookpoint, 130 Milton Park, Abingdon, Oxon OX14 4SB, United Kingdom *Tel:* (01235) 400 400 *Web Site:* bookpoint.wp.hachette.co.uk

Uitgeverij De Driehoek+
Imprint of Milinda Uitgevers
Mathenesserlaan 326, 3021 HX Rotterdam
Mailing Address: Postbus 61220, 3002 HE Rotterdam
Tel: (010) 4113867 *Fax:* (010) 4113932
E-mail: info@milinda.nl
Web Site: www.milinda-uitgevers.nl/driehoek/actueel
Key Personnel
Contact: Reinoud Douwes
Founded: 1933
Subjects: Asian Studies, Health, Nutrition, Medicine, Nursing, Dentistry, Religion - Buddhist
ISBN Prefix(es): 978-90-6030

De Vier Windstreken+
Amperelaan 3, 2289 CD Rijswijk
Tel: (070) 4131191 *Fax:* (070) 4131181
E-mail: info@vierwindstreken.com
Web Site: www.vierwindstreken.com

Key Personnel
Dir & Publisher: Bob Markus *E-mail:* bob.markus@vierwindstreken.com
Editor & Promotion: Cindy van Kester *E-mail:* cindy@vierwindstreken.com
Domestic Sales: Susana Abascal *E-mail:* susana@vierwindstreken.com
Founded: 1996
ISBN Prefix(es): 978-90-5579; 978-90-5116
Number of titles published annually: 50 Print

Derksen, Van Egmond & Derksen, *imprint of* Overamstel Uitgevers

Dienstboek, *imprint of* Boekencentrum Uitgevers BV

Van Dishoeck, *imprint of* Uitgeverij Unieboek|Het Spectrum BV

Dominicus, *imprint of* Gottmer Uitgevers Groep

Uitgeverij Ad Donker BV+
Koningin Emmaplein 1, 3016 AA Rotterdam
Tel: (010) 4363009
E-mail: donker@bart.nl
Web Site: www.uitgeverijdonker.nl
Key Personnel
Dir & Publisher: Willem A Donker
Founded: 1938
Subjects: Biography, Memoirs, Education, Fiction, History, Psychology, Psychiatry, Social Sciences, Sociology
ISBN Prefix(es): 978-90-6100
Number of titles published annually: 25 Print
Total Titles: 150 Print
Imprints: Wilkerdon

Uitgeverij Dwarsstap, *imprint of* Uitgeverij SUN Architecture

Uitgeverij Edu'Actief BV+
Zomerdijk 9e, 7942 JR Meppel
Mailing Address: Postbus 1056, 7940 KB Meppel
Tel: (0522) 235235; (0522) 235270 *Fax:* (0522) 235222
E-mail: info@edu-actief.nl
Web Site: www.edu-actief.nl
Key Personnel
Mng Dir: Jannes Hessels
Founded: 1848
Specialize in educational books for primary, secondary, vocational & adult education.
Membership(s): Groep Educatieve Uitgeverijen (GEU).
Subjects: Communications, Economics, Education, Foreign Countries, Geography, Geology, Management, Marketing, Nonfiction (General), Vocational Education
ISBN Prefix(es): 978-90-5117; 978-90-372; 978-90-5766; 978-90-6053
Parent Company: Koninklijke Boom Uitgevers

Elektor, *imprint of* Elektor International Media BV

Elektor Elektronics, *imprint of* Elektor International Media BV

Elektor International Media BV+
Subsidiary of Zhomer
Allee 1, 6141 AV Limbricht
Mailing Address: Postbus 11, 6114 ZG Susteren
Tel: (046) 4389444 *Fax:* (046) 4370161
E-mail: info@elektor.nl
Web Site: www.elektor.nl
Key Personnel
Mng Dir & Publisher: Don Akkermans
Founded: 1961

Subjects: Electronics, Electrical Engineering, Philosophy, Science (General)
ISBN Prefix(es): 978-90-5381; 978-90-70160
Imprints: Elektor; Elektor Elektronics; Publitronic

Uitgeverij Elmar+
Molslaan 131A, 2611 RL Delft
Tel: (015) 7370138
E-mail: info@uitgeverijelmar.nl
Web Site: www.uitgeverijelmar.nl
Key Personnel
Dir: Ton van Poelgeest *Tel:* (06) 18140678
  E-mail: tonvanpoelgeest@uitgeverijelmar.nl
Publisher: Kees van Bommel *E-mail:* kees@
  uitgeverijelmar.nl; Herman Masthoff
  E-mail: masthoff@uitgeverijelmar.nl
Founded: 1961
Subjects: Biography, Memoirs, Health, Nutrition,
  History, How-to, Humor, Nonfiction (General),
  Sports, Athletics, Travel & Tourism
ISBN Prefix(es): 978-90-6120; 978-90-389; 978-
  90-5814; 978-90-8553

Enterbooks, *imprint of* Uitgeverij De Toorts BV

Europa Law Publishing
PO Box 6047, 9702 HA Groingen
Tel: (050) 526 3844 *Fax:* (084) 832 5076
E-mail: info@europalawpublishing.com
Web Site: www.europalawpublishing.com
Key Personnel
Publisher: Dr Jacqueline Lensink
Subjects: Law, Environmental Law, International
  Law, International Trade
ISBN Prefix(es): 978-90-76871; 978-90-8952

Falkplan BV
Anderlechtstr 15, 5628 WB Eindhoven
Tel: (040) 26 45 104 *Fax:* (040) 26 45 115
E-mail: helpdesk@falk.nl; info@falk.nl; media@
  falk.nl; fietsplanner@falk.nl
Web Site: www.falk.nl
ISBN Prefix(es): 978-90-287

Fantom, *imprint of* Ars Scribendi Uitgeverij BV

Flash, *imprint of* Ars Scribendi Uitgeverij BV

De Fontein, *imprint of* Uitgeverij De
Fontein|Tirion

De Fontein Jeugd, *imprint of* Uitgeverij De
Fontein|Tirion

Uitgeverij De Fontein|Tirion
Subsidiary of Veen Bosch & Keuning Uitgevers-
  groep BV
Herculesplein 96, 3584 AA Utrecht
Mailing Address: Postbus 8049, 3503 AA Utrecht
Tel: (088) 700 26 00; (030) 252 85 00
E-mail: info@defonteintirion.nl
Web Site: www.defonteintirion.nl
Founded: 2009
Membership(s): The Combo Group.
Subjects: Animals, Pets, Cookery, Crafts, Games,
  Hobbies, Fiction, History, Humor, Mysteries,
  Suspense, Nonfiction (General), Science (Gen-
  eral), Sports, Athletics, Technology, Women's
  Studies
ISBN Prefix(es): 978-90-325; 978-90-261; 978-
  90-5121; 978-90-5210; 978-90-439
Imprints: De Fontein; De Fontein Jeugd; De
  Kern; Tirion Art & Creatief; Tirion Natuur;
  Tirion Sport
Foreign Rep(s): Veen Bosch & Keuning (Bel-
  gium)

Fontes Pers, *imprint of* Holland University Press
BV

Fw:Books
Laagte Kadijk 148, 1018 ZD Amsterdam
Tel: (020) 4282047
E-mail: info@fw-photography.nl
Web Site: fw-photography.nl
Subjects: Art, Photography
ISBN Prefix(es): 978-94-90119
Distributed by Idea Books

Gaberbocchus Press+
Postbus 3547, 1001 AH Amsterdam
Tel: (020) 6245181 *Fax:* (020) 6230672
E-mail: info@deharmonie.nl
Web Site: www.gaberbocchus.nl
Key Personnel
Rights Manager: Elsbeth Louis *E-mail:* elouis@
  deharmonie.nl
Founded: 1948
Subjects: Literature, Literary Criticism, Essays
ISBN Prefix(es): 978-90-6169; 978-0-85247
Total Titles: 26 Print
Parent Company: Uitgeverij De Harmonie
Orders to: Athenaeum Booksellers, Spui 14-
  16, 1012 XA Amsterdam *Tel:* (020) 6384901
  E-mail: info@athenaeum.nl

Uitgeverij Van Gennep BV+
Nieuwezijds Voorburgwal 330, 1012 RW Amster-
  dam
Tel: (020) 6247033 *Fax:* (020) 6247035
E-mail: info@vangennep-boeken.nl
Web Site: www.vangennep-boeken.nl
Key Personnel
Publisher: Chris ten Kate *E-mail:* chris@
  vangennep-boeken.nl
Editor: Nadia Ramer *E-mail:* nadia@vangennep-
  boeken.nl; Rebecca Wilson *E-mail:* rebecca@
  vangennep-boeken.nl
Founded: 1969
Subjects: Art, Fiction, Foreign Countries, Govern-
  ment, Political Science, History, Literature, Lit-
  erary Criticism, Essays, Philosophy, Psychol-
  ogy, Psychiatry, Religion - Buddhist, Religion -
  Catholic, Religion - Hindu, Religion - Islamic,
  Religion - Jewish, Religion - Protestant, Reli-
  gion - Other, Social Sciences, Sociology
ISBN Prefix(es): 978-90-6012; 978-90-5515
Imprints: Sara

Uitgeverij De Geus BV
Oude Vest 9, 4811 HR Breda
Mailing Address: Postbus 1878, 4801 BW Breda
Tel: (076) 522 81 51 *Fax:* (076) 522 25 99
E-mail: email@degeus.nl
Web Site: www.degeus.nl
Key Personnel
Dir & Publisher: Eric Visser
Publisher, Dutch Literature & Nonfiction/Rights:
  Sander van Vlerken *E-mail:* s.v.vlerken@
  degeus.nl
Founded: 1983
Specialize in international & Dutch literature,
  crime & nonfiction.
Subjects: Fiction, Nonfiction (General), Crime
  Literature
ISBN Prefix(es): 978-90-5226; 978-90-6222; 978-
  90-70610; 978-90-445
Number of titles published annually: 100 Print
Branch Office(s)
Meierij 68, 9660 Brakel-Michelbeke, Belgium
  Tel: (055) 420 676 *Fax:* (055) 420 835; (047)
  4837 367 *E-mail:* r.vanlitsenburg@degeus.de

Global Oriental, *imprint of* Brill

Global Oriental+
Imprint of Brill
Planttijnstr 2, 2321 JC Leiden
Mailing Address: Postbus 9000, 2300 PA Leiden
Tel: (071) 53 53 500 *Fax:* (071) 53 17 532
E-mail: sales-nl@brill.nl; marketing@brill.nl

Web Site: www.brill.com
Key Personnel
Publisher: Albert Hoffstadt *E-mail:* hoffstadt@
  brill.nl
Marketing Manager: Gerda Danielsson Coe
  E-mail: danielsson@brill.com
Founded: 1996
Subjects: Art, Asian Studies, Biography, Mem-
  oirs, Geography, Geology, History, Language
  Arts, Linguistics, Literature, Literary Criti-
  cism, Essays, Religion - Other, Social Sciences,
  Sociology, Transportation, Travel & Tourism,
  Women's Studies, China-General Reference,
  Comparative & Cultural Studies, Japan-General
  Reference, Korea-General Reference, Lafcadio
  Hearn Studies, Martial Arts, Media & Cultural
  Studies, Mongolia-General Reference
ISBN Prefix(es): 978-1-901903; 978-1-905246;
  978-1-906876
Number of titles published annually: 10 Print
Total Titles: 200 Print
Distribution Center: Brill, c/o Turpin Distribu-
  tion, Stratton Business Park, Pegasus Dr, Big-
  gleswade, Beds SG18 8TQ, United Kingdom
  Tel: (01767) 604-954 *Fax:* (01767) 601-640
  E-mail: brill@turpin-distribution.com (outside
  North America)
Brill, c/o Turpin Distribution, 143 West St, New
  Milford, CT 06776, United States *Tel:* 860-
  350-0041 *Fax:* 860-350-0039 *E-mail:* brillna@
  turpin-distribution.com (North America)

Gloriae, *imprint of* A W Bruna Uitgevers BV

Van Goor, *imprint of* Uitgeverij Unieboek|Het
Spectrum BV

Van Goor+
Imprint of Uitgeverij Unieboek|Het Spectrum BV
Papiermolen 14-24, 3994 DK Houten
Mailing Address: Postbus 97, 3990 DB Houten
Tel: (030) 799 83 00 *Fax:* (030) 799 83 98
E-mail: info@unieboekspectrum.nl
Web Site: www.unieboekspectrum.nl
Key Personnel
Sales Manager: Ruurd Woudstra *E-mail:* ruurd.
  woudstra@unieboekspectrum.nl
Foreign Rights: Mrs Geri Brandjes *Tel:* (020) 615
  3473 *E-mail:* geri@boek-pr.nl
Associate Companies: Standaard; Unieboek
  E-mail: info@unieboek.nl *Web Site:* www.
  unieboek.nl

Goose Press, *imprint of* Architectura & Natura

Gottmer, *imprint of* Gottmer Uitgevers Groep

Gottmer Uitgevers Groep (Gottmer Publishing
Group)+
Zijlweg 308, 2015 CN Haarlem
Mailing Address: Postbus 317, 2000 AH Haarlem
Tel: (023) 54 111 90; (023) 54 116 09 (foreign
  rights) *Fax:* (023) 52 744 04
E-mail: info@gottmer.nl
Web Site: www.gottmer.nl
Key Personnel
Dir: Melanie Lasance
Head, Sales: Marius van Campen
Founded: 1938
Subjects: Crafts, Games, Hobbies, Fiction, House
  & Home, Inspirational, Spirituality, Nonfiction
  (General), Religion - Other, Science (General),
  Sports, Athletics, Travel & Tourism, Body-
  Mind-Spirit, Lifestyle, Nautical
ISBN Prefix(es): 978-90-257; 978-90-230; 978-
  90-6834
Imprints: Altamira (body, mind & spirit); Becht
  (cookery & crafts); Dominicus (travel guides);
  Gottmer (children's & juvenile books); Hollan-
  dia (nautical books)

De Groot Goudriaan, *imprint of* Uitgeverij Kok

B R Gruener Publishing Co, *imprint of* John Benjamins Publishing Co

Happinez, *imprint of* A W Bruna Uitgevers BV

Uitgeverij De Harmonie (De Harmonie Publishers)+
Postbus 3547, 1001 AH Amsterdam
Tel: (020) 6245181 *Fax:* (020) 6230672
E-mail: info@deharmonie.nl
Web Site: www.deharmonie.nl
Key Personnel
Rights & Permissions: Elsbeth Louis
 E-mail: elouis@deharmonie.nl
Founded: 1972
Specialize in translated literature, poetry, comics & children's books.
Subjects: Fiction, Humor, Literature, Literary Criticism, Essays, Poetry, Comics
ISBN Prefix(es): 978-90-6169; 978-90-803481; 978-90-76168; 978-90-76174
Number of titles published annually: 35 Print
Total Titles: 1,200 Print; 6 Audio
Subsidiaries: Gaberbocchus Press

HarperCollins Holland
Division of HarperCollins Publishers
Kabelweg 37, 1014 BA Amsterdam
Tel: (020) 662 6646
E-mail: info@harpercollins.nl
Web Site: www.harpercollins.nl
Key Personnel
Publisher: Jacqueline de Jong
Mng Dir: Jan-Joris Keijzer
Subjects: Mysteries, Suspense, Romance, Science Fiction, Fantasy
ISBN Prefix(es): 978-90-347

Historische Uitgeverij+
Westersingel 37, 9718 CC Groningen
Tel: (050) 3181700
E-mail: info@historischeuitgeverij.nl; bestel@historischeuitgeverij.nl (orders); international@historischeuitgeverij.nl (international rights)
Web Site: www.historischeuitgeverij.nl
Key Personnel
Publisher: Patrick Everard *E-mail:* p.everard@historischeuitgeverij.nl
Founded: 1986
Subjects: History, Journalism, Literature, Literary Criticism, Essays, Nonfiction (General), Philosophy, Poetry, Psychology, Psychiatry, Mysticism, Nature
ISBN Prefix(es): 978-90-6554
Number of titles published annually: 20 Print
Total Titles: 150 Print
Foreign Rep(s): Van Halewyck (Jan Halsberghe) (Belgium); Gerald Pels Boekdiensten (Gerard Pels) (Netherlands)

Van Holkema & Warendorf, *imprint of* Uitgeverij Unieboek|Het Spectrum BV

Uitgeverij Holland
Spaarne 110, 2011 CM Haarlem
Tel: (023) 5323061 *Fax:* (023) 5342908
E-mail: info@uitgeverijholland.nl
Web Site: www.uitgeverijholland.nl
Key Personnel
Publisher: Ruurt van Ulzen
Founded: 1921
Subjects: Fiction, Philosophy, Poetry, Science (General), Travel & Tourism
ISBN Prefix(es): 978-90-251

Holland University Press BV (Holland Universiteits Pers BV)
Subsidiary of APA (Academic Publishers Associated)
Archangelkade 2-A, 1013 BE Amsterdam
Tel: (068) 1472742 (cell)
E-mail: orders@apa-publishers.com
Web Site: www.apa-publishers.com
Subjects: History, Human Relations, Language Arts, Linguistics, Law, Maritime, Theology
ISBN Prefix(es): 978-90-6037; 978-90-302; 978-90-6039; 978-90-6042
Imprints: Fontes Pers

Hollandia, *imprint of* Gottmer Uitgevers Groep

Hollandia+
Imprint of Gottmer Uitgevers Groep
Zijlweg 308, 2015 CN Haarlem
Mailing Address: Postbus 317, 2000 AH Haarlem
Tel: (023) 5411190 *Fax:* (023) 5274404
E-mail: info@gottmer.nl
Web Site: www.gottmer.nl/watersportboeken
Key Personnel
Publisher: Ben Rutte
Foreign Rights: Renee Ferment *Tel:* (023) 5411609 *E-mail:* rf@gottmer.nl
Founded: 1899
Subjects: Fiction, Maritime, Sports, Athletics, Transportation, Travel & Tourism
ISBN Prefix(es): 978-90-6410; 978-90-6045

Hollands Diep, *imprint of* Overamstel Uitgevers

Hotei Publishing, *imprint of* Brill

House of Books, *imprint of* Overamstel Uitgevers

The House of Books
Paul van Vlissingenstr 18, 1096 BK Amsterdam
Mailing Address: Postbus 107, 4130 EC Vianen
Tel: (0347) 379585; (020) 462 4300 *Fax:* (0347) 379271
E-mail: info@thehouseofbooks.com
Web Site: www.thehouseofbooks.com
Key Personnel
Publishing Dir: Heleen Buth
Founded: 2000
Subjects: Fiction, Mysteries, Suspense, Nonfiction (General)
ISBN Prefix(es): 978-90-443

ImageBooks Factory BV
Member of ImageGroup Holland BV
Doornhoek 3742, 5465 TA Veghel
Tel: (0413) 38 72 72 *Fax:* (0413) 38 72 71
E-mail: sales@imagebooks.nl; info@imagegroupholland.nl
Web Site: www.imagebooks.nl
Key Personnel
Chief Executive Officer & Publisher: Michael van Tinteren
International Sales Dir: Maurice Zant
 E-mail: maurice@imagebooks.nl
Subjects: Cookery, Crafts, Games, Hobbies, Literature, Literary Criticism, Essays
ISBN Prefix(es): 978-90-5964
Foreign Rights: KB Books & Music Publishing (Central America, North America, South America); Lenz-Mulligan Rights & Co-editions (worldwide)
Distribution Center: Allmedia Uitgeverij BV *Tel:* (0413) 38 72 92; (0413) 38 72 93 *E-mail:* verkoop@imagebooks.nl *Web Site:* www.allmedia.nl

International Books, *imprint of* Uitgeverij Jan van Arkel

Uitgeverij International Theatre & Film Books+
Johan Hofmanstr 262, 1069 KE Amsterdam
Tel: (020) 662 52 42
E-mail: info@itfb.nl
Web Site: www.itfb.nl
Key Personnel
Contact: Marlies Oele
Founded: 1975
Specialize in theatre & film books.
Subjects: Drama, Theater, Film, Video, Music, Dance
ISBN Prefix(es): 978-90-6403
Number of titles published annually: 25 Print
Total Titles: 500 Print
Distribution Center: Centraal Boekhuis, Erasmusweg 10, Postbus 125, 4100 AC Culemborg *Tel:* (0345) 47 59 11 *E-mail:* service@cb-logistics.nl *Web Site:* www.cb-logistics.nl

Uitgeverij Intertaal bv
Transistorstr 80, 1322 CH Almere
Mailing Address: Postbus 60081, 1320 AB Almere
Tel: (036) 547 16 40 *Fax:* (036) 547 15 82
E-mail: uitgeverij@intertaal.nl
Web Site: www.intertaal.nl
Key Personnel
Publisher: Wouter de Vries
Founded: 1962
Specialize in language learning products for education & business.
Also importer & distributor.
Subjects: Language Arts, Linguistics
ISBN Prefix(es): 978-90-70885; 978-90-5451; 978-90-800002
Branch Office(s)
Bisschoppenhoflaan 383, 2100 Deurne, Belgium *Tel:* (03) 220 65 00 *Fax:* (03) 226 81 86 *E-mail:* uitgeverij@intertaal.be
Showroom(s): Inter L, Schuttershofstr 43, 2000 Antwerp, Belgium
Warehouse: Lemelerbergweg 21-22, 1101 AJ Amsterdam

IOS Press BV+
Nieuwe Hemweg 6B, 1013 BG Amsterdam
Tel: (020) 688 3355 *Fax:* (020) 687 0019
E-mail: info@iospress.nl
Web Site: www.iospress.nl
Key Personnel
Dir: Dr Einar Fredriksson; Popke Huizinga
Contact: Astrid Engelen *E-mail:* a.engelen@iospress.nl
Founded: 1987
Subjects: Biological Sciences, Chemistry, Chemical Engineering, Computer Science, Electronics, Electrical Engineering, Environmental Studies, Health, Nutrition, Language Arts, Linguistics, Management, Mathematics, Mechanical Engineering, Medicine, Nursing, Dentistry, Physics, Technology
ISBN Prefix(es): 978-90-6275; 978-90-407; 978-90-5199; 978-1-58603; 978-0-9673355; 978-1-60750; 978-90-298; 978-1-61499
Number of titles published annually: 90 Print
Total Titles: 2,000 Print
Subsidiaries: IOS Press Inc (USA)
Branch Office(s)
Xiaguangli 66, Beijing 100027, China *Toll Free Tel:* 0400 661 8717 *Fax:* (010) 8446 7947 *E-mail:* china@iospress.cn
c/o Ohmsha Ltd, 3-1 Kanda Nishiki-cho, Chiyoda-ku, Tokyo 101, Japan *Tel:* (03) 3233 0641 *Fax:* (03) 3233 6224 *E-mail:* chokuhan@ohmsha.co.jp
U.S. Office(s): West Point Commons, 1816 West Point Pike, Suite 125, Lansdale, PA 19446, United States *Tel:* 215-393-5026 *Fax:* 215-660-5042 *E-mail:* iospress@accucoms.com
6751 Tepper Dr, Clifton, VA 20124, United States *Tel:* 703-830-6300 *Fax:* 703-830-2300 *E-mail:* sales@iospress.com

Foreign Rep(s): Continental Contacts (Roy de Boo) (Benelux, Germany); Disvan Enterprises (India); Michael Goh (Southeast Asia); Jahan Adib Publishing (Farhad Maftoon) (Iran); Marek Lewinson (Eastern Europe); Mare Nostrum Publishing Consultants (Cristina de Lara Ruiz) (Portugal, Spain); Princeton Selling Group (Robert K Meehan) (North America); Linda Sametz Remba (Middle America, South America)

Uitgeverij IT&FB, see Uitgeverij International Theatre & Film Books

Jap Sam Books
Hoge Heijningsedijk 5, 4794 AA Heijningen
Tel: (087) 8755579 *Fax:* (084) 2150921
E-mail: info@japsambooks.nl
Web Site: www.japsambooks.nl
Key Personnel
Publisher: Eleonoor Jap Sam
Subjects: Architecture & Interior Design, Art, Fashion, Film, Video, Philosophy, Photography, Design
ISBN Prefix(es): 978-94-90322
Foreign Rep(s): Art Data (France, Ireland, Japan, UK); RAM Publications (Canada, USA); Vice Versa Distribution (Austria, Germany, Italy, Switzerland)
Distribution Center: Centraal Boekhuis, Erasmusweg 10, PO Box 125, 4100 AC Culemborg *Tel:* (0345) 47 59 11 *Fax:* (0345) 47 53 43 *E-mail:* info@cb-logistics.nl *Web Site:* www. cb-logistics.nl

Uitgeverij Jes!, *imprint of* Boekencentrum Uitgevers BV

Karakter Uitgevers BV (Character Publishers BV)
Postbus 70, 1420 AB Uithoorn
Tel: (0297) 38644
E-mail: info@karakteruitgevers.nl; bestelservice@ karakteruitgevers.nl
Web Site: www.karakteruitgevers.nl
Key Personnel
Account Manager: Remko Polack *E-mail:* remko. polack@karakteruitgevers.nl; Eric Winkel *E-mail:* eric.winkel@karakteruitgevers.nl
Marketing & Foreign Rights: Martien Elema *E-mail:* martien.elema@karakteruitgevers.nl
Specialize in commercial fiction, practical nonfiction, computer software, books & audiobooks.
Subjects: Fiction, Nonfiction (General)
ISBN Prefix(es): 978-90-6112; 978-90-452

De Kern, *imprint of* Uitgeverij De Fontein|Tirion

KITLV Press+
Division of Royal Netherlands Academy of Arts & Science (KNAW)
Reuvensplaats 2, 2311 BE Leiden
Mailing Address: Postbus 9515, 2300 RA Leiden
Tel: (071) 527 2295 *Fax:* (071) 527 2638
E-mail: kitlv@kitlv.nl
Web Site: kitlv.nl/publications
Key Personnel
Dir: Dr Gert Oostindie *E-mail:* oostindie@kitlv.nl
Head, Publications & Personnel: Rosemarijn Hoefte *Tel:* (071) 527 2291 *E-mail:* hofte@ kitlv.nl
Founded: 1851
Subjects: Anthropology, Asian Studies, Economics, Environmental Studies, History, Language Arts, Linguistics, Social Sciences, Sociology, Women's Studies, Caribbean Studies
ISBN Prefix(es): 978-90-6718
Number of titles published annually: 20 Print; 2 Online
Total Titles: 250 Print

Distributed by The Asian Experts (Australia); Institute of Southeast Asian Studies (Singapore & Malaysia); United Publishers Services (Japan); University of Washington Press (USA & Canada)

Uitgeverij Klement, *imprint of* Boekencentrum Uitgevers BV

Kloof Booksellers & Scientia Verlag
Limmerick 7, 1046 AR Amsterdam
Tel: (020) 6223828
E-mail: kloof@xs4all.nl
Web Site: www.scientia-verlag-aalen.de; www. dekloof.com
Founded: 1953
Subjects: Archaeology, Economics, Education, History, Law, Philosophy, Religion - Other, Social Sciences, Sociology, Theology
ISBN Prefix(es): 978-3-511

Uitgeverij Kluitman Alkmaar BV (Kluitman Alkmaar Publishing Inc)
Jan Ligthartstr 11B, 1817 MR Alkmaar
Mailing Address: Postbus 9000, 1800 GR Alkmaar
Tel: (072) 52 75 075 *Fax:* (072) 52 09 400
E-mail: info@kluitman.nl; marketing@kluitman.nl
Web Site: www.kluitman.nl
Key Personnel
Publisher: Mariska Budding
Dir, Publishing: Piero Stanco
Marketing: Otto Wolring *Tel:* (072) 52 75 081
Founded: 1864
ISBN Prefix(es): 978-90-206
Imprints: Blossom Books

Kluwer Law International+
Zuidpoolsingel 2, 2408 ZE Alpen aan den Rijn
Mailing Address: Postbus 316, 2400 AH Alphen aan den Rijn
Tel: (0172) 64 1500 *Fax:* (0172) 64 1555
E-mail: sales@kluwerlaw.com
Web Site: www.kluwerarbitration.com; www.kluwercompetitionlaw.com; www.kluwerlawonline.com
Key Personnel
Marketing Dir: Joyce M Rivers
Founded: 1995
Subjects: Law, Antitrust/Competition Law, Arbitration/Litigation, Intellectual Property, International Taxation, International Trade Law
ISBN Prefix(es): 978-90-411; 978-90-6544
Number of titles published annually: 100 Print; 2 Online
Total Titles: 3,000 Print; 30 Online
Parent Company: Wolters Kluwer Law & Business
U.S. Office(s): Wolters Kluwer Law & Business, 76 Ninth Ave, 7th floor, New York, NY 10011, United States *Tel:* 212-771-0600
Distribution Center: Turpin Distribution Ltd, Stratton Business Park, Pegasus Dr, Biggleswade, Beds SG18 1BTQ, United Kingdom *Tel:* (01767) 604958 *Fax:* (0845) 0095880 *E-mail:* kluwerlaw@turpin-distribution.com (worldwide exc Canada, Central America, South America, USA)
7201 McKinney Circle, Frederick, MD 21704, United States *Tel:* 301-698-7100 (non-US customers) (Canada, Central America, South America, USA)

Kluwer Uitgeverij BV
Staverenstr 15, 7418 CJ Deventer
Mailing Address: Postbus 23, 7400 GA Deventer
Tel: (0570) 647111; (0570) 673555 (customer service) *Fax:* (0570) 634740
Web Site: www.wolterskluwer.nl
Founded: 1987

Subjects: Accounting, Business, Economics, Law, Technology, Taxes
ISBN Prefix(es): 978-90-267; 978-90-6500; 978-90-5576; 978-90-5577; 978-90-13; 978-90-14; 978-90-201; 978-90-6501
Parent Company: Wolters Kluwer NV
Branch Office(s)
Zuidpoolsingel 2, Postbus 4, 2400 MA Alphen aan den Rijn *Tel:* (0172) 466 633 *Fax:* (0172) 475 933
Lange Voorhout 84, 2514 EJ The Hague

KNNV Uitgeverij
Blvd 12, 3707 BM Zeist
Mailing Address: Postbus 310, 3700 AH Zeist
Tel: (030) 69 29 020; (030) 233 3544; (0411) 65 71 98 (customer service) *Fax:* (030) 236 8907
E-mail: info@knnvuitgeverij.nl; knnv@support. hexspoor.nl (customer service)
Web Site: www.knnvuitgeverij.nl
Key Personnel
Publisher & Assistant Dir: Rijnvis van Wirdum *E-mail:* rijnvis@knnvuitgeverij.nl
Publisher: Jack Folkers *E-mail:* folkers@ knnvuitgeverij.nl
Mng Dir: Paul Kemmeren *E-mail:* kemmeren@ knnvuitgeverij.nl
Marketing & Promotion: Kathrin Ohrmann *E-mail:* ohrmann@knnvuitgeverij.nl
Sales: Monique Lochtenberg *E-mail:* lochtenberg@knnvuitgeverij.nl
Subjects: Biological Sciences, Geography, Geology, Travel & Tourism, Conservation, Ecology, Hydrobiology, Marine Biology, Nature, Vegetation Science, Wildlife
ISBN Prefix(es): 978-90-5011
Foreign Rep(s): Davidsfonds Belgie (Joeri Dewallef) (Belgium); Jan Smit (Netherlands)

Koenen, *imprint of* Van Dale Uitgevers

Kok, *imprint of* Uitgeverij Kok

Uitgeverij Kok+
Subsidiary of Veen Bosch & Keuning Uitgeversgroep BV
Herculesplein 96, 3584 AA Utrecht
Mailing Address: Postbus 13288, 3507 LG Utrecht
Tel: (088) 700 2600 *Fax:* (088) 700 2999
E-mail: promotie@kok.nl
Web Site: www.kok.nl
Key Personnel
Sales Manager: Emiel Hendriks *Tel:* (06) 200 381 53 (cell) *E-mail:* ehendriks@vbkmedia.nl
Account Manager: Rene Slotboom *Tel:* (06) 1553 9719 (cell) *E-mail:* rslotboom@vbkmedia.nl
Founded: 1894
Subjects: Art, Behavioral Sciences, Biblical Studies, Biography, Memoirs, Environmental Studies, Fiction, History, Human Relations, Inspirational, Spirituality, Journalism, Philosophy, Poetry, Psychology, Psychiatry, Religion - Buddhist, Religion - Catholic, Religion - Hindu, Religion - Islamic, Religion - Jewish, Religion - Protestant, Religion - Other, Romance, Science (General), Self-Help, Social Sciences, Sociology, Theology, Women's Studies
ISBN Prefix(es): 978-90-266; 978-90-242; 978-90-6140; 978-90-297; 978-90-435; 978-90-205; 978-90-391; 978-90-304
Imprints: Callenbach; Citerreeks; De Groot Goudriaan; Kok; Voorhoeve; Zomer & Keuning

Kosmos Uitgevers
Subsidiary of Veen Bosch & Keuning Uitgeversgroep BV
Herculesplein 96, 3584 AA Utrecht
Mailing Address: Postbus 13288, 3507 LG Utrecht

Tel: (088) 700 2600 *Fax:* (088) 700 2699
E-mail: info@kosmosuitgevers.nl; promotie@
kosmosuitgevers.nl
Web Site: www.kosmosuitgevers.nl
Subjects: Cookery, Gardening, Plants, Health,
Nutrition, History, Inspirational, Spirituality,
Travel & Tourism, Wine & Spirits, Current Af-
fairs, Family, Leisure, Living, Personal Growth
ISBN Prefix(es): 978-90-210; 978-90-6117; 978-
90-6077; 978-90-6325; 978-90-215
Branch Office(s)
Ternesselei 326, 2160 Wommelgem, Belgium,
Marketing: Christine van Steerteghem *Tel:* (03)
355 28 36 *Fax:* (03) 355 28 40 *E-mail:* c.
vansteerteghem@vbku.be

Kugler Publications+
Imprint of SPB Academic Publishing BV
Nieuwe Hemweg 7, Hal P, Bedrijvenpark Hem-
point, Westpoortnummer 2551, 1013 BG Ams-
terdam
Mailing Address: Postbus 20538, 1001 NM Ams-
terdam
Tel: (020) 68 45 700 *Fax:* (020) 68 47 788
E-mail: info@kuglerpublications.com
Web Site: www.kuglerpublications.com
Key Personnel
Mng Dir: Simon Bakker
Founded: 1974
Subjects: Medicine, Nursing, Dentistry, Ophthal-
mology, Otorhinolaryngology
ISBN Prefix(es): 978-90-6299
Number of titles published annually: 10 Print
Total Titles: 200 Print
Foreign Rep(s): Princeton Selling Group (USA)
Distribution Center: American International Dis-
tribution Corp (AIDC), PO Box 2249, Willis-
ton, VT 05495, United States *Fax:* 802-864-
7626 *E-mail:* kug.orders@aidcvt.com

Kwintessens NZV Uitgevers
Berkenweg 11, 3818 LA Amersfoort
Mailing Address: Postbus 1492, 3800 BL Amers-
foort
Tel: (033) 460 19 40
E-mail: info@kwintessens.nl
Web Site: www.kwintessens.nl
Key Personnel
Dir: Ron Rijnbende
Founded: 1865
Specialize in the religious education of children.
Subjects: Crafts, Games, Hobbies, Philosophy,
Religion - Catholic, Religion - Protestant
ISBN Prefix(es): 978-90-5788
Parent Company: UnieNzv

Lannoo, *imprint of* Uitgeverij TerraLannoo BV

Lebowski Publishers, *imprint of* Overamstel
Uitgevers

Lebowski Publishers
Imprint of Overamstel Uitgevers
Paul van Vlissingenstr 18, 1096 BK Amsterdam
Mailing Address: Postbus 3626, 1001 AK Ams-
terdam
Tel: (020) 4624300
E-mail: stijn.devries@lebowskipublishers.nl
Web Site: www.lebowskipublishers.nl
Key Personnel
Publisher: Oscar van Gelderen
Mng Dir: Martijn Griffioen
Sales Manager: Willem Verduijn
E-mail: willem@overamstel.com
Subjects: Literature, Literary Criticism, Essays,
Nonfiction (General), Narrative, True Crime,
Urban Culture
ISBN Prefix(es): 978-90-488
Foreign Rights: WME (worldwide exc Holland)

Leiden University Press (LUP), *imprint of*
Amsterdam University Press BV (AUP)

Uitgeverij Lemniscaat+
Vijverlaan 48, 3062 HL Rotterdam
Mailing Address: Postbus 4066, 3006 AB Rotter-
dam
Tel: (010) 206 29 29 *Fax:* (010) 41 41 560
E-mail: info@lemniscaat.nl; verkoop@lemniscaat.
nl; foreignrights@lemniscaat.nl
Web Site: www.lemniscaat.nl
Key Personnel
Founder & Dir: Jean Christophe Boele van Hens-
broek
Rights: Elaine Michon
Sales: Robin van der Gaag
Founded: 1963
Subjects: Fiction, Psychology, Psychiatry, Social
Sciences, Sociology
ISBN Prefix(es): 978-90-6069; 978-90-5637
Total Titles: 380 Print
Foreign Rights: Bestun Korea Literary Agent
(Korea); Bookcosmos Agency (Korea); In-
spirees International BV (Zhou Yu) (China);
Japan UNI Agency Inc (Japan); Kids Mind
Agency (Korea); Momo Agency (Korea); Top-
pan Printing Co America Inc (Japan); Eric
Yang Agency (Korea)

Uitgeverij Leopold
Subsidiary of WPG Uitgevers
Singel 262, 1016 AC Amsterdam
Mailing Address: Postbus 3879, 1001 AR Ams-
terdam
Tel: (020) 5511250; (020) 5511262 (rights)
Fax: (020) 4204699
E-mail: info@leopold.nl; rights@leopold.nl
Web Site: www.leopold.nl
Key Personnel
Publisher: Manja Heerze *E-mail:* m.heerze@
leopold.nl
Dir: Paulien Loerts
Sales Manager: Vanessa Storm de Grave
Editor: Ria Turkenburg *E-mail:* r.turkenburg@
leopold.nl
Foreign Rights: Dania van Dishoeck *E-mail:* d.
van.dishoeck@leopold.nl
Founded: 1923
Subjects: Fiction, History, Nonfiction (General)
ISBN Prefix(es): 978-90-258
Associate Companies: BV Uitgeverij de Arbeider-
spers

LeV, *imprint of* A W Bruna Uitgevers BV

Van Loghum Slaterus, see Uitgeverij Bohn
Stafleu Van Loghum BV

Ludion, *imprint of* Uitgeverij De Bezige Bij BV

Luitingh-Sijthoff
Subsidiary of Veen Bosch & Keuning Uitgevers-
groep BV
Oostenburgervoorstr 168, 1018 MR Amsterdam
Mailing Address: Postbus 289, 1000 AG Amster-
dam
Tel: (020) 530 73 40 *Fax:* (020) 626 26 51
E-mail: info@lsamsterdam.nl; verkoop@
lsamsterdam.nl
Web Site: www.lsamsterdam.nl
Key Personnel
Publisher: Tom Harmsen
Publisher, Children's & Young Adult: Thille Dop
Editor, Children's & Young Adult: Hannerlie
Modderman
Commercial Manager: Cor Nieuwendijk
E-mail: cnieuwendijk@lsamsterdam.nl
Foreign Rights Manager: Annelies Sijmons
E-mail: asijmons@lsamsterdam.nl

Subjects: Fiction, Mysteries, Suspense, Nonfiction
(General), Science Fiction, Fantasy
ISBN Prefix(es): 978-90-245; 978-90-218

Magnum, *imprint of* Ars Scribendi Uitgeverij BV

Uitgeverij Malmberg BV
Magistratenlaan 138, 5223 MB Den Bosch
Mailing Address: Postbus 233, 5201 AE Den
Bosch
Tel: (073) 628 88 11 *Fax:* (073) 621 05 12
E-mail: malmberg@malmberg.nl
Web Site: www.malmberg.nl
Key Personnel
Marketing Manager: Ingmar Volmer
Founded: 1885
Subjects: Biological Sciences, Chemistry, Chem-
ical Engineering, Education, Mathematics,
Physics
ISBN Prefix(es): 978-90-208; 978-90-345
Distribution Center: De Beverspijken 5, Postbus
233, 5201 AE Den Bosch *Tel:* (073) 628 8811
Fax: (073) 631 2931

Mana, *imprint of* Uitgeverij Unieboek|Het
Spectrum BV

Maven Publishing
Willem Fenengastr 2L, 1096 BN Amsterdam
Tel: (020) 7371065
E-mail: info@mavenpublishing.nl
Web Site: www.mavenpublishing.nl
Key Personnel
Publisher: Sander Ruys *Tel:* (06) 39752551
E-mail: sander@mavenpublishing.nl
Editor: Emma Punt *E-mail:* emma@
mavenpublishing.nl
Marketing: Lydia Busstra *E-mail:* lydia@
mavenpublishing.nl
Subjects: Psychology, Psychiatry, Science (Gen-
eral)
ISBN Prefix(es): 978-94-90574
Distributed by Uitgeverij Epo (Belgium)
Orders to: Centraal Boekhuis, Erasmusweg 10,
4104 AK Culemborg *Tel:* (0345) 475866
Fax: (0345) 375896

Uitgeverij Medema
Postbus 484, 8440 AL Heerenveen
Tel: (055) 301446; (0655) 201227 (cell)
E-mail: henk@medema.nl
Web Site: www.medema.nl
Key Personnel
Publisher: Henk P Medema
E-mail: henkpmedema@gmail.com
Founded: 1952
Subjects: Inspirational, Spirituality, Religion -
Protestant
ISBN Prefix(es): 978-90-6353
Parent Company: Uitgeversgroep Jongbloed

Uitgeverij Meinema, *imprint of* Boekencentrum
Uitgevers BV

Uitgeverij Meinema+
Imprint of Boekencentrum Uitgevers BV
Goudstr 50, 2718 RC Zoetermeer
Mailing Address: Postbus 29, 2700 AA Zoeter-
meer
Tel: (079) 361 54 81; (079) 362 82 82 (sales)
Fax: (079) 361 54 89
E-mail: info@boekencentrum.nl; verkoop@
boekencentrum.nl
Web Site: www.uitgeverijmeinema.nl
Subjects: Inspirational, Spirituality, Philosophy,
Religion - Catholic, Religion - Protestant, The-
ology, Travel & Tourism, Lifestyle
ISBN Prefix(es): 978-90-211
Number of titles published annually: 40 Print
Total Titles: 220 Print

Distribution Center: Denis & Co, Industriepark Noord 5a, 9100 Sint-Niklaas, Belgium, Press: Katrien Hebb *Tel:* (03) 760 3075 *Fax:* (03) 760 3007 *E-mail:* info@denis.be

Meis & Maas
Meeuwenlaan 98-100, 1021 JL Amsterdam
Tel: (020) 303 50 10
E-mail: info@meisenmaas.nl
Web Site: www.meisenmaas.nl
Key Personnel
Owner: Marijn Koets *Tel:* (020) 303 50 11
    E-mail: marijn@meisenmaas.nl; Sanneke van
    de Pas *Tel:* (020) 303 50 11 *E-mail:* sanneke@
    meisenmaas.nl
Manufacturing & Logistics Coordinator:
    Birgit van Melick *Tel:* (020) 303 50 12
    E-mail: birgit@meisenmaas.nl
Administration: Herman Bon *Tel:* (020) 303 50
    16 *E-mail:* herman@meisenmaas.nl
Bookstore Accounts: Bibi Rumping *Tel:* (06)
    154591 54 *E-mail:* bibi@meisenmaas.nl
Design: Marina Zurel *Tel:* (020) 303 50 12
    E-mail: marina@meisenmaas.nl
Marketing & Public Relations: Ingelien Poutsma
    Tel: (020) 303 50 13 *E-mail:* ingelien@
    meisenmaas.nl
Special Sales: Marianne Slagter *Tel:* (06) 525463
    57 *E-mail:* marianne@meisenmaas.nl
Specialize in magazines & books for children &
    teens, including brands such as Lego®, Star
    Wars© & Minecraft™.
Subjects: Crafts, Games, Hobbies
ISBN Prefix(es): 978-90-305

Mercis Publishing BV
Johannes Vermeerplein 3, 1071 DV Amsterdam
Tel: (020) 675 8036 *Fax:* (020) 672 1924
E-mail: info@mercis.nl
Web Site: www.mercispublishing.nl
ISBN Prefix(es): 978-90-5647; 978-90-73991
Imprints: Dick Bruna

Uitgeverij Meulenhoff Boekerij+
Herengracht 507, 1017 BV Amsterdam
Tel: (020) 535 31 35; (020) 535 31 22 (sales)
    Fax: (020) 535 31 30
E-mail: info@meulenhoffboekerij.nl;
    bestellingen@meulenhoffboekerij.nl (sales)
Web Site: www.meulenhoffboekerij.nl
Key Personnel
Publishing Dir: Maaike le Noble
    E-mail: mlenoble@meulenhoffboekerij.nl
Foreign Rights: Karen Bikkel *E-mail:* kbikkel@
    meulenhoffboekerij.nl
Founded: 1986
Subjects: Biography, Memoirs, Fiction, Myster-
    ies, Suspense, Nonfiction (General), Romance,
    Science Fiction, Fantasy, Dutch Fiction
ISBN Prefix(es): 978-90-225; 978-90-6974
Parent Company: Uitgeverij Lannoo Groep
Distribution Center: Uitgeverij Lannoo, Kasteel-
    str 97, 8700 Tielt, Belgium *Tel:* (051) 424 211
    Fax: (051) 401 152 *E-mail:* info@lannoo.be

Meulenhoff/Manteau, *imprint of* Uitgeverij
    Meulenhoff

Uitgeverij Meulenhoff+
Herengracht 507, 1017 BV Amsterdam
Tel: (020) 535 31 35 *Fax:* (020) 535 31 30
E-mail: info@meulenhoff.nl
Web Site: www.meulenhoff.nl
Founded: 1895
Subjects: Biography, Memoirs, Fiction, History,
    Journalism, Literature, Literary Criticism, Es-
    says, Nonfiction (General), Poetry
ISBN Prefix(es): 978-90-290
Total Titles: 1,000 Print
Parent Company: Uitgeverij Meulenhoff Boekerij

Ultimate Parent Company: Uitgeverij Lannoo
    Groep
Imprints: Meulenhoff/Manteau
Subsidiaries: Meulenhoff International
Distribution Center: Uitgeverij Lannoo, Kasteel-
    str 97, 8700 Tielt, Belgium *Tel:* (051) 424 211
    Fax: (051) 401 152 *E-mail:* info@lannoo.be

Middernacht Pers
Keizer Ottoweg 17, 1412 ED Naarden
Tel: (035) 6950931 *Fax:* (035) 5824327
E-mail: kinderboek@middernachtpers.nl
Web Site: www.middernachtpers.nl
Key Personnel
Contact: Maaike Sigar
Founded: 1986
ISBN Prefix(es): 978-90-72259

Ministerie van Infrastructuur en Milieu
Plesmanweg 1-6, 2597 JG The Hague
Mailing Address: Postbus 20901, 2500 EX The
    Hague
Tel: (070) 456 00 00 *Fax:* (070) 456 11 11
Web Site: www.rijksoverheid.nl/ministeries
Key Personnel
Minister: Melanie Schultz van Haegen-Maas
    Geesteranus
Subjects: Transportation
ISBN Prefix(es): 978-90-369

Mistral Uitgevers (Mistral Publishers)
Imprint of Overamstel Uitgevers
Paul van Vlissingenstr 18, 1096 BK Amsterdam
Mailing Address: Postbus 3626, 1001 AK Ams-
    terdam
Tel: (020) 4624300
E-mail: redactiemistral@dutch-media.nl
Web Site: www.uitgeverijmistral.nl
Key Personnel
Publisher: Harold de Croon *Tel:* (06) 27 65 29 26
    E-mail: harold.decroon@dutch-media.nl
Editor: Hanneke Wijte *E-mail:* hanneke.wijte@
    dutch-media.nl
Founded: 2007
Subjects: Biography, Memoirs, Fiction, History,
    Literature, Literary Criticism, Essays, Nonfic-
    tion (General)
ISBN Prefix(es): 978-90-4995
Number of titles published annually: 22 Print
Distribution Center: Agora, Ninovesteenweg 24,
    9320 Aalst/Erembodegem, Belgium *Tel:* (053)
    78 87 00 *Fax:* (053) 78 26 91 *Web Site:* www.
    agorabooks.com

Uitgeverij mo'media
Oude Vest 9, 4811 HR Breda
Mailing Address: Postbus 3936, 4800 DX Breda
Tel: (076) 523 90 90 *Fax:* (076) 587 91 89
E-mail: info@momedia.nl
Web Site: www.momedia.nl
Key Personnel
Dir: Rene Bego *E-mail:* rene@momedia.nl
Publisher: Joyce Enthoven *Tel:* (076) 523 90 88
    E-mail: joyce@momedia.nl
Head, Sales & Marketing: Esther Frazer
    Tel: (076) 523 90 95 *E-mail:* esther@momedia.
    nl
Founded: 1997
Subjects: Cookery, Nonfiction (General), Travel &
    Tourism, Leisure
ISBN Prefix(es): 978-90-5767

Mometrix Media LLC, see Uitgeverij mo'media

Uitgeverij Moon+
Imprint of Overamstel Uitgevers
Paul van Vlissingenstr 18, 1096 BK Amsterdam
Mailing Address: Postbus 3626, 1001 AK Ams-
    terdam
Tel: (020) 4624 000 *Fax:* (020) 531 7460
Web Site: www.uitgeverijmoon.nl

Key Personnel
Publisher: Thille Dop *E-mail:* thille.dop@
    uitgeverijmoon.nl
Commissioning Editor: Hannerlie Modderman
    E-mail: hannerlie.modderman@uitgeverijmoon.
    nl
Subjects: Fiction, Nonfiction (General)
ISBN Prefix(es): 978-90-488

Moon Uitgevers, *imprint of* Overamstel Uitgevers

Uitgeverij Mozaiek, *imprint of* Boekencentrum
    Uitgevers BV

nai010 Uitgevers
Mauritsweg 23, 3012 JR Rotterdam
Mailing Address: Postbus 21927, 3001 AX Rot-
    terdam
Tel: (010) 20 10 133 *Fax:* (010) 20 10 130
E-mail: info@nai010.com
Web Site: www.nai010.com
Key Personnel
Publisher & Dir: Eelco van Welie
Art Publisher: Barbera van Kooij
Editor & Production: Mehgan Bakhuizen
Finance: Peter Pols
Public Relations & Marketing: Esmeralda Eggen
Sales & Distribution: Jan Verhagen *E-mail:* jan@
    nai010.com
Founded: 1994
Publisher of books about architecture, art & urban
    design in Dutch & English.
Subjects: Architecture & Interior Design, Art,
    Photography, Urban Design
ISBN Prefix(es): 978-90-6450; 978-94-6208
Foreign Rep(s): Art Data (Ireland, UK); Ed-
    win Chu (China, Hong Kong); Coen Sligting
    Bookimport (Germany, Greece, Italy, Portugal,
    Spain); DAP (Central America, North America,
    South America); Idea Books (all other terri-
    tories); Julie Onishi (Asia, Japan); Padovani
    Books Ltd (Penny Padovani) (Greece, Italy,
    Portugal, Spain); Robyn Realton (Australia,
    New Zealand); Sebastien Richard (France,
    Switzerland); Bo Rudin (Scandinavia)
Bookshop(s): NAi Boekver Kopers, Museumpark
    25, 3015 CB Rotterdam *Tel:* (010) 440 12 03
    E-mail: info@naibooksellers.nl
Distribution Center: CB, Erasmusweg 10,
    4104 AK Culemborg *Tel:* (0345) 475 911
    Fax: (0345) 475 343 *Web Site:* www.cb-
    logistics.nl

Narratio Theologische Uitgeverij (Theological
    Publishing House Narratio)+
Kwakernaat 10, 4205 PK Gorinchem
Mailing Address: Postbus 1006, 4200 CA Gor-
    inchem
Tel: (0183) 62 81 88 *Fax:* (084) 739 29 45
E-mail: info@narratio.nl
Web Site: www.narratio.nl
Key Personnel
Contact: Leen van den Herik *E-mail:* lvdherik@
    narratio.nl; Dullyna van den Herik van der
    Weit
Founded: 1988
Subjects: Biblical Studies, History, Religion
    - Catholic, Religion - Protestant, Theology,
    Women's Studies
ISBN Prefix(es): 978-90-5263
Number of titles published annually: 20 Print; 2
    CD-ROM; 3 Online; 2 Audio
Total Titles: 220 Print; 10 CD-ROM; 6 Online; 5
    E-Book; 5 Audio
Associate Companies: Docete-Utrecht
Warehouse: Kon Emmastr 44a, Gorinchem

Uitgeverij NBD Biblion
Huygensstr 1, 2721 LT Zoetermeer
Mailing Address: Postbus 437, 2260 AK Leid-
    schendam

Tel: (079) 3440 345; (079) 3440 344
E-mail: info@nbdbiblion.nl
Web Site: www.nbdbiblion.nl
Publish books, journals, loose-leaf works & digital products for library & education markets.
Subjects: Fiction, Literature, Literary Criticism, Essays, Nonfiction (General)
ISBN Prefix(es): 978-90-5483; 978-90-6252
Parent Company: Groep Educatieve Uitgevers

Uitgeverij Nieuw Amsterdam
Subsidiary of WPG Uitgevers
Jahannes Vermeerstr 63, 1071 DN Amsterdam
Mailing Address: Postbus 15511, 1001 NA Amsterdam
Tel: (020) 5706100 *Fax:* (020) 5706199
E-mail: info@nieuwamsterdam.nl
Web Site: www.nieuwamsterdam.nl
Key Personnel
Publishing Dir: Lidewijde Paris *E-mail:* lparis@nieuwamsterdam.nl
Publisher: Henk ter Borg *Tel:* (020) 5706118 *E-mail:* hterborg@nieuwamsterdam.nl
Account Manager: Ruth van Gessel *E-mail:* rvangessel@nieuwamsterdam.nl
Founded: 2005
Subjects: Business, Cookery, Government, Political Science, Literature, Literary Criticism, Essays, Management, Music, Dance, Poetry, Sports, Athletics, Media, Men's Interest
ISBN Prefix(es): 978-90-468

Uitgeverij Nieuwe Stad
Abdijlaan 24, 5253 VP Niewkuijk
Tel: (073) 5113656
E-mail: nieuwe.stad@focolare.nl
Founded: 1960
Subjects: Economics, Inspirational, Spirituality, Philosophy
ISBN Prefix(es): 978-90-71734

Uitgeverij Nijgh & Van Ditmar+
Spui 10, 1012 WZ Amsterdam
Tel: (020) 76 07 210
E-mail: info@nijghenvanditmar.nl
Web Site: www.singeluitgeverijen.nl/nijgh-van-ditmar
Key Personnel
Publicity: Maartje Lugtenborg
Founded: 1837
Subjects: Fiction, Humor, Literature, Literary Criticism, Essays, Mysteries, Suspense, Nonfiction (General), Poetry, Social Sciences, Sociology
ISBN Prefix(es): 978-90-388
Parent Company: Singel Uitgeverijen
Bookshop(s): CB Vlaanderen, Wezelsebaan 4, 2900 Schoten, Belgium *Tel:* (03) 658-80-60 *Fax:* (03) 658-80-80
Distribution Center: Centraal Boekhuis, Erasmusweg 10, 4104 AK Culemburg *Tel:* (0345) 47 59 11 *Fax:* (0345) 47 53 43

Noordhoff Uitgevers BV+
Winschoterdiep 70A, 9723 AB Groningen
Mailing Address: Postbus 58, 9700 MB Groningen
Tel: (050) 52 26 922; (088) 52 26 888
Web Site: www.noordhoffuitgevers.nl
Key Personnel
General Manager: Arjen Holl
Publishing Dir: Marchien van Doorn
Commercial Dir: Joost de Ridder
Founded: 1836
Part of Wolters Kluwer Nederland.
ISBN Prefix(es): 978-90-01
Subsidiaries: Martinus Nijhoff Publishers
Branch Office(s)
Het Spoor 8-14, Postbus 342, 3990 GC Houten
Tel: (030) 6383 333

Oog en Blik, *imprint of* Uitgeverij De Bezige Bij BV

Uitgeverij Van Oorschot bv+
Herengracht 613, 1017 CE Amsterdam
Tel: (020) 6231484 *Fax:* (020) 6254083
E-mail: contact@vanoorschot.nl
Web Site: www.vanoorschot.nl
Key Personnel
Dir: Mark Pieters
Publisher: Menno Hartman
Editor: Merijn de Boer
Sales, Promotion & Publicity: Ilona van den Berg
Production: Jaap Blansjaar
Editing & Publishing Assistant: Marko van der Wal
Founded: 1945
Membership(s): Koninklijke Nederlandse Uitgeversbond (KNUB).
Subjects: Literature, Literary Criticism, Essays, Nonfiction (General), Poetry
ISBN Prefix(es): 978-90-282

Oriental Press
Subsidiary of APA (Academic Publishers Associated)
Archangelkade 2-A, 1013 BE Amsterdam
Tel: (068) 1472742 (cell)
E-mail: info@apa-publishers.com
Web Site: www.apa-publishers.com
Subjects: Asian Studies, Language Arts, Linguistics, Religion - Islamic
ISBN Prefix(es): 978-90-6023

Uitgeverij Orlando
Middenweg 82a, 1097 BS Amsterdam
Tel: (020) 6611397
E-mail: info@uitgeverijorlando.nl
Web Site: www.uitgeverijorlando.nl
Key Personnel
Publishing Dir: Jacqueline Smit *Tel:* (062) 5045678 (cell) *E-mail:* jacquelinesmit@uitgeverijorlando.nl
Founded: 2010
Subjects: Fiction
ISBN Prefix(es): 978-94-9208

Overamstel Uitgevers
Paul van Vlissingerstr 18, 1096 BK Amsterdam
Mailing Address: Postbus 3626, 1001 AK Amsterdam
Tel: (020) 4624 300
E-mail: info@overamstel.com
Web Site: www.overamsteluitgevers.nl
Key Personnel
Dir: Martijn Griffioen
Marketing: Meike Wensink *E-mail:* meike.wensink@overamstel.com
Founded: 2007
Subjects: Fiction, Mysteries, Suspense, Nonfiction (General), Science Fiction, Fantasy
ISBN Prefix(es): 978-90-488; 978-90-495
Imprints: Uitgeverij Carrera; Derksen, Van Egmond & Derksen; Hollands Diep; House of Books; Lebowski Publishers; Moon Uitgevers

Pallas Publications, *imprint of* Amsterdam University Press BV (AUP)

Uitgeverij Paris BV
Waterstr 5, 7201 HM Zutphen
Mailing Address: Postbus 4083, 7200 BB Zutphen
Tel: (0575) 514299 *Fax:* (0575) 514509
E-mail: info@uitgeverijparis.nl
Web Site: www.uitgeverijparis.nl
Key Personnel
Publisher: Antoine Paris
Founded: 2002
Legal publisher.
Subjects: Law

ISBN Prefix(es): 978-90-77320; 978-94-6251; 978-94-90962
Number of titles published annually: 20 Print
Total Titles: 60 Print

Partners Training & Innovatie, see CED Rotterdam

Uitgeverij Passage+
Boterdiep 117, 9712 LM Groningen
Mailing Address: Postbus 216, 9700 AE Groningen
Tel: (050) 5271332
E-mail: info@uitgeverijpassage.nl
Web Site: www.uitgeverijpassage.nl
Key Personnel
Publisher: Anton Scheepstra *E-mail:* antonscheepstra@uitgeverijpassage.nl
Founded: 1991
Specialize in Dutch literature.
Membership(s): KVB; Nederlands Uitgeversverbond (GAU).
Subjects: Drama, Theater, History, Music, Dance, Nonfiction (General), Poetry, Science (General), Travel & Tourism, Dutch Literature
ISBN Prefix(es): 978-90-5452
Total Titles: 60 Print
Distributed by Maklu
Foreign Rep(s): Maklu (Belgium)

Pearson Benelux
Vossiusstr 54-55, 1071 AK Amsterdam
Mailing Address: Postbus 75598, 1070 AN Amsterdam
Tel: (020) 575 5800 *Fax:* (020) 664 5334
E-mail: amsterdam@pearson.com; klantenservice@pearson.com; marketing.benelux@pearson.com
Web Site: www.pearsoneducation.nl
Key Personnel
General Dir: Rita Snaddon
Founded: 1942
Subjects: Business, Computer Science, Economics, Education, Management, Technology
ISBN Prefix(es): 978-0-201
Parent Company: Pearson PLC

The Pepin Press BV+
PO Box 10349, 1001 EH Amsterdam
Tel: (020) 4202021 *Fax:* (020) 4201152
E-mail: mail@pepinpress.com; sales@pepinpress.com
Web Site: pepinpress.com
Key Personnel
Publisher & International Rights: Mr Pepin van Roojen
Founded: 1990
Specialize in high quality art publications.
Subjects: Antiques, Archaeology, Architecture & Interior Design, Art, Asian Studies, Fashion, History, Photography
ISBN Prefix(es): 978-90-5496; 978-90-5768; 978-94-6009

Philo Press - van Heusden - Hissink & Co CV
Subsidiary of APA (Academic Publishers Associated)
Archangelkade 2-A, 1013 BE Amsterdam
Tel: (068) 1472742 (cell)
E-mail: info@apa-publishers.com; orders@apa-publishers.com
Web Site: www.apa-publishers.com
Founded: 1963
Firm incorporates Gerard Th van Heusden (APA) & G W Hissink & Co (APA).
Subjects: Art, Asian Studies, Biblical Studies, History, Human Relations, Language Arts, Linguistics, Religion - Islamic, Religion - Jewish, Science (General), Theology
ISBN Prefix(es): 978-90-6022

Plateau, *imprint of* Uitgeverij Vuurbaak

Ploegsma, *imprint of* Uitgeverij Ploegsma BV

Uitgeverij Ploegsma BV+
Singel 262, 1016 AC Amsterdam
Tel: (020) 5511250 *Fax:* (020) 6203509
E-mail: info@ploegsma.nl
Web Site: www.ploegsma.nl
Key Personnel
Foreign Rights Manager: Dania van Dishoeck
Founded: 1901
Subjects: Child Care & Development, Fiction,
   How-to, Nonfiction (General), Science (Gen-
   eral)
ISBN Prefix(es): 978-90-216
Imprints: De Brink (adult books); Ploegsma (chil-
   dren's books)

Uitgeverij Podium BV+
Willem Fenengastr 2A, 1096 BN Amsterdam
Tel: (020) 421 38 30 *Fax:* (020) 421 37 76
E-mail: post@uitgeverijpodium.nl; publiciteit@
   uitgeverijpodium.nl; contact@2seaagency.com
   (rights)
Web Site: www.uitgeverijpodium.nl
Key Personnel
Publisher: Joost Nijsen
Foreign Rights: Merijn Hollestelle *E-mail:* mh@
   uitgeverijpodium.nl
Founded: 1997
Specialize in contemporary literature & quality
   nonfiction.
Subjects: Anthropology, Fiction, History, Liter-
   ature, Literary Criticism, Essays, Nonfiction
   (General), Poetry, Social Sciences, Sociology,
   Travel & Tourism
ISBN Prefix(es): 978-90-5759
Number of titles published annually: 30 Print; 1
   E-Book
Total Titles: 250 Print; 1 E-Book
Foreign Rights: The Susijn Agency Ltd (world-
   wide)

Poema Pocket
Leidsegracht 105a, 1017 ND Amsterdam
Mailing Address: Postbus 289, 1000 AG Amster-
   dam
Tel: (020) 530 73 40 *Fax:* (020) 626 26 51
E-mail: info@lsamsterdam.nl; verkoop@
   lsamsterdam.nl
Web Site: www.lsamsterdam.nl
Key Personnel
Sales: Janneke Dee
Founded: 1994
Subjects: Fiction, Mysteries, Suspense, Nonfiction
   (General), Romance, Science Fiction, Fantasy
ISBN Prefix(es): 978-90-210
Parent Company: Luitingh-Sijthoff

Post Editions
Sourystr 18a, 3039 ST Rotterdam
Tel: (010) 4666 260
E-mail: mail@post-editions.com
Web Site: www.post-editions.com
Key Personnel
Publisher: Nina Post *E-mail:* nina@post-editions.
   com
Founded: 2002
Independent publisher dedicated to the task of ini-
   tiating, producing & distributing special books
   on contemporary art, photography, graphic de-
   sign & architecture. Works in collaboration
   with renowned artists, photographers, muse-
   ums, art institutes, editors, translators, graphic
   designers & distributors. Publisher's catalog includes autonomous publications, theory books,
   magazines, artist's books & special editions.
Subjects: Architecture & Interior Design, Art,
   Photography, Cultural Theory, Graphic Design
ISBN Prefix(es): 978-94-6083
Number of titles published annually: 25 Print

Total Titles: 100 Print
Foreign Rep(s): Art Data (Ireland, UK); Idea
   Books; RAM publications + distribution
   (Canada, USA)

Prisma, *imprint of* Uitgeverij Unieboek|Het
Spectrum BV

Uitgeverij Prometheus/Bert Bakker
Subsidiary of WPG Uitgevers
Herengracht 540, 1017 CG Amsterdam
Mailing Address: Postbus 1662, 1000 BR Amster-
   dam
Tel: (020) 6241934 *Fax:* (020) 6225461; (020)
   5210592
E-mail: info@pbo.nl
Web Site: uitgeverijprometheus.nl
Key Personnel
Publisher & Owner: Mai Spijkers
Foreign Rights Manager: Ronit Palache *E-mail:* r.
   palache@pbo.nl
Founded: 1893
Subjects: Art, Fiction, Government, Political
   Science, History, Language Arts, Linguistics,
   LGBTQ, Literature, Literary Criticism, Essays,
   Nonfiction (General), Philosophy, Poetry, Psy-
   chology, Psychiatry, Science (General), Social
   Sciences, Sociology
ISBN Prefix(es): 978-90-6019; 978-90-5333; 978-
   90-351
Number of titles published annually: 300 Print
Associate Companies: Ooievaar
Orders to: Ivec, Postbus 154, 1380 AD Weesp

Publitronic, *imprint of* Elektor International
Media BV

Uitgeverij Q
Spui 10, 1012 WZ Amsterdam
Tel: (020) 76 07 210
E-mail: info@uitgeverijq.nl
Web Site: www.singeluitgeverijen.nl/uitgeverij-q
Founded: 2007
Subjects: Mysteries, Suspense, Nonfiction (Gen-
   eral), Science Fiction, Fantasy
ISBN Prefix(es): 978-90-214
Parent Company: Singel Uitgeverijen

Uitgeverij Querido
Spui 10, 1012 WZ Amsterdam
Tel: (020) 76 07 210
E-mail: info@querido.nl
Web Site: www.singeluitgeverijen.nl/querido
Key Personnel
Media: Janne Colenbrander
Founded: 1915
Subjects: Art, Biography, Memoirs, Drama, The-
   ater, Fiction, History, Mathematics, Nonfiction
   (General), Poetry, Romance
ISBN Prefix(es): 978-90-214
Parent Company: Singel Uitgeverijen

Rainbow Essentials, *imprint of* Uitgeverij
Rainbow BV

Rainbow Pocketboek, *imprint of* Uitgeverij
Rainbow BV

Uitgeverij Rainbow BV+
Herengracht 555, 1017 BW Amsterdam
Tel: (020) 6205905 *Fax:* (020) 3200338
E-mail: info@rainbow.nl
Web Site: www.rainbow.nl
Key Personnel
Publisher: Danielle Vermeulen
   E-mail: dvermeulen@rainbow.nl
Editorial/Production: Susan Derksen
   E-mail: sderksen@rainbow.nl
Founded: 1983

Subjects: Biography, Memoirs, Fiction, History,
   Humor, Literature, Literary Criticism, Essays,
   Nonfiction (General), Self-Help
ISBN Prefix(es): 978-90-6766; 978-90-417; 978-
   90-464
Imprints: Rainbow Essentials; Rainbow Pocket-
   boek
Distribution Center: Van Halewyck, Diestsesteen-
   weg 71A, 3010 Leuven, Belgium *Tel:* (016)
   35 33 06 *Fax:* (016) 35 33 07; (016) 35 33
   08 *Toll Free Fax:* info@vanhalewycke.be *Web
   Site:* www.vanhalewycke.be

Thomas Rap, *imprint of* Uitgeverij De Bezige
Bij BV

Rebo Publishers+
Leidsevaart 123, 2211 VS Noordwukerhout
Tel: (0252) 431 566 *Fax:* (0252) 431 567
E-mail: info@rebo-publishers.com; orders@rebo-
   publishers.com
Web Site: www.rebo-publishers.com
Key Personnel
Chief Executive Officer: Jacqueline Wagner
   Tel: (0627) 014 534 *Fax:* (0252) 431 555
Product Development & International Sales:
   Jenny van der Knaap *E-mail:* jenny@rebo-
   publishers.com
Founded: 1983
Subjects: Animals, Pets, Art, Cookery, Crafts,
   Games, Hobbies, Environmental Studies, Gar-
   dening, Plants, Health, Nutrition, Environmen-
   tal Science
ISBN Prefix(es): 978-90-366
Subsidiaries: Rebo Productions SRO; Celetna ii

Van Reemst, *imprint of* Uitgeverij Unieboek|Het
Spectrum BV

RELX NV+
Radarweg 29, 1043 NX Amsterdam
Tel: (020) 485 2222 *Fax:* (020) 485 2032
E-mail: amsterdam@reedelsevier.com
Web Site: www.reedelsevier.com
Subjects: Science (General)

**Royal Netherlands Institute of Southeast Asia
& Caribbean Studies**, see KITLV Press

Uitgeverij Rubinstein
Prinseneiland 43, 1013 LL Amsterdam
Tel: (020) 4200 772 *Fax:* (020) 4200 882
E-mail: info@rubinstein.nl
Web Site: www.rubinstein.nl
Founded: 1985
ISBN Prefix(es): 978-90-476
Distributed by Uitgeverij Van Halewyck

Salome, *imprint of* Amsterdam University Press
BV (AUP)

Samsom Stafleu, see Uitgeverij Bohn Stafleu Van
Loghum BV

Sara, *imprint of* Uitgeverij Van Gennep BV

Schilt Publishing
Peter Martensstr 121, 1087 NA Amsterdam
Tel: (020) 528 69 12
E-mail: press@schiltpublishing.com; sales@
   schiltpublishing.com
Web Site: www.schiltpublishing.com
Key Personnel
Publisher: Maarten Schilt; Maria Louise Schilt
Press & Marketing, Europe: Yasmin Keel
   E-mail: yasmin@schiltpublishing.com
Press & Marketing, North America: Mary Bisbee-
   Beek *E-mail:* bisbee-beek@schiltpublishing.
   com

Founded: 2009
Specialize in high quality photo books.
This publisher has indicated that 50% of their
product line is author subsidized.
Subjects: Art, Photography
ISBN Prefix(es): 978-90-5330
Number of titles published annually: 12 Print
Foreign Rep(s): Ingram Publisher Services
(Canada (English-speaking), USA); Luster
(Belgium); Coen Sligting Bookimport (Nether-
lands); Thames & Hudson (worldwide exc
Netherlands & North America)
Distribution Center: Central Boekhuis (CB),
Erasmusweg 10, PO Box 125, 4100
AC Culemborg Tel: (0345) 47 58 88
E-mail: detailhandel@centraal.boekhuis.nl

Scientia Verlag, see Kloof Booksellers &
Scientia Verlag

Scriptum Art, imprint of Uitgeverij Scriptum

Scriptum Management, imprint of Uitgeverij
Scriptum

Scriptum Topography, imprint of Uitgeverij
Scriptum

Uitgeverij Scriptum+
Nieuwe Haven 151, 3117 AA Schiedam
Tel: (010) 4271022 Fax: (010) 4736625
E-mail: info@scriptum.nl
Web Site: www.scriptum.nl
Key Personnel
Publisher: Hans Ritman E-mail: ritman@
scriptum.nl
Press & Promotion: Thea Duijvenbooden
E-mail: thea@scriptum.nl
Founded: 1985
Subjects: Antiques, Art, Business, Cookery,
Health, Nutrition, Management, Marketing,
Psychology, Psychiatry
ISBN Prefix(es): 978-90-71542; 978-90-5594
Number of titles published annually: 25 Print
Total Titles: 200 Print
Imprints: Scriptum Art; Scriptum Management;
Scriptum Topography
Foreign Rep(s): Ruud Binkhorst
Distribution Center: Elkedag Boeken, Joden-
str 16, 2000 Antwerp, Belgium Tel: (03)
3456040 E-mail: info@elkedagboeken.be Web
Site: www.elkedagboeken.be

SDU Uitgeverij
Prinses Beatrixlaan 116, 2595 AL The Hague
Mailing Address: Postbus 20025, 2500 EA The
Hague
Tel: (070) 378 99 11; (070) 378 98 60; (070) 378
09 00; (070) 378 98 80 Fax: (070) 385 43 21;
(070) 799 98 98
E-mail: boekhandels@sdu.nl
Web Site: www.sdu.nl
Key Personnel
Chief Executive Officer: Sam van Oostrom
General Dir: Sandra Kroon
Commercial Dir: Jeroen Kuerble
Founded: 1991
Subjects: Business, Finance, Government, Politi-
cal Science, Law
ISBN Prefix(es): 978-90-5409; 978-90-12; 978-
90-399; 978-90-5332; 978-90-5261; 978-90-
5903; 978-90-395; 978-90-6233
Branch Office(s)
Nachtwachtlaan 20, 1058 EA Amsterdam

SEMAR Publishers SRL+
1e Sweelinckstr, 16C, 2517 GC The Hague
SAN: 136-5967
Tel: (062) 5472413 (cell)
E-mail: info@semar.org; orders@semar.org
Web Site: www.semar.org

Key Personnel
President & Chief Executive Officer: Luciano
Sahlan Momo, PhD E-mail: momo@semar.org
Founded: 1986
Specialize in editions with sustainable conserva-
tion criteria.
Membership(s): AIE; NUV.
Subjects: Anthropology, Archaeology, Art, Asian
Studies, Drama, Theater, Education, Environ-
mental Studies, Human Relations, Language
Arts, Linguistics, Literature, Literary Criticism,
Essays, Philosophy, Photography, Poetry, Psy-
chology, Psychiatry, Religion - Buddhist, Re-
ligion - Hindu, Religion - Islamic, Religion -
Jewish, Social Sciences, Sociology, Theology
ISBN Prefix(es): 978-88-7778
Number of titles published annually: 15 Print; 2
CD-ROM; 3 Online; 5 E-Book; 2 Audio
Total Titles: 420 Print; 10 CD-ROM; 44 Online;
5 E-Book; 5 Audio
Imprints: Spanda Publishing
Distribution Center: Gazelle Book Services,
White Cross Mill, Lancaster LA1 4XS, United
Kingdom Tel: (01524) 68765 Fax: (01524)
63232 E-mail: sales@gazellebooks.co.uk Web
Site: www.gazellebooks.co.uk

Serena Libri
Vossiusstr 21, 1071 AD Amsterdam
Tel: (020) 664 24 26 Fax: (020) 664 24 26
E-mail: info@serenalibri.nl
Web Site: www.serenalibri.nl
Key Personnel
Founder: Annaserena Ferruzzi
Founded: 1997
Subjects: Fiction, Mysteries, Suspense
ISBN Prefix(es): 978-90-76270

Signatuur, imprint of A W Bruna Uitgevers BV

Slaughterhouse Books, imprint of Uitgeverij De
Bezige Bij BV

Sociaal en Cultureel Planbureau (SCP) (Social
& Cultural Planning Office)+
Rijnstr 50, 2511 XP The Hague
Mailing Address: Postbus 16164, 2500 BD The
Hague
Tel: (070) 3407000 Fax: (070) 3407044
E-mail: info@scp.nl
Web Site: www.scp.nl
Key Personnel
Dir: Dr Kim Putters
Deputy Dir: Dr Rob Bijl Tel: (070) 3407702
Founded: 1973
Subjects: Child Care & Development, Criminol-
ogy, Education, Ethnicity, Government, Politi-
cal Science, Health, Nutrition, Radio, TV, Real
Estate, Social Sciences, Sociology, Women's
Studies, Labor Market, Social Security, Welfare
ISBN Prefix(es): 978-90-377
Parent Company: Ministerie van Volksgezond-
heid, Welzijn en Sport

Spanda Publishing, imprint of SEMAR
Publishers SRL

Spectrum, imprint of Uitgeverij Unieboek|Het
Spectrum BV

Uitgeverij Unieboek|Het Spectrum BV
Papiermolen 14-24, 3994 DK Houten
Mailing Address: Postbus 97, 3990 DB Houten
Tel: (030) 7998300
E-mail: info@unieboekspectrum.nl
Web Site: www.unieboekspectrum.nl
Key Personnel
Sales Manager: Ruurd Woudstra E-mail: ruurd.
woudstra@unieboekspectrum.nl
Foreign Rights: Mrs Geri Brandjes Tel: (020) 615
3473 E-mail: geri@boek-pr.nl

Founded: 1935
Subjects: Astrology, Occult, Computer Science,
Criminology, Environmental Studies, History,
Literature, Literary Criticism, Essays, Manage-
ment, Mysteries, Suspense, Nonfiction (Gen-
eral), Travel & Tourism
ISBN Prefix(es): 978-90-315; 978-90-274
Number of titles published annually: 50 Online
Total Titles: 800 Print
Parent Company: LannooMeulenoff BV
Ultimate Parent Company: Uitgeverij Lannoo
Groep
Imprints: Van Dishoeck; Van Goor; Van Holkema
& Warendorf; Mana; Prisma; Van Reemst;
Spectrum; Winkler Prins; Vantoen.nu
Foreign Rep(s): Kris Nelissen (Belgium)

Staudt Verlag
Interdisc Trading BV, Pompmolenlaan 5, 3447
GK Woerden
Tel: (01516) 5420365
E-mail: info@staudt-verlag.de; vertrieb@staudt-
verlag.de
Web Site: www.staudt-verlag.de
Founded: 2006
ISBN Prefix(es): 978-3-9523504; 978-3-9397850
Distribution Center: RungeVA, Bergstr 2, 33803
Steinhagen, Germany
Verlags-Service Imfeld, Bruenigstr 24, 6055 Alp-
nachdorf, Switzerland

Stedelijk Van Abbemuseum
Bilderdijklaan 10, 5611 NH Eindhoven
Mailing Address: Postbus 235, 5600 AE Eind-
hoven
Tel: (040) 238 10 00; (040) 238 10 47 (shop)
Fax: (040) 246 06 80
E-mail: info@vanabbemuseum.nl;
museumwinkel@vanabbemuseum.nl
Web Site: www.vanabbemuseum.nl
Key Personnel
Dir: Charles Esche
Press: Ilse Cornelius Tel: (040) 238 10 19
E-mail: pressoffice@vanabbemuseum.nl
Founded: 1936
Subjects: Art, Library & Information Sciences,
Contemporary Art
ISBN Prefix(es): 978-90-70149

Steltman Galleries
Jan Luijkenstr 16, 1017 CN Amsterdam
Tel: (020) 622 8683
E-mail: steltman@steltman.com
Web Site: www.steltman.com
Key Personnel
Owner: Gerrit Steltman
Founded: 1982
Specialize in art design.
Subjects: Art
ISBN Prefix(es): 978-90-71867
U.S. Office(s): Steltman, 369 Montezuma Ave,
No 448, Santa Fe, NM 87501, United States
Tel: 505-986-9622 Fax: 505-988-9961

Stichting Evangelische Uitgeverij H Medema,
see Uitgeverij Medema

Studio Kers
Prins Hendrikkade 124A, 3071 KL Rotterdam
Mailing Address: Bakhuis 6, 3262 CB Oud-
Beijerland
Tel: (06) 5495 6704
Web Site: studiokers.nl
Key Personnel
Owner: Pieter Kers
Subjects: Art, Photography, Regional Interests
ISBN Prefix(es): 978-94-91835

Uitgeverij SUN Architecture
Prinsengracht 747, 1017 JX Amsterdam

Mailing Address: Postbus 15970, 1001 NL Amsterdam
Tel: (020) 5218938 *Fax:* (020) 6253327
E-mail: info@uitgeverijboom.nl
Web Site: www.uitgeverijboom.nl/boeken/architectuur
Key Personnel
Assistant Publisher: Daan de Kuyper
Founded: 1969
Subjects: Architecture & Interior Design, Art, Ethnicity, History, Management, Philosophy, Psychology, Psychiatry, Landscape Design, Urban Construction
ISBN Prefix(es): 978-90-6168; 978-94-6105
Parent Company: Boom Uitgevers Amsterdam
Imprints: Uitgeverij Dwarsstap
Foreign Rep(s): Idea Books (Asia, Australia, Europe, New Zealand, North America)
Distribution Center: CB, Postbus 125, 4100 AC Culemborg *Tel:* (0345) 47 59 11 *Fax:* (0345) 47 53 43 *E-mail:* info@cb-logistics.nl
Boom Distributiecentrum, Postbus 400, 7940 AK Meppel *Tel:* (0522) 23 75 55 *Fax:* (0522) 25 38 64 *E-mail:* info@boomdistributiecentrum.nl

Uitgeverij SWP BV (SWP Publishing Co)+
Spaklerweg 79, 1114 AE Amsterdam
Mailing Address: Postbus 12010, 1100 AA Amsterdam
Tel: (020) 3307200
Web Site: www.swppublishing.com; www.swpbook.com
Key Personnel
Dir & Publisher: Paul Roosenstein
Founded: 1982
Specialize in early childhood education, health issues & social welfare.
Subjects: Child Care & Development, Criminology, History, Management, Psychology, Psychiatry, Religion - Other, Social Sciences, Sociology
ISBN Prefix(es): 978-90-6665
Number of titles published annually: 150 Print; 1 CD-ROM
Total Titles: 300 Print; 2 CD-ROM

Syntax Publishers, *imprint of* Tilburg University

Uitgeverij Synthese+
Imprint of Milinda Uitgevers
Mathensserlaan 326, 3021 HX Rotterdam
Mailing Address: Postbus 61220, 3002 HE Rotterdam
Tel: (010) 411 38 67 *Fax:* (010) 411 39 32
E-mail: info@milinda.nl
Web Site: www.milinda-uitgevers.nl/synthese/actueel
Key Personnel
Dir: Reinoud Douwes
Assistant Editor: Natacha Weber
Founded: 1976
Subjects: Art, Astrology, Occult, Education, Language Arts, Linguistics, Philosophy, Psychology, Psychiatry, Religion - Other, Science (General)
ISBN Prefix(es): 978-90-6271; 978-90-6229
Number of titles published annually: 25 Print
Total Titles: 250 Print
Distributed by Denis & Co
Orders to: Centraal Boekhuis, Postbus 125, 4100 AC Culemborg *Tel:* (0345) 475888 *E-mail:* service@cb-logistics.nl *Web Site:* www.cb-logistics.nl

Uitgeverij Ten Have+
Subsidiary of Veen Bosch & Keuning Uitgeversgroep BV
Herculesplein 96, 3584 AA Utrecht
Mailing Address: Postbus 13288, 3507 LG Utrecht
Tel: (088) 700 2600 *Fax:* (088) 700 2699
E-mail: promotie@uitgeverijtenhave.nl

Web Site: www.uitgeverijtenhave.nl
Key Personnel
Publisher: Regine Dugardyn
Brand Manager: Willemijn Crombeecke
  Tel: (088) 700 2748 *E-mail:* wcrombeecke@uitgeverijtenhave.nl
Founded: 1831
Subjects: Biblical Studies, Inspirational, Spirituality, Philosophy, Psychology, Psychiatry, Religion - Jewish, Religion - Protestant, Religion - Other, Theology
ISBN Prefix(es): 978-90-259
Total Titles: 300 Print
Branch Office(s)
Uitgeverij Ten Have Belgie, c/o VBK Belgie, Katwilgweg 2, 2050 Antwerp, Belgium
  Tel: (03) 355 28 36 *Fax:* (03) 355 28 40

Uitgeverij TerraLannoo BV+
Member of LannooMeulenoff
Papiermolen 14-24, 3994 DK Houten
Mailing Address: Postbus 97, 3990 DB Houten
Tel: (030) 300 04 00 *Fax:* (030) 799 83 98
E-mail: info@terralannoo.nl
Web Site: www.terralannoo.nl
Founded: 1971
Publishing & import for Lannoo, Michelin & Betaplus in Netherlands.
Subjects: Architecture & Interior Design, Art, Cookery, Crafts, Games, Hobbies, Gardening, Plants, Health, Nutrition, Nonfiction (General), Poetry, Psychology, Psychiatry
ISBN Prefix(es): 978-90-6255; 978-90-209; 978-90-5897; 978-90-76124; 978-90-5837; 978-90-77880; 978-90-8568; 978-90-8989
Number of titles published annually: 90 Print
Total Titles: 2,200 Print; 1 E-Book
Imprints: Lannoo (Belgium)
Warehouse: Terra Magazijn, Distrimedia NV, Meulenbeeksesteenweg 20, 8700 Tielt, Belgium *Tel:* (051) 42 38 60 *Fax:* (051) 42 38 68 *E-mail:* distrimedia@lannoo.com

ThiemeMeulenhoff+
Smallepad 30, 3811 MG Amersfoort
Mailing Address: Postbus 400, 3800 AK Amersfoort
Tel: (033) 448 30 00 *Fax:* (033) 448 39 99
E-mail: info@thiememeulenhoff.nl
Web Site: www.thiememeulenhoff.nl
Key Personnel
Chief Executive Officer: Eric Razenberg
Founded: 2000
Subjects: Education
ISBN Prefix(es): 978-90-03; 978-90-238; 978-90-06; 978-90-433
Subsidiaries: NIB-Software

Uitgeverij Thoeris (Thoeris Publishers)
De Lairessestr 37 sous, 1071 NS Amsterdam
Tel: (020) 616 32 30; (061) 36 069 39 (cell)
E-mail: info@thoeris.nl
Web Site: thoeris.nl
Key Personnel
Publishing Dir: Mariel Croon *E-mail:* mcroon@thoeris.nl
Subjects: Nonfiction (General)
ISBN Prefix(es): 978-90-72219; 978-90-808113
Distribution Center: C de Vries-Brouwers, Haantjeslei 80, 2018 Antwerp, Belgium *Tel:* (03) 237 41 80 *Fax:* (03) 237 40 01 *E-mail:* devries@village.uunet.be

Uitgeverij Thoth+
Nieuwe's-Gravelandseweg 3, 1405 HH Bussum
Tel: (035) 694 41 44 *Fax:* (035) 694 32 66
E-mail: info@thoth.nl
Web Site: www.thoth.nl
Key Personnel
Publisher: Kees van den Hoek *E-mail:* kees@thoth.nl
Editor: Marja Jager *E-mail:* marja@thoth.nl

Publicity: Sabien Stols *E-mail:* sabien@thoth.nl
Founded: 1985
Subjects: Architecture & Interior Design, Art, History, Literature, Literary Criticism, Essays, Nonfiction (General), Photography, Landscape Architecture, Urban Planning
ISBN Prefix(es): 978-90-6868; 978-90-77699
Foreign Rep(s): Art Books International (UK); EPA (Belgium); Idea Books (Asia, Europe, USA); John Smith Books (Netherlands)

Boekencentrum Tijdschriften, *imprint of* Boekencentrum Uitgevers BV

De Tijdstroom Uitgeverij BV+
Janskerkhof 26, 3512 BN Utrecht
Mailing Address: Postbus 775, 3500 AT Utrecht
Tel: (030) 2364450 *Fax:* (030) 2369354
E-mail: info@tijdstroom.nl
Web Site: www.tijdstroom.nl
Key Personnel
Dir & Publisher: Dr M R C Kole; Dr N F van't Zet
Production: Dr H Klein Haneveld
Founded: 1921
Subjects: Health, Nutrition, Management, Medicine, Nursing, Dentistry, Philosophy, Physics, Psychology, Psychiatry, Social Sciences, Sociology
ISBN Prefix(es): 978-90-5898

Tilburg University
Warandelaan 2, 5037 AB Tilburg
Mailing Address: Postbus 90153, 5000 LE Tilburg
Tel: (013) 466 9111 *Fax:* (013) 466 2996
E-mail: info@tilburguniversity.edu
Web Site: www.tilburguniversity.edu
Key Personnel
Publicity: Tineke Bennema *Tel:* (013) 466 8998 *E-mail:* c.e.bennema@tilburguniversity.edu
Subjects: Behavioral Sciences, Biblical Studies, Economics, Language Arts, Linguistics, Library & Information Sciences, Philosophy, Psychology, Psychiatry, Theology
ISBN Prefix(es): 978-90-361
Imprints: Syntax Publishers

Tirion Art & Creatief, *imprint of* Uitgeverij De Fontein|Tirion

Tirion Natuur, *imprint of* Uitgeverij De Fontein|Tirion

Tirion Sport, *imprint of* Uitgeverij De Fontein|Tirion

De Toorts, *imprint of* Uitgeverij De Toorts BV

Uitgeverij De Toorts BV+
Conradkade 6, 2031 CL Haarlem
Mailing Address: Postbus 9585, 2003 LN Haarlem
Tel: (023) 553 29 20
E-mail: bestellingen@toorts.nl
Web Site: www.toorts.nl
Key Personnel
Dir & Publisher: Joost Hesseling; Madeleine Klis
Founded: 1936
Subjects: Behavioral Sciences, Child Care & Development, Health, Nutrition, Human Relations, Music, Dance, Psychology, Psychiatry, Self-Help
ISBN Prefix(es): 978-90-6020
Imprints: Enterbooks; De Toorts
Foreign Rep(s): Hans Bellingwout (Netherlands)
Orders to: Uitgeverij EPO, Lange Postoorstr 25-27, Berchem/Antwerp, Belgium *Tel:* (03) 239 68 74 *Fax:* (03) 218 46 04 *E-mail:* orders@epo.be *Web Site:* www.epo.be (Belgium orders)

Uniepers Uitgevers+
Postbus 352, 1620 AJ Hoorn
Tel: (0229) 236466; (065) 3147716 (cell)
E-mail: info@uniepersuitgevers.nl
Web Site: www.uniepersuitgevers.nl
Founded: 1961
Also book packagers.
Membership(s): Koninklijke Vereniging van het
  Boekenvak (KVB).
Subjects: Anthropology, Antiques, Archaeology,
  Architecture & Interior Design, Art, Ethnicity,
  Health, Nutrition, History, Music, Dance, Nat-
  ural History, Photography, Regional Interests,
  Culture, Nature
ISBN Prefix(es): 978-90-6825

Valiz
Gebouw Het Sieraad, Studio K34-K36, Post-
  jesweg 1, 1057 DT Amsterdam
Tel: (020) 6764144 *Fax:* (020) 6764126
E-mail: info@valiz.nl
Web Site: www.valiz.nl
Key Personnel
Dir: Astrid Vostermans
Subjects: Architecture & Interior Design, Art,
  Fashion, Photography
ISBN Prefix(es): 978-90-808185; 978-90-78088

De Grote Van Dale, *imprint of* Van Dale
  Uitgevers

**Van Dale Grote Woordenboeken voor
  hedendaags taalgebruik**, *imprint of* Van Dale
  Uitgevers

Van Dale Handbibliotheek, *imprint of* Van Dale
  Uitgevers

Van Dale Handwoordenboeken, *imprint of* Van
  Dale Uitgevers

Van Dale Kinderwoordenboeken, *imprint of* Van
  Dale Uitgevers

Van Dale Uitgevers (Van Dale Publishing)
Subsidiary of Veen Bosch & Keuning Uitgevers-
  groep BV
Herculesplein 96, 3584 AA Utrecht
Mailing Address: Postbus 13288, 3507 LG
  Utrecht
Tel: (088) 700 2600 *Fax:* (088) 700 2999
E-mail: helpdesk@vandale.nl
Web Site: www.vandale.nl
Founded: 1976
ISBN Prefix(es): 978-90-6648
Imprints: Koenen; De Grote Van Dale; Van Dale
  Grote Woordenboeken voor hedendaags taal-
  gebruik; Van Dale Handbibliotheek; Van Dale
  Handwoordenboeken; Van Dale Kinderwoor-
  denboeken
Branch Office(s)
Katwilgweg 2, 2050 Antwerp, Belgium *Tel:* (03)
  355 28 38 *Fax:* (03) 355 28 41

Uitgeverij van Wijnen+
Zilverstr 14, 8801 KC Franeker
Tel: (0517) 394588 *Fax:* (0517) 397179
E-mail: info@uitgeverijvanwijnen.nl
Web Site: www.uitgeverijvanwijnen.nl
Key Personnel
Publisher: Albert de Vos
Founded: 1988
Subjects: Government, Political Science, History,
  Maritime, Philosophy, Religion - Other, Theol-
  ogy, Maritime History
ISBN Prefix(es): 978-90-5194

Uitgeverij Vantilt
St Annastr 99, 6524 EK Nijmegen

Mailing Address: Postbus 1411, 6501 BK Ni-
  jmegen
Tel: (024) 3602294
E-mail: info@vantilt.nl; verkoop@vantilt.nl;
  promotie@vantilt.nl
Web Site: www.vantilt.nl
Key Personnel
Publicity: Judith Bosch *Tel:* (024) 3297863
Founded: 1996
Subjects: Architecture & Interior Design, Film,
  Video, History, Philosophy, Poetry, Science
  (General), Avant-garde, Cultural Studies, Her-
  itage
ISBN Prefix(es): 978-90-75697; 978-90-77503
Foreign Rep(s): Idea Book (worldwide exc
  Belgium, Luxembourg & Netherlands); Van
  Halewyck (Belgium (Dutch-speaking))

Vantoen.nu, *imprint of* Uitgeverij Unieboek|Het
  Spectrum BV

VBK, see Veen Bosch & Keuning Uitgeversgroep
  BV

Veen Bosch & Keuning Uitgeversgroep BV+
Herculesplein 94, 3584 AA Utrecht
Mailing Address: Postbus 8049, 3503 RA Utrecht
Tel: (088) 700 2600
E-mail: info@vbku.nl
Web Site: www.vbku.nl
Key Personnel
Chief Executive Officer & Publisher:
  Wiet de Bruijn *Tel:* (088) 700 2800
  E-mail: wdebruijn@vbku.nl
Chief Operating Officer: Bert Endedijk *Tel:* (088)
  700 2611 *E-mail:* bendedijk@vbku.nl
Commercial Dir: Caroline Mouwens *Tel:* (088)
  700 2612 *E-mail:* cmouwens@vbku.nl
Independent trade publisher of books, magazines,
  dictionaries & CD-ROMs.
ISBN Prefix(es): 978-90-246; 978-90-263; 978-
  90-266; 978-90-213; 978-90-259; 978-90-204;
  978-90-245; 978-90-218; 978-90-215; 978-90-
  254
Number of titles published annually: 2,000 Print;
  30 CD-ROM; 600 Online; 2,000 E-Book
Total Titles: 10,000 Print; 100 CD-ROM; 8,000
  E-Book
Subsidiaries: Ambo|Anthos Uitgevers;
  AnkhHermes; Atlas Contact; Uitgeverij De
  Fontein|Tirion; Uitgeverij Houtekiet; Uitgeverij
  Kok; Kosmos Uitgevers; Uitgeverij Luitingh-
  Sijthoff; Omniboek; Uitgeverij Ten Have; Van
  Dale Uitgevers; VBK Belgie; Veen Magazines
Branch Office(s)
Maliebaan 74, 3581 CV Utrecht *Tel:* (030) 234
  92 11
Luebeckweg 2, 9723 HE Groningen *Tel:* (050)
  584 44 44

Veltman Uitgevers BV
Energieweg 3, 3542 DZ Utrecht
Tel: (0346) 284 242 *Fax:* (0346) 284 282
E-mail: info@veltman-uitgevers.nl
Web Site: www.veltman-uitgevers.nl
Founded: 2001
Subjects: Animals, Pets, Cookery, Crafts, Games,
  Hobbies, Erotica, Gardening, Plants, Health,
  Nutrition, History, Military Science, Trans-
  portation, Travel & Tourism, Esotericism,
  Leisure, Nature, Pregnancy
ISBN Prefix(es): 978-90-483; 978-90-5920

Uitgeverij Verloren (Verloren Publishers)
Torenlaan 25, 1211 JA Hilversum
Tel: (035) 6859856 *Fax:* (035) 6836557
E-mail: info@verloren.nl
Web Site: www.verloren.nl
Key Personnel
President: Thys VerLoren van Themaat
Founded: 1979

Subjects: Biography, Memoirs, Genealogy, His-
  tory
ISBN Prefix(es): 978-90-6550; 978-90-8704; 978-
  90-70403; 978-90-72131
Number of titles published annually: 70 Print; 5
  CD-ROM
Total Titles: 1,100 Print; 10 CD-ROM

VIP, *imprint of* A W Bruna Uitgevers BV

Visual Steps BV
Postbus 70, 1420 AB Uithoorn
Tel: (0297) 386444
E-mail: info@visualsteps.nl
Web Site: www.visualsteps.nl
Subjects: Computer Science, Computers
ISBN Prefix(es): 978-90-5905

Voetbal International, *imprint of* A W Bruna
  Uitgevers BV

Voetbal International Boeken
Postbus 575, 2800 AN Gouda
Tel: (0182) 599377
Web Site: www.vi-boeken.nl
Subjects: Sports, Athletics, Football
ISBN Prefix(es): 978-90-71359; 978-90-6797
Orders to: Assist, Oranjeplein 4, 4455 AA
  Nieuwdorp *Tel:* (0113) 613044; (06) 30883125
  E-mail: assist@debuitenspelers.nl

Voorhoeve, *imprint of* Uitgeverij Kok

Vossiupers UvA, *imprint of* Amsterdam
  University Press BV (AUP)

VU Boekhandel+
De Boelelaan 1105, 1081 HV Amsterdam
Tel: (020) 598 40 00 *Fax:* (020) 646 27 19
E-mail: info@vuboekhandel.nl
Web Site: www.vuboekhandel.nl
Key Personnel
Dir: Pier Rienks
Founded: 1967
Subjects: Biological Sciences, Economics,
  History, Language Arts, Linguistics, Law,
  Medicine, Nursing, Dentistry, Philosophy, Psy-
  chology, Psychiatry, Public Administration,
  Science (General), Social Sciences, Sociology,
  Theology
ISBN Prefix(es): 978-90-6256; 978-90-5383; 978-
  90-8659
Imprints: VU Uitgeverij; VU University Press

VU Uitgeverij, *imprint of* VU Boekhandel

VU University Press, *imprint of* VU Boekhandel

Uitgeverij Vuurbaak (The Lighthouse)+
Hermesweg 20, 3771 ND Barneveld
Mailing Address: Postbus 257, 3770 AG Barn-
  eveld
Tel: (0342) 41 17 31
E-mail: info@vuurbaak.nl
Web Site: www.vuurbaak.nl
Founded: 1965
Subjects: Fiction, Literature, Literary Criticism,
  Essays, Religion - Protestant, Theology
ISBN Prefix(es): 978-90-6015; 978-90-5560; 978-
  90-5804; 978-94-6005
Number of titles published annually: 60 Print; 2
  CD-ROM
Total Titles: 300 Print; 4 CD-ROM
Parent Company: Nedag Uitgevers BV
Associate Companies: Telos
Imprints: Brandaan; Plateau

Waanders Uitgevers (Waanders Publishers)+
Faradaystr 17, 8013 PH Zwolle
Mailing Address: Postbus 1129, 8001 BC Zwolle
Tel: (038) 337 79 96; (038) 421 53 92

E-mail: info@waanders.nl
Web Site: www.waanders.nl
Key Personnel
Owner: Wim Waanders
Founded: 1836
Subjects: Antiques, Art, Ethnicity, History
ISBN Prefix(es): 978-90-6630; 978-90-400; 978-90-70072
Associate Companies: Uitgeverij de Kunst
Bookshop(s): Achter de Broeren 1-3,
8011 VA Zwolle *Tel:* (038) 421 53 92
E-mail: info@waandersindebroeren.nl *Web Site:* waandersindebroeren.nl

Wageningen Academic Publishers+
Marijkeweg 22, 6709 PG Wageningen
Mailing Address: Postbus 220, 6700 AE Wageningen
Tel: (0317) 47 65 16; (0317) 47 65 14 (sales)
Fax: (0317) 45 34 17
E-mail: info@wageningenacademic.com
Web Site: www.wageningenacademic.com
Key Personnel
Mng Dir: Mike Jacobs *E-mail:* jacobs@wageningenacademic.com
Technical Dir: Enrico Kunst *Tel:* (0317) 47 65 10
E-mail: kunst@wageningenacademic.com
Desk Editor & Technical Support: Marijn van der Gaag *Tel:* (0317) 47 65 11
E-mail: vandergaag@wageningenacademic.com
Lay-out & Format Editor: Jessica van Wijngaarden *Tel:* (0317) 47 65 12
E-mail: vanwijngaarden@wageningenacademic.com
Marketing: Inge Sahuleka *Tel:* (0317) 47 65 17
E-mail: sahuleka@wageningenacademic.com
Sales: Leslie Engbers *E-mail:* engbers@wageningenacademic.com
Founded: 2002
Publisher of scientific & technical books. Specialize in life sciences.
Publish scientific journals as well as monographs, textbooks & proceedings.
Subjects: Agriculture, Social Sciences, Sociology, Animal & Veterinary Science, Environmental Science, Food Science, Life Sciences, Plant Science
ISBN Prefix(es): 978-90-74134; 978-90-6754; 978-90-76998; 978-90-8686
Total Titles: 80 Print

Uitgeversmaatschappij Walburg Pers
Zaadmarkt 86, 7201 DE Zutphen
Mailing Address: Postbus 4159, 7200 BD Zutphen
Tel: (0575) 510522; (0575) 590336 (press)
Fax: (0575) 542289
E-mail: info@walburgpers.nl; publiciteit@walburgpers.nl
Web Site: www.walburgpers.nl
Key Personnel
Dir & Publisher: Pieter Schriks
Press & Publicity: Winnie Urban
Founded: 1961
Subjects: Architecture & Interior Design, Art, Drama, Theater, Ethnicity, History, Law, Culture
ISBN Prefix(es): 978-90-6011; 978-90-5730

Uitgeverij Wereldbibliotheek+
Jahannes Vermeerstr 63, 1071 DN Amsterdam
Tel: (020) 5706100 *Fax:* (020) 5706199
E-mail: info@wereldbibliotheek.nl; verkoop@wereldbibliotheek.nl; publiciteit@wereldbibliotheek.nl
Web Site: www.wereldbibliotheek.nl
Key Personnel
Publicity: Machteld de Vos
Sales: Fred Teunissen
Founded: 1905
Subjects: Anthropology, Fiction, History, Literature, Literary Criticism, Essays, Music, Dance,

Nonfiction (General), Philosophy, Poetry, Psychology, Psychiatry, Public Administration, Science (General), Science Fiction, Fantasy
ISBN Prefix(es): 978-90-284
Total Titles: 250 Print

Wilkerdon, *imprint of* Uitgeverij Ad Donker BV

Winkler Prins, *imprint of* Uitgeverij Unieboek|Het Spectrum BV

World Editions Ltd
Imprint of Libella Publishing Group
Weteringschans 259, 1017 XJ Amsterdam
E-mail: info@worldeditions.org
Web Site: www.worldeditions.org
Key Personnel
Publisher/Dir: Judith Uyterlinde
Dir, Business Development, Sales & Public Relations: Karin Wessel *E-mail:* k.wessel@worldeditions.org
Editor-in-Chief: Lydia Unsworth
Additional offices in London & New York.
ISBN Prefix(es): 978-94-6238
Orders to: Publishers Group Canada, c/o Raincoast Books, 2440 Viking Way, Richmond, BC V6V 1N2, Canada *E-mail:* customerservice@raincoast.com
Ingram Publisher Services, 210 American Dr, Jackson, TN 38301, United States *E-mail:* ipsjacksonorders@ingramcontent.com
Ingram Publisher Services, One Ingram Blvd, Mail Stop 512, La Vergne, TN 37086, United States *E-mail:* ips@ingramcontent.com (independent bookstores, higher education & gift account inquiries)
Returns: Publishers Group Canada, c/o Raincoast Books, 2440 Viking Way, Richmond, BC V6V 1N2, Canada *E-mail:* customerservice@raincoast.com; Ingram Publisher Services, 1210 Ingram Dr, Chambersburg, TN 17202, United States (independent bookstores, higher education & gift account inquiries); Ingram Publisher Services, 193 Edwards Dr, Jackson, TN 38301, United States

Xander Uitgevers
Hamerstr 3, 1021 JT Amsterdam
Tel: (020) 3033950
Web Site: www.xanderuitgevers.nl
Key Personnel
Publisher & Dir: Sander Knol *E-mail:* sander.knol@xanderuitgevers.nl
Editor: Hedi de Vree *E-mail:* hedi.de.vree@xanderuitgevers.nl
Marketing & Public Relations: Marieke Hofstede *E-mail:* marieke.hofstede@xanderuitgevers.nl
Founded: 2012
Subjects: Fiction, Nonfiction (General)
ISBN Prefix(es): 978-94-016

Zoem, *imprint of* Uitgeverij De Bezige Bij BV

Zomer & Keuning, *imprint of* Uitgeverij Kok

Uitgeverij Zwijsen BV
Subsidiary of WPG Uitgevers
Kantorencomplex Het Laken, Hart van Brabantlaan 18, 5038 JL Tilburg
Mailing Address: Postbus 805, 5000 AV Tilburg
Tel: (013) 583 88 00; (013) 583 88 88 (customer service) *Fax:* (013) 583 88 80
E-mail: klantenservice@zwijsen.nl; zwijsenwebshop@wpg.nl
Web Site: www.zwijsen.nl
Founded: 1982
Subjects: Fiction, Mysteries, Suspense
ISBN Prefix(es): 978-90-6692; 978-90-276

New Zealand

General Information

Capital: Wellington
Language: English
Religion: Predominantly Christian (mostly Anglican & Roman Catholic)
Population: 3.3 million
Bank Hours: 0930-1600 Monday-Friday
Shop Hours: Vary. Most open 6-7 days a week
Currency: 100 cents = 1 New Zealand dollar
Export/Import Information: No tariffs on books and advertising. No import licenses, but literature which is indecent, advocates violence, lawlessness, disorder or seditiousness is prohibited. No special exchange controls.
Copyright: UCC, Berne, Florence (see Copyright Conventions, pg viii)

ABA Resources Ltd
2d/6 Brooklyn Rd, Claudelands, Hamilton 3214
Mailing Address: PO Box 11-099, Hamilton 3251
Tel: (07) 854 9360 *Fax:* (07) 854 9361
Web Site: www.abaresources.co.nz
Key Personnel
Dir: Graeme Abbott *E-mail:* graeme@abaresources.co.nz
Founded: 1986
Educational book publishers.
Subjects: Accounting, Agriculture, Biological Sciences, Business, Chemistry, Chemical Engineering, Crafts, Games, Hobbies, Economics, Education, Fashion, Language Arts, Linguistics, Physical Sciences, Physics, Science (General), Sports, Athletics
ISBN Prefix(es): 978-1-877311; 978-1-877386; 978-1-877545

Arrow, *imprint of* Random House Books New Zealand (RHNZ)

Auckland University Press+
University of Auckland, Anzac Ave entrance, 1-11 Short St, Auckland 1010
Mailing Address: University of Auckland, Private Bag 92019, Auckland 1142
Tel: (09) 373 7528 *Fax:* (09) 373 7465
E-mail: press@auckland.ac.nz; pressorders@auckland.ac.nz
Web Site: www.press.auckland.ac.nz
Key Personnel
Dir: Dr Sam Elworthy *E-mail:* s.elworthy@auckland.ac.nz
Production Manager: Katharina Bauer *E-mail:* k.bauer@auckland.ac.nz
Design & Production: Katrina Duncan *E-mail:* k.duncan@auckland.ac.nz
Marketing & Sales Manager: Andrew Long *E-mail:* a.long@auckland.ac.nz
Editorial & Marketing Assistant: Louisa Kasza *E-mail:* l.kasza@auckland.ac.nz
Founded: 1966
Subjects: Anthropology, Archaeology, Art, Biography, Memoirs, Business, Government, Political Science, Health, Nutrition, History, Literature, Literary Criticism, Essays, Medicine, Nursing, Dentistry, Natural History, Poetry, Science (General)
ISBN Prefix(es): 978-1-86940
Number of titles published annually: 25 Print
Total Titles: 250 Print
Distributed by Eurospan (Europe & UK); Inbooks (Australia); Independent Publishers Group (IPG) (USA & Canada)
Orders to: Craig Potton Publishing, 98 Vickerman St, Port Nelson 7010 *Tel:* (03) 548 9009 *Fax:* (03) 548 9456 *E-mail:* info@cpp.co.nz
Web Site: www.craigpotton.co.nz
Inbooks, 114 Old Pittwater Rd, Unit 3, Brookvale, NSW 2100, Australia *Tel:* (02) 8988 5082

Fax: (02) 8988 5090 *E-mail:* orders@inbooks.com.au *Web Site:* www.inbooks.com.au
Eurospan Group, 3 Henrietta St, Convent Garden, London WC2E 8LU, United Kingdom *Tel:* (01767) 604972 *Fax:* (01767) 601640 *E-mail:* eurospan@turpin-distribution.com *Web Site:* www.eurospanbookstore.com/auckland
River North Editions from IPG, 814 N Franklin St, Chicago, IL 60610, United States *Tel:* 312-337-0747 *Fax:* 312-337-5985 *E-mail:* frontdesk@ipgbook.com *Web Site:* www.ipgbook.com

Auto Media Group Ltd+
PO Box 105010, Auckland 1043
Tel: (09) 309 2444 *Fax:* (09) 309 2449
Web Site: autotalk.co.nz
Key Personnel
Publisher: Vern Whitehead *E-mail:* vern@automediagroup.co.nz
Mng Editor: Richard Edwards *E-mail:* richard@automediagroup.co.nz
Sales Manager: Dale Stevenson *E-mail:* dale@automediagroup.co.nz
Founded: 1972
Publishers for the auto industry including newsletters, manuals, stock lists & pricing guides.
Subjects: Automotive
Number of titles published annually: 1 Print; 2 Online; 1 E-Book
Total Titles: 2 Print; 2 Online; 1 E-Book

Bantam, *imprint of* Random House Books New Zealand (RHNZ)

David Bateman Ltd+
30 Tarndale Grove, Albany, Auckland 0632
Mailing Address: North Shore Mail Centre, PO Box 100-242, Auckland 0745
Tel: (09) 415 7664 *Fax:* (09) 415 8892
E-mail: bateman@bateman.co.nz; info@bateman.co.nz
Web Site: www.batemanpublishing.co.nz; www.bateman.co.nz
Key Personnel
Mng Dir: Paul Bateman
Sales Manager: Bryce Gibson *E-mail:* bryceg@bateman.co.nz
Founded: 1979
Also acts as agent for overseas publishers.
Membership(s): Book Publishers Association of New Zealand; Booksellers New Zealand.
Subjects: Art, Business, Cookery, Crafts, Games, Hobbies, Gardening, Plants, History, Natural History, Outdoor Recreation, Travel & Tourism
ISBN Prefix(es): 978-1-86953; 978-0-908610
Total Titles: 250 Print
Imprints: Bateman Publishing

Bateman Publishing, *imprint of* David Bateman Ltd

Beatnik Publishing
11 New North Rd, Eden Terrace, Auckland 1021
Mailing Address: PO Box 8276, Symonds St, Auckland 1150
Tel: (09) 365 2223
Web Site: www.beatnikpublishing.com; www.facebook.com/beatnikpublishing
Key Personnel
Founder, Creative Dir, Designer & Photographer: Sally Greer
Associate Dir, Production Manager & Designer: Kitki Tong
Graphic Designer, Marketing Assistant & Copywriter: Kyle Ranudo
Publishing Assistant: Alena Kavka
Publicist & Author Management: Karen McKenzie
Editor & Proofreader-in-Chief: Janet McAllister

Subjects: Art, Cookery, Photography, Poetry
ISBN Prefix(es): 978-0-473
Distribution Center: David Bateman Ltd, 30 Tarndale Grove, Albany, Auckland 0632
Tel: (09) 415 7664 *Fax:* (09) 415 8892
E-mail: info@bateman.co.nz *Web Site:* www.bateman.co.nz (New Zealand)
Dennis Jones & Associates, Unit 1/10 Melrich Rd, Bayswater, Victoria 3153, Australia *Tel:* (03) 9762 9100 *Fax:* (03) 9762 9200 *E-mail:* theoffice@dennisjones.com.au *Web Site:* www.dennisjones.com.au (Australia)

BIOZONE International Ltd
32 Somerset St, Hamilton 3204
Mailing Address: PO Box 5002, Hamilton 3242
Tel: (07) 856 8104 *Fax:* (07) 856 9243
E-mail: info@biozone.co.nz; sales@biozone.co.nz
Web Site: www.biozone.co.nz
Key Personnel
Chief Executive Officer: Richard Allan
Sales Dir: Nadege Stoffel
Founded: 1988
Specialize in student & teacher resources for senior biology.
Subjects: Biological Sciences, Environmental Studies, Science (General), Anatomy, Physiology
ISBN Prefix(es): 978-1-877329; 978-1-877462
Branch Office(s)
BIOZONE Learning Media Australia, 4/35 Township Dr, West Burleigh, Qld 4219, Australia *Tel:* (07) 5535 4896 *Fax:* (07) 5508 2432 *E-mail:* info@biozone.com.au
BIOZONE Learning Media (UK) Ltd, Greenline Business Park, Wellington St, Burton-upon-Trent DE14 2AS, United Kingdom *Tel:* (01283) 530 366 *Fax:* (01283) 530 961 *E-mail:* sales@biozone.co.uk (UK, Europe & Middle East)

Black Swan, *imprint of* Random House Books New Zealand (RHNZ)

Blackwell & Ruth
Formerly PQ Blackwell
116 Symonds St, Auckland 1010
Mailing Address: PO Box 37 692, Parnell, Auckland 1151
Tel: (09) 300 9955 *Fax:* (09) 300 9959
E-mail: contact@pqblackwell.com
Web Site: www.pqblackwell.com
Key Personnel
Chief Executive Officer & Publisher: Geoff Blackwell
Editor-in-Chief: Ruth Hobday
Licensing: Michelle Langstone *E-mail:* michelle.langstone@pqblackwell.com
ISBN Prefix(es): 978-0-473

Book Island Ltd
49 Poplar Ave, Reumati South 5032
Tel: (04) 905 0482
E-mail: info@bookisland.co.nz
Web Site: www.bookisland.co.nz
Key Personnel
Publisher: Greet Pauwelijn
Founded: 2012
ISBN Prefix(es): 978-0-9876696
Distribution Center: Greene Phoenix Marketing, PO Box 5585, Terrace End, Palmerston North 4441, Sales Representative: Paul Greenberg *Tel:* (06) 356 4470; (021) 722 210 (cell) *Fax:* (06) 356 4471 *E-mail:* paul.gpm@xtra.co.nz
Dennis Jones & Associates Pty Ltd, 1/10 Melrich Rd, Bayswater, Victoria 3153, Australia *Tel:* (03) 9762 9100 *Fax:* (03) 9762 9200 *E-mail:* theoffice@dennisjones.com.au *Web Site:* dennisjones.com.au
Central Books Ltd, One Heath Park Industrial Estate, Freshwater Rd, Dagenham RM8

1RX, United Kingdom *Tel:* (020) 8525 8800 *Fax:* (020) 8599 2694 *E-mail:* contactus@centralbooks.com *Web Site:* www.centralbooks.com (UK & Ireland)

Brookers Ltd, see Thomson Reuters New Zealand Ltd

Brookfield Press
8 Napa Court, Howick, Auckland 2016
Tel: (09) 535 2344 (cell)
E-mail: esp@psychic.co.nz
Web Site: www.psychic.co.nz
Key Personnel
Mng Dir, Editorial: Richard Webster
E-mail: richard.webster@psychic.co.nz
Sales & Publicity: Don Kaye *E-mail:* don@psychic.co.nz
Founded: 1971
Subjects: Astrology, Occult, How-to, Parapsychology, Philosophy
ISBN Prefix(es): 978-0-86467
Number of titles published annually: 6 Print
Total Titles: 87 Print
Parent Company: Brookings Bookshop 1971 Ltd
Distributed by Peaceful Living Publications (New Zealand)

Bush Press Communications Ltd
41 Hauraki Rd, Takapuna, Auckland 0622
Mailing Address: PO Box 33-029, Takapuna, Auckland 0740
Tel: (09) 486 2667
E-mail: bush.press@clear.net.nz
Web Site: www.bushpress.com
Key Personnel
Mng Dir: Gordon Ell
Founded: 1979
Specializes in titles concerning the natural & historic heritage of New Zealand. Also offers publishing services.
Subjects: Archaeology, Geography, Geology, History, Natural History, Regional Interests, Historic & Natural Heritage of New Zealand
ISBN Prefix(es): 978-0-908608; 978-0-9864564
Number of titles published annually: 5 Print
Total Titles: 10 Print
Imprints: The Bush Press of New Zealand
Divisions: Bush Films; The Bush Press
Warehouse: David Bateman Ltd, 30 Tarndale Groove, off Bush Rd, North Shore, Auckland 0064 *Tel:* (09) 415 7664 *Fax:* (09) 415 8892
Distribution Center: David Bateman Ltd, 30 Tarndale Groove, off Bush Rd, North Shore, Auckland 0064 *Tel:* (09) 415 7664 *Fax:* (09) 415 8892

The Bush Press of New Zealand, *imprint of* Bush Press Communications Ltd

BWB, see Bridget Williams Books Ltd (BWB)

Calico Publishing Ltd
2A Heywood Crescent, Epsom, Auckland 1023
Tel: (09) 6245674
Web Site: calicopublishing.co.nz
Key Personnel
Publishing Dir: Linda Cassells *E-mail:* linda@calicopublishing.co.nz
Founded: 2003
Subjects: Biography, Memoirs, Gardening, Plants, Health, Nutrition, Nonfiction (General), Self-Help
ISBN Prefix(es): 978-1-877429

Canterbury University Press+
Alice Candy House, One Arts Rd, Ilam, Christchurch 8140
Mailing Address: Private Bag 4800, Christchurch 8140
Tel: (03) 369 3335
E-mail: universitypress@canterbury.ac.nz

Web Site: www.cup.canterbury.ac.nz
Key Personnel
Publisher: Catherine Montgomery *Tel:* (03)
369 3371 *E-mail:* catherine.montgomery@
canterbury.ac.nz
Founded: 1964
Subjects: Art, Biography, Memoirs, Biological
Sciences, History, Natural History, Nonfic-
tion (General), Poetry, Marine Biology, New
Zealand & Pacific History
ISBN Prefix(es): 978-0-900392; 978-0-908812;
978-1-877257; 978-1-927145
Number of titles published annually: 12 Print
Foreign Rep(s): Independent Publishers Group
(worldwide exc New Zealand)
Distribution Center: Nationwide Book Distributors, PO Box 65, Oxford, North Canterbury
7443 *Tel:* (03) 312 1603 *Toll Free Tel:* 0800
990 123 (New Zealand only) *Fax:* (03) 312
1604 *E-mail:* info@nationwidebooks.co.nz *Web
Site:* www.nationwidebooks.co.nz

Cape Catley Ltd+
PO Box 34 963, Birkenhead, Auckland 0746
Tel: (09) 480 5454
E-mail: cape.catley@gmail.com
Web Site: www.capecatleybooks.co.nz
Key Personnel
Publisher: Jenny Cole
Founded: 1973
Subjects: Biography, Memoirs, Fiction, Gov-
ernment, Political Science, Health, Nutrition,
History, Literature, Literary Criticism, Essays,
Mysteries, Suspense, Nonfiction (General), Po-
etry, Self-Help, Women's Studies, Feminism,
Social Justice
ISBN Prefix(es): 978-1-877340; 978-1-908561
Number of titles published annually: 5 Print
Total Titles: 100 Print
Distribution Center: Publishers Distribution
Ltd *Tel:* (09) 828 2999 *Fax:* (09) 828 2399
E-mail: orders@pubdist.co.nz

CaxEd, see Caxton Educational Ltd (CaxEd)

Caxton Educational Ltd (CaxEd)
2 Stark Dr, Wigram, Christchurch 8042
Mailing Address: PO Box 37-153, Halswell,
Christchurch 8245
Tel: (03) 366 7091 *Toll Free Tel:* 0800 628 474
E-mail: caxton@caxed.co.nz
Web Site: www.caxed.co.nz
Key Personnel
Dir: Bruce Bascand *Tel:* (03) 366 8516
E-mail: bruce@caxton.co.nz; Peter Watson
Tel: (03) 353 0734 *E-mail:* peter@caxton.co.nz
Manager: Mel Watson *E-mail:* mel@caxed.co.nz
Founded: 1988
Publisher of comprehensive mathematics re-
sources.
Subjects: Mathematics
ISBN Prefix(es): 978-0-908563; 978-0-908911

The Caxton Press
2 Stark Dr, Wigram, Christchurch 8042
Mailing Address: PO Box 36411, Merivale,
Christchurch 8146
Tel: (03) 366 8516
Web Site: www.caxton.co.nz
Key Personnel
Mng Dir: Bruce Bascand *E-mail:* bruce@caxton.
co.nz
Dir: Peter Watson *Tel:* (03) 353 0734
E-mail: peter@caxton.co.nz
Dir/Sales Manager: Bridget Batchelor *Tel:* (03)
353 0730 *E-mail:* bridget@caxton.co.nz
Founded: 1935
Subjects: Biography, Memoirs, Gardening, Plants,
Nonfiction (General)
ISBN Prefix(es): 978-0-908563; 978-0-908660;
978-1-877303

CCH New Zealand Ltd
129-157 Hurstmere Rd, Level 5, Takapuna 0622
Mailing Address: PO Box 2378, Shortland St,
Auckland 1140
Tel: (09) 488 2760 *Toll Free Tel:* 0800 500 224
(New Zealand only) *Fax:* (09) 477 0779
Toll Free Fax: 0800 555 602
E-mail: nzsales@cch.co.nz; nzorders@cch.co.nz;
support@cch.co.nz
Web Site: www.cch.co.nz
Key Personnel
Account Manager: Grant Cartwright *Tel:* (021)
430 712 *E-mail:* gcartwright@cch.co.nz
Regional Sales Manager: Danya Reinsfield
Tel: (09) 488 6927 *E-mail:* dreinsfield@cch.
co.nz
Founded: 1973
Subjects: Accounting, Business, Law
ISBN Prefix(es): 978-0-86475; 978-0-86903; 978-
1-77547
Parent Company: Wolters Kluwer NV

CheekyBird Press, *imprint of* Magari Publishing

Clean Slate Press Ltd
9 George St, Mount Eden, Auckland 1024
Mailing Address: PO Box 137183, Parnell, Auck-
land 1151
Tel: (09) 6300382 *Fax:* (09) 6300387
E-mail: info@cleanslatepress.com
Web Site: www.cleanslatepress.com
Subjects: Education, Fiction, Nonfiction (General)
ISBN Prefix(es): 978-1-877454; 978-1-877499;
978-1-927185; 978-1-927130

Clerestory Press+
PO Box 21-120, Christchurch 8001
Tel: (03) 355 3588
E-mail: young.writers@xtra.co.nz
Key Personnel
Contact: Dr Glyn Strange
Founded: 1994
Membership(s): Book Publishers Association of
New Zealand (BPANZ).
Subjects: Archaeology, Biography, Memoirs,
Drama, Theater, Education, Genealogy, History,
Law, Literature, Literary Criticism, Essays, Re-
gional Interests, Women's Studies
ISBN Prefix(es): 978-0-9583706; 978-0-9582201;
978-0-9582888; 978-0-9922517
Shipping Address: 31 Mersey St, Christchurch

Craig Potton Publishing+
98 Vickerman St, Port Nelson 7010
Mailing Address: PO Box 555, Nelson 7040
Tel: (03) 548 9009 *Fax:* (03) 548 9456
E-mail: info@cpp.co.nz
Web Site: www.craigpotton.co.nz
Key Personnel
Executive Dir & Publisher: Robbie Burton
E-mail: robbie@cpp.co.nz
Mng Dir: Emma Radcliffe *Tel:* (03) 989 5053
E-mail: emma@cpp.co.nz
National Sales Manager: Pauline Esposito
Tel: (03) 989 5051 *E-mail:* pauline@cpp.co.nz
Founded: 1987
Specialize in wilderness photography & writing
& high-quality, illustrated nonfiction; also acts
as book packagers, produce calendars, posters,
postcards.
Subjects: Architecture & Interior Design, Art, Bi-
ography, Memoirs, Biological Sciences, Crafts,
Games, Hobbies, History, Natural History,
Nonfiction (General), Outdoor Recreation, Pho-
tography, Travel & Tourism
ISBN Prefix(es): 978-0-908802; 978-1-877333;
978-1-877517; 978-1-877288; 978-1-927213

Craigs Design & Print Ltd
122 Yarrow St, Invercargill 9840
Mailing Address: PO Box 99, Invercargill 9840

Tel: (03) 211-0393; (03) 211-8618 (showroom)
Fax: (03) 214-9930
E-mail: www@craigprint.co.nz
Web Site: www.craigprint.co.nz
Key Personnel
Chief Executive & Dir: Tony Wills *Tel:* (027)
672-7147 (cell) *E-mail:* tony@craigprint.co.nz
Dir & Administration: Eleanor Wills *Tel:* (027)
284-6524 (cell) *E-mail:* eleanor@craigprint.co.
nz
Dir & Promotional/Digital Manager:
Richard Wills *Tel:* (021) 264-2772 (cell)
E-mail: richard@craigprint.co.nz
Dir & Sales Manager: Rodger Wills *Tel:* (027)
434-2757 (cell) *E-mail:* rodger@craigprint.co.
nz
Print Services Manager: Alan Shirley *Tel:* (027)
681-5240 (cell) *E-mail:* alan@craigprint.co.nz
Production Manager: Brent Hollingworth
Tel: (027) 221-2083 (cell) *E-mail:* brent@
craigprint.co.nz
Founded: 1876
Subjects: Aeronautics, Aviation, History, Non-
fiction (General), Regional Interests, Travel &
Tourism
ISBN Prefix(es): 978-0-908629; 978-0-9597554

Curly Tales, *imprint of* Magari Publishing

Current Pacific Ltd+
7 La Roche Pl, Northcote, Auckland 0627
Mailing Address: PO Box 36-536, Auckland,
Northcote 0748
Tel: (09) 480-1388
E-mail: info@cplnz.com; cpl_nz@hotmail.com
Web Site: www.cplnz.com
Key Personnel
Mng Dir: Charles Lau
Dir: Amy Yeung
Founded: 1992
Publisher of *New Zealand Trade Directory*, a
business/trade directory containing more than
6,000 firms including manufacturers, importers,
exporters, distributors, food processors, banks
& financial firms, tourism services, trade pro-
motion organizations, government departments,
tertiary & secondary education institutions, pro-
fessional institutions, libraries, etc.
Subjects: Business

Dollars & Sense, *imprint of* Pursuit Publishing
(NZ) Ltd

Duck Creek Press, *imprint of* David Ling
Publishing

Dunmore Publishing Ltd+
PO Box 28387, Auckland 1541
Tel: (09) 521 3121
E-mail: books@dunmore.co.nz
Web Site: www.dunmore.co.nz
Founded: 1975
Subjects: Accounting, Business, Economics, Edu-
cation, Ethnicity, History, Nonfiction (General)
ISBN Prefix(es): 978-0-908564; 978-0-86469
Number of titles published annually: 25 Print
Total Titles: 180 Print
Parent Company: Thomson Learning
Foreign Rep(s): Federation Press (Australia)

ESA Publications (NZ) Ltd+
Unit 14, 180 Montgomerie Rd, Airport Oaks,
Auckland 2022
Mailing Address: Box 9453, Newmarket, Auck-
land 1023
Tel: (09) 256 0831 *Toll Free Tel:* (0800) 372 266
Fax: (09) 256 9412 *Toll Free Fax:* (0800) 329
372
E-mail: info@esa.co.nz
Web Site: www.esa.co.nz

Key Personnel
Publisher & Mng Dir: Mark Sayes
  E-mail: mark@esa.co.nz
Office Manager & Accounts: Andrea Tamatea
  E-mail: andrea@esa.co.nz
Sales & Marketing: Julie Lubich *E-mail:* julie@
  esa.co.nz
Founded: 1985
Publisher of New Zealand educational books for
  primary & secondary school ages.
Membership(s): Book Publishers Association of
  New Zealand (BPANZ).
Subjects: Accounting, Agriculture, Art, Biologi-
  cal Sciences, Chemistry, Chemical Engineering,
  Computer Science, Drama, Theater, Economics,
  English as a Second Language, Geography,
  Geology, Health, Nutrition, History, Mathe-
  matics, Physics, Science (General), Social Sci-
  ences, Sociology, Sports, Athletics, Technology,
  French, Graphics, Horticulture, Japanese, Me-
  dia Studies, Physical Education
ISBN Prefix(es): 978-0-908756; 978-0-9597692;
  978-1-877234; 978-1-877291; 978-1-877366;
  978-1-877401; 978-1-877459; 978-1-877530;
  978-1-927194; 978-1-927245; 978-1-877153
Number of titles published annually: 55 Print
Total Titles: 155 Print

Essential Resources
PO Box 5036, Waikiwi, Invercargill 9843
Toll Free Tel: 0800 087 376 *Toll Free Fax:* 0800
  937 825
E-mail: info@essentialresources.co.nz
Web Site: www.essentialresources.co.nz
Key Personnel
Mng Dir: Nicola Smith
Subjects: Art, Education, Health, Nutrition, Lan-
  guage Arts, Linguistics, Mathematics, Science
  (General), Social Sciences, Sociology
ISBN Prefix(es): 978-1-877300; 978-1-877390;
  978-0-9582285; 978-1-877440; 978-1-927143;
  978-1-927190; 978-1-927221; 978-1-877478;
  978-1-877536; 978-1-877498; 978-1-877523
Branch Office(s)
PO Box 906, Strawberry Hill, NSW 2012 *Toll
  Free Tel:* 1800 005 068 *Toll Free Fax:* 1800
  981 213
Units 8-10 Parkside, Shortgate Lane, Laughton
  BN8 6DG, United Kingdom *Tel:* (0845) 3636
  147 *Fax:* (0845) 3636 148

Evagean Publishing Ltd+
28 Wyborn Rd, RD 2, Te Aroha 3392
Tel: (07) 884-8783; (07) 884-8594
Web Site: www.evagean.co.nz
Key Personnel
Owner: Alison Honeyfield *E-mail:* alison@xtra.
  co.nz; Andrew Honeyfield
Founded: 1990
Specialize in compiling, publishing & marketing
  family histories & genealogies.
Subjects: Genealogy
ISBN Prefix(es): 978-0-9577412; 978-0-9579080;
  978-0-908951; 978-0-9597991; 978-0-909032;
  978-1-877342; 978-1-877194; 978-1-877262;
  978-1-877558
Branch Office(s)
14 Kaweka Pl, Havelock North, Hawkes Bay,
  Contact: Jim Kelly *Tel:* (06) 877 1210
  Fax: (06) 877-1212
12 McCrae St, Wakefield 7025, Contact: Yvonne
  Lash *Tel:* (03) 541-9757 *E-mail:* ylash@xtra.
  co.nz
18 Waygrove Ave, Earlwood, NSW 2206, Australia, Contact: Trissia Waddingham *Tel:* (02)
  9789-4550 *Fax:* (02) 9789-4550
PO Box 1167, South Perth, WA 6951, Australia,
  Contact: Susan Chylek *Tel:* (08) 367-6578
  Fax: (08) 367-6578 *E-mail:* chylek@space.
  net.au

Fraser Books
53 Essex St, Masterton 5810
Tel: (06) 3771359
Key Personnel
Partner: Diane Grant *E-mail:* degrant@xtra.co.nz;
  Ian F Grant *E-mail:* ifgrant@xtra.co.nz
Founded: 1980
Specialize in history, politics, biography & car-
  toon histories. Some novels & children's pic-
  ture books.
This publisher has indicated that 50% of their
  product line is author subsidized.
Subjects: Agriculture, Biography, Memoirs, Eco-
  nomics, Government, Political Science, History,
  Regional Interests, Social Sciences, Sociology
ISBN Prefix(es): 978-0-9582617 (Wairarapa
  Archive); 978-0-9582645; 978-0-9582320 (NZ
  Carton Archive)
Number of titles published annually: 10 Print
Total Titles: 150 Print
Shipping Address: Nationwide Book Distributors,
  351 Kiri Kiri Rd, PO Box 65, Oxford 7495
  Web Site: www.nationwidebooks.co.nz
Warehouse: Nationwide Book Distributors, 351
  Kiri Kiri Rd, PO Box 65, Oxford 7495 *Web
  Site:* www.nationwidebooks.co.nz
Distribution Center: Nationwide Book Distrib-
  utors, 351 Kiri Kiri Rd, PO Box 65, Oxford
  7495 *Web Site:* www.nationwidebooks.co.nz
Orders to: Nationwide Book Distributors, 351
  Kiri Kiri Rd, PO Box 65, Oxford 7495 *Web
  Site:* www.nationwidebooks.co.nz
Returns: Nationwide Book Distributors, 351
  Kiri Kiri Rd, PO Box 65, Oxford 7495 *Web
  Site:* www.nationwidebooks.co.nz

Gecko Press+
9A Holland St, Level 1, Wellington 6011
Mailing Address: PO Box 9335, Marion Sq,
  Wellington 6141
Tel: (04) 801 9333
E-mail: info@geckopress.com
Web Site: www.geckopress.co.nz
Key Personnel
Publisher: Julia Marshall
Assistant Publisher: Petra Westropp
Publishing Manager: Rachel Lawson
Founded: 2005
New Zealand based independent publisher of chil-
  dren's books from around the world.
ISBN Prefix(es): 978-0-9582598; 978-0-9582787;
  978-0-9582720; 978-1-877467; 978-1-877579;
  978-1-927271; 978-1-77657
Number of titles published annually: 17 Print; 8
  E-Book
Total Titles: 97 Print; 37 E-Book
Distributed by Lerner Publishing Group Inc (USA
  & Canada); Scholastic Australia Pty Ltd (Aus-
  tralia); Upstart Press (New Zealand)
Foreign Rights: Bookman (Lillian Hsao) (China,
  Taiwan); Mundt Agency (Anja Mundt) (world-
  wide exc Australia, Canada, China, Ireland,
  New Zealand, UK & USA)
Distribution Center: Upstart Press, PO Box
  302-749, North Harbor, Auckland 0751
  Tel: (09) 280 3199 *Fax:* (09) 281 3090 *Web
  Site:* upstartpress.co.nz
Scholastic Australia, 76-80 Railway Crescent,
  Lisarow, NSW 2250, Australia *Tel:* (02) 4329
  9473 *E-mail:* customer_service@scholastic.
  com.au *Web Site:* www.scholastic.com.au
Bounce! Sales & Marketing, 320 City Rd, Lon-
  don EC1V 2NZ, United Kingdom *Tel:* (020)
  7138 3650 *E-mail:* sales@bouncemarketing.co.
  uk *Web Site:* www.bouncemarketing.co.uk
Lerner Publishing Group Inc, 241 First Ave
  N, Minneapolis, MN 55401, United States
  E-mail: info@lernerbooks.com *Web Site:* www.
  lernerbooks.com
Orders to: Archetype Book Agents, 17 Cascade
  Ave, Waiatarua, Auckland 0604, Contact: Neil
  Brown *Tel:* (09) 814 9455 *Fax:* (09) 814 9453
  E-mail: neilb@archetype.co.nz *Web Site:* www.
  archetype.co.nz

Gnostic Press Ltd
100 Riverland Rd, RD 2, Kumeu, Auckland 0892
Tel: (09) 412 7054 *Fax:* (09) 412 6476
E-mail: gnosticpress@ihug.co.nz
Web Site: www.gnosticpress.co.nz
Founded: 1978
Created for the disbursement of the works of Ab-
  dullah Dougan (Sufi teacher).
Subjects: Inspirational, Spirituality, Philosophy,
  Religion - Buddhist, Religion - Hindu, Religion
  - Islamic, Religion - Other, Self-Help
ISBN Prefix(es): 978-0-9597566

Godwit, *imprint of* Random House Books New
  Zealand (RHNZ)

Grantham House Publishing+
6/9 Wilkinson St, Oriental Bay, Wellington 6011
Tel: (04) 381 3071 *Fax:* (04) 381 3067
Web Site: www.granthamhouse.co.nz
Key Personnel
Publisher: Graham Stewart *E-mail:* graham@
  ghbil.com
Founded: 1985
Specialize in railways, tramways, aviation, ship-
  ping, Royal New Zealand Navy, Royal New
  Zealand Air Force & New Zealand history.
Membership(s): Booksellers New Zealand.
Subjects: History, Regional Interests, Transporta-
  tion, Military
ISBN Prefix(es): 978-1-86934
Total Titles: 40 Print
Parent Company: Bookprint Consultants Ltd
Distribution Center: David Bateman Ltd, 30
  Tarndale Grove, Albany, Auckland 0632
  Tel: (09) 415 7664 *Fax:* (09) 415 8892
  E-mail: info@bateman.co.nz *Web Site:* www.
  bateman.co.nz (trade inquiries & customer ser-
  vice)

Halcyon Publishing Ltd
PO Box 1064, Cambridge 3450
Tel: (09) 489 5337
E-mail: info@halcyonpublishing.co.nz
Web Site: www.halcyonpublishing.co.nz
Key Personnel
Mng Dir, Sales: Graham Gurr *E-mail:* gurr@
  halcyonpublishing.co.nz
Founded: 1984
Subjects: Cookery, Crafts, Games, Hobbies, Mar-
  itime, Outdoor Recreation, Sports, Athletics
ISBN Prefix(es): 978-0-908685; 978-0-908689;
  978-1-877256
Number of titles published annually: 3 Print; 5 E-
  Book
Total Titles: 83 Print; 30 E-Book
Imprints: Halcyon Sporting Heritage
Subsidiaries: Halcyon Books; The Halcyon Press;
  Hole in the Bank Books
Distribution Center: David Bateman Ltd,
  30 Tarndale Grove, Albany, Auckland
  0632 *Tel:* (09) 415 7664 *Fax:* (09) 415
  8892 *E-mail:* janetteb@bateman.co.nz *Web
  Site:* www.bateman.co.nz

Halcyon Sporting Heritage, *imprint of* Halcyon
  Publishing Ltd

Harper Sports, *imprint of* HarperCollins
  Publishers New Zealand

HarperCollins New Zealand, *imprint of*
  HarperCollins Publishers New Zealand

HarperCollins Publishers New Zealand+
Division of HarperCollins Publishers
Shortland St, PO Box 1, Auckland 1140
Tel: (09) 443 9400 *Fax:* (09) 443 9403
E-mail: orders@harpercollins.com.au; publicity@
  harpercollins.co.nz; rights@harpercollins.com.
  au

Web Site: www.harpercollins.co.nz
Key Personnel
Chief Executive Officer: James Kellow
Publisher: Alex Hedley
National Sales Manager: Matthew Simpson
Marketing Manager: Dawn Allan
Operations Manager: Michelle Enoka
Publicity Manager: Sandra Noakes
Founded: 1888
Subjects: Art, Biography, Memoirs, Cookery,
  Fiction, Gardening, Plants, History, Humor,
  Natural History, Regional Interests, Self-Help,
  Sports, Athletics, Travel & Tourism
ISBN Prefix(es): 978-1-86950
Total Titles: 100 Print
Ultimate Parent Company: News Corp
Imprints: Harper Sports; HarperCollins New
  Zealand

Heritage Press Ltd
PO Box 1426, Palmerston North 4440
Tel: (06) 3568078
E-mail: heritagepressltd@xtra.co.nz
Web Site: www.heritagepress.co.nz
Key Personnel
Mng Editor: Alyson B Cresswell
Founded: 1984
Specialize in New Zealand social history.
Subjects: Biography, Memoirs, Genealogy, His-
  tory, Regional Interests
ISBN Prefix(es): 978-0-908708

Huia Publishers+
39 Pipitea St, Thorndon, Wellington 6011
Mailing Address: PO Box 12-280, Thorndon,
  Wellington, Aotearon 6144
Tel: (04) 473 9262 *Fax:* (04) 473 9265
E-mail: info@huia.co.nz; customer@huia.co.nz
  (sales)
Web Site: www.huia.co.nz
Key Personnel
Executive Dir: Brian Morris *E-mail:* brian.
  morris@huia.co.nz; Eboni Waitere
Production Manager: Waimatua Morris
  E-mail: waimatua.morris@huia.co.nz
Founded: 1991
Specializes in books about & by Maori & Pa-
  cific New Zealanders; educational resources
  in Maori language; children's books in En-
  glish & Maori; histories of colonization in New
  Zealand.
Subjects: Art, Biography, Memoirs, Drama,
  Theater, Education, Erotica, Ethnicity, Fic-
  tion, Government, Political Science, History,
  LGBTQ, Nonfiction (General), Poetry, Bicul-
  tural, English Language, Indigenous Studies,
  Maori, Maori Studies
ISBN Prefix(es): 978-0-908975; 978-1-86969;
  978-1-877266; 978-1-877241; 978-1-877283;
  978-0-9582517; 978-1-77550
Number of titles published annually: 100 Print
Total Titles: 1,000 Print
Parent Company: Huia (NZ) Ltd
Foreign Rep(s): Random House (NZ) Ltd (New
  Zealand); University of Hawaii Press (USA)
Distribution Center: University of Hawaii Press,
  2840 Kolowalu St, Honolulu, HI 96822, United
  States *Tel:* 808-956-8255 *Fax:* 808-988-6052
  E-mail: uhpbooks@hawaii.edu

Knowing Science, *imprint of* Magari Publishing

Kotuku Media Ltd+
PO Box 54-234, Plimmerton, Wellington
Tel: (04) 233 1842
E-mail: kotuku.media@xtra.co.nz
Key Personnel
Owner: Ross Miller
Founded: 1991
Subjects: Regional Interests
ISBN Prefix(es): 978-0-908967

Learning Media+
PO Box 90712, Victoria St West, Auckland 1142
Tel: (04) 472 5522 *Toll Free Tel:* 0800 800 565
  Fax: (04) 472 6444 *Toll Free Fax:* 0800 800
  570
E-mail: info@learningmedia.co.nz; sales@
  learningmedia.co.nz
Web Site: www.learningmedia.co.nz
Founded: 1993
Also provides contract publishing services, con-
  sultancy & professional development programs
  for the Ministry of Education, Ministry of
  Health & a diverse range of public & private
  sector organizations. Produce a range of world-
  class curriculum aligned materials for schools
  in English, Te Reo Maori & other Pacific Is-
  land languages. Develop & sell education re-
  sources to New Zealand schools & to a number
  of international markets.
Membership(s): New Zealand Book Publishers
  Association.
Subjects: Education, Health, Nutrition
ISBN Prefix(es): 978-0-478; 978-0-790
Total Titles: 2 CD-ROM
Distributed by Alinea (Denmark); Bonnier Utbild-
  ning (Sweden); Brightpoint Literacy (USA);
  Cappelen (Norway); Cheneliere Education
  (Canada); Dafola (Denmark); Gardner Edu-
  cation (UK); Intelligent Media (Africa); Kiwik
  International Ltd (Hong Kong); Learning Me-
  dia (Asia exc Hong Kong); Maaholm Forlag
  (Denmark); Modern Teaching Aids (Australia);
  Nelson Education Ltd (Canada); Richard C
  Own Publishers Ltd (USA); Read Pacific Ltd
  (Pacific Nations)

LexisNexis NZ Ltd
Level 1, 138 The Terrace, Wellington 6011
Mailing Address: PO Box 472, Wellington 6011
Toll Free Tel: 0800 800 986 (NZ only) *Fax:* (04)
  474 3401
E-mail: customer.service@lexisnexis.co.nz
Web Site: www.lexisnexis.co.nz
Key Personnel
Chief Executive Officer: T J Viljoen
Executive Dir: Rachel Travers
Executive Dir, Editorial Operations: Anupama
  Bhattacharya
Founded: 1914
Subjects: Law
ISBN Prefix(es): 978-0-409; 978-0-408; 978-1-
  877511; 978-1-927149; 978-1-927183; 978-1-
  927227; 978-1-927248
Parent Company: RELX Group PLC
Branch Office(s)
57-59 Fort St, Level 12, PO Box 2399, Auckland
  1140 *Fax:* (09) 368 9500
Third Cove, Unit 5, 144 Third Ave, Tauranga
  3110 *Tel:* (07) 577 5604 *Toll Free Tel:* 0800
  222 338 *Fax:* (07) 577 5619

Libro International, *imprint of* Oratia Media Ltd

David Ling Publishing+
33 Robert Hastie Dr, Mangawhai 0573
Mailing Address: PO Box 401106, Mangawhai
  Heads, Mangawhai 0541
Tel: (09) 431 4200
E-mail: davidling@xtra.co.nz
Web Site: www.davidling.co.nz
Key Personnel
Mng Dir: David Ling
Founded: 1992
Publisher & packager.
Membership(s): Booksellers New Zealand; Pub-
  lishers Association of New Zealand (PANZ).
Subjects: Aeronautics, Aviation, Art, Biography,
  Memoirs, Fiction, History, Maritime, Nonfic-
  tion (General), Poetry, Sports, Athletics, Travel
  & Tourism, Lifestyle
ISBN Prefix(es): 978-0-908990; 978-1-877378;
  978-1-927305

Number of titles published annually: 10 Print
Total Titles: 90 Print
Imprints: Duck Creek Press (children's books)
Distribution Center: David Bateman Ltd, 30
  Tarndale Grove, Albany, Auckland 0632
Tel: (09) 415 7664 *Fax:* (09) 415 8892
E-mail: info@bateman.co.nz *Web Site:* www.
  bateman.co.nz

Longacre Child, *imprint of* Random House
  Books New Zealand (RHNZ)

Macmillan Publishers New Zealand Ltd+
Subsidiary of Macmillan Publishers Ltd
24 The Warehouse Way, Northcote, Auckland
  0627
Tel: (09) 905 3200 *Fax:* (09) 905 3224
E-mail: customersupport@macmillan.co.nz
Founded: 1843
ISBN Prefix(es): 978-0-333; 978-0-908923; 978-
  1-86965
Ultimate Parent Company: Verlagsgruppe George
  von Holtzbrinck GmbH, Stuttgart, Germany
Associate Companies: Macmillan Education Aus-
  tralia; Pan Macmillan Australia

Magari Publishing+
PO Box 104, Taupo 2730
Tel: (07) 377 0169
E-mail: webmail@magari.co.nz
Web Site: www.magari.co.nz
Key Personnel
Publisher: Margaret Woodhouse *E-mail:* marg@
  magari.co.nz
Founded: 1985
Publishes humorous, fun titles some of which are
  stories featuring cats.
Subjects: Education, Humor, Self-Help
ISBN Prefix(es): 978-0-908801
Imprints: CheekyBird Press; Curly Tales; Know-
  ing Science
Warehouse: 14 The Point, Taupo

Manaaki Whenua Press
Gerald St, Lincoln 7608
Mailing Address: PO Box 69040, Lincoln 7640
Tel: (03) 321 9999 *Fax:* (03) 321 9998
E-mail: mwpress@landcareresearch.co.nz
Web Site: www.mwpress.co.nz; www.
  landcareresearch.co.nz
Key Personnel
Chief Executive Officer: Richard Gordon *Tel:* (03)
  321 9681
Chair: Peter Schuyt
Publisher: Catherine Montgomery
Public Relations Manager: Judy Grindell *Tel:* (03)
  321 9684
Founded: 1993
Specialize in natural history & scientific publica-
  tions.
Subjects: Animals, Pets, Biological Sciences,
  Earth Sciences, Gardening, Plants, Natural
  History, Science (General), Social Sciences,
  Sociology
ISBN Prefix(es): 978-0-477; 978-0-478
Parent Company: Landcare Research
Distributed by Balogh International Inc (USA)
Distributor for Csiro Publishing (Australia)
Distribution Center: Nationwide Book Dis-
  tributor, 351 Kiri Kiri Rd, PO Box 65, Ox-
  ford *Tel:* (03) 312 1603 *Fax:* (03) 312 1604
  E-mail: books@nationwidebooks.co.nz

Massey Defence & Security Series, *imprint of*
  Massey University Press

Massey Symposia Series & Academic Series,
  imprint of Massey University Press

Massey University Press
Private Bag 102904, North Shore Mail Centre,
Auckland 0745
Tel: (09) 212 7073
E-mail: editorial@masseypress.ac.nz
Web Site: www.masseypress.ac.nz
Key Personnel
Founder & Publisher: Nicola Legat
Founded: 2015
Subjects: Agriculture, Business, Education,
Health, Nutrition, History, Military Science,
Psychology, Psychiatry, Social Sciences, Soci-
ology, Veterinary Science, Creative Arts, Food
Research, Maori Studies
ISBN Prefix(es): 978-0-9941473; 978-1-9941300;
978-0-9941407
Imprints: Massey Defence & Security Series;
Massey Symposia Series & Academic Series;
MasseyTexts
Distribution Center: David Bateman Ltd, 30
Tarndale Grove, Albany, Auckland 0632
Tel: (09) 415 7664 *Fax:* (09) 415 8892
E-mail: info@bateman.co.nz *Web Site:* www.
bateman.co.nz
IPG Academic & Professional Publishing, 814
N Franklin St, Chicago, IL 60610, United
States *Tel:* 312-337-0747 *Fax:* 312-337-5985
E-mail: orders@ipgbook.com *Web Site:* www.
ipgbook.com

MasseyTexts, *imprint of* Massey University Press

Mills Group Ltd+
Level 3, James Smith Bldg, 55 Cuba St, Welling-
ton 6011
Mailing Address: PO Box 11 721, Wellington
6011
Tel: (04) 499 6770 *Fax:* (04) 499 6771
Web Site: www.millsonline.com
Key Personnel
Chief Executive Officer: Harry Mills
E-mail: harry.mills@millsonline.com
Founded: 1982
Subjects: Business, Communications, Manage-
ment, Marketing, Nonfiction (General)
ISBN Prefix(es): 978-0-908722

Milly, Molly Books
752 Gladstone Rd, Gisborne 4010
Mailing Address: PO Box 539, Gisborne 4040
Tel: (06) 868 7769 *Fax:* (06) 868 7767
E-mail: info@millymolly.com
Web Site: www.millymolly.com
Key Personnel
Mng Dir: John Pittar
Founded: 2000
ISBN Prefix(es): 978-0-9582208; 978-1-877297;
978-1-86972; 978-1-877337; 978-1-877336

Moss Associates Ltd
7 Dorset Way, Wilton, Wellington 6012
Tel: (04) 472 8226 *Fax:* (04) 472 8226
E-mail: moss@mossassociates.co.nz; moss@xtra.
co.nz
Web Site: www.mossassociates.co.nz
Key Personnel
Dir: Geoffrey R Moss
Founded: 1986
Subjects: Business, Career Development, Commu-
nications, Human Relations, Management
ISBN Prefix(es): 978-0-9583538; 978-0-9864550
Total Titles: 7 E-Book
Distributed by Ane Books (India); Bagolyvar
Publishing House (Hungary); BPB Publica-
tions (India); Business ONE Irwin (USA);
CCH Australia Ltd (Australia); Cengage Learn-
ing Asia (Singapore); Development Programme
(United Nations); Dragon's Eye Communica-
tions (Korea); Federal Publications (Singapore);
Francolin Publishers (Pty) Ltd (South Africa);
GP Publications Ltd (New Zealand); Institute
for Research, Extension & Training in Agricul-

ture (IRETA) (Samoa); Joint Publishing (Hong
Kong) Co Ltd (China); Kogan Page Ltd (UK);
LDI Training Pte Ltd (Indonesia); McGraw-
Hill Australia Pty Ltd (Australia); Ministry of
Agriculture & Fisheries (New Zealand); Prom-
mociones Jumerca SL (Spain); Qingdao Pub-
lishing House (China); SE-Education Public Co
Ltd (Thailand); Shanghai People's Publishing
House (China); Singapore Institute of Manage-
ment (Singapore & Malaysia); Tech Publica-
tions Pty Ltd (Singapore); Thomson Learning
& Vijay Nicole Imprints Pvt Ltd (India); Vikas
Publishing House Pvt Ltd (India); Window of
Times (Korea); Yale International Publishing
House (Taiwan); Yale Management & Publish-
ing Services Inc (Taiwan)

Mower, *imprint of* Upstart Press

New Holland Publishers (NZ) Ltd
39 Woodside Ave, Off 5, Northcote, Auckland
0627
Tel: (09) 481 0444
E-mail: books@nhp.co.nz
Web Site: nz.newhollandpublishers.com
Key Personnel
Publishing Manager: Christine Thomson
E-mail: cthomson@nhp.co.nz
Founded: 1998
Subjects: Art, Cookery, Fiction, Gardening,
Plants, History, House & Home, Natural His-
tory, Nonfiction (General), Photography, Sports,
Athletics, Travel & Tourism
ISBN Prefix(es): 978-1-86966; 978-0-908808;
978-1-877213; 978-1-877246

**New Zealand Council for Educational
Research (NZCER)+**
Education House, Level 10, West Block, 178-182
Willis St, Wellington 6011
Mailing Address: PO Box 3237, Wellington 6140
Tel: (04) 384 7939 *Fax:* (04) 384 7933
E-mail: sales@nzcer.org.nz
Web Site: www.nzcer.org.nz/nzcer-press
Key Personnel
Publishing Manager: David Ellis *E-mail:* david.
ellis@nzcer.org.nz
Senior Editor: John Huria *Tel:* (04) 802 1438
E-mail: john.huria@nzcer.org.nz
Founded: 1935
Subjects: Education, Maori Education
ISBN Prefix(es): 978-0-908567; 978-0-908916;
978-1-877140; 978-1-877293; 978-1-877398;
978-1-877396; 978-1-927151; 978-1-927231
Distributor for ACER Press; NFER; SCRE

NZCER, see New Zealand Council for
Educational Research (NZCER)

Oily Rag, *imprint of* Pursuit Publishing (NZ) Ltd

Oratia Media Ltd
783 West Coast Rd, Oratia, Auckland 0604
Tel: (09) 814 8993; (027) 614 8993 (cell)
Fax: (09) 814 8997
E-mail: info@oratia.co.nz
Web Site: www.oratia.co.nz
Key Personnel
Mng Dir: Peter Dowling *E-mail:* peter@oratia.co.
nz
Creative Dir: Alessandra Zecchini
E-mail: alessandra@oratia.co.nz
Editorial Dir: Carolyn Lagahetau
E-mail: carolyn@oratia.co.nz
Sales & Marketing Consultant: Belinda Cooke
E-mail: belinda@oratia.co.nz
Founded: 2000
Subjects: Biography, Memoirs, Business, Educa-
tion, History, Nonfiction (General), Self-Help,
Maori Culture
ISBN Prefix(es): 978-1-877514

Imprints: Libro International
Branch Office(s)
Via Cornarotta 17, 32032 Feltre BL, Italy

Otago University Press+
398 Cumberland St, Level 1, Dunedin 9016
Mailing Address: PO Box 56, Dunedin 9054
Tel: (03) 479 8807
E-mail: university.press@otago.ac.nz; publicity@
otago.ac.nz
Web Site: www.otago.ac.nz/press
Key Personnel
Publisher & International Rights: Rachel Scott
Tel: (03) 479 4194 *E-mail:* rachel.scott@otago.
ac.nz
Publicist: Victor Billot *Tel:* (03) 479 9094
Founded: 1958
Membership(s): International Association of
Scholarly Publishers (IASP); Publishers As-
sociation of New Zealand (PANZ).
Subjects: Anthropology, Art, Biography, Mem-
oirs, Education, Environmental Studies, Eth-
nicity, Government, Political Science, History,
Literature, Literary Criticism, Essays, Natural
History, Photography, Poetry, Psychology, Psy-
chiatry, Social Sciences, Sociology
ISBN Prefix(es): 978-0-908569; 978-1-877133;
978-1-877276; 978-1-877578; 978-0-947522;
978-1-927322
Number of titles published annually: 20 Print
Total Titles: 200 Print
Foreign Rep(s): Gazelle Book Services (UK);
Independent Publishers Group (IPG) (USA);
Oxford University Press (OUP) (Australia)

Pasifika Press+
PO Box 68-446, Newton, Auckland
Tel: (09) 377 6068
Key Personnel
Contact: Robert Holding
Founded: 1976
Subjects: History, Literature, Literary Criticism,
Essays, Regional Interests, Travel & Tourism
ISBN Prefix(es): 978-0-908597
Distributed by University of Hawaii Press
Distributor for University of Hawaii Press

Penguin Books (NZ) Ltd
67 Apollo Dr, Rosedale, Auckland 0632
Mailing Address: Private Bag 102 902, North
Shore Mail Centre, Auckland 0745
Tel: (09) 442 7400 *Fax:* (09) 442 7401
E-mail: communications@penguinrandomhouse.
co.nz; publishing@penguinrandomhouse.co.nz
(rights)
Web Site: www.penguin.co.nz
Founded: 1973
Subjects: Cookery, Fiction, Health, Nutrition,
Nonfiction (General), Romance, Science Fic-
tion, Fantasy
ISBN Prefix(es): 978-0-14
Parent Company: Penguin Group (NZ)
Ultimate Parent Company: Penguin Random
House
Distribution Center: Trafalgar Square Publishing
(USA)

Polygraphia, *imprint of* Polygraphia Ltd

Polygraphia Ltd
8 Kittyhawk Way, Hobsonville Point, Auckland
0618
Mailing Address: PO Box 167, Westpark Village,
West Harbour, Auckland 0661
Tel: (09) 416 1437 *Fax:* (09) 416 1438
E-mail: orders@polygraphianz.com
Web Site: www.polygraphianz.com
Key Personnel
Dir: Dr Calum Gilmour *E-mail:* cgilmour@
polygraphianz.com; Raewyn Gilmour
E-mail: rgilmour@polygraphianz.com
Founded: 1998

Publishing, editing & manuscript assessment. This publisher has indicated that 50% of their product line is author subsidized.
Subjects: Archaeology, Biblical Studies, Biography, Memoirs, Fiction, Genealogy, History, Nonfiction (General), Philosophy, Religion - Catholic, Religion - Protestant, Theology
ISBN Prefix(es): 978-0-9582056; 978-0-9582121; 978-0-9582211; 978-0-9582337; 978-1-877332; 978-1-927160
Number of titles published annually: 10 Print; 3 CD-ROM; 2 E-Book
Total Titles: 104 Print; 9 CD-ROM; 2 E-Book
Imprints: Polygraphia

PQ Blackwell, see Blackwell & Ruth

Pursuit Publishing (NZ) Ltd+
370 Matapouri Rd, Tutukaka, Whangarei 0173
Mailing Address: PO Box 984, Whangarei 0140
Tel: (09) 4343 836 *Fax:* (09) 4344 224
Web Site: www.pursuit.co.nz
Key Personnel
Dir: Frank Newman *E-mail:* frank@newman.co. nz
Founded: 1988
Specialize in investment books.
Subjects: Business, Finance
ISBN Prefix(es): 978-0-9597904; 978-0-9582170
Imprints: Dollars & Sense; Oily Rag
Distributed by Reed (NZ) Ltd (New Zealand)
Distribution Center: Books R Us Press, Unit 11, 101-111 Diana Dr, Glenfield, PO Box 33, Takapuna, Auckland 1071 *Tel:* (09) 444 4144 *Fax:* (09) 444 4518

Random House Books New Zealand (RHNZ)
18 Poland Rd, Wairau Valley, Auckland 0627
Mailing Address: Private Bag 102950, North Shore Mail Centre, Auckland 0725
Tel: (09) 444 7197; (09) 441 2710 (customer service) *Fax:* (09) 444 7524; (09) 441 2713 (customer service)
E-mail: admin@randomhouse.co.nz; rights@ randomhouse.com.au
Web Site: www.randomhouse.co.nz
Key Personnel
Publishing Dir: Debra Millar
Marketing & Publicity Dir: Siobhan Clare
Sales Dir: Carrie Welch
Subjects: Architecture & Interior Design, Art, Biography, Memoirs, Business, Cookery, Fiction, Gardening, Plants, History, Nonfiction (General), Photography, Poetry, Art History, Design, Natural History, Parenting, Social History
ISBN Prefix(es): 978-0-908877; 978-1-86941; 978-1-877178; 978-0-908821; 978-0-908884; 978-1-86962 (Godwit); 978-1-877298; 978-1-86954; 978-1-86979 (Arrow); 978-1-77553
Parent Company: Penguin Random House
Ultimate Parent Company: Bertelsmann
Imprints: Arrow; Bantam; Black Swan; Godwit; Longacre Child; Vintage
Distributor for Gecko Press; Hardie Grant Publishing; Huia Publishers; Te Papa Press
Distribution Center: Trafalgar Square Publishing (USA)

Resource Books Ltd+
238 Waikoukou Valley Rd, Waimauku 0882
Tel: (09) 411 9550
E-mail: info@resourcebooks.co.nz
Web Site: www.resourcebooks.co.nz
Key Personnel
Publisher & Dir: Peter Biggs
Founded: 1984
Subjects: Art, Computer Science, Education, Medicine, Nursing, Dentistry
ISBN Prefix(es): 978-0-908618; 978-1-877432; 978-1-877431
Distributed by Read Pacific

RHNZ, see Random House Books New Zealand (RHNZ)

River Press
12 Market St, Picton 7220
Tel: (03) 573 6942
E-mail: riverpress@xtra.co.nz
Web Site: riverpress.co.nz
Key Personnel
Mng Dir: Carol Dawber *E-mail:* carol.dawber@ xtra.co.nz
Founded: 1992
Also offers writing, editing, indexing & book packaging services.
Subjects: History, Maritime, Mysteries, Suspense, Nonfiction (General), Regional Interests, Romance, Travel & Tourism, Local History
ISBN Prefix(es): 978-0-9598041; 978-0-9582779; 978-0-9582252
Number of titles published annually: 2 Print
Total Titles: 14 Print
Parent Company: October Enterprises Ltd
Subsidiaries: Best Books

RSNZ Publishing
11 Turnbull St, Thorndon, Wellington 6011
Mailing Address: PO Box 598, Wellington 6140
Tel: (04) 974 8608
E-mail: publish@royalsociety.org.nz
Web Site: www.royalsociety.org.nz/publications
Key Personnel
Chief Executive: Andrew Cleland
Publications Manager: Jill Mellanby
Founded: 1991
Publishers of scientific research journals focusing on New Zealand, Australia, Southwest Pacific & Antarctica; scientific proceedings of symposia & workshops; science education resources within the Royal Society of New Zealand.
Subjects: Agriculture, Archaeology, Biological Sciences, Earth Sciences, Environmental Studies, Science (General), Technology
ISBN Prefix(es): 978-0-908654; 978-0-9597886; 978-1-877264; 978-1-877317
Parent Company: Royal Society of New Zealand

RSVP Publishing Co Ltd+
24 Tiri Rd, Oneroa, Waiheke Island, Auckland 1081
Mailing Address: PO Box 47-166, Ponsonby, Auckland 1144
Tel: (09) 372 8480
E-mail: info@rsvp-publishing.co.nz; orders@ rsvp-publishing.co.nz; sales@rsvp-publishing. co.nz
Web Site: www.rsvp-publishing.co.nz
Key Personnel
Publisher: Stephen Picard *E-mail:* publisher@ rsvp-publishing.co.nz
Sales/Marketing Manager: Chris Palmer *Tel:* (0274) 734-721 (cell)
Founded: 1990
Specialize in eclectic & metaphysical books, illustrated books.
Membership(s): Publishers Association of New Zealand (PANZ).
Subjects: Alternative, Astrology, Occult, Environmental Studies, Fiction, Law, Nonfiction (General), Photography, Social Sciences, Sociology, Travel & Tourism
ISBN Prefix(es): 978-0-9597948; 978-0-9582182; 978-0-9876587
Number of titles published annually: 3 Print
Total Titles: 18 Print; 18 Online

Scholastic New Zealand Ltd
21 Lady Ruby Dr, East Tamaki, Auckland 2013
Mailing Address: Private Bag 94407, Botany, Auckland 2163
Tel: (09) 274 8112 (customer service) *Fax:* (09) 274 8115

E-mail: enquiries@scholastic.co.nz
Web Site: www.scholastic.co.nz
ISBN Prefix(es): 978-0-86896; 978-1-86943; 978-0-908643; 978-1-77543

Seagull Press
PO Box 211, Otaki 5542
Tel: (06) 364-6577
Key Personnel
Author & Owner: Marion Rego *E-mail:* marion. rego@xtra.co.nz
Subjects: Poetry
ISBN Prefix(es): 978-0-908738; 978-0-9597686; 978-1-877278; 978-0-9582014

Spinal Publications New Zealand Ltd+
338A Rosetta Rd, Raumati Beach 5032
Tel: (04) 299 7020 *Toll Free Tel:* 0508 222 522 (New Zealand only) *Fax:* (04) 299 7010
E-mail: info@endpain.co.nz; order@ spinalpublications.co.nz
Web Site: www.spinalpublications.co.nz
Founded: 1980
Membership(s): Book Publishers Association of New Zealand (BPANZ).
Subjects: Health, Nutrition, Self-Help, Diagnosis & Treatment of Lumbar & Cervical Spine
ISBN Prefix(es): 978-0-9583647; 978-0-9598049; 978-0-9597746; 978-0-9582692

Statistics New Zealand
PO Box 2922, Wellington 6140
Tel: (04) 931 4600 *Toll Free Tel:* (0508) 525 525 (publications) *Fax:* (04) 931 4049
E-mail: info@stats.govt.nz
Web Site: www.stats.govt.nz
Founded: 1936
New Zealand's national statistical office.
Subjects: Agriculture, Business, Economics, Education, Finance, Mathematics, Women's Studies
ISBN Prefix(es): 978-0-478

Sunshine Books International Ltd+
PO Box 128-146, Remuera, Auckland 1541
Toll Free Tel: 0800 85 5000 *Toll Free Fax:* 0800 85 1000
Key Personnel
Owner & Dir: Jenny Aston
Subjects: English as a Second Language, Language Arts, Linguistics
ISBN Prefix(es): 978-0-9597734
Total Titles: 2 Print

Te Papa Press
c/o Museum of New Zealand Te Papa Tongarewa, 55 Cable St, Te Aro, Wellington 6011
Mailing Address: PO Box 467, Wellington 6140
Tel: (04) 381 7470 *Fax:* (04) 381 7230
E-mail: tepapapress@tepapa.govt.nz
Web Site: www.tepapa.govt.nz/tepapapress
Key Personnel
Publisher: Claire Murdoch
Senior Editor: Odessa Owens
Publicist: Angela Radford *Tel:* (027) 540 1104
Founded: 1997
Museum publisher.
Subjects: Art, Gardening, Plants, History, Natural History
Number of titles published annually: 6 Print
Total Titles: 6 Print

Thomson Reuters New Zealand Ltd
Level 4, NEC House, 40 Taranaki St, Wellington 6011
Mailing Address: PO Box 43, Wellington 6140
Tel: (04) 499 8178 *Toll Free Tel:* 0800 10 60 60 *Fax:* (04) 802 0300
E-mail: service@thomsonreuters.co.nz
Web Site: www.thomsonreuters.co.nz
Key Personnel
Chief Executive Officer: Jackie Rhodes

Country Manager: Haydn Davies
General Manager, Commercial: Nigel Royfee
General Manager, Publishing Operations:
   Matthew Heaphy
General Manager, Sales & Marketing: Paul Lane
Founded: 1910
Specialize in looseleaf & electronic legal, tax &
   professional information.
Subjects: Accounting, Business, Law
ISBN Prefix(es): 978-0-86472
Parent Company: The Thomson Corp
Branch Office(s)
16 College Hill Rd, Freemans Bay, PO Box
   147245, Ponsonby, Auckland 1144 *Fax:* (09)
   361 1414
Distributed by Carswell; Lawbook Co; Sweet &
   Maxwell; Westlaw
Distributor for Carswell; Lawbook Co; Sweet &
   Maxwell; Westlaw

Trans Pacific Marine
121 Beaumont St, Westhaven, Auckland 1010
Mailing Address: PO Box 90546, Auckland 1142
Tel: (09) 303 1459 *Toll Free Tel:* 0508 242 787;
   0800 422 427 *Fax:* (09) 307 8170
E-mail: sales@transpacific.co.nz
Web Site: www.transpacific.co.nz
Founded: 1963
Subjects: Crafts, Games, Hobbies, Electronics,
   Electrical Engineering, Fiction, How-to, Sports,
   Athletics, Travel & Tourism, Marine
Distributor for Adlard Coles; Fernhurst; Sheridan
   House; Stationery Office

transpress New Zealand+
12 Awanui Dr, Waikanae 5036
Tel: (04) 905 3011
E-mail: transpress@paradise.net.nz
Web Site: www.transpressnz.com
Key Personnel
Dir: Geoffrey Churchman
Founded: 1985
Subjects: History, Transportation, Practical &
   Technical
ISBN Prefix(es): 978-0-908876; 978-1-877418
Number of titles published annually: 10 Print
Total Titles: 36 Print
Distributed by Pacific Island Books (USA); John
   Reed Books (Australia)
Warehouse: 10 Tarndale Grove, Auckland 0632

Upstart, *imprint of* Upstart Press

Upstart Press+
15 Huron St, Level 4, Takapuna, Auckland 0622
Mailing Address: PO Box 33319, Takapuna,
   Auckland 0740 SAN: 903-2711
Tel: (09) 280 3199 *Fax:* (09) 281 3090
E-mail: editor@upstartpress.co.nz
Web Site: upstartpress.co.nz
Founded: 2013
Subjects: Cookery, Fiction, History, Humor, Lit-
   erature, Literary Criticism, Essays, Nonfiction
   (General), Sports, Athletics, Wine & Spirits
ISBN Prefix(es): 978-1-927262; 978-1-988516
Number of titles published annually: 22 Print; 7
   E-Book
Imprints: Mower; Upstart
Distributor for Archetype; Auckland University
   Press; Dreamboat Books; Gecko Press; One-
   Tree House; Te Papa Press; Victoria University
   Press
Warehouse: Upstart Distribution, 26 Greenpark
   Rd, Penrose, Auckland 1051 *Tel:* (09) 280
   3205 *E-mail:* orders@upstartpress.co.nz
Orders to: Upstart Distribution, 26 Greenpark Rd,
   Penrose, Auckland 1051 *Tel:* (09) 280 3205
   E-mail: orders@upstartpress.co.nz

Victoria University Press+
49 Rawhiti Terrace, Kelburn, Wellington 6012

Mailing Address: PO Box 600, Wellington 6140
Tel: (04) 463 6580 *Fax:* (04) 463 6581
E-mail: victoria-press@vuw.ac.nz
Web Site: vup.victoria.ac.nz
Key Personnel
Publisher: Fergus Barrowman
Editing & Production: Kyleigh Hodgson
Publicist: Kirsten McDougall
Founded: 1979
Membership(s): Booksellers New Zealand.
Subjects: Anthropology, Architecture & Interior
   Design, Art, Biography, Memoirs, Drama, The-
   ater, Fiction, Government, Political Science,
   History, Language Arts, Linguistics, Law, Lit-
   erature, Literary Criticism, Essays, Nonfiction
   (General), Poetry, Regional Interests, Religion
   - Other, Science (General), Social Sciences,
   Sociology
ISBN Prefix(es): 978-0-86473
Number of titles published annually: 25 Print
Total Titles: 200 Print
Distribution Center: Upstart Distribution
   E-mail: orders@upstart.co.nz
Orders to: Archetype/Allen & Unwin, PO Box
   105, Auckland 200 *Tel:* (09) 3773800 *Fax:* (09)
   3773811 *E-mail:* wellington@archetype.co.nz

Viking Sevenseas NZ Ltd
201a Rosetta Rd, Raumati 5032
Mailing Address: PO Box 152, Paraparaumu,
   Wellington 5254
Tel: (04) 902-8240 *Fax:* (04) 902-8240
E-mail: vikings@paradise.net.nz
Key Personnel
Mng Dir: Murdoch Riley
Founded: 1957
Subjects: Ethnicity, Natural History
ISBN Prefix(es): 978-0-85467
Number of titles published annually: 2 Print
Total Titles: 80 Print

Vintage, *imprint of* Random House Books New
   Zealand (RHNZ)

Bridget Williams Books Ltd (BWB)+
Anglican House, 32 Mulgrave St, Thorndon,
   Wellington 6011
Mailing Address: PO Box 12474, Wellington
   6144
Tel: (04) 473 8128
E-mail: info@bwb.co.nz
Web Site: www.bwb.co.nz
Key Personnel
Publisher & Dir: Bridget Williams
   E-mail: bridget.williams@bwb.co.nz
Publisher: Tom Rennie *E-mail:* tom.rennie@bwb.
   co.nz
Business Manager: John Schiff
   E-mail: johnschiff1@gmail.com
Publishing Coordinator: Megan Simpson
   E-mail: megan@bwb.co.nz
Editor & Researcher: Philip Rainer
   E-mail: philip@bwb.co.nz
Production Editor: Jo Scully *E-mail:* jo@bwb.co.
   nz
Founded: 1990
An independent publishing company focusing on
   New Zealand subjects, including Maori history
   & politics.
Subjects: Biography, Memoirs, Government, Po-
   litical Science, History, Nonfiction (General),
   Women's Studies
ISBN Prefix(es): 978-0-908912; 978-1-877242;
   978-1-927131; 978-1-927247; 978-1-927277;
   978-0-86861
Number of titles published annually: 10 Print
Total Titles: 30 Print
Distributor for NIL
Distribution Center: David Bateman Ltd, 30
   Tarndale Grove, Auckland 0632 *Tel:* (09) 415
   7664 *Fax:* (09) 415 8892 *E-mail:* janetteb@
   bateman.co.nz *Web Site:* www.bateman.co.nz

Wily Publications Ltd
302 Lake Terrace Rd, Shirley, Christchurch 8061
Tel: (03) 385 4754
E-mail: info@wily.co.nz
Web Site: www.wily.co.nz
Subjects: Art, Biography, Memoirs, Fiction, Non-
   fiction (General), Outdoor Recreation, Fishing
ISBN Prefix(es): 978-0-9582923; 978-1-927167

Nigeria

General Information

Capital: Abuja
Language: English (official), also Hausa, Yoruba,
   Ibo & Fulani
Religion: Islamic (mainly in north), Christian, and
   traditional beliefs
Population: 88.5 million
Bank Hours: 0800-1500 Monday; 0800-1300
   Tuesday-Friday
Shop Hours: Vary locally. 0800-1230, 1400-1630
   Monday-Friday; 0800-1230 Saturday
Currency: 100 kobo = 1 naira
Export/Import Information: No tariffs on books or
   advertising matter. Open general license. Ob-
   scene literature prohibited. Exchange controls.
Copyright: UCC, Berne, Florence (see Copyright
   Conventions, pg viii)

ABIC Books & Equipment Ltd+
No 21, Edozien St, Uwani, Enugu 400001
Tel: (0803) 552 7558 (cell)
E-mail: admin@abicbooks.com
Web Site: abicbooks.com
Founded: 1987
Specialize in reference books & children's books.
   Also bookseller & literary agent.
Membership(s): Nigerian Publishers' Association
   (NPA).
Subjects: Drama, Theater, History, Language
   Arts, Linguistics, Poetry
ISBN Prefix(es): 978-978-2269

ABU Press Ltd, see Ahmadu Bello University
   Press Ltd

AFP Ltd, see Africana First Publishers Ltd

Africana First Publishers Ltd+
One Africana First Dr, PMB 1639, Onitsha,
   Anambra State
Tel: (0803) 317 947; (0803) 477 0740; (0705)
   855 4025
Web Site: afpublishersplc.com
Key Personnel
Chief Executive Officer & Mng Dir: Mr Austine
   C Onwubiko
Founded: 1971
Also acts as a distributor.
Subjects: Chemistry, Chemical Engineering, Ed-
   ucation, Fiction, Geography, Geology, Govern-
   ment, Political Science, How-to, Mathematics,
   Religion - Other, Science (General), Social Sci-
   ences, Sociology
ISBN Prefix(es): 978-978-175
Number of titles published annually: 20 Print
Total Titles: 750 Print; 6 Audio
Branch Office(s)
Plot 365, Obafemi Awolowo Way, Jabi District,
   Abuja *Tel:* (0803) 786 5363; (09) 671 5638
House No B996/18, Nii Akram St, Accra, Ghana
   Tel: (0242) 357 425
218 Adu-Lad House, Ilesha Garage, Akure, Ondo
   Tel: (0803) 562 8652
13 Okhoro Rd, Off Lagos, Benin City *Tel:* (0803)
   708 6758; (0803) 390 4527
147 Zik Ave, Enugu *Tel:* (0803) 540 5364

Kilometre 9 Old Lagos Rd, Podo, PMB 5632, Ibadan, Oyo *Tel:* (022) 311 383; (0803) 585 1000
14 Zaria Rd, PO Box 1792, Jos *Tel:* (0803) 376 7100; (0803) 379 4086
Plot 5/7A, Odofin Park Estate, Oshodi-Apapa Expressway, By Ijesha Bus/stop, Lagos *Tel:* (0803) 721 8873; (0803) 567 8693
124A, Okigwe Rd, Owerri, Imo State *Tel:* (0803) 750 9568; (0803) 342 3815
No 3 Main St, Gidan Juma, Sabon Gari, Zaria *Tel:* (0803) 352 9350; (0803) 382 3475
No 62, Enwe St, Uyo, Akwa Ibom State *Tel:* (0803) 617 8044

Ahmadu Bello University Press Ltd+
Ahmed Talib Bldg, Ring Rd, PO Box 1094, Zaria
Tel: (0803) 4524194; (0803) 5971815
E-mail: abupresslimited2005@yahoo.co.uk; abupress2013@gmail.com
Web Site: www.abupress.org
Key Personnel
Mng Dir: Abdullahi Hassan Kofar Sauri
Founded: 1973
Publishing & printing.
Subjects: Biography, Memoirs, Education, Environmental Studies, Government, Political Science, History, Law, Literature, Literary Criticism, Essays, Religion - Other, Science (General), Social Sciences, Sociology, Sports, Athletics, Technology, Veterinary Science
ISBN Prefix(es): 978-978-125

Bookcraft Ltd
23 Adebajo St, Kongi Layout, Ibadan
Tel: (0803) 3447889 (cell); (0807) 3199967 (cell); (0803) 7220773 (cell); (02) 7577153
E-mail: info@bookcraftafrica.com; editor@bookcraftafrica.com
Web Site: www.bookcraftafrica.com
Subjects: Biography, Memoirs, Business, History, Literature, Literary Criticism, Essays, Nonfiction (General)
ISBN Prefix(es): 978-978-2030

Chosen Generation Books Ltd
13, Oyeleke St, Alausa Bus Stop, Off Kudirat Abiola Way, Alausa, Ikeja, Lagos State
Tel: (01) 474 4815
Key Personnel
Mng Dir: Adebisi Olagoke
Subjects: Biography, Memoirs, Business, Fiction, Health, Nutrition, Religion - Other, Christian Living, Parenting

Cowrie Comics, *imprint of* Literamed Publications (Nig) Ltd

CSS Bookshops Ltd, Printing & Publishing Division+
Bookshop House, 50/52 Broad St, Lagos
Mailing Address: PO Box 174, Lagos
Tel: (01) 462 2593
E-mail: css@cssbookshopslimited.com
Web Site: www.cssbookshopslimited.com
Key Personnel
Chairman: Segun Agbetuyi
Mng Dir & Chief Executive: Mr Dotun Adegboyega
Founded: 1913
Specialize in Christian books.
Subjects: Biblical Studies, Biography, Memoirs, Ethnicity, Foreign Countries, History, Law, Medicine, Nursing, Dentistry, Nonfiction (General), Religion - Protestant, Religion - Other, Science (General)
ISBN Prefix(es): 978-978-143; 978-978-2951; 978-978-32292; 978-978-8057; 978-978-8401

CSS Press, see CSS Bookshops Ltd, Printing & Publishing Division

Delta Publications (Nigeria) Ltd+
8B, Byoon Onyeama Close, New Haven, PO Box 1172, Enugu
Tel: (042) 256595
Key Personnel
Chief Executive Officer & Dir: Dillibe Onyeama
Founded: 1982
Subjects: Biography, Memoirs, Fiction
ISBN Prefix(es): 978-2-335
Bookshop(s): Enugu Airport Bookshop
Book Club(s): The Delta Book Club

ECWA Productions Ltd
Challenge Bookshop by Constitution Hill Rd, Jos
Web Site: www.facebook.com/ECWA-Productions-Limited-122200617966960
Key Personnel
President: Dr Jeremiah Gado
Vice President: Dr Yakubu Hassan
Subjects: Education, Religion - Protestant, Religion - Other
ISBN Prefix(es): 978-978-137
Parent Company: Evangelical Church Winning All (ECWA)

Egret Books, *imprint of* Paperback Publishers Ltd

Egret Stars Series, *imprint of* Paperback Publishers Ltd

Ethiope Publishing Corp+
Ring Rd, PO Box 1332, Benin City, Edo State
Tel: (052) 253036
Founded: 1970
Subjects: Fiction, Foreign Countries, History, Law, Social Sciences, Sociology
ISBN Prefix(es): 978-978-123
Total Titles: 55 Print

Evans Brothers (Nigeria Publishers) Ltd+
2, Jericho Rd, PMB 5164, Ibadan, Oyo State
Tel: (02) 873 8897 *Toll Free Tel:* 0803 123 4000 (Nigeria only)
E-mail: evans@evanspublishers.com
Web Site: www.evanspublishers.com
Key Personnel
Chief Executive Officer & Mng Dir: Wale Olaniawo
Executive Dir: Lukman Dauda
General Manager, Production Services: Gboyega Adewole
National Sales Manager: Samuel Kikiowo
Founded: 1966
Educational book publishing.
Membership(s): Nigerian Publishers' Association (NPA).
Subjects: Accounting, Agriculture, Child Care & Development, Civil Engineering, Drama, Theater, Economics, Education, Electronics, Electrical Engineering, Environmental Studies, Fiction, Geography, Geology, Government, Political Science, History, Journalism, Law, Literature, Literary Criticism, Essays, Management, Mathematics, Medicine, Nursing, Dentistry, Philosophy, Romance, Science (General), Self-Help, Social Sciences, Sociology, Sports, Athletics, Technology
ISBN Prefix(es): 978-978-020; 978-978-167
Subsidiaries: Nelson Publishers
Branch Office(s)
1c, Kafi St, Cosmic Bus stop, Alausa, Ikeja
No 1, Nworie Lane, Plot 351, Amakohia/Akwakuma, Owerri North, Imo State

Format Publishers (Nig) Ltd
84 Obiagu Rd, Enugu, Enugu State
Tel: (042) 256025
Founded: 1994

ISBN Prefix(es): 978-978-36499
Branch Office(s)
No 6 Orogbu St, PO Box 1220, Awka, Anambra State

Fountain Series, *imprint of* Paperback Publishers Ltd

Gbabeks Publishers Ltd
SW8/194, NEPA Bus-Stop, Ring Rd, Ibadan
Mailing Address: GPO Box 37252, Ibadan
Tel: (02) 2315705
Founded: 1982
Membership(s): National Publishers Association.
Subjects: Education, Language Arts, Linguistics, Science (General), Social Sciences, Sociology
ISBN Prefix(es): 978-978-2416

Goldland Business Co Ltd+
75, St Finbarrs College Rd, Akoka, Yaba, Lagos
Tel: (01) 5821203
Founded: 1982
Business consultants, researchers, trainers & publishers of books in business & related fields.
Subjects: Business, Finance, Government, Political Science, How-to, Management, Marketing, Technology
ISBN Prefix(es): 978-978-30035
Number of titles published annually: 1 Print
Total Titles: 8 Print

HEBN Publishers PLC
One Ighodaro Rd, Jericho, Ibadan
Mailing Address: PO Box 5205, Ibadan
Tel: (02) 2410747; (02) 2410943; (02) 2413096; (02) 2412268 *Fax:* (02) 2411089; (02) 2413237
E-mail: info@hebnpublishers.com
Web Site: www.hebnpublishers.com
Key Personnel
Chief Executive Officer: Mr Ayo Ojeniyi
Mng Dir: Mrs Olawepo Afueri Sogo
Sales & Marketing: Mallam S J Aliyu
Founded: 1962
Subjects: Education, Science (General)
ISBN Prefix(es): 978-978-129; 978-978-081; 978-978-2091

Houseofklass, *imprint of* Houseofklass Enterprises

Houseofklass Enterprises
14/16 Ekunjimi St, Sari-Iganmu, Lagos 101010
Tel: (0803) 526 1606
E-mail: houseofklass@yahoo.com
Web Site: www.facebook.com/HouseofklassEnterprises
Key Personnel
Mng Partner: Godwin Iheanacho Ihemenwa *E-mail:* goddy1817@yahoo.com
Founded: 2005
Registered business enterprise with the Corporate Affairs Commission (CAC) of Nigeria. Championing series of religious, education & business events & seminars. Audio productions on CD & creative book publishing.
Subsidy publisher.
Subjects: Biography, Memoirs, Career Development, Drama, Theater, Fiction, How-to, Literature, Literary Criticism, Essays, Nonfiction (General), Poetry, Religion - Other, Romance, Science Fiction, Fantasy, Self-Help
Imprints: Houseofklass

Hudahuda Publishing Co Ltd+
Samaru Rd, PO Box 984, Zaria
Founded: 1981
Membership(s): Nigerian Publishers' Association (NPA).
Subjects: Literature, Literary Criticism, Essays
ISBN Prefix(es): 978-978-2368

Associate Companies: Hodder & Stoughton Publishers, Mill Rd, Dunton Green, Sevenoaks, Kent TN13 2YA, United Kingdom
Bookshop(s): No 28 Sobon Gari, Zaria, Kaduna State

Ibadan University Press+
University of Ibadan, PMB 16, Ibadan, Oyo State
Tel: (0808) 3816013 (cell)
E-mail: iup_unibadan@yahoo.com
Web Site: ui.edu.ng/press
Founded: 1949
Subjects: Agriculture, Education, Ethnicity, Foreign Countries, History, Law, Medicine, Nursing, Dentistry, Philosophy, Psychology, Psychiatry, Science (General), Social Sciences, Sociology, Technology
ISBN Prefix(es): 978-978-121

Institute of African Studies
University of Nigeria, Nsukka
Tel: (0803) 548 3074
E-mail: ias.unn@unn.edu.ng
Web Site: unn.edu.ng/institutes/institute-african-studies
Key Personnel
Dir: Prof Sam Onuigbo *E-mail:* sam.onuigbo@unn.edu.ng
Founded: 1963
Subjects: Social Sciences, Sociology, African Studies, Humanities
ISBN Prefix(es): 978-978-2450; 978-978-31426

International Publishing & Research Co
711 Road, B Close, House 33, Festac City, Lagos
Mailing Address: PO Box 1210, Festac City, Lagos
Tel: (080) 2317-5915 *Fax:* (01) 4937131
Key Personnel
Executive Chairman: Dr M J A Iginla
Founded: 1990
Publishing & research for the book trade.
Subjects: Biography, Memoirs, Developing Countries, Philosophy, Religion - Islamic, Science Fiction, Fantasy, Social Sciences, Sociology, Theology, Women's Studies
ISBN Prefix(es): 978-978-30855; 978-978-2438
Number of titles published annually: 2 Print
Total Titles: 13 Print
Parent Company: Ipreco Group of Companies
Subsidiaries: Unity Publishing & Research Co Ltd

IUP, see Ibadan University Press

Lantern Books, *imprint of* Literamed Publications (Nig) Ltd

Learn Africa PLC
Felix Iwerebon House, 52, Oba Akran Ave, Ikeja, Lagos
Tel: (01) 7403967; (01) 4393111; (0805) 5064737 (cell) *Fax:* (01) 4964370
E-mail: connect@learnafricaplc.com; marketing@learnafricaplc.com; sales@learnafricaplc.com
Web Site: www.learnafricaplc.com
Key Personnel
Mng Dir & Chief Executive: Segun Jacob Oladipo
Publishing Dir: Gbola Aiyedun
Head, Distribution & Warehouse: Raphael Amanam
Head, Sales: Alhaji Hassan Bala
Head, Sales & Marketing: Tony Brown-West
Founded: 1961
Subjects: Agriculture, Biography, Memoirs, Business, Computer Science, Economics, Education, Engineering (General), Ethnicity, Fiction, Finance, Geography, Geology, History, Language Arts, Linguistics, Literature, Literary Criticism, Essays, Marketing, Nonfiction (General), Po-

etry, Psychology, Psychiatry, Religion - Other, Science (General), Social Sciences, Sociology, Technology, Travel & Tourism
ISBN Prefix(es): 978-978-139
Branch Office(s)
79 Bale St, Olodi Apapa, Lagos *Tel:* (0809) 9912501 (cell)
1264, Nnamdi Azikiwe Expressway, Katampe District, Abuja *Tel:* (0803) 6819669 (cell) (corporate off)
Okejebu Rd, beside Energy Filling Station, Akure, Ondo State *Tel:* (0803) 4074185 (cell)
25, James Watt Rd, Benin City, Edo State *Tel:* (0802) 8453779 (cell)
49, New Adeoyo Hospital Rd, off Ring Rd, Ibadan, Oyo State *Tel:* (0809) 9912544 (cell)
One Coca-Cola Rd, off Unity Rd, Ilorin, Kwara State *Tel:* (0803) 8272336 (cell)
One Zaria Rd, Bebeyi House, opposite Mobil Filling Station, Jos, Plateau State *Tel:* (0803) 5076258 (cell)
10, Maiduguri Rd, opposite Ruqayya House, Kano, Kano State *Tel:* (0809) 9912573 (cell)
53, Limca Rd, Onitsha, Anambra State *Tel:* (0809) 9912557 (cell)
KM 4, Gbongan-Ibadan Expressway, opposite Old Governor's Off, Ayegbaju Market, Osogbo, Osun State *Tel:* (0803) 3309258 (cell)
Plot 14, Aladinma Northern Ext, Owerri, Imo State *Tel:* (0803) 7766846 (cell)
15, Okomoko St, D Line, Port-Harcourt, Rivers State *Tel:* (0809) 9912528 (cell)
14, Umuleri St, Uwani Enugu, Enugu State *Tel:* (0809) 9912556 (cell)
One Sokoto Rd, opposite Zaria Hotel, Zaria, Kaduna State *Tel:* (0803) 4502075 (cell)

Literamed Publications (Nig) Ltd+
Lantern House, One Morrison Crescent, Off Kudirat Abiola Way, Ikeja, Lagos
Mailing Address: PMB 21068, Ikeja, Lagos
Tel: (01) 8980764; (01) 7901130; (01) 7901129
E-mail: information@lantern-books.com; orders@lantern-books.com
Web Site: www.lantern-books.com
Key Personnel
Communications Manager: Solape Farotimi
Account Officer: Omoleye Akinso
Founded: 1969
Membership(s): Nigerian Publishers' Association (NPA).
Subjects: Education, Government, Political Science, Religion - Other, Social Sciences, Sociology
ISBN Prefix(es): 978-978-142
Number of titles published annually: 25 Print
Total Titles: 120 Print
Imprints: Cowrie Comics; Lantern Books; Living Scrolls; Medipharm
Branch Office(s)
Literamed Publications (Gh) Ltd, Lantern House, Plot 2, Seventh St, South Odorkor Estate, Sakaman, Opposite Enso Nyame Ye Spot, Dansoman, Accra, Ghana *Tel:* (026) 6361718
E-mail: info.ghana@lantern-books.com

Living Scrolls, *imprint of* Literamed Publications (Nig) Ltd

Medipharm, *imprint of* Literamed Publications (Nig) Ltd

Nelson Publishers+
Subsidiary of Evans Brothers (Nigeria Publishers) Ltd
2 Jericho Rd, PMB 5164, Ibadan, Oyo State
Tel: (02) 873 8897
E-mail: evans@evanspublishers.com
Web Site: www.evanspublishers.com
Founded: 1965 (acquired by Evans Brothers in 2004)

Subjects: Fiction, Nonfiction (General), Science (General), Social Sciences, Sociology
ISBN Prefix(es): 978-978-126

NIALS, see Nigerian Institute of Advanced Legal Studies (NIALS)

Nigerian Institute of Advanced Legal Studies (NIALS)
University of Lagos Campus, PMB 12820, Lagos
Tel: (01) 821223; (01) 821711; (01) 821109
Fax: (01) 4976078; (01) 825558
E-mail: info.nials@gmail.com
Web Site: nials-nigeria.org
Key Personnel
Dir General: Prof Deji Adekunle
Librarian: Mrs Eteng Uwem
Institute Secretary: James Gekeme
Founded: 1979
Subjects: Law
ISBN Prefix(es): 978-978-31963; 978-978-2353; 978-978-31474; 978-978-31689
Branch Office(s)
Supreme Court of Nigeria Complex, Three Arms Zone Central District, Abuja *Tel:* (09) 2346504 *Fax:* (09) 2346505

Nigerian Institute of International Affairs (NIIA)
13/15 Kofo Abayomi St, Victoria Island, Lagos
Mailing Address: GPO Box 1727, Lagos
Tel: (01) 2615606; (01) 2615607; (01) 9500983 *Fax:* (01) 2611360
E-mail: director-general@niia.gov.ng; director-general1@hotmail.com; niia@servenigeria.com
Web Site: www.niia.gov.ng
Key Personnel
Dir General: Prof Bukar Bukarambe
Founded: 1961
Established as an independent, nonofficial, nonpolitical & nonprofit making organization. In August 1991, the Institute was taken over by the Nigerian government.
Encourage & facilitate the understanding of international affairs; circumstances, conditions & attitudes of foreign countries & their people. Provide & disseminate information upon international questions, as we also promote the study & investigation of such international questions through such fora as conferences, lectures, discussions, to compliment our publications, journals & records.
Subjects: Economics, Law
ISBN Prefix(es): 978-978-2276; 978-978-002

NIIA, see Nigerian Institute of International Affairs (NIIA)

OAU Press Ltd, see Obafemi Awolowo University Press Ltd

Obafemi Awolowo University Press Ltd+
c/o Obafemi Awolowo University, PMB 004, Ile-Ife, Osun State
Tel: (036) 230284
Founded: 1968
Specializes in professional texts.
Membership(s): International Publishers Association; National Publishers Association; Nigerian Publishers' Association (NPA).
Subjects: Biography, Memoirs, Education, Ethnicity, History, Law, Medicine, Nursing, Dentistry, Philosophy, Religion - Other, Social Sciences, Sociology
ISBN Prefix(es): 978-978-136
Number of titles published annually: 6 Print
Total Titles: 100 Print
Foreign Rep(s): ABC London (Europe, USA)

G O Onibonoje Press
Division of Onibonoje Press & Book Industry (Nig) Ltd

Felele Layout, Challenge Area, Ibadan
Mailing Address: PO Box 3109, Mapo Post Office, Ibadan
Tel: (02) 2313956
E-mail: info@goonibonoje.com
Web Site: www.goonibonoje.com
Founded: 1958
Branch offices throughout Nigeria.
Subjects: Biography, Memoirs, Ethnicity, Fiction, Foreign Countries, History, How-to, Nonfiction (General), Poetry, Religion - Other, Science (General), Social Sciences, Sociology
ISBN Prefix(es): 978-978-145
Bookshop(s): SW8/77 Oke-Ado, Ibadan

Paperback Publishers Ltd+
Akinyemi Way, Ring Rd, Ibadan
Mailing Address: UIPO Box 14470, Ibadan
Tel: (02) 2316006; (02) 2316008
Founded: 1985
Membership(s): Nigerian Publishers' Association (NPA).
Subjects: Education, Fiction
ISBN Prefix(es): 978-978-2432
Imprints: Egret Books; Egret Stars Series; Fountain Series

Rasmed Publications Ltd+
16, New Court Rd, Old Gbagi, Ibadan, Oyo State
Tel: (0802) 8030469 (cell); (0803) 3272753 (cell); (0803) 3283710 (cell)
E-mail: info@rasmedpublications.com
Web Site: www.rasmedpublications.com
Key Personnel
Publisher: Gbadega Adedapo
Founded: 1996
Publishing, printing & marketing.
Membership(s): African Publishers Network (AP-NET); Nigerian Publishers' Association (NPA).
Subjects: Agriculture, Chemistry, Chemical Engineering, Computer Science, Economics, Education, Engineering (General), Marketing, Medicine, Nursing, Dentistry, Physics
ISBN Prefix(es): 978-978-8516
Number of titles published annually: 25 Print
Total Titles: 25 Print
Foreign Rep(s): APH Publishing Corp (India, Nigeria, West Africa); Comos Publishers (Cameroon, Ghana); Educat Ltd (South Africa)
Foreign Rights: Adaex Educational Publications (Africa, Ghana, Nigeria, West Africa); Farrar, Straus & Giroux LLC (USA); Pagesetters Services (Singapore)

Spectrum Books Ltd+
Ring Rd, PMB 5612, Ibadan
Tel: (02) 2310145; (02) 2311215; (02) 2310058
Fax: (02) 2312705; (02) 2318502
Web Site: spectrumbookslimited.com
Key Personnel
Editor: Olayemi Onakunle
Founded: 1978
Subjects: Education, Fiction
ISBN Prefix(es): 978-978-029; 978-2-265
Associate Companies: Safari Books (Export) Ltd, 17 Bond St, 1st floor, St Helier, Jersey, Channel Islands, United Kingdom
Distributed by ABC Oxford

SU Press & Books Ltd
Oyo Rd (Opposite Old Airport), Ibadan, Oyo State
Mailing Address: UIPO Box 4011, Ibadan, Oyo State
Tel: (02) 8101867; (02) 8102334
E-mail: md.supb@sunigeria.org
Web Site: su-international.org
Key Personnel
Chairman: Isaac Itegboje
Mng Dir: Emmanuel Ekurumadu
General Manager: Goddy Egu
Assistant Production Manager: Franklin Agbai

Secretary/Administrative Officer: Mrs Olufunke Osho
Subjects: Biblical Studies, Religion - Other
ISBN Prefix(es): 978-978-2341
Parent Company: Scripture Union Nigeria

Unilag Press, see University of Lagos Press

University of Lagos Press+
Works & Physical Planning Complex, University of Lagos, Commercial Rd, Main Campus, Akoka, Lagos
Tel: (01) 4539983
E-mail: info@unilagpress.com
Web Site: unilagpress.com
Key Personnel
Chairman: Wahab Babatunde Dabiri
Dir: Oyediran Akin; Prof Adetokunbo Denloye
Head, Accounts: Jatto Kenneth
Customer Service Manager: Abimbola Emmanuel
Operations Manager: Murthada Lawal
Founded: 1980
Subjects: Biography, Memoirs, Education, Ethnicity, Foreign Countries, Human Relations, Law, Medicine, Nursing, Dentistry, Social Sciences, Sociology
ISBN Prefix(es): 978-978-2264; 978-978-017
Distributed by African Books Collective
Bookshop(s): Bookshop Bldg, Main Campus, University of Lagos, Akoka-Yaba, Lagos *Tel:* (07) 4539984 *E-mail:* info@unilagbookshop.com

University Press PLC
Three Crowns Bldg, PMB 5095, Jericho, Ibadan, Oyo State 23402
Tel: (02) 8738896; (070) 98823872
E-mail: info@universitypressplc.com
Web Site: www.universitypressplc.com
Key Personnel
Chairman: Dr Lalekan Are
Executive Dir, Publishing: Folakemi Bademosi
Mng Dir: Samuel Kolawole
General Manager: Akinsola Ishola
Founded: 1949
Subjects: Agriculture, Biography, Memoirs, Chemistry, Chemical Engineering, Computer Science, Mathematics, Physics, Social Sciences, Sociology
ISBN Prefix(es): 978-978-154; 978-978-030; 978-978-069; 978-978-978

University Publishing Co Ltd+
11, Central Schools Rd, Onitsha, Anambra State 430001
Tel: (046) 410013; (0803) 4041661
Founded: 1959
Membership(s): Nigerian Publishers' Association (NPA).
Subjects: Biography, Memoirs, Ethnicity, Foreign Countries, History, Nonfiction (General), Philosophy, Poetry, Religion - Other
ISBN Prefix(es): 978-978-160
Associate Companies: African Literature Bureau, Aba; Cynako International Press, Aba; Thomas Nelson (Nigeria) Ltd
Orders to: PO Box 386, Onitsha, Anambra State

Vantage Publishers International Ltd+
98A, Samonda, Oyo Rd, Secretariat PO Box 7669, Ibadan, Oyo State
Tel: (02) 8100341; (02) 8102830; (02) 8103803
Founded: 1983
Subjects: Biblical Studies, Biography, Memoirs, Biological Sciences, Business, Drama, Theater, Education, English as a Second Language, Fiction, Government, Political Science, Language Arts, Linguistics, Literature, Literary Criticism, Essays, Nonfiction (General), Poetry, Public Administration, Religion - Protestant, Social Sciences, Sociology

ISBN Prefix(es): 978-978-2458
Subsidiaries: Vantage Paper & Stationeries
Divisions: Vantage Productions
Bookshop(s): 98A Airport Area, Ibadan, Oyo State

WABP, see West African Book Publishers Ltd

West African Book Publishers Ltd+
28/32, Industrial Ave, Ilupeju Industrial Estate, Ilupeju, Lagos State
Tel: (01) 4702757
Founded: 1963
Membership(s): Nigerian Publishers' Association (NPA).
Subjects: Advertising, Agriculture, Chemistry, Chemical Engineering, Child Care & Development, Economics, Geography, Geology, Government, Political Science, Human Relations, Mathematics, Science (General)
ISBN Prefix(es): 978-978-153; 978-978-31973
Associate Companies: Academy Computers Ltd; Academy Press PLC; Lithotec Ltd; Richware Pottery Ltd
Branch Office(s)
One, Akwa St by Uzoakoli Rd, Umuahia, Abia State *Tel:* (0803) 7381117
5, Independence Rd, Bompai, Kano State *Tel:* (0802) 3575522
52, Liberty Rd, Oke Ado, Ibadan, Oyo State *Tel:* (0803) 3303965

North Korea

General Information

Capital: Pyongyang
Language: Korean
Religion: Buddhism, Christian & Chundo Kyo
Population: 22.2 million
Currency: 100 chon = 1 won
Export/Import Information: No tariff information; all importation and exportation must go through Korea Publications Export & Import Corporation, Pyongyang.

Foreign Languages Publishing House
Sochon dong, Sosong District, Pyongyang
Subjects: Asian Studies
ISBN Prefix(es): 978-9946-0

Norway

General Information

Capital: Oslo
Language: Norwegian. There are two distinct forms, Bokmal (sometimes called Riksmal) and Nynorsk (formerly called Landsmal) whose relative importance has changed in recent years. About 90% of Norwegian books are now published in Bokmal and it is the medium of instruction in most schools. Danish and Swedish are usually intelligible to speakers of Norwegian
Religion: Predominantly Evangelical Lutheran
Population: 4.3 million
Bank Hours: 0830-1530 Monday-Friday; 0830-1500 (summer)
Shop Hours: 0830 or 0900-1700 or 1800 Monday-Friday; 0830 or 0900-1400 or 1600 Saturday
Currency: 100 ore = 1 Norwegian krone
Export/Import Information: Member of the European Free Trade Association. No tariff on

books except children's picture books. Books exempt from VAT. No duty on advertising. No import license required. Nominal exchange controls.

Copyright: UCC, Berne, Florence (see Copyright Conventions, pg viii)

Aschehoug Forlag, see H Aschehoug & Co (W Nygaard) A/S

H Aschehoug & Co (W Nygaard) A/S
Sehestedsgate 3, 0164 Oslo
Mailing Address: Postboks 363 Sentrum, 0102 Oslo
Tel: 22 40 04 00 *Fax:* 22 20 63 95
E-mail: kundeservice.litteratur@aschehoug.no
Web Site: www.aschehoug.no
Key Personnel
Chief Executive Officer & Publisher: Mads Nygaard *Tel:* 22 40 03 00 *E-mail:* mads.nygaard@aschehoug.no
Vice President: Kari-Anne Haugen *Tel:* 22 40 03 51 *E-mail:* kari.anne.haugen@aschehoug.no
Communications Manager: Mona Ek *Tel:* 97732170 (cell) *E-mail:* mona.ek@aschehoug.no
Founded: 1872
Subjects: Antiques, Architecture & Interior Design, Art, Business, Child Care & Development, Crafts, Games, Hobbies, Economics, Education, Fiction, Gardening, Plants, Health, Nutrition, How-to, Language Arts, Linguistics, Law, Mathematics, Philosophy, Poetry, Science (General), Science Fiction, Fantasy, Self-Help, Social Sciences, Sociology, Travel & Tourism
ISBN Prefix(es): 978-82-03
Subsidiaries: Kirkelig Kulturverksted A/S; Kunnskapsforlaget (jointly owned with Gyldendal Norsk Forlag); Lydbokforlaget A/S; Forlaget Oktober AS; Olaf Norlis Bokhandel A/S (jointly owned with Norake Skog A/S); Tano A/S Forlaget; Universitetsforlaget A/S; Yrkesopplaring ANS
Book Club(s): Den Norske Bokklubben A/S (with three other Norwegian publishers)

Balzar Forlag, *imprint of* Cappelen Damm AS

Bazar Forlag
Imprint of Cappelen Damm AS
Akersgata 47/49, 0180 Oslo
E-mail: post@bazarforlag.com
Web Site: www.bazarforlag.no
Key Personnel
Publisher: Oyvind Hagen *E-mail:* oyvind.hagen@bazarforlag.com
Editorial Dir: Turid Lovskar *E-mail:* turid.lovskar@bazarforlag.com
Sales & Marketing Manager: Kristin Eick Viuf *Tel:* 92 66 45 47 *E-mail:* kristin.eick.viuf@bazarforlag.no
Founded: 2002
Subjects: Biography, Memoirs, Fiction, History, Humor, Religion - Other
ISBN Prefix(es): 978-82-8087

Cappelen Akademisk Forlag
Akersgata 47/49, 0180 Oslo
Tel: 21 61 65 00
E-mail: akademisk@cappelendamm.no
Web Site: www.cappelendammundervisning.no; www.cappelendamm.no
Key Personnel
Publishing Dir: Birgit Skaldehaug *Tel:* 991 52 728 (cell) *E-mail:* birgit.skaldehaug@cappelendamm.no
Marketing Dir: Cecilie von Hirsch Larsen *Tel:* 21 61 66 01 *E-mail:* cecilie.larsen@cappelendamm.no
Editorial Manager: Hilde Laerum *Tel:* 21 61 66 19 *E-mail:* hilde.larum@cappelendamm.no

Subjects: Economics, Management, Nonfiction (General)
ISBN Prefix(es): 978-82-7037; 978-82-456
Parent Company: Cappelen Damm AS

Cappelen Damm AS
Akersgata 47/49, 0180 Oslo
Mailing Address: Postboks 1900, 0055 Oslo
Tel: 21 61 65 00
E-mail: post@cappelendamm.no; bokhandel@cappelendamm.no; informasjonogpresse@cappelendamm.no
Web Site: www.cappelendamm.no; www.forlagsliv.no
Key Personnel
Chief Financial Officer: Heidi Antonsen *Tel:* 21 61 65 08
Dir: Tom Dahl *Tel:* 21 61 75 50
Administrative Dir: Tom Harald Jenssen *Tel:* 21 61 73 15
Founded: 1829
Subjects: Fiction, Nonfiction (General), Religion - Other
ISBN Prefix(es): 978-82-02
Number of titles published annually: 1,500 Print
Parent Company: Cappelen Damm Holding AS
Ultimate Parent Company: Bonnier AB (Sweden); Egmont International Holding AS
Imprints: Balzar Forlag; Larsforlaget
Subsidiaries: Aventura Forlag A/S; Bedriftsoekonomens Forlag A/S; Boksenteret A/S; Chr Grondahls Forlag A/S; Sentraldistribusson ANS
Book Club(s): Den Norske Bokklubben A/S (with three other Norwegian publishers)

Commentum Forlag AS
Gamleveien 87, 4315 Sandnes
Tel: 51 96 12 40 *Fax:* 51 96 12 51
E-mail: post@commentum.no
Web Site: www.commentum.no
Key Personnel
Mng Dir: Per G Jansen *E-mail:* per@commentum.no
Publishing Editor: Tom Gaudland *Tel:* 51 96 24 40 *E-mail:* tom@commentum.no
Press: Christian W Holst *E-mail:* christian@commentum.no
Founded: 2000
Subjects: Cookery, Criminology, Fiction, Health, Nutrition, History, Language Arts, Linguistics, Nonfiction (General), Poetry, Religion - Other, Documentary
ISBN Prefix(es): 978-82-8233; 978-82-9309

Credo, *imprint of* Genesis Forlag AS

Dreyers Forlag AS+
Dronningens gate 16, 0152 Oslo
Mailing Address: Postboks 461 Sentrum, 0105 Oslo
Tel: 23 13 69 38 *Fax:* 23 13 69 39
E-mail: post@dreyersforlag.no
Web Site: www.dreyersforlag.no
Key Personnel
Editor: Helle Sommerfelt *Tel:* 23 13 69 33 *E-mail:* sommerfelt@dreyersforlag.no; Edvard Thorup *Tel:* 23 13 69 32 *E-mail:* edvard.thorup@dreyersforlag.no
Marketing: Pal Sandbaek *E-mail:* pal@dreyersforlag.no
Founded: 1992
Membership(s): The Norwegian Publishers Association
Subjects: Antiques, Architecture & Interior Design, Art, Biography, Memoirs, History, How-to, Travel & Tourism, Cultural Heritage
ISBN Prefix(es): 978-82-8265
Number of titles published annually: 25 Print

Total Titles: 200 Print
Distribution Center: Sentraldistribusjon ANS, O Aker vei 61, 0581 Oslo *Tel:* 22 98 57 00
E-mail: kundeservice@sd.no

Eide Forlag AS+
Flintegata 2, 4016 Stavanger
Mailing Address: Postboks 8019, 4068 Stavanger
Tel: 51 86 90 00; 55 38 66 50 (orders) *Fax:* 55 38 88 39 (orders)
E-mail: post@eideforlag.no; ordre@eideforlag.no
Web Site: www.eideforlag.no
Key Personnel
Publishing Manager: Jan Stefan Bengtsson *Tel:* 93 21 15 87 *E-mail:* stefan.bengtsson@eideforlag.no
Subjects: Art, Education, Film, Video, History, Music, Dance, Radio, TV
ISBN Prefix(es): 978-82-514

Fagbokforlaget AS
Imprint of Forlagshuset Vigmostad & Bjorke
Kanalveien 51, 5068 Bergen
Mailing Address: Postboks 6050 Postterminalen, 5892 Bergen
Tel: 55 38 88 00; 55 38 88 38 (orders) *Fax:* 55 38 88 01; 55 38 88 39 (orders)
E-mail: fagbokforlaget@fagbokforlaget.no; ordre@fagbokforlaget.no; faktural@fagbokforlaget.no
Web Site: www.fagbokforlaget.no
Key Personnel
Publisher: Arnstein Bjorke *Tel:* 55 38 88 40 *E-mail:* arnstein.bjorke@fagbokforlaget.no
Distribution Dir: Espen Konglevoll *Tel:* 55 38 88 18 *E-mail:* espen.konglevoll@fagbokforlaget.no
Marketing: Lars Mausethagen *Tel:* 55 38 88 20 *E-mail:* lars.mausethagen@fagbokforlaget.no
Founded: 1992
Subjects: Gardening, Plants, Language Arts, Linguistics, Science (General), Technology
ISBN Prefix(es): 978-82-7674; 978-82-450; 978-82-90953
Associate Companies: Cantando Musikkforlag; Eide Forlag; John Grieg AS; Haugenbok.no
Branch Office(s)
St Olavs gate 12, 0165 Oslo
Nardo Rd 12, 7032 Trondheim
ul 3 Maja 54, 81-850 Sopot, Poland

Fonna Forlag L/L
Underhaugsveien 9A, 0354 Oslo
Mailing Address: Postboks 6912, St Olavs plass, 0130 Oslo
Tel: 22 69 10 10; 95 10 96 15 (cell)
E-mail: post@fonna.no; fonna@fonna.no
Web Site: www.fonna.no
Key Personnel
Manager: Roald Waktskjold
Founded: 1940
Subjects: Biography, Memoirs, Fiction, Poetry
ISBN Prefix(es): 978-82-513

Font Forlag
Universitetsgata 20, 0162 Oslo
Tel: 90 79 50 22
Web Site: fontforlag.no
Key Personnel
Publisher: Halfdan W Freihow *Tel:* 91 60 19 24 *E-mail:* halfdan@fontforlag.no; Knut Ola Ulvestad *E-mail:* knut@fontforlag.no
Media & Public Relations Dir: Silje K I Hammersland *Tel:* 90 08 09 16 *E-mail:* silje@fontforlag.no
Sales & Marketing Dir: Lene Lover *Tel:* 90 55 76 12 *E-mail:* lene@fontforlag.no
Founded: 2005
Subjects: Art, Fiction, History, Literature, Literary Criticism, Essays, Nonfiction (General), Science (General), Sports, Athletics, Norwegian History
ISBN Prefix(es): 978-82-8169

Genesis Forlag AS+
Trondheimsveien 50 D, 2007 Kjeller
Mailing Address: Postboks 83, 2027 Kjeller
Tel: 63 80 30 99 *Fax:* 63 81 69 22
Web Site: www.genesis.no
Founded: 1996
Specialize in Christian books.
Subjects: Animals, Pets, Biography, Memoirs, Economics, Fiction, Health, Nutrition, History, Human Relations, Inspirational, Spirituality, Law, Nonfiction (General), Psychology, Psychiatry, Religion - Protestant, Sports, Athletics, Theology, Nature, Society
ISBN Prefix(es): 978-82-476
Parent Company: Hermon Gruppen
Imprints: Credo

Gyldendal Akademisk+
Sehesteds gate 4, 0130 Oslo
Mailing Address: Postboks 6860, St Olavs plass, 0130 Oslo
Tel: 22 03 41 00 *Fax:* 22 03 41 05
E-mail: akademisk@gyldendal.no; gnf@gyldendal.no
Web Site: www.gyldendal.no/faglitteratur
Key Personnel
Publishing Dir: Paul Gerhard Hedlund *Tel:* 03 22 43 86 *E-mail:* paul.hedlund@gyldendal.no
Editor, Sales & Marketing: Grete Rygh *E-mail:* gry@gyldendal.no
Founded: 1988
Subjects: Accounting, Business, Economics, Education, Finance, Government, Political Science, Health, Nutrition, Law, Medicine, Nursing, Dentistry, Philosophy, Psychology, Psychiatry, Social Sciences, Sociology
ISBN Prefix(es): 978-82-05; 978-82-417
Number of titles published annually: 100 Print
Parent Company: Gyldendal Norsk Forlag
Ultimate Parent Company: Gyldendal ASA

Gyldendal Norsk Forlag+
Sehesteds gate 4, 0130 Oslo
Mailing Address: Postboks 6860, St Olavs plass, 0130 Oslo
Tel: 22 03 41 00 *Fax:* 22 03 41 05
E-mail: gnf@gyldendal.no
Web Site: www.gyldendal.no
Key Personnel
Dir: Unni Fjesme
Sales & Marketing Dir: Astrid Snipsoyr *Tel:* 22 03 43 93 *E-mail:* astrid.snipsoyr@gyldendal.no
Information Manager: Bjarne Buset *Tel:* 22 03 41 23 *E-mail:* bjarne.buset@gyldendal.no
Founded: 1925
Subjects: Art, Biography, Memoirs, Fiction, Government, Political Science, History, How-to, Music, Dance, Philosophy, Poetry, Psychology, Psychiatry, Religion - Other, Science Fiction, Fantasy, Social Sciences, Sociology
ISBN Prefix(es): 978-82-05; 978-82-478
Parent Company: Gyldendal ASA
Associate Companies: Gyldendal Akademisk; Gyldendal Litteratur; Gyldendal Rettsdata; Gyldendal Undervisning
Imprints: Kolon Forlag; Tiden Norsk Forlag; Versal Forlag
Book Club(s): Den Norske Bokklubben A/S (with three other Norwegian publishers)

Humanist Forlag AS (Humanist Publishers)
Brugata 19, 0186 Oslo
Mailing Address: Postboks 9076 Gronland, 0133 Oslo
Tel: 22 36 48 29; 936 31 648 *Fax:* 22 15 60 21
E-mail: forlag@human.no
Web Site: www.humanistforlag.no
Key Personnel
Publisher: Bente Pihlstrom *Tel:* 415 64 797 (cell) *E-mail:* bente.pihlstrom@human.no
Marketing Manager: Marianne Egerdal *Tel:* 936 31 648 *E-mail:* marianne.egerdal@human.no

Founded: 1995
Subjects: History, Nonfiction (General), Philosophy, Poetry, Religion - Other, Science (General), Documentary, Ethics, Folklore, Human Rights
ISBN Prefix(es): 978-82-90425; 978-82-90603; 978-82-92622
Distribution Center: Forlagssentralen ANS, Norway

Hurra Forlag
Monolitveien 12, 0375 Oslo
Tel: 41400645
E-mail: post@hurra.no
Web Site: www.hurra.no
Key Personnel
Publisher: Victoria Dahr
Membership(s): Norwegian Publishers Association.
Subjects: Art, Cookery, Fiction, Music, Dance, Nonfiction (General)
ISBN Prefix(es): 978-82-996466

Kagge Forlag AS
Stortingsgaten 12, 0161 Oslo
Tel: 23 11 82 80
E-mail: post@kagge.no
Web Site: www.kagge.no
Key Personnel
Chief Executive Officer: Anne Gaathaug *Tel:* 991 53 959 *E-mail:* anne@kagge.no
Manager: Katja Rugaas *E-mail:* katja@kagge.no
Chief Editor: Tuva Orbeck Sorheim *Tel:* 971 83 483 *E-mail:* tuva@kagge.no
Public Relations: Raymond Vik *Tel:* 22 47 14 94 *E-mail:* raymond@kagge.no
Subjects: Biography, Memoirs, Fiction, Health, Nutrition, History, Humor, Poetry
ISBN Prefix(es): 978-82-489; 978-82-91769
Number of titles published annually: 70 Print

Kolibri Forlag A/S
Postboks 44 Ovre Ullern, 0311 Oslo
Tel: 92 45 25 29
E-mail: post@kolibriforlag.no
Web Site: www.kolibriforlag.no
Key Personnel
Publisher: Else Lill Bjonnes
Founded: 1982
Membership(s): Den Norske Forleggerforening.
Subjects: Cookery, Health, Nutrition, Nonfiction (General), Psychology, Psychiatry, Science Fiction, Fantasy
ISBN Prefix(es): 978-82-7917; 978-82-90478

Kolon Forlag, *imprint of* Gyldendal Norsk Forlag

Kolon Forlag
Imprint of Gyldendal Norsk Forlag
Sehesteds gate 4, 0164 Oslo
Mailing Address: Postboks 6860, St Olavs plass, 0130 Oslo
E-mail: redaksjon@kolonforlag.no
Web Site: www.kolonforlag.no
Key Personnel
Publisher: Bjorn Aagenaes *Tel:* 93 02 95 84 *E-mail:* bjorn@kolonforlag.no
Principal Consultant: Torleiv Grue
Foreign Rights Manager: Anne Cathrine Eng *Tel:* 95 78 16 40 *E-mail:* anne.cathrine.eng@gyldendal.no
Founded: 1995
Subjects: Drama, Theater, Literature, Literary Criticism, Essays, Poetry
ISBN Prefix(es): 978-82-05; 978-82-417
Foreign Rights: Gyldendal Agency (Eva Lie-Nielsen)

Kunnskapsforlaget
Gullhaug torg 1, Nydalen, Oslo

Mailing Address: Postboks 4432, Nydalen, 0403 Oslo
Tel: 22 02 22 00 *Fax:* 22 02 22 05
E-mail: forhandlersalg@kunnskapsforlaget.no
Web Site: www.kunnskapsforlaget.no
Key Personnel
Publishing Dir: Thomas Nygaard *Tel:* 90691464 *E-mail:* thomasnygaard@kunnskapsforlaget.no
Publishing Coordinator: Bente Buer Johansen *Tel:* 90594278
Senior Editor: Oystein Eek *Tel:* 90783509 *E-mail:* oystein.eek@kunnskapsforlaget.no
Project Manager: Petter Henriksen *Tel:* 90746581 *E-mail:* petter.henriksen@kunnskapsforlaget.no
Sales: Karin Austeng *Tel:* 90746406 *E-mail:* karin.austeng@kunnskapsforlaget.no; Lena Formagei *Tel:* 90726639; Ellen Prebensen *Tel:* 90044276 *E-mail:* ellen.prebensen@kunnskapsforlaget.no
Founded: 1975
Specialize in encyclopedias, dictionaries & reference works in book & electronic form.
ISBN Prefix(es): 978-82-573
Parent Company: H Aschehoug & Co; Gyldendal ASA

Larsforlaget, *imprint of* Cappelen Damm AS

Libretto Forlag+
Ovre Vollgate 15, 0158 Oslo
Tel: 22 41 03 85 *Fax:* 22 20 42 81
E-mail: post@librettoforlag.no
Web Site: www.librettoforlag.no
Key Personnel
Publisher: Tom Thorsteinsen *E-mail:* tomthor@online.no
Founded: 1991
Subjects: History, Self-Help
ISBN Prefix(es): 978-82-91091; 978-82-7886

Lunde Forlag+
Sinsenveien 25, 0572 Oslo
Tel: 22 00 73 50
E-mail: post@lundeforlag.no
Web Site: www.lundeforlag.no
Key Personnel
Publisher: Tom Teien *E-mail:* tteien@lundeforlag.no
Chief Editor: Katrine Masvie *E-mail:* kmasvie@lundeforlag.no
Editor: Kathrine Vigdel *E-mail:* kathrine@lundeforlag.no
Production: Reidlum Lindheim *E-mail:* rlindheim@lundeforlag.no
Founded: 1905
Specialize in Christian literature.
Membership(s): Christian Booksellers Association; Evangelical Christian Publishers Association; Den Norske Forleggerforening; Norsk Forleggersamband.
Subjects: Biography, Memoirs, Education, Fiction, Poetry, Religion - Other, Theology
ISBN Prefix(es): 978-82-520
Number of titles published annually: 90 Print
Total Titles: 250 Print
Parent Company: Lunde Forlag AS
Ultimate Parent Company: Lunde Holding
Book Club(s): Bokklubben Perspektiv *Tel:* 22 00 73 35
Distribution Center: Forlagsentralen

Luther Forlag
Sinsenveien 25, 0572 Oslo
Tel: 22 00 73 63
E-mail: post@lutherforlag.no
Web Site: www.lutherforlag.no
Key Personnel
Publishing Dir: Kathrine Vigdel *Tel:* 924 90 543 (cell) *E-mail:* kathrine@lutherforlag.no
Mng Dir: Morten Dahle Staerk *Tel:* 957 90 957 (cell) *E-mail:* morten@lutherforlag.no
Founded: 1868

Subjects: Biography, Memoirs, Fiction, Inspirational, Spirituality, Religion - Protestant, Religion - Other, Theology, Documentary
ISBN Prefix(es): 978-82-531
Number of titles published annually: 40 Print
Total Titles: 250 Print
Parent Company: Lunde Forlag AS
Ultimate Parent Company: Lunde Holding

Magikon Forlag
Fjellveien 48A, 1410 Kolbotn
E-mail: post@magikon.no
Web Site: www.magikon.no
Key Personnel
Owner: Kristin Roskifte *Tel:* 900 75 491
  E-mail: kristin@magikon.no; Svein Storksen
  Tel: 977 50 060 *E-mail:* svein@magikon.no
Founded: 2007
Subjects: Fiction
ISBN Prefix(es): 978-82-92863

Mangschou Forlag
Vestre Torggaten 18, 5015 Bergen
Tel: 55 55 10 50 *Fax:* 55 55 10 51
E-mail: mangschou@mangschou.no
Web Site: www.mangschou.no
Key Personnel
Publisher & Executive Dir: Marianne Rieber
  Tel: 910 05 368 (cell) *E-mail:* marianne.
  rieber@mangschou.no
Sales & Marketing Manager: Evy Singstad
  Tel: 909 26 658 (cell) *E-mail:* evy.singstad@
  mangschou.no
Editor: Petra Jonsdatter Helgesen *Tel:* 909 95 877
  (cell) *E-mail:* petra.j.helgesen@mangschou.no
Founded: 1997
ISBN Prefix(es): 978-82-91948

NKI Nettstudier
Universitetsgata 10, 0164 Oslo
Mailing Address: Postboks 6674 St Olavs plass,
  0129 Oslo
Tel: 67 58 88 00 *Fax:* 67 58 89 94
E-mail: post@nki.no
Web Site: www.nki.no
Founded: 1959
Subjects: Chemistry, Chemical Engineering, Electronics, Electrical Engineering, English as a
  Second Language, Environmental Studies,
  Mathematics, Mechanical Engineering, Physics,
  Transportation
ISBN Prefix(es): 978-82-562

Det Norske Samlaget+
Jens Bjelkes gate 12, 0506 Oslo
Mailing Address: Postboks 4672 Sofienberg, 0506
  Oslo
Tel: 22 70 78 00
Web Site: www.samlaget.no
Key Personnel
Chief Executive Officer: Edmund Austigard
  Tel: 482 01 320 (cell) *E-mail:* e.austigard@
  samlaget.no
Chief Information Officer: Karin Helgoy *Tel:* 970
  19 865 (cell) *E-mail:* k.helgoy@samlaget.no
Head, Sales & Marketing: Anne Liv Tresselt
  Tel: 905 61 322 (cell) *E-mail:* a.tresselt@
  samlaget.no
Production Manager: Erling I Vindheim *Tel:* 913
  15 136 (cell) *E-mail:* e.vindheim@samlaget.no
Marketing Coordinator: Maren Ingeborg Hvamstad *Tel:* 412 26 449 (cell) *E-mail:* m.
  hvamstad@samlaget.no
Founded: 1868
Membership(s): Den Norske Forleggerforening.
Subjects: Art, Biography, Memoirs, Cookery, Education, Fiction, Health, Nutrition, History,
  Humor, Language Arts, Linguistics, Literature, Literary Criticism, Essays, Management,
  Nonfiction (General), Philosophy, Poetry, Psychology, Psychiatry, Religion - Other, Social

Sciences, Sociology, Theology, Culture, Pedagogy
ISBN Prefix(es): 978-82-521
Number of titles published annually: 200 Print
Associate Companies: Noregs Boklag L/L
Subsidiaries: Litteraturselskapet Det Norske Samlaget; Stiftinga Det Norske Samlaget
Foreign Rights: Hagen Agency (Eirin Haeen)
  (worldwide)

Novus Forlag+
Herman Foss' Gate 19, 0171 Oslo
Tel: 22 71 74 50 *Fax:* 22 71 81 07
E-mail: novus@novus.no
Web Site: novus.mamutweb.com
Founded: 1971
Subjects: Education, Science (General)
ISBN Prefix(es): 978-82-7099
Total Titles: 300 Print

NRK Aktivum AS
Subsidiary of Norsk Rikskringkasting AS
Bjornstjerne Bjornsons pl 1, 0340 Oslo
Mailing Address: Postboks 8500, 0340 Oslo
Tel: 23 04 25 20 *Fax:* 23 04 27 20
Web Site: nrkaktivum.no; nrkbutikken.no
Key Personnel
Administrative Dir: Kjell Frostrud Johnsen
  Tel: 95 70 40 70 *E-mail:* kjell.frostrud.
  johnsen@nrk.no
Dir, Events: Ann-Kristin Holen *Tel:* 91 37 58 30
  E-mail: ann-kristin.holen@nrk.no
Marketing Manager: Stine Temte *Tel:* 92 05 35
  07 *E-mail:* stine.temte@nrk.no
Product Manager, Books: Rasa Ziburkute *Tel:* 93
  49 75 64 *E-mail:* rasa.ziburkute@nrk.no
Product Manager, DVDs & Music: Silje Berg
  Tomter *Tel:* 41 50 85 45 *E-mail:* silje.tomter@
  nrk.no
Product Manager, Merchandise: Marthe Heir
  Stene *Tel:* 92 40 59 07 *E-mail:* marthe.heir.
  stene@nrk.no
Founded: 1997
Subjects: NRK Broadcasts
ISBN Prefix(es): 978-82-8178

Forlaget Oktober A/S
Subsidiary of H Aschehoug & Co (W Nygaard)
  A/S
Kristian Augusts gate 11, 3 etasje, 0164 Oslo
Mailing Address: Postboks 6848 St Olavs plass,
  0130 Oslo
Tel: 23 35 46 20 *Fax:* 23 35 46 21
E-mail: oktober@oktober.no
Web Site: www.oktober.no
Key Personnel
Publishing Dir: Ingeri Engelstad *Tel:* 23 35 46 22
  E-mail: ingeri.engelstad@oktober.no
Publisher: Geir Gulliksen *Tel:* 23 35 46 29
  E-mail: geir.gulliksen@oktober.no
Mng Dir: Geir Berdahl *Tel:* 23 35 46 25
  E-mail: geir.berdahl@oktober.no
Senior Editor: Kari Joynt *Tel:* 23 35 46 26
  E-mail: kari.joynt@oktober.no
Editor: Cathrine Narum *Tel:* 23 35 46 22
  E-mail: cathrine.narum@oktober.no; Signe
  Eriksdatter Russwurm *Tel:* 23 32 74 96
  E-mail: signe.russwurm@oktober.no
Marketing: Ellen Hogsnes *Tel:* 913 26 385
  E-mail: ellen.hogsnes@oktober.no
Consultant: Birgit Bjerck *E-mail:* birgit.bjerck@
  oktober.no
Founded: 1970
Subjects: Biography, Memoirs, Fiction, Government, Political Science, Nonfiction (General)
ISBN Prefix(es): 978-82-7094; 978-82-495
Foreign Rights: Aschehoug Agency (Froydis
  Stromme Jorve)

Omnipax, *imprint of* Pax Forlag AS

Pantagruel Forlag AS
Inkognitogaten 33, 0256 Oslo
Mailing Address: Postboks 2370 Solli, 0201 Oslo
Tel: 23 27 28 10 *Fax:* 23 27 28 15
E-mail: alle@pantagruel.no
Web Site: pantagruel.no
Key Personnel
Publisher: Alexander Elguren *E-mail:* alexander@
  pantagruel.no
Head, Public Relations: Ida C Rahbek Manholt
  E-mail: ida@pantagruel.no
Production Manager: Agathe Skappel
  E-mail: agathe@pantagruel.no
Sales & Marketing Manager: Kristin Monsen
  E-mail: kristin@pantagruel.no
Subjects: Cookery, Fiction, Health, Nutrition, Humor, Self-Help, Travel & Tourism
ISBN Prefix(es): 978-82-7900

Pax Forlag AS+
Filmens hus, 5 etasje, Dronningens gate 16, 0152
  Oslo
Mailing Address: Postboks 461 Sentrum, 0105
  Oslo
Tel: 23 13 69 00 *Fax:* 23 13 69 19
E-mail: pax@pax.no
Web Site: www.pax.no
Key Personnel
Publisher: Bjorn Smith-Simonsen *Tel:* 23 13 69
  13
Publishing Dir: Astrid de Vibe *Tel:* 23 13 69 12
  E-mail: vibe@pax.no
Marketing & Public Relations Manager: Karen S
  Jensen *Tel:* 23 13 69 18 *E-mail:* karen@pax.no
Sales Manager: Eline Willumsen *Tel:* 23 13 69 11
  E-mail: eline@pax.no
Founded: 1964
Subjects: Anthropology, Architecture & Interior
  Design, Art, Biography, Memoirs, Criminology,
  Fiction, Government, Political Science, Health,
  Nutrition, History, Language Arts, Linguistics, Law, Literature, Literary Criticism, Essays,
  Nonfiction (General), Philosophy, Psychology,
  Psychiatry, Religion - Other, Social Sciences,
  Sociology, Women's Studies
ISBN Prefix(es): 978-82-530
Imprints: Omnipax (children's books)

Forlaget Press AS
Kongensgate 2, 0153 Oslo
Tel: 22 82 32 40
E-mail: marked@fpress.no
Web Site: www.fpress.no
Founded: 1997
Subjects: Art, Fiction, Literature, Literary Criticism, Essays, Photography, Contemporary Culture, Design
ISBN Prefix(es): 978-82-7547

Sambaandet Forlag AS+
Steinsvikvegen 30, 5353 Straume
Tel: 56 31 42 40 (cell)
E-mail: forlaget@sambaandet.no
Web Site: www.sambaandetforlag.no
Founded: 1945
Specialize in Christian literature & media.
Subjects: Biblical Studies, Poetry, Religion -
  Protestant
ISBN Prefix(es): 978-82-7752

Sandviks AS+
Strandsvingen 14, 4032 Stavanger
Tel: 51 44 00 00
E-mail: hello@sandviks.com
Web Site: www.sandviks.com; www.linkedin.com/
  company/284100?trk=tyah; www.facebook.com/
  sandviksas
Key Personnel
President & Chief Executive Officer: Marius
  Sandvik *Tel:* 51 44 00 01 *E-mail:* marius@
  sandviks.com
Chief Financial Officer: Are Schroder-Nielsen
  Tel: 51 44 00 30 *E-mail:* are@sandviks.com

Business Development Manager: Jens Otto
Hansen *Tel:* 51 44 00 09 *E-mail:* jens.otto@
sandviks.com
Information Technology Manager: Amund Junge
Tel: 51 44 00 03 *E-mail:* amund@sandviks.
com
Project Manager: Tiziana Egli *E-mail:* tiziana.
egli@gobo-kinder.com
Founded: 1965
Subjects: Health, Nutrition, Maritime, Medicine,
Nursing, Dentistry
ISBN Prefix(es): 978-82-7106
Subsidiaries: Baby's First Book Club; Go'boken
Book Club, Helsingborg, Sweden & Stavanger;
The International Log Book, Bath (UK & Sta-
vanger)
Branch Office(s)
GoBo Kinderbuecher, Junkerstr 84, 78263
Buesingen, Germany *Tel:* (01803) 001 386 0
Fax: (01803) 001 386 1 *E-mail:* info@gobo-
kinder.de
Goboken AB, Box 197, 201 21 Malmo, Swe-
den *Tel:* (040) 660 68 00 *Fax:* (040) 660 68 10
E-mail: goboken@goboken.se
U.S. Office(s): Sandvik Innovations LLC, 460 E
Swedesford Rd, Suite 2030, Wayne, PA 19087,
United States, Contact: Ann Szamboti *Tel:* 610-
975-9238 *E-mail:* ann.szamboti@sandviks.com
Warehouse: DFU-huset, Figgjo

Scandinavian Academic Press, *imprint of*
Spartacus Forlag AS

Scandinavian University Press, see
Universitetsforlaget AS

SINTEF Akademisk Forlag
Forskningsveien 3B, 0314 Oslo
Mailing Address: Postboks 124 Blindern, 0314
Oslo
Tel: 40 00 38 38
E-mail: salg.byggforsk@sintef.no
Web Site: www.sintef.no/byggforsk; sintefbok.no
Key Personnel
Publishing Manager: Trond Haug *Tel:* 478 13 898
E-mail: trond.haug@sintef.no
Senior Editor: Solveig Oyri *Tel:* 452 64 770
E-mail: solveig.oyri@sintef.no; Ina Sandberg
Tel: 991 01 036 *E-mail:* ina.sandberg@sintef.
no
Editor: Ida Rambaek *Tel:* 993 52 912 *E-mail:* ida.
rambaek@sintef.no
Founded: 2011
Subjects: Architecture & Interior Design,
Medicine, Nursing, Dentistry, Science (Gen-
eral), Social Sciences, Sociology, Technology
ISBN Prefix(es): 978-82-14; 978-82-536

Snofugl Forlag (Snowbird Publisher)+
Radhusvegen 3, 7224 Melhus
Mailing Address: Postboks 95, 7221 Melhus
Tel: 72 87 24 11 *Fax:* 72 87 10 13
E-mail: snoefugl@online.no
Web Site: snofugl.no
Key Personnel
Publishing Manager: Asmund Snofugl
Founded: 1972
Membership(s): Den Norske Forleggerforening.
Subjects: Biography, Memoirs, Fiction, Govern-
ment, Political Science, History, Literature, Lit-
erary Criticism, Essays, Nonfiction (General),
Poetry, Social Sciences, Sociology
ISBN Prefix(es): 978-82-7083
Number of titles published annually: 15 Print
Total Titles: 400 Print
Associate Companies: A/S Bygdetrykk, 7221
Melhus

Solum Forlag A/S+
Postboks 6794 St Olavs plass, 0130 Oslo
Tel: 22 50 04 00 *Fax:* 22 19 14 26

E-mail: info@solumforlag.no; tore@solumforlag.
no; gunnar@solumforlag.no
Web Site: www.solumforlag.no
Founded: 1974
Also publisher of educational materials.
Subjects: Disability, Special Needs, Fiction, Lit-
erature, Literary Criticism, Essays, Nonfiction
(General), Poetry, Science (General), Humani-
ties
ISBN Prefix(es): 978-82-562; 978-82-560
Parent Company: Forlagsgruppen BVT
Distributed by International Specialized Book
Service (USA)

Spartacus Forlag AS
St Olavs gate 21B, 4 etg, 0165 Oslo
Mailing Address: Postboks 6673 St Olavs plass,
0129 Oslo
Tel: 22 44 56 70
E-mail: post@spartacus.no
Web Site: www.spartacus.no
Key Personnel
Publishing Manager: Per Nordanger *Tel:* 23 13 69
45 *E-mail:* per@spartacus.no
Editorial Dir: Nina Castracane Selvik *Tel:* 23 13
69 43 *E-mail:* nina@spartacus.no
Marketing: Linn Abrahamsen Blomfeldt *Tel:* 23
13 69 44 *E-mail:* linn@spartacus.no
Sales: Nichlas Cobb *Tel:* 23 13 69 48
E-mail: nichlas@spartacus.no
Founded: 1989
Subjects: Art, Biography, Memoirs, History, Non-
fiction (General), Philosophy, Science (Gen-
eral), Documentary, Popular Science
ISBN Prefix(es): 978-82-430
Imprints: Scandinavian Academic Press
Branch Office(s)
Fosswinckelsgt 11, 5007 Bergen
Foreign Rights: Hagen Agency (Eirin Hagen)

Stabenfeldt A/S+
Postboks 8054, 4068 Stavanger
Tel: 51 84 54 00
E-mail: info@stabenfeldt.com
Web Site: www.stabenfeldt.com
Key Personnel
General Manager: Kristin Eriksen Berg
Founded: 1913
Subjects: Fiction, Nonfiction (General)
ISBN Prefix(es): 978-82-532
Branch Office(s)
Stabenfeldt AB, Makelankatu 54 A 501, 00510
Helsinki, Finland
Meister Verlag GmbH, Postfach 40 16 80, 80716
Munich, Germany *Tel:* (089) 12 170 960
Stabenfeldt KFT, Bajnok u 13, Budapest 1063,
Hungary *Tel:* (01) 374 38 29
Stabenfeldt AB, PO Box 876, 201 80 Malmo,
Sweden *Tel:* (040) 665 41 00

J M Stenersens Forlag AS
Stortingsgaten 12, 0161 Oslo
Tel: 23 11 82 80
E-mail: post@jms.no
Web Site: www.jms.no
Key Personnel
Publishing Manager: Solveig Oye *Tel:* 470 26
022 *E-mail:* solveig@kagge.no
Sales Dir: Marit Johansen *Tel:* 975 86 229
Editor: A Audhild Solberg *Tel:* 991 51 552
E-mail: audhild@jms.no
Founded: 1892
Subjects: Architecture & Interior Design, Art,
Cookery, Crafts, Games, Hobbies, Fiction,
Health, Nutrition, Self-Help
ISBN Prefix(es): 978-82-7201
Parent Company: Kagge Forlag AS

Tell Forlag AS+
Slemmestadveien 416, 1390 Vollen
Tel: 66 78 09 18 *Fax:* 66 90 05 72
E-mail: post@tell.no

Web Site: www.tell.no
Key Personnel
Publisher: Tell-Chr Wagle *E-mail:* tell@tell.no
Founded: 1987
Subjects: Art, Cookery, Crafts, Games, Hob-
bies, Drama, Theater, Health, Nutrition, Music,
Dance, Psychology, Psychiatry, Social Sciences,
Sociology, Design
ISBN Prefix(es): 978-82-7522
Number of titles published annually: 25 Print

Tiden Norsk Forlag, *imprint of* Gyldendal Norsk
Forlag

Tiden Norsk Forlag
Imprint of Gyldendal Norsk Forlag
St Olavs gate 21B, 0165 Oslo
Mailing Address: Postboks 6704, St Olavs plass,
0130 Oslo
Tel: 23 32 76 60 *Fax:* 23 32 76 97
E-mail: tiden@tiden.no
Web Site: www.tiden.no
Key Personnel
Publishing Dir & Foreign Rights Manager:
Richard Aaro *Tel:* 23 32 76 82 *E-mail:* richard.
aaro@tiden.no
Sales & Marketing Dir: Bjorn Fredrik Drang-
sholt *Tel:* 23 32 76 77 *E-mail:* bjorn.fredrik.
drangsholt@tiden.no
Production Manager: Aase Forfang Rognved
Tel: 22 99 04 22 *E-mail:* aase.forfang.
rognved@gyldendal.no
Information Officer: Linn Rottem *Tel:* 23 32 76
69 *E-mail:* linn.rottem@tiden.no
Founded: 1933
Subjects: Fiction, Literature, Literary Criticism,
Essays, Management, Nonfiction (General),
Science Fiction, Fantasy
ISBN Prefix(es): 978-82-10; 978-82-990075
Book Club(s): Den Norske Bokklubben A/S (with
three other Norwegian publishers)

Universitetsforlaget AS+
Subsidiary of H Aschehoug & Co (W Nygaard)
A/S
Sehesteds gate 3, 0164 Oslo
Mailing Address: Postboks 508 Sentrum, 0105
Oslo
Tel: 24 14 75 00
E-mail: post@universitetsforlaget.no
Web Site: www.universitetsforlaget.no
Key Personnel
Publishing Manager: Svein Skarheim
Tel: 916 10 467 *E-mail:* svein.skarheim@
universitetsforlaget.no
Production Coordinator: Steinar Andersen
Tel: 466 30 455 *E-mail:* steinar.andersen@
universitetsforlaget.no
Founded: 1950
Publishers for Scandinavian Universities & other
institutions of higher learning, learned societies
of Scandinavia.
Membership(s): European Educational Publish-
ers Group (EEPG); European Union Publishers
Forum; International Association of STM Pub-
lishers; Norwegian Publishers' Association.
Subjects: Business, Communications, Economics,
Education, Health, Nutrition, History, Language
Arts, Linguistics, Law, Literature, Literary Crit-
icism, Essays, Management, Marketing, Me-
chanical Engineering, Medicine, Nursing, Den-
tistry, Philosophy, Religion - Other, Science
(General), Theology, Ethics, Health Care &
Modern Language, Pedagogy
ISBN Prefix(es): 978-82-00
Number of titles published annually: 140 Print
Total Titles: 1,100 Print; 10 CD-ROM; 35 Online;
20 Audio
Branch Office(s)
Copenhagen, Denmark
Stockholm, Sweden
Scandinavian University Press United King-
dom, 60 St Aldates, Oxford OX1 1ST, United

Kingdom, Contact: Mr George Drennan
Tel: (01865) 791 891 *Fax:* (01865) 791 891
Foreign Rights: Oslo Literary Agency (Norway)
Returns: Forlagsentralen ANS, Postboks 20, 1402
Ski
Membership(s): American Association of University Presses

Vega Forlag AS
St Olavs gate 21B, 0165 Oslo
Tel: 21 09 04 10 *Fax:* 22 37 15 50
E-mail: post@vegaforlag.no
Web Site: www.vegaforlag.no
Key Personnel
Publisher: Finn Jorgen Solberg *Tel:* 21 09 04 12
   E-mail: solberg@vegaforlag.no
Sales Manager: Eline Oppeboen *Tel:* 21 09 04 14
   E-mail: eline@vegaforlag.no
Editor: Magnus Skjaeraasen Aaro *Tel:* 21 09 04
   16 *E-mail:* magnus@vegaforlag.no
Marketing & Public Relations: Elen Zickfeldt
   Tel: 21 09 04 11 *E-mail:* elen@vegaforlag.no
Founded: 2003
Subjects: Fiction, Nonfiction (General)
ISBN Prefix(es): 978-82-8211

Verbum Forlag
Bernhard Getz' gate 3, 0165 Oslo
Mailing Address: Postboks 6624 St Olavs plass,
   0129 Oslo
Tel: 47 97 64 50 *Fax:* 47 97 64 51
E-mail: post@bibel.no; mcm@bibel.no
Web Site: www.bibel.no
Key Personnel
Chief Secretary & Rights Editor: Ingvild
   Ellingsen *Tel:* 47 97 64 61 *E-mail:* ine@bibel.
   no
Founded: 1820
Christian, values-based publisher.
Subjects: Fiction
ISBN Prefix(es): 978-82-543
Number of titles published annually: 30 Print

Versal Forlag, *imprint of* Gyldendal Norsk Forlag

Oman

General Information

Capital: Muscat
Language: Arabic, English in business
Religion: Predominantly Muslim (mostly Ibadi,
   some Sunni)
Population: 1.6 million
Currency: 1,000 baiza = 1 rial Omani

Apex Press & Publishing
PO Box 2616, 112 Ruwi, Muscat
Tel: 24 799388 *Fax:* 24 793316; 24 787573
Web Site: www.apexmedia.co.om
Key Personnel
Executive Chairman: Saleh Zakwani
Chief Executive Officer: Mohana Prabhakar
Creative Dir & Press Manager: Benoite Lopes
General Manager, Sales: Kalpesh Adhia
Founded: 1980
Specialize in books about Oman.
Subjects: Art, Business, Gardening, Plants, History, Outdoor Recreation, Photography, Travel
   & Tourism

Pakistan

General Information

Capital: Islamabad
Language: Urdu is national language but English
   is used extensively. Other principal languages
   are Punjabi, Pushto, Sindhi and Saraiki
Religion: Predominantly Islamic
Population: 121.7 million
Bank Hours: 0900-1300 Saturday-Wednesday;
   0900-1100 Thursday
Shop Hours: 0930-1300, 1500-2000 Saturday-
   Thursday
Currency: 100 paisa = 1 Pakistan rupee
Export/Import Information: No tariff on books,
   magazines and advertising matter. Import license issued freely if required. Anti-Islamic
   and obscene literature prohibited. Exchange
   controls.
Copyright: UCC, Berne, Buenos Aires, Florence
   (see Copyright Conventions, pg viii)

**Academy of Educational Planning &
   Management (AEPAM)**
Taleemi chowk, G-8/1, Islamabad 44000
Tel: (051) 926-0674 *Fax:* (051) 926-1359
E-mail: webinfo@aepam.edu.pk
Web Site: www.aepam.edu.pk
Key Personnel
Dir General: Dr Allah Bakhsh Malik
   E-mail: abmmalik@yahoo.com
Dir, Training: Dr Dawood Shah *Tel:* (051) 926-
   0610 *E-mail:* aepam_dawood@yahoo.com
Founded: 1982
Subjects: Computers, Economics, Education, English as a Second Language, Library & Information Sciences, Management
ISBN Prefix(es): 978-969-444
Parent Company: Ministry of Federal Education
   & Professional Training

AEPAM, see Academy of Educational Planning
   & Management (AEPAM)

Sheikh Ghulam Ali & Sons (Pvt) Ltd+
Curcular Rd, Chowk Anarkali, Lahore 54000
Tel: (042) 7323951 *Fax:* (042) 6315478
E-mail: info@niaz.com
Web Site: www.ghulamali.niaz.com
Founded: 1887
Subjects: Education, History, Poetry, Religion -
   Islamic
ISBN Prefix(es): 978-969-31
Number of titles published annually: 150 Print
Branch Office(s)
M A Jinnah Rd, Karachi *Tel:* (021) 2722784
Yadkar Line, Chotki Ghitti, Hyderabad, India
   Tel: (022) 3641831
U.S. Office(s): c/o Sudaif Niaz, 330 E 38 St,
   Apartment 23F, New York, NY 10016, United
   States *Tel:* 646-454-0738 *E-mail:* sudaif@
   gmail.com

Sheikh Shaukat Ali & Sons+
Urdu Bazar Ext, M A Jinnah Rd, Karachi 74200
Tel: (021) 32217767; (021) 32637577 *Fax:* (021)
   32637877
Subjects: Poetry, Religion - Islamic
ISBN Prefix(es): 978-969-440
Branch Office(s)
Mian Market, Ghazni St, Lahore

**Applied Socio-Economic Research/Institute of
   Women's Studies Lahore,** see ASR/IWSL

ASR/IWSL+
96-A, G block, Gulberg III, PO Box 3154, Lahore

Tel: (042) 35882617; (042) 35882618 *Fax:* (042)
   35883991
Key Personnel
International Rights: Nighat Said Khan
Subjects: Women's Studies
ISBN Prefix(es): 978-969-8217
Distributed by Mr Books; Saeed Book Bank

Beacon Books
49-A Block B, Gulgasht Colony, Golbagh, Multan
Tel: (061) 6520790; (061) 6520791; (030)
   08636091 (cell)
E-mail: beaconbooks786@gmail.com
Web Site: www.facebook.com/
   beaconbookspakistan
Founded: 1984
Subjects: History, Literature, Literary Criticism,
   Essays, Religion - Other
ISBN Prefix(es): 978-969-534
Branch Office(s)
Ghazni St, Urdu Bazar, Lahore *Tel:* (042)
   37320030

Book Centre+
96 Tipu Block New Garden Town, Lahore 54000
Tel: (042) 35837297 (editorial); (042) 37237503;
   (042) 37237520 *Fax:* (042) 37311063
E-mail: info@bookcentre.pk
Web Site: www.bookcentre.pk
Founded: 1952
Subjects: Art, Computers, Crafts, Games, Hobbies, Education, Geography, Geology, Language Arts, Linguistics, Mathematics, Religion
   - Islamic, Science (General), Social Sciences,
   Sociology, English Language, Urdu Grammar
   & Writing
ISBN Prefix(es): 978-969-436
Showroom(s): 49 The Mall (Hall Rd Corner), Lahore

Caravan Book House (Maktab-e-Karwan)
2 Kachehri Rd Anarkali, Lahore
Tel: (042) 37122955
E-mail: caravanbookslhr@gmail.com
Web Site: www.caravanbookhouse.com.pk
Founded: 1946
Subjects: Chemistry, Chemical Engineering, Fiction, Language Arts, Linguistics, Mathematics,
   Medicine, Nursing, Dentistry, Physics, Urdu
   Literature
ISBN Prefix(es): 978-969-478

Centre for South Asian Studies
Quaid-i-Azam Campus, University of the Punjab,
   Lahore 54590
Mailing Address: PO Box 54590, Lahore
Web Site: www.pu.edu.pk
Key Personnel
Dir: Dr Umbreen Javaid *Tel:* (042) 99231143
   E-mail: director.csas@pu.edu.pk
Founded: 1973
Subjects: Asian Studies, Economics, Ethnicity,
   Government, Political Science, Social Sciences,
   Sociology, Foreign Affairs, South Asia
ISBN Prefix(es): 978-969-471

Classic Publishers+
42 The Mall, Lahore 54000
Tel: (042) 7312977 *Fax:* (042) 7323963
Key Personnel
Mng Dir, Editorial, Production, Permissions:
   Agha Amir Hussain
Founded: 1957
Subjects: Art, Fiction
ISBN Prefix(es): 978-969-28; 978-969-8136
Associate Companies: Menarva Publications, Lahore
Subsidiaries: Classic Bookshop; Shish Mahal
   Kitab Ghar

Fazlee Sons (Pvt) Ltd+
F-42, Hub River Rd, SITE, Karachi 75700
Tel: (021) 32563971; (021) 32572210 *Fax:* (021)
32571688
E-mail: contact@fazlee.com; tfazlee@gmail.com
Web Site: www.fazlee.com
Key Personnel
Contact: Adnan Saeed *Tel:* (0334) 3655887 (cell)
Founded: 1948
Membership(s): Pakistan Booksellers & Publishers Association (PBSPA).
Subjects: Literature, Literary Criticism, Essays, Religion - Other
ISBN Prefix(es): 978-969-441
Associate Companies: Printing Services (Pvt) Ltd
Subsidiaries: IS Asia
Bookshop(s): Fazlee Book Supermarket, 4 Mama Parsi Bldg, Temple Rd, Urdu Bazar, Karachi 74200
Orders to: 1-K-5/A, Commercial Area, Nazimabad No 1, Karachi *Tel:* (021) 66222125

Ferozsons
60-Shahrah-e-Quaid-e-Azam, Lahore
Tel: (042) 111-62-62-62 *Fax:* (042) 636-9204
E-mail: support@ferozsons.com.pk
Web Site: www.ferozsons.com.pk
Founded: 1894
Subjects: Architecture & Interior Design, Art, Biography, Memoirs, Biological Sciences, Business, Chemistry, Chemical Engineering, Computers, Cookery, Economics, Education, Engineering (General), Fashion, Fiction, Finance, Government, Political Science, Health, Nutrition, History, Language Arts, Linguistics, Law, Literature, Literary Criticism, Essays, Management, Mathematics, Medicine, Nursing, Dentistry, Mysteries, Suspense, Philosophy, Physics, Poetry, Psychology, Psychiatry, Regional Interests, Religion - Islamic, Self-Help, Sports, Athletics, Travel & Tourism
ISBN Prefix(es): 978-969-0
Bookshop(s): 51-54 Gaddafi Stadium, Lahore *Tel:* (042) 571-2250; (042) 571-2276 *Fax:* (042) 571-2020; H Block, DHA, Lahore *Tel:* (042) 574-2804; (042) 574-2805; Pearl Continental Hotel Shop No 9, Lahore *Tel:* (042) 636-0210; Urdu Bazzar, Lahore *Tel:* (042) 722-7086; Z Block, DHA, Lahore *Tel:* (042) 573-5662; (042) 573-5663; Clifton, Karachi, Manager: Ms Gul Afshan *Tel:* (021) 111-62-62-62 *Fax:* (042) 582-5170; Peshawar Rd, Rawalpindi *Tel:* (042) 62-62-62 *Fax:* (042) 556-4273

Hamdard Foundation Pakistan
Al-Majeed, Hamdard Centre, Nazimabad, No 3, Karachi 74600
Tel: (021) 6616001; (021) 6620945 *Fax:* (021) 6611755
E-mail: hfp@hamdardfoundation.org
Web Site: hamdardfoundation.org
Key Personnel
President: Mrs Sadia Rashid
Vice President: Dr Navaid ul Zafar
Founded: 1964
Service of humanity through medical, scientific, educational & cultural activities.
Subjects: Biography, Memoirs, Education, Health, Nutrition, History, Literature, Literary Criticism, Essays, Religion - Islamic
ISBN Prefix(es): 978-969-412
Parent Company: Hamdard Laboratories (Waqf) Pakistan
Bookshop(s): Hamdard Kitabistan, Seva Kunj Bldg, Shahrah-e-Liaquat, Karachi *Tel:* (021) 2213371

IIIT, see International Institute of Islamic Thought

International Institute of Islamic Thought+
28, Main Double Rd, F-10/2, Islamabad
Mailing Address: PO Box 1959, Islamabad
Tel: (051) 229-3734 *Fax:* (051) 228-0489
Web Site: www.iiit.org
Founded: 1981
Subjects: Ethnicity, Religion - Islamic
ISBN Prefix(es): 978-969-462

IRI, see Islamic Research Institute (IRI)

Islamic Publications (Pvt) Ltd
Mansoorah, Multan Rd, Lahore 54000
Tel: (042) 35417074 *Fax:* (042) 37214974
Founded: 1959
Specialize in literature on Islam.
Membership(s): Lahore Chamber of Commerce & Industry; Pakistan Publishers & Booksellers Association.
Subjects: Religion - Islamic
ISBN Prefix(es): 978-969-423
Number of titles published annually: 20 Print
Total Titles: 700 Print

Islamic Research Institute (IRI)
(Idara-e-Tehqiqat-e-Islami)+
Affiliate of International Islamic University, Islamabad
Editing & Publishing Bureau, Faisal Mosque Complex, Islamabad
Tel: (051) 2281289; (051) 9261761-5 (ext 207 & 222); (051) 2254874 (orders) *Fax:* (051) 2250821; (051) 9260769 (orders)
Web Site: iri.iiu.edu.pk
Key Personnel
Dir General: Dr Zia ul Haq *E-mail:* dgiri@iiu.edu.pk
Deputy Dir: Sohail Hassan
Founded: 1959
Publish research periodicals & books dealing with Islam, its history, thought, culture & civilization.
Subjects: Religion - Islamic
ISBN Prefix(es): 978-969-408
Number of titles published annually: 10 Print; 10 Online
Total Titles: 200 Print

Kazi Publications
121-Zulqarnain Chambers, Ganpat Rd, Lahore
Tel: (042) 37311359 *Fax:* (042) 37350805
E-mail: kazip@brain.net.pk
Web Site: www.brain.net.pk/~kazip/
Founded: 1978
Subjects: Islam

Kitabistan Publishing Co+
38 Urdu Bazar, Lahore
Tel: (042) 37230608; (042) 37313615
Key Personnel
Owner: Abdul Hamid Khan; Abdul Samad Khan
Founded: 1967
Subjects: Literature, Literary Criticism, Essays, Religion - Islamic
ISBN Prefix(es): 978-969-431; 978-969-34
Warehouse: 4C Mela Ram Darbar Market, Lahore

Library Promotion Bureau+
Karachi University Campus, PO Box 8421, Karachi 75270
Tel: (021) 3632-1959
E-mail: lpb_pakistan_66@yahoo.com
Key Personnel
President: Dr Ghaniul Akram Sabzwari
Deputy Chief Editor: Muhammad Wasil Usmani
Contact: Prof Liaquat Ali Khan
Founded: 1966
Subjects: Library & Information Sciences
ISBN Prefix(es): 978-969-459

U.S. Office(s): 4213 Heritage Way Dr, Fort Worth, TX 76137, United States
Distributed by M S Royal Book Co

Maktaba-i-Danial, *imprint of* Pakistan Publishing House

Malik Sirajuddin & Sons+
Kashmiri Bazar, 48-C, Lower Mall, Lahore
Tel: (042) 37225809; (042) 37225812 *Fax:* (042) 37224586
E-mail: sirajco@brain.net.pk
Founded: 1934
Subjects: Biography, Memoirs, Fiction, How-to, Psychology, Psychiatry, Religion - Islamic
ISBN Prefix(es): 978-969-29
Associate Companies: Gul I Khandan, Urdu Monthly, Kashmiri Baza, Lahore 8; Islamic Juntri, Kashmiri Baza, Lahore 8
Subsidiaries: Siraj Mohammadi Press; Ayaz Book Binding Works
Branch Office(s)
Chowk Urdu Bazar, Lahore *Tel:* (042) 7666226; (042) 7669062 *Fax:* (042) 7224586
18-19 M J Hospital (WAQF), O/S Mori Gate, Circular Rd, Lahore

Maqbool Academy+
10 Dayal Singh Mansion, Mall Rd, Lahore 54000
Tel: (042) 7357058 *Fax:* (042) 7238241
E-mail: maqboolbooks@gmail.com
Web Site: www.maqboolbooks.com
Founded: 1954
Membership(s): Lahore Chamber of Commerce & Industries.
Subjects: Asian Studies, Cookery, Drama, Theater, Education, Fashion, Fiction, Gardening, Plants, Government, Political Science, History, Humor, Literature, Literary Criticism, Essays, Poetry, Religion - Islamic, Religion - Other, Romance, Science (General)
ISBN Prefix(es): 978-969-442; 978-969-9059
Total Titles: 100 Print
Branch Office(s)
14-A, Pak Block, Allama Iqbal Town, Lahore *Tel:* (042) 37807518
130 Lower Ground floor, Siddiq Trade Centre, Gulberg, Lahore *Tel:* (042) 5781766
Distribution Center: Book Centre, Express House, White Abbey Rd, Bradford, West Yorks BD8 8EJ, United Kingdom *Tel:* (01274) 727 864 *Fax:* (01274) 728 136

Minhaj-ul-Quran Publications
365M, Model Town, Lahore 54700
Tel: (042) 111140140 *Fax:* (042) 5169114
Web Site: www.minhaj.biz
Subjects: Law, Philosophy, Religion - Other, Science (General), Urdu Literature
ISBN Prefix(es): 978-969-32

National Book Foundation+
6-Mauve Area, G-8/4, Taleemi Chowk, Islamabad 44000
Tel: (051) 9261533; (051) 2255572; (0961) 9280129 (bookshop); (041) 2648179 (bookshop); (051) 9314004 (bookshop) *Fax:* (051) 2264283; (051) 9261534
E-mail: books@nbf.org.pk
Web Site: www.nbf.org.pk
Key Personnel
Mng Dir: Dr Inam ul Haq Javeid
Secretary: Mr Ishtiaq Ahmed Malik
Founded: 1972
Making books available to the public & students at moderate prices. Also responsible for book development, book promotion, promotion of reading habit & printing of Braille books for the visually impaired. Works in collaboration with Asia/Pacific Cultural Centre for UNESCO, Tokyo, Japan; UNESCO; Pakistan National

Commission for UNESCO; Intellectual Property Organization (IPO), Pakistan.
Membership(s): Asia/Pacific Publishers Association.
Subjects: Accounting, Agriculture, Behavioral Sciences, Biological Sciences, Business, Career Development, Chemistry, Chemical Engineering, Civil Engineering, Computer Science, Economics, Education, Engineering (General), Language Arts, Linguistics, Law, Mathematics, Medicine, Nursing, Dentistry, Poetry, Psychology, Psychiatry, Religion - Islamic, Information Technology
ISBN Prefix(es): 978-969-37
Number of titles published annually: 617 Print
Total Titles: 7,116 Print
Parent Company: Government of Pakistan
Branch Office(s)
1st floor, Public Library, Jalal Baba Auditorium, Abbottabad *Tel:* (0992) 9310291
Garhi Khatta, University of Sindh, Hyderabad *Tel:* (022) 9200251
D C Chow, Quaid-i-Azam Rd, Jacobabad *Tel:* (0722) 650817
Liaquat Memorial Library Premises, Ground floor, Stadium Rd, Karachi *Tel:* (021) 99231806; (021) 99231089 *Fax:* (021) 99231089
Lower Ground floor, Bldg No 1, Aiwan-e-Iqbal Complex, Egerton Rd, Lahore *Tel:* (042) 99203863; (042) 99203864; (042) 99203865 *Fax:* (042) 99203864
Chandka Medical College, Main Gate, Larkana *Tel:* (0741) 9410229
Plot 4-5-6, MDA Rd, Near Multan Arts Council, Multan *Tel:* (061) 9201281
Public Library, Old Sukkur *Tel:* (071) 9310892
Plot 36-37, Sector B-2, Phase V, Hayatabad, Peshawar *Tel:* (091) 9217273 *Fax:* (091) 9217273
Natha Singh St, House No 3-9/9, Quetta *Tel:* (081) 9201570 *Fax:* (081) 9201869

National Institute of Historical & Cultural Research, Centre of Excellence
New Campus, Quaid-e-Azam University, Shahdara Rd, Islamabad 45320
Tel: (051) 2896153 (ext 102) *Fax:* (051) 2896152
E-mail: nihcr@yahoo.com
Web Site: www.nihcr.edu.pk
Key Personnel
Dir: Dr Khurram Qadir *Tel:* (051) 2896151
E-mail: dirnihcr@gmail.com
Publication Officer: Munir Khawar *Tel:* (051) 2896153 ext 141 *E-mail:* mmmunir60@yahoo.com
Officer in Charge: Dr Sajid Mahmood Awan *Tel:* (051) 2896153 ext 127
E-mail: smawan2222@gmail.com
Founded: 1973
Specialize in history & culture of South Asia with special emphasis on Pakistan.
Subjects: Biography, Memoirs, Ethnicity, History, Regional Interests
ISBN Prefix(es): 978-969-415

NIHCR, see National Institute of Historical & Cultural Research, Centre of Excellence

Oxford University Press Pakistan
No 38, Sector 15, Korangi Industrial Area, Karachi 74900
Mailing Address: PO Box 8214, Karachi 74900
Tel: (021) 35071580; (021) 35071587 *Fax:* (021) 35055072
E-mail: central.marketing.pk@oup.com
Web Site: www.oup.com.pk
Key Personnel
Mng Dir: Ameena Saiyid
Marketing Dir: Raheela Fahim Baqai *Tel:* (023) 362334647
Regional Sales Dir: Salma Adil *Tel:* (021) 35071580

Founded: 1952
Bookshop(s): Park Towers, Sharae Firdousi, Clifton, Karachi 75400, Contact: Roshan Zameer *Tel:* (021) 35875355; White Palace Tower, Khalid bin Waleed Rd, PECHS, Karachi 75400, Contact: Mishal Gul *Tel:* (021) 34380495; Shop No B-7, Robson Rd, Urdu Bazaar, Karachi 75300, Contact: Nasir Husain *Tel:* (021) 32219698; (021) 32219699; Sir Syed Urdu Bazaar, Nazimabad No 1, Karachi, Contact: Sabahat Qamar *Tel:* (021) 35441406; Shop No 13/14, Mian Yousaf, Jamal Plaza, Supply Bazar, Main Mansehra Rd, Abbottabad, Contact: Tauseef Zafar *Tel:* (099) 333042; 21-P, Malik Plaza, Main Kotwali Rd, Outside Aminpur Bazar, Faisalabad, Contact: Annas Mirza *Tel:* (041) 2620124; (041) 2620125; Faujdari Rd, Near St Mary's School, Hyderabad, Contact: Muhammad Ibrahim *Tel:* (040) 3038570; 7, Shalimar Plaza, Jinnah Ave, 99 West, Blue Area, Islamabad 44000, Regional Sales Dir, Northern Region: Fayyaz Raja *Tel:* (051) 38317022 *Fax:* (051) 32347266 *E-mail:* fayyaz.raja@oup.com; 17-L, Mini Market, Gulberg II, Lahore, Regional Sales Dir, Central Region: Tariq Haq *Tel:* (042) 35778601; (042) 35778602 *Fax:* (042) 35778680 *E-mail:* tariq.haq@oup.com; 31-B, Gulgasht Colony, Opposite Gole Bagh, Near National Bank of Pakistan, Multan, Contact: Mubasher Manzoor *Tel:* (061) 6511971; Samad Tower, Ground floor, Tahkal, University Rd, Peshawar, Contact: Bushra Shahab *Tel:* (091) 5840484; (091) 5854067; No 2-11/6A, Near Mannan Chowk, M A Jinnah Rd, Quetta, Contact: Imran Latif *Tel:* (081) 2827577; No 35/36, Trust Colony, Jamia Al Farooq Rd, Rahimyar Khan, Contact: Abdul Khaliq Shaheed *Tel:* (068) 5874213; (068) 5874214; New Urdu Bazar, Sargodha, Contact: Raheel Ahmed *Tel:* (048) 3713331; Neem ki Chari, Urdu Bazar, Sukkur, Contact: Ishfaq Ali *Tel:* (071) 5015299

Pak Company Pakistan
17-Urdu Bazar, Lahore 54000
Tel: (042) 37230555; (042) 37352427 *Fax:* (042) 37120077
E-mail: pakcompany@hotmail.com
Web Site: www.pakcompany.com.pk
Key Personnel
Dir: Syed Ahmed Shah
Founded: 1932
Also government printers.
Subjects: Religion - Islamic
ISBN Prefix(es): 978-969-434

Pakistan Institute of Development Economics (PIDE)
Quaid-i-Azam University Campus, PO Box 1091, Islamabad 44000
Tel: (051) 9248069 *Fax:* (051) 9248065
E-mail: publications@pide.org.pk; pide@pide.org.pk
Web Site: www.pide.org.pk
Key Personnel
Senior Publications Officer: Mr Imran Ul Haq
Assistant Publications Officer: Zafar Ehsan
Founded: 1957
University devoted to teaching & research in social science fields. Offers advanced degree programmes & serves as a policy think-tank; focal point of several international organizations like the World Bank, International Labour Organization, Asian Development Bank, International Development Research Centre, South Asia Network of Economic Research Institutes, GDN, etc.
Subjects: Agriculture, Anthropology, Business, Developing Countries, Economics, Environmental Studies, Finance, Health, Nutrition, Labor, Industrial Relations, Management, Marketing, Social Sciences, Sociology, Women's

Studies, Demography, Econometrics, Population Studies
ISBN Prefix(es): 978-969-461
Total Titles: 70 Print

Pakistan Law House
Pakistan Chowk, GPO Box 90, Karachi
Tel: (021) 32212455; (021) 32639558 *Fax:* (021) 32627549
E-mail: pak_law_house@hotmail.com
Web Site: www.pakistanlawhouse.com
Key Personnel
Owner: Kamran Noorani
Founded: 1950
Subjects: Law
ISBN Prefix(es): 978-969-8372

Pakistan Publishing House+
Victoria Chambers, 2, Abdullah Haroon Rd, Karachi 74400
Tel: (021) 35681457 *Fax:* (021) 3627549
E-mail: pak_law_house@hotmail.com
Key Personnel
Owner: Ms Hoori Noorani
Manager: Aamir Hussain
Founded: 1966
Subjects: History, Law, Literature, Literary Criticism, Essays
ISBN Prefix(es): 978-969-419
Associate Companies: Pakistan Law House, Pakistan Chowk, GPO Box 90, Karachi 1
Imprints: PPH; Maktaba-i-Danial

PIDE, see Pakistan Institute of Development Economics (PIDE)

PPH, *imprint of* Pakistan Publishing House

Quaid-i-Azam University Department of Biological Sciences
Quaid-i-Azam University, Dept of Plant Sciences, Islamabad 45320
Tel: (051) 90640000
E-mail: info@qau.edu.pk
Web Site: www.qau.edu.pk
Key Personnel
Dean, Faculty of Biological Sciences: Dr Asghari Bano *Tel:* (051) 90643096
E-mail: banoasghari@gmail.com
Founded: 1972
Subjects: Chemistry, Chemical Engineering, Social Sciences, Sociology
ISBN Prefix(es): 978-969-8329

Research Society of Pakistan
University of the Punjab, PO Box 54590, Lahore
Tel: (042) 99231176
Web Site: pu.edu.pk
Key Personnel
President: Dr Mujahid Kamran *E-mail:* vc@pu.edu.pk
Subjects: Culture, Heritage
ISBN Prefix(es): 978-969-425
Total Titles: 111 Print

Royal Book Co+
BG-5, Rex Centre, Fatima Jinnah Rd, Saddar, Karachi 75530
Tel: (021) 35653418; (021) 35684244; (021) 37015471; (021) 37011123 *Fax:* (021) 37015472
E-mail: info@royalbook.com.pk; royalbook@hotmail.com
Web Site: www.royalbook.com.pk
Key Personnel
Proprietor: Jamshed Mirza
Founded: 1964
Subjects: Accounting, Biography, Memoirs, Economics, Education, Engineering (General), Finance, Geography, Geology, Government, Political Science, History, Law, Literature, Literary Criticism, Essays, Management, Marketing,

Medicine, Nursing, Dentistry, Philosophy, Psychology, Psychiatry, Social Sciences, Sociology
ISBN Prefix(es): 978-969-407
Showroom(s): 402 Rehman Centre, Zaibunisa St, Karachi 74400
Warehouse: 402 Rehman Centre, Zaibunisa St, Karachi 74400

Sang-e-Meel Publications+
25 Lower Mall (Shahrah-e-Pakistan), Lahore 54000
Tel: (042) 37220100; (042) 37228143 *Fax:* (042) 37245101
E-mail: smp@sangemeel.com
Web Site: www.sang-e-meel.com
Founded: 1962
Membership(s): Lahore Chamber of Commerce & Industry; Pakistan Publishers & Booksellers Association.
Subjects: Agriculture, Anthropology, Archaeology, Architecture & Interior Design, Art, Asian Studies, Biography, Memoirs, Criminology, Drama, Theater, Fiction, Health, Nutrition, History, Humor, Journalism, Literature, Literary Criticism, Essays, Poetry, Religion - Islamic, Social Sciences, Sociology, Travel & Tourism
ISBN Prefix(es): 978-969-35
Imprints: SMP

SMP, *imprint of* Sang-e-Meel Publications

Vanguard Books Ltd+
No 52-53, Main Guru Mangat Rd, Gulberg II, Lahore
Tel: (042) 5754276
E-mail: inquiry@vanguardbooks.com; sales@vanguardbooks.com
Web Site: www.vanguardbooks.com
Key Personnel
Chief Executive Officer & International Rights: Najam Sethi
Sales, Marketing & Publicity: Jugnu Mohsin
Founded: 1978
Membership(s): Pakistan Publishers & Booksellers Association.
Subjects: Agriculture, Art, Asian Studies, Astronomy, Biography, Memoirs, Business, Chemistry, Chemical Engineering, Cookery, Drama, Theater, Economics, Fiction, History, Law, Poetry, Regional Interests, Religion - Islamic, Sports, Athletics, Travel & Tourism
ISBN Prefix(es): 978-969-402
Number of titles published annually: 30 Print
Total Titles: 325 Print
Branch Office(s)
Mukhtar Plaza, Kayani Rd, Barakahu, Islamabad *Tel:* (051) 2304246; (051) 2304247
E-mail: vblisb@vanguardbooks.com
Distributor for Blackwell; Macmillan Press; Penguin Books (UK); Pluto Press; Routledge; I B Tauris; Zed Press
Foreign Rep(s): Curzon Press (UK); Zed Press (UK)
Showroom(s): Lok Virsa Bldg, Super Market, F-6 Markaz, Islamabad *Tel:* (051) 2270317; (051) 2270328 *E-mail:* vblisb@vanguardbooks.com

Panama

General Information

Capital: Panama
Language: Spanish (English widely used)
Religion: Roman Catholic
Population: 2.7 million
Bank Hours: 0800-1600 Monday-Friday; 0900-1200 Saturday
Shop Hours: 0900-1800 Monday-Saturday

Currency: 100 centismos = 1 balboa. US currency also used
Export/Import Information: No tariffs on books and advertising matter. No import licenses or exhange controls.
Copyright: UCC, Buenos Aires (see Copyright Conventions, pg viii)

EUPAN, *imprint of* Editorial Universitaria Carlos Manuel Gasteazoro

Focus Publications (Int) SA
PO Box 0819-06908, El Dorado
Tel: 225-6638 *Fax:* 225-0466
E-mail: focusint@cableonda.net; focusint507@gmail.com
Web Site: www.focuspublicationsint.com
Key Personnel
Publisher: Kenneth Jones
Founded: 1970
Subjects: Marketing, Travel & Tourism
ISBN Prefix(es): 978-958-95276

Editorial Universitaria Carlos Manuel Gasteazoro
c/o Universidad de Panama, Calle principal Manuel Espinosa Batista, Panama
Tel: 523-5174; 523-5173 *Fax:* 523-5172
Web Site: www.editorial.up.ac.pa
Key Personnel
Secretary General: Dr Miguel Angel Candanedo
E-mail: secretaria.general@up.ac.pa
Founded: 1969
Subjects: Architecture & Interior Design, Art, Biological Sciences, Education, Environmental Studies, Geography, Geology, Government, Political Science, History, Law, Literature, Literary Criticism, Essays, Medicine, Nursing, Dentistry, Philosophy, Poetry, Psychology, Psychiatry, Science (General), Social Sciences, Sociology, Environmental Science
ISBN Prefix(es): 978-9962-53
Total Titles: 250 Print
Imprints: EUPAN

Papua New Guinea

General Information

Capital: Port Moresby
Language: Tok Pisin, English and Hiri Motu (all official)
Religion: Predominantly Christian
Population: 4 million
Bank Hours: 0900-1400 Monday-Thursday; 0900-1700 Friday
Shop Hours: 0900-1800 Monday-Friday; 0900-1200 Saturday
Currency: 100 teoa = 1 kina
Export/Import Information: No tariff on books and advertising but import tax on non-educational books. No import license for books, but no obscene literature permitted.
Copyright: No copyright law

Melanesian Institute
PO Box 571, Goroka 441 EHP
Tel: 732 1777 *Fax:* 732 1214
E-mail: info@mi.org.pg; info1.emmai@gmail.com
Web Site: www.mi.org.pg
Key Personnel
Dir: Fr Geovanne Bustos *E-mail:* director@mi.org.pg
Publications Dept: Lorraine Basse
E-mail: lorraine.basse@mi.org.pg
Founded: 1970

Subjects: Anthropology, Religion - Catholic, Religion - Protestant, Religion - Other, Social Sciences, Sociology, Theology
ISBN Prefix(es): 978-9980-65

National Research Institute of Papua New Guinea
Goro-Kaeaga Rd & Waigani Dr, Port Moresby
Mailing Address: PO Box 5854, Boroko 111 NCD
Tel: 326 0061; 326 0300; 7031 1044 (cell); 7031 1045 (cell) *Fax:* 326 0213
Key Personnel
Dir: Dr Thomas Webster
Founded: 1975
Applied research & policy making.
Subjects: Anthropology, Criminology, Developing Countries, Economics, Education, Environmental Studies, Government, Political Science, Social Sciences, Sociology
ISBN Prefix(es): 978-9980-75
Number of titles published annually: 20 Print
Total Titles: 500 Print

Papua New Guinea Institute of Medical Research (PNGIMR)
PO Box 60, Goroka 441 EHP
Tel: 532 2800; 531 4200 *Fax:* 532 1998
E-mail: info@pngimr.org.pg
Web Site: www.pngimr.org.pg
Key Personnel
Dir: Prof Peter Siba
Deputy Dir, Science: Dr William Pomat
Deputy Dir, Corporate & Support Services: Samson Akunaii
Founded: 1968
Produces *PNG Bibliography on Medicine.*
Subjects: Anthropology, Medicine, Nursing, Dentistry, Social Sciences, Sociology
ISBN Prefix(es): 978-0-909531; 978-9980-71
Number of titles published annually: 1 Print
Branch Office(s)
PO Box 378, Madang 511 EHP *Tel:* 422 2909; 422 2962 *Fax:* 422 3289
PO Box 400, Maprik 533 ESP *Tel:* 458 1294; 458 1414 *Fax:* 458 1257
PO Box 7891, Port Moresby 121 NCD *Tel:* 325 7470 *Fax:* 325 4120

PNGIMR, see Papua New Guinea Institute of Medical Research (PNGIMR)

Summer Institute of Linguistics+
Subsidiary of SIL International
PO Box 418, Ukarumpa 444 EHP
Tel: 537-4431 *Fax:* 537-3507
E-mail: do-dlp@sil.org.pg
Web Site: www.pnglanguages.org
Founded: 1956
Subjects: Anthropology, Language Arts, Linguistics, Regional Interests, Papua New Guinea Studies
ISBN Prefix(es): 978-9980-0; 978-0-909456; 978-0-7263
Total Titles: 24,000 Print

University of Papua New Guinea Press & Bookshop
Division of University of Papua New Guinea
Administration Area, University of Papua New Guinea, Waigani Campus, Port Moresby 134 NCD
Mailing Address: PO Box 413, University Post Office 134 NCD
Tel: 3267675 *Fax:* 3267187 (university)
E-mail: upngbooks@gmail.com
Web Site: www.pngbuai.com/buybooks
Key Personnel
Manager, Bookshop & Publications: John Evans
Tel: 3267375
Founded: 1995

Unified bookselling, distribution & publishing venture. Books on & about Papua New Guinea in all subjects.
Subjects: Agriculture, Anthropology, Biography, Memoirs, Economics, Education, Fiction, History, Language Arts, Linguistics, Law, Literature, Literary Criticism, Essays, Medicine, Nursing, Dentistry, Regional Interests, Religion - Other, Science (General), Social Sciences, Sociology, Travel & Tourism
ISBN Prefix(es): 978-9980-84; 978-0-909975
Number of titles published annually: 20 Print
Total Titles: 300 Print; 10 CD-ROM
Imprints: UPNG Press
Foreign Rep(s): Masalai Press (T H Slone) (USA)

UPNG Press, *imprint of* University of Papua New Guinea Press & Bookshop

Paraguay

General Information

Capital: Asuncion
Language: Spanish & Guarani (both official)
Religion: Predominantly Roman Catholic
Population: 5.6 million
Bank Hours: 0930-1145 Monday-Friday
Shop Hours: 0900-2000 Monday-Saturday
Currency: Guarani
Export/Import Information: Member of Southern Cone Common Market (MERCOSUR); ALADI; GATT & WTO. Children's picture books and atlases are dutied, plus added tax and compensatory tax. Advertising catalogs subject to added tax compensatory tax. Additional taxes on all goods; also Consular fee. No import licenses required. Exchange controls; foreign exchange surcharge.
Copyright: UCC, Berne, Buenos Aires (see Copyright Conventions, pg viii)

Intercontinental Editora SA+
Caballero 270 c/Mcal Estigarribia, Asuncion
Tel: (021) 496 991; (021) 449 738 *Fax:* (021) 448 721
Web Site: www.libreriaintercontinental.com.py
Key Personnel
Dir: Sr Alejandro Gatti *E-mail:* agatti@ libreriaintercontinental.com.py
Founded: 1987
Subjects: Computer Science, Economics, Government, Political Science, History, Language Arts, Linguistics, Law, Literature, Literary Criticism, Essays, Parapsychology, Poetry, Self-Help
ISBN Prefix(es): 978-99925-41; 978-99925-59; 978-99925-72
Number of titles published annually: 50 Print
Total Titles: 600 Print

Peru

General Information

Capital: Lima
Language: Spanish, Quechua & Aymara (all official)
Religion: Predominantly Roman Catholic
Population: 22.8 million
Bank Hours: January-December 0900-1500 Monday-Friday
Shop Hours: 1000-1500 Monday- Friday
Currency: 100 centisimos = 1 new sol

Export/Import Information: Children's picture books and advertising matter dutied per kg plus VAT, sales tax applies on advertising matter. No freight tax on books, but there is a wholesaler's tax. No import licenses required. No exhange controls.
Copyright: UCC, Berne, Buenos Aires (see Copyright Conventions, pg viii)

Aprende Digital Norma, *imprint of* Carvajal Soluciones Educativas

Asociacion Editorial Bruno+
Av Arica 751, Brena, Lima 5
Tel: (01) 202 4747
E-mail: informes@editorialbruno.com.pe
Web Site: www.editorialbruno.com.pe; www. brunoeditorial.com.pe
Key Personnel
Dir: Miguel Luna Garcia *E-mail:* mluna@ editorialbruno.com.pe
General Manager: Federico Diaz Tineo *E-mail:* gerencia@editorialbruno.com.pe
Founded: 1950
Subjects: Education, Religion - Catholic
ISBN Prefix(es): 978-9972-01
Associate Companies: McGraw-Hill Interamericana, Mexico
Branch Office(s)
Av Ricardo Palma 108, Umacollo, Arequipa
Tel: (054) 274 519

Coleccion Buenas Noches, *imprint of* Carvajal Soluciones Educativas

Bulletin de l'Institut Francais d'Etudes Andines, *imprint of* Instituto Frances de Estudios Andinos (IFEA)

Cara y Cruz, *imprint of* Carvajal Soluciones Educativas

Carvajal Soluciones Educativas (Carvajal Educational Solutions)
Member of Grupo Carvajal SA
Avda Canaval y Moreira 345, San Isidro, Lima 27
Tel: (01) 710 30 00 *Fax:* (01) 710 30 00 (ext 51703)
E-mail: servicioalclientenorma@edicionesnorma. com
Web Site: www.edicionesnorma.com
ISBN Prefix(es): 978-9972-745
Imprints: Aprende Digital Norma; Coleccion Buenas Noches; Cara y Cruz; Educa Inventia; Fuera de Serie; Franklin la Tortuga; Greenwich; Golu; Editorial Norma; Sol y Luna; Torre de Papel Amarillo; Torre de Papel Azul; Coleccion Torre de Papel; Torre de Papel Naranja; Torre de Papel Rojo; Zona Libre

Catalogo, *imprint of* Ediciones PEISA Sac

Centro de la Mujer Peruana Flora Tristan (Peruvian Women's Centre Flora Tristan)
Parque Hernan Velarde N° 42, Lima 1
Tel: (01) 433-2000; (01) 433-0694; (01) 433-2765; (01) 433-1457 *Fax:* (01) 433-9500
E-mail: postmast@flora.org.pe
Web Site: www.flora.org.pe
Key Personnel
Executive Dir: Blanca Fernandez
Founded: 1979
Feminist institution. Specialize in issues on communication, development, feminism, gender, health, library, research, tell-stories, violence, women's rights, history, literature & poetry.
Subjects: Government, Political Science, Health, Nutrition, History, Literature, Literary Criticism, Essays, Poetry, Science (General), Social Sciences, Sociology, Women's Studies

ISBN Prefix(es): 978-9972-610
Number of titles published annually: 10 Print; 5 Online
Total Titles: 50 Print

Educa Inventia, *imprint of* Carvajal Soluciones Educativas

Fondo Editorial de la Pontificia Universidad Catolica del Peru
Avda Universitaria 1801, San Miguel, Lima 32
Tel: (01) 626 2650
E-mail: feditor@pucp.edu.pe
Web Site: www.fondoeditorial.pucp.edu.pe; www. pucp.edu.pe
Subjects: Anthropology, Archaeology, Art, Computer Science, Economics, Education, Engineering (General), Ethnicity, History, Language Arts, Linguistics, Law, Literature, Literary Criticism, Essays, Philosophy, Physical Sciences, Psychology, Psychiatry, Science (General), Social Sciences, Sociology, Theology
ISBN Prefix(es): 978-9972-42

Fondo Editorial Universidad de Lima+
Av Javier Prado, cuadra 46 s/n, Urb Monterrico, Lima 33
Tel: (01) 437-6767; (01) 436-0500 *Fax:* (01) 437-8066
E-mail: fondoeditorial@ulima.edu.pe
Web Site: www.ulima.edu.pe
Key Personnel
Executive Dir: Jose Valdizan Ayala
Founded: 1962
Subjects: Communications, Computer Science, Economics, Engineering (General), Film, Video, Finance, Journalism, Law, Management, Marketing, Photography, Psychology, Psychiatry, Radio, TV, Science (General)
ISBN Prefix(es): 978-84-89358; 978-9972-45
Number of titles published annually: 40 Print
Total Titles: 500 Print

Franklin la Tortuga, *imprint of* Carvajal Soluciones Educativas

Fuera de Serie, *imprint of* Carvajal Soluciones Educativas

Golu, *imprint of* Carvajal Soluciones Educativas

Greenwich, *imprint of* Carvajal Soluciones Educativas

Editorial Horizonte
Av Nicolas de Pierola 995, Lima 1
Tel: (01) 427-9364 *Fax:* (01) 427-4341
Founded: 1968
Subjects: Anthropology, Art, Economics, Education, History, Language Arts, Linguistics, Literature, Literary Criticism, Essays, Philosophy, Social Sciences, Sociology
ISBN Prefix(es): 978-84-89307; 978-9972-699
Associate Companies: Codice Ediciones, Casilla 2118, Lima 100

IEP, see Instituto de Estudios Peruanos (IEP)

IFEA, see Instituto Frances de Estudios Andinos (IFEA)

Instituto de Estudios Peruanos (IEP)+
Horacio Urteaga 694, Jesus Maria, Lima 11
Tel: (01) 3326194 *Fax:* (01) 3326173
E-mail: libreria@iep.org.pe
Web Site: www.iep.org.pe
Key Personnel
Dir General: Roxana Barrantes *E-mail:* roxbarrantes@iep.org.pe
Founded: 1964

Subjects: Anthropology, Archaeology, Developing Countries, Economics, Education, Ethnicity, Government, Political Science, Health, Nutrition, History, Social Sciences, Sociology, Technology, Women's Studies
ISBN Prefix(es): 978-9972-51

Instituto Frances de Estudios Andinos (IFEA)
Av Arequipa 4595, 2° piso, Miraflores, Lima 18
Tel: (01) 447-6070; (01) 243-6090 *Fax:* (01) 445-7650
E-mail: biblioteca@ifea.org.pe
Web Site: www.ifeanet.org
Key Personnel
Dir: Georges Lomne
Founded: 1948
Research institution.
Subjects: Agriculture, Anthropology, Archaeology, Earth Sciences, Geography, Geology, History, Language Arts, Linguistics, Social Sciences, Sociology
ISBN Prefix(es): 978-9972-623
Number of titles published annually: 15 Print
Total Titles: 4 E-Book
Imprints: Bulletin de l'Institut Francais d'Etudes Andines; Travaux de l'Institut Francais d'Etudes Andines

Los Libros Mas Pequenos del Mundo
Jr Los Pelitres 1784, Urb San Hilarion, Lima 36
Tel: (01) 459-8363 *Fax:* (01) 458-4590
E-mail: ventas@minibooks.com.pe
Web Site: www.minibooks.com.pe
Founded: 1970
Subjects: Astrology, Occult, Business, Health, Nutrition, Self-Help, Sports, Athletics, Travel & Tourism
ISBN Prefix(es): 978-9972-206; 978-9972-886; 978-9972-9970; 978-9972-9988; 978-612-4013
Foreign Rep(s): Latifa Ahmed Abderrahaman (Spain); Yuri Angeles Perez (Spain); Neptali Angulo Moya (Spain); Elias Berrezueta Berrezueta (Spain); Briceno Chaves Julio Alberto (Spain); Luis Alberto Briceno Chavez (Chile); Elva Vilma Briceno Polo (Argentina, Spain); Oscar Briceno Polo (Spain); Raul Briceno Polo (Spain); Lester Alberto Briceno Tordoya (USA); Ludy Oriely Briceno Tordoya (USA, Uruguay); Rebeca Caceres de Canete (USA); Caramel (USA); Carrion Vuele Marcelo Roman (Ecuador); Cerna Auero Tobias Ciro (Ecuador); Ciex Cautivo Importacao e Exportacao Ltda (Brazil); Circulo Mundial del Libro (Ecuador); Consorcio Ecuatoriano del Libro Cedelibro CIA Ltda (Ecuador); Alejandrina Diaz Rojas (Spain); Libreria Donatina (USA); Dreaming Books (Colombia); Libreria Espanola Cia Ltda (Ecuador); Euroamericana de Ediciones Corp (Puerto Rico); Exitos Ilimitados SA de CV (Mexico); Andres Sergio Garcia Garin (Spain); Victoria Garin (Spain); Marcial Iza Chicaiza (Ecuador); Editorial Juridica Multilibro (Bolivia); Libreria Juridica Selecta (Ecuador); Angelica Lange de Loayza (Ecuador); Libro en Su Casa (Paraguay); Libreria y Papeleria LYM (Colombia); Wilson Rodrigo Meza Salazar (Libreria Mewil Promociones) (Ecuador); Mini Books World (USA); Morevalue Inc (USA); Mosca HNOS SA (Uruguay); Rosas Moscoso Hernan (Ecuador); Luis Alberto Nanez Meza (Bolivia, Costa Rica, Cuba, Dominican Republic, El Salvador, Guatemala, Honduras, Nicaragua, Panama); Nur Libros/Los Libros Mas Pequenos del Mundo (Mexico); Ernesto Olmos Morales (Spain); Paco Comercial Industrial (Ecuador); Simon Pena Vega (Ecuador); Mauro Benitez Pereira Das Neves (Uruguay); Publicaciones Nuevo Extremo SA (Chile); Florencio Rodriguez Gil (Spain); Libreria San Antonio (Honduras); Carlos Francisco Sanchez Ltda (CAFSA Ltda) (Chile); Libreria Shalom (USA); Juan Ramon Sosa Pena (Spain); Tello's

Professional Service (USA); Bertha Cecilia Unda Camacho (Ecuador); Paulo Cesar Zelada Delgado (Colombia)

Editorial Lima 2000 SAC
Av Arequipa 2625, Lince, Lima 14
Tel: (01) 440-3486 *Fax:* (01) 440-3480
E-mail: info@lima2000.com
Web Site: www.lima2000.com.pe
Founded: 1980
Subjects: Cartography
ISBN Prefix(es): 978-9972-654

Lluvia Editores SRL+
Av Inca Garcilaso de la Vega 1976, Oficina 501J, Piso 5, Lima
Tel: (01) 332-6641
Key Personnel
Contact: Esteban Quiroz Cisneros
Founded: 1978
Subjects: Literature, Literary Criticism, Essays
ISBN Prefix(es): 978-9972-627

Editorial Norma, *imprint of* Carvajal Soluciones Educativas

Grupo Editorial Norma SAC, see Carvajal Soluciones Educativas

Palestra Editores SAC
Plaza de La Bandera N° 125, Lima 21
Tel: (01) 637-8902; (01) 637-8903
E-mail: palestra@palestraeditores.com
Web Site: www.palestraeditores.com
Founded: 1996
Subjects: Law
ISBN Prefix(es): 978-9972-733

Ediciones PEISA Sac
Av Las Camelias 511, Oficina 601, San Isidro, Lima 27
Tel: (01) 2215988; (01) 2215992 *Fax:* (01) 4425906
E-mail: editor@peisa.com.pe
Web Site: www.peisa.com.pe
Key Personnel
Mng Dir: German Coronado Vallenas
E-mail: gcoronado@peisa.com.pe
Founded: 1968
Subjects: Foreign Countries
ISBN Prefix(es): 978-9972-40; 978-9972-721
Imprints: Catalogo
Distributor for Aranco (Spain); Concorcio Natuzart (Spain); Folio (Spain); Tres Torres (Spain)

Sol y Luna, *imprint of* Carvajal Soluciones Educativas

Sur Casa de Estudios del Socialismo
Av Brasil 1329 dep 201 Jesus Maria, Lima 11
Tel: 996262884 (cell)
E-mail: casasur@casasur.org
Web Site: www.casasur.org
Key Personnel
Dir: Gonzalo Portocarrero
Executive Coordinator: Nelson Manrique
Founded: 1986
Subjects: Anthropology, Developing Countries, Economics, History, Literature, Literary Criticism, Essays, Philosophy, Social Sciences, Sociology
ISBN Prefix(es): 978-9972-619

Tarea Asociacion de Publicaciones Educativas+
Parque Osores 161, Pueblo Libre, Lima 21
Tel: (01) 424 0997 *Fax:* (01) 332 7404
E-mail: postmast@tarea.org.pe
Web Site: tarea.org.pe

Key Personnel
President: Liliam Teresa Hidalgo Collazos
E-mail: lhidalgo@tarea.org.pe
Executive Dir: Julio Cesar del Valle Ramos
Founded: 1974
Subjects: Education
ISBN Prefix(es): 978-9972-618

Torre de Papel Amarillo, *imprint of* Carvajal Soluciones Educativas

Torre de Papel Azul, *imprint of* Carvajal Soluciones Educativas

Coleccion Torre de Papel, *imprint of* Carvajal Soluciones Educativas

Torre de Papel Naranja, *imprint of* Carvajal Soluciones Educativas

Torre de Papel Rojo, *imprint of* Carvajal Soluciones Educativas

Travaux de l'Institut Francais d'Etudes Andines, *imprint of* Instituto Frances de Estudios Andinos (IFEA)

Universidad de San Martin de Porres
Av Las Calandrias 151-291, Santa Anita, Lima 43
Tel: (01) 3620064
E-mail: fondoeditorial@usmp.pe
Web Site: www.usmp.edu.pe/fondo_editorial
Key Personnel
President & Dir: Juan De la Puente Mejia
General Editor: Luis Suarez Berenguela
Subjects: Architecture & Interior Design, Economics, Engineering (General), Law, Medicine, Nursing, Dentistry, Psychology, Psychiatry, Science (General), Travel & Tourism, Humanities
ISBN Prefix(es): 978-9972-607; 978-612-4088

Universidad Nacional Mayor de San Marcos, Fondo Editorial
Jr German Amezaga S/N, Biblioteca Central 4° piso, Ciudad Universitaria, Puerta N° 4, Lima
Tel: (01) 619-7000
E-mail: fondoedit@unmsm.edu.pe; fondo.editorial.unmsm@gmail.com
Web Site: biblioteca.unmsm.edu.pe/fondoeditorial/index.asp
Key Personnel
Dir: Emma Patricia Victorio Canovas
Founded: 1952
Subjects: Engineering (General), Law, Literature, Literary Criticism, Essays, Medicine, Nursing, Dentistry, Science (General)
ISBN Prefix(es): 978-9972-46
Bookshop(s): Av Nicolas de Pierola 1222, Lima 1

Universidade Peruana de Ciencias Aplicada (UPC)
Prolongacion Primavera 2390, Monterrico, Lima 33
Tel: (01) 313-3333 *Fax:* (01) 313-3344
E-mail: fondoeditorial@upc.edu.pe
Web Site: www.upc.edu.pe
Founded: 1998
Subjects: Architecture & Interior Design, Communications, Economics, Mathematics, Medicine, Nursing, Dentistry, Music, Dance, Psychology, Psychiatry, Humanities
ISBN Prefix(es): 978-9972-676

UPC, see Universidade Peruana de Ciencias Aplicada (UPC)

YachayPucllayPacha
Alameda Las Palmas 155, La Encantada, Chorillos, Lima 09
Tel: (02) 54 05 42

Web Site: yachaypucllaypacha.pe
Key Personnel
Founder: Carmen Pachas Pielago *E-mail:* carmen.
pachas.pielago@gmail.com
Subjects: Animals, Pets, Cookery, Culture, Nature

Zona Libre, *imprint of* Carvajal Soluciones
Educativas

Philippines

General Information

Capital: Quezon City
Language: Filipino (based on Tagalog) is the na-
tive national language. English widely used.
Nine other major languages of the Malayo-
Polynesian group, and about 60 other languages, are also spoken
Religion: Predominantly Roman Catholic and
some Islamic
Population: 67.1 million
Bank Hours: 0900-1600 Monday-Friday
Shop Hours: Vary. Many open 0900-1200, 1400-
1930 Monday-Saturday (some close 1730;
some open Sunday)
Currency: 100 centavos = 1 Philippine peso
Export/Import Information: Duty on books except
those which are philosophical, historical, economic, scientific, technical or vocational, approved by Department of Education for use of
certain institutions (not exceeding 10 copies for
an institution, or two for an individual) or for
encouragement of sciences or fine arts; no tariffs on Bibles and similar religious books. No
duty on advertising matter. No import licenses,
but no obscene or immoral literature permitted.
Release certificate issued on behalf of Central
Bank required to clear goods. Imports subject
to sales tax. No formal exchange controls but
most imports need Letter of Credit (over $100
in any month, for example).
Copyright: UCC (see Copyright Conventions, pg
viii)

Abiva Publishing House Inc+
851G Araneta Ave, 1113 Quezon City
Tel: (02) 7120245; (02) 7406603 *Fax:* (02)
7120486
E-mail: info@abiva.com.ph
Web Site: www.abiva.com.ph
Key Personnel
National Sales Manager: Joseph de Mesa
E-mail: jdemesa@abiva.com.ph
SRA Manager: Covina Belen *E-mail:* covs_sra@
abiva.com.ph
Founded: 1936
Membership(s): Book Development Association
of the Philippines (BDAP); National Book De-
velopment Board (NBDB); Philippine Book
Publishing Development Federation (Philbook);
Philippine Educational Publishers Association
(PEPA); Publishers Association of the Philip-
pines Inc (PAPI).
Subjects: Education, History, Religion - Other,
Science (General)
ISBN Prefix(es): 978-971-553
Total Titles: 1 CD-ROM; 1 Audio
Subsidiaries: ACG Asian Tradelinks Inc; Hiyas
Press
Branch Office(s)
2/F, Cebu Holdings Cente, Cebu Business Park,
6000 Cebu City
127 MacArthur Highway, Matina, 8000 Davao
City
Distributor for McGraw-Hill Education Editorial
Edinumen

ADB, see Asian Development Bank (ADB)

Anvil Publishing Inc+
Quad Alpha Centrum Bldg, 7th floor, 125 Pioneer
St, 1550 Mandaluyong City
Tel: (02) 4774752; (02) 4774755; (02) 4774756;
(02) 4774757 *Fax:* (02) 7471622
E-mail: publishing@anvilpublishing.com;
anvilsalesonline@anvilpublishing.com
Web Site: www.anvilpublishing.com
Key Personnel
Marketing Manager: Gwenn Galvez
Publishing Manager: Karina A Bolasco
Founded: 1990
Also acts as wholesaler & distributor of paper-
backs & tradebooks from the UK & USA.
Subjects: Art, Cookery, Crafts, Games, Hobbies,
Fiction, Gardening, Plants, Health, Nutrition,
History, How-to, Humor, Language Arts, Lin-
guistics, Law, Literature, Literary Criticism,
Essays, Mysteries, Suspense, Photography, Re-
ligion - Catholic, Romance, Science Fiction,
Fantasy, Self-Help, Travel & Tourism, Western
Fiction, Women's Studies
ISBN Prefix(es): 978-971-27
Number of titles published annually: 150 Print
Total Titles: 600 Print
Parent Company: National Book Store Inc
Associate Companies: Megastrat Inc
Shipping Address: 8007-B Pioneer St, Brgy,
Kapitolyo, 1600 Pasig City *Tel:* (02) 637-
5692; (02) 637-3621 *Fax:* (02) 637-6084
E-mail: anvilsales@eudoramail.com
Warehouse: 8007-B Pioneer St, Brgy, Kapitolyo,
1600 Pasig City *Tel:* (02) 637-5692; (02) 637-
3621 *Fax:* (02) 637-6084 *E-mail:* anvilsales@
eudoramail.com

Asian Development Bank (ADB)
6 ADB Ave, 1550 Mandaluyong City
Tel: (02) 632-4444 *Fax:* (02) 636-2649; (02) 636-
2444
E-mail: adbpub@adb.org
Web Site: www.adb.org/publications
Key Personnel
Dir, Dept External Relations: Omana Nair
Founded: 1966
Subjects: Agriculture, Economics, Education, En-
ergy, Health, Nutrition, Management
ISBN Prefix(es): 978-971-561; 978-92-9254
Foreign Rep(s): Asiatype Distribution Inc (ADI)
(Philippines); CV Ada Utama (Indonesia);
Everest Media International Services (P) Ltd
(Nepal); Far Eastern Booksellers (Nobuyuki
Namekawa) (Japan); Hong Kong Book Cen-
tre Ltd (Mandy Ho) (China, Hong Kong);
Lake House Bookshop (Pvt) Ltd (Miles Bo-
hier) (Sri Lanka); MDC Publishers Printers
Sdn Bhd (Ahmad Hussein) (Malaysia); Midas
Centre (Bangladesh); Press International Pvt
Ltd (Nepal); Renouf Publishing Co Ltd (Gor-
don Grahame) (Canada); Select Books Pte Ltd
(Chris Tevar) (Singapore); Tmecca Korea Inc
(T J Kim) (Korea)

Ateneo de Manila University Press+
Bellarmine Hall, ADMU Campus, Katipunan Ave,
Loyola Heights, 1108 Quezon City
Tel: (02) 426-5984; (02) 426-6001 (ext 4613)
Fax: (02) 426-5909
E-mail: unipress@admu.edu.ph
Web Site: www.ateneopress.org; www.ateneo.edu
Key Personnel
Dir: Rica Bolipata-Santos
Head of Publications: Cristina G Castro
Founded: 1972
Membership(s): Book Development Association
of the Philippines; International Association of
Scholarly Publishers.
Subjects: Anthropology, Archaeology, Architec-
ture & Interior Design, Asian Studies, Behav-
ioral Sciences, Biography, Memoirs, Drama,

Theater, Economics, Education, Environmental
Studies, Fiction, Government, Political Science,
History, Literature, Literary Criticism, Essays,
Philosophy, Poetry, Psychology, Psychiatry, Re-
ligion - Catholic, Social Sciences, Sociology,
Theology, Women's Studies, Social Sciences
ISBN Prefix(es): 978-971-550
Number of titles published annually: 25 Print
Total Titles: 150 Print
Distributed by University of Hawaii Press

Bestseller, *imprint of* Precious Pages Corp (PPC)

Bookman Inc+
2/F Bookman Bldg, 373 Quezon Ave, 1114 Que-
zon City
Tel: (02) 712-4813; (02) 712-4868; (02) 712-3587
Key Personnel
President: Lina P Enriquez
Founded: 1945
Also printer.
Subjects: Education, English as a Second Lan-
guage, Mathematics, Nonfiction (General), Sci-
ence (General)
ISBN Prefix(es): 978-971-712
Associate Companies: Missionbook Publishing
Inc, Bookman Bldg, Mezzanine floor, 375 Que-
zon Ave, 1114 Quezon City *Tel:* (02) 712-4818
Fax: (02) 712-4843

Bookman Printing & Publishing House Inc, see
Bookman Inc

The Bookmark Inc+
264 Pablo Ocampo Sr Ave, San Antonio Village,
1203 Makati City
Tel: (02) 8958061 *Fax:* (02) 8970824
E-mail: bookmark@
bookmarkthefilipinobookstore.com;
bookmark1945@gmail.com
Web Site: www.bookmarkthefilipinobookstore.com
Key Personnel
President: Bienvenido A Tan, Jr
General Manager: Dr Anna Maria Tan-Delfin
Founded: 1945
Membership(s): Book Development Association
of the Philippines (BDAP).
Subjects: Art, Child Care & Development, Cook-
ery, Environmental Studies, Government, Polit-
ical Science, Health, Nutrition, History, Math-
ematics, Music, Dance, Nonfiction (General),
Publishing & Book Trade Reference, Religion
- Catholic, Religion - Other, Science (General),
Self-Help, Sports, Athletics, Travel & Tourism,
Ecology, Fitness, Mother Tongue, Social Stud-
ies
ISBN Prefix(es): 978-971-569
Warehouse: Brgy Uno General Malvar St, Santo
Tomas, 1203 Batangas, Makati City, Warehouse
Manager: Romulo R Riso *Tel:* (043) 7783723
Fax: (043) 7783725

Don Bosco Press Inc+
Don Bosco Compound, Antonio Arnaiz Ave, Cor-
ner of Chino Roces Ave, 1260 Makati City,
Metro Manila
Tel: (02) 816-1519; (02) 892-1888
E-mail: info@donboscopress.ph
Web Site: www.donboscopress.ph
Key Personnel
Chief Finance Officer: Gerardo Enginco
Founded: 1979
Membership(s): Philippine Educational Publishers
Association (PEPA).
Subjects: Communications, Computer Science,
Earth Sciences, Human Relations, Language
Arts, Linguistics, Literature, Literary Criti-
cism, Essays, Mathematics, Physics, Religion
- Catholic, Science (General), Social Sciences,
Sociology, Technology
ISBN Prefix(es): 978-971-522
Book Club(s): Philippine Bookfair Association;
National Book Development Board

Cinderella, *imprint of* Precious Pages Corp (PPC)

Claretian Communications Foundation Inc+
8 Mayumi St, UP, 1101 Diliman, Quezon City
Mailing Address: PO Box 4, 1101 Diliman, Quezon City
Tel: (02) 921-3984 *Fax:* (02) 921-7429
E-mail: ccfi@claretianpublications.com
Web Site: www.claretianpublications.com
Key Personnel
Executive Dir, Rights & Permissions: Fr Dennis Tamayo
Founded: 1983
Subjects: Biblical Studies, Environmental Studies, Law, Theology, Women's Studies
ISBN Prefix(es): 978-971-501
Bookshop(s): Claretian Publications (CP) Bookstore *Tel:* (02) 924-6835

De La Salle University-Dasmarinas+
Student Publications Off, Gregoria Montoya Hall, Room 115, 4115 Dasmarinas, Cavite
Tel: (046) 416-4531 (ext 3122)
Web Site: www.dlsud.edu.ph
Key Personnel
Dir: Ma Luisa A Ongcol *E-mail:* maongcol@dlsud.edu.ph
Founded: 1983
Membership(s): International Association of Scholarly Publishers.
Subjects: Asian Studies, Business, Education, Fiction, Literature, Literary Criticism, Essays, Philosophy, Poetry, Religion - Catholic
ISBN Prefix(es): 978-971-92082

De La Salle University Publishing House (DLSUPH)
Yuchengco Hall, Room 601, 2401 Taft Ave, 1004 Manila
Tel: (02) 524-4611 (loc 271) *Fax:* (02) 523-4281
E-mail: dlsupublishinghouse@dlsu.edu.ph; dlsupublishinghouse@gmail.com
Web Site: www.dlsu.edu.ph/offices/publishing-house/
Key Personnel
Executive Publisher: Dr David Jonathan Y Bayot
Administrative Assistant: Joanne T Castanares
ISBN Prefix(es): 978-971-555

Easy to Learn Books, *imprint of* Lampara Publishing House Inc

The First Time Ever I Saw Your Face, *imprint of* Precious Pages Corp (PPC)

Gems, *imprint of* Precious Pages Corp (PPC)

Illigan Institute of Technology, see Mindanao State University - Illigan Institute of Technology

Inspirasyon, *imprint of* Precious Pages Corp (PPC)

International Rice Research Institute (IRRI)
Los Banos, Laguna
Mailing Address: DAPO Box 7777, 1301 Metro Manila
Tel: (02) 580 5600; (02) 845 0563 *Fax:* (02) 580 5699; (02) 845 0606
E-mail: info@irri.org
Web Site: irri.org
Key Personnel
Dir General: Robert S Zeigler
Founded: 1960
A nonprofit agricultural research & training institute established to improve the well-being of present generations of rice farmers & consumers, particularly with low incomes.

Membership(s): Consultative Group on International Agricultural Research (CGIAR).
Subjects: Agriculture
ISBN Prefix(es): 978-971-22
Imprints: IRRI

IRRI, *imprint of* International Rice Research Institute (IRRI)

IRRI, see International Rice Research Institute (IRRI)

JC Palabay Enterprises Inc+
67 General Ordonez St, Marikina Heights, 1800 Marikina City, Metro Manila
Tel: (02) 9424512 *Fax:* (02) 9424513
E-mail: mely@jcpalabay.com; palabaydev@gmail.com
Web Site: jcpalabay.com
Key Personnel
President: Jescie L Palabay
Founded: 1974
Also importer of science laboratory equipment & globes.
Subjects: Journalism
ISBN Prefix(es): 978-971-13
Associate Companies: Four J Arts; Instructional Material Council, Meralco Ave, Pasig City; Mhelle L Publications

Jewels, *imprint of* Precious Pages Corp (PPC)

Lampara Books, *imprint of* Lampara Publishing House Inc

Lampara Publishing House Inc
83 Sgt E Rivera St, San Francisco del Monte Brgy Manresa, 1115 Quezon City
Tel: (02) 367-6222 *Fax:* (02) 367-6222
E-mail: inquiry@lamparabooks.com
Web Site: www.lamparabooks.com.ph
Key Personnel
Publisher: Segundo Matias, Jr; Richard Reynante
ISBN Prefix(es): 978-971-518
Imprints: Easy to Learn Books; Lampara Books

Last Trip, *imprint of* Precious Pages Corp (PPC)

Logos Publications Inc+
Catholic Trade Bldg, 1916 Oroquieta St, 1000 Santa Cruz, Manila
Tel: (02) 7111323 *Fax:* (02) 7322736
E-mail: logospublications@yahoo.com.ph
Key Personnel
Dir: Fr Carlos Maria De Guzman, Jr
Production Officer: Josephine S Sarmiento
Founded: 1987
Subjects: Business, Communications, Education, Religion - Other
ISBN Prefix(es): 978-971-510
Total Titles: 5 Audio
Parent Company: Society of the Divine Word

Love & Magic, *imprint of* Precious Pages Corp (PPC)

Love Cafe, *imprint of* Precious Pages Corp (PPC)

Marren Publishing House Inc
G F Marren Bldg, 1157 Quezon Ave, 1003 Quezon City
Tel: (02) 3728939 *Fax:* (02) 3728940
Subjects: Cookery, Fiction
ISBN Prefix(es): 978-971-649
Subsidiaries: MRE Trading Inc

MBI, see Mutual Books Inc

Men in Blue, *imprint of* Precious Pages Corp (PPC)

Mindanao State University - Illigan Institute of Technology
Andres Bonifacio Ave, Tibanga, 9200 Iligan City
Tel: (063) 2214071; (063) 2232343; (063) 4921173 *Fax:* (063) 2233794
E-mail: ovcre@g.msuiit.edu.ph
Web Site: www.msuiit.edu.ph
Key Personnel
Vice Chancellor for Research & Extension: Jinky B Bornales, PhD *E-mail:* jinky.bornales@msuiit.edu.ph
Subjects: Art, Education, Engineering (General), Mathematics, Science (General), Social Sciences, Sociology, Technology
ISBN Prefix(es): 978-971-8708

Modern Girl, *imprint of* Precious Pages Corp (PPC)

Mutual Books Inc+
Jovan Condominium, Room 208, 600 Shaw Blvd, Mandaluyong City
Tel: (02) 532-9656; (02) 534-2664 *Fax:* (02) 534-2665
Web Site: mutualbooks.com
Founded: 1959
Subjects: Accounting, Business, Computer Science, Economics, Management, Mathematics
ISBN Prefix(es): 978-971-587
Associate Companies: Alfredo S Nicdao Jr Inc
Shipping Address: PO Box 245, Greenhills, San Juan, 1502 Metro Manila

My Love My Hero, *imprint of* Precious Pages Corp (PPC)

My Lovely Bride, *imprint of* Precious Pages Corp (PPC)

National Book Store Inc (NBSI)
125 Pioneer St, 1550 Mandaluyong City
Tel: (02) 631-8061
E-mail: customerservice@nationalbookstore.com.ph
Web Site: www.nationalbookstore.com.ph
Founded: 1945
Firm reprints over 300 titles annually for foreign publishers.
Subjects: Art, Fiction, Health, Nutrition, How-to, Music, Dance, Nonfiction (General), Religion - Other, Travel & Tourism
ISBN Prefix(es): 978-971-08

National Historical Commission of the Philippines
TM Kalaw St, 1000 Ermita, Manila
Tel: (02) 2547482
E-mail: records@nhcp.gov.ph; rphd@nhcp.gov.ph
Web Site: nhcp.gov.ph
Key Personnel
Chief, Research, Publications & Heraldry Division: Alvin Alcid *Tel:* (02) 2547482 ext 123
Subjects: Biography, Memoirs, History
ISBN Prefix(es): 978-971-538

National Museum of the Philippines
(Pambansang Museo ng Pilipinas)
Padre Burgos Dr, Rizal Park, 1000 Manila
Tel: (02) 527 12 15 *Fax:* (02) 527 03 06
E-mail: nationalmuseumph@yahoo.com
Web Site: www.nationalmuseum.gov.ph
Key Personnel
Dir: Jeremy Barns
Founded: 1901
The National Museum collects, identifies, preserves & exhibits the country's rich cultural heritage.
Also publishes guidebooks, monographs & newsletters.

Subjects: Anthropology, Archaeology, Art, Biological Sciences, Geography, Geology, Natural History, Botanical, Visual Arts, Zoological Collections
ISBN Prefix(es): 978-971-567
Total Titles: 50 Print; 5 CD-ROM; 1 Online; 1 E-Book; 2 Audio

NBSI, see National Book Store Inc (NBSI)

New Day Publishers+
11-C Tierra Evelina Homes, 1128 Quezon City
Mailing Address: PO Box 1167, 1100 Quezon City
Tel: (02) 928-8046; (02) 404-0934 *Fax:* (02) 791-8610
E-mail: info@newdaypublishers.com; sales@newdaypublishers.com; marketing@newdaypublishers.com; editorial@newdaypublishers.com
Web Site: www.newdaypublishers.com
Key Personnel
Executive Dir: Mrs Bezalie Bautista Uc-Kung
  E-mail: bezalie@newdaypublishers.com
Founded: 1969
Membership(s): Book Development Association of the Philippines; Book Exporters Association of the Philippines; National Book Development Board; World Association for Christian Communication.
Subjects: Anthropology, Asian Studies, Behavioral Sciences, Biblical Studies, Biography, Memoirs, Business, Career Development, Communications, Cookery, Economics, Education, Ethnicity, Fiction, History, How-to, Human Relations, Humor, Labor, Industrial Relations, Literature, Literary Criticism, Essays, Management, Marketing, Nonfiction (General), Philosophy, Poetry, Religion - Catholic, Religion - Protestant, Romance, Science Fiction, Fantasy, Self-Help, Theology
ISBN Prefix(es): 978-971-10
Number of titles published annually: 20 Print
Total Titles: 500 Print

Pambansang Komisyong Pangkasaysayan ng Pilipinas, see National Historical Commission of the Philippines

PHR Classics, *imprint of* Precious Pages Corp (PPC)

Precious Hearts Romances, *imprint of* Precious Pages Corp (PPC)

Precious Pages Corp (PPC)
83 Sgt E Rivera St, San Francisco del Monte Brgy Manresa, 1115 Quezon City
Tel: (02) 414-6188 *Fax:* (02) 367-6222
E-mail: admin@phr.com.ph; info@preciousshop.com.ph
Web Site: www.phr.com.ph; www.preciousshop.com.ph; www.facebook.com/PreciousPagesCorp/
Founded: 1992
Membership(s); Book Development Association of the Philippines Inc; Book Exporter Association of the Philippines Inc.
Subjects: Cookery, Mysteries, Suspense, Romance
ISBN Prefix(es): 978-971-02; 978-971-609; 978-971-627
Number of titles published annually: 600 Print
Associate Companies: Lampara Publishing House Inc
Imprints: Bestseller; Cinderella; The First Time Ever I Saw Your Face; Gems; Inspirasyon; Jewels; Last Trip; Love & Magic; Love Cafe; Men in Blue; Modern Girl; My Love My Hero; My Lovely Bride; PHR Classics; Precious Hearts Romances; Working Girl

RBSI, see REX Book Store Inc

REX Book Store Inc
Member of The REX Group of Companies
Rex Knowledge Center, 109 Sen M Cuenco Sr, 1114 Quezon City
Tel: (02) 857-7777
E-mail: wecare@rexpublishing.com.ph
Web Site: www.rexpublishing.com.ph
Key Personnel
Chief Operating Officer: Don Timothy I Buhain
President: Dominador D Buhain
  E-mail: ddbuhain@rexpublishing.com.ph
Marketing Dir: Jeanne Marie Fontelera-Tordesillas
Founded: 1950
Membership(s): Asia/Pacific Publishers Association; International Publishers Association.
Subjects: Accounting, Agriculture, Anthropology, Archaeology, Behavioral Sciences, Biological Sciences, Business, Child Care & Development, Cookery, Criminology, Economics, Education, Environmental Studies, Finance, History, Human Relations, Labor, Industrial Relations, Law, Maritime, Marketing, Mathematics, Parapsychology, Physics, Psychology, Psychiatry, Science (General), Social Sciences, Sociology, Theology, Travel & Tourism
ISBN Prefix(es): 978-971-23
Number of titles published annually: 100 Print
Branch Office(s)
REX Book Store Cubao, Unit 10 UGF Dona Consolacion Bldg, Gen Santos Ave, Araneta Center, Cubao, Quezon City *Tel:* (02) 911-1070
REX Book Store Angeles, Unit H, JMS Bldg, McArthur Hi-way, Brgy Salapungan, Angeles City *Tel:* (045) 887-5371
REX Book Store Bacolod, No 28 Barangay-36 Purok Immaculada, Quezon Ave, Bacolod City *Tel:* (034) 707-5825
REX Hall Baguio, Upper Gen Luna cor A Bonifacio St, 2600 Baguio City *Tel:* (074) 422-0574
REX Book Store Batanes, L Lopez St, Kayvaluganan, Basco, Batanes *Tel:* (02) 681-9085; (02) 330-4937
REX Book Store, Brgy Salong, National Hi-way, Calapan City, Oriental Mindoro *Tel:* (043) 288-1650
REX Book Store Cavite, Block 4, Lot 20 Don Gregorio Heights 2 Zone, 1-A Aguinaldo Hi-way, Dasmarinas Cavite, Cavite *Tel:* (046) 416-1824
REX Book Store Cebu, 11 Sanciangko St, Cebu City *Tel:* (032) 254-6773; (032) 416-9684; (032) 505-4313
REX Book Store Davao, 156-A CM Recto St, Davao City *Tel:* (082) 300-5422; (082) 305-5772; (082) 221-0272
REX Book Store General Santos, Aparinte St, Dadiangas Heights, General Santos City *Tel:* (083) 304-8512; (083) 554-7102
REX Book Store Iloilo, No 75 Brgy San Isidro Lopez-Jaena, Jaro, Iloilo City *Tel:* (033) 329-0332; (033) 329-0336
REX Book Store Legaspi, Unit 6, 3rd floor, A Bichara Silverscreen, Legazpi City, Albay *Tel:* (052) 480-2244
REX Book Store Makati, Unit UG-2, Star Centrum Bldg, Sen Gil Puyat Ave, Makati City *Tel:* (02) 818-5363; (02) 893-3744
REX Book Store Rockwell, Ateneo Professional School, 1st floor, Rockwell Center, Bel-Air, Makati City
REX Book Store Morayta, 856 Nicanor Reyes Sr St, Sampaloc, Manila *Tel:* (02) 736-0169; (02) 736-4191; (02) 733-6746
REX Book Store Recto, 161-65 Freedom Bldg, C M Recto Ave, Sampaloc, Manila *Tel:* (02) 522-4521; (02) 522-4305; (02) 522-4107; (02) 733-8637
REX Book Store Naga, 1-1A Geronimo Bldg, Barlin St, Sta Cruz, Naga City *Tel:* (054) 811-6878

REX Book Store Ortigas, EC-02D East Tower, Ground floor, Philippine Stock Exchange Condominium (Tektite Tower) Ortigas, Pasig City
REX Book Store Tacloban, Brgy 78 Marasbaras, Tacloban City *Tel:* (053) 323-8976; (053) 523-1784
REX Book Store Tuguerarao, 10 Arellano Ext St, Barangay Ugac Sur, Tuguerarao, Cagayan *Tel:* (078) 844-8072
REX Book Store Urdaneta, Zone 6, Pinmaludpod, Urdaneta City, Pangasinan *Tel:* (075) 568-3975
REX Book Store Zamboanga, San Francisco Loop, Mayor Agan Ave, Camino Nuevo, Zamboanga City *Tel:* (088) 858-6775; (088) 309-5881
Book Club(s): Phil Educational Publishers Association, Contact: Dominador D Buhain

Saint Mary's Publishing Corp+
10/F Unit 1006 Park Trade Centre Centre, 1716 Investment Dr, Madrigal Business Park, Ayala Alabang, Muntilupa City
Tel: (02) 822 3543; (02) 823 0012; (02) 556 7312 *Fax:* (02) 555 1856
E-mail: smpc@smpc.com.ph; corp@smpc.com.ph
Web Site: www.smpc.com.ph
Key Personnel
President: Jerry Vicente S Catabijan
Administration: Joseph H Sebua
Editorial: Mary Rozelle N Amadure
Sales Operations: May J Catabijan
Founded: 1995
Membership(s): Book Development Association of the Philippines (BDAP); Children's Literature Association of the Philippines (CLAPI); Philippine Educational Publishers Association (PEPA).
Subjects: Economics, Education, English as a Second Language, Geography, Geology, History, Language Arts, Linguistics, Mathematics, Science (General), Social Sciences, Sociology
ISBN Prefix(es): 978-971-509

SIBS Publishing House Inc
Member of Sibal group of companies
Phoenix Bldg, 927 Quezon Ave, Quezon City
Tel: (02) 376 4041 *Toll Free Tel:* 800-1-888-7427 *Fax:* (02) 376 4034
Web Site: www.sibs.com.ph
Founded: 1996
Membership(s): International Publishers Association; Philippine Educational Publishers Association.
Subjects: Art, Biological Sciences, Economics, Education, English as a Second Language, Environmental Studies, History, Journalism, Language Arts, Linguistics, Literature, Literary Criticism, Essays, Mathematics, Nonfiction (General), Religion - Other, Science (General), Social Sciences, Sociology, Christian Living Education, Civics & Culture, English, Filipino, Preschool Books - Reading, Language, Math & Art, Values Education
ISBN Prefix(es): 978-971-791
Branch Office(s)
Mayor Maximo V Patalinghug Ave, Barangay Pajo, 6015 Lapu-Lapu City *Tel:* (032) 340-6809 *Fax:* (032) 340-6808

Silsilah Publication
137 Gov Alvarez St, Buenavista St, 7000 Zamboanga City
Tel: (062) 991-5663 *Fax:* (062) 983-0952
E-mail: silsilahdialogue@gmail.com
Web Site: www.silsilahdialogue.com
Key Personnel
Dir: Aminda E Sano
Subjects: Inspirational, Spirituality, Religion - Other
ISBN Prefix(es): 978-971-31

Sinag-Tala Publishers Inc+
GMA Loubel Plaza, 6th floor, C Roces Ave, Corner Bagtikan St, San Antonio Village, 1203 Makati City
Tel: (02) 861-7084; (02) 897-1161; (02) 897-1162
Fax: (02) 896-9626
E-mail: sinagtal@gmail.com
Web Site: sinagtalapublishers.wordpress.com
Key Personnel
Mng Dir: Luis A Uson
Founded: 1969
Subjects: Business, Economics, Education, Inspirational, Spirituality, Philosophy, Religion - Catholic, Ethics, Family Life, Mariology
ISBN Prefix(es): 978-971-554

Solidaridad Publishing House
531 Padre Faura, Ermita, 1000 Manila, Metro Manila
Tel: (02) 254 1086 *Fax:* (02) 254 1068
E-mail: solidbookshop@yahoo.com
Key Personnel
Owner: F Sionil Jose
Founded: 1965
Subjects: Biography, Memoirs, Fiction, History
ISBN Prefix(es): 978-971-8845

University of the Philippines Press+
Unit of University of the Philippines System
E de los Santos St, Diliman, 1101 Quezon City
Mailing Address: PO Box 328, Diliman, Quezon City 1101
Tel: (02) 9266642; (02) 9284391; (02) 9253243
Fax: (02) 9282558
E-mail: uppresseditorial@gmail.com (editorial); press@up.edu.ph (marketing); up_press@yahoo.com (adminstrative); uppressbooks@gmail.com (book enquiries)
Web Site: press.up.edu.ph
Key Personnel
Dir: Jose Neil C Garcia
Deputy Dir, Editorial: Gerardo Los Banos
Marketing Supervisor: Anna Jhorie P Arciga
Founded: 1965
Subjects: Art, Business, Education, Fiction, Government, Political Science, Law, Medicine, Nursing, Dentistry, Music, Dance, Philosophy, Psychology, Psychiatry, Religion - Other, Science (General), Social Sciences, Sociology, Technology
ISBN Prefix(es): 978-971-542
Number of titles published annually: 40 Print
Total Titles: 300 Print
Bookshop(s): 2/F Isabelo delos Reyes Bldg, UP Baguio, Baguio City *Tel:* (0956) 280-7065
E-mail: museokordilyera.upbaguio@up.edu.ph; G/F Arts & Sciences Bldg, UP Cebu College, Lahug, Cebu City *Tel:* (032) 233-9034

University of San Carlos Press
P Del Rosario St, 6000 Cebu City
Tel: (032) 253 1000 (ext 175) *Fax:* (032) 255 4341
E-mail: uscpress@usc.edu.ph; sancarlospublications@yahoo.com
Web Site: usc.edu.ph/usc-press
Founded: 1973
Membership(s): Council of Editors of Learned Journals; International Association of Scholarly Publishers.
Subjects: Anthropology, Archaeology, Biological Sciences, History, Social Sciences, Sociology
ISBN Prefix(es): 978-971-539
Number of titles published annually: 2 Print; 1 Online
Total Titles: 26 Print; 1 Online

University of Santo Tomas Publishing House (USTPH)+
Beato Angelico Bldg, Espana St, Sampaloc, 1015 Manila

Tel: (02) 406-1611 (ext 8252); (02) 406-1611 (ext 8278) *Fax:* (02) 731-3522
E-mail: ustpublishing@gmail.com
Web Site: publishinghouse.ust.edu.ph
Key Personnel
Dir: Prof John Jack G Wigley
E-mail: jackwigley2004@yahoo.com
Deputy Dir: Ailil B Alvarez
Founded: 1996
Subjects: Architecture & Interior Design, Asian Studies, Biblical Studies, Biological Sciences, Business, Chemistry, Chemical Engineering, Economics, Education, English as a Second Language, Health, Nutrition, History, Literature, Literary Criticism, Essays, Medicine, Nursing, Dentistry, Philosophy, Poetry, Religion - Catholic, Social Sciences, Sociology, Theology
ISBN Prefix(es): 978-971-506
Parent Company: University of Santo Tomas
Distributor for The Bookmark Inc; Heritage; Rarebook; Solidaridad Publishing House
Book Club(s): Asian Catholic Publishers; Book Development Association of the Philippines

USC Press, see University of San Carlos Press

USTPH, see University of Santo Tomas Publishing House (USTPH)

Vibal Publishing House Inc (VPHI)
Corner of G Araneta Ave & Ma Clara St, Quezon City
Tel: (02) 712-9156; (02) 712-2722; (02) 712-9157; (02) 712-9158; (02) 712-9159 *Fax:* (02) 711-8852
E-mail: inquire@vibalpublishing.com
Web Site: www.vibalpublishing.com
Key Personnel
Vice President: Nila V Mala
Founded: 1953
Subjects: Ethnicity, Foreign Countries, Language Arts, Linguistics, Mathematics, Religion - Other, Science (General), Social Sciences, Sociology
ISBN Prefix(es): 978-971-07
Parent Company: Nasionale Boekhandel Ltd
Subsidiaries: ASN Graphics; SD Publications
Branch Office(s)
Pride Rock Business Park, Bldg A, Unit 4, Gusa, Cagayan de Oro City *Tel:* (082) 273-3630
E-mail: cdo@vibalpublishing.com
VPHI Cebu Branch, 0290 Unit 202 Cebu Holding Center, Cebu Business Park, Cardinal Rosales A, Cebu City *Tel:* (032) 233-0173; (032) 233-0176; (032) 233-2568 *Fax:* (032) 233-2983
E-mail: vpcebu@vibalpublishing.com
Corner of First & Calamansi Sts, Juna Subdivision, Matina, Davao City *Tel:* (082) 297-5226 *Fax:* (082) 297-8550 *E-mail:* vpdavao@vibalpublishing.com
Unit 6, 144 M H del Pilar St, Molo, Lloilo City *Tel:* (033) 335-8291

VPHI, see Vibal Publishing House Inc (VPHI)

Working Girl, *imprint of* Precious Pages Corp (PPC)

Poland

General Information

Capital: Warsaw
Language: Polish and some German. English also used, especially among young people
Religion: Predominantly Roman Catholic

Population: 38.4 million
Bank Hours: 0800-1900 Monday-Friday, 0800-1600 Saturday
Shop Hours: 1100-1900 Monday-Friday; 0900-1300 Saturday
Currency: 100 groszy = 1 zloty
Export/Import Information: Import of books and newspapers, duty free, no tax. Individual private importers allowed to act. Advertising may be placed through AGPOL Foreign Trade Advertising agency, ul Kierbedzia 4, 7, 00-957 Warsaw. No import licenses as such required. All overseas trade is conducted in foreign currency. Small quantities of advertising materials duty free.
Copyright: UCC, Berne (see Copyright Conventions, pg viii)

ABC, *imprint of* Wolters Kluwer SA

Wydawnictwo Albatros Andrzej Kurylowicz+
ul Hlonda 2A/25, 02-972 Warsaw
Tel: (22) 253 89 65 *Fax:* (22) 251 22 72
E-mail: biuro@wydawnictwoalbatros.com
Web Site: www.wydawnictwoalbatros.com
Key Personnel
Co-Owner, Publisher & Foreign Rights: Aleksandra Saluga; Renata Kurylowicz
Mng Editor: Marzena Wasilewska-Ginalska
E-mail: redakcja@wydawnictwoalbatros.com
Founded: 1994
Subjects: Fiction, Nonfiction (General)
ISBN Prefix(es): 978-83-7359; 978-83-88087; 978-83-904774
Number of titles published annually: 80 Print
Total Titles: 350 Print; 1 Audio
Distribution Center: Firma Ksiegarska Olesiejuk Spolka z ograniczona odpowiedzialnoscia Spolka jawna, Poznanska 91, 05-850 Warsaw *Tel:* (22) 721 30 00 *Fax:* (22) 721 30 01 *Web Site:* www.olesiejuk.pl

Ameet Sp z oo
ul Nowe Sady 6, 94-102 Lodz
Tel: (42) 676-27-78 *Fax:* (42) 676-28-19
E-mail: ameet@ameet.pl
Web Site: www.ameet.pl
Founded: 1991
Subjects: Art, Education, Literature, Literary Criticism, Essays
ISBN Prefix(es): 978-83-7214; 978-83-86116; 978-83-253

Wydawnicza Anagram Sp z oo
ul Walecznych 12/7, 03-916 Warsaw
Tel: (22) 698 70 70 *Fax:* (22) 698 70 70
E-mail: anagram@adres.pl
Web Site: www.anagram.com.pl
Founded: 1991
Subjects: Poetry, Women's Studies
ISBN Prefix(es): 978-83-203; 978-83-86086; 978-83-609; 978-83-60422; 978-83-939105

APOSTOLICUM Wydawnictwo Ksiezy Pallotynow
ul Wilcza 8, 05-091 Zabki
Tel: (22) 771 52 30; (22) 771 52 14 *Fax:* (22) 771 52 07
E-mail: sekretariat@apostolicum.pl; sklep@apostolicum.pl
Web Site: www.apostolicum.pl
Key Personnel
Dir: Jozef Nowak
Deputy Dir & Editor-in-Chief: Grzegorz Radzikowski *E-mail:* redaktor@apostolicum.pl
Subjects: Education, History, Inspirational, Spirituality, Religion - Catholic, Theology, Family
ISBN Prefix(es): 978-83-7031

Wydawnictwo Arkady+
ul Dobra 28, 00-344 Warsaw

Tel: (22) 444 86 97 Fax: (22) 444 86 87
E-mail: arkady@arkady.info; sklep@arkady.info
Web Site: www.arkady.info
Key Personnel
President & Dir: Janina Krysiak
Editor-in-Chief: Elzbieta Leszczynska Tel: (22) 444 86 52
Production Dir: Wieslaw Pyszka Tel: (22) 444 86 53
Founded: 1957
Subjects: Antiques, Architecture & Interior Design, Art, Crafts, Games, Hobbies, Environmental Studies, Photography
ISBN Prefix(es): 978-83-213

Bajka Sp z oo
ul Angorska 27 lok 1, 03-913 Warsaw
Tel: (22) 740 42 51 Fax: (22) 616 30 31
E-mail: handel@bajkizbajki.pl (sales); promocja@bajkizbajki.pl (marketing)
Web Site: bajkizbajki.pl
Key Personnel
President: Piotr Krolikowski E-mail: p.krolikowski@bajkizbajki.pl
Editor-in-Chief: Katarzyna Szantyr-Krolikowski E-mail: k.szantyr@bajkizbajki.pl
Founded: 2009
ISBN Prefix(es): 978-83-61824

Bellona SA+
ul Bema 87, 01-233 Warsaw
Tel: (22) 457 04 02 Fax: (22) 652 26 95
E-mail: biuro@bellona.pl
Web Site: www.bellona.pl
Key Personnel
Chairman: Jozef Skrzypiec
Publishing Dir: Zbigniew Czerwinski
Editor-in-Chief: Boguslaw Brodecki
Marketing Dir: Waldemar Michalski
Sales Dir: Katarzyna Szymanska
Subjects: Animals, Pets, Biography, Memoirs, Business, Cookery, Education, Gardening, Plants, Health, Nutrition, History, Humor, Regional Interests, Sports, Athletics
ISBN Prefix(es): 978-83-11
Bookshop(s): Pl Europejski 3, 00-844 Warsaw
Tel: (22) 45 70 306; (22) 45 70 378; (22) 45 70 302 Fax: (22) 652 27 01 E-mail: handel@bellona.pl Web Site: ksiegarnia.bellona.pl

Wydawnictwo Bernardinum Sp z oo
ul Bpa Dominika 11, 83-130 Pelplin
Tel: (58) 536-17-57; (58) 536-43-76 (customer service); (58) 531-64-81 (sales) Fax: (58) 536-43-76
E-mail: biuroobslugi@bernardinum.com.pl; zakupy@bernardinum.com.pl (sales)
Web Site: www.bernardinum.com.pl
Founded: 1993
Subjects: Biography, Memoirs, Cookery, Geography, Geology, History, Inspirational, Spirituality, Music, Dance, Poetry, Religion - Other, Science (General), Theology, Travel & Tourism, Adventure, Ministry, Prose
ISBN Prefix(es): 978-83-62994; 978-83-7380; 978-83-87668; 978-83-88487; 978-83-88935; 978-83-7823

Bialy Kruk Sp z oo
ul Szwedzka 38, 30-324 Krakow
Tel: (12) 260-32-90; (12) 260-34-50; (12) 260-32-40 Fax: (12) 260-32-90; (12) 260-34-50; (12) 260-32-40
E-mail: biuro@bialykruk.pl
Web Site: www.bialykruk.pl
Key Personnel
Founder & Publisher: Leszek Sosnowski
Founded: 1996
Subjects: Architecture & Interior Design, Biography, Memoirs, Film, Video, History, Poetry, Regional Interests, Religion - Catholic, Sports,

Athletics, Church History, Comics, Europe, Nature, Poland
ISBN Prefix(es): 978-83-88918; 978-83-907760; 978-83-912165; 978-83-7553; 978-83-60292; 978-83-914021

Biblioteka Narodowa w Warszawie (National Library of Poland)
al Niepodleglosci 213, 02-086 Warsaw
Tel: (22) 608 29 99; (22) 608 22 11 (bookshop); (22) 608 25 39 (sales) Fax: (22) 825 52 51; (22) 608 25 52 (sales)
E-mail: kontakt@bn.org.pl; bndyrekt@bn.org.pl; promocja@bn.org.pl
Web Site: www.bn.org.pl
Key Personnel
Dir: Dr Tomasz Makowski Tel: (22) 608 22 33
E-mail: dyrektor@bn.org.pl
Manager: Krzysztof Alberski Tel: (22) 608 23 66
E-mail: k.alberski@bn.org.pl
Librarian: Zofia Zurawinska
Founded: 1928
Membership(s): AIB; ASLIB; FID; IAM; International Federation of Library Associations & Institutions (IFLA).
Subjects: Library & Information Sciences
ISBN Prefix(es): 978-83-7009

Wydawnictwo BOSZ (BOSZ Publishing House)+
ul Przemyslowa 14, 38-600 Lesko
Tel: (13) 469 90 00; (13) 469 90 10 Fax: (13) 469 61 88
E-mail: biuro@bosz.com.pl
Web Site: www.bosz.com.pl
Key Personnel
Dir: Bogdan Szymanik
Deputy Dir: Barbara Szymanik
Marketing Dir: Aleksandra Falkowska-Dziedzic
Founded: 1994
Subjects: Architecture & Interior Design, Art, Film, Video, Literature, Literary Criticism, Essays, Music, Dance, Photography, Travel & Tourism, Theatre
ISBN Prefix(es): 978-83-87730; 978-83-7576

Wydawnictwo Czarna Owca Sp z oo
Ul Alzacka 15A, 03-972 Warsaw
Tel: (22) 616 12 72 (orders); (22) 616 29 20 (editorial); (22) 616 29 36 (sales)
E-mail: sklep@czarnaowca.pl (orders); redakcja@czarnaowca.pl (editorial); handel@czarnaowca.pl (sales)
Web Site: www.czarnaowca.pl
Founded: 1991
Subjects: Anthropology, Erotica, Fiction, Inspirational, Spirituality, Literature, Literary Criticism, Essays, Mysteries, Suspense, Nonfiction (General), Philosophy, Psychology, Psychiatry, Social Sciences, Sociology, Atheism
ISBN Prefix(es): 978-83-60207; 978-83-89763; 978-83-7554; 978-83-8015

Wydawnictwo Czarne
Wolowiec 11, 38-307 Sekowa
Tel: (18) 351 00 70 Fax: (18) 352 04 75
E-mail: redakcja@czarne.com.pl
Web Site: czarne.com.pl
Key Personnel
Publisher & Editor-in-Chief: Andrzej Stasiuk; Monika Sznajderman
Mng Editor: Magdalena Budzinska
E-mail: magda@czarne.com.pl
Founded: 1996
Specialize in contemporary Polish & Eastern-European prose, essays, documentaries & nonfiction.
Subjects: Literature, Literary Criticism, Essays, Nonfiction (General)
ISBN Prefix(es): 978-83-87391; 978-83-89755; 978-83-7536
Foreign Rights: Polish Rights (Magdalena Debowska)

Spoldzielnia Wydawnicza "Czytelnik"+
ul Wiejska 12a, 00-490 Warsaw
Tel: (22) 58 31 400; (22) 628 14 41 Fax: (22) 628 31 78
E-mail: sekretariat@czytelnik.pl; redakcja@czytelnik.pl
Web Site: www.czytelnik.pl
Key Personnel
Chief Executive Officer: Marek Zakowski
Tel: (22) 628 95 08
Publishing Dir: Anna Rucinska Tel: (22) 628 24 12
Manager, Administration: Anna Jankuc-Rudzka
Tel: (22) 58 31 404
Founded: 1944
Subjects: Biography, Memoirs, Fiction, Journalism, Poetry, Social Sciences, Sociology
ISBN Prefix(es): 978-83-07
Number of titles published annually: 60 Print

Wydawnictwo Debit SpJ
ul Gorkiego 20, 43-300 Bielsko-Biala
Tel: (33) 810 08 20 Fax: (33) 814 51 81
E-mail: wyddebit@bb.onet.pl; sklep.debit@onet.pl (sales); zamowienia.debit@onet.pl (orders); handlowy.debit@onet.pl (trade sales)
Web Site: www.wydawnictwo-debit.pl
Founded: 1991
Subjects: Automotive, Biological Sciences, Engineering (General), Fiction, Physics, Science (General)
ISBN Prefix(es): 978-83-7167; 978-83-85298

Wydawnictwo DiG Spj (DiG Publishing)+
ul Dankowicka 16 C lok 2, 01-987 Warsaw
Tel: (22) 8390838 Fax: (22) 8390838
E-mail: biuro@dig.com.pl
Web Site: www.dig.com.pl
Founded: 1991
Independent publishing company specializing in history & humanities.
Membership(s): Polska Izba Ksiazki (Polish Book Chamber).
Subjects: Antiques, Archaeology, Art, Biography, Memoirs, Genealogy, History, Language Arts, Linguistics, Library & Information Sciences, Literature, Literary Criticism, Essays
ISBN Prefix(es): 978-83-7181; 978-83-85490
Number of titles published annually: 80 Print; 2 CD-ROM; 2 Online; 2 E-Book
Total Titles: 250 Print
Distributed by Polnische Buchhandlung; Orbis Book Ltd
Bookshop(s): Al Niepodleglosci 213, 02-086 Warsaw

DKSW, see Wydawnictwo Swiety Wojciech (Drukarnia i Ksiegarnia Sw Wojciecha Sp z oo)

Wydawnictwo Dolnoslaskie+
ul Podwale 62, 50-010 Wroclaw
Tel: (71) 785 90 40 Fax: (71) 785 90 66
E-mail: wydawnictwodolnoslaskie@publicat.pl
Web Site: publicat.pl/wydawnictwo-dolnoslaskie.html
Key Personnel
Editorial Dir: Monika Kaczmarek-Klose
Founded: 1986
Membership(s): Polish Book Chamber.
Subjects: Biography, Memoirs, Fiction, History, Literature, Literary Criticism, Essays, Mysteries, Suspense, Nonfiction (General), Science Fiction, Fantasy, Travel & Tourism
ISBN Prefix(es): 978-83-7384; 978-83-7023
Number of titles published annually: 120 Print
Parent Company: Publicat SA
Associate Companies: Elipsa; Papilon; Wydawnictwo Ksiaznica
Orders to: Ars Polona SAV, Krakowskie Przedmiescie 7, 00-950 Warsaw

Wydawnictwo Sonia Draga Sp z oo
Pl Grunwaldzki 8-10, 40-127 Katowice
Tel: (32) 782 64 77 *Fax:* (32) 253 77 28
E-mail: info@soniadraga.pl
Web Site: www.soniadraga.pl
Key Personnel
President & Editor-in-Chief: Sonia Draga
Marketing Dir: Agnieszka Jedlinska
   E-mail: agnieszka@soniadraga.com.pl
Sales Dir: Danuta Czarnowska *E-mail:* danuta@
   soniadraga.com.pl
Mng Editor: Slawomir Call
Subjects: Biography, Memoirs, Business, Eco-
   nomics, History, Literature, Literary Criticism,
   Essays, Mysteries, Suspense, Nonfiction (Gen-
   eral), Poetry, Romance, Science Fiction, Fan-
   tasy, Travel & Tourism
ISBN Prefix(es): 978-83-7508

Wydawnictwo Dwie Siostry Sp z oo
Al 3 Maja 2 m 183, 00-391 Warsaw
Tel: (22) 618 25 30
E-mail: biuro@wydawnictwodwiesiostry.pl
Web Site: www.wydawnictwodwiesiostry.pl
Key Personnel
Publisher & Foreign Rights: Jadwiga Jedryas
   E-mail: jadzia@wydawnictwodwiesiostry.pl
Publisher: Joanna Rzyska
Editor: Magdalena Cicha-Klak *E-mail:* m.cicha@
   wydawnictwodwiesiostry.pl
ISBN Prefix(es): 978-83-63696; 978-83-60850;
   978-83-922807

Wydawnictwo Edukacyjne Parpamedia
ul Szczotkarska 48a, 01-382 Warsaw
Tel: (22) 666-09-79
Founded: 2003
Subjects: Psychology, Psychiatry, Addiction, Re-
   covery
ISBN Prefix(es): 978-83-7760; 978-83-89566;
   978-83-61849

Edycja Swietego Pawla
ul sw Pawla 13/15, 42-221 Czestochowa
Tel: (34) 362 06 89; (34) 372 34 34 (bookshop)
   Fax: (34) 362 09 89
E-mail: edycja@edycja.pl
Web Site: www.edycja.pl
Key Personnel
Publishing Dir: Daniel Luka *E-mail:* redakcja@
   edycja.pl
Dir of Trade & Distribution: Tadeusz
   Chmielewski
Production Manager: Miroslaw Dabrowski
   Tel: (34) 362 05 12 *E-mail:* produkcja@edycja.
   com.pl
Subjects: Biography, Memoirs, Economics, Psy-
   chology, Psychiatry, Religion - Other, Theology
ISBN Prefix(es): 978-83-7168; 978-83-7424; 978-
   83-85438

Elsevier Urban & Partner Sp z oo+
ul Kosciuszki 29, 50-011 Wroclaw
Tel: (71) 330 61 61; (42) 680 44 09 (orders)
   Fax: (71) 330 61 60; (42) 680 44 86 (orders)
E-mail: biuro@elsevier.com; zamowienia@
   elsevier.com (orders)
Web Site: www.elsevier.pl
Founded: 2003
Medical publishers.
Subjects: Medicine, Nursing, Dentistry, Psychol-
   ogy, Psychiatry
ISBN Prefix(es): 978-83-85842; 978-83-87944;
   978-83-89581; 978-83-60290; 978-83-7609
Parent Company: Elsevier
Branch Office(s)
ul Migdalowa 4 lok 59, 02-796 Warsaw *Tel:* (22)
   546 38 20 *Fax:* (22) 546 38 21

ExpressMap Polska Sp z oo
ul Miejska 4a, 01-352 Warsaw

Tel: (22) 666 04 05 *Fax:* (22) 666 04 05
E-mail: sprzedaz@e-map.pl
Web Site: www.comfortmap.com/pl
Subjects: Travel & Tourism, Travel Guides
ISBN Prefix(es): 978-83-7546

Fundacja Centrum Fotografii (Foundation
   Centre for Photography)+
Rynek 11, 43-300 Bielsko-Biala
Tel: (33) 814 09 55
Web Site: www.fundacja-centrum-fotografii.org
Key Personnel
President: Andrzej Baturo
Vice President: Inez Baturo
Founded: 1992
Membership(s): PIK; Polish Association of Book
   Publishers; Polish Book Chamber; PTWK.
Subjects: Animals, Pets, Architecture & Interior
   Design, Gardening, Plants, How-to, Photogra-
   phy
ISBN Prefix(es): 978-83-900579; 978-83-905021
Number of titles published annually: 5 Print

**Gdanskie Wydawnictwo Psychologiczne Sp z
   oo** (Gdansk Psychology Publishing Ltd)+
ul Bema 4/1A, 81-753 Sopot
Tel: (58) 555 71 89; (58) 555 71 94 *Fax:* (58)
   550 16 04
E-mail: sekretariat@gwp.pl; handel@gwp.pl
   (sales); redakcja@gwp.pl
Web Site: www.wydawnictwogwp.pl; www.gwp.pl
Key Personnel
Editor-in-Chief: Patrycja Pacyniak
Founded: 1991
Publishes exclusively psychology books: aca-
   demic textbooks, counselling books for psy-
   chotherapists & practical psychology for the
   general market.
Subjects: Anthropology, Education, Literature,
   Literary Criticism, Essays, Psychology, Psychi-
   atry, Science (General), Self-Help, Social Sci-
   ences, Sociology, Popular Science, Psychother-
   apy, Speech Therapy
ISBN Prefix(es): 978-83-85416; 978-83-87957;
   978-83-60577; 978-83-7489
Number of titles published annually: 20 Print
Total Titles: 100 Print

Wydawnictwo Harmonia
ul Szczodra 6, 80-283 Gdansk
Tel: (58) 348 09 50 *Fax:* (58) 348 09 00
E-mail: harmonia@harmonia.edu.pl
Web Site: www.harmonia.edu.pl
Key Personnel
Editor-in-Chief: Jozef Czescik *E-mail:* jozef.
   czescik@harmonia.edu.pl
Assistant Editor-in-Chief: Renata Wiecek
Chief Technical Editor: Witold Preyss *E-mail:* w.
   preyss@harmonia.edu.pl
Head, Commercial: Aleksandra Starczewska
Warehouse Manager: Roman Szykowski *Tel:* (58)
   735 02 95 *E-mail:* magazyn@harmonia.edu.pl
Marketing: Michal Szczepanski *E-mail:* m.
   szczepanski@harmonia.edu.pl
Founded: 1993
Subjects: Education, Dyslexia, Early Childhood
   Learning, Pedagogy, Speech Therapy
ISBN Prefix(es): 978-83-7134

HarperCollins Polska sp z oo
ul Staroscinska 1B lokal 24-25, 02-516 Warsaw
Tel: (22) 8565757
E-mail: info@harpercollins.pl
Web Site: www.harpercollins.pl
Key Personnel
Media: Agata Roznowska *E-mail:* agata.
   roznowska@harpercollins.pl
Founded: 1991
Subjects: Romance
ISBN Prefix(es): 978-83-7149; 978-83-7070; 978-
   83-238; 978-83-276

Wydawnictwo Hokus-Pokus
ul Wandy 10 A/4, 03-949 Warsaw
Tel: (22) 895 03 28 *Fax:* (22) 895 03 28
E-mail: redakcja@hokus-pokus.pl
Web Site: www.hokus-pokus.pl
Key Personnel
Contact: Marta Lipczynska-Gil *E-mail:* marta@
   hokus-pokus.pl
Founded: 2003
ISBN Prefix(es): 978-83-60402

Oficyna Wydawnicza Impuls+
Ul Fatimska 53 B, 31-831 Krakow
Tel: (12) 422-41-80 *Fax:* (12) 422-59-47
E-mail: impuls@impulsoficyna.com.pl
Web Site: www.impulsoficyna.com.pl
Key Personnel
Dir & Editor-in-Chief: Wojciech Sliwerski
   E-mail: wojciech.sliwerski@impulsoficyna.com.
   pl
Head of Publications: Danuta Porebska
   E-mail: danuta.porebska@impulsoficyna.com.pl
Founded: 1989
Membership(s): Polish Book Chamber.
Subjects: Education, Environmental Studies, Lit-
   erature, Literary Criticism, Essays, Philosophy,
   Religion - Catholic, Social Sciences, Sociology
ISBN Prefix(es): 978-83-86994; 978-83-85543;
   978-83-88030; 978-83-7308; 978-83-7850; 978-
   83-7587

Institute for Art Historical Research, see IRSA
   (Institute for Art Historical Research)

Instytut Historii Nauki PAN (Institute for the
   History of Science, PAS)+
Unit of Polish Academy of Sciences
ul Nowy Swiat 72, Pok 9, 00-330 Warsaw
Tel: (22) 826 87 54; (22) 65 72 746 *Fax:* (22)
   826 61 37
E-mail: ihn@ihnpan.waw.pl
Web Site: www.ihnpan.waw.pl
Key Personnel
Dir: Prof Leszek Zasztowt, PhD
Deputy Dir: Dr Jaroslaw Wlodarczyk, PhD
Subjects: Astronomy, Biography, Memoirs, Bi-
   ological Sciences, Chemistry, Chemical Engi-
   neering, Earth Sciences, Education, Geography,
   Geology, History
ISBN Prefix(es): 978-83-900065; 978-83-900482;
   978-83-900891; 978-83-86062
Total Titles: 10 Print
Branch Office(s)
ul Slawkowska 17, 31-016 Krakow
   E-mail: ihnpan.krakow@neostrada.pl

Instytut Meteorologii i Gospodarki Wodnej
   (Institute of Meteorology & Water
   Management)
ul Podlesna 61, 01-673 Warsaw
Tel: (22) 56-94-100 *Fax:* (22) 83-41-801
E-mail: imgw@imgw.pl
Web Site: www.imgw.pl
Key Personnel
Dir: Dr Ing Mieczyslaw S Ostojski *Tel:* (22) 56-
   94-301 *E-mail:* m.ostojski@imgw.pl
Founded: 1945
Subjects: Earth Sciences, Environmental Stud-
   ies, Foreign Countries, Geography, Geology,
   Library & Information Sciences, Physical Sci-
   ences, Hydrology, Meteorology, Oceanology,
   Water Engineering, Water Management, Water
   Quality
ISBN Prefix(es): 978-83-61102
Number of titles published annually: 20 Print
Parent Company: Ministry of Environment
Branch Office(s)
Gdynia
Krakow
Poznan
Wroclaw

Instytut Pamieci Narodowej - Komisja Scigania Zbrodni przeciwko Narodowi Polskiemu (Institute of National Remembrance - Commission for the Prosecution of Crimes Against the Polish Nation)
ul Woloska 7, 02-675 Warsaw
Tel: (22) 431 82 87
Web Site: ipn.gov.pl
Key Personnel
Contact: Maciej Steppa *E-mail:* maciej.steppa@ipn.gov.pl
Subjects: History, Polish History
ISBN Prefix(es): 978-83-89078; 978-83-915983
Bookshop(s): ul Marszalkowska 21/25, 00-628 Warsaw *Tel:* (22) 576 30 05

Instytut Techniki Budowlanej, Dzial Wydawniczy
ul Ksawerow 21, 02-656 Warsaw
Tel: (22) 825-04-71 *Fax:* (22) 825-52-86
E-mail: instytut@itb.pl
Web Site: www.itb.pl
Founded: 1945
Subjects: Civil Engineering
ISBN Prefix(es): 978-83-7130; 978-83-7226; 978-83-7290; 978-83-7321; 978-83-7370; 978-83-249; 978-83-7413
Imprints: ITB
Bookshop(s): ul Filtrowa 1, 00-611 Warsaw
E-mail: ksiegarnia@itb.pl

Instytut Wydawniczy Pax+
ul Wspolna 25, 00-519 Warsaw
Tel: (22) 586-51-00; (22) 625-23-01 (sales)
Fax: (22) 586-51-87; (22) 625-23-01 (sales)
E-mail: iwpax@inco.pl; kontakt.iwpax@inco.pl
Web Site: www.iwpax.pl
Key Personnel
Dir: Krzysztof Przestrzelski *Tel:* (22) 586-51-41
E-mail: krzysztof.przestrzelski@inco.pl
Editor-in-Chief: Zbigniew Borowik *Tel:* (22) 586-51-42 *E-mail:* zbigniew.borowik@inco.pl
Founded: 1949
Subjects: Biblical Studies, Education, Fiction, History, Inspirational, Spirituality, Literature, Literary Criticism, Essays, Philosophy, Poetry, Religion - Catholic, Religion - Other, Social Sciences, Sociology, Theology
ISBN Prefix(es): 978-83-211
Total Titles: 50 Print
Parent Company: Grupa Inco SA
Bookshop(s): Piekna 16b, 00-449 Warsaw
Orders to: ul Wybrzeze Kosciuszkowskie 21, 00-390 Warsaw

IRSA (Institute for Art Historical Research)+
Pl Matejki 7/8, 31-157 Krakow
Tel: (12) 421 90 30 *Fax:* (12) 421 48 07
E-mail: irsa@irsa.com.pl
Web Site: irsa.com.pl
Key Personnel
Founder & Dir: Jozef Grabski, PhD
Founded: 1979
Specialize in history of art.
Subjects: Antiques, Architecture & Interior Design, Art, Asian Studies, Film, Video, History, Philosophy, Photography, Religion - Catholic, Women's Studies
ISBN Prefix(es): 978-83-89831; 978-83-908675; 978-83-915130; 978-83-918454
Bookshop(s): Zamek Wawel 5, 31-001 Krakow
Tel: (12) 421 58 85

IRSA Publishing House, see IRSA (Institute for Art Historical Research)

Wydawnictwo Iskry Sp z oo (Iskry Publishing House Ltd)+
al Wyzwolenia 18, 00-570 Warsaw
Tel: (22) 827 94 15
E-mail: iskry@iskry.com.pl; promocja@iskry.com.pl
Web Site: www.iskry.com.pl
Key Personnel
President: Wieslaw Uchanski *E-mail:* w.uchanski@iskry.com.pl
Dir: Krzysztof Oblucki *E-mail:* k.oblucki@iskry.com.pl
Promotion & Marketing Dir: Mirela Tomczyk
Founded: 1952
Subjects: Aeronautics, Aviation, Biography, Memoirs, Cookery, Fiction, History, Literature, Literary Criticism, Essays, Maritime, Mysteries, Suspense, Nonfiction (General), Parapsychology, Philosophy, Regional Interests, Science Fiction, Fantasy, Self-Help, Travel & Tourism
ISBN Prefix(es): 978-83-207
Distribution Center: Dictum Sp z oo, ul Kabaretowa 21, 01-942 Warsaw *E-mail:* wysylka@dictum.pl

ITB, *imprint of* Instytut Techniki Budowlanej, Dzial Wydawniczy

Wydawnictwo IUVI
Marr Business Park Hala B1.1, ul Nad Drwina 10, 30-741 Krakow
E-mail: handlowy@iuvi.pl; redakcja@iuvi.pl
Web Site: iuvi.pl
Subjects: Biography, Memoirs, Mysteries, Suspense, Science Fiction, Fantasy
ISBN Prefix(es): 978-83-7966

Katolicki Uniwersytet Lubelski Jana Pawla II, see Wydawnictwo KUL

KAW (Kresowa Agencja Wydawnicza)
ul Kamienna 5/25, 15-021 Bialystok
Tel: (85) 732 43 47 *Fax:* (85) 732 43 47
E-mail: kaw@kaw.com.pl
Web Site: www.kaw.com.pl
Founded: 1974
Membership(s): RSW.
Subjects: Education, Ethnicity, Government, Political Science, Science (General), Travel & Tourism
ISBN Prefix(es): 978-83-03; 978-83-88072
Number of titles published annually: 30 Print
Branch Office(s)
ul Podedwornego 12a, 15-269 Bialystok
ul sw Ducha 111/113, 80-801 Gdansk
ul 3 Maja 36, 40-097 Katowice
ul Florianska 33, 31-019 Krakow
ul Sienkiewicza 3/5, 90-113 Lodz
ul Buczka 28, 20-076 Lublin
ul Slowackiego 22, 60-823 Poznan
ul Komunistow 10, 35-030 Rzeszow
ul Orla Bialego 5, 70-562 Szczecin
pl Solny 14, 50-062 Wroclaw

Komputerowa Oficyna Wydawnicza HELP+
Gorna 3a, 05-805 Kanie
Tel: (22) 759 35 60
Web Site: besthelp.pl
Key Personnel
Mng Dir: Piotr Gomolinski
Founded: 1989
Specialize in computer books.
Subjects: Computer Science
ISBN Prefix(es): 978-83-87211
Number of titles published annually: 15 Print
Total Titles: 200 Print

Wydawnictwa Komunikacji i Lacznosci Sp z oo (Transport & Communications Publishers)+
ul Kazimierzowska 52, 02-546 Warsaw 12
Tel: (22) 849 27 51; (22) 849 23 04 (warehouse); (22) 849 20 32 (bookshop) *Fax:* (22) 849 23 22
E-mail: wkl@wkl.com.pl
Web Site: www.wkl.com.pl

Key Personnel
General Dir: Jerzy Kozlowski *Tel:* (22) 849 23 14
Editor-in-Chief: Krzysztof Wisniewski *Tel:* (22) 849 23 24 *E-mail:* krzysztof.wisniewski@wkl.com.pl
Commercial Manager: Ewa Berus *Tel:* (22) 849 23 45 *Fax:* (22) 849 23 45 *E-mail:* ewa.berus@wkl.com.pl
Founded: 1949
Subjects: Aeronautics, Aviation, Automotive, Communications, Electronics, Electrical Engineering, Mechanical Engineering, Radio, TV, Transportation
ISBN Prefix(es): 978-83-206

Kresowa Agencja Wydawnicza, see KAW (Kresowa Agencja Wydawnicza)

Wydawnictwo Krytyka Polityczna
ul Foksal 16, IIP, 00-372 Warsaw
Tel: (22) 505 66 90 *Fax:* (22) 505 66 84
E-mail: editorial@krytykapolityczna.pl
Web Site: www.krytykapolityczna.pl
Key Personnel
President: Maciej Kropiwnicki *E-mail:* maciej.kropiwnicki@krytykapolityczna.pl
Promotion: Agata Diduszko-Zyglewska *E-mail:* agata.diduszko@poczta.krytykapolityczna.pl
Founded: 2007
Subjects: Government, Political Science, Philosophy, Culture & Society
ISBN Prefix(es): 978-83-63855; 978-83-61006; 978-83-62467
Total Titles: 200 Print

Spoldzielnia Wydawniczo-Handlowa 'Ksiazka i Wiedza'+
ul Smolna 13, 00-375 Warsaw
Tel: (22) 827-54-01; (22) 827-94-16; (22) 827-94-14 (sales) *Fax:* (22) 827-94-16; (22) 827-94-14 (sales)
Key Personnel
President & Editor-in-Chief: Wlodzimierz Galaska
Vice President: Maria Bialek-Krezalowska
Founded: 1948
Membership(s): RSW.
Subjects: Animals, Pets, Biography, Memoirs, Economics, Fiction, Government, Political Science, Health, Nutrition, History, Law, Literature, Literary Criticism, Essays, Philosophy, Poetry, Science (General), Social Sciences, Sociology, Travel & Tourism
ISBN Prefix(es): 978-83-05

Wydawnictwo Ksiaznica Sp z oo+
ul Powstancow 30/401, 40-039 Katowice
Tel: (32) 757 2216 *Fax:* (32) 757 2217
Specialize in encyclopedic thematic dictionaries.
Membership(s): Polish Chamber of Books.
Subjects: Fiction, Health, Nutrition, Nonfiction (General), Romance
ISBN Prefix(es): 978-83-85348; 978-83-7132

Wydawnictwo KUL+
ul Konstantynow 1 H, pok 702, 20-827 Lublin
Tel: (81) 740 93 45 *Fax:* (81) 740 93 51
E-mail: wydawnictwo@kul.lublin.pl
Web Site: www.kul.pl/1114.html; wydawnictwokul.lublin.pl/sklep (online bookstore)
Key Personnel
Publications Dir: Beata Pyc
Sales Manager: Beata Duma *Tel:* (81) 740 93 44
Founded: 2002
Subjects: Biblical Studies, History, Law, Mathematics, Philosophy, Psychology, Psychiatry, Religion - Catholic, Social Sciences, Sociology, Theology, Humanities, Natural Sciences
ISBN Prefix(es): 978-83-228; 978-83-7702
Imprints: RW-KUL

Wydawnictwo LektorKlett Sp z oo
Division of Ernest Klett AG
ul Polska 114, 60-401 Poznan
Tel: (61) 8496 201 *Fax:* (61) 8496 202
E-mail: bok@lektorklett.com.pl (orders)
Web Site: www.lektorklett.com.pl
ISBN Prefix(es): 978-83-7429; 978-83-88507;
   978-83-88894; 978-83-89427

Lex, *imprint of* Wolters Kluwer SA

Wydawnictwo Literackie Sp z oo+
ul Dluga 1, 31-147 Krakow
Tel: (12) 619 27 40 *Fax:* (12) 422 54 23
E-mail: sekretariat@wydawnictwoliterackie.pl;
   handel@wydawnictwoliterackie.pl; promocja@
   wydawnictwoliterackie.pl
Web Site: www.wydawnictwoliterackie.pl
Key Personnel
Chairman of the Board: Anna Zaremba-Michalska
President: Vera Michalski-Hoffman
Finance Dir: Dariusz Kurdziel
Dir, Sales: Greg Glodkowski
Rights Manager: Joanna Dawbrowska
   Tel: (12) 619 27 62 *E-mail:* j.dawbrowska@
   wydawnictwoliterackie.pl
Editor-in-Chief: Margaret Nycz
Founded: 1953
Subjects: Art, Biography, Memoirs, Drama, The-
   ater, Film, Video, History, Literature, Literary
   Criticism, Essays
ISBN Prefix(es): 978-83-08

Agencja Wydawnicza Liwona Sp z oo
ul Rakuszanki 5, 02-496 Warsaw
Tel: (22) 867 88 66; (60) 090 43 91 (cell)
   Fax: (22) 867 64 64
E-mail: liwona@liwona.pl
Web Site: www.liwona.pl
Key Personnel
Sales Dir: Agnieszka Sobieszek *Tel:* (60) 669 48
   80 (cell)
Founded: 1996
Subjects: Automotive, Fiction, Educational Driv-
   ing Materials
ISBN Prefix(es): 978-83-7570

Ludowa Spoldzielnia Wydawnicza (People's
   Cooperative Publishing)+
ul Ciolka 15 lokal 8 Ip, 01-445 Warsaw
Tel: (22) 620 54 24 *Fax:* (22) 620 57 18
E-mail: biuro@lsw.pl; sklep@lsw.pl (sales)
Web Site: www.lsw.pl
Key Personnel
Editorial: Jerzy Dobrzanski *Tel:* (22) 620 57 18
Founded: 1949
Subjects: Agriculture, Biography, Memoirs, His-
   tory, Literature, Literary Criticism, Essays, Po-
   etry
ISBN Prefix(es): 978-83-205

Wydawnictwo Mag
ul Krypska 21 m 63, 04-082 Warsaw
Tel: (22) 813-47-43 *Fax:* (22) 813-47-60
E-mail: handel@mag.com.pl
Web Site: www.mag.com.pl
Key Personnel
Copyright: Andrzej Miszkurka *E-mail:* kurz@
   mag.com.pl
Promotion & Marketing: Katarzyna Rodek
   E-mail: k.rodek@mag.com.pl
Founded: 1993
Subjects: Fiction, History, Humor, Literature, Lit-
   erary Criticism, Essays, Science Fiction, Fan-
   tasy, Horror
ISBN Prefix(es): 978-83-7480

Wydawnictwo Magnum Sp z oo (Magnum
   Publishing House Ltd)+
ul Narbutta 25a, 02-536 Warsaw

Tel: (22) 646-00-85; (22) 848-55-05 *Fax:* (22)
   848-55-05
E-mail: magnum@it.com.pl
Web Site: www.wydawnictwo-magnum.com.pl
Key Personnel
President: Jolanta Woloszanska
Vice President: Marcin Jarek
Founded: 1992
Membership(s): Polish Chamber of Books.
Subjects: Biography, Memoirs, Government, Po-
   litical Science, History
ISBN Prefix(es): 978-83-85852; 978-83-63986;
   978-83-89656

Mamania, *imprint of* Grupa Wydawnicza Relacja

Media Rodzina Sp z oo
ul Pasieka 24, 61-657 Poznan
Tel: (61) 827 08 60; (61) 827 08 50 *Fax:* (61)
   827 08 66
E-mail: mediarodzina@mediarodzina.pl;
   handlowy@mediarodzina.pl (sales)
Web Site: www.mediarodzina.com.pl
Key Personnel
Founder: Robert Gamble
Founded: 1992
Subjects: Fiction, Government, Political Science,
   History, Psychology, Psychiatry
ISBN Prefix(es): 978-83-7278; 978-83-85594;
   978-83-8008
Parent Company: Harbor Point Sp z oo

MedPharm Polska Sp z oo
ul Powstancow Slaskich 28-30, 53-333 Wroclaw
Tel: (71) 33 50 360 *Fax:* (71) 33 50 361
E-mail: info@medpharm.pl
Web Site: www.medpharm.pl
Founded: 2005
Subjects: Medicine, Nursing, Dentistry, Veteri-
   nary Science, Cosmetology, Human Anatomy,
   Pharmacy, Veterinary Medicine
ISBN Prefix(es): 978-83-60466; 978-83-7846

Agencja Wydawnicza Jerzy Mostowski
Janki K Warszawy, ul Wspolna 17a, 05-090
   Raszyn
Tel: (22) 720 35 99 *Fax:* (22) 720 34 90
E-mail: awm@morex.com.pl
Web Site: www.awm.waw.pl
Key Personnel
Owner: Jerzy Mostowski
Editor-in-Chief: Martyna Maron
Sales: Sylwester Golebiewski
Founded: 1990
Subjects: Animals, Pets, Cookery, Education,
   Health, Nutrition, History
ISBN Prefix(es): 978-83-7250; 978-83-85904;
   978-83-86510; 978-83-86848

Wydawnictwo Muchomor Sp z oo
ul Wachocka 11/13 m 1, 03-934 Warsaw
Tel: (22) 839 49 68 *Fax:* (22) 839 49 68
E-mail: muchomor@muchomor.pl
Web Site: www.muchomor.pl
Key Personnel
Sales: Tomasz Podgorski
Founded: 2002
ISBN Prefix(es): 978-83-89774; 978-83-917214;
   978-83-918667; 978-83-919311

Muza SA+
ul Marszalkowska 8, 00-590 Warsaw
Tel: (22) 621 17 75; (22) 621 50 58 *Fax:* (22)
   629 23 49
E-mail: muza@muza.com.pl; info@muza.com.pl
Web Site: www.muza.com.pl
Key Personnel
President: Marcin Garlinski *E-mail:* m.garlinski@
   muza.com.pl
Vice President: Malgorzata Czarzasty
Founded: 1991

Subjects: Art, Cookery, Education, Fiction, History, House & Home, Literature, Literary Criticism, Essays, Nonfiction (General), Social Sciences, Sociology, Sports, Athletics, Travel &
   Tourism
ISBN Prefix(es): 978-83-7079; 978-83-7200; 978-
   83-85325; 978-83-7319; 978-83-7495; 978-83-
   7758
Imprints: Redakcja Ksiazki Kolorowej; Sport I
   Turystyka; Warszawskie Wydawnictwo Literackie
Book Club(s): Klub Czytelnikow Muza SA
Warehouse: ul Cybernetyki 9, 02-677 Warsaw

Wydawnictwo Nasza Ksiegarnia Sp z oo (Nasza
   Ksiegarnia Publishing House)+
ul Sarabandy 24c, 02-868 Warsaw
Tel: (22) 643 93 89 *Fax:* (22) 643 70 28
E-mail: naszaksiegarnia@nk.com.pl
Web Site: nk.com.pl
Key Personnel
Dir, Publishing & Promotion: Dariusz Sedek
   E-mail: d.sedek@nk.com.pl
Head, Promotion & Advertising: Agata Janaszek
   E-mail: a.janaszek@nk.com.pl
Commercial Dir: Marek Dobrowolski *E-mail:* m.
   dobrowolski@nk.com.pl
Production Dir: Malgorzata Wieladek *E-mail:* m.
   wieladek@nk.com.pl
Founded: 1921
Subjects: Education, Fiction, Literature, Literary
   Criticism, Essays, Science (General)
ISBN Prefix(es): 978-83-10

Oficyna Naukowa
ul Mokotowska 65/3, 00-533 Warsaw
Tel: (22) 622 02 41 *Fax:* (22) 622 02 42
E-mail: oficyna.naukowa@data.pl
Web Site: www.oficyna-naukowa.com.pl
Key Personnel
Publisher: Elzbiety Nowakowskiej-Soltan; Ewy
   Pajestki-Kojder
Founded: 1992
Subjects: Economics, History, Law, Literature,
   Literary Criticism, Essays, Philosophy, Psy-
   chology, Psychiatry, Social Sciences, Sociology,
   Culture Studies, Social Anthropology
ISBN Prefix(es): 978-83-7459; 978-83-85505;
   978-83-88164; 978-83-7737

Norbertinum+
ul Dluga 5, 20-346 Lublin
Tel: (81) 744 11 58 *Fax:* (81) 744 11 48
E-mail: norbertinum@norbertinum.pl
Web Site: www.norbertinum.pl
Key Personnel
President & Editor-in-Chief: Piotr Sanetra
   Tel: (81) 744 11 58 ext 27 *E-mail:* piotr.
   sanetra@norbertinum.pl
Founded: 1989
Subjects: Biography, Memoirs, Fiction, History,
   Literature, Literary Criticism, Essays, Poetry,
   Religion - Catholic, Science (General), Social
   Sciences, Sociology, Theology
ISBN Prefix(es): 978-83-85131; 978-83-86837;
   978-83-7222

Oficyna, *imprint of* Wolters Kluwer SA

Firma Ksiegarska Olesiejuk
ul Poznanska 91, 05-850 Ozarow Mazowiecki
Tel: (22) 721 30 00 *Fax:* (22) 721 30 01
E-mail: internet@olesiejuk.pl
Web Site: www.olesiejuk.pl
Founded: 2003
ISBN Prefix(es): 978-83-274; 978-83-7512
Distributor for Koenemann; Parragon

Ossolineum, see Zaklad Narodowy im
   Ossolinskich - Wydawnictwo we Wroclawiu Sp
   z oo

Wydawnictwo Otwarte Sp z oo
ul Smolki 5 lok 302, 30-513 Krakow
Tel: (12) 427 12 00
E-mail: otwarte@otwarte.eu
Web Site: www.otwarte.eu
Founded: 2006
Subjects: Biography, Memoirs, Fiction, Nonfiction
(General)
ISBN Prefix(es): 978-83-7515
Number of titles published annually: 30 Print

**Pallottinum Wydawnictwo Stowarzyszenia
Apostolstwa Katolickiego+**
ul Przybyszewskiego 30, 60-959 Poznan
Mailing Address: skr pocztowa 23, 60-959 Poz-
nan
Tel: (61) 867 52 33 *Fax:* (61) 867 52 38
E-mail: pallottinum@pallottinum.pl
Web Site: www.pallottinum.pl
Key Personnel
Dir: Zbigniew Rembisz
Deputy Dir: Krzysztof Oleszczak
Production Manager: Aleksander Pikosz
Founded: 1948
Publishers of the Catholic Apostolate Association.
Subjects: Biblical Studies, Inspirational, Spiri-
tuality, Literature, Literary Criticism, Essays,
Philosophy, Religion - Catholic, Theology
ISBN Prefix(es): 978-83-7014

Panstwowe Wydawnictwo Rolnicze i Lene+
ul Malownicza 14, 02-272 Warsaw
Tel: (22) 8684529
E-mail: pwril@pwril.com; warszawa@pwril.com
Web Site: www.pwril.com
Founded: 1947
State agricultural & forestry publishers.
Subjects: Agriculture, Environmental Studies,
Gardening, Plants, Health, Nutrition, Veterinary
Science
ISBN Prefix(es): 978-83-09
Branch Office(s)
ul Marszalkowska 23, 60-327 Poznan
E-mail: poznan@pwril.com

Panstwowy Instytut Wydawniczy (PIW)
(National Publishing Institute)+
ul Foksal 17, 00-372 Warsaw
Tel: (22) 826 02 01; (22) 826 02 02 *Fax:* (22)
826 15 36
E-mail: piw@piw.pl; produkcja@piw.pl;
promocja@piw.pl
Web Site: www.piw.pl
Key Personnel
Dir, Sales & Marketing: Malgorzata Stawida
E-mail: mstawida@piw.pl
Head, Production: Agata Mularczyk
Head, Promotion & Public Relations: Kamil Pi-
wowarski
Founded: 1946
State publishing institute.
Subjects: Biography, Memoirs, Drama, Theater,
Ethnicity, Fiction, History, Literature, Literary
Criticism, Essays, Poetry, Science (General)
ISBN Prefix(es): 978-83-06
Number of titles published annually: 60 Print

Wydawnictwo Papierowy Ksiezyc (Paper Moon
Publishing)
Skr Poczt 220, 76-215 Slupsk 12
Tel: (59) 727 34 20 *Fax:* (59) 727 34 21
E-mail: wydawnictwo@papierowyksiezyc.pl
Web Site: www.papierowyksiezyc.pl
Founded: 2008
Subjects: Literature, Literary Criticism, Essays,
Mysteries, Suspense, Nonfiction (General), Sci-
ence Fiction, Fantasy, Horror, Paranormal
ISBN Prefix(es): 978-83-61386

Pearson Central Europe Sp z oo
ul Jana Olbrachta 94, 01-102 Warsaw

Tel: (22) 533 15 33; (22) 725 43 21 (orders)
Toll Free Tel: 800 12 00 76 *Fax:* (22) 533 15
34
E-mail: office@pearson.com; pearson@
eduksiazka.pl (orders)
Web Site: www.pearson.pl
Key Personnel
Vice President, Finance & Operations: Marcin
Rudnik *Tel:* (22) 533 15 51 *Fax:* (22) 533 15
56
Founded: 1991
Subjects: English as a Second Language, History,
Language Arts, Linguistics
ISBN Prefix(es): 978-83-88291; 978-83-61243;
978-83-7600
Parent Company: Pearson Education

PIW, see Panstwowy Instytut Wydawniczy (PIW)

Poligrafia PWM, *imprint of* Polskie
Wydawnictwo Muzyczne SA

Polish Scientific Publishers, see Wydawnictwo
Naukowe PWN SA

**Oficyna Wydawnicza Politechniki
Wroclawskiej** (Wroclaw University of
Technology Press)
Pl Grunwaldzki 13, 50-377 Wroclaw
Mailing Address: Wybrzeze Wyspianskiego 27,
50-370 Wroclaw
Tel: (71) 328 29 40; (71) 320 38 23; (71) 320 29
94 *Fax:* (71) 328 29 40
E-mail: oficwyd@pwr.wroc.pl
Web Site: www.oficyna.pwr.wroc.pl; www.pwr.
wroc.pl
Founded: 1968
Subjects: Architecture & Interior Design, Chem-
istry, Chemical Engineering, Computer Science,
Computers, Economics, Electronics, Electrical
Engineering, Engineering (General), Environ-
mental Studies, Language Arts, Linguistics,
Management, Mathematics, Physical Sciences,
Physics, Science (General), Social Sciences,
Sociology, Technology, Thermal Energy
ISBN Prefix(es): 978-83-7493; 978-83-7085
Number of titles published annually: 120 Print

Egmont Polska Sp z oo
ul Dzielna 60, 01-029 Warsaw
Tel: (22) 838 41 00 *Fax:* (22) 838 42 00
E-mail: poczta@egmont.pl
Web Site: www.egmont.pl
Key Personnel
Mng Dir: Beata Lewandowska-Kaftan
Tel: (22) 838 41 00 ext 126 *E-mail:* beata.
lewandowska@egmont.pl
Marketing Dir: Magdalena Kosch-
Mackowiak *Tel:* (22) 838 41 00 ext 172
E-mail: magdalena.mackowiak@egmont.pl
Press Officer: Aleksandra Chaberska *Tel:* (22) 838
41 00 ext 201 *E-mail:* aleksandra.chaberska@
egmont.pl
Founded: 1990
ISBN Prefix(es): 978-83-237; 978-83-7123; 978-
83-85396

Polskie Wydawnictwo Ekonomiczne SA+
ul Canaletta 4, 00-099 Warsaw
Tel: (22) 827 80 01 *Fax:* (22) 827 55 67
E-mail: pwe@pwe.com.pl; redakcje@pwe.com.pl
Web Site: www.pwe.com.pl
Key Personnel
President & Editor-in-Chief: Alicja Rutkowska
Dir: Mariola Rozmus *Tel:* (22) 826 41 82
E-mail: mrozmus@pwe.com.pl
Founded: 1949
Polish economics publishers.
Membership(s): Polish Chamber of Books.

Subjects: Accounting, Advertising, Business, Eco-
nomics, Environmental Studies, Finance, Man-
agement, Marketing
ISBN Prefix(es): 978-83-208
Number of titles published annually: 70 Print
Total Titles: 5,000 Print

Polskie Wydawnictwo Muzyczne SA (Polish
Music Publishers)+
al Krasinskiego 11a, 31-111 Krakow
Tel: (12) 422 70 44; (12) 422 73 28 (sales)
Fax: (12) 422 01 74
E-mail: pwm@pwm.com.pl; sales@pwm.com.pl
Web Site: www.pwm.com.pl
Key Personnel
President of the Management Board & Dir-in-
Chief: Adam Radzikowski *Tel:* (12) 422 70 44
ext 117 *E-mail:* adam_radzikowski@pwm.com.
pl
Editor-in-Chief: Daniel Cichy *Tel:* (12) 422-70-44
ext 117 *E-mail:* daniel_cichy@pwm.com.pl
Editorial Dir: Irena Stachel
Commercial Trade Dir: Sylwia Religa
Head of Management Rights: Janina Warzecha
Founded: 1945
Subjects: Music, Dance
ISBN Prefix(es): 978-83-224
Number of titles published annually: 150 Print;
100 Online; 10 E-Book; 1 Audio
Total Titles: 12,000 Print; 150 Online; 20 E-
Book; 1 Audio
Imprints: Poligrafia PWM
Subsidiaries: Biblioteka Materialow Orkie-
strowych (PWM hire dept)
Branch Office(s)
ul Fredry 8, 00-097 Warsaw
U.S. Office(s): Theodore Presser, 588 N Gulph
Rd, King of Prussia, PA 19406, United
States *Tel:* 610-592-1222 *Fax:* 610-592-1229
E-mail: sales@presser.com *Web Site:* www.
presser.com
Distributed by Kalmus (Great Britain Common-
wealth); Leduc (France); Schott (Germany &
Switzerland); Universal Edition AG (Austria)
Distributor for Baerenreiter Verlag; Boosey &
Hawkes; Schott; Universal Edition AG

**Wydawnictwo Polskiej Prowincji Dominikanow
W Drodze Sp z oo**
ul Kosciuszki 99, 61-716 Poznan
Tel: (61) 850 47 13; (61) 850 47 21; (61) 852 39
62 (sales) *Fax:* (61) 850 17 82
E-mail: esprzedaz@wdrodze.pl; redakcja@
wdrodze.pl
Web Site: www.wdrodze.pl
Subjects: Biography, Memoirs, Inspirational, Spir-
ituality, Literature, Literary Criticism, Essays,
Psychology, Psychiatry, Theology, Ecumeni-
cal, Prayer & Spirituality, Psychology & Faith,
Social Teaching of Church
ISBN Prefix(es): 978-83-7033; 978-83-85008

PROMIC Sp z oo
ul sw Bonifacego 9/1, 02-914 Warsaw
Tel: (22) 642 50 82; (22) 651 90 54 (sales)
Fax: (22) 651 90 55
E-mail: sprzedaz@wydawnictwo.pl; sekretariat@
wydawnictwo.pl
Web Site: www.wydawnictwo.pl
Key Personnel
Dir: Adam Stankiewicz
Editor-in-Chief: Krzysztof R Jaskiewicz
Head, Marketing: Aneta Zbieska
Founded: 1987
Subjects: Theology, Church & Society, Ecu-
menism, Liturgy
ISBN Prefix(es): 978-83-7502

Proszynski i S-ka SA
ul Rzymowskiego 28, 02-697 Warsaw
Tel: (22) 278 17 40 *Fax:* (22) 843 52 15
E-mail: proszynskimedia@proszynskimedia.pl

Web Site: www.proszynski.pl
Key Personnel
President: Maciej Makowski
Vice President & Dir, Marketing: Anna Deren-
gowska
Vice President: Mieczyslaw Proszynski; Tomasz
Woyda
Publishing Dir: Elzbieta Kwiatkowska *Tel:* (22)
278 17 49 *E-mail:* elzbietakwiatkowska@
proszynskimedia.pl
Dir, Production: Tomasz Szczepanik
E-mail: tomaszszczepanik@proszynski.pl
Dir, Sales: Anna Gajewska
Founded: 1990
Subjects: Biography, Memoirs, Cookery, Crimi-
nology, Education, History, Literature, Literary
Criticism, Essays, Mysteries, Suspense, Nonfic-
tion (General), Science (General), Social Sciences, Sociology
ISBN Prefix(es): 978-83-85661; 978-83-7180;
978-83-7255; 978-83-86669; 978-83-900062;
978-83-7337; 978-83-7469; 978-83-916854;
978-83-917389; 978-83-917852; 978-83-86868;
978-83-7839; 978-83-7648

Publicat SA+
ul Chlebowa 24, 61-003 Posnan
Tel: (61) 6529252 *Fax:* (61) 6529200
E-mail: publicat@publicat.pl; office@publicat.pl
Web Site: publicat.pl
Key Personnel
Dir: Anna Sojka-Leszczynska *E-mail:* a.sojka-
leszczynska@publicat.pl
Product Manager: Aleksandra Gospadarek
E-mail: a.gospadarek@publicat.pl
Founded: 1990
Specialize also in read-alongs & popular scien-
tific.
Subjects: Crafts, Games, Hobbies, Education, His-
tory, How-to, Poetry, Science (General)
ISBN Prefix(es): 978-83-85165; 978-83-7083;
978-83-7212

PWE, see Polskie Wydawnictwo Ekonomiczne
SA

Wydawnictwo Naukowe PWN SA (Polish
Scientific Publishers)+
ul G Daimlera 2, 02-460 Warsaw
Tel: (22) 6954321 *Fax:* (22) 6954288
Web Site: www.pwn.pl; www.ksiegarnia.pwn.pl
(online orders)
Key Personnel
President: Barbara Jozwiak *E-mail:* barbara.
jozwiak@pwn.com.pl
Foreign Rights Manager: Tomasz Berezinski
Tel: (22) 6954180 *E-mail:* tomasz.berezinski@
pwn.com.pl
Founded: 1951
Publisher of reference, science, the humanities
& multimedia. Provider of encyclopaedic &
illustrational content. Reference & academic
publisher. Cooperates with foreign publishers.
Membership(s): International Association of Sci-
entific, Technical & Medical Publishers (STM).
Subjects: Agriculture, Anthropology, Art, Biblical
Studies, Computer Science, Economics, Educa-
tion, Engineering (General), English as a Sec-
ond Language, Environmental Studies, Finance,
Geography, Geology, History, Language Arts,
Linguistics, Marketing, Mathematics, Nonfic-
tion (General), Philosophy, Psychology, Psy-
chiatry, Science (General), Social Sciences,
Sociology, Technology
ISBN Prefix(es): 978-83-01
Number of titles published annually: 400 Print
Associate Companies: School Publishers PWN, ul
Swietojerska 5/7, 00-236 Warsaw
Subsidiaries: All-Poland Distribution System-
AZYMUT; pwn.pl (multimedia subsidiary);
PZWL Wydawnictwo Lekarskie Ltd (medical

& health); School Publishers PWN; Yurincom
Inter (Ukrainian joint-venture)
Bookshop(s): Ksiegarnia PWN, Warsaw
E-mail: ksiegarnia.warszawa@pwn.com.pl;
Ksiegarnia PWN, ul Korzenna 33/35, 80-851
Gdansk *E-mail:* ksiegarnia.gdansk@pwn.com.
pl; Ksiegarnia PWN, ul Pilsudzkiego 3/1, 31-
110 Krakow *E-mail:* ksiegarnia.krakow@pwn.
com.pl; Ksiegarnia PWN, ul Wieckowskiego
13, 90-721 Lodz *E-mail:* ksiegarnia.lodz@pwn.
com.pl; Ksiegarnia PWN, ul Kuznicza 56, 50-
138 Wroclaw *E-mail:* ksiegarnia.wroclaw@
pwn.com.pl

PZWL Wydawnictwo Lekarskie Ltd (PZWL
Medical Publishers Ltd)+
Unit of PWN Scientific Publishers Group
ul Gottlieba Daimlera 2, 02-460 Warsaw
Tel: (22) 6954033 *Fax:* (22) 6954032
E-mail: pzwl@pzwl.pl
Web Site: www.wydawnictwopzwl.pl
Key Personnel
Publishing Dir: Ewelina Szyszkowska *Tel:* (22)
6954050 *E-mail:* ewelina.szyszkowska@pzwl.pl
Editor-in-Chief: Agata Solecka *Tel:* (22) 6954041
E-mail: agata.solecka@pzwl.pl
Founded: 1945
Subjects: Biological Sciences, Child Care & De-
velopment, Health, Nutrition, Medicine, Nurs-
ing, Dentistry, Psychology, Psychiatry
ISBN Prefix(es): 978-83-200
Number of titles published annually: 120 Print
Total Titles: 400 Print; 2 CD-ROM
Distributed by PWN Scientific Publishers Group
Warehouse: OSDW "AZYMUT", Park Tulipan,
Smolice 1F, 95-010 Strykow *Tel:* (42) 6804400

Wydawnictwo REA
Kosciuszki 21, 05-510 Konstancin-Jeziorna
Tel: (22) 673 28 16; (22) 631 94 23 *Fax:* (22)
673 28 16
E-mail: handylowy@rea-sj.pl
Web Site: www.rea-sj.pl
Key Personnel
Dir, Sales: Jacek Koceluch
Marketing: Karolina Jasiaczyk
Founded: 1995
Subjects: Language Arts, Linguistics, Culinary,
Entertainment, Esoteric
ISBN Prefix(es): 978-83-7141; 978-83-7544

Dom Wydawniczy REBIS Sp z oo
ul Zmigrodzka 41/49, 60-171 Poznan
Tel: (61) 867 81 40; (61) 867 47 08; (61) 882 38
21 (sales) *Fax:* (61) 867 37 74; (61) 882 38 19
(sales)
E-mail: rebis@rebis.com.pl; sprzedaz@rebis.com.
pl
Web Site: www.rebis.com.pl
Founded: 1990
Subjects: Art, Biography, Memoirs, Business,
Health, Nutrition, History, Literature, Literary
Criticism, Essays, Mysteries, Suspense, Psy-
chology, Psychiatry, Science Fiction, Fantasy,
Contemporary History, Dalai Lama, Historical
Novels, History of Art, 19th Century, Polish
Contemporary Literature
ISBN Prefix(es): 978-83-7120; 978-83-7301; 978-
83-85202; 978-83-85696; 978-83-7510; 978-83-
7818

Redakcja Ksiazki Kolorowej, *imprint of* Muza
SA

Relacja, *imprint of* Grupa Wydawnicza Relacja

Grupa Wydawnicza Relacja
Slowicza 27a, 02-170 Warsaw
Tel: (22) 464 82 73
E-mail: biuro@mamania.pl
Web Site: www.mamania.pl

Founded: 2012
Subjects: Nonfiction (General), Parenting
ISBN Prefix(es): 978-83-62829; 978-83-65087;
978-83-64270; 978-83-930598; 978-83-939019
Imprints: Mamania; Relacja

Wydawnictwo RM Sp z oo+
ul Minska 25, 03-808 Warsaw
Mailing Address: Skr Poczt 179, 00-987 Warsaw
Tel: (22) 870 60 24 *Fax:* (22) 870 05 33
E-mail: rm@rm.com.pl; sklep@rm.com.pl
Web Site: www.rm.com.pl
Key Personnel
President: Piotr Kieryl *Tel:* (22) 870 60 24 ext
151 *E-mail:* piotr.kieryl@rm.com.pl
Vice President: Tomasz Zajbt *E-mail:* tomasz.
zajbt@rm.com.pl
Founded: 1996
Subjects: Animals, Pets, Computer Science, Com-
puters, Cookery, Crafts, Games, Hobbies, Eco-
nomics, Education, Fiction, Gardening, Plants,
Health, Nutrition, History, Literature, Literary
Criticism, Essays, Outdoor Recreation, Self-
Help, Sports, Athletics, Travel & Tourism
ISBN Prefix(es): 978-83-85769; 978-83-7147;
978-83-87216; 978-83-900451; 978-83-7773;
978-83-7243
Number of titles published annually: 100 Print

Rosikon Press+
Al Debow 4, 05-080 Izabelin-Warsaw
Tel: (22) 722-61-01; (22) 722-66-66 *Fax:* (22)
722-66-67
E-mail: biuro@rosikonpress.com; handel@
rosikonpress.com (sales); promocja@
rosikonpress.com; rights@rosikonpress.com
Web Site: www.rosikonpress.com
Key Personnel
Mng Dir: Grazyna Kasprzycka-Rosikon
Founded: 1990
Membership(s): Polish Chamber of Books.
Subjects: Art, History, Photography, Poetry, Reli-
gion - Catholic, Travel & Tourism
ISBN Prefix(es): 978-83-88848
Number of titles published annually: 5 Print
Total Titles: 15 Print

RW-KUL, *imprint of* Wydawnictwo KUL

Wydawnictwo Sejmowe (Sejm Publishing
Office)
Division of Chancellery of the Sejm
ul Zagorna 3, 00-441 Warsaw
Tel: (22) 694-13-30; (22) 694-15-97 (sales)
Fax: (22) 694-10-04 (sales)
E-mail: wydawnictwo@sejm.gov.pl
Web Site: wydawnictwo.sejm.gov.pl
Founded: 1990
Subjects: Government, Political Science, History,
Law, Legal & Political Issues, Parliamentarism
ISBN Prefix(es): 978-83-7666; 978-83-7059

Wydawnictwo SIC+
ul Chelmska 27/23, 00-724 Warsaw
Tel: (22) 840 07 53 *Fax:* (22) 840 07 53
E-mail: biuro@wydawnictwo-sic.com.pl; info@
wydawnictwo-sic.com.pl
Web Site: www.wydawnictwo-sic.com.pl
Key Personnel
Mng Dir: Elzbieta Czerwirlska
Promotion & Public Relations Officer: Zofia
Gebert *Tel:* (22) 851 06 01
Founded: 1993
Subjects: Human Relations, Self-Help
ISBN Prefix(es): 978-83-86056; 978-83-88807;
978-83-61967
Total Titles: 50 Print

**Przedsiebiorstwo Wydawniczo-Handlowe
Siedmiorog Sp z oo+**
ul Krakowska 90, 50-427 Wroclaw

Tel: (71) 377 24 01; (71) 377 24 59 *Fax:* (71) 377 24 21
E-mail: biuro@siedmiorog.pl; wysylka@ siedmiorog.pl
Web Site: www.siedmiorog.pl
Subjects: Philosophy, Science Fiction, Fantasy
ISBN Prefix(es): 978-83-7162; 978-83-85193; 978-83-7254; 978-83-85959; 978-83-86685; 978-83-7791
Number of titles published annually: 100 Print
Total Titles: 570 Print

Wydawnictwo Sine Qua Non, see Wydawnictwo SQN

Slask Sp Z oo (Slask Ltd)+
ul Juliusza Ligonia 7, 40-036 Katowice
Tel: (32) 258 07 56; (32) 258 19 13 *Fax:* (32) 258 32 29
E-mail: biuro@slaskwn.com.pl; redakcja@ slaskwn.com.pl
Web Site: www.slaskwn.com.pl
Key Personnel
President: Dr Tadeusz Sierny
Manager: Bogumila Cyron; Ana Pilsniak
Editor-in-Chief: Dr Dariusz Pohl
Sales Specialist: Mariola Wosko
Founded: 1954
Membership(s): The Polish Chamber of the Book.
Subjects: Advertising, English as a Second Language, History, Literature, Literary Criticism, Essays, Nonfiction (General), Poetry, Regional Interests, Science (General)
ISBN Prefix(es): 978-83-900705; 978-83-900814; 978-83-85831; 978-83-7164; 978-83-60781

wydawnictwo slowo/obraz terytoria
ul Pniewskiego 4/1, 80-246 Gdansk
Tel: (58) 345 47 07 *Fax:* (58) 520 80 63
E-mail: redakcja@terytoria.com.pl; slowo-obraz@ terytoria.com.pl
Web Site: terytoria.com.pl
Key Personnel
President: Stanislaw Rosiek
Vice President: Maria Gospodarek
Editor: Daria Majewska; Piotr Sitkiewicz
   Tel: (58) 341 44 13
Marketing & Public Relations: Sandra Slawinska
   E-mail: s.slawinska@terytoria.com.pl
Trade: Elizabeth Brach *E-mail:* e.brach@terytoria. com.pl
Sales: Lukaszem Strachota *Tel:* (58) 520 89 83
   E-mail: l.strachota@terytoria.com.pl
Promotion: Iwona Korszanska *Tel:* (60) 377 29 47
   E-mail: i.korszanska@terytoria.com.pl
Founded: 1995
Subjects: Anthropology, Art, Drama, Theater, Education, History, Literature, Literary Criticism, Essays, Music, Dance, Philosophy, Photography, Poetry, Pop Culture, Social Sciences, Sociology
ISBN Prefix(es): 978-83-7453; 978-83-89405; 978-83-87316; 978-83-88560; 978-83-905063

Spoldzielnia Wydawnicza Anagram, see Wydawnicza Anagram Sp z oo

Spoleczny Instytut Wydawniczy Znak+
ul Kosciuszki 37, 30-105 Krakow
Tel: (12) 61 99 500 *Fax:* (12) 61 99 502
E-mail: kontakt@znak.com.pl
Web Site: www.znak.com.pl
Key Personnel
Dir: Danuta Skora *E-mail:* skora@znak.com.pl
Editor-in-Chief: Jerry Illg *E-mail:* illg@znak.com. pl
Dir, Marketing: Sylwia Wcislo *Tel:* (12) 61 99 551 *E-mail:* wcislo@znak.com.pl
Founded: 1959
Subjects: Film, Video, History, Philosophy, Religion - Other, Social Sciences, Sociology

ISBN Prefix(es): 978-83-7006; 978-83-240
Bookshop(s): ul Slawkowska 1, 31-007 Krakow

Sport I Turystyka, *imprint of* Muza SA

Wydawnictwo SQN
ul Tyniecka 35, 30-323 Krakow
Tel: (12) 261-17-49
E-mail: biuro@wsqn.pl; marketing@wsqn.pl
Web Site: www.wsqn.pl
Founded: 2010
Subjects: Music, Dance, Pop Culture, Sports, Athletics
ISBN Prefix(es): 978-83-7924

Wydawnictwo Studio EMKA
ul Krolowej Aldony 6/2a, 03-928 Warsaw
Tel: (22) 616 00 67 *Fax:* (22) 628 08 38
E-mail: wydawnictwo@studioemka.com.pl
Web Site: www.studioemka.com.pl
Key Personnel
Owner: Klara Molnar
Editor-in-Chief: Jacek Marciniak
Marketing: Agnieszka Kornilow
   E-mail: agnieszka@studioemka.com.pl
Sales: Katarzyna Malinowska *E-mail:* katarzyna@ studioemka.com.pl
Founded: 1996
Subjects: Biography, Memoirs, Business, Economics, Fiction, Literature, Literary Criticism, Essays, Poetry, Psychology, Psychiatry, Theology, Esoteric, Prose
ISBN Prefix(es): 978-83-62304

Swiat Ksiazki sp z oo
ul Hankiewicza 2, 02-103 Warsaw
Tel: (22) 46 00 610
Web Site: wydawnictwoswiatksiazki.pl
Key Personnel
Dir, Publishing & Editor-in-Chief: Daria Kielan
Sales: Katarzyna Polakowska *E-mail:* katarzyna. polakowska@swiatksiazki.pl
Founded: 1994
Subjects: Biography, Memoirs, Business, Cookery, Economics, History, Literature, Literary Criticism, Essays, Nonfiction (General), Poetry, Religion - Other, Romance, Science (General), Technology, Foreign Classic Literature, Humanities, Modern Polish Literature
ISBN Prefix(es): 978-83-7799; 978-83-7943
Parent Company: Bukowy Las
Distribution Center: Firma Ksiegarska Olesiejuk, ul Poznanska 91, 05-850 Ozarow, Mazowiecki *Tel:* (22) 721 30 00 *Fax:* (22) 721 30 01 *Web Site:* www.olesiejuk.pl

Wydawnictwo Swiety Wojciech (Drukarnia i Ksiegarnia Sw Wojciecha Sp z oo)
ul Chartowo 5, 61-245 Poznan
Tel: (61) 659 37 00; (61) 659 37 55 (orders); (61) 659 37 67 (marketing) *Fax:* (61) 659 37 01
E-mail: sklep@swietywojciech.pl; marketing@ swietywojciech.pl
Web Site: www.swietywojciech.pl
Key Personnel
Editor-in-Chief: Jerzy Stranz *Tel:* (61) 659 37 12
   E-mail: stranz@swietywojciech.pl
Founded: 1895
Subjects: Biblical Studies, Biography, Memoirs, Poetry, Religion - Catholic, Theology
ISBN Prefix(es): 978-83-7015; 978-83-7516
Bookshop(s): St Adalbert's Bookshop

Oficyna Wydawnicza Szkola Glowna Handlowa w Warszawie (Warsaw School of Economics Publishing House)+
al Niepodleglosci 162, p 023 bud glowny SGH, 02-554 Warsaw
Tel: (22) 564 94 77; (22) 564 95 46; (22) 564 94 86; (22) 564 94 98; (22) 564 98 37
E-mail: wydawnictwo@sgh.waw.pl

Web Site: www.sgh.waw.pl; www.wydawnictwo. sgh.waw.pl
Key Personnel
Editor-in-Chief: Stanislaw Konarski
Head, Marketing: Danuta Jastrzebska
Founded: 1917
Subjects: Agriculture, Business, Computer Science, Economics, English as a Second Language, Finance, Government, Political Science, History, Law, Management, Marketing, Mathematics, Philosophy, Psychology, Psychiatry, Public Administration, Social Sciences, Sociology, Travel & Tourism, Pedagogy
ISBN Prefix(es): 978-83-86689; 978-83-7225; 978-83-7378

Wydawnictwa Szkolne i Pedagogiczne (WSIP) (Polish Educational Publishers)+
Al Jerozolimskie, 96, 00-807 Warsaw
Tel: (22) 576 25 00 *Toll Free Tel:* 801-220 555
E-mail: wsip@wsip.com.pl; sklep@wsip.com.pl
Web Site: www.wsip.pl
Key Personnel
Chief Financial Officer: Michal Seider
Dir, Sales: Marcin Stawowczyk
Founded: 1945
Membership(s): European Educational Publishers Group; Polish Chamber of the Book.
Subjects: Education, Psychology, Psychiatry
ISBN Prefix(es): 978-83-02

Wydawnictwo Tatarak
Filtrowa 79/43, 02-032 Warsaw
E-mail: biuro@tatarak.com
Web Site: tatarak.com
Key Personnel
Publisher: Monika Wrobel-Lutz *Tel:* (60) 443 47 48
Marketing & Advertising: Lidia Drechny *Tel:* (50) 713 54 39 *E-mail:* lidia@tatarak.com
Sales: Lucyna Wrobel *Tel:* (60) 155 00 00
   E-mail: lucyna@tatarak.com
ISBN Prefix(es): 978-83-93256

Towarzystwo Autorow i Wydawcow Prac Naukowych Universitas
ul Slawkowska 17, 31-016 Krakow
Tel: (12) 423 26 05 *Fax:* (12) 422 02 08
Web Site: www.universitas.com.pl
Key Personnel
Management: Andrzej Nowakowski
   E-mail: andrzej@universitas.com.pl
Marketing: Marta Olszewska *E-mail:* marta@ universitas.com.pl
Founded: 1989
Specialize in scientific & popular science scientific books in humanities, particularly history of literature, theory of language & literature, history of philosophy & sociology.
Subjects: Art, Drama, Theater, Economics, Film, Video, Government, Political Science, History, Journalism, Language Arts, Linguistics, Law, Philosophy, Psychology, Psychiatry, Religion - Other, Science (General), Social Sciences, Sociology, Culture
ISBN Prefix(es): 978-83-7052; 978-83-242

Towarzystwo Naukowe w Toruniu
ul Wysoka 16, 87-100 Torun
Tel: (56) 622 39 41
E-mail: tnt.biuro@wp.pl; tnt.zamowienia@wp.pl
Web Site: www.tnt.torun.pl
Key Personnel
Editor-in-Chief: Prof Grazyna Halkiewicz-Sojak
Founded: 1875
Specialize in humanities.
Subjects: Archaeology, Art, Astronomy, Biological Sciences, Education, Geography, Geology, History, Language Arts, Linguistics, Law, Medicine, Nursing, Dentistry, Physical Sciences, Regional Interests, Humanities
ISBN Prefix(es): 978-83-85196; 978-83-87639

Wydawnictwa Uniwersytetu Warszawskiego (WUW) (University of Warsaw Press)+
ul Nowy Swiat 4, 00-497 Warsaw
Tel: (22) 55 31 318
E-mail: wuw@uw.edu.pl; dz.handlowy@uw.edu.pl
Web Site: www.wuw.pl
Key Personnel
Dir: Anna Szemberg *E-mail:* anna.szemberg@uw.
   edu.pl
Editor-in-Chief: Anna Kedziorek *E-mail:* anna.
   kedziorek@uw.edu.pl
Head, Sales: Anna Duracz *Tel:* (22) 55 31 344
   E-mail: a.duracz@uw.edu.pl
Foreign Rights Manager: Anna Raiter-Rosinska
   E-mail: a.rosinska@uw.edu.pl
Production Coordinator: Martyna Choluj *Tel:* (22)
   55 31 339 *E-mail:* martyna.choluj@uw.edu.pl
Marketing: Monika Wielga *E-mail:* m.wielga@
   uw.edu.pl
Founded: 1956
A leading Polish university publisher publishing
   monographs, scientific dissertations, textbooks
   for students & scholarly journals in many aca-
   demic areas.
Subjects: African American Studies, Agriculture,
   Americana, Regional, Anthropology, Archaeol-
   ogy, Art, Asian Studies, Behavioral Sciences,
   Biography, Memoirs, Biological Sciences,
   Chemistry, Chemical Engineering, Economics,
   Education, English as a Second Language, En-
   vironmental Studies, Ethnicity, Genealogy, Ge-
   ography, Geology, Government, Political Sci-
   ence, History, Medicine, Nursing, Dentistry,
   Science (General), Social Sciences, Sociology
ISBN Prefix(es): 978-83-230; 978-83-235
Number of titles published annually: 70 Print
Total Titles: 2,319 Print
Orders to: Centrala Handlu Zagranicznego, Ars
   Polona SA, ul Obroncow 25, 00-933 War-
   saw *Tel:* (22) 5098638 *Fax:* (22) 5098637
   E-mail: arspolona@arspolona.com.pl

**Wydawnictwo Uniwersytetu Wroclawskiego Sp
z oo**
pl Uniwersytecki 15, 50-137 Wroclaw
Tel: (71) 375 28 09; (71) 375 28 85 (orders)
   Fax: (71) 375 27 35
E-mail: biuro@wuwr.com.pl
Web Site: www.wuwr.com.pl
Key Personnel
President & Editor-in-Chief: Marek Gorny
Sales: Lidia Palka
Founded: 1996
Scientific handbooks for students of Wro-
   clawskiego University.
ISBN Prefix(es): 978-83-229

Verbinum Wydawnictwo Ksiezy Werbistow
(Verbinum-Publishing House of the Divine
Word Missionaries)+
ul Klasztorna 4, 86-134 Dragacz
Tel: (52) 330 63 03
E-mail: wydawnictwo@verbinum.pl
Web Site: www.verbinum.pl
Founded: 1982
Subjects: Developing Countries, Philosophy, Po-
   etry, Religion - Catholic, Religion - Other, The-
   ology
ISBN Prefix(es): 978-83-85009; 978-83-85762;
   978-83-7192
Parent Company: Verbinum
Subsidiaries: Verbinum, Dzial Kolportazu

Videograf II Sp z oo
Al Harcerska 3C, 41-500 Chorzow
Tel: (32) 348-31-33; (32) 348-31-35 *Fax:* (32)
   348-31-25
E-mail: office@videograf.pl; admin@videograf.pl
Web Site: www.videograf.pl
Founded: 1996

Subjects: Biography, Memoirs, Education, Fic-
   tion, Film, Video, Gardening, Plants, Mysteries,
   Suspense, Photography
ISBN Prefix(es): 978-83-7183; 978-83-86831;
   978-83-7835
Distribution Center: DICTUM Sp z oo,
   ul Kabaretowa 21, 01-942 Warsaw
   Tel: (22) 663-43-09 *Fax:* (22) 663-98-12
   E-mail: dystrybucja@dictum.pl *Web Site:* www.
   dictum.pl

Oficyna Wydawnicza Vocatio (Vocatio
Publishing House)+
ul Polnej Rozy 1, 02-798 Warsaw
Tel: (22) 648-54-50 *Fax:* (22) 648-03-79
E-mail: vocatio@vocatio.com.pl; ksiegarnia@
   vocatio.com.pl
Web Site: www.vocatio.com.pl
Key Personnel
Publisher: Piotr Waclawik *E-mail:* wydawca@
   vocatio.com.pl
Founded: 1991
Membership(s): ECPA; ICCC.
Subjects: Biblical Studies, Health, Nutrition, Mu-
   sic, Dance, Religion - Catholic, Religion -
   Protestant, Theology
ISBN Prefix(es): 978-83-85435; 978-83-7146;
   978-83-7492

Wydawnictwo WAB (WAB Publishers)
ul Foksal 17, 00-372 Warsaw
Tel: (22) 826 08 82; (22) 828 98 08 *Fax:* (22)
   380 18 01
E-mail: biuro@gwfoksal.pl
Web Site: www.wab.com.pl
Key Personnel
Dir, Publishing: Anita Musiol *E-mail:* anita.
   musiol@gwfoksal.pl
Dir, Sales: Lukasz Miczek
Promotion Dir: Edyta Woznica *E-mail:* edyta.
   woznica@gwfoksal.pl
Head, Production: Iwona Skwierczynska
   E-mail: iwona.skwierczynska@gwfoksal.pl
Founded: 1991
Specialize in promoting & publishing Polish con-
   temporary poetry & literary fiction, as well as
   translations.
Subjects: Fiction, Health, Nutrition, Human Rela-
   tions, Nonfiction (General), Poetry
ISBN Prefix(es): 978-83-87021; 978-83-88221;
   978-83-85554; 978-83-7414; 978-83-7747; 978-
   83-89291; 978-83-280
Number of titles published annually: 120 Print
Total Titles: 800 Print
Parent Company: Grupa Wydawnicza Foksal Sp z
   oo

Wydawnictwo WAM
ul Kopernika 26, 31-501 Krakow
Tel: (12) 629 32 00 *Fax:* (12) 429 50 03
E-mail: wam@wydawnictwowam.pl
Web Site: www.wydawnictwowam.pl
Key Personnel
Editor-in-Chief: Jacek Siepsiak *Tel:* (12) 629 32
   48 *E-mail:* j.siepsiak@wydawnictwowam.pl
Founded: 1872
Subjects: Art, Biography, Memoirs, Cookery, His-
   tory, Inspirational, Spirituality, Philosophy,
   Psychology, Psychiatry, Religion - Other, So-
   cial Sciences, Sociology, Theology, Travel &
   Tourism, Catechism, Cracovia, Culture, Peda-
   gogy, Popes, Prayer
ISBN Prefix(es): 978-83-7505; 978-83-7097; 978-
   83-7318; 978-83-85032; 978-83-85304

Warszawskie Wydawnictwo Literackie, *imprint
of* Muza SA

WEMA Wydawnictwo-Poligrafia Sp z oo+
ul Rolna 191/193, 02-729 Warsaw

Tel: (22) 827 21 17; (22) 827 54 59 *Fax:* (22)
   828 57 79
Web Site: www.wp-wema.pl
Founded: 1967
Also printer.
Subjects: Electronics, Electrical Engineering, Me-
   chanical Engineering
ISBN Prefix(es): 978-83-85250

Wydawnictwo Widnokrag
ul Jana Matejki 14, 05-501 Piaseczno
Tel: (60) 227 21 29
E-mail: kontakt@wydawnictwo-widnokrag.pl
Web Site: www.wydawnictwo-widnokrag.pl
ISBN Prefix(es): 978-83-61213; 978-83-932984;
   978-83-938652; 978-83-942952

Wydawnictwo Wiedza Powszechna Sp z oo+
ul Szeligowska 40a, 01-320 Warsaw
Tel: (22) 720 06 10
E-mail: kontakt@wiedza.pl; sklep@wiedza.pl
Web Site: www.wiedza.pl
Founded: 1952
Specialize in foreign language dictionaries & text-
   books.
Subjects: Language Arts, Linguistics, Science
   (General)
ISBN Prefix(es): 978-83-214

Wydawnictwo Wilga Sp z oo (Wilga Publishing
Ltd)+
ul Foksal 17, 00-372 Warsaw
Tel: (22) 826 08 82; (22) 828 98 08 *Fax:* (22)
   380 18 01
E-mail: biuro@gwfoksal.pl
Web Site: sklep.gwfoksal.pl
Key Personnel
Commercial Dir: Izabela Jakubiak
Production Dir: Dariusz Mroz
Promotion Dir: Edyta Woznica *E-mail:* edyta.
   woznica@gwfoksal.pl
Founded: 1993
Subjects: Education, Fiction
ISBN Prefix(es): 978-83-7156; 978-83-86664;
   978-83-901029; 978-83-903028; 978-83-7375;
   978-83-259
Number of titles published annually: 300 Print
Total Titles: 1,200 Print
Parent Company: Grupa Wydawnicza Foksal Sp z
   oo
Subsidiaries: Wilga Marketing
Warehouse: Panstwowe Magazyny Ustugowe,
   Przejazdowa 25, 05-800 Pruszkow

WNT Publisher+
ul Jaworzynska 4, 00-634 Warsaw
Tel: (22) 240 40 20; (22) 240 40 21
Web Site: wnt.pl
Founded: 1949
Subjects: Architecture & Interior Design, Biologi-
   cal Sciences, Chemistry, Chemical Engineering,
   Computer Science, Computers, Economics, Ed-
   ucation, Electronics, Electrical Engineering,
   Management, Mathematics, Mechanical Engi-
   neering, Medicine, Nursing, Dentistry, Physics,
   Technology, Ecology
ISBN Prefix(es): 978-83-204; 978-83-7926; 978-
   83-2043; 978-83-63623
Parent Company: M-Partner

Wolters Kluwer SA
ul Przyokopowa 33, 01-208 Warsaw
Tel: (22) 535 88 00
E-mail: handel@wolterskluwer.pl
Web Site: www.wolterskluwer.pl
Subjects: Business, Economics, Law
ISBN Prefix(es): 978-83-7526
Imprints: ABC; Lex; Oficyna

WSIP, see Wydawnictwa Szkolne i Pedagogiczne
   (WSIP)

Wytwornia
ul Welniana 31F, 02-833 Warsaw
E-mail: wytwornia@wytwornia.com
Web Site: wytwornia.com
Key Personnel
Publisher: Magdalena Klos-Podsiadlo *Tel:* (50)
991 43 57 *E-mail:* magdalenaklos@wytwornia.
com
Founded: 2005
ISBN Prefix(es): 978-83-921964

Zaklad Narodowy im Ossolinskich - Wydawnictwo we Wroclawiu Sp z oo+
ul Szewska 37, 50-139 Wroclaw
Tel: (71) 335 64 97
E-mail: wydawnictwo@ossolineum.pl
Web Site: www.ossolineum.pl
Key Personnel
Head, Publishing: Dr Dorota Szechinska
Founded: 1817
Subjects: Archaeology, Architecture & Interior
Design, Art, Biography, Memoirs, Biological Sciences, Environmental Studies, History, Language Arts, Linguistics, Literature, Literary Criticism, Essays, Medicine, Nursing, Dentistry, Philosophy, Poetry, Science (General), Social Sciences, Sociology, Humanities, Mythology
ISBN Prefix(es): 978-83-04
Bookshop(s): ul Kollataja 16, 50-007 Wroclaw; Sw Marka 12, 31-018 Krakow; ul Piotrkowska 181, 90-447 Lodz; ul Marcinkowskiego 30, 61-745 Poznan

Zaklad Wydawnictw Statystycznych (Statistical Publishing Establishment)
al Niepodleglosci 208, 00-925 Warsaw
Tel: (22) 608 31 45; (22) 608 32 10 (sales); (22) 608 38 10 (sales); (22) 608 37 37 (orders); (22) 608 30 87 (orders) *Fax:* (22) 608 31 83; (22) 608 38 67 (sales)
E-mail: zws-sprzedaz@stat.gov.pl; zwssek@stat.gov.pl
Web Site: zws.stat.gov.pl
Founded: 1957
Statistical Publications Board of the Central Statistical Office.
Also printer.
Subjects: Economics, Mathematics, Social Sciences, Sociology
ISBN Prefix(es): 978-83-7027

Wydawnictwo Zielona Sowa Sp z oo
Al Jerozolimskie 96, bud Equator II, 00-807 Warsaw
Tel: (22) 576 25 50 *Fax:* (22) 576 25 51
E-mail: wydawnictwo@zielonasowa.pl
Web Site: www.zielonasowa.pl
Founded: 1995
Subjects: Education, Fiction
ISBN Prefix(es): 978-83-7220; 978-83-7623; 978-83-86740; 978-83-7389; 978-83-7895; 978-83-265; 978-83-7435; 978-83-7983
Number of titles published annually: 400 Print

Zysk i S-ka Wydawnictwo
ul Wielka 10, 61-774 Poznan
Tel: (61) 853 27 51; (61) 853 27 67 *Fax:* (61) 852 63 26
E-mail: sekretariat@zysk.com.pl; marketing@zysk.com.pl
Web Site: www.zysk.com.pl
Key Personnel
Dir, Sales: Adam Nowicki *E-mail:* nowicki@zysk.com.pl
Foreign Rights: Aleksandra Basinska
E-mail: aleksandra.basinska@zysk.com.pl
Subjects: Fiction, Nonfiction (General), Psychology, Psychiatry, Religion - Catholic, Science (General), Sports, Athletics, Travel & Tourism
ISBN Prefix(es): 978-83-7785; 978-83-7506

Portugal

General Information

Capital: Lisbon
Language: Portuguese
Religion: Predominantly Roman Catholic, some Protestant
Population: 10 million
Bank Hours: 0830-1500 Monday-Friday
Shop Hours: 0900-1300, 1500-1900 Monday-Friday (some do not close midday); 0900-1300 Saturday. Generally closed Monday morning October-November
Currency: 100 Eurocents = 1 Euro
Export/Import Information: Member of European Union. Foreign language books from most countries dutied per kg (free from UK and reduced from EU); atlases and children's picture books have higher tariff rate and children's picture books have an import surcharge. 5% VAT on books. Small quantity of advertising duty-free. No import license required for goods not exceeding a certain value, otherwise license including permission to transfer foreign exchange required.
Copyright: UCC, Berne (see Copyright Conventions, pg viii)

Academia das Ciencias de Lisboa
R Academia das Ciencias 19 1º, 1249-122 Lisbon
Tel: 213 219 730
E-mail: geral@acad-ciencias.pt
Web Site: www.acad-ciencias.pt
Subjects: Art, History, Literature, Literary Criticism, Essays, Philosophy, Science (General), Theology
ISBN Prefix(es): 978-972-623

Academia do Livro
Member of Grupo LeYa
Rua Cidade de Cordova, 2, 2610-038 Alfragide
Tel: 21 427 2200 *Fax:* 21 427 2201
E-mail: comunicacao@leya.com
Web Site: www.academiadolivro.com.pt
Founded: 2008
Subjects: Cookery, Economics, Education, Government, Political Science, Health, Nutrition, Management, Nonfiction (General), Social Sciences, Sociology
ISBN Prefix(es): 978-989-8194

Actual Editora
Ave Fontes Pereira de Melo, 31-3º C, 1050-117 Lisbon
Tel: 213190240 *Fax:* 213190249
E-mail: info@actualeditora.com
Web Site: www.actualeditora.com
Founded: 2005
Subjects: Business, Economics, Management, Marketing
ISBN Prefix(es): 978-989-694
Parent Company: Editoras Grupo Almedina

Edicoes Afrontamento Lda+
Rua Costa Cabral, 859, 4200-225 Porto
Tel: 225074220 *Fax:* 225074229
E-mail: editorial@edicoesafrontamento.pt; comercial@edicoesafrontamento.pt
Web Site: www.edicoesafrontamento.pt
Key Personnel
Mng Dir, Editorial, Production: Jose Sousa Ribeiro
Founded: 1963
Subjects: Film, Video, Government, Political Science, Literature, Literary Criticism, Essays, Social Sciences, Sociology
ISBN Prefix(es): 978-972-36
Number of titles published annually: 40 Print
Total Titles: 900 Print

Edicoes Almedina SA
Rua Fernandes Tomas 76-80, 3000-167 Coimbra
Tel: 239 851 903 *Fax:* 239 851 901
E-mail: editora@grupoalmedina.net
Web Site: www.almedina.net
Key Personnel
Mng Dir: Joaquim Machado
Founded: 1955
Subjects: Architecture & Interior Design, Art, Economics, Education, History, Law, Literature, Literary Criticism, Essays, Music, Dance, Photography, Science (General)
ISBN Prefix(es): 978-972-40
Associate Companies: Edicoes Globo Ltda, Rua Sao Filipe Nery 37A, 1250-225 Lisbon; Porto Ltda, Rua de Ceuta 79, 4050 Oporto
Warehouse: Livraria Almedina, Parque Empresarial de Eiras, Lote 2, 3020-265 Coimbra
Tel: 239 436 281; 239 436 266 *Fax:* 239 436 267 *E-mail:* vendas@almedina.net

Edicoes Antigona
Rua Gustavo de Matos Sequeira, nº 39-1º, 1250-120 Lisbon
Tel: 21 324 41 70 *Fax:* 21 324 41 71
E-mail: info@antigona.pt
Web Site: www.antigona.pt
Founded: 1979
Subjects: Fiction, Government, Political Science, History, Literature, Literary Criticism, Essays, Social Sciences, Sociology
ISBN Prefix(es): 978-972-608
Number of titles published annually: 8 Print
Total Titles: 193 Print

Apostolado da Oracao Secretariado Nacional
Rua de S Barnabe, 32, 4710-309 Braga
Tel: 253 689 440 *Fax:* 253 689 441
E-mail: livros@snao.pt; geral@apostoladodaoracao.pt
Web Site: www.apostoladodaoracao.pt
Founded: 1874
Subjects: Biography, Memoirs, Poetry, Religion - Other, Theology
ISBN Prefix(es): 978-972-39

Areal Editores SA
Rua da Torrinha, 228 H-3º Andar, 4050-610 Porto
Tel: 223393900 *Fax:* 223393901
Web Site: www.arealeditores.pt
Subjects: Education, Literature, Literary Criticism, Essays
ISBN Prefix(es): 978-989-647; 978-972-627
Parent Company: Grupo Porto Editora

Arquivo Universidade de Coimbra
Rua S Pedro, No 2, 3000-370 Coimbra
Tel: 239 859 855; 239 859 800 *Fax:* 239 820 987
E-mail: secauc@ci.uc.pt; auc-geral@auc.uc.pt
Web Site: www.uc.pt/auc
Subjects: History
ISBN Prefix(es): 978-972-594

Arteplural Edicoes
Imprint of Grupo Bertrand Circulo
Rua Prof Jorge da Silva Horta, 1, 1500-499 Lisbon
Tel: 21 762 60 00 *Fax:* 21 762 32 50
Web Site: www.arteplural.pt
Subjects: Child Care & Development, Cookery, Education, Erotica, Health, Nutrition, Medicine, Nursing, Dentistry, Self-Help, Social Sciences, Sociology, Sports, Athletics, Travel & Tourism, Wine & Spirits
ISBN Prefix(es): 978-989-692

Edicoes Arvore
Rua Azevedo de Albuquerque, nº 1, 4050-076
Porto
Tel: 222 076 010 *Fax:* 222 076 019
E-mail: geral@arvorecoop.pt; direccao@
arvorecoop.pt
Web Site: www.arvorecoop.pt
Key Personnel
President: Amandio Fernandes Secca
Vice President: Jose Rodrigues
Founded: 1963
Subjects: Architecture & Interior Design, Art
ISBN Prefix(es): 978-972-9089

Edicoes ASA
Member of Grupo LeYa
Rua Cidade de Cordova nº 2, 2610-038 Alfragide
Tel: 214272200 *Fax:* 214272201
E-mail: comunicacao@leya.com
Web Site: www.asa.pt
Founded: 1951
Subjects: Architecture & Interior Design, Art, Ed-
ucation, Health, Nutrition, Literature, Literary
Criticism, Essays, Poetry, Science (General),
Sports, Athletics, Travel & Tourism, Gastron-
omy
ISBN Prefix(es): 978-989-23
Branch Office(s)
Rua Caminho do Senhor nº 230, 4410-083
Serzedo VNG *Tel:* 227537800

Assirio & Alvim
Edificio Grupo Bertrand Circulo, Rua Prof Jorge
da Silva Horta, 1, 1500-499 Lisbon
Tel: 217626000
Web Site: www.assirio.pt
Founded: 1972
Subjects: Art, Cookery, Health, Nutrition, History,
Literature, Literary Criticism, Essays, Photogra-
phy, Religion - Other, Science (General), Self-
Help, Wine & Spirits
ISBN Prefix(es): 978-972-37
Distribution Center: Porto Editora, Rua
da Restauracao, 365, Porto 4099-023
Tel: (022) 6088312 *Fax:* (022) 6088313
E-mail: depcomercial@portoeditora.pt

Bertrand Editora+
Imprint of Grupo Bertrand Circulo
Rua Prof Jorge da Silva Horta, 1, 1500-499 Lis-
bon
Tel: 21 762 60 00 *Fax:* 21 762 61 50
Web Site: www.bertrandeditora.pt
Subjects: Art, Computer Science, Economics,
Health, Nutrition, History, Law, Literature, Lit-
erary Criticism, Essays, Medicine, Nursing,
Dentistry, Religion - Other, Self-Help, Social
Sciences, Sociology, Sports, Athletics, Travel &
Tourism, Comics, Esoteric
ISBN Prefix(es): 978-972-25
Bookshop(s): Picoas Plaza, Loja C.0.9, Rua
Tomas Ribeiro/Rua Viriato, 1050-227 Lisbon
Tel: 707 31 50 00 *Fax:* 21 342 42 75

Biblioteca Geral da Universidade de Coimbra
(University of Coimbra General Library)
Largo da Porta Ferrea, 3000-447 Coimbra
Tel: 239 859 831; 239 859 800; 239 859 900
Fax: 239 827 135
E-mail: secretaria@bg.uc.pt
Web Site: www.uc.pt/bguc
Key Personnel
Dir: Jose Augusto Cardoso Bernardes
E-mail: director@bg.uc.pt
Deputy Dir: Antonio Eugenio Maia do Amaral
E-mail: aemaia@bg.uc.pt
Subjects: Education, History, Library & Informa-
tion Sciences, Literature, Literary Criticism,
Essays, Music, Dance, Religion - Catholic, Re-
ligion - Other
ISBN Prefix(es): 978-972-616
Parent Company: Universidade de Coimbra

Biblioteca Publica Municipal do Porto (Porto
Municipal Public Library)
Rua de D Joao IV 17, 4049-017 Porto
Tel: 225 193 480 *Fax:* 225 193 488
E-mail: bpmp@cm-porto.pt
Web Site: bmp.cm-porto.pt/bpmp
Founded: 1833
Subjects: Art, Biological Sciences, Geography,
Geology, History, Literature, Literary Criti-
cism, Essays, Psychology, Psychiatry, Religion
- Other
ISBN Prefix(es): 978-972-634

Editorial Bizancio Lda
Largo Luis Chavez, 11-11A, 1600-487 Lisbon
Tel: 217 550 228; 217 524 548 *Fax:* 217 520 072
E-mail: bizancio@editorial-bizancio.pt
Web Site: www.editorial-bizancio.pt
Founded: 1998
ISBN Prefix(es): 978-972-53

BPMP, see Biblioteca Publica Municipal do
Porto

Camara Municipal Viana do Castelo
Passeio das Mordomas de Romaria, 4904-877
Viana do Castelo
Tel: 258 809 300 *Fax:* 258 809 347
E-mail: cmviana@cm-viana-castelo.pt
Web Site: www.cm-viana-castelo.pt
Subjects: Antiques, Archaeology, Architecture &
Interior Design, Art, History, Poetry
ISBN Prefix(es): 978-972-588
Associate Companies: Biblioteca Municipal,
Museo Municipal
Subsidiaries: Livraria Municipal

Editorial Caminho SA+
Member of Grupo LeYa
Rua Cidade de Cordoba, nº 2, 2610-038 Alfragide
Tel: 214272200 *Fax:* 214272201
E-mail: comunicacao@leya.com
Web Site: www.caminho.leya.com
Key Personnel
Publications: Jaime Ramalho *E-mail:* jramalho@
caminho.leya.com
Founded: 1975
Subjects: Art, Fiction, Government, Political Sci-
ence, History, Poetry, Science (General)
ISBN Prefix(es): 978-972-21
Book Club(s): Club Caminho Fantastico
E-mail: fantastico@caminho.leya.com

CAPU
Ave Almirante Gago Coutinho, Nº 158, 1700-033
Lisbon
Tel: 218429190 *Fax:* 218409361
E-mail: capu@capu.pt; lojaonline@livrariacapu.
com
Web Site: www.capu.pt; www.livrariacapu.com
Subjects: Inspirational, Spirituality, Religion -
Other
ISBN Prefix(es): 978-972-580

Casa das Letras+
Member of Grupo LeYa
Rua Cidade de Cordova, 2, 2610-038 Alfragide
Tel: 214272200 *Fax:* 2104272201
E-mail: info@oficinadolivro.leya.com;
comunicacao@leya.com
Web Site: casadasletras.leya.com
Founded: 1985
Also acts as editor, distributor & bookseller.
Subjects: Cookery, Fiction, History, Journalism,
Law, Religion - Other, Self-Help
ISBN Prefix(es): 978-972-46
Total Titles: 90 Print
Associate Companies: Oficina Do Livro
Bookshop(s): Avenida Euro 2004, 2890-154 Al-
cochete; Centro Comercial Glicinias, Loja 37,
3810-498 Aveiro; Rua do Hospital Velho, 44,

Santa Maria Maior, 9000-129 Funchal; Praca
D Pedro IV, 11, 1100-199 Lisbon; Praca D Pe-
dro IV, 23, 1100-199 Lisbon; Rua Bento Jose
Morais, 13, 9500-772 Ponta-Delgada

**Casa Publicadora das Assembleias de Deus em
Portugal**, see CAPU

Centro de Estudos Geograficos (Center of
Geographical Studies)
Edificio da Faculdade de Letras Alameda de Uni-
versidade, 1600-214 Lisbon
Tel: 21 7940218
E-mail: ceg@campus.ul.pt
Web Site: www.ceg.ul.pt
Key Personnel
Dir: Dr Diogo de Abreu
Founded: 1943
Subjects: Geography, Geology, Social Sciences,
Sociology
ISBN Prefix(es): 978-972-636

Editora Cidade Nova Lda
Apdo 10, 2584-905 Abrigada
Tel: 263 799 090
E-mail: info@focolares.org.pt
Founded: 1970
Subjects: Art, Economics, Education, Environ-
mental Studies, Government, Political Science,
Inspirational, Spirituality, Philosophy, Theology
ISBN Prefix(es): 978-972-9159

Publicacoes Ciencia e Vida Lda+
Praca de Alvalade, No 9, 4º andar-sala 4.7, 1700-
037 Lisbon
Tel: 214787850 *Fax:* 214020750
E-mail: pub@cienciaevida.pt
Web Site: www.cienciaevida.pt
Founded: 1976
Subjects: Agriculture, Animals, Pets, Environmen-
tal Studies, Medicine, Nursing, Dentistry
ISBN Prefix(es): 978-972-590

Civilizacao Editora+
Rua Alberto Aires de Gouveia nº27, 4050-023
Porto
Tel: 226 050 917 *Fax:* 226 050 999
E-mail: info@civilizacao.pt
Web Site: www.civilizacao.pt
Key Personnel
President: Pedro Moura Bessa
Founded: 1921
Subjects: Art, Economics, Fiction, Government,
Political Science, History, Religion - Other, So-
cial Sciences, Sociology, Travel & Tourism
ISBN Prefix(es): 978-972-26

Classica Editora+
Rua do Vale Formoso, 37, 1959-006 Lisbon
E-mail: suporte@polytechnica.pt
Web Site: classicaeditora.pt
Key Personnel
President: Francisco Paulo
Subjects: Behavioral Sciences, Business, Com-
munications, Drama, Theater, Fiction, History,
Management, Science Fiction, Fantasy, Social
Sciences, Sociology, Wine & Spirits
ISBN Prefix(es): 978-972-561; 978-989-604
Parent Company: Grupo Escolar

Coimbra Editora Lda+
Rua Ferreira Borges 77-79, 3000-180 Coimbra
Tel: 239 85 2650 *Fax:* 239 85 2651
E-mail: editorial@coimbraeditora.net;
comercial@coimbraeditora.net; encomendas@
coimbraeditora.net
Web Site: www.coimbraeditora.net
Founded: 1920

Subjects: Education, Language Arts, Linguistics, Law, Literature, Literary Criticism, Essays, Psychology, Psychiatry
ISBN Prefix(es): 978-972-32; 978-989-96672
Bookshop(s): Livraria Juridica da AAC, Rua Padre Antonio Vieira, Edificio AAC, 3000-315 Coimbra *Tel:* 239 098 985 *Fax:* 239 098 985 *E-mail:* aac@livrariajuridica.com; Livraria Juridica Ferreira Borges, Rua Ferreira Borges, 77-79, 3000-180 Coimbra *Tel:* 239 099 002 *Fax:* 239 090 352 *E-mail:* ferreiraborges@livrariajuridica.com; Livraria Juridica Coimbra Editora, Edificio Arnado-Centro Comercial do Arnado-Loja 18, Rua Joao de Ruao, nº 12, 3000-229 Coimbra *Tel:* 239 83 7275 *Fax:* 239 83 7275 *E-mail:* arnado@livrariajuridica.com; Livraria Juridica Arco-Iris, Centro Commercial Arco-Iris, Av Julio Dinis, 6A, Lj 30, 36, 37 e 38, 1069-215 Lisbon *Tel:* 21 780 0468 *Fax:* 21 780 0469 *E-mail:* arcoiris@livrariajuridica.com; Livraria Juridica do Chiado, Rua Nova do Almada, 90, 1200-290 Lisbon *Tel:* 21 342 4917 *Fax:* 21 347 1464 *E-mail:* chiado@livrariajuridica.com; Livraria Juridica da Faculdade de Direito da Universidade Nova de Lisbon, Campus de Campolide, 1099-032 Lisbon *Tel:* 213 832 361 *Fax:* 213 832 362 *E-mail:* unl@livrariajuridica.com; Livraria Juridica da Faculdade de Direito de Lisboa, Alameda da Universidade, 1649-014 Lisbon *Tel:* 21 796 3122 *Fax:* 21 780 0763 *E-mail:* fdul@livrariajuridica.com; Livraria Juridica da Faculdade de Direito do Porto, Rua dos Bragos, 223, 4050-123 Porto *Tel:* 22 339 0587 *Fax:* 22 339 0588 *E-mail:* fdup@livrariajuridica.com; Livraria Juridica da ULP, Rua Dr Lopo de Carvalho, Edificio E, 4369-006 Porto *Tel:* 22 549 05 71 *Fax:* 22 549 05 72 *E-mail:* ulp@livrariajuridica.com

Edicoes Colibri+
Apdo 42 001, Telheiras, 1601-801 Lisbon
Tel: 21 796 40 38 *Fax:* 21 796 40 38
E-mail: colibri@edi-colibri.pt
Web Site: www.edi-colibri.pt
Key Personnel
Mng Dir: Fernando Mao de Ferro
Founded: 1991
Membership(s): Portuguese Association of Publishers & Booksellers (APEL).
Subjects: Archaeology, Environmental Studies, Geography, Geology, Government, Political Science, History, Literature, Literary Criticism, Essays, Philosophy, Social Sciences, Sociology
ISBN Prefix(es): 978-972-772; 978-972-8047; 978-972-8288
Number of titles published annually: 50 Print
Total Titles: 400 Print; 400 Online
Distributed by Dinapress; Sodiexpor; Sodilivros (only in Portugal)
Bookshop(s): Livraria Colibri-Faculdade de Ciencias Sociais e Humanas da Universidade Nova de Lisboa, Av de Berna, 26-C, 1069-061 Lisbon *Tel:* 21 795 11 89 *Fax:* 21 795 11 89

Comissao para a Cidadania e a Igualdade de Genero (Commission for Citizenship & Gender Equality)+
Ave Republica 32-1º, 1050-193 Lisbon
Tel: 217 983 000 *Fax:* 217 983 098
E-mail: cig@cig.gov.pt; cid@cig.gov.pt
Web Site: www.cig.gov.pt
Key Personnel
President: Fatima Duarte
Founded: 1977
Subjects: Women's Studies
ISBN Prefix(es): 978-972-597

Edicoes Joao Sa da Costa+
Av Brasil 120, 1º - E, 1700-074 Lisbon
Tel: 218400428

Founded: 1984
ISBN Prefix(es): 978-972-9230

Didactica Editora
Ave de Berna, 31 Loja, 1069-054 Lisbon
Tel: 21 797 92 78 *Fax:* 21 795 40 19
E-mail: geral@didacticaeditora.pt; mkt@didacticaeditora.pt; comercial@didacticaeditora.pt
Web Site: www.didacticaeditora.pt
Founded: 1944
Membership(s): Portuguese Association of Publishers & Booksellers (APEL).
Subjects: Astrology, Occult, Astronomy, Electronics, Electrical Engineering, Health, Nutrition, History, Mathematics, Philosophy, Physical Sciences, Science (General), Biology
ISBN Prefix(es): 978-972-650
Parent Company: Platano Editora SA
Branch Office(s)
Rua Manuel Ferreira, 1 A-B-C, Quinta das Lagoas, 2855-597 Santa Marta de Corroios *Tel:* 21 255 99 70 *Fax:* 21 253 40 68
Rua Guerra Junqueiro, 452, 4150-387 Porto *Tel:* 22 606 13 00 *Fax:* 22 606 13 05

Editora Difel+
Imprint of Grupo Editorial Record
Campo de Santa Clara, 160 C/D, 1100-475 Lisbon
Tel: 21 885 50 30 *Fax:* 21 887 50 50
Founded: 1982
Subjects: Fiction, Nonfiction (General)
ISBN Prefix(es): 978-972-29
Warehouse: Travessa da Sao Jose, 11, Armazem 7, 2715-116 Pero Pinheiro *Tel:* 21 927 16 03 *Fax:* 21 967 25 29 *E-mail:* armazem.pp@medialivros.pt

Dinalivro+
Rua Joao Ortigao Ramos, 17-A, 1500-362 Lisbon
Tel: 217 122 210; 217 107 081 *Fax:* 217 153 774
E-mail: comercial@dinalivro.com
Web Site: www.facebook.com/dinalivroedicoes
Founded: 1969
Also distributor.
Subjects: Accounting, Aeronautics, Aviation, Architecture & Interior Design, Art, Astronomy, Biological Sciences, Computer Science, Education, Electronics, Electrical Engineering, Engineering (General), Gardening, Plants, Geography, Geology, Health, Nutrition, History, Language Arts, Linguistics, Literature, Literary Criticism, Essays, Medicine, Nursing, Dentistry, Philosophy, Photography, Physics, Psychology, Psychiatry, Science (General), Social Sciences, Sociology, Theology
ISBN Prefix(es): 978-972-576
Bookshop(s): Livraria Centro Cultural Brasileiro, Largo Dr Antonio de Sousa de Macedo, 5A, 1500-153 Lisbon *Tel:* 21 396 1374 *E-mail:* ccbrasileiro@dinalivro.com; Nova Fronteira-Shopping Center Brasilia, 5 Piso-Loja 505-A, 4000 Porto
Distribution Center: Dinapress *E-mail:* info.dinapress@dinalivro.com

Edicoes Tecnicas e Profissionais (ETEP), *imprint of* Lidel Edicoes Tecnicas Lda

11x17
Imprint of Grupo Bertrand Circulo
Rua Prof Jorge da Silva Horta, 1, 1500-499 Lisbon
Tel: 21 762 60 00 *Fax:* 21 762 32 50
Web Site: www.11x17.pt
Founded: 2008
Subjects: Education, Erotica, Fiction, Health, Nutrition, History, Management, Medicine, Nursing, Dentistry, Mysteries, Suspense, Nonfiction (General), Poetry, Romance, Science Fiction,

Fantasy, Self-Help, Social Sciences, Sociology, Travel & Tourism
ISBN Prefix(es): 978-972-25

Editorial Estampa Lda+
Rua da Escola do Exercito, 9, R/C-Dto, 1169-090 Lisbon
Tel: 213 555 663 *Fax:* 213 141 911
E-mail: estampa@estampa.pt
Web Site: www.estampa.pt
Key Personnel
Editorial Dir: Antonio Carlos Manso Pinheiro
Founded: 1960
Subjects: Anthropology, Antiques, Architecture & Interior Design, Art, Astrology, Occult, Cookery, Drama, Theater, Economics, Education, Fiction, Geography, Geology, Government, Political Science, Health, Nutrition, History, Law, Literature, Literary Criticism, Essays, Medicine, Nursing, Dentistry, Nonfiction (General), Parapsychology, Philosophy, Psychology, Psychiatry, Religion - Other, Romance, Science (General), Social Sciences, Sociology, Sports, Athletics
ISBN Prefix(es): 978-972-33
Warehouse: Ave Santa Iria, 1, 2690-379 Santa Iria Azoia

Estrela Polar
Member of Grupo LeYa
Rua Cidade de Cordova, 2, 2610-038 Alfragide
Tel: 21 041 74 10 *Fax:* 21 471 77 37
E-mail: comunicacao@leya.com
Web Site: www.estrelapolar.leya.com
Subjects: Biography, Memoirs, Health, Nutrition, Inspirational, Spirituality, Management, Psychology, Psychiatry, Religion - Other, Self-Help, Social Sciences, Sociology, Lifestyle, Personal Development
ISBN Prefix(es): 978-989-8206; 978-972-8929

EuroImpala Books Lda
Rua de Impala, 33A-Abrunheira, Sao Pedro de Penaferrim, 2710-070 Sintra
Tel: 219238246 (orders) *Fax:* 219238463 (orders)
E-mail: vendadireta@euroimpalabooks.com
Web Site: www.euroimpalabooks.com
Founded: 1983
Membership(s): AIND; APCT.
Subjects: Astronomy, Biography, Memoirs, Career Development, Child Care & Development, Computers, Cookery, Economics, Education, Fashion, Gardening, Plants, Geography, Geology, How-to, Humor, Literature, Literary Criticism, Essays, Music, Dance, Photography, Radio, TV, Sports, Athletics, Women's Studies
ISBN Prefix(es): 978-972-574; 978-972-766

Publicacoes Europa-America Lda
Rua Francisco Lyon de Castro, 2, Apdo 8, 2725-354 Mem Martins
Tel: 21 926 77 00 *Fax:* 21 926 77 71
E-mail: secretariado@europa-america.pt
Web Site: www.europa-america.pt
Founded: 1945
Subjects: Art, Biography, Memoirs, Education, Engineering (General), Fiction, History, How-to, Medicine, Nursing, Dentistry, Music, Dance, Philosophy, Poetry, Psychology, Psychiatry, Science (General), Social Sciences, Sociology, Technology
ISBN Prefix(es): 978-972-1
Subsidiaries: Publicacoes Alfa SA; Edicoes Cetop; Lyon Edicoes
Bookshop(s): Arcadas do Parque Nascente, 2, 2765-266 Estoril *Tel:* 214 683 935 *E-mail:* pea.lojaestoril@europa-america.pt; Praca Ferreira de Almeida, 30, 8000-172 Faro *Tel:* 289 813 138 *E-mail:* pea.lojafaro@europa-america.pt; Ave Marques de Tomar, 1B, 1050-152 Lisbon *Tel:* 213 563 791 *E-mail:* pea.lojamtomar@europa-america.pt; Rua Jose Relvas, 15 B/C,

2775-222 Parede *Tel:* 214 581 645 *E-mail:* pea.
lojaparede@europa-america.pt; Rua 31 de
Janeiro, 221, 4000-543 Porto *Tel:* 222 055 658

**Europress Editores e Distribuidores de
Publicacoes Lda+**
Rua Joao Saraiva, 10-A, 1700-249 Lisbon
Tel: 218444340 *Fax:* 218492061
E-mail: geral@europress.pt; europress@mail.
telepac.pt
Web Site: www.europress.pt; www.
europresseditora.pt
Founded: 1986
Also acts as national & international distributor,
exporter & printer.
Membership(s): APIGT; UEP (Uniao dos Editores
Portugueses).
Subjects: Chemistry, Chemical Engineering,
Drama, Theater, Fiction, Health, Nutrition,
History, Humor, Law, Literature, Literary Crit-
icism, Essays, Medicine, Nursing, Dentistry,
Nonfiction (General), Poetry, Religion - Other,
Romance, Science (General), Sports, Athletics,
Western Fiction
ISBN Prefix(es): 978-972-559
Number of titles published annually: 50 Print
Total Titles: 600 Print
Associate Companies: Pentaedro-Publicidade e
Artes Graficas Lda, Praceta da Republica, Lote
A-1, Loja B, 2675 Povoa Santo Adriao, Odive-
las
Branch Office(s)
Cidade Da Praia, Cabo Verde
Maputo, Mozambique
Distributor for Ed-Maputo (Mozambique);
Livraria LEIA
Bookshop(s): Bolsonoite I-Livraria Bar Lda, Ave
Rainha D Leonor 25-A, 1600 Lisbon
Warehouse: Praceta de Republica, 15, 2620-
162 Pavoa da Santo Adriao *Tel:* 219381450
Fax: 219381452

Everest Editora
Parque Industrial Meramar II, Armazem n°1 & 2,
Cabra Figa, 2635-047 Rio do Mouro
Tel: 219152483; 219152510 *Fax:* 219152525
Key Personnel
Marketing & Communication Manager: Alexan-
dra Sofia Silva Fernandes
Founded: 1994
Subjects: Cookery, Travel & Tourism
ISBN Prefix(es): 978-972-750; 978-989-50

FCA-Editora de Informatica, *imprint of* Lidel
Edicoes Tecnicas Lda

FCA Editora de Informatica Lda
Ave Praia da Vitoria, 14A, 1000-247 Lisbon
Tel: 21 351 14 48 *Fax:* 21 317 32 59
E-mail: fca@fca.pt
Web Site: www.fca.pt
Founded: 1991
Subjects: Computer Science
ISBN Prefix(es): 978-972-722

Livraria Editora Figueirinhas
Rua do Almada 47, 4050-036 Porto
Tel: 223 325 300 *Fax:* 223 325 907
Founded: 1944
Subjects: Literature, Literary Criticism, Essays
ISBN Prefix(es): 978-972-661
Branch Office(s)
Rua do Olival, 120, 1200-743 Lisbon
Distributor for Pe de Pagina Editores; Edicoes
Universidade Fernando Pessoa

Editorial Franciscana+
Apdo 1217, Montariol, 4711-856 Braga
Tel: 253 253 490 *Fax:* 253 619 735
E-mail: edfranciscana@editorialfranciscana.org
Web Site: www.editorialfranciscana.org

Key Personnel
Mng Dir: Fr Jose Antonio Correia Pereira
Founded: 1924
Membership(s): Portuguese Association of Pub-
lishers & Booksellers (APEL).
Subjects: Art, Biography, Memoirs, History, Mu-
sic, Dance, Philosophy, Religion - Other, The-
ology
ISBN Prefix(es): 978-972-9190; 978-972-784;
978-972-8447
Subsidiaries: Delegacao da Editorial Franciscana
Bookshop(s): Livraria Editorial Francis-
cana, Rua de Cedofeita, 350, 4050-123
Porto *Tel:* 222 052 148 *Fax:* 222 052 148
E-mail: livrariafranciscana@gmail.com

Fronteira do Caos Editores Lda
Apdo 52028, 4202-801 Porto
Tel: 225 025 005
E-mail: fronteiradocaos@netcabo.pt
Web Site: www.fronteiradocaoseditores.pt
Founded: 2005
Subjects: Fiction, History, Management, Self-Help
ISBN Prefix(es): 978-989-95063; 978-989-8070
Distribution Center: Gradiva Publicacoes Lda,
Rua Almeida e Sousa, n° 21, R/C - esquina,
1399-041 Lisbon *Tel:* 213 974 067; 213 971
357 *E-mail:* geral@gradiva.mail.pt

**Gabinete de Especializcao e Cooperacao
Tecnica Internacional Lda,** see GECTI
(Gabinete de Especializacao e Cooperacao
Tecnica Internacional Lda)

Edicoes Gailivro SA
Member of Grupo LeYa
Rua Cidade de Cordova n° 2, 2610-038 Alfragide
Tel: 21 427 22 00; 707 252 252 (customer ser-
vice) *Fax:* 21 427 22 01; 707 289 289 (cus-
tomer service)
E-mail: comunicacao@leya.com
Web Site: www.gailivro.pt
Founded: 1987
Subjects: Education, Fiction, Mathematics, Sci-
ence Fiction, Fantasy
ISBN Prefix(es): 978-972-8473; 978-972-8723;
978-972-9443; 978-989-3200; 978-989-2321;
978-989-557

**GECTI (Gabinete de Especializacao e
Cooperacao Tecnica Internacional Lda)+**
Ave Republica 47, 6°-d, 1050-188 Lisbon
Tel: 217968877 *Fax:* 217963465
Founded: 1963
Subjects: Business, Marketing, Public Administra-
tion
ISBN Prefix(es): 978-972-9012

Gestao Plus
Imprint of Grupo Bertrand Circulo
Rua Prof Jorge da Silva Horta, 1, 1500-499 Lis-
bon
Tel: 21 762 60 00 *Fax:* 21 762 32 50
Web Site: www.gestaoplus.pt
Subjects: Accounting, Business, Communications,
Economics, Finance, Health, Nutrition, Litera-
ture, Literary Criticism, Essays, Management,
Marketing, Medicine, Nursing, Dentistry, Hu-
man Resources
ISBN Prefix(es): 978-989-8115

Girassol Edicoes Lda+
Rua das Macarocas, Abrunneira Business Center,
Arm N° 9-I, 2710-056 Sintra
Tel: 21 915 15 40
E-mail: editorial@girassoledicoes.com
Web Site: www.girassoledicoes.com
Founded: 1994
Subjects: Art, Cookery, History, How-to, Self-
Help
ISBN Prefix(es): 978-972-756; 978-989-633

Number of titles published annually: 120 Print
Total Titles: 590 Print
Imprints: Multinova; Susaeta Ediciones
Branch Office(s)
Banco Espirito Santo *Tel:* 21 4185367
Banco Santander *Tel:* 21 4588390
Alameda Pucurui, 51-59, Bloco B, 1° andar, Conj
1010, Sala 02, 06460-100 Tambore, Barueri-SP,
Brazil *Tel:* (011) 4196-6699 *Fax:* (011) 4196-
6690 *E-mail:* girassol@girassolbrasil.com.br
Web Site: www.girassolbrasil.com.br

Gradiva Publicacoes SA+
Rua Almeida e Sousa, 21 R/C esquina, 1399-041
Lisbon
Tel: 21 397 40 67; 21 397 40 68; 21 397 13 57;
21 395 34 70 *Fax:* 21 395 34 71
E-mail: geral@gradiva.mail.pt; encomendas@
gradiva.mail.pt (orders); gradivapublicacoessa@
gmail.com
Web Site: www.gradiva.pt
Founded: 1981
Specialize in science books.
Subjects: Anthropology, Asian Studies, Astron-
omy, Behavioral Sciences, Biological Sciences,
Communications, Computer Science, Crafts,
Games, Hobbies, Earth Sciences, Economics,
Education, Engineering (General), Environ-
mental Studies, Fiction, Geography, Geology,
Government, Political Science, History, Hu-
man Relations, Humor, Journalism, Literature,
Literary Criticism, Essays, Management, Math-
ematics, Natural History, Nonfiction (General),
Philosophy, Physics, Psychology, Psychiatry,
Romance, Science (General), Science Fiction,
Fantasy, Self-Help, Social Sciences, Sociology
ISBN Prefix(es): 978-972-662
Number of titles published annually: 80 Print
Total Titles: 700 Print
Distributor for Sinais de Fogo
Warehouse: Praca Sao Joao Bosco, 22-C, 1350-
297 Lisbon *Fax:* 21 397 14 11 *E-mail:* apoio@
gradiva.mail.pt

Guerra & Paz Editores SA
R Conde Redondo, 8-5° esquina, 1150-105 Lis-
bon
Tel: 21 314 44 88 *Fax:* 21 314 44 89
E-mail: guerraepaz@guerraepaz.net
Web Site: www.guerraepaz.net
Key Personnel
Editorial Dir: Manuel S Fonseca
Communication & Public Relations: Vania Custo-
dio
Design & Production: Ilidio Vasco
Founded: 2006
Subjects: Education, Fiction, Nonfiction (General)
ISBN Prefix(es): 978-989-8014; 978-989-8174;
978-989-702
Foreign Rights: Pontas Agency
Distribution Center: VASP Distribuidora de Pub-
licacoes SA *Tel:* 21 433 70 00

Livros Horizonte+
Rua das Chagas 17, 1° Dt°, 1200-106 Lisbon
Tel: 213466917 *Fax:* 213541852
E-mail: geral@livroshorizonte.pt
Web Site: www.livroshorizonte.pt
Founded: 1953
Subjects: Architecture & Interior Design, Art,
Economics, Education, Engineering (General),
History, Psychology, Psychiatry, Social Sci-
ences, Sociology, Sports, Athletics
ISBN Prefix(es): 978-972-24

Ideias de Ler
Rua da Restauracao n°365, 4099-023 Porto
Tel: 22 608 83 42 *Fax:* 22 608 83 43
Web Site: www.ideiasdeler.pt
Founded: 2006
Subjects: Fiction, Literature, Literary Criticism,
Essays, Nonfiction (General)

ISBN Prefix(es): 978-972-0
Parent Company: Grupo Porto Editora

IICT, see Instituto de Investigacao Cientifica
Tropical I P

Imprensa Nacional-Casa da Moeda SA
Ave Antonio Jose de Almeida, 1000-042 Lisbon
Tel: 217 810 700; 217 810 870 (customer service)
Fax: 217 810 745; 217 810 754
E-mail: cdi-mail@incm.pt; editorial.
apoiocliente@incm.pt; incm@incm.pt
Web Site: www.incm.pt
Key Personnel
President: Rui Carp
Founded: 1768
Subjects: Anthropology, Archaeology, Art, Biog-
raphy, Memoirs, Economics, Ethnicity, Gov-
ernment, Political Science, History, Language
Arts, Linguistics, Law, Literature, Literary Crit-
icism, Essays, Medicine, Nursing, Dentistry,
Philosophy, Poetry, Public Administration, So-
cial Sciences, Sociology
ISBN Prefix(es): 978-972-27
Bookshop(s): Rua da Escola Politecnica, 137,
1250-100 Lisbon *Tel:* 213 945 700; 213 945
729 *Fax:* 213 945 758 *E-mail:* livraria.r.
escola@incm.pt; Rua de D Filipa de Vilhena
12, 12A, 1000-136 Lisbon *Tel:* 217 904 030
Fax: 217 904 037 *E-mail:* livraria.f.vilhena@
incm.pt; Ave de Fernao de Magalhaes, 486,
3000-173 Coimbra *Tel:* 239 856 400 *Fax:* 239
856 416 *E-mail:* livraria.coimbra@incm.pt;
Praca de Gomes Teixeira (Leoes), 1 a 7, 4050-
290 Porto *Tel:* 223 395 820 *Fax:* 223 395 823
E-mail: livraria.porto@incm.pt; Galerias Lu-
mier, Rua de Jose Falcao, loja B-17, 4050-317
Porto *Tel:* 220 933 641 *E-mail:* livraria.outlet.
porto@incm.pt

INCM, see Imprensa Nacional-Casa da Moeda
SA

Instituto de Investigacao Cientifica Tropical I P
(Institute of Tropical Scientific Research)
Rua da Junqueira, 86-1°, 1300-344 Lisbon
Tel: 21 361 63 40 *Fax:* 21 363 14 60
E-mail: iict@iict.pt
Web Site: www.iict.pt
Key Personnel
President: Jorge Braga de Macedo
Founded: 1883
Specialize in tropical subjects.
Subjects: Agriculture, Anthropology, Archaeol-
ogy, Biological Sciences, Earth Sciences, En-
vironmental Studies, Ethnicity, Geography,
Geology, History, Social Sciences, Sociology,
Veterinary Science
ISBN Prefix(es): 978-972-672
Number of titles published annually: 23 Print
Bookshop(s): Imprensa Nacional-Casa da Moeda,
Ave Antonio Jose de Almeida, 1092-042 Lis-
bon *Tel:* 21 710 77 00 *Fax:* 21 781 07 45
E-mail: dco@incm.pt
Orders to: CDI-Centro de Documentacao e In-
formacao, Rua General Joao de Almeida, 15,
Palacio dos Condes da Calheta, 1300-266
Lisbon *Tel:* 21 361 97 30 *Fax:* 21 361 97 39
E-mail: cdi@iict.pt

Instituto Piaget Divisao Editorial
R Eng Cunha Leal, 1900-678 Lisbon
Tel: 218 364 020 *Fax:* 218 364 021
E-mail: infoeditora@ipiaget.pt
Web Site: www.ipiagetdeditora.com
Founded: 1988
Subjects: Biography, Memoirs, Economics, Gov-
ernment, Political Science, Health, Nutrition,
History, Law, Medicine, Nursing, Dentistry,
Philosophy, Poetry, Romance, Science (Gen-

eral), Technology, Ecology, Epistemology &
Society, Human Rights
ISBN Prefix(es): 978-972-771; 978-989-659; 978-
972-8245; 978-972-8329; 978-972-8407; 978-
972-9295

Jacaranda
Estrada das Palmeiras, 59, Queluz de Baixo,
2730-132 Barcarena
Tel: 214347001
E-mail: info@jacaranda.pt
Web Site: www.jacaranda.pt
Key Personnel
Editorial: Susana Lima *E-mail:* susana@
jacaranda.pt
Marketing & Communication: Vanessa Gama
E-mail: vanessa@jacaranda.pt
Subjects: Cookery, Crafts, Games, Hobbies, Fic-
tion, Health, Nutrition, Mysteries, Suspense,
Nonfiction (General), Romance
ISBN Prefix(es): 978-989-8752
Parent Company: Grupo Editorial Presenca

Lidel Edicoes Tecnicas Lda+
Rua Dona Estefania 183 r/c Dto, 1049-057 Lis-
bon
Tel: 21 351 14 48 *Fax:* 21 352 26 84
E-mail: lidel@lidel.pt
Web Site: www.lidel.pt
Key Personnel
Editorial Dir, Management & Technology: Fred-
erico Annes
Editorial Dir, Medicine & Science: Manuela
Annes
Founded: 1963
Membership(s): Publishers & Booksellers Por-
tuguese Association.
Subjects: Computer Science, Labor, Industrial Re-
lations, Language Arts, Linguistics
ISBN Prefix(es): 978-972-9018; 978-972-757;
978-989-752
Imprints: Edicoes Tecnicas e Profissionais
(ETEP); FCA-Editora de Informatica
Bookshop(s): Ave Praia da Vitoria, 14, 1000-247
Lisbon *Tel:* 21 354 14 18 *Fax:* 21 317 32 59
E-mail: livraria@lidel.pt
Warehouse: Rua Dona Luis de Noronha 25 A/B,
1050-071 Lisbon

Editora Livros do Brasil
Edificio GBC, A/C Libros do Brasil, Rua Prof
Jorge Silva Horta, n° 1, 1500-499 Lisbon
Tel: 217 626 000
Web Site: www.livrosdobrasil.pt
Founded: 1944
Subjects: Biography, Memoirs, Government, Po-
litical Science, History, Philosophy, Science
(General), Science Fiction, Fantasy
ISBN Prefix(es): 978-972-38
Associate Companies: Editores Associados Lda
Branch Office(s)
Rua de Ceuta, 80, 4050-189 Porto *Tel:* 222 052
541 *Fax:* 222 086 020
Distribution Center: Porto Editora, Rua da
Restauracao, 365, 4099-023 Porto

Lucerna, *imprint of* Principia Editora

Lucerna
Imprint of Principia Editora
Rua Vasco da Gama, n° 60 C, 2775-297 Parede
Tel: 21 467 87 10 *Fax:* 21 467 87 19
E-mail: principia@principia.pt
Web Site: www.principia.pt
Founded: 2003
Subjects: Religion - Catholic
ISBN Prefix(es): 978-972-8835; 978-989-8516

Marcador Editora
Rua Augusto Gil 35 A, 1049-043 Lisbon
Tel: 21 269 39 60

E-mail: info@marcador.pt
Web Site: www.marcador.pt
Key Personnel
Founder & Publisher: Joao Goncalves
Project Manager: Marina Oliveira
Designer: Marina Costa
Editorial Consultant: Hugo Goncalves
Subjects: Biography, Memoirs, Child Care &
Development, Cookery, Education, Fiction,
Health, Nutrition, History, Humor, Inspira-
tional, Spirituality, Literature, Literary Criti-
cism, Essays, Management, Romance, Science
(General), Travel & Tourism, History of Portu-
gal, Investigation, Personal Development
ISBN Prefix(es): 978-989-75

Editorial Minerva & Livraria+
Rua Luz Soriano, 31-33-35/1°, 1200-246 Lisbon
Tel: 213468288
E-mail: minerva.geral@sapo.pt; editorial.
minerva@gmail.com
Web Site: www.facebook.com/editorial.minerva
Key Personnel
Publisher & Manager: Narcisa Fernandes
Founded: 1927
Subjects: Fiction
ISBN Prefix(es): 978-972-591
Branch Office(s)
Grafica Minerva, Rua da Alegria, 30, 1250-007
Lisbon *Tel:* 213224950 *Fax:* 213224952

Edicoes Minervacoimbra+
Torre do Arnado, Rua Joao de Ruao, 12 - 1° -
Esc 63, 3000-229 Coimbra
Tel: 239701117
E-mail: info@minervacoimbra.pt;
minervacoimbra@gmail.com
Web Site: www.minervacoimbra.pt
Founded: 1986
Subjects: Architecture & Interior Design, Art, Bi-
ography, Memoirs, Communications, Computer
Science, Drama, Theater, Economics, Educa-
tion, Engineering (General), Fiction, Finance,
Geography, Geology, History, Humor, Jour-
nalism, Literature, Literary Criticism, Essays,
Management, Medicine, Nursing, Dentistry,
Philosophy, Poetry, Romance, Social Sciences,
Sociology
ISBN Prefix(es): 978-972-8318; 978-972-798;
978-972-9316
Total Titles: 25 Print
Distributed by Livraria Minerva
Bookshop(s): Livraria Minerva, Rua de Macau,
52, 3030-059 Coimbra

Monitor - Projectos e Edicoes Lda+
Av da Igreja, n° 66 - 3° Esq°, 1700-240 Lisbon
Tel: 217973656
E-mail: depeditorial@monitor.pt; depcomercial@
monitor.pt
Web Site: www.monitor.pt
Specialize in technical areas including manage-
ment, training & behavior, focusing on personal
& professional development.
Subjects: Career Development, Engineering (Gen-
eral), Human Relations, Management, Self-
Help
ISBN Prefix(es): 978-972-9413; 978-972-95278
Total Titles: 65 Print

Multinova, *imprint of* Girassol Edicoes Lda

Musicoteca Lda
Rua Joao Pereira da Rosa, 8, 1200-000 Lisbon
Tel: 213220130 *Fax:* 213476957
Founded: 1990
Subjects: Music, Dance
ISBN Prefix(es): 978-972-9449

Nova Acropole+
Ave Antonio Augusto de Aguiar, 17-4º esq, 1050-012 Lisbon
Tel: 213 523 056; 911 929 561
E-mail: lisboa@nova-acropole.pt
Web Site: www.nova-acropole.pt
Key Personnel
Dir: Jose Carlos Fernandez
Founded: 1979
Specialize in human sciences & esoterism.
Subjects: Anthropology, Archaeology, Astrology, Occult, History, Philosophy
ISBN Prefix(es): 978-972-9026
Branch Office(s)
Rua Tenente Resende, Nº 15º 1º B, 3800 Aveiro
Tel: 916 842 100 *E-mail:* aveiro@nova-acropole.pt
Rua do Brasil, 194 - R/c, 3030-775 Coimbra *Tel:* 239 108 209; 933 931 022
E-mail: coimbra@nova-acropole.pt
Ave da Boavista, 1057, 4100-129 Porto *Tel:* 22 600 92 77 *E-mail:* porto@nova-acropole.pt

Nova Vega Editora Lda+
Rua do Poder Local, nº 2-sobreloja A, 1675-156 Pontinha, Lisbon
Tel: 217 781 028
Web Site: www.novavegaeditorial.blogspot.com; www.facebook.com/novavega.editora
Founded: 1975
Subjects: Anthropology, Architecture & Interior Design, Art, Astrology, Occult, Behavioral Sciences, Biography, Memoirs, Child Care & Development, Communications, Computer Science, Cookery, Drama, Theater, Economics, Education, Fashion, Fiction, Government, Political Science, History, Humor, Language Arts, Linguistics, Law, LGBTQ, Literature, Literary Criticism, Essays, Philosophy, Photography, Poetry, Psychology, Psychiatry, Religion - Buddhist, Religion - Other, Romance, Science Fiction, Fantasy, Social Sciences, Sociology, Sports, Athletics, Esoteric Sciences, Media
ISBN Prefix(es): 978-972-699

Novagaia
Member of Grupo LeYa
Rua Cidade de Cordova, 2, 2610-038 Alfragide
Tel: 210 417 410 *Fax:* 214 717 737
E-mail: comunicacao@leya.com
Web Site: www.novagaia.pt
Founded: 1985
Subjects: Education, Fiction
ISBN Prefix(es): 978-972-712
Distribution Center: Livraria Papelaria 115, Estrada Lisboa-Palheira-Assafarge, 3040-692 Coimbra *Tel:* 239 810 150 *Fax:* 239 810 152 *E-mail:* liv115@mail.telepac.pt
Fundacao Livraria Esperanca, Rua dos Ferreiros, 119, 9000-082 Funchal *Tel:* 291 221 116 *Fax:* 291 221 348 *Web Site:* www.livraria-esperanca.pt
JB-Artigos Papelaria Lda, Zona Industrial Varziela, Rua 3, Lote 16 - Arvore, 4480-071 Vila do Conde *Tel:* 252 248 168 *Fax:* 252 637 311 *Web Site:* www.jb-cash.com

Observatorio Astronomico de Lisboa
Tapada da Ajuda, 1349-018 Lisbon
Tel: 21 361 6730 *Fax:* 21 361 6750
E-mail: info@oal.ul.pt
Web Site: www.oal.ul.pt
Key Personnel
Dir: Prof Rui Jorge Agostinho
Subjects: Astronomy
ISBN Prefix(es): 978-972-573

Oficina do Livro
Member of Grupo LeYa
Rua Cidade de Cordova, nº 2, 2610-038 Alfragide
Tel: 21 427 22 00 *Fax:* 21 427 22 01
E-mail: info@oficinadolivro.leya.com

Web Site: www.oficinadolivro.pt
Founded: 1999
Subjects: Biography, Memoirs, Economics, Fiction, Health, Nutrition, History, Humor, Literature, Literary Criticism, Essays, Management, Travel & Tourism
ISBN Prefix(es): 978-989-555; 978-989-7411

Edicoes Ora & Labora
Rua Mosteiro de Singeverga, 4795-309 Roriz, Santo Tirso
Tel: 252941176 *Fax:* 252872947
Founded: 1950
Membership(s): Society of Portuguese Publishers & Booksellers.
Subjects: Anthropology, Biography, Memoirs, Religion - Catholic, Theology
ISBN Prefix(es): 978-972-9278

Paulinas Editora+
Rua Francisco Salgado Zenha, Lote 11, 2685-332 Prior Velho
Tel: 219 405 640 *Fax:* 219 405 649
E-mail: editora@paulinas.pt
Web Site: www.paulinas.pt
Founded: 1950
Subjects: Biblical Studies, Biography, Memoirs, Human Relations, Literature, Literary Criticism, Essays, Psychology, Psychiatry, Religion - Catholic, Romance, Science Fiction, Fantasy, Securities
ISBN Prefix(es): 978-972-751
Bookshop(s): Paulinas Multimedia, Rua do Municipio, 12, 8000-398 Faro *Tel:* 289 823 027 *Fax:* 289 805 679 *E-mail:* liv.faro@paulinas.pt; Paulinas Multimedia, Rua Dr Fernao de Ornelas, 37, 9050-021 Funchal *Tel:* 291 235 699 *Fax:* 291 233 617 *E-mail:* liv.funchal@paulinas.pt; Paulinas Multimedia, Rua Morais Soares, 56-A, 1900-348 Lisbon *Tel:* 218 139 038 *Fax:* 218 133 933 *E-mail:* liv.lisboa@paulinas.pt; Paulinas Multimedia, Praca do Municipio, 18, 7300-110 Portalegre *Tel:* 245 308 165 *E-mail:* liv.portalegre@paulinas.pt; Paulinas Multimedia, Rua de Cedofeita, 355, 4050-181 Porto *Tel:* 222 054 956 *E-mail:* liv.porto@paulinas.pt; Paulinas Multimedia, Rua Fran Pacheco, 107, 2900-376 Setubal *Tel:* 265 548 500 *Fax:* 265 509 099 *E-mail:* liv.setubal@paulinas.pt

Paulus Editora
Rua Dom Pedro de Cristo, 10-12, 1749-092 Lisbon
Tel: 21 84 37 620 *Fax:* 21 84 37 629
E-mail: editor@paulus.pt; comercial@paulus.pt
Web Site: www.paulus.pt
Key Personnel
Editorial Dir: Darlei Zanon
Subjects: Biblical Studies, Inspirational, Spirituality, Philosophy, Psychology, Psychiatry, Religion - Catholic, Theology, Catechesis, Current Affairs, Family Life, Pedagogy
ISBN Prefix(es): 978-972-30
Orders to: Estrada de Sao Paulo, 2680-294 Apelacao *Tel:* 21 94 88 870 *Fax:* 21 94 88 875 *E-mail:* sede@paulus.pt

Peres-Soctip Industrias Graficas SA
Estrada Nacional nº 10, Km 108, 3 Porto Alto, 2135-114 Samora Correia
Tel: 263009900 *Fax:* 263009999
Founded: 1936
Subjects: Art
ISBN Prefix(es): 978-972-9435

Editora Pergaminho
Imprint of Grupo Bertrand Circulo
Rua Prof Jorge da Silva Horta, 1, 1500-499 Lisbon
Tel: 21 762 60 00 *Fax:* 21 762 61 50

Web Site: www.pergaminho.pt
Founded: 1990
Subjects: Art, Fiction, History, Inspirational, Spirituality, Management, Music, Dance, Nonfiction (General), Psychology, Psychiatry, Radio, TV, Self-Help, Humanities, Inspirational Fiction
ISBN Prefix(es): 978-972-711; 978-989-687
Distribution Center: Pergaminho Distribuidora de Livros e Audiovisuais Lda, Rua da Alegria, 486-A, Amoreira, 2645-167 Cascais
E-mail: pergaminhodistr@netcabo.pt

Livraria Petrony
Rua do Vale Formoso, 37, 1959-006 Lisbon
E-mail: suporte@polytechnica.pt
Web Site: www.petrony.pt
Founded: 1955
Subjects: Accounting, Architecture & Interior Design, Business, Computers, Economics, Engineering (General), Genealogy, Government, Political Science, History, Law, Social Sciences, Sociology
ISBN Prefix(es): 978-972-685
Parent Company: Grupo Escolar

Planeta Editora Lda+
Member of Grupo Planeta
Rua do Loreto, 16, 1º D, 1200-242 Lisbon
Tel: 213 408 520
E-mail: info@planeta.pt
Web Site: www.planeta.pt
Subjects: Astrology, Occult, Astronomy, Biblical Studies, Earth Sciences, Fiction, Mysteries, Suspense, Science Fiction, Fantasy
ISBN Prefix(es): 978-972-731; 978-989-657

Planeta Tangerina
Rua das Rosas, nº 20, Alto dos Lombos, 2775-683 Carcavelos
Tel: 214 680 844 *Fax:* 214 680 844
E-mail: editora@planetatangerina.com
Web Site: www.planetatangerina.com/pt
Key Personnel
Dir, Foreign Rights: Isabel Minhos Martins
E-mail: isabel.minhos@planetatangerina.com
Bookstore Orders: Cristina Lopes
Founded: 1999
ISBN Prefix(es): 978-989-8145

Platano Editora SA+
Ave de Berna, 31-Loja, 1069-054 Lisbon
Tel: 21 797 92 78 *Fax:* 21 795 40 19
E-mail: geral@platanoeditora.pt; mkt@platanoeditora.pt; comercial@platanoeditora.pt
Web Site: www.platanoeditora.pt
Founded: 1972
Membership(s): Portuguese Association of Publishers & Booksellers.
Subjects: Art, Astronomy, Business, Computers, Drama, Theater, Health, Nutrition, History, Literature, Literary Criticism, Essays, Poetry, Science (General), Self-Help, Nature
ISBN Prefix(es): 978-972-621; 978-972-707; 978-972-770
Subsidiaries: Alicerce Editora Lda; Didactica Editora Lda; Editora de Ensino a Distancia Lda; Paralelo Editora Lda; Platano Edicoes Tecnicas Lda
Branch Office(s)
Rua Manuel Ferreira, 1 A-B-C, Quinta das Lagoas, Santa Marta de Corrois, 2855-597 Corroios *Tel:* 21 255 99 70 *Fax:* 21 253 40 68
Rua Guerra Junqueiro, 452, 4150-387 Porto
Tel: 22 606 13 00 *Fax:* 22 609 53 79

Porto Editora Lda+
Rua da Restauracao, nº 365, 4099-023 Porto
Tel: 22 608 83 00 *Fax:* 22 608 83 01
Web Site: www.portoeditora.pt
Key Personnel
Chief Executive Officer & Dir: Vasco Teixeira
Founded: 1944

Subjects: Art, Economics, Education, History, Language Arts, Linguistics, Literature, Literary Criticism, Essays, Nonfiction (General), Religion - Other, Self-Help
ISBN Prefix(es): 978-972-0
Parent Company: Grupo Porto Editora
Associate Companies: Empresa Literaria Fluminense Lda
Subsidiaries: Livraria Arnado Lda
Bookshop(s): Rua da Fabrica 90, 4050-246 Porto *Tel:* 22 208 76 69; Praca D Filipa de Lencastre, 42, 4050-259 Porto *Tel:* 22 208 76 81

Portugalmundo Editora+
Rua Goncalves Crespo, 47, R/C, 1150-184 Lisbon
Tel: 213304685; 213304687 *Fax:* 213590420
E-mail: editoraportugalmundo@gmail.com
Web Site: www.editoraportugalmundo.com
Founded: 1976
Membership(s): Portuguese Association of Publishers & Booksellers (APEL).
Subjects: Drama, Theater, Law, Literature, Literary Criticism, Essays, Music, Dance, Poetry
ISBN Prefix(es): 978-972-9288

Editorial Presenca+
Estrada das Palmeiras, 59, Queluz de Baixo, 2730-132 Barcarena
Tel: 214347000 *Fax:* 214346502
E-mail: info@presenca.pt
Web Site: www.presenca.pt
Key Personnel
Finance Executive: Hugo Moura
Administration: Joao Espadinha
Founded: 1960
Subjects: Animals, Pets, Architecture & Interior Design, Art, Astrology, Occult, Biography, Memoirs, Business, Child Care & Development, Computer Science, Cookery, Crafts, Games, Hobbies, Economics, Education, Fiction, Gardening, Plants, Government, Political Science, Health, Nutrition, History, How-to, Human Relations, Inspirational, Spirituality, Language Arts, Linguistics, Management, Marketing, Mysteries, Suspense, Nonfiction (General), Philosophy, Poetry, Psychology, Psychiatry, Religion - Buddhist, Science (General), Self-Help, Social Sciences, Sociology, Sports, Athletics, Travel & Tourism, Art Techniques, Esoterics, Leisure
ISBN Prefix(es): 978-972-23

Principia Editora
Rua Vasco da Gama, no 60 c, 2775-297 Parede
Tel: 21 467 87 10 *Fax:* 21 467 87 19
E-mail: principia@principia.pt
Web Site: principia.pt
Founded: 1997
Subjects: Art, Education, Fiction, Maritime, Music, Dance, Religion - Other, Science (General), Sports, Athletics, Technology, Travel & Tourism
ISBN Prefix(es): 978-989-95168; 978-989-8131; 978-972-8818; 978-972-8835
Imprints: Lucerna; Casa Sassetti; Sete Mares; Sopade Letras; Tribuna
Distributed by Ahab; Centro de Estudos de Historia Religiosa da Universidade Catolica Portuguesa; Coisas de Ler; Consolata; Convenio; Diel; Edicoes Pedago; Fragmenta Editorial; Humus; Letras d'Ouro; Operaomnia; Paleta de Letras; Pearlbooks; Proliber; Scribe; Libreria Editrice Vaticana

Quetzal+
Imprint *of* Grupo Bertrand Circulo
Rua Prof Jorge da Silva Horta, 1, 1500-499 Lisbon
Tel: 21 762 60 00 *Fax:* 21 762 61 50
Web Site: www.quetzaleditores.pt
Founded: 1987

Subjects: Art, Biography, Memoirs, Drama, Theater, Economics, History, Literature, Literary Criticism, Essays, Music, Dance, Poetry, Religion - Other, Self-Help
ISBN Prefix(es): 978-972-564; 978-989-722

Quid Juris - Sociedade Editora+
Rua Sarmento Beires, nº 45G, Apdo 9803, 1911-701 Lisbon
Tel: 218405420 *Fax:* 218405423
E-mail: geral@quidjuris.pt; comercial@quidjuris.pt
Web Site: www.quidjuris.pt
Founded: 1989
Subjects: Criminology, Economics, Government, Political Science, History, Journalism, Law, Literature, Literary Criticism, Essays, Management, Mathematics, Psychology, Psychiatry, Social Sciences, Sociology, International Relations & Diplomacy
ISBN Prefix(es): 978-972-724
Bookshop(s): Universidade Autonoma de Lisboa (UAL), Rua de Santa Marta nº56, 1150-023 Lisbon *Tel:* 213158327 *Fax:* 213570514 *E-mail:* livraria@quidjuris.pt; Universidade Lusiada de Lisboa, Rua Pinto Ferreira nº 19 a 21, Edificio G, Sala G1, 1349-001 Lisbon *Tel:* 213630531 *Fax:* 213630513 *E-mail:* livralusiada@quidjuris.pt

Quimera Editores+
Rua do Vale Formoso, 37, 1959-006 Lisbon
E-mail: suporte@polytechnica.pt
Web Site: www.quimera-editores.com
Founded: 1987
Subjects: Architecture & Interior Design, Art, Biography, Memoirs, Cookery, Drama, Theater, Fiction, History, Literature, Literary Criticism, Essays
ISBN Prefix(es): 978-972-589

Quinta Essencia
Member of Grupo LeYa
Rua Cidade de Cordova, 2, 2610-038 Alfragide
Tel: 210 417 410 *Fax:* 214 717 737
E-mail: quintaessencia@oficinadolivro.leya.com
Web Site: www.quintaessencia.com.pt
Founded: 2008
Subjects: Fiction, Romance, Self-Help, Mind, Body & Spirit
ISBN Prefix(es): 978-989-8228; 978-989-95788

Publicacoes Dom Quixote+
Member of Grupo LeYa
Rua Cidade de Cordova, nº 2, 2610-038 Alfragide
Tel: 21 427 22 00; 70 725 22 52 (customer service) *Fax:* 21 427 22 01; 70 728 92 89 (customer service)
E-mail: info@dquixote.pt
Web Site: www.dquixote.pt
Founded: 1965
Subjects: Art, Economics, Education, Fiction, History, Philosophy, Poetry, Science (General), Social Sciences, Sociology
ISBN Prefix(es): 978-972-20
Warehouse: Estrada de Paco de Arcos nº 39/41, 2735 Cacem

Raiz Editora
Rua Prof Jorge de Silva Horta 1, 1500-499 Lisbon
Tel: 218 430 910 *Fax:* 218 430 911
Web Site: www.raizeditora.pt
Subjects: Education
ISBN Prefix(es): 978-972-680; 978-989-744
Parent Company: Grupo Porto Editora
Distribution Center: Porto Editora, Rua da Restauracao, 365, 4099-023 Porto *Tel:* 226 088 312 *Fax:* 226 088 313 *E-mail:* depcomercial@portoeditora.pt

Edicoes Saida de Emergencia
Rua Adelino Mendes, nº 152, Quinta do Choupal, 2765-082 Sao Pedro do Estoril
Tel: 214 583 770
E-mail: geral@saidadeemergencia.com
Web Site: www.saidadeemergencia.com
Founded: 2003
Subjects: Erotica, Literature, Literary Criticism, Essays, Mysteries, Suspense, Nonfiction (General), Romance
ISBN Prefix(es): 978-989-637

Edicoes Salesianas
Rua Dr Alves da Veiga, 124, Apdo 5281, 4022-001 Porto
Tel: 225 365 750 *Fax:* 225 365 800
E-mail: edisal@edicoes.salesianos.pt
Web Site: www.edisal.salesianos.pt
Key Personnel
Editorial Dir: Rui Alberto
Founded: 1947
Subjects: Biography, Memoirs, Education, Humor, Inspirational, Spirituality, Music, Dance, Psychology, Psychiatry, Religion - Other
ISBN Prefix(es): 978-972-690
Bookshop(s): Rua Dr Fernandes Tomas, 375, 4000-217 Porto *Tel:* 225 365 750 *E-mail:* livraria.porto@salesianos.pt; Largo Luis de Camoes, 7, 7000-766 Evora *Tel:* 266 704 570 *Fax:* 266 704 570 *E-mail:* livraria.evora@salesianos.pt; Rua Saraiva de Carvalho, 275, 1399-020 Lisbon *Tel:* 213 909 065 *E-mail:* livraria.salesianos@salesianos.pt

Santillana
Rua Mario Castelhano, 40, 2734-502 Barcarena
Tel: 214 246 901 *Fax:* 214 246 907
E-mail: apoioaoprofessor@santillana.com
Web Site: www.santillana.pt
Founded: 1989
Subjects: Art, Astronomy, Biological Sciences, Chemistry, Chemical Engineering, Earth Sciences, Economics, Education, Energy, English as a Second Language, Geography, Geology, History, Language Arts, Linguistics, Mathematics, Music, Dance, Natural History, Philosophy, Physical Sciences, Social Sciences, Sociology, Technology
ISBN Prefix(es): 978-972-761
Parent Company: Grupo Santillana
Branch Office(s)
Rua da Venezuela, 177, 4150-744 Porto *Tel:* 226 099 195 *Fax:* 226 007 277

Casa Sassetti, *imprint of* Principia Editora

Sebenta Editora
Member of Grupo LeYa
Rua Cidade de Cordova, nº 2, 2610-038 Alfragide
Tel: 21 427 22 00 *Fax:* 21 427 22 01
E-mail: escolar@sebenta.com
Web Site: www.sebenta.pt
Founded: 1986
Subjects: Biological Sciences, Chemistry, Chemical Engineering, Education, Geography, Geology, History, Mathematics, Philosophy, Physics, English, Portuguese
ISBN Prefix(es): 978-972-799

Sete Mares, *imprint of* Principia Editora

Edicoes 70+
Av Engenheiro Arantes e Oliveira, 11-3º C, 1900-221 Lisbon
Tel: 21 319 02 40 *Fax:* 21 319 02 49
E-mail: geral@edicoes70.pt; comercial@edicoes70.pt
Web Site: www.edicoes70.pt
Founded: 1970
Subjects: Anthropology, Architecture & Interior Design, Art, Biography, Memoirs, Education,

History, Language Arts, Linguistics, Literature, Literary Criticism, Essays, Music, Dance, Nonfiction (General), Philosophy, Photography, Psychology, Psychiatry, Social Sciences, Sociology
ISBN Prefix(es): 978-972-44
Number of titles published annually: 24 Print
Total Titles: 1,000 Print
Parent Company: Grupo Almedina

Edicoes Silabo Lda+
Rua Cidade de Manchester, 2, 1170-100 Lisbon
Tel: 218130345 *Fax:* 218166719
E-mail: silabo@silabo.pt
Web Site: www.silabo.pt
Key Personnel
Marketing Dir & Editor: Manuel Robalo
    E-mail: manuel.robalo@silabo.pt
Founded: 1983
Membership(s): Portuguese Association of Publishers & Booksellers (APEL).
Subjects: Computer Science, Economics, History, Management, Mathematics, Philosophy, Physics, Psychology, Psychiatry, Science (General), Self-Help
ISBN Prefix(es): 978-972-618

Sopade Letras, *imprint of* Principia Editora

Susaeta Ediciones, *imprint of* Girassol Edicoes Lda

Editorial Teorema+
Member of Grupo LeYa
Rua Cidade de Cordova, 2, 2610-038 Alfragide
Tel: 21 427 22 00 *Fax:* 21 427 22 01
E-mail: teorema@leya.com
Web Site: www.editorialteorema.pt
Founded: 1978
Subjects: Anthropology, Biography, Memoirs, Economics, Fiction, Government, Political Science, History, Literature, Literary Criticism, Essays, Nonfiction (General), Philosophy, Poetry, Psychology, Psychiatry, Romance, Science (General), Social Sciences, Sociology
ISBN Prefix(es): 978-972-695

Edicoes Texto & Grafia
Calcada do Tijolo, Nº 28, 1º Esq, 1200-465 Lisbon
Tel: 217 977 066
E-mail: texto.grafia@gmail.com; texto-grafia@texto-grafia.pt
Web Site: www.texto-grafia.blogspot.com
Founded: 2008
Subjects: Biography, Memoirs, Fashion, Film, Video, History, Psychology, Psychiatry, Social Sciences, Sociology, Humanities
ISBN Prefix(es): 978-989-8285

Texto Editora SA+
Member of Grupo LeYa
Rua Cidade de Cordova, nº 2, 2610-038 Alfragide
Tel: 21 427 22 00 *Fax:* 21 427 22 01
E-mail: comunicacao@leya.com
Web Site: www.texto.pt
Founded: 1977
Subjects: Cookery, Education, Fiction, Health, Nutrition, Humor, Management, Romance, Self-Help
ISBN Prefix(es): 978-972-47

Tribuna, *imprint of* Principia Editora

Edificio Turinta
Rua Marques de Pombal, 347, Murches, 2755-247 Alcabideche Cascais
Tel: 21 487 94 20 *Fax:* 21 487 20 99
E-mail: info@turinta.pt
Web Site: www.turinta.pt

Founded: 1976
Membership(s): International Map Industry Association (IMIA).
Subjects: Travel & Tourism
ISBN Prefix(es): 978-972-8134; 978-989-556
Distributed by Map Link (USA)

Editora Ulisseia Lda+
Av Antonio Augusto de Aguiar, 148 – 1º, 1050-021 Lisbon
Tel: 21 380 11 00 *Fax:* 21 386 53 96
Founded: 1950
Subjects: Literature, Literary Criticism, Essays
ISBN Prefix(es): 978-972-568
Warehouse: Alto da Bela Vista, Apdo 10, 2736-952 Calem *Tel:* 21 426 49 39 *Fax:* 21 426 49 41

Zero a Oito
Rua Castilho, 57-1º Direito, 1250-068 Lisbon
Tel: 213 713 130 *Fax:* 213 713 139
E-mail: geral@zeroaoito.pt
Web Site: www.zeroaoito.pt
Founded: 1999
ISBN Prefix(es): 978-989-648

Puerto Rico

General Information

Capital: San Juan
Language: Spanish and English
Religion: Predominantly Roman Catholic
Population: 3.6 million
Bank Hours: 0900-1430 Monday-Friday
Shop Hours: 0900-1730 or 1800 Monday-Saturday
Currency: US currency used: 100 cents = 1 US dollar
Export/Import Information: No tariff on books and advertising matter. No import licenses required.
Copyright: UCC (see Copyright Conventions, pg viii)

Editorial Cordillera Inc
Calle Mexico 17, Oficina 1-A, Hato Rey 00917
Mailing Address: PO Box 192363, San Juan 00919-2363
Tel: (787) 767-6188 *Fax:* (787) 767-8646
Founded: 1962
Subjects: Literature, Literary Criticism, Essays, Social Sciences, Sociology
ISBN Prefix(es): 978-0-88495
Associate Companies: Editorial Plaza Mayor

EDUPR, see University of Puerto Rico Press (EDUPR)

Libros-Ediciones Homines+
Apdo 191293, San Juan 00919-1293
Tel: (787) 250-1912 *Fax:* (787) 250-0782
Key Personnel
Dir & Editor: Aline Frambes Buxeda de Alzerreca
Editor: Sylvia Enid Arocho Velazquez
Founded: 1977
Subjects: Behavioral Sciences, Government, Political Science, Regional Interests, Social Sciences, Sociology, Women's Studies
ISBN Prefix(es): 978-0-9623590
Number of titles published annually: 2 CD-ROM
Total Titles: 45 Print; 7 CD-ROM
Parent Company: Universidad Interamericana de Puerto Rico

Ediciones Huracan Inc+
874 Baldorioty de Castro, Rio Piedras 00925
Tel: (787) 763-7407 *Fax:* (787) 753-1486
Key Personnel
Contact: Carmen Rivera-Izcoa
Founded: 1975
Subjects: Behavioral Sciences, Biography, Memoirs, Economics, Government, Political Science, History, Labor, Industrial Relations, LGBTQ, Literature, Literary Criticism, Essays, Poetry, Psychology, Psychiatry, Religion - Catholic, Social Sciences, Sociology, Women's Studies
ISBN Prefix(es): 978-0-940238; 978-0-929157; 978-1-932913

Instituto de Cultura Puertorriquena (Institute of Puerto Rican Culture)
Programa de Publicaciones y Grabaciones, Apdo 9024184, San Juan 00902-4184
Tel: (787) 724-0700; (787) 724-0700 (ext 1341, editorial); (787) 724-0700 (ext 1349, sales) *Fax:* (787) 724-8393
E-mail: editorial@icp.gobierno.pr
Web Site: www.icp.gobierno.pr/programas/editorial
Key Personnel
Editorial Dir: Gloria Tapia
Founded: 1955
Subjects: Anthropology, History, Literature, Literary Criticism, Essays, Music, Dance, Poetry
ISBN Prefix(es): 978-0-86581
Bookshop(s): Convento de los Dominicos, Galeria Nacional, San Juan *Tel:* (787) 721-5105; Casa Armstrong Pouventud, Ponce *Tel:* (787) 724-0700 ext 3062; Centro Ceremonial Caguana, Utuado *Tel:* (787) 724-0700 ext 3045

Ediciones Puerto+
Calle Hoare No 658 Miramar, San Juan 00907
Tel: (787) 721-0844 *Fax:* (787) 725-0861
E-mail: puertomailing@gmail.com
Web Site: www.edicionespuerto.com
Key Personnel
President: Jose Carvajal
Founded: 1971
Subjects: Poetry, Social Sciences, Sociology
ISBN Prefix(es): 978-0-942347; 978-1-933352; 978-1-934461
Number of titles published annually: 50 Print
Distributor for Ediciones Doce Calles SL (Spain); Ollero (Spain); Ediciones Siglo XXI (Mexico)

University of Puerto Rico Press (EDUPR) (La Editorial Universidad de Puerto Rico)
North UPR Botanical Garden, Highway 1, Km 12.0, San Juan 00927
Mailing Address: PO Box 23322, San Juan 00931-3322
Tel: (787) 250-0550; (787) 250-0435
Toll Free Tel: 877-338-7788 *Fax:* (787) 753-9116
E-mail: info@laeditorialupr.com
Web Site: www.upr.edu
Key Personnel
Editor: Rosa V Otero *E-mail:* rosa.otero1@upr.edu
Founded: 1932
Subjects: Art, Behavioral Sciences, Biography, Memoirs, Cookery, Education, Fiction, History, Law, Literature, Literary Criticism, Essays, Mathematics, Nonfiction (General), Philosophy, Poetry, Psychology, Psychiatry, Science (General), Social Sciences, Sociology
ISBN Prefix(es): 978-0-8477
Number of titles published annually: 30 Print; 1 CD-ROM; 5 E-Book
Distributed by Fernandez Editores
Foreign Rep(s): Baker & Taylor (USA); Fernandez Editores (Mexico)
Warehouse: Planta Piloto de Ron, Rd No 1 to Caguas, San Juan

Qatar

General Information

Capital: Doha
Language: Arabic (English used commercially)
Religion: Islamic
Population: 484,000
Bank Hours: 0730-1130 Saturday-Wednesday, 0730-1100 Thursday
Shop Hours: 0730-1200, 1630-2000 Saturday-Thursday
Currency: 100 dirhams = 1 Qatar riyal
Export/Import Information: No tariff on books or advertising matter. No import license; no obscenity permitted.

Hamad Bin Khalifa University Press+
Subsidiary of Hamad Bin Khalifa University
Student Center, Al Huqoul St, Education City, PO Box 5825, Doha
Tel: 4454 2431 *Fax:* 4454 2438
E-mail: info@hbkupress.com
Web Site: books.hbkupress.com
Founded: 2010
Strives to be a cornerstone of Qatar's knowledge-based economy by providing a unique local & international platform for literature, literacy, scholarship, discovery & learning. Publishes peer reviewed journals, monographs, reference books, fiction & nonfiction titles for adults & children.
Subjects: Fiction, Nonfiction (General)
ISBN Prefix(es): 978-99921-788

HBKU Press, see Hamad Bin Khalifa University Press

Reunion

General Information

Capital: Saint-Denis
Language: French
Religion: Predominantly Roman Catholic
Population: 626,000
Bank Hours: 0800-1500
Currency: 100 Eurocents = 1 Euro
Export/Import Information: No tariff on books and advertising. Books have reduced VAT. No import license. Nominal exchange control over certain value.
Copyright: Berne (see Copyright Conventions, pg viii)

Ocean Editions
305 rue de la Communaute, 97440 Saint-Andre
Tel: 0262 58 84 00 *Fax:* 0262 58 84 10
E-mail: ocean@ocean-editions.fr; maud. oceaneditions@gmail.com
Web Site: www.ocean-editions.fr
Key Personnel
Development: Yahel Bouaziz
Founded: 1987
Subjects: Animals, Pets, Architecture & Interior Design, Cookery, Education, History, Photography, Poetry, Social Sciences, Sociology
ISBN Prefix(es): 978-2-907064; 978-2-36247; 978-2-916533
Distributor for ARS-Terres Creoles; CNH; CRI

Romania

General Information

Capital: Bucharest
Language: Romanian
Religion: Predominantly Romanian Orthodox
Population: 23.2 million
Bank Hours: 0900-1200, 1300-1500 Monday-Friday; 0900-1200 Saturday
Shop Hours: 0900-1900 Monday-Friday; early closing Saturday
Currency: 100 bani = 1 leu
Export/Import Information: Import licenses required. Exchange controls: terms of payment established in the sales contract.
Copyright: Berne (see Copyright Conventions, pg viii)

Editura Academiei Romane (Romanian Academy Publishing House)
Calea 13 Septembrie nr 13, sector 5, 050711 Bucharest
Tel: (021) 318 81 46; (021) 318 81 06 *Fax:* (021) 318 24 44
E-mail: edacad@ear.ro
Web Site: www.ear.ro
Key Personnel
Dir General: Radu Dumitru Popescu
Deputy Dir, Economics: Liliana Ionescu
Technical Assistant Dir: Elena Popescu
Editor-in-Chief: Dolna Argeseanu
Founded: 1948
Subjects: Anthropology, Archaeology, Art, Astronomy, Biological Sciences, Chemistry, Chemical Engineering, Computer Science, Earth Sciences, Economics, Electronics, Electrical Engineering, Energy, Foreign Countries, History, Language Arts, Linguistics, Law, Literature, Literary Criticism, Essays, Mathematics, Medicine, Nursing, Dentistry, Philosophy, Physical Sciences, Physics, Psychology, Psychiatry, Science (General), Social Sciences, Sociology, Technology
ISBN Prefix(es): 978-973-27
Parent Company: Academiei Romane
Orders to: Orion Press Impex 2000 SRL, CP 77-19, Sector 3, Bucharest *Tel:* (021) 610 67 65; (021) 210 67 87 *Fax:* (021) 610 67 65; (021) 210 67 87 *E-mail:* office@orionpress.ro

Ad Libri
Str Rumeoara, nr 31, Sector 2, 024063 Bucharest
Tel: (021) 2123567; (021) 2108864 *Fax:* (021) 2123567
E-mail: adlibri@adlibri.ro; adlibri2@adlibri.ro; adlibri@b.astral.ro
Web Site: www.adlibri.ro
Key Personnel
Dir: Florin Andreescu
Founded: 2001
Subjects: Geography, Geology, Travel & Tourism, Leisure
ISBN Prefix(es): 978-973-7887; 978-973-85518; 978-973-86220; 978-973-86781
Number of titles published annually: 25 Print
Total Titles: 70 Print

Editura Aion+
Str Ion Cantacuzino nr 8F, bl PB 18, ap 7, 410430 Oradea, Bihor
Tel: (0359) 401 697; (0359) 401 751
E-mail: editura.aion@gmail.com
Web Site: edituraaion.ro
Founded: 1996
Subjects: Anthropology, Communications, How-to, Human Relations, Journalism, Philosophy, Psychology, Psychiatry, Religion - Other, Social Sciences, Sociology
ISBN Prefix(es): 978-973-97662; 978-973-99943; 978-973-87480

Editura Aius+
Str Pascani, nr 9, 200151 Craiova, Dolj
Tel: (0251) 596 136 *Fax:* (0251) 596 136
E-mail: editura_aius@yahoo.com
Web Site: aius.ro
Key Personnel
Founder: Nicolae Marinescu
Executive Manager: George Sorin Singer
Founded: 1991
Subjects: Economics, History, Literature, Literary Criticism, Essays, Medicine, Nursing, Dentistry
ISBN Prefix(es): 978-973-9251; 978-973-95229; 978-973-96340; 978-973-96913; 978-973-97385
Total Titles: 3 Print

Alcor Edimpex SRL+
BD Mihalache ion, nr 45 bl 16 B+C sc D et 7 ap 116, 011173 Bucharest
Tel: (021) 223 71 06 *Fax:* (021) 223 71 06
E-mail: ed_alcor@yahoo.com
Web Site: www.editura-alcor.ro
Founded: 1994
Subjects: Art, Crafts, Games, Hobbies, History, Literature, Literary Criticism, Essays, Religion - Other, Travel & Tourism
ISBN Prefix(es): 978-973-96752; 978-973-97200; 978-973-97901; 978-973-98341; 978-973-95673; 978-973-96304; 978-973-98935; 978-973-8160; 978-973-87068; 978-973-870
Number of titles published annually: 10 Print
Imprints: Arta Grafica Printing House, ao; Editura CNI Coresi

Editura ALL+
Bd Constructorilor, 20A, sector 6, 260512 Bucharest
Tel: (021) 402 26 00; (021) 402 26 30 (sales); (021) 402 26 34 (sales) *Fax:* (021) 402 26 10
E-mail: info@all.ro
Web Site: www.all.ro
Key Personnel
President: Mihail Penescu
Founded: 1991
Subjects: Computer Science, Education, Fiction, History, Medicine, Nursing, Dentistry, Nonfiction (General), Science (General)
ISBN Prefix(es): 978-973-96090; 978-973-9156; 978-973-571; 978-973-684; 978-973-8171
Number of titles published annually: 300 Print
Total Titles: 1,800 Print

Editura Amaltea
Str Spatarului nr 31, sector 2, 020773 Bucharest
Tel: (021) 210 45 55; (021) 210 65 22 *Fax:* (031) 816 19 29
E-mail: secretariat@amaltea.ro
Web Site: www.amaltea.ro
Key Personnel
President: Mihai Cristian Popescu
Editorial Dir: George Stanca
Founded: 1992
Subjects: Communications, Economics, Inspirational, Spirituality, Management, Medicine, Nursing, Dentistry, Psychology, Psychiatry, Science Fiction, Fantasy, Social Sciences, Sociology, Culture
ISBN Prefix(es): 978-973-7780; 978-973-9397; 978-973-96286; 978-973-97507; 978-973-98167
Number of titles published annually: 30 Print
Total Titles: 178 Print

Antet XX Press SRL
Str Max Heberlin nr 677, 107250 Filipestii de Targ
Tel: (021) 2221245
E-mail: comenzi@antet.ro
Web Site: www.antet.ro
Key Personnel
President: Turturel Nastase
Sales Dir: Crenguta Nastase
Founded: 1995

Subjects: Education, Management, Military Science, Philosophy, Psychology, Psychiatry, Culture
ISBN Prefix(es): 978-973-636; 978-973-8167; 978-973-8203; 978-973-9936; 978-973-96045; 978-973-96470; 978-973-96893
Number of titles published annually: 40 Print
Total Titles: 500 Print

Editura Aquila '93 SRL
Str Americii nr 41, 410554 Oradea, judetul Bihor
Tel: (0259) 453511; (0259) 419776; (0359) 402343 *Fax:* (0259) 414885; (0359) 402343
E-mail: editorial@edituraaquila93.ro
Web Site: www.edituraaquila93.ro; www.aquilashop.ro
Key Personnel
President: Vanyolos Merk Raymond
Editorial Dir: Diana Tautan
Founded: 1993
Subjects: Architecture & Interior Design, Astronomy, Chemistry, Chemical Engineering, Mathematics, Physics, Civilization, Culture
ISBN Prefix(es): 978-973-914; 978-973-8250; 978-973-9319; 978-973-9494; 978-973-96506; 978-973-97372; 978-973-97744
Number of titles published annually: 180 Print

Ararat+
Bd Carol I, nr 43, Bucharest
Tel: (021) 314 67 83 *Fax:* (021) 314 67 83
E-mail: redactia@araratonline.com
Web Site: www.araratonline.com
Key Personnel
Editor: Mihai Stepan-Cazazian
Founded: 1994
Also book manufacturer.
Subjects: History, Literature, Literary Criticism, Essays, Philosophy, Social Sciences, Sociology
ISBN Prefix(es): 978-973-9310; 978-973-97869; 978-973-97127; 978-973-96682; 978-973-7727
Distributed by Humanitas (Romania)

Ars Longa Publishing House+
Str Elena Doamna nr 2, 700398 Iasi
Tel: (0232) 215078; (0724) 516581 (cell)
Fax: (0232) 215078
E-mail: ars.longa@live.com; arslonga@mail.dntis.ro
Web Site: www.arslonga.ro
Key Personnel
President: Christian Tamas
Dir: Brandusa Tamas
Founded: 1994
Subjects: Anthropology, Art, Behavioral Sciences, Education, Fiction, History, Language Arts, Linguistics, Law, Literature, Literary Criticism, Essays, Medicine, Nursing, Dentistry, Philosophy, Physics, Poetry, Psychology, Psychiatry, Religion - Catholic, Religion - Islamic, Religion - Jewish, Social Sciences, Sociology, Theology
ISBN Prefix(es): 978-973-96681; 978-973-97252; 978-973-9325; 978-973-8912; 978-973-148
Number of titles published annually: 100 Print
Total Titles: 1,250 Print

Arta Grafica Printing House, ao, *imprint of* Alcor Edimpex SRL

Editura Artemis
Str Barbu Delavrancea nr 24, Sector 1, 013701 Bucharest
Tel: (021) 318 83 44; (021) 311 49 36 (distribution) *Fax:* (021) 318 83 44; (021) 311 49 36 (distribution)
E-mail: office@semneartemis.ro; difuzare@semneartemis.ro; semneartemis@yahoo.ro
Web Site: www.semneartemis.ro
Founded: 1991

Subjects: Art, Biography, Memoirs, History, Nonfiction (General), Religion - Other
ISBN Prefix(es): 978-973-566

Editura ASAB
B-dul Unirii 14, sector 4, 040106 Bucharest
Tel: (021) 3363895 *Fax:* (021) 3363893
E-mail: comercial@asab.ro
Web Site: www.asab.ro
Key Personnel
Head, Sales Dept: Magdalena Dobrescu
Founded: 2001
Subjects: Agriculture, Biological Sciences, Chemistry, Chemical Engineering, Computer Science, Management, Mathematics, Psychology, Psychiatry, Religion - Other, Technology
ISBN Prefix(es): 978-973-7725; 978-973-85247; 978-973-85643; 978-973-86010; 978-973-86011
Number of titles published annually: 36 Print
Total Titles: 124 Print

Bastion
Str Corbului nr 6, 300239 Timisoara
Tel: (0256) 214805; (0356) 102018 *Fax:* (0256) 214805
Founded: 2007
Subjects: Architecture & Interior Design, Economics, Fiction, Law, Medicine, Nursing, Dentistry, Philosophy, Culture, Pharmacy
ISBN Prefix(es): 978-973-88780; 978-973-1980
Number of titles published annually: 80 Print
Total Titles: 200 Print

Editura Brandbuilders
Str Vlad Dracul, 21-23, sector 3, 031195 Bucharest
Tel: (021) 3231985 *Fax:* (031) 8178779
E-mail: office@brandbuilders.ro
Web Site: www.brandbuilders.ro
Key Personnel
President: Gabriela Ciucurovschi
Founded: 2003
Subjects: Advertising, Communications, Economics, Public Relations
ISBN Prefix(es): 978-973-86481; 978-973-87488; 978-973-88156
Number of titles published annually: 12 Print
Total Titles: 30 Print

Callisto Comexim SRL
Str Elena nr 54, sector 2, 023482 Bucharest
Tel: (021) 2420791 *Fax:* (021) 2433022
E-mail: office@callisto.ro
Web Site: www.callisto.ro
Key Personnel
President: Gheorghe P Cuculici
Founded: 1998
Subjects: Biological Sciences, Chemistry, Chemical Engineering, Medicine, Nursing, Dentistry, Psychology, Psychiatry, Veterinary Science
ISBN Prefix(es): 978-973-85991; 978-973-87261; 978-973-98612
Number of titles published annually: 12 Print
Total Titles: 1,500 Print

Editura Cartea Romaneasca
Calea Victoriei nr 133 (Intrarea prin str Sfintii Voievozi nr 61), Bucharest
Tel: (021) 319 65 99 *Fax:* (021) 319 65 99
E-mail: ecr@cartearomaneasca.ro (editorial); sales@polirom.ro (sales)
Web Site: www.cartearomaneasca.ro
Key Personnel
Editor-in-Chief: Madalina Ghiu
Commercial Dir: Viorel Cordun *E-mail:* viorel.cordun@polirom.ro
Dir, Promotion & Public Relations: Claudia Fitcoschi *E-mail:* claudia.fitcoschi@polirom.ro
Sales Dir: Silvia Bucur *E-mail:* silvia.bucur@polirom.ro

Founded: 1919
Subjects: Drama, Theater, Fiction, Literature, Literary Criticism, Essays, Poetry
ISBN Prefix(es): 978-973-23

Editura Casa Radio
Str General Berthelot, nr 60-64, 010165 Bucharest
Tel: (021) 3031753 *Fax:* (021) 3031884
E-mail: editura.cr@rornet.ro; comenzi_editura@rornet.ro
Web Site: www.edituracasaradio.ro
Key Personnel
Distribution: Florea Mihaela; Florentina Popescu
Founded: 1912
ISBN Prefix(es): 978-973-7902; 978-973-98662; 978-973-99057; 978-973-99190
Parent Company: Romanian Broadcasting Co
Distribution Center: Str General Berthelot, nr 71 etaj 1, 010165 Bucharest *Tel:* (021) 3031772

Presa Universitara Clujeana (Cluj University Press)
Str Hasdeu, nr 51, 400371 Cluj-Napoca
Tel: (0264) 405300; (0264) 597401; (0264) 406451
E-mail: editura@editura.ubbcluj.ro; comenzi@editura.ubbcluj.ro
Web Site: www.editura.ubbcluj.ro
Key Personnel
Dir: Codruta Sacelean *E-mail:* c.sacelean@editura.ubbcluj.ro
Distribution Manager: Filip Pop *E-mail:* f.pop@editura.ubbcluj.ro
Founded: 1993
Subjects: Agriculture, Biological Sciences, Chemistry, Chemical Engineering, Computer Science, Education, Geography, Geology, Law, Mathematics, Philosophy, Sports, Athletics, Travel & Tourism, Culture, Ethics
ISBN Prefix(es): 978-973-595; 978-973-610; 978-973-9261; 978-973-9354; 978-973-96280; 978-973-97535; 978-973-97783
Number of titles published annually: 150 Print

Editura Clusium+
Piata Unirii nr 1, Cluj-Napoca
Tel: (0264) 596940 *Fax:* (0264) 596940
E-mail: clusium@cluj.astral.ro
Founded: 1990
Subjects: Art, Biography, Memoirs, Computer Science, Engineering (General), Fiction, History, Humor, Literature, Literary Criticism, Essays, Medicine, Nursing, Dentistry, Nonfiction (General), Philosophy, Poetry, Religion - Other, Science (General), Social Sciences, Sociology, Technology
ISBN Prefix(es): 978-973-555

Editura CNI Coresi, *imprint of* Alcor Edimpex SRL

Editura Codecs
Str Agricultori nr 37-39, Sector 2, 021492 Bucharest
Mailing Address: PO Box 62-67, 021482 Bucharest
Tel: (021) 2525182 *Fax:* (021) 2525613
E-mail: sales@codecs.ro
Web Site: www.codecs.ro
Key Personnel
President: Gehrig Schultz
General Dir: Ionut Florentin Mihailescu *E-mail:* ionut.mihailescu@codecs.ro
Sales Dir: Silviu Barbalat *E-mail:* silviu.barbalat@codecs.ro
Founded: 1998
Subjects: Communications, Economics, Education, Management, Public Administration, Public Relations

ISBN Prefix(es): 978-973-8060; 978-973-96596; 978-973-98490; 978-973-98491
Number of titles published annually: 15 Print
Total Titles: 50 Print

Editura Comunicare.ro
Str Povernei nr 6, sector 1, 010643 Bucharest
Tel: (021) 3135895; (021) 3100718 *Fax:* (021) 3135895
E-mail: editura@comunicare.ro
Web Site: www.editura.comunicare.ro
Key Personnel
Dir: Paul Dobrescu
Editorial Dir: Lucian Pricop
Editor: Dan Flonta
Founded: 2000
Subjects: Computer Science, Fiction, Law, Management, Philosophy, Psychology, Psychiatry, Social Sciences, Sociology, Culture, Politics
ISBN Prefix(es): 978-973-711; 978-973-8309; 978-973-8376; 978-973-85205; 978-973-99502; 978-973-99986
Number of titles published annually: 30 Print
Total Titles: 100 Print

Editura Coresi+
CP 1-477, 014700 Bucharest
Tel: (021) 223 2015; (021) 223 2012 *Fax:* (021) 260 0125
E-mail: coresi@coresi.net
Web Site: www.coresi.net
Key Personnel
Contact: Vasile Poenaru *Tel:* 0722 330 971 (cell)
   E-mail: vasile.poenaru@coresi.net
Founded: 1989 (during the Romanian Revolution)
Specialize in children's literature & educational publications as well as digital books.
Subjects: Career Development, English as a Second Language, Language Arts, Linguistics
ISBN Prefix(es): 978-973-608; 978-973-137
Number of titles published annually: 30 Print; 3 CD-ROM; 30 E-Book; 3 Audio
Total Titles: 1,000 Print; 3 CD-ROM; 35 E-Book; 3 Audio

Grupul Editorial Corint+
Str Mihai Eminescu nr 54A, Sector 1, Bucharest
Tel: (021) 319 47 97; (021) 319 88 22 (sales); (021) 319 88 33 (sales) *Fax:* (021) 319 48 20; (021) 319 88 66 (sales); (021) 310 15 30 (sales)
E-mail: office@edituracorint.ro; copyright@edituracorint.ro; vanzari@edituracorint.ro
Web Site: www.grupulcorint.ro
Key Personnel
Chief Executive Officer: Cristian Gresanu; Daniel Penescu; Luiza Penescu
Sales Dir: Roxana Liritis *E-mail:* roxana.liritis@edituracorint.ro
Public Relations Manager: Diana Bogdan
   E-mail: diana.bogdan@edituracorint.ro
Copyright Dept: Ioana Mogosanu *E-mail:* ioana.mogosanu@edituracorint.ro
Founded: 2004
Specialize in scholarly books.
Subjects: Art, Astrology, Occult, Behavioral Sciences, Biblical Studies, Biography, Memoirs, Business, Computers, Crafts, Games, Hobbies, Earth Sciences, Economics, Education, English as a Second Language, Fiction, Foreign Countries, Gardening, Plants, Geography, Geology, Government, Political Science, Health, Nutrition, History, House & Home, How-to, Human Relations, Humor, Language Arts, Linguistics, Literature, Literary Criticism, Essays, Management, Marketing, Mathematics, Mysteries, Suspense, Natural History, Nonfiction (General), Outdoor Recreation, Physics, Poetry, Religion - Other, Romance, Science (General), Science Fiction, Fantasy, Self-Help, Social Sciences, Sociology, Travel & Tourism, Western Fiction, Women's Studies

ISBN Prefix(es): 978-973-653; 978-973-9281; 978-973-9413; 978-973-97054; 978-973-97397; 978-973-97588; 978-973-97792
Number of titles published annually: 300 Print; 30 E-Book
Total Titles: 4,000 Print

Curtea Veche Publishing
Str Aurel Vlaicu, nr 35, Sector 2, 020091 Bucharest
Tel: (021) 260 22 87; (021) 222 57 26; (021) 222 47 65 *Fax:* (021) 223 16 88
E-mail: redactie@curteaveche.ro (editorial); marketing@curteaveche.ro; distributie@curteaveche.ro; pr@curteaveche.ro
Web Site: www.curteaveche.ro
Key Personnel
Public Relations Manager: Alina Dolea
Founded: 1998
Subjects: Fiction, Literature, Literary Criticism, Essays, Nonfiction (General)
ISBN Prefix(es): 978-973-669; 978-973-8120; 978-973-8356; 978-973-99127; 978-973-99444; 978-973-99592

Editura Dacia
Andrei Saguna, NR:36 Cluj, 400103 Cluj-Napoca
Tel: (0364) 149 797 *Fax:* (0364) 149 797
Web Site: edituradacia.ro
Key Personnel
Exec Dir: Nadia Farcas
Sales Dir: Geanina Dumitrescu
Administrator: Ion Vadan
Founded: 1969
Subjects: Astrology, Occult, Biological Sciences, Chemistry, Chemical Engineering, Education, Electronics, Electrical Engineering, Fiction, Finance, Geography, Geology, Literature, Literary Criticism, Essays, Poetry, Literary History
ISBN Prefix(es): 978-973-35

Editura Didactica si Pedagogica RA+
Str Spiru Haret nr 12, sector 1, 010176 Bucharest
Tel: (021) 315 73 98; (021) 312 28 85
E-mail: comenzi@edituradp.ro; comercial@edituradp.ro
Web Site: www.edituradp.ro
Founded: 1951
Subjects: Drama, Theater, Economics, Education, History, Literature, Literary Criticism, Essays, Medicine, Nursing, Dentistry, Music, Dance, Philosophy, Theology
ISBN Prefix(es): 978-973-30
Number of titles published annually: 300 Print

Editura Adevar Divin SRL
Str Zizinului nr 48, parter ap 7, 500414 Brasov
Tel: (0268) 324 970 *Fax:* (0368) 462 076
E-mail: contact@divin.ro
Web Site: www.divin.ro
Key Personnel
President: Catalin Parfene
Founded: 2005
Subjects: Ethnicity, Philosophy, Psychology, Psychiatry, Religion - Other
ISBN Prefix(es): 978-973-87595
Number of titles published annually: 10 Print
Total Titles: 15 Print

Editurii Eikon
Str Bucuresti, nr 3A, 400138 Cluj-Napoca
Tel: (0364) 117246 *Fax:* (0364) 117246
E-mail: eikondifuzare@yahoo.com; edituraeikon@gmail.com
Web Site: www.edituraeikon.ro
Founded: 2003
Subjects: Theology
ISBN Prefix(es): 978-973-7833; 978-973-7987; 978-973-86182; 978-973-86312; 978-973-86470

Editura Eminescu
Piata Presei Libere nr 1, corp C, et 3, cam 360, sector 1, Bucharest
Tel: (031) 805 8938 *Fax:* (031) 805 8938
Key Personnel
President: Ion Cristoiu
Dir General: Vlad Pufu
Sales Agent: George Mischie
Founded: 1969
Membership(s): World Publishing Industry.
Subjects: History, Inspirational, Spirituality, Literature, Literary Criticism, Essays, Philosophy, Poetry, Psychology, Psychiatry
ISBN Prefix(es): 978-973-22

Editura Enciclopedia RAO, *imprint of* Grupul Editorial RAO

Editura Enciclopedica+
Str Luigi Cazzavillan nr 17, sector 1, Bucharest
Tel: (021) 3179035 *Fax:* (0378) 105718
Founded: 1968
Subjects: Antiques, Archaeology, Biography, Memoirs, Biological Sciences, Economics, History, Religion - Other
ISBN Prefix(es): 978-973-45
Number of titles published annually: 40 Print
Total Titles: 290 Print

Editura Erc Press
Blvd Iuliu Maniu, nr 7, corp 1, et 1, sector 6, 061072 Bucharest
Tel: (021) 5699011 *Fax:* (021) 5699012
E-mail: office@ercpress.ro
Web Site: www.ercpress.ro
Key Personnel
Dir: Ciprian Ene
Founded: 1993
Subjects: Geography, Geology, Literature, Literary Criticism, Essays, Travel & Tourism, Leisure
ISBN Prefix(es): 978-973-706; 978-973-7977; 978-973-8403; 978-973-85548; 978-973-98697; 978-973-99549
Number of titles published annually: 500 Print
Total Titles: 1,200 Print

EST-Samuel Tastet Editeur+
Bd Uverturii nr 57-69, Bl 10, Sc C, Ap 87, Sector 6, 060933 Bucharest
Tel: (021) 326 57 03; 0722 225 180 (cell)
   Fax: (021) 326 57 03
E-mail: edest@rdslink.ro; edest@hotmail.com
Web Site: www.est-editura.ro
Founded: 1995
Subjects: Art, Biography, Memoirs, Drama, Theater, Fiction, Literature, Literary Criticism, Essays, Poetry
ISBN Prefix(es): 978-973-96902; 978-973-98094; 978-973-8346; 978-973-85477

Editura Etna
Str Anton Pann, nr 18A, Ap 1, sector 3, 030796 Bucharest
Tel: (0727) 317 800 (cell) *Fax:* (031) 8105942
Web Site: www.etna.ro
Key Personnel
President: Ioana Soare *E-mail:* ioanasoare5@gmail.com
Subjects: Health, Nutrition, Medicine, Nursing, Dentistry, Pharmacy
ISBN Prefix(es): 978-973-85719; 978-973-87046

Editura Excelsior Art+
Affiliate of Federatia Editorilor din Romania
Str Episcop Augustin Pacha nr 2/28, 300055 Timisoara
Mailing Address: CP 262, of 1, 300054 Timisoara
Tel: (0256) 201078
E-mail: editura@excelsiorart.ro
Web Site: www.excelsiorart.ro
Key Personnel
Dir & Editor: Corina Victoria Sein Badulescu

Tel: (0726) 708609 E-mail: seincorina@yahoo.
com
Founded: 1990
Editing, book distribution & publishing.
Membership(s): Asociatia Editorilor din Romania
(AER) (Publishers Association in Romania).
Subjects: Anthropology, Archaeology, Biblical
Studies, Biography, Memoirs, Business, Com-
munications, Cookery, Crafts, Games, Hob-
bies, Drama, Theater, Economics, Education,
Ethnicity, Fiction, Health, Nutrition, History,
Human Relations, Humor, Journalism, Lan-
guage Arts, Linguistics, Library & Information
Sciences, Literature, Literary Criticism, Es-
says, Mechanical Engineering, Medicine, Nurs-
ing, Dentistry, Mysteries, Suspense, Nonfiction
(General), Parapsychology, Philosophy, Poetry,
Psychology, Psychiatry, Publishing & Book
Trade Reference, Regional Interests, Religion -
Other, Science (General), Science Fiction, Fan-
tasy, Social Sciences, Sociology, Technology,
Western Fiction
ISBN Prefix(es): 978-973-592
Number of titles published annually: 50 Print; 3
CD-ROM; 6 E-Book; 1 Audio
Total Titles: 1,200 Print; 9 CD-ROM; 12 E-Book;
1 Audio
Imprints: SC Bistra
Distributor for Aletheia-Bistrita; Compact-
Brasov; Derex Com SRL; Libris-Galati; Li-
braria Mihai Eminescu; Librarii-TG Mures;
Prolibris-Ramnicu Valcea; SC Bibliostar SRL;
Sedcomlibris-Iasi; Sedcomlibris-Suceava; Tim-
libris Timisoara

Elena Francisc Publishing SRL
Sos Bucuresti-Targoviste, nr 22G, Sector 1,
Bucharest
Tel: (031) 014254
E-mail: office@elenafrancisc.ro
Web Site: www.elenafrancisc.ro
Subjects: Psychology, Psychiatry, Religion -
Other, Spirituality
ISBN Prefix(es): 978-973-87062; 978-973-87574

Editura Fundatia Culturala Ideea Europeana
Str Blanari nr 21, Et 1, sector 3, 014780
Bucharest
Mailing Address: OP 22, CP 113, sector 1,
014780 Bucharest
Tel: (021) 2125692; (021) 3106618 Fax: (021)
2125692
E-mail: office@ideeaeuropeana.ro;
fcideeaeuropeana@yahoo.com
Web Site: www.ideeaeuropeana.ro
Key Personnel
President: Andrei Potlog
Editorial Dir: Aura Christi
Founded: 2003
Subjects: Art, Fiction, Film, Video, Music, Dance,
Philosophy, Psychology, Psychiatry, Religion -
Other, Travel & Tourism, Culture
ISBN Prefix(es): 978-973-86721; 978-973-86970;
978-973-86971; 978-973-86972
Number of titles published annually: 100 Print
Total Titles: 185 Print

Editura Fundatia Romania de Maine
Bd Timisoara nr 58, sector 6, 061317 Bucharest
Tel: (021) 444 20 91 Fax: (021) 444 20 91
E-mail: editurafrm@yahoo.com
Web Site: www.edituraromaniademaine.ro
Key Personnel
President: Georgeta Mitran
Founded: 1992
Subjects: Architecture & Interior Design, Art,
Computer Science, Drama, Theater, Economics,
Education, Geography, Geology, History, Jour-
nalism, Language Arts, Linguistics, Law, Liter-
ature, Literary Criticism, Essays, Management,
Mathematics, Medicine, Nursing, Dentistry,
Music, Dance, Philosophy, Psychology, Psychi-

atry, Social Sciences, Sociology, Sports, Athlet-
ics, Veterinary Science, Culture, Folklore
ISBN Prefix(es): 978-973-582; 978-973-9202;
978-973-95602; 978-973-96128; 978-973-
96794
Number of titles published annually: 300 Print
Total Titles: 1,000 Print
Orders to: Splaiul Independentei nr 313, Sector 6,
Bucharest Tel: (021) 316 97 80 Fax: (021) 316
97 80 E-mail: difuzare@edituraromaine.ro

Editura Gama SRL
Sos Pacurari, nr 93-95, Bl 474, Tr B, Parter,
700293 Iasi
Tel: (0232) 230212; (0232) 231776 Fax: (0232)
231776
E-mail: office@edituragama.ro
Web Site: www.edituragama.ro
Key Personnel
General Manager: Diana Mocanu
Founded: 1994
Subjects: Literature, Literary Criticism, Essays
ISBN Prefix(es): 978-973-7824; 978-973-9382;
978-973-95120; 978-973-96339; 978-973-
97937; 978-973-97952
Number of titles published annually: 40 Print
Total Titles: 110 Print

Editura Gramar SRL
Str C-tin Radulescu Motru, nr 25, sector 4,
Bucharest
Tel: (021) 2112500; (021) 2104013 (editorial)
Fax: (021) 2112500
E-mail: comenzi@gramar.ro
Web Site: www.gramar.ro
Key Personnel
President: Daniel Tutunel
Administrator: Cristina Tutunel
Founded: 1994
Subjects: Art, Fiction, Geography, Geology,
Medicine, Nursing, Dentistry, Philosophy, Psy-
chology, Psychiatry, Travel & Tourism, Culture,
Folklore
ISBN Prefix(es): 978-973-591; 978-973-9004;
978-973-9223; 978-973-96206; 978-973-96251;
978-973-97032; 978-973-97033
Number of titles published annually: 100 Print

Editura Gryphon+
Division of Gryphon Filter Ltd
Str I L Caragiale no 6-Inrarea Gryphon, 500413
Brasov
Tel: (0722) 609253 (cell) Fax: (0268) 312888
E-mail: gryphon@gryphon.ro
Web Site: www.gryphon.ro
Key Personnel
President & General Manager: Dr Eugen Ioan
Popa, PhD
Founded: 1990
Specialize in importing books, provider for li-
braries & universities.
Subjects: Art, Civil Engineering, Earth Sciences,
Health, Nutrition, Medicine, Nursing, Dentistry,
Science (General), Technology, Veterinary Sci-
ence, Water Treatment
ISBN Prefix(es): 978-973-604
Number of titles published annually: 6 Print
Total Titles: 20 Print
Distributor for Grolier Inc USA

Gryphon Publishing Ltd, see Editura Gryphon

Editura Hamangiu SRL
Str Colonel Corneliu Popeia, nr 36, Sector 5,
051802 Bucharest
Mailing Address: OP5, CP 91, 051802 Bucharest
Tel: (021) 3360443; (031) 8058020 Fax: (031)
8058021
E-mail: office@hamangiu.ro; redactie@hamangiu.
ro
Web Site: www.hamangiu.ro

Key Personnel
Editorial Dir: Dorel Padurariu
Founded: 2006
Subjects: Law
ISBN Prefix(es): 978-973-8957

Hasefer Publishing House
Str Maria Rosetti nr 17, ap 5-6 interfon 005,
020481 Bucharest
Tel: (021) 308 62 08 Fax: (021) 308 62 08
E-mail: difuzare@hasefer.ro
Web Site: www.hasefer.ro
Subjects: Biblical Studies, Education, History,
Literature, Literary Criticism, Essays, Religion
- Other
ISBN Prefix(es): 978-973-8056
Number of titles published annually: 30 Print
Parent Company: Federation of Jewish Communi-
ties of Romania

Editura Herald
Str Ienachita Vacarescu, nr 18, sector 4, 040157
Bucharest
Mailing Address: OP 10, CP 33, sector 2, 024220
Bucharest
Tel: (021) 3194060; (021) 3194061 Fax: (021)
3194059
E-mail: office@edituraherald.ro; marketing@
edituraherald.ro; sales@edituraherald.ro
Web Site: www.edituraherald.ro
Key Personnel
President & Editorial Dir: Aurelian Scrima
Founded: 1994
Subjects: Fiction, History, Philosophy, Psychol-
ogy, Psychiatry, Religion - Other, Culture
ISBN Prefix(es): 978-973-7970; 978-973-9453;
978-973-96861; 978-973-97577; 978-973-
98399
Number of titles published annually: 60 Print
Total Titles: 160 Print

Editura Hora
Str N D Cocea, nr 9, 550370 Sibiu
Tel: (0269) 211839 Fax: (0269) 211839
E-mail: office@hora-verlag.ro
Web Site: www.hora-verlag.ro
Key Personnel
Owner: Dr Wolfgang Hoeppner; Dr Marie Luise
Roth-Hoeppner E-mail: roth-hoeppner@hora-
verlag.ro
Founded: 1997
Subjects: Fiction, Poetry, Religion - Other, Travel
& Tourism
ISBN Prefix(es): 978-973-8226; 978-973-98263;
978-973-98681; 978-973-99187

House of Guides SRL
Str Presei Libere, nr 1, Casa Presei, Corp
C3, Etaj 3, camera 15-17, sector 1, 013701
Bucharest
Mailing Address: OP 33, CP 123, 013701
Bucharest
Tel: (021) 2243183 Fax: (021) 2243186
E-mail: office@houseofguides.ro; dtp@
houseofguides.ro
Web Site: www.houseofguides.ro
Founded: 2001
Subjects: Geography, Geology, Religion - Other,
Travel & Tourism, Culture, Politics
ISBN Prefix(es): 978-973-7975; 978-973-85423;
978-973-86412; 978-973-86413
Number of titles published annually: 120 Print

Editura Humanitas (Humanitas Publishing
House)+
Piata Presei Libere nr 1, OP 33, 013701
Bucharest 1
Tel: (021) 408 83 50 Fax: (021) 408 83 51
E-mail: secretariat@humanitas.ro
Web Site: www.humanitas.ro
Key Personnel
Production Manager: Alexandru Nitu Tel: (021)
408 83 55 Fax: (021) 408 83 55

Copyright: Gabriela Nica *E-mail:* gabriela.nica@ humanitas.ro
Editorial Secretary: Mariana Clinciu *Tel:* (021) 408 83 56
Founded: 1990
Specialize in humanities & fiction.
Subjects: Biography, Memoirs, Fiction, Government, Political Science, History, Literature, Literary Criticism, Essays, Philosophy, Psychology, Psychiatry, Religion - Buddhist, Religion - Catholic, Religion - Hindu, Religion - Islamic, Religion - Jewish, Science (General), Social Sciences, Sociology, Theology, Humanities
ISBN Prefix(es): 978-973-28; 978-973-50
Parent Company: Grupul Humanitas
Associate Companies: Societatea Comerciala Librariile Humanitas
Subsidiaries: Societatea Comerciala Librariile Humanitas; Societate franco romana de difuzare a cartii SA
Bookshop(s): Libraria din Fundul Curtii, Calea Victoriei, nr 120, Bucharest, Contact: Tina Olea *Tel:* (021) 317 18 28 *Fax:* (021) 317 18 28 *E-mail:* gds@humanitas.ro; Libraria Humanitas Auchan, Str 1 Decembrie 1918 nr 33 A (Centrul Comercial Auchan Titan), Bucharest, Contact: Dan Dumitru *Tel:* (021) 345 22 02 *Fax:* (021) 345 22 02 *E-mail:* auchan@ humanitas.ro; Libraria Humanitas Kretzulescu, Calea Victoriei nr 45, Bucharest, Librarian: Monica Serban *Tel:* (021) 313 50 35 *Fax:* (021) 313 50 35 *E-mail:* kretzulescu@humanitas. ro; Str 1 Decembrie 1918, bl M10, Alba Iulia, Contact: Klara Baies *Tel:* (0258) 826 007 *Fax:* (0258) 826 007 *E-mail:* alba@humanitas. ro; Str Universitatii nr 4, Cluj-Napoca, Contact: Laura Man *Tel:* (0264) 439 475 *Fax:* (0264) 439 475 *E-mail:* cluj@humanitas.ro; Str Domneasca nr 45, Galati, Contact: Daniel Radu *Tel:* (0236) 468 822 *Fax:* (0236) 468 822 *E-mail:* galati@humanitas.ro; Piata Unirii nr 6, Iasi, Contact: Ionuta Necula *Tel:* (0232) 215 568 *Fax:* (0232) 215 568 *E-mail:* iasi1@ humanitas.ro; Libraria Humanitas din Centrul Comercial Felicia, Str Bucium nr 36, Iasi, Contact: Anca Jalba *Tel:* (0232) 239 698 *Fax:* (0232) 239 698 *E-mail:* iasi3@ humanitas.ro; Libraria Humanitas "Mircea Eliade", Bulevardul Republicii nr 5, Oradea, Contact: Orsolya Schmaus *Tel:* (0259) 472 955 *Fax:* (0259) 472 955 *E-mail:* oradea@ humanitas.ro; Piata Stefan cel Mare nr 15, Piatra Neamt, Contact: Dragos Vatra *Tel:* (0233) 212 015 *Fax:* (0233) 212 015 *E-mail:* piatra@ humanitas.ro; Piata Victoriei nr 3, Ploiesti, Contact: Alexandru Dragomir *Tel:* (0244) 519 475 *Fax:* (0244) 519 475 *E-mail:* ploiesti@ humanitas.ro; Str Calea lui Traian nr 147, bl D2, Ramnicu Valcea, Contact: Elena Isabelle Teodorescu *Tel:* (0250) 738 733 *Fax:* (0250) 738 733 *E-mail:* valcea@humanitas.ro; Str Nicolae Balcescu nr 16, Sibiu, Contact: Marian Coman *Tel:* (0269) 211 434 *Fax:* (0269) 211 434 *E-mail:* sibiu@humanitas.ro; Libraria Humanitas "Emil Cioran", Str Mercy nr 1, Timisoara, Contact: Manuela Zvic *Tel:* (0256) 433 180 *Fax:* (0256) 433 180 *E-mail:* timisoara1@humanitas.ro

Idea Design & Print SRL
Str Dorobanti, nr 12, 400117 Cluj-Napoca
Tel: (0264) 594634; (0264) 431661 *Fax:* (0264) 431603
E-mail: oferte@idea.ro
Web Site: www.idea.ro
Key Personnel
President & Editorial Dir: Timotei Nadasan
Executive Dir: Peter Nagy
Founded: 1993
Subjects: Film, Video, Philosophy, Photography
ISBN Prefix(es): 978-973-7913; 978-973-85126; 978-973-85541; 978-973-85788

Number of titles published annually: 10 Print
Total Titles: 59 Print

Infarom Publishing+
2, Nicolae Titulescu Str, Craiova
Mailing Address: PO Box 1 - 230, 200850 Craiova
Tel: (07) 21872518 (cell) *Fax:* (03) 51441303
E-mail: office@infarom.com
Web Site: www.infarom.com; www.infarom.ro
Key Personnel
Marketing & Rights Manager: George Fota
Founded: 1993
Technical & scientific publisher. Specialize in applied & scholarly mathematics. Publishes all genres, in English, Spanish, French, Italian, German & Romanian. Running international publishing projects with open participation & acquires Romanian rights for titles that are suitable for the Romanian market.
Subjects: Alternative, Animals, Pets, Art, Astrology, Occult, Astronomy, Business, Career Development, Computer Science, Computers, Crafts, Games, Hobbies, Education, Fiction, Health, Nutrition, History, How-to, Human Relations, Inspirational, Spirituality, Language Arts, Linguistics, Literature, Literary Criticism, Essays, Management, Marketing, Mathematics, Mysteries, Suspense, Nonfiction (General), Parapsychology, Philosophy, Photography, Physical Sciences, Physics, Psychology, Psychiatry, Publishing & Book Trade Reference, Romance, Science (General), Science Fiction, Fantasy, Self-Help, Social Sciences, Sociology, Sports, Athletics, Travel & Tourism, Western Fiction
ISBN Prefix(es): 978-973-87520; 978-973-88550; 978-973-1991
Number of titles published annually: 12 Print
Total Titles: 57 Print

Editura Institutul Cultural Roman
Aleea Alexandru, nr 38, sector 1, 011824 Bucharest
Tel: (031) 7100627; (031) 7100606 *Fax:* (031) 7100607
E-mail: icr@icr.ro
Web Site: www.icr.ro
Key Personnel
President: Andrei Marga
Dir: Bartha Csaba; Gabriela Matei; Bogdan Popescu *E-mail:* bogdan.popescu@icr.ro
Founded: 2003
Subjects: Architecture & Interior Design, Art, Music, Dance, Philosophy, Photography, Social Sciences, Sociology, Culture, Folklore
ISBN Prefix(es): 978-973-9155; 978-973-577; 978-973-9132; 978-973-95332
Number of titles published annually: 50 Print
Total Titles: 1,000 Print

Editura Institutul European (European Institute Publishing)+
Str Grigore Ghica Voda nr 13 et 9, 700469 Iasi
Tel: (0232) 233 800; (0232) 230 197; (0374) 073 833 *Fax:* (0232) 230 197
E-mail: editura_ie@yahoo.com; euroedit@ hotmail.com
Web Site: www.euroinst.ro
Key Personnel
Dir: Anca Untu-Dumitrescu
Chief Editor: Sorin Parvu
Sales: Cristina Vieru
Founded: 1991
Membership(s): Asociatia Editorilor din Romania (AER) (Publishers Association in Romania).
Subjects: Anthropology, Education, English as a Second Language, Government, Political Science, History, Literature, Literary Criticism, Essays, Medicine, Nursing, Dentistry, Philosophy, Religion - Other, Theology, European Studies, Literary Theory

ISBN Prefix(es): 978-973-9148; 978-973-95528; 978-973-586; 978-973-95671; 978-973-611; 978-973-95870
Distributed by Humanitas
Distributor for Ceu Press (Budapest)

Editura Junimea+
Str Pictorului, nr 14 (Ateneul Tatarasi), 700320 Iasi
Tel: (0232) 410427 *Fax:* (0232) 410427
E-mail: junimeais@yahoo.com
Web Site: www.editurajunimea.ro
Key Personnel
Dir: Simona Modreanu
Founded: 1969
Subjects: Literature, Literary Criticism, Essays, Technology
ISBN Prefix(es): 978-973-37

Editura Lider+
Oficiul postal 5, CP 15, sector 4, Bucharest
Tel: (021) 316 32 55; (0744) 530 970 (cell) *Fax:* (021) 316 32 55
E-mail: office@edituralider.ro
Web Site: www.edituralider.ro
Key Personnel
President & International Rights: Casandra Enescu
Editorial Dir: Gabriela Tatarau
Founded: 1994
Subjects: Art, History, Language Arts, Linguistics, Literature, Literary Criticism, Essays, Medicine, Nursing, Dentistry, Philosophy, Romance
ISBN Prefix(es): 978-973-8117; 978-973-97836

Editura Litera International
Calea Floreasca nr 60, et 5, 014462 Bucharest
Tel: (031) 425 16 19; (021) 319 63 93 *Fax:* (031) 425 16 20
E-mail: info@litera.ro
Web Site: www.litera.ro
Key Personnel
Executive Dir: Marin Vidrascu *E-mail:* m. vidrascu@litera.ro
Sales Manager: Costel Irimia *E-mail:* c.irimia@ litera.ro
Marketing Coordinator: Raluca Tirnauceanu *E-mail:* r.tirnauceanu@litera.ro
Public Relations Coordinator: Georgiana Sandu *E-mail:* g.sandu@litera.ro
Sales: Constanta Cristache
Subjects: Literature, Literary Criticism, Essays
ISBN Prefix(es): 978-973-43

Editura Lumen
Str Tepes Voda, nr 2, bl V1, Sc F, ap 14, 700714 Iasi
Mailing Address: OP3, CP 780, Iasi
Tel: (0332) 450133 *Fax:* (0332) 811551
E-mail: edituralumen@gmail.com; prlumen@ gmail.com (editorial)
Web Site: www.edituralumen.ro
Key Personnel
Chairman: Dr Antonio Sandu *E-mail:* antonio1907@yahoo.com
Editor: Bianca Beatrice Vlasa *E-mail:* beatrice_vsl@yahoo.com
Founded: 2001
Subjects: Art, Engineering (General), Geography, Geology, Philosophy, Poetry, Science (General), Social Sciences, Sociology, Culture
ISBN Prefix(es): 978-973-7766; 978-973-85194; 978-973-85922

Editura MAST+
Sirene nr 22, Bucharest
Tel: (021) 4101945; 0723536196 (cell) *Fax:* (021) 4101945
E-mail: mast@xnet.ro
Web Site: www.edituramast.ro
Founded: 1994

Subjects: Agriculture, Animals, Pets, Antiques, Astrology, Occult, Gardening, Plants, Medicine, Nursing, Dentistry, Veterinary Science
ISBN Prefix(es): 978-973-97297; 978-973-97867; 978-973-97868; 978-973-8011

Matrix Rom
Str Politehnicii 3, Bl 12, Ap 1, 060811 Bucharest
Mailing Address: CP 16-162, 062510 Bucharest
Tel: (021) 4113617; (021) 4012438 *Fax:* (021) 4114280
E-mail: office@matrixrom.ro
Web Site: www.matrixrom.ro
Key Personnel
President: Iancu Ilie
Editorial Dir: Gina Vacarescu
Founded: 1993
Subjects: Architecture & Interior Design, Computer Science, Economics, Engineering (General), Law, Mathematics, Medicine, Nursing, Dentistry, Science (General), Sports, Athletics, Pharmacy, Statistics
ISBN Prefix(es): 978-973-685; 978-973-9254; 978-973-9390; 978-973-97004; 978-973-97314; 978-973-97494
Number of titles published annually: 350 Print
Total Titles: 600 Print

Editura Medicala (Medical Publishing House)+
Str Episcop Radu 15A, Sector 2, Bucharest
Tel: (021) 252 51 86 *Fax:* (021) 252 51 89
E-mail: office@ed-medicala.ro
Web Site: www.ed-medicala.ro
Key Personnel
Administrator: Dr Alexandru Oproiu
Dir: Maria Neamt
Editorial: Dr Irina Dobrescu *Tel:* (021) 252 92 28
    E-mail: irina.dobrescu@ed-medicala.ro
Founded: 1954
Subjects: Medicine, Nursing, Dentistry
ISBN Prefix(es): 978-973-39
Number of titles published annually: 30 Print; 2 CD-ROM

Meteor Press
Str Bahluiului nr 1, sector 1, 011281 Bucharest
Tel: (021) 2228380; (021) 2223312 (distribution)
    Fax: (021) 2228380
E-mail: editura@meteorpress.ro
Web Site: www.meteorpress.ro
Key Personnel
President: Gigi Alecu
Founded: 1999
Subjects: Accounting, Chemistry, Chemical Engineering, Law, Management, Mathematics, Philosophy, Physics, Travel & Tourism, Culture
ISBN Prefix(es): 978-973-728; 978-973-8339; 978-973-8355; 978-973-85065; 978-973-85264; 978-973-99633
Number of titles published annually: 100 Print
Total Titles: 320 Print

Editura Militara (Military Publishing)+
Blvd Iuliu Maniu 13, Sector 6, 061074 Bucharest
Tel: (021) 314 91 61; (021) 319 58 88 *Fax:* (021) 314 91 61
Web Site: www.edituramilitara.ro
Key Personnel
Dir & Publications Manager: Adrian Pandea
    E-mail: adrian.pandea@edituramilitara.ro
Founded: 1950
Subjects: Education, Electronics, Electrical Engineering, Engineering (General), History, Military Science, Mysteries, Suspense, Social Sciences, Sociology
ISBN Prefix(es): 978-973-32

Millennium Press
Str General Victor Popescu, nr 7, 440021 Satu Mare
Tel: (0371) 388260

Web Site: www.millenniumpress.ro
Key Personnel
Owner: Bogdan Bucheru; Horia Nicola Ursu
    E-mail: horiaursu@gmail.com
Founded: 2005
Subjects: Fiction
ISBN Prefix(es): 978-973-88934; 978-973-88585; 978-973-87590

Editura Minerva+
B-dul Metalurgiei, nr 32-44, sector 4, 041831 Bucharest
Mailing Address: OP 82, CP 92, 041831 Bucharest
Tel: (021) 461 08 08; (021) 461 08 10; (021) 461 08 11; (021) 461 08 12; (021) 461 08 13; (021) 461 08 14; (021) 461 08 15; (021) 461 08 16; (021) 461 08 17 *Fax:* (021) 461 08 09; (021) 461 08 19
E-mail: office@edituraminerva.ro; edituraminerva@megapress.ro
Web Site: www.edituraminerva.ro
Key Personnel
Dir: Vasile Horinceanu
Editor: Ana Munteanu
Copyright: Mihaela Badara
Founded: 1970
Subjects: Astrology, Occult, Biography, Memoirs, Computer Science, Education, Film, Video, Finance, Library & Information Sciences
ISBN Prefix(es): 978-973-21
Parent Company: Megapress Holding
Subsidiaries: Series Biblioteca Pentru Toti

Misiunea Crestina Noua Speranta SRL
Zona Ion Ionescu de la Brad, Bloc A105, ap 1, 300245 Timisoara
Mailing Address: OP 14, CP 1129, 300940 Timisoara
Tel: (0256) 214487; (0744) 471214 (cell)
    Fax: (0256) 214487
E-mail: nosp@mail.dnttm.ro
Web Site: www.nouasperanta.ro
Key Personnel
Dir: Tinu Leontiuc
Publishing Dir: Tavi Verlan
Founded: 1992
Subjects: Religion - Other
ISBN Prefix(es): 978-973-7986; 978-973-85438; 978-973-97545; 978-973-98868
Number of titles published annually: 7 Print
Total Titles: 30 Print

Editura Mix SRL+
Str George Cosbuc nr 24, 507055 Cristian, jud Brasov
Tel: (0720) 499494 *Fax:* (0268) 257811
E-mail: comenzi@edituramix.ro
Web Site: www.edituramix.ro
Key Personnel
General Manager: Florin Zamfir *Tel:* (0722) 370057 *E-mail:* florin@edituramix.ro
Founded: 2000
Subjects: Biography, Memoirs, Education, Fiction, Medicine, Nursing, Dentistry, Philosophy, Psychology, Psychiatry, Religion - Other, Social Sciences, Sociology, Culture, Ethics
ISBN Prefix(es): 978-973-8471; 978-973-85646; 978-973-97337; 978-973-98504; 978-973-99946
Number of titles published annually: 12 Print
Total Titles: 110 Print

Mondo Vitale, *imprint of* Editura Univers SA

Regia Autonoma Monitorul Oficial+
Str Parcului nr 65, Sector 1, 012329 Bucharest
Tel: (021) 318 51 28; (021) 318 51 29; (021) 318 51 31 *Fax:* (021) 318 51 15 (marketing)
E-mail: ramo@ramo.ro; marketing@ramo.ro; editura@ramo.ro

Web Site: www.monitoruloficial.ro
Key Personnel
Editor: Alexandru Dranca
Founded: 1832
Subjects: Law
ISBN Prefix(es): 978-973-567
Bookshop(s): Sos Panduri nr 1, bl P33, parter, Sector 5, Bucharest

Editura Muzicala SRL
Calea Victoriei nr 141, Sector 1, Bucharest
Tel: (021) 312 98 67 *Fax:* (021) 312 98 67
E-mail: em@edituramuzicala.ro
Web Site: www.edituramuzicala.ro
Key Personnel
Dir: Silviu Deaconescu
Editorial Secretary, Distribution: Costin Aslam
Founded: 1957
Books, musical scores, compact discs & CD-ROMs.
Subjects: Biography, Memoirs, Music, Dance
ISBN Prefix(es): 978-973-42

Editura National
Str Straja 6, sector 4, 040864 Bucharest
Tel: (021) 4500362 *Fax:* (021) 4500362
Web Site: www.editura-national.ro
Founded: 1995
Subjects: Economics, Fiction, History, Law, Medicine, Nursing, Dentistry, Public Administration
ISBN Prefix(es): 978-973-659; 978-973-8194; 978-973-9308; 978-973-97574; 978-973-97767; 978-973-97768
Number of titles published annually: 150 Print

Editura Nemira+
Str Chiscani no 25-27, Grant Center, sector 1, 011573 Bucharest
Tel: (021) 201 79 64; (021) 201 79 65 (sales)
    Fax: (021) 222 16 56
E-mail: redactie@nemira.ro; office@nemira.ro; secretariat@nemira.ro
Web Site: www.nemira.ro
Key Personnel
Dir General: Valentin Nicolau
Editorial Dir: Dana Moroiu
Public Relations & Marketing Manager: Maria Galan *E-mail:* maria.galan@nemira.ro
Founded: 1991
Subjects: Economics, Education, Government, Political Science, Literature, Literary Criticism, Essays, Marketing, Science Fiction, Fantasy, Social Sciences, Sociology
ISBN Prefix(es): 978-973-569; 978-973-9301; 978-973-9144; 978-973-95576; 978-973-95169; 978-973-9177; 978-973-96255; 978-606-579
Associate Companies: Nemira & Co; Nemira Multimedia
Book Club(s): Clubul cartii

Editura Niculescu+
Bd Regiei 6D, 060204 Bucharest
Tel: (021) 312 97 82 *Fax:* (021) 312 97 83
E-mail: editura@niculescu.ro; club@niculescu.ro (book club)
Web Site: www.niculescu.ro
Key Personnel
Dir: Alina Pantazi
Development Manager: Andrei Niculescu
Founded: 1993
Subjects: Accounting, Biography, Memoirs, Biological Sciences, Business, Career Development, Child Care & Development, Cookery, Economics, Education, Engineering (General), English as a Second Language, Fiction, Film, Video, Gardening, Plants, Geography, Geology, Government, Political Science, Health, Nutrition, History, House & Home, Humor, Language Arts, Linguistics, Law, Management, Marketing, Mathematics, Mysteries, Suspense, Natural History, Nonfiction (General), Outdoor Recreation, Philosophy, Physics, Science (Gen-

eral), Self-Help, Social Sciences, Sociology,
Wine & Spirits, Reference Work
ISBN Prefix(es): 978-973-568; 978-973-748
Number of titles published annually: 180 Print;
18 CD-ROM
Total Titles: 70 Print; 12 CD-ROM

Editura Orizonturi SRL (Orizonturi Publishing
House)+
Bd Libertatii nr 4, bl 117, et 7, ap 20, sector 4,
040128 Bucharest
Tel: (021) 3177679 *Fax:* (021) 3177678
E-mail: orizonturi@editura-orizonturi.ro
Web Site: www.editura-orizonturi.ro
Key Personnel
General Manager: Ioan Enescu
Publishing Rights Manager: Mirela Stoian
Tel: (0744) 531333 (cell)
Founded: 1991
Also acts as a bookseller.
This publisher has noted that 20% of its product
line is author subsidized.
Subjects: Astrology, Occult, Behavioral Sciences,
Biography, Memoirs, Biological Sciences,
Communications, Cookery, Fiction, Govern-
ment, Political Science, History, Literature, Lit-
erary Criticism, Essays, Mysteries, Suspense,
Philosophy, Western Fiction
ISBN Prefix(es): 978-973-736; 978-973-9154;
978-973-9342; 978-973-95333; 978-973-95583;
978-973-95986
Total Titles: 540 Print

Editura Paideia+
Piata Unirii, Nr 1, 030119 Bucharest
Tel: (021) 316 82 10
E-mail: comenzi@paideia.ro
Web Site: www.paideia.ro
Key Personnel
President: Ion Bansoiu
Founded: 1990
Nonprofit organization. Publication of books, spe-
cializing in arts & architecture, cultural studies,
essays, exact sciences, history, literature, phi-
losophy, religion, social sciences & sociology.
Subjects: Anthropology, Architecture & Interior
Design, Art, History, Literature, Literary Crit-
icism, Essays, Medicine, Nursing, Dentistry,
Philosophy, Religion - Other, Social Sciences,
Sociology, Culture
ISBN Prefix(es): 978-973-9131; 978-973-95306;
978-973-9368; 978-973-9393; 978-973-596
Number of titles published annually: 60 Print; 10
CD-ROM
Total Titles: 30 Print; 6 CD-ROM; 4 Audio
Foreign Rep(s): Anca Chelaru (USA)
Foreign Rights: Radu Lungu (France)

**Pallas-Akademia Konyvkiado es
Konyvkereskedes**
Csikszereda, Petofi u 4 sz, Pf 140, 530210 Har-
gita megye
Tel: (0266) 371036; (0745) 005544 (cell)
Fax: (0266) 371036
E-mail: konyvkiado@pallasakademia.ro
Web Site: www.pallasakademia.ro
Key Personnel
Mng Dir: Josef Gyula Tozser
Chief Editor: Maria Kozma
Founded: 1993
Subjects: Biography, Memoirs, Computer Science,
Engineering (General), Ethnicity, Fiction, Jour-
nalism, Literature, Literary Criticism, Essays,
Regional Interests, Religion - Catholic, Science
(General), Social Sciences, Sociology, Technol-
ogy, Art History
ISBN Prefix(es): 978-973-96702; 978-973-665
Number of titles published annually: 30 Print
Distributed by Aligator kft Koenyvkereskedes
(Cluj-Napoca, Romania); Babits Kiado
(Szekszard, Hungary); Carthographia Ki-
ado (Budapest, Hungary); Casa de Presa

(Bucharest, Romania); Custos Koenyvk-
ereskedes (Bucharest, Romania); Editura Huma-
nitas (Targu-Mures, Romania); Editura Lyra
(Targu-Mures, Romania); Sc Bon Ami (Stantu-
Gheorghe, Romania); Sc Cartimpex Koenyvke-
seskedes (Cluj-Napoca, Romania); Sc Libris
srl (Satu-Mare, Romania); Sc Samlibris (Satu-
Mare, Romania); Sc Zalanta Prest (Salonta,
Romania)
Distributor for Akademiai Kiado (Budapest,
Hungary); Babits Kiado (Szekszard, Hun-
gary); Bagolyvar Kiado (Budapest, Hungary);
Carthogrphia Kiado (Budapest, Hungary); Ed-
itura Dacia (Cluj-Napoca, Romania); Euro pa
Kiado (Budapest, Hungary); Editura Humanita
(Bucharest, Romania); Editura Ion Creanga
(Bucharest, Romania); Editura Komp-Press
(Cluj-Napoca, Romania); Kossuth Kiado (Bu-
dapest, Hungary); Magveto Kiado (Budapest,
Hungary); Magyar Koenyvklubb (Budapest,
Hungary); Mentor Kiado (Targu-Mures, Ro-
mania); Mora Ferenc Kiado (Budapest, Hun-
gary); Osiris Kiado (Budapest, Hungary); Park
Kiado (Budapest, Hungary); Polis Kiado (Cluj-
Napoca, Romania); Editura Rao (Bucharest,
Romania); Sprinter Koenyvkereskedes (Bu-
dapest, Hungary); Szent Istvan Tarsulat (Bu-
dapest, Hungary); Szukits Kiado (Szeged, Hun-
gary)
Bookshop(s): Petofi u 4 sz, 530210 Csikszereda
Tel: (0266) 371036; Szabadsag ter 20, 535500
Gyergyoszentmiklos *Tel:* (0266) 361321;
Rozsak tere 57 sz, 540053 Marosvasarhely
Tel: (0265) 250491; Arnika Libri Konyves-
bolt, Kossut u 15 sz, Szekelyudvarhely; Korona
Konyveshaz, Szabadsag ter 20 foldszint, Szat-
marnemeti, Hungary
Distribution Center: Lovolde ter 4, Budapest
1068, Hungary *Tel:* (01) 351-4733 *Fax:* (01)
321-3287 *E-mail:* xantusz@interware.hu *Web
Site:* www.xantusz.hu

Editura Paralela 45
Str Fratii Golesti, nr 130, 110174 Pitesti, jud
Arges
Tel: (0248) 21 45 33; (0248) 63 14 92; (0248) 63
14 39 *Fax:* (0248) 21 45 33
E-mail: office@edituraparalela45.ro;
redactie@edituraparalela45.ro; comenzi@
edituraparalela45.ro
Web Site: www.edituraparalela45.ro
Key Personnel
Dir General: Calin Vlasie *E-mail:* vlasie@
edituraparalela45.ro
Sales Dir: Mihai Minea *E-mail:* mmihai@
edituraparalela45.ro
Editor-in-Chief: Cristina Brostianu
E-mail: cbrostianu@edituraparalela45.ro
Founded: 1994
Subjects: Education, Fiction, Geography, Geol-
ogy, Law, Mathematics, Philosophy, Physics,
Religion - Other, Social Sciences, Sociology,
Culture
ISBN Prefix(es): 978-973-593; 978-973-697; 978-
973-9273; 978-973-9291; 978-973-9433; 978-
973-96923; 978-973-97463; 978-973-97480
Number of titles published annually: 241 Print
Branch Office(s)
Str Intrarea General Grigore Ipatescu, Nr 5, Et
1, Ap 2, Sector 2, Bucharest *Tel:* (021) 317
90 28 *Fax:* (021) 317 90 28 *E-mail:* depbuc@
edituraparalela45.ro
Str Ion Popescu-Voltesti 1-3, bl D, sc 3, ap 43,
Jud Cluj, 400153 Cluj-Napoca *Tel:* (0264) 43
40 31 *Fax:* (0264) 43 40 31 *E-mail:* depcluj@
edituraparalela45.ro

Editura Marcela Penes SRL
Str Andrei Barseanu nr 14, 031091 Bucharest
Mailing Address: OP 4, CP 54, 031091 Bucharest
Tel: (021) 3239966; (021) 3237018; (021)
3236989 *Fax:* (0374) 091660
E-mail: comenzi@edituraana.ro

Web Site: www.marcelapenes.ro
Founded: 1998
Subjects: Biological Sciences, Education, Envi-
ronmental Studies, Mathematics, Music, Dance,
Fine Arts
ISBN Prefix(es): 978-973-7660; 978-973-8072;
978-973-98916; 978-973-99040; 978-973-
99289
Number of titles published annually: 186 Print

Editura Petrion+
Str Mircea Vulcanescu nr 153B, Sector 1, 010819
Bucharest
Mailing Address: CP 1-310, Bucharest
Tel: (021) 310 34 07 *Fax:* (021) 212 65 50
Key Personnel
Founder: Prof Petrica Ion
Founded: 1990
Subjects: Computer Science, Computers, Edu-
cation, Literature, Literary Criticism, Essays,
Mathematics, Physics
ISBN Prefix(es): 978-973-9116

Editura Polirom+
Bd Copou nr 4, 700506 Iasi
Mailing Address: CP 266, Iasi
Tel: (0232) 214 100; (0232) 214 111; (0232) 217
440; (0232) 218 363 *Fax:* (0232) 214 100;
(0232) 214 111; (0232) 217 440; (0232) 218
363
E-mail: office@polirom.ro
Web Site: www.polirom.ro
Key Personnel
Dir General: Silviu Lupescu
Assistant Dir General: Mihaela Vieru
Editorial Dir: Adrian Serban *E-mail:* adrian.
serban@polirom.ro
Sales Dir: Vlad Vinatoru *E-mail:* vlad.vinatoru@
polirom.ro
Founded: 1995
Subjects: Anthropology, Communications, His-
tory, Journalism, Literature, Literary Criticism,
Essays, Management, Marketing, Medicine,
Nursing, Dentistry, Philosophy, Psychology,
Psychiatry, Social Sciences, Sociology
ISBN Prefix(es): 978-973-9248; 978-973-97108;
978-973-97410; 978-973-97522; 978-973-683;
978-973-681
Branch Office(s)
Splaiul Unirii nr 6, Bl B3A, sc 1, et 1, Sector 4,
CP 15-728, 040031 Bucharest *Tel:* (021) 313
89 78; (021) 313 89 77 *Fax:* (021) 313 89 78
E-mail: office.bucuresti@polirom.ro

Editura Princeps Edit
Str Pacurari, nr 4, 700511 Iasi
Tel: (0332) 409829 *Fax:* (0332) 409830
Key Personnel
Dir: Filomena Corbu
Founded: 2001
Subjects: Literature, Literary Criticism, Essays,
Poetry
ISBN Prefix(es): 978-973-7730; 978-973-85706;
978-973-86275; 978-973-86652

Grupul Editorial RAO (RAO Publishing
Group)+
Str Turda Nr 117-119, Bl 6, parter, 011322
Bucharest
Tel: (021) 224 12 31; (021) 224 14 72; (031) 228
62 04 *Fax:* (021) 224 12 31; (021) 224 14 72;
(031) 228 62 04
E-mail: office@raobooks.com
Web Site: www.raobooks.com
Key Personnel
President: Anca Enculescu
Contact: Ovidiu Enculescu
Founded: 1993
Membership(s): Asociatia Editorilor din Romania
(AER) (Publishers Association in Romania);
IBBY.
Subjects: Biography, Memoirs, Education, Fiction,
History, Nonfiction (General), Science Fiction,

Fantasy, Self-Help, Classic & Contemporary Fiction
ISBN Prefix(es): 978-973-576; 978-973-98762; 978-973-98626
Total Titles: 280 Print
Imprints: Editura Enciclopedia RAO; RAO International Publishing Co
Book Club(s): Club Cartii Rao
Warehouse: Str Tiate Mics 4, Sibiu Fax: (069) 215605 E-mail: rao.sb@bx.logicnet.ro
Orders to: RAO International Publishing Co, PO Box 2-124, Bucharest, Contact: Catalina Manolache

RAO International Publishing Co, imprint of Grupul Editorial RAO

RAO International Publishing Co+
Imprint of Grupul Editorial RAO
Str Turda nr 117-119, bl 6, parter, 011322 Bucharest
Tel: (021) 224 14 72; (021) 224 12 31; (031) 228 62 04 Fax: (021) 224 12 31
E-mail: office@raobooks.com; club@raobooks.com
Web Site: www.raobooks.com
Key Personnel
Dir General: Ovidiu Enculescu
Copyright: Maxim Valentina
Founded: 1993
Subjects: Biography, Memoirs, Fiction, Literature, Literary Criticism, Essays, Mysteries, Suspense, Nonfiction (General), Religion - Other, Romance, Science Fiction, Fantasy
ISBN Prefix(es): 978-973-576; 978-973-9164; 978-973-96203; 978-973-96204; 978-973-98653; 978-973-98760; 978-973-98761; 978-973-98950; 978-973-98951
Subsidiaries: Rao Educational
Book Club(s): Clubul Cartii RAO

Realitatea Casa de Edituri Productie Audio-Video Film+
Bdul Dacia nr 126, 020056 Bucharest
Tel: (021) 610 56 59 Fax: (021) 312 15 08
Key Personnel
President: Corneliu Leu
Founded: 1990
Specialize in film production & video cassettes.
Membership(s): Romanian Copyright Society.
Subjects: Education, Government, Political Science, Literature, Literary Criticism, Essays, Nonfiction (General), Philosophy, Romance
ISBN Prefix(es): 978-973-9025
Parent Company: Realitatea-Publishers & Producers Ltd
Bookshop(s): Bucharest; Busteni; Iassi; Timisoara

Rentrop & Straton Grup de Editura si Consultanta in Afaceri+
Bdul Natiunile Unite nr 4, "Gemenii" Sitraco bl 107A, Sector 5, 050122 Bucharest
Tel: (021) 209 45 45; (021) 209 45 12 Fax: (021) 205 57 30
E-mail: rs@rs.ro; comenzi@rs.ro
Web Site: www.rs.ro
Key Personnel
President: George Straton
Founded: 1995
Subjects: Accounting, Advertising, Business, Career Development, Child Care & Development, Communications, Computer Science, Economics, Finance, How-to, Law, Management, Marketing, Nonfiction (General), Self-Help, Travel & Tourism
ISBN Prefix(es): 978-973-97748; 978-973-98033; 978-973-8154; 978-973-98232; 978-973-722
Associate Companies: VNR Verlag fuer die Deutsche Wirtschaft AG, Bonn, Germany
Bookshop(s): Libraria Rentrop & Straton, ROM-EXPO, pavilion 35, 53-57, Marasti Blvd, Sec-

tor 1, Bucharest; Librariile Rentrop & Straton, B-dul Natiunile Unite Nr 3-5, Sector 5, Bucharest

S C Editura Prut SRL
str Campia Libertatii 42, bl B2, sc C, ap 87, Sector 3, 030374 Bucharest
Tel: (021) 324 74 45 Fax: (021) 324 74 45
Web Site: www.prut.ro
Key Personnel
Executive Dir: Angela Garnet
Editorial: Gabriela Ionescu
Sales: Gheorghe Ene
Subjects: Crafts, Games, Hobbies, Education, Fiction, Literature, Literary Criticism, Essays, Poetry, Prose
ISBN Prefix(es): 978-973-8956

Grup Editorial Saeculum IO+
Str Teodosie Rudeanu, nr 29, sector 1, 011258 Bucharest
Tel: (021) 222 8597; (021) 222 8645 Fax: (021) 222 8597
E-mail: contact@saeculum.ro
Web Site: www.saeculum.ro
Key Personnel
Dir General: Prof Ionel Oprisan, PhD
    E-mail: director@saeculum.ro
Founded: 1994
Membership(s): SER (Publishers' Society of Romania).
Subjects: Anthropology, Art, Biography, Memoirs, Fiction, History, Literature, Literary Criticism, Essays, Mysteries, Suspense, Parapsychology, Philosophy, Poetry, Romance, Theology
ISBN Prefix(es): 978-973-9211; 978-973-9399; 978-973-642
Associate Companies: Editura Saeculum Vizual; Editura Vestala, Str Ciucea, 5, sector 3, bl L19, ap 216, of po 72, Bucharest

SC Bistra, imprint of Editura Excelsior Art

Editura Scrisul Romanesc SA (Romanian Writing Publishing PLC)
Str Mihai Viteazu nr 4, 200759 Craiova
Tel: (0351) 404 988; (0722) 753922 Fax: (0351) 404 988
E-mail: office@revistascrisulromanesc.ro
Web Site: www.revistascrisulromanesc.ro
Key Personnel
Editor: Prof Florea Firan
Founded: 1927
Subjects: Government, Political Science, Literature, Literary Criticism, Essays, Social Sciences, Sociology
ISBN Prefix(es): 978-973-38

Editura Semne
Str Barbu Delavrancea, nr 24, sector 1, 011355 Bucharest
Tel: (021) 3188344 Fax: (021) 3188344
E-mail: office@semneartemis.ro
Web Site: www.semneartemis.ro
Key Personnel
Dir General: Stefan Dulu
Founded: 1994
Subjects: Economics, Education, Fiction, Philosophy, Religion - Other, Social Sciences, Sociology, Culture
ISBN Prefix(es): 978-973-624; 978-973-654; 978-973-9318; 978-973-9446; 978-973-97340; 978-973-97998
Number of titles published annually: 150 Print
Total Titles: 550 Print

Samuel Tastet Editeur, see EST-Samuel Tastet Editeur

Editura Tehnopress
Str Gh Asachi nr 13, 700047 Iasi

Tel: (0232) 260092 Fax: (0232) 260092
E-mail: tehnopress@yahoo.com
Web Site: www.tehnopress.ro
Key Personnel
President: Ionel Sacaleanu
Founded: 1997
Subjects: Biological Sciences, Education, Engineering (General), Environmental Studies, Fiction, History, Medicine, Nursing, Dentistry, Philosophy, Physics, Religion - Other, Science (General), Culture
ISBN Prefix(es): 978-973-702; 978-973-8048; 978-973-8377; 978-973-98277; 978-973-98864; 978-973-98865
Number of titles published annually: 100 Print
Total Titles: 150 Print

Editura Teora+
Calea Mosilor 211, sector 2, 020863 Bucharest
Tel: (021) 212 40 53 Fax: (021) 210 38 28
E-mail: sediu@teora.ro
Web Site: www.teora.ro
Key Personnel
Dir: Teodor Raducanu
Founded: 1990
Subjects: Advertising, Art, Astrology, Occult, Astronomy, Biography, Memoirs, Biological Sciences, Business, Career Development, Child Care & Development, Communications, Computer Science, Computers, Cookery, Economics, Education, Electronics, Electrical Engineering, English as a Second Language, Fashion, Fiction, Gardening, Plants, Geography, Geology, Government, Political Science, Health, Nutrition, History, House & Home, How-to, Language Arts, Linguistics, Law, Literature, Literary Criticism, Essays, Management, Marketing, Mathematics, Medicine, Nursing, Dentistry, Music, Dance, Natural History, Nonfiction (General), Outdoor Recreation, Parapsychology, Philosophy, Photography, Psychology, Psychiatry, Science (General), Science Fiction, Fantasy, Self-Help, Social Sciences, Sociology, Sports, Athletics, Technology, Travel & Tourism
ISBN Prefix(es): 978-973-601; 978-973-20

Editura Tracus Arte
Str Pictor Sava Hentia nr 2, sector 1, 011162 Bucharest
Tel: (021) 223 41 11
E-mail: office@edituratracusarte.ro
Web Site: www.tracusarte.ro
Founded: 2008
Subjects: Literature, Literary Criticism, Essays, Poetry
ISBN Prefix(es): 978-606-664

Editura Trei
Str Sfantul Constantin nr 9, ap 1, sector 1, 270490 Bucharest
Tel: (021) 300 60 90 Fax: (0372) 25 20 20
Web Site: www.edituratrei.ro
Key Personnel
General Dir: Vasile Dem Zamfirescu
Executive Dir: Silviu Dragomir
Editorial Dir: Magdalena Marculescu-Cojocea
Rights Manager: Crina Draghici
Press: Teodora Ivan E-mail: teodora.ivan@edituratrei.ro
Founded: 1994
Subjects: Cookery, Fiction, Gardening, Plants, Psychology, Psychiatry
ISBN Prefix(es): 978-973-707; 978-973-8291; 978-973-9419; 978-973-96847; 978-973-97429; 978-973-98034; 978-973-98375
Number of titles published annually: 80 Print

Tritonic Media SRL
Str Coacazelor, nr 5, sector 2, 022651 Bucharest
Mailing Address: OP 71, CP 41, 022651 Bucharest
Tel: (0726) 738724

E-mail: editura@tritonic.ro
Web Site: www.tritonic.ro
Key Personnel
General Dir: Bogdan Hrib
Founded: 1993
Subjects: Fiction, History, Management, Psychology, Psychiatry, Social Sciences, Sociology
ISBN Prefix(es): 978-973-733; 978-973-8051; 978-973-8497; 978-973-96344; 978-973-97702; 978-973-98351; 978-973-98774
Number of titles published annually: 120 Print
Total Titles: 200 Print

Editura Univers SA (Universe Publishing House)+
Str Suvenir, nr 4, ap 3, Sector 2, 020741 Bucharest
Tel: (021) 315 33 08 *Fax:* (021) 315 33 07
E-mail: office@edituraunivers.ro
Web Site: www.edituraunivers.ro
Key Personnel
Owner: Sergiu Crupenschi
President: Diana Crupenschi
Founded: 1969
Subjects: Biography, Memoirs, Education, Fiction, Literature, Literary Criticism, Essays, Philosophy, Poetry, Romance, Science Fiction, Fantasy
ISBN Prefix(es): 978-973-34
Imprints: Mondo Vitale
Subsidiaries: Univers Informatic

Editura Univers Enciclopedic
Str Luigi Cazzavillan nr 17, sector 1, 010784 Bucharest
Tel: (0318) 211100 *Fax:* (0378) 105718
E-mail: office@universenciclopedic.ro
Web Site: www.universenciclopedic.ro
Key Personnel
President: Vlad Radu Popa
Dir, Marketing: Paula-Alina Dumitrescu
Founded: 1994
Subjects: Literature, Literary Criticism, Essays, Philosophy, Psychology, Psychiatry, Religion - Other, Art History, Culture
ISBN Prefix(es): 978-973-637; 978-973-9243; 978-973-9436; 978-973-96989; 978-973-97230; 978-973-97391
Number of titles published annually: 50 Print
Total Titles: 250 Print

Editura Universitara
Bd Nicolae Balcescu, nr 27-33, sector 1, 010045 Bucharest
Tel: (021) 3153247
E-mail: secretariat@edituauniversitara.ro
Web Site: www.editurauniversitara.ro
Key Personnel
Dir: Vasile Muscalu *E-mail:* muscalu@ editurauniversitara.ro
Sales Manager: Crisu Maria
Editorial: Angelica Malaescu
Founded: 2001
Subjects: Communications, Computer Science, Fiction, Geography, Geology, History, Management, Medicine, Nursing, Dentistry, Philosophy, Psychology, Psychiatry, Social Sciences, Sociology, Travel & Tourism, Pharmacy
ISBN Prefix(es): 978-973-749; 978-973-7787; 978-973-8499; 978-973-85744; 978-973-86067; 978-973-99615
Number of titles published annually: 120 Print
Total Titles: 400 Print

Editura Universitatii Alexandru Ioan Cuza
Str Pinului nr 1A, 700109 Iasi
Tel: (0232) 314 947 *Fax:* (0232) 314 947
E-mail: editura@uaic.ro
Web Site: www.editura.uaic.ro
Key Personnel
Dir: Andrei Corbea-Hoise *Tel:* (0232) 201 102 ext 2388

Editor-in-Chief: Dana Lungu *Tel:* (0232) 201 102 ext 2328
Marketing & Public Relations Coordinator: Andrian Acatrinei *Tel:* (0723) 975 876
Founded: 1990
Subjects: Biological Sciences, Chemistry, Chemical Engineering, Education, Environmental Studies, Government, Political Science, Law, Mathematics, Philosophy, Physics, Culture
ISBN Prefix(es): 978-973-703; 978-973-9149; 978-973-9312; 978-973-8243
Number of titles published annually: 100 Print
Total Titles: 300 Print

Editura Universitatii din Bucuresti
Soseaua Panduri 90-92, sector 5, 050663 Bucharest
Tel: (021) 4102384 *Fax:* (021) 4102384
E-mail: editura@unibuc.ro; editura_unibuc@ yahoo.com; editura_unibuc@gmail.com
Web Site: www.editura.unibuc.ro
Key Personnel
President & Editorial Dir: Ion Mihai
Editor-in-Chief: Alexander Calmacu
Founded: 1993
Subjects: Biological Sciences, Chemistry, Chemical Engineering, Computer Science, Fiction, Geography, Geology, Language Arts, Linguistics, Mathematics, Physics, Psychology, Psychiatry, Public Administration, Religion - Other, Art History, Culture
ISBN Prefix(es): 978-973-575; 978-973-9160; 978-973-96254; 978-973-737
Number of titles published annually: 200 Print
Total Titles: 362 Print

Editura Vellant SRL
Splaiul Independentei nr 319, Complex SEMA PARC, OP 84, 060044 Bucharest
Tel: (021) 2117741; (031) 8059825 *Fax:* (021) 2117741; (031) 8059825
E-mail: distributie@vellant.ro; editorial@vellant. ro; comenzi@vellant.ro
Web Site: www.vellant.ro
Key Personnel
Executive Dir: Dan Plesa *E-mail:* dan@vellant.ro
Editorial Dir: Simona Rauta *E-mail:* simona@ vellant.ro
Editor-in-Chief: Anca Lepadatu *E-mail:* anca@ vellant.ro
Press & Events: Oana Dumitru *E-mail:* oana@ vellant.ro
Subjects: Art, Literature, Literary Criticism, Essays, Philosophy, Politics
ISBN Prefix(es): 978-973-1984; 978-973-88759

Editura de Vest+
Str Sfantu Gheorghe nr 1-3, 300085 Timisoara, Timis
Tel: (0785) 255 033; (0356) 004 023 *Fax:* (0356) 816165
E-mail: edvtm@yahoo.com
Web Site: www.edituradevest.ro
Founded: 1972
Subjects: Art, Fiction, Science (General), Technology
ISBN Prefix(es): 978-973-36

Editura Vestala+
Str Ciucea nr 5, sector 3, bl L19, ap 216, of postal 72, Bucharest
Tel: (021) 222 85 97
E-mail: contact@saeculum.ro
Web Site: www.saeculum.ro
Key Personnel
Dir General: Dr Ionel Oprisan
Founded: 2002
Membership(s): Asociatia Editorilor din Romania (AER) (Publishers Association in Romania).
Subjects: Art, Biography, Memoirs, History, Literature, Literary Criticism, Essays, Mysteries, Suspense, Parapsychology, Philosophy

ISBN Prefix(es): 978-973-9200; 978-973-96063; 978-973-96421; 978-973-96817; 978-973-9418
Number of titles published annually: 30 Print
Total Titles: 120 Print
Parent Company: Grup Editorial Saeculum IO
Associate Companies: Saeculum Vizual

Editura Vivaldi
Str Polona, nr 92, bl 17A-B, sc 1, ap 1, sector 1, 010496 Bucharest
Tel: (021) 2108897; (021) 2101013
E-mail: contact@edituravivaldi.ro
Web Site: www.edituravivaldi.ro
Key Personnel
General Dir: Rodica Sava
Editorial Dir: Sanda Popa
Founded: 1991
Subjects: Fiction, History, Philosophy, Psychology, Psychiatry, Travel & Tourism, Politics
ISBN Prefix(es): 978-973-9139; 978-973-9473; 978-973-95310
Number of titles published annually: 20 Print
Total Titles: 70 Print

Editura Vox+
Str Petru Maior nr 32, Sector 1, 011264 Bucharest
Tel: (021) 222 02 13 *Fax:* (021) 222 02 13
E-mail: vox@edituravox.ro
Web Site: www.edituravox.ro
Key Personnel
General Manager: Lucia Ovezea
Contact: Cornelia Macarie *Tel:* (021) 222 02 14
    E-mail: cornelia_macarie@yahoo.com
Founded: 1994
Subjects: Art, Cookery, Economics, Gardening, Plants, Health, Nutrition, Literature, Literary Criticism, Essays, Psychology, Psychiatry
ISBN Prefix(es): 978-973-96922; 978-973-97848; 978-973-98159; 978-973-9381; 978-973-7811

Editura Vremea SRL (Vremea Publishers Ltd)+
Str Constantin Daniel nr 14, sector 1, 010631 Bucharest
Tel: (021) 335 81 31 *Fax:* (0378) 106 497
E-mail: office@edituravremea.ro
Web Site: www.edituravremea.ro
Key Personnel
Editorial Dir: Silvia Colfescu
Commercial Dir: Anda Simian
Public Relations: Roxana Vlasceanu
Founded: 1990
Membership(s): Asociatia Editorilor din Romania (AER) (Publishers Association in Romania).
Subjects: Art, Astrology, Occult, Biography, Memoirs, Child Care & Development, Education, Fiction, Health, Nutrition, History, Literature, Literary Criticism, Essays, Medicine, Nursing, Dentistry, Parapsychology, Philosophy, Poetry, Religion - Other, Science Fiction, Fantasy, Social Sciences, Sociology
ISBN Prefix(es): 978-973-9162; 978-973-95063; 978-973-95581
Number of titles published annually: 50 Print
Total Titles: 250 Print

Russia

General Information

Capital: Moscow
Language: Russian
Religion: Predominantly Christian (mostly Russian Orthodox), also Islam and Buddhist
Population: 149.5 million
Bank Hours: Generally open for short hours between 0930-1230 Monday-Friday

Shop Hours: Generally 0900-1800 Monday-Friday; often open weekends
Currency: 100 kopeks = 1 rubl
Export/Import Information: According to Ukrainian quotas and customs duties, companies engaged in trade should register with the Ukraine Ministry of Foreign Economic Relations. Licenses for export and import are also required for trade with Russia.
Copyright: UCC, Berne, Florence (see Copyright Conventions, pg viii)

Agni Publishing House
23 Michurin Str, 443110 Samara
Tel: (846) 270-32-90; (846) 270-20-11 *Fax:* (846) 270-20-11
E-mail: support@agniart.ru
Web Site: www.agniart.com
Key Personnel
Manager: Gennady Karev *Tel:* (846) 270-23-85 *Fax:* (846) 270-23-85 *E-mail:* gekarev@yandex.ru
Sales Manager: Julia Fenkova *Tel:* (846) 270-23-77 *Fax:* (846) 270-23-77
Founded: 1989
Also produce fine art prints, posters, landscape photographs, art albums & books.
Subjects: Art, History, Philosophy
ISBN Prefix(es): 978-5-89850

AGT Geocenter Ltd
Khersonskaya Str, 41a, 117246 Moscow
Tel: (495) 331-4005
E-mail: mail@geocenter.ru
Web Site: www.geocenter.ru
Subjects: Cartography, Russia
ISBN Prefix(es): 978-5-93014; 978-5-94050
Bookshop(s): 10, Bolshaya, Semyonovskaya St, Moscow *Tel:* (495) 727-0593

Airis Press+
Prospect Mira, Bldg 104, 2nd floor, 129626 Moscow
Tel: (495) 785 1530
E-mail: office@airis.ru; editor@airis.ru; trade@airis.ru
Web Site: www.airis.ru
Founded: 1996
Specialize in educational literature, books helping school-leavers & students to prepare for the exams, handbooks & textbooks in foreign languages, popular educational books, reference books.
Subjects: Business, Career Development, Child Care & Development, Cookery, Crafts, Games, Hobbies, Education, English as a Second Language, Gardening, Plants, Health, Nutrition, How-to, Language Arts, Linguistics, Medicine, Nursing, Dentistry
ISBN Prefix(es): 978-5-7836; 978-5-8112
Number of titles published annually: 70 Print; 3 Audio
Total Titles: 180 Print; 3 Audio
Distributor for Foulsham; New Market Press; Parenting Press

Aletheia Publishing House
Parkhomenko 37-43, 194021 St Petersburg
Tel: (812) 577-48-72; (921) 951-98-99 (sales)
E-mail: aletheia92@mail.ru
Key Personnel
Editor-in-Chief: Igor Savkin *Tel:* (905) 20-20-139
Founded: 1992
Subjects: Archaeology, Art, Economics, History, Language Arts, Linguistics, Music, Dance, Philosophy, Psychology, Psychiatry, Science (General), Social Sciences, Sociology
ISBN Prefix(es): 978-5-89329; 978-5-91419; 978-5-903354

ARGO-RISK
ul Staryj Gaj 6-1-419, 111402 Moscow

Tel: (495) 4768538
Key Personnel
Founder: Dmitry Kuzmin
Founded: 1993
Subjects: LGBTQ, Literature, Literary Criticism, Essays, Poetry
ISBN Prefix(es): 978-5-900506; 978-5-86856

Arkaim Publishing House
38 Karl Marx, Off 413, 454091 Chelyabinsk
Tel: (351) 239-15-26 *Fax:* (351) 239-15-26
Subjects: Cookery, Health, Nutrition, Nonfiction (General)
ISBN Prefix(es): 978-5-8029

Armada Ao+
a/r 4, 125565 Moscow
Tel: (495) 641-36-58
E-mail: adm@armada.ru; sale@armada.ru; mvn@armada.ru
Web Site: www.armada.ru
Founded: 1992
Subjects: Animals, Pets, Fiction, Mysteries, Suspense, Romance, Science Fiction, Fantasy
ISBN Prefix(es): 978-5-7632

Aspect Press Ltd
Zelenyi prospect, 3/10, Bldg 15, 111141 Moscow
Tel: (495) 3067801; (495) 3068371
Web Site: www.aspectpress.ru
Key Personnel
Dir General: Leonid Shipov *E-mail:* shipov@aspectpress.ru
Chief Editor: Lyudmila Shipova *E-mail:* shipova@aspectpress.ru
Founded: 1992
University textbooks in humanities.
Subjects: Government, Political Science, History, Journalism, Management, Radio, TV, International Relations
ISBN Prefix(es): 978-5-7567
Number of titles published annually: 50 Print
Total Titles: 780 Print

AST Press
dom 13, stroenie 4, Perevedenovsky pereulok, 105082 Moscow
Tel: (495) 276 01 11 *Fax:* (495) 276 09 60
E-mail: astpress@astpress.ru
Web Site: www.astpress.ru
Founded: 1990
Subjects: Art, Cookery, Fiction, History, How-to, Literature, Literary Criticism, Essays, Science (General), Self-Help
ISBN Prefix(es): 978-5-94776

Azbooka, *imprint of* Azbooka-Atticus Publishing Group

Azbooka-Atticus Publishing Group
5 Donskoy proezd, 15, korp 4, 119334 Moscow
Tel: (495) 933-76-01; (495) 933-76-00 (sales); (495) 933-76-20 (sales) *Fax:* (495) 933-76-19
E-mail: sales@atticus-group.ru
Web Site: www.atticus-group.ru
Founded: 1995
Subjects: Art, Biography, Memoirs, Fiction, History, Nonfiction (General), Science Fiction, Fantasy, Cultural Studies
ISBN Prefix(es): 978-5-389; 978-5-18
Imprints: Azbooka; CoLiblri (Russian authors & nonfiction); Inostranka (translated fiction); Machaon (children's books)

Azbookvarik Group Publishing House Ltd
Mamonovsky pereulok 4, Bldg 1, Off 3, 123001 Moscow
Tel: (495) 984 8004
E-mail: azbookvarik@bk.ru
Web Site: www.azbookvarik.com

Subjects: Crafts, Games, Hobbies, Education, Music, Dance, Fairy Tales
ISBN Prefix(es): 978-5-402
Branch Office(s)
Myasnikova 70, Off 607, 220030 Minsk, Belarus

N E Bauman (Moscow State Technical University Publishers)+
2nd Baumanskaya Str, 5, Bldg 1, 105005 Moscow
Tel: (499) 263-60-45 *Fax:* (495) 261-45-97
E-mail: info@baumanpress.ru; bauman@bmstu.ru; press@bmstu.ru (sales)
Web Site: baumanpress.ru
Founded: 1989
Subjects: Biblical Studies, Business, Communications, Computer Science, Computers, Earth Sciences, Economics, Education, Electronics, Electrical Engineering, Energy, Engineering (General), Law, Management, Mathematics, Mechanical Engineering, Physical Sciences, Science (General), Technology
ISBN Prefix(es): 978-5-7038
Parent Company: Moscow State Technical University

The BKL (BINOM Knowledge Laboratory) Publishers
3 Proezd Aeroporta, 125167 Moscow
Tel: (499) 157-52-72; (499) 157-79-77; (499) 157-19-02
E-mail: info@pilotlz.ru
Web Site: pilotlz.ru
Key Personnel
Production Manager: Lesya Galan
Subjects: Biological Sciences, Chemistry, Chemical Engineering, Computer Science, Economics, Engineering (General), Management, Mathematics, Medicine, Nursing, Dentistry, Physics, Academic, Nanotechnology, Pedagogics
ISBN Prefix(es): 978-5-94774; 978-5-9963

CLEVER Publishing
16, 3rd Monetchikovsky per, Bldg 1, 115054 Moscow
Tel: (495) 744 03 31
E-mail: info@clever-publishing.com
Web Site: clever-publishing.com; www.clever-media.ru
Key Personnel
Chief Executive Officer: Alexander Alperovich
Foreign Rights Dir: Olga Utkina *E-mail:* outkina@clever-media.ru
Foreign Rights Manager: Petula Chaplin *E-mail:* p.chaplin@clever-media.ru
Editor-in-Chief: Elena Izmaylova *E-mail:* e.izmaylova@clever-media.ru
Distributed by Quarto Publishing Group USA Inc

CoLiblri, *imprint of* Azbooka-Atticus Publishing Group

Izdatelstvo Detskaya Literatura (Children's Literature Publishing)+
ul Chernyakhovskogo 4, 125319 Moscow
Tel: (495) 601-22-68 *Fax:* (495) 601-22-68
E-mail: dl@detlit.ru; tk@detlit.ru
Web Site: www.detlit.ru
Key Personnel
Dir: Vishnyakov Oleg Voldmarovich
Founded: 1933
Subjects: Art, Fiction, History, Language Arts, Linguistics, Literature, Literary Criticism, Essays, Poetry, Science Fiction, Fantasy
ISBN Prefix(es): 978-5-08
Subsidiaries: Detskaya Literatura Publishers
Branch Office(s)
Dom Detskoy Knigi, I Tverskaya-Yamskaya 13, Moscow

Dobraya Kniga Publishers+
11 Petrovsky blvd, 127051 Moscow
Tel: (495) 694-20-78; (495) 694-16-81; (495) 694-20-94; (495) 650-46-38; (495) 650-44-34
E-mail: mail@dkniga.ru
Web Site: www.dkniga.ru
Founded: 2001
Books for highly effective life to help people & communities achieve worthwhile purposes through continuous learning & self-development.
Subjects: Advertising, Animals, Pets, Anthropology, Behavioral Sciences, Business, Career Development, Economics, Education, English as a Second Language, Human Relations, Humor, Management, Marketing, Psychology, Psychiatry, Self-Help, Social Sciences, Sociology
ISBN Prefix(es): 978-5-98124
Number of titles published annually: 200 Print; 25 Audio
Total Titles: 450 Print; 25 Audio

DROFA
Sushevsky Val St 49/1, 127018 Moscow
Tel: (495) 795-0550; (495) 795-0551
   Toll Free Tel: 800-2000-550 *Fax:* (495) 795-0552
E-mail: info@drofa.ru; marketing@drofa.ru; sales@drofa.ru
Web Site: www.drofa.ru
Founded: 1991
Specialize in teaching & education.
Subjects: Education
Number of titles published annually: 150 Print; 12 CD-ROM; 15 Audio
Total Titles: 3,500 Print; 47 CD-ROM; 37 Audio
Associate Companies: Dik; Drofa-Media; Drofa-Plus; Russkiy Yazyk Media; Shkolnik

Egmont Russia Ltd
Subsidiary of Egmont International Holding A/S
8/6, Olsufievsky per, 119021 Moscow
Tel: (495) 933-72-50 *Fax:* (495) 933-72-51
E-mail: info@egmont.ru
Web Site: www.egmont.ru
Key Personnel
Dir General: Lev Elin
Deputy Dir General & Chief Editor: Mikhail Morozov
Founded: 1992

Izdatelstvo 'Ekonomika'
Berezhkovskaia naberezhnaya 6, 123995 Moscow
Tel: (499) 240-48-77; (499) 240-48-48; (499) 240-48-17 *Fax:* (499) 240-48-17; (499) 240-48-48
E-mail: info@economizdat.ru
Web Site: www.economizdat.ru
Founded: 2000
Economics publishing house.
Subjects: Accounting, Agriculture, Business, Cookery, Economics, Education, Finance, Law, Literature, Literary Criticism, Essays, Management, Natural History, Science (General)
ISBN Prefix(es): 978-5-282

Eksmo Publishing House
Zorge 1, 123308 Moscow
Tel: (495) 411-68-86
E-mail: info@eksmo.ru
Web Site: eksmo.ru
Founded: 1991
Subjects: Cookery, Education, Fiction, Health, Nutrition, History, Literature, Literary Criticism, Essays, Poetry
ISBN Prefix(es): 978-5-699; 978-5-85585; 978-5-8153; 978-5-94700; 978-5-9955

Far Eastern Federal University (FEFU)+
8 Suhanova St, 690950 Vladivostok
Web Site: www.dvfu.ru

Founded: 1982
Subjects: Human Relations, Mathematics
ISBN Prefix(es): 978-5-7444
Number of titles published annually: 300 Print

Finansy i Statistika Publishing House (Finance & Statistics Publishing House)+
Pokrovka 7, 101000 Moscow
Tel: (495) 625-47-08; (495) 625-35-02; (495) 625-36-28; (495) 621-86-57 *Fax:* (495) 625-09-57
E-mail: mail@finstat.ru
Web Site: www.finstat.ru
Key Personnel
Mng Dir & Editor-in-Chief: Alevtina Nikolaevna Zvonova
Founded: 1924
Membership(s): Guild of Russian Financiers; Russian Association of Book Publishers; Russian Association of Booksellers
Subjects: Accounting, Business, Career Development, Computer Science, Computers, Economics, Education, Environmental Studies, Finance, Foreign Countries, Human Relations, Law, Library & Information Sciences, Management, Marketing, Mathematics, Public Administration, Real Estate, Regional Interests, Securities, Travel & Tourism, Women's Studies
ISBN Prefix(es): 978-5-279
Distributed by INFRA-M Izdatel 'skij dom
Distributor for INFRA-M Izdatel 'skij dom

Fiton +
2 Magistralny tupik, 7a, 123007 Moscow
Tel: (499) 256-67-20; (499) 256-25-75 (wholesale) *Fax:* (499) 256-67-20
E-mail: fiton@fiton-knigi.ru; sales@fiton-knigi.ru; curaren@cea.ru
Web Site: www.phytonflowers.ru; plantarya.ru
Subjects: Gardening, Plants, Floriculture, Horticulture, Landscape Design, Russian Flora
ISBN Prefix(es): 978-5-93457

Izdatelstvo Fizkultura i Sport+
ul Dolgorukovskaya, 27, 12703 Moscow
Tel: (495) 2582690
Founded: 1923
Subjects: Outdoor Recreation, Sports, Athletics
ISBN Prefix(es): 978-5-278

Fizmatlit Publishing Co+
ul Profsojuznaja 90, 117997 Moscow
Tel: (495) 334-74-21 *Fax:* (495) 334-76-20
E-mail: fizmat@maik.ru
Web Site: www.fml.ru
Key Personnel
Dir General: Andreeva Maria Nikolaevna
Founded: 1931
Subjects: Astronomy, Communications, Computer Science, Computers, Mathematics, Mechanical Engineering, Physical Sciences, Physics
ISBN Prefix(es): 978-5-9221
Parent Company: MAIK Nauka Publishers

Izdatelstvo Galart (Galart Publishing)
ul Chernyahovskogo 4a, 125319 Moscow
Tel: (499) 151-25-02; (499) 151-02-31; (499) 151-12-41 (sales); (499) 151-87-07 (production) *Fax:* (495) 151-25-02
E-mail: galart-books@yandet.ru; galart@m9com.ru
Web Site: www.galart-moscow.ru
Founded: 1969
Subjects: Art
ISBN Prefix(es): 978-5-269

Gidrometeoizdat Publishing
(Hydrometeorological Publishing)
ul Beringa, 38, 199397 St Petersburg
Tel: (812) 3520815; (812) 9836404 (English)
Fax: (812) 3520815

Founded: 1934 (as a Soviet Union state publishing house)
Professional editing & publishing of hydrological, meteorological, environmental & special purpose literature. Relations with professionals from research centers, monitoring posts & universities (including Arctic & Antarctic). Localization of titles to/from foreign languages. Publishing rights trading.
Membership(s): Federal Service for Hydrometeorology & Environmental Monitoring.
Subjects: Agriculture, Biography, Memoirs, Earth Sciences, Education, Environmental Studies, Geography, Geology, Science (General), Technology
ISBN Prefix(es): 978-5-286
Number of titles published annually: 50 Print; 1 CD-ROM; 1 Online
Total Titles: 7,125 Print; 1 CD-ROM; 1 Online

INFRA-M Izdatel 'skij dom (INFRA-M Academic Publishing House)+
Polyarnaya str, 31B, 127282 Moscow
Tel: (495) 280-7685 *Fax:* (495) 280-3629
E-mail: books@infra-m.ru
Web Site: www.infra-m.ru; www.znanium.com (electronic publications)
Key Personnel
Dir General: Albina Nikolaevna Nesterova *Tel:* (495) 280-7685 ext 461
Editor-in-Chief: Dr Vladimir Michailovich Prudnikov *Tel:* (495) 280-7685 ext 291 *E-mail:* prudnik@infra-m.ru
Deputy Editor-in-Chief (Foreign Rights): Victor Pavlovich Vymenets, Esq *Tel:* (495) 280-7685 ext 204 *E-mail:* wvym@infra-m.ru
Head, Sales: Anna Mikhaylovna Tokmadzhyan *Tel:* (495) 363-4260 ext 213 *E-mail:* nancy@infra-m.ru
Founded: 1992
Publisher of business books in accounting, management, law, public sector & produces audio & video courses of foreign languages. Also provides print-on-demand services & electronic library system.
Subjects: Accounting, Advertising, Behavioral Sciences, Business, Civil Engineering, Computer Science, Economics, Education, Finance, Government, Political Science, History, Language Arts, Linguistics, Law, Management, Marketing, Mathematics, Medicine, Nursing, Dentistry, Public Administration, Social Sciences, Sociology, Technology
ISBN Prefix(es): 978-5-86225; 978-5-16
Number of titles published annually: 1,000 Print

INFRA-M Nauchno-izdatel 'skij centr, see INFRA-M Izdatel 'skij dom

Inostranka, *imprint of* Azbooka-Atticus Publishing Group

Izdatelstvo Iskusstvo+
Kislovskiy M Lane, 3, 125009 Moscow
Tel: (495) 2035872 *Fax:* (495) 2918882
Key Personnel
Contact: Damian Lomonosov
Founded: 1938 (as Izogiz & Iskusstvo)
Publishing house for art literature.
Subjects: Architecture & Interior Design, Art, Drama, Theater, Film, Video, History, Philosophy
ISBN Prefix(es): 978-5-210
Distributed by Calmann & King (UK)
Distributor for Booth-Clibborn Editions; Giunti (Italy); Jaca Book (Italy)

IVM, see Izdatelstvo Ves Mir (IVM)

Izvestiya
Pushkinskaya Pl, 5, 127006 Moscow
Founded: 1927

Subjects: Agriculture, Business, Economics, Government, Political Science, Law, Public Administration, Social Sciences, Sociology, Sports, Athletics
ISBN Prefix(es): 978-5-206; 978-5-902422

JSC Interbook-Business
Spiridonievskij per, d 12/9, of 11, 12, 123104 Moscow
Tel: (495) 956-1392; (495) 650-67-66 (sales); (495) 650-1788 (secretary) *Fax:* (495) 956-3752
E-mail: info-interbook@mail.ru; real-interbook@mail.ru
Web Site: interbook-art.ru
Founded: 1992
Publisher of coffee table books.
Subjects: Art, Cookery, Crafts, Games, Hobbies, Gardening, Plants, Health, Nutrition, History, Regional Interests, Sports, Athletics
ISBN Prefix(es): 978-5-89164

Izdatel'stvo Kazanskogo Universiteta (Kazan Federal University Publishing House)+
18 Kremlyovskaya St, 420008 Kazan Respublika Tatarstan
Tel: (843) 233-71-09 *Fax:* (843) 292-44-48
E-mail: public.mail@kpfu.ru
Web Site: kpfu.ru
Founded: 1957
Subjects: Chemistry, Chemical Engineering, Criminology, Economics, Environmental Studies, Mathematics
ISBN Prefix(es): 978-5-7464

Izdatelstvo Khudozhestvennaya Literatura+
Nov Basmannaya ul 19, 107996 Moscow
Tel: (499) 261 88 65; (499) 261 88 63 *Fax:* (499) 261 83 00
E-mail: realisihl@mail.ru; redhudlit@mail.ru; hudizdat@yandex.ru
Web Site: hudlit.com
Founded: 1930 (as The State Publishers of Fiction)
Publishing house for fiction, poetry & literary biography.
Subjects: Biography, Memoirs, Fiction, Literature, Literary Criticism, Essays, Music, Dance, Poetry
ISBN Prefix(es): 978-5-280

Izdatelstvo Kniga+
ul Tverskaja 50, 125047 Moscow
Tel: (495) 2516003
Founded: 1964
Subjects: Library & Information Sciences, Publishing & Book Trade Reference
ISBN Prefix(es): 978-5-212
Subsidiaries: Business Week (Russian Language Edition) (owned jointly by Kniga Publishers, Russia & McGraw-Hill Corp, USA); The Culture Center at Bolshaya Polianka (owned jointly by Russia & USA); Kniga Printshop (owned jointly by Kniga Publishers, Russia & Fargo Group, Toronto, Ontario, Canada)

KompasGid
Lubianskiy 5, str 1, 101000 Moscow
Tel: (499) 707 74 75 *Fax:* (495) 624 24 28
E-mail: book.kompasgid@gmail.com
Web Site: kompasgid.ru; www.facebook.com/kompasguide
Key Personnel
Editor-in-Chief: Vitali Ziusko
Mng Editor & Foreign Rights: Marina Kadetova
E-mail: kgd.rights@gmail.com
Founded: 2008
Subjects: Child Care & Development, Education, Poetry, Science (General), Science Fiction, Fantasy
ISBN Prefix(es): 978-5-904561

Total Titles: 170 Print
Foreign Rights: Chengdu Tongzhou Culture Communication Co Ltd (George Zheng) (China); Japan Uni Agency (Japan)

KompasGuide Publishing House, see KompasGid

Izdatelskij dom Kompozitor
ul Sadovaja-Triumfal'naja d 12/14, 127006 Moscow
Tel: (495) 650-1670
E-mail: kompozitor@ikompozitor.ru
Web Site: ikompozitor.ru
Key Personnel
Chief Executive Officer & Chief Editor: Dr Boris Petrovich Jurgenson *Tel:* (495) 650-2980
Founded: 1957
Subjects: Biography, Memoirs, Education, Music, Dance
ISBN Prefix(es): 978-5-85285

Ladomir, Naucno-izdatelskij Centr+
ul Zavodskaja d 6a, 124681 Moscow
Tel: (495) 537-98-33 *Fax:* (495) 537-47-42
Founded: 1990
Subjects: Antiques, Asian Studies, Fiction, Government, Political Science, History, Philosophy, Religion - Buddhist, Religion - Hindu, Religion - Islamic, Science Fiction, Fantasy, Sports, Athletics
ISBN Prefix(es): 978-5-86218

Limbus Press+
Izmailovsky prosp, 14, 190005 St Petersburg
Tel: (812) 712-65-47; (812) 712-66-06
E-mail: limb@limbuspress.ru; limbusbooks@gmail.com; limbus.info@gmail.com; limbus.foreign.rights@gmail.com
Web Site: www.limbuspress.ru
Key Personnel
Foreign Rights Dir: Olga Tublina
Sales Dir: Victor Kuznestsov
Editor-in-Chief: Vadim Leventhal
Founded: 1990
Subjects: Biography, Memoirs, Fiction, Nonfiction (General)
ISBN Prefix(es): 978-5-8370
Number of titles published annually: 60 Print
Branch Office(s)
Moscow
Foreign Rep(s): Anna Benn (England); Catherine Fzagou (Greece); Anastasia Lester (France); Christian Marti-Menzel (Spain)

Machaon, *imprint of* Azbooka-Atticus Publishing Group

Izdatelstvo Mashinostroenie+
Stromynskij pereulok 4, 107076 Moscow
Tel: (499) 268-38-58; (499) 269-52-98 *Fax:* (499) 269-48-97
E-mail: mashpubl@mashin.ru; realiz@mashin.ru (sales, marketing & advertising)
Web Site: www.mashin.ru
Key Personnel
Dir: Olga N Rumyantseva
Founded: 1931
Publishing house for mechanical engineering.
Subjects: Aeronautics, Aviation, Automotive, Biography, Memoirs, Computer Science, Economics, Engineering (General), Environmental Studies, Mathematics, Mechanical Engineering, Technology
ISBN Prefix(es): 978-5-217
Associate Companies: Aspect

Izdatelstvo Medicina+
Verkhnyaya Krasnosel'skaya, 17 A, Bldg 1B, 107140 Moscow
Tel: (499) 264-70-43 *Fax:* (499) 264-70-43

E-mail: imlaw@list.ru
Web Site: www.medlit.ru
Key Personnel
Dir: Efim M Shifman, MD *Tel:* (499) 264-99-33
Founded: 1918
Publishing house for medicine.
Subjects: Health, Nutrition, Medicine, Nursing, Dentistry, Psychology, Psychiatry, Science (General)
ISBN Prefix(es): 978-5-225
Associate Companies: Association for Medical Literature

Mescerjakova Izdatel'skij dom ZAO
Novaya Basmannaya, 23, Bldg 2, Off 213, 107078 Moscow
Tel: (499) 265-3208; (499) 265-6658; (499) 265-1490; (499) 267-0402
E-mail: podpiska@idmkniga.ru; idmsale@idmkniga.ru
Web Site: www.idmkniga.ru
Key Personnel
Head: Vadim Meshcheryakov
Founded: 2005
Subjects: Art, Biography, Memoirs, Fiction, Literature, Literary Criticism, Essays, Nonfiction (General), Psychology, Psychiatry
ISBN Prefix(es): 978-5-91045

Izdatelstvo Mezdunarodnye Otnoshenia (International Relations Publishing House)+
Stoljarnyi Lane 3, Bldg 5, 123022 Moscow
Tel: (499) 253-15-31; (495) 978-31-63 (sales); (499) 253-13-24 (sales)
E-mail: info@inter-rel.ru
Web Site: www.inter-rel.ru
Key Personnel
Dir General: Kovalkov Andrey
Founded: 1957
Subjects: Biography, Memoirs, Economics, Education, Government, Political Science, History, Law, Contemporary Politics, Diplomacy, Foreign & International Law, International Economic Relations, World & National Culture, World Economy
ISBN Prefix(es): 978-5-7133
Parent Company: Goscomizdat, Strastnoi bul 5, 101409 Moscow

Ministerstvo Kul 'tury RF+
pereulok Malyy Gnezdnikovskiy 7/6, ctp 1,2, 125993 Moscow
Tel: (495) 629-20-08
E-mail: press@mkrf.ru; kultura@mkrf.ru
Web Site: mkrf.ru
Membership(s): International Federation of Library Associations & Institutions (IFLA).
Subjects: Genealogy, History, Library & Information Sciences, Social Sciences, Sociology
ISBN Prefix(es): 978-5-7196

Izdatelstvo Mir (Mir Publishers)+
1-j Rizskij per 2, 129626 Moscow
Tel: (495) 2861783 *Fax:* (495) 288-95-22
E-mail: info@vesmirbooks.ru
Web Site: www.vesmirbooks.ru
Key Personnel
Dir: Oleg Zimarin
Rights Manager: Larissa Troitskaya
Marketing & Distribution: Marina Dyadyunova
Founded: 1946 (under name Mir since 1964)
Translation & publication of scientific & technical books.
Membership(s): ASKI (Book Publishers Association of Russia).
Subjects: Aeronautics, Aviation, Animals, Pets, Astronomy, Biological Sciences, Chemistry, Chemical Engineering, Communications, Computer Science, Computers, Earth Sciences, Electronics, Electrical Engineering, Engineering (General), Environmental Studies, Fiction, Geography, Geology, Health, Nutrition, Mathematics, Mechanical Engineering, Physical Sci-

ences, Physics, Psychology, Psychiatry, Science (General), Science Fiction, Fantasy, Self-Help, Technology
ISBN Prefix(es): 978-5-03
Number of titles published annually: 50 Print
Total Titles: 370 Print

Mir Knigi+
4th Kabelnaya Str, 6A, 111024 Moscow
Tel: (495) 974 2976 *Fax:* (495) 234 4920
E-mail: info@mirknigi.ru; order@mirknigi.ru
Web Site: mirknigi.com
Key Personnel
General Dir: Ilya Polezhaev
Founded: 1989
Publisher of *Mir Knigi* magazine.
Subjects: Electronics, Electrical Engineering, Fiction, Health, Nutrition, House & Home, Music, Dance, Nonfiction (General), Sports, Athletics, Beauty
ISBN Prefix(es): 978-5-7043

Izdatelstvo Molodaya Gvardia (Young Guard Publishing House)
21 Sushchevskaya Str, 127055 Moscow
Tel: (495) 787-6385; (495) 787-95-59 (bookstore); (495) 787-62-88; (495) 787-62-85
Fax: (495) 978-1286; (495) 978-65-27
E-mail: info@gvardiya.ru; mg@gvardiya.ru; dsel@gvardiya.ru
Web Site: gvardiya.ru
Key Personnel
Dir & Chief Editor: Audrey V Petrov
General Manager: Valentin F Yurkin
Founded: 1922
Publishing house of the Young Communist League Central Committee.
Subjects: Art, Biography, Memoirs, Government, Political Science, History, Literature, Literary Criticism, Essays, Poetry, Social Sciences, Sociology, Sports, Athletics
ISBN Prefix(es): 978-5-235

Izdatelstvo Mordovskogo gosudarstvennogo universiteta (Publishing House of Mordovia State University)
Bolshevik, d 68, Mordovia, 430005 Saransk
Tel: (8342) 47-29-13; (8342) 29-05-45; (8342) 23-37-55 *Fax:* (8342) 47-29-13
E-mail: dep-general@adm.mrsu.ru; dep-mail@adm.mrsu.ru
Web Site: www.mrsu.ru
Key Personnel
Editor-in-Chief: Prof Makarkin Nikolai Petrovich
Tel: (8342) 24-48-88 *Fax:* (8342) 32-75-27
E-mail: makarkin@mrsu.ru
Founded: 1990
Specialize in scientific & educational publications for higher school.
Subjects: Agriculture, Civil Engineering, Economics, Education, Engineering (General), Geography, Geology, History, Language Arts, Linguistics, Literature, Literary Criticism, Essays, Mathematics, Medicine, Nursing, Dentistry, Philosophy, Social Sciences, Sociology
ISBN Prefix(es): 978-5-7103
Total Titles: 1,098 Print
Parent Company: Mordovia N P Ogarev State University

Moscow House of Photography, see Mul'timedijnyj Kompleks Aktual'nyh Iskusstv

Moscow State University Press, see Izdatel'stvo Moskovskogo Gosudarstvennogo Universiteta im M V Lomonosova

Izdatel'stvo Moskovskogo Gosudarstvennogo Universiteta im M V Lomonosova (Publishing House of M V Lomonosov Moscow State University)+

Ul Bolshaya Nikitskaya, 5/7, 125009 Moscow
Tel: (495) 629-5091; (495) 939-3323 (sales)
Fax: (495) 697-6671
E-mail: izd_mgu@yandex.ru; secretary-msu-press@yandex.ru; secretary@msupublishing.ru
Web Site: msupublishing.ru
Key Personnel
Dir: Matveeva Alla Nikolaevna
Editor-in-Chief: Mirantsev Valery Georgievitch
Founded: 1755
Membership(s): University Press Council.
Subjects: Education, Mathematics, Medicine, Nursing, Dentistry, Science (General), Sports, Athletics
ISBN Prefix(es): 978-5-211
Branch Office(s)
Rights & Permissions: VAAP, Bolshaya Bronnaya 6a, 103670 Moscow

Mozaika Sintez Education Publishing House
Mnevniki St 7, Bldg 1, 123308 Moscow
Tel: (499) 728-3610; (495) 663-9402 (online sales) *Fax:* (499) 728-3610
E-mail: info@msbook.ru; redactor@msbook.ru (editorial); marketing@msbook.ru; shop@msbook.ru
Web Site: www.msbook.ru
Key Personnel
Head, Sales: Dorofeyev Denis Yu
E-mail: zakaz@msbook.ru
Dir, Online Store: Khlyustov Konstantin
Subjects: Art, Child Care & Development, Education, Poetry
ISBN Prefix(es): 978-5-86775

Mul'timedijnyj Kompleks Aktual'nyh Iskusstv (Multimedia Complex of Actual Arts)
16 Ostozhenka Str, Bldg 1, 119034 Moscow
Tel: (495) 637-1100; (495) 637-11-22 (ext 247)
E-mail: books@mdf.ru
Web Site: www.mamm-mdf.ru
Subjects: Fashion, History, Photography, History of Russian Photography
ISBN Prefix(es): 978-5-93977

Izdatelstvo Muzyka (Music Publishing House)+
ul Bol'shaya Sadavoya d 2/46, 123001 Moscow
Tel: (499) 254-6598 *Fax:* (499) 503-7737
E-mail: tus@music-izdat.ru; sale@music-izdat.ru
Web Site: www.music-izdat.ru
Key Personnel
Executive Dir: Anna Safonov
E-mail: asafonova@music-izdat.ru
General Manager: Mark A Zilberquit *Tel:* (499) 254-9130
Editor-in-Chief: Valentina V Rubtsov *Tel:* (499) 254-5736 ext 140
Marketing & Distribution Head: Shataeva Lubov
Founded: 1861
Subjects: Education, Music, Dance
ISBN Prefix(es): 978-5-7140; 978-5-87356
Number of titles published annually: 150 Print
Distributor for Schott
Showroom(s): ul Petrovka 26, 127051 Moscow
Bookshop(s): Music World, ul B Nikitskaja, 13, 103871 Moscow
Warehouse: ul Petrovka 26, 127051 Moscow
Orders to: ul Petrovka 26, 127051 Moscow

Izdatelstvo Mysl+
Leninskij prospekt 15, 119071 Moscow
Tel: (495) 952-50-65 *Fax:* (495) 9550458
Founded: 1963
Subjects: Economics, Geography, Geology, History, Philosophy, Science (General)
ISBN Prefix(es): 978-5-244

Nauka Publishers (Science Publishers)+
B-485, Profsoyuznaya ul 90, 117997 Moscow
Tel: (495) 334-71-51; (495) 932-75-00; (495) 334-98-59 (sales) *Fax:* (495) 724-89-24

E-mail: secret@naukaran.com
Web Site: www.naukaran.com
Key Personnel
Dir General: Vladimir Vasiliev
Deputy Dir General: Akram Dzhaparovich Bobrovichi *Tel:* (499) 241-93-02; Vladimir I Krylov *Tel:* (495) 334-73-51
Deputy Dir General, International Affairs: Aleksandr Y Mozdakov *Tel:* (495) 335-36-00
Deputy Dir of Publishing: Tatiana Yefimovna Filippova *Tel:* (495) 336-10-22
Founded: 1727
Scientific books & journals in all fields of knowledge, university textbooks, popular science, academic monographs.
There are six self-supporting branches of Nauka in Moscow, two divisions in Novosibirsk & St Petersburg, Akademkniga Book selling firm & four printshops. The firm's other business activities include direct mail & advertising.
Subjects: Aeronautics, Aviation, Archaeology, Art, Asian Studies, Astronomy, Biological Sciences, Chemistry, Chemical Engineering, Communications, Computer Science, Computers, Earth Sciences, Economics, Education, Electronics, Electrical Engineering, Energy, Engineering (General), Environmental Studies, Geography, Geology, Government, Political Science, Health, Nutrition, History, Language Arts, Linguistics, Law, Library & Information Sciences, Literature, Literary Criticism, Essays, Management, Marketing, Mathematics, Mechanical Engineering, Medicine, Nursing, Dentistry, Natural History, Physics, Psychology, Psychiatry, Radio, TV, Science (General), Social Sciences, Sociology, Technology
ISBN Prefix(es): 978-5-02
Number of titles published annually: 1,500 Print
Subsidiaries: Akademkniga Booktrading Co; Oriental Literature Publishing Co Nauka; Science-Press
Branch Office(s)
Siberian Publishing Co Nauka, Sovetskaya Ul 18, 630099 Novosibirsk, Dir: Ye A Lazarchuk *Tel:* (3832) 22-51-81 *Fax:* (3832) 23-35-02
St Petersburg Publishing Co Nauka, Mendeleevskaya Liniya 1, 199164 St Petersburg, Dir: S V Val'chuk *Tel:* (812) 328-39-12 *Fax:* (812) 328-00-51
Bookshop(s): Shubinsky Per 6, 121009 Moscow, GSP *Tel:* (495) 241 0309 *Fax:* (495) 241 0277 *E-mail:* akademkniga@g23.relcom.ru *Web Site:* www.ak-book.naukaran.ru
Shipping Address: Nauka-Export Booktrading Co, Profsoyuznaya ul 90, 117997 Moscow, Dir: V V Bogomolov *Tel:* (495) 334-7479; (495) 334-7140 *Fax:* (495) 334-7479; (495) 334-7140 *E-mail:* nauka@naukae.msk.ru

Izdatelstvo Nedra+
Tverskaja Zastava 3, 125047 Moscow
Tel: (495) 228-34-74
E-mail: biblioteka@nedrainform.ru
Web Site: www.nedrainform.ru
Key Personnel
Chairman, Editorial Board: Albert I Vladimirov
Founded: 1964
Natural resources publishing house.
Subjects: Business, Earth Sciences, Energy, Geography, Geology
ISBN Prefix(es): 978-5-247; 978-5-8365

Izdatel'stvo Nizhegorodskogo Gosudarstvennogo Universiteta (University of Nizhni Novgorod Publishing House)
23 Prospekt Gagarina, 603950 Nizhni Novgorod
Tel: (831) 462-30-90; (831) 462-31-06 (public relations) *Fax:* (831) 462-30-85
E-mail: pr@unn.ru; rector@unn.ru
Web Site: www.unn.ru
Founded: 1990
Subjects: Archaeology, Biological Sciences, Chemistry, Chemical Engineering, Computer

Science, Computers, Economics, Education, Electronics, Electrical Engineering, Engineering (General), English as a Second Language, Environmental Studies, Government, Political Science, History, Law, Marketing, Mathematics, Mechanical Engineering, Philosophy, Physical Sciences, Physics, Psychology, Psychiatry, Social Sciences, Sociology
ISBN Prefix(es): 978-5-680; 978-5-91326
Parent Company: Lobachevsky State University of Nizhni Novgorod

Novoe Literaturnoe Obozrenie (New Literary Observer Publishing House)
Tverskoj Blvd, Bldg 13, 127422 Moscow
Mailing Address: PO Box 55, 129626 Moscow
Tel: (495) 229-91-03 *Fax:* (495) 229-91-03
E-mail: info@nlo.magazine.ru
Web Site: www.nlobooks.ru
Key Personnel
Chief Editor & Publisher: Irina Prokhorova
Rights Dir: Olga Kaufman
Public Relations Manager: Olga Vinogradova
Assistant Editor: Anna Reshetova
Founded: 1992
Subjects: Fiction, History, Literature, Literary Criticism, Essays, Nonfiction (General), Poetry, Cultural Studies
ISBN Prefix(es): 978-5-86793

Novosti Izdatelstvo (News Publishing House)+
ul Bolsaja Poctovaja 7, 105082 Moscow
Tel: (499) 265-52-81; (499) 265-52-08
E-mail: mail@novosty.ru
Web Site: novosty.ru
Key Personnel
General Manager: Anton Popov *E-mail:* popov@novosty.ru
Editor-in-Chief: Alexander Proskurin *E-mail:* proskurin@novosty.ru
Founded: 1961
Subjects: Art, Economics, Fiction, Government, Political Science, History, Nonfiction (General), Philosophy, Social Sciences, Sociology
ISBN Prefix(es): 978-5-7020

Izdatel'stvo Patriot
Olimpijskij prospekt 22, 129110 Moscow
Tel: (495) 688-49-04; (903) 612-77-89
E-mail: mail@patriot-izdat.ru
Web Site: www.patriot-izdat.ru
Founded: 1925
Voluntary society for the promotion of the Army, Air Force & Navy.
Subjects: Military Science
ISBN Prefix(es): 978-5-7030

Planeta Publishers+
ul Petrovka 8-11, 103031 Moscow
Tel: (495) 9230470; (495) 9238147 *Fax:* (495) 2005246
Founded: 1969
Subjects: Architecture & Interior Design
ISBN Prefix(es): 978-5-85250
Associate Companies: Interprint
Subsidiaries: Jupiter

Prakticheskaya Meditsina
Str 5, 23 Kashirskoe Shosse, 115446 Moscow
Tel: (499) 324-93-29
Web Site: www.medprint.ru
Founded: 2004
Subjects: Medicine, Nursing, Dentistry, Oncology
ISBN Prefix(es): 978-5-98811

Profizdat+
St Myasnitskaya 13, str 18-18a, 101000 Moscow
Tel: (495) 333-35-29; (499) 125-83-50; (499) 128-05-64 *Fax:* (495) 334-24-22
E-mail: profizdat@profizdat.ru
Web Site: www.profizdat.ru

Key Personnel
Dir: Vladimir Solovev
Founded: 1930
Information & publishing house.
Subjects: Art, Cookery, Crafts, Games, Hobbies, Fiction, Gardening, Plants, Health, Nutrition, Labor, Industrial Relations, Nonfiction (General), Poetry, Sports, Athletics, Fairy Tales
ISBN Prefix(es): 978-5-255

Prometej Izdatelstvo
ul Kibal'cica d 6 str 2, 129278 Moscow
Tel: (495) 238-40-65; (495) 238-53-60
Key Personnel
Dir: Kirillova Elena Sergeevna
Founded: 1987
Subjects: Art, History, Literature, Literary Criticism, Essays, Philosophy, Psychology, Psychiatry, Science (General), Technology
ISBN Prefix(es): 978-5-7042; 978-5-8300

Izdatelstvo Prosveshchenie+
3-j proezd Marinoi Roshchi 41, 127521 Moscow
Tel: (495) 789-30-40 *Fax:* (495) 789-30-41
E-mail: prosv@prosv.ru; pressa@prosv.ru
Web Site: www.prosv.ru
Key Personnel
Dir General: Alexander M Kondakov
Founded: 1930
Educational books & products.
Membership(s): European Educational Publishers Group (EEPG).
Subjects: Astronomy, Biological Sciences, Chemistry, Chemical Engineering, Computer Science, Cookery, Crafts, Games, Hobbies, Earth Sciences, Education, Geography, Geology, History, Literature, Literary Criticism, Essays, Mathematics, Music, Dance, Physical Sciences, Physics, Poetry
ISBN Prefix(es): 978-5-09
Number of titles published annually: 700 Print; 10 CD-ROM; 20 Audio
Total Titles: 80,000 Print; 15 CD-ROM; 60 Audio
Associate Companies: Prosveshchenie Media

Pushkinskij Dom Verlag
nab Makarova 4, 199034 St Petersburg
Tel: (901) 315-49-11
E-mail: pushkindom2008@yandex.ru
Web Site: www.pushkindom.ru
Key Personnel
Editorial Dir: Elena Goncharova
Founded: 2007
Subjects: History, Literature, Literary Criticism, Essays, Science (General), Culture
ISBN Prefix(es): 978-5-91476

Russian Ancestry Research Services RUSSIA+
Russkoe Geographicheskoe Obschestvo, Pereulok Grivtsova, 10, 190000 St Petersburg
Tel: (812) 436-9405
E-mail: rublitz@gmail.com
Web Site: feefhs.org/resource/russia-blitz
Key Personnel
Owner & Manager: Elena Tsvetkova
Founded: 1992
Specializes in various archival references, catalogs, historical books & monographies.
Subjects: Biography, Memoirs, Drama, Theater, Fiction, History, Maritime, Nonfiction (General), Poetry, Religion - Other, Romance, Science (General), Science Fiction, Fantasy, Sports, Athletics, Archival Research, Genealogy Research
ISBN Prefix(es): 978-5-86789
Total Titles: 70 Print
U.S. Office(s): Russian Ancestry Research Services USA, 907 Mission Ave, San Rafael, CA 94901-2910, United States, Contact: Kristin Nute *Tel:* 415-453-3579 *Fax:* 415-453-0343 *E-mail:* enute@igc.org

St Andrew's Biblical Theological Institute+
Jerusalem St, 3, 109316 Moscow
Tel: (495) 670-2200; (495) 670-7644 *Fax:* (495) 670-7644; (495) 670-2200
E-mail: standrews@standrews.ru; info@standrews.ru
Web Site: www.standrews.ru
Key Personnel
Rector: Dr Alexei Bodrov *E-mail:* abodrov@standrews.ru
Contact: Mikhail Tolstoluzhenko
Founded: 1993
Independent theological college & publishing house. Textbooks on Biblical studies & themes & two journals.
Subjects: Archaeology, Art, Biblical Studies, Child Care & Development, Education, History, Philosophy, Publishing & Book Trade Reference, Religion - Other, Theology, Inter-Faith, Inter-Religion
ISBN Prefix(es): 978-5-89647
Number of titles published annually: 25 Print
Total Titles: 150 Print

Severnyj Palomnik (Northern Pilgrim Publishing House)
Ul Trifonovskaya, 2, 127055 Moscow
Tel: (495) 721-4980; (926) 821-1131
E-mail: npilgrim@mail.ru
Web Site: www.npilgrim.ru
Subjects: Art, History, Culture, Embroidery, Russian Art, Russian History
ISBN Prefix(es): 978-5-94431

Slovo Publishing House
41 Vorontsovskaya St, 109147 Moscow
Tel: (495) 911-69-04; (495) 911-61-33 *Fax:* (495) 911-61-33
E-mail: slovo@slovo-pub.ru
Web Site: www.slovo-online.ru
Founded: 1989
Subjects: Art, Fashion, Fiction, History, Culture
ISBN Prefix(es): 978-5-85050; 978-5-387

Sovershenno Sekretno
Ul Kompozitorskaya, d 17, 121099 Moscow
Tel: (495) 544 3044 *Fax:* (495) 544 3041
E-mail: sekretnosov@gmail.com
Web Site: www.sovsekretno.ru
Founded: 1993
Subjects: Biography, Memoirs, Fiction, Nonfiction (General), Travel & Tourism
ISBN Prefix(es): 978-5-85275; 978-5-91179

Sredne-Uralskoe Knizhnoe Izatel'stvo (Middle Ural Publishing House)+
ul Malyseva 24, 620014 Ekaterinburg
Tel: (343) 3765742 *Fax:* (343) 3765748
Key Personnel
Executive Dir: Chiglintsev Sergey *Tel:* (343) 3765961 *Fax:* (343) 3765643
Founded: 1920
Subjects: Fiction, Literature, Literary Criticism, Essays
ISBN Prefix(es): 978-5-7529
Warehouse: Artinskaya St 23B, 620046 Ekaterinburg

Izdatelstvo Standartov+
Nakhimovsky prospect, 31 Bldg 2, 117418 Moscow
Tel: (495) 531-26-46; (495) 531-26-08 (sales)
E-mail: klp@gostinfo.ru (sales)
Web Site: www.standards.ru
Founded: 1926
Official publications of the State Service on Standard Data.
Subjects: Advertising, Law
ISBN Prefix(es): 978-5-7050

Stroyizdat
Bumazhnyy Proyezd, d 14, B 2, Moscow
Tel: (495) 664-27-61
E-mail: podpiska@panor.ru
Web Site: panor.ru
Key Personnel
Deputy General Manager: Gregory K Moskalenko
　E-mail: gk@panor.ru
Editor-in-Chief: Leonid A Ivanov *Tel:* (495) 664-
　27-91 *E-mail:* ivanov@panor.ru
Executive Secretary: Alex S Bukin
　E-mail: pirs2007@list.ru
Founded: 1932
Subjects: Architecture & Interior Design, Civil
　Engineering, Geography, Geology, Mechani-
　cal Engineering, Social Sciences, Sociology,
　Construction, Housing
ISBN Prefix(es): 978-5-274

Izdatelstvo Sudostroenie (Publishing House for
　Shipbuilding)+
ul Malaya Morskaya, 8, 191186 St Petersburg
Tel: (812) 312 44 79 *Fax:* (812) 312 08 21
Founded: 1940
Subjects: Advertising, Education, Engineering
　(General), History, Maritime, Mechanical En-
　gineering, Military Science, Science (General),
　Technology, Transportation
ISBN Prefix(es): 978-5-7355

Teorija Verojatnostej i ee Primenenija (TVP
　Science Publishers)+
ul Hahimovsky, 47, Room 802, 117418 Moscow
Tel: (499) 724 2437 *Fax:* (499) 724 2437
E-mail: tvp@tvp.ru
Web Site: www.tvp.ru
Founded: 1990
Specialize in mathematical applied sciences. Also
　acts as research laboratories & as a distribu-
　tion center for western scientific & professional
　editions & software.
Subjects: Communications, Economics, Mathe-
　matics, Military Science, Physics, Securities
ISBN Prefix(es): 978-5-85484
Subsidiaries: TBIMC; TEV PLC; TVP-Interkniga
Distributed by SIAM USA; VSP (Netherlands)
Distributor for Academic Press; Blackwell; Cam-
　bridge University Press; Chapman & Hall; Har-
　court Brace; O'Reilly; Pitman; Prentice Hall;
　John Wiley & Sons (all Russia)
Showroom(s): TVP, 1921 Nakhimovskii prosp 47,
　117418 Moscow
Orders to: TVP, 1921 Nakhimovskii prosp 47,
　117418 Moscow

Text Publishers Ltd+
7, Cosmonavta Volkava Str, 127299 Moscow
Tel: (499) 150-04-72; (499) 150-04-82 *Fax:* (499)
　150-04-72; (499) 150-04-82
E-mail: text@textpubl.ru; text-publ@yandex.ru;
　pr@textpubl.ru
Web Site: www.textpubl.ru
Key Personnel
Dir: Olgert Markovic Libkin
Editor-in-Chief: Valery Isaakovich Genkin
Senior Sales Manager: Julia Vinogradova
Public Relations: Ludmila Tarasova
Rights & Licenses: Alexander Nagy
Founded: 1988
Membership(s): Association of Russian Publish-
　ers.
ISBN Prefix(es): 978-5-7516; 978-5-87106
Shipping Address: 56 Proezd Cherepanovykh,
　125183 Moscow
Warehouse: 56 Proezd Cherepanovykh, 125183
　Moscow
Orders to: 56 Proezd Cherepanovykh, 125183
　Moscow

Tsentrpoligraf+
1st ul Entuziastov 15, 111024 Moscow
Tel: (495) 781-45-46 *Fax:* (495) 673-41-55

E-mail: cnpol@cnpol.ru
Web Site: www.cnpol.ru
Founded: 1991
Subjects: Biography, Memoirs, Fiction, History,
　Literature, Literary Criticism, Essays, Myster-
　ies, Suspense, Nonfiction (General), Poetry,
　Russian Fiction
ISBN Prefix(es): 978-5-7001; 978-5-218; 978-5-
　227
Bookshop(s): ul Oktyabr'skaya 18, 127018
　Moscow

**Izdatel'stvo Ural'skogo gosudarstvennogo
　universiteta+**
prosp Lenina, 13b, 620219 Ekaterinburg
Founded: 1986
Specialize in monographs & handbooks.
Subjects: Literature, Literary Criticism, Essays,
　Mathematics, Philosophy
ISBN Prefix(es): 978-5-7525

Izdatelstvo Ves Mir (IVM)
Mohovaya ul 11-3B, 125993 Moscow
Tel: (495) 276-0292
E-mail: rights@vesmirbooks.ru
Web Site: www.vesmirbooks.ru
Key Personnel
Dir: Oleg Zimarin
Foreign Rights: Larisa Troitskaya
Founded: 1994
Academic publisher specializing in the humanities
　& social sciences.
Subjects: Government, Political Science, History,
　Philosophy, Psychology, Psychiatry, Social Sci-
　ences, Sociology, Globalization, International
　Affairs
ISBN Prefix(es): 978-5-7777

**Izdatel'stvo Voroneskogo Gosudarstvennogo
　Universiteta** (Voronezh State University
　Publishers)
ul Engel'sa 8, 394000 Voronezh
Tel: (473) 2560481; (473) 2530481 *Fax:* (473)
　2208755
Founded: 1958
Subjects: Biological Sciences, Chemistry, Chem-
　ical Engineering, Economics, Geography, Ge-
　ology, Language Arts, Linguistics, Literature,
　Literary Criticism, Essays, Mathematics, Social
　Sciences, Sociology
ISBN Prefix(es): 978-5-7455
Total Titles: 540 Print

Izdatelstvo Vysshaya Shkola (High School
　Publishing House)+
ul Neglinnaja 29/14, 127994 Moscow
Tel: (495) 694-0456 (reception); (495) 694-1973
　(sales) *Fax:* (495) 694-04-56; (495) 694-3486
　(sales)
E-mail: secretar@vshkola.ru; sales_vshkola@
　mail.ru
Web Site: www.vshkola.ru
Key Personnel
Dir: Leonid Alexeev
Deputy Dir for Public Planning: Ludmila I
　Kravtsova *Tel:* (495) 694-6868
Head, Sales: Anastasia Kazakova *Tel:* (495) 229-
　6759 *E-mail:* abrisd@textbook.ru
Founded: 1939
Membership(s): Publishers' Association of the
　Russian Federation.
Subjects: Biological Sciences, Chemistry, Chemi-
　cal Engineering, Economics, Engineering (Gen-
　eral), History, Language Arts, Linguistics, Law,
　Literature, Literary Criticism, Essays, Mathe-
　matics, Philosophy, Physics, Technology
ISBN Prefix(es): 978-5-06

Znanie Izdatelstvo+
Lubjanskij pr d 4, 101990 Moscow

Tel: (495) 628-15-31; (495) 237-03-08 *Fax:* (495)
　237-03-08; (495) 621-24-47
Founded: 1951
Subjects: Business, Child Care & Development,
　Fiction, Science (General), Science Fiction,
　Fantasy, Self-Help
ISBN Prefix(es): 978-5-07

Rwanda

General Information

Capital: Kigali
Language: Kinyarwanda (a Bantu tongue) and
　French (both official) and Kiswahili
Religion: Traditional beliefs (about 50%), most of
　rest Roman Catholic
Bank Hours: 0800-1800 Monday-Friday; 0800-
　1300 Saturday
Shop Hours: 0800-1900 Monday-Saturday
Currency: 100 centimes = 1 Rwanda franc
Export/Import Information: No tariff on books
　and advertising, but statistical tax. Import li-
　cense, for statistical purposes, and Foreign Ex-
　change License required. Application to Na-
　tional Bank, through authorized bank.
Copyright: UCC, Berne (see Copyright Conven-
　tions, pg viii)

Diocese de Kabgayi, see Imprimerie de Kabgayi

Imprimerie de Kabgayi+
BP 66, Gitarama, Kigali
Founded: 1932
Subjects: Government, Political Science, History,
　Religion - Catholic
Associate Companies: Diocese de Kabgayi
　ASBL; Editions Bibliques et Liturgiques

Samoa

General Information

Capital: Apia
Language: Samoan, English
Religion: Predominantly Christian (Congrega-
　tional, Roman Catholic & Methodist)
Population: 165,000
Bank Hours: 0930-1500 Monday-Friday
Shop Hours: 0800-1200, 1330-1630 Monday-
　Friday; 0800-1230 Saturday
Currency: 100 sene = 1 tala (western Samoan
　dollar)
Export/Import Information: No tariff on most
　books, printed advertising generally free but
　some subject to duty. No import license or ex-
　change controls.

**Institute for Research Extension and Training
　in Agriculture (IRETA)**
c/o The University of the South Pacific, Faculty
　of Business & Economics, Private Bag, Apia
Tel: 22350; 21671
E-mail: enquiries@samoa.usp.ac.fj
Web Site: www.usp.ac.fj/ireta
Key Personnel
Dir: Mohammed Umar *Tel:* 21671 ext 204
　E-mail: umar_m@samoa.usp.ac.fj
Publication Officer: Dolly Autufuga *Tel:* 21671
　ext 304 *E-mail:* autufugadolly@gmail.com
Founded: 1980
Research, information dissemination & capacity
　building activities in agriculture are the key ar-
　eas of IRETA's work with emphasis on food
　security, income generation & climate change.

IRETA runs the USP-IRETA Agriculture Farm that produces commercial crops & livestock as well as providing practical training to the community & students of agriculture at the School of Agriculture & Food Technology (SAFT).
Subjects: Agriculture
Parent Company: The University of the South Pacific

IRETA, see Institute for Research Extension and Training in Agriculture (IRETA)

San Marino

General Information

Capital: San Marino
Language: Italian
Religion: Roman Catholic
Population: 33,020
Currency: 100 Eurocents = 1 Euro

Gaby Books SRL
Str di Paderna, 2, 47895 Domagnano
Tel: (0549) 910133
E-mail: info@gabybooks.com
Web Site: www.gabybooks.com
Key Personnel
Contact: Gabriella Canazza *E-mail:* gabriella. canazza@gabybooks.com

Saudi Arabia

General Information

Capital: Riyadh
Language: Arabic (English widely understood)
Religion: Islamic (officially) with about 85% of the Sunni sect
Population: 16.9 million
Bank Hours: 0830-1200, 1700-1900 Saturday-Wednesday; 0830-1130 Thursday. During Ramadan: 1000-1330 Saturday-Thursday
Shop Hours: 0900-1200, 1600-2100 Saturday-Thursday. During Ramadan closed until sunset, then open until 0200
Currency: 100 halalahs = 20 qurush = 1 Saudi riyal
Export/Import Information: No tariffs on books; advertising matter subject to ad valorem duty but if total duty on one consignment is less than 50 riyals, matter can enter free. Catalogues distributed gratis, usually admitted free. All printed matter except textbooks subject to censorship. No import licenses required.
Copyright: UCC (see Copyright Conventions, pg viii)

Al Jazirah Organization for Press, Printing, Publishing
King Fahad Highway, PO Box 354, Riyadh 11411
Tel: (011) 4870000; (011) 4870911 (customer service) *Fax:* (011) 4871063; (011) 4871064; (011) 4871175
E-mail: aljazirah@al-jazirah.com.sa; ccs@al-jazirah.com.sa
Web Site: www.al-jazirah.com.sa
Key Personnel
Chairman: Mutlaq Abdullah Al-Mutlaq *E-mail:* president@al-jazirah.com.sa
General Manager: Abdul Latif Bin Saad Al-Ateeq *Tel:* (011) 4870959 *Fax:* (011) 4871202

Editor-in-Chief: Khalid Bin Hamed Al-Malik *Tel:* (011) 4871016 *Fax:* (011) 4871017
E-mail: chief@al-jazirah.com.sa
Founded: 1960
Subjects: Government, Political Science, Law
ISBN Prefix(es): 978-9960-9190

Dar Al-Mirrikh (Mars Publishing House)
PO Box 10720, Riyadh 11443
Tel: (011) 4647531; (011) 4658523; (011) 2934096; (011) 2934091 (ext 24) *Fax:* (011) 4657939
Key Personnel
Owner & General Dir: Abdullah Ali R Almajid
Mng Dir: Mohamed Sayed Mostafa; Abdul Hameed Noor
Finance Dir: Adel Said Elnahrawy
Founded: 1976
Publisher, international library suppliers & subscription agents.
Subjects: Accounting, Agriculture, Art, Behavioral Sciences, Biological Sciences, Business, Civil Engineering, Communications, Computer Science, Economics, Education, Electronics, Electrical Engineering, Engineering (General), Health, Nutrition, Management, Marketing, Mathematics, Medicine, Nursing, Dentistry
ISBN Prefix(es): 978-9960-24

Dar Al-Rayah for Publishing & Distribution
PO Box 40124, Riyadh
Tel: (011) 4454746 *Fax:* (011) 4931869
Founded: 1979
Subjects: Literature, Literary Criticism, Essays
ISBN Prefix(es): 978-9960-661

King Saud University+
PO Box 22480, Riyadh 11495
Tel: (011) 4676176 *Fax:* (011) 4676162
E-mail: acksupress@ksu.edu.sa
Web Site: ksupress.ksu.edu.sa
Key Personnel
President: Prof Abdullah A Alothman *E-mail:* alothman@ksu.edu.sa
Academic Publishing & Press Supervisor: Dr Ali M Al-Turki *E-mail:* aturki@ksu.edu.sa
Deputy Supervisor: Dr Saeed Ali Alghailani *Tel:* (011) 4675530 *E-mail:* ghailani@ksu.edu.sa
Founded: 1957
Subjects: Agriculture, Behavioral Sciences, Biological Sciences, Chemistry, Chemical Engineering, Geography, Geology, Language Arts, Linguistics, Mathematics, Medicine, Nursing, Dentistry, Technology
ISBN Prefix(es): 978-9960-05

Mars Publishing House, see Dar Al-Mirrikh

Obeikan Publishing+
Division of Obeikan Education
PO Box 67622, Riyadh 11517
Tel: (011) 4808654 (ext 275); (011) 4808654 (ext 278) *Fax:* (011) 4808095
Web Site: www.obeikanpublishing.com
Key Personnel
Head, Commercial Publishing: Saria Alkhateeb *Tel:* (050) 8474527 (cell) *E-mail:* saria@obeikan.com.sa
Publishing Manager: Mohammed Abdullah Alfriah *Tel:* (050) 3732505 (cell) *E-mail:* malfriah@obeikan.com.sa
Deputy Publishing Manager: Aref A Atia *Tel:* (050) 0604594 (cell) *E-mail:* a.atia@obeikan.com.sa
Founded: 1995
Publishing, translation & localization.
This publisher has indicated that 75% of their product line is author subsidized.
Membership(s): Saudi Publishers Association.

Subjects: Business, Computers, Finance, Government, Political Science, Health, Nutrition, Literature, Literary Criticism, Essays, Management
ISBN Prefix(es): 978-603-503
Number of titles published annually: 300 Print; 1,500 E-Book; 5 Audio
Total Titles: 3,000 Print; 200 E-Book; 10 Audio
Ultimate Parent Company: Obeikan Investment Group, PO Box 355023, Riyadh 11452

Saudi Publishing & Distribution House+
PO Box 2043, Jeddah 21451
Tel: (012) 6294039
Founded: 1966
Also act as importers & distributors of English & Arabic books (academic, reference & general).
Subjects: Literature, Literary Criticism, Essays, Religion - Other, Science (General)
ISBN Prefix(es): 978-9960-26
Branch Office(s):
PO Box 899, Riyadh 31952 *Tel:* (011) 464 7894 *Fax:* (011) 465 1464
Bookshop(s): Hyat Plaza Complex, King Saud St, Dammam Dhahran St Near Governorate, Dammam *Tel:* (013) 832 3515; Zouman Shopping Centre, Opposite S Fakhee Hospital, Jeddah *Tel:* (012) 6608964

Senegal

General Information

Capital: Dakar
Language: French
Religion: About 90% Islamic, 5% Christian (mostly Roman Catholic), the rest follow traditional beliefs
Population: 8.2 million
Bank Hours: Generally 0800-1115, 1430-1630 Monday-Friday
Shop Hours: Vary, and some open Sunday morning, some close Monday morning. Generally are 0800-1200, 1430-1800 Monday-Saturday
Currency: 100 centimes = 1 CFA franc
Export/Import Information: Member of West African Economic Community. No tariff on books except atlases. Added taxes apply to atlases. Advertising matter (more than one copy) subject to fiscal and customs duty plus added taxes. Import licenses and exchange controls apply for imports from outside European Union, USA and Canada.
Copyright: Berne, UCC (see Copyright Conventions, pg viii)

ADP, see Agence de Diffusion de Presse (ADP)

Agence de Diffusion de Presse (ADP)
Km 2,500 bd du Centenaire de la Commune, Dakar
Mailing Address: BP 374, Dakar
Tel: 33 831 00 53 *Fax:* 33 832 49 15
Key Personnel
Dir: Laurent Gouttenoire *E-mail:* direction@adp.sn
Founded: 1943
Parent Company: NMPP, Paris, France

Bibliotheque Lecture Developpement
rue DSM No 670, Sicap Mbao - Route de Rufisque, Dakar
Mailing Address: BP 1046, Dakar
Tel: 33 834 34 94
E-mail: bld@bldsn.org
Web Site: www.bldsn.org
ISBN Prefix(es): 978-2-916859; 978-2-9524874; 978-2-9527685

BLD Editions, see Bibliotheque Lecture
Developpement

CAEC, see Khoudia

**Centre Africain d'Animation et d'Echanges
Culturels**, see Khoudia

Centre de Linguistique Appliquee (CLAD)
Universite Cheikh Anta Diop, Faculte des Lettres
et Sciences Humaines, Dakar-Fann
E-mail: clad@ucad.sn
Web Site: clad.ucad.sn
Key Personnel
Dir: Cherif Mbodj
Founded: 1963
Subjects: Language Arts, Linguistics, Literature,
Literary Criticism, Essays

CLAD, see Centre de Linguistique Appliquee
(CLAD)

CODESRIA, see Council for the Development of
Social Science Research in Africa
(CODESRIA)

**Council for the Development of Social Science
Research in Africa (CODESRIA)+**
Ave Cheikh Anta Diop X Canal IV, 18524 Dakar
Mailing Address: BP 3304, 18524 Dakar
Tel: 33 825 98 22; 33 825 98 23; 33 825 98 14
(publications) *Fax:* 33 824 12 89; 33 864 01 43
(publications)
Web Site: www.codesria.org
Key Personnel
Head, Dept Publications & Dissemination:
Alexander Bangirana
Mng Editor: Oyekunle Oyediran
E-mail: oyekunle.oyediran@codesria.sn
Marketing & Distribution Officer: Yves Eric
Elouga *E-mail:* yves.elouga@codesria.sn
Founded: 1973
Publish in four languages: English, French, Por-
tuguese & Arabic. Specialize in social sciences.
Also acts as a coordinator of social science re-
search in Africa.
Membership(s): International Research Councils.
Subjects: Behavioral Sciences, Developing Coun-
tries, Economics, Education, Environmental
Studies, Ethnicity, Government, Political Sci-
ence, History, Labor, Industrial Relations, So-
cial Sciences, Sociology, Women's Studies
ISBN Prefix(es): 978-1-870784; 978-2-86978
Number of titles published annually: 10 Print
Total Titles: 186 Print
Warehouse: Karthala, Edition Diffusion, 22-24
Blvd Arago, 75013 Paris, France
African Books Collective Ltd, The Jam Factory,
27 Park End St, Oxford 0X1 1KU, United
Kingdom *E-mail:* abc@africanbookscollective.
com

EDJA, *imprint of* Editions Juridiques Africaines

Enda Tiers Monde
Complex SICAP Point E, Batiment B, 1 er etage,
Ave Cheikh Anta Diop X Canal IV, 3370
Dakar
Tel: 33 869 99 48; 33 869 99 49 *Fax:* 33 860 51
33
E-mail: se@endatiersmonde.org
Web Site: endatiersmonde.org
Key Personnel
President: Cheikh Hamidou Kane
Executive Secretary: Jacques Bugnicourt
Founded: 1972
Subjects: Environmental Studies

**Environment & Development Action in the
Third World**, see Enda Tiers Monde

Institut Fondamental d'Afrique Noire (IFAN)
(African Institute of Basic Research)
BP 206, Dakar
Tel: 33 824 16 52 *Fax:* 33 824 49 18
E-mail: ifan@ucad.edu.sn
Web Site: ifan.ucad.sn
Key Personnel
Dir: Abdoulaye Toure *E-mail:* abdoulaye.toure@
ucad.edu.sn
Founded: 1936
Subjects: Animals, Pets, Biological Sciences, Gar-
dening, Plants, Language Arts, Linguistics,
Botany, Animal Biology, Civilization, Humani-
ties

IFAN, see Institut Fondamental d'Afrique Noire
(IFAN)

Editions Juridiques Africaines
18, rue Raffenel, 22057 Dakar-Ponty
Tel: 33 823 00 71; 33 821 66 89 *Fax:* 33 823 27
53
E-mail: edja.ed@orange.sn
Web Site: www.edja.sn
Founded: 1987
Subjects: Foreign Countries, Law
ISBN Prefix(es): 978-2-87838
Imprints: EDJA
Branch Office(s)
24, rue de l'Echiquier, 75010 Paris, France
Tel: 01 42 46 09 01; 06 28 40 05 56 *Fax:* 01
42 46 09 07

Editions Kalaama
Immeuble ABC, Rond-Point Jet d'eau n° 44B,
Dakar
Mailing Address: BP 1331, Dakar
Tel: 33 864 43 37 *Fax:* 33 864 43 37
E-mail: ufce.senegal@gmail.com; kalaama@
hotmail.com
Web Site: www.ufce-senegal.org/kalaama
Key Personnel
President: Nicole Gakou
Founded: 2003
Subjects: Education, Language Arts, Linguistics,
Science (General), Foreign Languages
ISBN Prefix(es): 978-2-915343

Khoudia+
CAEC-HLM Fass- Paillote, Immeuble 7, Dakar
Mailing Address: BP 5332, Dakar
Tel: 33 821 10 23
Key Personnel
Dir: Aminata Sow Fall
Founded: 1989
Subjects: Anthropology, Drama, Theater, Edu-
cation, Ethnicity, Fiction, Literature, Literary
Criticism, Essays, Poetry
ISBN Prefix(es): 978-2-87895
Distributed by Edilis (Ivory Coast); Presence
Africaine (France)
Distributor for Edilis (Ivory Coast); Haho (Togo)

NEAS, see Nouvelles Editions Africaines du
Senegal (NEAS)

**Nouvelles Editions Africaines du Senegal
(NEAS)+**
10 rue Amadou Assane Ndoye, Dakar
Mailing Address: BP 260, Dakar
Tel: 33 822 15 80; 33 821 13 81 *Fax:* 33 822 36
04
E-mail: neas@orange.sn
Key Personnel
Dir: Seydou Sow
Founded: 1989
Subjects: Literature, Literary Criticism, Essays,
Social Sciences, Sociology
ISBN Prefix(es): 978-2-7236
Distributed by African Imprint Library Services

Serbia

General Information

Capital: Belgrade
Language: Serbian (official)
Religion: Predominantly Serbian Orthodox, some
Catholic, Protestant and Muslim
Population: 10.1 million
Currency: Serbian dinars

Agape+
Cara Dusana 4, 21000 Novi Sad
Tel: (021) 469 474 *Fax:* (021) 469 382
E-mail: agape@eunet.rs
Web Site: www.agape.hu
Key Personnel
Dir: Dr Harmath Karoly
Founded: 1977
Membership(s): Association of Hungarian
Catholic Publishers; ELCE; International As-
sociation of Franciscan Publishers; Union
Catholique Internationale de la Presse (UCIP).
Subjects: Religion - Catholic, Theology
ISBN Prefix(es): 978-86-463
Number of titles published annually: 50 Print
Parent Company: Agape Kft, Szeksosi ut 16,
Szeged 6791, Hungary

Akademska Misao doo
Bulevar kralja Aleksandra 73, 11120 Belgrade
Tel: (011) 3218 354; (063) 301 075 (cell); (063)
301 065 (cell)
E-mail: office@akademska-misao.rs; knjizara@
akademska-misao.rs
Web Site: www.akademska-misao.rs
Founded: 1999
Subjects: Architecture & Interior Design, Chem-
istry, Chemical Engineering, Computer Science,
Education, Electronics, Electrical Engineering,
Energy, Engineering (General), Mathematics,
Mechanical Engineering, Medicine, Nursing,
Dentistry, Science (General), Social Sciences,
Sociology
ISBN Prefix(es): 978-86-7466

Alfa Narodna Knjiga
Safarikova 11, 11000 Belgrade
Tel: (011) 322-91-58 *Fax:* (011) 322-74-26
E-mail: info@narodnaknjiga.rs
Web Site: www.narodnaknjiga.rs
Key Personnel
Dir: Milicko Mijovic
Foreign Rights Manager: Tea Jovanovic
Founded: 1955 (privatized in 1995)
Membership(s): Association of Educational Pub-
lishers (AEP)
Subjects: Art, Astrology, Occult, Child Care &
Development, Cookery, Criminology, Fiction,
Government, Political Science, Health, Nutri-
tion, History, How-to, Journalism, Language
Arts, Linguistics, Literature, Literary Criticism,
Essays, Medicine, Nursing, Dentistry, Myster-
ies, Suspense, Nonfiction (General), Philoso-
phy, Poetry, Psychology, Psychiatry, Religion -
Other, Science (General), Self-Help
ISBN Prefix(es): 978-86-331
Number of titles published annually: 300 Print
Total Titles: 1,000 Print
Branch Office(s)
Batajnicki drum 293, Belgrade *Tel:* (011) 848
7035
Cara Dusana 158, Belgrade *Tel:* (011) 214 3752
Cetinjska 6, Belgrade *Tel:* (011) 322 6427
Knez Mihajlova 40, Belgrade *Tel:* (011) 636 208
Masarikova 5, Belgrade *Tel:* (011) 361 6965
Nikole Spasica 2, Belgrade *Tel:* (011) 303 4935

Pozeska 37, Belgrade *Tel:* (011) 305 8434
Pozeska 128a, Belgrade *Tel:* (011) 305 8424

BIGZ, *imprint of* BIGZ Publishing

BIGZ Publishing
Bulevar Vojvode Misica 17/111, 11000 Belgrade
Tel: (011) 3691 259; (011) 3690 518 (commercial) *Fax:* (011) 3690 519; (011) 3690 512
(commercial)
E-mail: bigz@bigz-publishing.co.rs;
komercijala@bigzskolstvo.rs
Web Site: www.bigz-publishing.co.rs
Founded: 1831
Subjects: Philosophy, Poetry, Social Sciences, Sociology
ISBN Prefix(es): 978-86-13
Imprints: BIGZ
Bookshop(s): Kosovska 37, Belgrade *Tel:* (011)
3221 250; (011) 3230 627; Pozeska 136, Belgrade *Tel:* (011) 3558 226; (011) 3573 607
Book Club(s): Book Lovers' Club

Evro Giunti
Dimitrija Tucovica 41, 11000 Belgrade
Tel: (011) 344 6618; (011) 344 7328 (marketing)
Fax: (011) 244 5926
E-mail: marketing@evro-giunti.com; office@evro-giunti.com; redakcija@evro-giunti.com
Web Site: www.evro-giunti.com
Key Personnel
Dir General: Novica Jevtic *E-mail:* novica@evrobook.com
Foreign Rights Manager: Zoran Miodrag
Tel: (011) 344 6618 ext 106 *E-mail:* zoran@evro-giunti.com
Editorial: Dimitrija Tucovica
Sales Manager: Mijodrag Zivkovic *Tel:* (011) 307
7771 *E-mail:* mijodrag@evrobook.com
Founded: 1989
Subjects: Cookery, Fiction, Literature, Literary Criticism, Essays, Medicine, Nursing, Dentistry, Poetry, Psychology, Psychiatry, Religion - Other, Natural Medicine, Prose, Serbian Classics, Serbian Fiction
ISBN Prefix(es): 978-86-505

Forum Konyvkiado
Vojvode Misica 1, 21000 Novi Sad
Tel: (021) 457 216 *Fax:* (021) 456 742
E-mail: direktor@forumliber.rs
Web Site: www.forumliber.rs
Key Personnel
Dir & Editor-in-Chief: Gabor Virag
Founded: 1957
Subjects: Fiction, Government, Political Science
ISBN Prefix(es): 978-86-323

Izadavacko Preduzece Gradevinska Knjiga
Trg Nikole Pasica 8/II, 11000 Belgrade
Tel: (011) 32 47 662; (011) 32 33 565 *Fax:* (011)
32 33 234
Web Site: www.gk.izlog.org
Key Personnel
Dir & Editor-in-Chief: Stana Sehalic
E-mail: stana.gk@stylos.rs
Editor: Milica Tasovac *E-mail:* milica.gk@stylos.rs
Commercial Representative: Nebojsa Stanojevic
E-mail: nebojsa.gk@stylos.rs
Commercial Officer: Dijana Drobac
E-mail: dijana.gk@stylos.rs
Founded: 1948
Subjects: Architecture & Interior Design, Engineering (General), Science (General)
ISBN Prefix(es): 978-86-395
Bookshop(s): ul Kralice Natalije br 14, Belgrade
Tel: (011) 2646-170; ul Kraljice Marije br 15,
Belgrade *Tel:* (011) 3221-147

Izdavacko Preduzece Vuk Karadzic+
Brankova 28, 11000 Belgrade
Tel: (011) 3342329
Founded: 1956
Subjects: Art, History, Philosophy, Psychology, Psychiatry, Science (General), Social Sciences, Sociology
ISBN Prefix(es): 978-86-307

Kreativni Centar (Creative Center)
Gradistanska 8, 11120 Belgrade
Tel: (011) 38 20 464; (011) 38 20 483; (011) 38
20 659 *Fax:* (011) 38 20 464; (011) 38 20 483;
(011) 38 20 659
E-mail: info@kreativnicentar.rs; rights@kreativnicentar.rs
Web Site: www.kreativnicentar.rs; www.kcknjizara.rs
Key Personnel
Rights Dir: Dejan Begovic *E-mail:* dejan.begovic@kreativnicentar.rs
Founded: 1989
Membership(s): European Educational Publishers Group (EEPG)
Subjects: Animals, Pets, Child Care & Development, Crafts, Games, Hobbies, Education, Fiction, Human Relations, Humor, Physics, Poetry
ISBN Prefix(es): 978-86-7781
Book Club(s): Klub knijizara

Kultura
XIV Vojvodanske udarne brigade 4-6, 21470
Backi Petrovac
Tel: (021) 780144; (021) 780156 *Fax:* (021)
780291
ISBN Prefix(es): 978-86-7103
Bookshop(s): Backi Petrovac Bodvis Jan

Laguna
Resavska 33, 11000 Belgrade
Tel: (011) 71-55-055 *Fax:* (011) 71-55-085
E-mail: info@laguna.rs
Web Site: www.laguna.rs
Founded: 1998
Subjects: Art, Biography, Memoirs, Cookery, Fiction, Literature, Literary Criticism, Essays, Management, Music, Dance, Mysteries, Suspense, Philosophy, Poetry, Psychology, Psychiatry, Science Fiction, Fantasy, Sports, Athletics, Popular Science
ISBN Prefix(es): 978-86-521; 978-86-7436

Male Majstorije Computer Book+
Danteova 36, 11060 Belgrade
Tel: (011) 2785-745 *Fax:* (011) 2776-298
Web Site: www.malemajstorije.com
Key Personnel
Sales Manager: Mr Nikola Gavric *E-mail:* nikola.gavric@malemajstorije.com
Founded: 1990
Publish cookbooks & magazines.
Subjects: Cookery, Health, Nutrition
Number of titles published annually: 20 Print
Total Titles: 240 Print

Izdavacko Centar Matica Srpska (Matica
Serbian Publishing Center)+
One Matica Srpska St, 21000 Novi Sad
Tel: (021) 527 855; (021) 527 622 *Fax:* (021) 528
901
E-mail: ms@maticasrpska.org.rs; glasnik@maticasrpska.org.rs
Web Site: www.maticasrpska.org.rs; www.icms.rs
Key Personnel
Dir & Mng Editor: Miro Vuksanovic
E-mail: miro@bms.ns.ac.rs
Founded: 1826
Subjects: History, Human Relations, Literature, Literary Criticism, Essays, Poetry
ISBN Prefix(es): 978-86-363

Bookshop(s): Trg Toz Markovica 24, Novi Sad,
Contact: Zdravko Gaseric *Tel:* 29-307; Zmaj
Jovina 4, Novi Sad, Contact: Milenko Ranin
Tel: 29-436

Narodna Biblioteka Srbije (National Library of
Serbia)
Skerliceva 1, 11000 Belgrade
Tel: (011) 2451 242 *Fax:* (011) 2451 289
E-mail: nbs@nb.rs
Web Site: www.nb.rs
Key Personnel
Head, Publishing: Dragan Puresic
E-mail: puresic@nb.rs
Deputy Dir & Manager, Finance: Branislav
Stankovic *Tel:* (011) 2438 607
E-mail: bstankovic@nb.rs
Deputy Dir & Manager, Virtual Library:
Vesna Stevanovic *Tel:* (011) 2459 473
E-mail: vesnas@nb.rs
Founded: 1832
Subjects: History
ISBN Prefix(es): 978-86-7035

Nolit AD+
Terazije 27/II, 11000 Belgrade
Tel: (011) 3245-017; (011) 3779-651; (011) 3232-
420; (011) 3248-322 (editorial) *Fax:* (011)
3248-322
Key Personnel
Dir: Slavica Sas
Founded: 1928
Subjects: Agriculture, Art, Fiction, History, Philosophy, Psychology, Psychiatry, Social Sciences, Sociology
ISBN Prefix(es): 978-86-19

Partenon MAM Sistem AD+
Simina 9a, 11000 Belgrade
Tel: (011) 3739-722; (011) 3167-918
E-mail: partenonsistem@gmail.com
Web Site: www.partenon.rs
Key Personnel
Dir: Momcilo Mitrovic
Subjects: Agriculture, Fiction, Language Arts, Linguistics, Literature, Literary Criticism, Essays, Psychology, Psychiatry, Science (General), Culture, Popular Psychology
ISBN Prefix(es): 978-86-7157
Number of titles published annually: 30 Print

Izdavacko preduzece Prosveta
Kneza Mihaila 12, 11000 Belgrade
Tel: (011) 26 39 714
E-mail: redakcija.ipprosveta@eunet.rs;
komercijala@prosveta.rs (sales); prosveta.
redakcija@gmail.com (returns)
Web Site: www.prosveta.rs
Founded: 1901
Subjects: Art, Biography, Memoirs, Cookery, Economics, Erotica, Health, Nutrition, How-to, Human Relations, Humor, Literature, Literary Criticism, Essays, Marketing, Poetry, Psychology, Psychiatry, Religion - Other, Social Sciences, Sociology
ISBN Prefix(es): 978-86-07

RAD ad, see Izdavacko Preduzece RAD

Izdavacko Preduzece RAD
Decanska 12, 11000 Belgrade
Tel: (011) 3239-758; (011) 3239-998 *Fax:* (011)
3230-923
Subjects: Biography, Memoirs, Economics, Engineering (General), Government, Political Science, Philosophy, Poetry, Social Sciences, Sociology
ISBN Prefix(es): 978-86-09
Bookshop(s): Papirus, Terazije 26, Belgrade;
Frankopanska 5, Zagreb, Croatia

Singapore

Republicki Zavod za Unapredivanje Vaspitanja i Obrazovanja ID (Institute for the Advancement of Education)
Fabrisova 10, 11000 Belgrade
Tel: (011) 206-80-000 *Fax:* (011) 206-80-18
E-mail: office@zuov.gov.rs
Web Site: www.zuov.gov.rs
Key Personnel
Dir: Dr Scepan Uscumlic *Tel:* (011) 206-80-05
  E-mail: scepan.uscumlic@zuov.gov.rs
Deputy Dir: Gordana Mijatovic *Tel:* (011) 206-80-22 *E-mail:* gordana.mijatovic@zuov.gov.rs
Founded: 1973
Subjects: Education
ISBN Prefix(es): 978-86-80871
Bookshop(s): Knjizara Zavoda, Kneza Milosa 101, 11000 Belgrade

Savez Inzenjera i Tehnicara Srbije (SITS)
  (Union of Engineers & Technicians of Serbia)+
Kneza Milosa 7, 11000 Belgrade
Tel: (011) 3230-067; (011) 3237-363 *Fax:* (011) 3230-067; (011) 3237-363
E-mail: office@sits.rs
Web Site: www.sits.org.rs
Key Personnel
President: Dr Igor Maric *E-mail:* igor@iaus.org.rs
Secretary General: Branislav Vujinovic
Founded: 1868
Membership(s): European Federation of National Engineering Associations (FEANI); Permanent Conference of Engineers of South-East Europe (COPISEE); World Federation of Engineering Organizations; World Federation of Scientific Workers.
Subjects: Civil Engineering, Communications, Economics, Electronics, Electrical Engineering, Engineering (General), Mechanical Engineering, Science (General), Technology

Savremena Administracija AD
ul Crnotravska 7-9, 11010 Belgrade
Tel: (011) 2663-733 *Fax:* (011) 2667-522; (011) 2667-633
E-mail: office@savremena-ad.com
Web Site: www.savremena-ad.com
Founded: 1954
Subjects: Economics, Law, Medicine, Nursing, Dentistry
ISBN Prefix(es): 978-86-387

SITS, see Savez Inzenjera i Tehnicara Srbije (SITS)

Srpska Knjizevna Zadruga (Serbian Literary Association)
Kralja Milana 19, 11000 Belgrade
Tel: (011) 32 30 305; (011) 32 31 593 (bookshop); (011) 32 38 218 (sales) *Fax:* (011) 32 31 593 (bookshop)
E-mail: skz@beotel.rs
Web Site: www.srpskaknjizevnazadruga.com
Key Personnel
Manager: Nina Novicevic *Tel:* (011) 32 32 379
Editor: Dragan Lakicevic *Tel:* (011) 33 45 403
Founded: 1892
Subjects: History, Poetry
ISBN Prefix(es): 978-86-379

Izdavacko Preduzece Svetovi (The Worlds)+
Arse Teodorovica 11, 21000 Novi Sad
Tel: (021) 528 032 *Fax:* (021) 528 036
Founded: 1951
Subjects: Anthropology, Art, Fiction, Philosophy, Poetry
ISBN Prefix(es): 978-86-7047
Number of titles published annually: 40 Print
Total Titles: 2,000 Print
Bookshop(s): Pasiceva 32, Novi Sad *Tel:* (021) 23-071

Tehnicka Knjiga NOVA+
Vojvode Stepe 89, 11000 Belgrade
Tel: (011) 2491-931; (011) 2492-075; (063) 8661-799 (cell) *Fax:* (011) 2492-075
Web Site: www.tehnicka-knjiga.com
Subjects: Automotive, Computer Science, Electronics, Electrical Engineering, Engineering (General), How-to, Science (General), Technology
ISBN Prefix(es): 978-86-325; 978-86-88429

Tehnika, see Savez Inzenjera i Tehnicara Srbije (SITS)

Turisticka Stampa AD+
Djure Djakovica 100, 11000 Belgrade
Tel: (011) 275 0740 *Fax:* (011) 762 236
Founded: 1953
Subjects: Art
ISBN Prefix(es): 978-86-7041

VINC, *imprint of* Vojnoizdavacki Zavod Vojna Knjiga

Vojnoizdavacki Zavod Vojna Knjiga (Military Publishing Institute)+
Balkanska 53, 11000 Belgrade
Tel: (011) 3612-390; (011) 3612-657 *Fax:* (011) 3612-506
Founded: 1945
Subjects: Military Science
ISBN Prefix(es): 978-86-335; 978-86-80641
Imprints: VINC
Bookshop(s): Poslovni biro "Vojna Knjiga", Vase Carapica 22, 11000 Belgrade

Vulkan Izdavastvo doo
Gospodara Vucica 245, 11000 Belgrade
Tel: (011) 3087-515 *Fax:* (011) 3087-614
E-mail: office@vulkani.rs
Web Site: www.vulkani.rs
Founded: 2013
Subjects: Biography, Memoirs, Erotica, Fiction, Mysteries, Suspense, Psychology, Psychiatry, Romance, Science Fiction, Fantasy
ISBN Prefix(es): 978-86-10

Zavod za izdavanje udzbenika
Obilicev venac 5, 11000 Belgrade
Tel: (011) 2637 433; (011) 2638 463; (011) 3051 900 (marketing & sales) *Fax:* (011) 2637 426; (011) 996 3051 (marketing & sales)
E-mail: kontakt@zavod.co.rs
Web Site: www.zavod.co.rs
Key Personnel
Acting Dir & Editor: Dragoljub Kojcic
Editorial Dir: Milorad Marjanovic
Dir, Marketing & Sales: Goran Pavlovic
Founded: 1958
Subjects: Education
ISBN Prefix(es): 978-86-17

Zavod za udzbenike
Obilicev venac 5, 11000 Belgrade
Tel: (011) 2637 433; (011) 2638 463; (011) 3051 900 (sales) *Fax:* (011) 2637 426; (011) 3051 996 (sales)
E-mail: kontakt@zavod.co.rs; reklamacije@zavod.co.rs
Web Site: www.zavod.co.rs
Key Personnel
Acting Dir & Editor: Dragoljub Kojcic
Editorial Dir: Milorad Marjanovic
Dir, Marketing & Sales: Goran Pavlovic
Founded: 1957
Subjects: Education
ISBN Prefix(es): 978-86-17
Bookshop(s): Kosovska 45, 11000 Belgrade; Vukasoviceva 50, 11090 Belgrade

General Information

Capital: Singapore
Language: Malay (national and official), also Chinese (Mandarin), Tamil and English (all official)
Religion: Daoism, Buddhist, Islamic, Christian, Hindu and Taoism
Population: 2.8 million
Bank Hours: 1000-1500 Monday-Friday; 930-1130 Saturday
Shop Hours: 0900-1800 Monday-Saturday
Currency: 100 cents = 1 Singapore dollar
Export/Import Information: No tariffs on books and advertising. Import licenses; no seditious publications permitted. Normal exchange control.
Copyright: Florence (see Copyright Conventions, pg viii)

Alkem Co (S) Pte Ltd
One, Sunview Rd 01-27, Singapore 627615
Tel: 6265 6666 *Fax:* 6261 7875
E-mail: enquiry@alkem.com.sg
Web Site: www.alkem.com.sg
Founded: 1999
Distributor & publisher for books, training materials, digital learning, educational aids, multimedia, research software & training kits.
Subjects: Education
ISBN Prefix(es): 978-981-08

Alkem Distribution Center, see Alkem Co (S) Pte Ltd

Angsana Books, *imprint of* Flame of the Forest Publishing Pte Ltd

APA Publications GmbH & Co Verlag KG+
Member of Langenscheidt Verlagsgruppe
38 Joo Koon Rd, Singapore 628990
Tel: 6865 1600; 6861 6438 (sales) *Fax:* 6861 6438
Key Personnel
Mng Dir: Agnieszka Mizak
Founded: 1971
Subjects: Travel & Tourism
ISBN Prefix(es): 978-9971-925; 978-9971-982; 978-981-234; 978-981-246; 978-981-4120; 978-981-258; 978-981-4137; 978-981-268; 978-981-282
Imprints: Berlitz Publishing; Insight Guides (English titles); Insight Pocket Guides; Insight Topics; Polygott (German titles); Rough Guides
Branch Office(s)
APA Publications (HK) Ltd, Unit C & D, 1/F Lladro Centre, 72-80 Hoi Yuen Rd, Kwun Tong, Kowloon, Hong Kong *Tel:* 2357 4883 *Fax:* 2344 8331 *E-mail:* apapubhk@netvigator.com
APA Publications (Thailand) Ltd, 1173, 1175, 1177, 1179 Srinakharin Rd, Suan Luang, Bangkok 10250, Thailand *Tel:* (02) 322 3678 *Fax:* (02) 271 1639
Distributor for Langenscheidt (Asia)

APAC Publishers Services Pte Ltd+
8 Lorong Bakar Batu No 05-02, Singapore 348743
Tel: 6844 7333 *Fax:* 6747 8916
Founded: 1990
Subjects: Architecture & Interior Design, Business, Chemistry, Chemical Engineering, Civil Engineering, Computer Science, Economics, Engineering (General), Environmental Studies, Management, Medicine, Nursing, Dentistry,

Science (General), Social Sciences, Sociology, Technology
ISBN Prefix(es): 978-981-3045
Distributor for American Academy of Ophthalmology; American Academy of Pediatrics; American Medical Association; Anthem Press; Blackwell Publishing; Verlag Barbara Budrich; Cabi; Chandos Publishing Ltd; Cold Spring Harbor Lab Press; CSIRO Publishing; DEStech Publications; ICFAI University Press; IET; IGI; Informa Healthcare; Island Press; Joint Commission International; Juta & Co; S Karger; Lippincott Williams & Wilkins; McGraw-Hill; MD Publications; New York University Press; W W Norton; Pearson; A K Peters; Purdue University Press; Lynne Rienner Publishers; RSC; M E Sharpe; Smithers & Rapra Technology; Springer Verlag; State University of New York Press; Thomas Telford; University of Michigan Press; University of New South Wales Press Ltd; University of Pennsylvania Press; University of Toronto Press; Wiley; Woodhead Publishing

Armour Publishing Pte Ltd
Block 1003 Bukit Merah Central, No 02-07, Singapore 159836
Tel: 6276 9976 *Fax:* 6276 7564
E-mail: enquiries@armourpublishing.com; mail@armourpublishing.com; sales@armourpublishing.com
Web Site: www.armourpublishing.com
Key Personnel
Publisher: Christina Lim
Publishing Dir: Chua Hong Koon
Founded: 1991
Subjects: Biography, Memoirs, Business, Education, Health, Nutrition, Management, Medicine, Nursing, Dentistry, Religion - Other, Christianity, Devotionals, Discipleship, Family, Missionaries, Parenting
ISBN Prefix(es): 978-981-04; 978-981-4138; 978-981-4305

Asiapac Books Pte Ltd+
996 Bendemeer Rd No 06-09, Singapore 339944
Tel: 6392 8455 *Fax:* 6392 6455
E-mail: info@asiapacbooks.com
Web Site: www.asiapacbooks.com
Key Personnel
Publishing Dir: Lydia Lum
Customer Service: Mr Ramesh Vakkiprath
Contact: Lim Li-Kok
Founded: 1983
Specialize in publishing & distribution.
Membership(s): Singapore Book Publishers Association.
Subjects: Asian Studies, History, Humor, Philosophy
ISBN Prefix(es): 978-9971-985; 978-981-3029; 978-981-3068; 978-981-229
Number of titles published annually: 50 Print
Total Titles: 600 Print; 4 Audio
Foreign Rep(s): Asia Books Co Ltd (Thailand); Bookplus (Indonesia); Caves Books Ltd (Taiwan); China Book Import Centre (China); China Books (Australia); China Books & Periodicals Inc (USA); China National Publications (China); Eastwind Books & Arts Inc (USA); Eastwind Books of Berkeley (USA); EDU Press & Media (Canada); Oliver Evers China Book Trading (Germany); Goodwill Trading Co Inc (Philippines); Kinokuniya Bookstores of Taiwan Co Ltd (Taiwan); Kyobo Book Centre Co Ltd (Korea); National Bookstore Inc (Philippines); P T Gramedia Asri Media (Indonesia); Peace Books Co Ltd (Hong Kong)

Bamboo Books, *imprint of* Flame of the Forest Publishing Pte Ltd

Berlitz Publishing, *imprint of* APA Publications GmbH & Co Verlag KG

Cannon International+
Blk 86 Marine Parade Central, No 03-213, Singapore 440086
Tel: 6344 7801 *Fax:* 6447 0897
Key Personnel
Mng Dir: Mr Tan Wu Cheng
Founded: 1975
Subjects: Education, Language Arts, Linguistics, Literature, Literary Criticism, Essays
ISBN Prefix(es): 978-9971-84; 978-9971-83; 978-981-00; 978-9971-941; 978-9971-943; 978-981-04
Imprints: Kingsway Publishers
Subsidiaries: Kingsway Publishers
Distributor for Robert Gibson (Singapore)

Celebrity Educational Publishers
474 Tampines St 43, No 01-108, Singapore 520474
Tel: 6785 7274 *Fax:* 6785 1977
Founded: 1983
Subjects: Language Arts, Linguistics, Science (General)
ISBN Prefix(es): 978-981-201
Subsidiaries: Willet Children's Books Australia

Chikubooks, *imprint of* Flame of the Forest Publishing Pte Ltd

China Knowledge Press+
119 Genting Lane, HB@119 Genting No 06-03, Singapore 349570
Tel: 6235 8468 *Fax:* 6235 2374
E-mail: info@chinaknowledge.com
Web Site: www.chinaknowledge.com
Founded: 2000
Provides independent insight, analysis & information to foreign investors to help them explore opportunities & determine values in the China market.
Specialize in translation projects, investment & consultancy services for the China market.
Subjects: Business
ISBN Prefix(es): 978-981-04; 978-981-4163; 978-981-4187
Number of titles published annually: 6 Print
Total Titles: 13 Print; 2 Online
Branch Office(s)
20 Millstream Close, Hitchin, Herts SG4 0D4, United Kingdom, Contact: Ms Weai-Hunt Yap *Tel:* (0146) 442230 *E-mail:* ywhunt@chinaknowledge.com

DL Publishing, *imprint of* World Scientific Publishing Co Pte Ltd

Earlybird Books, *imprint of* Federal Publications (S) Pte Ltd

EDM, see Editions Didier Millet (EDM)

Elsevier (Singapore) Pte Ltd+
Winsland House 1, 3 Killiney Rd No 08-01, Singapore 239519
Tel: 6349 0200 *Fax:* 6733 1510
E-mail: asiabkinfo@elsevier.com; sginfo@elsevier.com
Web Site: www.elsevier.com; asia.elsevier.com
Key Personnel
Vice President: Thomas Reller
Dir, Corporate Relations: Chris Capot
Founded: 1986
Membership(s): Afro Asian Book Council; Singapore Book Publishers Association.
Subjects: Biological Sciences, Chemistry, Chemical Engineering, Computer Science, Electronics, Electrical Engineering, Engineering (General), Law, Physical Sciences, Physics, Science (General), Social Sciences, Sociology, Technology, Travel & Tourism
ISBN Prefix(es): 978-981-259
Parent Company: Elsevier BV, Radarweg 29, 1043 NX Amsterdam, Netherlands
Ultimate Parent Company: RELX Group PLC, 1-3 Strand, London WC2N 5JR, United Kingdom

Epigram Books
1008 Toa Payoh North, 03-08, Singapore 318996
Tel: 6292 4456
E-mail: enquiry@epigrambooks.sg; rights@epigrambooks.sg; sales@epigrambooks.sg
Web Site: www.epigrambooks.sg
Key Personnel
Sales: Sarah Lee
Rights & Permissions: Req Ang
Subjects: Art, Cookery, Fiction, Nonfiction (General), Poetry
ISBN Prefix(es): 978-981-4757; 978-981-07
Distribution Center: APD Singapore Pte Ltd, 52 Genting Lane, No 06-05, Singapore 349560, Contact: Amnah Tan *Tel:* 6749 3551 *Fax:* 6749 3552 *E-mail:* th@apdsing.com *Web Site:* apdsing.com (Brunei, Cambodia, Indonesia, Laos, Malaysia, Myanmar, Philippines, Singapore & Thailand)

Federal Publications (S) Pte Ltd+
Imprint of Times Publishing Group
Times Centre, One New Industrial Rd, Singapore 536196
Tel: 6213 9288 *Fax:* 6284 4733; 6288 1186
E-mail: tpl@tpl.com.sg
Web Site: www.timespublishing.sg; www.tpl.com.sg
Founded: 1968
Subjects: Education
ISBN Prefix(es): 978-981-01; 978-9971-4
Associate Companies: Federal Publications (HK) Ltd, Hong Kong; Federal Publications Sdn Bhd, Malaysia
Imprints: Earlybird Books; Times Academic Press
Distributor for Chambers Harrap Publishers Ltd

Flame of the Forest Publishing Pte Ltd+
Blk 5 Ang Mo Kio Industrial Park 2A, No 07-22/23, AMK Tech II, Singapore 567760
Tel: 6484 8887 *Fax:* 6484 2208
E-mail: mail@flameoftheforest.com; editor@flameoftheforest.com; sales@flameoftheforest.com; rights@flameoftheforest.com
Web Site: www.flameoftheforest.com
Key Personnel
Publisher: Alex Amos Chacko
General Manager: Sarah Abraham Chia
Founded: 1989
Subjects: Cookery, Fiction, Humor, Nonfiction (General)
ISBN Prefix(es): 978-981-3056; 978-981-4193
Number of titles published annually: 20 Print
Total Titles: 200 Print
Imprints: Angsana Books; Bamboo Books; Chikubooks

Global Publishing Co, *imprint of* World Scientific Publishing Co Pte Ltd

Gordon & Breach, *imprint of* International Publishers Direct (S) Pte Ltd (IPD)

Graham Brash Pte Ltd
45 Kian Teck Dr, Block 1, Level 2, Singapore 628859
Tel: 6262 4843 *Fax:* 6262 1519
E-mail: sales@grahambrash.com.sg
Web Site: www.grahambrash.com.sg
Key Personnel
Chief Executive Officer: Chuan Campbell
E-mail: chuan@grahambrash.com.sg

General Manager: Evelyn Lee *E-mail:* evelyn@grahambrash.com.sg
Founded: 1926
Subjects: Biography, Memoirs, Business, Education, Ethnicity, Fiction, Government, Political Science, History, Nonfiction (General), Religion - Other, Self-Help, Sports, Athletics, Travel & Tourism, Culture, Nature, New Age, Pastimes
ISBN Prefix(es): 978-9971-947; 978-981-218; 978-9971-9901; 978-981-4115
Number of titles published annually: 36 Print
Total Titles: 600 Print
Foreign Rep(s): Asia Books Co Ltd (Thailand); BookaZine (Thailand); Booker International (Brunei); BookMark Inc (Philippines); Caves Books Ltd (Taiwan); China Books (Australia); The Commercial Press (HK) Ltd (Hong Kong); Dymocks Franchise Systems (Hong Kong); Far East Media (HK) Ltd (Hong Kong); Gazelle Book Services Ltd (UK); Goodwill Trading Co Inc (Philippines); Heian International Inc (USA); Hong Kong Book Centre (Hong Kong); Hushion House (Canada); Java Books (Indonesia); Kelly & Walsh Ltd (Hong Kong); National Book Store Inc (Philippines); PageOne The Bookshop (Hong Kong, Philippines); Pansing Distribution Sdn Bhd (Singapore); Peace Book Co Ltd (Hong Kong); Editions Le Printemps Lte (Mauritius); SAP Group (Singapore); W H Smith (Hong Kong); Swindon Book Co (Hong Kong); Times/Federal Publication (Hong Kong)

Harwood Academic Publishers, *imprint of* International Publishers Direct (S) Pte Ltd (IPD)

Hillview Publications Pte Ltd+
55 Ayer Rajah Crescent, No 05-08/9, Singapore 139949
Tel: 6334 8996 *Fax:* 6334 8997
Key Personnel
Mng Dir: Ms Ng Lai Mien
Founded: 1984
Membership(s): Singapore Book Publishers Association.
Subjects: Accounting, Economics, Education, English as a Second Language, Geography, Geology, Mathematics, Physics, Social Sciences, Sociology
ISBN Prefix(es): 978-981-202; 978-981-3052; 978-981-4013; 978-981-4041; 978-981-4073; 978-981-4099

Insight Guides, *imprint of* APA Publications GmbH & Co Verlag KG

Insight Pocket Guides, *imprint of* APA Publications GmbH & Co Verlag KG

Insight Topics, *imprint of* APA Publications GmbH & Co Verlag KG

Institute of Southeast Asian Studies+
30 Heng Mui Keng Terrace, Pasir Panjang, Singapore 119614
Tel: 6870 2447 *Fax:* 6775 6259
E-mail: publish@iseas.edu.sg
Web Site: www.iseas.edu.sg; bookshop.iseas.edu.sg
Key Personnel
Dir: Mr Chin Tiong Tan
Deputy Dir: Dr Kee Beng Ooi *E-mail:* keebeng@iseas.edu.sg
Head of Publications: Kok Kiong Ng
Senior Editor: Rahilah Yusuf *E-mail:* rahilah@iseas.edu.sg
Founded: 1968
Scholarly publishers.

Conduct post-doctoral research on politics, economics & social issues pertaining to the Asia-Pacific.
Subjects: Asian Studies, Economics, Energy, Environmental Studies, Finance, Foreign Countries, Government, Political Science, Social Sciences, Sociology
ISBN Prefix(es): 978-9971-902; 978-981-3035; 978-981-230; 978-981-3016; 978-981-3055; 978-9971-988; 978-981-4620; 978-981-4515; 978-981-4695; 978-981-4459; 978-981-4519
Number of titles published annually: 60 Print; 50 E-Book
Total Titles: 2,000 Print; 4 CD-ROM; 890 E-Book
Imprints: ISEAS
Distributed by Asia Books (Germany); Capital Books Pvt Ltd (India); Eurospan/ EDS (Europe); InBooks (Australia & New Zealand); PT Javabooks Indonesia (Indonesia); United Publishers Services Ltd (Japan)

International Publishers Direct (S) Pte Ltd (IPD)+
Entrepreneur Centre 02-11a, 50 Tagore Lane, Singapore 787494
Tel: 6741 6933
Founded: 1989
Subjects: Art, Education, Medicine, Nursing, Dentistry, Science (General), Social Sciences, Sociology, Technology, Theology, Humanities, STM
Total Titles: 3,000 Print
Parent Company: Omnistar Corp Pte Ltd
Imprints: Gordon & Breach; Harwood Academic Publishers
U.S. Office(s): PO Box 20029, River Front Plaza Station, Newark, NJ 07102-0301, United States

IPD, see International Publishers Direct (S) Pte Ltd (IPD)

ISEAS, *imprint of* Institute of Southeast Asian Studies

KH Biotech Services Pte Ltd, *imprint of* World Scientific Publishing Co Pte Ltd

Kingsway Publishers, *imprint of* Cannon International

LexisNexis
3 Killiney Rd, No 08-08 Winsland House One, Singapore 239519
Tel: 6733 1380; 6349 0110 (sales) *Fax:* 6733 1175
E-mail: help.sg@lexisnexis.com
Web Site: www.lexisnexis.com.sg
Key Personnel
Associate Dir, Sales: Angie Ong *E-mail:* angie.ong@lexisnexis.com
Associate Dir, Marketing: Vivian Sia *Tel:* 7882 3555 *E-mail:* vivian.sia@lexisnexis.com
Founded: 1982
Subjects: Law
Parent Company: RELX Group PLC

Lingzi Media Pte Ltd
Blk 48, Toh Guan Rd E, No 06-106, Enterprise Hub, Singapore 608586
Tel: 6293 5677 *Fax:* 6293 3575
E-mail: info@lingzi.com.sg
Web Site: www.lingzi.com.sg
Key Personnel
Mng Dir: Sandy Chen *E-mail:* sandy@lingzi.com.sg
Dir: Wendy Wenxu Chen *E-mail:* wenxu@lingzi.com.sg
Chief Editor: Denon Denan Lim *E-mail:* denon@lingzi.com.sg
Founded: 1993

Subjects: Cookery, Fiction, Finance, Health, Nutrition, History, Poetry, Culture
ISBN Prefix(es): 978-981-4243; 978-981-4127; 978-981-4157

Marshall Cavendish Books, *imprint of* Marshall Cavendish International (Asia) Pte Ltd

Marshall Cavendish Business, *imprint of* Marshall Cavendish International (Asia) Pte Ltd

Marshall Cavendish Continuity Sets, *imprint of* Marshall Cavendish International (Asia) Pte Ltd

Marshall Cavendish Cuisine, *imprint of* Marshall Cavendish International (Asia) Pte Ltd

Marshall Cavendish Editions, *imprint of* Marshall Cavendish International (Asia) Pte Ltd

Marshall Cavendish International (Asia) Pte Ltd+
Times Centre, One New Industrial Rd, Singapore 536196
Tel: 6213 9300 *Fax:* 6285 4871
E-mail: genref@sg.marshallcavendish.com; genrefsales@sg.marshallcavendish.com
Web Site: www.marshallcavendish.com/genref
Key Personnel
Corporate Sales Manager: Glenn Wray *E-mail:* glennwray@sg.marshallcavendish.com
Founded: 1975
Subjects: Architecture & Interior Design, Art, Biography, Memoirs, Business, Career Development, Cookery, Fiction, Gardening, Plants, Health, Nutrition, History, Humor, Literature, Literary Criticism, Essays, Management, Marketing, Nonfiction (General), Religion - Islamic, Self-Help, Travel & Tourism, Culture, Heritage, International Interests, Parenting
ISBN Prefix(es): 978-981-204; 978-2-85700; 978-981-232; 978-981-261
Associate Companies: Marshall Cavendish Books Ltd
Imprints: Marshall Cavendish Books; Marshall Cavendish Business; Marshall Cavendish Continuity Sets; Marshall Cavendish Cuisine; Marshall Cavendish Editions; les editions du Pacifique; Times Books International; Times Editions
Branch Office(s)
Times Subang, Lot 46, Persiaran Teknologi Subang, Subang Hi-Tech Industrial Park, Batu Tiga, 40000 Shah Alam, Selangor, Malaysia *Tel:* 5635 2191 *Fax:* 5635 2706 *E-mail:* cchong@my.marshallcavendish.com
Times Books International, Malaysia

Marshall Cavendish International (Singapore) Pte Ltd
Subsidiary of Marshall Cavendish Publishing Group
Times Centre, One New Industrial Rd, Singapore 536196
Tel: 6213 9300 *Fax:* 6266 3677
E-mail: tmesales@sg.marshallcavendish.com; enquiry@sg.marshallcavendish.com
Web Site: www.marshallcavendish.com
Subjects: Education
Ultimate Parent Company: Times Publishing Ltd

Math Paper Press
Imprint of BooksActually
No 9 Yong Siak St, Tiong Bahru, Singapore 168645
Tel: 6222 9195
E-mail: shop@booksactually.com

Web Site: www.booksactuallyshop.com/
collections/math-paper-press
Key Personnel
Owner: Kenny Leck
Subjects: Cookery, Fiction, Poetry
ISBN Prefix(es): 978-981-07; 978-981-11

McGallen & Bolden Pte Ltd+
Subsidiary of McGallen & Bolden Group
20 Maxwell Rd, No 04-01F, Maxwell House, Sin-
gapore 069113
Tel: 6871-4078
E-mail: postmaster@mcgallen.com
Web Site: mcgallen.net
Founded: 1991
Subjects: Advertising, Art, Biography, Mem-
oirs, Biological Sciences, Business, Chemistry,
Chemical Engineering, Child Care & Devel-
opment, Communications, Computer Science,
Economics, Education, Fiction, Geography,
Geology, History, Language Arts, Linguistics,
Medicine, Nursing, Dentistry, Philosophy, Psy-
chology, Psychiatry, Religion - Other, Social
Sciences, Sociology
ISBN Prefix(es): 978-981-04
Number of titles published annually: 2 Print; 2
CD-ROM; 10 Online; 2 Audio
Total Titles: 10 Print; 6 CD-ROM; 13 Online; 5
Audio
U.S. Office(s): McGallen & Bolden PR Corp,
1901 60 Pl, Suite L1029, Bradenton, FL
34203-5076, United States, Editor: Dr Seamus
Phan *E-mail:* sales@mcgallen.com

McGraw-Hill Education (Asia)
60 Tuas Basin Link, Jurong 638775
Tel: 6863 1580; 6868 8188 (customer service)
Fax: 6862 3354
E-mail: permissions_asia@mcgraw-hill.com
Web Site: www.mheducation.asia
Founded: 1970
Regional offices in China, Hong Kong, India, In-
donesia, Japan, Korea, Malaysia/Brunei, Philip-
pines, Singapore, Taiwan, Thailand & Vietnam.
Subjects: Business, Computer Science, Crafts,
Games, Hobbies, Economics, Education, En-
gineering (General), Mathematics, Medicine,
Nursing, Dentistry, Social Sciences, Sociology,
Sports, Athletics, Humanities, Statistics

Editions Didier Millet (EDM)+
121 Telok Ayer St No 03-01, Singapore 068590
Tel: 6324 9620; 6922 9610 *Fax:* 6324 9261
E-mail: edm@edmbooks.com.sg; farokh@
edmbooks.com.sg
Web Site: www.edmbooks.com
Key Personnel
Chairman & Publisher: Didier Millet
Editorial Dir: Douglas Amrine
General Manager: Charles Orwin
Founded: 1989
Subjects: Architecture & Interior Design, Art,
Asian Studies, Cookery, Crafts, Games, Hob-
bies, History, Literature, Literary Criticism,
Essays, Natural History, Photography, Travel &
Tourism, Southeast Asia
ISBN Prefix(es): 978-981-3018; 978-981-4260
Number of titles published annually: 30 Print
Total Titles: 150 Print
Associate Companies: Les Editions du Pacifique
Branch Office(s)
25 Jl Pudu Lama, 50200 Kuala Lumpur, Malaysia
Tel: (03) 2031 3805 *Fax:* (03) 2031 6298
E-mail: edmbooks@edmbooks.com.my
Distributor for Abrams (USA); Anaya Touring
Club (Spain); Atrium (Netherlands); Cassell
(UK); Christian Verlag (Germany); Chronicle
(USA); Bibliotheca Cullinaria (Italy); Dalian
University of Technology Press (China); Du-
mont (Germany); Gallimard (France); Ger-
stenburg (Germany); Good Cook Publishing
(Netherlands); Gradiva (Portugal); Hachette

(France); HarperCollins (UK); Harvard Uni-
versity Press (USA); Hawaii University Press
(USA); Kosmos (Netherlands); Kuperard (UK);
Liaoning & Technology Publishing House
(China); Little, Brown (UK); Logos (Italy);
La Martinere (France); Oxford University Press
(India); Penguin (India); Publifolha (Brazil);
Rizzoli (USA); St Martin's Press (USA); Terra
Lannoo (Netherlands); Thames & Hudson
(UK); Tuttle (USA); Vendome (USA); Wei-
denfeld & Nicolson (UK)
Foreign Rep(s): Asia Books Co Ltd (Ms Sita
Charoenpinitnan) (Thailand); Bookcourt
Bagatelle (Andy Lam) (Mauritius); Tim Bur-
land (Japan); China Publishers Marketing (Ben-
jamin Pan) (China); CSI Group (Mr Terry
Wybel) (North America); Editions Didier
Millet Pte Ltd (Mr Farokh Fan) (Singapore);
Editions Didier Millet Sdn Bhd (Mr Suresh
Sekaran) (Malaysia); Monument Books (Mr
Men Sambo) (Cambodia, Laos, Vietnam); Na-
tional Book Store (Philippines); B K Norton
Ltd (Lillian Hsiao) (Korea, Taiwan); Penguin
Books India Pvt Ltd (Mr Anantha Padman-
abhan) (India); Editions Le Printemps (Mrs
Madhvi) (Mauritius); PT Java Books Indonesia
(Indonesia); Roundhouse Group (Alan Good-
worth) (UK); Swindon Book Co Ltd (Liza
Lai & Elyse Wong) (Hong Kong); Thames &
Hudson (Mr Andrius Juknys) (UK); Thames &
Hudson Australia (Ms Saraid Banahan) (Aus-
tralia, New Zealand)

Newscom Pte Ltd+
Blk 105, Boon Keng Rd, No 04-17, Kallang
Basin Industrial Estate, Singapore 339776
Tel: 6291 9861 *Fax:* 6293 1445
Founded: 1987
Acts as media representative.
Membership(s): The BPA & ABC (UK).
Subjects: Publishing & Book Trade Reference,
Technology
Parent Company: Newsources Investments Ltd,
13 Wan Chai Rd, Wan Chai, Hong Kong
Associate Companies: Newsteam Sdn Bhd, 87-
89 Jl Ipoh, 3rd floor, 51200 Kuala Lumpur,
Malaysia *Tel:* (03) 4044-8599 *Fax:* (03) 4044-
9599

NUS Press Pte Ltd+
National University of Singapore, 3 Arts Link,
Singapore 117569
Tel: 6776 1148 *Fax:* 6774 0652
E-mail: nusbooks@nus.edu.sg; orders.nuspress@
nus.edu.sg
Web Site: www.nus.edu.sg/npu
Key Personnel
Acting Dir: Paul Kratoska
Founded: 1971
Publishing house of the National University of
Singapore.
Specialize in Southeast Asian & Asia-Pacific ti-
tles (scholarly & academic).
Membership(s): IASP; Singapore Book Publishers
Association (SBPA).
Subjects: Architecture & Interior Design, Asian
Studies, Business, Economics, Environmental
Studies, Finance, Government, Political Sci-
ence, History, Language Arts, Linguistics, Law,
Literature, Literary Criticism, Essays, Man-
agement, Maritime, Mathematics, Medicine,
Nursing, Dentistry, Science (General), Social
Sciences, Sociology, Technology, Singapore
Studies, Society
ISBN Prefix(es): 978-9971-69
Number of titles published annually: 30 Print
Total Titles: 1 CD-ROM; 1 Online
Imprints: Ridge Books
Distributed by APD Singapore Pte Ltd

Foreign Rep(s): Eurospan Group (Europe, UK);
University of Hawaii Press (Latin America,
North America, South America)
Foreign Rights: Hotaka Book Co Ltd (Japan); B
K Norton (China, South Korea, Taiwan)

les editions du Pacifique, *imprint of* Marshall
Cavendish International (Asia) Pte Ltd

Page One Publishing
20 Kaki Bukit View, Kaki Bukit Techpark II, Sin-
gapore 415956
Tel: 6742 2088 *Fax:* 6744 2088
Web Site: www.pageonegroup.com
Key Personnel
Publisher & Chief Executive Officer: Mark Tan
E-mail: mark_tan@pageonegroup.com
Founded: 1983
Subjects: Architecture & Interior Design, Art,
Cookery, Crafts, Games, Hobbies, Fash-
ion, Health, Nutrition, Photography, Travel
& Tourism, Design, Graphic & Visual Arts,
Lifestyle
Branch Office(s)
Room 303, Tower B, No 3 Bldg, North Area,
Pingguo Community, No 32, Baiziwan Rd,
Chaoyang District, Beijing 100022, China
Tel: (010) 5971 3119 *Fax:* (010) 5971 2606
E-mail: carling_chen@pageonegroup.com
Room B, 9/F, Roxy Industrial Centre, Tai Lin Pai
Rd, Kwai Chung, Hong Kong
Bookshop(s): Shop 3B201, Zone 3, China
World Mall, No 1 JianGuoMenWai Ave,
Chaoyang District, Beijing 100020, China
Tel: (010) 8535 1055 *Fax:* (010) 8535 1022
E-mail: page1_cwtc@pageonegroup.com; Shop
LG50, Indigo Mall, No 18 Jiuxianqiao Rd,
Chaoyang District, Beijing 100016, China
Tel: (010) 8426 0408 *Fax:* (010) 8426 0406
E-mail: page1_indigo@pageonegroup.com;
Units S2-14a-b, 1-2F, Taikoo Li Sanlitun, No
19 Sanlitun Rd, Chaoyang District, Beijing
100027, China *Tel:* (010) 6417 9582 *Fax:* (010)
6417 0322 *E-mail:* page1_slt@pageonegroup.
com; Units S2-14a-b, 2F, Taikoo Li Sanli-
tun, No 19 Sanlitun Rd, Chaoyang District,
Beijing 100027, China *Tel:* (010) 6417 9582
Fax: (010) 6417 5682 *E-mail:* woodhouse_slt@
pageonegroup.com; Cheng Du Interna-
tional Finance Centre IFS, Shop L510 &
L511B, IFS, No 1, Section 3, Hongxing Rd,
Jinjiang District, Chengdu 610021, China
Tel: (028) 8658 6510 *Fax:* (028) 8658 6810
E-mail: page1_cdifs@pageonegroup.com; Shop
488, 4F, MixC Mall, No 701, Fuchun Rd,
Jianggan District, Hangzhou 310020, China
Tel: (0571) 8970 5758 *Fax:* (0571) 8970 5768
E-mail: page1_hz@pageonegroup.com

Pan Asia Publishing Pte Ltd+
Raffles City, PO Box 677, Singapore 911723
Tel: 6316 1788 *Fax:* 6291 0500
E-mail: pa@panasiabooks.com
Web Site: shop.panasiabooks.com; panasia.exfree.
com
Key Personnel
Copyright: Evelyn Chia *E-mail:* evelyn@
panasiabooks.com
Founded: 1984
Publisher of children's illustrated story books
in English, Chinese & bilingual (English-
Chinese).
Membership(s): Singapore Book Publishers Asso-
ciation (SBPA).
Subjects: Education, Language Arts, Linguistics
ISBN Prefix(es): 978-9971-989; 978-981-3007;
978-981-222

Pan Pacific Publications (S) Pte Ltd+
Cpf Jurong Bldg, 21 Jurong East St 13, No 04-
00, Singapore 609646
Tel: 6261 6288 *Fax:* 6261 6088

Founded: 1971
Subjects: Education
ISBN Prefix(es): 978-981-208; 978-9971-63
Parent Company: Pan Pacific Public Co Ltd
Associate Companies: Eastview Publications Sdn
Bhd, Malaysia
Subsidiaries: Manhattan Press (HK) Ltd; Manhattan Press (S) Pte Ltd

Pearson Education South Asia Pte Ltd
23/25 First Lok Yang Rd, Jurong 629733
Tel: 6319 9388 *Fax:* 6265 1033
E-mail: info@pearsoned.com.sg; contacttrade@
pearson.com
Web Site: www.pearson.sg
Key Personnel
Mng Dir: Andrew Fong
Marketing Manager: Juliana Lim
Sales Manager: Tech Chuan
Founded: 1965
Subjects: Education, Language Arts, Linguistics,
English Language Teaching
ISBN Prefix(es): 978-981-247; 978-981-4063;
978-981-4069; 978-981-4075; 978-981-4079;
978-981-4080; 978-981-4083; 978-981-4085;
978-981-4087; 978-981-4088; 978-981-4093;
978-981-4096; 978-981-4098; 978-981-4105;
978-981-4110; 978-981-4114; 978-981-4119
Parent Company: Pearson Education

PN, *imprint of* Pustaka Nasional Pte Ltd

Polygott, *imprint of* APA Publications GmbH &
Co Verlag KG

Pustaka Nasional Pte Ltd+
Blk 1001 Eunos Ave 8, No 02-06, Singapore
409496
Tel: 6745 4321 *Fax:* 6745 2417
E-mail: enquiry@pustaka.com.sg
Web Site: www.pustaka.com.sg; www.pustaka.
com.sg/kedai/ (online book store)
Key Personnel
Dir: Syed Ali Semait *E-mail:* syed_ali@pustaka.
com.sg
Founded: 1963
Publisher, library supplier & typesetter.
Membership(s): Singapore Book Publishers Association (SBPA).
Subjects: Foreign Countries, Religion - Islamic
ISBN Prefix(es): 978-9971-77
Number of titles published annually: 12 Print; 10
E-Book; 3 Audio
Total Titles: 900 Print; 70 E-Book; 18 Audio
Associate Companies: Pustaka Islamiyah
Sdn Bhd, No 25 Jl TIB 1/21, Taman Industri Bolton, 68100 Batu Caves, Selangor, Malaysia, Dir: Syed Ali Semait
Tel: (03) 61889605 *Fax:* (03) 61882964
E-mail: pustakaislamiyah@me.com
Imprints: PN
Distributor for Dewan Bahasa Dan Pustaka
(Malaysia)

Ridge Books, *imprint of* NUS Press Pte Ltd

Rough Guides, *imprint of* APA Publications
GmbH & Co Verlag KG

SAP, *imprint of* Singapore Asian Publications Pte
Ltd

SAP Kids, *imprint of* Singapore Asian
Publications Pte Ltd

Scholastic Learners
26 Sin Ming Lane, No 05-127, Midview City,
Singapore 573971
Tel: 6454 8707 *Fax:* 6454 8504
E-mail: education@scholastic.com.sg

Web Site: scholasticlearners.com
Specialize in English & Chinese language learning materials.
ISBN Prefix(es): 978-981-4070; 978-981-4107;
978-981-4133; 978-981-4147; 978-981-4151

Select Publishing Pte Ltd+
65A, Jl Tenteram, No 02-06, St Michael's Industrial Estate, Singapore 328958
Tel: 6251 3798 *Fax:* 6251 3380
E-mail: info@selectbooks.com.sg; orders@
selectbooks.com.sg; marketing@selectbooks.
com.sg; publishing@selectbooks.com.sg
Web Site: www.selectbooks.com.sg
Key Personnel
Contact: Mr Seow Hwye Min
Founded: 1976
Specialize in books on Asia, particularly Southeast Asia & China.
Membership(s): Singapore Book Publishers Association (SBPA).
Subjects: Alternative, Architecture & Interior Design, Art, Asian Studies, Business, Developing
Countries, Drama, Theater, Economics, Education, Fiction, Geography, Geology, Government, Political Science, History, Law, Literature, Literary Criticism, Essays, Philosophy,
Religion - Other, Social Sciences, Sociology,
Technology, Travel & Tourism, Culture & People
ISBN Prefix(es): 978-981-4022
Total Titles: 30 Print
Parent Company: Select Books Pte Ltd
Distributed by Asia Books (Thailand)
Distributor for Cross Time Matrix Sdn Bhd;
Serindia; SIRD; Spore Heritage Society
Bookshop(s): 51, Armenian St, Singapore 179939
Tel: 6337 9319

Shing Lee Publishers Pte Ltd+
Member of Shing Lee Group
120 Hillview Ave, No 05-06/07 Kewalran
Hillview, Singapore 669594
Tel: 6760 1388 *Fax:* 6762 5684
E-mail: info@shinglee.com.sg
Web Site: www.shinglee.com.sg
Key Personnel
Executive Dir: Soh-Ngoh Peh *E-mail:* sohngoh@
shinglee.com.sg
General Manager: Mr Peh Shing Woei
Marketing Dir: Joe Neo *E-mail:* joeneo@shinglee.
com.sg
Founded: 1935
Subjects: Child Care & Development, Cookery,
Education
ISBN Prefix(es): 978-9971-61
Subsidiaries: Booktree; Concorde Publishers
Pte Ltd; Dragon Investment PL; Dragon Link
Granite PL; First Dragon Development PL;
Qingdao Huashan International Country Club;
Second Dragon Development PL; Shing Lee
Bookstore Pte Ltd; Shing Lee Investment Pte
Ltd; Shing Lee Realty Pte Ltd; Super Food Investment International PL; Tech Media; Third
Dragon Development PL; Third Dragon Holdings PL

Singapore Asian Publications Pte Ltd+
Henderson Industrial Park, 219 Henderson Rd No
10-04, Singapore 159556
Tel: 6276 8280 *Fax:* 6276 8292
E-mail: info@sapgrp.com
Web Site: www.sapgrp.com
Key Personnel
Chief Executive Officer: Kelvin Yoo
E-mail: kelvinyoo@sapgrp.com
Chief Publisher: Michelle Yoo
E-mail: michelleyoo@sapgrp.com
Founded: 1977
Publisher of academic & supplementary materials
for students age 6-19 years. Also library sup-

plier, importer, exporter, distributor & wholesaler.
Subjects: Education
Number of titles published annually: 300 Print
Total Titles: 700 Print
Imprints: SAP; SAP Kids; teachers@work
Subsidiaries: SAP Publications (HK) Ltd (Hong
Kong); SAP Publications (M) Sdn Bhd
(Malaysia); Singapore Asia Publishers (PH)
Inc (Philippines)

Star Publishing Pte Ltd
Block 115A, Commonwealth Dr, No 05-12, Tanglin Halt Industrial Park, Singapore 149596
Tel: 6479 6800 *Fax:* 6474 1080
E-mail: contactus@starpub.com.sg
Web Site: www.starpub.com.sg
Founded: 2002
Publish, market & distribute educational books &
materials in Singapore, China & Asia.
Subjects: Education, Geography, Geology, Language Arts, Linguistics, Mathematics, Music,
Dance, Science (General), English Language,
Home Economics
ISBN Prefix(es): 978-981-4176
Subsidiaries: Star Publishing Ltd

Success Publications Pte Ltd+
Blk 3013 Bedok Industrial Park E, No 04-2102,
Singapore 489979
Tel: 6443 1003 *Fax:* 6445 3156
E-mail: succpub@singnet.com.sg
Key Personnel
Mng Dir: Steven Khoo *E-mail:* tbkhoo@ymail.
com
Founded: 1983
Distributing, importing, exporting & publishing
of educational books & materials; reading program; assessment books; Chinese.
Subjects: Education, English as a Second Language, Mathematics, Science (General)
ISBN Prefix(es): 978-981-216; 978-981-3017;
978-981-3088; 978-981-4030; 978-981-4117;
978-981-4124; 978-981-4135; 978-981-262;
978-981-4146; 978-981-4152; 978-981-4158
Subsidiaries: Steven Tuition Centre
Orders to: Bowker-Saur Ltd, Windsor Court, E
Grinstead House, E Grinstead, West Sussex
RH19 1XA, United Kingdom *Tel:* (01342)
326972 *Fax:* (01342) 336198

Taylor & Francis Asia Pacific+
Member of Taylor & Francis Group, an Informa
Business
60 MacPherson Rd, Blk 1 No 06-09 Siemens
Centre, Singapore 348615
Tel: 6508 2888 *Fax:* 6742 9356
E-mail: info@tandf.com.sg
Web Site: www.taylorandfrancis.com.sg
Key Personnel
Mng Dir: Barry D Clarke *E-mail:* barry.clarke@
tandf.com.sg
Founded: 1979
Specialize in book distribution, publisher services,
conferences & author support.
Subjects: Agriculture, Anthropology, Architecture
& Interior Design, Art, Asian Studies, Biological Sciences, Business, Child Care & Development, Criminology, Economics, Education,
Engineering (General), Environmental Studies, Ethnicity, Government, Political Science,
History, Law, Library & Information Sciences,
Management, Mathematics, Medicine, Nursing,
Dentistry, Philosophy, Photography, Physical
Sciences, Physics, Psychology, Psychiatry, Religion - Other, Science (General), Social Sciences, Sociology, Veterinary Science
Ultimate Parent Company: Informa PLC
Distributor for American Psychological Association/Magination Press (USA); Bloomsbury
Academic (UK); Brookings Institution (USA);
Edinburgh University Press (UK); Edward El-

gar (UK); Facet Publishing (UK); Guilford Press (USA); IB Tauris Publishing (UK); Information Age Publishing Inc (USA); ISEAS (Singapore); Jessica Kingsley Publishers (UK); Pluto Press (UK); Springer Publishing Co (USA); Transaction Publishers (USA); World Bank Publications (USA)
Foreign Rep(s): ICK (South Korea)

teachers@work, *imprint of* Singapore Asian Publications Pte Ltd

Tech Publications Pte Ltd+
10 Jl Besar, No 1-39 Sim Lim Tower, Singapore 208787
Tel: 6291 4595 *Fax:* 6299 1550
Key Personnel
Owner: Rajiv Jain
Founded: 1984
Subjects: Computer Science, Electronics, Electrical Engineering
ISBN Prefix(es): 978-981-214; 978-981-3005; 978-981-3091
Associate Companies: Micro Tech Publications, Dubai, United Arab Emirates
Bookshop(s): 04-35 Funan Digitalife Mall, 109 North Bridge Rd, Singapore 179097
Warehouse: Henderson Bldg No 02-11, 211 Henderson Rd, Singapore 159552

Times Academic Press, *imprint of* Federal Publications (S) Pte Ltd

Times Books International, *imprint of* Marshall Cavendish International (Asia) Pte Ltd

Times Editions, *imprint of* Marshall Cavendish International (Asia) Pte Ltd

John Wiley & Sons (Asia) Pte Ltd+
One Fusionopolis Walk, No 07-01 Solaris South Tower, Singapore 138628
Tel: 6643 8000; 6302 9835 (returns) *Fax:* 6643 8008; 6265 6237 (returns)
E-mail: returnsasia@wiley.com; csd_ord@wiley.com
Web Site: www.wiley.com
Key Personnel
Chief Operating Officer Professional/Trade: Mark Allin
Publisher: Nick Wallwork
Foreign Rights Executive: Ira Tan
Founded: 1807
Subjects: Accounting, Business, Computer Science, Cookery, Education, Engineering (General), Geography, Geology, Language Arts, Linguistics, Mathematics, Psychology, Psychiatry, Science (General), Statistics
Number of titles published annually: 20 Print
Parent Company: John Wiley & Sons Inc, 111 River St, Hoboken, NJ 07030-5774, United States

World Scientific Publishing Co Pte Ltd+
5 Toh Tuck Link, Singapore 596224
Tel: 6466 5775 *Fax:* 6467 7667
E-mail: wspc@wspc.com.sg; sales@wspc.com.sg; editor@wspc.com.sg; mkt@wspc.com.sg; rights@wspc.com.sg
Web Site: www.worldscientific.com
Key Personnel
Co-Founder & Mng Dir: Doreen Liu
Dir & Publisher: Mrs Sook Cheng Lim
Founded: 1981
Develop products & services for the academic, scientific, professional, research & student communities worldwide.
Membership(s): International Association of STM Publishers; Singapore Book Publishers Association (SBPA).

Subjects: Architecture & Interior Design, Asian Studies, Biological Sciences, Chemistry, Chemical Engineering, Civil Engineering, Computer Science, Economics, Electronics, Electrical Engineering, Engineering (General), Environmental Studies, Finance, Management, Mathematics, Mechanical Engineering, Medicine, Nursing, Dentistry, Physics, Technology
ISBN Prefix(es): 978-981-02; 978-9971-950; 978-9971-966; 978-9971-978; 978-981-238; 978-981-256
Number of titles published annually: 400 Print
Total Titles: 6,000 Print
Imprints: DL Publishing; Global Publishing Co; KH Biotech Services Pte Ltd (Singapore)
Subsidiaries: ACES (India); Global Business Management Centre; Global Consultancy (Shanghai, China); Imperial College Press (UK); Meeting Matters International; World Century Publishing Co (US)
Branch Office(s)
World Scientific Publisher (Beijing), School of Mathematical Sciences Bldg No 2526W, Peking University, Beijing 100871, China
Tel: (010) 62759359 *Fax:* (010) 62759359
E-mail: wspbj@wspc.com
Global Consultancy (Shanghai) Pte Ltd, Room 2003, Shanghai Bund International Tower, No 99, Huangpu Rd, Shanghai 200080, China
Tel: (021) 63254982 *Fax:* (021) 63254985
E-mail: shanghai@worldscientific.com.cn
World Scientific Publishing (Tianjin), Room 309, Chern Institute of Mathematics, Nankai University, Weijin Rd 94, Nankai District, Tianjin 300071, China *Tel:* (022) 23509343
E-mail: wspbj@wspc.com
World Scientific Publishing (HK) Co Ltd, PO Box 72482, Kowloon Central Post Office, Kowloon, Hong Kong *Tel:* 2771 8791 *Fax:* 2771 8155 *E-mail:* hongkong@worldscientific.com.hk
World Scientific Publishing Co Pte Ltd, No 16 SW Boag Rd, T Nagar, Chennai 600 017, India
Tel: (044) 52065464 *E-mail:* mkt@wspc.com
World Scientific Publishing Company, Kiriat Hatikshort-Neve Ilan, Suite 226, 90805 Harei Yehuda, Israel *Tel:* (054) 4403728; (02) 5791532; (02) 5791533 *Fax:* (02) 5791532; (02) 5791533 *E-mail:* rspindel@wspc.com
World Scientific Publishing Co Pte Ltd, 8F, No 162 Sec 4, Roosevelt Rd, Taipei 10091, Taiwan *Tel:* (02) 2369-1366 *Fax:* (02) 2366-0460
E-mail: wsptw@ms13.hinet.net
World Scientific Publishing (UK) Ltd, 57 Shelton St, London WC2H 9HE, United Kingdom
Tel: (020) 7836-0888 *Fax:* (020) 7836-2020
E-mail: sales@wspc.co.uk
U.S. Office(s): World Scientific Publishing Co Inc, 27 Warren St, Suite 401-402, Hackensack, NJ 07601, United States *Tel:* 201-487-9655 *Fax:* 201-487-9656 *E-mail:* wspc_us@wspc.com
Distributor for Imperial College Press (UK); The National Academy Press, USA (Asia-Pacific exc Australia, Japan, New Zealand)
Foreign Rep(s): James Bennett (Australia, New Zealand); Cambridge University Press India Pvt Ltd Cambridge House (Afghanistan, Bangladesh, Bhutan, India, Maldives, Nepal, Pakistan, Sri Lanka); Colin Flint Ltd (Ben Greig) (Denmark, Finland, Iceland, Norway, Sweden); Cranbury International LLC (Ethan Atkins) (Caribbean, Central America, South America); Frauke Feldmann & Mare Nostrum (Austria, Germany, Switzerland); Hill/Martin Associates (Duke Hill) (Western USA); International Publishing Services Ltd (Zoe Kaviani) (Algeria, Libya, Morocco, Tunisia); Kemper Conseil Publishing (Dineke & Enno Kemper) (Belgium, Netherlands); Kinokuniya Co Ltd (Japan); Lum Tim Leng (Philippines, Thailand, Vietnam); Marek Lewinson (Eastern Europe); Marcello sas Publishers' Representatives (Flavio Marcello) (France, Greece, Italy, Portu-

gal, Spain); Maruzen Co Ltd (Japan); Quantum Publishing Solutions (Jim Chalmers) (UK); Scholarly Book Services Inc (Laura Rust) (Canada); Ben Schrager (Mid-Atlantic States, New England, USA); P C Tham (Indonesia, Malaysia); Trim Associates (Gary Trim) (Midwestern States)

Slovakia

General Information

Capital: Bratislava
Language: Slovak
Religion: Predominantly Roman Catholic, some Lutheran
Population: 5.3 million
Currency: 100 Eurocents = 1 Euro
Export/Import Information: Member of the European Union. There are plans to establish custom-free zones to stimulate foreign investment. 6% VAT on books.
Copyright: UCC, Berne (see Copyright Conventions, pg viii)

AB Art press vydavateľstvo a fotoagentura
Lichardova 51, 976 13 Slovenska Lupca
Tel: (048) 41 87 181; (048) 41 36 942 *Fax:* (048) 41 87 181
E-mail: barta@abartpress.sk
Web Site: www.abartpress.sk
Founded: 1990
Subjects: Cookery, Travel & Tourism, Bratislava, Slovakia, Tourist Guides
ISBN Prefix(es): 978-80-88817; 978-80-900433; 978-80-966998

Vydavateľstvo ARCHA+
Kvacalova 14/15, 821 08 Bratislava
Tel: (0903) 583 724 (cell)
Key Personnel
Contact: Pavol Skorvanek
Subjects: Government, Political Science, History, Law, Philosophy, Science (General), Social Sciences, Sociology
ISBN Prefix(es): 978-80-7115; 978-80-90192; 978-80-971321

Arkus Vydavaleľstvo sro
L Svoboda 1359/10, 905 01 Senica
Tel: (034) 6574868
E-mail: vydarkus@vydarkus.eu
Web Site: www.vydarkus.sk
Founded: 1992
Subjects: Fiction, Nonfiction (General)
ISBN Prefix(es): 978-80-88822; 978-80-900465; 978-80-967215

Aspekt ad
Mytna 38, 811 07 Bratislava
Tel: (02) 5249 1639; (0918) 479 677 *Fax:* (02) 5249 139
E-mail: aspekt@aspekt.sk; administrativa@aspekt.sk
Web Site: www.aspekt.sk
Founded: 1993
Subjects: Fiction, Nonfiction (General), Social Sciences, Sociology, Women's Studies, Humanities
ISBN Prefix(es): 978-80-85549

AV Studio SRO Reklamno-vydavatelska agentura
Lykovcova 7, 841 04 Bratislava
Tel: (02) 654 262 97 *Fax:* (02) 654 262 97
E-mail: avstudio@avstudio.sk
Web Site: www.avstudio.sk
Founded: 1990

Subjects: Health, Nutrition, Religion - Other
ISBN Prefix(es): 978-80-88779

Vydavatel'stvo Buvik sro
Partizanska 2, 811 03 Bratislava
Mailing Address: Mierova 28, 821 05 Bratislava
Tel: (02) 544 160 92
E-mail: buvik@buvik.sk
Web Site: www.buvik.sk
Key Personnel
Manager: Milica Matejkova
Editor-in-Chief: Maria Stevkova
Founded: 1991
Subjects: Biography, Memoirs, Poetry, Fairy Tales
ISBN Prefix(es): 978-80-85507; 978-80-89028

Dajama Vydavatel'stvo
Ljubljana 2, 831 02 Bratislava
Tel: (02) 44631702 *Fax:* (02) 44631702
E-mail: info@dajama.sk
Web Site: www.dajama.sk
Founded: 1995
Subjects: Geography, Geology, Travel & Tourism
ISBN Prefix(es): 978-80-89226

EDIS-Printing House of the University of Zilina
Univerzitna 1, 010 26 Zilina
Tel: (041) 513 49 00 *Fax:* (041) 562 00 23
Web Site: www.uniza.sk
Key Personnel
Dir: Miroslav Pfliegel, PhD *E-mail:* pfliegel@nic.uniza.sk
Founded: 1990
ISBN Prefix(es): 978-80-7100; 978-80-8070

Ikar as
Member of DirectGroup Bertelsmann
Kukuricna 13, 831 03 Bratislava 3
Tel: (02) 49 104 33; (02) 49 104 341
E-mail: ikar@ikar.sk; redakcia@ikar.sk
Web Site: www.ikar.sk
Key Personnel
President: Andreas Kaulfuss
Sales Dir: Vavra Juraj *Tel:* (02) 492 097 44
     E-mail: vavra.juraj@ikar.sk
Founded: 1990
Subjects: Criminology, Economics, Fiction, Government, Political Science, History, Language Arts, Linguistics, Nonfiction (General), Romance, Science Fiction, Fantasy, Travel & Tourism, Adult Fiction, Adventure, Crime
ISBN Prefix(es): 978-80-551; 978-80-7118

Jaga Group sro
Imricha Karvasa 2, 811 07 Bratislava
Tel: (02) 502 002 00; (02) 529 259 89 (bookshop) *Fax:* (02) 502 002 10
E-mail: objednavky@jagastore.sk
Web Site: www.jagastore.sk
Founded: 1993
Subjects: Architecture & Interior Design, Civil Engineering, Construction, Housing

Vydavatelstvo Junior sro+
Zadunajska cesta 8, 851 01 Bratislava
Tel: (02) 6820 4712; (02) 6820 4713 *Fax:* (02) 6820 4726
E-mail: obchod@junior.sk
Web Site: www.junior.sk
Founded: 1994
ISBN Prefix(es): 978-80-7146
Associate Companies: Nakladatelstvi Junior, Prague, Czech Republic
Distributor for Slowakei

Kalligram spol sro+
Staromestska 6/D, 810 00 Bratislava 1
Mailing Address: PO Box 223, 810 00 Bratislava 1
Tel: (02) 544-15-028 *Fax:* (02) 544-15-028

E-mail: kalligram@kalligram.sk; distribucia@kalligram.sk
Web Site: www.kalligram.com
Key Personnel
Dir: Laszlo Szigeti *E-mail:* vydavatelstvo@kalligram.sk
Editor: Karol Chmel *E-mail:* chmel@kalligram.sk; Ingrid Hrubanicova *E-mail:* vydavatelstvo@kalligram.sk
Founded: 1991
Subjects: Art, Cookery, Fiction, History, Language Arts, Linguistics, Literature, Literary Criticism, Essays, Philosophy, Science (General), Social Sciences, Sociology
ISBN Prefix(es): 978-80-7149
Number of titles published annually: 70 Print
Total Titles: 800 Print
Subsidiaries: Slovak Literature SAS
Branch Office(s)
Pesti Kalligram Konyvkiado es Konyvterjeszto Kft, Tuzolto utca 8, felemelet 2, Budapest 1094, Hungary *Tel:* (01) 216-68-75 *Fax:* (01) 216-68-75 *E-mail:* kalligram@interware.hu

Kniha Mikula
Nam Hraniciarov 35, 851 03 Bratislava
Tel: (09) 05150416 (cell)
E-mail: mikula@knihy-mikula.sk
Web Site: www.knihy-mikula.sk
Key Personnel
Dir: Vojtech Mikula
Founded: 1992
Subjects: Language Arts, Linguistics
ISBN Prefix(es): 978-80-88814
Total Titles: 77 Print; 2 CD-ROM

LIC, see Literarne Informacne Centrum

Literarne Informacne Centrum (The Centre for Information on Literature)
Nam SNP 12, 812 24 Bratislava
Tel: (02) 2047 3506 *Fax:* (02) 5296 4563
E-mail: lic@litcentrum.sk
Web Site: www.litcentrum.sk
Key Personnel
Dir: Miroslava Vallova *Tel:* (02) 2047 3505
     E-mail: miroslava.vallova@litcentrum.sk
Secretary: Brigita Drabova *E-mail:* brigita.drabova@litcentrum.sk
Subjects: Literature, Literary Criticism, Essays, Contemporary Slovakia Literature
ISBN Prefix(es): 978-80-88878; 978-80-89222

Luc vydavatelske druzstvo+
Kozicova 2, 841 10 Bratislava
Tel: (02) 60421233; (02) 60421237 (distribution & sales)
E-mail: recepcia@luc.sk
Web Site: www.luc.sk
Founded: 1989
Membership(s): Association of Slovak Catholic Publishers; Publishers of Catholic Libraries of Europe.
Subjects: Biography, Memoirs, Education, History, Philosophy, Poetry, Religion - Catholic, Theology
ISBN Prefix(es): 978-80-7114

Marencin PT spol sro
Jelenia 6, 811 05 Bratislava 1
Tel: (02) 20 723 752 *Fax:* (02) 20 723 752
E-mail: marencin@marencin.sk
Web Site: www.marencin.sk
Founded: 1993
Subjects: Fiction, Nonfiction (General)
ISBN Prefix(es): 978-80-8114

Vydavatelstvo MATYS sro
Starhradska 8, 851 01 Bratislava
Tel: (02) 556 423 97; (02) 556 423 98 *Fax:* (02) 554 102 82

E-mail: matys@matys.sk
Web Site: www.matys.sk
Key Personnel
Management: Jaroslav Jankovic; Lydia Matuskova
Founded: 1994
Subjects: Fiction, Nonfiction (General)
ISBN Prefix(es): 978-80-8088; 978-80-89147
Warehouse: Area VUZ, Racianska 71, 832 59 Bratislava, Contact: Olga Sabova *Tel:* (02) 492 462 028 *Fax:* (02) 492 462 028

Vydavatelstvo Obzor sro+
Spitalska 35, 811 07 Bratislava
Mailing Address: PO Box 64, 820 12 Bratislava
Tel: (02) 52961251
E-mail: obzor@obzor.sk
Web Site: www.obzor.sk
Founded: 1953
Horizon: Slovak Book & Periodical Publishing House for People's Education.
Subjects: Archaeology, Art, Health, Nutrition, Law, Literature, Literary Criticism, Essays, Medicine, Nursing, Dentistry, Mysteries, Suspense, Parapsychology
ISBN Prefix(es): 978-80-215

Perfekt as
Karpatska 7, 811 05 Bratislava
Tel: (02) 524 99 783; (02) 524 44 070 (bookstore); (02) 524 99 784; (02) 524 99 785 *Fax:* (02) 524 99 788
E-mail: knihy@perfekt.sk; odbyt@perfekt.sk (sales); marketing@perfekt.sk; knihkupectvovz@perfekt.sk (bookstore)
Web Site: www.perfekt.sk
Subjects: Architecture & Interior Design, Fiction, History, How-to, Nonfiction (General), Parenting
ISBN Prefix(es): 978-80-8046; 978-80-85261

Vydavatel'stvo Priroda sro (Priroda Publishing sro)+
Kocelova 17, 821 08 Bratislava 2
Tel: (02) 55 42 51 60 *Fax:* (02) 20 74 96 33
E-mail: priroda@priroda.sk
Web Site: www.priroda.sk
Key Personnel
Contact: Mikulas Jankovits *Tel:* (0905) 685077
     E-mail: jankovits@priroda.sk
Founded: 1949
Subjects: Animals, Pets, Business, Gardening, Plants, House & Home, How-to, Language Arts, Linguistics, Management, Outdoor Recreation, Self-Help, Travel & Tourism, Veterinary Science, Nature
ISBN Prefix(es): 978-80-07
Number of titles published annually: 100 Print; 5 CD-ROM
Total Titles: 9,000 Print; 10 CD-ROM; 1 E-Book
Distributed by Belimex (Slovakia); EUROMEDIA Bertelsmann Group (Czech Republic); LB Story (Slovakia); Modul (Slovakia); Panta Rhei (Slovakia); Pemic (Slovak & Czech Republic); Slovartstore (Slovakia)
Warehouse: Sustekova 5-7, 851 01 Bratislava
     Tel: (0905) 757 860 *E-mail:* skad@priroda.sk

Vydavatel'stvo Q111
JC Hronskeho 4, 831 02 Bratislava
Tel: (02) 444 57057
E-mail: q111@q111.sk; q111@stonline.sk
Web Site: www.q111.sk
Key Personnel
Publisher: Kvetusa Daskova
Founded: 1990
Subjects: Fiction, Literature, Literary Criticism, Essays, Nonfiction (General), Poetry
ISBN Prefix(es): 978-80-85401; 978-80-89092

Vydavatel'stvo RAK
J Holceka 65, 900 86 Budmerice
Tel: (033) 6448 119 *Fax:* (033) 6448 119

Web Site: www.vydavatelstvorak.sk
Key Personnel
Founder & Owner: Dr Pavel Dvorak
   E-mail: dvorak@vydavatelstvorak.sk
Sales: Daniela Dvorakova
   E-mail: danieladvorakova@nextra.sk
Founded: 1991
Subjects: History
ISBN Prefix(es): 978-80-85501

Vydavatelstvo Serafin (Serafin Publishing
   House)+
Frantiskanska 2, 811 01 Bratislava
Tel: (0915) 700 581 *Fax:* (02) 544 343 42
E-mail: serafin@serafin.sk
Web Site: www.serafin.sk
Founded: 1990
Membership(s): Zdruzenie katolickych vydavatel-
   stiev Slovenska (Association of Catholic Pub-
   lishers in Slovakia).
Subjects: Foreign Countries, Inspirational, Spir-
   ituality, Medicine, Nursing, Dentistry, Poetry,
   Religion - Catholic, Theology
ISBN Prefix(es): 978-80-85310; 978-80-88944
Number of titles published annually: 15 Print
Total Titles: 125 Print
Bookshop(s): Frantisek

Vydavatel'stvo Slovart spol sro
Bojnicka 10, 830 00 Bratislava 3
Mailing Address: PO Box 70, 830 00 Bratislava 3
Tel: (02) 49 20 18 00 *Fax:* (02) 49 20 18 99
E-mail: objednavky@slovart.sk
Web Site: www.slovart.sk
Key Personnel
Dir: Juraj Heger
Assistant Dir: Kristina Nemcova
   E-mail: nemcova@slovart.sk
Export Manager: Sona Wells *Tel:* (02) 49 20 18
   16 *E-mail:* wells@slovart.sk
Foreign Rights: Elena Hudakova *Tel:* (02) 49 20
   18 01 *E-mail:* hudakova@slovart.sk
Marketing & Promotion: Sasa Petrasova *Tel:* (02)
   49 20 18 33 *E-mail:* petrasova@slovart.sk
Subjects: Architecture & Interior Design, Art,
   Fiction, Photography, Science Fiction, Fantasy,
   Fine Art, Graphic Design
ISBN Prefix(es): 978-80-7145; 978-80-8085; 978-
   80-556

Slovenska Narodna Galeria
Riecna 1, 815 13 Bratislava 1
Tel: (02) 59226113 *Fax:* (02) 54433971
E-mail: sng@sng.sk
Web Site: www.sng.sk
Key Personnel
General Dir: Alexandra Kusa, PhD
Subjects: Art, History
ISBN Prefix(es): 978-80-8059; 978-80-85188

Slovenska Narodna Kniznica, Martin (Slovak
   National Library, Martin)+
Division of The National Bibliography Institute
Nam J C Hronskeho 1, 036 01 Martin
Tel: (043) 2451 125; (043) 2451 140 (ISBN
   Agency)
E-mail: snk@snk.sk
Web Site: www.snk.sk
Key Personnel
Dir General: Katarina Kristofova, PhD *Tel:* (043)
   2451 131 *E-mail:* katarina.kristofova@snk.sk
Founded: 1863
Subjects: Biography, Memoirs, Ethnicity, Geneal-
   ogy
ISBN Prefix(es): 978-80-7090

**Slovenske pedagogicke nakladatelstvo - Mlade
   leta sro+**
Sasinkova 5, 811 08 Bratislava
Tel: (02) 502 272 25; (02) 50 227 323 (sales)
E-mail: spn@spn.sk; odbyt@spn.sk (sales)

Web Site: www.mladeleta.sk
Founded: 1920
Slovak publishing house for educational litera-
   ture, textbooks, dictionaries, encyclopedias,
   children's & juvenile literature.
Specialize in languages: English, French, German,
   Hungarian, Russian & Slovak.
Subjects: Education, English as a Second Lan-
   guage, History, Language Arts, Linguistics,
   Mathematics, Music, Dance, Physics, Psychol-
   ogy, Psychiatry
ISBN Prefix(es): 978-80-06; 978-80-10
Number of titles published annually: 300 Print; 2
   CD-ROM
Bookshop(s): Krizna 13, 811 07 Bratislava
   Tel: (02) 554 255 04 *E-mail:* predajna@spn.sk
Warehouse: Pristavna 1, 821 09 Bratislava
   Tel: (02) 53 41 41 01 *E-mail:* sklad@spn.sk

Vydavatel'stvo Slovenskej Akademie Vied
   (Publishing House of the Slovak Academy of
   Sciences)
Dubravska cesta 9, 845 02 Bratislava
Tel: (02) 2092 0203
E-mail: vedasav@savba.sk
Web Site: veda.sav.sk
Key Personnel
Dir: Dr Milan Brnak *Tel:* (02) 2092 0200
   E-mail: brnak@savba.sk
Editor-in-Chief: Pavol Krsak, PhD *Tel:* (02) 2092
   0232 *E-mail:* pavol.krsak@savba.sk
Production Manager: Ema Zovinkova
   E-mail: ema.zovinkova@savba.sk
Sales Manager: Anna Markova *Tel:* (02) 2092
   0206 *E-mail:* anna.markova@savba.sk
Founded: 1942
Subjects: Archaeology, Biological Sciences, Earth
   Sciences, Economics, Gardening, Plants, Geog-
   raphy, Geology, Government, Political Science,
   History, Language Arts, Linguistics, Law, Lit-
   erature, Literary Criticism, Essays, Nonfiction
   (General), Philosophy, Psychology, Psychiatry,
   Regional Interests, Science (General), Social
   Sciences, Sociology, Technology, Art History,
   Botany, Ecology, Ethnology, Statistics
ISBN Prefix(es): 978-80-224
Bookshop(s): Stefanikova 3, 811 06
   Bratislava *Tel:* (02) 2092 0233
   E-mail: vedaknihkupectvo@savba.sk;
   Rybníkova 13/A, sudentsky domov Pe-
   tra Pazmana, Trnava *Tel:* (033) 593 9816
   E-mail: vedatrnava@savba.sk

Slovensky Spisovatel as+
Vajnorska 128, 831 04 Bratislava 3
Tel: (02) 44 44 12 39; (02) 44 45 30 21 *Fax:* (02)
   44 44 12 39
E-mail: slovenskyspisovatel@slovenskyspisovatel.
   sk
Web Site: www.slovenskyspisovatel.sk
Key Personnel
Dir: Martin Chovanec
Founded: 1951
Subjects: Criminology, Fiction, Literature, Liter-
   ary Criticism, Essays, Poetry, Romance, Crime
   Fiction
ISBN Prefix(es): 978-80-220
Bookshop(s): Laurinska 2, 813 67 Bratislava
   Tel: (02) 54 37 60 *Fax:* (02) 54 37 60
   E-mail: knihkupectvo@slovenskyspisovatel.sk
Book Club(s): KMP (Kruh milovnikov poezie);
   SPKK (Spolocnost'priatel'ov krasnych knih)

Vydavatelstvo SOFA+
PO Box 4, 820 11 Bratislava 211
Tel: (02) 555 626 44 *Fax:* (02) 555 626 44
E-mail: sofa@sofanet.sk
Web Site: www.sofanet.sk
Key Personnel
Dir: Dr Robert Farbula
Founded: 1992

Subjects: Child Care & Development, Economics,
   Health, Nutrition, Human Relations, Library &
   Information Sciences, Philosophy, Physics, Psy-
   chology, Psychiatry, Publishing & Book Trade
   Reference, Social Sciences, Sociology
ISBN Prefix(es): 978-80-85752; 978-80-89033

Vydavatelstvo Tatran spol sro
Klariska 16, 815 82 Bratislava
Tel: (02) 5443 5849; (0915) 772 399 (cell)
   Fax: (07) 5443 5777
E-mail: info@slovtatran.sk
Web Site: www.slovtatran.sk
Founded: 1947
Slovak publishing house of belles lettres.
Subjects: Art, Drama, Theater, Literature, Literary
   Criticism, Essays, Nonfiction (General), Poetry,
   Regional Interests
ISBN Prefix(es): 978-80-222

**Vydavatel'stvo Technicka Univerzita vo
   Zvolene** (Publishing House of Technical
   University in Zvolen)
ul T G Masaryka 24, 960 53 Zvolen
Tel: (045) 520 61 11 *Fax:* (045) 533 00 27
E-mail: info@tuzvo.sk
Web Site: www.tuzvo.sk
Key Personnel
Head, Publishing: Dr Eva Fekiacova
   Tel: (045) 520 6170 *Fax:* (045) 532 2051
   E-mail: fekiacovae@is.tuzvo.sk
Deputy Head: Iveta Malisova *Tel:* (045) 520 173
   E-mail: malisova@is.tuzvo.sk
Founded: 1997
Subjects: Agriculture, Animals, Pets, Architecture
   & Interior Design, Economics, Education, En-
   vironmental Studies, Science (General), Tech-
   nology
ISBN Prefix(es): 978-80-228

Tranoscius AS
Tranovskeho 1, 031 80 Liptovsky Mikulas
Tel: (044) 552 30 70 *Fax:* (044) 552 22 06
E-mail: sefradaktor@tranoscius.sk; odbyt@
   tranoscius.sk
Web Site: www.tranoscius.sk
Key Personnel
Dir: Lubomir Turcan *E-mail:* lubomir.turcan@
   tranoscius.sk
Sales & Marketing: Marcela Haborakova
   E-mail: marcela.haborakova@tranoscius.sk
Subjects: Poetry, Religion - Other
ISBN Prefix(es): 978-80-7140

Trio Publishing
Trajanova 3A, 851 10 Bratislava
E-mail: infotrio@mail.t-com.sk; info@
   triopublishing.sk
Web Site: www.triopublishing.sk
Key Personnel
Publisher: Magdalena Fazekasova *Tel:* (0908) 756
   855 (cell) *E-mail:* magdalena.trio@mail.t-com.
   sk
Mng Editor: Jozef Rundes *Tel:* (0917) 964 401
   (cell)
Sales Assistant: Veronika Kissova
Subjects: Architecture & Interior Design, Edu-
   cation, Fiction, History, Nonfiction (General),
   Poetry, Science (General)
ISBN Prefix(es): 978-80-89552; 978-80-969444;
   978-80-967324; 978-80-968705

UIPS, see Ustav informacii a prognoz skolstva

Ustav informacii a prognoz skolstva+
Stare Grunty 52, 842 44 Bratislava 4
Tel: (02) 692 95 111 *Fax:* (02) 654 26 180
E-mail: uips@uips.sk
Web Site: www.uips.sk
Key Personnel
Mng Dir: Peter Jakub *Tel:* (02) 692 95 101

Founded: 1989
Subjects: Career Development, Computer Science, Computers, Education, Labor, Industrial Relations, Library & Information Sciences, Management, Outdoor Recreation, Psychology, Psychiatry, Social Sciences, Sociology
ISBN Prefix(es): 978-80-7098
Associate Companies: Slovenska pedagogicka kniznica

VEDA, see Vydavatel'stvo Slovenskej Akademie Vied

Zilinska Univerzita, see EDIS-Printing House of the University of Zilina

ZSVTS, see Zvazu Slovenskych Vedeckotechnickych Spolocnosti sro

Zvazu Slovenskych Vedeckotechnickych Spolocnosti sro (Association of Slovak Scientific & Technological Societies)
Kocelova 15, 815 94 Bratislava
Tel: (02) 5020 7649 *Fax:* (02) 5020 7656
E-mail: zsvts@zsvts.sk
Web Site: www.zsvts.sk
Key Personnel
President: Dr Dusan Petras
Founded: 1990
Subjects: Business, Finance, Management, Marketing, Mechanical Engineering, Science (General), Technology
ISBN Prefix(es): 978-80-230; 978-80-233; 978-80-236

Slovenia

General Information

Capital: Ljubljana
Language: Slovenian and Serbo-Croat
Religion: Predominantly Roman Catholic
Population: 2 million
Bank Hours: 0730-1800 Monday-Friday and 0730-1200 Saturday
Shop Hours: 0800-1900 Monday-Friday; 0800-1300 Saturday, some open Saturday afternoon
Currency: 100 Eurocents = 1 Euro
Export/Import Information: Member of the European Union. 3% VAT on books.
Copyright: UCC, Berne (see Copyright Conventions, pg viii)

Beletrina, Zavod za Zaloznisko Dejavnost
Kersnikova ul 4, SI-1000 Ljubljana
Tel: (01) 200 37 00 *Fax:* (01) 252 26 18
E-mail: info@zalozba.org
Web Site: www.knjigarna-beletrina.com
Key Personnel
Dir & Editor: Mitja Cander
Founded: 1996
Subjects: Literature, Literary Criticism, Essays, Nonfiction (General), Poetry
ISBN Prefix(es): 978-961-242
Bookshop(s): Novi trg 2, SI-1000 Ljubljana
   Tel: (040) 922 521 *E-mail:* beletrina@galarna.si

Center za slovensko knjizevnost (Center for Slovenian Literature)
Metelkova 6, SI-1000 Ljubljana
Tel: (01) 505 1674 *Fax:* (01) 505 1674
E-mail: litcenter@mail.ljudmila.org
Web Site: www.ljudmila.org/litcenter
Key Personnel
Chairman: Matej Bogataj
Founded: 1999

Subjects: Fiction, Literature, Literary Criticism, Essays, Poetry
ISBN Prefix(es): 978-961-6036

Zalozba /*cf+
Slomskova 15, SI-1000 Ljubljana
Mailing Address: Kersnikova 4/IV, SI-1000 Ljubljana
Tel: (01) 43 444 31; (01) 230 65 80 (orders); (01) 31 43 444 (editorial) *Fax:* (01) 230 65 85 (orders)
E-mail: info@zalozbacf.si; zalozba@t-2.net; buca@siol.net
Web Site: www.zalozbacf.si
Key Personnel
Dir: Alvina Zuraj
Editor: Zoja Skusek
Founded: 1997
Subjects: Art, Astrology, Occult, Astronomy, Biblical Studies, Child Care & Development, Communications, Drama, Theater, English as a Second Language, Fiction, Foreign Countries, Government, Political Science, History, Journalism, Language Arts, Linguistics, Literature, Literary Criticism, Essays, Medicine, Nursing, Dentistry, Parapsychology, Philosophy, Photography, Psychology, Psychiatry, Regional Interests, Religion - Buddhist, Religion - Catholic, Self-Help, Social Sciences, Sociology, Theology, Travel & Tourism
ISBN Prefix(es): 978-961-6271
Showroom(s): Dunajska 23, SI-1000 Ljubljana
Bookshop(s): Dunajska 23, SI-1000 Ljubljana
Book Club(s): MOLJ
Orders to: Dunajska 23, SI-1000 Ljubljana

Didakta doo
Gorenjska cesta 33c, SI-4240 Radovljica
Tel: (04) 53 20 200; (041) 308 300 *Fax:* (04) 53 20 211
E-mail: zalozba@didakta.si
Web Site: www.didakta.si
Founded: 1989
Subjects: Economics, Fiction, Medicine, Nursing, Dentistry, Nonfiction (General), Technology, Travel & Tourism, Information Technology, Pedagogy
ISBN Prefix(es): 978-86-7707; 978-86-7749; 978-961-6214; 978-961-6363

Zalozba Goga
Glavni trg 6, SI-8000 Novo Mesto
Tel: (07) 393 08 01 *Fax:* (07) 393 08 00
E-mail: goga@goga.si
Web Site: www.goga.si
Key Personnel
Dir: Mitja Licen *E-mail:* mitja.licen@goga.si
Editor: Jelka Ciglenecki *Tel:* (07) 393 08 10
   E-mail: jelka.ciglenecki@goga.si
Marketing Manager: Nastja Mohorko
   E-mail: nastja.mohorko@goga.si
Founded: 1998
Subjects: Fiction, Music, Dance, Nonfiction (General)
ISBN Prefix(es): 978-961-6421; 978-961-90796

Zalozba Krtina
Hrenova 13, SI-1000 Ljubljana
Tel: (01) 251 5585 *Fax:* (01) 620 8713
E-mail: urednistvo@zalozbakrtina.si
Web Site: www.zalozbakrtina.si
Subjects: Art, Economics, Education, Government, Political Science, Language Arts, Linguistics, Religion - Other, Social Sciences, Sociology, Humanities, Nature
ISBN Prefix(es): 978-961-260; 978-961-6174

Zalozba Litera
Miklosiceva ul 4, SI-2000 Maribor
Tel: (02) 250 10 39 *Fax:* (02) 620 87 42
E-mail: info@knjigarna-litera.org

Web Site: www.zalozba-litera.org
Key Personnel
Dir & Chief Editor: Orlando Ursic *E-mail:* ursic.litera@gmail.com
Dir: Jana Skaza *E-mail:* jana.skaza@zalozba-litera.org
Founded: 2001
Subjects: Fiction, History, Literature, Literary Criticism, Essays, Nonfiction (General), Science (General), Ancient World, Humanities, Prose, Slovenia, Slovenian Poets & Writers
ISBN Prefix(es): 978-961-6604

Literarno-umetnisko drustvo Literatura
Erjavceva 4, SI-1000 Ljubljana
Tel: (01) 251 43 69 *Fax:* (01) 426 97 60
E-mail: ludliteratura@yahoo.com
Web Site: www.ludliteratura.si
Key Personnel
Editor: Andrej Hocevar *E-mail:* andrej.hocevar@ludliteratura.si
Assistant to the Editor: Urban Vovk
   E-mail: urban.vovk@ludliteratura.si
Subjects: Drama, Theater, Fiction, Literature, Literary Criticism, Essays, Nonfiction (General), Poetry
ISBN Prefix(es): 978-961-6717; 978-961-6098

LUD Literatura, see Literarno-umetnisko drustvo Literatura

Zalozba Mis
Gorjusa 33, SI-1233 Dob pri Domzalah
Tel: (01) 721 45 40 *Fax:* (01) 729 31 65
E-mail: info@zalozbamis.com
Web Site: www.zalozbamis.com
Key Personnel
Publisher: Janez Mis
Founded: 2003
Subjects: Fiction, Nonfiction (General), Poetry
ISBN Prefix(es): 978-961-6630
Number of titles published annually: 30 Print

Mladika Zaloznisko Podjetje
Vojkova Cesta 48, SI-1000 Ljubljana
Tel: (01) 420 52 10 *Fax:* (01) 420 51 16
E-mail: knjigarna@zalozbamladika.si
Web Site: www.zalozbamladika.si
Key Personnel
Dir: Primoz Music *E-mail:* primoz.music@zalozbamladika.si
Editor-in-Chief: Barbara Music *E-mail:* barbara.music@zalozbamladika.si
Founded: 1990
Subjects: Art, Fiction, History
ISBN Prefix(es): 978-86-7063; 978-961-205

Mladinska knjiga Zalozba dd+
Slovenska cesta 29, SI-1000 Ljubljana
Tel: (01) 241 30 00; (01) 588 74 80 (orders); (01) 241 32 89 (rights) *Fax:* (01) 425 28 66; (01) 425 22 94 (rights)
E-mail: info@mladinska.com; intsales@mkz-lj.si (international rights & trade); emka@emka.si (orders)
Web Site: www.mladinska.com
Key Personnel
Chairman: Peter Tomsic
Member of the Board: Marco Rucigaj
Office of the Board: Nadja Pipan *E-mail:* nadja.pipan@mkz.si
Founded: 1945
Subjects: Art, Astrology, Occult, Biblical Studies, Biography, Memoirs, Biological Sciences, Chemistry, Chemical Engineering, Child Care & Development, Cookery, Crafts, Games, Hobbies, Drama, Theater, Education, Fiction, Gardening, Plants, Health, Nutrition, History, House & Home, How-to, Language Arts, Linguistics, Literature, Literary Criticism, Essays, Mathematics, Military Science, Mysteries, Suspense, Nonfiction (General), Physics, Poetry, Psychology, Psychiatry, Regional Interests,

Romance, Science (General), Science Fiction, Fantasy, Self-Help, Travel & Tourism, Women's Studies
ISBN Prefix(es): 978-86-11
Number of titles published annually: 400 Print
Total Titles: 3,474 Print
Parent Company: Mladinska Knjiga Group
Foreign Rep(s): The Clark Agency Ltd; Verlags Agentur Prahl (Germany)

Moderna galerija Ljubljana (Museum of Modern Art)+
Tomsiceva 14, SI-1000 Ljubljana
Tel: (01) 2416800; (01) 2416834 *Fax:* (01) 2514120
E-mail: info@mg-lj.si
Web Site: www.mg-lj.si
Key Personnel
Dir: Ms Zdenka Badovinac *E-mail:* zdenka. badovinac@mg-lj.si
Administration: Ana Zan *E-mail:* ana.zan@mg-lj. si
Curator: Marko Jenko
Founded: 1948
Subjects: Art, Photography, Drawing, Graphics, Media Art, Painting, Sculpture, Video
ISBN Prefix(es): 978-961-206
Total Titles: 5 Print

Modrijan Zalozba doo
Poljanska cesta 15, SI-1000 Ljubljana
Tel: (01) 236 46 00 *Fax:* (01) 236 46 01
E-mail: modrijan@modrijan.si; urednistvo@ modrijan.si
Web Site: www.modrijan.si
Key Personnel
Dir: Branimir Nesovic
Editor-in-Chief: Bronislava Aubelj
Foreign Rights: Metod Bocko *Tel:* (01) 236 46 09 *E-mail:* metod.bocko@modrijan.si
Sales & Marketing: Ales Glad *Tel:* (01) 0236 46 17
Founded: 1996
Subjects: Art, Biological Sciences, Chemistry, Chemical Engineering, Environmental Studies, Fiction, Geography, Geology, History, Language Arts, Linguistics, Literature, Literary Criticism, Essays, Mathematics, Nonfiction (General), Physics, Science (General), Technology, Slovenian Language
ISBN Prefix(es): 978-961-241; 978-961-6183; 978-961-6357; 978-961-6465

Nova Revija Zalozba
Cankarjeva cesta 10 B, SI-1000 Ljubljana
Tel: (01) 24 44 560 *Fax:* (01) 24 44 586
E-mail: info@nova-revija.si
Web Site: www.nova-revija.si
Key Personnel
Dir: Tomaz Zalaznik
Founded: 1990
Subjects: Art, Biography, Memoirs, History, Law, Literature, Literary Criticism, Essays, Music, Dance, Philosophy, Social Sciences, Sociology, History of Art, Mythology, Politics, Religious Studies
ISBN Prefix(es): 978-961-6017; 978-961-6352

Zalozba Obzorja dd+
Partizanska cesta 5, SI-2000 Maribor
Tel: (02) 23 48 102 *Fax:* (02) 23 48 135
E-mail: info@zalozba-obzorja.si; narocila@ zalozba-obzorja.si (orders)
Web Site: www.zalozba-obzorja.si
Key Personnel
Dir: Nevenka Richter Pece
Founded: 1950
Subjects: Animals, Pets, Anthropology, Biography, Memoirs, Biological Sciences, Business, Chemistry, Chemical Engineering, Child Care & Development, Cookery, Crafts, Games, Hobbies, Criminology, Drama, Theater, Earth Sci-

ences, Economics, Education, English as a Second Language, Environmental Studies, Fiction, Gardening, Plants, Health, Nutrition, History, Journalism, Language Arts, Linguistics, Law, LGBTQ, Literature, Literary Criticism, Essays, Management, Marketing, Mathematics, Medicine, Nursing, Dentistry, Music, Dance, Nonfiction (General), Philosophy, Photography, Physics, Poetry, Psychology, Psychiatry, Regional Interests, Religion - Other, Science (General), Self-Help, Social Sciences, Sociology, Travel & Tourism
ISBN Prefix(es): 978-86-377; 978-961-230
Divisions: Zalozba Obzorja po Maribor
Bookshop(s): Zalozba Obzorja-Knjigarna, Gosposka 24 SLO, SI-2000 Maribor
Warehouse: Mlinska 22, SI-2000 Maribor
E-mail: skladisce.zom@siol.net

Zalozba Rokus Klett doo
Member of Klett Gruppe
Stegne 9b, SI-1000 Ljubljana
Tel: (01) 513 46 00; (01) 513 46 46 (orders) *Fax:* (01) 513 46 79
E-mail: rokus@rokus-klett.si; narocila@rokus-klett.si (orders)
Web Site: www.rokus.com
Key Personnel
Mng Dir: Marusa Kmet
Financial Dir: Adrijana Japelj *Tel:* (01) 513 46 81 *Fax:* (01) 513 46 89 *E-mail:* adrijana.japelj@ rokus-klett.si
Production Dir: Klemen Fedran *Tel:* (01) 513 46 21 *Fax:* (01) 513 46 99 *E-mail:* klemen. fedran@rokus-klett.si
Head, Marketing: Wojtek Grudzinski *Tel:* (01) 513 46 41 *E-mail:* wojtek.grudzinski@rokus-klett.si
Head, Sales: Matija Karlovsek *Tel:* (01) 513 46 71 *E-mail:* matic.karlovsek@rokus-klett.si
Head, Warehousing: Tomaz Vagaja *Tel:* (01) 513 46 90 *E-mail:* tomaz.vagaja@rokus-klett.si
Editorial Project Coordinator: Jelka Miranda Razpotnik *Tel:* (01) 513 46 94 *E-mail:* jelka. razpotnik@rokus-klett.si
Founded: 1991
Subjects: English as a Second Language, Literature, Literary Criticism, Essays, Mathematics
ISBN Prefix(es): 978-961-209
Subsidiaries: Izdavacka Kuca Klett doo (Belgrade); Klett Verlag doo (Zagreb, Croatia)

Zalozba Sanje doo (Dreams Publishing Ltd)
Leskoskova 12, SI-1000 Ljubljana
Tel: (01) 51-41-628; (01) 51-41-629
E-mail: info@sanje.si
Web Site: www.sanje.si
Key Personnel
Dir: Rok Zavrtanik *E-mail:* rok.zavrtanik@sanje. si
Editor-in-Chief: Tjasa Koprivec *E-mail:* tjasa. koprivec@sanje.si
International Book Sales: Matjaz Juricak *E-mail:* sales@sanje.si
Subjects: Criminology, Erotica, Fiction, Nonfiction (General), Sports, Athletics, Crime, Short Story
ISBN Prefix(es): 978-961-6387; 978-961-90573; 978-961-274
Bookshop(s): Trubarjeva 29, SI-1000 Ljubljana *Tel:* (01) 230-14-26 *E-mail:* knjigarna. tavcarjeva@sanje.si

Slovenska matica
Kongresni trg 8, SI-1000 Ljubljana
Tel: (01) 422 43 40 *Fax:* (01) 422 43 44
E-mail: slovenskamatica@siol.net
Web Site: www.slovenska-matica.si
Key Personnel
President: Dr Milcek Komelj *Tel:* (01) 422 43 45

Editor-in-Chief & Secretary: Drago Jancar *Tel:* (01) 422 43 42 *E-mail:* drago.jancar@siol. net
Chief Editor: Katja Kleindienst *Tel:* (01) 422 43 45 *E-mail:* katja.kleindienst@siol.net
Sales Manager: Mateja Rizvic *Fax:* (01) 422 43 44
Founded: 1864
Subjects: Literature, Literary Criticism, Essays, Philosophy, Science (General), Technology
ISBN Prefix(es): 978-86-80933; 978-961-213

Zalozba Sophia
Slomskova ul 6, SI-1000 Ljubljana
Tel: (01) 434 49 35
E-mail: info@zalozba-sophia.si
Web Site: www.zalozba-sophia.si
Key Personnel
Publishing Dir: Tanja Velagic *E-mail:* tanja. velagic@zalozba-sophia.si
Editor: Uros Zorman *E-mail:* uros.zorman@ zalozba-sophia.si
Subjects: Art, Communications, Economics, Education, Government, Political Science, History, Literature, Literary Criticism, Essays, Philosophy, Psychology, Psychiatry, Religion - Other, Social Sciences, Sociology
ISBN Prefix(es): 978-961-6768

Studia HumanitatiS
Knafljev prehod 11, SI-1000 Ljubljana
Tel: (01) 4250-475 *Fax:* (01) 4251-846
E-mail: studia.humanitatis@guest.arnes.si
Web Site: www.studia-humanitatis.si
Key Personnel
Editor-in-Chief: Neda Pagon
Editor: Jernej Habjan; Janez Justin
Founded: 1985
Subjects: Behavioral Sciences, Regional Interests
ISBN Prefix(es): 978-961-6262

Tehniska Zalozba Slovenije+
Lepi pot 6, SI-1000 Ljubljana
Tel: (01) 47-902-11 *Fax:* (01) 47-902-30
E-mail: info@tzs.si
Web Site: www.tzs.si
Key Personnel
President: Blaz De Costa *Tel:* (01) 47-902-12 *E-mail:* blaz.decosta@tzs.si
Head, Marketing: Bernarda Zuzek *Tel:* (01) 47-902-28 *E-mail:* bernarda.zuzek@tzs.si
Founded: 1948
Subjects: Cookery, Education, Health, Nutrition, Nonfiction (General), Leisure
ISBN Prefix(es): 978-961-251
Number of titles published annually: 100 Print

TZS, see Tehniska Zalozba Slovenije

Univerza v Ljubljani Ekonomska Fakulteta (University of Ljubljana Faculty of Ecomonics)+
Kardeljeva ploscad 17, SI-1000 Ljubljana
Tel: (01) 5892-400 *Fax:* (01) 5892-698
E-mail: info@ef.uni-lj.si
Web Site: www.ef.uni-lj.si
Key Personnel
Dean: Dusan Mramor, PhD *Tel:* (01) 5892-403 *E-mail:* dusan.mramor@ef.uni-lj.si
Coordinator: Dr Irena Ograjensek *Tel:* (01) 5892-505 *E-mail:* irena.ograjensek@ef.uni-lj.si
Founded: 1946
Subjects: Accounting, Advertising, Business, Economics, Finance, Government, Political Science, Language Arts, Linguistics, Law, Management, Marketing, Mathematics, Securities
ISBN Prefix(es): 978-86-398; 978-961-6081; 978-961-6273; 978-961-6343; 978-961-6430; 978-961-240; 978-86-389

Uradni list Republike Slovenije doo
Dunajska cesta 167, SI-1000 Ljubljana
Tel: (01) 425-14-19; (01) 200 18 21 *Fax:* (01)
425-01-99
E-mail: info@uradni-list.si; prodaja@uradni-list.si
(orders)
Web Site: www.uradni-list.si
Key Personnel
Dir: Spela Munih Stanic
Consultant Dir: Irene Nebec
Marketing & Sales: Mojca Samotorcan
Founded: 1946
Subjects: Law, Legislation
ISBN Prefix(es): 978-86-7085; 978-961-204

Zalozba ZRC+
Unit of Scientific Research Centre of the Slove-
nian Academy of Sciences & Arts
Gosposka ul 13/2nd floor, SI-1001 Ljubljana
Mailing Address: PO Box 306, SI-1001 Ljubljana
Tel: (01) 470 64 74 *Fax:* (01) 425 77 94
E-mail: zalozba@zrc-sazu.si; narocanje@zrc-sazu.
si
Web Site: zalozba.zrc-sazu.si; www.zrc-sazu.si
Key Personnel
Dir: Oto Luther
Mng Editor: Ales Pogacnik *Tel:* (01) 470 64 77
E-mail: ales.pogacnik@zrc-sazu.si
Assistant Editor: Barbara Sustar *E-mail:* sustar@
zrc-sazu.si
Founded: 1994
Subjects: Anthropology, Archaeology, Art, Bio-
logical Sciences, Geography, Geology, History,
Language Arts, Linguistics, Literature, Liter-
ary Criticism, Essays, Philosophy, Humanities,
Natural Sciences
ISBN Prefix(es): 978-961-6182; 978-961-6358;
978-961-6500; 978-961-6568; 978-961-254
Number of titles published annually: 70 Print; 1
CD-ROM; 2 Audio
Total Titles: 300 Print; 2 CD-ROM; 12 Audio
Bookshop(s): Azil Bookstore
Book Club(s): Bookclub of ZRC Publishing -
Azil

South Africa

General Information

Capital: Pretoria
Language: Afrikaans and English (both official),
11 other official languages exist
Religion: Predominantly Christian. Politically
most important is the Dutch Reformed Church
(about 30% of the white population). Also
many Methodist, Anglican and African Independent Churches among African Christians
Population: 41.25 million
Bank Hours: 0900-1530 Monday-Friday
Shop Hours: Vary province to province. Often
0900-1700 Monday-Friday
Export/Import Information: Printed books,
brochures, leaflets and similar matter (tariff
heading 49.01) are free of duty and surcharge
with the exception of directories, guide books,
yearbooks, Christmas annuals and handbooks
relating to South Africa which attract duty at
a rate of 20% or 11c/Kg. No objectionable or
undesirable literature permitted. No import permit required. Trade advertising matter, commercial catalogues and the like (tariff heading 4911.10.10 to 4911.10.30) are free of duty
(otherwise 25% and 20% duty respectively).
5% surcharge is payable in all instances. 14%
VAT on books. No import permit is required.

AA The Motorist Publications, *imprint of*
Reader's Digest South Africa

Acacia Books, *imprint of* Via Afrika

Afritech, *imprint of* Via Afrika

Afro, *imprint of* Via Afrika

Anansi Publishers/Uitgewers+
25 Church St, Durbanville 7550
Tel: (021) 976 8411 *Fax:* (021) 976 9698
E-mail: info@anansibooks.co.za
Web Site: www.anansibooks.co.za
Key Personnel
Mng Dir, Editorial: Dr Lydia Snyman
Mng Dir, Financial: Andre Conradie
Administration & Sales: Mariaan Conradie
Founded: 1989
ISBN Prefix(es): 978-1-86843; 978-0-947454;
978-1-874885

Atlas, *imprint of* Via Afrika

Jonathan Ball Publishers
10-14 Watkins St, Denver, Ext 4, Johannesburg
2094
Mailing Address: PO Box 6836, Roggebaai 8012
Tel: (011) 601 8000 *Fax:* (011) 601 8183
Web Site: www.jonathanball.co.za
Key Personnel
Mng Dir: Jonathan Ball *E-mail:* jball@
jonathanball.co.za
Publishing Dir: Jeremy Boraine
E-mail: jboraine@jbp.co.za
Sales Dir: Eugene Ashton *E-mail:* eashton@
jonathanball.co.za
Founded: 1977
Subjects: Biography, Memoirs, Cookery, Fiction,
Government, Political Science, History, Sports,
Athletics
ISBN Prefix(es): 978-1-86842; 978-1-874959;
978-0-86850; 978-0-947464; 978-0-9583751
Parent Company: Media 24 Ltd
Imprints: Delta Books; Ad Donker Publications
Branch Office(s)
Off C4, The District, 41 Sir Lowry Rd, Wood-
stock 7925, Contact: Sophy Kohler *Tel:* (021)
469-8900
KwaZulu-Natal, Sales Manager: Andrew Smith
Tel: (031) 465 4914

Bateleur, *imprint of* Via Afrika

Best Books, *imprint of* NB Publishers

Best Red, *imprint of* Human Sciences Research
Council Press

Bible Society of South Africa
134 Edward St, Bellville 7530
Mailing Address: PO Box 5500, Tyger Valley
7536
Tel: (021) 910-8777 *Fax:* (021) 910-8799
E-mail: biblia@biblesociety.co.za
Web Site: www.biblesociety.co.za; www.
bybelgenootskap.co.za
Key Personnel
Chief Executive Officer: Rev Dirk Gevers
Founded: 1820 (as auxiliary of British & Foreign
Bible Society, 1965 as autonomous body)
The Society translates, publishes & distributes
Bibles in all the languages spoken in South
Africa.
Subjects: Publishing & Book Trade Reference,
Religion - Catholic, Religion - Protestant
ISBN Prefix(es): 978-0-7982
Imprints: Bybelgenootskap
Branch Office(s)
Bible House, 134 Edward St, Bellville 7530,
Regional Head, Western Cape: Dr Quintus
Heine *Tel:* (021) 910-8777 *Fax:* (021) 910-
8771 *E-mail:* bibcpt@biblesociety.co.za

Bible House, 220 Nelson Mandela Dr, Bloemfontein 9324, Regional Head, Free State: Rev
Gerrie van Dyk *Tel:* (051) 444-5980 *Fax:* (051)
444-4988 *E-mail:* bibbfn@biblesociety.co.za
Bible House, 70-76 Ramsay Ave, Mayville,
Durban 4058, Regional Head, KwaZulu-
Natal: Rev Clive van Rooyen *Tel:* (031) 207-
4933 *Fax:* (031) 207-1058 *E-mail:* bibdbn@
biblesociety.co.za
Bible House, 8 Annemoon Rd, Glen Marais Ext
1, Kempton Park, Gauteng 1619, Contact: Rev
Shane Fraser *Tel:* (011) 970-4010 *Fax:* (011)
970-2506 *E-mail:* bibjhg@biblesociety.co.za
Bible House, 49 Madeira St, PO Box 265,
Mthatha 5099, Regional Head, Transkei:
Mveleli Saliwa *Tel:* (047) 532 6402 *Fax:* (047)
532 5719 *E-mail:* bibumt@biblesociety.co.za
Bible House, 31 Cotswold Ave, Cotswold, Port
Elizabeth 6045, Regional Head, Eastern Cape:
Rev Ben Fourie *Tel:* (041) 364-1138 *Fax:* (041)
365-2634 *E-mail:* bibpe@biblesociety.co.za

The Brenthurst Press (Pty) Ltd
Brenthurst Estate, Federation Rd, Parktown, Jo-
hannesburg
Mailing Address: PO Box 87184, Houghton, Jo-
hannesburg 2041
Tel: (011) 544-5400 *Fax:* (011) 486-1651
E-mail: info@brenthurst.org.za; orders@
brenthurst.co.az
Web Site: www.brenthurst.org.za
Key Personnel
Dir: Sally MacRoberts
Founded: 1974
Subjects: Art, History, Natural History, Regional
Interests
ISBN Prefix(es): 978-0-909079

Briza Academic Books, *imprint of* Briza
Publications

Briza Publications
121 Soutpansberg Rd, Riviera, Pretoria 0084
Mailing Address: PO Box 11050, Queenswood,
Pretoria 0121
Tel: (012) 329-3896 *Fax:* (012) 329-4525
E-mail: books@briza.co.za
Web Site: www.briza.co.za
Founded: 1990
Subjects: Animals, Pets, Gardening, Plants, Natu-
ral History, Travel & Tourism, Ecology, South
African Grasses
ISBN Prefix(es): 978-1-875093
Imprints: Briza Academic Books; Marula Books
Distribution Center: Namibia Book Market, Con-
tact: Angela Hofmeyer *Tel:* (061) 236 938
E-mail: orders@namibiabooks.com

Butterfly Books, *imprint of* Shuter & Shooter
Publishers (Pty) Ltd

Bybelgenootskap, *imprint of* Bible Society of
South Africa

Bybelkor, *imprint of* Lux Verbi

Killie Campbell Africana Library, *imprint of*
University of KwaZulu-Natal Press

CCR, see The Centre for Conflict Resolution

The Centre for Conflict Resolution
Coornhoop, 2 Dixon Rd, Observatory, Cape Town
7925
Mailing Address: PO Box 14047, Mowbray 7705
Tel: (021) 689 1005 *Fax:* (021) 689 1003
E-mail: mailbox@ccr.uct.ac.za
Web Site: www.ccr.org.za
Key Personnel
Senior Project Officer, Fundraising & Communi-

cations: Rosaline Daniel *E-mail:* rdaniel@ccr.
org.za
Founded: 1968
Specialize in conflict management.
Subjects: Human Relations, Social Sciences, Sociology
ISBN Prefix(es): 978-0-7992
Number of titles published annually: 10 Print
Total Titles: 24 Print

Centre for the Book
Unit of National Library of South Africa
62 Queen Victoria St, Cape Town
Mailing Address: PO Box 15254, Vlaeberg 8018
Tel: (021) 423 2669 *Fax:* (021) 424 1484
E-mail: cbreception@nlsa.ac.za
Web Site: www.nlsa.ac.za
Key Personnel
Executive Head: Mandlakayise Matyumza
  E-mail: mandla.matyumza@nlsa.ac.za
Deputy Program Manager: Anita Shaw
  E-mail: anita.shaw@nlsa.ac.za
Subjects: Fiction, How-to, Publishing & Book
  Trade Reference, Self-Help
Number of titles published annually: 15 Print; 10
  Online
Total Titles: 15 Print; 10 Online
Orders to: Blue Weaver Marketing, PO
  Box 30370, Tokai, Cape Town 7966
  E-mail: orders@blueweaver.co.za

Chart Studio Publishing Pty Ltd
Imprint of Chart Studio (Pty) Ltd
396 Lansdowne Rd, Landsdowne, Cape Town
7780
Mailing Address: PO Box 46870, Glosderry 7702
Tel: (021) 697 3669 *Fax:* (021) 697 0968
E-mail: educatorders@mgh.co.za; sales@mgh.co.
za
Web Site: www.chartstudio.com; www.educat.co.
za (orders)
Key Personnel
Chief Executive Officer: Keith C Blair
Export Dir: Kally Benitto *E-mail:* kally@mgh.co.
za
Sales, South Africa Management: Ricardo Stanley
Children's publishing company that produces
  novelty-based & educational products for a
  global children's market.
Subjects: Biblical Studies, Education, Mathematics, Science (General), Bible Stories
ISBN Prefix(es): 978-1-86902; 978-1-86913; 978-
  1-919735; 978-1-919745; 978-1-4151; 978-1-
  919736; 978-1-919744
Number of titles published annually: 11 CD-ROM
Total Titles: 12 Audio
Distributed by Advance Marketing Services
  (AMS)

Christian Art Publishers (Christelike
  Uitgewersmaatskappy)
Smutslaan 20, Vereeniging 1939
Mailing Address: PO Box 1599, Vereeniging
  1930
Tel: (016) 440 7000 *Fax:* (016) 421 1748
Web Site: www.cumuitgewers.co.za
Founded: 1939
Subjects: Law, Religion - Other
ISBN Prefix(es): 978-0-86984; 978-1-86829; 978-
  1-86832
Bookshop(s): CUM Books

Clever Books+
Melrose Arch Piazza, 2nd floor, 34 Whiteley Rd,
  Johannesburg 2116
Mailing Address: Private Bag X19, Northlands
  2116
Tel: (011) 731 3300 *Fax:* (011) 731 3535
E-mail: customerservices@macmillan.co.za
Web Site: www.macmillan.co.za
Key Personnel
Joint Group Mng Dir: Mandla Balisa *Tel:* (011)

731 3357 *E-mail:* balisam@macmillan.
co.za; John Keddle *Tel:* (011) 731 3338
E-mail: keddle@macmillan.co.za
Sales & Marketing Dir: Terence Ball *Tel:* (011)
  731 3364
Founded: 1981
Specialize in educational & language teaching
  books.
Membership(s): Publishers' Association of South
  Africa (PASA); Southern African Book Dealers
  Association (SABDA).
Subjects: Biological Sciences, Education, English
  as a Second Language, Language Arts, Linguistics, Mathematics, Physical Sciences, Science (General)
ISBN Prefix(es): 978-0-947056; 978-1-86897
Total Titles: 1,200 Print; 12 CD-ROM
Parent Company: Macmillan Education South
  Africa

Delta Books, *imprint of* Jonathan Ball Publishers

Delta Books (Pty) Ltd+
Imprint of Jonathan Ball Publishers
PO Box 33977, Jeppestown 2043
Tel: (011) 601 8000; (011) 601 8088 (customer
  services) *Fax:* (011) 622 3553; (011) 601 8183
  (customer services)
E-mail: services@jonathanball.co.za; orders@
  jonathanball.co.za; jonathanballreturns@
  jonathanball.co.za (returns)
Web Site: www.jonathanball.co.za; jonathanball.
  bookslive.co.za
Key Personnel
Publisher: Ingeborg Pelser
Publishing Dir: Jeremy Boraine
Sales Dir: Eugene Ashton *E-mail:* eashton@
  jonathanball.co.za
Sales & Marketing: Nicky Stubbs *Tel:* (021) 469
  8900 *E-mail:* nicky.stubbs@bookpro.co.za
Founded: 1976
Subjects: Government, Political Science, History,
  Nonfiction (General), Current Affairs, General
  South African
ISBN Prefix(es): 978-0-908387
Associate Companies: Ad Donker (Pty) Ltd
Warehouse: Jonathan Ball Publishers, 10-14
  Watkins St, Denver Ext 4, Johannesburg 2094

Ad Donker Publications, *imprint of* Jonathan
Ball Publishers

Ad Donker Publishers+
Imprint of Jonathan Ball Publishers
PO Box 33977, Jeppestown, Johannesburg 2043
Tel: (011) 601-8000 *Fax:* (011) 601-8183
E-mail: services@jonathanball.co.za; orders@
  jonathanball.co.za
Web Site: www.jonathanball.co.za; jonathanball.
  bookslive.co.za
Key Personnel
Mng Dir: Jonathan Ball
Publishing Dir: Jeremy Boraine
Sales Dir: Eugene Ashton
Services Dir: Keri Blackmore
Founded: 1976
Subjects: Nonfiction (General), General South
  African
ISBN Prefix(es): 978-0-86852; 978-0-949937
Associate Companies: Delta Books (Pty) Ltd
Warehouse: Jonathan Ball Publishers (Pty) Ltd,
  10-14 Watkins St, Denver Ext 4, Johannesburg
  2094

eKhaya, *imprint of* Random House Struik (Pty)
Ltd

Fanele, *imprint of* Jacana Media (Pty) Ltd

Fantasi Books (Pty) Ltd
65 Kremetart St, Val de Grace, Pretoria 0184

Mailing Address: PO Box 36881, Menlo Park,
  Pretoria 0102
Tel: (012) 804 2616 *Fax:* (012) 804 0480
E-mail: fantasi@ffg.net
Web Site: fantasi.co.za
Key Personnel
Contact: Frans Maree
ISBN Prefix(es): 978-1-919764; 978-1-919765
Imprints: Fantasidigi; Fundi Books

Fantasidigi, *imprint of* Fantasi Books (Pty) Ltd

Fernwood Press, *imprint of* Random House
Struik (Pty) Ltd

Fernwood Press CC+
3 Victory Close, Simonskloof, Simon's Town
  7975
Mailing Address: PO Box 481, Simon's Town
  7995
Tel: (021) 786 2460 *Fax:* (021) 786 2478
Key Personnel
Contact: Pam Struik; Pieter Struik
Founded: 1991
Subjects: Art, History, Natural History, Nonfiction (General), Regional Interests, Travel &
  Tourism, Wine & Spirits
ISBN Prefix(es): 978-1-874950; 978-0-9583154
Number of titles published annually: 5 Print
Distributed by Central Books Ltd (UK)
Distribution Center: Booksite Afrika, Tygerberg
  Business Park, 6 Koets St, Parow Industria
  7493 *Tel:* (021) 950 5900 *Fax:* (021) 950 5999

Fundi Books, *imprint of* Fantasi Books (Pty) Ltd

Gecko Poetry, *imprint of* University of
KwaZulu-Natal Press

Government Printer
149 Bosman St, Private Bag X85, Pretoria 0001
Tel: (012) 334-4500; (012) 334-4508; (012) 334-
  4509; (012) 334-4510 *Fax:* (012) 323-0009
E-mail: info@gpw.gov.za
Web Site: www.gpwonline.co.za
Key Personnel
Chief Executive Officer: Prof A D Mbewu
Founded: 1888
Subjects: Education, Geography, Geology
ISBN Prefix(es): 978-0-621
Branch Office(s)
Cape Town *Tel:* (021) 465-7531

Hadeda Books, *imprint of* University of
KwaZulu-Natal Press

**Heinemann Educational Publishers Southern
  Africa+**
Division of Pearson Education Group
Grayston Off Park, 128 Peter Rd, Bldg 5, Sandton 2146
Mailing Address: PO Box 781940, Sandton 2146
Tel: (011) 322 8600 *Fax:* (086) 687 7822
E-mail: customerliaison@heinemann.co.za
Web Site: www.heinemann.co.za
Key Personnel
Publishing Dir: Rebecca Pretorius
Mng Dir: Naett Atkinson
Sales Dir: Sweetie Mapukata
Customer Service Manager: Molly Veeran
Founded: 1986
Membership(s): Publishers' Association of South
  Africa (PASA).
Subjects: Economics, Education, English as a
  Second Language, Mathematics, Mechanical
  Engineering
ISBN Prefix(es): 978-1-86813; 978-0-908379;
  978-0-947034; 978-0-947472; 978-1-86853;
  978-1-874820; 978-1-874914; 978-0-7962; 978-
  1-874925

Branch Office(s)
Heinemann Educational Botswana (Publishers) (Pty) Ltd, Plot 20695, Unit 4, Magochanyama Rd, Western Bypass, PO Box 10103, Village Post Office, Gaborone, Botswana, Contact: Wynter Mmolotsi *Tel:* 397 2305 *Fax:* 397 1832 *E-mail:* allstaffbotswana@heinemann.co.za
Heinemann Lesotho, Christian Council Bldg, 2nd floor, 160 Constitute Rd, PO Box 1307, Maseru 100, Lesotho, Contact: Leomile Nthabane *Tel:* 22 32 2984 *Fax:* 22 323 913
Editions de l'Ocean Indien Ltd, Stanley, Rose Hill, Mauritius *Tel:* 464 6761 *Fax:* 464 3445
Knight Owl Publishers, Old Power Station Bldg, Shop 34, Corner of Nobel & Armstrong Sts, Windhoek 9000, Namibia *Tel:* (061) 220 352 *Fax:* (081) 283 3332 *E-mail:* cynthia.adams@ heinemann.co.za
Maiden Publishing House, Cheetah Rd, Showgrounds, PO Box 51276, Ridgeway, Lusaka, Zambia, Contact: Christine Kasonde *Tel:* (021) 1256571 *E-mail:* maiden@zamnet.zm
Warehouse: Mirabel Industrial Park, Unit 6, Corner of Maple & Mirabel Rds, Pomona, Kempton Park *Tel:* (082) 339 2012; (083) 322 3883

Hippogriff Press+
19 The Valley Rd, Westcliff, Gauteng, Johannesburg 2193
Mailing Address: PO Box 47191, Parklands, Johannesburg 2121
Tel: (011) 6464229 *Fax:* (011) 6464229
Founded: 1989
Membership(s): IPASA (Independent Publishers Association of South Africa).
Subjects: Fiction, Poetry
ISBN Prefix(es): 978-0-9583122

Homeros, *imprint of* Tafelberg Publishers Ltd

HSRC Press, see Human Sciences Research Council Press

HSRC Publishers, *imprint of* Human Sciences Research Council Press

Hugenote Uitgewers, *imprint of* Lux Verbi

Human & Rousseau (Pty) Ltd, *imprint of* NB Publishers

Human & Rousseau (Pty) Ltd+
Imprint of NB Publishers
Naspers, 12th floor, 40 Heerengracht, Roggebaai 8012
Mailing Address: PO Box 5050, Cape Town 8000
Tel: (021) 406 3033 *Fax:* (021) 406 3812
E-mail: nb@nb.co.za
Web Site: www.humanrousseau.com; www.nb.co.za
Key Personnel
General Manager: Kerneels Breytenbach
Founded: 1959
Subjects: Anthropology, Architecture & Interior Design, Art, Biography, Memoirs, Business, Child Care & Development, Communications, Cookery, Crafts, Games, Hobbies, Drama, Theater, Economics, Fiction, Gardening, Plants, History, House & Home, How-to, Language Arts, Linguistics, Literature, Literary Criticism, Essays, Management, Marketing, Music, Dance, Natural History, Nonfiction (General), Philosophy, Poetry, Religion - Protestant, Romance, Self-Help, Sports, Athletics
ISBN Prefix(es): 978-0-7981
Branch Office(s)
Johannesburg
Pretoria
Orders to: On the Dot, PO Box 487, Bellville 7535 *Tel:* (021) 918 8603 *Toll Free Tel:* 0800

220 224 *Fax:* (021) 951 4903; (021) 951 4633 *E-mail:* customerservices@onthedot.co.za *Web Site:* www.onthedot.co.za

Human Sciences Research Council, *imprint of* Human Sciences Research Council Press

Human Sciences Research Council Press+
Private Bag X9182, Cape Town 8000
Tel: (021) 466 8000 *Fax:* (021) 461 0836
E-mail: vjoshua@hsrc.ac.za
Web Site: www.hsrcpress.ac.za
Founded: 1965
Nonprofit publisher committed to the dissemination of high quality social science publications, in print & electronic form. The Press publishes the research output of the Human Sciences Research Council, as well as some externally authored works.
This publisher has indicated that 50% of their product line is author subsidized.
Subjects: Behavioral Sciences, Career Development, Criminology, Developing Countries, Education, Government, Political Science, Human Relations, Nonfiction (General), Philosophy, Psychology, Psychiatry, Regional Interests, Social Sciences, Sociology, Women's Studies, African Studies
ISBN Prefix(es): 978-0-7969; 978-0-86965; 978-1-928
Number of titles published annually: 40 Print; 50 Online; 50 E-Book
Total Titles: 275 Print; 300 Online; 300 E-Book
Parent Company: Human Sciences Research Council, Pleinpark Bldg, 16th floor, 69-83 Plein St, Cape Town 8001
Imprints: Best Red (nonfiction); HSRC Publishers; Human Sciences Research Council
Foreign Rep(s): BlueWeaver (Africa); Eurospan Group (Europe); Independent Publishers Group (IPG) (North America)

Ithemba! Publishing
58 Auckland Ave, Auckland Park 2092
Tel: (011) 726 6529
E-mail: firechildren@icon.co.za
Key Personnel
Dir: Bronwen Jones
Founded: 1994
Publisher of South African produced books only.
Membership(s): Publishers' Association of South Africa (PASA); South African Children's Book Forum (SACBF).
Subjects: Biography, Memoirs, Fiction, Regional Interests
ISBN Prefix(es): 978-0-9583900; 978-0-9584107; 978-0-9584412
Number of titles published annually: 1 Print
Total Titles: 12 Print
Distribution Center: Africa Book Centre, 266 Banbury Rd, Oxford OX2 7DL, United Kingdom

Jacana Media (Pty) Ltd+
10 Orange St, Sunnyside, Auckland Park, Johannesburg 2092
Mailing Address: PO Box 291784, Melville, Johannesburg 2109
Tel: (011) 628 3200 *Fax:* (011) 482 7280; (011) 482 7282 (sales)
E-mail: marketing@jacana.co.za; sales@jacana.co.za
Web Site: www.jacana.co.za
Founded: 1991
Independent publisher specializing in books, maps & guides, second language publications & contract publishing.
Subjects: Architecture & Interior Design, Art, Biography, Memoirs, Business, Child Care & Development, Cookery, Fiction, Government, Political Science, History, Humor, Inspirational, Spirituality, LGBTQ, Literature, Literary Crit-

icism, Essays, Medicine, Nursing, Dentistry, Natural History, Nonfiction (General), Poetry, Religion - Catholic, Religion - Islamic, Religion - Jewish, Religion - Other, Self-Help, Travel & Tourism, Women's Studies, Current Affairs, True Crime
ISBN Prefix(es): 978-1-874955; 978-1-919777; 978-1-919931; 978-1-77009
Imprints: Fanele
Branch Office(s)
1st floor, 33 Protea Rd, Claremont, Cape Town 7708 *Tel:* (021) 671 6852; (021) 671 1332 *Fax:* (021) 679 7954
Orders to: On the Dot *Tel:* (021) 918 8810 *Fax:* (021) 918 8815 *E-mail:* orders@onthedot.co.za

Janssen Publishers CC
PO Box 404, Simon's Town 7995
Fax: (021) 786 2468
E-mail: info@janssenbooks.co.za
Web Site: www.janssenbooks.co.za
Key Personnel
Founder: Volker Janssen
Founded: 1979
Specialize in photo & art books of the male nude & local photo books of South Africa.
Subjects: Architecture & Interior Design, Art, Erotica, LGBTQ, Photography, Landscape, Wildlife of South Africa
ISBN Prefix(es): 978-1-919901; 978-0-9584314
Number of titles published annually: 10 Print
Total Titles: 120 Print
Foreign Rep(s): Edition Habit Press Pty Ltd (Australia); Independent Publishers Group/Art Stock Books (USA); Kaktus Buecher & Comics (Switzerland); Turnaround Publisher Service Ltd (UK)
Distribution Center: Suedost Verlags Service GmbH, Am Steinfeld 4, 94065 Waldkirchen, Germany *Web Site:* www.suedost-verlags-service.de (retail only, Germany & worldwide exc Australia, Great Britain, South Africa, Switzerland & USA)

Jasmyn, *imprint of* Tafelberg Publishers Ltd

Johannesburg Art Gallery
Corner of Klein & King George St, Box 23561, Joubert Park, Johannesburg 2044
Tel: (011) 725-3130; (011) 725-3180 *Fax:* (011) 720-6000
E-mail: jag@joburg.org.za; friend@friendsofjag.org
Web Site: friendsofjag.org
Founded: 1910
Friends of JAG bookshop on site.
Membership(s): AAM; ICOM; SAMA.
Subjects: Art, Education, Photography
ISBN Prefix(es): 978-1-874836
Total Titles: 20 Print

Juta & Co (Pty) Ltd+
Sunclare Bldg, 1st floor, 21 Dreyer St, Claremont 7708
Mailing Address: PO Box 14373, Lansdowne 7779
Tel: (021) 659 2300; (087) 820 5882 (bookshop) *Fax:* (021) 659 2360 (customer service); (021) 659 2752 (bookshop)
E-mail: companysecretary@juta.co.za; orders@juta.co.za; cserv@juta.co.za
Web Site: www.juta.co.za
Founded: 1853
Publisher of academic & professional information.
Membership(s): PASA.
Subjects: Accounting, Art, Biography, Memoirs, Business, Communications, Education, Engineering (General), Environmental Studies, Fiction, Health, Nutrition, Human Relations, Humor, Labor, Industrial Relations, Law, Management, Marketing, Medicine, Nursing, Den-

tistry, Photography, Psychology, Psychiatry, Self-Help, Social Sciences, Sociology, Sports, Athletics, Technology, Travel & Tourism, Wine & Spirits
ISBN Prefix(es): 978-0-7021
Number of titles published annually: 500 Print; 5 CD-ROM; 5 Online
Total Titles: 55 CD-ROM; 46 Online
Divisions: Juta Academic (further education & training; higher education); Juta Law (legal & regulatory publications); UCT Press (scholarly publications)
Branch Office(s)
Clifton Pl, Off 101A, 1st floor, 19 Hurst Grove, Musgrave, Durban 4001 *Tel:* (031) 201 0671 *Fax:* (031) 201 0898
Norfolk House, Sandton Close 2, 3rd floor, c/o Fifth & Norwich Rd, Sandton 2196 *Tel:* (011) 217 7200 *Fax:* (011) 883 8169
Foreign Rep(s): Gaunt Inc (USA); William S Hein & Co Inc (USA); Helaine Distributors Inc (Canada); Law Africa Publishing Ltd (Africa); The Law Shop (Australia); Mkuki na Nyota Publishers (Africa); Wildy & Sons Ltd (UK)

Juta Law
Division of Juta & Co Ltd
Sunclare Bldg, 1st floor, 21 Dreyer St, Claremont 7708
Mailing Address: PO Box 24299, Lansdowne 7779
Tel: (021) 659 2300; (021) 670 6680 (bookshop) *Fax:* (021) 659 2360; (021) 670 6795 (bookshop)
E-mail: lawmarketing@juta.co.za; cserv@juta.co.za; claremontbooks@juta.co.za (bookshop)
Web Site: www.jutalaw.co.za
Key Personnel
Publisher: Marlene Chetty *Tel:* (021) 659 2313 *E-mail:* mchetty@juta.co.za
Product Marketing Coordinator: Paula Whitaker *Tel:* (021) 763 2440 *E-mail:* pwhitaker@juta.co.za
Subjects: Accounting, Business, Criminology, Human Relations, Labor, Industrial Relations, Law
Foreign Rights: Gaunt Inc (Florida); William S Hein & Co Inc (New York); Helaine Distributors Inc (Toronto); Law Africa Publishing Ltd (Kenya); The Law Shop (Australia); Mkuki na Nyota Publishers (Tanzania); Wildy & Sons Ltd (London, UK)
Bookshop(s): University of Johannesburg (RAU), Shop 21, Entrance 6, Student Centre, 1st floor, Academica Rd, Auckland Park 2092, Contact: Asham Singh *Tel:* (011) 482 3566; (011) 489 3463 *Fax:* (011) 482 3565 *E-mail:* ujbooks@juta.co.za; Unit 1 & 2 Parow Business Park, Jean Simonis St (Next to UNISA Parow), Cape Town 7500 *Tel:* (021) 911 2411 *Fax:* (021) 911 2415 *E-mail:* pabooks@juta.co.za; Level 3, Steve Biko Bldg, University of Cape Town, Chemistry Lane, Upper Campus, Cape Town 7700 *Tel:* (021) 650 2486 *Fax:* (021) 650 5771 *E-mail:* uctbooks@juta.co.za; Hatfield Plaza, 1st floor, 1122 Burnett St, Hatfield 0083 *Tel:* (012) 362 5799 *Fax:* (012) 362 5744 *E-mail:* ptabooks@juta.co.za; Shop 231, Lower Level, Carlton Centre, 111 Commissioner St, Johannesburg 2001 *Tel:* (011) 331 5140 *Fax:* (011) 331 5079 *E-mail:* jhbbooks@juta.co.za; Tshwane University of Technology, Pretoria West Campus, State Artillery Rd, Bldg 4, No G51, Pretoria West 0183 *Tel:* (012) 382 5918 *Fax:* (012) 382 5499 *E-mail:* tutbooks@juta.co.za; University of Stellenbosch, Shop 4, Stelmont, c/o Andringa & Beyers St, Stellenbosch 7600 *Tel:* (021) 882 9068 *Fax:* (021) 882 8903 *E-mail:* stelbooks@juta.co.za

Kagiso Education, *imprint of* Maskew Miller Longman

Kagiso Education
Imprint of Maskew Miller Longman
Corner of Logan Way & Forest Dr, Pinelands 7405
Mailing Address: PO Box 396, Cape Town 8000
Tel: (021) 532 6000; (021) 531 4049 (orders) *Fax:* (021) 531 0716
E-mail: customerservices@mml.co.za
Web Site: www.mml.co.za
Key Personnel
Head, Marketing: Camilla Costa *E-mail:* camilla.costa@pearson.com
Marketing Coordinator: Karen Morris *E-mail:* karen.morris@pearson.com
Founded: 1894 (as HAUM)
Subjects: Education, Literature, Literary Criticism, Essays, Religion - Other
ISBN Prefix(es): 978-0-7986
Ultimate Parent Company: Pearson Southern Africa (PSA)

Kima Global Publishers Ltd+
50 Clovelly Rd, Clovelly, Cape Town 7975
Mailing Address: PO Box 22404, Fish Hoek, Cape Town 7974
Tel: (021) 782 4463 *Fax:* (021) 782 4982
Web Site: www.kimabooks.com
Key Personnel
Founder & Mng Dir: Mr Robin Beck
Editorial Dir: Nadia van der Veen *Tel:* (021) 782 7451 *E-mail:* nadinemay@global.co.za
Founded: 1992
Specialize in body, mind & spirit books.
Membership(s): PMA.
Subjects: Alternative, Astrology, Occult, Behavioral Sciences, How-to, Human Relations, Psychology, Psychiatry, Religion - Other, Self-Help, Body, Mind, Spirit
ISBN Prefix(es): 978-0-9584
Number of titles published annually: 10 Print; 10 Online; 10 E-Book
Total Titles: 70 Print; 70 Online; 25 E-Book
Imprints: Perfect Planet (global issues); Power of Words (fiction)
Distributor for Expansions Publishing Co (USA); Floris Books (Scotland); Heartspace Books (Australia)
Foreign Rep(s): Heartspace Books (Australia)
Foreign Rights: Rightol (China)
Warehouse: Lightning Source AUS, Unit A1/A3 7, Janine St, Scoresby, Victoria 3179, Australia
Lightning Source, Chapter House, Pitfield, Kiln Farm, Milton Keynes, United Kingdom *Web Site:* www.lightningsource.com
Lightning Source, 1246, Heil Quaker Blvd, La Vergne, TN 37086, United States *Web Site:* www.lightningsource.com
Distribution Center: Ingram Content Group (USA)

Kwela Books, *imprint of* NB Publishers

KZN Books, *imprint of* Via Afrika

LAPA Uitgewers+
Bosmanstr 380, Pretoria 0002
Mailing Address: Posbus 123, Pretoria 0001
Tel: (012) 401 0700 *Fax:* (086) 720 1583
E-mail: lapa@lapa.co.za; bestellings@lapa.co.za
Web Site: www.lapa.co.za
Founded: 1943
Publisher & bookseller.
Subjects: Fiction, Law, Nonfiction (General), Philosophy, Religion - Other
ISBN Prefix(es): 978-0-7993; 978-0-86969
Number of titles published annually: 140 Print
Parent Company: ATKV, h/v Doverstraat en Surreylaan, Ferndale, Randburg 2125
Imprints: Symbol Books
Branch Office(s)
Winkel 1, Cascades 1, Tyger Waterfront, Carl

Cronjerylaan, Bellville 7530 *Tel:* (021) 914 0936; (021) 914 0481 *Fax:* (086) 603 6624
Book Club(s): Eike-Boekklub; Keurbiblioteek; President Boekklub; Romankeur; Symbol; Treffer-Boekklub

LexisNexis South Africa
215 North Ridge Rd, Morningside, Durban 4001
Tel: (031) 268 3111; (031) 268 3100; (0860) 765 432 (customer support); (031) 268 3007 (customer support); (031) 268 3284 (media)
E-mail: customercare@lexisnexis.co.za; media@lexisnexis.co.za
Web Site: www.lexisnexis.co.za
Key Personnel
Chief Executive Officer: William John Last
Chief Financial Officer: Paul Worsnip
Technology & Operations: Terrance Naidoo
Commercial Dir: Thabo Molefe
Founded: 1934
Subjects: Economics, Education, Law
ISBN Prefix(es): 978-0-409
Parent Company: LexisNexis (Dayton, Ohio, USA)
Ultimate Parent Company: RELX Group plc
Distributor for Butterworth-Heinemann

Lux Verbi, *imprint of* NB Publishers

Lux Verbi+
Imprint of NB Publishers
Naspers Centre, 12th floor, 40 Heerengracht, Cape Town 8001
Mailing Address: Posbus 551, Cape Town 8000
Tel: (021) 406 3033
E-mail: enquiries@nb.co.za
Web Site: www.luxverbi.co.za
Key Personnel
Mng Dir: Stephan Spies *Tel:* (021) 864 8210
Founded: 1956
Subjects: Religion - Other, Theology
ISBN Prefix(es): 978-0-86997; 978-0-7963
Imprints: Bybelkor; Hugenote Uitgewers; NG Kerk-Uitgewers; Protea-Uitgewers; Waterkant-Uitgewers

Marula Books, *imprint of* Briza Publications

Maskew Miller Longman+
Subsidiary of Pearson Southern Africa
Corner of Logan Way & Forest Dr, Pinelands 7405
Mailing Address: PO Box 396, Cape Town 8000
Tel: (021) 532 6000 *Fax:* (021) 531 0716; (021) 531 4049 (orders)
E-mail: customerservices@mml.co.za; orders@mml.co.za
Web Site: www.mml.co.za
Key Personnel
Chief Executive Officer: Fathima Dada
Marketing Dir: Ginny Felps
Founded: 1893
Educational publisher of textbooks & a variety of learning materials for primary & high schools in South Africa.
Subjects: Education, Language Arts, Linguistics, Literature, Literary Criticism, Essays
ISBN Prefix(es): 978-0-623; 978-0-636
Imprints: Kagiso Education; Phumelela
Subsidiaries: Longman Botswana Pty Ltd; Longman Kenya Ltd; Longman Lesotho Ltd; Longman Namibia Pty Ltd; Longman Zambia Ltd; Longman Zimbabwe Pvt Ltd
Branch Office(s)
Off 127, Bloem Plaza, 1st floor, Corner of Maitland & East Burger Sts, Bloemfontein 9301, Contact: Donald Bojang *Tel:* (051) 448 0424 *Fax:* (051) 430 4130 *E-mail:* Donald.Bojang@mml.co.za (Free State off)
Brackengate Business Park, 12 London Circle, Brackenfell 7560, Contact: Gaynor Higgs

Tel: (021) 980 9500 *Fax:* (021) 555 4071
E-mail: Gaynor.Higgs@pearson.com (Western
Cape & Northern Cape off)
Central Park, Block H, 400 16 Rd, Midrand
1685 *Tel:* (011) 347 0700 *Fax:* (011) 315 2343
(Gauteng publishing off)
Laeveldtrust, 20 Russel St, Nelspruit 1200, Con-
tact: Gertrude Ncongwane *Tel:* (013) 752
5936 *Fax:* (013) 752 5980 *E-mail:* Gertrude.
Ncongwane@pearson.com (Mpumalanga off)
Unit F102, Park Row Bldg, 4/10 School Rd,
Pinetown 3620, Contact: Mbali Mkhize
Tel: (031) 701 8813 *Fax:* (031) 702 9627
E-mail: Mbali.Mkhize@pearson.com
(KwaZulu-Natal off)
25 Bodenstein St, Polokwane 0699, Contact:
Ngaka Kekana *Tel:* (015) 295 9194 *Fax:* (015)
295 6012 *E-mail:* Ngaka.Kekana@pearson.com
(Limpopo off)
61 B Boom St, Rustenburg 0299, Contact:
Xoliswa Sebitlo *Tel:* (071) 602 0263 *Fax:* (018)
381 6029 *E-mail:* Xoliswa.Sebitlo@pearson.
com (Northwest off)
Grayston Office Park, Bldg 5, 128 Peter Rd,
Athol Ext, Sandton 2146, Contact: Rekina
Makanyane *Tel:* (011) 322 8600 *Fax:* (011) 322
8611 *E-mail:* Rekina.Makanyane@pearson.com
(Gauteng sales off)
4 Kings St, Southernwood 5200, Sales Assistant: Vuyokazi Nkamisa *Tel:* (043) 722
7989 *Fax:* (043) 742 5113 *E-mail:* Vuyokazi.
Nkamisa@mml.co.za (King William's Town
off)

Media House Publications (PTY) Ltd+
161 Ninth Rd, Johannesburg 2090
Mailing Address: PO Box 782395, Sandton 2146
Tel: (011) 882-6237 *Fax:* (011) 882-9652
Founded: 1983
Subjects: Humor, Nonfiction (General)
ISBN Prefix(es): 978-0-9583080

The Methodist Publishing House
Unit of The Methodist Church of Southern Africa
PO Box 13128, Woodstock 7915
Tel: (021) 4483640 *Fax:* (021) 4483716
E-mail: enquiries@methbooks.co.za; marketing@
ccrc.co.za
Web Site: www.methodist.org.za/work/publishing/
methodist-publishing-house
Key Personnel
General Manager: George G Vine
Marketing Manager: Rev Ken Leverton
Founded: 1894
Christian books & supplies.
Subjects: Religion - Protestant
ISBN Prefix(es): 978-0-949942; 978-0-947450;
978-1-919883
Total Titles: 30 Print
Distributor for Abingdon (South Africa); Concor-
dia (South Africa); Dayspring (South Africa);
Eagle (South Africa); Highland (South Africa);
Paraclete Press (South Africa); WCC (South
Africa); Westminster/John Knox (South Africa)
Bookshop(s): Christian Connexion Resource Cen-
tre, c/o Charles & Wes Burger, Shop C18,
Middestad Shopping Centre, Bloemfontein
9301, Contact: Velile Booi *Tel:* (051) 430 5589
Fax: (051) 430 5577 *E-mail:* bloem@ccrc.
co.za; Christian Connexion Resource Cen-
tre, Methodist Church, 115 Grosvenor Rd,
Bryanston 2191, Contact: Vicky van der Merwe
Tel: (011) 463 0942 *Fax:* (011) 463 0946
E-mail: vicky@methbooks.co.za; Christian
Connexion Resource Centre, Shop No 1, Union
Castle Bldg, 6 Hout St, Cape Town 8001,
Contact: Samantha Lawrence *Tel:* (021) 426
1110 *Fax:* (021) 426 0120 *E-mail:* ctown@
methbooks.co.za; Christian Connexion Re-
source Centre, 216 Anton Lembede St (formerly Smith St), Durban 4001, Contact: Jackie
Gregory *Tel:* (031) 332 8656 *Fax:* (031) 337
3922 *E-mail:* durban@methbooks.co.za; Chris-

tian Connexion Resource Centre, 24 Mal-
comess Park Shopping Centre, Gately St,
East London 5201, Contact: Nomsa Mququ
Tel: (043) 722 0708 *Fax:* (043) 722 0708
E-mail: el@ccrc.co.za; Christian Connexion
Resource Centre, Central Methodist Church,
Smal St, Johannesburg 2001, Contact: Elaine
Bala *Tel:* (011) 337 2600 *Fax:* (011) 336 0379
E-mail: jhb@methbooks.co.za; Christian Con-
nexion Resource Centre, Shop 12, Kimpark
Shopping Centre, Lennox St, Kimberley 8301,
Contact: Elizabeth Fairweather *Tel:* (053) 831
1638 *Fax:* (053) 831 2977 *E-mail:* kim@
methbooks.co.za; Christian Connexion Re-
source Centre, Shop 8A, City Centre Complex,
York Rd, Mthatha 5100, Manager: Nomawethu
Ntwanambi *Tel:* (047) 531 2212 *Fax:* (047)
534 2212 *E-mail:* mthatha@methbooks.co.za;
Christian Connexion Resource Centre, 164
Peter Kerschoff St, Pietermaritzburg 3201,
Contact: Ylonda May *Tel:* (033) 394 2222
Fax: (033) 345 0723 *E-mail:* pmb@methbooks.
co.za; Christian Connexion Resource Centre,
Shop 4, Park Towers, Rink St, Port Elizabeth
6001, Contact: Liz Wilmot *Tel:* (041) 582 1611
Fax: (041) 586 3437 *E-mail:* pe@ccrc.co.za;
Christian Connexion Resource Centre, Shop
5, Orion Bldg, 482 Myburgh St, Capital Park,
Pretoria 0084, Contact: Veronica Koekemoer
E-mail: pta@ccrc.co.za

Metz Press
One Cameronians Ave, Welgemoed 7535
Mailing Address: PO Box 7322, Welgemoed
7538
Tel: (021) 913 7557; (087) 802 5266 *Fax:* (021)
913 5102; (086) 575 5769
E-mail: info@metzpress.co.za
Web Site: www.metzpress.co.za
Key Personnel
Publisher: Wilsia Metz
Subjects: Crafts, Games, Hobbies, Gardening,
Plants, Life, Parenting
ISBN Prefix(es): 978-1-920268
Foreign Rights: Bridges Agency (Europe exc Por-
tugal & Spain, UK, USA); Illustrata (Portugal,
Spain)
Warehouse: On the Dot *Tel:* (021) 918 8584
Fax: (021) 918 88 15 *E-mail:* info@onthedot.
co.za *Web Site:* www.onthedot.co.za
Distribution Center: Blue Weaver Marketing &
Distribution *Tel:* (021) 701 4477 *Fax:* (021)
701 7302 *E-mail:* info@blueweaver.co.za *Web
Site:* www.blueweaver.co.za

Modjaji Books (Pty) Ltd
PO Box 385, Athlone, Cape Town 7760
Web Site: www.modjajibooks.co.za; www.modjaji.
bookslive.co.za
Key Personnel
Publisher: Colleen Higgs *Tel:* 27 72 7743546
(cell) *E-mail:* cdhiggs@gmail.com
Founded: 2007
Subjects: Fiction, Nonfiction (General), Poetry
ISBN Prefix(es): 978-1-920397
Orders to: On the Dot, PO Box 30370, Tokai
7966 *Tel:* (021) 7014477

Nasou Via Afrika Pty Ltd, see Via Afrika

National Inquiry Services Centre, see NISC

NB Publishers
Division of Media24 Books
Naspers Centre, 12th floor, 40 Heerengracht,
Cape Town 8001
Mailing Address: PO Box 879, Cape Town 8000
Tel: (021) 406 3033 *Fax:* (021) 406 3812
E-mail: nb@nb.co.za
Web Site: www.nb.co.za
Founded: 1950

Subjects: Biography, Memoirs, Business, Cook-
ery, Education, Fiction, History, Nonfiction
(General)
ISBN Prefix(es): 978-0-7981
Ultimate Parent Company: Naspers Ltd
Imprints: Best Books; Human & Rousseau (Pty)
Ltd; Kwela Books; Lux Verbi; Pharos; Queil-
lerie; Tafelberg Publishers Ltd
Book Club(s): Leserskring (Leisure Books)

New Africa Books (Pty) Ltd+
6 Spin St, Cape Town 8001
Mailing Address: PO Box 46962, Glosderry 7702
Tel: (021) 467 5860 *Fax:* (086) 500 2550 (orders)
E-mail: orders@newafricabooks.co.ca
Key Personnel
Mng Dir: Mr P Dadlana
Founded: 1971
Membership(s): Publishers' Association of South
Africa (PASA).
Subjects: Agriculture, Anthropology, Archaeol-
ogy, Architecture & Interior Design, Art, Biog-
raphy, Memoirs, Child Care & Development,
Cookery, Developing Countries, Drama, The-
ater, Economics, Education, English as a Sec-
ond Language, Environmental Studies, Fiction,
Government, Political Science, History, Humor,
Literature, Literary Criticism, Essays, Natu-
ral History, Nonfiction (General), Photography,
Poetry, Publishing & Book Trade Reference,
Regional Interests, Social Sciences, Sociology,
Sports, Athletics, Travel & Tourism, Women's
Studies
ISBN Prefix(es): 978-1-919876; 978-1-86928;
978-1-919888
Imprints: New Africa Education; David Philip;
Spearhead
Distributor for Africa World Press Inc; James
Currey; Christopher Hurst & Co (Publishers)
Ltd; Oneworld Publications; Ian Randle Publi-
cations; Zed Books
Distribution Center: Africa Book Centre, 38
King St, London WC2E 8JT, United Kingdom
Tel: (020) 7240 6649 *Fax:* (020) 7497 0309
International Publishers Marketing, 22841 Quick-
silver Dr, Dulles, VA 20166, United States
Tel: 703-661-1586 *Fax:* 703-661-1547 *Web
Site:* www.internationalpubmarket.com

New Africa Education, *imprint of* New Africa
Books (Pty) Ltd

New Spin, *imprint of* Shuter & Shooter
Publishers (Pty) Ltd

NG Kerk-Uitgewers, *imprint of* Lux Verbi

NISC
One Dundas St, Grahamstown 6140
Mailing Address: PO Box 377, Grahamstown
6140
Tel: (046) 622 9698 *Fax:* (046) 622 9550
E-mail: sales@nisc.co.za
Web Site: www.nisc.co.za
Key Personnel
Mng Dir: Margaret Crampton
Publishing Manager: Mike Schramm
Founded: 1995
Academic publishers of bibliographic databases,
scientific journals & books.
Subjects: Developing Countries, Earth Sciences,
Engineering (General), Environmental Studies,
Health, Nutrition, Language Arts, Linguistics,
LGBTQ, Mathematics, Regional Interests, Sci-
ence (General), Social Sciences, Sociology,
Technology, Women's Studies
Number of titles published annually: 10 Print
Total Titles: 13 Print; 38 CD-ROM; 49 Online
Associate Companies: NISC India; NISC USA

North-West University+
Hoffman St, Potchefstroom 2520

Mailing Address: Private Bag X6001, Potchef-
stroom 2520
Tel: (018) 299-1111; (018) 299-2222 *Fax:* (018)
299-2799
Web Site: www.nwu.ac.za
Key Personnel
Manager: Amanda van der Merwe
Founded: 1962
Subjects: Anthropology, Art, Biblical Studies, De-
veloping Countries, Education, Government,
Political Science, Religion - Protestant, Theol-
ogy, Women's Studies
ISBN Prefix(es): 978-0-86990; 978-1-86822

Oceanographic Research Institute (ORI)
Division of South African Association of Marine
Biological Research (SAAMBR)
PO Box 10712, Marine Parade, Durban 4056
Tel: (031) 3288222 *Fax:* (031) 3288188
E-mail: ori@saambr.org.za
Web Site: www.ori.org.za
Key Personnel
Dir: Dr Larry Oellermann
Deputy Dir: Prof Michael Schleyer
Founded: 1958
Library services, exchange of scientific publica-
tions.
Subjects: Biological Sciences, Environmental
Studies, Natural History, Science (General),
Coastal Management, Conservation, Fisheries,
Marine Biology, Pollution Studies
ISBN Prefix(es): 978-0-86989
Total Titles: 1 Print
Associate Companies: Sea World, Durban
Tel: (031) 3288222 *Fax:* (031) 3288188

Pearson Southern Africa
Phoenix House, 4 Glen Roy (off Forest Dr),
Pinelands 7405
Mailing Address: PO Box 396, Cape Town 8000
Tel: (021) 532 6009 *Toll Free Tel:* 0800 444 338
Fax: (021) 531 0716
E-mail: enquiries@pearsoned.co.za
Web Site: www.pearson.co.za
Key Personnel
Chief Executive Officer: Fathima Dada
Marketing Dir: Ginny Felps
Founded: 1994
Specialize in education.
Subjects: Education
ISBN Prefix(es): 978-1-86891
Subsidiaries: Maskew Miller Longman

Perfect Planet, *imprint of* Kima Global
Publishers Ltd

Pharos, *imprint of* NB Publishers

David Philip, *imprint of* New Africa Books (Pty)
Ltd

Phumelela, *imprint of* Maskew Miller Longman

Power of Words, *imprint of* Kima Global
Publishers Ltd

Protea Boekhuis
Burnettstr 1067, Hatfield, Pretoria 0083
Mailing Address: PO Box 35110, Menlo Park,
Pretoria 0102
Tel: (012) 343 6279 *Fax:* (012) 344 2653
Web Site: www.proteaboekhuis.com
Key Personnel
Publicity: Louis Smit *E-mail:* louis@
proteaboekhuis.co.za
Contact: Martie Eloff *Tel:* (012) 343 3897
E-mail: martie@proteaboekhuis.co.za
Subjects: Art, Biography, Memoirs, Drama, The-
ater, Fiction, Genealogy, Government, Political
Science, History, Law, Music, Dance, Philoso-

phy, Photography, Poetry, Psychology, Psychi-
atry, Science (General), Self-Help, Theology,
Travel & Tourism, Academics, Politics
ISBN Prefix(es): 978-1-86919; 978-1-919825

Protea-Uitgewers, *imprint of* Lux Verbi

PSA, see Pearson Southern Africa

Queillerie, *imprint of* NB Publishers

Random House Struik (Pty) Ltd+
Wembley Sq, 1st floor, Solan Rd, Gardens, Cape
Town 8001
Mailing Address: PO Box 1144, Cape Town 8000
Tel: (021) 460 5400
Web Site: www.randomstruik.co.za
Key Personnel
Mng Dir: Steve Connolly
General Manager, Sales & Marketing: Rinette
Verster *E-mail:* rinettev@randomstruik.co.za
Publisher-Struik Lifestyle: Linda de Villiers
E-mail: lindad@randomstruik.co.za
Publisher-Struik Nature, Struik Travel & Her-
itage & Fernwood Press: Pippa Parker
E-mail: pippap@randomstruik.co.za
Publisher-Umuzi: Fourie Botha *E-mail:* fourieb@
randomstruik.co.za
Publisher-Zebra Press: Marlene Fryer
E-mail: marlenef@randomstruik.co.za
Sales: Lucille Bester *E-mail:* lucilleb@
randomstruik.co.za; Anthea Branders
E-mail: antheab@randomstruik.co.za
Founded: 1962
Subjects: Business, Child Care & Development,
Cookery, Environmental Studies, Fiction, Gar-
dening, Plants, Government, Political Science,
Humor, Management, Military Science, Natural
History, Nonfiction (General), Regional Inter-
ests, Self-Help, Travel & Tourism, Women's
Studies, African Countries/Interests, Lifestyle,
Military History, Women's Interest
ISBN Prefix(es): 978-0-86977; 978-0-947458
Parent Company: Penguin Random House
Associate Companies: Struik Christian Books
Tel: (021) 462 4360 *Fax:* (021) 461 3612 *Web
Site:* www.struikchristianmedia.co.za
Imprints: eKhaya (digital); Fernwood Press;
Struik Lifestyle; Struik Nature; Struik Travel
& Heritage; Umuzi; Zebra Press
Distribution Center: Booksite Afrika, Tyger-
berg Business Park, 6 Koets St, Parow In-
dustria, Cape Town 7493 *Tel:* (021) 950 5900
Fax: (021) 950 5999 *E-mail:* inquiry@booksite.
co.za
Trafalgar Square Publishing (USA)

Reader's Digest South Africa+
PO Box 146, Cape Mail 8003
Toll Free Tel: 0860 111 462
E-mail: customercare_sa@readersdigest.com
Web Site: www.facebook.com/
ReadersDigestSouthAfrica/
Founded: 1922
Direct mail books & catalogs.
Subjects: Computer Science, Cookery, Garden-
ing, Plants, Health, Nutrition, Medicine, Nurs-
ing, Dentistry, Nonfiction (General), Travel &
Tourism
ISBN Prefix(es): 978-1-874912; 978-1-919750
Number of titles published annually: 5 Print
Total Titles: 53 Print
Parent Company: Trusted Media Brands Inc, 750
Third Ave, 3rd floor, New York, NY 10017,
United States
Imprints: AA The Motorist Publications

Renaissance, *imprint of* Tafelberg Publishers Ltd

RHS, see Random House Struik (Pty) Ltd

SAIIA, see South African Institute of
International Affairs

N F Saliwa Publishing cc
5 Coriander Crescent, Vredenberg, Bellville 7530
Tel: (083) 336 9639 *Fax:* (086) 425 9626
E-mail: info@nfsaliwa.co.za
Web Site: www.nfsaliwa.co.za
Key Personnel
Founder: Ncebakazi Faith Saliwa-Mogale
E-mail: ncebakazi@nfsaliwa.co.za
ISBN Prefix(es): 978-0-620; 978-0-9802661; 978-
1-92034; 978-0-9802660; 978-0-9814107; 978-
0-9802778; 978-0-9814106

SANBI, see South African National Biodiversity
Institute (SANBI)

Sasavona Books, *imprint of* Sasavona Publishers
and Booksellers (Pty) Ltd

Sasavona Publishers and Booksellers (Pty) Ltd
18 Kastania Corner Fosteri St, Next to Magaba
Total Garage, Burgersfort 1150
Mailing Address: PO Box 1944, Burgersfort 1150
Tel: (013) 231-8494; (087) 802-6110; (082) 402-
7267 (orders) *Fax:* (086) 726-5523
E-mail: info@sasavona.co.za
Web Site: www.sasavona.co.za
Key Personnel
Mng Dir: Nkosinathi D Lowan *E-mail:* dunstan@
sasavona.co.za
Manager: Justice Singita Ndabane
E-mail: justice@sasavona.co.za
Founded: 2012
Subjects: Education, Literature, Literary Criti-
cism, Essays, Religion - Other
ISBN Prefix(es): 978-0-907985; 978-0-949985;
978-0-949981
Number of titles published annually: 5 Print; 1
Online; 10 E-Book; 5 Audio
Total Titles: 15 Print; 1 Online; 10 E-Book; 15
Audio
Imprints: Sasavona Books
Bookshop(s): PO Box 242, Khomanani 0933

Shuter, *imprint of* Shuter & Shooter Publishers
(Pty) Ltd

Shuter & Shooter, *imprint of* Shuter & Shooter
Publishers (Pty) Ltd

Shuter & Shooter Publishers (Pty) Ltd
Shuters House, 110 CB Downes Rd, Pietermar-
itzburg, KwaZulu-Natal 3201
Tel: (033) 846 8700 *Fax:* (033) 846 8701
Web Site: www.shuters.com
Key Personnel
Publishing Dir, Indigenous Languages: Ray Wela
Tel: (033) 846 8767
Publishing Dir, General Books: Heather Hann-
away *Tel:* (033) 846 8777
Publishing Manager, Education: Sabelo Zulu
Tel: (033) 846 8770
National Marketing Manager: Patricia Khumalo
Tel: (033) 846 8738
International Rights & Production Manager: Julie
Titchmarsh *Tel:* (033) 846 8754
Founded: 1925
Also major book dealer.
Membership(s): Publishers' Association of South
Africa (PASA).
Subjects: Biography, Memoirs, Ethnicity, History,
Nonfiction (General), Science (General), Social
Sciences, Sociology, Technology
ISBN Prefix(es): 978-0-947476; 978-0-7960; 978-
0-86985; 978-0-947475; 978-1-919778
Parent Company: The Natal Witness (Pty) Ltd
Associate Companies: Reach Out Publishers
Imprints: Butterfly Books; New Spin; Shuter;
Shuter & Shooter; Songololo

Subsidiaries: Shuter & Shooter (Gazankulu) (Pty) Ltd; Shuter & Shooter (Transkei) (Pty) Ltd
Branch Office(s)
54 Alexandar Rd, King Williams Town, Eastern Cape *Tel:* (043) 642 2849; (043) 642 3279 *Fax:* (043) 642 2778
23 Gleneagles Rd, Greenside, Johannesburg, Gauteng *Tel:* (011) 782 1641; (011) 782 3348 *Fax:* (011) 782 8981
Warehouse: Herschenson Rd, Plessislaer, Pietermaritzbung, KwaZulu-Natal *Tel:* (033) 398 1019 *Fax:* (033) 398 1332

Lannice Snyman Publishers+
PO Box 26344, Hout Bay, Cape Town 7872
Tel: (021) 790 3367 *Fax:* (021) 790 1055
E-mail: tamsin@lannicesnyman.com
Web Site: www.lannicesnyman.com
Key Personnel
Special Project Manager: Tamsin Snyman
Distribution & Public Relations: Courtenay Snyman
Founded: 1995
Subjects: Cookery, House & Home
ISBN Prefix(es): 978-0-620
Number of titles published annually: 5 Print
Total Titles: 11 Print

Songololo, *imprint of* Shuter & Shooter Publishers (Pty) Ltd

South African Institute of International Affairs+
University of the Witwatersrand, Jan Smuts House, East Campus, Johannesburg
Mailing Address: PO Box 31596, Braamfontein, Johannesburg 2017
Tel: (011) 339-2021 *Fax:* (011) 339-2154
E-mail: info@saiia.org.za; pubs@saiia.org.za
Web Site: www.saiia.org.za
Key Personnel
Publications Specialist: Alexandra Begg
Founded: 1934
Subjects: Economics, Foreign Countries, Government, Political Science, Military Science
ISBN Prefix(es): 978-0-908371; 978-0-909239; 978-1-874890; 978-1-919810; 978-1-919969
Branch Office(s)
Vunani Chambers, 1st floor, 33 Church St, Cape Town 8001 *Tel:* (021) 422-0717 *Fax:* (021) 426-1455
37 Paterson St, East London 5201, Chairperson: Jonathan Schewitz *Tel:* (043) 722-5421; (043) 722-5422; (043) 722-5423 *Fax:* (043) 743-0181 *E-mail:* atlasfil@iafrica.com
Pietermaritzburg, Chairperson: Melanie Veness *E-mail:* pcb@pcb.org.za
PO Box 454, Plumstead, Western Cape 7800, Contact: Pippa Segall *Tel:* (083) 305 2339 *E-mail:* saiia.admin@telkomsa.net

South African Institute of Race Relations
2 Clamart Rd, Richmond, Johannesburg 2092
Tel: (011) 482-7221 *Fax:* (011) 482-7690
E-mail: prisca@sairr.org.za
Web Site: www.sairr.org.za
Key Personnel
Chief Executive Officer: John Kane-Berman
Business Development Manager: Sherwin van Blerk
Founded: 1929
Specialize in human rights.
Subjects: Agriculture, Business, Ethnicity, Government, Political Science, Human Relations, Law, Public Administration, Social Sciences, Sociology, Human Rights
ISBN Prefix(es): 978-0-86982

South African National Biodiversity Institute (SANBI)
2 Cussonia Ave, Brummeria, Pretoria

Mailing Address: Private Bag X101, Pretoria 0001
Tel: (012) 843 5000 *Fax:* (012) 804 3211
E-mail: info@sanbi.org; bookshop@sanbi.org
Web Site: www.sanbi.org
Founded: 2004
Publishes popular & scientific books on plants of Southern Africa & related topics.
Subjects: Biological Sciences, Environmental Studies, Gardening, Plants, Natural History, Science (General), Biodiversity
ISBN Prefix(es): 978-0-9583205; 978-1-874907; 978-1-919684; 978-1-919795; 978-1-919976
Total Titles: 100 Print
Branch Office(s)
SANBI Private Bag X7, Claremont 7735
Tel: (021) 779 8800 *Fax:* (021) 762 3229
Distributor for Briza Publications (South Africa)

Spearhead, *imprint of* New Africa Books (Pty) Ltd

Struik, see Random House Struik (Pty) Ltd

Struik Lifestyle, *imprint of* Random House Struik (Pty) Ltd

Struik Nature, *imprint of* Random House Struik (Pty) Ltd

Struik Travel & Heritage, *imprint of* Random House Struik (Pty) Ltd

Symbol Books, *imprint of* LAPA Uitgewers

Tafelberg Publishers Ltd, *imprint of* NB Publishers

Tafelberg Publishers Ltd+
Imprint of NB Publishers
Naspers, 12th floor, 40 Heerengracht, Kaapstad, Cape Town 8001
Mailing Address: PO Box 879, Cape Town 8000
Tel: (021) 406 3033 *Fax:* (021) 406 3812
E-mail: nb@nb.co.za
Web Site: www.tafelberg.com
Founded: 1951
Publishes forms in African literature, author & political publications, books for young children & young readers in all the official languages & a wide variety of illustrated nonfiction.
Subjects: Cookery, Crafts, Games, Hobbies, Fiction, Gardening, Plants, Government, Political Science, Literature, Literary Criticism, Essays, Nonfiction (General), Romance
ISBN Prefix(es): 978-0-624
Number of titles published annually: 100 Print; 1 CD-ROM
Total Titles: 1,200 Print; 1 CD-ROM
Imprints: Homeros; Jasmyn; Renaissance
Orders to: On the Dot, PO Box 487, Bellville 7535 *Tel:* (021) 918 8603 *Toll Free Tel:* 0800 220 224 *Fax:* (021) 951 4903; (021) 951 4633 *E-mail:* customerservices@onthedot.co.za *Web Site:* www.onthedot.co.za

Umuzi, *imprint of* Random House Struik (Pty) Ltd

UNISA Press+
University of South Africa, Muckleneuk Campus, Preller St, Muckleneuk, Pretoria
Mailing Address: PO Box 392, Unisa 0003
Tel: (012) 429 3515; (012) 429 3448 *Fax:* (012) 429 3449
E-mail: unisa-press@unisa.ac.za; thearl@unisa.ac.za (orders); morodjm@unisa.ac.za
Web Site: www.unisa.ac.za

Key Personnel
Publications Assistant: Sharon Boshoff *Tel:* (012) 429 3316 *E-mail:* boshosm@unisa.ac.za
Founded: 1956
University press specializing in scholarly & academic publications.
Membership(s): Publishers' Association of South Africa (PASA)
Subjects: Architecture & Interior Design, Art, Developing Countries, Economics, Education, Fiction, History, Language Arts, Linguistics, Law, Literature, Literary Criticism, Essays, Nonfiction (General), Psychology, Psychiatry, Social Sciences, Sociology, Theology
ISBN Prefix(es): 978-0-86981; 978-1-86888
Number of titles published annually: 30 Print
Parent Company: University of South Africa
Distributed by Brill (Imagined SA series); Michigan State University Press (titles from ABC)
Foreign Rep(s): Eurospan (Europe); International Specialized Book Services (ISBS) (Canada, USA)
Distribution Center: Blue Weaver, PO Box 30370, Tokai 7966, Contact: Lorna van Romburgh *Tel:* (021) 701 4477 *Fax:* 0865242139 *E-mail:* info@blueweaver.co.za *Web Site:* www.blueweaver.co.za

University of KwaZulu-Natal Press+
Private Bag X01, Scottsville 3209
Tel: (033) 260 5226 *Fax:* (033) 260 5801
E-mail: books@ukzn.ac.za
Web Site: www.ukznpress.co.za
Key Personnel
Publisher: Debra Primo *E-mail:* primod@ukzn.ac.za
Editor: Sally Hines *E-mail:* hiness@ukzn.ac.za
Associate Editor: Elana Bregin *E-mail:* bregin@ukzn.ac.za
Finance & Administration: Shevoun Pillay *E-mail:* pillays10@ukzn.ac.za
Marketing: Adele Branch *E-mail:* brancha@ukzn.ac.za
Customer Service: Edwin Ramthew *E-mail:* ramthew@ukzn.ac.za
Founded: 1947
Membership(s): Publishers' Association of South Africa (PASA).
Subjects: Agriculture, Animals, Pets, Archaeology, Art, Biography, Memoirs, Biological Sciences, Drama, Theater, Economics, Education, Genealogy, Government, Political Science, Health, Nutrition, History, Literature, Literary Criticism, Essays, Photography, Poetry, Psychology, Psychiatry, Regional Interests, Social Sciences, Sociology, Women's Studies, African Literature, Military History, Natural Science
ISBN Prefix(es): 978-0-86980; 978-1-86914; 978-1-86840; 978-1-874897
Number of titles published annually: 20 Print; 1 CD-ROM
Imprints: Killie Campbell Africana Library; Gecko Poetry; Hadeda Books
Distributor for Deep South
Foreign Rep(s): Eurospan Ltd (Europe, UK); International Specialized Book Services (ISBS) (USA)
Distribution Center: On the Dot

Van Schaik Publishers+
1059 Francis Baard St, 1st floor, Hatfield 0083
Mailing Address: PO Box 12681, Hatfield 0028
Tel: (012) 342-2765 *Fax:* (012) 430-3563
E-mail: vanschaik@vanschaiknet.com
Web Site: www.vanschaiknet.com
Key Personnel
Chief Executive Officer: Leanne Martini *E-mail:* lmartini@vanschaiknet.com
Founded: 1915
Specialize in publishing high-quality academic texts at affordable prices. Aim to provide academic content in any form, combination or format.

Subjects: Accounting, Behavioral Sciences, Biological Sciences, Business, Career Development, Child Care & Development, Communications, Criminology, Economics, Education, Environmental Studies, Film, Video, Finance, Government, Political Science, History, Labor, Industrial Relations, Language Arts, Linguistics, Law, Library & Information Sciences, Management, Marketing, Mathematics, Medicine, Nursing, Dentistry, Psychology, Psychiatry, Public Administration, Social Sciences, Sociology, Technology
ISBN Prefix(es): 978-0-627; 978-0-86874
Number of titles published annually: 30 Print; 3 CD-ROM; 2 Online; 1 E-Book
Total Titles: 260 Print; 3 CD-ROM; 2 Online; 1 E-Book
Parent Company: Media24
Warehouse: On the Dot Distribution, PO Box 487, Bellville 7535 *Tel:* (021) 918 8811 *Fax:* (021) 918 8888 *E-mail:* orders@onthedot.co.za
Orders to: PO Box 487, Bellville 7535 *Tel:* (0861) 668 368 *Fax:* (021) 918 8888

Via Afrika+
40 Heerengracht, Cape Town 8001
Mailing Address: PO Box 5197, Cape Town 8000
Tel: (021) 406-3528 *Fax:* (021) 406-3086
E-mail: customerservices@viaafrika.com; info@viaafrika.com
Web Site: viaafrika.com
Key Personnel
Chief Executive Officer: Christina Watson
    E-mail: christina.watson@viaafrika.com
Group Content Manager: Michael Goodman
    E-mail: michael.goodman@viaafrika.com
Operations Manager: Carmen Kallis
    E-mail: carmen.kallis@viaafrika.com
Founded: 1970
Owned by Media24 & Thebe Investments.
Publisher of educational textbooks & related materials.
Subjects: Education, Fiction, Poetry, Science (General), Social Sciences, Sociology, Technology
ISBN Prefix(es): 978-0-77004; 978-0-625; 978-0-7994
Total Titles: 1,500 Print
Imprints: Acacia Books; Afritech; Afro; Atlas; Bateleur; KZN Books
Bookshop(s): 15 Kraal St, East End, PO Box 1097, Bloemfontein 9300, Contact: Patrick Bidi *Tel:* (051) 447-9334 *Fax:* (051) 447-1754 *E-mail:* pbidi@nasou.com; 6 Derby Rd, 5241 Berea, PO Box 1163, East London 5200, Contact: Wynand Schoeman *Tel:* (043) 721-0897; (043) 741-0879 *Fax:* (043) 741-0887 *E-mail:* mwschoem@mweb.co.za; Hatfield Sq, 2nd floor, 1115 Burnette St, PO Box 11943, Hatfield 0028, Contact: Henk Visser *Tel:* (012) 362-1141 *Fax:* (012) 362-4658 (marketing); (012) 362-8671 (publishing) *E-mail:* hvisser@nasou.com; Tarentaal Centre, Corner of Kaapsehoop Rd & N4, PO Box 2400, Nelspruit 1200, Contact: Stanley Mzuzu *Tel:* (013) 741-1936 *Fax:* (013) 741-3086 *E-mail:* smzuzu@nasou.com; Shop 3, Wakefield House, 75 Crompton St, PO Box 2505, Pinetown 3600, Contact: Manie Mtshali *Tel:* (031) 702-6184 *Fax:* (031) 702-6189; (031) 701-0001 *E-mail:* maniemtshali@mweb.co.za; Nedbank Bldg, 10th floor, Off No 1001, 59-60 Landros Mare St, Polokwane North 0750, Contact: Gloria Monakhisi *Tel:* (015) 291-4978; (015) 291-5328 *Fax:* (015) 291-5250 *E-mail:* nafrika@mweb.co.za; 49 Steen St, Room No 10, PO Box 9749, Rustenburg 0300, Contact: Lance Mamogale *Tel:* (014) 594-0514 *Fax:* (014) 594-0337 *E-mail:* lancemamogale@mweb.co.za

Distribution Center: On the Dot Distribution, PO Box 487, Bellville 7535 *Tel:* (021) 918-8500 *Fax:* (021) 918-8807 *E-mail:* sjoubert1@onthedot.co.za

Vivlia Publishers & Booksellers (Pty) Ltd+
One Amanda Ave, Lea Glen, Florida, Roodepoort 1709
Tel: (011) 472-3912 *Fax:* (011) 472-4904
E-mail: headoffice@vivlia.co.za
Web Site: www.vivlia.co.za
Key Personnel
Chairman & Mng Dir: Albert N Nemukula
    E-mail: sitholet@vivlia.co.za
Publisher: Phathu Nemukula *Tel:* (083) 308-2352
    E-mail: phathu@vivlia.co.za
Publishing Dir: Jerome M Mogashoa
    E-mail: jerome@vivlia.co.za
Sales & Marketing Dir: Zanele Maqabuka
    Tel: (082) 286-0917 *E-mail:* zanele@vivlia.co.za
Publishing Manager: Timothy Sibeko *Tel:* (083) 252-2407 *E-mail:* timothy@vivlia.co.za; Faith Sirayi *Tel:* (083) 267-0379 *E-mail:* faith@vivlia.co.za; Moira Strydom *Tel:* (083) 452-0213 *E-mail:* moira@vivlia.co.za
Warehouse & Distribution Manager: Sipho Sibiya
    E-mail: sipho@vivlia.co.za
Production Coordinator: Priya Sookdeo *Tel:* (083) 252-2418 *E-mail:* priya@vivlia.co.za
Founded: 1989
Services schools & libraries.
Membership(s): Publishers' Association of South Africa (PASA); South African Booksellers Association.
Subjects: Accounting, Agriculture, Biography, Memoirs, Biological Sciences, Business, Economics, Education, English as a Second Language, Geography, Geology, History, Literature, Literary Criticism, Essays, Mathematics, Physical Sciences, Poetry, Science (General), Social Sciences, Sociology, Technology, Travel & Tourism
ISBN Prefix(es): 978-0-9583125; 978-1-86867; 978-1-874868; 978-1-77024; 978-1-77006
Total Titles: 15 Print
Branch Office(s)
Shop 8B, York Rd, Umtata 5100, Sales & Marketing Dir: Zanele Maqabuka *Tel:* (047) 531 4225/5051 *Fax:* (047) 532 6239 *E-mail:* umtata@vivlia.co.za
Distributor for Africa World Press Inc (USA)
Showroom(s): Africa Book Centre, Unit 13, Preston Park Business Centre, 36 Robertson Rd, Brighton BN1 5NL, United Kingdom *Tel:* (01273) 560 474

Waterkant-Uitgewers, *imprint of* Lux Verbi

Wits University Press+
PO Wits, Johannesburg 2050
Tel: (011) 717 8700; (011) 717 8701 *Fax:* (011) 717 8708
E-mail: witspress@wup.wits.ac.za
Web Site: witspress.co.za
Key Personnel
Publisher: Veronica Klipp *E-mail:* veronica.klipp@wits.ac.za
Commissioning Editor: Roshan Cader
    E-mail: roshan.cader@wits.ac.za
Digital Publisher: Andrew Joseph *E-mail:* andrew.joseph@wits.ac.za
Marketing Coordinator: Corina van der Spoel
    E-mail: corina.vanderspoel@wits.ac.za
Founded: 1922
Scholarly publisher specializing in the humanities.
Membership(s): Publishers' Association of South Africa (PASA).
Subjects: Anthropology, Archaeology, Art, Biography, Memoirs, Business, Crafts, Games, Hobbies, Drama, Theater, Economics, Education, Ethnicity, Finance, Government, Political

Science, History, Language Arts, Linguistics, Law, Literature, Literary Criticism, Essays, Medicine, Nursing, Dentistry, Natural History, Religion - Jewish, Science (General), Humanities
ISBN Prefix(es): 978-0-85494; 978-1-86814
Number of titles published annually: 20 Print
Total Titles: 160 Print
Orders to: Blue Weaver, PO Box 30370, Tokai (Cape Town) 7966 *Tel:* (021) 701 4477 *E-mail:* orders@blueweaver.co.za *Web Site:* www.blueweaver.co.za (Africa)
The Eurospan Group, Gray's Inn House, 127 Clerkenwell Rd, London EC1R 5DB, United Kingdom *Tel:* (020) 7240 0856 *E-mail:* info@eurospangroup.com *Web Site:* eurospangroup.com (Australia, India, UK/Europe)
Independent Publishers Group (IPG), 814 N Franklin St, Chicago, IL, United States *Fax:* 312-337-5985 *E-mail:* orders@ipgbook.com *Web Site:* www.ipgbook.com (China, North America, South America)

Zebra Press, *imprint of* Random House Struik (Pty) Ltd

South Korea

General Information

Capital: Seoul
Language: Korean (English also spoken in business)
Religion: Predominantly Mahayana Buddhist and Christian
Population: 44.1 million
Bank Hours: 0930-1600 Monday-Friday; 0930-1300 Saturday
Shop Hours: 1000-1900 Monday-Saturday
Currency: 100 chun = 10 hwan = 1 won
Export/Import Information: No tariffs on books and advertising matter. Authorizations for import of books and publications are reviewed annually by the Korean government. Import licenses are required. Exchange controls; prior deposits required at present.
Copyright: UCC (see Copyright Conventions, pg viii)

A&C Publishing Co Ltd
A&C Bldg, 736-44 Yeoksam-dong, Gangnam-nu, Seoul 135-080
Tel: (02) 538-7333 *Fax:* (02) 558-0338
Web Site: www.ancbook.com
Founded: 1971
Subjects: Architecture & Interior Design
ISBN Prefix(es): 978-89-7212

Agaworld
Agaworld Bldg, 1357-74 Seocho-dong, Seocho-gu, Seoul 137-070
Tel: (02) 2191-2073 *Fax:* (02) 2191-2077
E-mail: cosmo@agaworld.com
Web Site: eng.agaworld.com
Key Personnel
Chairman: Suk-ho Lee
Founded: 1980
Subjects: Education, Language Arts, Linguistics

Ahn Graphics Ltd+
24, Yanghwa-ro 8-gil, Mapo-gu, Seoul 04044
Tel: (02) 743 8065 *Fax:* (02) 744 3251
E-mail: contact@ag.co.kr
Web Site: www.ag.co.kr
Founded: 1985
Specialize in art books.
Membership(s): Korean Publishers Association.

Subjects: Architecture & Interior Design, Art, Computer Science, Travel & Tourism
ISBN Prefix(es): 978-89-7059

Alice, *imprint of* Munhakdongne Publishing Group

Anibooks, *imprint of* Munhakdongne Publishing Group

Archiworld Co Ltd
5F Archiworld Bldg, 256 Neungdong-ro, Gwangjn-gu, Seoul 04990
Tel: (02) 422-7392 (ext 110) *Fax:* (02) 422-7396; (02) 422-7399
E-mail: aid@archiworld1995.com
Web Site: archiworld1995.com
Key Personnel
President: Mr Kwang-young Jeong
Founded: 1995
Subjects: Architecture & Interior Design, Environmental Studies, Construction, Landscape Design, Urban Design
ISBN Prefix(es): 978-89-5770; 978-89-87223

Artbooks, *imprint of* Munhakdongne Publishing Group

Aurum, *imprint of* Munhakdongne Publishing Group

Bawoosol, *imprint of* Grass & Wind Publishing

BCM Media Inc+
Language Center, 7F Yuchang Bldg, 1305-7 Seocho-dong, Seocho-gu, Seoul 137-070
Tel: (02) 3482-0584 *Fax:* (02) 3482-0585
E-mail: info@bcm.co.kr
Web Site: www.spworks.co.kr; corp.bcm.co.kr
Key Personnel
Chairman: Dr Byoung-Chul Min
Founded: 1980
Distributes English, Japanese & Chinese educational materials.
Subjects: Education, Language Arts, Linguistics
ISBN Prefix(es): 978-89-7512
Total Titles: 100 Print
Parent Company: BCM Educational Group
Distributor for Child's Play; Houghton Mifflin; Steck-Vaughn
Shipping Address: 752-27 Yuksam-Dong, B1 Jeil Bldg, Gangnam-gu, Seoul 135-080
Warehouse: 752-27 Yuksam-Dong, B1 Jeil Bldg, Gangnam-gu, Seoul 135-080
Returns: 752-27 Yuksam-Dong, B1 Jeil Bldg, Gangnam-gu, Seoul 135-080

BIR Publishing Co Ltd, *imprint of* Minumsa Publishing Co Ltd

BIR Publishing Co Ltd+
Imprint of Minumsa Publishing Group
4F Gangnam Publishing Culture Center, 506 Sinsa-dong, Gangnam-gu, Seoul 135-887
Tel: (02) 3443-4318; (02) 3443-4319 *Fax:* (02) 3442-4661
E-mail: bir@bir.co.kr
Web Site: www.bir.co.kr
Key Personnel
President & Chief Executive Officer: Sanghee Park *Tel:* (02) 515-2003
Founded: 1994
Picture & story books for young children.
ISBN Prefix(es): 978-89-491
Number of titles published annually: 120 Print; 40 E-Book
Imprints: Gorilla Box (fiction for ages 7-12 & comic books)

Booknomad, *imprint of* Munhakdongne Publishing Group

Bori Publishing Co Ltd+
498-11, Pajubookcity, Munbal-ri, Gyoha-eup, Paju-si, Gyeonggi-do 413-756
Tel: (031) 955 3535
E-mail: bori@boribook.com
Web Site: www.boribook.com
Founded: 1991
Specialize in books about education, value of labour & harmony with nature for infants, children, juveniles & adults.
Subjects: Child Care & Development, Education, Labor, Industrial Relations, Literature, Literary Criticism, Essays
ISBN Prefix(es): 978-89-85494; 978-89-8428
Associate Companies: Dotori Publishing Co; Jakenchak Publishing Co

Borim Press+
515-2 Pajubookcity, Munbal-ri, Paju-si, Gyeonggi-do 413-756
Tel: (031) 955-3456 *Fax:* (031) 955-3500
E-mail: borimbook@borimpress.com
Web Site: www.borimpress.com
Key Personnel
President: Kwon Jong-Taek
Founded: 1976
Specialize in picture books.
Subjects: Animals, Pets, Fiction, History, Nonfiction (General), Science (General)
ISBN Prefix(es): 978-89-433
Distribution Center: Network International Inc, PO Box 1081, Northbrook, IL 60065-1081, United States (exclusive distribution for Canada & USA)

Braille Publishing Co Ltd
303 Myeongil Mega Town, 325-11 Myeongil-dong, Gangdong-gu, Seoul 134-070
Tel: (02) 3426-7500; (02) 3426-7511 *Fax:* (02) 3426-7502
E-mail: kbraille@naver.com; kbraille1@gmail.com
Web Site: www.kbraille.net; bfbooks.koreasme.com

Bricks Education
17, World Cup buk-ro 12-gil, Mapo-gu, Seoul 121-844
Tel: (02) 326-1182; (02) 326-1168 *Fax:* (02) 326-3173
E-mail: ake@ebricks.co.kr; aslee@ebricks.co.kr; jwkim@ebricks.co.kr
Web Site: www.ebricks.co.kr
Founded: 2004
ISBN Prefix(es): 978-89-6435

Bumhan Book Corp, see Pan Korea Book Corp

Bumwoosa Co Ltd
525-2 Munhalli Publishing Cultural Information Industrial Complex, Gyohaeup Pajusi, Gyeonggi-do, Seoul 413-256
Tel: (031) 955-6900 *Fax:* (031) 955-6905
E-mail: bumwoosa@chol.com; bumwoosa1966@naver.com
Web Site: www.bumwoosa.co.kr
Key Personnel
Chief Executive: Hyung-Doo Yoon
Founded: 1966
Subjects: Communications, Drama, Theater, Fiction, History, Literature, Literary Criticism, Essays, Philosophy, Publishing & Book Trade Reference, Social Sciences, Sociology
ISBN Prefix(es): 978-89-08
Associate Companies: Yoon Communications

Cham Kae, *imprint of* Oneull Publishing Co Ltd

Changbi Publishers Inc
513-11 Munbal-ri, Gyoha-eup, Gyeonggi-do, Paju 413-756
Tel: (031) 955-3333 *Fax:* (031) 955-3400
Web Site: www.changbi.com; en.changbi.com
Key Personnel
Editor: Paik Nak-chung *E-mail:* paiknc@snu.ac.kr
Founded: 1966
Subjects: Art, Biography, Memoirs, Fiction, History, Poetry, Science (General), Social Sciences, Sociology, Humanities
ISBN Prefix(es): 978-89-364
Total Titles: 1,500 Print

The Chosun Ilbo Co Ltd
62-4, Taepyeongro 1-ga, Jung-gu, Seoul 04519
Tel: (02) 724-5114
E-mail: englishnews@chosun.com
Web Site: www.chosun.com; english.chosun.com
Key Personnel
President & Chief Executive Officer: Sang-Hun Bang
Founded: 1920
Subjects: Business, Government, Political Science, Health, Nutrition, Sports, Athletics
ISBN Prefix(es): 978-89-7365
Subsidiaries: Chogwang Publishing Printing; Digital Chosun Ilbo; Monthly Chosun; Sports Chosun
Branch Office(s)
Shop 4, 324 Burwood Rd, Belmore, NSW, Australia *Tel:* (02) 9740-3592 *Fax:* (02) 9750-2241
331A-4501 North Rd, Bumavy, BC V3N 4R7, Canada *Tel:* 604-877-1158 *Fax:* 604-877-1128
Qingdao, China *Tel:* (0532) 583-0333 *Fax:* (0532) 582-1333
Guente-Vogt-Ring 55, 60437 Frankfurt, Germany *Tel:* (069) 508-30859 *Fax:* (069) 508-30860
PO Box 23425, GMF 96921, Guam *Tel:* 671-646-8032 *Fax:* 671-649-1021
11th floor, Block 40, Baguio Villa, 550 Victoria Rd, Hong Kong, Hong Kong *Tel:* 2542 0270 *Fax:* 2541 8755
Jl Raden Salehraya No 64, Jakarta-Pusat 10330, Indonesia *Tel:* (0221) 3150-815 *Fax:* (0221) 3151-028
Togin Bldg, Room 517, 1-4-2, Marunouchi, Chiyoda-ku, Tokyo 100-0005, Japan *Tel:* (03) 3216-2711 *Fax:* (03) 3214-1080
461 Lake Rd, Takapuna, Auckland, New Zealand *Tel:* (09) 357-6170 *Fax:* (09) 358-3218
Room 303 Executive Bldg Center Sen, Corner of Gil Puyat Ave & Makati Ave, Metro Manila, Philippines *Tel:* (01) 896-3926 *Fax:* (02) 897-8976
Bil 80, Jl Daud No 05-04 Windy Heights, Singapore 419591, Singapore *Tel:* 744 9208 *Fax:* 744 9078
Taipei, Taiwan *Tel:* (02) 738-8943 *Fax:* (02) 838-1860
Sukumvit 39, Bangkok, Thailand *Tel:* (02) 480-4290 *Fax:* (02) 662-7640
One, Ground floor, 14 Westbourne Crescent, London W2 3DB, United Kingdom *Tel:* (020) 8399-9977 *Fax:* (020) 8399-9940
U.S. Office(s): 9840 Main St, Suite 100, Fairfax, VA 22031, United States *Tel:* 703-865-8310 *Fax:* 703-204-0104

The Christian Literature Society of Korea
169-1 Samsung-Dong, Gangnam-gu, Seoul 135-090
Tel: (02) 553-0870 *Fax:* (02) 555-7721
E-mail: clsk@clsk.org
Web Site: www.clsk.org
Founded: 1890
Subjects: Theology
ISBN Prefix(es): 978-89-511

ChungRim Publishing Co Ltd
Imprint of ChungRim Interactive Co Ltd
63, Nonhyun-dong, Gangnam-gu, Seoul
Tel: (02) 546-4341 *Fax:* (02) 546-8053

E-mail: webmaster@chungrim.com
Web Site: www.chungrim.com
Key Personnel
Contact: M Koh Youngsoo *E-mail:* cr@chungrim.
com
Founded: 1973
Subjects: Accounting, Advertising, Art, Behavioral Sciences, Biography, Memoirs, Business, Career Development, Child Care & Development, Communications, Computer Science, Crafts, Games, Hobbies, Economics, Education, Electronics, Electrical Engineering, English as a Second Language, Fiction, Finance, Health, Nutrition, History, How-to, Human Relations, Humor, Journalism, Labor, Industrial Relations, Law, Literature, Literary Criticism, Essays, Management, Marketing, Music, Dance, Nonfiction (General), Philosophy, Psychology, Psychiatry, Real Estate, Religion - Protestant, Romance, Science (General), Science Fiction, Fantasy, Social Sciences, Sociology, Sports, Athletics, Technology, Travel & Tourism, Women's Studies
ISBN Prefix(es): 978-89-352
Number of titles published annually: 80 Print; 3 CD-ROM; 6 Online; 6 E-Book
Total Titles: 1,300 Print; 3 CD-ROM; 6 Online; 6 E-Book
Associate Companies: Kolis Co Ltd; Pan Rae Wolbo SA; Woo Jin Publishing Co

C3 Publishing Co
72-9 GongHang-dong, GangSeo-gu, Seoul 157-182
Tel: (02) 2661 2811 *Fax:* (02) 2661 2456
E-mail: biz@c3p.kr (distribution); editor@c3p.kr (editorial); subs@c3p.kr (subscriptions)
Web Site: www.c3p.kr
Key Personnel
Publisher: JaeHong Lee
Editorial Dir: Uje Lee
Art Dir: YilGui Yoo
Mng Editor: YuMi Hyun
Editor: HyoJin Jeon; JiMin Lee; HyunA Jo
Founded: 1984
Subjects: Architecture & Interior Design, Landscape, Urban Design
ISBN Prefix(es): 978-89-86780
Foreign Rep(s): Art Data (Ireland, UK); Bookport (Southern Europe); Anna Eriksson (Scandinavia); Phillip Galgiani (Canada, USA); Kerstin Heyen (Austria, Germany); Julie Onishi (Japan); Perimeter Books (Australia, New Zealand); Sebastien Richard (France, Switzerland)
Distribution Center: Idea Books, Nieuwe Herengracht 11, 1011 RK Amsterdam, Netherlands *Tel:* (020) 6226154 *Fax:* (020) 6209299 *E-mail:* idea@ideabooks.nl *Web Site:* www.ideabooks.nl

Daewonsa+
358-17, Huam-dong, Yongsan-gu, Seoul 140-190
Tel: (02) 757-6717; (02) 757-6718; (02) 757-6719; (02) 757-6711 *Fax:* (02) 775-8043
Web Site: daewonsa.co.kr
Key Personnel
Vice President: S W Chang
Founded: 1986
Subjects: Antiques, Architecture & Interior Design, Art, Cookery, Crafts, Games, Hobbies, Environmental Studies, Health, Nutrition, History, Philosophy, Religion - Buddhist, Science (General), Travel & Tourism
ISBN Prefix(es): 978-89-369

Dahl, *imprint of* Munhakdongne Publishing Group

Damdi Publishing Co
2F, 79 Samgaksan-ro, Gangbuk-gu, Seoul 01036
Tel: (02) 900-0652 *Fax:* (02) 900-0657

E-mail: dd@damdi.co.kr; m.damdi_book@naver.com
Web Site: www.damdi.co.kr
Founded: 2002
Subjects: Architecture & Interior Design, Landscape Architecture
ISBN Prefix(es): 978-89-91111; 978-89-953598
Foreign Rep(s): Art Data (Ireland, UK); Berend Bosch (Belgium, Netherlands); Phillip Galgiani (Canada, USA); Julie Onishi (Asia, Japan); Eric Poll (France, Switzerland); Josef Portelli (Southern Europe); Robyn Ralton (Australia, New Zealand); Bo Rudin (Scandinavia); Kurt Salchii (Austria, Germany)
Distribution Center: Idea Books, Nieuwe Herengracht 11, 1011 RK Amsterdam, Netherlands *Tel:* (020) 6226154 *Fax:* (020) 6209299 *E-mail:* idea@ideabooks.nl *Web Site:* www.ideabooks.nl

Dankook University Press
152, Jukjeon-ro, Suji-gu, Yongin-si, Gyeonggi-do 16890
Tel: (031) 1899-3700
Web Site: www.dankook.ac.kr
Key Personnel
President: Hosung Chang, PhD
Founded: 1967
Academic & reference series as well as individual texts.
Subjects: History, Literature, Literary Criticism, Essays
ISBN Prefix(es): 978-89-7092
Total Titles: 280 Print

Dong-hwa Publishing Co
130-4 1ga Wonhyo-ro, Yongsan-ku, Seoul 140-846
Tel: (02) 713-5411 *Fax:* (02) 701-7041
Founded: 1968
Subjects: Art, History, Literature, Literary Criticism, Essays, Philosophy
ISBN Prefix(es): 978-89-431

Dong-A Publishing Co Ltd
Eunhengro 30, 9th & 10th floors, Youngdeunpo-gu, Seoul
Tel: (02) 2229 7275 *Fax:* (02) 2229 7309
Web Site: www.dongapublishing.com
Founded: 1980
ISBN Prefix(es): 978-89-00

Econ, *imprint of* Munhakdongne Publishing Group

Eulyoo Publishing Co Ltd+
51-4, Jongno-gu, Seoul 03144
Tel: (02) 7338151; (02) 7338152; (02) 7338153 *Fax:* (02) 7329154
E-mail: eulyoo1945@eulyoo.co.kr
Web Site: www.eulyoo.co.kr
Founded: 1945
Subjects: History, Language Arts, Linguistics, Literature, Literary Criticism, Essays, Philosophy
ISBN Prefix(es): 978-89-324
Distributor for UN Publications

Ewha Womans University Press (EWUP)
Hanuesol Bldg A, 4th floor, Seongsan-ro, Seodaemun-gu, Seoul 03721
Tel: (02) 362-6076; (02) 3277-3242 (sales); (02) 3277-3164 (sales) *Fax:* (02) 312-4312
E-mail: press@ewha.ac.kr
Web Site: www.ewhapress.com
Key Personnel
Mng Dir: Hye-ryen Kim *Tel:* (02) 3277-3162
Dir: Min Suk Choe *Tel:* (02) 3277-3621
Founded: 1949
Subjects: Art, Education, History, Human Relations, Language Arts, Linguistics, Literature, Literary Criticism, Essays, Music, Dance, Phi-

losophy, Psychology, Psychiatry, Religion - Other, Science (General), Social Sciences, Sociology, Nature
ISBN Prefix(es): 978-89-7300

EWUP, see Ewha Womans University Press (EWUP)

Geulhangari, *imprint of* Munhakdongne Publishing Group

Gimm-Young Publishers Inc+
63-3 Bukchon-ro, Jongro-gu, Seoul 110-260
Tel: (02) 745 4823 *Fax:* (02) 745 4827
E-mail: bestbook@gimmyoung.com
Web Site: en.gimmyoung.com/main/index.aspx
Key Personnel
President: Ms Eun-Ju Park
Foreign Rights Manager: Ms Jinhee Cha *Tel:* (02) 3668 3203 *E-mail:* jinhee@gimmyoung.com
Founded: 1979
Publish in every category including current affairs, business, self-improvement, history, popular science, religion, spirituality, lifestyles & literary novels. International authors include Stephen R Covey, Jim Collins, Richard Dawkins, Matt Ridley, His Holiness the Dalai Lama, Thich Nhat Hanh, Malcolm Gladwell & Michael Sandel. Domestic authors include Koh Eun, Kim Dae-jung, Seong Cheol & Ahn Cheol-soo.
Subjects: Behavioral Sciences, Business, Child Care & Development, English as a Second Language, Fiction, History, Inspirational, Spirituality, Literature, Literary Criticism, Essays, Nonfiction (General), Philosophy, Pop Culture, Religion - Other, Science (General), Self-Help, Social Sciences, Sociology, Current Affairs, Lifestyles, Popular Science
ISBN Prefix(es): 978-89-349
Number of titles published annually: 200 Print; 50 E-Book
Total Titles: 3,000 Print; 200 E-Book
Imprints: VICHE (fiction imprint)

Golden Bough Publishing Co Ltd, *imprint of* Minumsa Publishing Co Ltd

GoldenCompass, *imprint of* Minumsa Publishing Co Ltd

Gomdori, *imprint of* Woongjin ThinkBig Co Ltd

Gorilla Box, *imprint of* BIR Publishing Co Ltd

Grass & Wind Publishing
3F, 514-5 Mubal-ri, Gyoha-eup, Paju-si, Gyeonggi-do, Paju 413-756
Tel: (031) 955-1515 *Fax:* (031) 955-1517
E-mail: grassandwind@hanmail.net
Web Site: www.grassandwind.com
Founded: 1998
Subjects: Art, Fiction, History, Philosophy, Science (General)
ISBN Prefix(es): 978-89-8389
Imprints: Bawoosol

Hainaim Publishing Co Ltd
5-6 F Hainaim Bldg, 368-4 Seogyo-dong, Mapo-gu, Seoul 121-210
Tel: (02) 326-1600 *Fax:* (02) 326-1624
Web Site: www.hainaim.com
Founded: 1982
Subjects: Education, Fiction, History, Nonfiction (General), Science (General), Comics
ISBN Prefix(es): 978-89-7337

Hakgojae+
50 Samcheong-ro, Jongno-gu, Seoul 110-200
Tel: (02) 720 1524-6 *Fax:* (02) 720 1527

E-mail: info@hakgojae.com
Web Site: www.hakgojae.com
Key Personnel
Contact: Chan-Kyu Woo
Founded: 1991
Subjects: Archaeology, Architecture & Interior Design, Art, Asian Studies, Foreign Countries, History, Literature, Literary Criticism, Essays, Photography, Korean Studies
ISBN Prefix(es): 978-89-85846; 978-89-5625
Book Club(s): Kyobo Book Club

Hakmunsa Publishing Co+
198 Naeja-dong, Jongno-gu, Seoul 110-053
Tel: (02) 738-5118 *Fax:* (02) 733-8998
E-mail: hakmun@hakmun.co.kr
Web Site: www.hakmun.co.kr
Key Personnel
Contact: Ki-Hyoung Kim
Founded: 1963
Subjects: Business, Child Care & Development, Computer Science, Education, Engineering (General), English as a Second Language, Science (General), Social Sciences, Sociology, Technology
ISBN Prefix(es): 978-89-467; 978-89-87510
Branch Office(s)
Pusan *Tel:* (051) 502-8104
Taegu *Tel:* (053) 422-5000

Hangil Art
520-11, Munbal-li, Gyoha-eup, Paju-si Gyeonggi-do 413-832
Tel: (031) 955-2000; (031) 955-2034 (editorial dept) *Fax:* (031) 955-2005
E-mail: hangilsaone@hangilsa.co.kr
Web Site: www.hangilart.co.kr
Key Personnel
Chief Executive: Euon-Ho Kim
Founded: 1976
Subjects: History, Literature, Literary Criticism, Essays, Philosophy, Photography, Social Sciences, Sociology, Travel & Tourism
ISBN Prefix(es): 978-89-88360; 978-89-91636

Hansol Education Co Ltd
1653 Sangam-dong, floors 18-29, Mapo-gu, Seoul 121-604
Web Site: www.eduhansol.co.kr
Key Personnel
Representative Dir & Chairman: Byun Jae Yong
Founded: 1991
Subjects: Education, Mathematics, Science (General), Sports, Athletics
ISBN Prefix(es): 978-89-535

Hanul MPlus+
Hanul Seesaw Bldg 3F, Gwanginsa-gil 153, Paju-si, Gyeonggi-do 10881
Tel: (031) 955 0655; (031) 955 0615 *Fax:* (031) 955 0656
E-mail: hanul@hanulbooks.co.kr; edit@hanulbooks.co.kr; marketing@hanulbooks.co.kr
Web Site: www.hanulmplus.kr
Key Personnel
Chief Executive Officer: Kim Chong-Soo
Founded: 1980
Subjects: Asian Studies, Economics, Education, Geography, Geology, Health, Nutrition, History, Journalism, Law, Library & Information Sciences, Literature, Literary Criticism, Essays, Medicine, Nursing, Dentistry, Philosophy, Pop Culture, Science (General), Social Sciences, Sociology, Technology, Theology, Women's Studies
ISBN Prefix(es): 978-89-460; 978-89-7058
Number of titles published annually: 200 Print
Total Titles: 3,000 Print
Associate Companies: Seoul M Co; Siinsa Publishing Co

Happy House Co Ltd
Imprint of Darakwon
141 Songwol-dong, Jongno-gu, Seoul 110-101
Tel: (02) 736-2031 *Fax:* (02) 736-2037
E-mail: luna1001@darakwon.co.kr
Web Site: www.ihappyhouse.co.kr
Key Personnel
Mng Dir: Mi-Kyung Kim *E-mail:* moon@darakwon.co.kr
Founded: 2002
ISBN Prefix(es): 978-89-5655; 978-89-86171

Haseo Publishing Co+
370-27, Shindang-dong, Chung-ku, Seoul 100-454
Tel: (02) 2237-8161 *Fax:* (02) 2237-6575
Web Site: www.haseo.co.kr
Founded: 1964
Subjects: Literature, Literary Criticism, Essays, Nonfiction (General), Self-Help, Social Sciences, Sociology
ISBN Prefix(es): 978-89-7330
Subsidiaries: Jigyung Publishing Co

Hollym Corp Publishers
13-13 Gwancheol-dong, Jongno-gu, Seoul 110-111
Tel: (02) 735-7551; (02) 735-7554; (02) 735-7552; (02) 735-7553 *Fax:* (02) 730-5149
E-mail: info@hollym.co.kr
Web Site: www.hollym.co.kr
Key Personnel
President: Rhimm Sang-Bek
Sales Dir: Ki Lee
Founded: 1963
Subjects: Art, Cookery, Economics, Fiction, Government, Political Science, History, Literature, Literary Criticism, Essays, Photography, Poetry, Religion - Buddhist, Sports, Athletics, Travel & Tourism
ISBN Prefix(es): 978-0-930878; 978-1-56591; 978-89-7094
U.S. Office(s): Hollym International Corp, 18 Donald Pl, Elizabeth, NJ 07208, United States *Tel:* 908-353-1655 *Fax:* 908-353-0255 *Web Site:* www.hollym.com
Foreign Rep(s): Aladdin US (USA); British Library (UK); Ehon House Publishing Inc (Japan); Hakutei-sha Co Ltd (Japan); Hansol Korean Books/Ram Tech Australia Pty Ltd (Australia); Korea Language Center (Japan); Korean Book Services (Helmut Hetzer) (Germany); Koryo Books Importing Inc (USA); Master Communications Inc (USA); Qing's Media (Singapore); Sanshusha Publishing Co Inc (Japan); Andy Spate (Australia)

ILCHOKAK Publishing Co Ltd+
1-335 Sinmunno 2-ga, Jongro-gu, Seoul 110-062
Tel: (02) 7335430; (02) 7335431 *Fax:* (02) 7385857
E-mail: ilchokak@hanmail.net
Web Site: www.ilchokak.co.kr
Key Personnel
President: Si-Yeon Kim
Founded: 1953
Subjects: Anthropology, Education, Engineering (General), History, Law, Medicine, Nursing, Dentistry, Psychology, Psychiatry, Science (General), Social Sciences, Sociology
ISBN Prefix(es): 978-89-337

Jigyungsa Ltd+
790-14, Yoksam-dong, Kangnam-gu, Seoul 135-929
Tel: (02) 557-6351 *Fax:* (02) 557-6352
E-mail: copyright@jigs.co.kr
Web Site: www.jigyung.co.kr
Founded: 1978
Subjects: Fiction, History, Language Arts, Linguistics, Mathematics, Nonfiction (General), Science (General)
ISBN Prefix(es): 978-89-319

Number of titles published annually: 100 Print
Total Titles: 2,100 Print
Subsidiaries: Miraejungbosa
Divisions: Walt Disney Books & Magazines

Kemongsa Publishing Co Ltd+
772 Yoksam-dong, Kangnam-gu, Seoul 135-080
Tel: (02) 531-5500 *Fax:* (02) 531-5550
E-mail: kmcc@kemongsa.co.kr
Web Site: www.kemongsa.co.kr
Key Personnel
President: Choon-sik Kim
Mng Dir: Jong-uk Lee
Assistant Manager, Foreign Rights: Park Yeon
Founded: 1946
Specialize in children's books.
Subjects: Biography, Memoirs, English as a Second Language, Fiction, Geography, Geology, Nonfiction (General), Science (General)
ISBN Prefix(es): 978-89-06
Subsidiaries: EMI - Kemongsa Co Ltd; Kemong Enterprise Co Ltd; Young Printing Co Ltd

KONG & PARK Inc
85, Gwangnaru-ro 56-gil, Prime-center 1518, Gwangjin-gu, Seoul 05116
Tel: (02) 565 1531 *Fax:* (02) 3445 1080
E-mail: info@kongnpark.com
Web Site: www.kongnpark.com
Founded: 2000
Research & publish books for studying Chinese characters.
Subjects: Education, Language Arts, Linguistics
ISBN Prefix(es): 978-89-97134
Branch Office(s)
KONG & PARK Chile SpA, Av Providencia 1208, No 1603, Providencia, 7500571 Santiago, Chile *Tel:* (022) 833 9055 *E-mail:* martin.moon@kongnpark.com
No 401, Unit 1, Bldg 6, Xihucincun, Beiqijazhen, Changping District, Beijing 102200, China *Tel:* (0186) 1257 4230
U.S. Office(s): KONG & PARK USA Inc, 1480 Renaissance Dr, Suite 412, Park Ridge, IL 60068, United States *Tel:* 847-241-4845 *Fax:* 312-757-5553 *E-mail:* usaoffice@kongnpark.com SAN: 990-1922
Distribution Center: Fitzhenry & Whiteside Ltd, 195 Allstate Parkway, Markham, ON L3R 4T8, Canada *Tel:* 905-477-9700 *E-mail:* bookinfo@fitzhenry.ca *Web Site:* www.fitzhenry.ca
Hemybooks Libros de Idiomas, Lazaro Cardenas No 407, Colonia Emiliano Zapata, 64390 Monterrey NL, Mexico *Tel:* (0181) 8123-4423 *Toll Free Tel:* 01800-822-5770 *E-mail:* ventasweb@hemybooks.com *Web Site:* www.hemybooks.com
Canet Educacion, Calle Tambo Real 332|334, Urb Matellini, Chorrillos, Lima 09, Peru *E-mail:* canet@canet.pe *Web Site:* www.panasiabooks.com
Pan Asis Publishing Pte Ltd, Raffles City, PO Box 677, Singapore 911723, Singapore *Tel:* 9660 1088 *Fax:* 6291 0500 *E-mail:* pa@panasiabooks.com *Web Site:* www.panasiabooks.com
Kodansha Europe Ltd, 40 Stockwell St, Greenwich, London SE10 8EY, United Kingdom *Tel:* (020) 8293 0111 *Fax:* (020) 8293 5533 *E-mail:* info@kodansha.eu *Web Site:* www.kodansha.eu (UK, Africa & Middle East)

Kookminbooks Co Ltd
Gwangin Sagil 63, 514-4 Munhwa-dong, Paju-si, Gyeonggi-do 413-832
Tel: (070) 4330-7853 *Fax:* (070) 4330-7855
Web Site: www.kmbooks.com; www.kookminbooks.co.kr
Founded: 1961
Subjects: Social Sciences, Sociology
ISBN Prefix(es): 978-89-11

Koonja Publishing Inc
6F Dongwon B/D 112-1 Inui-dong, Jongno-gu, Seoul 110-717
Tel: (02) 762-9193 *Fax:* (02) 764-0209
E-mail: copyright@koonja.co.kr
Web Site: koonja.co.kr
Key Personnel
Foreign Rights: Joseph Kim
Founded: 1980
Subjects: Health, Nutrition, Medicine, Nursing, Dentistry, Oriental Medicine, Orthopedics
ISBN Prefix(es): 978-89-7089; 978-89-627
Total Titles: 1,500 Print

Korea Britannica Corp
Jeilsangho B/D 7th floor, 1-117 Jangchung-dong, Jung-gu, Seoul 100-391
Tel: (02) 1588-1768 *Fax:* (02) 2278-9983
E-mail: webmaster@britannica.co.kr
Web Site: www.britannica.co.kr
Founded: 1968
Subjects: Art, Education, English as a Second Language, Mathematics, Science (General)
ISBN Prefix(es): 978-89-7544
Parent Company: Encyclopaedia Britannica Inc, 325 N LaSalle St, Suite 200, Chicago, IL 60654-2682, United States

Korea University Press
1-2 Anam-dong 5-ga, Seongbuk-gu, Seoul 136-701
Tel: (02) 3290-4232 *Fax:* (02) 923-6311
E-mail: kupress@korea.ac.kr
Web Site: www.kupress.com
Founded: 1956
Subjects: Agriculture, Earth Sciences, Education, Engineering (General), History, Language Arts, Linguistics, Literature, Literary Criticism, Essays, Philosophy, Poetry, Psychology, Psychiatry, Social Sciences, Sociology
ISBN Prefix(es): 978-89-7641

Korean Publishers Association+
105-2, Sagan-Dong, Jongno-gu, Seoul 110-190
Tel: (070) 7126-4720 *Fax:* (02) 738-5414; (02) 735-5653
E-mail: webmaster@kpa21.or.kr
Web Site: www.kpa21.or.kr
Key Personnel
President: Sok-Ghee Baek
Secretary General: Jong Jin Jung
Founded: 1947
Subjects: Publishing & Book Trade Reference
ISBN Prefix(es): 978-89-85231

Kumsung Publishing Co Ltd+
23, Mili-ri, Mapo-gu, Seoul
Tel: (080) 969-1000 (customer service); (02) 2077-8145 (purchase inquiry)
E-mail: webmaster@kumsung.co.kr
Web Site: www.kumsung.co.kr
Founded: 1965
Subjects: Art, English as a Second Language, Fiction, Geography, Geology, History, Mathematics, Music, Dance, Nonfiction (General), Science (General), Physical Education
ISBN Prefix(es): 978-89-07
Subsidiaries: Kumsung Textbook Co Ltd; Kumsung Artcom

Kyobo Book Centre Co Ltd
1 Jongno 1-Ga, Jongno-gu, Seoul 03154
Tel: (02) 1544 1900 *Fax:* (0502) 987 5711
E-mail: privacy@kyobobook.co.kr
Web Site: www.kyobobook.co.kr
Key Personnel
Chief Executive Officer: Lee Han-woo
Subjects: Business, Government, Political Science, Law, Literature, Literary Criticism, Essays
ISBN Prefix(es): 978-89-7085

Kyohaksa Printing & Publishing Co Ltd+
105-67 Gongduk-dong, Mapo-gu, Seoul 152-020
Tel: (010) 8480-8830 *Fax:* (02) 854-6006
Web Site: www.kyohakpublishing.com
Key Personnel
Chief Executive Officer & Founder: Chul-Woo Yang
Founded: 1951
Subjects: Business, Nonfiction (General)

Kyungnam University Press
7 Kyungnamdaehak-ro, Masanhappo-gu, Changwon-si, Cyeongsangnam-do 51767
Tel: (055) 245-5000 *Fax:* (055) 246-6184
Web Site: www.kyungnam.ac.kr
Key Personnel
President: Dr Jae Kyu Park
Subjects: Philosophy, Social Sciences, Sociology
ISBN Prefix(es): 978-89-8421; 978-89-86696

Literature Academy Publishing (Munhak Akademi)
133, Ihwa-dong, Jongno-gu, Seoul 110-500
Tel: (02) 764-5057 *Fax:* (02) 745-8516
Founded: 1988
Subjects: Art, Language Arts, Linguistics, Literature, Literary Criticism, Essays, Poetry
ISBN Prefix(es): 978-89-400
Total Titles: 280 Print

Minjisa Publishing Co+
673-3 Mia-Dong, Gangbug-gu, Seoul 142-819
Tel: (02) 980-6382; (02) 985-8034 *Fax:* (02) 986-1531
Web Site: www.minjisa.co.kr
Key Personnel
President: Tae Seung Lee
Founded: 1982
Subjects: Child Care & Development, Education, Health, Nutrition, History, Literature, Literary Criticism, Essays, Psychology, Psychiatry
ISBN Prefix(es): 978-89-7362
Number of titles published annually: 10 Print
Total Titles: 160 Print

Minjungseorim Bobmunsa Ltd
526-3 Munbal-ri, Gyoha-eup, Paju-si, Gyeonggi-do 413-832
Tel: (031) 955-6500 *Fax:* (031) 955-6525
E-mail: editmin@minjungdic.co.kr
Web Site: www.minjungdic.co.kr
Key Personnel
President: Chul Hwan Kim
Founded: 1979
Subjects: Business, Economics, Government, Political Science, Law, Public Administration, Social Sciences, Sociology
ISBN Prefix(es): 978-89-387
Parent Company: Beupmun Sa Publishing Co

Minumin Publishing, *imprint of* Minumsa Publishing Co Ltd

Minumsa Publishing Co Ltd+
5F Gangnam Publishing Culture Center, 62, Dosan-daero 1-gil, Gangnam-gu, Seoul 06027
Tel: (02) 515-2000 *Fax:* (02) 3444-5185
Web Site: www.minumsa.com
Key Personnel
Vice President: Park Geun-sup; Park Sang-Jun
Sales: Jung Dae Yong
Foreign Rights Manager: Michelle Nam *Tel:* (02) 515-2003 ext 206 *E-mail:* michellenam@minumsa.com
Founded: 1966
Publishes a literary magazine, *World Literature*.
Subjects: Fiction, History, Literature, Literary Criticism, Essays, Nonfiction (General), Philosophy, Science (General), Social Sciences, Sociology
ISBN Prefix(es): 978-89-374

Total Titles: 200 Print
Imprints: BIR Publishing Co Ltd; Golden Bough Publishing Co Ltd; GoldenCompass; Science-Books; SemiColon; Minumin Publishing

Mirae N Co Ltd
321 Sinbanpo-ro, Seocho-gu, Seoul 137-905
Fax: (02) 541-8158
Web Site: www.mirae-n.com
Key Personnel
President: Kim Young-jin
Manager: Ji Young Park *Tel:* (02) 3475-3870
E-mail: park.jiyoung@mirae-n.com
Founded: 1948
Subjects: Advertising, Agriculture, Antiques, Architecture & Interior Design, Art
ISBN Prefix(es): 978-89-378

Mirinae Publishing Co+
63-84 3ga, Hangang-ro, Yongsan-ku, Seoul 152-880
Tel: (02) 2279-2669 *Fax:* (02) 2279-2665
Subjects: Literature, Literary Criticism, Essays, Poetry
ISBN Prefix(es): 978-89-7082

Moonye Publishing Co Ltd+
6 North Rd, Bldg 401, Mapo-gu, Seoul 121-819
Tel: (02) 393-5681 *Fax:* (02) 393-5685
E-mail: info@moonye.com
Web Site: www.moonye.com; www.facebook.com/moonyepublishing
Key Personnel
Chief Executive: Byung-Suk Chun
Founded: 1966
Subjects: Art, Fiction, History, Literature, Literary Criticism, Essays, Nonfiction (General), Philosophy, Social Sciences, Sociology, Women's Studies
ISBN Prefix(es): 978-89-310

Munhakdongne Children's, *imprint of* Munhakdongne Publishing Group

Munhakdongne Publishing Group
210, Hoedong-gil, Paju-si, Gyeonggi-do 413-120
Tel: (031) 955 8888; (031) 955 2635 *Fax:* (031) 955 8855
E-mail: rights@munhak.com
Web Site: www.munhak.com
Key Personnel
Chief Executive Officer: Kang Byoungsun
Foreign Rights Associate: Kate Han
Founded: 1993
Subjects: Art, Business, Economics, Education, Fiction, Health, Nutrition, History, Literature, Literary Criticism, Essays, Nonfiction (General), Philosophy, Psychology, Psychiatry, Science (General), Self-Help, Comics, Fine Arts, Fitness, Humanities, Liberal Arts, Parenting
ISBN Prefix(es): 978-89-8281; 978-89-546; 978-89-85712
Imprints: Alice; Anibooks; Artbooks; Aurum; Booknomad; Dahl; Econ; Geulhangari; Munhakdongne Children's

Munundang Publishing Co
45-3 Myeongnyun-dong 1-ga, Jongro-gu, Seoul 110-521
Tel: (02) 762-6010 *Fax:* (02) 745-0265
E-mail: munun2@chol.com
Web Site: munundang.co.kr
Founded: 1962
Subjects: Engineering (General), Science (General)
ISBN Prefix(es): 978-89-7393

Nanam Publishing House+
518-4, Munbal-ri, Paju-si, Gyeonggi-do 413-756
Tel: (031) 955-4600 *Fax:* (031) 955-4555
E-mail: webmaster@nanam.net; post@nanam.net

Web Site: www.nanam.net
Key Personnel
Chief Executive: Sang-Ho Cho
Founded: 1979
Subjects: Advertising, Art, Communications, Journalism, Literature, Literary Criticism, Essays, Poetry, Social Sciences, Sociology
ISBN Prefix(es): 978-89-300
Parent Company: Korea Society Review

Oneull Publishing Co Ltd+
Seonyugol 67, Yangpyeong-dong 2-ga, Sindonga High Palace 102-dong 201, Yeongdeungpo-gu, Seoul 150-102
Tel: (02) 716-2811 *Fax:* (02) 712-7392
E-mail: oneull@hanmail.net
Web Site: www.on-publications.com
Key Personnel
Mng Editor: Kim Jin Mi
Founded: 1980
Subjects: Child Care & Development, Fiction, History, House & Home, Mysteries, Suspense, Nonfiction (General), Poetry, Religion - Other, Women's Studies
ISBN Prefix(es): 978-89-355
Number of titles published annually: 10 Print
Total Titles: 900 Print
Imprints: Cham Kae

Oruem Publishing House+
1596-6 Socho-dong, Socho-ku, Seoul
Tel: (02) 585-9122 *Fax:* (02) 584-7952
Founded: 1993
Subjects: Asian Studies, Business, Communications, Economics, Education, Government, Political Science, Public Administration, Social Sciences, Sociology
ISBN Prefix(es): 978-89-7778

Pagijong Press
129-162, Yongdu-dong, Dongdaemun-gu, Seoul 130-070
Tel: (02) 922-1192; (02) 922-1193
E-mail: pijbook@naver.com
Web Site: www.pjbook.com
Key Personnel
Chief Executive Officer: Chan-Ik Park
Founded: 1989
Subjects: Art, Language Arts, Linguistics, Literature, Literary Criticism, Essays, Social Sciences, Sociology
ISBN Prefix(es): 978-89-7878

Pakyoungsa Publishing Co
Hoedong-gil, 37-9, Gyeonggi-do, Paju-si 413-120
Tel: (031) 955-4071 *Fax:* (031) 955-4076
E-mail: pys@pybook.co.kr
Web Site: www.pybook.co.kr
Founded: 1952
Subjects: Accounting, Business, Economics, Finance, Government, Political Science, History, Law, Management, Marketing, Psychology, Psychiatry, Real Estate, Social Sciences, Sociology
ISBN Prefix(es): 978-89-10

Pan Korea Book Corp
1-222, 2-Ga, Shinmun-Ro, Jungro-Gu, Seoul 110-601
Tel: (02) 733-2011; (02) 733-2014 *Fax:* (02) 733-2016
E-mail: info@bumhanbook.co.kr; text@bumhanbook.co.kr
Web Site: www.bumhanbook.co.kr
Key Personnel
President: Mr Yoon-Sun Kim
Founded: 1956
Also book importer & distributor.
Subjects: Chemistry, Chemical Engineering, Engineering (General), Language Arts, Linguistics,

Literature, Literary Criticism, Essays, Technology
ISBN Prefix(es): 978-89-7129

Panmun Book Co Ltd+
CPO Box 1016, 40, Changro 1-ka, Seoul
Tel: (02) 2653 5131; (02) 2653 5301 *Fax:* (02) 2653 2454
Key Personnel
Chairman & Chief Executive Officer: Mr S K Liu
E-mail: skliu@epublic.co.kr
Founded: 1955
Subjects: Cookery, Education, Language Arts, Linguistics, Literature, Literary Criticism, Essays, Management, Medicine, Nursing, Dentistry, Science (General), Social Sciences, Sociology, Children, English Education, Fitness
Number of titles published annually: 100 Print; 30 CD-ROM; 10 Online; 10 E-Book
Total Titles: 500 Print; 100 CD-ROM; 50 Online; 20 E-Book
Parent Company: Epublic
Associate Companies: Language World, Seoul Telecom Bldg, 14th floor, 923-12, Mok 1-dong, Yangcheonku, Seoul, Mng Dir: Hannah Lee *E-mail:* halee@languageworld.co.kr *Web Site:* www.lwbooks.co.kr
Subsidiaries: Bummun Education
Branch Office(s)
Kwangju
Pusan
Taegu
Taejon
Warehouse: Paju, Kyunggido

Pearson Education Korea Ltd+
8th floor, A-dong, Times Sq, Tower 442, Yeongdeungpo-dong 4-ga, Yeongdeung po-gu, Seoul 150-798
Tel: (02) 2014 8800 *Fax:* (02) 2014 8801
E-mail: koreaelt@pearson.com
Web Site: www.pearsonelt.com
Founded: 1998
Subjects: Computer Science, Engineering (General), English as a Second Language
ISBN Prefix(es): 978-89-450
Number of titles published annually: 30 Print
Total Titles: 500 Print
Parent Company: Pearson Education, 225 River St, Hoboken, NJ 07030-4772, United States
Ultimate Parent Company: Pearson PLC

PoChinChai Printing Co Ltd, Publishing Division
250, Jikji-gil, Paju-si, Gyeonggi-do 10881
Tel: (031) 955-1114; (031) 955-1130 *Fax:* (031) 696-6324
Web Site: www.pochinchai.co.kr
Key Personnel
Chairman: Kim Joon-Ki
President: Kim Jung-Sun
Founded: 1961
Subjects: Art, History, Social Sciences, Sociology, Technology

St Pauls Publications+
7 Hyunno-ro, Gangbuk-gu, Seoul
Tel: (02) 945-2972 *Fax:* (02) 986-1365
E-mail: bookclub@paolo.net
Web Site: www.paolo.kr
Founded: 1991
Publication of literary, children's books, theology & philosophy books, religious books. Publishes *My Friends,* monthly comic magazine.
Subjects: Biblical Studies, Fiction, Human Relations, Inspirational, Spirituality, Literature, Literary Criticism, Essays, Philosophy, Poetry, Religion - Catholic, Theology
Total Titles: 150 Print; 30 Audio
Book Club(s): St Pauls Book Club *Tel:* (02) 986-1361; (02) 986-1365

Sakyejul Publishing Ltd
Gyeonggi-do 252, Paju-si, Gongdong-gu 10881
Tel: (031) 955-8588; (031) 955-8558 *Fax:* (031) 955-8595; (031) 955-8596
E-mail: skj@sakyejul.co.kr
Web Site: www.sakyejul.net
Founded: 1982
Subjects: Art, Business, Economics, Fiction, History, Nonfiction (General), Social Sciences, Sociology, Business Administration, Humanities, Natural Science
ISBN Prefix(es): 978-89-5828; 978-89-7196

Samsung Publishing Co Ltd+
1516-2, Seocho-dong, Seocho-gu, Seoul 137-070
Tel: (02) 3470-6800
Web Site: www.ssbooks.com
Key Personnel
Chief Executive Officer & Dir: Jin Yong Kim
Mng Dir: Yeong Ryeol Kim
Founded: 1951
Subjects: Art, Business, Crafts, Games, Hobbies, Engineering (General), History, Literature, Literary Criticism, Essays, Science (General), Women's Studies
ISBN Prefix(es): 978-89-15
Orders to: 60-32 Garibong-dong, Guro-gu, Seoul

ScienceBooks, *imprint of* Minumsa Publishing Co Ltd

Sejong Taewang Kinyom Saophoe (King Seijong The Great Memorial Society)
1-157 Cheongnyangni-dong, Dongdaemun-gu, Seoul 130-866
Tel: (02) 969-8851; (02) 969-8852; (02) 969-8853 *Fax:* (02) 969-8854
E-mail: sejong@sejongkorea.org
Web Site: sejongkorea.org
Subjects: History, Religion - Other
ISBN Prefix(es): 978-89-8275

Sekwang Music Publishing Co+
232-32 Seogye-Dong, Yongsan-gu, Seoul 140-140
Tel: (02) 719-2652 *Fax:* (02) 719-2191
E-mail: sekwang@sekwang.co.kr
Web Site: www.sekwang.co.kr
Key Personnel
President & Chairman: Shin-Joon Park
Founded: 1953
Subjects: Art, Music, Dance
ISBN Prefix(es): 978-89-03

SemiColon, *imprint of* Minumsa Publishing Co Ltd

Seogwangsa+
77-12 Hoedong-gil, Paju-si, Gyeonggi-do 10881
Tel: (031) 955-4331; (031) 955-4335 (editorial off) *Fax:* (031) 955-4336
E-mail: phil6161@chol.com
Web Site: seokwangsa.or.kr
Founded: 1974
Subjects: Anthropology, Asian Studies, Education, Philosophy, Religion - Buddhist, Religion - Catholic, Religion - Hindu, Religion - Other
ISBN Prefix(es): 978-89-306

Seoul National University Press
One Gwanak-ro, Gwanak-gu, Seoul 08826
Tel: (02) 880-5252 *Fax:* (02) 888-4148; (02) 889-0785
E-mail: snubook@snu.ac.kr
Web Site: www.snu.ac.kr; www.snupress.com
Key Personnel
Dir: Sung-dong Kim *Tel:* (02) 880-5217
E-mail: sungdong@snu.ac.kr
Marketing Dir: Kyu-Lli Lee *Tel:* (02) 880-7995
E-mail: kyuill@snu.ac.kr
Founded: 1961
Subjects: Architecture & Interior Design, Art, Earth Sciences, History, Language Arts, Lin-

guistics, Literature, Literary Criticism, Essays, Medicine, Nursing, Dentistry, Philosophy, Science (General), Social Sciences, Sociology
ISBN Prefix(es): 978-89-7096; 978-89-521

Seoul Selection
6, Samcheong-ro, 2nd floor, Jongno-gu, Seoul 110-190
Tel: (070) 5038-5034; (070) 4060-5064 (direct)
Fax: (070) 8668-1090
E-mail: atoz@seoulselection.com
Web Site: www.seoulselection.com
Founded: 2003
Subjects: Business, Economics, Education, Government, Political Science, History, Language Arts, Linguistics, Literature, Literary Criticism, Essays, Photography, Travel & Tourism, Culture, Korea
ISBN Prefix(es): 978-89-91913

Shinkwang Publishing Co
278-1 Bomun-Dong 6-ga, Sungbuk-ku, Seoul 136-086
Tel: (02) 925 5051; (02) 925 5053 *Fax:* (02) 925 5054
E-mail: shkpub7@naver.com
Web Site: www.shinkwangpub.com
Founded: 1972
Subjects: Cookery, Medicine, Nursing, Dentistry, Science (General)

SNU Press, see Seoul National University Press

Sogang University Press
35 Baekbeom-ro, Mapo-gu, Seoul 04107
Tel: (02) 705-8212
Web Site: www.sogang.ac.kr
Founded: 1978
Subjects: Art, History, Language Arts, Linguistics, Literature, Literary Criticism, Essays, Science (General), Social Sciences, Sociology
ISBN Prefix(es): 978-89-7273

Soohaksa
1586-4 Seocho 3-dong, Seocho-ku, Seoul 137-876
Tel: (02) 584-4642 *Fax:* (02) 521-1458
Web Site: www.soohaksa.co.kr
Key Personnel
President: Lee Young-Ho
Founded: 1953
Subjects: Fashion, Health, Nutrition, House & Home
ISBN Prefix(es): 978-89-7140
Total Titles: 143 Print
Book Club(s): KPA

VICHE, *imprint of* Gimm-Young Publishers Inc

Woongjin ThinkBig Co Ltd+
535-1, Munbal-ri, Gyoha-eup, Paju-si, Gyeonggi-do 413-756
Tel: (031) 956-7111; (031) 956-7365 *Fax:* (031) 956-7579
Web Site: www.wjthinkbig.com
Key Personnel
Chairman: Seok-keum Yoon
Chief Executive Officer & Dir: Jae-Jin Lee
Chief Financial Officer & Dir: Cheon-Shin Park
Chief Scientific Officer & Dir: Sae-bom Yoon
Mng Dir: Hyung-deok Yoon
Founded: 1980
Specialize in multimedia packages, educational & home videos, CAI-software, compact discs.
Subjects: Business, Fiction, History, Nonfiction (General), Science (General)
ISBN Prefix(es): 978-89-01; 978-89-02
Imprints: Gomdori
Subsidiaries: Woongjin (USA) Inc
Book Club(s): Woongjin Book Club

Word of Life Press+
Division of TEAM Mission Korea
69 Saemunan-ro, Jongno-gu, Seoul 03175
Tel: (02) 595 3545 *Fax:* (02) 591 9103
E-mail: int@lifebook.co.kr; shopping@lifebook.co.kr
Web Site: www.lifebook.co.kr
Key Personnel
President: Chang-Young Kim
Founded: 1953
Specialize in Christian book publishing.
Subjects: Religion - Protestant, Missionary Work
ISBN Prefix(es): 978-89-04
Number of titles published annually: 510 Print
Total Titles: 2,000 Print
U.S. Office(s): Word of Life Books, 9838 W Garden Grove Blvd, Garden Grove, CA 92844, United States *Tel:* 714-530-2211
Word of Life Books, 8884 N Milwaukee Ave, Niles, IL 60714, United States *Tel:* 847-296-3160 *Fax:* 847-296-3164
Word of Life Books, 4113 John Marr Dr, Annandale, VA 22003, United States *Tel:* 703-256-3444

YBM+
104 Jongno, Jongno-gu, Seoul 110-772
Tel: (02) 2000-0509; (02) 2000-0515; (02) 2000-0592
E-mail: suite@ybmsisa.com
Web Site: www.ybm.co.kr; www.ybmbooks.com
Key Personnel
Founder & Chairman: Y B Min
President & Chief Executive Officer: Dong-Hyun Lee
Founded: 1961
Book & magazine publishing, language schools, testing activities, music company, IT business, ELT materials, multimedia publications, online publishing, English language study materials, TOETL & TOEIC prep books.
Membership(s): ABC; FIPP; IPA.
Subjects: Economics, English as a Second Language, Literature, Literary Criticism, Essays, Music, Dance, Photography, Science (General), Travel & Tourism
ISBN Prefix(es): 978-89-17
Number of titles published annually: 1,000 Print; 24 CD-ROM; 48 Online; 100 E-Book; 600 Audio
Total Titles: 13,000 Print; 50 CD-ROM; 89 Online; 199 E-Book; 6,500 Audio
Branch Office(s)
Beijing City Chaoyang District Waisi Language Training Center, America School of English, China Merchants Onward Center, 4th floor, No 118, Chaoyang District Jianguo Rd, Beijing 100022, China *Tel:* (010) 6566 0786
YBM/ELS Language Centers, 549 Howe St, 6th floor, Vancouver, BC V6C 2C2, Canada, Dir: Stephen Muhleisen *Tel:* 604-684-9577 *E-mail:* info@elscanada.com *Web Site:* www.elscanada.com
YBM/ELS Language Centers, 36 Victoria St, Toronto, ON M5C 1H3, Canada, Dir: Zbigniew Andrzejcuk *Tel:* 416-203-6466 *E-mail:* info@elscanada.com *Web Site:* www.elscanada.com
U.S. Office(s): Young & Son Global, 3250 Wilshire Blvd, Suite 2007, Los Angeles, CA 90010, United States *E-mail:* hylee58@ybmsisa.com
Distributor for Barron's; ETS/Chauncey; Macmillan; McGraw-Hill; National Geographic Society; Newsweek International; Pearson; Peterson's; Reader's Digest; Simon & Schuster

YeaRimDang Publishing Co Ltd
Yearim Bldg, 153, Samseong-dong, Gangnam-gu, Seoul 135-090
Tel: (02) 566 1004 *Fax:* (02) 567 9660
E-mail: yearim@yearim.co.kr
Web Site: www.yearim.co.kr

Key Personnel
President: Na Sung-Hun
Dir, Editorial Dept: Yoo In-Hwa
Dir, International Affairs & Publication Planning Dept: Mr Derrick Kim *Tel:* (02) 3404 9247 *E-mail:* derrick@yearim.co.kr
Foreign Copyrights Coordinator: Claire Ko *Tel:* (02) 3404 9248 *E-mail:* rights@yearim.co.kr
Founded: 1973
Subjects: Cookery, Education, Fiction, Nonfiction (General), Science (General), Nature
ISBN Prefix(es): 978-89-507; 978-89-302; 978-89-87941; 978-89-8449
Subsidiaries: Haenggan, Between Lines Publisher Inc; JB Books Co; Nungin Book Co; Yearim Education Co

Yeha Publishing Co+
736-37, Yoksam-dong, Kangnam-ku, Seoul 135-080
Tel: (02) 553-5933 *Fax:* (02) 552-5149
Founded: 1987
Membership(s): Korean Publishers Association.
Subjects: Business, Literature, Literary Criticism, Essays, Music, Dance
ISBN Prefix(es): 978-89-7359

Yeowon Media
1420-6 Seocho-dong, Seocho-gu, Seoul 137-864
Tel: (02) 523-6660 *Fax:* (02) 588-8060
E-mail: info@tantani.com
Web Site: www.tantani.com; eng.tantani.com
Key Personnel
Dir General: Dong-hwi Kim
Subjects: Art, Fiction, Science (General)
ISBN Prefix(es): 978-89-5570; 978-89-89636

Yonsei University Press
Yonsei University, 50 Yonsei-ro, Bldg 704 (Housing Off), 4-Haksa, Seodaemun-ro, Seoul 03722
Tel: (02) 2123-3380 *Fax:* (02) 2123-8673
E-mail: press@yonsei.ac.kr (editorial); ysup@yonsei.ac.kr (marketing); webmaster@yonsei.ac.kr
Web Site: press.yonsei.ac.kr
Key Personnel
Executive Dir: So Young Sohn *Tel:* (02) 2123-4014 *E-mail:* sohns@yonsei.ac.kr
Deputy Dir: Jong Ho Lee *Tel:* (02) 2123-8473 *E-mail:* leejh@yonsei.ac.kr
Founded: 1955
Subjects: Art, History, Medicine, Nursing, Dentistry, Philosophy, Religion - Other, Science (General), Social Sciences, Sociology, Technology
ISBN Prefix(es): 978-89-7141

Youlhwadang Publisher+
520-10, Paju Bookcity, Munbal-Ri, Gyoha-Eup, Paju-Si, Gyeonggi-do
Tel: (031) 955-7000-6 *Fax:* (031) 955-7010
E-mail: yhdp@youlhwadang.co.kr
Web Site: youlhwadang.co.kr
Key Personnel
President: Ki-Ung Yi
Editor & Foreign Rights: Soojung Yi *E-mail:* ysj0710@youlhwadang.co.kr
Founded: 1971
Specialize in Korean traditional art.
Subjects: Antiques, Architecture & Interior Design, Art, Crafts, Games, Hobbies, Film, Video, Literature, Literary Criticism, Essays, Music, Dance, Photography, Korean Art
ISBN Prefix(es): 978-89-301
Number of titles published annually: 20 Print
Total Titles: 500 Print; 7 E-Book

Spain

General Information

Capital: Madrid
Language: Castilian Spanish (official) is the most widely used. Also Basque in the north, Catalan in the northeast, Galician in the northwest
Religion: Roman Catholic
Population: 40 million
Bank Hours: 0900-1400 Monday-Friday; 0900-1300 Saturday
Shop Hours: 0900-1300, 1700-2000 Monday-Saturday
Currency: 100 Eurocents = 1 Euro
Export/Import Information: Member of European Union. Tariffs on books same as other EU members. 4% VAT on books. Import license not required; foreign books subject to censorship. No exchange controls.
Copyright: UCC, Berne, Florence (see Copyright Conventions, pg viii)

Aache Ediciones
C/ Malvarrosa, 2 (Las Lomas), 19005 Guadalajara
SAN: 000-006X
Tel: 949 220 438 *Fax:* 949 491 160
E-mail: editorial@aache.com
Web Site: www.aache.com
Key Personnel
Dir: Antonio Herrera Casado
Founded: 1990
Specialize in Guadalajara (Spain) books.
Subjects: Archaeology, History, Regional Interests
ISBN Prefix(es): 978-84-87743; 978-84-95179; 978-84-96236

Abada Editores SL
Calle del Gobernador, 18, 28014 Madrid
Tel: 914 296 882 *Fax:* 914 297 507
Web Site: www.abadaeditores.com
Subjects: Architecture & Interior Design, Art, Government, Political Science, History, Language Arts, Linguistics, Literature, Literary Criticism, Essays, Music, Dance, Philosophy, Religion - Other, Science (General)
ISBN Prefix(es): 978-84-96258

Publicacions de l'Abadia de Montserrat SA
Carrer Ausias Marc, 92-98, 08013 Barcelona
Tel: 932 450 303
E-mail: informacio@pamsa.cat
Web Site: www.pamsa.cat
Key Personnel
Administrator: Jordi Ubeda i Baulo
Dir: Josep Massot i Muntaner
Founded: 1499
Subjects: Art, Biography, Memoirs, Fiction, History, Language Arts, Linguistics, Literature, Literary Criticism, Essays, Music, Dance, Philosophy, Religion - Catholic, Theology
ISBN Prefix(es): 978-84-7202; 978-84-7826; 978-84-8415; 978-84-9883
Total Titles: 3,000 Print

Academia de la Llingua Asturiana
Apartau de Correos 574, 33080 Uvieu
SAN: 000-0205
Tel: 985 21 18 37 *Fax:* 985 22 68 16
E-mail: alla@asturnet.es
Web Site: www.academiadelallingua.com
Founded: 1981
Subjects: Anthropology, Language Arts, Linguistics, Literature, Literary Criticism, Essays
ISBN Prefix(es): 978-84-8168; 978-84-86936
Number of titles published annually: 30 Print
Total Titles: 550 Print; 3 Online
Orders to: Albora Llibros, Pz Romualdo Alvargonzalez 5, 33202 Xixon *Tel:* 985 354 213 *Fax:* 985 354 213

Acantilado+
Subsidiary of Quaderns Crema SA
Muntaner, 462, 08006 Barcelona
Tel: 934 144 906 *Fax:* 934 147 107
E-mail: correo@acantilado.com; rights@acantilado.es
Web Site: www.acantilado.es
Key Personnel
Mng Dir: Jaume Vallcorba
Press Dept: Sr Sergi Masferrer
Founded: 1999
Subjects: History, Literature, Literary Criticism, Essays, Poetry, Narratives
ISBN Prefix(es): 978-84-95359; 978-84-930657; 978-84-96489; 978-84-96136; 978-84-96834
Number of titles published annually: 50 Print
Total Titles: 100 Print
Distributed by Compania Caribena de Libros (Puerto Rico); Centro Cuesta Nacional (Dominica Republic); El Hombre de la Mancha (Panama); Libreria La Tertulia (Puerto Rico); VDL Books (Venezuela)
Foreign Rep(s): Fernandez De Castro SA (Chile); Colofon SA de CV (Mexico); Gussi Libros (Uruguay); Libreria Internacional (Costa Rica); Libri Mundi SA (Ecuador); Grupo Penta Distribuidores SAS (Colombia); Sophos SA (Guatemala); Libreria El Virrey (Peru); Distribuidora Waldhuter (Argentina)

Editorial Acanto SA
c/ Can Guiu, 9, 08188 Vallromanes, Barcelona
SAN: 022-2322
Tel: 93 572 98 39; 93 572 97 75
E-mail: acanto@dtinf.net
Web Site: www.editorialacanto.com
Key Personnel
Commercial, Printing & Marketing: Isabel Casadevall Oliver *E-mail:* acantoisabel@dtinf.net
Production & Purchasing Rights: Silvia Blume Bruns
Founded: 1987
Subjects: Art, Cookery, Crafts, Games, Hobbies, Fashion, Film, Video, Gardening, Plants, Health, Nutrition, Photography, Sports, Athletics
ISBN Prefix(es): 978-84-86673; 978-84-95376
Foreign Rep(s): Libreria Artemis Edinter (Guatemala); Editorial Ceiba SA de CB (El Salvador); Editorial Contrapunto (Chile); Cuesta - Centro del Libro (Dominican Republic); Desarrollos Culturales Costarricenses DCC SA (Costa Rica); DH Libros CA (Venezuela); Distribudora La Familia (Peru); Fondo Cultural Iberoamericano (Colombia); Gussi Libros (Uruguay); Hispamer SA (Nicaragua); El Hombre de la Mancha (Panama); El Libro Cia Ltda (Ecuador); Litexsa Boliviana (Bolivia); Distribuciones Marin (Mexico); MS Books Inc (Puerto Rico); Riverside Agency SAC (Argentina); Ediciones Tec Paraguayas (Paraguay); Zamboni Books (Brazil)
Distribution Center: Naturart SA, Av Mare de Deu de Lorda, 20, 08034 Barcelona *Tel:* 93 205 40 00 *Fax:* 93 205 14 41 *E-mail:* info@blume.net (Spain, Latin America & Portugal)

Acervo Editorial SL+
Ronda General Mitre, 200, 08006 Barcelona
SAN: 022-2349
Tel: 93 2122664 *Fax:* 93 4174425
E-mail: info@editorialacervo.es
Web Site: editorialacervo.es
Founded: 1954
Subjects: History, Law, Literature, Literary Criticism, Essays, Mysteries, Suspense, Religion - Catholic, Science Fiction, Fantasy
ISBN Prefix(es): 978-84-7002
Total Titles: 1 Print

Editorial Acribia SA+
C/ Royo Urieta, 23, 50006 Zaragoza

SAN: 022-2357
Mailing Address: Apdo Postal 466, 50080 Zaragoza
Tel: 976 232 089 *Fax:* 976 219 212
E-mail: acribia@editorialacribia.com
Web Site: www.editorialacribia.com
Key Personnel
Mng Dir: Maria Josefa Lopez Buesa
Founded: 1957
Subjects: Agriculture, Medicine, Nursing, Dentistry, Natural History, Science (General), Veterinary Science
ISBN Prefix(es): 978-84-200; 978-84-370
Number of titles published annually: 30 Print
Total Titles: 980 Print
Foreign Rep(s): Libreria Eduardo Albers Ltda (Chile); Avances Clinicos (Uruguay); Livraria Canuto Ltda (Brazil); Libreria Cervantes Cia Ltda (Ecuador); Miguel Concha SA (Chile); Cuspide Libros SA (Argentina); Didaclibros Ltda (Colombia); Librerias Artemis Edinter SA (Guatemala); Edit Agropecuaria Hemisferio Sur (Uruguay); Fundacion Libro Universitario Libun (Peru); Hispamer (Nicaragua); Editorial Hispano Andina (Colombia); Libreria Del Ingeniero Ltda (Colombia); Lea Book Distributors (USA); Lectorum Publication (USA); Libreria Lehmann SA (Costa Rica); El Libro Cia Ltda (Ecuador); Livraria Lopes Da Silva Editora (Portugal); Losa Libros Ltda (Uruguay); Meditec SA (Panama); Ediciones Menvi (Bolivia); Libri Mundi (Ecuador); La Odisea (El Salvador); Libreria Papiros (Ecuador); Prata Rodrigues Publicacoes Lda (Portugal); Ediciones el Profesional Ltda (Colombia); Publindus Tria-Producao de Comunicacao LT (Portugal); Editorial Reverte Colombiana SA (Colombia); RGS Libros SA de CV (Mexico); Libreria San Cristobal SAC (Peru); Tecni-ciencia Libros (Venezuela); Libreria Tecnica Santa Teresa CA (Venezuela); Ediciones Tecnicas Paraguayas (Paraguay); Libreria Universal Carlos Federspiel & Co SA (Costa Rica); Distribuidora Universal Text CA (Venezuela); Franz Wald Bacharel (Panama); Zamboni-Comercio De Livros Ltda (Brazil)

ACTAR Publishing
Roca i Batlle 2, 08023 Barcelona
Tel: 93 417 49 93 *Fax:* 93 418 67 07
E-mail: info@actar.com; editorial@actar.com
Web Site: www.actar.com
Founded: 1931
Subjects: Architecture & Interior Design, Contemporary Art, Graphic Design
ISBN Prefix(es): 978-84-89698; 978-84-920718; 978-84-95273; 978-84-95951; 978-84-89771; 978-84-96954
U.S. Office(s): 151 Grand St, 5th floor, New York, NY 10013, United States *Tel:* 212-966-2207 *Fax:* 212-966-2214 *E-mail:* officeusa@actard.com
Bookshop(s): RAS Gallery Barcelona, Doctor Dou 10, 08001 Barcelona *Tel:* 93 412 71 99 *E-mail:* rasbcn@rasbcn.com *Web Site:* www.rasbcn.com
Distribution Center: Ingram Publisher Services, One Ingram Blvd, La Vergne, TN 37086, United States *E-mail:* ips@ingramcontent.com *Web Site:* www.ingramcontent.com

ACV Ediciones
Imprint of ACV Global
Diputacio, 238-244, 08007 Barcelona
Tel: 933042980
E-mail: info@acvglobal.com
Web Site: www.acvedicions.com; www.acvglobal.com
Key Personnel
Mng Dir: Sergi Roses Collado
Founded: 1987

Subjects: Health, Nutrition
ISBN Prefix(es): 978-84-88907; 978-84-89589

ADE, see Asociacion de Directores de Escena de Espana (ADE)

AECID, see Agencia Espanola de Cooperacion Internacional para el Desarrollo

AENOR Internacional SAU+
Calle Genova no 6, 28004 Madrid
Tel: 914 326 000 *Fax:* 913 104 043
E-mail: editorial@aenor.com
Web Site: www.aenor.es
Key Personnel
Publishing Manager: Eva Maria Lopez
General Dir: Rafael Garcia Meiro
Founded: 1986
This publisher has indicated that 90% of their product line is author subsidized.
Membership(s): CEN; CENELEC; COPANT; ETSI; GENE; IEC; IQNET; ISO.
Subjects: Aeronautics, Aviation, Agriculture, Automotive, Business, Civil Engineering, Computer Science, Electronics, Electrical Engineering, Engineering (General), Environmental Studies, Management, Marketing, Mechanical Engineering, Technology, Transportation, Business Certification, International Standards, National Standards
ISBN Prefix(es): 978-84-8143; 978-84-86688
Number of titles published annually: 15 Print; 20 E-Book

Editorial Afers SL+
Av Doctor Gomez Ferrer, 55, 1r-5a, Apartat de Correus 267, 46470 Catarroja (Pais Valencia)
Tel: 961 26 93 94
E-mail: afers@editorialafers.cat
Web Site: www.editorialafers.com
Key Personnel
Publishing Dir: Vicent Olmos *E-mail:* vicent.olmos@editorialafers.cat
Rights & Marketing: Dr Miquel Rossello, PhD *E-mail:* miquel.rossello@telefonica.net
Founded: 1983
Subjects: History, Regional Interests, Social Sciences, Sociology
ISBN Prefix(es): 978-84-95916; 978-84-86574; 978-84-92542
Number of titles published annually: 30 Print
Total Titles: 300 Print

Agata, *imprint of* Editorial Libsa SA

Agencia Espanola de Cooperacion Internacional para el Desarrollo
Ciudad Universitaria, Ave de Reyes Catolicos, 4, 28040 Madrid
SAN: 001-6446
Tel: 915 838 100; 915 838 598; 915 838 599 *Fax:* 915 838 310; 915 838 311; 915 838 313
E-mail: centro.informacion@aecid.es
Web Site: www.aecid.es
Key Personnel
Contact: Hector Cuesta *Tel:* 915 823 430 *E-mail:* hector.cuesta@aecid.es
Subjects: Art, Biography, Memoirs, Drama, Theater, Economics, Education, History, Law, Literature, Literary Criticism, Essays, Poetry, Social Sciences, Sociology
ISBN Prefix(es): 978-84-7232; 978-84-8347

Ediciones Agrotecnicas SL
Plaza Espana, 10 5° Izq, 28008 Madrid
Tel: 91 547 35 15 *Fax:* 91 547 45 06
E-mail: info@terralia.com
Web Site: www.terralia.com
Subjects: Agriculture, Civil Engineering
ISBN Prefix(es): 978-84-87480
Subsidiaries: ISLA Agricola SA

Editorial Agua Clara SL+
C/ Rosello, 55, 03010 Alicante
SAN: 002-242X
Tel: 965 24 00 64 *Fax:* 965 25 93 02
E-mail: info@traduccionesaguaclara.com; aguaclara@editorialaguaclara.es
Web Site: www.traduccionesaguaclara.com; www.editorialaguaclara.com
Founded: 1982
Subjects: Fiction, Literature, Literary Criticism, Essays, Poetry, Religion - Catholic
ISBN Prefix(es): 978-84-86234; 978-84-8018

Editorial Agustiniana Revista
Paseo de la Alameda, 39, 28440 Guadarrama, Madrid
Tel: 918 549 590 *Fax:* 918 549 612
E-mail: editorial@agustiniana.es
Web Site: www.agustiniana.es
Key Personnel
Dir: Pedro Luis Morais Anton
Administrator: Felix Rodriguez Olmo
Founded: 1960
Subjects: Biblical Studies, History, Law, Philosophy, Religion - Catholic, Social Sciences, Sociology, Theology
ISBN Prefix(es): 978-84-86898; 978-84-95745
Foreign Rep(s): Casalini Libri SpA (Italy)

AITIM (Asociacion de Investigacion Tecnica de las Industrias de la Madera)+
Calle de la Flora, 3, 2° dcha, 28013 Madrid
Tel: 91 542 58 64 *Fax:* 91 559 05 12
E-mail: informame@aitim.es; carla@aitim.es (publications)
Web Site: www.infomadera.net
Key Personnel
Dir: Fernando Peraza Sanchez *E-mail:* f.peraza@aitim.es; J Enrique Peraza Sanchez *E-mail:* e.peraza@aitim.es
Founded: 1962
Subjects: Architecture & Interior Design, Technology
ISBN Prefix(es): 978-84-87381

Aizkorri, *imprint of* Editorial Everest SA

Ediciones Akal SA+
Imprint of Akal Grupo Editorial
Sector Foresta n° 1, 28760 Tres Cantos, Madrid
SAN: 001-5326
Tel: 918 061 996 *Fax:* 918 044 028
E-mail: pedidos.blume@akal.com; edicion@akal.com; universidad@akal.com; educacion@akal.com; prensa@akal.com; atencion.cliente@akal.com
Web Site: www.akal.com
Founded: 1972
Subjects: Anthropology, Archaeology, Architecture & Interior Design, Art, Asian Studies, Behavioral Sciences, Economics, Education, English as a Second Language, Film, Video, Law, Philosophy, Psychology, Psychiatry, Social Sciences, Sociology
ISBN Prefix(es): 978-84-460; 978-84-7339; 978-84-7600
Associate Companies: Foca; H Blume; Ediciones Istmo; Siglo XXI de Espana

Editorial Alas+
C/ Villarroel, n° 124, 08011 Barcelona
SAN: 002-2446
Tel: 934 537 506 *Fax:* 934 537 506
E-mail: info@editorial-alas.com
Web Site: www.editorial-alas.com
Key Personnel
Editor: Jordi Sala
Founded: 1923
Specialize in sports subjects with emphasis on martial arts.

Subjects: Health, Nutrition, Parapsychology, Religion - Buddhist, Sports, Athletics, Martial Arts
ISBN Prefix(es): 978-84-203

Alba, *imprint of* Editorial Libsa SA

Alba Editorial SLU
Baixada de Sant Miguel, 1, bajos, 08002 Barcelona
Tel: 934152929 *Fax:* 934157493
E-mail: info@albaeditorial.es
Web Site: www.albaeditorial.es
Founded: 1993
Subjects: Art, Biography, Memoirs, Fiction, Geography, Geology, Philosophy, Social Sciences, Sociology, Recreation
ISBN Prefix(es): 978-84-88730; 978-84-89846; 978-84-8428

Alberdania+
Istillaga Pl, 2 behea C, 20304 Irun, Gipuzkoa
SAN: 000-1201
Tel: 943 63 28 14 *Fax:* 943 63 80 55
E-mail: alberdania@alberdania.net
Web Site: www.alberdania.net
Key Personnel
Editor: Jorge Gimenez Bech
Founded: 1933
Subjects: Anthropology, Art, Government, Political Science, Literature, Literary Criticism, Essays, Philosophy, Social Sciences, Sociology, Culture
ISBN Prefix(es): 978-84-88669; 978-84-95589; 978-84-96310

Albur Producciones Editoriales SL
Carrer de Sant Joan de Malta 39, 08018 Barcelona
Tel: 933 076 850
Key Personnel
Editorial Dir: Fernando Diego Garcia *E-mail:* zr.fernando.dg@gmail.com
Editor: Alejandro Garcia Schnetzer *E-mail:* zr.alejandro.gs@gmail.com
ISBN Prefix(es): 978-84-933361; 978-84-933976; 978-84-934032; 978-84-96509
Imprints: Libros del Zorro Rojo

Formacion Alcala SL
Pol Ind El Retamar-Parcela 6-Vial B, 23687 Alcal la Real, Jaen
Tel: 902 108801 *Fax:* 953 585331
E-mail: info@formacionalcala.es
Web Site: www.formacionalcala.es
Founded: 2000
Subjects: Health, Nutrition
ISBN Prefix(es): 978-84-931695; 978-84-95658; 978-84-96224

El Aleph Editores
Imprint of grup62
C/ Pedro i Pons, 9-11, 11a planta, puertas 1 i 2, 08034 Barcelona
Tel: 93 443 71 00
E-mail: info@elalepheditores.com
Web Site: www.elalepheditores.com
Founded: 1973
Subjects: Fiction
ISBN Prefix(es): 978-84-931977
Distributed by Ediciones Oceano (Argentina, Bolivia, Chile, Colombia, Costa Rica, Panama & Paraguay); Editorial Oceano (Ecuador, Mexico, Peru, Uruguay & Venezuela)
Distribution Center: Comercial Planeta, Avda Diagonal 662, 08034 Barcelona *Tel:* 902 121 020 *Fax:* 902 121 029 *Web Site:* www.comercial.planeta.es

Ediciones Alfar SA
P I La Chaparrilla, 34-36, 41016 Seville
SAN: 001-544X

Tel: 954 406 100 *Fax:* 954 402 580
E-mail: alfar@edicionesalfar.es
Web Site: www.edicionesalfar.web
Founded: 1982
Subjects: Anthropology, Archaeology, Behavioral Sciences, Fiction, History, Literature, Literary Criticism, Essays, Mathematics, Medicine, Nursing, Dentistry, Philosophy, Social Sciences, Sociology
ISBN Prefix(es): 978-84-7898; 978-84-8248; 978-84-86256

Institucio Alfons el Magnanim+
Carrer Corona, 36, 46003 Valencia
SAN: 002-0923
Tel: 963 883 169 *Fax:* 963 883 170
E-mail: iam@alfonselmagnanim.com
Web Site: www.alfonselmagnanim.net
Key Personnel
President: Alfonso Rus Terol
Vice President: Maria Jesus Puchalt Farinos
Dir: Ricard Bellveser Icardo
Subjects: Ethnicity, Government, Political Science, History, Social Sciences, Sociology
ISBN Prefix(es): 978-84-7822
Distribution Center: J A Morcillo Distribudor SL, Ctra Benetusser, 62, 46200 Paiporta (Valencia) *Tel:* 963 974 474 *Fax:* 963 975 273 *E-mail:* jamorcillo@morcillolibros.com

Algaida Editores SA
Avda San Francisco Javier, 22, Edif Hermes, pl 4º, mod 6, 41018 Seville
Tel: 954652311 *Fax:* 954656254
E-mail: algaida@algaida.es
Web Site: www.algaida.es
Subjects: Education
ISBN Prefix(es): 978-84-7647; 978-84-8433
Parent Company: Grupo Anaya SA

Algar Editorial
Apdo de Correos 225, 46600 Alzira
Tel: 962459091 *Fax:* 962403191
E-mail: algar@algareditorial.com
Web Site: www.algareditorial.com
Subjects: Fiction, Literature, Literary Criticism, Essays, Science (General)
ISBN Prefix(es): 978-84-923853; 978-84-931382; 978-84-95722; 978-84-96514

Editorial Algazara SL+
San Milan, 27, 1aº 2a, 29013 Poblacion, Malaga
Tel: 952358284 *Fax:* 952333175
Founded: 1991
Membership(s): Editors Association of Andalucia.
Subjects: History, Literature, Literary Criticism, Essays
ISBN Prefix(es): 978-84-87999

Editorial Alhulia SA
Plaza de Rafael Alberti, 1, 18680 Salobrena (Granada)
Tel: 958828301 *Fax:* 958828301
E-mail: alhulia@alhulia.es
Web Site: www.alhulia.es
Founded: 1997
Subjects: Archaeology, Education, Literature, Literary Criticism, Essays, Poetry
ISBN Prefix(es): 978-84-96641; 978-84-923063; 978-84-95136; 978-84-96083
Imprints: Arqueologia del Paisaje; Aquinoktium; Catalogo; Catalogo General; El Carro de Madera; Ex Corde; Crisalida; Kaleidoskop; Mirto Academia; Nakla; Narrativa SA; Palabras Mayores; Poesta SA; TE-Temas Educativos; Vigia

Alianza Editorial SA+
C/ Juan Ignacio Luca de Tena, 15, 28027 Madrid
SAN: 000-1570
Tel: 91 393 88 88 *Fax:* 91 320 74 80

E-mail: alianzaeditorial@alianzaeditorial.es
Web Site: www.alianzaeditorial.es
Founded: 1966
Specialize in books for adults.
Subjects: Art, Fiction, Government, Political Science, History, Mathematics, Music, Dance, Philosophy, Poetry, Science (General), Social Sciences, Sociology
ISBN Prefix(es): 978-84-206
Parent Company: Grupo Anaya SA
Associate Companies: Alianza Editorial Mexicana SA de CV, Remacimiento No 180, Col San Juan Tlihuaca, 02400 Azcapotzalco, Mexico, Mng Dir: Alberto E Diaz *Tel:* (0155) 53 54 31 00 *Fax:* (0155) 53 54 91 01

Alienta Editorial
Centro de Libros PAPF, Av Diagonal 662-664, 08034 Barcelona
Tel: 934926956
E-mail: info@centrolibrospapf.es
Web Site: www.planetadelibros.com
Subjects: Business, Fiction, Nonfiction (General), Self-Help, Social Sciences, Sociology, Humanities, Narrative
ISBN Prefix(es): 978-84-92414
Parent Company: Editorial Planeta SA

Ediciones Aljibe SL
C/ Canteros 3-5, 29300 Archidona (Malaga)
Tel: 952714395 *Fax:* 952754342
Web Site: www.edicionesaljibe.com
Key Personnel
Dir General: Reyes Bautista
Content Manager: Daniel Gomez
 E-mail: dgomez@edicionesaljibe.com
Founded: 1990
Subjects: Education, Psychology, Psychiatry
ISBN Prefix(es): 978-84-9700; 978-84-87767; 978-84-95212

Editorial Alma
Av Diagonal 440, 08037 Barcelona
Tel: 93 238 43 43
E-mail: info@editorialalma.com
Web Site: www.editorialalma.com
Subjects: Nonfiction (General)
ISBN Prefix(es): 978-84-15618
Distribution Center: IPG Spanish Books, c/o Independent Publishers Group (IPG), 814 N Franklin St, Chicago, IL 60610, United States (USA & Canada)

Almadraba Editorial
Imprint of Hermes Editora General SAU
Infantas, 6 Bajos, local posterior, 28922 Alcorcon, Madrid
Tel: 91 616 01 92 *Fax:* 902 10 68 32; 932 15 66 80 (orders)
E-mail: info@almadrabainforma.com; ediciones@almadrabaeditorial.com; administracio@hermeseditora.com; pedidos@hermeseditora.com (orders)
Web Site: www.almadrabaeditorial.com
Founded: 1994
Subjects: Art, History, Language Arts, Linguistics, Literature, Literary Criticism, Essays, Mathematics, Philosophy, Social Sciences, Sociology, Art History, Humanities
ISBN Prefix(es): 978-84-8308; 978-84-89475

Editorial Almed
Av Divina Pastora 7, Local 18, 18012 Granada
Tel: 958806005; 958291581 *Fax:* 958282435
E-mail: almed@almed.net
Web Site: www.almed.net
Founded: 1996
Subjects: History
ISBN Prefix(es): 978-84-931194; 978-84-934215; 978-84-935857; 978-84-936685

Ediciones El Almendro de Cordoba SL+
C/ El Almendro, 6 Bajo, 14006 Cordoba
SAN: 001-6810
Mailing Address: Apdo 5.066, 14006 Cordoba
Tel: 957 082 789; 957 274 692 *Fax:* 957 274 692
E-mail: ediciones@elalmendro.org
Web Site: elalmendro.org
Founded: 1982
Also book packager.
Subjects: Biblical Studies, Religion - Catholic, Religion - Jewish, Religion & Judaism
ISBN Prefix(es): 978-84-8005; 978-84-86077
Subsidiaries: PI El Guijar
Foreign Rep(s): Libreria Agape (Argentina); Alma Roma (Italy); Asociacion Libreria Editorial Salesiana (Peru); Casa de la Biblia (Mexico); Libreria Catolica (Panama); Libreria Catolica Ave Maria (Puerto Rico); Editorial Claretiana (Argentina); Disliber Spes Mejico (Mexico); Distal Libros (Argentina); Hijas de San Pablo (Dominican Republic, El Salvador, Paraguay, Peru, Portugal, Puerto Rico, Uruguay, Venezuela); Libreria Hispanoamericana (Nicaragua); Livro Ibero Americano Ltda (Brazil); Editorial Letraviva (Brazil); Distribuidora Loyola (Brazil); Libreria Manantial (Italy); Manantial, Libreria Loyola (Guatemala); Nueva Libreria Parroquial (Mexico); Libreria Juan Pablo II (Dominican Republic, Honduras); Libreria Parroquial (Mexico); Paulinas (Brazil, Colombia, Ecuador, Italy, USA, Venezuela); Libreria Pontificia Universita Gregoriana (Italy); Libreria Proa Ltda (Chile); Rubaisen S EN cs (Argentina); Libreria Salesiana (El Salvador); San Pablo (Costa Rica, Italy); Libreria San Pablo (Colombia, Costa Rica, Panama, USA); Libreria Sole (Italy); Libreria Sorgente (Italy); Spanish Speaking Bookstore Distributions (USA); Editorial Verbo Divino (Bolivia, Ecuador); Fundacion Verbo Divino (Colombia); Libreria Verbum (Mexico); Verdad y Vida - Libreria Diocesana (Paraguay); Libreria Verdade e Vida (Portugal)
Distribution Center: America Ediexport, Pol Ind Ventorro del Cano, Vereda de los Barros, 77, 28925 Alcorcon (Madrid) *Tel:* 916 323 288 *Fax:* 916 334 821 *E-mail:* americaediexport@yahoo.es
Azteca Distribuidora de Publicaciones, Marquesa de Argueso 36, 28019 Madrid *Tel:* 915 604 360 *Fax:* 915 652 922 *E-mail:* azteca@aztecadist.es

Editorial Almuzara
Imprint of Grupo Almuzara
Ctra Palma del Rio, km 4, C/8, Nave L2, Modulos 6 y 7, Buzon nº 3, 14005 Cordoba
Tel: 957467081 *Fax:* 957461463
E-mail: info@editorialalmuzara.com
Web Site: www.editorialalmuzara.com
Key Personnel
Editorial Dir: Manuel Pimentel
Founded: 2004
Subjects: Art, Economics, Education, Fiction, Science (General), Technical
ISBN Prefix(es): 978-84-96968; 978-84-933378; 978-84-933901; 978-84-96416; 978-84-88586
Distributed by Ediciones Urano (Chile, Colombia, Mexico, Uruguay & Venezuela)
Foreign Rep(s): Baker & Taylor (USA); The Book Annex Ltd (Europe); Distribuciones del Futuro (Argentina); Sochepress (Arab Middle East)
Foreign Rights: Anthea Agency (Bulgaria); Anne Confuron (France); Agencja Literacka Graal (Poland); Grandi & Associati (Italy); The Deborah Harris Agency (Israel); Ilidio da Fonseca Matos (Portugal); Indent Literary Agency (USA); Japan UNI Agency Inc (Japan); Nurcihan Kesim Literary Agency (Turkey); Maxima Creative Agency; Prava i prevodi (Baltic States, Russia); Read n' Right Agency (Greece);

Agencia Riff (Brazil); Livia Stoia Literary Agency (Romania); Undercover (Germany, Holland, Scandinavia)

Editorial Alpina SL
c/Princesa 67, 08401 Granollers, Barcelona
Tel: 93 879 50 83
E-mail: info@editorialalpina.com
Web Site: www.editorialalpina.com
Founded: 1946
Subjects: Outdoor Recreation, Hiking Guides, Topography
ISBN Prefix(es): 978-84-8090

Editorial Alreves
Passeig Manuel Girona 52, 5° 5a, 08034 Barcelona
Tel: 93 203 5258
E-mail: info@alreveseditorial.com; lector@alreveseditorial.com; prensa@alreveseditorial.com
Web Site: www.alreveseditorial.com
Subjects: Fiction, Nonfiction (General)
ISBN Prefix(es): 978-84-937435; 978-84-937920
Foreign Rep(s): Cauce Libros (Latin America exc Chile & Colombia); Cuarto Propio (Chile); Independent Publishers Group (IPG) (USA); El Libro Universal (Colombia)

Alta Fulla Editorial
Passatge d'Alio, 10, 08037 Barcelona
SAN: 000-1694
Tel: 934 590 708 *Fax:* 932 075 203
E-mail: afweb@altafulla.com
Web Site: www.altafulla.com
Key Personnel
Editor & Dir: Josep J Moli Cambray
Founded: 1977
Specialize in linguistics & paperback books.
Subjects: Anthropology, Architecture & Interior Design, Cookery, Crafts, Games, Hobbies, Economics, Pop Culture, Social Sciences, Sociology, Ethnography, Folklore, Mythology
ISBN Prefix(es): 978-84-85403; 978-84-86556; 978-84-7900
Foreign Rep(s): Canal 2 de Distribuciones (Colombia); La Casa Verde (Peru); Centro Nacional Cuesta (Dominican Republic); Librerias Crisol (Peru); Cultural Portobelo (Panama); Editora y Distribuidora Azteca (Mexico); Ideal Foreign Books (USA); Libreria Guadalquivir (Argentina); Metales Pesados (Chile); Mr Books (Ecuador); Nueva Decada (Costa Rica); Libreria Nueva Imagen (Ecuador); Libreria El Quijote (Paraguay); Libreria Sophos (Guatemala); Librerias La Tertulia (Puerto Rico); Libreria Ulises (Chile); Libreria El Virrey (Peru); Libreria Yachaywasi (Bolivia); Zamboni Books (Brazil)

Altera Ediciones+
Formerly Altera 2005 SL
Member of Grupo Comunicacion y Publicaciones Caudal
C/ Marcenado, 14 Loc 28002, 28002 Madrid
Tel: 910 378 428
Web Site: www.edicionesaltera.com
Key Personnel
Dir: Javier Ruiz Portella
Management & Production: Ingrid Valdes
Founded: 1995
Subjects: Literature, Literary Criticism, Essays
ISBN Prefix(es): 978-84-920659; 978-84-89779; 978-84-96840
Number of titles published annually: 8 Print
Total Titles: 34 Print
Distribution Center: Distrifer, Calle Valle de Tobalina, 32, 28021 Madrid *Tel:* 917 954 935

Altera 2005 SL, see Altera Ediciones

Alvarellos Editora
Rua de Sempre en Galiza, 4, 15706 Santiago de Compostela-Galicia
Tel: 981522137; 609908852 (cell)
Fax: 981522137
E-mail: correo@alvarellos.info; editora@alvarellos.info
Web Site: alvarellos.info
Key Personnel
Dir & Editor: Henrique Alvarellos Casas
Founded: 1977
Subjects: History, Literature, Literary Criticism, Essays, Regional Interests, Culture
ISBN Prefix(es): 978-84-85311; 978-84-89323

Ediciones Amara
Apdo de Correos 995, 07760 Ciutadella de Menorca (Illes Balears)
Tel: 971385756
E-mail: edicionesamara@gmail.com
Web Site: www.ediciones-amara.net
Subjects: Religion - Buddhist, Meditation, Yoga
ISBN Prefix(es): 978-84-920119; 978-84-95094

Ambit Serveis Editorials SA+
Balmes, 195, 08006 Barcelona
Tel: 934880150
Founded: 1981
Subjects: Art, Cookery, Geography, Geology, Photography, Craftsmanship, Fine Arts, Nature
ISBN Prefix(es): 978-84-89681; 978-84-87342; 978-84-86147; 978-84-96645

Amnistia Internacional Editorial SL
Secretariado Estatal, Fernando VI, 8, 1° izda, 28004 Madrid
SAN: 002-2608
Tel: 902 119 133; 91 310 12 77 *Fax:* 91 319 53 34
E-mail: info@es.amnesty.org
Web Site: www.es.amnesty.org
Founded: 1987
Subjects: Developing Countries, Education, Foreign Countries, Government, Political Science, Law, Nonfiction (General), Regional Interests, Social Sciences, Sociology
ISBN Prefix(es): 978-84-86874
U.S. Office(s): AI-USA, 304 Pennsylvania Ave SE, Washington, DC 20003, United States
Distributed by La Catarata; El Pais Aguilar

AMV Ediciones, see A Madrid Vicente Ediciones

Editorial Anagrama SA+
Pedro de la Creu, 58, 08034 Barcelona
SAN: 022-2616
Tel: 932 037 652 *Fax:* 932 037 738
E-mail: anagrama@anagrama-ed.es
Web Site: www.anagrama-ed.es
Key Personnel
Founder, Editor & Dir: Jorge Herralde
Founded: 1969
Subjects: Anthropology, Literature, Literary Criticism, Essays, Philosophy, Psychology, Psychiatry, Social Sciences, Sociology
ISBN Prefix(es): 978-84-339
Total Titles: 2,000 Print
Foreign Rep(s): Fernandez de Castro Ltd (Chile); Colofon SA (Mexico); Gussi Libros (Uruguay); Editorial Oceano SL (Panama, Peru); Grupo Penta Distribuidores (Colombia, Ecuador); Riverside Agency SAC (Argentina)

Grupo Anaya SA
C/ Juan Ignacio Luca de Tena, 15, 28027 Madrid
Tel: 913 938 800 *Fax:* 917 426 631
E-mail: administrador@anaya.es
Web Site: www.anaya.es
Founded: 1959

ISBN Prefix(es): 978-84-207; 978-84-667
Parent Company: Hachette Livre

Anaya-Touring Club+
C/ Juan Ignacio Luca de Tena, 15, 28027 Madrid
Tel: 91 393 86 00 *Fax:* 91 320 91 29
E-mail: administrador@anayatouring.com
Web Site: www.anayatouring.es
Key Personnel
Publisher: Pedro Pardo
Founded: 1989
Specialize in travel books, guides, phrase books.
Subjects: Travel & Tourism, Travel Guides
ISBN Prefix(es): 978-84-8165
Number of titles published annually: 30 Print
Total Titles: 280 Print
Parent Company: Grupo Anaya SA
Imprints: Guia Viva; Guiarama; Guiatotal

Andana Editorial
C/ Valencia, 56, B, 46680 Algemesi, Valencia
Tel: 649 539 205 *Fax:* 962 484 382
E-mail: andana@andana.net
Web Site: www.andana.net
ISBN Prefix(es): 978-84-940802; 978-84-941757

Angle Editorial
c/Mutaner, 200, atic 8a, 08036 Barcelona
Tel: 933630823 *Fax:* 933630824
E-mail: angle@angleeditorial.com
Web Site: www.angleeditorial.com
Founded: 1992
Subjects: Art, Biography, Memoirs, Humor, Literature, Literary Criticism, Essays, Photography
ISBN Prefix(es): 978-84-15307; 978-84-15695; 978-84-88811; 978-84-96521; 978-84-96970; 978-84-16139
Parent Company: N9u Grup Editorial

Anroart Ediciones
C/ General Vives, 2 6a planta, puerta 21, 35006 Las Palmas de Gran Canaria (Islas Canarias)
Tel: 928339021 *Fax:* 928249436
E-mail: anroart_ediciones@yahoo.es
Web Site: www.anroart.com
Key Personnel
Executive Dir: Jorge A Liria
Commercial Dir: Noelia E Liria
Founded: 2004
Subjects: Geography, Geology, History, Literature, Literary Criticism, Essays, Culture
ISBN Prefix(es): 978-84-96577; 978-84-934168; 978-84-934211; 978-84-934336; 978-84-934504; 978-84-934582

Anthropos Editorial-Narino SL+
C/ Diputacio 266, 08007 Barcelona
SAN: 000-2313
Tel: 93 697 22 96
E-mail: info@anthropos-editorial.com; anthropos@anthropos-editorial.com
Web Site: www.anthropos-editorial.com
Key Personnel
Dir: Ramon Gabarros Cardona
Founded: 1981
Subjects: Inspirational, Spirituality
ISBN Prefix(es): 978-84-7658; 978-84-85887

APD, see Asociacion para el Progreso de la Direccion (APD)

Apila Ediciones
Mosen Felix Lacambra 36B, 50630 Alagon, Zaragoza
Tel: 617 227 843; 976 610 339
E-mail: apila@apilaediciones.com
Web Site: www.apilaediciones.com
Founded: 2007
Subjects: Fiction
ISBN Prefix(es): 978-84-939736

Aquinoktium, *imprint of* Editorial Alhulia SA

Ara Llibres Sccl
C Corders 22-28, 08911 Barcelona
Tel: 933 899 542 *Fax:* 933 899 460
E-mail: info@arallibres.cat
Web Site: www.arallibres.cat
Key Personnel
Chief Executive Officer: Izaskun Arretxe
Editor: Eduard Hurtado
Communication & Marketing: Roser Sebastia
Founded: 2002
Subjects: Fiction, Health, Nutrition, Nonfiction
   (General), Self-Help
ISBN Prefix(es): 978-84-96767
Associate Companies: Alisis Llibres; Amsterdam
   Llibres

Arambol SL+
C/ Garcia de Paredes, 86, 28010 Madrid
SAN: 002-2713
Tel: 913194057
E-mail: arambolsl@hotmail.com
Founded: 1988
Subjects: Music, Dance
ISBN Prefix(es): 978-84-88128
Distributed by Piles; Seemsa
Distributor for Schell Music

Aran Ediciones
C/Castello 128, 1º, 28006 Madrid
Tel: 917820030 *Fax:* 915615787
Web Site: www.grupoaran.com
Subjects: Health, Nutrition, Medicine, Nursing,
   Dentistry, Psychology, Psychiatry, Pharmacy
ISBN Prefix(es): 978-84-86725; 978-84-95913

Arantzazu Ediciones Franciscanas
Castillo de Villamonte, 2, 01007 Vitoria-Gasteiz
SAN: 000-2682
Tel: 945 14 72 24 *Fax:* 945 14 72 24
E-mail: info@edicionesfranciscanasarantzazu.com
Web Site: www.edicionesfranciscanasarantzazu.
   com
Subjects: Biography, Memoirs, History, Inspira-
   tional, Spirituality, Religion - Other
ISBN Prefix(es): 978-84-7240

L'Arca, *imprint of* Ediciones Robinbook SL

ArCiBel Editores
Infni 10, 41012 Seville, Andalucia
Tel: 699931670
E-mail: editorial@arcibel.es
Web Site: www.arcibel.es
Founded: 2003
Subjects: Language Arts, Linguistics, Poetry, Cul-
   ture
ISBN Prefix(es): 978-84-933318; 978-84-934085;
   978-84-934508; 978-84-935374; 978-84-
   935747; 978-84-935905; 978-84-96980

Arco Libros SL+
C/ Juan Bautista de Toledo, 28, 28002 Madrid
Tel: 91 415 36 87; 91 416 13 71 *Fax:* 91 413 59
   07
E-mail: arcolibros@arcomuralla.com
Web Site: www.arcomuralla.com
Key Personnel
Mng Dir: Lidio Nieto Jimenez
Founded: 1984
Subjects: Art, History, Language Arts, Linguis-
   tics, Library & Information Sciences, Litera-
   ture, Literary Criticism, Essays, Librarian Stud-
   ies, Philology
ISBN Prefix(es): 978-84-7635

Arete, *imprint of* Penguin Random House Grupo
   Editorial

Editorial Arguval SA+
C/ Maria Malibran, 16, Trevenez, 1a Fase, 29590
   Malaga
SAN: 002-2780
Tel: 952 31 87 84 *Fax:* 952 17 85 63
E-mail: editorial@arguval.com
Web Site: www.arguval.com
Key Personnel
Dir: Francisco Arguelles
Founded: 1982
Subjects: Biography, Memoirs, Business, Child
   Care & Development, Cookery, Fiction, Health,
   Nutrition, Literature, Literary Criticism, Essays,
   Nonfiction (General)
ISBN Prefix(es): 978-84-86167; 978-84-89672;
   978-84-95948; 978-84-96912

Editorial Ariel SA+
Member of Grupo Planeta
Edificio Planeta, Avda Diagonal 662-664, 08034
   Barcelona
Tel: 93 496 70 30
E-mail: editorial@ariel.es
Web Site: www.planetadelibros.com/editorial-
   editorial-ariel-2.html
Key Personnel
Foreign Rights Manager: Daniel Cladera *Tel:* 93
   492 80 08 *E-mail:* dcladera@planeta.es
Press: Laura Gamundi *Tel:* 93 492 89 47
   E-mail: lgamundi@planeta.es
Founded: 1942
Subjects: Economics, Geography, Geology, His-
   tory, Literature, Literary Criticism, Essays, Phi-
   losophy, Psychology, Psychiatry, Science (Gen-
   eral), Social Sciences, Sociology
ISBN Prefix(es): 978-84-344
Number of titles published annually: 80 Print; 80
   Online; 80 E-Book
Total Titles: 700 Online; 700 E-Book
Associate Companies: Editorial Seix Barral SA

Arqueologia del Paisaje, *imprint of* Editorial
Alhulia SA

Art 62, *imprint of* grup62

As de Diamante, *imprint of* Ediciones Robinbook
   SL

Asklepios Medical Atlas
Calle del Doctor Carulla 76, 1.1, 08017
   Barcelona
Tel: 931882070; 625 562 179 (cell)
E-mail: info@asklepiosmedicalatlas.com
Web Site: www.asklepiosmedicalatlas.com
Key Personnel
Publisher & General Manager: Jordi Vigue
Commercial Dir: Charly Spasov
Scientific Dir: Diana Bohorquez
Chief Coordinator Medical Publication: Dr Jordi
   Rancano
Subjects: Medicine, Nursing, Dentistry, Science
   (General)
Parent Company: Apex

**Asociacion de Directores de Escena de Espana
   (ADE)**
C/ Costanilla de los Angeles 13, Bajo lzq, 28013
   Madrid
Tel: 915591246 *Fax:* 915483012
E-mail: asociacion@adeteatro.com
Web Site: www.adeteatro.com
Key Personnel
Dir: Juan Antonio Hormigon
Publishing Coordinator: Carlos Rodriguez Alonso
Subjects: Drama, Theater, Literature, Literary
   Criticism, Essays
ISBN Prefix(es): 978-84-87591; 978-84-95576;
   978-84-92639

**Asociacion de Investigacion Tecnica de las
   Industrias de la Madera**, see AITTIM
(Asociacion de Investigacion Tecnica de las
   Industrias de la Madera)

**Asociacion para el Progreso de la Direccion
   (APD)**
Montalban, 3, 28014 Madrid
SAN: 000-3662
Tel: 915237900
E-mail: apd@mad.apd.es
Web Site: www.apd.es
Key Personnel
Chairman: Rafael Miranda Robredo
Dept of Program: Irene Perez *Tel:* 915221331
   E-mail: iperez@apd.es
Communication: Blanca Leon *Tel:* 915322265
   E-mail: bleon@mad.apd.es
Sales Dept: Paula Allende *Tel:* 915227579
   E-mail: pallende@apd.es
Founded: 1956
Specialize in business management.
Subjects: Business, Education, Management,
   Business Education, Business Management
ISBN Prefix(es): 978-84-7019; 978-84-89379

Libros del Asteroide
Avio Plus Ultra 23, bajos, 08017 Barcelona
Tel: 932802524 *Fax:* 933969699
E-mail: editorial@librosdelasteroide.com (foreign
   rights); prensa@librosdelasteroide.com (press
   & communications)
Web Site: www.librosdelasteroide.com
Founded: 2005
Subjects: Fiction, Literature, Literary Criticism,
   Essays, Nonfiction (General)
ISBN Prefix(es): 978-84-935448; 978-84-934315;
   978-84-935018; 978-84-92663; 978-84-935914;
   978-84-936597
Foreign Rep(s): Distribuidora de Libros Heraldos
   Negros (Peru); Hueders SL (Chile); Indepen-
   dent Publishers Group (USA); La Panoplia
   Export (Latin America exc Argentina, Chile,
   Mexico & Peru); Sexto Piso Distribuciones
   (Mexico); Distribuidora Waldhuter (Argentina)

Astiberri Ediciones
Apdo 485, 48080 Bilbao
E-mail: info@astiberri.com
Web Site: www.astiberri.com
Founded: 2001
Publisher of comic books.
Subjects: Fiction, History, Humor, Nonfiction
   (General)
ISBN Prefix(es): 978-84-92769; 978-84-96815;
   978-84-95825; 978-84-15163
Distribution Center: SD, c/ Montsia 9-11
   Pol Ind Can Bernades, 08130 Barcelona
   Tel: 933 001 022 *Fax:* 933 007 301
   E-mail: distribucion@sddistribuciones.com *Web
   Site:* sddistribuciones.com
UDL Libros, Av del Acero, 4, Azuqueca
   de Henares, 19200 Madrid *Tel:* 949 267
   648 *E-mail:* info@udllibros.com *Web
   Site:* udllibros.com

Atico de los Libros
Calle Mallorca 303, 2º 1a, 08037 Barcelona
E-mail: info@aticodeloslibros.com
Web Site: aticodeloslibros.com
Founded: 2010
Subjects: Fiction, History, Nonfiction (General)
ISBN Prefix(es): 978-84-16222; 978-84-937809;
   978-84-939720
Foreign Rep(s): Lecturalia SA de CV (Mexico);
   Ediciones Oceano Argentina SA (Argentina);
   Ediciones Oceano de Chile SA (Chile); Edi-
   ciones Oceano de Colombia SA (Colom-
   bia); Ediciones Oceano de Costa Rica SA
   (Costa Rica); Ediciones Oceano de Panama SA
   (Panama); Ediciones Oceano de Paraguay SA
   (Paraguay); Editorial Oceano de Guatemala SA

(Guatemala); Editorial Oceano de Venezuela SA (Venezuela); Editorial Oceano del Uruguay SA (Uruguay); Editorial Oceano Ecuatoriana SA (Ecuador); Editorial Oceano Peruana SA (Peru)

Distribution Center: Les Punxes Distribuidora SL, c/ Sardenya, 75-81, 08018 Barcelona *Tel:* 93 485 63 80 *Fax:* 93 300 90 91 *E-mail:* punxes@punxes.es (Spain exc Madrid)

Red Books Canarias, Pol Ind Arinaga, fase 1, C/ Canal Izquierdo, 29, 35118 Aguimes-Gran Canaria *Tel:* 928 50 39 57 *E-mail:* info@redbookspain.com

Machado Grupo de Distribucion SL, Pol Ind Prado del Espino, c/ Labradores, Manzana 15, Parcela 3, Sector 01, 28660 Boadilla del Monte (Madrid) *Tel:* 91 632 48 93; 91 632 61 10 *Fax:* 91 632 65 13; 91 633 02 48 *E-mail:* machadolibros@machadolibros.com

L'Avenc
Passig de Sant Joan, 26, 2n, 1º, 08010 Barcelona
Tel: 93 245 79 21 *Fax:* 93 265 44 16
E-mail: lavenc@lavenc.cat
Web Site: www.lavenc.cat
Key Personnel
Dir: Josep M Munoz *E-mail:* jmmunoz@lavenc.cat
Founded: 1977
Subjects: Geography, Geology, History, Philosophy, Social Sciences, Sociology
ISBN Prefix(es): 978-84-88839; 978-84-95905

Editorial Avgvstinvs
General Davila 5, bajo D, 28003 Madrid
SAN: 000-443X
Tel: 915342070
Web Site: www.agustinosrecoletos.com
Key Personnel
Dir: Enrique A Eguiarte
Founded: 1956
Subjects: Philosophy, Theology
ISBN Prefix(es): 978-84-85096
Number of titles published annually: 5 Print
Total Titles: 200 Print

Ediciones B, *imprint of* Penguin Random House Grupo Editorial

Ediciones B+
Imprint of Penguin Random House Grupo Editorial
Consell de Cent, 425-427, 08009 Barcelona
SAN: 001-5911
Tel: 93 484 66 00 *Fax:* 93 232 46 60
Web Site: www.megustaleer.com/editoriales/ediciones-b/eb
Key Personnel
Dir General: Roman de Vicente
Dir, Marketing/Special Sales: Mercedes Lopez-Molina
Copyright/Foreign Rights: Tatiana Espin
Founded: 1986
Subjects: Biography, Memoirs, Cookery, Fiction, Health, Nutrition, Humor, Nonfiction (General), Romance
ISBN Prefix(es): 978-84-406; 978-84-7735; 978-84-666
Imprints: Vergara
Branch Office(s)
C/ Orduna, 3, 28034 Madrid *Tel:* 91 586 33 00; 91 586 33 02 *Fax:* 91 586 34 11
Paseo Colon, 221, 6º Piso 1399, Buenos Aires, Argentina *Tel:* (011) 4343 7510 *Web Site:* www.edicionesb-argentina.com
Avda Las Torres 1375-A, Huechuraba, Santiago, Chile *Tel:* (02) 27295400 *Fax:* (02) 27295430
Carrera 15 No 52 A-33, Bogota DC, Colombia *Tel:* (01) 212 40 12 *Fax:* (01) 248 02 64 *Web Site:* www.edicionesb.com.co
Bradley 52 esquina Gutemberg, Delegacion Miguel Hidalgo Colonia Anzures, 11590

Mexico, DF, Mexico *Tel:* (0155) 254 51 50 *Fax:* (0155) 254 64 54 *Web Site:* www.edicionesb-mexico.com
Constituyente, 2032, 11200 Montevideo, Uruguay *Tel:* 2419 86 03 *Fax:* 2418 90 05 *Web Site:* www.edicionesb.com.uy
Av Romulo Gallegos, c/c Rep Dominicana, Edif Vista, Mezzanina, Boleita Norte, Caracas 1050, A, Venezuela *Tel:* (0212) 235 31 34 *Fax:* (0212) 235 58 55 *E-mail:* brozados@edicionesb.com.ve

Ediciones B Mexico SA de CV, *imprint of* Penguin Random House Grupo Editorial

BAC, see Biblioteca de Autores Cristianos

Backlist
Member of Grupo Planeta
Av Diagonal, 662-664, 08034 Barcelona
Tel: 93 492 89 28
E-mail: cdlom@planeta.es
Web Site: www.planetadelibros.com/editorial-backlist-6.html
Founded: 2008
Subjects: Fiction, Nonfiction (General), Classics, Contemporary Fiction, Contemporary Nonfiction
ISBN Prefix(es): 978-84-08

Baia Edicions
Pol Pocomaco, 2a Avda Parcela A2/22, 15190 A Coruna
Tel: 981174296 *Fax:* 981915698
E-mail: comercial@baiaedicions.net
Web Site: www.baiaedicions.net
Key Personnel
Dir General: Belen Lopez Vazquez
Founded: 1990
Subjects: Literature, Literary Criticism, Essays, Philosophy, Gastronomy
ISBN Prefix(es): 978-84-87674; 978-84-89803; 978-84-96128

Ediciones Baile del Sol+
Apdo de Correos 133, 38280 Tegueste-Tenerife, Canary Islands
SAN: 001-0103
Tel: 922 570 196
E-mail: info@bailedelsol.org
Web Site: bailedelsol.org
Key Personnel
General Coordinator: Tito Exposito
Founded: 1992
Subjects: Alternative, History, Poetry, Self-Help
ISBN Prefix(es): 978-84-88671; 978-84-95309; 978-84-96225; 978-84-96687
Foreign Rep(s): Baker & Taylor (USA); Panoplia Export SL (Latin America)

Bainet Media SA
Uribitarte 18, 6th floor, 48001 Bilbao
Tel: 944 010 750 *Fax:* 944 010 757
E-mail: comercial@bainet-editorial.com; prensa@bainet-editorial.com
Web Site: www.bainet-editorial.com
Key Personnel
Editorial Dir: Javier Colomo *Tel:* 635 70 76 28 *Fax:* 93 308 85 82
Special Operations: Eduardo Aduna
Subjects: Cookery, Gardening, Plants, Health, Nutrition, How-to, Travel & Tourism, Decorations
ISBN Prefix(es): 978-84-932768; 978-84-96177

Editorial Bambu, *imprint of* Editorial Casals SA

Ediciones Barataria
Gran Via Corts Catalanes 523 5º 1a, 08011 Barcelona
Tel: 622434594

E-mail: info@barataria-ediciones.com; administracion@barataria-ediciones.com
Web Site: www.barataria-ediciones.com
Founded: 2000
Subjects: Narrative
ISBN Prefix(es): 978-84-95764
Distribution Center: Sociedad General Espanola de Libreria SA, Av Valdelaparra, 29, 28108 Alcobendas (Madrid) *Tel:* 916576900 *Fax:* 916576928 *Web Site:* www.sgel.es

Editorial Barcanova SA+
Mallorca 45 4a Planta, 08029 Barcelona
SAN: 022-2985
Tel: 932 172 054 *Fax:* 932 373 469
E-mail: barcanova@barcanova.cat
Web Site: www.barcanova.es; www.barcanovadigital.cat
Key Personnel
Dir General: Ramon Besora Oliva
Founded: 1980
Subjects: Education, Literature, Literary Criticism, Essays
ISBN Prefix(es): 978-84-7533; 978-84-489; 978-84-85923; 978-84-485; 978-84-95103; 978-84-95184
Parent Company: Grupo Anaya SA, Madrid
Associate Companies: Ediciones Anaya SA
Branch Office(s)
Mallorca, 45, pl baixa, 08029 Barcelona
Tel: 934 948 590 *Fax:* 934 190 297
E-mail: comandescat@cga.es
Montfalgars, 1, local C, 17005 Girona *Tel:* 972 243 814 *Fax:* 972 400 086 *E-mail:* plastra@cga.es
Cristofor de Boleda, 6, 25006 Lleida *Tel:* 973 273 388 *Fax:* 973 274 719 *E-mail:* jsans@cga.es
Francesc Vallduvi, 18, local 1, Poligon can Enetgistes, 07011 Palma *Tel:* 971 253 000 *Fax:* 971 253 003 *E-mail:* dllambias@cga.es
Domenech i Soberano, 7-9 baixos, 43203 Reus *Tel:* 650 661 014 *E-mail:* jgonzalezs@cga.es

Barcelona eBooks
Avinguda Marques de l'Argentera 17, Pral, 08003 Barcelona
E-mail: info@barcelonaebooks.com
Web Site: www.barcelonaebooks.com
Key Personnel
Chief Executive Officer: Blanca Rosa Roca
ISBN Prefix(es): 978-1-4532
Associate Companies: Open Road Integrated Media

Editorial Barcino SA+
Carrer Acacies, 15, 08027 Barcelona
SAN: 002-3000
Tel: 933 495 935
E-mail: barcino@editorialbarcino.cat
Web Site: www.editorialbarcino.cat
Founded: 1924
Subjects: Literature, Literary Criticism, Essays
ISBN Prefix(es): 978-84-7226

Edicions Baula
C Salvador Espriu, 79, baixos 2a, 08005 Barcelona
Tel: 933 540 399 *Fax:* 933 540 489
E-mail: comercialbaula@baula.com
Web Site: baula.com
Founded: 1993
Subjects: Animals, Pets, Education, Language Arts, Linguistics, Catalan Language
ISBN Prefix(es): 978-84-479
Parent Company: Grupo Editorial Luis Vives

Beascoa, *imprint of* Penguin Random House Grupo Editorial

Beascoa SA Ediciones
Imprint of Penguin Random House Grupo Editorial

Travessera de Gracia 47-49, 08021 Barcelona
SAN: 001-5997
Tel: 93 366 03 00 *Fax:* 93 366 04 49
Web Site: penguinrandomhousegrupoeditorial.
com/
Key Personnel
Foreign Rights Manager: Justyna Rzewuska
Tel: 93 366 02 91
Founded: 2001
ISBN Prefix(es): 978-84-488; 978-84-7546
Associate Companies: Sol-Jouem, Lisbon, Portugal
Subsidiaries: Beascoa Internacional

Belio Magazine & Books SL
Calle Argente 14, 28053 Madrid
Tel: 914 782 528 *Fax:* 914 782 526
E-mail: info@beliomagazine.com
Web Site: beliomagazine.com
Key Personnel
Dir: Javier Iglesias Algora; Pablo Iglesias Algora
Founded: 1999
Subjects: Art, Contemporary Art, Graphic Design, Illustration, Street Art

Ediciones Bellaterra SL
Navas de Tolosa, 289 bis, 08026 Barcelona
SAN: 001-6004
Tel: 933 408 976 *Fax:* 933 520 851
E-mail: info@ed-bellaterra.com
Web Site: www.ed-bellaterra.com
Founded: 1973
Subjects: Anthropology, Chemistry, Chemical Engineering, Science (General), Social Sciences, Sociology, Technology, Applied Sciences
ISBN Prefix(es): 978-84-7290
Total Titles: 250 Print
Foreign Rep(s): L'Alebrije (Latin America); Aparicio Distributor (Puerto Rico); Libros de la Arena (Uruguay); Libreria Baum (Costa Rica); Libreria Casa del Saber (Peru); Casalini Libri SpA (Europe); Distripal SA de CV (Mexico); Forsa Editores Inc (Puerto Rico); Libros sin Fronteras (USA); Fundacion del Libro Universitario - Libun (Puerto Rico); Libreria Guadalquivir (Proeme) (Argentina); El Hombre de la Mancha (Panama); Ibero A & G (Peru); Karma (Chile); Libun (Peru); Mr Books (Ecuador); La Panoplia Export SL (Latin America); Editorial Plaza & Janes - Bibliografica (Colombia); Libreria Profetica-Casa de la Lectura (Mexico); Pujol & Amado SLL (Latin America); Sophos (Guatemala); El Virrey Libreria (Peru); Waldhuter Distribuidores (Argentina); Libreria Yachaywasi (Bolivia)

Editorial Berenice
Imprint of Grupo Almuzara
Ctra Palma del Rio, km 4, C/8, Nave L2, Modules 6 & 7, Buzon nº 3, 14005 Cordoba
Tel: 957467081 *Fax:* 957461413
E-mail: info@editorialberenice.com; prensa@editorialberenice.com
Web Site: www.editorialberenice.com
Founded: 2005
Subjects: Fiction, Classics
ISBN Prefix(es): 978-84-934466; 978-84-934881; 978-84-96756; 978-84-935047
Foreign Rep(s): Baker & Taylor (USA); The Book Annex Ltd (Europe); Distribuciones del Futuro (Argentina); Sochepress (Morocco); Ediciones Urano Colombia Ltda (Colombia); Ediciones Urano Chile (Chile); Ediciones Urano Uruguay SA (Uruguay); Ediciones Urano Venezuela (Venezuela)
Foreign Rights: Anthea Agency (Bulgaria); Anne Confuron (France); Agencja Literacka Graal (Poland); Grandi & Associati (Italy); The Deborah Harris Agency (Israel); Ilidio da Fonseca Matos (Portugal); Indent Literary Agency (USA); Japan Uni Agency Inc (Japan); Nurcihan Kesim Literary Agency Inc (Turkey);

Maxima Creative Agency (Indonesia); Prava i prevodi (Baltic States, Russia); Read n' Right Agency (Greece); Agencia Riff (Brazil); Livia Stoia Literary Agency (Romania); Undercover (Germany, Holland, Scandinavia)

Beta Editorial SA
Rosari, 10, 08017 Barcelona
SAN: 000-5746
Tel: 93 2804640 *Fax:* 93 2806320
E-mail: beta@betabarcelona.es
Web Site: www.betaeditorial.com; www.facebook.com/betaeditorial
Founded: 1943
Subjects: Cookery, Fiction, Health, Nutrition, Nonfiction (General)
ISBN Prefix(es): 978-84-7091

Biblioteca de Autores Cristianos+
Anastro 1, 3º, 28033 Madrid
SAN: 003-9004
Tel: 91 343 97 91; 91 343 96 76 *Fax:* 91 343 96 65
E-mail: secretariadireccion@bac-editorial.com; administracion.editoriales@conferenciaepiscopal.es
Web Site: www.bac-editorial.com
Founded: 1945
Subjects: Astrology, Occult, History, Philosophy, Religion - Other, Theology
ISBN Prefix(es): 978-84-7914; 978-84-220
Foreign Rep(s): Agape Libros (Argentina); Apuntes Libros (Argentina); Librerias Artemis Edinter (Guatemala); Asociacion Hijas de San Pablo (Peru); Asociacion Instituto Misionero de San Pablo (Costa Rica); Asociacion Manatial de la Cultura (Guatemala); Libreria Beityala SA de CV (Mexico); Libreria Benedetto XVI (Mexico); Canal Buenos Aires (Argentina); Casa San Paolo della Societa Figlie (Mexico); Casalini Libri (Mexico); Libreria Catolica Arquidiocesana (Panama); Libreria Catolica Ave Maria (Puerto Rico); Libreria Catolica de Colores-Casa San Pablo (Dominican Republic); Libreria Catolica Gethesemani (USA); Libreria Catolica Mater et Magistra (Guatemala); Libreria Catolica Sicomoro (Colombia); Editoriales La Ceiba SA de CV (El Salvador); Ediciones CEM AR (Mexico); Centro Biblico Verbo Divino (Ecuador); Centro Cuesta Nacional (Dominican Republic); Libreria Coletti (Mexico); Comunidad Siervos de Cristo Vivo (Dominican Republic); Conferencia Episcopal Ecuatoriana (Ecuador); Conferencia Episcopal Peruana (Peru); Congregacion Hijas de San Pablo (Chile); Corporacion Ediciones Paulinas (Ecuador); Diel-Distribuidores e Livreiros Lda (Portugal); Disliber Spes Mexico (EDICEP) (Mexico); Distritexto (Colombia); Distribuidora de Estudios (Venezuela); Libreria Familia de Nazareth (Chile); Libreria de la Familia (Paraguay); Libreria Universal Carlos Federspiel & Co (Costa Rica); Frente y Vuelta SA de CV (Mexico); Fundacion de Editores Verbo Divino (Colombia); Libreria Norberto Gonzalez (Puerto Rico); Iglesia Catolica Apostolica y Romana (El Salvador); Institucion Salesiana (El Salvador); Instituto Misionero de Sociedad de San Pablo (Honduras, Puerto Rico); Instituto Misionero Hijas de San Pablo (Argentina, Ecuador); Instituto Misionero Sociedad de San Pablo (Chile, Costa Rica, El Salvador, Guatemala); Fundacion Jesus de la Misericordia (Ecuador); Katholicos SA (Costa Rica); Libreria Sor Virginia Laporte (Dominican Republic); Libreria Leoniana (Mexico); Liberalia (Chile); Distribuidora Loyola (Brazil); Ministerio Biblico Verbo Divino (USA); Editorial Nueva Decada (Costa Rica); La Nueva Libreria Parroquial de Claveria (Mexico); Obra Nacional de la Buena Prensa (Mexico); Libreria Juan Pablo II (Dominican Republic); Libreria Papiros (Ecuador); Paulinas (Brazil); Pauli-

nas Centro Multimedia (Puerto Rico); Paulinas-Instituto Misionero Hijas de San Pablo (Colombia); Libreria Paulinas (Argentina, Dominican Republic, Paraguay, Uruguay, Venezuela); Paulinas Multimedia (Portugal); Paulus Editora (Brazil); Empresa Periodistica Mundo Ltda (Chile); Pia Sociedad San Pablo (Chile); Proveeduria Conferencia Episcopal (Costa Rica); Libreria Quijote (Paraguay); Libreria San Pablo (Nicaragua, Panama, Venezuela); Libreria di San Paolo SSP (Mexico); Sociedad de San Pablo (Colombia, Peru); Libreria Sole (Mexico); Tecnicas Paraguayas (Paraguay); Libreria la Tertulia (Puerto Rico); Libreria Universidad Centroamericana J Simeon Canas (El Salvador); USA Madrid Books (USA); Libreria Verbo Divino (Costa Rica); Verbum Libreria Catolica (Mexico); Verdad y Vida (Paraguay); Verdade e Vida-Livraria e Distribuidora (Portugal)
Warehouse: San Rafael, 6, 28108 Alcobendas, Madrid *Tel:* 91 484 03 27 *Fax:* 91 661 72 82 *E-mail:* pedidos.editoriales@conferenciaepiscopal.es

Biblioteca de Catalunya (National Library of Catalonia)
Carrer de l'Hospital, 56, 08001 Barcelona
Tel: 93 270 23 00 *Fax:* 93 270 23 04
E-mail: bustia@bnc.cat
Web Site: www.bnc.cat
Key Personnel
Dir: Eugenia Serra Aranda *Tel:* 93 270 2300 ext 84013122 *E-mail:* eserra@bnc.cat
Head, Administration: Margarita Valverde *Tel:* 93 270 2300 ext 84013106 *E-mail:* mvalverd@bnc.cat
Founded: 1914
Subjects: Art, History, Library & Information Sciences, Literature, Literary Criticism, Essays, Music, Dance
ISBN Prefix(es): 978-84-7845
Number of titles published annually: 6 Print
Parent Company: Department de Cultura
Ultimate Parent Company: Generalitat De Catalunya
Distribution Center: Distribuciones de Enlace SA, Carrer Reina Amalia, 20-22, 08001 Barcelona
Tel: 902 109 431

Biblioteca 'NT', *imprint of* EUNSA (Ediciones Universidad de Navarra SA)

Editorial Biblioteca Nueva SL
c/ Almagro, 38, 28010 Madrid
SAN: 002-3086
Tel: 91 310 04 36 *Fax:* 91 319 82 35
E-mail: editorial@bibliotecanueva.es
Web Site: www.bibliotecanueva.es
Founded: 1920
Subjects: Biography, Memoirs, Economics, History, Poetry, Psychology, Psychiatry
ISBN Prefix(es): 978-84-7030; 978-84-9742
Number of titles published annually: 140 Print
Total Titles: 3,895 Print
Distribution Center: Adonay Llibres, Poligono Industrial La Pahilla, c/ Fuente Forraje, 170, 46370 Chiva *Tel:* 90 215 46 43 *Fax:* 96 252 17 39 *E-mail:* info@adonay.com
Babel Libros SL, Polg San Cristobal, c/ Magnesio, 24, 47012 Valladolid *Tel:* 98 320 97 73 *Fax:* 98 320 33 49 *E-mail:* babel@trevenque.es

Blackie Books
Esglesia 4-10, 4º, 08024 Barcelona
Tel: 934 160 959
E-mail: info@blackiebooks.org
Web Site: www.blackiebooks.org
Key Personnel
Press: Raul Sanchez-Serrano *E-mail:* raul@blackiebooks.org
Subjects: Biography, Memoirs, Fiction, Inspirational, Spirituality

ISBN Prefix(es): 978-84-16290; 978-84-17059; 978-84-937362; 978-84-938272; 978-84-938745; 978-84-938817; 978-84-940019; 978-84-941676; 978-84-942247; 978-84-942580
Imprints: Blackie Little
Foreign Rep(s): Catalonia Editorial (Chile); Centro Cuesta Nacional (Dominican Republic); Colofon SA de CV (Mexico); Del Nuevo Extremo Grupo Editorial (Argentina, Paraguay, Uruguay); Desarrollos Culturales Costarricenses (Costa Rica); Oceano Panama (Panama); Editorial Oceano Peruana SA (Peru); Rey & Naranjo Editorial (Colombia); Libreria Sophos (Guatemala)
Distribution Center: Les Punxes Distribuidora SL, Sardenya, 75-81, 08018 Barcelona *Tel:* 902 107 581 *Fax:* 933 009 091 *E-mail:* punxes@ punxes.es (exc Castilla-La Mancha & Madrid)
Antonio Machado SA, Labradores s/n, PI Prado del Espino, 28660 Boadilla de Monte *Tel:* 916 324 893 *Fax:* 916 326 513 *E-mail:* machadolibros@machadolibros.com (Castilla-La Mancha & Madrid)

Blackie Little, *imprint of* Blackie Books

Blex Ideas
Avda 3 de Mayo, 77, Edif Residencial Maritimo, Nivel 1, Oficina 4, 38005 Santa Cruz de Tenerife
Tel: 922653401 *Fax:* 922653801
E-mail: info@blexideas.com
Web Site: www.blexideas.com
Key Personnel
Dir General: Francisco Javier Bello Lecuona
Subjects: Geography, Geology, History, Science (General)
ISBN Prefix(es): 978-84-934694

Editorial Blume/Naturart SA
Av Mare de Deu de Lorda, 20, 08034 Barcelona
Tel: 932054000 *Fax:* 932051441
E-mail: info@blume.net; export@blume.net; rights@blume.net
Web Site: www.blume.net
Key Personnel
International Sales Manager: Teresa Fernandez Pena
Administration: Aroa Borlan Martinez
Foreign Rights: Elsa Gasoliba Encado
Press & Marketing: Laura Lanuza Buil *E-mail:* laura@blume.net
Subjects: Architecture & Interior Design, Art, Health, Nutrition, History, Photography, Sports, Athletics, Travel & Tourism, Ecology
ISBN Prefix(es): 978-84-8076; 978-84-87535

Boletin Oficial del Estado
Ave de Manoteras, 54, 28050 Madrid
SAN: 000-6254
Tel: 91 111 43 58; 91 111 40 00 *Fax:* 91 111 42 97
Web Site: www.boe.es
Founded: 1661
Subjects: Law, Public Administration
ISBN Prefix(es): 978-84-340
Branch Office(s)
C/ Trafalgar, 27, 28010 Madrid
Distributed by Edisofer SL; Distribuidora Juridica Espanola (DIJUSA); Marcial Pons Librero SL; Reydis Libros; Sociedad General Espanola de Libreria SA (SGEL)

Bon Vivant, *imprint of* Ediciones Robinbook SL

Books4pocket, *imprint of* Ediciones Urano SA

Antoni Bosch Editor SA+
Palafolls, 28, 08017 Barcelona
Tel: 93 206 07 30 *Fax:* 932 520 379
E-mail: info@antonibosch.com

Web Site: www.antonibosch.com
Founded: 1978
Subjects: Economics, Music, Dance, Science (General)
ISBN Prefix(es): 978-84-85855; 978-84-95348
Associate Companies: Bon Ton
Distributed by Editorial Byblos Ltda (Uruguay); Libreria Editorial Juventud (Bolivia); Lectorum Publications (USA); Mayol Ediciones SA (Colombia); Ediciones Tecnicas Paraguayas (Paraguay)
Distributor for Bon Ton
Foreign Rep(s): Editorial Byblos Ltda (Uruguay); Cuspide Libros SA (Argentina); EDISA (Costa Rica); Fernandez de Castro Libros (Chile); Fundacion del Libro Universitario (LIBUN) (Peru); Hispamer SA (Nicaragua); Libreria y Editorial Juventud SRL (Bolivia); Libros y Editoriales SA de CV (Mexico); Libri Mundi SA (Ecuador); Ediciones Tecnicas Paraguayas (Paraguay); RGS Libros SA de CV (Mexico); Libreria Universidad Centroamericana UCA (El Salvador); Universidad de Panama, Libreria Universitaria (Panama)

J M Bosch Editor+
C/Mayor, 337 1º 2a, 08759 Barcelona
Tel: 93 683 13 44 *Fax:* 93 412 27 64
E-mail: info@libreriabosch.es
Web Site: www.editorial.libreriabosch.com; www.libreriabosch.es
Founded: 1889
Subjects: Astronomy, Law, Medicine, Nursing, Dentistry, Music, Dance
ISBN Prefix(es): 978-84-7698
Number of titles published annually: 35 Print; 3 CD-ROM; 30 Online; 3 E-Book
Total Titles: 530 Print
Parent Company: Libreria Bosch SL

Editorial Maria Jesus Bosch SL
Calle Villarroel 39, 08011 Barcelona
SAN: 006-6435
Tel: 934 512 335 *Fax:* 934 539 717
Subjects: Criminology, Law
ISBN Prefix(es): 978-84-89591

Editorial Bosch SA+
Avda Carrilet, 3 Edificio D 9a planta, 08902 Barcelona
SAN: 000-6297
Tel: 902 250 500 *Fax:* 93 205 52 02
E-mail: clientes@wke.es
Web Site: www.wolterskluwer.es/nuestras-marcas/bosch
Key Personnel
Mng Dir: Albert Ferre
Head, Publications: Santiago Gales
Founded: 1934
Focus is on law books & legal matters.
Membership(s): Publishers Association of Catalonia.
Subjects: Criminology, Journalism, Language Arts, Linguistics, Law, Literature, Literary Criticism, Essays, Public Administration, Radio, TV
ISBN Prefix(es): 978-84-7162; 978-84-7676

Editorial Boveda
C/ Juan Ignacio Luca de Tena, 15, 28027 Madrid
Tel: 913 938 800 *Fax:* 917 426 631
Web Site: www.editorialboveda.com
Subjects: Fiction, History, Mysteries, Suspense, Science Fiction, Fantasy, Historical Fiction
ISBN Prefix(es): 978-84-936684

Brau Edicions
C/ Dinamarca, 1, 17600 Figueres
Tel: 972 670 417 *Fax:* 972 670 417
E-mail: brau@brauedicions.com
Web Site: www.brauedicions.com

Founded: 1993
Subjects: Architecture & Interior Design, Fiction, Humor, Travel & Tourism, Classics, Comedy, Cultural Heritage, Nature
ISBN Prefix(es): 978-84-95946; 978-84-88589

Editorial Brief SL+
c/ Daniel Balaciart, 5 bajo, 46020 Valencia
Tel: 96 310 60 37 *Fax:* 96 362 00 77
E-mail: info@editorialbrief.com
Web Site: editorialbrief.com
Key Personnel
Dir General: Sonsoles Sancho
Dir, Administration & Sales: Lidia Martinez
Dir, Editorial Dept & Production: Inma Arlandis
Founded: 2000
Publications go out to pedagogic innovations & projects which influence a person's whole training. Parents & teachers can find supporting didactic material.
Membership(s): Asociacion de Editores de Espana (Spain Publishing Association).
Subjects: Education, Fiction, Poetry
ISBN Prefix(es): 978-84-95895
Number of titles published annually: 8 Print; 1 CD-ROM; 1 Online; 2 E-Book
Total Titles: 37 Print; 1 CD-ROM; 2 Online; 4 E-Book

Edicions Bromera SL+
Poli Industrial I, Ronda dels Tintorers 10, 46600 Alzira
SAN: 002-0974
Mailing Address: PO Box 147, 46600 Alzira
Tel: 962 402 254 *Fax:* 962 403 191
E-mail: adm@bromera.com; bromera@bromera.com; comunicacio@bromera.com; comercial@bromera.com
Web Site: www.bromera.com
Key Personnel
Foreign Rights: Carol Borras *E-mail:* carol@bromera.com
Founded: 1986
Membership(s): Valencia Publishers' Association.
Subjects: Education, Language Arts, Linguistics, Literature, Literary Criticism, Essays, Culture, Ecology
ISBN Prefix(es): 978-84-7660; 978-84-7658; 978-84-9824

Ediciones del Bronce
Av Diagonal, 662-664, 08034 Barcelona
Tel: 93 496 70 01 *Fax:* 93 217 77 48
E-mail: comunicacioneditorialplaneta@planeta.es
Web Site: www.planeta.es
Founded: 1996
Subjects: Literature, Literary Criticism, Essays, Nonfiction (General), Current Affairs
ISBN Prefix(es): 978-84-8453; 978-84-89854
Parent Company: Editorial Planeta SA

Grupo Editorial Bruno SL+
C/ Juan Ignacio Luca de Tena, 15, 28027 Madrid
SAN: 002-3175
Tel: 91 724 48 00 *Fax:* 91 725 83 59
E-mail: asesoriapedagogica@editorial-bruno.es
Web Site: www.editorial-bruno.es
Founded: 1898
Subjects: Communications, Education, Religion - Catholic
ISBN Prefix(es): 978-84-216
Branch Office(s)
Mallorca, 45, 08029 Barcelona *Tel:* 93 485 85 90
Warehouse: Av Castilla, 15-17, Pol Ind S Fernando 1, 28850 Torrejon de Ardoz (Madrid)

By Architect Publications
Pla dels avellaners 6, nave 3, 08210 Barcelona
E-mail: info@by-architect.com
Web Site: www.by-architect.com
Subjects: Architecture & Interior Design
ISBN Prefix(es): 978-84-941915

Caballo de Troya, *imprint of* Penguin Random House Grupo Editorial

Caballo de Troya
Imprint of Penguin Random House Grupo Editorial
Agustin de Betancourt, 19, 28003 Madrid
Tel: 91 535 8190 *Fax:* 91 535 8939
Founded: 2004
Subjects: Fiction, Nonfiction (General)
ISBN Prefix(es): 978-84-96594

Cabildo de Gran Canaria, Dept de Ediciones
(Grand Canary Council Island, Publishing Dept)
c/ Cano 24, 1a, 35002 Las Palmas de Gran Canaria
SAN: 000-6793
Tel: 928 381 020; 928 381 083 *Fax:* 928 381 627
E-mail: ediciones@grancanaria.com
Web Site: www.grancanaria.com
Key Personnel
President: Jose Miguel Bravo de Laguna Bermudez
Founded: 1955
Subjects: Geography, Geology, History, Natural History, Regional Interests
ISBN Prefix(es): 978-84-8103; 978-84-86127; 978-84-87832

Edicions Cadi, *imprint of* Editorial Everest SA

Caelus Books, *imprint of* Ediciones Urano SA

Calambur Editorial SL+
Calle Maria Teresa, 17-1° D, 28028 Madrid
Tel: 91 725 92 49 *Fax:* 91 298 11 94
E-mail: calambur@calambureditorial.com
Web Site: www.calambureditorial.com
Founded: 1991
Subjects: Art, Fiction, History, Language Arts, Linguistics, Literature, Literary Criticism, Essays, Poetry, Romance
ISBN Prefix(es): 978-84-88015
Number of titles published annually: 12 Print
Total Titles: 86 Print
Distributed by Adonay; Babel Libros; Baker & Taylor; Besai Llibres; Bitarte; Liberia Guadalquivir; Cal-Malaga; Celesa; E/A Libros; Gaia Libros; Icaro Distribuidora; KRK Ediciones; LiTeca; Lopez Caballero Libros; Editorial Moll; Puvill Libros; Tarahumara SL; Teran Libros

Editorial Calamo
C/Pintor Aparicio, 13, 03003 Alicante
SAN: 002-3213
Tel: 965130581; 965115345
E-mail: editorial@edcalamo.com
Web Site: www.edcalamo.com
Key Personnel
Contact: Ana C Baidal Lopez
Founded: 1990
Subjects: Fiction, Human Relations, Literature, Literary Criticism, Essays, Religion - Islamic, Travel & Tourism, Arab & Mediterranean Culture
ISBN Prefix(es): 978-84-87839

Editorial La Calesa+
Juan de Herrera, 26, 47151 Boecillo, Valladolid
SAN: 002-5119
Tel: 983 548 102 *Fax:* 983 548 024
E-mail: editorial@lacalesa.es
Web Site: www.araleditores.es
Key Personnel
Manager: Jacinto Altes-Bustelo
Founded: 1989
Subjects: Education, Language Arts, Linguistics, Mathematics

ISBN Prefix(es): 978-84-8105; 978-84-87463; 978-84-89556
Subsidiaries: Boecillo Editora Multimedia SA

Edicions Camacuc SL+
Calle Doctor Maranon, 30-21, 46200 Valencia
SAN: 002-0990
Tel: 961 293 440
Founded: 1987
Subjects: History, Literature, Literary Criticism, Essays, Science Fiction, Fantasy
ISBN Prefix(es): 978-84-86970; 978-84-89938

Edicions La Campana+
Ave 49 Baixos, 08021 Barcelona
Tel: 934 531 665 *Fax:* 934 518 918
E-mail: info@lacampanaeditorial.com
Web Site: lacampanaeditorial.com
Founded: 1985
Subjects: Fiction, Nonfiction (General)
ISBN Prefix(es): 978-84-96735; 978-84-86491; 978-84-88791; 978-84-95616
Number of titles published annually: 18 Print
Total Titles: 18 Print
Distribution Center: Les Punxes SL, Sardenya, 75-81, 08018 Barcelona *Tel:* 93 485 63 20 *Fax:* 93 300 90 91 *E-mail:* punxes@punxes.es
Gea Llibres SL, Pol Ind Oliveral, Carrer G - Nau 6, 46190 Riba-roja de Turia *Tel:* 96 166 52 56 *Fax:* 96 168 52 49 *E-mail:* gea@xpress.es

Campgrafic Editors SL
Matias Perello, 17, 6°, 46005 Valencia
Tel: 646 314 862
E-mail: campgrafic@campgrafic.com
Web Site: www.campgrafic.com
Subjects: Printing (typography)
ISBN Prefix(es): 978-84-931677; 978-84-933446
Distribution Center: Asunto Impreso, Pasaje Rivarola, 169, C1015AAA Buenos Aires, Argentina *Tel:* (011) 4383-5152 *Fax:* (011) 4383-6262 *Web Site:* www.asuntoimpreso.com
Editorial RM, Rio Panuco, 141, Colonia Cuauhtemoc, 06500 Mexico, DF, Mexico *Tel:* (0155) 5533-5658 *Fax:* (0155) 5514-6799 *E-mail:* info@editorialrm.com

Editorial Caritas Espanola
C/ Embajadores 162, 28045 Madrid
Tel: 914441000 *Fax:* 915934882
E-mail: correo@caritas.es; publicaciones@caritas.es
Web Site: www.caritas.es
Subjects: Religion - Other, Social Sciences, Sociology
ISBN Prefix(es): 978-84-89733; 978-84-8440; 978-84-920386

El Carro de Madera, *imprint of* Editorial Alhulia SA

Carroggio SA de Ediciones+
Rambla Catalunya, 38, 08007 Barcelona
SAN: 000-7439
Tel: 93 494 99 22 *Fax:* 93 494 99 23
E-mail: editorial@carroggio.es
Web Site: www.carroggio.es
Key Personnel
General Administrator: Santiago Carroggio
Founded: 1911
Specialize in art & educational books.
Subjects: Art, History, Literature, Literary Criticism, Essays, Natural History
ISBN Prefix(es): 978-84-7254
Total Titles: 2,000 Print
Branch Office(s)
San Ignacio de Loyola, 4, 46008 Valencia
Tel: 963 854 377 *Fax:* 963 820 159

Instituto Cartografico Latino, *imprint of* Ediciones Vicens Vives SA

Casa de Velazquez+
Ciudad Universitaria, C/ Paul Guinard, 3, 28040 Madrid
SAN: 000-7471
Tel: 914 551 580; 914 551 624 (orders) *Fax:* 914 551 625
E-mail: publications@casadevelazquez.org (orders & publications rights)
Web Site: www.casadevelazquez.org; www.casadevelazquez.org/en/publications/online-bookshop (orders)
Key Personnel
Dir: Michel Bertrand
Publications Coordinator: Richard Figuier
  E-mail: richard.figuier@casadevelazquez.org
Contact: German Huelamo
Founded: 1920
Membership(s): AFPU-D (Association Francaise des Presses d'Universite-Diffusion); UNE Union de Editoriales Universitarias Espanolas.
Subjects: Archaeology, Art, Geography, Geology, History, Literature, Literary Criticism, Essays
ISBN Prefix(es): 978-84-86839; 978-84-95555; 978-84-96820; 978-84-15636; 978-84-9096
Number of titles published annually: 15 Print; 2 Online; 10 E-Book
Total Titles: 250 Print; 26 Online; 51 E-Book
Distribution Center: Celesa, Laurel 21, 28005 Madrid *Tel:* 915 170 170 *Fax:* 915 173 481 *E-mail:* celesa@celesa.com *Web Site:* www.celesa.com
Puvill, Estany, 13, Nave D-1, 08038 Barcelona *Tel:* 932 988 960 *Fax:* 932 988 961 *E-mail:* info@puvill.com *Web Site:* www.puvill.com
Distriforma, C/ Oficio, 16, 28906 Getafe *Tel:* 916 845 628 *Fax:* 925 137 566 *E-mail:* distriforma@distriforma.es *Web Site:* www.distriforma.es (Spain only)
Sodis, 128, av du Marechal Lattre-de-Tassigny, BP 142, 77403 Lagny-sur-Marne Cedex, France *Tel:* 01 60 07 82 00 *Fax:* 01 64 30 92 22 *Web Site:* www.sodis.fr

Editorial Casals SA+
Casp, 79, 08013 Barcelona
Tel: 902 107 007 *Fax:* 932 656 895
E-mail: casals@editorialcasals.com; export@editorialcasals.com
Web Site: www.editorialcasals.com
Key Personnel
Dir General: Ramon Casals Roca
Contact: Pere Mateo *E-mail:* pere.mateo@editorialcasals.com
Founded: 1870
Subjects: Art, Education, Literature, Literary Criticism, Essays, Mathematics, Music, Dance, Philosophy, Religion - Catholic, Science (General), Social Sciences, Sociology, Culture
ISBN Prefix(es): 978-84-218; 978-84-7864; 978-84-265 (Editorial Magisterio Espanol); 978-84-7552 (Editorial Onda); 978-84-88017; 978-84-8343 (Editorial Bambu); 978-84-934826 (Editorial Bambu); 978-84-9825; 978-84-7684
Number of titles published annually: 225 Print
Total Titles: 2,150 Print
Associate Companies: Editorial Magisterio Espanol, SA
Imprints: Editorial Bambu; Combel Editorial SA; Biografia Joven; Letras Mayusculas; Novelas y Cuentos; Punto Juvenil
Warehouse: Juli Galve i Brusons 72-74, 08912 Badalona

Ediciones Castalia
Av Diagonal, 519-521, 2° piso, 08029 Barcelona
SAN: 002-3345
Tel: 934949720
E-mail: info@castalia.es
Web Site: www.castalia.es
Key Personnel
Mng Dir: Amparo Soler

Sales Dir: Federico Ibanez
Founded: 1946
Specialize in editions of the classics.
Subjects: Education, Literature, Literary Criticism, Essays
ISBN Prefix(es): 978-84-7039; 978-84-9740
Foreign Rep(s): Colophon (Mexico); Edhasa (Argentina)
Distribution Center: Celesa, Moratines, 22 1° B, 28005 Madrid *Tel:* 91 517 01 70 *Fax:* 91 517 34 81 *E-mail:* pedidos@celesa.es (Africa, Asia, Europe, Oceania, USA)

Castellnou Edicions
Imprint of Hermes Editora General SAU
Pau Claris, 184, 08037 Barcelona
Tel: 93 496 14 00 *Fax:* 93 487 55 35
E-mail: info@hermeseditora.com
Web Site: www.castellnouedicions.com
Founded: 1994
Specialize in education.
Subjects: Education, Language Arts, Linguistics, Literature, Literary Criticism, Essays, Mathematics, Psychology, Psychiatry, Science (General), Social Sciences, Sociology, Catalan Classic Literature, Catalan Language, Spanish Language
ISBN Prefix(es): 978-84-8287; 978-84-88901; 978-84-9804

Castellnou Editora Valenciana
Imprint of Hermes Editora General SAU
Atenas 2004, 11B Puerta 6, 46900 Valencia
Tel: 96 317 00 38
E-mail: info@hermeseditora.com
Web Site: www.castellnouedival.com
Subjects: Education, Environmental Studies, Geography, Geology, History, Language Arts, Linguistics, Literature, Literary Criticism, Essays, Mathematics, Music, Dance, Science (General), Social Sciences, Sociology, Valenciana Language
ISBN Prefix(es): 978-84-89625

Edicios do Castro
O Castro, s/n, 15168 Sada, A Coruna
SAN: 001-4605
Tel: 902246644 *Fax:* 982557804
E-mail: sargadelos@sargadelos.com
Web Site: www.sargadelos.com
Key Personnel
Dir: Angel Vazquez Mosquera *Tel:* 981620937 *Fax:* 981623804 *E-mail:* ocastro@sargadelos.com
Founded: 1963
Subjects: Art, Drama, Theater, Economics, Geography, Geology, History, Literature, Literary Criticism, Essays, Poetry, Science (General), Social Sciences, Sociology
ISBN Prefix(es): 978-84-7492; 978-84-8485; 978-84-85134
Imprints: Graficas do Castro/Moret
Foreign Rep(s): Abr Imports LLC (USA); Arlanzon Technologies Inc (USA); Atelier Gourmed Ltda (Portugal); Bernardina de Sousa Pereira (Portugal); El Corte Ingles (Portugal); Galeria Marco Polo 2000 CA (Venezuela); Glrow Co Ltd (Japan); Franziska Hartz (Germany); Iberica Imports LLC (USA); Nihon Ceraty Co Ltd (Japan); Outra-Western Lighthouse SL (Belgium, Luxembourg, Netherlands)

Graficas do Castro/Moret, *imprint of* Edicios do Castro

Catalogo, *imprint of* Ediciones Maeva

Catalogo, *imprint of* Editorial Alhulia SA

Catalogo General, *imprint of* Editorial Alhulia SA

Ediciones Catedra SA+
Juan Ignacio Luca de Tena, n° 15, 28027 Madrid
SAN: 001-6144
Tel: 91 393 87 87 *Fax:* 91 741 21 18
E-mail: catedra@catedra.com
Web Site: www.catedra.com
Key Personnel
Dir: Josune Garcia
Rights & Permissions: Marisa Barreno
Founded: 1973
Subjects: Art, Film, Video, History, Human Relations, Language Arts, Linguistics, Literature, Literary Criticism, Essays, Music, Dance, Philosophy, Poetry, Women's Studies
ISBN Prefix(es): 978-84-376
Parent Company: Grupo Anaya
Associate Companies: Algaida; Ediciones Anaya SA; Piramide
Bookshop(s): Iriarte 4, 28028 Madrid
Warehouse: Avda Ferrocarril s/n, 28346 Madrid
Orders to: Comercial Grupo Anaya, SA Calle Iriaste, 4, 28028 Madrid *Tel:* 913 597 600 *Fax:* 913 559 403

CCG, see Consello da Cultura Galega (CCG)

Editorial CCS, see Central Catequistica Salesiana (CCS)

Ediciones CEAC+
Av Diagonal, 662-664, 08034 Barcelona
SAN: 003-357X
Tel: 93 492 69 56
Web Site: www.planetadelibros.com/editorial-para-dummies-16.html; www.paradummies.es
Founded: 1947
Subjects: Education, Science Fiction, Fantasy, Technology
ISBN Prefix(es): 978-84-329
Parent Company: Planeta de Agostini Profesional y Formacion
Ultimate Parent Company: Grupo Planeta
Imprints: Libros Cupula; Timun Mas

Edicions Cedel+
c/Rossend Arus 16, 08014 Barcelona
Mailing Address: Apdo de Correos 99066, 08014 Barcelona
Tel: 93 421 18 80; 93 331 10 42 *Fax:* 93 422 89 71
E-mail: cedel@kadex.com
Web Site: www.kadex.com/cedel
Founded: 1956
Subjects: Agriculture, Biological Sciences, Environmental Studies, Health, Nutrition
ISBN Prefix(es): 978-84-352

CEDMA, see Centro de Ediciones de la Diputacion de Malaga (CEDMA)

CEIC Alfons El Vell
Marques de Campo 3, 46701 Gandia
Tel: 96 295 95 64; 96 295 95 62 *Fax:* 96 295 95 66
E-mail: ceicalfonselvell@gandia.org
Web Site: www.alfonselvell.com
Key Personnel
President: Arturo Torro Chisvet
Vice President: Vicent Gregori Acosta
Dir: Rafael Delgado Artes
Subjects: History, Regional Interests
ISBN Prefix(es): 978-84-96839
Distribution Center: Sendra Distribuidor, C/ Taronja, 16, 46210 Picanya (Valencia) *Tel:* 96 159 08 41

Central Catequistica Salesiana (CCS)
Alcala 166, 28028 Madrid
SAN: 002-3701
Tel: 91 725 20 00 *Fax:* 91 726 25 70

E-mail: sei@editorialccs.com; apedidos@editorialccs.com (national orders); apedidos2@editorialccs.com (international orders)
Web Site: www.editorialccs.com
Founded: 1944
Subjects: Biblical Studies, Biography, Memoirs, Crafts, Games, Hobbies, Drama, Theater, Education, Religion - Catholic
ISBN Prefix(es): 978-84-7043; 978-84-8316

Centre d'Informacio i Documentacio Internacionals de Barcelona (CIDOB)
C/ Elisabets 12, 08001 Barcelona
Tel: 93 302 64 95
E-mail: cidob@cidob.org
Web Site: www.cidob.org
Key Personnel
Executive Coordinator: Anna Estrada Bertran *E-mail:* aestrada@cidob.org
Publications: Elisabet Mane *E-mail:* bmane@cidob.org
Press: Esther Masclans *E-mail:* emasclans@cidob.org
Subjects: Philosophy, Social Sciences, Sociology
ISBN Prefix(es): 978-84-87072

Centro de Ediciones de la Diputacion de Malaga (CEDMA) (Publications Center - County Hall of Malaga)
Av de los Guindos, 48, 29004 Malaga
Tel: 952 069 207 *Fax:* 952 069 215
E-mail: cedma@malaga.es
Web Site: cedma.es
Key Personnel
Publication Dir: Victoria Rosado *E-mail:* vrosado@malaga.es
Founded: 1973
Subjects: Anthropology, Archaeology, Art, Drama, Theater, Geography, Geology, History, Literature, Literary Criticism, Essays, Poetry
ISBN Prefix(es): 978-84-7785
Number of titles published annually: 20 Print; 1 CD-ROM; 4 Online
Total Titles: 1,000 Print; 2 CD-ROM; 142 Online

Centro de Estudios Adams-Ediciones Valbuena SA
C/ Ayala 128, bajo, 28006 Madrid
Tel: 902 333 543 *Fax:* 915 774 221
E-mail: adams@adams.es
Web Site: www.adams.es
Key Personnel
Dir General: Manuel Pereira
Founded: 1957
Subjects: Accounting, Career Development, Computer Science, Labor, Industrial Relations, Psychology, Psychiatry, Public Administration, Transportation
ISBN Prefix(es): 978-84-7357; 978-84-8303; 978-84-9731; 978-84-8061; 978-84-9818

Centro de Estudios Avanzados en Ciencias Sociales (CEACS) del Instituto Juan March de Estudios e Investigaciones (Center for Advanced Study in the Social Science of the Juan March Institute for Studies & Research)
Castello, 77, 28006 Madrid
Tel: 91 435 42 40 *Fax:* 91 576 34 20
E-mail: info@march.es
Web Site: www.march.es/ceacs/ceacs.asp
Key Personnel
President: Juan March Delgado
Vice President: Carlos March Delgado
Dir: Javier Goma Lanzon *E-mail:* direccion@march.es
Founded: 1955
Subjects: Science (General), Social Sciences, Sociology

Centro de Estudios Politicos Y Constitucionales+
Plaza de la Marina Espanola 9, 28071 Madrid
SAN: 000-8109
Tel: 91 540 19 50 *Fax:* 91 541 95 74
E-mail: cepc@cepc.es
Web Site: www.cepc.es
Key Personnel
Dir: Benigno Pendas Garcia *Tel:* 91 547 85 45
　E-mail: direccion@cepc.es
Deputy Dir, Publications & Documentation:
　Angel Sanchez Navarro *Tel:* 91 422 89 33
　E-mail: publicdirector@cepc.es
Deputy Dir, Studies & Research: Isabel
　Wences Simon *Tel:* 91 422 89 48
　E-mail: secrestudios@cepc.es
Manager: Israel Pastor Sainz-Pardo *Tel:* 91 548
　01 18 *E-mail:* gerente@cepc.es
Founded: 1939
Subjects: Government, Political Science, History,
　Law, Philosophy, Social Sciences, Sociology
ISBN Prefix(es): 978-84-259

Centro de Investigaciones Sociologicas (CIS)
C/ Montalban, 8, 28014 Madrid
Tel: 915807607 *Fax:* 915807619
E-mail: cis@cis.es; publicaciones@cis.es
Web Site: www.cis.es
Key Personnel
President: Requena Santos *E-mail:* presidencia@
　cis.es
Dir General: Cristina Rodriguez Vela
Subjects: Social Sciences, Sociology
ISBN Prefix(es): 978-84-7476

Centro de la Cultura Popular Canaria
C/ Daute, esquina Cruz de Candelaria, 38203 La
　Laguna
Tel: 922 827 800 *Fax:* 922 827 801
E-mail: centrodelacultura@centrodelacultura.com
Web Site: www.centrodelacultura.com
Key Personnel
Dir General: Cesar Rodriguez Placeres
Editorial Dir: Remedios Sosa Diaz
Founded: 1977
Subjects: Biography, Memoirs, Economics, His-
　tory, Photography, Poetry, Folklore, Nature
ISBN Prefix(es): 978-84-7926

Centro de Publicaciones del Ministerio de Sanidad, Servicios Sociales e Igualdad
P° del Prado, 18-20, 28014 Madrid
Tel: 91 596 11 52; 91 596 40 60 *Fax:* 91 596 11
　41
E-mail: publicaciones@msssi.es
Web Site: www.msssi.gob.es/biblioPublic/
　publicaciones/centroPub.htm
Subjects: Health, Nutrition
ISBN Prefix(es): 978-84-351

Centro de Tecnologia Educativa+
Via Augusta 4, 6a Planta, 08006 Barcelona
SAN: 000-9040
Tel: 93 217 74 00; 93 217 75 01 *Fax:* 93 217 62
　53
E-mail: info@centrocte.com
Web Site: www.centrocte.com
Founded: 1983
Specialize in books for teaching & training needs
　of the business world.
Membership(s): ANCED; EADL (European Asso-
　ciation for Distance Learning).
Subjects: Business, Education, Management
ISBN Prefix(es): 978-84-7608
Warehouse: Puig-gari, 21, 08014 Barcelona

Centro UNESCO de San Sebastian
C/ Paseo de Colon 9-1°C, 20002 San Sebastian
Tel: 943 29 31 68 *Fax:* 943 29 31 68
E-mail: unescoeskola@ibercom.com
Web Site: www.unescoeskola.org

Founded: 1992
Specialize in Unesco training courses, manuals &
　student books.
Subjects: Education
Total Titles: 107 Print; 7 Online; 5 E-Book; 310
　Audio
Parent Company: UNESCO

Editorial Grupo Cero
C/ Princesa 13, 1° Izq, 28008 Madrid
Tel: 91 758 19 40
E-mail: actividades@grupocero.info; central@
　grupocero.info
Web Site: www.editorialgrupocero.com
Key Personnel
Dir: Miguel Oscar Menassa
Founded: 1976
Subjects: Art, Drama, Theater, Literature, Literary
　Criticism, Essays, Medicine, Nursing, Den-
　tistry, Poetry, Psychology, Psychiatry, Social
　Sciences, Sociology, Psychoanalysis
ISBN Prefix(es): 978-84-85498; 978-987-9196;
　978-84-9755

CEU Ediciones
Imprint of Fundacion Universitaria San Pablo
　CEU
Julian Romea, 18, 28003 Madrid
Tel: 91 514 05 73 *Fax:* 91 514 04 30
E-mail: ceuediciones@ceu.es
Web Site: www.ceuediciones.es
Subjects: Art, Economics, Education, History,
　Law, Philosophy, Science (General), Social Sci-
　ences, Sociology, Bullfighting
ISBN Prefix(es): 978-84-92456; 978-84-92989

CIDOB, see Centre d'Informacio i Documentacio
　Internacionals de Barcelona (CIDOB)

Ediciones El Cipres
C/ Molino de Cela s/n, 24395 Nistal, Leon
Tel: 987 053 952; 629 016 361 (cell) *Fax:* 987
　600 502
E-mail: info@edicioneselcipres.com
Web Site: www.edicioneselcipres.com
Subjects: Poetry, Narrative
ISBN Prefix(es): 978-84-613
Distribution Center: La Casa del Libro *Web
　Site:* www.casadellibro.com

Circe Ediciones SA+
Calle Milanesat, 25-27, 4-2a, 08017 Barcelona
Tel: 93 204 09 90 *Fax:* 93 204 11 83
E-mail: info@oceano.com
Web Site: www.oceano.com
Founded: 1986
Subjects: Biography, Memoirs, Fiction, Literature,
　Literary Criticism, Essays, Nonfiction (General)
ISBN Prefix(es): 978-84-7765
Parent Company: Grupo Oceano

Circulo de Bellas Artes
C/ Alcala, 42, 28014 Madrid
Tel: 91 360 54 00
E-mail: info@circulobellasartes.com; prensa@
　circulobellasartes.com
Web Site: www.circulobellasartes.com
Key Personnel
Dir: Juan Barja
Subjects: Fiction, Nonfiction (General), Humani-
　ties
ISBN Prefix(es): 978-84-87619; 978-84-86418

CIS, see Centro de Investigaciones Sociologicas
　(CIS)

Editorial Ciudad Nueva
C/ Jose Picon, 28, 28028 Madrid
Tel: 91 725 95 30; 91 356 96 12 *Fax:* 91 713 04
　52

E-mail: editorial@ciudadnueva.com; revista@
　ciudadnueva.com
Web Site: www.ciudadnueva.com
Founded: 1964
Subjects: Religion - Other
ISBN Prefix(es): 978-950-586; 978-84-86987;
　978-84-85159; 978-84-89651; 978-84-9715
Parent Company: Citta Nuova Editrice, Italy
Subsidiaries: Ciutat Nova (Publicaciones en
　lengua Catalana)
U.S. Office(s): Living City Office, 202 Cardi-
　nal Rd, Hyde Park, NY 12538, United States
　Tel: 845-229-0230 ext 180 *Fax:* 845-229-0496
Foreign Rep(s): Ciudad Nueva de la Sefoma (Ar-
　gentina); Pia Sociedade de Sao Paulo (Brazil);
　USA Madrid Books (USA); Fundacion Editores
　Verbo Divino (Colombia)

Ciudadela Libros SL
Lopez de Hoyos 327, 1-5, 28043 Madrid
Tel: 911 859 800 *Fax:* 911 859 806
E-mail: info@ciudadela.es
Web Site: www.ciudadela.es
Key Personnel
Dir: Antonio Arcones *E-mail:* editor@ciudadela.
　es
Foreign Rights: Carlos Rego *E-mail:* rego@
　ciudadela.es
Founded: 2005
Subjects: Biography, Memoirs, History, Literature,
　Literary Criticism, Essays
ISBN Prefix(es): 978-84-96836; 978-84-934669;
　978-84-935173

Civitas Ediciones SL
Camino de Galar, n° 15, 31190 Cizur Menor,
　Navarra
SAN: 002-3205
Tel: 902 40 40 47 *Fax:* 902 40 00 10
E-mail: atencionclientes@thomsonreuters.com
Web Site: www.tienda.aranzadi.es
Key Personnel
President & Counselor: Eduardo Garcia de Enter-
　ria
Founded: 1970
Subjects: Economics, Law, Public Administration
ISBN Prefix(es): 978-84-470; 978-84-7398
Bookshop(s): General Pardinas, 24, 28001 Madrid

Editorial Claret SA+
Roger de Lluria, 5, 08010 Barcelona
Tel: 93 301 08 87
E-mail: libreria@claret.es
Web Site: www.claret.cat
Key Personnel
Dir General: Jesep Ma Cervera i March
Communication: Marta Rodriguez Torras
Founded: 1926
Subjects: Religion - Other
ISBN Prefix(es): 978-84-7263; 978-84-8297

Publicaciones Claretianas
C/ Juan Alvarez Mendizabal, 65 dpdo 3°, 28008
　Madrid
Tel: 91 540 12 65 *Fax:* 91 540 00 66
E-mail: publicaciones@claret.org; comercial-
　ventas@claret.org; edicionpcl@claret.org
Web Site: www.publicacionesclaretianas.com
Key Personnel
Dir: Fr Fernando Prado Ayuso
Editorial: Ruth Guerrero
Sales: Pilar Veiga *Tel:* 91 540 12 67
Publishing service of the Missioneros Claretianos
　de la Provincia de Santiago, Espana.
Membership(s): Asociacion de Editores Catolicos
　de Espana; Federacion de Gremios de Editores
　de Espana.
Subjects: Inspirational, Spirituality, Religion -
　Other, Theology
ISBN Prefix(es): 978-84-7966; 978-84-85167;
　978-84-86425
Parent Company: Claret Publishing Group

Editorial Clie+
Ferrocarril, 8, 08232 Viladecavalls
SAN: 004-0010
Tel: 93 788 4262 *Fax:* 93 780 0514
E-mail: clie@clie.es
Web Site: clie.es
Key Personnel
Executive Dir: Alfonso Trivino
Founded: 1924
Subjects: Biblical Studies, History, Religion -
Catholic, Religion - Protestant, Theology
ISBN Prefix(es): 978-84-7645; 978-84-7228; 978-
84-8267
Distributed by HarperCollins Christian Publishing
(outside Spain)

Cofas SA, *imprint of* Vindicacion Feminista
Publicaciones

Ediciones Colegio De Espana (ECE)+
C/ Compania, Nº 65, 37002 Salamanca
Tel: 923 214 788 *Fax:* 923 218 791
E-mail: info@colegioespana.com
Web Site: www.colegioespana.com
Founded: 1987
Subjects: Art, Language Arts, Linguistics, Litera-
ture, Literary Criticism, Essays
ISBN Prefix(es): 978-84-86408
Number of titles published annually: 20 Print
Total Titles: 50 Print

COLEX, see Constitucion y Leyes SA Editorial
COLEX

Collins, *imprint of* Penguin Random House
Grupo Editorial

Columna Edicions, *imprint of* grup62

Columna Edicions+
Imprint of grup62
C/ Pedro i Pons, 9-11, 11a planta, portes 1 i 2,
08034 Barcelona
Tel: 93 443 71 00
Web Site: www.grup62.cat/editorial-columna-
edicions-83.html
Key Personnel
Editor: Pema Maymo Veny
Founded: 1985
Subjects: Fiction, Nonfiction (General), Poetry
ISBN Prefix(es): 978-84-7809; 978-84-8300; 978-
84-86433; 978-84-664
Subsidiaries: Aea

Editorial Comares
Poligono Juncaril, Parcela 208, 18220 Albolote
(Granada)
Tel: 958 465 382
E-mail: pedidos@comares.com
Web Site: www.comares.com
Founded: 1983
Subjects: Art, History, Poetry, Humanities
ISBN Prefix(es): 978-84-8151; 978-84-8444; 978-
84-86509; 978-84-87708

Combel Editorial+
Imprint of Editorial Casals SA
Casp, 79, 08013 Barcelona
Tel: 932 449 550 *Fax:* 932 656 895
E-mail: combel@editorialcasals.com; rights@
combeleditorial.com
Web Site: www.combeleditorial.com
Key Personnel
Foreign Rights: Maite Etcheto *E-mail:* maite.
etcheto@editorialcasals.com
Founded: 1989
ISBN Prefix(es): 978-84-7864; 978-84-9825
Number of titles published annually: 50 Print

Total Titles: 800 Print
Foreign Rep(s): Independent Publishers Group-
Chicago (USA)

Combel Editorial SA, *imprint of* Editorial Casals
SA

Comunicacion Social Ediciones y Publicaciones
Plaza de Barcelona, s/n Local 2, 37004 Sala-
manca
Tel: 923 626 722
E-mail: info@comunicacionsocial.es; prensa@
comunicacionsocial.es
Web Site: www.comunicacionsocial.es
Key Personnel
Press: Pepa Pelaez *Tel:* 923 626 722 ext 35
Subjects: Art, Geography, Geology, History, Lit-
erature, Literary Criticism, Essays, Mass Com-
munication
ISBN Prefix(es): 978-84-96082; 978-84-932251

**Comunidad Autonoma de Madrid, Servicio de
Documentacion**
Libreria Institucional de la Comunidad de
Madrid, calle Fortuny, 51, 28010 Madrid
SAN: 001-0820
Tel: 917 027 625 *Fax:* 913 195 055
E-mail: centrodocumentacion.economia@madrid.
org
Web Site: www.madrid.org/next
Founded: 1983
Subjects: Agriculture, Animals, Pets, Archaeol-
ogy, Architecture & Interior Design, Art, Bi-
ological Sciences, Business, Communications,
Cookery, Crafts, Games, Hobbies, Economics,
Education, Film, Video, Gardening, Plants,
History, Law, Management, Medicine, Nurs-
ing, Dentistry, Music, Dance, Natural History,
Poetry, Science (General), Sports, Athletics,
Transportation, Travel & Tourism, Wine &
Spirits
ISBN Prefix(es): 978-84-451

Conecta, *imprint of* Penguin Random House
Grupo Editorial

**Consejo Superior de Investigaciones
Cientificas+**
C/ Vitruvio, 8, 28006 Madrid
SAN: 001-1347
Tel: 915 159 670 *Fax:* 915 614 851
E-mail: publ@csic.es
Web Site: editorial.csic.es; www.csic.es/publica
Key Personnel
Dir: Ramon B Rodriguez
Manager: Maria Soledad Alvarez Gonzalez
Editorial Production: Jose Manuel Prieto Bernabe
Founded: 1939
Subjects: Science (General)
ISBN Prefix(es): 978-84-00
Bookshop(s): Libreria Cientifica Del CSIC,
Duque de Medinaceli, 6, 28014 Madrid
Tel: 913 697 253 *Fax:* 913 697 253
E-mail: libreria@ch.csic.es

Consello da Cultura Galega (CCG)
Pazo de Raxoi, 2º andar, 15705 Santiago de Com-
postela, A Coruna
SAN: 001-141X
Tel: 981 95 72 02 *Fax:* 981 95 72 05
E-mail: correo@consellodacultura.org
Web Site: www.consellodacultura.org
Founded: 1983
Subjects: Anthropology, Architecture & Interior
Design, Art, Biological Sciences, Journalism,
Law, Photography
ISBN Prefix(es): 978-84-87172

Constitucion y Leyes SA Editorial COLEX
Ctra de Pozuelo a Majadahonda nº 52, 28220
Majadahonda, Madrid

Tel: 915 811 502 *Fax:* 911 736 870
E-mail: info@colex.es; colexeditor@interbook.net
Web Site: www.colex.es
Founded: 1981
Subjects: Economics, Government, Political Sci-
ence, Law, Management
ISBN Prefix(es): 978-84-7879; 978-84-86123;
978-84-8342

Ex Corde, *imprint of* Editorial Alhulia SA

Editorial Corimbo SL
Av Pla del Vent, 56, 08970 Sant Joan Despi,
Barcelona
Tel: 93 373 34 84 *Fax:* 93 373 34 84
E-mail: corimbo@corimbo.es
Web Site: www.corimbo.es
Key Personnel
Dir General: Rafael Ros
ISBN Prefix(es): 978-84-95150; 978-84-8470

Corner Editorial, *imprint of* Roca Editorial

Cossetania Edicions
Carrer de la Violeta, 6, 43800 Valls
Tel: 977602591 *Fax:* 977614357
E-mail: cossetania@cossetania.com
Web Site: www.cossetania.com
Key Personnel
Press & Communication: Raquel Estrada
E-mail: restrada@cossetania.com
Foreign Rights: Judit Juncosa *E-mail:* jjuncosa@
cossetania.com
Founded: 1996
Subjects: Cookery, Travel & Tourism
ISBN Prefix(es): 978-84-95684; 978-84-89890;
978-84-921476; 978-84-96035; 978-84-9791
Parent Company: N9u Grup Editorial

Costaisa SA+
Pau Alcover, 33, 08017 Barcelona
Tel: 932 536 100 *Fax:* 932 057 917
E-mail: costaisa@costaisa.com
Web Site: www.costaisa.com
Key Personnel
Dir General: Mauricio Recolons de Arquer
Founded: 1968
Specialize in multimedia, CD-ROM & the Inter-
net.
Subjects: Health, Nutrition, Management, Tech-
nology
Branch Office(s)
Euterpe, 11, 08017 Barcelona
Pau Alcover, 52, 08017 Barcelona
Foreign Rep(s): Aplicacao de Informatica Ltda
(Brazil); APTRA Consultadoria em Sistemas
de Informacao (Portugal); Ayssa (El Salvador);
Disprol (Uruguay); E C SA (Paraguay); No-
vasys (Peru); Red Colombia SA (Colom-
bia); Software AG Brazil (Brazil); Software
AG Chile (Chile); Software AG Costa Rica
(Costa Rica); Software AG Mexico (Mex-
ico); Software AG Panama (Panama); Software
AG Puerto Rico (Puerto Rico); Software AG
Venezuela (Venezuela)

Creotz Ediciones SL
Arquitecto Gomez Roman, 69, 36390 Vigo, Pon-
tevedra
Tel: 986 498 628
E-mail: info@creotz.com
Web Site: www.creotz.com
Subjects: Poetry
ISBN Prefix(es): 978-84-941473
Distribution Center: IPG Spanish Books, c/o
Independent Publishers Group (IPG), 814 N
Franklin St, Chicago, IL 60610, United States

Crisalida, *imprint of* Editorial Alhulia SA

Ediciones Cristiandad+
C/ Jose Ortega y Gasset 40, 7º izq, 28006 Madrid
Tel: 91 781 9970 *Fax:* 91 781 9977
E-mail: info@edicionescristiandad.es
Web Site: www.edicionescristiandad.es
Subjects: Biblical Studies, History, Philosophy,
  Religion - Catholic, Social Sciences, Sociology
ISBN Prefix(es): 978-84-7057

Editorial Critica SA+
Member of Grupo Planeta
Avda Diagonal, 662-664, 08034 Barcelona
Tel: 93 496 70 31
E-mail: editorial@ed-critica.es
Web Site: www.planetadelibros.com/editorial-
  editorial-critica-1.html
Key Personnel
Foreign Rights Manager: Daniel Cladera
  E-mail: dcladera@planeta.es
Press Officer: Laura Gamundi *Tel:* 93 492 89 47
  E-mail: lgamundi@planeta.es
Founded: 1976
Subjects: Fiction, Nonfiction (General), Culture
ISBN Prefix(es): 978-987-9317

Editorial Cruilla SA+
Subsidiary of Ediciones SM
C Balmes 245, 4t, 08006 Barcelona
Tel: 902 12 33 36; 932 922 172 *Fax:* 902 241
  222
E-mail: contacte@cruilla.com
Web Site: www.cruilla.cat; www.llegircruilla.cat
Key Personnel
Dir General: Enric Masllorens
Founded: 1984
Publishes only in the Catalan language.
ISBN Prefix(es): 978-84-7629; 978-84-8286; 978-
  84-661
Total Titles: 1,152 Print

CSIC, see Consejo Superior de Investigaciones
  Cientificas

CTE, see Centro de Tecnologia Educativa

Cuadernos del Vigia
Apdo correos 503, 18080 Granada
Tel: 958 210 444; 615 114 177
E-mail: editorial@cuadernosdelvigia.com
Web Site: www.acceda.com/host/
  cuadernosdelvigia/index.htm
Key Personnel
Dir: Miguel Angel Arcas *E-mail:* miguelangel.
  arcas@cuadernosdelvigia.com
Editorial Coordinator: Jesus Ortega *E-mail:* jesus.
  ortega@cuadernosdelvigia.com
Founded: 1997
Subjects: Fiction, Poetry
ISBN Prefix(es): 978-84-923391; 978-84-95430

Cuento de Luz
Calle Claveles 10, Urb, Monteclaro, Pozuelo de
  Alarcon, 28223 Madrid
Tel: 913 51 01 35
E-mail: info@cuentodeluz.com
Web Site: www.cuentodeluz.com
Founded: 2009
ISBN Prefix(es): 978-84-937814; 978-84-15241;
  978-84-938240; 978-84-15503; 978-84-15619;
  978-84-15784
Foreign Rep(s): Antartica Libros (Chile); Colofon
  SA de CV (Mexico); Ediciones Continente (Ar-
  gentina); Grupo Editorial Monserrate (Colom-
  bia); Publishers Group West (Canada, USA);
  Pujol & Amado (Peru, Puerto Rico)

Editorial Cultural y Espiritual Popular SL, see
  Editorial EDICEP CB

Edicions do Cumio
Pol Ind A Reigosa, Parcela 19, 36827 Ponte
  Caldelas, Pontevedra
Tel: 986 761 045 *Fax:* 986 761 022
E-mail: cumio@cumio.com
Web Site: www.cumio.com
Key Personnel
Dir General: Xose Maria Arguibay Torres
Editorial Dir: Francisco Villegas Belmonte
Founded: 1988
Subjects: Biography, Memoirs, Fiction, Music,
  Dance, Travel & Tourism
ISBN Prefix(es): 978-84-8286; 978-84-8289; 978-
  84-87126

Ediciones La Cupula SL+
Plaza Beates 3, Entlo, 08003 Barcelona
SAN: 001-8066
Tel: 932 682 805 *Fax:* 932 680 765
E-mail: consultas@lacupula.com
Web Site: www.lacupula.com
Key Personnel
Editor: Jose Maria Berenguer
Production: Emilio Bernandez
Founded: 1979
Subjects: Erotica, Humor, Young & Adult Comics
  (Humor & Sex)
ISBN Prefix(es): 978-84-7833; 978-84-85733

Curial Edicions Catalanes SA
Consolat de Mar, 9, 08395 Sant Pol de Mar
SAN: 001-2181
Tel: 93 760 22 87
E-mail: info@curial.cat
Web Site: www.curial.cat
Subjects: Art, Ethnicity, Geography, Geology,
  History, Literature, Literary Criticism, Essays
ISBN Prefix(es): 978-84-7256

DAC Editions
PO Box 57, 08870 Sitges, Barcelona
E-mail: art7@dac-editions.com
Web Site: www.dac-editions.com
Key Personnel
Sales Manager: Daniela Sampietro
Founded: 1998
Subjects: Art, Science Fiction, Fantasy, Dragons,
  Fantasy Art
ISBN Prefix(es): 978-84-931278

Rafael Dalmau Editor
Carrer del Pi, n'um 13 1r 1a, 08002 Barcelona
SAN: 004-7295
Tel: 93 317 33 38 *Fax:* 93 317 33 38
E-mail: rafaeldalmau@rafaeldalmaueditor.cat
Web Site: www.rafaeldalmaueditor.cat
Founded: 1959
Subjects: Anthropology, Biography, Memoirs,
  Ethnicity, Geography, Geology, History
ISBN Prefix(es): 978-84-232
Number of titles published annually: 14 Print
Total Titles: 1,000 Print
Distributor for Garsineu

Ediciones Daly SL+
C/ Cordoba, 11-2ºF, 29640 Fuengirola (Malaga)
SAN: 001-6527
Tel: 952 58 25 69 *Fax:* 952 58 36 19
E-mail: daly@edicionesdaly.es
Web Site: www.edicionesdaly.es
Key Personnel
General Manager: Hugo Quiroga Capovilla
  E-mail: hugoquiroga@edicionesdaly.es
Dir of Sales: David Fernandez Garcia
  E-mail: davidf@edicionesdaly.es
Founded: 1986
Membership(s): Association of Andalusia Publish-
  ers.
Subjects: Architecture & Interior Design, Art,
  Cookery, Crafts, Games, Hobbies, Education,
  Engineering (General), Gardening, Plants, Lan-
guage Arts, Linguistics, Philosophy, Technol-
  ogy, Carpentry, Furniture Manufacturing, Hair-
  dressing, Hotel Management, Leather Industry,
  Wrought Iron
ISBN Prefix(es): 978-84-86584; 978-84-89738;
  978-84-95818
Total Titles: 320 Print; 30 CD-ROM
Distributed by Michael Beerman Books Inc (NT)
Warehouse: Poligono Industrial La Vega, 29650
  Mijas-Costa (Malaga)

Daly Technical Books Publishers Ltda, see
  Ediciones Daly SL

Dastin SL
Poligono Europolis Calle M Nº 9, 28230 Las
  Rozas, Madrid
Tel: 91 637 52 54; 91 637 36 86 *Fax:* 91 636 12
  56
E-mail: info@dastin.es
Web Site: www.dastin.es
Key Personnel
Chief Executive Officer: Raul Gonzalez Gomez
Commercial Dir: Juan Carlos Ponce Ruiz
Editorial Dir: Daniel Dorronsoro Perez
Founded: 1992
Subjects: Art, Biography, Memoirs, Geography,
  Geology, History, Social Sciences, Sociology
ISBN Prefix(es): 978-84-492; 978-84-96249; 978-
  84-96410

Debate, *imprint of* Penguin Random House
  Grupo Editorial

Debolsillo, *imprint of* Penguin Random House
  Grupo Editorial

Editorial Deimos SL
Glorieta del Puente de Segovia, Nº 3, 28011
  Madrid
Tel: 914 792 342; 669 316 406
E-mail: editorial@academiadeimos.es
Web Site: www.academiadeimos.es
Subjects: History, Mathematics, Religion -
  Catholic
ISBN Prefix(es): 978-84-86379
Number of titles published annually: 6 Print
Total Titles: 46 Print

Editorial Demipage
C/Pez, 12, 28004 Madrid
Tel: 91 563 88 67 *Fax:* 91 563 00 38
E-mail: madrid@demipage.com
Web Site: www.demipage.com
Key Personnel
Editor: David Villanueva
Founded: 2003
Subjects: Fiction, Poetry
ISBN Prefix(es): 978-84-92719; 978-84-933801

Editorial de Derecho Financiero, *imprint of*
  Editoriales de Derecho Reunidas SA
  (EDERSA)

**Editoriales de Derecho Reunidas SA
  (EDERSA)**
Leganitos, 15, 28013 Madrid
SAN: 001-4451
Tel: 915 210 246
Founded: 1913
Subjects: Biography, Memoirs, History, Law, Phi-
  losophy, Social Sciences, Sociology
ISBN Prefix(es): 978-84-7130; 978-84-8494
Imprints: Editorial de Derecho Financiero; Edi-
  ciones Pegaso; Editorial Revista de Derecho
  Privado

Editorial Desclee De Brouwer SA+
Henao, 6 3º, 48009 Bilbao
SAN: 002-4090
Tel: 944 246 843 *Fax:* 944 237 594

E-mail: info@edesclee.com; edicion@desclee.
com
Web Site: www.edesclee.com
Key Personnel
President & Commercial Dir: Javier Gogeas-
coechea
Editorial Dir: Manuel Guerrero
Financial Dir: Fernando Isasi
Founded: 1945
Subjects: Biblical Studies, Education, Man-
agement, Psychology, Psychiatry, Religion -
Protestant, Religion - Other, Self-Help, Busi-
ness Management, Humanities
ISBN Prefix(es): 978-84-330
Warehouse: Poligono Ugaldeguren II -
Nave 16, 48170 Zamudio *Tel:* 944522790
Fax: 944522798

Ediciones Desnivel SL
Calle San Victorino, 8, 28025 Madrid
SAN: 001-2858
Tel: 913 602 242 *Fax:* 913 602 264
E-mail: edicionesdesnivel@desnivel.es; editorial@
desnivel.com
Web Site: www.edicionesdesnivel.com; www.
desnivel.com
Key Personnel
Dir: Dario Rodriguez *E-mail:* dario@desnivel.
com
Editorial Dir: Maria Carmen Samper
Dir, Publicity: Ana Vinuesa *E-mail:* ana.vinuesa@
desnivel.com
Coordinator: Ana Fernandez Soto *E-mail:* ana.
soto@desnivel.com
Founded: 1991
Subjects: Sports, Athletics, Travel & Tourism
ISBN Prefix(es): 978-84-87746; 978-84-89969;
978-84-95760
Bookshop(s): Libreria Desnivel, Pza Matute
6, 28012 Madrid *Tel:* 902 24 8848 *Web
Site:* www.libreriadesnivel.com

Ediciones Destino SA, *imprint of* grup62

Ediciones Destino SA+
Imprint of grup62
Avda Diagonal 662-664, 7a, 08034 Barcelona
Tel: 93 492 80 04
E-mail: edicionesedestino@edestino.es;
comunicaciondestino@edestino.es
Web Site: www.planetadelibros.com/editorial-
ediciones-destino-7.html; www.planeta.es
Key Personnel
Press: Fite Alba Navarro *Tel:* 93 492 80 27
E-mail: afite@edestino.es
Founded: 1942
Subjects: Architecture & Interior Design, Art,
Fiction, History, Literature, Literary Criticism,
Essays, Nonfiction (General)
ISBN Prefix(es): 978-84-233; 978-84-9710
Ultimate Parent Company: Grupo Planeta

Destino Infantil & Juvenil, *imprint of* grup62

Deusto
Member of Grupo Planeta
Centro de Libros PAPF, Av Diagonal, 662-664,
08034 Barcelona
Tel: 93 492 69 56
E-mail: info@centrolibrospapf.es
Web Site: www.planetadelibros.com/editorial-
deusto-14.html
Founded: 1960
Subjects: Accounting, Finance, Law, Management
ISBN Prefix(es): 978-84-234

Diabolo Ediciones
Apdo 40171, 28007 Madrid
E-mail: diaboloediciones@diaboloediciones.com;
diaboloediciones@gmail.com
Web Site: www.diaboloediciones.com

Key Personnel
Editor: Lorenzo Pascual
Founded: 2006
Comic book publisher.
ISBN Prefix(es): 978-84-15153; 978-84-15839;
978-84-16217; 978-84-934949; 978-84-936151;
978-84-936764; 978-84-937422; 978-84-
937933; 978-84-942625
Distribution Center: IPG Spanish Books, 814 N
Franklin St, Chicago, IL 60610, United States

Diada Editora SL
C/ Londres, 24, 41012 Seville
Tel: 954129216
E-mail: editorial@diadaeditora.com
Web Site: diadaeditora.com
Key Personnel
General Dir: Paloma Espejo Roig
E-mail: paloma@diadaeditora.com
Founded: 1989
ISBN Prefix(es): 978-84-87118
Warehouse: Pgno Ind Los Alamos, C/ Abedul
Nave 14, Fuente del Rey Dos Hermanas, 41700
Seville

Ediciones Diaz de Santos SA+
C/ Albasanz 2, 28037 Madrid
SAN: 001-6519
Tel: 917 434 890
E-mail: ediciones@editdiazdesantos.com
Web Site: www.editdiazdesantos.com
Key Personnel
Publishing Dir: Joaquin Vioque Lozano
E-mail: jvioque@editdiazdesantos.com
Commercial Dir: Alejandro Zuniga Lopez
E-mail: azl@editdiazdesantos.com
Production Dir: Jose Manuel Diaz Gomez
E-mail: jmdiaz@editdiazdesantos.com
Founded: 1986
Subjects: Business, Computer Science, Eco-
nomics, Management, Medicine, Nursing, Den-
tistry, Science (General)
ISBN Prefix(es): 978-84-87189; 978-84-86251;
978-84-7978
Distributed by Grupo Editorial Iberoamerica
(Mexico)
Foreign Rep(s): Cuspide Libros SA (Argentina);
EOS Libros (Chile); Ediciones Granica SA
(Uruguay); Ediciones Diaz de Santos Argentina
SA (Argentina); Diaz de Santos de Colom-
bia (Colombia); Diaz de Santos de Mexico SA
(Mexico)
Bookshop(s): Diaz de Santos SA - Libreria
Cientifico-Tecnica, Lagasca, 95, 28006 Madrid

Didaco SA+
C/Regas, 3 bajos, 08006 Barcelona
Tel: 93 237 64 00 *Fax:* 93 218 92 77
Founded: 1986
Producers of multimedia English courses.
Subjects: Biological Sciences, English as a Sec-
ond Language, Health, Nutrition, Language
Arts, Linguistics, Nonfiction (General)
ISBN Prefix(es): 978-84-86983; 978-84-89712
Total Titles: 9 CD-ROM

Difusion
Trafalgar, 10-Entresuelo 1a, 08010 Barcelona
Tel: 932 680 300 *Fax:* 933 103 340
E-mail: info@difusion.com
Web Site: www.difusion.com
ISBN Prefix(es): 978-84-8443; 978-84-87099;
978-84-89344

Dinsic Publicacions Musicals SL
Santa Anna 10, E 3a, 08002 Barcelona
Tel: 93 318 06 05 *Fax:* 93 412 05 01
E-mail: dinsic@dinsic.com
Web Site: www.dinsic.com; www.dinsic.es; www.
dinsic.cat

Key Personnel
General Dir & Dir, Pedagogy: Francesca Galofre
Technical Dir: Daniel Maso
Public Relations: Silvia Bonet
Founded: 1988
Subjects: Education, Music, Dance
ISBN Prefix(es): 978-84-86949; 978-84-95055

Diputacion de Cordoba
Plaza colon 15, 14001 Cordoba
SAN: 001-3307
Tel: 957 211 100; 957 212 848; 957 211 101
Fax: 957 211 290
E-mail: infodipu@dipucordoba.es
Web Site: www.dipucordoba.es
Founded: 1967
Subjects: Architecture & Interior Design, Envi-
ronmental Studies, Social Sciences, Sociology,
Engineering & Urban Planning, Purification &
Environmental Control, Social Welfare
ISBN Prefix(es): 978-84-8154; 978-84-87034

Ediciones Diputacion de Salamanca
Division of Diputacion de Salamanca
Unidad de Ediciones, Dept de Cultura, C/ Felipe
Espino, nº 1, 37002 Salamanca
SAN: 001-348X
Tel: 923 29 3100 *Fax:* 923 293 256
E-mail: informacion@lasalina.es
Web Site: www.dipsanet.es
Key Personnel
President: Anibal Lozano Jimenez
Founded: 1982
Subjects: Geography, Geology, History, Regional
Interests
ISBN Prefix(es): 978-84-7797
Distributed by Distribuciones Breogan

**Diputacion Provincial de Sevilla, Servicio de
Publicaciones**
Av Menendez y Pelayo, 32, 41071 Seville
SAN: 001-3501
Tel: 954 55 00 00; 954 55 24 64
E-mail: oficinaatencionciudadana@dipusevilla.es
Web Site: www.dipusevilla.es
Key Personnel
President: Fernando Rodriguez Villalobos
Tel: 954 55 24 03 *Fax:* 954 55 00 44
Founded: 1967
Subjects: History, Literature, Literary Criticism,
Essays, Social Sciences, Sociology
ISBN Prefix(es): 978-84-7798

Editorial Dirigido Por SL
Casanova 136-138, Esc A 1º 6a, 08036 Barcelona
Tel: 93 323 87 04
E-mail: redaccion@dirigidopor.com
Web Site: www.dirigidopor.com
Key Personnel
Dir General: Joan Padrol
Editorial: Tomas Fernandez Valenti
Founded: 1972
Subjects: Art, Outdoor Recreation, Cinematogra-
phy
ISBN Prefix(es): 978-84-87270

Disfruto y Hago, *imprint of* Editorial Paidotribo

Ediciones Doce Calles SL+
Affiliate of Gremio de Editores de Madrid
Calle de la Ribera 36, 28300 Aranjuez, Madrid
SAN: 001-6659
Tel: 91 892 22 34
E-mail: docecalles@docecalles.com
Web Site: www.docecalles.com
Key Personnel
Manager & Chief Editor: Pedro Miguel Sanchez
Moreno
Founded: 1988
Specializes in works of investigation & reference
on America, natural history, mechanical history,

art, sanitation, bibliophilism, facsimile editions, landscapes & historical gardening, among other subjects. Its intention is to spread the historical memory of Spain's scientific patrimony whilst contributing with new analyses & approaches: social, ethnographic, technological & ethical.

This publisher has indicated that 25% of their product line is author subsidized.

Subjects: African American Studies, Anthropology, Architecture & Interior Design, Art, Biography, Memoirs, Civil Engineering, Gardening, Plants, Geography, Geology, Health, Nutrition, History, Mechanical Engineering, Medicine, Nursing, Dentistry, Natural History, Poetry, Science (General), Social Sciences, Sociology, Technology, Travel & Tourism, Art History, Bibliophile, Historical Gardening, Landscaping History, Natural History

ISBN Prefix(es): 978-84-87111; 978-84-89796; 978-84-9744

Number of titles published annually: 6 Print

Total Titles: 142 Print

Foreign Rep(s): L'Alebrije (Europe); Antiquus Editores (Colombia); Libreria Bonilla Y Asociados SA de CV (Mexico); Booksellers - Libreros Reunidos (France, USA); Celesa (Europe); Iberoamericana Vervuert (Germany); Latin American Book Source Inc (USA); Ediciones Puerto (Puerto Rico); Puvill Libros SA (Europe)

Editorial Donostiarra SA+
Pokopandegi, 4, 20009 San Sebastian, Guipuzcoa
SAN: 002-3825
Tel: 943 215 737; 943 213 011 *Fax:* 943 219 521
E-mail: info@editorialdonostiarra.com
Web Site: editorialdonostiarra.com
Founded: 1965
Subjects: Accounting, Computer Science, Economics, Engineering (General), Film, Video, Finance, Health, Nutrition, Technology
ISBN Prefix(es): 978-84-7063
Distributor for EGA-Donostiarra-Profesores-Editores, SA; Larrauri Editorial SA
Book Club(s): Anele

Dorleta SA+
C/ San Isidro 13, 48007 Bilbao
SAN: 001-4133
Tel: 944456597 *Fax:* 944274512
Founded: 1985
Subjects: Sports, Athletics
ISBN Prefix(es): 978-84-87812

Editorial Dossat SA
Calle de Velazquez 39, 28001 Madrid
SAN: 002-3833
Tel: 914 317 479
Subjects: Architecture & Interior Design, Automotive, Civil Engineering, Disability, Special Needs, Electronics, Electrical Engineering, Engineering (General), Journalism, Medicine, Nursing, Dentistry, Science (General)
ISBN Prefix(es): 978-84-237
Bookshop(s): Libreria Ingenieria y Arte
E-mail: info@ingenieriayarte.com *Web Site:* www.ingenieriayarte.com

Doyma, see Elsevier Doyma SL

Duomo Ediciones
Av del Principe de Asturias, 20 3º B, 08012 Barcelona
Tel: 93 181 01 53
E-mail: info@duomoediciones.com
Web Site: www.duomoediciones.com
Founded: 2009
ISBN Prefix(es): 978-84-15355; 978-84-16261; 978-84-92723
Parent Company: Gruppo Editoriale Mauri Spagnol

Foreign Rep(s): Ediciones Oceano de Mexico SA de CV (Mexico); Editorial Oceano Argentina SA (Argentina); Editorial Oceano de Chile SA (Chile); Editorial Oceano de Colombia SA (Colombia); Editorial Oceano de Costa Rica SA (Costa Rica); Editorial Oceano de Panama SA (Panama); Editorial Oceano de Venezuela SA (Venezuela); Editorial Oceano del Paraguay SA (Paraguay); Editorial Oceano del Uruguay SA (Uruguay); Editorial Oceano Ecuatoriana SA (Ecuador); Editorial Oceano Peruana SA (Peru)

Durvan SA de Ediciones+
Subsidiary of SA de Promocion y Ediciones
Avda de Manoteras 50, 28050 Madrid
SAN: 001-4214
Tel: 913 842 022 (sales)
E-mail: editorial@durvan.com
Web Site: www.durvan.com
Key Personnel
Editorial Dir: Javier Pereda Prado
Founded: 1960
Subjects: Geography, Geology, History, Language Arts, Linguistics
ISBN Prefix(es): 978-84-85001; 978-84-7677
Number of titles published annually: 2 Print; 1 CD-ROM; 1 Online
Total Titles: 42 Print; 3 CD-ROM; 1 Online
Associate Companies: Durclub SA de Ediciones
Distributor for Club Internacional del Libro; SA de Promocion y Ediciones

Dykinson SL+
C/ Melendez Valdes, 61, 28015 Madrid
Tel: 91 544 28 46; 91 544 28 69 *Fax:* 91 544 60 40
E-mail: info@dykinson.com
Web Site: www.dykinson.com
Key Personnel
Dir: Rafael Tigeras Sanchez
Administrator: Gabriel Tigeras Sanchez
Founded: 1973
Subjects: Economics, Education, Law, Psychology, Psychiatry
ISBN Prefix(es): 978-84-88030; 978-84-8155; 978-84-86133; 978-84-88038; 978-84-9772; 978-84-9849; 978-84-9790
Total Titles: 850 Print

EADOP, see Generalitat de Catalunya, Entitat Autonoma del Diari Oficial i de Publicacions

ECE, see Ediciones Colegio De Espana (ECE)

Editorial ECIR SA
Sequia de Calvera, 41, 46910 Sedavi, Valencia
Tel: 963 186 007 *Fax:* 963 186 432
E-mail: info@tabarcallibres.com
Web Site: www.tabarcallibres.com/va
Key Personnel
Dir: Maria Teresa Olmos Lopez
Manager: Rafael Dominguez Perez
Founded: 1942
Subjects: Art, Biological Sciences, Child Care & Development, Earth Sciences, Economics, Education, Geography, Geology, History, Literature, Literary Criticism, Essays, Mathematics, Science (General)
ISBN Prefix(es): 978-84-9826; 978-84-89886; 978-84-96321; 978-84-7065
Number of titles published annually: 100 Print; 10 CD-ROM; 3 E-Book
Total Titles: 1,000 Print; 30 CD-ROM; 3 E-Book

Editorial EDAF SA+
Jorge Juan 68, 1a planta, 28009 Madrid
SAN: 002-3884
Tel: 91 435 82 60 *Fax:* 91 431 52 81
E-mail: edaf@edaf.net
Web Site: www.edaf.net

Key Personnel
President: Luciano Fossati
Dir: Jose Antonio Fossati
Publicity: Gerardo Fossati
Editorial/Rights Dept: Deanna Lyles
Founded: 1959
Subjects: Astrology, Occult, Biography, Memoirs, Health, Nutrition, History, Literature, Literary Criticism, Essays, Self-Help
ISBN Prefix(es): 978-84-414; 978-84-7166; 978-84-7640; 978-84-96107
Number of titles published annually: 150 Print
Total Titles: 3,000 Print
Branch Office(s)
Edaf del Plata SA, Chile, 2222, C1227AAJ Buenos Aires, Argentina *Tel:* (011) 43 08 52 22 *E-mail:* edafdelplata@edaf.net
EDAF Chile SA, Coyancura 2270, Oficina 914, Santiago, Chile *Tel:* (02) 335 75 11; (02) 334 84 17 *E-mail:* edafchile@edaf.net
EDAF Mexico, Algaba Ediciones, SA de CV, 21 Poniente 33-23, 72180 Puebla, Mexico *Tel:* (0155) 580 23 71 *E-mail:* edafmexicoclaien@yahoo.com.mx
EDAF Antillas Inc, Av JT Pinero, 1594, Caparra Terrace, San Juan 00921-1413, Puerto Rico *Tel:* (787) 707-1792 *Fax:* (787) 707-1797 *E-mail:* edafantillas@edaf.net
Warehouse: Poligno Azque, Ctra de Daganzo KM, 3400 Naves 2Y3-Alcala de Henares, Madrid, Contact: Horacio Mallo *Tel:* 918 809 514 *Fax:* 918 893 851

Grupo Edebe+
Paseo San Juan Bosco 62, 08017 Barcelona
SAN: 001-4435
Tel: 932 037 408 *Fax:* 932 054 670
E-mail: rights@edebe.net; editorial@edebe.net; audiovisual@edebe.net; edebedigital@edebe.net
Web Site: www.edebe.com
Key Personnel
General Manager: Antonio Garrido Gonzalez
Literature Publication Dir: Reina Duarte
Educational Product Manager: Esteban Lorenzo
Rights Manager: Georgia Picanyol-Bullo *Tel:* 695 352 656 *Fax:* 932 041 577 *E-mail:* gpicanyol@edebe.net
Founded: 1888
Children & young adult literature, school textbooks, educational platforms, audiovisual producer, licensing.
Membership(s): Federacion de Gremios de Editores de Espana (FGEE).
Subjects: Education, Fiction, Religion - Catholic, Science Fiction, Fantasy
ISBN Prefix(es): 978-84-236 (Edebe); 978-84-96352 (Rodeira); 978-84-8118 (Giltza); 978-84-8117 (Guadiel); 978-84-8115 (Marjal)
Number of titles published annually: 850 Print
Total Titles: 2,000 Print
Associate Companies: Edebe SA, Don Bosco 4069, C1206ABM Buenos Aires, Argentina *Tel:* (011) 4883-0111 *Fax:* (011) 4883-0115 *E-mail:* info@edebe.com.ar *Web Site:* edebe.com.ar; Don Bosco Editora, Av Libertador Bernardo O'Higgins 2373, 8350708 Santiago de Chile, Chile *Tel:* (02) 24378050 *Fax:* (02) 24378059 *E-mail:* contacto@edebe.cl *Web Site:* www.edebe.cl; Edebe Ediciones Internacionales SA de CV, Ignacio Mariscal, No 8, Col Tabacalera, 06030 Mexico, DF, Mexico *Tel:* (0155) 5535-7557 *Web Site:* www.edebe.com.mx
Subsidiaries: Giltza; Guadiel; Marjal; Rodeira

Edelsa Grupo Didascalia SA
Pl Ciudad de Salta 3, 28043 Madrid
SAN: 001-4443
Tel: 91 416 55 11 *Fax:* 91 416 54 11
E-mail: edelsa@edelsa.es
Web Site: www.edelsa.es
Key Personnel
Dir General: Federica Angel Toro Garcia

Marketing: Laurent Bereau *E-mail:* lbereau@
edelsa.es
Founded: 1986
Spanish publisher exclusively specialized in methods & materials of Spanish as a foreign language.
Subjects: Education, Language Arts, Linguistics
ISBN Prefix(es): 978-84-85786; 978-84-7711;
978-84-389
Parent Company: Hachette-Livre, del Grupo de
Comunicaciones Lagardere

Edelvives, see Editorial Luis Vives (Edelvives)

EDERSA, see Editoriales de Derecho Reunidas
SA (EDERSA)

Edex, Centro de Recursos Comunitarios
Indautxu, 9, 48011 Bilbao
Tel: 94 442 57 84 *Fax:* 94 441 75 12
E-mail: edex@edex.es
Web Site: www.edex.es
Key Personnel
Editor: Itxaso Gonzalez
Founded: 1973
Subjects: Child Care & Development, Education
ISBN Prefix(es): 978-84-88300; 978-84-9726;
978-84-95189; 978-84-89504
Number of titles published annually: 67 Print; 3
CD-ROM; 1 Audio
Total Titles: 121 Print; 5 CD-ROM; 3 Audio

**EDHASA (Editora y Distribuidora
Hispanoamericana SA)+**
C/ Disputacion, 262, 2a 1a, 08007 Barcelona
Tel: 934 949 720 *Fax:* 934 194 584
E-mail: info@edhasa.es; comercial@edhasa.es
Web Site: www.edhasa.es
Founded: 1946
Subjects: Fiction, History, Literature, Literary
Criticism, Essays
ISBN Prefix(es): 978-84-350
Number of titles published annually: 60 Print
Total Titles: 600 Print
Foreign Rep(s): Colofon SA (Mexico); Cuspide
Libros SA (Argentina); Herder Editorial y Libreria (Colombia)
Distribution Center: IPG Spanish Books, 814 N
Franklin St, Chicago, IL 60610, United States

Edibesa
Madre de Dios, 35 bis, 28016 Madrid
Tel: 91 345 19 92 *Fax:* 91 350 50 99
E-mail: info@edibesa.com
Web Site: www.edibesa.com
Key Personnel
Dir General: Jose Antonio Martinez Puche
Subjects: Literature, Literary Criticism, Essays,
Religion - Other
ISBN Prefix(es): 978-84-8407; 978-84-85803;
978-84-89761
Foreign Rep(s): Baker & Taylor Publisher Services (USA)

Editorial EDICEP CB+
C/ Almirante Cadarso, 11, 46005 Valencia
SAN: 001-0480
Tel: 963 952 045; 963 957 293 *Fax:* 963 952 297
E-mail: edicep@edicep.com
Web Site: www.edicep.com
Key Personnel
Owner: Mora Pilar Taroncher
Founded: 1964
Subjects: Biblical Studies, History, Law, Philosophy, Religion - Catholic
ISBN Prefix(es): 978-84-7050; 978-84-9925

Edigol Ediciones SA+
Calle Sant Gabriel, 50, 08950 Esplugues de Llobregat, Barcelona
SAN: 002-144X

Tel: 93 372 6304
E-mail: info@edigol.com; informacion@edigol.
com; administracion@edigol.com
Web Site: www.edigol.com
Key Personnel
Mng Dir: Jorge Onrubia
Founded: 1976 (as Edigol Ediciones Cartograficas)
School cartography & educational wall charts: human anatomy, biology, natural sciences, early
reading-writing.
Subjects: Astronomy, Biological Sciences, Chemistry, Chemical Engineering, Earth Sciences,
Geography, Geology, Physical Sciences, Science (General), Social Sciences, Sociology,
Educational Cartography
ISBN Prefix(es): 978-84-85406

EDIKAMED SL+
C/ Josep Tarradellas, 52, 08029 Barcelona
SAN: 002-1490
Tel: 93 454 96 00 *Fax:* 93 323 48 03
E-mail: info@edikamed.com
Web Site: www.edikamed.com
Key Personnel
Manager: Dolores Gandia
Founded: 1988
Specialize in medical literature.
Membership(s): Grenio Publications.
Subjects: Health, Nutrition, Medicine, Nursing,
Dentistry, Psychology, Psychiatry, Emergency
Medicine, Gastroenterology, Pharmaceutics,
Physical Therapy, Trauma
ISBN Prefix(es): 978-84-7877
Foreign Rep(s): Editorial Atlante Argentina SRL
(Argentina); Distribuidora Intersistemas SA
de CV (Mexico); Logista SA (Spain); Libros
Medicos (Javier Cuadrado) (Uruguay)

Ediciones Edilux SL+
C/ Los Juncos 7, Bajo, 18006 Granada
SAN: 003-8245
Tel: 958 082000 *Fax:* 958 082000
E-mail: edilux@edilux.es
Web Site: www.andaluciabooks.com
Founded: 1983
Specializes in guidebooks about Andalusia.
Subjects: Art, Photography, Travel & Tourism
ISBN Prefix(es): 978-84-87282; 978-84-95856

Edimat Libros SA+
Primavera 35, Poligono Industrial el Malvar,
28500 Arganda del Rey, Madrid
SAN: 004-0908
Tel: 918 719 088 *Fax:* 918 719 071
E-mail: edimat@edimat.es
Key Personnel
Dir of International Affairs: Katherine Wright
E-mail: cathy.wright@edimat.es
Founded: 1992
Specialize in children's & general interest books.
Subjects: Art, Biography, Memoirs, Cookery,
Crafts, Games, Hobbies, Fiction, Health, Nutrition, Literature, Literary Criticism, Essays,
Mysteries, Suspense, Nonfiction (General),
Wine & Spirits
ISBN Prefix(es): 978-84-495
Number of titles published annually: 70 Print
Total Titles: 500 Print; 25 Audio
Imprints: Estudio Didactico

EDIMSA - Editores Medicos SA+
Alsasua, 16, 28023 Madrid
SAN: 002-1601
Tel: 913 768 140 *Fax:* 913 739 907
Subjects: Medicine, Nursing, Dentistry
ISBN Prefix(es): 978-84-87054; 978-84-95076;
978-84-7714
Branch Office(s)
Rafael de Casanovas, 1, 08950 Barcelona

Editorial Edinumen
C/ Jose Celestino Mutis, 4, 28028 Madrid
Tel: 913 085 142 *Fax:* 913 199 309
E-mail: edinumen@edinumen.es
Web Site: www.edinumen.es
Subjects: Education, English as a Second Language, Literature, Literary Criticism, Essays,
Culture
ISBN Prefix(es): 978-84-95986; 978-84-89756;
978-84-9848
Foreign Rep(s): Abiva Publishing House (Philippines); Algoritam Ltd (Croatia); Allecto Ltd
(Estonia); Attica (France); AVA (Switzerland); Beijing Publications Import & Export
Corp (China); Bierman & Bierman ApS (Denmark); Books & Books Ltda (Colombia); Britannia ELT (Russia); Cambridge University
Press (Canada, USA); Carpe Librum (Sweden); Carturesti (Romania); Caves Books Ltd
(Taiwan); CELESA (worldwide); Cervantes Libreria (Morocco); Ciudad Real Sarl (Morocco);
Colibri Ltd (Bulgaria); Data status (Serbia);
Librairie Decitre (France); Educational Centre (Bulgaria); English Center (Denmark); The
European Bookshop (UK); Express Publishing (Greece); Filigranes (Belgium); Librairie
Michel Fortin Inc (Canada); Griffin (Lebanon);
Libreria Hernandez (Austria); Highlands Books
SA de CV (Mexico); Ibercultura (Switzerland);
ILC Czechoslovakia sro (Czechia); INKAS
(Turkey); International Books (Ireland); Interspain Ltd (Japan); Intertaal Boekhandel (Holland); Intertaal BV (Belgium); Intext Book
Co (Australia); Kyobo Book Centre Co Ltd
(Korea); LaroMedia Bokhandel Orebro AB
(Sweden); Letraviva (Brazil); Lia Editora Ltda
(Brazil); Libra Books (Hungary); LibRomania
(Switzerland); Las Lilas (Singapore); Lingva
Store IP Savastyuk EI (Belarus); MHM Ltd
(Japan); Mladinska knijiga Trgovina ddo Center
Oxford (Slovenia); Librairie Mollat (France);
Nowela Sp z oo (Poland); Osiris Bookshop
(Egypt); Oxico jazykove knihy (Slovakia);
Pearson Education do Brasil Ltda (Brazil);
Petersen Buchimport GmbH (Austria, Germany); Thu Trang Piefke (Vietnam); Piefke
Trading (Indonesia, Malaysia, Myanmar, Singapore, Thailand); Pioli Uhak Center (Korea); Practicum Educatief (Holland); Prosvetno
Delo AD (Macedonia); Protea Boekhuis (South
Africa); Pt Chev Bookshop & Resource Room
(New Zealand); RCS Libri Education (Italy);
Alberto Renteria (Israel); El Rincon del Libro
(Holland); Sprakbokhandeln (Sweden); Stirling en Espanol (UK); Stockmann Akateeminen
Kirjakauppa (Finland); Sunny Publishing Co
(Taiwan); TSP (Ukraine); Boekhandel Walry
(Belgium)
Distribution Center: Cambridge University
Press, C/ Jose Abascal, 56, 1° Planta, 28003
Madrid *Tel:* 913604565 *Fax:* 913604570
E-mail: iberia@cambridge.org

Editorial Editex SA+
Via dos Castillas, 33, Complejo Empresarial Atica
7, Edificio 3-Planta 3a, of B, 28224 Pozuelo de
Alarcon, Madrid
SAN: 002-3914
Tel: 91 799 20 40; 91 799 20 60 (orders) *Fax:* 91
715 04 44 (orders)
E-mail: comercial@editex.es; correo@editex.es
Web Site: www.editex.es
Key Personnel
Dir General: Severino Basarrate Elorrieta
Founded: 1946
Subjects: Child Care & Development, Health, Nutrition, Management
ISBN Prefix(es): 978-84-7131

Editora y Distribuidora Hispanoamericana SA,
see EDHASA (Editora y Distribuidora
Hispanoamericana SA)

Editores Educatori+
C/ Guevara Pozo 2 bajo, 18001 Granada
Tel: 958 290 577
E-mail: educatori@educatori.es
Web Site: www.educatori.es
Founded: 1990
Subjects: History, Language Arts, Linguistics, Law, Literature, Literary Criticism, Essays, Regional Interests
ISBN Prefix(es): 978-84-92483; 978-84-92782

Educaula62, *imprint of* grup62

Egales Editorial+
C/ Cervantes, 2, 08002 Barcelona
Tel: 934 12 52 61
E-mail: info@editorialegales.com
Web Site: www.editorialegales.com
Founded: 1995
Subjects: LGBTQ
ISBN Prefix(es): 978-84-95346; 978-84-88052; 978-84-920857
Number of titles published annually: 24 Print
Total Titles: 125 Print
Branch Office(s)
C/ Hortaleza, 64, 28004 Madrid *Tel:* 915 22 55 99 *Fax:* 915 23 12 79
Foreign Rep(s): ASP Wholesale (USA); Baker & Taylor (USA); Bella Books Inc (USA); Grupal Logistica y Distribucion SA (Argentina); El Placard (Colombia); Voces en Tinta (Mexico)

Edicions de l'Eixample SL+
Llull, 27-39, 3r 8a, 08005 Barcelona
SAN: 002-0737
Tel: 93 4584600
E-mail: eixample@ed-eixample.com
Web Site: www.ed-eixample.com
Key Personnel
Founder: Salvador Saura; Ramon Torrente
Founded: 1983
Subjects: Art, Fiction, Culture
ISBN Prefix(es): 978-84-86279

Ediciones El Viso
C/ Castello 128-1°, 28006 Madrid
SAN: 001-690X
Tel: 91 519 65 76
E-mail: elviso@edicioneselviso.com
Web Site: www.edicioneselviso.com
Key Personnel
Contact: Casilda Ybarra *E-mail:* c.ybarra@edicioneselviso.com
Founded: 1981
Subjects: Art, Photography
ISBN Prefix(es): 978-84-86022; 978-84-95241; 978-84-940325
Branch Office(s)
C/ Durango, 149, Col Roma Norte, 06700 Mexico, DF, Mexico, Contact: Carmen Robles *Tel:* (0155) 65 47 22 16 *E-mail:* c.robles@edicioneselviso.com
Distributed by Les Punxes SL; Visor Distibuciones SL

Electa, *imprint of* Penguin Random House Grupo Editorial

Ediciones Elfos SL+
c/ Alberes, 34, 08017 Barcelona
Tel: 934 069 479 *Fax:* 934 069 006
Key Personnel
Mng Dir: Rita Schnitzer
Founded: 1980
Subjects: Cookery, Health, Nutrition, Humor, Decorative Art
ISBN Prefix(es): 978-84-85791; 978-84-87251; 978-84-88990; 978-84-8423

Number of titles published annually: 18 Print
Orders to: Naturart, SA, Avda Mare de Deu de Lorda, 20, 08034 Barcelona *Tel:* 932 054 000 *Fax:* 932 051 441

Editorial Elkar+
Portuetxe, 88 bis, 20018 Donostia, Gipuzkoa
Tel: 943 310 267
E-mail: elkarargitaletxea@elkar.eus
Web Site: www.elkarlanean.eus
Founded: 1975
Specialize in student languages.
Subjects: Education, Literature, Literary Criticism, Essays
ISBN Prefix(es): 978-84-7529; 978-84-7917; 978-84-85485; 978-2-903421; 978-2-913156
Warehouse: Zabaltzen, Igarabidea, 88 bis, Donostia *Tel:* 943 212 144; 943 212 033 *Fax:* 943 212 192

Ellago Ediciones SL
Pol Ind A Reigosa, Parcela 19, 36827 Ponte Caldelas, Pontevedra
Tel: 986 761 045 *Fax:* 986 761 022
E-mail: ellagoediciones@ellagoediciones.com
Web Site: www.ellagoediciones.com
Founded: 2001
Subjects: Art, Biography, Memoirs, Fiction, Geography, Geology, History, Religion - Other, Social Sciences, Sociology
ISBN Prefix(es): 978-84-95881

ELR Ediciones
Travesia de Andres Mellado 9, 28015 Madrid
SAN: 001-8317
Tel: 91 543 46 46
E-mail: produccion@elr.es
Web Site: www.elr.es
Founded: 1971
Subjects: Art, History, Photography, Poetry, Science Fiction, Fantasy
ISBN Prefix(es): 978-84-87607

Elsevier Doyma SL+
Travesera de Gracia, 17-21, 08021 Barcelona
SAN: 001-6675
Tel: 932 418 800 *Fax:* 932 419 020
Web Site: www.elsevier.es
Founded: 1971
Subjects: Medicine, Nursing, Dentistry
ISBN Prefix(es): 978-84-85285; 978-84-7592; 978-84-8086; 978-84-8174
Parent Company: Elsevier BV
Branch Office(s)
Jose Abascal, 45, 3rd floor, 28003 Madrid *Tel:* 914 021 212 *Fax:* 914 251 131

Emece Editores+
Member of Grupo Planeta
Av Diagonal, 662-664, 08034 Barcelona
Tel: 934928000
E-mail: info@planeta.es
Web Site: www.planeta.es; www.planetadelibros.com/editorial-emece-editores-12.html
Founded: 1939
Subjects: Art, Biography, Memoirs, Fiction, History, Literature, Literary Criticism, Essays, Mysteries, Suspense, Nonfiction (General)
ISBN Prefix(es): 978-84-95908
Number of titles published annually: 120 Print

Empresa Activa, *imprint of* Ediciones Urano SA

Editorial Empuries, *imprint of* grup62

Editorial Empuries
Imprint of grup62
Peu de la Creu, 4, 08001 Barcelona
Tel: 93 505 70 06 *Fax:* 93 505 70 59
E-mail: info@editorialempuries.cat

Web Site: www.grup62.cat/editorial-editorial-empuries-80.html
Key Personnel
Contact: Silvia Buzzi *E-mail:* sbuzzi@grup62.com
Founded: 1983
Subjects: Art, Cookery, Economics, Fiction, History, Humor, Poetry, Romance, Science Fiction, Fantasy, Travel & Tourism
ISBN Prefix(es): 978-84-7596; 978-84-9787
Ultimate Parent Company: Grupo Planeta
Distribution Center: Un per Un, Solucions Comercials SA, C/ Agusti Duran i Sanpere, 1, 08001 Barcelona *Tel:* 93 505 62 00 *Fax:* 93 505 62 31 *E-mail:* info@unperun.cat

Enciclopedia Catalana SAU (Catalan Encyclopedia)+
Subsidiary of Fundacio Enciclopedia Catalana
Josep Pla, 95, 08019 Barcelona
Tel: 93 412 00 30 *Fax:* 93 301 48 63
E-mail: secedit@enciclopedia.cat
Web Site: www.enciclopedia.cat
Key Personnel
Editorial Dir: Jesus Giralt
Rights & Export Dir: Iolanda Bethencourt *E-mail:* ibethencourt@grec.cat
Founded: 1965
Subjects: Art, Cookery, Education, English as a Second Language, Geography, Geology, Health, Nutrition, History, Literature, Literary Criticism, Essays, Natural History, Publishing & Book Trade Reference, Religion - Catholic, Travel & Tourism
ISBN Prefix(es): 978-84-412; 978-84-7739; 978-84-85194
Imprints: La Galera SAU Editorial

enClave ELE
Paseo Marques de Zafra 38, bis, 28028 Madrid
Tel: 914 316 714
E-mail: info@enclave-ele.com
Web Site: www.enclave-ele.com
Founded: 2005
Subjects: Education, Language Arts, Linguistics, Spanish Language
ISBN Prefix(es): 978-84-935792; 978-84-96942; 978-84-935805

Ediciones Encuentro SA
Ramirez de Arellano 17, 10°, 28043 Madrid
Tel: 902 999 689; 915 322 607 *Fax:* 915 322 346
E-mail: encuentro@ediciones-encuentro.es
Web Site: www.ediciones-encuentro.es
Key Personnel
President: Jose Miguel Oriol
Mng Dir: Carmen Salgado *E-mail:* csalgado@ediciones-encuentro.es
Editorial, Rights & Permissions: Manuel Oriol *E-mail:* moriol@ediciones-encuentro.es
Production: Antonio Valenzuela *E-mail:* avalenzuela@ediciones-encuentro.es
Sales: Inmaculada Garcia Balbuena *E-mail:* igbalbuena@ediciones-encuentro.es
Founded: 1978
Subjects: Anthropology, Art, Economics, History, Literature, Literary Criticism, Essays, Philosophy, Social Sciences, Sociology, Theology
ISBN Prefix(es): 978-84-7490; 978-84-9920
Number of titles published annually: 70 Print; 20 E-Book
Total Titles: 1,000 Print
Foreign Rep(s): Libreria Agape (Argentina); Alma Roma SRL (Italy); Casa San Paolo della Pia Societa delle Figlie di San Paolo (Italy); Catholic University of Puerto Rico Bookstore - Libreria (Puerto Rico); Libreria Catolica (Panama); Cuesta Centro del Libro (Dominican Republic); Disliber-Spws-Mexico SA de CV (Mexico); Libreria Espiritual (Ecuador); Hispamer (Nicaragua); Itacalibri (Italy); Libri Mundi - Libreria Internacional

(Ecuador); Libreria Juan Pablo II (Dominican Republic); Paulinas (Colombia, Peru); Paulinas Centro Multimedia (Puerto Rico); Paulinas Distribuidora (USA); Libreria Proa (Chile); Libreria Sorgente (Italy); Libreria Studium (Ecuador); Libreria Vida Nueva (Ecuador); Yenny Libros (Argentina)

Ediciones Endymion
C/ Cruz Verde, 22-bajo, 28004 Madrid
SAN: 001-6977
Tel: 91 522 22 10
E-mail: ediendymion@yahoo.es
Web Site: edicionesendymion.es
Founded: 1986
Subjects: Poetry
ISBN Prefix(es): 978-84-7731

Entramat, *imprint of* Ediciones Urano SA

EOS Gabinete de Orientacion Psicologica
Avda Reina Victoria, 8, 2º A, 28003 Madrid
Tel: 915 541 204
E-mail: eos@eos.es
Web Site: www.eos.es
Key Personnel
Dir General: Miguel Martinez Garcia
Founded: 1966
Subjects: Psychology, Psychiatry
ISBN Prefix(es): 978-84-85851; 978-84-9727; 978-84-89967

Equipo Difusor del Libro SL
Ave Quitapesares, 33 -Local 11, Villa Viciesa de Odon, 28670 Madrid
Tel: 91 616 23 11 *Fax:* 91 616 61 98
E-mail: libros@equipodifusor.com
Web Site: www.equipodifusor.com
Subjects: Literature, Literary Criticism, Essays
ISBN Prefix(es): 978-84-95593
Distributed by Luis Carcamo; Editorial Mirach SL

Erein Argitaletxea+
Tolosa Etorbidea 107, 20018 Donostia
SAN: 002-8436
Tel: 943 21 83 00 *Fax:* 943 21 83 11
E-mail: erein@erein.com
Web Site: www.erein.com
Founded: 1976
Specialize in Basque literature.
Subjects: Education, Literature, Literary Criticism, Essays, Poetry, Culture
ISBN Prefix(es): 978-84-7568; 978-84-85324; 978-84-9746

Esencia
Member of Grupo Planeta
Av Diagnol 662-664, 7a planta, 08034 Barcelona
Tel: 934928130 *Fax:* 934967051
E-mail: infoesencia@planetadelibros.com
Web Site: www.planetadelibros.com/editorial/esencia/24
Founded: 2007
Subjects: Romance
ISBN Prefix(es): 978-84-080; 978-987-1388

La Esfera de los Libros SL
Av San Luis, 25, 28033 Madrid
Tel: 912 960 200
E-mail: laesfera@esferalibros.com
Web Site: www.esferalibros.com
Key Personnel
Dir General: Ymelda Navajo
Editorial Dir & Foreign Rights: Carmen Fernandez de Blas *E-mail:* carmen.fernandez@esferalibros.com
Communications Dir: Mercedes Pacheco
Marketing: Ricardo Tejedor
Production: Alberto Fernandez

Subjects: Biography, Memoirs, Fiction, Health, Nutrition, History, Literature, Literary Criticism, Essays, Nonfiction (General), Psychology, Psychiatry, Religion - Other, Sports, Athletics, Current Affairs
ISBN Prefix(es): 978-84-9734
Distribution Center: Logintegral 2000 SAU, C/ Pradillo 42, 28002 Madrid *Tel:* 901 022 900 *Fax:* 915 864 313 *E-mail:* pedidoslibros@logintegral.com *Web Site:* www.logintegral-libros.com

Esic Editorial
Avda Valdenigrales s/n, 28224 Pozuelo de Alarcon, Madrid
Tel: 914 524 100; 91 452 41 33 (rights)
E-mail: info.madrid@esic.es; derechos@esic.es (rights)
Web Site: www.esic.es
Key Personnel
Contact: Maria Jesus Merino Sanz
E-mail: mariajesus.merino@esic.es
Founded: 1970
Specializes in economy, marketing & enterprise.
Subjects: Accounting, Business, Economics, Marketing
ISBN Prefix(es): 978-84-7356

Insituto Espanol de Comercio Exterior (ICEX)
Paseo de la Castellana 14, 28046 Madrid
Tel: 913 496 223 *Fax:* 914 311 442
E-mail: edicion@icex.es
Web Site: www.icex.es
Key Personnel
Head, Editorial Dept: Francisco Meno Galindez
E-mail: francisco.meno@icex.es
Subjects: Finance, Foreign Trade, Investments
ISBN Prefix(es): 978-84-7811
Foreign Rep(s): Alfaomega Colombiana SA (Colombia); Arcadia Libros (Argentina); Editora y Distribuidora Azteca (Mexico); Baker & Taylor (USA); Internacional Libros SA (Chile); Libreria Universitaria de Buenos Aires (Argentina); Probooks (Mexico)
Distribution Center: Mundi-Prensa Barcelona, Apdo Postal 33388, 08080 Barcelona *Tel:* 629 262 328 *Fax:* 933 063 499 *E-mail:* barcelona@mundiprensa.es *Web Site:* www.mundiprensa.es
Puvill Libros, Estany, 13 y 17, nave D-1, 08038 Barcelona *Tel:* 932 988 960 *Fax:* 932 988 961 *E-mail:* info@puvill.com *Web Site:* www.puvill.com
Mundi-Prensa Libros SA, Castello, 37, 28001 Madrid *Tel:* 914 363 700 *Fax:* 915 753 998 *E-mail:* libreria@mundiprensa.es *Web Site:* www.mundiprensa.com

Espasa+
Member of Grupo Planeta
Av Diagonal, 662-664, 08034 Barcelona
Web Site: www.planetadelibros.com/editorial-espasa-5.html
Founded: 1860
Subjects: Art, Biography, Memoirs, Child Care & Development, Cookery, English as a Second Language, Fiction, History, Literature, Literary Criticism, Essays, Nonfiction (General), Science Fiction, Fantasy, Self-Help, Social Sciences, Sociology
ISBN Prefix(es): 978-84-339; 978-84-239; 978-84-670; 978-84-8326

Editorial de Espiritualidad
C/ Triana, 9, 28016 Madrid
Tel: 913 504 922 *Fax:* 913 504 922
E-mail: info@editorialdeespiritualidad.com; editorial@editorialdeespiritualidad.com
Web Site: www.editorialdeespiritualidad.com
Founded: 1948
Subjects: History, Inspirational, Spirituality, Music, Dance, Poetry, Religion - Catholic

ISBN Prefix(es): 978-84-7068
Distribution Center: Azteca Distribuidora SL, Marquesa de Argueso, 36, 28019 Madrid *Tel:* 915 604 360 *Fax:* 915 652 922

Estrella Polar, *imprint of* grup62

Estudio Didactico, *imprint of* Edimat Libros SA

Institut d'Estudis Regionals i Metropolitans de Barcelona (Barcelona Institute of Regional & Metropolitan Studies)
Universitat Autonoma de Barcelona, Campus de Bellaterra, Placa Nord, edifici MRA, 1/c planta 2, 08193 Bellaterra (Cerdanyola del Valles)
Tel: 93 586 88 80 *Fax:* 93 581 44 33
E-mail: iermb@uab.es
Web Site: www.iermb.uab.es
Key Personnel
President: Xavier Trias i Videl de Llobatera
Dir: Joan Trullen Thomas *Tel:* 93 581 22 44 *Fax:* 93 581 22 92 *E-mail:* joan.trullen@uab.es
Founded: 1984
Subjects: Environmental Studies
ISBN Prefix(es): 978-84-88068
Branch Office(s)
Carrer 62, num 16, edifici B, planta 0, Zona Franco, 08040 Barcelona *Tel:* 93 223 42 14 *Fax:* 93 223 47 07 *E-mail:* iermb@amb.es

Publicaciones Etea (ETEA Publishing)
C/ Escritor Castilla Aguayo, 4, PO Box 439, 14004 Cordoba
SAN: 002-8724
Tel: 957 222 100 *Fax:* 957 222 182
E-mail: comunica@etea.com; cordoba@etea.com
Web Site: www.etea.com/web/etea/publicaciones-etea
Key Personnel
Dir: Ildefonso Camacho; Pilar Tirado
Founded: 1963
University education.
Subjects: Business, Economics, Labor, Industrial Relations, Law, Business Management
Number of titles published annually: 20 Print
Parent Company: ETEA - Institucion Universitaria de la Compania de Jesus
Distributed by Desclee de Brouwer
Foreign Rights: Desclee de Brouwer (Spain)

Eumo Editorial+
Pedro i Pons, 9-11, 11a planta, 08034 Barcelona
Tel: 93 889 28 18
E-mail: eumoeditorial@eumoeditorial.com
Web Site: www.eumoeditorial.com
Key Personnel
Dir: Montse Ayats
Founded: 1979
Subjects: Archaeology, Education, History, Journalism, Language Arts, Linguistics, Library & Information Sciences, Literature, Literary Criticism, Essays, Nonfiction (General), Poetry, Women's Studies, Advertising
ISBN Prefix(es): 978-84-7602; 978-84-9766
Number of titles published annually: 50 Print
Total Titles: 1,300 Print
Parent Company: N9u Grup Editorial

EUNSA (Ediciones Universidad de Navarra SA)+
Plaza de los Sauces, 1 y 2, 31010 Baranain-Navarra
Tel: 948 256 850 *Fax:* 948 256 854
E-mail: eunsa@eunsa.es
Web Site: www.eunsa.es
Key Personnel
Editorial Dir: Jose Martinez Echalar
Founded: 1967
Subjects: Architecture & Interior Design, Biological Sciences, Business, Economics, Education, Engineering (General), History, Journalism,

Language Arts, Linguistics, Law, Library &
Information Sciences, Literature, Literary Crit-
icism, Essays, Medicine, Nursing, Dentistry,
Philosophy, Religion - Other, Theology
ISBN Prefix(es): 978-84-313
Imprints: Biblioteca 'NT' (number of paperback
series covering the arts & sciences, current af-
fairs, religion & philosophy, etc)
Branch Office(s)
C/ Na Sa de Lujan 5, esc dcha, bajo, 28016
Madrid *Tel:* 913 506 815 *Fax:* 913 506 830
Foreign Rep(s): Agape (Argentina); Apuntes (Ar-
gentina); Atenas (Paraguay); Baker & Tay-
lor (USA); Libreria Beityala (Mexico); Canal
Buenos Aires (Argentina); Libreria Catolica
Gethesemani (USA); Libros la Ceiba (El Sal-
vador); Edisa (Costa Rica, Nicaragua); Equo
(Peru); Gandhi (Mexico); Ediciones Iberoamer-
icanas (Costa Rica, Nicaragua); Libreria Ka-
tolicos (Costa Rica, Nicaragua); Liberalia
(Chile); Limerin (Ecuador); Libreria Loyola
(Guatemala); Manatial (Brazil); Minos Ter-
cer Milenio (Mexico); Nueva Libreria Parro-
quial (Mexico); Paoline Multimedia (Italy);
Papiros (Ecuador); Libreria Parroquial (Mex-
ico); Paulinas (Brazil, Colombia, Dominican
Republic, Ecuador, Paraguay, Peru, Puerto
Rico, Venezuela); Libreria PROA (Chile);
Procodes (Colombia); Quadrante (Brazil); Li-
breria San Cristobal (Peru); San Pablo (Colom-
bia, Venezuela); Libreria San Pablo (Bolivia);
Soluciones Bibliograficas (Mexico); Urbaniana
(Italy); USAMadrid (Puerto Rico, USA); V&D
Distribuidores (Peru); Verbo Divino (Colom-
bia); J Waldhuter Ediciones (Argentina)

**Euskaltzaindia-Royal Academy of the Basque
Language**
Plaza Barria 15, 48005 Bilbao
Tel: 944 15 81 55 *Fax:* 944 15 81 44
E-mail: info@euskaltzaindia.net
Web Site: www.euskaltzaindia.eus
Founded: 1919
Subjects: Language Arts, Linguistics, Literature,
Literary Criticism, Essays, Classical Basque
Literature, Dialectology, Grammar, Onomastics,
Sociolinguistics
ISBN Prefix(es): 978-84-85479; 978-84-95438

Everest Editora, *imprint of* Editorial Everest SA

Editorial Everest SA+
Carretera Leon-La Coruna, Km 5, 24080 Leon
Mailing Address: Apdo 339, 24080 Leon
Tel: 987 844 200 *Fax:* 987 844 202
E-mail: info@everest.es
Web Site: www.everest.es
Key Personnel
Publication Dir: Raquel Lopez Varela
Founded: 1958
Subjects: Animals, Pets, Astrology, Occult, Cook-
ery, Crafts, Games, Hobbies, Gardening, Plants,
History, Physics, Religion - Catholic
ISBN Prefix(es): 978-84-241; 978-972-750
Parent Company: Grupo Editorial Everest
Associate Companies: Lectorum Publications Inc,
205 Chubb Ave, Lyndhurst, NJ 07071, United
States (USA distributor)
Imprints: Aizkorri; Edicions Cadi; Everest Gali-
cia; Everest Editora; Ediciones Gaviota; Turpial
Orders to: Everest de Ediciones & Distribu-
cion SL, Carretera Leon-Coruna, Km 5, Apdo
339, 24080 Leon, Manager: Javier Atienza
E-mail: pedidos@distribucion.everest.es

Everest Galicia, *imprint of* Editorial Everest SA

Everest Galicia SL
Imprint of Editorial Everest SA
Avda de Arteixo, 15, 15004 A Coruna
Tel: 981 142 939 *Fax:* 981 143 190

Web Site: www.everest.es
Key Personnel
Publishing Dir: Irene Penas Murias
  E-mail: ipenas@galicia.everest.es
Dir General: Jose Antonio Lopez Martinez
Founded: 1994
ISBN Prefix(es): 978-84-403
Ultimate Parent Company: Grupo Editorial Ever-
est

Extramuros Edicion SL
Brujula, 10, Parque Industrial PISA, 41927
Mairena del Aljarafe, Seville
Tel: 955 60 21 02 *Fax:* 955 60 24 73
E-mail: extramuros@extramuros.es
Web Site: www.extramuros.es
Subjects: Agriculture, Architecture & Interior
Design, Art, Biography, Memoirs, Biological
Sciences, Economics, Education, Engineering
(General), Gardening, Plants, Literature, Liter-
ary Criticism, Essays, Mathematics, Medicine,
Nursing, Dentistry, Philosophy, Religion -
Other, Veterinary Science, Botany, Folklore
ISBN Prefix(es): 978-84-96784

La Fabrica Editorial
C/ Veronica 13, 28014 Madrid
Tel: 91 360 13 20 *Fax:* 91 360 13 22
E-mail: info@lafabrica.com; edicion@lafabrica.
com
Web Site: www.lafabrica.com
Key Personnel
Dir: Alberto Anaut
Publishing Dir: Camino Brasa
Publishing Coordinator: Domenico Chiappe
Development Dir: Fernando Paz
Sales Dir: Chelo Lozano
Head, Publicity: Pilar Amores
Distribution: Raul Munoz
Production: Rufino Diaz
Founded: 1995
Subjects: Art, Photography, Culture
ISBN Prefix(es): 978-84-95471; 978-84-96466;
  978-84-15691
Foreign Rep(s): Buchart Verlagsvertretungen
(Austria, Germany, Switzerland); DAP (Dis-
tributed Art Publishers) (USA); Grupo Oceano
(Latin America); Pollen Diffusion (France);
Publishers International Marketing (Asia);
Roundhouse Group (Europe, UK)

**Facultad de Ciencias de la Actividad Fisica y
del Deporte (INEF)** (Faculty of Sciences for
Physical Activity & Sport)
Ciudad Universitaria de Madrid, C/ Martin Fierro,
7, 28040 Madrid
Tel: 913 364 001
Web Site: www.inef.upm.es
Founded: 1961
Subjects: Sports, Athletics

Fanbooks, *imprint of* grup62

Fantascy, *imprint of* Penguin Random House
Grupo Editorial

Barbara Fiore Editora SL
Calle Huetor Vega, 11, Poligono Juncaril, 18220
Albolote
Tel: 958 175 303; 958 569 833
Web Site: www.barbara-fiore.es
ISBN Prefix(es): 978-84-933980; 978-84-15208
Foreign Rep(s): L'Alebrije scp (Chile); Calibro-
scopio Ediciones (Argentina); Colofon SA de
CV (Mexico); Liberalia Ediciones Ltda (Chile);
Ediciones Monserrate Ltda (Colombia); Pu-
jol & Amado (Argentina, Central America,
Chile, Colombia, Mexico, South America,
USA, Venezuela)

Fondo de Cultura Economica de Espana SA+
C/ Fernando el Catolico, 86, 28015 Madrid
SAN: 003-0562
Tel: 91 763 28 00 *Fax:* 91 763 51 33
E-mail: info@fondodeculturaeconomica.es
Web Site: www.fcede.es
Key Personnel
Management: Francisco Ruiz Bar-
  bosa *E-mail:* francisco.ruiz@
  fondodeculturaeconomica.es
Founded: 1934
Subjects: Anthropology, Economics, Government,
Political Science, History, Language Arts, Lin-
guistics, Law, Literature, Literary Criticism,
Essays, Philosophy, Psychology, Psychiatry,
Science (General), Social Sciences, Sociology,
Technology
ISBN Prefix(es): 978-84-375
Parent Company: Fondo de Cultura Economica,
Mexico
U.S. Office(s): Fondo de Cultura Economica USA
Inc, 2293 Verus St, San Diego, CA 92154,
United States *Tel:* 619-429-0455 *Fax:* 619-651-
9684 *E-mail:* dbase@fceusa.com

**Fondo de Publicaciones del Gobierno de
Navarra**
Calle de las Navas de Tolosa, 21, 31002 Pam-
plona, Navarra
Tel: 848 42 7121 *Fax:* 848 42 7123
E-mail: fondo.publicaciones@navarra.es
Web Site: www.publicaciones.navarra.es
ISBN Prefix(es): 978-84-235

Libreria Fragua
C/ Andres Mellado, 64, 28015 Madrid
Tel: 91 544 22 97; 91 549 18 06 *Fax:* 91 543 17
  94
E-mail: pedidos@fragua.es
Web Site: www.fragua.es
Founded: 1972
Subjects: Advertising, Communications, Journal-
ism, Language Arts, Linguistics, Library &
Information Sciences, Philosophy, Photography,
Radio, TV, Technology
ISBN Prefix(es): 978-84-7074; 978-84-7974
Bookshop(s): Facultad de Ciencias de la Informa-
cion, Planta Baja, Universidad Complutense de
Madrid, Avda de la Complutense, s/n, 28040
Madrid *Tel:* 91 544 18 05 *Fax:* 91 543 17 94
E-mail: fragualibros@fragua.es

Fundacio Espais d'Art Contemporani
Carrer del Pou Rodo, 7, 17004 Girona
Tel: 972 202530 *Fax:* 972 412301
Founded: 1987
Subjects: Art, Culture, Contemporary Art
ISBN Prefix(es): 978-84-930566

Fundacion Coleccion Thyssen-Bornemisza
Paseo del Prado 8, 28014 Madrid
Tel: 914 203 944
E-mail: mtb@museothyssen.org
Web Site: www.museothyssen.org
Key Personnel
Publications: Ana Cela
Founded: 1988
Subjects: Art
ISBN Prefix(es): 978-84-88474; 978-84-96233;
  978-84-15113
Distributed by Lunwerg SA

Fundacion Confemetal
C/ Principe de Vergara, 74, 28006 Madrid
Tel: 91 782 36 30 *Fax:* 91 563 17 41
E-mail: informacion@fundacionconfemetal.es;
  editorial@fundacionconfemetal.es
Web Site: www.fundacionconfemetal.com
Key Personnel
Dir General: Luis Asencio Sanchez
Founded: 1985

Subjects: Finance, Labor, Industrial Relations, Law, Management, Technology, Commerce, Production
ISBN Prefix(es): 978-84-96169; 978-84-89786; 978-84-921339; 978-84-95428
Branch Office(s)
C/ Arregui y Aruej 25-27, 28007 Madrid *Tel:* 91 564 95 36

Fundacion de Estudios Libertarios Anselmo Lorenzo
C/ Penuelas, 41, 28005 Madrid
Tel: 91 473 82 48
E-mail: fal@cnt.es
Web Site: fal.cnt.es
Founded: 1987
Subjects: Biography, Memoirs, Economics, History, Labor, Industrial Relations, Literature, Literary Criticism, Essays, Social Sciences, Sociology, Anarchism, Trade Unionism
ISBN Prefix(es): 978-84-86864
Number of titles published annually: 4 Print
Distributor for Lucina; Nossa y Jara Editores

Fundacion de los Ferrocarriles Espanoles
(Spanish Railways Foundation)
Calle Santa Isabel, 44, 28012 Madrid
Tel: 911 511 002; 911 511 071 *Fax:* 911 511 068
E-mail: palacio@ffe.es; fugeu02@ffe.es
Web Site: www.ffe.es
Key Personnel
Mng Dir: Juan Pedro Pastor *Tel:* 911 511 070
  E-mail: gerente@ffe.es
Founded: 1985
Promote knowledge & use of rail transport.
Subjects: Transportation, Railways
ISBN Prefix(es): 978-84-88675; 978-84-89649; 978-84-9000

Fundacion Gratis Date
Apdo 2154, 31080 Pamplona
Tel: 948 123612 *Fax:* 948 123612
E-mail: fundacion@gratisdate.org
Web Site: www.gratisdate.org
Subjects: Theology
ISBN Prefix(es): 978-84-87903

Fundacion Jose Manuel Lara
Ave de Jerez s/n Edif Indotorre, 41012 Seville
Tel: 954 50 11 40 *Fax:* 954 50 11 44
E-mail: fundacionjmlara@fundacionjmlara.es
Web Site: www.fundacionjmlara.es
Key Personnel
Dir General: Ana Gavin Martin
Communications Dir: Carmen Carballo Aguilar
  E-mail: ccarballo@fundacionjmlara.es
Subjects: History, Literature, Literary Criticism, Essays
ISBN Prefix(es): 978-84-96556; 978-84-931995; 978-84-96152

Fundacion Juan March
Castello, 77, 28006 Madrid
Tel: 91 435 42 40 *Fax:* 91 576 34 20
E-mail: prensa@march.es
Web Site: www.march.es
Key Personnel
President: Juan March Delgado
Vice President: Carlos March Delgado
Dir: Javier Goma Lanzon *E-mail:* direccion@march.es
Founded: 1955
Subjects: Art
ISBN Prefix(es): 978-84-7075

Fundacion la Caixa
Av Diagonal, 621, torre 2, planta 2, 08028 Barcelona
SAN: 003-1240
Tel: 93 404 67 35
E-mail: info@fundaciolacaixa.org

Web Site: obrasociallacaixa.org
Key Personnel
President: Isidre Faine Casas
Dir General: Jaume Lanaspa Gatnau
Press Officer: Jesus N Arroyo Gonzalez
Founded: 1904
Subjects: Child Care & Development, Disability, Special Needs, Education, Health, Nutrition, Psychology, Psychiatry, Social Sciences, Sociology, Women's Studies
ISBN Prefix(es): 978-84-7664

Fundacion Legado Andalusi
Pabellon de al-Andalus la Ciencia, Parque de las Ciencias de Granada, Avda de la Ciencia, s/n, 18006 Granada
Tel: 958 225 995 *Fax:* 958 228 644
E-mail: info@legadoandalusi.es
Web Site: www.legadoandalusi.es
Subjects: History, Culture
ISBN Prefix(es): 978-84-96395; 978-84-930615; 978-84-932051; 978-84-932923

Fundacion Marcelino Botin
c/ Pedrueca 1, 39003 Santander
Tel: 942 22 60 72 *Fax:* 942 36 04 94
E-mail: becas@fundacionmbotin.org; prensa@fundacionmbotin.org
Web Site: www.fundacionmbotin.org
Key Personnel
President: Emilio Botin
Press: Isabel Cubria
Founded: 1964
Subjects: Art, Environmental Studies, History, Science (General)
ISBN Prefix(es): 978-84-87678; 978-84-95516; 978-84-96655
Number of titles published annually: 7 Print; 1 CD-ROM
Branch Office(s)
C/ Castello, 18C, 28001 Madrid *Tel:* 917 81 41 32
Distributed by Emiliano Garcia de la Torre (Spain)

Fundacion Pablo Iglesias
Calle Ferraz 35, 1° Izq, 28008 Madrid
Tel: 91 310 43 13
Web Site: www.fpabloiglesias.es
Key Personnel
President: Alfonso Guerra
Subjects: Government, Political Science, History
ISBN Prefix(es): 978-84-85691; 978-84-95886

Fundacion Rosacruz+
Camino del Pesebre, s/n, 50162 Villamayor (Zaragoza)
Tel: 976589100 *Fax:* 976589161
E-mail: comercial@fundacionrosacruz.org; secretaria@fundacionrosacruz.org
Web Site: www.fundacionrosacruz.org; tienda.fundacionrosacruz.org
Founded: 1993
Subjects: Literature, Literary Criticism, Essays, Mysteries, Suspense, Philosophy, Religion - Other
ISBN Prefix(es): 978-84-87055
Showroom(s): C/ D Juan de Aragon, 12, 50001 Zaragoza *Tel:* 97 620 49 76; C/ San Juan de Malta, 219, 08018 Barcelona *Tel:* 93 218 43 68; C/ Francisco de Ricci, 7, 28015 Madrid *Tel:* 91 559 59 92; C/ Padre Rico 8, Bajo derecha, 46008 Valencia *Tel:* 96 385 77 08

Editorial Fundamentos+
c/ Caracas, 15-3° ctro dcha, 28010 Madrid
Tel: 913 199 619; 913 194 378 *Fax:* 913 195 584
E-mail: fundamentos@editorialfundamentos.es
Web Site: www.editorialfundamentos.es
Key Personnel
Publisher: Juan Serraller *E-mail:* jserraller@editorialfundamentos.es

Founded: 1970
Subjects: Alternative, Crafts, Games, Hobbies, Drama, Theater, Fiction, Film, Video, Government, Political Science, Literary Criticism, Essays, Music, Dance, Philosophy, Psychology, Psychiatry, Social Sciences, Sociology
ISBN Prefix(es): 978-84-245
Bookshop(s): PAE Madrid Este 1- Nave B16, Carretera M-119 hacia Alcala de Henares km 2,8, 28816 Camarma de Esteruelas, Madrid

Gadir Editorial
Calle Jazmin, 22, 28033 Madrid
Tel: 913835646 *Fax:* 913835647
E-mail: gadir@gadireditorial.com
Web Site: www.gadireditorial.com
Subjects: Biography, Memoirs, Fiction
ISBN Prefix(es): 978-84-936033; 978-84-933767; 978-84-934045; 978-84-934439; 978-84-935382; 978-84-96974; 978-84-934748; 978-84-935237
Foreign Rep(s): Comercial Grupo Anaya (Bolivia, Brazil, Costa Rica, Ecuador, Guatemala, Honduras, Nicaragua, USA); Grupal Distribuidora (Argentina); Liberalia Ediciones Ltda (Chile); Plaza & Janes Colombia (Colombia); Sexto Piso Distribucion (Mexico)

Editorial Galaxia SA+
Av de Madrid, 44, 36204 Vigo
Tel: 986 43 21 00 *Fax:* 986 22 32 05
E-mail: galaxia@editorialgalaxia.es
Web Site: www.editorialgalaxia.es
Key Personnel
Dir General: Victor F Freixanes
Founded: 1950
Subjects: Art, History, Literature, Literary Criticism, Essays, Philosophy, Poetry, Social Sciences, Sociology, Travel & Tourism
ISBN Prefix(es): 978-84-7154; 978-84-8288; 978-84-9865
Distribution Center: Travesia de Vigo, 71, soto, 36206 Vigo *Tel:* 986 37 22 79 *Fax:* 986 26 27 34 *E-mail:* pedidos@editorialgalaxia.com

La Galera SAU Editorial, *imprint of* Enciclopedia Catalana SAU

La Galera SAU Editorial+
Imprint of Enciclopedia Catalana SAU
Josep Pla, 95, 08019 Barcelona
Tel: 93 412 00 30 *Fax:* 93 301 48 63
E-mail: lagalera@grec.cat
Web Site: www.lagaleraeditorial.com; www.facebook.com/editoriallagalera
Key Personnel
Rights Dir: Iolanda Bethencourt *Tel:* 93 505 76 02 *E-mail:* ibethencourt@lagaleraeditorial.com
Founded: 1963
Subjects: Child Care & Development, Education, Fiction, Comics
ISBN Prefix(es): 978-84-246; 978-84-7515; 978-84-85297
Number of titles published annually: 200 Print

Galland Editorial Books
C/ Estaciuon, 41 ent B, 47004 Valladolid
Tel: 983 116 527; 983 290 774 *Fax:* 983 116 528
E-mail: pedidos@gallandbooks.com
Web Site: www.gallandbooks.com
Subjects: Warfare (Spain)
ISBN Prefix(es): 978-84-936251

Vicent Garcia Editores SA
C/ Guardia Civil, 22 Torre 3a, piso 1°, 3a, 46020 Valencia
SAN: 005-318X
Tel: 62 759 65 73; 96 369 15 89 *Fax:* 96 111 90 20
E-mail: vgesa@combios.es

Web Site: www.vgesa.com
Key Personnel
Dir General: Ricardo J Vicent
Founded: 1974
Specialize in facsimiles of manuscripts, incunabula & antique books.
Subjects: Antiques, Art, Gardening, Plants, History, Language Arts, Linguistics, Law, Religion - Catholic, Travel & Tourism
ISBN Prefix(es): 978-84-85094; 978-84-87988; 978-84-88093; 978-84-923358; 978-84-932929; 978-84-15182
Book Club(s): Club Konrad Haebler

Ediciones Gaviota, *imprint of* Editorial Everest SA

Ediciones Gaviota+
Imprint of Editorial Everest SA
C/ Manuel Tovar, 8, 28034 Madrid
Tel: 91 358 01 08 *Fax:* 91 729 38 58
E-mail: ventas@ediciones-gaviota.com
Key Personnel
Mng Dir: Jose Antonio Lopez Martinez
Founded: 1983
Specialize in children's & juvenile books.
Licensed publishing.
ISBN Prefix(es): 978-84-392
Associate Companies: Lectorum Publications Inc (USA distributor)
Subsidiaries: Everest de Ediciones y Distribucion
Orders to: Everest de Ediciones y Distribucion

Editorial Gedisa SA+
Av del Tibidabo, 12, 3°, 08022 Barcelona
Tel: 93 253 09 04
E-mail: informacion@gedisa.com
Web Site: www.gedisa.com
Key Personnel
Founder & President: Victor Landman
Dir General: Alfredo Landman
Founded: 1977
Subjects: Biography, Memoirs, Education, Human Relations, Nonfiction (General), Philosophy, Psychology, Psychiatry, Social Sciences, Sociology, Sports, Athletics
ISBN Prefix(es): 978-84-7432
Subsidiaries: Editorial Celtia SA; Editorial Gedisa Mexicana
Distributed by Ediciones Oceano de Chile SA (Chile); Ediciones Oceano de Colombia SA (Colombia); Edisa Distribuidores (Venezuela); Editorial Oceano Peruana SA (Peru); Editorial Oceano del Uruguay SA (Uruguay)
Foreign Rep(s): EDISA Distribuidores (Venezuela)

Gemser Publications SL
Castell 38, 08329 Teia, Barcelona
Tel: 935 401 353 *Fax:* 935 401 346
E-mail: info@mercedesros.com
Web Site: www.mercedesros.com
Key Personnel
Publisher: Mercedes Ros
Contact: Merce Segarra *E-mail:* merce@mercedesros.com
Founded: 1999
Subjects: Art, Cookery, Fiction, Geography, Geology, History, Nonfiction (General), Religion - Other, Science (General), Mythology
ISBN Prefix(es): 978-84-96346

Generalitat de Catalunya, Entitat Autonoma del Diari Oficial i de Publicacions
(Government of Catalonia, Autonomous Unit of Official Journal & Publications)+
Avinguda de Josep Tarradellas, 20, 2a planta, 08029 Barcelona
Tel: 932 925 400 *Fax:* 932 925 435
Web Site: www20.gencat.cat/portal/site/portaldogc

Key Personnel
Editorial Coordinator: Pilar Vallugera Balana
Commercial: Pere Artasu i Peris *E-mail:* pere.artasu@gencat.cat
Publishing Service: Lluis Prat i Francisco *E-mail:* lluis.prat@gencat.cat
Founded: 1977
Official journal & public publishing services.
At the Government of Catalonia Online Bookshop you can buy the saleable publications of the Catalan government's departments, autonomous bodies & other attached entities. They include both technical & non-specialist publications concerning the areas dealt with by the departments of the Catalan government (culture, the economy, education, the environment, health, tourism, cartography, etc).
Subjects: Agriculture, Archaeology, Art, Economics, Education, Energy, Environmental Studies, Government, Political Science, Health, Nutrition, History, Language Arts, Linguistics, Law, Photography, Public Administration, Social Sciences, Sociology, Transportation, Public Administration
ISBN Prefix(es): 978-84-393
Parent Company: Generalitat de Catalunya
Bookshop(s): Llibreria de la Generalitat de Catalunya (Government of Catalonia Bookshop), Rambla dels Estudis 118, 08002 Barcelona, Head, Bookshop: Ferran Tur *Tel:* 933 026 462 *Fax:* 933 186 221 *E-mail:* llibrbcn@gencat.net *Web Site:* llibreria.gencat.cat; Llibreria de la Generalitat de Catalunya, Joan Maragall, 2, 17002 Girona, Contact: Carmina Solano *Tel:* 972 227 267 *Fax:* 972 227 315 *E-mail:* llibrgi@gencat.net *Web Site:* llibreria.gencat.cat; Llibreria de la Generalitat de Catalunya, Dr Fleming 19, 25006 Lleida, Head, Bookshop: Teresa Freixa *Tel:* 973 281 930 *Fax:* 973 261 056 *E-mail:* llibrlle@gencat.net *Web Site:* llibreria.gencat.cat; Llibreria de la Generalitat, c Major, 37, 43003 Tarragona, Head, Bookshop: Carme Benitez *Tel:* 977 21 17 97 *Fax:* 977 22 01 27 *E-mail:* llibrtar@gencat.cat *Web Site:* llibreria.gencat.cat
Distribution Center: Un per Un, Solucions Comercials, SA *Tel:* 902 109 431 *E-mail:* mroig@agorallibres.cat
Orders to: Llibreria de la Generalitat de Catalunya (Government of Catalonia Bookshop), Rambla dels Estudis 118, 08002 Barcelona, Head, Bookshop: Ferran Tur *Tel:* 933 026 462 *Fax:* 933 186 221 *E-mail:* llibrbcn@gencat.net *Web Site:* llibreria.gencat.cat
Government of Catalonia Online Bookshop *Tel:* 932 925 417 *E-mail:* suport.llibreria@gencat.cat *Web Site:* llibreria.gencat.cat
Un per Un, Solucions Comercials, SA *Tel:* 902 109 431 *E-mail:* mroig@agorallibres.cat

Gestion 2000+
Member of Grupo Planeta
Centro de Libros PAPF, Av Diagonal, 662-664, 08034 Barcelona
Tel: 93 492 69 56
E-mail: info@centrolibrospapf.es
Web Site: www.planetadelibros.com/editorial-gestion-2000-13.html
Key Personnel
Foreign Rights Manager: Daniel Cladera *Tel:* 93 492 80 08 *E-mail:* dcladera@planeta.es
Communication: Sira Coll *Tel:* 93 492 82 03 *E-mail:* scoll@planeta.es
Founded: 1987
Specialize in business management.
Subjects: Accounting, Advertising, Business, Career Development, Communications, Computer Science, Economics, Finance, Human Relations, Management, Marketing, Technology, Human Resources, Sales

ISBN Prefix(es): 978-84-86703; 978-84-8088; 978-84-86582; 978-84-96612; 978-84-96426
Total Titles: 400 Print; 10 CD-ROM
Distributed by Aboitiz Asociados SA de CV (Mexico); Contemporanea de Ediciones (Venezuela); Editorial Planeta Argentina (Argentina); Editorial Planeta Chilena SA (Chile); Editorial Planeta Colombiana (Bolivia, Colombia, Ecuador & Peru); Editorial Planeta SA (Uruguay); Planeta Publishing Corp (Caribbean, Central America & USA); Quijote (Paraguay); Ediciones Tecnicas Paraguayas (Paraguay)
Bookshop(s): Libreria de la Empresa, Muntaner, 90, 08008 Barcelona *E-mail:* libreria.empresa@gestion2000.com

Ediciones Gigamesh
Ronda de San Pedro, 08010 Barcelona
Tel: 933019434 *Fax:* 933171559
E-mail: media@gigamesh.com
Web Site: www.gigamesh.com
Key Personnel
Founder: Alejo Cuervo
Founded: 1999
Subjects: Fiction, Mysteries, Suspense, Science Fiction, Fantasy
ISBN Prefix(es): 978-84-96208; 978-84-930663; 978-84-932250; 978-84-932702
Bookshop(s): Paseo San Juan, 2, local 5 (esquina Av Vilanova), 08010 Barcelona *Tel:* 932 462 121; Rda San Pedro, 53, 08010 Barcelona *Tel:* 932 466 359 *Fax:* 932 327 708
Distribution Center: Asgard Distribuciones, P° de la Reforma, 42, 1°, of A46, Col Centro Deleg Cuauhtemoc, 06010 Mexico, DF, Mexico *Tel:* (0155) 939 839 *E-mail:* contacto@asgarddistribuciones.com.mx *Web Site:* www.asgarddistribuciones.com.mx

Editorial Gustavo Gili SL+
Rossello, 87-89, 08029 Barcelona
Tel: 93 322 81 61 *Fax:* 93 322 92 05
E-mail: info@ggili.com
Web Site: ggili.com
Key Personnel
Mng Dir & Editor-in-Chief: Monica Gili
Mng Dir & Marketing: Gabriel Gili
Foreign Rights: Elena Llobera *E-mail:* elena@ggili.com
Founded: 1902
Specialize in architectural & design books & magazines, fashion & urbanism. Also subscription & periodical publications.
Subjects: Architecture & Interior Design, Art, Fashion, Photography, Urbanism
ISBN Prefix(es): 978-84-252
Number of titles published annually: 60 Print
Total Titles: 1,200 Print
Associate Companies: Editorial Gustavo Gili de Mexico SA; Editorial Gustavo Gili Sociedade Unipessoal Lda
Distributor for Colegio De Arquitectos de Almeria; Collegio De Arquitectos de Madrid; Loft Publicacions SL; Mao Mao Publications SL; Instituto Monsa de Ediciones SA

Gobierno de Canarias - Consejeria de Cultura, Deportes, Politicas Sociales y Vivienda
Edif El Cabo, planta 5a, C/ Leoncio Rodriguez, n° 3, 38071 Santa Cruz de Tenerife
Tel: 922 47 70 00 *Fax:* 922 47 70 56
E-mail: contacto.cepsv@gobiernodecanarias.org
Web Site: www.gobiernodecanarias.org/ccdpsv
Subjects: Government, Political Science, Social Sciences, Sociology
ISBN Prefix(es): 978-84-7947; 978-84-87137; 978-84-87317

Miguel Gomez Ediciones
P° Reading, 45 1° 4B, 29015 Malaga
Tel: 952 602 873

E-mail: mge@miguelgomezediciones.com
Web Site: miguelgomezediciones.com;
    miguelgomezediciones.com/editorial.php
Key Personnel
Dir: Maria Navarro
Editor: Jacobo Gomez; Miguel Gomez Pena
Founded: 1993
Subjects: Education, Literature, Literary Criti-
    cism, Essays, Poetry
ISBN Prefix(es): 978-84-88326
Foreign Rep(s): Proeme (Argentina)
Distribution Center: Latorre Literaria SA, C°
    Boca Alta, naves 8 y 9 Poligono El Malvar,
    28500 Arganda del Rey (Madrid) *Tel:* 918
    719 379 *Fax:* 918 719 408 *E-mail:* info@
    latorreliteraria.com *Web Site:* www.
    latorreliteraria.com

Grupo Gourmets (Progourmet)
Aniceto Marinas, 92, 28008 Madrid
Tel: 915489651 *Fax:* 915487133
E-mail: gourmets@gourmets.net
Web Site: www.gourmets.net
Key Personnel
Dir General: Francisco Lopez Canis
    E-mail: lcanis@gourmets.net; Francisco Lopez
    Lopez-Bago *E-mail:* lopezbago@gourmets.net
Subjects: Cookery, Travel & Tourism, Food
ISBN Prefix(es): 978-84-931168; 978-84-95754

Grafalco Ediciones SL
Division of Navneet Education Limited
Calle Maldonado, 26, 28006 Madrid
Tel: 91 620 02 03
E-mail: inquiry@navneet.com
ISBN Prefix(es): 978-84-7773

Gran Enciclopedia Asturiana SA
Poligono Maximino Vega, nave 8, 33211 Tre-
    manes Gijon, Asturias
SAN: 004-9476
Tel: 985 349 684 *Fax:* 985 349 542
E-mail: gea_edi@yahoo.es
Founded: 1970
Subjects: Regional Interests
ISBN Prefix(es): 978-84-7286
Parent Company: GEA Distribuciones Graficas
    2000 SL

Editorial Gran Via
Plaza de Aragon 9, Bajo, 09001 Burgos
Tel: 636 64 6496
E-mail: eduardomunguia@editorialgranvia.es
Web Site: www.editorialgranvia.es
Subjects: Art, Poetry, Burgos Heritage & Culture
ISBN Prefix(es): 978-84-937453
Distribution Center: Utopos Libros, C/ Juan Ra-
    mon Jimenez-Pentasa III-Nave 163, 09007 Bur-
    gos *Tel:* 947 48 06 43 *Fax:* 947 48 12 43
Egartorre SL, C/ Primavera, 2 (Nave 31) - Pol
    Ind El Malvar, Arganda del Rey, 28500 Madrid
    Tel: 91 872 93 90 *Fax:* 91 871 93 99 *Web
    Site:* www.egartorre.com

Grao Editorial+
Hurtado, 29, 08022 Barcelona
Tel: 93 408 04 64 *Fax:* 93 352 43 37
E-mail: grao@grao.com; info@grao.com
Web Site: www.grao.com
Key Personnel
Rights Manager: Sara Cardona
Administration: Anna M Garcia *E-mail:* agarcia@
    irif.es
Production: Anna Martinez
Sales: Anna Macias
Founded: 1977
Subjects: Child Care & Development, Education,
    Geography, Geology, History, Language Arts,
    Linguistics, Mathematics, Music, Dance, Social
    Sciences, Sociology, Sports, Athletics
ISBN Prefix(es): 978-84-7827; 978-84-85729

Number of titles published annually: 50 Print
Total Titles: 800 Print
Divisions: Interactiva

Editorial Gredos SA+
Imprint of RBA Libros
C/ Lopez de Hoyos 141, 28002 Madrid
Tel: 902 213 413; 902 026 898
E-mail: tienda@editorialgredos.com
Web Site: www.editorialgredos.com
Founded: 1944
Subjects: Economics, Education, History, Liter-
    ature, Literary Criticism, Essays, Philosophy,
    Psychology, Psychiatry, Social Sciences, Soci-
    ology, Greco-Roman, Humanities, Lexicogra-
    phy
ISBN Prefix(es): 978-84-249

Grijalbo, *imprint of* Penguin Random House
Grupo Editorial

Grijalbo Mondadori SA+
Imprint of Penguin Random House Grupo Edito-
    rial
Arago 385, 08013 Barcelona
Tel: 93 476 71 00 *Fax:* 93 476 71 21
E-mail: export@rhm.es; pedidos@rhm.es
Web Site: www.megustaleer.com/editoriales/
    grijalbo/gj
Founded: 1962
Subjects: Architecture & Interior Design, Fiction,
    Gardening, Plants, Human Relations, Humor,
    Literature, Literary Criticism, Essays, Nonfic-
    tion (General), Poetry
ISBN Prefix(es): 978-84-7515; 978-84-8441; 978-
    84-85297
Number of titles published annually: 400 Print
Divisions: Grijalbo Mondadori SA Junior
Branch Office(s)
Grijalbo SA, Av Belgrano, 1256/64, 1093 Buenos
    Aires, Argentina *E-mail:* info@grijalbo.com.ar
Distribuidora Exclusiva Grijalbo SA, Centro In-
    dustiral Eldorado, Calle 64, 88 A-06, inte-
    rior 1-2, Bogota DE, Colombia *Tel:* (0224)
    74 28; (0252) 26 75 *Fax:* (0252) 95 97
    E-mail: grijalbo@cdl.telecom.com.co
Editorial Grijalbo SA, Almirante Barroso, 27,
    Santiago De Chile, Chile *Tel:* (0672) 30
    27 *Fax:* (0672) 18 50 *E-mail:* mondadori@
    entelchile.net
Editorial Grijalbo SA de CV, Av Homero, No
    544, Col Chapultepec-Morales, 11570 Mex-
    ico, DF, Mexico *Tel:* (0155) 2030660; (0155)
    2030955 *Fax:* (0155) 2547683
Ap Correos, 106-62260 Chacao, Av Principal
    Diego Cisnero, Edificio colegial Bolivari-
    ana, piso 2, local 2-2 Los Ruices, Caracas,
    Venezuela *Tel:* (0238) 13 22 *Fax:* (0239) 03
    08 *E-mail:* griven@etheron.net
Distributor for Dedicersa De Cervantes Ediciones
    SA; Editorial Amazonas SA; Electa Espana
    SA; Forza Editores Inc
Foreign Rights: Ros Ramsay (UK); Mary Anne
    Thompson

Grijalbo Mondadori SA Junior+
Division of Grijalbo Mondadori SA
Arago 385, 08013 Barcelona
Tel: 93 476 71 00 *Fax:* 93 476 71 21
Web Site: www.megustaleer.com
Key Personnel
Foreign Rights Manager: Maria Reina de la
    Puebla *Tel:* 93 366 03 12 *E-mail:* mariareina.
    delapuebla@penguinrandomhouse.com
Founded: 1974
Subjects: Humor, Comics
ISBN Prefix(es): 978-84-253; 978-84-7419; 978-
    84-7423; 978-84-397; 978-84-478
Ultimate Parent Company: Penguin Random
    House Grupo Editorial

Grijaldo Ilustrados, *imprint of* Penguin Random
House Grupo Editorial

Grupo Comunicar
Apdo Correos 527, 21080 Huelva
Tel: 959248380 *Fax:* 959248380
E-mail: info@grupocomunicar.com
Web Site: www.grupocomunicar.com
Key Personnel
President & Dir: Jose Ignacio Aguaded Gomez
    E-mail: director@grupocomunicar.com
Vice President: Enrique Martinez-Salanova
    Sanchez *E-mail:* emsalanova@ono.com
Founded: 1989
Subjects: Communications, Education
ISBN Prefix(es): 978-84-920218; 978-84-930045;
    978-84-932380
Number of titles published annually: 4 Print; 3
    CD-ROM; 4 Online; 2 E-Book
Total Titles: 40 Print; 5 CD-ROM; 4 Online; 5 E-
    Book
Distributor for Abis & Books; Amares; A-Z Dis-
    libros; Carrer de Llibres; Centro Andaluz del
    Libro; Andres Garcia; Grial; Ikuska; Lemus

grup62+
Member of Grupo Planeta
Av Diagonal, 662-664, 08034 Barcelona
Tel: 93 443 71 00 *Fax:* 93 443 71 30
E-mail: correu@grup62.com
Web Site: www.grup62.cat
Key Personnel
Foreign Rights Manager: Pilar Lafuente *Tel:* 93
    492 82 44 *E-mail:* plafuente@planeta.es
Founded: 1962
Subjects: Art, Biography, Memoirs, Drama, The-
    ater, Fiction, History, Language Arts, Linguis-
    tics, Literature, Literary Criticism, Essays,
    Nonfiction (General), Parapsychology, Philos-
    ophy, Poetry, Psychology, Psychiatry, Science
    (General), Travel & Tourism
ISBN Prefix(es): 978-84-297 (Peninsula Edi-
    cions); 978-84-87254; 978-84-95808; 978-84-
    89999 (Difusio Editorial SL); 978-84-9762;
    978-84-8307; 978-84-930548; 978-84-95571;
    978-84-96149
Imprints: Art 62; Columna Edicions; Ediciones
    Destino SA; Destino Infantil & Juvenil; Ed-
    ucaula62; Editorial Empuries; Estrella Polar;
    Fanbooks; Labutxaca; Lecturanda62; Edi-
    ciones Luciernaga; Ediciones Peninsula; Edi-
    torial Planeta SA; Editorial Portic SA; Edicions
    Proa SA; Salsa Books (Castella); Salsa Books
    (Catala); Edicions 62
Distributed by Agora Solucions Logistiques SL;
    Enlaces Editorials; Solucions Comercials
Foreign Rep(s): Grupo Editorial Norma (South
    America, USA)

Guadalquivir Ediciones SL
Calle Asuncion, 61, 41011 Seville
SAN: 003-3863
Founded: 1979
Subjects: Art, History, Literature, Literary Criti-
    cism, Essays
ISBN Prefix(es): 978-84-8093; 978-84-86080
Subsidiaries: Varflora
Orders to: Varflora, 17 Bajo, 41001 Seville

Guadiel
Subsidiary of Grupo Edebe
Poligono Tecnologico, nave 93, 18151 Ogijares
    (Granada)
Tel: 958 507333 *Fax:* 958 507240
E-mail: contacta@edebe.net
Web Site: www.edebe.com/grupo_edebe/guadiel.
    asp
ISBN Prefix(es): 978-84-8117

Guia Viva, *imprint of* Anaya-Touring Club

Guiarama, *imprint of* Anaya-Touring Club

Guiatotal, *imprint of* Anaya-Touring Club

Editorial Gulaab
C/ Alquimia, 6, 28933 Mostoles (Madrid)
Tel: 916145849 *Fax:* 916184012
E-mail: alfaomega@alfaomega.es
Web Site: www.alfaomega.es
Subjects: Human Relations, Philosophy, Religion
- Buddhist, Religion - Hindu, Religion - Other,
Women's Studies
ISBN Prefix(es): 978-84-86797
Parent Company: Alfaomega
Foreign Rep(s): Alfaomega SL (Colombia); Del-
lare SA (MUSEO) (Guatemala); Desarrollos
Culturales Costarricenses DCC SA (Costa
Rica); Edaf Chile (Chile); Grupal Logistica
y Distrbucion SA (Argentina); Gussi Libros
(Uruguay); Editorial Oceano de Mexico SA de
CV (Mexico); Sipan CA (Venezuela)

H Blume
Imprint of Akal Grupo Editorial
Sector Foresta nº 1, 28760 Tres Cantos, Madrid
SAN: 005-1721
Tel: 918 061 996 *Fax:* 918 044 028
E-mail: pedidos.blume@akal.com; edicion@akal.
com; universidad@akal.com; educacion@akal.
com; prensa@akal.com; atencion-cliente@akal.
com
Web Site: www.akal.com
Founded: 1978
Also book illustrator.
Membership(s): la Camara, federacion y gremio
de Editore.
Subjects: Advertising, Architecture & Interior
Design, Art, Child Care & Development, Cook-
ery, Crafts, Games, Hobbies, Disability, Spe-
cial Needs, Environmental Studies, Garden-
ing, Plants, Health, Nutrition, Outdoor Recre-
ation, Photography, Self-Help, Sports, Athletics, Travel & Tourism, Fine Arts
ISBN Prefix(es): 978-84-87756; 978-84-89840
Associate Companies: Ediciones Akal SA; Foca;
Ediciones Istmo; Siglo XXI de Espana
Warehouse: Poligono Industrial Las Monjas C/In-
vierno S/N Naves 14-15, Torrejon, Madrid

Harlequin Iberica SA
Calle de Nunez de Balboa, 56, 28001 Madrid
Tel: 914 358 623 *Fax:* 914 310 484
E-mail: atencion_al_cliente@harpercollinsiberica.
com
Web Site: www.harpercollinsiberica.com
Founded: 1982
Subjects: Romance
ISBN Prefix(es): 978-84-396; 978-84-671
Parent Company: Harlequin Enterprises Ltd,
Toronto, ON, Canada

Hercules de Ediciones SA
Member of Grupo Hercules Global
Edificio Hercules, C/ Cordeleria, 32, 15003
Coruna
Tel: 981 220 585 *Fax:* 981 220 717
E-mail: info@herculesediciones.es
Web Site: www.herculesediciones.es
Key Personnel
Founder & President: Francisco Rodriguez Igle-
sias
Founded: 1985
Subjects: Anthropology, Art, Child Care & Devel-
opment, Economics, Education, Environmental
Studies, Genealogy, Geography, Geology, Law,
Literature, Literary Criticism, Essays, Culture,
Ecology, Nature
ISBN Prefix(es): 978-84-87244; 978-84-89468;
978-84-96314
Warehouse: Rua Chinto Crespo, 2, A Gandara,
San Pedro, La Coruna

Herder Editorial SL+
c/ Provenca, 388, 08025 Barcelona

Tel: 93 476 26 26 *Fax:* 93 207 34 48
E-mail: herder@herdereditorial.com; pedido@
herdereditorial.com; prensa@herdereditorial.
com; foreignrights@herdereditorial.com
Web Site: www.herdereditorial.com
Key Personnel
Editor: Raimund Herder
Founded: 1944
Subjects: Economics, Education, History, Lan-
guage Arts, Linguistics, Medicine, Nursing,
Dentistry, Philosophy, Psychology, Psychiatry,
Religion - Other, Social Sciences, Sociology,
Theology
ISBN Prefix(es): 978-84-254
Associate Companies: Verlag Herder & Co, Aus-
tria; Herder und Herder GmbH, Germany; Ver-
lag Herder GmbH & Co KG, Germany; Herder
AG Basel, Switzerland; Herder & Herder/The
Crossroads Publishing Co, United States
Foreign Rep(s): Agape Libros (Argentina);
Ciberlibros CA (Venezuela); Gussi Libros
(Uruguay); Editorial y Libreria Herder (Mex-
ico); Liberalia Ediciones (Chile); Ediciones
Manantial (Argentina); Siglo del Hombre Edi-
tores (Colombia)

Hermetica, *imprint of* Ediciones Robinbook SL

Ediciones Hiperion SL+
Calle de Salustiano Olozaga, 14, 28001 Madrid
Tel: 91 577 60 15; 91 577 60 16 *Fax:* 91 435 86
90
E-mail: info@hiperion.com
Web Site: www.hiperion.com
Key Personnel
Mng Dir, Editorial: Jesus Munarriz
Founded: 1975
Subjects: Language Arts, Linguistics, Literature,
Literary Criticism, Essays, Poetry, Religion -
Islamic, Religion - Jewish
ISBN Prefix(es): 978-84-7517; 978-84-85272
Number of titles published annually: 30 Print
Total Titles: 700 Print

Hiru Argitaletxea SL
Apdo Correos 184, 20280 Hondarribia, Gipuzkoa
Tel: 943641087
E-mail: hiru@euskalnet.net; hiru@hiru-ed.com
Web Site: www.hiru-ed.com
Subjects: Drama, Theater, History
ISBN Prefix(es): 978-84-95786; 978-84-87524;
978-84-89753

Hispabooks Publishing
Caminho de los Vinateros, 106, 28030 Madrid
Tel: 91 430 88 97; 690 21 36 73
E-mail: editorial@hispabooks.com
Web Site: www.hispabooks.com
Key Personnel
Mng Dir: Ana Perez Galvan
Editorial Dir: Gregorio Doval
Founded: 2011
Focus on contemporary Spanish fiction in English
language translation.
Subjects: Fiction
ISBN Prefix(es): 978-84-942284; 978-84-940948;
978-84-941744; 978-84-942830
Distribution Center: Dennis Jones & Associates,
Unit 1/10 Melrich Rd, Bayswater, Victoria
3153, Australia *Tel:* (03) 9762 9100 *Fax:* (03)
9762 9200 *E-mail:* theoffice@dennisjones.com.
au
Central Books, One Heath Park Industrial Estate,
Freshwater Rd, Dagenham RM8 1RX, United
Kingdom *Tel:* (020) 8525 8800 *Fax:* (020)
8599 2694 *E-mail:* orders@centralbooks.com
Web Site: www.centralbooks.com (Ireland &
UK)
Consortium Book Sales & Distribution LLC,
34 13 Ave NE, Suite 101, Minneapolis, MN
55413-1007, United States *Tel:* 612-746-2600
Fax: 612-746-2606 (Canada & USA)

Editorial Hispano Europea SA+
Primer de Maig 21, Pol Ind Gran Via Sud, 08908
L'Hospitalet, Barcelona
Tel: 93 201 85 00 *Fax:* 93 414 26 35
E-mail: hispanoeuropea@hispanoeuropea.
com; admin@hispanoeuropea.com;
export@hispanoeuropea.com; comercial@
hispanoeuropea.com
Web Site: www.hispanoeuropea.com
Key Personnel
Mng Dir, Editorial & Publicity: Jorge J Prat
Administration: Merche Terrades
Production: Bernat Peso
Sales: Xavier Espia
Founded: 1953
Subjects: Animals, Pets, Business, Cookery, Gar-
dening, Plants, Health, Nutrition, Sports, Ath-
letics, Fitness
ISBN Prefix(es): 978-84-255
Number of titles published annually: 80 Print
Total Titles: 650 Print

Historial Enigmas, *imprint of* Ediciones
Robinbook SL

Ibaizabal SA+
Barrio San Miguel, s/n, 48340 Amorebieta,
Bizkaia
Tel: 946 308 036; 944 532 009 (ordering)
Fax: 946 308 028; 944 532 091 (ordering)
E-mail: info@ibaizabal.biz
Web Site: www.ibaizabal.com
Key Personnel
Dir: Sabin Gorrotxategi Zelaieta
Founded: 1990
Materials for school teaching literary editions in
Basque.
Subjects: Education, Literature, Literary Criti-
cism, Essays, Religion - Catholic
ISBN Prefix(es): 978-84-8325; 978-84-7992; 978-
84-8394
Number of titles published annually: 152 Print
Total Titles: 2,200 Print

Editorial Iberia SA+
Imprint of Ediciones Omega SA
c/ Plato, 26, 08006 Barcelona
Tel: 93 201 05 99; 93 201 38 07; 93 201 21 44
Fax: 93 209 73 62
E-mail: omega@ediciones-omega.es
Web Site: www.ediciones-omega.es
Key Personnel
Administrator: Antonio Paricio Larrea
Founded: 1945
Subjects: Art, Biography, Memoirs, Education,
Fiction, Health, Nutrition, Literature, Literary
Criticism, Essays, Physics, Psychology, Psy-
chiatry, Science (General), Self-Help, Travel &
Tourism, Customs
ISBN Prefix(es): 978-84-282; 978-84-7082
Associate Companies: Ediciones Medici SA

IC Editorial, *imprint of* Innovacion y
Cualificacion

Icaria Editorial SA+
Arc de Sant Cristofol, 11-23, 08003 Barcelona
Tel: 93 301 17 23; 93 301 17 26 *Fax:* 93 295 49
16
E-mail: icaria@icariaeditorial.com; comandes@
icariaeditorial.com (orders)
Web Site: www.icariaeditorial.com
Key Personnel
Mng Dir, Editorial, Rights & Permissions: Anna
Monjo
Founded: 1977
Subjects: Anthropology, Cookery, Developing
Countries, Economics, Energy, Environmental
Studies, Literature, Literary Criticism, Essays,
Poetry, Social Sciences, Sociology, Women's

Studies, Analysis of International Politics, Critical Economy, Ecology, Relations of the North-South, Voices & Proposals
ISBN Prefix(es): 978-84-7426; 978-84-9888
Foreign Rep(s): Euroamericana de Ediciones (Venezuela); Editorial Juventud (Mexico); Liberalia Ediciones (Chile); Libri Mundi (Ecuador); Merino y Sanchez (Puerto Rico); Proeme (Argentina); Siglo del Hombre (Colombia); Sophos (Guatemala)
Warehouse: Lepanto, 135-7, 08013 Barcelona

Publicaciones ICCE (Calasanz Institute of Education Sciences Center)+
Calle Jose Picon Nº 7, 28028 Madrid
SAN: 003-6277
Tel: 91 725 72 00 *Fax:* 91 361 10 52
E-mail: info@icceciberaula.es
Web Site: www.icceciberaula.es
Key Personnel
Dir: Juan Yzuel
Founded: 1967
Subjects: Education, History, Psychology, Psychiatry, Religion - Other, Social Sciences, Sociology, Pedagogy
ISBN Prefix(es): 978-84-7278
Number of titles published annually: 10 Print
Total Titles: 85 Print
Parent Company: Calasanzian Fathers
Foreign Rep(s): A G Internacional (Chile); Ediciones Barcelona (Peru); Servicios Intergrales Calasanz (Mexico); Ediciones Libro Amigo (Peru); Libreria Studium (Ecuador)

ICEX, see Insdtuto Espanol de Comercio Exterior (ICEX)

Ideaspropias Editorial SL
Padre Sarmiento 19, Bajo, 36204 Vigo, Pontevedra
Tel: 902 100 938; 986 415 241
E-mail: comercial@ideaspropiaseditorial.com
Web Site: www.ideaspropiaseditorial.com
Key Personnel
Dir General: Pedro Lopez Gomez
Specialize in the development of educational material for training centers & departments.
Subjects: Business, Computer Science, Education, Health, Nutrition, Language Arts, Linguistics, Management, Marketing, Travel & Tourism, Manufacturing
ISBN Prefix(es): 978-84-96578; 978-84-934547; 978-84-934553; 978-84-934594; 978-84-934607

iermB, see Institut d'Estudis Regionals i Metropolitans de Barcelona

Imagen y Deporte SL+
Urbanizacion el Faro, 31, Marina del Este, 18697 La Herradura-Almunecar (Granada)
Tel: 958640891 *Fax:* 958640891
E-mail: imagenydeporte@imagenydeporte.com; internacional@imagenydeporte.com
Web Site: www.imagenydeporte.com
Key Personnel
International Operations: Carlos Torres
National Operations: Elisa de Pedro
Founded: 1988
Production & distribution company of physical education & sports related educational products & books.
Subjects: Education, Sports, Athletics
ISBN Prefix(es): 978-84-89117

Editorial Impedimenta SL
Benito Gutierrez, 8, 28008 Madrid
Tel: 916 091 542
Key Personnel
Editor: Enrique Redel *E-mail:* enriqueredel@impedimenta.es

Founded: 2007
Subjects: Fiction, Literature, Literary Criticism, Essays, Classical Literature, Modern Literature
ISBN Prefix(es): 978-84-15
Foreign Rep(s): Hueders SL (Chile); La Panoplia Export (Latin America exc Chile & Mexico); SP Distribuciones (Mexico)
Distribution Center: UDL Libros, C/ Belfast 15, Naves 3-4-5-6, Pol Ind Las Mercedes, 28022 Madrid *Tel:* 91 748 11 90 *Fax:* 91 329 25 85
E-mail: info@udllibros.com *Web Site:* www.udllibros.com

INAP, see Instituto Nacional de Administracion Publica (INAP)

INDE Editorial
Pl Sant Pere 4 bis, baixos 2º, 08003 Barcelona
Tel: 93 319 97 99 *Fax:* 93 319 09 54
E-mail: editorial@inde.com
Web Site: www.inde.com
Key Personnel
Editorial Dir: Nuria Domedel Matemales
Subjects: Education, Health, Nutrition, Sports, Athletics, Physical Education
ISBN Prefix(es): 978-84-9729; 978-84-87330; 978-84-95114
Foreign Rep(s): Alfaomega Colombiana SA (Colombia); Artemis Edinter (Guatemala); Biblo-Informatica 2000 (Puerto Rico); Editoriales La Ceiba (El Salvador); Ediciones Continente (Argentina); Edisa (Costa Rica); Edufisa Ltda (Costa Rica); Euroamericana de Ediciones (Venezuela); Gussi Libros (Uruguay); Hispamer (Nicaragua); Liberalia Ediciones Ltda (Chile); Grupo Libros & Editoriales (Mexico); Distribuidora Marin SA de CV (Mexico); Omniservicos (Portugal); Ediciones Tecnicas Paraguayas (Paraguay); V&D Peru (Peru)

Index Book
Arago, 174 16-3, 08011 Barcelona
Tel: 93 454 55 47 *Fax:* 93 454 84 38
Key Personnel
Dir General: Joan Antoni Canal
Founded: 1993
Subjects: Advertising, Architecture & Interior Design, Communications, Fashion, Marketing, Photography, Graphic Design, Interactive Design, Typography, Visual Communication
ISBN Prefix(es): 978-84-89994; 978-84-96309; 978-84-96774; 978-84-92643

INEF Madrid, see Facultad de Ciencias de la Actividad Fisica y del Deporte (INEF)

Innovacion y Cualificacion+
Poligono Industrial de Antequera, Avda El Romeral, 2, 29200 Antequera, Malaga
Tel: 952 706 004 *Fax:* 952 845 503
E-mail: innova@innovacionycualificacion.com
Web Site: www.innovacionycualificacion.com
Key Personnel
General Manager: Miguel Angel Sanchez Maza
Founded: 1985
Educational software, edition & printing.
Subjects: Computer Science, Education, Management
ISBN Prefix(es): 978-84-95733
Number of titles published annually: 10 Print; 8 CD-ROM
Total Titles: 200 Print; 60 CD-ROM
Parent Company: Grupo Antakira
Imprints: IC Editorial
Foreign Rep(s): CPI Ediciones (Mexico)

INSHT, see Instituto Nacional de Seguridad e Higiene en el Trabajo (INSHT)

Institucion Fernando el Catolico de la Excma Diputacion de Zaragoza
Plaza de Espana, 2, 50071 Zaragoza
Tel: 976 28 88 78; 976 28 88 79 *Fax:* 976 28 88 69
E-mail: ifc@dpz.es; infodpz@dpz.es
Web Site: ifc.dpz.es
Key Personnel
President: Luis Maria Beamonte Mesa
Founded: 1943
Subjects: Agriculture, Archaeology, Art, Geography, Geology, History, Law, Literature, Literary Criticism, Essays, Music, Dance
ISBN Prefix(es): 978-84-7820; 978-84-936442; 978-84-9911
Branch Office(s)
Centro de Estudios Borjanos, Casa de Aguilar, Borja
Centro de Estudios Bibilitanos, Puerta de Terrer, Calatayud
Grupo Cultural Caspolino, Palacio Barberan, 50700 Caspe
Centro de Estudios Darocenses, Puerta Baja, 50360 Daroca
Centro de Estudios Cinco Villas, Ramon y Caja, 17, 50600 Ejea Caballeros
Centro de Estudios Turiasonenses, Apdo 39, 50500 Tarazona

El Institute de Trabajo Social y de Servicios Sociales
Villarroel 45, entlo, 08011 Barcelona
Tel: 932 172 664 *Fax:* 932 373 634
E-mail: intressbar@intress.org
Web Site: www.intress.org
Key Personnel
Dir General: Edita Navarro
Founded: 1984
Subjects: Social Sciences, Sociology
ISBN Prefix(es): 978-84-87400
Branch Office(s)
Maria de Molina 64, 1ºB, 28006 Madrid
Tel: 915 621 050 *Fax:* 915 612 247
E-mail: intressmad@intress.org
La Rambla 15, 07003 Palma de Mallorca *Tel:* 971 715 029 *Fax:* 971 712 200 *E-mail:* intressib@intress.org

Instituto Alicantino de Cultura Juan Gil-Albert+
C/ San Fernando 44, Casa Bardin, 03001 Alicante
Tel: 965 121 214; 965 121 216 *Fax:* 965 921 824
E-mail: galbert@dip-alicante.es
Web Site: www.dip-alicante.es/gilalbert/pub/inicio.asp
Key Personnel
Chairwoman: Luisa Pastor Lillo
Dir: Jose Luis Vicente Ferris
Founded: 1983
Also acts as council for scientific research.
Subjects: Art, Poetry, Regional Interests, Social Sciences, Sociology
ISBN Prefix(es): 978-84-7784

Instituto de Estudios Altoaragoneses
C/ Parque, 10, 22002 Huesca
Tel: 974 294 120 *Fax:* 974 294 122
E-mail: iea@iea.es
Web Site: www.iea.es
Key Personnel
President: Antonio Cosculluela Bergua
Vice President: Elisa Sanjuan Castan
Founded: 1949
Subjects: Language Arts, Linguistics, Literature, Literary Criticism, Essays, Philosophy, Social Sciences, Sociology
ISBN Prefix(es): 978-84-8127; 978-84-86856

Instituto de Estudios Economicos (Institute for Economic Studies)
C/ Castello, 128, 6a Planta, 28006 Madrid
Tel: 91 782 05 80 *Fax:* 91 562 36 13

E-mail: iee@ieemadrid.com
Web Site: www.ieemadrid.es
Key Personnel
General Manager: Joaquin Trigo
Manager: Semur Almudena
Administrator: Jose Maria Goizueta
Editor: Jose Maria Perez de Tudela
Press Office: Erica Alonso
Publication: Pablo Hernandez
Founded: 1979
Subjects: Economics, Social Sciences, Sociology
ISBN Prefix(es): 978-84-85719; 978-84-88533

Instituto de Estudios Fiscales (Institute for
   Fiscal Studies)+
Avda Cardenal Herrera Oria, 378, 28035 Madrid
Tel: 91 339 88 00
E-mail: informacion.ief@ief.minhap.es
Web Site: www.ief.es
Key Personnel
Dir General: Jose Antonio Martinez Alvarez
   Tel: 91 339 89 14 *Fax:* 91 339 89 64
   E-mail: direccion.general@ief.minhap.es
Subjects: Accounting, Economics, Law, Public
   Administration
ISBN Prefix(es): 978-84-8008
Parent Company: Ministerio de Economia y Ha-
   cienda
Warehouse: Centro de Publicaciones del Min-
   isterio de Economia y Hacienda, Plaza del
   Campillo del Mundo Nuevo, 3, 28005 Madrid
Orders to: Centro de Publicaciones del Ministerio
   de Economia y Hacienda, Plaza del Campillo
   del Mundo Nuevo, 3, 28005 Madrid

Instituto de Estudios Riojanos
C/ Portales, nº 2, 26001 Logrono
Tel: 941 29 11 81; 941 29 11 87 (publication)
   Fax: 941 29 19 10
E-mail: ier@larioja.org; publicaciones.ier@larioja.
   org
Web Site: www.larioja.org/ier
Key Personnel
Dir: Jose Luis Perez Pastor
Founded: 1946
Membership(s): Confederacion Espanola de Cen-
   tros de Estudios Locales (CECEL).
Subjects: Archaeology, Art, Biological Sciences,
   Chemistry, Chemical Engineering, Earth Sci-
   ences, Geography, Geology, History, Language
   Arts, Linguistics, Literature, Literary Criticism,
   Essays, Mathematics, Physical Sciences, Re-
   gional Interests, Social Sciences, Sociology
ISBN Prefix(es): 978-84-87252; 978-84-89362;
   978-84-95747; 978-84-96637

**Instituto de la Mujer Ministerio de Sanidad,
   Servicios Sociales e Igualdad** (Institute of
   Women, Ministry of Health, Social Services &
   Equality)
C/ Condesa de Venadito, nº 34, 28027 Madrid
Tel: 900 191010; 91 452 86 59 *Fax:* 91 452 87
   86
E-mail: inmujer@inmujer.es
Web Site: www.inmujer.gob.es
Key Personnel
Dir General: Carmen Plaza Martin
Founded: 1983
Subjects: Education, Health, Nutrition, Discrimi-
   nation Against Women, Unemployment
ISBN Prefix(es): 978-84-7799

Instituto de las Identidades
Plaza de Colon, 4, 37001 Salamanca
SAN: 000-7951
Tel: 923 293 255
E-mail: ides@lasalina.es
Web Site: www.institutodelasidentidades.es
Key Personnel
Dir: Juan Francisco Blanco Gonzalez *Tel:* 923 29
   32 54 *E-mail:* pblanco@lasalina.es

Subjects: Regional Interests, Botany, Meteorology
ISBN Prefix(es): 978-84-87339

Instituto Juan de Herrera
Ave Juan de Herrera, No 4, Ciudad Universitaria,
   28040 Madrid
Tel: 913364251
E-mail: sedhc.es@gmail.com
Web Site: www.aq.upm.es/instituciones/jherrera/
   inicio.html
Subjects: Architecture & Interior Design
ISBN Prefix(es): 978-84-89977; 978-84-920297;
   978-84-95365; 978-84-9728

**Instituto Nacional de Administracion Publica
   (INAP)**
Calla Atocha, 106-1a planta, 28012 Madrid
Tel: 91 273 91 00 *Fax:* 91 273 92 87
E-mail: publicaciones@inap.es
Web Site: www.inap.es
Key Personnel
Dir: Manuel Arenilla Saez *Tel:* 91 273 91 47
   Fax: 91 273 91 60 *E-mail:* direccion@inap.es
Head, Dept of Publications: Guadalupe Herranz
   Escudero *Tel:* 91 273 92 11 *Fax:* 91 273 92 87
Subjects: Economics, Finance, Government, Po-
   litical Science, Law, Public Administration,
   Social Sciences, Sociology
ISBN Prefix(es): 978-84-7088; 978-84-7351

Instituto Nacional de Estadistica (National
   Institute of Statistics)
Paseo de la Castellana, 183, 28071 Madrid
Tel: 91 583 91 00; 91 583 94 38 (bookshop)
   Fax: 91 583 91 58; 91 583 45 65 (bookshop)
E-mail: indice@ine.es (bookshop)
Web Site: www.ine.es
Key Personnel
President: Gregorio Izquierdo Llanes
Specialize in statistical information of Spanish
   society.
Subjects: Agriculture, Economics, Finance, Sci-
   ence (General), Technology, Demography,
   Statistics
ISBN Prefix(es): 978-84-260
Distributed by Libreria Lines-Chiel; Mundi-
   Prensa Libros SA

**Instituto Nacional de Seguridad e Higiene en el
   Trabajo (INSHT)** (National Institute for Safety
   & Health at Work)
Servicios de Ediciones y Publicaciones, C/ Torre-
   laguna, 73, 28027 Madrid
SAN: 003-6668
Tel: 913 634 100 *Fax:* 913 634 327
E-mail: edicionesinsht@insht.meyss.es
Web Site: www.insht.es
Subjects: Labor, Industrial Relations, Industrial
   Security
ISBN Prefix(es): 978-84-7425
Parent Company: Ministerio de Trabajo e Immi-
   gracion

**Publicaciones del Instituto Provincial de
   Investigaciones y Estudios Toledanos
   (IPIET)+**
Plaza de la Merced, 4, 45002 Toledo
SAN: 003-536X
Tel: 925 259 442; 925 259 300 (ext 367)
   Fax: 925 259 404
E-mail: publicaciones@diputoledo.es
Web Site: www.diputoledo.es/publicaciones
Key Personnel
President: D Arturo Garcia-Tizon Lopez
Founded: 1963
Subjects: Archaeology, Art, Biological Sciences,
   Cookery, Drama, Theater, Ethnicity, Geogra-
   phy, Geology, History, Poetry, Social Sciences,
   Sociology
ISBN Prefix(es): 978-84-87103; 978-84-95432
Distributed by Pedro Alcantarilla (Spain)

Instituto Tecnologico de Galicia (ITG)
Poligono Industrial Pocomaco, Sector 1, Portal 5,
   15190 A Coruna
Tel: 981 173 206 *Fax:* 981 173 223
E-mail: itg@itg.es
Web Site: www.itg.es
Key Personnel
Manager: Carlos Bald Orosa
Founded: 1991
Subjects: Business, Energy, Management, Tech-
   nology
ISBN Prefix(es): 978-84-89473

Instituto Universitario Ortega y Gasset
C/ Fortuny, 53, 28010 Madrid
Tel: 91 700 4100 *Fax:* 91 700 3530
E-mail: comunicacion@fog.es
Web Site: www.ortegaygasset.edu
Subjects: Geography, Geology, History, Philoso-
   phy, Social Sciences, Sociology, Humanities
ISBN Prefix(es): 978-84-922562; 978-84-95048

Instituto Vasco de Criminologia
Elhuyar Plaza, 2, 20018 Donostia-San Sebastian
Tel: 943 017 484 *Fax:* 943 017 474
E-mail: ivac-krei@ehu.es
Web Site: www.sc.ehu.es/ivac; www.ivac.ehu.es
Founded: 1976
Subjects: Criminology, Human Rights
ISBN Prefix(es): 978-84-920328

Ediciones Internacionales Universitarias SA+
Travesia Doctor Fleming 16-2, 2º izqda, 28036
   Madrid
Tel: 91 577 5715
E-mail: teconte@edicionesteconte.com
Web Site: edicionesteconte.com
Founded: 1967
Subjects: Architecture & Interior Design, Biog-
   raphy, Memoirs, Communications, Economics,
   Education, Journalism, Language Arts, Lin-
   guistics, Literature, Literary Criticism, Essays,
   Nonfiction (General), Philosophy, Theology,
   Family
ISBN Prefix(es): 978-84-87155; 978-84-8469;
   978-84-89893; 978-84-87115
Branch Office(s)
Plaza de los Sauces, 1 y 2, 31010 Baranain,
   Navarra *Tel:* 948 256 850 *Fax:* 948 256 854
Foreign Rep(s): Atenas (Paraguay); Baker & Tay-
   lor (USA); Libreria Beityala (Mexico); Libre-
   ria Catolica Gethesemani (USA); Edisa (Costa
   Rica, Nicaragua); Equo (Peru); Gandhi (Mex-
   ico); Ediciones Iberoamericanas (Costa Rica,
   Nicaragua); Libreria Katholicos (Costa Rica,
   Nicaragua); Liberalia (Chile); Libros La Ceiba
   (El Salvador); Limerin (Ecuador); Libreria
   Loyola (Guatemala); Manantial (Brazil); Mi-
   nos Tercer Milenio (Mexico); Nueva Libre-
   ria Parroquial (Mexico); Paoline Multimedia
   (Italy); Libreria Papiros (Ecuador); Libreria
   Parroquial (Mexico); Paulinas (Brazil, Colom-
   bia, Dominican Republic, Ecuador, Paraguay,
   Peru, Puerto Rico, Venezuela); Libreria PROA
   (Chile); Procodes (Colombia); Quadrante
   (Brazil); Libreria San Cristobal (Peru); San
   Pablo (Colombia, Venezuela); Libreria San
   Pablo (Bolivia); Soluciones Bibliograficas
   (Mexico); Libreria Sorgente (Italy); Urbaniana
   (Italy); USA Madrid (Puerto Rico, USA); V&D
   Distribuidores (Peru); Verbo Divino (Colom-
   bia); J Waldhuter Ediciones (Argentina)

INTRESS, see El Institute de Trabajo Social y de
   Servicios Sociales

IPIET, see Publicaciones del Instituto Provincial
   de Investigaciones y Estudios Toledanos
   (IPIET)

Ir Indo Edicions SA
Ave Florida, 30, 36210 Vigo

Tel: 986 21 12 12 *Fax:* 986 21 11 33
E-mail: administracion@irindo.com
Web Site: www.irindo.com
Key Personnel
Dir: Bieito Ledo
Founded: 1985
Subjects: Biography, Memoirs, Government, Political Science, History, Religion - Catholic
ISBN Prefix(es): 978-84-7680

Editorial Iralka SL+
c/ Ametzagana, 21-Local 10, 20012 Donostia-San Sebastian
Tel: 943 32 30 14
E-mail: iralka@euskalnet.net
Web Site: www.euskalnet.net/iralka
Key Personnel
Editor & Publisher: Manu Muner Sorazu
Founded: 1993
Subjects: Anthropology, Literature, Literary Criticism, Essays, Philosophy, Poetry, Social Sciences, Sociology, Humanities
ISBN Prefix(es): 978-84-89806; 978-84-920202; 978-84-920963
Number of titles published annually: 5 Print
Total Titles: 50 Print
Distribution Center: Puvill Libros SA, Estany, 13-17 Nave D-1, 08038 Barcelona *Tel:* 93 298 89 60 *Fax:* 93 298 89 61 *E-mail:* info@puvill. com *Web Site:* www.puvill.com
Virus Editorial, c/ Aurora, 23, bajos, 08001 Barcelona *Tel:* 93 441 38 14 *E-mail:* virus@ pangea.org (Catalonia)
Bitarte, Pol Berriaiz Calle B, nave 44, 31195 Berriozar, Navarra *Tel:* 948 30 22 39 (Basque Country)

IRIF, see Grao Editorial

Editorial Iru SL+
C/ Roger de Flor, 91, 08013 Barcelona
Tel: 932 318032 *Fax:* 932 653670
Founded: 1982
Subjects: Cookery, Humor
ISBN Prefix(es): 978-84-8065; 978-84-86819

Ediciones Istmo SA+
Imprint of Akal Grupo Editorial
Sector Foresta nº 1, 28760 Tres Contos, Madrid
SAN: 001-7817
Tel: 918 061 996 *Fax:* 918 044 028
E-mail: pedidos.blume@akal.com; edicion@akal. com; universidad@akal.com; educacion@akal. com; prensa@akal.com; atencion.cliente@akal. com
Web Site: www.akal.com
Founded: 1966
Subjects: Anthropology, Art, History, Language Arts, Linguistics, Literature, Literary Criticism, Essays, Philosophy, Social Sciences, Sociology
ISBN Prefix(es): 978-84-7090
Associate Companies: Ediciones Akal SA; Foca; H Blume; Siglo XXI de Espana

ITG, see Instituto Tecnologico de Galicia (ITG)

Biografia Joven, *imprint of* Editorial Casals SA

Junta de Castilla y Leon Consejeria de Cultura y Turismo
Monasterio de Prado, Avda del Monasterio de Nuestra Senora de Prado, s/n, 47071 Valladolid
Web Site: www.jcyl.es
Founded: 1983
Subjects: Archaeology, Art, Biography, Memoirs, History, Literature, Literary Criticism, Essays, Poetry, Regional Interests, Science (General), Travel & Tourism
ISBN Prefix(es): 978-84-7846; 978-84-9718; 978-84-87884

Distribution Center: Lidiza, Avda de Soria, 15, 47193 La Cisterniga (Vallodolid) *Tel:* 983 40 30 60 *Fax:* 983 40 30 70
Latorre Literaria SA, Camino Boca Alta, Poligono Ind El Mavar Naves 8 y 9, 28500 Arganda del Rey (Madrid) *Tel:* 91 871 93 79; 91 871 93 72 *Fax:* 91 871 94 08

Editorial Juventud SA (Youth Publishing)+
C/ Provenca, 101, 08029 Barcelona
Tel: 93 444 18 00 *Fax:* 93 439 83 83
E-mail: info@editorialjuventud.es
Web Site: www.editorialjuventud.es
Key Personnel
Dir General: Luis Zendrera Duniau
Founded: 1923
Subjects: Accounting, Aeronautics, Aviation, Animals, Pets, Architecture & Interior Design, Art, Biography, Memoirs, Fiction, History, Language Arts, Linguistics, Sports, Athletics, Travel & Tourism
ISBN Prefix(es): 978-84-261
Associate Companies: Editorial Juventud SA de CV, Herodoto, 42 Col Anzures, 11590 Mexico, DF, Mexico *Tel:* (0155) 52 03 97 49 *E-mail:* juventud@editorialjuventud.com.mx *Web Site:* www.editorialjuventud.com.mx
Subsidiaries: Editorial Juventud de Espana Ltd
Distributor for Editorial Corimbo; Editorial Parsifal
Foreign Rep(s): Alianza Distribuidora de Colombia Ltda (Colombia); America Latina Ltda (Uruguay); Aparicio Distributors Inc (Puerto Rico); Ediciones Continente SRL (Argentina); Desarrollos Culturales Costarricenses DCC SA (Costa Rica); J Garraio & Ca Lda (Portugal); Editorial Juventud SA de CV (Mexico); Lectorum Publications Inc (USA); Liberalia Ediciones Ltda (Chile); V&D Distribuidores SA (Peru)

Kailas Editorial
C/ Tutor 51 7, 28008 Madrid
Tel: 911400740 *Fax:* 911309883
Web Site: www.kailas.es
Key Personnel
General Coordinator: Marta Alonso Dorrego *E-mail:* martaalonso@kailas.es
Communications Coordinator: Cristina Fernandez Fermoselle *E-mail:* cristina@kailas.es
Editor: Angel Fernandez Fermoselle *E-mail:* angel@kailas.es
Subjects: Fiction, Literature, Literary Criticism, Essays, Nonfiction (General)
ISBN Prefix(es): 978-84-934491

Editorial Kairos SA+
C/ Numancia, 117-121, 08029 Barcelona
Tel: 93 494 94 90 *Fax:* 93 410 51 66
E-mail: info@editorialkairos.com
Web Site: www.editorialkairos.com
Key Personnel
Dir & Editorial: Agustin Paniker
Administration: Meritxel Ferrer; Patricia Malagarriga
Copyright: Anna Ayesta
Production: Isabel Asensio
Founded: 1964
Publishes a growing range of new consciousness titles.
Subjects: Philosophy, Psychology, Psychiatry, Religion - Other, Social Sciences, Sociology
ISBN Prefix(es): 978-84-7245
Foreign Rep(s): Centro Cuesta Nacional (Dominican Republic); Ediciones Continente (Argentina); Dellare (Guatemala); Desarrollos Culturales Costarricenses DCCSA-Libreria Internacional (Costa Rica); Libros Gussi (Uruguay); IPG Independent Publishers Group (USA); Distribuciones Mediterraneo SAC (Peru); Mr Books (Ecuador); Nirvana Libros (Mexico); Ediciones Urano (Chile, Colombia)

Kalandraka Editora
C/ Pastor Diaz 1, 4º A, 36001 Pontevedra
Tel: 986 86 02 76 *Fax:* 986 10 02 80
E-mail: editora@kalandraka.com
Web Site: www.kalandraka.com
Key Personnel
Dir General: Xose Ballesteros
Subjects: Art, Fiction, Literature, Literary Criticism, Essays
ISBN Prefix(es): 978-84-96388; 978-84-933755; 978-84-933759; 978-84-933780
Branch Office(s)
Kalandraka Cataluna, C/ Guillem Tell, 27-piso 1º-despacho 1, 08006 Barcelona *Tel:* 932 189 877 *E-mail:* catalunya@kalandraka.com
Espacio Kalandraka, C/ Santa Maria (Barrio de las Letras), 16-bajo dcha, 28014 Madrid *Tel:* 915 330 028 *E-mail:* espacio@kalandraka. com
Kalandraka Andalucia, C/ Avion Cuatro Vientos, 7-bajo, 41013 Seville *Tel:* 954 095 558; 607 688 620 (cell) *E-mail:* andalucia@kalandraka. com
Kalandraka Italia, Piazzale Donatello, 29, 50132 Florence FI, Italy *Tel:* (055) 38 40 340 *E-mail:* info@kalandraka.it *Web Site:* www. kalandraka.it
Kalandraka Mexico, Libros para sonar, Camino a la Hacienda Grande Nº 14, Colonia Hacienda Grande, 76799 Tequisquiapan, Queretaro, Mexico *E-mail:* lpsmexico@kalandraka.com
Kalandraka Portugal, Rua Alfredo Cunha, 37, Sala 34, 4450-023 Matosinhos, Portugal *Tel:* 229 375 718; 961 954 396 (cell) *E-mail:* editora@kalandraka.pt *Web Site:* www. kalandraka.pt
Foreign Rep(s): Aparicio Distributors Inc (Puerto Rico); Baker & Taylor (USA); The Bilingual Publications Company (USA); Brodart Co (USA); Celesa (Europe); Doukeisha Co Ltd (Japan); Ediciones Iamique (Argentina); Lectorum Publications Inc (USA); Let's Read in Spanish! (USA); Liberalia Ediciones Ltda (Chile); Ediciones Monserrate Ltda (Colombia); Pujol & Amado SLL (Latin America exc Argentina, Chile, Colombia, Mexico & Puerto Rico); Ediciones Tecolote (Mexico)

Kaleidoskop, *imprint of* Editorial Alhulia SA

Editorial Kokinos
Sagasta 30, 28004 Madrid
Tel: 915934204 *Fax:* 915934204
E-mail: cuentanos@editorialkokinos.com; editorial@editorialkokinos.com
Web Site: www.editorialkokinos.com
Key Personnel
Contact: Eva Domenech Martin
Founded: 1992
Subjects: Literature, Literary Criticism, Essays
ISBN Prefix(es): 978-84-88342; 978-84-96629
Foreign Rep(s): Aparicio Distributors Inc (Puerto Rico); Calibroscopio Ediciones y el Libro de Arena (Argentina); Centro Cuesta Nacional (Dominican Republic); El Hombre de La Mancha (Panama); El Hormiguero 20 (Guatemala); Libreria Internacional (Costa Rica); Lectorum Publications Inc (USA); Liberalia (Chile); Libros de la Arena (Uruguay); Litexa Boliviana (Bolivia); Losa Libros Ltda (Uruguay); Mosca Hnos (Ecuador); Mr Books (Ecuador); Editorial Plaza & Janes (Colombia); Sophos (Guatemala); V & D Distribuidores SA (Peru); Libreria El Virrey (Peru)
Distribution Center: IPG Spanish Language

Ediciones La Salle+
C/ Marques de Mondejar, 32, 28028 Madrid
SAN: 001-9720
Tel: 917 262 817 *Fax:* 913 552 727
E-mail: ediciones@lasalle.es
Web Site: www.lasalleediciones.es

Key Personnel
Dir: Joaquin Gasca
Founded: 1967
Subjects: Biblical Studies, Education, Philosophy, Religion - Catholic, Social Sciences, Sociology, Theology
ISBN Prefix(es): 978-84-7221
Number of titles published annually: 25 Print
Total Titles: 315 Print

Labutxaca, *imprint of* grup62

Editorial Laertes+
C/ Virtut nº 8 bajos, 08012 Barcelona
Tel: 93 218 70 20; 93 218 55 58 *Fax:* 93 217 47 51
E-mail: laertes@laertes.es
Web Site: laertes.es
Key Personnel
Mng Dir & Editorial: Eduardo Suarez Alonso
Sales & Publicity: Carmen Miret
Founded: 1975
Subjects: Anthropology, Archaeology, Biography, Memoirs, Education, Fiction, Film, Video, LGBTQ, Literature, Literary Criticism, Essays, Medicine, Nursing, Dentistry, Philosophy, Travel & Tourism, Pedagogy
ISBN Prefix(es): 978-84-85346; 978-84-7584
Total Titles: 525 Print
Foreign Rep(s): Ediciones de Aguazul (Argentina); Libreria America Latina (Uruguay); Clasicos Roxsil (El Salvador); Editorial Juventud (Mexico); Livraria Leonardo da Vinci (Brazil); Liberalia Ediciones Ltda (Chile); LibriMundi (Ecuador); Papiros (Ecuador); Plaza y Janes Editores Colombia SA (Colombia); Libreria Prosa & Politica (Chile); Melanio Rosas Cueva (Peru); Unilibros (Dominican Republic)

Edicions Laiovento SL+
Rua do Horreo, 60, Apdo 1 072, 15072 Santiago de Compostela, Galiza, UE
Tel: 981 887 570 *Fax:* 981 572 239
E-mail: laiovento@laiovento.com
Web Site: www.laiovento.com
Key Personnel
President: Afonso Ribas Fraga
Founded: 1989
Subjects: Drama, Theater, Economics, Education, History, Literature, Literary Criticism, Essays, Poetry, Science (General), Science Fiction, Fantasy, Social Sciences, Sociology, Technology, Humanities
ISBN Prefix(es): 978-84-87847; 978-84-89896
Imprints: Lengua Gallega Y Portuguesa
Distributor for Ninguna

Larousse Editorial SL+
C/ Mallorca 45, 3a planta, 08029 Barcelona
Tel: 93 241 35 05 *Fax:* 93 241 35 11
E-mail: larousse@larousse.es
Web Site: www.larousse.es
Key Personnel
Communications Manager: Eva Zamora
E-mail: ezamora@larousse.es
Foreign Rights: Esther Franch *Fax:* 93 241 35 07
E-mail: esther.franch@larousse.es
Founded: 1852
ISBN Prefix(es): 978-84-8016
Parent Company: Grupo Anaya
Subsidiaries: Grandes De La Cite International

Las Ediciones de Arte, see LEDA (Las Ediciones de Arte)

Lectio Ediciones
Calle de la Violeta, 6, 43800 Valls
Tel: 977602591 *Fax:* 977604357
E-mail: lectio@lectio.es
Web Site: www.lectio.es

Key Personnel
Communications: Raquel Estrada
E-mail: restrada@cossetania.com
Administration: Emma Alcazar *E-mail:* ealcazar@cossetania.com
Foreign Rights: Judit Juncosa *E-mail:* jjuncosa@cossetania.com
Founded: 2006
Subjects: Cookery, Health, Nutrition, Sports, Athletics
ISBN Prefix(es): 978-84-16012; 978-84-96757; 978-84-15088
Number of titles published annually: 30 Print
Parent Company: N9u Grup Editorial
Foreign Rep(s): Editorial Catalonia Ltda (Chile); La Familia Distribuidora de Libros SA (Peru); Fondo Cultural Iberoamericano (Colombia); Libros Gussi (Uruguay); Independent Publishers Group (USA); El Libro Cia Ltda (Ecuador); Distribuidora Marin SA de CV (Mexico)

Lecturanda62, *imprint of* grup62

LEDA (Las Ediciones de Arte)+
Riera de Sant Miguel, 37, 08006 Barcelona
Tel: 932 379 389 *Fax:* 932 155 273
Founded: 1942
Subjects: Advertising, Architecture & Interior Design, Art, Child Care & Development, Crafts, Games, Hobbies
ISBN Prefix(es): 978-84-7095

Legua Editorial SL
Paseo de los Melancolicos, 28036 Madrid
E-mail: comunicacion@leguaeditorial.es
Web Site: leguaeditorial.com
ISBN Prefix(es): 978-84-93858; 978-84-93884

Lengua de Trapo
Calle del Acuerdo, 20, 28015 Madrid
Tel: 915210813 *Fax:* 9153226777
E-mail: ldt@lenguadetrapo.com
Web Site: www.lenguadetrapo.com; twitter.com/lenguadetrapo?lang=en
Founded: 1995
ISBN Prefix(es): 978-84-8381; 978-84-96080; 978-84-89618

Lengua Gallega Y Portuguesa, *imprint of* Edicions Laiovento SL

Ediciones Leonesas SA+
Camino Cuesta Luzar, nº 37, 24010 Leon
SAN: 001-8198
Tel: 987800905 *Fax:* 987840028
E-mail: edilesa@edilesa.es
Web Site: www.edilesa.es
Key Personnel
Dir: Jesus Vicente Pastor Benavides
Founded: 1981
Subjects: Architecture & Interior Design, Art, Cookery, Literature, Literary Criticism, Essays, Photography, Travel & Tourism
ISBN Prefix(es): 978-84-8012; 978-84-86013
Distributor for Fundacion Hullera Vasco-Leonesa
Book Club(s): Club Bibliofilo Leones

Letras Mayusculas, *imprint of* Editorial Casals SA

Grupo Lettera
Poligono Industrial La Red Norte, C/ 6, parcela 54, nave 13, 41500 Seville
Tel: 954 424 300 *Fax:* 954 424 300
E-mail: lettera@letteranet.com
Web Site: www.letteranet.com
Key Personnel
President: Joaquin Fernandez Cepedello
Founded: 1989

Subjects: Equine (horses)
ISBN Prefix(es): 978-84-931896; 978-84-96060

Liber Ediciones SA
Av Zaragoza, 45, 31005 Pamplona
Tel: 948 177 488 *Fax:* 948 176 667
E-mail: info@liberediciones.com
Web Site: www.liberediciones.com
Founded: 1989
Subjects: Art
ISBN Prefix(es): 978-84-89339

Ediciones Libertarias+
C Carpinteros, 5 - Nave 13, 28200 San Lorenzo de El Escorial (Madrid)
Tel: 91 890 46 10 *Fax:* 91 890 46 10
E-mail: libertarias@libertarias.com
Web Site: www.libertarias.com
Key Personnel
Publisher: Carmelo Martinez Garcia
Communication Dir: Annamaria Duran
Founded: 1979
Subjects: Cookery, Government, Political Science, Health, Nutrition, History, Literature, Literary Criticism, Essays, Poetry, Psychology, Psychiatry, Science Fiction, Fantasy, Social Sciences, Sociology
ISBN Prefix(es): 978-84-7954; 978-84-87095; 978-84-85641; 978-84-7683; 978-84-86943
Distributed by Conty SA de CV (Central America); Libertarias Prodhufi, SA

Libros Cupula, *imprint of* Ediciones CEAC

Libsa, *imprint of* Editorial Libsa SA

Editorial Libsa SA+
C/ San Rafael, 4, 28108 Alcobendas, Madrid
Tel: 916 572 580 *Fax:* 916 572 583
E-mail: libsa@libsa.es
Web Site: www.libsa.es
Key Personnel
President: Amado Sanchez *E-mail:* asanchez@libsa.es
Sales Dir: Emilio Mata *E-mail:* emata@libsa.es
Foreign Rights Executive: Alberto Boix
E-mail: aboix@libsa.es
Foreign Rights Manager: Francisco Saavedra
E-mail: fsaavedra@libsa.es
Founded: 1980
Publisher of children/adult lists, leisure & practical guides.
Subjects: Art, Cookery, Crafts, Games, Hobbies, Gardening, Plants, Health, Nutrition, History, House & Home, Language Arts, Linguistics, Literature, Literary Criticism, Essays, Nonfiction (General), Photography, Self-Help
ISBN Prefix(es): 978-84-7630; 978-84-662
Imprints: Agata; Alba; Libsa

LID Editorial Empresarial (LID Business Publisher)+
Musgo 3, 28023 Madrid
SAN: 004-010X
Tel: 91 372 90 03
E-mail: info@lideditorial.com
Web Site: www.lideditorial.com
Key Personnel
President: Marcelino Elosua de Juan
E-mail: marcelino.elosua@lideditorial.com
Founded: 1993
Also publishes specialized business dictionaries.
Membership(s): Gremio de Editores de Madrid.
Subjects: Biography, Memoirs, Business, Career Development, Economics, Finance, Language Arts, Linguistics, Marketing, Self-Help, Spanish Business History
ISBN Prefix(es): 978-84-88717; 978-84-8356
Number of titles published annually: 12 Print; 1 CD-ROM
Total Titles: 50 Print; 2 CD-ROM

Branch Office(s)
Roger de Lluria 118, 08037 Barcelona *Tel:* 93
252 14 01 *E-mail:* info@lideditorial.com
LID Editorial Mexicana, Homero 109, Despa-
cho 1405, Col Chapultec Morales, 11570
Mexico, DF, Mexico *Tel:* (0155) 5255 4883
E-mail: info@lideditorial.com.mx
LID Editorial Mexicana, Zaragoza 345A, San Pe-
dro Garzagarcia, 66230 Nuevo Leon, Mexico
Tel: (081) 8336 6834 *E-mail:* info@lideditorial.
com.mx
LID Publishing Ltd, 6-8 Underwood St, Reino
Unido, London N1 7JQ, United King-
dom *Tel:* (020) 8374 0719 *E-mail:* lid@
lidpublishing.com
U.S. Office(s): LID Publishing Inc, 37 E 18 St,
8th floor, New York, NY 10003, United States
Tel: 646-957-3767 *E-mail:* info@lidpublishing.
com
Distribution Center: LOGISTA (Spain)

La Liebre de Marzo
Arizala 1, entresuelo 1a, 08028 Barcelona
Tel: 934 485 605 *Fax:* 934 498 070
E-mail: info@liebremarzo.com
Web Site: www.liebremarzo.com
Subjects: Inspirational, Spirituality, Religion -
Buddhist, Chinese Medicine, Psychotherapy,
Shamanism, Tai Chi, Yoga, Zen
ISBN Prefix(es): 978-84-87403
Foreign Rep(s): Distribuciones Continente (Ar-
gentina); Karma Libros (Chile); El Libro Uni-
versal (Colombia); Nirvana Libros SA de CV
(Mexico)

Links Books
Jonqueres No 10, 1-5, 08003 Barcelona
Tel: 93 301 21 99 *Fax:* 93 301 00 21
E-mail: info@linksbooks.net
Web Site: www.linksbooks.net
Subjects: Architecture & Interior Design, Graphic
Design, Landscape
ISBN Prefix(es): 978-84-96969; 978-84-921606;
978-84-89861; 978-84-96263; 978-84-96424;
978-84-15123; 978-84-92796
Foreign Rep(s): Continental Sales Inc (USA)

Llibres del Segle+
Pujada de la Torrassa, 2, 17007 Girona
Tel: 616661011; 659497063
Web Site: www.llibresdelsegle.com
Key Personnel
Management: Marta Costa-Paz *E-mail:* martacp@
llibresdelsegle.com
Founded: 1995
Subjects: Art, Education, History, Literature, Lit-
erary Criticism, Essays, Nonfiction (General),
Poetry, Social Sciences, Sociology
ISBN Prefix(es): 978-84-89885; 978-84-920952;
978-84-8128
Total Titles: 12 Print
Distributor for L'Arc de Bera

Loft Publications SL
Via Laietana nº 32, piso 4, of 92, 08003
Barcelona
Tel: 93 268 80 88 *Fax:* 93 268 70 73
E-mail: loft@loftpublications.com
Web Site: www.loftpublications.com
Founded: 1997
Subjects: Architecture & Interior Design, Com-
mercial Spaces, Houses, Lifestyle
ISBN Prefix(es): 978-84-931598; 978-84-95832;
978-84-96936; 978-84-92731; 978-84-9936

Loguez Ediciones+
Carretera de Madrid, nº 128, 37900 Santa Marta
de Tormes (Salamanca)
SAN: 003-8849
Tel: 923 138 541 *Fax:* 923 138 586
E-mail: loguez@loguezediciones.com

Web Site: www.loguezediciones.es
Key Personnel
Foreign Rights: Mabel Garcia *E-mail:* mabelgm@
loguezediciones.com
Founded: 1977
Specialize in children's literature & musical
books.
Subjects: Art, Earth Sciences, Education, Fiction,
LGBTQ, Literature, Literary Criticism, Essays,
Music, Dance, Religion - Catholic, Religion -
Other, Self-Help, Theology
ISBN Prefix(es): 978-84-85334; 978-84-89804;
978-84-96646
Number of titles published annually: 12 Print; 3
CD-ROM
Distributed by America Latina (Uruguay); Apari-
cio Distributors (Puerto Rico); Librerias
Artemis Edinter SA (Guatemala); Calibro-
scopio Ediciones (Argentina); Colofon SA de
CV (Mexico); EDISA (Costa Rica); El Hom-
bre de la Mancha (Panama); Lectorum Publi-
cations Inc (USA); Liberalia Ediciones Ltda
(Chile); Plaza y Janes Editores de Colombia
SA (Colombia)
Foreign Rep(s): Aparicio Distributors (Puerto
Rico)

Ediciones Luciernaga, *imprint of* grup62

Ediciones Luciernaga
Imprint of grup62
Diagonal, 662, 08034 Barcelona
Tel: 93 443 71 00 *Fax:* 93 443 71 30
E-mail: info@edicionesluciernaga.com
Web Site: www.planetadelibros.com/editorial-
edicions-luciernaga-72.html
Key Personnel
Foreign Rights Manager: Daniel Cladera *Tel:* 93
492 80 08 *E-mail:* dcladera@planeta.es
Founded: 1988
Specialize in books on spirituality & personal
growth.
Subjects: Health, Nutrition, Inspirational, Spiritu-
ality, Self-Help
ISBN Prefix(es): 978-84-87232; 978-84-89957
Distributed by Edoca SA (Guatemala); Edi-
ciones Oceano Argentina (Argentina); Edi-
ciones Oceano Boliviana SL (Bolivia); Edi-
ciones Oceano de Chile SA (Chile); Edi-
ciones Oceano de Colombia SA (Colombia);
Ediciones Oceano de Costa Rica SA (Costa
Rica); Editorial Oceano de Mexico SA de CV
(Mexico); Ediciones Oceano de Panama SA
(Panama); Ediciones Oceano de Paraguay SA
(Paraguay); Editorial Oceano de Venezuela SA
(Venezuela); Editorial Oceano del Uruguay SA
(Uruguay); Editorial Oceano Ecuatoriana SA
(Ecuador); Editorial Oceano Peruana SA (Peru-
ana)
Distribution Center: Enlaces Editoriales, Ram-
bla de Catalunya, 135, 3a planta, 08008
Barcelona *Tel:* 93 218 50 20 *Fax:* 93 218 55
30 *E-mail:* enlaces@enlaceseditoriales.com

Lumen, *imprint of* Penguin Random House
Grupo Editorial

Lumen+
Imprint of Penguin Random House Grupo Edito-
rial
Travessera de Gracia 47-49, 08021 Barcelona
Tel: 93 366 03 00 *Fax:* 93 366 04 49
Web Site: penguinrandomhousegrupoeditorial.com
Founded: 1960
Subjects: Art, Fiction, Humor, Literature, Liter-
ary Criticism, Essays, Poetry, Social Sciences,
Sociology
ISBN Prefix(es): 978-84-264

Lumen Infantil, *imprint of* Penguin Random
House Grupo Editorial

Lunwerg Editores SA+
Member of Grupo Planeta
Beethoven, 12, 08021 Barcelona
SAN: 004-072X
Tel: 93 201 59 33 *Fax:* 93 201 15 87
E-mail: lunwerg@lunwerg.com
Web Site: www.planetadelibros.com/editorial-
lunwerg-editores-31.html
Key Personnel
Press: Lola Escudero *Tel:* 91 423 37 11
E-mail: lescudero@planeta.es
Founded: 1979
Subjects: Archaeology, Architecture & Interior
Design, Art, Cookery, Drama, Theater, History,
Maritime, Photography, Transportation, Travel
& Tourism, Wine & Spirits
ISBN Prefix(es): 978-84-7782; 978-84-85983;
978-84-9785
Number of titles published annually: 60 Print

Lynx Edicions+
Montseny, 8, 08193 Bellaterra, Barcelona
Tel: 93 594 77 10 *Fax:* 93 592 09 69
E-mail: lynx@hbw.com
Web Site: www.lynxeds.com
Key Personnel
Contact: Elisa Badia *E-mail:* ebadia@hbw.com
Founded: 1989
Specialize in ornithology & natural history books.
Subjects: Biological Sciences, Natural History,
Ornithology
ISBN Prefix(es): 978-84-87334; 978-84-96553
U.S. Office(s): c/o Postal Express & Fulfillment
Center Inc, 265 Sunrise Highway, Suite 1,
No 252, Rockville Centre, NY 11570, United
States

Ma Non Troppo, *imprint of* Ediciones
Robinbook SL

Libreria Antonio Machado
C/ Marques de Casa Riera, 2, 28014 Madrid
Tel: 915 237 066; 913 190 594
E-mail: web@machadolibros.com; libreria@
machadolibros.com
Web Site: www.machadolibros.com
Founded: 1971
Publisher of books, magazines, journals & news-
papers.
Subjects: Architecture & Interior Design, Art,
Drama, Theater, Education, Government, Po-
litical Science, History, Language Arts, Lin-
guistics, Literature, Literary Criticism, Essays,
Music, Dance, Philosophy, Psychology, Psy-
chiatry, Publishing & Book Trade Reference,
Regional Interests, Self-Help, Social Sciences,
Sociology, Cultural History, Performing Arts
ISBN Prefix(es): 978-84-7644

Macmillan ELT (English Language Teaching)
Muguet, 6-4º C, 28044 Madrid
Tel: 915 17 85 40 *Fax:* 915 17 85 54
E-mail: madrid@macmillan.es
Web Site: www.macmillanelt.es
Founded: 1987
Specialize in the publication of core curriculum
texts for primary, junior secondary school &
senior secondary school.
Subjects: Education, Language Arts, Linguistics,
English Language Teaching
ISBN Prefix(es): 978-1-4050; 978-0-333
Parent Company: Macmillan Education Ltd
Ultimate Parent Company: Macmillan Publishers
Ltd
Branch Office(s)
Jose Luis Bugallal Marchesi, 20-1º dcha, 15008
A Coruna *Tel:* 981 20 89 87 *Fax:* 981 21 12 30
E-mail: coruna@macmillan.es
Silla del Rey, nº 4-2º P, 33013 Oviedo, As-
turias *Tel:* 985 24 59 21 *Fax:* 985 27 64 85
E-mail: asturias@macmillan.es

Valencia, 307-3r, 2a, 08009 Barcelona
Tel: 932 41 33 01 *Fax:* 932 09 99 49
E-mail: barcelona@macmillan.es
Simon Bolivar, 27 Dpto 12, 48013 Bilbao
Tel: 944 27 13 14 *Fax:* 944 41 92 70
E-mail: bilbao@macmillan.es
Hoya de la Mora, 11-Local 9, 18008 Granada
Tel: 958 22 04 30 *Fax:* 958 22 01 10
E-mail: granada@macmillan.es
Betania, 25 Local, Lomo los Frailes, 35018
Las Palmas de Gran Canaria *Tel:* 928 43 34
93 *Fax:* 928 37 17 66 *E-mail:* canarias@
macmillan.es
Kandinsky, 10-bloque 3, 1° B, Edificio Ala-
zor, 29010 Malaga *Tel:* 952 30 95 30
E-mail: malaga@macmillan.es
Salitre 35-1° F, 30150 La Alberca, Mur-
cia *Tel:* 968 84 69 84 *Fax:* 968 84 69 69
E-mail: murcia@macmillan.es
Son Oliva, 10 baixos, 07004 Palma de Mal-
lorca *Tel:* 971 75 82 73 *Fax:* 971 76 00 44
E-mail: illesbalears@macmillan.es
Avda Hytasa, 36-Edificio Toledo II, 4a planta,
mods 2, 3 y 4, 41006 Seville *Tel:* 954 28 04 00
Fax: 954 28 46 03 *E-mail:* sevilla@macmillan.
es
Avda Tamarindos, 21-pta 1a Of 7, Edificio
Vaymer III, 46015 Valencia *Tel:* 963 41 27
33 *Fax:* 963 41 72 79 *E-mail:* valencia@
macmillan.es
Paseo de Sagasta 32-38, Esc 2a, 1° F, 50006
Zaragoza *Tel:* 976 20 42 17 *Fax:* 976 39 17
98 *E-mail:* zaragoza@macmillan.es

Editorial MAD+
Plg Empresarial Merka C/ Merka Cuatro, naves
1-15, 41500 Alcala de Guadaira, Seville
Mailing Address: Apdo 8910, 41080 Seville
Tel: 902 452 900; 955 635 900 *Fax:* 955 630 713
E-mail: infomad@mad.es; marketing@mad.es
Web Site: www.mad.es
Key Personnel
General Dir: Narciso Sanchez-Valdenaura
Founded: 1983
Subjects: Business, Education, Health, Nutrition,
Law
ISBN Prefix(es): 978-84-86526; 978-84-665; 978-
84-8311; 978-84-88834; 978-84-89464

Madrasa Editorial+
Mezquita Mayor de Granada, Plaza de San Nico-
las s/n, 18010 Granada
Tel: 958202526; 958202331 *Fax:* 958296195
E-mail: info@madrasaeditorial.com
Web Site: www.madrasaeditorial.com
Founded: 2008
Islamic classical books published in Spanish lan-
guage.
This publisher has indicated that 50% of their
product line is author subsidized.
Membership(s): Agency of Publications of the
Islamic Community in Spain.
Subjects: Biography, Memoirs, History, Inspira-
tional, Spirituality, Law, Religion - Islamic
ISBN Prefix(es): 978-84-85973; 978-84-93051
(Kutubia)
Number of titles published annually: 5 Print; 1 E-
Book
Total Titles: 50 Print; 5 E-Book

Ediciones Maeva+
Benito de Castro, 6, 28028 Madrid
Tel: 91 355 95 69 *Fax:* 91 355 19 47
E-mail: emaeva@maeva.es
Web Site: www.maeva.es
Key Personnel
Publisher: Maite Cuadros
Founded: 1985
Subjects: Anthropology, Biography, Memoirs,
Fiction, Foreign Countries, History, Literature,
Literary Criticism, Essays, Nonfiction (Gen-

eral), Regional Interests, Travel & Tourism,
Crime Fiction, Family Sagas, Historial Fiction
ISBN Prefix(es): 978-84-86478; 978-84-95354;
978-84-15120; 978-84-92695; 978-84-96231;
978-84-96748
Imprints: Catalogo
Subsidiaries: Editoriales Exclusivas
Distributed by Ediciones Oceano (Argentina,
Chile, Colombia, Costa Rica, Guatemala,
Ecuador, Mexico, Panama, Paraguay, Peru,
Uruguay, Venezuela)
Orders to: SGEL, c/o Avda Valdelaparda, 29,
Poligono Industrial, 28108 Alcobendas-
Madrid *Tel:* 902 194 752 *Fax:* 949 277 266
E-mail: peddos.libros@sgel.es

Magoria, *imprint of* Ediciones Obelisco SA

La Magrana+
Imprint of RBA Libros
Avda Diagonal, 189, 08018 Barcelona
Tel: 93 415 73 74
E-mail: atencion-clienterba@rbalibros.es
Web Site: www.magrana.cat; www.rbalibros.com
Founded: 1975
Subjects: Biography, Memoirs, Cookery, Fiction,
Literature, Literary Criticism, Essays, Philoso-
phy, Science (General), Social Sciences, Soci-
ology
ISBN Prefix(es): 978-84-7410; 978-84-8264

Malpaso Ediciones SLU
Diputacion 327, ppal 1a, 08009 Barcelona
Tel: 932 720 850
E-mail: hola@malpasoed.com; editorial@
malpasoed.com
Web Site: malpasoed.com
Key Personnel
Editorial Dir: Malcolm Otero
Editor: Julian Vinuales
Marketing Coordinator: Berta Monge
Founded: 2013
Subjects: Fiction, Literature, Literary Criticism,
Essays, Music, Dance, Pop Culture
ISBN Prefix(es): 978-84-16420

Malsinet Editor, *imprint of* Ediciones Robinbook
SL

Mandala Ediciones+
C/ Tarragona, 23, 28045 Madrid
SAN: 004-1114
Tel: 914 678 528
E-mail: info@mandalaediciones.com; fernando@
mandalaediciones.com
Web Site: www.mandalaediciones.com
Key Personnel
Mng Dir: Fernando Cabal
Founded: 1980
Subjects: Architecture & Interior Design, Astrol-
ogy, Occult, Behavioral Sciences, Cookery,
Earth Sciences, Environmental Studies, Film,
Video, Health, Nutrition, Inspirational, Spiri-
tuality, Medicine, Nursing, Dentistry, Music,
Dance, Psychology, Psychiatry, Religion - Bud-
dhist, Religion - Hindu, Religion - Islamic,
Biological Agriculture, Biological Medicine,
Chinese Medicine, Dietetic Natural, Ecological
Architecture, Ecology, Homeopathy, Manual
Medicine, Massage, Natural Health, Relaxation
ISBN Prefix(es): 978-84-86961; 978-84-88769;
978-84-95052
Total Titles: 210 Print

Editorial Mapfre SA
Carr de Pozuelo, 52, Majadahonda, 28220 Madrid
Tel: 91 581 53 57 *Fax:* 91 581 18 83
E-mail: edimap@mapfre.com
Web Site: www.editorialmapfre.com
Founded: 1970

Subjects: Medicine, Nursing, Dentistry, Financial
Security & Services, Insurances
ISBN Prefix(es): 978-84-7100
Foreign Rep(s): Ciceron Editores (Colombia);
CPL Contacto Profesional (Argentina); Im-
portadora Centrolibros (Chile); Itsemap Portu-
gal (Portugal); Eduardo Morales & Asociados
(Dominican Republic); Luis Perez Bustamante
(Ecuador); RGS Libros (Mexico); Libreria STA
Teresa (Venezuela); Libreria Technica Dieguez
(Venezuela)

Marbot Ediciones
Passeig de Sant Joan, 199, 3° 1a, 08037
Barcelona
Tel: 933014218
E-mail: marbot@marbotediciones.com
Web Site: www.marbotediciones.com
Founded: 2007
Subjects: Fiction
ISBN Prefix(es): 978-84-92728; 978-84-936411
Distributed by Panoplia de Libros
Foreign Rep(s): El Libro Universal SAS (Colom-
bia); La Panoplia Export SL (Latin America
exc Argentina, Colombia & Mexico); Sexto
Piso Distribuciones (Mexico); Distribuidora
Waldhuter (Argentina)

Marcial Pons Ediciones Juridicas SA+
C/ San Sotero, 6, 28037 Madrid
Tel: 91 304 33 03 *Fax:* 91 327 23 67
E-mail: edicionesjuridicas@marcialpons.es;
atencion@marcialpons.es (customer service)
Web Site: www.marcialpons.es
Founded: 1989
Subjects: Economics, History, Law, Public Ad-
ministration, Social Sciences, Sociology
ISBN Prefix(es): 978-84-7248; 978-84-95379;
978-84-9768; 978-84-96467
Number of titles published annually: 80 Print
Total Titles: 1,600 Print
Bookshop(s): Derecho-Economia-Empresa,
C/ Barbara de Braganza, 11, 28004 Madrid
Tel: 91 319 42 50; 91 308 56 49 *Fax:* 91
319 43 73 *E-mail:* derecho@marcialpons.
es; Libreria de Humanidades y Ciencias So-
ciales, Plz Conde del Valle de Suchil, 8, 28015
Madrid *Tel:* 91 448 47 97 *Fax:* 91 593 13
29 *E-mail:* humanidades@marcialpons.es;
Juridico-Economica, C/ Provenza, 249, 08008
Barcelona *Tel:* 93 487 39 99 *Fax:* 93 488 19
40 *E-mail:* llibreter@marcialpons.es

Marcombo SA+
Gran Via de les Corts Catalanes No 594, 08007
Barcelona
Tel: 93 318 00 79 *Fax:* 93 318 93 39
E-mail: info@marcombo.com
Web Site: www.marcombo.com
Key Personnel
Dir: Josep M Boixareu Vilaplana
Founded: 1945
Subjects: Anthropology, Automotive, Business,
Chemistry, Chemical Engineering, Child Care
& Development, Civil Engineering, Commu-
nications, Computer Science, Computers, Eco-
nomics, Electronics, Electrical Engineering,
Energy, Engineering (General), Environmen-
tal Studies, Finance, Management, Marketing,
Mathematics, Psychology, Psychiatry, Radio,
TV, Science (General), Social Sciences, Sociol-
ogy
ISBN Prefix(es): 978-84-267
Foreign Rep(s): Alfaomega Grupo Editor
(Chile, Colombia, Costa Rica, Ecuador, El
Salvador, Guatemala, Honduras, Mexico,
Nicaragua); Cuspide Libros SA (Argentina);
Edisa SA (Costa Rica); Global Ediciones SA
(Venezuela); Losa Libros Ltda (Uruguay); Pub-
lindustria (Portugal); Sr Libro (Bolivia); Tecni-
Ciencia Libros (Venezuela)
Bookshop(s): Libreria Hispano Americana

Editorial Marfil SA+
Sequia de Calvera, 41, 46910 Sedavi, Valencia
Tel: 963 186 007 *Fax:* 963 186 432
E-mail: info@tabarcallibres.com
Web Site: www.editorialmarfil.com; www.
  tabarcallibres.com
Founded: 1947
Subjects: Education, Literature, Literary Criticism, Essays, Psychology, Psychiatry
ISBN Prefix(es): 978-84-268

Marge Books
Valencia 558, atico 2a, 08026 Barcelona
Tel: 932449130 *Fax:* 932310865
E-mail: marge@margebooks.com
Web Site: www.marge.es
Key Personnel
Dir General: Jose Manuel Montagud; David Soler
Founded: 1982
Subjects: History, Medicine, Nursing, Dentistry, Science (General), Technology, Culture
ISBN Prefix(es): 978-84-86684; 978-84-92442
Foreign Rep(s): Alfaomega Colombiana SA (Colombia); Alfaomega Grupo Editor (Argentina, Chile); Alfaomega Grupo Editor SAB (Mexico); Eculibros (Ecuador); Oferta Exportable (Paraguay); Plaza & Janes Editores Colombia SA (Colombia); Representaciones Nacional Book SA (Panama); Libreria San Cristobal SAC (Peru); Ediciones Trecho (Uruguay); Unilibros (Dominican Republic)

Editorial Marin SA+
Av Diagonal 505, Piso Primero, Primera, 08029
  Barcelona
Tel: 934536955 *Fax:* 965523496
Founded: 1900
Subjects: Art, Medicine, Nursing, Dentistry, Nonfiction (General)
ISBN Prefix(es): 978-84-7102
Branch Office(s)
Anaxagoras 1400, Colonia Santa Cruz Atoyac, 03310 Mexico, DF, Mexico
Warehouse: Calle Industria 5/n, Polzono Industrial, El Papiol

Marova SL+
Ramirez Arellano, 17, 28043 Madrid
SAN: 004-1610
Tel: 915 322 607 *Fax:* 915 225 123
Key Personnel
Mng Dir: Jose Miguel Oriol
Founded: 1956 (70% owned by Ediciones Encuentros since 1984)
Subjects: Education, Psychology, Psychiatry, Religion - Other, Social Sciences, Sociology, Theology
ISBN Prefix(es): 978-84-269

Ediciones Martinez Roca SA+
Member of Grupo Planeta
Pº Recoletos, 4 3a planta, 28001 Madrid
SAN: 001-8406
Tel: 91 423 03 14 *Fax:* 91 423 03 06
E-mail: info@mrediciones.es
Web Site: www.planetadelibros.com/editorial-ediciones-martinez-roca-11.html
Key Personnel
Communication: Ana Gazquez Morales *Tel:* 91 423 03 76 *E-mail:* agazquez@mrediciones.es
Founded: 1965
Subjects: Animals, Pets, Astrology, Occult, Biography, Memoirs, Crafts, Games, Hobbies, Fiction, Health, Nutrition, How-to, Literature, Literary Criticism, Essays, Nonfiction (General), Psychology, Psychiatry, Romance, Science Fiction, Fantasy, Self-Help, Sports, Athletics
ISBN Prefix(es): 978-84-270; 978-84-8327

Editorial La Mascara SL+
Pza Juan Pablo II, 46015 Valencia

SAN: 002-5127
Tel: 963 486 500 *Fax:* 963 487 440
Founded: 1991
Subjects: Biography, Memoirs, Music, Dance, Poetry
ISBN Prefix(es): 978-84-7974
Subsidiaries: La Mascara France Sarl

Masterclass, *imprint of* Ediciones Robinbook SL

McGraw-Hill/Interamericana de Espana SL+
C/ Basauri 17, 1a Planta, 28023 Aravaca, Madrid
Tel: 91 180 30 00; 91 180 32 40 (bookstore)
  Fax: 91 180 30 55 (bookstore)
E-mail: educador@mcgraw-hill.com;
  pedidos_es@mcgraw-hill.com (bookstore)
Web Site: www.mcgraw-hill.es
Key Personnel
General Manager: Alvaro Garcia
  E-mail: alvaro_garcia@mcgraw-hill.com
Editorial Dir: Juan Francisco Ocana
  E-mail: juanfrancisco.ocana@mheducation.com
Editorial Dept: Cristina Sanchez
  E-mail: cristina_sanchez@mcgraw-hill.com
Commercial Supervisor: Daniel Fernandez
  E-mail: daniel_fernandez@mcgraw-hill.com
Founded: 1974
Subjects: Biological Sciences, Education, Health, Nutrition, Medicine, Nursing, Dentistry, Science (General), Technology
ISBN Prefix(es): 978-84-7615; 978-84-85240; 978-84-481; 978-84-486
Parent Company: The McGraw-Hill Companies, 1221 Avenue of the Americas, New York, NY 10020, United States
Branch Office(s)
C/ Entenca, 95 5a Planta, 08015 Barcelona, Editorial Manager: Josep Oriol
  Tel: 93 228 98 88 *Fax:* 93 289 01 70
  E-mail: joseporiol_magrina@mcgraw-hill.com

Media Vaca
C/ Salamanca 49, pta 13, 46005 Valencia
Tel: 963 956 927 *Fax:* 963 956 927
E-mail: mediavaca@mediavaca.net;
  administracion@mediavaca.net
Web Site: www.mediavaca.com
Key Personnel
Publisher: Vicente Ferrer Azcioti; Begona Lobo Abascal
Founded: 1998
ISBN Prefix(es): 978-84-932004; 978-84-930221; 978-84-934038

Editorial Medica JIMS SL
Via Augusta, 48-54, 7º 2a, 08006 Barcelona
SAN: 008-3003
Tel: 649 479 445 *Fax:* 932 11 87 65
E-mail: jims@es.inter.net
Web Site: www.jimsmedica.com
Founded: 1956
Subjects: Health, Nutrition, Medicine, Nursing, Dentistry, Physiotherapy
ISBN Prefix(es): 978-84-922442; 978-84-95062

Editorial Medica Panamericana SA+
C/ Quintanapalla, No 8, 4ºB, 28050 Madrid
Tel: 911317800 *Fax:* 914570919
E-mail: info@medicapanamericana.es
Web Site: www.medicapanamericana.com
Founded: 1953
Subjects: Biological Sciences, Education, Medicine, Nursing, Dentistry, Psychology, Psychiatry, Ecology
ISBN Prefix(es): 978-950-06
Branch Office(s)
Carrera 7a A Nº 69-19, Bogota DC, Colombia
  Tel: (01) 345-4508; (01) 314-5014 *Fax:* (01) 314-5015; (01) 345-0019 *E-mail:* infomp@ medicapanamericana.com.co

Hegel Nº 141, 2º piso, Col Chapultepec Morales, Del Miguel Hidalgo, 11570 Mexico, DF, Mexico *Tel:* (0155) 5250-0664; (0155) 5262 9470 *Fax:* (0155) 2624-2827 *E-mail:* infomp@ medicapanamericana.com.mx
Editorial Medica Panamericana CA, Edificio Polar, Torre Oeste, Piso 6, Oficina 6-C Plaza Venezuela, Urbanizacion Los Caobos, Parroquia El Recreo, Municipio Libertador, Caracas Distrito Federal, Venezuela *Tel:* (0212) 793-6906; (0212) 793-1666; (0212) 793-5985; (0212) 793-2857; (0212) 793-9889; (0212) 794-3065 *Fax:* (0212) 793-5885 *E-mail:* info@ medicapanamericana.com.ve
Warehouse: Almacen Editorial Medica Panamericana, C Paeque, 10, Alalpardo, 28130 Madrid
Returns: Almacen Editorial Medica Panamericana, C Paeque, 10, Alalpardo, 28130 Madrid

Ediciones Medici SA+
Imprint of Ediciones Omega SA
c/Plato, 26, 08006 Barcelona
Tel: 93 201 05 99; 93 201 38 07; 93 201 21 44
  Fax: 93 209 73 62
E-mail: omega@ediciones-omega.es
Web Site: www.ediciones-omega.es
Key Personnel
Mng Dir: Gabriel Paricio Larrea
Founded: 1983
Subjects: Child Care & Development, Cookery, Education, Health, Nutrition, Human Relations, Medicine, Nursing, Dentistry, Nonfiction (General), Pregnancy
ISBN Prefix(es): 978-84-86193; 978-84-89778; 978-84-9799

Editorial Mediterrania SL+
Casp 108, 8e, 08010 Barcelona
Tel: 93 218 34 58 *Fax:* 93 265 65 23
E-mail: editorial@editorialmediterrania.cat
Web Site: editorialmediterrania.net
Key Personnel
Editorial Dir: Monica Estruch
Communication: Francesc Buxeda
Founded: 1980
Membership(s): Association of Editors in the Catalan Language; Editors Guild of Catalunya.
Subjects: Art, Health, Nutrition, History, Literature, Literary Criticism, Essays, Outdoor Recreation, Photography, Religion - Catholic, Sports, Athletics, Travel & Tourism
ISBN Prefix(es): 978-84-85984; 978-84-88591; 978-84-8334; 978-84-89622
Branch Office(s)
Juan Hurtado de Mendoza, 19, 28036 Madrid
  Tel: 913 598 534 *E-mail:* editorial@ editorialmediterrania.net
Distribution Center: Museum Line SL, C/ Montevideo 5, nave 15, Poligono Industrial Camporroso, 28806 Alcala de Henares *Tel:* 91 830 03 88 *Fax:* 91 830 03 71 *E-mail:* museumline@ museumline.com
L'Arc de Bera, C Belgica 47-49, Poligon Montigala, 08917 Badalona *Tel:* 93 465 30 08 *Fax:* 93 465 87 90 *E-mail:* arc@arcdebera.com
  Web Site: www.arcdebera.com
Elite 1976 SA, C/ Jaume Ferran 72 A, 07004 Palma de Mallorca *Tel:* 971 910 210; 971 910 234 *Fax:* 971 910 232 *E-mail:* distribuidora@ elite-distribucions.com *Web Site:* www.elite-distribucions.com

Menoscuarto Ediciones
Pza Cardenal Almaraz, 4-1º F, 34005 Palencia
Tel: 979701250 *Fax:* 979701250
E-mail: correo@menoscuarto.es
Web Site: www.menoscuarto.es
Subjects: Fiction
ISBN Prefix(es): 978-84-96675; 978-84-933823; 978-84-934653
Foreign Rep(s): Asgard Distribuciones (Mexico); El Virrey (Peru); Laregold SA (Uruguay);

Liberalia Ediciones Ltda (Chile); Plaza & Janes Colombia SA (Colombia); Libreria Prosa&Politica (Chile); Distribuidora Waldhuter Libros (Argentina)
Distribution Center: FI-REX 21 SL, Andorra, 23 (Poligono Fonolla Sud), 08830 Sant Boi de Llobregat, Barcelona *Tel:* 936 354 120 *Fax:* 915 040 824 *E-mail:* firex21@firex21.com
Web Site: www.firex21.com

Ediciones Mensajero+
Sancho de Azpeitia, 2 Bajo, 48014 Bilbao
SAN: 001-852X
Tel: 944 470 358 *Fax:* 944 472 630
E-mail: mensajero@mensajero.com
Web Site: www.mensajero.com
Key Personnel
Dir: Jose Manuel Diaz Oses
Mng Editor: Josu Leguina Echeberria
Founded: 1915
Subjects: Education, How-to, Inspirational, Spirituality, Philosophy, Psychology, Psychiatry, Religion - Catholic, Social Sciences, Sociology
ISBN Prefix(es): 978-84-271
Distributor for Universidad de Deusto
Foreign Rep(s): Agape Libros (Argentina); Libreria Artemis Edinter SA (Guatemala); Asociacion Hijas de San Pablo (Chile, Colombia, Ecuador, Peru); Asociacion Manantial de la Cultura (Guatemala); Libreria Catolica Ave Maria (Puerto Rico); Editoriales La Ceiba (El Salvador); Libreria Centro Paulinas (Venezuela); Congregacion Hijas de San Pablo (Chile); Grupo Copages Libreria (Ecuador); Corporacion Ediciones Paulinas (Ecuador); Distribuidora de Estudios (Venezuela); Libreria Familia de Nazareth (Chile); Fundacion Jesus de la Misericordia (Ecuador); Instituto Misionero Hijas de San Pablo (Bolivia, Colombia, Ecuador); Paulinas (Dominican Republic, Paraguay, Uruguay); Paulinas Centro Multimedia (Puerto Rico); Paulinas - Instituto Misionero Hijas de San Pablo (Bolivia, Colombia, Ecuador); Pia Sociedad San Pablo (Chile); San Pablo (Costa Rica, El Salvador); Libreria San Pablo (Guatemala, Puerto Rico, USA); Sociedad de San Pablo (Argentina, Colombia, Peru); Libreria Studium (Ecuador)

Editorial Milenio+
Calle Sant Salvador, 8, 25005 Lleida
Tel: 973 23 66 11 *Fax:* 973 24 07 95
E-mail: editorial@edmilenio.com; rights@ edmilenio.com
Web Site: www.edmilenio.com
Key Personnel
Dir: Lluis Pages i Marigot
Founded: 1996
Specialize in Spanish & Latin American books.
Subjects: Anthropology, Art, Biography, Memoirs, Cookery, Drama, Theater, Education, Fiction, History, Humor, Literature, Literary Criticism, Essays, Philosophy, Photography, Psychology, Psychiatry, Romance, Theology, Travel & Tourism, Women's Studies, Narrative
ISBN Prefix(es): 978-84-9743; 978-84-921502
Total Titles: 40 Print
Associate Companies: Pages Editors SL
Distributed by L'Arc De Bera; Arclogi
Foreign Rep(s): Distribuidora Alexandria (Costa Rica); Casalini Libri SpA (Italy); Colofon SA de CV (Mexico); Digitalia (USA); Ediciones Gaviota (Colombia); Ibero Librerias (Peru); Liberalia Ediciones (Chile); Losa Libros (Uruguay); Distribuidora Waldhuter (Argentina)
Book Club(s): Eventualmente

Editorial del Ministerio de Educacion Culture y Deporte (Publisher of the Ministry of Education, Culture & Sports)
San Agustin, 5, 28014 Madrid
SAN: 004-2323

Tel: 91 701 83 52 (education & sports)
E-mail: publicaciones.educacion@mecd.es
Web Site: sede.educacion.gob.es/publiventa/inicio.action
Subjects: Education, Film, Video, Health, Nutrition, Literature, Literary Criticism, Essays, Music, Dance, Sports, Athletics, Culture, Performing Arts, Sports History, Sports Science
ISBN Prefix(es): 978-84-368; 978-84-369
Branch Office(s)
Abdon Terradas, 7, 28015 Madrid *Tel:* 91 543 93 66 *E-mail:* publicaciones.cultura@mecd.es

Ministerio de Hacienda y Administraciones Publicas
C/ Alcala, 9, 28071 Madrid
SAN: 004-2315
Tel: 91 595 58 08 *Fax:* 91 583 76 25
E-mail: ventas.publicaciones@minhap.es
Web Site: www.minhap.gob.es/en-gb/publicaciones
Subjects: Accounting, Economics, Finance, Public Administration
ISBN Prefix(es): 978-84-460; 978-84-476; 978-84-7196; 978-84-85482

Ministerio de Justicia, Centro de Publicaciones
San Bernardo, 62, 28015 Madrid
SAN: 004-234X
Tel: 91 390 44 29; 91 390 20 82; 91 390 20 97 *Fax:* 91 390 20 92
E-mail: tienda.publicaciones@mjusticia.es
Web Site: www.mjusticia.gob.es
Founded: 1947
Subjects: Law
ISBN Prefix(es): 978-84-7787
Distributed by BOE; Diputacion de Barcelona; Edisofer SL; Marcial Pons; Reydis Libros, Lazaro Pascual Yague SL
Warehouse: C/Ocana, 151-28047 Madrid

Ministerio de Sanidad, Servicios Sociales e Igualdad, see Centro de Publicaciones del Ministerio de Sanidad, Servicios Sociales e Igualdad

Ediciones Minotauro+
Member of Grupo Planeta
Diagonal, 662-664 7a planta, 08034 Barcelona
Tel: 93 4967001 *Fax:* 93 4967011
E-mail: scyla@planetadelibros.com
Web Site: www.planetadelibros.com/editorial-minotauro-21.html
Key Personnel
Foreign Rights Manager: Daniel Cladera *Tel:* 93 4928008 *E-mail:* dcladera@planeta.es
Founded: 1956
Specialize in fantasy & science fiction.
Subjects: Biography, Memoirs, Fiction, Literature, Literary Criticism, Essays, Science Fiction, Fantasy
ISBN Prefix(es): 978-84-450
Number of titles published annually: 35 Print
Total Titles: 270 Print
Imprints: Zenith (self-help, spirituality & history)

Editorial Minuscula SL
Av Republica Argentina, 163, 3° 1a, 08023 Barcelona
Tel: 93 254 13 64 *Fax:* 93 254 13 64
E-mail: minuscula@editorialminuscula.com
Web Site: www.editorialminuscula.com
Founded: 2000
Subjects: Fiction, Geography, Geology, History, Literature, Literary Criticism, Essays, Biology, Recreation
ISBN Prefix(es): 978-84-95587

Mira Editores SA
C/ Dalia, 11, 50012 Zaragoza
SAN: 004-2471
Tel: 976 460 505 *Fax:* 976 460 446

E-mail: info@miraeditores.com
Web Site: www.miraeditores.com
Founded: 1987
Subjects: Psychology, Psychiatry, Social Sciences, Sociology
ISBN Prefix(es): 978-84-86778; 978-84-88688; 978-84-89859; 978-84-8465

Mirto Academia, *imprint of* Editorial Alhulia SA

Miscelanea Editorial, *imprint of* Roca Editorial

M Moleiro Editor SA+
Travesera de Gracia, 17-21, 08021 Barcelona
Tel: 93 240 20 91 *Fax:* 93 201 50 62
E-mail: mmoleiro@moleiro.com
Web Site: www.moleiro.com
Key Personnel
President: Manuel Moleiro
Founded: 1992
Specialize in facsimile editions of medieval illuminated manuscripts & maps.
Subjects: Art, Biblical Studies, Medicine, Nursing, Dentistry, Natural History, First Editions, Rare Books
ISBN Prefix(es): 978-84-88526

Molino+
Imprint of RBA Libros
Avda Diagonal, 189, 08018 Barcelona
Tel: 93 415 73 74
E-mail: atencion-clienterba@rbalibros.es
Web Site: www.editorialmolino.com; www.rbalibros.com
Founded: 1933
Subjects: Education, Fiction, Mysteries, Suspense, Sports, Athletics
ISBN Prefix(es): 978-84-272
Number of titles published annually: 100 Print
Total Titles: 1,345 Print

Editorial Moll SL (Moll Publisher)+
Can Valero, 25, Poligon Can Valero, 07011 Palma de Mallorca, Balearic Islands
SAN: 002-5631
Tel: 971 72 41 76 *Fax:* 971 72 62 52
E-mail: info@editorialmoll.cat
Web Site: www.editorialmoll.cat
Founded: 1934
Also acts as book distributor to the Balearic Islands.
Subjects: Art, Biography, Memoirs, Fiction, History, Language Arts, Linguistics, Literature, Literary Criticism, Essays, Natural History, Poetry, Regional Interests, Social Sciences, Sociology, Travel & Tourism
ISBN Prefix(es): 978-84-273
Number of titles published annually: 60 Print
Total Titles: 1,200 Print
Bookshop(s): Libres Mallorca, Esglesia de Santa Eulalia, 11, 07001 Palma de Mallorca, Contact: Alex Martinez *Tel:* 971 728 453 *Fax:* 971 728 453

Mondadori, *imprint of* Penguin Random House Grupo Editorial

Monsa Publications
Calle Gravina, Sant Adria de Besos, 08930 Barcelona
Tel: 93 381 00 50
E-mail: info@monsashop.com; press@monsa.com
Web Site: www.monsa.com; monsashop.com/es
Subjects: Architecture & Interior Design, Art, Fashion, Gardening, Plants, Health, Nutrition, Advertising Design, Floral Art, Graphic Design, Fashion Design, Hairdressing, Hairstyle, Industrial Design, Web Design
ISBN Prefix(es): 978-84-95275; 978-84-86426; 978-84-96429; 978-84-96823

Montagud Editores SA
C/ Ausias March, 25 1°, 08010 Barcelona
Tel: 933182082
E-mail: montagud@montagud.com; infoweb@
montagud.com
Web Site: www.libreriagastronomica.com
Founded: 1906
Subjects: Cookery, Bakery, Cuisine, Gastronomy,
Sweet Pastry
ISBN Prefix(es): 978-84-7212
Foreign Rep(s): Editions BPI (France); Capitulo 2
Sa (Argentina); Librairie Gourmande (Canada);
Gout (Argentina); Editorial Juventud SA de CV
(Mexico); De Kookboekhandel (Netherlands);
Editorial Omeba (Argentina); Vandenberg Edizioni SRL (Italy); Virtue Books NZ Ltd (New
Zealand)

Editorial Monte Carmelo
Paseo del Empecinado, 1, Apdo, 19, 09001 Burgos
SAN: 002-5658
Tel: 947 256 061 *Fax:* 947 256 062
E-mail: editorial@montecarmelo.com; direccion@
montecarmelo.com; comercial@montecarmelo.
com (sales); pedidos@montecarmelo.com
(orders)
Web Site: www.montecarmelo.com
Founded: 1900
Subjects: Inspirational, Spirituality, Religion -
Catholic
ISBN Prefix(es): 978-84-7239

Montena, *imprint of* Penguin Random House
Grupo Editorial

Ediciones Morata SL+
C/ Mejia Lequerica, 12, 28004 Madrid
Tel: 914 48 09 26 *Fax:* 914 48 09 25
E-mail: morata@edmorata.es
Web Site: www.edmorata.es
Key Personnel
Mng Dir: Paulo Cosin
Founded: 1920
Subjects: Behavioral Sciences, Child Care & Development, Disability, Special Needs, Education, Human Relations, Philosophy, Psychology,
Psychiatry, Self-Help, Social Sciences, Sociology, Women's Studies
ISBN Prefix(es): 978-84-7112
Total Titles: 300 Print
Foreign Rep(s): A B Representaciones Generales (Peru); Alfabeta (Guatemala); Alfomega
Grupo Editor (Colombia); America Latina
(Uruguay); Los Amigos Del Libro (Bolivia);
Axis SA (El Salvador); Bibliomarketing SA
(Dominican Republic); Bilingual Publications
Co (USA); Boriken Libros Inc (Puerto Rico);
Editorial Don Bosco (Paraguay); Libreria Don
Bosco (Bolivia); Capitulo 2 SA (Argentina); La
Ceiba SA de CV (El Salvador); CELI Srl Distribuidora e Importadora (Peru); Libreria Cervantes (Ecuador); Libreria Editorial Ciencias
(Uruguay); Libreria Cientifica Ltda (Colombia); Grupo Editorial Circulo (Puerto Rico);
Clasicos Roxsil SA (El Salvador); Colofon
SA (Mexico); Libreria Cosmos (Guatemala);
Cuesta Centro Del Libro (Dominican Republic); Cultural Panamena (Panama); DISESA-Distribuidora Escolar Libreria Didactic (Dominican Republic); Distribuidora Comercial
Didactica Ltda (Colombia); EDISA-Ediciones
y Distribuciones del ISTMO SA (Costa Rica);
Edudacta CA (Venezuela); Distribuidora Estudios SRL (Venezuela); Libreria Universal
Carlos Federspiel & Co (Costa Rica); Fondo
de Cultura Economica (Mexico); Libreria
Gandhi (Mexico); Editorial Geminis (Panama);
Global Ediciones SA (Venezuela); Hispamer
(Nicaragua); Hispamer SA de CU (El Salvador); Intercontinental Libreria (Paraguay); Internacional Libros Miguel Concha SA (Chile);

Inversiones Mojave (Venezuela); Latin American Book Source (USA); Lectorum Publications Inc (USA); Libreria Lehman (Costa
Rica); Liberalia Ediciones Ltda (Chile); El Libro Cia Ltda (Ecuador); LIBUN-Fundacion
del Libro Universitario (Peru); Losa Libros
Ltda (Uruguay); Libreria Loyola (Guatemala);
Livraria Editora Maneco (Brazil); Martinez Acchini Ltda (Bolivia); Libreria Mateca (Dominican Republic); Livraria Minho (Puerto Rico);
Mr Books (Ecuador); Libreria Navarro (Honduras); Editorial Nueva Decada (Costa Rica);
Especializada Olejnik Libreria (Chile); Papiros
(Ecuador); El Parnaso de Coyoacan (Mexico);
Libreria Parroquial (Mexico); Libreria De La
Paz (Argentina); Piedrasanta y Gare de Creacion (Guatemala); Prata & Rodrigues Publicacoes Lda (Portugal); Proeme SL (Argentina);
Libreria Prosa & Politica (Chile); Publicaciones
Educativas Inc (Puerto Rico); Editorial Pueblo
y Educacion (Cuba); RevisLibros (Venezuela);
Importadora Rubaisen (Argentina); Libreria San
Cristobal (Peru); Servicio Lewis Internacional
(Panama); Libreria Studium (Ecuador); Ediciones Tecnicas Paraguayas SRL (Paraguay);
Thesaurus (Dominican Republic); Editorial
Verbo Divino (Bolivia); Vida Nueva Libreria (Ecuador); El Virrey (Peru); Distribuidora
Waldhuter (Argentina); Libreria Yachaywasi
(Bolivia)

Anaya & Mario Muchnik+
c/ Juan Ignacio Luca de Tena, 15, 28027 Madrid
Tel: 913 938 800 *Fax:* 917 426 631
E-mail: cga@anaya.es; administrador@anaya.es
Web Site: www.anaya.es
Founded: 1990
Subjects: Literature, Literary Criticism, Essays
ISBN Prefix(es): 978-84-7979
Parent Company: Grupo Anaya SA
Distributor for America Latina

Multimedica Ediciones Veterinarias
Av Corts Catalanes, 2, Edificio 2, Planta 3a, local
10, 08173 Sant Cugat del Valles, Barcelona
Tel: 93 674 61 08 *Fax:* 93 674 72 67
E-mail: info@multimedica.es
Web Site: www.multimedica.es
Subjects: Veterinary Science
ISBN Prefix(es): 978-84-96344
Foreign Rep(s): Avances Clinicos (Uruguay);
Ediciones Diaz de Santos Mexico (Mexico);
Disinlimed, C A (Venezuela); Hipocratico S
A (Argentina); Librerias Lehmann S A (Costa
Rica); Libun SA (Peru); Libreria El Profesional Ltda (Colombia); Ediciones Tecnicas
Paraguays (Paraguay); Libreria E Insumos Veterinarios (Bolivia)

Mundi-Prensa Libros SA+
Calle Velazquez no 31, 3° Derecha, 28001 Madrid
Tel: 914 463 350 *Fax:* 914 456 218
E-mail: info@paraninfo.es
Web Site: www.mundiprensa.com
Key Personnel
Editorial Dir: Jose Maria Hernandez
Founded: 1948
Subjects: Agriculture, Animals, Pets, Biological
Sciences, Economics, Gardening, Plants, Mechanical Engineering, Technology, Veterinary
Science
ISBN Prefix(es): 978-84-7114; 978-84-8476
Parent Company: Grupo Editorial Paraninfo

Editorial Mundo Negro+
Arturo Soria, 101, 28043 Madrid
SAN: 002-5690
Tel: 914 152 412 *Fax:* 915 192 550
Web Site: www.combonianos.es
Founded: 1959
Subjects: Anthropology, Art, Biography, Memoirs,
Developing Countries, Ethnicity, Foreign Coun-

tries, History, Religion - Catholic, Religion -
Other, Theology, Africa
ISBN Prefix(es): 978-84-7295
Parent Company: Misioneros Combonianos

Munoz Moya Editores+
Affiliate of Grupo Agrinar
c/ Estacada del Pozo 79, 41940 Tomares, Seville
Tel: 95 565 30 58
E-mail: editorial@mmoya.es
Web Site: www.mmoya.es
Founded: 1984
Specialize in biblioteca Americana.
Subjects: Anthropology, Astrology, Occult, History, Literature, Literary Criticism, Essays,
Mysteries, Suspense, Poetry, Religion - Buddhist, Religion - Catholic, Religion - Jewish
ISBN Prefix(es): 978-84-8010; 978-84-86335;
978-84-931192; 978-84-932439; 978-84-96074
Number of titles published annually: 24 Online;
24 E-Book
Total Titles: 45 Online; 45 E-Book

Editorial la Muralla SA+
C/ Constancia, 33, 28002 Madrid
SAN: 002-5143
Tel: 91 415 36 87; 91 416 13 71 *Fax:* 91 413 59
07
E-mail: muralla@arcomuralla.com
Web Site: www.arcomuralla.com
Key Personnel
Mng Dir: Lidio Nieto Jimenez
Founded: 1966
Subjects: Art, Biological Sciences, Education, Geography, Geology, History, Language Arts, Linguistics, Literature, Literary Criticism, Essays,
Mathematics, Music, Dance, Physical Sciences,
Physics, Technology
ISBN Prefix(es): 978-84-7133
Associate Companies: Arco/Libros SL, C/ Juan
Bautista de Toledo, 28, 28002, Madrid
E-mail: arcolibros@arcomuralla.com
Distributed by Logista Libros

Editorial NA+
Pizarro 19, bajo dcha, 28004 Madrid
SAN: 004-3850
Tel: 915 218 863 *Fax:* 915 312 952
E-mail: info@editorial-na.com
Web Site: www.editorial-na.com
Founded: 1957
Subjects: Anthropology, Archaeology, Art, Astrology, Occult, Astronomy, History, Parapsychology, Philosophy, Religion - Other, Culture,
Esoteric, Humanism
ISBN Prefix(es): 978-84-85982; 978-84-96369

Ediciones y Publicaciones El Nadir Tres SL
Guillen de Castro 77, 11a, 46008 Valencia
Tel: 687 541 263 *Fax:* 649 114 723
Web Site: www.elnadir.es
Subjects: Biological Sciences, Fiction, Literature,
Literary Criticism, Essays
ISBN Prefix(es): 978-84-934029; 978-84-922194;
978-84-931761
Foreign Rep(s): Azteca Difusora del Libro SL
(Italy, Latin America, Portugal)

Nakla, *imprint of* Editorial Alhulia SA

Naque Editora+
Pasaje Gutierrez Ortega, 1, 13001 Ciudad Real
Tel: 926 216714 *Fax:* 926 216714
E-mail: naque@naque.es
Web Site: www.naque.es; www.libreriadeteatro.
com; www.momentodc.es
Key Personnel
Dir: Fernando Bercebal
Founded: 1995
Specialize in bimonthly magazines & translations.

Subjects: Art, Drama, Theater, Education, Literature, Literary Criticism, Essays, Cultural Management, Performing Arts, Theatre Pedagogy
ISBN Prefix(es): 978-84-89987; 978-84-920844
Number of titles published annually: 10 Print
Total Titles: 69 Print
Distributor for Arbole Marionetas; IGDEM
Bookshop(s): Libreriadeteatro, San Mateo, 30, 28004 Madrid *Tel:* 91 3080018 *Fax:* 91 3080018 *E-mail:* info@libreriadeteatro.com
Web Site: www.libreriadeteatro.com

Narcea SA de Ediciones+
Paseo Imperial, 53-56, 28005 Madrid
Tel: 91 554 64 84; 91 554 61 02 (distribution)
    Fax: 91 554 64 87
E-mail: narcea@narceaediciones.es
Web Site: www.narceaediciones.es
Key Personnel
Rights & Permissions: Monica Gonzalez Navarro
    E-mail: derechos@narceaediciones.es
Founded: 1968
Subjects: Education, Psychology, Psychiatry, Religion - Other, Social Sciences, Sociology
ISBN Prefix(es): 978-84-277
Total Titles: 1,500 Print

Narrativa SA, *imprint of* Editorial Alhulia SA

Ediciones Nauta Credito SA+
C/ Josep Tarradellas, 123-127 5º, 08029 Barcelona
Tel: 934 392 204 *Fax:* 934 107 314
Founded: 1962
Also book packager.
Subjects: Art, Nonfiction (General)
ISBN Prefix(es): 978-84-8259; 978-84-89140
Warehouse: N Sra Montserrat 84-86, 08020 Barcelona

Editorial Nerea SA+
Aldamar nº 36, Bajo, 20003 Donostia-San Sebastian
Tel: 943 432 227 *Fax:* 943 433 379
E-mail: nerea@nerea.net; prensa@nerea.net
Web Site: www.nerea.net
Key Personnel
Chief Executive Officer & Secretary, Board of Directors: Marta Casares Bidasoro
President: Juan Bertran Berges
Dir: Rafael Casares Bidasoro
Founded: 1987
Subjects: Architecture & Interior Design, Art, History, Women's Studies, Art History
ISBN Prefix(es): 978-84-86763; 978-84-89569; 978-84-96431
Foreign Rep(s): Fondo Cultural Iberoamericano (Colombia); Idea Books (Netherlands); IPG/Independent Publishers Group (USA); Loggilibro (Portugal, Spain); Riverside Agency (Argentina); Ediciones Trecho SA (Uruguay)

Edicions de 1984 SA
C/ Trafalgar 10, 08010 Barcelona
Tel: 93 300 32 71 *Fax:* 93 485 43 75
E-mail: 1984@edicions1984.cat
Web Site: www.edicions1984.cat
Founded: 1984
Subjects: Literature, Literary Criticism, Essays, Nonfiction (General), Poetry
ISBN Prefix(es): 978-84-96061; 978-84-86540; 978-84-15835
Number of titles published annually: 300 Print

Ediciones Nobel SA
Centro Covico Comercial, C/ Comandante Caballero s/n of 6, 33005 Oviedo, Asturias
Tel: 985 27 74 83 *Fax:* 985 27 74 85
E-mail: nobel@edicionesnobel.com
Web Site: www.edicionesnobel.com

Key Personnel
Dir General: Pelayo Garcia Cervero
Founded: 1989
Subjects: Biological Sciences, Cookery, Fiction, Literature, Literary Criticism, Essays, Psychology, Psychiatry, Juvenile
ISBN Prefix(es): 978-84-8459; 978-84-87531; 978-84-89770

Noguer y Caralt Editores SA+
C/ Santa Amelia, 22, 08034 Barcelona
SAN: 004-0568
Tel: 93 280 13 99 *Fax:* 93 280 19 93
Founded: 1942
Subjects: Art, Astrology, Occult, Biography, Memoirs, Cookery, Fiction, Geography, Geology, History, Literature, Literary Criticism, Essays, Nonfiction (General), Outdoor Recreation
ISBN Prefix(es): 978-84-279; 978-84-217
Associate Companies: Editorial Noguer SA

Nordica Libros
C/ Fuerte de Navidad, 11 1º B, 28044 Madrid
Tel: 685104101
E-mail: info@nordicalibros.com
Web Site: www.nordicalibros.com
Founded: 2006
Subjects: Literature, Literary Criticism, Essays
ISBN Prefix(es): 978-84-92683; 978-84-934854; 978-84-935578; 978-84-936213; 978-84-936693
Foreign Rep(s): Heraldos Negros (Peru); Independent Publishers Group (USA); Liberalia Ediciones Ltda (Chile); La Panoplia Export (Latin America exc Argentina, Chile, Mexico & Peru); Sexto Piso Distribuciones (Mexico); Distribuidora Waldhuter (Argentina)

Ediciones Norma-Capitel+
Parque Europolis, c/ Bruselas (V), 16B, 28232 Las Rozas, Madrid
Tel: 91 637 74 14; 627 405 777 *Fax:* 91 637 74 14
E-mail: rpa@norma-capitel.com
Web Site: www.norma-capitel.com
Key Personnel
Contact: Rafael Perez Alonso
Founded: 1976
Subjects: Alternative, Career Development, Child Care & Development, Cookery, Health, Nutrition, How-to, Medicine, Nursing, Dentistry, Self-Help, Fine Arts
ISBN Prefix(es): 978-84-7487; 978-84-8451; 978-84-931104
Associate Companies: Ediciones Eilea SA
Subsidiaries: Eilea SA; Libros Gamma
Foreign Rep(s): Ediciones-Distribuciones Universum (Mexico); Importaciones PH Lugo Libros (Venezuela); LCM Libros Ciencias Medicas (Chile); Ediciones Medicas Ecuatorians (Ecuador); Redactores en Red (Argentina); Libreria Tecnica Prata Oliveira (Portugal); Ediciones Tecnicas Paraguayas (Paraguay)
Showroom(s): Ronda de la Plazuela 8, 28230 Las Rozas, Madrid
Bookshop(s): Ronda de la Plazuela 8, 28230 Las Rozas, Madrid
Shipping Address: Ronda de la Plazuela 8, 28230 Las Rozas, Madrid
Warehouse: Ronda de la Plazuela 8, 28230 Las Rozas, Madrid
Orders to: Ronda de la Plazuela 8, 28230 Las Rozas, Madrid

Norma Editorial
Passeig de Sant Joan 7, 08010 Barcelona
Tel: 933036820 *Fax:* 933036831
E-mail: norma@normaeditorial.com; info@normacomics.com
Web Site: www.normaeditorial.com

Key Personnel
Publications: Flor Castellanos *Tel:* 93 303 68 29; Dolors Romero *Tel:* 93 303 68 30
Export: Irene Garcia
Rights: Sylvie Poulain *Tel:* 93 303 68 33
Founded: 1977
Subjects: Fiction, Comics
ISBN Prefix(es): 978-84-7904; 978-84-8431; 978-84-85475; 978-84-86595

Nova Galicia Edicions SL
Avda Ricardo Mella, 143, Nave 3, 36330 Vigo
Tel: 986 46 21 11 *Fax:* 986 46 21 18
E-mail: novagalicia@novagalicia.com
Web Site: www.novagalicia.com
Key Personnel
Dir: Jose Manuel Cabo Pelaez
Editorial Dir: Carlos del Pulgar
Founded: 1984
Subjects: Architecture & Interior Design, Art, History
ISBN Prefix(es): 978-84-96070; 978-84-87755; 978-84-96293

Novelas y Cuentos, *imprint of* Editorial Casals SA

Ediciones Nowtilus SL
Camino de Vinateros 40, Local 90, 28030 Madrid
Tel: 912426594
E-mail: administracion@nowtilus.com; ventas@nowtilus.com
Web Site: www.nowtilus.com
Key Personnel
Founder & Editor: Santos Rodriguez
Subjects: Biography, Memoirs, Business, Fiction, History, Literature, Literary Criticism, Essays, Religion - Other, Science Fiction, Fantasy, Technology
ISBN Prefix(es): 978-84-9763; 978-84-932221; 978-84-932527; 978-84-9967
Foreign Rep(s): Alejandria (Ignacio Camarillo Ruiz) (Mexico); Artemis Edinter (Guatemala); Baker & Taylor Publisher Services (Canada, USA); The Bilingual Publications Co (USA); Brodart Co (USA); La Casita (El Salvador); CCN Libreria Cuesta (Dominican Republic); La Ceiba (Juan Luis Bolanos) (El Salvador); Contento (Israel); Cuspide (Argentina); Libreria Ediciones (Chile); Ediciones Gaviota (Colombia); Gussi Distribuidora de Libros (Gustavo Fuentes) (Uruguay); HISPAMER (Jesus de Santiago) (Nicaragua); Inspirees International BV (Yu Tony Zhou) (China); Lectorum Publications Inc (USA); Libreria Lehmann SA (Mario Cordero) (Costa Rica); Distribuidora Lewis (Panama); Librimundi (Juan Leon Mera) (Ecuador); Libro-Express, Distribuidora Lectorum (Ecuador); Litexsa Boliviana (Carla Maria Berdegue) (Bolivia); Metromedia (Eleonora Gomez) (Honduras); Mr Books SA (Cathy Wright) (Ecuador); Libreria Navarro (Agustin Montes) (Honduras); Distribuciones Plaza Mayor (USA); Quijote, Musica y Libros (Paraguay); El Regalo Universal (Ivan Nino) (Venezuela); Sophos (Philippe Hunziker) (Guatemala); Libreria Spagnola (Italy); Tecni - Ciencia Librios (Venezuela); Thesaurus (Dominican Republic); El Virrey (Brunilda Koffler) (Peru); Yenny (Marcella Nulchis) (Argentina); Ediciones Zeta (Peru)

Nube de Tinta, *imprint of* Penguin Random House Grupo Editorial

NubeOcho Ediciones
Calle del Factor, 10, 28013 Madrid
E-mail: info@nubeocho.com
Web Site: www.nubeocho.com
ISBN Prefix(es): 978-84-942360; 978-84-942929
Branch Office(s)
Calle San Juan de Letran, 4-3º A, 29012 Malaga
Foreign Rights: S B Rights Agency

Distribution Center: Consortium Book Sales & Distribution *Toll Free Tel:* 800-283-3572 *Toll Free Fax:* 800-351-5073 *Web Site:* www.cbsd. com

Nueva Acropolis, see Editorial NA

Editorial Ob Stare
Apdo de Correos 122, 38280 Tegueste, Tenerife
Tel: 922540513 *Fax:* 922546131
E-mail: obstare@obstare.com
Web Site: www.obstare.com
Key Personnel
Dir General: Eva Darias Esteban
Founded: 2001
Subjects: Medicine, Nursing, Dentistry, Gynecology, Obstetrics
ISBN Prefix(es): 978-84-933314

Ediciones Obelisco SA (Obelisco Publishing)+
C/ Pedro IV, 78, 3°, 5a, 08005 Barcelona
SAN: 001-8872
Tel: 93 309 85 25
E-mail: info@edicionesobelisco.com
Web Site: www.edicionesobelisco.com
Founded: 1981
Subjects: Alternative, Astrology, Occult, Biblical Studies, Crafts, Games, Hobbies, Education, Fiction, Health, Nutrition, How-to, Human Relations, Inspirational, Spirituality, Medicine, Nursing, Dentistry, Nonfiction (General), Parapsychology, Psychology, Psychiatry, Religion - Buddhist, Religion - Catholic, Religion - Hindu, Religion - Islamic, Religion - Jewish, Religion - Protestant, Religion - Other, Self-Help, Alternative Psychology, Judaica, New Age, Spiritualism
ISBN Prefix(es): 978-84-7720; 978-84-9777; 978-84-8600
Number of titles published annually: 60 Print
Total Titles: 900 Print
Imprints: Magoria
Foreign Rep(s): Editoriales La Ceiba (El Salvador); Centro Cuesta Nacional (Dominican Republic); Dellare SA (Guatemala); Desarrollos Culturales Constarricenses DCC SA (Costa Rica); Disbook SL (Spain); Distribuciones Mediterraneo (Peru); Distribuciones del Futuro (Argentina); Ediciones Gaviota (Colombia); Libreria Hispamer (Nicaragua); Metro Nova SA de CV (Honduras); Mr Books (Ecuador); Editorial Pomaire (Venezuela); Sophos SA (Guatemala); Spanish Publishers LLC (Puerto Rico, USA); Ediciones Urano SA (Chile); Ediciones Urano Mexico SA de CV (Mexico); Ediciones Urano Uruguay SA (Uruguay)

Oberta UOC Publishing SLU, see Editorial UOC

Ocean Ambar-Circe-Guias Oceano, *imprint of* Oceano Grupo Editorial SA

Oceano/ergon-Ocean Multimedia-Ocean-Digital, *imprint of* Oceano Grupo Editorial SA

Oceano Grupo Editorial SA+
c/ Milanesado, 21-23, 08017 Barcelona
Tel: 93 280 20 20 *Fax:* 93 204 10 73
E-mail: info@oceano.com
Web Site: www.oceano.com
Key Personnel
Mng Dir: Jose Lluis Monreal
Founded: 1950
Subjects: Art, Education, Fiction, Geography, Geology, History, Literature, Literary Criticism, Essays, Management, Science (General)
ISBN Prefix(es): 978-84-7069
Associate Companies: Ediciones Centrum Tecnicas y Cientificas SA, Milanesat, 21-23, 08017

Barcelona; Circe Ediciones SA, Milanesat, 21-23, 08017 Barcelona; Ediciones Manfer SA, Milanesat, 21-23, 08017 Barcelona
Imprints: Ocean Ambar-Circe-Guias Oceano; Oceano/ergon-Ocean Multimedia-Ocean-Digital; Oceano-Instituto Gallach-Oceano/Centrum
Subsidiaries: Instituto Gallach de Libreria y Ediciones SL
Branch Office(s)
Carlos Pellegrini, 855 pisos 12 y 13, 1009 Buenos Aires, Argentina *Tel:* (011) 4021 92 00 *Fax:* (011) 5811 44 62 *E-mail:* oceano@ oceano.com.ar *Web Site:* www.oceano.com.ar
Av Cnel Manuel M Franco, n° 24, entre SV Guzman y Julio A Gutierrez, Barrio Mc-Donalds, Santa Cruz de la Sierra, Bolivia *Tel:* (01) 33 44 91 75 *Fax:* (01) 33 44 91 74 *E-mail:* distribucion@oceano.com.bo
Rua Tabapua, 422, 4° andar, Conj 41, Bairro Itaim Bibi, 04536-070 Sao Paulo-SP, Brazil *Tel:* (011) 3071-1331 *Fax:* (011) 3071-1537 *E-mail:* dirgral@ocelivros.com.br *Web Site:* brasil.oceano.com
Edificio Oceano, C/ San Diego, N° 81, Santiago Centro, Santiago, Chile *Tel:* (02) 450 13 00 *Fax:* (02) 450 13 60 *E-mail:* info@oceanochile.cl *Web Site:* www.editorialoceano.cl
Av Carrera 45, N° 108, A-50, Oficina 404, Edificio Bosch, Bogota DC, Colombia *Tel:* (01) 405 00 44 *Fax:* (01) 412 10 81 *E-mail:* ocelibros@edicionesoceano.com.co
Sabana Norte, del ICE, 350 m al Noreste, San Jose, Costa Rica *Tel:* 2210-2000 *Fax:* 2210-2061 *E-mail:* ocecor@racsa.co.cr
C/ J, esquina calle L, Edif Calidad a tiempo, piso 2, Santo Domingo, Dominican Republic *Tel:* (809) 537-08 32 *Fax:* (809) 537-51 87 *E-mail:* info@oceano.com.do
c/ De Las Retamas, E1-136X, y Av 10 de Agosto, Quito, Ecuador *Tel:* (02) 240 58 88; (02) 241 27 94 *Fax:* (02) 240 65 26 *E-mail:* ecua-libro@oceano.com.ec
Calle Circunvalacion No 120, Colonia San Benito, San Salvador, El Salvador *Tel:* 2521-7200 *Fax:* 2521-7207 *E-mail:* editorial@oceano.com.sv
Av La Reforma, 9-55, Zona 10, edificio Reforma 10, Nivel 4, Oficina 409, Guatemala, Guatemala *Tel:* 24 96 81 00 *Fax:* 23 85 24 02 *E-mail:* oceano@intelnet.net.gt
Colonia Alameda, Avda Juan M Galvez, Alameda Casa 1232, Tegucigalpa, Honduras *Tel:* 235 72 97; 235 60 41 *Fax:* 2235-6254 *E-mail:* edoca-honduras@globalnet.hn
C/ Eugenio Sue, 55, Colonia Chapultepec Polanco Del Miguel Hidalgo, 11560 Mexico, DF, Mexico *Tel:* (0155) 5279 9000 *Fax:* (0155) 5281 3805 *E-mail:* info@oceano.com.mx *Web Site:* www.oceano.com.mx
Blvd M Avila Camacho N° 76 Piso 10, Colonia Lomas de Chapultepec Del Miguel Hidalgo, 11000 Mexico DF, Mexico *Tel:* (0155) 9178 5100 *E-mail:* info@oceano.com.mx *Web Site:* www.oceano.com.mx
Km 7 1/2 carretera a Masaya, Contigua Nitalsa, Managua, Nicaragua *Tel:* 2276 13 72 *Fax:* 2276 14 43 *E-mail:* info@oceano.com.ni
Corregimiento de Bethania, Av La Paz (Calle del Ingenio), Edificio N° 7, Panama, Panama *Tel:* 261 68 08 *Fax:* 261 04 62 *E-mail:* ediciones@oceanopanama.com
C/ General Maximo Santos, 2000 esquina Pirisal, Asuncion, Paraguay *Tel:* (021) 302 600 *Fax:* (021) 301 826 *E-mail:* oceano@oceano.com.py *Web Site:* www.oceano.com.py
Calle 41, n° 894, pisco 2°, San Isidro, Lima, Peru *Tel:* (01) 719 0777 *Fax:* (01) 225 7592 *E-mail:* oceanoperuana@oceano.com.pe
Portugal *E-mail:* info@oceano.pt
C/ Salvador Ferrer Serra, 1966, Montevido, Uruguay *Tel:* 24036090 *Fax:* 24036090 *E-mail:* oceano@oceanouruguay.com

Edificio El Condor, calle 8, entre calles 4 y 5, 1060, A La Urbina, Caracas, Venezuela *Tel:* (0212) 242 05 08; (0212) 242 01 09 *Fax:* (0212) 242 05 16 *E-mail:* info@oceano.com.ve
U.S. Office(s): Editorial Oceano Inc, 10843 NW 29 St, Doral, FL 33172, United States *Tel:* 305-436-1008 *Fax:* 305-436-0502 *E-mail:* info@oceanousa.com *Web Site:* www.oceanousa.com
Orders to: Ediciones Oceano, SA, Paseo de Gracia, 26, 08007 Barcelona

Oceano-Instituto Gallach-Oceano/Centrum, *imprint of* Oceano Grupo Editorial SA

Editorial Octaedro
C/ Bailen 5, 08010 Barcelona
Tel: 93 246 40 02 *Fax:* 93 231 18 68
E-mail: octaedro@octaedro.com
Web Site: www.octaedro.com
Key Personnel
Dir General: Juan Leon
Founded: 1992
Subjects: Art, Education, Language Arts, Linguistics, Literature, Literary Criticism, Essays, Science (General), Sports, Athletics
ISBN Prefix(es): 978-84-8063; 978-84-9921
Branch Office(s)
Pol Virgen de las nieves, Paseo del Lino, 6, 18110 Las Gabias, Granada *Tel:* 95 895 83 82; 95 855 33 24 *Fax:* 98 555 33 07 *E-mail:* magina@octaedro.com
Foreign Rep(s): AB Representaciones Generales SRL (Peru); Ediciones de Aguazul SA (Argentina); Editorial Juventud SA de CV (Mexico); Libreria Papiris Codices Cia LTC (Ecuador); Siglo del Hombre Editores (Colombia); Ediciones Trecho (Uruguay)
Distribution Center: Distrifer Libros, C/ Valle de Tobalina, n 32 Naves 5-6, 28021 Madrid *Tel:* 91 796 27 09 *E-mail:* distrifer@retemail.es

Oikos-Tau SA Ediciones+
Montserrat, 12-14, 08340 Vilassar de Mar
Tel: 937590791 *Fax:* 937506825
Founded: 1963
Membership(s): Editors Guild of Cataluna; Federation of Editors of Spain.
Subjects: Agriculture, Anthropology, Architecture & Interior Design, Behavioral Sciences, Biography, Memoirs, Biological Sciences, Earth Sciences, Economics, Education, Geography, Geology, History, Language Arts, Linguistics, Literature, Literary Criticism, Essays, Marketing, Medicine, Nursing, Dentistry, Poetry, Psychology, Psychiatry, Social Sciences, Sociology
ISBN Prefix(es): 978-84-281

Ediciones Olimpic SL+
Ronda d'Altafulla, 14, 43893 Altafulla
Tel: 977 650 885 *Fax:* 977 650 885
E-mail: edolimpic@yahoo.es
Key Personnel
Administrator: Rafael Barberan
Contact: Angels Gimeno
Founded: 1987
Specialize in legal books for universities.
Subjects: Fiction, Law, Science Fiction, Fantasy, Social Sciences, Sociology, Western Fiction
ISBN Prefix(es): 978-84-7750

El Olivo Azul
C/ Diego Serrano 21, local, 14005 Cordoba
Tel: 957 450897; 957 452811
Key Personnel
Founder: Eduardo Moreno; Jose Castillo; Francisco Rincon
Founded: 2007
Subjects: Literature, Literary Criticism, Essays
ISBN Prefix(es): 978-84-92698; 978-84-935900
Foreign Rep(s): Panoplia de Libros (Latin America)

Ediciones Omega SA+
c/ Plato, 26, 08006 Barcelona
Tel: 93 201 05 99; 93 201 38 07; 93 201 21 44
Fax: 93 209 73 62
E-mail: omega@ediciones-omega.es
Web Site: www.ediciones-omega.es
Key Personnel
Mng Dir: Antonio Paricio; Gabriel Paricio
Founded: 1948
Also specialize in field guides.
Subjects: Agriculture, Biological Sciences, Chemistry, Chemical Engineering, Film, Video, Geography, Geology, Literature, Literary Criticism, Essays, Medicine, Nursing, Dentistry, Music, Dance, Natural History, Photography, Science (General), Technology
ISBN Prefix(es): 978-84-282; 978-84-7082
Associate Companies: Editorial Iberia SA; Ediciones Medici SA

Omnicon SA+
Seis de diciembre, s/n, Local 25, 28023 Madrid
SAN: 004-4164
Tel: 91 740 20 81 *Fax:* 91 357 92 95
E-mail: revistafv@omnicon.es
Web Site: www.omnicon.es
Key Personnel
Dir & International Rights: Juan M Varela
Founded: 1988
Subjects: Photography, Photography & Imaging Technical Books
ISBN Prefix(es): 978-84-88914

Opera Tres Ediciones Musicales SL+
Daza Valdes, 7 Nave 6-7, 28914 Madrid
SAN: 004-4210
Tel: 916801505 *Fax:* 916807626
E-mail: operatres@operatres.com
Web Site: www.operatres.com
Publication & distribution of printed music, books & recordings.
Subjects: Music, Dance, Spanish Classical Guitar
ISBN Prefix(es): 978-84-7893

OQO Editora
Alemana 72, 36162 Pontevedra
Tel: 986 109 270 *Fax:* 986 109 356
Web Site: www.oqo.es
Key Personnel
Owner: Eva Mejuto
Founded: 2005
Subjects: Literature, Literary Criticism, Essays
ISBN Prefix(es): 978-84-934499; 978-84-934516; 978-84-96788
Foreign Rep(s): Agence du livre (Canada); Altera (Belgium); Baker & Taylor (USA); The Bilingual Publications Co (USA); Brodart Co (USA); CELESA (worldwide); Chulainn Publishing Corp (USA); Colofon (Mexico); Editorial Comunicarte (Argentina); Doukeisha Co Ltd (Japan); Italia Shobo (Japan); O bichinho de conto (Portugal); Olf (Switzerland); Penguin Books (Portugal); Roundhouse Group (UK); Vilo (France)

Ediciones del Oriente y del Mediterraneo+
C/ Prado Luis, 11, 28440 Guadarrama, Madrid
Tel: 918 543 428
E-mail: info@orienteymediterraneo.com
Web Site: www.orienteymediterraneo.com
Key Personnel
Dir: Inmaculada Jimenez Morell
Founded: 1989
Subjects: Asian Studies, Biography, Memoirs, Developing Countries, Education, Ethnicity, Fiction, Foreign Countries, History, Literature, Literary Criticism, Essays, Nonfiction (General), Philosophy, Poetry, Religion - Islamic, Social Sciences, Sociology, Women's Studies
ISBN Prefix(es): 978-84-87198; 978-84-96327
Number of titles published annually: 12 Print; 8 E-Book

Total Titles: 149 Print; 64 E-Book
Distribution Center: La Panoplia Export SL, C/Andorra 69, 28043 Madrid *Tel:* 913004390 *Fax:* 913886518 *E-mail:* export@panopliadelibros.com *Web Site:* www.panopliadelibros.com
L'Alebrije, C/Gosol, 39, 08017 Barcelona *Tel:* 932800677 *Fax:* 932057724 *E-mail:* alebrije@alebrije.e.telefonica.net
Baker & Taylor, 1120 Route 22 E, Bridgewater, NJ 08807-0885, United States *Tel:* 908-541-7464 *Fax:* 908-541-7862

Editorial Alfredo Ortells SL
C/ Carboner, 44, Parque Empresarial Destro Junto PI Fuente del Jarro, 46980 Paterna (Valencia)
SAN: 002-2500
Tel: 96 134 54 84 *Fax:* 96 134 54 85
E-mail: editorial@ortells.com
Web Site: www.ortells.com
Key Personnel
Mng Dir: Alfredo Ortells
Founded: 1952
Subjects: Poetry
ISBN Prefix(es): 978-84-7189; 978-84-9748

Oxford University Press Espana SA+
Edificio Atenas, Parque empresarial San Fernando, 28830 Madrid
Tel: 902 876 878
E-mail: contactoprofesor@oupe.es; prensa@oupe.es
Web Site: www.oup.es
Key Personnel
Mng Dir: Jesus Lezcano
Founded: 1992
Subjects: Education, Language Arts, Linguistics, English Language Teaching
ISBN Prefix(es): 978-84-8104
Total Titles: 93 Print
Parent Company: Oxford University Press, United Kingdom

Pages Editors+
Sant Salvador, 8, 25005 Lleida
SAN: 004-4636
Tel: 973 23 66 11 *Fax:* 973 24 07 95
E-mail: editorial@pageseditors.cat
Web Site: www.pageseditors.cat
Key Personnel
Dir: Lluis Pages Marigot
Editor: Ramon Badia
Founded: 1990
Specialize in Catalan & Spanish books.
Subjects: Agriculture, Anthropology, Drama, Theater, Ethnicity, Fiction, History, Nonfiction (General), Philosophy, Psychology, Psychiatry, Religion - Catholic, Social Sciences, Sociology
ISBN Prefix(es): 978-84-7935; 978-84-9779
Associate Companies: Editorial Milenio Arts Grafiques Bobala, SL
Distributed by L'Arc de Bera

La Pagina Ediciones SL
C/ Sauco 8, 38360 El Sauzal (Tenerife)
Tel: 649 190 093
Key Personnel
Dir General: Domingo-Luis Hernandez
Dir: S D Suria *Tel:* 629 257 644
Subjects: Literature, Literary Criticism, Essays
ISBN Prefix(es): 978-84-931032; 978-84-932868
Branch Office(s)
Av del Manzanares 62, 4° D, 28026 Madrid

Editorial Paginas de Espuma SL
C/ Madera 3, 1° izq, 28004 Madrid
Tel: 91 522 72 51; 91 522 49 48
E-mail: prensa@ppespuma.com; ventas@ppespuma.com; ppespuma@arrakis.es
Web Site: paginasdeespuma.com

Key Personnel
Editor: Juan Casamayor; Encarnacion Molina
Subjects: Biography, Memoirs, Fiction, Literature, Literary Criticism, Essays, Philosophy, Social Sciences, Sociology
ISBN Prefix(es): 978-84-95642; 978-84-931243
Foreign Rep(s): L'Alebrije (Spain); Baker & Taylor Inc (USA); The Bilingual Books (USA); Brodart Co (USA); Casalini Libri (Spain); Celesa SA (Spain); Colofon SA (Mexico); Libreria Cuesta/Centro Cuesta Nacional (Dominican Republic); Desarrollos Culturales Costarricenses DCC SA Libreria Internacional (Costa Rica); DL Libros (Venezuela); Exedra Books (Panama); La Familia Distribuidora de Libros (Peru); Gea Llibres SL (Spain); Libros Gussi (Uruguay); El Hombre de la Mancha (Panama); Ibero Librerias (Peru); Libreria La Ceiba (El Salvador); Latin American Book Source Inc (USA); Lectorum Publications Inc (USA); Libreria Lehmann SA (Costa Rica); LibriMundi (Ecuador); Mr Books (Ecuador); La Panoplia (Spain); Plaza & Janes Colombia SA (Colombia); Premia SL (Spain); Proeme/Libreria Guadalquivir (Argentina); Pujol & Amado SLL (Spain); Puvill Libros SA (Spain); Libreria Santa Fe (Argentina); Sophos (Guatemala); Ediciones Tecnicas Paraguayas SRL (Paraguay); Libreria La Tertulia (Puerto Rico); La Tierra Libros SL (Spain); El Virrey (Peru); Jorge Waldhuter Distribuidor (Argentina); Liberalia Distribuidora Yachaywasi (Bolivia); Librerias Yenny/El Ateneo (Argentina); Ediciones Zeta (Peru)

Paginos Libros de Magia
C/ Silva, 13 3°-A, 28004 Madrid
Tel: 915 411 611 *Fax:* 639 472 625
E-mail: info@librosdemagia.com
Web Site: www.librosdemagia.com
Founded: 1992
Subjects: Magic
ISBN Prefix(es): 978-84-89749

Ediciones Paidos Iberica SA+
Member of Grupo Planeta
Av Diagonal, 662-664, 08034 Barcelona
Tel: 93 241 92 50
E-mail: paidos@paidos.com
Web Site: www.planetadelibros.com/editorial-ediciones-paidos-3.html
Key Personnel
Press Officer: Anna Portabella *Tel:* 93 492 89 61 *E-mail:* aportabella@planeta.es
Founded: 1945
Specialize in humanities & social sciences.
Subjects: Communications, Film, Video, Government, Political Science, Health, Nutrition, History, Philosophy, Psychology, Psychiatry, Self-Help, Social Sciences, Sociology, Humanities, Parenting, Pedagogy, Popular Science
ISBN Prefix(es): 978-84-7509; 978-84-493
Associate Companies: Editorial Paidos SAICF, Av Indepencia 1682/1686, C1100ABQ Buenos Aires, Argentina *Tel:* (011) 4124 9100 *Web Site:* www.paidosargentina.com.ar; Editorial Paidos Mexicana SA, Av Presidente Masarik, Col Chapultepec Morales, 11570 Mexico, DF, Mexico *Tel:* (0155) 3000-6200; (0155) 3000-6202 (sales) *E-mail:* ventaspaidos@paidos.com.mx *Web Site:* www.paidos.com.mx
Distributed by Editorial Paidos SAICF; Editorial Planeta Chilena SA; Editorial Planeta Colombiana SA; Editorial Planeta Del Ecuador; Editorial Paidos Mexicana SA; Editorial Planeta Peru; Sara Grecco Editorials; Editorial Planeta Uruguay; Editorial Planeta Venezolana SA

Editorial Paidotribo
Poligono Les Guixeres, C/ de la Energia, 19-21, 08915 Badalona
Tel: 93 323 33 11 *Fax:* 93 453 50 33

E-mail: paidotribo@paidotribo.com
Web Site: www.paidotribo.com
Key Personnel
Dir General: Emilio Ortega Gomez
Foreign Rights Dir: Remei Piqueras
Founded: 1985
Subjects: Crafts, Games, Hobbies, Education,
Health, Nutrition, Medicine, Nursing, Dentistry,
Sports, Athletics, Veterinary Science, Anatomy,
Physiology
ISBN Prefix(es): 978-84-8019; 978-84-86475;
978-84-9910
Number of titles published annually: 100 Print; 1
CD-ROM; 35 E-Book
Total Titles: 1,020 Print; 6 CD-ROM; 120 E-
Book
Imprints: Disfruto y Hago (crafts); Parramon
Paidotribo (sports, medicine, health & physi-
cal education)
Branch Office(s)
Adolfo Alsina 1537, C1088AAM Buenos Aires,
Argentina *Tel:* (011) 4383-6454 *Fax:* (011)
4383-0135 *E-mail:* paidotribo.argentina@
paidotribo.com *Web Site:* www.paidotribo.com.
ar
Calle Lago Viedma 81, 03020 Mexico, DF,
Mexico *Tel:* (0155) 55239670 *Fax:* (0155)
55239670 *E-mail:* paidotribo.mexico@
paidotribo.com *Web Site:* www.paidotribo.com.
mx
Foreign Rep(s): Paidotribo Mexico (Mexico)

Ediciones El Pais SA
Gran Via, 32, 4a planta, 28013 Madrid
SAN: 001-6888
Tel: 91 337 82 00; 91 536 55 00 *Fax:* 91 304 87
66; 91 536 55 55
E-mail: prisabs@prisabs.com; deports@elpais.es
Web Site: elpais.com
Founded: 1976
Subjects: How-to, Journalism, Language Arts,
Linguistics, Nonfiction (General), Self-Help,
Travel & Tourism
ISBN Prefix(es): 978-84-86459; 978-84-95595

El Paisaje Editorial+
Arangoiti, 8, 48850 Aranguren
SAN: 002-7774
Tel: 946390774
Founded: 1981
Subjects: Biography, Memoirs, Drama, Theater,
Fiction, Literature, Literary Criticism, Essays,
Music, Dance, Poetry
ISBN Prefix(es): 978-84-7697; 978-84-7541; 978-
84-85956

Ediciones Palabra SA+
Pº de la Castellana, 210, 28046 Madrid
Tel: 91 350 77 39; 91 350 77 20 *Fax:* 91 359 02
30
E-mail: palabra@palabra.es
Web Site: www.palabra.es
Founded: 1965
Subjects: Biography, Memoirs, Education, His-
tory, Philosophy, Religion - Other, Theology,
Family, Leisure Time
ISBN Prefix(es): 978-84-7118; 978-84-8239; 978-
84-9840
Number of titles published annually: 80 Print; 1
CD-ROM
Total Titles: 500 Print; 1 CD-ROM

Palabras Mayores, *imprint of* Editorial Alhulia
SA

Ediciones Paraninfo SA+
Calle Velazquez no, 31º, 28001 Madrid
Tel: 902 995 240; 985 27 46 96 (press) *Fax:* 914
456 218
E-mail: info@paraninfo.com; comunicacion@
paraninfo.es

Web Site: www.paraninfo.es
Key Personnel
Dir: Manuel Montalban Velasco
Founded: 1948
Subjects: Biological Sciences, Business, Com-
puter Science, How-to, Management, Physical
Sciences, Science (General), Technology
ISBN Prefix(es): 978-84-283; 978-84-9732
Bookshop(s): Melendez Valdes 65, Madrid 28015

Parlamento Vasco
Becerro de Bengoa, 01005 Vitoria-Gasteiz
Tel: 945 00 40 00 *Fax:* 945 13 54 06
E-mail: legebiltzarra@legebiltzarra.eus
Web Site: www.legebiltzarra.eus
Subjects: History, Law, Social Sciences, Sociol-
ogy
ISBN Prefix(es): 978-84-87122

Parramon Paidotribo, *imprint of* Editorial
Paidotribo

Parramon Paidotribo SL+
Imprint of Editorial Paidotribo
C/ de la Energia, 19-21, 08915 Badalona
Tel: 93 323 33 11 *Fax:* 93 453 50 33
E-mail: foreignrights.parramon@paidotribo.com;
paidotribo@paidotribo.com
Web Site: www.paidotribo.com; www.parramon.
com
Key Personnel
General Dir: Emilio Ortega
Foreign Rights Dir: Ms Remei Piqueras
Subjects: Architecture & Interior Design, Art,
Crafts, Games, Hobbies, Education, Fashion,
Fiction, Health, Nutrition, How-to, Medicine,
Nursing, Dentistry, Music, Dance, Nonfic-
tion (General), Self-Help, Sports, Athletics,
Technology, Parenting, Practical Art, Sports
Medicine
ISBN Prefix(es): 978-84-8019; 978-84-342; 978-
84-9910
Foreign Rep(s): Aletea (Uruguay); Libreria Arca-
dia (Peru); Artemis Edinter (Guatemala); Libre-
rias Artemis (Guatemala); Bibliografica Interna-
cional (Chile); Libreria Lehmann (Costa Rica);
Distribuidora Lewis (Panama); Del Monte
SRL (Argentina); Galo Moreno (Ecuador);
Paidotribo Mexico (Mexico); Editorial Reverte
Colombiana SA (Colombia)

Editorial El Pasaje de las Letras
Teresa Gil 16, Entreplanta, 47002 Valladolid
Tel: 983 33 29 61
Founded: 2004
ISBN Prefix(es): 978-84-936761; 978-84-935402

Centre de Pastoral Liturgica+
Napols 346, 1, 08025 Barcelona
Tel: 933 022 235 *Fax:* 933 184 218
E-mail: cpl@cpl.es
Web Site: www.cpl.es
Key Personnel
President: Jaume Fontbona Misse
Founded: 1966
Subjects: Literature, Literary Criticism, Essays,
Religion - Other, Theology
ISBN Prefix(es): 978-84-7467; 978-84-9805
Warehouse: Pujudes, 77-79, Barcelona

Ediciones Patrimonio
C/ Martin el Humano, 12, 46008 Valencia
Tel: 96 382 18 34
E-mail: admin@patrimonio-ediciones.com; info@
patrimonioediciones.com
Web Site: www.patrimonio-ediciones.com
Specialize in facsimiles of medieval codices.
Subjects: Art, History, Religion - Other, Theology

ISBN Prefix(es): 978-84-95061
Branch Office(s)
C/ Villanueva, 2 esc 3-6ºA (esquina Pº Recolectos
18), 28001 Madrid *Tel:* 607 72 35 65

Pearson Educacion SA+
Ribera del Loira, 28, 28042 Madrid
SAN: 002-2527
Tel: 91 382 83 00 *Fax:* 91 382 83 29
E-mail: pearson.educacion@pearson.com
Web Site: pearson.es
Key Personnel
President: John Fallon
Founded: 1942
Subjects: Art, Education, History, Language Arts,
Linguistics, Medicine, Nursing, Dentistry, Phi-
losophy, Psychology, Psychiatry, Science (Gen-
eral)
ISBN Prefix(es): 978-84-205
Parent Company: Pearson PLC, United Kingdom

Ediciones Pegaso, *imprint of* Editoriales de
Derecho Reunidas SA (EDERSA)

Penguin Random House Grupo Editorial
Travessera de Gracia 47-49, 08021 Barcelona
Tel: 93 366 03 00; 90 030 01 27 (orders); 93 663
30 30 (orders) *Fax:* 93 366 04 49
Web Site: penguinrandomhousegrupoeditorial.com
Key Personnel
CEO: Nuria Cabuti
Foreign Rights Manager: Maria Reina de la
Puebla *Tel:* 93 366 03 12 *E-mail:* mariareina.
delapuebla@penguinrandomhouse.com
Subjects: Business, Fiction, Literature, Literary
Criticism, Essays, Nonfiction (General), Ro-
mance, Science Fiction, Fantasy
Parent Company: Penguin Random House (USA)
Imprints: Arete; Ediciones B; Ediciones B Mex-
ico SA de CV; Beascoa; Caballo de Troya;
Collins; Conecta; Debate; Debolsillo; Electa;
Fantascy; Grijalbo; Grijaldo Ilustrados; Lumen;
Lumen Infantil; Mondadori; Montena; Nube
de Tinta; Plaza y Janes; Random; Reservoir
Books; RHM Flash (ebooks); Rosa dels Vents;
Sudamericana
Branch Office(s)
Agustin de Betancourt, 19, 28003 Madrid *Tel:* 91
535 8190 *Fax:* 91 535 8939
Distributed by Penguin Random House (USA)
Foreign Rights: xyz

Ediciones Peninsula, *imprint of* grup62

Ediciones Peninsula
Imprint of grup62
Pº de Recoletos, 4, 28001 Madrid
E-mail: info@edicionespeninsula.com
Web Site: www.planetadelibros.com/editorial-
ediciones-peninsula-73.html
Key Personnel
Editor: Ester Pujol *E-mail:* epujol@grup62.com
Founded: 1964
Subjects: Biography, Memoirs, History, Philoso-
phy, Social Sciences, Sociology, Humanities
ISBN Prefix(es): 978-84-9942
Distribution Center: Enlaces Editoriales, Rambla
de Catalunya, 135 3a planta, 08008 Barcelona
Tel: 93 218 50 20 *Fax:* 93 218 55 30

Pentalfa Ediciones+
Division of Grupo Helicon SA
Apdo 360, 33080 Oviedo
Tel: 985 985 386 *Fax:* 985 985 512
E-mail: pentalfa@helicon.es
Web Site: www.helicon.es/index.htm
Founded: 1974
Subjects: Anthropology, Philosophy
ISBN Prefix(es): 978-84-85422; 978-84-7848
Total Titles: 3 Print; 2 CD-ROM

Perea Ediciones+
Calle Velazquez 31, 13620 Pedro Munoz
Tel: 926586386
Founded: 1987
Subjects: Astrology, Occult, Literature, Literary
   Criticism, Essays
ISBN Prefix(es): 978-84-7729

Editorial Peregrino SL
La Almazara, 19, Apdo 19, 13350 Moral de Cala-
   trava, Ciudad Real
Tel: 926 349 634 *Fax:* 926 319 459
E-mail: info@editorialperegrino.com
Web Site: www.editorialperegrino.com
Key Personnel
Dir: Demetrio Canovas *E-mail:* director@
   editorialperegrino.com
Founded: 1979
Editing & distributing religious literature.
Subjects: Biblical Studies, Biography, Memoirs,
   Religion - Protestant
ISBN Prefix(es): 978-84-86589; 978-84-96562
Number of titles published annually: 24 Print
Total Titles: 170 Print
Distributed by Distribuidora Bereana (USA);
   Cristianismo Historico (USA)
Distributor for El Estandarte de la Verdad; Faro
   de Gracia; Libros Desafio
Book Club(s): Club Peregrino, La Almazara, 19,
   Apdo 19, 13350 Moral de Calatrava, Ciudad
   Real

Editorial Perfils
Joaquim Costa 38, 25110 Alpicat, Lleida
Mailing Address: Apdo de Correos, 2, 25110
   Alpicat (Lleida)
Tel: 973 738175; 696 300774
E-mail: editorial@perfils.info
Web Site: www.perfils.info
Key Personnel
Dir: Mario Arque *E-mail:* mario@perfils.info
Subjects: Aeronautics, Aviation, Sports, Athletics,
   Hang Gliding, Paragliding, Thermal Flying
ISBN Prefix(es): 978-84-87695

Editorial Periferica
Apdo de Correos 293, 10001 Caceres
Tel: 915 390 249; 692 148 294 (cell)
E-mail: info@editorialperiferica.com
Web Site: www.editorialperiferica.com
Key Personnel
Editorial Dir: Julian Rodriguez
Founded: 2006
Subjects: Fiction
ISBN Prefix(es): 978-84-935492; 978-84-936926;
   978-84-92865
Foreign Rep(s): Independent Publishers Group
   (USA); Liberalia Ediciones (Chile); Dis-
   tribuidora de Libros Heraldos Negros (Peru);
   La Panoplia Export (Latin America exc Ar-
   gentina, Chile, Mexico & Peru); SP Distribu-
   ciones (Mexico); Distrbuidora Waldhuter (Ar-
   gentina)

Publicaciones Permanyer SL+
Mallorca, 310, 08037 Barcelona
Tel: 93 207 5920 *Fax:* 93 457 6642
E-mail: permanyer@permanyer.com
Web Site: www.permanyer.com
Founded: 1973
Specialize in medical publications in Spanish,
   Portuguese & English.
Subjects: Medicine, Nursing, Dentistry, Veterinary
   Science
Branch Office(s)
Paseo del Prado, 14, 2°-E, 28014 Madrid
   E-mail: madrid@permanyer.com
Av Engenheiro LC Berrini, 1461, An-
   dar 4, 04571-011 Sao Paulo-SP, Brazil
   E-mail: brasil@permanyer.com

Temistocles, 315-Colonia Polanco, Delegacion
   Miguel Hidalgo, 11560 Mexico, DF, Mexico
   E-mail: mexico@permanyer.com
Avda Duque d'Avila n° 92, 7° E, 1050-084 Lis-
   bon, Portugal *E-mail:* portugal@permanyer.com
Chemain du Molan, 6, 1295 Tannay, Switzerland
   E-mail: suisse@permanyer.com

Editorial Perpetuo Socorro+
C/ Covarrubias, 19, 28010 Madrid
Tel: 91 445 51 26 *Fax:* 91 445 51 27
E-mail: perso@pseditorial.com
Web Site: www.pseditorial.com
Founded: 1899
Membership(s): Catholic Association of Publish-
   ers of Spain (AECE).
Subjects: Behavioral Sciences, Biblical Studies,
   Biography, Memoirs, Education, Music, Dance,
   Religion - Catholic, Religion - Other, Theology
ISBN Prefix(es): 978-84-284

Pintar-Pintar Editorial
C/ Rosal n°6 2°-3, 33009 Oviedo
Tel: 985 22 91 55
E-mail: info@pintar-pintar.com
Web Site: www.pintar-pintar.com
Key Personnel
Partner & Dir General: Angela Sanchez
Founded: 2005
Subjects: Children's Literature
ISBN Prefix(es): 978-84-937325; 978-84-936266

Ediciones Piramide+
Calle Juan Ignacio Luca de Tena, n° 15, 28027
   Madrid
Tel: 91 393 89 89 *Fax:* 91 742 36 61
E-mail: piramide@anaya.es
Web Site: www.edicionespiramide.es
Founded: 1973
Subjects: Business, Economics, Psychology, Psy-
   chiatry, Science (General), Technology, Out-
   reach & Training
ISBN Prefix(es): 978-84-368
Parent Company: Grupo Anaya

Pirene Editorial SAL+
Calle Ausias Marc, 16, 3r la, 08010 Barcelona
SAN: 004-5314
Tel: 933 187 794 *Fax:* 933 178 242
Founded: 1987
Editions in Spanish & Catalan.
Specialize in infants' & children's books.
Subjects: Biography, Memoirs, Education, Fiction,
   Humor
ISBN Prefix(es): 978-84-7766

Pirueta Editorial, *imprint of* Roca Editorial

Editorial Planeta SA, *imprint of* grup62

Editorial Planeta SA+
Member of Grupo Planeta
Av Diagonal, 662-664, 08034 Barcelona
Tel: 93 496 70 01 *Fax:* 93 496 70 11
E-mail: atencionalcliente@planeta.es
Web Site: www.planetadelibros.com/editorial-
   editorial-planeta-8.html
Key Personnel
Chief Executive Officer: Jose Lara Garcia
President: Joseph Creuheras Margenat
Executive Vice President: Carlos Fernandez
   Sanchiz
Dir, Communication: Laura Franch *Tel:* 91 423
   03 03 *E-mail:* lfranch@planeta.es
Founded: 1945
Subjects: Fiction, Nonfiction (General)
ISBN Prefix(es): 978-84-320; 978-84-8460; 978-
   84-395; 978-84-08; 978-970-37
Associate Companies: Planeta/Agostini (Forum
   y Fasciculos Planeta), Aribau 185, 08021
   Barcelona; Sudamericana/Planeta SA (Edi-

tores), Argentina; Lord Cochrane SA, Ave
   Providencia 727, Santiago, Chile; Editorial
   Artemisa SA, Ave Cuauhtemoc 1236 - 4, Colo-
   nia Vertiz Narvarte, Delegacion Benito Juarez,
   03600 Mexico, DF, Mexico; Editorial Joaquin
   Mortiz SA, Mexico
Imprints: Zenith

Del Planeta Rojo Ediciones
Imprint of Planeta Rojo Comunicacion
C/Salvador Dali, 7 Bloque, 2, 1° B, 29620 Torre-
   molinos, Malaga
Tel: 951 13 74 81
Key Personnel
Administration: Begona Romero
Editorial & Production: David Tejeiro
Subjects: Fiction, Poetry, Narrative
ISBN Prefix(es): 978-84-611; 978-84-612; 978-
   84-937061

Plata, *imprint of* Ediciones Urano SA

Plataforma Editorial SL
C/ Muntaner, 269 Entlo 1a, 08021 Barcelona
Tel: 93 494 79 99 *Fax:* 93 419 23 14
E-mail: info@plataformaeditorial.com;
   prensa@plataformaeditorial.com; rights@
   plataformaeditorial.com
Web Site: www.plataformaeditorial.com
Key Personnel
Dir: Jordi Nadal
Press: Miriam Malagrida
Rights: Sandra Naharro
Founded: 2007
Subjects: Career Development, Cookery, Fiction,
   History
ISBN Prefix(es): 978-84-15750; 978-84-15115
Total Titles: 200 Print

Play Attitude
C/ Historiador Maians n° 20 bajos, 08026
   Barcelona
Tel: 943 357 888 *Fax:* 943 568 310
E-mail: info@playattitude.com
Web Site: playattitude.com
ISBN Prefix(es): 978-84-15149
Parent Company: Play Creatividad SL

Plaza y Janes, *imprint of* Penguin Random
   House Grupo Editorial

Plaza y Janes Editores SA+
Imprint of Penguin Random House Grupo Edito-
   rial
Travessera de Gracia 47-49, 08021 Barcelona
Tel: 93 366 03 00 *Fax:* 93 200 22 19
Web Site: www.megustaleer.com/sello/PJ/plaza-
   janes
Founded: 1959
Subjects: Biography, Memoirs, Fiction, History,
   Nonfiction (General)
ISBN Prefix(es): 978-84-01
Number of titles published annually: 100 Print
Total Titles: 500 Print

Pleniluni Edicions SA+
Riera Fosca, 7, 08328 Barcelona
Tel: 93 5552851
Founded: 1979
Membership(s): Association of Editors in Llen-
   gua, Catalana & Gremi.
Subjects: Crafts, Games, Hobbies, Science Fic-
   tion, Fantasy, Sports, Athletics
ISBN Prefix(es): 978-84-85752; 978-84-89467

Editorial Pliegos+
Veronica 8 bajo C, 28014 Madrid
SAN: 002-6247
Tel: 914 291 545 *Fax:* 914 291 545
E-mail: pliegos@pliegoseditorial.com

Web Site: www.pliegoseditorial.com
Key Personnel
Dir: Cesar Leante Gonzalez
Founded: 1982
Subjects: Drama, Theater, Fiction, Journalism,
Literature, Literary Criticism, Essays, Poetry
ISBN Prefix(es): 978-84-88435; 978-84-86214;
978-84-96045

Plot Ediciones SA+
San Rogelio, 8, 28039 Madrid
Tel: 914 505 770 *Fax:* 914 505 770
Web Site: www.eirelink.com/plot/catalogo.htm
Key Personnel
Dir: Jesus Rodriguez Trueba
Founded: 1987
Subjects: Film, Video
ISBN Prefix(es): 978-84-86702
Number of titles published annually: 4 Print

La Poesia, Senor Hidalgo
Leiva 25, bajos, 08014 Barcelona
Tel: 934211897 *Fax:* 934211897
E-mail: poesia@poesiahidalgo.com
Web Site: www.poesiahidalgo.com
Key Personnel
Dir: Juan Ramon Ortega Ugena
Subjects: Poetry
ISBN Prefix(es): 978-84-95976
Foreign Rep(s): La Panoplia Export (worldwide
exc Spain)

Poesta SA, *imprint of* Editorial Alhulia SA

Ediciones Polifemo
Avda de Bruselas, 44, 28028 Madrid
SAN: 001-9313
Tel: 917 257 101 *Fax:* 913 556 811
E-mail: libros@polifemo.com
Web Site: www.polifemo.com
Founded: 1980
Subjects: Anthropology, Archaeology, Asian Stud-
ies, History, Travel & Tourism, American His-
tory, History of the Philippines, History of
Spain, History of Travel
ISBN Prefix(es): 978-84-86547; 978-84-96813
Total Titles: 45 Print

Ediciones Poligrafa+
Balmes 54 entlo 2a, 08007 Barcelona
Tel: 93 396 88 46 *Fax:* 93 467 21 72
E-mail: info@edicionespoligrafa.com;
ventas@edicionespoligrafa.com; export@
edicionespoligrafa.com
Web Site: www.edicionespoligrafa.com
Founded: 1962
Specialize in the graphic arts.
Subjects: Architecture & Interior Design, Art,
Photography
ISBN Prefix(es): 978-84-343
Foreign Rep(s): Asia Publishers Services (Ed-
ward Summerson) (China, Hong Kong, Ko-
rea, Philippines, Taiwan); Book Bird Publish-
ers (Anwer Iqbal) (Pakistan); Coen Sligting
Bookimport (Netherlands); Elisabeth Harder-
Kreimann (Scandinavia); IMA InterMedi-
aAmericana (Africa exc South Africa); Inter-
art (France); Jacana Media (Pty) Ltd (Shay
Heydenrych) (South Africa); Josef Kolar Publishers' Representative (Eastern Europe exc
Russia); Lonnie Kahn Ltd (Aviva Karlinski)
(Israel); Prestel Verlag (Reegan Koester) (Austria, Germany, Switzerland); Publishers' Export (Sandro Salucci) (Greece); Gabrielle Redmond (Ireland); Sales East (Peter Couzens)
(Southeast Asia); Signature Book Representation (Mel Howells) (East Anglia, England,
Southeast UK); Signature Book Representation
(Jim Sheehan) (Midlands, North UK, Northern Wales, Scotland); TBI - Publisher & Distributors (Raavi Sabharwal) (Bhutan, India,

Nepal, Sri Lanka); Henry Thompson (London);
United Publishers Services Ltd (Japan); Uni-
versity Presses Marketing (Andrew Gilman)
(Southern Wales, Southwest England); Peter
Ward Book Exports (Richard Ward) (Eastern
Mediterranean, Middle East, North Africa)
Distribution Center: LOGGILIBRO, Rosello,
87-89, 08029 Barcelona *Tel:* 933 228 161
Fax: 933 229 205 *E-mail:* pedidos@ggili.com
(Spain, Brazil & Portugal)
ASPPAN SL, Calle de la Fundicion, 15, Pol In-
dustrial Santa Ana, 28529 Rivas Vaciamadrid,
Madrid *Tel:* 916665001 *Fax:* 913012683
E-mail: asppan@asppan.com (Argentina,
Bolivia, Chile, Ecuador, Paraguay, Peru &
Uruguay)
Peribo Pty Ltd, 58 Beaumont Rd, Mount Kuring-
gai, NSW 2080, Australia *Tel:* (02) 9457 0011
Fax: (02) 9457 0022 *E-mail:* info@peribo.com.
au
Siglo del Hombre, Carrera 31A No 25B-50,
Santa Fe de Bogota, Colombia *Tel:* (01) 337
7700 *Fax:* (01) 337 7665 *E-mail:* info@
siglodelhombre.com
Gustavo Gili Mexico, Av Valle de Bravo No 21,
Col Fracc El Mirador, 53050 Naucalpan, Mex-
ico *Tel:* (0155) 60 60 11 *Fax:* (0153) 60 14 56
E-mail: ggili@prodigy.net.mx
Macmillan Distribution (MDL), Brunel Rd,
Houndmills, Basingstoke, Hants RG21 6XS,
United Kingdom *Tel:* (0845) 070 5656 (UK);
(01256) 302692 (European); (01256) 329242
(non-European) *Fax:* (01256) 812558 (UK cus-
tomer service); (01256) 842084 (export customer service) *E-mail:* orders@macmillan.co.uk
Web Site: www.macmillandistribution.co.uk
Prestel Publishing Ltd, 14-17 Wells St, London
W1T 3PD, United Kingdom *Tel:* (020) 7323
5004 *Fax:* (020) 7323 0271 *E-mail:* sales@
prestel-uk.co.uk *Web Site:* www.prestel.com
Artbook/DAP, 155 Sixth Ave, New York, NY
10013, United States *E-mail:* orders@dapinc.
com *Web Site:* www.artbook.com (USA &
Canada)

Editorial Popular+
Doctor Esquerdo, 173 6° Izda, 28007 Madrid
SAN: 002-6263
Tel: 91 409 35 73 *Fax:* 91 573 41 73
E-mail: popular@editorialpopular.com
Web Site: www.editorialpopular.com
Founded: 1973
Subjects: Education, Government, Political Sci-
ence, Literature, Literary Criticism, Essays,
Self-Help, Social Sciences, Sociology, Chinese
Culture
ISBN Prefix(es): 978-84-85016; 978-84-86524;
978-84-7884

Porcia Ediciones SL
C/ Aragon, 621, 4° 1a, 08026 Barcelona
Tel: 93 245 54 76 *Fax:* 93 245 54 76
Web Site: www.edicionesporcia.com
Subjects: Astrology, Occult, Inspirational, Spiri-
tuality, Religion - Other, Angels, Macrobiotics,
Meditation
ISBN Prefix(es): 978-84-95513; 978-84-930812
U.S. Office(s): Porcia Publishing Corp, 13155
SW 123 Ave, Unit 11, Miami, FL 33186-5943,
United States *Tel:* 305-364-0035; 305-395-7716
Fax: 786-573-0000
Foreign Rep(s): Baker & Taylor (USA); Edi-
ciones Cerro Manquehue SA (Chile); Cesar
Arrocha Graell y Cia SA (Panama); Dellare
SA (Guatemala); Downtown Book Center
Inc (USA); Grupo Federspiel (Costa Rica);
Ediciones Gaviota (Colombia); Distribuidora
Gilavil (Venezuela); Giron Distribuidores
(USA); Distribuidora Grupal (Argentina); Lec-
torum SA de CV (Mexico); Lectorum USA
(USA); Porica Publishing (USA); Spanish Pe-
riodical & Book Sale (USA); Distribuidora
Tarots del Mundo (Mexico)

Editorial Portic SA, *imprint of* grup62

Editorial Portic SA+
Imprint of grup62
C/ Peu de la Creu, 4, 08001 Barcelona
Tel: 93 443 71 00 *Fax:* 93 443 71 30
E-mail: correu@grup62.com
Web Site: www.grup62.cat/editorial-editorial-
portic-68.html
Key Personnel
Foreign Rights: Pilar Lafuente *Tel:* 93 492 82 44
E-mail: plafuente@planeta.es
Founded: 1963
Subjects: Biography, Memoirs, History, Jour-
nalism, Literature, Literary Criticism, Essays,
Nonfiction (General), Travel & Tourism, Guide
Books, Historic Monographs
ISBN Prefix(es): 978-84-7306; 978-84-9809

Edicions Positivas SL
Rua das Carretas, 18, Baixo, 15705 Santiago de
Compostela, Galiza
Tel: 981553051
E-mail: positivas@edicionspositivas.com
Web Site: www.edicionspositivas.com
Key Personnel
Dir General: Francisco Macias
Founded: 1990
Subjects: Literature, Literary Criticism, Essays
ISBN Prefix(es): 978-84-87783; 978-84-921162

PPC Editorial+
Imprint of Grupo SM
Impresores, 2, Urbanizacion Prado del Espino,
28660 Boadilla de Monte, Madrid
Tel: 91 422 62 09; 91 422 66 99 *Fax:* 91 428 65
91; 91 422 61 20
E-mail: pedidoppc@ppc-editorial.com
Web Site: www.ppc-editorial.com
Key Personnel
President: Antonio Montero
Dir: Luis Aranguren
Communication: Ana Prieto *Tel:* 91 422 63 12
Founded: 1955
Subjects: Education, Philosophy, Religion - Other
ISBN Prefix(es): 978-84-288

Editorial Pre-Textos+
Luis Santangel 10, 1-C, 46005 Valencia
SAN: 001-4354
Tel: 963 333 226 *Fax:* 963 955 477
E-mail: info@pre-textos.com
Web Site: www.pre-textos.com
Key Personnel
Management Dir: Silvia Pratdesaba Lafuente
E-mail: spratdesaba@pre-textos.com
Foreign Rights: Manuel Ramirez Gimenez
E-mail: mramirez@pre-textos.com
Founded: 1976
Subjects: Biography, Memoirs, Fiction, Language
Arts, Linguistics, Literature, Literary Criticism,
Essays, Music, Dance, Nonfiction (General),
Philosophy, Poetry
ISBN Prefix(es): 978-84-85081; 978-84-87101;
978-84-8191
Number of titles published annually: 60 Print
Total Titles: 970 Print
Foreign Rep(s): Editora y Distribuidora Azteca
(Mexico); Fondo de Cutltura Economica
(Colombia); Liberalia Ediciones Ltda (Chile);
Libreria Prosa & Politica (Chile); Distribuidora
Waldhuter (Argentina)
Foreign Rights: Saskia von Hoegen (Literarische
Agentur) (Germany); Sylvia Meucci Agencia
Literaria (worldwide exc Germany)

Prensas Universitarias de Zaragoza+
Edificio de Ciencias Geologicas, Calle Pedro Cer-
buna, 12, 50009 Zaragoza
Tel: 976 761 330; 976 761 000 *Fax:* 976 761 063
E-mail: puz@unizar.es

Web Site: puz.unizar.es
Key Personnel
Editorial Dir: Peter Rujula Lopez *E-mail:* rujula@
unizar.es
Manager: Jose M Arbex Benavides
  E-mail: arbex@unizar.es
Distribution & Sales: Alejandro Aguelo Floria
  E-mail: alaguelo@unizar.es
Founded: 1542
Subjects: History, Literature, Literary Criticism,
  Essays, Science (General), Social Sciences, So-
  ciology, Academic
ISBN Prefix(es): 978-84-7733; 978-84-92774;
  978-84-15538; 978-84-15770
Distributed by Bitacora

Editorial Presencia Gitana
C/ Valderrodrigo, 76 y 78, bajos A, 28039
  Madrid
Tel: 91 373 62 07 *Fax:* 91 373 44 62
E-mail: presenciagitana@presenciagitana.org
Web Site: www.presenciagitana.org
Founded: 1987
Subjects: Anthropology, Biography, Memoirs, Ed-
  ucation, Ethnicity, History, Humor, Social Sci-
  ences, Sociology, Antiracism, Gypsies (Culture,
  Language, Story)
ISBN Prefix(es): 978-84-87347

Editorial Primerapersona
Plaza de Pontevedra nº 6 A, 15003 Coruna
Tel: 981 145 520 *Fax:* 981 913 479
E-mail: info@primerapersona.com;
  comunicacion@primerapersona.com
Web Site: www.primerapersona.com
Key Personnel
Editorial Manager: Yesica Herranz Mesa
Founded: 2000
Subjects: History, Photography, Self-Help
ISBN Prefix(es): 978-84-95923
Parent Company: Monllor y Gey Editores SL
Foreign Rep(s): Baker & Taylor Publisher Ser-
  vices (Canada, USA); Pujol i Amado (Latin
  America)
Distribution Center: IPG Spanish Books, c/o
  Independent Publishers Group (IPG), 814 N
  Franklin St, Chicago, IL 60610, United States

Edicions Proa SA, *imprint of* grup62

Edicions Proa SA+
Imprint of grup62
C/ Peu de la Creu, 4, 08001 Barcelona
Tel: 93 443 71 00 *Fax:* 93 443 71 30
E-mail: original@grup62.com
Web Site: www.grup62.cat/editorial-editorial-proa-
  69.html
Key Personnel
Head, Marketing: Gloria Gasch
Press Officer: Xavier Gafarot
Editorial Manager: Josep Llunch
Editor: Merce Ubach
Founded: 1928
Subjects: Fiction, Literature, Literary Criticism,
  Essays, Poetry, Social Sciences, Sociology
ISBN Prefix(es): 978-84-8256; 978-84-8437; 978-
  84-7588
Bookshop(s): Proa Espais, Diputacio 250, 08007
  Barcelona
Distribution Center: Un Per Un, Solucions Com-
  ercials, c/ d'Agusti Duran i Sanpere, 1, 08001
  Barcelona *Tel:* 93 505 62 00 *Fax:* 93 505 62
  31 *E-mail:* info@unperun.cat

Progensa Editorial+
Parque Industrial PISA-Edificio Censolar, c/
  Comercio 12, 41927 Mairena del Aljarafe,
  Seville
Tel: 954 186 200 *Fax:* 954 186 111
E-mail: progensa@progensa.com
Web Site: www.progensa.es

Founded: 1980
Publishers of technical books.
Subjects: Electronics, Electrical Engineering, En-
  ergy, How-to, Technology
ISBN Prefix(es): 978-84-86505; 978-84-95693
Total Titles: 2 Print; 1 CD-ROM

Promocion Popular Cristiana, see PPC Editorial

Ediciones Pronaos SA+
Mayor 39, 28013 Madrid
SAN: 001-9364
Tel: 676808196
E-mail: edicionespronaos@yahoo.es; pedidos@
  pronaos.net
Web Site: pronaos.net
Subjects: Architecture & Interior Design, Art,
  Gardening, Plants
ISBN Prefix(es): 978-84-85941
Total Titles: 2 CD-ROM
Bookshop(s): Naos-Libros, Quintana-12, 28013
  Madrid *Tel:* 915 473 916

PS Editorial, see Editorial Perpetuo Socorro

Publicaciones de la Universidad de Alicante
Campus San Vicente del Raspeig, s/n, Aulario
  General II, planta baja, 03080 Alicante
Tel: 965 903 480
E-mail: publicaciones.web@ua.es
Web Site: publicaciones.ua.es
Key Personnel
Editor: Vincent M Navarro Bertomeu *Tel:* 965
  909 576
Sales: Diego M Candela Jaen *Tel:* 965 909 445
Founded: 1978
Subjects: Agriculture, Chemistry, Chemical Engi-
  neering, Economics, Literature, Literary Crit-
  icism, Essays, Medicine, Nursing, Dentistry,
  Regional Interests, Science (General), Social
  Sciences, Sociology
ISBN Prefix(es): 978-84-7908; 978-84-86809;
  978-84-940403; 978-84-9717
Distributed by Distribuciones de Enlace SA
Foreign Rep(s): Celesa (Centro de Exportacion de
  Libros Espanoles) (all other territories); Dig-
  italia (Lluis Claret) (USA); Pujol & Amado
  (Latin America); Universitaria de Buenos Aires
  (Argentina); Universo Bibliografico SA de CV
  (Mexico); Jorge Walduther Distribucion de Li-
  bros (Argentina)
Distribution Center: Breogan SL, C/ Lanuza,
  11, 28028 Madrid *Tel:* 917 259 072
  E-mail: breogan@breogan.org

**Publicaciones de la Universidad Pontificia
Comillas-Madrid**
Alberto Aguilera, 23, 28015 Madrid
Tel: 91 542 28 00 *Fax:* 91 559 65 69
E-mail: oia@oia.upcomillas.es
Web Site: www.upco.es
Key Personnel
Dir, Publications Service: Belen Recio Godoy
  E-mail: brecio@pub.upcomillas.es
Founded: 1975
Subjects: Business, Economics, Engineering
  (General), History, Law, Medicine, Nursing,
  Dentistry, Philosophy, Social Sciences, Sociol-
  ogy, Theology, Women's Studies, Humanities
ISBN Prefix(es): 978-84-87840; 978-84-89708;
  978-84-8468; 978-84-85281
Distributed by Edisofer; Ikuska Libros; Melisa;
  Odon Molina; Sal Terrae; Sendra Marco
Foreign Rep(s): Fondos de Publicaciones de
  Iberoamerica y Europa SA (Mexico); Sal Ter-
  rae (Latin America); Jorge Waldhuter (Ar-
  gentina)
Orders to: Universidad Comillas, 3, 28049
  Madrid *Tel:* 91 734 39 50

**Publicacions i Edicions de la Universitat de
Barcelona+**
c/ Adolf Florensa 8, 08028 Barcelona
Tel: 93 403 54 39 *Fax:* 93 403 54 46
E-mail: comandes.ediciones@ub.edu
Web Site: www.publicacions.ub.es
Key Personnel
Dir: Meritxell Carrillo *Tel:* 93 403 54 44
Sales & Marketing: Lidia Cuenca *Tel:* 93 403 47
  61
Founded: 1935
Membership(s): Gremi d'Editors de Catalunya;
  Asociacion Editoriales Universitarias Es-
  panoles.
Subjects: Art, Economics, Education, History,
  Law, Mathematics, Science (General), Social
  Sciences, Sociology
ISBN Prefix(es): 978-84-475; 978-84-7875; 978-
  84-7528
Bookshop(s): Balmes-21, 08071 Barcelona
Warehouse: Baldiri I Reixac, 08028 Barcelona

Publicacions Universitat Rovira i Virgili (URV)
Campus Centre, Av Catalunya, 35, 43005 Tarrag-
  ona
Tel: 977 558 474 *Fax:* 977 558 393
E-mail: publicacions@urv.cat
Web Site: www.urv.cat/publicacions
Key Personnel
Head, Publications: John Bates *Tel:* 977 558 372
  E-mail: infosl@urv.cat
Technical Publications: Jaume Llambrich Brull
Subjects: Art, Language Arts, Linguistics, Liter-
  ature, Literary Criticism, Essays, Philosophy,
  Religion - Other, Science (General), Social Sci-
  ences, Sociology
ISBN Prefix(es): 978-84-8424; 978-84-88693;
  978-84-89866

Puck, *imprint of* Ediciones Urano SA

Puentepalo
C/ Parroco Parer, 1, (trasera de la iglesia), 35260
  Aguimes, Gran Canaria
Tel: 607 949 637
E-mail: editorialpuentepalo@hotmail.com
Web Site: www.puentepalo.com
Key Personnel
Dir General: Juan Ramon Tramunt
Editorial Dir: Maria Jesus Alvarado
Founded: 2001
Subjects: Art, Fiction, Literature, Literary Criti-
  cism, Essays
ISBN Prefix(es): 978-84-611; 978-84-612

Pulso Ediciones SL+
Rambla del Celler, 117-119, 08172 Sant Cugat
  del Valles, Barcelona
Tel: 93 589 62 64 *Fax:* 93 589 50 77
E-mail: info@pulso.com; comercial@pulso.com;
  production@pulso.com
Web Site: www.pulso.com
Key Personnel
Editorial Dir: Beatriz Gallart
Founded: 1978
Subjects: Animals, Pets, Architecture & Inte-
  rior Design, Behavioral Sciences, Computer
  Science, Health, Nutrition, Medicine, Nurs-
  ing, Dentistry, Psychology, Psychiatry, Science
  (General), Veterinary Science
ISBN Prefix(es): 978-84-86671
Branch Office(s)
C/ Cronos, 24, Bloque 1 Bajo E-14, 28037
  Madrid *Tel:* 91 320 58 27 *Fax:* 91 741 81 22

Punto Juvenil, *imprint of* Editorial Casals SA

PUV, see Publicacions de la Universitat de
  Valencia (PUV)

PUZ, see Prensas Universitarias de Zaragoza

Quaderns Crema SA+
Muntaner, 462, 08006 Barcelona
Tel: 934 144 906 *Fax:* 934 147 107
E-mail: correu@quadernscrema.com; rights@
quadernscrema.com
Web Site: www.quadernscrema.com
Key Personnel
Mng Dir: Jaume Vallcorba
Founded: 1979
Membership(s): Gremi D'Editors De Catalunya
(Guild of Editors of Catalonia).
Subjects: History, Literature, Literary Criticism,
Essays, Poetry, Narratives
ISBN Prefix(es): 978-84-85704; 978-84-7727;
978-84-930657; 978-84-96489; 978-84-96136
Number of titles published annually: 60 Print
Total Titles: 907 Print
Subsidiaries: Acantilado
Distributed by Gea Llibres SL; Les Punxes SL
Foreign Rights: Undercover Literary Agents
(Alexander Doboer) (Denmark, Finland, Ger-
many, Netherlands, Norway, Sweden)

RA-MA SA Editorial y Publicaciones
c/Jarama, 3A, Poligno Industrial lgarsa, 28860
Paracuellos de Jarama, Madrid
Tel: 91 658 42 80 *Fax:* 91 662 81 39
E-mail: editorial@ra-ma.com; info@ra-ma.com
Web Site: www.ra-ma.es
Key Personnel
Production: Jesus R Galan *E-mail:* jesusrg@ra-
ma.com
Sales: Luis San Jose *E-mail:* lsanjose@ra-ma.
com; Julio Santoro *E-mail:* jsantoro@ra-ma.
com
Founded: 1985
Subjects: Computer Science, Computers
ISBN Prefix(es): 978-84-7897
Number of titles published annually: 90 Print
Total Titles: 2,100 Print
Foreign Rep(s): Libreria Eduardo Albers Ltda
(Chile); Artemis Edinter (Guatemala); CODEU
(La Corporacion para el Desarrollo de la Ed-
ucacion Universitaria (Ecuador); Librerias
CRISOL SAC (Peru); Cuspide Libros SA
(Argentina); Ecoe Ediciones Ltda (Colom-
bia); Edisa (Costa Rica); Global Ediciones SA
(Venezuela); Hispamer-Libreria Hispanoameri-
cana (Nicaragua); El Hombre de la Mancha
(Panama); INGELSI Cia Ltda (Ecuador); Lib-
rimundi (Ecuador); Limerin (Ecuador); Losa
Libros Ltda (Uruguay); Omniprom SA de CV
(Mexico); Libreria Papiros (Paraguay); Edi-
ciones Tecnicas Paraguayas SRL (Paraguay);
Ediciones de la U (Colombia); Ediciones Zeta
SRL (Peru)

Random, *imprint of* Penguin Random House
Grupo Editorial

Random House Mondadori, see Penguin
Random House Grupo Editorial

Editora Region de Murcia - ERM
Avda de la Fama, 15, 30006 Murcia
Tel: 968 27 98 01
Web Site: www.carm.es
Key Personnel
Contact: Angel Penalver Martinez *E-mail:* angel.
penalver@carm.es
Founded: 1980
Subjects: Anthropology, Archaeology, Architec-
ture & Interior Design, Art, Cookery, Crafts,
Games, Hobbies, Economics, Education, Envi-
ronmental Studies, Gardening, Plants, Geogra-
phy, Geology, History, Literature, Literary Crit-
icism, Essays, Music, Dance, Outdoor Recre-
ation, Philosophy, Poetry, Regional Interests,
Religion - Islamic
ISBN Prefix(es): 978-84-7564
Distributed by Distribuidora M Atenea SL;
Carisma Libros; Distribuciones Cimadevilla; M

Alonso Estravis Distribuidora; Herro Ediciones;
Icaro Distribuidora SL; Lidiza; Servei del Lli-
bre; Distribuciones Lyra; Distribuidora Literaria
de Editorial Siglo XXI; Miguel Sanchez Libros; La Tierra Libros; Troquel; Viuber
Orders to: Siglo XXI, c/Plaza 5, 28043 Madrid
Tel: 917 591 809

Editorial Renacimiento SA
Poligono Nave Expo, nº 17, 41907 Valencina de
la Concepcion, Seville
Tel: 955 998 232
E-mail: editorial@editorialrenacimiento.com
Web Site: www.editorialrenacimiento.com
Key Personnel
Dir: Abelardo Linares Crespo
Contact: Pedro Gonzalbes Alonso
Founded: 1977
Subjects: Art, History, Language Arts, Linguis-
tics, Literature, Literary Criticism, Essays,
Music, Dance, Philosophy, Poetry, Travel &
Tourism
ISBN Prefix(es): 978-84-8472; 978-84-86307;
978-84-89371

Reservoir Books, *imprint of* Penguin Random
House Grupo Editorial

Editorial Reus SA
C/ Preciados, 23, 2º, 28013 Madrid
Tel: 915 213 619; 915 223 054 *Fax:* 914 451 126
E-mail: reus@editorialreus.es
Web Site: www.editorialreus.es
Founded: 1852
Subjects: Law
ISBN Prefix(es): 978-84-290
Distributed by Edisofer
Warehouse: Avda Democracia 7, Nave 305,
28031 Madrid

Editorial Reverte SA+
C/ Loreto 13-15 Local B, 08029 Barcelona
Tel: 93 419 33 36 *Fax:* 93 419 51 89
E-mail: reverte@reverte.com; export@reverte.com
Web Site: www.reverte.com
Key Personnel
Dir & Rights & Permission: Javier Reverte
Editorial: Julio Bueno
Founded: 1947
Subjects: Architecture & Interior Design, Chem-
istry, Chemical Engineering, Engineering (Gen-
eral), Environmental Studies, Mathematics,
Physics, Science (General), Social Sciences,
Sociology
ISBN Prefix(es): 978-84-291
Number of titles published annually: 30 Print
Total Titles: 1,200 Print
Foreign Rep(s): Editorial Antartica (Chile); Bis
Salvado (El Salvador); Cuesta (Dominican
Republic); Libreria Cultural Panamena SA
(Panama); Cuspide Libros (Argentina); His-
pamer SA (Nicaragua); IGA (Guatemala); Li-
breria Lehmann SA (Costa Rica); Libun (Peru);
Losa Libros Ltd (Uruguay); Distribuidora
Origen (Jorge Saracini) (Uruguay); Libreria
Papiros Codice Cia Ltd (Randini Gonzalez)
(Ecuador); Corporacion Pilatus SA (Pahola
Paz); Policromia (Costa Rica); Distribuciones
Ramirez (Guatemala); Editorial Reverte Colom-
biana SA (Colombia); Reverte Ediciones SA
de CV (Mexico); San Cristobal Libreria (Peru);
Spanish Book Co (Puerto Rico); Special Book
Services (Peru); Sr Libro (Bolivia); Ediciones
Tecnicas Paraguayas SRL (Paraguay); Text
Book SA (Panama); Distribuidora Universal
Text (Venezuela); Zamboni Comercio de Livros
Ltda (Brazil)

Editorial Revista de Derecho Privado, *imprint
of* Editoriales de Derecho Reunidas SA
(EDERSA)

RHM Flash, *imprint of* Penguin Random House
Grupo Editorial

Ediciones Rialp SA+
Alcala 290, 28027 Madrid
Tel: 91 326 05 04 *Fax:* 91 326 13 21
E-mail: ediciones@rialp.com; foreignrights@
rialp.com; pedidos@rialp.com
Web Site: www.rialp.com
Key Personnel
Chief Executive Officer: Santiago Herraiz
Dir General: Miguel Arango
Dir, Finance: Eduardo Miron
Sales Dir: Julio Aguilar
Founded: 1949
Membership(s): Commerce Association of Spain;
Editors Association of Spain.
Subjects: Art, Cookery, Economics, Education,
Gardening, Plants, Health, Nutrition, History,
Inspirational, Spirituality, Literature, Literary
Criticism, Essays, Military Science, Music,
Dance, Philosophy, Poetry, Religion - Other,
Science (General), Social Sciences, Sociology
ISBN Prefix(es): 978-84-321; 978-84-320
Branch Office(s)
Via Augusta, No 6, 08006 Barcelona
Warehouse: Logistica de Ediciones, SA, Bem-
bibre, 28-30, Polg Cobo Calleja, 28940 Fuen-
labrada, Madrid *Tel:* 916 420 086 *Fax:* 916 421
696
Orders to: Cauce, Distribuidora de Ediciones SA,
Sebastian Elcano, 30, 28012 Madrid *Tel:* 914
672 666 *Fax:* 915 302 537

Robin Book, *imprint of* Ediciones Robinbook SL

Ediciones Robinbook SL
Industria, 11, Pol Industrial Buvisa, 08329 Teia,
Barcelona
Tel: 935551411 *Fax:* 935404092
E-mail: contacto@robinbook.com
Web Site: www.robinbook.com
Key Personnel
Dir General: Manuel Martinez Alsinet
Founded: 1990
Subjects: Art, Drama, Theater, Geography, Geol-
ogy, Health, Nutrition, History, Music, Dance,
Alternative Health
ISBN Prefix(es): 978-84-7927
Imprints: L'Arca; As de Diamante; Bon Vivant;
Hermetica; Historial Enigmas; Malsinet Edi-
tor; Ma Non Troppo; Masterclass; Robin Book;
Rouge; Swing; Victor

Roca Bolsillo, *imprint of* Roca Editorial

Roca Editorial
Av Marques de l'Argentera 17, pral 3, 08003
Barcelona
Tel: 932 687 275 *Fax:* 932 688 591
E-mail: info@rocaeditorial.com
Web Site: www.rocaeditorial.com
Key Personnel
Chief Financial Officer: Angel Molina
Dir: Blanca Rosa Roca
Assistant Dir: Gloria Martinez
Dir, Marketing: Jose Antonio Bernal
Editorial Dir: Patricia Escalona
Editorial Coordinator: Beatriz Jambrina
Manager: Carlos Ramos
Subjects: Biography, Memoirs, Fiction, Mysteries,
Suspense, Nonfiction (General), Sports, Athlet-
ics
ISBN Prefix(es): 978-84-96791; 978-84-96284;
978-84-96544; 978-84-15242; 978-84-15410;
978-84-9918; 978-84-938644; 978-84-1523;
978-84-9283; 978-84-92567
Imprints: Corner Editorial; Miscelanea Editorial;
Pirueta Editorial; Roca Bolsillo; Roca Junior;

Roca Juvenil; Tempus Editorial; Terciopelo Editorial; Editorial Vive Bien
Distribution Center: UDL Libros *Tel:* 918 823 280 *Fax:* 918 800 658 *E-mail:* info@udllibros.com *Web Site:* www.udllibros.com

Roca Junior, *imprint of* Roca Editorial

Roca Juvenil, *imprint of* Roca Editorial

Rodeira
Subsidiary of Grupo Edebe
Rafael Alberti, nº 11, Sector A2, nave 16, 15008 A Coruna
Tel: 981 133290; 981 133294 *Fax:* 981 133216
E-mail: rodeira@edebe.net
Web Site: www.edebe.com/grupo_edebe/rodeira. asp
Subjects: Education
ISBN Prefix(es): 978-84-96352; 978-84-8116

Ediciones Joaquin Rodrigo
General Yague 11, 4 J, 28020 Madrid
Tel: 91 5552728 *Fax:* 91 5564335
E-mail: info@joaquin-rodrigo.com
Web Site: www.joaquin-rodrigo.com
Key Personnel
General Manager: Cecilia Rodrigo
Founded: 1989
Specialize in classical music.
Subjects: Music, Dance
ISBN Prefix(es): 978-84-88558

Ediciones ROL SA+
Peris i Mencheta, 50, 08032 Barcelona
Tel: 93 200 80 33 *Fax:* 93 200 27 62
E-mail: rol@e-rol.es
Web Site: www.e-rol.es
Key Personnel
Mng Dir: Julia Martinez Saavedra
Founded: 1977
Membership(s): The Spanish Association of Technical Press.
Subjects: Health, Nutrition, Human Relations, Medicine, Nursing, Dentistry, Psychology, Psychiatry, Science (General), Social Sciences, Sociology
ISBN Prefix(es): 978-84-85535

Rosa dels Vents, *imprint of* Penguin Random House Grupo Editorial

Rouge, *imprint of* Ediciones Robinbook SL

Editorial Rueda SL+
Fisicas 5, Pi Urtinsa Ii, 28923 Alcorcon, Madrid
Tel: 916 192 779 *Fax:* 916 102 855
E-mail: comercial@editorialrueda.es
Web Site: www.editorialrueda.es
Key Personnel
Contact: Rafael Rueda Sanchez
Founded: 1970
Subjects: Agriculture, Architecture & Interior Design, Biological Sciences, Civil Engineering, Earth Sciences, Environmental Studies, Gardening, Plants, Geography, Geology
ISBN Prefix(es): 978-84-7207

SAEM Thales, see Sociedad Andaluza de Educacion Matematica Thales

Publicaciones y Ediciones Salamandra SA+
Almogavers 56, 7º 2º, 08018 Barcelona
Tel: 932 151 199 *Fax:* 932 154 636
E-mail: ventas@salamandra.es
Web Site: www.salamandra.info; www. salamandra.es
Key Personnel
Contact: Sigrid Kraus de Carril

Founded: 1989
Subjects: Child Care & Development, Fiction, History, Romance
ISBN Prefix(es): 978-84-7888; 978-84-86033
Distributed by Editorial EDHASA (Argentina); Gussi Books (Uruguay); Ediciones Oceano Boliviana SL (Bolivia); Ediciones Oceano de Chile SA (Chile); Ediciones Oceano de Colombia SA (Colombia); Ediciones Oceano de Costa Rica SA (Costa Rica); Editorial Oceano Ecuatoriana SA (Ecuador); Editorial Oceano de Mexico SA de CV (Mexico); Ediciones Oceano de Panama SA (Panama); Ediciones Oceano de Paraguay SA (Paraguay); Editorial Oceano Peruana SA (Peru); Editorial Oceano Venezuela SA (Venezuela)

Ediciones Saldana SA
Poligono Lintzirin-gaina, B-3, 20180 Oiarzun, Guipuzcoa
Tel: 943 490 943 *Fax:* 943 493 208
E-mail: info@edicionessaldana.com
Web Site: www.edicionessaldana.com
Key Personnel
Commercial Dir: Fermin Saldana Ayerra
Founded: 1956
ISBN Prefix(es): 978-84-7297

Salsa Books (Castella), *imprint of* grup62

Salsa Books (Catala), *imprint of* grup62

Editorial Salvat SL+
c/ Mallorca, 45, 08029 Barcelona
Mailing Address: PO Box 178 FD, 08080 Barcelona
Tel: 902 101 262
E-mail: lopt@salvat.es
Web Site: www.salvat.es; www.salvat.com
Founded: 1923
Subjects: Education, Literature, Literary Criticism, Essays
ISBN Prefix(es): 978-84-345
Parent Company: Hachette Livre SA, Paris, France
Branch Office(s)
Salvat Editores Portugal, Av da Republica Nº 59, 10º andar, 1050-189 Lisbon, Portugal *Tel:* 21 355 08 66 *Fax:* 21 352 22 46 *E-mail:* salvat@ salvat.pt
Salvat Brasil, Rua Purpurina, 05435-030 Sao Paulo-SP, Brazil

Editorial Miguel A Salvatella SA
Santa Agusti 8, 08012 Barcelona
Tel: 932 189 026 *Fax:* 932 177 437
E-mail: editorial@salvatella.com
Web Site: www.salvatella.com
Founded: 1922
Subjects: Education, Origami
ISBN Prefix(es): 978-84-7210; 978-84-8412

Editorial San Esteban
Division of Dominicanos de la Provincia de Espana
Plaza Concilio de Trento sn, 37001 Salamanca
Mailing Address: Apdo 17, 37080 Salamanca
Tel: 923 264 781; 923 215 000 *Fax:* 923 265 480
E-mail: info@sanestebaneditorial.com; ediciones@sanestebaneditorial.com
Web Site: www.sanestebaneditorial.com
Founded: 1964
Subjects: Education, History, Philosophy, Religion - Other, Theology
ISBN Prefix(es): 978-84-8260; 978-84-85045; 978-84-87557

Editorial San Martin SL+
C/ Arenal, 23-2, 28013 Madrid
Tel: 915 483 590
Founded: 1854

Subjects: Aeronautics, Aviation, History, Military Science
ISBN Prefix(es): 978-84-7140
Bookshop(s): Libreria San Martin, Puerta del Sol 6, 28013 Madrid
Warehouse: Libreria San Martin, Puerta del Sol 6, 28013 Madrid

Editorial San Pablo+
C/ Protasio Gomez, 15, 28027 Madrid
SAN: 001-9739
Tel: 917 425 113; 917 987 752
E-mail: comunicacion@sanpablo.es; attencioncliente@sanpablo.es
Web Site: www.sanpablo.es
Founded: 1934
Subjects: Biography, Memoirs, Education, Religion - Other, Theology
ISBN Prefix(es): 978-84-285
Number of titles published annually: 100 Print
Total Titles: 1,500 Print
Parent Company: Sociedad de San Pablo
Warehouse: San Pablo Comunicacion, Resina, 1, 28021 Madrid *Tel:* 917 987 426; 917 987 427 *Fax:* 915 052 050
Orders to: San Pablo Comunicacion, Resina, 1, 28021 Madrid *Tel:* 917 987 426; 917 987 427 *Fax:* 915 052 050 *E-mail:* ventas@sanpablo.es
Returns: San Pablo Comunicacion, Resina, 1, 28021 Madrid *Tel:* 917 987 426; 917 987 427 *Fax:* 915 052 050

Ediciones Miguel Sanchez
Marques de Mondejar, 44, 18004 Grenada
Tel: 958253268 *Fax:* 958253174
E-mail: info@edicionesmiguelsanchez.com
Web Site: www.edicionesmiguelsanchez.com
Founded: 1950
Subjects: Architecture & Interior Design, History, Photography, Travel & Tourism
ISBN Prefix(es): 978-84-7169

Grupo Santillana de Ediciones SL+
Av de los Artesanos 6, 28760 Madrid
Tel: 917449060 *Fax:* 917449019
E-mail: grupo@santillana.es; comunicacion@ santillana.es
Web Site: www.gruposantillana.com
Key Personnel
Dir, Global Trade Publishing: Armando Collazos
Dir, Communications: Rosa Junquera Santiago
E-mail: rjunquera@santillana.com
Founded: 1960
Subjects: Fiction, Nonfiction (General)
ISBN Prefix(es): 978-84-294; 978-84-668
Parent Company: PRISA
Associate Companies: Ave Leandro N Alem 720, C1001AAP Buenos Aires, Argentina *Tel:* (011) 4119 5000 *Fax:* (011) 4119 5021 *E-mail:* info@santillana.com.ar; Calle 13 esquina Av Julio Patino Nº 8078, Zona Calacoto, La Paz, Bolivia *Tel:* (02) 2774242 *Fax:* (02) 2771056 *E-mail:* info@santillana.com.bo; Rua Padre Adelino, 758, 03303-904 Sao Paulo-SP, Brazil *Tel:* (011) 2790 1300 *Fax:* (011) 2790 1501 *E-mail:* contato@gruposantillana.com.br; Dr Anibal Ariztia 1444, Providencia, Santiago, Chile *Tel:* (02) 384 30 00 *Fax:* (02) 384 30 80 (editorial); (02) 384 30 30 (sales) *E-mail:* info@santillana.cl; Carrera 11 A, Nº 98-50, Off 501, Bogota, Colombia *Tel:* (01) 705 77 77 *E-mail:* gerencia@santillana.com.co *Web Site:* www.santillana.com.co; La Uruca, nº 78, 1150 San Jose de Costa Rica, Costa Rica *Tel:* 22204242; 22204770 *Fax:* 22202002; 22201320 *E-mail:* santilla@santillana.co.cr; Calle Juan Sanchez Ramirez No 9, Gazcue, Santo Domingo, DN, Dominican Republic *Tel:* (809) 682-1382 *Fax:* (809) 689-1022 *E-mail:* santillana@santillana.com.do; Av Eloy Alfaro N 33-347, Y Av 6 de Diciembre, Quito, Ecuador *Tel:* (02) 244 66 56; (02) 244 21 54 *Fax:* (02) 244 87 91 *E-mail:* melsan2e@

santillana.com.ec; Calle Siemens 48, Zona Industrial Santa Elena, Antiguo Cuscatlan La Libertad, El Salvador *Tel:* 2505 8920 *Fax:* 2270 6066 *E-mail:* santillana@santillana. com.gt; 26 Av 2-20 Zona 14, Guatemala, CA, Guatemala *Tel:* 242 94300 *Fax:* 242 94343 *E-mail:* santillana@santillana.com.gt; Blvd Suyapa, Complex Metropolis, 20501 Tegucigalpa, Honduras *Tel:* 2270-7100; Av Rio Mixcoac, No 274, Colonia Acacias, Mexico, DF, Mexico *Tel:* (0155) 5420 7530 *E-mail:* mexico@santillana.com.mx; Urbanizacion Industrial Orillac, Via Transistmica, Calle 2da Local No 9, Apdo Postal 0823-03803, Panama, Panama *Tel:* 378 2200 *Fax:* 378 2200; Venezuela, 276 (entre Mariscal Lopez y Espana), Asuncion, Paraguay *Tel:* (021) 202942 *Fax:* (021) 202942 *E-mail:* general@santillana.com.py; Avda Primavera 2160, Santiago de Surco, Lima 33, Peru *Tel:* (01) 313 40 00 *Fax:* (01) 313 40 01 *E-mail:* santillana@santillana.com.pe; Ave Roosvelt 1506, Guaynabo, San Juan, Puerto Rico *Tel:* (787) 781-9800 *Fax:* (787) 782-6149 *E-mail:* grupo_santillana@santillanapr.net; Juan Manuel Blanes 1132, 11200 Montevideo, Uruguay *Tel:* 2410 7342 *E-mail:* edicion@ santillana.com.uy; Av Romulo Gallegos Sector Montecristo, Edificio Zulia, piso 1, Boleita Norte, Caracas 1071, Venezuela *Tel:* (0212) 235 30 33 *Fax:* (0212) 239 10 51 *E-mail:* info@santillana.com.ve
Divisions: Aguilar; Alfaguara; Punto de Lectura; Richmond Publisning (UK); Suma de Letras; Taurus
U.S. Office(s): 2023 NW 84 Ave, Doral, FL 33122, United States *Tel:* 305-591-9522 *Fax:* 305-591-9145 *E-mail:* customerservice@ santillanausa.com

Editorial Saure SL
Poligono Industrial de Goiain, Ave San Blas, 11, 01171 Legutiano
Tel: 945 465 825
Founded: 2002
Educational graphic novels in Spanish for young people.
Subjects: Fiction
ISBN Prefix(es): 978-84-95225; 978-84-922086
Total Titles: 50 Print

Ediciones Scriba SA+
Affiliate of Libreria Martinez Perez
Valencia, 246, 08007 Barcelona
SAN: 001-9763
Tel: 932 151 933 *Fax:* 934 873 766
Key Personnel
Mng Dir: Manuel Martinez Bravo
Founded: 1890
Subjects: Art, Medicine, Nursing, Dentistry, Science (General)
ISBN Prefix(es): 978-84-85835

Sd.edicions
Provenca 183, 5e 4a, 08036 Barcelona
Tel: 934 514 557 *Fax:* 934 514 557
E-mail: info@sdedicions.com
Web Site: www.sdedicions.com
ISBN Prefix(es): 978-84-92607

Editorial Secretariado Trinitario+
Av Filiberto Villalobos 80, 37007 Salamanca
Tel: 923235602 *Fax:* 923235602
E-mail: editorialst@secretariadotrinitario.org
Web Site: www.secretariadotrinitario.org
Key Personnel
Mng Dir & Rights & Permissions: Juan Pujana Ascorbebeitia
Founded: 1967
Subjects: Religion - Catholic, Religion - Other, Theology

ISBN Prefix(es): 978-84-88643; 978-84-85376; 978-84-96488
Parent Company: Orden de la Santisima Trinidad

Editorial Seix Barral+
Member of Grupo Planeta
Avda Diagonal 662-664, 7a, 08034 Barcelona
Tel: 93 492 89 01
E-mail: editorial@seix-barral.es
Web Site: www.planetadelibros.com/editorial-seix-barral-9.html
Key Personnel
Dir, Communication: Nahir Gutierrez
  E-mail: ngutierrez@seix-barral.es
Founded: 1911
Subjects: Art, Biography, Memoirs, Drama, Theater, Geography, Geology, Literature, Literary Criticism, Essays, Mysteries, Suspense, Poetry, Science (General), Science Fiction, Fantasy, Social Sciences, Sociology, Travel & Tourism, Humanities; Historical novels
ISBN Prefix(es): 978-84-322

Septem Ediciones SL
C/ Cimadevilla 15, esc A 1° C, 33003 Oviedo, Asturias
Tel: 985 20 85 12
E-mail: info@septemediciones.com
Web Site: www.septemediciones.com
Key Personnel
Dir General: Marta Magadan
Founded: 2000
Subjects: Anthropology, Art, Biography, Memoirs, Cookery, Economics, Energy, Geography, Geology, Government, Political Science, History, Mathematics, Medicine, Nursing, Dentistry, Philosophy, Physics, Poetry, Psychology, Psychiatry, Science (General), Social Sciences, Sociology, Travel & Tourism
ISBN Prefix(es): 978-84-95687; 978-84-96491

Ediciones del Serbal SA+
Francesc Tarrega, 12, 08027 Barcelona
Tel: 93 408 08 34 *Fax:* 93 408 07 92
E-mail: serbal@ed-serbal.es
Web Site: edicionesdelserbal.com
Key Personnel
President: Jose Maria Riano de Castro
Founded: 1979
Subjects: Art, Science (General), Humanities, Physical Education
ISBN Prefix(es): 978-84-85800; 978-84-7628
Foreign Rep(s): Ediciones del Aguazul SA (Argentina); Artemis Libros Ltda (Colombia); Editora y Distribuidora Azteca SA (Mexico); La Panoplia de Libros SL (worldwide exc Argentina & Mexico)

Servei de Publicitat, Difusio i Projectes Editorials Diputacion Provincial de Barcelona
Rbla Catalunya, 126, 2a planta, Edifici can Serra, 08008 Barcelona
Tel: 934 022 116 *Fax:* 934 022 272
E-mail: comunicacio.diba@diba.cat
Web Site: www.diba.cat; www.diba.es
Key Personnel
Head: Angels Prats Nadal
Founded: 1991
Subjects: Economics, Education, Environmental Studies, Government, Political Science, Health, Nutrition, Public Administration, Social Sciences, Sociology, Sports, Athletics, Travel & Tourism
ISBN Prefix(es): 978-84-7794

Servicio Central de Publicaciones
Division of Gobierno Vasco
Libreria, C/ Donostia-San Sebastian, 1, 01010 Vitoria-Gasteiz (Alava)
SAN: 003-2964

Tel: 945 01 68 66 *Fax:* 945 01 87 09
E-mail: ejgvpublicaciones@ej-gv.es
Web Site: www.jusap.ejgv.euskadi.net
Key Personnel
Contact: Idoia Mendia Cueva
Founded: 1980
Subjects: Agriculture, Art, Business, Education, Health, Nutrition, History, Law, Public Administration, Social Sciences, Sociology
ISBN Prefix(es): 978-84-457; 978-84-7542
Number of titles published annually: 200 Print; 10 CD-ROM
Total Titles: 3,450 Print; 30 CD-ROM
Distribution Center: Elkar Banaketa, Portuetxe kalea 88, 20009 Donastia-San Sebastian *Tel:* 943 310 301 *Web Site:* www.elkarbanaketa.com
Egartorre, Primavera 31, PI Malvar, 28500 Arganda del Rey, Madrid *Tel:* 918 729 390 *Web Site:* www.egartorre.com

Servicio de Publicaciones Universidad de Cordoba+
Campus Universitario de Rabanales Ctra Nacional IV, km 396, 14071 Cordoba
Tel: 957 21 81 26 (administration) *Fax:* 957 21 81 96
E-mail: publicaciones@uco.es
Web Site: www.uco.es/organiza/servicios/publica
Key Personnel
Dir, Publications: Fernando Lopez Mora *Tel:* 957 21 20 33
Founded: 1972
Subjects: Agriculture, Archaeology, Biological Sciences, Computer Science, Economics, Education, Geography, Geology, Law, Veterinary Science
ISBN Prefix(es): 978-84-7801

Servicio de Publicaciones y Difusion Cientifica de la Universidad de Las Palmas de Gran Canaria
Parque Cientifico-Tecnologico, Edificio Polivalente II, C/ Practicante Ignacio Rodriguez, s/n Campus Universitario de Tafira, 35017 Las Palmas de Gran Canaria
Tel: 928 452 707 *Fax:* 928 458 950
E-mail: serpubli@ulpgc.es
Web Site: www.servicios.ulpgc.es/publicaciones
Key Personnel
Dir: Eloisa Llavero Ruiz *Tel:* 928 459 922
Founded: 1992
Subjects: Education, English as a Second Language, Geography, Geology, History, Mathematics, Science (General), Social Sciences, Sociology, Technology
ISBN Prefix(es): 978-84-89728; 978-84-88412; 978-84-95792; 978-84-95286; 978-84-96131; 978-84-96502; 978-84-96971

Editorial Sexto Piso Espana
Los Madrazo 24, semisotano izqda, 28014 Madrid
Tel: 91 532 56 72
Web Site: www.sextopiso.es
Subjects: Literature, Literary Criticism, Essays, Philosophy
ISBN Prefix(es): 978-84-96867; 978-84-935204

Ediciones Seyer+
Cueva de Menga, 22, 29018 Malaga
SAN: 001-9798
Tel: 952 320 887
Key Personnel
Dir: Antonio Abad
Founded: 1979
Subjects: Art, Literature, Literary Criticism, Essays, Maritime, Music, Dance, Poetry, Science Fiction, Fantasy, Sports, Athletics
ISBN Prefix(es): 978-84-86975
Warehouse: San Millan, 15 29013 Malaga

SGEL, see Sociedad General Espanola de Libreria SA (SGEL)

Sieteleguas Ediciones SL
C/Lugo 22, 28430 Alpedrete, Madrid
Tel: 91 857 27 45 *Fax:* 91 857 27 45
E-mail: info@sieteleguas.es
Web Site: www.sieteleguas.es
Key Personnel
Dir General: Pedro Rubio
Founded: 2004
Subjects: Kamishibai, Paper Theater
ISBN Prefix(es): 978-84-934008

Siglo XXI de Espana Editores SA+
Imprint of Akal Grupo Editorial
Sector Foresta nº 1, 28760 Tres Cantos, Madrid
Tel: 918 061 996 *Fax:* 918 044 028
E-mail: atencion.cliente@akal.com
Web Site: www.sigloxxieditores.com
Founded: 1967
Subjects: Anthropology, Government, Political
    Science, History, Literature, Literary Criticism,
    Essays, Philosophy, Psychology, Psychiatry,
    Social Sciences, Sociology
ISBN Prefix(es): 978-84-323
Associate Companies: Ediciones Akal SA
    (Spain); Foca; H Blume; Ediciones Istmo
Branch Office(s)
Siglo Veintiuno Editores, Guatemala 4824,
    C1425BUP Buenos Aires, Argentina, Edi-
    torial Dir: Carlos E Diaz *Tel:* (011) 4770-
    9090 *Fax:* (011) 4770-9090 *E-mail:* info@
    sigloxxieditores.com.ar *Web Site:* www.
    sigloxxieditores.com.ar
Siglo Veintiuno Editores, Cerro del Agua 248,
    Col Romero de Terreros, 01000 Mexico, DF,
    Mexico, General Manager: Jose Maria Cas-
    tro Mussot *Tel:* (0155) 5658-7999 *Fax:* (0155)
    5658-7599 *E-mail:* ventas@sigloxxieditores.
    com.mx *Web Site:* www.sigloxxieditores.com.
    mx
Distributed by Ediciones Akal SA (Spain);
    Casalini Libri SpA (Italy); Ediciones Mil Hojas
    (Chile); Siglo del Hombre Editores (Colombia);
    Siglo Veintiuno Editores (Argentina & Mex-
    ico); Siglo XXI Iberoamericana (Argentina);
    Ediciones Trecho SA (Uruguay)
Foreign Rep(s): Alianza Distribuidora Ecuatoriana
    C Ltda (Ecuador); Baker & Taylor Inc (USA);
    La Familia Distribuidora de Libros SA (Peru);
    Inversiones Codice CA (Venezuela)

Signatura Ediciones de Andalucia SL
Calle Astronomia, nº 1, Torre 2, planta 9, of 14,
    41015 Seville
Tel: 95 495 11 19 *Fax:* 95 494 88 76
E-mail: signatura@signaturaediciones.com
Web Site: www.signaturaediciones.com
Founded: 1996
Subjects: Anthropology, Culture
ISBN Prefix(es): 978-84-96210; 978-84-922279;
    978-84-95122

Ediciones Sigueme SA+
Garcia Tejado, 23-27, 37007 Salamanca
Tel: 923 218 203 *Fax:* 923 270 563
E-mail: ediciones@sigueme.es
Web Site: www.sigueme.es
Founded: 1948
Subjects: Biblical Studies, Biography, Memoirs,
    History, Philosophy, Religion - Catholic, Reli-
    gion - Protestant, Theology
ISBN Prefix(es): 978-84-301
Total Titles: 1,600 Print
Distributed by Augsburg Fortess (USA &
    Canada)

Silex Ediciones+
Alcala 202 1º C, 28028 Madrid
Tel: 91 356 69 09
E-mail: silex@silexediciones.com
Web Site: www.silexediciones.com
Key Personnel
Editorial Dir: Cristina Pineda

Editor: Jose Luis Ibanez
Founded: 1972
Subjects: Aeronautics, Aviation, Archaeology,
    Art, Biography, Memoirs, History, Maritime,
    Photography, Travel & Tourism
ISBN Prefix(es): 978-84-85041; 978-84-7737
Distribution Center: Pujol & Amado SLL, C/ Mi-
    lans, 13-1º-1a, Sant Feliu de, 17220 Guixols
    (Girona) *Tel:* 972 327 453 *Fax:* 971 327 454
    E-mail: bernat@pujolamado.com (North &
    South America)

Editorial Sintesis SA+
Calle Vallehermoso 34, 28015 Madrid
Tel: 91 593 20 98; 91 593 49 61 (orders) *Fax:* 91
    445 86 96
E-mail: sintesis@sintesis.com; info@sintesis.com
Web Site: www.sintesis.com
Key Personnel
Chief Executive Officer: Francisco Belloso
    Cruzado *E-mail:* fbelloso@sintesis.com
President: Felisa Cedenilla Lorente
    E-mail: fcedenilla@sintesis.com
Dir General: Alfredo Molina Abril
    E-mail: amolina@sintesis.com
Commercial Dept: Javier Rojas Garcia
    E-mail: comercial2@sintesis.com
Rights & Permissions: Carolina Centeno Diaz
    E-mail: carolina@sintesis.com
Founded: 1986
Provides high quality scientific & academic texts
    for university students in all areas of study.
Subjects: Biography, Memoirs, Biological Sci-
    ences, Chemistry, Chemical Engineering, Com-
    munications, Computer Science, Earth Sci-
    ences, Economics, Education, Engineering
    (General), Geography, Geology, History, Jour-
    nalism, Language Arts, Linguistics, Library
    & Information Sciences, Literature, Literary
    Criticism, Essays, Management, Mathematics,
    Mechanical Engineering, Nonfiction (General),
    Philosophy, Physical Sciences, Psychology,
    Psychiatry, Science (General), Social Sciences,
    Sociology, Travel & Tourism
ISBN Prefix(es): 978-84-7738; 978-84-9756
Number of titles published annually: 100 Print
Foreign Rep(s): A B Representaciones Gen-
    erales SRL (Peru); Alfaomega Colombiana SA
    (Colombia); Baker & Taylor Books (USA);
    Libreria Ciencia Medica (Bolivia); Miguel de
    la Concha (Chile); Crambury Services Cia
    Ltda (Ecuador); Desarrollas Culturales Cas-
    tarricenses SA (Costa Rica); Distribuciones
    Cifuentes SA de CV (Mexico); Distribuidora
    FERLE CA (Venezuela); Duran San Martin
    y Compania Ltda (Chile); Ediciones Tecni-
    cas Paraguayes SRL (Paraguay); Ediciones
    y Distribuciones Istmo SA (Costa Rica); Efs-
    tathiadis Group SA (Greece); Fundacion Li-
    bro Universitario - LIBUN (Peru); Hispamer
    SA (Nicaragua); Libreria Lehmann SA (Costa
    Rica); Libreria Proa Ltd (Chile); Libreriwa Pa-
    piros Codices CIA Ltd (Ecuador); Losa Libros
    (Uruguay); Editorial Nueva Decada SA (Costa
    Rica); Prata y Rodrigues Public Ltda (Por-
    tugal); Promolibro (Colombia); Libreria San
    Cristobal Sac (Peru); Sophos SA - Guatemala
    (Guatemala); Tecni-Books CA (Venezuela)

Editorial Sirio SA
C/ Rosa de los Vientos, 64, 29006 Malaga
Tel: 952 23 52 90 *Fax:* 952 23 74 35
E-mail: sirio@editorialsirio.com
Web Site: www.editorialsirio.com
Subjects: Astrology, Occult, Health, Nutrition,
    Psychology, Psychiatry, Religion - Other, The-
    ology, Alternative Health
ISBN Prefix(es): 978-84-7808; 978-84-86221
Foreign Rep(s): Artemis Edinter Libros
    (Guatemala); Dellare SA (Guatemala); De-
    sarrollos Culturales Costarricenses DCC SA
    (Costa Rica); Distribuciones Del Futuro (Ar-
    gentina); Hispamer SA (Nicaragua); Distribu-

ciones Mediterraneo (Peru); Mister Books SA
    (Ecuador); Nirvana Libros SA de CV (Mex-
    ico); Editorial Pomaire (Venezuela); Sophos
    SA (Guatemala); Spanish Publishers (USA);
    Thesaurus (Dominican Republic); Ediciones
    Urano SA (Chile, Colombia); Ediciones Urano
    Uruguay SA (Uruguay)

Equipo Sirius+
Antequera, 2-local, 28041 Madrid
Tel: 917 107 349
Founded: 1985
Subjects: Archaeology, Astronomy, Crafts,
    Games, Hobbies, Education, Photography,
    Physical Sciences, Science (General)
ISBN Prefix(es): 978-84-86639; 978-84-95495
Distributed by Editorial Hispano Andina Ltda
    (Colombia); Cuspide Libros SA (Argentina);
    Libreria Escolar Editora (Portugal); Reverte
    Ediciones SA de CV (Mexico); Sousa, So-
    brinho y Freixo (Portugal)

Siruela Ediciones SA+
c/ Almagro 25, ppa dcha, 28010 Madrid
Tel: 91 355 57 20 *Fax:* 91 355 22 01
E-mail: siruela@siruela.com
Web Site: www.siruela.com
Key Personnel
Editorial: Elena Garcia-Aranda
    E-mail: egaranda@siruela.com
Press & Communications: Elena F Palacios
    E-mail: epalacios@siruela.com
Sales: Manuel Gil *E-mail:* mgil@siruela.com
Founded: 1982
Subjects: Animals, Pets, Art, Biography, Mem-
    oirs, Fiction, Humor, Inspirational, Spirituality,
    Literature, Literary Criticism, Essays, Myster-
    ies, Suspense, Nonfiction (General), Philoso-
    phy, Poetry, Religion - Buddhist, Religion -
    Catholic, Religion - Hindu, Religion - Islamic,
    Religion - Jewish, Religion - Other, Social Sci-
    ences, Sociology, Theology, Art Theory, Me-
    dieval European Literature
ISBN Prefix(es): 978-84-7844; 978-84-85876
Foreign Rights: ACER Literary Agency (Laure
    Merle d'Aubigne) (France); The English
    Agency (Corinne Shioji) (Japan); Literarische
    Agentur Michael Gaeb (Germany); Indent
    Literary Agency (Andrea Montejo) (USA);
    Iris Agency (Catherine Frafou) (Greece); Sil-
    via Meucci Agenzia Letteraria (Italy); Sapere
    Critico Agencia Literaria (David Lopez-del
    Amo) (China, South Korea, Taiwan)

Editorial Sistema
C/Fuencarral, 127, 1º, 28010 Madrid
Tel: 91 448 73 19 *Fax:* 91 448 73 39
Web Site: www.fundacionsistema.com
Key Personnel
Dir: Jose Felix Tezanos
Subjects: Government, Political Science, History,
    Philosophy, Social Sciences, Sociology
ISBN Prefix(es): 978-84-86497
Parent Company: Fundacion Sistema

Edicions 62, *imprint of* grup62

Edicions 62+
Imprint of grup62
C/ Peu de la Creu, 4, 08001 Barcelona
Tel: 93 443 71 00 *Fax:* 93 443 71 30
E-mail: correu@grup62.com
Web Site: www.edicions62.cat/editorial-ediciones-
    62-64.html
Key Personnel
Foreign Rights Manager: Pilar Lafuente *Tel:* 93
    492 82 44 *E-mail:* plafuente@planeta.es
Founded: 1962
Subjects: Art, Biography, Memoirs, Drama, The-
    ater, Fiction, History, Literature, Literary Criti-
    cism, Essays, Music, Dance, Nonfiction (Gen-

eral), Philosophy, Poetry, Social Sciences, Sociology, Travel & Tourism
ISBN Prefix(es): 978-84-297

Ediciones SM+
c/ Impresores, 2, 28660 Madrid
Tel: 902 13 12 23
E-mail: ayudaaldocente@grupo-sm.com
Web Site: www.grupo-sm.com
Key Personnel
Dir General: Javier Cortes Soriano
Founded: 1938
Specialize in publication of children's, juveniles, young adults & textbooks.
Subjects: Biography, Memoirs, Education, Humor, Literature, Literary Criticism, Essays, Philosophy, Religion - Other, Social Sciences, Sociology, Theology, Children's Literature
ISBN Prefix(es): 978-84-348; 978-84-675
Parent Company: Grupo SM
Associate Companies: Editorial Cruilla SA, C/ Balmes nº 245, 08006 Barcelona
  E-mail: contacte@cruilla.com *Web Site:* www.cruilla.cat
Subsidiaries: Acento Editorial; Editorial PPC
Orders to: CESMA SA, Av de la Marina, 54, Poligon Can Calderon, 08830 Sant Boi de Llobregat

Sociedad Andaluza de Educacion Matematica Thales
Facultad de Matematicas, Apdo 1160, 41080 Seville
Tel: 954 623 658 *Fax:* 954 236 378
E-mail: thales@cica.es
Web Site: thales.cica.es
Key Personnel
President: Sixto Romero Sanchez
Vice President: Francisco Espana Perez
Founded: 1981
Subjects: Education, Mathematics
ISBN Prefix(es): 978-84-920056

Sociedad General Espanola de Libreria SA (SGEL)
Avda Valdelaparra, 29, 28108 Alcobendas, Madrid
Tel: 916 576 900; 916 576 914 (retail); 916 576 902 (distribution) *Fax:* 916 576 928
E-mail: libros@sgel.es; tiendas@sgel.es
Web Site: www.sgel.es
Key Personnel
Dir, Books Division: Luis Angel Fernandez
  E-mail: fernandez.la@sgel.es
Dir, Publishing: Javier Lahuerta *E-mail:* lahuerta.j@sgel.es
Dir, International Press: Christophe Grandjean
  E-mail: grandjean.c@sgel.es
Dir, Marketing: Carlos Hernandez
  E-mail: hernandez.c@sgel.es
Dir, Sales & Marketing: Jose Luis del Val
  E-mail: delval.j@sgel.es
Founded: 1914
Subjects: English as a Second Language, French as a Second Language, Spanish as a Second Language
ISBN Prefix(es): 978-84-7143
Parent Company: HDS

Editorial Sol90
Ravella, 10, bajos 3a, 08021 Barcelona
Tel: 93 445 87 00
E-mail: email@sol90.com
Web Site: www.sol90.com
Founded: 1990
Subjects: Art, Biography, Memoirs, Computers, History, Language Arts, Linguistics, Science (General), Humanities
ISBN Prefix(es): 978-84-93110; 978-84-95594; 978-84-95978; 978-84-96118; 978-84-96247; 978-84-96412

Branch Office(s)
Av Leandro N Alem 896 Piso 6º, CABA, C1001AAQ Buenos Aires, Argentina *Tel:* (011) 4328 5484
Av Angelica, 2163, Conjunto 31, Consolacao, 01227-200 Sao Paulo-SP, Brazil *Tel:* (011) 2129 7442
Wilhelm-Hoegner-str 7, 81737 Munich, Germany *Tel:* (089) 67 97 47 03
288 Bishopsgate, Reino Unido, London EC2M 4QP, United Kingdom *Tel:* (020) 7666 3046
U.S. Office(s): 175 SW Seventh St, Suite 1604, Miami, FL 33130-2992, United States *Tel:* 786-439-3292

Sotelo Blanco Edicions SL+
San Marcos, 77, 15820 Santiago de Compostela
Tel: 981 582 571 *Fax:* 981 587 290
Web Site: www.soteloblancoedicions.com
Key Personnel
President & Founder: Olegario Sotelo Blanco
Founded: 1980
Subjects: Drama, Theater, Fiction, Language Arts, Linguistics, Literature, Literary Criticism, Essays, Poetry, Science Fiction, Fantasy, Women's Studies
ISBN Prefix(es): 978-84-7824; 978-84-86021
Total Titles: 600 Print

SPUS, see Secretariado de Publicaciones de la Universidad de Sevilla

Stanley Publishing+
Mendula, 15, 20280 Hondarribia
SAN: 002-6786
Tel: 943 640 412 *Fax:* 943 643 863
E-mail: editorial@stanleypublishing.es
Web Site: www.stanleypublishing.es
Founded: 1991
Specialize in languages.
Subjects: History, Language Arts, Linguistics
ISBN Prefix(es): 978-84-7873; 978-84-86859
Total Titles: 100 Print
Distributor for ELI
Warehouse: Popigono Olivares, c/o Sierra de Albarracin 3, 28500 Arganda del Rey, Madrid

Editorial Rudolf Steiner SA+
Calle Guipuzcoa Nº11 1º, 28020 Madrid
SAN: 002-6603
Tel: 91 553 14 81 *Fax:* 911 850 798
E-mail: pedidos@editorialrudolfsteiner.com
Web Site: www.editorialrudolfsteiner.com
Key Personnel
President: Isabel Novillo Gavin
Founded: 1975
Subjects: Agriculture, Education, Inspirational, Spirituality, Medicine, Nursing, Dentistry, Philosophy, Psychology, Psychiatry, Religion - Other, Self-Help, Anthroposophy
ISBN Prefix(es): 978-84-89197; 978-84-85370
Number of titles published annually: 12 Print

Sua Edizioak
Epalza Kalea 8-4º, 48007 Bilbao
Tel: 944169430 *Fax:* 944166976
E-mail: cliente@sua-ediciones.com; sua@sua-ediciones.com
Web Site: www.sua.eus
Key Personnel
Dir: Javier Pascual Otalora
Administration: David Vargas *E-mail:* dvargas@sua-ediciones.com
Founded: 1987
Subjects: Outdoor Recreation, Sports, Athletics, Travel & Tourism, Hiking, Mountaineering, Northern Spain, Pyrenees Mountains
ISBN Prefix(es): 978-84-8216; 978-84-87187

Sudamericana, *imprint of* Penguin Random House Grupo Editorial

Susaeta Ediciones SA
c/ Campezo, 13, 28022 Madrid
SAN: 005-0431
Tel: 91 300 91 00 *Fax:* 91 300 91 18
E-mail: general@susaeta.com
Web Site: www.editorialsusaeta.com
Key Personnel
Dir: Jose Ignacio Susaeta Erburu
Founded: 1963
Subjects: Biblical Studies, Cookery, Crafts, Games, Hobbies, Fiction, Gardening, Plants, Travel & Tourism
ISBN Prefix(es): 978-84-305; 978-84-677

Swing, *imprint of* Ediciones Robinbook SL

T&B Editores (T&B Publishers)+
C/Barquillo, 15A, 2ºA, 28004 Madrid
Tel: 91 523 27 04 *Fax:* 91 532 02 44
E-mail: tbeditores@cinemitos.com
Web Site: www.cinemitos.com/tbeditores
Key Personnel
Dir & Copyright: Juan Tejero
Editor, Production & Marketing: Carmen Bayod
Founded: 1998
Specialize in the cinema world.
Subjects: Biography, Memoirs, Film, Video, Cinema
ISBN Prefix(es): 978-84-96576
Number of titles published annually: 20 Print
Total Titles: 92 Print
Parent Company: Cineprint SL
Warehouse: c/ Brouce, 4, Poligono Industrial Sur, 28770 Colmenar Viejo, Madrid

Tandem Edicions SL
Pl Espana 2, puerta 2, 46007 Valencia
Tel: 963 172 047 *Fax:* 963 172 201
E-mail: tandem@tandemedicions.com
Web Site: www.tandemedicions.com
Key Personnel
Editorial Dir: Rosa Serrano
Founded: 1990
Subjects: Biological Sciences, Fiction, Poetry
ISBN Prefix(es): 978-84-8131; 978-84-87693
Foreign Rep(s): Lectorum Publications Inc (USA); Ediciones Monserrate Ltda (Colombia); Pujol I Amado (Latin America, USA)

Ediciones Tarraco
San Francisco, 10, 43003 Tarragona
SAN: 002-0001
Tel: 977 233 813; 977 233 806
Founded: 1976
Subjects: Art, Education
ISBN Prefix(es): 978-84-7320
Parent Company: F Sugranes Editors SA

TE-Temas Educativos, *imprint of* Editorial Alhulia SA

TEA Ediciones SA+
Fray Bernardino Sahagun, 24, 28036 Madrid
Tel: 912 705 000 *Fax:* 913 458 608
E-mail: madrid@teaediciones.com
Web Site: web.teaediciones.com
Key Personnel
Sales: Marian Angeles Perez *E-mail:* marian.perez@teaediciones.com
Founded: 1957
Subjects: Psychology, Psychiatry
ISBN Prefix(es): 978-84-7174
Number of titles published annually: 15 Print
Total Titles: 300 Print
Parent Company: TEA-Cegos SA
Branch Office(s)
Paris, 211 - piso 2º, 08008 Barcelona *Tel:* 932 379 590 *Fax:* 932 377 382 *E-mail:* barcelona@teaediciones.com

Bidebarrieta, 12, 48008 Bilbao *Tel:* 944 163 032
Fax: 944 163 032 *E-mail:* bibao@teaediciones.
com
Avda Ramon y Cajal, 5, la Planta - Mod 2, 41005
Seville *Tel:* 954 933 216 *Fax:* 954 643 045
E-mail: sevilla@teaediciones.com
Paseo Independencia 22 9°, 50004 Zaragoza
Tel: 976 218 306 *E-mail:* zaragoza@
teaediciones.com
Foreign Rep(s): Editorial Atlante SRL (Argentina); Editorial Buenas Noticias 78 CA
(Venezuela); CEGOC-TEA (Portugal); Miguel
Concha SA (Chile); Desarrollo SRL (Dominican Republic); E-Trading & Supply SAC
(Peru); Euroamericana de Ediciones Corp
(Puerto Rico); Libreria Lehmann (Costa Rica);
Machon y Vejarano SA de CV "Liberia la Casita" (El Salvador); Libreria Matriz (Ecuador);
Meditec (Panama); PSEA SAS (Psicologos Especialistas Asociados SAS) (Colombia); Selcap
(Chile); Libreria Studium (Ecuador); Ediciones
Tecnicas Paraguayas SRL (Paraguay); Universidad del Valle de Guatemala (Guatemala);
Libreria Universo S de RL de CV (Honduras);
Universo SA (Nicaragua); Vesalius SA de CV
(Mexico)

Ediciones Tecnicas REDE SA
Ecuador, 91, 08029 Barcelona
Tel: 93 4302872 *Fax:* 93 4392813
E-mail: info@redeweb.com
Subjects: Electronics, Electrical Engineering
ISBN Prefix(es): 978-84-247

Editorial Tecnos SA+
C/ Juan Ignacio Luca de Tena, 15, 28027 Madrid
Tel: 913 938 600
E-mail: foro_tecnos@anaya.es
Web Site: www.tecnos.es
Key Personnel
Dir: Manuel Gonzalez Moreno
Founded: 1947
Subjects: Art, Business, Economics, Education,
History, Law, Literature, Literary Criticism,
Essays, Philosophy, Psychology, Psychiatry,
Science (General), Social Sciences, Sociology,
Technology
ISBN Prefix(es): 978-84-309
Parent Company: Grupo Anaya
Associate Companies: Ediciones Anaya SA

Editorial Teide SA
Viladomat, 291, 08029 Barcelona
Tel: 902 23 30 30 *Fax:* 93 321 26 46
E-mail: info@editorialteide.com
Web Site: www.teidenet.org; www.editorialteide.es
Founded: 1942
Subjects: Education
ISBN Prefix(es): 978-84-307
Branch Office(s)
Calle Hierbabuena 50, 28039 Madrid *Tel:* 915
707 920
Warehouse: Tambor del Bruch 8, 08970 San Juan
Despi

Editorial Pila Telena SL+
C/ Pozo Nuevo, 12, 28430 Alpedrete, Madrid
Tel: 609 25 20 82
E-mail: pilatelena@pilatelena.com
Web Site: www.pilatelena.com
Key Personnel
Chief Executive Officer: Marco Pila
Founded: 1972
Specialize in physical education & sports.
Subjects: Education, Sports, Athletics, Physical
Education
ISBN Prefix(es): 978-84-85514; 978-84-922803;
978-84-922838; 978-84-923778; 978-84-95353

Ediciones Temas de Hoy SA+
Member of Grupo Planeta

P° Recoletos, 4, 4a planta, 28001 Madrid
Tel: 91 423 03 33
E-mail: temasdehoy@planetadelibros.es
Web Site: www.planetadelibros.com/editorial-
ediciones-temas-de-hoy-10.html
Key Personnel
Press: Isabel Santos *E-mail:* isantos@temasdehoy.
es
Founded: 1987
Subjects: Biography, Memoirs, History, How-to,
Humor, Literature, Literary Criticism, Essays,
Self-Help
ISBN Prefix(es): 978-84-7880; 978-84-86675;
978-84-8460

Tempus Editorial, *imprint of* Roca Editorial

Tendencias, *imprint of* Ediciones Urano SA

Editorial Tenov SL
C/ Casp 147, 3er 2a, Barcelona 08013
Tel: 93 265 34 29
E-mail: tenov@editorialtenov.com
Web Site: www.editorialtenov.com
ISBN Prefix(es): 978-84-939231
Distributed by University of Chicago Press (Europe)
Orders to: Chicago Distribution Center, 11030 S
Langley Ave, Chicago, IL 60628, United States
Tel: 773-702-7000 *Fax:* 773-702-7212 (worldwide exc Spain & Europe)

Terciopelo Editorial, *imprint of* Roca Editorial

Editorial Sal Terrae+
Poligono de Raos Parcela 14-I, 39600 Maliano
(Cantabria)
Mailing Address: Apdo 77, 39080 Santander
(Cantabria)
Tel: 942 369 198 *Fax:* 942 369 201
E-mail: salterrae@salterrae.es
Web Site: www.salterrae.es
Key Personnel
Dir: Antonio Allende Felgueroso
    E-mail: aallendefelgueroso@gmail.com
Administrative Dir: Antonio Obregon Ruiz
    E-mail: obregon@salterrae.es
Publications: Jesus Garcia-Abril
    E-mail: garciabril@salterrae.es
Founded: 1912
Subjects: Anthropology, Biography, Memoirs,
History, Human Relations, Literature, Literary
Criticism, Essays, Medicine, Nursing, Dentistry, Philosophy, Psychology, Psychiatry, Religion - Other, Theology, Family, Letters, Love,
Sexuality
ISBN Prefix(es): 978-84-293

TF Editores+
Poligono Industrial de Alcobendas, C/ Aragoneses
2, Acceso 11, 28108 Madrid
Tel: 914 841 870 *Fax:* 91 661 00 82
E-mail: editorial@tfeditores.com; tfonline@
tfonline.es
Web Site: www.tfeditores.com
Key Personnel
International Distribution: Gabriela Torres
Editor: Paco Bastida; Ignacio Fernandez del Amo;
Chusa Hernandez
Founded: 1994
Publisher & printer.
Subjects: Architecture & Interior Design, Art, Literature, Literary Criticism, Essays, Photography
ISBN Prefix(es): 978-84-89162; 978-84-95183;
978-84-96209; 978-84-92441; 978-84-15253
Number of titles published annually: 40 Print
Total Titles: 215 Print
Parent Company: Tf Artes Graficas
Distributed by Distriforma SA

Editorial Thassalia SA
Muntaner, 50, 08006 Barcelona
SAN: 005-4372
Tel: 934 512 232
Founded: 1994
Subjects: Fiction, History, Nonfiction (General),
Religion - Buddhist, Religion - Hindu, Religion
- Islamic, Spirituality
ISBN Prefix(es): 978-84-8237
Orders to: Distribuciones Prologo, Mascaro 35,
08032 Barcelona *Tel:* 933 472 511 *Fax:* 934
599 506

Grupo Editorial 33
Avda Manuel Agustin Heredia 12, 1° dcha, 29001
Malaga
Tel: 952226281; 655 963 644
E-mail: inma@grupoeditorial33.com
Web Site: www.grupoeditorial33.com
Key Personnel
Editor: Inma Benitez
Founded: 2001
Subjects: History, Literature, Literary Criticism,
Essays, Medicine, Nursing, Dentistry
ISBN Prefix(es): 978-84-932611; 978-84-96257

Thomson Reuters Aranzadi
Camino de Galar, n° 15, 31190 Cizur Menor
(Navarra)
SAN: 002-273X
Tel: 902 40 40 47; 948 29 72 97 *Fax:* 902 40 00
10
E-mail: atencionclientes@thomsonreuters.com
Web Site: www.aranzadi.es
Key Personnel
General Dir: Jose Ruiz Cerrillo; Fernando Lopez
Lorente
Founded: 1929
Loose leaf publications, books & online products.
Subjects: Finance, Law, Management
ISBN Prefix(es): 978-84-7016; 978-84-8193; 978-
84-9767; 978-84-8410; 978-84-9903
Total Titles: 25 CD-ROM; 15 Online
Branch Office(s)
Avda La Paz n° 24D, 09004 Buergos
Paseo Recoletos n° 37, 2a planta, 28004 Madrid
C/ General Solchaga 3, 47008 Valladolid

3C3, see tresCtres Editores

Thule Ediciones
C/ Alcala de Guadaira, 26, 08020 Barcelona
Tel: 932 080 898 *Fax:* 932 080 064
E-mail: info@thuleediciones.com
Web Site: www.thuleediciones.com
Key Personnel
Foreign Rights: Jose Diaz
Founded: 2003
ISBN Prefix(es): 978-84-96473; 978-84-933734
Foreign Rep(s): Babel Libros (Colombia); Cajon
de Sastre (Chile); Caliroscopio Ediciones (Argentina); Independent Publishers Group (USA);
Ediciones Tecolote (Mexico)

Timun Mas, *imprint of* Ediciones CEAC

Editorial Tirant lo Blanch+
Artes Graficas 14, Bajo dcha, 46010 Valencia
SAN: 002-6964
Tel: 96 361 00 48; 96 361 00 50 *Fax:* 96 369 41
51
E-mail: tlb@tirant.es; atencioncliente@tirant.es
Web Site: www.tirant.com
Founded: 1976
Subjects: Biography, Memoirs, Criminology, Education, Labor, Industrial Relations, Language
Arts, Linguistics, Law, Management, Music,
Dance, Philosophy, Psychology, Psychiatry,
Religion - Other, Social Sciences, Sociology,
Theology, Humanities, Philology

ISBN Prefix(es): 978-84-8002; 978-84-86558; 978-84-8442; 978-84-8456; 978-84-9849; 978-84-2047; 978-84-9245; 978-84-9985
Branch Office(s)
Ciudad de la Justicia, Av del Saler, 14, 46013 Valencia *Tel:* 96 350 40 47 *Fax:* 96 350 40 46
Gravador Esteve, 5, 46004 Valencia *Tel:* 96 374 98 40 *Fax:* 96 334 18 35
Ramon Llull 31, Bajo izda, 46021 Valencia
Tel: 96 389 02 61 *Fax:* 96 389 02 62

Titania, *imprint of* Ediciones Urano SA

Ediciones de la Torre+
Minipoligono San Jose, nave 16, 28320 Pinto, Madrid
Tel: 916 922 034 *Fax:* 916 924 855
E-mail: info@edicionesdelatorre.com
Web Site: www.edicionesdelatorre.com
Founded: 1976
Subjects: Advertising, Child Care & Development, Communications, Drama, Theater, Education, Geography, Geology, History, Human Relations, Journalism, Literature, Literary Criticism, Essays, Nonfiction (General), Philosophy, Physics, Poetry, Radio, TV, Science (General), Social Sciences, Sociology
ISBN Prefix(es): 978-84-7960; 978-84-85866; 978-84-85277; 978-84-86587
Warehouse: C/Sorgo, 45, 28029 Madrid
Orders to: C/Sorgo, 45, 28029 Madrid

Ediciones Torremozas SL
Paseo de la Castellana, 190, 28046 Madrid
Mailing Address: Apdo 19032, 28080 Madrid
Tel: 913 590 315
E-mail: ediciones@torremozas.com
Web Site: www.torremozas.com
Key Personnel
Dir: Luzamaria Jimenez Faro
Founded: 1982
Specialize in poetry.
Subjects: Literature, Literary Criticism, Essays, Poetry, Women's Studies
ISBN Prefix(es): 978-84-7839; 978-84-86072
Distributed by Maidhisa SL

Editorial Toxosoutos
Cruceiro do Rego, 2 Obre, 15217 Noia, A Coruna
Tel: 981 823 855 *Fax:* 981 821 690
E-mail: editorial@toxosoutos.com
Web Site: www.toxosoutos.com
Subjects: Biography, Memoirs, History, Literature, Literary Criticism, Essays
ISBN Prefix(es): 978-84-89129; 978-84-95622; 978-84-96259

Ediciones Trabe SL
C/ Foncalada 10, 2u A, 33002 Oviedo, Asturias
Tel: 985 208 206 *Fax:* 985 208 206
E-mail: ediciones@trabe.org
Web Site: www.trabe.org
Key Personnel
Dir General: Inaciu Iglesias Fernandez
Founded: 1992
Subjects: Art, Biography, Memoirs, Cookery, Literature, Literary Criticism, Essays, Philosophy, Religion - Other
ISBN Prefix(es): 978-84-8053

Trama Editorial
C/ Blanca de Navarra 6, 28010 Madrid
Tel: 917 024 154
E-mail: trama@tramaeditorial.es
Web Site: www.tramaeditorial.es; www.facebook.com/Trama.Texturas
Subjects: Art, Literature, Literary Criticism, Essays
ISBN Prefix(es): 978-84-89239; 978-9978-30

Trapella Books
Imprint of ACV Global
Diputacio, 238-244, 6-8, 08007 Barcelona
Tel: 933042980
E-mail: info@acvglobal.com
Web Site: www.trapellabooks.com
Key Personnel
Mng Dir: Sergi Roses Collado
Founded: 2009
ISBN Prefix(es): 978-84-92880

Trea Ediciones SL+
Pol Industrial de Somonte, Maria Gonzalez La Pondala, 98, nave D, 33393 Cenero, Gijon, Asturias
Tel: 985 303 801 *Fax:* 985 303 712
E-mail: trea@trea.es; prensa@trea.es; pedidos@trea.es
Web Site: www.trea.es
Key Personnel
Manager: Miguel A Blanco Vazquez
Editor: Alvaro Diaz Huici
Founded: 1991
Subjects: Art, Biological Sciences, Cookery, Education, Fiction, Geography, Geology, History, Library & Information Sciences, Literature, Literary Criticism, Essays, Nonfiction (General), Photography, Poetry, Public Administration, Social Sciences, Sociology, Travel & Tourism
ISBN Prefix(es): 978-84-87733; 978-84-89427; 978-84-9704; 978-84-95178
Associate Companies: Edicions Nigra Trea SL

Edicions Tres i Quatre+
Apdo 134, La Canyada, Paterna, 46182 Valencia
Tel: 680 437 157
E-mail: tresiquatre@tresiquatre.cat
Web Site: www.tresiquatre.cat/3i4/editorial
Key Personnel
Editor: Eliseu Climent
Founded: 1968
Subjects: Biography, Memoirs, Drama, Theater, Language Arts, Linguistics, Poetry
ISBN Prefix(es): 978-84-85211; 978-84-7502

tresCtres Editores
Jose Villar Granjel, 35, 1a planta, Poligono de Boisaca, 15890 Santiago de Compustela
Tel: 981 535 960 *Fax:* 981 818 799
E-mail: info@tresctres.com
Web Site: www.tresctres.com
Key Personnel
Editorial Dir: Amancio Linares Giraut; Antonio Puentes Chao
Founded: 2001
Subjects: Agriculture, Biography, Memoirs, Drama, Theater, Economics, Government, Political Science, Literature, Literary Criticism, Essays, Music, Dance, Poetry, Ecology
ISBN Prefix(es): 978-84-934890; 978-84-932667; 978-84-932136

Trito Edicions SL
Enamorats 35-37, baixos, 08013 Barcelona
Tel: 93 342 61 75 *Fax:* 93 302 26 70
E-mail: info@trito.es
Web Site: www.trito.es
Founded: 1992
Subjects: Art, Music, Dance
ISBN Prefix(es): 978-84-88955

Editorial Trivium SA+
Calle Molina, 20, 28029 Madrid
SAN: 002-7006
Tel: 913 147 495 *Fax:* 915 422 862
Founded: 1982
Subjects: Economics, Law
ISBN Prefix(es): 978-84-7855; 978-84-86440
Bookshop(s): Tapia Libreria Juridica
Warehouse: Pintores, 30 (Polig Urtinsa II), 28925 Alcorcon Madrid

Trotta Editorial SA+
Ferraz, 55, 28008 Madrid
Tel: 915430361 *Fax:* 915431488
E-mail: editorial@trotta.es
Web Site: www.trotta.es
Key Personnel
President: Alejandro Sierra Benayas
Founded: 1990
Subjects: History, Law, Literature, Literary Criticism, Essays, Philosophy, Psychology, Psychiatry, Religion - Catholic, Religion - Islamic, Religion - Jewish, Religion - Other, Social Sciences, Sociology, Theology
ISBN Prefix(es): 978-84-87699; 978-84-8164; 978-84-9879
Number of titles published annually: 60 Print
Total Titles: 700 Print

Editorial Ttarttalo
Portuetxe, 88 bis, 20018 Donostia
Tel: 943 31 02 67
E-mail: ttarttalo@ttarttalo.com
Web Site: www.ttarttalo.com
Subjects: Anthropology, Cookery, Geography, Geology, History, Literature, Literary Criticism, Essays
ISBN Prefix(es): 978-84-8091; 978-84-86202
Parent Company: Fundacion Elkar

Ediciones Turner, see Turner Publicaciones

Turner Publicaciones+
Rafael Calvo, 42-2° esc izda, 28010 Madrid
SAN: 002-029X
Tel: 913 083 336
E-mail: contactosweb@turnerlibros.com; turner@turnerlibros.com
Web Site: www.turnerlibros.com
Key Personnel
Publisher: Santiago F de Cayela
Mng Dir: Rafael Ramirez
Editorial Dir: Laura Estevez
Distribution & Sales: Carolina Faustmann
Press: Lola Martin
Founded: 1973
Specialize in production of catalogues & illustrated books; publishes general nonfiction.
Subjects: Architecture & Interior Design, Art, History, Literature, Literary Criticism, Essays, Nonfiction (General), Philosophy, Photography, Poetry, Regional Interests, Museum Catalogues
ISBN Prefix(es): 978-84-7506; 978-84-85137
Number of titles published annually: 120 Print
Total Titles: 400 Print; 5 Audio
Subsidiaries: Editorial Turner de Mexico SA
Foreign Rep(s): Art Data (UK); Dap (Distributed Art Publishers) (Canada, USA); Ideabooks (Europe); Oceano (Latin America)

Turpial, *imprint of* Editorial Everest SA

Tusquets Editores SA+
Diagonal 604, 1° 1a, 08021 Barcelona
Tel: 93 253 04 00; 93 362 33 79 *Fax:* 93 417 67 03; 93 209 89 19
E-mail: general@tusquets-editores.es
Web Site: www.tusquetseditores.com
Key Personnel
Founder & Editorial Dir: Beatriz de Moura
Foreign Rights Acquisitions: Carmen Corral
Production: Orencio Sales
Sales: Rosa Maria Segala
Founded: 1968
Subjects: Biography, Memoirs, Fiction, History, Literature, Literary Criticism, Essays, Nonfiction (General), Science (General)
ISBN Prefix(es): 978-84-7223; 978-84-8310; 978-84-8383; 978-84-96171
Branch Office(s)
Venezuela, 1664, 1096 Buenos Aires, Argentina, Press: Paola Lucantis *Tel:* (011) 4381 45 20

Fax: (011) 4381 17 60 *E-mail:* info@tusquets.com.ar

Av Presidente Masaryk No III, Piso 2, Col Chapultec Morales, Delegacion Miguel Hildalgo, 11570 Mexico, DF, Mexico *Tel:* (0155) 5574 63 79; (0155) 3000 62 00 *E-mail:* info@tusquetsmexico.com

Warehouse: Carretera del Prat 39, Poligono Industrial Almeda nave n 5, 08940 Cornella, Barcelona

Ediciones Tutor SA+
Marques de Urquijo, 34-2° izda, 28008 Madrid
SAN: 002-0303
Tel: 915 599 832; 915 420 935 *Fax:* 915 410 235
E-mail: info@edicionestutor.com;
atencionalcliente@edicionestutor.com;
edicion@edicionestutor.com; comercial@edicionestutor.com
Web Site: www.edicionestutor.com
Key Personnel
President: Jesus Domingo Garcia
Editorial Dir & Rights & Permissions: David Domingo Yanes *E-mail:* daviddomingo@edicionestutor.com
Marketing, Public Relations: Vivas Francisco Rubira
Founded: 1988
Subjects: Animals, Pets, Career Development, Cookery, Crafts, Games, Hobbies, Gardening, Plants, Health, Nutrition, Humor, Outdoor Recreation, Sports, Athletics, Leisure
ISBN Prefix(es): 978-84-7902
Associate Companies: Editorial El Drac SL
Warehouse: ADT, c/o Pelaya ue4, Poligono Industrial Rio de Janeiro, 28110 Algete *Tel:* 916 280 606
Orders to: I Taca SA Distribuciones Editoriales, Lopez de Hoyos, 141, 28002 Madrid *Tel:* 913 224 400 *Fax:* 913 224 370

Ediciones 29+
c/ Francesc Vila, nau 14, Poligono Industrial Can Magi, 08190 Sant Cugat del Valles, Barcelona
Tel: 936 754 135 *Fax:* 935 900 440
E-mail: ediciones29@comunired.com
Key Personnel
Mng Dir: Alfredo Llorente Diez
Founded: 1968
Subjects: Astrology, Occult, Cookery, Erotica, Fiction, Geography, Geology, History, Literature, Literary Criticism, Essays, Poetry, Religion - Catholic, Self-Help
ISBN Prefix(es): 978-84-7175
Total Titles: 200 Print

Editorial Txalaparta
San Isidro, 35-1 A, 31300 Tafalla, Navarra, Basque
Tel: 948703934
E-mail: txalaparta@txalaparta.com
Web Site: www.txalaparta.com
Key Personnel
Editorial Dir: Mikel Soto *E-mail:* mikel@txalaparta.com
Subjects: Biography, Memoirs, Fiction, Geography, Geology, History, Social Sciences, Sociology
ISBN Prefix(es): 978-84-8136; 978-84-86597; 978-84-86957

Editorial Txertoa Argitaletxera+
Portuetxe 88 bis, 20018 Donostia
SAN: 002-7022
Tel: 943 310 267 *Fax:* 943 460 941
E-mail: txertoa@txertoa.com
Web Site: www.txertoa.com
Founded: 1968
Subjects: Anthropology, Art, Biography, Memoirs, Ethnicity, Geography, Geology, History, Language Arts, Linguistics, Literature, Literary Criticism, Essays, Philosophy, Regional

Interests, Religion - Other, Science (General), Social Sciences, Sociology, Ethnography
ISBN Prefix(es): 978-84-7148
Number of titles published annually: 12 Print
Total Titles: 250 Print

UAM Ediciones, see Universidad Autonoma de Madrid-Servicio de Publicaciones

Edicions UIB
Universitat de les Illes Balears, Cra de Valldemossa, km 7.5, 07122 Palma
Tel: 971173000; 971172499; 971173357
E-mail: info.edicions@uib.es
Web Site: www.uib.cat
Key Personnel
Dir: Joan Munoz Gomila
Head, Promotion & Publishing Projects: Joan Vives Riera
ISBN Prefix(es): 978-84-7632; 978-84-8384

Umbriel, *imprint of* Ediciones Urano SA

Universidad Autonoma de Madrid-Servicio de Publicaciones
Edificio Rectorado, 2a Entreplanta, Carretera Colmenar Km 15, 28049 Madrid
Tel: 914 974 233 *Fax:* 914 975 169
E-mail: servicio.publicaciones@uam.es
Web Site: www.uam.es
Key Personnel
Dir: Juan Manuel Gillem Mesado
Marketing & Communication: Beatriz Dorado Perez
ISBN Prefix(es): 978-84-8344; 978-84-922229; 978-84-7477

Universidad Complutense de Madrid Servicio de Publicaciones+
Ciudad Universitaria, C/ Obispo Trejo, 3, 28040 Madrid
Tel: 913 941 127 *Fax:* 913 941 126
E-mail: servicio.publicaciones@rect.ucm.es
Web Site: www.ucm.es/servicio-de-publicaciones
Founded: 1986
Subjects: Anthropology, Biological Sciences, Economics, History, Psychology, Psychiatry, Social Sciences, Sociology
ISBN Prefix(es): 978-84-669; 978-84-8466; 978-84-95215; 978-84-688

Universidad de Alcala Servicio de Publicaciones
Plaza San Diego s/n, 28801 Alcala de Henares
Tel: 918854066; 918854106
E-mail: serv.publicaciones@uah.es
Web Site: publicaciones.uah.es
Key Personnel
Dir: Francisco J Gomez *Tel:* 918854470
E-mail: franciscoj.gomez@uah.es
Administrative: Nuria Boyarizo *E-mail:* nuria.boyarizo@uah.es
ISBN Prefix(es): 978-84-16133; 978-84-8138

Editorial Universidad de Almeria
Ctra Sacramento s/n, La Canada de San Urbano, 04120 Almeria
Tel: 950 015459; 950 015182 *Fax:* 950 214435
E-mail: publicac@ual.es
Web Site: cms.ual.es/UAL/es/universidad/serviciosgenerales/editorial/index.htm (Spanish); cms.ual.es/UAL/en/universidad/serviciosgenerales/editorial/index.htm (English)
Key Personnel
Dir: Gabriel Nunez Ruiz *Tel:* 950 015861
E-mail: gnunez@ual.es
Founded: 1994
Subjects: Economics, History, Law, Literature, Literary Criticism, Essays, Philosophy, Psychology, Psychiatry, Social Sciences, Sociology, Technology, Humanities

ISBN Prefix(es): 978-84-8240
Distribution Center: Dogma SL, Plaza Santa Isabel, 11, 04009 Almeria *Tel:* 950 262855 *Fax:* 950 268371 *E-mail:* dogma@dogmalibros.com
Bitacora, Olzinelles, 5, 08014 Barcelona
Tel: 93 4222215 *Fax:* 93 4321493
E-mail: bitacorarte@bitacorarte.com *Web Site:* www.bitacorarte.com (international)
Pujol & Amado SL, Industria, 49, 08025 Barcelona *Tel:* 93 2080048 *Fax:* 93 2080639 *E-mail:* bernat@pujolamado.com (international)
Breogan SL, Lanuza, 11-Local dcha, 28028 Madrid *Tel:* 91 7259072 *Fax:* 91 7130631

Universidad de Cadiz Servicio de Publicaciones+
Edificio de Servicios Centrales Andres Segovia, C/ Dr Maranon, N° 3, 11002 Cadiz
Tel: 956 015 268 *Fax:* 956 015 634
E-mail: publicaciones@uca.es
Web Site: minerva.uca.es/publicaciones/asp/default.asp
Key Personnel
Dir: Gonzalo Butron Prida
Manager: Pedro Cervera Corbacho; Ana Maria Vega Moreno
Founded: 1980
Subjects: Chemistry, Chemical Engineering, Education, Engineering (General), History, Law, Literature, Literary Criticism, Essays, Medicine, Nursing, Dentistry, Science (General), Technology, Culture
ISBN Prefix(es): 978-84-7786; 978-84-96274; 978-84-9828
Distributed by Libreria Telmatica Espanola
Distributor for L'Alebrije (USA)
Foreign Rep(s): L'Alebrije (Latin America, Mexico); Bitacora-Arte y Humanidades SL (Europe); Pujol i Amado (all other territories, Latin America); Puvill Libros (all other territories, Latin America)

Ediciones de la Universidad de Castilla-La Mancha
Calle Camino del Pozuelo, s/n, 16071 Cuenca
Tel: 969179100 *Fax:* 969179111
E-mail: publicaciones@uclm.es
Web Site: publicaciones.uclm.es
Key Personnel
Dir General: Carmen Vazquez Varela
Editorial Dir: Carlos Julian Martinez Soria
Founded: 1988
Membership(s): Genueve Ediciones y de CEDRO; La Union de Editoriales Universitarias Espanolas.
Subjects: Geography, Geology, History, Language Arts, Linguistics, Literature, Literary Criticism, Essays, Philosophy, Social Sciences, Sociology
ISBN Prefix(es): 978-84-8427; 978-84-88255; 978-84-89492; 978-84-89958

Universidad de Deusto, Dpto de Publicaciones
Av de las Universidades 24, 48007 Bilbao
Tel: 944139000; 944139162 *Fax:* 944456817
E-mail: publicaciones@deusto.es; web@deusto.es
Web Site: www.deusto-publicaciones.es
Key Personnel
Editorial Dir: Javier Torres Ripa
Founded: 1972
Subjects: Archaeology, Economics, Engineering (General), History, Language Arts, Linguistics, Law, Philosophy, Psychology, Psychiatry, Social Sciences, Sociology, Theology, Travel & Tourism, Ethics
ISBN Prefix(es): 978-84-7485; 978-84-9830
Foreign Rep(s): Agape Libros (Argentina); Libreria Artemis Edinter SA (Guatemala); Asociacion Hijas de San Pablo (Peru); Asociacion Manantial de la Cultura (Guatemala); Libreria Catolica Ave Maria (Puerto Rico); Editoriales La Ceiba (El Salvador); Libreria Centro Paulinas (Venezuela); Congregacion

Hijas de San Pablo (Chile); Grupo Copages Libreria (Ecuador); Corporacion Ediciones Paulinas (Ecuador); Distribuidora de Estudios (Venezuela); Libreria Familia de Nazareth (Chile); Fundacion Jesus de la Misericordia (Ecuador); Instituto Misionero Hijas de San Pablo (Bolivia, Ecuador); Paulinas (Dominican Republic, Paraguay, Uruguay); Paulinas Centro Multimedia (Puerto Rico); Paulinas-Instituto Misionero Hijas de San Pablo (Colombia); Pia Sociedad San Pablo (Chile); San Pablo (Costa Rica, El Salvador); Libreria San Pablo (Guatemala, Puerto Rico, USA); Sociedad de San Pablo (Argentina, Colombia, Peru); Libreria Studium (Ecuador)

Universidad de Extremadura-Servicio de Publicaciones
Edificio Rectorado, Plaza de Caldereros 1, 10071 Caceres
Tel: 927 257 041 *Fax:* 927 257 046
E-mail: publicac@unex.es
Web Site: www.unex.es/publicaciones
Key Personnel
Dir: Manuel Rojas Gabriel *Tel:* 927 257 041 ext 51115 *E-mail:* mrojas@unex.es
ISBN Prefix(es): 978-84-7723

Editorial Universidad de Granada (University of Granada Publishing)
Antiguo Colegio Maximo, Campus Universitario de Cartuja, Universidad de Granada, 18071 Granada
Tel: 958 246 220; 958 506 722 *Fax:* 958 243 931
E-mail: pedidos@editorialugr.com
Web Site: www.editorialugr.com
Key Personnel
Dir: Maria Isabel Cabrera Garcia *Tel:* 958 243 932 *E-mail:* direccioneug@ugr.es
Communication & Marketing: Yolanda Ortiz Alejo *Tel:* 958 242 827 *E-mail:* yortiz@ugr.es
Founded: 1997
Subjects: Anthropology, Archaeology, Art, Behavioral Sciences, Biography, Memoirs, Biological Sciences, Chemistry, Chemical Engineering, Civil Engineering, Earth Sciences, Economics, Education, Engineering (General), English as a Second Language, Environmental Studies, Foreign Countries, Geography, Geology, Government, Political Science, Health, Nutrition, History, Language Arts, Linguistics, Law, Library & Information Sciences, Literature, Literary Criticism, Essays, Mathematics, Medicine, Nursing, Dentistry, Music, Dance, Philosophy, Physical Sciences, Poetry, Religion - Catholic, Science (General), Social Sciences, Sociology, Theology, Women's Studies
ISBN Prefix(es): 978-84-338

Universidad de Jaen, Servicio de Publicaciones
Campus de las Lagunillas, s/n, Edif Biblioteca 2a planta, 23071 Jaen
Tel: 953 21 23 55 *Fax:* 953 21 23 55
E-mail: servpub@ujaen.es
Web Site: www10.ujaen.es/conocenos/servicias-unidades/servpub
Key Personnel
Head: Maria Rosalia Tudela Caballero *Tel:* 953 21 23 52 *Fax:* 953 21 23 35 *E-mail:* mrtudela@ujaen.es
Membership(s): CEDRO; DILVE; UNE.
Subjects: Art, Biography, Memoirs, Geography, Geology, History, Language Arts, Linguistics, Literature, Literary Criticism, Essays, Philosophy, Social Sciences, Sociology
ISBN Prefix(es): 978-84-8439; 978-84-88942; 978-84-89869

Universidad de Malaga+
Avda Cervantes, 2, 29071 Malaga
SAN: 005-2310
Tel: 952 13 10 00

E-mail: redessociales@uma.es
Web Site: www.uma.es
Key Personnel
Head, Publications: Eva Alarcon Fanjul *Tel:* 952 13 72 25 *E-mail:* eva@uma.es
Founded: 1974
Subjects: Agriculture, Art, Earth Sciences, Economics, Education, History, Law, Medicine, Nursing, Dentistry, Philosophy, Social Sciences, Sociology
ISBN Prefix(es): 978-84-7496; 978-84-9747
Distributed by Distribuciones de Enlace SA

Ediciones Universidad de Navarra SA, see EUNSA (Ediciones Universidad de Navarra SA)

Universidad de Oviedo Servicio de Publicaciones
Campus de Humanidades, Edificio de Servicios, 33011 Oviedo
Tel: 985 10 95 04; 985 10 95 05 *Fax:* 985 10 95 07
E-mail: servipub@uniovi.es
Web Site: www.uniovi.es/publicaciones
Key Personnel
Dir: Ana Isabel Gonzalez
Administration: Carmen del Rosal Areces *Tel:* 985 10 95 03
Subjects: Behavioral Sciences, Language Arts, Linguistics, Physical Sciences, Science (General), Social Sciences, Sociology
ISBN Prefix(es): 978-84-7468; 978-84-8317

Ediciones Universidad de Salamanca+
Plaza de San Benito, nº 2, 37008 Salamanca
Tel: 923 294 598; 923 294 500 (ext 4598) *Fax:* 923 262 579
E-mail: pedidos@universitas.usal.es; eusal@usal.es; comunicacion.eusal@usal.es
Web Site: www.eusal.es
Key Personnel
Dir: Maria jose Rodriguez Sanchez de Leon *E-mail:* direccion.eusal@usal.es
Promotion: Luciano Alonso Alonso *E-mail:* laa@usal.es
Sales: Juan Vicente Vicente *E-mail:* jvv@usal.es
Founded: 1486
Subjects: Education, History, Literature, Literary Criticism, Essays, Philosophy, Science (General)
ISBN Prefix(es): 978-84-7880; 978-84-7481; 978-84-7800
Number of titles published annually: 100 Print
Foreign Rep(s): L'Alebrije (Latin America); Pujol & Amado (Latin America); Puvill Libros (USA); Studia Humanitatis (USA); Jorge Waldhuter (Latin America)

Universidad de Santiago de Compostela
Servicio de Publicaciones e Intercambio Cientifico, Campus Vida, 15782 Santiago de Compostela
SAN: 005-2728
Tel: 881 812 391
E-mail: sepinter@usc.es
Web Site: www.usc.es/en/servizos/publicacions
Key Personnel
Dir: Juan Luis Blanco Valdes *Tel:* 981 563 100 ext 12392 *E-mail:* juanluis.blanco@usc.es
Editor: Natalia Villar Conde *Tel:* 981 563 100 ext 12390 *E-mail:* natalia.villar@usc.es
Administration: V Manuel Fernandez Martinez *Tel:* 881 815 010 *E-mail:* vmanuel.fernandez@usc.es
Founded: 1945
Membership(s): Association of Spanish Editorial University.
Subjects: Art, Education, Electronics, Electrical Engineering, Geography, Geology, History, Language Arts, Linguistics, Law, Philosophy,

Physics, Science (General), Social Sciences, Sociology
ISBN Prefix(es): 978-84-7191; 978-84-8121; 978-84-9750; 978-84-9887; 978-84-15876; 978-84-16183
Number of titles published annually: 50 Print; 200 Online; 20 E-Book
Total Titles: 1,700 Print; 1,450 Online; 200 E-Book

Secretariado de Publicaciones de la Universidad de Sevilla
C/ Porvenir, 27, 41013 Seville
Tel: 954 487 444; 954 487 450 *Fax:* 954 48 74 43; 954 487 447
E-mail: secpub2@us.es
Web Site: editorial.us.es
Key Personnel
Dir: Dr Antonio Francisco Caballos Rufino *E-mail:* directoreus@us.es
Head, Publications Unit: Sara Fernandez Rendon
Publications Manager: Angel Martinez Perez *Tel:* 954 487 478 *E-mail:* secpub6@us.es
Founded: 1938
ISBN Prefix(es): 978-84-472; 978-84-7405; 978-84-86783
Distributed by Centro Andaluz del Libro SA; Distribuciones de Enlace SA; Laforre Literaria SA

Universidad de Valladolid Secretariado de Publicaciones e Intercambio Editorial+
Servicios Centrales, C/ Juan Mambrilla, 14, 47003 Valladolid
Tel: 98318-7810 *Fax:* 98318-7812
E-mail: secretariado.publicaciones@uva.es
Web Site: www.publicaciones.uva.es
Key Personnel
Dir: Pedro Pablo; Conde Parrado *Tel:* 98318-7809 *E-mail:* direccion.publicaciones@uva.es
Founded: 1949
Subjects: Accounting, Archaeology, Architecture & Interior Design, Art, Business, Chemistry, Chemical Engineering, Computer Science, Economics, Education, Electronics, Electrical Engineering, Engineering (General), Geography, Geology, Government, Political Science, History, Law, Literature, Literary Criticism, Essays, Medicine, Nursing, Dentistry, Philosophy, Physics, Psychology, Psychiatry, Science (General), Social Sciences, Sociology, Humanities
ISBN Prefix(es): 978-84-7762; 978-84-8448; 978-84-86192

Universidad del Pais Vasco (University of the Basque Country)
PO Box 1397, 48080 Bilbao
Tel: 94 601 2227; 94 601 7944 (rights) *Fax:* 94 601 2333
E-mail: info.editorial@ehu.eus
Web Site: www.ehu.eus/es/web/argitalpen-zerbitzua/home
Founded: 1982
Subjects: Biological Sciences, Communications, Economics, Education, Engineering (General), History, Journalism, Language Arts, Linguistics, Law, Literature, Literary Criticism, Essays, Medicine, Nursing, Dentistry, Philosophy, Psychology, Psychiatry, Science (General), Social Sciences, Sociology
ISBN Prefix(es): 978-84-7585; 978-84-8373; 978-84-9860
Number of titles published annually: 150 Print; 15 CD-ROM; 25 Online
Total Titles: 1,623 Print
Distributed by Celesa (Spain); Pujol & Amado (Spain)

Universidad Nacional de Educacion a Distancia (UNED)
C/ Bravo Murillo, 38 (Metro Canal), 28015 Madrid

Tel: 91 398 60 00; 91 398 66 00 *Fax:* 91 398 75 27
E-mail: infouned@adm.uned.es
Web Site: www.uned.es/publicaciones
Key Personnel
Editorial Dir: Herminia Calero
Founded: 1972
Subjects: Biography, Memoirs, English as a Second Language, Geography, Geology, History, Language Arts, Linguistics, Literature, Literary Criticism, Essays, Philosophy, Science (General)
ISBN Prefix(es): 978-84-362
Bookshop(s): C/ Senda del Rey, Nº 5 (Edificio de la Biblioteca Central), 28040 Madrid *Tel:* 91 398 73 73 *E-mail:* libreria-sr@adm.uned.es; C/ Tribulete, 14 (Escuelas Pias), 28012 Madrid *Tel:* 91 527 10 98 *E-mail:* libreriaep@adm.uned.es

Universidad Pontificia de Salamanca
C/ Compania, 5, 37002 Salamanca
Tel: 923 277 128 *Fax:* 923 277 129
E-mail: publicaciones@upsa.es
Web Site: www.upsa.es/publicaciones
Key Personnel
Dir: Alberto Pedrero Esteban, PhD
 E-mail: director.publicaciones@upsa.es
Subjects: Advertising, Art, Behavioral Sciences, Biblical Studies, Computer Science, Computers, Disability, Special Needs, Education, Film, Video, Finance, History, Inspirational, Spirituality, Journalism, Law, Marketing, Medicine, Nursing, Dentistry, Music, Dance, Philosophy, Psychology, Psychiatry, Radio, TV, Religion - Catholic, Religion - Other, Science (General), Social Sciences, Sociology, Technology, Theology, Wine & Spirits, Women's Studies, Culture, Family Studies
ISBN Prefix(es): 978-84-7299

Universidade de Burgos, Servicio de Publicaciones
C/ Don Juan de Austria, no 1, 09001 Burgos
Tel: 947258880
E-mail: serv.publicaciones@ubu.es
Web Site: www.ubu.es/publicaciones
Key Personnel
President: Jose Antonio Fernandez Florez
Secretary: Fernando Somoza Lopez
Founded: 1996
Subjects: Education, Law, Psychology, Psychiatry, Science (General), Humanities
ISBN Prefix(es): 978-84-922382; 978-84-95211; 978-84-96394

Universidade de Vigo, Servizo de Publicacions
Edificio de Biblioteca Central Lagoas-Marcosende s/n, 36310 Vigo
Tel: 986812235
E-mail: sep@uvigo.es
Web Site: publicacions.uvigo.es/publicacions_es
Key Personnel
Dir: Julia Castro Mencia
Founded: 1993
Membership(s): Spanish Association of University Publishers.
Subjects: Language Arts, Linguistics, Public Administration, Science (General), Technology, Humanities
ISBN Prefix(es): 978-84-8158
Total Titles: 200 Print

Editorial Universitas SA
Nunez de Balboa 5º I, 28006 Madrid
Tel: 915643652 *Fax:* 915633652
Web Site: www.universitas.es
Key Personnel
President: Carlos Agullo-Campos
Subjects: Communications, Economics, Education, Geography, Geology, Government, Political Science, Health, Nutrition, History, Language Arts, Linguistics, Law, Literature, Literary Criticism, Essays, Psychology, Psychiatry, Social Sciences, Sociology
ISBN Prefix(es): 978-84-7991; 978-84-933377

Universitat Autonoma de Barcelona
Edificio A, Bellaterra, 08193 Cerdanyola del Valles-Barcelona
Tel: 93 581 10 22 *Fax:* 93 581 32 39
E-mail: sp@uab.cat
Web Site: publicacions.uab.es
Key Personnel
Management: Joan Carles Marset *Tel:* 93 581 2130 *E-mail:* joancarles.marset@uab.cat
Administration: Nuria Mateos *Tel:* 93 581 1715 *E-mail:* nuria.mateos@uab.cat
Publications: Xavier Tortajada *Tel:* 93 581 2129 *E-mail:* xavier.tortajada@uab.cat
Membership(s): Union de Editoriales Universitarias Espanolas; Xarxa Vives d'Universitats.
Subjects: Anthropology, Art, Biography, Memoirs, Biological Sciences, Economics, History, Language Arts, Linguistics, Literature, Literary Criticism, Essays, Mathematics, Medicine, Nursing, Dentistry, Science (General), Social Sciences, Sociology, Technology, Egyptian Studies
ISBN Prefix(es): 978-84-7929; 978-84-490; 978-84-7488

Publicacions de la Universitat de Valencia (PUV) (Valencia University Press)+
C/ Arts Grafiques, 13, 46010 Valencia
Tel: 963 864 115 *Fax:* 963 864 067
E-mail: publicacions@uv.es
Web Site: puv.uv.es
Key Personnel
Dir: Josep Lluis Canet *E-mail:* jose.canet@uv.es
Manager: Lluis Miro *E-mail:* lluis.miro@uv.es
Editor: Vicent Olmos *E-mail:* vicent.olmos@uv.es; Maite Simon *E-mail:* maite.simon@uv.es
Marketing: Maria Ferrer *E-mail:* maria.ferrer-martorell@uv.es; Amparo Jesus-Maria *E-mail:* amparo.jesus@uv.es
Subjects: Biography, Memoirs, Biological Sciences, Economics, Education, History, Law, Literature, Literary Criticism, Essays, Medicine, Nursing, Dentistry, Philosophy, Social Sciences, Sociology
ISBN Prefix(es): 978-84-370
Number of titles published annually: 226 Print
Total Titles: 4,300 Print
Foreign Rep(s): Corporacion Bibliografica SA de CV (Mexico); Fundacion Libro Universitario-Libun (Peru); Siglo del Hombre Editores (Colombia); Jorge Waldhuter (Argentina)

Editorial de la Universitat Politecnica de Catalunya SL
C Jordi Girona, 31, 08034 Barcelona
Tel: 93 401 5885 *Fax:* 93 405 4101
E-mail: edicions-upc@upc.edu; edicions.virtuals@upc.es
Web Site: www.edicionsupc.es; www.upc.edu; www.upc.edu/idp
Key Personnel
Dir: Jordi Prats *E-mail:* jordi.prats@upc.edu
Founded: 1994
Subjects: Architecture & Interior Design, Chemistry, Chemical Engineering, Civil Engineering, Computer Science, Electronics, Electrical Engineering, Engineering (General), Science (General)
ISBN Prefix(es): 978-84-7653

Editorial de la Universitat Politecnica de Valencia
Camino de Vera, s/n, 46022 Valencia
Tel: 963 877 012; 963 877 901 *Fax:* 963 877 912
E-mail: edicion@editorial.upv.es; pedidos@editorial.upv.es
Web Site: www.upv.es/entidades/AEUPV

Founded: 1986
Subjects: Agriculture, Architecture & Interior Design, Communications, Economics, Engineering (General), Language Arts, Linguistics, Mathematics, Physics, Biotechnology, Urban Affairs
ISBN Prefix(es): 978-84-9705; 978-84-7721

UNWTO, see World Tourism Organization (UNWTO)

Editorial UOC
Rambla del Poblenou, No 156, 08018 Barcelona
Tel: 93 486 39 40 *Fax:* 93 451 30 16
E-mail: ediuoc@uoc.edu
Web Site: www.editorialuoc.cat
Key Personnel
Dir General: Lluis Pastor
Subjects: Economics, Education, Finance, Geography, Geology, History, Literature, Literary Criticism, Essays, Psychology, Psychiatry, Religion - Other, Science (General), Technology, Travel & Tourism, Administration
ISBN Prefix(es): 978-84-9788; 978-84-8318; 978-84-8429; 978-84-89382; 978-84-922767; 978-84-95131

Editions UPC SL, see Editorial de la Universitat Politecnica de Catalunya SL

Editorial UPV, see Editorial de la Universitat Politecnica de Valencia

Urano, *imprint of* Ediciones Urano SA

Ediciones Urano SA+
Aribau, 142 pral, 08036 Barcelona
Tel: 902 131 315 *Fax:* 934 153 796
E-mail: infoes@edicionesurano.com; atencion@edicionesurano.com
Web Site: www.edicionesurano.es
Key Personnel
Manager: Joaquin Sabate
Founded: 1983
Subjects: Alternative, Astrology, Occult, Business, Fiction, Health, Nutrition, How-to, Management, Medicine, Nursing, Dentistry, Mysteries, Suspense, Psychology, Psychiatry, Romance, Self-Help
ISBN Prefix(es): 978-84-7953; 978-84-86344; 978-84-95618; 978-84-95752; 978-84-95787; 978-84-96711
Number of titles published annually: 74 Print
Total Titles: 561 Print
Imprints: Books4pocket; Caelus Books; Empresa Activa; Entramat; Plata; Puck; Tendencias; Titania; Umbriel; Urano
Branch Office(s)
Paracas 59, C1275AFA Buenos Aires, Argentina
 Tel: (011) 4305 0633 *Fax:* (011) 4304 7820
 E-mail: infoar@edicionesurano.com.ar
Av Francisco Bilbao, 2790, Providencia, Santiago, Chile *Tel:* (02) 3417232 *Fax:* (02) 2233896
 E-mail: infoch@edicionesurano.com
Calle 144, Nº 49-40, Bogota DC, Colombia *Tel:* (01) 6146252 *Fax:* (01) 5221481
 E-mail: infoco@edicionesurano.com.co
Vito Alessio Robles, No 175, Col Hacienda Guadalupe de Chimalistac, 01050 Mexico, DF, Mexico *Tel:* (0155) 5661-7590 *Fax:* (0155) 5663-0913 *E-mail:* infome@edicionesurano.com
Calle Blvd 162 Oficina 504-Edificio Metropolis, Santiago de Surco, Lima, Peru *Tel:* (01) 4361413 *Fax:* (01) 4361530 *E-mail:* infope@edicionesurano.com
C/ Uruguay 1579, 11200 Montevideo, Uruguay *Tel:* 24028469 *Fax:* 24085293 *E-mail:* infour@edicionesurano.com
4ta transversal de los cortijos de lourdes, Piso 4 este, 1071 Caracas, Venezuela *Tel:* (0212) 2395914 *Fax:* (0212) 2392968 *E-mail:* jlgarcia@edicionesurano.com

U.S. Office(s): 8871 SW 129 Terrace, Miami, FL 33176, United States *Tel:* 305-233-3365 *Fax:* 305-251-1310 *E-mail:* infousa@edicionesurano.com
Foreign Rep(s): Franklin & Siegal Associates (Kalah McCaffrey)

Urmo SA de Ediciones+
C/ Berbiqui 17-19, Rivas Vaciamadrid, 28522 Madrid
SAN: 005-2841
Tel: 916702189 *Fax:* 913012939
E-mail: ismaroto@hotmail.com
Web Site: www.urmo.com
Founded: 1963
Subjects: Computers, Engineering (General), Science (General)
ISBN Prefix(es): 978-84-314
Total Titles: 210 Print
Foreign Rep(s): Livraria Publindustria (Portugal)

URV, see Publicacions Universitat Rovira i Virgili (URV)

Ediciones Valbuena, see Centro de Estudios Adams-Ediciones Valbuena SA

Editorial Valdemar (Enokia SL)
Gran Via 69, 28013 Madrid
Tel: 915 428 897
E-mail: valdemar@valdemar.com
Web Site: www.valdemar.com
Subjects: Art, Biography, Memoirs, Fiction, Geography, Geology, History, Literature, Literary Criticism, Essays, Philosophy, Religion - Other, Social Sciences, Sociology
ISBN Prefix(es): 978-84-7702
Foreign Rep(s): Alejandria Libros (Chile); Librerias Crisol (Peru); Grupo Cultural Lizma (Mexico); Los Heraldos Negros (Peru); Librerias Ibero (Peru); Libreria Kalathos (Venezuela); Libreria Lehmann SA (Costa Rica); Librerias Proa (Chile); Libreria Prologo (Chile); Promolibro (Colombia); Puro Verso (Uruguay); Libreria Sophos (Guatemala); Libreria Takk (Chile); Libreria La Tertulla (Puerto Rico); Libreria el Virrey (Peru)

Vaso Roto Ediciones
c/ Alacala 85, 7° izda, 28009 Madrid
Tel: 915 779 152
E-mail: vasoroto@vasoroto.com
Web Site: www.vasoroto.com
Founded: 2003
Subjects: Art, Drama, Theater, Literature, Literary Criticism, Essays, Poetry
ISBN Prefix(es): 978-84-15168; 978-84-935842; 978-84-16193; 978-84-936423; 978-84-938087
Branch Office(s)
Gruta Azul 147, Col Valle de San Angel, 66290 San Pedro Garza Garcia, Mexico *Tel:* (0181) 8303 4247
Distribution Center: IPG Spanish Books, 814 N Franklin St, Chicago, IL 60610, United States

Editorial Verbo Divino+
Avda Pamplona, 41, 31200 Estella (Navarra)
Tel: 948 55 65 11 *Fax:* 948 55 45 06
E-mail: ventas@verbodivino.es
Web Site: www.verbodivino.es
Key Personnel
Sales Dir: Martin Esparza
Founded: 1959
Subjects: Biblical Studies, Religion - Catholic, Social Sciences, Sociology, Theology
ISBN Prefix(es): 978-84-7151; 978-84-8169; 978-84-9945
Parent Company: Grupo Editorial Verbo Divino
Subsidiaries: Editorial Guadalupe
Foreign Rep(s): A Coruna (Spain); Distribuciones El Buho Azul (Spain); Libreria Catolica Geth-

esemani (USA); Libreria Centro Biblico Divino (Paraguay); Centro Biblico Verbo Divino (Nicaragua); Libreria Centro Biblico Verbo Divino (Ecuador); Claret Llibres Distribucio SLU (Spain); Emaus Libros SL (Spain); Garbi Distribuciones Editoriales SL (Spain); Editorial Guadalupe (Argentina); Libreria Hispamer SA (Nicaragua); Icaro Distribuidora SL (Spain); Libreria Loyola (Guatemala); Ministerio Biblico Verbo Divino (USA); Distribuidora Paulinas (Venezuela); Paulinas Filhas de Sao Paulo (Brazil); Libreria Paulinas (Bolivia, Peru); Unicornio Musica y Letras SL (Spain); Vallejo (Spain); Editorial Verbo Divino (Bolivia, Colombia, Costa Rica); Libreria Verbo Divino (Chile, Colombia); Libreria Verbum Guadalajara (Mexico); Libreria Verbum Mexico DF (Mexico)

Editorial Verbum SL+
Manzana 9, bajo unico, 28015 Madrid
Tel: 914 468 841
E-mail: gestor.ed.verbum@gmail.com; editorialverbum@gmail.com
Web Site: www.verbumeditorial.com
Founded: 1990
Specialize in Spanish for foreigners, translation from Korean into Spanish.
Subjects: Drama, Theater, Fiction, Language Arts, Linguistics, Literature, Literary Criticism, Essays, Music, Dance, Philosophy, Poetry, Spanish as a Second Language
ISBN Prefix(es): 978-84-7962
Number of titles published annually: 30 Print; 450 Online
Total Titles: 501 Print; 501 Online; 1 Audio
Foreign Rep(s): Librairie Las Americas (Canada); Grupo Editorial Atlas (Paraguay); Interlogos SRL (Italy); Latin American Book Source Inc (USA); La Libreria (Germany); Libreria Espanola Nikolopoulos (Greece); Libreria Hernandez Paez OG (Austria); Puvill Libros SA (worldwide); Libreria Universal (USA)

Vergara, *imprint of* Ediciones B

Veron Editor+
Carrer de Tarragona, 97, Prat de Llobregat, 08820 Barcelona
Tel: 934781908
Founded: 1965
Subjects: Literature, Literary Criticism, Essays, Nonfiction (General)
ISBN Prefix(es): 978-84-7255

Editorial Versos y Trazos
C/ Fray Junipero Serra, 70, 3° Bajo izq, 46014 Valencia
Tel: 962 061 121
E-mail: literaria@versosytrazos.com
Web Site: www.versosytrazos.com
Key Personnel
Commercial Dir: Neus Flores
Founded: 2004
Membership(s): Associacio D'Editors del Pais Valencia.
Subjects: Literature, Literary Criticism, Essays
ISBN Prefix(es): 978-84-935727
Foreign Rep(s): Librerias Artemis Edinter (Guatemala); Azteca (Mexico); Baker & Taylor (USA); Lapanopliaexport (Latin America); Libreria El Virrey (Peru)

Vicens Basica, *imprint of* Ediciones Vicens Vives SA

Vicens Universidad, *imprint of* Ediciones Vicens Vives SA

Ediciones Vicens Vives SA+
Av de Sarria 130, 08017 Barcelona

Tel: 93 252 37 00 *Fax:* 93 252 37 11
E-mail: e@vicensvives.es; administracion@vicensvives.es; cm@vicensvives.com
Web Site: www.vicensvives.es; www.vicensvives.com
Key Personnel
President: Roser Rahola; Pere Vicens
Dir: Albert Vicens; Anna Vicens
Founded: 1942
Subjects: Education, Ethnicity, Fiction, History, Language Arts, Linguistics, Literature, Literary Criticism, Essays, Mathematics, Science (General)
ISBN Prefix(es): 978-84-316
Imprints: Instituto Cartografico Latino; Vicens Basica; Vicens Universidad

A Madrid Vicente Ediciones+
Calle Almansa, 94, 28040 Madrid
Tel: 915 336 926; 915 349 368 *Fax:* 915 530 286
E-mail: amadrid@amvediciones.com
Web Site: www.amvediciones.com
Key Personnel
Manager: Antonio Madrid Vicente
Founded: 1986
Specialize also in cooling, heating & construction.
Subjects: Agriculture, Electronics, Electrical Engineering, Engineering (General), Gardening, Plants, Health, Nutrition, Medicine, Nursing, Dentistry, Science (General), Technology, Wine & Spirits, Food Technology
ISBN Prefix(es): 978-84-89922; 978-84-96709
Number of titles published annually: 15 Print; 110 Online; 1 E-Book
Total Titles: 110 Print; 10 CD-ROM; 110 Online; 1 E-Book

Victor, *imprint of* Ediciones Robinbook SL

El Viejo Topo
c/ Sant Antoni 86, puerta 9, 08301 Mataro
Tel: 93 755 08 32 *Fax:* 93 755 41 42
E-mail: info@elviejotopo.com
Web Site: www.elviejotopo.com
Key Personnel
Dir General: Miguel Riera
Subjects: Economics, Government, Political Science, Social Sciences, Sociology, Culture
ISBN Prefix(es): 978-84-922573; 978-84-95224
Foreign Rep(s): Cajon de Sastre (Chile); Colofon SA (Mexico); MS Books (Maritza Santos) (Puerto Rico); Siglo del Hombre Editores SA (Colombia); Distribuidora Venezolana de la Cultura (Venezuela); Jorge Waldhuter (Argentina)

Viena Edicions (Viena Publishing)+
c/ Tuset 13 ext 1st-3rd, 08006 Barcelona
Tel: 93 453 55 00 *Fax:* 93 209 81 68
E-mail: viena@vienaeditorial.com
Web Site: www.vienaeditorial.com
Key Personnel
Publisher: Isabel Monso
Founded: 1991
Membership(s): Gremi d'Editors de Catalunya.
Subjects: Animals, Pets, Art, Cookery, Health, Nutrition, Inspirational, Spirituality, Nonfiction (General), Photography, Poetry, Psychology, Psychiatry, Religion - Other, Self-Help
ISBN Prefix(es): 978-84-8330; 978-84-89553
Number of titles published annually: 40 Print
Total Titles: 409 Print

Ediciones del Viento SL
Alfredo Vicenti, 32-9, 15004 La Coruna
Tel: 981 244 468; 649 095 533 (cell) *Fax:* 981 244 468
E-mail: info@edicionesdelviento.es
Web Site: www.edicionesdelviento.es
Key Personnel
Dir General: Eduardo Riestra
Founded: 2003

Subjects: Biography, Memoirs, Fiction, Literature, Literary Criticism, Essays
ISBN Prefix(es): 978-84-933001; 978-84-934060

Vigia, *imprint of* Editorial Alhulia SA

Vindicacion Feminista Publicaciones+
C/ Magdalena 29, 1° A, 28012 Madrid
Tel: 91 369 4488 *Fax:* 91 369 4488
Key Personnel
Dir: Lidia Falcon
Founded: 1976
Subjects: Anthropology, Biography, Memoirs, Drama, Theater, Fiction, Literature, Literary Criticism, Essays, Nonfiction (General), Poetry, Women's Studies, Feminism
ISBN Prefix(es): 978-84-88217
Imprints: Cofas SA
Divisions: Aconcagua Publishing
Distributed by Aconcagua Publishing; Editorial Hacer; Kira Edit

Editorial VIS-A-VIA SL
C/ Vilamari 81, 8° 1a, 08015 Barcelona
Tel: 931633562 *Fax:* 935393565
E-mail: info@vis-a-via.com
Web Site: www.vis-a-via.com
Subjects: Education, Fiction, Poetry, Spanish Language
ISBN Prefix(es): 978-84-95982

Visor Distribuciones SA+
Tomas Breton, 55, 28045 Madrid
Tel: 915301136
Founded: 1987
Subjects: Art, Education, Literature, Literary Criticism, Essays, Philosophy, Psychology, Psychiatry
ISBN Prefix(es): 978-84-7774

Visor Libros SL+
Isaac Peral, 18, 28015 Madrid
Tel: 91 549 26 55 *Fax:* 91 544 86 95
E-mail: visor-libros@visor-libros.com
Web Site: www.visor-libros.com
Key Personnel
Dir: Jesus Garcia Sanchez *E-mail:* jesus@visor-libros.com
Founded: 1970
Subjects: Language Arts, Linguistics, Literature, Literary Criticism, Essays, Poetry
ISBN Prefix(es): 978-84-7522

Editorial Vive Bien, *imprint of* Roca Editorial

Editorial Luis Vives (Edelvives)
Xaudaro, 25, 28034 Madrid
Tel: 913 344 884
E-mail: info@edelvives.es
Web Site: www.edelvives.com
Key Personnel
Mng Dir: Antonio Gimenez de Baguees
Commercial Dir: Jose Luis Illana
Founded: 1889
Subjects: Education
ISBN Prefix(es): 978-84-263
Number of titles published annually: 200 Print
Total Titles: 35,000 Print; 6 CD-ROM; 3 Audio
Branch Office(s)
Ctra de Madrid, km 315,700, 50012 Zaragoza
Tel: 976 304 030

Vox
Mallorca, 45, 3a, 08029 Barcelona
Tel: 93 241 35 05 *Fax:* 93 241 35 11
E-mail: vox@vox.es
Web Site: www.vox.es
ISBN Prefix(es): 978-84-85750
Parent Company: Larousse Editorial SL
Ultimate Parent Company: Grupo Anaya

Vulcano Ediciones SL+
C/ Matilde Hernandez, 71, bajo local 6, 28025 Madrid
SAN: 003-3812
Tel: 91 500 16 49
Founded: 1980
Subjects: Literature, Literary Criticism, Essays, Poetry, Technology, Travel & Tourism
ISBN Prefix(es): 978-84-7828

Wolters Kluwer Espana SA
c/ Collado Mediano, 9, 28230 Las Rozas, Madrid
Tel: 916 020 000
E-mail: clientes@laley.es
Web Site: www.wolterskluwer.es
Key Personnel
Marketing & Sales Dir: Pablo Villanueva Zamora
Press: Cristina Sancho Ferran *E-mail:* csancho@wke.es
Subjects: Accounting, Education, Finance, Health, Nutrition, Law, Management
ISBN Prefix(es): 978-84-87670
Parent Company: Wolters Kluwer NV, Netherlands

World Tourism Organization (UNWTO)
Capitan Haya 42, 28020 Madrid
Tel: 91 567 81 00 *Fax:* 91 571 37 33
E-mail: info@unwto.org
Web Site: www.unwto.org
Subjects: Education, Finance, Marketing, Travel & Tourism, Culture
ISBN Prefix(es): 978-92-844
Parent Company: United Nations
Foreign Rep(s): Balogh International Inc (USA); Bernan Associates (USA); Renouf Publishing Co Ltd (Canada); The Stationery Office (UK)

Ediciones Xandro+
Ave del Mediterraneo, 18, 28007 Madrid
SAN: 002-0591
Tel: 91 552 02 61 *Fax:* 91 501 41 45
E-mail: soespgraf@soespgraf.com
Web Site: www.soespgraf.com
Founded: 1987
Subjects: Psychology, Psychiatry, Graphology
ISBN Prefix(es): 978-84-88665

Edicions Xerais de Galicia
Doutor Maranon, 12, 36211 Vigo
SAN: 001-4591
Tel: 986 214 888; 986 214 880 *Fax:* 986 201 366
E-mail: xerais@xerais.es; xeraispedidos@xerais.es (orders)
Web Site: www.xerais.es
Key Personnel
Dir General: Manuel Bragado Rodriguez *Tel:* 986 214 890 *E-mail:* mbragado@xerais.es
Mng Dir: Xose M Garcia Crego *Tel:* 986 214 884 *E-mail:* xcrego@xerais.es
Promotion Dir: Celia Torres Bouzas *Tel:* 986 214 893 *E-mail:* ctorres@xerais.es
Founded: 1979
Subjects: Education, Fiction, History, Language Arts, Linguistics, Poetry, Social Sciences, Sociology
ISBN Prefix(es): 978-84-7507; 978-84-8302; 978-84-9782; 978-84-9914
Distribution Center: Comercial Grupo Anaya, Poligono Pocomaco, Ave 3, Edifico Diana, nave 4, baixo, 15009 A Coruna *Tel:* 981 171 641 *Fax:* 981 171 647

Xunta de Galicia
San Caetano s/n, 15704 Santiago de Compostela
Tel: 981 54 54 00
E-mail: 012@xunta.es
Web Site: www.xunta.gal/portada
Key Personnel
President: Alberto Nunez Feijoo

Subjects: Agriculture, Animals, Pets, Art, Biological Sciences, Business, Economics, Education, Fiction, Finance, Geography, Geology, Health, Nutrition, History, Law, Literature, Literary Criticism, Essays, Management, Maritime, Marketing, Military Science, Public Administration, Science (General), Sports, Athletics, Design, Graphic Arts
ISBN Prefix(es): 978-84-453

Editorial Verena Zech, see Zech Verlag

Zech Verlag
Carretera Provincial, 59-Edificio Aurora I, n° 17, 38390 Santa Ursula
Tel: 922 302596 *Fax:* 922 302596
E-mail: info@editorial-zech.com; info@zech-verlag.com
Web Site: www.editorial-zech.es
Key Personnel
Publisher: Verena Zech
Founded: 2001
Subjects: History, Language Arts, Linguistics, Travel & Tourism, English Language, German Language, Spanish Language
ISBN Prefix(es): 978-84-933108; 978-84-934857
Foreign Rep(s): Paulsen Buchimport (Germany)

Zenith, *imprint of* Ediciones Minotauro

Zenith, *imprint of* Editorial Planeta SA

Libros del Zorro Rojo, *imprint of* Albur Producciones Editoriales SL

Libros del Zorro Rojo
Imprint of Albur producciones editoriales SL
Sant Joan de Malta 39, 2° 2a, 08018 Barcelona
Tel: 933 076 850; 931 853 412 *Fax:* 931 853 412
E-mail: info@librosdelzorrorojo.com; rights@librosdelzorrorojo.com; export@librosdelzorrorojo.com
Web Site: www.librosdelzorrorojo.com
Key Personnel
Editorial Dir: Fernando Diego Garcia
Art Dir: Sebastian Garcia Schnetzer
Editor: Alejandro Garcia Schnetzer *E-mail:* zr.alejandro.gs@gmail.com
Export: Jesus Miranda Rayo
Foreign Rights: Ruth Ruyffelaere
Founded: 2004
Subjects: Fiction, Mysteries, Suspense
ISBN Prefix(es): 978-84-92412
Foreign Rep(s): CELESA (Centro de Exportacion de Libros Espanoles) (all other territories, Europe); Del Nuevo Extremo Grupo Editorial (Argentina); La Panoplia de Libros (Latin America exc Argentina & Spain)

Sri Lanka

General Information

Capital: Colombo
Language: Sinhala & Tamila (official & national) & English (national)
Religion: Predominantly Buddhism
Population: 17.6 million
Bank Hours: 0900-1300 Monday-Friday
Shop Hours: 0800-1730 Monday-Friday
Currency: 100 cents = 1 Sri Lanka rupee
Export/Import Information: No tariff on books or advertising. Import license required for most book importation. Exchange controls.
Copyright: UCC, Berne, Florence (see Copyright Conventions, pg viii)

Bay Owl Press, *imprint of* Perera-Hussein Publishing House

Buddhist Publication Society Inc
No 54 Sangharaja Mawatha, Kandy
Mailing Address: PO Box 61, Kandy
Tel: (081) 223 7283; (081) 223 8901 *Fax:* (081) 222 3679
E-mail: bps@bps.lk
Web Site: www.bps.lk
Founded: 1958
Subjects: Religion - Buddhist
ISBN Prefix(es): 978-955-24
Foreign Rep(s): Buddhist Merit & Wisdom Service (Hong Kong); Dhamma Books (Australia); Evergreen Buddhist Culture Service (Singapore); Mahamakuta Rajavidyalaya Foundation (Thailand); Pariyatti (USA); Petaling Jaya Outlet (Malaysia); Sukhi Hotu (Malaysia); Vipassana Publications Aotearoa (New Zealand)

The Ceylon Chamber of Commerce
50, Navam Mawatha, Colombo 02
Tel: (011) 2421745-7; (011) 558880 *Fax:* (011) 2437477; (011) 2449352; (011) 2381012
E-mail: info@chamber.lk
Web Site: www.chamber.lk
Key Personnel
Chairman: Suresh Shah *E-mail:* suresh.shah@ lionbeer.com
Vice Chairman: Mr Samantha Rantunga
 E-mail: samantha@cic.lk
Deputy Vice Chairman: Mr Rajendra Theagarajah
 E-mail: thearev@yahoo.com
Chief Executive Officer: Dhara Wijayatilake
 E-mail: mbpyapa@chamber.lk
Founded: 1839
Subjects: Agriculture, Business, Economics, Government, Political Science
ISBN Prefix(es): 978-955-604

Department of Census & Statistics
104/A, Kithulwatta Rd, Colombo 08
Tel: (011) 2694666; (011) 2147488 (sales)
 Fax: (011) 2697634
E-mail: publication@statistics.gov.lk; data. requests@statistics.gov.lk (sales)
Web Site: www.statistics.gov.lk
Key Personnel
Dir General: Dr A J Satharasinghe *E-mail:* amara. satharasinghe@statistics.gov.lk
Founded: 1947
Government publisher.
Subjects: Agriculture, National Accounts, Population & Demography, Prices & Wages, Survey Reports, Trade & Industry, Yearbooks
ISBN Prefix(es): 978-955-577
Number of titles published annually: 12 Print; 2 CD-ROM
Total Titles: 40 Print; 10 CD-ROM

Department of National Museums
PO Box 854, Sir Marcus Fernando Mawatha, Colombo 07
Tel: (011) 2695366 *Fax:* (011) 2692092
E-mail: nmdep@slt.lk
Web Site: www.museum.gov.lk
Key Personnel
Secretary: Nanda Wickramasinghe
Founded: 1877
Subjects: Anthropology, Antiques, Natural History
ISBN Prefix(es): 978-955-578
Subsidiaries: Dutch Museum; Folk Museum; Independence Memorial Museum; National Maritime Museum; National Museum (Galle); National Museum (Kandy); National Museum of Natural History; National Museum (Ratnapura)
Divisions: School Conservation Museum; School Cultural Museum; School Library Museum; School Publication Museum; School Science Museum

Gihan Book Shop
144C, Sir D B Jayathilaka Mawatha, Dehiwala
Tel: (011) 2730152 *Fax:* (011) 2730152
Web Site: www.gihanbookshop.lk; www.facebook. com/GihanBookshop
Founded: 1984
Subjects: Mathematics
ISBN Prefix(es): 978-955-593
Imprints: Sanjana Offset

M D Gunasena & Co Ltd
No 217, Olcott Mawatha, Colombo 11
Tel: (011) 2323981; (011) 2323982; (011) 2323983; (011) 2323984 *Fax:* (011) 2323336
E-mail: info@mdgunasena.com; publishinginfo@ mdgunasena.com; publishingmgr@mdgunasena. com
Web Site: www.mdgunasena.com
Founded: 1913
Associated imprints include Ananda Books Ltd, Sirisara Vidyalaya.
ISBN Prefix(es): 978-955-21

Inter-Cultural Book Promoters+
21G4 Peramuna Mawatha, Eldeniya, Kadawatha
Tel: (011) 2925359
E-mail: inculture@sltnet.lk
Founded: 1985
Subjects: Language Arts, Linguistics, Philosophy, Religion - Buddhist, Religion - Catholic, Religion - Hindu, Religion - Islamic, Religion - Jewish, Religion - Protestant, Religion - Other
ISBN Prefix(es): 978-955-9036
Number of titles published annually: 2 Print
Parent Company: Inter-cultural Research Center

International Centre for Ethnic Studies+
No 2, Kynsey Terrace, Colombo 08
Tel: (011) 2679745; (011) 2674884 *Fax:* (011) 2688929
Web Site: www.ices.lk
Key Personnel
Chairman: Mr Tissa Jayatilaka
Executive Dir: Dr Mario Gomez *E-mail:* mario@ ices.lk
Founded: 1982
A social science & policy research institute.
Subjects: Ethnicity, Women's Studies
ISBN Prefix(es): 978-955-580
Total Titles: 20 Print
Branch Office(s)
554/6A, Peradeniya Rd, Mulgampola (Kandy)
 Tel: (081) 2234892; (081) 2232381 *Fax:* (094) 2234892
Distributed by St Martin's Press
Distributor for Frances Pinter (UK)

Dayawansa Jayakody & Co+
No 86, 101, 110 & 112, Ven S Mahinda Himi Mawatha, Maradana, Colombo 10
Tel: (011) 2695773; (011) 2696653 *Fax:* (011) 2696653; (011) 2695773
E-mail: dayawansa@sltnet.lk; dayawansa@ dayawansajayakody.com
Web Site: dayawansajayakody.com
Key Personnel
Chairman & Mng Dir: Dayawansa Jayakody
Founded: 1960
Membership(s): APPA; IPA; Sri Lanka Book Publishers Association.
Subjects: Drama, Theater, Fiction, Literature, Literary Criticism, Essays, Poetry
ISBN Prefix(es): 978-955-551
Number of titles published annually: 200 Print; 200 Online
Total Titles: 4,450 Print; 1,500 Online
Associate Companies: Helabima Publishers
U.S. Office(s): Dayawansa Jayakody & Co (USA), Windy Oaks Rd, No 4405, Louisville, KY 40241, United States *Tel:* 502-442-7632 *Fax:* 502-442-7632 (USA sales)
Distributor for Helabima Publishers

Warehouse: 163/4, Siri Dhamma Mawatha, Colombo
Distribution Center: Lanka Hands *Web Site:* lankahands.de

Karunaratne & Sons (Pvt) Ltd+
67, UDA Industrial Estate, Homagama
Tel: (0114) 887 227; (0112) 855 520 *Fax:* (0114) 440 313
E-mail: info@karusons.com
Web Site: www.karusons.com
Key Personnel
Chairman & Mng Dir: Ravi Karunaratne
Founded: 1971
Membership(s): Sri Lanka Association of Publishers.
Subjects: Archaeology, Economics, Education, Ethnicity, History, Philosophy, Religion - Buddhist, Social Sciences, Sociology, Women's Studies
ISBN Prefix(es): 978-955-9098
Associate Companies: Calcey Technologies; Impressions Labels; Timeplan Diairies & Agendas

Lake House Printers & Publishers PLC+
41 W A D Ramanayake Mawatha, Colombo 02
Tel: (011) 2433271; (011) 2433272; (011) 2433273 *Fax:* (011) 2449504
Key Personnel
Dir: R C Samarasinghe
Founded: 1965
Specialize in textbooks on science & law, both in Sinhala & English.
Subjects: Education, Fiction, History, Law, Medicine, Nursing, Dentistry, Music, Dance, Science (General), Sports, Athletics
ISBN Prefix(es): 978-955-552
Divisions: Chitrafoto; Lake House Bookshop; Lakexpo
Bookshop(s): Colombo University Bookshop, Colombo University, Cumarathuga Munidasa Mawatha, Colombo; Lake House Bookshop, 100 Chittampalam Gardinar Mawatha, Colombo

Ministry of Culture & the Arts
Dept of Cultural Affairs, Sethsiripaya, 8th floor, Battaramulla
Tel: (011) 2872035 *Fax:* (011) 2872035
E-mail: dcanews@sltnet.lk
Web Site: www.culturaldept.gov.lk
Key Personnel
Dir: Anusha Gokula Fernando
Founded: 1971
Subjects: Art, Ethnicity, Literature, Literary Criticism, Essays, Religion - Other
ISBN Prefix(es): 978-955-9117
Bookshop(s): No 275, Kaduwela Rd, Battaramulla

Ministry of Education, Educational Publications Dept+
Isurupaya, Battaramulla 10120
Tel: (011) 2784815 *Fax:* (011) 2784815
E-mail: commissioner_epd@yahoo.com
Web Site: www.edupub.gov.lk
Key Personnel
Commissioner General: Mr Tissa Hewawithana
 Tel: (011) 2784815 ext 1108 *Fax:* (011) 2784815
Administrative Officer: B C Jayawardhana
 Tel: (011) 2784307 ext 1126
Subjects: Accounting, Agriculture, Chemistry, Chemical Engineering, Computer Science, Geography, Geology, Mathematics, Physics, Science (General)
ISBN Prefix(es): 978-955-28

Ministry of Internal Affairs, North-Western Development & Cultural Affairs, see Ministry of Culture & the Arts

National Library & Documentation Services Board
No 14, Independence Ave, Colombo 07
Tel: (011) 2698847; (011) 2685197; (011) 2685199 *Fax:* (011) 2685201
E-mail: nldsb@mail.natlib.lk; nldc@mail.natlib.lk
Web Site: www.natlib.lk
Key Personnel
Chairman: Dr W A Abeysinghe *Tel:* (011) 2685198 *E-mail:* ch@mail.natlib.lk
Dir General: Mr W Sunil *Tel:* (011) 2687581 *E-mail:* dg@mail.natlib.lk
Dir, Finance & Administration: Mr K Waduge *Tel:* (011) 3056211 *E-mail:* dirfinadm@mail.natlib.lk
Dir, Library Development, Standardization & Publications: Ms Senani Bandara *Tel:* (011) 2687584 *E-mail:* dirlibserv@mail.natlib.lk
Deputy Dir, Administration: Ms D R Jayasinghe *Tel:* (011) 2688926 *E-mail:* ddiradm@mail.natlib.lk
Founded: 1990
Membership(s): ACCU; AMIC; CDNLAO; COMLA; International Federation of Library Associations & Institutions (IFLA).
Subjects: Communications, Computer Science, Ethnicity, Human Relations, Library & Information Sciences, Literature, Literary Criticism, Essays, Regional Interests, Social Sciences, Sociology
ISBN Prefix(es): 978-955-9011
Total Titles: 2 CD-ROM

NLDSB, see National Library & Documentation Services Board

Perera-Hussein, *imprint of* Perera-Hussein Publishing House

Perera-Hussein Publishing House+
No 80A, Dharmapala Mawatha, Colombo 07
Tel: (011) 4858 972
E-mail: info@pererahussein.com
Web Site: www.pererahussein.com
Founded: 2003
Subjects: Biography, Memoirs, Erotica, Fiction, Humor, Nonfiction (General), Poetry, Travel & Tourism
ISBN Prefix(es): 978-955-8897 (Perera-Hussein); 978-955-1723 (Bay Owl Press); 978-955-0041 (Popsicle Books); 978-955-7743 (Sailfish)
Number of titles published annually: 10 Print; 10 Online; 8 E-Book
Total Titles: 100 Print
Imprints: Bay Owl Press; Perera-Hussein (fiction); Popsicle Books (children's stories); Sailfish

Popsicle Books, *imprint of* Perera-Hussein Publishing House

Sailfish, *imprint of* Perera-Hussein Publishing House

Samayawardhana Printers (Pvt) Ltd+
53, Hikkaduwe Sri Sumangala Na-himi, Mawatha (Maligakanda Rd), Maradana, Colombo 10
Tel: (011) 2694 682; (011) 2687 904; (011) 2683 525; (011) 2698 977
E-mail: info@samayaprinters.com; samaya@samayaprinters.com
Web Site: www.samayaprinters.com
Key Personnel
Mng Dir: Ariyadasa Abeywickrama Weeraman
Founded: 1965
Membership(s): Asia Pacific Book Publishers Association; Sri Lanka Book Publishers Association.
Subjects: Education, English as a Second Language, Nonfiction (General), Philosophy, Religion - Buddhist
ISBN Prefix(es): 978-955-570

Bookshop(s): Samayawardhana Book Shop (Pvt) Ltd, No 61-63, Ven Hikkaduwe Sri Sumangala Nahimi Mw, Colombo *Tel:* (011) 2677539; (011) 2698977 *E-mail:* samaybooks@sltnet.lk

Sanjana Offset, *imprint of* Gihan Book Shop

SLJI, see Sri Lanka Jama'ath-e-Islami (SLJI)

Sri Lanka Jama'ath-e-Islami (SLJI)
Darul Iman, No 77, Dematagoda Rd, Maradana, Colombo 09
Tel: (011) 2687091 *Fax:* (011) 2687091
Web Site: www.sljipr.blogspot.com
Subjects: Nonfiction (General), Religion - Islamic
ISBN Prefix(es): 978-955-608

Sudan

General Information

Capital: Khartoum
Language: Arabic (official), English also used
Religion: Muslims (north), Animists or Christians (south)
Population: 28.3 million
Bank Hours: 0830-1200 Sunday-Thursday
Shop Hours: 0800-1300, 1700-2000 Saturday-Thursday
Currency: 1,000 milliemes = 100 piastres = 1 Sudanese pound
Export/Import Information: No tariff on books; some advertising matter may be dutied. Import licenses required. Exchange controls; annual foreign exchange budget.

ACADI, see Arab Organization for Agricultural Development (AOAD)

AOAD, see Arab Organization for Agricultural Development (AOAD)

Arab Center for Agricultural Documentation, see Arab Organization for Agricultural Development (AOAD)

Arab Organization for Agricultural Development (AOAD)
Amarat St 7, 11111 Khartoum
Mailing Address: PO Box 474, 11111 Khartoum
Tel: (01) 83472176; (01) 83472177; (01) 83472178; (01) 83472179; (01) 83472180; (01) 83472181; (01) 83472182; (01) 83472183 *Fax:* (01) 83471402; (01) 83471050
E-mail: info@aoad.org
Web Site: www.aoad.org
Key Personnel
Dir General: Prof Ibrahim Adam El Dukhiri
Founded: 1970
Subjects: Agriculture, Economics, Regional Interests
Parent Company: Arab League

University of Khartoum Press
PO Box 321, 11115 Khartoum
Web Site: www.uofk.edu
Founded: 1968
Subjects: Biography, Memoirs, Education, Engineering (General), Environmental Studies, Ethnicity, Fiction, Government, Political Science, History, Management, Marketing, Medicine, Nursing, Dentistry, Nonfiction (General), Philosophy, Poetry, Religion - Other, Science (General), Social Sciences, Sociology, Technology
ISBN Prefix(es): 978-99942-50

Bookshop(s): University of Khartoum Bookshop, Gamhorya St, 11115 Khartoum *Tel:* (01) 23023195 *Fax:* (01) 83780558 *E-mail:* k.u.press@sudanmail.net

Suriname

General Information

Capital: Paramaribo
Language: Dutch. Hindustani and Javanese also spoken
Religion: Christian, Hindu and Islamic
Population: 410,000
Bank Hours: 0730-1400 Monday-Friday
Shop Hours: 0730-1630 Monday-Friday; 0730-1300 Saturday
Currency: 100 cents = 1 Suriname gulden or florin
Export/Import Information: No tariff on books except children's picture books; none on small quantities of advertising matter. Added taxes charged. Import licenses liberally granted. Exchange controls.
Copyright: Berne (see Copyright Conventions, pg viii)

Stichting Wetenschappelijke Informatie (SWI)
(Foundation for Information & Development)+
Prins Hendrikstr 38, Paramaribo
Tel: 475232 *Fax:* 422195
Web Site: www.swi77.org
Key Personnel
Chairman: Jack Menke *E-mail:* menkejack@yahoo.com
Vice Chairman: Jerry Egger
Treasurer: Wonnie Boedhoe
Founded: 1977
Subjects: Anthropology, Developing Countries, Ethnicity, Government, Political Science, History, Labor, Industrial Relations, Literature, Literary Criticism, Essays, Science (General), Social Sciences, Sociology, Women's Studies
ISBN Prefix(es): 978-99914-900
Distributor for Local Surinamese Publications

SWI, see Stichting Wetenschappelijke Informatie (SWI)

Vaco NV+
Domineestr 26, Paramaribo
Mailing Address: PO Box 1841, Paramaribo
Tel: 472545 *Fax:* 410563
Web Site: www.vaco.sr
Founded: 1952
Subjects: History, Regional Interests
ISBN Prefix(es): 978-99914-0
Parent Company: Interfund NV

Swaziland

General Information

Capital: Mbabane
Language: Siswati, English used in business
Religion: Christian (about 60%), most others follow traditional beliefs
Population: 913,000
Bank Hours: Until 1100 Saturday
Shop Hours: 0700-1800
Currency: 100 cents = 1 lilangeni = 1 South African rand
Export/Import Information: Same as South Africa.

Boleswa, *imprint of* Macmillan Boleswa
Publishers (Pty) Ltd

Macmillan Boleswa Publishers (Pty) Ltd
Plot 230/231, First Ave, Matsapa Industrial Estate, Manzini
Mailing Address: PO Box 1235, Manzini
Tel: 518 45 33 *Fax:* 518 52 47
Web Site: www.macmillan-africa.com
Key Personnel
Mng Dir: Elias Nwandwe
Founded: 1978
Subjects: Education
ISBN Prefix(es): 978-0-333; 978-0-7978
Parent Company: Macmillan Publishers Ltd,
United Kingdom
Imprints: Boleswa
Subsidiaries: Macmillan Boleswa Publishers
(Lesotho) Ltd; Macmillan Botswana Publishing Co Ltd; Macmillan South Africa (Pty) Ltd;
Macmillan Swaziland National Publishing Co
Branch Office(s)
Matsapa

Sweden

General Information

Capital: Stockholm
Language: Swedish. Some Finnish and Lapp also spoken
Religion: Evangelical Lutheran Church of Sweden
Population: 8.8 million
Bank Hours: 0930-1500 Monday-Friday
Shop Hours: 0900-1800 Monday-Friday (later Friday); 0900-1400 or 1600 Saturday
Currency: 100 oere = 1 Swedish korona
Export/Import Information: Member of the European Free Trade Association. No tariff on books. Advertising tax. 25% VAT on books. No import licenses. No exchange controls.
Copyright: UCC, Berne, Florence (see Copyright Conventions, pg viii)

Acta Universitatis Gothoburgensis
Renstromsgatan 4, 405 30 Gothenburg
Mailing Address: PO Box 222, 405 30 Gothenburg
Tel: (031) 7861000 *Fax:* (031) 16 37 97
E-mail: acta@ub.gu.se
Web Site: www.ub.gu.se/service/acta
Key Personnel
Administration: Anna Lindstrom *Tel:* (031) 786 17 64
Contact: Fredrik Cordenius *Tel:* (031) 786 19 32; Maja Pelling *Tel:* (031) 786 11 65
Publishes only works produced at or connected with Gothenburg University.
Subjects: Art, Education, Language Arts, Linguistics, Literature, Literary Criticism, Essays, Social Sciences, Sociology, Women's Studies
ISBN Prefix(es): 978-91-7346
Parent Company: Gothenburg University Library

Alfabeta Audio, *imprint of* Alfabeta Bokforlag
AB

Alfabeta Bokforlag AB+
Fiskargatan 8, 102 66 Stockholm
Mailing Address: PO Box 4284, 102 66 Stockholm
Tel: (08) 714 36 30 *Fax:* (08) 643 24 31
E-mail: info@alfabeta.se
Web Site: www.alfabeta.se
Key Personnel
Chief Executive Officer & Publisher: Dag Hernried *Tel:* (08) 714 36 33 *E-mail:* dag@alfabeta.se

Publisher, Children's Books: Lotta Lyssarides
Tel: (08) 714 36 42 *E-mail:* lotta.lyssarides@alfabeta.se
Editor, Children's Books: Anna Bogaeus *Tel:* (08) 714 36 36 *E-mail:* anna@alfabeta.se
Editor, Non-Fiction: Jacob Swedberg *Tel:* (08) 714 36 37 *E-mail:* jacob@alfabeta.se
Foreign Rights: AnnaKaisa Danielsson *Tel:* (08) 714 36 32 *E-mail:* annakaisa@alfabeta.se
Marketing: Pelle Olofsson *Tel:* (070) 828 91 75 *E-mail:* pelle.olofsson@alfabeta.se
Founded: 1978
Subjects: Art, Ethnicity, Fiction, Film, Video, Music, Dance, Nonfiction (General), Psychology, Psychiatry, Travel & Tourism
ISBN Prefix(es): 978-91-7712; 978-91-85328; 978-91-501
Imprints: Alfabeta Audio
Subsidiaries: Gammafon AB (audio cassettes)

Allt om Hobby AB+
Box 90 120, 120 08 Stockholm
Tel: (08) 999 333; (08) 999 060
E-mail: order@hobby.se; redaktion@hobby.se
Web Site: www.hobby.se
Key Personnel
Editor: Rutger Friberg
Founded: 1966
Subjects: Aeronautics, Aviation, Communications, Crafts, Games, Hobbies, Electronics, Electrical Engineering, History, Maritime, Military Science, Photography, Transportation, Boats, Cars, Military Aircraft, Model Aircraft, Model Railroad, Scale Modeling, Trains
ISBN Prefix(es): 978-91-85496; 978-91-7243
Book Club(s): Allt om Hobbys Bokklubb; Flygboklubben

Almqvist & Wiksell, *imprint of* Liber AB

Alvina Forlag och Produktion AB
c/o Alviks Strand Kontorshotell AB, Gustavslundsvagen 143, 167 51 Bromma
Tel: (070) 22 81 903
E-mail: info@alvinaforlag.se
Web Site: www.alvinaforlag.se
Key Personnel
Dir: Kristina Hoas
Founded: 2009
ISBN Prefix(es): 978-91-86391

Apotekarsocieteten Forlag (Swedish Academy of Pharmaceutical Sciences)
Wallingatan 26A, 111 81 Stockholm
Mailing Address: Box 1136, 111 81 Stockholm
Tel: (08) 723 50 00 *Fax:* (08) 20 55 11
E-mail: info@apotekarsocieteten.se
Web Site: www.swepharm.se
Key Personnel
Mng Dir: Karin Meyer *Tel:* (08) 723 50 61 *E-mail:* karin.meyer@apotekarsocieteten.se
Communications: Birgitta Karpesjo *Tel:* (08) 723 50 42 *E-mail:* birgitta.karpesjo@apotekarsocieteten.se
Founded: 1971
Subjects: Medicine, Nursing, Dentistry, Medicinal Chemistry, Pharmaceuticals

ArcanumSkolan+
Lilla Lyckevagen 7, Brastad
Mailing Address: Box 83, 454 21 Brastad
Tel: (0523) 47700; (0768) 648000
E-mail: arcanum.utbildning@gmail.com
Web Site: arcanum-homeopati.se
Founded: 1970
Subjects: Medicine, Nursing, Dentistry, Alternative Medicine, Homeopathy, Iridology
ISBN Prefix(es): 978-91-85690

Argument Forlag
Annebergsvaegen 4, 432 48 Varberg

Tel: (0340) 69 80 00 *Fax:* (0340) 69 80 10
E-mail: info@argument.se; order@argument.se
Web Site: www.argument.se
Key Personnel
Chief Executive Officer: Christer Brosche *Tel:* (0340) 69 80 14 *E-mail:* christer@argument.se
Publisher/Manager: Kristina Reftel *Tel:* (0340) 69 80 13 *E-mail:* kristina@argument.se
Press Officer & Editor: Pierre Eriksson *Tel:* (0340) 69 80 17 *E-mail:* pierre@argument.se
Subjects: Crafts, Games, Hobbies, Mathematics, Music, Dance, Poetry, Religion - Other, Science (General), Social Sciences, Sociology, English, Ethics, Sweden
ISBN Prefix(es): 978-91-7315

Arkitektur Forlag AB
Fiskargatan 8, 116 20 Stockholm
Mailing Address: PO Box 4296, 102 66 Stockholm
Tel: (08) 702 78 50
E-mail: redaktionen@arkitektur.se
Web Site: www.arkitektur.se
Key Personnel
Chief Executive Officer: Tommy Rundqvist
Publisher & Chief Editor: Dan Hallemar *E-mail:* dan.hallemar@arkitektur.se
Editor: Matilda Stannow *E-mail:* matilda.stannow@arkitektur.se
Graphic Design: Marianne Lundqvist *E-mail:* marianne.lundqvist@arkitektur.se
Founded: 1901
Publisher of *Arkitektur* magazine.
Subjects: Architecture & Interior Design
ISBN Prefix(es): 978-91-86050
Number of titles published annually: 4 Print

Arvinius Forlag AB
Upplandsgatan 41, 113 28 Stockholm
Mailing Address: PO Box 6040, 102 31 Stockholm
Tel: (08) 32 00 15 *Fax:* (08) 32 00 95
E-mail: info@arvinius.se
Web Site: www.arvinius.se
Key Personnel
President & Founder: Marie Arvinius *Tel:* (070) 527 7015 (cell) *E-mail:* marie@arvinius.se
Editor: Esther Whang *E-mail:* esther@arvinius.se
Founded: 1995
Subjects: Architecture & Interior Design, Crafts, Games, Hobbies, Contemporary Nordic Architecture
ISBN Prefix(es): 978-91-85689; 978-91-85213

Assessio Sverige AB+
Hornsbruksgatan 28, 117 34 Stockholm
Mailing Address: Box 470 54, 100 74 Stockholm
Tel: (08) 775 09 00
E-mail: info@assessio.se
Web Site: assessio.com; assessio.se
Key Personnel
Owner: Hunter Mabon
Mng Dir: Mattias Elg
Founded: 1954
Specialize in psychometric tests.
Subjects: Education, Psychology, Psychiatry
ISBN Prefix(es): 978-91-7418
Associate Companies: GlobeSoft

Bokforlaget Atlantis AB+
Sturegatan 24, 114 36 Stockholm
Tel: (08) 545 660 70 *Fax:* (08) 545 660 71
E-mail: info@atlantisbok.se; folj@atlantisbok.se
Web Site: www.atlantisbok.se
Key Personnel
Publishing Dir: Elin Sennero Kaunitz *E-mail:* elin.sennero.kaunitz@atlantisbok.se
Editorial & Production Manager: Hanna Hedman *E-mail:* hanna.eliasson.hedman@atlantisbok.es
Founded: 1977

Subjects: Art, Cookery, Fiction, Health, Nutrition, History, Nonfiction (General)
ISBN Prefix(es): 978-91-7486; 978-91-7353
Associate Companies: Bokforlaget Signum
Book Club(s): Bokforlaget Signum

Bokforlaget Axplock (Axplock Publishers)+
Subsidiary of Hans Richter Laromedel (Educational publishers)
Hospitalsgatan 5B, 645 30 Strangnas
Tel: (0152) 15060
E-mail: post@axplock.se
Web Site: www.axplock.se
Key Personnel
Publisher: Hans Richter
Founded: 1982
Subjects: Business, Drama, Theater, Education, Fiction, Gardening, Plants, History, How-to, Humor, Language Arts, Linguistics, Music, Dance, Mysteries, Suspense, Nonfiction (General), Poetry, Self-Help
ISBN Prefix(es): 978-91-86436; 978-91-85385; 978-91-87119; 978-91-88523
Number of titles published annually: 24 Print; 10 Online; 25 E-Book
Total Titles: 250 Print; 40 E-Book
Imprints: Richbook (ebooks)
Warehouse: StjarnDistribution AB, Hastskovagen 12, 813 33 Hofors *Tel:* (0290) 76 76 76 *E-mail:* info@sdist.se *Web Site:* www.sdist.se

BBB Bokklubben Bra Bocker, *imprint of* Bra Bocker AB

BBT, see Bhaktivedanta Book Trust (BBT)

Berghs Forlag AB
Observatoriegatan 10, 104 30 Stockholm
Mailing Address: PO Box 45084, 104 30 Stockholm
Tel: (08) 31 65 59 *Fax:* (08) 32 77 45
E-mail: info@berghsforlag.se
Web Site: www.berghsforlag.se
Key Personnel
President & Publishing Dir: Lena Andersson *E-mail:* lena.andersson@berghsforlag.se
Editorial: Linda Pelenius *E-mail:* linda.pelenius@berghsforlag.se; Eva Viden *E-mail:* eva.viden@berghsforlag.se
Founded: 1954
Subjects: Crafts, Games, Hobbies, Nonfiction (General)
ISBN Prefix(es): 978-91-502
Distribution Center: ForlagsSystem AB, Lovasvagen 26, 791 45 Falun
Orders to: ForlagsSystem AB, PO Box 30195, 104 30 Stockholm *Tel:* (08) 657 19 90 *Fax:* (08) 657 19 95

Bhaktivedanta Book Trust (BBT)
Korsnas Gard, 147 92 Grodinge
Tel: (08) 53029800 *Fax:* (08) 53025062
E-mail: info@bbt.se
Web Site: www.bbt.se
Founded: 1987
Subjects: Cookery, Music, Dance, Philosophy, Religion - Hindu, Religion - Other
ISBN Prefix(es): 978-91-7149; 978-91-85580
U.S. Office(s): BBT, 3764 Watseka Ave, Los Angeles, CA 90034, United States *Tel:* 310-836-2676

Bibliotekstjaenst AB
Scheelevagen 18, 221 82 Lund
Tel: (046) 18 00 00
E-mail: btj@btj.se; info@btj.se
Web Site: www.btj.se
Key Personnel
Owner & Chairman: Per Samuelson
Chief Executive Officer: Hans Persson
Founded: 1951

Subjects: Library & Information Sciences
ISBN Prefix(es): 978-91-7018
Associate Companies: BTJ Finland Oy
Subsidiaries: BTJ Tryck AB
Divisions: BTJ Database; BTJ Media

Bilda Forlag & Ide
Vastberga Alle 5, 126 13 Stockholm
Mailing Address: Box 42053, 126 13 Stockholm
Tel: (08) 709 04 00; (0290) 76 76 88 (customer service)
E-mail: info@bildaforlag.se; kundtjanst@bildaforlag.se
Web Site: www.bildaforlag.se
Key Personnel
Chief Executive Officer: Bengt Fasth *Tel:* (08) 709 04 50
Manager, Publishing: Ingrid Persson *Tel:* (08) 709 04 04 *E-mail:* ingrid.persson@bildaforlag.se
Founded: 1919
Subjects: Biography, Memoirs, Geography, Geology, Health, Nutrition, History, Language Arts, Linguistics, Maritime, Religion - Other, Travel & Tourism, Cultural History, Democracy, Social Issues, Social Movement
ISBN Prefix(es): 978-91-574; 978-91-7026
Number of titles published annually: 15 Print
Total Titles: 200 Print

Bonnier Audio+
Sveavagen 56, 103 63 Stockholm
Mailing Address: Box 3159, 103 63 Stockholm
Tel: (08) 696 87 60; (08) 696 84 10 (customer service) *Fax:* (08) 696 87 58 (orders)
E-mail: info@bonnieraudio.se
Web Site: www.bonnieraudio.se
Key Personnel
Publishing Manager: Johanna Hansen *Tel:* (08) 696 84 44 *E-mail:* johanna.hansen@bonnieraudio.se
Marketing: Torgny Lundin *Tel:* (08) 696 80 92 *E-mail:* torgny.lundin@bonnierforlagen.se
Editor: Yvonne Wiking *Tel:* (08) 696 82 26 *E-mail:* yvonne.wiking@bonnieraudio.se
Founded: 1986
Specialize in audiobooks.
Subjects: Fiction
ISBN Prefix(es): 978-91-7950
Number of titles published annually: 35 Print
Total Titles: 350 Print
Parent Company: Bonnierforlagen

Bonnier Carlsen Bokforlag
Sveavagen 56, Stockholm
Mailing Address: Box 3159, 103 63 Stockholm
Tel: (08) 696 89 30; (08) 696 84 10 (orders) *Fax:* (08) 696 89 31; (08) 696 83 58 (orders)
E-mail: info@carlsen.bonnier.se; kundservice@bonnierforlagen.se
Web Site: www.bonniercarlsen.se
Key Personnel
Publishing Manager: Jonas Bystrom *Tel:* (08) 696 80 38 *E-mail:* jonas.bystrom@bonnierforlagen.se
Sales Manager: Alexandra Torstendahl *Tel:* (08) 799 30 81 *E-mail:* alexandra.torstendahl@bonnierforlagen.se
Mng Editor: Ulrika Caperius *Tel:* (08) 696 87 25 *E-mail:* ulrika.caperius@bonnierforlagen.se
Head, Corporate Communications: Katarina Arborelius *Tel:* (08) 696 66 90 *E-mail:* katarina.arborelius@bonnierforlagen.se
Founded: 1968
Subjects: Animals, Pets, Erotica, Fiction, Health, Nutrition, History, Humor, Mysteries, Suspense, Romance, Science Fiction, Fantasy, Social Sciences, Sociology, Sports, Athletics, Adventure, Cartoons, Child Care, Classics, Comics, Fantasy, Fairy Tales, Holidays, Horror & Ghost, Love & Sexuality, Social Situations

ISBN Prefix(es): 978-91-510; 978-91-48; 978-91-638
Parent Company: Bonnierforlagen

Albert Bonniers Forlag
Sveavagen 56, 103 63 Stockholm
Mailing Address: Box 3159, 103 63 Stockholm
Tel: (08) 696 86 20
E-mail: info@abforlag.bonnier.se
Web Site: www.albertbonniersforlag.se
Key Personnel
Publishing Dir: Eva Bonnier *Tel:* (08) 696 86 21 *E-mail:* eva.bonnier@abforlag.bonnier.se
Publishing Manager: Jesper Monthan *Tel:* (08) 696 82 18 *E-mail:* jesper.monthan@bonnierforlagen.se
Mng Editor: Helena Ljungstrom *Tel:* (08) 696 86 36 *E-mail:* helena.ljungstrom@abforlag.bonnier.se
Marketing Manager: Martin Ahlstrom *Tel:* (08) 696 86 61 *E-mail:* martin.ahlstrom@bonnierforlagen.se
Founded: 1837
Subjects: Art, Cookery, Fiction, Nonfiction (General)
ISBN Prefix(es): 978-91-7458; 978-91-0; 978-91-34; 978-91-85015
Total Titles: 150 Print
Parent Company: Bonnierfoerlagen AB
Warehouse: Samdistribution, PO Box 449, S-191 04 Sollentuna

Bookhouse, *imprint of* Volante

Bra Bocker AB
Angbatsbron 1, Box 892, 201 80 Malmo
Tel: (040) 665 46 00 *Fax:* (040) 665 46 22
E-mail: stockholm@stockholmtext.com
Web Site: www.bbb.se
Key Personnel
Chief Executive Officer: Niclas Ek
Editor-in-Chief: Doe Mena-Berlin
Founded: 1965
Subjects: Fiction, Geography, Geology, History, Nonfiction (General)
ISBN Prefix(es): 978-91-7024; 978-91-7119; 978-91-7133; 978-91-7002
Parent Company: International Masters Publishers AB, PO Box 814, 201 80 Malmo
Imprints: BBB Bokklubben Bra Bocker

Brombergs Bokforlag AB+
Hantverkargatan 26, 112 21 Stockholm
Tel: (08) 562 620 80 *Fax:* (08) 562 620 85
E-mail: info@brombergs.se
Web Site: brombergs.se
Key Personnel
Chief Executive Officer & Dir: Dorotea Bromberg *E-mail:* dorotea.bromberg@brombergs.se
Production Manager: Ylva Aberg *Tel:* (08) 562 620 86 *E-mail:* ylva.aberg@brombergs.se
Founded: 1975
Subjects: Fiction, Nonfiction (General)
ISBN Prefix(es): 978-91-7608; 978-91-7337; 978-91-85251; 978-91-85342
Number of titles published annually: 25 Print

BTJ, see Bibliotekstjaenst AB

Carlsson Bokforlag AB+
Stora Nygatan 31, Gamla Stan, 111 27 Stockholm
Mailing Address: PO Box 2112, 103 13 Stockholm
Tel: (08) 545 254 80 *Fax:* (08) 657 95 00
E-mail: info@carlssonbokforlag.se
Web Site: www.carlssonbokforlag.se
Key Personnel
Publisher: Trygve Carlsson *Tel:* (08) 545 254 85
Finance Manager & Editor: Ellinor Olander *Tel:* (08) 545 254 81

Marketing & Public Relations Manager: Adina Pierrou *Tel:* (08) 545 254 86
General Editor: Eva Sjostrom *Tel:* (08) 545 254 84
Founded: 1983
Subjects: Anthropology, Architecture & Interior Design, Art, Biography, Memoirs, Fiction, Government, Political Science, Health, Nutrition, History, Journalism, Language Arts, Linguistics, Literature, Literary Criticism, Essays, Psychology, Psychiatry, Travel & Tourism, Women's Studies, Ethnology, Media, Nature
ISBN Prefix(es): 978-91-7798; 978-91-7203; 978-91-7331
Warehouse: Foerlagssystem, Loevasvagen 26, 791 45 Falun

Citadell, *imprint of* Raben och Sjogren Bokforlag

Cordia, *imprint of* Verbum Forlag AB

Corona Forlag
Nobelvagen 135, Box 5, 201 20 Malmo
Tel: (040) 28 61 61 *Fax:* (040) 28 61 62
E-mail: kundservice@cor.se
Web Site: www.cor.se
Founded: 1961
Subjects: Education, Fiction, Nonfiction (General)
ISBN Prefix(es): 978-91-564; 978-91-7034
Associate Companies: Codex-Koncernen; Forlagshuset Nordens Grafiska Ab

Dahlia Books HB
Kalsangsgrand 4B, 753 19 Uppsala
Mailing Address: Box 1025, 751 40 Uppsala
Tel: (070) 897 02 17
Founded: 1973
Major function of this company is bookselling (antiquarian & new).
ISBN Prefix(es): 978-91-974094; 978-91-972293; 978-91-975840

Dar Al Muna
PO Box 127, 182 05 Djursholm
Tel: (08) 21 05 65 *Fax:* (08) 622 61 51
E-mail: info@daralmuna.com
Web Site: www.daralmuna.com
Founded: 1984
Subjects: Fiction
ISBN Prefix(es): 978-91-88356

8tto, *imprint of* Volante

Ellerstroms Forlag+
Stora Fiskaregatan 91, 222 24 Lund
Tel: (046) 32 32 95
E-mail: info@ellerstroms.se
Web Site: www.ellerstroms.se
Key Personnel
Manager: Jonas Ellerstrom
Editor: Erik Magntorn *E-mail:* erik@ellerstroms.se; Klara Rasmussen *E-mail:* klara@ellerstroms.se
Founded: 1983
Publisher of fiction, prose & poetry. Swedish & translations.
Subjects: Fiction, Literature, Literary Criticism, Essays, Poetry
ISBN Prefix(es): 978-91-7247; 978-91-86488; 978-91-86489
Number of titles published annually: 20 Print
Total Titles: 220 Print

Filur, *imprint of* Massolit Forlag AB

Bokforlaget Fischer & Co+
Imprint of Lind & Co
Svartmangatan 18, 2tr, 111 29 Stockholm
Mailing Address: Box 2036, 103 11 Stockholm
Tel: (08) 643 38 46 *Fax:* (08) 643 38 98

E-mail: info@lindco.se
Web Site: www.lindco.se; forlaggare.se/content/bokforlaget-fischer-co
Founded: 1987
Subjects: Biography, Memoirs, Fiction, History, Nonfiction (General)
ISBN Prefix(es): 978-91-7054; 978-91-85183
Total Titles: 1 Audio
Book Club(s): Bockernas Klubb

Folkuniversitetets forlag
Magle Lilla Kyrkogata 4, 223 51 Lund
Tel: (046) 14 87 20
E-mail: info@folkuniversitetsforlag.se
Web Site: www.folkuniversitetet.se
Key Personnel
President: Annika Dolk *Tel:* (046) 19 77 00 *E-mail:* annika.dolk@folkuniversitetet.se
Publishing Manager: Henrik Killander *Tel:* (046) 14 87 35 *E-mail:* henrik.killander@folkuniversitetetsforlag.se
Founded: 1972
Subjects: Education, Language Arts, Linguistics, Swedish as Second Language, Swedish for Immigrants
ISBN Prefix(es): 978-91-7434
Number of titles published annually: 10 Print; 1 CD-ROM; 2 Audio
Total Titles: 205 Print; 5 CD-ROM; 50 Audio

Foreningen Svenskt naringsliv
Storgatan 19, 114 82 Stockholm
Tel: (08) 553 430 00 *Fax:* (08) 553 430 99
Web Site: www.svensktnaringsliv.se
Key Personnel
Manager: Kjell Frykhammar *Tel:* (08) 553 430 51 *E-mail:* kjell.frykhammar@svensktnaringsliv.se
Subjects: Economics, Economy
ISBN Prefix(es): 978-91-7152
Branch Office(s)
Rue de Luxembourg 3, 1000 Brussels, Belgium *Tel:* (02) 501 53 00 *Fax:* (02) 501 53 20 *E-mail:* bryssel@svensktnaringsliv.se

Bokforlaget Forum AB+
Sveavagen 56, 4tr, 103 63 Stockholm
Mailing Address: PO Box 3159, 103 63 Stockholm
Tel: (08) 696 84 40 *Fax:* (08) 696 83 58
E-mail: info@forum.se; kundservice@bonnierforlagen.se
Web Site: www.forum.se
Key Personnel
Publisher: Karin Linge Nordh *Tel:* (08) 696 84 63 *E-mail:* karin.linge.nordh@forum.se; Anders Sjoqvist *Tel:* (08) 696 87 02 *E-mail:* anders.sjoqvist@forum.se
Literary Manager & Publisher: Adam Dahlin *Tel:* (08) 696 84 64 *E-mail:* adam.dahlin@forum.se
Public Relations & Communications Manager: Annelie Eldh *Tel:* (08) 696 84 51 *Fax:* (08) 696 83 47 *E-mail:* annelie.eldh@bonnierforlagen.se
Mng Editor: Asa Ernflo *Tel:* (08) 696 86 86 *E-mail:* asa.ernflo@forum.se
Marketing: Hakan Kohler *Tel:* (08) 696 84 41 *E-mail:* hakan.kohler@bonnierforlagen.se
Founded: 1944
Subjects: Fiction, Nonfiction (General)
ISBN Prefix(es): 978-91-37; 978-91-7160; 978-91-7161
Number of titles published annually: 125 Print
Parent Company: Bonnierforlagen

Fri Tanke
Box 3020, 181 03 Lidingo
Tel: (08) 411 14 60
E-mail: info@fritanke.se
Web Site: www.fritanke.se

Key Personnel
Publishing Manager & Editor-in-Chief: Chris Sturmark
Founded: 2006
Subjects: Philosophy, Science (General), Social Sciences, Sociology, Culture, Ethics
ISBN Prefix(es): 978-91-86061

C E Fritzes AB
Fritzes/Norstedts Juridik AB, Kundservice, 106 47 Stockholm
Tel: (08) 598 191 90; (08) 598 191 00 *Fax:* (08) 598 191 91
E-mail: kundservice@nj.se
Web Site: www.nj.se/cms/pub/fritzes
Key Personnel
Chief Executive Officer: Olov Sundstrom *Tel:* (08) 598 191 22 *E-mail:* olov.sundstrom@nj.se
Sales & Marketing Dir: Bjorn Candler *Tel:* (08) 598 191 14 *E-mail:* bjorn.candler@nj.se
Publishing Consultant: Lotta Bjornstrom *Tel:* (08) 598 191 47 *E-mail:* lotta.bjornstrom@nj.se
Founded: 1837
Official publications from Swedish government & authorities.
Subjects: Agriculture, Business, Communications, Criminology, Economics, Education, Energy, Environmental Studies, Health, Nutrition, Law, Medicine, Nursing, Dentistry, Real Estate, Technology, Transportation
ISBN Prefix(es): 978-91-38; 978-91-7052; 978-91-7050
Parent Company: Norstedts Juridik
Ultimate Parent Company: Wolters Kluwer Scandinavia

Galago Forlag, *imprint of* Ordfront Forlag AB

Gehrmans Musikforlag AB
Vastberga alle 5, 126 30 Hagersten
Mailing Address: PO Box 42 026, 126 12 Stockholm
Tel: (08) 610 06 00 *Fax:* (08) 610 06 27
E-mail: info@gehrmans.se; order@gehrmans.se
Web Site: www.gehrmans.se
Key Personnel
Chief Executive Officer: Gunnar Helgesson *Tel:* (08) 610 06 12 *E-mail:* gunnar.helgesson@gehrmans.se
Senior Advisor: Kettil Skarby *Tel:* (0736) 20 99 33 *E-mail:* kettil.skarby@gehrmans.se
Founded: 1893
Music publisher specializing in folk music & ballads, music with Christian lyrics, accordion music, orchestral music for brass & woodwinds, contemporary music, classical music, music for choirs, educational publications, sheet music publications & compilations, sheet wholesale distributions. Orchestral parts rental.
Subjects: Music, Dance
ISBN Prefix(es): 978-91-7748
Number of titles published annually: 80 Print
Total Titles: 7,000 Print
Branch Office(s)
Fennica Gehrman oy, PL 158, Lonnrotinkatu 20 B, 00121 Helsinki, Finland, Publishing Manager: Ari Nieminen *Tel:* (09) 1038 7122 0 *Fax:* (09) 1038 7122 1 *E-mail:* info@fennicagehrman.fi

Gidlunds forlag
Orlinge 111, 733 99 Moklinta
E-mail: info@gidlunds.se
Web Site: www.gidlunds.se
Key Personnel
Contact: Sara Gidlund *Tel:* (0224) 83140; Anders Svedin *Tel:* (070) 6204426 *E-mail:* anders.svedin@gidlunds.se
Founded: 1968

Subjects: Art, Biography, Memoirs, History, Philosophy, Social Sciences, Sociology, Humanities
ISBN Prefix(es): 978-91-7844
Number of titles published annually: 30 Print
Total Titles: 1,000 Print

Gilla Bocker, *imprint of* Lilla Piratforlaget

Gilla Bocker
Imprint of Lilla Piratforlaget
Kaptensgatan 6, 114 57 Stockholm
Tel: (08) 545 678 54 *Fax:* (08) 545 678 56
E-mail: info@lillapiratforlaget.se
Web Site: www.gillabocker.se
Key Personnel
Publisher: Ada Wester *Tel:* (0736) 70 37 47
    E-mail: ada@lillapiratforlaget.se
Editor: Klara Bjelkenas *Tel:* (0707) 77 51 96
    E-mail: klara@lillapiratforlaget.se
Marketing Coordinator: Kajsa Olofsson
    E-mail: kajsa@lillapiratforlaget.se
Founded: 2010
ISBN Prefix(es): 978-91-86634
Number of titles published annually: 10 Print

Gothia Fortbildning+
Kungsholmstorg 5, 112 21 Stockholm
Mailing Address: Box 22543, 104 22 Stockholm
Tel: (08) 462 26 60; (08) 462 26 70 (orders)
    Fax: (08) 644 46 67
E-mail: info@gothiafortbildning.se
Web Site: www.gothiafortbildning.se
Key Personnel
President & Group Publisher: Anders Jonasson
    Tel: (08) 462 26 61 *E-mail:* anders.jonasson@
    gothiafortbildning.se
Mng Editor: Ingrid Sundqvist *Tel:* (08) 462 26 67
    E-mail: ingrid.sundqvist@gothiafortbildning.se
Press Contact & Promotion Manager: Pia Leufstedt *Tel:* (08) 462 26 10 *E-mail:* pia.leufstedt@
    gothiafortbildning.se
Production Manager: Mimma Almstrom *Tel:* (08)
    462 26 73 *E-mail:* mimma.almstrom@
    gothiafortbildning.se
Founded: 1981
Subjects: Child Care & Development, Education, Health, Nutrition, Medicine, Nursing, Dentistry, Psychology, Psychiatry, Regional Interests, Social Care
ISBN Prefix(es): 978-91-526; 978-91-7205; 978-91-85174; 978-91-86028; 978-91-7728; 978-91-85232; 978-91-85660

Hallgren & Fallgren Studieforlag AB
Box 92 192, 120 09 Stockholm
Tel: (08) 37 66 98; (0175) 266 11 (orders)
    Fax: (08) 87 33 21; (0175) 266 10 (orders)
E-mail: info@hallgren-fallgren.se
Web Site: www.hallgren-fallgren.se
Founded: 1973
Book for teachers & students in multicultural classes with emphasis on language-oriented teaching in all subjects.
Subjects: Education, Fiction, Literature, Literary Criticism, Essays, Science (General)
ISBN Prefix(es): 978-91-7382

Halsoforlaget, *imprint of* Massolit Forlag AB

Harlequin, *imprint of* HarperCollins Nordic AB

HarperCollins Nordic, *imprint of* HarperCollins Nordic AB

HarperCollins Nordic AB
Subsidiary of HarperCollins Publishers
Box 49005, 100 28 Stockholm
E-mail: kundservice@harlequin.se
Web Site: harpercollins.se

Key Personnel
Mng Dir & Publisher: Anette Ekstrom
Publishing & Marketing Dir: Carina Nunstedt
Sales Dir: Pauline Riccius
Subjects: Biography, Memoirs, Mysteries, Suspense, Romance, Paranormal
ISBN Prefix(es): 978-91-509; 978-91-507
Imprints: Harlequin; HarperCollins Nordic

Bokforlaget Hegas AB
Ronnowsgatan 8 DA, 252 25 Helsingborg
Tel: (042) 33 03 40
E-mail: info@hegas.se
Web Site: www.hegas.se
Key Personnel
Publishing Manager: Anna Hjerpe
Founded: 1983
Specialize in easy-to-read books.
ISBN Prefix(es): 978-91-86650; 978-91-86651; 978-91-973287; 978-91-973620; 978-91-973621

Hermods AB+
Warfvinges vag 33, 112 51 Stockholm
Tel: (08) 410 251 00 *Fax:* (08) 619 04 28
E-mail: info@hermods.se
Web Site: www.hermods.se
Founded: 1898
Specialize in educational & business publishing & distance education.
Membership(s): Euro Business Publishing Network.
Subjects: Accounting, Business, Chemistry, Chemical Engineering, Communications, Computers, Geography, Geology, Health, Nutrition, History, Journalism, Marketing, Mathematics, Philosophy, Physics, Social Sciences, Sociology, Technology
ISBN Prefix(es): 978-91-21; 978-91-23
Branch Office(s)
Foreningsgatan 26, 211 52 Malmo *Tel:* (040) 631 67 00 *Fax:* (040) 97 35 66

Hillelforlaget (Hillel Publishing House)+
Box 7427, 103 91 Stockholm
Tel: (08) 587 858 04 *Fax:* (08) 587 858 58
E-mail: hillelforlaget@jfst.se
Web Site: www.hillelforlaget.se
Founded: 1963
Subjects: Regional Interests, Religion - Jewish
ISBN Prefix(es): 978-91-85164
Number of titles published annually: 3 Print
Total Titles: 20 Print

Historiska Media
Bantorget 3, 222 29 Lund
Mailing Address: Box 1206, 221 05 Lund
Tel: (046) 33 34 50
E-mail: info@historiskamedia.se
Web Site: www.historiskamedia.se
Key Personnel
Chief Executive Officer: Erik Osvalds
    Tel: (046) 33 34 53 *E-mail:* erik.osvalds@
    historiskamedia.se
Publisher: Lena Amuren *Tel:* (046) 33 34 64
    E-mail: lena.amuren@historiskamedia.se
Senior Editor: Asa Bjorck *Tel:* (046) 33 34 70
    E-mail: asa.bjorck@historiskamedia.se; Hakan Peterson *Tel:* (046) 33 34 52 *E-mail:* hakan.
    peterson@historiskamedia.se; Christina Sejte *Tel:* (046) 33 34 78 *E-mail:* christina.sejte@
    historiskamedia.se
Marketing & Public Relations Manager: Christina Haugen *Tel:* (046) 33 34 76 *E-mail:* christina.
    haugen@historiskamedia.se
Subjects: Fiction, History, Mysteries, Suspense, Nonfiction (General)
ISBN Prefix(es): 978-91-85057; 978-91-88930; 978-91-89442; 978-91-971992
Number of titles published annually: 25 Audio

K Hjelm Forlag AB
Bolandsgatan 10, 753 23 Uppsala
Mailing Address: Box 1405, 751 42 Uppsala
Tel: (018) 127888 *Fax:* (018) 135497
E-mail: info@hjelms.se
Web Site: www.hjelms.com
Key Personnel
President: Ivan Hjelm *Tel:* (018) 105783
    E-mail: ivan@hjelms.se
Chief Executive Officer: Karin Hjelm
    E-mail: karin@hjelms.se
Marketing Dir: Erika McDonald *Tel:* (018)
    105782 *E-mail:* erika@hjelms.se
Editor: Fredrik Hjelm *Tel:* (018) 105786
    E-mail: fredrik@hjelms.se; Jonas Hjelm
    Tel: (018) 105785 *E-mail:* jonas@hjelms.se
ISBN Prefix(es): 978-91-85275; 978-91-87922

Informationsforlaget AB
Sveavagen 61, 113 86 Stockholm
Mailing Address: PO Box 6884, 113 86 Stockholm
Tel: (08) 545 560 50 *Fax:* (08) 31 39 03
E-mail: red@informationsforlaget.se
Web Site: www.informationsforlaget.se
Key Personnel
Chief Executive Officer & Publisher: Ulf Heimdahl *E-mail:* ulf.heimdahl@
    informationsforlaget.se
Publisher & Project Manager: Christian Reimers
Project Manager: Martin Andreasson
Mng Editor: Kirsi Ylioja
Marketing: Charlotte Porat
Founded: 1979
Specialize in sponsored books in cooperation with Swedish industry & authorities.
Subjects: Cookery, How-to, Wine & Spirits
ISBN Prefix(es): 978-91-7736
Associate Companies: Kulturhistoriska Bokforlaget

Ingenjorsforlaget AB+
Master Samuelsgatan 56, 111 21 Stockholm
Tel: (08) 796 66 90; (08) 796 66 00 *Fax:* (08)
    789 62 24
Founded: 1970
Subjects: Science (General)
ISBN Prefix(es): 978-91-7284; 978-91-85804; 978-91-973810; 978-91-85834

Interskol Forlag AB
Schaktugnsgatan 2, 216 16 Limhamn
Tel: (040) 51 01 95 *Fax:* (040) 15 06 25
E-mail: info@interskol.se; order@interskol.se
Web Site: www.interskol.se
Founded: 1975
Specialize in school books.
Subjects: Education, Literature, Literary Criticism, Essays, Science (General), Social Sciences, Sociology
ISBN Prefix(es): 978-91-7306

Invandrarfoerlaget
c/o Emigranternas Hus Packhusplatsen 7, 411 13 Gothenburg
E-mail: migrant@immi.se
Web Site: www.immi.se
Key Personnel
Contact: Miguel Benito *E-mail:* miguel.benito@
    immi.se
Founded: 1973
Subjects: Education, Ethnicity, Migrants, Racism, Refugees
ISBN Prefix(es): 978-91-85242; 978-91-7906
Total Titles: 180 Print
Parent Company: Immigrant-institutet

Isaberg Forlag ab
Mogatan 26, 330 27 Hestra
Tel: (0370) 33 63 10 *Fax:* (0370) 33 63 20
E-mail: info@isaberg.nu
Web Site: www.isaberg.nu

Key Personnel
Chief Executive Officer: Jan Mansson *Tel:* (070)
758 15 15 *E-mail:* jan@isaberg.nu
Publisher: Eva Mansson *Tel:* (070) 785 84 25
E-mail: eva@isaberg.nu
Sales & Administration: Renee Schultz
E-mail: renee@isaberg.nu
Founded: 1903
Subjects: Fiction, History, Language Arts, Linguistics, Music, Dance, Nonfiction (General), Regional Interests, Civics, English, Local History, Swedish
ISBN Prefix(es): 978-91-7694

Iustus Forlag AB
Ostra Agatan 9, 753 22 Uppsala
Mailing Address: Box 1994, 751 49 Uppsala
Tel: (018) 65 03 30 *Fax:* (018) 69 30 99
E-mail: kundtjanst@iustus.se
Web Site: www.iustus.se
Key Personnel
Chief Executive Officer & Publishing Dir: Pia
Wahren *E-mail:* pia.wahren@iustus.se
Customer Service: Gunilla Jakobsson
E-mail: gunilla.jakobsson@iustus.se
Founded: 1973
Specialize in law books, aimed at both university level & practicing lawyers, judges, civil servants.
Subjects: Business, Economics, Finance, Government, Political Science, Law, Management, Public Administration
ISBN Prefix(es): 978-91-7678
Number of titles published annually: 40 Print
Total Titles: 200 Print

IVA, see Kungl IngenjorsVetenskapsAkademien (IVA)

Jannersten Forlag AB+
Banergaten 15, 752 37 Uppsala
Tel: (018) 52 13 00 *Fax:* (018) 52 13 03
E-mail: bridge@jannersten.com; order@jannersten.com
Web Site: www.jannersten.se
Key Personnel
Chief Executive Officer: Per Jannersten
Founded: 1939
Subjects: Crafts, Games, Hobbies
ISBN Prefix(es): 978-91-85024

Kabusa Bocker
Erik Dahlbergsgatan 9, 411 26 Gothenburg
Tel: (031) 85 95 80 *Fax:* (031) 12 84 45
E-mail: red@kabusabocker.se
Web Site: www.kabusabocker.se
Founded: 2002
Subjects: Fiction
ISBN Prefix(es): 978-91-89680; 978-91-7355

Kalla Kulor Forlag
Gotlandsgatan 71, 116 38 Stockholm
E-mail: info@kallakulor.com
Web Site: kallakulor.com
Key Personnel
Publishing Dir: Hans-Olov Oberg *E-mail:* hoo@kallakulor.com
Editorial Dir: Katarina Sandart *E-mail:* katarina@kallakulor.com
Public Relations Manager: Cecilia Ahrfeldt
E-mail: cecilia@kallakulor.com
Founded: 2001
ISBN Prefix(es): 978-91-87879; 978-91-85535; 978-91-974278; 978-91-975361
Warehouse: ForlagsSystem AB, Tunavagen 90, 791 61 Falun

Liber Kartor, *imprint of* Liber AB

Klassikerforlaget Steniq AB
Blaklocksvagen 19, 139 35 Varmdo

Tel: (08) 716 35 28 *Fax:* (08) 716 35 28
E-mail: info@klassikerforlaget.com
Web Site: klassikerforlaget.com
Key Personnel
Owner: Stefan Mattsson
Founded: 1994
Subjects: Drama, Theater, Fiction, Literature, Literary Criticism, Essays, Poetry, Classic Literature
ISBN Prefix(es): 978-91-88680; 978-91-8868
Orders to: Forlagssystem AB, Warfvinges vag 30, Box 30195, 104 25 Stockholm *Tel:* (08) 657 19 00 *Fax:* (08) 618 34 70 *Web Site:* www.forlagssystem.se
Pocketgrossisten AB, Sveavagen 56, Box 3159, 103 63 Stockholm *Tel:* (08) 441 15 20 *Fax:* (08) 654 53 35 *E-mail:* info@pocketgrossisten.se *Web Site:* www.pocketgrossisten.se

Kungl IngenjorsVetenskapsAkademien (IVA)
(Royal Swedish Academy of Engineering Sciences)
Grev Turegatan 16, 102 42 Stockholm
Mailing Address: PO Box 5073, 102 42 Stockholm
Tel: (08) 791 29 00 *Fax:* (08) 611 56 23
E-mail: info@iva.se
Web Site: www.iva.se
Key Personnel
Chief Executive Officer: Bjorn O Nilsson
Tel: (08) 791 29 71 *E-mail:* bjorn.o.nilsson@iva.se
Dir, Communications: Camilla Koebe *Tel:* (08) 791 29 85 *E-mail:* camilla.koebe@iva.se
Founded: 1919
Subjects: Management, Science (General), Technology
ISBN Prefix(es): 978-91-7082

LAMANICA Logistikservice AB
Tradgardsgatan 31, 641 23 Katrineholm
Mailing Address: Industrilitteratur, Box 345, 641 23 Katrineholm
Tel: (150) 133 30
E-mail: info@industrilitteratur.se
Web Site: www.industrilitteratur.se
Founded: 1887
Subjects: Ethnicity, Marketing, Public Administration
ISBN Prefix(es): 978-91-7548; 978-91-7176
Parent Company: Mentor Communications AB

Hans Richter Laromedel+
Box 100, 645 22 Strangnas
SAN: 105-0893
Tel: (0152) 15060
E-mail: post@richbook.se
Web Site: www.richbook.se
Key Personnel
Publisher: Hans Richter
Founded: 1964
Also acts as agent. Mail order distribution & direct marketing to businesses & schools. E-learning material.
Subjects: Education, English as a Second Language, History, Language Arts, Linguistics, Psychology, Psychiatry, Self-Help, Technology
ISBN Prefix(es): 978-91-7884
Subsidiaries: Bokforlaget Axplock
Distributor for Bokforlaget Axplock

Bokforlaget Robert Larson AB+
Paternostervagen 49, 121 49 Johanneshov
Mailing Address: Box 6074, 121 06 Johanneshov
Tel: (08) 732 84 60
E-mail: info@larsonforlag.se
Web Site: www.larsonforlag.se
Founded: 1971
Subjects: Inspirational, Spirituality, Nonfiction (General)
ISBN Prefix(es): 978-91-514

Legenda, *imprint of* Bokforlaget Natur och Kultur

Leopard Forlag
St Paulsgatan 11, 118 46 Stockholm
Tel: (08) 20 31 40
E-mail: info@leopardforlag.se
Web Site: www.leopardforlag.se
Key Personnel
Chief Executive Officer/Publisher: Dan Israel
E-mail: dan.israel@leopardforlag.se
Publishing Dir: Moa Elf Karlen *E-mail:* moa.elf.karlen@leopardforlag.se
Founded: 2001
Subjects: Fiction, History, Literature, Literary Criticism, Essays, Nonfiction (General), Science (General)
ISBN Prefix(es): 978-91-7343

Lethe Forlag, *imprint of* Massolit Forlag AB

Liber, *imprint of* Liber AB

Liber AB+
Rasundavagen 18, Solna
Tel: (08) 690 90 00; (08) 690 93 30 (customer service) *Fax:* (08) 690 93 36
E-mail: kundservice.liber@liber.se
Web Site: www.liber.se
Key Personnel
President & Chief Executive Officer: Jerker Nilsson
Sales & Marketing Dir: Patrik von Bergen
Production Manager: Kenneth Olsson
Founded: 1973
Subjects: Business, Economics, Education, English as a Second Language, Geography, Geology, Health, Nutrition, History, Language Arts, Linguistics, Law, Mathematics, Medicine, Nursing, Dentistry, Science (General), Social Sciences, Sociology, Technology, Taxation
ISBN Prefix(es): 978-91-22; 978-91-21; 978-91-38; 978-91-7084; 978-91-7157; 978-91-40; 978-91-634; 978-91-47; 978-91-7171; 978-91-7012; 978-91-87182
Parent Company: Infinitas Learning
Imprints: Almqvist & Wiksell; Liber; Liber Kartor
Subsidiaries: Liber Distribution
Branch Office(s)
Kalendegatan 26, Malmo

Libris Forlag+
Kungsholmstorg 5, 112 21 Stockholm
Mailing Address: Box 121 11, 102 23 Stockholm
Tel: (019) 20 84 00
E-mail: info@libris.se; order@forlagssystem.se
Web Site: www.libris.se; www.facebook.com/pages/Libris-Förlag/178044889003180
Key Personnel
Publishing Manager: Jennie Sjostrom
E-mail: jennie.sjostrom@libris.se
Publisher: Peter Eriksson *E-mail:* peter.eriksson@libris.se
Marketing & Sales Manager: Anders Daleskog
E-mail: anders.daleskog@libris.se
Founded: 1916
Subjects: Fiction, Music, Dance, Theology, Christian Music
ISBN Prefix(es): 978-91-7194; 978-91-7195; 978-91-7218; 978-91-7837
Book Club(s): Libris Bok & Musikklubb

Lilla Piratforlaget
Kaptensgatan 6, 114 57 Stockholm
Tel: (08) 54567854
E-mail: info@lillapiratforlaget.se
Web Site: www.lillapiratforlaget.se
Key Personnel
President & Publishing Dir: Erik Titusson

Founded: 2011
ISBN Prefix(es): 978-91-87027
Number of titles published annually: 25 Print
Associate Companies: Piratforlaget AB
Imprints: Gilla Bocker

Massolit Forlag AB
Tradgardstvargrand 2, 111 31 Stockholm
Tel: (08) 410 45 857
E-mail: info@massolit.se
Web Site: www.massolit.se
Key Personnel
Chief Executive Officer: Jan Nilstadius
    E-mail: jan@massolit.se
Publishing Dir: Marta Hedener *E-mail:* marta.
    hedener@massolit.se
Founded: 2010
Subjects: Art, Biography, Memoirs, Cookery,
    Crafts, Games, Hobbies, History, Humor, Pho-
    tography
ISBN Prefix(es): 978-91-74431; 978-91-86649;
    978-91-97881
Imprints: Filur; Halsoforlaget; Lethe Forlag

Modernista Books
Kvarngatan 10, Garaget, 118 47 Stockholm
Tel: (08) 702 04 11 *Fax:* (08) 714 78 50
E-mail: info@modernista.se
Web Site: www.modernista.se
Subjects: Biography, Memoirs, Fiction, Nonfiction
    (General), Poetry
ISBN Prefix(es): 978-91-85453; 978-91-88748

Mondial
Vidargatan 4, 113 27 Stockholm
E-mail: office@mondial.se
Web Site: mondial.se/forlaget
Key Personnel
Publisher & Marketing: Simon Brouwers
    Tel: (073) 444 47 36 *E-mail:* simon@mondial.
    se
Publisher & Production: Olle Grundin *Tel:* (073)
    654 12 05 *E-mail:* olle@mondial.se
Design & Art Dir: Gustav Schiring *Tel:* (073) 504
    37 85 *E-mail:* gustav@mondial.se
Economics & Administration: Marianne Stenst-
    edt *Tel:* (070) 262 36 84 *E-mail:* marianne@
    mondial.se
Founded: 2017
Subjects: Biography, Memoirs, Fiction, Journal-
    ism, Current Affairs
ISBN Prefix(es): 978-91-88671
Number of titles published annually: 30 Print

Bokforlaget Natur och Kultur+
Karlavagen 31, 102 54 Stockholm
Mailing Address: PO Box 27 323, 102 54 Stock-
    holm
Tel: (08) 453 86 00 *Fax:* (08) 453 87 90
E-mail: info@nok.se
Web Site: www.nok.se
Key Personnel
Chief Executive Officer: Per Almgren
Dir, Educational Publishing: Helena Holmstrom
Dir, General Literature: Richard Herold
Foreign Rights: Eva Schonning *E-mail:* eva.
    schonning@nok.se
Founded: 1922
Subjects: Biography, Memoirs, Fiction, History,
    Nonfiction (General), Psychology, Psychiatry,
    Science (General), Social Sciences, Sociology
ISBN Prefix(es): 978-91-27; 978-91-582; 978-91-
    7136; 978-91-36; 978-91-7008
Number of titles published annually: 250 Print
Total Titles: 5,000 Print; 12 CD-ROM; 60 Audio
Imprints: Legenda (commercial fiction & sus-
    pense novels)
Subsidiaries: Natur och Kultur/Fakta etc

Book Club(s): Boeckernas Klubb, Box 3317, 103
    66 Stockholm; Natur och Kultur Direkt
Warehouse: Forlagsystem, Box 30195, 104 25
    Stockholm *Tel:* (08) 657 95 00 *E-mail:* order@
    forlagsystem.se *Web Site:* www.fsbutiken.se

Norstedts Forlag+
Subsidiary of Norstedts Forlagsgrupp AB
Tryckerigatan 4, 103 12 Stockholm
Mailing Address: PO Box 2052, 103 12 Stock-
    holm
Tel: (010) 744 22 00; (010) 744 20 20 (customer
    service) *Fax:* (010) 744 22 14 (customer ser-
    vice)
Web Site: www.norstedts.se
Key Personnel
Publishing Dir: Eva Gedin *Tel:* (010) 744 20 10
    E-mail: eva.gedin@norstedts.se
Production & Information Technology Dir:
    Peder Hagerstrom *Tel:* (010) 744 21 62
    E-mail: peder.hagerstrom@norstedts.se
Mng Editor, Fiction: Helena Lindstedt *Tel:* (010)
    744 20 49 *E-mail:* helena.lindstedt@norstedts.
    se
Mng Editor, Nonfiction: Henrik Sjoberg
    Tel: (010) 744 20 52 *E-mail:* henrik.sjoberg@
    norstedts.se
Communications Manager: Fanny Birath
    Tel: (010) 744 21 45 *E-mail:* fanny.birath@
    norstedts.se
Founded: 1823
Subjects: Fiction, Nonfiction (General)
ISBN Prefix(es): 978-91-1
Number of titles published annually: 100 Print
Foreign Rights: Norstedts Agency

Norstedts Forlagsgrupp AB
Tryckerigatan 4, 10312 Stockholm
Mailing Address: PO Box 2052, 103 12 Stock-
    holm
Tel: (010) 744 22 00
Web Site: www.norstedts.se
Key Personnel
President: Otto Sjoberg *E-mail:* otto.sjoberg@
    norstedts.se
Publishing Manager: Eva Gedin *E-mail:* eva.
    gedin@norstedts.se
Communications Manager: Olle Lidbom
    E-mail: olle.lidbom@norstedts.se
Founded: 1823
Subjects: Cookery, Fiction, Health, Nutrition,
    Mysteries, Suspense, Nonfiction (General), Po-
    etry
Parent Company: Storytel
Subsidiaries: Norstedts Forlag; Raben & Sjogren;
    Norstedts Ordbok
Divisions: Norstedts Agency
Foreign Rights: Norstedts Agency
Book Club(s): Barnens Bokklubb (partially owned
    with Bokforlaget Opal); Bockernas Klubb;
    Clio (partially owned with Atlantis); Hem &
    Tradgard; Manadens Bok (partially owned with
    Bonnierforlagen); Nautiska Bokklubben

Norstedts Juridik AB
Warfvinges vag 39, 11251 Stockholm
Tel: (08) 598 191 00; (08) 598 191 90
E-mail: kundservice@nj.se
Web Site: www.nj.se
Key Personnel
President: Olov Sundstrom *Tel:* (08) 598 191 22
    E-mail: olov.sundstrom@nj.se
Sales & Marketing Dir: Bjorn Candler *Tel:* (08)
    598 191 14 *E-mail:* bjorn.candler@nj.se
Customer Service Manager: Tina Andersson
    Tel: (08) 598 193 05 *E-mail:* tina.andersson@
    nj.se
Subjects: Law
ISBN Prefix(es): 978-91-38; 978-91-7598; 978-
    91-87364; 978-91-39; 978-91-88134; 978-91-
    970450; 978-91-970756

Parent Company: Wolters Kluwer
Branch Office(s)
Amerikaskjulet, 414 63 Gothenburg *Tel:* (031)
    775 17 00

Norstedts Ordbok AB
Subsidiary of Norstedts Forlagsgrupp AB
Tryckerigatan 4, 103 12 Stockholm
Mailing Address: PO Box 2052, 103 12 Stock-
    holm
Tel: (010) 744 22 00
E-mail: infoord@norstedts.se
Web Site: www.ord.se; www.norstedts.se
Key Personnel
Head: Ann Skold Nilsson *E-mail:* ann.skold@
    rabensjogren.se
Editor: Britt-Marie Berglund *E-mail:* britt-
    marie.berglund@norstedts.se; Mathias Thiel
    E-mail: mathias.thiel@norstedts.se; Mona
    Wiman *E-mail:* mona.wiman@norstedts.se
Founded: 2005
Specialize in dictionaries & academic titles & is
    tailored to these lines of publishing & particu-
    lar marketing & information requirements.
ISBN Prefix(es): 978-91-7227
Ultimate Parent Company: KF Media

Bokforlaget Nya Doxa AB+
Kungsgatan 5, 713 31 Nora
Mailing Address: Box 113, 713 23 Nora
Tel: (0587) 12905; (0587) 104 16 (orders)
    Fax: (0587) 14257
E-mail: info@nya-doxa.se
Web Site: www.nya-doxa.se
Key Personnel
Publisher: David Stansvik *E-mail:* david.
    stansvik@nya-doxa.se
Founded: 1990
Also distribution & sales for Bokforlaget Thales,
    Sweden.
Subjects: Art, Biblical Studies, Communications,
    Ethnicity, History, Literature, Literary Criti-
    cism, Essays, Nonfiction (General), Philosophy,
    Science (General), Social Sciences, Sociology,
    Theology, Women's Studies, Humanities
ISBN Prefix(es): 978-91-88248; 978-91-578; 978-
    91-85318
Number of titles published annually: 20 Print
Total Titles: 200 Print

Odins Forlag AB
Tranhusgatan 29, 621 55 Visby
Tel: (0498) 24 93 18
E-mail: info@odinsforlag.se
Web Site: www.odinsforlag.se
Founded: 1978
Subjects: Art, History, Regional Interests, Art
    History, Culture, Military History, Russian Art,
    Wooden Sculpture
ISBN Prefix(es): 978-91-85716

Olika Forlag AB
Kindagatan 31, 582 47 Linkoping
E-mail: info@olika.nu
Web Site: www.olika.nu/olika-forlag
Key Personnel
Publisher & Editor: Karin Salmson *Tel:* (0733) 38
    24 27 *E-mail:* karin@olika.nu; Marie Tomicic
    Tel: (0708) 62 28 08 *E-mail:* marie@olika.nu
Founded: 2007
ISBN Prefix(es): 978-91-85845
Parent Company: Olika AB

Bokforlaget Opal AB
Tegelbergsvagen 31, 168 66 Bromma
Mailing Address: Box 20113, 161 02 Bromma
Tel: (08) 28 21 79
E-mail: opal@opal.se
Web Site: www.opal.se
Key Personnel
Publisher & Foreign Rights Manager: Catrine
    Christell

Mng Dir: Bengt Christell
Business Editor: Jacqueline Sietses
Editor: Dorothea Hygrell; Sara Ruder
Marketing: Melina Nordstrand
Founded: 1973
Subjects: Animals, Pets, Fiction, Humor, Literature, Literary Criticism, Essays, Social Sciences, Sociology, Sports, Athletics, Adventure, Classics, Horror & Ghost, Nature
ISBN Prefix(es): 978-91-7270; 978-91-7299
Orders to: PO Box 30 195, 104 30 Stockholm
   Tel: (08) 657 95 00 Fax: (08) 657 19 95
   E-mail: order@fsys.se

Ordalaget Bokforlag AB
Nockeby Torg 6, 167 74 Bromma
Mailing Address: Box 17018, 167 17 Bromma
Tel: (08) 80 88 48 Fax: (08) 80 88 49
E-mail: bok@ordalaget.se
Web Site: www.ordalaget.se
Key Personnel
Publisher: Margot Henrikson E-mail: margot@ordalaget.se
Publisher & Editor: Mattias Henrikson
   E-mail: mattias@ordalaget.se
Editor & Marketing: Anna Nolgren
   E-mail: annanolgren@ordalaget.se
Founded: 1992
Subjects: Cookery, Gardening, Plants, History
ISBN Prefix(es): 978-91-7469

Ordfront Forlag AB (Ordfront Publishing House)+
Hogbergsgatan 18, nb, 118 91 Stockholm
Mailing Address: PO Box 17506, 118 91 Stockholm
Tel: (070) 410 20 84
E-mail: forlaget@ordfrontforlag.se; info@ordfront.se
Web Site: www.ordfrontforlag.se
Key Personnel
President & Publisher: Pelle Andersson Tel: (070) 525 21 99 E-mail: pelle@ordfrontforlag.se
Marketing & Public Relations Manager: Jenny Bjarnar Tel: (0708) 53 99 03 E-mail: jenny@ordfrontforlag.se
Production Manager: Goran Skarbrandt Tel: (070) 410 20 85 E-mail: goran@ordfrontforlag.se
Founded: 1969
Specialize in history, politics, journalism & fiction.
Membership(s): Swedish Publishers Association.
Subjects: Fiction, History, Journalism, Publishing & Book Trade Reference, Social Sciences, Sociology
ISBN Prefix(es): 978-91-7324; 978-91-7037
Total Titles: 50 Print
Imprints: Galago Forlag
Book Club(s): Ordfront Bookclub
Distribution Center: Forlagssystem AB, PO Box 30195, 104 25 Stockholm

Pagina Forlags AB+
Vegagatan 2, 172 34 Sundbyberg
Mailing Address: Box 2103, 174 02 Sundbyberg
Tel: (08) 564 218 00 Fax: (08) 564 218 19
E-mail: info@pagina.se
Web Site: www.pagina.se
Key Personnel
Publisher: Christian Reimers Tel: (070) 586 02 67
Mng Dir & Head, Sales & Marketing: Ivan Wase Tel: (08) 564 218 03
Publishing Manager: Kenneth Ekholm Tel: (08) 564 218 05
Founded: 1978
Subjects: Computer Science
ISBN Prefix(es): 978-91-86200; 978-91-86201; 978-91-636
Parent Company: Pagina AB
Subsidiaries: Pagina Oy
Orders to: Forlagssystem AB, Box 30195, 104 25 Stockholm Tel: (08) 657 95 00 Fax: (08) 657 19 95 E-mail: order@fsys.se

Pilgrim, imprint of Verbum Forlag AB

Piratforlaget AB
Kaptensgatan 6, 114 57 Stockholm
Tel: (08) 412 13 50 Fax: (08) 545 678 58
E-mail: info@piratforlaget.se
Web Site: www.piratforlaget.se
Key Personnel
Chief Executive Officer & Publisher: Ann-Marie Skarp Tel: (08) 412 13 54 E-mail: ann-marie@piratforlaget.se
Publisher: Sofia Brattselius Thunfors Tel: (08) 412 13 53 E-mail: sofia@piratforlaget.se
Editor/Production: Mattias Bostrom Tel: (08) 412 13 51 E-mail: mattias@piratforlaget.se
Editor: Anna Hirvi Sigurdsson Tel: (08) 545 678 40 E-mail: anna@piratforlaget.se
Marketing: Cherie Fusser Tel: (08) 412 13 52 E-mail: cherie@piratforlaget.se
Public Relations & Information: Christina Kivi Tel: (08) 412 13 58 E-mail: christina@piratforlaget.se
Founded: 1999
Subjects: Fiction
ISBN Prefix(es): 978-91-642; 978-91-89426
Associate Companies: Lilla Piratforlaget

Printz Publishing
Stora Nygatan 21A, 111 27 Stockholm
E-mail: info@printzpublishing.se
Web Site: www.printzpublishing.se
Key Personnel
Publisher: Pia Printz Tel: (0767) 86 87 99
   E-mail: pia@printzpublishing.se
Marketing Manager: Anna Levahn Tel: (0723) 19 89 00 E-mail: anna@printzpublishing.se
Project & Event Manager: Frida Hedene Tel: (070) 370 50 93 E-mail: frida@printzpublishing.se
Publishing Coordinator & Ebook Manager: Madeleine Ahlberg Tel: (073) 511 97 88 E-mail: madde@printzpublishing.se
Founded: 2010
ISBN Prefix(es): 978-91-87343
Distribution Center: Forlagssystem AB, Warfvinges vag 30, 112 51 Stockholm Tel: (08) 657 19 00 Fax: (08) 618 34 70

R & S Books, imprint of Raben och Sjogren Bokforlag

Raben och Sjogren Bokforlag+
Subsidiary of Norstedts Forlagsgrupp AB
Tryckerigatan 4, 103 12 Stockholm
Mailing Address: PO Box 2052, 103 12 Stockholm
Tel: (010) 744 23 00
E-mail: info@rabensjogren.se
Web Site: www.rabensjogren.se
Key Personnel
Publishing Manager: Ann Skold Nilsson Tel: (010) 744 20 79 E-mail: ann.skold.nilsson@rabensjogren.se
Public Relations Manager: Karin Rowland Tel: (010) 744 21 55 E-mail: karin.rowland@norstedts.se
Sales Manager: Anders Toll Tel: (010) 744 21 41 E-mail: anders.toll@norstedts.se
Founded: 1942
Subjects: Nonfiction (General)
ISBN Prefix(es): 978-91-29
Ultimate Parent Company: Storytel
Imprints: Citadell; R & S Books; Tiden
Book Club(s): Barnens Bokklubb (jointly owned)

Bokforlaget Rediviva
Brantingsgatan 41, 115 35 Stockholm
Tel: (08) 25 70 07
E-mail: mail@rediviva.nu
Web Site: www.rediviva.nu
Founded: 1968

Subjects: Crafts, Games, Hobbies, Geography, Geology, History, Science (General), Travel & Tourism, Design
ISBN Prefix(es): 978-91-7120

Richbook, imprint of Bokforlaget Axplock

Ruta Ett DVD AB
Tullkammaregatan 12, 791 31 Falun
Tel: (023) 702 20 33
E-mail: info@rutaett.com
Web Site: www.rutaett.com
Key Personnel
Chief Executive Officer: Pelle Ferner
Dir, Sales & Licensing: Lennart Blixt
ISBN Prefix(es): 978-91-978340

NYA Samsprak Forlags AB
Stortorget 6, 702 11 Orebro
Tel: (019) 13 24 45 Fax: (019) 18 72 55
Founded: 1980
Subjects: Communications, Education
ISBN Prefix(es): 978-91-86020; 978-91-88052
Total Titles: 10 Print; 1 CD-ROM; 14 Audio

Sanoma Utbildning AB
Astromergatan 12, 104 25 Stockholm
Mailing Address: Box 30091, 104 25 Stockholm
Tel: (08) 587 642 10 Fax: (08) 587 642 02
E-mail: kundtjanst@sanomautbildning.se; info@sanomautbildning.se
Web Site: www.sanomautbildning.se
Key Personnel
Chief Executive Officer: Erik Larsson Tel: (08) 587 642 11 E-mail: erik.larsson@sanomautbildning.se
Marketing & Sales Manager: Christer Carlberg Tel: (08) 587 642 98 E-mail: christer.carlberg@sanomautbildning.se
Founded: 1993
Specialize in school books.
Subjects: Education, Language Arts, Linguistics, Law, Mathematics, Philosophy, Social Sciences, Sociology
ISBN Prefix(es): 978-91-622

Schibsted Forlag AB+
Vaktgatan 1B, 254 56 Helsingborg
Tel: (042) 136415 Fax: (042) 147132
E-mail: info@boknoje.se
Web Site: www.boknoje.se
Key Personnel
Publisher: Peter Stenson
Founded: 1982
Subjects: Animals, Pets, Biography, Memoirs, Business, Career Development, History, Human Relations, Management, Nonfiction (General), Philosophy, Psychology, Psychiatry, Self-Help
ISBN Prefix(es): 978-91-7738
Parent Company: Schibsted ASA
Book Club(s): Bokklubben Liv & Ledarskap

Bokforlaget Semic AB
Esplanaden 3B, 172 25 Sundbyberg
Mailing Address: Box 1243, 172 25 Sundbyberg
Tel: (08) 799 30 50; (08) 696 84 10 (orders) Fax: (08) 799 30 64; (08) 696 83 58 (orders)
E-mail: info@semic.se; kundenservice@bonnierforlagen.se (orders)
Web Site: www.semic.se
Key Personnel
Publisher & Mng Editor: Annelie Lindqvist Tel: (08) 799 30 36 E-mail: annelie.lindqvist@semic.se
Chief Executive Officer: Rickard Ekstrom Tel: (08) 799 30 65
Founded: 1945
Subjects: Animals, Pets, Architecture & Interior Design, Cookery, Crafts, Games, Hobbies, Fiction, Gardening, Plants, House & Home, Hu-

mor, Nonfiction (General), Outdoor Recreation, Sports, Athletics
ISBN Prefix(es): 978-91-552
Parent Company: Semic International AB

Bokforlaget Settern AB+
Drakabygget, 286 92 Orkelljunga
Tel: (0435) 804 70 *Fax:* (0435) 804 00
E-mail: order@settern.se; info@settern.se
Web Site: www.settern.se
Key Personnel
Customer Service & Orders: Joergen Wahlen
  E-mail: jw@settern.se
Editor: Tomas Wahlen *Tel:* (0430) 539 33
  E-mail: tomas@settern.se
Founded: 1974
Specialize in hunting & fishing books.
Membership(s): NOFF.
Subjects: Nonfiction (General), Outdoor Recreation, Dogs, Hunting & Fishing, Nature
ISBN Prefix(es): 978-91-7586; 978-91-85274
Number of titles published annually: 10 Print
Total Titles: 600 Print
Book Club(s): Bokklubben Jakt & Fiske

Sjostrands Forlag AB
Agatan 24, 172 62 Sundbyberg
Tel: (08) 29 75 99
Founded: 1978
Subjects: Astrology, Occult, Fiction, Nonfiction (General), Science Fiction, Fantasy
ISBN Prefix(es): 978-91-7574

SNS Forlag+
Jakobsbergsgatan 18, 111 44 Stockholm
Mailing Address: Box 5629, 114 86 Stockholm
Tel: (08) 507 025 00 *Fax:* (08) 507 025 25
E-mail: info@sns.se
Web Site: www.sns.se
Key Personnel
Editor: Gabriella Stjarnborg *Tel:* (08) 507 025 19
  E-mail: gabriella.stjarnborg@sns.se
Founded: 1948
Subjects: Economics, Social Sciences, Sociology
ISBN Prefix(es): 978-91-7150; 978-91-85355; 978-91-85695; 978-91-86203

Sober Forlag AB
Box 12825, 112 97 Stockholm
Tel: (08) 672 60 00 *Fax:* (08) 672 60 01
E-mail: info@iogt.se
Web Site: iogt.se/soberforlag
Key Personnel
Communications: Karin Friberg *Tel:* (08) 672 60 24 *E-mail:* karin.friberg@iogt.se
Founded: 1973
Subjects: Health, Nutrition, Social Sciences, Sociology, Alcohol & Drug Policy, Alcohol Counseling
ISBN Prefix(es): 978-91-7296
Parent Company: IOGT-NTO och Nykterhetsorelsens Bildnings verksamhet (NBV)
Orders to: IOGT-NTO, Metallvagen 4, 435 83 Molnlycke *Tel:* (031) 338 28 73 *Fax:* (031) 338 04 50

Frank Stenvalls Forlag+
Foreningsgatan 12, Oppet mand-fred 10-18, 200 10 Malmo
Mailing Address: Box 17111, 200 10 Malmo
Tel: (040) 127703 *Fax:* (040) 127706
E-mail: info@stenvalls.com
Web Site: www.stenvalls.com/shop
Key Personnel
Mng Dir: Frank Stenvall
Founded: 1966
Subjects: Aeronautics, Aviation, History, Maritime, Music, Dance, Transportation, Military History, Motor, Railway
ISBN Prefix(es): 978-91-7266
Number of titles published annually: 5 Print

Total Titles: 60 Print
Book Club(s): Swedish Military Bookclub

Stiftelsen Kursverksamhetens Forlag, see Folkuniversitetets forlag

Stockholm Text
King's St 58, 3rd floor, 111 22 Stockholm
Tel: (0721) 666 933
E-mail: stockholm@stockholmtext.com
Web Site: stockholmtext.com
Key Personnel
Founder & Publisher: Claes Ericson
  E-mail: claes.ericson@stockholmtext.com
Founded: 2011
Subjects: Fiction, Nonfiction (General)
ISBN Prefix(es): 978-91-87173
U.S. Office(s): 19820 82 Pl NE, Seattle, WA 98028, United States *E-mail:* seattle@stockholmtext.com

Stromberg Brunnhages+
Olofsgatan 18, 103 64 Stockholm
Mailing Address: Box 3211, 103 64 Stockholm
Tel: (08) 620 19 00
E-mail: gunilla.segerdahl@stromberg.se
Web Site: www.stromberg.se
Founded: 1944
Subjects: Cookery, Economics, Education, Law, Nonfiction (General), Regional Interests, Sports, Athletics, Football, Olympics, Soccer
ISBN Prefix(es): 978-91-7151; 978-91-7148
Warehouse: Seelig & Co, Box 1308, Solna
Orders to: Seelig & Co, Box 1308, Solna

Studentlitteratur AB+
Akergranden 1, 226 60 Lund
Mailing Address: Box 141, 221 00 Lund
Tel: (046) 31 20 00 *Fax:* (046) 30 53 38
E-mail: info@studentlitteratur.se
Web Site: www.studentlitteratur.se
Key Personnel
President: Stefan Persson *Tel:* (046) 31 22 77
  E-mail: stefan.persson@studentlitteratur.se
Marketing Dir & Vice President: Magnus Pettersson Roos *Tel:* (046) 31 21 50 *E-mail:* magnus.pettersson.roos@studentlitteratur.se
Publishing Dir: Ronny Pettersson *Tel:* (046) 31 21 74 *E-mail:* ronny.pettersson@studentlitteratur.se; Johanna Thulesius *Tel:* (046) 31 21 35 *E-mail:* johanna.thulesius@studentlitteratur.se
Press: Annie Nyblom *Tel:* (046) 31 21 80
  E-mail: annie.nyblom@studentlitteratur.se
Founded: 1963
Subjects: Accounting, Behavioral Sciences, Biological Sciences, Business, Chemistry, Chemical Engineering, Computer Science, Education, Engineering (General), Government, Political Science, History, Language Arts, Linguistics, Law, Management, Mathematics, Medicine, Nursing, Dentistry, Philosophy, Physical Sciences, Psychology, Psychiatry, Social Sciences, Sociology, Technology
ISBN Prefix(es): 978-91-44; 978-91-88618; 978-91-971791; 978-91-7990
Number of titles published annually: 300 Print
Total Titles: 3,500 Print; 200 Online
Parent Company: Bratt International AB, Lund

Svenska Institutet+
Slottsbacken 10, 103 91 Stockholm
Mailing Address: Box 7434, 103 91 Stockholm
Tel: (08) 453 78 00 *Fax:* (08) 20 72 48
E-mail: si@si.se
Web Site: si.se
Key Personnel
General Dir: Annika Rembe *Tel:* (08) 453 78 10
  E-mail: annika.rembe@si.se
Founded: 1945

Specialize in information about Swedish culture & society in many languages.
Subjects: Environmental Studies, Fashion, Film, Video, Literature, Literary Criticism, Essays, Music, Dance, Photography, Social Sciences, Sociology
ISBN Prefix(es): 978-91-520

Foreningen Svenska Laromedel (FSL) (The Swedish Association of Educational Publishers)
Norrtullsgatan 6, 6 tr, 113 29 Stockholm
Tel: (08) 588 314 00
E-mail: info@svenskalaromedel.se
Web Site: svenskalaromedel.se
Key Personnel
Dir: Rickard Vinde *E-mail:* rickard.vinde@svenskalaromedel.se
Founded: 1974
Publish educational materials in the form of printed educational material, audiovisual educational material, electronic educational material & similar materials.
Membership(s): The Educational Publishers Forum; Federation of European Publishers.
Subjects: Education
ISBN Prefix(es): 978-91-85386; 978-91-633

Tiden, *imprint of* Raben och Sjogren Bokforlag

Tidkort Tryckeriforlaget AB+
Hantverkarvagen 11, 187 66 Taby
Tel: (08) 756 70 90
Subjects: Antiques, Mysteries, Suspense, Wine & Spirits
ISBN Prefix(es): 978-91-970081; 978-91-971201; 978-91-972765

Timbro
Kungsgatan 60, 111 22 Stockholm
Mailing Address: PO Box 3037, 103 61 Stockholm
Tel: (08) 587 898 00
E-mail: info@timbro.se
Web Site: www.timbro.se
Key Personnel
President: Markus Uvell
Founded: 1978
Subjects: Economics, Government, Political Science, Nonfiction (General), Social Sciences, Sociology, Free Enterprise
ISBN Prefix(es): 978-91-7566
Number of titles published annually: 15 Print
Total Titles: 950 Print; 3 E-Book; 1 Audio
Parent Company: Stiftelsen Fritt Naringsliv

Trots Allt, *imprint of* Verbum Forlag AB

Var Skola Forlag AB+
Skarpovagen 2, 185 91 Vaxholm
Tel: (08) 541 301 60 *Fax:* (08) 541 306 90
Subjects: Nonfiction (General)
ISBN Prefix(es): 978-91-7396

Verbum, *imprint of* Verbum Forlag AB

Verbum Forlag AB+
Subsidiary of Berling Media AB
Kungsholmstorg 5, 112 21 Stockholm
Mailing Address: Box 22543, 104 22 Stockholm
Tel: (08) 743 65 00; (08) 743 65 10 (customer service) *Fax:* (08) 644 56 04
E-mail: info@verbum.se
Web Site: webshop.verbumforlag.se
Key Personnel
Publishing Manager: Jonas Eek *Tel:* (08) 743 65 51 *E-mail:* jonas.eek@verbum.se
Business Development & Project Manager: Andreas Stromberg *Tel:* (08) 743 65 04
  E-mail: andreas.stromberg@verbum.se
Founded: 1911
Publisher of theological literature.
Membership(s): FSL; IPA; SBF; Worlddidac.

Subjects: Music, Dance, Religion - Other, Theology
ISBN Prefix(es): 978-91-7098; 978-91-526; 978-91-7852; 978-91-7070; 978-91-7114
Associate Companies: Gleerups Forlag; Forlagshuset Gothia
Imprints: Cordia; Pilgrim; Trots Allt; Verbum
Subsidiaries: Libraria Konsthantverk AB
Bookshop(s): V Hamngatan 21, 411 17 Gothenburg

Volante
Stora Nygatan 7, 111 27 Stockholm
Tel: (08) 702 15 19
E-mail: info@volante.se; press@volante.se
Web Site: volante.se
Key Personnel
President & Group Publisher: Tobias Nielsen
  E-mail: tobias@volante.se
Foreign Rights & Permissions: Simon Brouwers
  E-mail: simon@volante.se
Public Relations: Janna Granesjo *E-mail:* janna@volante.se
Subjects: Fiction, Nonfiction (General)
ISBN Prefix(es): 978-91-87419
Imprints: Bookhouse (management & business); 8tto (research & debate)

Wahlstrom & Widstrand+
Sveavagen 58, nb, 103 63 Stockholm
Mailing Address: Box 3159, 103 63 Stockholm
Tel: (08) 696 84 80 *Fax:* (08) 696 83 80
E-mail: info@wwd.se
Web Site: www.wwd.se
Key Personnel
Deputy, Head of Publishing: Jesper Monthan
  Tel: (08) 696 82 18 *E-mail:* jesper.monthan@bonnierforlagen.se
Marketing: Katarina Arborelius *Tel:* (08) 696 86 84 *E-mail:* katarina.arborelius@bonnierforlagen.se
Founded: 1884
Specialize in novels, poetry, illustrated nature books, travel guides, health, psychology.
Subjects: Fiction, Health, Nutrition, Nonfiction (General), Poetry, Psychology, Psychiatry, Travel & Tourism
ISBN Prefix(es): 978-91-46; 978-91-500; 978-91-614
Parent Company: Bonnierforlagen AB
Foreign Rights: Bonnier Group Agency (worldwide)

B Wahlstroms Bokforlag+
Tryckerigatan 4, 111 28 Stockholm
Mailing Address: PO Box 24167, 104 51 Stockholm
Tel: (08) 728 23 00
Web Site: www.wahlstroms.se
Key Personnel
Chief Executive Officer: Jonas Tellander
  E-mail: jonas.tellander@storytel.com
Head of Print Publishing: Marta Hedener
  E-mail: marta.hedener@wahlstroms.se
Principal Publisher, Children's & Youth Literature: Maja Lindqvist *E-mail:* maja.lindqvbist@wahlstroms.se
Editorial Coordinator: Jill Sundkvist *E-mail:* jill.sundkvist@wahlstroms.se
Founded: 1911
Subjects: Fiction, Nonfiction (General)
ISBN Prefix(es): 978-91-32
Number of titles published annually: 200 Print
Parent Company: Storytel
Associate Companies: Damm Forlag (adult fiction); Ica Bokforlag (nonfiction); Ponto Pocket (paperback)
Branch Office(s)
Jungmansgatan 12, 211 19 Malmo *Tel:* (021) 475 75 00

Book Club(s): Bokklubben Skapargladje; Fantasy Klubben; LivsEnergi/Vitalis
Warehouse: Loevasvaegen 26, 791 29 Falun

Weyler Forlag
Tyska Brinken 19, Gamla stan, 103 16 Stockholm
Mailing Address: PO Box 2262, 103 16 Stockholm
Tel: (08) 648 76 56; (08) 657 95 00
E-mail: info@weylerforlag.se
Web Site: www.weylerforlag.se
Key Personnel
Publisher: Svante Weyler *E-mail:* svante@weylerforlag.se
Production Manager: Cilla Sjoblom
  E-mail: cilla@weylerforlag.se
Marketing, Press & Sales: Maria Sathe
  E-mail: maria@weylerforlag.se
Founded: 2007
Subjects: Fiction, Nonfiction (General), Swedish
ISBN Prefix(es): 978-91-85849

Zindermans Forlag
Ovre Hagnavagen 21, 436 51 Hovas
Tel: (031) 775 04 00 *Fax:* (031) 12 06 60
Key Personnel
Mng Dir: Leif Stigsjoo
Founded: 1960
Subjects: Biography, Memoirs, Fiction, Government, Political Science, History, How-to, Nonfiction (General), Psychology, Psychiatry, Social Sciences, Sociology
ISBN Prefix(es): 978-91-528

Switzerland

General Information

Capital: Bern
Language: 3 official: German, French and Italian
Religion: Protestant and Roman Catholic
Population: 6.8 million
Bank Hours: 0800 or 0830-1200 or 1230, 1300 or 1330-1630 Monday-Friday
Shop Hours: 0800-1200, 1330-1830 Monday-Friday; in most cities, closed Monday morning; 0800-1200, 1330-1600 or 1700 Saturday
Currency: 100 rappen (centimes) = 1 Swiss franc
Export/Import Information: Member of the European Free Trade Association. No tariff on books. Most books exempt from Turnover Tax. Advertising matter usually dutiable, some exempt from Turnover Tax. 2% VAT on books. No import licenses required. No exchange controls.
Copyright: UCC, Berne, Florence (see Copyright Conventions, pg viii)

Abegg-Stiftung
Werner Abeggstr 67, 3132 Riggisberg
Mailing Address: Postfach, 3132 Riggisberg
Tel: (031) 808 12 01 *Fax:* (031) 808 12 00
E-mail: info@abegg-stiftung.ch
Web Site: www.abegg-stiftung.ch
Key Personnel
Contact: Dr Henry Hohmann *E-mail:* hohmann@abegg-stiftung.ch
Founded: 1961
Subjects: Art, Textile Art
ISBN Prefix(es): 978-3-905014

Academic Press Fribourg+
Perolles 42, 1700 Fribourg
Tel: (026) 426 43 31 *Fax:* (026) 426 43 11
E-mail: info@paulusedition.ch
Web Site: www.paulusedition.ch/academic_press
Key Personnel
Dir: Jean-Bernard Repond

Assistant Dir: Maurice Greder
Publishing Dir: Hans Thomas
Sales Manager: Manon Catillaz
Founded: 1873
Subjects: Art, Economics, Ethnicity, Government, Political Science, History, Law, Literature, Literary Criticism, Essays, Medicine, Nursing, Dentistry, Music, Dance, Philosophy, Psychology, Psychiatry, Religion - Other, Social Sciences, Sociology, Theology
ISBN Prefix(es): 978-3-7278; 978-2-8271
Parent Company: Paulus Verlag-Editions Saint-Paul Fribourg
Bookshop(s): Librairie et Edition de la Suisse Romande

ADIRA+
Rue du Rhone 29, 1204 Geneva
Tel: (022) 312 25 43 *Fax:* (022) 312 26 13
E-mail: adira@adira.net
Web Site: www.adira.net
Key Personnel
President: Dominique Mottas
Author: Michel Potay
Founded: 1985
Also acts as distributor.
Subjects: Inspirational, Spirituality, Philosophy, Religion - Other, Self-Help
ISBN Prefix(es): 978-2-901821 (Maison de la Revelation); 978-2-9700584 (ADIRA)
Number of titles published annually: 2 Print
Total Titles: 12 Print
Parent Company: Editions Michel Potay
Ultimate Parent Company: Maison de la Revelation
U.S. Office(s): ADIRA Inc, 590 Madison Ave, 21st floor, New York, NY 10022, United States
Distributed by Biramo Books (Australia & New Zealand); Gazelle Book Services (North Europe & UK); Ingram (USA); Pathway Book Service (North America)

Adonia-Verlag+
Trinerweg 3, 4805 Brittnau
Tel: (062) 746 86 46 *Fax:* (062) 746 86 47
E-mail: info@adonia.ch; order@adonia.ch
Web Site: www.adonia.ch
Key Personnel
Mng Dir: Markus Hottiger *Tel:* (062) 746 86 41
  E-mail: markus.hottiger@adonia.ch
Founded: 1986
Specialize in music performance materials.
Membership(s): SBVV; SSV.
Subjects: Music, Dance, Poetry, Women's Studies
ISBN Prefix(es): 978-3-905009
Branch Office(s)
CP 3923, 64052-970 Teresina-PL, Brazil
  E-mail: info@adonia.com.br *Web Site:* www.adonia.com.br
Windelbachstr 9, 76228 Karlsruhe, Germany, Contact: Markus Heusser *Tel:* (0721) 5600 99 10 *Fax:* (0721) 5600 99 110 *E-mail:* info@adonia.de *Web Site:* www.adonia.de
Rua da Ingreja Matriz, lote 5, Urbanizacao dos Carvalhos, 2950-422 Palmela, Portugal *Tel:* 210 887 638 *Fax:* 210 887 638 *E-mail:* info@adonia.pt *Web Site:* www.adonia.pt

Editions L'Age d'Homme
2-4, ave du Theatre, 1002 Lausanne
Mailing Address: CP 5076, 1002 Lausanne
Tel: (021) 312 00 95 *Fax:* (021) 320 84 40
E-mail: info@agedhomme.com; admin@agedhomme.com
Web Site: www.lagedhomme.com
Founded: 1966
Subjects: Art, Biography, Memoirs, Drama, Theater, Fiction, Film, Video, Literature, Literary Criticism, Essays, Music, Dance, Philosophy, Poetry, Psychology, Psychiatry, Regional Interests, Religion - Other, Science Fiction, Fantasy, Social Sciences, Sociology

ISBN Prefix(es): 978-2-8251
Branch Office(s)
5, rue Ferou, 75006 Paris, France *Tel:* 01
55 42 79 79 *Fax:* 01 40 51 71 02
E-mail: lagedhomme@orange.fr
Bookshop(s): Librairie Rameau d'Or, 17, blvd
Georges-Favon, 1204 Geneva *Tel:* (022) 310 26
33 *Fax:* (022) 781 45 90 *E-mail:* rameaudor@
bluewin.ch
Distribution Center: Les Belles Lettres, 25, rue
du General Leclerc, 94270 Le Kremlin Bicetre,
France *Tel:* 01 45 15 19 70 *Fax:* 01 45 15 19
80 (Belgium & France)
Edipresse Inc, 945, ave Beaumont, Montreal,
QC H3N 1W3, Canada *Tel:* 514-273-6141
Fax: 514-273-7021 *E-mail:* information@
edipresse.ca (Canada)

Akanthus
Boendlerstr 49, 8802 Kilchberg
Tel: (044) 715 59 73 *Fax:* (044) 715 37 34
E-mail: akanthus@bluewin.ch
Web Site: www.akanthus.ch
Founded: 1989
Subjects: Archaeology, History, Ancient Cultural
History
ISBN Prefix(es): 978-3-905083

Allinti Verlag GmbH
Baslerstr 31, 4123 Allschwil
E-mail: verlag@allinti.ch
Web Site: www.allinti.ch
Key Personnel
Owner: Anouk Claes
Publishing Manager: Eckhard Graf *E-mail:* eg@
allinti.ch
Founded: 2006
Subjects: Inspirational, Spirituality, Self-Help
ISBN Prefix(es): 978-3-905836

Appenzeller Verlag
Kasernenstr 64, 9101 Herisau
Mailing Address: Postfach 61, 9101 Herisau
Tel: (071) 354 64 64 *Fax:* (071) 354 64 65
E-mail: verlag@appenzellerverlag.ch
Web Site: www.appenzellerverlag.ch
Key Personnel
Publisher: Marcel Steiner *Tel:* (071) 354 64 04
Fax: (071) 354 64 05 *E-mail:* marcel.steiner@
appenzellerverlag.ch
Production: Josef Scheuber *Tel:* (071) 354 64 60
Fax: (071) 354 64 87 *E-mail:* josef.scheuber@
appenzellerverlag.ch
Administration: Christine Burkart *Tel:* (071) 354
64 37 *Fax:* (071) 354 64 05 *E-mail:* christine.
burkart@appenzellerverlag.ch
Founded: 1974
Subjects: Animals, Pets, Art, Biography, Mem-
oirs, Cookery, History, Regional Interests, Na-
ture
ISBN Prefix(es): 978-3-85882
Distribution Center: Herold Auslieferung und
Service GmbH, Raiffeisenallee 10, 82041
Oberhaching, Germany *Tel:* (089) 61 38 71-
0 *Fax:* (089) 61 38 71-20 *E-mail:* herold@
herold-va.de *Web Site:* www.herold-va.de (Austria & Germany)
Schweizer Buchzentrum, Industriestra Ost
10, 4614 Hagendorf *Tel:* (062) 209 27
04 *Fax:* (062) 209 27 60 *E-mail:* aerni@
buchzentrum.ch *Web Site:* www.buchzentrum.ch
(Switzerland)

aracari verlag ag
Schuetzengasse 4, 8001 Zurich
Tel: (043) 497 69 79
E-mail: mails@aracari.ch
Web Site: www.aracari.ch; www.facebook.com/
aracariverlag/
Key Personnel
Founder & Publisher: Andreas Gerber *E-mail:* a.
gerber@aracari.ch

Founded: 2009
ISBN Prefix(es): 978-3-905945
Foreign Rep(s): Buchnetzwerk Verlagsvertretung
(Guenther Staudinger & Marlene Pobegen)
(Austria)
Distribution Center: AVA Verlagsauslieferung
AG, Centralweg 16, 8910 Affoltern am Al-
bis *Tel:* (044) 762 42 00 *Fax:* (044) 762 42 10
E-mail: avainfo@ava.ch
Mohr Morawa Buchvertrieb GmbH, Sulzengasse
2, 1230 Vienna, Austria *Tel:* (01) 680 14-
0 *Fax:* (01) 688 71 30 *E-mail:* bestellung@
mohrmorawa.at
Runge Verlagsauslieferung GmbH, Bergstr 2,
33803 Steinhagen, Germany *Tel:* (05204) 998
124 *Fax:* (05204) 998 114 *E-mail:* team4@
rungeva.de

Archivio Storico Ticinese
Via del Bramantino 3, 6500 Bellinzona
Tel: (091) 820 0101 *Fax:* (091) 825 1874
E-mail: info@archiviostoricoticinese.ch
Web Site: www.archiviostoricoticinese.ch
Key Personnel
Co-Founder & Editor: Libero Casagrande
Founded: 1960
Subjects: Art, Economics, History, Literature, Lit-
erary Criticism, Essays
ISBN Prefix(es): 978-88-7714
Parent Company: Edizioni Casagrande SA

AS Verlag
Turbinenweg 6, 8866 Ziegelbruecke
Tel: (044) 300 23 23 *Fax:* (044) 300 23 24
E-mail: mail@as-verlag.ch
Web Site: www.as-verlag.ch
Key Personnel
Publishing Dir, Administration & Sales: Iris
Becher *Tel:* (044) 300 23 21 *E-mail:* becher@
as-verlag.ch
Publishing Dir, Graphics & Book Design: Urs
Bolz *Tel:* (044) 300 23 22 *E-mail:* bolz@as-
verlag.ch
Publishing Dir, Production & Sales: Matthias We-
ber *Tel:* (044) 300 39 08 *E-mail:* weber@as-
verlag.ch
Publisher: Heinz von Arx *Tel:* (044) 300 39 09
E-mail: vonarx@as-verlag.ch; Peter Schnyder
Tel: (044) 300 23 22 *E-mail:* schnyder@as-
verlag.ch
Founded: 1991
Subjects: Art, Photography, Sports, Athletics
ISBN Prefix(es): 978-3-905111; 978-3-909111
Distribution Center: Baumgartner Buecher
AG, c/o AVA Verlagsauslieferung, Cen-
tralweg 16, Postfach 74, 8910 Affoltern
Tel: (044) 762 42 80 *Fax:* (044) 762 42 85
E-mail: baumgartner@ava.ch
AS-Hoeller GmbH Verlagsservice, Schrackgasse
11 a, 8650 Kindberg, Austria *Tel:* (03865)
44880 *Fax:* (03865) 44880-77 *E-mail:* office@
ashoeller.com
PROLIT Verlagsauslieferung GmbH, Siemensstr
16, 35463 Fernwald-Annerod, Germany
Tel: (0641) 943 93 201 *Fax:* (0641) 943 93
89 *E-mail:* g.lemuth@prolit.de

**Association pour la Diffusion Internationale de
la Revelation d'Ares**, see ADIRA

Astrodata AG+
Chilenholzstr 8, 8907 Wettswill
Tel: (043) 343 33 33 *Fax:* (043) 343 33 43
E-mail: info@astrodata.ch
Web Site: www.astrodata.com
Key Personnel
Owner & Founder: Claude Weiss
Founded: 1978
Subjects: Astrology, Occult, Psychology, Psychia-
try

ISBN Prefix(es): 978-3-907029
Distributor for Edition Astrodata; Edition As-
troterra

AT Verlag+
Division of AZ Fachverlage AG
Bahnhofstr 41, 5000 Aarau
Tel: (058) 200 44 00 *Fax:* (058) 200 44 01
E-mail: info@at-verlag.ch
Web Site: www.at-verlag.ch
Key Personnel
Editorial Dir: Urs Hunziker *E-mail:* urs.
hunziker@azmedien.ch
Editorial: Monika Schmidhofer *E-mail:* monika.
schmidhofer@azmedien.ch
Production: Adrian Pabst *E-mail:* adrian.pabst@
azmedien.ch; Heidy Schuppisser *E-mail:* heidy.
schuppisser@azmedien.ch; Tanja Weber
E-mail: tanja.weber@azmedien.ch
Sales: Christine Gutknecht *E-mail:* christine.
gutknecht@azmedien.ch
Sales & Marketing: Anne-Catherine Schuermann
E-mail: anne-catherine@azmedien.ch
Press: Brigitte Bosshard Bordoni *E-mail:* brigitte.
bosshard@azmedien.ch
Founded: 1967
Book publishing section of Aargauer Zeitung AG.
Subjects: Cookery, Health, Nutrition, How-to, Re-
gional Interests
ISBN Prefix(es): 978-3-905214; 978-3-85502;
978-3-03800
Number of titles published annually: 50 Print; 10
E-Book
Total Titles: 480 Print; 72 E-Book; 2 Audio
Branch Office(s)
AT Verlag Deutschland/Oesterreich, Fruchthof,
Gotzinger Str 52b, Munich 750 199, Germany,
Contact: Dr Michael Guenther *Tel:* (089) 767
567 10 *Fax:* (089) 767 567 11 *E-mail:* michael.
guenther@atverlag.de
Warehouse: Grafische Betriebe Aargauer Zeitung
AG, Neumattstr 1/Betrieb Telli, 5004 Aarau
Distribution Center: Buchzentrum AG,
Industriestr Ost 10, Haegendorf 4614
Tel: (062) 209 25 25 *Fax:* (062) 209 26 27
E-mail: kundendienst@buchzentrum.ch *Web
Site:* www.buchzentrum.ch
Dr Franz Hain Verlagsauslieferungen, Dr-
Otto-Neurath-Gasse 5, Vienna 1220, Austria
Tel: (01) 282 65 77 *Fax:* (01) 282 52 82
E-mail: bestell@hain.at
Brockhaus/Commission, Kreidlerstr 9, Kornwes-
theim 70806, Germany *Tel:* (07154) 13 27
0 *Fax:* (07154) 13 2713 *E-mail:* atverlag@
brocom.de *Web Site:* www.brocom.de

Atlantis Musikbuch-Verlag AG+
Subsidiary of Schott Musik GmbH & Co KG
Zollikerstr 87, 8008 Zurich
Tel: (043) 499 86 60; (043) 499 86 61 *Fax:* (043)
499 86 62
E-mail: info@atlantismusik.ch
Web Site: www.atlantismusik.ch
Key Personnel
Contact: Nicole Froidevaux *E-mail:* nicole.
froidevaux@atlantismusik.ch
Founded: 1976
Subjects: Music, Dance
ISBN Prefix(es): 978-3-254

Atlantis Verlag, *imprint of* Orell Fuessli Verlag
AG

Atlantis-Verlag AG
Imprint of Orell Fuessli Verlag AG
Dietzingerstr 3, 8036 Zurich
Tel: (044) 466 77 11 *Fax:* (044) 466 74 12
E-mail: info@ofv.ch
Web Site: www.ofv.ch
Key Personnel
Mng Dir: Dr Matti Schuesseler *E-mail:* matti.
schuesseler@ofv.ch

Editor: Hans ten Doornkaat *E-mail:* hans.
tendoornkaat@ofv.ch
Founded: 1930
Subjects: Art, Geography, Geology, Nonfiction
(General), Parenting
ISBN Prefix(es): 978-3-7611

AURA Foto Film Verlag GmbH
Gerliswilstr 23, 6020 Emmenbruecke
Tel: (041) 420 65 65
E-mail: info@aura.ch
Web Site: www.aura.ch; www.aurabooks.ch
Key Personnel
Publisher: Emanuel Ammon *E-mail:* emanuel.
ammon@aura.ch
Subjects: Photography
ISBN Prefix(es): 978-3-9523375; 978-3-906105
Total Titles: 12 Print

Aurora Production AG
Tellsgasse 18, 6460 Altdorf
Tel: (041) 7201531 *Fax:* (041) 7106745
E-mail: info@auroraproduction.com; aurora@
auroraproduction.com
Web Site: www.auroraproduction.com
Founded: 1999
Subjects: Education, Inspirational, Spirituality
ISBN Prefix(es): 978-3-03730; 978-3-905332
Foreign Rep(s): Activated Ministries (USA);
Aurora Print SRL (Romania); Big Thot Pub-
lications (South Africa); Channel of Hope
(Philippines); Coloring the World Produc-
tions (Canada); Comece Cedo Comercio
Ltda (Brazil); Conectate AC (Mexico); Es-
Futuro (Spain); Masterlight Co Ltd (Japan);
Red Conectate (Chile); TreasureChest-Verlag-
Christian Krieg (Switzerland)

Editions de la Baconnière SA+
Division of Groupe Medecine & Hygiene
4 rue Maunoir, 1207 Geneva
Tel: (079) 653 69 17
Web Site: www.editions-baconnierre.ch
Key Personnel
Contact: Laurence Gudin *E-mail:* laurence.
gudin@editions-baconniere.ch
Founded: 1927
Subjects: Art, Biography, Memoirs, History, Mu-
sic, Dance, Philosophy, Poetry, Social Sciences,
Sociology
ISBN Prefix(es): 978-2-8252; 978-2-915306

Baeschlin Buecher AG+
Hauptstr 32, 8750 Glarus
Tel: (055) 640 11 25 *Fax:* (055) 640 65 94
E-mail: office@baeschlin.ch
Web Site: www.lesestoff.ch
Founded: 1853
Subjects: General
ISBN Prefix(es): 978-3-85546
Showroom(s): Schiffslaende 26, 2 Stock, 8001
Zurich Tel: (044) 209 91 11 Fax: (044) 209 91
12
Warehouse: Schiffslaende 26, 2 Stock, 8001
Zurich Tel: (044) 209 91 11 Fax: (044) 209
91 12

Baobab Books
Jurastr 49, 4053 Basel
Tel: (061) 333 27 27; (061) 333 27 25 *Fax:* (061)
333 27 26
E-mail: info@baobabbooks.ch
Web Site: www.baobabbooks.ch
Key Personnel
Editor: Sonja Matheson
Press: Lydia Zimmer
Founded: 1983
Editor of children's books from Africa, Asia &
Latin America.
Subjects: Literature, Literary Criticism, Essays,
Picture Books

Number of titles published annually: 3 Print
Total Titles: 60 Print
Distribution Center: Buchzentrum AG,
Industriestr Ost 10, 4614 Haegendorf
Tel: (062) 209 26 26 *Fax:* (062) 209 26 27
E-mail: kundendienst@buchzentrum.ch
Medienlogistik Pichler-OEBZ GmbH & Co KG,
IZ-NOE Sued, Str 1, Objekt 34, 2355 Wiener
Neudorf, Austria *Tel:* (02236) 635 352 90
Fax: (02236) 635 352 43 *E-mail:* bestellen@
medien-logistik.at
MSR Runge Verlagsauslieferung GmbH, Bergstr
2, 33803 Steinhagen, Germany *Tel:* (05204)
998 123 *Fax:* (05204) 998 111 *E-mail:* msr@
rungeva.de

Belser Reich Verlag AG+
Werchlaubengaessli 8, 6004 Lucerne
Tel: (041) 4103721 *Fax:* (041) 4103227
Key Personnel
Mng Dir: Alfons Wueest
Founded: 1974
Subjects: Photography
ISBN Prefix(es): 978-3-7243
Number of titles published annually: 8 Print
Total Titles: 60 Print

Benteli Verlag AG+
Member of bsmediagroup
Steinackerstr 8, 8583 Sulgen
Tel: (071) 644 91 31 *Fax:* (071) 644 91 39
E-mail: info@benteli.ch
Web Site: www.benteli.ch
Key Personnel
Publisher: Markus Sebastian Braun
E-mail: braun@benteli.ch
Chief Editor: Chris van Uffelen *E-mail:* uffelen@
benteli.ch
Editorial: Sophie Steybe *E-mail:* steybe@benteli.
ch
Sales & Distribution: Stephan Goetz
E-mail: goetz@benteli.ch
Founded: 1899
Subjects: Art, History, Photography, Culture
ISBN Prefix(es): 978-3-7165
Number of titles published annually: 35 Print
Total Titles: 350 Print
Associate Companies: Archithese; Heer Druck;
Neue Anzeiger; Verlag Niggili AG; SmartPub-
lishing
Foreign Rep(s): Hans Frieden (Germany); Gio-
vanni Ravasio (Switzerland); Helga Schuster
(Austria)
Distribution Center: AVA / buch 2000 Ver-
lagsauslieferung, Centralweg 16, 8910 Af-
foltern am Albis *Tel:* (044) 762 42 60
Fax: (044) 762 42 10 *E-mail:* verlagsservice@
ava.ch
GVA Goettingen GmbH & Co KG, Post-
fach 2021, 37010 Goettingen, Germany
Tel: (0551) 487 177 *Fax:* (0551) 41 392
E-mail: bestellung@gva-verlage.de (Germany
& Austria)
Interart Sarl, One, rue de l'Est, 75020 Paris,
France *Tel:* 01 43 49 36 60 *Fax:* 01 43 49 41
22 *E-mail:* commercial@interart.fr
Coen Sligting Bookimport, Groot Nieuwland 27,
1811 ET Alkmaar, Netherlands *Tel:* (072) 511
92 20 *Fax:* (072) 511 70 29 *E-mail:* sligting@
xs4all.nl
ACC, 6 West 18 St, 4th floor, New York, NY
10011, United States *Tel:* 212-645-1111
Fax: 212-989-3205 *E-mail:* sales@antiquecc.
com (USA & Canada)
ACC, Sandy Lane, Old Martlesham, Wood-
bridge, Suffolk IP12 4SD, United Kingdom
Tel: (01394) 389 950 *Fax:* (01394) 389 999
E-mail: sales@antique-acc.com (all other countries)

Beobachter Buchverlag, see Jean Frey AG,
Beobachter Buchverlag

Berchtold Haller Verlag (BHV)+
Laengackerweg 18, 3048 Worblaufen
Mailing Address: PO Box 101, 3048 Worblaufen
Tel: (031) 330 46 44 *Fax:* (031) 330 46 40
E-mail: verlag@egw.ch
Web Site: www.egw.ch; www.theologische.ch
Key Personnel
President: Thomas Gerber
Publishing Dir: Peter Schranz *E-mail:* peter.
schranz@egw.ch
Founded: 1848
Subjects: Religion - Protestant, Romance, Theol-
ogy
ISBN Prefix(es): 978-3-85570
Number of titles published annually: 3 Print
Total Titles: 40 Print; 13 Audio
Parent Company: Evangelisches Gemeinschaf-
swerk (EGW)

Bergli Books AG+
Falknerstr 13, 4001 Basel
Tel: (061) 373 27 77 *Fax:* (061) 373 27 78
E-mail: info@bergli.ch
Web Site: www.bergli.ch
Key Personnel
Mng Dir: Dianne Dicks
Founded: 1990
Publisher of books in English that focus on life in
Switzerland, collections of writing that explain
the essence of living in Switzerland & thriving
on diversity.
Subjects: Behavioral Sciences, Cookery, Ethnicity,
Foreign Countries, Human Relations, Humor,
Language Arts, Linguistics, Literature, Liter-
ary Criticism, Essays, Nonfiction (General),
Regional Interests, Travel & Tourism, Cultural
Diversity
ISBN Prefix(es): 978-3-9520002; 978-3-905252

Beroea-Verlag
Zellerstr 61, 8038 Zurich
Tel: (044) 480 13 13 *Fax:* (044) 480 13 12
E-mail: info@beroea.ch
Web Site: www.beroea.ch
Founded: 1957
Subjects: Biblical Studies, Religion - Protestant
ISBN Prefix(es): 978-3-905335; 978-3-905336;
978-3-909337

Editions Medicales Roland Bettex
Rue des Fontenailles 3, 1000 Lausanne 6
Tel: (021) 616 66 10; (076) 334 76 92 (cell)
E-mail: rbettex@comedition.ch
Web Site: www.comedition.ch
Key Personnel
Founder: Bettex Roland
Subjects: Genealogy, Medicine, Nursing, Den-
tistry, Psychology, Psychiatry
ISBN Prefix(es): 978-2-88113

Galerie Beyeler AG
Baeumleingasse 101, 4125 Riehen
Tel: (061) 206 97 00 *Fax:* (061) 206 97 19
E-mail: kommunikation@fondationbeyeler.ch;
publikationen@fondationbeyeler.ch; info@
fondationbeyeler.ch
Web Site: www.fondationbeyeler.ch
Key Personnel
Owner: Ernst Beyeler
Head, Publications: Delia Ciuha
Publications Assistant: Franziska Stegmann
Founded: 1967
Subjects: Art
ISBN Prefix(es): 978-3-85575; 978-3-9520156

BHV, see Berchtold Haller Verlag (BHV)

Bibellesebund eV+
Industriestr 1, Postfach, 8404 Winterthur
Tel: (052) 245 14 45 *Fax:* (052) 245 14 46
E-mail: info@bibellesebund.ch

Web Site: www.bibellesebund.ch
Key Personnel
Dir: Markus Giger *Tel:* (052) 245 14 40
    E-mail: markus.giger@bibellesebund.ch
Public Relations & Assistant Mng Dir: Sonja
    Meier *E-mail:* sonja.meier@bibellesebund.ch
Founded: 1930
Scripture union of Switzerland & Germany.
Subjects: Religion - Protestant
ISBN Prefix(es): 978-3-87982
Branch Office(s)
Industriestr 2, 51709 Marienheide, Germany
    Tel: (02264) 40434-0 *Fax:* (02264) 40434-39
    E-mail: info@bibellesebund.de *Web Site:* www.
    bibellesebund.de

La Bibliotheque des Arts+
Ave de Rumine 55, 1005 Lausanne
Tel: (021) 312 36 67 *Fax:* (021) 312 36 15
E-mail: webmaster@bibliotheque-des-arts.com
Web Site: www.bibliotheque-des-arts.com
Founded: 1954
Subjects: Architecture & Interior Design, Art,
    Literature, Literary Criticism, Essays, Poetry,
    Travel & Tourism
ISBN Prefix(es): 978-2-85047; 978-2-88453
Distribution Center: Volumen, 69, rue de Vaugi-
    rard, 75006 Paris, France *Tel:* 01 44 10 75 75
    E-mail: volumen@volumen.fr

bilgerverlag GmbH
Josefstr 52, 8005 Zurich
Tel: (044) 271 81 46 *Fax:* (044) 271 14 44
E-mail: info@bilgerverlag.ch; presse@
    bilgerverlag.ch
Web Site: www.bilgerverlag.ch
Key Personnel
Owner & Mng Dir: Ricco Bilger *E-mail:* bilger@
    bilgerverlag.ch
Subjects: Literature, Literary Criticism, Essays,
    Swiss Literature
ISBN Prefix(es): 978-3-908010; 978-3-03762
Distribution Center: Buchzentrum AG, Indus-
    triestr East 10, 4614 Haegendorf, Contact:
    Regula Aerni *Tel:* (062) 209 27 04 *Fax:* (062)
    209 27 60 *E-mail:* aerni@buchzentrum.ch *Web
    Site:* www.buchzentrum.ch
GVA Gemeinsame Verlagsauslieferung, Post-
    fach 2021, 37010, Goettingen, Germany
    Tel: (0551) 48 71 77 *Fax:* (0551) 4 13 92
    E-mail: bestellungen@gva-verlage.de

Birkhauser Verlag GmbH+
Imprint of Walter de Gruyter GmbH & Co KG
Allschwilerstr 10, 4055 Basel
Toll Free Tel: (061) 306 17 00 *Fax:* (061) 306 17
    01
E-mail: editorial@birkhauser.ch
Web Site: www.birkhauser.com
Key Personnel
Senior Editorial Dir Art & Architecture:
    Dr Ulrich Schmidt *Tel:* (061) 306 17 02
    E-mail: ulrich.schmidt@birkhauser.ch
Editor: Annette Gref *Tel:* (061) 306 17 05
    E-mail: annette.gref@birkhauser.ch; Alexander
    Felix *Tel:* (061) 306 17 04 *E-mail:* alexander.
    felix@birkhauser.ch; David Marold *Tel:* (01)
    353 60 00-35 *E-mail:* david.marold@
    birkhauser.ch
Editor / Project Editor: Angela Foessl *Tel:* (01)
    353 60 00-31 *E-mail:* angela.foessl@
    birkhauser.ch
Project Editor: Angelika Heller *Tel:* (01) 353
    60 00-33 *E-mail:* angelika.heller@birkhauser.
    ch; Katharina Kulke *Tel:* (061) 306 17 07
    E-mail: katharina.kulke@birkhauser.ch; Odine
    Osswald *Tel:* (061) 306 17 06 *E-mail:* odine.
    osswald@birkhauser.ch; Petra Schmid
    Tel: (061) 306 17 10 *E-mail:* petra.schmid@
    birkhauser.ch
Assistant: Florina Ionescu *Tel:* (061) 306 17 03
    E-mail: florina.ionescu@birkhauser.ch

Founded: 1879
Subjects: Architecture & Interior Design, Biolog-
    ical Sciences, Computer Science, Engineering
    (General), Environmental Studies, Mathematics,
    Physics, History of Science
ISBN Prefix(es): 978-0-8176; 978-3-7643; 978-3-
    0346; 978-3-03821
Number of titles published annually: 200 Print
Associate Companies: Lars Mueller Publish-
    ers GmbH, Stadtturmstr 19, 5400, Baden
    Tel: (056) 430 17 40 *Fax:* (056) 430 17 41
    E-mail: books@lars-muller.ch *Web Site:* www.
    lars-muller-publishers.com
U.S. Office(s): Birkhauser Publishing Ltd, 233
    Spring St, New York, NY 10013, United
    States, Product Manager: Linda Lorusso
    Tel: 212-460-1500 *E-mail:* service@birkhauser.
    com *Web Site:* www.birkhauser.com
Distributor for Princeton Architectural Press
    (Asia, UK & USA)

Blaukreuz-Verlag Bern+
Lindenrain 5a, 3012 Bern
Tel: (031) 300 58 66 *Fax:* (031) 300 58 69
E-mail: verlag@blaueskreuz.ch
Web Site: www.blaukreuzverlag.ch
Key Personnel
Publishing Dir: Lars Lepperhoff
Founded: 1884
Publishes for the Blue Cross health & religious
    movement.
Subjects: Biography, Memoirs, Health, Nutrition,
    Religion - Protestant, Religion - Other, Addic-
    tion Problems
ISBN Prefix(es): 978-3-85580
Parent Company: Blaues Kreuz der deutschen
    Schweiz

Theodor Boder Verlag
Rifeldweg 18, 4322 Mumpf
Tel: (079) 566 81 84 *Fax:* (079) 566 81 84
E-mail: info@boderverlag.ch
Web Site: www.boderverlag.ch
Key Personnel
Owner: Theodor Boder
Manager: Susanna Schlegel
Founded: 2004
Subjects: Drama, Theater, Fiction, Mysteries, Sus-
    pense
ISBN Prefix(es): 978-3-9521993; 978-3-905802

Bohem Press AG+
Ramistr 5, 8001 Zurich
Tel: (044) 253 6270 *Fax:* (043) 268 2299
E-mail: info@bohem.ch; ruland@bohem.ch
Web Site: www.bohem.ch
Key Personnel
Board: Hartmut Fromm; Alexander Herbert
Founded: 1973
Subjects: Animals, Pets, Art, Child Care & De-
    velopment, Fiction
ISBN Prefix(es): 978-3-85581
Number of titles published annually: 10 Print
Total Titles: 120 Print

Braun Publishing AG
Arenenbergstr 2, 8268 Salenstein
Tel: (044) 586 11 97 *Fax:* (071) 664 31 32
E-mail: info@braun-publishing.ch
Web Site: www.braun-publishing.ch
Key Personnel
Publisher: Markus Sebastian Braun
Sales & Distribution: Stephan Goetz
    E-mail: goetz@braun-publishing.ch
Founded: 2000
Subjects: Architecture & Interior Design, Con-
    temporary History, Design, Urban Planning
ISBN Prefix(es): 978-3-938780

Braun Publishing AG
Arenenbergstr 2, 8268 Salenstein

Tel: (044) 586 11 97 *Fax:* (071) 664 31 32
E-mail: info@braun-publishing.ch
Web Site: www.braun-publishing.ch
Key Personnel
Publisher: Markus Sebastian Braun
Head, Sales & Distribution: Stephan Goetz
    E-mail: goetz@braun-publishing.ch
Subjects: Architecture & Interior Design, Design,
    Urban Development
ISBN Prefix(es): 978-3-03768
Distribution Center: Leipziger Kommissions- und
    Grossbuchhandelsgesellschaft mbH (LKG), An
    der Suedspitze 1-12, 04571 Roetha, Germany,
    Contact: Martina Koernig *Tel:* (034206) 65 10-
    6 *Fax:* (034206) 65 17-41 *E-mail:* mkoernig@
    lkg-service.de *Web Site:* www.lkg-va.de

Briefmarken Zumstein & Cie (Stamps Zumstein
    & Co)
Zeughausgasse 24, 3000 Bern 7
Tel: (031) 312 00 55 *Fax:* (031) 312 23 26
E-mail: post_zumstein@briefmarken.ch
Web Site: www.briefmarken.ch
Key Personnel
Contact: Christoph Hertsch
Founded: 1905
Subjects: Crafts, Games, Hobbies, Philately
ISBN Prefix(es): 978-3-909278; 978-3-85994

Brunnen Verlag Basel+
Wallstr 6, 4051 Basel
Tel: (061) 295 60 00 *Fax:* (061) 295 60 69
E-mail: info@brunnen-verlag.ch
Web Site: www.brunnen-verlag.ch
Key Personnel
Chief Executive Officer & Publisher: Dr Dominik
    Klenk
Head, Editorial Dept: Christian Meyer
Founded: 1921
Christian books.
Subjects: Biography, Memoirs, Child Care & De-
    velopment, Fiction, How-to, Nonfiction (Gen-
    eral), Religion - Other, Self-Help
ISBN Prefix(es): 978-3-7655
Bookshop(s): Buchhandlung Pilgermission,
    Spalenweg 20, 4002 Basel; Sunnaewirbel,
    Buecher & Geschenke, Olympstr 4, 6440
    Brunnen; Brunnen-Buchhandlung, Marktgasse
    31, 8180 Buelach; Brunnen-Buchhandlung,
    St Gallerstr 6, 8500 Frauenfeld; Senfkorn-
    Laden, Hauptstr 33, 5262 Frick; Libreria La
    Fonte, Viale Stazione 1, 6512 Giubiasco;
    Buechegge AG, Loewengasse 37, 8810 Hor-
    gen; Christlicher Buecherladen zur Arche,
    Amtshausgasse 10, 4410 Liestal; Evange-
    lische Buchhandlung, Haupstr 25, 5734
    Reinach AG; Christliche Buchhandlung, Ave
    Mercier de Molin 1, 3960 Sierre; Christliche
    Buchhandlung, Bahnhofstr 42, 6210 Sursee;
    Christliche Buchhandlung, Susann-Muellerstr
    14, 9630 Wattwil; Christliche Buchhandlung
    "Brunne-Stube", Schmidstr 3, 8570 Wein-
    felden; Brunnen-Buchhandlung, untere Bah-
    nofstr 20, 9500 Wil; Christliche Buchhandlung,
    Herti-Zentrum, 6300 Zug

Nadja Brykina Gallery AG
Sihlstr 91, 8001 Zurich
Tel: (044) 222 05 05
E-mail: info@brykina.com
Web Site: www.brykina.com
Subjects: Art, Modern Russian Art
ISBN Prefix(es): 978-3-9523523
Branch Office(s)
Myasnitskaja 24, 101000 Moscow, Russia
    Tel: (495) 669 17 34

Bundesamt fuer Landestopografie, Swisstopo
Seftigenstr 264, Postfach, 3084 Wabern
Tel: (058) 469 01 11 *Fax:* (058) 469 04 59
E-mail: info@swisstopo.ch; mapsales@swisstopo.
    ch
Web Site: www.swisstopo.ch

Subjects: Outdoor Recreation, Sports, Athletics, Hiking, Switzerland
ISBN Prefix(es): 978-3-302; 978-3-7176
Branch Office(s)
METAS Bldg, Lindenweg 50, 3084 Wabern
Tel: (058) 464 73 03 *Fax:* (058) 469 02 97
E-mail: infovd@swisstopo.ch
Militaerflugplatz, 8600 Duebendorf
Tel: (044) 801 14 60 *Fax:* (044) 801 14 69
E-mail: flugdienst@swisstopo.ch

Les Cahiers de la Renaissance Vaudoise
Pl Grand-St-Jean 1, 1002 Lausanne
Mailing Address: CP 6724, 1002 Lausanne
Tel: (021) 312 19 14 *Fax:* (021) 312 67 14
E-mail: courrier@ligue-vaudoise.ch
Web Site: www.ligue-vaudoise.ch
Key Personnel
President: Olivier Delacretaz
Founded: 1926
Subjects: Government, Political Science, History
ISBN Prefix(es): 978-2-88017
Orders to: CP 142, 1814 La Tour-de-Peilz

Cantate Domino, see Editions Schola Cantorum
- Charles Huguenin-Pro Arte - Cantate Domino

Cardun AG+
Obergasse 34 Postfach, 8402 Winterthur
Tel: (052) 232 2442 *Fax:* (052) 232 2592
E-mail: info@cardun.ch
Web Site: www.cardun.ch
Key Personnel
Mng Dir: Heiner Duebi
Founded: 1991
Subjects: Biography, Memoirs, History, Literature, Literary Criticism, Essays, Theology
ISBN Prefix(es): 978-3-907803; 978-3-905270; 978-3-906348; 978-3-906349

Carl-Huter-Verlag GmbH
Ohm-Str 14, 8050 Zurich
Tel: (044) 3117471 *Fax:* (044) 3117485
E-mail: verlag@carl-huter.ch
Web Site: www.carl-huter.ch
Key Personnel
Founder & Publishing Dir: Fritz Aerni
Management: Elisabeth Aerni
Founded: 1982
Subjects: Economics, Education, Medicine, Nursing, Dentistry, Psychology, Psychiatry, Physiognomy
ISBN Prefix(es): 978-3-906598; 978-3-03741; 978-3-89677; 978-3-906417
Branch Office(s)
Pommernstr 29, 79761 Waldshut-Tiengen, Germany *Web Site:* www.carl-huter.de

Editions du CAS
Monbijoustr 61, Postfach, 3000 Berne
Tel: (031) 370 18 18 *Fax:* (031) 370 18 00
E-mail: info@sac-cas.ch
Web Site: www.sac-verlag.ch
Subjects: Education, Outdoor Recreation, Travel & Tourism, Alpine Hiking, Nature, Skiing, Snowshoe Tours
ISBN Prefix(es): 978-3-85902
Parent Company: Schweizer Alpen-Club SAC

Edizioni Casagrande SA+
Via Quatorta 15, 6533 Lumino
Mailing Address: Casella postale 1291, 6501 Bellinzona
Tel: (091) 820 0101 *Fax:* (091) 825 1874
E-mail: edizioni@casagrande-online.ch
Web Site: www.edizionicasagrande.com
Key Personnel
Co-Founder & Editor: Libero Casagrande
Founded: 1972
Subjects: Art, History, Literature, Literary Criticism, Essays

ISBN Prefix(es): 978-88-7713
Subsidiaries: Archivio Storico Ticinese; Istituto Editoriale Ticinese; Istituto Grafico Casagrande SA
Bookshop(s): Libreria Casagrande, Via Stazione 1, 6500 Bellinzona *Tel:* (091) 825 1888 *Fax:* (091) 825 2231 *E-mail:* libreria@casagrande-online.ch

Caux Edition SA
Luzernerstr 94, 6010 Kriens
Mailing Address: PO Box 3909, 6002 Lucerne
Tel: (041) 310 12 61 *Fax:* (041) 311 22 14
E-mail: info@caux.ch
Web Site: www.caux.iofc.org/fr/caux-edition
Key Personnel
Dir: Andrew Stallybrass *Tel:* (022) 749 16 22 *Fax:* (022) 733 02 67
Manager: Graziella Falconnier *Tel:* (021) 962 94 68 *Fax:* (021) 962 94 67
Founded: 1965
Subjects: Biography, Memoirs, Drama, Theater, Religion - Other, Social Sciences, Sociology
ISBN Prefix(es): 978-3-85601; 978-2-88037; 978-2-85233
Parent Company: CAUX-Initiatives of Change
Branch Office(s)
One, rue de Varembe, PO Box 3, 1211 Geneva 20 *Tel:* (022) 749 16 20 *Fax:* (022) 733 02 67

Chamaeleon Verlag AG
Riehentorstr 15, 4058 Basel
Tel: (061) 261 83 85 *Fax:* (061) 261 83 05
E-mail: info@armin-vogt.ch; chamaeleon@armin-vogt.ch
Web Site: www.armin-vogt.ch
Founded: 1985
Subjects: Cultural Issues
ISBN Prefix(es): 978-3-905274; 978-3-9523175; 978-3-9523074

Chasa Editura Rumantscha ScRL
Via de la Plessur 47, Chascha Postala, 7001 Cuira
Tel: (081) 250 40 46
E-mail: info@chasaeditura.ch
Web Site: www.chasaeditura.ch
Key Personnel
Dir: Anita Capaul
Founded: 2010
Subjects: Fiction, Literature, Literary Criticism, Essays, Poetry
ISBN Prefix(es): 978-3-905956

Christoph Merian Verlag+
Rittergasse 35, 4051 Basel
Mailing Address: St Alban-Vorstadt 5, Postfach, 4002 Basel
Tel: (061) 226 33 25 *Fax:* (061) 226 33 45
E-mail: verlag@merianstiftung.ch
Web Site: www.christoph-merian-verlag.ch
Key Personnel
Mng Dir: Oliver Bolanz *Tel:* (061) 226 33 48 *E-mail:* o.bolanz@merianstiftung.ch
Production Manager: Claus Donau *Tel:* (061) 226 33 54 *E-mail:* c.donau@merianstiftung.ch
Advertising & Public Relations: Andrea Bikle *Tel:* (061) 226 33 50 *E-mail:* a.bikle@merianstiftung.ch
Founded: 1976
Subjects: Art, History, Literature, Literary Criticism, Essays, Photography, Regional Interests
ISBN Prefix(es): 978-3-85616
Total Titles: 80 Print
Parent Company: Christoph Merian Stiftung Basel
Distribution Center: buch 2000/AVA, Centralweg 16, Postfach 27, 8910 Affoltern am Albis *Tel:* (044) 762 42 60 *Fax:* (044) 762 42 10 *E-mail:* avainfo@ava.ch *Web Site:* www.ava.ch
Mohr Morawa Buchvertrieb GmbH, Sulzengasse 2, 1230 Vienna, Austria *Tel:* (01) 68 01 40 *Fax:* (01) 688 71 30 *E-mail:* momo@

mohrmorawa.at *Web Site:* www.mohrmorawa.at (audiobooks)
GVA Gemeinsame Verlagsauslieferung Goettingen GmbH & Co KG, Postfach 2021, 37010 Goettingen, Germany *Tel:* (0551) 4871 77 *Fax:* (0551) 41 392 *E-mail:* bestellung@gva-verlage.de *Web Site:* www.gva-verlage.de (Austria & Germany)
VVA-Vereinigte Verlagsauslieferung arvato media GmbH, Auftragsbearbeitung, An der Autobahn, 33334 Guetersloh, Germany *Tel:* (05241) 80 19 89 *Fax:* (05241) 46 75 0 *E-mail:* marion.riediger@bertelsmann.de (audiobooks)
Idea Books, Nieuwe Herengracht 11, 1011 Amsterdam, Netherlands *Tel:* (020) 622 61 54 *Fax:* (020) 620 92 99 *E-mail:* idea@ideabooks.nl *Web Site:* www.ideabooks.nl (Africa, Asia, Australia, Europe & USA)

Chronos Verlag+
Eisengasse 9, 8008 Zurich
Tel: (044) 265 4343 *Fax:* (044) 265 4344
E-mail: info@chronos-verlag.ch
Web Site: www.chronos-verlag.ch
Founded: 1985
Specialize in history, gender studies, philosophy, media & theatre studies.
Subjects: Drama, Theater, Government, Political Science, History, Language Arts, Linguistics, Nonfiction (General), Philosophy, Social Sciences, Sociology, Women's Studies
ISBN Prefix(es): 978-3-905312; 978-3-905314; 978-3-905315; 978-3-905313; 978-3-905311; 978-3-905278; 978-3-0340
Number of titles published annually: 50 Print
Total Titles: 800 Print
Orders to: AVA, Centralweg 16, Postfach 27, 8910 Affoltern am Albis *Tel:* (044) 762 4260 *Fax:* (044) 762 4210 (Liechtenstein, Switzerland)
GVA, Postfach 2021, 37010 Goettingen, Germany *Tel:* (0551) 48 71 77 *Fax:* (0551) 4 13 92 (European Union, Germany)

editions clandestin
Hoeheweg 73, 2502 Biel/Bienne
Tel: (032) 377 21 31 *Fax:* (032) 377 21 32
E-mail: edition.clandestin@bluewin.ch
Web Site: www.edition-clandestin.ch
Key Personnel
Publisher: Judith Luks
Founded: 1989
Subjects: Art
ISBN Prefix(es): 978-3-905297

CMS Verlagsgesellschaft mbH
Hertizentrum 14, 6300 Zug
Tel: (071) 669 19 56 *Fax:* (071) 669 19 54
E-mail: info@cms-verlag.ch
Web Site: cms-verlag.ch
Key Personnel
Publisher: Marlies Schmidt *E-mail:* marlies.schmidt@cms-verlag.ch
Subjects: Biography, Memoirs, Fiction, Health, Nutrition, Mysteries, Suspense, Nonfiction (General), Religion - Other, Romance
ISBN Prefix(es): 978-3-905968

Compendio Bildungsmedien AG
Neunbrunnenstr 50, 8050 Zurich
Tel: (044) 368 21 11 *Fax:* (044) 368 21 70
E-mail: postfach@compendio.ch
Web Site: www.compendio.ch
Key Personnel
Head, Marketing, Communications & Sales: Diana Widmer *Tel:* (044) 368 21 18 *E-mail:* d.widmer@compendio.ch
Subjects: Accounting, Business, Computer Science, Economics, Education, Language Arts, Linguistics, Law, Management, Mathematics, Science (General), Banking, Humanities, Staff Management
ISBN Prefix(es): 978-3-7155

Conseil oecumenique de Eglises, see World Council of Churches (WCC Publications)

Consejo Mundial de Iglesias, see World Council of Churches (WCC Publications)

Conzett Verlag
Verena-Conzett-Str 7, 8004 Zurich
Tel: (044) 242 76 53 *Fax:* (044) 242 76 86
Web Site: conzettverlag.ch
Founded: 1944
Subjects: Fiction, History, Literature, Literary Criticism, Essays, Philosophy, Poetry
ISBN Prefix(es): 978-3-7175; 978-3-9520804
Total Titles: 350 Print
Parent Company: Sunflower Foundation

Cornelsen Schulverlage Schweiz AG+
Verlagshaus Baecherstr, 8832 Wollerau
Tel: (044) 786 72 00 *Toll Free Tel:* (0800) 44 22 00 *Fax:* (044) 786 72 09
E-mail: verlag@cornelsen.ch
Web Site: www.cornelsen.ch
Key Personnel
Dir: Urs Schupp
Founded: 1807
Subjects: Education
ISBN Prefix(es): 978-3-464; 978-3-7941; 978-3-06; 978-3-0345
Total Titles: 300 Print; 30 CD-ROM
Parent Company: Franz Cornelsen Bildungsgruppe

COSA-Verlag+
Giusep Condrau SA, Via Cavardiras 1, 7180 Disentis
Tel: (081) 947 64 64 *Fax:* (081) 947 63 52
E-mail: condrau@cosa.ch
Web Site: www.cosa.ch
Founded: 1953
Subjects: Art

Cosmos Verlag AG+
Kraeyigenweg 2, 3074 Muri-Bern
Tel: (031) 950 64 64 *Fax:* (031) 950 64 60
E-mail: info@cosmosverlag.ch
Web Site: www.cosmosverlag.ch
Key Personnel
Dir: Reto M Aeberli
Contact: Regina Haener
Founded: 1923
Subjects: Accounting, Business, Fiction, Finance, Management, Regional Interests
ISBN Prefix(es): 978-3-85621; 978-2-8296; 978-3-305
Number of titles published annually: 12 Print

Comite international de la Croix-Rouge (CICR) (International Committee of the Red Cross)
19 Ave de la Paix, 1202 Geneva
Tel: (022) 734 60 01 *Fax:* (022) 733 20 57
E-mail: shop@icrc.org (publications & films)
Web Site: www.icrc.org
Key Personnel
Head, Public Communication: Sebastien Carliez *Tel:* (022) 730 28 81
Founded: 1863
Subjects: History, Law
ISBN Prefix(es): 978-2-88145; 978-2-88077
Total Titles: 4 Print; 2,000 Online
U.S. Office(s): International Committee of the Red Cross, 780 Third Ave, 28th floor, New York, NY 10017, United States

Cultur Prospectiv Edition
Muehlebachstr 35, 8008 Zurich
Tel: (044) 260 69 01 *Fax:* (044) 260 69 29
Web Site: www.culturprospectiv.ch

Key Personnel
Management: Dr Hans-Peter Meier-Dallach *E-mail:* hanspeter.meier@culturprospectiv.ch
Founded: 1990
Subjects: Economics, Psychology, Psychiatry, Social Sciences, Sociology, Social Psychology
ISBN Prefix(es): 978-3-905345

Armando Dado Editore
Via Orelli 29, 6600 Locarno
Mailing Address: CP 563, 6601 Locarno
Tel: (091) 751 48 02 *Fax:* (091) 752 10 26
E-mail: info@editore.ch
Web Site: www.editore.ch
Key Personnel
Mng Dir: Armando Dado
Founded: 1961
Subjects: Art, History, Literature, Literary Criticism, Essays, Photography
ISBN Prefix(es): 978-88-85115; 978-88-86315; 978-88-8281
Total Titles: 700 Print

Daimon Verlag AG+
Hauptstr 85, 8840 Einsiedeln
Tel: (055) 412 22 66 *Fax:* (055) 412 22 31
E-mail: daimon@daimon.ch
Web Site: www.daimon.ch
Key Personnel
Publisher: Dr Robert Hinshaw
Founded: 1979
Specialize in dream interpretation.
Membership(s): Swiss Booksellers & Publishers Association (SBVV).
Subjects: Environmental Studies, History, Human Relations, Poetry, Psychology, Psychiatry, Personal Development
ISBN Prefix(es): 978-3-85630
Distributor for Chiron; Eranos; Parabola; Sounds True Rec; Spring Publication & Spring Audio/Journal
Orders to: Beyer Verlag, Langgasse 2, 96142 Hollfeld, Germany *Tel:* (09274) 95051 *Fax:* (09274) 95053 *E-mail:* info@beyerverlag.de *Web Site:* www.beyerverlag.de
Gazelle Book Services Ltd, White Cross Mills, High Town, Lancaster, Lancs LA1 4XS, United Kingdom *Tel:* (01524) 68765 *Fax:* (01524) 63232 *E-mail:* sales@gazellebooks.co.uk *Web Site:* www.gazellebooks.co.uk
Baker & Taylor Publisher Services, 30 Amberwood Parkway, Ashland, OH 44805, United States *Tel:* 567-215-0030 *E-mail:* info@btpubservices.com *Web Site:* www.btpubservices.com

Daphnis-Verlag
Kappelistr 15, 8002 Zurich
Tel: (044) 2025271 *Fax:* (044) 2014231
Key Personnel
Mng Dir: Juerg Fischlin
Founded: 1959
Subjects: Poetry
ISBN Prefix(es): 978-3-85631

Deutsch Wyss & Partner
Effingerstr 17, 3001 Bern
Mailing Address: Postfach 5860, 3001 Bern
Tel: (031) 381 44 25 *Fax:* (031) 381 48 21
Web Site: www.advobern.ch
Key Personnel
Dir: Christoph Wyss *E-mail:* chr.wyss@advobern.ch
Founded: 1849
Subjects: Art, History, Law
ISBN Prefix(es): 978-3-7285

diaphanes AG
Hardstr 69, 8004 Zurich
Tel: (043) 322 07 83 *Fax:* (043) 322 07 84
Web Site: www.diaphanes.net

Key Personnel
Contact: Michael Heitz
Founded: 2001
Subjects: Computer Science, Fiction, Government, Political Science, History, Literature, Literary Criticism, Essays, Music, Dance, Philosophy, History of Science, Humanities
ISBN Prefix(es): 978-3-935300; 978-3-03734
Number of titles published annually: 50 Print
Distributed by University of Chicago Press
Distribution Center: AVA, Centralweg 16, 8910 Affoltern am Albis, Contact: Barbara Joss *Tel:* (044) 762 42 57 *Fax:* (044) 762 42 10 *E-mail:* b.joss@ava.ch *Web Site:* www.ava.ch
Prolit Verlagsauslieferung GmbH, Siemensstr 16, 35463 Fernwald-Annerod, Germany, Contact: Andrea Willenberg *Tel:* (0641) 943 93 35 *Fax:* (0641) 943 93 39 *E-mail:* a.willenberg@prolit.de *Web Site:* www.prolit.de (Germany & Austria)

Dike Verlag AG
Weinbergstr 41, 8006 Zurich
Tel: (044) 251 58 30 *Fax:* (044) 251 58 29
E-mail: verlag@dike.ch; auslieferung@dike.eu (orders)
Web Site: www.dike.ch
Key Personnel
Publisher: Werner Stocker
Head, Production: Benon Eugster
Founded: 1985
Subjects: Economics, Law, Literature, Literary Criticism, Essays, Science (General), Social Sciences, Sociology, Interdisciplinary Literature
ISBN Prefix(es): 978-3-03751

Diogenes Verlag AG+
Sprecherstr 8, 8032 Zurich
Tel: (044) 254 85 11 *Fax:* (044) 252 84 07
E-mail: info@diogenes.ch
Web Site: www.diogenes.ch
Key Personnel
Publisher: Daniel Keel
Publicity & Promotion: Ruth Geiger *E-mail:* rg@diogenes.ch
Sales & Marketing: Ulrich Richter *E-mail:* ur@diogenes.ch
Foreign Rights & Permissions: Susanne Bauknecht *E-mail:* bau@diogenes.ch
Founded: 1952
Subjects: Art, Drama, Theater, Fiction, Literature, Literary Criticism, Essays, Mysteries, Suspense, Philosophy
ISBN Prefix(es): 978-3-257

Doerlemann Verlag AG
Forchstr 21, 8032 Zurich
Tel: (044) 251 00 25 *Fax:* (044) 251 89 09
E-mail: verlag@doerlemann.com
Web Site: www.doerlemann.com
Key Personnel
Publisher: Sabine Doerlemann *E-mail:* sabine.doerlemann@doerlemann.com
Production: Mike Bierwolf *Tel:* (044) 251 88 80 *E-mail:* mb@doerlemann.com
Subjects: Literature, Literary Criticism, Essays, Nonfiction (General)
ISBN Prefix(es): 978-3-908777; 978-3-908778
Foreign Rep(s): Ravasio GmbH (Giovanni Ravasio) (Switzerland); Helga Schuster (Austria)
Distribution Center: Prolit Verlagsauslieferung GmbH, Siemensstr 16, Postfach 9, 35461 Fernwald (Annerod), Germany, Contact: Heike Schenk-Schwarzer *Tel:* (0641) 943 93 0; (0641) 943 93 203 *Fax:* (0641) 943 93 39; (0641) 943 93 199 *E-mail:* h.schenk-schwarzer@prolit.de *Web Site:* www.prolit.de
AVA Verlagsauslieferung AG, Centralweg 16, 8910 Affoltern am Albis, Contact: Barbara Joss *Tel:* (044) 762 42 50 *Fax:* (044) 762 42 10 *E-mail:* b.joss@ava.ch *Web Site:* www.ava.ch

Librairie Droz SA+
11 rue Massot, 1211 Geneva 12
Mailing Address: BP 389, 1211 Geneva 12
Tel: (022) 346 66 66 *Fax:* (022) 347 23 91
E-mail: droz@droz.org
Web Site: www.droz.org
Key Personnel
Mng Dir, Rights & Permissions: Max Engammare
Founded: 1924
Subjects: Antiques, History, Literature, Literary
  Criticism, Essays, Religion - Protestant, Social
  Sciences, Sociology, French Literature, Human-
  ism, Renaissance
ISBN Prefix(es): 978-2-600
Number of titles published annually: 80 Print; 2
  CD-ROM; 2 E-Book
Total Titles: 80 Print; 4 CD-ROM; 2 E-Book

Duboux Editions SA+
Frutigenstr 6, 3600 Thun
Tel: (033) 225 60 60 *Fax:* (033) 225 60 66
E-mail: duboux@duboux.ch
Web Site: duboux.ch
Key Personnel
Owner & Publisher: Jean-Pierre Duboux
Founded: 1988
Subjects: Cookery, Language Arts, Linguistics,
  Travel & Tourism
ISBN Prefix(es): 978-3-907950

Gottlieb Duttweiler Institute
Langhaldenstr 21, 8803 Rueschlikon, Zurich
Mailing Address: Postfach 531, 8803 Ruesch-
  likon, Zurich
Tel: (044) 724 61 11 *Fax:* (044) 724 62 62
E-mail: info@gdi.ch
Web Site: www.gdi.ch
Key Personnel
Chief Executive Officer: Dr David Bosshart
  Tel: (044) 724 62 01 *E-mail:* david.bosshart@
  gdi.ch
Head, Communications: Alain Egli *Tel:* (044) 724
  62 78 *E-mail:* alain.egli@gdi.ch
Head, Sales & Events: Laura de Wolf *Tel:* (044)
  724 62 12 *E-mail:* laura.dewolf@gdi.ch
Manager, Sales & Events: Silke Kroehnert
  Tel: (044) 724 62 08 *E-mail:* silke.kroehnert@
  gdi.ch
Founded: 1963
Subjects: Economics, Management, Marketing,
  Social Sciences, Sociology
ISBN Prefix(es): 978-3-7184
Parent Company: Stiftung Im Grueene
Imprints: GDI

Echtzeit Verlag GmbH
Murbacherstr 34, 4056 Basel
Tel: (061) 322 45 00
E-mail: info@echtzeit.ch
Web Site: echtzeit.ch
Subjects: Fiction, Nonfiction (General)
ISBN Prefix(es): 978-3-905800

Edition Limonade
Route de Burtigny 28A, 1268 Begnins
E-mail: info@editions-limonade.com
Web Site: www.editions-limonade.com
Key Personnel
Dir: Delphine Murano *E-mail:* delphine.murano@
  editions-limonade.com
Founded: 2010
ISBN Prefix(es): 978-2-940456
Distribution Center: OLF SA, ZI3 Corminboeuf,
  PO Box 1152, 1701 Fribourg *Tel:* (026) 467 51
  11 *Fax:* (026) 467 54 66 *E-mail:* information@
  olf.ch *Web Site:* www.olf.ch
Volumen, 25 bd Romain Rolland-CS 21418,
  75993 Paris Cedex 14, France *Tel:* 01 41 48
  84 60 *E-mail:* volumen@volumen.fr *Web
  Site:* www.volumen.fr (Belgium, Canada &
  France)

eFeF-Verlag+
Berninastr 4, 5430 Wettingen
Tel: (056) 426 06 18 *Fax:* (056) 427 04 61
E-mail: info@efefverlag.ch
Web Site: www.efefverlag.ch
Key Personnel
Publishing Dir: Doris Stump
Founded: 1988
Subjects: Biography, Memoirs, Fiction, Nonfiction
  (General), Women's Studies, Feminist Science,
  Gender Studies
ISBN Prefix(es): 978-3-905493; 978-3-9521022;
  978-3-905561
Distribution Center: AVA Verlagsauslieferung,
  Centralweg 16, Postfach 27, 8910 Affoltern am
  Albis *Tel:* (044) 762 42 60 *Fax:* (044) 762 42
  10
Sozialistische Verlagsauslieferung, Philip-
  Reis-Str 17, 63477 Maintal, Germany
  Tel: (06811) 9088072 *Fax:* (06811) 9088073
  E-mail: sovaffm@t-online.de

Edition 8
Quellenstr 25, 8005 Zurich
Tel: (044) 271 80 22
E-mail: info@edition8.ch
Web Site: www.edition8.ch
Founded: 1998
Subjects: Biography, Memoirs, Cookery, Myster-
  ies, Suspense, Poetry, Travel & Tourism
ISBN Prefix(es): 978-3-85990

elfundzehn Verlag
Member of Verlagsgruppe Baeschlin
Oberdorfstr 32, 8024 Eglisau
Mailing Address: Postfach 412, 80024 Eglisau
Tel: (041) 726 97 21
E-mail: info@lesestoff.ch
Web Site: verlag.lesestoff.ch/verlag
Key Personnel
Publishing Dir: Gaby Ferndriger *Tel:* (055) 640
  99 40 *E-mail:* gaby.ferndriger@baeschlin.ch
Subjects: Biography, Memoirs
ISBN Prefix(es): 978-3-905769
Distribution Center: Vertrieb und Ausliefer-
  ung Baeschlin-Verlage, Turbinenweg 6,
  8866 Ziegelbruecke *Tel:* (044) 209 91 95
  E-mail: vertrieb@lesestoff.ch
Ennsthaler Gesellschaft mbH & Co KG,
  Stadtplatz 26, 4400 Steyr, Austria
  Tel: (07252) 52053 21 *Fax:* (07252) 52053 22
  E-mail: auslieferung@ennsthaler.at
Koch, Neff & Volckmar GmbH, Industriestr
  23, 70565 Stuttgart, Germany *Tel:* (0711)
  78 60 45 45 *Fax:* (0711) 78 60 28 01
  E-mail: bestellungen.bs@knv.de

Elster Verlagsbuchhandlung AG
Hofackerstr 13, 8032 Zurich
Tel: (044) 385 55 10 *Fax:* (044) 385 55 19
E-mail: info@elsterverlag.ch
Web Site: www.elsterverlag.ch
Key Personnel
Owner: Rio bei Elster
Subjects: Cookery, Economics, Government, Po-
  litical Science, History, Literature, Literary
  Criticism, Essays, Philosophy, Psychology,
  Psychiatry, Social Sciences, Sociology, Sports,
  Athletics
ISBN Prefix(es): 978-3-907668

Elvetica Edizioni SA+
C so San Gottardo, 34, CP 2429, 6830 Chiasso
Tel: (091) 683 50 56 *Fax:* (091) 683 76 05
E-mail: info@elveticaedizioni.com;
  amministrazione@elveticaedizioni.com
Founded: 1967
Membership(s): Association Europeenne des Edi-
  teurs d'Annuaires; Schweizer Adressbuch Ver-
  leger Verband; Societa Editori Svizzera Ital-
  iana.

Subjects: Economics, Fiction, Literature, Literary
  Criticism, Essays
ISBN Prefix(es): 978-88-86639
Total Titles: 1 CD-ROM; 1 E-Book

EMH Schweizerischer Aerzteverlag AG (EMH
  Swiss Medical Publishers Ltd)
Farnsburgerstr 8, 4132 Muttenz
Tel: (061) 467 85 55 *Fax:* (061) 467 85 56
E-mail: verlag@emh.ch
Web Site: www.emh.ch
Key Personnel
Chief Executive Officer: Ruedi Bienz *Tel:* (061)
  467 85 65 *E-mail:* rbienz@emh.ch
Mng Editor: Dr Katharina Blatter-Schwedler
  Tel: (061) 467 85 25 *E-mail:* kblatter@emh.ch
Head, Publications: Dr Natalie Marty *Tel:* (061)
  467 85 50 *E-mail:* nmarty@emh.ch
Subjects: Medicine, Nursing, Dentistry
ISBN Prefix(es): 978-3-03754

EPFL Press, *imprint of* Presses Polytechniques et
  Universitaires Romandes (PPUR)

Edition Epoca+
Kramgasse 58, 3011 Bern
Tel: (031) 772 10 10 *Fax:* (031) 772 10 11
E-mail: info@epoca.ch
Web Site: www.epoca.ch
Key Personnel
Contact: Urs Kummer
Founded: 1995
Subjects: Fiction, Literature, Literary Criticism,
  Essays, Philosophy, Social Sciences, Sociology
ISBN Prefix(es): 978-3-905513
Number of titles published annually: 7 Print
Distribution Center: buch 2000 c/o AVA, Cen-
  tralweg 16, 8910 Affoltern am Albis *Tel:* (044)
  762 42 60 *Fax:* (044) 762 42 10
Verlagsauslieferungen Dr Franz Hain GmbH, Dr-
  Otto-Neurath-Gasse 5, 1220 Vienna, Austria
  Tel: (01) 282 65 65 0 *Fax:* (01) 282 5 282
SOVA, Friesstr 20-24, 60388 Frankfurt am Main,
  Germany *Tel:* (069) 41 02 11 *Fax:* (069) 41 02
  80

ETH Zurich-Institute fuer Geschichte und
  Theorie der Architektur, see gta Verlag

Evangelische Buchhandlungen und Basileia
  Verlag GmbH
Martinskirchplatz 2, 4051 Basel
Tel: (061) 260 21 20 *Fax:* (061) 260 22 68
Subjects: Religion - Other, Social Sciences, Soci-
  ology
ISBN Prefix(es): 978-3-85555

Ekkehard Faude Verlag
Sternengarten 6, 8574 Lengwil
Mailing Address: Postfach 10 05 24, 78405 Kon-
  stanz, Germany
Tel: (04171) 688 35 55 *Fax:* (04171) 688 35 65
E-mail: info@libelle.ch
Web Site: www.libelle.ch
Key Personnel
Contact: Ekkehard Faude *E-mail:* faude@libelle.
  ch; Elisabeth Tschiemer *E-mail:* tschiemer@
  libelle.ch
Founded: 1979
Subjects: Art, Drama, Theater, Education, History,
  Humor, Literature, Literary Criticism, Essays,
  Mongolia, Natural Sciences
ISBN Prefix(es): 978-3-922305
Parent Company: Libelle Verlag
Foreign Rep(s): Markus Wieser (Switzerland)
Distribution Center: AVA Verlagsauslieferungen
  AG, Centralweg 16, 8910 Affoltern am Albis,
  Contact: Helene Amsler *Tel:* (044) 762 42 52
  Fax: (044) 762 42 10 *E-mail:* h.amsler@ava.ch
Leipziger Kommissions- und Grossbuchhan-
  delsgesellschaft mbH (LKG), An der Sued-
  spitze 1-12, 04571 Roetha, Germany, Con-

tact: Katharina Hillmann *Tel:* (034206) 65-280 *Fax:* (034206) 65-1762 *E-mail:* khillmann@ lkg-service.de *Web Site:* www.lkg-va.de (Germany & Austria)

Editions Favre SA
29, rue de Bourg, 1002 Lausanne
Tel: (021) 312 17 17 *Fax:* (021) 320 50 59
E-mail: lausanne@editionsfavre.com
Web Site: www.editionsfavre.com
Key Personnel
Editor: Pierre-Marcel Favre; Jean-Louis Gouraud; Lidiane Quaglia; Sophie Rossier
Founded: 1986
Subjects: Art, Biography, Memoirs, Cookery, Government, Political Science, Health, Nutrition, History, Literature, Literary Criticism, Essays, Photography, Sports, Athletics, Travel & Tourism, Wine & Spirits, Equestrian, Leisure, Nature, Political & Social Issues, Wellness
ISBN Prefix(es): 978-2-8289
Number of titles published annually: 50 Print
Distribution Center: OLF, Rte Andre Piller 39, 1720 Corminboeuf-Fribourg
Interforum, Rte de Sermaises 46, 45330 Malesherbes-Paris, France (France, Belgium & Canada)

Edition Fink
Waffenplatzstr 39a, 8002 Zurich
Tel: (044) 280 55 62 *Fax:* (044) 280 55 63
E-mail: verlag@editionfink.ch
Web Site: www.editionfink.ch
Key Personnel
Publisher: Georg Rutishauser
E-mail: rutishauser@editionfink.ch
Founded: 1994
Subjects: Art, Contemporary Art
ISBN Prefix(es): 978-3-906086

FONA Verlag AG
Aarauerstr 25, 5600 Lenzburg
Tel: (062) 886 91 91 *Fax:* (062) 886 91 99
E-mail: info@fona.ch
Web Site: www.fona.ch
Key Personnel
Publisher: Alfred Haefeli
Marketing: Eva-Marie Wilhelm *Tel:* (062) 886 91 81
Subjects: Cookery
ISBN Prefix(es): 978-3-907108

Fontis - Brunnen Basel
Steinentorstr 23, 4010 Basel
Tel: (061) 295 60 00 *Fax:* (061) 295 60 68
E-mail: info@fontis-verlag.ch
Web Site: www.fontis-verlag.com
Key Personnel
Publishing Dir & Chief Executive Officer: Dominik Klenk
Head, Editorial Dept: Christian Meyer
Sales Manager: Roland Sigrist
Founded: 1921
Subjects: Biography, Memoirs, Fiction, Nonfiction (General), Faith, Family
ISBN Prefix(es): 978-3-03848

Fotorotar AG/EGG ZH, *imprint of*
Schweizerisches Jugendschriftenwerk (SJW)

Foundation Simon I Patino, see Editions Patino

Jean Frey AG, Beobachter Buchverlag
Foerrlibuckstr 70, Postfach, 8021 Zurich
Tel: (043) 444 53 07; (043) 444 53 01 *Fax:* (043) 444 53 09; (043) 444 53 53
E-mail: edition@beobachter.ch
Web Site: www.beobachter.ch; www.axelspringer.ch
Key Personnel
Publishing Dir: Roland Wahrenberger *Tel:* (043)

444 53 00 *E-mail:* roland.wahrenberger@beobachter.ch
Production Manager: Mario Guedel
E-mail: mario.guedel@beobachter.ch
Chief Editor: Andres Buechi *Tel:* (043) 444 52 50
E-mail: andres.buechi@beobacter.ch
Subjects: Cookery, Economics, Finance, Government, Political Science, Health, Nutrition, House & Home, Law, Regional Interests
ISBN Prefix(es): 978-3-85569
Total Titles: 60 Print
Parent Company: Axel Springer Schweiz AG
Branch Office(s)
Industriestr 54, Postfach 8152, Glattbrugg-Zurich

Edition Patrick Frey
Limmatstr 268, 8005 Zurich
Tel: (044) 381 51 02
E-mail: mail@editionpatrickfrey.ch
Web Site: www.editionpatrickfrey.com
Key Personnel
Press: Gloria Wismer *E-mail:* wismer@editionpatrickfrey.ch
Text Editor: Miriam Wiesel
Translation: Miriamne Fields
Founded: 1986
Subjects: Art, Photography, Pop Culture
ISBN Prefix(es): 978-3-905509
Distribution Center: AVA Verlagsauslieferung, Centralweg One, Centralweg 10, 8919 Affoltem *Tel:* (044) 762 42 00 *Fax:* (044) 762 42 10 *E-mail:* avainfo@ava.ch *Web Site:* www.ava.ch (Switzerland)
Ravasio GmbH, Postfach 554, CH-8037 Zurich, Contact: Giovanni Ravasio *Tel:* (044) 260 61 31 *Fax:* (044) 260 61 32 *E-mail:* g.ravasio@bluewin.ch (Switzerland)
Perimeter Distribution, 748 High St, Thornbury, Melbourne, Victoria 3071, Australia *Tel:* (03) 9484 8101 *E-mail:* hello@perimeterdistribution.com (Australia)
GVA Gemeinsame Verlagsauslieferung Goettingen GmbH & Co KG, Postfach 2021, 37010 Goettingen, Germany *Tel:* (0551) 487177 *Fax:* (0551) 41392 *E-mail:* bestellung@gva-verlage.de *Web Site:* www.gva-verlage.de (Germany & Austria)
Les presses du reel, 35 rue Colson, 21000 Dijon, France *Tel:* (03) 80 30 75 23 *Fax:* (03) 80 30 59 74 *E-mail:* info@lespressesdureel.com (France, Belgium & Luxembourg)
Marginal Press, 5C 1-14-12, 150-0011 Higashi Shibuya-ku, Tokyo, Japan *Tel:* (080) 67123832 *E-mail:* hello@marginal-press.com (Japan)
Antenne Books Limited, Unit 55, Hackney Downs Studios, 17 Amhurst Terrace, London E8 2BT, United Kingdom *Tel:* (020) 3582 8257 *E-mail:* bryony@antennebooks.com (UK)
RAM publications & distribution inc, 2525 Michigan Ave, Bldg A2, Santa Monica, CA 90404, United States *Tel:* 310-453-0043 *E-mail:* orders@rampub.com (USA)

Orell Fuessli Verlag AG+
Dietzingerstr 3, 8036 Zurich
Tel: (044) 466 74 45 *Fax:* (044) 466 74 12
E-mail: info@ofv.ch
Web Site: www.ofv.ch
Key Personnel
Mng Dir: Dr Matti Schuesseler *E-mail:* matti.schuesseler@ofv.ch
Founded: 1519
Subjects: Accounting, Art, Biography, Memoirs, Business, Economics, Education, Geography, Geology, History, How-to, Law
ISBN Prefix(es): 978-3-280; 978-3-7249
Parent Company: Orell Fuessli Holding Ltd
Imprints: Atlantis Verlag; Globi Verlag; Verlag Huber; Orell Fuessli Kinderbuch; Photoglob; Rentsch Verlag; Scola Verlag
Bookshop(s): Orell Fuessli Buchhandlungs AG

Futurum Verlag
Im Ackermannshof, St Johanns-Vorstadt 19/21, 4056 Basel
Tel: (061) 706 91 30 *Fax:* (061) 706 91 49
E-mail: info@futurumverlag.com
Web Site: www.futurumverlag.com; www.steinerverlag.com
Subjects: Art, History, Anthroposophy, Cultural History, Current Affairs
ISBN Prefix(es): 978-3-85636
Parent Company: Rudolf Steiner Verlag AG

Galerie Kornfeld Verlag AG
Laupenstr 41, 3008 Bern
Tel: (031) 381 46 73 *Fax:* (031) 382 18 91
E-mail: galerie@kornfeld.ch
Web Site: www.kornfeld.ch
Key Personnel
General Partner: Dr Eberhard W Kornfeld
Limited Partner: Christine E Stauffer
Founded: 1864
Subjects: Art
ISBN Prefix(es): 978-3-85773

Garuda-Verlag Eisenegger & Eisenegger+
Lindenweg 3, 6288 Schongau, Lucerne
Tel: (041) 917 02 45 *Fax:* (041) 917 02 46
E-mail: garuda@bluewin.ch
Key Personnel
Dir: P Eisenegger; K Eisenegger
Founded: 1985
Also acts as book distributor & agent.
Subjects: Religion - Buddhist
ISBN Prefix(es): 978-3-906139
Distributor for Diamant Verlag; Fabri-Verlag

Gasser Verlag
Regula Gasser-Stebler Hirzbrunnenallee 29, 4058 Basel
Tel: (079) 542 67 66
E-mail: regulagasser@gmx.ch
Web Site: www.brunogasser.ch
Key Personnel
Mng Dir: Bruno Gasser
Subjects: Art, Film, Video, Photography, Grass
ISBN Prefix(es): 978-3-905504; 978-3-906210

GDI, *imprint of* Gottlieb Duttweiler Institute

Genossenschaft Edition Exodus
Rotseehoehe 4, 6006 Lucerne
Tel: (041) 422 04 63 *Fax:* (041) 422 04 62
E-mail: editionexodus@bluewin.ch
Key Personnel
President: Odilo Noti
Executive Vice President: Florian Flohr
Founded: 1982
Subjects: History, Philosophy, Religion - Catholic, Religion - Protestant, Social Sciences, Sociology, Theology
ISBN Prefix(es): 978-3-905575; 978-3-905577

Georg Editeur SA+
46, chemin de la Mousse, 1225 Chene-Bourg
Tel: (022) 702 93 11 *Fax:* (022) 702 93 55
E-mail: livres@medhyg.ch
Web Site: www.georg.ch
Key Personnel
Dir: Dr Bertrand Kiefer *Tel:* (022) 702 93 36
E-mail: bertrand.kiefer@medhyg.ch
Head, Publishing: Michael Balavoine *Tel:* (022) 702 93 53 *E-mail:* michael.balavoine@medhyg.ch
Administration: Gaelle Bryand *Tel:* (022) 702 93 22 *E-mail:* gaelle.bryand@medhyg.ch
Founded: 1857
Subjects: Economics, Environmental Studies, Ethnicity, Government, Political Science, History, Language Arts, Linguistics, Law, Music, Dance, Philosophy, Psychology, Psychiatry, Religion - Other, Science (General), Social Sciences, Sociology

ISBN Prefix(es): 978-2-8257
Number of titles published annually: 35 Print
Total Titles: 450 Print; 1 CD-ROM
Parent Company: Groupe Medecine & Hygiene
Associate Companies: Editions Eshel, Paris,
France
Imprints: Editions Medecine et Hygiene
Distribution Center: Vilo Distribution, 25 rue Gi-
noux, 75015 Paris, France *Tel:* 01 45 77 08 05
Fax: 01 45 75 75 53

Georg et Cie SA, see Georg Editeur SA

Der Gesunde Menschenversand GmbH
Neuweg 10, 6003 Lucerne
Tel: (041) 360 65 05 *Fax:* (041) 210 32 00
E-mail: info@menschenversand.ch
Web Site: www.menschenversand.ch
Key Personnel
Owner: Matthias Burki
ISBN Prefix(es): 978-3-905825
Distribution Center: AVA Verlagsauslieferung,
Centralweg 16, Postfach 27, 8910 Affoltern
am Albis *Tel:* (044) 762 42 00 *Fax:* (040)
762 42 10 *E-mail:* verlagsservice@ava.ch *Web
Site:* www.ava.ch (Switzerland)
SOVA GmbH, Philipp-Reis-Str 17, 63477
Maintal, Germany *Tel:* (06181) 9088072
Fax: (06181) 9088073 *E-mail:* sovaffm@t-
online.de (Germany & Austria)

Giger Verlag
Bubental 51, 8852 Altendorf
Tel: (055) 442 68 48 *Fax:* (055) 442 68 42
E-mail: info@gigerverlag.ch
Web Site: www.gigerverlag.ch
Key Personnel
Chief Executive Officer: Sabine Giger
Founded: 2000
Subjects: Art, Inspirational, Spirituality, Music,
Dance
ISBN Prefix(es): 978-3-9523532; 978-3-905958;
978-3-9523202
Distribution Center: Buchzentrum AG,
Industriestr Ost 10, 4614 Haegendorf
Tel: (062) 209 25 25 *Fax:* (062) 209 26 27
E-mail: kundendienst@buchzentrum.ch
Dr Franz Hain GmbH, Dr-Otto-Neurath-Gasse 5,
1220 Vienna, Austria *Tel:* (01) 282 65 65-24
Fax: (01) 282 65 65-49 *E-mail:* vertrieb@hain.
at
Brokhaus GmbH, Kreidlerstr 9, 70806 Kornwest-
heim, Germany *E-mail:* m.baum@brocom.de

Globi Verlag, *imprint of* Orell Fuessli Verlag AG

Globi Verlag AG
Imprint of Orell Fuessli Verlag AG
Dietzingerstr 3, 8036 Zurich
Tel: (044) 466 73 18 *Fax:* (044) 466 74 12
E-mail: info@globi.ch
Web Site: www.globi.ch
Key Personnel
Publishing Manager: Gisela Klinkenberg
Production Manager: Sarah Zollinger-Keiser
Sales & Marketing: Katja Hug
Founded: 1944
Subjects: Humor, Comic
ISBN Prefix(es): 978-3-85703
Distribution Center: Buchzentrum AG,
Industriestr Ost 10, 4614 Haegendorf
Tel: (062) 209 26 26 *Fax:* (062) 209 26 27
E-mail: kundendienst@buchzentrum.ch
Mohr Morawa Buchvertrieb GmbH, Sulzen-
gasse 2, 1230 Vienna, Austria *Tel:* (01) 68
01 40 *Fax:* (01) 68 87 130 *E-mail:* momo@
mohrmorawa.at *Web Site:* www.mohrmorawa.at
Koch, Neff & Oetinger Verlagsauslieferung
GmbH, Industriestr 23, 70565 Stuttgart, Ger-
many *E-mail:* dtv@kno-va.de

Verlag am Goetheanum+
Huegelweg 53, 4143 Dornach
Mailing Address: Postfach 131, 4143 Dornach
Tel: (061) 706 42 00 *Fax:* (061) 706 42 01
E-mail: info@vamg.ch
Web Site: vamg.ch
Key Personnel
Head, Publishing: Dr Christiane Haid *Tel:* (061)
706 42 03 *E-mail:* haid@vamg.ch
Accounting & Licences: Max Savin *Tel:* (061)
706 42 02 *E-mail:* savin@vamg.ch
Sales & Production: Anna S Fischer
E-mail: fischer@vamg.ch
Founded: 1924
Subjects: Art, Education, Literature, Literary Crit-
icism, Essays, Mathematics, Medicine, Nursing,
Dentistry, Philosophy, Religion - Other, Science
(General), Theology
ISBN Prefix(es): 978-3-7235
Subsidiaries: Rudolf Geering Verlag; Natura Ver-
lag; Ogham Verlag
Distribution Center: Buchzentrum AG (BZ), In-
dustriestr Ost 10, 4614 Haegendorf, Germany
Tel: (062) 209 26 26 *Fax:* (062) 209 26 27
E-mail: kundendienst@buchzentrum.ch
Koch, Neff & Oetinger Verlagsauslieferung
GmbH, Industriestr 23, 70565 Stuttgart, Ger-
many *E-mail:* goetheanum@kno-va.de

Goldfish Verlag, *imprint of* Midas Verlag AG

Goldschmidt Basel AG
Mostackerstr 17, 4051 Basel
Tel: (061) 261 61 91 *Fax:* (061) 261 61 23
E-mail: info@goldschmidt-basel.ch
Web Site: www.victorgoldschmidt.ch
Founded: 1902
Membership(s): Swiss Booksellers & Publishers
Association (SVBB).
Subjects: Religion - Jewish, Judaica & Hebraica,
English, French, German, Hebrew & Yiddish
ISBN Prefix(es): 978-3-85705

Govinda-Verlag GmbH (Govinda Press)
Postfach 769, 8053 Zurich
Tel: (043) 321 66 77 *Fax:* (043) 321 66 77
E-mail: info@govinda.ch
Web Site: www.govinda.ch
Key Personnel
Publisher & General Manager: Ronald Zuerrer
E-mail: rz@govinda.ch
Founded: 1989
This publisher has indicated that 50% of their
product line is author subsidized.
Subjects: Astrology, Occult, Mysteries, Suspense,
Parapsychology, Philosophy, Poetry, Religion -
Hindu, Religion - Other
ISBN Prefix(es): 978-3-906347; 978-3-905831
Number of titles published annually: 5 Print
Total Titles: 100 Print

Graduate Institute Publications
20 rue Rothschild, 1202 Geneva
Mailing Address: Postfach 136, 1211 Geneva 21
Tel: (022) 908 43 60 *Fax:* (022) 908 62 73
E-mail: publications@graduateinstitute.ch
Web Site: www.graduateinstitute.ch/publications
Key Personnel
President: Marc Galvin *Tel:* (022) 908 43 61
E-mail: marc.galvin@graduateinstitute.ch
Founded: 2008
Subjects: Anthropology, Economics, Government,
Political Science, History, Law, International
Economics, International Law
ISBN Prefix(es): 978-2-88247; 978-2-940415

Terra Grischuna Buchverlag+
Zwinglistr 6, 8750 Glarus
Tel: (055) 645 28 64
Web Site: www.terragrischuna.ch

Key Personnel
Publishing Dir: Eva Zopfi *E-mail:* ezopfi@
suedostschweiz.ch
Founded: 1942
Subjects: Geography, Geology, Natural History,
Regional Interests, Romance, Travel & Tourism
ISBN Prefix(es): 978-3-7298; 978-3-908133
Distributed by Baumgartner Bucher AG (Switzer-
land); Herold Verlagsauslieferung GmbH (Ger-
many)
Orders to: Suedostschweiz Buchvertrieb
Tel: (055) 645 28 70 *E-mail:* buchvertrieb@
suedostschweiz.ch

gta Verlag
Wolfgang Pauli-Str 15, 8093 Zurich
Tel: (044) 633 2458 *Fax:* (044) 633 1581
E-mail: verlag@gta.arch.ethz.ch
Web Site: www.verlag.gta.arch.ethz.ch
Key Personnel
Publishing Dir: Dr Veronika Darius *Tel:* (044)
633 2896 *E-mail:* veronika.darius@gta.arch.
ethz.ch
Editorial Management: Ulrike Steiner *Tel:* (044)
633 2925 *E-mail:* ulrike.steiner@gta.arch.ethz.
ch
Marketing Management: Ursula Bein
E-mail: ursula.bein@gta.arch.ethz.ch
Subjects: Architecture & Interior Design, Photog-
raphy
ISBN Prefix(es): 978-3-85676

Guides-Olizane Decouverte, *imprint of* Editions
Olizane

Th Gut Verlag
Oberdorfstr 32, 8001 Zurich
Mailing Address: Postfach 412, 8024 Zurich
Tel: (044) 209 91 11
E-mail: admin@baeschlin.ch
Web Site: www.lesestoff.ch/verlage/gutverlag
Key Personnel
Publishing Dir: Gaby Ferndriger *E-mail:* gaby.
ferndriger@baeschlin.ch
Press & Marketing: Hansrudolf Frey
E-mail: verlag@baeschlin.ch
Founded: 1944
Subjects: Ethnicity, Government, Political Sci-
ence, Regional Interests
ISBN Prefix(es): 978-3-85717
Parent Company: Baeschlin Buecher AG, Haupstr
32, 8750 Glarus
Distribution Center: Turbinenweg 6, 8866 Ziegel-
bruecke *Tel:* (044) 209 91 11 *Fax:* (044) 209
91-12

Hallwag Kuemmerly+Frey AG+
Grubenstr 109, 3322 Schoenbuehl
Tel: (031) 850 31 31; (031) 850 31 10 (orders)
Fax: (031) 850 31 00
E-mail: info@swisstravelcenter.ch
Web Site: www.swisstravelcenter.ch
Key Personnel
Chief Executive Officer: Markus Schneider
Special Editions Production: Adolf Amacher
Marketing & Public Relations: Danielle Zingg
Sales Manager, Export: Lorenz Beer
Sales: Fritz Ruchti
Founded: 1912
Subjects: Animals, Pets, Art, Cookery, Geog-
raphy, Geology, History, How-to, Nonfiction
(General), Outdoor Recreation, Science (Gen-
eral), Sports, Athletics, Travel & Tourism
ISBN Prefix(es): 978-3-259 (Kuemmerly+Frey);
978-3-8283 (Hallwag); 978-3-905755 (Hallwag
AG); 978-3-444 (Hallwag)

Haupt Verlag AG+
Falkenplatz 14, 3012 Bern
Tel: (031) 309 09 00 *Fax:* (031) 309 09 90
E-mail: info@haupt.ch; bestellung@haupt.ch
Web Site: www.haupt.ch

Key Personnel
Mng Dir, Permissions: Matthias Haupt
E-mail: matthias.haupt@haupt.ch
Dir: Regine Balmer *E-mail:* regine.balmer@haupt.
ch; Frank Heins *E-mail:* frank.heins@haupt.ch
Founded: 1906
Subjects: Art, Biological Sciences, Crafts, Games,
Hobbies, Economics, Education, How-to, Science (General), Social Sciences, Sociology
ISBN Prefix(es): 978-3-258
Number of titles published annually: 150 Print
Total Titles: 1,000 Print; 5 CD-ROM

Heile Dich Selbst Verlag
Suot Crastas, 7514 Sils Maria
Tel: (081) 834 21 22; (081) 834 20 03 *Fax:* (081)
834 20 04; (081) 834 21 24
Web Site: www.heile-dich-selbst.ch
Key Personnel
Publisher: Annemarie Troost
Subjects: Astrology, Occult, Health, Nutrition,
Self-Help, Healing
ISBN Prefix(es): 978-3-905794

Max Heindel, see Rosenkreuzer Philosophie
Verlag & Buecherecke

Helbing Lichtenhahn Verlag+
Elisabethenstr 8, 4051 Basel
Tel: (061) 228 90 70 *Fax:* (061) 228 90 71
E-mail: info@helbing.ch
Web Site: www.helbing.ch
Key Personnel
Dir: Men Haupt; Alexander Jaeger
Marketing & Press: Priska Hutterli *Tel:* (061) 228
91 58 *E-mail:* priska.hutterli@helbing.ch
Founded: 1822
Subjects: Anthropology, Economics, Environmental Studies, Government, Political Science,
History, Language Arts, Linguistics, Law, Management
ISBN Prefix(es): 978-3-7190
Associate Companies: Sauerlaender AG

Helden Verlag
Geibelstr 33, 8037 Zurich
Tel: (044) 240 44 70 *Fax:* (044) 240 44 41
Key Personnel
Publisher: Katharina Blarer
Marketing: Stefan Bar
Press: Urs Bernet
Subjects: Nonfiction (General), Culture
ISBN Prefix(es): 978-3-905748
Parent Company: Die Buechermacher GmbH
Distribution Center: GVA Gemeinsame Verlagsauslieferung Goettingen GmbH & Co KG,
Postfach 2021, 37010 Goettingen, Germany
Tel: (0551) 384200-0 *Fax:* (0551) 384200-10
E-mail: admin@gva-verlage.de (Austria & Germany)
Worldwide Booksearch Service, One Chelsea
Court, Westport, CT 06880, United States
Tel: 917-669-7833 *E-mail:* orders.helden@
gmail.com (USA & other countries)

Verlag Helvetica Chimica Acta
Subsidiary of Wiley-VCH Verlag GmbH & Co
KGaA
Hofwiesenstr 26, Postfach, 8042 Zurich
Tel: (044) 360 24 34 *Fax:* (044) 360 24 35
E-mail: vhca@vhca.ch
Web Site: www.vhca.ch
Key Personnel
Editor-in-Chief: Dr M Volkan Kisakuerek
Founded: 1917
Publisher of *Helvetica Chimica Acta & Chemistry
& Biodiversity.*
Subjects: Chemistry, Chemical Engineering
ISBN Prefix(es): 978-3-85727; 978-3-906390
Orders to: Wiley-VCH, Customer Service Dept,
PO Box 101161, 69451 Weinheim, Germany

Tel: (06201) 606-400 *Fax:* (06201) 606-184
E-mail: service@wiley-vch.de *Web Site:* www.
wiley-vch.de (Germany, Austria & Switzerland)
John Wiley & Sons Ltd, Customer Service Dept,
One Oldlands Way, Bognor Regis, West Sussex PO22 9SA, United Kingdom *Tel:* (01243)
843-294 *Fax:* (01243) 843-296 *Web Site:* www.
wileyeurope.com (Africa, Asia, Middle East &
rest of Europe)
Customer Care-Wiley, 10475 Crosspoint
Blvd, Indianapolis, IN 45256, United States
E-mail: custserv@wiley.com *Web Site:* www.
wiley.com (Central, North & South America)

hep verlag AG+
Gutenbergstr 31, 3001 Bern
Mailing Address: Postfach 6607, 3001 Bern
Tel: (031) 310 29 29 *Fax:* (031) 318 31 35
E-mail: info@hep-verlag.ch
Web Site: www.hep-verlag.ch
Key Personnel
Publishing Dir & Chairman: Peter Egger
Tel: (031) 310 29 20 *E-mail:* peter.egger@hep-
verlag.ch
Vice President: Dr Men Haupt *E-mail:* men.
haupt@hep-verlag.ch
Marketing: Gisela Fluehmann *Tel:* (031) 310 29
17 *E-mail:* gisela.fluehmann@hep-verlag.ch
Marketing & Sales: Rahel Wenger *Tel:* (031) 310
29 21 *E-mail:* rahel.wenger@hep-verlag.ch
Founded: 2000
Subjects: Business, Earth Sciences, Economics,
Gardening, Plants, Geography, Geology, Management, Military Science, Nonfiction (General), Sports, Athletics
ISBN Prefix(es): 978-3-7225; 978-3-85942; 978-
3-03905; 978-3-905905
Distribution Center: Brockhaus Kommissionsgeschaeft GmbH, Kreidlerstr 9, 70806 Kornwestheim, Germany *Tel:* (071) 54 13 27 0
Fax: (071) 54 13 27 13 *E-mail:* info@brocom.
de *Web Site:* www.brocom.de (Austria & Germany)

Herder AG Basel Verlagsauslieferungen
Muttenzerstr 109, 4133 Pratteln 1
Tel: (061) 827 90 60 *Fax:* (061) 827 90 67
Key Personnel
Sales: Chantal Metzger
Subjects: Philosophy, Religion - Other, Theology
ISBN Prefix(es): 978-3-906371; 978-3-906372
Associate Companies: Verlag Herder & Co, Austria; Verlag Herder GmbH & Co KG, Germany; Herder und Herder GmbH, Germany;
Verlag A G Ploetz GmbH & Co KG, Germany;
Editorial Herder SA, Spain

Edition Hier & Jetzt, *imprint of* Synergia Verlag

**Hier + Jetzt Verlag fuer Kultur & Geschichte
GmbH**
Langacker 16, 5405 Baden-Daettwil
Tel: (056) 470 03 00
E-mail: admin@hierundjetzt.ch
Web Site: www.hierundjetzt.ch
Founded: 1998
Subjects: Agriculture, Biography, Memoirs, Economics, Environmental Studies, History, Music,
Dance, Photography, Culture, Museology
ISBN Prefix(es): 978-3-03919; 978-3-906419
Distribution Center: AVA Verlagsauslieferung AG, Centralweg 16, Postfach 27, 8910
Affoltern am Albis *Tel:* (044) 762 42 51
Fax: (044) 762 42 10 *E-mail:* e.laub@ava.ch
(Switzerland book trade)
Brockhaus/Commission, Kreidlerstr 9, 70806 Kornwestheim, Germany *Tel:* (07154) 13 27 0
Fax: (07154) 13 27 13 *E-mail:* heirundjetzt@
brocom.de (abroad, book trade & private)

Hogrefe AG+
Member of Hogrefe Verlagsgruppe

Laenggass-Str 76, 3000 Bern 9
Tel: (031) 300 45 00 *Fax:* (031) 300 45 90
E-mail: verlag@hogrefe.ch
Web Site: www.hogrefe.ch
Key Personnel
Chief Executive Officer/Publisher: Dr G-Juergen
Hogrefe *E-mail:* juergen.hogrefe@hogrefe.ch
Marketing: Christian Liengme *Tel:* (031) 300 46
37 *E-mail:* christian.liengme@hogrefe.ch
Founded: 1927 (as Verlag Hans Huber)
Specialize in psychology, psychotherapy & psychiatry.
Subjects: Education, Medicine, Nursing, Dentistry, Psychology, Psychiatry
ISBN Prefix(es): 978-3-456; 978-3-8017
Subsidiaries: Hogrefe Publishing Corp (Boston,
MA, USA & Toronto, ON, Canada); Psychodiagnostika Brno sro (Brno, Czech Republic);
Testzentrale der Schweizer Psychologen AG
(Bern, Switzerland)
U.S. Office(s): Hogrefe Publishing Corp,
7 Bulfinch Pl, Suite 202, Boston, MA
02114, United States *Fax:* 617-354-6875
E-mail: customerservice@hogrefe-publishing.
com *Web Site:* us.hogrefe.com
Bookshop(s): Schanzenstr 1, 3000 Bern 9
Tel: (031) 3004646 *Fax:* (031) 3004656
E-mail: contactbern@huberlang.com; Zeltweg
6, 8032 Zurich *Tel:* (044) 268 39 39 *Fax:* (044)
268 39 20 *E-mail:* contactzurich@huberlang.
com
Distribution Center: Buchzentrum AG (BZ), Industriestr Ost 10, 4614 Haegendorf *Tel:* (062)
209 25 25 *E-mail:* kundendienst@buchzentrum.
ch
Brockhaus Kommissionsgeschaeft GmbH, Kreidlerstr 9, 70806 Kornwestheim, Germany
Tel: (0715) 413 27 34 *E-mail:* hanshuber@
brocom.de

Edition Howeg
Burglistr 21, 8002 Zurich
Tel: (044) 201 0650; (078) 771 0806 (cell)
E-mail: edition_howeg@datacomm.ch
Web Site: www.editionhoweg.ch
Subjects: Art, Poetry
ISBN Prefix(es): 978-3-85736

Verlag Huber, *imprint of* Orell Fuessli Verlag
AG

Hug Musikverlage+
Grossmuensterplatz 7, 8001 Zurich
Mailing Address: Limmatquai 28-30, Postfach,
8022 Zurich
Tel: (044) 269 41 40 *Fax:* (044) 269 41 06
E-mail: info@hug-musikverlage.ch
Web Site: www.hug-musikverlage.ch
Key Personnel
Dir: Erika Hug
Founded: 1807
Subjects: Music, Dance
ISBN Prefix(es): 978-3-909415
Associate Companies: Edition Foetisch-Foetisch
Freres, 1002 Lausanne
Distribution Center: Musica Viva Musikalien-
und Buchgrosshandel, Schuetzenmattstr 14-16,
8180 Buelach *Tel:* (044) 864 41 50 *Fax:* (044)
864 41 51 *E-mail:* office@musicaviva.ch *Web
Site:* www.musicaviva.ch
Orders to: Alphonse Leduc & Cie, 175, rue
Saint-Honore, 75040 Paris Cedex 01, France
Tel: 01 42 96 89 11 *Fax:* 01 42 86 02 83
E-mail: alphonseleduc@wanadoo.fr *Web
Site:* www.alphonseleduc.com
Ancora Verlagsservice Halbig eK, Schreinerstr 8,
85077 Manching, Germany *Tel:* (08459) 3249-
0 *Fax:* (08459) 3249-15 *E-mail:* vertrieb@
ancora-verlagsservice.de *Web Site:* www.
ancora-verlagsservice.de (worldwide exc France
& Switzerland)

Charles Huguenin-Pro Arte, see Editions Schola Cantorum - Charles Huguenin-Pro Arte - Cantate Domino

Idegraf SA
28 Route de Chancy, 1213 Petit-Lancy
Tel: (022) 792 03 96 *Fax:* (022) 793 63 30 (orders)
E-mail: info@formez-vous.com; sales@formez-vous.com
Web Site: www.formez-vous.com
Subjects: Education, Language Arts, Linguistics
ISBN Prefix(es): 978-2-88259

Editions Ides et Calendes SA+
Ave de Rumine 55, 1005 Lausanne
Tel: (032) 725 38 61
E-mail: info@idesetcalendes.com
Web Site: www.idesetcalendes.com
Key Personnel
Chief Executive: Alain Bouret
Founded: 1941
Subjects: Art, Law, Photography
ISBN Prefix(es): 978-2-8258

IHEID, see Institut de Hautes etudes Internationales et du Developpment

ILO Publications
4 route des Morillons, 1211 Geneva 22
Tel: (022) 799 6111 *Fax:* (022) 798 8685
E-mail: communication@ilo.org; ilo@ilo.org; infom@ilo.org
Web Site: www.ilo.org
Subjects: Labor, Industrial Relations, Law, Management, Child Labor, Employment, Gender Issues, Labor Issues, Labor Law, Labor Statistics, Occupational Safety & Health, Social Protection, Training
ISBN Prefix(es): 978-92-2
Distribution Center: Turpin Distribution, Stratton Business Park, Pegasus Dr, Biggleswade, Beds SG18 8TQ, United Kingdom *Tel:* (01767) 604951 *Fax:* (01767) 601640 *E-mail:* ilo@turpin-distribution.com

Infel AG
Militaerstr 36, 8004 Zurich
Tel: (044) 299 41 41
E-mail: welcome@infel.ch
Web Site: www.infel.ch
Key Personnel
Chief Executive Officer: Alfredo Trasatti
E-mail: trasatti@infel.ch
Publishing Dir: Michael Frischkopf *Tel:* (044) 299 41 36 *E-mail:* frischkopf@infel.ch
Subjects: Electronics, Electrical Engineering
Branch Office(s)
Waisenhausplatz 22, 3011 Bern *Tel:* (031) 320 13 13

Infolio Edition
En Crausaz, 1124 Gollion
Tel: (021) 863 22 47 *Fax:* (021) 863 22 49
E-mail: info@infolio.ch
Web Site: www.infolio.ch
Founded: 1999
Subjects: Archaeology, Architecture & Interior Design, Art, History, Photography
ISBN Prefix(es): 978-2-88474
Branch Office(s)
15, rue de Tournon, 75006 Paris, France
Tel: 01 45 48 62 70 *Fax:* 01 45 48 62 70
E-mail: comm@infolio.ch
Distribution Center: OLF SA, Route Andre Piller 39, Z I Corminboeuf, 1701 Fribourg
Tel: (026) 467 51 11 *Fax:* (026) 467 54 44
E-mail: commandes@olf.ch
Volumen, 13, rue du General Leclerc, 91165 Ballainvilliers Cedex, France *Tel:* 01 69 10 89 09 *Fax:* 01 69 48 49 63 (France & Belgium)

Ink Press GmbH
Langstr 94, 8004 Zurich
Tel: (079) 768 63 76
E-mail: info@ink-press.ch
Web Site: ink-press.ch
Key Personnel
Publisher: Susanne Schenzle *E-mail:* schenzle@ink-press.ch
Subjects: Art, Literature, Literary Criticism, Essays
ISBN Prefix(es): 978-3-906811

InnoVatio Verlags AG
Alte Jonastr 48, 8640 Rapperswil
Tel: (043) 25519-20 *Fax:* (043) 25519-29
Web Site: www.innovatio.de
Key Personnel
Contact: Roland Schatz *E-mail:* r.schatz@innovatio.de
Founded: 1985
Specialize in monthly & quarterly newsletters on media content analysis.
Subjects: Business, History
ISBN Prefix(es): 978-3-906501
Total Titles: 25 Print

Institut de Hautes etudes Internationales et du Developpment (Graduate Institute of International & Development Studies)+
Maison de la Paix, Chemin, Eugene-Rigot 2, 1211 Geneva
Mailing Address: CP 136, 1211 Geneva 21
Tel: (022) 908 57 00 *Fax:* (022) 908 57 10
E-mail: info@graduateinstitute.ch; publications@hei.unige.ch; webmaster@graduateinstitute.ch
Web Site: graduateinstitute.ch
Key Personnel
Dir: Philippe Burrin
Head, Publications: Marc Galvin *E-mail:* marc.galvin@graduateinstitute.ch
Press Officer: Michael Savage *Tel:* (022) 908 4373 *E-mail:* michael.savage@graduateinstitute.ch
Founded: 1927
Publishes only works originating from the Institute.
Subjects: Economics, History, Law, International Affairs, International Relations
Number of titles published annually: 10 Print
Total Titles: 12 Print
Distributed by Kegan Paul International (UK); Kluwer (The Hague); Presses Universitaires de France (PUF) (France)

International Labour Office, see ILO Publications

International Organization for Migration (IOM)
Publications Unit, 17 Route des Morillons, 1211 Geneva 19
Tel: (022) 717 9111 *Fax:* (022) 798 6150
E-mail: pubsales@iom.int; hq@iom.int; info@iom.int
Web Site: www.iom.int
Key Personnel
Dir General: William Lacy Swing
Deputy Dir General: Laura Thompson
Founded: 1951
Subjects: Migration
ISBN Prefix(es): 978-92-9068

International Union for Conservation of Nature, see IUCN (International Union for Conservation of Nature)

IOM, see International Organization for Migration (IOM)

Istituto Editoriale Ticinese
Via del Bramantino 3, 6500 Bellinzona

Tel: (091) 825 6622 *Fax:* (091) 825 1874
E-mail: casagrande@casagrande-online.ch
Web Site: www.casagrande-online.ch/Edizioni/iet
Key Personnel
Co-Founder & Editor: Libero Casagrande
Founded: 1900
Subjects: Fiction, Literature, Literary Criticism, Essays, Poetry
ISBN Prefix(es): 978-88-7713
Parent Company: Edizioni Casagrande SA

IUCN (International Union for Conservation of Nature)
Publishing Division, Rue Mauverney 28, 1196 Gland
Tel: (022) 999 0000 *Fax:* (022) 999 0002
E-mail: publications@iucn.org
Web Site: www.iucn.org/publications
Key Personnel
Publications Officer: Sarina van der Ploeg
Tel: (022) 999 0119 *E-mail:* sarina.vanderploeg@iucn.org
Founded: 1948
Subjects: Earth Sciences, Environmental Studies, Law
ISBN Prefix(es): 978-2-8317; 978-2-88032
Number of titles published annually: 100 Print
Total Titles: 1,100 Print
Distributed by Island Press
Orders to: Earthprint Ltd, Cavendish House, Cavendish Rd, Stevenage, Herts SG1 2EQ, United Kingdom *E-mail:* orders@earthprint.co.uk *Web Site:* www.earthprint.com
Island Press, University of Chicago Distribution Center, 11030 S Langley Ave, Chicago, IL 60628, United States *E-mail:* custserv@press.uchicago.edu *Web Site:* www.islandpress.org

Editions La Joie de Lire SA
5, Chemin Neuf, 1207 Geneva
Tel: (022) 807 33 99 *Fax:* (022) 807 33 92
E-mail: info@lajoiedelire.ch
Web Site: www.lajoiedelire.ch
Key Personnel
Dir: Francine Bouchet
Foreign Rights: Carina Solari *E-mail:* carina.solari@lajoiedelire.ch
Founded: 1987
Subjects: Art, Education, Entertainment
ISBN Prefix(es): 978-2-88258
Distribution Center: OLF-Office du Livre, ZI 3 Corminboeuf, 1701 Fribourg *Tel:* (026) 467 51 11 *Fax:* (026) 467 54 44 *E-mail:* information@olf.ch (Switzerland)
Heidiffusion, Rue de la Mercirie 14, 1003 Lausanne *Tel:* (021) 601 65 19 *Fax:* (078) 686 54 68 *E-mail:* l.feugere@heidiffusion.ch
Dimedia Diffusion, 539, Blvd Lebeau, Saint-Laurent, QC, Canada *Tel:* 514-336-3941 *Fax:* 514-331-3916
Harmonia Mundi, BP 20150, 13631 Arles Cedex, France *Tel:* 04 90 49 58 05 *Fax:* 04 90 49 58 35 *E-mail:* adv-livre@harmonia-mundi.com

Jordanverlag AG+
Steffenstr 1, 8052 Zurich
Tel: (044) 302 36 76
Founded: 1984
Interdenominational Christian belles-lettres & nonfiction books in standard German. Also 9 biblical books translated from Greek or Hebrew into Zurich dialect.
Subjects: Biblical Studies, Religion - Catholic, Religion - Protestant
ISBN Prefix(es): 978-3-906561
Total Titles: 50 Print

JPM Guides+
Ave William-Fraisse 12, 1006 Lausanne
Tel: (021) 617 75 61 *Fax:* (021) 616 12 57
Web Site: www.jpmguides.com

Key Personnel
Chief Executive Officer: Guy Minder *E-mail:* guy.
minder@jpmguides.com
Founded: 1992
Subjects: Travel & Tourism
ISBN Prefix(es): 978-2-88452
U.S. Office(s): JPM Publications, 245 E 19 St,
Suite 3D, New York, NY 10003, United States,
Contact: Dorsey Smith *Tel:* 212-777-1179
Fax: 212-777-1115 *E-mail:* dorsey.smith@
jpmguides.com
Distributed by Hunter Publishing
Foreign Rep(s): Daphne-Diffusion SA (Belgium);
Gazelle Book Services Ltd (UK); IMA (East
Africa); India Book Distributors (Bombay) Ltd
(India); K P Kyriakow Bookshop (Cyprus); Lit-
tle Hills Press Pty Ltd (Australia); Miller Dis-
tributors Ltd (Malta); Nouveau Quartier Latin
(France); Othmar Edelmann GmbH (Austria);
Pan Macmillan South Africa (South Africa);
Pansing Distribution Sdn Bhd (Singapore);
Photoglob AG (Switzerland); S G E L Cen-
tral Libros (Spain); Guides de Voyage Ulysse
(Canada)

JRP|Ringier Kunstverlag AG
Limmatstr 270, 8005 Zurich
Tel: (043) 311 27 50 *Fax:* (043) 311 27 51
E-mail: info@jrp-ringier.com
Web Site: www.jrp-ringier.com
Key Personnel
Publisher: Lionel Bovier *E-mail:* lionel.bovier@
jrp-ringier.com
Sales & Distribution: Lukas Haller *E-mail:* lukas.
haller@jrp-ringier.com
Subjects: Art, Contemporary Art
ISBN Prefix(es): 978-2-940271; 978-3-905701;
978-3-905770; 978-3-03764; 978-3-905829

Editions Nicolas Junod
12 rue Robert-de-Traz, 1206 Geneva
Tel: (022) 347 02 42 *Fax:* (022) 347 02 42
Key Personnel
Owner: M Nicolas Junod *E-mail:* nicolas.junod@
bluewin.ch
Founded: 1977
Subjects: Art, Cookery, Government, Political
Science, Health, Nutrition, History, Humor, Ra-
dio, TV
ISBN Prefix(es): 978-2-8297
Parent Company: SA de la Tribune de Geneve

S Karger AG+
Allschwilerstr 10, 4009 Basel
Tel: (061) 306 11 11 *Fax:* (061) 306 12 34
E-mail: karger@karger.com; permission@karger.
com
Web Site: www.karger.com
Key Personnel
President: Dr Thomas Karger
Dir, Sales & Marketing: Moritz Thommen
  E-mail: m.thommen@karger.com
Rights & Permissions: Silvia Meier
Founded: 1890
Specialize in the biomedical sciences, basic &
  clinical research, reviews & textbooks.
Subjects: Biological Sciences, Medicine, Nursing,
  Dentistry, Psychology, Psychiatry, Veterinary
  Science
ISBN Prefix(es): 978-3-8055; 978-3-318
Associate Companies: Karger China, 51F Raffles
  City Centre, 268 Xi Zang Middle Rd, Shang-
  hai 200001, China, Contact: Raymond Chew
  Tel: (021) 2312 7673 *Fax:* (021) 2312 7777
  E-mail: service@karger.cn *Web Site:* www.
  karger.cn; Enter & Read, 23, rue du Depart,
  75014 Paris, France *Tel:* 06 81 04 76 85
  E-mail: albertineluginbuhl@orange.fr; S Karger
  GmbH, Wilhelmstr 20A, 79098 Freiburg, Ger-
  many *Tel:* (0761) 45 20 70 *Fax:* (0761) 45
  20 714 *E-mail:* information@karger.com *Web
  Site:* www.karger.de; Karger India, Plot No

17, Yusuf Sarai Market, BL Glass Bldg, 2nd
floor, Sri Aurobindo Marg, New Delhi 110
016, India *Tel:* (011) 46029 633 *Fax:* (011)
46029 634 *E-mail:* r.kumar@kargerindia.com;
Karger Japan Inc, Shiba Daimon Asahi Bldg
2F, 1-2-23 Shiba Daimon, Minato-ku, Tokyo
105-0012, Japan *Tel:* (03) 6435 6242 *Fax:* (03)
6435 6244 *E-mail:* publisher@karger.jp; Karger
Regional Office (Malaysia), Level 28-03-03A,
PJ Exchange, No 16A, Persiaran Barat, 46050
Petaling Jaya, Malaysia *Tel:* (03) 7962 0158
Fax: (03) 7962 0001 *E-mail:* service@karger.
cn; S Karger Publishers Inc, 26 West Avon Rd,
PO Box 529, Unionville, CT 06085, United
States *Tel:* 860-675-7834 *Fax:* 860-675-7302
E-mail: karger@snet.net
Foreign Rep(s): dot.lib (Argentina, Brazil, Chile,
Uruguay); S Karger (Thailand); Tahir M Lodhi
Publishers' Consultants & Representatives
(Pakistan); Guy Simpson (Africa exc North
& South Africa)
Bookshop(s): Karger Libri AG, Petersgraben 31,
4009 Basel *Tel:* (061) 306 15 15 *Fax:* (061)
306 15 16 *E-mail:* info@libri.karger.ch *Web
Site:* www.libri.ch

Kein & Aber AG
Baeckerstr 52, 8026 Zurich
Tel: (044) 297-12-33 *Fax:* (044) 297-12-30
E-mail: info@keinundaber.ch; presse@
keinundaber.ch
Web Site: www.keinundaber.ch
Key Personnel
Publisher: Peter Haag
Media & Public Relations: Laurin Jaeggi
Sales: Hanna Boes *E-mail:* h.boes@keinundaber.
ch
Founded: 1997
Subjects: Fiction, Nonfiction (General)
ISBN Prefix(es): 978-3-0369; 978-3-906547

Editions Ketty & Alexandre+
chemin des Mules 6, 1063 Chapelle-sur-Moudon
Tel: (021) 9051111
Founded: 1975
Subjects: History
ISBN Prefix(es): 978-2-88114

Klett und Balmer AG Verlag
Grabenstr 17, 6341 Zug
Mailing Address: Postfach 1464, 6341 Baar
Tel: (041) 726 28 00 *Fax:* (041) 726 28 01
E-mail: info@klett.ch
Web Site: www.klett.ch
Key Personnel
Mng Dir: Irene Schuepfer *Tel:* (041) 726 28 33
  E-mail: irene.schuepfer@klett.ch
Assistant Manager & Finance: Beni Marty-Gisler
  Tel: (041) 726 28 13 *E-mail:* beni.marty@klett.
  ch
Sales & Marketing: Martin Laeuppi *Tel:* (041)
  726 28 15 *E-mail:* martin.laeuppi@klett.ch
Founded: 1967
Subjects: Education, Government, Political Sci-
  ence, Philosophy, Science (General)
ISBN Prefix(es): 978-3-264
Parent Company: Klett Gruppe, Rotebuehlstr 77,
70178 Stuttgart, Germany

Knapp Verlag AG
Gartenstr 25, 4600 Olten
Tel: (062) 296 50 48 *Fax:* (062) 296 51 27
E-mail: buch@knapp-verlag.ch
Web Site: www.knapp-verlag.ch
Key Personnel
Head, Publishing: Thomas Knapp
Founded: 2005
Subjects: Nonfiction (General)
ISBN Prefix(es): 978-3-905848
Distribution Center: Buchzentrum AG (BZ), In-
dustriestr Ost 10, 4614 Haegendorf *Tel:* (062)

209 25 25 *Fax:* (062) 209 26 27 *Web
Site:* www.buchzentrum.ch
GVA Gemeinsame Verlagsauslieferung GmbH
& Co KG, Postfach 2021, 37010 Goettingen,
Germany *Tel:* (0551) 487 177 *Fax:* (0551) 413
92 *Web Site:* www.gva-verlage.de (Germany &
Austria)

Kober Verlag AG
Postfach 1051, 8640 Rapperswil
Tel: (055) 214 11 34 *Fax:* (055) 214 11 32
E-mail: info@koberverlag.ch
Web Site: www.kober-verlag.ch
Founded: 1816
Subjects: Inspirational, Spirituality, Philosophy,
  Religion - Other, Theology
ISBN Prefix(es): 978-3-85767
Associate Companies: The Kober Press, 2534
  Chilton Way, Berkeley, CA 94704, United
  States *Tel:* 510-540-7309 *Fax:* 510-548-2411
  E-mail: koberpress@mindspring.com *Web
  Site:* www.kober.com
Distribution Center: Verlagsauslieferung Duran,
  Ernst-Sach-Str 4b, 78467 Konstanz, Germany
  Tel: (075) 31 59 90 0 *Fax:* (075) 31 59 90 19
  E-mail: manuel@duran-auslieferung.de *Web
  Site:* www.duran-auslieferung.de (Germany &
  Austria)

Kolumbus-Verlag+
Muehlebuehlstr 10, 5737 Menziken
Tel: (062) 771 13 70
Key Personnel
Mng Dir: Dr Phil G van den Bergh
Founded: 1945
Subjects: Language Arts, Linguistics, Philosophy
ISBN Prefix(es): 978-3-85769

Kommode Verlag+
Anemonenstr 40G, 8047 Zurich
Tel: (079) 246 5914 (cell)
E-mail: info@kommode-verlag.ch; vertrieb@
kommode-verlag.ch; pr@kommode-verlag.ch
Web Site: www.kommode-verlag.ch
Key Personnel
Publishing Dir: Annette Beger
Marketing/Distribution: Fr Somea Hurlimann
Public Relations/Communication: Fr Nani Khak-
shouri
Subjects: Architecture & Interior Design, Art,
  Drama, Theater, History, Literature, Literary
  Criticism, Essays, Music, Dance
ISBN Prefix(es): 978-3-9523768
Distribution Center: AVA Verlagsauslieferung
  AG, Centralweg 16, 8910 Affoltern am Albis
  Tel: (044) 762 42 00 *E-mail:* avainfo@ava.ch
GVA Gemeinsame Verlagsauslieferung Goet-
  tingen, Postfach 2021, 37010 Goettingen,
  Germany *Tel:* (0551) 384200-0 *Fax:* (0551)
  384200-10 *E-mail:* bestellung@gva-verlage.de
Central Books Ltd, One Heath Park Indus-
  trial Estate, Freshwater Rd, Dagenham RM8
  1RX, United Kingdom *Tel:* (020) 8525 8800
  Fax: (020) 8599 2694 *E-mail:* contactus@
  centralbooks.com *Web Site:* www.centralbooks.
  com

**Kranich-Verlag, Dres Alice Gertrud und Hans
  Rudolf Bosch-Gwalter**
Dufour Str 30, 8702 Zollikon
Tel: (044) 391 84 84 *Fax:* (086) 5695699
E-mail: buecher@kranichverlag.com
Web Site: www.kranichverlag.com
Key Personnel
Founder: Hans Rudolf Bosch-Gwalter; Alice
  Gertrud Bosch-Gwalter
Founded: 1958
Specialize in prints & bibliophile editions.
Subjects: Architecture & Interior Design, Art,
  Biblical Studies, Biography, Memoirs, Busi-
  ness, Economics, History, Language Arts, Lin-
  guistics, Law, Literature, Literary Criticism,
  Essays, Philosophy, Poetry, Psychology, Psychi-

atry, Religion - Catholic, Religion - Protestant,
Theology, Travel & Tourism
ISBN Prefix(es): 978-3-906640; 978-3-909194
Number of titles published annually: 5 Print
Total Titles: 164 Print; 2 CD-ROM

Kuemmerly+Frey, see Hallwag
Kuemmerly+Frey AG

Edition Kunzelmann GmbH
Gruetstr 28, 8134 Adliswil
Tel: (044) 710 36 81 *Fax:* (044) 710 38 17
E-mail: edition@kunzelmann.ch
Web Site: www.kunzelmann.ch
Key Personnel
Mng Dir: Irene Kunzelmann
Rights: Daniela Jordi
Sales: Maurizio Olori
Founded: 1945
Subjects: Education, Music, Dance
ISBN Prefix(es): 978-3-85662; 978-3-9521049
Distributor for Edition Musica Budapest; Music-
Partner; Edition Peters
Foreign Rep(s): Edition Peters Frankfurt (Eu-
rope); Edition Peters London (Europe); Edition
Peters New York (USA)

Labor et Fides SA+
One rue Beauregard, 1204 Geneva
Tel: (022) 311 32 69 *Fax:* (022) 781 30 51
E-mail: contact@laboretfides.com
Web Site: www.laboretfides.com
Key Personnel
Dir: Gabriel de Montmollin
Dir, Administration: Guy Burnier
Founded: 1924
Protestant French language publisher.
Subjects: Biblical Studies, Religion - Protestant,
Social Sciences, Sociology, Theology, Ethics
ISBN Prefix(es): 978-2-8309
Distribution Center: OLF, Zl 3 Corminboeuf,
1701 Fribourg *Tel:* (026) 467 51 11 *Fax:* (026)
467 54 66 *E-mail:* information@olf.ch
Dimedia, 539, bl Lebeau, Montreal, Quebec, QC
H4N 1S2, Canada *Tel:* 514-336-3941 *Fax:* 514-
331-3916 *Web Site:* www.dimedia.qc.ca/index.
php
Union Distribution (UD), Siege Social 106 rue
Petit Leroy, 94550 Chevilly-Larue, France *Web
Site:* www.ud-net.com (France & Belgium)

Les Editions de l'Aire
rue de l'Union, 15, 1800 Vevey
Mailing Address: CP 57, 1800 Vevey
Tel: (021) 923 68 36 *Fax:* (021) 923 68 23
E-mail: editionaire@bluewin.ch
Web Site: www.editions-aire.ch
Key Personnel
Dir: Michel Moret
Founded: 1978
Subjects: History, Literature, Literary Criticism,
Essays, Poetry
ISBN Prefix(es): 978-2-88108

Peter Lang AG+
Hochfeldstr 32, 3012 Bern
Mailing Address: PO Box 350, 2542 Pieterlen
Tel: (032) 376 17 17 *Fax:* (032) 376 17 27
E-mail: info@peterlang.com
Web Site: www.peterlang.com
Key Personnel
Chairman of the Board: Claude Begle
Chief Executive Officer & Deputy Chairman of
the Board: Kelly Shergill
Chief Financial Officer: Vanessa Weber
Head, Warehouse & Logistics: Abdurahman Kay-
maz
Founded: 1977
Specialize in academic publications.
Subjects: Art, History, Language Arts, Linguis-
tics, Law, Literature, Literary Criticism, Essays,

Philosophy, Social Sciences, Sociology, Theology
ISBN Prefix(es): 978-0-8204; 978-3-631; 978-
3-906750; 978-3-906751; 978-3-906752; 978-
3-906753; 978-3-906754; 978-3-906755; 978-
3-906757; 978-3-906758; 978-3-906759; 978-
3-906756; 978-3-906760; 978-3-906761; 978-
3-906762; 978-3-906763; 978-3-906764; 978-
3-906765; 978-3-906766; 978-3-906767; 978-
3-906768; 978-3-906769; 978-3-03910; 978-
3-03769; 978-3-03911; 978-3-0343; 978-3-
906770
Subsidiaries: Peter Lang GmbH; Peter Lang Publishing Inc; PIE-Peter Lang SA

Lenos Verlag+
Spalentorweg 12, 4003 Basel
Tel: (061) 261 34 14
E-mail: lenos@lenos.ch
Web Site: www.lenos.ch
Key Personnel
Contact: Christoph Blum; Tom Forrer
Founded: 1970
Subjects: Government, Political Science, Journal-
ism, Nonfiction (General)
ISBN Prefix(es): 978-3-85787
Distribution Center: AVA Verlagsaulieferung
AG, Centralweg 16, 8910 Affoltern am Al-
bis *Tel:* (044) 762 42 60 *Fax:* (044) 762 42 10
E-mail: verlagsservice@ava.ch *Web Site:* www.
ava.ch
Prolit Verlagsauslieferung GmbH, Postfach 9,
35461 Fernwald, Germany, Contact: Nina
Kallweit *Tel:* (0641) 943 93 24 *Fax:* (0641)
943 93 89 *E-mail:* n.kallweit@prolit.de *Web
Site:* www.prolit.de (Germany & Austria)

Leonis Verlag Ag+
Hurdackerstr 3, 8600 Duebendorf
Key Personnel
Proprietor, Mng Dir: Dr Wolfgang M Metz
Founded: 1976
Subjects: How-to, Religion - Other, Self-Help
ISBN Prefix(es): 978-3-7210
Associate Companies: Doulos Verlag

Librairie Bernard Letu+
2, rue Calvin, 1204 Geneva
Tel: (022) 310 47 57 *Fax:* (022) 310 84 92
E-mail: arts@letubooks.com
Web Site: www.letubooks.com
Founded: 1973
Subjects: Art, Photography
ISBN Prefix(es): 978-2-88051

Les Editions de l'Hebe SA
Chemin du Lac 39, 1637 Charmey
Mailing Address: CP 45, 1637 Charmey
Tel: (026) 927 50 30 *Fax:* (026) 927 26 61
E-mail: info@lhebe.ch
Web Site: www.lhebe.ch
Key Personnel
Dir: Jean-Philippe Ayer *E-mail:* jp.ayer@lhebe.ch;
Eleonora Gualandris *E-mail:* e.gualandris@
lhebe.ch
Subjects: Biography, Memoirs, Nonfiction (Gen-
eral)
ISBN Prefix(es): 978-2-88485; 978-2-940063
Distribution Center: OLF, Rte Andre Piller 39,
1720 Corminboeuf, Fribourg

Lia Rumantscha
Via da la Plessur 47, 7001 Cuira
Tel: (081) 258 32 22
E-mail: info@rumantsch.ch
Web Site: www.liarumantscha.ch
Key Personnel
Communication & Media: Andreas Gabriel
Founded: 1919
Company also gives financial support to other
publications in Romansh in the Romansh-
speaking area.

Subjects: History, Language Arts, Linguistics,
Literature, Literary Criticism, Essays, Music,
Dance, Poetry, Regional Interests, Religion -
Other
ISBN Prefix(es): 978-3-906680
Branch Office(s)
Via Curtin pign 35, 7031 Laax *Tel:* (081) 920 80
70
Stradung 23, 7460 Savognin *Tel:* (081) 684 28 11
Via Sura 79, 7530 Zernez *Tel:* (081) 860 07 61
Plazza da posta, 7432 Ziran *Tel:* (081) 258 32 22

Libelle Verlag AG
Sternengarten 6, 8574 Lengwil
Mailing Address: Postfach 10 05 24, 78405 Kon-
stanz
Tel: (071) 688 35 55 *Fax:* (071) 688 35 65
E-mail: info@libelle.ch
Web Site: www.libelle.ch
Key Personnel
Editorial & Press: Ekkehard Faude
E-mail: faude@libelle.ch; Elisabeth Tschiemer
E-mail: tschiemer@libelle.ch
Founded: 1979
Subjects: Art, Drama, Theater, History, Humor,
Literature, Literary Criticism, Essays, Myster-
ies, Suspense, Science (General)
ISBN Prefix(es): 978-3-909081; 978-3-905707
Foreign Rep(s): Indiebook (Nicole Grabert, Judith
Heckel, Christiane Krause) (Germany); Markus
Wieser (Switzerland)
Distribution Center: AVA Verlagsauslieferung
AG, Centralweg 16, Postfach 119, 8910 Af-
foltern am Albis, Contact: Helene Amsler
Tel: (044) 762 41 68 *Fax:* (044) 762 42 10
E-mail: h.amsler@ava.ch
Leipziger Kommissions- und Grossbuchhandels-
gesellschaft mbH (LKG), An der Suedspitze 1-
12, 04571 Roetha, Germany, Contact: Veronika
Reumann *Tel:* (034206) 65-288 *Fax:* (034206)
65-1762 *E-mail:* vreumann@lkg-service.de *Web
Site:* www.lkg-va.de (Germany & Austria)

Lichtwelle-Verlag
Oberdorfstr 28, 8024 Zurich
Mailing Address: Postfach 770, 8024 Zurich
Tel: (044) 252 68 78 *Fax:* (044) 252 68 60
E-mail: info@lichtwelle-verlag.ch
Web Site: www.lichtwelle-verlag.ch
Key Personnel
Chief Executive Officer: Wolfgang Jaeger
Management: Charlot van Stuijvenberg
Subjects: Inspirational, Spirituality
ISBN Prefix(es): 978-3-950878

Licorne-Verlag/Verlag Alpenhorn-Kalender
Ryf 54, Postfach, 3280 Murten
Tel: (026) 670 21 50 *Fax:* (026) 670 33 91
E-mail: info@licorne.ch
Web Site: www.licorne.ch
Founded: 1845
Subjects: Architecture & Interior Design, Art,
Fiction, Geography, Geology, History, Photog-
raphy, Regional Interests
ISBN Prefix(es): 978-3-85654
Orders to: Postfach, 3550 Langnau

Limmat Verlag
Quellenstr 25, 8005 Zurich
Mailing Address: Postfach, 8031 Zurich
Tel: (044) 44 5 80 80 *Fax:* (044) 44 5 80 88
E-mail: presse@limmatverlag.ch; vertrieb@
limmatverlag.ch
Web Site: www.limmatverlag.ch
Key Personnel
Publishing Dir: Juerg Zimmerli
E-mail: zimmerli@limmatverlag.ch
Founded: 1975
Subjects: Art, Biography, Memoirs, Fiction, Film,
Video, Government, Political Science, Litera-
ture, Literary Criticism, Essays, Poetry, Social
Sciences, Sociology, Women's Studies
ISBN Prefix(es): 978-3-85791

Number of titles published annually: 30 Online
Total Titles: 500 Print
Foreign Rep(s): Beat Eberle (Switzerland); Herrn
(Hans Frieden) (Germany); Markus Wieser
(Switzerland)
Distribution Center: AVA Verlagsauslieferung
AG, Centralweg 16, 8910 Affoltern am Al-
bis *Tel:* (044) 762 42 50 *Fax:* (044) 762 42 10
E-mail: verlagsservice@ava.ch
GVA Gemeinsame Verlagsauslieferung, Post-
fach 20212, 37010 Goettingen, Germany
Tel: (0551) 48 71 77 *Fax:* (0551) 41 39 2
E-mail: bestellung@gva-verlage.de (Germany,
Austria & rest of world)

Lokwort Buchverlag
Aegertenstr 73, 3000 Bern 6
Mailing Address: Postfach 260, 3000 Bern 6
Tel: (031) 351 48 48 *Fax:* (031) 351 48 49
E-mail: verlag@lokwort.ch
Web Site: www.lokwort.ch
Key Personnel
Publisher: Bernard Engler
Founded: 1995
Subjects: Inspirational, Spirituality
ISBN Prefix(es): 978-3-906786

LZ Fachverlag AG
Sihlbruggstr 105a, 6341 Baar
Tel: (041) 767 76 76 *Fax:* (041) 767 79 11
E-mail: info@lzfachverlag.ch
Web Site: www.lzfachverlag.ch
Key Personnel
Publishing Dir: Renate Kucher *E-mail:* renate.
kucher@lzmedien.ch
Founded: 1959
Subjects: Biography, Memoirs, History, Maritime
ISBN Prefix(es): 978-3-9520027; 978-3-9520756;
978-3-906970; 978-3-9522033
Branch Office(s)
Forchstr 60, Postfach 1474, 8032 Zurich
Tel: (044) 388 99 66 *Fax:* (044) 388 99 60

Maihof Verlag, see LZ Fachverlag AG

La Maison de la Bible+
Praz-Roussy 4 bis, 1032 Romanel-sur-Lausanne
Mailing Address: BP 151, 1032 Romanel-sur-
Lausanne
Tel: (021) 867 10 10; (021) 867 10 20 (customer
service) *Fax:* (021) 867 10 15
E-mail: info@bible.ch; ventes@maisonbible.net
Web Site: www.maisonbible.net
Key Personnel
Dir: Jean-Pierre Bezin
Contact: Olivia Festal; Stefan Waldmann
Founded: 1917
Specialize in publishing & translating bibles,
books, audio & CD-ROM.
Membership(s): CBA; ECPA.
Subjects: Biblical Studies, Biography, Memoirs,
Human Relations, Religion - Protestant, Theol-
ogy, Family
ISBN Prefix(es): 978-2-8260; 978-2-608
Number of titles published annually: 25 Print
Total Titles: 340 Print; 4 CD-ROM; 47 Audio
Parent Company: Geneva Bible Society
Imprints: Editions Ourania
Distributed by Haenssler/Bolanz/C L Verlag (Ger-
many); Service d'Orientation Biblique (Canada)
Distributor for Crossway; Focus on the Family;
Harvest House; Lion, OM; Moody (USA);
Thomas Nelson (USA); STL; Zondervan
(USA)
Bookshop(s): Rebgasse 21, 4058 Basel *Tel:* (061)
681 33 21 *E-mail:* basel@hausderbibel.ch; Rue
de Rive 11, 1204 Geneva, Manager: Medhat
Eskandar *Tel:* (022) 310 52 59 *Fax:* (022) 311
05 67 *E-mail:* geneve@maisonbible.net; Rue
Bournot 25, 2400 Le Locle, Manager: Francine
Houriet *Tel:* (032) 931 26 66 *E-mail:* lelocle@
maisonbible.net; Baeckerstr 10, 8004 Zurich

Tel: (044) 201 29 41 *Fax:* (044) 201 12
40 *E-mail:* zurich@hausderbibel.ch *Web
Site:* www.haus-der-bibel.ch; Rue de Mul-
house 61, 90000 Belfort, France *Tel:* 03 84 28
81 50 *Fax:* 03 84 28 81 50 *E-mail:* belfort@
maisonbible.net; 115, cours d'Alsace-Lorraine,
33000 Bordeaux, France *Tel:* 05 56 52 46
92 *E-mail:* bordeaux@maisonbible.net; 7,
Grand'Rue, 67500 Haguenau, France *Tel:* 03
88 06 15 15 *E-mail:* haguenau@maisonbible.
net; 130, Ave Thiers, 69006 Lyon, France
Tel: 04 37 48 49 85; 09 51 48 49 85 *Fax:* 09
56 48 49 85 *E-mail:* lyon@maisonbible.net;
184, ave de la Rose, 13013 Marseille, France
Tel: 04 91 78 69 69 *E-mail:* marseille@
maisonbible.net; 78, Grand Rue, 54000 Nancy,
France *Tel:* 03 83 35 08 97 *E-mail:* nancy@
maisonbible.net; 135, Blvd Saint-Michel, 75005
Paris, France *Tel:* 01 43 26 80 53 *Fax:* 01 46
33 90 22 *E-mail:* paris@maisonbible.net; Via
Balbi, 125 R, 16126 Genoa, Italy *Tel:* (010)
247 21 94 *E-mail:* genova@maisonbible.net;
Via Falcone 1, 97100 Ragusa, Italy *Tel:* (0932)
713 146 *E-mail:* ragusa@maisonbible.net; Via
Massari 189/B, 10148 Turin, Italy *Tel:* (011)
205 23 86 *E-mail:* torino@maisonbible.net

Editions M+H, see Editions Medecine &
Hygiene

Manufacture of Art
Seestr 105, 9326 Horn
Tel: (071) 888 6663 *Fax:* (071) 888 6664
E-mail: info@manufacture-of-art.com
Web Site: www.manufacture-of-art.com
Key Personnel
Mng Dir: Sabine Irion
Founded: 2009
Subjects: Art
ISBN Prefix(es): 978-3-9523607

Manus Verlag AG
Bergstr 90, 8708 Maennedorf
Tel: (044) 920 27 27 *Fax:* (044) 920 27 40
Web Site: www.manus.ch
Key Personnel
Manager: Kurt Borer
Founded: 1968
Subjects: Art
ISBN Prefix(es): 978-3-907003; 978-3-906982;
978-3-906956; 978-3-907956

Markt & Technik AG, see Pearson Schweitz AG

Editions de la Matze
Route des Ronquoz 86, 1950 Sion
Tel: (027) 327 72 34 *Fax:* (027) 327 72 44
E-mail: info@editionsmatze.ch
Web Site: www.editionsmatze.ch
Founded: 1975
Subjects: Archaeology, Art, Fiction, History, Mili-
tary Science
ISBN Prefix(es): 978-2-88025

Editions Medecine & Hygiene
46, chemin de la Mousse, 1225 Chene-Bourg
Tel: (022) 702 93 11 *Fax:* (022) 702 93 55
E-mail: admin@medhyg.ch
Web Site: www.medhyg.ch
Key Personnel
Dir: Dr Bertrand Kiefer *Tel:* (022) 702 93 36
E-mail: bertrand.kiefer@medhyg.ch
Founded: 1943
Subjects: Medicine, Nursing, Dentistry, Psychol-
ogy, Psychiatry, Science (General)
ISBN Prefix(es): 978-2-88049
Bookshop(s): Librairie Ellipse, 14 rue Rousseau,
1201 Geneva

Editions Medecine et Hygiene, *imprint of* Georg
Editeur SA

Memory/Cage Editions
Flurstr 93 (Hof), 8047 Zurich
Tel: (044) 281 35 65 *Fax:* (044) 281 35 66
E-mail: mail@memorycage.com
Web Site: www.memorycage.com
Founded: 1994
Subjects: Art, Literature, Literary Criticism, Es-
says, Photography
ISBN Prefix(es): 978-3-907053
Orders to: DAP, 155 Sixth Ave, New York, NY
10013, United States, Contact: Amy Lozada
Tel: 212-627-1999 *Fax:* 212-627-9484

Editions H Messeiller SA
St-Nicolas 11, 2006 Neuchatel
Mailing Address: CP 95, 2006 Neuchatel
Tel: (032) 725 12 96 *Fax:* (032) 724 19 37
E-mail: admin@messeiller.ch
Web Site: www.messeiller.ch
Key Personnel
Dir: Raphael Gambarini
Founded: 1887
Subjects: Art, Education, Law, Psychology, Psy-
chiatry, Public Administration, Religion - Other
ISBN Prefix(es): 978-2-8261

Midas Computer Verlag, *imprint of* Midas
Verlag AG

Midas Management Verlag, *imprint of* Midas
Verlag AG

Midas Verlag AG
Dunantstr 3, 8044 Zurich
Tel: (044) 242 61 02 *Fax:* (044) 242 61 05
E-mail: kontakt@midas.ch
Web Site: www.midas.ch
Key Personnel
Publishing Dir: Gregory C Zaech
Subjects: Computers, Management, Marketing,
Nonfiction (General), Graphics & Design
ISBN Prefix(es): 978-3-907020; 978-3-907100
Imprints: Goldfish Verlag; Midas Computer Ver-
lag; Midas Management Verlag
Distribution Center: Balmer Buecherdienst AG,
Im Kobiboden, 8840 Einsiedeln, Contact: Petra
Wolf *Tel:* (055) 418 89 22 *Fax:* (055) 418 89
58 *E-mail:* petra.wolf@balmer-bd.ch
Dr Franz Hain Verlagsauslieferungen GmbH, Dr-
Otto-Neurath-Gasse 5, 1220 Vienna, Austria,
Contact: Michaela Puchberger *Tel:* (01) 282 65
65 77 *Fax:* (01) 282 52 82 *E-mail:* bestell@
hain.at
Prolit Verlagslauslieferung GmbH, Siemensstr 16,
35463 Fernwald, Germany, Contact: Jens Vogt
Tel: (0641) 943 932 31 *Fax:* (0641) 943 93 39
E-mail: j.vogt@prolit.de

Verlag Minerva International Bern+
Wabersackerstr 31a, 3097 Liebefed
Tel: (031) 372 62 23 *Fax:* (031) 372 62 23
E-mail: info@minervaint.ch; verlag.minerva.int@
bluewin.ch
Web Site: www.minervaint.ch
Key Personnel
Editor: Louis R Jenzer
Founded: 1991
Membership(s): Bern Writers Association; Pen
Club; Swiss Booksellers & Publishers Associa-
tion (SBVV); Swiss Writers Association.
ISBN Prefix(es): 978-3-9520216; 978-3-906555
Total Titles: 15 Print; 8 Audio
Distributor for Prodest SA Lugano; WerdtVerlag
Zuerich
Book Club(s): Penclub; Swisswriter

Edition Moderne AG
Eglistr 8, 8004 Zurich
Tel: (044) 491 96 82 *Fax:* (044) 401 19 44
E-mail: post@editionmoderne.ch

Web Site: www.editionmoderne.ch
Key Personnel
Design: Joe Zimmermann
Editor: David Basler
Founded: 1981
ISBN Prefix(es): 978-3-03731
Number of titles published annually: 20 Print
Total Titles: 200 Print
Distribution Center: AVA Verlagsauslieferung
AG/Scheidegger & Co AG, Centralweg 16,
8910 Affoltern am Albis *Tel:* (044) 762 42 00
Fax: (044) 762 42 10 *E-mail:* verlagsservice@
ava.ch *Web Site:* www.ava.ch
Pictopia Comics, Lichtensteinstr 64, 1090 Vi-
enna, Austria, Contact: Sebastian Broskwa
Tel: (0676) 93 00 789 *E-mail:* office@pictopia.
at *Web Site:* www.pictopia.at
LKG Leipziger Kommissions- und Grossbuchhan-
delsgesellschaft mbH, An der Suedspitze 1-12,
04571 Roetha, Germany, Contact: Elisabeth
Kaiser *Tel:* (034206) 65-100 *Fax:* (034206)
65-110 *E-mail:* ekaiser@lkg-service.de *Web
Site:* www.lkg-va.de

Lars Mueller Publishers GmbH+
Pfingstweidstr 6, 8005 Zurich
Tel: (044) 274 37 40 *Fax:* (044) 274 37 41
E-mail: info@lars-mueller.ch; editorial@lars-
muller.ch; marketing@lars-muller.ch; sales@
lars-muller.ch
Web Site: www.lars-mueller-publishers.com
Key Personnel
Owner: Lars Mueller *E-mail:* lars@lars-mueller-
publishers.com
Marketing & Press/Communications: Julia Sumi
E-mail: julia@lars-muller.ch
Sales: Susanne Schenzle *E-mail:* susanne@lars-
muller.ch
Founded: 1983
Membership(s): Motovun Group of International
Publishers (MGIP); Swiss Independent Publish-
ers (SWIPS).
Subjects: Architecture & Interior Design, Art,
Photography, Graphic Design, Typography
ISBN Prefix(es): 978-3-906700; 978-3-907044;
978-3-907078; 978-3-03778
Number of titles published annually: 20 Print
Foreign Rep(s): Asia Publishers Service (Ed-
ward Summerson) (China, Hong Kong, Ko-
rea, Philippines, Taiwan); Book Bird Publish-
ers Representatives (Pakistan); Book City Co
(Iran); Canadian Manda Group (Canada); Elisa-
beth Harder-Kreimann (Scandinavia); Idea SRL
(Italy); Interart Ltd (France); Jocanda Media
(Pty) Ltd (Shay Heydenrych) (South Africa);
Books International di Piretti Massimiliano
(Italy); Nationwide Book Distributors (Andrew
Tizzard) (New Zealand); Peribo (Australia);
Prestel Publishing Ltd (Japan, UK, USA); Pub-
lishers International Marketing (Chris Ash-
down) (Southeast Asia); Gabrielle Redmond
(Ireland); Representaciones Editoriales (Nicolas
Friedmann) (Caribbean, Latin America); Tapas
Dutta (Bhutan, India, Nepal, Sri Lanka); Timuri
Books (Joseph Makope) (Africa exc South
Africa); Ward International (Book Export) Ltd
(Richard Ward) (Eastern Mediterranean, Israel,
Middle East, North Africa)
Distribution Center: AVA Verlagsauslieferung
AG, Centralweg 16, 8910 Affoltern am Albis,
Contact: Karin Schiemann *Tel:* (044) 762 42 02
Fax: (044) 762 42 10 *E-mail:* k.schiemann@
ava.ch

Nachtschatten Verlag
Kronengasse 11, 4502 Solothurn
Mailing Address: Postfach 448, 4502 Solothurn
Tel: (032) 621 89 49 *Fax:* (032) 621 89 47
E-mail: info@nachtschatten.ch
Web Site: www.nachtschatten.ch
Key Personnel
Publishing Dir: Roger Liggenstorfer
  E-mail: roger@nachtschatten.ch

Public Relations & Communications: David
Hoener *Tel:* (076) 426 66 14 *E-mail:* david@
nachtschatten.ch
Founded: 1984
ISBN Prefix(es): 978-3-03788; 978-3-907080
Foreign Rep(s): Richard Bhend (Switzerland);
Gmunden (Alfred Trux) (Austria); Ines Schae-
fer (Germany)
Distribution Center: AVA Verlagsauslieferung
AG, Centralweg 16, 8910 Affoltern am Albis
Tel: (01) 762 42 00
Leipziger Kommissions- und Grossbuchhandels-
gesellschaft mbH (LKG), An der Suedspitze 1-
12, 04571 Roetha, Germany *Tel:* (034206) 65-
100 *Fax:* (034206) 65-100 *E-mail:* lkg@lkg-
service.de *Web Site:* www.lkg-va.de (Germany
& Austria)

Georges Naef Editeur+
33, Quai Wilson, 1211 Geneva 21
Tel: (022) 731 50 00 *Fax:* (022) 738 42 24
E-mail: naef@kister.ch
Web Site: www.georgesnaef.com; www.kister.ch
Key Personnel
Contact: Georges Naef
Founded: 1986
Also offers Internet development.
Subjects: History, Travel & Tourism, Culture
ISBN Prefix(es): 978-2-8313
Total Titles: 24 CD-ROM
Parent Company: Naef-Kister SA
Subsidiaries: Naef Diffusion

Verlag Nagel & Kimche AG+
Subsidiary of Carl Hanser Verlag GmbH & Co
KG
Neptunestr 20, 8032 Zurich
Tel: (044) 366 66 80 *Fax:* (044) 366 66 88
E-mail: info@nagel-kimche.ch
Web Site: www.hanser-literaturverlage.de/verlage/
nagel-und-kimche.html
Key Personnel
Publishing Dir: Dr Dirk Vaihinger
Founded: 1983
Subjects: Fiction, Literature, Literary Criticism,
Essays, Nonfiction (General), Contemporary
Swiss Literature
ISBN Prefix(es): 978-3-312
Associate Companies: Hanser Berlin; Hanser
Kinderbuch; Sanssouci Verlags; Zsolnay und
Deuticke

Neptun Verlag AG
Rietwiesenstr 26, 8593 Kesswil
Tel: (071) 463 30 23 *Fax:* (071) 463 39 30
E-mail: neptun@bluewin.ch
Web Site: www.neptunart.ch
Key Personnel
Manager: Herbert Berchtold
Event Manager: Peter John
Founded: 1946
Subjects: Crafts, Games, Hobbies, Fiction, His-
tory, Travel & Tourism
ISBN Prefix(es): 978-3-85820

Buchverlag Neue Zuercher Zeitung, see NZZ
Libro

Verlag Niggli AG
Gemeindestr 25, 8032 Zurich
Tel: (044) 586 7968
E-mail: info@niggli.ch
Web Site: www.niggli.ch
Key Personnel
Publisher: Markus Sebastian Braun
  E-mail: braun@niggli.ch
Editorial: Sophie Steybe *E-mail:* steybe@niggli.
ch; Chris van Uffelen *E-mail:* uffelen@niggli.
ch
Sales & Distribution: Stephan Goetz
  E-mail: goetz@niggli.ch

Founded: 1950
Subjects: Architecture & Interior Design, Art, Ty-
pography
ISBN Prefix(es): 978-3-7212
Parent Company: bnb media gmbh
Associate Companies: Benteli Verlag AG
Distribution Center: AVA Verlagsausliefer-
ung AG, Centralweg 16, Postfach 27, 8910
Affoltern am Albis *Tel:* (044) 762 42 60
Fax: (044) 762 42 10 *E-mail:* verlagsservice@
ava.ch *Web Site:* www.ava.ch
Interart Paris, One rue de l'est, 75020 Paris,
France *Tel:* 01 43 49 36 60 *Fax:* 01 43 49
41 22 *E-mail:* commercial@interart.fr *Web
Site:* interartparis.free.fr
GVA Goettingen GmbH & Co KG, Post-
fach 2021, 37073 Goettingen, Germany
E-mail: bestellung@gva-verlage.de *Web
Site:* www.gva-verlage.de
Coen Sligting Bookimport, Groot Nieuw-
land 27, 1811 ET Alkmaar, Netherlands
E-mail: sligting@xs4all.nl
Antique Collector's Club, Sandy Lane, Old
Martlesham, Woodbridge, Suffolk IP12 4SD,
United Kingdom *E-mail:* sales@antique-acc.
com
RAM publications + distributions inc, 2525
Michigan Ave, Bldg A2, Santa Monica, CA
90404, United States *E-mail:* info@rampub.
com *Web Site:* www.rampub.com

Nimbus, Kunst und Buecher AG
Villa zum Abendstern, Buerglistr 37, 8820 Wae-
denswil
Tel: (044) 680 3704 *Fax:* (044) 680 3703
E-mail: verlag@nimbusbooks.ch; gelinek@
nimbusbooks.ch
Web Site: www.nimbusbooks.ch
Key Personnel
Founder & Mng Dir: Bernhard Echte
Board President: Walter Maria Feilchenfeldt
Founded: 1996
Subjects: Art
ISBN Prefix(es): 978-3-907142

NordSud Verlag AG (North-South Publishers
Inc)
Heinrichstr 249, 8005 Zurich
Tel: (044) 936 68 68 *Fax:* (044) 936 68 00
E-mail: info@nord-sued.com
Web Site: www.nord-sued.com
Key Personnel
Chief Executive Officer & Publisher: Herwig
Bitsche
Assistant Publisher: Andrew Rushton
  E-mail: andrew.rushton@nord-sued.com
Foreign Rights Manager: Louise Pachtner
  E-mail: louise.pachtner@nord-sued.com
Press & Public Relations: Nina Gruen-
berger *Tel:* (044) 936 68 88 *E-mail:* nina.
gruenberger@nord-sued.com
Production: Henrike Judwitt *E-mail:* henrike.
judwitt@nord-sued.com
Founded: 1961
ISBN Prefix(es): 978-3-85825; 978-3-314; 978-3-
03733
Subsidiaries: Editions NordSud
Distribution Center: AVA Verlagsauslieferung,
Centralweg 16, 8910 Affoltern am Albis
Tel: (044) 762 42 00 *Fax:* (044) 762 42 10
E-mail: avainfo@ava.ch
Runge Verlagsauslieferung GmbH, Bergstr 2,
33803 Steinhagen, Germany *Tel:* (05204) 99
81 21 *Fax:* (05204) 99 81 11 *E-mail:* nord-
sued@rungeva.de (Germany & Austria)

Editions Notari
One rue Rene-Louis-Piachaud, 1204 Geneva
Tel: (022) 310 55 35
Web Site: www.editionsnotari.ch
Key Personnel
Publisher: Luca Notari *E-mail:* luca@

editionsnotari.ch; Paola Notari *E-mail:* paola@
editionsnotari.ch
Founded: 2006
Subjects: Art
ISBN Prefix(es): 978-2-9700532; 978-2-940408
Distribution Center: Servidis SA, Chemin
des Chalets, 1279 Chavannes-de-Bogis
Tel: (022) 960 95 10 *Fax:* (022) 776 35 27
E-mail: admin@servidis.ch *Web Site:* www.
servidis.ch
Belles Lettres, 25, rue du General Leclerc, 94270
Le Kremlin-Bicetre, France *Tel:* 01 45 15
19 70 *Fax:* 01 45 15 19 80 *E-mail:* bldd@
lesbelleslettres.com *Web Site:* www.bldd.fr
(France & international)

NZZ Libro+
Zurich Str 39, 8952 Schlieren
Mailing Address: Postfach, 8021 Zurich
Tel: (044) 258 15 05 *Fax:* (044) 258 13 99
E-mail: nzz.libro@nzz.ch
Web Site: www.nzz-libro.ch
Key Personnel
Publishing Dir: Hans-Peter Thuer *Tel:* (044) 258
19 90 *Fax:* (044) 258 29 90
Advertising & Public Relations: Simon Ruttimann
Tel: (044) 258 19 92 *Fax:* (044) 258 29 92
Production: Beate Becker *Tel:* (044) 258 13 94
Fax: (044) 258 23 94
Founded: 1927
Book publishing division of Zurich daily newspaper.
Subjects: Architecture & Interior Design, Art, Biography, Memoirs, Economics, Government, Political Science, History, Language Arts, Linguistics
ISBN Prefix(es): 978-3-85823; 978-3-03823; 978-3-907092
Total Titles: 200 Print; 10 CD-ROM
Distribution Center: Buchzentrum AG,
Industriestr Ost 10, 4614 Haegandorf
Tel: (062) 209 25 25 *Fax:* (062) 209 27 27
E-mail: geissbuehler@buchzentrum.ch
Koch, Neff & Oetinger Verlagsauslieferung
GmbH, Industriestr 23, 70565 Stuttgart, Germany *E-mail:* nzz-buchverlag@kno-va.de

Objectif Terre, *imprint of* Editions Olizane

Oekumenischer rat der Kirchen, see World
Council of Churches (WCC Publications)

Oesch Verlag AG+
Verena-Cozett-Str 7, 8036 Zurich
Tel: (044) 305 70 60 *Fax:* (044) 242 76 86
E-mail: info@oeschverlag.ch
Web Site: www.oeschverlag.ch
Key Personnel
Dir: Dr Juerg Conzett
Contact: Ursula Kohler *E-mail:* ursula.kohler@
sunflower.ch
Founded: 1935
Subjects: Career Development, Health, Nutrition, Nonfiction (General), Self-Help
ISBN Prefix(es): 978-3-926955; 978-3-85833; 978-3-7263; 978-3-0350; 978-3-905267; 978-3-909101
Number of titles published annually: 40 Print
Total Titles: 1 Audio
Parent Company: Sunflower Foundation
Associate Companies: Conzett Verlag *Web Site:* conzettverlag.ch
Distribution Center: Oesch Verlag, c/o FO-Publishing GmbH, Gewerbestr 18, 8132 Egg
ZH, Contact: Sabrina Ravazzolo *Tel:* (044) 986
35 70 *Fax:* (044) 986 35 71 *E-mail:* verlag@
fo-publishing.ch *Web Site:* www.fo-publishing.ch
Mohr Morawa Buchvertrieb GmbH, Sulzengasse,
Postfach 26, 1101 Vienna, Austria *Tel:* (01)
680 145 *Fax:* (01) 688 71 30 *E-mail:* momo@
mohrmorawa.at *Web Site:* www.mohrmorawa.at

Brockhaus/Commission GmbH, Kreidlerstr 9, 70806 Kornwestheim, Germany
Tel: (07154) 13 27-9210 *Fax:* (07154) 13 27-
13 *E-mail:* oesch@brocom.de *Web Site:* www.
brocom.de

Offizin Zurich Verlag GmbH
Stockerstr 60, 8002 Zurich
Tel: (078) 714 14 32 *Fax:* (044) 202 08 11
E-mail: info@offizin.ch
Web Site: www.offizin.ch
Key Personnel
Mng Dir: Manfred Hiefner *E-mail:* manfred.
hiefner@offizin.ch
Founded: 1989
Subjects: Art, Photography, Ethnology, Local History
ISBN Prefix(es): 978-3-907496; 978-3-907495

OFL SA
ZI3, Corminboeuf, 1701 Fribourg
Mailing Address: PO Box 1152, 1701 Fribourg
Tel: (026) 467 51 11; (0848) 653 653 (customer
service) *Fax:* (026) 467 54 66
E-mail: information@olf.ch; serviceclients@olf.ch
Web Site: www.olf.ch
Key Personnel
Dir General: Patrice Fehlmann *Tel:* (026) 467 51
00 *E-mail:* p.fehlmann@olf.ch
Dir, English & German Books: Barbara Humm
Fax: (026) 467 54 44 *E-mail:* b.humm@olf.ch
Sales & Marketing: Andrea Barthel *Tel:* (026)
467 51 31 *E-mail:* a.barthel@olf.ch
Founded: 1947
Subjects: Antiques, Architecture & Interior Design, Art, Asian Studies, Crafts, Games, Hobbies, Sports, Athletics
ISBN Prefix(es): 978-3-7215; 978-2-8264

Editions Olizane+
11, rue des Vieux-Grenadiers, 1205 Geneva
Tel: (022) 328 52 52 *Fax:* (022) 328 57 96
E-mail: guides@olizane.ch
Web Site: www.olizane.ch
Key Personnel
Mng Dir: Matthias Huber
Founded: 1981
Subjects: Ethnicity, Photography, Travel & Tourism
ISBN Prefix(es): 978-2-88086
Number of titles published annually: 20 Print
Total Titles: 150 Print
Imprints: Guides-Olizane Decouverte (Guides
Olizane Aventure); Objectif Terre
Foreign Rep(s): Altair (Spain); Centre Cartographique (Belgium); Harmonia Mundi
(France); Servidis (Switzerland); Ulysse
(Canada)
Foreign Rights: Hagenbach & Bender (worldwide)

Edition Olms AG+
Subsidiary of Georg Olms AG - Verlag
Willikonerstr 10a, 8618 Oetwil am See/Zurich
Tel: (043) 8449777 *Fax:* (043) 8449778
E-mail: info@edition-olms.com
Web Site: www.edition-olms.com
Founded: 1977
Subjects: Art, Film, Video, Humor, Literature, Literary Criticism, Essays, Music, Dance, Chess
ISBN Prefix(es): 978-3-283; 978-3-03766 (Edition
Skylight)
Imprints: Edition Skylight (photography)
Foreign Rep(s): AVA Verlagsauslieferung AG
(Switzerland); Bookport Associates (Joe
Portelli) (Gibraltar, Greece, Italy, Portugal,
Spain); Peter Couzens (Asia, Israel); Everybody's Books (Warren Halford) (South Africa);
Gazelle Book Services Ltd (Ireland, UK); Edition Habit Press Pty Ltd (Bernard Eisenbeis)
(Australia); IMA Ltd (Africa, Eastern Eu-

rope); Maya Publishers Pvt Ltd (India); Mohr
Morawa Buchvertrieb GmbH (Austria); Jan
Smit (Netherlands); David Towle (Baltic States,
Scandinavia); Trafalgar Square from Independent Publishers Group (Canada, Latin America,
USA); VVA - Vereinigte Verlagsauslieferung
GmbH (Germany)

Ediciones de la OMS, see World Health
Organization (WHO)

Editions de l'OMS, see World Health
Organization (WHO)

Open Door Verlag
Amlehnhalde 23a, 6010 Kriens
Tel: (041) 312 14 45 *Fax:* (041) 312 14 42
E-mail: info@opendoorverlag.ch
Web Site: www.opendoorverlag.ch
Key Personnel
Publisher: Stephan Laeuppi
ISBN Prefix(es): 978-3-9521998

Orell Fuessli Kinderbuch, *imprint of* Orell
Fuessli Verlag AG

Organisation Mundial de la Sante, see World
Health Organization (WHO)

orte-Verlag
Wirtschaft Rutegg, 9413 Oberegg
Tel: (071) 888 15 56
E-mail: info@orteverlag.ch
Web Site: www.orteverlag.ch
Key Personnel
Editor & Publisher: Werner Bucher
Subjects: Fiction, Poetry, Crime Novels
ISBN Prefix(es): 978-3-85830
Distribution Center: Scheidegger & Co AG, Centralweg 16, 8910 Affoltern am Albis *Tel:* (044)
762 42 50 *Fax:* (044) 762 42 10 *E-mail:* info@
scheidegger-buecher.ch
GVA Gemeinsame Verlagsauslieferung Goettingen GmbH & Co KG, Postfach 2021, 37010
Goettingen, Germany *Tel:* (0551) 487177
Fax: (0551) 41392

Ostschweiz Druck AG
Hofstetstr 14, 9300 Wittenbach
Tel: (071) 292 29 29 *Fax:* (071) 292 29 38
E-mail: info@ostschweizdruck.ch; sekretariat@
ostschweizdruck.ch
Web Site: www.ostschweizdruck.ch
Key Personnel
Owner & Mng Dir: Urs Kolb *Tel:* (071) 292 29
20 *E-mail:* u.kolb@ostschweizdruck.ch
Sales Manager: Elmar Broder *Tel:* (071) 292
29 13 *E-mail:* e.broder@ostschweizdruck.ch;
Bruno Sivec *Tel:* (071) 292 29 18 *E-mail:* b.
sivec@ostschweizdruck.ch
Founded: 1892
Subjects: Art, History, Music, Dance, Poetry, Social Sciences, Sociology
ISBN Prefix(es): 978-3-85837

Editions Ourania, *imprint of* La Maison de la
Bible

Pano Verlag, *imprint of* Theologischer Verlag
Zurich (TVZ)

Park Books AG
Affiliate of Scheidegger & Spiess AG
Niederdorfstr 54, 8001 Zurich
Tel: (044) 262 16 62 *Fax:* (044) 262 16 63
E-mail: info@park-books.com; publisher@park-books.com; publicity@park-books.com; sales@
park-books.com
Web Site: www.park-books.com

Key Personnel
Publishing Dir: Thomas Kramer *Tel:* (044) 253 64 54
Marketing: Patrick Schneebeli
Marketing & Press: Domenica Schulz *Tel:* (044) 253 64 56
Founded: 2012
Subjects: Architecture & Interior Design, Art
ISBN Prefix(es): 978-3-906027

Parkett Publishers Inc+
Quellenstr 27, 8005 Zurich
Tel: (044) 271 81 40 *Fax:* (044) 272 43 01
E-mail: info@parkettart.com
Web Site: www.parkettart.com
Key Personnel
Publisher: Dieter von Graffenried *E-mail:* d.v. graffenried@parkettart.com
Editor-in-Chief: Bice Curiger *E-mail:* b.curiger@parkettart.com
Founded: 1984
Subjects: Art
ISBN Prefix(es): 978-3-907509; 978-3-907582
U.S. Office(s): Parkett Publishers, 145 Avenue of the Americas at Spring St, New York, NY 10013, United States *Tel:* 212-673-2660 *Fax:* 212-271-0704

Editions Parole et Silence+
17 route du Muveran, 1880 Les Plans sur Bex
Tel: (024) 498 23 01 *Fax:* (024) 498 23 11
E-mail: paroleetsilence@omedia.ch
Web Site: www.paroleetsilence.com
Key Personnel
Editorial Dir: Sabine Larive
Press: Jean-Philippe Bertrand *Tel:* 01 40 46 54 30 *E-mail:* jpbertrand@ddbeditions.fr
Subjects: Inspirational, Spirituality, Philosophy, Religion - Catholic, Theology
ISBN Prefix(es): 978-2-84573; 978-2-911940

Editions du Parvis
Route de l'Eglise 71, 1648 Hauteville
Tel: (026) 915 93 93 *Fax:* (026) 915 93 99
E-mail: librairie@parvis.ch
Web Site: www.parvis.ch
Key Personnel
Executive: Jean-Marie Castella *Tel:* (026) 915 93 90 *E-mail:* jm.castella@parvis.ch
Founded: 1969
Subjects: Health, Nutrition, Religion - Catholic
ISBN Prefix(es): 978-2-88022; 978-3-907523; 978-3-907524; 978-3-907525
Number of titles published annually: 20 Print
Distributed by Gallus (Austria)
Distributor for Centro Editoriale Valtortiano (Europe)

Editions Patino+
8, rue Giovanni-Gambini, 1206 Geneva
Tel: (022) 3470211 *Fax:* (022) 7891829
E-mail: info@fondationpatino.org
Web Site: www.edipatino.com; fundacionpatino. org
Key Personnel
Contact: John Dubouchet
Founded: 1986
Subjects: Fiction, Philosophy, Poetry
ISBN Prefix(es): 978-2-88213
Orders to: Vilo L'Amateur, 25 rue Ginoux, 75015 Paris, France *Fax:* 01 45 75 75 53

Paulusverlag
Perolles 42, 1700 Fribourg
Tel: (026) 4264331 *Fax:* (026) 4264330
E-mail: info@paulusedition.ch
Web Site: www.paulusedition.ch
Key Personnel
Assistant Dir: Maurice Greder
Founded: 2003
Subjects: Philosophy, Theology, Social History

ISBN Prefix(es): 978-3-7228; 978-3-7278; 978-2-8271
Parent Company: Saint-Paul SA, 42, blvd Perolles, CP 150, 1705 Fribourg
Ultimate Parent Company: Academic Press Fribourg
Associate Companies: Editions la Sarine, 42, blvd Perolles, CP 150, 1705 Fribourg *E-mail:* contact@lasarine.ch *Web Site:* www.lasarine.ch
Bookshop(s): Librairie Saint-Paul, Perolles 38, 1700 Fribourg *E-mail:* librairie@st-paul.ch; Librairie du Vieux Comte, rue de Vevey, 1630 Bulle *E-mail:* contact@vieux-comte.ch *Web Site:* www.vieux-comte.ch

Pearson Schweitz AG+
Subsidiary of Pearson PLC
Chollerstr 37, 6300 Zug
Tel: (041) 747 47 47 *Fax:* (041) 747 47 77
E-mail: mailbox@pearson.ch
Web Site: www.pearson.ch
Founded: 1983
Subjects: Computer Science, Economics, Education, Language Arts, Linguistics
Distributor for Adobe Press; BradyGames; Hayden Books; M&T Books & Software; New Riders; Que; Sams; Sams.net; Waite Group Press; Ziff-Davis Press

Pedrazzini Tipografia SA
Via B Varenna, 7, 6601 Locarno
Tel: (091) 751 77 34 *Fax:* (091) 751 51 18
E-mail: print@pedrazzinitipografia.ch
Web Site: pedrazzinitipografia.com
Founded: 1880
Subjects: Education, History, Literature, Literary Criticism, Essays, Publishing & Book Trade Reference, Religion - Other
ISBN Prefix(es): 978-88-7404

Verlag Edizioni Periferia
Museggstr 31, 6004 Lucerne
Tel: (041) 410 88 79 *Fax:* (041) 410 88 79
E-mail: mail@periferia.ch
Web Site: www.periferia.ch
Key Personnel
Dir: Flurina Paravicini-Toenz; Gianni Paravicini-Toenz
Founded: 1992
Subjects: Art
ISBN Prefix(es): 978-3-9520474; 978-3-907474; 978-3-9522474

Verlag Johannes Petri
Imprint of Druck- und Verlaghauses Schwabe
Steinentorstr 13, 4010 Basel
Tel: (061) 278 95 60 *Fax:* (061) 278 95 66
E-mail: verlag@verlag-johannes-petri.ch
Web Site: www.verlag-johannes-petri.ch
Key Personnel
Owner: Ruedi Bienz
Dir: Thomas Gierl
Marketing & Press: Cecilia Baechlin *Tel:* (061) 278 98 25 *E-mail:* c.baechlin@verlag-johannes-petri.ch
Subjects: Fiction, Poetry, Science (General)
ISBN Prefix(es): 978-3-03784

Photoglob, *imprint of* Orell Fuessli Verlag AG

Pizzicato Verlag Helvetia
Division of Music & Copyright Consulting GmbH
Schaerbaechlistr 3, 8810 Horgen
Tel: (044) 710 62 52 *Fax:* (044) 710 61 53
E-mail: info@pizzicato.ch
Web Site: www.pizzicato.ch
Founded: 1985

Subjects: Biography, Memoirs, Ethnicity, Music, Dance
ISBN Prefix(es): 978-88-7736

PPUR, see Presses Polytechniques et Universitaires Romandes (PPUR)

Presses Polytechniques et Universitaires Romandes (PPUR)+
EPFL-Rolex Learning Center, 1015 Lausanne
Mailing Address: CP 119, 1015 Lausanne
Tel: (021) 693 21 30 *Fax:* (021) 693 40 27
E-mail: ppur@epfl.ch
Web Site: www.ppur.org
Key Personnel
Mng Dir, Editorial: Olivier Babel *Tel:* (021) 693 41 34 *E-mail:* oliver.babel@epfl.ch
Publisher: Frederick F Fenter *Tel:* (021) 693 69 58 *E-mail:* frederick.fenter@epfl.ch
Production Manager: Christophe Borlat *Tel:* (021) 693 27 31 *E-mail:* christophe.borlat@epfl.ch
Promotion: Sylvain Collette *Tel:* (021) 693 41 40 *E-mail:* sylvain.collette@epfl.ch
Promotion & Marketing: Gabriel Hussy *Tel:* (021) 693 27 30 *E-mail:* gabriel.hussy@epfl.ch
Press: Ingrid Crisinel *Tel:* (021) 693 41 42 *E-mail:* ingrid.crisinel@epfl.ch
Founded: 1980
Also acts as book packager
Subjects: Architecture & Interior Design, Biological Sciences, Chemistry, Chemical Engineering, Civil Engineering, Computer Science, Earth Sciences, Education, Electronics, Electrical Engineering, Engineering (General), Management, Mathematics, Mechanical Engineering, Physics, Science (General), Technology, Construction
ISBN Prefix(es): 978-2-88074; 978-2-940222
Number of titles published annually: 30 Print
Imprints: EPFL Press
Distribution Center: Patrimoine SPRL, Ave Milcamps 119, 1030 Brussels, Belgium *Tel:* (02) 736 68 47 *Fax:* (02) 736 68 47 *E-mail:* patrimoine@telenet.be (Belgium, Luxembourg & Netherlands)
Presses Internationales Polytechnique, PO Box 6079 succ Centre-ville, Monteal, QC H3C 3A7, Canada *Tel:* 514-340-3286 *Fax:* 514-340-5882 *E-mail:* pip@polymtl.ca *Web Site:* www.pressespoly.ca (Canada & USA)
GEODIF, 61 Bd Saint-Germain, 75240 Paris Cedex 05, France *Tel:* 01 44 41 11 11 *Fax:* 01 44 41 11 44 (France & Morocco)
Sodis, 128 Ave du Marechal de Lattre de Tassigny, 77400 Lagny sur Marne, France *Tel:* 01 60 07 82 00 *Fax:* 01 64 30 92 22 *E-mail:* portail@sodis.fr *Web Site:* www.sodis.fr (France & Morocco)
CPC Press of the Taylor & Francis Group, 6000 Broken Sound Parkway, NW, Suite 300, Boca Raton, FL 33487, United States (EPFL Press worldwide)

Pro Juventute Verlag+
Thurgauerstr 39, 8050 Zurich
Tel: (044) 256 77 77 *Fax:* (044) 256 77 78
E-mail: info@projuventute.ch
Web Site: www.projuventute.ch
Key Personnel
Dir: Katja Wiesendanger *E-mail:* katja.wiesendanger@projuventute.ch
ISBN Prefix(es): 978-3-7152

Verlag Pro Libro Luzern GmbH
Adligenswilerstr 30, 6006 Lucerne
Tel: (041) 210 24 03
E-mail: info@prolibro.ch; prolibro@bluewin.ch
Web Site: www.prolibro.ch
Key Personnel
Publisher: Peter Schulz *E-mail:* prolibro@bluewin.ch
Editor: Dr Thomas Goetz *E-mail:* thomas.goetz@swissonline.ch

Media & Public Relations: Eva Holz *E-mail:* eva.
holz@textbueroholtz.ch
Publisher Secretary: Therese Schilter
   E-mail: sekretariat@prolibro.ch
Founded: 2006
ISBN Prefix(es): 978-3-905927; 978-3-9523163

Promoedition SA+
Member of Quorum Communication Group
35 rue des Bains, 1211 Geneva 11
Mailing Address: CP 5615, 1211 Geneva 11
Tel: (022) 809 94 94 *Fax:* (022) 809 94 00
E-mail: info@quorum-com.ch
Web Site: www.promoedition.ch
Key Personnel
President: Roland Ray *Tel:* (022) 809 94 45
   E-mail: roland.ray@quorum-com.ch
Editing & Production: Maryse Avidor *Tel:* (022)
   809 94 75 *E-mail:* maryse.avidor@quorum-
   com.ch
Founded: 1972
Subjects: Business, Communications, Fashion,
   Film, Video, Finance
ISBN Prefix(es): 978-2-88129

**Publications de l'Institut de hautes etudes
internationales et du developpment**, see
Graduate Institute Publications

Punktum AG Buchredaktion und Bildarchiv+
Klusstr 50, 8032 Zurich
Tel: (044) 422 45 40
E-mail: punktum@punktum.ch
Web Site: www.punktum.ch
Specialize in Swiss topics.
Subjects: Art, Ethnicity, History, Travel &
   Tourism
ISBN Prefix(es): 978-3-907577; 978-3-9523577
Divisions: Punktum Buchredoktion (packaging);
   Punktum Bildarchiv (picture library)

Quart Verlag GmbH
Denkmalstr 2, 6006 Lucerne
Tel: (041) 420 20 82 *Fax:* (041) 420 20 92
E-mail: books@quart.ch
Web Site: www.quart.ch
Key Personnel
Publisher: Heinz Wirz
Founded: 1999
Subjects: Architecture & Interior Design, Art,
   Landscape Architecture
ISBN Prefix(es): 978-3-907631

Quaternio Verlag
Obergrundstr 98, 6005 Lucerne
Tel: (041) 318 40 20 *Fax:* (041) 318 40 25
E-mail: info@quaternio.ch
Web Site: www.quaternio.ch
Key Personnel
Head of Production & Marketing: Gunter Tampe
   Tel: (041) 318 40 23 *E-mail:* gunter.tampe@
   quaternio.ch
Sales Dir & Marketing: Ernst Erni *Tel:* (041) 318
   40 29 *E-mail:* ernst.erni@quaternio.ch
Advertising & Marketing: Arne Domroes
   Tel: (041) 318 40 28 *E-mail:* arne.domroes@
   quaternio.ch
Editorial & Public Relations: Clarissa Rothacker
   Tel: (041) 318 40 27 *E-mail:* clarissa.
   rothacker@quaternio.ch
Specialize in fine art facsimile editions.
Subjects: Art

Rauhreif Verlag
Postfach 2562, 8033 Zurich
Tel: (044) 350 88 08; (079) 257 04 00 (cell)
E-mail: info@nimrodundrauhreif.ch
Web Site: nimrodundrauhreif.ch
Key Personnel
Owner & Mng Dir: Elle Niksic

Subjects: Literature, Literary Criticism, Essays
ISBN Prefix(es): 978-3-907764

Verlag fuer Recht und Gesellschaft AG
Ringstr 75, 4106 Therwil
Tel: (061) 726 26 26 *Fax:* (061) 726 26 27
E-mail: info@vrg-verlag.ch
Web Site: www.vrg-verlag.ch
Founded: 1933
Subjects: Accounting, Law
ISBN Prefix(es): 978-3-7242
Associate Companies: Sciamed Verlag AG

Friedrich Reinhardt Verlag
Missionsstr 36, 4012 Basel
Mailing Address: Postfach 393, 4012 Basel
Tel: (061) 264 64 50 *Fax:* (061) 264 64 88
E-mail: verlag@reinhardt.ch
Web Site: www.reinhardt.ch
Key Personnel
Publisher: Alfred Ruedisuehli *E-mail:* a.
   ruedisuehli@reinhardt.ch
Deputy Head, Publishing & Editorial: Claudia Le-
   uppi *Tel:* (061) 264 64 80 *E-mail:* c.leuppi@
   reinhardt.ch
Marketing & Communications: Kerstin Hessel
   Tel: (061) 264 64 40 *E-mail:* k.hessel@
   reinhardt.ch
Rights & Licenses: Beatrice Rubin *Tel:* (061) 264
   64 60 *E-mail:* b.rubin@reinhardt.ch
Founded: 1900
Subjects: Art, Biography, Memoirs, Environmen-
   tal Studies, Fiction, History, How-to, Religion -
   Other, Theology
ISBN Prefix(es): 978-3-7177; 978-3-7245; 978-3-
   497
Subsidiaries: Eular Verlag; Reinhardt Communi-
   cations

Rentsch Verlag, *imprint of* Orell Fuessli Verlag
AG

Rex Verlag Luzern
Arsenalstr 24, 6011 Kriens
Tel: (041) 419 47 19 *Fax:* (041) 419 47 11
E-mail: info@rex-verlag.ch
Web Site: www.rex-verlag.ch; www.rex-buch.ch
Key Personnel
Mng Dir: Markus Kappeler *Tel:* (041) 419 47 01
   E-mail: m.kappeler@rex-verlag.ch
Production Manager: Martin Vollmeier *Tel:* (041)
   318 34 83 *Fax:* (041) 318 34 00 *E-mail:* m.
   vollmeier@bag.ch
Sales Manager: Claudia Lapierre-Ruckli
   Tel: (041) 318 34 77 *E-mail:* c.lapierre@bag.ch
Founded: 1931
Subjects: Education, Fiction, Religion - Catholic
ISBN Prefix(es): 978-3-7252
Parent Company: Brunner Media AG
Bookshop(s): Rex Buchladen, St Karliquair 12,
   Postfach 5266, 6000 Lucerne

Riverfield Verlag
Postfach 459, 4010 Basel
E-mail: info@riverfield-verlag.ch
Web Site: www.riverfield-verlag.ch
Founded: 2014
Subjects: Biography, Memoirs, Fiction, Adventure
ISBN Prefix(es): 978-3-9524523; 978-3-9524463

Editiones Roche
c/o F Hoffmann-La Roche Ltd, Grenzacherstr
   124, 4070 Basel
Tel: (061) 688 1111; (061) 688 8888 *Fax:* (061)
   691 9391
E-mail: basel.webmaster@roche.com
Web Site: www.roche.com; www.roche.ch
Key Personnel
Chief Executive Officer: Severin Schwan
Head, Media Relations: Alexander Klauser
Founded: 1971

Subjects: Art, Health, Nutrition, Natural History,
   Science (General)
ISBN Prefix(es): 978-3-907770; 978-3-907946

Rodana Verlag AG, see Schweizer Spiegel
   Verlag mit Rodana Verlag AG

Romantik Verlag
Risistr 11, 8488 Turbenthal
Tel: (052) 503 98 09
E-mail: info@romantik-verlag.ch; info@
   zauberblume.ch
Web Site: www.romantik-verlag.ch
Key Personnel
Publisher: Ariane Costantini
Rights: Matthias Czerny
Founded: 2013
Subjects: Fiction, Romance
ISBN Prefix(es): 978-3-906246
Imprints: Zauberblume Verlag

Rondo Verlag
Hittenbergstr 1, 8636 Wald
Tel: (055) 2463937 *Fax:* (055) 2464293
Subjects: Music, Dance
ISBN Prefix(es): 978-3-907935

**Rosenkreuzer Philosophie Verlag &
Buecherecke**
Suot Crastas, 7514 Sils Maria
Tel: (081) 834 20 03 *Fax:* (081) 834 20 04
Web Site: heile-dich-selbst.ch/index.php?id=103
Key Personnel
Publisher: Annemarie Troost
Subjects: Philosophy
ISBN Prefix(es): 978-3-906414
Distribution Center: Buchzentrum AG, Indus-
   triestr Ost 10, 4614 Haegendorf *Tel:* (062) 209
   25 25 *Fax:* (062) 209 26 27 *Web Site:* www.
   buchzentrum.ch

Roth et Sauter SA
Rte de la Pale 1, 1026 Denges
Tel: (021) 811 36 36 *Fax:* (021) 811 36 37
E-mail: info@rothsauter.ch
Web Site: www.rothsauter.ch
Key Personnel
Dir: Jean-Michel Borel
Founded: 1890
Subjects: Art
ISBN Prefix(es): 978-2-88075
Imprints: Editions du Verseau

Rotpunktverlag+
Hohlstr 86A, 8004 Zurich
Tel: (044) 405 44 88 *Fax:* (044) 405 44 89
E-mail: info@rotpunktverlag.ch
Web Site: www.rotpunktverlag.ch
Key Personnel
Sales & Marketing Manager: Thomas Heil-
   mann *Tel:* (044) 405 44 80 *E-mail:* thomas.
   heilmann@rotpunktverlag.ch
Press: Daniela Koch *Tel:* (044) 405 44 85
   E-mail: daniela.koch@rotpunktverlag.ch
Founded: 1977
Membership(s): Swiss Booksellers & Publishers
   Association (SBVV).
Subjects: Alternative, Developing Countries, Fic-
   tion, Government, Political Science, History,
   Nonfiction (General), Outdoor Recreation,
   Travel & Tourism
ISBN Prefix(es): 978-3-85869
Distribution Center: AVA Verlagsauslieferung
   AG, Centralweg 16, 8910 Affoltern am Al-
   bis *Tel:* (044) 762 42 00 *Fax:* (044) 762 60 10
   E-mail: avainfo@ava.ch
Prolit Verlagsauslieferung, Postfach 9, 35461
   Fernwald, Germany *Tel:* (0641) 943 93 24
   Fax: (0641) 943 93 89 *E-mail:* n.kallweit@
   prolit.de (Germany & Austria)

Willems Adventure, Honderdland 120, 2676
LT Maasdijk, Netherlands *Tel:* (088) 599
01 40 *Fax:* (088) 599 01 41 *E-mail:* info@
willemsadventure.nl

Rotten Verlag AG
Pomonastr 12, 3930 Visp
Tel: (027) 948 30 32 *Fax:* (027) 948 30 33
E-mail: shop@rottenverlag.ch
Web Site: www.1815.ch/rottenverlag
Key Personnel
Head: Rico Erpen *E-mail:* rico.erpen@
rottenverlag.ch
Founded: 1973
Subjects: Regional Interests, Culture
ISBN Prefix(es): 978-3-907816; 978-3-907624

Edition Rueegger+
Zwinglistr 6, 8750 Glarus
Web Site: www.somedia-buchverlag.ch/edition/
edition-rueegger
Specialize in economics, politics, sociology, ecol-
ogy & educational research.
Subjects: Business, Criminology, Economics,
Education, Environmental Studies, Govern-
ment, Political Science, Management, Psychol-
ogy, Psychiatry, Social Sciences, Sociology,
Women's Studies
ISBN Prefix(es): 978-3-7253
Number of titles published annually: 30 Print
Parent Company: Somedia Buchverlag
Distribution Center: Buchzentrum AG, Indus-
triestr Ost 10, 4614 Haegendorf *Tel:* (062) 209
25 25 *Fax:* (062) 209 26 27 *Web Site:* www.
buchzentrum.ch

SAB, see Schweizerische Arbeitsgemeinschaft
fuer die Berggebiete (SAB)

SAC-Verlag
Monbijoustr 61, Postfach, 3000 Bern 23
Tel: (031) 370 18 83 *Fax:* (031) 370 18 90
E-mail: verlag.edition@sac-cas.ch
Web Site: www.sac-cas.ch
Key Personnel
Mng Dir: Andreas Mathyer
Founded: 1863
Subjects: Education, Outdoor Recreation, Alpine
Hiking, Climbing, Nature, Skiing, Snowshoe
Tours, Swiss Alps
ISBN Prefix(es): 978-3-85902
Parent Company: Schweizer Alpen-Club SAC
Distribution Center: SAC-Auslieferung, Alpen-
str 58, 3052 Zollikofen *Tel:* (031) 919 13 08
Fax: (031) 919 13 14 *E-mail:* eshop@sac-cas.
ch

Editions Saint-Augustin+
CP 51, 1890 Saint-Maurice
Tel: (024) 486 05 04; (024) 486 05 06 *Fax:* (024)
486 05 23
E-mail: editions@staugustin.ch; editions.livres@
staugustin.ch
Web Site: www.st-augustin.ch
Key Personnel
General Dir: Dominique-Anne Puenzieux
Founded: 1934
Subjects: Religion - Catholic, Theology
ISBN Prefix(es): 978-2-88011; 978-2-940145
Bookshop(s): Librairie Saint-Augustin, Rue de
Lausanne 88, 1700 Fribourg *Tel:* (026) 322 36
82 *Fax:* (026) 322 69 70 *E-mail:* librairiefr@
staugustin.ch; Librairie Saint-Augustin, Ave
de la Gare 1, 1890 St-Maurice *Tel:* (024) 486
05 51; (024) 486 05 55 *Fax:* (024) 486 05 56
E-mail: librairievs@staugustin.ch

Editions Saint-Paul, see Paulusverlag

Salis Verlag AG
Motorenstr 14, 8005 Zurich

Tel: (044) 381 51 01 *Fax:* (044) 381 51 05
E-mail: info@salisverlag.com
Web Site: www.salisverlag.com
Key Personnel
Chief Executive Officer & Publisher: Andre
Gstettenhofer
Finance & Mng Dir: Roger Ingold
Editor: Patrick Schaer
Founded: 2006
Subjects: Criminology, Fiction, Nonfiction (Gen-
eral)
ISBN Prefix(es): 978-3-905801

Salvioni arti grafiche SA
Via Ghiringhelli 9, 6500 Bellinzona
Tel: (091) 821 11 11 *Fax:* (091) 821 11 12
E-mail: tecnica@salvioni.ch
Web Site: www.salvioni.ch
Key Personnel
Dir: Ivan Patelli *E-mail:* ivan@salvioni.ch
Founded: 1850
Subjects: Art
ISBN Prefix(es): 978-88-7967

editions des sauvages
3 route de Meyrin, 1202 Geneva
Tel: (022) 320 12 01
Web Site: www.editionsdessauvages.ch
Key Personnel
Publisher: Valerie Solano *E-mail:* valerie@
editionsdessauvages.ch
Founded: 2008
Subjects: Drama, Theater, Fiction
ISBN Prefix(es): 978-2-9700583

Verlag Scheidegger & Spiess AG
Niederdorfstr 54, 8001 Zurich
Tel: (044) 262 16 62 *Fax:* (044) 262 16 63
E-mail: info@scheidegger-spiess.ch
Web Site: www.scheidegger-spiess.ch
Key Personnel
Publishing Dir: Thomas Kramer *Tel:* (044) 253
64 54 *E-mail:* t.kramer@scheidegger-spiess.ch
Marketing: Domenica Schulz *Tel:* (044) 253 64
56 *E-mail:* d.schulz@scheidegger-spiess.ch
Press: Monique Zumbrunn *Tel:* (044) 253 64 52
E-mail: m.zumbrunn@scheidegger-spiess.ch
Sales: Patrick Schneebeli *Tel:* (044) 253 64 53
E-mail: p.schneebeli@scheidegger-spiess.ch
Subjects: Architecture & Interior Design, Art,
Photography
ISBN Prefix(es): 978-3-85881

Schnellmann-Verlag+
Rotackerstr 49, 8645 Jona
Tel: (055) 211 14 72 *Fax:* (055) 211 14 77
E-mail: schnellmann-verlag@bluewin.ch
Web Site: www.dictionaries.ch
Founded: 1973
Publisher of bilingual dictionaries.
Subjects: Language Arts, Linguistics
ISBN Prefix(es): 978-3-85542

Verlag fuer Schoene Wissenschaften
Albert Steffen-Stiftung, Unterer Zielweg 36, 4143
Dornach
Tel: (061) 701-39-11 *Fax:* (061) 701-14-17
E-mail: info@albert-steffen.ch
Web Site: steffen.com/verlag-fuer-schoene-
wissenschaften/
Founded: 1928
Subjects: Art, Drama, Theater, Fiction, Literature,
Literary Criticism, Essays, Poetry
ISBN Prefix(es): 978-3-85889
Parent Company: Albert Steffen-Stiftung

**Editions Schola Cantorum - Charles
Huguenin-Pro Arte - Cantate Domino**
rue du Sapin 2a, 2114 Fleurier
Tel: (032) 861 37 19 *Fax:* (032) 861 27 27
E-mail: schola@sysco.ch

Web Site: www.schola-editions.com
Music scores for organ or harmonium.
Subjects: Music, Dance
Parent Company: Schola Cantorum-Triton

Schulthess Juristische Medien AG
Zwingli Platz 2, 8022 Zurich
Tel: (044) 200 29 29 *Fax:* (044) 200 29 28
E-mail: verlag@schulthess.com
Web Site: www.schulthess.com
Key Personnel
Executive Publisher: Dr Karen Schobloch
Tel: (044) 200 29 99 *E-mail:* karen.
schobloch@schulthess.com
Publisher: Maria Iskic *Tel:* (044) 200 29 42
Fax: (044) 200 29 08 *E-mail:* maria.iskic@
schulthess.com
Head, Marketing: Juerg Strebel *Tel:* (044) 200
29 56 *Fax:* (044) 200 29 08 *E-mail:* juerg.
strebel@schulthess.com
Founded: 1791
Subjects: Business, Law, Social Sciences, Sociol-
ogy
ISBN Prefix(es): 978-3-7255
Distribution Center: AVA Verlagsauslieferung
AG, Centralweg 16, 8910 Affoltern am Al-
bis *Tel:* (044) 762 42 00 *Fax:* (044) 762 42 10
E-mail: avainfo@ava.ch

Schwabe AG
Steinentorstr 13, 4010 Basel
Tel: (061) 278 95 65 *Fax:* (061) 272 95 66
E-mail: verlag@schwabe.ch
Web Site: www.schwabe.ch
Key Personnel
Owner & Chief Executive Officer: Ruedi Bienz
Publishing Dir: Dr Wolfgang Rother
Head, Marketing & Sales: Anne Rose Fischer
Tel: (061) 278 98 21
Marketing Dir: Thomas Gierl *Tel:* (061) 278 98
20
Founded: 1488
Subjects: Archaeology, Art, History, Language
Arts, Linguistics, Literature, Literary Criticism,
Essays, Medicine, Nursing, Dentistry, Philos-
ophy, Photography, Psychology, Psychiatry,
Science (General), Theology, Psychotherapy
ISBN Prefix(es): 978-3-7965
Branch Office(s)
Farnsburgerstr 8, 4132 Muttenz *Tel:* (061) 467 85
85 *Fax:* (061) 467 85 86
Bookshop(s): Das Narrenschiff, Im Schmiedenhof
10, 4001 Basel *Tel:* (061) 261 1982 *Fax:* (061)
263 9184

**Schweizer Spiegel Verlag mit Rodana Verlag
AG+**
Hammerstr 24, 8008 Zurich
Tel: (044) 2115000
Key Personnel
President: Anna von Senger
Subjects: Education, Psychology, Psychiatry
ISBN Prefix(es): 978-3-7270; 978-3-85863

**Schweizerische Arbeitsgemeinschaft fuer die
Berggebiete (SAB)+**
Seilerstr 4, 3001 Bern
Mailing Address: Postfach 7836, 3001 Bern
Tel: (031) 382 10 10 *Fax:* (031) 382 10 16
E-mail: info@sab.ch
Web Site: www.sab.ch
Key Personnel
Dir: Thomas Egger *E-mail:* thomas.egger@sab.ch
Founded: 1943
Subjects: Agriculture, Architecture & Interior De-
sign, Economics, Energy, Environmental Stud-
ies, Labor, Industrial Relations, Regional In-
terests, Social Sciences, Sociology, Travel &
Tourism, Mountain & Rural Areas, Mountain
Population

Schweizerische Stiftung fuer Alpine Forschung
(Swiss Foundation for Alpine Research)
Stadelhoferstr 42, 8001 Zurich
Tel: (044) 253 12 00 *Fax:* (044) 253 12 01
Web Site: www.alpineresearch.ch; www.alpinfo.ch
Key Personnel
President: Etienne Gross
Mng Dir: Thomas Weber-Wegst
Founded: 1939
Subjects: Biological Sciences, Environmental
Studies, Geography, Geology, Sports, Athlet-
ics
ISBN Prefix(es): 978-3-85515

Schweizerisches Jugendschriftenwerk (SJW)+
Uetlibergstr 20, 8045 Zurich
Tel: (044) 462 49 40 *Fax:* (044) 462 69 13
E-mail: office@sjw.ch
Web Site: www.sjw.ch
Key Personnel
Publishing Dir: Regula Malin *E-mail:* r.malin@
sjw.ch
Founded: 1956
ISBN Prefix(es): 978-3-7269
Number of titles published annually: 30 Print
Total Titles: 300 Print
Imprints: Fotorotar AG/EGG ZH
Orders to: BD Bucherdienst/Einsiel

Verlag Schweizerisches Katholisches Bibelwerk
Bederstr 76, 8002 Zurich
Tel: (044) 205 99 60 *Fax:* (044) 205 99 60
E-mail: info@bibelwerk.ch
Web Site: www.bibelwerk.ch
Membership(s): AMB.
Subjects: Religion - Catholic
ISBN Prefix(es): 978-3-7203

Scola Verlag, *imprint of* Orell Fuessli Verlag AG

Secession Verlag fuer Literatur GmbH
Merkurstr 27, 8032 Zurich
Tel: (044) 586 22 26
E-mail: info@secession-verlag.com
Web Site: www.secession-verlag.com
Key Personnel
Publisher, Press & Rights: Christian Ruzicska
Tel: (030) 325 346 63 *E-mail:* ruzicska@
secession-verlag.com
Publisher, Sales & Marketing: Joachim von Ze-
pelin *Tel:* (030) 702 425 18 *E-mail:* zepelin@
secession-verlag.com
Subjects: Literature, Literary Criticism, Essays,
International Literature
ISBN Prefix(es): 978-3-905951
Branch Office(s)
Potsdamer Str 98a, 10785 Berlin, Germany
Tel: (030) 325 346 63 *Fax:* (030) 325 346 64
Distribution Center: Buchzentrum AG, Indus-
triestr Ost 10, 4614 Haegendorf, Contact: Mar-
ion Haeni *Tel:* (062) 209 26 44 *Fax:* (062) 209
27 88 *E-mail:* haeni@buchzentrum.ch
Medienlogistik Pichler OEBZ GmbH & Co KG,
IZ NOE Sued, Str 1, Objekt 34, 2355 Wiener
Neudorf, Austria *Tel:* (02236) 635 35 290
Fax: (02236) 635 35 243 *E-mail:* bestellen@
medien-logistik.at *Web Site:* www.medien-
logistik.at
Prolit Verlagsauslieferung GmbH, Siemensstr 16,
35463 Fernwald Annerod, Germany, Contact: Alexandra Reichel *Tel:* (0641) 943 93
36 *Fax:* (0641) 943 93 29 *E-mail:* a.reichel@
prolit.de

Seismo Verlag
Zaehringerstr 26, 8001 Zurich
Tel: (044) 261 10 94 *Fax:* (044) 251 11 94
E-mail: buch@seismoverlag.ch
Web Site: www.seismoverlag.ch
Founded: 1989
Subjects: Social Sciences, Sociology

ISBN Prefix(es): 978-3-03777
Distribution Center: AVA Verlagsauslieferung
AG, Centralweg 16, 8910 Affoltern am Al-
bis *Tel:* (044) 762 42 00 *Fax:* (044) 762 42 10
E-mail: avainfo@ava.ch *Web Site:* www.ava.ch
(German-speaking Switzerland)
Albert le Grand SA, 20, Route de Beaumont,
1701 Fribourg *Tel:* (026) 425 85 95 *Fax:* (026)
425 85 90 *E-mail:* diffusion@albert-le-grand.
ch *Web Site:* www.albert-le-grand.ch (French-
speaking Switzerland)
FMSH-diffusion, 18, rue Robert-Schuman, CS
90003, 94227 Charenton-le-Pont, France
Tel: 01 53 48 56 30 *Fax:* 01 53 48 20 95
E-mail: cid@msh-paris.fr *Web Site:* www.
lcdpu.fr
GVA Gemeinsame Verlagsauslieferung Goettingen GmbH & Co AG, Postfach 2021, 37010
Goettingen, Germany *Tel:* (0551) 384200 0
Fax: (0551) 384200 10 *E-mail:* info@gva-
verlage.de *Web Site:* www.gva-verlage.de

SEWES Verlagsgenossenschaft
Wichlernweg 7, 6010 Kriens
Tel: (041) 320 19 79 *Fax:* (041) 320 19 79
E-mail: kontakt@sewes.ch
Web Site: www.sewes.ch
Key Personnel
Owner: Rosmarie Schneeberger *E-mail:* ar-ro.
schneeberger@hispeed.ch
Founded: 2009
Subjects: Philosophy
ISBN Prefix(es): 978-3-9523632

Sinwel Buchhandlung und Verlag
Lorrainestr 10, 3013 Bern
Tel: (031) 332 52 05 *Fax:* (031) 333 13 76
E-mail: sinwel@sinwel.ch
Web Site: www.sinwel.ch
Founded: 1978
Subjects: Crafts, Games, Hobbies, Outdoor Recre-
ation
ISBN Prefix(es): 978-3-85911

SJW, see Schweizerisches Jugendschriftenwerk
(SJW)

**SKAT (Swiss Resource Centre & Consultancies
for Development)**
Vadianstr 42, 9000 St Gallen
Tel: (071) 228 54 54 *Fax:* (071) 228 54 55
E-mail: publications@skat.ch; info@skat.ch
Web Site: www.skat.ch
Key Personnel
Mng Dir: Juerg Christen *E-mail:* juerg.christen@
skat.ch
Founded: 1978
Consulting, documentation & project implementa-
tion of water supply, sanitation & urban devel-
opment.
Subjects: Agriculture, Environmental Studies,
Management, Transportation
ISBN Prefix(es): 978-3-908001
Number of titles published annually: 10 Print
Total Titles: 66 Print
Distributed by IT Publications Ltd

Edition Skylight, *imprint of* Edition Olms AG

Slatkine Reprints
5, rue des Chaudronniers, 1211 Geneva 3
Mailing Address: CP 3625, 1211 Geneva 3
Tel: (022) 776 25 51 *Fax:* (022) 960 95 78
E-mail: slatkine@slatkine.ch
Web Site: www.slatkine.com
Key Personnel
Dir: Ivan Slatkine *Tel:* (022) 960 95 35
E-mail: islatkine@slatkine.com; Michel-Igor
Slatkine *E-mail:* mislatkine@slatkine.com
Founded: 1918

Subjects: History, Language Arts, Linguistics,
Literature, Literary Criticism, Essays, French
History & Literature
ISBN Prefix(es): 978-2-05; 978-2-8321
Number of titles published annually: 30 Print
Total Titles: 5,000 Print
Branch Office(s)
7, ch des Chalets, 1279 Chavannes-de-Bogis
Distributor for Editions Honore Champion (out-
side of Belgium & France)

Solothurn Zeitung AG+
Zuchwilerstr 21, 4501 Solothurn
Tel: (058) 200 47 74 *Fax:* (058) 200 47 71
E-mail: redaktion@solothurnerzeitung.ch
Web Site: www.solothurnerzeitung.ch
Key Personnel
Publisher: Peter Wanner
Founded: 1906
Specialize in periodicals.
Subjects: Architecture & Interior Design, Chem-
istry, Chemical Engineering, Electronics, Elec-
trical Engineering, Technology, Transportation
ISBN Prefix(es): 978-3-85962
Subsidiaries: Jeger Moll Druck und Verlag AG

Speer Verlag AG
Limmatstr 130, 8049 Zurich
Tel: (044) 341 42 56 *Fax:* (044) 342 45 31
E-mail: buchbestellung@speerverlag.ch
Web Site: www.speerverlag.ch
Key Personnel
Mng Dir: Ernst Pfluger
Founded: 1944
Subjects: Fiction, Mysteries, Suspense, Philoso-
phy, Poetry, Psychology, Psychiatry
ISBN Prefix(es): 978-3-85916

Sphinx GmbH
Andreasplatz 12, 4051 Basel
Tel: (061) 261 92 92 *Fax:* (061) 261 92 21
E-mail: sphinx@sphinx-book.ch
Web Site: www.sphinx-book.ch
Founded: 1975
Subjects: Astrology, Occult, Fiction, Health, Nu-
trition, Philosophy, Psychology, Psychiatry, Sci-
ence (General)
ISBN Prefix(es): 978-3-85914
Associate Companies: Sauerlaender AG

Staempfli Verlag AG+
Woelflistr 1, 3001 Bern
Mailing Address: Postfach 5662, 3001 Bern
Tel: (031) 300 66 44; (031) 300 66 66; (031) 300
66 77 (orders) *Fax:* (031) 300 66 88
E-mail: verlag@staempfli.com; order@staempfli.
com
Web Site: www.staempfliverlag.ch; www.
staempfli.com
Key Personnel
Chairman of the Board: Peter Staempfli
Mng Dir: Dr Manfred Hiefner *Tel:* (031) 300 63
10 *E-mail:* manfred.hiefner@staempfli.com
Publisher: Dr Rudolf Staempfli *Tel:* (031) 300 62
01 *E-mail:* rudolf.staempfli@staempfli.com
Program Manager: Stephan Grieb *Tel:* (031) 300
63 14 *E-mail:* stephan.grieb@staempfli.com
Head, Marketing & Sales: Andrea Kueng
Tel: (031) 300 63 21 *E-mail:* andrea.kueng@
staempfli.com
Founded: 1799
Membership(s): Law Books in Europe.
Subjects: Government, Political Science, Law
ISBN Prefix(es): 978-3-7272
Parent Company: Staempfli AG
Branch Office(s)
Leutschenbachstr 95, PO Box 145, 8050 Zurich
Tel: (044) 309 90 90 *Fax:* (044) 309 90 92
Foreign Rep(s): Brochhaus/Commission (Austria,
Germany)

Stahlbau Zentrum Schweiz (SZS)
Seefeldstr 25, 8008 Zurich
Tel: (044) 261 89 80 *Fax:* (044) 262 09 62
E-mail: info@szs.ch
Web Site: www.szs.ch
Key Personnel
Publications: Stefan Hunger *Tel:* (044) 285 10 75
Subjects: Engineering (General)

Rudolf Steiner Verlag AG
Im Ackermannshof, St Johanns-Vorstadt 19/21,
    4056 Basel
Tel: (061) 706 91 30 *Fax:* (061) 706 91 49
E-mail: verlag@steinerverlag.com
Web Site: www.steinerverlag.com
Key Personnel
Publishing Dir: Jonathan Stauffer
    E-mail: jonathan.stauffer@steinerverlag.com
Sales & Press: Claudia Zangger *E-mail:* claudia.
    zangger@steinerverlag.com
Editor: Mr Taja Gut *E-mail:* taja.gut@
    steinerverlag.com
Founded: 1949
Administrators of the Rudolf Steiner Literary Es-
    tate.
Subjects: Philosophy
ISBN Prefix(es): 978-3-7274
Total Titles: 700 Print

Swedenborg-Verlag+
Apollostr 2, 8032 Zurich
Tel: (0411) 383 59 44 *Fax:* (0411) 382 29 44
E-mail: info@swedenborg.ch
Web Site: www.swedenborg.ch
Key Personnel
Editor: Pfarrer Thomas Noack *E-mail:* pfarrer@
    swedenborg.ch
Founded: 1952
Subjects: Theology
ISBN Prefix(es): 978-3-85927
Distribution Center: pg medien GmbH,
    Muehlweg 2, 82054 Sauerlach, Germany
    E-mail: bestsellung@pg-va.de
Orders to: Schweizer Buchzentrum, Olten

**Swiss Resource Centre & Consultancies for
    Development**, see SKAT (Swiss Resource
    Centre & Consultancies for Development)

Swisstopo, see Bundesamt fuer Landestopografie,
    Swisstopo

Synergia Verlag
Unit of Sentovision GmbH
Venedigstr 35, 4142 Basel-Muenchenstein
Tel: (061) 511 21 91
E-mail: info@synergia-verlag.ch
Web Site: synergia-verlag.ch
Key Personnel
Graphic Design, Public Relations & Edito-
    rial: Alex Beckmann *E-mail:* a.beckmann@
    synergia-verlag.ch
Public Relations & Editorial: Carol Chiffelle
    E-mail: c.chiffelle@synergia-verlag.ch
Subjects: Art, Astrology, Occult, Business,
    Drama, Theater, Government, Political Science,
    Health, Nutrition, Inspirational, Spirituality,
    Literature, Literary Criticism, Essays, Music,
    Dance, Philosophy, Psychology, Psychiatry, Re-
    ligion - Other, Science (General), Nature
ISBN Prefix(es): 978-3-940392; 978-3-9523057
    (Wolfbach Verlag); 978-3-906643; 978-3-
    906873; 978-3-944615
Imprints: Edition Hier & Jetzt; Wolfbach Verlag;
    Edition ZhanDao
Distribution Center: Synergia Auslieferung
    GmbH, Industriestr 20, 64380 Rossdorf, Ger-
    many *Tel:* (06154) 60 39 5-0 *Fax:* (06154) 60
    39 5-10 *E-mail:* info@synergia-auslieferung.de
    Web Site: synergia-auslieferung.de

SZS, see Stahlbau Zentrum Schweiz (SZS)

edition taberna kritika
Gutenbergstr 47, 3011 Bern
Tel: (033) 534 9308
E-mail: info@etkbooks.com
Web Site: www.etkbooks.com
Subjects: Fiction, Photography, Poetry
ISBN Prefix(es): 978-3-905846

Tamaron Verlag
Postfach 50, 6078 Lungern
Tel: (041) 679 78 79 *Fax:* (041) 679 78 71
E-mail: info@tamaron.ch
Web Site: www.tamaron.ch
ISBN Prefix(es): 978-3-908530

Theologischer Verlag Zurich (TVZ)+
Badenerstr 73, 8004 Zurich
Tel: (044) 299 33 55 *Fax:* (044) 299 33 58
E-mail: tvz@ref.ch
Web Site: www.tvz.ref.ch
Key Personnel
Dir, Rights & Licences: Lisa Briner *E-mail:* lisa.
    briner@ref.ch
Dir, Sales & Finance: Hansruedi Hausherr
    E-mail: hansruedi.hausherr@ref.ch
Press, Marketing & Editing: Corinne Auf der
    Maur *E-mail:* corinne.aufdermaur@ref.ch
Founded: 1946
Subjects: Religion - Catholic
ISBN Prefix(es): 978-3-290
Number of titles published annually: 4 Print
Imprints: Pano Verlag
Distribution Center: AVA Verlagsauslieferung
    AG, Centralweg 16, 8910 Afflotern am Al-
    bis *Tel:* (044) 762 42 50 *Fax:* (044) 762 42 10
    E-mail: verlagsservice@ava.ch *Web Site:* www.
    ava.ch
Brockhaus/Commission, Kreidlerstr 9, 70806
    Kornwestheim, Germany *Tel:* (07154) 1327 0
    Fax: (07154) 1327 13 *E-mail:* info@brocom.de
    Web Site: www.brocom.de
ISD Distributor of Scholarly Books, 70 Enter-
    prise Dr, Suite 2, Bristol, CT 06010, United
    States *Tel:* 860-584-6546 *Fax:* 860-540-
    1001 *E-mail:* orders@isdistribution.com *Web
    Site:* www.isdistribution.com

Tobler Verlag AG+
KLV Kaufmaennischer Lehrmittelverlag AG,
    Quellenstr 4e, 9402 Moerschwil
Tel: (071) 845 20 10 *Fax:* (071) 845 20 91
E-mail: info@klv.ch
Web Site: www.tobler-verlag.ch
Key Personnel
Publishing Dir: Sascha Gloor
Subjects: Health, Nutrition, Law, Management,
    Marketing, Nonfiction (General), Parapsychol-
    ogy, Philosophy, Photography, Psychology, Psy-
    chiatry
ISBN Prefix(es): 978-3-907506; 978-3-85612

Trans Tech Publications Ltd
Kreuzstr 10, 8635 Durnten-Zurich
Tel: (044) 922 10 22 *Fax:* (044) 922 10 33
E-mail: info@ttp.net; ttp@ttp.net
Web Site: www.ttp.net
Key Personnel
Chief Operating Officer & President: Anne-
    Kristin Wohlbier
Founded: 1967
Specialize in materials science & engineering.
Subjects: Chemistry, Chemical Engineering, En-
    gineering (General), Mechanical Engineering,
    Physics, Science (General), Materials Science
ISBN Prefix(es): 978-0-87849; 978-3-908158;
    978-3-908454; 978-3-908053; 978-3-908452;
    978-3-908451; 978-3-908450; 978-3-03785
Number of titles published annually: 30 Print
Total Titles: 412 Print

U.S. Office(s): Trans Tech Publications Inc, 234
    May St, PO Box 699, Enfield, NH 03748,
    United States *Tel:* 603-632-7377 *Fax:* 603-632-
    5611 *E-mail:* usa-ttp@ttp.net *Web Site:* www.
    ttp.net
Foreign Rep(s): ABE Marketing (Poland); Ac-
    cess Information Services Co (Taiwan); Ja-
    han Adib Publishing (Iran); ALKEM Com-
    pany (S) Pte Ltd (Singapore); Allied Publishers
    Ltd (India); Ane Books (India); L'Appel du
    Lvre (France); Arbert Int'l Book Co Ltd (Tai-
    wan); ARS Polona (Poland); Baker & Taylor
    Inc (USA); James Bennett Pty Limited (Aus-
    tralia); Blackwell North America (USA); Books
    Import-Export SA (Switzerland); Buecherecke
    AG (Switzerland); Caglayan Kitabevi (Turkey);
    Livraria Canuto Ltda (Brazil); Capital Books
    Pvt Ltd (India); Cenfor International (Italy);
    China Educational Publications Import & Ex-
    port Corp (China); China International Book
    Trading Corp (China); China National Publica-
    tions (Germany); China National Publications
    Import & Export Corporations (China); China
    Publishers Services Ltd (China, Hong Kong);
    China Science Publishing Group (China);
    Chips Books (USA); Co-op Information Ser-
    vices (Australia); Curran Associates Inc (USA);
    Dawson France (France); Dawson UK, Daw-
    son Books (UK); DEA (Italy); Buchand-
    lung DECIUS (Germany); Diaz de Santos
    SA (Spain); C V Djakarta Raya (Indonesia);
    DKG Info Systems (China, Hong Kong); Di-
    etmar Dreier (Germany); Erasmus Boekhan-
    del BV (Netherlands); Ex Libris (Germany);
    Julio L Figueiredo Lda (Portugal); Gambit
    COiS sp z o o (Poland); Green Po Book Inc
    (Taiwan); Haksul Intelligence (South Korea);
    Harrassowitz Buchhandlung (Germany); Ul-
    rico Hoepli (Italy); A Houtschild (Netherlands);
    Impact Korea (South Korea); Ingressus BV
    (Netherlands); International Publishing Ser-
    vice (Poland); Librairie Interphiliv (France);
    Intes Praha (Czechia); Inthanon Publishing
    Ltd (Thailand); Izmir Tip Kitabevi (Turkey);
    Karger Libri AG (Switzerland); Kinokuniya
    Company Ltd (Japan); KL Books Distributor
    (Malaysia); Koch, Neff & Volckmar GmbH
    (Germany); Kyobo Book Centre Co Ltd (South
    Korea); H Lang & Cie AG (Switzerland); Li-
    brairie Lavosier-Technique & Documentation
    (France); Lehmanns Fachbuchhandlung (Ger-
    many); LEVANT Distributors Sarl (Lebanon);
    Leykam Buchhandelsges mbH (Austria); Ex
    Libris (Germany); Licitec Libros SLL (Spain);
    Licosa (Italy); Lindsay & Croft (UK); Tahir
    Lodhi (Pakistan); LSR Libros Servicios y Rep-
    resentaciones SA de CV (Mexico); Massmann
    Internationale Buchhandlung (Germany); May-
    ersche Buchhandlung (Germany); The Midori
    Book Store Co (Japan); John Mihalopoulos
    & Son International Booksellers (Greece);
    Minerva Wissenschaftliche Buchhandlung
    GmbH (Austria); Neutrino Inc (Japan); OLF
    SA (Switzerland); Osaka Oviss Inc (Japan);
    Pak Book Corp (Pakistan); Pan Korea Book
    Corp (South Korea); PMS Publishers Services
    Pte Ltd (Malaysia, Singapore); Progressive In-
    ternational Agencies (Pvt) Ltd (Pakistan); Red
    Pepper Books (South Africa); Sara Books Pvt
    Ltd (India); Buchhandlung Schreiber (Switzer-
    land); Schweitzer Sortiment oHG (Germany);
    Shankar's Book Agency Pvt Ltd (India); Sin-
    minchu Publishing Co Ltd (Hong Kong); Sis-
    temas Bibli002;informa SA de CV (Mexico);
    Solochek Libros SL (Spain); The Standard
    Book Company (India); Starkmann Ltd (UK);
    Buchhaus Stern-Verlag (Germany); Stockmann
    Akateeminen Kirjakauppa (Finland); Ta Tong
    Book Co Ltd (Taiwan); Tapir (Norway); Thalia
    Buecher AG (Switzerland); Trans Tech Pub-
    lications Inc (USA); Transmedia BV (Nether-
    lands); Unifacmanu Trading Co Ltd (Taiwan);
    Librairie Universitaire (Belgium); Konrad Wit-
    twer Buchhandlung (Germany); Wouters NV

(Belgium); Yankee Book Peddler (USA); YOO REE Information Co (South Korea); YPiJ-BOOKS.com Sdn Bhd (Malaysia); YUHA Associates Sdn Bhd (Malaysia)

Editions du Tricorne+
14 rue Lissignol, 1201 Geneva
Tel: (022) 738 83 66
Web Site: www.editionstricorne.net
Key Personnel
Mng Dir: Serge Kaplun
Founded: 1976
Subjects: Environmental Studies, Government, Political Science, Development, Global Issues, Human Rights, Humanitarian, International Relations
ISBN Prefix(es): 978-2-8293
Number of titles published annually: 12 Print
Total Titles: 300 Print
Distributed by Presses Universitaires de France (PUF)

TVZ, see Theologischer Verlag Zurich (TVZ)

Unionsverlag
Rieterstr 18, 8002 Zurich
Mailing Address: Postfach 2188, 8027 Zurich
Tel: (044) 283 20 00 *Fax:* (044) 283 20 01
E-mail: webmail_3@unionsverlag.ch; presse@ unionsverlag.ch
Web Site: www.unionsverlag.com
Key Personnel
Publisher & Editorial: Lucien Leitess *Tel:* (044) 283 20 07
Editorial: Iris Wiederkehr *Tel:* (044) 283 20 06
Press & Public Relations: Ulla Steffan *Tel:* (044) 283 20 03 *E-mail:* ulla.steffan@unionsverlag.ch
Sales & Marketing: Sven Baier *Tel:* (044) 283 20 10
Subjects: Criminology, Fiction, Romance, Travel & Tourism
ISBN Prefix(es): 978-3-293
Foreign Rep(s): b+i buch und information ag (Dagmar Bhend) (Switzerland); Buchkontor (Ulla Harms & Christiane Eblinger) (Austria)
Distribution Center: Schweizer Buchzentrum AG (BZ), Industriestr Ost 10, 4614 Haegendorf *Tel:* (062) 209 25 25 *Fax:* (062) 209 26 27 *E-mail:* kundendienst@buchzentrum.ch
Medienlogistik Pichler-OEBZ GmbH & Co KG, IZ-NOE S, Str 1, Objekt 34, 2355 Wiener Neudorf, Austria, Contact: Eva Maria Prinz *Tel:* (02236) 63535 245 *Fax:* (02236) 63535 271 *E-mail:* eva.prinz@medien-logistik.at
Prolit Verlagsauslieferung GmbH, Siemensstr 16, 35463 Fernwald, Germany, Contact: Andrea Willenberg *Tel:* (0641) 943 93 35 *Fax:* (0641) 943 93 39 *E-mail:* a.willenberg@prolit.de

The United Nations Office at Geneva (UNOG)
Ave del la Paix 8-14, 1211 Geneva 10
Tel: (022) 917 1234 *Fax:* (022) 917 0123
E-mail: webmaster@unog.ch
Web Site: www.unog.ch
Key Personnel
Dir General: Michael Moller
Subjects: International Affairs
ISBN Prefix(es): 978-92-1
U.S. Office(s): UN Sales & Marketing Section, 300 E 42 St, 9th floor, IN-919J, New York, NY 10017, United States, Contact: Nicolas Bovay *E-mail:* permissions@un.org
Bookshop(s): United Nations Bookshop, Palais des Nations, Door 40, 1211 Geneva 10 *Tel:* (022) 917 48 72 *Fax:* (022) 917 06 10 *E-mail:* unogbookshop@unog.ch

UNOG, see The United Nations Office at Geneva (UNOG)

vdf Hochschulverlag AG an der ETH Zurich
VOB D, Voltastr 24, 8092 Zurich
Tel: (044) 632 42 42 *Fax:* (044) 632 12 32
E-mail: verlag@vdf.ethz.ch
Web Site: vdf.ch
Key Personnel
Publishing Dir: Ernst Schaerer *E-mail:* schaerer@ vdf.ethz.ch
Marketing & Editorial: Claudia Signer *Tel:* (044) 632 77 74 *E-mail:* signer@vdf.ethz.ch
Founded: 1992
Subjects: Agriculture, Archaeology, Architecture & Interior Design, Astronomy, Biological Sciences, Business, Chemistry, Chemical Engineering, Civil Engineering, Communications, Computer Science, Computers, Earth Sciences, Economics, Electronics, Electrical Engineering, Energy, Engineering (General), Environmental Studies, Gardening, Plants, Geography, Geology, Government, Political Science, History, Law, Management, Marketing, Mathematics, Medicine, Nursing, Dentistry, Military Science, Physics, Psychology, Psychiatry, Real Estate, Science (General), Social Sciences, Sociology, Technology
ISBN Prefix(es): 978-3-7281
Number of titles published annually: 30 Print; 1 Online; 25 E-Book
Total Titles: 650 Print; 8 CD-ROM; 3 Online; 220 E-Book; 4 Audio
Orders to: Brokhaus Kommissionsgeschaeft, Postfach 1220, 70806 Kornwestheim, Germany

Verkehrshaus der Schweiz (Swiss Museum of Transport)
Lidostr 5, 6006 Lucerne
Tel: (041) 370 44 44 *Fax:* (041) 370 61 68
E-mail: mail@verkehrshaus.ch
Web Site: www.verkehrshaus.ch
Key Personnel
Dir: Martin Buetikofer *Tel:* (041) 375 74 01 *E-mail:* martin.buetikofer@verkehrshaus.ch
Head, Marketing & Sales: Jacqueline Schleier *Tel:* (041) 375 74 03 *E-mail:* jacqueline. schleier@verkehrshaus.ch
Subjects: Communications, Transportation
ISBN Prefix(es): 978-3-85954
Branch Office(s)
Museum of Transportation & Communication

Editions du Verseau, *imprint of* Roth et Sauter SA

Versus Verlag AG
Merkurstr 45, 8032 Zurich
Tel: (044) 251 08 92 *Fax:* (044) 262 67 38
E-mail: info@versus.ch
Web Site: www.versus.ch
Key Personnel
Manager: Anne Buechi; Judith Henzmann
Founded: 1993
Subjects: Accounting, Business, Economics, Finance, Human Relations, Labor, Industrial Relations, Law, Management, Marketing, Public Administration
ISBN Prefix(es): 978-3-908143; 978-3-909066; 978-3-03909
Foreign Rep(s): Axel Kueppers (Germany); Giovanni Ravasio (Switzerland)
Distribution Center: Buch 2000, c/o AVA, Centralweg 16, Affoltern am Albis *Tel:* (044) 762 42 60 *Fax:* (044) 762 42 10 *E-mail:* buch2000@ava.ch
G Umbreit GmbH & Co KG, Mundelsheimer Str 3, 74321 Bietigheim-Bissingen, Germany *Tel:* (07154) 596 373 *Fax:* (07154) 596 387 *E-mail:* thomas.duchardt@umbreit.de (Germany & Austria)

Vexer Verlag+
Brauerstr 27b, 9000 St Gallen
Tel: (071) 245 79 66

E-mail: info@vexer.ch
Web Site: www.vexer.ch
Key Personnel
Contact: Josef Felix Mueller
Founded: 1985
Subjects: Art, Film, Video, Literature, Literary Criticism, Essays
ISBN Prefix(es): 978-3-909090
Total Titles: 80 Print
Branch Office(s)
Koepenicker Str 154, 10997 Berlin, Germany, Contact: Vera Ida Mueller *E-mail:* mail@ vexerberlin.de
Distributed by Buchhandlung Walther Koenig

Verlag A Vogel AG
Haetschen, 9053 Teufen
Mailing Address: Postfach 63, 9053 Teufen
Tel: (071) 335 66 66 *Fax:* (071) 335 66 88
E-mail: info@verlag-avogel.ch
Web Site: www.avogel.ch
Key Personnel
Publishing Dir: Clemens Umbricht
Subjects: Health, Nutrition, Medicine, Nursing, Dentistry, Alternative Medicine, Herbal Medicine, Natural Health, Naturopathy
ISBN Prefix(es): 978-3-906404; 978-3-909106
Number of titles published annually: 1 Print

Verlag die Waage
Zielackerstr 13, 8603 Schwerzenbach
E-mail: bestellungen@verlagdiewaage.ch
Web Site: www.verlagdiewaage.ch
Key Personnel
Publisher: Claudia Wiesner Eymard
Founded: 1951
Subjects: Art, Asian Studies, Culture
ISBN Prefix(es): 978-3-85966

Waldgut Verlag & Atelier Bodoni+
Industriestr 23, 8500 Frauenfeld
Tel: (052) 728 89 28 *Fax:* (052) 728 89 27
E-mail: info@waldgut.ch; bestellung@waldgut.ch
Web Site: www.waldgut.ch
Key Personnel
Publishing Dir: Beat Brechbuehl
Press & Sales: Berrit Fuhrmann-Stiehler *E-mail:* pressundvertrieb@waldgut.ch
Founded: 1980
Subjects: Developing Countries, Education, Ethnicity, Foreign Countries, Music, Dance, Poetry
ISBN Prefix(es): 978-3-7294; 978-3-03740
Branch Office(s)
Gottlieber Str 44, Postfach 50 53, 78429 Konstanz, Germany
Distribution Center: AVA Verlagsauslieferung AG, Centralweg 16, 8910 Affoltern am Albis *Tel:* (044) 7624200 *Fax:* (044) 7624210 *E-mail:* avainfo@ava.ch
SOVA GmbH, Phillipp-Reis-Str 17, 63477 Maintal, Germany *Tel:* (06181) 9088072 *Fax:* (06181) 9088073 *E-mail:* sovaffm@t-online.de

WCC Publications, see World Council of Churches (WCC Publications)

Weka Business Media AG+
Hermetschloostr 77, Postfach, 8010 Zurich
Tel: (044) 434 88 34 *Fax:* (044) 434 89 99
E-mail: info@weka.ch
Web Site: www.weka.ch
Key Personnel
Mng Dir: Stephen Bernhard
Founded: 1978
Specialize in loose-leaf publications.
Subjects: Engineering (General), Environmental Studies, Finance, Law, Management, Medicine, Nursing, Dentistry, Construction, Human Resources, Information Science, Tax Law
ISBN Prefix(es): 978-3-297
Parent Company: WEKA MEDIA GmbH & Co KG, Roemerstr 4, 86438 Kissing, Germany

Weltrundschau Verlag AG+
Oberneuhofstr 1, 6341 Baar
Tel: (041) 761 54 31 *Fax:* (041) 761 44 04
E-mail: info@wrs.ch
Web Site: www.wrs.ch
Key Personnel
Mng Dir: Franz Truniger
Founded: 1959
Subjects: Government, Political Science, Sports,
Athletics
ISBN Prefix(es): 978-3-7283
Associate Companies: Jeunesse Verlagsanstal,
Kirchstr 1, Vaduz, Liechtenstein (Rights & Per-
missions)

Werd & Weber Verlag AG
Gwattstr 125, 3645 Thun-Gwatt
Tel: (033) 336 55 55 *Fax:* (033) 336 55 56
E-mail: mail@weberverlag.ch; buecher@
werdverlag.ch
Web Site: www.weberverlag.ch; www.werdverlag.
ch; www.weberag.ch
Key Personnel
Publishing Manager: Annette Weber *Tel:* (033)
336 44 44 *E-mail:* a.weber@weberag.ch
Communications & Sales Manager: Bernhard
Hunziker *Tel:* (033) 334 50 15 *E-mail:* b.
hunziker@weberag.ch
Subjects: Cookery, Regional Interests, Travel &
Tourism, Nature
ISBN Prefix(es): 978-3-85932; 978-3-906033

Werner Druck & Medien AG
Kanonengasse 32, 4001 Basel
Tel: (061) 270 15 15 *Fax:* (061) 270 15 16
E-mail: info@wd-m.ch
Web Site: www.wd-m.ch
Key Personnel
Owner & Mng Dir: Roger Kessler *Tel:* (061) 279
15 40 *E-mail:* r.kessler@wd-m.ch
Founded: 1862
Subjects: Art
ISBN Prefix(es): 978-3-85979

WHO Press, see World Health Organization
(WHO)

WMO, see World Meteorological Organization
(WMO)

Woerterseh Verlag
Im Langstuck 14, 8044 Gockhausen
Tel: (044) 368 33 68
E-mail: verlag@woerterseh.ch
Web Site: www.woerterseh.ch
Key Personnel
Publisher: Gabriella Baumann-von Arx
Tel: (044) 368 33 62 *E-mail:* baumannvonarx@
woerterseh.ch
Founded: 2004
Subjects: Biography, Memoirs, Nonfiction (Gen-
eral)
ISBN Prefix(es): 978-3-03763

Wolfau-Druck AG
Lagerstr 6, 8570 Weinfelden
Tel: (071) 622 53 53 *Fax:* (071) 622 30 04
E-mail: wolfau-druck@bluewin.ch
Key Personnel
Owner: Christof Muehlemann; Erika Muehlemann
Founded: 1949
ISBN Prefix(es): 978-3-85809; 978-3-9523610

Wolfbach Verlag, *imprint of* Synergia Verlag

J E Wolfensberger AG
Stallikonerstr 79, 8903 Birmensdorf
Mailing Address: Postfach 474, 8903 Birmensdorf
Tel: (044) 285 78 78 *Fax:* (044) 285 78 79
E-mail: office@wolfensberger-ag.ch

Web Site: www.wolfensberger-ag.ch
Key Personnel
General Manager: Benni Wolfensberger *Tel:* (044)
285 78 00 *E-mail:* benni.wolfensberger@
wolfensberger-ag.ch
Lithography & Publishing: Thomi Wolfensberger
E-mail: thomi.wolfensberger@wolfensberger-
ag.ch
Founded: 1902
Subjects: Art, Lithographs, Limited editions,
signed & numbered

**World Council of Churches (WCC
Publications)+**
150 route de Ferney, 1211 Geneva
Mailing Address: PO Box 2100, 1211 Geneva
Tel: (022) 791 6171 *Fax:* (022) 791 6346
E-mail: publications@wcc-coe.org
Web Site: www.oikoumene.org; publications.
oikoumene.org
Founded: 1948
Subjects: Religion - Other, Theology
ISBN Prefix(es): 978-2-8254
U.S. Office(s): 777 UN Plaza, Suite 9D, New
York, NY 10017, United States, Advocacy Of-
ficer: Geronimo Desumala, III *Tel:* 212-867-
5890
Foreign Rep(s): Alban Books (UK & the con-
tinent); Christian Literature Society of Korea
(Korea); ISBS (Canada, USA)

World Health Organization (WHO)
1211 Geneva 27
Tel: (022) 791 32 64 *Fax:* (022) 791 48 57
E-mail: bookorders@who.int; publications@who.
int
Web Site: www.who.int/bookorders
Subjects: Environmental Studies, Health, Nutri-
tion, Human Relations, Medicine, Nursing,
Dentistry, Veterinary Science
ISBN Prefix(es): 978-92-4; 978-92-9031; 978-92-
832; 978-92-890; 978-92-9020; 978-92-9021;
978-92-9022; 978-92-9023; 978-92-9036; 978-
92-9061; 978-92-9173
Branch Office(s)
World Health Organization Regional Office for
Africa, PO Box 6, Brazzaville, Congo (Braz-
zaville) *Tel:* 63 72 05; 81 15 53; 81 12 60
Fax: 81 19 39; 81 14 09 *E-mail:* afro@who.org
Web Site: www.whoafr.org
World Health Organization Regional Office for
Europe, Marmorvej 51, 2100 Copenhagen
O, Denmark *Tel:* 45 33 70 00 *Fax:* 45 33
70 01 *E-mail:* postmaster@euro.who.int *Web
Site:* www.euro.who.int
World Health Organization Regional Office for
the Eastern Mediterranean, WHO Post Of-
fice, Abdul Razzak Al Sanhouri St, Naser
City, Cairo 11371, Egypt *Tel:* (02) 2670 25
35 *Fax:* (02) 2670 24 92; (02) 2670 24 94
E-mail: dsa@emro.who.int *Web Site:* www.
emro.who.int
World Health Organization Regional Office for
Southeast Asia, World Health House, In-
draprastha Estate, Mahatma Gandhi Rd, New
Delhi 110 002, India *Tel:* (011) 43040 103;
(011) 43040 104; (011) 43040 105 *Fax:* (011)
23370197 *E-mail:* sebookshop@who.int *Web
Site:* www.searo.who.int/publications-sales
World Health Organization Regional Office
for the Western Pacific, PO Box 2932, 1099
Manila, Philippines *Tel:* (02) 528 80 01
Fax: (02) 521 1036; (02) 536 0279; (02) 536
0362 *E-mail:* publications@wpro.who.int *Web
Site:* www.wpro.who.int
U.S. Office(s): Pan American Health Organization,
525 23 St NW, Washington, DC 20037, United
States *Tel:* 202-974-3000 *Fax:* 202-974-3663
E-mail: sales@paho.org *Web Site:* www.paho.
org
Orders to: Stylus Publishing LLC, PO Box
605, Herndon, VA 20172-0605, United

States *Tel:* 703-661-1581 *Fax:* 703-661-1501
E-mail: stylusmail@presswarehouse.com *Web
Site:* www.styluspub.com

World Meteorological Organization (WMO)
7bis, ave de la Paix, 1211 Geneva
Mailing Address: Case postale 2300, 1211
Geneva 2
Tel: (022) 730 81 11 *Fax:* (022) 730 81 81
E-mail: cpa@wmo.int
Web Site: www.wmo.int
Key Personnel
Secretary General: Petteri Taalas
Deputy Secretary General: Jeremiah Lengoasa
Subjects: Science (General), Technology, Meteo-
rology
ISBN Prefix(es): 978-92-63

Edition Xanthippe
Zaehringerstr 26, 8001 Zurich
Tel: (044) 251 03 02; (079) 230 84 43 (cell)
E-mail: info@xanthippe.ch
Web Site: www.xanthippe.ch
Key Personnel
Publisher: Dr Yvonne-Denise Koechli
Subjects: Biography, Memoirs, Economics, Gov-
ernment, Political Science, Social Sciences,
Sociology
ISBN Prefix(es): 978-3-9522868
Branch Office(s)
Xanthippe Verlag, Rechte Wien Zeile 39, 1040
Vienna, Austria
Distribution Center: Xanthippe Verlag, Men-
zingerstr 121, 80997 Munich-Obermenzing,
Germany
AVA Verlagsauslieferung, Centralweg 16, Post-
fach 27, 8910 Affoltern am Albis *Tel:* (044)
762 42 60 *Fax:* (044) 762 42 10 *E-mail:* h.
amsler@ava.ch
GVA Gemeinsame Verlagsvertretung Goettingen
GmbH, Postfach 2021, 37010 Goettingen, Ger-
many *Tel:* (0551) 48 71 77 *Fax:* (0551) 4 13
92 *E-mail:* frester@gva-verlage.de (Germany &
Austria)

Editions Xenia SA
Route des Ronquoz 86, 1950 Sion
Mailing Address: Case postale 429, 1951 Sion
Tel: (027) 327 53 67 *Fax:* (027) 327 53 66
E-mail: info@editions-xenia.com
Web Site: www.editions-xenia.com
Key Personnel
Owner & Chief Executive Officer: Slobodan
Despot *E-mail:* despot@editions-xenia.com
Founded: 2006
Subjects: History, Literature, Literary Criticism,
Essays
ISBN Prefix(es): 978-2-88892
Distribution Center: OLF SA, ZI 3, Corminboeuf,
CP 1152, 1701 Fribourg, Contact: Armand Car-
ruzzo *Tel:* (026) 467 51 11 *Fax:* (026) 467 54
66 *E-mail:* armand.carruzzo@olf.ch
CED, 73, quai Auguste-Deshaies, 94854 Ivry-
sur-Seine, France, Sales Dir: Dorothee Per-
rault *Tel:* 01 46 58 38 40 *Fax:* 01 46 71 25 59
E-mail: d-perrault@wanadoo.fr
Les Belles Lettres, 25, rue du General-Leclerc,
94270 Le Kremlin-Bicetre, France, Con-
tact: Marc Leymarios *Tel:* 01 45 15 19 78
Fax: 01 45 15 19 80 *E-mail:* m.leymarios@
lesbelleslettres.com

Zauberblume Verlag, *imprint of* Romantik
Verlag

Edition ZhanDao, *imprint of* Synergia Verlag

Editions Zoe
11, rue des Moraines, 1227 Carouge-Geneva
Tel: (022) 309 36 06 *Fax:* (022) 309 36 03

E-mail: info@editionszoe.ch; commandes@
  editionszoe.ch
Web Site: www.editionszoe.ch
Key Personnel
Founder & Editorial Advisor: Marlyse Pietri
Dir: Caroline Coutau
Distribution: Dominique Fries
Representative: Manuella Mounir
Founded: 1975
Subjects: History, Literature, Literary Criticism,
  Essays, Social Sciences, Sociology
ISBN Prefix(es): 978-2-88182
Foreign Rep(s): Dimedia (Canada); Harmonia
  Mundi (Belgium, France)

Zuercher Oberland Medien AG
Rapperswilerstr 1, 8620 Wetzikon
Mailing Address: Postfach 1425, 8620 Wetzikon
Tel: (044) 933 32 54 *Fax:* (044) 933 32 58
E-mail: info@zo-shop.ch
Web Site: www.zo-medien.ch; www.zo-shop.ch
Key Personnel
Chief Executive Officer & Mng Dir: Dani Sigel
  E-mail: daniel.sigel@zol.ch
Editor-in-Chief: Christian Braendli
  E-mail: christian.braendli@zol.ch
Subjects: Environmental Studies, Fiction, History,
  Poetry, Nature
ISBN Prefix(es): 978-3-85981

Zumstein & Cie, see Briefmarken Zumstein &
  Cie

Zytglogge Verlag AG
Schoren 7, 3653 Oberhofen
Tel: (033) 244 00 30 *Fax:* (033) 244 00 33
E-mail: info@zytglogge.ch
Web Site: www.zytglogge.ch
Key Personnel
Publishing Dir: Bettina Kaelin Ramseyer
  E-mail: bettina.kaelin@zytglogge.ch; Hugo
  Ramseyer *E-mail:* hugo.ramseyer@zytglogge.ch
Press & Sales: Anne Riesen *E-mail:* anne.
  riesen@zytglogge.ch
Founded: 1965
Subjects: Art, Language Arts, Linguistics, Litera-
  ture, Literary Criticism, Essays, Music, Dance,
  Nonfiction (General), Photography, Comics
ISBN Prefix(es): 978-3-7296
Number of titles published annually: 20 Print; 15
  CD-ROM
Total Titles: 600 Print; 500 CD-ROM

Syria

General Information

Capital: Damascus
Language: Arabic and some Kurdish
Religion: Islamic (mostly of the Sunni sect) and
  Christian
Population: 13.7 million
Bank Hours: 0800-1400 Saturday-Thursday
Shop Hours: 1000-1900. Closed Friday. Generally
  long closing at lunchtime
Currency: 100 piastres = 1 Syrian pound
Export/Import Information: No tariffs on books
  except children's picture books, with additional
  taxes; most advertising matter is dutied. State
  organization for control and execution of publicity and advertising within Syria is Arab Advertising Organization, Damascus. The General
  Advertising Institute, 2842, must get samples
  of commercial advertising and promotional materials before distribution permitted. Import
  license must be submitted to Commercial Bank
  of Syria in order to obtain exchange license.
Copyright: No copyright conventions signed

Dar Al-Fikr
PO Box 962, Damascus
Tel: (011) 2211166 *Fax:* (011) 2239716
E-mail: fikr@fikr.net; mailus@fikr.net
Web Site: www.fikr.com
Founded: 1957
ISBN Prefix(es): 978-1-57547; 978-1-59239

Dar Al Maarifah (House of Knowledge)
29 Ayar St, Damascus
Mailing Address: PO Box 30268, Damascus
Tel: (098) 635559 *Fax:* (011) 2241615
E-mail: info@easyquran.com
Web Site: www.easyquran.com
Key Personnel
General Manager: Subhi Taha *E-mail:* manager@
  easyquran.com
Founded: 1986
Also printer & distributor.
Membership(s): Arab Publishers Association.
Subjects: Religion - Islamic
Number of titles published annually: 1 CD-ROM
Total Titles: 240 Print; 5 CD-ROM

Dar Al Rowad Lil Nashr, see Pioneers
  Publishing House (Dar Al Rowad Lil Nashr)

IFPO, see Institut Francais du Proche-Orient
  (IFPO)

Institut Francais du Proche-Orient (IFPO)
  (French Institute of the Near East)
Abou Roummaneh, Damascus
Mailing Address: BP 344, Damascus
Tel: (011) 333 02 14 *Fax:* (011) 332 78 87
E-mail: diffusion-ifpo@ifporient.org; secretariat@
  ifporient.org
Web Site: www.ifporient.org
Key Personnel
Head, Publications: Nadine Meouchy *E-mail:* n.
  meouchy@ifporient.org
Founded: 2003
Specialize in ancient & modern civilization of the
  Near East.
Subjects: Anthropology, Archaeology, Geography,
  Geology, History, Language Arts, Linguistics,
  Literature, Literary Criticism, Essays, Philoso-
  phy, Religion - Islamic, Social Sciences, Soci-
  ology, Humanities
ISBN Prefix(es): 978-2-901315; 978-2-84128
Number of titles published annually: 8 Print
Total Titles: 292 Print
Parent Company: Direction Generale des Rela-
  tions Culturelles Scientifiques et Techniques,
  Ministere des affaires Etrangeres, Paris, France
Distributed by Al-Jaffan et al Jabi (Middle East)
Distribution Center: Leila Books, 39 Kasr El-
  Nil St, 2nd floor, Daher, Cairo 11271, Egypt
  E-mail: leilabks@intouch.com
Librairie-Boutique de l'ima, One rue des Fos-
  ses, St-Bernard, 75236 Paris Cedex 05,
  France *E-mail:* bookshop@imarabe.org *Web
  Site:* www.imarabe.org
Librairie d'Amerique et d'Orient (Adrien Maison-
  neuve), 11, rue St-Sulpice, 75006 Paris, France
  E-mail: maisonneuve@maisonneuve-adrien.com
  Web Site: www.maisonneuve-adrien.com
Orders to: Librairie d'Amerique et d'Orient
  (Adrien Maisonneuve), 11, rue St-Sulpice,
  75006 Paris, France *Tel:* 01 43 26 86 35
  Fax: 01 43 54 59 54 *E-mail:* maisonneuve@
  maisonneuve-adrien.com *Web Site:* www.
  maisonneuve-adrien.com

**Pioneers Publishing House (Dar Al Rowad Lil
  Nashr)**
Halbouni, Musallam al Baroudi St, 4943 Damas-
  cus
Tel: (011) 222 8261 *Fax:* (011) 222 8261
E-mail: info@rowadpub.com
Web Site: www.rowadpub.com

Key Personnel
Dir General: Kassem Terrace *Tel:* (093) 2886087
  (cell) *E-mail:* kassem@rowadpub.com
Sales Manager: Ammar Terrace *Tel:* (093)
  3650977 (cell)
Founded: 1986
Subjects: Art, Computer Science, Geography, Ge-
  ology, History, Language Arts, Linguistics, Lit-
  erature, Literary Criticism, Essays, Philosophy,
  Psychology, Psychiatry, Religion - Other, Sci-
  ence (General), Rhetoric
ISBN Prefix(es): 978-9933-401

Taiwan

General Information

Capital: Taipei
Language: Northern Chinese (Mandarin)
Religion: Predominantly Buddhist, also Muslim,
  Daoist & Christian
Population: 20.9 million
Bank Hours: 0900-1530 Monday-Friday; 0900-
  1200 Saturday
Shop Hours: 1000-2130 Monday-Saturday
Currency: 100 cents = 1 new Taiwan dollar
Export/Import Information: No tariffs on books
  and advertising. Import licenses required; ex-
  change available when license is presented at
  authorized bank. Publications approved for im-
  port will not violate the Republic of China's
  basic national policy, undermine public morality or contravene special regulations.
Copyright: No copyright conventions signed.
  Copyright is protected by the Copyright Law.
  Companies and individuals, including foreigners, can register their works with the Ministry of the Interior for protection. An amendment broadening the scope of the Republic of
  China's Copyright Law was passed 28 June
  1985 by the Legislative Yuan and put into effect on 12 July 1985. The amendment, aimed
  at curbing pirating activities, sharply increases
  the maximum sentence for violating copyrights
  from three to five years and the maximum fine
  from US $75 to US $11,250, and brings computer software and video tapes under the scope
  of the law. Publications printed in Taiwan must
  acquire approval from the copyright holder before export.

Aichi Book Co Ltd
235, Chien Fu St, Chien Cheng District, Kaohsi-
  ung 806
Tel: (07) 8121571 *Fax:* (07) 8121534
E-mail: mail@aichi.com.tw
Web Site: www.aichibooks.com.tw; www.achi.
  com.tw
Founded: 1978
Subjects: Child Care & Development, Literature,
  Literary Criticism, Essays
ISBN Prefix(es): 978-957-608

Art Book Publishing+
4F, 18, Lane 283, Roosevelt Rd, Taipei 106
Tel: (02) 23620578 *Fax:* (02) 23623594
E-mail: artbook@ms43.hinet.net
Web Site: artbookho.com
Key Personnel
Publisher: Kung-Shang Ho
Founded: 1972
Specialize in fine arts.
Subjects: Antiques, Art, Biblical Studies, History,
  How-to
ISBN Prefix(es): 978-957-672; 978-957-9045

The Artist Publishing Co
6F, 147, Chongqing South Rd, Sec 1, Taipei 100

Tel: (02) 23886715 *Fax:* (02) 23317096
E-mail: artvenue@seed.net.tw
Founded: 1975
Subjects: Art
ISBN Prefix(es): 978-957-9500; 978-957-8273;
  978-957-9530; 978-986-7487; 978-986-7957

Asian Culture Co Ltd+
6F, 21 Nanking East Rd, Sec 3, Zhongshan District, Taipei 10487
Tel: (02) 2507-2606 *Fax:* (02) 2507-4260
E-mail: asian.culture@msa.hinet.net; ycwh1982@gmail.com
Web Site: www.asianculture.com.tw
Founded: 1982
Subjects: Archaeology, Art, Asian Studies, Biography, Memoirs, Business, Fiction, Health, Nutrition, History, Law, Literature, Literary Criticism, Essays, Military Science, Music, Dance, Philosophy, Photography, Romance, Self-Help, Women's Studies
ISBN Prefix(es): 978-957-8983; 978-957-9027; 978-957-9449; 978-957-03

Bookman Books Ltd+
3F, 60 Roosevelt Rd, Sec 4, Taipei 100
Tel: (02) 2368-4938; (02) 2365-8617 (customer service)
E-mail: bkservice@bookman.com.tw
Web Site: www.bookman.com.tw
Founded: 1977
Subjects: Fiction, History, Language Arts, Linguistics, Literature, Literary Criticism, Essays, Philosophy, Poetry, Travel & Tourism, Humanities
ISBN Prefix(es): 978-957-586
Number of titles published annually: 80 Print; 10 CD-ROM
Total Titles: 2,000 Print; 100 CD-ROM

Campus Evangelical Fellowship Press+
3F, 22 Luosifu Rd, Sec 4, Taipei 10090
Tel: (02) 2368-2361; (02) 2365-3665 *Fax:* (02) 2367-2139
E-mail: info@cef.tw; publish@campus.org.tw;
  mis@campus.org.tw; sales@campus.org.tw;
  bks@campus.org.tw
Web Site: www.cef.tw; www.campus.org.tw
Founded: 1965
Subjects: Biblical Studies, Biography, Memoirs, Child Care & Development, Human Relations, Religion - Protestant
ISBN Prefix(es): 978-957-587
U.S. Office(s): Campus Evangelical Fellowship-Overseas Campus Magazine (CEF-OCM), 365 Du Pahze St, Naperville, IL 60565, United States *Tel:* 630-983-7708 *E-mail:* usacef@gmail.com

Cheng Chung Book Co Ltd
4F, No 43, Fu-Hsin Rd, Hsin-Tien City, Taipei
Tel: (02) 8667-6565 (ext 120) *Fax:* (02) 2218-5172
E-mail: service@ccbc.com.tw
Web Site: www.ccbc.com.tw
Founded: 1931
Subjects: Biography, Memoirs, Business, Fiction, Government, Political Science, Health, Nutrition, History, Language Arts, Linguistics, Literature, Literary Criticism, Essays, Science (General)
ISBN Prefix(es): 978-957-09

Cheng Wen Publishing Co Ltd
3F-B, No 277, Roosevelt Rd, Sec 3, Taipei 106
Tel: (02) 23628032 *Fax:* (02) 23660806; (02) 23660826
E-mail: book@chengwen.com.tw;
  chengwenpub@hotmail.com
Web Site: www.chengwen.com.tw
Founded: 1965

Subjects: History, Literature, Literary Criticism, Essays, Philosophy
ISBN Prefix(es): 978-957-07

Chien Chen Publishing Co Ltd+
56 Ford Rd, Kaohsiung City 802
Tel: (07) 7268399 *Fax:* (07) 7268058
E-mail: services@cncgp.com.tw
Web Site: www.cncgp.com.tw
Founded: 1977
Subjects: Accounting, Agriculture, Animals, Pets, Behavioral Sciences, Biological Sciences, Business, Career Development
ISBN Prefix(es): 978-957-9574; 978-957-704

Chin-Chin Publications Ltd Inc+
9F, No 8, Wenhe St, WenShan District, Taipei 11653
Tel: (02) 22397890 *Fax:* (02) 22392790
E-mail: ivy@kissnature.com.tw
Web Site: www.kissnature.com.tw
Key Personnel
General Manager: LinPin Ou Yang
Founded: 1981
ISBN Prefix(es): 978-957-9427
Number of titles published annually: 30 Print; 10 CD-ROM
Total Titles: 658 Online

China Times Publishing Co (Shibao Wenhua Chuban)+
5F, 240 Hoping West Rd, Sec 3, Wanhua District, Taipei 10803
Tel: (02) 2304-7103; (02) 2306-6600 *Fax:* (02) 2304-6858
E-mail: newstudy@readingtimes.com.tw;
  newlife@readingtimes.com.tw
Web Site: www.readingtimes.com.tw
Founded: 1975
Subjects: Art, Astrology, Occult, Biography, Memoirs, Business, Fashion, Fiction, Finance, Government, Political Science, Health, Nutrition, History, Inspirational, Spirituality, Photography, Psychology, Psychiatry, Social Sciences, Sociology
ISBN Prefix(es): 978-957-13

Chu Liu Book Co+
2F-2, 57 Wufu First Rd, Kaohsiung City 80252
Tel: (07) 223-6780; (07) 226-5267 *Fax:* (07) 223-3073
E-mail: chuliu@liwen.com.tw
Web Site: www.liwen.com.tw
Founded: 1973
Subjects: Art, Child Care & Development, Education, History, Human Relations, Literature, Literary Criticism, Essays, Philosophy, Psychology, Psychiatry, Social Sciences, Sociology
ISBN Prefix(es): 978-957-732; 978-957-9464

Commonwealth Publishing Co Ltd+
2F, No 1, Lane 93, Sung Chiang Rd, Taipei 104
Tel: (02) 26620012 *Fax:* (02) 26620007
E-mail: service@cwgv.com.tw
Web Site: www.bookzone.com.tw; www.cwgv.com.tw
Key Personnel
Founder & Chairman: Dr Charles H C Kao
Founder & Chief Executive Officer: Cora L S Wang
Founder: Tso-ching Chang
Rights Dir: Grace Chang *E-mail:* gracechang@cwgv.com.tw
Founded: 1982
General trade & translated titles.
Subjects: Biography, Memoirs, Business, Child Care & Development, Economics, Fiction, Health, Nutrition, Management, Nonfiction (General), Science (General), Self-Help
ISBN Prefix(es): 978-957-621
Number of titles published annually: 150 Print

Parent Company: Commonwealth Publishing Group
Associate Companies: CommonWealth Magazine, 4F, No 87, Sung Chiang Rd, Taipei 104
Tel: (02) 2507 8627; Global Views Monthly Magazine

Dog House Press Co Ltd+
No 15 Longjiang Rd, Lane 71, Taipei 104
Tel: (02) 27765889 *Fax:* (02) 27712568
E-mail: love@doghouse.com.tw
Web Site: love.doghouse.com.tw
Membership(s): Republic of China Publisher's Association.
Subjects: Fiction, Journalism, Literature, Literary Criticism, Essays, Mysteries, Suspense, Romance
ISBN Prefix(es): 978-957-593; 978-957-812; 978-957-491; 978-957-8410; 978-957-98772; 978-957-8519
Parent Company: Lin Pai Publishing Co Ltd
Shipping Address: 271 Chungyang Rd, Nan Gang, Taipei
Warehouse: 6F3 Lane 327, Sec 2, Jongshan Rd, Jongher, Taipei Shiang

Echo Publishing Co Ltd+
105 Bade Rd, Section 4, Lane 72, Alley 16, 1st floor, Taipei 105
Tel: (02) 2763-1452 *Fax:* (02) 2766-8709
E-mail: gifts@mail.echogroup.com.tw
Web Site: www.hanshenggifts.com
Founded: 1970
Subjects: Anthropology, Antiques, Archaeology, Architecture & Interior Design, Art, Asian Studies, Child Care & Development, Crafts, Games, Hobbies
ISBN Prefix(es): 978-957-588
Associate Companies: Echo Communications Co Ltd
Distributed by Charles E Tuttle Co (USA & UK)

The Far East Book Co Ltd+
66 Chungking S Rd, Sec 1, Taipei
Tel: (02) 2311-8740 *Fax:* (02) 2311-4184
E-mail: service@mail.fareast.com.tw
Web Site: www.fareast.com.tw
Founded: 1950
Subjects: Art, Education, History, Language Arts, Linguistics, Literature, Literary Criticism, Essays, Physics, Poetry, Chinese Language Education, English Language Education
ISBN Prefix(es): 978-957-612
Distributed by US International Publishing Inc

Farseeing Publishing Co Ltd+
Member of Farseeing Publishing Group
7F, No 50-2, Section 1, Hsin-Sheng S Rd, Zhongzheng District, Taipei 10059
Tel: (02) 2392-1167; (02) 2392-1167 (ext 722, customer service) *Fax:* (02) 2322-5455
E-mail: fars@ms6.hinet.net
Web Site: www.farseeing.com.tw
Key Personnel
Dir: Julia K Hsiao
Founded: 1983
Specialize in nursing & health science.
Subjects: English as a Second Language, Health, Nutrition, Medicine, Nursing, Dentistry
ISBN Prefix(es): 978-957-640; 978-957-9506; 978-957-99215; 978-957-99266
Associate Companies: Far Du Publishing Co Ltd; Hua Cheng Publishing Co Ltd; Wey Far Books Co Ltd

The Grand East Book Co Ltd, *imprint of* San Min Book Co Ltd

Grimm Press Ltd+
3F, No 2, Sec 2, Hsin-Sheng S Rd, Taipei

Tel: (02) 23517251; (02) 23515222 (customer service)
E-mail: grimm_service@grimmpress.com.tw
Web Site: www.grimmpress.com.tw; www.
facebook.com/pages/Grimm-Press/
133569776716353 (English)
Key Personnel
Foreign Rights Manager: Diane Ho
Founded: 1993
Publishes world-class illustrated children's books.
ISBN Prefix(es): 978-957-745

Heavenly Lotus Publishing Co, Ltd
2F, 168, Chungcheng Rd, Sec 2, Taipei 111
Tel: (02) 2873-6629 *Fax:* (02) 2873-6709
Founded: 1977
Buddism books, life protection books, vegetarian recipe, biography of eminent.
Subjects: Religion - Buddhist
ISBN Prefix(es): 978-957-665; 978-957-9397

Ho-Chi Book Publishing Co+
No 1 Xiping Rd, Section 2, Xizhi District, New Taipei City 221
Tel: (02) 8646-1828 *Fax:* (02) 8646-1866
E-mail: hochi@ms12.hinet.net
Web Site: www.hochitw.com
Founded: 1962
Subjects: Behavioral Sciences, Biological Sciences, Child Care & Development, Health, Nutrition, Medicine, Nursing, Dentistry, Psychology, Psychiatry, Veterinary Science, Life Science
ISBN Prefix(es): 978-957-666; 978-957-9097
Number of titles published annually: 120 Print
Total Titles: 2,350 Print
Distributor for Elsevier Ltd; Lippincott Williams & Wilkins; McGraw-Hill
Bookshop(s): 249 Wu-Hsing St, Taipei 110
Tel: (02) 2723-9404 *Fax:* (02) 2723-0997; 120 Shih-Pai Rd, Sec 2, Taipei 112 *Tel:* (02) 2826-5375 *Fax:* (02) 2823-9604; 7 Lane 12, Roosevelt Rd, Sec 4, Taipei 100 *Tel:* (02) 2365-1544 *Fax:* (02) 2367-1266; 632 Chung-Shan Rd, Hualien 970 *Tel:* (03) 846-3459 *Fax:* (03) 846-3424; 1 Pei-Peng 1st St, Kaohsiung 807 *Tel:* (07) 322-6177 *Fax:* (07) 323-5118; 24 Yu-Der Rd, Taichung 404 *Tel:* (04) 2203-0795 *Fax:* (04) 2202-5093

Honya Book Co Ltd, *imprint of* San Min Book Co Ltd

Hsin Yi Publications+
75, Chung Ching S Rd, Sec 2, Taipei 100
Tel: (02) 2391-3384
Web Site: www.hsin-yi.org.tw
Key Personnel
Chief Executive Officer: Sing-ju Chang
Publisher: Show Chung Ho
Chief Editor: Sin-Ju Ho
Founded: 1971
ISBN Prefix(es): 978-957-642; 978-957-9526
Total Titles: 1,000 Print
Parent Company: Hsin Yi Foundation
Associate Companies: Hsinex International Corp
Distribution Center: Shen's Books & Supplies, 8625 Hubbard Rd, Auburn, CA 95602, United States

Jillion Publishing Co+
5F, No 9, Lane 12, Nanking W Rd, Taipei 104
Tel: (02) 2571-0558; (02) 2521-6904 (bookshop)
Fax: (02) 2523-1891; (02) 2511-8182 (bookshop)
E-mail: jillion.lanbri@msa.hinet.net
Web Site: www.jlbooks.com.tw
Key Personnel
Chief Executive: Ai Tien-Shi
Founded: 1985

Subjects: Career Development, English as a Second Language, How-to, Language Arts, Linguistics, Japanese Language Teaching
ISBN Prefix(es): 978-957-9415; 978-957-786

Kwang Fu Book Enterprises Co Ltd+
6F, No 38, Fu Hsing N Rd, Taipei 104
Tel: (02) 2771 6622 *Fax:* (02) 2721 8230
Key Personnel
President: Mr Chun Hui Lin
Founded: 1962
Also specializing in distance learning.
Subjects: Art, Education, Fiction, Health, Nutrition, History, Literature, Literary Criticism, Essays, Medicine, Nursing, Dentistry, Science (General)
ISBN Prefix(es): 978-957-42
Total Titles: 2,000 Print; 80 CD-ROM
Subsidiaries: Kwang Toong Book Department Store Co Ltd
Book Club(s): New Reader's Book Club, Contact: Lola Tiao *E-mail:* bookclub@kfgroup.com.tw

Li Ming Cultural Enterprise Co Ltd
1F, 49, Chung-ching S Rd, Sec 1, Taipei 100
Tel: (02) 23310557; (02) 23116829 (bookshop); (02) 23820613 (ext 201) *Fax:* (02) 23821240; (02) 23817230 (bookshop)
E-mail: liming2f@ms15.hinet.net
Web Site: www.limingbook.com.tw
Subjects: Art, History, Literature, Literary Criticism, Essays, Music, Dance, Science (General), Social Sciences, Sociology, Culture, Humanities
ISBN Prefix(es): 978-957-16
Subsidiaries: Tai-Chung Kaohsiung/Two Cities

Linking Publishing Co Ltd+
4F, No 180, Keelung Rd, Sec 1, Taipei 180
Tel: (02) 8787-6242 (ext 203) *Fax:* (02) 2756-7668
E-mail: linking@udngroup.com; bookcs@udngroup.com; linkingrights@udngroup.com
Web Site: www.linkingbooks.com.tw
Founded: 1974
Subjects: Art, Asian Studies, Biography, Memoirs, Business, Career Development, Child Care & Development, Cookery, Economics, English as a Second Language, Fiction, Health, Nutrition, History, Human Relations, Literature, Literary Criticism, Essays, Management, Nonfiction (General), Self-Help, Travel & Tourism, Wine & Spirits, Women's Studies
ISBN Prefix(es): 978-957-08

Liwil Publishing Co Ltd+
2F-4, 110, Zhongshan Rd, Sec 3, Chungho 235
Tel: (02) 7731-5050 *Fax:* (02) 7731-6060; (02) 2799-1984
E-mail: liwil.tw@gmail.com; leo@liwil.com.tw; leoshiao@gmail.com
Web Site: www.liwil.com.tw
Founded: 1987
Subjects: Computer Science, How-to, Labor, Industrial Relations, Language Arts, Linguistics
ISBN Prefix(es): 978-957-441
Number of titles published annually: 20 Print
Total Titles: 300 Print

Locus Publishing
11F, No 25, Sec 4, Nan-King E Rd, Taipei 105
Tel: (02) 8712-3898 *Toll Free Tel:* 0800-322-220 *Fax:* (02) 8712-3897
E-mail: service@locuspublishing.com; locus@locuspublishing.com
Web Site: www.locuspublishing.com
Founded: 1996
Subjects: Art, Biography, Memoirs, Business, Fiction, History, Journalism, Literature, Literary Criticism, Essays, Philosophy, Religion - Other,

Science (General), Self-Help, Social Sciences, Sociology, Applied Sciences, World History
ISBN Prefix(es): 978-957-8468
Parent Company: Locus International

National Museum of History
49 Nan Hai Rd, Taipei 100
Tel: (02) 2361-0270 *Fax:* (02) 2331-1086
Web Site: www.nmh.gov.tw
Key Personnel
Dir: Chang Yui-Tan
Subjects: Antiques, Art, Asian Studies, History

National Palace Museum+
No 221, Sec 2, Zhishan Rd, Shilin District, Taipei 11143
Tel: (02) 2881-2021; (02) 6610-3600
E-mail: service01@npm.gov.tw
Web Site: www.npm.gov.tw
Key Personnel
Dir: Jeng-yi Lin *E-mail:* jasperlin0520@npm.gov.tw
Founded: 1983
Subjects: Antiques, Archaeology, Art, History
ISBN Prefix(es): 978-957-562
Number of titles published annually: 25 Print; 5 CD-ROM
Total Titles: 108 Print
U.S. Office(s): World Journal Book Store, 379 Broadway, New York, NY 10013, United States
Bookshop(s): Paragon Books, 1507 S Michigan Ave, Chicago, IL 60605, United States

Pearson Education Taiwan
11F, Room D, No 219, Beixin Rd, Sec 3, Xindian District, New Taipei City 231
Tel: (02) 2918-8368 *Fax:* (02) 2913-3258
Web Site: www.pearsoned.com.tw
Subjects: Education, English as a Second Language
Parent Company: Pearson Education Asia Ltd

Rye Field Publications
5F, No 141, Sec 2, Minsheng E Rd, Taipei 10483
Tel: (02) 25007696 *Fax:* (02) 25001966
Web Site: ryefield.pixnet.net
Founded: 1992
Subjects: Biography, Memoirs, Fiction, Health, Nutrition, History, Literature, Literary Criticism, Essays, Military Science, Philosophy, Science (General), Science Fiction, Fantasy, Social Sciences, Sociology, Humanities, Lifestyle, Mind, Body & Spirit
ISBN Prefix(es): 978-957-708; 978-957-469; 978-986-7413; 978-986-7252; 978-986-7537; 978-986-7691; 978-986-7782; 978-986-7895; 978-986-173
Parent Company: Cite Publishing Ltd

San Min Book Co Ltd+
386 Fushing North Rd, Taipei 104
Tel: (02) 2500-6600 *Fax:* (02) 2506-4000
E-mail: editor@sanmin.com.tw
Web Site: www.sanmin.com.tw
Key Personnel
President: Chen-Chiang Liu
Deputy General Manager: Peter Li
Rights & Permissions: Allie Hwang
Founded: 1953
Also acts as bookseller.
Subjects: Accounting, Advertising, Agriculture, Anthropology, Architecture & Interior Design, Art, Asian Studies, Business, Career Development, Chemistry, Chemical Engineering, Child Care & Development, Communications, Computer Science, Crafts, Games, Hobbies, Drama, Theater, Earth Sciences, Economics, Education, Electronics, Electrical Engineering, English as a Second Language, Environmental Studies, Fiction, Finance, Geography, Geology, Government, Political Science, Health, Nutrition, His-

tory, Human Relations, Humor, Language Arts, Linguistics, Law, Literature, Literary Criticism, Essays, Management, Marketing, Mathematics, Music, Dance, Nonfiction (General), Philosophy, Physics, Poetry, Psychology, Psychiatry, Public Administration, Publishing & Book Trade Reference, Religion - Buddhist, Religion - Hindu, Religion - Islamic, Religion - Other, Science (General), Social Sciences, Sociology, Technology, Travel & Tourism, Women's Studies
ISBN Prefix(es): 978-957-14; 978-957-19
Number of titles published annually: 400 Print
Total Titles: 8,000 Print
Imprints: The Grand East Book Co Ltd; Honya Book Co Ltd
Branch Office(s)
No 61, Chungking S Rd, Sec 1, Taipei 100
Tel: (02) 2361-7511

Senate Books Co Ltd+
6F-2, No 98, Jen Ai Rd, Sec 2, Taipei 100
Tel: (02) 23213054 *Fax:* (02) 23214041
Founded: 1985
Subjects: Law
ISBN Prefix(es): 978-957-789
Distributor for Matthew Bender

Shy Mau Publishing Co+
5F, 19 Minsheng Rd, Xindian District, New Taipei City 23150
Tel: (02) 2218-3277 *Fax:* (02) 2218-3239
E-mail: service@coolbooks.com.tw
Web Site: www.coolbooks.com.tw
Founded: 1982
Subjects: Biological Sciences, Business, Child Care & Development, Computer Science, Gardening, Plants, Health, Nutrition, History, How-to, Journalism, Law, Management, Psychology, Psychiatry, Real Estate, Science (General), Self-Help, Social Sciences, Sociology, Travel & Tourism, Entertainment, Zoology
ISBN Prefix(es): 978-957-776; 978-957-529

SMC Publishing Inc+
1F, No 14, Alley 14, Lane 283, Roosevelt Rd, Sec 3, Taipei 106
Tel: (02) 2362-0190 *Fax:* (02) 2362-3834
E-mail: smc@smcbook.com.tw
Web Site: www.smcbook.com.tw
Key Personnel
Manager: Wei Te-wen *E-mail:* weitw@smcbook.com.tw
Founded: 1976
Publish in English, Chinese, Japanese & Tibetan.
Subjects: Anthropology, Architecture & Interior Design, Art, Asian Studies, Biological Sciences, History, Medicine, Nursing, Dentistry, Religion - Buddhist
ISBN Prefix(es): 978-957-638; 978-957-9482

Torch of Wisdom+
10, Lane 270, Chien Kuo S Rd, Taipei 10656
Tel: (02) 27075802 *Fax:* (02) 27085054
E-mail: tow.wisdom@msa.hinet.net
Web Site: www.towisdom.org.tw
Founded: 1951
Subjects: Asian Studies, Health, Nutrition, Religion - Buddhist
ISBN Prefix(es): 978-957-518

Transoxania Int'l Co Ltd
4 F-3, No 27, Sec 2, Fuxing S Rd, Da'an District, Taipei 106
Tel: (02) 27 02 82 15
E-mail: hezhong@transoxania.com.tw
Web Site: www.transoxania.com.tw
Founded: 2003
Subjects: Education, Literature, Literary Criticism, Essays, Military Science, Social Sciences, Sociology, Culture

The World Book Co Ltd+
99, Chung Ching S Rd, Sec 1, Taipei 100
Tel: (02) 2311-0183; (02) 2311-3834 *Fax:* (02) 2331-7963
E-mail: wbc.ltd@msa.hinet.net
Web Site: worldbook.com.tw
Founded: 1916
Subjects: Art, Drama, Theater, History, Language Arts, Linguistics, Literature, Literary Criticism, Essays, Medicine, Nursing, Dentistry, Philosophy, Poetry, Social Sciences, Sociology, Chinese Classics
ISBN Prefix(es): 978-957-06

Wu Nan Book Co Ltd+
4F, No 339, Sec 2, Ho-Ping E Rd, Taipei 106
Tel: (02) 27055066 *Fax:* (02) 27066100
E-mail: wunan@wunan.com.tw
Web Site: www.wunan.com.tw
Key Personnel
Management: Rong-Chuan Yang
Founded: 1968
Subjects: Anthropology, Biography, Memoirs, Biological Sciences, Business, Computer Science, Crafts, Games, Hobbies, Engineering (General), Environmental Studies, Finance, Geography, Geology, History, Language Arts, Linguistics, Law, Literature, Literary Criticism, Essays, Military Science, Music, Dance, Religion - Other, Science (General), Technology, Administration, Entertainment, Esoteric
ISBN Prefix(es): 978-957-11
Associate Companies: Kao-Une Publishing House; Shu-Chuan Publishing House; Taiwan Bookhouse Publishing Co Ltd

Yee Wen Publishing Co Ltd+
4F-3, No 253, Roosevelt Rd, Sec 3, Taipei 106
Tel: (02) 2362-6012 *Fax:* (02) 2366-0977
E-mail: yeewen@ms9.hinet.net
Founded: 1953
Subjects: Archaeology, Art, Asian Studies, Ethnicity, Geography, Geology, History, Literature, Literary Criticism, Essays, Philosophy, Regional Interests, Religion - Other, Science (General)
ISBN Prefix(es): 978-957-520
Number of titles published annually: 12 Print
Total Titles: 3,000 Print
U.S. Office(s): 518 Oak Park Way, Emerald Hills, CA 94062-4038, United States *Tel:* 650-367-5020

Yi Hsien Publishing Co Ltd+
2F, No 3, Lane 7, Baogao Rd, Hsintien, Taipei 231
Tel: (02) 2918-2288 *Fax:* (02) 2917-2266
E-mail: service@yihsient.com.tw
Web Site: www.yihsient.com.tw
Founded: 1975
Subjects: Agriculture, Animals, Pets, Biological Sciences, Chemistry, Chemical Engineering, Earth Sciences, Health, Nutrition, Medicine, Nursing, Dentistry, Psychology, Psychiatry, Publishing & Book Trade Reference, Science (General), Veterinary Science
ISBN Prefix(es): 978-957-616
Bookshop(s): No 3, Lane 316, Roosevelt Rd, Sec 3, Taipei *Tel:* (02) 2367-6824 *Fax:* (02) 2365-0346; No 178, Wu-ch'ang St N, Taichung *Tel:* (04) 2206-8119 *Fax:* (04) 2206-8120

Youth Cultural Publishing Co+
3F, 66-1 Chungching S Rd, Sec 1, Taipei 10045
Tel: (02) 2311-2836 *Fax:* (02) 2311-5368
E-mail: customer@youth.com.tw
Web Site: www.youth.com.tw
Founded: 1958
Subjects: Cookery, Crafts, Games, Hobbies, Education, Fashion, Language Arts, Linguistics, Literature, Literary Criticism, Essays, Psychol-

ogy, Psychiatry, Science (General), Travel & Tourism, Entertainment, Food/Drink
ISBN Prefix(es): 978-957-530; 978-957-574
Parent Company: China Youth Corps
Showroom(s): No 219, Sung Chiang Rd, Taipei *Tel:* (02) 2502-5858
Bookshop(s): No 157, Fu Hsing South Rd, Kaohsiung; No 2-1, Feng Chia Rd, Taichung; No 6, Heng Yang Rd, Taipei
Warehouse: No 21, Lane 111, Chung Ying St, Su Lin Town, Taipei

Yuan-Liou Publishing Co Ltd+
6F, No 81, Sec 2, Nanchang Rd, Taipei 100
Tel: (02) 2392-6899 *Fax:* (02) 2392-6658
E-mail: ylib@ylib.com
Web Site: www.ylib.com
Key Personnel
Publisher: Jung-Wen Wang
Founded: 1975
Subjects: Art, Business, Fiction, Health, Nutrition, History, How-to, Psychology, Psychiatry, Self-Help
ISBN Prefix(es): 978-957-32
Associate Companies: Meta Media International Co

Tajikistan

General Information

Capital: Dushanbe
Language: Tajik
Population: 5.7 million
Bank Hours: Generally open for short hours between 0930-1230 Monday-Friday
Shop Hours: Generally 0900-1800 Monday-Friday; often open weekends
Currency: 100 kopeks = 1 rubl
Export/Import Information: According to Ukrainian quotas and customs duties, companies engaged in trade should register with the Ukraine Ministry of Foreign Economic Relations. Licenses for export and import are also required for trade with Russia
Copyright: UCC (see Copyright Conventions, pg viii)

Irfon (Knowledge)
17, Negmat Karabaev Ave, 734018 Dushanbe
Tel: (372) 333906; (372) 336254
Founded: 1925
Subjects: Agriculture, Economics, Fiction, Government, Political Science, Medicine, Nursing, Dentistry, Philosophy, Social Sciences, Sociology, Technology
ISBN Prefix(es): 978-5-667

Tanzania

General Information

Capital: Dodoma (legislative); Dar es Salaam (administrative)
Language: Swahili and English are both official languages
Religion: Islamic, Christian (mostly Roman Catholic), Hindu, the rest follow traditional beliefs
Population: 27.8 million
Bank Hours: Mainland Tanzania: 0900-1200 Monday-Friday; 0900-1100 Saturday. Zanzibar: 0830-1130 Monday-Friday; 0830-1000 Saturday

Shop Hours: 0800-1200, 1400-1715 or 1800
  Monday-Saturday
Currency: 100 cents = 1 Tanzanian shilling
Export/Import Information: No tariff on books or
  advertising matter. Import license and exchange
  controls.
Copyright: Berne, Florence (see Copyright Con-
  ventions, pg viii)

Ben & Co Ltd+
Plot 3, Samora Ave, Box 3164, Dar es Salaam
Tel: (022) 2134401; (022) 2115147 *Fax:* (022)
  2112440
E-mail: benandco@mail.com
Founded: 1981
Specialize in Kiswahili, arts & crafts (life skills).
Membership(s): Publishers Association of Tanza-
  nia (PATA).
Subjects: English as a Second Language, Mathe-
  matics, Science (General)
ISBN Prefix(es): 978-9976-920
Total Titles: 72 Print

Bilal Muslim Mission of Tanzania+
Plot No 2239, Libya St, Dar es Salaam
Mailing Address: PO Box 20033, Dar es Salaam
Tel: (022) 2120111; (022) 2112419
E-mail: bilaltz@africafederation.org
Web Site: www.bilaltz.org
Founded: 1968
An autonomous subsidiary of Shia Ithnaashery
  Supreme Council of Africa.
Subjects: Literature, Literary Criticism, Essays
ISBN Prefix(es): 978-9976-956
Total Titles: 158 Print

Central Tanganyika Press+
Makay House, PO Box 15, Dodoma
Tel: (026) 232 4518
Web Site: www.anglicancommunion.org
Founded: 1954
Promotes Christian faith & increase knowledge
  through publishing & distribution of Christian
  literature that meets human needs.
Subjects: Biblical Studies, Biography, Memoirs,
  Child Care & Development, Religion - Protes-
  tant, Theology, Family & Social Life
ISBN Prefix(es): 978-9976-66
Total Titles: 150 Print
Branch Office(s)
UZIM Press, PO Box 48127, Nairobi 00100,
  Kenya *E-mail:* uzima@wanachi.com

Dar es Salaam University Press Ltd (DUP)+
PO Box 35091, Dar es Salaam
Web Site: udsm.ac.tz
Key Personnel
Vice Chancellor: Prof Rwekaza S Mukandala
  Tel: (022) 2410700 *Fax:* (022) 2410078
  E-mail: vc@admin.udsm.ac.tz
Dir, Press: Albert Kanuya
Founded: 1979
Also book packager.
Membership(s): Tanzania Publishers Association.
Subjects: Accounting, Biological Sciences, Chem-
  istry, Chemical Engineering, Civil Engineering,
  Developing Countries, Drama, Theater, Elec-
  tronics, Electrical Engineering, History, Lan-
  guage Arts, Linguistics, Mathematics, Mechan-
  ical Engineering, Medicine, Nursing, Dentistry,
  Physical Sciences, Physics, Women's Studies
ISBN Prefix(es): 978-9976-60

DUP, see Dar es Salaam University Press Ltd
  (DUP)

Eastern Africa Publications Ltd
PO Box 1002, Arusha
Tel: (057) 26708
Founded: 1979

Subjects: Biography, Memoirs, Geography, Ge-
  ology, Government, Political Science, History,
  Nonfiction (General), Poetry, Science (General)
ISBN Prefix(es): 978-9976-2

Emmaus Bible School
PO Box 1424, Dodoma
Tel: (026) 2350911
E-mail: emmaus.dodoma@kanisa-la-biblia.org
Specialize in correspondence courses.
Membership(s): Tanzania Evangelical Literature
  Ministry (TELM).
Subjects: Biblical Studies
ISBN Prefix(es): 978-9976-80
Associate Companies: Kanisa la Biblia (KLB)
  Publishers
Imprints: Emmaus Shule ya Biblia
Branch Office(s)
PO Box 9322, Dar es Salaam
Distributor for Everyday Publications Inc
  (Canada)

Emmaus Shule ya Biblia, *imprint of* Emmaus
  Bible School

IKS, see Institute of Kiswahili Studies

Institute of Kiswahili Studies
PO Box 35110, Dar es Salaam
Tel: (022) 2410757 *Fax:* (022) 2410328
E-mail: ikr@udsm.ac.tz
Web Site: www.iks.udsm.ac.tz; www.udsm.ac.tz
Key Personnel
Head, Dept of Literature, Communications &
  Publishing: S S Sewangi
Founded: 1930
Subjects: Language Arts, Linguistics, Literature,
  Literary Criticism, Essays
ISBN Prefix(es): 978-9976-911; 978-9987-442

Kanisa la Biblia Publishers
PO Box 1424, Dodoma
Tel: (075) 3656342 (cell); (071) 3609166 (cell)
E-mail: contact@klb-publishers.org
Web Site: klb-publishers.org
Key Personnel
Manager: Miss Inge Danzeisen
Founded: 1979
Specialize in Bible teaching books for lay people
  in Swahili.
Membership(s): Booksellers Association of Tan-
  zania (BSAT); Tanzania Evangelical Literature
  Ministry (TELM).
Subjects: Biblical Studies, Education, Religion -
  Protestant, Theology
ISBN Prefix(es): 978-9976-74
Number of titles published annually: 5 Print
Total Titles: 50 Print; 1 E-Book; 4 Audio
Showroom(s): KLB Publishers Bookshop, Em-
  maus Ipagala, Block E, Dodoma

Kiswahili, *imprint of* Press & Publicity Centre

Mkuki na Nyota Publishers+
47 Samora Ave, Dar es Salaam
Mailing Address: PO Box 4246, Dar es Salaam
Tel: (078) 755 8448 (cell)
E-mail: publishing@mkukinanyota.com; buy@
  mkukinanyota.com (sales & marketing)
Web Site: www.mkukinanyota.com
Founded: 1991
Subjects: Accounting, Business, Education, En-
  glish as a Second Language, Fiction, Medicine,
  Nursing, Dentistry
ISBN Prefix(es): 978-9987-449; 978-9976-973
Associate Companies: Nyota Consultancy Co Ltd

National Bureau of Statistics+
Kivukoni Front, PO Box 796, Dar es Salaam

Tel: (022) 2122722; (022) 2122723 *Fax:* (022)
  2130852
E-mail: dg@nbs.go.tz
Web Site: www.nbs.go.tz
Founded: 1961
Subjects: Agriculture, Economics, Education

Oxford University Press Tanzania Ltd
Mickocheni "B" Plot, 149 Mwai Kibaki Rd, Dar
  es Salaam
Tel: (022) 781403
Web Site: global.oup.com
Founded: 1969
Subjects: Literature, Literary Criticism, Essays,
  Poetry
ISBN Prefix(es): 978-9976-4
Parent Company: Oxford University Press, United
  Kingdom

Press & Publicity Centre+
PO Box 20910, Dar es Salaam
Tel: (022) 2122765
Founded: 1981
Membership(s): Publishers Association of Tanza-
  nia (PATA).
Subjects: Agriculture, Astrology, Occult, Com-
  puter Science, Education, Environmental Stud-
  ies, Fiction, Geography, Geology, Health, Nu-
  trition, Language Arts, Linguistics, Literature,
  Literary Criticism, Essays, Science (General)
ISBN Prefix(es): 978-9976-916
Total Titles: 30 Print
Imprints: Kiswahili
Distributed by Tepusa
Distributor for Africa Book Collective Ltd (UK)
Bookshop(s): Aggrey Street Shop, Nkrumah St,
  Dar es Salaam

Readit Books Ltd+
NK Bldg, 5th floor, Msimbazi/Sikukuu St, Kari-
  akoo
Mailing Address: PO Box 20986, Dar es Salaam
Tel: (022) 2184077 *Fax:* (022) 2181077
E-mail: readit@raha.com
Web Site: readitbooks.web.com
Key Personnel
Mng Dir: Abdullah Saiwaad
Sales Dir: Khalfan Abdallah
Founded: 1993
Subjects: Astronomy, Economics, Fiction, Science
  (General)
ISBN Prefix(es): 978-9987-21

Standard Book Numbering Agency, see
  Tanzania Library Services Board

Tanzania Library Services Board
Unit of Ministry of Education & Vocational
  Training
National Central Library, PO Box 9283, Dar es
  Salaam
Tel: (022) 2150048; (022) 2150049 *Fax:* (022)
  2151100
E-mail: tlsb@africaonline.co.tz
Web Site: www.tlsb.or.tz
Key Personnel
Dir General: Dr Alli Mcharazo
Founded: 1963
Subjects: Library & Information Sciences
ISBN Prefix(es): 978-9976-65

Tanzania Publishing House+
PO Box 2138, Dar es Salaam
Tel: (022) 213 0669
Founded: 1966
Membership(s): African Books Collective; Pub-
  lishers Association of Tanzania (PATA).
Subjects: Accounting, Agriculture, Animals, Pets,
  Art, Child Care & Development, Drama, The-
  ater, English as a Second Language, Fiction,
  Gardening, Plants, Geography, Geology, Gov-

ernment, Political Science, Health, Nutrition, History, Journalism, Labor, Industrial Relations, Language Arts, Linguistics, Law, Management, Mathematics, Nonfiction (General), Photography, Physics, Poetry, Public Administration, Science (General), Sports, Athletics
ISBN Prefix(es): 978-9976-1
Parent Company: Tanzania Karatasi Associated Industries, Box 2418 DSM

Tema Publisher Ltd+
PO Box 63115, Dar es Salaam
Tel: (022) 211-3608
Founded: 1994
Also publish educational supplementary books.
Membership(s): African Publishers Network (AP-NET); Afro-Asian Book Council (AABC); Publishers Association of Tanzania (PATA).
Subjects: Education, Environmental Studies, Fiction, Mathematics, Nonfiction (General), Women's Studies
ISBN Prefix(es): 978-9987-25
Total Titles: 42 Print
Distributed by Tanzania Publishing House
Foreign Rep(s): African Books Collective (Canada, Europe, USA)

TLSB, see Tanzania Library Services Board

Thailand

General Information

Capital: Bangkok
Language: Thai is official language. English is widely used in government and commercial circles
Religion: Predominantly Buddhist of the Hinaya form
Population: 57.6 million
Bank Hours: 0830-1500 Monday-Friday
Shop Hours: Vary. Those catering to tourists generally open 0830-1800 or later
Currency: 100 satangs = 1 baht
Export/Import Information: No tariff on books but Standard Profit Tax and Business Tax apply (also a Municipal Tax of percentage of Business Tax). Advertising subject to same taxes and ad valorem percentage of import duty. No import licenses for books, but special permit required by importer for orders over a certain sum. Certificate of payment (from Exchange Control Authority) required.
Copyright: Berne, Florence (see Copyright Conventions, pg viii)

Aksorn Charoen Tat ACT Co Ltd
142, Tanao Rd, Sancchoaphosua, Pranakorn, Bangkok 10200
Tel: (02) 622 2999 *Fax:* (02) 622 2999 (ext 1390)
E-mail: webmaster@aksorn.com
Web Site: www.aksorn.com
Key Personnel
President: Mr Tawan Dheva-Aksorn
   E-mail: tawan@aksorn.com
Founded: 1935
Subjects: Education
ISBN Prefix(es): 978-974-405; 978-974-406; 978-974-9689; 978-974-9690; 978-974-9691; 978-974-9869; 978-974-9890

Amarin Printing & Publishing Public Co Ltd
378 Chaiyaphruk Rd, Taling Chan, Bangkok 10170
Tel: (02) 422-9999 *Fax:* (02) 434-3555; (02) 434-3777
Web Site: www.amarin.co.th

Key Personnel
Chief Executive Officer: Mrs Rarin Utakapan Punjarungroj
President: Mrs Metta Utakapan
Executive Dir: Ms Ussanee Viratkaphan
Dir, Amarin Publishing Services: Mrs Pattrawan Pultawekiat
Publishing Management Dir: Ms Chatchda Phomlert
Assistant Mng Dir: Mr Ongaj Jira-on
Founded: 1976
Subjects: Cookery, Geography, Geology, Health, Nutrition
ISBN Prefix(es): 978-974-387; 978-974-9931

Asian Manga, *imprint of* Praphansarn Publishing Co Ltd

Asian Wisdom, *imprint of* Praphansarn Publishing Co Ltd

Banlue Publications Co Ltd
955 Soi Suthiporn, Prachasongkroh Rd, Dindaeng, Bangkok 10400
Tel: (02) 6419955
Web Site: www.banluegroup.com
Founded: 1955
Membership(s): Publishers & Booksellers Association of Thailand.
Subjects: Fiction, Science Fiction, Fantasy
ISBN Prefix(es): 978-616-90842; 978-616-7134; 978-616-90803

Booknet Co Ltd
Member of iGroup (Asia Pacific) Ltd
8 Soi Krungthep Kreetha 8 Yaek 8, Huamark, Bangkapi, Bangkok 10240
Tel: (02) 769-3888 *Fax:* (02) 379-5183
E-mail: booknet@book.co.th
Web Site: www.booknet.co.th
Founded: 1997
Subjects: Agriculture, Business, Cookery, Engineering (General), Language Arts, Linguistics, Management, Medicine, Nursing, Dentistry, Science (General), Social Sciences, Sociology, Administration, Asian Cooking, Asian Culture, Asian Language
ISBN Prefix(es): 978-974-89009

Chiang Mai University Library
239 Huay Kaew Rd, Muang District, Chiang Mai 50200
Tel: (053) 94-4531 *Fax:* (053) 22-2766
Web Site: lib.cmu.ac.th; library.cmu.ac.th
Key Personnel
Dir: Ms Wararak Hanbanchaphong *Tel:* (053) 94-4501 *E-mail:* wararak@lib.cmu.ac.th
Founded: 1964
Subjects: Agriculture, Behavioral Sciences, Business, Economics, Education, Finance, Government, Political Science, Medicine, Nursing, Dentistry, Physics
ISBN Prefix(es): 978-974-565; 978-974-656; 978-974-657; 978-974-658

Chokechai Thewet+
57-59 Ti Thong Rd, Pranakhorn District, Bangkok 10200
Tel: (02) 222-666-0
Key Personnel
Mng Dir: Mr Wichai Rojjanaprapayon
Marketing Executive: Rujira Rojjanaprapayon, PhD *Tel:* (089) 766-3131 *E-mail:* rujira2@yahoo.com
Founded: 1963
Subjects: Fiction, Nonfiction (General), Romance, Science Fiction, Fantasy
ISBN Prefix(es): 978-974-420

Duang Kamol Co Ltd
244-6 Siam Sq, Soi 2, Bangkok 10330

Tel: (02) 251-6335 *Fax:* (02) 250-1262
Key Personnel
Manager: Somkwaon Somwanawat
ISBN Prefix(es): 978-974-210

Karusapa Business Organization (Suksapanpanit)
2249 Landprao Rd, Wangthonglang, Bangkok 10310
Tel: (02) 5383033 *Fax:* (02) 5393215
E-mail: suksapan99@hotmail.com; suksapanpress@hotmail.com
Web Site: www.suksapan.or.th
Founded: 1950
ISBN Prefix(es): 978-974-8101
Branch Office(s)
69 Bldg 9 Rachdamnoeng Klang Rd, Bawuannives Pranakhon, Bangkok 10200 *Tel:* (02) 2817822 *Fax:* (02) 2803680

Odeon Store
218/10-12 Siam Square Rd Soi 1, Bangkok 10330
Tel: (02) 251-4476
Key Personnel
Manager: Mrs Pornpimol Amornworanat
Founded: 1947
Subjects: Nonfiction (General)
ISBN Prefix(es): 978-974-275

Pass Education Co Ltd+
248 Sirinthorn Rd, Bang Phlat, Bangkok 10700
Tel: (02) 881 2840 *Fax:* (02) 434 4572
E-mail: info@passeducation.com; copyrights@passeducation.com
Web Site: www.passeducation.com
Key Personnel
Mng Dir: Suchada Sahasakul
Founded: 2003
ISBN Prefix(es): 978-974-8389
Imprints: Pass@Kids; Pass@Teen; Pass2Learn

Pass@Kids, *imprint of* Pass Education Co Ltd

Pass@Teen, *imprint of* Pass Education Co Ltd

Pass2Learn, *imprint of* Pass Education Co Ltd

Pearson Education Indochina Ltd
498/16 Nonsee Rd, Chongnonsee Sub-District Yannawa, Bangkok 10120
Tel: (02) 681-5515 *Fax:* (02) 681-5517; (02) 681-5518
E-mail: cserve@pearson.com
Web Site: www.edexcel.com; www.pearsonelt.com
Founded: 1998
Formed through the merger of Simon & Schuster & Addison Wesley Longman.
Subjects: Education
Parent Company: Pearson PLC

Plan for Kids Co Ltd
1/999 Phoomsnan Bldg, Kampaengpetch 6 Rd, Don Muang, Bangkok 10210
Tel: (02) 575 25 59 *Fax:* (02) 575 26 59
E-mail: info@planforkids.com; happykids@happykids.com; cs@planforkids.com (customer services); mkt@planforkids.com; pr@planforkids.com (public relations); webadmin@planforkids.com
Web Site: www.planforkids.com
ISBN Prefix(es): 978-974-91872; 978-974-91895

Praphansarn Publishing Co Ltd+
222 Buddhamontol 2 Rd, Saladhammasop, Thaweewattana, Bangkok 10170
Tel: (02) 448-0658; (02) 448-0659; (02) 448-0312 *Fax:* (02) 448-0393
E-mail: editor@praphansarn.com; admin@praphansarn.com; distri@praphansarn.com
Web Site: www.praphansarn.com; www.praphansarnasia.com

Key Personnel
Mng Dir: Arthorn Techatada *E-mail:* arthorn@
praphansarn.com
Founded: 1960
Publisher, distributor & exporter of Asian licenses.
Membership(s): The Publishers & Booksellers
Association of Thailand (PUBAT).
Subjects: Fiction, Nonfiction (General), Asian
Cultures
ISBN Prefix(es): 978-611-510; 978-616-510
Number of titles published annually: 112 Print
Associate Companies: Perfect Prints & Advertising Co Ltd
Imprints: Asian Manga (cartoon); Asian Wisdom
(popular nonfiction); Rainbow (fantasy & fiction); Woman Publisher (beauty & health, do-it-yourself)

Rainbow, *imprint of* Praphansarn Publishing Co
Ltd

River Books
396 Maharaj Rd, Tatien, Bangkok 10200
Tel: (02) 222 1290; (02) 224 6686 *Fax:* (02) 225
3861
E-mail: order@riverbooksbk.com
Web Site: www.riverbooksbk.com
Subjects: Archaeology, Architecture & Interior
Design, Art, Cookery, History, Asian Art &
Culture, Burma, Contemporary Thai Culture,
Ethnography, Guidebooks, Thai Art & Architecture, Thai History
ISBN Prefix(es): 978-974-8363; 978-974-8225;
978-974-89007; 978-974-9863; 978-616-7339

Ruamsarn (1977) Co Ltd+
864 Mahachai Rd, Bangkok 10200
Tel: (02) 221-6483; (02) 226-3808 *Fax:* (02) 222-
2036
Web Site: www.ruamsarn.com
Founded: 1977
Subjects: Fiction, History
ISBN Prefix(es): 978-974-245; 978-974-246; 978-
974-9556; 978-974-9557

Sangdad Publishing Co Ltd+
320 Soi Ladphrao 94, Ladphrao Rd, Wangthonglang, Bangkok 10310
Tel: (02) 934-4414 *Fax:* (02) 934-4415
E-mail: marketing@sangdad.com
Web Site: www.sangdad.com
Key Personnel
Rights: Mr Nan Hongvivatana *E-mail:* nanh@
sangdad.com
Founded: 1984
Largest cookery book publisher in Thailand.
Subjects: Art, Child Care & Development, Cookery, History, Travel & Tourism
ISBN Prefix(es): 978-974-7162; 978-616-7016
Total Titles: 250 Print
Parent Company: Sangdad Group

Silkworm Books+
6 Sukkasem Rd, T Suthep, Chiang Mai 50200
Tel: (053) 226161 *Fax:* (053) 226643
E-mail: info@silkwormbooks.com; orders@
silkwormbooks.com
Web Site: www.silkwormbooks.com
Key Personnel
Publisher & Dir: Trasvin Jittidecharak
E-mail: trasvin@silkwormbooks.com
Founded: 1991
Subjects: Asian Studies
ISBN Prefix(es): 978-974-7047; 978-974-954;
978-974-9511
Total Titles: 12 Print
Distributed by University of Washington Press
(North America & UK)
Distributor for Nordic Institute of Asian Studies

Foreign Rep(s): The Asia Bookroom (Australia,
New Zealand); Combined Academic Publishers Ltd (Nicholas Esson) (Europe, UK); Select
Books (Brunei, Indonesia, Malaysia, Singapore)

Suan Nguen Mee Ma Co Ltd
77, 79 Fuang Nakorn Rd, Wat Rajabopit,
Bangkok 10200
Tel: (02) 622-0955; (02) 622-0966; (02) 622-2495
Fax: (02) 222 9540; (02) 622-3228
E-mail: publishers@suan-spirit.com; shopping@
suan-spirit.com
Web Site: www.suan-spirit.com
Key Personnel
Co-Owner: Hans van Willenswaard
Subjects: Government, Political Science, Social
Sciences, Sociology
ISBN Prefix(es): 978-974-260
Number of titles published annually: 24 Print
Bookshop(s): Suksit Siam Bookshop *Tel:* (02)
225-9531 *Fax:* (02) 225-9532

Suksapanpanit, see Karusapa Business
Organization (Suksapanpanit)

Thai Watana Panich Co Ltd+
1991/129-130, Sukhumvit 77 Rd, Bangkok 10250
Tel: (02) 320 3721-6 *Fax:* (02) 320 3729-32
E-mail: admin@twp.co.th
Web Site: www.twp.co.th
Key Personnel
Mng Dir: Mrs Intira Bunnag *E-mail:* intira@twp.
co.th
Founded: 1936
Publisher & distributor.
Subjects: Agriculture, Art, Biography, Memoirs, Education, Government, Political Science,
Health, Nutrition, History, Language Arts, Linguistics, Management, Marketing, Mathematics,
Music, Dance, Philosophy, Psychology, Psychiatry, Religion - Buddhist, Science (General),
Social Sciences, Sociology, Egnlish as Second
Language, English Language Teaching
ISBN Prefix(es): 978-974-07; 978-974-08
Distributor for Blake; Cengage Learning; Falcon;
Kernerman; Kyowon; McGraw-Hill; Mileskelly;
Oxford; Pearson Education; Wendy Pye; Sejer

**UNESCO Bangkok, Asia & Pacific Regional
Bureau for Education**
Mom Luang Pin Malakul, Centenary Bldg, 920
Sukhumvit Rd, Prakanong, Klongtoey, Bangkok
10110
Tel: (02) 3910577 *Fax:* (02) 3910866
E-mail: bangkok@unesco.org
Web Site: www.unescobkk.org
Key Personnel
Dir: Mr Gwang-Jo Kim
Founded: 1961
Subjects: Communications, Education, Human
Relations, Social Sciences, Sociology
ISBN Prefix(es): 978-974-680; 978-92-9223

Watana Phanit Printing & Publishing Co Ltd
31/1-2-32/23 Mahachai Rd, Samran Rat, Phra
Nakhon, Samranrasd, Pranakorn, Bangkok
10200
Tel: (02) 222 9394 *Fax:* (02) 225 6556; (02) 225
6557
E-mail: info@wpp.co.th
Web Site: www.wpp.co.th
Key Personnel
Rights: Ms Sirintra Chongpipatanasook
Founded: 1939
ISBN Prefix(es): 978-974-250; 978-974-02

White Lotus Co Ltd+
145/3-6 Soi Huay Yai Chin, Huay Yai Pattaya,
Banglamung, Chonburi 20150
Tel: (038) 239-883; (038) 239-886; (038) 239-884
Fax: (038) 239-885

E-mail: ande@loxinfo.co.th
Web Site: whitelotusbooks.com
Founded: 1972
Out-of-print & new books, antiquarian maps. Specialize in books on Asia (Southeast).
Subjects: Animals, Pets, Antiques, Archaeology,
Asian Studies, Ethnicity, Gardening, Plants,
Geography, Geology, Language Arts, Linguistics, Military Science, Music, Dance, Natural
History, Nonfiction (General), Religion - Buddhist, Travel & Tourism, Ceramics, Ecology,
Flora & Fauna, Performing Arts, Textiles
ISBN Prefix(es): 978-974-8495; 978-974-8496;
978-974-4800; 978-974-8434; 978-974-7534;
978-974-4801
Number of titles published annually: 15 Print
Distributor for Orientations (Hong Kong)

Woman Publisher, *imprint of* Praphansarn
Publishing Co Ltd

Togo

General Information

Capital: Lome
Language: French, Kabiye and Ewe are official
languages
Religion: About half follow traditional beliefs,
Christian (about 35%) and Muslim (about 15%)
Population: 4 million
Bank Hours: 0730-1130, 1430-1600 Monday-
Friday
Shop Hours: 0800-1200, 1430 or 1500-1730 or
1800 Monday-Friday; 0730-1230 Saturday
Currency: 100 centimes = 1 CFA franc
Export/Import Information: No tariff on books;
advertising catalogs dutied. Additional taxes:
Tax Forfaitaire, Statistical Tax, and Customs
Stamp Tax of percentage of duties and added
taxes; Small Wharfage Tax. Import license required for goods from non-franc zones above a
certain value; from franc zone, need authorization of Togolese Government Office. Exchange
controls on non-franc zone.
Copyright: Berne (see Copyright Conventions, pg
viii)

Editogo
5, Ave Leopold Sedar Senghor, BP 891, Lome
Tel: 221 37 18; 221 61 08 *Fax:* 222 14 89
E-mail: editogo@cafe.tg
Web Site: www.editogo.tg
Founded: 1961
Subjects: Economics, Education, Language Arts,
Linguistics, Science (General), Sports, Athletics, Culture

Editions Haho
One, rue du Commerce, BP 378, Lome
Tel: 9046745
Key Personnel
Dir: Tompy Kudzo Nakou
ISBN Prefix(es): 978-2-906718; 978-2-913746

Societe Nationale des Editions du Togo, see
Editogo

Presses de l'Universite de Lome
Direction des Affaires Academiques et Scolaires,
BP 1515, Lome
Tel: 225 48 44 *Fax:* 225 87 84
Subjects: Medicine, Nursing, Dentistry, Science
(General)
ISBN Prefix(es): 978-2-909886

Trinidad and Tobago

General Information

Capital: Port of Spain
Language: English (officially). French, Spanish, Hindi and Chinese also spoken
Religion: Roman Catholic and Anglican, also Hindu and Muslim
Population: 1.3 million
Bank Hours: 0800-1400 Monday-Thursday; 0800-1200, 1500-1700 Friday
Shop Hours: 0800-1630 Monday-Friday; 0800-1200 Saturday
Currency: 100 cents = 1 Trinidad and Tobago dollar
Export/Import Information: No tariff on books; duty and postal fee on advertising matter. No import license required for books; no obscene literature permitted. Exchange controls.
Copyright: UCC, Berne (see Copyright Conventions, pg viii)

Caribbean Telecommunications Union

4 Mary St, St Clair, Port of Spain
Tel: (868) 628-0281; (868) 628-6359 *Fax:* (868) 622-6523
E-mail: info@ctu.int
Web Site: www.ctu.int
Key Personnel
Secretary General: Bernadette Lewis
   E-mail: bernadette.lewis@ctu.int
Telecommunications Specialist: Nigel Cassimire
   E-mail: nigel.cassimire@ctu.int
Telecommunications Strategist: Selby Wilson
   E-mail: selby.wilson@ctu.int
Founded: 1989
Caribbean intergovernmental agency responsible for telecommunications & Information & Communications Technologies (ICT) policy formulation, capacity development, project coordination for the Caribbean.
Membership(s): International Telecommunications Union (ITU).
Subjects: Communications, Public Administration, Technology, Internet Governance, National ICT Policy, Strategy & Implementation Plan, Open Data, Spectrum Management, Technical Advice

Charran Educational Publishers+

No 8, Lot 2C Chootoo Rd, El Socorro South
Tel: (868) 638-9205 *Fax:* (868) 674-0817
E-mail: sales@charran.com; siras@charranpublishers.com
Web Site: www.charranpublishers.com
Key Personnel
President: Reginald Charran
Founded: 1986
Subjects: Education, Language Arts, Linguistics, Foreign Language Teaching
ISBN Prefix(es): 978-976-613; 978-976-646
Bookshop(s): 58 Western Main Rd, Port of Spain *Tel:* (868) 622-3832; 12 Main Rd, Chaguanas *Tel:* (868) 671-1244; 53 Eastern Main Rd, Tunapuna *Tel:* (868) 663-1884

CTU, see Caribbean Telecommunications Union

Karnak House+

CB 03184, Tunapuna Post Office, Tunapuna
Tel: (868) 351-3447 (Trinidad & North America); (020) 8830 8301 (UK)
E-mail: karnakhouse@aol.com
Key Personnel
Publisher & Editorial Dir: Amon Saba Sakaana, PhD
UK Contact: Aniba Saakana

Founded: 1979
Specialize in African & Caribbean studies worldwide.
This publisher has indicated that 100% of their product line is author subsidized.
Subjects: Anthropology, Education, Fiction, History, Language Arts, Linguistics, Music, Dance, Nonfiction (General), Philosophy, Poetry, Religion - Other, Science (General), Women's Studies, Egyptology
ISBN Prefix(es): 978-0-907015; 978-1-872596
Number of titles published annually: 4 Print
Total Titles: 100 Print; 100 Online
Orders to: Frontline Distribution International, 5206 S Harper Ave, Chicago, IL 60615, United States *Tel:* 773-288-7718 *E-mail:* info@frontlinedistribution.com *Web Site:* www.frontlinedistribution.com

Prospect Press

Imprint of Media & Editorial Projects (MEP) Ltd
6 Prospect Ave, Maraval, Port of Spain
Tel: (868) 622-3821; (868) 622-5813; (868) 622-6138 *Fax:* (868) 628-0639
E-mail: web-queries@meppublishers.com
Web Site: www.meppublishers.com
Key Personnel
General Manager: Halcyon Salazar
   E-mail: hsalazar@meppublishers.com
Sales & Marketing Manager: Denise Chin
   Tel: (868) 683-0832 *E-mail:* dchin@meppublishers.com
Production & Distribution: Jacqueline Smith
Subjects: Art, Biography, Memoirs, Fiction, Natural History
ISBN Prefix(es): 978-976-9508

University of the West Indies (Trinidad and Tobago)

St Augustine Campus, St Augustine
Tel: (868) 662-2002 *Fax:* (868) 663-9684
Web Site: sta.uwi.edu
Subjects: Agriculture, Art, Education, Engineering (General), History, Law, Literature, Literary Criticism, Essays, Science (General), Social Sciences, Sociology
ISBN Prefix(es): 978-976-620

Tunisia

General Information

Capital: Tunis
Language: Arabic. French widely used
Religion: Islam
Population: 8.4 million
Bank Hours: 0800-1200/1400-1800 Monday-Friday
Shop Hours: 0800-1300/1500-1900 Monday-Saturday
Currency: 1,000 millimes = 1 Tunisian dinar
Export/Import Information: Tunisia had preferred tariffs and European Union agreement but most books are dutied. Advertising matter free. Custom formalities tax per 1,000 kg or less gross weight, with minimum rate. Consumption tax on and duty tax paid of percentage of duty and tax paid. Imports liberalized but in practice licenses granted dependent on foreign exchange position.
Copyright: UCC, Berne (see Copyright Conventions, pg viii)

Academie Tunisienne des Sciences, des Lettres et des Arts Beit al-Hikma (Tunisian Academy of Sciences, Letters & Arts)+

25, Ave de la Republique, 2016 Carthage
Tel: 71 277 275

Web Site: www.beitalhikma.tn; www.facebook.com/BeitalhikmaTunisie
Founded: 1983
Subjects: Art, Biography, Memoirs, Drama, Theater, Geography, Geology, History, Journalism, Language Arts, Linguistics, Law, Literature, Literary Criticism, Essays, Mathematics, Medicine, Nursing, Dentistry, Music, Dance, Philosophy, Physics, Poetry, Religion - Islamic, Social Sciences, Sociology, Veterinary Science
ISBN Prefix(es): 978-9973-929; 978-9973-911
Distributed by Afrique Culture; Dar Souhnoun; Demeter

Editions Ali Bouslama et Fils+

15, Ave de France, 1000 Tunis
Tel: 71240056 *Fax:* 71343100
Founded: 1959
Subjects: History
ISBN Prefix(es): 978-9973-714
Branch Office(s)
15 bis rue Lamine el Abassi, Tunis

Les Editions de l'Arbre

17, rue Mohamed Karboub, Manar II, 2092 Tunis
Tel: 71887927 *Fax:* 71887927
Founded: 1993
Subjects: Animals, Pets, Archaeology, Gardening, Plants, History, House & Home, Humor, Language Arts, Linguistics, Literature, Literary Criticism, Essays, Natural History, Outdoor Recreation, Poetry, Publishing & Book Trade Reference, Self-Help
ISBN Prefix(es): 978-9973-772

CAEU, *imprint of* Editions Med Ali

Dar el Maaref Edition

ZI Route de Tunis, KM 131, 4022 Sousse
Mailing Address: BP 215, 4000 Sousse
Tel: 73 309 235; 24 241 395 *Fax:* 73 309 472
E-mail: edition@darelmaaref.com.tn
Web Site: www.darelmaaref.com/edition/fr
Subjects: Language Arts, Linguistics, Literature, Literary Criticism, Essays, Science (General)
ISBN Prefix(es): 978-9973-60
Bookshop(s): 55 Rue Kheireddine Bacha, Tunis

Demeter Editions

36 av Fattouma Bourguiba, Sidi Fraj, 2036 La Soukra
Tel: 71 94 52 42; 71 94 53 15 *Fax:* 71 94 51 99
E-mail: demeter@planet.tn
Key Personnel
Contact: Moncef Guellaty
Subjects: Art, History
ISBN Prefix(es): 978-9973-706

Faculte des Sciences Humaines et Sociales de Tunis

94, Blvd du 9 avnl 1938, 1007 Tunis
Tel: 71 560 840 *Fax:* 71 567 551
E-mail: fshst@fshst.rnu.tn
Web Site: www.fshst.rnu.tn
Founded: 1956
Arabic & Latin languages.
Subjects: Archaeology, Ethnicity, Geography, Geology, History, Language Arts, Linguistics, Literature, Literary Criticism, Essays, Philosophy, Psychology, Psychiatry, Social Sciences, Sociology
ISBN Prefix(es): 978-9973-922

Fondation Temimi pour la Recherche Scientifique et l'Information

Centre Urbain Nord, Immeuble Al-Imtiaz, 1003 Tunis
Tel: 71 23 14 44; 71 75 11 64 *Fax:* 71 23 66 77
E-mail: fondationtemimi@gnet.tn; fondationtemimi@yahoo.fr
Web Site: temimi.refer.org

Key Personnel
President: Prof Abdeljelil Temimi
Founded: 1986
Subjects: Archaeology, History, Library & Information Sciences, Social Sciences, Sociology
ISBN Prefix(es): 978-9973-719; 978-9973-32
Number of titles published annually: 15 Print
Total Titles: 154 Print

FTERSI, see Fondation Temimi pour la Recherche Scientifique et l'Information

Imprimerie Officielle de la Republique Tunisienne (IORT) (Official Printing Office of the Republic of Tunisia)
40 ave Farhat Hached, 2098 Rades
Tel: 71 43 42 11 *Fax:* 71 43 42 34
E-mail: iort@iort.gov.tn
Web Site: www.iort.gov.tn
Subjects: Law
ISBN Prefix(es): 978-9973-906; 978-9973-946; 978-9973-39

IORT, see Imprimerie Officielle de la Republique Tunisienne (IORT)

Maison d'Edition Mohamed Ali Hammi, see Editions Med Ali

Edition Maison du Livre
Rue malaga Manar, 2092 Tunis
Mailing Address: BP 245, 2092 Tunis
Tel: (071) 87 40 31
E-mail: maisondulivre@planet.tn
Web Site: www.maisondulivretn.com
Subjects: Economics, Government, Political Science, Law, Marketing, Philosophy
ISBN Prefix(es): 978-9938-872

Editions Med Ali+
3 Rue Mohamed Chaabouni, Immueble Zarkaa Yamam, 3027 Sfax
Tel: 74407440 *Fax:* 74407441
E-mail: edition.medali@tunet.tn
Web Site: www.edition-medali.com
Key Personnel
Owner: Nouri Abid
Founded: 1983
Subjects: History, Language Arts, Linguistics, Literature, Literary Criticism, Essays, Mathematics, Philosophy
ISBN Prefix(es): 978-9973-727; 978-9973-33
Imprints: CAEU
Distributor for Centre Culturel Arabic (Liban); El Farabi (Liban)

Scientifique et l'Information-TRSI, see Fondation Temimi pour la Recherche Scientifique et l'Information

Sud Editions
79, Rue de Palestine, 1002 Tunis
Tel: 71 785 179; 71 782 991 *Fax:* 71 848 664
E-mail: sud.edition@planet.tn
Founded: 1976
Subjects: Art, Language Arts, Linguistics, Literature, Literary Criticism, Essays
ISBN Prefix(es): 978-9973-703; 978-9973-844
Warehouse: La Soukra, Km 15, 2036 Tunis

Editions Techniques Specialisees
28, av Habib Bourguiba, BP 734, 2078 Marsa Safsaf, Tunis
Tel: 71 74 61 61; 71 74 70 04 *Fax:* 71 74 61 60
E-mail: commercial@pagesjaunes.com.tn
Founded: 1978
ISBN Prefix(es): 978-9973-711
Subsidiaries: Redaction

Turkey

General Information

Capital: Ankara
Language: Turkish
Religion: Predominantly Sunni Muslim
Population: 63.9 million
Bank Hours: 0900-1730 Monday-Friday
Shop Hours: 0800-1900 Monday-Saturday
Currency: Turkish lira
Export/Import Information: Books, magazines and similar publications are freely imported. International copyright laws enforced. 1% VAT on books.
Copyright: Berne, Florence (see Copyright Conventions, pg viii)

ABC Yayin Grubu Egitim Hizmetleri san ve Tic Ltd Sti
Cirpici Mah 1, Tasocagi Sok No 61/A, Zeytinburnu, Istanbul
Tel: (0212) 416 06 05 *Fax:* (0212) 416 06 05
Founded: 1976
Subjects: Art, Child Care & Development, Education, Language Arts, Linguistics
ISBN Prefix(es): 978-975-09

Agora Kitapligi Basim Yayim Ltd Sti
Kuloglu Mah Turnacibasi Cad No 54, 34420 Beyoglu, Istanbul
Tel: (0212) 243 96 26; (0212) 251 37 04; (0212) 293 83 72; (0212) 503 82 95
E-mail: agora@agorakitapligi.com
Web Site: www.agorakitapligi.com
Key Personnel
Editor: Osman Akinhay
Art Dir: Mithat Cinar
Founded: 2003
Subjects: Government, Political Science, Literature, Literary Criticism, Essays, Women's Studies, Cinema, Culture, Feminism, Turkish Literature, World Literature
ISBN Prefix(es): 978-605-103

Alfa Basim Yayim Dagitim Ltd Sti
Ticarethane sk No 53, 34410 Cagaloglu, Istanbul
Tel: (0212) 511 53 03 *Fax:* (0212) 519 33 00
E-mail: info@alfakitap.com
Web Site: www.alfakitap.com
Subjects: Art, Biography, Memoirs, Business, Cookery, Education, Fiction, Government, Political Science, History, Law, Literature, Literary Criticism, Essays, Management, Medicine, Nursing, Dentistry, Philosophy, Poetry, Sports, Athletics, Contemporary Turkish Literature, World Literature
ISBN Prefix(es): 978-9944-486; 978-975-289; 978-975-252; 978-975-8733; 978-975-253; 978-975-7368; 978-975-8052
Imprints: Artemis; Buyulu Fener; Everest; Kapi

Alkim Kitapcilik Yayincilik+
Caferaga Mah Damga Sok No 23-25, Kadikoy, Istanbul
Tel: (0216) 450 20 08 (sales)
Membership(s): Basar Arslan.
Subjects: Astrology, Occult, Business, Child Care & Development, Computer Science, Computers, Cookery, Crafts, Games, Hobbies, Drama, Theater, Economics, Finance, How-to, Law, Management, Marketing, Nonfiction (General), Psychology, Psychiatry, Sports, Athletics
ISBN Prefix(es): 978-975-337; 978-975-6363

Altin Kitaplar
Goztepe Mah Kazim Karabekir Cad, No 32 Mahmutbey-Bagcilar, Istanbul
Tel: (0212) 446 38 88

E-mail: iletisim@altinkitaplar.com.tr; pr@altinkitaplar.com.tr
Web Site: www.altinkitaplar.com.tr
Key Personnel
Editor-in-Chief: Batu Bozkurt; Erden Heper
Editorial: Alpar Oya
Founded: 1959
Subjects: Criminology, Economics, Fiction, History, Nonfiction (General), Philosophy, Psychology, Psychiatry, Regional Interests, Science Fiction, Fantasy
ISBN Prefix(es): 978-975-7620
Showroom(s): Celal ferdi Goekcay SK, Nebio Is Hani, Istanbul

Antik Classics, *imprint of* Timas Yayinlari

April Yayincilik
Tarik Zafer Tunaya Sokak Oniz, Apartment 21/3, Beyoglu, Istanbul
Tel: (0212) 252 94 38 *Fax:* (0212) 252 94 39
E-mail: bilgi@aprilyayincilik.com
Web Site: www.aprilyayincilik.com
Subjects: Fiction
ISBN Prefix(es): 978-975-6006

Arkadas Yayinevi Ltd+
Yuva Mahallesi 3702, Sokak No 4, 06105 Yenimahalle, Ankara
Tel: (0312) 396 0111 *Fax:* (0312) 396 0141
E-mail: info@arkadas.com.tr; musterihizmetleri@arkadas.com.tr
Web Site: www.arkadas.com.tr
Key Personnel
Chairman & Owner: Cumhur Ozdemir
Editor: Miss Zeynep Kopuzlu
Founded: 1980
Specialize in computer books & textbooks. Also acts as book distributor & bookshop. Authorized software replicator of Microsoft EMEA (Europe, Middle East & Africa).
Subjects: Animals, Pets, Archaeology, Computer Science, Cookery, Crafts, Games, Hobbies, English as a Second Language, Environmental Studies, Fiction, Health, Nutrition, History, Mathematics, Medicine, Nursing, Dentistry, Music, Dance, Physics, Psychology, Psychiatry, Social Sciences, Sociology
ISBN Prefix(es): 978-975-509
Number of titles published annually: 100 Print
Total Titles: 600 Print
Distributor for Microsoft Press
Foreign Rep(s): Microsoft Press (Turkey)
Bookshop(s): Atlantis Alisveris Merkezi, Kent-Koop Mahallesi Baskent Blvd, No 213 C3 Batikent Yenimahalle, Ankara *Tel:* (0312) 255 5044; Kentpark Alisveris Merkezi, Eskisehir Yolu 7 km No 164/2 Kat No 103 06520, Ankara *Tel:* (0312) 219 9244 *Fax:* (0312) 219 9247; One Tower Alisveris Merkezi, Oran Mahallesi Kudus Cad No 6 Cankaya, Ankara *Tel:* (0312) 503 0062

Arkeoloji Ve Sanat Yayinlari (Archaeology & Art Publications)+
Hayriye Cad, Cezayir Sok, Mateo Mratovic, Apartment No 5/2, 34425 Beyoglu, Istanbul
Tel: (0212) 293 03 78 *Fax:* (0212) 245 68 77
E-mail: info@arkeolojisanat.com; editor@arkeolojisanat.com
Web Site: www.arkeolojisanat.com
Key Personnel
Publisher: Nezih Basgelen
Founded: 1978
Publish books on archaeology, history & art history of Turkey. With titles in Turkish, English, German & French, the company's list includes publications ranging from specialized scholarly monographs to popular guides to Turkey's famed tourist sites.
Also publishes *Arkeoloji ve Sanat*, a bimonthly journal presenting the academic contributions

of the world's leading scholars of Anatolian archaeology & art.

Subjects: Anthropology, Antiques, Archaeology, Architecture & Interior Design, Art, History, Photography, Travel & Tourism

ISBN Prefix(es): 978-975-7538; 978-975-6899; 978-605-396; 978-975-6561; 978-9944-75

Number of titles published annually: 20 Print

Total Titles: 100 Print

U.S. Office(s): Archaeology & Art Publications (AAP), 8 South Eighth St, Suite 200, Richmond, IN 47374, United States, Mng Dir: Ahmet Basgelen *Tel:* 765-277-6773 *E-mail:* info@aapbl.com *Web Site:* www.aapbl.com

Bookshop(s): Arkeopera, Yenicarsi Cad Peter Han No 66/A, Galatasaray, 34433 Istanbul *Tel:* (0212) 249 92 26 *Fax:* (0212) 244 31 64 *E-mail:* info@arkeopera.com *Web Site:* www.arkeopera.com

Artemis, *imprint of* Alfa Basim Yayim Dagitim Ltd Sti

Ataturk Kultur, Dil ve Tarih, Yuksek Kurumu
Ataturk Bulvari, No 217, 06680 Kavaklidere, Ankara
Tel: (0312) 457 52 00 *Fax:* (0312) 468 07 83
E-mail: bilgi@tdk.gov.tr; katki@tdk.org.tr; isaretdili@tdk.org.tr
Web Site: www.tdk.gov.tr
Key Personnel
President: Dr Derya Ors
Subjects: Archaeology, Ethnicity, History, Language Arts, Linguistics
ISBN Prefix(es): 978-975-16
Branch Office(s)
Ataturk Arastirma Merkezi (Ataturk Research Center)
Ataturk Kultur Merkezi (Ataturk Culture Center)
Turk Tarih Kurumu (Turkish Historical Society)
Turk Dil Kurumu (Turkish Language Society)

Ataturk Universitesi+
25240 Erzurum
Tel: (0442) 231 11 11 *Fax:* (0442) 236 10 14
E-mail: ata@atauni.edu.tr
Web Site: www.atauni.edu.tr
Key Personnel
Library & Documentation: Mustafa Ozyurek
E-mail: mustafaozyurek@atauni.edu.tr
Founded: 1957
Subjects: Agriculture, Architecture & Interior Design, Art, Communications, Earth Sciences, Economics, Education, Engineering (General), Law, Medicine, Nursing, Dentistry, Science (General), Theology, Travel & Tourism, Veterinary Science
ISBN Prefix(es): 978-975-442

Aydin Yayinlari+
Haymana Yolu 5 km, Karsiyaka Mah 577 Sokak No 1, Golbasi, Ankara
Tel: (0312) 498 25 25 *Fax:* (0312) 498 24 46
Web Site: aydinegitim.com
Key Personnel
Founder: Nesibe Aydin
Founded: 1984
Subjects: Mathematics, Science (General)
ISBN Prefix(es): 978-975-7948
Subsidiaries: Aydin Web Tesisleri (printing)
Book Club(s): Yayincilar Birligi
Warehouse: 100 yil Bolvari, Gl Sok, No 29, Ostim

Ayrinti Yayinlari
Cemal Nadir Sok No 3, 34112 Cagaloglu, Istanbul
Tel: (0212) 512 15 00 *Fax:* (0212) 512 15 11
E-mail: info@ayrintiyayinlari.com.tr
Web Site: www.ayrintiyayinlari.com.tr

Subjects: Art, Biography, Memoirs, Literature, Literary Criticism, Essays, Philosophy, Art Theory
ISBN Prefix(es): 978-975-539

Bilden Bilgisayar
Ziverbey Kasap Ismail Sok, Sadikoglu-4 Is Merkezi No 13 Buro No 41, 81040 Kadikoy/Istanbul
Tel: (0216) 449 52 50 *Fax:* (0216) 449 52 51
Key Personnel
General Manager: Sukru Korman
Founded: 1983
Specializes in the development of educational software on CD-ROM for ages 3-18.
Subjects: Education, Language Arts, Linguistics, Mathematics, Science (General), Social Sciences, Sociology
Distributor for Encyclopaedia Britannica Co; LangMaster

Bilgi Yayinevi
Mesrutiyet Caddesi No 46/A, Kizilay, 06420 Yenisehir, Ankara
Tel: (0312) 431 81 22 *Fax:* (0312) 431 77 58
E-mail: info@bilgiyayinevi.com.tr; rights@bilgiyayinevi.com.tr
Web Site: www.bilgiyayinevi.com.tr
Founded: 1965
Subjects: Biography, Memoirs, Drama, Theater, Fiction, Poetry, Anthology, Food, Narrative
ISBN Prefix(es): 978-975-494; 978-975-22

Birsen Yayinevi (Birsen Publishers)+
Cagaloglu Yokusu Evren Carsisi, 29/13 Eminonu PK, 34555 Istanbul
Tel: (0212) 527 85 78 *Fax:* (0212) 527 08 95
E-mail: info@birsenyayinevi.com
Web Site: www.birsenyayinevi.com
Founded: 1973
ISBN Prefix(es): 978-975-511

Blue Dome Press, *imprint of* Kaynak Publishing Group

Boyut Yayin Grubu
Yuzyil Mah Matbaacilar Sitesi 1 Cad No 115, 34204 Bagcilar, Istanbul
Tel: (0212) 413 33 33 *Fax:* (0212) 413 33 34
Web Site: www.boyutstore.com
Subjects: Architecture & Interior Design, Art, Computers, Education, Fiction, Geography, Geology, Government, Political Science, Health, Nutrition, History, Humor, Language Arts, Linguistics, Literature, Literary Criticism, Essays, Poetry, Sports, Athletics, Research
ISBN Prefix(es): 978-975-521; 978-975-23

Buyulu Fener, *imprint of* Alfa Basim Yayim Dagitim Ltd Sti

Cagri Yayinlari
Binbirdirek Meydani Sok, Han No:3 Kat:1 D:8, Sultanahmet Fatih, 34122 Istanbul
Tel: (0212) 516-20-80 *Fax:* (0212) 516-20-82
E-mail: cagri@cagri.com.tr
Web Site: www.cagri.com.tr; www.facebook.com/groups/116886788342035
Subjects: Art, Cookery, Drama, Theater, Fiction, Government, Political Science, Law, Literature, Literary Criticism, Essays, Poetry, Religion - Islamic, Historical Novels
ISBN Prefix(es): 978-975-454
Number of titles published annually: 8 Print
Total Titles: 242 Print

Can Cocuk
Yenicarsi Cad No 74, 34430 Galatasaray, Istanbul
Tel: (0212) 245 82 92 *Fax:* (0212) 245 60 82
E-mail: cancocuk@cancocuk.com

Web Site: www.cancocuk.com
Founded: 1981
Subjects: Biography, Memoirs, Literature, Literary Criticism, Essays, Thrillers
ISBN Prefix(es): 978-975-07

Can Sanat Yayinlari
Hayriye Cad No 2, 34430 Galatasaray, Istanbul
Tel: (0212) 252 59 88 *Fax:* (0212) 252 72 33
E-mail: yayinevi@canyayinlari.com; rights@canyayinlari.com
Web Site: www.canyayinlari.com
Founded: 1981
Subjects: Biography, Memoirs, Drama, Theater, Literature, Literary Criticism, Essays, Poetry, Children's Literature, Classics, Contemporary Turkish Literature, Contemporary World Literature, Modern Classics
ISBN Prefix(es): 978-975-510; 978-975-8440

Carpe Diem Publishing, *imprint of* Timas Yayinlari

Cep Kitaplari, *imprint of* Varlik Yayinlari AS

Cep Kitaplari+
Imprint of Varlik Yayinlari AS
Perpa Ticaret Merkezi, B-Block K 5 No 484, 34384 Sisli, Istanbul
Tel: (0212) 221 31 71 *Fax:* (0212) 320 06 46
E-mail: varlik@varlik.com.tr; varlik@isbank.net.tr (sales)
Web Site: www.varlik.com.tr
Key Personnel
Publisher: Ms Filiz Deniztekin *Tel:* (0532) 791 3424 *E-mail:* fnayir54@gmail.com; Mr Osman Cetin Deniztekin *Tel:* (0532) 700 0172 *E-mail:* odeniztekin@gmail.com
Founded: 1982
Membership(s): Turkish Publishers Association.
Subjects: Fiction, Nonfiction (General), Religion - Islamic, Science (General), Science Fiction, Fantasy, Women's Studies
ISBN Prefix(es): 978-975-480
Number of titles published annually: 5 Print
Total Titles: 60 Print
Distributed by Varlik Yayinlari AS

Citlembik Publications+
Division of Citlembik Film Video Yapim Ceviri Egitim Yayincilik Turizm ve Gida san ve Tic Ltd Sti
Seyh Bender Sok 18/5, Asmalimescit, Tunel, 80050 Istanbul
Tel: (0212) 292 30 32; (0212) 252 31 63 *Fax:* (0212) 293 34 66
E-mail: kitap@citlembik.com.tr
Web Site: www.citlembik.com.tr; www.nettleberry.com
Key Personnel
Owner: Mustafa Ozturk
Dir: Nancy Ozturk
Founded: 1992
American/Turkish publishing company working in conjunction with Nettleberry LLC, Eden, South Dakota, USA.
Specialize in books with a multicultural focus & publishes books in both English & Turkish. English publications include travel books (in-depth guides to some aspect of Turkey); autobiographies, biographies & memoirs (primarily related to Turkey, the Middle East or Central Asia); cookbooks on Turkish cuisine; children's books with a multicultural focus; translations of Turkish literature into English.
Membership(s): PMA; Turkish Publishers Association.
Subjects: Architecture & Interior Design, Biography, Memoirs, Cookery, Developing Countries, Fiction, Foreign Countries, Government, Political Science, History, LGBTQ, Literature, Literary Criticism, Essays, Nonfiction (General), Philosophy, Psychology, Psychiatry, Religion

- Islamic, Science (General), Social Sciences, Sociology, Travel & Tourism, Women's Studies
ISBN Prefix(es): 978-975-6663; 978-9944-424
Number of titles published annually: 20 Print
Total Titles: 140 Print
U.S. Office(s): Nettleberry LLC, 44030 123 St, Eden, SD 57232, United States *Fax:* 605-448-2699 *E-mail:* info@nettleberry.com
Foreign Rep(s): National Book Network (Australia, Canada, New Zealand, UK, USA)
Distribution Center: National Book Network, 15200 NBN Way, Blue Ridge Summit, PA 17214, United States *Tel:* 717-794-3800 *Fax:* 717-794-3828

Cosku Yayinlari, *imprint of* Zambak Yayinlari

Damla Yayinevi
Prof Kazim Ismail Gurkan Cd, No 8, 34110 Cagaloglu, Istanbul
Tel: (0212) 514 28 28 *Fax:* (0212) 514 28 34
E-mail: iletisim@damlayayinevi.com.tr
Web Site: www.damlayayinevi.com.tr; www.damlapublishing.com
Founded: 1974
Specialize in foreign language study focusing on English language teaching.
Subjects: Child Care & Development, Criminology, Education, Health, Nutrition, Mysteries, Suspense, Nonfiction (General), Classics, Diet, Fitness, Foreign Language Study
ISBN Prefix(es): 978-975-381
Parent Company: Damla Publishing Group

Daral Nile, *imprint of* Kaynak Publishing Group

Deger Yayinlari, *imprint of* Zambak Yayinlari

Dergah Yayinlari (Dergah Publications)+
Binbirdirek Mah Klodfarer Cad, No 3/20, Altan Is Merkezi, 34122 Sultanahmet, Istanbul
Tel: (0212) 518 95 78 *Fax:* (0212) 518 95 81
E-mail: bilgi@dergahyayinlari.com
Web Site: www.dergahyayinlari.com
Key Personnel
Founder: Ezel Erverdi
Dir: Asim Onur Erverdi
Editorial: Ismail Kara; Mustafa Kutlu
Editor & Foreign Rights: Isil Erverdi
Founded: 1977
Subjects: Economics, Government, Political Science, History, Literature, Literary Criticism, Essays, Philosophy, Religion - Other, Social Sciences, Sociology, Theology, Mysticism
ISBN Prefix(es): 978-975-7462; 978-975-7032; 978-975-6611
Number of titles published annually: 40 Print
Total Titles: 400 Print
Subsidiaries: Ulke Yayin Haber Tic Ltd Sti
Bookshop(s): Ulke Yayin Haber Tic Ltd Sti

Destek Yayinevi (Support Publishing House)
Abdi ipek cad 31/5 Nisantasi Sisli, Istanbul
Tel: (0212) 252 22 42 *Fax:* (0212) 252 22 43
E-mail: info@destekyayinlari.com
Web Site: www.destekdukkan.com
Key Personnel
Contact: Asli Perker
Founded: 2006
Subjects: Biography, Memoirs, Government, Political Science, Health, Nutrition, History, Literature, Literary Criticism, Essays, Mysteries, Suspense, Psychology, Psychiatry, Religion - Other, Science Fiction, Fantasy, Self-Help, Travel & Tourism
ISBN Prefix(es): 978-605-4455; 978-605-4607; 978-605-4771; 978-605-4994; 978-605-9913; 978-9944-298; 978-605-311

Dogan Egmont Yayincilik ve Yapimcilik AS (Dogan Egmont Publishing & Production Inc)
19 Mayis Mahallesi Golden Plaza No 1, Kat 10, 34360 Sisli, Istanbul
Tel: (0212) 373 77 00; (0212) 373 77 77
Fax: (0212) 246 66 66
Web Site: www.de.com.tr
Key Personnel
Advertising & Business Development Coordinator: Irem Akkaya *E-mail:* iakkaya@de.com.tr
Advertising Sales & Business & Development Manager: Damia Cebeci Saridede *E-mail:* dcebeci@de.com.tr
Founded: 1996
Subjects: Education, Fiction
ISBN Prefix(es): 978-975-323

Dokuz Eylul Universitesi
Cumhuriyet Bulvari No 144, Alsancak, 35210 Izmir
Tel: (0232) 412 12 12 *Fax:* (0232) 464 81 35
Web Site: www.deu.edu.tr
Key Personnel
President: Dr Mehmet Fuzun *E-mail:* mehmet.fuzun@deu.edu.tr
Founded: 1982
Subjects: Law
ISBN Prefix(es): 978-975-441

Dost Kitabevi Yayinlari+
Paris Caddesi No 76/7, Kavaklidere, 06680 Ankara
Tel: (0312) 435 93 70; (0312) 435 79 02
Fax: (0312) 435 79 02
E-mail: bilgi@dostyayinevi.com
Web Site: www.dostyayinevi.com
Key Personnel
Chief Executive Officer: Erdal Akalin
Finance Manager: Gunay Okumus
Publishing Coordinator: Ali Karabayram
Founded: 1979
Chain of bookshops. Started publishing books in 1997. Co-editions with Dorling Kindersley, Franco Maria Ricci.
Membership(s): Turkish Publishers Association.
Subjects: Art, History, Social Sciences, Sociology, Travel & Tourism, Culture, Translated Fiction
ISBN Prefix(es): 978-975-7501; 978-975-298
Number of titles published annually: 60 Print
Total Titles: 80 Print

Editions Dunil, *imprint of* Kaynak Publishing Group

Dus Degirmeni, *imprint of* Erdem Yayinlari

Elma Yayinevi
Aziziye Mah Portakal Cigegi Sokak 37/7, 06690 Cankaya, Ankara
Tel: (0312) 417 72 73; (0312) 417 27 77
Fax: (0312) 417 36 46
E-mail: elmayayinevi@elmayayinevi.com; bilgi@elmayayinevi.com
Web Site: www.elmayayinevi.com
Key Personnel
Mng Dir: Mustafa Besturk
Editor-in-Chief: Seyra Faralyali Erdaloglu
Sales & Marketing Officer: Timucin Karakus
Subjects: Business, Education, Management, Self-Help
ISBN Prefix(es): 978-975-6093

Epsilon Yayinevi
Osmanli Sk Osmanli Is Merkezi 18/4, Beyoglu, Istanbul
Tel: (0212) 252 38 21 *Fax:* (0212) 252 63 98
E-mail: epsilon@epsilonyayinevi.com
Web Site: www.epsilonyayinevi.com
Founded: 1988
Subjects: Fiction, Mysteries, Suspense, Romance, Science Fiction, Fantasy

ISBN Prefix(es): 978-9944-82
Number of titles published annually: 130 Print
Total Titles: 1,300 Print

Erdem, *imprint of* Erdem Yayinlari

Erdem Cocuk, *imprint of* Erdem Yayinlari

Erdem Yayinlari
Uncular Cad Mimar Sinan, Mah Eksioglu Is Merzeki No 22 Kat 3 Daire 45/B, 34672 Uskudar
Tel: (0216) 492 55 55-15 *Fax:* (0216) 201 14 80
E-mail: bilgi@erdemyayinlari.com
Web Site: www.erdemyayinlari.com
Key Personnel
Editor-in-Chief: Dr Melike Gunyuz
Founded: 1984
Subjects: Education, Fiction
ISBN Prefix(es): 978-975-501 (Erdem); 978-605-349 (Erdem & Erdem Cocuk); 978-975-8739 (Dus Degirmeni); 978-605-4890 (Minik Ada); 978-605-90 (UMP)
Imprints: Erdem; Erdem Cocuk; Dus Degirmeni; Minik Ada; UMP

Eren Yayincilik Kitap, Dagitim Ltd+
Tunel, Istiklal Cad, Sofyali Sk 24, 34430 Beyoglu, Istanbul
Tel: (0212) 252 05 60; (0212) 251 28 58
Fax: (0212) 243 30 16
E-mail: eren@eren.com.tr
Web Site: www.eren.com.tr
Founded: 1939
Membership(s): Istanbul Chamber of Commerce; Turkey Young Businessmen Association; Turkish Publishers Association.
Subjects: Engineering (General)
ISBN Prefix(es): 978-975-7622; 978-975-9916; 978-975-2639
Associate Companies: Ottomania

Erkam Publishing
Ikitelli Organize Sanayi Bolgesi, Turgut Ozal Caddesi No 117/2-A, Basaksehir, Istanbul
Tel: (0212) 671 07 00 *Fax:* (0212) 671 07 17
Web Site: store.erkamyayinlari.com
Key Personnel
Owner: Dogan Gokmen
Founded: 1980
Specialize in works on moral & spiritual development.
Subjects: Religion - Islamic
ISBN Prefix(es): 978-975-6247; 978-975-6736
Parent Company: Erkam Yayinlari San Tic AS

Everest, *imprint of* Alfa Basim Yayim Dagitim Ltd Sti

Evrensel Basim Yayin
Kamerhatun Mahallesi, Alhatun Sokak, No 25, 34980 Beyoglu, Istanbul
Tel: (0212) 255 25 46 *Fax:* (0212) 255 25 87
E-mail: info@evrenselbasim.com
Web Site: www.evrenselbasim.com
Founded: 1988
Subjects: Government, Political Science, History, Literature, Literary Criticism, Essays, Philosophy, Poetry, Science (General), Socialistic Theory
ISBN Prefix(es): 978-975-6865; 978-975-7837; 978-975-6525; 978-605-4156

Editorial La Fuente, *imprint of* Kaynak Publishing Group

Gunisigi Kitapligi
Profilo Plaza, Cemal Sahir Sok 26/28 B3, 34387 Mecidiyekoy, Istanbul
Tel: (0212) 212 99 73 *Fax:* (0212) 217 91 74
E-mail: info@gunisigikitapligi.com; satis@gunisigikitapligi.com

Web Site: gunisigikitapligi.com
Key Personnel
Foreign Rights: Hande Demirtas *E-mail:* hande@
gunisigikitapligi.com
Founded: 1996
Subjects: History, Literature, Literary Criticism,
Essays, Poetry, Science Fiction, Fantasy
ISBN Prefix(es): 978-975-6227; 978-975-8142

Hayrat Nesriyat Sanyi ve Ticaret AS
Cumhuriyet Mah Asik Veysel Cad No 72/A,
34290 Kucukcekmece, Istanbul
Tel: (0212) 624 24 34; (0850) 333 99 66
Fax: (0212) 424 49 32
E-mail: info@hayrat.com
Web Site: www.hayrat.com.tr
Key Personnel
General Manager: Metin Kilitcioglu
Marketing Manager: Omer Kemaloglu
Subjects: Inspirational, Spirituality, Religion - Is-
lamic, Qur'an
ISBN Prefix(es): 978-975-9023
Branch Office(s)
Ankara Cad No 41, Uygur is Hani, Eminonu, Is-
tanbul *Tel:* (0212) 527 72 44 *Fax:* (0212) 424
49 32
Haci Bayram Mh Saribay Sok No 37, Ulus,
Ankara *Tel:* (0312) 309 97 18 *Fax:* (0312) 309
97 18
Pazaryolu Mevkii Atabey Yolu Kavsagi, Kuleonu
Kasabasi, Isparta *Tel:* (0246) 259 46 20
Fax: (0246) 259 44 99

IkiNokta Bilisim Teknolojileri AS+
Icerenkoy Mh Ali Nihat Tarlan Cad, Eryilmazlar
Sk Teknikhan No 7 K 5 D 6, 34752 Atasehir,
Istanbul
Tel: (0216) 575 05 05 *Fax:* (0216) 577 51 79
E-mail: bilgi@ikinokta.com
Web Site: www.ikinokta.com
Founded: 1985
Specialize in geographic information.
Subjects: Archaeology, Communications, Geogra-
phy, Geology, History
ISBN Prefix(es): 978-975-340
Number of titles published annually: 130 Print; 5
CD-ROM; 1 Online; 1 E-Book

Iletisim Yayinlari+
Binbirdirek Meydani Sok Iletisim Han 3, 34122
Istanbul
Tel: (0212) 5162260 *Fax:* (0212) 5161258
E-mail: iletisim@iletisim.com.tr
Web Site: www.iletisim.com.tr
Key Personnel
Contact: Nihat Tuna; Osman Yener
Founded: 1980
Subjects: Ethnicity, Fiction, Government, Political
Science, History, Literature, Literary Criticism,
Essays, Nonfiction (General), Philosophy, Sci-
ence Fiction, Fantasy, Social Sciences, Sociol-
ogy
ISBN Prefix(es): 978-975-470
Associate Companies: Birikim Yayinlari
Branch Office(s)
Selanik Caddesi, Tankut Is Merkezi, 82/17, 06640
Ankara *Tel:* (0312) 425 36 00; (0312) 425 20
71 *Fax:* (0312) 425 14 18

Imge Kitabevi
Konur SK No 17, Kizilay, Ankara
Tel: (0312) 419 93 10; (0312) 419 93 11
E-mail: info@paraf.com.tr
Web Site: www.imgekitabevi.com; www.imge.
com.tr
Key Personnel
Owner: Refik Tabakci
Mng Dir: Ozge Atalay
Founded: 1987
Subjects: Anthropology, Archaeology, Art, Bi-
ography, Memoirs, Business, Child Care &
Development, Computers, Crafts, Games, Hob-

bies, Economics, Education, Government, Polit-
ical Science, Health, Nutrition, History, Humor,
Language Arts, Linguistics, Law, Philosophy,
Religion - Other, Social Sciences, Sociology,
Travel & Tourism
ISBN Prefix(es): 978-975-533
Parent Company: Imge Kitabevi Ltd
Divisions: Imge Kitabevi Yayinlari

Inkilap Publishers Ltd
Cohancesme Mah Cad, Altay Sokak No 8, 34196
Yenibosna, Istanbul
Tel: (0212) 496 11 11 *Fax:* (0212) 496 11 12
(customer service)
E-mail: siparis@inkilap.com
Web Site: www.inkilap.com
Key Personnel
Owner: Nazar Fikri
Mng Dir: Arman Fikri
Foreign Rights: Sema Diker
Founded: 1927
Subjects: Animals, Pets, Archaeology, Art, Busi-
ness, Child Care & Development, Cookery,
Drama, Theater, Economics, Electronics, Elec-
trical Engineering, Fiction, Gardening, Plants,
Humor, Management, Mathematics, Music,
Dance, Philosophy, Photography, Physics, Po-
etry, Psychology, Psychiatry, Religion - Islamic
ISBN Prefix(es): 978-975-10
Number of titles published annually: 150 Print
Total Titles: 3,000 Print
Parent Company: Inkilap Kitabevi
Associate Companies: Inkas, Ingilizce Nesriyat
Kitapcilik AS, Ankara Cad 95, Sirkeci, Istanbul
Branch Office(s)
Yeni Zaman Kitabevi, Ankara Cad 155, Sirkeci,
Istanbul (correspondence to Inkilap)
Bookshop(s): Inkilap Kitabevi Bagdat Caddesi,
Bagdat Cad No 416, No 1, Kadikoy-Istanbul
Tel: (0216) 658 85 11 *Fax:* (0216) 658 85 07;
Metrocity Nkilap Kitabevi, Buyukdere Cad No
171, Levent, Istanbul, Contact: Arman Fikri
Tel: (0212) 3440296 *Fax:* (0212) 3440297;
Inkilap Mah B061 Carrefour Ticaret merkezi
Uemraniye, Istanbul *Tel:* (0216) 525 12 95
Fax: (0216) 525 12 97; Yeni Havaalani Cad
No 40 Kipa Alisveris Merkezi Cigli, Izmir
Tel: (0232) 386 50 70 *Fax:* (0232) 386 50 70

Insan Yayinlari
Istiklal Caddesi No 96, Beyoglu, Istanbul
Tel: (0212) 249 55 55 *Fax:* (0212) 249 55 56
Founded: 1984
Subjects: Economics, History, Language Arts,
Linguistics, Literature, Literary Criticism, Es-
says, Medicine, Nursing, Dentistry, Philosophy,
Psychology, Psychiatry, Religion - Other, So-
cial Sciences, Sociology
ISBN Prefix(es): 978-975-574; 978-975-7732

The ISIS Press+
Yazmaci Emine Sokak No:4/a, Burhaniye-
Beylerbeyi, 34676 Istanbul
Tel: (0216) 321-3851; (0216) 321-6600
Fax: (0216) 321-8666
E-mail: isis@theisispress.org
Web Site: www.theisispress.org
Key Personnel
Owner: Sinan Kuneralp
Founded: 1983
Subjects: History, Social Sciences, Sociology
ISBN Prefix(es): 978-975-428
Number of titles published annually: 25 Print

Istanbul Bilgi Universitesi Yayinlari
1st Bilgi Universitesi Kustepe Kampusu, Inonu
Cad No 6, 34387 Kustepe, Istanbul
Tel: (0212) 311 61 47 *Fax:* (0212) 216 24 15
(sales & marketing)
E-mail: yayin@bilgiyay.com
Web Site: www.bilgiyay.com

Key Personnel
Publisher: H Pinar Mutlu
Editor-in-Chief: Fahri Aral
Sales: Sinasi Korkutur
Founded: 2000
Subjects: Art, Biography, Memoirs, Communica-
tions, Economics, Education, Finance, Govern-
ment, Political Science, History, Law, Litera-
ture, Literary Criticism, Essays, Mathematics,
Philosophy
ISBN Prefix(es): 978-605-399

Kaknus Yayinlari
Krzkulesi Kultur Merkezi Selman Aga mh, Se-
lami Ali Efendi Cad No 11, 34672 Uskudar,
Istanbul
Tel: (0216) 341 08 65; (0212) 520 49 27 (orders)
Fax: (0216) 334 61 48; (0212) 520 49 28 (or-
ders)
E-mail: info@kaknus.com.tr
Web Site: www.kaknus.com.tr
Founded: 1997
Subjects: Anthropology, Biography, Memoirs, Ed-
ucation, History, Poetry, Psychology, Psychiatry
ISBN Prefix(es): 978-975-256; 978-975-6963;
978-975-94832; 978-975-6698
Total Titles: 300 Print
Orders to: Catalcesme Sokak Defne Han No 27/
3, Cagaloglu, Istanbul

Kapi, *imprint of* Alfa Basim Yayim Dagitim Ltd
Sti

Kaynak Publishing Group
Bulgurlu Mah Bagcilar Cad No 1, Uskudar, Istan-
bul
Tel: (0216) 522 1144 (ext 3481); (0216) 522
1144 (ext 3402)
E-mail: kaynak@kaynakpublishing.com
Web Site: www.kaynakpublishing.com
Subjects: History, Inspirational, Spirituality, Reli-
gion - Islamic, Islamic History & Arts, Islamic
Spirituality & Traditions
ISBN Prefix(es): 978-975-343; 978-975-278; 978-
975-315
Imprints: Blue Dome Press; Daral Nile; Editions
Dunil; Editorial La Fuente; Main Donau Ver-
lag; Noviysvet Izdat; Tughra Books
Foreign Rep(s): Fountain Books (Singapore);
Gazelle Book Services Ltd (Europe); IPG-
Independent Publishers Group (Canada, USA);
Nile Publishing (Middle East)

Kok Yayincilik+
Incesu Cad Nu 10, 06670 Kolej, Ankara
Tel: (0312) 435 04 97; (0533) 647 46 96 (cell)
Fax: (0312) 430 26 22
E-mail: kokbilgi@kokyayincilik.com.tr
Web Site: www.kokyayincilik.com.tr
Founded: 1987
Subjects: Animals, Pets, Child Care & Develop-
ment, Education, Health, Nutrition, House &
Home, Human Relations, Mathematics, Music,
Dance
ISBN Prefix(es): 978-975-499
Imprints: Offset
Branch Office(s)
Perpa Yp Merkezi, B Blok 11 kat Nu
1926, Okmeydany, Istanbul *Tel:* (0212)
222 61 66 *Fax:* (0212) 222 61 66-114
E-mail: kokistanbul@kokyayincilik.com.tr
1412 Sok 14-A, Kahramanlar, Izmir *Tel:* (0232)
483 70 63 *Fax:* (0232) 483 60 82
E-mail: kokizmir@kokyayincilik.com.tr

Komsu Yayinevi
Rasimpasa Mah, Iskele Sk, No 54, Alibey Apart-
ment, floor 1, Apartment 4, 34716 Kadikoy
Istanbul
Tel: (0216) 414 33 31 *Fax:* (0216) 414 33 31
E-mail: editor@yasakmeyve.com
Web Site: www.yasakmeyve.com

Key Personnel
Owner: Ali Enver Ercan
Editorial Dir: Ozge Ercan
Founded: 2002
Subjects: Biography, Memoirs, Poetry
ISBN Prefix(es): 978-605-5497

KRP Yayincilik Matbaacilik Ltd
Turan Gunes Blvd 100/20, 06550 Ankara
Tel: (0312) 213 44 04 *Fax:* (0312) 213 44 04
E-mail: info@krpyayincilik.com
Web Site: krpcocuk.com
Founded: 2007
Subjects: Fiction, Science (General), Metaphysics
ISBN Prefix(es): 978-605-6339

Kubbealti Akademisi Kultur ve Sasat Vakfi
(Academy of Culture & Arts Foundation
Kubbealti)+
Koprulu Medresesi, Peykhane Sokagi, No 3,
34400 Cemberlitas, Istanbul
Tel: (0212) 516 23 56; (0212) 518 92 09
Fax: (0212) 638 02 72
E-mail: info@kubbealti.org.tr
Web Site: www.kubbealti.org.tr
Founded: 1970
Subjects: Architecture & Interior Design, Art,
Biography, Memoirs, Environmental Studies,
History, Literature, Literary Criticism, Essays,
Music, Dance, Religion - Islamic, Culture
ISBN Prefix(es): 978-975-7663; 978-975-6444
Distributor for Istanbul Fetih Cemiyeti's Yayinlari
Bookshop(s): Yeniceriler Cad No 43, 34490 Car-
sikapi, Istanbul

Kultur Sanat Yayincilik, see Yapi Kredi Kultur
Sanat ve Yayincilik AS

L&M Publishing, *imprint of* Timas Yayinlari

Main Donau Verlag, *imprint of* Kaynak
Publishing Group

Marti Yayin Grubu
Maltepe Mahallesi Davutpasa Caddessi, 34010
Istanbul
Tel: (0212) 483 27 37 *Fax:* (0212) 483 27 38
E-mail: info@martiyayinlari.com
Web Site: www.martiyayinlari.com
Founded: 2006
Subjects: Economics, Literature, Literary Criti-
cism, Essays, Self-Help
ISBN Prefix(es): 978-605-348

Mavi Agac Kultur Sanat Yayincilik Tic Ltd Sti
Catalcesme Sk Mericli, Apartment No 52, K3,
Cagaloglu, 34410 Istanbul
Tel: (0212) 000 0000; (0212) 640 0123
Fax: (0212) 514 4512
Web Site: www.maviagac.com
Key Personnel
General Coordinator: Munir Ostun
Editor-in-Chief: Cem Kucuk
Editor: Elif Avci
Founded: 1999
Subjects: Drama, Theater, Fiction, Literature, Lit-
erary Criticism, Essays, Poetry, Sports, Athlet-
ics, Vampires
ISBN Prefix(es): 978-975-996

Mavibulut Yayincilik Tic ve San Ltd
Perpa Ticaret Merkezi B Blok Kat 5 No 477,
34384 Okmeydani, Istanbul
Tel: (0212) 320 21 30 *Fax:* (0212) 320 21 33
E-mail: mavibulut@mavibulut.com.tr
Web Site: www.mavibulut.com.tr
Founded: 1980
ISBN Prefix(es): 978-975-310; 978-975-7549

Metis Yayincilik Ltd (Metis Publishers)+
Ipek Sokak No 5, 34433 Beyoglu, Istanbul
Tel: (0212) 2454696 *Fax:* (0212) 2454519
E-mail: bilgi@metiskitap.com; rights@
metisbooks.com
Web Site: www.metiskitap.com
Founded: 1982
Publisher of psychiatry, literature, politics & phi-
losophy. Also acts as Verso agent in Turkey.
Membership(s): Turkish Publishers Association.
Subjects: Government, Political Science, Liter-
ature, Literary Criticism, Essays, Nonfiction
(General), Philosophy, Poetry, Psychology, Psy-
chiatry, Science Fiction, Fantasy, Social Sci-
ences, Sociology, Western Fiction, Women's
Studies
ISBN Prefix(es): 978-975-342; 978-975-7650
Number of titles published annually: 40 Print
Total Titles: 600 Print

Minik Ada, *imprint of* Erdem Yayinlari

Morpa Kultur Yayinlari
Ankara Cad No 16/1, 34112 Cagaloglu, Istanbul
Tel: (0212) 512 62 09
E-mail: info@morpa.com.tr
Web Site: www.morpa.com.tr
Founded: 1980
Subjects: Health, Nutrition, Language Arts, Lin-
guistics, Mathematics, Music, Dance, Psychol-
ogy, Psychiatry, Science (General), Social Sci-
ences, Sociology, Sports, Athletics, Technology,
Classical Music, Educational Technology, En-
glish Language, E-learning, Life Sciences
ISBN Prefix(es): 978-605-390

Nesil Yayinlari (Nesil Publications)+
Sanayi Cad Bilge Sok No 2, 34196 Yenibosna,
Istanbul
Tel: (0212) 551 32 25 *Fax:* (0212) 551 26 59
Web Site: www.nesilyayinlari.com
Key Personnel
Editor-in-Chief: Ikram Arslan
E-mail: ikramarslan@nesil.com.tr
Founded: 1968
This publisher has indicated that 40% of their
product line is author subsidized.
Subjects: Education, Fiction, Health, Nutrition,
History, Poetry, Self-Help, Travel & Tourism
ISBN Prefix(es): 978-975-6401; 978-975-6503;
978-975-7055; 978-975-8499; 978-975-269;
978-605-183
Number of titles published annually: 50 Print
Total Titles: 2,000 Print
Parent Company: Nesil Yayin Grubu

**Nobel Akademik Yayincilik Egetim
Danismanlik Tic Ltd Sti**
Kultur Mah Mithatpasa Cad No 74B-01/02, Ko-
catepe Camii Yani Kultur Merkezi Ici, 06420
Cankaya, Ankara
Tel: (0312) 418 20 10 *Fax:* (0312) 418 30 20
E-mail: dagitim@nobelyayin.com
Web Site: www.nobelyayin.com
Key Personnel
Editor-in-Chief: Nevzat Argun *E-mail:* nargun@
nobelyayin.com
General Distribution Manager: Volkan Kurt
E-mail: volkankurt@nobelyayin.com
Founded: 1997
Subjects: Agriculture, Architecture & Interior De-
sign, Business, Education, Government, Po-
litical Science, Medicine, Nursing, Dentistry,
Psychology, Psychiatry, Humanities
ISBN Prefix(es): 978-975-591
Total Titles: 2,000 Print

Noviysvet Izdat, *imprint of* Kaynak Publishing
Group

Nuans Kitapcilik San Tic Ltd Sti
Selanik Cad 25/1, 06650 Kizilay, Ankara
Tel: (0312) 419 8096; (0312) 419 8492
Fax: (0312) 418 4512
E-mail: info@nuanskitabevi.com
Web Site: www.nuanskitabevi.com
ISBN Prefix(es): 978-975-7103
Distributor for Ahead Books; Alma Edizioni;
Build & Grow; Compass Publishing; Edizioni
Edilingua; HarperCollins; Marshall Cavendish;
Mundo Espanol
Bookshop(s): Camlik Mah Selcuklu Cad Mini-
point Sitesi No 26/88, 34912 Kurtkoy, Istan-
bul *Tel:* (0216) 450 1708; 858 Sokak Paykoc
Ishani No 9, Kat 2, Daire 207, Konak, Izmir
Tel: (0232) 482 0971

Offset, *imprint of* Kok Yayincilik

Oglak Yayinlari
Zambak Sokak, 21, 34435 Beyoglu, Istanbul
Tel: (0212) 251 71 08-09 *Fax:* (0212) 212 293 65
50
E-mail: oglakkitap@oglak.com; oglak@oglak.
com (sales); info@oglak.com
Key Personnel
Editor-in-Chief: Senay Haznedaroglu
E-mail: senayh@oglak.com
Editor: Nilufer Altinel *E-mail:* nilufer@oglak.com
Sales: Huseyin Yurttas; Kadir Yurttas
Founded: 1992
Subjects: Cookery, Fiction, Poetry, Social Sci-
ences, Sociology, Historical Novels, Turkish
Classics
ISBN Prefix(es): 978-975-329

Oguz Yayinlari
Babiali Cad Seyhan Ishani No 30/7, 34410 Caga-
loglu, Istanbul
Tel: (0212) 5113418 *Fax:* (0212) 5114695
Subjects: Religion - Islamic, Theology
ISBN Prefix(es): 978-975-538

Omega Yayinlari, *imprint of* Say Yayinlari

Otuken Nesriyat
Istiklal Caddesi, Ankara Han, No 65, Kat 3,
34435 Beyoglu, Istanbul
Tel: (0212) 251 0350; (0212) 293 8871
Fax: (0212) 251 0012
E-mail: otuken@otuken.com.tr
Web Site: www.otuken.com.tr
Founded: 1964
Subjects: Fiction, History, Poetry, Social Sciences,
Sociology, Travel & Tourism
ISBN Prefix(es): 978-975-437

Pan Yayincilik+
Barbaros Bulvari, 18/4, Besiktas, 34353 Istanbul
Tel: (0212) 261 80 72; (0212) 227 56 75
Fax: (0212) 227 56 74
E-mail: pankitap@pankitap.com (orders)
Web Site: www.pankitap.com
Key Personnel
Editor: Isik Tabar Gencer
Foreign Rights: Ferruh Gencer
Founded: 1986
Subjects: Fiction, Music, Dance, Science (Gen-
eral)
ISBN Prefix(es): 978-975-7652

Parantez Gazetecilik ve Yayincilik+
Asmaly Mescid Mah Tunel Meydany, Tunel
Gecidi Ishany C Block, D:424 Beyoglu, Is-
tanbul
Tel: (0212) 252 65 16 *Fax:* (0212) 252 65 16
E-mail: parantez@yahoo.com; parantez@
parantez.net
Web Site: www.parantez.net
Key Personnel
International Rights: Metin Zeynioglu
Founded: 1991

Membership(s): Turkish Pen Club; Turkish Publishers Association.
Subjects: Biography, Memoirs, Fiction, Film, Video, Humor, LGBTQ
ISBN Prefix(es): 978-975-7939; 978-975-8441
Distribution Center: Punto Kitap Hizmetleri, Cobancepme Mah Altay Sk No 8, 34196 Yenibosna, Istanbul *Tel:* (0212) 496 1050
E-mail: punto@puntokitap.com

Pearson Egitim Cozumleri Tic Ltd Sti+
Barbaros Bulvari No 149, Dr Orhan Birman Is Merkezi Kat 3, Gayrettepe Besiktas, Istanbul
Tel: (0212) 288 69 41 *Fax:* (0212) 267 18 51
E-mail: pearson.turkey@pearson.com; istanbul@pearson.com
Web Site: www.pearsonelt.com
Founded: 1995
Subjects: English as a Second Language
ISBN Prefix(es): 978-975-7015
Parent Company: Pearson Education
Ultimate Parent Company: Pearson PLC
Branch Office(s)
Istiklal Mah Bakimyurdu Cad No 180, Seyhan, Adana *Tel:* (0322) 432 28 62 *Fax:* (0322) 432 29 24 *E-mail:* adana@pearson.com
Yuzuncuyil Mah Hatir Sok Ardasa Apartment, floor 2, No 27/5 GOP, Ankara *Tel:* (0312) 437 77 80; (0312) 437 77 81 *Fax:* (0312) 437 77 22 *E-mail:* ankara@pearson.com
Nalbantoglu Mah Taskapi Cad, Altinova Is Hani No 9/C Heykel, Bursa *Tel:* (0224) 225 18 23 *Fax:* (0224) 225 04 42 *E-mail:* bursa@pearson.com
Kibris Sehitleri Cad No 48/A-B, Izmir *Tel:* (0232) 463 23 01; (0232) 462 23 03 *Fax:* (0232) 463 23 02 *E-mail:* izmir@pearson.com
Evren Pasa Cad M Dereli Is Merkezi, B Blok No 2 Yenikent, Lefkosa *Tel:* (0392) 223 99 80 *Fax:* (0392) 223 99 94 *E-mail:* guy.elders@pearson.com
Distributor for Langenscheidt

Pegasus Yayinlari
Gumussuyu Mah Osmanli Sok No 11/9, 34437 Taksim-Istanbul
Tel: (0212) 244 23 50 *Fax:* (0212) 244 23 46
E-mail: info@pegasusyayinlari.com
Web Site: www.pegasusyayinlari.com
Founded: 2006
Subjects: Fiction, Romance, Science Fiction, Fantasy, Self-Help
ISBN Prefix(es): 978-605-4263; 978-605-343; 978-605-5943

Redhouse, see SEV Yayincilik Egitim Ticaret AS

Remzi Kitabevi AS+
Akmerkez E3 Blok Kat 14, 34337 Etiler, Istanbul
Tel: (0212) 282 2080 *Fax:* (0212) 282 2090
E-mail: post@remzi.com.tr
Web Site: www.remzi.com.tr
Key Personnel
Mng Dir: Erol Erduran
Dir: Ahmet Erduran
Production Manager: Omer Erduran
Founded: 1927
Subjects: Art, Biography, Memoirs, Education, Fiction, History, Nonfiction (General), Philosophy, Psychology, Psychiatry, Science (General), Social Sciences, Sociology
ISBN Prefix(es): 978-975-14
Subsidiaries: Evrim Matbaacilik Ltd
Branch Office(s)
Akmerkez Is Hani, Nispetiye Cad No 223, 80600 Etiler, Istanbul *Tel:* (0212) 282 2575; (0212) 282 2576 *Fax:* (0212) 282 2577
Kanyon AVM Levent, Istanbul *Tel:* (0212) 353 0500; (0212) 353 0501 *Fax:* (0212) 353 0505
Migros Alisveris Merkezi Istinye, Istanbul *Tel:* (0212) 323 5833 *Fax:* (0212) 323 5835

Armada Alisveris Merkezi Sogutozu, Ankara *Tel:* (0312) 219 1112 *Fax:* (0312) 219 1114
Carrefour Ticaret Merkezi, 80120 Icerenkoy, Istanbul *Tel:* (0216) 448 0373; (0216) 448 0374 *Fax:* (0216) 448 0375
Agora Alisveris Merkezi Balcova, Izmir *Tel:* (0232) 279 1966 *Fax:* (0232) 279 1932
Konak Pier Alisveris Merkezi, Izmir *Tel:* (0232) 489 5325; (0232) 489 5355 *Fax:* (0232) 489 5006
Profilo Alisveris Merkezi, 80470 Mecidiyekoy, Istanbul *Tel:* (0212) 217 1225 *Fax:* (0212) 216 8288
Rumeli Cad No 44, 80220 Nisantasi, Istanbul *Tel:* (0212) 234 5475; (0212) 234 5476 *Fax:* (0212) 232 5934
Bagdat Caddesi No 452, Suadiye, Istanbul *Tel:* (0216) 361 9071 *Fax:* (0216) 416 2065

Republic of Turkey - Ministry of Culture & Tourism+
Ataturk Blvd No 29, 06050 Opera, Ankara
Tel: (0312) 309 08 50 *Fax:* (0312) 312 43 59
E-mail: sosyalmedya@kultur.gov.tr
Web Site: www.kultur.gov.tr
Founded: 1973
Subjects: Archaeology, Art, Drama, Theater, History, Literature, Literary Criticism, Essays
ISBN Prefix(es): 978-975-17
Distributed by Dosimm

Ruh ve Madde Yayinlari (Spirit & Matter Publications)+
Hasnun Galip Sokak Pembe Cikmazi No 4, D6, 80060 Beyoglu, Istanbul
Tel: (0212) 243 18 14 *Fax:* (0212) 252 07 18
Founded: 1994
Subjects: Alternative, Astrology, Occult, Earth Sciences, Nonfiction (General), Parapsychology, Philosophy, Religion - Islamic, Religion - Other, Self-Help
ISBN Prefix(es): 978-975-8007; 978-975-6377
Number of titles published annually: 25 Print
Total Titles: 300 Print
Parent Company: Foundation for Spreading the Knowledge to Unify Humanity (BILYAY)
Distributed by EGE META
Distributor for EGE META

Say Yayinlari
Ankara Caddesi Pamir Han No 22/4, 34110 Sirkeci, Istanbul
Tel: (0212) 512 21 58; (0212) 528 17 54 *Fax:* (0212) 512 50 80
E-mail: satisdestek@saykitap.com
Web Site: www.saykitap.com
Founded: 1978
Subjects: Architecture & Interior Design, Art, Business, Computer Science, Education, Health, Nutrition, History, Literature, Literary Criticism, Essays, Music, Dance, Religion - Other, Self-Help
ISBN Prefix(es): 978-975-468
Imprints: Omega Yayinlari

Seckin Yayincilik Sanayi Ve Ticaret AS (Seckin Publishing Industry & Trading Co Ltd)
Saglik Sokak 21, Sihhiye, 06410 Ankara
Tel: (0312) 435 30 30; (0533) 770 50 99 *Fax:* (0312) 435 24 72
E-mail: seckin@seckin.com.tr
Web Site: www.seckin.com.tr
Founded: 1959
Membership(s): Ankara Chamber of Commerce; Association of Broadcasters; Turkish Publishers Association.
Subjects: Accounting, Computer Science, Criminology, Economics, Engineering (General), Government, Political Science, Language Arts, Linguistics, Law, Management, Marketing, Mathematics, Public Administration
ISBN Prefix(es): 978-975-347; 978-975-02

Number of titles published annually: 280 Print
Total Titles: 1,100 Print
Branch Office(s)
Ankara Adliye Sarayi, K Blok Zemin Kat Sihhiye, Ankara *Tel:* (0312) 309 52 48 *E-mail:* adliyesube@seckin.com.tr
Strazburg Cad 23/B, Sihhiye, Ankara *Tel:* (0312) 230 56 62 *Fax:* (0312) 230 52 62 *E-mail:* ankarasube@seckin.com.tr
Abide-i Hurriyet Caddesi No 193 A, Istanbul *Tel:* (0212) 234 34 77 *Fax:* (0212) 231 24 69 *E-mail:* sislisube@seckin.com.tr
C Blok Zemin Kat No 29 Kartal, Istanbul *Tel:* (0216) 303 11 23 *Fax:* (0216) 303 11 23 *E-mail:* kartalsube@seckin.com.tr

Sel Yayincilik
Piyerloti Caddesi, Saka Ishani No 11, Kat 3, 34122 Cemberlitas, Istanbul
Tel: (0212) 516 96 85 *Fax:* (0212) 516 97 26
E-mail: posta@selyayincilik.com
Web Site: www.selyayincilik.com
Key Personnel
Contact: Bilge Sanci *E-mail:* bilgesanci@selyayincilik.com
Founded: 1990
Provide Turkish readers with both the original & translated works of contemporary writers.
Subjects: History, Literature, Literary Criticism, Essays, Poetry, Women's Studies, Turkish Culture
ISBN Prefix(es): 978-975-570

Selt-Dilset Yayinlari, *imprint of* Zambak Yayinlari

SEV Yayincilik Egitim Ticaret AS (SEV Publishing Education & Trade Inc)+
Nuhkuyusu Cad, No 197 Uskudar Is Merkezi, Kat 3, 34664 Baglarbasi, Uskudar, Istanbul
Tel: (0216) 474 23 41; (0216) 474 23 42; (0216) 474 23 43; (0216) 474 23 44 *Fax:* (0216) 474 23 45
E-mail: info@redhouse.com.tr
Web Site: www.redhouse.com.tr
Founded: 1997
Subjects: Education
ISBN Prefix(es): 978-975-413; 978-975-8176

SEV-YAY, see SEV Yayincilik Egitim Ticaret AS

Sistem Yayincilik
Tarlabasi Blvd, Utarit Sokak No 7, Taksim-Beyoglu, 34427 Istanbul
Tel: (0212) 2938372 *Fax:* (0212) 2936671
Key Personnel
Executive Editor: Erdogan Yenice *E-mail:* erdogan@sistem.com.tr
Editor: Ilyas Burak *E-mail:* ilyas@sistem.com.tr; Zuhal Dogan *E-mail:* dizgi@sistem.com.tr
Public Relations: Yildiz Ekin
Founded: 1991
Subjects: Education, Psychology, Psychiatry, Self-Help, Social Sciences, Sociology
ISBN Prefix(es): 978-975-322; 978-975-7397

Sufi Book, *imprint of* Timas Yayinlari

Sule Yayinlari
Alemdar Mh Alaykosku Cd No 2-4 F 3 Eminonu, 34110 Istanbul
Tel: (0212) 5282357 *Fax:* (0212) 5282589
E-mail: iletisim@suleyayinlari.com
Web Site: www.suleyayinlari.com
Founded: 1990
Subjects: Communications, History, Literature, Literary Criticism, Essays, Poetry, Modern Eastern Literature, Qur'an Studies, Turkish & World Classics
ISBN Prefix(es): 978-975-6446; 978-975-6841; 978-975-7796

Timas Yayinlari (Timas Publishing Group)
Alaykosku Cd No 11, 34410 Cagaloglu, Istanbul
Tel: (0212) 513 84 15; (0212) 511 24 24
  Fax: (0212) 512 40 00
Web Site: www.timaspublishing.com; www.timas.
  com.tr
Key Personnel
Foreign Rights: Nefise Atcakarlar
  E-mail: nefiseatcakarlar@timas.com.tr
Subjects: Art, Biography, Memoirs, Government,
  Political Science, History, Literature, Literary
  Criticism, Essays, Poetry, Psychology, Psychia-
  try, Religion - Islamic
ISBN Prefix(es): 978-975-263; 978-975-362; 978-
  605-114; 978-605-08
Imprints: Antik Classics; Carpe Diem Publishing;
  L&M Publishing; Sufi Book

Toker Yayinlari Ltd Sti+
Cennet Mah Yavuz Selim Cd No 25, Kucukcek-
  mece, Istanbul
Tel: (0212) 601 00 35 *Fax:* (0212) 592 40 38
E-mail: yatoker@yahoo.com
Web Site: www.tokeryayinlari.com
Founded: 1962
Membership(s): Turkish Publishers Association.
Subjects: Ethnicity, History, Literature, Literary
  Criticism, Essays
ISBN Prefix(es): 978-975-445
U.S. Office(s): C E M Toker, PO Box 39652,
  Phoenix, AZ 85069, United States

Tudem
1476/1 Sokak No 10/51, 35220 Alsancak Izmir
Tel: (0232) 463 46 38; (0232) 463 46 39; (0232)
  463 46 40 *Fax:* (0232) 464 18 47
E-mail: tudem@tudem.com; siparis@tudem.com
Web Site: www.tudem.com
ISBN Prefix(es): 978-9944-69
Branch Office(s)
Ankara Cad No 51/83, 34110 Cagaloglu Istan-
  bul *Tel:* (0212) 514 33 70; (0212) 514 33
  71; (0212) 514 33 72 *Fax:* (0212) 514 62 89
  E-mail: istanbul@tudem.com

Tughra Books, *imprint of* Kaynak Publishing
  Group

Turkiye is Bankasi Kultur Yayinlari
Istiklal Caddesi Meselik Sokak No 2 Kat 4, Be-
  yoglu, Istanbul
Tel: (0212) 252 39 91 *Fax:* (0212) 252 39 95
E-mail: info@iskultur.com.tr
Web Site: alisveris.iskulturyayinlari.com.tr
Key Personnel
General Manager: Ahmet Salcan *E-mail:* ahmet.
  salcan@iskultur.com.tr
Sales Manager: Harun Yilmaz *E-mail:* harun.
  yilmaz@iskultur.com.tr
Founded: 1956
Subjects: Art, Fiction, History, Literature, Literary
  Criticism, Essays, Science (General)
ISBN Prefix(es): 978-605-360

Turkuvaz Kitapcilik Yayincilik AS
Barbaros Bulvari No 153, 34349 Balmumcu-
  Besiktas Istanbul
Tel: (0212) 354 30 00 *Fax:* (0212) 288 50 67
E-mail: info@turkuvazkitap.com.tr
Web Site: www.turkuvazkitap.com
Subjects: Biography, Memoirs, Criminology, His-
  tory, Literature, Literary Criticism, Essays,
  Classics, Turkish Literature
ISBN Prefix(es): 978-605-5596

Ufuk Yayinlari, see Yaran Yayincilik Tic Ltd

UMP, *imprint of* Erdem Yayinlari

Varlik Yayinlari AS+
Perpa Ticaret Merkezi, B-Blok K 5 No 484,
  34384 Sisli, Istanbul
Tel: (0212) 221 31 71 *Fax:* (0212) 320 06 46
E-mail: varlik@varlik.com.tr
Web Site: www.varlik.com.tr
Key Personnel
Founder: Yasar Nabi Nayir
Mng Editor: Ms Filiz Nayir Deniztekin
  Tel: (0532) 791 34 24 *E-mail:* fnayir54@gmail.
  com
Representative: Mr Osman Cetin Deniztekin
  Tel: (0532) 700 01 72 *E-mail:* odeniztekin@
  gmail.com
Founded: 1933
Membership(s): Turkish Publishers Association.
Subjects: Fiction, Nonfiction (General), Philoso-
  phy, Poetry, Science (General), Self-Help, So-
  cial Sciences, Sociology, Women's Studies
ISBN Prefix(es): 978-975-434
Number of titles published annually: 30 Print; 10
  E-Book
Total Titles: 250 Print; 40 E-Book
Imprints: Cep Kitaplari
Foreign Rights: Akcali Copyright Agency (world-
  wide)

Yapi-Endustri Merkezi (YEM) (Building
  Information Center)+
Fulya Mah Yesilcimen, Sok No 12/430 (Polat
  Kulesi Yani), 34394 Fulya, Istanbul
Tel: (0212) 266 70 70 *Fax:* (0212) 266 70 10
E-mail: yem@yem.net
Web Site: www.yem.net
Founded: 1968
Also acts as bookshop & book importer.
Membership(s): Association of Trade Press Pub-
  lishers; Building Materials & Manufactures
  Association (IMSAD); Fair Turkey Producer's
  Association (TFYD); Foreign Economic Rela-
  tions Board (DEIK); The Global Association of
  the Exhibition Industry (UFI); INDER; Interna-
  tional Confederation of Architectural Museums
  (ICAM); International Union of Construction
  (UICB); Turkey Construction Technology Plat-
  form (TCTP); Turkish Green Building Council
  (GBC); Turkish Publishers Association.
Subjects: Architecture & Interior Design, Art,
  Civil Engineering, Photography, Cultural Her-
  itage, Industrial Design, Urban Development
ISBN Prefix(es): 978-975-7438; 978-975-8599
Distributor for Melissa (Greece)

Yapi Kredi Kultur Sanat ve Yayincilik AS
  (Yapi Kredi Cultural Activities, Arts &
  Publishing Inc)
Istiklal Cad No 142, 34433 Beyoglu, Istanbul
Tel: (0212) 252 47 00 *Fax:* (0212) 293 07 23
E-mail: ykkultur@ykykultur.com.tr; hulya.kaya@
  ykykultur.com.tr (sales)
Web Site: www.ykykultur.com.tr
Founded: 1944
Subjects: Art, Geography, Geology, Literature,
  Literary Criticism, Essays, Poetry
ISBN Prefix(es): 978-975-08
Bookshop(s): Istiklal Cad No 16, 34433 Beyoglu,
  Istanbul *Fax:* (0212) 251 71 95; Tavus Sokak
  No 24/A, 34710 Kadikoy, Istanbul *Tel:* (0216)
  337 72 04; Ataturk Bulvari No 65/B, Sahinbey,
  Gaziantep *Tel:* (0342) 371 71 46; Gazi Bulvari
  No 3, Egehan-Pasaport, Izmir *Tel:* (0232) 441
  82 90; Ataturk Bulvari No 93, 06422 Kizilay
  Tel: (0312) 435 85 94; Kuvaimilliye Caddesi
  No 8/A, Akdeniz, Mersin *Tel:* (0324) 232 42
  75

Yaran Yayincilik Tic Ltd
Rasimpasa Mh Rihtim Cd, Derya Is Merkezi No
  28/39-48, 34710 Kadikoy, Istanbul
Tel: (0216) 449 49 09 *Fax:* (0216) 449 49 11
Founded: 2002

Subjects: Government, Political Science, History,
  Religion - Other, Science (General)
ISBN Prefix(es): 978-605-5314; 978-605-6240

Literatur Yayincilik Ltd
Istiklal Cad Emgen Han No 47/4, 34433 Beyoglu,
  Istanbul
Tel: (0212) 292 41 20
E-mail: literatur@literatur.com.tr
Web Site: www.literatur.com.tr
Key Personnel
Editor-in-Chief: Kenan Kocaturk
Founded: 1988
Subjects: Architecture & Interior Design, Art,
  Business, Cookery, Economics, Engineering
  (General), Science (General), Social Sciences,
  Sociology, Technology, Transportation, Culture
ISBN Prefix(es): 978-975-8431; 978-975-04

Domingo Yayinevi
Sahkulu Mah Buyuk Hendek Cad Brot Apartment
  No 4/10 Beyoglu, 34421 Istanbul
Tel: (0212) 2450839 *Fax:* (0212) 2455474
E-mail: domingo@domingo.com.tr
Web Site: www.domingo.com.tr
Founded: 2007
Subjects: Architecture & Interior Design, History,
  Science (General), Self-Help
ISBN Prefix(es): 978-605-4729; 978-9944-0837

Kabalci Yayinevi Dagitim Pazarlama Ltd Sti
Gulbahar Mah Cemal Sahir Sok Celic Is, Merkezi
  D Blok No 16, Mecidiyekoy, Istanbul
Tel: (0212) 347 54 51 *Fax:* (0212) 347 54 64
E-mail: yayinevi@kabalci.com.tr
Web Site: www.kabalci.com.tr/kabalci-yayinevi
Key Personnel
Owner: Sabri Kabalci
Dir: Mustafa Kuepuesodlu
Founded: 1984
Membership(s): Turkish Publishers Association.
Subjects: Anthropology, Archaeology, Art,
  Drama, Theater, Fiction, History, Literature,
  Literary Criticism, Essays, Nonfiction (Gen-
  eral), Philosophy, Poetry, Science (General),
  Social Sciences, Sociology, Contemporary
  French Thought
ISBN Prefix(es): 978-975-7942; 978-975-997;
  978-975-8240
Bookshop(s): Ortabahce Cad No 22-24, Besiktas,
  Istanbul *Tel:* (0212) 327 33 22 *Fax:* (0212) 261
  82 54 *E-mail:* info@kabalci.com.tr

Alev Yayinlari+
Alemdar Mah Divanyolu Caddesi, Ercelik Is Hani
  No 54/102, 34110 Eminonu, Istanbul
Tel: (0212) 519 56 35
Founded: 1989
Specialize in Alevite-Islamic culture & philoso-
  phy.
Subjects: Ethnicity, Government, Political Sci-
  ence, Literature, Literary Criticism, Essays,
  Philosophy
ISBN Prefix(es): 978-975-335
Parent Company: Genel Ajans B D O Ltd sti
Distributed by Baris; Papiruea; Say; Yoen
Distributor for CAN; Pencere
Book Club(s): Cumhuriyet Book Club

YEM, see Yapi-Endustri Merkezi (YEM)

**Yetkin Basim Yayim ve Dagitim San ve Tic
  AS+**
Strasburg Cad No 31/A, 06430 Sihhiye, Ankara
Tel: (0312) 232 03 43; (0312) 231 42 34; (0312)
  231 42 35 *Fax:* (0312) 229 87 85
E-mail: yetkin@yetkin.com.tr
Web Site: www.yetkin.com.tr
Key Personnel
Chairman: Yusuf Ziya Gulkok
Mng Dir: Muharrem Baser; Ahmet Gulkok

Founded: 1984
Subjects: Accounting, Computer Science, Law,
Management
ISBN Prefix(es): 978-975-464
Divisions: Kazimkarahekir Cd (Printing)
Bookshop(s): Gulkok Bookstore, Kocabeyoglu Pst
74, Kizilay, Ankara

Yuce Yayim+
Nato Caddesi No 23, Kat 3, Seyrantepe, 34418
Istanbul
Mailing Address: PK 17 Levent, 34330 Istanbul
Tel: (0212) 279 10 26 *Fax:* (0212) 279 18 64
E-mail: bilgi@yuceyayim.com.tr
Web Site: www.yuceyayim.com.tr
Key Personnel
Editor: Metin Erdogan *E-mail:* metin.erdogan@
publika.com.tr
Founded: 1982
Subjects: Computer Science, Electronics, Electri-
cal Engineering, Medicine, Nursing, Dentistry
ISBN Prefix(es): 978-975-411
Subsidiaries: A F M Yayincilik-Tanitim
Warehouse: Dizdariye Cesme Sok 6 Emre Han,
Kat: 1, 34400 Sultanahmet, Istanbul

Zafer Basin Yayin
Mahmutbey Mah Devekaldirimi Cad, Gelincik
Sok No 6, 34217 Bagcilar, Istanbul
Tel: (0212) 446 21 00 *Fax:* (0212) 446 01 39
E-mail: zafer@zafer.com
Web Site: www.zafer.com
Key Personnel
Chief Editor: Ergun Ur *E-mail:* ergun@zafer.com
Publishing Editor: Ozkan Oze *E-mail:* ozkan@
zafer.com
Sales & Marketing Manager: Ibrahim Halil Temel
Tel: (0532) 495 73 49 *E-mail:* ibrahim@zafer.
com; Hizir Ali Velioglu *Tel:* (0533) 648 00 21
E-mail: hizir@zafer.com
Subjects: History, Literature, Literary Criticism,
Essays, Current Affairs
ISBN Prefix(es): 978-975-7762

Zambak Yayinlari
Mahmutbey Mah Soguksu, Cad Teker Is Merkezi
No 31, 34217 Bagcilar, Istanbul
Tel: (0212) 604 21 00 *Fax:* (0212) 445 85 40
Founded: 1998
Subjects: Biological Sciences, Chemistry, Chemi-
cal Engineering, Computer Science, Mathemat-
ics, Physics
ISBN Prefix(es): 978-605-112; 978-975-266
Imprints: Cosku Yayinlari; Deger Yayinlari; Selt-
Dilset Yayinlari

Uganda

General Information

Capital: Kampala
Language: English is official language
Religion: Predominantly Christian (about 60%)
and some Muslim
Population: 19.4 million
Bank Hours: 0830-1400 Monday-Friday
Shop Hours: 0830-1230, 1400-1630 or longer;
0800-1230 Saturday
Currency: 100 cents = 1 new Uganda shilling
Export/Import Information: No tariff on books
or advertising matter but subject to sales tax.
Import license and exchange controls (granted
automatically with import licenses).

Centre for Basic Research
Affiliate of Network of Ugandan Researchers &
Research Users (NURRU)

Plot 15 Baskerville Ave, Kololo, Kampala
Mailing Address: PO Box 9863, Kampala
Tel: (0414) 342987 *Fax:* (0414) 235413
E-mail: cbr@cbr.ug; library@cbr.ug
Key Personnel
Executive Dir: Josephine Ahikire, PhD
Founded: 1988
New publications covering topics on civil soci-
ety, human rights, foreign investment, taxation
federalism in Uganda, trade unions & gender.
Formed a partnership with ActionAid to un-
dertake critical case studies on the relevance,
access, quality & equity dimensions of univer-
sal primary education (UPE) in Uganda.
Membership(s): Council for the Develop-
ment of Social Science Research in Africa
(CODESRIA).
Subjects: Agriculture, Environmental Studies,
Ethnicity, Geography, Geology, Government,
Political Science, History, Labor, Industrial
Relations, Law, Social Sciences, Sociology,
Women's Studies, Humanities
ISBN Prefix(es): 978-9970-877; 978-9970-516
Total Titles: 121 Print

Fountain, *imprint of* Fountain Publishers Ltd

Fountain Publishers Ltd+
Fountain House, 55 Nkrumah Rd, Kampala
Mailing Address: PO Box 488, Kampala
Tel: (0414) 259163; (0414) 251112; (0414)
312 263041; (0414) 312 263042 *Fax:* (0414)
251160
E-mail: publishing@fountainpublishers.co.ug;
sales@fountainpublishers.co.ug
Web Site: www.fountainpublishers.net
Key Personnel
Group Chief Accountant: Moses Mugasa
Founded: 1988
Membership(s): African Publishers Network (AP-
NET); Uganda Publishers & Booksellers Asso-
ciation (UPABA).
Subjects: Agriculture, Anthropology, Biography,
Memoirs, Career Development, Communica-
tions, Cookery, Economics, Education, Fiction,
Government, Political Science, Health, Nutri-
tion, History, Humor, Language Arts, Linguis-
tics, Law, Literature, Literary Criticism, Essays,
Mathematics, Nonfiction (General), Physical
Sciences, Poetry, Psychology, Psychiatry, Re-
ligion - Other, Science (General), Social Sci-
ences, Sociology, Sports, Athletics, Travel &
Tourism, Women's Studies
ISBN Prefix(es): 978-9970-02; 978-9970-25
Number of titles published annually: 40 Print
Total Titles: 500 Print
Imprints: Fountain
Distributed by African Books Collective (ABC)
(Australia, Europe, UK & USA); James Currey
Ltd (UK)
Distributor for James Currey Ltd (UK); Food
Agricultural Organization (FAO) (Italy);
Christopher Hurst (UK); Lion Publishers PLC
(UK); Oxfam GB (UK); Princeton University
Press; Scholastic Inc (USA); Zed Books Ltd
(UK)
Foreign Rep(s): The African Books Collective
(ABC) (worldwide exc North America); Michi-
gan State University Press (Canada, USA)
Foreign Rights: The African Books Collective
(ABC)
Bookshop(s): University Bookshop Makerere,
Contact: Catherine Tugaineyo *Tel:* (0414)
543442

Ukraine

General Information

Capital: Kiev
Language: Ukrainian
Religion: Predominantly Christian (mostly
Ukrainian Orthodox)
Population: 52 million
Bank Hours: Generally open for short hours be-
tween 0930-1230 Monday-Friday
Shop Hours: Generally 0900-1800 Monday-
Friday; often open weekends
Currency: 100 kopeks = 1 rubl
Export/Import Information: According to
Ukrainian quotas and customs duties, compa-
nies engaged in trade should register with the
Ukraine Ministry of Foreign Economic Re-
lations. 28% VAT on books. Licenses for ex-
port and import are also required for trade with
Russia.
Copyright: UCC (see Copyright Conventions, pg
viii)

A-BA-BA-HA-LA-MA-HA Publishers
1/2 Baseyna St, Kiev 01004
Tel: (044) 234 11 31 *Fax:* (044) 235 01 05
Web Site: ababahalamaha.com.ua
Key Personnel
Founder: Ivan Malkovych *E-mail:* ivanababa@i.ua
ISBN Prefix(es): 978-617-585

Anetta Publishers+
12 ap, 32-B, Gogolivska str, Kiev 01054
Tel: (066) 988 40 85 (cell)
E-mail: anetta@anetta-publishers.com
Web Site: anetta-publishers.com
Key Personnel
Dir: Anetta Antonenko
Founded: 2013 (1991 as Calvaria)
Specialize in contemporary Ukranian literature.
Subjects: Government, Political Science, Liter-
ature, Literary Criticism, Essays, Philosophy,
Social Sciences, Sociology
ISBN Prefix(es): 978-966-7092; 978-966-663
Number of titles published annually: 60 Print; 5
CD-ROM; 30 Online; 60 E-Book; 5 Audio
Total Titles: 300 Print; 20 CD-ROM; 100 Online;
100 E-Book; 20 Audio

ASK LLC+
3, Nesterova Str, Kiev 03057
Tel: (044) 456-84-40; (044) 455-58-94 *Fax:* (044)
456-84-40; (044) 455-58-94
Key Personnel
General Dir: Ihor Sologub
Editor-in-Chief: Anatoliy Moskalyuk
Sales: Ihor Ternov
Founded: 1991
Subjects: Accounting, Astrology, Occult, Biblical
Studies, Business, Career Development, Child
Care & Development, Computer Science, Com-
puters, Cookery, Economics, English as a Sec-
ond Language, Fiction, Gardening, Plants, Law,
Marketing, Nonfiction (General), Parapsychol-
ogy, Science Fiction, Fantasy, Social Sciences,
Sociology, Western Fiction
ISBN Prefix(es): 978-966-539
Number of titles published annually: 230 Print
Total Titles: 750 Print

BHV Publishing Group
21, Poliova St, Off 221, Kiev 03056
Tel: (063) 593-74-27; (063) 237-08-05 (cell)
E-mail: market@osvita.info
Web Site: kiev.bhv-osvita.com
Key Personnel
Chief Executive Officer: Alexander Polyakov
Computer & business literature, e-learning & e-
publishing.

Subjects: Art, Astronomy, Biological Sciences, Computer Science, English as a Second Language, Geography, Geology, Science (General)
ISBN Prefix(es): 978-966-552

Dnipro
42 Volodymyrska Str, Kiev 01034
Tel: (044) 234-31-82 *Fax:* (044) 234-92-40
Key Personnel
Dir: Volodymyr Voytovych
Founded: 1919
Subjects: Fiction, Literature, Literary Criticism, Essays, Folklore, Modern Ukranian & Foreign Authors, World Classics
ISBN Prefix(es): 978-5-308; 978-966-578

Factor Publishing House
ul Sumskaia 106-a, Kharkiv 61002
Tel: (057) 719-41-09; (057) 717-52-71 (sales)
   Fax: (057) 719-41-09
E-mail: office@factor.ua; pr@factor.ua
Web Site: www.factor.ua
Key Personnel
President: Sergey Potitychiy
Founded: 1991
Subjects: Accounting, Business, Law
ISBN Prefix(es): 978-966-180; 978-617-690
Number of titles published annually: 185 Print
Parent Company: Factor Group of Companies

Family Leisure Club
Gagarina Ave 20-A, Kharkiv 61140
Mailing Address: PO Box 84, Kharkiv 61001
Tel: (057) 783 8888 *Toll Free Tel:* 0800 30 10 90
E-mail: publish@bookclub.ua (manuscripts)
Web Site: www.ksd.ua
Founded: 2000
Subjects: Business, Cookery, History, Literature, Literary Criticism, Essays, Mysteries, Suspense, Psychology, Psychiatry, Self-Help
ISBN Prefix(es): 978-5-9910; 978-617-12

Fountain of Fairy Tales+
Yaroslaviv Val 13/2-B, Kiev 01054
Tel: (044) 33 111 33
E-mail: info@fontan-book.com; rights@fontan-book.com
Web Site: www.fontan-book.com
Key Personnel
Foreign Rights: Oleg Rybalka
Founded: 2014
Subjects: Fiction, Poetry, Science Fiction, Fantasy
ISBN Prefix(es): 978-617-7262; 978-966-97422
Number of titles published annually: 30 Print
Foreign Rep(s): Roman Rybalka (Poland)

Institute of Advanced Technologies Kiev
Popudrenka Str 54, Room 203, Kiev 02660
Tel: (044) 292-20-27
E-mail: iat@antex.kiev.ua
Web Site: www.iat.kiev.ua
Founded: 1996
Membership(s): International Cartographic Association.
ISBN Prefix(es): 978-966-455

Kamenyar
3 Pidvalna str, Lviv 79000
Tel: (0322) 35-59-49 *Fax:* (0322) 35-59-49
E-mail: vyd@kamenyar.com.ua
Web Site: www.kamenyar.com.ua
Brochures, "Dzvin" magazine, wholesale of printed materials.
Subjects: Fiction, History, Poetry
ISBN Prefix(es): 978-5-7745; 978-966-7255; 978-966-607

Lybid+
32, Pushkinska Str, Kiev 01004
Tel: (044) 278 58 04 (sales); (044) 279 11 71
   Fax: (044) 279 11 71

E-mail: info@lybid.org.ua; lybid.zbut@gmail.com (sales)
Web Site: www.lybid.org.ua
Key Personnel
Dir: Elene A Boyko
Deputy Dir & Marketing/Sales: Mary Kurhak
Heritage of Ukranian people, national-cultural rebirth of independent Ukraine. Famous series: *Monuments of Historical Thought of Ukraine*; *Literary Monuments of Ukraine*.
Subjects: Business, Chemistry, Chemical Engineering, Economics, Education, Geography, Geology, Government, Political Science, History, Language Arts, Linguistics, Law, Literature, Literary Criticism, Essays, Mathematics, Philosophy, Physics, Psychology, Psychiatry, Science (General)
ISBN Prefix(es): 978-966-06

Mystetstvo Publishers+
11, Zolotovoritska St, Kiev 01034
Tel: (044) 235-53-92; (044) 234-91-01; (044) 234-63-30; (044) 758-83-93 *Fax:* (044) 279-05-64
E-mail: mystetstvo@ukr.net
Key Personnel
Dir: Nina D Prybega
Editor-in-Chief: Alla Vakulenko *Tel:* (044) 234-32-72
Sales: Kateryna Sprogis *Tel:* (044) 234-91-01
Founded: 1932
Subjects: Art, Drama, Theater, Ethnicity, Film, Video, History, Literature, Literary Criticism, Essays, Travel & Tourism
ISBN Prefix(es): 978-5-7715; 978-966-577

Naukova Dumka Publishers
Division of National Academy of Sciences of Ukraine
Ul Tereshchenkivska 3, Kiev 01601
Tel: (044) 235-41-70; (044) 235-42-78 (orders); (044) 235-53-09 *Fax:* (044) 235-41-70
E-mail: info@ndumka.kiev.ua
Web Site: www.ndumka.kiev.ua
Key Personnel
Dir General: Igor Alekseenko Rostislavovich *Tel:* (044) 234-40-68
Production Dir: Nellie A Chukhnov *Tel:* (044) 234-61-16
Founded: 1922
Subjects: Agriculture, Biological Sciences, Chemistry, Chemical Engineering, Computer Science, Earth Sciences, Economics, Environmental Studies, Geography, Geology, Health, Nutrition, History, Language Arts, Linguistics, Law, Literature, Literary Criticism, Essays, Mathematics, Mechanical Engineering, Medicine, Nursing, Dentistry, Natural History, Philosophy, Photography, Physical Sciences, Psychology, Psychiatry
ISBN Prefix(es): 978-5-12; 978-966-00
Number of titles published annually: 60 Print
Total Titles: 12 Print
Distributed by ASK; Oberegi Publishers; Osnova

Osnovy, see Solomii Pavlychko Osnovy

Osvita (Education)
5 George Kotsyubinskogo Str, Kiev 04053
Tel: (044) 456-08-35 *Fax:* (044) 456-08-37
E-mail: osvitapublish_ok@ukr.net
Web Site: www.osvitapublish.gov.ua
Founded: 1920
Membership(s): Pan Educational Publishers Club (PEP-Club).
Subjects: Education, Foreign Countries, Literature, Literary Criticism, Essays, Mathematics, Children's Literature, English, German, Russian, Ukrainian
ISBN Prefix(es): 978-966-04
Number of titles published annually: 108 Print

Rodovid Press
17 Khreschatyk St, r 45, Kiev 01001
Tel: (044) 279 46 12
E-mail: rodovid2@gmail.com
Web Site: www.rodovid.net
Key Personnel
Owner, Dir & Editor-in-Chief: Lidia Lykhach
   E-mail: lidia.lykhach@rodovid.net
Owner & Art Dir: Iryna Pasichnyk *E-mail:* iryna.pasichnyk@rodovid.net
Distribution Manager: Olena Kukhta
   E-mail: olena.kukhta@rodovid.net
Subjects: Art, Fiction, Ethnography, Folk Art, Sculpture
ISBN Prefix(es): 978-966-7845; 978-966-95114

Solomii Pavlychko Osnovy+
7 St George St, 3rd floor, Kiev 01030
Tel: (044) 331 02 49
E-mail: osnovypublishing@gmail.com
Web Site: osnovypublishing.com
Founded: 1992
Subjects: Art, Business, Economics, Fiction, Finance, Government, Political Science, History, Language Arts, Linguistics, Law, Literature, Literary Criticism, Essays, Management, Philosophy, Photography, Poetry, Public Administration, Social Sciences, Sociology, Women's Studies
ISBN Prefix(es): 978-966-500
Total Titles: 300 Print

SSPE Kartografiya, see State Scientific & Production Enterprise "Kartografiya"

Vydavnytstvo Starogo Leva (Old Lion Publishing House)
Lemkivska, 15a, Lviv 79008
Tel: (032) 240 47 98 *Fax:* (032) 240 47 98
E-mail: zbut@starlev.com.ua; lev@starlev.com.ua
Web Site: www.starylev.com.ua
Key Personnel
Foreign Rights: Ivan Fedechko *Tel:* (097) 696 07 03 *E-mail:* ivan.fedechko@starlev.com.ua
Founded: 2001
Subjects: Cookery, Education, Fiction, Poetry
ISBN Prefix(es): 978-617-679

State Scientific & Production Enterprise "Kartografiya"+
54 Popudrenka Str, Kiev 02094
Tel: (044) 292-4033; (044) 292-3124 (sales)
E-mail: admin@ukrmap.com.ua; zbut@ukrmap.com.ua (sales)
Web Site: www.ukrmap.com.ua
Founded: 1944
Development, production & realization of cartographic production.
Subjects: Education, Geography, Geology, Travel & Tourism, Cartography
ISBN Prefix(es): 978-966-631; 978-966-7085
Number of titles published annually: 400 Print; 10 CD-ROM
Parent Company: State Service of Geodesy, Cartography & Cadastre of Ukraine
Ultimate Parent Company: Ministry of Environment & Natural Resources of Ukraine, 35 Uritskogo, Kiev
Distributor for Freytag (Austria); GiziMap (Hungary); Hallwag (Switzerland); Ravenstein (Germany)

Veselka Publishers+
63, Melnikova str, Kiev 04655
Tel: (044) 483-95-01; (044) 483-13-11; (044) 483-92-65 *Fax:* (044) 483-33-59
Key Personnel
Dir: Yarema Goyan
Editor-in-Chief: Iryna Boyko *Tel:* (044) 483-92-35
Sales: Hanna Burkovska *Tel:* (044) 483-33-83

Founded: 1934
Subjects: Fiction, Literature, Literary Criticism,
Essays
ISBN Prefix(es): 978-5-301; 978-966-01
Bookshop(s): Toronto, ON, Canada; Prague,
Czech Republic; Frankfurt am Main, Germany;
Munich, Germany; Chicago, IL, United States

Publishing House Vesna
Ave Gargarina 20, Off 1406, Kharkov 61001
Tel: (057) 260 23 89 *Fax:* (057) 260 23 89
Subjects: Education, Fiction, Nonfiction (General)

Vivat Publishing Ltd
Gomonenko St 10, Kharkov 61037
Tel: (057) 714-91-73
E-mail: ishop@vivat.factor.ua
Web Site: www.vivat-book.com.ua
Key Personnel
Editorial: Nadezhda Varakina *E-mail:* n.
varakina@vivat.factor.ua
Founded: 2013
Subjects: Cookery, Fiction, Government, Polit-
ical Science, Journalism, Literature, Literary
Criticism, Essays, Nonfiction (General), Poetry,
Psychology, Psychiatry, Humanities
ISBN Prefix(es): 978-617-690
Parent Company: Factor Group of Companies

United Arab Emirates

General Information

Capital: Abu Dhabi
Language: Arabic and English
Religion: Islamic
Population: 2.23 million
Bank Hours: 0800-1200 Saturday-Thursday (1100
Thursday in Abu Dhabi)
Shop Hours: Abu Dhabi: Summer: 0800-1300,
1600-dusk Saturday-Thursday; Winter: 0800-
1300, 1530-1900 Saturday-Thursday. Northern
Emirates: Summer: 0900-1300, 1630-2000 or
2100 Saturday-Thursday: Winter: 0900-1300,
1600-2000 or 2100 Saturday-Thursday
Currency: 100 fils = 1 UAE dirham
Export/Import Information: No tariff on books or
advertising matter, except duty on imports in
Dubai and ad valorem rates in Ras al Khaimah
anf Sharjah. No import licenses requires except
for obscene publications in Dubai.

Arabian Heritage Books, *imprint of* Motivate
Publishing

**The Emirates Center for Strategic Studies &
Research**
PO Box 4567, Abu Dhabi
Tel: (02) 4044541 *Fax:* (02) 4044542
E-mail: pubdis@ecssr.ac.ae; books@ecssr.ae
Web Site: www.ecssr.com
Key Personnel
President: Mohammed Bin Zayed Al Nahyan
Dir General: Jamal Sanad Al-Suwaidi
Founded: 1994
Subjects: Communications, Economics, Environ-
mental Studies
ISBN Prefix(es): 978-0-86372

Government of Sharjah Department of Culture
Publications Dept, PO Box 5119, Sharjah
Tel: (06) 5123333; (06) 5671116; (06) 5673139
Fax: (06) 5123303; (06) 5662126; (06)
5660535
E-mail: sdci@sdci.gov.ae
Web Site: www.sdci.gov.ae/english/index1.html

Key Personnel
Head: Dr Sultan Bin Mohammed Al Qasimi
Founded: 1982
Subjects: Poetry, Regional Interests

Gulf Business Books, *imprint of* Motivate
Publishing

Kalimat
PO Box 21969, 21969 Sharjah
Tel: (06) 5566696 *Fax:* (06) 5566691
E-mail: info@kalimat.ae
Web Site: www.kalimat.ae
ISBN Prefix(es): 978-9948-03

Motivate Publishing+
Media One Tower, 34th floor, Dubai Media City
Mailing Address: PO Box 2331, Dubai
Tel: (04) 427 3000 *Fax:* (04) 428 2274
E-mail: motivate@motivate.ae
Web Site: www.motivatepublishing.com
Key Personnel
Mng Partner & Group Editor: Ian Fairservice
E-mail: executive@motivate.ae
Editorial Dir: Gina Johnson *E-mail:* gina@
motivate.ae
General Manager, Administration: Urvashi Kadam
General Manager, Books: John Deykin
General Manager, Finance: Gopi Krishnan
E-mail: gopik@motivate.ae
General Manager, Group Sales: Anthony Milne
E-mail: anthony@motivate.ae
General Manager, Information Technology: Grish
Chouhan *E-mail:* grish@motivate.ae
General Manager, Motivate Val Morgan: Avinash
Udeshi *E-mail:* avinash@motivate.ae
Founded: 1979
Subjects: Biography, Memoirs, Business, Cook-
ery, Foreign Countries, History, Natural His-
tory, Travel & Tourism
ISBN Prefix(es): 978-1-873544; 978-1-86063
Imprints: Arabian Heritage Books; Gulf Business
Books
Subsidiaries: Stewart's Court
Branch Office(s)
Media City Motivate Publishing FZ LLC, 5th
floor, Office 508, Bldg No 8, Dubai Media City
Tel: (04) 390 3550 *Fax:* (04) 390 4845
PO Box 43072, Abu Dhabi *Tel:* (02) 677 2005
Fax: (02) 677 0124
Motivate Publishing Ltd, Acre House 11/15
William Rd, London NWI 3ER, United King-
dom
Orders to: Book Representation & Distribution
Ltd, 244A London Rd, Hadleigh, Essex S57
2DE, United Kingdom *Tel:* (020) 7552912
Fax: (020) 7556095

Zam Zam Publishing
Shop 14, Murjanet Al Khaleej Bldg, Abu Baker
Siddique Rd, Deira, Dubai
Mailing Address: PO Box 182161, Dubai
Tel: (04) 2699 604 *Fax:* (04) 2699 731
E-mail: info@zamzampublishing.com;
zamzampublishing@yahoo.com
Web Site: www.zamzampublishing.com
Founded: 2004
Subjects: Accounting, Business, Management
Distributor for BPP Learning Media (UK)

United Kingdom

General Information

Capital: London
Language: English; Welsh in most of Wales
(where it is used alongside English for official
purposes). About 80,000 speak Scots Gaelic
(in Highlands and Islands of Scotland). Irish is
used in parts of Northern Ireland
Religion: Protestant (The Church of England) officially, Roman Catholic, Methodist, United
Reformed and Baptist have significant numbers
of adherents
Population: 57.8 million
Bank Hours: 0900-1730 Monday-Friday
Shop Hours: 0900-1730 Monday-Saturday
Currency: 100 pence = 1 pound sterling
Export/Import Information: No tariffs on books;
advertising matter dutiable over a certain
weight. No import licenses required; nominal
exchange controls. Advertising in the UK is
regulated by statutes and voluntary codes; for
information contact The Advertising Standards
Authority Ltd, Mid City Place, 71 High Hol-
born, London WC1V 6QT
Copyright: UCC, Berne, Florence (see Copyright
Conventions, pg viii)

AA Publishing+
Fanum House UG, Basing View, Basingstoke,
Hants RG21 4EA
Tel: (01256) 495969
E-mail: aapublish@theaa.com
Web Site: www.theaa.com
Key Personnel
Senior Public Relations Officer: Katie Stephens
Founded: 1908
Subjects: Outdoor Recreation, Travel & Tourism,
Car Accessories, Cycling, Driving, Leisure,
Walking
ISBN Prefix(es): 978-0-86145; 978-0-7495; 978-
0-901088; 978-1-872163
Total Titles: 530 Print
Parent Company: The Automobile Association
Orders to: Littlehampton Book Services Ltd,
Faraday Close, Durrington, Worthing, West
Sussex BN13 3RB *Tel:* (01903) 828500;
(01903) 828501 (customer service) *Web
Site:* lbsltd.wp.hachette.co.uk

AAAI Press, *imprint of* The MIT Press

Aardvark Bureau, *imprint of* Gallic Books

Abacus, *imprint of* Little, Brown Book Group

Abbotsford Publishing+
20 Havefield Ave, Lichfield, Staffs WS14 9XS
Tel: (01543) 258903
Web Site: www.abbotsfordpublishing.com
Key Personnel
Owner: Kathy Simmons *E-mail:* kathysimmons@
outlook.com
Founded: 1992
Subjects: History, Poetry, Regional Interests,
Travel & Tourism, Mind/Body/Spirit, Minia-
ture Railways
ISBN Prefix(es): 978-1-899596; 978-0-9503563
Number of titles published annually: 3 Print; 3
Online
Total Titles: 12 Print; 12 Online

Aber Education, *imprint of* GLMP Ltd

Aber Publishing, *imprint of* GLMP Ltd

Ablex, *imprint of* Intellect Ltd

Absolute Press, *imprint of* Bloomsbury Publishing Plc

Absolute Press+
Imprint of Bloomsbury Publishing PLC
Scarborough House, 29 James St W, Bath, Avon BA1 2BT
Tel: (01225) 316 013 *Fax:* (01225) 445 836
E-mail: office@absolutepress.co.uk; info@ absolutepress.co.uk
Web Site: www.absolutepress.co.uk
Key Personnel
Publisher: Jon Croft
Founded: 1979
Also acts as agent in UK & Europe for Smith & Kraus Publishers Inc & Streetwise Maps.
Subjects: Biography, Memoirs, Cookery, LGBTQ, Travel & Tourism, Wine & Spirits
ISBN Prefix(es): 978-0-948230; 978-0-9506785; 978-1-899791; 978-1-904573; 978-1-906650
Foreign Rep(s): Answers & Insights Inc (North America); Compass DSA Ltd (UK); Compass Independent Book Sales Ltd (Ireland); Edgeler Book Services (Caribbean, Cyprus, Greece, Middle East, Netherlands, North Africa, Scandinavia); Peter Hyde Associates (South Africa); Peribo Pty Ltd (Australia)
Distribution Center: Central Books Ltd, One Heath Park Industrial Estate, Freshwater Rd, Dagenham RM8 1RX *Tel:* (020) 8525 8800 *Fax:* (020) 8599 2694 *E-mail:* contactus@ centralbooks.com *Web Site:* www.centralbooks. com

Academic Cell Press, *imprint of* Elsevier Ltd

Academic Press, *imprint of* Elsevier Ltd

Acair Ltd+
An Tosgan, 54 Seaforth Rd, Stornoway, Isle of Lewis HS1 2SD
Tel: (01851) 703020
E-mail: info@acairbooks.com
Web Site: www.acairbooks.com
Key Personnel
Manager: Agnes Rennie *E-mail:* agnes@ acairbooks.com
Founded: 1976
Publish a wide range of Gaelic, English & Bilingual books.
Subjects: Biography, Memoirs, Environmental Studies, Fiction, History, Poetry, Regional Interests
ISBN Prefix(es): 978-0-86152
Orders to: Booksource, 50 Cambuslang Rd, Glasgow G32 8NB *Tel:* (0845) 370 0067 *Fax:* (0845) 370 0068 *E-mail:* orders@ booksource.net

ACC Art Books, see ACC Publishing Group

ACC Editions, *imprint of* ACC Publishing Group

ACC Publishing Group+
Formerly Antique Collectors' Club Ltd
Sandy Lane, Old Martlesham, Woodbridge, Suffolk IP12 4SD
Tel: (01394) 389950 *Fax:* (01394) 389999
E-mail: sales@accpublishinggroup.com
Web Site: www.accpublishinggroup.com/uk; www. accartbooks.com/uk
Key Personnel
Dir: Vanessa Shorten
Marketing Dir: Sarah Smye *Tel:* (01394) 389966 *E-mail:* sarah.smye@accpublishinggroup.com
Founded: 1966

Subjects: Antiques, Architecture & Interior Design, Art, Fashion, Gardening, Plants, Photography
ISBN Prefix(es): 978-1-85149; 978-0-907462; 978-0-902028; 978-0-9504269; 978-1-905377
Number of titles published annually: 40 Print
Total Titles: 200 Print
Parent Company: Australia Images Publishing Group
Imprints: ACC Editions; Antique Collectors' Club; Garden Art Press
Divisions: ACC Book Distribution Ltd
U.S. Office(s): 6 W 18 St, Suite 4B, New York, NY 10011, United States *Tel:* 212-645-1111 *Fax:* 212-989-3205 *E-mail:* ussales@ accpublishinggroup.com
Foreign Rep(s): Academic Book Promotions (Fred Hermans) (Belgium, Holland, Luxembourg); APD Kuala Lumpur (Lilian Koe) (Malaysia); APD Singapore Pte Ltd (Ian Pringle) (Brunei, Cambodia, Indonesia, Singapore, Southeast Asia, Thailand, Vietnam); Asia Publishers Services Ltd (Edward Summerson) (China, Far East, Hong Kong, Philippines, Taiwan); Avicenna Partnership (Claire de Gruchy) (Algeria, Cyprus, Jordan, Malta, Morocco, Palestine, Tunisia, Turkey); Avicenna Partnership (Bill Kennedy) (Bahrain, Egypt, Iraq, Kuwait, Lebanon, Libya, Oman, Qatar, Saudi Arabia, Sudan, Syria, United Arab Emirates); Bookreps NZ Ltd (Susan Holmes) (New Zealand); Elisabeth Harder-Kreimann (Scandinavia); Peter Hyde Associates (South Africa); IMA/InterMediaAmericana Ltd (David Williams) (Caribbean, Latin America); Interart Sarl (France); IPR (Nicholas Nicolaou) (Israel); Adriana & Cristian Juncu (Albania, Armenia, Azerbaijan, Bulgaria, Croatia, Czechia, Estonia, Georgia, Hungary, Latvia, Lithuania, Moldova, Poland, Romania, Slovakia, Slovenia, Ukraine); Michael Klein (Austria, Germany, Switzerland); Yasy Murayama (Japan, South Korea); Padovani Books Ltd (Penny Padovani) (Greece, Italy); Padovani Books Ltd (Jenny Padovani) (Portugal, Spain); Peribo (Michael Coffey) (Australia); Ralph & Sheila Summers (Japan, South Korea); Robert Towers (Ireland); Vijeh Nashr Co International Book & Journal Services (Iran)

Accent Press, *imprint of* Accent Press Ltd

Accent Press Ltd
Ty Cynon House, Navigation Park, Abercynon CF44 4SN
Tel: (01443) 710930 *Fax:* (01443) 710940
E-mail: info@accentpress.co.uk
Web Site: www.accentpress.co.uk
Key Personnel
Founder & Foreign Rights: Hazel Cushion *E-mail:* hazel@accentpress.co.uk
Founded: 2003
Subjects: Biography, Memoirs, Cookery, Education, Erotica, Fiction, Health, Nutrition, Nonfiction (General), Self-Help, Crime, Thrillers, Writing
ISBN Prefix(es): 978-0-9544899; 978-0-9547092; 978-1-905170; 978-0-9548673; 978-1-906373; 978-1-907726; 978-1-907016; 978-1-906125
Imprints: Accent Press; Cariad; Xcite Books; Ya Cafe
Foreign Rep(s): Adbox Book Distributors (Philippines); Iberian Book Services (Gibraltar, Portugal, Spain); Maya Publishers Pvt Ltd (India); Penguin Singapore & Malaysia (Malaysia, Singapore); Phambdi Agencies CC (South Africa); SCB Distributors (Canada, USA); Butler Sims Ltd (Ireland); Southern Publishers Group (Australia, New Zealand)
Distribution Center: Macmillan Distribution (MDL), Brunel Rd, Houndmills, Basingstoke, Hants RG21 6XT *Tel:* (01256) 302692 *E-mail:* mdlqueries@macmillan.co.uk

Acorn Editions, *imprint of* The Lutterworth Press

Actinic Press, *imprint of* Cressrelles Publishing Co Ltd

ACU, see Association of Commonwealth Universities (ACU)

Adam Matthew Publications
Imprint of Adam Matthew Digital Ltd
c/o Adam Matthew Digital Ltd, Pelham House, London Rd, Marlborough, Wilts SN8 2AG
Tel: (01672) 511921 *Fax:* (01672) 511663
E-mail: info@ampltd.co.uk
Web Site: www.ampltd.co.uk
Key Personnel
Publishing Dir: Martha Fogg *Tel:* (01672) 518315 *E-mail:* martha@amdigital.co.uk
Mng Dir: Khal Rudin *Tel:* (01672) 518324 *E-mail:* khal@amdigital.co.uk
Editorial Dir: Jennifer Kemp *Tel:* (01672) 518316 *E-mail:* jennifer@amdigital.co.uk
Founded: 1990
Original manuscript collections, rare printed books & other primary source material in microform & electronic format.
Subjects: African American Studies, Architecture & Interior Design, Art, Asian Studies, Drama, Theater, Economics, Ethnicity, Foreign Countries, History, Literature, Literary Criticism, Essays, Music, Dance, Religion - Jewish, Religion - Other, Science (General), Social Sciences, Sociology, Technology, Women's Studies
ISBN Prefix(es): 978-1-85711
Number of titles published annually: 7 Online
Ultimate Parent Company: SAGE Publications
Distributed by Maruzen Co Ltd (Japan only); Transmission Books & Microinfo Co Ltd (TBMC) (Taiwan)

Addison-Wesley, *imprint of* Pearson Education Ltd

Adelphi Papers, *imprint of* International Institute for Strategic Studies

Adlard Coles Nautical+
Imprint of A&C Black Publishers Ltd
50 Bedford Sq, London WC1B 3DP
Tel: (020) 7631 5600 *Fax:* (020) 7631 5800
E-mail: adlardcoles@bloomsbury.com
Web Site: www.bloomsbury.com
Key Personnel
Dir: Janet Murphy
Rights Dir: Joanna Everard
Founded: 1947
Specialize in nautical books for the leisure market.
Subjects: Outdoor Recreation, Sports, Athletics, Boating
ISBN Prefix(es): 978-0-7136; 978-1-4081; 978-1-904358; 978-0-229; 978-1-4729
Number of titles published annually: 40 Print
Total Titles: 320 Print; 1 CD-ROM
Ultimate Parent Company: Bloomsbury Publishing PLC
Associate Companies: Thomas Reed Publications
Distribution Center: Macmillan Distribution (MDL), Brunel Rd, Houndmills, Basingstoke, Hants RG21 6XS *Tel:* (01256) 302699 *Fax:* (01256) 812521; (01256) 812558 *E-mail:* orders@macmillan.co.uk
Orders to: Macmillan Distribution (MDL), Brunel Rd, Houndmills, Basingstoke, Hants RG21 6XS *Tel:* (01256) 302699 *Fax:* (01256) 812521; (01256) 812558 *E-mail:* orders@ macmillan.co.uk

Adlib, *imprint of* Scholastic Ltd

African Books Collective
PO Box 721, Oxford OX1 9EN

Fax: (01865) 412341
E-mail: orders@africanbookscollective.com
Web Site: www.africanbookscollective.com
Key Personnel
Chief Executive Officer: Justin Cox
E-mail: justin.cox@africanbookscollective.com
Dir: David Brooks; Mary Jay
Nonprofit worldwide marketing & distribution
outlet for scholarly, literature & children's
books.
Subjects: Art, Business, Economics, Education,
Environmental Studies, Fiction, Government,
Political Science, Law, Literature, Literary Crit-
icism, Essays, Management, Public Adminis-
tration, Social Sciences, Sociology, African Lit-
erature, African Studies, Culture, Humanities,
Human Rights, International Affairs
ISBN Prefix(es): 978-0-9521269; 978-0-9542030;
978-0-9545384; 978-1-904855; 978-9966-9615
Distributed by Michigan State University Press
(North America)

Afterall Books, *imprint of* The MIT Press

Age UK
Tavis House, 1-6 Tavistock Sq, London WC1H
9NA
Toll Free Tel: 0800 169 6565
E-mail: contact@ageuk.org.uk
Web Site: www.ageuk.org.uk/publications
Key Personnel
Chief Executive: Tom Wright *E-mail:* t.wright@
ageuk.org.uk
Mng Dir: Gordon Morris
Founded: 1971
Specialize in practical books providing expert
guidance & information for the over 50s, their
careers & professionals working with older
people.
Subjects: Computer Science, Crafts, Games, Hob-
bies, Finance, Health, Nutrition, Photography,
Self-Help, Travel & Tourism
ISBN Prefix(es): 978-0-86242
Total Titles: 50 Print
Foreign Rep(s): Books for Europe (Europe)
Orders to: Orca Book Services, Stanley House, 3
Fleets Lane, Poole, Dorset BH15 3AJ, Contact:
Carol Guerrier *Tel:* (01202) 665432

De Agostini UK Ltd
Battersea Studios 2, 82 Silverthorne Rd, London
SW8 3HE
Tel: (0844) 493 5440
E-mail: customercare@deagostini.co.uk
Web Site: www.deagostini.co.uk
Founded: 1959
Subjects: Crafts, Games, Hobbies, Health, Nutri-
tion, How-to, Inspirational, Spirituality
ISBN Prefix(es): 978-1-86212; 978-1-899883

AHG Books, see Adam Gordon Books

Airlife Publishing Ltd, *imprint of* The Crowood
Press Ltd

AK Press & Distribution+
33 Tower St, Leith, Edinburgh EH6 7BN
Mailing Address: PO Box 12766, Edinburgh EH8
9YE
Tel: (0131) 555 5165 *Fax:* (0131) 555 5215
E-mail: ak@akedin.demon.co.uk
Web Site: www.akuk.com
Founded: 1991
Anarchist & radical book publishers & distribu-
tors.
Subjects: Art, Biography, Memoirs, Fiction, Mu-
sic, Dance, Nonfiction (General), Philosophy,
Poetry, Religion - Other, Science (General),
Social Sciences, Sociology, Animal Rights
ISBN Prefix(es): 978-1-873176; 978-1-902593;
978-1-904859; 978-1-84935

U.S. Office(s): 674-A 23 St, Oakland, CA 94612,
United States *Tel:* 510-208-1700 *Fax:* 510-208-
1701 *E-mail:* info@akpress.org
Distributed by Bookspeed (UK); Counter Productions (UK); Turnaround (UK)

Aladdin Books+
PO Box 53987, London SW15 25F
Tel: (020) 3174 3090 *Fax:* (020) 8780 3939
E-mail: sales@aladdinbooks.co.uk
Web Site: www.aladdinbooks.co.uk
Key Personnel
Dir: Eleanor P Whittaker
Mng Dir: Charles Nicholas
Founded: 1979
Subjects: Art, Environmental Studies, Geography,
Geology, Nonfiction (General), Science (Gen-
eral), Natural History

Aladdin Children's Books, see Aladdin Books

Ian Allan Publishing+
Member of Ian Allan Group
12 Ethel St, Birmingham B2 4BG
Tel: (01932) 266600; (0844) 245 6944
E-mail: info@ianallanpublishing.co.uk;
enquiries@ianallandirect.co.uk
Web Site: www.ianallanpublishing.com; www.
ianallan.com
Key Personnel
Chairman: David Allan
Marketing Dir: Nicholas Lerwill
Founded: 1942
Subjects: Aeronautics, Aviation, Architecture &
Interior Design, Automotive, Cookery, Garden-
ing, Plants, History, Maritime, Photography,
Transportation, Military
ISBN Prefix(es): 978-0-7110; 978-0-86364
Associate Companies: Ian Allan Motors Ltd; Ian
Allan Printing Ltd; Ian Allan Travel Ltd; Chase
Organics Ltd; Lewis Masonic
Imprints: Dial House
Distributor for Mill Stream; Runpast; World of
Transport; Yore Publications
Foreign Rep(s): Bill Bailey Publishers' Repre-
sentatives (Austria, Belgium, Bulgaria, Croa-
tia, Cyprus, Czechia, Estonia, France, Ger-
many, Gibraltar, Greece, Hungary, Italy, Latvia,
Liechtenstein, Lithuania, Luxembourg, Malta,
Monaco, Montenegro, Netherlands, Poland,
Portugal, Romania, Serbia, Slovenia, Spain,
Switzerland); Baker & Taylor Publisher Ser-
vices (USA); D Richard Bowen (Scandinavia);
Combined Books (USA); DLS Australia Pty
Ltd (Australia, New Zealand, Papua New
Guinea); Electra Media Group Pty Ltd (Brunei,
China, Eastern Asia, Hong Kong, Japan, Ko-
rea, Malaysia, Philippines, Singapore, Taiwan,
Thailand); PIM (India, Middle East, Pakistan);
Vanwell Publishing Ltd (Canada)
Bookshop(s): 12 Ethel St, Birmingham B2 4BG
Tel: (0121) 643 2496 *Fax:* (0121) 643 6855
E-mail: bcc@ianallanpublishing.co.uk; Main
Terminal Bldg, 3rd floor, Birmingham In-
ternational Airport, Birmingham B26 3QJ
Tel: (0121) 781 0921 *Fax:* (0121) 781 0928;
45-46 Lower Marsh, Waterloo, London SE1
7SG *Tel:* (020) 7401 2100 *Fax:* (020) 7401
2887 *E-mail:* waterloo@ianallanpublishing.co.
uk; 5 Piccadilly Station, Approach, Manchester
M1 2GH *Tel:* (0161) 237 9840 *Fax:* (0161) 237
9921 *E-mail:* manchester@ianallanpublishing.
co.uk
Warehouse: Littlehampton Book Services Ltd,
Faraday Close, Durrington, Worthing, West
Sussex BN13 3RB *Tel:* (01903) 828500;
(01903) 828501 (customer service) *Web
Site:* lbsltd.wp.hachette.co.uk

J A Allen, *imprint of* The Crowood Press Ltd

Alligator Publishing Ltd
314 Regents Park Rd, 2nd floor, Finchley, London
N3 2JX
Tel: (020) 8371 6622 *Fax:* (020) 8371 6633
E-mail: sales@alligatorbooks.co.uk
Web Site: www.alligatorbooks.co.uk
Key Personnel
Publishing & Sales Dir: Andrew H Rabin
Commercial Dir: Neil Rodol
Sales Manager: Paul Taylor
Regional Sales Agent: Michael Kenley
Founded: 1999
Subjects: Fiction, Nonfiction (General)
ISBN Prefix(es): 978-1-84239; 978-1-84750; 978-
0-85726
Parent Company: International Greetings PLC
Imprints: Cupcake; Pinwheel

Allison & Busby Ltd
Subsidiary of Editorial Prensa Iberica
12 Fitzroy Mews, London W1T 6DW
Tel: (020) 7580 1080 *Fax:* (020) 7580 1180
Web Site: www.allisonandbusby.com
Key Personnel
Publishing Dir: Susie Dunlop *E-mail:* susie@
allisonandbusby.com
Digital & Online Marketing Manager: Lesley
Crooks *E-mail:* lesley@allisonandbusby.com
Founded: 1967
Subjects: Biography, Memoirs, Fiction, History,
Humor, Mysteries, Suspense, Nonfiction (Gen-
eral), Pop Culture, Science Fiction, Fantasy,
Travel & Tourism, Contemporary & Literary
Fiction, Crime Fiction
ISBN Prefix(es): 978-0-85031; 978-0-7490; 978-
1-902809
Number of titles published annually: 80 Print; 20
E-Book
Total Titles: 300 Print; 30 E-Book
Foreign Rep(s): Jonathan Ball (South Africa);
DLS Australia Pty Ltd (Australia, New
Zealand); Faber Factory Plus (Europe); George-
town Publications (Canada); IMA (Africa, Cen-
tral Europe, Eastern Europe); International Pub-
lishers Marketing (USA); Maya Publishers Pvt
Ltd (India)
Foreign Rights: Marshall Rights (USA)
Distribution Center: Turnaround Publisher
Services, Olympia Trading Estate, Unit 3,
Coburg Rd, London N22 6TZ *Tel:* (020) 8829
3000 *Fax:* (020) 8881 5088 *E-mail:* orders@
turnaround-uk.com

Alloway Publishing Ltd, *imprint of* Stenlake
Publishing Ltd

Allyn & Bacon, *imprint of* Pearson Education
Ltd

Alma Books Ltd+
3 Castle Yard, Richmond, Surrey TW10 6TF
Tel: (020) 8940 6917 *Fax:* (020) 8948 5599
E-mail: info@almabooks.com
Web Site: www.almabooks.com
Key Personnel
Owner & Publisher: Alessandro Gallenzi
Owner: Elisabetta Minervini
Founded: 2005
Subjects: Drama, Theater, Fiction, Nonfiction
(General), Poetry
ISBN Prefix(es): 978-1-84688; 978-0-9517497
Number of titles published annually: 70 Print
Total Titles: 50 Print
Imprints: Alma Classics; Calder Publications;
Overture Publications
Foreign Rep(s): Jonathan Ball Publishers (South
Africa); Bloomsbury Publishing PLC (Algeria,
Austria, France, Germany, Morocco, Pakistan,
Sri Lanka, Tunisia); Bloomsbury Publishing
Pty Ltd (Australia, New Zealand); Blooms-
bury USA (USA); Penguin Books India (India);
Penguin Books Malaysia (Malaysia); Penguin
Books SA (Portugal, Spain); Penguin Books

Singapore (Singapore); Penguin Group (Arabia) (Middle East); Penguin Group Canada (Canada); Penguin International Sales (Africa, Asia, Malta, Scandinavia, Southeast Europe, Switzerland); Penguin Italia SRL (Italy); Penguin Poland (Central Europe, Eastern Europe); RepForce Ireland (Ireland)
Distribution Center: Macmillan Distribution, Houndmills, Basingstoke, Hants RG21 6XS *Tel:* (01256) 302 692 *Fax:* (01256) 812 521 *E-mail:* mdl@macmillan.co.uk

Alma Classics, *imprint of* Alma Books Ltd

Alpha Science International Ltd+
Oxford Business Park North, 7200 The Quorum, Garsington Rd, Oxford OX4 2JZ
Tel: (01865) 481433 *Fax:* (01865) 481482
E-mail: info@alphasci.com; editorial@alphasci.com; rights@alphasci.com; sales@alphasci.com (orders)
Web Site: www.alphasci.com
Founded: 2000
Publisher of textbooks & professional & post-graduate books in all areas of science, technology, engineering, mathematics & medicine.
Subjects: Biological Sciences, Chemistry, Chemical Engineering, Computer Science, Earth Sciences, Engineering (General), Environmental Studies, Management, Mathematics, Medicine, Nursing, Dentistry, Physics, Science (General), Technology, Life Sciences
ISBN Prefix(es): 978-1-84265
Number of titles published annually: 80 Print
Total Titles: 400 Print
Distribution Center: Marston Book Services Ltd, 160 Eastern Ave, Milton Park, Abingdon, Oxon OX14 4SB *Tel:* (01235) 465500 *Fax:* (01235) 465555 *E-mail:* direct.orders@marston.co.uk *Web Site:* www.marston.co.uk (worldwide exc Canada, Mexico, North & South America)
STM Book Distribution, 40 Oak View Dr, San Rafael, CA 94903, United States (Canada, Mexico, North & South America)

Alun Books
3 Crown St, Port Talbot, W Glam SA13 1BG
Tel: (01639) 886186
E-mail: enquiries@alunbooks.co.uk; orders@alunbooks.co.uk
Web Site: www.alunbooks.co.uk
Key Personnel
Editor: Sally Roberts Jones
Founded: 1977
Publish books about Wales +/or by Welsh authors.
Subjects: Biography, Memoirs, Fiction, History, Poetry, Regional Interests, Travel & Tourism
ISBN Prefix(es): 978-0-907117; 978-0-9505643
Total Titles: 60 Print
Imprints: Barn Owl Press (children's books); Goldleaf Publishing (local history)
Distributor for Port Talbot Historical Society

Amadeus Press, *imprint of* Timber Press

Amateur Winemaker, *imprint of* Special Interest Model Books Ltd

Amber Books Ltd+
74-77 White Lion St, London N1 9PF
Tel: (020) 7520 7600 *Fax:* (020) 7520 7606
E-mail: enquiries@amberbooks.co.uk
Web Site: www.amberbooks.co.uk
Key Personnel
Mng Dir: Stasz Gynch *E-mail:* stasz@amberbooks.co.uk
Rights Dir: Sara McKie *E-mail:* sara@amberbooks.co.uk
Rights Executive: Melody Travers
E-mail: melody@amberbooks.co.uk

Production Manager: Peter Thompson
E-mail: peter@amberbooks.co.uk
Publishing Manager: Charles Catton
E-mail: charles@amberbooks.co.uk
Founded: 1989
Packager of illustrated nonfiction for international co-editions.
Subjects: Aeronautics, Aviation, Astronomy, Automotive, Cookery, Crafts, Games, Hobbies, Criminology, Gardening, Plants, Health, Nutrition, History, How-to, Maritime, Medicine, Nursing, Dentistry, Military Science, Music, Dance, Nonfiction (General), Science (General), Sports, Athletics, Transportation, Mind, Body & Spirit, Nature, Social History
ISBN Prefix(es): 978-1-897884; 978-0-9543125; 978-1-904687; 978-0-9544356; 978-1-905704; 978-1-906626
Number of titles published annually: 60 Print
Total Titles: 500 Print
Distributed by Casemate UK; Sterling Publishing Co (Canada & USA)

Amberwood Publishing Ltd+
The Herb Place, Culpeper Close, Medway City Estate, Rochester, Kent ME2 4HN
Tel: (01634) 290 115 *Fax:* (01634) 290 761
E-mail: info@amberwoodpublishing.com
Web Site: www.amberwoodpublishing.com
Key Personnel
Dir: Henry Crisp; June Crisp
Founded: 1991
Specialize in natural/health publications, herbs, vitamins, minerals & self-medication.
Subjects: Health, Nutrition, Aromatherapy, Herbal Medicine
ISBN Prefix(es): 978-1-899308; 978-0-9517723
Number of titles published annually: 3 Print
Total Titles: 32 Print

Amnesty International Publications
Human Rights Action Centre, 17-25 New Inn Yard, London EC2A 3EA
Tel: (020) 7033 1500
E-mail: sct@amnesty.org.uk
Web Site: www.amnesty.org.uk
Key Personnel
Head, Media, Public Relations & Supporter Care: Niall Couper *Tel:* (020) 7033 6414
E-mail: niall.couper@amnesty.org.uk
Founded: 1961
Subjects: Human Rights
ISBN Prefix(es): 978-0-86210; 978-0-900058; 978-1-873328
Branch Office(s)
Amnesty International Northern Ireland, 397 Ormeau Rd, Belfast BT7 3GP, Press Contact: Patrick Corrigan *Tel:* (028) 9064 3000 *E-mail:* nireland@amnesty.org.uk
Amnesty International Wales, Temple Court, Cathedral Rd, Cardiff CF11 9HA, Press Contact: Cathy Owens *Tel:* (029) 2078 6415 *Fax:* (029) 2078 6416 *E-mail:* wales@amnesty.org.uk
Amnesty International Scotland, MWB Business Exchange, 9-10 St Andrew's Sq, Edinburgh EH2 2AF, Press Contact: Pauline Kelly *Tel:* (0131) 718 6076 *E-mail:* scotland@amnesty.org.uk
Orders to: PO Box 4, Rugby, Warwicks CV21 1RU *Tel:* (01788) 545553 *Fax:* (01788) 579244

Amsco Publications, *imprint of* Omnibus Press

And Other Stories
91 Tadros Court, High Wycombe, Bucks HP13 7GF
Tel: (01494) 443797
E-mail: info@andotherstories.org
Web Site: www.andotherstories.org
Key Personnel
Publisher: Stefan Tobler

Head, Publicity UK: Nicci Praca
Publicity Dir, North America: Justin Hargett
Senior Editor: Sophie Lewis
Editor: Tara Tobler
Founded: 2010
Subjects: Fiction
ISBN Prefix(es): 978-1-908276
U.S. Office(s): 511 Avenue of the Americas, Suite 112, New York, NY 10011, United States
Warehouse: Consortium Perseus Distribution, 210 American Dr, Jackson, TN 38301, United States *Tel:* 731-423-1550 *Fax:* 731-423-1335 *E-mail:* orderentry@perseusbooks.com (North America)
Distribution Center: Faber Factory Plus, Bloomsbury House, 74-77 Great Russell St, London WC1B 3DA, Sales Dir: Ian West *Tel:* (020) 7927 3808 *E-mail:* ian.west@faber.co.uk
Repforce Ireland, 7 Seapoint Terrace, Irishtown, Dublin 4, Ireland *Tel:* (01) 6349927 *Fax:* (01) 6697449 *E-mail:* info@repforce.ie
Consortium Book Sales & Distribution, 34 13 Ave NE, Suite 101, Minneapolis, MN 55413-1006, United States *Tel:* 612-746-2600 *Fax:* 612-746-2606 *E-mail:* info@cbsd.com (North America)

Andersen Paperback Picture Books, *imprint of* Andersen Press Ltd

Andersen Press Board Books, *imprint of* Andersen Press Ltd

Andersen Press Ltd
Affiliate of Penguin Random House
20 Vauxhall Bridge Rd, London SW1V 2SA
Tel: (020) 7840 8701 *Fax:* (020) 7233 6263
E-mail: andersoneditorial@penguinrandomhouse.co.uk
Web Site: www.andersenpress.co.uk
Key Personnel
Publisher & Chairman: Klaus Flugge
Tel: (020) 7840 8702 *E-mail:* kflugge@penguinrandomhouse.co.uk
Senior Rights Manager: Liz White
Tel: (020) 7840 7381 *E-mail:* lwhite@penguinrandomhouse.co.uk
Rights & Permissions: Sarah Vanden-Abeele
Tel: (020) 7840 8729 *E-mail:* svandenabeele@penguinrandomhouse.co.uk
Founded: 1976
Subjects: Fiction
ISBN Prefix(es): 978-0-86264; 978-0-905478
Number of titles published annually: 90 Print; 80 E-Book
Total Titles: 800 Print; 350 E-Book; 12 Audio
Imprints: Andersen Paperback Picture Books; Andersen Press Board Books; Andersen Young Readers Library
Distributed by Penguin Random House (worldwide)
Foreign Rep(s): Penguin Random House (worldwide)
Foreign Rights: The Bardon Chinese Media Agency (China); Big Apple Agency Inc (Malaysia, Thailand, Vietnam); Book Publishers Association of Israel (Israel); Agencja Literacka Graal (Poland); Katai & Bolza Literary Agents (Hungary); Simona Kessler Agency (Romania); Maxima Creative Agency (Indonesia); Andrew Nurnberg Agency (ANA Sofia Ltd) (Bulgaria); Andrew Nurnberg Associates Russia (Russia); Kristin Olson Literary Agency sro (Czechia, Slovakia); RDC Agency (Spanish); Seibel Publishing Services (Patricia Seibel) (Brazil); Tuttle-Mori Agency Inc (Japan); Eric Yang Agency (Korea)
Warehouse: The Book Service Ltd, Distribution Centre, Colchester Rd, Frating Green, Colchester, Essex CO7 7DW *Tel:* (01206) 256000 *Fax:* (01206) 255715 *Web Site:* www.thebookservice.co.uk

Orders to: The Book Service Ltd, Distribution Centre, Colchester Rd, Frating Green, Colchester, Essex CO7 7DW *Tel:* (01206) 255678 *Fax:* (01206) 255930

Andersen Young Readers Library, *imprint of* Andersen Press Ltd

Chris Andrews Publications Ltd
15 Curtis Yard, North Hinksey Lane, Oxford, Oxon OX2 0LX
Tel: (01865) 723404
E-mail: enquiries@cap-ox.com
Web Site: www.cap-ox.com
Key Personnel
Contact: C M Andrews
Founded: 1982
Membership(s): BAPLA; IPG.
Subjects: Travel & Tourism, Channel Islands (Guernsey & Sark, Cotswolds, Peak District, Stratford upon Avon, Thames & Chilterns, Worcestershire), Henley on Thames, Herm & Alderney, Life Under the Seas of Guernsey & Jersey, Oxford-Universities & Colleges
ISBN Prefix(es): 978-0-9509643; 978-0-9540331; 978-1-905385; 978-1-906725
Number of titles published annually: 8 Print
Total Titles: 25 Print
Imprints: Oxford Picture Library

Angels' Share, *imprint of* Neil Wilson Publishing Ltd

Angry Robot Ltd
Imprint of Watkins Media Ltd
20 Fletcher Gate, Nottingham, Notts NG1 2FZ
Tel: (0115) 933 8456
E-mail: incoming@angryrobotbooks.com
Web Site: angryrobotbooks.com
Key Personnel
Mng Dir & Publisher: Marc Gascoigne
Marketing Manager: Caroline Lambe *Tel:* (0115) 933 8421
North American Sales & Marketing Manager (USA): Mike Underwood *Tel:* 812-606-8098 *E-mail:* mike.underwod@angryrobotbooks.com
Editor: Phil Jourdan *Tel:* (0790) 184 8784
Founded: 2009
Subjects: Science Fiction, Fantasy
ISBN Prefix(es): 978-0-85766
Foreign Rep(s): Nationwide Book Distributors (New Zealand); Pansing (Far East, Singapore); Penguin Random House (Canada, USA); Simon & Schuster Australia (Australia)
Distribution Center: Grantham Book Services Ltd, Trent Rd, Grantham, Lincs NG31 7XQ

Ankara Press, *imprint of* Cassava Republic Press

Anness Publishing Ltd
Algores Way, Wisbech, Cambs PE13 2TQ
E-mail: info@anness.com
Web Site: www.annesspublishing.com
Key Personnel
Mng Dir: Paul Anness *E-mail:* panness@anness.com
Publisher: Joanna Lorenz *E-mail:* jlorenz@anness.com
Founded: 1988
Subjects: Animals, Pets, Art, Cookery, Crafts, Games, Hobbies, Fiction, Gardening, Plants, Health, Nutrition, History, How-to, Music, Dance, Nonfiction (General), Photography, Poetry, Sports, Athletics
ISBN Prefix(es): 978-0-7548; 978-1-901688
Imprints: Armadillo; Lorenz Books; Peony Press; Practical Pictures; Southwater
Foreign Rep(s): David Bateman Ltd (Bryce Gibson) (New Zealand); Gunnar Lie & Associates Ltd (Guillame Ferrand) (Belgium, Central America, Eastern Europe, France, Gibraltar,

Italy, Luxembourg, Malta, Portugal, South America, Spain); Gunnar Lie & Associates Ltd (Africa, Indian subcontinent, Southeast Asia); Gunnar Lie & Associates Ltd (John Edgeler) (Caribbean, Cyprus, Egypt, Greece, Iran, Iraq, Israel, Jordan, Kuwait, Netherlands, Scandinavia, Syria, Turkey, United Arab Emirates); The Manning Partnership Ltd (Ireland, UK); Marketing Services for Publishers (Lorie Ocampo) (China, Hong Kong, Japan, Korea, Philippines, Taiwan); Publishers Services (Gabriele Kern) (Austria, Germany, Switzerland); John Reed Book Distribution (Australia); Research Press (Ajay Parmar) (India); Trinity Books (Nigel Hargreaves) (South Africa)
Distribution Center: Book Trade Services, Blaby Rd, Wigston, Leics LE18 4SE
Tel: (0116) 2759086 *Fax:* (0116) 2759090
E-mail: uksales@booktradeservices.com (UK & Ireland)
National Book Network (NBN), 4501 Forbes Blvd, Suite 200, Lanham, MD 20706, United States *Tel:* 301-459-3366 *Fax:* 301-429-5746
Web Site: www.nbnbooks.com (USA trade & Canada)

Anshan Ltd
6 Newlands Rd, Tunbridge Wells, Kent TN4 9AT
Mailing Address: The Control Center, 11 Little Mount Sion, Tunbridge Wells, Kent TN1 1YS
Tel: (01892) 557767
E-mail: info@anshan.co.uk; shan@anshan.co.uk
Web Site: www.anshan.co.uk
Subjects: Chemistry, Chemical Engineering, Engineering (General), Health, Nutrition, Mathematics, Physics, Science (General), Health Science, Natural & Applied Sciences
ISBN Prefix(es): 978-1-904798; 978-1-905740; 978-1-84829

Anthem Press+
Imprint of Wimbledon Publishing Co
75-76 Blackfriars Rd, London SE1 8HA
Tel: (020) 7401 4200 *Fax:* (020) 7401 4225
E-mail: info@anthempress.com
Web Site: www.anthempress.com
Key Personnel
Publisher: Tej P S Sood
Editor: Brian Stone
Founded: 1993
Specialize in political science & humanities plus gift & humor books for the discerning wit.
Subjects: Asian Studies, Biography, Memoirs, Biological Sciences, Business, Economics, Education, Film, Video, Finance, Government, Political Science, Health, Nutrition, History, Humor, Language Arts, Linguistics, Literature, Literary Criticism, Essays, Self-Help, Social Sciences, Sociology, Women's Studies, Humanities
ISBN Prefix(es): 978-1-898855; 978-1-84331; 978-0-85728; 978-1-78308
Number of titles published annually: 50 Print
Total Titles: 150 Print
U.S. Office(s): 244 Madison Ave No 116, New York, NY 10016, United States *Tel:* 646-736-7908 *Fax:* 646-839-2934
Distribution Center: Marston Book Services Ltd, 160 Eastern Ave, Milton Park, Abingdon, Oxon OX14 4SB *Tel:* (01235) 465500 *Fax:* (01235) 465555 *E-mail:* direct.orders@marston.co.uk
Web Site: www.marston.co.uk
Books International, PO Box 605, Herndon, VA 20172-0605, United States *Tel:* 703-661-1570 *Fax:* 703-661-1501 *E-mail:* bimail@presswarehouse.com *Web Site:* www.bookintl.com

Antique Collectors' Club, *imprint of* ACC Publishing Group

Antique Collectors' Club Ltd, *see* ACC Publishing Group

Anvil Press Poetry Ltd
Neptune House, 70 Royal Hill, London SE10 8RF
Tel: (020) 8469 3033
E-mail: anvil@anvilpresspoetry.com
Web Site: www.anvilpresspoetry.com
Key Personnel
Founder, Editorial & Production Dir: Peter Jay
Founded: 1968
Specialize in contemporary poetry in English & translated poetry from all periods, sometimes in bilingual editions.
Subjects: Poetry
ISBN Prefix(es): 978-0-85646; 978-0-900977
Number of titles published annually: 12 Print
Imprints: Poetica
Foreign Rep(s): Ted Dougherty (Austria, Benelux, France, Germany, Switzerland); Iberian Book Services (Peter Prout) (Portugal, Spain); IMA (Eastern Europe, Greece, Israel); Robert Towers (Ireland, Northern Ireland); Turnaround Publisher Services Ltd (England, Scotland, Wales)
Distribution Center: National Book Network (NBN), Thornbury Rd, Plymouth, Devon PL6 7PP *Tel:* (01752) 20230 *Fax:* (01752) 202333 *E-mail:* orders@nbninternational.com *Web Site:* www.nbninternational.com
Eleanor Brasch Enterprises, PO Box 586, Artarmon, NSW 2064, Australia, Owner: Eleanor Brasch *Tel:* (02) 9419 8717 *Fax:* (02) 9419 7930 *E-mail:* brasch2@aol.com (Australia & New Zealand)
Consortium Book Sales & Distribution *Toll Free Tel:* 800-283-3572 *Web Site:* www.cbsd.com (USA, select titles)

Apex Publishing Ltd+
12A St John's Rd, Clacton-on-Sea, Essex CO15 4BP
Mailing Address: PO Box 7086, Clacton-on-Sea, Essex CO15 5WN
Tel: (01255) 428500 *Fax:* (0871) 918 4756
E-mail: mail@apexpublishing.co.uk
Web Site: www.apexpublishing.co.uk
Key Personnel
Mng Dir: Chris Cowlin
Founded: 2002
Membership(s): The Publishers Association.
Subjects: Animals, Pets, Biography, Memoirs, Cookery, Crafts, Games, Hobbies, Education, Fiction, Film, Video, Health, Nutrition, History, Inspirational, Spirituality, Music, Dance, Nonfiction (General), Philosophy, Poetry, Radio, TV, Religion - Other, Science Fiction, Fantasy, Self-Help, Sports, Athletics, True Crime
ISBN Prefix(es): 978-1-904444; 978-1-906358; 978-1-907792; 978-1-910295; 978-1-908382; 978-1-908548; 978-1-909949; 978-1-908752
Total Titles: 85 Print
Foreign Rep(s): Andrews UK Ltd (UK); Bertram Books (UK); Central Book Services Pty Ltd (Australia, New Zealand, Southeast Asia); Gardners Books Ltd (UK); Mayfield Books & Gifts (UK); Oakridge Books & Gifts (UK); SG Distributors (South Africa); Unifacmanu Trading Co Ltd (Taiwan)
Foreign Rights: Chengdu Rightol Media & Advertisement Co Ltd (China, Hong Kong, Macau, Malaysia, Singapore, Taiwan); Salkind Literary Agency (USA)
Distribution Center: Gardners Books Ltd, One Whittle Dr, Eastbourne, Sussex BN23 6QH *Tel:* (01323) 521777 *Fax:* (01323) 521666 *E-mail:* custcare@gardners.com *Web Site:* www.gardners.com
Andrews UK Ltd, The Hat Factory, 65-67 Bute St, Suite 4, Luton, Beds LU1 2EY *Tel:* (01582) 522610 *E-mail:* info@andrewsuk.com *Web Site:* www.andrewsuk.com (ebooks)

Apollos, *imprint of* Inter-Varsity Press

Apple Press+
Member of Quarto International Co-Editions Group
74-77 White Lion St, Islington, London N1 9PF
Tel: (020) 7284 9300
E-mail: info@quartouk.com
Web Site: www.quartoknows.com/apple-press
Founded: 1984
Produces illustrated & narrative books focused on history, entertainment & sports.
Subjects: Animals, Pets, Antiques, Art, Cookery, Crafts, Games, Hobbies, Fashion, Health, Nutrition, History, House & Home, Nonfiction (General), Photography, Sports, Athletics, Transportation, Art Instruction, Beauty, Body/Mind/Spirit, Design, Diet, Entertainment, Fitness, Food & Drink, Lifestyle
ISBN Prefix(es): 978-1-85076; 978-1-84092; 978-1-84543
Number of titles published annually: 25 Print
Total Titles: 500 Print
Ultimate Parent Company: The Quarto Group Inc
Foreign Rep(s): APD (Hong Kong, Malaysia, Singapore, Thailand); Bill Bailey Publishers Representatives (Europe); Arturo Guiterrez Hernandez (Central America, Mexico); Humphrys Roberts Associates (Chris Humphrys) (Caribbean); IMA (David Williams) (Latin America); International Publishing Services (Zoe Kaviani) (Africa exc South Africa, Middle East); Benjie Ocampo (China, Japan, Korea, Philippines, Taiwan); Real Books (South Africa)
Distribution Center: Littlehampton Book Services Ltd, Faraday Close, Durrington, Worthing, West Sussex BN13 3RB *Tel:* (01903) 828500; (01903) 828501 (customer service) *Web Site:* lbsltd.wp.hachette.co.uk

Appletree Press Ltd+
Roycroft House, 164 Malone Rd, Belfast BT9 5LL
Tel: (028) 9024 3074 *Fax:* (028) 9024 6756
E-mail: reception@appletree.ie
Web Site: www.appletree.ie
Key Personnel
Mng Dir: John D Murphy
Sales: Alison Osborne *E-mail:* osborne@appletree.ie
Founded: 1974
Publishers of gift & guidebooks in eight languages, including French, Russian, Japanese, Greek & Spanish. Also creates books for co-publishers.
Subjects: Art, Biography, Memoirs, Cookery, Crafts, Games, Hobbies, Fiction, Genealogy, History, Humor, Literature, Literary Criticism, Essays, Music, Dance, Photography, Poetry, Regional Interests, Religion - Other, Social Sciences, Sociology, Sports, Athletics, Travel & Tourism, Celtic, Nature
ISBN Prefix(es): 978-0-904651; 978-0-86281; 978-1-84758
Total Titles: 300 Print
Foreign Rep(s): Compass Ireland Independent Book Sales (Ireland); John Fitzgerald & Associates (USA); Peter Hyde Associates (South Africa); IMA (Caribbean, Cyprus, Eastern Europe, Greece, Israel, South America); Independent Publishers Group (USA); Peribo Pty Ltd (Australia); Publishers Group UK (England, Wales); Seol Ltd (Scotland)
Distribution Center: Book Source, 50 Cambuslang Investment Park, Glasgow G32 8NB *Tel:* (0845) 370 0063 *Fax:* (0141) 370 0064
Gill Distribution, Hume Ave, Park West, Dublin D12 YV96, Ireland *Tel:* (01) 500 9500 *Web Site:* www.gilldistribution.ie

Arcadia Books Ltd+
139 Highlever Rd, London W10 6PH
Tel: (020) 8960 4967
E-mail: info@arcadiabooks.co.uk

Web Site: www.arcadiabooks.co.uk
Key Personnel
Dir: Sam Parker; Piers Russell-Cobb
Founded: 1996
Subjects: African American Studies, Biography, Memoirs, Fiction, LGBTQ, Literature, Literary Criticism, Essays, Nonfiction (General), Travel & Tourism, Women's Studies, Crime, Gender Studies, Translated Fiction
ISBN Prefix(es): 978-1-900850; 978-1-905147; 978-1-906413; 978-1-908129; 978-1-910050
Number of titles published annually: 25 Print
Total Titles: 170 Print
Parent Company: MediaFund
Imprints: BlackAmber; Bliss Books; EuroCrime; The Maia Press Ltd
Foreign Rep(s): Horizon Books (Brunei, Hong Kong, Indonesia, Malaysia, Philippines, Singapore, Thailand); Independent Publisher's Group (Canada, USA); InterMedia Americana (Caribbean, Latin America); InterMediaAfrica (Sub-Saharan Africa); Maya Publishers (India); New South Books (Australia); Quartet Sales & Marketing (South Africa); Steimatzky Ltd (Israel); Turnaround Publisher Services Ltd (Europe, UK)
Foreign Rights: Eulama SRL (Germany, Italy); The Marsh Agency (worldwide exc Germany & Italy)
Distribution Center: Macmillan Distribution Ltd (MDL), Brunel Rd, Houndmills, Basingstoke, Hants RG21 6XS *Tel:* (01256) 302692 *Fax:* (01256) 812558 *E-mail:* orders@macmillan.co.uk (UK, Europe & Ireland)
NewSouth Books, c/o TL Distribution, 15-23 Helles Ave, Moorebank, NSW 2170, Australia *Tel:* (02) 8778 9999 *Fax:* (02) 8778 9944 *E-mail:* orders@tldistribution.com.au *Web Site:* www.newsouthbooks.com.au (Australia & New Zealand)
Feel Books Pvt Ltd, 4381/4 Ansari Rd, Darya Ganj, New Delhi 110 002, India *E-mail:* india@feelbooks.net *Web Site:* www.feelbooks.net
Dufour Editions, PO Box 7, Chester Springs, PA 19425, United States *Tel:* 610-458-5005 *E-mail:* orders@dufoureditions.com *Web Site:* www.dufoureditions.com (USA & Canada)

Architectural Association Publications+
Subsidiary of Architectural Association Inc
36 Bedford Sq, London WC1B 3ES
Tel: (020) 7887 4021; (020) 7887 4000 *Fax:* (020) 7414 0783
E-mail: publications@aaschool.ac.uk
Web Site: www.aaschool.ac.uk/publications
Key Personnel
Dir: Brett Steele
Publications Editor: Pamela Johnston
Marketing & Distribution: Kirsten Morphet
Founded: 1847
Also acts as a school of architecture.
Subjects: Architecture & Interior Design, Art, Engineering (General), History, Philosophy, Photography, Landscape, Urbanism
ISBN Prefix(es): 978-1-870890; 978-0-904503; 978-1-902902
Foreign Rep(s): Basheer Graphic Books (Hong Kong, Indonesia, Singapore, Thailand); Bookport Associates (Joe Portelli) (Croatia, Montenegro, Serbia, Slovenia, Southern Europe); Berend Bosch (Belgium, Netherlands); Muriel Fischer (France); Robyn Ralton (Australia, New Zealand); Kurt Salchli (Austria, Germany); United Publishers Services Ltd (Japan)

Architectural Press, *imprint of* Elsevier Ltd

Arcturus Publishing Ltd+
26/27 Bickels Yard, 151-153 Bermondsey St, London SE1 3HA

Tel: (020) 7407 9400 *Fax:* (020) 7407 9444
E-mail: info@arcturuspublishing.com
Web Site: www.arcturuspublishing.com
Key Personnel
Sales Dir: Paul Byers
Marketing Manager: Charles Cooper
Founded: 1994
ISBN Prefix(es): 978-1-84193; 978-1-900032; 978-1-84837; 978-1-84858; 978-1-78212
Number of titles published annually: 70 Print
Total Titles: 300 Print; 2 Audio
Foreign Rep(s): Gunnar Lie & Associates Ltd (Gunnar Lie) (Africa, Asia, Indian subcontinent); Gunnar Lie & Associates Ltd (John Edgeler) (Caribbean, Cyprus, Greece, Middle East, Netherlands, Scandinavia); Gunnar Lie & Associates Ltd (Guillaume Ferrand) (Belgium, Central America, Eastern Europe, France, Gibraltar, Italy, Luxembourg, Malta, Portugal, South America, Spain); Benjie Ocampo (China, Hong Kong, Japan, Korea, Philippines, Taiwan); Publisher's Services (Gabriele Kern) (Austria, Germany, Switzerland); Research Press (Ajay Parmer) (India)
Distribution Center: Macmillan Distribution Ltd, Brunel Rd, Houndmills, Basingstoke, Hants RG21 6XS *Tel:* (01256) 302692 *Fax:* (01256) 812558; (01256) 812521 *E-mail:* orders@macmillan.co.uk *Web Site:* www.macmillandistribution.co.uk

Arden Shakespeare, *imprint of* A&C Black Publishers Ltd

Ardis, *imprint of* Gerald Duckworth & Co Ltd

Arena Books+
6 Southgate Green, Bury St Edmunds, Suffolk IP33 2BL
Tel: (01284) 754123 *Fax:* (01284) 754123
E-mail: arenabooks@tiscali.co.uk
Web Site: www.arenabooks.co.uk
Key Personnel
Dir: James Farrell
Founded: 2000
Subjects: Art, Biography, Memoirs, Business, Economics, Education, Fiction, Foreign Countries, Government, Political Science, History, Labor, Industrial Relations, Literature, Literary Criticism, Essays, Nonfiction (General), Philosophy, Psychology, Psychiatry, Religion - Other, Social Sciences, Sociology, Travel & Tourism
ISBN Prefix(es): 978-0-9543161; 978-0-9556055; 978-0-9538460; 978-1-906791; 978-1-909421
Number of titles published annually: 12 Print; 12 E-Book
Total Titles: 83 Print; 68 E-Book
Foreign Rep(s): Silvia Bastos (Spain); Dar Alsalam (Egypt); Agencja Literacka Graal (Poland); Iris Literary Agency (Greece)
Distribution Center: Lightning Source UK Ltd, Chapter House, Pitfield, Kiln Farm, Milton Keynes MR11 3LW
Ingram International, One Ingram Blvd, PO Box 3006, La Vergne, TN 37086-1986, United States

Arena Sport, *imprint of* Birlinn Ltd

Argus Books, *imprint of* Special Interest Model Books Ltd

Argyll Publishing
Glendaruel, Argyll PA22 3AE
Tel: (0845) 463 6759
E-mail: inf@argyllpublishing.co.uk
Web Site: www.argyllpublishing.co.uk
Founded: 1992
Subjects: Biography, Memoirs, Fiction, Health, Nutrition, History, Inspirational, Spirituality, Literature, Literary Criticism, Essays, Maritime,

Poetry, Self-Help, Sports, Athletics, Current
Affairs, Nature, Scottish Interest, Wildlife
ISBN Prefix(es): 978-1-874640; 978-1-902831;
978-0-906938; 978-1-906134; 978-1-908931
Imprints: Thirsty Books (fiction)
Distribution Center: Central Books Ltd, One
Heath Park Industrial Estate, Freshwater
Rd, Dagenham RM8 1RX *Tel:* (020) 8525
8800 *Fax:* (020) 8599 2694 *E-mail:* orders@
centralbooks.com *Web Site:* www.centralbooks.
com

Arkana, *imprint of* Penguin Books Ltd

Armadillo, *imprint of* Anness Publishing Ltd

Armchair Traveller, *imprint of* Haus Publishing

Arrow, *imprint of* The Random House Group
Ltd, a Penguin Random House Company

Artech House+
Subsidiary of Horizon House Publications Inc
16 Sussex St, London SW1V 4RW
Tel: (020) 7596 8750 *Fax:* (020) 7630 0166
E-mail: artech-uk@artechhouse.com
Web Site: www.artechhouse.com
Key Personnel
Sales & Marketing Manager: Maiken Fjellstad
Tel: (020) 7596 8761 *E-mail:* mfjellstad@
artechhouse.co.uk
Acquisitions Editor: Aileen Storry
E-mail: astorry@artechhouse.co.uk
Founded: 1969
Publisher of professional books for engineers &
managers.
Subjects: Communications, Computer Science,
Electronics, Electrical Engineering, Engineering
(General), Management, Radio, TV, Science
(General), Technology, Transportation
ISBN Prefix(es): 978-0-89006; 978-1-58053; 978-
1-59693; 978-1-60807; 978-1-60783; 978-1-
6381
Number of titles published annually: 70 Print; 5
CD-ROM
U.S. Office(s): 685 Canton St, Norwood, MA
02062, United States

Arts Council of England
21 Bloomsbury St, London WC1B 3HF
Tel: (0845) 300 6200; (0161) 934 4428
Fax: (0161) 934 4426
E-mail: enquiries@artscouncil.org.uk
Web Site: www.artscouncil.org.uk
Key Personnel
Chief Executive: Darren Henley
E-mail: chiefexecutive@artscouncil.org.uk
Communications Officer: Nick Tapper *Tel:* (020)
7268 9653 *E-mail:* nick.tapper@artscouncil.org.
uk
Founded: 1946
Specialize in arts policy, arts management & re-
search.
Subjects: Art, Drama, Theater, Music, Dance,
Photography, Visual Arts
ISBN Prefix(es): 978-0-7287; 978-0-900085
Distribution Center: Marston Book Services Ltd,
160 Eastern Ave, Milton Park, Abingdon, Oxon
OX14 4SB *Tel:* (01235) 465500 *Fax:* (01235)
465555 *E-mail:* direct.orders@marston.co.uk
Web Site: www.marston.co.uk

Ashgrove Publishing+
27 John St, London WC1N 2BX
Tel: (020) 7242 4820
E-mail: ashgrovepublishing@gmail.com
Web Site: ashgrovebooks.vpweb.co.uk
Key Personnel
Dir: Alan Smith; Brad Thompson
Founded: 1970

Subjects: Cookery, Drama, Theater, Fiction,
Health, Nutrition, History, Humor, Mysteries,
Suspense, Religion - Other, Self-Help, Sports,
Athletics, Detective & Crime, Military
ISBN Prefix(es): 978-0-906798; 978-1-85398
Number of titles published annually: 8 Print; 5 E-
Book
Total Titles: 40 Print; 1 CD-ROM; 20 E-Book
Parent Company: Hollydata Publishers Ltd
Imprints: 'Round Midnight (detective & crime);
Thin Red Line (military & related books);
Zephyr (literary fiction)
Distribution Center: Orca Book Services,
Unit A3, Fleets Corner Industrial Estate, off
Nuffield Rd, Fleetsbridge, Poole, Dorset BH17
0HL *Tel:* (01235) 465500 *E-mail:* orders@
orcabookservices.co.uk
Orders to: Star Book Sales, PO Box 20,
Whimple Exeter EX5 2WY, Sales Dir:
Dennis Buckingham *Tel:* (0845) 156 7082
E-mail: dennisbuckingham@starbooksales.com
Web Site: www.starbooksales.com

Ashmolean Museum Publications+
Beaumont St, Oxford, Oxon OX1 2PH
Tel: (01865) 278010 *Fax:* (01865) 278106
E-mail: publications@ashmus.ox.ac.uk
Web Site: www.ashmolean.org; www.ashmolean.
org/services/publications
Key Personnel
Commercial Services Manager: Declan McCarthy
Deputy Publishing Manager: Emily Jolliffe
Founded: 1683
Publishing & retail sales.
Subjects: Archaeology, Art, Asian Studies, Crafts,
Games, Hobbies, History, Regional Interests,
Travel & Tourism
ISBN Prefix(es): 978-0-907849; 978-1-85444;
978-0-900090
Number of titles published annually: 15 Print
Parent Company: University of Oxford
Imprints: Griffith Institute
Distributed by Antique Collectors Club
Orders to: Antique Collectors' Club, Sandy Lane,
Old Martlesham, Woodbridge, Suffolk IP12
4SD *Tel:* (01394) 389950 *Fax:* (01394) 389999
E-mail: sales@antique-acc.com (UK/European
trade orders)
Inbooks, Locked Bag 535, Frenchs Forest, NSW
2086, Australia *Tel:* (02) 8988 5082 *Fax:* (02)
8988 5090 *E-mail:* orders@inbooks.com.au
(Australian trade orders)
Antique Collectors' Club Ltd, Eastworks, 116
Pleasant St, Suite 60B, Easthampton, MA
01027, United States *E-mail:* info@antiquecc.
com (USA trade orders)

Ashton & Denton Publishing Co (CI) Ltd
Kensington Chambers, 46/50 Kensington Pl, St
Helier, Jersey, Channel Islands JE1 1ET
Key Personnel
Editorial: Yvonne Aston
Founded: 1948
Specialize in Channel Islands publications.
Subjects: Business, Finance, Regional Interests
ISBN Prefix(es): 978-0-85053
Number of titles published annually: 6 Print
Total Titles: 8 Print

Asia Ink
One Alma Terrace, London W8 6QY
Tel: (020) 7938 4476
E-mail: sales@asiainkbooks.com
Web Site: asiainkbooks.com
Key Personnel
Publisher & Editor: Sherry Buchanan
Founded: 2002
Subjects: History, Culture, Museums
ISBN Prefix(es): 978-0-9537839
Distributed by Paragon Asia (Thailand); Thames
& Hudson (Asia exc Thailand & Europe); Uni-
versity of Chicago Press (North America)

**ASLIB, The Association for Information
Management+**
Howard House, Wagon Lane, Bingley BD16 1WA
Tel: (01274) 777700 *Fax:* (01274) 785201
E-mail: support@aslib.com
Web Site: www.aslib.com
Key Personnel
Publications & Training Manager: Diane Heath
E-mail: dheath@aslib.com
Editor-in-Chief: Graham Coult *E-mail:* gcoult@
aslib.com
Founded: 1924
Membership(s): The Association of Learned
& Professional Society Publishers (ALPSP);
ECIA; FID; ICSTI.
Subjects: Business, Law, Library & Information
Sciences, Management, Technology
ISBN Prefix(es): 978-0-85142
Distributed by Allied Publishers Pvt Ltd; DA
Books & Journals Pty (Australia); Kinoku-
niyiya (Japan); Portland Press Ltd (worldwide
exc Australia & Japan)
Orders to: Portland Press Ltd, Commerce Way,
Whitehall Industrial Estate, Colchester CO2
8HP

ASLS, see Association for Scottish Literary
Studies

Aspects of Portugal, *imprint of* Carcanet Press
Ltd

The Association for Information Management,
see ASLIB, The Association for Information
Management

Association for Science Education+
College Lane, Hatfield, Herts AL10 9AA
Tel: (01707) 283000; (01707) 283001 (sales)
Fax: (01707) 266532
E-mail: info@ase.org.uk; booksales@ase.org.uk
Web Site: www.ase.org.uk
Key Personnel
Chief Executive: Shaun Reason
Coordinator, Journals: Jane R Hanrott
E-mail: janehanrott@ase.org.uk
Founded: 1901
Subjects: Biological Sciences, Chemistry, Chemi-
cal Engineering, Computer Science, Disability,
Special Needs, Education, Energy, Physics, Sci-
ence (General)
ISBN Prefix(es): 978-0-86357; 978-0-902786
Number of titles published annually: 5 Print; 1
CD-ROM; 2 Online
Total Titles: 25 Print; 1 CD-ROM; 2 Online

Association for Scottish Literary Studies
c/o Scottish Literature, University of Glasgow, 7
University Gardens, Glasgow G12 8QH
Tel: (0141) 330 5309 *Fax:* (0141) 330 5309
E-mail: office@asls.org.uk (orders)
Web Site: asls.arts.gla.ac.uk
Key Personnel
President: Prof Alison Lumsden
Treasurer: Tom Ralph
Secretary: Dr Ronnie Young
Dir: Duncan Jones
Founded: 1970
Educational charity supporting the study, teaching
& writing of Scottish literature & languages.
Subjects: Language Arts, Linguistics, Literature,
Literary Criticism, Essays, Scottish Literature
& Linguistics
ISBN Prefix(es): 978-0-948877; 978-0-9502629;
978-1-906841; 978-1-908980 (Scottish Litera-
ture International)
Number of titles published annually: 8 Print; 1 E-
Book; 1 Audio
Total Titles: 2 Online; 1 E-Book; 7 Audio
Imprints: Scottish Literature International
Warehouse: Book Source, 50 Cambuslang
Rd, Clyde Industrial Estate, Glasgow G32

8NB *Tel:* (0845) 370 0063 *Fax:* (0845) 370 0064 *E-mail:* orders@booksource.net *Web Site:* www.booksource.net

Association of Commonwealth Universities (ACU)
Woburn House, 20-24 Tavistock Sq, London WC1H 9HF
Tel: (020) 7380 6700 *Fax:* (020) 7387 2655
E-mail: info@acu.ac.uk
Web Site: www.acu.ac.uk
Key Personnel
Secretary General: Prof John Wood
Deputy Secretary General: Dr John Kirkland
Founded: 1913
Specialize in promoting, in various practical ways, contact & cooperation between its member institutions. The association's membership includes 500 universities in 37 countries/regions in the Commonwealth.
Membership(s): Directory & Database Publishers Association.
Subjects: Developing Countries, Education, Higher Education
ISBN Prefix(es): 978-0-85143
Number of titles published annually: 4 Print; 1 Online
Total Titles: 8 Print; 1 Online
Distributed by Palgrave Macmillan

Atebol Ltd
Fagwyr Bldgs, Llandre, Aberystwyth, Ceredigion SY24 5AQ
Tel: (01970) 832 172 *Fax:* (01970) 832 259
E-mail: atebol@atebol.com
Web Site: www.atebol.com
Subjects: Education, Language Arts, Linguistics, Learning Skills
ISBN Prefix(es): 978-0-9547578; 978-1-905255

Atelier Books
6 Dundas St, Edinburgh EH3 6HZ
Tel: (0131) 5574050 *Fax:* (0131) 5578382
E-mail: art@bournefineart.com
Web Site: www.bournefineart.com/publications
Founded: 1991
Subjects: Art, Biography, Memoirs
ISBN Prefix(es): 978-1-873830
Distribution Center: BookSource, 50 Cambuslang Rd, Cambuslang, Glasgow G32 8NB *Tel:* (0845) 370 0067 *Fax:* (0845) 370 0068 *E-mail:* orders@booksource.net *Web Site:* www.booksource.net
ACC Publishing Group, Sandy Lane, Old Martlesham, Woodbridge, Suffolk IP12 4SD *Tel:* (01394) 389950 *Fax:* (01394) 389999 *E-mail:* info@antique-acc.com *Web Site:* www.accdistribution.com

Atlantic Books
Ormond House, 26-27 Boswell St, London WC1N 3JZ
Tel: (020) 7269 1610; (020) 7269 1628 (sales); (020) 7269 0249 (rights) *Fax:* (020) 7430 0916
E-mail: enquiries@atlantic-books.co.uk; sales@atlantic-books.co.uk; rights@atlantic-books.co.uk
Web Site: atlantic-books.co.uk
Key Personnel
Publisher & Mng Dir: Will Atkinson
Publishing Dir: Margaret Stead
Founded: 2000
Subjects: Biography, Memoirs, Fiction, Government, Political Science, History, Current Affairs
ISBN Prefix(es): 978-1-78239
Imprints: Corvus
Distributor for Allen & Unwin
Distribution Center: The Book Service Ltd, Distribution Centre, Colchester Rd, Frating Green, Colchester, Essex CO7 7DW *Tel:* (01206) 256000 *Fax:* (01206) 255715 *E-mail:* sales@

tbs-ltd.co.uk *Web Site:* www.thebookservice.co.uk
Trafalgar Square Publishing, c/o Independent Publishers Group (IPG), 814 N Franklin St, Chicago, IL 60610, United States *Tel:* 312-337-0747 *Fax:* 312-337-5985 *E-mail:* orders@ipgbook.com

Atlas Press+
BCM Atlas Press, 27 Old Gloucester St, London WC1N 3XX
Tel: (020) 7490 8742 *Fax:* (021) 7490 8742
E-mail: enquiries@atlaspress.co.uk
Web Site: www.atlaspress.co.uk
Key Personnel
Chief Editor: Alastair Brotchie
German Language & Series Editor: Malcolm Green
French Language & Series Editor: Antony Melville
Copy Editor & Proofreader: Chris Allen
Founded: 1983
Specialize in extremist & avant-garde prose writing from 1890s to the present day.
Subjects: Alternative, Art, Biography, Memoirs, Drama, Theater, Erotica, Fiction, Art History, European Avant-Garde Literature & Art, Limited Editions
ISBN Prefix(es): 978-0-947757; 978-1-900565
Number of titles published annually: 8 Print
Total Titles: 75 Print
Imprints: The Printed Head
Distributed by Exact Change (trade titles only); Marginal Distribution (Canada); Peribo Pty Ltd (Australia)
Distributor for Cymbalum Pataphysicum
Foreign Rep(s): Exact Exchange (USA)
Orders to: Turnaround Publisher Services, Olympia Trading Estate, Unit 3, Coburg Rd, London N22 6TZ *Tel:* (0181) 8829 3002 *E-mail:* customercare@turnaround-uk.com (UK & Europe)
Distributed Art Publishers Inc, 155 Sixth Ave, 2nd floor, New York, NY 10013, United States *Tel:* 212-627-1999 *Fax:* 212-627-9484 *E-mail:* orders@artbook.com

Atom, *imprint of* Little, Brown Book Group

Audio Books, *imprint of* Carcanet Press Ltd

Augener, *imprint of* Stainer & Bell Ltd

Aureus Publishing Ltd+
Castle Court, Castle-upon-Alun, St Bride's Major, Vale of Glamorgan CF32 0TN
Tel: (01656) 880033 *Fax:* (01656) 880033
E-mail: info@aureus.co.uk
Web Site: www.aureus.co.uk
Key Personnel
Dir: Meuryn Hughes
Founded: 1993
Publisher of rock biographies, music biographies, sport & related titles.
Subjects: Biography, Memoirs, Music, Dance, Sports, Athletics, Popular Music
ISBN Prefix(es): 978-1-899750
Number of titles published annually: 3 Print
Total Titles: 50 Print
Distribution Center: Gardners Books Ltd

Aurora Metro Books
67 Grove Ave, Twickenham TW1 4HX
Tel: (020) 3261 0000 *Fax:* (020) 8898 0735
E-mail: info@aurorametro.com; submissions@aurorametro.com; orders@aurorametro.com
Web Site: www.aurorametro.com
Key Personnel
Publisher: Cheryl Robson *E-mail:* cheryl@aurorametro.com

Mng Editor: Andrew Walby *E-mail:* andrew@aurorametro.com
Editor: Simon Smith *E-mail:* editor@aurorametro.com
Marketing: Ellen Cheshire *E-mail:* ellenaurorametro@gmail.com
Founded: 1989
Independent publisher of print & ebooks - fiction, nonfiction, humour, teen fiction, drama, cookery & biography.
Membership(s): IPG; SOA.
Subjects: Biography, Memoirs, Cookery, Drama, Theater, Fiction, Humor, Nonfiction (General)
ISBN Prefix(es): 978-0-9546912; 978-0-9551566; 978-1-906582; 978-0-9566329; 978-0-9515877; 978-0-9536757; 978-0-9542330
Number of titles published annually: 10 Print; 20 Online; 20 E-Book
Total Titles: 230 Print; 150 Online; 150 E-Book
Imprints: Supernova Books
Foreign Rep(s): Central Books Ltd (Europe, UK); Consortium (Canada, USA); Andrew Durnell (Europe); INT Books Pty Ltd (Australia, New Zealand); PMS (Malaysia, Singapore); Signature Publishing Services (UK)
Foreign Rights: Theatre Communications Group (TCG) (USA)
Distribution Center: Central Books Ltd, One Heath Park Industrial Estate, Freshwater Rd, Dagenham RM8 1RX *Tel:* (020) 8525 8800 *Fax:* (020) 8599 2694 *E-mail:* orders@centralbooks.com *Web Site:* www.centralbooks.com
Consortium Book Sales Inc, c/o Two Rivers Distribution, 1094 Flex Dr, Jackson, TN 38301, United States *Tel:* 731-423-1550 *Fax:* 731-423-1335 *E-mail:* orders@cbsd.com *Web Site:* www.cbsd.com

Aurora Northern Classics, *imprint of* Orkney Press Ltd

Aurum Press, *imprint of* Quarto Publishing Group UK

Aurum Press+
Imprint of Quarto Publishing Group UK
74-77 White Lion St, Islington N1 9PF
Tel: (020) 7284 9300 *Fax:* (020) 7485 0490
E-mail: publicity@aurumpress.co.uk; sales@aurumpress.co.uk
Web Site: www.quartoknows.com/aurum-press
Key Personnel
Publisher: Richard Green
Head, Marketing: Sam Shone
Head, Production: Laura Grandi
Head, Special Sales: Simon Fox
Foreign Rights Dir: Valerie Saint-Pierre
Mng Editor: Jessica Halliwell
Senior Marketing Manager: Jessica Clarke
Founded: 1976
Subjects: Architecture & Interior Design, Art, Biography, Memoirs, Film, Video, History, Humor, Military Science, Music, Dance, Nonfiction (General), Photography, Sports, Athletics, Transportation, Travel & Tourism, Current Affairs, General Adult Nonfiction
ISBN Prefix(es): 978-1-85410; 978-0-948149; 978-1-84513; 978-0-906053; 978-1-78131
Number of titles published annually: 75 Print
Total Titles: 250 Print
Ultimate Parent Company: The Quarto Group Inc
Foreign Rep(s): APD (Malaysia, Singapore); Bookwise International Pty Ltd (Australia); Fitzhenry & Whiteside Ltd (Canada); Hachette Livre (New Zealand); Nilsson & Lamm (Netherlands); Publishers Associates Ltd (Hong Kong); Quayside Publishing Group (USA); Trinity Books (South Africa)
Orders to: Littlehampton Book Services Ltd, Faraday Close, Durrington, Worthing, West

Sussex BN13 3HD *Tel:* (01903) 828500; (01903) 828501 (customer service) *Web Site:* lbsltd.wp.hachette.co.uk

Authentic Media
52 Presley Way, Crown Hill, Milton Keynes MK8 0ES
Tel: (01908) 268500
E-mail: info@authenticmedia.co.uk; orders@authenticmedia.co.uk
Web Site: www.authenticmedia.co.uk
Key Personnel
Mng Dir: Steve Mitchell
Operations Manager: Donna Harris
Publishing Manager: Malcolm Down
Marketing Manager: Kate Beaton
Paternoster Commissioning Editor: Mike Parsons
Editorial Supervisor: Liz Williams
Accounts Administrator: Wendy Tyler
Christian publishing house.
Subjects: Theology
ISBN Prefix(es): 978-0-85364; 978-1-85078; 978-0-948902; 978-0-9630908; 978-1-884543; 978-0-903843; 978-1-86024; 978-1-932805; 978-1-934068; 978-1-60657
Imprints: Paternoster

Autumn Publishing Ltd
Imprint of Bonnier Publishing
c/o Igloo Books Ltd, Cottage Farm, Mears Ashby Rd, Sywell, Northants NN6 0BJ
Tel: (01604) 741116 *Fax:* (01604) 670495
E-mail: info@igloobooks.com; customerservice@igloobooks.com
Web Site: igloobooks.com; www.facebook.com/AutPub/?ref=page_internal
Key Personnel
Creative Dir: Helen Wicks
Foreign Rights Manager: Cecilia Fanucci
Sales Manager: Tony Cleugh
Founded: 1976
ISBN Prefix(es): 978-0-946593; 978-1-85997; 978-1-84531; 978-1-84958; 978-1-78296
Ultimate Parent Company: Bonnier AB
Imprints: Smellessence

AVA Publishing, *imprint of* Bloomsbury Publishing Plc

Avon, *imprint of* HarperCollins UK

Award Publications Ltd+
The Old Riding School, Welbeck Estate, Worksop, Notts S80 3LR
Tel: (01909) 478 170 *Fax:* (01909) 484 632
E-mail: info@awardpublications.co.uk
Web Site: www.awardpublications.co.uk
Key Personnel
Mng Dir: Anna Wilkinson *E-mail:* anna@awardpublications.co.uk
International Sales Manager: Richard Carman *E-mail:* richardcarman@awardpublications.co.uk
Production Manager: Adam Wilde
UK Sales Manager: David Meggs *E-mail:* davidmeggs@awardpublications.co.uk
Founded: 1972
ISBN Prefix(es): 978-0-86163; 978-1-84135; 978-1-899762; 978-1-78270
Imprints: Horus Editions; Picthall & Gunzi

Axis Mundi Books, *imprint of* O Books

Ayni Books, *imprint of* O Books

b small publishing ltd+
27 Sladedale Rd, London SE18 1PY
Web Site: www.bsmall.co.uk

Key Personnel
Publisher: Sam Hutchinson *E-mail:* sh@bsmall.co.uk
Founded: 1990
Specialize in general children's interactive nonfiction & foreign language learning books.
No submissions accepted.
ISBN Prefix(es): 978-1-874735; 978-1-902915; 978-1-905710; 978-1-908164; 978-1-909767
Foreign Rep(s): Bardon Chinese Media Agency (Jian-Mei Wang or Cynthia Chang) (China, Taiwan); IMC Agencia Literaria (Spain); Alexander Korzhenevski Agency (Russia)
Foreign Rights: Big Leap Ltd (Gwen Bennet) (Australia, Brazil, Canada (English-speaking), New Zealand, South Africa, Spanish Latin America, Turkey, USA, Wales); Capricorn International Rights (Rachel Pidcock) (Eastern Europe, France, Germany, Netherlands, Scandinavia)
Distribution Center: Grantham Book Services Ltd, Trent Rd, Grantham, Lincs NG31 7XQ *Tel:* (01476) 541080 *Fax:* (01476) 541061 *E-mail:* orders@gbs.tbs-ltd.co.uk *Web Site:* www.granthambookservices.co.uk
Orders to: Bounce! Sales & Marketing Ltd, 320 City Rd, London EC1V 2NZ *Tel:* (020) 7138 3650 *Fax:* (020) 7138 3658 *E-mail:* sales@bouncemarketing.co.uk *Web Site:* www.bouncemarketing.com (trade orders in UK & export markets)
Intext Book Co, Kew East, Victoria, Australia *Tel:* (03) 9819 4500 *Fax:* (03) 9819 4511 *E-mail:* jillian@intextbook.com.au *Web Site:* www.intextbook.com.au
South Pacific Book Distributors Ltd, North Harbour, Auckland, New Zealand *Tel:* (09) 448 1591 *Fax:* (09) 448 1592 *E-mail:* sales@soupacbooks.co.nz *Web Site:* www.soupacbooks.co.nz
Phambili Agencies, Germiston, South Africa, Contact: Maria Lastrucci *Tel:* (011) 8733461 *Fax:* (011) 8734263 *E-mail:* phambili@icon.co.za

Bernard Babani (Publishing) Ltd+
The Grampians, Shepherds Bush Rd, London W6 7NF
Tel: (020) 7603 2581 *Fax:* (020) 7603 8203
E-mail: enquiries@babanibooks.com
Web Site: www.babanibooks.com
Key Personnel
Mng Dir: Michael H Babani
Founded: 1977
Subjects: Computer Science, Electronics, Electrical Engineering, Radio, TV
ISBN Prefix(es): 978-0-85934; 978-0-900162
Associate Companies: Babani Press

Babel Guides, *imprint of* Boulevard Books/The Babel Guides

BackPage Press Ltd
Anniesland Rd, Glasgow G13 2TL
E-mail: backpage@backpagepress.co.uk
Web Site: backpagepress.co.uk
Key Personnel
Rights: Neil White *E-mail:* neil.white@backpagepress.co.uk
Founded: 2010
Subjects: Sports, Athletics
ISBN Prefix(es): 978-0-9564971
Distributed by Trafalgar Square Publishing

Bailliere Tindall Ltd, *imprint of* Elsevier Ltd

Charles Baker Books Ltd
47 Bury New Rd, Prestwich, Manchester M25 9JY
Tel: (020) 7612 4342 *Fax:* (020) 7182 6764
E-mail: sales@charlesbaker.co.uk

Web Site: www.charlesbaker.co.uk
Founded: 2000
Subjects: Computer Science, Fiction, Classics
ISBN Prefix(es): 978-1-84665

The Banner of Truth Trust+
The Grey House, 3 Murrayfield Rd, Edinburgh EH12 6EL
Tel: (0131) 337 7310 *Fax:* (0131) 346 7484
E-mail: info@banneroftruth.co.uk
Web Site: www.banneroftruth.co.uk
Key Personnel
General Manager: John Rawlinson
General Editorial: Jonathan Watson
Founded: 1957
Historic Christianity through literature.
Subjects: Biography, Memoirs, History, Religion - Protestant, Theology
ISBN Prefix(es): 978-0-85151
U.S. Office(s): PO Box 621, Carlisle, PA 17013, United States *Tel:* 717-249-5747 *Fax:* 717-249-0604 *E-mail:* info@banneroftruth.org

Bantam, *imprint of* Transworld Publishers

Bantam Children, *imprint of* The Random House Group Ltd, a Penguin Random House Company

Bantam Press, *imprint of* Transworld Publishers

The Banton Press
Dippin Cottage, Kildonan, Isle of Arran KA27 8SB
Tel: (01770) 820671
E-mail: bantonpress@ndo.co.uk
Web Site: www.bantonpress.ndo.co.uk
Key Personnel
Contact: Mark Brown
Founded: 1988
Subjects: Astrology, Occult, Biography, Memoirs, History, Mysteries, Suspense, Philosophy, Religion - Other, Celts/Druids, Folklore, Kaballa/Tarot
ISBN Prefix(es): 978-1-85652
Number of titles published annually: 4 Print
Total Titles: 180 Print

Barbet Books, *imprint of* Helm Information

Barefoot Books+
294 Banbury Rd, Oxford OX2 7ED
Tel: (01865) 311100 *Toll Free Tel:* 0800 328 2640 (sales) *Fax:* (01865) 51496524
E-mail: help@barefootbooks.com; salessupport@barefootbooks.com
Web Site: www.barefootbooks.com/uk
Key Personnel
Owner, Co-Founder & Chief Executive Officer: Nancy Traversy
Co-Founder, Editor-in-Chief: Tessa Strickland *E-mail:* tessa.strickland@barefootbooks.co.uk
Founded: 1993
ISBN Prefix(es): 978-1-901223; 978-1-902283; 978-1-84148; 978-1-84686; 978-1-905236; 978-1-989000
Branch Office(s)
89 Thoreau St, Concord, MA 01742, United States *Tel:* 978-369-1770 *E-mail:* concord.store@barefootbooks.com
Foreign Rep(s): A-Z Africa Book Services (Anita Zih) (Africa exc South Africa); Conor Hackett (Ireland); JCC Enterprises Inc (Caribbean, Central America, South America); Peribo Pty Ltd (Australia, New Zealand); Publishers International Marketing (Ru Ashdown) (Middle East); Publishers International Marketing (Chris Ashdown) (Asia); Kyle & Stephanie Tucker (Canada)
Orders to: Littlehampton Book Services Ltd, Faraday Close, Durrington, Worthing, West

Sussex BN13 3RB *Tel:* (01903) 828500; (01903) 828501 (customer service) *Web Site:* lbsltd.wp.hachette.co.uk

Baring & Rogerson Books, *imprint of* Eland Publishing Ltd

Barn Dance Publications Ltd+
20, Shirley Ave, Old Coulsdon CR5 1QU
Tel: (020) 8668 5714 *Fax:* (020) 8645 6923
E-mail: info@barndancepublications.co.uk
Web Site: shop.barndancepublications.co.uk
Key Personnel
Dir: Derek L Jones
Founded: 1984
Supplier of barn dance/ceilidh books, cassettes & CDs.
Membership(s): Book Data.
Subjects: Music, Dance, Folk Dance
ISBN Prefix(es): 978-0-9514285; 978-1-874565
Total Titles: 20 Print; 16 Audio

Barn Owl Press, *imprint of* Alun Books

Barnabas, *imprint of* Bible Reading Fellowship

Barrington Stoke
18 Walker St, Edinburgh EH3 7LP
Tel: (0131) 225 4113
E-mail: barrington@barringtonstoke.co.uk
Web Site: www.barringtonstoke.co.uk
ISBN Prefix(es): 978-1-84299; 978-1-902260
Distribution Center: Grantham Book Services, Trent Rd, Grantham, Lincs NG31 7XQ
Tel: (01476) 541080 *E-mail:* orders@gbs.tbs-ltd.co.uk (trade customers)
Orders to: Bounce! Sales & Marketing, 320 City Rd, London EC1V 2NZ *Tel:* (020) 7138 3650
E-mail: sales@bouncemarketing.co.uk (UK & export trade exc Australia, Malaysia, New Zealand, Singapore & South Africa)

Batsford, *imprint of* Pavilion Books

Colin Baxter, *imprint of* Colin Baxter Photography Ltd

Colin Baxter Photography Ltd+
Achnagonalin Industrial Estate, Unit 9 1/2, Grantown-on-Spey, Moray PH26 3TA
Tel: (01479) 873999 *Fax:* (01479) 873888
E-mail: sales@colinbaxter.co.uk
Web Site: www.colinbaxter.co.uk
Key Personnel
Mng Dir: Colin Baxter
Founded: 1982
Subjects: Natural History, Photography, Travel & Tourism
ISBN Prefix(es): 978-0-948661; 978-1-900455; 978-1-84107
Number of titles published annually: 20 Print
Total Titles: 80 Print
Imprints: Colin Baxter; Worldlife Library
Distributed by Voyageur Press (USA)
Foreign Rep(s): Ted Dougherty (Austria, Belgium, France, Germany, Greece, Italy, Luxembourg, Netherlands, Switzerland); Theo Philips (Brunei, Hong Kong, Malaysia, Philippines, Singapore, Thailand); Peter Prout (Spain); Voyageur Press Inc (USA)
Orders to: Freepost, PO Box 1, Grantown-on-Spey, Moray PH26 3YA

BBC Active, *imprint of* Pearson Education Ltd

BBC Active English Language Learning+
80 Strand, London WC2R 0RL
Tel: (020) 7010 2754 *Fax:* (020) 7010 6965
E-mail: bbcactive.languages.admin@pearson.com

Web Site: www.bbcactivelanguages.com; www.bbcactiveenglish.com; www.bbcactive.com
Key Personnel
Contact: Vito D'Onghia *E-mail:* vito.d'onghia@pearson.com
Founded: 1943
Subjects: English as a Second Language
ISBN Prefix(es): 978-1-85497; 978-0-946675
Parent Company: Pearson Education Group

BBC Books, *imprint of* Ebury Publishing

BBC Books+
Imprint of Ebury Publishing
c/o The Random House Group Ltd, 20 Vauxhall Bridge Rd, London SW1V 2SA
Tel: (020) 7840 8400 *Fax:* (020) 7233 8791
Web Site: www.eburypublishing.co.uk
Key Personnel
Publishing Dir: Albert De Petrillo
Commissioning Editor: Yvonne Jacobs
Founded: 1925
Subjects: Cookery, Gardening, Plants, History, Humor, Natural History, Travel & Tourism
ISBN Prefix(es): 978-1-84990
Ultimate Parent Company: The Random House Group Ltd, a Penguin Random House Company

BC Books, *imprint of* Birlinn Ltd

BCS, The Chartered Institute for IT
Block D, North Star House, 1st floor, North Star Ave, Swindon, Wilts SN2 1FA
Tel: (01739) 417417; (01793) 417440 (bookshop) *Fax:* (01793) 417444
E-mail: bcspublishing@hq.bcs.org.uk
Web Site: www.bcs.org/books
Key Personnel
Group Chief Executive: Paul Fletcher
Group Finance Dir: Philip Jones
Dir, BCS Academy of Computing: Bill Mitchell
Dir, Business Technology: Carl Harris
Dir, Membership: David Evans
Dir, Professionalism, Communications & Public Affairs: Adam Thilthorpe
Head, Customer Service: Chris Butcher
Head, Media Relations: Adrian Oldman
    Tel: (01793) 417531 *E-mail:* adrian.oldman@bcs.uk
Press Officer: Amanda Matheson *Tel:* (01793) 417625 *E-mail:* amanda.matheson@bcs.org.uk
Subjects: Business, Information Technology
ISBN Prefix(es): 978-1-902505; 978-0-901865; 978-1-906124
Foreign Rep(s): Apex Knowledge Sdn Bhd (Brunei, Malaysia); Booknet Co Ltd (Cambodia, Laos, Thailand, Vietnam); ChoiceTEXTS (Asia) Pte Ltd (Indonesia, Singapore); Compass Academic (Europe, UK); iCaves Ltd (Hong Kong); IG Knowledge Services Ltd (Taiwan); iGroup Press Co Ltd (Frank Wang) (China); Information Development Consultancy Asia (IDCA), Korea (Korea); Ingram Book Co (USA); MegaTEXTS Phil Inc (Philippines); Viva Books (Bangladesh, India, Pakistan, Sri Lanka); Woodslane Pty Ltd (Australia, New Zealand)
Distribution Center: Turpin Distribution, Stratton Business Park, Pegasus Dr, Biggleswade, Beds SG18 8TQ *Tel:* (01767) 604951 *E-mail:* bcs@turpin-distribution.com (UK & Europe)

Ruth Bean Publishers, *imprint of* The Crowood Press Ltd

John Beaufoy Publishing Ltd
11 Blenheim Court, 316 Woodstock Rd, Oxford OX2 7NS
Tel: (01865) 510920
Web Site: www.johnbeaufoy.com

Key Personnel
Owner: John Beaufoy *E-mail:* johnb@johnbeaufoy.com
Founded: 2008
Membership(s): Independent Publishers Guild; Motovun Group of International Publishers (MGIP).
Subjects: Cookery, Fiction, History, Maritime, Natural History, Nonfiction (General), Travel & Tourism, Adventure, Classics, Diving, Natural Science, Southeast Asia
ISBN Prefix(es): 978-0-620; 978-1-906780; 978-1-909612
Foreign Rep(s): A-Z Africa Book Services (Anita Zih-De Haan) (Indian Ocean Islands, Sub-Saharan Africa); European Publishers Representation (Joe Portelli) (Continental Europe exc Gibraltar, Portugal & Spain); Humphrys Roberts Associates (Christopher Humphrys) (Caribbean, Central America, Gibraltar, Mexico, Portugal, Spain); Chris McClaren (Cyprus, Middle East, North Africa, Turkey); Midpoint Trade Books Inc (USA); Pansing Distribution Pte Ltd (Brunei, Malaysia, Singapore); South Pacific Book Distributors (New Zealand); Star Book Sales (Dennis Buckingham) (Ireland, UK); Wild Dog Publishing CC (Southern Africa); Woodslane Pty Ltd (Australia)
Warehouse: Orca Book Services, Unit A3, Fleets Corner, Poole, Dorset BH17 0HL *Tel:* (01202) 665432 *E-mail:* orders@orcabookservices.co.uk
Distribution Center: Orca Book Services, Unit A3, Fleets Corner, Poole, Dorset BH17 0HL *Tel:* (01202) 665432 *E-mail:* orders@orcabookservices.co.uk

Mitchell Beazley, *imprint of* Octopus Publishing Group Ltd

Mitchell Beazley+
Imprint of Octopus Publishing Group
Endeavour House, 189 Shaftesbury Ave, London WC2H 8JY
Tel: (020) 7632 5400 *Fax:* (020) 7632 5405
E-mail: info@octopusbooks.co.uk; sales@octopusbooks.co.uk
Web Site: www.octopusbooks.co.uk
Founded: 1969
Subjects: Antiques, Cookery, Gardening, Plants, House & Home, Natural History, Wine & Spirits
ISBN Prefix(es): 978-0-85533; 978-1-85732; 978-1-84000; 978-0-86134; 978-0-905879; 978-1-84533
Orders to: Littlehampton Book Services Ltd, Faraday Close, Durrington, Durrington, Worthing, Worthing, West Sussex BN13 3RB
Tel: (01903) 828500; (01903) 828501 (customer service) *Web Site:* lbsltd.wp.hachette.co.uk

Bedford Square Books
6 Bayley St, Bedford Sq, London WC1B 3HE
Tel: (020) 7304 4100 *Fax:* (020) 7304 4111
Web Site: www.bedfordsquarebooks.com
Key Personnel
Contact: Edina Imrik *E-mail:* edina@edvictor.com
Ebook & print on demand publishing venture from the Ed Victor Literary Agency.
Subjects: Fiction, Nonfiction (General)

Bedroom Books, *imprint of* O Books

Belknap, *imprint of* Harvard University Press

Bene Factum Publishing
10 Elm Quay Ct, Nine Elms Lane, London SW8 5DE
Tel: (020) 7720 6767
E-mail: inquiries@bene-factum.co.uk
Web Site: bene-factum.co.uk

Key Personnel
Owner: Anthony Weldon
Subjects: Biography, Memoirs, Business, Cookery, Nonfiction (General), Travel & Tourism
ISBN Prefix(es): 978-1-903071; 978-0-9522754
Foreign Rep(s): Adbox (Edwin Makabenta) (Philippines); Bookreps NZ Ltd (New Zealand); Ted Dougherty (Western Europe); Phambili (South Africa); Research Press Pvt Ltd (India); Trafalgar Square - Independent Publishers Group (Canada, USA); David Williams (Caribbean, Central America, South America); Woodslane Pty Ltd (Australia)
Distribution Center: Faber Factory, Bloomsbury House, 74-77 Great Russell St, London WC1B 3DA *Tel:* (020) 7927 3800 *Web Site:* www. faberfactory.co.uk (ebooks)
Combined Book Services, Paddock Wood Distribution Centre, Unit D, Paddock Wood, Tonbridge, Kent TN12 6UU *Tel:* (01892) 837171 *Fax:* (01892) 837272 *E-mail:* orders@combook.co.uk *Web Site:* www.combook.co.uk (books)

Berghahn Books Ltd (UK)+
3 Newtec Pl, Magdalen Rd, Oxford, Oxon OX4 1RE
Tel: (01865) 250011 *Fax:* (01865) 250056
E-mail: info@berghahnbooks.com
Web Site: www.berghahnbooks.com
Key Personnel
Publisher & Editor-in-Chief (Books): Dr Marion Berghahn, PhD *E-mail:* publisher@berghahnbooks.com
Mng Dir & Editorial Dir (Journals): Vivian Berghahn *E-mail:* editorial@journals.berghahnbooks.com
International Sales Dir: Rubert Jones Parry
Publicity & Marketing Executive: Ben Parker *E-mail:* publicityuk@berghahnbooks.com
General Manager, Sales & Marketing Manager: Leigh Waite
Production Editor, Journals: Charlotte Mosedale
Founded: 1994
Independent scholarly publisher in humanities & social sciences.
Subjects: Anthropology, Economics, Government, Political Science, History, Literature, Literary Criticism, Essays, Military Science, Religion - Jewish, Social Sciences, Sociology, Women's Studies, Cultural & Media Studies, Gender, Humanities, International Relations, Migration Studies
ISBN Prefix(es): 978-1-57181; 978-0-436; 978-1-84545; 978-0-85745; 978-1-85745; 978-1-78238
Number of titles published annually: 100 Print; 15 Online
Total Titles: 600 Print; 1 CD-ROM; 15 Online
U.S. Office(s): Berghahn Books Inc, 150 Broadway, Suite 812, New York, NY 10038, United States *Tel:* 212-233-6004 *Fax:* 212-233-6007
Foreign Rep(s): The African Moon Press (Chris Reinders) (South Africa); Avicenna Partnership Ltd (Claire de Gruchy) (Algeria, Cyprus, Greece, Jordan, Malta, Morocco, Palestine, Tunisia, Turkey); Avicenna Partnership Ltd (Bill Kennedy) (Middle East); Co Info Pty Ltd (Australia, New Zealand); Cranbury International LLC (Ethan Atkin) (Caribbean, Central America, Latin America); D T International (David Towle) (Scandinavia); Laszlo Horvath (Central Europe, Eastern Europe); Iberian Book Services (Peter Prout) (Portugal, Spain); Impact Korea (Korea); K L Books Distributor (K L Lee) (Malaysia, Southeast Asia); Flavio Marcello (France, Italy); Missing Link (Germany); Efrat Saad (Israel); Sagun Enterprises Inc (Philippines); Sara Books Pvt Ltd (Ravindra Sazena) (Indian subcontinent); Ian Taylor Associates Ltd (China); Unifacmanu Trading Co Ltd (Celine Li) (Taiwan); United Publisher Services (Japan)

Orders to: Turpin Distribution, Pegasus Dr, Statton Business Park, Biggleswade, Beds SG18 8TQ *Tel:* (01767) 604976 *Fax:* (01767) 601640 *E-mail:* berghahnbooks@turpin-distribution.com (UK & Europe, Africa, India, Middle East)
Books International, 22883 Quicksilver Dr, Dulles, VA 20166, United States *Tel:* 703-661-1500 *Fax:* 703-661-1501 *E-mail:* berghahnmail@presswarehouse.com (USA, Asia-Pacific, Australia & China)

Berlitz Publishing+
c/o Apa Publications UK Ltd, Magdalen House, 1st floor West, 136-148 Tooley St, London SE1 2TU
Tel: (020) 7403 0284
E-mail: london@berlitzpublishing.com; comments@berlitzpublishing.com
Web Site: www.berlitzpublishing.com
Founded: 1970
Specialize in phrase books, dictionaries, audio, video & children's language products, travel guides & language reference. Also provides translation & interpreting services.
Subjects: Travel & Tourism
ISBN Prefix(es): 978-0-7511; 978-1-78004
Total Titles: 375 Print
Distributed by Dorling Kindersley Ltd (UK, Europe & Ireland)
Distribution Center: Woodslane, 10 Apollo St, Warriewood, NSW 2102, Australia *Tel:* (02) 8445 2300 *Fax:* (02) 9997 5850 *E-mail:* info@woodslane.com.au (Australia & New Zealand)
Ingram Publisher Services, One Ingram Blvd, PO Box 3006, La Vergne, TN 37086, United States *E-mail:* ips@ingramcontent.com (USA & Canada)

Betterway, *imprint of* David & Charles Ltd

Between The Lines (BTL), *imprint of* The Waywiser Press

BFBS, *imprint of* Bible Society

BFI Publishing+
c/o Palgrave Macmillan, 4 Crinan St, London N1 9XW
Tel: (020) 7833 4000
Web Site: www.bfi.org.uk; www.palgrave.com/page/bfi-publishing
Key Personnel
Publisher: Jenna Steventon *E-mail:* j.steventon@palgrave.com
Founded: 1980
Subjects: Film, Video, Radio, TV, Social Sciences, Sociology, Women's Studies
ISBN Prefix(es): 978-0-85170; 978-0-900212; 978-1-84457; 978-1-903786
Number of titles published annually: 30 Print
Total Titles: 280 Print
Distributed by Bloomsbury Academic

Bible Distributors, *imprint of* Chapter Two

Bible Reading Fellowship+
15 The Chambers, Vineyard, Abingdon, Oxon OX14 3FE
Tel: (01865) 319700 *Fax:* (01865) 319701
E-mail: enquiries@brf.org.uk
Web Site: www.brf.org.uk; www.brfonline.org.uk
Key Personnel
Chief Executive: Richard Fisher *E-mail:* richard.fisher@brf.org.uk
Deputy Chief Executive: Karen Laister *E-mail:* karen.laister@brf.org.uk
Marketing Coordinator: Kevin Ball
Commissioning Editor: Naomi Starkey *E-mail:* naomi.starkey@brf.org.uk
Founded: 1922

Subjects: Biblical Studies, Education, Religion - Protestant, Theology
ISBN Prefix(es): 978-0-7459; 978-1-84101; 978-0-900164; 978-0-85746
Number of titles published annually: 40 Print
Total Titles: 300 Print; 50 Online
Imprints: Barnabas

Bible Society+
Stonehill Green, Westlea, Swindon, Wilts SN5 7DG
Tel: (01793) 418100
E-mail: contactus@biblesociety.org.uk
Web Site: www.biblesociety.org.uk; lc.bfbs.org.uk
Key Personnel
Group Chief Executive: James Catford
Deputy Chief Executive Officer: Paul Woolley
Founded: 1804
Subjects: Biblical Studies
ISBN Prefix(es): 978-0-564
Imprints: BFBS

Biblica Europe
The Mount Business Centre, 2 Woodstock Link, Belfast BT6 8DD
Tel: (028) 9073 5875
E-mail: europe@biblica.com
Web Site: www.biblicaeurope.com
Key Personnel
Dir for Partnerships & Publishing: Mark Finnie
ISBN Prefix(es): 978-91-7165; 978-91-87412
Parent Company: International Bible Society, 1820 Jet Stream Dr, Colorado Springs, CO 80921, United States

Joseph Biddulph Publisher+
32 Stryd Ebeneser, Pontypridd CF37 5PB
Tel: (01443) 662559
Web Site: www.dickgrune.com/Biddulph
Key Personnel
Sole Proprietor: Joseph Biddulph
Contact: Dick Grune *E-mail:* dick@dickgrune.com
Founded: 1991
Subjects: Language Arts, Linguistics, Poetry, Heraldry
ISBN Prefix(es): 978-1-897999; 978-0-948565
Total Titles: 50 Print
Imprints: Languages Information Centre

Big Picture Press, *imprint of* Templar Publishing

BILD Publications
Birmingham Research Park, 97 Vincent Dr, Edgbaston, Birmingham B15 2SQ
Tel: (0121) 415 6960 *Fax:* (0121) 415 6999
E-mail: enquiries@bild.org.uk
Web Site: www.bild.org.uk
Key Personnel
Chief Executive: Ann Chivers
Publications Officer: Tracey Tindell *Tel:* (0121) 415 6982 *E-mail:* t.tindell@bild.org.uk
Founded: 1972
Subjects: Behavioral Sciences, Child Care & Development, Disability, Special Needs, Health, Nutrition
ISBN Prefix(es): 978-1-873791; 978-0-906054; 978-1-902519; 978-1-904082; 978-1-905218
Orders to: BookSource, 50 Cambuslang Rd, Cambuslang, Glasgow G32 8NB *Tel:* (0845) 370 0067 *Fax:* (0845) 370 0068 *E-mail:* orders@booksource.net *Web Site:* www.booksource.net

BINDT, see British Institute of Non-Destructive Testing (BINDT)

Bio Scientifica, *imprint of* Society for Endocrinology

Birlinn, *imprint of* Birlinn Ltd

Birlinn Ltd+
West Newington House, 10 Newington Rd, Edinburgh EH9 1QS
Tel: (0131) 668 4371 *Fax:* (0131) 668 4466
E-mail: info@birlinn.co.uk
Web Site: www.birlinn.co.uk
Key Personnel
Mng Dir: Hugh Andrew *E-mail:* hugh@birlinn.co.uk
Publishing Dir: Neville Moir *E-mail:* neville@birlinn.co.uk
Editorial Dir: Andrew Simmons *E-mail:* andrew@birlinn.co.uk
Finance Dir: Joanne Macleod *E-mail:* joanne@birlinn.co.uk
Sales Dir: Laura Poynton *E-mail:* laura@birlinn.co.uk
Production Manager: Liz Short *E-mail:* liz@birlinn.co.uk
Founded: 1992
Membership(s): Scottish Publishers Association.
Subjects: Biography, Memoirs, Fiction, History, Military Science, Regional Interests, Sports, Athletics
ISBN Prefix(es): 978-1-874744; 978-0-85976; 978-1-898410; 978-1-86232; 978-1-84158; 978-1-84341; 978-1-84697; 978-0-85790; 978-1-78027
Number of titles published annually: 80 Print
Associate Companies: Maclean Press
Imprints: Arena Sport; BC Books; Birlinn; John Donald; Polygon
Distributor for Maclean Press
Foreign Rep(s): Bill Bailey Publishers Representatives (Northern Europe); Compass IPSL (England, Wales); Export Sales Agency (Ted Dougherty) (Southern Europe); Independent Publishers Group (IPG) (Canada, China, USA); New South Books (Australia, New Zealand); Seol Ltd (Scotland)
Foreign Rights: Script Agency (Maria White)
Distribution Center: Casemate I IPM, 1950 Lawrence Rd, Havertown, PA 19083, United States *Tel:* 610-853-9131 *Fax:* 610-853-9146 *E-mail:* casemate@casematepublishers.com *Web Site:* www.casemateipm.com (US, print; North America, ebooks)
Orders to: BookSource, 50 Cambuslang Rd, Cambuslang, Glasgow G32 8NB *Tel:* (0845) 370 0067 *E-mail:* customerservice@booksource.net *Web Site:* www.booksource.net

Biteback Publishing
Westminster Tower, 3 Albert Embankment, 10th floor, London SE1 7SP
Tel: (020) 7091 1260
E-mail: info@bitebackpublishing.com
Web Site: www.bitebackpublishing.com
Key Personnel
Deputy Chief Executive: James Stephens
Mng Dir: Iain Dale
Publicity Dir: Suzanne Sangster
Mng Editor: Olivia Beattie
Editor-at-Large: Michael Smith
Founded: 2009
Britain's leading publisher of political & current affairs titles. Also publish espionage, general, nonfiction & sport.
Subjects: Economics, Government, Political Science, History, Current Affairs
ISBN Prefix(es): 978-1-84954; 978-1-906447
Imprints: Biteback Sport; Dialogue; The Robson Press; Total Politics
Foreign Rep(s): Brookside Publishing Services (Ireland, Northern Ireland); Ted Dougherty (Austria, Belgium, France, Germany, Greece, Italy, Luxembourg, Malta, Netherlands, Switzerland); Iberian Book Services (Peter Prout) (Portugal, Spain); IMA (Central Europe, Eastern Europe, Russia, Sub-Saharan Africa exc South Africa); Pansing Distribution Pte Ltd (Brunei, Malaysia, Singapore); TowerToo & NewSouth Books (Australia, New Zealand);

Trinity Books (South Africa); The White Partnership (Andrew White) (Hong Kong, India, Japan, Korea, Pakistan, Philippines, Sri Lanka, Taiwan, Thailand)
Foreign Rights: Sheil Land Associates (Gaia Banks)
Distribution Center: Marston Book Services Ltd, 160 Eastern Ave, Milton Park, Abingdon, Oxon OX14 4SD *Tel:* (01235) 465500 *Fax:* (01235) 465509 *E-mail:* trade.orders@marston.co.uk *Web Site:* www.marston.co.uk
Consortium Book Sales & Distribution, The Keg House, 34 13 Ave NE, Suite 101, Minneapolis, MN 55413, United States *Tel:* 612-746-2600 *Fax:* 612-746-2606 *E-mail:* info@cbsd.com *Web Site:* www.cbsd.com

Biteback Sport, *imprint of* Biteback Publishing

Bitter Lemon Press Ltd
47 Wilmington Sq, London WC1X 0ET
Tel: (020) 7278 3738
E-mail: books@bitterlemonpress.com
Web Site: www.bitterlemonpress.com
Founded: 2003
Subjects: Fiction, Contemporary Crime Fiction, Thrillers
ISBN Prefix(es): 978-1-904738
Imprints: Wilmington Square Books
Distribution Center: Turnaround Publisher Services, Unit 3, Olympia Trading Estate, Coburg Rd, Wood Green, London N22 6TZ *Tel:* (020) 8829 3000 *E-mail:* info@turnaround-uk.com (UK & rest of Europe)
TL Distribution, 15-23 Helles Ave, Moorebank, NSW 2170, Australia *Tel:* (02) 8778 9999 *E-mail:* orders@tldistribution.com.au (Australia)
Consortium Book Sales & Distribution, 34 13 Ave NE, Suite 101, Minneapolis, MN 55413, United States *Tel:* 612-746-2600 *E-mail:* sales@cbsd.com (USA & Canada)

BL Publishing
Division of Games Workshop Ltd
Willow Rd, Lenton, Nottingham NG7 2WS
Tel: (0115) 900 4069
E-mail: contact@blacklibrary.com
Web Site: www.blacklibrary.com
Subjects: Science Fiction, Fantasy
ISBN Prefix(es): 978-0-7434; 978-1-84154; 978-1-84416; 978-1-84970
Imprints: The Black Library
Distributed by Simon & Schuster

A&C Black Publishers Ltd+
Subsidiary of Bloomsbury Publishing PLC
50 Bedford Sq, London WC1B 3DP
Tel: (020) 7631 5600 *Fax:* (020) 7631 5800
E-mail: contact@bloomsbury.com
Web Site: www.bloomsbury.com
Key Personnel
Dir: Janet Murphy
Founded: 1807
Subjects: Art, Crafts, Games, Hobbies, Drama, Theater, Education, Maritime, Music, Dance, Natural History, Nonfiction (General), Sports, Athletics, Ornithology, Visual Arts
ISBN Prefix(es): 978-0-7136; 978-0-212; 978-1-4081; 978-1-4729
Total Titles: 1,800 Print
Imprints: Arden Shakespeare; Andrew Brodie; Adlard Coles Nautical; Christopher Helm (Publishers) Ltd; Herbert Press Ltd; Methuen Drama; T & A D Poyser Ltd; Thomas Reed
Distributor for Magi Children's Books; Sheridan House; Sunflower Books; V&A Publications
Distribution Center: Macmillan Distribution (MDL), Brunel Rd, Houndmills, Basingstoke, Hants RG21 6XS *Tel:* (01256) 302699 *Fax:* (01256) 81252; (01256) 812558 *E-mail:* orders@macmillan.co.uk

Orders to: Macmillan Distribution (MDL), Brunel Rd, Houndmills, Basingstoke, Hants RG21 6XS *Tel:* (01256) 302699 *Fax:* (01256) 81252; (01256) 812558 *E-mail:* orders@macmillan.co.uk

Black Ace Books+
PO Box 7547, Perth PH2 1AU
Tel: (01821) 642 822 *Fax:* (01821) 642 101
Web Site: www.editor.net/blackace
Key Personnel
Publisher: Hunter Steele
Founded: 1991
Specialize in high quality fiction.
Subjects: Fiction, History, Philosophy
ISBN Prefix(es): 978-1-872988
Number of titles published annually: 5 Print
Total Titles: 30 Print
Associate Companies: Maran Steele Music

Black & White Publishing Ltd
29 Ocean Dr, Edinburgh EH6 6JL
Tel: (0131) 625 4500
E-mail: mail@blackandwhitepublishing.com
Web Site: www.blackandwhitepublishing.com
Key Personnel
Mng Dir: Campbell Brown
Marketing Dir: Alison McBride
Founded: 1999
Membership(s): Publishing Scotland.
Subjects: Biography, Memoirs, Cookery, Fiction, Humor, Nonfiction (General), Romance, Sports, Athletics, Classics, Crime Fiction
ISBN Prefix(es): 978-1-873631; 978-0-9515151; 978-1-902927; 978-1-903265; 978-1-84502
Imprints: Itchy Coo

Black Lace, *imprint of* Ebury Publishing

The Black Library, *imprint of* BL Publishing

Black Spring Press Ltd+
Curtain House, 134-146 Curtain Rd, London EC2A 3AR
Tel: (020) 7613 3066 *Fax:* (020) 7613 0028
E-mail: enquiries@blackspringpress.co.uk; info@blackspringpress.co.uk
Web Site: www.blackspringpress.co.uk
Founded: 1985
Subjects: Biography, Memoirs, Fiction, Music, Dance, Cinema
ISBN Prefix(es): 978-0-948238; 978-0-931181
Number of titles published annually: 5 Print
Orders to: Turnaround Publisher Services, Olympia Trading Estate, Unit 3, Coburg Rd, Wood Green, London N22 TZ *Tel:* (020) 8829 3000 *Fax:* (020) 8881 5088 *E-mail:* orders@turnaround-uk.com *Web Site:* www.turnaround-uk.com

Black Swan, *imprint of* Transworld Publishers

Black Swan Ireland, *imprint of* The Random House Group Ltd, a Penguin Random House Company

BlackAmber, *imprint of* Arcadia Books Ltd

Blackbirch Press, *imprint of* Gale

Blackfriars, *imprint of* Little, Brown Book Group

Blackstaff Press+
Member of The Baird Group
4D Weavers Court, Linfield Rd, Belfast BT12 5GH
Tel: (028) 9034 7510
E-mail: info@blackstaffpress.com
Web Site: www.blackstaffpress.com

Key Personnel
General Manager & Mng Editor: Patricia Horton
Mng Dir: Anne Tannahill
Marketing Executive: Sarah Bowers
  E-mail: sarah.bowers@blackstaffpress.com
Production & Rights: Michelle Griffin
  E-mail: michelle.griffin@blackstaffpress.com
Publicity: Jim Meredith *E-mail:* jim.meredith@
  blackstaffpress.com
Founded: 1971
Subjects: Art, Biography, Memoirs, Cookery,
  Drama, Theater, Fiction, Government, Political
  Science, History, Humor, Literature, Literary
  Criticism, Essays, Music, Dance, Natural His-
  tory, Nonfiction (General), Photography, Poetry,
  Regional Interests, Religion - Buddhist, Reli-
  gion - Catholic, Religion - Hindu, Religion -
  Islamic, Religion - Jewish, Religion - Protes-
  tant, Religion - Other, Sports, Athletics, Travel
  & Tourism
ISBN Prefix(es): 978-0-85640
Foreign Rep(s): Dufour Editions (Canada, USA);
  O'Brien Press (Ireland, Northern Ireland); Ox-
  ford Publicity Partnership (England, Scotland,
  Wales)
Foreign Rights: Andreas Brunner Literary Agency
  (Austria, Germany, Switzerland); The Susijn
  Agency (Nicola Barr) (worldwide exc Austria,
  Germany & Switzerland)
Distribution Center: Gill Distribution, Hume Ave,
  Park West, Dublin D12 YV96, Ireland *Tel:* (01)
  500 9500 *Web Site:* www.gilldistribution.ie
Orders to: Gill Distribution, Hume Ave, Park
  West, Dublin D12 YV96, Ireland *Tel:* (01) 500
  9500 *Web Site:* www.gilldistribution.ie
Dufour Editions Inc, Byers Rd, PO Box 7,
  Chester Springs, PA 19425-0007, United
  States *Tel:* 610-458-5005 *Fax:* 610-458-7103
  E-mail: info@dufoureditions.com

Blackwell Futura, *imprint of* Wiley-Blackwell
Ltd

Blackwell Munksgaard, *imprint of*
Wiley-Blackwell Ltd

Blackwell Publishing, *imprint of*
Wiley-Blackwell Ltd

Blackwell Publishing Asia, *imprint of*
Wiley-Blackwell Ltd

John Blake Publishing Ltd+
3 Bramber Court, 2 Bramber Rd, London W14
9PB
Tel: (020) 7381 0666
E-mail: help@johnblakebooks.com
Web Site: johnblakebooks.com
Key Personnel
Editorial Dir: Toby Buchan *E-mail:* toby@blake.
  co.uk
Publishing Dir: Kelly Ellis
Publicity Dir: Liz Mallett *E-mail:* liz@blake.co.
  uk
Head, UK Sales & Digital: Stuart Finglass
  E-mail: sfinglass@blake.co.uk
Commissioning Editor: Anna Marx
  E-mail: anna@blake.co.uk
Editor: Chris Mitchell *E-mail:* chris@blake.co.uk
Editorial Manager: James Hodgkinson
  E-mail: james@blake.co.uk
Digital Marketing & Public Relations Manager:
  Lorna Mackinnon *E-mail:* lorna@blake.co.uk
Senior Accounts Executive: Aleksandra Bil
  E-mail: alex@blake.co.uk
Founded: 1991
Subjects: Animals, Pets, Biography, Memoirs,
  Business, Cookery, Criminology, Fiction, Film,
  Video, Health, Nutrition, History, Humor, Law,
  Military Science, Nonfiction (General), Radio,
  TV, Science (General), Self-Help, Sports, Ath-

letics, Travel & Tourism, Mind, Body & Spirit,
  Popular Science, True Crime
ISBN Prefix(es): 978-1-85782; 978-1-900512
  (Metro Publishing); 978-0-905846; 978-1-
  903402; 978-1-904034; 978-1-84358 (Metro
  Publishing); 978-1-84454; 978-1-84241 (Metro
  Publishing); 978-1-78219; 978-1-78418
Number of titles published annually: 60 Print
Parent Company: Bonnier
Imprints: Blake Publishing; Dino Books; Metro
  Publishing; Music Press Books
Distributed by Chris Ashdown (Far East); New-
  South Books (Australia & New Zealand); Peter
  Hyde Associates (South Africa); Peter Newsom
  (Europe); Ru Ashdown (Middle East); Trafal-
  gar Square Publishing (Canada & USA)
Distribution Center: The Book Service Ltd, Dis-
  tribution Centre, Colchester Rd, Frating Green,
  Colchester, Essex CO7 7DW *Tel:* (01206)
  256000 *Fax:* (01206) 255715 *E-mail:* sales@
  tbs-ltd.co.uk *Web Site:* www.thebookservice.co.
  uk
Pansing Distribution Pte Ltd, 438, Ang Mo
  Kio Indiustrial Park 1, Level 1, Singapore
  569619, Singapore *Tel:* 6715 7300 *Fax:* 6715
  4348 *E-mail:* infomags@pansing.com *Web
  Site:* www.pansingmag.com (Asia Pacific)

Blake Publishing, *imprint of* John Blake
Publishing Ltd

Blink Publishing, *imprint of* Kings Road
Publishing

Blink Publishing
Imprint of Kings Road Publishing
2.08 The Plaza, 535 Kings Rd, London SW10
0SZ
Tel: (020) 3770 8888
E-mail: info@blinkpublishing.co.uk
Web Site: www.blinkpublishing.co.uk
Key Personnel
Chief Executive Officer: Perminder Mann
Mng Dir: Benn Dunn
Acquisitions & Rights Dir: Clare Tillyer
  E-mail: clare.tillyer@blinkpublishing.co.uk
Commercial Dir: Lisa Hoare *E-mail:* lisa.hoare@
  blinkpublishing.co.uk
Head, Digital: Nick Coveney *E-mail:* nick.
  coveney@blinkpublishing.co.uk
Head, Public Relations: Karen Browning
  E-mail: karen.browning@blinkpublishing.co.uk
Production Manager: Yolanta Motylinska
  E-mail: yolanta.motylinska@blinkpublishing.
  co.uk
Public Relations Manager: Lizzie Dorney-
  Kingdom *E-mail:* lizzie.dorney@
  blinkpublishing.co.uk
Rights Manager: Eryl Humphrey-Jones
  E-mail: eryl.humphreyjones@blinkpublishing.
  co.uk
Social Media Manager: Michelle Tish Tilley
  E-mail: michelle.tilley@blinkpublishing.co.uk
Editor: Joel Simons *E-mail:* joel.simons@
  blinkpublishing.co.uk
Junior Designer: Emily Rough *E-mail:* emily.
  rough@blinkpublishing.co.uk
Finance & Social Media Assistant: Lisa Hellyer
  E-mail: lisa.hellyer@blinkpublishing.co.uk
Subjects: Sports, Athletics, Entertainment, Style
ISBN Prefix(es): 978-1-910536; 978-1-905825
Ultimate Parent Company: Bonnier Publishing
Ltd
Distributed by Trafalgar Square Publishing

Bliss Books, *imprint of* Arcadia Books Ltd

Bloodaxe Books Ltd
Eastburn, South Park, Hexham NE46 1BS
Tel: (01434) 611 581 *Fax:* (01434) 611 586

E-mail: editor@bloodaxebooks.com; publicity@
  bloodaxebooks.com; sales@bloodaxebooks.
  com; rights@bloodaxebooks.com; finance@
  bloodaxebooks.com
Web Site: www.bloodaxebooks.com
Key Personnel
Chairman: Simon Thirsk *E-mail:* simon@
  bloodaxebooks.com
Mng Dir & Editor: Dr Neil Astley
Finance Manager: Bethan Jones
Publicity Manager: Christine Macgregor
Rights & Permissions Manager: Dr Suzanne
  Fairless-Aitken
Founded: 1978
Not-for-profit arts council funded poetry pub-
  lisher.
Subjects: Poetry
ISBN Prefix(es): 978-0-906427; 978-1-85224;
  978-1-78037
Number of titles published annually: 30 Print
Total Titles: 500 Print
Distributed by Dufour Editions Inc (Canada &
  USA)
Orders to: Grantham Distribution Services (GBS),
  Trent Rd, Grantham NG31 7XQ *Tel:* (01476)
  541080 *E-mail:* orders@gbs.tbs-ltd.co.uk

Bloomsbury Academic
Imprint of Bloomsbury Publishing PLC
50 Bedford Sq, London WC1B 3DP
Tel: (020) 7631 5600 *Fax:* (020) 7631 5800
E-mail: academic@bloomsbury.com
Web Site: www.bloomsbury.com/uk/academic
Key Personnel
Global Head, Academic Publishing: Jenny Ridout
Head, Publishing: Rob Winter
Mng Dir: Jonathan Glasspool *E-mail:* jonathan.
  glasspool@bloomsbury.com
Academic Rights Manager: Elizabeth White
  E-mail: elizabeth.white@bloomsbury.com
Subjects: Anthropology, Drama, Theater, Educa-
  tion, Fashion, Government, Political Science,
  History, Literature, Literary Criticism, Essays,
  Philosophy, Religion - Other, Social Sciences,
  Sociology, Theology, Design, Humanities
Distributor for BFI Publishing
Foreign Rep(s): Jonathan Ball Publishers
  (Botswana, Lesotho, Namibia, Southern Africa,
  Swaziland); Bookbird (M Anwer Iqbal) (Pak-
  istan); Codasat Canada Ltd (Canada); Colin
  Flint Ltd (Denmark, Finland, Iceland, Norway,
  Sweden); Iberian Book Services (Gibraltar,
  Portugal, Spain); Information & Culture Ko-
  rea (South Korea); International Publishers Ser-
  vices (Malta, Middle East exc Israel, North
  Africa); Jacek Lewinson (Central Europe,
  Eastern Europe); Penguin Group (Canada)
  (Canada); Taylor & Francis Asia Pacific (Asia-
  Pacific, Brunei, China, Hong Kong, Malaysia,
  Taiwan, Thailand); Tula Publishing Ltd (Africa
  exc South Africa); Tyers Book Sales Ltd (Aus-
  tria, Cyprus, Greece, Israel)
Distribution Center: Macmillan Distribu-
  tion (MDL), Brunel Rd, Houndsmill, Basingstoke, Hants RG21 6XS *Tel:* (01256)
  302692 *Fax:* (01256) 812521; (01256) 812558
  E-mail: orders@macmillan.co.uk

Bloomsbury Arden Shakespeare, *imprint of*
Bloomsbury Publishing Plc

Bloomsbury China, *imprint of* Bloomsbury
Publishing Plc

Bloomsbury Circus, *imprint of* Bloomsbury
Publishing Plc

Bloomsbury Continuum, *imprint of* Bloomsbury
Publishing Plc

Bloomsbury Professional, *imprint of* Bloomsbury
Publishing Plc

Bloomsbury Professional Ltd
41-43 Boltro Rd, Haywards Heath, West Sussex
RH16 1BJ
Tel: (01444) 416119 *Fax:* (01444) 440426
E-mail: customerservices@
bloomsburyprofessional.com
Web Site: www.bloomsburyprofessional.com
Key Personnel
Mng Dir: Jonathan Glasspool
New Business Dir: Kathryn Earle
Subjects: Accounting, Law, Tax
ISBN Prefix(es): 978-1-84766; 978-1-84592
Parent Company: Bloomsbury Publishing Plc
Branch Office(s)
9/10 St Andrew Sq, Edinburgh *Tel:* (0131) 718
6073 *Fax:* (0131) 718 6100
Fitzwilliam Business Centre, 26 Upper Pem-
broke St, Dublin 2, Ireland *Tel:* (01) 637 3920
Fax: (01) 662 0365
Distribution Center: Gill Distribution, Hume Ave,
Park West, Dublin D12 YV96, Ireland *Tel:* (01)
500 9500 *Web Site:* www.gilldistribution.ie
Orders to: Marston Book Services Ltd, 160 East-
ern Ave, Milton Park, Abingdon, Oxon OX14
4SB *Tel:* (01235) 465500 *Fax:* (01235) 465555
E-mail: direct.orders@marston.co.uk *Web
Site:* www.marston.co.uk

Bloomsbury Publishing Plc+
50 Bedford Sq, London WC1B 3DP
Tel: (020) 7631 5600 *Fax:* (020) 7631 5800
E-mail: contact@bloomsbury.com; sales@
bloomsbury.com
Web Site: www.bloomsbury.com
Key Personnel
Chief Executive Officer: Nigel Newton
Executive Dir: Richard Charkin
Executive Dir, Bloomsbury Information Ltd: Mike
Bryan
Mng Dir, Bloomsbury Consumer Publishing:
Emma Hopkin
Mng Dir, Bloomsbury Information Ltd: Kathy
Rooney
Publisher, Sports & Wisden: Charlotte Atyeo
Editorial Dir, Fiction, Bloomsbury Children's:
Ellen Holgate
Editorial Dir, Bloomsbury Crime: Alison Hen-
nessey
Group Fin Dir: Penny Scott-Bayfield
Group Sales & Marketing Dir: Kathleen Farrar
Group Adult Editor-in-Chief: Alexandra Pringle
Publishing Dir: Alexis Kirschbaum
Publishing Dir, Children's Books: Rebecca Mc-
Nally
Rights Executive: Jenna Brown *Tel:* (020) 7631
5871 *E-mail:* jenna.brown@bloomsbury.com
Rights Dir: Ruth Logan
Global Head, Contracts: Christelle Chamouton
Head, International Sales: Jacqueline Sells
Tel: (020) 7631 5869 *E-mail:* jacqueline.sells@
bloomsbury.com
Senior Fiction Editor: Alexa von Hirschberg
Academic Sales Manager: Phil Prestianni
Tel: (07733) 328663 *E-mail:* phil.prestianni@
bloomsbury.com
Founded: 1986
Subjects: Cookery, Fiction, Humor, Nonfiction
(General)
ISBN Prefix(es): 978-0-333; 978-0-7136; 978-
0-510; 978-0-948230; 978-0-9506785; 978-0-
85496; 978-1-85973; 978-0-7475; 978-0-85177;
978-0-7156; 978-1-85399; 978-1-86176; 978-
0-245; 978-1-85691; 978-0-485; 978-0-85314;
978-0-212; 978-1-899791; 978-2-88479; 978-
1-84520; 978-1-84486; 978-1-84113; 978-1-
901362; 978-1-84731; 978-1-4081; 978-1-
84788; 978-1-904573; 978-1-906650; 978-
2-940373; 978-2-940439; 978-1-84946; 978-
0-86292; 978-0-906515; 978-0-907582; 978-
0-85146; 978-0-85147; 978-0-85317; 978-0-
86019; 978-0-946716; 978-0-9507160; 978-
1-897737; 978-0-9524867; 978-1-902233;
978-1-904187; 978-1-904970; 978-1-905019;

978-1-4088; 978-1-84930; 978-1-84966; 978-
2-940411; 978-1-78093; 978-0-85785; 978-1-
78043; 978-2-940496; 978-1-78225
Number of titles published annually: 1,000 Print
Imprints: Absolute Press; AVA Publishing;
Bloomsbury Arden Shakespeare; Bloomsbury
China (English-language); Bloomsbury Cir-
cus; Bloomsbury Continuum; Bloomsbury Pro-
fessional; Bloomsbury Reader; Bloomsbury
Sigma; Bloomsbury Spark; Hart Publishing
Ltd; Rouleur Books (cycling)
Subsidiaries: A & C Black Publishing Ltd
Branch Office(s)
Bloomsbury Publishing Pty Ltd, 387 George
St, Level 4, Sydney, NSW 2000, Australia
Tel: (02) 8820 4900 *E-mail:* au@bloomsbury.
com *Web Site:* www.bloomsburyanz.com
Bloomsbury Publishing India Pvt Ltd, VISHRUT
Bldg, Bldg No 3, DDA Complex, Ground
floor, Pocket C 6&7, Vasant Kunj, New
Delhi 110 070, India *Tel:* (011) 40574957
E-mail: marketing-in@bloomsbury.com
U.S. Office(s): Bloomsbury Publishing Inc,
1385 Broadway, 5th floor, New York, NY
10018, United States *Tel:* 212-419-5300
E-mail: marketingusa@bloomsbury.com
Foreign Rep(s): Jonathan Ball (Botswana,
Lesotho, Namibia, South Africa, Swaziland);
Bloomsbury Qatar Foundation Publishing (Mid-
dle East exc United Arab Emirates, North
Africa); Book Bird (M Anwer Iqbal) (Pak-
istan); Codasat Canada Ltd (academic titles)
(Canada); Colin Flint Ltd (Denmark, Finland,
Iceland, Norway, Sweden); Iberian Book Ser-
vices (Gibraltar, Portugal, Spain); Informa-
tion & Culture Korea (South Korea); Inter-
national Publishers Services (Malta, Middle
East exc Israel, North Africa); Jacek Lewin-
son (Central Europe, Eastern Europe); Penguin
Books Malaysia (Malaysia, Singapore); Pen-
guin Books SA (Italy, Portugal, Spain); Pen-
guin Books Singapore (Malaysia, Singapore);
Penguin Group (Canada) (special interest titles)
(Canada); Taylor & Francis Asia Pacific (Asia-
Pacific, Brunei, China, Hong Kong, Indonesia, Malaysia, Singapore, Taiwan, Thailand);
Tula Publishing Ltd (Julian Russ) (Africa exc
South Africa); Tyers Book Sales Ltd (Austria,
Cyprus, Greece, Israel)
Orders to: Macmillan Distribution Ltd, Brunel
Rd, Houndmills, Basingstoke, Hants RG21
6XS *Tel:* (01256) 302699 *Fax:* (01256)
812521; (01256) 812558 *E-mail:* orders@
macmillan.co.uk

Bloomsbury Reader, *imprint of* Bloomsbury
Publishing Plc

Bloomsbury Sigma, *imprint of* Bloomsbury
Publishing Plc

Bloomsbury Spark, *imprint of* Bloomsbury
Publishing Plc

Blorenge Books+
Blorenge Cottage, Church Lane, Llanfoist, Aber-
gavenny, Monmouthshire NP7 9NG
Tel: (01873) 856114
E-mail: cbarber010@aol.com
Web Site: blorenge-books.co.uk
Key Personnel
Proprietor: Chris Barber
Co-Owner: Anne Marie Barber
Founded: 1985
Subjects: Fiction, History, Mysteries, Suspense,
Outdoor Recreation, Travel & Tourism
ISBN Prefix(es): 978-0-9510444; 978-1-872730
Number of titles published annually: 3 Print
Total Titles: 12 Print

Blue Door, *imprint of* HarperCollins UK

Bluebird, *imprint of* Pan Macmillan

BMI Research+
Senator House, 85 Queen Victoria St, London
EC4V 4AB
Tel: (020) 7248 0468 *Fax:* (020) 7248 0467
E-mail: enquiry@bmiresearch.com
Web Site: www.bmiresearch.com
Key Personnel
Chief Executive Officer: Richard Hall
Chief Financial Officer: Simon Longfield
Chief Marketing & Technology Officer: Jon Ew-
ing
Global Head, Sales: Greg Davis
Head, Strategic Analysis & Production Develop-
ment: Matthew Brooks
Marketing Manager: Leila Scott *Tel:* (020) 7246
5131 *E-mail:* leila.scott@bmiresearch.com
Founded: 1984
Specialize in essential news, data, analysis &
forecasts on economic, business & political
developments in global emerging markets coun-
tries.
Subjects: Business, Chemistry, Chemical Engi-
neering, Developing Countries, Economics, En-
ergy, Engineering (General), Finance, Foreign
Countries, Government, Political Science, Jour-
nalism, Securities, Social Sciences, Sociology
Number of titles published annually: 80 Print; 28
CD-ROM; 68 Online
Total Titles: 80 Print; 28 CD-ROM; 68 Online
Parent Company: Fitch Group
Ultimate Parent Company: Hearst Corp & Fi-
malac SA
Associate Companies: Commercial Intelligence
Service
Branch Office(s)
OUE Downtown 2, No 12-09, 6 Shenton Way,
Singapore 068809, Singapore *Tel:* 6576 5820
Fax: 6576 5821
Lougardia Bldg, Suite 403, 4th floor, Corner of
Hendrik Verwoerd & Embankment, Centurion
0046, South Africa *Tel:* (012) 679 2600 *Toll
Free Fax:* (0800) 982 275
U.S. Office(s): 777 Third Ave, New York, NY
10017, United States *Tel:* 646-368-1319
Fax: 212-202-5062

BMJ Publishing Group Ltd+
Subsidiary of British Medical Association
BMA House, Tavistock Sq, London WC1H 9JR
Tel: (020) 7387 4410; (020) 7111 1105 (customer
service)
E-mail: support@bmj.com
Web Site: group.bmj.com
Key Personnel
Chief Executive Officer: Tim Brooks
Chief Operating Officer: Patrick Spencer
Editor-in-Chief: Dr Fiona Godlee
Commercial Dir: Angus Metcalfe *Tel:* (020) 7383
6187 *E-mail:* ametcalfe@bmj.com
Marketing Dir: Caroline Hird *Tel:* (020) 7874
7397 *E-mail:* chird@bmj.com
Publishing Dir, Journals: Peter Ashman *Tel:* (020)
7874 7026 *E-mail:* pashman@bmj.com
Founded: 1857
Subjects: Medicine, Nursing, Dentistry
ISBN Prefix(es): 978-1-905545; 978-0-9548965
Subsidiaries: Professional & Scientific Publica-
tions (PSP)

BMM, *imprint of* SportsBooks Ltd

Bobcat Books, *imprint of* Omnibus Press

Bodleian Library Publishing
Osney One, Osney Mead, Oxford OX2 0EW
Tel: (01865) 283850
E-mail: publishing@bodleian.ox.ac.uk; orders@
bodleianshop.co.uk; customerservice@
bodleianshop.co.uk
Web Site: www.bodleianshop.co.uk

Founded: 1602
Subjects: Art, Gardening, Plants, History, Humor, Literature, Literary Criticism, Essays, Military Science, Sports, Athletics, Botany, General Interest
ISBN Prefix(es): 978-1-85124; 978-0-900177
Foreign Rep(s): APD Singapore Pte Ltd (Brunei, Cambodia, Indonesia, Laos, Malaysia, Myanmar, Philippines, Singapore, Thailand, Vietnam); Avicenna Partnership Ltd (Claire de Gruchy & Bill Kennedy) (Cyprus, Malta, Middle East, North Africa, Turkey); Book Marketing Services (S Janakiraman) (India, Sri Lanka); Footprint Books Pty Ltd (Australia, New Zealand); Christopher Humphrys (Gibraltar, Portugal, Spain); Information & Culture Korea (Se-Yung Jun) (Korea); Ewa Ledochowicz (Central Europe, Eastern Europe); Uwe Luedemann (Austria, France, Germany, Switzerland); Mirjam Mayenburg (Belgium, Luxembourg, Netherlands); Padovani Books Ltd (Greece, Italy); Robert Towers (Ireland); University of Chicago Press (North America); University Presses Marketing (Helena Svojsikova) (Denmark, Finland, Iceland, Norway, Sweden); World Press (Saleem Malik) (Pakistan)
Foreign Rights: Edwards Fuglewicz Literary Agency (Julia Forrest)
Distribution Center: John Wiley & Sons Ltd, European Distribution Centre, New Era Estate, Oldlands Way, Bognor Regis, West Sussex PO22 9NQ Tel: (01243) 843291 Fax: (01243) 843303 E-mail: customer@wiley.com

Bodley Head, imprint of The Random House Group Ltd, a Penguin Random House Company

Bodley Head Children's, imprint of The Random House Group Ltd, a Penguin Random House Company

Book Guild Publishing Ltd+
The Werks, 45 Church Rd, Hove BN3 2BE
Tel: (01273) 720900 Fax: (01273) 723122
E-mail: info@bookguild.co.uk
Web Site: www.bookguild.co.uk
Key Personnel
Mng Dir: Carol Biss E-mail: carol@bookguild.co.uk
Production Dir: Janet Wrench E-mail: janet@bookguild.co.uk
Head, Marketing & Publicity: Louise Campbell E-mail: louise@bookguild.co.uk
Mng Editor: Joanna Bently E-mail: joanna@bookguild.co.uk
Founded: 1982
Membership(s): IPG; Publishers' Association.
Subjects: Art, Biography, Memoirs, Fiction, History, Literature, Literary Criticism, Essays, Military Science, Nonfiction (General), Travel & Tourism
ISBN Prefix(es): 978-1-85776; 978-0-86332; 978-1-84624; 978-1-909716
Number of titles published annually: 100 Print
Foreign Rep(s): Angell Eurosales (Denmark, Finland, Iceland, Norway, Scandinavia, Sweden); Ashton International Marketing Services (Brunei, China, Hong Kong, Indonesia, Japan, Malaysia, Philippines, Singapore, Southeast Asia, Taiwan, Thailand); Bookport Associates (Joe Portelli) (Greece, Italy, Malta, Portugal, Southern Europe, Spain); DLS Distribution Services, Victoria (Australia, New Zealand); European Marketing Services (Anselm Robinson) (Austria, Belgium, France, Germany, Switzerland, Western Europe); Everybody's Books CC (Warren Halford) (South Africa); IMA (InterMediaAmericana) (Caribbean, Central America, South America); Trans-Atlantic Publications Inc (USA)

Distribution Center: Orca Book Services, 160 Eastern Ave, Milton Park, Abingdon, Oxon OX14 4SD Tel: (01235) 465500 E-mail: tradeorders@orcabookservices.co.uk Web Site: www.orcabookservices.co.uk (UK & Ireland)

Book House, imprint of The Salariya Book Co Ltd

Book Works Publishing
19 Holywell Row, London EC2A 4JB
Tel: (020) 7247 2203 Fax: (020) 7247 2540
Web Site: www.bookworks.org.uk
Key Personnel
Dir: Jane Rolo E-mail: jane@bookworks.org.uk
Marketing Manager & Editor: Gavin Everall E-mail: gavin@bookworks.org.uk
Sales & Distribution: Paul Sammut E-mail: paul@bookworks.org.uk
Founded: 1984
Subjects: Art
ISBN Prefix(es): 978-1-870699
Foreign Rep(s): RAM Publications Distributions Inc (USA)

Bookmarks Publications+
One Bloomsbury St, London WC1B 3QE
Tel: (020) 7637 1848 Fax: (020) 7637 3416
E-mail: info@bookmarksbookshop.co.uk
Web Site: www.bookmarksbookshop.co.uk
Founded: 1979
Socialist publisher & bookshop.
Subjects: Economics, Government, Political Science, History, Labor, Industrial Relations
ISBN Prefix(es): 978-0-906224; 978-1-898876; 978-1-905192

Boosey & Hawkes Music Publishers Ltd+
Aldwych House, 71-91 Aldwych, London WC2B 4HN
Tel: (020) 7054 7200 Fax: (020) 7054 7290
E-mail: musicshop@boosey.com
Web Site: www.boosey.com
Key Personnel
Chief Executive: John Minch E-mail: john.minch@boosey.com
Mng Dir: Janis Susskind E-mail: janis.susskind@boosey.com
Head of Publishing: James Eggleston Tel: (020) 7054 7260
Senior Editor: Jeremy Allen Tel: (020) 7054 7262; Sally Cox Tel: (020) 7054 7261
Founded: 1890
Also distributes musical background books for other music companies & book publishers.
Subjects: Music, Dance
ISBN Prefix(es): 978-0-85162
Parent Company: Boosey & Hawkes PLC
Divisions: B & H Inc, Printed Music
Branch Office(s)
Boosey & Hawkes Bote & Bock GmbH & Co KG, Anton J Benjamin GmbH, Luetzowufer 26, 10787 Berlin, Germany Tel: (030) 2500 1300 Fax: (030) 2500 1399 E-mail: musikverlag@boosey.com
U.S. Office(s): Boosey & Hawkes Inc, 229 W 28 St, 11th floor, New York, NY 10001, United States Tel: 212-358-5300 Fax: 212-358-5305 E-mail: composers.us@boosey.com
Returns: Music Exchange (Manchester) Ltd, Claverton Rd, Manchester M23 9AZ

The Borough Press, imprint of HarperCollins UK

Borthwick Institute for Archives
University of York, Heslington, York YO10 5DD
Tel: (01904) 321166
E-mail: borthwick-institute@york.ac.uk
Web Site: www.york.ac.uk/borthwick

Key Personnel
Keeper of Archives: Christopher C Webb E-mail: chris.webb@york.ac.uk
Founded: 1950
Subjects: Archaeology, Genealogy, History, Law, Palaeography
ISBN Prefix(es): 978-0-900701; 978-0-903857; 978-1-904497
Number of titles published annually: 10 Print
Total Titles: 100 Print
Parent Company: University of York

Boulevard Books/The Babel Guides+
71 Lytton Rd, Oxford, Oxon OX4 3NY
Tel: (01865) 712931
E-mail: info@babelguides.co.uk
Web Site: babelguides.co.uk
Key Personnel
Owner: Ray Keenoy E-mail: ray.keenoy@gmail.com
Founded: 1989
Publish contemporary world fiction in English translation, popular guides to fiction in translation.
Subjects: Fiction, Literature, Literary Criticism, Essays
ISBN Prefix(es): 978-1-899460
Number of titles published annually: 4 Print
Total Titles: 30 Print
Imprints: Babel Guides; Boulevard Books UK
Distribution Center: Gardners Books, One Whittle Dr, Eastbourne, East Sussex BN23 6QH Tel: (01323) 521777 Fax: (01323) 521666 E-mail: sales@gardners.com Web Site: www.gardners.com

Boulevard Books UK, imprint of Boulevard Books/The Babel Guides

Bounty Books, imprint of Octopus Publishing Group Ltd

Bounty Books+
Imprint of Octopus Publishing Group Ltd
Endeavor House, 189 Shaftesbury Ave, London WC2H 8JY
Tel: (020) 7632 5400
E-mail: info@octopusbooks.co.uk; sales@octopusbooks.co.uk
Web Site: www.octopusbooks.co.uk
Key Personnel
Publishing & International Sales Dir: Polly Manguel
Publisher of promotional titles.
Subjects: Animals, Pets, Antiques, Cookery, Crafts, Games, Hobbies, Fiction, Gardening, Plants, History, Natural History, Religion - Other, Sports, Athletics, Transportation
Distribution Center: Littlehampton Book Services Ltd, Faraday Close, Durrington, Worthing, West Sussex BN13 3RB Tel: (01903) 828500; (01903) 828501 (customer service) Web Site: lbsltd.wp.hachette.co.uk

Bowker, an affiliate of ProQuest
Division of R R Bowker LLC
3 Dorset Rise, 5th floor, London EC4Y 8EN
Tel: (020) 7832 1700
E-mail: sales@bowker.co.uk
Web Site: www.bowker.com
Subjects: Library & Information Sciences, Publishing & Book Trade Reference
ISBN Prefix(es): 978-1-85739; 978-0-8352; 978-0-85935; 978-0-86290; 978-0-907150
Ultimate Parent Company: Cambridge Information Group, 7200 Wisconsin Ave, Suite 601, Bethesda, MD 20814, United States
Distributed by Thorpe-Bowker
Distributor for R R Bowker LLC

Boxer Books Ltd
70 Cowcross St, London EC1M 6EJ

Tel: (020) 7138 3650
E-mail: info@boxerbooks.com; sales@ boxerbooks.com
Web Site: www.boxerbooksltd.co.uk
Founded: 2005
Subjects: Fiction
ISBN Prefix(es): 978-1-905417; 978-0-9547373; 978-1-910126
Distributed by Frances Lincoln (UK); Sterling Publishing Co Inc (USA)
Distribution Center: Bounce Sales & Marketing, 320 City Rd, London EC1V 2NZ *Tel:* (020) 7138 3650 *E-mail:* sales@bouncemarketing.co.uk

Boxtree, *imprint of* Pan Macmillan

Boxtree Ltd+
Imprint of Pan Macmillan
20 New Wharf Rd, London N1 9RR
Tel: (020) 7014 6000 *Fax:* (020) 7014 6001
E-mail: webqueries@macmillan.co.uk
Web Site: www.panmacmillan.com
Key Personnel
Sales Dir: Christine Jones *Tel:* (020) 7014 6344 *E-mail:* christine.jones@macmillan.com
Founded: 1986
Specialize in film & TV tie-ins, pop music, sport, biographies & humor.
Subjects: Biography, Memoirs, Film, Video, Humor, Music, Dance, Radio, TV
ISBN Prefix(es): 978-1-85283; 978-0-7522
Ultimate Parent Company: Macmillan Group
Distributor for Museum Quilts (UK); Piccadilly (UK); Rosendale (UK); Smith Gryphon (UK)

Boydell & Brewer Ltd+
Bridge Farm Business Park, Top St, Martlesham IP12 4RB
Tel: (01394) 610600 *Fax:* (01394) 610316
E-mail: editorial@boydell.co.uk; marketing@ boydell.co.uk; production@boydell.co.uk
Web Site: www.boydellandbrewer.com
Key Personnel
Head of Sales & Marketing: Michael Richards *E-mail:* mrichards@boydell.co.uk
Founded: 1969
Publish & distribute academic & trade history & literature studies. Also publish Hispanic & German studies, plus music, philosophy, film & African studies.
Subjects: African American Studies, Film, Video, History, Literature, Literary Criticism, Essays, Music, Dance, Philosophy, Travel & Tourism
ISBN Prefix(es): 978-0-85115; 978-0-85991; 978-1-85566; 978-1-878822; 978-1-58046; 978-1-57113; 978-1-900639; 978-1-84383; 978-1-84384; 978-1-879751; 978-0-938100
Number of titles published annually: 200 Print; 5 CD-ROM
Imprints: Camden House; James Currey
U.S. Office(s): Boydell & Brewer Inc, 668 Mount Hope Ave, Rochester, NY 14620-2731, United States *Tel:* 585-275-0419 *Fax:* 585-271-8778 *E-mail:* boydell@boydellusa.net
Distributed by Casemate | publishers (North & South America)
Foreign Rep(s): Jim Blaho (Malta); Blue Weaver (Natasha Store & Lorna van Romburgh) (South Africa, Zimbabwe); Casemate UK (Ireland, UK); Co Info Pty Ltd (Australia); Colin Flint Ltd (Ben Greig) (Iceland, Scandinavia); Govinda Book House (Mr Govinda Berry) (India); Iberian Book Services (Peter & Charlotte Prout) (Portugal, Spain); Inbooks (Australia); Marek Lewinson (Baltic States, Eastern Europe, Russia); Mare Nostrum (Katie Machin) (Belgium, France, Luxembourg, Netherlands); Mare Nostrum (Francesca Pollard) (Italy); Mare Nostrum (Frauke Feldmann) (Austria, Germany, Switzerland); Publishers International Marketing (Chris Ashdown) (Asia); Pub-

lishers International Marketing (Edwin Makabenta) (Philippines); Scholarly Book Services Inc (Canada); TML (Tahir Lodhi) (Pakistan); United Publishers Services Ltd (Japan)

BPP Publishing Ltd
BPP House, Aldine Pl, 142-144 Uxbridge Rd, London W12 8AA
Tel: (020) 8740 2222 *Fax:* (020) 8740 1111
E-mail: learningmedia@bpp.com
Web Site: www.bpp.com
Founded: 1976
Subjects: Accounting, Business, Economics, Marketing
ISBN Prefix(es): 978-0-7517; 978-0-86277; 978-1-871824; 978-1-84438; 978-1-4453; 978-1-4727

BPS Blackwell (British Psychological Society)
Imprint of Wiley-Blackwell Ltd
St Andrew's House, 48 Princess Rd E, Leicester LE1 7DR
Tel: (0116) 252 9568
E-mail: enquiries@bps.org.uk
Web Site: psychsource.bps.org.uk
Founded: 2002
Subjects: Behavioral Sciences, Education, Management
ISBN Prefix(es): 978-0-631; 978-0-901715; 978-1-85433; 978-1-4051
Number of titles published annually: 7 Print
Total Titles: 118 Print
Ultimate Parent Company: John Wiley & Sons Inc
U.S. Office(s): Wiley-Blackwell, Commerce Pl, 350 Main St, Malden, MA 02148, United States *Tel:* 781-388-8200 *Fax:* 781-388-8210

BPS Blackwell (British Psychological Society), *imprint of* Wiley-Blackwell Ltd

Bradford Books, *imprint of* The MIT Press

Bradt Travel Guides Ltd+
IDC House, 1st floor, The Vale, Chalfont St Peter, Bucks SL9 9RZ
Tel: (01753) 893444 *Fax:* (01753) 892333
E-mail: info@bradtguides.com
Web Site: www.bradtguides.com
Key Personnel
Founder: Hilary Bradt
Senior Sales Executive: Deborah Gerrard *Tel:* (01753) 480634 *E-mail:* deborah.gerrard@ bradtguides.com
Marketing Executive: Hugh Collins *Tel:* (01753) 480633 *E-mail:* hugh.collins@bradtguides.com
Mng Dir: Adrian Phillips *E-mail:* adrian.phillips@bradtguides.com
Head, Editorial: Anna Moores
Mng Editor: Claire Strange
Production Manager: Sue Cooper
Commissioning Editor: Rachel Fielding *Tel:* (01753) 480639 *E-mail:* rachel.fielding@ bradtguides.com
Founded: 1972
Publisher of travel guides.
Subjects: Outdoor Recreation, Travel & Tourism
ISBN Prefix(es): 978-0-946983; 978-1-898323; 978-1-84162; 978-0-9505797
Number of titles published annually: 50 Print
Total Titles: 115 Print
Associate Companies: The Globe Pequot Press, PO Box 480, 246 Goose Lane, Guilford, CT 06437-0480, United States *Tel:* 203-458-4500 *Fax:* 203-458-4601 *E-mail:* info@globepequot.com
Foreign Rep(s): A-Z Africa Book Services (Anita Zih-De Haan) (Africa exc South Africa); Al Manahil International LLC & Educational Consultancy (Oman); Altair (Spain); Angell Eurosales (Denmark, Finland, Iceland, Nor-

way, Sweden); Cartotheque EGG (France); Lale Colakoglu (Turkey); Craenen bvba (Belgium, Netherlands); Durnell Marketing (Belarus, Belgium, Cyprus exc North Cyprus, Estonia, France, Germany, Greece, Italy, Latvia, Lithuania, Luxembourg, Malta, Netherlands, Russia, Ukraine); Feel Books Pvt Ltd (India); Freytag-Berndt (Austria); InterMediaAmericana Ltd (Latin America); Jacana Media (Pty) Ltd (South Africa); Cristian Juncu (Albania, Armenia, Azerbaijan, Bosnia and Herzegovina, Bulgaria, Croatia, Czechia, Georgia, Hungary, Kazakhstan, Kyrgyzstan, Moldova, Montenegro, Poland, Romania, Serbia, Slovakia, Slovenia, Tajikistan, Turkmenistan, Uzbekistan); National Book Network (Canada, USA); OLF SA (Switzerland); Pansing Distribution (Malaysia, Singapore); Platypus (Finland, Norway, Sweden); Publishers International Marketing (China, Hong Kong, Indonesia, Japan, Korea, Mongolia, Philippines, Taiwan, Thailand, Vietnam); Humphrys Roberts Associates (Portugal); Scanvik Books A/S (Denmark, Norway); Steinhart Sharav Publishers Ltd (Israel); Ward International Book Export Ltd (Bahrain, Egypt, Iran, Jordan, Kuwait, Lebanon, Oman, Qatar, Saudi Arabia, Syria, United Arab Emirates, Yemen); Woodslane Pty Ltd (Australia, New Zealand)
Distribution Center: Grantham Book Services, Trent Rd, Grantham NG31 7XQ *Tel:* (01476) 541080 (UK customers); (01476) 541082 (non-UK customers) *E-mail:* orders@gbs.tbs-ltd.co.uk (UK & Ireland)

BrandBooks
Division of G&M Brand Publications Ltd
PO Box 174, Brighton BN51 9FA
Tel: (0845) 676 9254 *Fax:* (0845) 075 3702
E-mail: sales@brandbooks.co.uk
Web Site: www.spellingmadeeasy.co.uk
Key Personnel
Founder: Geoffrey Brand; Michael Brand
General Manager: David Kraft *E-mail:* david@ brandbooks.co.uk
Founded: 2002
Subjects: Education, Fiction
ISBN Prefix(es): 978-1-904421
Associate Companies: R Smith Music Publishing Co

Nicholas Brealey Publishing, *imprint of* John Murray Press

Nicholas Brealey Publishing+
Imprint of John Murray (Publishers) Ltd
3-5 Spafield St, Clerkenwell, London EC1R 4QB
Tel: (020) 7239 0360 *Fax:* (020) 7239 0370
E-mail: sales@nicholasbrealey.com; rights@nicholasbrealey.com; publicity@ nicholasbrealey.com; translations@ nicholasbrealey.com
Web Site: nicholasbrealey.com
Key Personnel
Rights Manager: Gail Blackhall
Founded: 1992
Membership(s): IPG.
Subjects: Business, Career Development, Economics, Finance, Foreign Countries, Language Arts, Linguistics, Management, Psychology, Psychiatry, Self-Help, Travel & Tourism, Foreign Countries
ISBN Prefix(es): 978-0-89106; 978-1-85788; 978-1-904838; 978-0-9839558; 978-1-941176
Total Titles: 100 Print
U.S. Office(s): Nicholas Brealey Publishing, 20 Park Plaza, Suite 610, Boston, MA 02116, United States, Sales Manager: Melissa Carl *Tel:* 617-523-3801 *Fax:* 617-523-3708 *E-mail:* sales-us@nicholasbrealey.com
Distributed by Hachette Book Group (North America)

Distributor for Intercultural Press Inc (outside USA)

Foreign Rep(s): A-Z Africa Book Services (Anita Zih) (East Africa); Allen & Unwin (Pty) Ltd (Australia, New Zealand); Angell Eurosales (Denmark, Finland, Iceland, Norway, Sweden); APD Singapore Pte Ltd (Brunei, Cambodia, Indonesia, Laos, Myanmar, Philippines, Singapore, Thailand, Vietnam); Michael Geoghegan (Austria, Belgium, Croatia, Czechia, France, Germany, Hungary, Netherlands, Poland, Slovakia, Slovenia, Switzerland); Iberian Book Services (Charlotte Prout) (Gibraltar, Portugal, Spain); Research Press (India); DJ Segrue Ltd (Ireland, UK); The White Partnership (Hong Kong, Japan, South Korea, Taiwan); Wild Dog Press (South Africa)

Distribution Center: The Book Service Ltd, Distribution Center, Colchester Rd, Frating Green, Colchester, Essex C07 7DW Tel: (01206) 256000 Fax: (01206) 255715 E-mail: sales@tbs-ltd.co.uk Web Site: www.thebookservice.co.uk (UK & Ireland)

Breslich & Foss Ltd+
2A, Union Court, 20-22 Union Rd, London SW4 6JP
Tel: (020) 7819 3990
E-mail: sales@breslichfoss.co.uk
Web Site: www.breslichfoss.co.uk
Key Personnel
Mng Dir: Paula Breslich
Rights Manager: Janet Ravenscroft
Founded: 1978
Also acts as an independent packager of co-edition books for the international market.
Subjects: Cookery, Crafts, Games, Hobbies, Fiction, Gardening, Plants, Health, Nutrition, Wine & Spirits

Brewin Books, imprint of Brewin Books Ltd

Brewin Books Ltd+
Doric House, 56 Alcester Rd, Studley, Warwicks B80 7LG
Tel: (01527) 854228; (01527) 853624 Fax: (01527) 852746
E-mail: admin@brewinbooks.com
Web Site: www.brewinbooks.com
Key Personnel
Mng Dir: Alan Brewin
Dir: Alistair Brewin
Secretary: Julie Brewin
Founded: 1976
Publish a range of nonfiction titles including hospital, health, housing, police, education, transport, local history, biographies & some military history. Distribute for several local authorities for walking guides & local history books.
Also publishers of Local History Magazine, a national history magazine established in 1984, published bimonthly.
Subjects: Biography, Memoirs, Education, Fiction, Genealogy, Health, Nutrition, History, Military Science, Nonfiction (General), Regional Interests, Transportation, Travel & Tourism
ISBN Prefix(es): 978-0-9505570; 978-0-947731; 978-1-85858
Number of titles published annually: 30 Print
Total Titles: 325 Print
Associate Companies: SupaPrint (Redditch) Ltd, Enfield Estate, Unit 19, Redditch, Worcs B97 6BY Tel: (01527) 8562212 Fax: (01527) 8560451 Web Site: www.supaprint.com
Imprints: Brewin Books; Alton Douglas Books; History-into-Print
Distributor for City of Birmingham Libraries & Leisure; Hereford City Council
Warehouse: SupaPrint (Redditch) Ltd, Enfield Estate, Unit 19, Redditch, Worcs B97 6BY Tel: (01527) 62212 Fax: (01527) 60451 Web Site: www.supaprint.com

Bridge Books
Pear Tree Cottage, The Orchard, Worthenbury, Wrexham LL13 0BF
Tel: (01948) 770125
E-mail: books@bridgebooks.co.uk
Web Site: www.bridgebooks.co.uk
Founded: 1983
Specialist publisher of Welsh, military & aviation history. Also performs contract publishing.
Subjects: Aeronautics, Aviation, Biography, Memoirs, Ethnicity, Genealogy, History, Maritime, Military Science, Regional Interests, Sports, Athletics, Military & Welsh History
ISBN Prefix(es): 978-1-872424; 978-0-9508285; 978-1-84494
Number of titles published annually: 12 Print
Total Titles: 350 Print; 2 CD-ROM
Subsidiaries: Maelor Interactive Publishing Ltd

Brilliant Publications+
Sparrow Hall Farm, Unit 10, Edlesborough, Dunstable LU6 2ES
Tel: (01525) 222292 Fax: (01525) 222720
E-mail: sales@brilliantpublications.co.uk
Web Site: www.brilliantpublications.co.uk
Key Personnel
Publisher: Priscilla Hannaford E-mail: priscilla@brilliantpublications.co.uk
Founded: 1993
Specialize in educational books for 3-13 year olds.
Membership(s): IPG; Publishers Association.
Subjects: Art, Education, Language Arts, Linguistics, Mathematics, Science (General), English, Modern Foreign Languages
ISBN Prefix(es): 978-1-897675; 978-1-903893; 978-1-905780; 978-0-85747
Number of titles published annually: 20 Print; 20 E-Book
Total Titles: 300 Print; 100 E-Book
Distribution Center: Trade Counter Distribution Ltd, Mendlesham Industrial Estate, Norwich Rd, Mendlesham IP14 5ND, Contact: Louise Ward Tel: (01449) 766629 Fax: (01449) 767122 E-mail: orders@tradecounter.co.uk Web Site: www.tradecounter.co.uk

Britannia Press, imprint of East-West Publications (UK) Ltd

The British Academy+
10-11 Carlton House Terrace, London SW1Y 5AH
Tel: (020) 7969 5200 Fax: (020) 7969 530
E-mail: pubs@britac.ac.uk
Web Site: www.britac.ac.uk
Key Personnel
President: Prof Nick Stern
Chief Executive: Alun Evans Tel: (020) 7969 5255 E-mail: chiefexec@britac.ac.uk
Dir: Tim Brassell Tel: (020) 7969 5253 E-mail: t.brassell@britac.ac.uk
Head of Publications: James Rivington Tel: (020) 7969 5261
Head, Press & Communications: Kate Rosser Frost Tel: (020) 7969 5263 E-mail: k.rosserfrost@britac.ac.uk
Founded: 1902
National organization for the humanities & social sciences.
Subjects: Archaeology, Art, History, Literature, Literary Criticism, Essays, Philosophy, Social Sciences, Sociology
ISBN Prefix(es): 978-0-85672 (British Academy Policy Centre reports); 978-0-902732; 978-0-19 (published for the British Academy by Oxford University Press)
Orders to: Oxford University Press, North Kettering Park, Hipwell Rd, Kettering NN14 1VA Tel: (01536) 452640 Fax: (01536) 454518 E-mail: bookorders.uk@oup.com Web Site: ukcatalogue.oup.com (new & recent titles)

Oxbow Books, Park End Pl, Oxford OX1 1HN
Tel: (01865) 241249 Fax: (01865) 794449
E-mail: oxbow@oxbowbooks.com Web Site: www.oxbowbooks.com (older titles)

The British & Foreign Bible Society, see Bible Society

British Film Institute, see BFI Publishing

British Institute of Learning Disabilities, see BILD Publications

British Institute of Non-Destructive Testing (BINDT)
Newton Bldg, St George's Ave, Northampton NN2 6JB
Tel: (01604) 89 3811 Fax: (01604) 89 3861
E-mail: info@bindt.org
Web Site: www.bindt.org
Key Personnel
Deputy Chief Executive Officer & Head of Media: David Gilbert E-mail: david.gilbert@bindt.org
Publishing, Media & Marketing Manager: Corinne Mackle E-mail: corinne.mackle@bindt.org
Subjects: Engineering (General), Science (General), Technology
ISBN Prefix(es): 978-0-903132

British Library Publishing+
Imprint of The British Library
96 Euston Rd, London NW1 2DB
Tel: (020) 7412 7294 (editorial & sales)
E-mail: publishing_editorial@bl.uk; publishing_sales@bl.uk
Web Site: bl.uk/publishing
Key Personnel
Head, Commercial Brand Development & Sales: Rebecca Nuotio
Mng Editor: Robert Davies
Founded: 1979
Publish books based on the British Library collection - illustrated nonfiction, classic crime, exhibition catalogues, gift books & more.
Subjects: Art, Fiction, History, Literature, Literary Criticism, Essays, Nonfiction (General)
ISBN Prefix(es): 978-0-7123
Number of titles published annually: 50 Print; 15 E-Book
Total Titles: 300 Print; 40 E-Book
Distributed by Trafalgar Square Publishing (North America)
Foreign Rep(s): Angell Eurosales (Scandinavia); Isabella Curtis (Greece); Ted Dougherty (Austria, Belgium, France, Germany, Luxembourg, Netherlands, Switzerland); Surit Mitra (India); Padovani Books Ltd (Jenny Padovani) (Portugal, Spain); Padovani Books Ltd (Penny Padovani) (Italy); D J Segrue Ltd (UK); Robert Towers (Ireland); Trafalgar Square Publishing (Canada, USA); David Williams (Caribbean, South America)
Foreign Rights: Edwards Fuglewicz (worldwide)
Distribution Center: NBN International, 10 Thornbury Rd, Plymouth PL6 7PP Tel: (01752) 202301 Fax: (01752) 202333 E-mail: orders@nbninternational.com

British Museum Press+
Division of The British Museum Co Ltd
38 Russell Sq, London WC1B 3QQ
Tel: (020) 7323 1234 Toll Free Tel: 0800 218 2222 (customer services) Fax: (020) 7436 7315
E-mail: reception@britishmuseum.co.uk; sales@britishmuseum.co.uk
Web Site: www.britishmuseum.org
Key Personnel
Dir: Neil McGregor
Dir, Publishing: Rosemary Bradley

Press: Hattie Clarke *E-mail:* hclarke@
britishmuseum.co.uk
Rights: Katie Poupard *E-mail:* kpoupard@
britishmuseum.co.uk
Founded: 1973
Subjects: Antiques, Archaeology, Art, Asian Stud-
ies, Cookery, Crafts, Games, Hobbies, Ethnic-
ity, History, Natural History, Religion - Other
ISBN Prefix(es): 978-0-71
Distributed by Thames & Hudson (exc USA)

British Psychological Society, see BPS
Blackwell (British Psychological Society)

British Tourist Authority
Sanctuary Bldg, 20 Great Smith St, Westminster
SW1P 3BT
Tel: (020) 7578 1000
E-mail: industry.relations@visitbritain.org
Web Site: www.visitbritain.org
Key Personnel
Chief Executive Officer: Sally Balcombe
Tel: (020) 7578 1020 *E-mail:* sally.balcombe@
visitbritain.org
Overseas Network Dir: Keith Beechham
Marketing Dir: Joss Croft
Strategy & Communications Dir: Patricia Yates
Founded: 1969
Subjects: Travel & Tourism
ISBN Prefix(es): 978-0-7095; 978-0-85630; 978-
0-900225

Broad Leys Publications Ltd
Midas House, The Conge, Great Yarmouth, Nor-
folk NR29 3QG
Tel: (01493) 249 160
Web Site: broadleys.org
Key Personnel
Owner: Nigel Bowerbank
Business Dir: David Thear
Founded: 2001
Publishers of books on poultry, livestock & small-
holdings.
Subjects: Agriculture, Animals, Pets, Gardening,
Plants, Organic Gardening
ISBN Prefix(es): 978-0-906137
Number of titles published annually: 2 Print
Total Titles: 14 Print

Andrew Brodie, *imprint of* A&C Black
Publishers Ltd

Brookemead Associates Ltd
PO Box 58230, London N1 1RP
Tel: (020) 7700 7517 *Fax:* (020) 7607 5705
E-mail: info@brookemead-elt.co.uk
Web Site: www.brookemead-elt.co.uk
Subjects: Education, Language Arts, Linguistics,
ELT
ISBN Prefix(es): 978-1-905248
U.S. Office(s): Brookemead ELT USA, 3450
Sacramento St, PO Box 135, San Francisco,
CA 94118, United States
Foreign Rep(s): Alokke A/S (Denmark); Attica,
Librairie des Langues (France); BEBC Distri-
bution (UK); BELT de Mexico (Mexico); An-
drew Betsis ELT (Greece); Book Editions (S)
Pte Ltd (Singapore); Calliope The Language
Bookshop (Morocco); Caves Books (Taiwan);
CIDEB Black Cat (Italy); Compass Publish-
ing (Korea); DZS Solski Epicenter (Slovenia);
Educational Centre (Moldova, Montenegro,
Romania, Serbia); English Language Services
(Colombia); FLB Bookery Pty Ltd (Australia);
4kids Books (China); ILC Czechoslovakia Ltd
(Czechia); International Books (Ireland); Inter-
taal Belgium (Belgium); Intertaal BV (Holland,
Netherlands); Koolibri Publishers (Estonia);
Korinor Skoleavdelingen (Norway); Macmillan
Language House (Japan); Middle East Publish-
ing & Distribution (Egypt); Nuans Publishing

(Turkey); Oxford Centre (Albania, Bulgaria);
Oxico (Slovakia); Polanglo Sp z oo/Akademia
Bookshops (Poland); Sanoma Utbildning (Sweden); Libreria SBS Peru (Peru); SBS Libreria y Editora Ltda (Chile); SBS Libros de Idiomas (Argentina); SBS Special Book Services
(Brazil); Titul Publishers (Russia); Universi-
texts Ltd (Thailand); WSOY (Finland)

Brooklands Books Ltd
PO Box 146, Cobham, Surrey KT11 1LG
Tel: (01932) 865051 *Fax:* (01932) 868803
E-mail: sales@brooklands-books.com
Web Site: brooklandsbooks.co.uk
Key Personnel
Founder: John Dowdeswell
Mng Dir: Ian Dowdeswell
Subjects: Automotive, Military, Motorcycles, Rac-
ing
ISBN Prefix(es): 978-0-906589; 978-0-907073;
978-0-946489; 978-0-948207; 978-1-85520;
978-1-869826; 978-1-870642
Number of titles published annually: 50 Print
Total Titles: 800 Print
Branch Office(s)
Brooklands Books Australia, 3/37-39 Green St,
Banksmeadow, NSW 2019, Australia *Tel:* (02)
9695 7055 *Fax:* (02) 9695 7355
U.S. Office(s): CarTech, 39966 Grand Ave, North
Branch, MN 55056, United States *Tel:* 651-
277-1200 *Fax:* 651-277-1203
Distributor for Robert Bentley Inc

Brown Bear Books, *imprint of* Windmill Books
Ltd

Brown, Son & Ferguson Ltd
Unit 1A, 426 Drumoyne Rd, Glasgow G51 4DA
Tel: (0141) 883 0141 *Fax:* (0141) 810 5931
E-mail: info@skipper.co.uk
Web Site: www.skipper.co.uk
Key Personnel
Chairman & Production: T Nigel Brown
Dir & Secretary: Wendy Brown
Dir: Richard Brown
Mng Dir: L Ingram-Brown
Founded: 1832
Nautical publishers & printers.
Subjects: Drama, Theater, Maritime, Scottish
Plays, Nautical Publications
ISBN Prefix(es): 978-0-85174; 978-1-84927; 978-
0-85347
Number of titles published annually: 10 Print; 1
CD-ROM
Total Titles: 1 CD-ROM
Subsidiaries: James Munro & Co

Brown Watson
The Old Mill, 76 Fleckney Rd, Kibworth
Beauchamp, Leics LE8 0HG
Tel: (0116) 279 6333 *Fax:* (0116) 279 6303
E-mail: books@brownwatson.co.uk; sales@
brownwatson.co.uk
Web Site: www.brownwatson.co.uk
Key Personnel
Production Manager: Emily Betts *E-mail:* emily@
brownwatson.co.uk
Foreign Rights: Barbara Friedberger
E-mail: barbara@brownwatson.de
Sales: Hannah Clipston
Founded: 1980
ISBN Prefix(es): 978-0-7097; 978-0-7027; 978-0-
85175

Bryntirion Press+
Bryntirion, Bridgend, M Glam CF31 4DX
Tel: (01656) 655912 *Fax:* (01656) 665919
E-mail: bridgendbookshop@emw.org.uk
Web Site: www.bryntirionpress.com; www.emw.
org.uk

Key Personnel
Press Manager: Huw Kinsey
Founded: 1955
Publish books in Welsh & English.
Also distribute for other publishers.
Subjects: Biblical Studies, Biography, Memoirs,
History, Religion - Protestant, Theology
ISBN Prefix(es): 978-0-900898; 978-1-85049
Total Titles: 80 Print
Parent Company: Evangelical Movement of
Wales
Imprints: Evangelical Library of Wales
Distributed by Evangelical Press (English lan-
guage titles)

Buried River Press, *imprint of* The Crowood
Press Ltd

Burleigh Dodds Science Publishing
82 High St, Sawston, Cambs CB22 3HJ
Tel: (01223) 839365
E-mail: info@bdspublishing.com
Web Site: www.bdspublishing.com
Key Personnel
Mng Dir: Rob Burleigh *E-mail:* rob.burleigh@
bdspublishing.com
Editorial Dir: Francis Dodds
Sales Dir: John Parsons
Product Delivery Manager: Jenny Wheeler
Founded: 2015
Publisher of agricultural science books, in print &
online.
Subjects: Agriculture, Science (General)

Business Books, *imprint of* O Books

Buster Books, *imprint of* Michael O'Mara Books
Ltd

Butterworth Heinemann Ltd, *imprint of*
Elsevier Ltd

CABI
Division of CAB International
Nosworthy Way, Wallingford, Oxon OX10 8DE
Tel: (01491) 832111 *Fax:* (01491) 833508
E-mail: enquiries@cabi.org; sales@cabi.org
Web Site: www.cabi.org
Key Personnel
Chief Executive Officer: Trevor Nicholls
Chief Financial Officer: Ian Barry
Executive Dir, Commercial: Caroline McNamara
Executive Dir, Publishing: Andrea Powell
Publishing Sales Dir: Adam Gardner
Production Manager: Michael Bodinham
Founded: 1928
Provide information & apply scientific expertise
to solve problems in agriculture & the environ-
ment worldwide.
Subjects: Agriculture, Animals, Pets, Biological
Sciences, Engineering (General), Environmen-
tal Studies, Gardening, Plants, Health, Nutri-
tion, Medicine, Nursing, Dentistry, Science
(General), Travel & Tourism, Veterinary Sci-
ence, Agricultural Economics, Animal Breed-
ing, Biodiversity, Biological Control, Breeding,
Crop Production & Protection, Dairy Science,
Ecology, Engineering & Entomology, Forestry,
Genetics & Pathology, Horticulture, Medici-
nal Plants, Nematology, Nutrition & Produc-
tion, Parasitology & Infectious Diseases, Plant
Biotechnology, Postharvest, Rural Develop-
ment, Sugar Industry, Weed Science
ISBN Prefix(es): 978-0-85198; 978-0-85199; 978-
1-84593
Total Titles: 350 Print; 430 E-Book
U.S. Office(s): 38 Chauncy St, Suite 1002,
Boston, MA 02111, United States *Fax:* 617-
354-6875 *E-mail:* cabi-nao@cabi.org
Distributed by Quantum Publishing Solutions Ltd
(UK); Stylus Publishing (USA)

Foreign Rep(s): ABE Marketing Sp z oo (Piotr Antczak) (Poland); Academic Marketing Services (Pty) Ltd (Michael Brightmore) (South Africa); Access Dunia Sdn Bhd (Malaysia); Albertina icome Bratislava (Mr Ladislav Svrsek/Lucia Lazarova) (Slovakia); Albertina Icome Praha sro (Jakub Petrik) (Czechia); Alex Centre for Multimedia & Librairies (Dr Shawky Salem) (Egypt); Book Promotion & Service Co Ltd (iGroup) (Thailand); Tim Burland (Japan); CABI (Chris Edmeades) (Australia, Japan, New Zealand, Papua New Guinea); CABI (Sarah Pollard) (Austria, Belgium, France, Germany, Greece, Ireland, Netherlands, Portugal, Spain, Switzerland); CABI North America (Canada, USA); CABI South Asia (Manish Singh) (Bangladesh, India, Pakistan, Sri Lanka); Data Status (Marina Jovanovic) (Serbia); DEA SpA (Paola Piretta) (Italy); DotLib Informacao Profissional (Federico Agostino) (Argentina); DotLib Informacao Profissional (Marcelo Dias, Marcos Criado, Celso Carvalho & Rafael Borowski) (Brazil); E-nformation (Victor Voican) (Romania); Fenice Distribuzione SRL (Italy); Colin Flint Ltd (Ben Greig) (Denmark, Finland, Iceland, Norway, Sweden); GreenData (Carolina Mazzoleni) (Spain); Kevin van Hasselt (Africa); IG Knowledge Services Ltd (Taiwan); iGroup (Asia Pacific) Ltd (Vietnam); Info Access & Distribution (Hong Kong) Ltd (Hong Kong); Infoestrategica Latina SA de CV (Marco Antonio Bringas) (Mexico); InfoLink Ltda (Gonzalo Galvez Clderon) (Chile); INFONET (South Korea); PT Jasaraya Tama Jaya Buana (Indonesia); Levant Distributors (Lebanon); Jacek Lewison (Central Europe, Eastern Europe); Library Information for Marketing & Services (Mahmoud Hussein) (Egypt); LKCG LLC (Juan Cristobal Zulueta) (Puerto Rico); LM Tietopalvelut Oy (Janne Jarvinen) (Denmark, Finland, Iceland, Norway, Sweden); Lusodoc Documentacao Tecnico-Cientifica (Miguel Silva) (Portugal); MegaTEXTS Phil Inc (Philippines); Catharine Nel Naseej (United Arab Emirates); Mr Abdulrahman Al Kreedes Naseej (Middle East exc Iran, Saudi Arabia); Probook (Israel); Publiciencia Ltda (Jair Saavedra Angulo) (Colombia, Costa Rica, Ecuador, Peru); Quantum Publishing Solutions Ltd (UK); Shabake Tajhiz Danesh Co (Mehran Jalali) (Iran); Shinwon Datanet Inc (South Korea); STM-Info (Mehmet T Haseki) (Turkey); Stylus Publishing (USA)

Cadmos Publishing Ltd
Subsidiary of Cadmos Verlag GmbH
2, Sheen Rd, Richmond TW91 AE
Tel: (020) 8973 2685 *Fax:* (020) 8973 2301
E-mail: info@cadmos.co.uk; rights@cadmos-books.com
Web Site: www.cadmos.co.uk
Key Personnel
Rights: Lisa Metzemacher
Founded: 2002
Subjects: Agriculture, Animals, Pets, Gardening, Plants, Health, Nutrition, Dog Training, Equestrian
ISBN Prefix(es): 978-0-85788
Ultimate Parent Company: Oesterreichischer Agrarverlag
Foreign Rep(s): Bookreps NZ Ltd (New Zealand); Capricorn Link (Aust) Pty Ltd (Australia); Independent Publishers Group (USA); Target Sales (Robert Ertle) (Europe, Ireland, UK); Trinity Books (South Africa)
Distribution Center: Central Books Ltd, One Heath Park Industrial Estate, Freshwater Rd, Dagenham RM8 1RX *Tel:* (020) 8525 8800 *Fax:* (020) 8599 2694 *E-mail:* orders@centralbooks.com *Web Site:* www.centralbooks.com

Caffeine Nights Publishing+
4 Eton Close, Walderslade, Chatham, Kent ME5 9AT
Tel: (01634) 681432
E-mail: info@caffeinenights.com
Web Site: caffeinenights.com
Founded: 2007
Crime & horror fiction publisher of work from UK based authors.
Subjects: Fiction, Mysteries, Suspense
ISBN Prefix(es): 978-0-9554070; 978-1-907565; 978-1-910720
Number of titles published annually: 20 Print; 20 E-Book; 5 Audio
Total Titles: 55 Print; 1 CD-ROM; 60 E-Book; 6 Audio

Calder Publications, *imprint of* Alma Books Ltd

Cambridge University Press+
University Printing House, Shaftesbury Rd, Cambridge CB2 8BS
Tel: (01223) 358331; (01223) 326070 (journals) *Fax:* (01223) 325150
E-mail: information@cambridge.org; press@cambridge.org; editorial@cambridge.org; rights@cambridge.org
Web Site: www.cambridge.org
Key Personnel
Chief Executive: Peter Phillips
Global Operations Dir: Iain Harrison
Mng Dir, Academic: Mandy Hill
Mng Dir, English Language Teaching & Americas: Michael Peluse
Mng Dir, Education: Rod Smith
Rights Sales Manager: Katie Scarff
Permissions: Linda Nicol
Founded: 1534
Subjects: Agriculture, Archaeology, Architecture & Interior Design, Art, Asian Studies, Astronomy, Behavioral Sciences, Biblical Studies, Biological Sciences, Business, Chemistry, Chemical Engineering, Computer Science, Drama, Theater, Earth Sciences, Engineering (General), Environmental Studies, Geography, Geology, Government, Political Science, Language Arts, Linguistics, Law, Literature, Literary Criticism, Essays, Medicine, Nursing, Dentistry, Physical Sciences, Psychology, Psychiatry, Science (General), Technology
ISBN Prefix(es): 978-0-521
Number of titles published annually: 1,600 Print; 50 CD-ROM; 500 Online; 1,000 E-Book; 50 Audio
Total Titles: 50,000 Print; 500 CD-ROM; 550 Online; 3,000 E-Book; 200 Audio
Imprints: Greenwich Medical Media; Law in Context
Divisions: Cambridge University Press - Printing Division
Branch Office(s)
477 Williamstown Rd, Port Melbourne, Victoria 3207, Australia *Tel:* (03) 8671 1400 *Fax:* (03) 9676 9955 *E-mail:* melbourne@cambridge.org
Web Site: www.cambridge.org/aus
Lower Ground floor, Nautica Bldg, The Water Club, Beach Rd, Granger Bay, Cape Town 8005, South Africa *Toll Free Tel:* (021) 412 7800 *Fax:* (021) 419 0594 *E-mail:* capetown@cambridge.org
Basilica 17, 1, 28020 Madrid, Spain *Tel:* 91 360 4565 *Fax:* 91 360 4570 *E-mail:* madrid@cambridge.org
U.S. Office(s): One Liberty Plaza, 20th floor, New York, NY 10006, United States *Tel:* 212-337-5000 *E-mail:* newyork@cambridge.org
Distributor for The Asser Press (worldwide)
Foreign Rights: Bardon-Chinese Media Agency (Hong Kong, Macau, Taiwan); Bestun Korea Agency (Korea)
Showroom(s): One & 2 Trinity St, Cambridge CB2 1SU

Camden House, *imprint of* Boydell & Brewer Ltd

Camden Press Ltd+
Albany House, 2nd floor, 14 Bishopric, Horsham, West Sussex RH12 1QN
Tel: (020) 7226 4673
Key Personnel
Publisher: Robert Borzello
Mng Dir: Peter Allez
Founded: 1985
Subjects: Art, Biography, Memoirs, Health, Nutrition, Social Sciences, Sociology, Women's Studies
ISBN Prefix(es): 978-0-948491

Cameron & Hollis+
Imprint of Cameron Books
2 Sunnybank, Old Edinburgh Rd, Moffat, Dumfries & Galloway DG10 9RU
Tel: (01683) 220808
Web Site: www.cameronbooks.co.uk
Key Personnel
Dir: Jill Hollis *E-mail:* jh@cameronbooks.co.uk
Founded: 1976
Also a book production company.
Subjects: Architecture & Interior Design, Art, Environmental Studies, Film, Video, Natural History, Nonfiction (General)
ISBN Prefix(es): 978-0-906506
Number of titles published annually: 5 Print

Campbell Books, *imprint of* Macmillan Children's Books

Campbell Books, *imprint of* Pan Macmillan

Candle Books, *imprint of* Lion Hudson PLC

C&R, *imprint of* Little, Brown Book Group

Canongate Books+
14 High St, Edinburgh EH1 1TE
Tel: (0131) 557 5111 *Fax:* (0131) 557 5211
E-mail: support@canongate.co.uk
Web Site: www.canongate.co.uk
Key Personnel
Chairman: David Young
Chief Executive: Jamie Byng
Chief Operating Officer: Kate Gibb
Campaigns Dir: Katie Moffat
Editorial Dir: Simon Thorogood
Production Dir: Caroline Gorham
Publishing Dir: Francis Bickmore
Rights Dir: Andrea Joyce *E-mail:* andrea.joyce@canongate.co.uk
Head, Brand & Events: Angela Robertson
Head, Publicity: Anna Frame
E-mail: annaframe@canongate.co.uk
Head, Sales: Sian Gibson *E-mail:* sian.gibson@canongate.co.uk
Senior Commissioning Editor: Hannah Knowles
Assistant Editor: Jo Dingley
Founded: 1973
Subjects: Art, Biography, Memoirs, Business, Cookery, Fiction, Government, Political Science, History, Humor, Literature, Literary Criticism, Essays, Music, Dance, Mysteries, Suspense, Nonfiction (General), Philosophy, Poetry, Regional Interests, Religion - Other, Romance, Self-Help, Travel & Tourism, Nature
ISBN Prefix(es): 978-0-86241; 978-1-84195; 978-1-84767; 978-0-903937; 978-0-85786; 978-1-78211
Number of titles published annually: 65 Print
Total Titles: 350 Print
Imprints: Canongate Classics; Walker Canongate (young adult)
Distributed by Grove Atlantic (USA)
Foreign Rep(s): A-Z Africa Book Services (Anita Zih) (Africa exc Botswana & South Africa);

Allen & Unwin (Miranda Van Asch) (Australia); Ashton International Marketing Services (Julian Ashton) (Far East); Faber & Faber Ltd (Bridget Lane) (Belgium, Denmark, Finland, Ireland, Northern Europe, Norway, Sweden, Switzerland); Faber & Faber Ltd (Suzy Jenner) (Austria, France, Germany); Cristian Juncu (Central Europe, Eastern Europe); Penguin Random House India (Bangladesh, India, Nepal); Penguin Random House South Africa (Angela Thomson) (South Africa); Repforce Ireland Ltd (Ireland); Trafalgar Square (Brooke O'Donnell) (Canada, USA)

Foreign Rights: AnatoliaLit Agency (Amy Spangler, Eda Caca & Secil Kivrak) (Turkey); The English Agency (Japan) Ltd (Hamish Macaskill) (Japan); Japan Uni Agency (Miko Yamanouchi) (Japan); Andrew Nurnberg Associates Baltic (Tatjana Zoldnere & Kristine Shatrovska) (Estonia, Latvia, Lithuania); Andrew Nurnberg Associates Budapest (Blanka Daroczi & Kriszta Makk) (Croatia, Hungary); Andrew Nurnberg Associates International Ltd (Jackie Huang & Whitney Hsu) (China, Taiwan); Andrew Nurnberg Associates Prague (Jitka Nemeckova) (Czechia, Slovakia, Slovenia); Andrew Nurnberg Associates Sofia (Mira Droumeva) (Bulgaria, Romania, Serbia); Owls Agency Inc (Mario Tauchi) (Japan); Tuttle-Mori Agency (Thananchai Pandey) (Thailand); The Van Lear Agency (Liz Van Lear & Olga Rogozina) (Russia); Eric Yang Agency (Sue Yang) (Korea)

Orders to: The Book Service Ltd (TBS), Distribution Centre, Colchester Rd, Frating Green, Colchester, Essex CO7 7DW Tel: (01206) 256060 Fax: (01206) 255715 E-mail: sales@tbs-ltd.co.uk Web Site: www.thebookservice.co.uk

Canongate Classics, *imprint of* Canongate Books

Canterbury Press, *imprint of* Hymns Ancient & Modern Ltd

Capall Bann Publishing Ltd+
Auton Farm, Milverton, Somerset TA4 1NE
Tel: (01823) 401528
E-mail: enquiries@capallbann.co.uk
Web Site: www.capallbann.co.uk
Key Personnel
Publisher: Jon Day; Julia Day
Founded: 1993
Subjects: Alternative, Animals, Pets, Archaeology, Astrology, Occult, Environmental Studies, Gardening, Plants, Music, Dance, Mysteries, Suspense, Parapsychology, Philosophy, Psychology, Psychiatry, Religion - Other, Self-Help, Women's Studies, Alternative Healing, Mind, Body & Spirit
ISBN Prefix(es): 978-1-898307; 978-1-86163
Number of titles published annually: 40 Print
Total Titles: 310 Print
Distribution Center: Brumby Books, 10 Southfork Dr, Kilsyth South, Victoria 3137, Australia *Tel:* (03) 9761 5535 *Fax:* (03) 9761 7095 *E-mail:* brumby@hotkey.net.au
New Leaf Distributing Co, 401 Thornton Rd, Lithia Springs, GA 30122-1557, United States *Tel:* 770-948-7845 *Fax:* 770-944-2313 *E-mail:* sales@newleaf-dist.com *Web Site:* www.newleaf-dist.com
Holmes Publishing Group, PO Box 2370, Sequim, WA, United States, Contact: Mr J D Holmes *Tel:* 360-681-2900 *E-mail:* jdholmes@fastmail.fm *Web Site:* www.jdholmes.com

Jonathan Cape, *imprint of* The Random House Group Ltd, a Penguin Random House Company

Jonathan Cape Children's, *imprint of* The Random House Group Ltd, a Penguin Random House Company

Jonathan Cape (PB), *imprint of* The Random House Group Ltd, a Penguin Random House Company

Capstone Publishing Ltd+
Subsidiary of John Wiley & Sons Ltd
The Atrium, Southern Gate, Chichester, West Sussex PO19 8SQ
Tel: (01243) 843294
Web Site: www.thisiscapstone.com
Key Personnel
Publisher: Ian Campbell
Mng Dir: Doug Pocock
Executive Commissioning Editor: Holly Bennion
Development Editor: Jenny Ng
Commissioning Editor: Jonathan Shipley
Assistant Editor: Vicky Kinsman
    E-mail: vkinsman@wiley.com
Senior Marketing Manager: Michael Friedberg
    E-mail: mfriedbe@wiley.com; Megan Saker
    E-mail: msaker@wiley.com
Marketing Manager: Emily Bryczkowski; Lauren Noens *E-mail:* lnoens@wiley.com
Content Editor: Grace O'Byrne
Founded: 1996
Membership(s): IPG.
Subjects: Business, Economics, Management
ISBN Prefix(es): 978-1-900961; 978-1-84112
Number of titles published annually: 20 Print
Total Titles: 90 Print
Foreign Rights: Susie Adams Rights Agency (UK)
Orders to: John Wiley & Sons, Ltd Service & Distribution Centre, New Era Estate, One Odlands Way, Bognor Regis, West Sussex PO22 9NQ *Tel:* (01243) 779 777 *Fax:* (01243) 843 274 *E-mail:* customer@wiley.com

Capuchin Classics, *imprint of* Stacey International

Carcanet Fiction, *imprint of* Carcanet Press Ltd

Carcanet Film, *imprint of* Carcanet Press Ltd

Carcanet Merchandise, *imprint of* Carcanet Press Ltd

Carcanet Poetry, *imprint of* Carcanet Press Ltd

Carcanet Press Ltd+
Alliance House, 4th floor, 30 Cross St, Manchester M2 7AQ
Tel: (0161) 834 8730 *Fax:* (0161) 832 0084
E-mail: info@carcanet.co.uk
Web Site: www.carcanet.co.uk
Key Personnel
Editorial & Mng Dir: Michael Schmidt
    E-mail: schmidt@carcanet.co.uk
Finance Dir: Christine Steel *E-mail:* christine@carcanet.co.uk
Mng Editor: Luke Allan *E-mail:* luke@carcanet.co.uk
Marketing Manager: Alice Kate Mullen
    E-mail: alice@carcanet.co.uk
Sales Manager: Katie Caunt *E-mail:* katie@carcanet.co.uk
Founded: 1962
Independent poetry & fiction translation publisher.
Subjects: Fiction, Literature, Literary Criticism, Essays, Poetry
ISBN Prefix(es): 978-0-85635; 978-0-902145; 978-1-85754; 978-1-903039; 978-1-84777; 978-1-903101; 978-1-906188; 978-1-905583
Number of titles published annually: 40 Print
Total Titles: 1,000 Print; 20 Audio

Parent Company: Folio Holdings Ltd
Associate Companies: Folio Society
Imprints: Aspects of Portugal; Audio Books; Carcanet Fiction; Carcanet Film; Carcanet Merchandise; Carcanet Poetry; Comma Press; Fyfield Books; Lintott Press; Lives & Letters; Northern House; OxfordPoets; PN Review; Sheep Meadow Press
Distributor for Comma Press
Foreign Rep(s): Melanie Boesen (Denmark, Finland, Iceland, Sweden); Brookside Publishing Services (Michael Darcy) (Ireland); Ted Dougherty (Austria, Belgium, France, Germany, Greece, Italy, Netherlands, Switzerland); Iberian Book Services (Peter Prout) (Portugal, Spain)
Distribution Center: NBN International, 10 Thornbury Rd, Plymouth, Devon PL6 7PP
Tel: (01752) 202301 *Fax:* (01752) 202333
    E-mail: orders@nbninternational.com
Eleanor Brasch Enterprises, PO Box 586, Artarmon, NSW 2064, Australia *Tel:* (02) 9419 8717 *Fax:* (02) 9419 7930 *E-mail:* brasch2@aol.com (Australia & New Zealand)
Independent Publishers Group, Order Dept, 814 N Franklin St, Chicago, IL 60610, United States *Tel:* 312-337-0747 *Fax:* 312-337-5985 *E-mail:* frontdesk@ipgbook.com (USA & Canada, Caribbean, Korea, Latin America, Micronesia, Philippines & South America)

Cardiff Academic Press+
St Fagans Rd, Fairwater, Cardiff CF5 3AE
Tel: (029) 2056 0333 *Fax:* (029) 2055 4909
E-mail: enquiries@drakeed.com
Founded: 1979
Subjects: Biography, Memoirs, Education, Literature, Literary Criticism, Essays, Regional Interests, Religion - Other, Social Sciences, Sociology, Women's Studies, Welsh Studies
ISBN Prefix(es): 978-1-899025; 978-1-870495
Parent Company: Drake Group
Distributor for ILSI Press (USA); Plantin Publishers (UK)

Cariad, *imprint of* Accent Press Ltd

Caribbean Modern Classics, *imprint of* Peepal Tree Press Ltd

Carina Press, *imprint of* Harlequin Mills & Boon

Carlton, *imprint of* Carlton Publishing Group

Carlton Kids, *imprint of* Carlton Publishing Group

Carlton Publishing Group+
20 Mortimer St, London W1T 3JW
Tel: (020) 7612 0400 *Fax:* (020) 7612 0401
E-mail: enquires@carltonbooks.co.uk; sales@carltonbooks.co.uk
Web Site: www.carltonbooks.co.uk
Key Personnel
Publisher & Chairman: Jonathan Goodman
Editorial Dir: Piers Murray Hill
    E-mail: pmurrayhill@carltonbooks.co.uk
International Sales Dir: Jo Wort
Commercial Dir: Jim Greehough *Tel:* (020) 7612 0414 *E-mail:* jgreehough@carltonbooks.co.uk
UK Sales & Marketing Dir: Owen Hazell
    Tel: (020) 7612 0433 *E-mail:* ohazell@carltonbooks.co.uk
Head, Marketing: Helen Churchill *Tel:* (020) 7612 0474 *E-mail:* hchurchill@carltonbooks.co.uk
Marketing Manager: Anthony Grant
    E-mail: agrant@carltonbooks.co.uk
Head, Publicity: Carol Farley *Tel:* (020) 7612 0416 *E-mail:* cfarley@carltonbooks.co.uk
Royalty & Rights: Nicholas Brink *Tel:* (020) 7612 0448 *E-mail:* royaltyacc@carltonbooks.co.uk

Founded: 1992
Publisher of illustrated books.
Subjects: Antiques, Architecture & Interior Design, Art, Biography, Memoirs, Criminology, Erotica, Fashion, Film, Video, Health, Nutrition, History, Humor, Music, Dance, Natural History, Radio, TV, Sports, Athletics, Wine & Spirits
ISBN Prefix(es): 978-1-85868; 978-1-84222; 978-1-84732; 978-1-78097
Number of titles published annually: 100 Print
Total Titles: 1,000 Print
Parent Company: Jonathan Goodman Publishing Ltd
Imprints: Carlton; Carlton Kids; Andre Deutsch; Goodman; Goodman Fiell; Prion
Foreign Rep(s): Gunnar Lie & Associates Ltd (Gunnar Lie) (Africa, Asia, Indian subcontinent); Gunnar Lie & Associates Ltd (Guillaume Ferrand) (Belgium, Central America, Eastern Europe, France, Gibraltar, Italy, Luxembourg, Malta, Portugal, South America, Spain); Gunnar Lie & Associates Ltd (John Edgeler) (Caribbean, Cyprus, Greece, Middle East, Netherlands, Scandinavia); Lorie Ocampo (China, Hong Kong, Japan, Korea, Philippines, Taiwan); Publishers Services (Gabriele Kern) (Austria, Germany, Switzerland); Research Press (Ajay Parmer) (India)
Distribution Center: HarperCollins Distribution Services, Customer Services Dept, Westerhill Rd, Bishopbriggs, Glasgow G64 2QT
Tel: (0141) 306 3100 *Fax:* (0141) 306 3261
E-mail: uk.orders@harpercollins.co.uk
Hardie Grant Books, 658 Church St, Ground floor, Bldg 1, Richmond, Victoria 3121, Australia, Contact: Clare Morrison
Tel: (03) 8520 644 *Fax:* (03) 8520 6422
E-mail: claremorrison@hardiegrant.com.au
Web Site: www.hardiegrant.com.au (Australia & New Zealand)
Sterling Publishing Co Inc, 1166 Avenue of the Americas, New York, NY 10036, United States
E-mail: custservice@sterlingpublishing.com
(Carlton Books)

Carrick Media
89 Mount Pleasant Way, Kilmarnock KA3 1HJ
Tel: (01563) 521839
Web Site: whoswhoinscotland.com
Founded: 1983
Specialize in Scotland & British media.
Subjects: Regional Interests
ISBN Prefix(es): 978-0-946724; 978-0-9546631; 978-0-9565748

Casemate UK
The Old Music Hall, 106-108 Cowley Rd, Oxford OX4 1JE
Tel: (01865) 241249 *Fax:* (01865) 794449
E-mail: casemate-uk@casematepublishing.co.uk
Web Site: www.casematepublishing.co.uk
Key Personnel
Chairman & Chief Executive Officer: David Farnsworth
Mng Dir: Simone Drinkwater *E-mail:* simone.drinkwater@casematepublishing.co.uk
Publishing Dir: Claire Litt
Founded: 2007
Military history publisher & distributor.
Subjects: History, Military Science, Military History
ISBN Prefix(es): 978-0-9711709; 978-1-932033; 978-1-935149; 978-1-61200
Associate Companies: Casemate | publishers, 1950 Lawrence Rd, Havertown, PA 19083, United States *Tel:* 610-853-9131 *Fax:* 610-853-9146 *E-mail:* casemate@casematepublishers.com *Web Site:* www.casematepublishers.com
Distributor for AFV Modeller; AJ Press; Amber Books; Andrea Press; Brookhurst Press; Casemate Publishers; Ch Links; Compendium Films; Concord Publications; D-Day Publish-

ing; Emperor's Press; Enigma Books; Formac Lorimer Books; Foundry Publications; Editions Heimdal; Helion & Company; Histoire & Collections; History Facts; Kagero; Lancer International; Leandoer & Ekholm; Medals of America; National Maritime Museum; Naval Institute Press; OREP; Paladin Press; Periscopio Publications; Philedition; Presidio Press; Quiron; Ryton Publications; RZM Publications; Savas Beatie; Scoval Publishing; S I Publicaties; Stackpole Books; Stevens International; Ken Trotman Books; Warlord Games
Foreign Rep(s): Angell Eurosales (Denmark, Finland, Iceland, Norway, Sweden); Books for Europe (Sandro Salucci) (Gibraltar, Greece, Italy, Portugal, Spain); Mary Campbell (Ireland, Northern Ireland); Kerrin Cocks (South Africa); European Marketing Services (Anselm Robinson) (Austria, Belgium, Germany, Switzerland); Horizon Books Pte Ltd (Singapore); Horizon Books Sdn Bhd (Malaysia); KW Publishers Pvt Ltd (India); Peribo Pty Ltd (Michael Coffey) (Australia); Publishers International Marketing (Ray Potts & Chris Ashdown) (Far East, Middle East); South Pacific Books (Liza Raybould) (New Zealand); Tuttostoria (Ermanno Albertelli) (Italy); Vanwell Publishing (Simon Kooter) (Canada)
Distribution Center: Bookpoint Ltd, 130 Milton Park, Abingdon, Oxon OX14 4SB *Tel:* (01235) 400 400 *Web Site:* bookpoint.wp.hachette.co.uk

Cassava Crime, *imprint of* Cassava Republic Press

Cassava Republic Press
26a Pepys Rd, London SE14 5SB
E-mail: info@cassavarepublic.biz
Web Site: www.cassavarepublic.biz
Founded: 2006
Subjects: Criminology, Fiction, Mysteries, Suspense, Nonfiction (General), Science Fiction, Fantasy
ISBN Prefix(es): 978-978-950; 978-1-911115
Number of titles published annually: 20 Print
Imprints: Ankara Press (romance); Cassava Crime
Distribution Center: Central Books Ltd, One Heath Park Industrial Estate, Freshwater Rd, Dagenham RM8 1RX *Tel:* (020) 8525 8800 *Fax:* (020) 8599 2694 *E-mail:* orders@centralbooks.com *Web Site:* www.centralbooks.com

Cassell Illustrated, *imprint of* Octopus Publishing Group Ltd

Caterpillar Books, *imprint of* Little Tiger Press Group

The Catholic Truth Society+
42-46 Harleyford Rd, Vauxhall, London SE11 5AY
Tel: (020) 7640 0042 *Fax:* (020) 7640 0046
E-mail: orders@ctsbooks.org
Web Site: www.ctsbooks.org
Key Personnel
General Secretary & Publisher: Fergal Martin *E-mail:* f.martin@ctsbooks.org
Mng Editor: Pierpaolo Finaldi *E-mail:* p.finaldi@ctsbooks.org
Founded: 1868
Subjects: Education, Religion - Catholic
ISBN Prefix(es): 978-0-85183; 978-1-86082
Imprints: CTS Publications
Distributor for Liberia Editrice Vaticana; L'Osservatore Romano Newspaper
Bookshop(s): 25 Ashley Pl, London SW1P 1LT *Tel:* (020) 7834 1363 *Fax:* (020) 7821 7398 *E-mail:* bookshop@ctsbooks.org
Book Club(s): CTS Readers' Club

Distribution Center: St Pauls Publications, PO Box 906, Strathfield, NSW 2135, Australia *Tel:* (02) 9394 3400 *Fax:* (02) 9746 1140 *E-mail:* sales@stpauls.com.au *Web Site:* www.stpauls.com.au

Catnip Publishing Ltd+
320 City Rd, London EC1V 2NZ
Tel: (020) 7138 3650
Web Site: www.catnippublishing.co.uk
Key Personnel
Editorial: Liz Bankes *Tel:* (020) 7138 3695 *E-mail:* liz.bankes@catnippublishing.co.uk
Founded: 2005
ISBN Prefix(es): 978-1-899248; 978-1-903285; 978-1-905117; 978-1-84647; 978-1-903207; 978-1-904700
Number of titles published annually: 40 Print
Total Titles: 129 Print
Imprints: Happy Cat Books
Foreign Rights: Caroline Hill-Trevor
Distribution Center: Grantham Book Services, Trent Rd, Grantham, Lincs NG31 7XQ *Tel:* (01476) 541080 *Fax:* (01476) 541061 *E-mail:* orders@gbs.tbs-ltd.co.uk
Orders to: Grantham Book Services, Trent Rd, Grantham, Lincs NG31 7XQ *Tel:* (01476) 541080 *Fax:* (01476) 541061 *E-mail:* orders@gbs.tbs-ltd.co.uk

Cat's Pyjamas Books
Headlands Business Centre, 10 Headlands, Kettering, Northants NN15 7HP
Tel: (01536) 525817
Web Site: www.catspyjamasbooks.com
Key Personnel
Partner: John Moulder; Jeffrey Nobbs
Vice President, Sales: Sarah Fereday
Sales Executive: Tahlia Bellamy
Editorial Dir: Gail Penston
Art Dir: Owen Lee
Rights Manager: Sarah See
ISBN Prefix(es): 978-1-902319

CCH+
145 London Rd, Kingston upon Thames, Surrey KT2 6SR
Tel: (020) 8247 1100 *Toll Free Tel:* 0844 561 8166 (customer services); 0844 561 8167 (online support) *Fax:* (020) 8547 2638
E-mail: uk-customer.services@wolterskluwer.com
Web Site: www.cch.co.uk
Founded: 1982
Subjects: Business, Law
ISBN Prefix(es): 978-0-86325
Parent Company: Wolters Kluwer (UK) Ltd

Cengage Learning (EMEA) Ltd
Cheriton House, North Way, Walworth Business Park, Andover, Hants SP10 5BE
Tel: (01264) 332424 *Fax:* (01264) 342763
E-mail: emea.enquiries@cengage.com; emea.customerservices@cengage.com; emea.edureply@cengage.com
Web Site: edu.cengage.co.uk; www.cengage.co.uk
Key Personnel
UK & Europe Sales Manager: Matthew Keown *Tel:* (07768) 220186 *E-mail:* matthew.keown@cengage.com
Subjects: Business, Economics, Education, Language Arts, Linguistics, Mathematics, Science (General), Social Sciences, Sociology
ISBN Prefix(es): 978-0-15; 978-1-84480; 978-1-86152; 978-1-85032; 978-1-4080; 978-1-4737

Centaur Books, *imprint of* Old Vicarage Publications

Centaur Press, *imprint of* Open Gate Press Ltd

Center for Advanced Welsh & Celtic Studies
National Library of Wales, Aberystwyth, Ceredigion SY23 3HH
Tel: (01970) 636543
Web Site: www.wales.ac.uk/en/
CentreforAdvancedWelshCelticStudies
Key Personnel
Dir: Prof Dafydd Johnston, PhD *E-mail:* d.r.
johnston@wales.ac.uk
Editorial Officer: Gwen Gruffudd *E-mail:* g.
gruffudd@wales.ac.uk
Founded: 1985
Specialize in academic & celtic.
Subjects: History, Literature, Literary Criticism,
Essays
ISBN Prefix(es): 978-0-947531
Parent Company: University of Wales, King Edward VII Ave, Cardiff CF10 3NS

Centre for Alternative Technology+
Machynlleth, Powys SY20 9AZ
Tel: (01654) 705980; (01654) 705959 (mail order); (01654) 705993 (CAT shop) *Fax:* (01654) 703409 (mail order)
E-mail: info@cat.org.uk; mail.order@cat.org.uk
Web Site: www.cat.org.uk
Key Personnel
Publisher: Allan Shepherd *E-mail:* allan.
shepherd@cat.org.uk
Production Designer: Graham Preston
E-mail: graham.preston@cat.org.uk
Publishing Assistant: Annika Faircloth
E-mail: annika.faircloth@cat.org.uk
Founded: 1974
Publisher of DIY titles for environmentalists.
Registered charity.
Subjects: Energy, Environmental Studies, Gardening, Plants, How-to, Nonfiction (General), Technology, Sustainable Lifestyles
ISBN Prefix(es): 978-1-902175; 978-1-898049; 978-0-9514504
Number of titles published annually: 2 Print
Total Titles: 81 Print; 60 Online
Distributed by New Society Publishers (Canada & USA)
Foreign Rep(s): New Society Publishers (Canada, USA)
Distribution Center: Central Books Ltd, One Heath Park Industrial Estate, Freshwater Rd, Dagenham RM8 1RX *Tel:* (020) 8525 8800 *Fax:* (020) 8599 2694 *E-mail:* orders@ centralbooks.com *Web Site:* www.centralbooks. com

Century, *imprint of* The Random House Group Ltd, a Penguin Random House Company

CF4Kids, *imprint of* Christian Focus Publications Ltd

CGP, see Coordination Group Publications Ltd (CGP)

Chancellor Publications Ltd
5-7 Highgate Rd, London NW5 1JY
Tel: (020) 7324 0020 *Fax:* (020) 7324 0021
E-mail: mail@chancellorpublication.com
Web Site: www.chancellorpublication.com
Key Personnel
Mng Dir: Jonathan Bloch *E-mail:* j.bloch@
exchange-data.com
Founded: 1994
Supplier of legal & financial texts for practitioners & laymen.
Subjects: Finance, Law
ISBN Prefix(es): 978-1-899217; 978-0-9569986
Number of titles published annually: 1 Print
Total Titles: 9 Print; 2 E-Book
Parent Company: Information Publishing Plc (iPP), 5-7 Highgate Rd, London NW5 1JY

Chandos Publishing, *imprint of* Elsevier Ltd

Chandos Publishing+
Imprint of Elsevier Ltd
The Boulevard, Langford Lane, Kidlington, Oxford OX5 1GB
Tel: (01865) 843000 *Fax:* (01865) 843010
Web Site: store.elsevier.com/chandos-publishing
Key Personnel
Publisher: Dr Glyn Jones
Founded: 1998
Specialize in academic books.
Subjects: Asian Studies, Business, Civil Engineering, Computer Science, Economics, Education, Engineering (General), Finance, Labor, Industrial Relations, Law, Library & Information Sciences
ISBN Prefix(es): 978-1-902375; 978-1-84334
Number of titles published annually: 50 Print
Total Titles: 300 Print
Ultimate Parent Company: RELX Group
Foreign Rep(s): Apac Publishers Services Pte Ltd (Steven Goh) (Hong Kong, Malaysia, Philippines, Singapore, Thailand); Avicenna Partnership Ltd (Claire de Gruchy) (Algeria, Cyprus, Jordan, Malta, Morocco, Palestine, Tunisia, Turkey); Avicenna Partnership Ltd (Bill Kennedy) (Bahrain, Egypt, Iraq, Kuwait, Lebanon, Libya, Oman, Qatar, Saudi Arabia, Sudan, Syria, United Arab Emirates, Yemen); CRW Marketing Services for Publishers Inc (Tony Sagun) (Philippines); Dr Laszlo Horvath (Eastern Europe, Russia); ICK (Information & Culture Korea) (Se-Yung Jin) (South Korea); IMA/Intermediaamericana (David Williams) (Caribbean); Ingram Publishing Services (USA); JN Publishers' Representative (Jan Norbye) (Scandinavia); Ben Kato (Japan); Kowkab Publishers (Iran); Cristina de Lara Ruiz (Portugal, Spain); Tahir M Lodhi Publishers' Representatives (Pakistan); LSR Libros Servicios Representaciones Vsa de CV (Linda Sametz de Walerstein) (Argentina, Chile, Colombia, Mexico); Mare Nostrum (David Pickering) (France, Italy); Robbert J Pleysier (Austria, Belgium, Germany, Luxembourg, Netherlands, Switzerland); Sara Books Pvt Ltd (Ravindra Saxena) (Bangladesh, India, Sri Lanka); Ian Taylor Associates Ltd (Chile); Unifacmanu Trading Co Ltd (Celine Li) (Taiwan)

Changemakers Books, *imprint of* O Books

Channel 4 Books, *imprint of* The Random House Group Ltd, a Penguin Random House Company

Channel View Publications, *imprint of* Multilingual Matters Ltd

Channel View Publications Ltd
Imprint of Multilingual Matters Ltd
St Nicholas House, 31-34 High St, Bristol BS1 2AW
Tel: (0117) 3158562 *Fax:* (0117) 3158563
E-mail: info@channelviewpublications.com
Web Site: www.channelviewpublications.com
Key Personnel
Mng Dir: Tommi Grover *E-mail:* tommi@
channelviewpublications.com
Editorial Manager & Foreign Rights: Anna Roderick *E-mail:* anna@channelviewpublications.
com
Marketing Manager: Elinor Robertson
E-mail: elinor@channelviewpublications.com
Production Manager: Sarah Williams
E-mail: sarah@channelviewpublications.com
Subjects: Travel & Tourism, Sustainability
ISBN Prefix(es): 978-1-873150; 978-1-84541
Foreign Rep(s): Aromix Books Co Ltd (Nick Woon) (Hong Kong); James Bennett (Australia,

New Zealand); China Publishers Services Ltd (Sarah Zhao) (China); Eureka Press (Japan); Govinda Book House (India); ICK (Se-Yung Jun) (Korea); KVH Books (Kelvin van Hasselt) (Caribbean, Sub-Saharan Africa); Publishers Marketing Services (Malaysia, Singapore); The White Partnership (Andrew White) (Philippines, Taiwan)
Distribution Center: Marston Book Services Ltd, 160 Eastern Ave, Milton Park, Abingdon, Oxon OX14 4SB *Tel:* (01235) 465550 *Fax:* (01235) 465555 *E-mail:* direct.orders@marston.co.uk
Web Site: www.marston.co.uk
UTP Distribution, 5201 Dufferin St, North York, ON M3H 5T8, Canada *Tel:* 416-667-7791 *Fax:* 416-667-7832 *E-mail:* utpbooks@utpress. utoronto.ca
UTP Distribution, 2250 Military Rd, Tonawanda, NY 14150, United States *Tel:* 416-667-7791 *Fax:* 416-667-7832 *E-mail:* utpbooks@utpress. utoronto.ca

Paul Chapman Publishing, *imprint of* SAGE Publications Ltd

Chapter Two+
Fountain House, 3 Conduit Mews, London SE18 7AP
Tel: (020) 8316 5389 *Fax:* (020) 8854 5963
E-mail: info@chaptertwobooks.org.uk
Web Site: www.chaptertwobooks.org.uk; www.
biblecentre.org
Key Personnel
Publisher: Simon Attwood
Founded: 1976
Publisher & bookseller.
Specialize in Plymouth Brethren literature & their history.
Subjects: History, Language Arts, Linguistics, Religion - Protestant, Theology
ISBN Prefix(es): 978-1-85307; 978-0-947588
Number of titles published annually: 20 Print
Total Titles: 205 Print; 1 CD-ROM; 500 Online
Imprints: Bible Distributors
U.S. Office(s): 16 Vincent St, Cambridge, MA 02140, United States
Bookshop(s): 199 Plumstead Common Rd, Plumstead Common, London SE18 2UJ *Tel:* (020) 8316 4972

Deborah Charles Publications+
173 Mather Ave, Liverpool L18 6JZ
Tel: (0151) 724 2500
E-mail: dcp@deborahcharles.co.uk
Web Site: www.legaltheory.demon.co.uk
Key Personnel
Contact: Prof B S Jackson
Founded: 1988
Subjects: Law, Philosophy, Religion - Jewish, Social Sciences, Sociology, Jewish Law of Divorce (Agunah), Jewish Studies, Legal Theory
ISBN Prefix(es): 978-0-9528938; 978-1-9513793; 978-1-9067310
Distributor for Jewish Law Association

Charnwood Library Series, see Ulverscroft Large Print Books Ltd

The Chartered Institute of Building
One Arlington Sq, Downshire Way, Bracknell RG12 1WA
Tel: (01344) 630700 *Fax:* (01344) 306430
E-mail: reception@ciob.org.uk
Web Site: www.ciob.org
Key Personnel
Chief Executive: Chris Blythe
Deputy Chief Executive: Bridget Bartlett
Subjects: Architecture & Interior Design, Environmental Studies, Law, Management, Regional Interests

ISBN Prefix(es): 978-0-906600; 978-1-85380;
978-0-901822
Associate Companies: American Institute of Constructors

**The Chartered Institute of Public Finance &
Accountancy**
77 Mansell St, London E1 8AN
Tel: (020) 7543 5601 *Fax:* (020) 7543 5607
E-mail: customerliasion@cipfa.org; publications@
cipfa.org
Web Site: www.cipfa.org
Key Personnel
Subscriptions & Publications Manager: Steve
Crackett
Subjects: Accounting, Finance
ISBN Prefix(es): 978-1-85229; 978-1-84508
Branch Office(s)
Lesley Exchange 2, 3rd floor, 22 East Bridge
St, Belfast BT1 3NR *Tel:* (028) 9026 6770
Fax: (028) 9026 6771 *E-mail:* nitraining@
cipfa.org
Local Government House, Drake Walk, Cardiff
CF10 4LG *Tel:* (029) 2046 8701 *Fax:* (029)
2052 3470 *E-mail:* wales@cipfa.org
160 Dundee St, Edinburgh EH11 1DQ
Tel: (0131) 221 8640 *E-mail:* scotland@cipfa.
org

Chartwell-Yorke Ltd+
114 High St, Belmont Village, Bolton, Lancs BL7
8AL
Tel: (01204) 811001 *Fax:* (01204) 811008
E-mail: info@chartwellyorke.com; orders@
chartwellyorke.com
Web Site: www.chartwellyorke.com
Key Personnel
Owner: Philip Yorke *E-mail:* philip.yorke@
chartwellyorke.com
Founded: 1997
Also software & book distributor.
Specialize in secondary mathematics ICT.
Subjects: Mathematics
ISBN Prefix(es): 978-1-904506
Number of titles published annually: 1 Print; 2
CD-ROM; 1 E-Book
Total Titles: 2 Print; 4 CD-ROM; 1 E-Book

Chatham House, see Royal Institute of
International Affairs

Chatham Publishing+
Imprint of Pen & Sword Books Ltd
c/o Pen & Sword Books, 47 Church St, Barnsley,
S Yorks S70 2AS
Tel: (01226) 734222 *Fax:* (01226) 734438
E-mail: enquiries@pen-and-sword.co.uk
Web Site: www.pen-and-sword.co.uk
Founded: 1996
Small publishing house concerned principally
with maritime history & narrative history.
Subjects: Maritime, Nonfiction (General), Narrative History, Nautical Archaeology, Naval or
Mercantile History & Biography, Ship Modelling
ISBN Prefix(es): 978-1-86176
Number of titles published annually: 30 Print
Total Titles: 150 Print
Distributed by Pen & Sword Books Ltd (USA)

Chatto & Windus, *imprint of* The Random
House Group Ltd, a Penguin Random House
Company

Cheeky Monkey Publishing Ltd
Braeside, 101 Higher Ainsworth Rd, Radcliffe,
Manchester M26 4JJ
Tel: (0161) 762 0321
E-mail: info@cheekymonkeypublishing.com
Web Site: www.cheekymonkeypublishing.com

Key Personnel
Production Dir: Peter Balderson
ISBN Prefix(es): 978-0-9555020
Foreign Rights: Leaf & Page (Robert Woodcock) (Canada, USA); TMA (Tom McGorry)
(Australia, New Zealand, UK); Verok Agency
(Veronique Kirchhoff) (Canada (French-speaking), France, Germany, Italy)

Cherrytree Books+
2A Portman Mansions, Chiltern St, London W1U
6NR
Tel: (020) 7487 0920 *Fax:* (020) 7487 0921
Founded: 1988
Publish illustrated information books for children
ages 5-15 years, mainly for the school library.
ISBN Prefix(es): 978-0-7451; 978-0-7540; 978-1-
84234
Associate Companies: Chivers Press Ltd; Zero to
Ten Ltd
Distributed by Cengage Learning Services

Chicken House Publishing Ltd
2 Palmer St, Frome, Somerset BA11 1DS
Tel: (01373) 454488 *Fax:* (01373) 454499
E-mail: chickenhouse@doublecluck.com
Web Site: www.doublecluck.com
Key Personnel
Publisher & Mng Dir: Barry Cunningham
Deputy Mng Dir: Rachel Hickman
Editorial Dir: Rachel Leyshon
Rights Dir: Elinor Bagenal *E-mail:* elinor@
doublecluck.com
Senior Editor: Imogen Cooper
Founded: 2000
ISBN Prefix(es): 978-1-903434; 978-1-904442;
978-1-905294; 978-1-906427; 978-1-908435
Parent Company: Scholastic Inc
Foreign Rep(s): Joyce Agyare (West Africa);
Sarah Ailsby (Austria, Germany, UK); James
Allen (Gibraltar, Portugal, Spain); Bampisaki
Amos (Burundi, Rwanda, Southern Sudan,
Tanzania, Uganda); Yolanda Banuet (Mexico); Joyce Bautista (Philippines); Alexis Chao
(China); Lenore Chciuk (American Samoa,
Guam, Northern Mariana Islands, Virgin Islands); Amanda Clarke (Middle East); Sonia
Dung (Taiwan); Carole Figueiredo (Bermuda);
Soo Jung Hyun (Hong Kong); Independent
Publishers Representatives (Jordan, Lebanon);
Cristian Juncu (Baltic States, Eastern Europe);
Dennis Koay (Indonesia, Thailand); Sjenka
Leslie (Benelux, France, Liechtenstein, Scandinavia, Switzerland); Hon-Mun Liew (Malaysia,
Singapore); Alana Lyell (Cyprus, Greece, Israel, Italy, Malta, Turkey); Silvana Moscoso
(Bolivia); Sharon Neita (Caribbean, Jamaica);
Axel Norrild (Argentina, Chile, Paraguay, Peru,
Uruguay); Beatriz Perez Colin (Qatar); Carey
Phillipps (Barbados, Grenada, Trinidad and Tobago); Ranai Pinsuwan (Myanmar, Thailand,
Vietnam); Oscar Reyes (Colombia, Venezuela);
Elizabeth Robinson (Cuernavaca, Morelos,
Mexico); Carol Sakoian (Gulf States, North
Africa); Lidia Scaldaferri (Ecuador); Melinda
Schoeman (Coastal Southern Africa); Kozue
Sekiguchi (Japan); Marjorie Solorzano (Costa
Rica, El Salvador, Guatemala, Honduras,
Nicaragua, Panama); Helena Theodoro da Silva
(Brazil); Darlene Vazquez (Puerto Rico); Joan
Wamae (Kenya); Estelle Whitby (Johannesburg,
South Africa); Helen Yang (Korea)
Foreign Rights: Rights People (worldwide)
Distribution Center: HarperCollins Publishers,
103 Westerhill Rd, Bishopbriggs, Glasgow G64
2QT *Tel:* (0844) 576 8121 *Fax:* (0844) 576
8131 *E-mail:* uk.orders@harpercollins.co.uk

Child's Play (International) Ltd+
Ashworth Rd, Bridgemead, Swindon, Wilts SN5
7YD
Tel: (01793) 616286 *Fax:* (01793) 512795

E-mail: office@childs-play.com
Web Site: www.childs-play.com
Key Personnel
Publisher & Chief Executive Officer: Neil Burden
E-mail: neil@childs-play.com
Sales Manager: Paul Gerrish *E-mail:* paul@
childs-play.com
Editor: Sue Baker *E-mail:* sue@childs-play.com
Founded: 1972
Specialize in early years education.
Membership(s): IPG.
Subjects: Education
ISBN Prefix(es): 978-0-85953; 978-1-904550;
978-1-84643; 978-1-78628
Total Titles: 400 Print; 45 Audio
Branch Office(s)
Child's Play Australia Pty Ltd, 10/20 Narabang
Way, Belrose, NSW 2085, Australia, President:
Garry McManus *Tel:* (02) 9450 2050 *Fax:* (02)
9486 3225 *E-mail:* office@childsplay.com.au
Web Site: www.childsplay.com.au
U.S. Office(s): Child's Play USA, 250 Minot Ave,
Auburn, ME 04210, United States, Contact:
Laurie Reynolds *Tel:* 207-784-7252 *Fax:* 207-
784-7358 *Web Site:* www.childsplayusa.com
Child's Play Inc, 71 S Orange Ave, South Orange, NJ 07079, United States, Vice President, Sales: Joseph Gardner *Tel:* 973-761-4555
Fax: 973-761-1555 *E-mail:* joe@childsplayusa.
com *Web Site:* www.childsplayusa.com
Foreign Rep(s): Ecogreens Marketing Services
Inc (Philippines); Hello Book Club (Taiwan);
JeF Diffusion (Jeff Mclean) (France); JYbooks
(J Y Park) (Korea); Monarch Books of Canada
Ltd (Canada); Moonjinmedia Co Ltd (H K
Lee) (Korea); Nationwide Book Distributors
(Andrew Tizzard) (New Zealand); Phambili
Agencies CC (Maria Lastrucci) (South Africa);
Special Needs (Singapore); Special Needs Co
Ltd (Thailand); Yasmy International Marketing
(Yasy Murayama) (Japan)

Choc Lit Ltd
Penrose House, Crawley Dr, Camberley, Surrey
GU15 2AB
Tel: (01276) 27492
E-mail: info@choc-lit.com
Web Site: www.choc-lit.com
Founded: 2009
Subjects: Fiction, History, Literature, Literary
Criticism, Essays, Romance, Historical Fiction,
Women's Literature
ISBN Prefix(es): 978-1-906931
Foreign Rep(s): International Publishers Marketing (North America); Peribo Pty Ltd (Australia); South Pacific Book Distributors Ltd
(New Zealand)
Distribution Center: Orca Book Services
Tel: (01202) 665432 *E-mail:* orders@
orcabookservices.co.uk

CHP, see Church House Publishing

Christian Alternative, *imprint of* O Books

Christian Education+
1020 Bristol Rd, Selly Oak, Birmingham B29
6LB
Tel: (0121) 472 4242 *Fax:* (0121) 472 7575
E-mail: editorial@christianeducation.org.uk;
sales@christianeducation.org.uk
Web Site: shop.christianeducation.org.uk
Key Personnel
Chief Executive Officer: Zoe Keens *E-mail:* ceo@
christianeducation.org.uk
Mng Editor: Anstice Hughes
Design & Production Controller: Azhar Lodhi
Sales: Paul Broadhurst
Office Manager: Diane Horton
Founded: 1809

Subjects: Biblical Studies, Crafts, Games, Hobbies, Drama, Theater, Education, Religion - Protestant
ISBN Prefix(es): 978-0-7197; 978-0-85213
Imprints: Hillside
Subsidiaries: International Bible Reading Association (IBRA)
Bookshop(s): NCEL Bookroom

Christian Education Movement, see Christian Education

Christian Focus, *imprint of* Christian Focus Publications Ltd

Christian Focus Publications Ltd+
Geanies House, Fearn, Tain, Ross-shire IV20 1TW
Tel: (01862) 871 011 *Fax:* (01862) 871 699
E-mail: info@christianfocus.com
Web Site: www.christianfocus.com
Key Personnel
Mng Dir: William Mackenzie
Production Manager: Jonathan Dunbar
Children's Editor: Catherine Mackenzie
Founded: 1979
Evangelical publisher.
Membership(s): Christian Booksellers Association; Evangelical Christian Publishing Association.
Subjects: Biblical Studies, Biography, Memoirs, Fiction, Inspirational, Spirituality, Religion - Protestant, Theology
ISBN Prefix(es): 978-0-906731; 978-1-871676; 978-1-85792; 978-1-84550
Number of titles published annually: 90 Print
Total Titles: 800 Print; 1 CD-ROM; 1 Audio
Parent Company: Balintore Holdings PLC
Imprints: CF4Kids; Christian Focus; Christian Heritage; Mentor
Foreign Rep(s): Publisher's International Marketing (Chris Ashdown) (Far East)
Distribution Center: Reformers Bookshop, 140 Albany Rd, Stanmore, NSW 2048, Australia *Tel:* (029) 564 3555 *Fax:* (029) 569 8039 *E-mail:* dave.hann@reformers.com.au *Web Site:* www.reformers.com.au
Koorong, 4-8 Vicki St, Blackburn South, Victoria 3130, Australia *Web Site:* www.koorong.com.au
Word Australia, 11-13 Moncrief Rd, Nunawading, Victoria 3131, Australia, Contact: Graeme Dwight *Tel:* (03) 9894 2027 *Fax:* (03) 9894 3099 *E-mail:* wa@word.com.au *Web Site:* www.word.com.au
Soul Distributors, PO Box 107025, 10 Andrew Baxter Dr, Mangere, Auckland, New Zealand *E-mail:* orders@souldistributors.co.nz
Struik Christian Media, PO Box 1144, Capetown 8000, South Africa *Tel:* (021) 462 4360 *Fax:* (021) 461 3612 *E-mail:* sharon@struik.co.za *Web Site:* www.struikchristianmedia.co.za
Sola Scriptura Ministries International, 271 Shoemaker St, Unit 3, Kitchener, ON, Canada *E-mail:* info@sola-scriptura.ca *Web Site:* www.sola-scriptura.ca
STL North America, 100 Biblica Way/Frank Schaffer Way, Elizabethton, TN 37643, United States *E-mail:* sherry.engle@stl-distribution.com *Web Site:* www.stl-distribution.com

Christian Heritage, *imprint of* Christian Focus Publications Ltd

Christian Large Print, *imprint of* Gale

Christian Research Association
Trinity Business Center, Storehill Green, Westlea, Swindon SN5 7DG
Tel: (01793) 418388
E-mail: admin@christian-research.org.uk
Web Site: www.christian-research.org.uk

Key Personnel
Dir: Benita Hewitt
Founded: 1993
Provide resources & undertaking research for Christian leaders.
Subjects: Management, Religion - Catholic, Religion - Protestant
ISBN Prefix(es): 978-1-85321
Number of titles published annually: 5 Print; 1 Online
Total Titles: 19 Print; 1 Online

Chronos Books, *imprint of* O Books

Church House Publishing+
Imprint of The Archbishop's Council of the Church of England
Church House, Great Smith St, London SW1P 3AZ
Tel: (01603) 785 923
Web Site: www.chpublishing.co.uk
Key Personnel
Publishing Manager: Dr Thomas Allain Chapman
Sales & Marketing Controller: Josie Gunn
Commissioning Editor: Christine Smith
Rights & Permissions: Rebecca Goldsmith
Official publisher of the Church of England.
Subjects: Religion - Other
ISBN Prefix(es): 978-0-7151
Number of titles published annually: 40 Print; 1 CD-ROM
Total Titles: 300 Print; 1 CD-ROM; 1 Audio
Bookshop(s): 31 Great Smith St, London SW1P 3BN *Tel:* (020) 7799 4064 *Fax:* (020) 7340 9997 *E-mail:* bookshop@chbookshop.co.uk *Web Site:* www.chbookshop.co.uk
Orders to: Norwich Books & Music, 13a Hellesdon Park Rd, Norwich, Norfolk NR6 5DR *Tel:* (01603) 785900 *Fax:* (01603) 785915 *E-mail:* orders@norwichbooksandmusic.co.uk *Web Site:* norwichbooksandmusic.hymnsam.co.uk

Church Literature Association, *imprint of* The Church Union

Church Society
Dean Wace House, 16 Rosslyn Rd, Watford, Herts WD18 0NY
Tel: (01923) 235111 *Fax:* (01923) 800362
E-mail: admin@churchsociety.org
Web Site: www.churchsociety.org
Key Personnel
Dir: Dr Lee Gatiss
Administrator: David Meager
Founded: 1835 (present company started in 1950 as an amalgamation of two other similar organizations)
Specialize in books & booklets. Publishers of *Churchman*, quarterly since 1879. A society founded to keep the Church of England faithful to its formularies.
Subjects: Religion - Protestant
ISBN Prefix(es): 978-0-85190
Total Titles: 4 Print

The Church Union
c/o Additional Curates Society, Gordon Browning House, 8 Spitfire Rd, Birmingham B24 9PB
Tel: (0121) 382 5533
E-mail: info@additionalcurates.co.uk
Web Site: www.churchunion.co.uk; www.additionalcurates.co.uk
Founded: 1859
Specialize in religious books.
Also acts as bookseller.
Membership(s): The Booksellers Association.
Subjects: Religion - Catholic, Religion - Protestant, Religion - Other
ISBN Prefix(es): 978-0-85191
Imprints: Church Literature Association; Tufton Books

Churchill Livingstone, *imprint of* Elsevier Ltd

Cicada
76 Lissenden Mansions, Lissenden Gardens, London NW5 1PR
Tel: (07890) 431 037
E-mail: info@cicadabooks.co.uk
Web Site: www.cicadabooks.co.uk
Key Personnel
Owner: Ziggy Hanaor *E-mail:* ziggy@cicadabooks.co.uk
Founded: 2009
Specialize in high-end art & design books.
Subjects: Art, Crafts, Games, Hobbies, Design
ISBN Prefix(es): 978-0-9562053; 978-1-908714
Distribution Center: Publishers Group UK (PGUK), 63-66 Hatton Garden, London EC1N 8LE *Tel:* (020) 7405 1105 *Fax:* (020) 7242 3725 *E-mail:* sales@pguk.co.uk *Web Site:* www.pguk.co.uk (worldwide)
DAP (Distributed Art Publishers), 115 Sixth Ave, 2nd floor, New York, NY 10013, United States *Tel:* 212-627-1999 *Fax:* 212-627-9484 *Web Site:* www.artbook.com

Cicerone Press
2 Police Sq, Milnthorpe, Cumbria LA7 7PY
Tel: (01539) 562 069 *Fax:* (01539) 563 417
E-mail: info@cicerone.co.uk
Web Site: www.cicerone.co.uk
Key Personnel
Owner: Jonathan E Williams *E-mail:* jonathan@cicerone.co.uk; Mrs Lesley Williams *E-mail:* lesley@cicerone.co.uk
Founded: 1969
Publish specialized guides to walking, trekking, climbing, mountaineering & biking in the UK, Europe & other world regions.
Subjects: Outdoor Recreation, Travel & Tourism
ISBN Prefix(es): 978-0-902363; 978-1-85284; 978-1-84965; 978-1-78362 (ebook)
Number of titles published annually: 30 Print
Total Titles: 350 Print; 300 E-Book
Warehouse: Booksource, 50 Cambuslang Rd, Cambuslang, Glasgow G32 8NB *Tel:* (0141) 6429192 *Fax:* (0141) 6429181
Distribution Center: Midpoint Trade Books, 27 W 20 St, Suite 1102, New York, NY 10011, United States *Tel:* 212-727-0190 *Fax:* 212-727-0195

CICO Books, *imprint of* Ryland Peters & Small

CICO Books+
Imprint of Ryland Peters & Small
20-21 Jockey's Fields, London WC1R 4BW
Tel: (020) 7025 2200 *Fax:* (020) 7025 2201
E-mail: sales@rps.co.uk; publicity@rps.co.uk
Web Site: www.rylandpeters.com
Key Personnel
Rights Dir: Denise Lie
Subjects: Animals, Pets, Cookery, Crafts, Games, Hobbies, Gardening, Plants, Health, Nutrition, House & Home, How-to, Humor, Nonfiction (General), Body, Mind & Spirit
ISBN Prefix(es): 978-1-84172; 978-1-84597; 978-1-900518; 978-1-906525; 978-1-903116; 978-1-904991; 978-1-906094; 978-1-907030; 978-1-907563; 978-1-84975; 978-1-78249; 978-1-908170; 978-1-908862
U.S. Office(s): 341 E 116 St, New York, NY 10029, United States *Tel:* 646-791-5410 *Fax:* 646-861-3518
Distribution Center: Macmillan Distribution Ltd, Brunel Rd, Houndmills, Basingstoke, Hants RG21 6XS *Tel:* (01256) 302 692 *Fax:* (01256) 812 521 *E-mail:* orders@macmillan.co.uk (trade)

Orders to: Macmillan Distribution Ltd, Brunel Rd, Houndmills, Basingstoke, Hants RG21 6XS *Tel:* (01256) 302 692 *Fax:* (01256) 812 521 *E-mail:* orders@macmillan.co.uk (trade)

Cinderella, *imprint of* Novello & Co

CIPFA, see The Chartered Institute of Public Finance & Accountancy

Circle Books, *imprint of* O Books

CIRIA
Griffin Court, 15 Long Lane, London EC1A 9PN
Tel: (020) 7549 3300 *Fax:* (020) 7549 3349
E-mail: enquiries@ciria.org
Web Site: www.ciria.org
Key Personnel
Chief Executive: Bill Healy
Research Dir: Owen Jenkins
Finance Dir: Roy Seger
CIRIA is the construction industry research & information association.
Subjects: Civil Engineering, Environmental Studies, Management, Maritime
ISBN Prefix(es): 978-0-86017; 978-0-901208
Branch Office(s)
c/o University of Dundee, Dundee DD1 4HN
Tel: (01382) 386085 *E-mail:* martin.squibbs@ciria.org

Cisco Press, *imprint of* Pearson Education Ltd

City Noir, *imprint of* Dedalus Ltd

Clarendon Press, *imprint of* Oxford University Press (OUP)

James Clarke & Co Ltd+
PO Box 60, Cambridge CB1 2NT
Tel: (01223) 350865 *Fax:* (01223) 366951
E-mail: publishing@jamesclarke.co.uk
Web Site: www.jamesclarke.co.uk
Key Personnel
Mng Dir: Adrian Brink
Founded: 1859
A long-established British academic publisher. Specialize in historical & theological books, as well as reference material. Associated with the Lutterworth Press since 1984.
Membership(s): IPG; The Publishers Association.
Subjects: Biblical Studies, Biography, Memoirs, History, Library & Information Sciences, Literature, Literary Criticism, Essays, Philosophy, Religion - Catholic, Religion - Protestant, Religion - Other, Theology
ISBN Prefix(es): 978-0-227
Number of titles published annually: 120 Print; 120 E-Book
Total Titles: 500 Print; 1 CD-ROM; 230 E-Book
Associate Companies: The Lutterworth Press
Distribution Center: Casemate | academic, PO Box 511, Oakville, CT, United States *Tel:* 860-945-9329 *Fax:* 860-945-9468 *E-mail:* info@casemateacademic.com *Web Site:* www.casemateacademic.com
Orders to: Gardners Books, One Whittle Dr, Eastbourne, East Sussex BN23 6QH *Tel:* (01323) 521555 *Fax:* (01323) 525504 *E-mail:* sales@gardners.com *Web Site:* www.gardners.com

Clarkson Research Services Ltd
Commodity Quay, St Katharine Docks, London E1W 1BF
Tel: (020) 7334 3134 *Fax:* (020) 7522 0330
E-mail: sales.crs@clarksons.com
Web Site: www.crsl.com; www.oilpubs.com
Key Personnel
Chief Executive: Andi Case

Sales Manager: Matt Lovering
Founded: 1996
Publish specialist reference maps, books & vessel registers for the international offshore oil & gas industry.
Subjects: Energy, Maritime
ISBN Prefix(es): 978-1-870945; 978-1-902157
Branch Office(s)
15 The Homend, Ledbury, Herts HR8 1BN
Tel: (01531) 634561
1303-1304, Standard Chartered Tower, 201 Century Ave, Pudong New Area, Shanghai 200120, China *Tel:* (021) 6103 0100

Class Publishing+
The Exchange, Express Park, Bristol Rd, Bridgewater TA6 4RR
Tel: (01278) 427800
E-mail: info@class.co.uk; post@class.co.uk
Web Site: www.classhealth.co.uk
Key Personnel
Mng Dir: Richard Warner
Founded: 1989
Membership(s): IPG.
Subjects: Health, Nutrition, Medicine, Nursing, Dentistry, Self-Help, Chronic Disease
ISBN Prefix(es): 978-0-7637; 978-1-85487; 978-0-86242; 978-1-872362; 978-1-84119; 978-0-9528823; 978-1-85959
Book Club(s): BCA
Distribution Center: Macmillan Distribution Ltd, Basingstoke, Hants *Tel:* (01256) 302699

The Clerkenwell Press, *imprint of* Profile Books Ltd

Clinical Publishing
Imprint of Atlas Medical Publishing Ltd
110 Innovation House, Parkway Court, Oxford OX4 2JY
Tel: (01865) 811116
E-mail: info@clinicalpublishing.co.uk
Web Site: www.clinicalpublishing.co.uk
Founded: 2000
Subjects: Medicine, Nursing, Dentistry, Psychology, Psychiatry, Accident & Emergency, Allergy, Anesthesia, Cardiovascular Medicine, Dermatology, Diabetes, Endocrinology, Gastroenterology, Geriatric Medicine, Hematology, Hepatology, Imaging, Immunology, Infectious Diseases, Inflammatory Disease, Musculoskeletal Medicine, Neurology, Obstetrics & Gynecology, Oncology, Pediatrics, Urology
ISBN Prefix(es): 978-1-904392; 978-0-9537339; 978-1-84692
Distribution Center: Marston Book Services Ltd, 160 Eastern Ave, Milton Park, Abingdon, Oxon OX14 4SD *Tel:* (01235) 465500 *Fax:* (01235) 465555 *E-mail:* trade.orders@marston.co.uk *Web Site:* www.marston.co.uk (worldwide exc Canada & USA)
Baker & Taylor Publisher Services, 30 Amberwood Parkway, Ashland, OH 44805, United States *Tel:* 567-215-0030 *E-mail:* info@btpubservices.com *Web Site:* www.btpubservices.com (USA & Canada)

CLP, see College of Law Publishing (CLP)

Coachwise Ltd
Chelsea Close, off Amberley Rd, Armley, Leeds LS12 4HP
Tel: (0113) 231 1310 *Fax:* (0113) 231 9606
E-mail: enquiries@coachwise.ltd.uk
Web Site: www.coachwise.ltd.uk
Key Personnel
Chief Operating Officer: Kath Leonard
Mng Dir: Dr Anthony Byrne
Business Development Dir: Phil Collier
Marketing Dir: Melanie Mallinson
Head, Publications & Design: Martin Betts

Founded: 1989
Specialize in leisure management & coaching targeting sports professionals.
Membership(s): Direct Marketing Association (UK) Ltd.
Subjects: Health, Nutrition, Music, Dance, Outdoor Recreation, Sports, Athletics
Total Titles: 40 Print; 1 CD-ROM; 1 Audio
Parent Company: National Coaching Foundation

Cogent OA, *imprint of* Taylor & Francis Group, an Informa Business

Adlard Coles Nautical, *imprint of* A&C Black Publishers Ltd

The Collector's Library, *imprint of* CRW Publishing Ltd

The Collector's Library, *imprint of* Pan Macmillan

College of Law Publishing (CLP)
Braboeuf Manor, Portsmouth Rd, St Catherines, Guildford, Surrey GU3 1HA
Tel: (01235) 465500 (orders)
E-mail: info@clponline.co.uk; clp@bebc.co.uk; orders@orcabookservices.co.uk (orders)
Web Site: www.clponline.co.uk
Key Personnel
Editorial: David Stott *Tel:* (0750) 706 4900 *E-mail:* david.stott@virgin.net
Sales & Marketing: Sue Hall *Tel:* (0797) 750 8162 *E-mail:* sue@clponline.co.uk
Subjects: Law
ISBN Prefix(es): 978-0-905835; 978-1-905391

Collins, *imprint of* HarperCollins UK

Collins & Brown, *imprint of* Pavilion Books

William Collins, *imprint of* HarperCollins UK

Colonsay Books, *imprint of* House of Lochar

ColorCards, *imprint of* Speechmark Publishing Ltd

Colourpoint Creative Ltd+
Colourpoint House, Jubilee Business Park, 21 Jubilee Rd, Newtownards, Co Down BT23 4YH
Tel: (028) 9182 6339 *Fax:* (028) 9182 1900
E-mail: info@colourpoint.co.uk
Web Site: www.colourpoint.co.uk
Key Personnel
Dir: Malcolm Johnston *E-mail:* malcolm@colourpoint.co.uk
Publisher: Sheila M Johnston *E-mail:* sheila@colourpoint.co.uk; Dr Wesley Johnston *E-mail:* wesley@colourpoint.co.uk
Founded: 1993
Specializes in educational textbooks/resources, transport titles, books of Irish interest.
Membership(s): Irish Educational Publishers' Association.
Subjects: Biography, Memoirs, Disability, Special Needs, Education, Government, Political Science, History, Humor, Maritime, Religion - Other, Transportation, Travel & Tourism
ISBN Prefix(es): 978-1-898392
Number of titles published annually: 25 Print
Total Titles: 165 Print
Parent Company: Colourpoint Group
Imprints: Plover Fiction
Distributed by Bookworld (England, Scotland & Wales)
Distributor for Martin Bairston (Ireland); Bus Enthusiast Publishing; KRB Publishing (Ireland)
Orders to: MiMO Distribution *Tel:* (028) 9182 0505 *E-mail:* sales@mimodistribution.co.uk

Comma Press, *imprint of* Carcanet Press Ltd

Commonwealth Secretariat
Marlborough House, Pall Mall, London SW1Y
5HX
Tel: (020) 7747 6342
E-mail: publications@commonwealth.int
Web Site: books.thecommonwealth.org
Key Personnel
Publications Manager: Sherry Dixon
Publications Coordinator: Nicola Perou *E-mail:* n.
perou@commonwealth.int
Founded: 1965
Intergovernmental organization with responsibility
for the work & all activities of the Common-
wealth.
Membership(s): Independent Publishers Guild;
The Publishers Association.
Subjects: Agriculture, Developing Countries,
Earth Sciences, Economics, Education, Energy,
Environmental Studies, Finance, Government,
Political Science, Law, Management, Public
Administration, Social Sciences, Sociology,
Technology, Women's Studies
ISBN Prefix(es): 978-0-85092; 978-1-84859 (e-
books); 978-1-84929
Number of titles published annually: 40 Print; 2
CD-ROM; 10 E-Book
Total Titles: 250 Print; 4 CD-ROM; 20 E-Book; 2
Audio
Distributed by Nexus Strategic Partnerships; Tay-
lor & Francis Journals
Foreign Rep(s): Avicenna (Algeria, Armenia,
Cyprus, Egypt, Greece, Iran, Iraq, Jordan,
Kuwait, Lebanon, Libya, Malta, Morocco,
Oman, Palestine, Saudi Arabia, Syria, Tunisia,
Turkey, United Arab Emirates); Book Bird
(Pakistan); Booker International (Brunei);
Buma Kor & Co Ltd (Cameroon); E & D
Limited (Tanzania); Livraria Escolar Editora
(Mozambique); Colin Flint Ltd Publishers
Scandinavian Consultancy (Denmark, Fin-
land, Iceland, Norway, Sweden); Globe Enter-
prises (Malaysia); Hargraves Library Services
(South Africa); Iberian Book Services (Portu-
gal, Spain); Karim International (Bangladesh);
Lake House Bookshop (Sri Lanka); Parrot
Reads Publishers Pvt Ltd (India); Prestige
Books (Zimbabwe); Reimmer Book Services
(Ghana); Renouf Publishing Company Ltd
(Canada); Select Books Pte Ltd (Singapore);
Stylus Publishing LLC (USA); Transglobal
Publishers Service Ltd (Hong Kong)
Distribution Center: Turpin Distribution Ser-
vices Ltd, Stratton Business Park, Pegasus Dr,
Biggleswade SG18 8TQ *Tel:* (01767) 604951
Fax: (01767) 601640 *E-mail:* custserv@
turpin-distribution.com *Web Site:* www.turpin-
distribution.com

Compass Books, *imprint of* O Books

Compass Maps Ltd
Subsidiary of Morris Communications Co LLC
6 Riverside Court, Lower Bristol Rd, Bath BA2
3DZ
Tel: (01225) 406440 *Fax:* (01225) 469461
E-mail: info@popoutmaps.com
Web Site: www.popoutproducts.co.uk
Key Personnel
Commercial Dir: Patrick Dawson
General Manager: Linda Flynn
Custom Account Manager: Marie Cepek
Production Manager: Tiina Wastie
Publishing Manager: Helen Baker
Trade Product Manager: Diane McEntee
Sales & Marketing Manager: Shelly Bufton
Sales Manager: Paul Bew; Tania Ross
Project Coordinator: Easter Lam
Foreign Rep(s): Affecto Finland Ltd (Finland);
Bill Bailey Publishers' Representatives (Eu-
rope); DDP Diffusion (Asia); Espasa Calpe

SA (Spain); Exlibriz AS (Norway); Geo-
Center (Germany); Grantham Book Services
Ltd (GBS) (UK); InterMedia Americana
(Caribbean, Latin America); Minumsa/Golden
Compass (South Korea); OLF SA (Switzer-
land); Paperclip Pte Ltd (Malaysia, Singapore);
Popout Products (North America); Santillana
Ediciones Generales (Spain); Schibsted Forlag
(Norway); 62 Damrak (Netherlands); UBS Pub-
lishers' Distributors Pvt Ltd (India); Woodslane
Pty Ltd (Australia, New Zealand)

Concept Books, *imprint of* Dedalus Ltd

The Concrete Society
Riverside House, 4 Meadows Business Park, Sta-
tion Approach, Blackwater, Camberley, Surrey
GU17 9AB
Tel: (01276) 607140; (07004) 607777 (sales)
Fax: (01276) 607141
E-mail: enquiries@concretebookshop.com
Web Site: www.concrete.org.uk
Key Personnel
Manager, Information Services: Edwin A R Trout
E-mail: e.trout@concrete.org.uk
Founded: 1935
Subjects: Civil Engineering, Engineering (Gen-
eral), Cement, Concrete
ISBN Prefix(es): 978-0-946691; 978-1-904482

Condor Books, *imprint of* Souvenir Press Ltd

Connections Book Publishing, *imprint of*
Eddison Sadd Editions Ltd

Conran Octopus, *imprint of* Octopus Publishing
Group Ltd

Conran Octopus+
Imprint of Octopus Publishing Group
Endeavour House, 189 Shaftesbury Ave, London
WC2H 8JY
Tel: (020) 7632 5400 *Fax:* (020) 7632 5405
E-mail: info@octopusbooks.co.uk
Web Site: www.octopusbooks.co.uk
Key Personnel
Group Art Dir: Jonathan Christie
UK Key Accounts Dir: Kevin Hawkins
Founded: 1984
Subjects: Architecture & Interior Design, Cook-
ery, Crafts, Games, Hobbies, Gardening, Plants
ISBN Prefix(es): 978-1-85029; 978-1-84091; 978-
0-7064
Foreign Rep(s): APD Kuala Lumpur (Lilian
Koe) (Malaysia); APD Singapore Ptd Ltd (Ian
Pringle) (Singapore); Bill Bailey Publishers'
Representatives (Austria, Baltic States, Bel-
gium, Cyprus, Eastern Europe, France, Ger-
many, Iceland, Malta, Netherlands, Russia,
Scandinavia, Switzerland); Jonathan Ball Pub-
lishers (South Africa); Canadian Manda Group
(Canada); Everest International Publishing
Services (Wei Zhao) (China); Vanessa Forbes
(Algeria, Bahrain, Comoros, Djibouti, Egypt,
Finland, Germany, Iraq, Italy, Jordan, Kuwait,
Lebanon, Libya, Mauritania, Morocco, Oman,
Palestine, Qatar, Saudi Arabia, Somalia, Sudan,
Syria, Tunisia, Turkey, United Arab Emirates,
Yemen); Arturo Gutierrez Hernandez (Central
America); Hachette Australia (Australia); Ha-
chette Book Group Ireland (Ireland, Northern
Ireland); Hachette Book Publishing India Pvt
Ltd (Kapil Agrawal) (Bangladesh, India, Sri
Lanka); Hachette Livre NZ (New Zealand); Ha-
chette UK Ltd (Paul Kenny) (Cambodia, Guam,
Hong Kong, Indonesia, Japan, Laos, Myan-
mar, Papua New Guinea, Philippines, South
Korea, Taiwan, Thailand, Vietnam); Hachette
UK Ltd (Matt Cowdery) (Israel, Middle East,
North Africa); Chris Humphrys & Linda Hop-
kins (Caribbean); InterMedia Americana Ltd

(David Williams) (South America); Octopus
Books USA (USA); Octopus Publishing Group
(all other territories); Padovani Books Ltd
(Jenny Padovani) (Gibraltar, Portugal, Spain);
Padovani Books Ltd (Penny Padovani) (Greece,
Italy); Anita Zih-De Haan (Sub-Saharan Africa)
Foreign Rights: Lana de Lucia (Central Europe,
Eastern Europe, Greece); Vanessa Forbes (Fin-
land, Germany, Italy, Turkey); Marco Rodino
(Asia exc Japan); John Saunders-Griffiths
(Brazil, France, Iceland, Japan, Norway, Que-
bec, Canada); Veronique de Sutter (Denmark,
Latin America, Netherlands, Portugal, South
Africa, Spain, Sweden); Ros Webber (North
America)
Distribution Center: Littlehampton Book Ser-
vices Ltd, Faraday Close, Durrington, Wor-
thing, West Sussex BN13 3RB *Tel:* (01903)
828500; (01903) 828501 (customer service)
Web Site: lbsltd.wp.hachette.co.uk

Conservative Policy Forum
4 Matthew Parker St, London SW1H 9HQ
Tel: (020) 7222 9000
E-mail: cpf@conservatives.com
Web Site: www.conservativepolicyforum.com;
www.conservativesabroad.org
Key Personnel
Voluntary National Dir: Hannah David
Manager: Dr John Hayward
Founded: 1945 (as Conservative Political Forum)
Subjects: Economics, Government, Political Sci-
ence
ISBN Prefix(es): 978-0-85070

Constable, *imprint of* Little, Brown Book Group

Constable+
Imprint of Little, Brown Book Group
Carmelite House, 50 Victoria Embankment, Lon-
don EC4Y 0DZ
Tel: (020) 3122 7000
E-mail: info@littlebrown.co.uk
Web Site: www.littlebrown.co.uk
Key Personnel
Group Sales Dir: Robert Manser
Publicity Manager: Florence Partridge *Tel:* (020)
7911 8132 *E-mail:* florence.partridge@
littlebrown.co.uk
Press Officer: Grace Vincent *Tel:* (020) 7911
8124 *E-mail:* grace.vincent@littlebrown.co.uk
Founded: 1795
Subjects: Archaeology, Art, Astrology, Occult,
Behavioral Sciences, Criminology, Erotica,
Fiction, Health, Nutrition, History, Humor,
LGBTQ, Literature, Literary Criticism, Essays,
Military Science, Nonfiction (General), Photog-
raphy, Psychology, Psychiatry, Science Fiction,
Fantasy, Self-Help, Travel & Tourism, Current
Affairs
ISBN Prefix(es): 978-1-85487; 978-0-09; 978-
0-948164; 978-1-84119; 978-1-85004; 978-1-
84529; 978-1-84901
Number of titles published annually: 130 Print
Foreign Rights: Anthea Literary Agency (Katalina
Sabewa) (Bulgaria); Tassy Barham Associates
(Tassy Barham) (Brazil); Big Apple Agency
Inc (Lily Chen) (Mainland China); Big Apple
Agency Inc (Vincent Lin) (Taiwan); Agencja
Literacka Graal (Dominika Bojanowska)
(Poland); International Copyright Agency
(Simona Kessler) (Romania); Katai & Bolza
Literary Agents (Katalin Katai) (Hungary);
Kristin Olson Literary Agency (Kristin Olson)
(Czechia); Nova Littera Ltd (Sergei Chere-
dov) (Russia); Prava i prevodi (Nada Popvic)
(Bosnia and Herzegovina, Croatia, Kosovo,
Macedonia, Montenegro, Serbia, Slovenia)
Orders to: LBS Ltd, Faraday Close, Durrington,
Worthing, West Sussex BN13 3RB *Tel:* (01903)
828500 *E-mail:* mailorders@lbsltd.co.uk

Construction Industry Research & Information Association, see CIRIA

David C Cook+
26-28 Lottbridge Drove, Eastbourne, East Sussex BN23 6NT
Tel: (01323) 437700 *Fax:* (01323) 411970
E-mail: office@kingsway.co.uk
Web Site: www.kingsway.co.uk
Key Personnel
Chief Executive Officer: John Paculabo
Publishing Dir: Rev Richard Herkes
Founded: 1977
Publisher & supplier of Christian books, music & gifts.
Subjects: Religion - Protestant, Religion - Other, Theology
ISBN Prefix(es): 978-0-86065; 978-0-85476; 978-0-902088; 978-1-84291
Parent Company: Kingsway Communications Ltd
Distributor for Barbour; Charisma House; Moody Press

Leo Cooper, *imprint of* Pen & Sword Books Ltd

Leo Cooper+
Imprint of Pen & Sword Books Ltd
47 Church St, Barnsley, S Yorks S70 2AS
Tel: (01226) 734222 *Fax:* (01226) 734438
E-mail: enquiries@pen-and-sword.co.uk; publicity@pen-and-sword.co.uk
Web Site: www.pen-and-sword.co.uk
Key Personnel
Marketing & Publicity: Jonathan Wright
Founded: 1990
Subjects: Biography, Memoirs, History, Maritime, Military Science, Nonfiction (General), Travel & Tourism
ISBN Prefix(es): 978-0-7232; 978-0-85052; 978-1-84415; 978-1-84468; 978-1-84832; 978-1-84884; 978-1-78159; 978-1-78383; 978-1-4738
Number of titles published annually: 100 Print
Total Titles: 350 Print
Associate Companies: Wharncliffe Publishing
Distributed by Combined Books (USA); Vanwell Publishing Ltd (Canada)

Coordination Group Publications Ltd (CGP)
Broughton House, Griffin St, Broughton In Furness, Cumbria LA20 6HH
Tel: (0870) 750 1262; (0870) 750 1242 (orders) *Fax:* (0870) 750 1292
E-mail: customerservices@cgpbooks.co.uk
Web Site: www.cgpbooks.co.uk
Founded: 1995
Subjects: Education, Mathematics, Science (General), GCSE, SATs, Test Preparation
ISBN Prefix(es): 978-1-84146; 978-1-84762

Copper Beech Publishing Ltd+
PO Box 159, East Grinstead, Sussex RH19 4FS
Tel: (01342) 314734
E-mail: ventouxbooks@gmail.com
Web Site: www.ventouxbooks.co.uk
Key Personnel
Dir: Jan Barnes
Membership(s): IPG.
Subjects: Etiquette, Food & Drink, Victoriana
ISBN Prefix(es): 978-0-9516295; 978-1-898617

CoramBAAF Adoption & Fostering Academy+
41 Brunswick Sq, London WC1N 1AZ
Tel: (020) 7520 7517 (orders)
E-mail: pubs.sales@corambaaf.org.uk
Web Site: www.corambaaf.org.uk
Key Personnel
Mng Dir: Shaila Shah *E-mail:* shaila.shah@corambaaf.org.uk
Marketing Manager: Michelle Bell *Tel:* (020) 7520 7516 *E-mail:* michelle.bell@corambaaf.org.uk

Publishing Manager: Jo Francis *Tel:* (020) 7520 7513 *E-mail:* jo.francis@corambaaf.org.uk
Commissioning Editor, Adoption & Fostering (Journal): Roger Bullock
Founded: 2015
Membership organization dedicated to improving outcomes for children & young people in care by supporting the agencies & professionals who work with them.
Primarily in the UK but also international.
Subjects: Child Care & Development, Social Sciences, Sociology, Adoption, Fostering
ISBN Prefix(es): 978-0-903534; 978-1-873868; 978-0-9506807; 978-1-903699; 978-1-905664; 978-1-907585; 978-1-910039
Number of titles published annually: 25 Print
Total Titles: 250 Print
Distribution Center: Turnaround Publisher Services, Hertford Distribution Centre, Foxholes Business Park, John Tate Rd, Hertford SG13 7YH, Dir: Claire Thompson *Tel:* (020) 8829 3000 *Fax:* (020) 8881 5088 *E-mail:* orders@turnaround-uk.com *Web Site:* www.turnaround-uk.com

Cordee Ltd+
Dodwells Bridge Industrial Estate, 11 Jacknell Rd, Hinckley LE10 3BS
Tel: (01455) 611 185 *Fax:* (01455) 635 687
E-mail: info@cordee.co.uk
Web Site: www.cordee.co.uk
Key Personnel
Co-Owner & Dir: Chris Balic; Jim Wilson
Founded: 1973
Specialist publisher, distributor & wholesaler (worldwide).
Subjects: Outdoor Recreation, Sports, Athletics, Travel & Tourism
ISBN Prefix(es): 978-1-871890; 978-0-904405; 978-1-904207

Corgi, *imprint of* Transworld Publishers

Corgi Children's, *imprint of* The Random House Group Ltd, a Penguin Random House Company

Cornerhouse Publications, see HOME

Cornerstone, *imprint of* The Random House Group Ltd, a Penguin Random House Company

Coronet, *imprint of* Hodder & Stoughton Ltd

Corsair, *imprint of* Little, Brown Book Group

Corvus, *imprint of* Atlantic Books

Corvus Books
Imprint of Atlantic Books
c/o Atlantic Books, Ormond House, 26-27 Boswell St, London WC1N 3JZ
E-mail: enquiries@atlantic-books.co.uk
Web Site: www.atlantic-books.co.uk
Key Personnel
Editorial Dir: Sara O'Keeffe
Subjects: Fiction, Science Fiction, Fantasy, Crime, Historical Fiction, Women's Fiction
ISBN Prefix(es): 978-0-85789; 978-1-84887; 978-1-78239
Distribution Center: The Book Services Ltd, Distribution Centre, Colchester Rd, Frating Green, Colchester, Essex CO7 7DW *Tel:* (01206) 256000 *Fax:* (01206) 255717 *E-mail:* sales@tbs-ltd.co.uk *Web Site:* www.thebookservice.co.uk

Corwin Press, *imprint of* SAGE Publications Ltd

Cosmic Egg Book, *imprint of* O Books

Cottage Publications
Imprint of Laurel Cottage Ltd
c/o Laurel Cottage Ltd, 15 Ballyhay Rd, Donaghadee, Co Down BT21 0NG
Tel: (028) 9188 8033
E-mail: info@cottage-publications.com
Web Site: www.cottage-publications.com
Key Personnel
Dir: Timothy Johnston *E-mail:* tim@cottage-publications.com
Founded: 1990
Specialize in illustrated books on Ireland.
Subjects: Art, Biography, Memoirs, Fiction, History, Music, Dance, Nonfiction (General), Regional Interests
ISBN Prefix(es): 978-0-9516402; 978-1-900935
Number of titles published annually: 10 Print
Total Titles: 60 Print
Associate Companies: Ballyhay Books

Council for British Archaeology
Beatrice de Cardi House, 66 Bootham, York YO30 7BZ
Tel: (01904) 671417 *Fax:* (01904) 671384
E-mail: info@archaeologyuk.org
Web Site: www.archaeologyuk.org
Key Personnel
Dir: Dr Mike Heyworth *E-mail:* mikeheyworth@archaeologyuk.org
Founded: 1944
This publisher has indicated that 50% of their product line is author subsidized.
Subjects: Archaeology, Education
ISBN Prefix(es): 978-0-900312; 978-0-906780; 978-1-872414; 978-1-902771
Number of titles published annually: 10 Print
Total Titles: 50 Print

Countryman Press, *imprint of* W W Norton & Co Ltd

Countryside Books
Highfield House, 2 Highfield Ave, Newbury, Berks RG14 5DS
Tel: (01635) 43816 *Fax:* (01635) 551004
E-mail: info@countrysidebooks.co.uk
Web Site: www.countrysidebooks.co.uk
Key Personnel
Mng Dir, Editorial, Sales & Production: Nicholas Battle
Publicity, Rights & Permissions: Suzanne Battle
Founded: 1976
Publisher of regional interest books within UK. Specialize in walking guides.
Subjects: Aeronautics, Aviation, Genealogy, History, Humor, Maritime, Mysteries, Suspense, Photography, Regional Interests, Transportation, Airfields & Aviation, Folklore, Ghosts & Supernatural, Railways, Walking & Cycling
ISBN Prefix(es): 978-0-905392; 978-0-86368; 978-1-85306; 978-1-84674
Number of titles published annually: 60 Print
Total Titles: 500 Print

The Covenant Publishing Co Ltd
121 Low Etherley, Bishop Auckland, Co Durham DL14 0HA
Tel: (01388) 835 753
E-mail: admin@covpub.co.uk
Web Site: www.covpub.co.uk; www.britishisrael.co.uk
Key Personnel
Chairman: Mr M A Clark
Administrator: Talia Creed
Founded: 1922
Subjects: Archaeology, Biblical Studies, History, Religion - Protestant

ISBN Prefix(es): 978-0-85205
Parent Company: The British-Israel-World Federation

Richard & Erika Coward Writing & Publishing Partnership+
16 Queensway, King's Lynn PE30 4AW
Tel: (01553) 764946
Key Personnel
Author: Richard Coward *E-mail:* randecoward@googlemail.com
Business Manager: Erika Coward
Subjects: Mysteries, Suspense
ISBN Prefix(es): 978-0-9515019

CRC Press, *imprint of* Taylor & Francis Group, an Informa Business

Creative Essentials, *imprint of* Oldcastle Books Ltd

Crecy Publishing Ltd
1A Ringway Trading Estate, Shadowmoss Rd, Manchester M22 5LH
Tel: (0161) 499 0024 *Fax:* (0161) 499 0298
E-mail: enquiries@crecy.co.uk
Web Site: www.crecy.co.uk
Key Personnel
Mng Dir: Jeremy M Pratt
Sales & Editorial: Gill Richardson
Sales & Publicity: Nathan Connolly
Subjects: Aeronautics, Aviation, History, Airplanes, Naval, Pilots, War
ISBN Prefix(es): 978-0-85979; 978-0-947554
Foreign Rep(s): Bookport Associates (Southern Europe); European Marketing Services (Anselm Robinson) (Northern Europe exc Scandinavia); IMA (Eastern Europe)
Distribution Center: J B Wholesalers, 30 Biscayne Way, Unit 1, 6164 Jandakot, WA, Australia *Tel:* (08) 9434 9100 *Fax:* (08) 9434 9195 *E-mail:* sales@jbwholesalers.com.au *Web Site:* www.jbwholesalers.com.au
Vanwell Publishing, PO Box 2131, One Northrup Crescent, St Catharines, ON L2R 7S2, Canada *Tel:* 905-937-3100 *Fax:* 905-937-1760 *E-mail:* sales@vanwell.com *Web Site:* www.vanwell.com
South Pacific Books, PO Box 303 243, North Harbour, Auckland 1330, New Zealand *Tel:* (09) 448 1591 *Fax:* (09) 448 1592 *E-mail:* sales@soupacbooks.co.nz *Web Site:* www.soupacbooks.co.nz
Specialty Press, 39966 Grand Ave, North Branch, MN 55056, United States *Tel:* 651-277-1400 *Fax:* 651-277-1203 *E-mail:* info@specialtypress.com *Web Site:* www.specialtypress.com

Cressrelles Publishing Co Ltd+
Industrial Estate, 10 Station Rd, Colwall, Malvern, Herts WR13 6RN
Tel: (01684) 540154
Web Site: www.cressrelles.co.uk
Key Personnel
Mng Dir: Leslie Smith
Business Manager: Simon Smith *E-mail:* simon@cressrelles.co.uk
Founded: 1973
Subjects: Drama, Theater
ISBN Prefix(es): 978-0-85956
Number of titles published annually: 3 Print
Total Titles: 48 Print
Imprints: Actinic Press (chiropody); Kenyon-Deane (plays); J Garnet Miller (plays); New Playwrights' Network (plays)
Distributed by Empire Publishing Services
Distributor for Anchorage Press Inc

The Crime Vault, *imprint of* Little, Brown Book Group

Crimson, *imprint of* Crimson Publishing Ltd

Crimson Publishing Ltd
Westminster House, Kew Rd, Richmond, Surrey TW9 2ND
Tel: (020) 8334 1600 *Fax:* (020) 8334 1601
E-mail: info@crimsonpublishing.co.uk
Web Site: www.crimsonpublishing.co.uk
Key Personnel
Founder & Mng Dir: David Lester
Advertising: Lee Scott *Tel:* (020) 8445 3391 *E-mail:* lees@crimsonpublishingservices.co.uk
Editorial: Hugh Burne *E-mail:* hughb@crimsonpublishing.co.uk
Marketing: Sam Bacon *E-mail:* samb@crimsonpublishing.co.uk; Helena Cole *Tel:* (01225) 584 962 *E-mail:* helenac@crimsonpublishing.co.uk
Founded: 2007
Subjects: Business, Travel & Tourism, Guidebooks, Living Abroad, Personal Growth
ISBN Prefix(es): 978-0-907638; 978-1-85458; 978-0-901205; 978-0-9548219; 978-1-905410; 978-0-9543914; 978-1-78059; 978-1-907087
Imprints: Crimson; Pathfinder; Pocket Bibles; Trotman; Vacation Work; White Ladder
Branch Office(s)
19-21C Charles St, Bath BA1 1HX *Tel:* (01225) 584 950
6-8 Cole St, London SE1 4YH *Tel:* (020) 3627 1865
Foreign Rights: Letter Soup Rights Agency (Allison Olson)

Paul H Crompton Ltd+
94 Felsham Rd, London SW15 1DQ
Tel: (020) 8780 1063 *Fax:* (020) 8780 1063
E-mail: cromptonph@aol.com
Key Personnel
Dir: Paul Crompton
Founded: 1968
Also produce martial arts videos & DVDs.
Subjects: Self-Help, Sports, Athletics, Martial Arts
ISBN Prefix(es): 978-0-901764; 978-1-874250
Orders to: Publishers Group UK (PGUK), 63-66 Hatton Garden, London EC1N 8LE *Tel:* (020) 7405 1105 *Fax:* (020) 7242 3725 *E-mail:* orders@pguk.co.uk *Web Site:* www.pguk.co.uk

Croner
145 London Rd, Kingston upon Thames, Surrey KT2 6SR
Tel: (020) 8547 3333
E-mail: enquiries@croner.co.uk
Web Site: croner.co.uk
Founded: 1941
Subjects: Business, Finance, Health, Nutrition, Labor, Industrial Relations, Law, Transportation
ISBN Prefix(es): 978-0-900319; 978-1-85524
Parent Company: Wolters Kluwer (UK) Ltd
Ultimate Parent Company: Wolters Kluwer NV, Netherlands
Subsidiaries: CCH Editions (Bicester)
Branch Office(s)
272 Bath St, Glasgow G2 4JR *Tel:* (0141) 354 1563
Croner House, Wheatfield Way, Hinckley, Leics LE10 1YG *Tel:* (01455) 897000
Reward House, Diamond Way, Stone Business Park, Stone, Staffs ST15 0SD *Tel:* (01785) 813566

Crossway, *imprint of* Inter-Varsity Press

Crown House Publishing Ltd+
Crown Bldgs, Bancyfelin, Carmarthen SA33 5ND
Tel: (01267) 211345 *Fax:* (0844) 500 7211
E-mail: books@crownhouse.co.uk
Web Site: www.crownhouse.co.uk

Key Personnel
Mng Dir: David Bowman *E-mail:* dbowman@crownhouse.co.uk
Publishing Dir: Caroline Lenton *E-mail:* clenton@crownhouse.co.uk
Sales, Marketing & Rights Manager: Rosalie Williams *E-mail:* rwilliams@crownhouse.co.uk
Founded: 1992
Subjects: Business, Education, Health, Nutrition, Psychology, Psychiatry, Self-Help, Business Training & Development, Green Living, Mind/Body/Spirit, Psychotherapy
ISBN Prefix(es): 978-1-899836; 978-1-904424; 978-1-84590; 978-0-9823573; 978-1-935810; 978-1-78135
Number of titles published annually: 40 Print; 1 CD-ROM; 40 E-Book
Total Titles: 335 Print; 166 E-Book
Imprints: Independent Thinking Press (education)
Divisions: Crown House Publishing Co LLC
U.S. Office(s): Crown House Publishing Co LLC, 6 Trowbridge Dr, Suite 5, Bethel, CT 06801, United States *Tel:* 203-778-1300 *Fax:* 203-778-9100 *E-mail:* info@chpus.com *Web Site:* www.chpus.com
Foreign Rep(s): Geoff Bryan (Ireland, Northern Ireland); European Chinese Publishers Promotion Center (China); Footprint Books Pty Ltd (Australasia); Rance Fu (China); Charles Gibbes (Cyprus, Greece); Iberian Book Services (Gibraltar, Portugal, Spain); IJ Sagun Enterprises Inc (Korea, Philippines, Taiwan); InterMediaAmericana Ltd (David Williams) (Caribbean, Latin America); Juta & Co Ltd (Botswana, Lesotho, Namibia, South Africa, Swaziland, Zimbabwe); Litmus Education (Middle East); Publishers International Marketing (Ru Ashdown) (Middle East, Turkey); Publishers International Marketing (Chris Ashdown) (Indonesia, Thailand); Publishers Marketing Services Pte Ltd (Malaysia, Singapore); Research Press (India)
Orders to: Grantham Book Services Ltd, Trent Rd, Grantham, Lincs NG31 7XQ *Tel:* (01476) 541080 *Fax:* (01476) 541061 *E-mail:* orders@gbs.tbs-ltd.co.uk

The Crowood Press Ltd+
The Stable Block, Crowood Lane, Ramsbury, Wilts SN8 2HR
Tel: (01672) 520320 *Fax:* (01672) 520280
E-mail: enquiries@crowood.com
Web Site: www.crowood.com; www.facebook.com/TheCrowoodPress; twitter.com/crowoodpress
Key Personnel
Owner & Chairman: John F Dennis
Sales Office Manager: Julie Sankey
Founded: 1982
Subjects: Aeronautics, Aviation, Agriculture, Animals, Pets, Art, Automotive, Crafts, Games, Hobbies, Drama, Theater, Film, Video, Gardening, Plants, Health, Nutrition, How-to, Maritime, Music, Dance, Natural History, Outdoor Recreation, Photography, Sports, Athletics, Farming & Land Use, Horology, Martial Arts, Military History
ISBN Prefix(es): 978-0-946284; 978-1-85223; 978-1-86126; 978-1-84797; 978-1-78500
Number of titles published annually: 70 Print
Total Titles: 900 Print
Imprints: Airlife Publishing Ltd; J A Allen; Ruth Bean Publishers; Buried River Press; Helmsman Guides; NAG Press
Foreign Rep(s): Angell Eurosales (Scandinavia); Bookport Associates (Joe Portelli) (Southern Europe); European Marketing Services (Anselm Robinson) (Austria, Belgium, France, Germany, Luxembourg, Switzerland); Kevin van Hasselt (Africa, Caribbean); Peter Hyde Associates (South Africa); Edwin G Makabenta (Philippines, Thailand); Motorbooks International (Canada, USA); Peribo Pty Ltd (Australia,

New Zealand); Publishers Marketing Services (Singapore); Publishers Marketing Services Pte Ltd (Malaysia); Trafalgar Square Publishing (Canada, USA)
Distribution Center: Grantham Book Services, Trent Rd, Grantham, Lincs NG31 7XQ
Tel: (01476) 541080 *Fax:* (01476) 541060
E-mail: orders@gbs.tbs-ltd.co.uk

Crucible Publishers+
4 Monmouth Paddock, Norton St Philip, Bath BA2 7LA
Tel: (01373) 834900 *Fax:* (01373) 834900
E-mail: cruciblepublishers@gmail.com
Web Site: www.cruciblepublishers.com
Key Personnel
Mng Dir & Publisher: Mr Robin Campbell
  E-mail: robin@cruciblepublishers.com
Founded: 2002
Subjects: Environmental Studies, Fiction, Health, Nutrition, Inspirational, Spirituality, Body/Mind, Healing
ISBN Prefix(es): 978-1-902733
Number of titles published annually: 4 Print
Total Titles: 12 Print
Distribution Center: Gazelle Book Services, White Cross Mills, Hightown, Lancaster, Lancs LA1 4XS *Tel:* (01524) 68765 *Fax:* (01524) 63232 *E-mail:* sales@gazellebooks.co.uk
New Leaf Distributing Co, 401 Thornton Rd, Lithia Springs, GA 30122, United States
  Tel: 770-948-7845

CRW Publishing Ltd
6 Turville Barns, Eastleach, Cirencester, Glos GL7 3QB
Tel: (01367) 850448
Web Site: www.collectors-library.com
Key Personnel
Editorial Dir: Marcus Clapham
Sales: Clive Reynard
Subjects: Classics
ISBN Prefix(es): 978-1-904633; 978-1-904919; 978-1-905716; 978-1-907360
Imprints: The Collector's Library
Branch Office(s)
69 Gloucester Crescent, London NW1 7EG
Orders to: Macmillan Distribution, Brunel Rd, Basingstoke, Hants RG21 6XS *Tel:* (01256) 302692; (0845) 0705656 (orders) *Fax:* (01256) 812558 *E-mail:* orders@macmillan.co.uk (trade)

CTBI Publications
39 Eccleston Sq, London SW1V 1BX
Tel: (0845) 680 6851 *Fax:* (0845) 680 6852
E-mail: info@ctbi.org.uk
Web Site: www.ctbi.org.uk
Key Personnel
General Secretary: Rev Bob Fyffe *E-mail:* bob.fyffe@ctbi.org.uk
Founded: 1940 (as BCC Publications)
Subjects: Biblical Studies, Biography, Memoirs, Computers, Education, Environmental Studies, History, Religion - Catholic, Religion - Protestant, Religion - Other, Theology, Women's Studies
ISBN Prefix(es): 978-0-85169
Parent Company: Churches Together in Britian & Ireland
Distributor for World Council of Churches (UK & Ireland)
Bookshop(s): Church House Bookshop, 31 Great Smith St, London SW1P 3BN *Tel:* (020) 7898 1306 *Fax:* (020) 7898 1305 *E-mail:* bookshop@c-of-e.org.uk
Distribution Center: Norwich Books & Music, 13a Hellesdon Park Rd, Norwich, Norfolk NR6 5DR *Tel:* (01603) 785925 *Fax:* (01603) 785915

CTS Publications, *imprint of* The Catholic Truth Society

Culture Smart!, *imprint of* Kuperard

Benjamin Cummings, *imprint of* Pearson Education Ltd

Cupcake, *imprint of* Alligator Publishing Ltd

Curiad
Capel Salem, Talysarn, Caernarfon, Gwynedd LL54 6AB
Tel: (01286) 882166
E-mail: curiad@curiad.co.uk
Web Site: www.curiad.co.uk
Founded: 1992
Subjects: Music, Dance
ISBN Prefix(es): 978-1-897664
Orders to: Active Music Services (AMS), Heulwen, Hirwaun Rd, Hirwaun, Aberdare *Tel:* (01685) 813318 *E-mail:* info@activemusicservices.co.uk *Web Site:* www.activemusicservices.co.uk

James Currey, *imprint of* Boydell & Brewer Ltd

James Currey+
Imprint of Boydell & Brewer Ltd
Bridge Farm Business Park, Top St, Martlesham, Suffolk IP12 4RB
Tel: (01394) 610 600 *Fax:* (01394) 610 316
E-mail: trading@boydell.co.uk; marketing@boydell.co.uk
Web Site: boydellandbrewer.com/james-currey
Key Personnel
Mng Editor & Commissioning Editor, Literature, Film & Music: Lynn Taylor *E-mail:* ltaylor@boydell.co.uk
Commissioning Editor: Jaqueline Mitchell *Tel:* (01865) 881 790 *E-mail:* jmitchell@boydell.co.uk
Founded: 1984
Publisher of academic books on Africa.
Subjects: Agriculture, Anthropology, Archaeology, Biography, Memoirs, Developing Countries, Drama, Theater, Economics, Education, Environmental Studies, Ethnicity, Foreign Countries, Government, Political Science, History, Law, Literature, Literary Criticism, Essays, Philosophy, Social Sciences, Sociology, Africa, Film Studies, Gender Studies, Third World Bibliographies
ISBN Prefix(es): 978-0-85255; 978-1-84701
Number of titles published annually: 35 Print
Total Titles: 470 Print
Foreign Rep(s): Abraham Associates Inc (Midwestern States); African Connection (Guy Simpson) (Africa); Chris Ashdown (Asia); Jim Blaho (Malta); Blue Weaver (Natasha Store & Lorna van Romburgh) (South Africa); Chesapeake & Hudson Inc (Mid-Atlantic States); CoInfo Pty Ltd (Australia); Leonidas Diamantopoulos (Cyprus, Greece); Colin Flint Inc (Ben Greig) (Denmark, Faroe Islands, Finland, Greenland, Iceland, Norway, Sweden); Global Book Marketing Ltd (Anthony Zurbrugg) (Ireland, Northern Ireland); Govinda Book House (Govinda Berry) (India); Claire de Gruchy (Middle East, North Africa, Turkey); Iberian Book Services (Peter & Charlotte Prout) (Portugal, Spain); Marek Lewinson (Baltic States, Eastern Europe, Russia); Mare Nostrum (Francesca Pollard) (Italy); Mare Nostrum (Frauke Feldmann) (Austria, Germany, Switzerland); Mare Nostrum (Lauren Keane) (Belgium, France, Luxembourg, Netherlands); Publishers International Marketing (Edwin Makabenta) (Philippines); Bob Rosenberg Group (Western USA); Scholarly Book Services Inc (Canada); Southeastern Book Travelers LLC (Southeast USA); TML (Tahir Lodhi) (Pakistan)
Orders to: Wiley European Distribution Centre, New Era Estate, Oldlands Way, Bog-

nor Regis PO22 9NQ *Tel:* (01243) 843 291
E-mail: customer@wiley.com (worldwide exc North & South America)
Boydell & Brewer Inc, 668 Mount Hope Ave, Rochester, NY 14620-2731, United States *Tel:* 585-275-0419 *Fax:* 585-271-8778 *E-mail:* boydell@boydellusa.net (North & South America)

Cutting Edge Press
116 West Heath Rd, London NW3 7TU
Tel: (020) 8731 9040
E-mail: info@cuttingedgepress.co.uk; sales@cuttingedgepress.co.uk; rights@cuttingedgepress.co.uk; submissions@cuttingedgepress.co.uk
Web Site: www.cuttingedgepress.co.uk
Founded: 2010
Subjects: Fiction, Nonfiction (General)
ISBN Prefix(es): 978-1-903813
Distribution Center: Turnaround Publisher Services Ltd, Unit 3, Olympia Trading Estate, Coburg Rd, Wood Green, London N22 6TZ *Tel:* (020) 8829 3000 *Web Site:* www.turnaround-uk.com
Independent Publishers Group, 814 North Franklin St, Chicago, IL 60610, United States *Tel:* 312-337-0747 *Web Site:* www.ipgbook.com

Cv Publications
Albion House, 49 Park Rd, Hampton Wick, Kingston Upon Thames KT1 4AS
Tel: (020) 8943 9697
E-mail: cvpub@ision.co.uk
Web Site: www.tracksdirectory.ision.co.uk
Key Personnel
Publisher: Nicholas James
Editor: Janet Barber; Sarah James
Founded: 1992
Subjects: Art, Career Development, Crafts, Games, Hobbies, Human Relations, Social Sciences, Sociology, Travel & Tourism
ISBN Prefix(es): 978-1-904727; 978-0-9512784; 978-1-901161; 978-1-908419
Number of titles published annually: 40 Print
Total Titles: 200 Print
Distributed by Ebsco Publishing
Distribution Center: Central Books Ltd, One Heath Park Industrial Estate, Freshwater Rd, Dagenham RM8 1RX *Tel:* (020) 8525 8800 *Fax:* (020) 8599 2694 *E-mail:* contactus@centralbooks.com *Web Site:* www.centralbooks.com
Bookwire.de, Kaiserstr 56, 60329 Frankfurt am Main, Hessen, Germany *Web Site:* www.bookwire.de (ebooks)

CWR
Waverley Abbey House, Waverley Lane, Farnham, Surrey GU9 8EP
Tel: (01252) 784 700 *Fax:* (01252) 784 734
Web Site: www.cwr.org.uk
Subjects: Biblical Studies
ISBN Prefix(es): 978-1-74401; 978-1-78259; 978-1-85345
Distribution Center: Baker & Taylor Publisher Services, 30 Amberwood Parkway, Ashland, OH 44805, United States *Tel:* 567-215-0030 *E-mail:* info@btpubservices.com *Web Site:* www.btpubservices.com

Cyfres y Gair, *imprint of* Cyhoeddiadau'r Gair

Cyhoeddiadau Barddas
Bod Aeron, Heol Pen-sarn, Y Bala, Gwynedd LL23 7SR
Tel: (01678) 520378 *Fax:* (01678) 521051
Web Site: www.barddas.com
Key Personnel
Administrative Officer: Elwyn Edwards

Publications Editor: Elena Gruffudd *Tel:* (01970) 625659
Founded: 1976
Specialize in Welsh language & literature.
Subjects: Literature, Literary Criticism, Essays, Poetry
ISBN Prefix(es): 978-1-900437

Cyhoeddiadau FBA, *imprint of* FBA Group

Cyhoeddiadau'r Gair (Work Publications)+
Ael y Bryn, Chwilog, Pwllheli, Gwynedd LL53 6SH
Tel: (01766) 819120
Web Site: ysgolsul.com
Key Personnel
Dir: Aled Davies *E-mail:* aled@ysgolsul.com
Founded: 1992
Specialize in Welsh language Christian books, cards & systems.
Subjects: Biblical Studies, Religion - Protestant
ISBN Prefix(es): 978-1-85994; 978-1-874410
Total Titles: 300 Print; 2 CD-ROM
Parent Company: Cyngor Ysgolion Sul
Imprints: Cyfres y Gair
Subsidiaries: Cardiau'r Gair Gifts
Distributed by Welsh Books Council
Distributor for Curaid; Gwasg Efeng yl Aidd Cymru
Bookshop(s): Canolfan Addysg Grefyddol, Bangor
Warehouse: Libanus, Bontnewydd

Cynulliad Cenedlaethol Cymru, see National Assembly for Wales

CYPI Press
79 College Rd, Harrow, Middx HA1 1BD
Tel: (020) 3178 7279 *Fax:* (020) 8626 7064
E-mail: sales@cypi.net; editor@cypi.net
Web Site: www.cypi.net
Founded: 2007
Subjects: Art, Photography, Travel & Tourism, Chinese Art & Culture, Design
ISBN Prefix(es): 978-0-9556057
Parent Company: CYP International Ltd

Dance Books Ltd+
Southwold, Isington Rd, Binsted, Hants GU34 4PH
Tel: (01420) 525 299
Web Site: www.dancebooks.co.uk
Key Personnel
Mng Dir: David Leonard *E-mail:* dwl@dancebooks.co.uk
Sales Dir: Richard Holland
Founded: 1960
Also bookseller.
Subjects: Music, Dance
ISBN Prefix(es): 978-0-903102; 978-1-85273
Number of titles published annually: 10 Print
Total Titles: 130 Print
Distributed by Australia Footprint Books Pty; Princeton Book Co
Distributor for Princeton Book Co
Distribution Center: Vine House Distribution, The Old Mill House, Mill Lane, Uckfield, East Sussex TN22 5AA *Tel:* (01825) 767 396 *Fax:* (01825) 765 649 *E-mail:* sales@vinehouseuk.co.uk *Web Site:* www.vinehouseuk.co.uk

D&B Ltd, see Dun & Bradstreet Ltd

Darf Publishers Ltd
277 West End Lane, West Hampstead, London NW6 1QS
Tel: (020) 7431 7009 *Fax:* (020) 7431 7655
E-mail: info@darfpublishers.co.uk; orders@darfpublishers.co.uk
Web Site: darfpublishers.co.uk

Key Personnel
Mng Dir: Ghassan Fergiani *E-mail:* ghassan@darfpublishers.co.uk
Project Manager: Fergus McKeown *E-mail:* fergusmck@darfpublishers.co.uk
Founded: 1983
Specialize in reprints of out-of-print & rare books written in the 18th & 19th centuries.
Subjects: Archaeology, Geography, Geology, History, Literature, Literary Criticism, Essays, Outdoor Recreation, Religion - Islamic, Sports, Athletics, Theology, Travel & Tourism, Cricket, Culture, Horse Racing
ISBN Prefix(es): 978-1-85077
Number of titles published annually: 10 Print
Total Titles: 200 Print

Dark Masters, *imprint of* Dedalus Ltd

Darton, Longman & Todd Ltd+
One Spencer Court, 140-142 Wandsworth High St, London SW18 4JJ
Tel: (020) 8875 0155 *Fax:* (020) 8875 0133
E-mail: editorial@darton-longman-todd.co.uk
Web Site: www.darton-longman-todd.co.uk; www.dltbooks.com
Key Personnel
Editorial Dir: David Maloney *E-mail:* davidm@darton-longman-todd.co.uk
Marketing & Publicity Dir: Will Parkes *Tel:* (020) 8875 2811 *E-mail:* willp@darton-longman-todd.co.uk
Production Dir: Ken Ruskin *E-mail:* kenr@darton-longman-todd.co.uk
Mng Editor: Helen Porter *E-mail:* helenp@darton-longman-todd.co.uk
Finance: Kamal Singh *E-mail:* kamals@darton-longman-todd.co.uk
Sales: Ian Matthews *E-mail:* ian@darton-longman-todd.co.uk
Founded: 1959
Subjects: Biblical Studies, Biography, Memoirs, Fiction, Humor, Inspirational, Spirituality, Religion - Catholic, Religion - Protestant, Religion - Other, Theology
ISBN Prefix(es): 978-0-232
Foreign Rep(s): Alban Books (Europe exc Malta); Garrett Publishing (Australia); Novalis (Canada); Pleroma Christian Supplies (New Zealand); Preca Library (Malta)
Distribution Center: Norwich Books & Music Distribution, 13a Hellesdon Park Rd, Norwich, Norfolk NR6 5DR *Tel:* (01603) 785 925 *Fax:* (01603) 785 915 *E-mail:* orders@norwichbooksandmusic.co.uk *Web Site:* www.norwichbooksandmusic.co.uk

David & Charles Ltd+
Imprint of F+W Media Inc
Brunel House, Forde Close, Newton Abbot, Devon TQ12 4PU
Tel: (01626) 323 200 *Fax:* (01626) 323 319
E-mail: info@fwmedia.co.uk
Web Site: www.fwcommunity.com/uk
Key Personnel
Mng Dir: James Woollam *Tel:* (01626) 323 243 *E-mail:* james.woollam@fwmedia.com
Senior Rights Manager: Fallon Sheffield *Tel:* (01626) 323 303 *E-mail:* fallon.sheffield@fwmedia.com
Head, International Sales: Sam Vallance *E-mail:* sam.vallance@fwmedia.com
Head, UK Sales: Annabel Youldon *E-mail:* annabel.youldon@fwmedia.com
Founded: 1960
Subjects: Animals, Pets, Art, Cookery, Crafts, Games, Hobbies, Gardening, Plants, Health, Nutrition, How-to, Maritime, Outdoor Recreation, Photography, Transportation, Travel & Tourism
ISBN Prefix(es): 978-0-7153; 978-1-4463
Associate Companies: Levinson

Imprints: Betterway; How Design; North Light; Popular Woodworking; Writer's Digest
Divisions: The Readers' Union
Distributed by David Bateman Ltd (New Zealand); F+W Media Inc (USA & Canada); Kirby Book Distribution (Australia); Trinity Books (South Africa)
Foreign Rep(s): Angell Eurosales (Belgium, Denmark, Finland, France, Iceland, Netherlands, Norway, Sweden); Pat Bence (Botswana, Caribbean, The Gambia, Kenya, Mauritius); Candida Buckley (Denmark, Finland, Netherlands, Norway, Switzerland); Michelle Morrow Curreri (Asia, Latin America, Middle East); Lora Fountain (France); Gabriele Kern (Austria, Germany, Switzerland); Surit Mitra (Bangladesh, Indonesia, Nepal, Sri Lanka); Padovani Books Ltd (Penny Padovani) (France, Gibraltar, Greece, Italy, Spain); Marta Schooler (Asia, Latin America, Middle East)
Book Club(s): Readers Union Ltd
Orders to: Grantham Book Services, Trent Rd, Grantham, Lincs NG31 7QX *Tel:* (01476) 541080 *Fax:* (01476) 541061 *E-mail:* orders@gbs.tbs-ltd.co.uk

Christopher Davies Publishers Ltd+
PO Box 403, Swansea, W Glam SA1 4YF
Tel: (01792) 648825 *Fax:* (01792) 648825
Key Personnel
Dir: Emyr Nicholas
Founded: 1949
Subjects: Cookery, Health, Nutrition, History, Natural History
ISBN Prefix(es): 978-0-7154; 978-0-85339

Debrett's Ltd+
16 Charles St, London W1J 5DS
Tel: (020) 7290 5950
E-mail: people@debretts.com; publications@debretts.com; press@debretts.com; enquiries@debretts.com
Web Site: www.debretts.com
Founded: 1769
All matters of etiquette, social occasions, people of distinction & fine style.
Subjects: Biography, Memoirs, Genealogy
ISBN Prefix(es): 978-1-870520; 978-0-905649; 978-0-9929348
Distribution Center: Trafalgar Square Publishing (Canada & USA)
Orders to: Vinehouse Distribution Ltd, Waldenbury, North Common, Chailey, East Sussex BN27 3RP *Tel:* (01825) 723 398 *Fax:* (01825) 724 188

Decadence from Dedalus, *imprint of* Dedalus Ltd

Dedalus Anthologies, *imprint of* Dedalus Ltd

Dedalus Euro Shorts, *imprint of* Dedalus Ltd

Dedalus Europe 1992-2012, *imprint of* Dedalus Ltd

Dedalus European Classics, *imprint of* Dedalus Ltd

Dedalus Ltd+
Langford Lodge, St Judith's Lane, Sawtry, Cambs PE28 5XE
Tel: (01487) 832382 *Fax:* (01487) 832382
E-mail: info@dedalusbooks.com
Web Site: www.dedalusbooks.com
Key Personnel
Mng Dir: Eric Lane
Editorial Dir: Robert Irwin
Founded: 1983

Specialize in new English literary fiction, translated European contemporary fiction & neglected European classics.
Membership(s): Arts Council England.
Subjects: Fiction, Literature, Literary Criticism, Essays, Nonfiction (General), English Literary Fiction, European Classics, European Contemporary Fiction
ISBN Prefix(es): 978-0-946626; 978-1-873982; 978-1-903517; 978-1-904556; 978-1-906614
Imprints: City Noir; Concept Books; Dark Masters; Decadence from Dedalus; Dedalus Anthologies; Dedalus European Classics; Dedalus Europe 1992-2012; Dedalus Euro Shorts; Dedalus Nobel Prize Winner; Empire of the Senses; Original English Language Fiction
Foreign Rep(s): Angell Eurosales (Gill Angell & Stewart Siddall) (Scandinavia); Michael Geoghegan (Austria, Belgium, France, Germany, Holland, Switzerland); Padovani Books Ltd (Penny Padovani) (Greece, Italy, Portugal, Spain); Peribo Pty Ltd (Australia, New Zealand); SCB Disributors (Canada, USA)
Distribution Center: Central Books Ltd, One Heath Park Industrial Estate, Freshwater Rd, Dagenham RM8 1RX Tel: (020) 8525 8800 Fax: (020) 8599 2694 E-mail: orders@centralbooks.com Web Site: www.centralbooks.com

Dedalus Nobel Prize Winner, *imprint of* Dedalus Ltd

Definitions, *imprint of* The Random House Group Ltd, a Penguin Random House Company

Del Rey, *imprint of* Ebury Publishing

Delancey Press Ltd+
23 Berkeley Sq, London W1J 6HE
Tel: (020) 7665 6605 *Fax:* (020) 7665 6650
E-mail: delanceypress@aol.com
Web Site: www.delanceypress.co.uk
Key Personnel
Mng Dir: Tatiana Wilson
Membership(s): The Booksellers Association.
Subjects: Fiction, Humor
ISBN Prefix(es): 978-0-9539119; 978-1-907205
Number of titles published annually: 2 Print
Total Titles: 4 Print
Distributed by The Book Guild Ltd
Orders to: Central Books Ltd, One Heath Park Industrial Estate, Freshwater Rd, Dagenham RM8 1RX *Tel:* (020) 8525 8800 *Fax:* (020) 8599 2694 *E-mail:* orders@centralbooks.com *Web Site:* www.centralbooks.com

Delectation, *imprint of* Delectus Books

Delectus Books+
27 Old Gloucester St, London WC1N 3XX
Tel: (020) 8963 0979 *Fax:* (020) 8963 0979
E-mail: mgdelectus@aol.com
Web Site: www.delectusbooks.co.uk
Key Personnel
Publisher: Michael R Goss *E-mail:* mgdelectus@aol.com
Founded: 1988
Also acts as a bookseller.
Subjects: Anthropology, Criminology, Erotica, LGBTQ, Psychology, Psychiatry, Dada, Decadence, Drugs & Alcohol, Ethnology, Fantasy, Folklore, Gothic & Horror, Occult & Witchcraft, Psychoanalysis, Scotland & Ireland, Sexology, Surrealism, Symbolists & the 1890s, True Crime, Vampires & Werewolves
ISBN Prefix(es): 978-1-897767
Number of titles published annually: 3 Print
Total Titles: 15 Print
Imprints: Delectation

Delta Alpha Publishing Ltd
19H John Spencer Sq, London N1 2LZ
Tel: (020) 7359 1822 *Fax:* (020) 7359 1822
Web Site: www.deltaalpha.com
Founded: 1998
Membership(s): IBPA, the Independent Book Publishers Association; Independent Publishers Guild (IPG).
Subjects: Business, Law, Real Estate
ISBN Prefix(es): 978-0-9668946
Number of titles published annually: 2 Print; 1 CD-ROM; 1 Online
Total Titles: 4 Print; 1 CD-ROM
Branch Office(s)
16 Casteways Close, Kewarra Beach, Qld 4879, Australia
U.S. Office(s): 35 Ash Dr, Kimball, MI 48074, United States
Distribution Center: Port City Fulfillment, 35 Ash Dr, Kimball, MI 48074, United States *Tel:* 810-388-9500 *Fax:* 810-388-9502
Orders to: Port City Fulfillment, 35 Ash Dr, Kimball, MI 48074, United States *Tel:* 810-388-9500 *Fax:* 810-388-9502

Delta Publishing
Quince Cottage, Hoe Lane, Peaslake, Surrey GU5 9SW
Tel: (01306) 731770 *Fax:* (01306) 731770
E-mail: info@deltapublishing.co.uk
Web Site: www.deltapublishing.co.uk
Key Personnel
Mng Dir: Nick Boisseau *E-mail:* nick.boisseau@deltapublishing.co.uk
Founded: 1997
Publishers of English language teaching materials.
Subjects: English as a Second Language
ISBN Prefix(es): 978-1-900783; 978-1-905085; 978-1-953309
Number of titles published annually: 10 Print; 2 CD-ROM
Total Titles: 100 Print; 8 CD-ROM
Distributed by Algoritam (Croatia); Allecto AS (Estonia); Forlaget Alokke A/S (Denmark); Attica (France); Audiovox (Belgium); Bohemian Ventures Spol SRO (Czech Republic); Books.ba (Bosnia and Herzegovina); Cengage Learning (Argentina, Brazil & Chile); Cengage Learning Asia Pvt Ltd (China, Malaysia, Singapore & Taiwan); Cengage Learning Hong Kong Ltd (Hong Kong); Cengage Learning KK (Japan); Cengage Learning Korea Ltd (Korea); Cengage Learning (Thailand) Ltd (Thailand); Educational Center Albania (Albania); Educational Centre Bulgaria (Bulgaria); English Central (Canada); EQ opciones en Educacion (Uruguay); FLB Bookery (Australia); Helbling Languages (Austria & Germany); Raamatukauplus Krisostomus (Estonia); Megabooks (Czech Republic); Nowa Era (Poland); Char J Philippides & Son Ltd (Cyprus); Solonion Book Centre (Cyprus); Stockmann Academic Bookstore (Finland); VBZ Ltd (Croatia)

Denor Press Ltd+
925 Finchley Rd, London NW11 7PE
Tel: (07768) 855 995 *Fax:* (020) 8446 4504
E-mail: denorgroup@gmail.com
Web Site: www.denorpress.com
Founded: 1997
Also provides promotion & marketing services.
Membership(s): The Publishers Association.
Subjects: Fiction, Health, Nutrition, Medicine, Nursing, Dentistry, Music, Dance, Nonfiction (General)
ISBN Prefix(es): 978-0-9526056
Total Titles: 4 Print; 4 Online; 4 E-Book

JM Dent, *imprint of* Orion Publishing Group Ltd

Andre Deutsch, *imprint of* Carlton Publishing Group

Andre Deutsch+
Imprint of Carlton Publishing Group
20 Mortimer St, London W1T 3JW
Tel: (020) 7612 0400 *Fax:* (020) 7612 0401
E-mail: sales@carltonbooks.co.uk
Web Site: www.carltonbooks.co.uk
Key Personnel
Mng Dir: Frank Chambers *Tel:* (020) 7612 0407 *E-mail:* fchambers@carltonbooks.co.uk
UK Sales & Marketing Dir: Owen Hazell *Tel:* (020) 7612 0433 *E-mail:* ohazell@carltonbooks.co.uk
Head, Marketing: Helen Churchill *Tel:* (020) 7612 0474 *E-mail:* hchurchill@carltonbooks.co.uk
Head, Publicity: Carol Farley *Tel:* (020) 7612 0416 *E-mail:* cfarley@carlton.books.co.uk
Founded: 1951
Subjects: Art, Biography, Memoirs, Government, Political Science, History, Humor, Music, Dance, Natural History, Photography, Psychology, Psychiatry, Sports, Athletics, Travel & Tourism, Current Affairs
ISBN Prefix(es): 978-0-233; 978-1-85375 (Prion)
Foreign Rep(s): Gunnar Lie & Associates Ltd (Gunnar Lie) (Africa, Indian subcontinent, Southeast Asia); Gunnar Lie & Associates Ltd (Guillaume Ferrand) (Belgium, Central America, Eastern Europe, France, Gibraltar, Italy, Luxembourg, Malta, Portugal, South America, Spain); Gunnar Lie & Associates Ltd (John Edgeler) (Caribbean, Cyprus, Greece, Middle East, Netherlands, Scandinavia); Michael & Lorie Ocampo (China, Hong Kong, Japan, Korea, Philippines, Taiwan); Publishers Services (Gabriele Kern) (Austria, Germany, Switzerland); Research Press (Ajay Parmar) (India)
Distribution Center: HarperCollins Distribution Services, Westerhill Rd, Bishopbriggs, Glasgow G64 2QT *Tel:* (0141) 306 3100 *Fax:* (0141) 306 3261 *E-mail:* uk.orders@harpercollins.co.uk

Andre Deutsch Children's Books, *imprint of* Scholastic Ltd

Diagram Visual Information Ltd+
34 Elaine Grove, London NW5 4QH
Tel: (020) 7485 5941 *Fax:* (020) 7485 5941
E-mail: info@diagramgroup.com
Web Site: www.diagramgroup.com
Key Personnel
Mng Dir: Bruce Robertson *E-mail:* brucerobertson@diagramgroup.com
Administration: Eva Flores *E-mail:* evaflores@diagramgroup.com
Founded: 1960
Book designer & creator.
Subjects: Art, Crafts, Games, Hobbies, Earth Sciences, Environmental Studies, Health, Nutrition, History, House & Home, Science (General), Sports, Athletics, Africa Studies, Family, Pre-History, Science/Humanities, Self-Knowledge
ISBN Prefix(es): 978-1-900121; 978-0-9574028
Number of titles published annually: 10 Print
Total Titles: 500 Print
Foreign Rights: Big Apple Agency Inc (Lily Chen) (China); Big Apple Agency Inc (Mathilde Wang) (Taiwan); DS Budapest Kft (Margit Gruber) (Hungary); DS Rights & Co-Editions Ltd (Richard Elman) (Lithuania); DS Warszawa (Anna Kolendarska-Fidyk) (Poland); Eva Flores (UK) (Tatjana Wanjat) (Russia); ICSTI (Tatjana Wanjat) (Russia); KCC - Korea Copyright Center Inc (Ms Hong Misook) (Korea); Hani & Dar Kreidieh (Algeria, Bahrain, Comoros, Djibouti, Egypt, Iraq, Jordan, Kuwait, Lebanon, Libya, Mauritius, Morocco, Oman, Qatar, Saudi Arabia, Somalia, Sudan, Syria, Tunisia, United Arab Emirates, Yemen); Nika Literary Agency (Vania Kadiyska) (Bulgaria); Livia Stoia Literary Agency (Livia Stoia) (Moldova, Roma-

nia); Tuttle-Mori Agency Inc (Naomi Mizuno) (Japan); Tuttle-Mori Agency Inc (Ms Pimol-porn Yutisri) (Thailand)

Dial House, *imprint of* Ian Allan Publishing

Dialogue, *imprint of* Biteback Publishing

Dialogue Books, *imprint of* Little, Brown Book Group

Dickens Publishing Ltd
Subsidiary of Pelangi Publishing Group
Davina House, Suite G2, Goswell Rd, 137-149 London EC1V 7ET
Tel: (020) 72 53 68 88 *Fax:* (0560) 310 24 59
Web Site: www.dickenspublishing.co.uk
ISBN Prefix(es): 978-1-907580

Digital Leaf Ltd+
200 St Leonards Rd, Richmond, London SW14 7BN
Tel: (020) 8404 2225
E-mail: hello@digitalleaf.co.uk
Web Site: www.digitalleaf.co.uk
Key Personnel
Founder & Mng Dir: Neil Jeffries *Tel:* (07904) 517248
Founder & Chief Editor: Dustin Brooks *Tel:* (07981) 699498
Founded: 2011
This publisher has indicated that 40% of their product line is author subsidized.
ISBN Prefix(es): 978-0-9573087; 978-1-909428
Number of titles published annually: 4 Print; 4 E-Book
Total Titles: 15 Print; 10 E-Book

Digital Press, *imprint of* Elsevier Ltd

DIME, *imprint of* Tarquin Publications

Dinas, *imprint of* Y Lolfa Cyf

Dino Books, *imprint of* John Blake Publishing Ltd

Discovery Walking Guides Ltd+
10 Tennyson Close, Northampton, Northants NN5 7HJ
Tel: (01604) 244869
E-mail: ask.discovery@ntlworld.com
Web Site: www.dwgwalking.co.uk
Key Personnel
Company Secretary: David Brawn
Contact: Ros Brawn
Founded: 1993
Specialize in walking guides, tour & trail maps.
Subjects: Regional Interests, Travel & Tourism
ISBN Prefix(es): 978-1-899554; 978-1-78275; 978-1-904946
Number of titles published annually: 8 Print
Total Titles: 45 Print
Imprints: Tour & Trail Maps; Warm Island Walking Guides
Distribution Center: Gardners Books, One Whittle Dr, Eastbourne BN23 6QH *Tel:* (01323) 521555

Disney, *imprint of* Ladybird Books Ltd

DK Ltd+
Division of The Penguin Group (UK)
80 Strand, London WC2R 0LR
Tel: (020) 7010 3000 *Fax:* (020) 7010 6060
E-mail: sales@uk.dk.com
Web Site: www.dk.com

Key Personnel
Chairman: Peter Kindersley
Chief Executive: Ian Hudson
Mng Dir, Multi-Media: Alan Buckingham
Publishing Dir, Travel: Georgina Dee
Founded: 1974
Subjects: Art, Child Care & Development, Cookery, Crafts, Games, Hobbies, Gardening, Plants, Health, Nutrition, History, House & Home, Music, Dance, Nonfiction (General), Photography, Self-Help, Sports, Athletics, Wine & Spirits
ISBN Prefix(es): 978-0-7894; 978-0-86318; 978-0-7513; 978-0-7547; 978-0-7566; 978-1-4053
Ultimate Parent Company: Penguin Random House
Imprints: Funfax; Hugo
Subsidiaries: DKP Inc; DK Family Library
Branch Office(s)
DK Australia & New Zealand, Melbourne, Australia
DK Canada, Toronto, ON, Canada
DK Germany, Munich, Germany
DK India, Delhi, India
U.S. Office(s): DK Publishing, 345 Hudson St, 2nd floor, New York, NY 10014, United States *Tel:* 646-674-4000
Distributed by Penguin Books Ltd
Bookshop(s): 10-13 King St, London WC2E 8HN
Warehouse: International Book Distributors Ltd, Magna Park, Coventry Rd, Butterworth, Leics LE17 4XH

The Do Book Co
63 Redchurch St, London E2 7DJ
Tel: (020) 3287 2665
E-mail: info@thedobook.co
Web Site: thedobook.co
Key Personnel
Founder & Publisher: Miranda West *Tel:* (07957) 597 540 *E-mail:* miranda@thedobook.co
Founded: 2013
Subjects: Inspirational, Spirituality, Self-Help
ISBN Prefix(es): 978-1-907974
Total Titles: 15 Print
Foreign Rep(s): Ingram Content Group (USA); Perimeter Distribution (Australia, New Zealand)
Distribution Center: Publishers Group UK, 63-66 Hatton Garden, London EC1N 8LE *Tel:* (020) 7405 1105 *Fax:* (020) 7242 3725 *E-mail:* orders@pguk.co.uk *Web Site:* www.pguk.co.uk
Orders to: Grantham Book Services *Tel:* (01476) 541080 *E-mail:* orders@gbs.tbs-ltd.co.uk (UK & Ireland book trade)

Dobro Publishing
Bloomsbury Therapy Centre, 80 A Southampton Row, London WC1B 4BB
Tel: (020) 8346 4010
E-mail: dobropublishing@aol.com
Web Site: www.drsandradelroy.com
Key Personnel
Contact: Dr Sandra Delroy *Tel:* (07956) 297054 (cell) *E-mail:* psychologist@drsandradelroy.com
Subjects: Health, Nutrition, Medicine, Nursing, Dentistry, Psychology, Psychiatry
ISBN Prefix(es): 978-0-9527520

Dodona Books, *imprint of* O Books

Dod's Parliamentary Communications Ltd
21 Dartmouth St, London SW1H 9BP
Tel: (020) 7593 5500 *Fax:* (020) 7593 5501
E-mail: information@dods.co.uk
Web Site: www.dods.co.uk
Founded: 1832
Publisher of UK Parliamentary Reference.
Subjects: Foreign Countries, Government, Political Science

ISBN Prefix(es): 978-0-905702; 978-0-9530664; 978-1-908232
Branch Office(s)
Rue du Trone 60, 1050 Brussels, Belgium *Tel:* (02) 741 8201 *E-mail:* info@dods.eu

Dog 'n' Bone, *imprint of* Ryland Peters & Small

Dog 'n' Bone
Imprint of Ryland Peters & Small
20-21 Jockey's Fields, London WC1R 4BW
Tel: (020) 7025 2200 *Fax:* (020) 7025 2201
E-mail: sales@rps.co.uk; publicity@rps.co.uk
Web Site: www.rylandpeters.com
Key Personnel
Rights Dir: Denise Lie
Gift & humor.
Subjects: Humor
ISBN Prefix(es): 978-1-909313; 978-0-957140; 978-1-911026

The Dolmen Press Ltd, see Colin Smythe Ltd

John Donald, *imprint of* Birlinn Ltd

Dorling Kindersley Ltd, see DK Ltd

Doubleday, *imprint of* Transworld Publishers

Doubleday Childrens, *imprint of* The Random House Group Ltd, a Penguin Random House Company

Alton Douglas Books, *imprint of* Brewin Books Ltd

Drake Educational Associates Ltd+
St Fagans Rd, Fairwater, Cardiff CF5 3AE
Tel: (029) 2056 0333
E-mail: enquiries@drakeed.com
Web Site: www.drakeed.com
Key Personnel
Marketing Dir: Heather Williams
Editor: Barbara Cargill
Founded: 1970
Specialize in literacy & numeracy educational resources for primary & middle schools.
Subjects: Disability, Special Needs, Education
ISBN Prefix(es): 978-0-86174
Parent Company: Drake Group
Distributor for Highsmith Press (USA); Pembroke Publishers (Canada)

Dramatic Lines Publishers+
PO Box 201, Twickenham, Middx TW2 5RQ
Tel: (020) 8296 9502 *Fax:* (020) 8296 9503
E-mail: mail@dramaticlines.co.uk
Web Site: www.dramaticlines.co.uk
Founded: 1994
Small independent press founded to promote drama.
Membership(s): The Publishers Association.
Subjects: Drama, Theater, Education
ISBN Prefix(es): 978-0-9522224; 978-0-9537770; 978-1-904557; 978-0-9533980
Number of titles published annually: 6 Print
Distributor for Janus Publishing; Playhouse Books; Playtime Productions

Dref Wen+
28 Church Rd, Whitchurch, Cardiff CF14 2EA
Tel: (029) 2061 7860
E-mail: post@drefwen.com
Web Site: www.drefwen.com
Key Personnel
Mng Dir, Editorial: Roger Boore
Founded: 1970
Welsh language publishers.
Membership(s): Union of Welsh Publishers & Booksellers.

ISBN Prefix(es): 978-0-946962; 978-0-904910; 978-1-85596
Number of titles published annually: 50 Print; 4 Audio
Total Titles: 450 Print; 15 Audio

Gerald Duckworth & Co Ltd+
30 Calvin St, London E1 6NW
Tel: (020) 7490 7300 *Fax:* (020) 7490 0080
E-mail: info@duckworth-publishers.co.uk
Web Site: www.ducknet.co.uk
Key Personnel
Mng Dir: Peter Mayer
Editorial Dir: Gesche Ipsen
Publicity Manager: Thogdin Ripley
  E-mail: publicity@duckworth-publishers.co.uk
Sales & Marketing Manager: Matt Casbourne
  E-mail: sales@duckworth-publishers.co.uk
Contracts, Rights & Permissions Manager: David Marshall *E-mail:* david@duckworth-publishers.co.uk
Production Manager: Robin Forrester
Founded: 1898
Specialize in Greek & Latin classics.
Subjects: Biography, Memoirs, Fiction, History, Language Arts, Linguistics, Literature, Literary Criticism, Essays, Maritime, Nonfiction (General), Philosophy, Psychology, Psychiatry, Religion - Other, Science (General), Classics
ISBN Prefix(es): 978-0-7156; 978-1-86176
Number of titles published annually: 300 Print
Total Titles: 1,500 Print
Associate Companies: The Overlook Press, 141 Wooster St, New York, NY 10012, United States
Imprints: Ardis (English translations of Russian literature); Duckworth Overlook
Distribution Center: Macmillan Distribution Ltd, Houndmills, Basingstoke, Hants RG21 6XS
  Tel: (01256) 302 692 *Fax:* (01256) 812 521
  E-mail: orders@macmillan.co.uk

Duckworth Overlook, *imprint of* Gerald Duckworth & Co Ltd

Dun & Bradstreet Ltd
Marlow International Parkway, Marlow, Bucks SL7 1AJ
Tel: (0808) 278 9942
E-mail: enquiries@dnb.com
Web Site: www.dnb.co.uk
Founded: 1841
Membership(s): Booksellers Association; Business Information Network; Directory Publishers Association, European Association of Directory Publishers.
ISBN Prefix(es): 978-0-901491; 978-0-900714; 978-1-86071; 978-0-900625
Parent Company: D&B Corp, 103 JFK Parkway, Short Hills, NJ 07078, United States
Branch Office(s)
The Leadenhall Bldg, 30th floor, 122 Leadenhall St, London EC3V 4AB
The Chase, 4th floor, Carmanhall Rd, Sandyford, Dublin 18, Ireland

Dunedin Academic Press
Hudson House, 8 Albany St, Edinburgh EH1 3QB
Tel: (0131) 473 2397
E-mail: mail@dunedinacademicpress.co.uk
Web Site: www.dunedinacademicpress.co.uk
Key Personnel
Dir: Anthony Kinahan *E-mail:* anthony@dunedinacademicpress.co.uk
Founded: 2000
Independent academic publishing house. Publishes works of scholarship & utility from undergraduate & equivalent level through to postgraduate & professional levels.
Membership(s): The Publishers Association; Publishing Scotland.

Subjects: Earth Sciences, Environmental Studies, Geography, Geology
ISBN Prefix(es): 978-1-903765; 978-1-906716; 978-1-78046; 978-1-903544 (Terra Publishing)
Number of titles published annually: 15 Print
Total Titles: 120 Print; 50 E-Book
Imprints: Terra Publishing
Foreign Rep(s): Brookside (Ireland); China Publishers Services Ltd (China, Taiwan); International Specialized Book Services (Canada, USA); Missing Link (Germany); David Towle (Baltic States, Iceland, Scandinavia); Transglobal Publishers Services Ltd (Hong Kong, Macau); The White Partnership (Bangladesh, India, Indonesia, Japan, Malaysia, Pakistan, Singapore, Sri Lanka, Thailand)
Distribution Center: Turpin Distribution, Pegasus Dr, Biggleswade SG18 8TQ
  Tel: (01767) 604951 *Fax:* (01767) 601640
  E-mail: custserv@turpin-distribution.com

Gwasg Dwyfor
Stad Ddiwydiannol, Penygroes, Gwynedd LL54 6DB
Tel: (01286) 881 911 *Fax:* (01286) 881 952
Key Personnel
Partner & Mng Dir: Dafydd Owen
Partner & Dir: M P Roberts
Founded: 1981
Subjects: Nonfiction (General)
ISBN Prefix(es): 978-1-870394; 978-0-9562585; 978-0-9573033

Eaglemoss Publishing Group Ltd+
Beaumont House, 1st floor, Kensington Village, Avonmore Rd, London W14 8TS
Tel: (020) 7605 1200 *Fax:* (020) 7605 1201
Web Site: www.eaglemoss.com
Key Personnel
Chief Executive: Andrew Jarvis
Financial Dir: Cecile Marret
Editorial Dir: Maggie Calmels
Digital Marketing Manager: Emma Thackara
Founded: 1979
Specialize in publication of Partworks.
Subjects: Art, Computer Science, Cookery, Crafts, Games, Hobbies, Criminology, Gardening, Plants, History, Outdoor Recreation, Photography, Sports, Athletics, Technology, Transportation, Nature, Parenting
ISBN Prefix(es): 978-0-947837; 978-1-85167; 978-1-85629; 978-1-85875

EAL, *imprint of* Training Publications Ltd

Earth Books, *imprint of* O Books

EarthDancer Books, *imprint of* Findhorn Press Ltd

East-West Publications (UK) Ltd+
8 Caledonia St, London N1 9DZ
Tel: (020) 7837 5061 *Fax:* (020) 7278 4429
Founded: 1976
Subjects: Music, Dance, Religion - Other
ISBN Prefix(es): 978-0-85692
Associate Companies: Cromwell Book Services Ltd
Imprints: Britannia Press; Gallery Children's Books
Warehouse: East-West & Britannia, c/o The Book Service, Ltd, Distribution Centre, Colchester Rd, Frating Green, Colchester, Essex CO7 7DW *Tel:* (01206) 256000 *Fax:* (01206) 255715 *E-mail:* sales@tbs-ltd.co.uk *Web Site:* www.thebookservice.co.uk
Gallery: The Trade Counter, The Airfield, Norwich Rd, Mendlesham IP14 5NA

Ebury Press, *imprint of* Ebury Publishing

Ebury Publishing
Division of The Random House Group Ltd, a Penguin Random House Company
c/o The Random House Group Ltd, 20 Vauxhall Bridge Rd, London SW1V 2SA
Tel: (020) 7840 8400
Web Site: www.eburypublishing.co.uk
Key Personnel
Mng Dir: Rebecca Smart
Deputy Mng Dir & Publisher: Jake Lingwood
Deputy Publisher, Vermilion, Virgin & WH Allen: Joel Rickett
Subjects: Biography, Memoirs, Cookery, Erotica, Fiction, Gardening, Plants, Government, Political Science, Health, Nutrition, History, Humor, Inspirational, Spirituality, Music, Dance, Natural History, Nonfiction (General), Philosophy, Psychology, Psychiatry, Romance, Science Fiction, Fantasy, Self-Help, Sports, Athletics, Travel & Tourism, Wine & Spirits, Current Affairs
ISBN Prefix(es): 978-0-426; 978-1-85227; 978-0-7535; 978-0-09; 978-0-7126; 978-0-86369; 978-0-903446; 978-1-905042; 978-1-904978; 978-1-84670; 978-0-85223; 978-0-907080; 978-0-427; 978-1-905264
Imprints: BBC Books; Black Lace; Del Rey; Ebury Press; Fodor's; Rider Books; Time Out Guides; Vermilion; Virgin Books; WH Allen

The Economist Intelligence Unit+
20 Cabot Sq, London E14 4QW
Tel: (020) 7576 8181
E-mail: london@eiu.com
Web Site: www.eiu.com
Key Personnel
Mng Dir: Mr Robin Bew
Founded: 1954
Subjects: Automotive, Business, Developing Countries, Economics, Finance, Management, Travel & Tourism
ISBN Prefix(es): 978-0-85058; 978-0-86218; 978-0-900351
Parent Company: The Economist Group
Branch Office(s)
6001 Central Plaza, 18 Harbour Rd, Wan Chai, Hong Kong *Tel:* 2802 7288 *E-mail:* asia@eiu.com
U.S. Office(s): 750 Third Ave, 5th floor, New York, NY 10017, United States *Tel:* 212-698-9717 *E-mail:* americas@eiu.com
Foreign Rep(s): Albertina icome Praha (Czechia, Slovakia); Bharat Book Bureau (M K Chettiar) (India); Jose Casio do Val (Brazil); e-Tech Solutions de Ecuador SA (Felipe Dominguez) (Ecuador); e-Technologies Solutions Corp (Cristina Lara de Rowe) (Panama); Viktor Herman (Bosnia and Herzegovina, Croatia, Montenegro, Serbia, Slovenia); Infoestrategica SA de CV (Luis Alberto Dominguez) (Mexico); Tae Hyun Kim (South Korea); Dariusz Kuzminski (Poland, Ukraine); Latin Knowledge Consulting (Martha Orellana) (Venezuela); Quantec Research (Pty) Ltd (Claude van der Merwe) (South Africa); Jerry Rabas (Australia); Rose Systems (Iran); Sezen Tan (Turkey); Jorge Andres Toledo Medina (Colombia); Patrick Vlaskovits (Hungary)
Warehouse: PO Box 200, Harold Hill, Romford RM3 8UX

Eddison Sadd Editions Ltd+
St Chads House, 148 King's Cross Rd, London WC1X 9DH
Tel: (020) 7837 1968 *Fax:* (020) 7837 2025
E-mail: info@eddisonsadd.com
Web Site: www.eddisonsadd.com
Key Personnel
Mng Dir: Nick Eddison
Editorial Dir: Ian Jackson
Rights Manager: Cara Clapham
Founded: 1982

Packagers of illustrated books, kits & gift titles for international co-edition markets.
Subjects: Alternative, Animals, Pets, Astrology, Occult, Crafts, Games, Hobbies, Erotica, Health, Nutrition, How-to, Human Relations, Inspirational, Spirituality, Nonfiction (General), Self-Help, Sex
ISBN Prefix(es): 978-1-85906
Imprints: Connections Book Publishing

Edinburgh University Press Ltd
The Tun - Holyrood Rd, 12 (2f) Jackson's Entry, Edinburgh EH8 8PJ
Tel: (0131) 650 4218 *Fax:* (0131) 650 3286
E-mail: editorial@eup.ed.ac.uk; marketing@eup.ed.ac.uk
Web Site: www.euppublishing.com
Key Personnel
Non-Executive Chair: Ivon Asquith
Dir: Timothy Wright
Deputy Chief Executive & Head, Book Publishing: Jackie Jones *Tel:* (0131) 650 4217 *E-mail:* jackie.jones@eup.ed.ac.uk
Head, Finance: Jan Thomson *E-mail:* jan.thomson@eup.ed.ac.uk
Head, Journals: Sarah Edwards *E-mail:* sarah.edwards@eup.ed.ac.uk
Head, Production: Ian Davidson *E-mail:* ian.davidson@eup.ed.ac.uk
Head, Sales & Marketing: Anna Glazier *E-mail:* anna.glazier@eup.ed.ac.uk
Marketing Executive: Naomi Farmer *E-mail:* naomi.farmer@eup.ed.ac.uk
Marketing Manager: Carla Hepburn *E-mail:* carla.hepburn@eup.ed.ac.uk
Digital Sales Manager: Avril Cuthbert *E-mail:* avril.cuthbert@eup.ed.ac.uk
Project Manager: Rebecca Mackenzie *E-mail:* rebecca.mackenzie@eup.ed.ac.uk
Senior Commissioning Editor: Nicola Ramsey *E-mail:* nicola.ramsey@eup.ed.ac.uk
Commissioning Editor: Gillian Leslie *E-mail:* gillian.leslie@eup.ed.ac.uk; Carol Macdonald *E-mail:* carol.macdonald@eup.ed.ac.uk; John Watson *E-mail:* john.watson@eup.ed.ac.uk
Assistant Commissioning Editor: Jenny Daly *E-mail:* jenny.daly@eup.ed.ac.uk; Michelle Houston *E-mail:* michelle.houston@eup.ed.ac.uk
Journals Production Editor: Ann Vinnicombe *E-mail:* ann.vinnicombe@eup.ed.ac.uk
Mng Desk Editor: James Dale *E-mail:* james.dale@eup.ed.ac.uk; Eddie Clark *E-mail:* edward.clark@eup.ed.ac.uk
Production Controller: Gavin Jack *E-mail:* gavin.jack@eup.ed.ac.uk
Founded: 1948
Registered charity.
Membership(s): The Association of Learned & Professional Society Publishers; The Independent Publishers Guild; The Publishers Association; Publishing Scotland
Subjects: Film, Video, Government, Political Science, History, Language Arts, Linguistics, Law, Literature, Literary Criticism, Essays, Philosophy, Religion - Islamic, Botany, Classics, Film & Media Studies, Scottish History, Scottish Studies
ISBN Prefix(es): 978-0-85224; 978-0-7486
Parent Company: The University of Edinburgh
Foreign Rep(s): Academic Marketing Services (Michael Brightmore) (South Africa); Avicenna Partnership (Bill Kennedy) (Arab Middle East, North Africa, Turkey); Brookside Publishing Services (Ireland); Compass Academic (England, Wales); Kemper Consell Publishing (Dineke Kemper) (Benelux, Netherlands); Colin Flint Ltd (Scandinavia); ICK (Se-Yung Jun) (Korea); InterMedia Africa Ltd (Tony Moggach) (Sub-Saharan Africa); Marek Lewinson (Eastern Europe); Mare Nostrum (Frauke Feldmann) (Austria, Germany, Switzerland); Mare

Nostrum Publishing (Cristina de Lara) (Portugal, Spain); Mare Nostrum Publishing Consultants (David Pickering) (France, Italy); Maya Publishers Pvt Ltd (Surit Mitra) (India); Oxford University Press (North America); Seol Ltd (Scotland); Taylor & Francis Asia Pacific (Malaysia); Ian Taylor Associates Ltd (China); Turnkey Projects (UK) Ltd (Charles Gibbes) (Cyprus, Greece); United Publishers Services Ltd (Japan); World Press (Saleem A Malik) (Pakistan)
Distribution Center: Macmillan Distribution (MDL), Brunel Rd, Houndmills, Basingstoke, Hants RG21 6XS

Educational Explorers (Publishers) Ltd
Unit 5, Feidr Castell Business Park, Fishguard, Pembrokeshire SA65 9BB
Tel: (01348) 874890 *Fax:* (01348) 874925
E-mail: enquiries@cuisenaire.co.uk
Web Site: www.cuisenaire.co.uk
Key Personnel
Chairman: D M Gattegno
Mng Dir: M J Hollyfield
Founded: 1960
Subjects: Language Arts, Linguistics, Mathematics, Psychology, Psychiatry
ISBN Prefix(es): 978-0-85225
Parent Company: Educational Solutions (UK) Ltd
Associate Companies: The Cuisenaire Co; Educational Explorers Film Co

EG Books, see Estates Gazette Books

Egmont UK Ltd
The Yellow Bldg, 1st floor, One Nicholas Rd, London W11 4AN
Tel: (020) 3220 0400 *Fax:* (020) 3220 0401
E-mail: pressoffice@euk.egmont.com
Web Site: www.egmont.co.uk
Key Personnel
Chief Executive Officer, International: Rob McMenemy
Chief Financial Officer: Alan Hurcombe
Mng Dir, Egmont Publishing: Cally Poplak
Mng Dir, Magazines: Gillian Laskier
Consumer Insight Dir: Alison David
Production & Distribution Dir: Alison Kennedy
Public Relations Dir: Katy Cattell
Public Relations Manager: Alice Hill
Public Relations Officer: Maggie Eckel
Public Relations Executive: Emily Thomas
ISBN Prefix(es): 978-0-7497; 978-0-416; 978-0-603; 978-0-7498; 978-1-4052
Parent Company: Egmont Group
Imprints: Electric Monkey (young adult); Red Shed
Divisions: Egmont Books; Egmont Magazines
Distribution Center: Macmillan Distribution, Brunel Rd, Houndmills, Basingstoke, Hants RG21 6XS *Tel:* (01256) 302692 *Fax:* (01256) 812558; (01256) 812521 (UK)

EIC, see Energy Information Centre

EITB, *imprint of* Training Publications Ltd

Eland Publishing Ltd
61 Exmouth Market, London EC1R 4QL
Tel: (020) 7833 0762 *Fax:* (020) 7833 4434
E-mail: info@travelbooks.co.uk
Web Site: www.travelbooks.co.uk
Key Personnel
Owner: Rose Baring; John Hatt; Barnaby Rogerson *E-mail:* barnaby@travelbooks.co.uk
Publicity Dir: Stephanie Allen
Founded: 1982
Subjects: Biography, Memoirs, Fiction, Travel & Tourism
ISBN Prefix(es): 978-0-907871; 978-0-9550105; 978-1-906011

Imprints: Baring & Rogerson Books; Sickle Moon Books
Foreign Rep(s): Dufour Editions (Canada, USA); NewSouth Books (Australia); Publishers Group UK (UK)
Warehouse: Grantham Book Services (GBS), Trent Rd, Grantham, Lincs NG31 7QX
Tel: (01476) 541080 *Fax:* (01476) 541061
E-mail: orders@gbs.tbs-ltd.co.uk
Orders to: Grantham Book Services (GBS), Trent Rd, Grantham, Lincs NG31 7QX *Tel:* (01476) 541080 *Fax:* (01476) 541061 *E-mail:* orders@gbs.tbs-ltd.co.uk

ELB Publishing
31 George St, Brighton BN2 1RH
Tel: (01273) 604864 *Fax:* (01273) 687280
Web Site: www.elbpublishing.co.uk
Subjects: ELT
ISBN Prefix(es): 978-0-9522808
Parent Company: English Language Bookshop (ELB Brighton)
Distributed by Crane Publishing (Taiwan); Melting Pot Press (Australia); Zenith Publishing (New Zealand)
Foreign Rep(s): English Central (Canada, USA)

ELC International
5 Five Mile Dr, Oxford OX2 8HT
Tel: (01865) 513 186
E-mail: snyderpub@aol.com
ISBN Prefix(es): 978-0-948058; 978-0-948281
Branch Office(s)
43 Ave Paola, 1330 Rixensart, Belgium *Tel:* (026) 520284 *Fax:* (026) 530180 *E-mail:* nigel.hunt@skynet.be

Electric Monkey, *imprint of* Egmont UK Ltd

11:9, *imprint of* Neil Wilson Publishing Ltd

Edward Elgar Publishing Ltd
The Lypiatts, 15 Lansdown Rd, Cheltenham, Glos GL50 2JA
Tel: (01242) 226934 *Fax:* (01242) 262111
E-mail: info@e-elgar.co.uk; sales@e-elgar.co.uk
Web Site: www.e-elgar.co.uk
Key Personnel
Chairman: Edward Elgar *E-mail:* edward@e-elgar.co.uk
Mng Dir: Tim Williams *E-mail:* tim@e-elgar.co.uk
Sales & Marketing Manager: Hilary Quinn *E-mail:* hquinn@e-elgar.co.uk
Founded: 1986
A privately owned scholarly publisher with a focus on economics, business & law.
Subjects: Accounting, Agriculture, Business, Developing Countries, Economics, Energy, Environmental Studies, Finance, Government, Political Science, Labor, Industrial Relations, Law, Management, Marketing, Public Administration, Social Sciences, Sociology, Transportation, Women's Studies
ISBN Prefix(es): 978-1-85898; 978-1-85278; 978-1-84064; 978-1-84376; 978-1-84542; 978-1-84844; 978-1-78347; 978-1-78100; 978-1-78254; 978-1-78195
Number of titles published annually: 250 Print; 150 E-Book
Total Titles: 4,000 Print; 400 E-Book
Branch Office(s)
Heatherley House, 10 Heatherley Rd, Chamberley, Surrey GU15 3LW *Tel:* (01276) 459050 *Fax:* (01276) 685898
U.S. Office(s): Edward Elgar Publishing Inc, 9 Dewey Court, Northampton, MA 01060-3815, United States *Tel:* 413-584-5551 *Fax:* 413-584-9933 *E-mail:* elgarinfo@e-elgar.com
Foreign Rep(s): Edward Elgar Publishing Inc (North America, South America); Taylor & Francis Asia Pacific (East Asia, Malaysia,

Southeast Asia); United Publishers Services Ltd (Japan)
Orders to: Marston Book Services Ltd, 160 Eastern Ave, Milton Park, Abingdon, Oxon OX14 4SB *Tel:* (01235) 465500 *Fax:* (01235) 465555 *E-mail:* trade.orders@marston.co.uk
Web Site: www.marston.co.uk

Elkin, *imprint of* Novello & Co

Elliott & Thompson+
27 John St, London WC1N 2BX
Tel: (020) 7831 5013
E-mail: info@eandtbooks.com
Web Site: www.eandtbooks.com
Key Personnel
Chairman: Lorne Forsyth
Dir: Olivia Bays *E-mail:* olivia@eandtbooks.com
Publisher: Jennie Condell *E-mail:* jennie@eandtbooks.com
Operations Manager: Marianne Thorndahl
Senior Editor: Pippa Crane
Publicist: Alison Menzies *E-mail:* alison@eandtbooks.com
Founded: 2009
Literary works & belles lettres.
Subjects: Art, Biography, Memoirs, Fiction, History, Humor, Music, Dance, Religion - Islamic, Religion - Jewish, Sports, Athletics, Western Fiction, Food & Drink
ISBN Prefix(es): 978-1-904027; 978-1-907642; 978-1-908739; 978-1-909653; 978-1-78396
Number of titles published annually: 10 Print
Total Titles: 55 Print
Imprints: Elliott & Thompson Gold Editions; Spitfire; Spitfire Originals; Young Spitfire
Foreign Rights: InkWell Management (USA)
Distribution Center: Macmillan Distribution, Houndmills, Basingstoke, Hants RG21 6XS *Tel:* (0845) 0705656 *E-mail:* trade@macmillan.co.uk *Web Site:* pubeasy.books.macmillan-mdl.co.uk

Elliott & Thompson Gold Editions, *imprint of* Elliott & Thompson

Elm Bank Press, *imprint of* Intellect Ltd

Elsevier, *imprint of* Elsevier Ltd

Elsevier/Geo Abstracts, *imprint of* Elsevier Ltd

Elsevier Ltd+
The Boulevard, Langford Lane, Kidlington, Oxford, Oxon OX5 1GB
Tel: (01865) 843000
Web Site: www.elsevier.com
Founded: 1971
Subjects: Agriculture, Architecture & Interior Design, Behavioral Sciences, Biological Sciences, Business, Chemistry, Chemical Engineering, Communications, Computer Science, Earth Sciences, Economics, Education, Electronics, Electrical Engineering, Energy, Environmental Studies, Health, Nutrition, Library & Information Sciences, Mechanical Engineering, Medicine, Nursing, Dentistry, Technology
ISBN Prefix(es): 978-0-08; 978-0-85334; 978-1-85166; 978-1-85861; 978-0-4430
Parent Company: Elsevier BV, Amsterdam, Netherlands
Ultimate Parent Company: RELX Group PLC, Radarweg 29, 1043 NX Amsterdam, Netherlands
Imprints: Academic Cell Press; Academic Press; Architectural Press; Bailliere Tindall Ltd; Butterworth Heinemann Ltd; Chandos Publishing; Churchill Livingstone; Digital Press; Elsevier; Elsevier/Geo Abstracts; Gulf Professional Publishing; JAI; Made Simple Books; Morgan

Kauffman; Mosby; Newnes; North Holland; Saunders; William Andrew
Branch Office(s)
20-22 E London St, Edinburgh EH7 34BQ
Tel: (0131) 524 1700 *Fax:* (0131) 524 1800
32 Jamestown Rd, London NW1 7BY *Tel:* (020) 7424 4200 *Fax:* (020) 7483 2293
84 Theobald's Rd, London WC1X 8RR *Tel:* (020) 7611 4500 *Fax:* (020) 7611 4501
Linacre House, Jordan Hill, Oxford, Oxon OX2 8DP *Tel:* (01865) 310366 *Fax:* (01865) 314541
Warehouse: Elsevier Editora Ltda, Rua Sao Januario, 581, Sao Christavao, 20291-004 Rio de Janeiro-RJ, Brazil *Tel:* (021) 3970 9300 *Fax:* (021) 2507 1991

Elwin Street Productions
3 Percy St, London W1T 1DE
Tel: (020) 7637 3273
E-mail: info@elwinstreet.com
Web Site: www.elwinstreet.com
Key Personnel
Publisher: Silvia Langford *E-mail:* silvia@elwinstreet.com
Foreign Rights Manager: Elena Battista
E-mail: elena@elwinstreet.com
Co-edition publisher.
Subjects: Advertising, Astronomy, Cookery, Fashion, Health, Nutrition, Humor, Language Arts, Linguistics, Literature, Literary Criticism, Essays, Mathematics, Natural History, Outdoor Recreation, Philosophy, Psychology, Psychiatry, Science (General), Sports, Athletics, Wine & Spirits, Forensics
ISBN Prefix(es): 978-1-906761 (Modern Books); 978-0-9546309 (Modern Books); 978-0-9556421
Imprints: Modern Books

Emerald Group Publishing Ltd
Howard House, Wagon Lane, Bingley, W Yorks BD16 1WA
Tel: (01274) 777700 *Fax:* (01274) 785201
E-mail: emerald@emeraldinsight.com; editorial@emeraldinsight.com
Web Site: www.emeraldgrouppublishing.com
Key Personnel
Executive Chairman: Richard Bevan
Chief Executive Officer: Vicky Williams
Chief Technology Officer: Phill Jones
Publisher: Jenny McCall
Publishing Dir: Tony Roche
Editorial Dir, Social Science Books & Publisher, Sociology, Criminology & Social Policy: Philippa Grand, PhD
Editorial Dir & Head, Business, Finance & Economic Books: Pete Baker
Operations Dir: Brian McDermott
Finance Dir: Simon Cox
Head, Books Marketing: Amy Potter
Founded: 1967
Subjects: Business, Education, Engineering (General), Human Relations, Language Arts, Linguistics, Library & Information Sciences, Management, Marketing, Social Sciences, Sociology, Audiology, Public Policy
ISBN Prefix(es): 978-1-84544; 978-1-84663; 978-1-84855; 978-1-84950; 978-0-85724; 978-1-78052; 978-1-78350; 978-1-78441; 978-1-78190

The Emma Press
118 Bathurst, Winnerst, Wokingham, Berks RG41 5JF
E-mail: queries@theemmapress.com
Web Site: theemmapress.com
Key Personnel
Founder & Publisher: Emma Wright
Co-Editor: Rachel Piercey
Founded: 2012
Subjects: Poetry
ISBN Prefix(es): 978-0-9574596; 978-1-910139

Associate Companies: Valley Press
Distribution Center: Central Books Ltd, One Heath Park Industrial Estate, Freshwater Rd, Dagenham RM8 1RX *Tel:* (020) 8525 8800 *Fax:* (020) 8599 2694 *E-mail:* orders@centralbooks.com *Web Site:* www.centralbooks.com

Empire of the Senses, *imprint of* Dedalus Ltd

Encyclopaedia Britannica (UK) Ltd
Subsidiary of Encyclopaedia Britannica Inc
Unity Wharf, 2nd floor, Mill St, London SE1 2BH
Tel: (020) 7500 7800 *Fax:* (020) 7500 7878
E-mail: enquiries@britannica.co.uk
Web Site: britannica.co.uk
Key Personnel
Senior Vice President: Michael Ross
Mng Dir, EMEA: Khurshid Khan
International Business Development Dir, EMEA: Caroline Kennard *E-mail:* ckennard@britannica.co.uk
Finance Dir, EMEA: Ed Downey
Technical/Product Development Manager: Adrian Murray *E-mail:* amurray@britannica.co.uk
ISBN Prefix(es): 978-1-61535
Associate Companies: Encyclopaedia Britannica (Australia) Ltd, Level 1, 9 Help St, Chatswood, NSW 2067, Australia *Tel:* (02) 9915 8800 *Fax:* (02) 9419 5247 *E-mail:* sales@eb.com.au *Web Site:* edu.eb.com; Encyclopaedia Britannica (India) Pvt Ltd, A-41, Mohan Co-Operative Industrial Estate, Mathura Rd, New Delhi 110 044, India *Tel:* (011) 4715 4100 *Fax:* (011) 4715 4116 *E-mail:* online@ebindia.com *Web Site:* www.britannicaindia.com; Britannica Japan Co Ltd, Da Vinci Nishi-Gotanda 2F, 8-3-16 Nishi-Gotanda, Shinagawa-ku, Tokyo 141-0031, Japan *Tel:* (03) 5436 1390 *Fax:* (03) 5436 1380 *E-mail:* info@britannica.co.jp *Web Site:* www.britannica.co.jp; Korea Britannica Corp, Younghan B/D 7F, 59-23 Chungmuro 3ga, Joong-gu, Seoul 100-013, South Korea *Tel:* (02) 1588 1768 *Fax:* (02) 2278 9983 *E-mail:* webmaster@britannica.co.kr *Web Site:* www.britannica.co.kr
Foreign Rep(s): ABE Marketing International (Marek Nowakowski) (Poland); Akademischer Lexikadienst (Hans-Dieter Blatter) (Austria, Germany, Luxembourg, Switzerland); Avicenna Partnership (Claire de Gruchy) (Cyprus, Greece, Malta, North Africa, Turkey); Avicenna Partnership (Bill Kennedy) (Middle East); Calamo (Pedro Tejerina) (Spain); CenterCom (Darya Anashkina) (Russia); Ted Dougherty (Austria, Germany, Netherlands, Switzerland); EEP Book Services (Gibrine Adam) (Ghana); Encyclopaedia Britannica France (Universalis) (Belgium, France); Colin Flint Ltd (Ben Greig) (Scandinavia); Folio Ltd (Dima Mozhzhukhin) (Ukraine); Havilah Procurement (Lanre Adesuyi) (Nigeria); Iberian Book Services (Peter Prout) (Gibraltar, Portugal, Spain); IMA (Eastern Europe, Sub-Saharan Africa); International Book Distributor (Michal Wapinski) (Poland); Jacklin Enterprises (Pty) Ltd (Liesl Smit) (South Africa); Mare Nostrum (David Pickering) (Italy); Negar-e-Soraya Co Ltd (Soraya Imani) (Iran); Nobis Gorjup & Sauperl DNO (Gorazd Gorjup) (Slovenia); Omega Marketing (Essam Saad) (Egypt); Prior Books (Ion Arzoiu) (Romania); Sabra (Dagmar Al-Salman) (Czechia); Salvesen International References (Inge Salvesen) (Norway); Training Club (Valter Bozzoli) (Italy)
Distribution Center: Combined Book Services *Tel:* (01892) 839814 *Fax:* (01892) 837272 *E-mail:* britannica@combook.co.uk

Endeavour London Ltd
21-31 Woodfield Rd, London W9 2BA

Tel: (020) 7604 8624 *Fax:* (020) 7604 8645
Web Site: www.endeavourlondon.com
Subjects: Architecture & Interior Design, Art, Fashion, History, Photography, Sports, Athletics, Design, Entertainment
ISBN Prefix(es): 978-1-908271; 978-1-873913
Total Titles: 55 Print

Energy Information Centre+
Ravens Court, Ravensbank Business Park, Redditch B98 9EY
Tel: (01527) 511 700 *Fax:* (01527) 512 712
E-mail: theenergyexperts@eic.co.uk
Web Site: www.eic.co.uk
Key Personnel
Mng Dir: Simon Butterfield
Founded: 1975
Subjects: Energy
ISBN Prefix(es): 978-0-905332; 978-1-874334
Parent Company: Utilitywise PLC
Branch Office(s)
Linden Sq, Kings Rd, Bury St Edmunds, Suffolk IP33 3DJ

English Heritage
The Engine House, Fire Fly Ave, Swindon SN2 2EH
Tel: (01793) 414700 *Fax:* (01793) 414707
E-mail: customers@english-heritage.org.uk
Web Site: www.english-heritage.org.uk
Key Personnel
Chairman: Sir Tim Laurence
Chief Executive: Kate Mavor
Marketing Dir: Luke Whitcomb
Commercial Dir: Shirley Jackson
Finance Dir: Jon Bullen
Operations Manager: Becky Smith
Subjects: Archaeology, Architecture & Interior Design, History, Sports, Athletics, Architectural History, Guidebooks, Social History, Sporting Heritage
ISBN Prefix(es): 978-1-85074; 978-1-873592; 978-1-905624; 978-1-84802

Enitharmon Press
10 Bury Pl, London WC1A 2JL
Tel: (020) 7430 0844
E-mail: info@enitharmon.co.uk
Web Site: www.enitharmon.co.uk
Key Personnel
Artistic Dir: Stephen Stuart-Smith
  E-mail: stephen@enitharmon.co.uk
Business Dir: Isabel Brittain *E-mail:* isabel@enitharmon.co.uk
Gallery Manager: Kathryn McCandless
  E-mail: kathryn@enitharmon.co.uk
Sales & Production: Lavinia Singer
  E-mail: info@enitharmon.co.uk
Bookkeeper: Alison Barker *E-mail:* accounts@enitharmon.co.uk
Founded: 1967
Subjects: Biography, Memoirs, Literature, Literary Criticism, Essays, Poetry
ISBN Prefix(es): 978-0-905289; 978-1-870612; 978-0-901111; 978-1-904634; 978-1-900564
Associate Companies: Enitharmon Editions

Entice, *imprint of* Little, Brown Book Group

Entra, *imprint of* Training Publications Ltd

EP Books, see Evangelical Press

Equinox Publishing Ltd+
415, The Workstation, 15 Paternoster Row, Sheffield S1 2BX
Tel: (0114) 221 0285 *Fax:* (0114) 279 6522
Web Site: www.equinoxpub.com
Key Personnel
Editorial & Marketing Manager: Val Hall
  E-mail: vhall@equinoxpub.com

Founded: 2003
Independent publisher of academic books & journals in the humanities. Trade historic cookery & popular music list.
Subjects: Anthropology, Archaeology, Biblical Studies, Biography, Memoirs, Cookery, History, Language Arts, Linguistics, Music, Dance, Pop Culture, Religion - Buddhist, Religion - Catholic, Religion - Hindu, Religion - Islamic, Religion - Jewish, Religion - Protestant, Religion - Other, Theology, Women's Studies
ISBN Prefix(es): 978-1-84553; 978-1-904768; 978-1-908049; 978-1-78179; 978-1-870962
Number of titles published annually: 50 Print; 50 E-Book
Total Titles: 300 Print; 200 E-Book
Imprints: Southover Press (historic cookery)
Foreign Rep(s): APD Singapore (Brunei, Cambodia, Indonesia, Laos, Malaysia, Philippines, Singapore, Thailand, Vietnam); Avicenna Partnership (Middle East, North Africa, Turkey); Tim Burland (Japan); Colin Flint Ltd (Scandinavia); Charles Gibbes (Cyprus, Greece, Malta); Laslo Horvath (Eastern Europe); ISD (Ian Stevens) (North America); Maya Publishers Pvt Ltd (Bangladesh, India, Sri Lanka); Quantum Publishing Solutions (Ireland, UK); Ian Taylor Associates Ltd (China, Hong Kong, Korea, Taiwan)
Foreign Rights: Eulana SRL (France, Germany, Italy, Japan, Korea, Portugal, Spain)
Warehouse: Macmillan Distribution Ltd, Brunel Rd, Houndmills, Basingstoke, Hants RG21 6XS *Tel:* (01256) 302692 *Fax:* (01256) 812558 *E-mail:* orders@macmillan.co.uk (book trade, worldwide exc Australia, New Zealand & North America)
ISD, 70 Enterprise Dr, Suite 2, Bristol, CT 06010, United States, Contact: Ian Stevens *Tel:* 860-584-6546 *Fax:* 860-540-1001 *E-mail:* ian@isdistribution.com (Canada, Mexico & USA)
Distribution Center: Macmillan Distribution Ltd, Brunel Rd, Houndmills, Basingstoke, Hants RG21 6XS *Tel:* (01256) 302692 *Fax:* (01256) 812558 *E-mail:* orders@macmillan.co.uk (book trade, worldwide exc Australia, New Zealand & North America)
Kinokuniya Co Ltd, Book Import Dept, Shin-Mizonokuchi Bldg 2F, 5-7, Hisamoto 3-Chome, Takatsu-ku, Kawasaki, Kanagawa 213-8506, Japan *Tel:* (044) 874-9642 *Fax:* (044) 829-1025 *E-mail:* bkimp@kinokuniya.co.jp
MHM Ltd, 1-1-13-4F Kanda Jimbocho, Chiyoda-ku, Tokyo 101-0051, Japan, Contact: Mark Gresham *Tel:* (03) 3518 9181 *E-mail:* gresham@mhmlimited.co.jp
Maruzen Co Ltd, 1-9-18, Kaigan, Minato-ku, Tokyo 105-0022, Japan *Tel:* (03) 3272-3851 *Fax:* (03) 3272-3920 *E-mail:* promote@maruzen.co.jp
ISD, 70 Enterprise Dr, Suite 2, Bristol, CT 06010, United States, Contact: Ian Stevens *Tel:* 860-584-6546 *Fax:* 860-540-1001 *E-mail:* ian@isdistribution.com (Canada, Mexico & USA)
Orders to: Macmillan Distribution Ltd, Brunel Rd, Houndmills, Basingstoke, Hants RG21 6XS *Tel:* (01256) 302692 *Fax:* (01256) 812558 *E-mail:* orders@macmillan.co.uk (book trade, worldwide exc Australia, New Zealand & North America)
ISD, 70 Enterprise Dr, Suite 2, Bristol, CT 06010, United States, Contact: Ian Stevens *Tel:* 860-584-6546 *Fax:* 860-540-1001 *E-mail:* ian@isdistribution.com (Canada, Mexico & USA)
Returns: Macmillan Distribution Ltd, Brunel Rd, Houndmills, Basingstoke, Hants RG21 6XS *Tel:* (01256) 302692 *Fax:* (01256) 812558 *E-mail:* orders@macmillan.co.uk (book trade, worldwide exc Australia, New Zealand & North America); ISD, 70 Enterprise Dr, Suite

2, Bristol, CT 06010, United States *Tel:* 860-584-6546 *Fax:* 860-540-1001 (Canada, Mexico & USA)

Ernest Press
17 Carleton Dr, Glasgow G46 6AQ
Tel: (0141) 637 1410
Web Site: www.ernest-press.co.uk
Key Personnel
Proprietor: Joy Hodgkiss
Founded: 1985
Subjects: Outdoor Recreation, Mountain Biking Guides, Mountaineering
ISBN Prefix(es): 978-0-948153
Warehouse: Cordee Ltd, 11 Jacknell Rd, Dodwells Bridge Industrial Estate, Hinckley, Leics LE10 3BS *Tel:* (01455) 611185 *E-mail:* info@cordee.co.uk *Web Site:* www.cordee.co.uk

Ernst & Young+
One More London Pl, London SE1 2AF
Tel: (020) 7951 2000 *Fax:* (020) 7951 1345
Web Site: www.ey.com/uk
Key Personnel
Chairman: Steve Varley
Also chartered accountants & business advisers.
Subjects: Accounting, Foreign Countries, Management
ISBN Prefix(es): 978-0-9505745; 978-1-873278
Branch Office(s)
Becket House, One Lambeth Palace Rd, London SE1 7EU

The Erskine Press Ltd+
The White House, Sandfield Lane, Eccles, Norwich NR16 2PB
Tel: (01953) 88 72 77 *Fax:* (01953) 88 83 61
E-mail: books@erskine-press.com
Web Site: www.erskine-press.com
Key Personnel
Chief Executive: Crispin de Boos
Founded: 1986
Specialize in literature on Antarctic exploration.
Subjects: Architecture & Interior Design, Art, Astronomy, Cookery, History, Travel & Tourism, World War II
ISBN Prefix(es): 978-1-85297; 978-0-948285; 978-0-9506104
Total Titles: 58 Print

ESB, see European Schoolbooks Ltd (ESB)

Essential Works
29 Clerkenwell Green, London EC1R 0DU
Tel: (020) 7017 0890 *Fax:* (020) 7014 3169
Web Site: www.essentialworks.co.uk
Key Personnel
Mng Dir: John Conway
Subjects: Art, How-to, Music, Dance, Nonfiction (General), Photography
ISBN Prefix(es): 978-0-9545493; 978-1-906615
Imprints: Rocket 88 Books

Estates Gazette Books
The Eye, One Proctor St, London WC1V 6EU
Tel: (020) 7911 1701 *Fax:* (020) 7911 1798
E-mail: info@estatesgazette.com
Web Site: www.estatesgazette.com
Key Personnel
Head, Marketing: Ben Colclough *Tel:* (020) 7911 1716 *E-mail:* ben.colclough@estatesgazette.com
Founded: 1858
Leading providers of property information.
ISBN Prefix(es): 978-0-08; 978-0-7282; 978-0-900361
Parent Company: Reed Business Information Ltd

Ethics International Press Ltd+
St Andrews Castle, St Andrews St South, Bury St Edmunds, Suffolk IP33 3PH
Tel: (01954) 710086 *Fax:* (01954) 710103

E-mail: info@ethicspress.com
Web Site: www.ethicspress.com
Founded: 1993
Specialize in academic, business, government, law, accounting & banking.
Membership(s): The Publishers Association.
Subjects: Business, Environmental Studies, Government, Political Science, Philosophy, Public Administration, Anti-corruption, Banking, Corporate Social Responsibility, Environmental Ethics, Ethics in Business, Government Ethics
ISBN Prefix(es): 978-1-871891
Number of titles published annually: 3 Print; 6 E-Book
Total Titles: 10 Print; 6 E-Book
Associate Companies: Ethics International Multimedia Ltd *Web Site:* www.ethicsmultimedia.co.uk

EuroCrime, *imprint of* Arcadia Books Ltd

Euromonitor International Ltd+
60-61 Britton St, London EC1M 5UX
Tel: (020) 7251 8024 *Fax:* (020) 7608 3149
E-mail: info@euromonitor.com
Web Site: www.euromonitor.com
Key Personnel
Founder: Robert Senior
Executive Chairman: Trevor Fenwick
Chief Executive: Tim Kitchin
Founded: 1972
Provider of global business intelligence & strategic market analysis.
Membership(s): European Directory Publishers Association; UK Directory Publishers Association.
Subjects: Business, Economics, Marketing, Publishing & Book Trade Reference, Demographics
ISBN Prefix(es): 978-0-903706; 978-0-86338; 978-1-84264
Number of titles published annually: 25 Print
Branch Office(s)
Euromonitor International (Australia) Pty Ltd, 134 William St, Suite 401, Level 4, Sydney, NSW 2011, Australia *Tel:* (02) 9581 9200 *Fax:* (02) 9581 9299 *E-mail:* info-australia@euromonitor.com
Euromonitor International Research & Consulting Ltda, Alameda Xingu, 350, Edifico I-Tower, 16th floor, conj 1603, Alphaville - Barueri, Sao Paulo-SP 06455-030, Brazil *Tel:* (011) 2970 2150 *Fax:* (011) 2970 2155 *E-mail:* info-brazil@euromonitor.com
Euromonitor International, Ave Apoquindo 4501, 11th floor, Off 1102 Las Condes, Santiago 7580125, Chile *Tel:* (02) 29157200 *Fax:* (02) 29157201 *E-mail:* info@euromonitor.cl
Euromonitor International (Shanghai) Co Ltd, Unit 01-08, 11/F Cross Tower, 318 Fuzhou Rd, Shanghai 200001, China *Tel:* (021) 6032 1088 *Fax:* (021) 6032 1080 *E-mail:* info@euromonitor.com.cn
Euromonitor Research and Consulting (India) Pvt Ltd, Unit No N1503, 15th floor, World Trade Center, Brigade Gateway Campus, 26/1 Dr Rajkumar Rd, Malleswaram-Rajinagar, Bangalore 560055, India *Tel:* (080) 4904 0500 *Fax:* (080) 4904 0501 *E-mail:* info-india@euromonitor.com
Level 34, Shiroyama Trust Tower, 4-3-1 Toranomon, Minato-ku, Tokyo 105-6016, Japan *Tel:* (03) 3436 2100 *Fax:* (03) 3436 2199 *E-mail:* info-japan@euromonitor.com
Euromonitor International, Jogailos St 4, Vilnius LT-01116, Lithuania *Tel:* (05) 243 1577 *Fax:* (05) 243 1599 *E-mail:* info@euromonitor.lt
Euromonitor International (Asia) Pte Ltd, ABI Plaza, 11 Keppel Rd, No 06-00, Singapore 089057, Singapore *Tel:* 6429 0590 *Fax:* 6324 1855 *E-mail:* info@euromonitor.com.sg

Euromonitor International, One Waterford Pl, Century Blvd, Century City, Capetown 7441, South Africa *Tel:* (021) 524 3000 *Fax:* (021) 552 7071
Euromonitor International, Dubai Silicon Oasis, F-Wing, Off 606-607, PO Box 341155, Dubai, United Arab Emirates *Tel:* (04) 372 4363 *Fax:* (04) 372 4370 *E-mail:* info-mena@euromonitor.com
U.S. Office(s): Euromonitor International Inc, 224 S Michigan Ave, Suite 1500, Chicago, IL 60604, United States *Tel:* 312-922-1115 *Fax:* 312-922-1157 *E-mail:* insight@euromonitorintl.com
Distributed by Gale Research

Europa Editions UK
8 Blackstock Mews, Islington, London N4 2BT
E-mail: info@europaeditions.com
Web Site: www.europaeditions.com
Key Personnel
Dir: Daniela Petracco
Subjects: Fiction, Nonfiction (General)
ISBN Prefix(es): 978-1-933372; 978-1-60945
Associate Companies: Europa Editions, Via Camozzi, 1, 00195 Rome RM, Italy, Contact: Simona Olivito *Tel:* (06) 37 22 829 *Fax:* (06) 37 35 1096 *E-mail:* info@europaeditions.com
U.S. Office(s): Europa Editions, 214 W 29 St, Suite 1003, New York, NY 10001, United States *Tel:* 212-868-6844 *Fax:* 212-868-6845
Orders to: Turnaround Publisher Services Ltd, Unit 3, Olympia Trading Estate, Coburg Rd, Wood Green, London N22 6TZ *Tel:* (020) 8829 3000 *E-mail:* orders@turnaround-uk.com (UK & Ireland)
Pearson Canada Distribution Centre, 195 Harry Walker Parkway N, New Market, ON L3Y 7B4, Canada *Tel:* 905-713-3852
Penguin Group (USA) Inc, 405 Murray Hill Parkway, East Rutherford, NJ 07073-2136, United States *E-mail:* orders@us.penguingroup.com

European Schoolbooks Ltd (ESB)
The Runnings, Cheltenham GL51 9PQ
Tel: (01242) 245252 *Fax:* (01242) 224137
E-mail: direct@esb.co.uk
Web Site: www.eurobooks.co.uk
Founded: 1964
Also act as distributor for European publishers.
Subjects: Economics, Environmental Studies, Foreign Countries, Geography, Geology, Language Arts, Linguistics, Social Sciences, Sociology
ISBN Prefix(es): 978-0-85048; 978-0-85233
Subsidiaries: European Schoolbooks Publishing
Bookshop(s): The European Bookshop & Young Europeans Bookstore, 5 Warwick St, London W1B 5LU *Tel:* (020) 7734 5259 *Fax:* (020) 7287 1720 *E-mail:* mrg@esb.co.uk; The Italian Bookshop, 123 Gloucester Rd, London SW7 4TE *Tel:* (020) 7240 1634 *Fax:* (020) 7370 3129 *E-mail:* italian@esb.co.uk

Evangelical Library of Wales, *imprint of* Bryntirion Press

Evangelical Press
Venture House, 1st floor, 5 & 6 Silver Court Watchmead, Welwyn Garden City, Herts AL7 1TS
Tel: (0333) 772 0214
E-mail: sales@epbooks.org
Web Site: www.epbooks.org
Founded: 1967
International publisher of Christian, Evangelical & Reformed literature.
Membership(s): Affinity (UK); CBA; ECPA.
Subjects: Biblical Studies, Religion - Protestant, Theology
ISBN Prefix(es): 978-0-85234
Number of titles published annually: 25 Print
Total Titles: 350 Print

Subsidiaries: Europresse Sarl (French publisher)
Distributor for Bryntirion Press; Carey Publications; Grace Publications Trust
Distribution Center: JPL Fulfillment, 3741 Linden Ave SE, Wyoming, MI 49548, United States *E-mail:* sales@jplbooks.com

Evans Mitchell Books
184-192 Drummond St, 4th floor, London NW1 3HP
Tel: (020) 7650 1640
E-mail: info@embooks.co.uk
Web Site: www.embooks.co.uk
Key Personnel
Chief Executive Officer: Caroline Minshell
Subjects: Cookery, Natural History, Photography, Wildlife
ISBN Prefix(es): 978-1-901268
Foreign Rep(s): A-Z Africa Book Services (Anita Zih) (Africa); AG Distribution (Gerald Wratten) (South Africa); Chris Ashdown (Asia, Middle East); Bookport Associates Ltd (Continental Europe); Canadian Manda Group (Canada); Intermedia Americana Ltd (David Williams) (Latin America); Pansing Distribution Pte Ltd (Brunei, Malaysia, Singapore); Peribo Pty Ltd (Michael Coffey) (Australia, New Zealand); Quayside Publishing Group (USA)
Distribution Center: Orca Book Services, Fleets Corner, Unit A3, Poole, Dorset BH17 0LA *Tel:* (01202) 665432 *E-mail:* orders@orcabookservices.co.uk

Evidence Press, *imprint of* Totally Entwined Group Ltd

Ex Libris Press+
11 Regents Pl, Bradford on Avon, Wilts BA15 1ED
Tel: (01225) 865191; (07980) 356081 (cell)
Fax: (01225) 865191
Web Site: www.ex-librisbooks.co.uk
Key Personnel
Proprietor: Roger Jones *E-mail:* roger.jones@ex-librisbooks.co.uk
Founded: 1981
Local & regional press covering west country & Channel Islands. Primarily paperbacks as well as an occasional hardcover.
Subjects: Biography, Memoirs, Geography, Geology, History, Literature, Literary Criticism, Essays, Countryside & Walking Guides
ISBN Prefix(es): 978-0-9506563; 978-0-948578; 978-1-903341
Number of titles published annually: 4 Print
Total Titles: 130 Print
Imprints: Ex Libris Self Publishing (ELSP); Seaflower Books

Ex Libris Self Publishing (ELSP), *imprint of* Ex Libris Press

Excellent Press, *imprint of* Quiller Publishing Ltd

Helen Exley Giftbooks+
16 Chalk Hill, Watford, Herts WD19 4BG
Tel: (01923) 474480
E-mail: enquiries@helenexley.com
Web Site: www.helenexleygiftbooks.com
Key Personnel
Chief Executive Officer: Helen Exley
Dir: Lincoln Exley; Richard Exley
Creative Dir: Dalton Exley
Founded: 1976
Specializes in giftbooks, family & relationships, inspirational & biographies.
Subjects: Biography, Memoirs, Human Relations, Humor, Inspirational, Spirituality, Nonfiction (General)

ISBN Prefix(es): 978-1-85015; 978-1-86187; 978-0-905521; 978-1-905130; 978-1-84634
Total Titles: 400 Print
Associate Companies: Exley SA, 13 rue de Genval, B-1301 Bierges, Belgium; Exley Handels GmbH, Kreuzherrenstr 14, 52379 Langerwehe, Germany *Tel:* (02423) 7210 *Fax:* (02423) 5219
Subsidiaries: Exley Giftbooks
Distributed by Exley Handel GmbH (Germany); Exley SA (Belgium)

Exley Publications Ltd, see Helen Exley Giftbooks

Expert, *imprint of* The Random House Group Ltd, a Penguin Random House Company

Express Publishing
Liberty House, Greenham Business Park, Newbury, Berks RG19 6HW
Tel: (01635) 817 363 *Fax:* (01635) 817 473
E-mail: inquiries@expresspublishing.co.uk
Web Site: www.expresspublishing.co.uk
Founded: 1988
Subjects: Education, Language Arts, Linguistics, ELT
ISBN Prefix(es): 978-1-84216; 978-1-903128; 978-1-84325; 978-1-84466

Eye Books+
8 Peacock Yard, Iliffe St, London SE17 3LH
Tel: (0845) 4508870 *Fax:* (020) 7708 2942
Web Site: eye-books.com
Key Personnel
Founder, Sales & Marketing: Dan Hiscocks
    Tel: (07973) 861 869 *E-mail:* dan@eye-books.com
Editor-in-Chief: Martha Ellen Zenfell
Production: Jenny Orr
Founded: 1996
Membership(s): IPG.
Subjects: Biography, Memoirs, Inspirational, Spirituality, Cycling
ISBN Prefix(es): 978-1-903070; 978-1-908646
Foreign Rep(s): Independent Publishers Group (IPG) (Canada, USA); NewSouth Books (Australia, New Zealand)
Distribution Center: Littlehampton Book Services Ltd, Faraday Close, Durrington, Worthing, West Sussex BN13 3RB *Tel:* (01903) 828500; (01903) 828501 (customer service)
    Web Site: lbsltd.wp.hachette.co.uk

FAB Press+
2 Farleigh, Ramsden Rd, Godalming, Surrey GU7 1QE
Tel: (01483) 527293
E-mail: info@fabpress.com
Web Site: www.fabpress.com
Key Personnel
Owner & Editorial Dir: Harvey Fenton
    E-mail: harvey@fabpress.com
Founded: 1997
Subjects: Alternative, Art, Asian Studies, Biography, Memoirs, Erotica, Film, Video, Music, Dance, Photography, Pop Culture, Television
ISBN Prefix(es): 978-0-9529260; 978-1-903254
Number of titles published annually: 6 Print
Total Titles: 40 Print; 1 E-Book
Distribution Center: Turnaround Publisher Services, Olympia Trading Estate, Unit 3, Coburg Rd, London N22 6TZ *Tel:* (020) 8829 3002
    E-mail: customercare@turnaround-uk.com *Web Site:* www.turnaround-uk.com (UK & Europe)
SCB Distributors, 15608 S New Century Dr, Gardena, CA 90248, United States *Tel:* 310-532-9400 *E-mail:* scb@scbdistributors.com
    Web Site: www.scbdistributors.com (USA & Canada)

Faber & Faber Ltd+
Bloomsbury House, 74-77 Great Russell St, London WC1B 3DA
Tel: (020) 7927 3800 *Fax:* (020) 7927 3801; (020) 7927 3805 (sales)
E-mail: gasales@faber.co.uk
Web Site: www.faber.co.uk
Key Personnel
Chief Executive Officer & Publisher: Stephen Page
Dir, Publishing Services: Nigel Marsh
Publisher, Adult: Alex Bowler
Publisher, Children's: Leah Thaxton
Editorial Dir: Walter Donohue; Laura Hassan; Louisa Joyner
International & Digital Sales Dir: Miles Poynton
    Tel: (020) 7927 3870
Sales & Services Dir: Charlotte Robertson
    Tel: (020) 7927 3856
UK Sales Dir: Neal Price *Tel:* (020) 7927 3857
Commissioning Editor, Faber Children's: Alice Swan
Editor-at-Large: Jarvis Cocker
Founded: 1929
Also distributor.
Subjects: Art, Biography, Memoirs, Drama, Theater, Fiction, Film, Video, History, How-to, Literature, Literary Criticism, Essays, Music, Dance, Philosophy, Poetry, Psychology, Psychiatry, Radio, TV, Religion - Other, Social Sciences, Sociology, Wine & Spirits
ISBN Prefix(es): 978-0-571; 978-1-78335
Parent Company: Geoffrey Faber Holdings
Imprints: Faber Digital; Faber Finds; Faber Kids; Faber Modern Classics; Guardian Faber
U.S. Office(s): Faber & Faber Inc, 19 Union Sq W, New York, NY 10003, United States *Fax:* 212-633-9385
Foreign Rep(s): Allen & Unwin Pty Ltd (Australia, New Zealand); Jonathan Ball Publishers (South Africa); China Publishers Marketing (Benjamin Pan) (China); Gill Hess Ltd (Ireland); IMA (David Williams) (Caribbean, Latin America); Cristian Juncu (Eastern Europe); Penguin Books Canada Ltd (Tim Carter) (Canada); Penguin Books India (India, Sri Lanka); Penguin Books Malaysia Sdn Bhd (Malaysia); Penguin Books SA (Italy); Penguin Books Singapore (Singapore); Penguin Espana (Portugal, Spain)
Distribution Center: The Book Service Ltd, Distribution Centre, Colchester Rd, Frating Green, Colchester, Essex CO7 7DW *Tel:* (01206) 256000 *Fax:* (01206) 255715 *E-mail:* sales@tbs-ltd.co.uk *Web Site:* www.thebookservice.co.uk

Faber Digital, *imprint of* Faber & Faber Ltd

Faber Finds, *imprint of* Faber & Faber Ltd

Faber Kids, *imprint of* Faber & Faber Ltd

Faber Modern Classics, *imprint of* Faber & Faber Ltd

Fabian Society
61 Petty France, Westminster, London SW1H 9EU
Tel: (020) 7227 4900 *Fax:* (020) 7976 7153
E-mail: info@fabians.org.uk; bookshop@fabian-society.org.uk (orders)
Web Site: www.fabians.org.uk
Key Personnel
General Secretary: Andrew Harrop
    E-mail: andrew.harrop@fabians.org.uk
Editorial Dir: Ed Wallis *E-mail:* ed.wallis@fabians.org.uk
Dir, Operations: Phil Mutero *E-mail:* phil.mutero@fabians.org.uk

Media & Communications Manager: Claire Sewell *E-mail:* claire.sewell@fabians.org.uk
Founded: 1884
Subjects: Economics, Government, Political Science
ISBN Prefix(es): 978-0-7163
Subsidiaries: NCLC Publishing Society Ltd

Facet Publishing+
Imprint of Chartered Institute of Library & Information Professionals (CILIP)
7 Ridgmount St, London WC1E 7AE
Tel: (020) 7255 0590 *Fax:* (020) 7255 0591
E-mail: info@facetpublishing.co.uk
Web Site: www.facetpublishing.co.uk; www.cilip.org.uk
Key Personnel
Publishing Dir: Helen Carley *Tel:* (020) 7255 0592 *E-mail:* helen.carley@facetpublishing.co.uk
Marketing Manager: James Williams *Tel:* (020) 7255 0597 *E-mail:* james.williams@facetpublishing.co.uk
Production Manager: Kathryn Beecroft *Tel:* (020) 7255 0595 *E-mail:* kathryn.beecroft@facetpublishing.co.uk
Sales Manager & Permission Rights: Rohini Ramachandran *Tel:* (020) 7255 0594 *E-mail:* rohini.ramachandran@facetpublishing.co.uk
Commissioning Editor: Damian Mitchell *Tel:* (020) 7255 0593 *E-mail:* damian.mitchell@facetpublishing.co.uk
Founded: 1980
Specialize in library & information science.
Subjects: Computer Science, Library & Information Sciences, Management, Technology
ISBN Prefix(es): 978-0-85365; 978-1-85604; 978-1-872088
Foreign Rep(s): American Library Association (Canada, USA); Co Info Pty Ltd (Australia, New Zealand); Iberian Book Services (Portugal, Spain); International Publishing Services Ltd (Algeria, Bahrain, Cyprus, Egypt, Iran, Iraq, Israel, Jordan, Kuwait, Lebanon, Libya, Malta, Morocco, Oman, Qatar, Saudi Arabia, Syria, Tunisia, Turkey, United Arab Emirates, Yemen); Marek Lewinson (Albania, Armenia, Azerbaijan, Belarus, Bosnia and Herzegovina, Bulgaria, Croatia, Czechia, Estonia, Georgia, Hungary, Kazakhstan, Kyrgyzstan, Latvia, Lithuania, Macedonia, Moldova, Mongolia, Montenegro, Poland, Romania, Russia, Serbia, Slovakia, Slovenia, Tajikistan, Turkmenistan, Ukraine, Uzbekistan); Network Academic Book Agency (Belgium, Luxembourg, Netherlands); Taylor & Frances Asia Pacific (Cambodia, China, Hong Kong, Indonesia, Korea, Laos, Malaysia, Myanmar, Philippines, Singapore, Taiwan, Thailand, Vietnam); Tula Publishing (Africa); United Publishers Services Ltd (Japan)
Warehouse: Bookpoint Ltd, 130 Milton Park, Abingdon, Oxon OX14 4SB *Tel:* (01235) 400 400 *Web Site:* bookpoint.wp.hachette.co.uk
Orders to: Bookpoint Ltd, 130 Milton Park, Abingdon, Oxon OX14 4SB *Tel:* (01235) 400 400 *Web Site:* bookpoint.wp.hachette.co.uk

Fairacres Publications, *imprint of* SLG Press

Fairfield, *imprint of* Novello & Co

Famedram Publishers Ltd+
PO Box 3, Ellon, Aberdeenshire AB41 9EA
Tel: (01651) 842429 *Fax:* (01651) 842180
E-mail: info@famedram.com; orders@famedram.com; online@famedram.com
Web Site: www.famedram.com; www.northernbooks.co.uk; www.artwork.co.uk
Key Personnel
Dir: James Williams

Founded: 1983
Publisher of *ArtWork*, bimonthly arts newspaper for Scotland & Northern England.
Subjects: Art, Nonfiction (General), Transportation, Travel & Tourism, Wine & Spirits
ISBN Prefix(es): 978-0-905489; 978-0-9501944; 978-0-7179
Number of titles published annually: 3 Print; 1 CD-ROM
Total Titles: 60 Print; 4 CD-ROM
Imprints: Northern Books

Family Walks, *imprint of* Scarthin Books

Fand Music Press
Glenelg, 10 Avon Close, Petersfield, Hants GU31 4LG
Tel: (01730) 267341 *Fax:* (01730) 267341
E-mail: contact@fandmusic.com; orders@fandmusic.com
Web Site: www.fandmusic.com
Sheet music, books & CDs.
Subjects: Music, Dance
ISBN Prefix(es): 978-0-9535125

Fanny, *imprint of* Knockabout Comics

Far Far Away Books & Media Ltd
20-22 Bedford Row, London WC1 R4JS
Tel: (020) 7400 3375
E-mail: office@farfarawaybooksandmedia.co.uk
Web Site: www.farfarawaybooks.com
Key Personnel
Dir: Paula Mendonca
Founded: 2011
ISBN Prefix(es): 978-1-908786
Orders to: Central Books Ltd, One Heath Park Industrial Estate, Freshwater Rd, Dagenham RM8 1RX *Tel:* (020) 8525 8800 *Fax:* (020) 8599 2694 *E-mail:* orders@centralbooks.com *Web Site:* www.centralbooks.com

FBA Group+
4 The Science Park, Aberystwyth, Dyfed SY23 3AH
Tel: (01970) 636400
E-mail: info@fbagroup.co.uk
Web Site: fbagroup.wales
Key Personnel
Mng Dir: Meilyr Ceredig
Editor: Dr Denis Balsom
Founded: 1989
Publisher of *The Wales Yearbook*.
Subjects: Art, Government, Political Science, Health, Nutrition, Sports, Athletics
ISBN Prefix(es): 978-1-901862
Imprints: Cyhoeddiadau FBA; FBA Publications
Branch Office(s)
One Caspian Point, Cardiff Bay CF10 4DQ

FBA Publications, *imprint of* FBA Group

Fern House
19 High St, Haddenham, Ely, Cambs CB6 3XA
Tel: (01353) 740 222
E-mail: info@fernhouse.com
Web Site: www.fernhouse.com
Key Personnel
Owner: Rodney Dale
Founded: 1976
Subjects: Biography, Memoirs, Fiction, History, Nonfiction (General)
ISBN Prefix(es): 978-0-9524897; 978-1-902702

Fernhurst Books Ltd
62 Brandon Parade, Holly Walk, Leamington Spa, Warwicks CV32 4JE
Tel: (01926) 337488
Web Site: fernhurstbooks.com
Founded: 1979

Subjects: Outdoor Recreation, Sports, Athletics, Boating, Sailing, Water Sports
ISBN Prefix(es): 978-0-470; 978-1-909911
Distributed by John Wiley & Sons Ltd
Distribution Center: Casemate | IPM, 1950 Lawrence Rd, Havertown, PA 19083, United States *Tel:* 610-853-9131 *Fax:* 610-853-9146 *E-mail:* casemate@casematepublishers.com *Web Site:* www.casemateipm.com (North America)

David Fickling Books
31 Beaumont St, Oxford OX1 2NP
Tel: (01865) 339000
Web Site: www.davidficklingbooks.com
Key Personnel
Publisher: David Fickling
Mng Dir: Simon Mason
Sales & Marketing Dir: Phil Earle
Editor: Bella Pearson
Membership(s): Independent Alliance.
ISBN Prefix(es): 978-1-84992; 978-1-910200; 978-0-85756
Number of titles published annually: 20 Print

FIELL Publishing Ltd
Barley Mow, High St, Chipping Campden, Glos GU55 6AG
Tel: (01386) 840882
E-mail: info@fiell.com
Web Site: www.fiell.com
Key Personnel
Co-Founder: Charlotte Fiell; Peter Fiell
Subjects: Architecture & Interior Design, Art, Fashion, Natural History, Photography, Pop Culture, Design, Digital Culture, Ethics, Lifestyle
ISBN Prefix(es): 978-1-906863
Foreign Rep(s): A&J International Design Media Ltd (Helen Liyan) (China); Antique Collectors' Club Ltd (Elisabeth Harder-Kreimann) (Scandinavia); Antique Collectors' Club Ltd (James Smith) (Middle East, UK); APD Kuala Lumpur (Lilian Koe) (Malaysia); APD Singapore Pte Ltd (Ian Pringle) (Brunei, Cambodia, Indonesia, Singapore, Southeast Asia, Thailand, Vietnam); Asia Publishers Services Ltd (Edward Summerson) (Far East, Hong Kong, Philippines, Taiwan); Avicenna Partnership (Claire de Gruchy) (Cyprus, Jordan, Malta, Palestine, Turkey); Avicenna Partnership (Bill Kennedy) (Egypt, Gulf States, Iraq, Lebanon, Libya, Sudan, Syria); Depozitul de Carte Distributie srl (Dan Catalin Serban) (Romania); Distributed Art Publishers (Avery Lozada) (Canada, USA); The English Book (Aleksandar Ilic) (Serbia); Fortytwo Bookz Galaxy (Krishan Sharma) (India); Humanitas Ltd (Laisve Saduikiene) (Lithuania); Jahan Adib Publishing (Farhad Maftoon) (Iran); Padovani Books Ltd (Penny Padovani) (Greece, Italy); Peribo Pty Ltd (Jane Coffey) (Australia, New Zealand); SG Distributors (Giulietta Campanelli) (South Africa); Slovart Publishing Ltd (Ivana Stankova) (Czechia); Slovart Publishing Ltd (Anna Buzakova) (Slovakia); Steimatzky (2005) Ltd (Diane Levy) (Israel); Ralph & Sheila Summers (Yasy Murayama) (Japan, South Korea); Top Mark Centre (Zbyszek Duda) (Poland); Robert Towers (Ireland); Tzomet Sfarim (Arlette Perl) (Israel); VBZ Slovenia doo (Berta Mauhler) (Slovenia)

Fig Tree, *imprint of* Penguin Books Ltd

Fil Rouge Press
46 Voss St, London E2 6HP
Tel: (020) 3669 1922
Web Site: www.filrougepress.com
Key Personnel
Publisher & Foreign Rights: Judith More
E-mail: judithmore@filrougepress.com
Founded: 2007

Subjects: Cookery, Crafts, Games, Hobbies, Health, Nutrition, History, Pop Culture
ISBN Prefix(es): 978-0-9564382
Foreign Rights: I E Illustrata SL (Angela Reynolds) (Brazil, Portugal, Spain); International Book Marketing (Manuela Kerkhoff) (Germany, Russia, Scandinavia); Brigitte Perivier (France, Holland, Italy, worldwide French-speaking Territories)
Distribution Center: Search Press, Well, North Farm Rd, Turnbridge Wells, Kent TN2 3DR *Tel:* (01892) 510850 *E-mail:* su_h@searchpress.com *Web Site:* www.searchpress.co.uk
David Bateman Ltd, Tamdale Grove, Albany Business Park, Bush Rd, Auckland, New Zealand *Tel:* (09) 415 7664 *E-mail:* bryceg@bateman.co.nz *Web Site:* www.bateman.co.nz
Blue Weaver, PO Box 30370, Tokai 7966, South Africa *Tel:* (021) 701 4477 *E-mail:* mark@blueweaver.co.ca *Web Site:* www.blueweaver.co.ca

Finch Books, *imprint of* Totally Entwined Group Ltd

Findhorn Press Ltd+
Delft Cottage, Dyke, Forres IV36 2TF
Tel: (01309) 690582
E-mail: info@findhornpress.com
Web Site: www.findhornpress.com
Key Personnel
Editorial Dir: Sabine Weeke
Founded: 1971
Publishes books that bring hope, healing & inspiration to the world.
Subjects: Alternative, Animals, Pets, Astrology, Occult, Biography, Memoirs, Child Care & Development, Environmental Studies, Gardening, Plants, Health, Nutrition, How-to, Inspirational, Spirituality, LGBTQ, Music, Dance, Native American Studies, Parapsychology, Psychology, Psychiatry, Self-Help, Women's Studies, Alternative Health
ISBN Prefix(es): 978-0-905242; 978-1-899171; 978-1-84409
Number of titles published annually: 40 Print; 2 CD-ROM; 5 E-Book; 7 Audio
Total Titles: 220 Print
Parent Company: Inner Traditions/Bear & Co
Imprints: EarthDancer Books (primarily crystal healing titles)
Distributed by Simon & Schuster, Inc

Fine Wine Editions
Member of Quarto International Co-Editions Group
The Old Brewery, 6 Blundell St, London N7 9BH
Tel: (020) 7812 8645 *Fax:* (020) 7400 8066
Web Site: www.quartoknows.com/fine-wine-editions
Key Personnel
Publisher: Philip Cooper *E-mail:* philip.cooper@quarto.com
Produces wine books in collaboration with *The World of Fine Wine* magazine.
Subjects: Cookery, Wine & Spirits
ISBN Prefix(es): 978-1-906885
Ultimate Parent Company: The Quarto Group Inc

Firecrest Publishing Ltd
The Coach House, Church Farm, The Lee, Great Missenden, Bucks HP16 9LZ
Tel: (01296) 613800
E-mail: pfirecrest@aol.com; ps@firecrestbooks.net
Web Site: www.firecrestbooks.net
Co-edition book publisher.
Subjects: Crafts, Games, Hobbies, Geography, Geology, History, Natural History, Nonfiction (General), Science (General), Technology, Prehistoric Life
ISBN Prefix(es): 978-1-906174; 978-0-9560192

First & Best in Education Ltd+
c/o Hamilton House Mailings Ltd, Earlstrees
Court, Earlstrees Rd, Corby, Northants NN17
4HH
Tel: (01536) 399005 *Fax:* (01536) 399012
E-mail: sales@firstandbest.co.uk
Web Site: www.firstandbest.co.uk
Founded: 1979
Suppliers of educational photocopiable books &
books on disk for teachers & parents.
Subjects: Business, Education
ISBN Prefix(es): 978-0-906888; 978-1-898091;
978-1-86083
Number of titles published annually: 30 Print; 25
CD-ROM
Total Titles: 600 Print; 200 CD-ROM
Parent Company: Hamilton House Mailings Ltd
Imprints: School Improvement Reports

First Discovery, *imprint of* Moonlight Publishing
Ltd

First Discovery Art, *imprint of* Moonlight
Publishing Ltd

First Discovery Music, *imprint of* Moonlight
Publishing Ltd

Fitzcarraldo Editions
243 Knightsbridge, London SW7 1DN
Tel: (07772) 249942 (cell)
E-mail: info@fitzcarraldoeditions.com
Web Site: fitzcarraldoeditions.com
Founded: 2014
Subjects: Fiction, Literature, Literary Criticism,
Essays
ISBN Prefix(es): 978-1-910695; 978-0-9929747
Distribution Center: Grantham Book Services,
Trent Rd, Grantham NG31 7XQ *Tel:* (01476)
541080 *Fax:* (01476) 541061 *E-mail:* orders@
gbs.tbs-ltd.co.uk
Consortium Book Sales & Distribution, The Keg
House, 34 13 Ave NE, Suite 101, Minneapolis,
MN 55413-1007, United States *Tel:* 612-746-
2600 *Fax:* 612-746-2606 *E-mail:* info@cbsd.
com *Web Site:* www.cbsd.com

Five Star, *imprint of* Gale

Flame Tree Publishing+
Crabtree Hall, Crabtree Lane, Fulham, London
SW6 6TY
Tel: (020) 7386 4700 *Fax:* (020) 7386 4701
E-mail: info@flametreepublishing.com
Web Site: www.flametreepublishing.com
Key Personnel
Publisher & Creative Dir: Nick Wells
  E-mail: nick@flametreepublishing.com
Mng Dir: Frances Bodiam *E-mail:* frances@
flametreepublishing.com
Customer Services Manager: Birgitta Williams
  E-mail: birgitta@flametreepublishing.com
Founded: 1992
Publishers of books & stationery.
Membership(s): Independent Publishers Guild.
Subjects: Art, Cookery, Education, Fiction, His-
tory, Inspirational, Spirituality, Music, Dance,
Pop Culture, Religion - Other, Science Fiction,
Fantasy, Travel & Tourism
ISBN Prefix(es): 978-1-84451; 978-1-84786; 978-
1-874634; 978-1-78361; 978-1-904041; 978-1-
903817
Number of titles published annually: 25 Print
Total Titles: 200 Print
Parent Company: The Foundry Creative Media
Co Ltd
Foreign Rep(s): Baccara A/S (Mogens Mogensen)
(Norway); Editions des Blancs Manteaux (Em-
manuelle Trumeau-Donies) (France); Brown-
trout Publishers (USA); Browntrout Publishers
Canada (Canada); Decadence Nederland BV

(Geert Hoeberigs) (Benelux); Mesange (Hit-
omi Mazza) (Japan); Oxted Resources (Lucia
M Tubbs) (New Zealand); Putinki-Tukku Oy
(Anu Hartonen) (Finland); Q Cards & Co AB
(Birgitta Murray) (Sweden); SG Distributors
(Giulietta Campanelli) (South Africa); Waterlyn
Pty Ltd (David Pursley) (Australia)
Distribution Center: Marston Book Services Ltd,
160 Eastern Ave, Milton Park, Abingdon, Oxon
OX14 4SB *Tel:* (01235) 465500 *Fax:* (01235)
465555 *E-mail:* trade.orders@marston.co.uk
Web Site: www.marston.co.uk
Baker & Taylor Publisher Services, 30 Am-
berwood Parkway, Ashland, OH 44805,
United States *Tel:* 567-215-0030 *E-mail:* inf@
btpubservices.com *Web Site:* www.
btpubservices.com

Fleet, *imprint of* Little, Brown Book Group

Jo Fletcher Books, *imprint of* Quercus
Publishing PLC

Floris Books+
2a Robertson Ave, Edinburgh EH11 1PZ
Tel: (0131) 337 2372
E-mail: floris@florisbooks.co.uk
Web Site: www.florisbooks.co.uk
Key Personnel
Publisher: Katy Lockwood-Holmes
Head, Sales & Marketing: Chani McBain
Design & Production Manager: Leah McDowell
Editor: Christian Maclean; Christopher Moore;
Sally Polson
Founded: 1976
Membership(s): Scottish Publishers Association.
Subjects: Child Care & Development, Crafts,
Games, Hobbies, Fiction, Health, Nutrition,
Inspirational, Spirituality, Medicine, Nurs-
ing, Dentistry, Nonfiction (General), Religion
- Other, Science (General), Self-Help, Child
Health & Development, Community Living,
Holistic Health & Education, Organics
ISBN Prefix(es): 978-0-903540; 978-0-86315
Foreign Rep(s): Footprint Books (Australia);
Gryphon House Inc (USA); Mandragore
(Canada); Steiner Books Inc (USA); Rudolf
Steiner Productions SA (South Africa)
Distribution Center: Consortium Book Sales &
Distribution, an Ingram brand, The Keg House,
34 13 Ave NE, Suite 101, Minneapolis, MN
55413-1007, United States *Tel:* 612-746-2600
Fax: 612-746-2606 *E-mail:* info@cbsd.com
Web Site: www.cbsd.com SAN: 200-6049
Orders to: BookSource, 50 Cambuslang Rd,
Glasgow G32 8NB *Tel:* (0845) 370 0067
Fax: (0845) 370 0068 *E-mail:* orders@
booksource.net *Web Site:* www.booksource.net

Flying Eye Books, *imprint of* Nobrow Ltd

Flying Eye Books
Imprint of Nobrow Ltd
62 Great Eastern St, London EC2A 3QR
Tel: (020) 7033 4430
E-mail: sales@flyingeyebooks.com
Web Site: flyingeyebooks.com
Subjects: Fiction, Nonfiction (General)
ISBN Prefix(es): 978-1-909263
Foreign Rep(s): Belles Lettres Diffusion Distribu-
tion (Belgium, France, Switzerland); Consor-
tium Book Sales & Distribution (Ruth Berger)
(USA); Perimeter Distribution (Australia, New
Zealand, Tasmania); Publishers Group Canada
(Canada)
Distribution Center: Bounce Sales & Market-
ing Ltd, 320 City Rd, London EC1V 2NZ
Tel: (020) 7138 3650 *Fax:* (020) 7138 3658
E-mail: sales@bouncemarketing.co.uk *Web
Site:* www.bouncemarketing.co.uk

Grantham Book Services, Trent Rd, Grantham,
Lincs NG31 7XQ *Tel:* (01476) 541080;
(01476) 541082 (international orders)
Fax: (01476) 541061; (01476) 541068 (interna-
tional orders) *E-mail:* orders@gbs.tbs-ltd.co.uk
Penguin Random House Publisher Ser-
vices (PRHPS), 1745 Broadway,
New York, NY 10019, United States
E-mail: distribution@randomhouse.com *Web
Site:* penguinrandomhouse.biz/publisherservices

Focal Press, *imprint of* Routledge

Fodor's, *imprint of* Ebury Publishing

Footprint Travel Guides
Imprint of Peloton Grey Publishing
5 Riverside Court, Lower Bristol Rd, Bath BA2
3DZ
Tel: (01225) 469141 *Fax:* (01225) 469461
E-mail: contactus@morriscontentalliance.com
Web Site: www.footprinttravelguides.com
Subjects: Travel & Tourism
ISBN Prefix(es): 978-1-907263; 978-1-909268;
978-1-911082; 978-1-910120; 978-1-908207;
978-1-906098
Ultimate Parent Company: Compass Maps Ltd
Foreign Rep(s): Bill Bailey Publishers Repre-
sentatives (Central Europe, Eastern Europe,
Finland, France, Germany, Italy, Norway,
Portugal, Spain, Sweden); Geoff Bryan (Ire-
land); Craenen Cartografie (Belgium); Frey-
tag & Berndt (Austria); Intermedia Americana
(Caribbean, Latin America); National Book
Network (Canada, USA); OLF SA (Switzer-
land); OM Books (India); Pansing Distribution
Pte Ltd (Malaysia, Singapore); Publishers Sales
Agency (Don Morrison) (Scotland); Scanvik
Books (Denmark); 62Damrak (Netherlands);
Steinhart Sharav Publishers Ltd (Israel); Ward
International Book Exports (Greece, Middle
East, North Africa, Turkey); Woodslane Pty
Ltd (Australasia)
Foreign Rights: Crown International Rights
(Dionel Corona) (worldwide)
Distribution Center: Grantham Book Services
(GBS), Trent Rd, Grantham, Lincs NG31 7XQ
Tel: (01476) 541000 *Fax:* (01476) 541064 *Web
Site:* www.granthambookservices.co.uk
National Book Network, 15200 NBN Way,
Blue Ridge Summit, PA 17214, United States
Tel: 717-794-3800 *E-mail:* customercare@
nbnbooks.com *Web Site:* www.nbnbooks.com

Forbes Publications Ltd+
Epic House, 128 Fulwell Rd, Teddington, Middx
TW11 0RQ
Tel: (020) 8973 0040
Founded: 1992
Subjects: Business, Economics, Education,
Health, Nutrition, Human Relations, Science
(General), Technology
ISBN Prefix(es): 978-0-901762; 978-1-899527
Parent Company: The Rapport Group Ltd
Orders to: NBN International, Plymbridge
House, Estover Rd, Plymouth, Devon PL6
7PY *Tel:* (01752) 202301 *Fax:* (01752) 202333
E-mail: orders@nbninternational.com *Web
Site:* www.nbninternational.com

Forth Naturalist & Historian
c/o Information Services (The Library), Univer-
sity of Stirling, Stirling FK9 4LA
Tel: (01786) 467269
E-mail: fnh@stir.ac.uk
Web Site: www.fnh.natsci.stir.ac.uk
Key Personnel
Chairman: Prof Mike Thomas
Secretary: Marilyn Scott
Assistant Editor: Roy Sexton
  E-mail: roygravedigger@aol.com
Founded: 1975

An informal charitable body of the University of Stirling to promote the environment, heritage & wildlife of Central Scotland.
Specialize in maps & journals.
Membership(s): Scottish Publishers Association.
Subjects: Environmental Studies, History, Natural History
ISBN Prefix(es): 978-0-9506962; 978-0-9514147; 978-1-898008
Number of titles published annually: 1 Print
Total Titles: 30 Print
Distributor for CFSS (Clarkmannanshire Field Studies Society); Clarkmannanshire Libraries; Creag Darach; Falkirk Local History Society; RIAS/Rutland Press; Stirling District Libraries
Orders to: 22 Alexander Dr, Bridge of Allen FK9 4QB *Tel:* (01786) 833409

Fostering Network+
87 Blackfriars Rd, London SE1 8HA
Tel: (020) 7620 6400 *Fax:* (020) 7620 6401
E-mail: info@fostering.net
Web Site: www.fostering.net
Key Personnel
President: Jim Bond
Dir, Operations: Melissa Green
Dir, Communications & Public Affairs: Jackie Sanders
Founded: 1976
Subjects: Child Care & Development
ISBN Prefix(es): 978-1-897869; 978-0-946015

W Foulsham & Co Ltd+
The Old Barrel Store, Brewery Courtyard, Draymans Lane, Marlow, Bucks SL7 2FF
Tel: (01628) 400 631 *Fax:* (01753) 535003
E-mail: sales@foulsham.com
Web Site: www.foulsham.com
Key Personnel
Dir: B A R Belasco
Publicity Manager: Margaret Lashbrook
Tel: (01843) 299007 *E-mail:* lashbrook@foulsham.com
Founded: 1819
Subjects: Alternative, Antiques, Astrology, Occult, Cookery, Crafts, Games, Hobbies, Education, Film, Video, Finance, Gardening, Plants, Health, Nutrition, House & Home, How-to, Humor, Self-Help, Technology, Travel & Tourism, Wine & Spirits, Family Reference, Know How, Mind, Body, Spirit, Self Improvement
ISBN Prefix(es): 978-0-572
Number of titles published annually: 100 Print; 2 E-Book
Total Titles: 300 Print
Imprints: Quantum
Foreign Rep(s): Ashton International Marketing Services (Cambodia, Far East, Laos, Malaysia, Myanmar, Philippines, Singapore, Thailand, Vietnam); Associated Publishers Group (USA); Butler Sims Ltd (Brian Blennerhassett) (Ireland); Capricorn-Link (Australia) Pty Ltd (Australia); Codasat Canada Ltd (Canada); Inter Media Americana (David Williams) (Central America, South America); Inter Media Americana (Czechia, Hungary, Poland, Slovakia, Sub-Saharan Africa); Macmillan Caribbean Ltd (Caribbean); Maya Publishers Pvt Ltd (India); Robbert Pleysier (Austria, Belgium, Germany, Liechtenstein, Luxembourg, Netherlands, Switzerland); Southern Publishers Group (New Zealand); Trinity Books (South Africa)
Distribution Center: Macmillan Distribution Ltd, Brunel Rd, Houndmills, Basingstoke, Hants RG21 6XS *Tel:* (01256) 329 242 *Fax:* (01256) 812 558 *E-mail:* mdl@macmillan.co.uk *Web Site:* www.macmillandistribution.co.uk

4th Estate, *imprint of* HarperCollins UK

4th Estate+
Imprint of HarperCollins UK
The News Bldg, One London Bridge St, London SE1 9GF
Tel: (020) 8741 7070
E-mail: 4thestate.marketing@harpercollins.co.uk; 4thestate.publicity@harpercollins.co.uk
Web Site: www.harpercollins.co.uk
Key Personnel
Chief Executive Officer: Brian Murray
Publishing Dir: Helen Garnons-Williams; Louise Haines; Nicholas Pearson
Executive Publisher: David Roth-Ey
Publicity: Michelle Kane
Sales: Oliver Wright
Founded: 1984
Subjects: Architecture & Interior Design, Biography, Memoirs, Cookery, Fiction, History, Humor, LGBTQ, Literature, Literary Criticism, Essays, Radio, TV
ISBN Prefix(es): 978-0-947795; 978-1-872180; 978-1-84115; 978-1-85702; 978-0-00

Francis Balsom Associates Ltd, see FBA Group

Franklin Watts, *imprint of* Hachette Children's Books

Robert Frederick Ltd
4 N Parade, Bath BA1 1LF
Tel: (01225) 310107 *Fax:* (01225) 312878
E-mail: hello@robert-frederick.co.uk
Web Site: www.robert-frederick.co.uk
ISBN Prefix(es): 978-0-907781; 978-1-85081; 978-0-7554; 978-1-903437; 978-1-78373
Associate Companies: North Parade Publishing

Free Association Books Ltd+
One Angel Cottages, Milespit Hill, London NW7 1RD
E-mail: info@freeassociationpublishing.com
Web Site: www.freeassociationpublishing.com
Key Personnel
Chief Executive, Editorial & Mng Dir: Trevor Brown
Publishing Dir: Alice Solomons
Marketing Manager: Lisa Findley *E-mail:* lisa.findley@gmail.com
Founded: 1983
Subjects: Behavioral Sciences, Child Care & Development, Ethnicity, Human Relations, Philosophy, Psychology, Psychiatry, Social Sciences, Sociology, Parenting
ISBN Prefix(es): 978-0-946960; 978-1-85343
Foreign Rights: Cathy Miller Foreign Rights Agency (Cathy Miller)
Distribution Center: NBN International, Airport Business Centre, 10 Thornbury Rd, Plymouth PL6 7PP *Tel:* (01752) 202349 *Fax:* (01752) 202366 *Web Site:* www.nbninternational.com
Footprint Books Pty Ltd, 1/6A Prosperity Parade, Warriewood, NSW 2102, Australia *Tel:* (02) 9997 3973 *Fax:* (02) 9997 3185 *E-mail:* simonpl@footprint.com.au *Web Site:* www.footprint.com.au (Australia)
International Specialized Book Services, 920 NE 58 Ave, Suite 300, Portland, OR 97213-3786, United States *Tel:* 503-287-3093 *Web Site:* www.isbs.com (North America)

Freedom Press
Angel Alley, 84b Whitechapel High St, London E1 7QX
Tel: (020) 7247 9249
E-mail: shop@freedompress.org.uk; admin@freedompress.org.uk; editor@freedompress.org.uk
Web Site: www.freedompress.org.uk
Founded: 1886
Independent nonprofit publisher.

Subjects: Economics, Government, Political Science, History, Philosophy, Social Sciences, Sociology
ISBN Prefix(es): 978-0-900384; 978-1-904491
Number of titles published annually: 7 Print
Total Titles: 80 Print
Distributor for Calabria Press; Michael E Coughlin; Five Leaves Publications; Libertarian Education; Phoenix Press; Red Lion Press; See Sharp Press

Samuel French Ltd
24-37 Stephenson Way, London NW1 2HD
Tel: (020) 7387 9373
E-mail: customer.services@samuelfrench.co.uk
Web Site: www.samuelfrench.co.uk
Founded: 1830
Play publisher & licensing agents.
PMA.
Subjects: Drama, Theater, Theater Plays & Musicals
ISBN Prefix(es): 978-0-573
U.S. Office(s): Samuel French Inc, 235 Park Ave S, 5th floor, New York, NY 10003, United States *Tel:* 212-206-8990 *E-mail:* info@samuelfrench.com *Web Site:* www.samuelfrench.com
Foreign Rights: DALRO (Pty) Ltd (Botswana, Lesotho, Namibia, South Africa, Swaziland); Dingli Co International Ltd (Malta); Drama League of Ireland (Ireland, Northern Ireland); National Theatre Organization (Zimbabwe); Origin Theatrical (Australia); Phoenix Players (East Africa); Play Bureau (NZ) Ltd (New Zealand)
Bookshop(s): Samuel French Bookshop, The Royal Court Theatre, Sloane Sq, Chelsea, London SW1W 8AS *Tel:* (020) 7565 5024

Fretwork Editions
16 Teddington Park Rd, Teddington, Middx TW11 8ND
Tel: (020) 8977 0924
E-mail: publishing@fretwork.co.uk
Web Site: www.fretwork.co.uk/publishing
Key Personnel
Dir: William Hunt
Founded: 1989
Publisher of scholarly performing editions of music for viols.
Subjects: Music, Dance
ISBN Prefix(es): 978-1-898131
Number of titles published annually: 6 Print; 6 CD-ROM
Total Titles: 65 Print; 60 CD-ROM
Associate Companies: Voicebox

The Friday Project, *imprint of* HarperCollins UK

Friends of the Earth Ltd+
c/o The Printworks, 139 Clapham Rd, 1st floor, London SW9 0HP
Tel: (020) 7490 1555 *Fax:* (020) 7490 0881
Web Site: www.foe.co.uk
Key Personnel
Chief Executive Officer: Craig Bennett
Media Manager: Maria Castellina *Tel:* (020) 7566 1649 *E-mail:* maria.castellina@foe.co.uk
Founded: 1971
Environmental pressure group & charity.
Subjects: Environmental Studies, Climate, Corporate Accountability, Food, Transport, Waste
Number of titles published annually: 10 Print
Distributed by HarperCollins

Frontier Publishing Ltd+
Windetts, Seething Rd, Kirstead, Norwich NR15 1EG
Tel: (01508) 558174
E-mail: contact@frontierpublishing.co.uk

Web Site: www.frontierpublishing.co.uk
Key Personnel
Principal: Mr R Barnes
Founded: 1986
Membership(s): IPG; PMSA.
Subjects: Art, History, Nonfiction (General), Photography, Poetry, Travel & Tourism
ISBN Prefix(es): 978-1-872914; 978-0-9508701
Total Titles: 25 Print
Imprints: Frontier 2000 Series

Frontier 2000 Series, *imprint of* Frontier Publishing Ltd

Frontline Books, *imprint of* Pen & Sword Books Ltd

The Fruitmarket Gallery
45 Market St, Edinburgh EH1 1DF
Tel: (0131) 225 2383 *Fax:* (0131) 220 3130
E-mail: info@fruitmarket.co.uk; marketing@fruitmarket.co.uk; bookshop@fruitmarket.co.uk
Web Site: fruitmarket.co.uk
Key Personnel
Dir: Dr Fiona Bradley
Deputy Dir: Elizabeth McLean
    E-mail: elizabeth@fruitmarket.co.uk
Head, Development: Armida Taylor
    E-mail: armida@fruitmarket.co.uk
Bookshop Manager: Claire Leach
Press & Marketing Manager: Claire Rocha da Cruz
Exhibitions Organizer: Samantha Woods
    E-mail: sam@fruitmarket.co.uk
Founded: 1984
Mission: to bring the work of leading artists worldwide to Scotland & to exhibit the work of Scottish artists in an international context, engaging with contemporary issues.
Subjects: Art
ISBN Prefix(es): 978-0-947912
Number of titles published annually: 3 Print
Total Titles: 30 Print
Foreign Rep(s): Art Data (worldwide)

FT Publishing, *imprint of* Pearson Education Ltd

David Fulton Books+
Imprint of Routledge Education
Milton Park, 2 Park Sq, Abingdon, Oxon OX14 4RN
Tel: (020) 7017 6000 *Fax:* (020) 7017 6699
Web Site: www.routledge.com/teachers
Founded: 1987
Specialize in special education needs (SEN) books for teachers.
Subjects: Disability, Special Needs, Education
ISBN Prefix(es): 978-1-85346; 978-1-84312
Ultimate Parent Company: Taylor & Francis Group
Foreign Rep(s): Andrew Durnell (Europe, Ireland, Scandinavia); Karim International (Bangladesh); Viva Group (India); Yale Representation Ltd (England)
Foreign Rights: Book Promotions (Pty) Ltd (South Africa); Hemisphere Publication Services (Asia, The Pacific); Macmillan Academic & Reference (Australia); Macmillan Publishers New Zealand Ltd (New Zealand); Taylor & Francis Inc (North America)
Orders to: Bookpoint Ltd, 130 Milton Park, Abingdon, Oxon OX14 4SB *Tel:* (01235) 400 400 *Web Site:* bookpoint.wp.hachette.co.uk (Africa, Asia, Australia, Europe & UK)
Routledge, c/o Taylor & Francis Inc, 7625 Empire Dr, Florence, KY 41042-2919, United States *E-mail:* orders@taylorandfrancis.com (North & South America)

Funfax, *imprint of* DK Ltd

Fyfield Books, *imprint of* Carcanet Press Ltd

Gaia Books, *imprint of* Octopus Publishing Group Ltd

Gaia Books Ltd+
Imprint of Octopus Publishing Group
Carmelite House, 50 Victoria Embankment, London EC4Y 0DZ
Tel: (020) 3122 6400 *Fax:* (020) 8283 9704
E-mail: publisher@gaiabooks.co.uk
Web Site: www.octopusbooks.co.uk
Founded: 1982
Specialize in books that celebrate the vision of Gaia, the self-sustaining living Earth & seek to help their readers live in greater personal & planetary harmony; mainly four-color illustrated titles.
Subjects: Architecture & Interior Design, Environmental Studies, Gardening, Plants, Health, Nutrition, Mind, Body & Spirit, Natural Health & Living, Planetary Ecology
ISBN Prefix(es): 978-1-85675
Number of titles published annually: 12 Print
Total Titles: 110 Print; 5 Audio
Foreign Rep(s): APD Kuala Lumpur (Lilian Koe) (Malaysia); APD Singapore Pte Ltd (Singapore); Jonathan Ball Publishers (South Africa); Canadian Manda Group (Canada); Everest International Publishing Services (Wei Zhao) (China); Arturo Gutierrez Hernandez (Central America); Hachette Australia (Australia); Hachette Book Group Ireland (Ireland, Northern Ireland); Hachette Book Publishing India Pvt Ltd (Kapil Agrawal) (Bangladesh, India, Sri Lanka); Hachette Livre NZ (New Zealand); Hachette UK Ltd (Matt Cowdery) (Israel, Middle East, North Africa); Hachette UK Ltd (Paul Kenny) (Cambodia, Guam, Hong Kong, Indonesia, Japan, Laos, Myanmar, Papua New Guinea, Philippines, South Korea, Taiwan, Thailand, Vietnam); Lynda Hopkins (Caribbean); Chris Humphrys (Caribbean); InterMediaAmericana Ltd (David Williams) (South America); Octopus Books USA (USA); Octopus Export Sales (all other territories)
Orders to: Littlehampton Book Services Ltd, Faraday Close, Durrington, Worthing, West Sussex BN13 3RB *Tel:* (01903) 828500; (01903) 828501 (customer service) *Web Site:* lbsltd.wp.hachette.co.uk

Gale
Division of Cengage Learning
Cheriton House, North Way, Andover, Hants SP10 5BE
Tel: (01264) 332 424
E-mail: emea.galereply@cengage.com
Web Site: gale.cengage.co.uk
Key Personnel
Publisher, History & Politics: Julia de Mowbray *Tel:* (01264) 347 308 *E-mail:* julia.demowbray@cengage.com
Publisher, Media History: Seth Cayley *Tel:* (01264) 342 927 *E-mail:* seth.cayley@cengage.com
Founded: 1989
Subjects: Architecture & Interior Design, Art, Biography, Memoirs, Business, Child Care & Development, Drama, Theater, Fashion, Genealogy, History, Literature, Literary Criticism, Essays, Music, Dance, Women's Studies
ISBN Prefix(es): 978-0-15; 978-1-873477; 978-1-84480; 978-1-86152; 978-1-4080
Imprints: Blackbirch Press; Christian Large Print; Five Star; Graham & Whiteside; Greenhaven Press; GK Hall & Co; Kidhaven Press; Large Print Press; Lucent Books; Macmillan Reference USA; Oceano Grupo Editorial; Primary Source Microfilm; St James Press; Schirmer Reference; Scholarly Resources; Charles Scribner's Sons; Sleeping Bear Press; The TAFT

Group; Thorndike Press; Twayne Publishers; UXL; Wheeler Publishing
U.S. Office(s): 27500 Drake Rd, Farmington Hills, MI 48331, United States
Shipping Address: PO Box 699, Andover, Hants SP10 5YE
Warehouse: PO Box 699, Andover, Hants SP10 5YE
Orders to: PO Box 699, Andover, Hants SP10 5YE

Gallery Children's Books, *imprint of* East-West Publications (UK) Ltd

Galley Beggar Press
37 Dover St, Norwich NR2 3 LG
E-mail: info@galleybeggar.co.uk
Web Site: galleybeggar.co.uk
Key Personnel
Founder: Sam Jordison; Henry Layte; Eloise Millar
Founded: 2012
Subjects: Fiction
ISBN Prefix(es): 978-0-9571853; 978-1-910296

Galliard, *imprint of* Stainer & Bell Ltd

Gallic Books
59 Ebury St, London SW1W ONZ
Tel: (020) 7259 9336
E-mail: info@gallicbooks.com
Web Site: belgraviabooks.com/gb
Key Personnel
Mng Dir: Jane Aitken
Editorial Dir: Pilar Webb
Specialize in French literature translated to English.
Subjects: Cookery, Fiction
ISBN Prefix(es): 978-1-9083; 978-1-906040
Imprints: Aardvark Bureau
Foreign Rep(s): Michael Geoghegan (Austria, Belgium, Croatia, Czechia, France, Germany, Hungary, Netherlands, Poland, Slovakia, Slovenia, Switzerland); Gill Hess (Ireland); Humphrys Roberts Associates (Gibraltar, Portugal, Spain); Peribo (Australia, New Zealand); SG Distributors (South Africa); Peter Ward Book Exports (Algeria, Bahrain, Cyprus, Egypt, Greece, Iran, Iraq, Israel, Jordan, Kuwait, Lebanon, Libya, Malta, Morocco, Oman, Qatar, Saudi Arabia, Syria, Tunisia, Turkey, United Arab Emirates, Yemen); The White Partnership (Hong Kong, India, Indonesia, Japan, Korea, Malaysia, Pakistan, Philippines, Singapore, Taiwan, Thailand)
Distribution Center: Ingram Publisher Services, 52-54 St John St, 5th fl, Clerkenwell, London EC1M 4HF *E-mail:* ipsuk_enquiries@ingramcontent.com (UK, Europe & Ireland)
Consortium Book Sales & Distribution, The Keg House, 34 13 Ave NE, Suite 101, Saint Paul, MN 55413-1007, United States *Tel:* 612-746-2600 *E-mail:* sales@cbsd.com (USA & Canada)

Gaming Books, *imprint of* O Books

Garden Art Press, *imprint of* ACC Publishing Group

Garden Art Press+
Imprint of ACC Publishing Group
Sandy Lane, Old Martlesham, Woodbridge, Suffolk IP12 4SD
Tel: (01394) 389950 *Fax:* (01394) 389999
E-mail: sales@accpublishinggroup.com
Web Site: www.accpublishinggroup.com/uk
Subjects: Gardening, Plants
ISBN Prefix(es): 978-1-870673

U.S. Office(s): ACC Publishing Group, 6 W 18 St, Suite 4B, New York, NY 10011, United States *Tel:* 212-645-1111 *Fax:* 212-989-3205 *E-mail:* ussales@accpublishinggroup.com

Garland Science, *imprint of* Taylor & Francis Group, an Informa Business

Garland Science+
Imprint of Taylor & Francis Group, an Informa Business
2 Park Sq, Milton Park, Abingdon, Oxon OX14 4RN
Tel: (020) 7017 6000 *Fax:* (020) 7017 6699
E-mail: science@garland.com
Web Site: www.garlandscience.com
Key Personnel
Head of UK Sales: Nick Perry *Tel:* (020) 7017 6132 *Fax:* (020) 7017 6732 *E-mail:* nick.perry@tandf.co.uk
International Sales Dir: Graham Crossley *Tel:* (020) 7017 6048 *Fax:* (020) 7017 6748 *E-mail:* graham.crossley@tandf.co.uk
Foreign Rights: Adele Parker *E-mail:* adele.parker@tandf.co.uk
Founded: 1989
Publishers of Bios Instant Notes, The Basics, Clinic Handbooks, Advanced Texts, Advanced Methods, Key Topics series, Genomes 2, Human Molecular Genetics 2, Clinic Intensive Care, Medical Mycology, Biotechnic & Histochemistry.
Membership(s): International Federation of Reproductive Rights Organisations (IFRRO).
Subjects: Agriculture, Biological Sciences, Chemistry, Chemical Engineering, Medicine, Nursing, Dentistry, Science (General)
ISBN Prefix(es): 978-1-872748; 978-1-85996; 978-0-8240; 978-0-8153
U.S. Office(s): 711 Third Ave, 8th floor, New York, NY 10017, United States
Distributed by Springer Verlag New York Inc (North America); University of New South Wales (Australia & New Zealand); Viva Books (India)
Distributor for Experimental Biology Reviews; Horizon Scientific Press; Royal Microscopical Society (microscopy handbooks); Society of Experimental Biology
Foreign Rep(s): Book Bird (M Anwer Iqbal) (Pakistan); Book Promotions/Horizon Books Botswana (Arthur Oageng) (Botswana); Book Promotions Ltd (Michelle Symington) (Lesotho, Namibia, South Africa, Swaziland); Franklin's International (Rodney Franklin) (Israel, Palestine); ICK (Information & Culture Korea) (Se-Yung Jun) (Korea); IPS (Middle East) Ltd; Publishers Support Services Ltd (Chinke Ojiji) (Nigeria); Taylor & Francis Group (Hans Van Ess) (Japan); United Publishers Services Ltd (Japan)
Orders to: Bookpoint, 130 Milton Park, Abingdon, Oxon OX14 4SB *Tel:* (01235) 400 400 *Web Site:* bookpoint.wp.hachette.co.uk
Routledge, c/o Taylor & Francis Inc, 7625 Empire Dr, Florence, KY 41042-2919, United States *E-mail:* orders@taylorandfrancis.com

Garnet Education, *imprint of* Garnet Publishing Ltd

Garnet Publishing Ltd+
8 Southern Court, South St, Reading, Berks RG1 4QS
Tel: (0118) 959 7847 *Fax:* (0118) 959 7356
E-mail: info@garnetpublishing.co.uk
Web Site: www.garnetpublishing.co.uk
Key Personnel
Production, Sales & Marketing Manager: Pamela Park
Founded: 1991

Specialize in trade books, with a special interest in the Middle East.
Subjects: Anthropology, Archaeology, Architecture & Interior Design, Art, Biography, Memoirs, Cookery, Education, English as a Second Language, Fiction, Foreign Countries, Government, Political Science, History, Language Arts, Linguistics, Literature, Literary Criticism, Essays, Photography, Poetry, Religion - Islamic, Social Sciences, Sociology, Travel & Tourism, Women's Studies, Culture, Legends & Folklore, Middle East Studies, Myths
ISBN Prefix(es): 978-1-85964; 978-1-873938; 978-1-86372
Total Titles: 300 Print
Imprints: Garnet Education; Ithaca Press; South Street Press
Foreign Rep(s): All Prints Distributors & Publishers SAL (Middle East); InBooks (Australia); International Publishers Marketing (IPM) (North America); International Specialized Book Services (ISBS) (North America)
Foreign Rights: Compass Academic Ltd (Ireland, UK); Salt Way Publishing/Torpedo Global Sales Network (Chris McLaren) (Africa, Asia, Europe)
Distribution Center: Consortium Book Sales & Distribution (USA)
Orders to: Macmillan Distribution (MDL), Brunel Rd, Houndmills, Basingstoke, Hants RG21 6XS *Tel:* (01256) 302692 *Fax:* (01256) 812558; (01256) 812521 *E-mail:* orders@macmillan.co.uk *Web Site:* www.macmillandistribution.co.uk

Gateway, *imprint of* Orion Publishing Group Ltd

Gateway Books+
c/o Castlemilk High School, 223 Castlemilk Dr, Glasgow G45 9JY
Tel: (0141) 270 6110 *Fax:* (0141) 270 6122
E-mail: ceg@ceg.org.uk
Web Site: www.ceg.org.uk
Founded: 1982
Subjects: Anthropology, Earth Sciences, Environmental Studies, Health, Nutrition, Mysteries, Suspense, Philosophy, Psychology, Psychiatry, Religion - Other, Self-Help
ISBN Prefix(es): 978-0-946551; 978-1-85860
Distribution Center: Gill Distribution, Hume Ave, Park West, Dublin D12 YV96, Ireland *Tel:* (01) 500 9500 *Web Site:* www.gilldistribution.ie

Geddes & Grosset+
Academy Park, Bldg 4000, Gower St, Glasgow G51 1PR
Tel: (0141) 375 1998 *Fax:* (0141) 427 1791
E-mail: info@waverley-books.co.uk
Web Site: www.geddesandgrosset.com; www.waverley-books.co.uk
Key Personnel
Publisher: Ron B Grosset *E-mail:* ron@waverley-books.co.uk; Elizabeth Small *Tel:* (0141) 375 1996 *E-mail:* liz@waverley-books.co.uk
Executive Officer: Mike Miller
Founded: 1988
Specialize in reference books & illustrated children's books for the mass market.
Membership(s): Scottish Publishers Association.
Subjects: Health, Nutrition, History, Language Arts, Linguistics, Self-Help
ISBN Prefix(es): 978-1-85534; 978-1-84205
Number of titles published annually: 80 Print
Parent Company: The Gresham Publishing Company Ltd
Imprints: Waverley Books
Distributed by Interlink Publishing (USA)
Foreign Rep(s): Codasat (Canada); Jonathan Ng Publishers Agency (Malaysia)
Foreign Rights: AC2 Literary Agency (Anna Mioni) (Italy); Alexander Korzhenevski (Russia, Ukraine)

Distribution Center: Booksource, 50 Cambuslang Rd, Cambuslang, Glasgow G32 8NB
Tel: (0845) 370 0067 *Fax:* (0845) 370 0068
E-mail: customerservice@booksource.net

Genesis Publications Ltd+
2 Jenner Rd, Guildford, Surrey GU1 3PL
Tel: (01483) 540970 *Fax:* (01483) 304709
E-mail: info@genesis-publications.com; orders@genesis-publications.com
Web Site: www.genesis-publications.com
Key Personnel
Publisher: Catherine Roylance *E-mail:* catherine@genesis-publications.com; Nick Roylance *E-mail:* nick@genesis-publications.com
Subscriber & Relationship Manager: David Williams
Production Editor & Website Manager: Bruce Hopkins *E-mail:* bruce@genesis-publications.com
Editor: Sally Millard *E-mail:* sasha@genesis-publications.com
Accounts: Marguerite Rooke *E-mail:* marguerite@genesis-publications.com
Administration: Amanda Carter *E-mail:* amanda@genesis-publications.com
Founded: 1974
Publisher of fine limited editions.
Subjects: Art, History, Literature, Literary Criticism, Essays, Natural History, Poetry, Science (General)
ISBN Prefix(es): 978-0-904351; 978-1-905662

Geographers' A-Z Map Co Ltd
Unit 9, North Downs Business Park, Lime Pit Lane, Dunton Green, Sevenoaks, Kent TN13 2TL
Tel: (01732) 783422
Web Site: www.az.co.uk; www.facebook.com/azmaps; twitter.com/azmaps
Key Personnel
Joint Mng Dir: Steve Berger; Steve Egleton
Production Manager: Tim Heathfield
Sales Manager: Kieran Bartlett
Founded: 1936
ISBN Prefix(es): 978-0-85039; 978-1-84348

The Geographical Association+
160 Solly St, Sheffield S1 4BF
Tel: (0114) 296 0088 *Fax:* (0114) 296 7176
E-mail: info@geography.org.uk
Web Site: www.geography.org.uk
Key Personnel
Chief Executive: Alan Kinder *E-mail:* akinder@geography.org.uk
Head, Publishing: Elaine Anderson *E-mail:* eanderson@geography.org.uk
Senior Production Editor: Dorcas Brown *E-mail:* dbrown@geography.org.uk; Anna Grandfield *E-mail:* anna@geography.org.uk
Sales & Dispatch Coordinator: Carole Porter *E-mail:* cporter@geography.org.uk
Founded: 1893
National subject association for geography teachers with a membership of about 5,500.
Subjects: Geography, Geology
ISBN Prefix(es): 978-0-900395; 978-0-948512; 978-1-899085; 978-1-903448; 978-1-84377
Number of titles published annually: 12 Print; 5 CD-ROM; 5 Online
Total Titles: 200 Print; 60 CD-ROM; 5 Online

Geological Society Publishing House
Unit 7, Brassmill Enterprise Centre, Brassmill Lane, Bath BA1 3JN
Tel: (01225) 445046 *Fax:* (01225) 442836
E-mail: sales@geolsoc.org.uk
Web Site: www.geolsoc.org.uk
Key Personnel
Dir, Publishing: Neal Marriott

Commissioning Editor: Angharad Hills
  E-mail: angharad.hills@geolsoc.org.uk
Senior Production Editor: Sarah Gibbs
Head, Sales, Marketing & Distribution: Anne
  Davenport
Sales & Customer Services Supervisor: Dawn
  Angel
Sales Administrator: Victoria Randall
Marketing Coordinator: Jennifer Davey
Founded: 1807
Membership(s): Association of European Geolog-
  ical Societies; European Federation of Geolo-
  gists.
Subjects: Civil Engineering, Earth Sciences, Ge-
  ography, Geology, Science (General)
ISBN Prefix(es): 978-0-903317; 978-1-897799;
  978-1-86239
Number of titles published annually: 30 Print
Total Titles: 250 Print; 2 CD-ROM
Parent Company: The Geological Society,
  Burlington House, Piccadilly, London W1J
  0BG
Distributed by American Association of
  Petroleum Geologists (AAPG) (North Amer-
  ica)
Distributor for American Association of
  Petroleum Geologists (AAPG) (Europea); Ge-
  ological Society of America (Europe); Society
  for Sedimentary Geology (Europe)

George Ronald Publisher Ltd
3 Rosecroft Lane, Oaklands, Welwyn AL6 0UB
Tel: (01438) 716062
E-mail: sales@grbooks.com
Web Site: www.grbooks.com
Key Personnel
General Manager: Erica Leith *E-mail:* erica@
  grbooks.com
Founded: 1947
Subjects: Religion - Other
ISBN Prefix(es): 978-0-85398
Number of titles published annually: 8 Print; 10
  E-Book
Total Titles: 290 Print; 63 E-Book

E J W Gibb Memorial Trust
14 Avalon Way, Trumpington, Cambridge CB2
  9DX
Tel: (01223) 566630
E-mail: secretary@gibbtrust.org
Web Site: www.gibbtrust.org
Key Personnel
Secretary to the Trustees: Mr P R Bligh
Founded: 1902
A charity which supports & publishes books on
  the literature, religions, philosophy & history of
  the Persian, Turk & Arab people.
Subjects: History, Literature, Literary Criticism,
  Essays, Philosophy, Religion - Other
ISBN Prefix(es): 978-0-906094
Number of titles published annually: 2 Print; 2 E-
  Book
Total Titles: 45 Print; 15 E-Book
Distributed by Oxbow Books
Foreign Rep(s): Chris Ashdown (Far East exc
  Japan, Southeast Asia); Roy de Boo (Belgium,
  Germany, Netherlands); Casemate Academic
  (North America); Ray Potts (Middle East); Pe-
  ter Prout (Gibraltar, Portugal, Spain)
Distribution Center: Oxbow Books, The Old
  Music Hall, 106 Cowley Rd, Oxford, Oxon
  OX4 1JE *Tel:* (01865) 241249 *Fax:* (01865)
  794449 *E-mail:* oxbow@oxbowbooks.com *Web
  Site:* www.oxbowbooks.com
Casemate Academic, 1950 Lawrence Rd, Haver-
  town, PA 19083, United States *Fax:* 610-853-
  9146 *E-mail:* queries@dbbconline.com *Web
  Site:* www.casemateacademic.com
Orders to: Oxbow Books, The Old Music Hall,
  106 Cowley Rd, Oxford, Oxon OX4 1JE
  Tel: (01865) 241249 *Fax:* (01865) 794449
  E-mail: oxbow@oxbowbooks.com *Web
  Site:* www.oxbowbooks.com

Casemate Academic, 1950 Lawrence Rd, Havertown, PA 19083, United States *Fax:* 610-853-
  9146 *E-mail:* queries@dbbconline.com *Web
  Site:* www.casemateacademic.com

Stanley Gibbons Ltd
399 Strand, London WC2R 0LX
Tel: (020) 7836 8444 *Fax:* (020) 7836 7342
E-mail: help@stanleygibbons.com
Web Site: www.stanleygibbons.com; www.
  facebook.com/stanleygibbonsgroup
Key Personnel
Chief Executive Officer: Michael Hall
  Tel: (01534) 766711 *E-mail:* mhall@
  stanleygibbons.com
Chief Financial Officer: Donal Duff *Tel:* (01534)
  766711 *E-mail:* dduff@stanleygibbons.com
Business Development Dir: Tony Grodecki
  Tel: (01303) 762076 *E-mail:* agrodecki@
  benham.co.uk
Corporate Development Dir: John Byfield
  Tel: (01534) 766711 *E-mail:* jbyfield@
  stanleygibbons.com
Corporate Services Dir: Richard Purkis *Tel:* (020)
  7557 4428 *E-mail:* rpurkis@stanleygibbons.
  com
Group Investment Dir: Keith Heddle *Tel:* (020)
  7557 4449 *E-mail:* kheddle@stanleygibbons.
  com
Dir, Philately: Dr Phillip Kinns *Tel:* (020) 7557
  4420 *E-mail:* commonwealth@stanleygibbons.
  com
Dir, British Philately: Vince Cordell *Tel:* (020)
  7557 4414 *E-mail:* vcordell@stanleygibbons.
  com
Dir, UK Operations: Anthony Gee *Tel:* (020)
  7557 4409 *E-mail:* agee@stanleygibbons.com
Publisher: Robert Swain *Tel:* (01425) 481072
  E-mail: rswain@stanleygibbons.com
Retail Manager: Wayne Elliot *Tel:* (020) 7557
  4443 *E-mail:* welliot@stanleygibbons.com
Customer Services Manager: Kerry Finney
  Tel: (01425) 481048 *E-mail:* kfinney@
  stanleygibbons.com
Editor, Gibbons Stamp Monthly: Hugh Jefferies
  Tel: (01425) 481021 *E-mail:* hjefferies@
  stanleygibbons.com
Founded: 1856
Subjects: Crafts, Games, Hobbies, Philately
ISBN Prefix(es): 978-0-85259
Parent Company: Stanley Gibbons International
  Ltd
Branch Office(s)
7 Parkside, Ringwood, Hants BH24 3SH
  Tel: (01425) 472 363 *Fax:* (01425) 470 247
6 Minden Pl, St Helier, Jersey JE2 4WQ
  Tel: (01534) 766711 *Fax:* (01534) 766177
18-20 Le Bordage, St Peter Port, Guernsey GY1
  1DE *Tel:* (01481) 708 270

Gibson Square
47 Lonsdale Sq, London N1 1EW
Tel: (020) 7096 1100 *Fax:* (020) 7993 2214
E-mail: info@gibsonsquare.com
Web Site: www.gibsonsquare.com
Key Personnel
Publishing Dir: Martin Rynja
ISBN Prefix(es): 978-1-903933; 978-1-906142;
  978-1-908096

Ginger Fox Ltd
Stirling House, College Rd, Cheltenham GL53
  7HY
Tel: (01242) 241765
E-mail: sales@gingerfox.co.uk
Web Site: gingerfox.co.uk; www.millyandflynn.
  com
ISBN Prefix(es): 978-1-909290; 978-0-9557785
Parent Company: Hacche Retail Ltd
Imprints: Milly & Flynn

Gingko Library
70 Cadogan Pl, London SW1X 9AH
Tel: (020) 7838 9055 *Fax:* (020) 7584 9501
E-mail: gingko@gingkolibrary.com
Web Site: www.gingkolibrary.com
Key Personnel
Sales: Edoardo Braschi *E-mail:* edoardo@
  gingkolibrary.com
Founded: 2014
Subjects: Architecture & Interior Design, Art, Bi-
  ography, Memoirs, Economics, Government,
  Political Science, History, Literature, Literary
  Criticism, Essays, Music, Dance, Philosophy,
  Religion - Other, Science (General)
ISBN Prefix(es): 978-1-909942
Number of titles published annually: 5 Print
Total Titles: 7 Print
Distribution Center: Macmillan Distribution,
  Lye Industrial Estate, Pontarddulais, Swansea
  SA4 8QD *Tel:* (01256) 329242 *E-mail:* order@
  macmillan.co.uk (UK & Ireland)
Chicago Distribution Center, 11030 S Lang-
  ley Ave, Chicago, IL 60628, United States
  Tel: 773-702-7000 *E-mail:* orders@press.
  uchicago.edu (worldwide exc Ireland & UK)

Glasgow City Libraries Publications+
The Mitchell Library, North St, Glasgow G3 7DN
Tel: (0141) 287 2910 *Fax:* (0141) 287 2815
E-mail: archives@glasgowlife.org.uk
Founded: 1980
Specialize in local history fact books.
Membership(s): Publishing Scotland.
Subjects: History, Regional Interests
ISBN Prefix(es): 978-0-906169; 978-0-9517010

GLMP Ltd
PO Box 225, Abergele, Conwy County LL18
  9AY
Tel: (01745) 832863 *Fax:* (01745) 826606
Key Personnel
Publisher & Dir: Dr Graham Lawler
Specialize in educational books, creative writing
  guides & professional books.
ISBN Prefix(es): 978-1-84285
Imprints: Aber Education; Aber Publishing; Mr
  Educator; Studymates
Foreign Rep(s): Durnell Marketing Ltd (Eu-
  rope); Footprint Books Pty Ltd (Australia, New
  Zealand); HRA (Caribbean); Peter Hyde As-
  sociates (South Africa); IPS Ltd (Zoe Kaviani)
  (Middle East); Trans-Atlantic Publications Inc
  (USA); The White Partnership (Asia)

Global Book Publishing
Member of Quarto International Co-Editions
  Group
Ovest House, Level 1, 58 West St, Brighton BN1
  2RA
Tel: (01273) 716009
Web Site: www.quartoknows.com/global-book-
  publishing
Key Personnel
Publisher: Nigel Browning *E-mail:* nigel.
  browning@quarto.com
Founded: 1999 (in Sydney, Australia)
Subjects: Biblical Studies, Gardening, Plants,
  Wine & Spirits, Anatomy, Mythology
ISBN Prefix(es): 978-1-74048
Ultimate Parent Company: The Quarto Group Inc

Global Professional Publishing Ltd
Random Acres, Slip Mill Lane, Hawkhurst, Kent
  TN18 5AD
Key Personnel
Dir: Tracey Dobby
Subjects: Accounting, Business, Economics, Fi-
  nance, Law, Management, Marketing, Banking
  Services, Corporate Banking, Finance & Leas-
  ing, Insurance, Investment, IT & E-Commerce,
  Lending, Marketing & Sales, Multi-National
  Finance, Risk

ISBN Prefix(es): 978-1-906403; 978-1-908287; 978-1-909170

Foreign Rep(s): APD Singapore Pte Ltd (Indonesia, Japan, Malaysia, Philippines, Singapore, Vietnam); Asia Publishing Services Ltd (China, Hong Kong, Korea, Southeast Asia, Taiwan); Avicenna Partnership Ltd (Malta, Middle East, North Africa, Northern Cyprus); Domaine de Manses (Charles Gibbs) (Cyprus, Greece, Italy); Claire de Gruchy (Jordan, Malta, North Africa, Northern Cyprus, Turkey); Laszlo Horvath (Austria, Eastern Europe); Iberian Book Services (Peter Prout) (Gibraltar, Portugal, Spain); Just in Time Business Communications (Jos de Jong) (Belgium, Liechtenstein, Luxembourg, Netherlands); Bill Kennedy (Egypt, Gulf States, Iran, Iraq, Lebanon, Libya, Middle East, Sudan, Yemen); Palgrave Macmillan (South Africa); Stylus Publishing LLC (Canada, USA); David Towle International (Scandinavia); Woodslane Pty Ltd (Australia, New Zealand)

Distribution Center: Publishers Group UK, 63-66 Hatton Garden, London EC1N 8LE *Tel:* (020) 7405 1105 *Fax:* (020) 7242 3725 *E-mail:* orders@pguk.co.uk *Web Site:* www.pguk.co.uk (UK & Ireland)

Globe Law & Business
Division of Globe Business Publishing Ltd
New Hibernia House, Winchester Walk, London Bridge, London SE1 9AG
Tel: (020) 7234 0606
Web Site: www.globelawandbusiness.com
Key Personnel
Mng Dir: Sian O'Neill *E-mail:* sian@globelawandbusiness.com
Marketing & Publications Coordinator: Nicola Hornsby *E-mail:* nicola@globelawandbusiness.com
Commissioning Editor: Katherine Cowdrey *E-mail:* kcowdrey@gbp.co.uk
Founded: 2005
Subjects: Accounting, Business, Career Development, Finance
ISBN Prefix(es): 978-0-9533255; 978-1-905783; 978-0-9548706; 978-1-909416
Orders to: NBN International *Tel:* (01752) 202301 *E-mail:* orders@nbninternational.com

Glowworm Books Ltd+
Unit 2, 5 Youngs Rd, East Mains Industrial Estate, Broxburn, W Lothian EH52 5LY
Tel: (01506) 857570 *Fax:* (01506) 858100
Web Site: www.glowwormbooks.co.uk
Key Personnel
Dir: Gordon Allan; Katrena Allan
Founded: 1999
Specialize in publishing children's picture books. Also a school supplier for textbooks & libraries (in Scotland only).
Membership(s): Booksellers Association; Scottish Publishers Association.
ISBN Prefix(es): 978-1-871512; 978-0-9557559
Number of titles published annually: 3 Print
Total Titles: 43 Print

GMC Publications Ltd+
166 High St, Lewes, East Sussex BN7 1XU
Tel: (01273) 477374; (01273) 488005 (orders)
Fax: (01273) 478606
Web Site: www.thegmcgroup.com
Key Personnel
Contact: Helen Chrystie *E-mail:* helen.chrystie@thegmcgroup.com
Publish magazines, books & DVDs for general trade.
Subjects: Cookery, Crafts, Games, Hobbies, Gardening, Plants, How-to, Photography, Woodworking
ISBN Prefix(es): 978-0-946819; 978-1-86108
Total Titles: 120 Print

Distributor for Sterling Publishing Co Inc; Taunton Press Publishers
Warehouse: Mail International Ltd, Braybon Business Park, Consort Way, Burgess Hill, West Sussex

Godsfield Press, *imprint of* Octopus Publishing Group Ltd

Godsfield Press+
Imprint of Octopus Publishing Group Ltd
Endeavor House, 189 Shaftesbury Ave, London WC2H 8JY
Tel: (020) 7632 5400 *Fax:* (020) 7632 5405
E-mail: info@octopus-publishing.co.uk
Web Site: www.octopusbooks.co.uk
Founded: 1995
Subjects: Health, Nutrition, Humor, Nonfiction (General), Divination, Esoterics/New Age, Personal Growth, Sacred Living, Spiritual Wisdom
ISBN Prefix(es): 978-1-899434; 978-1-84181
Foreign Rep(s): APD Kuala Lumpur (Malaysia); APD Singapore Pte Ltd (Singapore); Bill Bailey Publishers Representatives (Austria, Baltic States, Belgium, Cyprus, Eastern Europe, France, Germany, Iceland, Malta, Netherlands, Russia, Scandinavia, Switzerland); Jonathan Ball Publishers (South Africa); Canadian Manda Group (Canada); Everest International Publishing Services (Asia, China); Arturo Gutierrez Hernandez (Central America); Hachette Book Publishing India Pvt Ltd (Sudipto Mookherjee) (Bangladesh, India, Sri Lanka); Hachette Livre Australia (Australia); Hachette Livre NZ (New Zealand); Hachette UK Ltd (Paul Kenny) (Cambodia, Guam, Hong Kong, Indonesia, Japan, Laos, Myanmar, Papua New Guinea, Philippines, South Korea, Taiwan, Thailand, Vietnam); Hachette UK Ltd (Matt Cowdery) (Israel, Middle East, North Africa); Chris Humphrys & Lynda Hopkins (Caribbean); IntermediaAmericana Ltd (South America); Benjie Ocampo (Korea, Philippines); Octopus Books USA (USA); Padovani Books Ltd (Jenny Padovani) (Gibraltar, Portugal, Spain); Padovani Books Ltd (Penny Padovani) (Greece, Italy); Anita Zih- De Haan (Sub-Saharan Africa)
Distribution Center: Littlehampton Book Services Ltd, Faraday Close, Durrington, Worthing, West Sussex BN13 3RB *Tel:* (01903) 828500; (01903) 828501 (customer service)
Web Site: lbsltd.wp.hachette.co.uk

Golden Dawn, *imprint of* Mandrake of Oxford

Goldleaf Publishing, *imprint of* Alun Books

Gollancz, *imprint of* Orion Publishing Group Ltd

Gomer Press Ltd+
Gwasg Gomer, Llandysul, Ceredigion SA44 4JL
Tel: (01559) 363090 (publishing); (01559) 362371 (printing); (01559) 363092 (orders) *Fax:* (01559) 363758
E-mail: gwasg@gomer.co.uk; orders@gomer.co.uk; sales@gomer.co.uk
Web Site: www.gomer.co.uk
Key Personnel
Mng Dir: Jonathan Lewis *E-mail:* jonathan@gomer.co.uk
Administrative Manager: Meryl Roberts *E-mail:* meryl@gomer.co.uk
Senior Editor: Sioned Lleinau *E-mail:* sioned@gomer.co.uk
Marketing Officer: Sioned Wyn Davies *E-mail:* sionedwyn@gomer.co.uk; Nia Jenkins *E-mail:* nia@gomer.co.uk
Founded: 1892
Specialize in books from Wales, about Wales, in Welsh & English.

Subjects: Biography, Memoirs, Education, Fiction, History, Language Arts, Linguistics, Literature, Literary Criticism, Essays, Music, Dance, Nonfiction (General), Poetry, Regional Interests, Religion - Other, Sports, Athletics, Transportation, Travel & Tourism, Culture, Literary Studies, Nature
ISBN Prefix(es): 978-0-86383; 978-0-85088; 978-1-85902; 978-1-84323; 978-1-84851
Number of titles published annually: 120 Print
Total Titles: 700 Print
Parent Company: Gomer Press Ltd, Parc Menter Llandysul, Llandysul, Ceredigion SA44 4JL
Imprints: Pont Books (English books for children)
Distribution Center: Welsh Books Council, The Distribution Centre Ceredigion, Glanyrafon Enterprise Park, Llanbadarn Fawr, Aberystwyth SY23 3AQ *Tel:* (01970) 624455 *Fax:* (01970) 625506 *E-mail:* distribution.centre@wbc.org.uk
Web Site: www.gwales.com
Orders to: Welsh Books Council, The Distribution Centre Ceredigion, Glanyrafon Enterprise Park, Llanbadarn Fawr, Aberystwyth SY23 3AQ *Tel:* (01970) 624455 *Fax:* (01970) 625505 *E-mail:* distribution.centre@wbc.org.uk *Web Site:* www.gwales.com

Goodman, *imprint of* Carlton Publishing Group

Goodman Fiell, *imprint of* Carlton Publishing Group

Adam Gordon Books
Kintradwell Farmhouse, Brora, Sutherland KW9 6LU
Tel: (01408) 622660
E-mail: adam@ahg-books.com
Web Site: www.ahgbooks.com
Key Personnel
Publisher: Adam Gordon
Founded: 1990
Specialize in tramways, trolley buses & railways. Publisher of new books & dealer in second-hand books & ephemera.
Subjects: Transportation, Buses, Railways
ISBN Prefix(es): 978-1-874422
Number of titles published annually: 8 Print
Total Titles: 72 Print

Gorilla Guides, *imprint of* Stacey International

Gracewing Publishing
2 Southern Ave, Leominster, Herts HR6 0QF
Tel: (01568) 616835 *Fax:* (01568) 613289
E-mail: gracewingx@aol.com
Web Site: www.gracewing.co.uk
Subjects: Religion - Catholic, Theology, Church Biography, Ecclesiastical History
ISBN Prefix(es): 978-0-85244
Number of titles published annually: 40 Print
Total Titles: 600 Print
Distributed by Morehouse (USA)
Distributor for Ampleforth Abbey Press; Hillenbrand; Ignatius Press; Midwest Theological Forum; Newman House; Our Sunday Visitor; Saint Michael's Abbey Press; Smyth & Helwys; Source; Templegate
Distribution Center: Freedom Publishing, 9 Malvern St, Bayswater, Victoria 3153, Australia *Tel:* (03) 9720 5288 *Fax:* (03) 9816 0899 *E-mail:* accountant@newsweekly.com.au *Web Site:* www.freedompublishing.com.au
Liturgy Training Publications, 3949 S Racine Ave, Chicago, IL 60609, United States *E-mail:* orders@ltp.com *Web Site:* www.ltp.com

Graffeg Ltd
24 Stradey Park Business Centre, Mwrwg Rd, Llangennech, Llanelli, Carmarthenshire SA14 8YP
Tel: (01554) 824000; (01554) 823489

E-mail: croeso@graffeg.com
Web Site: www.graffeg.com
Key Personnel
Mng Dir: Peter Gill
Head of Sales & Marketing: Matthew Howard
Founded: 2003
Subjects: Architecture & Interior Design, Art, Cookery, Gardening, Plants, Photography, Sports, Athletics, Culture, Heritage, Landscapes, Lifestyle
ISBN Prefix(es): 978-0-9544334; 978-1-905582
Distributed by Trafalgar Square Publishing

Graffito Books Ltd
32 Great Sutton St, London EC1V 0NB
Tel: (020) 3239 0968
E-mail: contact@graffitobooks.com
Web Site: www.graffitobooks.com
Publisher of visual, counter-cultural design, graphics, street art & fashion books.
Subjects: Art, Fashion
ISBN Prefix(es): 978-0-9560284; 978-1-909051

Graham & Whiteside, *imprint of* Gale

W F Graham (Northampton) Ltd
2 Pondwood Close, Moulton Park Industrial Estate, Northampton NN3 6RT
Tel: (01604) 645537 *Fax:* (01604) 648414
E-mail: books1@wfgraham.co.uk
Web Site: www.wfgraham.co.uk
Key Personnel
Mng Dir: Timothy Angus Graham
Founded: 1952
Publisher of children's coloring & activity books.
ISBN Prefix(es): 978-1-85128

Grange Books Ltd+
PO Box 700, Rochester, Kent ME1 9LX
Tel: (01634) 255502
Web Site: www.grangebooks.co.uk
Key Personnel
Consultant, Greenwich Book Co Ltd: Stephen Ash *E-mail:* stephen.ash@greenwichbooks.co.uk
Administrative Dir: Heather Staples *E-mail:* heather.staples@greenwichbooks.co.uk
Sales & Marketing Dir: Bob Siwecki *E-mail:* bob.siwecki@grangebooks.co.uk
Founded: 1972
Discount & promotional book publisher & distributor.
Subjects: Aeronautics, Aviation, Animals, Pets, Architecture & Interior Design, Art, Astronomy, Automotive, Cookery, Crafts, Games, Hobbies, Gardening, Plants, Natural History, Nonfiction (General), Transportation, Travel & Tourism, Wine & Spirits
ISBN Prefix(es): 978-1-85627; 978-1-84013; 978-0-9509620; 978-1-84804
Imprints: Park Lane (Art)
Bookshop(s): London
Distribution Center: Gardners Books Ltd, Whittle Dr, Eastbourne, East Sussex BN23 6QH *Tel:* (01323) 521777 *Fax:* (01323) 521666 *E-mail:* custcare@gardners.com

Granta Books+
12 Addison Ave, London W11 4QR
Tel: (020) 7605 1360 *Fax:* (020) 7605 1361
E-mail: info@grantabooks.com; rights@grantabooks.com; sales@grantabooks.com
Web Site: www.grantabooks.com
Key Personnel
Publisher: Sigrid Rausing
Editorial Dir: Bella Lacey
Editorial Dir, Granta & Portobello: Laura Barber
Editorial Dir, Granta & Portobello Books: Max Porter
Mng Editor: Christine Lo
Production Dir: Sarah Wasley

Publicity Dir: Pru Rowlandson
Rights Dir: Angela Rose
Sales, Marketing & Digital Dir: Iain Chapple
Editor: Ken Bradley; Anne Meadows
Ebook & Sales Operations Manager: Katie Hayward
Publicity Manager: Aidan ONeal
Founded: 1989
Subjects: Biography, Memoirs, Fiction, History, Literature, Literary Criticism, Essays, Nonfiction (General), Travel & Tourism
ISBN Prefix(es): 978-0-14; 978-1-86207; 978-1-84708; 978-1-78378
Number of titles published annually: 25 Print
Parent Company: Granta Publications
Imprints: Granta Magazine; Portobello Books
Distributed by Allen & Unwin (Australia & New Zealand); Faber & Faber Ltd (England, Scotland & Wales); House of Anansi (Canada); Penguin Random House (Indian subcontinent)
Foreign Rep(s): Allen & Unwin Pty Ltd (Australia, New Zealand); Book Promotions (South Africa); Faber & Faber (Melissa Elders) (Austria, China, France, Germany, Hong Kong, Indonesia, Japan, Malaysia, Philippines, Singapore, South Korea, Taiwan, Thailand); Faber & Faber (Bridget Lane) (Northern Europe); Faber & Faber (Hattie Castelberg) (Middle East, Southern Europe); Gill Hess Ltd (Ireland); House of Anansi (Canada); InterMedia Americana Ltd (Africa exc South Africa); Cristian Juncu (Eastern Europe); Penguin Random House (Indian subcontinent)
Warehouse: The Book Service Ltd, Distribution Centre, Colchester Rd, Frating Green, Colchester, Essex CO7 7DW *Tel:* (01206) 256000 *Fax:* (01206) 255717 *E-mail:* sales@tbs-ltd.co.uk *Web Site:* www.thebookservice.co.uk
Distribution Center: The Book Service Ltd, Distribution Centre, Colchester Rd, Frating Green, Colchester, Essex CO7 7DW *Tel:* (01206) 256000 *Fax:* (01206) 255715 *E-mail:* sales@tbs-ltd.co.uk *Web Site:* www.thebookservice.co.uk

Granta Magazine, *imprint of* Granta Books

Greater Manchester Arts Centre Ltd, see HOME

Alison Green Books, *imprint of* Scholastic Ltd

Green Print, *imprint of* The Merlin Press Ltd

W Green The Scottish Law Publisher+
21 Alva St, Edinburgh EH2 4PS
Tel: (0131) 225 4879; (0845) 600 9355 (orders); (0845) 082 1032 (trade customers) *Fax:* (0131) 225 2104; (020) 3285 7644 (orders)
E-mail: wgreen.enquiries@thomson.com
Web Site: www.sweetandmaxwell.co.uk
Key Personnel
Dir: Gilly Grant
Publisher: Janet Campbell
Head of Editorial Operations: Rebecca Standing
Marketing Manager: Alan Bett
Subjects: Law
ISBN Prefix(es): 978-0-414
Total Titles: 140 Print; 1 CD-ROM
Parent Company: Sweet & Maxwell, London
Ultimate Parent Company: Thomson Reuters
Foreign Rep(s): Barbara Gerken (Scotland)

Greenhaven Press, *imprint of* Gale

Greenwich Medical Media, *imprint of* Cambridge University Press

Griffith Institute, *imprint of* Ashmolean Museum Publications

Grub Street Publishing Ltd+
4 Rainham Close, London SW11 6SS
Tel: (020) 7924 3966 *Fax:* (020) 7738 1008
E-mail: post@grubstreet.co.uk
Web Site: www.grubstreet.co.uk
Key Personnel
Chief Executive: Anne Dolamore
Founded: 1986
Subjects: Cookery, Health, Nutrition, Nonfiction (General), Wine & Spirits, Military Aviation History
ISBN Prefix(es): 978-0-948817; 978-1-898697; 978-1-902304; 978-1-904010; 978-1-904943; 978-1-906502; 978-1-909808; 978-1-908117; 978-1-909166
Number of titles published annually: 35 Print
Total Titles: 170 Print
Foreign Rep(s): Capricorn Link (Australia); Casemate (USA); Casemate Publishing (Andrew Tarring) (Wales, West Midlands, UK); Casemate Publishing (Jean-Marc Evans) (London, Paris, Southern England); Casemate Publishing (Sheila Hilton) (Northern England, Scotland); Ted Dougherty (Austria, Belgium, France, Germany, Switzerland); John Edgeler (Belgium, Caribbean, Greece, Italy, Middle East, Near East, Netherlands, Scandinavia, Turkey); Fitzhenry & Whiteside (Canada); Vivienne Lavery (Ireland); Nationwide Books (Andrew Tizzard) (New Zealand); Publishers Marketing Services Pte Ltd (Far East, Singapore); Research Press (India); Humphrys Roberts Associates (Portugal, Spain); Trinity Books (South Africa)
Distribution Center: Littlehampton Book Services Ltd, Faraday Close, Durrington, Worthing, West Sussex BN13 3RB *Tel:* (01903) 828500; (01903) 828501 (customer service) *Web Site:* lbsltd.wp.hachette.co.uk

Guardian Faber, *imprint of* Faber & Faber Ltd

Guild of Master Craftsman Publications Ltd, see GMC Publications Ltd

Guinea Pig Education+
2 Cobs Way, New Haw, Surrey KT15 3AF
Tel: (01932) 336554
E-mail: info@guineapigeducation.co.uk
Web Site: www.guineapigeducation.co.uk
Key Personnel
Dir: Amanda Jones *E-mail:* amanda@guineapigeducation.co.uk; Sally Wake *E-mail:* sally@guineapigeducation.co.uk
Founded: 2008
Educational publisher of books, resources, textbooks & revision guides for use at primary & secondary levels. Publish a range of books that help children learn vital English & math skills at key stages 1-4 (ages 5-14) & to help those preparing for 11+ entrance exams to grammar school or other examinations.
Subjects: Education, English as a Second Language
ISBN Prefix(es): 978-0-9558315; 978-1-907733; 978-0-9561150
Number of titles published annually: 30 Print; 30 Online
Total Titles: 50 Print; 50 Online
Foreign Rep(s): Ashton International Marketing Services (Julian Ashton) (Far East); Continental Sales (Canada, USA); Innovative Logistics (Canada, USA); John Reed Book Distribution (Australia); Star Book Sales (Dennis Buckingham) (Ireland, UK)
Warehouse: Orca Book Services UK, Unit A3, Fleets Corner Industrial Estate, Fleetsbridge, Poole, Dorset BH17 0HL *Tel:* (01202) 665432

Guinness World Records Ltd
Division of The Jim Pattison Group

South Quay Bldg, 189 Marsh Wall, London E14
9SH
Tel: (020) 7891 4567 *Fax:* (020) 7891 4501
E-mail: enquiries@guinnessworldrecords.com
Web Site: www.guinnessworldrecords.com
Key Personnel
Global President: Alistair Richards
Senior Vice President, Records: Marco Frigatti
Editor-in-Chief: Craig Glenday
Editor, Garner's Edition: Stephen Daultrey
Founded: 1955
Subjects: Military Science, Music, Dance, Sports,
Athletics
ISBN Prefix(es): 978-0-900424; 978-0-85112;
978-1-892051; 978-1-904994
U.S. Office(s): Guinness World Records NA Inc,
45 W 45 St, Suite 902, New York, NY 10036,
United States, SVP, Americas: Peter Harper
Tel: 718-513-7270
Distributed by Macmillan (USA)
Warehouse: Macmillan Distribution, Brunel Rd,
Houndmills, Basingstoke, Hants RG21 6XS
Tel: (08450) 705 656 *Fax:* (01256) 812 558

Gulf Professional Publishing, *imprint of* Elsevier
Ltd

Gwasg Carreg Gwalch+
12 Iard yr Orsaf, Llanrwst, Dyffryn, Conwy LL26
0EH
Tel: (01492) 642031 *Fax:* (01492) 641502
E-mail: llanrwst@carreg-gwalch.com
Web Site: www.carreg-gwalch.co.uk
Key Personnel
Dir: Myrddin ap Dafydd
Founded: 1980
Privately owned publisher & printing company.
Subjects: Art, Crafts, Games, Hobbies, Outdoor
Recreation, Photography, Transportation, Travel
& Tourism, Walking & Mountaineering, Welsh
& Celtic Interest, Welsh Language
ISBN Prefix(es): 978-0-86381; 978-1-84524; 978-
1-84527
Number of titles published annually: 70 Print
Total Titles: 1,200 Print
Branch Office(s)
Ysgubor Plas, Llwyndyrys, Pwllheli, Gwynedd
LL53 6NG *Tel:* (01758) 750432 *Fax:* (01758)
750438 *E-mail:* llyfrau@carreg-gwalch.com
Distribution Center: Welsh Book Council,
Riverside Industrial Estate, Llanbadarn Fawr,
Aberystwyth SY23 2JB *Tel:* (01970) 624455

Hachette Audio, *imprint of* Little, Brown Book
Group

Hachette Children's Books+
Division of Hachette UK
Carmelite House, 50 Victoria Embankment, Lon-
don EC4Y 0DZ
Tel: (020) 3122 6000
E-mail: ad@hachettechildrens.co.uk
Web Site: www.hachettechildrens.co.uk
Key Personnel
Senior Publisher: Anne McNeil
Deputy Mng Dir: Clare Somerville
Editorial Dir, Fiction: Jon Appleton
Editorial Dir, Hodder & Quercus Children's:
Sarah Lambert
Commercial Dir: Clare Somerville
Trade Sales Dir: Paul Litherland
UK Sales Dir: Jason McKenzie
Founded: 1868
Subjects: Fiction, Nonfiction (General), Science
Fiction, Fantasy
ISBN Prefix(es): 978-0-340; 978-0-450; 978-1-
85998; 978-1-4449
Ultimate Parent Company: Lagardere
Imprints: Franklin Watts; Hodder Children's
Books; Hodder Silver (science fiction/fantasy);
Orchard Books; Wayland

Foreign Rep(s): Angell Eurosales (Gill Angell)
(Denmark, Finland, Iceland, Norway, Sweden);
Ted Dougherty (Belgium, France, Luxembourg,
Netherlands); Emkay Books International (Ar-
slan Matin Khan) (Pakistan); Everest Interna-
tional Publishing Services (Wei Zhao) (China);
Hachette Book Group Canada (Canada); Ha-
chette India (India); Hachette New Zealand
(New Zealand); Hachette UK Ltd (Paul Kenny)
(Hong Kong, Indonesia, Japan, Laos, Myan-
mar, South Korea, Taiwan, Thailand, Vietnam);
Hachette UK Ltd (Matt Cowdery) (Middle
East); Humphrys Roberts Associates (Christo-
pher Humphrys) (Caribbean, Central America);
IMA (David Williams) (Central America, South
America); Adriana Juncu (Eastern Europe);
Padovani Books Ltd (Penny Padovani) (Cyprus,
Gibraltar, Greece, Italy, Portugal, Spain); Pan
Macmillan SA (South Africa); Pansing Dis-
tribution Pte Ltd (Malaysia, Singapore); Pub-
lishers Services (Gabriele Kern) (Austria, Ger-
many, Switzerland)
Orders to: Bookpoint Ltd, 130 Milton Park,
Abingdon, Oxon OX14 4SB *Tel:* (01235) 400
400 *Web Site:* bookpoint.wp.hachette.co.uk

Hachette UK
Subsidiary of Hachette Livre
Carmelite House, 50 Victoria Embankment, Lon-
don EC4Y 0DZ
Tel: (020) 3122 6000
E-mail: enquiries@hachette.co.uk
Web Site: www.hachette.co.uk
Key Personnel
Chief Executive Officer: David Shelley
Chairman, Little, Brown Book Group: Ursula
Mackenzie
Chief Executive Officer, Hodder & Stoughton,
John Murray Press, Headline & Quercus/Dir,
Trade Publishing: Jamie Hodder-Williams
Chief Executive, Octopus Publishing Group: Ali-
son Goff
Deputy Chief Executive Officer: Richard Kitson
Group Chief Operating Officer: Chris Emerson
Publisher, Orion Publishing Group: Jon Wood
Mng Dir, Children's: Ruth Alltimes
Mng Dir, Distribution: Matt Wright
Mng Dir, Headline Publishing Group: Jane Mor-
peth
Brand Development Dir: Damian Horner
Finance Dir: Emily-Jane Taylor
Group Communications Dir: Clare Harington
Group Finance Dir: Pierre de Cacqueray
Group Human Resources Dir: Dominic Mahony
Digital & Development Dir: George Walkley
Dir, Subsidiary Rights: Jason Bartholomew
International Sales Dir: Ben Wright
Founded: 1986
ISBN Prefix(es): 978-0-340; 978-0-7131; 978-1-
84456; 978-0-7122; 978-0-7553; 978-1-84616;
978-1-85998
Ultimate Parent Company: Lagardere
Divisions: Chambers Harrap; Hachette Australia;
Hachette Book Publishing India Pvt Ltd; Ha-
chette Children's Books; Hachette Ireland;
Hachette New Zealand; Headline Publishing
Group; Hodder & Stoughton; Hodder Edu-
cation; Little, Brown Book Group; Octopus
Publishing Group; Orion Publishing Group;
Quercus
U.S. Office(s): Hachette Book Group USA, 1290
Avenue of the Americas, New York, NY
10104, United States
Distribution Center: Bookpoint Ltd, 130 Milton
Park, Abingdon, Oxon OX14 4SB *Tel:* (01235)
400 400 *Web Site:* bookpoint.wp.hachette.co.uk
Littlehampton Book Services Ltd, Faraday Close,
Durrington, Worthing, West Sussex BN13 3RB
Tel: (01903) 828500; (01903) 828501 (cus-
tomer service) *Web Site:* lbsltd.wp.hachette.co.
uk

Orders to: Bookpoint Ltd, 130 Milton Park,
Abingdon, Oxon OX14 4SB *Tel:* (01235) 400
400 *Web Site:* bookpoint.wp.hachette.co.uk
Littlehampton Book Services Ltd, Faraday Close,
Durrington, Worthing, West Sussex BN13 3RB
Tel: (01903) 828500; (01903) 828501 (cus-
tomer service) *Web Site:* lbsltd.wp.hachette.co.
uk

The Hakluyt Society
c/o Map Library, British Library, 96 Euston Rd,
London NW1 2DB
Tel: (01428) 641850 *Fax:* (01428) 641933
E-mail: office@hakluyt.com
Web Site: www.hakluyt.com
Key Personnel
President: Captain Michael Barritt
Founded: 1846
A registered charity inspired by & named af-
ter Richard Hakluyt (1552-1616), the famous
collector & editor of narratives of voyages &
travels & other documents relating to English
interests overseas.
Subjects: Geography, Geology, History, Travel &
Tourism
ISBN Prefix(es): 978-0-904180
Number of titles published annually: 2 Print
Distributed by Ashgate Publishing Direct Sales

Halban Publishers Ltd+
22 Golden Sq, London W1F 9JW
Tel: (020) 7437 9300 *Fax:* (020) 7431 9512
E-mail: books@halbanpublishers.com
Web Site: www.halbanpublishers.com
Key Personnel
Mng Dir: Martine Halban; Peter Halban
Founded: 1986
Membership(s): Independent Publishers Guild.
Subjects: Biography, Memoirs, Fiction, History,
Philosophy, Religion - Other
ISBN Prefix(es): 978-1-870015; 978-1-905559
Number of titles published annually: 10 Print
Total Titles: 60 Print
Foreign Rep(s): Orion (export sales dept)
Shipping Address: Littlehampton Book Ser-
vices Ltd, Faraday Close, Durrington, Wor-
thing, West Sussex BN13 3RB, Contact: Tim
Kinghorn *Tel:* (01903) 828500; (01903) 828501
(customer service) *Web Site:* lbsltd.wp.hachette.
co.uk
Warehouse: Littlehampton Book Services Ltd,
Faraday Close, Durrington, Worthing, West
Sussex BN13 3RB, Contact: Tim Kinghorn
Tel: (01903) 828500; (01903) 828501 (cus-
tomer service) *Web Site:* lbsltd.wp.hachette.co.
uk
Distribution Center: Littlehampton Book Services Ltd, Faraday Close, Durrington, Wor-
thing, West Sussex BN13 3RB *Tel:* (01903)
828500; (01903) 828501 (customer service)
Web Site: lbsltd.wp.hachette.co.uk
Orders to: Littlehampton Book Services Ltd,
Faraday Close, Durrington, Worthing, West
Sussex BN13 3RB, Contact: Rose Mellish
Tel: (01903) 828500; (01903) 828501 (customer service) *Web Site:* lbsltd.wp.hachette.co.
uk

Haldane Mason Ltd+
PO Box 34196, London NW10 3YB
Tel: (020) 8459 2131 *Fax:* (020) 8728 1216
E-mail: info@haldanemason.com
Web Site: www.haldanemason.com
Key Personnel
Editorial: Sydney Francis *E-mail:* sfrancis@
haldanemason.com
Production: Ron Samuel *E-mail:* rsamuel@
haldanemason.com
Rights: Andrew Duncan *E-mail:* aduncan@
haldanemason.com

Subjects: Crafts, Games, Hobbies, Health, Nutrition, Nonfiction (General), Sports, Athletics, Mind, Body, Spirit
ISBN Prefix(es): 978-1-902463; 978-1-905339
Imprints: Red Kite Books (children's)
Distribution Center: Orca Book Services, Fleets Corner Industrial Estate, Unit A3, Nuffield Rd, Dorset BH17 0HL *Tel:* (01235) 465521 *Fax:* (01235) 465555 *E-mail:* tradeorders@ orcabookservices.co.uk

GK Hall & Co, *imprint of* Gale

Halsted Press, *imprint of* John Wiley & Sons Ltd

Hamish Hamilton, *imprint of* Penguin Books Ltd

Hamish Hamilton+
Imprint of Penguin Books Ltd
80 Strand, London WC2R 0RL
Tel: (020) 7010 3000 *Fax:* (020) 7010 6692
E-mail: hamish@hamishhamilton.co.uk
Web Site: www.hamishhamilton.co.uk
Key Personnel
Publisher: Simon Prosser *Tel:* (020) 7010 3281 *E-mail:* simon.prosser@penguin.co.uk
Mng Dir: Tom Weldon *Tel:* (020) 7010 3280 *E-mail:* tom.weldon@penguin.co.uk
Founded: 1931
Subjects: Art, Biography, Memoirs, Fiction, Government, Political Science, Nonfiction (General), Philosophy, Travel & Tourism, Nature
ISBN Prefix(es): 978-0-14; 978-0-241
Warehouse: Central Park, Unit 1, 3 Castle Mound Way, Rugby, Warwicks CV23 0WB

Hamlyn, *imprint of* Octopus Publishing Group Ltd

Hamlyn+
Imprint of Octopus Publishing Group Ltd
Endeavor House, 189 Shaftesbury Ave, London WC2H 8JY
Tel: (020) 7632 5400 *Fax:* (020) 7632 5405
E-mail: info@octopus-publishing.co.uk
Web Site: www.octopusbooks.co.uk
Founded: 1947
International publisher of high quality illustrated, nonfiction for the general market.
Subjects: Architecture & Interior Design, Cookery, Crafts, Games, Hobbies, Fashion, Film, Video, Gardening, Plants, Health, Nutrition, History, Music, Dance, Natural History, Nonfiction (General), Sports, Athletics
ISBN Prefix(es): 978-0-600; 978-0-601
Foreign Rep(s): APD Kuala Lumpur (Lillian Koe) (Malaysia); APD Singapore Pte Ltd (Ian Pringle) (Cambodia, Guam, Hong Kong, Indonesia, Japan, Laos, Philippines, Singapore, South Korea, Taiwan, Thailand, Vietnam); Bill Bailey Publishers Representatives (Austria, Baltic States, Belgium, Eastern Europe, France, Germany, Iceland, Netherlands, Russia, Scandinavia, Switzerland); Jonathan Ball Publishers (South Africa); Canadian Manda Group (Canada); Arturo Gutierrez Hernandez (Central America); Hachette Book Group Ireland (Ireland, Northern Ireland); Hachette Book Publishing India Pvt Ltd (Kapil Agrawal) (Bangladesh, India, Sri Lanka); Hachette Livre Australia (Australia); Hachette Livre NZ (New Zealand); Hachette UK Ltd (Paul Kenny) (Myanmar, Papua New Guinea); Hachette UK Ltd (Matt Cowdery) (Cyprus, Israel, Middle East, North Africa); Chris Humphrys & Lynda Hopkins (Caribbean); Intermedia Americana Ltd (David Williams) (South America); Octopus Books USA (USA); Padovani Books Ltd (Jenny Padovani) (Gibraltar, Portugal, Spain); Padovani Books Ltd (Penny Padovani) (Greece, Italy); Anita Zih-De Haan (Sub-Saharan Africa)

Distribution Center: Littlehampton Book Services, Faraday Close, Durrington, Worthing, West Sussex BN13 3RB *Tel:* (01903) 828 511 *Fax:* (01903) 828 801

Hammer, *imprint of* The Random House Group Ltd, a Penguin Random House Company

Hammersmith Books Ltd+
4/4A Bloomsbury Sq, London WC1A 2RP
Tel: (01892) 839819 (book orders only)
Fax: (01892) 839819 (book orders only)
E-mail: info@hammersmithbooks.co.uk
Web Site: www.hammersmithbooks.co.uk
Founded: 2009
Publisher of health books & literary medicine.
Membership(s): Independent Publishers' Guild, UK.
Subjects: Biography, Memoirs, Health, Nutrition, Medicine, Nursing, Dentistry, Poetry, Self-Help
ISBN Prefix(es): 978-1-905140; 978-1-78161 (Hammersmith Health Books)
Number of titles published annually: 5 Print
Total Titles: 30 Print
Imprints: Hammersmith Health Books
Foreign Rep(s): Princeton Selling Group (USA); Sula Books (South Africa)
Foreign Rights: John Scott & Co (worldwide)
Warehouse: Combined Book Services (CBS) Ltd, Paddock Wood Distribution Centre, Unit D, Paddock Wood, Tonbridge TN12 6UU *Tel:* (01892) 837171 *Fax:* (01892) 837272 *E-mail:* orders@combook.co.uk *Web Site:* www.combook.co.uk
Distribution Center: Combined Book Services (CBS) Ltd, Paddock Wood Distribution Centre, Unit D, Paddock Wood, Tonbridge TN12 6UU *Tel:* (01892) 837171 *Fax:* (01892) 837272 *E-mail:* orders@combook.co.uk *Web Site:* www.combook.co.uk
Orders to: Combined Book Services (CBS) Ltd, Paddock Wood Distribution Centre, Unit D, Paddock Wood, Tonbridge TN12 6UU *Tel:* (01892) 837171 *Fax:* (01892) 837272 *E-mail:* orders@combook.co.uk *Web Site:* www.combook.co.uk

Hammersmith Health Books, *imprint of* Hammersmith Books Ltd

The Handsel Press+
35 Dunbar Rd, Haddington EH41 3PJ
Tel: (01620) 824896
Web Site: www.handselpress.co.uk; handselpress.org.uk
Key Personnel
Chairman: Fergus MacDonald
Editor: Rev Jock Stein *Tel:* (01620) 824896 *E-mail:* jstein@handselpress.org.uk
Founded: 1976
Subjects: Theology
ISBN Prefix(es): 978-0-905312; 978-1-871828

Happy Cat Books, *imprint of* Catnip Publishing Ltd

Hard Case Crime, *imprint of* Titan Books Ltd

Harden's Ltd
The Brew, Victoria House, Paul St, London EC2A 4NA
Tel: (020) 7839 4763
E-mail: editorial@hardens.com
Web Site: www.hardens.com
Key Personnel
Owner: Peter Harden
Founded: 1991
Publish consumer guides, restaurant guides in particular. Specialize in corporate gift editions.
Membership(s): IPG.
Subjects: Foreign Countries, Travel & Tourism

ISBN Prefix(es): 978-1-873721
Number of titles published annually: 5 Print; 2 E-Book
Total Titles: 10 Print; 2 E-Book

Harlequin Mills & Boon
Subsidiary of Harlequin Enterprises Ltd
Eton House, 18-24 Paradise Rd, Richmond, Surrey TW9 1SR
Tel: (020) 8288 2800 *Fax:* (020) 8288 2898
E-mail: info@millsandboon.co.uk
Web Site: www.millsandboon.co.uk
Key Personnel
Editorial Dir: Joanne Grant
Executive Editor, UK Acquisitions: Bryony Green
Senior Mng Editor: Samantha Walmsley
Assistant Mng Editor: Lucy Gough
Senior Editor: Linda Fildew; Sheila Hodgson
Senior Editor, Harlequin Presents/Mills & Boon Modern: Flo Nicoll
Editor, Harlequin Medical Romance & Harlequin Romance: Sareeta Domingo
Associate Editor: Carly Byrne; Suzanne Clark; Megan Haslam; Sarah Stubbs
Associate Editor, Harlequin Historical: Nicola Caws
Assistant Editor: Laurie Prescott
Assistant Editor, Harlequin Historical: Kathryn Cheshire
Founded: 1908
Subjects: Fiction, Romance
ISBN Prefix(es): 978-0-263; 978-0-373; 978-0-340; 978-0-204; 978-0-7783; 978-1-84845; 978-1-4089; 978-1-4720; 978-1-4740
Number of titles published annually: 120 Print
Imprints: Carina Press

Harper NonFiction, *imprint of* HarperCollins UK

HarperAudio, *imprint of* HarperCollins UK

HarperCollins Children's Books, *imprint of* HarperCollins UK

HarperCollins UK+
Division of HarperCollins Publishers
The News Bldg, One London Bridge St, London SE1 9GF
Tel: (020) 8741 7070
E-mail: uk.orders@harpercollins.co.uk; enquiries@harpercollins.co.uk
Web Site: www.harpercollins.co.uk
Key Personnel
Chief Executive Officer: Charlie Redmayne
Chief Information Officer: Laura Meyer
Chief Marketing Officer: Barnaby Dawe
Financial Controller: David Alford
Executive Publisher, Fiction & Nonfiction: Kate Elton
Executive Publisher, 4th Estate & William Collins: David Roth-Ey
Executive Publisher, HarperCollins Children's Books: Ann-Janine Murtagh
Publisher, Crime & Thrillers: Julia Wisdom
Publisher, Nonfiction: Natalie Jerome
Associate Publisher, HarperCollins Children's Books: Alison Ruane
Publishing Dir, Fiction & Nonfiction: Jack Fogg
Publishing Dir, HarperCollins Children's Books: Nick Lake
Publishing & Creative Dir, HarperCollins Children's Books: Rachel Denwood
Publishing Dir, The Borough Press: Suzie Doore
Deputy Publishing Dir, Voyager: Emma Coode
Audio Dir: Jo Forshaw
Communications Dir: Fiona Allen
Corporate Development Dir: Alex Beecroft
Dir, People: John Athanasiou
Editorial Dir, HarperCollins Children's Books: Harriet Wilson
Finance Dir: Ed Kielbasiewicz

Global Dir, Pricing & Analytics: Eloy Sasot
Group Sales Dir: Oliver Wright
European Sales Dir: Pauline Gilbert
International Sales Dir: Laura Christie
Insight Dir: Rufus Weston
Marketing Dir, HarperCollins Children's Books: Nicola Way
Public Relations & Communications Dir, Harper-Collins Children's Books: Geraldine Stroud
Special Projects Dir: Katie Fulford
Account Manager, Children's Sales: J P Hunting
Senior Communications Officer: James Lewis
Assistant Editor, HarperFiction: Claire Palmer
Founded: 1819
Membership(s): Publishers Association.
Subjects: Animals, Pets, Anthropology, Art, Astrology, Occult, Behavioral Sciences, Biblical Studies, Biography, Memoirs, Business, Child Care & Development, Cookery, Crafts, Games, Hobbies, English as a Second Language, Fiction, Film, Video, Finance, Foreign Countries, Gardening, Plants, Government, Political Science, Health, Nutrition, History, House & Home, How-to, Human Relations, LGBTQ, Literature, Literary Criticism, Essays, Management, Mysteries, Suspense, Natural History, Nonfiction (General), Outdoor Recreation, Philosophy, Psychology, Psychiatry, Romance, Science Fiction, Fantasy, Self-Help, Sports, Athletics, Theology, Travel & Tourism, Wine & Spirits, Women's Studies
ISBN Prefix(es): 978-0-06; 978-0-00; 978-0-246; 978-0-261; 978-0-586; 978-0-85152; 978-0-01; 978-0-411; 978-1-55468
Ultimate Parent Company: News Corp
Imprints: Avon; Blue Door; The Borough Press; Collins; William Collins; 4th Estate; The Friday Project; HarperAudio; HarperCollins Children's Books; HarperFiction; HarperImpulse; Harper NonFiction; Harper360; HarperVoyager; HQ; Thorsons; The Times Books
U.S. Office(s): 195 Broadway, New York, NY 10007, United States *Tel:* 212-207-7000
Distributor for Anova: Carlton Publishing; Collins Debden; Egmont Books; Folens Education; Harlequin Mills & Boon; Hinkler; Leckie & Leckie; Letts/Lonsdale; Luath Press; Simon & Schuster; Usborne Books at Home; Usborne Publishing
Distribution Center: Westerhill Rd, Bishopbriggs, Glasgow G64 2QT

HarperFiction, *imprint of* HarperCollins UK

HarperImpulse, *imprint of* HarperCollins UK

Harper360, *imprint of* HarperCollins UK

HarperVoyager, *imprint of* HarperCollins UK

Hart Publishing Ltd, *imprint of* Bloomsbury Publishing Plc

Hart Publishing Ltd+
Imprint of Bloomsbury Publishing PLC
16C Worcester Pl, Oxford, Oxon OX1 2JW
Tel: (01865) 517530 *Fax:* (01865) 510710
E-mail: mail@hartpub.co.uk
Web Site: www.hartpub.co.uk
Key Personnel
Publisher & General Manager: Sinead Moloney
   E-mail: sinead@hartpub.co.uk
Mng Editor: Mel Hamill *E-mail:* mel@hartpub.co.uk
Commissioning Editor: Bill Asquith
   E-mail: bill@hartpub.co.uk
Journals Manager: Ken Bruce *E-mail:* ken.bruce@bloomsbury.com
Production Manager: Tom Adams *E-mail:* tom@hartpub.co.uk

Marketing Coordinator: Jo Ledger *E-mail:* jo@hartpub.co.uk
Founded: 1996
Academic law publisher.
Subjects: Law
ISBN Prefix(es): 978-1-84113; 978-1-901362; 978-1-84731; 978-1-84946
Number of titles published annually: 65 Print
Total Titles: 700 Print; 400 E-Book
Distribution Center: Macmillan Distribution Ltd (MDL), Brunel Rd, Houndmills, Basingstoke, Hants RG21 6XS *Tel:* (01256) 302692 *Fax:* (01256) 812521 *E-mail:* orders@macmillan.co.uk (worldwide exc Australia, Canada & USA)
Bloomsbury Publishing Pty Ltd, 387 George St, Level 4, Sydney, NSW 2000, Australia *Tel:* (02) 8820 4900 *E-mail:* au@bloomsbury.com
Codasat Canada Ltd, 1153-56 St, PO Box 19150, Delta, BC V4L 2P8, Canada *Tel:* 604-228-9952 *Fax:* 604-222-2965 *E-mail:* info@codasat.com
ISBS (International Specialized Book Services), 920 NE 58 Ave, Suite 300, Portland, OR 97213-3786, United States *Tel:* 503-287-3093 *Fax:* 503-280-8832 *E-mail:* orders@isbs.com

Harvard University Press+
Vernon House, 23 Sicilian Ave, London WC1A 2QS
Tel: (020) 3463 2350 *Fax:* (020) 7831 9261
E-mail: info@harvardup.co.uk
Web Site: www.hup.harvard.edu
Key Personnel
Sales Dir, Trade: Richard Howells
   E-mail: rhowells@harvardup.co.uk
Marketing Manager: Rebekah White
   E-mail: rwhite@harvardup.co.uk
Founded: 1913
Subjects: Anthropology, Asian Studies, Behavioral Sciences, Biological Sciences, Business, Earth Sciences, Economics, Education, Film, Video, Government, Political Science, History, Law, Literature, Literary Criticism, Essays, Medicine, Nursing, Dentistry, Natural History, Nonfiction (General), Philosophy, Psychology, Psychiatry, Religion - Jewish, Science (General), Social Sciences, Sociology, Women's Studies
ISBN Prefix(es): 978-0-674
Imprints: Belknap
Subsidiaries: The Loeb Classical Library
U.S. Office(s): 79 Garden St, Cambridge, MA 02138, United States *Tel:* 617-495-2600 *Fax:* 617-495-5898 *E-mail:* contact_hup@harvard.edu
Orders to: John Wiley & Sons Ltd, Southern Cross Trading Estate, One Oldlands Way, Bognor Regis, West Sussex PO22 9SA *Tel:* (01243) 843291 *Fax:* (01243) 843303

Harvey Map Services Ltd+
12-22 Main St, Doune, Perthshire FK16 6BJ
Tel: (01786) 841202 *Fax:* (01786) 841098
E-mail: winni@harveymaps.co.uk; sales@harveymaps.co.uk
Web Site: www.harveymaps.co.uk
Key Personnel
Dir: Robin Harvey; Susan Harvey
Founded: 1977
Also acts as mapmakers.
Subjects: Education, Sports, Athletics
ISBN Prefix(es): 978-1-85137

Harvill Secker, *imprint of* The Random House Group Ltd, a Penguin Random House Company

Harvill Secker+
Imprint of The Random House Group Ltd, a Penguin Random House Company

c/o The Random House Group Ltd, 20 Vauxhall Bridge Rd, London SW1V 2SA
Tel: (020) 7840 8400 *Fax:* (020) 7233 8791
E-mail: enquiries@randomhouse.co.uk; harvillseckereditorial@randomhouse.co.uk; harvillseckerpublicity@randomhouse.co.uk
Web Site: www.randomhouse.co.uk/harvillsecker; www.vintage-books.co.uk/about-us/harvill-secker
Key Personnel
Mng Dir: Richard Cable
Deputy Mng Dir: Faye Brewster
Deputy Publishing Dir: Kate Harvey
Founded: 1946
Subjects: Anthropology, Biography, Memoirs, Fiction, Gardening, Plants, History, Literature, Literary Criticism, Essays, Mathematics, Natural History, Nonfiction (General), Philosophy, Photography, Poetry, Self-Help, Travel & Tourism, African Studies, Anthology, Art History, Crime Fiction, Current Affairs, Letters, Memoirs, Mythology, Politics, Russian Studies
ISBN Prefix(es): 978-1-86046; 978-1-84343
Total Titles: 800 Print

Hassle Free Press, *imprint of* Knockabout Comics

Haus Publishing
70, Cadogan Pl, London SW1X 9AH
Tel: (020) 7838 9055 *Fax:* (020) 7584 9501
E-mail: info@hauspublishing.com; sales@hauspublishing.com; publicity@hauspublishing.com
Web Site: www.hauspublishing.com; www.bookhaus.co.uk
Key Personnel
Owner: Dr Barbara Schwepcke
Associate Publisher: Harry Hall
Submissions: Emma Henderson *E-mail:* emma@hauspublishing.com
Founded: 2003
Subjects: Art, Biography, Memoirs, Drama, Theater, Fiction, Government, Political Science, History, Literature, Literary Criticism, Essays, Music, Dance, Nonfiction (General), Photography, Travel & Tourism, Sustainability History
ISBN Prefix(es): 978-1-905791; 978-1-906598; 978-1-904341; 978-1-904950; 978-1-910376; 978-1-909961; 978-1-907973; 978-1-907822
Imprints: Armchair Traveller
Distributed by University of Chicago Press
Distribution Center: Macmillan Distribution Ltd, Lye Industrial Estate, Pontardulais, Swansea SA4 8QD *Tel:* (01256) 329242 *E-mail:* order@macmillan.co.uk *Web Site:* www.macmillandistribution.co.uk

Hawker Publications Ltd+
Culvert House, Culvert Rd, London SW11 5DH
Tel: (020) 7720 2108 *Fax:* (020) 7498 3023
E-mail: info@hawkerpublications.com
Web Site: www.careinfo.org
Key Personnel
Dir: Richard Hawkins; Pat Petker
Founded: 1985
Provides a wide range of information to professionals working with elderly people & in the children's nursery sector.
Subjects: Child Care & Development, Medicine, Nursing, Dentistry
ISBN Prefix(es): 978-1-874790
Number of titles published annually: 12 Print
Total Titles: 18 Print
Warehouse: Plymbridge, Estover Rd, Plymouth PL6 7P2 *Fax:* (01752) 202330

Hawthorn Press+
Hawthorn House, One Lansdown Lane, Stroud, Glos GL5 1BJ
Tel: (01453) 757040 *Fax:* (01453) 751138
E-mail: info@hawthornpress.com

Web Site: www.hawthornpress.com
Key Personnel
Dir: Martin Large
Head, Design & Production: Claire Percival
Accounts & Foreign Rights Manager: Farimah
  Englefield
Founded: 1980
Membership(s): Independent Publishers Guild.
Subjects: Child Care & Development, Crafts,
  Games, Hobbies, Education, Inspirational, Spir-
  ituality, Philosophy, Psychology, Psychiatry,
  Women's Studies
ISBN Prefix(es): 978-1-869890; 978-1-903458;
  978-0-9507062; 978-1-902069; 978-1-907359
Number of titles published annually: 10 Print
Total Titles: 100 Print
Distributed by Ceres Books (New Zealand); Foot-
  print Books (Australia); Steiner Books (USA);
  Rudolf Steiner Publications (South Africa); Tri-
  fold Books (Canada)
Distribution Center: Trafalgar Square Publishing
  (Canada & USA)
Orders to: BookSource, 50 Cambuslang
  Rd, Glasgow G32 8NB *Tel:* (0845)
  370 0063 *Fax:* (0845) 370 0064
  E-mail: customerservice@booksource.net

Hay House UK Ltd+
33 Notting Hill Gate, London W11 3JQ
Tel: (020) 3675 2450 *Toll Free Tel:* 0 333 240
  2480 (customer service) *Fax:* (020) 3675 2451
Web Site: www.hayhouse.co.uk
Key Personnel
Founder: Louise L Hay
Commissioning Editor: Amy Kiberd
Founded: 1984
Subjects: Alternative, Health, Nutrition, Inspira-
  tional, Spirituality, Self-Help
ISBN Prefix(es): 978-1-84850; 978-1-78180
Branch Office(s)
Hay House Australia Pty Ltd, 18/36 Ralph St,
  Alexandria, NSW 2015, Australia *Tel:* (02)
  9669 4299 *Fax:* (02) 9669 4144 *Web
  Site:* www.hayhouse.com.au
Hay House Publishers India, Muskaan Complex,
  Plot No 3, B-2, Vasant Kunj, New Delhi 110
  070, India *Tel:* (011) 4176 1620 *Fax:* (011)
  4176 1630 *Web Site:* www.hayhouse.co.in
Hay House SA (Pty) Ltd, PO Box 990, Witkop-
  pen 2068, South Africa *Tel:* (011) 326 3449
  Fax: (011) 326 3449 *Web Site:* www.hayhouse.
  co.za
U.S. Office(s): Hay House Inc, PO Box 5100,
  Carlsbad, CA 92018-5100, United States *Web
  Site:* www.hayhouse.com
Hay House Inc, 250 Park Ave S, Suite 201, New
  York, NY, United States *Tel:* 646-484-4950
  Fax: 646-484-4956

Haynes Publishing+
Sparkford, Yeovil, Somerset BA22 7JJ
Tel: (01963) 440635; (01476) 541085 (trade)
  Fax: (01476) 541063 (trade)
Web Site: www.haynes.com
Key Personnel
Mng Dir, Haynes Consumer: Jeremy Yates-Round
Editorial Manager, Manuals Division: John Austin
Editorial Manager, Practical Lifestyle: Louise
  McIntyre
International Sales, Foreign Rights & Co-
  Editions: Graham Cook *Tel:* (01963) 442028
  E-mail: gcook@haynes.co.uk
Licensing & Client Publishing: Iain Wakefield
  E-mail: iwakefield@haynes.co.uk
Founded: 1960
Subjects: Aeronautics, Aviation, Animals, Pets,
  Automotive, Computer Science, Cookery, Gov-
  ernment, Political Science, Health, Nutrition,
  History, House & Home, How-to, Maritime,
  Outdoor Recreation, Technology, Transporta-
  tion, Car & Motorcycle Service & Repair, Mo-
  toring, Motorsports, Restoration

ISBN Prefix(es): 978-1-85010; 978-0-85696; 978-
  1-56392; 978-1-85960; 978-1-84425; 978-0-
  900550; 978-1-85260; 978-0-85733
Number of titles published annually: 100 Print
Total Titles: 2,280 Print
Parent Company: Haynes Publishing Group PLC
Branch Office(s)
Haynes Australia Pty Ltd, Willfox St, Unit
  8, Condell Park, NSW 2200, Australia
  Tel: (02) 8713 1400 *Fax:* (02) 9708 3070
  E-mail: sales@haynes.com.au *Web Site:* www.
  haynes.com.au
HaynesPro BV, Flankement 6, 3831 SM Leusden,
  Netherlands *Tel:* (035) 603 6270 *Fax:* (035)
  602 7597 *E-mail:* info@haynespro.com *Web
  Site:* www.haynespro.com
U.S. Office(s): Haynes Manuals Inc, 859
  Lawrence Dr, Newbury Park, CA 91320,
  United States *Tel:* 805-498-6703 *Fax:* 805-
  498-2867 *E-mail:* sales@haynes.com *Web
  Site:* www.haynes.com
Foreign Rep(s): Haynes Australia (Australia, New
  Zealand); Quarto (North America)
Distribution Center: Grantham Book Ser-
  vices, Trent Rd, Grantham NG31 7XQ
  E-mail: orders@gbs.tbs-ltd.co.uk

Hayward Gallery Publishing+
Southbank Centre, Belvedere Rd, London SE1
  8XX
Tel: (020) 7960 4200 *Fax:* (020) 7921 0607
E-mail: customer@southbankcentre.co.uk
Web Site: www.southbankcentre.co.uk
Key Personnel
Publications Sales Officer: Alex Glen *Tel:* (020)
  7921 0826 *E-mail:* alex.glen@southbankcentre.
  co.uk
Press & Marketing Coordinator: Diana Adell
  Tel: (020) 7960 4357 *E-mail:* diana.adell@
  southbankcentre.co.uk
Subjects: Architecture & Interior Design, Art,
  Music, Dance, Photography, Visual Arts
ISBN Prefix(es): 978-1-85332
Number of titles published annually: 8 Print
Foreign Rep(s): Cornerhouse Publications (world-
  wide exc North America); Distributed Art Pub-
  lishers (Central America, North America, South
  America)
Distribution Center: Cornerhouse Publications,
  70 Oxford St, Manchester M1 5NH *Tel:* (0161)
  228 7621 *E-mail:* publications@cornerhouse.
  org *Web Site:* www.cornerhouse.org
DAP/Distributed Art Publishers Inc, 818 S Broad-
  way, Suite 700, Los Angeles, CA 90014,
  United States *Tel:* 323-969-8985 *Fax:* 323-662-
  7896 *Web Site:* www.artbook.com
DAP/Distributed Art Publishers Inc, 155 Sixth
  Ave, 2nd floor, New York, NY 10013, United
  States *Tel:* 212-627-1999 *Fax:* 212-627-9484
  Web Site: www.artbook.com

HB Publications
PO Box 21660, London SW16 1WJ
Tel: (020) 8769 1585 *Fax:* (020) 8769 2320
E-mail: info@hbpublications.com
Web Site: www.hbpublications.com
Key Personnel
Owner: Lascelles Hussey
Founded: 1996
Specializes in the production of books for public
  sector managers.
Subjects: Accounting, Business, Finance, Man-
  agement, Marketing
ISBN Prefix(es): 978-1-899448
Parent Company: HB Consulting
Ultimate Parent Company: HB Group

Head of Zeus
45-47 Clerkenwell Green, London EC1R 0HT
Tel: (020) 7253 5557
E-mail: info@headofzeus.com
Web Site: headofzeus.com

Key Personnel
Chairman & Chief Executive Officer: Anthony
  Cheetham
Financial Dir: Ian Rutland
Digital Publisher & Deputy Mng Dir: Nicolas
  Cheetham
Publisher: Neil Belton
Publisher, Nonfiction: Richard Milbank
Publisher, Zephyr: Fiona Kennedy
Editorial Dir, Fiction: Laura Palmer
Mng Editor & Production Controller: Clemence
  Jacquinet
Senior Editor: Rosie de Courcy
Editor-at-Large: Maggie McKernan
Editor: Madeleine O'Shea
Digital Editor: Ellen Parna Velas
Publicity Dir: Suzanne Sangster
Rights Dir: Claire Nozieres
Sales Dir: Daniel Groenewald
Marketing & Digital Sales Dir: Kaz Harrison
Sales Manager: Victoria Reed
Founded: 2012
Subjects: Fiction, Nonfiction (General)
ISBN Prefix(es): 978-1-908800; 978-1-78185;
  978-1-78408
Imprints: Zephyr (children's)
Distributed by Trafalgar Square Publishing
Distributor for Mysterious Press
Foreign Rep(s): Jonathan Ball (South Africa); Gill
  Hess Ltd (Ireland); HarperCollins Publishers
  (Australia, New Zealand); Peter Newson (Eu-
  rope, Far East, Mideast); Pansing Distribution
  PTE Ltd (Singapore); Trafalgar Square/Inde-
  pendent Publishers Group (Canada, USA)
Distribution Center: Macmillan Distribution
  Ltd, Brunel Road, Houndmills, Basingstoke,
  Hants RG21 6XS *Tel:* (0845) 070 5656
  E-mail: trade@macmillan.co.uk

Headline, *imprint of* Headline Publishing Group
Ltd

Headline Publishing Group Ltd+
Division of Hachette Livre UK
Carmelite House, 50 Victoria Embankment, Lon-
  don EC4Y 0DZ
Tel: (020) 3122 7222
E-mail: enquiries@headline.co.uk
Web Site: www.headline.co.uk
Key Personnel
Chair: Jane Morpeth
Mng Dir: Mari Evans
Executive Publisher: Marion Donaldson
Publishing Dir: Imogen Taylor
Publishing Dir, Fiction: Jennifer Doyle
Publishing Dir, Nonfiction: Jonathan Taylor
Deputy Publishing Dir, Fiction: Vicki Mellor
Digital Publisher: Clare Foss
Publisher, Tinder Press: Mary-Anne Harrington
Associate Publisher, Tinder Press: Leah Wood-
  burn
Communications Dir: Georgina Moore
  E-mail: georgina.moore@headline.co.uk
Editorial Dir, Commercial Fiction: Toby Jones
Marketing Dir: Viviane Basset
Rights Dir: Jason Bartholomew *E-mail:* jason.
  bartholomew@hodder.co.uk
Sales Dir: Barbara Ronan
Digital Strategy Dir: Frances Doyle
Senior Commissioning Editor: Kate Stephenson
Commissioning Editor, Crossover Fiction: Frankie
  Gray
Founded: 1986
Subjects: Biography, Memoirs, Cookery, Fiction,
  Gardening, Plants, History, Nonfiction (Gen-
  eral), Sports, Athletics, Wine & Spirits
ISBN Prefix(es): 978-0-7472; 978-0-7553; 978-1-
  4722
Number of titles published annually: 410 Print

Imprints: Headline; Review; Tinder Press; Wild-fire
Orders to: Bookpoint Ltd, 130 Milton Park, Abingdon, Oxon OX14 4SB Tel: (01235) 400 400 Web Site: bookpoint.wp.hachette.co.uk

Headline Specials, *imprint of* Moorley's Print & Publishing Ltd

Headlions, *imprint of* Packard Publishing Ltd

William Heinemann, *imprint of* The Random House Group Ltd, a Penguin Random House Company

William Heinemann+
Imprint of Cornerstone
c/o The Random House Group Ltd, 20 Vauxhall Bridge Rd, London SW1V 2SA
Tel: (020) 7840 8400; (020) 7840 8707 (editorial) Fax: (020) 7233 6127 (editorial); (020) 7233 8791
Web Site: www.randomhouse.co.uk
Founded: 1890
Subjects: Biography, Memoirs, Fiction, Government, Political Science, History, Nonfiction (General), Travel & Tourism
ISBN Prefix(es): 978-0-434
Ultimate Parent Company: Penguin Random House UK
Orders to: The Book Service Ltd, Distribution Centre, Colchester Rd, Frating Green, Colchester, Essex CO7 7DW Tel: (01206) 256000 Fax: (01206) 255715 E-mail: sales@tbs-ltd.co.uk Web Site: www.thebookservice.co.uk

Helion & Co Ltd+
26 Willow Rd, Solihull, West Midlands B91 1UE
Tel: (0121) 705 3393 Fax: (0121) 711 4075
E-mail: info@helion.co.uk
Web Site: www.helion.co.uk
Key Personnel
Dir: Duncan Rogers E-mail: duncan@helion.co.uk
Founded: 1992
Specialize in military history.
Subjects: History, Military Science, Military History
ISBN Prefix(es): 978-1-874622; 978-1-906033
Number of titles published annually: 30 Print
Total Titles: 75 Print
Foreign Rep(s): Casemate Publishers (Sean Johnston) (Canada, USA); Casemate UK (Amy Himsworth/Simone Drinkwater) (Europe exc UK); DLS Australia Pty Ltd (Australia); Peter Hyde & Associates Pty Ltd (South Africa)
Distribution Center: Orca Book Services Ltd, Fleets Corner Industrial Estate, Unit A3, Fleetsbridge, Poole, Dorset BH17 0HL Tel: (01235) 465 500

Christopher Helm (Publishers) Ltd, *imprint of* A&C Black Publishers Ltd

Christopher Helm (Publishers) Ltd+
Imprint of A&C Black Publishers Ltd
50 Bedford Sq, London WC1B 3DP
Tel: (020) 7631 5600 Fax: (020) 7631 5800
E-mail: contact@bloomsbury.com
Web Site: www.bloomsbury.com
Key Personnel
Dir: Janet Murphy
Founded: 1986
Subjects: Natural History, Birds
ISBN Prefix(es): 978-0-7136; 978-0-7470; 978-1-873403; 978-1-903206; 978-1-4081
Number of titles published annually: 30 Print; 1 CD-ROM; 1 Audio
Total Titles: 200 Print; 1 CD-ROM; 2 Audio
Ultimate Parent Company: Bloomsbury Publishing PLC

Distribution Center: Macmillan Distribution (MDL), Brunel Rd, Houndmills, Basingstoke, Hants RG21 6XS Tel: (01256) 302699 Fax: (01256) 812521; (01256) 812558 E-mail: orders@macmillan.co.uk
Orders to: Macmillan Distribution (MDL), Brunel Rd, Houndmills, Basingstoke, Hants RG21 6XS Tel: (01256) 302699 Fax: (01256) 812521; (01256) 812558

Helm Information+
73 Springfield Rd, St Leonards-on-Sea TN38 0TU
Tel: (01424) 319685
Key Personnel
Dir: Amanda Helm E-mail: amandahelm@helm-information.co.uk
Founded: 1990
Membership(s): IPG (Independent Publisher's Guild).
Subjects: History, Literature, Literary Criticism, Essays
ISBN Prefix(es): 978-1-873403; 978-1-903206
Total Titles: 20 Print
Imprints: Barbet Books

Helmsman Guides, *imprint of* The Crowood Press Ltd

Hemming Information Services
32 Vauxhall Bridge Rd, London SW1V 2SS
Tel: (020) 7973 6400 Fax: (020) 7233 5056
E-mail: info@hgluk.com
Web Site: www.hgluk.com
Key Personnel
Chairman: Nicholas Service
Mng Dir: Graham Bond
Mng Editor: Dean Wanless E-mail: d.wanless@hemmings-group.co.uk
Production Dir: Linda Alderson
Sales Dir: Emma Sabin
Financial Dir & Accountant: M Joseph Dowling
Founded: 1939
Membership(s): DMA; DPA; EADP.
Subjects: Cookery, Government, Political Science, Marketing
ISBN Prefix(es): 978-0-7079; 978-0-900566
Parent Company: Hemming Group Ltd

Ian Henry Publications Ltd
20 Park Dr, Romford, Essex RM1 4LH
E-mail: info@ian-henry.com
Web Site: www.ian-henry.com
Founded: 1975
Specialize in books on Essex, towns & villages in Essex, Essex during wartime & the borough of Havering.
Subjects: Drama, Theater, Fiction, Genealogy, History, Humor, Regional Interests, Transportation, Planning, Wellness
ISBN Prefix(es): 978-0-86025
Number of titles published annually: 5 Print
Total Titles: 450 Print
U.S. Office(s): PO Box 1132, Studio City, CA 91604-0132, United States
Distributed by Players' Press (USA)
Distribution Center: Parish Chest Ltd, Credvill, Quakers Rd, Perranwell Station, Truro TR3 7PJ Tel: (01872) 864807 Fax: (01872) 870719 E-mail: parishchest@btconnect.com Web Site: www.parishchest.com

Herbert Press Ltd, *imprint of* A&C Black Publishers Ltd

Herbert Press Ltd+
Imprint of A&C Black Publishers Ltd
50 Bedford Sq, London WC1B 3DP
Tel: (020) 7631 5600 Fax: (020) 7631 5800
E-mail: contact@bloomsbury.com
Web Site: www.bloomsbury.com

Founded: 1975
Specialize in arts, crafts & art reference.
Subjects: Archaeology, Architecture & Interior Design, Art, Crafts, Games, Hobbies
ISBN Prefix(es): 978-0-7136; 978-0-906969; 978-1-871569; 978-1-408
Number of titles published annually: 10 Print
Total Titles: 100 Print; 3 E-Book
Ultimate Parent Company: Bloomsbury Publishing PLC
Distribution Center: Macmillan Distribution (MDL), Brunel Rd, Houndmills, Basingstoke, Hants RG21 6XS Tel: (01256) 302699 Fax: (01256) 812521; (01256) 812558 E-mail: orders@macmillan.co.uk
Orders to: Macmillan Distribution (MDL), Brunel Rd, Houndmills, Basingstoke, Hants RG21 6XS Tel: (01256) 302 699 Fax: (01256) 812521; (01256) 812558 E-mail: orders@macmillan.co.uk

Heritage, *imprint of* Osborne Books Ltd

Nick Hern Books Ltd+
The Glasshouse, 49a Goldhawk Rd, London W12 8QP
Tel: (020) 8749 4953 Fax: (020) 8735 0250
E-mail: info@nickhernbooks.co.uk
Web Site: www.nickhernbooks.co.uk
Key Personnel
Publisher: Nick Hern
Marketing Executive: Robin Booth E-mail: robin@nickhernbooks.co.uk
Mng Dir & Commissioning Editor: Matt Applewhite E-mail: matt@nickhernbooks.co.uk
Sales Manager: Ian Higham E-mail: ian@nickhernbooks.co.uk
Founded: 1988
Specialist performing arts publisher.
Subjects: Drama, Theater
ISBN Prefix(es): 978-1-85459; 978-1-84842
Number of titles published annually: 50 Print
Total Titles: 500 Print
Distributed by Currency Press (Australia & New Zealand); Playwrights Canada Press (Canada); Theatre Communications Group (USA)
Foreign Rep(s): Brookside Publishing (Ireland); Peter Hyde Associates (Peter Hyde) (South Africa); Iberian Book Services (Charlotte Prout) (Portugal, Spain)
Shipping Address: Grantham Book Services, Isaac Newton Way, Alma Park Industrial Estate, Grantham, Lincs NG31 9SD Tel: (01476) 541 080 Fax: (01476) 541 061
Warehouse: Grantham Book Services, Isaac Newton Way, Alma Park Industrial Estate, Grantham, Lincs NG31 9SD Tel: (01476) 541 080 Fax: (01476) 541 061
Orders to: Grantham Book Services, Isaac Newton Way, Alma Park Industrial Estate, Grantham, Lincs NG31 9SD Tel: (01476) 541 080 Fax: (01476) 541 061 E-mail: orders@gbs.tbs-ltd.co.uk Web Site: www.granthambookservices.co.uk

Heron Books, *imprint of* Quercus Publishing PLC

Hertfordshire Publications, *imprint of* University of Hertfordshire Press

Hesperus Press Ltd
28 Mortimer St, London W1W 7RD
Tel: (020) 7436 0869
Web Site: www.hesperuspress.com
Subjects: Biography, Memoirs, Fiction, Classics
ISBN Prefix(es): 978-1-84391; 978-1-78094
Distribution Center: Grantham Book Services, Trent Rd, Grantham, Lincs NG31 7XQ Tel: (01476) 541 080 Fax: (01476) 541 061 E-mail: orders@gbs.tbs-ltd.co.uk

Edition HH Ltd
68 West End, Launton, Bicester, Oxon OX26 5DG
Tel: (01869) 241672 *Fax:* (01869) 690013
E-mail: admin@editionhh.co.uk; sales@editionhh.co.uk
Web Site: www.editionhh.co.uk
Founded: 1996
Music publisher specializing in critical editions & contemporary music.
Membership(s): Music Publishers Association.
Subjects: Music, Dance
ISBN Prefix(es): 978-1-904229; 978-1-905779
Number of titles published annually: 30 Print
Total Titles: 250 Print
Distributed by Schott Music Ltd

Highland Books Ltd+
2 High Pines, Knoll Rd, Godalming GU7 2EP
Tel: (01483) 42 4560 *Fax:* (01483) 42 4388
E-mail: info@highlandbks.com
Web Site: www.highlandbks.com
Key Personnel
Dir: Philip Ralli
Founded: 1983
Publish books for Christian market, including "pick-me-ups" (books that encourage & restore).
Subjects: Biography, Memoirs, Fiction, Inspirational, Spirituality, Religion - Protestant, Science Fiction, Fantasy, Travel & Tourism, Evangelism, Prayer
ISBN Prefix(es): 978-0-946616; 978-1-897913
Number of titles published annually: 8 Print
Total Titles: 60 Print

Highstakes, *imprint of* Oldcastle Books Ltd

Hillside, *imprint of* Christian Education

Hippo, *imprint of* Scholastic Ltd

Hippopotamus Press+
22 Whitewell Rd, Frome, Somerset BA11 4EL
Tel: (01373) 466653 *Fax:* (01373) 466653
Key Personnel
Editor: R John *E-mail:* rjhippopress@aol.com; M Pargitter *E-mail:* mphippopress@aol.com
Foreign Editor: B A Martin *E-mail:* bajohn22@aol.com
Founded: 1974
Subjects: Literature, Literary Criticism, Essays, Poetry
ISBN Prefix(es): 978-0-904179
Number of titles published annually: 3 Print
Total Titles: 119 Print
Associate Companies: Outposts

History-into-Print, *imprint of* Brewin Books Ltd

The History Press, *imprint of* The History Press Ltd

The History Press Ltd+
The Mill, Brimscombe Port, Stroud, Glos GL5 2QG
Tel: (01453) 883300 *Fax:* (01453) 883233
Web Site: www.thehistorypress.co.uk
Key Personnel
Mng Dir: Gareth Swain *E-mail:* gswain@thehistorypress.co.uk
Publisher of history books - military, transport, local & general history.
Subjects: Aeronautics, Aviation, Archaeology, Biography, Memoirs, History, Maritime, Regional Interests, Transportation, Local History (UK), Military History, Rail
ISBN Prefix(es): 978-0-7524; 978-1-86077 (Phillimore); 978-0-7509; 978-1-84588; 978-1-8277

Imprints: The History Press; The Mystery Press; Phillimore & Co Ltd; THP Ireland
Distribution Center: Gill Distribution, Hume Ave, Park West, Dublin D12 YV96, Ireland *Tel:* (01) 500 9500 *Web Site:* www.gilldistribution.ie

Hobsons PLC+
44 Featherstone St, London EC1Y 8RN
Tel: (020) 7250 6600
Web Site: www.hobsons.com
Key Personnel
Regional Dir: Paul Clark
Founded: 1974
Subjects: Business, Career Development, Education, Science (General), Technology
ISBN Prefix(es): 978-1-86017; 978-0-86021; 978-1-85324; 978-0-903161; 978-1-904638
Parent Company: Daily Mail & General Trust PLC

Hodder & Stoughton Ltd
Division of Hachette UK
Carmelite House, 50 Victoria Enbankment, London EC4Y 0DZ
Tel: (020) 3122 6777
Web Site: www.hodder.co.uk
Key Personnel
Chief Executive Officer: Jamie Hodder-Williams
Publishing Dir: Carole Welch
Publishing Dir, Fiction: Carolyn Mays
Publisher: Nick Sayers *E-mail:* nick.sayers@hodder.co.uk
Publisher, Hodder Crime & Thriller: Ruth Tross
Publisher, Hodder Gen Fiction: Kate Howard
Publisher, Hodder Lifestyle & Yellow Kite: Liz Gough
Publisher, Hodder Nonfiction: Drummond Moir
Publisher, Nonfiction: Hannah Black; Rupert Lancaster
Associate Publisher: Oliver Johnson
Mng Dir, John Murray Press Division: Nick Davies
Deputy Mng Dir: Lisa Highton
Communications Dir: Eleni Lawrence *E-mail:* eleni.lawrence@hodder.co.uk
Communications Dir, John Murray Press Division: Rosie Gailer *E-mail:* rosie.gailer@hodder.co.uk
Group International Sales Dir: Ben Wright *E-mail:* ben.wright@hachette.co.uk
Group Sales Dir: Lucy Hale *E-mail:* lucy.hale@hodder.co.uk
Key Account Dir, Digital: Ben Gutcher
Dir, Publicity: Karen Geary *E-mail:* karen.geary@hodder.co.uk
Rights Dir: Jason Bartholomew *E-mail:* jason.bartholomew@hodder.co.uk
Publicity Manager, John Murray Press Division: Lyndsey Ng *E-mail:* lyndsey.ng@hodder.co.uk
Founded: 1868
Subjects: Biography, Memoirs, Child Care & Development, Cookery, Fiction, History, Humor, Military Science, Mysteries, Suspense, Self-Help, Sports, Athletics, Travel & Tourism
ISBN Prefix(es): 978-0-550; 978-0-340; 978-0-7131; 978-0-245; 978-1-84456; 978-0-7195; 978-1-84854; 978-1-85998; 978-1-444; 978-1-473; 978-1-84032; 978-1-4447; 978-1-4736
Total Titles: 5,000 Print; 300 Audio
Imprints: Coronet; Hodder Faith; Mulholland Books; John Murray; John Murray Learning; Saltyard Books; Sceptre; Two Roads; Yellow Kite
Divisions: John Murray Press; Quercus Publishing PLC
Foreign Rep(s): Jonathan Ball Publishers (South Africa); Everest International Publishing Services (Wei Zhao) (China); Hachette Australia (Australia); Hachette Book Group (Ireland); Hachette Book Publishing India Pvt Ltd (India); Hachette Canada (Canada); Hachette New Zealand (New Zealand); Hachette UK Ltd (Matthew Cowdery) (Middle East); Ha-

chette UK Ltd (Paul Kenny) (Southeast Asia); HRA (Christopher Humphrys & Lynda Hopkins) (Caribbean); Intermedia Americana Ltd (David Williams) (South America); Anna Martini (Eastern Europe); Pansing Distribution Pte Ltd (Malaysia, Singapore); Trafalgar Square Publishing (IPG) (USA)
Orders to: Bookpoint Ltd, 130 Milton Park, Abingdon, Oxon OX14 4SB *Tel:* (01235) 400 400 *Web Site:* bookpoint.wp.hachette.co.uk

Hodder Arnold, *imprint of* Hodder Education Group

Hodder Children's Books, *imprint of* Hachette Children's Books

Hodder Education Group
Division of Hachette UK
338 Euston Rd, London NW1 3BH
Tel: (020) 7873 6000 *Fax:* (020) 7873 6299
E-mail: educationenquiries@hodder.co.uk
Web Site: www.hoddereducation.co.uk
Key Personnel
Mng Dir: Lis Tribe
Business Operations Dir: Alyssum Ross
Founded: 1868
Subjects: Biblical Studies, Biological Sciences, Business, Career Development, Chemistry, Chemical Engineering, Computer Science, Crafts, Games, Hobbies, Engineering (General), Geography, Geology, Language Arts, Linguistics, Literature, Literary Criticism, Essays, Mathematics, Natural History, Photography, Physics, Science (General), Sports, Athletics, Theology
ISBN Prefix(es): 978-0-340; 978-0-7131; 978-1-84456; 978-0-7122
Imprints: Hodder Arnold; Hodder Gibson; Hodder Murray; Teach Yourself
Distribution Center: Ingram Publisher Services (IPS), One Ingram Blvd, La Vergne, TN 37086, United States *E-mail:* ips@ingramcontent.com SAN: 631-8630
Orders to: Bookpoint Ltd, 130 Park Dr, Milton Park, Abingdon, Oxon OX14 4SE *Tel:* (01235) 400 400 *Web Site:* bookpoint.wp.hachette.co.uk

Hodder Faith, *imprint of* Hodder & Stoughton Ltd

Hodder Gibson, *imprint of* Hodder Education Group

Hodder Murray, *imprint of* Hodder Education Group

Hodder Silver, *imprint of* Hachette Children's Books

Paul Holberton Publishing
89 Borough High St, London SE1 1NL
Tel: (020) 7407 0809
E-mail: press@paul-holberton.net
Web Site: www.paul-holberton.net
Key Personnel
Contact: Paul Holberton
Founded: 1999
Subjects: Architecture & Interior Design, Art, Fine Arts, Medieval
ISBN Prefix(es): 978-1-903470; 978-1-907372
Distributed by University of Washington Press (USA & Japan)

Holland Publishing PLC
18 Bourne Court, Southend Rd, Woodford Green, Essex IG8 8HD
Tel: (020) 8551 7711 *Fax:* (020) 8551 1266
Key Personnel
Mng Dir: Jonathan Holland
Founded: 1980

ISBN Prefix(es): 978-1-85038; 978-1-904699;
   978-1-84932
Imprints: Little Star Creations

HOME
2 Tony Wilson Pl, First St, Manchester M15 4FN
Tel: (0161) 228 7621
E-mail: info@homemcr.org
Web Site: homemcr.org
Key Personnel
Publications Manager: Debbie Fielding
Publications Officer: James Brady; Suzanne
   Davies
Publications Sales & Marketing Assistant: Eva
   Helen
Bookshop Manager: Tim Sheehan
Subjects: Art, Art Museums, Contemporary Art
ISBN Prefix(es): 978-0-948797; 978-1-897586;
   978-0-9550478

Honeyglen Publishing Ltd+
Durrels House, Flat 56, 28-46 Warwick Gardens,
   London W14 8QB
Tel: (020) 7602 2876 *Fax:* (020) 7602 2876
Key Personnel
Publisher: Nadja Poderegin
Dir: Jelena Poderegin-Harley
Founded: 1980
Subjects: Biography, Memoirs, Fiction, History,
   Philosophy of History
ISBN Prefix(es): 978-0-907855
Total Titles: 13 Print
Orders to: Vine House Distribution Ltd, The Old
   Mill House, Mill Lane, Uckfield, East Sussex
   TN22 5AA *Tel:* (01825) 767396 *Fax:* (01825)
   765649 *E-mail:* sales@vinehouseuk.co.uk *Web
   Site:* www.vinehouseuk.co.uk

Honno Fiction, *imprint of* Honno Welsh
Women's Press

Honno Voices, *imprint of* Honno Welsh Women's
Press

Honno Welsh Women's Press (Gwasg Menywod
Cymru)+
Creative Units, Unit 14, Aberystwyth Arts Centre,
   Aberystwyth, Ceredigion SY23 3GL
Tel: (01970) 623 150 *Fax:* (01970) 623 150
E-mail: post@honno.co.uk
Web Site: www.honno.co.uk
Key Personnel
Editor & Publisher: Caroline Oakley
Marketing Manager: Helena Earnshaw
Production Manager: Lesley Rice
Founded: 1986
Specialize in writings by women born or living in
   Wales or having a Welsh connection.
Membership(s): IPG.
Subjects: Biography, Memoirs, Fiction, Nonfiction
   (General), Regional Interests, Western Fiction,
   Anthologies, Classics
ISBN Prefix(es): 978-1-870206; 978-1-906784
Number of titles published annually: 7 Print
Total Titles: 80 Print
Imprints: Honno Fiction; Honno Voices; Welsh
   Women's Classics
Distribution Center: Welsh Books Council,
   Glanyrafon Enterprise Park, Llanbadarn
   Fawr, Aberystwyth, Ceredigion SY23 3AQ
   Tel: (01970) 624 455 *Fax:* (01970) 625 506
   Web Site: www.gwales.com (Wales only)
Turnaround Publisher Services Ltd, Unit 3,
   Olympia Trading Estate, Coburg Rd, London
   N22 6TZ *Tel:* (020) 8829 3000 *Fax:* (020)
   8881 5088 *E-mail:* orders@turnaround-uk.com
   Web Site: www.turnaround-uk.com (UK exc
   Wales)

Hood Hood Books Ltd
39 Thurloe Sq, London SW7 2SR

Tel: (020) 7584 7878
Founded: 1995
Children's Islamic publisher.
ISBN Prefix(es): 978-1-900251
Distributor for Goodword Books; Iman Publishing
Distribution Center: Central Books Ltd, One
   Heath Park Industrial Estate, Freshwater Rd,
   Dagenham RM8 1RX *Tel:* (020) 8525 8800
   Fax: (020) 8599 2694 *E-mail:* contactus@
   centralbooks.com *Web Site:* www.centralbooks.
   com
Returns: Central Books Ltd, One Heath Park In-
   dustrial Estate, Freshwater Rd, Dagenham RM8
   1RX *Tel:* (020) 8525 8800 *Fax:* (020) 8599
   2694 *E-mail:* contactus@centralbooks.com *Web
   Site:* www.centralbooks.com

Horus Editions, *imprint of* Award Publications
Ltd

Hot Key Books
Imprint of Bonnier Zaffre Ltd
Northburgh House, 10 Northburgh St, London
   EC1V 0AT
Tel: (020) 7490 3875
E-mail: enquiries@hotkeybooks.com
Web Site: www.hotkeybooks.com
Key Personnel
Art Dir: Jet Purdie
Rights Dir: Ruth Logan
Editor: Jenny Jacoby; Georgia Murray
Editor-at-Large: Emma Matthewson
Digital & Social Media Manager: Sanne Vliegen-
   thart
Production Controller: Tristan Hanks
Editorial Assistant: Monique Meledje
Subjects: Fiction
ISBN Prefix(es): 978-1-4714
Ultimate Parent Company: Bonnier Publishing
Distributed by Trafalgar Square Publishing

House of Lochar
Isle of Colonsay, Argyll PA61 7YR
Tel: (01951) 200232 *Fax:* (01951) 200232
E-mail: sales@houseoflochar.com
Web Site: www.houseoflochar.com
Key Personnel
Owner: Christa Byrne; Kevin Byrne
   E-mail: byrne@colonsay.org.uk
Subjects: Biography, Memoirs, Fiction, Geneal-
   ogy, History, Literature, Literary Criticism, Es-
   says, Maritime, Transportation, Roads & Rail-
   ways, Scotland
ISBN Prefix(es): 978-1-899863; 978-0-946537
Imprints: Colonsay Books; West Highland Series
Distributed by Natural Heritage (Canada); Scot-
   tish Book Source

House of Stratus
Lisandra House, Fore St, Looe, Cornwall PL13
   1AD
Tel: (0870) 3836922
E-mail: cust@houseofstratus.com
Web Site: www.houseofstratus.com
Subjects: Biography, Memoirs, Fiction, Humor,
   Mysteries, Suspense, Nonfiction (General), Po-
   etry, Romance, Science Fiction, Fantasy, War
ISBN Prefix(es): 978-1-84232; 978-0-7551
Distribution Center: Gardners Books Ltd, One
   Whittle Dr, Eastbourne, East Sussex BN23
   6QH *Tel:* (01323) 521555 *Fax:* (01323) 521666
   E-mail: sales@gardners.com
Baker & Taylor, 2550 W Tyvola Rd, Suite 300,
   Charlotte, NC 28217, United States *Tel:* 704-
   998-3100 *E-mail:* btinfo@btol.com

How Design, *imprint of* David & Charles Ltd

How To Books Ltd+
Imprint of Constable & Robinson

Carmelite House, 50 Victoria Embankment, Lon-
   don EC4Y 0DZ
Tel: (020) 3122 7000
E-mail: info@howtobooks.co.uk
Web Site: www.howtobooks.co.uk
Key Personnel
Publisher: Giles Lewis
Press & Publicity: Joanne Salt *E-mail:* joanne.
   salt@howtobooks.co.uk
Founded: 1991
Reference publisher.
Subjects: Business, Career Development, How-
   to, Management, Self-Help, Living & Working
   Abroad, Small Business, Successful Writing
ISBN Prefix(es): 978-1-85703; 978-1-84528
Number of titles published annually: 50 Print
Total Titles: 300 Print
Foreign Rep(s): Adaji Book Services (Nige-
   ria); Electra Media Group (Scott Brodie)
   (Philippines); Footprint Books (Australia, New
   Zealand); Kevin van Hasselt (Africa); IMA
   (Tony Moggach) (Eastern Europe, Greece);
   IMA (David Williams) (Caribbean, Latin
   America); Pansing Distribution Pte Ltd (East
   Asia); Parkwest Publications (Canada, USA);
   Phambili Agencies cc (South Africa); Robbert
   Pleysier (Austria, Benelux, Germany); Peter
   & Charlotte Prout (Gibraltar, Portugal, Spain);
   Publishers International Marketing (Chris Ash-
   down) (China, Japan); Publishers International
   Marketing Ltd (Ray Potts) (Middle East); John
   Wilson Booksales (Ireland, UK)
Warehouse: Grantham Book Services, Isaac
   Newton Way, Alma Park Industrial Estate,
   Grantham, Lincs NG31 9SD *Tel:* (01476)
   541080 *Fax:* (01476) 541061
Orders to: Grantham Book Services, Isaac
   Newton Way, Alma Park Industrial Estate,
   Grantham, Lincs NG31 9SD *Tel:* (01476)
   541080 *Fax:* (01476) 541061

HQ, *imprint of* HarperCollins UK

Hudson's Media Ltd
28 Whitehorse St, Baldock, Herts SG7 6QQ
Tel: (0844) 854 3432
E-mail: contact@hudsons-media.co.uk
Web Site: www.hudsons-media.co.uk
Key Personnel
Publishing Manager: Sarah Phillips
Founded: 1950
Specialize in guidebooks to stately homes, castles,
   museums, Cathedrals, etc, aimed at the tourist
   industry.
Publisher of *Hudson's Historic Houses & Gar-
   dens.*
Subjects: History, Regional Interests, Travel &
   Tourism
ISBN Prefix(es): 978-0-85101
Number of titles published annually: 9 Print
Total Titles: 88 Print

Hugo, *imprint of* DK Ltd

Human Horizons Series, *imprint of* Souvenir
Press Ltd

John Hunt Publishing Ltd, see O Books

Hurst & Co (Publishers) Ltd, see Hurst
Publishers

Hurst Publishers+
41 Great Russell St, London WC1B 3PL
Tel: (020) 7255 2201
E-mail: contact@hurstpub.co.uk
Web Site: www.hurstpublishers.com
Key Personnel
Publisher: Michael J Dwyer *E-mail:* michael@
   hurstpub.co.uk
Sales & Marketing Dir: Kathleen May
   E-mail: kathleen@hurstpub.co.uk

Mng Editor: Daisy Leitch *E-mail:* daisy@hurstpub.co.uk
Senior Editor: Jonathan de Peyer *E-mail:* jon@hurstpub.co.uk
Commissioning Editor: Mr Alasdair Craig *E-mail:* alasdair@hurstpub.co.uk
Publicist: Alison Alexanian *E-mail:* alison@hurstpub.co.uk
Founded: 1969
Subjects: Anthropology, Economics, Government, Political Science, History, Regional Interests, Religion - Other, Contemporary History, International Relations
ISBN Prefix(es): 978-0-7735; 978-0-905838; 978-0-903983; 978-0-900966; 978-1-85065; 978-1-84904
Number of titles published annually: 85 Print; 60 E-Book
Total Titles: 600 Print
Foreign Rep(s): Blue Weaver (Southern Africa); Tim Burland (Japan); Michael Geoghegan (Albania, Austria, Belgium, Bulgaria, Croatia, Czechia, France, Germany, Hungary, Netherlands, Poland, Romania, Serbia, Slovakia, Slovenia, Switzerland); Charles Gibbes (Cyprus, Greece); Ben Greig (Denmark, Finland, Iceland, Norway, Sweden); Claire de Gruchy (Algeria, Jordan, Morocco, Palestine, Tunisia, Turkey); Iberian Book Services (Charlotte Prout) (Portugal, Spain); IMA Ltd (Africa); Bill Kennedy (Middle East); Oxford University Press (North America); Russell Books (Ireland, Northern Ireland); Andrew White (Brunei, Indonesia, Malaysia, Philippines, Singapore, Thailand, Vietnam)
Distribution Center: Macmillan Distribution *Tel:* (0845) 070 5656 *E-mail:* orders@macmillan.co.uk

Hutchinson, *imprint of* The Random House Group Ltd, a Penguin Random House Company

Hutchinson Childrens, *imprint of* The Random House Group Ltd, a Penguin Random House Company

Hutton Grove, *imprint of* Kuperard

Hyden House Ltd, see Permanent Publications

Hymns Ancient & Modern Ltd+
Invicta House, 3rd floor, 108-114 Golden Lane, London EC1Y 0TG
Tel: (020) 7776 7540 *Fax:* (020) 7776 7556
Web Site: www.hymnsam.co.uk
Key Personnel
Group Chief Executive Officer: Dominic Vaughan *Tel:* (020) 7776 7541 *E-mail:* dominic@hymnsam.co.uk
Group Finance Dir: Sue Stapleford *Tel:* (01603) 785 908 *E-mail:* sue.stapleford@hymnsam.co.uk
Sales & Marketing Dir: Michael Addison *Tel:* (020) 7776 7551 *E-mail:* michael@hymnsam.co.uk
Publishing Dir: Christine Smith *Tel:* (020) 7776 7546 *E-mail:* christine@hymnsam.co.uk
Retail Sales Dir: Aude Pasquier *Tel:* (07831) 145964 *E-mail:* aude@hymnsam.co.uk
Sales & Marketing Controller: Josie Gunn *Tel:* (020) 7776 7555 *E-mail:* josie@hymnsam.co.uk
Customer Services Manager: Richard Pickett *Tel:* (01603) 785 907 *E-mail:* richard.pickett@hymnsam.co.uk
Editorial Manager: Mary Matthews *Tel:* (020) 7776 7548 *E-mail:* mary@hymnsam.co.uk
Production Manager: Stephen Rogers *Tel:* (020) 7776 7543 *E-mail:* stephen@hymnsam.co.uk

Rights & Permissions Manager: Rebecca Goldsmith *Tel:* (020) 7776 7547 *E-mail:* rebecca@hymnsam.co.uk
Senior Commissioning Editor: Dr Natalie K Watson *Tel:* (020) 7776 7545 *E-mail:* natalie@scmpress.co.uk
Founded: 1861 (public company 1975)
Membership(s): IPG.
Subjects: Religion - Other
ISBN Prefix(es): 978-0-334; 978-0-907547; 978-1-85311; 978-1-84825
Associate Companies: Church House Publishing; Saint Andrew Press
Imprints: Canterbury Press; SCM Press
Distributed by Morehouse Publishing (USA)
Bookshop(s): Church House Bookshop, 31 Great Smith St, London SW1P 3BN *Tel:* (020) 7799 4064 *E-mail:* bookshop@chbookshop.co.uk
Web Site: www.chbookshop.co.uk
Distribution Center: Norwich Books & Music, 13a Hellesdon Park Rd, Norwich, Norfolk NR6 5DR *Tel:* (01603) 785925 *Fax:* (01603) 785915 *E-mail:* orders@norwichbooksandmusic.co.uk
Web Site: www.norwichbooksandmusic.co.uk

i am a bookworm
Unit 1.1, Paintworks, Bath Rd, Bristol BS4 3EH
Tel: (0117) 9725173
Web Site: iamabookworm.co.uk
Key Personnel
Contact: Nick Ackland *Tel:* (07875) 221 750 *E-mail:* nick@iamabookworm.co.uk
Founded: 2011
ISBN Prefix(es): 978-0-9929108
Total Titles: 90 Print

Iaith Cyf
Aberarad Business Park, Unit 3, Newcastle Emlyn, Carmarthenshire SA38 9DB
Tel: (01239) 711668 *Fax:* (01239) 711698
E-mail: post@iaith.eu
Web Site: www.iaith.eu
Key Personnel
Chief Executive: Gareth Ioan
Senior Finance & Administrative Officer: Nigel Vaughn
Administrative Office/Language Services Officer: Kelly Davies
Founded: 1993
Subjects: Education, Welsh Language
ISBN Prefix(es): 978-0-9522905; 978-1-900563
Branch Office(s)
St Asaph Business Park, Unit 95, William Morgan Rd, St Asaph, Denbighshire LL17 0JE, Contact: Llys Bowen *Tel:* (01745) 585120

IBRA, see International Bee Research Association

IC Publications Ltd
7 Coldbath Sq, London EC1R 4LQ
Tel: (020) 7841 3210 *Fax:* (020) 7841 3211
E-mail: editorial@icpublications.com
Web Site: www.africasia.com
Key Personnel
Founder: Afif Ben Yedder
Group Publisher: Omar Ben Yedder
Founded: 1966
Specializes in current affairs, Middle East & Africa.
Subjects: Art, Business, Sports, Athletics
ISBN Prefix(es): 978-0-905268
Number of titles published annually: 4 Print
Subsidiaries: IC Publications (UK)
Branch Office(s)
609 Bat A 77 rue Bayen, 75017 Paris, France *Tel:* 01 44 30 81 11 *E-mail:* peter@icpublications.com
Foreign Rep(s): Nana Asiama Bekoe (Ghana); G&G Communications Inc (Gabshin Hwang) (South Korea); Hogan Media Services (Tania Licastro) (Australia); IC Publications (Sal-

iba Manneh) (France); IMR (Gisela Albrecht) (South Africa); Media Gateway International Ltd (Mary Yao) (China); MHI Ltd (Godfrey Wu) (Hong Kong, Malaysia, Singapore); NastaOne (Patricia Pal) (Spain); Antonio Scavone Jr (Brazil); Shinano International Inc (Kazuhiko Tanaka) (Japan); World Media (Conover Brown) (USA)

Icarus Arts Publishing, *imprint of* Maverick Arts Publishing Ltd

ICE Publishing
1-7 Great George St, London SW1P 3AA
Tel: (020) 7665 2019; (01892) 83 22 99 (orders)
E-mail: info@icepublishing.com; orders@icepublishing.com
Web Site: www.icevirtuallibrary.com; www.thomastelford.com
Key Personnel
Publishing: Gavin Jamieson *Tel:* (020) 7665 2477 *Fax:* (020) 7538 4101 *E-mail:* gavin.jamieson@icepublishing.com
Subjects: Energy, Engineering (General), Environmental Studies, Health, Nutrition, History, Law, Management, Maritime, Building Design, Contracts, Eurocode Guides, Innovation & Research, Municipal, Professional Development, Quality Systems, Safety, Waste Management
ISBN Prefix(es): 978-0-7277; 978-0-901948
Parent Company: Institution of Civil Engineers
Foreign Rep(s): APD Singapore Pte Ltd (Cambodia, Indonesia, Philippines, Singapore, Thailand, Vietnam); APDKL (Malaysia); Avicenna Partnership Ltd (Bill Kennedy & Claire de Gruchy) (Middle East); Tim Burland (Japan); Compass Academic (Ireland, UK); Cranbury International (David Rivera) (Puerto Rico); Cranbury International (Patrice Ammon-Jagdeo) (Trinidad and Tobago); Cranbury International LLC (Caribbean, Latin America); Marek Lewinson (Eastern Europe); Tahir Lodhi (Pakistan); Marcello SAS (Flavio Marcello) (France, Greece, Italy, Portugal, Spain); Netwerk Academic Book Agency (Belgium, Luxembourg, Netherlands); Publicaciones Educativas (Jose Rios) (Central America); ChongHo Ra (Korea); Renato Reichmann (Brazil); Sara Books Pvt Ltd (Ravindra Saxena) (Bangladesh, India, Sri Lanka); Science, Humanities, Social Sciences Publishers' Consultants & Representatives (Bernd Feldmann) (Austria, Germany, Switzerland); Silvermine International (John Atkin) (Caribbean); Ian Taylor Associates Ltd (Ms Zhang Pei) (China, Hong Kong, Taiwan)
Distribution Center: Paddock Wood Distribution Centre, Unit D, Tonbridge, Tonbridge, Kent TN12 6UU *Tel:* (01892) 832299 *Fax:* (01892) 837272 (UK & Ireland)
South African Institution of Civil Engineering, Thornhill Off Park, Bldg 19, Bekker St, Vorna Valley X21, Midrand 1686, South Africa *Tel:* (011) 805 5947 *Fax:* (011) 805 5971 *E-mail:* civilinfo@saice.org.za *Web Site:* saice.org.za
PSSC, 46 Development Rd, Fitchburg, MA 01420, United States *Tel:* 978-829-2544 *Fax:* 978-348-1233 *E-mail:* orders@pssc.com (USA & Canada)

IChemE, see Institution of Chemical Engineers (IChemE)

Icon Books Ltd
Omnibus Business Centre, 39-41 North Rd, London N7 9DP
Tel: (020) 7697 9695 *Fax:* (020) 7697 9501
E-mail: info@iconbooks.com; sales@iconbooks.com
Web Site: www.iconbooks.com
Key Personnel
Chairman: Peter Pugh

Marketing & Rights Executive: Steven White
  E-mail: steve@iconbooks.com
Mng Dir: Philip Cotterell *E-mail:* philip@
  iconbooks.com
Editorial Dir: Duncan Heath *E-mail:* duncan@
  iconbooks.com
Sales & Marketing Dir: Andrew Furlow
  E-mail: andrew@iconbooks.com
Assistant Editor: Nira Begum *E-mail:* nira@
  iconbooks.com
Founded: 1991
Subjects: Art, Biography, Memoirs, Business,
  Computers, Earth Sciences, Economics, En-
  gineering (General), Finance, Geography, Ge-
  ology, Government, Political Science, History,
  Humor, Language Arts, Linguistics, Litera-
  ture, Literary Criticism, Essays, Mathemat-
  ics, Medicine, Nursing, Dentistry, Nonfiction
  (General), Philosophy, Psychology, Psychiatry,
  Science (General), Self-Help, Social Sciences,
  Sociology, Technology
ISBN Prefix(es): 978-1-874166; 978-1-84046
Imprints: Totem Books
Foreign Rep(s): A-Z Africa Book Services (Anita
  Zih-De Haan) (Eastern Africa, West Africa);
  Allen & Unwin Pty Ltd (Australia, New
  Zealand); Jonathan Ball (South Africa); Faber
  & Faber (Melissa Elders) (Southern Europe);
  Faber & Faber (Bridget Lane) (Northern Eu-
  rope); Gill Hess Ltd (Ireland); Penguin Books
  India (India); Penguin Singapore (Malaysia,
  Singapore); Publishers Group Canada (Canada)
Foreign Rights: The Carol Mann Agency (USA);
  The Marsh Agency
Distribution Center: The Book Service Ltd, Dis-
  tribution Centre, Colchester Rd, Frating Green,
  Colchester, Essex CO7 7DW *Tel:* (01206)
  256000 *Fax:* (01206) 255715 *E-mail:* sales@
  tbs-ltd.co.uk *Web Site:* www.thebookservice.co.
  uk
Consortium Book Sales & Distribution, 34 13
  Ave NE, Suite 101, Minneapolis, MN 55413,
  United States *Tel:* 612-746-2600 *E-mail:* info@
  cbsd.com

ICSA Publishing
Subsidiary of Institute of Chartered Secretaries &
  Administrators (ICSA)
16 Park Crescent, London W1B 1AH
Tel: (020) 7612 7020
E-mail: publishing@icsa.org.uk; puborders@icsa.
  org.uk
Web Site: www.icsa.org.uk/bookshop
Key Personnel
Strategy Dir: Susan Richards
Publisher: Emma Reitano *E-mail:* ereitano@icsa.
  org.uk
Founded: 1981
Subjects: Business, Law, Management, Public
  Administration
ISBN Prefix(es): 978-1-86072; 978-0-902197;
  978-1-872860; 978-1-901498; 978-0-9559189
Number of titles published annually: 20 Print
Total Titles: 100 Print
Distribution Center: NBN International, 10
  Thornbury Rd, Plymouth PL6 7PP

IDS, see Institute of Development Studies

IEA, see Institute of Economic Affairs

IEE, *imprint of* The Institution of Engineering &
  Technology

Iff Books, *imprint of* O Books

**IFIS Publishing (International Food
  Information Service)**
Lane End House, Shinfield Rd, Shinfield, Reading
  RG2 9BB
Tel: (0118) 988 3895 *Fax:* (0118) 988 5065

E-mail: ifis@ifis.org; sales@ifis.org; a.ball@ifis.
  org
Web Site: foodinfo.ifis.org
Key Personnel
Mng Dir: Richard Hollingsworth
Head, Editorial & Production: Hilary Spencer
Head, Sales & Marketing: Rene Scholzel
Founded: 1968
Subjects: Health, Nutrition, Science (General),
  Technology
ISBN Prefix(es): 978-0-86014
Foreign Rep(s): Arabian Advanced Systems
  (AAS) (Middle East); DEA SpA (Italy); Green-
  data (Spain); Infoestrategica Latina SA de CV
  (Central America, South America, Southwest
  USA); Reiko Ohsawa (Japan)

Igloo Books Ltd
Imprint of Bonnier Publishing
Cottage Farm, Mears Ashby Rd, Sywell,
  Northants NN6 OBJ
Tel: (01604) 741116 *Fax:* (01604) 670495
E-mail: customerservice@igloobooks.com
Web Site: igloobooks.com
Key Personnel
Chief Executive Officer: Paul Gregory
Chief Operating Officer: Darren Witherall
Founded: 2003
Subjects: Cookery, Lifestyle, Trivia
ISBN Prefix(es): 978-1-84561; 978-1-84817; 978-
  1-84852
Ultimate Parent Company: Bonnier AB
Distributed by Simon & Schuster (North Amer-
  ica)
Distributor for DreamWorks Animation Publish-
  ing Group

IHS Jane's, IHS Global Ltd
Sentinel House, 163 Brighton Rd, Coulsdon, Sur-
  rey CR5 2YH
Tel: (01344) 328 300
Web Site: www.janes.com
Key Personnel
Chief Financial Officer & Dir: Michael Staton
Founded: 1898
Specializes in defence intelligence, terrorism &
  insurgency, geopolitics, risk assessment, tech-
  nical & infrastructure information. Full online
  subscription access & CD-ROMs.
Membership(s): AFA; AUSA; DMA Navy
  League.
Subjects: Aeronautics, Aviation, Foreign Coun-
  tries, Maritime, Military Science, Transporta-
  tion
ISBN Prefix(es): 978-0-7106
Total Titles: 200 Print; 200 CD-ROM; 200 Online
Branch Office(s)
Norwest Business Park, 14 Lexington Dr, Suite
  4.05, Bella Vista, NSW 2153, Australia
  Tel: (02) 8884 0000 *Fax:* (02) 8884 0099
  E-mail: oceania@ihsjanes.com
CERA51 Bldg 1-21-8 Ebisu, Shibuya-ku, Tokyo
  150-0013, Japan *Tel:* (03) 5791 9663 *Fax:* (03)
  5420 6402 *E-mail:* japan@ihsjanes.com
78 Shenton Way, No 12-01, Singapore 079120,
  Singapore *Tel:* 6576 5300 *Fax:* 6226 1185
  E-mail: asiapacific@ihsjanes.com
PO Box 502138, Dubai, United Arab Emi-
  rates *Tel:* (04) 390 2335 *Fax:* (04) 390 8848
  E-mail: mideast@janes.com
U.S. Office(s): Jane's Information Group Inc, 110
  N Royal St, Suite 200, Alexandria, VA 22314,
  United States *E-mail:* customer.servicesus@
  janes.com

Ilex Press, *imprint of* Octopus Publishing Group
Ltd

Ilex Press+
Imprint of Octopus Publishing Group Ltd
210 High St, Lewes, East Sussex BN7 2NS
Tel: (01273) 403 124 *Fax:* (01273) 487 441

Web Site: www.ilex.press
Key Personnel
Executive Publisher: Roly Allen *E-mail:* allen@
  ilex-press.com
Associate Publisher, Ilex Photo: Adam Juniper
  E-mail: juniper@ilex-press.com
Art Dir: Julie Weir *E-mail:* weir@ilex-press.com
Senior Project Editor: Natalia Price-Cabrera
  E-mail: price-cabrera@ilex-press.com
Senior Specialist Editor: Frank Gallaugher
  E-mail: fgallaugher@ilex-press.com
Commissioning Editor: Zara Larcombe
  E-mail: larcombe@ilex-press.com
Assistant Editor: Rachel Silverlight
  E-mail: silverlight@ilex-press.com
Founded: 2000
Subjects: Architecture & Interior Design, Art,
  Business, Crafts, Games, Hobbies, Fashion,
  Film, Video, Marketing, Nonfiction (General),
  Photography, Pop Culture, Science Fiction,
  Fantasy, Sports, Athletics, Technology, Creative
  Business, Web Design
ISBN Prefix(es): 978-1-904705; 978-1-905814;
  978-1-908150; 978-1-78157; 978-1-907579
Number of titles published annually: 30 Print
Total Titles: 250 Print; 50 E-Book
Ultimate Parent Company: Hachette UK
Associate Companies: The Ivy Press Ltd, 210
  High St, Lewes BN7 2NS, Publisher: Susan
  Kelly *E-mail:* susan@ivy-group.co.uk
Distributed by Thames & Hudson Ltd
Foreign Rep(s): Bookcity Co (Iran); Edgeler
  Book Services Ltd (John Edgeler) (Caribbean);
  Peter Hyde Associates (Botswana, Lesotho,
  Namibia, South Africa, Swaziland, Zimbabwe);
  Interart Sarl (France); Michael Klein (Austria,
  Germany exc South Germany); Levant Distrib-
  utors (Lebanon); Roli Books (Kapil Kapoor)
  (Bangladesh, Bhutan, India, Nepal); Thames
  & Hudson (Australia) Pty Ltd (Australia, New
  Zealand, Pacific Islands, Papua New Guinea);
  Thames & Hudson China Ltd (Hong Kong,
  Macau); Thames & Hudson China Ltd (He-
  len Lee) (Taiwan); Thames & Hudson China
  Ltd (Michelle Liu) (China); Thames & Hudson
  China Ltd (Ed Summerson) (Korea); Thames
  & Hudson Ltd (Scipio Stringer) (Japan, Pak-
  istan, Sri Lanka); Thames & Hudson Ltd (Bas
  van der Zee) (Belgium, Luxembourg, Nether-
  lands); Thames & Hudson Ltd (Stephen Em-
  brey) (Eastern Europe, Eastern Mediterranean,
  Egypt, Middle East); Thames & Hudson Ltd
  (Sara Ticci) (Southern Germany, Switzer-
  land); Thames & Hudson Ltd (Karim White)
  (Ireland); Thames & Hudson Ltd (Natasha
  Ffrench) (Central America, Italy, Mexico, Portugal, South America, Spain); Thames & Hudson Ltd (Per Burell) (Baltic States, Commonwealth of Independent States, Russia, Scandinavia); Thames & Hudson Ltd (Ian Bartley)
  (Africa exc South Africa); Thames & Hudson
  Pvt Ltd (Malaysia); Thames & Hudson Singapore (Singapore, Southeast Asia)
Foreign Rights: Ivy Press (Claire Kennedy)
Distribution Center: Littlehampton Book Services Ltd, Worthing, West Sussex, Worthing, West Sussex BN13 3RB *Tel:* (01903)
  828500; (01903) 828501 (customer service)
  Web Site: lbsltd.wp.hachette.co.uk
Thames & Hudson Australia Pty Ltd, 11 Central Blvd, Portside Business Park, Fisherman's Bend, Melbourne, Victoria 3207, Australia *Tel:* (03) 9646 7788 *Fax:* (03) 9646 8790
  E-mail: enquiries@thaust.com.au

Imagine That!, *imprint of* Top That Publishing
Ltd

IMIA, see International Map Industry Association
  (IMIA)

Imperial College Press+
57 Shelton St, Covent Garden, London WC2H 9HE
Tel: (020) 7836 3954; (020) 7836 0888 (sales & marketing) *Fax:* (020) 7836 2020 (sales & marketing)
E-mail: edit@icpress.co.uk; sales@wspc.co.uk; marketing@wspc.co.uk
Web Site: www.icpress.co.uk
Key Personnel
Commissioning Editor: Laurent Chaminade *E-mail:* laurent@icpress.co.uk; Kellye Curtis *E-mail:* kcurtiswspc@icpress.co.uk; Merlin Fox *E-mail:* mfox@icpress.co.uk; Alive Oven *E-mail:* aoven@icpress.co.uk; Jane Sayers *E-mail:* jsayers@icpress.co.uk; Lance Sucharov *E-mail:* lsucharov@icpress.co.uk
Founded: 1995
STM publisher of books & journals. Specialize in medicine.
Subjects: Architecture & Interior Design, Asian Studies, Biological Sciences, Business, Chemistry, Chemical Engineering, Computer Science, Economics, Electronics, Electrical Engineering, Engineering (General), Finance, Management, Mathematics, Medicine, Nursing, Dentistry, Physical Sciences, Physics, Science (General), Social Sciences, Sociology, Business Management, Environmental Science, Life Sciences, Materials Sciences, Nanoscience, Nanotechnology
ISBN Prefix(es): 978-1-86094; 978-1-84816; 978-1-78326; 978-1-908977; 978-1-908978; 978-1-908979
Number of titles published annually: 85 Print; 2 CD-ROM
Total Titles: 175 Print; 2 CD-ROM
Distributed by World Scientific Publishing (UK) Ltd (UK); World Scientific Publishing (Beijing) (China); World Scientific Publishing Co (Israel); World Scientific Publishing Co Inc (USA); World Scientific Publishing Co Pte Ltd (India, Singapore & Taiwan); World Scientific Publishing (HK) Co Ltd (Hong Kong); World Scientific Publishing (Tianjin) (China)
Orders to: Marston Book Services Ltd, 160 Eastern Ave, Milton Park, Abingdon, Oxon OX14 4SB *Tel:* (01235) 465500 *Fax:* (01235) 465555 *E-mail:* trade.orders@marston.co.uk *Web Site:* www.marston.co.uk (UK, Europe & Middle East)

Impress Books Ltd
Innovation Centre, University of Exeter, Rennes Dr, Devon EX4 4RN
Tel: (01392) 950910
E-mail: enquiries@impress-books.co.uk
Web Site: www.impress-books.co.uk
Key Personnel
Publisher: Richard Willis
Founded: 2004
ISBN Prefix(es): 978-0-9547586
Distribution Center: Central Books Ltd, One Heath Park Industrial Estate, Freshwater Rd, Dagenham RM8 1RX *Tel:* (020) 8525 8800 *Fax:* (020) 8599 2694 *E-mail:* orders@centralbooks.com *Web Site:* www.centralbooks.com

Imprint Academic Ltd+
Seychelles Farm, Upton Pyne, Exeter EX5 5HY
Mailing Address: PO Box 200, Exeter EX5 5YX
Tel: (01392) 851550 *Fax:* (01392) 851178
Web Site: www.imprint.co.uk
Key Personnel
Contact: Sandra Good *E-mail:* sandra@imprint.co.uk
Subjects: Communications, Education, Government, Political Science, Human Relations, Philosophy, Psychology, Psychiatry, Religion - Other, Social Sciences, Sociology
ISBN Prefix(es): 978-0-907845; 978-1-84540

Number of titles published annually: 30 Print; 30 E-Book
Total Titles: 250 Print; 250 E-Book

In Easy Steps Ltd+
16 Hamilton Terrace, Holly Walk, Warwicks CV32 4LY
Tel: (01926) 831557
E-mail: info@ineasysteps.com
Web Site: ineasysteps.com
Key Personnel
Dir: Sevanti Kotecha
Founded: 1991
Subjects: Business, How-to, Technology, Computers, Educational Software
ISBN Prefix(es): 978-1-874029; 978-1-84078
Total Titles: 60 Print; 10 E-Book
Distributed by McGraw-Hill Education (Asia) (Southeast Asia); Tata McGraw-Hill Education (Bangladesh, India, Nepal & Sri Lanka)
Foreign Rep(s): Intersoft (South Africa); Publishers Group West (USA); Woodslane Pty Ltd (Australia, New Zealand, Tasmania)

The In Pinn, *imprint of* Neil Wilson Publishing Ltd

Incorporated Catholic Truth Society, see The Catholic Truth Society

Independence Educational Publishers
The Studio, High Green, Great Shelford, Cambridge CB22 5EG
Tel: (01223) 550801 *Fax:* (01223) 550806
E-mail: issues@independence.co.uk
Web Site: www.independence.co.uk
Key Personnel
Mng Dir: Ken Sewell *E-mail:* ken.sewell@cambridge-media.com
Mng Editor: Cara Acred *E-mail:* cara@independence.co.uk
Assistant Editor: Christina Hughes *E-mail:* christina@independence.co.uk
Sales & Marketing: Mary Chapman *E-mail:* mary@independence.co.uk
Founded: 1989
Subjects: Alternative, Child Care & Development, Disability, Special Needs, Earth Sciences, Energy, Ethnicity, Finance, Government, Political Science, Health, Nutrition, Philosophy, Science (General), Social Sciences, Sociology, Transportation, Travel & Tourism, Contemporary Social Issues
ISBN Prefix(es): 978-1-86168; 978-1-872995
Parent Company: Cambridge Media Group

Independent Thinking Press, *imprint of* Crown House Publishing Ltd

Independent Voices, *imprint of* Souvenir Press Ltd

Indigo, *imprint of* Orion Publishing Group Ltd

Infinite Ideas Ltd
36 St Giles, Oxford, Oxon OX1 3LD
Tel: (01865) 514 888
E-mail: info@infideas.com
Web Site: www.infideas.com
Key Personnel
Mng Dir: Richard Burton *E-mail:* richard@infideas.com
Editorial Dir: Rebecca Clare
Foreign Rights: Catherine Holdsworth *E-mail:* catherine@infideas.com
Founded: 2004
Subjects: Art, Biography, Memoirs, Business, Career Development, Cookery, Crafts, Games, Hobbies, Finance, Health, Nutrition, History, Human Relations, Literature, Literary Criti-

cism, Essays, Music, Dance, Self-Help, Sports, Athletics, Wine & Spirits, Leisure, Lifestyle
ISBN Prefix(es): 978-1-904902; 978-1-905940; 978-1-906821; 978-1-908474; 978-1-907518
Orders to: Littlehampton Book Services Ltd, Faraday Close, Durrington, Worthing, West Sussex *Tel:* (01903) 828500; (01903) 828501 (customer service) *Web Site:* lbsltd.wp.hachette.co.uk

Informa Healthcare
Albert House, 1-4 Singer St, London EC2A 4BQ
Tel: (020) 7017 5000
Web Site: informahealthcare.com
Key Personnel
Sales Dir: John Purkis
Supplier of contact names for the pharmaceutical, biotechnical, medical device, diagnostics & service industries. Details of pharma, biotech, MD & service company addresses worldwide with named senior personnel.
ISBN Prefix(es): 978-1-61631
Parent Company: Informa PLC
U.S. Office(s): 52 Vanderbilt, 7th floor, New York, NY 10017, United States *Tel:* 212-520-2777

Informa Law from Routledge
2 Park Sq, Milton Park, Abingdon, Oxon OX14 4RN
Tel: (020) 7017 6000 *Fax:* (020) 7017 6699
E-mail: professional.enquiries@informa.com
Web Site: www.routledge.com/informalaw; www.taylorandfrancis.com/informalaw
Key Personnel
Senior Publisher: Fiona Briden *E-mail:* fiona.briden@tandf.co.uk
Associate Editor: Joshua Wells *E-mail:* joshua.wells@tandf.co.uk
Marketing Manager: Jane Williams *E-mail:* jane.williams@informa.com
Founded: 1973
Business to business international publishers.
Subjects: Finance, Law, Maritime, Insurance
ISBN Prefix(es): 978-0-415; 978-1-84214; 978-1-84311; 978-1-61631; 978-1-138
Parent Company: Taylor & Francis Group Ltd
Ultimate Parent Company: Informa PLC

Informa PLC
5 Howick Pl, London SW1P 1WG
Tel: (020) 7017 5000
E-mail: headoffice@informa.com
Web Site: www.informa.com
Key Personnel
Group Chief Executive Officer: Stephen A Carter
Group Finance Dir: Gareth Wright
Programme Dir: James Gareh
Public Relations: Kay Phelps *E-mail:* kay.phelps@informa.com
Subjects: Business, Economics, Social Sciences, Sociology
ISBN Prefix(es): 978-1-85044; 978-0-904093; 978-0-907432; 978-1-84311; 978-1-85978

INSPEC, *imprint of* The Institution of Engineering & Technology

Institute for Fiscal Studies
7 Ridgmount St, London WC1E 7AE
Tel: (020) 7291 4800 *Fax:* (020) 7323 4780
E-mail: mailbox@ifs.org.uk
Web Site: www.ifs.org.uk
Key Personnel
Dir: Paul Johnson *E-mail:* p_j@ifs.org.uk
Deputy Dir: Carl Emmerson *E-mail:* c.emmerson@ifs.org.uk
Research Dir: Richard Blundell *E-mail:* r.blundell@ucl.ac.uk
Deputy Research Dir: Rachel Griffith *E-mail:* rgriffith@ifs.org.uk
Research Fellow: Alissa Goodman
Head, Content: Emma Hyman *E-mail:* e.hyman@ifs.org.uk

Publications Manager: Stephanie Seavers
  E-mail: stephanie_seavers@ifs.org.uk
Founded: 1969
Independent research institute.
Publish research findings on all aspects of taxation & economic public policy.
Subjects: Economics, Finance, Public Administration, Working Papers (online only)
ISBN Prefix(es): 978-1-873357; 978-0-902992; 978-1-903274; 978-1-909463
Number of titles published annually: 5 Print; 10 Online
Total Titles: 200 Print; 100 Online

Institute of Clinical Research
10 Cedar Court, Grove Park, White Waltham Rd, Maidenhead SL6 3LW
Tel: (01628) 501700 Fax: (01628) 501709
E-mail: icrenquiries@yahoo.co.uk
Web Site: www.icr-global.org
Key Personnel
Head, Media: Andrew Smith Tel: (01628) 536975
  E-mail: asmith@icr-global.org
Founded: 1978
Subjects: Health, Nutrition, Medicine, Nursing, Dentistry, Clinical Research
ISBN Prefix(es): 978-0-9549345; 978-1-905238
Number of titles published annually: 5 Print; 1 E-Book
Total Titles: 31 Print; 4 E-Book

Institute of Development Studies
University of Sussex, Brighton, East Sussex BN1 9RE
Tel: (01273) 606261
E-mail: ids@ids.ac.uk
Web Site: www.ids.ac.uk
Key Personnel
Communications Dir: James Georgalakis
  Tel: (01273) 915781 E-mail: j.georgalakis@ids.ac.uk
Publications Manager: Alison Norwood
  Tel: (01273) 915641 E-mail: a.norwood@ids.ac.uk
Marketing & Database Coordinator: Gary Edwards Tel: (01273) 915637 E-mail: g.edwards@ids.ac.uk
Founded: 1966
Subjects: Agriculture, Developing Countries, Economics, Education, Environmental Studies, Government, Political Science, Public Administration, Women's Studies
ISBN Prefix(es): 978-0-903354; 978-0-903715; 978-1-85864
Number of titles published annually: 50 Print
Total Titles: 500 Print

Institute of Economic Affairs+
2 Lord North St, London SW1P 3LB
Tel: (020) 7799 8900 Fax: (020) 7799 2137
E-mail: iea@iea.org.uk
Web Site: www.iea.org.uk
Key Personnel
Chief Operating Officer: Chad Wilcox
  E-mail: cwilcox@iea.org.uk
Dir General: Mark Littlewood Tel: (020) 7799 8907 E-mail: mlittlewood@iea.org.uk
Deputy Editorial Dir: Dr Richard Wellings
  Tel: (020) 7799 8919 E-mail: rwellings@iea.org.uk
Editorial & Programme Dir: Prof Philip Booth
  Tel: (020) 7799 8912 E-mail: pbooth@iea.org.uk
Founded: 1955
Subjects: Economics, Education
ISBN Prefix(es): 978-0-255
Distribution Center: IPG, 814 N Franklin St, Chicago, IL 60610, United States

Institute of Education Press
20 Bedford Way, London WC1H 0AL
Fax: (020) 7612 6126

E-mail: admin@ucl-ioe-press.com
Web Site: www.ucl-ioe-press.com
Key Personnel
Publisher: Nicky Platt
Deputy Publishing Dir & Production Editor: Jonathan Dore
Mng Editor: Dr Nicole Edmondson
Commissioning Editor, Trentham Books: Dr Gillian Klein
Sales & Marketing: Sally Sigmund
Marketing Assistant: Margie Coughlin
Founded: 1902
Academic & professional publishing.
Membership(s): Independent Publishers Guild.
Subjects: Education, Social Sciences, Sociology
ISBN Prefix(es): 978-0-85473; 978-1-85856 (Trentham Books); 978-1-78277
Number of titles published annually: 30 Print; 1 CD-ROM; 90 E-Book
Total Titles: 685 Print; 3 CD-ROM; 350 E-Book
Imprints: Trentham Books
Distributed by Stylus Publishing (North America)
Distribution Center: Central Books Ltd, One Heath Park Industrial Estate, Freshwater Rd, Dagenham RM8 1RX Tel: (020) 8525 8800 Fax: (020) 8599 2694 E-mail: contactus@centralbooks.com Web Site: www.centralbooks.com
Orders to: Central Books Ltd, One Heath Park Industrial Estate, Freshwater Rd, Dagenham RM8 1RX Tel: (020) 8525 8800 Fax: (020) 8599 2694 E-mail: contactus@centralbooks.com Web Site: www.centralbooks.com

Institute of Employment Rights
Jack Jones House, 4th floor, One Islington, L3 8EG Liverpool L3 8EG
Tel: (0151) 207 5265 Fax: (0151) 207 5264
E-mail: office@ier.org.uk
Web Site: www.ier.org.uk
Key Personnel
Dir: Carolyn Jones E-mail: cad@ier.org.uk
Administration Officer: Treena Johnson
Founded: 1989
Subjects: Disability, Special Needs, Economics, Ethnicity, Government, Political Science, Law, Women's Studies
ISBN Prefix(es): 978-0-9543781; 978-1-873271; 978-0-9547562; 978-0-9551795; 978-1-906703
Number of titles published annually: 8 Print

The Institute of Faculty & Actuaries
Holborne Gate, 7th floor, 326-330 High Holborn, London WC1V 7PP
Tel: (020) 7632 2100 Fax: (020) 7632 2111
E-mail: education.services@actuaries.org.uk
Web Site: www.actuaries.org.uk
Founded: 1848
Subjects: Environmental Studies, Science (General), Technology
ISBN Prefix(es): 978-0-901066; 978-1-903965
Branch Office(s)
Exchange Crescent, Level 2, 7 Conference Sq, Edinburgh EH3 8RA Fax: (0131) 240-1313
Park Central, 1st floor, 40/41 Park End St, Oxford, Oxon OX1 1JD Fax: (01865) 268 211

Institute of Food Science & Technology
5 Cambridge Court, 210 Shepherds Bush Rd, London W6 7NJ
Tel: (020) 7603 6316
E-mail: info@ifst.org
Web Site: www.ifst.org
Key Personnel
Deputy Chief Executive: Jane Emry
Founded: 1964
Professional qualifying body & educational charity.
Subjects: Science (General), Technology, Food Science
ISBN Prefix(es): 978-0-905367

Number of titles published annually: 2 Print; 1 Online
Total Titles: 10 Print; 1 Online

Institute of Irish Studies, Queen's University Belfast+
Queen's University Belfast, 8 Fitzwilliam St, Belfast BT7 1NN
Tel: (028) 9097 3386 Fax: (028) 9097 3388
E-mail: irish.studies@qub.ac.uk
Web Site: www.qub.ac.uk/irishstudies
Key Personnel
Dir: Dr Dominic Bryan
Founded: 1987
A small press & publishing company which publishes academic & semi-academic books relative to all aspects of Irish studies.
Subjects: Anthropology, Archaeology, Art, Biography, Memoirs, Ethnicity, Film, Video, Geography, Geology, Government, Political Science, History, Language Arts, Linguistics, Regional Interests, Religion - Catholic, Religion - Protestant
ISBN Prefix(es): 978-0-85389
Number of titles published annually: 10 Print
Total Titles: 150 Print
Distributed by Dufour Editions (USA); P D Meaney (1 title only)
Distributor for Van Gorcum (North Ireland & Irish Republic for 1 book only)
Foreign Rep(s): Russell Book Representation (UK); Robert Towers (Ireland)
Distribution Center: Central Books Ltd, One Heath Park Industrial Estate, Freshwater Rd, Dagenham RM8 1RX Tel: (020) 8525 8800 Fax: (020) 8599 2694 E-mail: orders@centralbooks.com Web Site: www.centralbooks.com (Great Britain & Europe)
Irish Books & Media, 1433 Franklin Ave E, Minneapolis, MN 55404-2135, United States Tel: 612-871-3505 Fax: 612-871-3358
E-mail: irishbooks@aol.com

Institution of Chemical Engineers (IChemE)
Davis Bldg, Railway Terrace, Rugby CV21 3HQ
Tel: (01788) 578214 Fax: (01788) 560833
E-mail: customerservices@icheme.org
Web Site: www.icheme.org
Key Personnel
Executive: Claudia Flavell-White
Founded: 1922
Subjects: Chemistry, Chemical Engineering
ISBN Prefix(es): 978-0-85295
Branch Office(s)
One Portland Pl, London W1B 1PN Tel: (020) 7927 8200 Fax: (020) 7927 8181
7/455 Bourke St, Melbourne, Victoria 3000, Australia Tel: (03) 9642 4494 Fax: (03) 9642 4495 E-mail: austmembers@icheme.org Web Site: www.icheme.org/australia
Unit A-27-3A, Level 27, Tower A, Menara UOA Bangsar 5, JL Bangsar Utama 1, 59000 Bangsar, Kuala Lumpur, Malaysia Tel: (03) 2283 1381 Fax: (03) 2283 1382 E-mail: malaysianmembers@icheme.org Web Site: www.icheme.org/malaysia
PO Box 5714, Lambton Quay, Wellington 6145, New Zealand Tel: (04) 473 4398 E-mail: nzmembers@icheme.org Web Site: www.icheme.org/newzealand
4 Leng Kee Rd, No 04-02 SIS Bldg, Singapore 159088, Singapore Tel: 6471 5043 Fax: 6377 0879 E-mail: singaporemembers@icheme.org Web Site: www.icheme.org/singapore

The Institution of Engineering & Technology+
Michael Faraday House, Six Hills Way, Stevenage, Herts SG1 2AY
Tel: (01438) 313311 Fax: (01438) 765526
E-mail: books@theiet.org; postmaster@theiet.org; submissions@theiet.org
Web Site: www.theiet.org

Key Personnel
Chief Executive & Secretary: Nigel Fine
Dir of Knowledge: Tim Hamer
Communications Manager: Robert Beahan
Founded: 1871
Provides a range of leading publications & information services in the areas of engineering & technology.
Subjects: Aeronautics, Aviation, Business, Communications, Computer Science, Electronics, Electrical Engineering, Energy, History, Management, Physical Sciences, Technology
ISBN Prefix(es): 978-0-85296; 978-0-906048; 978-0-86341; 978-0-901223; 978-0-903748; 978-1-84919
Number of titles published annually: 30 Print
Total Titles: 240 Print
Imprints: IEE; INSPEC
Foreign Rep(s): Inspec Asia Pacific Office (Asia, The Pacific); Inspec Inc (Central America, North America, South America); Inspec, The IET (Africa, Europe, Middle East)

Intellect, *imprint of* Intellect Ltd

Intellect Ltd+
The Mill, Parnall Rd, Fishponds, Bristol BS16 3JG
Tel: (0117) 9589910 *Fax:* (0117) 9589911
E-mail: info@intellectbooks.com
Web Site: www.intellectbooks.com
Key Personnel
Publisher: Simon Baker
Mng Dir: Mark Lewis
Marketing Dir: Holly Rose
Founded: 1984
A multidisciplinary publisher for individual & institutional readers.
Membership(s): IPG.
Subjects: Art, Drama, Theater, Film, Video, Language Arts, Linguistics, Regional Interests, Women's Studies
ISBN Prefix(es): 978-1-871516; 978-1-84150; 978-1-78320
Number of titles published annually: 25 Print; 25 E-Book
Total Titles: 450 Print; 200 E-Book
Imprints: Ablex; Elm Bank Press; Intellect; Venton
U.S. Office(s): King Hall, Suite 103A, 601 S College Rd, Wilmington, NC 28403, United States *Tel:* 910-962-2609 *E-mail:* usinfo@intellectbooks.com
Foreign Rep(s): Inbooks (Australia, New Zealand); University of Chicago Press (Canada, USA)
Distribution Center: University of Chicago Press, c/o Wiley & Sons Ltd, European Distribution Centre, New Era Estate, Oldlands Way, Bognor Regis, West Sussex PO22 9NQ *Tel:* (01243) 779777 *Fax:* (01243) 820250 *E-mail:* cs-books@wiley.co.uk

Inter-Varsity Press+
IVP Book Centre, Norton St, Nottingham NG7 3HR
Tel: (0115) 978 1054 *Fax:* (0115) 942 2694
E-mail: sales@ivpbooks.com
Web Site: www.ivpbooks.com
Key Personnel
Chief Executive: Brian Wilson
Customer Services & Distribution Manager: Janet Hunter
Finance Manager: Chris Blainey
Marketing & Design Manager: Daryl Wearring
Operations Manager: George Russell
Production Manager: John Mansfield
Sales Development Manager: Tim Banting
Senior Commissioning Editor: Eleanor Trotter
Commissioning Editor: Sam Parkinson
Copy Editor: Kath Stanton
Theological Books Editor: Phil Duce

Information Technology Officer: David Cornish
International Sales Coordinator: Janet Wileman
Graphic Designer: Kev Jones
Founded: 1928
Publisher & distributor of evangelical Christian books.
Subjects: Education, History, Literature, Literary Criticism, Essays, Religion - Protestant
ISBN Prefix(es): 978-0-85110; 978-0-85111; 978-1-84474; 978-1-85684
Number of titles published annually: 50 Print
Total Titles: 650 Print; 3 CD-ROM; 8 Audio
Imprints: Apollos (academic books); Crossway (popular books); IVP (general books)
Distributor for Bible Society; Blue Bottle; DK Religious; Eagle Publishing; Good Book Company; I V Press; Matthias Media; Piquant

International Affairs, *imprint of* Royal Institute of International Affairs

International Bee Research Association+
Unit 6 Centre Court Main Ave, Treforest, RCT CF37 5YR
Tel: (029) 2037 2409
E-mail: mail@ibra.org.uk
Web Site: www.ibrabee.org.uk
Key Personnel
Publications Manager: Sarah Jones
Editor: Richard Jones
Founded: 1949
World information specialists on bees.
Membership(s): IUBS.
Subjects: Agriculture, Biological Sciences, Education, Natural History, Bees, Bee Science, Conservation, History of Apiculture, Pollination
ISBN Prefix(es): 978-0-86098; 978-0-900149
Number of titles published annually: 4 Print; 4 CD-ROM
Total Titles: 70 Print; 10 CD-ROM; 2 Online

International Biographical Centre, *imprint of* Melrose Press Ltd

International Communications, see IC Publications Ltd

International Institute for Strategic Studies+
Arundel House, 13-15 Arundel St, Temple Pl, London WC2R 3DX
Tel: (020) 7379 7676 *Fax:* (020) 7836 3108
Web Site: www.iiss.org
Key Personnel
Dir General & Chief Executive: Dr John Chipman
Dir of Editorial: Alexander Nicoll
Dir of Finance & Corporate Governance: Sally Taylor
Head of Publications: Gaynor Roberts
Founded: 1958
Subjects: Government, Political Science, Military Science
ISBN Prefix(es): 978-0-86079; 978-0-900492
Number of titles published annually: 12 Print
Imprints: Adelphi Papers; The Military Balance; Strategic Comments; Strategic Dossiers; Strategic Survey; Survival

International Map Industry Association (IMIA)
17 Tetbury Dr, Witney, Oxon OX28 5GF
Tel: (01993) 774519 *Fax:* (01993) 883096
Web Site: imiamaps.org
Key Personnel
Executive Dir: Howard Hudson *E-mail:* howard.hudson1@btinternet.com
Worldwide organization of the mapping, geospatial & geographic information industry.
Subjects: Geography, Geology
Branch Office(s)
147 Unley Rd, Unley, SA 5061, Australia, Executive Dir: Noleen Zander *Tel:* (08) 8357 1777

Fax: (08) 8357 3001 *E-mail:* imiaap@chariot.net.au (Australia, New Zealand & Asia Pacific)
U.S. Office(s): 23052 H Alicia Pkwy, No 602, Mission Viejo, CA 92692, United States, Executive Dir: Sanford J Hill *Tel:* 949-458-8200 *E-mail:* info@imiamaps.org (North America, South America, Mexico & Canada)

International Water Association Publishing, see IWA Publishing

Internationella bibelsaellskapet, see Biblica Europe

Interpet Publishing+
Vincent Lane, Dorking, Surrey RH4 3YX
Tel: (01306) 881 033
E-mail: customercare@interpet.co.uk
Web Site: www.interpet.co.uk
Key Personnel
Senior National Account Manager: Graeme McCartan *E-mail:* gmccartan@interpet.co.uk
Production & Contracts Manager: Hannah Turner *E-mail:* hturner@interpet.co.uk
Subjects: Animals, Pets, Gardening, Plants, Veterinary Science
ISBN Prefix(es): 978-1-900667; 978-0-948955; 978-1-86054; 978-1-84286; 978-1-902389; 978-1-903098; 978-1-85279; 978-0-9668592

Iona Community, see Wild Goose Publications

Ipso Books
Drury House, 34-43 Russell St, London WC2B 5HA
E-mail: hello@ipsobooks.com
Web Site: www.ipsobooks.com
Key Personnel
Associate Publisher: Kate Evans *Tel:* (020) 7344 1047 *E-mail:* kate@ipsobooks.com
Founded: 2015
Digital publisher of contemporary genre fiction & original nonfiction.
Subjects: Fiction, Nonfiction (General)
Parent Company: Peters Fraser & Dunlop

iSeek Ltd
One A Stairbridge Court, Bolney Grange Business Park, Haywards Heath, West Sussex RH17 5PA
Tel: (01444) 462860 *Fax:* (01444) 232142
Web Site: www.iseekcreative.com
Founded: 1997
ISBN Prefix(es): 978-1-902553; 978-1-905288; 978-1-906824

Isis Publishing Ltd+
Unit 7 Centremead, Osney Mead, Oxford, Oxon OX2 0ES
Tel: (01865) 250 333 *Toll Free Tel:* 0800 731 5637 (orders-UK only) *Fax:* (01865) 790 358
E-mail: new@isishousepub.com; sales@isis-publishing.co.uk
Web Site: www.isis-publishing.co.uk; www.isishousepub.com
Key Personnel
Co-Publisher: Justin Howard *E-mail:* jhoward@isishousepub.com; Traci Regula *E-mail:* tregula@isishousepub.com
Specialize in unabridged audio titles.
Subjects: Biography, Memoirs, Fiction, Health, Nutrition, Mysteries, Suspense, Nonfiction (General), Romance, Science Fiction, Fantasy, Self-Help, Travel & Tourism, Western Fiction, Adventure, Classical Literature, War
ISBN Prefix(es): 978-1-85089; 978-1-85695; 978-0-7531; 978-1-86042; 978-1-84559
Number of titles published annually: 192 Print; 192 Audio
U.S. Office(s): Ulverscroft Large Print (USA) Inc, 950 A Union Rd, Suite 427, PO Box 1230, West Seneca, NY 14224-1230, United

States *Tel:* 716-674-4270 *Fax:* 716-674-4195 *E-mail:* sales@ulverscroftusa.com *Web Site:* www.ulverscroftusa.com

Islam International Publications Ltd
118 London Rd, Morden, Surrey SM4 5AE
Tel: (020) 8687 7831
E-mail: info@islaminternationalpublications.com
Web Site: www.islaminternationalpublications.com
Key Personnel
National Sales Dir: Mohammed Arshad Ahmedi
Founded: 1889
Specialize in books on Islam, various translations & exegesis of Holy Quran in different languages.
Subjects: Religion - Islamic, Theology
ISBN Prefix(es): 978-1-85372

The Islamic Texts Society
Miller's House, Kings Mill Lane, Great Shelford, Cambridge CB22 5EN
Tel: (01223) 842425 *Fax:* (01223) 842425
E-mail: info@its.org.uk; orders@its.org.uk
Web Site: www.its.org.uk
Founded: 1981
Specialize in Islamic literature.
Membership(s): Publishers' Association.
Subjects: Art, Biography, Memoirs, History, Law, Natural History, Nonfiction (General), Philosophy, Poetry, Religion - Islamic
ISBN Prefix(es): 978-0-946621; 978-1-903682
Number of titles published annually: 6 Print
Total Titles: 50 Print
Foreign Rep(s): Eleanor Brasch Enterprises (Australia); Iberian Book Services (Portugal, Spain); IQRA Agencies (Sub-Saharan Africa); Publishers International Marketing Ltd (Southeast Asia); Quantum Publishing Solutions Ltd (UK); University Presses Marketing (Denmark, Finland, Iceland, Ireland, Norway, Sweden); Viva Books Pvt Ltd (India)
Distribution Center: Independent Publishers Group (IPG), 814 N Franklin St, Chicago, IL 60610, United States *Tel:* 312-337-0747 *Fax:* 312-337-5985 *E-mail:* frontdesk@ipgbook.com *Web Site:* www.ipgbook.com (North America)
Orders to: Orca Book Services Ltd, Unit A3, Fleets Corner, Poole, Dorset BH17 0HL
Tel: (01202) 665432 *Fax:* (01202) 666219
E-mail: orders@orcabookservices.co.uk

ISTE Ltd
Tuition House, 3rd floor, 27/37 St George's Rd, London SW19 4EU
Tel: (020) 8879 4580 *Toll Free Tel:* 0800 902 354 (within France)
E-mail: info@iste-editions.fr
Web Site: www.iste.co.uk; www.iste-editions.fr
Key Personnel
President & Mng Dir: Sami Menasce *E-mail:* s.menasce@iste.co.uk
Vice President: Raphael Menasce *Tel:* (020) 8879 4588 *E-mail:* r.menasce@iste.co.uk
General Administration: Chantal Menasce
Tel: (020) 8879 4582 *E-mail:* c.menasce@iste.co.uk
Production & Digital: Ludovic Moulard
Tel: (020) 8879 4584 *E-mail:* l.moulard@iste.co.uk
Founded: 2005
Scientific & technical publisher.
Subjects: Civil Engineering, Communications, Computer Science, Electronics, Electrical Engineering, Finance, Management, Mechanical Engineering, Science (General), Technology
ISBN Prefix(es): 978-1-903398; 978-1-905209; 978-1-84704; 978-1-78405
Number of titles published annually: 100 Print; 100 E-Book
Distributed by John Wiley & Sons (Asia) Pte Ltd (Asia/Pacific Region); John Wiley & Sons

Canada Ltd (Canada); John Wiley & Sons Inc (Mexico, South America & USA); John Wiley & Sons Ltd (Africa, Europe & Middle East)
Distribution Center: NBN International, 10 Thornbury Rd, Plymouth PL6 7PP *Tel:* (01752) 202301 *E-mail:* orders@nbninternational.com

Istros Books, *imprint of* Peter Owen Publishers

Istros Books
Imprint of Peter Owen Publishers
Conway Hall, 25 Red Lion Sq, London WC1R 4RL
Tel: (020) 7435 1540
E-mail: info@istrosbooks.com
Web Site: istrosbooks.com
Key Personnel
Contact: Susan Curtis-Kojakovic
Founded: 2011
Publish & promote literature in English translation from Southeast Europe & the Balkans.
ISBN Prefix(es): 978-1-908236
Distribution Center: Central Books Ltd, One Heath Park Industrial Estate, Freshwater Rd, Dagenham RM8 1RX *Tel:* (020) 8525 8800 *Fax:* (020) 8599 2694 *E-mail:* orders@centralbooks.com *Web Site:* www.centralbooks.com

Itchy Coo, *imprint of* Black & White Publishing Ltd

Ithaca Press, *imprint of* Garnet Publishing Ltd

IVP, *imprint of* Inter-Varsity Press

Ivy Kids
Member of Quarto International Co-Editions Group
Ovest House, 58 West St, Brighton BN1 2RA
Tel: (01273) 487440
Web Site: www.quartoknows.com/ivy-kids
Key Personnel
International Publishing Dir: Simon Gwynn
E-mail: simon.gwynn@quarto.com
Press & Publicity Officer: Graham Robson
E-mail: graham.robson@quarto.com
Trade Sales: Nikki Tilbury *E-mail:* nikki.tilbury@quarto.com
Subjects: Crafts, Games, Hobbies, Nonfiction (General)
ISBN Prefix(es): 978-1-78240
Ultimate Parent Company: The Quarto Group Inc

Ivy Press
Member of Quarto International Co-Editions Group
Ovest House, 58 West St, Brighton BN1 2RA
Tel: (01273) 487440
Web Site: www.quartoknows.com/ivy-press
Key Personnel
Founder & Co-Owner: Jenny Manstead
Publisher: Susan Kelly
International Publishing Dir: Simon Gwynn
E-mail: simon.gwynn@quarto.com
Group Rights Dir: Karine Marko *E-mail:* karine.marko@quarto.com
Creative Dir: Michael Whitehead
Financial Dir: Dan Logan
Production Dir: Simon Eaton
Press & Publicity Officer: Graham Robson
E-mail: graham.robson@quarto.com
Subjects: Animals, Pets, Cookery, Crafts, Games, Hobbies, Health, Nutrition, Humor, Science (General), Mind, Body & Spirit, Parenting, Popular Science
ISBN Prefix(es): 978-1-905695; 978-1-907332; 978-1-908005; 978-1-78240
Ultimate Parent Company: The Quarto Group Inc
Foreign Rep(s): Bookcity Co (Iran); Per Burell (Armenia, Azerbaijan, Baltic States, Belarus,

Kazakhstan, Kyrgyzstan, Moldova, Russia, Scandinavia, Tajikistan, Uzbekistan); Edgeler Book Services Ltd (Caribbean); Peter Hyde Associates (Botswana, Lesotho, Namibia, South Africa, Swaziland, Zimbabwe); Interart Sarl (France); Michael Klein (Austria, Germany, Switzerland); Levant Distributors (Lebanon); Roli Books (Kapil Kapoor) (Bangladesh, Bhutan, India, Nepal); Thames & Hudson (Australia) Pty Ltd (Australia, New Zealand, Pacific Islands, Papua New Guinea); Thames & Hudson China Ltd (China, Hong Kong, Macau); Thames & Hudson Ltd (Scipio Stringer) (Japan, Pakistan, Sri Lanka); Thames & Hudson Ltd (Stephen Embrey) (Eastern Mediterranean, Egypt, Middle East); Thames & Hudson Ltd (Ian Bartley) (Africa exc South Africa); Thames & Hudson Ltd (Natasha French) (Italy, Portugal, Spain); Thames & Hudson Ltd (Bas Van der Zee) (Belgium, Luxembourg, Netherlands); Thames & Hudson Ltd (Sara Ticci) (Eastern Europe); Thames & Hudson Ltd (Karim White) (Ireland); Thames & Hudson Singapore (Singapore, Southeast Asia); Thames & Hudson Singapore Pte Ltd (Malaysia)
Distribution Center: Littlehampton Book Services Ltd, Faraday Close, Durrington, Worthing, West Sussex BN13 3RB *Tel:* (01903) 828500; (01903) 828501 (customer service)
Web Site: lbsltd.wp.hachette.co.uk
Thames & Hudson Australia Pty Ltd, Portside Business Park, 11 Central Blvd, Fisherman's Bend, Victoria 3207, Australia *Tel:* (03) 9646 7788 *Fax:* (03) 9646 8790 *E-mail:* enquires@thaust.com.au (Australia & New Zealand)

IWA Publishing
Subsidiary of International Water Association
Alliance House, 12 Caxton St, London SW1H 0QS
Tel: (020) 7654 5500 *Fax:* (020) 7654 5555
E-mail: publications@iwap.co.uk
Web Site: www.iwapublishing.com
Key Personnel
Mng Dir: Rod Cookson
Marketing Manager: Ian Morgan
E-mail: imorgan@iwap.co.uk
Production Manager: Michelle Jones
Editor: Maggie Smith *E-mail:* msmith@iwap.co.uk
Subjects: Civil Engineering, Earth Sciences, Environmental Studies, Hydrology, Wastewater, Water
ISBN Prefix(es): 978-1-84339; 978-1-900222
Number of titles published annually: 50 Print; 1 CD-ROM
Total Titles: 250 Print; 5 CD-ROM
Foreign Rights: Aditya Books Pvt Ltd (Kailash Balani) (India, Korea, Malaysia, Vietnam); Co Info Pty Ltd (Australia, New Zealand); Martin P Hill Consulting (North America); iGroup (Asia Pacific) Ltd (Australia, China, Hong Kong, India, Indonesia, Japan, Korea, Malaysia, New Zealand, Philippines, Singapore, Taiwan, Thailand, Vietnam); iGroup Japan (Gina Jeong) (Japan); International Publishing Services Ltd (Zoe Kaviani) (Middle East); Tony Poh (China, Korea, Malaysia, Philippines, Singapore, Thailand, Vietnam); Ta Tong Books Ltd (Taiwan)
Distribution Center: Turpin Distribution Ltd., Stratton Business Park, Pegasus Dr, Biggleswade SG18 8TQ *Tel:* (01767) 604800 *Fax:* (01767) 601640 *E-mail:* iwap@turpin-distribution.com *Web Site:* www.turpin-distribution.com/turpinweb/content/home.aspx (worldwide exc North America)
Baker & Taylor Publisher Services, 30 Amberwood Parkway, Ashland, OH 44805, United States *Tel:* 567-215-0030 *E-mail:* info@btpubservices.com *Web Site:* www.btpubservices.com (North America)

JAI, *imprint of* Elsevier Ltd

Jane's Information Group, see IHS Jane's, IHS Global Ltd

Jawbone Press+
Imprint of Outline Press Ltd
Unit 2.1 Union Court, 20-22 Union Rd, London SW4 6JP
Tel: (020) 7720 3581 *Fax:* (020) 7819 3998
E-mail: info@jawbonepress.com
Web Site: jawbonepress.com
Key Personnel
Owner: Nigel Osborne
Founded: 2007
Music book publisher.
Also produces Backbeat-branded books for Hal Leonard.
Subjects: Music, Dance
ISBN Prefix(es): 978-1-906002
Number of titles published annually: 10 Print; 2 CD-ROM
Total Titles: 22 Print; 4 CD-ROM
U.S. Office(s): 1700 Fourth St, Berkeley, CA 94710, United States
Distribution Center: Publishers Group UK, 63-66 Hatton Garden, London EC1N 8LE
Tel: (020) 7405 1105 *Fax:* (020) 7242 3725
E-mail: orders@pguk.co.uk *Web Site:* www.pguk.co.uk (book trade)
First Line, 16 Teignbridge Business Centre, Cavalier Rd, Heathfield, Newton Abbott TQ12 6TZ, Contact: Jay Henson
Tel: (01626) 830336 *Fax:* (01626) 837001
E-mail: enquiries@firstlinemusic.co.uk *Web Site:* www.firstlinemusic.co.uk (music trade & mail order)
Music Sales, 14-15 Bernes St, London W1T 3LJ *Tel:* (020) 7612 7400 *Fax:* (020) 7612 7545 *E-mail:* music@musicsales.co.uk *Web Site:* www.musicsales.co.uk (music trade)
Publishers Group West, 1700 Fourth St, Berkeley, CA 94710, United States *Fax:* 510-528-3444 *Web Site:* www.pgw.com (book trade)
Hal Leonard Corp, 7777 W Bluemound Rd, PO Box 13819, Milwaukee, WI 53213, United States *Fax:* 414-774-3259 *E-mail:* halinfo@halleonard.com *Web Site:* www.halleonard.com (music trade)

JMD Media+
3 The Parker Centre, Mansfield Rd, Derby, Derbys DE21 4SZ
Tel: (07914) 647382
E-mail: sales@jmdmedia.co.uk
Web Site: www.jmdmedia.co.uk
Key Personnel
Mng Dir: Steve Caron *E-mail:* steve.caron@jmdmedia.co.uk
Founded: 1980
Subjects: Biography, Memoirs, Genealogy, History, Sports, Athletics
ISBN Prefix(es): 978-1-85983; 978-1-78091
Number of titles published annually: 60 Print
Total Titles: 500 Print

Joffe Books Ltd
The Stables, Enterprise House, Tudor Grove, London E9 7QL
Web Site: www.joffebooks.com
Key Personnel
Publisher: Jasper Joffe *E-mail:* jasper@joffebooks.com
Founded: 2012
Independent publisher of new fiction with a focus on thriller, mystery & romance. Print & Kindle editions.
Subjects: Fiction, Mysteries, Suspense, Romance
Number of titles published annually: 40 Print
Total Titles: 280 Print; 1 Audio

Jolly Grammar, *imprint of* Jolly Learning Ltd

Jolly Learning Ltd
Tailours House, High Rd, Chigwell, Essex IG7 6DL
Tel: (020) 8501 0405 *Fax:* (020) 8500 1696
E-mail: info@jollylearning.co.uk
Web Site: www.jollylearning.co.uk
Key Personnel
Mng Dir: Christopher Jolly *E-mail:* chris@jollylearning.co.uk
Founded: 1987
Phonics & grammar material for teaching reading to young children (age 3-7).
Subjects: Education
ISBN Prefix(es): 978-1-870946; 978-1-903619; 978-1-84414
Number of titles published annually: 10 Print; 1 CD-ROM
Total Titles: 100 Print; 3 Audio
Imprints: Jolly Grammar; Jolly Music; Jolly Phonics; Jolly Phonique (French); Jolly Readers
Distribution Center: AIDC, 82 Winter Sport Lane, Williston, VT 05495, United States
Fax: 802-864-7626 *E-mail:* jolly.orders@aidcvt.com

Jolly Music, *imprint of* Jolly Learning Ltd

Jolly Phonics, *imprint of* Jolly Learning Ltd

Jolly Phonique, *imprint of* Jolly Learning Ltd

Jolly Readers, *imprint of* Jolly Learning Ltd

Jordan Publishing Ltd
21 St Thomas St, Bristol BS1 6JS
Tel: (0117) 923 0600 *Fax:* (0117) 925 0486
E-mail: customerservice@jordanpublishing.co.uk
Web Site: www.jordanpublishing.co.uk
Key Personnel
Chief Executive Officer: Will Ricketts
Publishing Dir: Daniel Pollock
Publishing Manager: Kate Hather
Head, Publishing: Tony Hawitt
E-mail: tony_hawitt@jordanpublishing.co.uk
Head, Business Development: Mary Kenny
E-mail: mary_kenny@jordanpublishing.co.uk
Founded: 1863
Subjects: Accounting, Business, Law
ISBN Prefix(es): 978-0-85308; 978-1-84661; 978-0-85938
Parent Company: LexisNexis
Ultimate Parent Company: RELX Group PLC
Branch Office(s)
20-22 Bedford Row, London WC1R 4JS
Tel: (020) 7400 3307 *Fax:* (020) 7400 3366

Michael Joseph, *imprint of* Penguin Books Ltd

Richard Joseph Publishers Ltd
Priory Cottage, Frithelstock, Torrington, Devon EX38 8ZJ
Tel: (01805) 625750 *Fax:* (01805) 625376
E-mail: sales@sheppardsconfidential.com; office@sheppardsconfidential.com; info@sheppardsconfidential.com
Web Site: www.sheppardsconfidential.com
Key Personnel
Advertising: Rachel Heath
Editorial: Richard Joseph
Founded: 1990
Also publish the weekly book trade e-newsletter *Sheppard's Confidential*.
ISBN Prefix(es): 978-1-872699
Number of titles published annually: 8 Online
Total Titles: 2 Print
Imprints: Sheppard

Jossey-Bass, *imprint of* John Wiley & Sons Ltd

Kahn & Averill+
2-10 Plantation Rd, Amersham, Bucks HP6 6HJ
Tel: (01494) 725 525
E-mail: kahnandaverill@gmail.com
Web Site: www.kahnandaverill.co.uk
Founded: 1975
Publisher of essential books on music, including the highly acclaimed Yehudi Menuhin Music Guides.
Membership(s): Independent Publishers Guild (IPG).
Subjects: Music, Dance
ISBN Prefix(es): 978-0-900707; 978-1-871082
Number of titles published annually: 4 Print
Total Titles: 102 Print
Foreign Rep(s): Marissa Cote (Canada, USA)
Shipping Address: Central Books Ltd, One Heath Park Industrial Estate, Freshwater Rd, Dagenham RM8 1RX *Tel:* (020) 8525 8800 *Fax:* (020) 8599 2694 *E-mail:* contactus@centralbooks.com *Web Site:* www.centralbooks.com
Warehouse: Central Books Ltd, One Heath Park Industrial Estate, Freshwater Rd, Dagenham RM8 1RX *Tel:* (020) 8525 8800 *Fax:* (020) 8599 2694 *E-mail:* contactus@centralbooks.com *Web Site:* www.centralbooks.com
Orders to: Central Books Ltd, One Heath Park Industrial Estate, Freshwater Rd, Dagenham RM8 1RX *Tel:* (020) 8525 8800 *Fax:* (020) 8599 2694 *E-mail:* contactus@centralbooks.com *Web Site:* www.centralbooks.com

Kalimat Quarto, *imprint of* Quarto Publishing Group UK

KAMA Publishing
19a The Swale, Three Score, Norwich NR5 9HE
Tel: (01603) 749003; (07587) 178135 (cell)
E-mail: kamapublishing@gmail.com
Web Site: kamapublishing.co.uk
Key Personnel
Proprietor: Kevin Price
Founded: 2010
ISBN Prefix(es): 978-0-9567196
Distributed by MMS Publishing
Distribution Center: Orca Book Services Ltd, Unit A3, Fleets Corner, Poole BH17 0HL *Tel:* (01235) 465641 *E-mail:* orders@orcabookservices.co.uk

Kamera Books, *imprint of* Oldcastle Books Ltd

Kaplan Publishing
The Business Centre, Unit 2, Molly Millars Lane, Wokingham, Berks RG41 2QZ
Tel: (0118) 912 3000; (0118) 989 0629 *Fax:* (0118) 979 7455
E-mail: publishing@kaplan.co.uk
Web Site: kaplan-publishing.kaplan.co.uk
Founded: 1978
Publisher of accountancy study materials & business books.
Subjects: Accounting
ISBN Prefix(es): 978-1-85179; 978-1-84390
Orders to: Kaplan Financial Flexible Learning, West Gate, 6 Grace St, Leeds LS1 2RP
Tel: (0113) 200 6375 *Fax:* (0113) 243 0133
E-mail: flexiblelearning@kaplan.co.uk

Karnac Books Ltd+
118 Finchley Rd, London NW3 5HT
Tel: (020) 7431 1075 *Fax:* (020) 7435 9076
E-mail: shop@karnacbooks.com
Web Site: www.karnacbooks.com
Founded: 1950
Subjects: Psychology, Psychiatry, Social Sciences, Sociology

ISBN Prefix(es): 978-0-946439; 978-1-85575;
   978-0-9501647; 978-0-9507146; 978-1-84940;
   978-1-78049; 978-1-78220; 978-1-78241
Number of titles published annually: 40 Print
Imprints: Maresfield Lib
Distributed by Footprint Books (Australia & New
   Zealand); Stylus Publishing LLC (USA)
Distributor for Karnac Books; Harris Meltzer
   Trust; Zeig, Tucker & Theisen (UK & Europe
   only)
Foreign Rights: Cathy Miller Foreign Rights
   Agency

Kemps Publishing Ltd+
11 The Swan Courtyard, Charles Edward Rd,
   Yardley, Birmingham B26 1BU
Tel: (0121) 765 4144 *Fax:* (0121) 706 3491
E-mail: enquiries@kempspublishing.co.uk;
   sales@kempspublishing.co.uk
Web Site: www.kempspublishing.co.uk
Key Personnel
Executive Dir: Martin Jennings; Frank Markham
Founded: 1912
ISBN Prefix(es): 978-0-86259; 978-0-900273;
   978-0-901268; 978-0-905255

Kenilworth Press, *imprint of* Quiller Publishing
Ltd

Kenilworth Press Ltd+
Imprint of Quiller Publishing Ltd
Wykey House, Wykey, Shrewsbury, Salop SY4
   1JA
Tel: (01939) 261616 *Fax:* (01939) 261606
E-mail: admin@quillerbooks.com
Web Site: www.kenilworthpress.co.uk; www.
   countrybooksdirect.com
Key Personnel
Editorial & Foreign Rights: John Beaton
   E-mail: john@beaton.org.uk
Trade Sales: Jonathan Heath *E-mail:* jonathan@
   quillerbooks.com
Founded: 1989
Publisher of instructional equestrian books.
Also acts as official publisher to The British
   Horse Society.
Subjects: Animals, Pets, Natural History, Sports,
   Athletics, Veterinary Science
ISBN Prefix(es): 978-1-872082; 978-0-600; 978-
   0-901366; 978-1-872119; 978-1-905693; 978-1-
   910016
Number of titles published annually: 10 Print
Total Titles: 100 Print
Imprints: Threshold
Divisions: Threshold Books
Distributed by Half Halt Press Inc (USA)
Distributor for Half Halt Press Inc; The Pony
   Club; Trafalgar Square Publishing
Foreign Rep(s): Can-Pro Horse Equipment Ltd
   (Canada); Darragh Equestrian Solutions (Ire-
   land, Northern Ireland); DLS Australia Pty
   Ltd (Australia, New Zealand); IMA (Cen-
   tral Europe, Eastern Europe); Peribo Pty Ltd
   (Michael Coffey) (Australia, New Zealand);
   Robbert J Pleysier (Austria, Benelux, Germany,
   Switzerland); Sandro Salucci (France, Gibral-
   tar, Greece, Italy, Portugal, Spain); Stackpole
   Books Inc (USA); Trafalgar Square Publishing
   (USA); Trinity Books (South Africa)
Warehouse: Grantham Book Services, Trent Rd,
   Grantham, Lincs NG31 7XQ *Tel:* (01476)
   541080 *Fax:* (01476) 541061 *E-mail:* orders@
   gbs.tbs-ltd.co.uk

Kenyon-Deane, *imprint of* Cressrelles Publishing
Co Ltd

Kenyon-Deane+
Imprint of Cressrelles Publishing Co Ltd
Industrial Estate, 10 Station Rd, Colwall, Nr
   Malvern, Herts WR13 6RN

Tel: (01684) 540154
Web Site: www.cressrelles.co.uk
Key Personnel
Mng Dir: Leslie Smith
Business Manager: Simon Smith *E-mail:* simon@
   cressrelles.co.uk
Founded: 1930
Specialize in plays.
Subjects: Drama, Theater
ISBN Prefix(es): 978-0-7155
Number of titles published annually: 6 Print
Total Titles: 400 Print
Distributor for Anchorage Press (Europe)
Foreign Rights: Baker Plays (USA); DALRO
   (Southern Africa); Drama League of Ireland
   (Ireland); Origin Theatrical (Australia); Play
   Bureau (New Zealand)

Kew Publishing
Sir Joseph Banks Bldg, Royal Botanic Gardens,
   Kew, Richmond, Surrey TW9 3AE
Tel: (020) 8332 5715 *Fax:* (020) 8332 5646
E-mail: publishing@kew.org; info@kew.org;
   onlineshop@kew.org
Web Site: www.kew.org; shop.kew.org/
   kewbooksonline
Key Personnel
Head, Publishing: Gina Fullerlove
Publishing house of the Royal Botanic Gardens.
Subjects: Gardening, Plants, Science (General),
   Botanical Art, Botany, Conservation, Ecol-
   ogy, Flora & Fauna, Horticulture, Taxonomy,
   Wildlife
ISBN Prefix(es): 978-0-947643; 978-1-900347;
   978-0-85521; 978-1-84246
Distribution Center: Marston Book Services Ltd
   (UK & other territories)
University of Chicago Press (North America &
   Mexico)

Kidhaven Press, *imprint of* Gale

Killian Press, *imprint of* The MIT Press

Kingfisher, *imprint of* Pan Macmillan

Kingfisher+
Imprint of Pan Macmillan
20 New Wharf Rd, London N1 9RR
Tel: (020) 7014 6000 *Fax:* (020) 7014 6001
E-mail: childrensbooks@macmillan.co.uk;
   webqueries@macmillan.com
Web Site: www.panmacmillan.com/imprints/
   kingfisher
Key Personnel
International Dir: Jonathan Atkins *Tel:* (020) 7014
   6082 *E-mail:* j.atkins@macmillan.co.uk
Rights Dir: Harriet Sanders *Tel:* (020) 7014 6148
   E-mail: h.sanders@macmillan.co.uk
Head of International Sales, Exclusive Mar-
   kets: Leanne Williams *Tel:* (020) 7014 6223
   E-mail: leanne.williams@macmillan.com
Head of International Sales, Open Markets: Sarah
   McLean *E-mail:* s.mclean@macmillan.co.uk
Rights Assistant, Kingfisher & Macmillan Chil-
   dren's Books: Annabel El-Kerim *Tel:* (020)
   7014 6000 *E-mail:* annabel.el-kerim2@
   macmillan.com
Founded: 1974
Subjects: Biography, Memoirs, Fiction, Health,
   Nutrition, History, Literature, Literary Criti-
   cism, Essays, Regional Interests
ISBN Prefix(es): 978-0-7523; 978-0-86272; 978-
   1-85697; 978-0-7534
Number of titles published annually: 85 Print
Orders to: Pan Macmillan Ltd, Brunel Rd,
   Houndmills, Basingstoke, Hants RG21 6XS
   Tel: (01256) 329242 *Fax:* (01256) 812521 (re-
   tail); (01256) 812558 (wholesale)

The King's Fund+
11-13 Cavendish Sq, London W1G 0AN
Tel: (020) 7307 2400
E-mail: enquiry@kingsfund.org.uk
Web Site: www.kingsfund.org.uk
Key Personnel
Chief Executive: Chris Ham
Dir, Communications & Information: Rebecca
   Gray
Assistant Dir, Communications & External Af-
   fairs: Patrick South
Head, Marketing & Corporate Communications:
   Saul Harris
Publishing Manager: Mary Jean Pritchard
Founded: 1897
Health & social care titles mainly for profession-
   als, managers, academics & libraries.
Not-for-profit charitable foundation.
Subjects: Health, Nutrition, Social Sciences, Soci-
   ology
ISBN Prefix(es): 978-1-85551; 978-1-85717; 978-
   1-870551; 978-1-870607; 978-1-873883; 978-0-
   900889
Number of titles published annually: 30 Print
Total Titles: 200 Print

Kings Road Publishing
Division of Bonnier Publishing Ltd
Suite 2.08, The Plaza, 535 Kings Rd, London
   SW10 0SZ
Tel: (020) 3770 8888
E-mail: info@kingsroadpublishing.co.uk
Web Site: www.kingsroadpublishing.co.uk
Key Personnel
Mng Dir: Ben Dunn
Acquisitions Dir & Publisher: Natalie Jerome
Head, Children's Publishing: Helen Edwards
Brand, Licensing & Digital Dir: Kari Tavendale
Business Development & Group Licensing Dir:
   Helen Wicks
UK Sales & Marketing Dir: Andrew Sauerwine
Founded: 2015
Subjects: Fiction, Nonfiction (General)
Imprints: Blink Publishing; Studio Press; Templar
   Publishing; Weldon Owen Pty Ltd

Kingston University Press
Kingston University, Penrhyn Rd, Kingston upon
   Thames, Surrey KT1 2EE
Tel: (020) 8417 9000
E-mail: fass-kup@kingston.ac.uk
Web Site: fass.kingston.ac.uk/kup
Key Personnel
Dir: Dr David Rogers *E-mail:* d.rogers@kingston.
   ac.uk; Judith Watts *E-mail:* j.watts@kingston.
   ac.uk
Subjects: Biography, Memoirs, History, Literature,
   Literary Criticism, Essays
ISBN Prefix(es): 978-1-899999

Chris Kingston Publishing
Imprint of Optimus Education
St Mark's House, Shepherdess Walk, London N1
   7BQ
Tel: (0845) 450 6404 *Fax:* (0845) 450 6410
E-mail: customer.services@optimus-education.
   com
Web Site: www.teachingexpertise.com; www.
   optimus-education.com
Founded: 1995
Educational Publisher.
Membership(s): IPG; Publishers Association.
Subjects: Education, Geography, Geology
ISBN Prefix(es): 978-1-899857
Number of titles published annually: 5 Print; 2
   CD-ROM
Total Titles: 25 Print; 2 CD-ROM
Orders to: NBN International, c/o Optimus Edu-
   cation, Airport Business Centre, 10 Thornbury
   Rd, Plymouth PL6 7PP *Tel:* (0845) 450 6407
   E-mail: optimus.shop@optimus-education.com

Knockabout Comics+
42c Lancaster Rd, London W11 1QR
Tel: (020) 7243 2280
E-mail: info@knockabout.com
Web Site: www.knockabout.com
Key Personnel
Mng Dir: Tony Bennett
Founded: 1975
Specialize in comic books, graphic novels & drug information.
Subjects: Gardening, Plants, Health, Nutrition, Humor, Social Sciences, Sociology
ISBN Prefix(es): 978-0-86166
Number of titles published annually: 6 Print
Total Titles: 110 Print
Parent Company: Toskanex Ltd
Imprints: Fanny; Hassle Free Press
Distributor for Last Gasp (North America); Quick American Archives (North America); Quick Trading Co (North America); Rip Off Press (exc Canada & USA)
Foreign Rights: Lora Fountain (France, Germany, Netherlands, Spain)

Knox Robinson Publishing
34 New House, 67-68 Hatton Garden, London EC1N 8JY
Tel: (020) 8816 8630 *Fax:* (020) 8711 2334
E-mail: media@knoxrobinsonpublishing.com
Web Site: www.knoxrobinsonpublishing.com
Key Personnel
Mng Dir: Dr Dana Celeste Robinson
Founded: 2010
Specialize in historical fiction, historical romance & medieval fantasy.
Subjects: Fiction, Mysteries, Suspense, Romance, Science Fiction, Fantasy, War
ISBN Prefix(es): 978-0-9567901; 978-1-908483; 978-1-910282
Imprints: Mithras Books; Under the Maple Tree Books
U.S. Office(s): 244 Fifth Ave, Suite 1861, New York, NY 10001, United States *Tel:* 646-652-6980
Foreign Rep(s): Midpoint Trade Books (Australia, New Zealand, North America, South America)
Distribution Center: Marston Book Services Ltd, 160 Eastern Ave, Milton Park, Abingdon, Oxon OX14 4SB *Tel:* (01235) 465500 *Fax:* (01235) 465555 *E-mail:* direct.orders@marston.co.uk *Web Site:* www.marston.co.uk (UK, Europe & Ireland)

Kodansha Europe Ltd
40 Stockwell St, Greenwich, London SE10 8EY
Tel: (020) 8293 0111 *Fax:* (020) 8293 5533
E-mail: info@kodansha.eu
Web Site: www.kodansha.eu
Founded: 1990
Subjects: Archaeology, Architecture & Interior Design, Art, Biography, Memoirs, Fashion, Fiction, History, Language Arts, Linguistics, Literature, Literary Criticism, Essays, Philosophy, Poetry, Travel & Tourism, Japanese Culture
Distributor for HPH Publishing; Orchid Press; Purple Moon Publications; Serindia Publications; Visionary World

Kogan Page+
45 Gee St, London EC1V 3RS
Tel: (020) 7278 0433
E-mail: kpinfo@koganpage.com
Web Site: www.koganpage.com
Key Personnel
Mng Dir: Helen Kogan
Digital & Operations Dir: Martin Klopstock *E-mail:* mklopstock@koganpage.com
Rights Manager: Amy Joyner *E-mail:* kprights@koganpage.com
Founded: 1967
Independent publisher of business & management books.

Subjects: Business, Career Development, Education, Finance, Management, Marketing, Self-Help, Transportation
ISBN Prefix(es): 978-0-85038; 978-1-85091; 978-0-7494
Total Titles: 700 Print
Branch Office(s)
Kogan Page India, c/o Viva Books, 432713 Ansari Rd, New Delhi 110 002, India *Tel:* (011) 4224 2200 *E-mail:* viva@vivagroupindia.com *Web Site:* www.vivagroupindia.com
U.S. Office(s): Kogan Page USA, 1518 Walnut St, Philadelphia, PA 19102, United States *Tel:* 215-928-9112 *E-mail:* info@koganpage.com *Web Site:* www.koganpage.com
Distributed by Stylus Publishing Inc (USA)
Distributor for Kellogg School of Management, Northwestern University; Redline Wirtschaft; Stanford University Business Press
Foreign Rep(s): Book Promotions (South Africa); Durnell Marketing Ltd (Europe); EPP (Ghana); Footprint Books Pty Ltd (Australia, Fiji, New Zealand, Papua New Guinea); Ingram Publishers Services (USA); International Publishing Services (IPS) (Middle East, North Africa); Pansing (Malaysia, Singapore); Rombic Concepts Ltd (Nigeria); Ian Taylor Associates (China); Viva Books (Bangladesh, India, Pakistan, Sri Lanka); The White Partnership (Cambodia, Japan, Korea, Philippines, Taiwan)
Foreign Rights: Amo Agency (Korea); ANA (Albania, Bosnia and Herzegovina, Bulgaria, Macedonia, Romania, Serbia); Beijing International Rights Agency (China); Big Apple Agency Inc (China, Taiwan); The English Agency (Japan) Ltd (Japan); Agencja Literacka Graal (Croatia, Hungary, Poland); The Grayhawk Agency (Taiwan); Danny Hong Agency (Korea); Japan Uni Agency Inc (Japan); Nurcihan Kesim Literary Agency Inc (Turkey); Maxima Creative Agency (Indonesia); Andrew Nurnberg Associates Prague (Czechia, Slovakia, Slovenia); Silkroad Agency (Thailand); Julio F Yanez Agencia Literaria SL (Latin America, Spain, USA)
Distribution Center: The Book Service Ltd, Distribution Centre, Colchester Rd, Frating Green, Colchester, Essex CO7 7DW *Tel:* (01206) 256000 *Fax:* (01206) 255715 *E-mail:* koganpaged2c@tbs-ltd.co.uk *Web Site:* www.thebookservice.co.uk

Kube Publishing Ltd+
Markfield Conference Centre, Ratby Lane, Markfield, Leics LE67 9SY
Tel: (01530) 249 230 *Fax:* (01530) 249 656
E-mail: info@kubepublishing.com
Web Site: www.kubepublishing.com; www.islamic-foundation.com
Key Personnel
Mng Dir: Mr Haris Ahmad
Children's Editor: Mr Yosef Smyth
Founded: 1973
Research, publication, post-graduate education, training.
Subjects: Economics, Education, Fiction, Government, Political Science, History, Religion - Islamic, Science (General)
ISBN Prefix(es): 978-0-86037 (Islamic Foundation); 978-0-9503954 (Islamic Foundation); 978-1-84774
Number of titles published annually: 10 Print
Parent Company: Islamic Foundation, Markfield Conference Centre, Ratby Lane, Markfield, Leics LE67 9SY
Imprints: Revival Publications
Distributor for Ali Gator; Book Foundation; Hurst Books; International Institute of Islamic Thought (IIIT); Kazi Publications; Seerah Foundation; Tughra Books
Foreign Rep(s): CIEL (Bahrain, Egypt, Kuwait, Lebanon, Qatar, Saudi Arabia, United Arab

Emirates); Islamic Propagation Centre International (IPCI) (South Africa); Vijeh Nashr (Iran); Paradise Books & Distributors (Pakistan)
Distribution Center: Grantham Book Services, One Heath Park Industrial Estate, Trent Rd, Grantham, Lincs NG31 7XQ *Tel:* (01476) 541000 *Fax:* (01476) 541060 (UK & Europe)
Consortium Book Sales & Distribution, 34 13 Ave NE, Minneapolis, MN 55413-1002, United States *Web Site:* www.cbsd.com (USA & Canada)

Kudos, *imprint of* Top That Publishing Ltd

Kuperard+
59 Hutton Grove, London N12 8DS
Tel: (020) 8446 2440 *Fax:* (020) 8446 2441
E-mail: office@kuperard.co.uk
Web Site: www.kuperard.co.uk
Key Personnel
Publisher: Joshua Kuperard
Sales & Marketing: Martin Kaye *E-mail:* martin@kuperard.co.uk; Linda Tenenbaum *E-mail:* linda@kuperard.co.uk
Subjects: Education, Fiction, Religion - Other, Travel & Tourism
ISBN Prefix(es): 978-1-85733; 978-1-870668
Number of titles published annually: 30 Print
Total Titles: 300 Print
Imprints: Culture Smart!; Hutton Grove; Living Language; Simple Guides
Distribution Center: Orca Book Services, Unit A3, Fleets Corner Industrial Estate, Poole, Dorset BH17 7TD *Tel:* (01202) 665432 *Fax:* (01202) 785747

Kyle Books+
Formerly Kyle Cathie Ltd
Carmelite House, 50 Victoria Embankment, London EC4Y 0DZ
Tel: (020) 7692 7215
E-mail: general.enquiries@kylebooks.com
Web Site: www.kylebooks.com
Founded: 1991
Publisher of illustrated books specializing in health & beauty, mind, body & spirit & reference.
Subjects: Biography, Memoirs, Cookery, Crafts, Games, Hobbies, Gardening, Plants, Health, Nutrition, History, House & Home, Inspirational, Spirituality, Nonfiction (General), Philosophy, Regional Interests, Sports, Athletics, Travel & Tourism, Wine & Spirits, Health & Beauty, Lifestyle, Mind, Body & Spirit
ISBN Prefix(es): 978-1-85626
Number of titles published annually: 45 Print
Parent Company: Octopus Publishing Group
Ultimate Parent Company: Hachette UK
Distributed by New Holland (New Zealand); Penguin (India & South Africa); Simon & Schuster Pty Ltd (Australia)
Foreign Rep(s): Angell Eurosales (Gill Angell & Stewart Siddall) (Scandinavia); CLB Marketing Services (Adriana Junco) (Central Europe, Eastern Europe); John Fitzpatrick (Ireland, Northern Ireland); Michael Geoghegan (Belgium, France, Netherlands); Jacana Media Ltd (South Africa); National Book Network (NBN) (Richard Lowe) (Canada, USA); New Holland Publishers (NZ) Ltd (Belinda Cooke) (New Zealand); Padovani Books Ltd (Jenny Padovani) (Portugal, Spain); Padovani Books Ltd (Penny Padovani) (Greece, Italy); Page One (Singapore); Penguin Books India (India); Publishers Services (Gabriele Kern) (Austria, Germany, Switzerland); Simon & Schuster (Australia) Pty Ltd (Australia); David Williams (South America)
Distribution Center: Hachette Book Group, 121 N Enterprise Blvd, Lebanon, IN 46052, United States *Tel:* 765-483-9900 *Fax:* 765-483-0706 (North America)

Orders to: Littlehampton Book Services Ltd, Faraday Close, Durrington, Worthing, West Sussex BN13 3RB *Tel:* (01903) 828500; (01903) 828501 (customer service) *Web Site:* lbsltd.wp.hachette.co.uk

Kyle Cathie Ltd, see Kyle Books

Ladybird, *imprint of* Penguin Books Ltd

Ladybird Books Ltd+
Subsidiary of Penguin Books Ltd
80 Strand, London WC2R 0RL
Tel: (020) 7010 3000; (0845) 313 4444 (customer service) *Fax:* (020) 7010 6704
E-mail: ladybird@uk.penguingroup.com
Web Site: www.ladybird.co.uk
Key Personnel
International Rights Dir: Stefan Davey
Senior Publishing Operations Coordinator: Stephanie Tourbier
Editor: Nicola Bird
Marketing: Camilla Ray
Marketing Assistant: Shelley Warnaby
Subjects: Education, English as a Second Language, Fiction, History, Natural History, Nonfiction (General)
ISBN Prefix(es): 978-0-7214; 978-1-904351; 978-1-84422
Imprints: Disney
Divisions: Ladybird Disney Books
Foreign Rep(s): Ariel Balabat (Philippines); Jean Luc Morel (Algeria, France, Morocco, Tunisia); Penguin Books Deutchland GmbH (Austria, Germany); Penguin Books India Pvt Ltd (Bangladesh, Bhutan, India, Nepal, Sri Lanka); Penguin Books Malaysia Sdn Bhd (Malaysia); Penguin Books SA (Portugal, Spain); Penguin Books Singapore (Singapore); Penguin Group (Benelux); Penguin Group (Australia) (Australia); Penguin Group (Canada) (Canada); Penguin Group China (Azia Cheng) (China); Penguin Group (New Zealand) (New Zealand); Penguin Group (South Africa); Penguin Group (USA) (USA); Penguin Italia srl (Italy); Penguin Korea (Jeeyeon Oh) (South Korea); Penguin Random House UK (Eleanor O'Connor) (Cambodia, Hong Kong, Indonesia, Japan, Laos, Taiwan, Thailand, Vietnam); Penguin Random House UK (Jonathan Phillips) (Africa, Pakistan); Penguin Random House UK (Sarah Davidson-Aitkins) (Scandinavia, Switzerland); Penguin Random House UK (Olivia Hough) (Central Europe, Eastern Europe, Gibraltar, Malta, Southeast Europe); Grazyna Sosynska (Central Europe, Eastern Europe); Hector G Torres (Caribbean, Central America, Mexico, South America)

LAG, see Legal Action Group (LAG)

Allen Lane, *imprint of* Penguin Books Ltd

Allen Lane, *imprint of* Viking

Lang Syne Publishers Ltd+
79 Main St, Newtongrange, Midlothian EH22 4NA
Tel: (0131) 344 0414 *Fax:* (0845) 0756085
E-mail: info@lang-syne.co.uk
Web Site: www.langsyneshop.co.uk
Key Personnel
Owner & Dir: Kenneth W Laird
Founded: 1978
Publisher of Scottish interest nonfiction.
Subjects: Business, History, Humor, Music, Dance, Mysteries, Suspense
ISBN Prefix(es): 978-0-946264; 978-1-85217
Branch Office(s)
Scott's Highland Enterprises, 1646 Beckworth

Ave, London, ON N5V 2K7, Canada *Tel:* 519-453-0892 *Fax:* 519-453-6303
Scottish Flair, 168 Crawford St, Queanbeyan, NSW 2620, Australia *Tel:* (06) 2977-8780

Languages Information Centre, *imprint of* Joseph Biddulph Publisher

Lantana Publishing
65 Peak Hill, London SE26 4NS
E-mail: info@lantanapublishing.com; submissions@lantanapublishing.com; media@lantanapublishing.com
Web Site: www.lantanapublishing.com
Key Personnel
Founder & Publisher: Alice Curry *E-mail:* alice@lantanapublishing.com
Communications & Project Manager: Katrina Gutierrez *E-mail:* katrina@lantanapublishing.com
Membership(s): Independent Publishers Guild.
ISBN Prefix(es): 978-0-9932253; 978-1-911373
Foreign Rep(s): Roundhouse Group (Europe, UK)
Foreign Rights: Ashtar Publi Ltd (Europe, UK)
Distribution Center: Orca Book Services, 160 Eastern Ave, Milton Park, Abingdon, Oxon OX14 4SB *Tel:* (01235) 465500
E-mail: tradeorders@orcabookservices.co.uk
Web Site: www.orcabookservices.co.uk

Large Print Press, *imprint of* Gale

Laurel, *imprint of* Novello & Co

Laurence King Publishing Ltd+
361-373 City Rd, London EC1V 1LR
Tel: (020) 7841 6900 *Fax:* (020) 7841 6910
E-mail: enquiries@laurenceking.com; sales@laurenceking.com; rights@laurenceking.com
Web Site: www.laurenceking.com
Key Personnel
Mng Dir: Laurence King
Editorial Dir: Philip Cooper
Senior Production Manager: Felicity Awdry
Senior Publicist: Alex Coumbis
Publicity Assistant: Kristina Sumfleth
Founded: 1976
Design, produce & publish illustrated books.
Specialize in international co-editions.
Subjects: Architecture & Interior Design, Art, Fashion, History, Photography, Graphic Design
ISBN Prefix(es): 978-1-85669; 978-1-898113; 978-1-78067
Number of titles published annually: 60 Print
Total Titles: 200 Print
Subsidiaries: Laurence King Verlag (Germany)
Distributed by Chronicle Books (Canada, Mexico & USA); Thames & Hudson (worldwide exc Canada, Mexico & USA)

Law in Context, *imprint of* Cambridge University Press

Lawpack Publishing Ltd
76-89 Alscot Rd, London SE1 3AW
Tel: (020) 7394 4040 *Fax:* (020) 7394 4041
E-mail: enquiries@lawpack.co.uk
Web Site: www.lawpack.co.uk
Key Personnel
Mng Dir: Thomas Coles
Commissioning Editor: Jamie Ross
Founded: 1993
Self-help legal publisher.
Subjects: Business, How-to, Law, Management, Self-Help, Taxes
ISBN Prefix(es): 978-1-898217; 978-1-902646; 978-1-904053; 978-1-905261

Lawrence & Wishart Ltd+
99a Wallis Rd, London E9 5LN

Tel: (020) 8533 2506 *Fax:* (020) 8533 7369
E-mail: info@lwbooks.co.uk
Web Site: www.lwbooks.co.uk
Key Personnel
Mng Editor: Sally J Davison *E-mail:* sally@lwbooks.co.uk
Financial Dir: Avis Greenaway *E-mail:* avis@lwbooks.co.uk
Web Site Manager: Becky Luff *E-mail:* becky@lwbooks.co.uk
Promotions: Katharine Harris *E-mail:* katharine@lwbooks.co.uk
Founded: 1936
Independent radical publishing.
Subjects: Economics, Education, Environmental Studies, Ethnicity, Fiction, Film, Video, Government, Political Science, History, Human Relations, Labor, Industrial Relations, LGBTQ, Social Sciences, Sociology, Political Science
ISBN Prefix(es): 978-0-85315; 978-1-905007; 978-1-907103
Distributed by New York University Press
Distribution Center: Central Books Ltd, One Heath Park Industrial Estate, Freshwater Rd, Dagenham RM8 1RX *Tel:* (020) 8525 8800 *Fax:* (020) 8599 2694 *E-mail:* orders@centralbooks.com *Web Site:* www.centralbooks.com (UK)
Orders to: PO Box 7701, Latchingdon, Chelmsford CM3 6WL *Tel:* (01621) 741607
E-mail: landw@btinternet.com

LCCIEB, see London Chamber of Commerce & Industry Examinations Board (LCCIEB)

LDA+
2 Gregory St, Hyde SK14 4HR
Tel: (0845) 120 4776 *Toll Free Fax:* 0800 783 8648
E-mail: enquiries@ldalearning.com
Web Site: www.ldalearning.com
Founded: 1980
Publish learning materials covering language, literacy, ICT, teacher support, maths, numeracy & PSHE. For use with all children, including those with special needs, in the early years, primary or secondary classrooms.
Subjects: Health, Nutrition, Language Arts, Linguistics, Mathematics, ICT, Literacy, PSHE
ISBN Prefix(es): 978-1-85503; 978-0-905114
Parent Company: Findel Education Ltd
Branch Office(s)
Naas Road Business Park, Unit 11, Naas Rd, Dublin 12, Ireland *Tel:* (01) 427 3100 *Fax:* (01) 427 3118 *E-mail:* sales@findel-education.ie
Distribution Center: Chris Lloyd Sales & Marketing Services, 50a Willis Way, Dorset BH15 3SY *Tel:* (01202) 649930 *Fax:* (01202) 949950 *E-mail:* chrlloyd@globalnet.co.uk *Web Site:* www.chrislloydsales.co.uk

Leaping Hare Press
Member of Quarto International Co-Editions Group
Ovest House, 58 West St, Brighton BN1 2RA
Tel: (01273) 487440
Web Site: www.quartoknows.com/leaping-hare-press
Key Personnel
International Publishing Dir: Simon Gwynn *E-mail:* simon.gwynn@quarto.com
Press & Publicity Officer: Graham Robson *E-mail:* graham.robson@quarto.com
Trade Sales: Nikki Tilbury *E-mail:* nikki.tilbury@quarto.com
Subjects: Inspirational, Spirituality
ISBN Prefix(es): 978-1-78240
Ultimate Parent Company: The Quarto Group Inc

Learning & Work Institute+
21 De Montfort St, Leicester, Leics LE1 7GE
Tel: (0116) 204 4200 *Fax:* (0116) 204 6988

E-mail: press@learningandwork.org.uk;
enquiries@learningandwork.org.uk
Web Site: www.learningandwork.org.uk
Key Personnel
Chief Executive: Stephen Evans *E-mail:* stephen.
evans@learningandwork.org.uk
Founded: 2016 (merger of NIACE & CESI)
Independent policy & research organization dedicated to lifelong learning, full employment & inclusion.
Membership(s): Independent Publishers Guild (IPG).
Subjects: Education, Adult Education
ISBN Prefix(es): 978-1-872941; 978-1-86201; 978-0-900559
Number of titles published annually: 50 Print; 2 CD-ROM; 40 E-Book
Total Titles: 175 Print; 5 CD-ROM; 50 E-Book
Foreign Rep(s): Footprint Books (Australasia); International Specialized Book Services (ISBS) (Canada, USA)
Distribution Center: Marston Book Services Ltd, 160 Eastern Ave, Milton Park, Abingdon, Oxon OX14 4SB *Tel:* (01235) 465500 *Fax:* (01235) 465555 *E-mail:* direct.orders@marston.co.uk *Web Site:* www.marston.co.uk (worldwide exc Australasia & North America)
Footprint Books, 1/6a Prosperity Parade, Warriewood, NSW 2102, Australia *Tel:* (02) 9997 3973 *Fax:* (02) 9997 3185 *E-mail:* info@footprint.com.au *Web Site:* www.footprint.com.au (Australasia)
International Specialized Book Services (ISBS), 920 NE 58 Ave, Suite 300, Portland, OR 97213, United States *Fax:* 503-280-8832 *E-mail:* orders@isbs.com *Web Site:* www.isbs.com (North America)
Orders to: Marston Book Services Ltd, 160 Eastern Ave, Milton Park, Abingdon, Oxon OX14 4SB *Tel:* (01235) 465500 *Fax:* (01235) 465555 *E-mail:* direct.orders@marston.co.uk *Web Site:* www.marston.co.uk (worldwide exc Australasia & North America)

Learning Development Aids, see LDA

Learning Matters Ltd
One Oliver's Yard, 55 City Rd, London EC1Y 1SP
Tel: (020) 7324 8500 *Fax:* (020) 7324 8600
E-mail: market@sagepub.co.uk; orders@sagepub.co.uk
Web Site: www.uk.sagepub.com/learningmatters
Founded: 1999
Publishers of university course books for professional courses in education, health & social care.
Membership(s): IPG.
Subjects: Education, Social Sciences, Sociology
ISBN Prefix(es): 978-1-903300; 978-1-903337; 978-1-84445; 978-0-85725; 978-1-4739
Number of titles published annually: 80 Print; 80 E-Book
Total Titles: 300 Print; 250 E-Book
Parent Company: SAGE Publications Ltd
Warehouse: Unit 18 Fengate East, Titan Dr, Peterborough PE1 5XN *E-mail:* warehouse@sagepub.co.uk
Returns: Unit 18 Fengate East, Titan Dr, Peterborough PE1 5XN *Tel:* (0844) 412 5674 *Fax:* (0844) 412 5675 *E-mail:* warehouse@sagepub.co.uk

Learning Together+
18 Shandon Park, Belfast BT5 6NW
Tel: (028) 9040 2086 *Fax:* (028) 9040 2086
E-mail: info@learningtogether.co.uk
Web Site: www.learningtogether.co.uk
Key Personnel
Contact: Stephen McConkey
E-mail: smcconkey@learningtogether.co.uk
Founded: 1989

Eleven plus exams papers in verbal & nonverbal reasoning.
Membership(s): Educational Publishers Council; Publishers Association of Great Britain.
Subjects: Education, Mathematics, Science (General)
ISBN Prefix(es): 978-1-873385
Orders to: Orca Book Services, 160 Milton Park, Abingdon, Oxon OX14 4SB
E-mail: tradeorders@orcabookservices.co.uk
Web Site: www.orcabookservices.co.uk

Legal Action Group (LAG)+
Universal House, 3rd floor, 88-94 Wentworth St, London E1 7SA
Tel: (020) 7833 2931 *Fax:* (020) 7837 6094
E-mail: lag@lag.org.uk; books@lag.org.uk
Web Site: www.lag.org.uk
Key Personnel
Chair: Poonam Bhari
Publisher: Esther Pilger
Dir: Steve Hynes *E-mail:* shynes@lag.org.uk
Marketing Manager: Nim Moorthy *Tel:* (020) 7833 7430
Founded: 1972
Membership(s): Independent Publishers' Guild.
Subjects: Law
ISBN Prefix(es): 978-0-905099; 978-1-903307; 978-1-908407
Total Titles: 35 Print
Distribution Center: Marston Book Services Ltd, 160 Eastern Ave, Milton Park, Abingdon, Oxford OX14 4SB *Tel:* (01235) 465500 *Fax:* (01235) 465555 *E-mail:* trade.orders@marston.co.uk *Web Site:* www.marston.co.uk

Lemos & Crane+
64 Highgate High St, London N6 5HX
Tel: (020) 8348 8263
E-mail: info@lemosandcrane.co.uk
Web Site: www.lemosandcrane.co.uk
Key Personnel
Partner: Paul Crane; Gerard Lemos
Founded: 1994
Subjects: Law, Management
ISBN Prefix(es): 978-1-898001
Orders to: NBN International, Estover Rd, Plymouth PL6 7PZ *Tel:* (01752) 202301 *Fax:* (01752) 202333 *Web Site:* www.nbninternational.com

Lennard Publishing
Windmill Cottage, Mackerye End, Harpenden, Herts AL5 5DR
Tel: (01582) 715866
Key Personnel
Chief Executive: Adrian Stephenson
E-mail: stephenson@lennardqap.co.uk
Subjects: Biography, Memoirs, History, Nonfiction (General), Sports, Athletics
Parent Company: Lennard Associates Ltd

Letterland International Ltd
Riverbridge House, Guildford Rd, Leatherhead, Surrey KT22 9AD
Tel: (01223) 26 26 75 *Fax:* (01223) 26 41 26
E-mail: info@letterland.com
Web Site: www.letterland.com
Key Personnel
Mng Dir: Mark Wendon
Founded: 1985
Subjects: Education, Language Arts, Linguistics
ISBN Prefix(es): 978-0-907345; 978-1-86209
Distributed by HarperCollins Publishers (Ireland & UK)

Letts
Imprint of Collins Education
Westerhill Rd, Bishopbriggs, Glasgow G64 2QT
E-mail: education@harpercollins.co.uk
Web Site: collins.co.uk/pages/about-letts-revision

Founded: 1979
Educational publisher, including home study & classroom resources.
Subjects: Accounting, Computer Science, Economics, Finance, Labor, Industrial Relations, Law, Library & Information Sciences, Management, Marketing, Mathematics
ISBN Prefix(es): 978-1-85805; 978-1-85758; 978-1-84315
Number of titles published annually: 50 Print; 5 CD-ROM; 5 Online
Total Titles: 500 Print; 10 CD-ROM; 10 Online
Ultimate Parent Company: HarperCollins Publishers Ltd
Foreign Rep(s): APD Kuala Lumpur (Malaysia); APD Singapore (Brunei, Singapore); Book Promotions (Botswana, Lesotho, Namibia, South Africa, Swaziland); Chelis Bookazine (Nigeria); EPP Book Service (Benin, Cote d'Ivoire (Ivory Coast), Ghana, Liberia, Sierra Leone); EQ Opciones en Educacion (Uruguay); Evans Shepherd P/L trading as Schoolbooks 4 Africa (Zimbabwe); HarperCollins Canada (Canada); HarperCollins China (China); HarperCollins India (India); Librarie Ikirezie (Rwanda); KEL Ediciones (Argentina); Libromania (Chile); Lioncrest (primary) (Australia); Moses Mutumba (Uganda); Nelson Cengage Learning (secondary) (Australia); Editions Le Printemp (Mauritius); Publishers Marketing Associates (Pakistan); SBS - Special Book Services (Brazil); Schoolstoreng (Nigeria); Transglobal Publishers Services Ltd (Hong Kong); Unlimited Press (Egypt)

J D Lewis & Sons Ltd, see Gomer Press Ltd

John Libbey Publishing+
3 Leicester Rd, New Barnet, Herts EN5 5EW
E-mail: john.libbey@orange.fr
Web Site: www.johnlibbey.com
Key Personnel
Dir: Arporn Aunsuksan; John Libbey
Founded: 1979
Subjects: Communications, Fiction, Film, Video, Music, Dance, Cinema/Animation, Epilepsy, Media, Neurology, Nuclear Medicine
ISBN Prefix(es): 978-0-86196; 978-1-86462
Total Titles: 100 Print
Foreign Rep(s): East-West Export Books (Asia); Elsevier Australia (Australia, New Zealand); Indiana University Press (Asia, North America)
Distribution Center: East-West Export Books, University of Hawaii Press, 2840 Kolowalu St, Honolulu, HI 96822, United States *Tel:* 808-956-6214 *Fax:* 808-988-6052 *E-mail:* royden@hawaii.edu (Asia)
Indiana University Press, 601 N Morton St, Bloomington, IN 47404-3797, United States *Tel:* 812-855-4203 *Fax:* 812-855-8507 *Web Site:* www.iupress.indiana.edu/catalog (North America)
Orders to: Marston Book Services Ltd, 160 Eastern Ave, Milton Park, Abingdon, Oxon OX14 4SB *Tel:* (01235) 465500 *Fax:* (01235) 465509 *E-mail:* direct.orders@marston.co.uk *Web Site:* www.marston.co.uk

Liberty+
Liberty House, 26-30 Strutton Ground, London SW1P 2HR
Tel: (020) 7403 3888
Web Site: www.liberty-human-rights.org.uk
Key Personnel
Dir: Ms Shami Chakrabarti
Founded: 1934
Subjects: Law
ISBN Prefix(es): 978-0-901108; 978-0-946088
Associate Companies: Civil Liberties Trust

LID Publishing Ltd
Garden Studios, 71-75 Shelton St, Covent Garden, London WC2H 9JQ
Tel: (020) 7470 8801
E-mail: info@lidpublishing.com
Web Site: www.lidpublishing.com
Key Personnel
General Manager: Martin Liu *E-mail:* martin.liu@lidpublishing.com
Founded: 1993
Subjects: Business, History, Business History
ISBN Prefix(es): 978-1-907794
Number of titles published annually: 120 Print
U.S. Office(s): LID Publishing Inc, 31 W 34 St, Suite 8004, New York, NY 10001, United States, Contact: Andrew Mueller *E-mail:* contact@lidpublishing.com
Distribution Center: Marston Book Services Ltd, 160 Eastern Ave, Milton Park, Abingdon, Oxon OX14 4SB *Tel:* (01235) 465500 *Fax:* (01235) 465555 *E-mail:* trade.orders@marston.co.uk
Web Site: www.marston.co.uk

Frances Lincoln, *imprint of* Quarto Publishing Group UK

Frances Lincoln+
Imprint of Quarto Publishing Group UK
74-77 White Lion St, Islington, London N1 9PF
Tel: (020) 7284 9300 *Fax:* (020) 7485 0490
Web Site: www.quartoknows.com/frances-lincoln
Founded: 1977
Subjects: Architecture & Interior Design, Art, Biography, Memoirs, Child Care & Development, Crafts, Games, Hobbies, Gardening, Plants, Government, Political Science, Health, Nutrition, House & Home, Humor, Outdoor Recreation, Philosophy, Photography, Poetry, Religion - Other, Science (General), Sports, Athletics, Travel & Tourism, Nature
ISBN Prefix(es): 978-0-7112; 978-1-84507; 978-0-906459; 978-1-84780
Number of titles published annually: 100 Print
Total Titles: 500 Print
Ultimate Parent Company: The Quarto Group Inc
Distributor for Allen & Unwin; Barn Owl Books; Campfire; The Little Bookroom; The Natural History Museum Publishing; The New York Review Children's Collection; NYRB Classics; NYRB Collections; O'Brien Press
Foreign Rep(s): A-Z Africa Book Services (Anita Zih-de Haan) (Africa exc South Africa); Angell Eurosales (Gill Angell & Stewart Siddall) (Iceland, Scandinavia); Bill Bailey Publishers' Representatives (Eastern Europe, Russia); Ariel Balatbat (Guam, Philippines); Tim Burland (Japan); Ted Dougherty (Gallery Accounts) (Benelux, France); John Fitzpatrick & Siobhan Mullet (Ireland); Michael Geoghegan (Benelux, France); Hardy Bigfoss International Co Ltd (Cambodia, Indonesia, Laos, Myanmar, Thailand, Vietnam); IMA (David Williams) (Bermuda, Caribbean, Central America, Mexico, South America); International Publishing Services (Zoe Kaviani) (Middle East); Jacana (Shay Heydenrych) (South Africa); B K Norton (Chiafeng Peng) (Taiwan); Padovani Books Ltd (Penny Padovani) (Greece, Italy); Padovani Books Ltd (Jenny Padovani) (Gibraltar, Portugal, Spain); Benjamin Pan (China); Pan Macmillan India (India); Pansing Distribution PTE Ltd (Malaysia, Singapore); Publishers Group Canada (Canada); Publishers Group West (USA); Publishers' Services (Gabriel Kern) (Austria, Germany, Switzerland); Walker Books Australia (Australia, New Zealand)
Distribution Center: Littlehampton Book Services Ltd, Faraday Close, Durrington, Worthing, West Sussex BN13 3RB *Tel:* (01903) 828500; (01903) 828501 (customer service)
Web Site: lbsltd.wp.hachette.co.uk

Frances Lincoln Children's Books, *imprint of* Quarto Publishing Group UK

Frances Lincoln Children's Books
Imprint of Quarto Publishing Group UK
74-77 White Lion St, London N1 9PF
Tel: (020) 7284 9300 *Fax:* (020) 7485 0490
Web Site: www.quartoknows.com/frances-lincoln-childrens-books
Key Personnel
Publisher: Janetta Otter-Barry *E-mail:* janetta.otter-barry@quarto.com; Rachel Williams *E-mail:* rachel.williams@quarto.com
Editor: Katie Cotton *E-mail:* katie.cotton@quarto.com
Senior Designer: Andrew Watson *E-mail:* andrew.watson@quarto.com
Founded: 1983
Subjects: Fiction, Nonfiction (General)
ISBN Prefix(es): 978-1-84507; 978-1-84780
Ultimate Parent Company: The Quarto Group Inc

Linen Hall Library+
17 Donegall Sq N, Belfast BT1 5GB
Tel: (028) 9032 1707 *Fax:* (028) 9043 8586
E-mail: info@linenhall.com
Web Site: linenhall.com
Key Personnel
Dir: Julie Andrews *E-mail:* j.andrews@linenhall.com
Librarian: Samantha McCombe *E-mail:* s.mccombe@linenhall.com
Customer Services Manager: Marie Ryan *E-mail:* m.ryan@linenhall.com
Digital & Marketing Communications Specialist: Rachel Wetherall *E-mail:* r.wetherall@linenhall.com
Founded: 1788
Subjects: Biography, Memoirs, History, Library & Information Sciences, Literature, Literary Criticism, Essays
ISBN Prefix(es): 978-0-9508985; 978-1-900921
Number of titles published annually: 1 Print
Total Titles: 1 Print; 1 CD-ROM; 1 Online

Linford Mystery Library Series, see Ulverscroft Large Print Books Ltd

Linford Romance Library Series, see Ulverscroft Large Print Books Ltd

Linford Western Library Series, see Ulverscroft Large Print Books Ltd

Linguaphone Institute Ltd+
Member of Linguaphone Group
Liongate Enterprise Park, 80 Morden Rd, Mitcham, Surrey CR4 4PH
Tel: (020) 8687 6000; (020) 3603 6554
Fax: (020) 8687 6410
E-mail: info@linguaphonegroup.com; sales@linguaphone.co.uk; cst@linguaphone.co.uk (customer sales)
Web Site: www.linguaphonegroup.com
Key Personnel
Chief Executive Officer: Clive Sawkins
Head, Marketing: Charlotte Pritchard *Tel:* (020) 8687 6115
Founded: 1924
Provider of self-study & classroom language courses, products & services.
Subjects: Language Arts, Linguistics
ISBN Prefix(es): 978-0-7473
Number of titles published annually: 5 Print; 5 CD-ROM; 1 Audio
Total Titles: 50 Print; 10 CD-ROM; 5 Audio
Imprints: Linguatape
Subsidiaries: Linguapac Distributors Sdn Bhd

Linguatape, *imprint of* Linguaphone Institute Ltd

Lintott Press, *imprint of* Carcanet Press Ltd

Lion, *imprint of* Lion Hudson PLC

Lion Children's, *imprint of* Lion Hudson PLC

Lion Fiction, *imprint of* Lion Hudson PLC

Lion Hudson PLC+
Wilkinson House, Jordan Hill Rd, Oxford, Oxon OX2 8DR
Tel: (01865) 302750 *Fax:* (01865) 302757
E-mail: info@lionhudson.com; marketing@lionhudson.com; international@lionhudson.com; uksales@lionhudson.com
Web Site: www.lionhudson.com
Key Personnel
Mng Dir & International Dir: Nick Jones *E-mail:* nickj@lionhudson.com
Head, Hudson International: Chris Atkinson
Head, Lion International: Paul Whitton
Head, Export Sales: Robert Wendover
Sales & Development Manager: Anne Rogers
Founded: 2003
Specialize in adult religion & spirituality, illustrated reference, biography, health, gift books, children's books - Bible stories & prayers, information & reference, activity, novelty & picture books.
Subjects: Biblical Studies, Biography, Memoirs, Health, Nutrition, Inspirational, Spirituality, Nonfiction (General), Religion - Catholic, Religion - Protestant, Self-Help, Theology
ISBN Prefix(es): 978-0-7459; 978-0-85648; 978-1-85424 (Monarch); 978-1-85985 (Candle Books); 978-0-948902 (Candle Books); 978-0-85721; 978-1-899746 (Monarch)
Number of titles published annually: 200 Print
Total Titles: 800 Print
Imprints: Candle Books; Lion; Lion Children's; Lion Fiction; Monarch Books
Foreign Rep(s): ASAF EV (Netherlands); Campus Crusade Asia Ltd (Malaysia, Singapore); Canadian Manda (Canada); Christian Art (South Africa); David C Cook (Canada); Jacana Media Pty Ltd (South Africa); Keswick Books & Gifts Ltd (East Africa); Koorong Books (Australia); Kregel Publications (USA); New Holland Publishers (NZ) Ltd (New Zealand); OMF Literature Inc (Philippines); Soul Distributors (Christian Market) (New Zealand); Trafalgar Square Publishing (USA); Word Bookstore (Australia)
Distribution Center: Marston Book Services Ltd, 160 Eastern Ave, Milton Park, Abingdon, Oxon OX14 4SB *Tel:* (01235) 465500 *Fax:* (01235) 465509 *E-mail:* direct.orders@marston.co.uk
Web Site: www.marston.co.uk
Trafalgar Square Publishing, 814 N Franklin St, Chicago, IL 60610, United States *Tel:* 312-337-0747 *Fax:* 312-337-5985 (Canada, USA & ebooks worldwide)

Lippincott Williams & Wilkins (LWW)
Unit of Wolters Kluwer Health
250 Waterloo Rd, London SE1 8RD
Tel: (020) 7981 0600 *Fax:* (020) 7981 0601
E-mail: enquiry@lww.co.uk
Web Site: www.lww.co.uk
Founded: 1893
Subjects: Medicine, Nursing, Dentistry, Veterinary Science
ISBN Prefix(es): 978-0-397; 978-0-316; 978-0-683; 978-0-8121; 978-0-7817; 978-1-901831; 978-1-4698; 978-1-60929; 978-1-60831; 978-0-8067; 978-1-60547; 978-1-881063; 978-0-88167; 978-0-89004; 978-0-89313; 978-0-89640; 978-0-911216
Branch Office(s)
Lippincott Williams & Wilkins Pty Ltd, Suite 1801, Level 18, 9 Hunter St, Sydney, NSW

2000, Australia *Tel:* (02) 9276-6600 *Fax:* (02) 9231-1255

Lippincott Williams & Wilkins Asia Ltd, 15/F, W Square, 314-324 Hennessy Rd, Wan Chai, Hong Kong *Tel:* 2610 7000 *Fax:* 2610 7098

Wolterskluwer Health Japan, Forecast Mita 5F, 1-3-31 Mita, Minato-Ku, Tokyo 108-0073, Japan *Tel:* (03) 5427 1969 *Fax:* (03) 3451 2025

U.S. Office(s): Wolters Kluwer Health, 2700 Lake Cook Rd, Riverwoods, IL 60015, United States *Tel:* 847-580-5000

351 W Camden St, Baltimore, MD 21201, United States *Tel:* 410-528-4000

16522 Hunters Green Parkway, Hagerstown, MD 21740, United States *Tel:* 301-223-2300 *Fax:* 301-223-2400 *E-mail:* orders@lww.com

Healthcare Group, 333 Seventh Ave, 19th & 20th floors, New York, NY 10001, United States

Two Commerce Sq, 2001 Market St, Philadelphia, PA 19103, United States *Tel:* 215-521-8300 *Fax:* 215-521-8902 (head office)

Distribution Center: NBN International Ltd, Airport Business Centre, Thornbury Rd, Plymouth, Devon PL6 7PP *Tel:* (01752) 202-301 *E-mail:* lww.orders@nbninternational.com

LISU
Loughborough University, Loughborough, Leics LE11 3TU
Tel: (01509) 635680
E-mail: lisu@lboro.ac.uk
Web Site: www.lboro.ac.uk/departments/dis/lisu
Key Personnel
Dir: Claire Creaser *Tel:* (01509) 635682
  E-mail: c.creaser@lboro.ac.uk
Senior Research Associate: Helen Greenwood
  E-mail: h.r.greenwood@lboro.ac.uk
Research Associate: Valerie Spezi *E-mail:* v.c.l.
  spezi@lboro.ac.uk
Administrator: Sharon Fletcher *Tel:* (01509)
  635685 *E-mail:* s.fletcher@lboro.ac.uk
Assistant Statistician: Sonya White *E-mail:* s.u.
  white@lboro.ac.uk
Founded: 1987
Collect, analyse, interpret & publish statistical information for & about the library domain in the UK.
Subjects: Library & Information Sciences, Management, Public Administration
ISBN Prefix(es): 978-0-948848; 978-0-904924; 978-1-901786; 978-1-905499
Number of titles published annually: 4 Print; 4 CD-ROM; 3 Online
Total Titles: 134 Print; 4 CD-ROM; 27 Online
Ultimate Parent Company: Loughborough University

Little Bee, *imprint of* Weldon Owen Pty Ltd

Little, Brown, *imprint of* Little, Brown Book Group

Little, Brown Book Group
Division of Hachette UK
50 Victoria Embankment, London EC4Y 0DZ
Tel: (020) 3122 7000 *Fax:* (020) 8283 9706
E-mail: info@littlebrown.co.uk
Web Site: www.littlebrown.co.uk
Key Personnel
Chief Operating Officer: Ben Groves-Raines
Mng Dir: Charlie King
Group Sales: Robert Manser
Fiction Publisher, Little Brown UK/Abacus: Clare Smith
Publisher, Corsair & Atom: James Gurbutt
Publisher, Dialogue Books: Sharmaine Lovegrove
Publisher, Fleet: Ursula Doyle
Publisher, Orbit: Tim Holman
Publisher, Sphere Fiction, Crime & Thrillers: Catherine Burke
Publisher, Virago Press: Sarah Savitt
Deputy Publisher, Sphere Fiction: Maddie West

Publishing Dir, Constable: Andreas Campomar
Publishing Dir, Nonfiction, Little, Brown/Piatkus: Tim Whiting
Publishing Dir, Nonfiction, Sphere: Adam Strange
Publishing Dir, Robinson: Duncan Proudfoot
Publishing Dir, Sphere Fiction: Lucy Malagoni
Mng Dir, Little, Brown & Abacus: Richard Beswick
Head of Design/Creative Dir: Duncan Spilling
Editor-in-Chief, Commercial Division (Sphere & Piatkus): Antonia Hodgson
Editorial Dir, Crime Fiction, C&R: Krystyna Green
Editorial Dir, Piatkus Fiction: Emma Beswetherick
Editorial Dir, Piatkus Nonfiction: Zoe Bohm
Subsidiary Rights Dir: Laura Mamelok
Senior Subsidiary Rights Associate: Nel Malikova
Founded: 1988
Also acts as book distributor.
Subjects: Biography, Memoirs, Business, Fiction, History, Humor, Mysteries, Suspense, Nonfiction (General), Romance, Science Fiction, Fantasy, Travel & Tourism
ISBN Prefix(es): 978-0-316; 978-0-86068; 978-0-7515; 978-1-85723; 978-0-7499; 978-1-86049; 978-0-7088; 978-1-85381; 978-1-904233; 978-1-184149; 978-1-84408; 978-1-4055; 978-0-356; 978-0-349; 978-1-84744; 978-1-4087; 978-1-905654; 978-0-7481; 978-1-907411
Number of titles published annually: 500 Print; 4 CD-ROM; 600 E-Book; 100 Audio
Total Titles: 7,000 Print; 1,000 CD-ROM; 6,500 E-Book; 5,000 Audio
Ultimate Parent Company: Lagadere, France
Imprints: Abacus; Atom; Blackfriars; C&R; Constable; Corsair; The Crime Vault; Dialogue Books; Entice; Fleet; Hachette Audio; Little, Brown; Orbit; Piatkus; Robinson; Sphere; Trapdoor; Virago
Orders to: Littlehampton Book Services Ltd, Faraday Close, Durrington, Worthing, West Sussex BN13 3RB *Tel:* (01903) 828500; (01903) 828501 (customer service) *Web Site:* lbsltd.wp.hachette.co.uk

Little Star Creations, *imprint of* Holland Publishing PLC

Little Tiger Kids, *imprint of* Little Tiger Press Group

Little Tiger Press, *imprint of* Little Tiger Press Group

Little Tiger Press Group+
One The Coda Centre, 189 Munster Rd, London SW6 6AW
Tel: (020) 7385 6333 *Fax:* (020) 7385 7333
E-mail: sales@littletiger.co.uk; contact@littletiger.co.uk (publicity); rights@littletiger.co.uk; rights@stripespublishing.co.uk
Web Site: www.littletiger.co.uk; www.littletigerpress.com; www.stripespublishing.co.uk
Key Personnel
Editorial Dir: Barry Timms
Associate Publisher, Stripes Publishing: Jane Harris
Head, Marketing: Hayley Castle
Group Sales & Marketing Dir: David Bucknor
  Tel: (07967) 672906 (cell) *E-mail:* dbucknor@littletiger.co.uk
Group UK Sales Manager: Patricia Cooper
  Tel: (07950) 410320 (cell) *E-mail:* pcooper@littletiger.co.uk
Group Export Sales: Nik Bhatia *Tel:* (07786) 333889 (cell) *E-mail:* nbhatia@littletiger.co.uk
Senior Editor, Stripes Publishing: Ruth Bennett
Founded: 1987
Specialize in co-production of children's picture books.

Subjects: English as a Second Language, Fiction
ISBN Prefix(es): 978-1-870271; 978-1-85430; 978-1-84506; 978-1-84715 (Stripes); 978-1-84745 (Stripes); 978-1-84857; 978-1-84143; 978-1-84895
Imprints: Caterpillar Books; Little Tiger Kids; Little Tiger Press; Stripes Publishing
Foreign Rep(s): Butler Sims Ltd (Brian Blennerhassett) (Ireland)
Distribution Center: Macmillan Distribution Ltd (MDL), Brunel Rd, Houndmills, Basingstoke, Hants RG21 6XS *Tel:* (01256) 302 692 *Fax:* (01256) 812 558 *E-mail:* orders@macmillan.co.uk

The Littman Library of Jewish Civilization+
PO Box 645, Oxford OX2 0UJ
Tel: (01865) 790740
E-mail: info@littman.co.uk
Web Site: www.littman.co.uk
Key Personnel
Chief Executive Officer: Ludo Craddock
Dir: Glenn Hurstfield; Colette Littman; Joanna Littman
Editorial: Connie Webber *E-mail:* connie.webber@littmanlibrary.co.uk
Founded: 1965
Subjects: Art, Biography, Memoirs, Drama, Theater, Ethnicity, History, Literature, Literary Criticism, Essays, Philosophy, Poetry, Religion - Jewish, Social Sciences, Sociology, Theology, Women's Studies
ISBN Prefix(es): 978-1-874774; 978-1-904113; 978-1-906764; 978-1-909821
Distributed by The Hebrew University Magnes Press (exclusive distributor for Israel)
Warehouse: NBN International, 10 Thornbury Rd, Plymouth PL6 7PP *Tel:* (01752) 202000 *Fax:* (01752) 202333 *E-mail:* orders@nbninternational.com *Web Site:* www.nbninternational.com (UK & overseas)
Distribution Center: NBN International, 10 Thornbury Rd, Plymouth PL6 7PP *Tel:* (01752) 202301 *Fax:* (01752) 202333 *E-mail:* orders@nbninternational.com *Web Site:* www.nbninternational.com (UK & overseas)
Co-op Information Services, 200A Rooks Rd, Vermont, Victoria 3133, Australia *Tel:* (03) 9210 7777 *Fax:* (03) 9210 7788 *E-mail:* customerservice@coinfo.com.au *Web Site:* www.coinfo.com.au (Australia & New Zealand)
The Hebrew University Magnes Press, PO Box 39099, Jerusalem 91390, Israel *Toll Free Tel:* 800-200-217 *Fax:* (02) 5660341 *E-mail:* sales.israel@magnespress.co.il *Web Site:* www.magnespress.co.il
ISBS, 920 NE 58 Ave, Suite 300, Portland, OR 97213-3786, United States *Fax:* 503-280-8832 (USA & Canada)

Liverpool University Press+
4 Cambridge St, Liverpool L69 7ZU
Tel: (0151) 794 2233 *Fax:* (0151) 794 2235
E-mail: lup@liv.ac.uk
Web Site: www.liverpooluniversitypress.co.uk
Key Personnel
Mng Dir: Anthony Cond *E-mail:* acond@liv.ac.uk
Editorial Dir: Alison Welsby *E-mail:* a.welsby@liv.ac.uk
Sales & Marketing Dir: Jennifer Howard
  E-mail: jennifer.howard@liv.ac.uk
Production Manager: Patrick Brereton
  E-mail: patrick.brereton@liv.ac.uk
Founded: 1899
Subjects: Archaeology, Architecture & Interior Design, Art, Education, Environmental Studies, Geography, Geology, Government, Political Science, History, Labor, Industrial Relations, Literature, Literary Criticism, Essays, Maritime, Natural History, Poetry, Regional Interests, Science (General), Science Fiction, Fantasy, Social Sciences, Sociology, Veterinary Science, Art

History, Cultural Affairs, Current Events, Modern Language, Population Studies, Urban & Regional Planning
ISBN Prefix(es): 978-0-85323
Number of titles published annually: 40 Print
Total Titles: 200 Print
Distributed by University of Chicago Press (Caribbean, Central, North, Central & South America)
Foreign Rep(s): Avicenna Partnership Ltd (Middle East, North Africa, Turkey); Continental Contacts (Roy de Boo) (Benelux, Germany); Eureka Press (Akira Tanaka) (Japan); Laszlo Horvath (Central Europe, Eastern Europe, Former USSR); Iberian Book Services (Peter Prout) (Portugal, Spain); InterMedia Americana (David Williams) (Caribbean, Latin America exc Mexico); Overleaf (India); Quantum Publishing Solutions (Ireland, UK); STM Publisher Services Pte Ltd (Tony Poh) (China, Hong Kong, Korea, Southeast Asia, Taiwan); University Presses Marketing (France, Scandinavia)
Distribution Center: Turpin Distribution, Stratton Business Park, Pegasus Dr, Biggleswade, Beds SG18 8TQ *Tel:* (01767) 604977 *Fax:* (01767) 601640 *E-mail:* liverpool@turpin-distribution. co.uk *Web Site:* www.turpin-distribution.com
YUHA Associates Sdn Bhd, No 17, Jalan Bola Janing, 13/15 Seksyen 13, 40000 Shah Alam, Selangor Darul Ehsan, Malaysia, Contact: Ahmad Zahar Kamaruddin *Tel:* (03) 5511 9799 *E-mail:* yuha_sb@tm.net.my
Ta Tong Book Company Ltd, 162-44 Hsin Yi Rd, Section 3, Taipei 10658, Taiwan *Tel:* (02) 2701 5677 *E-mail:* tatong@tatong.com.tw
Oxford University Press, 2001 Evans Rd, Cary, NC 27513, United States *Tel:* 919-677-0977 *E-mail:* orders.cary@oup.com *Web Site:* global. oup.com/academic

Lives & Letters, *imprint of* Carcanet Press Ltd

Living Language, *imprint of* Kuperard

Locomotion Papers, *imprint of* Oakwood Press & Video Library

Y Lolfa Cyf+
Talybont, Aberystwyth, Ceredigion SY24 5HE
Tel: (01970) 832 304 *Fax:* (01970) 832 782
E-mail: ylolfa@ylolfa.com
Web Site: www.ylolfa.com
Key Personnel
Mng Dir, Production: Garmon Gruffudd
   E-mail: garmon@ylolfa.com
Chief Editor: Lefi Gruffudd *E-mail:* lefi@ylolfa. com
Founded: 1965
Publishers of Welsh books & English books of Welsh & Celtic interest.
Subjects: Art, Biography, Memoirs, Cookery, Crafts, Games, Hobbies, Government, Political Science, History, Humor, Language Arts, Linguistics, Music, Dance, Regional Interests, Sports, Athletics
ISBN Prefix(es): 978-0-86243; 978-0-904864; 978-0-9500178; 978-0-9555272; 978-1-84771; 978-0-9567031; 978-0-9560125
Number of titles published annually: 50 Print
Total Titles: 500 Print; 4 Audio
Imprints: Dinas

London Chamber of Commerce & Industry Examinations Board (LCCIEB)
Pearson LCCI International Account Services, One90 High Holborn, London WC1V 7BH
Web Site: qualifications.pearson.com/en/about-us/ qualification-brands/lcci.html
Publishing arm of the LCCI Examinations Board, publish support materials for students, candidates of LCCI exams (& their teachers), students financial textbooks & teachers handbooks. Specialize in English language for business & secretarial.
Subjects: Business, Finance
ISBN Prefix(es): 978-1-86247
Number of titles published annually: 10 Print
Total Titles: 60 Print

Lonely Planet Kids, *imprint of* Lonely Planet UK

Lonely Planet UK+
240 Blackfriars Rd, London SE1 8NW
Tel: (020) 3771 5100 *Fax:* (020) 3771 5101
Web Site: www.lonelyplanet.com
Key Personnel
Mng Dir, Publishing: Piers Pickard
Founded: 1991
Subjects: Travel & Tourism
ISBN Prefix(es): 978-1-55992; 978-0-908086; 978-0-86442; 978-1-86450; 978-1-74104; 978-1-74059; 978-1-76034; 978-1-74360; 978-1-74321; 978-0-9598080; 978-1-74179; 978-1-74220
Parent Company: Lonely Planet Publications Pty Ltd
Ultimate Parent Company: NC2 Media
Imprints: Lonely Planet Kids
Branch Office(s)
Lonely Planet Asia-Pacific, 90 Maribyrnong St, Footscray, Victoria 3011, Australia, Contact: Adam Bennett *Tel:* (03) 8379 8000 *Fax:* (03) 8379 8111 *E-mail:* adam.bennett@lonelyplanet. com.au
Lonely Planet India, 302 DLF City Court, Sikanderpur, Gurgaon 122 002, India *Tel:* (0124) 423 1645
U.S. Office(s): Lonely Planet USA, 150 Linden St, Oakland, CA 94607-2538, United States *Tel:* 510-250-6400 *Fax:* 510-893-8572 *E-mail:* press.usa@lonelyplanet.com
Lonely Planet USA, 230 Franklin Rd, Bldg 2B, Franklin, TN 37064, United States
Lonely Planet Kids, 315 W 36 St, 10th floor, New York, NY 10018, United States, Publisher: Hanna Otero
Warehouse: Grantham Book Services, Trent Rd, Grantham NG31 7XQ

Barry Long Books+
BCM Box 876, London WC1N 3XX
E-mail: contact@barrylongbooks.com
Web Site: www.barrylongbooks.com
Founded: 1994
Nonprofit educational company.
Specialize in the work of spiritual teacher Barry Long.
Subjects: Philosophy, Religion - Other, Self-Help, Spirituality
ISBN Prefix(es): 978-0-9508050; 978-1-899324
Number of titles published annually: 1 Print
Total Titles: 21 Print; 6 E-Book; 4 Audio
Parent Company: The Barry Long Foundation International, Box 838, Billinudgel, NSW 2483, Australia
Foreign Rep(s): Baker & Taylor Publisher Services (Canada, USA); Brumby Sunstate (Australia); Deep Books (UK)

Lorenz Books, *imprint of* Anness Publishing Ltd

Lorenz Books+
Imprint of Anness Publishing Ltd
Algores Way, Wisbech, Cambs PE13 2TQ
E-mail: info@anness.com
Web Site: www.anness.com
Key Personnel
Mng Dir: Paul Anness *E-mail:* panness@anness. com
Publisher: Joanna Lorenz *E-mail:* jlorenz@ anness.com
Subjects: Animals, Pets, Cookery, Crafts, Games, Hobbies, Gardening, Plants, Health, Nutrition, History, How-to, Nonfiction (General), Transportation, New Age
ISBN Prefix(es): 978-1-85967; 978-0-7548
Distributed by David Bateman Publishing (New Zealand); Macmillan (Australia); Parrot Reads Publishers (India)
Foreign Rep(s): Gabriele Kern Publishers Services (Austria, Germany, Switzerland); Gunnar Lie & Associates Ltd (Africa, Indian subcontinent, Southeast Asia); Gunnar Lie & Associates Ltd (John Edgeler) (Caribbean, Cyprus, Egypt, Greece, Iran, Iraq, Israel, Jordan, Kuwait, Netherlands, Scandinavia, Syria, Turkey, United Arab Emirates); Gunnar Lie & Associates Ltd (Guillaume Ferrand) (Belgium, Central America, Eastern Europe, France, Gibraltar, Italy, Luxembourg, Malta, Portugal, South America, Spain); Marketing Services for Publishers (Lorie Ocampo) (China, Hong Kong, Japan, Korea, Philippines, Taiwan); National Book Network (Canada, USA); John Reed Book Distribution (Australia); Research Press (Ajay Parmar) (India); Trinity Books (South Africa)
Distribution Center: Book Trade Services, Blaby Rd, Wigston, Leicester LE18 4SE *Tel:* (0116) 275 9086 *Fax:* (0116) 275 9090 *E-mail:* uksales@booktradeservices.com *Web Site:* www.booktradeservices.com
Trinity Books, PO Box 242, Randburg 2125, South Africa *Tel:* (011) 787 4010 *Fax:* (011) 787 8920 *E-mail:* trinity@iafrica.com
National Book Network (NBN), 4501 Forbes Blvd, Suite 200, Lanham, MD 20706, United States *Tel:* 301-459-3366 *Fax:* 301-429-5746 *E-mail:* customercare@nbnbooks.com *Web Site:* www.nbnbooks.com (USA & Canada)

Lorna, *imprint of* Novello & Co

Luath Press Ltd+
543/2 Castlehill, The Royal Mile, Edinburgh EH1 2ND
Tel: (0131) 225 4326 *Fax:* (0131) 225 4324
E-mail: sales@luath.co.uk
Web Site: www.luath.co.uk
Key Personnel
Dir: Gavin MacDougall *E-mail:* gavin. macdougall@luath.co.uk
Founded: 1981
Membership(s): Publishing Scotland.
Subjects: Biography, Memoirs, Fiction, Genealogy, Government, Political Science, History, Literature, Literary Criticism, Essays, Natural History, Nonfiction (General), Outdoor Recreation, Poetry, Regional Interests, Science Fiction, Fantasy, Sports, Athletics, Travel & Tourism, Wine & Spirits
ISBN Prefix(es): 978-0-946487; 978-1-84282; 978-1-905222; 978-1-906307; 978-1-906817; 978-1-908373; 978-1-910021
Number of titles published annually: 30 Print; 1 Audio
Total Titles: 200 Print; 4 Audio
Foreign Rep(s): Faber Factory (ebooks) (worldwide exc Canada & USA); Midpoint Trade Books (Canada, USA); Missing Link Ltd (Germany)
Foreign Rights: Big Apple Agency Inc (Lily Chen) (China); EJ International (Mayumi Finn) (Japan); Agenzia Letteraria Internazionale (Stefania Cattaneo) (Italy); Yanez Agencia Literaria SL (Montse F-Yanez & Julio F-Yanez) (Spain)
Distribution Center: BookSource, 50 Cambuslang Rd, Glasgow G32 8NB *Tel:* (0141) 642 9192 *E-mail:* orders@booksource.net (Australia, New Zealand & UK)

Lucent Books, *imprint of* Gale

Lucis Press Ltd
3 Whitehall Court, Suite 54, London SW1A 2EF
Tel: (020) 7839 4512 *Fax:* (020) 7839 5575
E-mail: london@lucistrust.org
Web Site: www.lucistrust.org
Key Personnel
Company Secretary: Christine Morgan
Dir: Helen Durant
Founded: 1938
Publisher of 24 books of esoteric philosophy by
Alice A Bailey.
Subjects: Astrology, Occult, Education, Philosophy, Religion - Other, Social Sciences, Sociology
ISBN Prefix(es): 978-0-85330
Total Titles: 38 Print; 1 CD-ROM
Parent Company: Lucis Publishing Co, 120 Wall
St, 24th floor, New York, NY 10005, United
States
Associate Companies: Lucis Trust, One rue de
Varembe (3e), Case Postale 26, 1211 Geneva
20, Switzerland *Tel:* (022) 734-1252 *Fax:* (022)
740-0911 *E-mail:* geneva@lucistrust.org (for
European translations)
Distributor for Agni Yoga Society
Foreign Rep(s): Sydney Goodwill (Australia); Lucis Press SA (South Africa)

Lucky Duck Books, *imprint of* SAGE
Publications Ltd

Lund Humphries+
2nd floor, Regus, 16 St Martin's Le Grand, London EC1A 4EN
Tel: (020) 7440 7530 *Fax:* (020) 7440 7545
E-mail: info@lundhumphries.com
Web Site: www.lundhumphries.com
Key Personnel
Mng Dir: Lucy Myers *E-mail:* lmyers@
lundhumphries.com
Head, Editorial & Production: Sarah Thorowgood
E-mail: sthorowgood@lundhumphries.com
Commissioning Editor: Lucy Clark
E-mail: lclark@lundhumphries.com
Marketing & Publicity Manager: Victoria Benjamin *E-mail:* vbenjamin@lundhumphries.com
Sales Manager: Eleanor Hooker
E-mail: ehooker@lundhumphries.com
Founded: 1939
Modern British art.
Subjects: Architecture & Interior Design, Art,
Crafts, Games, Hobbies, Photography, Art History, Contemporary Art
ISBN Prefix(es): 978-0-85331; 978-0-906909;
978-1-84822
Foreign Rep(s): Casemate UK Ltd (Jean-Marc
Evans) (England, France, Scotland, Wales);
Casemate UK Ltd (Andrew Tarring) (England,
Scotland, Wales); CRW Marketing Inc (Tony
Sagun) (Philippines); Ted Dougherty (Austria,
Belgium, Germany, Greece, Italy, Luxembourg,
Netherlands, Switzerland); Durnell Marketing
(Andrew Durnell) (Ireland, Northern Ireland,
Scandinavia); Dr Laszlo Horvath (Central Europe, Eastern Europe); Peter Hyde Associates
Pty Ltd (Peter Hyde) (South Africa); ICK (Se-Yung Jun) (Korea); IMA (David Williams)
(Caribbean, Latin America); Maya Publishers Pvt Ltd (Surit Mitra) (India); MHM Ltd
(Mark Gresham) (Japan); Michelle Moline &
Associates Inc (Michelle Moline) (Midwestern States, USA); Padovani Books Ltd (Penny
Padovani) (Portugal, Spain); South Pacific
Books (Liza Raybould) (New Zealand); YUHA
Associates Sdh Bhd (Ahmad Zahar Kamaruddin) (Malaysia)
Distribution Center: Bookpoint Ltd, 130 Park
Dr, Milton Park, Abingdon, Oxon OX14 4SE
Tel: (01235) 400 400 *Web Site:* bookpoint.wp.
hachette.co.uk (worldwide exc North America)
Art Stock Books, c/o Independent Publishers
Group (IPG), 814 N Franklin St, Chicago,

IL 60610, United States *Fax:* 312-337-5985
E-mail: orders@ipgbook.com *Web Site:* www.
ipgbook.com (North America)

The Lutterworth Press+
50-52 Kingston St, Cambridge CB1 2NU
Mailing Address: PO Box 60, Cambridge CB1
2NT
Tel: (01223) 350865 *Fax:* (01223) 366951
E-mail: publishing@lutterworth.com; sales@
lutterworth.com
Web Site: www.lutterworth.com
Key Personnel
Mng Dir: Adrian Brink
Founded: 1799
Membership(s): IPG; Publishers' Association.
Subjects: Antiques, Archaeology, Architecture &
Interior Design, Art, Biblical Studies, Biography, Memoirs, Child Care & Development,
Crafts, Games, Hobbies, Drama, Theater, Education, Health, Nutrition, History, Humor,
Inspirational, Spirituality, Literature, Literary Criticism, Essays, Music, Dance, Natural
History, Nonfiction (General), Philosophy, Regional Interests, Religion - Catholic, Religion - Protestant, Religion - Other, Theology, Travel
& Tourism
ISBN Prefix(es): 978-0-7188
Number of titles published annually: 120 Print;
120 E-Book
Total Titles: 800 Print; 1 CD-ROM; 230 E-Book
Associate Companies: James Clarke & Co
Imprints: Acorn Editions
Foreign Rep(s): Casemate Academic (USA)
Distribution Center: Casemate Academic,
PO Box 511, Oakville, CT 06779, United
States *Tel:* 860-945-9329 *Fax:* 860-945-9468
E-mail: info@casemateacademic.com *Web
Site:* www.casemateacademic.com
Orders to: Gardners Books, One Whittle
Dr, Eastbourne, East Sussex BN23 6QH
Tel: (01323) 521555 *Fax:* (01323) 525504
E-mail: sales@gardners.com *Web Site:* www.
gardners.com

LWW, see Lippincott Williams & Wilkins
(LWW)

Lyle Publications Ltd
c/o Sanderson Mcgraeth & Edney, 4 Quay Walls,
Berwick upon Tweed TD15 1HD
Tel: (01750) 23355
Key Personnel
Dir: Annette Curtis; Tony Curtis
Subjects: Antiques, Art
ISBN Prefix(es): 978-0-86248; 978-0-902921

Austin Macauley Publishers Ltd
CGC-33-01, 25 Canada Sq, Canary Wharf, London E14 5LQ
Tel: (020) 7038 8212 *Fax:* (020) 7038 8100
E-mail: mail@austinmacauley.com
Web Site: www.austinmacauley.com
Subjects: Biography, Memoirs, Fiction, Mysteries, Suspense, Nonfiction (General), Poetry,
Religion - Other, Romance, Science Fiction,
Fantasy, Travel & Tourism, Historical Romance
ISBN Prefix(es): 978-1-905609; 978-1-84963;
978-1-78455

MacLehose Press, *imprint of* Quercus Publishing
PLC

Macmillan, *imprint of* Pan Macmillan

Macmillan Bello, *imprint of* Pan Macmillan

Macmillan Children's Books, *imprint of* Pan
Macmillan

Macmillan Children's Books+
Imprint of Pan Macmillan
20 New Wharf Rd, London N1 9RR
Tel: (020) 7014 6000 *Fax:* (020) 7014 6001
E-mail: webqueries@macmillan.co.uk; direct@
macmillan.co.uk; childrensbooks@macmillan.
co.uk
Web Site: www.panmacmillan.com/imprints
Key Personnel
Publisher: Belinda Rasmussen
Publisher, Macmillan Over 6s: Venetia Gosling
Editorial Dir, Campbell & Nursery: Jackie Mc-Cann
Editorial Dir, Macmillan Over 6s: Rachel Petty
Editorial Dir, Poetry: Gaby Morgan
International Sales Dir: Jonathan Atkins
Subjects: Fiction, Nonfiction (General), Poetry
ISBN Prefix(es): 978-0-330; 978-0-333; 978-1-4050; 978-0-230
Number of titles published annually: 200 Print
Total Titles: 2,500 Print
Imprints: Campbell Books
Divisions: Macmillan Over 6s; Macmillan Under
6s
Distributed by Pan Macmillan (worldwide exc
Canada & Africa)
Foreign Rep(s): A-Z Africa Book Services (Anita
Zih) (Africa); H B Fenn & Co Ltd (Canada)

Macmillan Digital Audio, *imprint of* Pan
Macmillan

Macmillan Digital Audio+
Imprint of Pan Macmillan
20 New Wharf Rd, London N1 9RR
Tel: (020) 7014 6000 *Fax:* (020) 7014 6001
E-mail: webqueries@macmillan.co.uk;
audiobooks@macmillan.co.uk
Web Site: www.panmacmillan.com/imprints
Founded: 1995
Subjects: Art, Biography, Memoirs, Cookery, Fiction, History, Military Science, Mysteries, Suspense, Natural History, Poetry
ISBN Prefix(es): 978-1-4050; 978-0-230

Macmillan Ltd
The Macmillan Bldg, 4 Crinan St, London N1
9XW
Tel: (020) 7833 4000 *Fax:* (020) 7843 4640
E-mail: info@macmillan.com
Web Site: www.macmillan.com
Key Personnel
Global Chief Operating Officer, Macmillan Science & Education: Ken Michaels
Chief Financial Officer: Jonathan Wheeldon
Deputy Chairman: Michael Barnard
Executive Dir: Dominic Knight *E-mail:* d.
knight@macmillan.co.uk
Founded: 1843
An international company focusing on high quality academic, scholarly, education & trade publishing as well as publishing services for third
parties.
Subjects: Fiction, Nonfiction (General)
ISBN Prefix(es): 978-0-330; 978-0-333; 978-1-4050
Number of titles published annually: 5,000 Print;
20 CD-ROM; 1,000 Online; 100 Audio
Parent Company: Verlagsgruppe Georg von
Holtzbrinck, Gaensheidestr 26, 70184 Stuttgart,
Germany
U.S. Office(s): Macmillan, 175 Fifth Ave, New
York, NY 10010, United States *Tel:* 646-307-5151 *Web Site:* us.macmillan.com
Distribution Center: Macmillan Distribution (MDL), Brunel Rd, Houndmills, Basingstoke, Hants RG21 6XS
Tel: (01256) 329242 *Fax:* (01256) 479476
E-mail: mdlqueries@macmillan.co.uk *Web
Site:* www.macmillandistribution.co.uk

Macmillan New Writing, *imprint of* Pan
Macmillan

Macmillan Publishers Ltd+
Brunel Rd, Houndmills, Basingstoke, Hants RG21 6XS
Tel: (01256) 329242 *Fax:* (01256) 812558
Web Site: www.macmillan.com
Founded: 1843
Subjects: Fiction, Nonfiction (General)
ISBN Prefix(es): 978-0-333
Parent Company: Springer Nature
Associate Companies: The College Press plc, Zimbabwe; Macmillan India Ltd, India; Macmillan Publishers Nigeria Ltd, Nigeria; Pan Macmillan Ltd
Subsidiaries: College Press Pvt Ltd; Macmillan Boleswa Publishers Pty Ltd; Macmillan Children's Books Ltd; Macmillan Distribution Ltd; Macmillan Education Ltd; Macmillan General Books Ltd; Macmillan Language House Ltd; Macmillan Magazines Ltd; Macmillan New Asia Publishing Ltd; Macmillan Press Ltd; Macmillan Publishers Australia Pty Ltd; Macmillan Publishers (China) Ltd; Macmillan Publishers New Zealand Ltd; Macmillan Publishers SA de CV; Nature Japan KK; Nature Publishing Group; St Martin's Press Inc; Stockton Press Ltd; Stockton Press Netherlands BV; Stockton Press Netherlands Holdings BV
Orders to: Macmillan Distribution (MDL), Brunel Rd, Houndmills, Basingstoke, Hants RG21 6XS *Tel:* (01256) 329242 *Fax:* (01256) 479476 *E-mail:* mdlqueries@macmillan.co.uk

Macmillan Reference USA, *imprint of* Gale

Made Simple Books, *imprint of* Elsevier Ltd

Magna Large Print Books+
Magna House, Main St, Long Preston, Skipton, N Yorks BD23 4ND
Tel: (01729) 840225 *Fax:* (01729) 840683
E-mail: orders@magnaprint.co.uk
Web Site: www.ulverscroft.co.uk
Founded: 1973
ISBN Prefix(es): 978-0-86009; 978-1-85057; 978-1-85389; 978-0-7505; 978-1-84137; 978-1-78502
Number of titles published annually: 240 Print; 72 Audio
Total Titles: 1,000 Print
Parent Company: The Ulverscroft Group Ltd
Showroom(s): Trecerus Industrial Estate, Padstow, Cornwall PL28 8RW, Contact: Mark Merrill *Tel:* (07880) 506 505 (cell) *E-mail:* m.merrill@ulverscroft.co.uk; 3 Maple Grove Business Centre, Ground floor, Lawrence Rd, off Green Lane, Hounslow, Middx TW4 6DR, Contact: Jim Sacre *Tel:* (07767) 646 572 (cell) *E-mail:* j.sacre@ulverscroft.co.uk; Unit C, North Wing, Prospect Business Park, Leadgate, Consett, Co Durham DH8 6RR, Contact: Peter Douglas *Tel:* (07767) 646 576 (cell) *E-mail:* p.douglas@ulverscroft.co.uk; Unit 5/6 Automobile Palace, Temple St, Llandrindod Wells LD1 5HO, Contact: Mark Merrill *Tel:* (0788) 506 505 (cell) *E-mail:* m.merrill@ulverscroft.co.uk

Magnet & Steel Publishing
Vale Business Park, Unit 6, Llandow, Vale of Glamorgan GF71 7PF
Tel: (01446) 776 199 *Fax:* (01446) 776 127
Web Site: www.magnetandsteelpublishing.com
Subjects: Animals, Pets
ISBN Prefix(es): 978-1-906492; 978-1-907337
U.S. Office(s): Magnet & Steel Inc, 3311 Christina Dr, Dana Point, CA 92629, United States *Tel:* 949-874-1014

The Maia Press Ltd, *imprint of* Arcadia Books Ltd

The Maia Press Ltd
Imprint of Arcadia Books Ltd
c/o 15-16 Nassau St, London W1W 7AB
Tel: (020) 7436 9898
E-mail: info@arcadiabooks.co.uk
Web Site: www.maiapress.com
Key Personnel
Founder: Maggie Hamand; Jane Havell
Founded: 2003
Subjects: Fiction
ISBN Prefix(es): 978-1-904559
Foreign Rep(s): Angell Eurosales (Gill & Stewart Angell) (Scandinavia); Ashton International Marketing Services (Far East); Michael Geoghegan (Eastern Europe, Western Europe); Padovani Books Ltd (Penny Padovani) (Southern Europe); Turnaround Publisher Services (UK)
Distribution Center: Turnaround Publisher Services, Unit 3, Olympia Trading Estate, Coburg Rd, Wood Green, London N22 6TZ *Tel:* (020) 8829 3000 *Fax:* (020) 8881 5088 *E-mail:* andy@turnaround-uk.com (UK)
Tower Books, 2/17 Rodborough Rd, Frenchs Forest, NSW 2086, Australia *Tel:* (02) 9975 5566 *Fax:* (02) 9975 5599 *Web Site:* www.towerbooks.com (Australia)
Pansing Distribution Pte Ltd, 438 Ang Mo Kio Industrial Park 1, Ang Mo Kio Ave 10, Singapore 569619, Singapore *Tel:* 199939 *Fax:* 594930 *Web Site:* www.pansing.com (Singapore & Malaysia)
Dufour Editions Inc, PO Box 7, Chester Springs, PA 19425, United States *Tel:* 610-458-5005 *Fax:* 610-458-7103 *Web Site:* www.dufoureditions.com (North America)

Mainstream Publishing, *imprint of* The Random House Group Ltd, a Penguin Random House Company

Make Believe Ideas
The Wilderness, Berkhamsted, Herts HP4 2AZ
Tel: (01442) 874569 *Fax:* (01442) 878458
E-mail: enquiries@makebelieveideas.com
Web Site: www.makebelieveideas.com
Founded: 2003
ISBN Prefix(es): 978-1-905051; 978-1-84610; 978-1-84879; 978-1-78235; 978-1-78065

Making Sense of Science, *imprint of* Portland Press Ltd

Management Books 2000 Ltd+
36 Western Rd, Oxford OX1 4LG
Tel: (01865) 600 738
E-mail: info@mb2000.com
Web Site: www.mb2000.com
Key Personnel
Publisher: Nicholas Dale-Harris
Founded: 1986
Publisher & distributor of management guides, textbooks & references.
Subjects: Business, Career Development, Finance, Health, Nutrition, Management, Marketing, Technology, Health & Safety, Human Resources, Information Technology, Personal & Life Skills, Sales, Self-Improvement
ISBN Prefix(es): 978-1-85251; 978-1-85252; 978-1-85636
Number of titles published annually: 24 Print
Total Titles: 200 Print
Imprints: Mercury Books
Orders to: Combined Book Services Ltd, Paddock Wood Distribution Centre, Unit D, Paddock Wood, Tonbridge, Kent TN12 6UU *Tel:* (01892) 837171 *Web Site:* www.combook.co.uk

Management Pocketbooks Ltd+
Laurel House, Station Approach, Alresford, Hants SO24 9JH

Tel: (01962) 735 573 *Toll Free Tel:* 800 028 6217 *Fax:* (01962) 733 637
E-mail: sales@pocketbook.co.uk
Web Site: www.pocketbook.co.uk; www.teacherspocketbooks.co.uk
Key Personnel
Commissioning Editor: Ros Baynes *E-mail:* ros@pocketbook.co.uk
International Rights: Jenny Jones *E-mail:* jenny@pocketbook.co.uk
Founded: 1987
Small, highly accessible management guides written by trainers, full of graphics, mnemonics, bullet points for clarity & ease of recall.
Membership(s): Independent Publishers Guild (IPG).
Subjects: Business, Education, Finance, Management, Marketing, Personal Development
ISBN Prefix(es): 978-1-870471; 978-1-903776; 978-1-906610
Number of titles published annually: 10 Print
Total Titles: 140 Print; 2 CD-ROM; 135 E-Book
Imprints: Teachers' Pocketbooks
Distribution Center: c/o Ware-pak, 2427 Bond St, University Park, IL 60466, United States *Fax:* 708-534-7803 *E-mail:* mp.orders@ware-pak.com

Manchester University Press+
Reynold Bldg, floor J, Altrincham St, Manchester M1 7JA
Tel: (0161) 275 2310 *Fax:* (0161) 275 7711
E-mail: mup@manchester.ac.uk
Web Site: www.manchesteruniversitypress.co.uk
Key Personnel
CEO: Simon Ross
Editorial Dir & Commissioning Editor, History, Art History & Design: Emma Brennan *E-mail:* emma.brennan@manchester.ac.uk
Senior Commissioning Editor, Literature: Matthew Frost *E-mail:* m.frost@manchester.ac.uk
Senior Commissioning Editor, Politics, International Law & Economics: Tony Mason *E-mail:* t.mason@manchester.ac.uk
Sales & Marketing Executive: Rebecca Mortimer *E-mail:* rebecca.mortimer@manchester.ac.uk
Sales & Marketing Coordinator: Bethan Hirst *E-mail:* bethan.hirst@manchester.ac.uk
Founded: 1904
Subjects: Architecture & Interior Design, Art, Business, Economics, Film, Video, Finance, Government, Political Science, History, Law, Literature, Literary Criticism, Essays, Medicine, Nursing, Dentistry, Philosophy, Photography, Radio, TV, Religion - Other, Social Sciences, Sociology, Academic, Language, Medieval, Military, Theater
ISBN Prefix(es): 978-0-7190
Number of titles published annually: 145 Print
Imprints: Mandolin
Distributed by Footprint Books Pty Ltd (Australia & New Zealand); Palgrave Macmillan (USA); University of British Columbia Press (Canada)
Foreign Rep(s): Andrew B Durnell (Europe); Publishers International Marketing Ltd (Asia, Middle East); Publishers Marketing Services Pte Ltd (Malaysia, Singapore); Robert Towers (Ireland); United Publishers Services Ltd (Japan); The White Partnership (Andrew White) (India)
Distribution Center: NBN International, 10 Thornbury Rd, Plymouth, Devon PL6 7PP *Tel:* (01752) 202301 *Fax:* (01752) 202331; (01752) 202333 (orders) *E-mail:* orders@nbninternational.com *Web Site:* www.nbninternational.com

Mandolin, *imprint of* Manchester University Press

Mandrake, *imprint of* Mandrake of Oxford

Mandrake of Oxford+
PO Box 250, Oxford, Oxon OX1 1AP
Tel: (01865) 243671 *Fax:* (01865) 432929
E-mail: mandrake@mandrake.uk.net
Web Site: mandrake.uk.net
Key Personnel
Publisher: Mogg Morgan *E-mail:* mandox2000@
yahoo.com
Founded: 1986
Also acts as bookseller & mail-order subscription
agent.
Subjects: Art, Astrology, Occult, Criminology,
Fiction, Health, Nutrition, Mysteries, Suspense,
Parapsychology, Religion - Hindu, Religion -
Other, Science (General), Science Fiction, Fan-
tasy, Folklore
ISBN Prefix(es): 978-1-869928; 978-1-906958
Number of titles published annually: 10 Print
Total Titles: 100 Print
Imprints: Golden Dawn; Mandrake; Nuit-Isis
Orders to: Gazelle, White Crown Mills,
Hightown, Lancaster LA1 4XS
Tel: (01524) 68765 *Fax:* (01424) 63232
E-mail: sales@gazellebooks.co.uk *Web
Site:* gazellebookservices.co.uk
New Leaf, 401 Thornton Rd, Lithia Springs, GA
30057-1557, United States *Tel:* 770-948-7845
Fax: 770-944-2313 *Web Site:* www.newleaf-
dist.com

Mantle, *imprint of* Pan Macmillan

Mantra Lingua Ltd
Global House, 303 Ballards Lane, London N12
8NP
Tel: (020) 8445 5123 *Fax:* (020) 8446 7745
E-mail: info@mantralingua.com; sales@
mantralingua.com
Web Site: www.mantralingua.com
Key Personnel
Dir: Mishti Chatterji
Mng Dir: Robene Dutta
Subjects: Language Arts, Linguistics
ISBN Prefix(es): 978-0-947679; 978-1-84444;
978-1-84611; 978-1-85269

Maresfield Lib, *imprint of* Karnac Books Ltd

The Market Research Society (MRS)
The Old Trading House, 15 Northburgh St, Lon-
don EC1V 0JR
Tel: (020) 7490 4911 *Fax:* (020) 7490 0608
E-mail: info@mrs.org.uk; publications@mrs.org.
uk
Web Site: www.mrs.org.uk
Key Personnel
Chief Executive: Jane Frost
Mng Dir: Debrah Harding
Operations Dir: Nikki Bower
Digital Dir: Christian Walsh
Organization for professional researchers & oth-
ers engaged or interested in market, social &
opinion research.
ISBN Prefix(es): 978-0-906117

Mars Business Associates Ltd
16 Westbrook Green, Blewbury, Didcot, Oxon
OX11 9QD
Tel: (01367) 252 506 *Fax:* (01367) 252 506
Key Personnel
Contact: Dr John Robertson
Founded: 1988
Subjects: Accounting, Finance
ISBN Prefix(es): 978-1-873186

Marshall Editions+
Member of Quarto International Co-Editions
Group
The Old Brewery, 6 Blundell St, London N7 9BH
Tel: (020) 7700 6700 *Fax:* (020) 7700 8066
E-mail: info@quarto.com

Web Site: www.quartoknows.com/marshall-
editions
Key Personnel
Publisher: Samantha Warrington
E-mail: samantha.warrington@quarto.com
Founded: 1977
Also acts as book packager.
Subjects: Business, Cookery, Crafts, Games, Hob-
bies, Gardening, Plants, Geography, Geology,
Health, Nutrition, History, Management, Mili-
tary Science, Natural History, Religion - Other,
Science (General), Travel & Tourism, Wine &
Spirits
ISBN Prefix(es): 978-0-9507901; 978-1-84028
Ultimate Parent Company: The Quarto Group Inc

Marston House, *imprint of* Stenlake Publishing
Ltd

Marylebone House, *imprint of* The Society for
Promoting Christian Knowledge (SPCK)

Maverick Arts Publishing Ltd
City Business Centre, Studio 3A, 6 Brighton Rd,
Horsham, West Sussex RH13 5BB
Tel: (01403) 256941
E-mail: sales@maverick-arts.co.uk; submissions@
maverickbooks.co.uk
Web Site: www.maverickbooks.co.uk
Key Personnel
Mng Dir: Steve Bicknell
Finance Dir: Karen Bicknell
Editor: Kimara Nye
Founded: 2009
ISBN Prefix(es): 978-1-84886
Imprints: Icarus Arts Publishing (calendars)
Foreign Rep(s): New South Books (Australia);
South Pacific Books Ltd (New Zealand)
Foreign Rights: Rights People Ltd
Distribution Center: Orca Book Services
Ltd *Tel:* (01202) 665432 *E-mail:* orders@
orcabookservices.co.uk *Web Site:* www.
orcabookservices.co.uk

Mayhew-McCrimmon Ltd, see McCrimmon
Publishing Co Ltd

MCB University Press Ltd, see Emerald Group
Publishing Ltd

McCrimmon Publishing Co Ltd+
10-12 High St, Great Wakering, Essex SS3 0EQ
Tel: (01702) 218956 *Fax:* (01702) 216082
E-mail: info@mccrimmons.com
Web Site: www.mccrimmons.com
Key Personnel
Sales & Marketing Dir: Don McCrimmon
Production Dir: Nick Snode
Proprietor: Joan McCrimmon
Accounts, Royalties & Permissions: Sue Ander-
son
Founded: 1968
Specialize in music & liturgical publications &
artwork for Christians of all denominations.
Membership(s): MCPS, PRS.
Subjects: Art, Biblical Studies, Education, Music,
Dance, Religion - Catholic, Religion - Other,
Textbooks-Liturgy
ISBN Prefix(es): 978-0-85597
Number of titles published annually: 20 Print
Total Titles: 100 Print
Distributed by Liturgical Press (USA); Novalis
(Canada); Charles Paine Pty Ltd (Austria)
Distributor for A M Laverty; CJM; GIA; LTP
Publications; OCP; Pauline Books & Me-
dia; Printery Cards (USA); Printery House; St
Michael's Altar Breads
Foreign Rep(s): The Book Shop (France); Casa
San Paola Pia (Italy); The Catholic Bookshop
(Kenya, South Africa); Catholic Centre (Hong

Kong); John Garrett Publishing (Australia);
Pleroma Christian Supplies (New Zealand)
Bookshop(s): McCrimmons at All Saints Book-
shop, All Saints Pastoral Centre, Shenley Lane-
London Colney, Herts AL2 1AF *Tel:* (01727)
827612; (01727) 822010 *Fax:* (01727) 827612

McGraw-Hill Education+
Division of The McGraw-Hill Companies
Shoppenhangers Rd, Maidenhead, Berks SL6
2QL
Tel: (01628) 502500 *Fax:* (01628) 635895
E-mail: customer.service@mheducation.com;
enquiries@openup.co.uk; international_cs@
mheducation.com
Web Site: www.mheducation.com
Key Personnel
Sales & Marketing Dir: Jim Voute
Subjects: Accounting, Art, Business, Career De-
velopment, Economics, Engineering (General),
Finance, Geography, Geology, Government,
Political Science, Health, Nutrition, History,
Language Arts, Linguistics, Literature, Literary
Criticism, Essays, Mathematics, Music, Dance,
Psychology, Psychiatry, Science (General), So-
cial Sciences, Sociology, Technology
ISBN Prefix(es): 978-0-07; 978-0-335

McNidder & Grace
Bridge Innovation Centre, Pembrokeshire Science
& Technology Park, Pembroke Dock SA72
6UN
Tel: (01646) 689239
Web Site: www.mcnidderandgrace.co.uk
Key Personnel
Publisher: Andy Peden Smith *E-mail:* andy@
mcnidderandgrace.co.uk
Publicity & Events Manager: Linda MacFadyen
E-mail: linda@mcnidderandgrace.co.uk
Founded: 2011
Subjects: Art, Biography, Memoirs, Fiction, Mu-
sic, Dance, Nonfiction (General), Photography,
Pop Culture
ISBN Prefix(es): 978-1-904794; 978-0-85716
Foreign Rep(s): Bill Bailey Publishers' Represen-
tatives (Europe); Global Book Sales Ltd (David
Wightman) (North America); Publishers In-
ternational Marketing (Ru & Chris Ashdown)
(Middle East); Target Sales (Robert Ertle) (Ire-
land, UK)
Distribution Center: Orca Book Services, 160
Milton Park, Abingdon, Oxon OX14 4SD
Tel: (01235) 465521 *Fax:* (01235) 465555
E-mail: tradeorders@orcabookservices.co.uk
Web Site: www.orcabookservices.co.uk (Asia,
Europe, Ireland & UK)

McRae Publishing Ltd+
32 Campden Grove, London W8 4JQ
Tel: (020) 7937 6031
E-mail: info@mcraepublishing.com; info@
mcraepublishing.co.uk
Web Site: www.mcraepublishing.co.uk
Key Personnel
Publisher: Anne McRae; Marco Nardi
Founded: 1994
Also packagers of children's & adults illustrated
nonfiction books for the international co-edition
market.
Subjects: Art, Cookery, Geography, Geology, His-
tory, Nonfiction (General), Religion - Other,
Science (General)
ISBN Prefix(es): 978-88-88166; 978-88-900126;
978-88-900466; 978-88-89272; 978-88-6098

Media Research Publishing Ltd+
Lister House, 117 Milton Rd, Weston-super-Mare,
Avon BS23 2UX
Founded: 1992
Specialize in financial aspects of the music indus-
try.
Subjects: Accounting, Business, Music, Dance

ISBN Prefix(es): 978-0-9521414
Total Titles: 2 Print

The Medici Society Ltd
19-23 White Lion St, London N1 9PD
Tel: (020) 7713 8800 *Fax:* (020) 7837 7579
E-mail: info@medici.co.uk
Web Site: www.medici.co.uk
Founded: 1908
Subjects: Art, Poetry, Fine Art
ISBN Prefix(es): 978-0-85503
Bookshop(s): The Medici Gallerie, 26 Thurloe
St, London SW7 2LT *Tel:* (020) 7589 1363
Fax: (020) 7581 9758 *E-mail:* thurloe@medici.
co.uk

Melrose Press Ltd+
St Thomas' Pl, Ely, Cambs CB7 4GG
Tel: (01353) 646600 *Fax:* (01353) 646601
E-mail: tradesales@melrosepress.co.uk
Founded: 1969
Subjects: Biography, Memoirs
ISBN Prefix(es): 978-0-948875; 978-1-903986;
978-0-900332; 978-0-9501016; 978-0-900300
Imprints: International Biographical Centre

Mentor, *imprint of* Christian Focus Publications
Ltd

Merchiston Publishing
Scottish Centre for the Book, Edinburgh Napier
University, Merchiston Campus, Edinburgh
EH10 5DT
Tel: (0131) 455 6150
E-mail: scob@napier.ac.uk
Web Site: merchistonpublishing.com
Founded: 1987
In-house publishing arm of the Scottish Centre
for the Book & Edinburgh Napier University.
Membership(s): Scottish Publishers' Association.
Subjects: Publishing & Book Trade Reference,
Regional Interests
ISBN Prefix(es): 978-0-9511266; 978-1-872800;
978-0-9553561

Mercury Books, *imprint of* Management Books
2000 Ltd

#Merky Books, *imprint of* The Random House
Group Ltd, a Penguin Random House
Company

The Merlin Press Ltd+
Central Books Bldg, Freshwater Rd, London
RM8 1RX
Tel: (020) 8590 9700
E-mail: info@merlinpress.co.uk
Web Site: www.merlinpress.co.uk
Founded: 1956
Subjects: Economics, Government, Political Sci-
ence, History, Labor, Industrial Relations, Phi-
losophy, Social Sciences, Sociology
ISBN Prefix(es): 978-0-85036; 978-1-85425
Number of titles published annually: 10 Print
Imprints: Green Print
Foreign Rep(s): Blue Weaver Marketing (South
Africa); Eleanor Brasch (Australia); Global
Book Marketing (UK); Independent Publishers
Group (USA)
Distribution Center: Central Books Ltd,
Freshwater Rd, Dagenham RM8 1RX
Tel: (020) 8525 8800 *Fax:* (020) 8599 2694
E-mail: contactus@centralbooks.com *Web
Site:* www.centralbooks.com (UK)

Merlin Unwin Books Ltd
Palmers House, 7 Corve St, Ludlow, Salop SY8
1DB
Tel: (01584) 877 456 *Fax:* (01584) 877 457
E-mail: books@merlinunwin.co.uk

Web Site: www.merlinunwin.co.uk
Subjects: Cookery, Humor, Outdoor Recreation,
Field Sports, Fishing, Fly Tying, Shooting,
Wildlife
ISBN Prefix(es): 978-1-873674; 978-1-906122

Merrell Publishers Ltd+
70 Cowcross St, London EC1M 6EJ
Tel: (020) 7928 8880 *Fax:* (020) 7928 1199
Web Site: www.merrellpublishers.com
Key Personnel
Publisher: Hugh Merrell *E-mail:* hm@
merrellpublishers.com
Founded: 1993
Editing, design & production in collaboration
with authors, photographers, museums, foun-
dations, private collectors, brands & companies.
Illustrated books on art, design, photography, ar-
chitecture, fashion, gardens & interiors.
Subjects: Architecture & Interior Design, Art, Au-
tomotive, Cookery, Fashion, Gardening, Plants,
History, Photography, Travel & Tourism, Food
& Drink, Graphic Design & Illustration
ISBN Prefix(es): 978-1-85894
Number of titles published annually: 25 Print
Total Titles: 160 Print
Foreign Rep(s): Ashton International Marketing
Services (Julian Ashton) (China, Hong Kong,
Indonesia, Japan, Korea, Philippines, Tai-
wan, Thailand); Critiques Livres Distribution
(France); Elisabeth Harder-Kreimann (Scandi-
navia); Arturo Gutierrez Hernandez (Central
America); Humphrys Roberts Associates (Chris
Humphrys) (Caribbean); InterMediaAfrica
(Tony Moggach) (Sub-Saharan Africa); Inter-
MediaAmericana Ltd (Tony Moggach) (Esto-
nia, Latvia, Lithuania, Russia, Ukraine); Inter-
MediaAmericana Ltd (David Williams) (South
America); Adriana Juncu (Eastern Europe);
Gabriele Kern (Austria, Germany, Switzer-
land); Maya Publishers Pvt Ltd (Surit Mitra)
(Bangladesh, Bhutan, India, Nepal, Sri Lanka);
Padovani Books Ltd (Greece, Italy, Portugal,
Spain); Pansing Distribution Pte Ltd (Brunei,
Malaysia, Singapore); Peribo Pty Limited (Aus-
tralasia); Publishers Group Canada (Canada);
S G Distributors (Southern Africa); Van Dit-
mar Boekenimport (Belgium, Luxembourg,
Netherlands); Ward International Ltd (Cyprus,
Georgia, Israel, Malta, Middle East, Turkey)
Orders to: Marston Book Services Ltd, 160
Eastern Ave, Milton Park, Abingdon, Oxon
OX14 4SB *Tel:* (01235) 465500 *Fax:* (01235)
465555 *E-mail:* trade.orders@marston.co.uk
Web Site: www.marston.co.uk
Two Rivers Distribution, 193 Edwards Dr, Jack-
son, TN 38301, United States *Web Site:* www.
tworiversdistribution.com (Canada & USA)
Returns: Marston Book Services Ltd, 160 East-
ern Ave, Milton Park, Abingdon, Oxon OX14
4SB *Tel:* (01235) 465500 *Fax:* (01235) 465444
E-mail: returns@marston.co.uk *Web Site:* www.
marston.co.uk; Two Rivers Distribution, 193
Edwards Dr, Jackson, TN 38301, United States
Web Site: www.tworiversdistribution.com
(Canada & USA)

Methodist Publishing
Methodist Church House, 25 Marylebone Rd,
London NW1 5JR
Tel: (020) 7486 5502 (helpdesk); (0845) 0178220
(orders & customer service) *Fax:* (0845)
0178220 (orders & customer service)
E-mail: orders@norwichbooksandmusic.co.
uk (orders & customer service); helpdesk@
methodistchurch.org.uk
Web Site: www.methodistpublishing.org.uk (sales
& distribution)
Key Personnel
Dir, Publishing & Communications: Andy Jack-
son *Tel:* (020) 7467 5164 *E-mail:* jacksona@
methodistchurch.org.uk
Founded: 1733

Subjects: Biblical Studies, Religion - Protestant,
Theology
ISBN Prefix(es): 978-0-7162; 978-0-901027; 978-
0-946550; 978-1-85852
Number of titles published annually: 40 Print; 1
CD-ROM; 2 Audio
Total Titles: 200 Print; 1 CD-ROM; 10 Audio
Parent Company: The Methodist Church of Great
Britain
Distribution Center: Norwich Books & Music,
13a Hellesdon Park Rd, Norwich NR6 5DR
Tel: (0845) 0178220 *Fax:* (01603) 785915
E-mail: orders@norwichbooksandmusic.co.uk

Methuen Drama, *imprint of* A&C Black
Publishers Ltd

Methuen Publishing Ltd+
Orchard House, Railway St, Slingsby, York YO62
4AN
Tel: (01653) 628152; (01653) 628195
E-mail: editorial@methuen.co.uk; rights@
methuen.co.uk; sales@methuen.co.uk
Web Site: www.methuen.co.uk
Key Personnel
Dir: Peter Tummons
Founded: 1889
Subjects: Archaeology, Biography, Memoirs,
Drama, Theater, Fiction, History, Humor,
LGBTQ, Music, Dance, Nonfiction (General),
Poetry, Sports, Athletics, Travel & Tourism,
Discovery
ISBN Prefix(es): 978-0-413; 978-0-415; 978-0-
417; 978-0-416; 978-0-423
Total Titles: 500 Print
Foreign Rep(s): Independent Publishers Group
(Canada, USA)
Orders to: Grantham Book Services, Trent Rd,
Grantham, Lincs NG31 7XQ *Tel:* (01476)
541000 *Fax:* (01476) 541060 *E-mail:* sales@
tbs-ltd.co.uk *Web Site:* www.thebookservice.co.
uk

Metro Publishing Ltd, *imprint of* John Blake
Publishing Ltd

Metro Publishing Ltd+
Imprint of John Blake Publishing Ltd
3 Bramber Court, 2 Bramber Rd, London W14
9PB
Tel: (020) 7381 0666 *Fax:* (020) 7381 6868
E-mail: words@blake.co.uk; rosie@blake.co.uk
(foreign rights)
Web Site: www.johnblakepublishing.co.uk
Founded: 1995
Subjects: Biography, Memoirs, Business, Child
Care & Development, Cookery, Criminology,
Fiction, Film, Video, Gardening, Plants, Gov-
ernment, Political Science, Health, Nutrition,
History, Humor, Inspirational, Spirituality, Law,
Music, Dance, Nonfiction (General), Psychol-
ogy, Psychiatry, Science (General), Self-Help,
Sports, Athletics, Travel & Tourism, Military,
Pets, Popular Science
ISBN Prefix(es): 978-1-900512; 978-1-84358;
978-1-84241

Micelle Press+
12 Ullswater Crescent, Weymouth, Dorset DT3
5HE
Tel: (01305) 781574
E-mail: micellepress@gmail.com
Web Site: www.micellepress.com
Key Personnel
Proprietor: Anthony Hunting
Founded: 1984
Specialist publisher & bookseller of books on
cosmetics, toiletries, perfumes, surfactants &
other specialty materials.
Subjects: Biological Sciences, Chemistry, Chem-
ical Engineering, Health, Nutrition, Natural

History, Physical Sciences, Science (General), Technology
ISBN Prefix(es): 978-1-870228; 978-0-9608752
Number of titles published annually: 2 Print
Total Titles: 20 Print
Divisions: Janet Barber Translations
Distributor for Chemical Publishing Co; PCPC Inc (formerly CTFA); Verlag fuer chemische Industrie H Ziolkowsky GmbH

Michelin Travel Publications
Hannay House, 39 Clarendon Rd, Watford, Herts WD17 1JA
Tel: (01923) 205240 Fax: (01923) 205241
E-mail: travelpubsales@uk.michelin.com
Web Site: travel.michelin.co.uk
Founded: 1910
Subjects: Travel & Tourism
ISBN Prefix(es): 978-2-06
U.S. Office(s): One Parkway S, Greenville, SC 29615, United States E-mail: michelin.travel-publications-us@us.michelin.com
Distributed by Travel House Media GmbH
Foreign Rep(s): Librairie Al Kitab (Kamel Hmaidi) (Tunisia); ALPY PRAHA spol sro (Ondrej Jirasko) (Czechia); La Biblioteca SA - Libreria Francesa (Isabelle Morizon) (Chile); Bookshop SA (Laura Garcia) (Uruguay); Cartographia Ltd (Zsuzanna Kertesz) (Hungary); Livraria Cultura (Dionsius Amendola/ Aline Tieme) (Brazil); Faradawn cc (Marinda Swanepoel) (South Africa); Livraria Freebook (Brazil); Freytag-Berndt spol sro (Lenka Cirhanova) (Czechia, Slovakia); Jana Seta Map Shop Ltd (Aivars Beldavs) (Latvia); Kiwi Bookshop (Tomas Lejsek) (Czechia); Ksiegami Atlas (Tadeusz Przeslakiewicz) (Poland); Mapworld Ltd (Endre Kiss) (Hungary); Nakas Group (Mara Postali) (Greece); Norstedts Forlagsgrupp AB (Anders Lundstrom) (Sweden); Promoculture (Slim Jemmali) (Tunisia); Scanvik A/S (Trine Brehmer) (Denmark, Norway); Steinhart Sharav Publishers Ltd (Israel); Sklep Podroznika (Poland); Travel Bookstore (Elena Skoundi) (Greece); Universal Publishers (Australia, New Zealand)

Microform Academic Publishers
Division of Microform Imaging Ltd
Main St, East Ardsley, Wakefield, W Yorks WF3 2AP
Tel: (01924) 825700 Fax: (01924) 871005
E-mail: info@microform.co.uk
Web Site: www.microform.co.uk
Key Personnel
Mng Dir: Nigel Le Page
Founded: 1956
Archival publishing online & on microfilm.
Subjects: Accounting, African American Studies, Americana, Regional, Asian Studies, Developing Countries, Government, Political Science, History, Labor, Industrial Relations, Literature, Literary Criticism, Essays, Radio, TV, Regional Interests, Religion - Protestant, Social Sciences, Sociology, British India, Historical Newspapers, Missionary Archives, Socialism
ISBN Prefix(es): 978-0-7158; 978-1-85117
Number of titles published annually: 10 Print; 10 Online
Total Titles: 30 CD-ROM; 35 Online
Foreign Rights: Far Eastern Booksellers (Kyokuto Shoten Ltd) (Japan); Micrographics Data Pte Ltd (Singapore, Southeast Asia); PraXess (Canada, Mexico, USA)

Middleton Press
Easebourne Lane, Midhurst, West Sussex GU29 9AZ
Tel: (01730) 813169 Fax: (01730) 812601
E-mail: info@middletonpress.co.uk
Web Site: www.middletonpress.co.uk

Key Personnel
President & Editor: Vic Mitchell
Founded: 1981
Produce books for the railway & tramway enthusiast & modeller.
Subjects: Military Science, Regional Interests, Transportation, Railways, Tramways, Trolleybuses
ISBN Prefix(es): 978-0-906520; 978-1-873793; 978-1-901706; 978-1-904474
Number of titles published annually: 22 Print
Total Titles: 540 Print

Miles Kelly Publishing Ltd+
Harding's Barn, Bardfield End Green, Thaxted, Essex CM6 3PX
Tel: (01371) 832440 Fax: (01371) 831512
E-mail: info@mileskelly.net
Web Site: www.mileskelly.net
Key Personnel
Dir: Gerard Kelly
Foreign Rights Dir: Ruth Blakemore
Sales Dir: Richard Curry
Foreign Rights Executive: Sean Donelan
Promotional Sales Manager: Robert Grant
Trade & Export Sales Manager: Andrew Stafford
Founded: 1996
Subjects: Crafts, Games, Hobbies, Fiction, Non-fiction (General), Poetry
ISBN Prefix(es): 978-1-84236; 978-1-902947; 978-1-84810; 978-1-78209
Distribution Center: Trade Counter Distribution Ltd, Mendlesham Industrial Estate, Norwich Rd, Mendlesham, Suffolk IP14 5ND
Tel: (01449) 766629 Fax: (01449) 767122
E-mail: orders@tradecounter.co.uk

The Military Balance, imprint of International Institute for Strategic Studies

J Garnet Miller, imprint of Cressrelles Publishing Co Ltd

J Garnet Miller+
Imprint of Cressrelles Publishing Co Ltd
Industrial Estate, 10 Station Rd, Colwall, Malvern, Herts WR13 6RN
Tel: (01684) 540154
Web Site: www.cressrelles.co.uk
Key Personnel
Mng Dir: Leslie Smith
Business Manager: Simon Smith E-mail: simon@cressrelles.co.uk
Founded: 1955
Publisher of plays.
Subjects: Drama, Theater
ISBN Prefix(es): 978-0-85343
Number of titles published annually: 10 Print
Total Titles: 250 Print
Distributed by Empire Publishing Services (Africa & Asia)
Foreign Rights: Bakers Plays (USA); DALRO (Southern Africa); Drama League of Ireland (Ireland); Origin Theatrical (Australia); Play Bureau (New Zealand)

Miller's, imprint of Octopus Publishing Group Ltd

Miller's Publications
Subsidiary of Octopus Publishing Group Ltd
Endeavor House, 198 Shaftsbury Ave, London WC2H 8JY
Tel: (020) 7632 5400; (020) 7632 5488
Fax: (020) 7531 8650
E-mail: info@millersguides.com
Web Site: www.millersantiquesguide.com; www.octopusbooks.co.uk
Subjects: Antiques, Architecture & Interior Design

ISBN Prefix(es): 978-0-85533; 978-1-85732; 978-1-84000; 978-0-86134; 978-0-905879; 978-1-84533
Distributed by Antique Collectors Club (USA)

Milly & Flynn, imprint of Ginger Fox Ltd

Mind Publications+
15-19 Broadway, Stratford, London E15 4BQ
Tel: (020) 8519 2122 Fax: (020) 8522 1725; (020) 8534 6399 (orders)
E-mail: contact@mind.org.uk; publications@mind.org.uk (mail order)
Web Site: www.mind.org.uk
Key Personnel
Chief Executive: Paul Farmer
Dir, External Relations: Sophie Corlett
Head, Policy & Campaigns: Vicki Nash
Head, Information: Beth Murphy
Founded: 1946
Specialize in mental health, psychiatry, psychology.
Subjects: Psychology, Psychiatry, Self-Help, Women's Studies
ISBN Prefix(es): 978-1-874690; 978-0-900557; 978-1-903567
Number of titles published annually: 15 Print
Total Titles: 200 Print; 200 Online; 200 E-Book

The Mineralogical Society
12 Baylis Mews, Amyand Park Rd, Twickenham, Middx TW1 3HQ
Tel: (020) 8891-6600 Fax: (020) 8891-6599
E-mail: info@minersoc.org; admin@minersoc.org
Web Site: www.minersoc.org
Key Personnel
Executive Dir: Kevin Murphy Tel: (023) 8845401 E-mail: kevin@minersoc.org
Finance & Operations Manager: Russell Rajendra E-mail: russell@minersoc.org
Founded: 1876
To advance the knowledge of the science of mineralogy & its application to other subjects including crystallography, geochemistry, petrology, environmental science & economic geology.
Subjects: Environmental Studies, Geography, Geology, Crystallography, Environmental Science, Geochemistry, Mineralogy, Petrology
ISBN Prefix(es): 978-0-903056

Mr Educator, imprint of GLMP Ltd

The MIT Press
One Duchess St, Suite 2, London W1W 6AN
Tel: (020) 7306 0603
E-mail: info@mitpress.org.uk
Web Site: mitpress.mit.edu
Key Personnel
Promotion Manager: Judith Bullent E-mail: jbullent@mitpress.org.uk
Contact: Katie Stileman E-mail: kstileman@mitpress.org.uk
Founded: 1932
Subjects: Architecture & Interior Design, Art, Behavioral Sciences, Biological Sciences, Communications, Computer Science, Earth Sciences, Economics, Engineering (General), Environmental Studies, Finance, Government, Political Science, Language Arts, Linguistics, Mathematics, Philosophy, Physics, Psychology, Psychiatry, Science (General), Social Sciences, Sociology, Technology
ISBN Prefix(es): 978-0-262; 978-1-85209
Number of titles published annually: 250 Print
Imprints: AAAI Press; Afterall Books; Bradford Books; Killian Press; Semiotext(e); Zone Books
U.S. Office(s): One Rogers St, Cambridge, MA 02142-1209, United States

Orders to: John Wiley & Sons Ltd, New Era Estate, One Oldlands Way, Bognor Regis, West Sussex PO22 9NQ *Tel:* (01243) 779 777 *Fax:* (01243) 843 296 *E-mail:* cs-books@wiley.co.uk

Footprint Books Pty Ltd, 1/6a Prosperity Parade, Warriewood, NSW 2102, Australia *Tel:* (02) 9997 3973 *Fax:* (02) 9997 3185 *Web Site:* www.footprint.com.au

c/o Triliteral, 100 Maple Ridge Dr, Cumberland, RI 02864, United States *Tel:* 401-658-4226 *E-mail:* mitpress-orders@mit.edu

Returns: John Wiley & Sons Ltd, New Era Estate, One Oldlands Way, Bognor Regis, West Sussex PO22 9SA *Tel:* (01243) 779 777 *Fax:* (01243) 843 296 *E-mail:* cs-books@wiley.co.uk

Mithras Books, *imprint of* Knox Robinson Publishing

MM Publications
155A West Green Rd, London N15 5EA
Tel: (020) 7681 2913 *Fax:* (020) 7681 2913
E-mail: info@mmpublications.com
Web Site: www.mmpublications.com
Founded: 1993
Subjects: ELT, Grammar
ISBN Prefix(es): 978-960-379
Branch Office(s)
6/F, No 16, Songyuan Rd, Changning District, Shanghai 200336, China *Tel:* (021) 5151 8909 *E-mail:* china@mmpublications.com
41, Hermes St, 6023 Larnaka, Cyprus *Tel:* (024) 628404 *E-mail:* cyprus@mmpublications.com
Deligiorgi 58, Alimos, 17456 Athens, Greece *Tel:* 2109953680 *Fax:* 2109938393 *E-mail:* sales@mmpublications.com (marketing dept)
ul Armii Krajowej 2, 05-500 Piaseczno, Poland *Tel:* (22) 711 99 33 *E-mail:* sales-poland@mmpublications.com
85-10 Songpa dong, No 202, Songpa-gu, Seoul, South Korea *Tel:* (02) 3431-8202 *Fax:* (02) 3431 8203 *E-mail:* cen621@beltenglish.co.kr
Cevizlik Mahallesi Hafiz Cikmazi No 10B, Bakirkoy, Istanbul, Turkey *Tel:* (0212) 543 90 00 *Fax:* (0212) 583 36 59 *E-mail:* turkey@mmpublications.com
U.S. Office(s): PO Box 162953, Austin, TX 78716, United States *Tel:* 512-400-2656 *E-mail:* us-sales@mmpublications.com

Modern Books, *imprint of* Elwin Street Productions

Monarch Books, *imprint of* Lion Hudson PLC

Monarch Books+
Imprint of Lion Hudson PLC
Wilkinson House, Jordan Hill Rd, Oxford, Oxon OX2 8DR
Tel: (01865) 302750 *Fax:* (01865) 302757
E-mail: international@lionhudson.com; marketing@lionhudson.com; uksales@lionhudson.com
Web Site: www.lionhudson.com
Founded: 1988
Christian publisher producing up-market paperbacks, hardbacks & church resources for the international market.
Subjects: Biblical Studies, Biography, Memoirs, Education, Fiction, Humor, Psychology, Psychiatry, Religion - Protestant, Science (General), Self-Help, Theology
ISBN Prefix(es): 978-0-8254; 978-1-85424; 978-0-85721
Number of titles published annually: 40 Print
Total Titles: 150 Print
Distributed by Kregel Publications

Distributor for Abingdon Press; Baker Publishing Group; Cambridge University Press (Bibles); Charisma House; Darton Longman & Todd; Elevation; Instant Apostle; Kregel Publications
Warehouse: Kregel Publications, PO Box 2607, Grand Rapids, MI 49501-2607, United States *Tel:* 616-451-4775 *Fax:* 616-451-9330 *Web Site:* www.kregel.com
Orders to: Kregel Publications, PO Box 2607, Grand Rapids, MI 49501-2607, United States *Tel:* 616-451-4775 *Fax:* 616-451-9330 *Web Site:* www.kregel.com

Monsoon, *imprint of* Monsoon Books Ltd

Monsoon Books Ltd+
No 1, Duke of Windsor Suite, Burrough Court, Burrough on the Hill LE14 2QS
E-mail: sales@monsoonbooks.co.uk
Web Site: www.monsoonbooks.co.uk
Key Personnel
Publisher & Dir: Philip Tatham *E-mail:* phil@monsoonbooks.co.uk
Founded: 2003
Subjects: Asian Studies, Cookery, Erotica, Fiction, Humor, Literature, Literary Criticism, Essays, Nonfiction (General), Romance, Travel & Tourism, Wine & Spirits, Southeast Asia
ISBN Prefix(es): 978-981-05; 978-981-08; 978-1-912049
Number of titles published annually: 15 Print; 15 E-Book
Total Titles: 120 Print; 120 E-Book
Imprints: Monsoon
Foreign Rep(s): Monsoon Books (Australia, Indonesia, Thailand); National Book Network (NBN) (Canada, USA); Pansing Distribution (Brunei, Malaysia, Singapore); DJ Segrue (UK & the continent)

Monument Series, *imprint of* Witherby Publishing Group

Moon Books, *imprint of* O Books

Moonlight Publishing Ltd
The King's Manor, East Hendred, Oxon OX12 8JY
Tel: (01235) 821821 *Fax:* (01235) 821155
Web Site: www.moonlightpublishing.co.uk
Key Personnel
Contact: John Clement; Penny Clement
Founded: 1980
Specialize in illustrated nonfiction books for children.
Subjects: Animals, Pets, Art, Environmental Studies, History, Music, Dance, Nonfiction (General), Physical Sciences, Sports, Athletics, Technology, Culture, Ecology
ISBN Prefix(es): 978-1-85103; 978-0-907144
Imprints: First Discovery; First Discovery Art; First Discovery Music; Torchlights
Foreign Rep(s): Children's Publications (Taiwan); Dar al Shorouk (Bahrain, Egypt, Kuwait, Lebanon, Libya, Oman, Qatar, Saudi Arabia); ERA Publications (Australia); JYbooks (South Korea); Raincoast Books (Canada); Rupa & Co (India); Distribudora Vicens Vives (Spain); Wild Dog Press (Botswana, South Africa)
Distribution Center: Booksource, 50 Cambuslang Rd, Cambuslang, Glasglow G32 8NB (booksellers)

Moorley's Bible & Bookshop Ltd, see Moorley's Print & Publishing Ltd

Moorley's Print & Publishing Ltd
23 Park Rd, Ilkeston, Derbys DE7 5DA
Tel: (0115) 932 0643 *Fax:* (0115) 932 0643
E-mail: info@moorleys.co.uk
Web Site: www.moorleys.co.uk

Key Personnel
Dir: Patrick A Mancini *E-mail:* patrick@moorleys.co.uk; Peter R Newberry *E-mail:* peter@moorleys.co.uk
Founded: 1970 (as a Limited Co - traded since 1966 as Moorley's Bible & Bookshop)
Also printer.
Subjects: Biblical Studies, Drama, Theater, Music, Dance, Poetry, Religion - Protestant, Theology
ISBN Prefix(es): 978-0-901495; 978-0-86071
Number of titles published annually: 10 Print
Total Titles: 350 Print; 2 E-Book
Imprints: Headline Specials
Distributor for Cliff College Publishing; Nimbus Press; Pustaka Sufes Sdn Bhd; Social Work Christian Fellowship; T Young

Morgan Kauffman, *imprint of* Elsevier Ltd

Mosby, *imprint of* Elsevier Ltd

MP Publishing Ltd
12 Strathallan Crescent, Douglas, Isle of Man IM2 4NR
Tel: (01624) 618672 *Fax:* (01624) 620798
E-mail: info@skoobestore.com
Web Site: mppublishing.co.uk
Key Personnel
Owner: Mark Pearce *E-mail:* mark@mppublishing.co.uk
Founded: 2008
Subjects: Fiction, Nonfiction (General)
ISBN Prefix(es): 978-0-9555792; 978-1-84982
Foreign Rights: Akcali Copyright Agency (Kezban Akcali) (Turkey); BMSR (Laura Riff) (Brazil); The Deborah Harris Agency (Efrat Lev) (Israel); Licht & Burr Literary Agency (Trine Licht) (Scandinavia); Andrew Nurnberg Associates (Sofia Anna & Mira Droumeva) (Bulgaria, Romania, Serbia); Andrew Nurnberg Associates (Sarah Nundy & Daniela Petracco) (Italy, Spain); Andrew Nurnberg Associates (Claire Noziere) (France); Andrew Nurnberg Associates (Sabine Pfannenstiel-Wright) (Austria, Germany, Switzerland); Andrew Nurnberg Associates (Barbara Taylor); Andrew Nurnberg Associates Baltic (Ingrida Sniedze & Tatjana Zoldnere) (Estonia, Latvia, Lithuania, Ukraine); Andrew Nurnberg Associates Budapest (Judit Hermann) (Croatia, Hungary); Andrew Nurnberg Associates Prague (Petra Tobiskova) (Czechia, Slovakia, Slovenia); Andrew Nurnberg Associates Warsaw (Aleksandra Matuszak) (Poland); Andrew Nurnberg Literary Agency (Ludmilla Sushkova) (Russia); Owls Agency (Seiichiro Shimono) (Japan); Eric Yang Agency (Vince Baek) (Korea)

Mulholland Books, *imprint of* Hodder & Stoughton Ltd

Multilingual Matters Ltd+
St Nicholas House, 31-34 High St, Bristol BS1 2AW
Tel: (0117) 315 8562 *Fax:* (0117) 315 8563
E-mail: info@channelviewpublications.com
Web Site: www.multilingual-matters.com
Key Personnel
Mng Dir, Sales & Distribution: Tommi Grover *E-mail:* tommi@channelviewpublications.com
Editorial Manager & Rights & Permissions: Anna Roderick *E-mail:* anna@channelviewpublications.com
Marketing Manager: Elinor Robertson *E-mail:* elinor@channelviewpublications.com
Production Manager: Sarah Williams *E-mail:* sarah@channelviewpublications.com
Foreign Rights: Laura Longworth *E-mail:* laura@channelviewpublications.com
Founded: 1982

Specialize in bilingualism & bilingual education, second & foreign language learning, translation studies & creative writer's studies.
Membership(s): Independent Publishers Guild (IPG).
Subjects: Education, Environmental Studies, Geography, Geology, Government, Political Science, Language Arts, Linguistics, Social Sciences, Sociology, Travel & Tourism, Applied Linguistics, Creative Writing Studies, Tourism Research
ISBN Prefix(es): 978-0-905028; 978-1-85359; 978-1-873150; 978-1-84541 (Channel View); 978-1-84769
Number of titles published annually: 40 Print; 40 E-Book
Total Titles: 532 Print; 340 E-Book
Imprints: Channel View Publications
Foreign Rep(s): CPS (Sarah Zhao) (China); Eureka Press (Japan); Govinda Book House (India); ICK (Se-Yung Jun) (Korea); KVH Books (Kevin van Hasselt) (Caribbean, Sub-Saharan Africa); Andrew White (Malaysia, Philippines, Singapore, Taiwan)
Distribution Center: Marston Book Services Ltd, 160 Eastern Ave, Milton Park, Abingdon, Oxon OX14 4SB *Tel:* (01235) 465500 *Fax:* (01235) 465555 *E-mail:* direct.orders@marston.co.uk *Web Site:* www.marston.co.uk (UK, Europe & rest of the world)
James Bennett, 114 Old Pittwater Rd, Unit 3, Brookvale, NSW 2100, Australia *Tel:* (02) 8988 5000 *Fax:* (02) 8988 5031 *E-mail:* info@bennett.com.au (Australia & New Zealand)
UTP Distribution, 5201 Dufferin St, North York, ON M3H 5T8, Canada *Tel:* 416-667-7791 *Fax:* 416-667-7832 *E-mail:* utpbooks@utpress.utoronto.ca (Canada, USA)
Aromix Books Co Ltd, Unit 7, 8th floor, Block B Hoi Luen Industrial Centre, 55 Hoi Yuen Rd, Kwun Tong, Kowloon, Hong Kong *Tel:* 2749 1288 *E-mail:* enquiry@aromix.ath.cx (Hong Kong)
PMS Publishers Marketing Services Pte Ltd, 10-C Jl Ampas, No 07-01 Ho Seng Lee Flatted Warehouse, Singapore 329513, Singapore *Tel:* 62565166 *Fax:* 62530008 *E-mail:* info@pms.com.sg (Singapore & Malaysia)
UTP Distribution, 2250 Military Rd, Tonowanda, NY 14150, United States *Tel:* 416-667-7791 *Fax:* 416-667-7832 *E-mail:* utpbooks@utpress.utoronto.ca (USA)

James Munro & Co
Subsidiary of Brown, Son & Ferguson Ltd
4-10 Darnley St, Glasgow G41 2SD
Tel: (0141) 429 1234 *Fax:* (0141) 420 1694
E-mail: info@skipper.co.uk
Web Site: www.skipper.co.uk
Founded: 1832
Also acts as printer.
Subjects: Maritime
ISBN Prefix(es): 978-0-85174; 978-1-84927; 978-0-85347

John Murray, *imprint of* Hodder & Stoughton Ltd

John Murray Learning, *imprint of* Hodder & Stoughton Ltd

John Murray Learning, *imprint of* John Murray Press

John Murray Press+
Imprint of Hodder & Stoughton
338 Euston Rd, London NW1 3BH
Tel: (020) 7873 6000
E-mail: enquiries@johnmurrays.co.uk
Web Site: www.hodder.co.uk

Key Personnel
Publisher: Kate Parkin
Mng Dir: Nick Davies *E-mail:* nick.davies@johnmurrays.co.uk
Publishing Dir, Nonfiction: Eleanor Birne
Editorial Dir: Mark Richards
Communications Dir: Rosie Gailer *E-mail:* rosie.gailer@hodder.co.uk
Rights Dir: Jason Bartholomew *E-mail:* jason.bartholomew@hodder.co.uk
Sales Dir: Ben Gutcher *E-mail:* ben.gutcher@hodder.co.uk
Publicity Manager: Lyndsey Ng
Founded: 1768
Subjects: Fiction, Humor, Nonfiction (General)
ISBN Prefix(es): 978-0-7195; 978-1-84854; 978-1-473
Ultimate Parent Company: Hachette UK
Imprints: Nicholas Brealey Publishing; John Murray Learning
Foreign Rep(s): Jonathan Ball Publishers (South Africa); CLB Marketing Services (Csaba & Jackie Lengyel) (Eastern Europe); Hachette Australia (Australia); Hachette Book Group Ireland (Bernard Hoban) (Ireland); Hachette Book Publishing India Pvt Ltd (India); Hachette Canada (Canada); Hachette New Zealand (New Zealand); HRA (Christopher Humphrys & Lynda Hopkins) (Caribbean); Intermedia Americana Ltd (David Williams) (South America); Pansing Distribution Pte Ltd (Malaysia, Singapore); Trafalgar Square Publishing (IPG) (USA)
Orders to: Bookpoint Ltd, 130 Milton Park, Abingdon, Oxon OX14 4TD *Tel:* (01235) 400 400 *Web Site:* bookpoint.wp.hachette.co.uk

Music Press Books, *imprint of* John Blake Publishing Ltd

Myriad Editions
c/o New Internationalist, The Old Music Hall, 106-108 Cowley Rd, Oxford OX4 1JE
Tel: (01865) 403345
E-mail: info@myriadeditions.com
Web Site: www.myriadeditions.com
Founded: 1993
Publisher of *The State of the World Atlas.*
Subjects: Biography, Memoirs, Fiction, Government, Political Science, Mysteries, Suspense, Nonfiction (General)
ISBN Prefix(es): 978-0-9549309; 978-0-9562515
Distributed by Trafalgar Square Publishing (Australia, India, New Zealand, North & South America, South Africa)
Foreign Rep(s): ACER Literary Agency (Latin America, Portugal, Spain); Awax Literary Agency (Russia); Big Apple Agency (China, Taiwan, Thailand, Vietnam); The Book Publishers Association of Israel (Israel); Il Caduceo Literary Agency (Italy); EYA Literary Agency (Korea); Iris Literary Agency (Greece); Japan Uni (Japan); Anna Jarota Literary Agency (France); Nurcihan Kesim Literary Agency (Turkey); Kessler Agency (Romania); Plima Literary Agency (Croatia, Serbia); Torus-Books Agency (Hungary)
Foreign Rights: Louisa Pritchard Associates
Distribution Center: Faber Factory, Bloomsbury House, 74-77 Great Russell St, London WC1B 3DA *Tel:* (020) 7927 3800 *E-mail:* factory@faber.co.uk (ebooks)
Turnaround Publisher Services, Unit 3, Olympia Trading Estate, Coburg Rd, London N22 6TZ *Tel:* (020) 8829 3000 *Fax:* (020) 8881 5088 *E-mail:* orders@turnaround-uk.com (books)
Consortium Books Sales & Distribution, The Keg House, 34 13 Ave NE, Suite 101, Minneapolis, MN 55413, United States *Tel:* 612-746-2600 *Fax:* 612-746-2606 *E-mail:* info@cbsd.com *Web Site:* www.cbsd.com

Myrmidon Books Ltd
Rotterdam House, 116 Quayside, Newcastle upon Tyne NE1 3DY
Tel: (0191) 2064005 *Fax:* (0191) 2064001
E-mail: enquiries@myrmidonbooks.com
Web Site: myrmidonbooks.com
Key Personnel
Contact & Rights Manager: Edward Handyside *E-mail:* ed@myrmidonbooks.com
Membership(s): Independent Publishers Guild; The Publishers Association.
Subjects: Fiction
ISBN Prefix(es): 978-1-905802
Foreign Rep(s): Ashton International Marketing Services (Far East); Compass Ireland Booksales Ltd (Ireland); Iberian Book Services (Gibraltar, Portugal, Spain); Independent Publishers Group (Canada, USA); Pansing Distribution Pte Ltd (Malaysia, Singapore); Penguin Books (South Africa); Supernova Publishers (India)
Distribution Center: Littlehampton Book Services Ltd, Faraday Close, Durrington, Worthing, West Sussex BN13 3RB *Tel:* (01903) 828500; (01903) 828501 (customer service) *Web Site:* lbsltd.wp.hachette.co.uk

The Mystery Press, *imprint of* The History Press Ltd

NAG Press, *imprint of* The Crowood Press Ltd

NATE, see National Association for the Teaching of English (NATE)

National Assembly for Wales (Cynulliad Cenedlaethol Cymru)
The National Assembly for Wales, Cardiff Bay CF10 3NQ
Tel: (0300) 200 6565
E-mail: contact@assembly.wales
Web Site: wales.gov.uk; www.assembly.wales
Founded: 1981
Specialize in statistics on Wales.
Subjects: Business, Economics, Education, Government, Political Science, Health, Nutrition, Public Administration, Social Sciences, Sociology
ISBN Prefix(es): 978-0-7504; 978-0-86348; 978-0-903702; 978-0-904251
Total Titles: 35 Print

National Association for the Teaching of English (NATE)
Aizlewood Business Centre, Unit 410, Aizlewood's Mill Nursery St, Sheffield S3 8GG
Tel: (0114) 2823545 *Fax:* (0114) 2823150
E-mail: info@nate.org.uk
Web Site: www.nate.org.uk
Key Personnel
Dir: Paul Clayton *E-mail:* paul.clayton@nate.org.uk
Publishing Contact: Gary Snapper *E-mail:* gary@gabrielsnapper.co.uk
Founded: 1963
Specialize in English teaching.
Membership(s): Publishers' Association.
Subjects: Drama, Theater, Education, Film, Video, Literature, Literary Criticism, Essays, Poetry, English, Literacy, Information & Communication Technology
ISBN Prefix(es): 978-0-901291; 978-1-904709
Number of titles published annually: 5 Print; 1 CD-ROM
Total Titles: 50 Print
Distributed by Phoenix Education, Australia
Distributor for BFI Education; Cambridge University Press; Paul Chapman Publishing; Devon County Council; English & Media Centre; David Fulton; Nelsons; Open University Press; Phoenix Education, Australia; Routledge Publishers

National Council for Voluntary Organisations (NCVO)+

Society Bldg, 8 All Saints St, London N1 9RL
Tel: (020) 7713 6161 *Fax:* (020) 7713 6300
E-mail: ncvo@ncvo.org.uk
Web Site: www.ncvo.org.uk
Key Personnel
Chief Executive: Stuart Etherington
Dir, Enterprise: Richard Williams
Dir, Public Policy: Karl Wilding
External Relations Manager: Aidan Warner
 E-mail: aidan.warner@ncvo-vol.org.uk
Head, Policy & Public Services: Ruth Driscoll
Founded: 1919 (NCVO), 1969 (BSP), 1991 (NCVO Publications)
Also publish in association with other organizations.
Membership(s): IPG; Publishers' Association.
Subjects: Disability, Special Needs, Finance, Management, Marketing, Public Administration, Employment, Human Resources, Information & Communication Technology (ICT)
ISBN Prefix(es): 978-0-7199
Orders to: Hamilton House Mailings, 17 Staveley Way, Northampton NN6 7TX

National Extension College+

Michael Young Centre, Purbeck Rd, Cambridge, Cambs CB2 8HN
Tel: (01223) 400 200 *Toll Free Tel:* 0800 389 2839
E-mail: info@nec.ac.uk
Web Site: www.nec.ac.uk
Key Personnel
Chief Executive: Dr Ros Morpeth
Founded: 1963
Membership(s): EADL; NIACE.
Subjects: Accounting, Business, Child Care & Development, Education, Health, Nutrition, Language Arts, Linguistics, Management, Mathematics, Science (General), Self-Help
ISBN Prefix(es): 978-0-86082; 978-1-85356; 978-0-902404; 978-1-84308
Imprints: NEC

National Foundation for Educational Research

The Mere Upton Park, Slough, Berks SL1 2DQ
Tel: (01753) 574123 *Fax:* (01753) 691632
E-mail: enquiries@nfer.ac.uk
Web Site: www.nfer.ac.uk
Key Personnel
Chief Executive: Carole Willis *Tel:* (01753) 637350 *E-mail:* c.willis@nfer.ac.uk
Commercial Dir: Richard Birkett *Tel:* (01753) 637258 *E-mail:* r.birkett@nfer.ac.uk
Dir, Research: Lesley Duff
Dir, Research & Product Operations: Maria Charles *Tel:* (01753) 637341 *E-mail:* m.charles@nfer.ac.uk
Media & Press: Jane Parrack *Tel:* (01753) 637245 *E-mail:* j.parrack@nfer.ac.uk
Founded: 1946
Subjects: Education, Children's Services
ISBN Prefix(es): 978-0-7005; 978-0-7087; 978-0-85633; 978-0-901225; 978-1-903880; 978-1-905314; 978-1-910008
Number of titles published annually: 40 Print; 60 Online
Total Titles: 1 CD-ROM; 432 Online
Branch Office(s)
Genesis 4, Innovation Way, Heslington, York YO10 5DQ *Tel:* (01904) 433435 *Fax:* (01904) 433436 *E-mail:* north@nfer.ac.uk
Swansea Metropolitan University, Room TK128, Townhill Rd, Swansea SA2 0UT *Toll Free Tel:* (0300) 1231363 *Toll Free Fax:* (0300) 1231365 *E-mail:* scya@nfer.ac.uk

National Galleries of Scotland+

Scottish National Gallery of Modern Art, 73 Belford Rd, Edinburgh EH4 3DR
Tel: (0131) 624 6269 *Fax:* (0131) 623 7135
E-mail: publications@nationalgalleries.org
Web Site:. www.nationalgalleries.org/research/publishing
Key Personnel
Commissioning Publisher: Christine Thompson
Publications Project Manager: Sarah Worrall
Publishing Assistant: Mairi Lafferty
Subjects: Art, Photography
ISBN Prefix(es): 978-0-903598; 978-1-903278; 978-0-903148; 978-1-906270
Number of titles published annually: 15 Print
Total Titles: 90 Print; 1 CD-ROM
Distribution Center: ACC Distribution, Sandy Lane, Old Martlesham, Woodbridge, Suffolk IP12 4SD *Tel:* (01394) 4389950 *Fax:* (01394) 389999 *E-mail:* sales@antique-acc.com

National History Museum Publishing

Cromwell Rd, London SW7 5BD
Web Site: www.nhm.ac.uk/business-services/publishing.html; www.facebook.com/naturalhistorymuseum; twitter.com/NHM_London
Key Personnel
Head of Publishing: Colin Ziegler *Tel:* (020) 7942 5423
Publishing Marketing Manager: Howard Trent *Tel:* (020) 7942 5336
Founded: 1881
Publish books that reflect the museum's collections, scientific work & exhibitions.
Subjects: Animals, Pets, Art, Earth Sciences, Environmental Studies, Natural History, Botany, Dinosaurs, Evolution, Fossils, Nature
ISBN Prefix(es): 978-0-565
Distributed by Frances Lincoln Publishers (UK & Europe)
Distribution Center: Littlehampton Book Services Ltd, Faraday Close, Durrington, Worthing, West Sussex BN13 3RB *Tel:* (01903) 828500; (01903) 828501 (customer service) *Web Site:* lbsltd.wp.hachette.co.uk

National Institute for Health Care Excellence (NICE)

10 Spring Gardens, London SW1A 2BU
Tel: (0300) 323 0140 *Fax:* (0300) 323 0148
E-mail: nice@nice.org.uk
Web Site: www.nice.org.uk
Founded: 1999
Subjects: Child Care & Development, Health, Nutrition, Medicine, Nursing, Dentistry, Sports, Athletics, Women's Studies
ISBN Prefix(es): 978-1-84629
Branch Office(s)
Level 1A, City Tower, Piccadilly Plaza, Manchester M1 4BT

National Institute of Adult Continuing Education, see Learning & Work Institute

National Library of Scotland

George IV Bridge, Edinburgh EH1 1EW
Tel: (0131) 623 3700 *Fax:* (0131) 623 3701
E-mail: enquiries@nls.uk
Web Site: www.nls.uk
Key Personnel
National Librarian & Chief Executive: John Scally *Tel:* (0131) 623 3700 ext 3730 *E-mail:* john.scally@nls.uk
Subjects: History, Regional Interests
ISBN Prefix(es): 978-0-902220; 978-1-872116

National Library of Wales

Aberystwyth, Ceredigion SY23 3BU
Tel: (01970) 632 800 *Fax:* (01970) 615 709
E-mail: gofyn@llgc.org.uk
Web Site: www.llyfrgell.cymru; www.library.wales
Key Personnel
National Librarian: Linda Tomos *Tel:* (01970) 632 806 *E-mail:* linda.tomos@llgc.org.uk
Dir, Collections & Public Programs: Pedr ap Llwyd *Tel:* (01970) 632 952 *E-mail:* pedr.ap.llwyd@llgc.org.uk
Dir, Corporate Resources: David Michael *Tel:* (01970) 632 855 *E-mail:* david.michael@llgc.org.uk
Founded: 1911
Copyright/Legal Deposit Library.
Subjects: Art, Genealogy, Government, Political Science, Library & Information Sciences, Literature, Literary Criticism, Essays, Photography, Publishing & Book Trade Reference
ISBN Prefix(es): 978-0-907158; 978-0-901833; 978-1-86225

National Maritime Museum Publishing

Park Row, Greenwich, London SE10 9NF
Tel: (020) 8858 4422
E-mail: publishing@nmm.ac.uk
Web Site: www.nmm.ac.uk/business-and-hire/publishing
Key Personnel
Dir: Kevin Fewster
Deputy Dir: Margarette Lincoln
Museum Secretary: Christopher Gray
Subjects: Maritime
ISBN Prefix(es): 978-0-948065; 978-0-905555; 978-0-9501764; 978-1-906367
Orders to: Bookpoint, 130 Milton Park, Abingdon, Oxon OX14 4SB *Tel:* (01235) 400 400 *Web Site:* bookpoint.wp.hachette.co.uk (adult books)
Casemate UK, The Old Music Hall, 106-108 Cowley Rd, Oxford OX4 1JE *Tel:* (01226) 734350 *E-mail:* orders@casematepublishing.co.uk *Web Site:* www.casematepublishing.co.uk (adult books)
Grantham Book Services, Trent Rd, Grantham, Lincs NG31 7XQ *Tel:* (01206) 255678 *Fax:* (01476) 541060 *E-mail:* sales@tbs-ltd.co.uk *Web Site:* www.thebookservice.co.uk (children's books)
Bounce! Sales & Marketing Ltd, 14 Greville St, London EC1N 8SB *Tel:* (020) 7138 3650 *Fax:* (020) 7138 3658 *E-mail:* sales@bouncemarketing.co.uk *Web Site:* www.bouncemarketing.co.uk (children's books)

National Museum Wales Books (Llyfrau Amgueddfa Cymru)+

Imprint of Amgueddfa Cymru - National Museum Wales
Cathays Park, Cardiff CF10 3NP
Tel: (029) 2057 3177
E-mail: shop@museumwales.ac.uk
Web Site: www.museumwales.ac.uk
Key Personnel
Head, Publishing: Ms Mari Gordon *Tel:* (029) 2057 3235 *E-mail:* mari.gordon@museumwales.ac.uk
Founded: 1907
Museum.
Subjects: Archaeology, Art, Earth Sciences, Education, Geography, Geology, History, Maritime, Photography, Regional Interests, Folk History
ISBN Prefix(es): 978-0-7200
Number of titles published annually: 6 Print; 1 CD-ROM
Total Titles: 71 Print; 6 CD-ROM
Distributed by Welsh Books Council

National Museums Scotland Publishing, see NMS Enterprises Ltd - Publishing

National Portrait Gallery Publications+

St Martin's Pl, London WC2H 0HE
Tel: (020) 7306 0055; (020) 7321 6612 (publications); (020) 7312 2452 (press) *Fax:* (020) 7321 6657 (publications)
Web Site: www.npg.org.uk
Key Personnel
Dir: Sandy Nairne *E-mail:* snairne@npg.org.uk

Mng Editor: Christopher Tinker *E-mail:* ctinker@
npg.org.uk
Head, Trading: Robert Carr-Archer
E-mail: rcarrarcher@npg.org.uk
Production Manager: Ruth Muller-Wirth
E-mail: rmullerwirth@npg.org.uk
Founded: 1976 (book publishing division)
Also acts as picture library.
Membership(s): Independent Publishers Guild.
Subjects: Art, Biography, Memoirs, History, Photography
ISBN Prefix(es): 978-0-904017; 978-1-85514
Number of titles published annually: 12 Print
Total Titles: 40 Print
Distributed by Amsterdam University Press
(Netherlands); Antique Collector's Club (USA);
Grantham Book Services (UK); Peribo (Australia)
Foreign Rep(s): Bookcity Co (Iran); Edgeler
Book Services Ltd (John Edgeler) (Caribbean);
Peter Hyde Associates (Botswana, Lesotho,
Namibia, South Africa, Swaziland, Zimbabwe);
Interart Sarl (France); Michael Klein (Austria,
Germany exc South Germany); Levant Distributors (Lebanon); Thames & Hudson (Australia)
Pty Ltd (Australia, New Zealand, Pacific Islands, Papua New Guinea); Thames & Hudson China Ltd (China, Hong Kong, Macau);
Thames & Hudson Ltd (Scipio Stringer) (India,
Japan, Pakistan, Sri Lanka); Thames & Hudson
Ltd (Sara Ticci) (Southern Germany, Switzerland); Thames & Hudson Ltd (Karim White)
(Ireland); Thames & Hudson Ltd (Per Burell)
(Armenia, Azerbaijan, Baltic States, Belarus,
Kazakhstan, Kyrgyzstan, Moldova, Russia,
Scandinavia, Tajikistan, Uzbekistan); Thames
& Hudson Ltd (Ian Bartley) (Africa exc South
Africa); Thames & Hudson Ltd (Natasha
Ffrench) (Central America, Italy, Mexico, Portugal, South America, Spain); Thames & Hudson Ltd (Bas van der Zee) (Belgium, Luxembourg, Netherlands); Thames & Hudson Ltd
(Stephen Embrey) (Eastern Europe, Eastern
Mediterranean, Egypt, Middle East); Thames &
Hudson Pvt Ltd (Malaysia); Thames & Hudson
Singapore (Singapore, Southeast Asia); Zeenat
Book Supply Ltd (Bangladesh)
Distribution Center: Littlehampton Book Services Ltd, Faraday Close, Durrington, Worthing, West Sussex BN13 3RB *Tel:* (01903)
828500; (01903) 828501 (customer service)
Web Site: lbsltd.wp.hachette.co.uk

National Records of Scotland (NRS)

HM General Register House, 2 Princes St, Edinburgh EH1 3YY
Tel: (0131) 535 1314
Web Site: www.nrscotland.gov.uk; twitter.com/
natrecordsscot
Key Personnel
Chief Executive: Tim Ellis
Founded: 1774
General historical & educational publications designed to make the holdings of the NRS more
accessible.
Membership(s): Scottish Publishing.
Subjects: History
ISBN Prefix(es): 978-1-870874
Number of titles published annually: 1 Print
Total Titles: 30 Print; 5 CD-ROM

National Trust, *imprint of* Pavilion Books

The National Youth Agency

Eastgate House, 19-23 Humberstone Rd, Leicester, Leics LE5 3GJ
Tel: (0116) 242 7350
E-mail: nya@nya.org.uk
Web Site: www.nya.org.uk
Key Personnel
Chief Executive Officer: Fiona Blacke
Operations Dir: Jon Boagey

Communications Manager: Daisy Powell
Subjects: Career Development
ISBN Prefix(es): 978-0-86155; 978-0-902095
Number of titles published annually: 10 Print
Total Titles: 80 Print

NavyBooks

Lodge Hill, Liskeard, Cornwall PL30 3NA
Tel: (01579) 343663 *Fax:* (01579) 346747
E-mail: info@navybooks.com; sales@navybooks.
com
Web Site: www.navybooks.com
Key Personnel
Mng Dir: Ian Whitehouse
Founded: 1979
Specialize in books on the Royal Navy along
with naval books & videos from other publishers.
Subjects: Maritime
ISBN Prefix(es): 978-0-907771; 978-1-904459;
978-0-9506323
Total Titles: 51 Print
Subsidiaries: Warship World Magazine

NBS, *imprint of* RIBA Publishing

NCVO, see National Council for Voluntary Organisations (NCVO)

NEC, *imprint of* National Extension College

Neil Wilson Publishing Ltd+

226 King St, Castle Douglas DG7 1DS
Tel: (01556) 504119 *Fax:* (01556) 504065
E-mail: info@nwp.co.uk
Web Site: www.nwp.co.uk
Key Personnel
Publisher: Neil Wilson
Founded: 1992
Membership(s): Publishing Scotland.
Subjects: Biography, Memoirs, Cookery, Fiction, History, Humor, Music, Dance, Outdoor
Recreation, Regional Interests, Sports, Athletics, Travel & Tourism, Wine & Spirits
ISBN Prefix(es): 978-1-897784; 978-1-903238;
978-1-906476; 978-1-906000
Number of titles published annually: 6 Print; 25
E-Book
Total Titles: 225 Print; 120 E-Book
Imprints: Angels' Share (food, drink, cookery);
11:9 (contemporary Scottish fiction); The In
Pinn (travel, mountaineering & memoir, hillwalking); NWP (history, biography, reference,
true crime); The Vital Spark (Scottish humour)
Foreign Rep(s): Geoff Bryan (Ireland); Donald
Morrison (Scotland)
Warehouse: BookSource Ltd, 50 Cambuslang Rd, Cambuslang, Glasgow G32 5NB
Tel: (0845) 370 0067 *Fax:* (0845) 370 0068
E-mail: customerservices@booksource.net *Web
Site:* www.booksource.net
Distribution Center: BookSource Ltd, 50 Cambuslang Rd, Cambuslang, Glasgow G32 5NB
Tel: (0845) 370 0067 *Fax:* (0845) 370 0068
E-mail: customerservices@booksource.net *Web
Site:* www.booksource.net
Interlink Publishing, 46 Crosby St, Northampton,
MA 01060-1804, United States *E-mail:* info@
interlinkbooks.com *Web Site:* www.
interlinkbooks.com (USA)
Orders to: BookSource Ltd, 50 Cambuslang Rd, Cambuslang, Glasgow G32 5NB
Tel: (0845) 370 0067 *Fax:* (0845) 370 0068
E-mail: customerservices@booksource.net *Web
Site:* www.booksource.net

New Academic Science

27 Old Gloucester St, London WC1N 3AX
E-mail: info@newacademicscience.co.uk
Web Site: www.newacademicscience.co.uk

Subjects: Chemistry, Chemical Engineering, Economics, Engineering (General), Management,
Medicine, Nursing, Dentistry, Physics, Pharmacy, Statistics
ISBN Prefix(es): 978-1-906574; 978-1-78183
Distribution Center: Combined Book Services,
Paddock Distribution Centre, Unit D, Paddock Wood, Tonbridge, Kent TN12 6UU
Tel: (01892) 837171 *Fax:* (01892) 837272
E-mail: orders@combook.co.uk
Publishers Storage & Shipping Corp, 46 Development Rd, Fitchburg, MA 01420, United
States *Tel:* 978-345-2121 *Fax:* 978-348-1233
E-mail: orders@pssc.com

New Cavendish Books+

3 Denbigh Rd, London W11 2SJ
Tel: (020) 7229 6765 *Fax:* (020) 7792 0027
Founded: 1973
Specialize in books on collectable items.
Subjects: Nonfiction (General), Technology, Collecting, Popular Culture, Toys
ISBN Prefix(es): 978-0-904568; 978-1-872727;
978-1-904562
Number of titles published annually: 4 Print
Total Titles: 70 Print
Distributed by Antique Collectors Club (UK &
Europe); Antique Collectors Club (USA); Renniks (Australia)

New Era Publications UK Ltd+

Subsidiary of New Era Publications International
ApS
Crown House, 2nd floor, 37 High St, East Grinstead, West Sussex RH19 3AF
Key Personnel
Dir: Margaret Blunden; Luisella Novikov
Founded: 1985
Subjects: Business, Education, Fiction, Health,
Nutrition, Management, Nonfiction (General),
Philosophy, Religion - Other, Science Fiction,
Fantasy, Self-Help, Western Fiction
ISBN Prefix(es): 978-1-870451; 978-1-900944;
978-1-903820
Total Titles: 90 Print; 1 CD-ROM; 18 Audio
Associate Companies: Author Services Inc, 7051
Hollywood Blvd, Suite 400, Los Angeles,
CA 90028, United States *Tel:* 213-466-3310
E-mail: asi@earthlink.net
Branch Office(s)
New Era Publications Australia Pty Ltd, 16
Doraby St, Dundas, NSW 2177, Australia
Tel: (029) 638 30 88 *Fax:* (029) 898 15 88
E-mail: cploanzo@tpg.com.au
New Era Publications Deutschland GmbH, Hittfelder Kirchweg 5, 21220 Seevetal-Maschen,
Germany *Tel:* (041) 05 683 30 *Fax:* (049) 41
05 683 3 22 *E-mail:* neweragermany@t-online.
de
New Era Central Europe, Leonardo Da Vinci utca
8-12, Budapest 1084, Hungary *Tel:* (01) 210
46 13 *Fax:* (01) 210 46 13 *E-mail:* newera@
menthanet.hu
N E Publications India Pvt Ltd, 96 Gautam Nagar, New Delhi 110 049, India *Tel:* (011) 26 60
15 48 *E-mail:* tgoeldenitz@gmx.net
New Era Publications Italia, Via Cadorna, 61,
20090 Vimodrone (MI), Italy *Tel:* (02) 274
09272 *Fax:* (02) 274 09198 *E-mail:* sales@
newera.it
New Era Publications Japan Inc, Sakei SS Bldg
2F, 4-38-15, Higashi Ikebukuro, Toshima-Ku, Tokyo 170-0013, Japan *Tel:* (03) 5960
5660 *Fax:* (03) 5960 5561 *E-mail:* nepjp@
newerapublications.com
New Era Publications Group, Pr Mira, VVC Bldg
265, 129223 Moscow, Russia *Tel:* (495) 746 64
97 *E-mail:* info@new-era.ru
Continental Publications Pty Ltd, PO Box 27080,
Benerose, Johannesburg 2011, South Africa
Tel: (011) 331 66 21 *Fax:* (011) 331 66 21
E-mail: nepaf@newerapublications.com

Source Publications Co, 2nd floor 65, Section 4, Min-Shen East Rd, Taipei, Taiwan *Tel:* (062) 25 46 58 51 *Fax:* (062) 25 45 70 33 *E-mail:* nep.twn@msa.hinet.net
U.S. Office(s): Bridge Publications, 5600 E Olympic Blvd, Los Angeles, CA 90022, United States

New Holland Publishers (UK) Ltd+
The Chandlery, Unit 9, 50 Westminster Rd, London SE1 7QY
Tel: (020) 7953 7565
E-mail: enquiries@nhpub.co.uk
Web Site: newhollandpublishers.com/uk
Key Personnel
Finance Dir: Sandy Caven
Founded: 1956
Specialize in illustrated books.
Subjects: Cookery, Crafts, Games, Hobbies, House & Home, How-to, Natural History, Travel & Tourism
ISBN Prefix(es): 978-1-85368; 978-1-85974; 978-1-84330; 978-1-84537; 978-1-84773; 978-1-84636; 978-1-78009
Imprints: Reed New Holland
Branch Office(s)
66 Gibbes St, Unit 1, Chatswood, NSW 2067, Australia *Tel:* (02) 8986 4700 *E-mail:* orders@newholland.com.au *Web Site:* newhollandpublishers.com/au
New Holland Publishers (NZ) Ltd, 39 Woodside Ave, Off 5, Northcote, Auckland 0627, New Zealand *Tel:* (09) 481 0444 *E-mail:* books@nhp.co.nz *Web Site:* nz.newhollandpublishers.com
Distributor for La Belle Aurore; Complete Dive Guides; Juicy Books; Pilot Books; SCP Publishing; Southern Book Publishers (Europe, UK, North America & Asia); Stonebridge Press (Europe, UK & South Africa); Struik Publishers (Europe, UK & North America); Turtle Press; Weatherhill (Europe, UK & South Africa)
Foreign Rep(s): APD Malaysia (Malaysia); APD Singapore Pte Ltd (Southeast Asia); Ted Dougherty (Western Europe); The Globe Pequot Press (USA); Arturo Gutierrez Hernandez (Mexico); HRA (Christopher Humphrys) (Caribbean, Central America); HRA (Tony Moggach) (Eastern Europe, Russia); HRA (Terry Roberts) (South America); Iberian Book Services (Peter Prout) (Gibraltar, Portugal, Spain); Tahir M Lodhi, Publishers Representative (Pakistan); McNeish Publishing International (Katie McNeish) (Scandinavia); Midpoint (USA); Random House Struik (Central Africa, East Africa, Southern Africa); Research Press (India); United Century Book Services Ltd (China, Hong Kong)
Distribution Center: Publishers Group UK (PGUK), 63-66 Hatton Garden, London EC1N 8LE *Tel:* (020) 7405 1105 *Fax:* (020) 7242 3725 *E-mail:* orders@pguk.co.uk *Web Site:* www.pguk.co.uk
National Book Network (NBN), 15200 NBN Way, Blue Ridge Summit, PA 17214, United States *Tel:* 717-794-3800 *Fax:* 717-794-3828 *E-mail:* customercare@nbnbooks.com *Web Site:* www.nbnbooks.com

New Internationalist Publications Ltd
The Old Music Hall, 106-108 Cowley Rd, Oxford, Oxon OX4 1JE
Tel: (01865) 403345 *Fax:* (01865) 403346
E-mail: contracts@newint.org
Web Site: newint.org
Founded: 1971 (as Peter Adamson Communications)
Subjects: Fiction, Government, Political Science, Photography, Poetry, Current Affairs, Ethical Living, Food
ISBN Prefix(es): 978-1-869847; 978-1-904456; 978-0-9540499; 978-1-906523; 978-1-78026

Branch Office(s)
2446 Bank St, Suite 653, Ottawa, ON K1V 1A8, Canada
Distribution Center: Consortium Books Sales & Distribution, The Keg House, 34 13 Ave NE, Suite 101, Minneapolis, MN 55413, United States *Tel:* 612-746-2600 *Fax:* 612-746-2606 *E-mail:* info@cbsd.com *Web Site:* www.cbsd.com
Orders to: PO Box 61, Rotherham S63 9YG *Tel:* (01709) 513999 *Fax:* (01709) 881673 *E-mail:* help@newint.org

New Playwrights' Network, *imprint of* Cressrelles Publishing Co Ltd

New Playwrights' Network+
Imprint of Cressrelles Publishing Co Ltd
Industrial Estate, 10 Station Rd, Colwall, Malvern, Herts WR13 6RN
Tel: (01684) 540154
Web Site: www.cressrelles.co.uk
Key Personnel
Mng Proprietor: L G Smith
Business Manager: Simon Smith *E-mail:* simon@cressrelles.co.uk
Founded: 1972
Publisher of plays.
Subjects: Drama, Theater
ISBN Prefix(es): 978-0-86319; 978-0-903653; 978-0-906660
Number of titles published annually: 5 Print
Total Titles: 400 Print
Foreign Rights: Bakers Plays (USA); DALRO (Southern Africa); Drama League of Ireland (Ireland); Origin Theatrical (Australia); Play Bureau (New Zealand)

New Riders, *imprint of* Pearson Education Ltd

Newnes, *imprint of* Elsevier Ltd

Nexus Special Interests, *imprint of* Special Interest Model Books Ltd

NGS Publishing, see National Galleries of Scotland

NIACE, see Learning & Work Institute

NICE, see National Institute for Health Care Excellence (NICE)

Nielsen Book
Midas House, 3rd floor, 62 Goldsworth Rd, Woking, Surrey GU21 6LQ
Tel: (01483) 712 200 *Fax:* (01483) 712 201
E-mail: sales.bookdata@nielsen.com; marketing.book@nielsen.com; customerservices.book@nielsen.com
Web Site: www.nielsenbook.co.uk
Key Personnel
Senior Vice President & Mng Dir: Jonathan Stolper
Head, Product Leadership: Jon Windus
Founded: 1841
Leading provider of search, discovery, commerce, consumer research & retail sales analysis services globally. Nielsen runs the Registration Agencies (ISBN & SAN agencies for UK & Ireland, ISTC), provides search & discovery products through its Nielsen Book Discovery Solutions, electronic trading via Nielsen Book Commerce Solutions, retail sales analysis via Nielsen BookScan & consumer research through its Books & Consumer Survey. Nielsen Books' solutions portfolio brings deeper insights & improved efficiencies to the global book industry.

Branch offices in Australia, India, New Zealand & the US.
Subjects: Library & Information Sciences, Publishing & Book Trade Reference
ISBN Prefix(es): 978-0-85021
Parent Company: The Nielsen Co
Associate Companies: Nielsen Book Services Ltd, Midas House, 3rd floor, 62 Goldsworth Rd, Woking, Surrey GU21 6LQ, Global Mng Dir, Discovery & Commerce Solutions: Stephen Long; Nielsen Registration Agencies, Woking, Registration Services Manager: Diana Dalasini; Nielsen Book Research, 85 Broad St, New York, NY 10004, United States

NMM Publishing, see National Maritime Museum Publishing

NMS Enterprises Ltd - Publishing+
National Museums Scotland, Chambers St, Edinburgh EH1 1JF
Tel: (0131) 247 4026 *Fax:* (0131) 247 4012
E-mail: publishing@nms.ac.uk
Web Site: www.nms.ac.uk; shop.nms.ac.uk
Key Personnel
Dir: Dr Gordon Rintoul
Publishing Dir: Lesley A Taylor *E-mail:* ltaylor@nms.ac.uk
Administrator: Margaret Wilson *E-mail:* m.wilson@nms.ac.uk
Founded: 1985
Subjects: Archaeology, Art, Biography, Memoirs, Cookery, Geography, Geology, History, Natural History, Nonfiction (General), Poetry, Science (General), Technology, Photographic Archive, Scottish History & Culture
ISBN Prefix(es): 978-0-948636; 978-1-901663; 978-1-905267; 978-0-900733
Number of titles published annually: 8 Print
Total Titles: 75 Print

No Exit Press, *imprint of* Oldcastle Books Ltd

Nobrow Ltd
27 Westgate St, London E8 3RL
Tel: (020) 7033 4430
E-mail: info@nobrow.net; sales@nobrow.net; nobrowsubs@gmail.com (submissions)
Web Site: www.nobrow.net
Founded: 2008
ISBN Prefix(es): 978-1-907704
Imprints: Flying Eye Books (children's)
Foreign Rep(s): Belles Lettres Diffusion Distribution (Belgium, France, Switzerland); Consortium Book Sales & Distribution (USA); Perimeter Distribution (Australia, New Zealand, Tasmania); Publishers Group Canada (Canada)
Distribution Center: Grantham Book Services, Trent Rd, Grantham NG31 7XQ *Tel:* (01476) 541080 *Fax:* (01476) 541061 *E-mail:* orders@gbs.tbs-ltd.co.uk
Penguin Random House Publisher Services (PRHPS), 1745 Broadway, New York, NY 10019, United States *E-mail:* distribution@randomhouse.com *Web Site:* penguinrandomhouse.biz/publisherservices (North America)

North Holland, *imprint of* Elsevier Ltd

North Light, *imprint of* David & Charles Ltd

North Parade Publishing
4 North Parade, Bath BA1 1LF
Tel: (01225) 310107 *Fax:* (01225) 312878
E-mail: info@nppbooks.co.uk
Web Site: www.nppbooks.co.uk
Key Personnel
Chief Executive Officer & Dir: Peter Hicks
ISBN Prefix(es): 978-0-7554
Associate Companies: Robert Frederick Ltd

North York Moors National Park
The Old Vicarage, Bondgate, Helmsley, York YO62 5BP
Tel: (01439) 772700 *Fax:* (01439) 770691
E-mail: info@northyorkmoors.org.uk; press@northyorkmoors.org.uk
Web Site: www.northyorkmoors.org.uk
Key Personnel
Information & Countryside Interpretation: Michael Graham
Founded: 1952
Subjects: Archaeology, Geography, Geology, Natural History, Regional Interests
ISBN Prefix(es): 978-1-904622; 978-0-907480

Northcote House Publishers Ltd
Horndon House, Horndon, Tavistock, Devon PL19 9NQ
Tel: (01822) 810066; (01892) 837171 (sales)
Fax: (01822) 810034; (01892) 837272 (sales)
E-mail: admin@writersandtheirwork.co.uk
Web Site: www.writersandtheirwork.co.uk
Key Personnel
Publisher: Brian Hulme
General Editor: Prof Isobel Armstrong
Founded: 1994
Independent academic publisher.
Membership(s): IPG.
Subjects: Drama, Theater, Education, Literature, Literary Criticism, Essays, Music, Dance
ISBN Prefix(es): 978-0-7463
Number of titles published annually: 30 Print; 12 E-Book
Total Titles: 240 Print; 12 E-Book
Imprints: Writers & Their Work
Foreign Rep(s): Books & Volume (Australia, New Zealand); Casemate | academic (Canada, USA); Ted Dougherty (Austria, Belgium, Germany, Greece, Italy, Netherlands, Switzerland); InterMedia Americana (Africa, Eastern Europe); Hani Kreidieh (Middle East); Maya Publishers Pvt Ltd (Surit Mitra) (India); Peter Prout (Portugal, Spain); David Towle (Baltic States, Scandinavia)
Distribution Center: Casemate | academic (USA)
Orders to: Combined Book Services, Unit I/K, Paddock Wood Distribution Centre, Paddock Wood, Tonbridge, Kent TN12 6UU *Tel:* (01892) 837171 *Fax:* (01892) 837272 *E-mail:* orders@combook.co.uk *Web Site:* www.combook.co.uk

Northern Books, *imprint of* Famedram Publishers Ltd

Northern House, *imprint of* Carcanet Press Ltd

W W Norton & Co Ltd+
Castle House, 75/76 Wells St, London W1T 3QT
Tel: (020) 7323 1579 *Fax:* (020) 7436 4553
E-mail: office@wwnorton.co.uk
Web Site: www.wwnorton.co.uk
Key Personnel
President: W Drake McFeely
Mng Dir: Edward Crutchley
Dir, Sales: Judith Pamplin
Marketing Manager: Victoria Keown-Boyd
Founded: 1980
Subjects: Architecture & Interior Design, Art, Biography, Memoirs, Economics, Government, Political Science, History, Literature, Literary Criticism, Essays, Maritime, Music, Dance, Photography, Psychology, Psychiatry
ISBN Prefix(es): 978-0-393
Number of titles published annually: 120 Print; 20 CD-ROM
Total Titles: 4,000 Print
Parent Company: W W Norton & Company Inc, 500 Fifth Ave, New York, NY 10110, United States
Imprints: Countryman Press
Distributor for Kales Press; New Directions

Foreign Rep(s): The African Moon Press (Chris Reinders) (South Africa); Kelvin van Hasselt Publishing Services (Africa exc North & South Africa, Caribbean); International Publishers Representatives (Middle East, North Africa); Cristina de Lara Ruiz (Portugal, Spain); Russell Book Representation (Andrew Russell) (Ireland, Northern Ireland); Viva Books Pvt Ltd (Vinod Vasishta) (India, Sri Lanka); World Press (Saleem A Malik) (Pakistan)
Foreign Rights: Everest International Publishing Services (China); Pearson Education, New Zealand (New Zealand)
Orders to: John Wiley & Sons Ltd, One Oldlands Way, Bognor Regis, West Sussex PO22 9SA *Tel:* (01243) 779 777 *Fax:* (01243) 820 250 *E-mail:* cs-books@wiley.co.uk
W W Norton & Company Inc, 500 Fifth Ave, New York, NY 10110, United States *Tel:* 212-354-5500 *Fax:* 212-869-0856 (USA, Australasia & Far East)

Nosy Crow Ltd+
The Crow's Nest, 10a Lant St, London SE1 1QR
Tel: (020) 7089 7575 *Fax:* (020) 7089 7576
E-mail: hello@nosycrow.com
Web Site: nosycrow.com
Key Personnel
Operations Executive: Mary Berry
Sales Executive: Frances Sleigh
Mng Dir: Kate Wilson *E-mail:* kate@nosycrow.com
Commercial Dir: Adrian Soar *E-mail:* adrian@nosycrow.com
Editorial Dir: Camilla Reid *E-mail:* camilla@nosycrow.com
Head, Operations: Imogen Blundell
Head, Publicity: Dom Kingston
Head, Sales & Marketing: Catherine Stokes
Business Development Manager: Tom Bonnick
Editor: Ruth Symons
Founded: 2010
Publisher of children's books & apps.
Membership(s): The Independent Publishers Guild; The Publishers Association.
Subjects: Fiction, Nonfiction (General)
Number of titles published annually: 50 Print; 6 Online; 15 E-Book; 10 Audio
Total Titles: 100 Print; 15 Online; 40 E-Book; 10 Audio
Distribution Center: Grantham Book Services, Trent Rd, Grantham, Lincs NG31 7XQ *Tel:* (01476) 541 080 *Fax:* (01476) 541 061 *Web Site:* www.granthambookservices.co.uk
Orders to: Grantham Book Services, Trent Rd, Grantham, Lincs NG31 7XQ *Tel:* (01476) 541 080 *Fax:* (01476) 541 061 *Web Site:* www.granthambookservices.co.uk

Nourish
359 Goswell Rd, London EC1V 7JL
Tel: (020) 3468 0102
E-mail: enquiries@watkinspublishing.co.uk
Web Site: www.nourishbooks.com
Key Personnel
Publisher: Jo Lal
Associate Publisher: Chris Wold
Marketing & Publicity Dir: Vicky Hartley
E-mail: vicky.hartley@watkinspublishing.com
Senior Rights Manager: Alex Thomson
E-mail: alex.thomson@watkinspublishing.com
Rights Executive: Claudia Esteves
E-mail: claudia.esteves@watkinspublishing.com
Export & UK Sales Executive: Emma McArthur
E-mail: emma.mcarthur@watkinspublishing.com
UK Sales Manager: Sian Jones *E-mail:* sian.jones@watkinspublishing.com
Sales & Rights Assistant: Jared van den Aardweg
E-mail: jared.aardweg@watkinspublishing.com
Founded: 1992 (as Duncan Baird Publishers, rebranded as Nourish in 2014)
Subjects: Cookery, Health, Nutrition

ISBN Prefix(es): 978-1-84899
Parent Company: Watkins Media Ltd
Foreign Rep(s): A-Z Africa Book Services (Anita Zih) (Cameroon, Ethiopia, Ghana, Kenya, Malawi, Mauritius, Nigeria, Rwanda, Seychelles, Tanzania, Uganda, Zambia, Zimbabwe); Ashton International Marketing Services (Cambodia, China, Guam, Hong Kong, Indonesia, Japan, Korea, Myanmar, Philippines, Taiwan, Thailand, Vietnam); Bill Bailey Publishers' Representatives (Albania, Belarus, Belgium, Bosnia and Herzegovina, Bulgaria, Croatia, Czechia, Estonia, France, Georgia, Greece, Hungary, Kazakhstan, Latvia, Lithuania, Luxembourg, Macedonia, Montenegro, Poland, Romania, Russia, Serbia, Slovakia, Turkey, Ukraine); Hay House (South Africa); International Publishing Services (Melanie Boesen) (Denmark, Finland, Iceland, Norway, Sweden); Messinter SpA (Italy); Pansing Distribution Pte Ltd (Singapore); Research Press (Ajay Parmar) (India); Simon & Schuster (Australia, New Zealand)
Foreign Rights: Ilustrata (Angela Reynolds) (Portugal, Spain); Print Company (Gabriela Scolik) (Germany); Katia Schumer (Brazil)

Novello & Co+
14-15 Berners St, London W1T 3LJ
Tel: (020) 7612 7400 *Fax:* (020) 7612 7545
E-mail: promotion@musicsales.co.uk
Web Site: www.musicsalesclassical.com
Key Personnel
Mng Dir: James Rushton *E-mail:* james.rushton@musicsales.co.uk
Mng Editor: Howard Friend *E-mail:* howard.friend@musicsales.co.uk
Music Editor: Daniel Rollison *E-mail:* daniel.rollison@musicsales.co.uk; Laurence Scott *E-mail:* laurence.scott@musicsales.co.uk
European Promotion Dir: Gill Graham *E-mail:* gill.graham@musicsales.co.uk
Creative Manager: Kate Johnson *E-mail:* kate.johnson@musicsales.co.uk
Promotion Manager: Meg Monteith *E-mail:* meg.monteith@musicsales.co.uk
Founded: 1811
Subjects: Music, Dance
ISBN Prefix(es): 978-0-85360
Parent Company: The Music Sales Group
Imprints: Cinderella; Elkin; Fairfield; Laurel; Lorna; Paxton
Foreign Rep(s): Chester Music France (France); Edition Wilhelm Hansen AS (Denmark); KK Music Sales (Japan); Music Sales Classical Berlin (Germany); Music Sales Corp-G Schirmer Inc-Associated Music Publishers Inc (USA); Music Sales Pty Ltd (Australia); Union Musical Ediciones SL (Spain)
Distribution Center: Music Sales Distribution Centre, Newmarket Rd, Bury St Edmunds, Suffolk IP33 3YB *Tel:* (01284) 705705 *Fax:* (01284) 703401

Nuit-Isis, *imprint of* Mandrake of Oxford

NWP, *imprint of* Neil Wilson Publishing Ltd

O Books+
Laurel House, Station Approach, Alresford, Hants SO24 9JH
Web Site: www.o-books.com
Key Personnel
Publisher: Maria Barry; John Hunt
Founded: 2001
Membership(s): Independent Publishers Guild.
Subjects: Alternative, Biography, Memoirs, Fiction, History, Inspirational, Spirituality, Philosophy, Poetry, Psychology, Psychiatry, Religion - Buddhist, Religion - Hindu, Religion - Islamic, Religion - Jewish, Religion - Protestant, Religion - Other, Self-Help, Travel & Tourism,

Women's Studies, Culture, Educational, Mind, Body & Spirit, New Age
ISBN Prefix(es): 978-1-85608; 978-1-903019; 978-1-84928; 978-1-905047; 978-1-84694; 978-1-903816; 978-1-78099
Number of titles published annually: 100 Print
Total Titles: 600 Print
Imprints: Axis Mundi Books; Ayni Books; Bedroom Books; Business Books; Changemakers Books; Christian Alternative; Chronos Books; Circle Books; Compass Books; Cosmic Egg Book; Dodona Books; Earth Books; Gaming Books; Iff Books; Moon Books; Roundfire Books; 6th Books; Zero Books
Foreign Rep(s): Bookreps NZ Ltd (New Zealand); Brumby Books (Australia); Hay House SA (South Africa); NBN (National Book Network) (Canada, USA); Orca Book Services Ltd (Europe, UK); Pansing Distribution Pte Ltd (Brunei, Malaysia, Singapore)
Orders to: NBN, 15200 NBN Way, Blue Ridge Summit, PA 17214, United States Tel: 717-794-3800 E-mail: customercare@nbnbooks.com

Oakwood Library of Railway History, imprint of Oakwood Press & Video Library

Oakwood Press & Video Library
PO Box 13, Usk, Monmouthshire NP15 1YS
Tel: (01291) 650444 Fax: (01291) 650484
E-mail: sales@oakwoodpress.co.uk
Web Site: www.oakwoodpress.co.uk
Key Personnel
Proprietor, Mng Dir & Rights: Jane Kennedy
Founded: 1934
Specialist transport publisher.
Subjects: History, Transportation
ISBN Prefix(es): 978-0-85361
Number of titles published annually: 20 Print
Total Titles: 210 Print
Imprints: Locomotion Papers; Oakwood Library of Railway History
Divisions: Oakwood Visuals

Oberon Books Ltd
521 Caledonian Rd, London N7 9RH
Tel: (020) 7607 3637 Fax: (020) 7607 3629
E-mail: info@oberonbooks.com
Web Site: www.oberonbooks.com
Founded: 1985
Subjects: Biography, Memoirs, Drama, Theater, Fiction, Music, Dance, Performing Arts
ISBN Prefix(es): 978-1-78682; 978-1-84002; 978-1-870259; 978-1-84943; 978-1-78319
Distribution Center: Consortium Book Sales & Distribution, The Keg House, 34 13 Ave NE, Suite 101, Minneapolis, MN 55413-1007, United States Tel: 612-746-2600 Fax: 612-746-2606 E-mail: info@cbsd.com Web Site: www.cbsd.com SAN: 200-6049

Oceano Grupo Editorial, imprint of Gale

Octopus Publishing Group Ltd+
Division of Hachette UK
Endeavor House, 189 Shaftesbury Ave, London WC2H 8JY
Tel: (020) 7632 5400 Fax: (020) 7632 5405
E-mail: info@octopusbooks.co.uk; sales@octopus-publishing.co.uk
Web Site: www.octopusbooks.co.uk
Key Personnel
Chief Executive Officer: Alison Goff
Deputy Chief Executive Officer: Andrew Welham
Publisher of lifestyle books.
Subjects: Aeronautics, Aviation, Antiques, Architecture & Interior Design, Automotive, Cookery, Crafts, Games, Hobbies, Drama, Theater, Fiction, Film, Video, Gardening, Plants, Geography, Geology, Health, Nutrition, Literature, Literary Criticism, Essays, Music, Dance,

Mysteries, Suspense, Natural History, Nonfiction (General), Photography, Poetry, Science Fiction, Fantasy, Sports, Athletics, Travel & Tourism, Wine & Spirits
Ultimate Parent Company: Hachette Livre
Imprints: Mitchell Beazley; Bounty Books; Cassell Illustrated; Conran Octopus; Gaia Books; Godsfield Press; Hamlyn; Ilex Press; Miller's; Philip's; Spruce; Summersdale
Foreign Rep(s): APD Kuala Lumpur (Lillian Koe) (Malaysia); APD Singapore Pte Ltd (Ian Pringle) (Cambodia, Guam, Hong Kong, Indonesia, Japan, Laos, Philippines, Singapore, South Korea, Taiwan, Thailand, Vietnam); Bill Bailey Publishers' Representatives (Austria, Baltic States, Belgium, Cyprus, Eastern Europe, France, Germany, Iceland, Netherlands, Russia, Scandinavia, Switzerland); Jonathan Ball Publishers (South Africa); Canadian Manda Group (Canada); Arturo Gutierrez Hernandez (Central America); Hachette Book Group Ireland (Ireland, Northern Ireland); Hachette Book Publishing India Pvt Ltd (Kapil Agrawal) (Bangladesh, India, Sri Lanka); Hachette UK Ltd (Matt Cowdery) (Israel, Middle East, North Africa); Hachette UK Ltd (Paul Kenny) (Myanmar, Papua New Guinea); Chris Humphrys & Linda Hopkins (Caribbean); Intermedia Americana Ltd (David Williams) (South America); Octopus Books USA (USA); Padovani Books Ltd (Jenny Padovani) (Gibraltar, Portugal, Spain); Padovani Books Ltd (Penny Padovani) (Greece, Italy); Anita Zih-De Haan (Sub-Saharan Africa)
Orders to: Littlehampton Book Services Ltd, Faraday Close, Durrington, Worthing, West Sussex BN13 3RB Tel: (01903) 828500; (01903) 828501 (customer service) Web Site: lbsltd.wp.hachette.co.uk

Old Barn Books Ltd
Warren Barn, Bedham Rd, Fittleworth, Pulborough, West Sussex RH20 1JW
Tel: (01798) 865010
E-mail: info@oldbarnbooks.com
Web Site: www.oldbarnbooks.com
Key Personnel
Publisher: David Ellwand; Ruth Huddleston
E-mail: ruth@oldbarnbooks.com
Founded: 2015
ISBN Prefix(es): 978-1-91064
Number of titles published annually: 12 Print
Foreign Rep(s): Walker Books (Australia)
Distribution Center: Bounce Sales & Marketing Ltd, 320 City Rd, London EC1V 2NZ, Trade Sales Dir: Sam Webster Tel: (020) 7138 3650 E-mail: sales@bouncemarketing.co.uk Web Site: www.bouncemarketing.co.uk

Old House Books
Kemp House, Chawley Park, Botley, Cumnor Hill, Oxford OX2 9PH
Tel: (01865) 811332 Fax: (01865) 242009
Web Site: www.bloomsbury.com
ISBN Prefix(es): 978-1-873590; 978-1-908402
Distribution Center: The Book Service Ltd, Distribution Centre, Colchester Rd, Frating Green, Colchester, Essex CO7 7DW Tel: (01206) 256000 Fax: (01206) 255715 E-mail: orders@tbs-ltd.co.uk Web Site: www.thebookservice.co.uk
Random House Inc, 400 Hahn Rd, Westminster, MD 21157, United States

Old Pond Publishing Ltd
Benchmark House, 8 Smithy Wood Dr, Sheffield S35 1QN
Tel: (0114) 240 9930 Fax: (0114) 303 0085
Web Site: www.oldpond.com
Founded: 1998
Specialize in books in the land-based industries: farmers & smallholders, workers in the earth-

moving, forestry & heavy transport occupations.
Subjects: Agriculture, Animals, Pets, Transportation, Veterinary Science
ISBN Prefix(es): 978-1-903366; 978-1-905523; 978-0-9533651; 978-1-906853
Number of titles published annually: 15 Print
Total Titles: 100 Print
Parent Company: 5m Enterprises Ltd
Ultimate Parent Company: Benchmark

Old Street Publishing
c/o Parallel.net, 8 Hurlingham Business Park, Sullivan Rd, London SW6 3DU
Tel: (01874) 731 222
E-mail: info@oldstreetpublishing.co.uk
Web Site: www.oldstreetpublishing.co.uk
Key Personnel
Mng Dir: Ben Yarde-Buller
Founded: 2006
Subjects: Fiction, Nonfiction (General)
ISBN Prefix(es): 978-1-905847; 978-1-906964; 978-1-908699
Foreign Rep(s): Bill Bailey Publishers Representatives (Europe); Faber Factory Plus (Australia, South Africa, UK); Mullet Fitzpatrick (Ireland); Sales East (Asia)
Distribution Center: Grantham Book Services, Trent Rd, Grantham, Lincs NG31 7XQ
Tel: (01476) 541000 E-mail: orders@gbs.tbs-ltd.co.uk

Old Vicarage Publications
The Old Vicarage, Reades Lane, Dane in Shaw, Congleton, Cheshire CW12 3LL
Tel: (01260) 279276 Fax: (01260) 298649
Key Personnel
Proprietor: William Ball E-mail: wbbtov@gmail.com
Founded: 1983
Subjects: Ethnicity, Film, Video, Regional Interests, Travel & Tourism
ISBN Prefix(es): 978-0-900269; 978-0-947818; 978-0-9508635
Imprints: Centaur Books

Oldcastle Books Ltd+
PO Box 394, Harpenden, Herts AL5 1XJ
Tel: (01582) 766348 Fax: (01582) 766348
E-mail: info@noexit.co.uk
Web Site: www.oldcastlebooks.co.uk; www.noexit.co.uk
Key Personnel
Dir & Foreign Rights: Ion Mills
E-mail: ionmills@noexit.co.uk
Marketing Manager: Frances Teehan Tel: (07704) 371693 (cell)
Founded: 1985
No unsolicited manuscripts.
Subjects: Crafts, Games, Hobbies, Fiction, Mysteries, Suspense, Crime Fiction, Gambling, Noir Fiction
ISBN Prefix(es): 978-0-948353; 978-1-874061; 978-1-901982; 978-1-84243; 978-1-904915
Imprints: Creative Essentials; Highstakes; Kamera Books; No Exit Press; Pocket Essentials; Pulp! The Classics
Branch Office(s)
21 Great Ormond St, London WC1N 3JB
Tel: (020) 7430 1021 Fax: (020) 7430 0021
Web Site: www.thebigbookshop.co.uk
Foreign Rep(s): Codasat (Canada); John Fitzpatrick (Ireland); Gill (Paul Neilan) (Ireland); Gunnar Lie & Associates Ltd (John Edgeler) (Caribbean, Cyprus, Greece, Middle East, Netherlands, Scandinavia); Gunnar Lie & Associates Ltd (Guillaume Ferrand) (Belgium, Central America, Eastern Europe, France, Gibraltar, Italy, Luxembourg, Malta, Portugal, South America, Spain); Gunnar Lie & Associates Ltd (Africa, Indian subcontinent, Southeast Asia); New South Books (Australia, New

Zealand); Lorie Ocampo (China, Hong Kong, Japan, Korea, Philippines, Taiwan); Pansing Distribution Pte Ltd (Malaysia, Singapore); Publishers Services (Gabriele Kern) (Austria, Germany, Switzerland); Research Press (Ajay Parmer) (India); Trafalgar Square Publishing (USA); Turnaround (Andy Webb) (UK); Wild Dog Press (Nicola O'Flynn-Madden) (South Africa)
Foreign Rights: Biagi Rights Management (Linda Biagi) (USA)
Distribution Center: Turnaround, 3 Olympia Trading Estate, Coburg Rd, London N22 6TZ
Tel: (020) 8829 3000 *Fax:* (020) 8881 5088
E-mail: julie@turnaround-uk.com

The Oleander Press+
16 Orchard St, Cambridge, Cambs CB1 1JT
Tel: (01638) 500784
E-mail: editor@oleanderpress.com
Web Site: oleanderpress.com
Key Personnel
Mng Dir: Jon Gifford
Founded: 1960
Specialize in travel, local history & classic fiction.
Subjects: Biography, Memoirs, Crafts, Games, Hobbies, Drama, Theater, Fiction, History, Language Arts, Linguistics, Literature, Literary Criticism, Essays, Poetry, Regional Interests, Travel & Tourism, Arabian Peninsula, Monographs
ISBN Prefix(es): 978-0-900891; 978-0-902675; 978-0-906672; 978-1-909349; 978-1-909349; 978-1-909349
Number of titles published annually: 6 Print
Total Titles: 120 Print

Michael O'Mara Books Ltd+
9 Lion Yard, Tremadoc Rd, London SW4 7NQ
Tel: (020) 7720 8643 *Fax:* (020) 7627 3041 (UK sales/publicity); (020) 7627 4900 (foreign sales)
E-mail: enquiries@mombooks.com
Web Site: www.mombooks.com
Key Personnel
Chairman: Michael O'Mara
Mng Dir: Lesley O'Mara
Head, Publicity: Saskia Angenet
Head, UK Sales & Export: Louise Hall
E-mail: louise.hall@mombooks.com
UK Sales: Madeleine Ovenden
E-mail: madeleine.ovenden@mombooks.com
Foreign Sales Manager: Helen Pickford; Mauro Spagnol *E-mail:* mauro.spagnol@mombooks.com
Founded: 1985
Subjects: Art, Biography, Memoirs, Fiction, History, Humor, Nonfiction (General)
ISBN Prefix(es): 978-1-85479; 978-0-948397; 978-1-84317; 978-1-904613; 978-1-903840; 978-1-905158 (Buster Books); 978-1-906082 (Buster Books); 978-0-946429; 978-1-907151; 978-1-78243
Number of titles published annually: 80 Print
Imprints: Buster Books (juvenile list)
Foreign Rep(s): A-Z Africa Book Services (Anita Zih-De Haan) (Africa exc Algeria, Egypt, Libya, Morocco, South Africa & Tunisia); Jonathan Ball Publishers (Bradley Lutz) (South Africa); Everest International Publishing Services (Wei Zhao) (China); Hardie Grant Books (Australia, New Zealand); Little, Brown Book Group (Simon McArt) (worldwide exc Africa, Australia, Caribbean, China, Latin America, New Zealand & South Africa); David Williams (Caribbean, Latin America)
Distribution Center: Littlehampton Book Services Ltd, Faraday Close, Durrington, West Sussex BN13 3RB *Tel:* (01903) 828 800 *Fax:* (01903) 828 802 *E-mail:* orders@lbsltd.co.uk

Omnibus Press+
Imprint of Music Sales Group
14/15 Berners St, London W1T 3LJ
Tel: (020) 7612 7400; (01284) 705050 (orders)
Fax: (020) 7612 7545; (01284) 702595 (orders)
E-mail: info@omnibuspress.com; orders@musicsales.co.uk
Web Site: www.omnibuspress.com
Key Personnel
Editor-in-Chief: Chris Charlesworth *E-mail:* chris.charlesworth@musicsales.co.uk
Commercial Dir: Chris Hargrave *E-mail:* chris.hargrave@musicsales.co.uk
Rights Manager: Helen Donlon
E-mail: hdonlon@well.com
Founded: 1976
Subjects: Biography, Memoirs, Music, Dance
ISBN Prefix(es): 978-0-7119; 978-0-86001; 978-0-9657122; 978-1-84609; 978-1-84938; 978-1-78038; 978-1-78305
Imprints: Amsco Publications; Bobcat Books; Proteus; Vision On; WISE Publications; Zomba Books
U.S. Office(s): Music Sales Corp, 257 Park Ave S, New York, NY 10010, United States
Tel: 212-254-2100 *Fax:* 212-254-2013
E-mail: info@musicsales.com *Web Site:* www.musicsales.com
Distributor for BBC Music Guides; Firefly; Gramophone; OZONE; Parker Mead; RED Independent Music Press; Rogan House; Showcase Publications
Foreign Rep(s): Bosworth Music GmbH (Germany); Butler Sims Ltd (Ireland, Northern Ireland); Exhibitions International (Marleen Geukens) (Belgium, Luxembourg); Humphrys Roberts Associates (Chris Humphrys & Lynda Hopkins) (Caribbean, Central America, Costa Rica, Mexico); IMA/Intermediaamericana (David Williams) (South America); Ingram Publisher Services (USA); Gabriele Kern (Austria, Germany, Switzerland); Login Canada (Canada); Macmillan Publishers NZ Ltd (Australia, New Zealand); Katie McNeish (Scandinavia); Music Sales Corp (Canada, USA); Nilsson & Lamm (Els van Boggelen) (Netherlands); Padovani Books Ltd (Penny & Jenny Padovani) (Gibraltar, Italy, Portugal, Spain); Publishers International Marketing (Chris Ashdown) (North Asia, Southeast); Publishers International Marketing (Ray Potts) (South Asia); Dennis Segrue (UK); Trinity Books CC (South Africa); Peter Ward Book Exports (Cyprus, Greece, Malta, Middle East, Turkey)
Warehouse: Book Sales Ltd, Newmarket Rd, Bury St Edmunds, Suffolk IP33 3YB *Tel:* (01284) 702 600 *Fax:* (01284) 768 301
Distribution Center: Book Sales Ltd, Newmarket Rd, Bury St Edmunds, Suffolk IP33 3YB *Tel:* (01284) 702 600 *Fax:* (01284) 768 301

ONE, *imprint of* Pushkin Press

Oneworld Publications+
10 Bloomsbury St, London WC1B 3SR
Tel: (020) 7307 8900 *Fax:* (020) 7307 8900
E-mail: info@oneworld-publications.com; editorial@oneworld-publications.com; marketing@oneworld-publications.com; sales@oneworld-publications.com; submissions@oneworld-publications.com
Web Site: www.oneworld-publications.com
Key Personnel
Partner: Novin Doostdar; Juliet Mabey
Sales Executive: Cailin Neal *Tel:* (020) 7307 8906 *E-mail:* cneal@oneworld-publications.com
Editor, Nonfiction: Alex Christofi
Editor-at-Large, Nonfiction: Bill Swainson
Founded: 1986
Subjects: Biography, Memoirs, Business, Fiction, History, Nonfiction (General), Philosophy, Pop

Culture, Psychology, Psychiatry, Science (General)
ISBN Prefix(es): 978-1-85168; 978-1-78074
Number of titles published annually: 50 Print
Total Titles: 500 Print
Imprints: Rock the Boat (children's & young adult)
Foreign Rep(s): Bloomsbury Publishing Pty Ltd (Australia); Book Promotions (Jonathan Ball) (South Africa); China Publishers Services Ltd (Edwin Chu) (China); Pan Macmillan (Europe, Middle East); Penguin Books India (India); Penguin Books Singapore (Malaysia, Singapore); Publishers Group West (Canada, USA); Repforce Ireland (Ireland, Northern Ireland); Tula Publishing (Sub-Saharan Africa); United Book Distributors (UBD) (Australia); The White Partnership (Andrew White) (Cambodia, Hong Kong, Japan, Laos, Philippines, South Korea, Taiwan, Thailand, Vietnam)
Distribution Center: Grantham Book Services, Trent Rd, Grantham NG31 7XQ *Tel:* (01476) 541080 *Fax:* (01476) 541061 *E-mail:* orders@gbs.tbs-ltd.co.uk
Publishers Group West, 1700 Fourth St, Berkeley, CA 94710, United States *Web Site:* www.pgw.com (USA & Canada)

Onlywomen Press Ltd+
40d St Lawrence Terrace, London W10 5ST
Tel: (020) 8354 0796 *Fax:* (020) 8960 2817
Founded: 1974
Independent lesbian feminist publishers.
Subjects: Fiction, History, LGBTQ, Nonfiction (General), Poetry, Women's Studies
ISBN Prefix(es): 978-0-906500
Number of titles published annually: 3 Print
Total Titles: 45 Print
Foreign Rep(s): Bulldog Books Pty Ltd (Australia); Central Books Ltd (Europe, UK)

Open Gate Press Ltd+
51 Achilles Rd, London NW6 1DZ
Tel: (020) 7431 4391 *Fax:* (020) 7431 5129
E-mail: books@opengatepress.co.uk
Web Site: www.opengatepress.co.uk
Key Personnel
Dir: Jeannie Cohen; Sandra Lovell; Elizabeth Petersdorff
Founded: 1988
Subjects: Anthropology, Archaeology, Economics, Government, Political Science, Philosophy, Psychology, Psychiatry, Social Sciences, Sociology
ISBN Prefix(es): 978-0-900001; 978-1-871871
Imprints: Centaur Press
Distributor for Cambridge International Publishers
Orders to: Book Representation & Distribution Ltd, 244-A London Rd, Hadleigh, Essex SS7 2DE

Open University Press+
c/o McGraw-Hill House, Shoppenhangers Rd, Maidenhead, Berks SL6 2QL
Tel: (01628) 502500; (01628) 502720 (customer service) *Fax:* (01628) 635895 (customer service)
E-mail: enquiries@openup.co.uk; emea_orders@mcgraw-hill.com (orders); emea_queries@mcgraw-hill.com (customer service)
Web Site: www.mheducation.com; www.mcgrawhillcreate.com/openup
Key Personnel
Divisional Dir: Jim Voute
Head, Production: Beverley Shields
Founded: 1977
Subjects: Behavioral Sciences, Child Care & Development, Communications, Criminology, Education, Government, Political Science, Health, Nutrition, How-to, Journalism, Management, Medicine, Nursing, Dentistry, Psychology, Psy-

chiatry, Social Sciences, Sociology, Women's Studies
ISBN Prefix(es): 978-0-335
Parent Company: McGraw-Hill Education
Ultimate Parent Company: The McGraw-Hill Companies

Open University Worldwide Ltd+
East Perry Bldg, 1st floor, Walton Hall, Milton Keynes MK7 6AA
Tel: (01908) 274066 *Fax:* (01908) 858787
E-mail: general-enquiries@open.ac.uk
Web Site: www.open.ac.uk
Founded: 1977
Subjects: Architecture & Interior Design, Astronomy, Behavioral Sciences, Biological Sciences, Business, Chemistry, Chemical Engineering, Child Care & Development, Communications, Computer Science, Developing Countries, Disability, Special Needs, Earth Sciences, Economics, Education, Electronics, Electrical Engineering, Energy, Engineering (General), English as a Second Language, Environmental Studies, Geography, Geology, Government, Political Science, Health, Nutrition, History, Language Arts, Linguistics, Literature, Literary Criticism, Essays, Management, Marketing, Mathematics, Mechanical Engineering, Music, Dance, Natural History, Nonfiction (General), Philosophy, Physical Sciences, Physics, Poetry, Psychology, Psychiatry, Religion - Buddhist, Religion - Catholic, Religion - Hindu, Religion - Islamic, Religion - Jewish, Religion - Protestant, Religion - Other, Science (General), Social Sciences, Sociology, Technology, Theology, Art History, Arts & Humanities, Biology, Classical Studies, Cultural & Media Studies, Statistics
ISBN Prefix(es): 978-0-7492; 978-1-84873
Branch Office(s)
110 Victoria St, Belfast BT1 3GN *Tel:* (028) 9024 5025 *Fax:* (028) 9053 6208 *E-mail:* ireland@open.ac.uk
66 High St, Harborne, Birmingham B17 9NB *Tel:* (0121) 426 1661 *Fax:* (0121) 427 9484 *E-mail:* west-midlands@open.ac.uk
Cintra House, 12 Hills Rd, Cambridge, Cambs CB2 1PF *Tel:* (01223) 364721 *Fax:* (01223) 355207 *E-mail:* east-of-england@open.ac.uk
18 Custom House St, Cardiff CF10 1AP *Tel:* (029) 2047 1019 *Fax:* (029) 2038 8132 *E-mail:* wales@open.ac.uk
St James's House, 150 London Rd, East Grinstead RH19 1HG *Tel:* (01342) 327821 *Fax:* (01342) 317411 *E-mail:* south-east@open.ac.uk
10 Drumsheugh Gardens, Edinburgh EH3 7QJ *Tel:* (0131) 226 3851 *Fax:* (0131) 220 6730 *E-mail:* scotland@open.ac.uk
Abbots Hill, Baltic Business Quarter, Gateshead NE8 3DF *Tel:* (0191) 477 6100 *Fax:* (0191) 202 6968 *E-mail:* north@open.ac.uk
2 Trevelyan Sq, Boar Lane, Leeds LS1 6ED *Tel:* (0113) 2444431 *Fax:* (0113) 2341862 *E-mail:* yorkshire@open.ac.uk
1-11 Hawley Crescent, Camden Town, London NW1 8NP *Tel:* (020) 7485 6597 *Fax:* (020) 7556 6196 *E-mail:* london@open.ac.uk
Foxcombe Hall, Boars Hill, Oxford OX1 5HR *Tel:* (01865) 327000 *Fax:* (01865) 736288 *E-mail:* south@open.ac.uk
351 Altrincham Rd, Sharston, Manchester M22 4UN *Tel:* (0161) 998 7272 *Fax:* (0161) 945 3356 *E-mail:* north-west@open.ac.uk
Clarendon Park, Clumber Ave, Sherwood Rise, Nottingham, Notts NG5 1AH *Tel:* (0115) 962 5451 *Fax:* (0115) 971 5575 *E-mail:* east-midlands@open.ac.uk
Foreign Rep(s): Cinehollywood Srl (Italy); Films for the Humanities & Sciences (Canada, USA); GMR & Consulting Co Ltd (Korea); Insight Media Inc (USA); On Target Training Sdn Bhd (Malaysia, Singapore, Thailand); Technear Iberica SL (Argentina, Bolivia, Colom-

bia, Ecuador, Mexico, Paraguay, Peru, Spain, Uruguay, Venezuela); Video Education Australasia Pty Ltd (Australia, New Zealand)

Opus Book Publishing Ltd
20 The Strand, Steeple Ashton, Trowbridge, Wilts BA14 6EP
Tel: (01380) 871354 *Fax:* (01380) 871354
E-mail: opus@dmac.co.uk
Web Site: www.opusbooks.co.uk
Key Personnel
Contact: Diana van der Klugt
Specialize in publishing & promoting directories & guides for the boat & leisure industry in the UK & continental Europe.
Subjects: Maritime
ISBN Prefix(es): 978-1-898574

Opus Publishing Ltd
36 Camden Sq, London NW1 9XA
Tel: (020) 7267 1034
E-mail: opuspub@btconnect.com
Key Personnel
President: Martin Heller
Subjects: History
ISBN Prefix(es): 978-0-9535546

Orbit, *imprint of* Little, Brown Book Group

Orchard Books, *imprint of* Hachette Children's Books

Ordnance Survey
Explorer House, Adanac Dr, Southampton SO16 0AS
Tel: (03456) 05 05 05
E-mail: customerservices@os.uk
Web Site: www.ordnancesurvey.co.uk
Key Personnel
Acting Dir General & Chief Executive: Neil Ackroyd
Dir, Finance & Corporate Services: Ian Nunn
Dir, Products: Peter Ter Haar
Commercial Dir: Andrew Loveless
Dir, Marketing & Communications: Katie Powell
ISBN Prefix(es): 978-0-319

Orenda Books
16 Carson Rd, West Dulwich, London SE21 8HU
E-mail: info@orendabooks.co.uk
Web Site: orendabooks.co.uk
Key Personnel
Founder & Publisher: Karen Sullivan
Subjects: Fiction, Mysteries, Suspense
ISBN Prefix(es): 978-1-910633
Distribution Center: Faber Factory, 74-77 Great Russell St, London WC1B 3DA, Account Executive: Matthew Howard *Tel:* (020) 7927 3913 *E-mail:* factory@faber.co.uk *Web Site:* www.faberfactory.co.uk (international ebook sales)
Turnaround Publisher Services, Olympia Trading Estate, Unit 3, Coburg Rd, Wood Green, London N22 6TZ *Tel:* (020) 8829 3000 *Fax:* (020) 8881 5088 *E-mail:* orders@turnaround.uk.com *Web Site:* www.turnaround-uk.com (UK & Europe)
Trafalgar Square Publishing, c/o Independent Publishers Group (IPG), 814 N Franklin St, Chicago, IL 60610, United States *Tel:* 312-568-5448 *Fax:* 312-337-5985 *E-mail:* orders@ipgbook.com *Web Site:* www.ipgbook.com

Original English Language Fiction, *imprint of* Dedalus Ltd

Orion Books, *imprint of* Orion Publishing Group Ltd

Orion Children's, *imprint of* Orion Publishing Group Ltd

Orion Publishing Group Ltd+
Division of Hachette UK
Carmelite House, 50 Victoria Embankment, London EC4Y 0DZ
Tel: (020) 7873 6444
Web Site: www.orionbooks.co.uk
Key Personnel
Deputy Publisher: Amanda Harris
Publishing Dir: Anna Valentine
Publishing Dir, Gollancz: Gillian Redfearn
Associate Publisher, Gollancz: Simon Spanton
Mng Dir: Katie Espiner
Digital Marketing Dir: Marissa Hussey *E-mail:* marissa.hussey@orionbooks.co.uk
Editorial Dir, Fiction: Genevieve Pegg
Editorial Dir, Orion Children's: Helen Thomas
Group Marketing Dir: Sarah Benton
Deputy Marketing Dir, Fiction: Jessica Htay *E-mail:* jessica.htay@orionbooks.co.uk
Deputy Marketing Dir, Nonfiction: Claire Brett *E-mail:* claire.brett@orionbooks.co.uk
Group Publicity & Communications Dir: Helen Richardson *E-mail:* helen.richardson@orionbooks.co.uk
Deputy Publicity Dir, Fiction: Gaby Young *E-mail:* gaby.young@orionbooks.co.uk
Deputy Publicity Dir, Nonfiction: Elizabeth Allen *E-mail:* elizabeth.allen@orionbooks.co.uk
Sales Dir: Jo Carpenter
Head, Brand Development: Louisa Macpherson *E-mail:* louisa.macpherson@orionbooks.co.uk
Founded: 1991
Subjects: Antiques, Biography, Memoirs, Cookery, Criminology, Fashion, Fiction, Foreign Countries, Gardening, Plants, Geography, Geology, Health, Nutrition, History, House & Home, How-to, Humor, Military Science, Mysteries, Suspense, Natural History, Nonfiction (General), Outdoor Recreation, Photography, Poetry, Romance, Science Fiction, Fantasy, Self-Help, Sports, Athletics, Travel & Tourism, Western Fiction, Wine & Spirits, Women's Studies
ISBN Prefix(es): 978-0-304; 978-0-575; 978-1-85881; 978-0-460; 978-1-85797; 978-1-85798; 978-1-84188; 978-0-7528; 978-1-4091; 978-1-86047; 978-1-84255; 978-1-905619; 978-1-78062; 978-0-85782; 978-1-4072; 978-1-4719
Ultimate Parent Company: Lagardere Group
Associate Companies: Dent Children; Everyman; Millenium; Phoenix; Phoenix House
Imprints: JM Dent; Gateway (science fiction & fantasy); Gollancz (science fiction, fantasy & horror); Indigo (young adult science fiction & fantasy); Orion Books (fiction); Orion Children's (books for young readers); Spring (well-being & lifestyle); Trapeze (commercial fiction & nonfiction); Weidenfeld & Nicolson (fiction & nonfiction)
Foreign Rep(s): Jonathan Ball Publishers (South Africa); Everest International Publishing Services (China); Hachette Australia (Australia); Hachette Book Publishing India Pvt Ltd (India); Hachette Canada (Canada); Hachette Ireland (Ireland); Hachette Middle East (Matthew Cowdery) (Middle East); Hachette New Zealand (New Zealand); Hachette UK Ltd (Asia) (Paul Kenny) (Asia); Pansing Distribution Times Centre (Malaysia, Singapore)
Warehouse: Littlehampton Book Services Ltd, Faraday Close, Durrington, Worthing, West Sussex BN13 3RB *Tel:* (01903) 828500; (01903) 828501 (customer service) *Web Site:* lbsltd.wp.hachette.co.uk
Orders to: Littlehampton Book Services Ltd, Faraday Close, Durrington, Worthing, West Sussex BN13 3RB *Tel:* (01903) 828500; (01903) 828501 (customer service) *Web Site:* lbsltd.wp.hachette.co.uk

Orkney Press Ltd+
One Linksfield Court, Elgin, Morayshire IV30 5JB

Tel: (01343) 540844
Key Personnel
Dir: Howie Firth
Founded: 1981
Subjects: Anthropology, Archaeology, History, Maritime, Natural History, Philosophy, Science (General)
ISBN Prefix(es): 978-0-907618
Imprints: Aurora Northern Classics; Scottish Falcon

Orpheus Books Ltd+
6 Church Green, Witney, Oxon OX28 4AW
Tel: (01993) 774949 *Fax:* (01993) 700330
E-mail: info@orpheusbooks.com
Web Site: www.orpheusbooks.com
Key Personnel
Dir: Sarah Hartley
Founded: 1992
Create & produce illustrated nonfiction books for children.
Subjects: Animals, Pets, Astronomy, Earth Sciences, Geography, Geology, History, Natural History, Nonfiction (General), Science (General), Transportation
ISBN Prefix(es): 978-1-901323; 978-1-905473
Number of titles published annually: 12 Print; 40 E-Book
Total Titles: 250 Print; 40 E-Book
Associate Companies: Q-files Ltd *E-mail:* info@q-files.com *Web Site:* www.q-files.com (online encyclopedia for schools & libraries)
Foreign Rights: Rightol Media (China, Taiwan)

Osborne Books Ltd
Unit 1B, Everoak Estate, Bromyard Rd, Worcester, Worcs WR2 5HP
Tel: (01905) 748071 *Fax:* (01905) 748952
E-mail: books@osbornebooks.co.uk
Web Site: www.osbornebooks.co.uk
Key Personnel
Mng Editor: Michael Fardon
Accounts Manager: Mike Gilbert
Operations Manager: Jo Osborne
Production: Maz Loton
Sales & Marketing: Cathy Turner
Administration: Bee Pugh
Founded: 1987
Educational publisher of learning resources for accounting & business studies.
Subjects: Accounting, Business, History, Literature, Literary Criticism, Essays, Photography
ISBN Prefix(es): 978-1-872962; 978-0-9510650; 978-0-955074
Imprints: Heritage

Osprey Publishing Ltd+
Kemp House, Chawley Park, Cumnor Hill, Oxford OX2 9PH
Tel: (01865) 727022 *Fax:* (01865) 242009
E-mail: info@ospreypublishing.com
Web Site: www.ospreypublishing.com
Key Personnel
Mng Dir: Sarah Broadway
Rights Dir: Joanna Sharland
Illustrated military history from around the world with all-time greatest battles of land & air, from antiquity to the present day.
Subjects: Aeronautics, Aviation, Crafts, Games, Hobbies, History, Military Science
ISBN Prefix(es): 978-1-85532; 978-0-85045; 978-0-540; 978-1-902579; 978-1-84176; 978-1-84603; 978-1-84908; 978-0-9531399; 978-1-78096
Total Titles: 600 Print
Parent Company: Bloomsbury Publishing PLC
U.S. Office(s): Osprey Publishing Inc, 2 West 46 St, Suite 1408, New York, NY 10036, United States *Tel:* 718-433-4402
Distributor for Compendium Publishing
Distribution Center: The Book Service Ltd, Distribution Centre, Colchester Rd, Frating Green,

Colchester, Essex CO7 7DW *Tel:* (01206) 256000 *Fax:* (01206) 255715 *E-mail:* sales@tbs-ltd.co.uk *Web Site:* www.thebookservice.co.uk (worldwide exc Canada & USA)
Osprey Direct, Random House Customer Service, 400 Hahn Rd, Westminster, MD 21157, United States (USA & Canada)

Ossian Publications+
Imprint of Music Sales Group
14-15 Berners St, London W1T 3LJ
Tel: (020) 7612 7400 *Fax:* (020) 7612 7545
E-mail: music@musicsales.co.uk
Web Site: www.musicroom.com; www.musicsales.com/brands
Key Personnel
Group Chairman: Robert Wise
Group Head, Publishing & Rights: Chris Butler
Founded: 1989
Traditional Celtic music publisher, predominantly Irish.
Subjects: Ethnicity, How-to, Music, Dance, Traditional Celtic & Irish Music
ISBN Prefix(es): 978-0-946005; 978-1-900428; 978-1-84938; 978-1-78038; 978-1-78305
Distribution Center: Newmarket Rd, Bury St Edmunds, Suffolk 1P33 3YB *Tel:* (01284) 702600 *Fax:* (01284) 768301

Otter-Barry Books Ltd
Little Orchard, Burley Gate, Hereford HR1 3QS
Tel: (01432) 820972
E-mail: info@otterbarrybooks.com; sales@otterbarrybooks.com
Web Site: www.otterbarrybooks.com
Key Personnel
Publisher: Janetta Otter-Barry *E-mail:* janetta@otterbarrybooks.com
Art Dir: Judith Escreet
Sales & Marketing Dir: Gail Lynch
Head, Rights: Caterina Favaretto
Designer: Arianna Osti
Publicist: Nicky Potter
Subjects: History, Natural History, Culture
ISBN Prefix(es): 978-1-91095
Foreign Rep(s): Publishers Group Canada (Canada); Publishers Group West (USA); Walker Books (Australia, New Zealand)
Distribution Center: Bounce Sales & Marketing Ltd, 320 City Rd, London EC1V 2NZ *Tel:* (020) 7138 3650 *E-mail:* sales@bouncemarketing.co.uk *Web Site:* www.bouncemarketing.co.uk
Grantham Book Services *Tel:* (01476) 541080 *E-mail:* orders@gbs-tbs-ltd.co.uk

OUP, see Oxford University Press (OUP)

Overture Publications, *imprint of* Alma Books Ltd

Peter Owen Publishers+
81 Ridge Rd, London N8 9NP
Tel: (020) 8350 1775 *Fax:* (020) 8340 9488
E-mail: info@peterowen.com; sales@peterowen.com
Web Site: www.peterowenpublishers.com
Key Personnel
Publishing Dir: Antonia Owen
Mng Dir: Nick Kent
Founded: 1951
Subjects: Art, Biography, Memoirs, Drama, Theater, Fiction, Language Arts, Linguistics, LGBTQ, Literature, Literary Criticism, Essays, Music, Dance, Publishing & Book Trade Reference, Social Sciences, Sociology, Women's Studies
ISBN Prefix(es): 978-0-7206
Number of titles published annually: 25 Print; 30 Audio
Imprints: Istros Books

Foreign Rep(s): Angell Eurosales (Iceland, Scandinavia); Michael Geoghegan (Austria, Belgium, Croatia, Czechia, France, Germany, Hungary, Netherlands, Poland, Slovakia, Slovenia, Switzerland); Independent Publishers Group (Canada, USA); Maya Publishers Pvt Ltd (India); Peter Owen Ltd (UK exc Northern Ireland); Padovani Books Ltd (Cyprus, Gibraltar, Greece, Italy, Malta, Portugal, Spain); Stephan Phillips (Pty) Ltd (South Africa); Andrew Russell (Ireland, Northern Ireland)
Orders to: Central Books Ltd, One Heath Park Industrial Estate, Freshwater Rd, Dagenham RM8 1RX *Tel:* (020) 8525 8800 *Fax:* (020) 8599 2694 *E-mail:* orders@centralbooks.com
Web Site: www.centralbooks.com

Oxbow Books
The Old Music Hall, 106-108 Cowley Rd, Oxford, Oxon OX4 1JE
Tel: (01865) 241249 *Fax:* (01865) 794449
E-mail: orders@oxbowbooks.com; trade@oxbowbooks.com
Web Site: www.oxbowbooks.com
Key Personnel
Publishing Dir: Clare Litt *E-mail:* clare@oxbowbooks.com
Founded: 1983
Subjects: Archaeology, Environmental Studies, Classical World, Egyptology, Heritage, Middle Ages, Near Eastern Studies, Prehistory
ISBN Prefix(es): 978-0-946897; 978-1-900188; 978-1-84217; 978-1-78297
Number of titles published annually: 80 Print
Parent Company: Casemate | publishers
Foreign Rep(s): Casemate Academic (Canada, North America); Continental Contacts (Roy de Boo) (Belgium, Germany, Netherlands); Iberian Book Services (Peter Prout) (Gibraltar, Portugal, Spain); International Publishers Representatives (Middle East, Turkey); Flavio Marcello (France, Greece, Italy); Publishers International Marketing Ltd (Chris Ashdown) (Far East exc Japan, Southeast Asia)
Distribution Center: Orca Book Services Ltd, Order Dept, 160 Milton Park, Abingdon, Oxon OX14 4SB

Oxfam Publications+
Member of Oxfam International
Policy & Practice Communications Team, Oxfam House, John Smith Dr, Oxford, Oxon OX4 2JY
Tel: (020) 01292
E-mail: enquiries@oxfam.org.uk
Web Site: www.oxfam.org.uk
Key Personnel
Communications for Development: Robert Cornford
Founded: 1942
Subjects: Developing Countries, Economics, Education, Environmental Studies, Government, Political Science, Health, Nutrition, Social Sciences, Sociology, Women's Studies, Public Policy
ISBN Prefix(es): 978-0-85598; 978-971-91752
Total Titles: 130 Print
Distribution Center: Practical Action Publishing, The Schumacher Centre for Technology & Development, Bourton on Dunsmore, Rugby, Warwicks CV23 9QZ *Tel:* (01926) 634501 *Fax:* (01926) 634502 *E-mail:* publishinginfo@practicalaction.org.uk *Web Site:* www.practicalactionpublishing.org

Oxford International Centre for Publishing Studies
Richard Hamilton Bldg, Oxford Brookes University, Headington Campus, Oxford, Oxon OX3 0BP
Tel: (01865) 484967 *Fax:* (01865) 484082
E-mail: publishing@brookes.ac.uk
Web Site: www.publishing.brookes.ac.uk

Key Personnel
Dir: Angus Phillips *E-mail:* angus.phillips@
brookes.ac.uk
Founded: 1994
Graduate & undergraduate awards in book, mag-
azine & digital publishing. Publishing training,
research & consultancy.
Subjects: Journalism, Publishing & Book Trade
Reference

Oxford Picture Library, *imprint of* Chris
Andrews Publications Ltd

Oxford University Press (OUP)+
Great Clarendon St, Oxford, Oxon OX2 6DP
Tel: (01865) 556767 *Fax:* (01865) 556646
E-mail: webenquiry.uk@oup.com
Web Site: global.oup.com
Key Personnel
Chief Executive Officer: Nigel Portwood
Group Communications Dir: Rachel Goode
Group Finance Dir: Giles Spackman
Mng Dir, ELT Division: Peter Marshall
Mng Dir, Global Academic Publishing: Tim Bar-
ton
Mng Dir, OUP Spain: Jesus Lezcano
Mng Dir, Oxford Education Division: Kate Harris
Founded: 1478
Subjects: Accounting, African American Stud-
ies, Agriculture, Americana, Regional, Anthro-
pology, Archaeology, Architecture & Interior
Design, Art, Asian Studies, Astronomy, Be-
havioral Sciences, Biblical Studies, Biography,
Memoirs, Biological Sciences, Business, Career
Development, Chemistry, Chemical Engineer-
ing, Child Care & Development, Civil Engi-
neering, Communications, Computer Science,
Computers, Criminology, Developing Coun-
tries, Disability, Special Needs, Drama, The-
ater, Earth Sciences, Economics, Education,
Electronics, Electrical Engineering, Energy,
Engineering (General), English as a Second
Language, Environmental Studies, Ethnicity,
Fashion, Fiction, Film, Video, Finance, Foreign
Countries, Gardening, Plants, Geography, Ge-
ology, Government, Political Science, Health,
Nutrition, History, Human Relations, Jour-
nalism, Labor, Industrial Relations, Language
Arts, Linguistics, Law, Library & Information
Sciences, Literature, Literary Criticism, Essays,
Management, Maritime, Marketing, Mathe-
matics, Mechanical Engineering, Medicine,
Nursing, Dentistry, Military Science, Music,
Dance, Native American Studies, Natural His-
tory, Nonfiction (General), Philosophy, Pho-
tography, Physical Sciences, Physics, Poetry,
Psychology, Psychiatry, Public Administration,
Publishing & Book Trade Reference, Religion
- Buddhist, Religion - Catholic, Religion -
Hindu, Religion - Islamic, Religion - Jewish,
Religion - Protestant, Religion - Other, Science
(General), Social Sciences, Sociology, Tech-
nology, Theology, Transportation, Veterinary
Science, Women's Studies
ISBN Prefix(es): 978-0-19
Parent Company: University of Oxford
Associate Companies: The Chancellor Masters &
Scholars of the University of Oxford; Gapura
Cita (Malaysia); ITEXT Ltd; OELT Ltd
Imprints: Clarendon Press
Branch Office(s)
253 Normanby Rd, South Melbourne, Victoria
3205, Australia *Tel:* (03) 9934 9123 *Fax:* (03)
9934 9100 *E-mail:* cs.au@oup.com *Web
Site:* www.oup.com.au
Oxford University Press Canada, 8 Sampson
Mews, Suite 204, Don Mills, ON M3C 0H5,
Canada *Tel:* 416-441-2941 *Fax:* 416-444-0427
E-mail: customer.service.ca@oup.com *Web
Site:* www.oupcanada.com
Oxford University Press (China) Ltd, Warwick
House, 18th floor East, Taikoo Pl, 979 King's
Rd, Quarry Bay, Hong Kong *Tel:* 2516 3222

Fax: 2565 8491 *E-mail:* webmaster.hk@oup.
com *Web Site:* www.oupchina.com.hk
Oxford University Press India, YMCA Li-
brary Bldg, 1st floor, One, Jai Singh Rd,
Post Box 43, New Delhi 110 001, India
Tel: (011) 43600300 *Fax:* (011) 23360897
E-mail: northcare.in@oup.com *Web Site:* www.
oup.co.in
Oxford University Press Japan, 3F Sotetsu
Tamachi Bldg, 4-17-5 Shiba, Minato-ku, Tokyo
108-8386, Japan *Tel:* (03) 5444-5454 *Fax:* (03)
5444-6644 *Web Site:* www.oupjapan.co.jp
Oxford University Press East Africa Ltd, The Ox-
ford Pl, Elgon Rd, Upper Hill, PO Box 72532-
00200, Nairobi, Kenya *Tel:* (020) 2732047
Fax: (020) 2732009 *E-mail:* enq@oxford.co.ke
Web Site: www.oxford.co.ke
Oxford Fajar Sdn Bhd, No 4 Jl Pemaju U1/15,
Section U1, Hicom-Glenmarie Industrial Park,
40150 Shah Alam, Selangor Darul Ehsan,
Malaysia *Tel:* (03) 5629 4000 *Fax:* (03) 5629
4006 *E-mail:* dcs@oxfordfajar.com.my *Web
Site:* www.oxfordfajar.com.my
Oxford University Press Pakistan, No 38, Sec-
tor 15, Korangi Industrial Area, PO Box 8214,
Karachi 74900, Pakistan, Mng Dir: Ameena
Saiyid *Tel:* (0213) 5071580; (0213) 5071587
Fax: (0213) 5055072 *Web Site:* www.oup.com.
pk
Oxford University Press Southern Africa (Pty)
Ltd, Vasco Blvd, N1 City, Goodwood, Cape
Town 7460, South Africa *Tel:* (021) 596 2300
Fax: (021) 596 1234 *E-mail:* oxford.za@oup.
com *Web Site:* www.oxford.co.za
Oxford University Press Espana SA, Par-
que Empresarial San Fernando, Edificio
Atenas, Esc A Planta 1a, 28830 Madrid,
Spain *Tel:* 902876878 *Fax:* 902050447
E-mail: contactoprofesor@oupe.es *Web
Site:* www.oupe.es
U.S. Office(s): 198 Madison Ave, New York, NY
10016, United States
Bookshop(s): 116 High St, Oxford, Oxon OX1
4BZ *Tel:* (01865) 242913 *Fax:* (01865) 241701
E-mail: bookshop.uk@oup.com
Orders to: OUP Distribution Services, North Ket-
tering Business Park, Hipwell Rd, Kettering,
Northants NN14 1UA *Tel:* (01865) 556767
E-mail: bookquery.uk@oup.com

OxfordPoets, *imprint of* Carcanet Press Ltd

Packard Publishing Ltd+
14 Guilden Rd, Chichester, West Sussex PO19
7LA
Tel: (01243) 537977 *Fax:* (01243) 537977
E-mail: packardpublishing@gmail.com
Web Site: www.packardpublishing.com
Key Personnel
Mng Dir: Michael Packard
Founded: 1977
Academic book publisher & distributor.
Subjects: Agriculture, Architecture & Interior De-
sign, Biological Sciences, Environmental Stud-
ies, Gardening, Plants, Geography, Geology,
Language Arts, Linguistics, Natural History,
Elementary English & French, Landscape Ar-
chitecture
ISBN Prefix(es): 978-1-85341
Number of titles published annually: 6 Print
Total Titles: 28 Print
Imprints: Headlions; PPL

Packt Publishing Ltd
Livery Pl, 2nd floor, 35 Livery St, Birmingham
B3 2PB
Tel: (0121) 265 6484 *Fax:* (0121) 212 1419
E-mail: contact@packtpub.com; customercare@
packtpub.com; service@packtpub.com
Web Site: www.packtpub.com
Founded: 2004

Subjects: Career Development, Communications,
Computer Science, Computers, Technology
ISBN Prefix(es): 978-1-904811; 978-1-84719;
978-1-84968; 978-1-84951; 978-1-84969; 978-
1-78355; 978-1-78216; 978-1-78217; 978-1-
78328; 978-1-78398; 978-1-78439
Distributed by O'Reilly Media Inc (technology
ebook program)

Palazzo Editions Ltd+
15 Church Rd, London SW13 9HE
Tel: (01225) 326444 *Fax:* (01225) 330209
E-mail: info@palazzoeditions.com
Web Site: www.palazzoeditions.com
Key Personnel
Chief Executive Officer: Jon Rippon
E-mail: jon@palazzoeditions.com
Mng Dir: Rob Nichols *E-mail:* rob@
palazzoeditions.com
Mng Editor: Victoria Webb *E-mail:* victoria@
palazzoeditions.com
Foreign Rights: Pamela Webb *E-mail:* pam@
palazzoeditions.com
Founded: 2001
Specialize in high quality, illustrated co-editions.
Also packager.
Subjects: Architecture & Interior Design, Art, Bi-
ography, Memoirs, History
Foreign Rep(s): Bookport Associates Ltd (Joe
Portelli) (Europe)
Foreign Rights: Karlov Marketing Services Pty
Ltd (Georg Karlov) (Australia); Manuela
Kerkhoff (Germany)
Distribution Center: D J Segrue Ltd, 9 Church
Rd, 1st floor, Stanmore, Middx HA7 4AR,
Contact: David Segrue *Tel:* (020) 8420 6548
Fax: (020) 8420 6458 *E-mail:* info@djsegrue.
co.uk
Orders to: Orca Book Services, Unit A3, Fleets
Corner Industrial Estate, Poole, Dorset BH17
0HL *Tel:* (01202) 665432 *Fax:* (01202) 666219
E-mail: orders@orcabookservices.co.uk *Web
Site:* www.orcabookservices.co.uk

Palgrave Macmillan+
4 Crinan St, London N1 9XW
Tel: (020) 7833 4000
E-mail: customerservice@springernature.com;
rights@palgrave.com
Web Site: www.palgrave.com
Key Personnel
Editorial Dir, Humanities & Publisher, Theatre &
Performance: Felicity Plester *Tel:* (020) 7418
5782 *E-mail:* f.plester@palgrave.com
Editorial Dir, Politics & International Studies,
Publisher International Political Economy:
Christina M Brian *Tel:* (020) 7418 5757
E-mail: c.brian@palgrave.com
Editorial Dir, Social Science: Tamsine O'Riordan
Tel: (020) 7843 5733 *E-mail:* tamsine.
oriordan@palgrave.com
Publisher, Economics: Rachel Sangster *Tel:* (020)
7014 6549 *E-mail:* rachel.sangster@palgrave.
com
Publisher, International Relations & Security
Studies: Sarah Roughley *Tel:* (020) 7418 5783
E-mail: sarah.roughley@palgrave.com
Publisher, Literature: Ben Doyle *Tel:* (020) 7418
5714 *E-mail:* b.doyle@palgrave.com
Publisher, Philosophy: Brendan George *Tel:* (020)
7418 5798 *E-mail:* brendan.george@palgrave.
com
Publisher, Sociology & Social Policy: Sharla
Plant *Tel:* (020) 7843 4781 *E-mail:* sharla.
plant@palgrave.com
Head of Business & Publisher, Scholarly Busi-
ness & Management Business: Liz Barlow
Tel: (020) 7014 6441 *E-mail:* liz.barlow@
palgrave.com
Head, Science & Society & Publisher, Geography,
Environment & Sustainability: Rachael Ballard
Tel: (020) 7843 4725 *E-mail:* rachael.ballard@
palgrave.com

Subjects: Business, Computer Science, Economics, Engineering (General), Government, Political Science, History, Human Relations, Management, Science (General), Social Sciences, Sociology, Technology, Humanities
ISBN Prefix(es): 978-0-312; 978-0-333; 978-1-4039; 978-0-230; 978-1-137; 978-1-4641
Parent Company: Springer Nature
U.S. Office(s): One New York Plaza, Suite 4500, New York, NY 10004-1562, United States
Tel: 212-726-9200

Pallas Athene+
Archway Studios, Studio 11B, Bickerton House, 25-27 Bickerton Rd, London N19 5JT
Tel: (020) 7272 4282
E-mail: info@pallasathene.co.uk
Web Site: www.pallasathene.co.uk
Founded: 1991
Subjects: Art, Travel & Tourism
ISBN Prefix(es): 978-1-873429; 978-0-9529986
Number of titles published annually: 15 Print
Total Titles: 45 Print; 1 CD-ROM; 30 E-Book
Imprints: Pallas Guides; WOL Books
Foreign Rep(s): Iberian Book Services (Peter Prout) (Spain); IMA (Africa, Central Europe, Eastern Europe, Greece); Trafalgar Square Publishing (USA)
Distribution Center: Gardners Books, One Whittle Dr, Eastbourne, East Sussex BN23 6QH *Tel:* (01323) 521777 *Fax:* (01323) 521666 *E-mail:* custcare@gardners.com *Web Site:* www.gardners.com
Orca Book Services, Fleets Corner Industrial Estate, Unit A3, Off Nuffield Rd, Fleetsbridge, Poole, Dorset BH17 0HL *Tel:* (01202) 665432 (fulfillment UK & worldwide exc USA)
Trafalgar Square Publishing, 814 N Franklin St, Chicago, IL 60610, United States *Tel:* 312-337-0747 *Fax:* 312-337-5985

Pallas Guides, *imprint of* Pallas Athene

Pan Books, *imprint of* Pan Macmillan

Pan Books Ltd, see Pan Macmillan

Pan Macmillan+
20 New Wharf Rd, London N1 9RR
Tel: (020) 7014 6000 *Fax:* (020) 7014 6001
Web Site: www.panmacmillan.com
Key Personnel
Mng Dir: Anthony Forbes Watson
Nonfiction Publisher: Robin Harvie
Publisher, Macmillan Adult Books: Jeremy Trevathan
Publisher, Macmillan Children's Books: Belinda Rasmussen
Associate Publisher, Picador: Ravi Mirchandani
Digital & Communications Dir: Sara Lloyd
Editorial Dir, Adult Fiction Dept: Trish Jackson
Editorial Dir, Picador: Francesca Main
Communications Dir, Fiction & Partnerships: Emma Bravo
Communications Dir, Macmillan Children's Books: Katharine Smales
Communications Dir, Nonfiction & Events: Dusty Miller
Group Publicity Dir, Literary & Brands: Camilla Elworthy *E-mail:* c.elworthy@macmillan.co.uk
International Development Dir: Jonathan Atkins
Sales & Brand Dir: Anna Bond
Senior Commissioning Editor, Tor: Bella Pagan
Senior Content & Communities Editor: Rosanna Boscawen
Founded: 1947
No unsolicited manuscripts. Query first for appropriate contact details & submission process. New authors & agents for children's books should go through an agent.

Subjects: Biography, Memoirs, Education, Fiction, Health, Nutrition, History, Military Science, Mysteries, Suspense, Nonfiction (General), Poetry, Romance, Science Fiction, Fantasy, Self-Help
ISBN Prefix(es): 978-0-312; 978-0-330; 978-0-333; 978-0-283; 978-1-85283; 978-0-7522; 978-1-4050; 978-1-904633; 978-1-904919; 978-1-905716; 978-1-907360; 978-1-4472; 978-1-909621
Parent Company: Macmillan Publishers Ltd, Brunel Rd, Houndmills, Basingstoke, Hants RG21 6XS
Ultimate Parent Company: Verlagsgruppe Georg von Holtzbrinck GmbH
Associate Companies: Macmillan General Books Ltd
Imprints: Bluebird (wellness & lifestyle); Boxtree; Campbell Books (PreK); The Collector's Library (pocket hardcover classics); Kingfisher (illustrated books); Macmillan (hardcover); Macmillan Bello (digital); Macmillan Children's Books; Macmillan Digital Audio; Macmillan New Writing; Mantle; Pan Books (paperback); Picador; Sidgwick & Jackson (commercial & popular nonfiction); Tor (science fiction & fantasy)
Subsidiaries: Pan Macmillan (Australia) Pty Ltd; Pan Macmillan India
Orders to: Macmillan Distribution, Brunel Rd, Houndmills, Basingstoke, Hants RG21 6XS

Panaf Books
PO Box 1217, Bedford MK40 9AE
Tel: (01234) 340 430; (0870) 333 1192
E-mail: zakakembo@yahoo.co.uk
Web Site: www.panafbooks.com
Founded: 1968
Academic & general publications on African affairs.
Subjects: Biography, Memoirs, Government, Political Science, History
ISBN Prefix(es): 978-0-901787
Foreign Rep(s): Africa Book Centre Ltd (worldwide exc Africa); Foyles (worldwide exc Africa); Gardners Books (worldwide exc Africa); Hensteve Publications Ltd (Africa)

Papadakis Publisher
Kimber Studio, Winterbourne, Berks RG20 8AN
Tel: (0163) 524 8833 *Fax:* (0163) 524 8595
E-mail: info@papadakis.net
Web Site: news.papadakis.net
Key Personnel
Publishing Dir: Alexandra Papadakis
Founded: 1968
Specialize in books on architecture, nature, science & the visual arts.
Subjects: Architecture & Interior Design, Science (General), Nature, Visual Arts
ISBN Prefix(es): 978-1-901092; 978-1-906506
Parent Company: New Architecture Group Ltd
Bookshop(s): 11 Shepherd Market, London W1J 7PG *Tel:* (020) 7823 2323

Paperstyle Gift Line, *imprint of* Ryland Peters & Small

Parapress+
Flat 2, The Grange, 3 Broadwater Down, Tunbridge Wells, Kent TN2 5NJ
Tel: (01892) 512118 *Fax:* (01892) 512118
E-mail: office@parapress.myzen.co.uk
Web Site: www.parapresspublishing.co.uk
Founded: 1999
Specialize in animals, biography, history & militaria.
Membership(s): IPG.
Subjects: Animals, Pets, Biography, Memoirs, History, Literature, Literary Criticism, Essays, Maritime, Military Science, Music, Dance, Nonfiction (General)

ISBN Prefix(es): 978-1-898594
Number of titles published annually: 2 Print
Total Titles: 20 Print
Distributor for Whydown Books

Park Lane (Art), *imprint of* Grange Books Ltd

Parthian Books+
The Old Surgery, Napier St, Cardigan, Dyfed SA43 1ED
Tel: (01239) 615 888 *Fax:* (01239) 615 888
E-mail: parthianbooks@yahoo.co.uk; editor@parthianbooks.com
Web Site: www.parthianbooks.com
Key Personnel
Founding Partner & Commercial Dir: Richard Lewis Davies
Founding Partner & Financial Dir: Gillian Griffiths
Editor & Marketing Officer: Claire Houguez *E-mail:* c.houguez@gmail.com
Poetry Editor: Alan Kellermann
Publishing Editor: Susie Wild *E-mail:* susiewild@hotmail.com
Rights: Nikki Griffiths *E-mail:* nikkigriffiths21@yahoo.co.uk
Founded: 1993
Specialize in translations from Welsh to English.
Membership(s): Independent Publishers Group; Welsh Books Council.
Subjects: Drama, Theater, Fiction
ISBN Prefix(es): 978-0-9521558; 978-1-902638; 978-1-906998; 978-1-908946; 978-1-905762
Number of titles published annually: 6 Print
Total Titles: 26 Print
Branch Office(s)
426 Grove Ext, Swansea University, Singleton Park, Swansea SA2 8PP *Tel:* (01792) 606 605 (editorial & marketing)
Foreign Rep(s): IPG (Canada, USA)
Orders to: Central Books Ltd, One Heath Park Industrial Estate, Freshwater Rd, Dagenham RM8 1RX *Tel:* (020) 8525 8800 *Fax:* (020) 8599 2694 *E-mail:* orders@centralbooks.com
Web Site: www.centralbooks.com

Particular Books, *imprint of* Penguin Books Ltd

PasTest Ltd
Egerton Court, Parkgate Estate, Knutsford, Cheshire WA16 8DX
Tel: (01565) 752000 *Fax:* (01565) 650264
E-mail: enquiries@pastest.co.uk
Web Site: www.pastest.co.uk
Key Personnel
Market Development Manager: Hannah Brown
Founded: 1972
Subjects: Business, Medicine, Nursing, Dentistry
ISBN Prefix(es): 978-0-906896; 978-1-901198; 978-1-904627; 978-0-905635

Paternoster, *imprint of* Authentic Media

Pathfinder, *imprint of* Crimson Publishing Ltd

Pathfinder Books+
24E Fairways Business Park, Lammas Rd, London E10 7QT
Tel: (020) 7998 0959 *Fax:* (020) 7998 0959
E-mail: orders@pathfinderbooks.com
Web Site: www.pathfinderpress.com
Subjects: Developing Countries, Economics, Government, Political Science, History, Labor, Industrial Relations, Social Sciences, Sociology, Women's Studies
ISBN Prefix(es): 978-0-87348; 978-0-913460; 978-1-60488
Book Club(s): Pathfinder Readers Club
Orders to: Australia Pathfinder, Level 1, 3/281-287 Beamish St, Campsie, NSW 2194, Australia *Tel:* (02) 9718 9698 *Fax:* (02) 9718 9698 *E-mail:* pathfinderbooks@optusnet.com.au

(Australia, New Zealand, the Pacific, Southeast Asia)

Pathfinder Books/Livres Pathfinder, 6362 Fraser St, Suite 264, Vancouver, BC V5W 0A1, Canada *Fax:* 888-692-4939 *E-mail:* pathfinderbooks@telus.net (Canada)

Livres Pathfinder, BP 10130, 75723 Paris, France *Tel:* 01 40 10 28 37 *Fax:* 01 40 10 28 37 *E-mail:* livres.pathfinder@laposte.net

New Zealand Pathfinder, 188a Onehunga Mall, Onehunga, PO Box 3025, Auckland 1140, New Zealand *Tel:* (09) 636 3231 *E-mail:* pathnz@ xtra.co.nz

Pathfinder Press, PO Box 162767, Atlanta, GA 30321-2767, United States *Tel:* 404-669-0600 *Fax:* 707-667-1141 *E-mail:* orders@ pathfinderpress.com (USA, Caribbean, Latin America, East Asia; accepts online orders only)

PatrickGeorge
46 Vale Rd, Ramsgate, Kent CT11 9DA
Web Site: patrickgeorge.com
Key Personnel
Illustrator: Patrick George *Tel:* (07817) 913242 *E-mail:* patrick@patrickgeorge.com
Publisher & Rights Manager: Ann Scott *Tel:* (07773) 096080 *E-mail:* ann@ patrickgeorge.com
Founded: 2009
ISBN Prefix(es): 978-0-9562558; 978-1-908473
Foreign Rep(s): Peribo (Australia); Trafalgar Square Publishing (USA)
Distribution Center: Grantham Book Services (GBS), Trent Rd, Grantham, Lincs NG31 7XQ *Tel:* (01476) 541 080 *Fax:* (01476) 541 061 *E-mail:* orders@gbs.tbs-ltd.co.uk *Web Site:* www.granthambookservices.co.uk
Orders to: Grantham Book Services (GBS), Trent Rd, Grantham, Lincs NG31 7XQ *Tel:* (01476) 541 080 *Fax:* (01476) 541 061 *E-mail:* orders@gbs.tbs-ltd.co.uk *Web Site:* www.granthambookservices.co.uk

Pavilion, *imprint of* Pavilion Books

Pavilion Books+
One Gower St, London WC1E 6HD
Tel: (020) 7462 1500
E-mail: info@pavilionbooks.com; sales@ pavilionbooks.com
Web Site: www.pavilionbooks.com
Key Personnel
Owner & Publisher: Polly Powell
Mng Dir: David Graham
Head, Foreign Rights: Sinead Hurley *E-mail:* shurley@pavilionbooks.com
Head, International Sales: Peter Lee *E-mail:* plee@pavilionbooks.com
Head, Marketing & Publicity: Colette Whitehouse *E-mail:* cwhitehouse@pavilionbooks.com
Senior Marketing & Publicity Manager: Komal Patel *E-mail:* kpatel@pavilionbooks.com
Subjects: Architecture & Interior Design, Art, Biography, Memoirs, Cookery, Crafts, Games, Hobbies, Erotica, Fashion, Fiction, Film, Video, Gardening, Plants, History, House & Home, Humor, Nonfiction (General), Pop Culture, Radio, TV, Wine & Spirits
ISBN Prefix(es): 978-1-85753; 978-1-85561; 978-0-85177; 978-0-86283; 978-0-86288; 978-0-86101; 978-1-84138; 978-1-85585; 978-1-85028; 978-1-84065; 978-0-904609; 978-0-947553; 978-1-85833; 978-1-84333; 978-1-84340; 978-1-84411; 978-1-84458; 978-1-85600; 978-1-906388; 978-1-85470; 978-1-908449; 978-1-909397; 978-1-902616; 978-1-85993; 978-1-903954; 978-1-86222; 978-0-86124; 978-1-85841
Imprints: Batsford; Collins & Brown; National Trust; Pavilion; Pavilion Children's; Portico; Salamander

Bookshop(s): Books Pavilion, 34 Shorts Gardens, London WC2H 9PX *E-mail:* shop@ pavilionbooks.com
Distribution Center: HarperCollins Distribution, Customer Service Dept, Westerhill Rd, Bishopbriggs, Glasgow G64 2QT *Tel:* (0870) 787 1722 (UK orders); (0141) 396 3739 (export orders) *Fax:* (0970) 787 1725 (UK orders); (0141) 306 3422 (export orders) (e-mail for UK: uk.orders@harpercollins.co.uk; for export: international.orders@harpercollins.co.uk)
Orders to: HarperCollins Distribution, Customer Service Dept, Westerhill Rd, Bishopbriggs, Glasgow G64 2QT *Tel:* (0870) 787 1722 (UK orders); (0141) 396 3739 (export orders) *Fax:* (0970) 787 1725 (UK orders); (0141) 306 3422 (export orders) (e-mail for UK: uk.orders@harpercollins.co.uk; for export: international.orders@harpercollins.co.uk)

Pavilion Children's, *imprint of* Pavilion Books

Pavilion Publishing & Media Ltd
Rayford House, School Rd, Hove, East Sussex BN3 5HX
Tel: (01273) 434 943 *Fax:* (01273) 227 308
E-mail: info@pavpub.com
Web Site: www.pavpub.com
Founded: 1987
Subjects: Health, Nutrition, Medicine, Nursing, Dentistry, Social Sciences, Sociology, Disability, Special Needs
ISBN Prefix(es): 978-1-84196; 978-1-900600; 978-1-871080
Distributed by Gizmo
Distributor for Gizmo; NEC

Paxton, *imprint of* Novello & Co

Peachpit Press, *imprint of* Pearson Education Ltd

Pearson Assessment
Division of Pearson Education Ltd
Halley Court, Jordan Hill, Oxford, Oxon OX2 8EJ
Tel: (0845) 630 88 88 *Fax:* (0845) 630 55 55
E-mail: info@pearsonclinical.co.uk
Web Site: www.pearsonclinical.co.uk
Key Personnel
Manager: Alison Quainton
Founded: 1921
Subjects: Business, Disability, Special Needs, Education, Health, Nutrition, Language Arts, Linguistics, Psychology, Psychiatry, Bilingual Education, Special Education
ISBN Prefix(es): 978-0-749123
Foreign Rep(s): Artsberg Enterprise Ltd (Hong Kong); Brainworx (Ireland); Cegoc-TEA Lda (Portugal); Center za psihodiagnosticna sredstva doo (Slovenia); Chinese Behavioral Science Corp (Taiwan); ETC Consult (Ireland); InnovAct (South Africa); JvR Psychometrics (South Africa); Liban Test Editions (Lebanon); Mindmuzik Media (Pty) Ltd (South Africa); Motibo Publishing SA - Topos Greece (Greece); Naklada Slap (Croatia); OS Hungary KFT (Hungary); OS Organizzazioni Speciali SRL (Italy); Outside the Box Learning Resources Ltd (Ireland); Play & Schoolroom (PTY) Ltd (South Africa); PsychTech Ltd (Israel); Psykologien Kustannus Oy (Finland); Testcentrum Praha SRO (Czechia); Testzentrale der Schweizer (Switzerland))

Pearson Education Ltd+
Edinburgh Gate, Harlow, Essex CM20 2JE
Tel: (01279) 623623
Web Site: www.pearsoned.co.uk
Key Personnel
Contracts Dir: Brenda Gvozdanovic

Founded: 1998 (result of merger of Addison-Wesley Longman (Longman founded 1724), Financial Times Management & Prentice Hall Europe)
Multinational publisher of educational & academic textbooks & professional titles, language teaching materials & dictionaries.
Subjects: Accounting, Aeronautics, Aviation, Biological Sciences, Business, Career Development, Chemistry, Chemical Engineering, Computer Science, Criminology, Earth Sciences, Economics, Education, Electronics, Electrical Engineering, English as a Second Language, Environmental Studies, Geography, Geology, Government, Political Science, History, Language Arts, Linguistics, Literature, Literary Criticism, Essays, Management, Parenting, Personal Development
ISBN Prefix(es): 978-0-201; 978-0-582; 978-0-321; 978-0-273; 978-1-84479; 978-0-673; 978-1-4058; 978-1-84658; 978-1-84959; 978-1-84878; 978-1-84776; 978-1-4479; 978-1-292
Parent Company: Pearson UK
Ultimate Parent Company: Pearson PLC, 80 Strand, London WC2R 0RL
Imprints: Addison-Wesley; Allyn & Bacon; BBC Active; Cisco Press; Benjamin Cummings; FT Publishing; New Riders; Peachpit Press; Prentice Hall; QUE Publishing; SAMS Publishing; York Notes
U.S. Office(s): Pearson Education, 225 River St, Hoboken, NJ 07030-4772, United States
Distribution Center: Pearson Shared Services, Central Park, Unit 1, Castle Mound Way, Rugby, Warwicks CV23 0WB

Peepal Tree Press Ltd+
17 King's Ave, Leeds LS6 1QS
Tel: (0113) 245 1703
E-mail: contact@peepaltreepress.com
Web Site: www.peepaltreepress.com
Key Personnel
Mng Editor: Dr Jeremy Poynting, PhD *E-mail:* jeremy@peepaltreepress.com
Marketing Manager: Hannah Bannister *E-mail:* hannah@peepaltreepress.com
Founded: 1985
Specialize in Caribbean, African, South Asian & Black British fiction, poetry & criticism.
Subjects: Education, Fiction, History, Literature, Literary Criticism, Essays, Poetry, Social Sciences, Sociology
ISBN Prefix(es): 978-0-948833; 978-1-900715; 978-1-84523
Imprints: Caribbean Modern Classics
Foreign Rep(s): Independent Publishers Group (IPG) (Canada, USA); Intermediaamericana (David Williams) (Caribbean)
Orders to: Central Books Ltd, One Heath Park Industrial Estate, Freshwater Rd, Dagenham RM8 1RX *Tel:* (020) 8525 8800 *Fax:* (020) 8599 2694 *E-mail:* contactus@centralbooks.com *Web Site:* www.centralbooks.com

Peirene Press Ltd
17 Cheverton Rd, London N19 3BB
Tel: (020) 7686 1941
Web Site: www.peirenepress.com
Key Personnel
Founder, Publisher & Public Relations: Meike Ziervogel *E-mail:* meike.ziervogel@ peirenepress.com
Marketing: Maddy Pickard *E-mail:* maddy. pickard@peirenepress.com
Founded: 2008
Subjects: Literature, Literary Criticism, Essays, Contemporary European Literature
ISBN Prefix(es): 978-0-9562840
Distribution Center: Central Books Ltd, One Heath Park Industrial Estate, Freshwater Rd, Dagenham RM8 1RX *Tel:* (020) 8525

8800 *Fax:* (020) 8599 2694 *E-mail:* orders@centralbooks.com *Web Site:* www.centralbooks.com

Pelican History of Art, *imprint of* Yale University Press London

Pen & Sword Aviation, *imprint of* Pen & Sword Books Ltd

Pen & Sword Books Ltd+
47 Church St, Barnsley, S Yorks S70 2AS
Tel: (01226) 734222 *Fax:* (01226) 734438
E-mail: enquiries@pen-and-sword.co.uk
Web Site: www.pen-and-sword.co.uk
Key Personnel
Marketing & Business Development Manager: Jonathan Wright *E-mail:* bdm@pen-and-sword.co.uk
Sales & Rights Manager: Paula Hurst
E-mail: sales@pen-and-sword.co.uk
Founded: 1990
Subjects: Aeronautics, Aviation, History, Maritime, Military Science, Antiques & Collectibles, Family History, Local History, Military History, Nostalgia, True Crime
ISBN Prefix(es): 978-0-7232; 978-0-85052; 978-1-84415; 978-1-84468; 978-1-84832; 978-1-84884; 978-1-78159; 978-1-78383; 978-1-4738
Parent Company: The Barnsley Chronicle
Ultimate Parent Company: Acredula Group Ltd
Imprints: Leo Cooper; Frontline Books; Pen & Sword Aviation; Pen & Sword Maritime; Pen & Sword Military; Remember When; Seaforth Publishing; Wharncliffe Books

Pen & Sword Maritime, *imprint of* Pen & Sword Books Ltd

Pen & Sword Military, *imprint of* Pen & Sword Books Ltd

Penguin, *imprint of* Penguin Books Ltd

Penguin Books Ltd+
80 Strand, London WC2R 0RL
Tel: (020) 7010 3000
Web Site: www.penguin.co.uk
Key Personnel
Chairman of the Board: John Makinson
Chief Executive Officer: Tom Weldon
Group Communications Dir: Maureen Corish
Group Human Resources Dir: Neil Morrison
Group Legal Dir: Helena Peacock
Publishing Dir: Juliet Matthews
Mng Dir, Children's: Francesca Dow
Mng Dir, Penguin General Books: Joanna Prior
Publishing Dir, Michael Joseph: Maxine Hitchcock
Brand Dir & Creative Dir, Children's: Graham Sim
Communications Dir: Amelia Fairney
E-mail: afairney@penguinrandomhouse.co.uk
Digital Development Dir: Nathan Hull
Edit Dir, Portfolio: Martina O'Sullivan
Head, Licensing & Consumer Products: Susan Bolsover
Head, UK Rights: Alex Elam *E-mail:* aelam@penguinrandomhouse.co.uk
Acquisitions & New Business Manager, Children's: Richard Haines
Editor, Portfolio Penguin: Zoe Bohm
Editor, Puffin: Rebecca Lewis-Oakes
Founded: 1935
ISBN Prefix(es): 978-0-14; 978-0-670; 978-0-7181; 978-1-4059; 978-1-4093
Parent Company: Penguin Random House
Ultimate Parent Company: Bertelsmann & Pearson
Imprints: Arkana; Fig Tree; Hamish Hamilton; Michael Joseph; Ladybird; Allen Lane; Partic-

ular Books; Penguin; Penguin Life; Portfolio Penguin; Puffin Books; Ventura; Viking; Frederick Warne
U.S. Office(s): Penguin Group (USA) Inc, 375 Hudson St, New York, NY 10014, United States
Distribution Center: Trafalgar Square Publishing (USA)
Orders to: Penguin Group Distribution Ltd, Bath Rd, Harmondsworth, Middx UB7 0DA

Penguin Life, *imprint of* Penguin Books Ltd

Penguin Life
Imprint of Penguin Books Ltd
80 Strand, London WC2R 0RL
Tel: (020) 7010 3000
Web Site: www.penguin.co.uk
Key Personnel
Publishing Dir: Venetia Butterfield
Head, Communications: Richard Lennon
Tel: (020) 7010 4276 *E-mail:* rlennon@penguinrandomhouse.co.uk
Campaign Manager: Julia Murday
Tel: (020) 7010 3288 *E-mail:* jmurday@penguinrandomhouse.co.uk
Founded: 2016
Subjects: Health, Nutrition, Self-Help
ISBN Prefix(es): 978-0-241
Number of titles published annually: 10 Print
Ultimate Parent Company: Penguin Random House

The Penguin Press, *imprint of* Viking

The Pensions Management Institute
PMI House, 4/10 Artillery Lane, London E1 7LS
Tel: (020) 7247 1452; (020) 7392 7425
Fax: (020) 7375 0603
E-mail: pmiservices@pensions-pmi.org.uk
Web Site: www.pensions-pmi.org.uk
Key Personnel
Chief Executive: Vince Linnane
Professional body for employee benefit and retirement savings professionals.
Subjects: Public Administration
ISBN Prefix(es): 978-0-946242; 978-1-898785; 978-1-904120

Peony Press, *imprint of* Anness Publishing Ltd

Permanent Publications+
The Sustainability Centre, Droxford Rd, East Meon, Hants GU32 1HR
Tel: (01730) 823311 *Fax:* (01730) 823322
Web Site: www.permanentpublications.co.uk
Key Personnel
Co-Founder: Tim Harland
Publisher: Anthony Rollinson *E-mail:* tony@permaculture.co.uk
Founded: 1990
Specialize in permaculture & solutions for sustainable living.
Subjects: Agriculture, Earth Sciences, Environmental Studies, Gardening, Plants, Permaculture
ISBN Prefix(es): 978-1-85623
Number of titles published annually: 7 Print
Total Titles: 42 Print
Distributed by Chelsea Green Publishing Inc (North America)

Pesda Press Ltd
Victoria House, Plas Llwyd Terrace, Bangor, Gwynedd LL57 1UB
E-mail: info@pesdapress.com
Web Site: www.pesdapress.com
Key Personnel
Mng Dir: Franco Ferrero
Subjects: Outdoor Recreation, Canoeing, Climbing, Kayaking, Mountaineering

ISBN Prefix(es): 978-0-9531956; 978-0-9547061; 978-1-906095
Distributed by Cordee Ltd

Pevsner Architectural Guides, *imprint of* Yale University Press London

Phaidon Press Ltd+
Regent's Wharf, All Saints St, London N1 9PA
Tel: (020) 7843 1000 *Fax:* (020) 7843 1010
E-mail: enquiries@phaidon.com
Web Site: www.phaidon.com
Key Personnel
Chief Executive Officer: Keith Fox
Chairman & Chief Operating Officer: Andrew Price
Mng Dir: James Booth Clibborn
Editorial Dir: Emilia Terragni
Founded: 1923
Subjects: Architecture & Interior Design, Art, Biography, Memoirs, Cookery, Drama, Theater, Fashion, History, Photography, Travel & Tourism
ISBN Prefix(es): 978-0-275; 978-0-7148; 978-0-269
Branch Office(s)
Phaidon Sarl, 55 rue Traversiere, 75012 Paris, France *Tel:* 01 55 28 38 38 *Fax:* 01 55 28 38 39
Phaidon Verlag, Innstr 30, 10243 Berlin, Germany *Tel:* (030) 28 04 08 35 *Fax:* (030) 28 04 48 79
U.S. Office(s): Phaidon, 65 Bleecker St, 8th floor, New York, NY 10012, United States *Tel:* 212-652-5400 *Fax:* 212-652-5410 *E-mail:* ussales@phaidon.com
Foreign Rep(s): Book Promotions (South Africa); GBS (Ireland, UK); Kawade Kosan (Japan); Libridis Nederland (Belgium (Dutch-speaking), Netherlands); Logista Librodis (Spain); Messaggerie Libri (Italy, Switzerland (Italian-speaking)); Editorial Oceano de Mexico (Mexico); Grupo Oceano (Central America, South America exc Brazil); OLF SA (Switzerland); Penguin Group (Australia, New Zealand); Roli Books (India, Nepal, Pakistan, Sri Lanka); Vereinigte (Austria, Germany)

Pharmaceutical Press+
Division of The Royal Pharmaceutical Society
One Lambeth High St, London SE1 7JN
Tel: (020) 7735 9141 *Fax:* (020) 7572 2509
E-mail: pharmaceutical.press@rpharms.com
Web Site: www.pharmpress.com
Key Personnel
Chairman: Tom Moloney
Head, Publishing Services: John Wilson
Sales & Marketing Dir: Peter Goacher
UK Business Development Manager: Charlotte Mason
Founded: 1841
Subjects: Chemistry, Chemical Engineering, Health, Nutrition, Law, Medicine, Nursing, Dentistry, Veterinary Science, Pharmaceutical
ISBN Prefix(es): 978-0-85369; 978-0-85711
Number of titles published annually: 30 Print; 5 CD-ROM; 30 E-Book
Total Titles: 60 Print; 7 CD-ROM; 1 Online; 60 E-Book
U.S. Office(s): 1573 St Paul Ave, Gurnee, IL 60031, United States, Special Sales Manager: Neil Adams *Tel:* 847-623-4747 *Fax:* 847-244-6689 *E-mail:* orders_americas@pharmpress.com
Orders to: Macmillan Publishing Solutions, The Macmillan Bldg, 4 Crinan St, London N1 9XW (journals & subscriptions)

Philip's, *imprint of* Octopus Publishing Group Ltd

Philip's+
Imprint of Octopus Publishing Group
Endeavor House, 189 Shaftesbury Ave, London WC2H 8JY
Tel: (020) 7632 5400 *Fax:* (020) 7632 5405
E-mail: publisher@philips-maps.co.uk; rights@ philips-maps.co.uk; info@octopusbooks.co.uk
Web Site: www.octopusbooks.co.uk
Key Personnel
Rights & Co-Editions: Victoria Dawbarn
Founded: 1834
Specialize in world atlases, road & street atlases, astronomy, natural history & encyclopedias.
Membership(s): International Map Industry Association (IMIA); Royal Geographical Society.
Subjects: Astronomy, Geography, Geology, Natural History
ISBN Prefix(es): 978-0-540; 978-0-435; 978-1-84907
Total Titles: 300 Print
Ultimate Parent Company: Lagardere Group
Foreign Rep(s): APD Kuala Lumpur (Lilian Koe) (Malaysia); APD Singapore Pte Ltd (Ian Pringle) (Singapore); Bill Bailey Publishers Representatives (Austria, Baltic States, Belgium, Cyprus, Eastern Europe, France, Germany, Gibraltar, Greece, Iceland, Italy, Malta, Netherlands, Portugal, Russia, Scandinavia, Spain, Switzerland); Jonathan Ball Publishers (South Africa); Canadian Manda Group (Canada); Everest International Publishing Services (Wei Zhao) (China); Arturo Gutierrez Hernandez (Central America); Hachette Australia (Australia); Hachette Book Group Ireland (Ireland, Northern Ireland); Hachette Book Publishing India Pvt Ltd (Kapil Agrawal) (Bangladesh, India, Sri Lanka); Hachette Livre NZ (New Zealand); Hachette UK Ltd (Matt Cowdery) (Israel, Middle East, North Africa); Hachette UK Ltd (Paul Kenny) (Cambodia, Guam, Hong Kong, Indonesia, Japan, Laos, Myanmar, Papua New Guinea, Philippines, South Korea, Taiwan, Thailand, Vietnam); Chris Humphrys & Lynda Hopkins; Octopus Books USA (USA); Anita Zih-De Haan (Sub-Saharan Africa)
Distribution Center: InterMedia Americana Ltd, PO Box 8734, London SE21 7ZF, Contact: David Williams *Tel:* (020) 7274 7113 *Fax:* (020) 7274 7103 *E-mail:* david@ intermediaamericana.com

Phillimore & Co Ltd, *imprint of* The History Press Ltd

Piatkus, *imprint of* Little, Brown Book Group

Piatkus Books+
Imprint of Little, Brown Book Group
Carmelite House, 50 Victoria Embankment, London EC4Y 0DZ
Tel: (020) 7911 8000; (020) 3122 7000
Fax: (020) 7911 8100
E-mail: info@littlebrown.co.uk; sales@ littlebrown.co.uk
Web Site: www.littlebrown.co.uk/piatkus
Key Personnel
Chief Executive Officer: Ursula Mackenzie
Publishing Dir: Tim Whiting
Editorial Dir, Fiction: Emma Beswetherick
Group Sales & Marketing Dir: Robert Manser
Rights & Contracts Dir: Diane Spivey
Founded: 1979
Specialize in general trade nonfiction & popular fiction including mass market.
Subjects: Astrology, Occult, Biography, Memoirs, Business, Career Development, Cookery, Criminology, Fashion, Fiction, Health, Nutrition, Humor, Management, Nonfiction (General), Psychology, Psychiatry, Romance, Science Fiction, Fantasy, Self-Help

ISBN Prefix(es): 978-0-7499; 978-0-86188; 978-0-34940
Number of titles published annually: 180 Print
Total Titles: 3,000 Print
Ultimate Parent Company: Hachette UK
Imprints: Piatkus Entice (ebooks)
Distributed by Hachette (Australia) Pty Ltd (Australia); Hachette Canada (Canada); Hachette (India) (India); Jonathan Ball (South Africa)
Shipping Address: Littlehampton Book Services Ltd, Faraday Close, Durrington, Worthing, West Sussex BS13 3RB *Tel:* (01903) 828500; (01903) 828501 (customer service)
Web Site: lbsltd.wp.hachette.co.uk
Orders to: Littlehampton Book Services Ltd, Faraday Close, Durrington, Worthing, West Sussex BS13 3RB *Tel:* (01903) 828500; (01903) 828501 (customer service) *Web Site:* lbsltd.wp.hachette.co.uk

Piatkus Entice, *imprint of* Piatkus Books

Picador, *imprint of* Pan Macmillan

Piccadilly Press+
Imprint of Bonnier Zaffre Ltd
Northburgh House, 10 Northburgh St, London EC1V 0AT
Tel: (020) 7490 3875
E-mail: books@piccadillypress.co.uk
Web Site: www.piccadillypress.co.uk
Key Personnel
Rights Dir: Ruth Logan
Rights Executive: Alex Dickinson *E-mail:* a. dickinson@bonnierpublishing.co.uk
Public Relations Manager: Rosi Crawley
Marketing Campaign Manager: Jen Green
Head, UK Trade Sales: Geraldine McBride
Founded: 1983
Independent children's publisher. Specialize in picture books, teenage fiction, nonfiction & parental books.
Subjects: Fiction, Humor, Nonfiction (General), Parenting
ISBN Prefix(es): 978-1-85340; 978-1-84812
Number of titles published annually: 30 Print
Total Titles: 250 Print
Ultimate Parent Company: Bonnier Publishing
Distributed by Trafalgar Square Publishing
Foreign Rights: Akcali Copyright (Turkey); Luigi Bernabo Associates (Italy); The Book Publishers Association of Israel (Israel); The English Agency (Japan) Ltd (Japan); JLM Literary Agency (Greece); KCC (Korea); Andrew Nurnberg Associates (Baltic States, Bulgaria, Czechia, Hungary, Poland, Romania, Russia, Slovakia)
Orders to: The Book Service Ltd, Distribution Centre, Colchester Rd, Frating Green, Colchester, Essex CO7 7DW *Tel:* (01206) 256000 *Fax:* (01206) 522715 *E-mail:* orders@tbs-ltd.co.uk *Web Site:* www.thebookservice.co.uk
Peribo, 58 Beaumont Rd, Mount Kuring-Gai, NSW 2080, Australia *Tel:* (02) 9457 0011 *Fax:* (02) 9457 0022 *E-mail:* peribo@bigpond.com
Merlin Publishing, Newmarket Hall, Cork St, Dublin 8, Ireland, Contact: Chenile Keogh *Tel:* (01) 453 5866 *E-mail:* chenilek@merlin.ie
South Pacific Book Distributors, Unit 1/50, Tarndale Grove, Albany, North Shore, Auckland, New Zealand, Contact: Liza Raybould *Tel:* (09) 448 1591 *Fax:* (09) 448 1592 *E-mail:* sales@soupacbooks.co.nz *Web Site:* www.soupacbooks.co.nz

Picthall & Gunzi, *imprint of* Award Publications Ltd

Picthall & Gunzi
Imprint of Award Publications Ltd

The Old Riding School, The Welbeck Estate, Worksop S80 3LR
Tel: (01909) 478170 *Fax:* (01909) 484632
ISBN Prefix(es): 978-0-9537785; 978-1-904618; 978-1-905503; 978-1-907604; 978-1-906572; 978-1-909763
Distribution Center: Bounce Sales & Marketing Ltd, Quality Court, off Chancery Lane, London WC2A 1HR *Tel:* (020) 7138 3650 *Fax:* (020) 7138 3658 *E-mail:* sales@bouncemarketing.co. uk *Web Site:* www.bouncemarketing.co.uk

Piggyback Interactive Ltd
5 Westmont Court, Monmouth Rd, London W2 4UU
Tel: (020) 7313 9232 *Fax:* (020) 7681 3626
E-mail: service@piggyback.com
Web Site: www.piggyback.com
Founded: 1998
Videogame guides.
Subjects: Crafts, Games, Hobbies
ISBN Prefix(es): 978-0-9537112; 978-1-903511; 978-1-906064
Distributed by Simon & Schuster (USA & Canada)

Pikku Publishing
54 Ferry St, London E14 3DT
Tel: (020) 7093 1614
Web Site: www.pikkupublishing.com
Key Personnel
Publisher: Elena Sapsford *E-mail:* elena@ sapsfordmail.net
ISBN Prefix(es): 978-0-9928050
Warehouse: Orca Book Services Ltd, Fleets Corner, Unit A3, Industrial Estate, Fleetsbridge, Poole, Dorset BH17 0HL *Tel:* (01235) 465521 *E-mail:* tradeorders@orcabookservices.co.uk
Distribution Center: Orca Book Services Ltd, Fleets Corner, Unit A3, Industrial Estate, Fleetsbridge, Poole, Dorset BH17 0HL *Tel:* (01235) 465521 *E-mail:* tradeorders@ orcabookservices.co.uk

Pimlico, *imprint of* The Random House Group Ltd, a Penguin Random House Company

Pimpernel Press Ltd
22 Marylands Rd, London W9 2DY
Tel: (020) 7289 7100
E-mail: enquiries@pimpernelpress.com
Web Site: www.pimpernelpress.com
Key Personnel
Publisher: Jo Christian *Tel:* (07775) 917 202 (cell) *E-mail:* jo@pimpernelpress.com
Founded: 2013
Subjects: Art, Crafts, Games, Hobbies, Gardening, Plants, House & Home, Design
ISBN Prefix(es): 978-1-910258
Distribution Center: Grantham Book Services, Trent Rd, Grantham, Lincs NG31 7XQ *Tel:* (01476) 541000 *E-mail:* orders@gbs.tbs-ltd.co.uk

Pine Forge Press, *imprint of* SAGE Publications Ltd

Pinter & Martin Ltd
6 Effra Parade, London SW2 1PS
Tel: (020) 7737 6868
E-mail: info@pinterandmartin.com
Web Site: www.pinterandmartin.com
Key Personnel
Founder & Mng Dir: Martin Wagner *E-mail:* martin@pinterandmartin.com
Co-Founder: Maria Pinter *E-mail:* maria@ pinterandmartin.com
Publishing Manager: Zoe Blanc *E-mail:* zoe@ pinterandmartin.com
Marketing Manager: Gaby Moss *E-mail:* gaby@ pinterandmartin.com

Publishing Assistant: Zoe Hutton *E-mail:* office@
pinterandmartin.com
Founded: 1997
Subjects: Art, Biography, Memoirs, Fiction,
Health, Nutrition, Literature, Literary Criti-
cism, Essays, Medicine, Nursing, Dentistry,
Psychology, Psychiatry, Breastfeeding, Con-
ceptual Continuity, Gender Studies, Parenting,
Performing Arts, Plays, Pregnancy & Birth,
Sexuality, Yoga
ISBN Prefix(es): 978-0-9530964; 978-1-905177;
978-1-78066
Number of titles published annually: 12 Print
Foreign Rep(s): David Bateman Ltd (New
Zealand); Maya Publications Pvt Ltd (Surit Mi-
tra) (India); Tom McGorry (Africa); National
Book Network (Canada, USA); Penguin Books
Singapore (Malaysia, Singapore); Woodslane
Pty Ltd (Australia)
Distribution Center: Macmillan Distribution Ltd,
Brunel Rd, Houndmills, Basingstoke, Hants
RG21 6XS *Tel:* (01256) 302692 *Fax:* (01256)
812521; (01256) 812558 *E-mail:* orders@
macmillan.co.uk

Pinwheel, *imprint of* Alligator Publishing Ltd

Pinwheel Ltd+
Imprint of Alligator Books Ltd
314 Regents Park Rd, 2nd floor, Finchley, London
N3 2JX
Tel: (020) 8371 6622 *Fax:* (020) 8371 6633
E-mail: sales@alligatorbooks.co.uk
Web Site: www.alligatorbooks.co.uk/products/
pinwheel
Key Personnel
Publishing & Sales Dir: Andrew H Rabin
Commercial Dir: Neil Rodol
Founded: 1995
Children's novelty books for preschool age.
ISBN Prefix(es): 978-1-86199; 978-1-871869;
978-1-902249; 978-1-86233; 978-1-904921
Number of titles published annually: 15 Print
Total Titles: 60 Print

Pippbrook Books, *imprint of* Templar Publishing

Pitch Publishing Ltd
A2 Yeoman Gate, Yeoman Way, Worthing, Sus-
sex BN13 3QZ
E-mail: info@pitchpublishing.co.uk
Web Site: www.pitchpublishing.co.uk
Key Personnel
Contact: Jane Camillin *E-mail:* jane.camillin@
pitchpublishing.co.uk
Subjects: Sports, Athletics
ISBN Prefix(es): 978-1-905411; 978-0-9542460;
978-1-908051; 978-1-909178
Distribution Center: LBS Ltd, Faraday Close,
Worthing, West Sussex BN13 3RB *Tel:* (01903)
828905 *Fax:* (01903) 828802 *E-mail:* team4@
lbsltd.co.uk (UK & Northern Ireland)
Trafalgar Square Publishing, c/o Independent
Publishers Group (IPG), 814 N Franklin St,
Chicago, IL 60610, United States *Tel:* 312-337-
0747 *E-mail:* orders@ipgbook.com (USA &
Canada)

Pitkin Publishing+
Imprint of The History Press
The Mill, Brimscombe Port, Stroud, Glos GL5
2QG
Tel: (01453) 883300 *Fax:* (01453) 883233
Web Site: www.thehistorypress.co.uk
Founded: 1947
Subjects: Biography, Memoirs, History, Travel &
Tourism
ISBN Prefix(es): 978-0-85372; 978-1-871004;
978-0-9507291; 978-1-84165

Number of titles published annually: 10 Print; 1
CD-ROM
Total Titles: 280 Print; 1 CD-ROM; 270 Online;
1 E-Book

Planet
PO Box 44, Aberystwyth, Ceredigion SY23 3ZZ
E-mail: planet.enquiries@planetmagazine.org.uk
Web Site: www.planetmagazine.org.uk
Key Personnel
Editor: Emily Trahair *E-mail:* emily.trahair@
planetmagazine.org.uk
Founded: 1985
Subjects: Art, Drama, Theater, Government, Po-
litical Science, Literature, Literary Criticism,
Essays, Poetry, Women's Studies
ISBN Prefix(es): 978-0-9505188; 978-0-9540881;
978-1-872106
Total Titles: 7 Print
Parent Company: Berw Cyf

Plantin Publishers+
Imprint of Cardiff Academic Press
St Fagans Rd, Fairwater, Cardiff CF5 3AE
Tel: (01222) 560333 *Fax:* (01222) 554909
E-mail: info@drakeav.com
Web Site: www.drakeav.com
Key Personnel
Mng Dir: R G Drake
Dir: M Bass; J Smith; H Y Stewart; H C
Williams
Founded: 1987
Specialize in publishing reprints of out-of-print
titles, usually out-of-copyright.
Subjects: Biography, Memoirs, Literature, Liter-
ary Criticism, Essays
ISBN Prefix(es): 978-1-870495
Ultimate Parent Company: Drake Group

Platform 5 Publishing Ltd
52 Broadfield Rd, Sheffield S8 0XJ
Tel: (0114) 255 2625 *Fax:* (0114) 255 2471
E-mail: sales@platform5.com
Web Site: www.platform5.com
Key Personnel
Editor: David Haydock
Founded: 1984
Subjects: Transportation
ISBN Prefix(es): 978-0-906579; 978-1-872524;
978-1-902336
Distributor for Quail Map Co (UK exc South of
England); South Coast Transport Publishing

The Playwrights Publishing Co
70 Nottingham Rd, Burton Joyce, Notts NG14
5AL
Tel: (01159) 313356
E-mail: playwrightspublishingco@yahoo.com
Web Site: www.playwrightspublishing.co.uk
Key Personnel
Dir: Liz Breeze; Tony Breeze
Founded: 1990
Publisher of one-act & full-length plays on the
Internet.
Subjects: Drama, Theater
ISBN Prefix(es): 978-1-873130
Number of titles published annually: 12 Print; 12
E-Book
Total Titles: 45 Print; 12 E-Book

Plexus Publishing Ltd+
The Studio, Hillgate Pl, 18-20 Balham Hill, Lon-
don SW12 9ER
Tel: (020) 8673 9230 *Fax:* (020) 8675 9424
E-mail: plexus@plexusuk.demon.co.uk
Web Site: www.plexusbooks.com
Key Personnel
Dir: Sandra Wake
Founded: 1973
Publish illustrated nonfiction books specializing
in international co-editions with an empha-

sis on biography, popular music, rock 'n' roll,
popular culture, art, photography & cinema.
Subjects: Art, Biography, Memoirs, Drama, The-
ater, Fashion, Film, Video, Music, Dance, Non-
fiction (General), Photography, Radio, TV
ISBN Prefix(es): 978-0-85965
Number of titles published annually: 15 Print
Total Titles: 100 Print
Warehouse: Bookpoint Ltd, 130 Park Dr, Abing-
don, Oxon OX14 4SE *Tel:* (01235) 400 400
Web Site: bookpoint.wp.hachette.co.uk
Orders to: Bookpoint Ltd, 130 Park Dr, Abing-
don, Oxon OX14 4SE *Tel:* (01235) 400 400
Web Site: bookpoint.wp.hachette.co.uk
Publishers Group West, 1700 Fourth St, Berkeley,
CA 94710, United States *Tel:* 510-528-1444
Fax: 510-528-3444

Plover Fiction, *imprint of* Colourpoint Creative
Ltd

Pluto Press
345 Archway Rd, London N6 5AA
Tel: (020) 8348 2724 *Fax:* (020) 8348 9133
E-mail: pluto@plutobooks.com
Web Site: www.plutobooks.com
Key Personnel
Mng Dir & Commissioning Editor: Anne Beech
Tel: (020) 8374 2193 *E-mail:* beech@
plutobooks.com
Mng Editor: Robert Webb *Tel:* (020) 8374 2190
E-mail: robertw@plutobooks.com
Sales Dir: Simon Liebesny *Tel:* (020) 8374 2188
E-mail: simon@plutobooks.com
Ebook & Academic Marketing Manager: Chris
Browne *Tel:* (020) 8374 2194 *E-mail:* chrisb@
plutobooks.com
Marketing Manager: Emily Orford *Tel:* (020)
8374 6426 *E-mail:* emilyo@plutobooks.com
Publicity Manager: Kieran O'Connor *Tel:* (020)
8374 6424 *E-mail:* kierano@plutobooks.com
Rights Manager: Tania Palmieri *E-mail:* rights@
plutobooks.com
Senior Commissioning Editor: David Castle
Tel: (020) 8374 6425 *E-mail:* davidc@
plutobooks.com
Commissioning Editor: David Shulman *Tel:* (020)
8374 2192 *E-mail:* davids@plutobooks.com
Founded: 1969
Independent progressive publishing.
Subjects: African American Studies, Anthropol-
ogy, Biography, Memoirs, Criminology, De-
veloping Countries, Economics, Environmental
Studies, Ethnicity, Government, Political Sci-
ence, History, Journalism, Labor, Industrial
Relations, Law, Philosophy, Social Sciences,
Sociology, Women's Studies
ISBN Prefix(es): 978-0-85305; 978-0-86104; 978-
0-7453; 978-0-902818; 978-0-904383; 978-0-
9501165; 978-1-84964
Number of titles published annually: 60 Print; 55
E-Book
Total Titles: 1,000 Print; 500 E-Book
Associate Companies: Journeyman Press
Distributor for Paradigm Publishers
Foreign Rep(s): Amos Bampisaki (Burundi,
Ethiopia, Kenya, Rwanda, Southern Sudan,
Tanzania, Uganda); Brookside Publishing Ser-
vices (Ireland, Northern Ireland); Tim Burland
(Japan); Durnell Marketing (Cyprus, Europe,
Israel); Maya Publishers Pvt Ltd (Surit Mitra)
(India)
Warehouse: Marston Book Services Ltd, 160
Eastern Ave, Milton Park, Abingdon, Oxon
OX14 4SB *Tel:* (01235) 465500 *Fax:* (01235)
465555 *E-mail:* trade.orders@marston.co.uk
Web Site: www.marston.co.uk
Distribution Center: Brunswick Books, 20
Maud St, No 303, Toronto, ON M5V 2M5,
Canada *Tel:* 416-703-3598 *Fax:* 416-703-
6561 *E-mail:* info@brunswickbooks.ca *Web
Site:* www.brunswickbooks.ca

Jacana Media (Pty) Ltd, 10 Orange St, Sunny-side, Auckland Park, Johannesburg 2092, South Africa *Tel:* (011) 628 3200 *E-mail:* sales@jacana.co.za *Web Site:* www.jacana.co.za (Botswana, Lesotho, Namibia, South Africa, Swaziland & Zimbabwe)

University of Chicago Press, Chicago Distribution Center, 11030 S Langley Ave, Chicago, IL 60628, United States *Tel:* 773-702-7000 *Fax:* 773-702-7212 *E-mail:* custserv@press.uchicago.edu *Web Site:* www.press.uchicago.edu

Orders to: Marston Book Services Ltd, 160 Eastern Ave, Milton Park, Abingdon, Oxon OX14 4SB *Tel:* (01235) 465500 *Fax:* (01235) 465555 *E-mail:* trade.orders@marston.co.uk *Web Site:* www.marston.co.uk

PN Review, *imprint of* Carcanet Press Ltd

Pocket Bibles, *imprint of* Crimson Publishing Ltd

Pocket ColorCards, *imprint of* Speechmark Publishing Ltd

Pocket Essentials, *imprint of* Oldcastle Books Ltd

Poetica, *imprint of* Anvil Press Poetry Ltd

Point, *imprint of* Scholastic Ltd

Polarworld Ltd
11 Alverton Terrace, Penzance, Cornwall TR18 4JH
E-mail: hello@polarworld.co.uk
Web Site: www.polarworld.co.uk
Key Personnel
Mng Dir: Kari Herbert *E-mail:* kari@kariherbert.com
Editorial Dir: Dr Huw Lewis-Jones
Founded: 2007
Independent publishing company specializing in illustrated books about all aspects of polar, maritime & wilderness environments.
Subjects: Art, Maritime, Photography, Arctic, Polar
ISBN Prefix(es): 978-0-9555255

The Policy Press+
1-9 Old Park Hill, Clifton, Bristol BS2 8BB
Tel: (0117) 954 5940
E-mail: pp-info@bristol.ac.uk
Web Site: www.policypress.co.uk
Key Personnel
Dir: Alison Shaw *E-mail:* ali.shaw@bristol.ac.uk
Assistant Dir & Rights: Julia Mortimer
Tel: (0117) 954 5966 *E-mail:* julia.mortimer@bristol.ac.uk
Marketing Manager: Kathryn King *Tel:* (0117) 954 5952 *E-mail:* kathryn.king@bristol.ac.uk
Production Manager: Dave Worth *Tel:* (0117) 954 5942 *E-mail:* dave.j.worth@bristol.ac.uk
Sales & Distribution Manager: Ann Moore
Tel: (0117) 954 5067 *E-mail:* ann.moore@bristol.ac.uk
Permissions: Laura Vickers *Tel:* (0117) 954 5946 *E-mail:* laura.vickers@bristol.ac.uk
Senior Commissioning Editor: Emily Watt
E-mail: emily.watt@bristol.ac.uk
Commissioning Editor: Victoria Pittman
E-mail: victoria.pittman@bristol.ac.uk
Founded: 1996
A specialist social sciences publisher, publishing books, journals & reports from leading academics & researchers. Publications provide the latest research & teaching materials in accessible formats, reaching those who formulate or implement policy at executive & grass-roots levels, as well as academics & students.

Subjects: Criminology, Disability, Special Needs, Economics, Education, Ethnicity, Geography, Geology, Government, Political Science, Health, Nutrition, Labor, Industrial Relations, Management, Public Administration, Social Sciences, Sociology, Women's Studies
ISBN Prefix(es): 978-1-86134; 978-1-873575; 978-1-84742
Number of titles published annually: 80 Print
Total Titles: 400 Print
Associate Companies: The Joseph Rowntree Foundation
Foreign Rep(s): Blue Weaver Specialist Publishers' Representatives (Mark Hackney) (South Africa); Compass Academic Ltd (UK); Durnell Marketing Ltd (Europe, Northern Ireland); Tahir Lodhi (Pakistan); Maya Publishers Pvt Ltd (Surit Mitra) (Bangladesh, Bhutan, India, Nepal, Sri Lanka); STM Publishers Services Pte Ltd (Tony Poh & Leong Wah) (China, Hong Kong, Korea, Malaysia, Philippines, Singapore, Taiwan, Thailand, Vietnam)
Distribution Center: Marston Book Services Ltd, 160 Eastern Ave, Milton Park, Abingdon, Oxon OX14 4SB *Tel:* (01235) 465500 *Fax:* (01235) 465556 *E-mail:* direct.orders@marston.co.uk *Web Site:* www.marston.co.uk
UBSD Distribution Sdn Bhd, 3f-15, IOI Business Park, One Persiaran Puchong Jaya, Selatan, Bandar Puchong Jaya, 47100 Puchong, Selangor, Malaysia *Tel:* (03) 8076 3042 *Fax:* (03) 8076 3142 *E-mail:* enquiry@ubsd-dist.com *Web Site:* www.ubsd-dist.com (Malaysia & Brunei)
Unifacmanu Trading Co Ltd, 4F, 91, Ho-Ping East Rd Section 1, Taipei, Taiwan *Tel:* (02) 2394 2749 *Fax:* (02) 2394 3103 *E-mail:* unifacmu@ms34.hinet.net *Web Site:* www.unifacmanu.com.tw
University of Chicago Press, Chicago Distribution Center, 11030 S Langley Ave, Chicago, IL 60628, United States *E-mail:* custserv@press.uchicago.edu *Web Site:* www.press.uchicago.edu (North & South America)

Polybooks Ltd+
2 Caversham St, London SW3 4AH
Tel: (020) 7351 4995 *Fax:* (020) 7351 4995
Key Personnel
Mng Editor: James Hughes
Founded: 1964
Subjects: Art, Biography, Memoirs, Communications, Erotica, Fiction, History, Literature, Literary Criticism, Essays, Nonfiction (General), Wine & Spirits
ISBN Prefix(es): 978-0-284
Number of titles published annually: 10 Print
Total Titles: 20 Print
Parent Company: Christchurch Publishers Ltd
Associate Companies: Luxor Press

Polygon, *imprint of* Birlinn Ltd

Polygon+
Imprint of Birlinn Ltd
West Newington House, 10 Newington Rd, Edinburgh EH9 1QS
Tel: (0131) 668 4371 *Fax:* (0131) 668 4466
E-mail: info@birlinn.co.uk
Web Site: www.birlinn.co.uk
Key Personnel
Mng Dir: Hugh Andrew
Founded: 1969
Subjects: Biography, Memoirs, Drama, Theater, Fiction, Film, Video, History, Humor, Literature, Literary Criticism, Essays, Music, Dance, Nonfiction (General), Philosophy, Poetry, Women's Studies
ISBN Prefix(es): 978-0-85224; 978-0-7486; 978-0-904919; 978-0-948275; 978-0-9501890; 978-1-904598; 978-1-902930; 978-0-9544075

Number of titles published annually: 30 Print; 130 Online
Total Titles: 100 Print; 130 Online
Foreign Rep(s): Casemate (USA); Interlink Publishing (USA); IPG (Canada, USA); McArthur & Co (Canada); New South Books (Australia); Penguin SA (South Africa)
Distribution Center: Booksource, 50 Cambuslang Rd, Glasgow G32 8NB *Tel:* (0845) 370 0067; (0141) 642 9192 *E-mail:* customerservice@booksource.net

Pomegranate Europe Ltd
Unit 1, Heathcote Business Centre, Hurlbutt Rd, Warwick, Warwicks CV34 6TD
Tel: (01926) 430111 *Fax:* (01926) 430888
Web Site: www.pomegranate.com/poeult.html
Key Personnel
Sales & Marketing Dir: Ms Ley Bricknell
Founded: 1985
Also acts as distributor of books, calendars, cards, postcards, posters & social stationery throughout Europe.
Subjects: Animals, Pets, Architecture & Interior Design, Art, Astrology, Occult, Crafts, Games, Hobbies, Drama, Theater, Environmental Studies, Ethnicity, Gardening, Plants, Humor, Photography, Sports, Athletics, Travel & Tourism, Women's Studies, Metaphysics, Performing Arts
ISBN Prefix(es): 978-1-85257
Parent Company: Pomegranate Communications
Imprints: Pomegranate Kids

Pomegranate Kids, *imprint of* Pomegranate Europe Ltd

Pont Books, *imprint of* Gomer Press Ltd

Popular Woodworking, *imprint of* David & Charles Ltd

Portfolio Penguin, *imprint of* Penguin Books Ltd

Portico, *imprint of* Pavilion Books

Portland Press Ltd+
Subsidiary of The Biochemical Society
Charles Darwin House, 3rd floor, 12 Roger St, London WC1N 2JU
Tel: (020) 7685 2444; (020) 7685 2410 (editorial) *Fax:* (020) 7685 2468; (020) 7685 2469 (editorial)
E-mail: editorial@portlandpress.com; sales@portland-services.com
Web Site: www.portlandpress.com
Founded: 1990
Publisher of school to research level books.
Membership(s): The Association of Learned & Professional Society Publishers (ALPSP); IPG; UKSG.
Subjects: Biological Sciences, Chemistry, Chemical Engineering, Health, Nutrition, Medicine, Nursing, Dentistry, Physical Sciences, Science (General), Biochemistry & Molecular Biology
ISBN Prefix(es): 978-1-85578; 978-0-904498
Number of titles published annually: 5 Print; 2 Online
Total Titles: 128 Print; 18 Online; 3 Audio
Imprints: Making Sense of Science

Portobello Books, *imprint of* Granta Books

Portobello Books
Imprint of Granta Books
12 Addison Ave, London W11 4QR
Tel: (020) 7605 1380 *Fax:* (020) 7605 1361
E-mail: info@portobellobooks.com; sales@portobellobooks.com; publicity@portobellobooks.com; rights@portobellobooks.com
Web Site: www.portobellobooks.com

Key Personnel
Publisher: Sigrid Rausing
Editorial Dir: Laura Barber; Bella Lacey; Max Porter
Production Dir: Sarah Wasley
Publicity Dir: Pru Rowlandson
Rights Dir: Angela Rose
Sales, Marketing & Digital Dir: Iain Chapple
Ebook & Sales Operations Manager: Katie Hayward
Mng Editor: Christine Lo
Editor: Anne Meadows
Assistant Editor: Ka Bradley
Founded: 2005
Subjects: Literature, Literary Criticism, Essays, Nonfiction (General)
ISBN Prefix(es): 978-1-84627

T & A D Poyser Ltd, *imprint of* A&C Black Publishers Ltd

PPL, *imprint of* Packard Publishing Ltd

Practical Action Publishing Ltd+
The Shumacher Centre, Bourton-on-Dunsmore, Rugby, Warwicks CV23 9QZ
Tel: (01926) 634501 *Fax:* (01926) 634502
E-mail: publishinginfo@practicalaction.org.uk
Web Site: practicalactionpublishing.org; www.developmentbookshop.com (orders)
Key Personnel
Mng Dir: Toby Milner
Mng Editor: Clare Tawney
Founded: 1973
Subjects: Agriculture, Animals, Pets, Business, Developing Countries, Education, Finance, Health, Nutrition, Social Sciences, Sociology, Technology
ISBN Prefix(es): 978-0-903031; 978-0-946688; 978-1-85339
Number of titles published annually: 25 Print
Total Titles: 400 Print
Parent Company: Practical Action
Foreign Rep(s): Book Promotions/Horizon Books (Botswana, Lesotho, Namibia, South Africa, Swaziland); Booknet (Thailand); Tim Burland (Japan); DKG Info Systems (Dipak Kumar Guha) (China, Hong Kong); Colin Flint Ltd (Ben Grieg) (Denmark, Finland, Iceland, Norway, Sweden); Footprint Books Pty Ltd (Australia, Fiji, New Zealand, Oceania, Papua New Guinea); Iberian Book Services (Peter Prout) (Portugal, Spain); InterMediaAmericana Ltd (David Williams) (Caribbean, Latin America); Lake House Bookshop (Sri Lanka); Maya Publishers Pvt Ltd (Surit Mitra) (India); MegaTexts Phil Inc (Philippines); Mirza Book Agency (Pakistan); Renouf Publishing Co Ltd (Canada); STM Publishers Services Pte Ltd (Malaysia, Singapore, Thailand, Vietnam); Stylus Publishing LLC (USA)
Orders to: NBN International, 10 Thornbury Rd, Plymouth PL6 7PP *Tel:* (01752) 202300 *Fax:* (01752) 202333 *E-mail:* orders@nbninternational.com *Web Site:* www.nbninternational.com

Practical Pictures, *imprint of* Anness Publishing Ltd

Preface Publishing, *imprint of* The Random House Group Ltd, a Penguin Random House Company

Prentice Hall, *imprint of* Pearson Education Ltd

Priddy Books
Chancery House, 53-64 Chancery Lane, London WC2A 1QT
Tel: (020) 7418 5506 *Fax:* (020) 7418 5507
E-mail: website@priddybooks.com

Web Site: www.priddybooks.com
ISBN Prefix(es): 978-1-84332; 978-1-84915
Distributed by Macmillan Children's Publishing Group (USA); Macmillan Publishers New Zealand Ltd; Pan Macmillan Asia; Pan Macmillan Australia; Pan Macmillan Books India; Pan Macmillan South Africa; Raincoast Books
Foreign Rep(s): A-Z Africa Book Services (Anita Zih) (Ethiopia, Ghana, Kenya, Malawi, Mauritius, Rwanda, Seychelles, Tanzania, Uganda, Zambia)
Distribution Center: Macmillan Distribution Ltd, Brunel Rd, Houndmills, Basingstoke, Hants RG21 6XS *Tel:* (01256) 302692 *Fax:* (01256) 812558; (01256) 812521 *E-mail:* orders@macmillan.co.uk

Pride Publishing, *imprint of* Totally Entwined Group Ltd

Primary Source Microfilm, *imprint of* Gale

The Printed Head, *imprint of* Atlas Press

Prion, *imprint of* Carlton Publishing Group

Prion
Imprint of Carlton Publishing Group
20 Mortimer St, London W1T 3JW
Tel: (020) 7612 0400 *Fax:* (020) 7612 0411
E-mail: sales@carltonbooks.co.uk
Web Site: www.carltonbooks.co.uk
Key Personnel
Mng Dir: Frank Chambers *Tel:* (020) 7612 0407 *E-mail:* fchambers@carltonbooks.co.uk
Commercial Dir: Jim Greenhough *Tel:* (020) 7612 0414 *E-mail:* jgreenhough@carltonbooks.co.uk
UK Sales & Marketing Dir: Owen Hazell *Tel:* (020) 7612 0433 *E-mail:* ohazell@carltonbooks.co.uk
Head, Marketing: Helen Churchill *Tel:* (020) 7612 0474 *E-mail:* hchurchill@carltonbooks.co.uk
Head, Publicity: Carol Farley *Tel:* (020) 7612 0416 *E-mail:* cfarley@carltonbooks.co.uk
Founded: 1980
Specialize in military history, humor, nostalgia & entertainment.
Subjects: History, Humor, Entertainment, Military History, Nostalgia
ISBN Prefix(es): 978-1-85375
Number of titles published annually: 50 Print
Total Titles: 200 Print
Foreign Rep(s): Gunnar Lie & Associates Ltd (Gunnar Lie) (Africa, Asia, Indian subcontinent); Gunnar Lie & Associates Ltd (Guillaume Ferrand) (Belgium, Central America, Eastern Europe, France, Gibraltar, Italy, Luxembourg, Malta, Portugal, South America, Spain); Gunnar Lie & Associates Ltd (John Edgeler) (Caribbean, Cyprus, Greece, Middle East, Netherlands, Scandinavia); Lorie & Michael Ocampo (China, Hong Kong, Japan, Korea, Philippines, Taiwan); Publisher's Services (Gabriele Kern) (Austria, Germany, Switzerland); Research Press (Ajay Parmer) (India)
Distribution Center: HarperCollins Distribution Services, Customer Service Dept, Westerhill Rd, Bishopbriggs, Glasgow G64 2QT *Tel:* (0141) 306 3100 *Fax:* (0141) 306 3261 *E-mail:* uk.orders@harpercollins.co.uk
Trafalgar Square Publishing, c/o Independent Publishers Group (IPG), 814 N Franklin St, Chicago, IL 60610, United States *Tel:* 312-337-0747 *Fax:* 312-337-5985 *E-mail:* frontdesk@ipgbook.com *Web Site:* www.ipgbook.com

Profile Audio, *imprint of* Profile Books Ltd

Profile Books Ltd+
3 Holford Yard, Bevin Way, London WC1X 9HD

Tel: (020) 7841 6300 *Fax:* (020) 7833 3969
E-mail: info@profilebooks.co.uk
Web Site: www.profilebooks.com
Key Personnel
Publisher & Mng Dir: Andrew Franklin *E-mail:* andrew.franklin@profilebooks.com
Publisher, Serpent's Tail & Tindal Street Press: Hannah Westland *E-mail:* hannah.westland@profilebooks.com
Editorial Dir, Profile & Serpent's Tail: Rebecca Gray
Editorial Dir, Profile: Ed Lake
International Sales Dir: Sarah Ward *E-mail:* sarah.ward@profilebooks.com
Publicity Dir: Hannah Ross
Sales Dir: Claire Beaumont *E-mail:* claire.beaumont@profilebooks.com
Editor: Louisa Dunnigan
Editorial & International Rights: Penny Daniel *E-mail:* penny.daniel@profilebooks.com
Founded: 1996
Subjects: Biography, Memoirs, Business, Criminology, Developing Countries, Economics, Environmental Studies, Ethnicity, Finance, History, Management, Marketing, Nonfiction (General), Psychology, Psychiatry, Social Sciences, Sociology, Travel & Tourism, Current Affairs
ISBN Prefix(es): 978-1-86197; 978-0-85383
Number of titles published annually: 80 Print; 20 E-Book
Total Titles: 300 Print; 40 E-Book
Imprints: The Clerkenwell Press; Profile Audio (in partnership with Little, Brown UK); Serpent's Tail; Third Millennium; Tindal Street Press
Divisions: The Economist Books
Distributed by Little, Brown UK (Profile Audio)
Distributor for The Economist Books (worldwide exc North America)
Foreign Rep(s): Allen & Unwin (Australia, New Zealand); APD Singapore Pte Ltd (Indonesia, Malaysia, Singapore, Thailand, Vietnam); Book Promotions (South Africa); Consortium Book Sales & Distribution (Canada, USA); Faber & Faber (Europe, UK); Faber & Faber (Melissa Elders) (China, Hong Kong, Japan, Korea, Macau, Taiwan); Faber & Faber (Hattie Castelberg) (North Africa, Turkey); Hachette India (Bangladesh, Bhutan, India, Nepal, Pakistan, Sri Lanka); itsabook (Jim Papworth) (Caribbean, Latin America); Repforce Ireland (Ireland, Northern Ireland)
Orders to: The Book Service Ltd, Distribution Centre, Colchester Rd, Frating Green, Colchester, Essex CO7 7DW *Tel:* (01206) 256000 *Fax:* (01206) 255715 *E-mail:* sales@tbs-ltd.co.uk *Web Site:* www.thebookservice.co.uk

ProQuest LLC
Subsidiary of Cambridge Information Group Inc
The Quorum, Barnwell Rd, Cambridge, Cambs CB5 8SW
Tel: (01223) 215 512 *Fax:* (01223) 215 513
E-mail: customerservice@proquest.com; orders@proquest.com
Web Site: www.proquest.com
Founded: 1988
Online, CD-ROM & print publisher of reference tools & professional development texts for the library & information world & publishing industry.
Subjects: Library & Information Sciences, Publishing & Book Trade Reference
ISBN Prefix(es): 978-0-8352
Number of titles published annually: 7 Print
Total Titles: 164 Print
U.S. Office(s): 789 E Eisenhower Parkway, Ann Arbor, MI 48108, United States *Tel:* 734-761-4700 (headquarters)
Foreign Rep(s): Kai-Henning Gerlach (Austria, Central Europe, Eastern Europe, Finland, Germany, Switzerland)

Proteus, *imprint of* Omnibus Press

The Publishing Training Centre at Book House+
Crowne House, 56-58 Southwark St, London SE1 1UN
Tel: (020) 8874 2718
E-mail: publishing.training@bookhouse.co.uk
Web Site: www.train4publishing.co.uk
Key Personnel
Chief Executive: Peter McKay *E-mail:* peter@bookhouse.co.uk
Founded: 1976
Training for worldwide publishing community.
Membership(s): Association of Bookseller & Publisher Training Organisations in Europe (APBTOE).
Subjects: Career Development, Publishing & Book Trade Reference
ISBN Prefix(es): 978-0-907706

Puffin Books, *imprint of* Penguin Books Ltd

Pulp! The Classics, *imprint of* Oldcastle Books Ltd

Pushkin Press
71-75 Shelton St, London WC2H 9JQ
Tel: (020) 7470 8830
E-mail: books@pushkinpress.com
Web Site: www.pushkinpress.com
Key Personnel
Publisher & Mng Dir: Adam Freudenheim
Publicist: Tabitha Pelly
Commissioning Editor: Gesche Ipsen; Daniel Seton
Editor-at-Large: Sarah Odedina
Founded: 1997
Specialize in international classics & contemporary fiction in English.
Subjects: Fiction, Literature, Literary Criticism, Essays
ISBN Prefix(es): 978-1-901285; 978-1-906548; 978-1-782271
Number of titles published annually: 20 Print; 20 E-Book
Imprints: ONE
Distributed by Penguin Random House India (Indian subcontinent)
Foreign Rep(s): Angell Eurosales (Gill Angell & Stewart Siddall) (Denmark, Finland, Iceland, Norway, Sweden); Faber Factory Plus (Ireland, UK); Michael Geoghegan (Austria, Belgium, France, Germany, Netherlands, Switzerland); Cristian Juncu (Eastern Europe, Russia); Padovani Books Ltd (Penny Padovani) (Greece, Italy); Padovani Books Ltd (Jenny Padovani) (Gibraltar, Portugal, Spain); Random House (Canada, Central America, India, South Africa, South America, USA); Peter Ward Book Exports (Richard Ward) (Middle East, North Africa); The White Partnership (Andrew White) (Far East)
Distribution Center: Grantham Book Services, Trent Rd, Grantham NG31 7XQ *Tel:* (01476) 541080 *E-mail:* orders@gbs.tbs-ltd.co.uk

QEB Publishing
Member of Quarto International Co-Editions Group
The Old Brewery, 6 Blundell St, London N7 9BH
Tel: (020) 7812 8633 *Fax:* (020) 7700 8066
Web Site: www.quartoknows.com/qeb-publishing
Key Personnel
Group Publisher: Zeta Jones *E-mail:* zeta.jones@quarto.com
Publisher: Maxime Boucknooghe
E-mail: maxime.boucknooghe@quarto.com
ISBN Prefix(es): 978-1-59566; 978-1-60992; 978-1-68297
Ultimate Parent Company: The Quarto Group Inc

QED Publishing
Member of Quarto International Co-Editions Group
6 Blundell St, London N7 9BH
Tel: (020) 7700 6700 *Fax:* (020) 7700 4191
E-mail: qedpublishing@quarto.com
Web Site: www.quartoknows.com/qed-publishing
Key Personnel
Publisher: Zeta Jones *Tel:* (020) 7812 8633
E-mail: zeta.jones@quarto.com
Associate Publisher: Maxime Boucknooghe
Tel: (020) 7812 8636 *E-mail:* maxime.boucknooghe@quarto.com
Editorial Dir: Victoria Garrard *E-mail:* victoria.garrard@quarto.com
Foreign Rights Dir: Carine Delagrave
E-mail: carine.delagrave@quarto.com
Founded: 2003
Subjects: Art, Computer Science, Geography, Geology, History, Mathematics, Religion - Other, Science (General), Technology, Design, Literacy, Natural World, Physical Education
ISBN Prefix(es): 978-0-946544; 978-1-84538; 978-1-84835; 978-1-78171
Ultimate Parent Company: The Quarto Group Inc
Foreign Rep(s): A-Z Africa Book Services (Anita Zih-De Haan) (Central Africa, West Africa); Tim Burland (Japan); China Publishers Marketing (Benjamin Pan) (China); IMA/Intermediaamericana (David Williams) (Caribbean, Central America, Mexico, South America); IPS ME Ltd (Zoe Kaviani) (Middle East, North Africa); B K Norton (Chiafeng Peng) (Taiwan); P S Publishers Services (Gabriel Kern) (Austria, Belgium, Bosnia and Herzegovina, Czechia, Denmark, Germany, Hungary, Italy, Liechtenstein, Luxembourg, Poland, Romania, Slovakia, Switzerland, Ukraine); Padovani Books Ltd (Penny Padovani) (Greece, Italy, Portugal, Spain)
Distribution Center: Littlehampton Book Services Ltd, Faraday Close, Durrington, Worthing, West Sussex BN13 3RB *Tel:* (01903) 828500; (01903) 828501 (customer service)
Web Site: lbsltd.wp.hachette.co.uk

Quad Books
Member of Quarto International Co-Editions Group
Ovest House, Level 1, 58 West St, Brighton BN1 2RA
Tel: (01273) 716009
Web Site: www.quartoknows.com/quad-books
Key Personnel
Publisher: Nigel Browning *E-mail:* nigel.browning@quarto.com
Subjects: Medicine, Nursing, Dentistry, Anatomy
ISBN Prefix(es): 978-0-85762
Ultimate Parent Company: The Quarto Group Inc

Quadrille Publishing Ltd+
Imprint of Hardie Grant Books
Pentagon House, 52-54 Southwark St, London SE1 1UN
Tel: (020) 7601 7500
E-mail: enquiries@quadrille.co.uk; sales@quadrille.co.uk; publicity@quadrille.co.uk; internationalsales@quadrille.co.uk
Web Site: www.quadrille.co.uk
Key Personnel
Publishing Dir: Sarah Lavelle
Deputy Mng Dir & Production: Vincent Smith
Creative Dir: Helen Lewis
Finance Dir: Russell Barclay
International Sales Dir: Margaux Durigon
UK & Export Sales Dir: Inez Munsch
Founded: 1994
Subjects: Architecture & Interior Design, Art, Astrology, Occult, Biography, Memoirs, Cookery, Crafts, Games, Hobbies, Gardening, Plants, Health, Nutrition, House & Home, How-to, Self-Help, Travel & Tourism, Wine & Spirits, Lifestyles, Mind, Body & Spirit

ISBN Prefix(es): 978-1-84400; 978-1-899988; 978-1-902757; 978-1-903845; 978-1-906106; 978-1-84949
Number of titles published annually: 35 Print
Total Titles: 150 Print
Distributed by Chronicle Books (North America)
Foreign Rep(s): Bloomsbury Publishing India Pvt Ltd (India); Gabriele Kern Publisher's Services (Austria, Germany, Switzerland); Gunnar Lie & Associates (Gunnar Lie) (Africa, Indian subcontinent, Southeast Asia); Gunnar Lie & Associates (John Edgeler) (Caribbean, Cyprus, Greece, Middle East, Netherlands, Scandinavia); Gunnar Lie & Associates (Guillaume Ferrand) (Belgium, Central America, Eastern Europe, France, Gibraltar, Italy, Luxembourg, Malta, Portugal, South America, Spain); Lorie Ocampo (China, Hong Kong, Japan, Korea, Philippines, Taiwan); Pan Macmillan SA Pty Ltd (South Africa)
Orders to: Macmillan Distribution Ltd, Brunel Rd, Houndmills, Basingstoke, Hants RG21 6XS *Tel:* (01256) 329242 *Fax:* (01256) 327961

Quaker Books
Quaker Centre Bookshop, Friends House, 173-177 Euston Rd, London NW1 2BJ
Tel: (020) 7663 1000; (020) 7663 1030 (orders) *Fax:* (020) 7663 1001 (orders)
E-mail: quakercentre@quaker.org.uk
Web Site: www.quaker.org.uk/shop
Key Personnel
Communication & Services: Helen Griffith
Tel: (020) 7663 1161 *E-mail:* heleng@quaker.org.uk
Founded: 1882
Subjects: Religion - Other
ISBN Prefix(es): 978-0-85245
Parent Company: Religious Society of Friends

Quantum, *imprint of* W Foulsham & Co Ltd

Quantum Publishing
Member of Quarto International Co-Editions Group
The Old Brewery, 6 Blundell St, London N7 9BH
Tel: (020) 7700 6700 *Fax:* (020) 7700 4191
Web Site: www.quartoknows.com/quantum-publishing
Key Personnel
Publisher: Kerry Enzor *E-mail:* kerry.enzor@quarto.com
Subjects: Crafts, Games, Hobbies, Inspirational, Spirituality, Self-Help
ISBN Prefix(es): 978-1-84573; 978-1-86160
Ultimate Parent Company: The Quarto Group Inc

Quartet Books Ltd+
Member of Namara Group
27 Goodge St, London W1T 2LD
Tel: (020) 7636 3992
E-mail: info@quartetbooks.co.uk
Web Site: quartetbooks.co.uk
Key Personnel
Chairman: Naim Attallah
Founded: 1972
Subjects: Biography, Memoirs, Fiction, History, Music, Dance, Philosophy, Social Sciences, Sociology
ISBN Prefix(es): 978-0-7043
Associate Companies: Robin Clark Ltd
Subsidiaries: Namara Publications
Foreign Rep(s): Ted Dougherty (Europe); Interlink (USA); Turnaround Publisher Services Ltd (UK)
Orders to: NBN International, Airport Business Centre, 10 Thornbury Rd, Plymouth PL6 7PP *Tel:* (01752) 202300 *E-mail:* orders@nbninternational.com

Quarto Children's Books
Member of Quarto International Co-Editions Group
The Old Brewery, 6 Blundell St, London N7 9BH
Tel: (020) 7812 8633 *Fax:* (020) 7700 8066
Web Site: www.quartoknows.com/quarto-childrens-books
Key Personnel
Group Publisher: Zeta Jones *E-mail:* zeta.jones@quarto.com
Founded: 1990
Subjects: Animals, Pets, Astronomy, Nonfiction (General)
ISBN Prefix(es): 978-1-58209
Ultimate Parent Company: The Quarto Group Inc

Quarto Editora, *imprint of* Quarto Publishing Group UK

Quarto Iberoamericana, *imprint of* Quarto Publishing Group UK

Quarto Publishing
Member of Quarto International Co-Editions Group
The Old Brewery, 6 Blundell St, London N7 9BH
Tel: (020) 7700 6700 *Fax:* (020) 7700 8066
E-mail: quarto@quarto.com
Web Site: www.quartoknows.com/quarto-publishing
Key Personnel
Publisher: Samantha Warrington *Tel:* (020) 7700 8047 *E-mail:* samantha.warrington@quarto.com
Art Dir: Caroline Guest *E-mail:* caroline.guest@quarto.com
Creative Dir: Moira Clinch *E-mail:* moira.clinch@quarto.com
Editorial Dir: Kate Kirby *E-mail:* kate.kirby@quarto.com
Group Rights Dir: Karine Marko *E-mail:* karine.marko@quarto.com
Senior Manager, Foreign Rights Operations: Kate Essam *E-mail:* kate.essam@quarto.com
Subjects: Architecture & Interior Design, Art, Cookery, Crafts, Games, Hobbies, Fashion, Gardening, Plants, Health, Nutrition, House & Home, How-to, Music, Dance, Natural History, Sports, Athletics, Wine & Spirits
ISBN Prefix(es): 978-0-85762
Ultimate Parent Company: The Quarto Group Inc

Quarto Publishing Group UK+
Division of The Quarto Group Inc
The Old Brewery, 6 Blundell St, London N7 9BH
Tel: (020) 7700 6700 *Fax:* (020) 7700 8066
E-mail: info@quarto.com
Web Site: www.quartoknows.com
Key Personnel
Executive Chairman: Laurence Orbach
Chief Creative Officer: David Breuer
Chief Financial Officer: Michael Connole
Group Dir, Foreign Rights: Karine Marko *E-mail:* karine.marko@quarto.com
Group Dir, People: Sally Dwyer
Publisher-at-Large: Jacqui Small
Adult Marketing Dir: Jessica Axe
Children's Marketing Dir: Katherine Josselyn
Dir, Children's Sales: Tim Loynes
Sales Dir, UK & Europe: Andrew Stanley
Sales Dir, EMEA, Central Asia, Korea, Taiwan, India & Subcontinent: Monica Baggio *Tel:* (020) 7284 9328 *Fax:* (020) 7149 9958 *E-mail:* monica.baggio@quarto.com
Founded: 1976
Subjects: Alternative, Animals, Pets, Antiques, Architecture & Interior Design, Art, Astrology, Occult, Crafts, Games, Hobbies, Gardening, Plants, Health, Nutrition, History, House & Home, How-to, Natural History, Nonfiction (General), Outdoor Recreation, Self-Help
ISBN Prefix(es): 978-0-901105
Number of titles published annually: 150 Print

Total Titles: 5,000 Print
Imprints: Aurum Press; Frances Lincoln; Frances Lincoln Children's Books; Jacqui Small; Kalimat Quarto (Arab language); Quarto Editora (Brazilian language); Quarto Iberoamericana (Spanish language); Wide-Eyed Editions
Foreign Rep(s): A-Z Africa Book Services (Anita Zih-De Haan) (Sub-Saharan Africa); Allen & Unwin (Australia, New Zealand); Angell Eurosales (Denmark, Finland, Iceland, Norway, Sweden); APD Singapore Pte Ltd (Ian Pringle) (Brunei, Cambodia, Indonesia, Malaysia, Philippines, Singapore, Thailand, Vietnam); Bill Bailey Publishers' Representatives (Central Europe, Eastern Europe); Tim Burland (Japan); Canadian Manda Group (Canada); China Publishers Marketing (Benjamin Pan) (China); International Publishing Services Ltd (Zoe Kaviani) (Cyprus, Egypt, Malta, Middle East); JCC Enterprises Inc (Jerry Carrillo Ortiz) (Caribbean, Central America, Mexico, South America); B K Norton Ltd (Chiafeng Peng) (Taiwan); Padovani Books (Penny Padovani) (Greece, Italy); Padovani Books (Jenny Padovani) (Gibraltar, Portugal, Spain); Phambili Agencies (Botswana, Lesotho, Namibia, South Africa, Swaziland, Zimbabwe); Publishers' Services (Gabriele Kern) (Austria, Germany, Switzerland)
Distribution Center: Littlehampton Book Services Ltd, Faraday Close, Durrington, Worthing, West Sussex BN13 3RB *Tel:* (01903) 828500
Orders to: 74-77 White Lion St, London N1 9PF *Tel:* (020) 7284 9329 *Fax:* (020) 7485 4902 *E-mail:* sales@quartouk.com
Quarto Publishing Group USA, 400 First Ave N, Suite 400, Minneapolis, MN 55401, United States *Tel:* 612-344-8100 *Fax:* 612-344-8691 *E-mail:* sales@quartous.com

QUE Publishing, *imprint of* Pearson Education Ltd

Quercus Publishing PLC
Division of Hodder & Stoughton Ltd
Carmelite House, 50 Victoria Embankment, London EC4Y 0DZ
Tel: (020) 7291 7200
E-mail: enquiries@quercusbooks.co.uk
Web Site: www.quercusbooks.co.uk
Key Personnel
Mng Dir: Jon Butler
Publishing Dir, Nonfiction: Richard Milner
Publisher, Heron Books: Susan Watt
Publisher, Nonfiction: Katy Follain
Publisher, Quercus Fiction: Cassie Browne
Dir, Quercus US: Jason Bartholomew
Sales Dir: David Murphy *E-mail:* david.murphy@quercusbooks.co.uk
Head, Publicity: Hannah Robinson *E-mail:* hannah.robinson@quercusbooks.co.uk
Head, Rights & Co-Editions: Emma Thawley *E-mail:* emma.thawley@quercusbooks.co.uk
Senior Publicity Manager: Corinna Zifko *E-mail:* corinna.zifko@quercusbooks.co.uk
Media Communications Executive: Andrew Turner *E-mail:* andrew.turner@quercusbooks.co.uk
Founded: 2004
Subjects: Fiction, Mysteries, Suspense, Nonfiction (General)
ISBN Prefix(es): 978-1-84724; 978-1-906694; 978-1-905204
Ultimate Parent Company: Hachette UK
Imprints: Jo Fletcher Books; Heron Books; MacLehose Press
Branch Office(s)
55 Baker St, London W1U 8EW
E-mail: uksales@quercusbooks.co.uk
U.S. Office(s): 31 W 57 St, New York, NY 10019, United States

Foreign Rep(s): Matt Cowdrey (Middle East, North Africa); Hachette Australia (Australia); Hachette India (India); Hachette Ireland (Ireland); Hachette New Zealand (New Zealand); Andrew Hally (Belgium, Cyprus, France, Greece, Luxembourg, Malta, Turkey); Paul Kenny (East Asia); Anna Martini (Austria, Eastern Europe, Germany, Switzerland); Simon McArt (Indian subcontinent, South Africa); Abigail Mitchell (Baltic States, Scandinavia); Pansing Distribution Pte Ltd (Malaysia, Singapore); Eleanor Wood (Italy, Netherlands, Portugal, Spain, Sub-Saharan Africa exc South Africa); Wei Zhao (China, Taiwan)
Distribution Center: Bookpoint, 130 Park Dr, Milton Park, Abingdon, Oxon OX14 4SE *Tel:* (01235) 400 400 *Web Site:* bookpoint.wp.hachette.co.uk

Quest, *imprint of* Top That Publishing Ltd

Qu:id Publishing
Member of Quarto International Co-Editions Group
Ovest House, Level 1, 58 West St, Brighton BN1 2RA
Tel: (01273) 716009 *Fax:* (01273) 727269
E-mail: info@quidpublishing.com
Web Site: www.quartoknows.com/quid-publishing
Key Personnel
Publisher: Nigel Browning *E-mail:* nigel.browning@quarto.com
Founded: 2002
Subjects: Art, History, Humor, Mathematics, Natural History, Philosophy, Science (General), Culture
Ultimate Parent Company: The Quarto Group Inc

Quiller Press, *imprint of* Quiller Publishing Ltd

Quiller Publishing Ltd+
Wykey House, Wykey, Shrewsbury, Salop SY4 1JA
Tel: (01939) 261616 *Fax:* (01939) 261606
E-mail: admin@quillerbooks.com
Web Site: www.quillerbooks.com
Key Personnel
Mng Dir: Andrew Johnston
Editorial: Gilly Johnston *E-mail:* gilly@quillerbooks.com
Foreign Rights: John Beaton *E-mail:* john@beaton.org.uk
Sales & Marketing Manager: Matt Colllis *E-mail:* matt@quillerbooks.com
Founded: 2001
Specialize in sponsored books & adult nonfiction.
Subjects: Biography, Memoirs, Business, Cookery, History, House & Home, Humor, Nonfiction (General), Outdoor Recreation, Travel & Tourism, Country Sports, Equestrian, Falconry, Fishing, Shooting
ISBN Prefix(es): 978-1-904057; 978-1-84689
Number of titles published annually: 30 Print
Total Titles: 300 Print
Imprints: Excellent Press; Kenilworth Press; Quiller Press; The Sportsman's Press; Swan Hill Press
Distributed by Peribo Pty Ltd (Australia); Stackpole Books (USA)
Warehouse: Grantham Book Services, Trent Rd, Grantham, Lincs NG31 7QX *Tel:* (01476) 541080 *Fax:* (01476) 541061 *E-mail:* orders@gbs.tbs-ltd.co.uk
Orders to: Grantham Book Services, Trent Rd, Grantham, Lincs NG31 7QX *Tel:* (01476) 541080 *Fax:* (01476) 541061 *E-mail:* orders@gbs.tbs-ltd.co.uk

Quintessence Publishing Co Ltd+
Quintessence House, Grafton Rd, New Malden, Surrey KT3 3AB
Tel: (020) 8949-6087 *Fax:* (020) 8336-1484
E-mail: info@quintpub.co.uk

Web Site: www.quintpub.co.uk
Key Personnel
Publishing Dir: Johannes Wolters
  E-mail: wolters@quintessenz.de
General Manager: Susan Newbury
  E-mail: snewbury@quintpub.co.uk
Marketing Manager: Muriel Suma
  E-mail: msuma@quintpub.co.uk
Founded: 1949
Scientific & clinical information for dental practitioners, researchers & students.
Subjects: Medicine, Nursing, Dentistry
ISBN Prefix(es): 978-1-85097
Parent Company: Quintessenz Verlags-GmbH, Ifenpfad 2-4, 12107 Berlin, Germany
Associate Companies: Quintessence Editora Ltda, Rua Apeninos, 664-13° Andar-Conjunto 133 Paraiso, Sao Paulo-SP 01533-000, Brazil *Tel:* (011) 5574-1200 *Fax:* (011) 5539-3183 *E-mail:* yara@quintessenceditora.com.br; Quintessenz Nakladatelstvi spol sro, PO Box 66, 120 00 Prague 2, Czech Republic *Tel:* (02) 5732 8723 *Fax:* (02) 5732 8723 *E-mail:* info@quintessenz.cz *Web Site:* www.quintessenz.cz; Quintessence International Sarl, Le Chanzy, 18 Ave Winston Churchill, 94220 Charenton-le-Pont, France *Tel:* 01 43 78 40 50 *Fax:* 01 43 78 78 85 *E-mail:* knellesen@quintessence-international.fr *Web Site:* www.quintessence-international.fr; Quintessence Science Communications Pvt Ltd, 303-304, Virat Bhawan, Commercial Complex, Delhi 110 009, India *Tel:* (011) 2765 2341; (011) 2765 2369 *Fax:* (011) 2765 2658 *E-mail:* passip@ndb.vsnl.net.in *Web Site:* www.quintasia.com; Quintessenza Edizioni SRL, Via C Menotti 65, Passirana di Rho, 20017 Milan MI, Italy *Tel:* (02) 931 82 264 *Fax:* (02) 931 86 159 *E-mail:* info@quintessenzaedizioni.it *Web Site:* www.quintessenzaedizioni.it; Quint House Bldg, 3-2-6 Hongo, Bunkyo-ku, Tokyo 113-0033, Japan *Tel:* (03) 5842 2271 *Fax:* (03) 5800 7598 *E-mail:* info@quint-j.co.jp *Web Site:* www.quint-j.co.jp; Wydawnictwo Kwintescencja Sp z oo, ul Rozana 75, 02-569 Warsaw, Poland *Tel:* (22) 845 69 70 *Fax:* (22) 845 05 53 *E-mail:* wydawnictwo@kwintesencja.com.pl *Web Site:* www.kwintesencja.com.pl; Quintessence Publishing & Education SRL, Sos Nordului nr 62, Sector 1, 014104 Bucharest, Romania, Contact: Dr Octavian Fargaras *Tel:* (031) 102 43 80 *Fax:* (031) 102 43 81 *E-mail:* dr.fagaras@quintessence.ro *Web Site:* www.quintessence.ro; Quintessence Moscow, Bldg 1, Business Center, Off 14, Usacheva str, 62, 119048 Moscow, Russia *Tel:* (495) 245-5270 *Fax:* (495) 245-5279 *E-mail:* sash@quintessence.ru *Web Site:* www.quintessence.ru; Quintessence, RM 1003, Sangji B/D, No 326, Eulijiro-3GA, Choong-gu, Seoul, South Korea *Tel:* (02) 2262 4231-3 *Fax:* (02) 2262 4234; Editorial Quintessence SL, Gran Via Carles III, 84, 08028 Barcelona, Spain *Tel:* 934912300 *Fax:* 934091360 *E-mail:* javier@quintessence.es *Web Site:* www.quintessence.es; Quintessence Yayincilik Tanitim, Buyukdere Caddesi, Sakarya Apartment No 6/7, 34360 Sisli-Istanbul, Turkey *Tel:* (0212) 343 05 99 *Fax:* (0212) 230 34 19 *E-mail:* bilgi@quintessence.com.tr *Web Site:* www.quintessence.com.tr
U.S. Office(s): Quintessence Publishing Co Inc, 4350 Chandler Dr, Hanover Park, IL 60133, United States *Tel:* 630-736-3600 *Fax:* 630-736-3633 *E-mail:* service@quintbook.com *Web Site:* www.quintpub.com

Quintessentially Publishing Ltd
29 Portland Pl, London W1B 1QB
Tel: (020) 3073 6719
E-mail: info@quintessentiallycreative.com; sales@quintessentiallycreative.com
Web Site: quintessentiallycreative.com

Founded: 2006
Subjects: Architecture & Interior Design, Travel & Tourism
ISBN Prefix(es): 978-0-9558270
Branch Office(s)
Grosvenor Bldg, 6th floor, 14 Riverside, Nairobi, Kenya *E-mail:* theuri@quinessentially.com
Unit No 2705-2706, Indigo icon, Jumeriah, Dubai, United Arab Emirates *E-mail:* charleyb@quinessentially.com
G07 Ground floor, The Manor 2, 91 Nguyen Huu Canh, Binh Thanh, Vietnam *E-mail:* vicky.pester@quinessentially.com

Quintet Publishing+
Member of Quarto International Co-editions Group
Ovest House, 58 West St, Brighton BN1 2RA
Tel: (01273) 716000
Web Site: www.quartoknows.com/quintet-publishing
Key Personnel
Publisher: Mark Searle *E-mail:* mark.searle@quarto.com
Founded: 1984
Publishes co-edition books.
Subjects: Cookery, Crafts, Games, Hobbies, Fashion, Gardening, Plants, Geography, Geology, Health, Nutrition, History, House & Home, How-to, Maritime, Military Science, Music, Dance, Mysteries, Suspense, Natural History, Outdoor Recreation, Photography, Sports, Athletics, Technology, Transportation, Travel & Tourism, Wine & Spirits, Interior Design
ISBN Prefix(es): 978-1-86155
Number of titles published annually: 60 Print
Total Titles: 750 Print
Ultimate Parent Company: The Quarto Group Inc

Ragged Bears Ltd+
79 Acreman St, Sherborne, Dorset DT9 3PH
Tel: (01935) 816933
E-mail: books@ragged-bears.co.uk
Web Site: ragged-bears.com
Specialize in picture books for children.
ISBN Prefix(es): 978-1-85714; 978-1-870817
Imprints: Spindlewood
Distributor for ACC - Children's Classics; Allen & Unwin Children's Books; David Bennett Books; b small publishing; Children's Corner; Chronicle Books; Clunie Press; Era Publications; Gallery Children's Books; Key Porter Books; Lemniscaat; Lothian Books; Moonlight Publishing; North-South Books; Owl Man; Matthew Price Children's Books; R&S Books; Siphano Picture Books; Star Bright Books; Templar Publishing; Tundra Books; Upland Books; The Wordhouse
Warehouse: c/o The Trade Counter, The Airfield, Norwich Rd, Mendlesham, Suffolk IP14 5NA

Raintree
Brunel Rd, Houndmills, Basingstoke, Hants RG21 6XS
Mailing Address: Halley Court, Jordan Hill, Oxford, Oxon OX2 8EJ
Tel: (01256) 302699 *Fax:* (01256) 812521
E-mail: myorders@raintreepublishers.co.uk
Web Site: www.raintree.co.uk
Key Personnel
Mng Dir: Doug Pocock
Founded: 2004
Subjects: Art, Biography, Memoirs, Economics, Fiction, Geography, Geology, Government, Political Science, History, Mathematics, Music, Dance, Nonfiction (General), Science (General), Technology, Art Design, English, Literacy, Modern Languages, Physical Education
ISBN Prefix(es): 978-1-84443; 978-1-84421; 978-1-4062
Parent Company: Capstone Publishers

Ramakrishna Vedanta Centre
Blind Lane, Bourne End, Bucks SL8 5LF
Tel: (01628) 526 464
E-mail: vedantauk@talk21.com
Web Site: www.vedantauk.com
Key Personnel
Centre Leader: Swami Dayatmananda
Founded: 1948
Subjects: Philosophy, Religion - Hindu
ISBN Prefix(es): 978-0-902479; 978-0-7025
U.S. Office(s): 17 E 94 St, New York, NY 10128, United States *Tel:* 212-534-9445 *Fax:* 212-828-1618 *E-mail:* rvcenternewyork@gmail.com

Random House Audiobooks, *imprint of* The Random House Group Ltd, a Penguin Random House Company

Random House Books, *imprint of* The Random House Group Ltd, a Penguin Random House Company

The Random House Group Ltd, a Penguin Random House Company+
20 Vauxhall Bridge Rd, London SW1V 2SA
Tel: (020) 7840 8400 *Fax:* (020) 7233 8791; (020) 7840 8778
Web Site: www.penguin.co.uk
Key Personnel
Editorial Dir, Square Peg: Rosemary Davidson
Editorial Dir, Yellow Jersey Press: Matt Phillips
Associate Editorial Dir & Publicity Dir, Hutchinson: Emma Mitchell
Mng Dir, Cornerstone: Susan Sandon
Mng Dir, Ebury: Rebecca Smart
Deputy Mng Dir & Publisher, Ebury: Jake Lingwood
Mng Dir, Vintage Publishing: Richard Cable
Deputy Mng Dir, Vintage Publishing: Faye Brewster
Publishing Dir, Bodley Head: Stuart Williams
Publishing Dir, Century Editorial: Jenny Geras
Publishing Dir, Chatto & Windus: Clara Farmer
Publishing Dir, Jonathan Cape: Michal Shavit
Publishing Dir, Windmill: Stephanie Sweeney
Deputy Publishing Dir, Jonathan Cape: Bea Hemming
Publisher, Century & Arrow: Selina Walker
Publisher, Heinemann Editorial: Jason Arthur
Deputy Publisher, Arrow: Emily Griffin
Associate Publisher, Jonathan Cape: Robin Robertson
Group Commercial Dir: Nigel Waters
Group Deputy Sales Dir: Ed Christie
Group Operations Dir: Deborah Wright
Dir, Group Mktg & Audiences: Albert Hogan
International Dir: Simon Littlewood
International & Export Sales Dir: Rob Waddington
Publicity Dir, Jonathan Cape & Bodley Head: Joe Pickering
Strategy Dir: Philipp Bartscher
UK Sales Dir, Cornerstone: Aslan Byrne
Head, UK Communications: Rebecca Sinclair
Product Manager, Author Portal: Ami Greko
UK Sales Manager: Thomas Glover
UK Sales & Marketing Coordinator: Samuel Bonner
Founded: 1987
Subjects: Art, Astrology, Occult, Biography, Memoirs, Cookery, Fashion, Fiction, Government, Political Science, Health, Nutrition, Humor, Nonfiction (General), Philosophy, Poetry, Travel & Tourism
ISBN Prefix(es): 978-0-09; 978-1-85686; 978-0-7126; 978-1-86046; 978-0-224; 978-1-870516; 978-0-85265; 978-1-84657; 978-1-84655; 978-1-84853; 978-1-4881
Parent Company: Penguin Random House
Imprints: Arrow; Bantam Children; Black Swan Ireland; Bodley Head; Bodley Head Children's; Jonathan Cape; Jonathan Cape Chil-

dren's; Jonathan Cape (PB); Century; Channel 4 Books; Chatto & Windus; Corgi Childrens; Cornerstone; Definitions; Doubleday Childrens; Expert; Hammer; Harvill Secker; William Heinemann; Hutchinson; Hutchinson Childrens; Mainstream Publishing; #Merky Books; Pimlico; Preface Publishing; Random House Audiobooks; Random House Books; Red Fox; Red Fox Classics; RH AudioGo; RHCP Audio; Square Peg; Tamarind; Vintage; Vintage Children's Classics; Vintage Classics; Vintage Digital; Windmill; Yellow Jersey Press; Young Arrow
Divisions: Ebury Publishing
Orders to: The Book Service Ltd, Distribution Centre, Colchester Rd, Frating Green, Colchester, Essex CO7 7DW *Tel:* (01206) 256000 *Fax:* (01206) 255715 *E-mail:* sales@tbs-ltd.co. uk *Web Site:* www.thebookservice.co.uk

Random House UK, see The Random House Group Ltd, a Penguin Random House Company

Ransom Publishing Ltd+
Brocklands Farm, Unit 7, West Meon, Hants GU32 1JN
Tel: (01730) 829091 *Fax:* (05601) 148881
E-mail: ransom@ransom.co.uk; orders@ransom. co.uk; enquiries@ransom.co.uk
Web Site: www.ransom.co.uk
Key Personnel
Mng Dir: Jenny Ertle
Founded: 1995
Independent specialist publisher of books that encourage & help children & young adults to develop their reading skills.
ISBN Prefix(es): 978-1-900127; 978-1-84167; 978-1-84671; 978-1-78127
Number of titles published annually: 100 Print; 5 CD-ROM
Total Titles: 200 Print; 5 CD-ROM

Raven's Quill Ltd
63 High St, Billingshurst, West Sussex RH14 9QP
E-mail: info@ravensquill.com
Web Site: www.ravensquill.com
Subjects: Fiction, History, Romance, Science Fiction, Fantasy, Thriller
ISBN Prefix(es): 978-0-9555486
Imprints: The Shabby Tatter Press (children's books)

Ravette Publishing Ltd+
PO Box 876, Horsham, West Sussex RH12 9GH
Tel: (01403) 711443
Web Site: www.ravettepublishing.tel
Key Personnel
Mng Dir: Ingrid Parris *E-mail:* ingrid@ ravettepub.co.uk
Founded: 1980
Subjects: Fiction, Humor, Nonfiction (General)
ISBN Prefix(es): 978-1-85304; 978-1-84161
Number of titles published annually: 5 Print
Total Titles: 80 Print
Foreign Rep(s): Mr Julian Ashton (Far East); Richard Ward (Middle East)
Distribution Center: Orca Book Services, Unit A3, Fleets Corner, Poole, Dorset BH17 0HL, Contact: Trish Clapp *Tel:* (01202) 785716 *Fax:* (01202) 672076 *E-mail:* trish.clapp@ orcabookservices.co.uk *Web Site:* www. orcabookservices.co.uk

RCGP, see Royal College of General Practitioners (RCGP)

Reader's Digest UK
PO Box 7853, Ringwood BH24 9FH

Tel: (0844) 332 4884; (0844) 332 4994 (subscriptions)
E-mail: enquiries@readersdigest.co.uk
Web Site: www.readersdigest.co.uk
Founded: 1922
Subjects: Animals, Pets, Antiques, Archaeology, Architecture & Interior Design, Cookery, Crafts, Games, Hobbies, Earth Sciences, Fiction, Film, Video, Gardening, Plants, Health, Nutrition, House & Home, How-to, Mysteries, Suspense, Nonfiction (General), Science (General), Travel & Tourism
ISBN Prefix(es): 978-0-276; 978-1-78020

Reaktion Books Ltd+
33 Great Sutton St, London EC1V 0DX
Tel: (020) 7253 1071 *Fax:* (020) 7253 1208
E-mail: info@reaktionbooks.co.uk
Web Site: www.reaktionbooks.co.uk
Key Personnel
Founder & Publisher: Michael R Leaman
Mng Dir: David Hayden
Publicity Dir: Maria Kilcoyne *Tel:* (020) 7253 1208
Sales Manager: David Hoek
Designer: Simon McFadden
Founded: 1985
Specialize in nonfiction.
Subjects: Architecture & Interior Design, Art, Asian Studies, Film, Video, Geography, Geology, Government, Political Science, History, Language Arts, Linguistics, Literature, Literary Criticism, Essays, Nonfiction (General), Photography, Travel & Tourism
ISBN Prefix(es): 978-0-948462; 978-1-86189; 978-1-78023
Number of titles published annually: 80 Print
Total Titles: 600 Print
Foreign Rep(s): The African Moon Press (South Africa); APD Kuala Lumpur Ltd (Malaysia); APD Singapore Pte Ltd (Brunei, Cambodia, Indonesia, Philippines, Singapore, Thailand, Vietnam); Avicenna Partnership Ltd (Bill Kennedy) (Bahrain, Egypt, Iraq, Lebanon, Libya, Oman, Saudi Arabia, Sudan, United Arab Emirates, Yemen); Avicenna Partnership Ltd (Claire de Gruchy) (Algeria, Jordan, Malta, Morocco, Palestine, Tunisia, Turkey); Vivian Constantinopoulos (Greece); Everest International Publishing Services (Wei Zhao) (China, Hong Kong); Vernon Hous (Denmark, Finland, Iceland, Norway, Sweden); Christopher Humphrys (Portugal, Spain); Se-Yung Jun (Korea); Ewa Ledochowicz (Croatia, Czechia, Estonia, Hungary, Poland, Romania, Slovakia, Slovenia); Uwe Ludemann (Austria, Germany, Italy, Switzerland); Maruzen Co Ltd (Tim Burland) (Japan); Maya Publishers Pvt Ltd (Surit Mitra) (India); Mirjam Mayenburg (Belgium, Netherlands); NewSouth Books (Australia, New Zealand); Andrew Russell (Ireland, Northern Ireland); Signature Book Services Ltd (Catherine Bell) (England, Scotland, Wales); Unicfacmanu Trading Co (Taiwan); University of Chicago Press (Canada, South America, USA); World Press (Pakistan)
Distribution Center: Grantham Book Services Ltd, Trent Rd, Grantham, Lincs NG31 7XQ
Tel: (01476) 541 080 *Fax:* (01476) 541 061
E-mail: orders@gbs.tbs-ltd.co.uk

Real Reads
Knoll House, Burleigh, Stroud, Glos GL5 2PR
Tel: (01453) 882139
E-mail: enquiries@realreads.co.uk
Web Site: www.realreads.co.uk
Subjects: Literature, Literary Criticism, Essays, Mysteries, Suspense, Science Fiction, Fantasy, Classic Literature, Indian Classics, New Testament
ISBN Prefix(es): 978-1-906230; 978-1-911091
Foreign Rep(s): John Beaufoy Publishing Ltd (Australasia, East Asia, South Africa, South

Asia); SaltWay Global Ltd (Chris McLaren) (all other territories, UK)
Distribution Center: BookSource, 50 Cambuslang Rd, Cambuslang, Glasgow G32 8NB
Tel: (0845) 370 0063 *Fax:* (0845) 370 0064
E-mail: customerservice@booksource.net

Really Decent Books Ltd
191 Newbridge Rd, Bath BA1 3HH
Tel: (01225) 334747; (07525) 691671
E-mail: info@reallydecentbooks.co.uk
Web Site: www.reallydecentbooks.co.uk
Key Personnel
Publisher: Phil Dauncey
ISBN Prefix(es): 978-1-909090

Reardon Publishing+
PO Box 919, Cheltenham, Glos GL50 9AN
Tel: (01242) 231800
Web Site: www.reardon.co.uk; www. cotswoldbookshop.co.uk; www. antarcticbookshop.co.uk
Key Personnel
Co-Founder & Owner: Nicholas Reardon
Founded: 1976
Cotswolds maps, walking & cycling guides & books on history & folklore of the Cotswolds area.
Subjects: Asian Studies, Foreign Countries, History, Outdoor Recreation, Travel & Tourism, Chinese Language, History & Culture, Cotswolds England, Exploring Antarctica
ISBN Prefix(es): 978-0-950867; 978-1-873877; 978-1-874192
Number of titles published annually: 10 Print; 1 CD-ROM
Total Titles: 100 Print; 2 CD-ROM
Distributor for Cassel; Cicerone; Cordee; Estate Publications; Flukes UK; Harvey Maps; Ordnance Survey; Philips Maps; Video-Ex

Red Bird Publishing Ltd
Eastend Green, Brightlingsea, Colchester, Essex CO7 0SX
Tel: (01206) 303525 *Fax:* (01206) 304545
Web Site: www.red-bird.co.uk
Key Personnel
Sales Dir: Ian C Wallace
ISBN Prefix(es): 978-1-902626

Red Fox, *imprint of* The Random House Group Ltd, a Penguin Random House Company

Red Fox Classics, *imprint of* The Random House Group Ltd, a Penguin Random House Company

Red Kite Books, *imprint of* Haldane Mason Ltd

Red Lemon Press, *imprint of* Weldon Owen Pty Ltd

Red Shed, *imprint of* Egmont UK Ltd

Redcliffe Press Ltd+
81G Pembroke Rd, Clifton, Bristol BS8 3EA
Tel: (01179) 737 207 *Fax:* (01179) 238 991
E-mail: info@redcliffepress.co.uk
Web Site: www.redcliffepress.co.uk
Key Personnel
Publishing Dir: John Sansom
Production Dir: Clara Sansom
Sales Dir: Angela Sansom
Founded: 1976
Subjects: Art, Biography, Memoirs, Literature, Literary Criticism, Essays, Photography, Poetry, Regional Interests, Sports, Athletics

ISBN Prefix(es): 978-0-905459; 978-0-948265; 978-1-872971; 978-1-900178; 978-1-904537; 978-1-906593
Associate Companies: Art Directories Ltd; Sansom & Co Ltd

RedDoor Publishing Ltd

277 London Rd, Burgess Hill, West Sussex RH15 9QU
Tel: (01444) 240152
E-mail: hello@reddoorpublishing.com
Web Site: reddoorpublishing.com
Key Personnel
Publisher: Clare Christian *E-mail:* clare@reddoorpublishing.com
Publishing Manager & Editor: Heather Boisseau *E-mail:* heather@reddoorpublishing.com
Publishing Coordinator & Editor: Anna Burtt *E-mail:* anna@reddoorpublishing.com
Head, Rights: Flora McMichael *E-mail:* flora@reddoorpublishing.com
Digital Marketing Manager: Julia Pidduck *E-mail:* julia@reddoorpublishing.com
Subjects: Business, Fiction, Nonfiction (General)
ISBN Prefix(es): 978-1-910453
Foreign Rights: ACER Agencia Literaria (Latin America, Portugal, Spain); Big Apple Agency Inc (China, Taiwan, Thailand, Vietnam); Iris Literary Agency (Greece); Japan Uni Agency Inc (Japan); Nurcihan Kesim Literary Agency (Turkey); Silvia Meucci Literary Agency (Italy); Andrew Nurnberg Associates Budapest (Hungary); Andrew Nurnberg Literary Agency (Russia); Sue Yang (Korea)
Distribution Center: Central Books Ltd, One Heath Park Industrial Estate, Freshwater Rd, Dagenham RM8 18X *Tel:* (020) 8525 8800 *Fax:* (020) 8599 2694 *E-mail:* contactus@centralbooks.com *Web Site:* www.centralbooks.com
Trafalgar Square Publishing, 814 N Franklin St, Chicago, IL 60610, United States *Tel:* 312-337-0747 *Fax:* 312-337-5985

Redstone Press+

7a St Lawrence Terrace, London W10 5SU
Tel: (020) 8968 4302 *Fax:* (01625) 800077
E-mail: redstone.press@gmail.com
Web Site: www.redstonepress.co.uk
Key Personnel
Proprietor: Julian Rothenstein
Founded: 1986
Subjects: Art
ISBN Prefix(es): 978-1-870003
Associate Companies: Shambhala Publications (USA)
Subsidiaries: Shambhala Redstone Editions
Foreign Rep(s): Idea Books (Europe exc Spain); Distribuciones Loring (Spain); Polite Cards (UK); Signature Books Ltd (UK); Wild & Wolf Ltd (UK)
Bookshop(s): Redstone Shop, c/o Polite Company, Canalside 3, Clarence Mill, Bollington, Cheshire SK10 5JZ *Tel:* (01625) 560055 *E-mail:* redstone@politecompany.co.uk

Reed Business Information Ltd

Member of RELX Group PLC
Quadrant House, The Quadrant, Sutton, Surrey SM2 5AS
Tel: (020) 8652 3500 *Fax:* (020) 8652 8932
E-mail: enquiries@reedbusiness.com
Web Site: www.reedbusiness.com
Key Personnel
Chief Executive Officer: Dominic Feltham
Chief Executive Officer, Risk & Business: Mark Kelsey
Chief Financial Officer: Jamie O'Sullivan
Chief Product Officer: Mie-Yun Lee
Chief Technology Officer: Mark Wilmhurst
Global Strategy Dir: Paul White
Human Resources Dir: Graeme Roy

Marketing Dir: Lawrence Mitchell
Production & Editorial Systems Dir: Eric Lambert *E-mail:* eric.lambert@rbi.co.uk
Head, Finance & Accounting: Julie Dinnage
Subjects: Accounting, Aeronautics, Aviation, Agriculture, Engineering (General), Human Relations, Real Estate, Science (General), Technology, Community Care, Human Resources
ISBN Prefix(es): 978-0-610; 978-0-611; 978-0-948056
Branch Office(s)
One Changi Business Park Crescent, Tower A, 06-01, Singapore 486025, Singapore *Tel:* 6548 6066; 6789 8828
U.S. Office(s): 230 Park Ave, 7th floor, New York, NY 10169, United States *Tel:* 212-309-8100

Reed New Holland, *imprint of* New Holland Publishers (UK) Ltd

Thomas Reed, *imprint of* A&C Black Publishers Ltd

William Reed Business Media+

Broadfield Park, Crawley, West Sussex RH11 9RT
Tel: (01293) 613 400
Web Site: www.william-reed.co.uk
Key Personnel
Chief Financial Officer: Richard Oscroft *Tel:* (01293) 610 242
Group Mng Dir: Charles Reed *Tel:* (01293) 610 242
Marketing Dir: Paul Joyce *E-mail:* paul.joyce@wrbm.com
Production Dir: Christopher Reed *Tel:* (01293) 610 212 *E-mail:* christopher.reed@wrbm.com
Founded: 1991
Membership(s): DPA.
Subjects: Business, Catering, Food & Drink
ISBN Prefix(es): 978-1-903115; 978-0-901595; 978-1-906493
Associate Companies: Knowledge Store; William Reed International
Branch Office(s)
Le Belem, 355 rue Vendemiaire, 34000 Montpellier, France
U.S. Office(s): 183 Madison Ave, Suite 1516, New York, NY 10016, United States

Reel Art Press Ltd

Unit 2, 6a Foscote Mews, London W9 2HH
Tel: (07837) 978282
E-mail: info@reelartpress.com
Web Site: www.reelartpress.com
Key Personnel
Dir: Tony Nourmand
Head, Operations & Editorial: Alison Elangasinghe
Founded: 2010
Subjects: Art, Film, Video, Photography, Cinema
ISBN Prefix(es): 978-1-909526; 978-0-9572610; 978-0-9566487

Regency House Publishing Ltd+

The Manor House, High St, Buntingford, Herts SG9 9AB
Tel: (01763) 274666
E-mail: regency-house@btconnect.com
Web Site: www.regencyhousepublishing.com
Key Personnel
Mng Dir: Nicolette Trodd
Founded: 1991
Publisher & packager of mass market nonfiction.
Subjects: Animals, Pets, Architecture & Interior Design, Art, Automotive, Cookery, Crafts, Games, Hobbies, Humor, Military Science, Nonfiction (General), Photography, Poetry, Regional Interests, Transportation, Travel & Tourism
ISBN Prefix(es): 978-1-85361

RELX Group PLC

1-3 Strand, London WC2N 5JR
Tel: (020) 7166 5500 *Fax:* (020) 7166 5799
E-mail: london@relxgroup.com; press.office@reedelsevier.com
Web Site: www.relxgroup.com
Key Personnel
Chief Executive Officer: Erik Engstrom
Head, Corporate Communications: Paul Abrahams
Dir, Corporate Affairs: Youngsuk Chi
Innovations Manager: Maxim Khan
Subjects: Business, Law, Medicine, Nursing, Dentistry, Science (General), Technology

Remember When, *imprint of* Pen & Sword Books Ltd

Review, *imprint of* Headline Publishing Group Ltd

Revival Publications, *imprint of* Kube Publishing Ltd

RH AudioGo, *imprint of* The Random House Group Ltd, a Penguin Random House Company

RHCP Audio, *imprint of* The Random House Group Ltd, a Penguin Random House Company

RIAS Publishing+

15 Rutland Sq, Edinburgh EH1 2BE
Tel: (0131) 229 7545 *Fax:* (0131) 228 2188
E-mail: info@rias.org.uk; bookshop@rias.org.uk
Web Site: www.rias.org.uk
Founded: 1982
Subjects: Architecture & Interior Design, Travel & Tourism
ISBN Prefix(es): 978-1-873190; 978-0-9501462
Parent Company: Royal Incorporation of Architects in Scotland

RIBA Publishing+

Broad Street House, 55 Old Broad St, London EC2M 1RX
Tel: (020) 7496 8300
E-mail: enquiry@ribapublishing.com; marketing@ribabookshops.com
Web Site: www.ribapublishing.com
Key Personnel
Dir, Partnerships: Steven Cross *Tel:* (020) 7496 8308 *E-mail:* steven.cross@ribaenterprises.com
Founded: 1967
Publishing arm of the Royal Institute of British Architects.
Subjects: Architecture & Interior Design, Construction
ISBN Prefix(es): 978-0-900630; 978-0-947877; 978-1-85946
Parent Company: RIBA Enterprises Ltd
Imprints: NBS
Foreign Rep(s): Angell Eurosales (Gill Angell & Stewart Siddell) (Scandinavia); Michael Geoghegan (Austria, Belgium, France, Germany, Netherlands, Switzerland); IMA Ltd (David Williams) (Central America, South America); Momenta Publishing Ltd (Rob Leech) (UK); Padovani Books Ltd (Penny Padovani) (Greece, Italy); Peter Prout (Portugal, Spain); Publishers International Marketing (Ray Potts) (Middle East); Publishers International Marketing (Chris Ashdown) (Far East); Sara Books Pvt Ltd (Ravindra Saxena) (India)
Bookshop(s): RIBA Bookshop, The Old Post Office, St Nicholas St, Newcastle Upon Tyne NE1 1RH *Tel:* (0191) 244 5557 *Fax:* (0191) 244 5553 *E-mail:* sales@ribabookshops.com

Richmond Publishing Co Ltd+
The Cottage, Allerds Rd, Slough, Berks SL2 3TJ
Tel: (01753) 643104
E-mail: rpc@richmond.co.uk
Web Site: richmond.co.uk
Founded: 1970
Subjects: Environmental Studies, Natural History
ISBN Prefix(es): 978-84-668
Total Titles: 100 Print

RICS Books+
Parliament Sq, 12 Great George St, London
SW1P 3AD
Tel: (0870) 333 1600; (024) 7686 8555
Fax: (020) 7334 3811
E-mail: contactrics@rics.org; mailorder@rics.org
Web Site: www.rics.org
Key Personnel
Chief Executive Officer: Sean Tompkins
Executive Dir, Corporate Services & Chief Financial Officer: Violetta Parylo
Mng Dir, EMEA: Mark Walley
Founded: 1981
Specialize in surveying, property, construction &
environment.
Subjects: Architecture & Interior Design, Civil
Engineering, Earth Sciences, Environmental
Studies, Real Estate
ISBN Prefix(es): 978-0-85406; 978-0-900633;
978-1-84219

Rider Books, *imprint of* Ebury Publishing

Rising Stars UK Ltd
7 Hatchers Mews, Bermondsey St, London SE1
3GS
Mailing Address: PO Box 105, Rochester, Kent
ME2 4BE
Toll Free Tel: 0800 091 1602 *Toll Free Fax:* 0800
091 1603
E-mail: custcare@risingstars-uk.com
Web Site: www.risingstars-uk.com
Key Personnel
Founder & Mng Dir: Andrea Carr
Founded: 2002
Subjects: Disability, Special Needs, Education,
Fiction, Mathematics, Nonfiction (General),
Science (General), Foreign Languages, Literacy
ISBN Prefix(es): 978-0-9542202; 978-1-904591;
978-1-905056; 978-1-84680; 978-0-85769; 978-
1-78339
Distribution Center: Trade Counter Distribution Ltd, Mendlesham Industrial Estate, Norwich Rd, Mendlesham, Suffolk IP14 5ND
Tel: (01449) 766629 *Fax:* (01449) 767122
E-mail: tradeorders@risingstars-uk.com

John Ritchie Ltd
40 Beansburn, Kilmarnock KA3 1RL
Tel: (01563) 536394 *Fax:* (01563) 571191
Web Site: www.ritchiechristianmedia.co.uk
Key Personnel
Contact: Gillian Cairnie *E-mail:* gillian.cairnie@
johnritchie.co.uk
Subjects: Biblical Studies, Biography, Memoirs,
Fiction, Music, Dance, Theology
ISBN Prefix(es): 978-0-946351; 978-1-904064;
978-1-907731; 978-1-910513

Roadmaster Books
105 High St, Rochester, Kent ME1 1JS
Tel: (07813) 632623
E-mail: roadmasterbooks@blueyonder.co.uk
Web Site: www.roadmasterbooks.co.uk
Key Personnel
Contact: Malcolm Wright
Subjects: Automotive, Environmental Studies,
Geography, Geology, History, Natural History,
Regional Interests, Transportation
ISBN Prefix(es): 978-1-871814

Number of titles published annually: 2 Print
Total Titles: 9 Print

Robert Gordon University
Garthdee Rd, Aberdeen, Aberdeenshire AB10
7QB
Tel: (01224) 262000 *Fax:* (01224) 263553
E-mail: business@rgu.ac.uk
Web Site: www.rgu.ac.uk
Key Personnel
Dept Head, Dept Communication, Marketing &
Media: Jo Royle *E-mail:* j.royle@rgu.ac.uk
Founded: 1967
Subjects: Publishing & Book Trade Education &
Training
ISBN Prefix(es): 978-0-9506289; 978-0-9519114;
978-1-901085

Robinson, *imprint of* Little, Brown Book Group

Robinswood Press Ltd+
30 South Ave, Stourbridge, West Midlands DY8
3XY
Tel: (01384) 397475 *Fax:* (01384) 440443
E-mail: customers@robinswoodpress.com
Web Site: www.robinswoodpress.co.uk
Founded: 1985
Subjects: Disability, Special Needs, Education,
English as a Second Language, Fiction, Nonfiction (General)
Number of titles published annually: 70 Print
Total Titles: 130 Print
Subsidiaries: Robinswood Press (Dublin) Ltd

The Robson Press, *imprint of* Biteback
Publishing

The Robson Press
Imprint of Biteback Publishing
Westminster Tower, 3 Albert Embankment, London SE1 7SP
Tel: (020) 7091 1260
E-mail: info@bitebackpublishing.com
Web Site: www.bitebackpublishing.com
Key Personnel
Publisher: Jeremy Robson
Mng Dir: Iain Dale
Subjects: Biography, Memoirs, Fiction, Film,
Video, History, Humor, Mathematics, Music,
Dance, Nonfiction (General), Self-Help, Sports,
Athletics, Travel & Tourism, Arts & Culture,
Current Affairs, Lifestyle, Wildlife
ISBN Prefix(es): 978-1-906217; 978-1-84954;
978-1-906779
Foreign Rep(s): Brookside Publishing Services
(Ireland, Northern Ireland); Consortium Book
Sales & Distribution (Canada, USA); Ted
Dougherty (Austria, Belgium, France, Germany, Greece, Italy, Luxembourg, Malta,
Netherlands, Switzerland); Iberian Book Services (Peter Prout) (Portugal, Spain); IMA
(Central Europe, Eastern Europe, Russia, Sub-
Saharan Africa exc South Africa); TowerToo
& NewSouth Books (Australia, New Zealand);
Pansing Distribution Pte Ltd (Brunei, Malaysia,
Singapore); Trinity Books (South Africa); The
White Partnership (Andrew White) (Hong
Kong, India, Japan, Korea, Pakistan, Philippines, Sri Lanka, Taiwan, Thailand)
Distribution Center: Marston Book Services Ltd,
160 Eastern Ave, Milton Park, Abingdon, Oxon
OX14 4SB *Tel:* (01235) 465500 *Fax:* (01235)
465555 *E-mail:* direct.orders@marston.co.uk
Web Site: www.marston.co.uk

Rock the Boat, *imprint of* Oneworld Publications

Rocket 88 Books, *imprint of* Essential Works

Rockpool Children's Books Ltd
15 North St, Marton, Warwicks CV23 9RJ
Tel: (07711) 351 691
E-mail: rockpoolchildrensbookltd@gmail.com
Web Site: www.rockpoolchildrensbooks.co.uk
Key Personnel
Dir: Stuart Trotter
Founded: 2006
ISBN Prefix(es): 978-0-9553022

Rooster Books Ltd
69 Fluin Lane, Frodsham WA6 7QT
Toll Free Tel: 0800 009 6036 *Fax:* (0844) 357
7035
E-mail: info@roosterbooks.co.uk
Web Site: www.roosterbooks.co.uk
Key Personnel
Dir: Guy Garfit
Founded: 1978
Subjects: Fiction, Travel & Tourism
ISBN Prefix(es): 978-1-871510
Number of titles published annually: 3 Print
Bookshop(s): Large Print Bookshop
E-mail: info@largeprintbookshop.co.uk *Web
Site:* www.largeprintbookshop.co.uk

RotoVision SA
Member of Quarto International Co-Editions
Group
Ovest House, 4th floor, 58 West St, Brighton
BN1 2RA
Tel: (01273) 716000
Web Site: www.quartoknows.com/rotovision
Key Personnel
Publisher: Mark Searle *E-mail:* mark.searle@
quarto.com
Editorial Dir: Isheeta Mustafi *E-mail:* isheeta.
mustafi@quarto.com
Foreign Rights Dir: Nicole Kemble
E-mail: nicole.kemble@quarto.com
International Sales Dir: Adrian Greenwood *E-mail:* adrian.greenwood@
aurumpublishinggroup.com
Founded: 1974
Subjects: Advertising, Architecture & Interior Design, Crafts, Games, Hobbies, Photography,
Digital Design, Graphic Design, Illustration,
Visual Arts
ISBN Prefix(es): 978-2-88046; 978-2-940361;
978-2-940378; 978-2-88893
Ultimate Parent Company: The Quarto Group Inc
Foreign Rep(s): Abe Marketing (Poland); Accendo (Estonia); Akademibokhandeln Imports (Sweden); Al Ahram Distributon Agency
(Egypt); Al Shegray (Saudi Arabia); Algoritam
(Croatia); All Prints Distributors & Publishers (United Arab Emirates); Allecto (Estonia);
American Book Centre (Netherlands); American Bookstore (Poland); APD Singapore Pte
Ltd (Brunei, Cambodia, Indonesia, Malaysia,
Philippines, Singapore, Thailand, Vietnam);
APP-Holding (Russia); Art Land Book Co Ltd
(Taiwan); Artrodnick (Russia); Asia Books
(Thailand); Basheer Design Books (HK) Ltd
(Hong Kong); Baum SA (Costa Rica); Bertrand
(Portugal); Bilimsel (Turkey); Book City (Iran);
Book Corner (United Arab Emirates); Book
Merchants (New Zealand); Book World Enterprises (India); Books Import (Italy); Booksplus
(United Arab Emirates); Bookworm (Israel);
Arnold Busck (Denmark); Canadian Manda
(Canada); Casa Ono (Brazil); Cav Giovanni
Russano SAS (Italy); Centrecom (Russia); Chi
Maw Enterprise Co Ltd (Taiwan); China Book
Import Centre (China); CNPIEC New Book
Showroom (China); Creative Publishing International (USA); Livraria Cultura (Brazil);
Dar An Nashr for Universities (Egypt); Design
Books (Russia); Design Books International
(Switzerland); Dongnam Books Inc (Korea);
Elefheroudakis (Greece); The English Book
(Serbia); Eslite Bookshop (Taiwan); Euro Publications (Finland); FNAC Belgium (Belgium);

FNAC Brazil (Brazil); Fraktaly (Czechia); Global Books (Mexico); Grantham Book Services (UK); Humanitas (Lithuania); Hyperion Books (Greece); Idea Books (Italy); IMEC (Egypt); Index Book SL (Spain); India Book Distributors (India); Interart (France); IPS Media II (Serbia); Jaguar Book Group (Canada); Jashanmal & Co (United Arab Emirates); Jana Jerotic (Slovenia); Joint Publishing Co Ltd (Hong Kong); Jordan Book Centre (Jordan); Lonnie Kahn Ltd (Israel); Kapitalka Poznanska Ksiegarnia (Poland); Keng Seng Enterprises Ltd (Hong Kong); Keski Toolon Paperikauppa (KTP) (Finland); Knjigarna MK Konzoricij (Slovenia); Konstig AB (Sweden); Kopp Fachbuch- und Medienversand (Germany); The Kuwait Bookshop (Kuwait); Kyriakou (Cyprus); Liberty Books (Pakistan); Light Q sro (Czechia); Logosphera (Russia); Luth (Norway); Macgrudy's (United Arab Emirates); Magma (Russia); Mal & Menning HF (Iceland); Robert Matton (Sweden); MBR (United Arab Emirates); Mediterranean Publishers Services (Egypt); Mega Books (Czechia); Mladinska Knjiga Trgovina (Slovenia); MM Mukhi & Sons (India); Multi-Line Books (Pakistan); Nilsson & Lamm (Netherlands); Norli Import (Norway); Novak Bookstore (Slovenia); Obeikan Bookshop (Saudi Arabia); OM Book Service (India); Page One Bookshop (Malaysia); Page One The Bookshop Pte Ltd (Singapore); Page One The Designer's Bookshop (HK) Ltd (Hong Kong); Papasotiriu SA (Greece); Pendragon (Hungary); Penninn IB Press (Iceland); Prior Books (Romania); Profil (Croatia); Promotora de Prensa Internacional SA (Spain); Prosperos Books (Hungary); Publigraphics Ediciones (Colombia); Real Books (South Africa); RED (Italy); Firma Janis Roze (Latvia); Saeed & Samir Bookstore (Kuwait); SBD Subscription Services (India); Schibsteds Internasjonal (Norway); Seiseisha (Japan); Servicios Amar SC (Mexico); Sethi Books (Pakistan); Shimada & Co Inc (Japan); Slovart Publishing Ltd (Czechia, Slovakia); Somohano (Mexico); Specialty Academic Book Centre (Jordan); Steimatsky (Israel); Steinars (Iceland); Stockmann (Finland); Studio Book (Greece); Super Book House (India); Swindon Book Co (Hong Kong); Tamaris (Croatia); Tanum (Norway); Tenge Centre (Denmark); Thames & Hudson (Australia); Tongjin Chulpan Muyeok Co Ltd (Korea); Top Mark Center (Poland); Tower Books (Australia); Tripont (Hungary); United Publishers Services Ltd (Japan); Librairie Universelle (Syria); University Bookshop (Jordan); Vanguard Books (Pakistan); VBZ doo (Croatia); Vijeh Nashr (Iran); Virgin Megastore (Lebanon); Westland (India); Wilco International (India); Yapi (Turkey); Ediciones Zeta (Peru); Znanje (Croatia)

Rough Guides Ltd+
80 Strand, London WC2R 0RL
Tel: (020) 7010 3000; (020) 7010 3709 (press)
E-mail: mail@roughguides.com
Web Site: www.roughguides.com
Key Personnel
Publicity Executive: Hayley Cox *E-mail:* hayley.cox@uk.dk.com
Publicity Assistant: Sarah-Jane Wilson
	E-mail: sarah-jane.wilson@uk.dk.com
Founded: 1982
Specialize in worldwide travel guides, maps & phrasebooks for a range of independently minded travellers, including cultural & historical information. Also publish a Rough Guide to music & cultural reference titles.
Subjects: Developing Countries, Foreign Countries, Geography, Geology, History, Music, Dance, Outdoor Recreation, Travel & Tourism
ISBN Prefix(es): 978-1-85828; 978-1-84353; 978-1-906063; 978-1-84836

Parent Company: APA Publications
Distribution Center: Ingram Publisher Services, One Ingram Blvd, La Vergne, TN 37086, United States *E-mail:* ips@ingramcontent.com
Web Site: ingramcontent.com (North America)

Rouleur Books, *imprint of* Bloomsbury Publishing Plc

'Round Midnight, *imprint of* Ashgrove Publishing

Roundfire Books, *imprint of* O Books

Roundhouse Group
18 Marine Gardens, Unit B, Brighton BN2 1AH
Tel: (01273) 603 717 *Fax:* (01273) 697 494
E-mail: info@roundhousegroup.co.uk
Web Site: www.roundhousegroup.co.uk
Key Personnel
Mng Dir: Alan Goodworth *E-mail:* alan@roundhousegroup.co.uk
Dir, Sales & Marketing: Matt Goodworth
	E-mail: matthew@roundhousegroup.co.uk
Publicity: Angie Prysor-Jones *E-mail:* angie@roundhousegroup.co.uk
Founded: 1991
Major distributor of adult nonfiction & children's books throughout Great Britain & Europe.
Subjects: Architecture & Interior Design, Art, Asian Studies, Astrology, Occult, Biography, Memoirs, Business, Cookery, Crafts, Games, Hobbies, Criminology, Drama, Theater, Film, Video, Genealogy, Government, Political Science, Health, Nutrition, History, House & Home, Language Arts, Linguistics, Literature, Literary Criticism, Essays, Management, Marketing, Medicine, Nursing, Dentistry, Music, Dance, Photography, Self-Help, Sports, Athletics, Travel & Tourism, Graphic Art & Design, Lifestyle, Mind-Body-Spirit, Natural World
ISBN Prefix(es): 978-1-85710
Subsidiaries: Roundhouse Reference Books
Distributor for ABC Art Books Canada; ABC-Clio; About Pets; Allen & Unwin (Australia); AM Editores; Angelika Books; AWA Press; Boyds Mills Press; Breckling Press; Bunker Hill; Cameron & Hollis; Georgina Campbell Guides; C & T Publishing; Capstone Publishing (Compass Point, Picture Window, Red Brick, Stone Arch); Charta Art Books; Classroom Complete Press; Conde Nast Johansens; Crabtree Publishing Company; Creative Homeowner; Editions Didier Millet (selected titles); Fil Rouge Press; Free Spirit Publishing; Getty Publications; Giunti Editore; David Godine; Greenwood International; Gryphon House (UK & Europe); Health Direction; Hunter Publishing; Irish Museum of Modern Art (IMMA); Landauer; Learning Together; Martingale & Company; Monsa Publishing; National Gallery of Victoria; National Library of Australia; Northern Bee Books; One Peace Books; Open Road Publishing; Panache; Paragon House; Pelican Publishing; Portland Press; Prometheus Books; Pyr; Quality Medical Publishing; J Ross Publishing; Santana Books; Self-Counsel Press; Sinclair-Stevenson; Star Bright Books; University of Queensland Press; University Press of Mississippi; UWA Publishing; Vadehra Art Gallery; Watermark; Michael Wilcox (School of Colour); WRTH (World Radio TV Handbook); ABC Art Books Canada; Angelika Books; National Library of Australia; Pyr
Foreign Rep(s): Ted Dougherty; Pernille Larsen; Tony Moggach; Peter Prout
Orders to: Orca Book Services Ltd, Unit A3, Fleets Corner Industrial Estate, off Nuffield Rd, Fleetsbridge, Poole, Dorset BH17 0HL
Tel: (01235) 465 521 *Fax:* (01235) 465 555
E-mail: tradeorders@orcabookservices.co.uk

Routledge, *imprint of* Taylor & Francis Group, an Informa Business

Routledge+
Imprint of Taylor & Francis Group, an Informa Business
2-4 Park Sq, Milton Park, Abingdon, Oxon OX14 4RN
Tel: (020) 7017 6000 *Fax:* (020) 7017 6699
Web Site: www.routledge.com
Key Personnel
Head of Rights, UK: Adele Parker *E-mail:* adele.parker@tandf.co.uk
Founded: 1834
Subjects: Anthropology, Archaeology, Architecture & Interior Design, Asian Studies, Business, Communications, Developing Countries, Economics, Education, Environmental Studies, Film, Video, Geography, Geology, Government, Political Science, History, Language Arts, Linguistics, Law, Literature, Literary Criticism, Essays, Management, Philosophy, Physical Sciences, Psychology, Psychiatry, Religion - Other, Social Sciences, Sociology, Sports, Athletics, Travel & Tourism, Women's Studies
ISBN Prefix(es): 978-0-415
Number of titles published annually: 3,000 Print; 3 Online; 10,000 E-Book
Total Titles: 60,000 Print; 12 Online; 30,000 E-Book
Ultimate Parent Company: Informa PLC
Imprints: Focal Press; Routledge Education; Routledge Law; Routledge Mental Health; Routledge Reference; Routledge Sport; Routledge Strategic Studies
U.S. Office(s): 711 Third Ave, 8th floor, New York, NY 10017, United States *Tel:* 212-216-7800 *Fax:* 212-563-2269 *E-mail:* info@routledge-ny.com *Web Site:* www.routledge-ny.com
Orders to: Bookpoint Ltd, 130 Milton Park, Abingdon, Oxon OX14 4SB *Tel:* (01235) 400 400 *Fax:* (01235) 400 401 *Web Site:* www.hodderheadline.co.uk/bookpoint
Taylor & Francis Group LLC, 7625 Empire Dr, Florence, KY 41042-2919, United States *Tel:* 800-634-7064 *Fax:* 800-248-4724 *E-mail:* orders@taylorandfrancis.com (USA, Canada, North & South America)

Routledge Education, *imprint of* Routledge

Routledge Law, *imprint of* Routledge

Routledge Mental Health, *imprint of* Routledge

Routledge Reference, *imprint of* Routledge

Routledge Sport, *imprint of* Routledge

Routledge Strategic Studies, *imprint of* Routledge

Rowman & Littlefield International
Affiliate of Rowman & Littlefield
Unit A, Whitacre Mews, 26-34 Stannary St, London SE11 4AB
Web Site: www.rowmaninternational.com
Key Personnel
Chief Executive: Oliver Gadsby *Tel:* (01752) 202360 *E-mail:* ogadsby@rowman.com
Executive Dir: Ken Rhodes
Editorial Dir: Sarah Campbell *Tel:* (01752) 202362 *E-mail:* scampbell@rowman.com
Publisher: Martina O'Sullivan *Tel:* (01752) 202363 *E-mail:* mosullivan@rowman.com
Dir, International Sales & Marketing: Jennifer Cima *Tel:* (01752) 202374 *E-mail:* jcima@rowman.com

Dir, Rights & Permissions: Clare Cox
   E-mail: ccox@rowman.com
Marketing Manager: Claudia Buttler *Tel:* (01752)
   202382 *E-mail:* cbuttler@rowman.com
Subjects: Economics, Government, Political Science, Philosophy, Cultural Studies
ISBN Prefix(es): 978-1-78348
Distribution Center: NBN International, 10
   Thornbury Rd, Plymouth PL6 7PP *Tel:* (01752)
   202301 *E-mail:* orders@nbninternational.com
   (UK, Europe & rest of world)
National Book Network, 15200 NBN Way,
   Blue Ridge Summit, PA 17214, United
   States *Tel:* 717-794-3800 *Fax:* 717-794-3828
   E-mail: customercare@nbnbooks.com (Australia, Canada, Central America, Japan, South
   America, USA)

Royal Collection Publications
York House, St James's Palace, London SW1A
1BQ
Tel: (020) 7839 1377
E-mail: publishing@royalcollection.org.uk;
   press@royalcollection.org.uk
Web Site: www.royalcollection.org.uk
Key Personnel
Dir, Content & Audiences: Jemima Rellie
Press & Public Relations Officer: Emma Shaw
Communication Manager: Rachel Woollen
   Tel: (020) 7024 5607
Founded: 1987
Subjects: Art, Fashion, History
ISBN Prefix(es): 978-1-902163; 978-1-905686
Distributed by Thames & Hudson Ltd (Worldwide exc USA & Canada); University of
   Chicago Press (USA & Canada)

**Royal College of General Practitioners
(RCGP)+**
30 Euston Sq, London NW1 2FB
Tel: (020) 3188 7400 *Fax:* (020) 3188 7401
E-mail: info@rcgp.org.uk
Web Site: www.rcgp.org.uk
Key Personnel
Publications Manager: Helen Farrelly
   E-mail: hfarrelly@rcgp.org.uk
Founded: 1952
Subjects: Education, Health, Nutrition, Medicine,
   Nursing, Dentistry, Psychology, Psychiatry
ISBN Prefix(es): 978-0-85084
Warehouse: Bertrams, Norwich
Distribution Center: Bertrams, Norwich

The Royal College of Psychiatrists
21 Prescot St, London E1 8BB
Tel: (020) 7235 2351 *Fax:* (020) 3701 2761
E-mail: reception@rcpsych.ac.uk
Web Site: www.rcpsych.ac.uk
Subjects: Psychology, Psychiatry
ISBN Prefix(es): 978-0-902241; 978-1-901242
Foreign Rep(s): Compass Academic Ltd (Ireland,
   UK); Princeton Selling Group (Canada, USA);
   David Towle International (Estonia, Iceland,
   Scandinavia)
Distribution Center: Turpin Distribution, Stratton
   Business Park, Pegasus Dr, Biggleswade, Beds
   SG18 8TQ *Tel:* (01767) 604 951 *Fax:* (01767)
   601 640 *E-mail:* custserv@turpin-distribution.
   com
Footprint Books, 1/6A Prosperity Parade, Warriewood, NSW 2102, Australia *Tel:* (02) 9997
   3973 *Fax:* (02) 9997 3185 *E-mail:* info@
   footprint.com.au *Web Site:* www.footprint.com.
   au
Publishers Storage & Shipping Corp, 46 Development Rd, Fitchburg, MA 01420, United
   States *Tel:* 978-829-2560 *Fax:* 978-348-1233
   E-mail: orders@pssc.com

Royal Institute of International Affairs+
Chatham House, 10 St James's Sq, London
SW1Y 4LE

Tel: (020) 7957 5700 *Fax:* (020) 7957 5710
E-mail: contact@chathamhouse.org
Web Site: www.chathamhouse.org
Key Personnel
Publications Editor: Jake Statham
   E-mail: jstatham@chathamhouse.org
Deputy Editor: Joanne Maher *E-mail:* jmaher@
   chathamhouse.org
Dir, Communications: Keith Burnet *Tel:* (020)
   7314 2798 *E-mail:* kburnet@chathamhouse.org
Founded: 1920
Subjects: Asian Studies, Business, Developing
   Countries, Economics, Energy, Environmental Studies, Foreign Countries, Government,
   Political Science, International Law, Regional
   Interests
ISBN Prefix(es): 978-0-905031; 978-1-86203;
   978-1-899658
Number of titles published annually: 50 Print; 60
   Online
Imprints: International Affairs; The World Today
U.S. Office(s): Brookings Institution Press,
   1775 Massachusetts Ave NW, Washington, DC 20036, United States *Tel:* 202-536-
   3600 *Fax:* 202-536-3623 *E-mail:* bibooks@
   brookings.edu
Distributed by Brookings Institution Press
Warehouse: NBN International, 10 Thornbury Rd, Estover Plymouth, Devon PL6 7PP
   Tel: (01752) 202 301 *Fax:* (01752) 202 333
   E-mail: orders@nbninternational.com *Web
   Site:* www.nbninternational.com
Orders to: NBN International, 10 Thornbury
   Rd, Estover Plymouth, Devon PL6 7PP
   Tel: (01752) 202 301 *Fax:* (01752) 202 333
   E-mail: orders@nbninternational.com *Web
   Site:* www.nbninternational.com

Royal Institution of Chartered Surveyors, see
RICS Books

The Royal Society
6-9 Carlton House Terrace, London SW1Y 5AG
Tel: (020) 7839 5561; (020) 7451 2500
   Fax: (020) 7930 2170; (020) 7976 1837
E-mail: info@royalsoc.ac.uk; sales@royalsociety.
   org
Web Site: www.royalsoc.ac.uk
Key Personnel
President: Sir Paul Nurse
Executive Dir: Dr Julie Maxton
Head of Publishing: Stuart Taylor *E-mail:* stuart.
   taylor@royalsociety.org
Senior Manager, Publishing Operations: Charles
   Lusty *E-mail:* charles.lusty@royalsociety.org
Publisher: Phil Hurst *E-mail:* phil.hurst@
   royalsociety.org
Marketing: Debbie Vaughan *E-mail:* debbie.
   vaughan@royalsociety.org
Founded: 1660
Subjects: Education, Energy, Engineering (General), Geography, Geology, Mathematics,
   Mechanical Engineering, Physical Sciences,
   Physics, Psychology, Psychiatry, Science (General)
ISBN Prefix(es): 978-0-85403

The Royal Society of Chemistry+
Thomas Graham House, Science Park, Milton Rd,
   Cambridge CB4 0WF
Tel: (01223) 420066 *Fax:* (01223) 423623
E-mail: sales@rsc.org
Web Site: www.rsc.org
Key Personnel
Mng Dir, Publishing: Dr Robert Parker
   Tel: (01223) 432308 *Fax:* (01223) 432133
Manager, Editorial Production: Janet Dean
   Tel: (01223) 432292
Publisher, Books: Rohena Anand
Publisher, Journals: Emma Wilson *Tel:* (01223)
   432386

Publisher, Magazines: Bibiana Campos-Seijo
   Tel: (01223) 432247
Publisher, Journals Development: Liz Dunn
   Tel: (01223) 432404; Jamie Humphrey
   Tel: (01223) 432139
Founded: 1841
Subjects: Chemistry, Chemical Engineering, Engineering (General), Health, Nutrition, Mechanical Engineering
ISBN Prefix(es): 978-0-85186; 978-0-85404; 978-
   0-901886; 978-0-85990; 978-1-870343; 978-1-
   84755; 978-1-84973
Branch Office(s)
Burlington House, Piccadilly, London W1J 0BA
   Tel: (020) 7437 8656
British Consulate-General Sao Paulo, Rua Ferreira de Araujo 741, 05428-002 Sao Paulo,
   Brazil *Tel:* (011) 3094 1876 *Fax:* (011) 3094
   2712
South Block, Tower C, Raycom InfoTech Park,
   5th floor, 2 Kexueyuan South Road, Haidian
   District, Beijing 100190, China *Tel:* (010) 5982
   2341 *Fax:* (010) 5982 2336
Chong Hing Finance Center, Unit 1216, Level
   12, 288 Nanjing Rd West, Huangppu District,
   Shanghai 200003, China *Tel:* (021) 6133 7739
   Fax: (021) 6133 7999
Lindencorso, 5th floor, Unter den Linden 21,
   10117 Berlin, Germany *Tel:* (030) 20924177
N 301, 3rd floor, World Trade Center, Brigade
   Gateway Campus, 26/1 Dr Rajkumar Rd,
   Malleswaram, Bangalore 560055, India
   Tel: 9620155776 (cell)
Kagakukaikan 6F, 1-5 Kanda-Surugadai, Chiyoda-
   ku, Tokyo 101-0062, Japan *Tel:* (03) 5577 4360
   Fax: (03) 5577 4190
U.S. Office(s): University City Science Center,
   3711 Market St, Suite 800, Philadelphia, PA
   19104, United States *Tel:* 215-966-6157
1050 Connecticut Ave NW, 10th floor, Washington, DC 20036, United States
Distributed by Springer-Verlag New York Inc
   (North America)
Distribution Center: Ingram Publisher Services

Royal Society of Medicine Press Ltd+
Subsidiary of Royal Society of Medicine
One Wimpole St, London W1G 0AE
Tel: (020) 7290 2900
E-mail: info@rsm.ac.uk
Web Site: www.rsm.ac.uk
Key Personnel
Dir, Strategic Development: Jeremy Theobald
   E-mail: strategydirector@rsm.ac.uk
Media Manager: Rosalind Dewar *E-mail:* media@
   rsm.ac.uk
Subjects: Medicine, Nursing, Dentistry
ISBN Prefix(es): 978-1-85315; 978-0-905958;
   978-0-9501555
Number of titles published annually: 35 Print; 1
   E-Book
Total Titles: 500 Print; 1 E-Book
Foreign Rep(s): Bernd Feldmann (Austria, Germany, Switzerland); Frans Janssen (Belgium,
   Luxembourg, Netherlands); Zoe Kaviani
   (Africa, Gulf States, Middle East); Jan Norbye
   (Denmark, Finland, Iceland, Norway, Sweden);
   Jim Osgerby (Southeast England exc London,
   Southern England); Judith Rushby (Midlands,
   Northern England, Scotland)

RSM Press Ltd, see Royal Society of Medicine
Press Ltd

Rubicon Press, *imprint of* Stacey International

Michael Russell Publishing Ltd+
Wilby Hall, Wilby, Norwich NR16 2JP
Tel: (01953) 887776 *Fax:* (01953) 887762
Key Personnel
Mng Dir: Michael Russell
Founded: 1976

Subjects: Nonfiction (General)
ISBN Prefix(es): 978-0-85955
Number of titles published annually: 15 Print
Total Titles: 135 Print

Ryland Peters & Small+
20-21 Jockey's Fields, London WC1R 4BW
Tel: (020) 7025 2200 *Fax:* (020) 7025 2201
E-mail: info@rps.co.uk; sales@rps.co.uk;
    publicity@rps.co.uk
Web Site: www.rylandpeters.com
Key Personnel
President: David Peters
Art Dir: Leslie Harrington
Dir, Sales: Christina Noriega *E-mail:* christina.
    noriega@rylandpeters.com
Rights Dir: Denise Lie *E-mail:* denise.lie@rps.co.
    uk
UK & Export Sales Dir: Danny Parnes
    E-mail: danny.parnes@rps.co.uk
Senior Publicity Manager: Yvonne Doolan
    E-mail: yvonne.doolan@cicobooks.co.uk
Founded: 1995
Publish high quality illustrated books for the in-
    ternational market.
Subjects: Architecture & Interior Design, Cook-
    ery, Crafts, Games, Hobbies, Gardening, Plants,
    Health, Nutrition, House & Home, Self-Help,
    Wine & Spirits, Lifestyle
ISBN Prefix(es): 978-1-84172; 978-1-84597
    (RPS); 978-1-900518; 978-1-906525 (CICO);
    978-1-84975
Number of titles published annually: 120 Print
Total Titles: 1,000 Print
Imprints: CICO Books; Dog 'n' Bone (gift & hu-
    mor); Paperstyle Gift Line
U.S. Office(s): Ryland Peters & Small Inc, 341 E
    116 St, New York, NY 10029, United States
    Tel: 646-791-5410 *Fax:* 646-861-3518
Foreign Rep(s): A-Z Africa Book Services (Anita
    Zih) (Africa); Angell Eurosales (Gil Angell &
    Stewart Siddall) (Scandinavia); Bookreps NZ
    Ltd (Susan Holmes) (New Zealand); Fitzmull
    Books (John Fitzpatrick) (Ireland, Northern
    Ireland); Hardie Grant Books (Leilani Mason)
    (Australia); Peter Hyde Associates (Botswana,
    Lesotho, Namibia, South Africa, Swaziland);
    itsabook (James Papworth) (Caribbean, Latin
    America exc Argentina & Brazil); Padovani
    Books Ltd (Jenny Padovani) (Portugal, Spain);
    Padovani Books Ltd (Penny Padovani) (Italy);
    Padovani Books Ltd (Isabella Curtis) (Greece)
Distribution Center: Macmillan Distribution Ltd,
    Brunel Rd, Houndmills, Basingstoke, Hants
    RG21 6XS *Tel:* (01256) 302 692 *Fax:* (01256)
    812 251 *E-mail:* orders@macmillan.co.uk

Saffron Books+
Division of EAPGROUP International Media
PO Box 13666, London SW14 8WF
Tel: (020) 8392 1122 *Fax:* (020) 8392 1422
E-mail: saffronbooks@eapgroup.com
Web Site: www.saffronbooks.com; www.eapgroup.
    com
Key Personnel
Publisher & Editor-in-Chief: Sajid Rizvi
Founded: 1992
Subjects: Antiques, Archaeology, Architecture &
    Interior Design, Art, Asian Studies, Develop-
    ing Countries, Fiction, Film, Video, Foreign
    Countries, Gardening, Plants, History, Lan-
    guage Arts, Linguistics, Literature, Literary
    Criticism, Essays, Music, Dance, Religion -
    Other, Women's Studies, Art History, Con-
    temporary International Art, Current Affairs,
    Gender Issues
ISBN Prefix(es): 978-1-872843
Number of titles published annually: 6 Print; 3
    Online
Total Titles: 40 Print

SAGE Publications Ltd+
One Oliver's Yard, 55 City Rd, London EC1Y
    1SP
Tel: (020) 7324 8500 *Fax:* (020) 7324 8600
E-mail: market@sagepub.co.uk
Web Site: www.uk.sagepub.com
Key Personnel
Founder, Publisher & Chairman: Sarah Miller
    McCune
Chief Operating Officer: Katharine Jackson
Chief Information Officer: Phil Denvir
President, Sage International: Stephen Barr
Deputy Mng Dir & Executive Vice President/
    Global Publishing: Ziyad Marar
Editorial Dir: Karen Phillips
Finance Dir: Richard Thame
Global Marketing Dir: Clive Parry
Human Resources Dir: Carol Irwin
International Sales Dir: Tony Histed *E-mail:* tony.
    histed@sagepub.co.uk
Production Dir: Richard Fidczuk
Head, Product Innovation: Ian Mulvany
Founded: 1965
Membership(s): IPG.
Subjects: Anthropology, Archaeology, Art, Behav-
    ioral Sciences, Biological Sciences, Business,
    Chemistry, Chemical Engineering, Communi-
    cations, Computer Science, Criminology, Eco-
    nomics, Education, Engineering (General), En-
    vironmental Studies, Ethnicity, Finance, Geog-
    raphy, Geology, Government, Political Science,
    Health, Nutrition, History, Human Relations,
    Language Arts, Linguistics, Management, Mar-
    keting, Mathematics, Medicine, Nursing, Den-
    tistry, Philosophy, Physics, Psychology, Psy-
    chiatry, Religion - Protestant, Social Sciences,
    Sociology, Theology, Women's Studies, Arts &
    Humanities, Cultural Studies, Psychoanalysis,
    Psychotherapy
ISBN Prefix(es): 978-0-8039; 978-0-7619; 978-
    1-903300; 978-1-84445; 978-1-4129; 978-0-
    85725; 978-1-84860; 978-1-4739; 978-1-84641;
    978-1-4462; 978-0-85702; 978-1-84787
Imprints: Paul Chapman Publishing; Corwin
    Press; Lucky Duck Books; Pine Forge Press;
    Sage Science Press
Divisions: Scolari
Branch Office(s)
SAGE Publications India Pvt Ltd, B 1/I 1 Mohan
    Cooperative Industrial Area, Mathura Rd, New
    Delhi 110 044, India *Tel:* (011) 4053 9222
    Fax: (011) 4053 9234 *E-mail:* info@sagepub.in
SAGE Publications Asia-Pacific Pte Ltd, 3
    Church St, No 10-04, Samsung Hub, Singapore
    049483, Singapore, Head, Sales & Marketing:
    Rosalia da Garcia *Tel:* 6220 1800 *Fax:* 6438
    1008 *E-mail:* sagebooks@sagepub.co.uk
U.S. Office(s): SAGE Publications Inc, 2455
    Teller Rd, Thousand Oaks, CA 91320, United
    States *Tel:* 805-499-0721 *Fax:* 805-499-0871
    E-mail: info@sagepub.com
Foreign Rep(s): Academic Marketing Services
    (Southern Africa); Amin Al-Abini (Middle East
    exc Iran, North Africa); CRW Marketing Ser-
    vices for Publishers Inc (Tony Sagun) (Philip-
    pines); Footprint Books Pty Ltd (Australia,
    New Zealand); Impact Korea (ChongHo Ra)
    (Korea); Koro Komori (Japan); Marek Lewin-
    son (Eastern Europe); Helen Li (China); Mare
    Nostrum Publishing Consultants (Frauke Feld-
    mann) (Austria, Germany, Switzerland); Mare
    Nostrum Publishing Consultants (David Picker-
    ing) (France, Italy); Mare Nostrum Publishing
    Consultants (Cristina de Lara Ruiz) (Portu-
    gal, Spain); Vikrum Mehta (Benelux); SAGE
    Publications Ltd (Malaysia); Zitsa Seraphimidi
    (Cyprus, Greece, Malta)

Sage Science Press, *imprint of* SAGE
Publications Ltd

Saint Andrew Press+
121 George St, Edinburgh EH2 4YN

Tel: (0131) 225 5722
Web Site: www.standrewpress.com; twitter.
    com/standrewpress
Founded: 1954
Publishing house of the Church of Scotland.
Membership(s): Publishing Scotland.
Subjects: History, Regional Interests, Religion -
    Protestant, Religion - Other, Theology
ISBN Prefix(es): 978-0-7152; 978-0-86153
Number of titles published annually: 12 Print; 3
    CD-ROM
Total Titles: 200 Print; 3 CD-ROM
Distributor for Church of Scotland Stationery
Foreign Rep(s): Christian Publishers Representa-
    tives
Distribution Center: Marston Book Services Ltd,
    160 Eastern Ave, Milton Park, Abingdon, Oxon
    OX14 4SB *Tel:* (01235) 465579 *Fax:* (01235)
    465518 *E-mail:* christian.orders@marston.co.uk
    Web Site: www.marston.co.uk

St David's Press, *imprint of* Welsh Academic
Press

St James Press, *imprint of* Gale

St Pauls Publishing+
Morpeth Terrace, London SW1P 1EP
Tel: (020) 7828 5582 *Fax:* (020) 7828 3329
E-mail: sales@stpauls.org.uk
Web Site: www.stpauls.org.uk
Founded: 1967
Subjects: Biblical Studies, Human Relations, Re-
    ligion - Catholic, Theology
ISBN Prefix(es): 978-0-85439
Number of titles published annually: 20 Print
Total Titles: 450 Print
Parent Company: Society of St Paul, Via
    Alessandro Savero 56, 00145 Rome, Italy
Bookshop(s): St Chad's Queensway, Birmingham,
    W Midlands B4 6ET *Tel:* (0121) 236 6336;
    25 Cookridge St, Leeds, W Yorks LS2 3AG
    Tel: (0113) 245 0850; 62 Headingley Lane,
    Leeds, W Yorks LS6 2BX *Tel:* (0113) 275
    4043; 5 King's Sq, York, N Yorks YO1 8BH
    Tel: (01904) 541729
Distribution Center: Redemptorist Publications,
    Alphonsus House, Chawton, Hants GU34 3HQ
    Tel: (01420) 88222 *E-mail:* sales@rpbooks.co.
    uk *Web Site:* www.rpbooks.co.uk (UK & Ire-
    land)
St Pauls Distribution, Moyglare Rd, Maynooth,
    Co Kildare, Ireland *Tel:* (01) 6285933
    Fax: (01) 6289330 *E-mail:* sales@stpauls.ie
    Web Site: www.stpauls.ie (outside of UK)

Salamander, *imprint of* Pavilion Books

The Salariya Book Co Ltd+
25 Marlborough Pl, Brighton, East Sussex BN1
    1UB
Tel: (01273) 603306 *Fax:* (01273) 621619
E-mail: salariya@salariya.com
Web Site: www.salariya.com
Key Personnel
Mng Dir: David Salariya
Founded: 1989
Illustrated children's books for international co-
    edition market.
Subjects: Architecture & Interior Design, Fic-
    tion, Foreign Countries, Geography, Geology,
    History, Natural History, Science (General),
    Technology
ISBN Prefix(es): 978-1-904194; 978-1-906370;
    978-1-905638; 978-1-906714; 978-1-907184;
    978-1-908177; 978-1-908759; 978-1-908973;
    978-1-904642; 978-1-905087; 978-1-909645
Total Titles: 150 Print
Imprints: Book House; Scribblers; Scribo

Salt Publishing Ltd
12 Norwich Rd, Cromer Norfolk NR27 0AX
Tel: (01263) 511011
E-mail: sales@saltpublishing.com
Web Site: www.saltpublishing.com
Key Personnel
Dir: Linda Bennett; Chris Hamilton-Emery
   Tel: (020) 8816 7604 *E-mail:* chris@
   saltpublishing.com; Jen Hamilton-Emery
   Tel: (020) 8816 8669 *E-mail:* jen@
   saltpublishing.com; John Skelton
Founded: 1990
Subjects: Biography, Memoirs, Literature, Literary Criticism, Essays, Poetry
ISBN Prefix(es): 978-1-876857; 978-1-901994;
   978-1-84471
Branch Office(s)
c/o Irish Pages, Unit 1, 129 Ormeau Rd, Belfast
   BT7 1SH, Ireland, Contact: Chris Agee
Distribution Center: Grantham Book Services,
   Trent Rd, Grantham, Lincs NG31 7XQ
   Tel: (01476) 541080 *Fax:* (01476) 541061
   E-mail: orders@gbs.tbs-ltd.co.uk
Ingram Book Group, One Ingram Blvd, La
   Vergne, TN 37086-1986, United States
   E-mail: orders@ingrambooks.com (North
   America)

The Saltire Society
9 Fountain Close, 22 High St, Edinburgh EH1
   1TF
Tel: (0131) 556 1836
E-mail: saltire@saltiresociety.org.uk
Web Site: www.saltiresociety.org.uk
Key Personnel
Executive Dir: Jim Tough *E-mail:* jim.tough@
   saltiresociety.org.uk
President: Magnus Linklater
Founded: 1936
Subjects: History, Literature, Literary Criticism,
   Essays
ISBN Prefix(es): 978-0-85411
Number of titles published annually: 3 Print
Total Titles: 3 Print

Saltyard Books, *imprint of* Hodder & Stoughton
Ltd

Salvationist Publishing & Supplies Ltd
Division of Salvation Army Trading Company
   Ltd
One Tiverton St, London SE1 6NT
Tel: (020) 7367 6588; (01933) 445 445 (web/mail
   orders) *Fax:* (01933) 445 415
E-mail: sales@sps-shop.com
Web Site: www.sps-shop.com
Key Personnel
Mng Dir: Trevor Caffull
Subjects: Music, Dance, Religion - Other
ISBN Prefix(es): 978-0-85412
Branch Office(s)
66-78 Denington Rd, Denington Industrial Estate,
   Wellingborough, Northants NN8 2QH

SAM Publications
Media House, 12 Kingsway, Bedford MK42 9BJ
Tel: (01234) 211 245 *Fax:* (01234) 325 927
E-mail: mail@sampublications.com
Web Site: www.sampublications.com
Key Personnel
Advertising Sales: Rebecca Harris
   E-mail: rebecca@sampublications.com
Editor: Andy Evans *E-mail:* andyevans@
   sampublications.com; David Francis
   E-mail: david@sampublications.com
Subjects: Aeronautics, Aviation
ISBN Prefix(es): 978-0-9533465; 978-0-9551858;
   978-1-906959

SAMS Publishing, *imprint of* Pearson Education
Ltd

Sangam Books Ltd+
57 London Fruit Exchange, Brushfield St, London
   E1 6EP
Tel: (020) 7377 6399 *Fax:* (020) 7375 1230
Founded: 1981
Subjects: Fiction, Medicine, Nursing, Dentistry,
   Nonfiction (General), Science (General), Social
   Sciences, Sociology, Technology
ISBN Prefix(es): 978-0-86131; 978-0-86311; 978-
   0-86125; 978-0-86132
Number of titles published annually: 30 Print

Saqi Books+
26 Westbourne Grove, London W2 5RH
Tel: (020) 7221 9347 *Fax:* (020) 7229 7492
Web Site: www.saqibooks.com
Key Personnel
Publisher: Lynn Gaspard *E-mail:* lynn@
   saqibooks.com
Founded: 1983
Independent publishing house of quality general
   interest & academic books on North Africa &
   the Middle East. Saqi's links with cutting edge
   & authoritative voices have led to a rigorous
   reassessment of Arab cultural heritage.
Subjects: Art, Asian Studies, Biography, Memoirs, Cookery, Developing Countries, Ethnicity, Fiction, Foreign Countries, Government, Political Science, History, Humor, Language Arts, Linguistics, Literature, Literary Criticism, Essays, Music, Dance, Nonfiction (General), Photography, Social Sciences, Sociology, Travel & Tourism, Wine & Spirits, Middle Eastern Studies
ISBN Prefix(es): 978-0-86356; 978-1-90890 (The
   Westbourne Press); 978-1-84659 (Telegram)
Number of titles published annually: 15 Print
Total Titles: 450 Print
Imprints: Telegram Books (fiction); The Westbourne Press (nonfiction)
Foreign Rep(s): Consortium Book Sales & Distribution (Canada, USA); Durnell Marketing (Andrew Durnell) (Europe, Ireland, Northern Ireland); Liberty Books Ltd (Saleem Hussain) (Pakistan); Maya Publishers Pvt Ltd (Surit Mitra) (India); The White Partnership (Hong Kong, Japan, Korea, Malaysia, Philippines, Singapore, Taiwan, Thailand); Yale Representation (Andrew Jarmain) (UK)
Distribution Center: Marston Book Services Ltd,
   160 Eastern Ave, Milton Park, Abingdon, Oxon
   OX14 4SB *Tel:* (01235) 465500 *Fax:* (01235)
   465555 *E-mail:* direct.orders@marston.co.uk
   Web Site: www.marston.co.uk

Saraband Ltd
98 Woodlands Rd, Suite 202, Glasgow G3 6HB
Tel: (0141) 339 5030 *Fax:* (0141) 332 1864
E-mail: hermes@saraband.net
Web Site: www.saraband.net
Subjects: Architecture & Interior Design, Art,
   Environmental Studies, Fiction, History, Nonfiction (General), Dreams, Heritage, Mythology,
   Nature, Symbols, Wildlife
ISBN Prefix(es): 978-1-887354
Distribution Center: Gardners Books, One
   Whittle Dr, Eastbourne, East Sussex BN23
   6QH *Tel:* (01323) 521777 *Fax:* (01323)
   521666 *E-mail:* sales@gardners.com *Web
   Site:* gardners.com

Saunders, *imprint of* Elsevier Ltd

Steve Savage Publishers Ltd+
The Old Truman Brewery, 91 Brick Lane, London E1 6QL
Tel: (020) 7770 6083
E-mail: sales@savagepublishers.com
Web Site: www.savagepublishers.com
Founded: 2001
Membership(s): Independent Publishers Guild.

Subjects: Fiction, Humor, Literature, Literary
   Criticism, Essays, Nonfiction (General)
ISBN Prefix(es): 978-1-904246; 978-0-903065
Branch Office(s)
213 Portobello High St, Edinburgh EH15 1EU
Orders to: Book Source, 50 Cambuslang Rd,
   Cambuslang, Glasgow G32 8NB *Tel:* (0845)
   370 0067; (0141) 642 9192 *Fax:* (0845) 370
   0068; (0141) 642 9182 *E-mail:* orders@
   booksource.net

Savannah Publications
90 Dartmouth Rd, Forest Hill, London SE23 3HZ
Tel: (020) 8244 4350 *Fax:* (020) 8244 2448
Web Site: www.savannahpublications.com
Subjects: History, Military Science, Military Genealogy
ISBN Prefix(es): 978-1-902366
Total Titles: 100 Print

Alastair Sawday Publishing Co Ltd
Merchants House, Wapping Rd, Bristol BS1 4RW
Tel: (01172) 047 810
E-mail: hello@sawdays.co.uk; press@sawdays.co.
   uk
Web Site: www.sawdays.co.uk
Key Personnel
Chairman: Alastair Sawday
Mng Dir: Toby Sawday
Head, Marketing & Brand: Nada Matti-Leighton
Subjects: Environmental Studies, Regional Interests, Travel & Tourism
ISBN Prefix(es): 978-1-901970; 978-1-906136;
   978-0-9521954

Scala Arts & Heritage Publishers
10 Lion Yard, Tremadoc Rd, London SW4 7NQ
Tel: (020) 7808 1550
E-mail: info@scalapublishers.com
Web Site: www.scalapublishers.com
Key Personnel
Contact: Jenny McKinley *E-mail:* jmckinley@
   scalapublishers.com
Specialize in books on museums, art galleries,
   cathedrals, historic monuments & religious &
   heritage sites.
Subjects: Architecture & Interior Design, Art, Regional Interests, Religion - Other
ISBN Prefix(es): 978-1-85759; 978-1-870248
U.S. Office(s): Scala Arts Publishers Inc, 141
   Wooster St, Suite 4D, New York, NY 10012,
   United States, Contact: Jennifer Wright Norman *Tel:* 212-477-0748 *E-mail:* jnorman@
   scalapublishers.com
Foreign Rep(s): Inbooks (Australia)
Distribution Center: ACC Distribution, Sandy
   Lane, Old Martlesham, Woodbridge, Suffolk
   IP12 4SD *Tel:* (01394) 389950 *Fax:* (01394)
   389999 *E-mail:* sales@antique-acc.com
ACC Distribution, 6 W 18 St, Suite 4B, New
   York, NY 10011, United States *E-mail:* sales@
   antiquecc.com

Scarthin Books+
The Promenade Scarthin, Cromford, Derbys DE4
   3QF
Tel: (01629) 823272 *Fax:* (01629) 825094
E-mail: nickscarthin@gmail.com
Web Site: www.scarthinbooks.com
Key Personnel
Proprietor: Dave J Mitchell
General Manager: David Booker
New Books Buyer: Guy N Cooper
Founded: 1981
Membership(s): Booksellers Association of Great
   Britain & Ireland (BAGBI).
Subjects: History, Outdoor Recreation
ISBN Prefix(es): 978-0-907758; 978-1-900446
Number of titles published annually: 5 Print
Total Titles: 110 Print
Imprints: Family Walks

Sceptre, *imprint of* Hodder & Stoughton Ltd

Schirmer Reference, *imprint of* Gale

Schofield & Sims Ltd+
Dogley Mill, Fenay Bridge, Huddersfield, W
Yorks HD8 0NQ
Tel: (01484) 607080 *Fax:* (01484) 606815
E-mail: post@schofieldandsims.co.uk
Web Site: www.schofieldandsims.co.uk
Key Personnel
Trade Sales & Marketing Dir: Harriet Platts
Tel: (020) 7833 1783
Senior Mng Editor: Dawn Phillips
E-mail: dawn@schofieldandsims.co.uk
Sales Manager: David Nesbitt *Tel:* (01484)
601718 *E-mail:* david@schofieldandsims.co.uk
Founded: 1901
Membership(s): IPG.
Subjects: Mathematics, Music, Dance, Science
(General), Literacy
ISBN Prefix(es): 978-0-7217

Scholarly Resources, *imprint of* Gale

Scholastic Ltd+
Euston House, 24 Eversholt St, London NW1
1DB
Tel: (020) 7756 7756; (0845) 6039091 (customer
service)
E-mail: contactus@scholastic.co.uk; enquiries@
scholastic.co.uk
Web Site: www.scholastic.co.uk
Key Personnel
Co-Group Mng Dir: Catherine Bell; Steve
Thompson
Publisher, Alison Green Books: Alison Green
Publisher, Children's & Global Nonfiction:
Miriam Farbey
Publisher, Fiction & Picture Books: Samantha
Smith
Editorial Dir, Nonfiction & Media: Elizabeth
Scoggins
Group Marketing & Public Relations Dir: Rachel
Partridge
Commissioning Editor: David Maybury
Desk Editor, Fiction: Peter Matthews
Founded: 1964
Subjects: Fiction, Nonfiction (General)
ISBN Prefix(es): 978-0-590; 978-0-439; 978-0-
9536420 (Alison Green Books)
Parent Company: Scholastic Inc, 557 Broadway,
New York, NY 10012, United States
Imprints: Adlib; Andre Deutsch Children's Books;
Alison Green Books; Hippo; Point
Branch Office(s)
Scholastic Book Clubs, Freepost RRGT-TRTJ-
CHTR, Windrush Park, Range Rd, Wit-
ney, Oxon OX29 0YZ *Tel:* (01993) 893456
E-mail: bookclubs@scholastic.co.uk
Scholastic Book Fairs, Westfield Rd, Southam,
Warwicks CV47 0RA *Tel:* (01926) 813910
E-mail: info@scholastic.co.uk
Scholastic Education, Freepost RRGT-TRTJ-
CHTR, Windrush Park, Range Rd, Witney,
Oxon OX29 0YZ *Tel:* (01993) 893456

School Improvement Reports, *imprint of* First &
Best in Education Ltd

The School of Life
70 Marchmont St, London WC1N 1AB
Tel: (020) 7833 1010
E-mail: shop@theschooloflife.com
Web Site: www.theschooloflife.com
Subjects: Self-Help
ISBN Prefix(es): 978-1-9997471
Distribution Center: Consortium Book Sales
& Distribution, The Keg House, 34 13 Ave
NE, Suite 101, Minneapolis, MN 55413-1007,

United States *Tel:* 612-746-2600 *Fax:* 612-746-
2606 *E-mail:* info@cbsd.com *Web Site:* www.
cbsd.com (USA & Canada) SAN: 200-6049

School of Oriental & African Studies (SOAS)+
University of London, Thornhaugh St, Russell Sq,
London WC1H 0XG
Tel: (020) 7637 2388 *Fax:* (020) 7898 4009
E-mail: marketing@soas.ac.uk
Web Site: www.soas.ac.uk
Key Personnel
Dir: Paul Webley *E-mail:* pw2@soas.ac.uk
Founded: 1916
Subjects: Art, History, Language Arts, Linguis-
tics, Literature, Literary Criticism, Essays, Reli-
gion - Other, Asia & Africa
ISBN Prefix(es): 978-0-901877; 978-0-7286

SchoolPlay Productions Ltd
15 Inglis Rd, Colchester Essex CO3 3HU
Tel: (01206) 540111
Web Site: www.schoolplayproductions.co.uk
Key Personnel
Administrator: Chrissie Wenden
E-mail: chrissie@schoolplayproductions.co.uk
Founded: 1989
Specialize in publishing plays & musicals for
performance by youth groups & schools; play
scripts & musical scores.
Membership(s): The Publishers Association.
Subjects: Drama, Theater, Music, Dance
ISBN Prefix(es): 978-1-872475; 978-1-902472
Total Titles: 160 Print; 140 Online

Science & Technology Letters, *imprint of*
Science Reviews 2000 Ltd

Science Navigation Group+
Middlesex House, 34-42 Cleveland St, London
W1T 4LB
Tel: (020) 7323 0323 *Fax:* (020) 7022 1664
E-mail: info@sciencenavigation.com
Web Site: sciencenavigation.com
Key Personnel
Chairman: Vitek Tracz *E-mail:* vitek@
sciencenow.com
Chief Executive: Andrew Crompton
E-mail: andrew@sciencenow.com
Mng Dir: Anne Greenwood *E-mail:* anne@
sciencenow.com
Finance Dir: David Menashy *E-mail:* david.
menashy@sciencenow.com
Human Resources Manager: Kate Walenkamp
E-mail: kate.walenkamp@sciencenow.com
Founded: 1979
Subjects: Biological Sciences, Medicine, Nursing,
Dentistry, Science (General)
ISBN Prefix(es): 978-1-870485; 978-1-85922
Subsidiaries: Current Drugs Ltd; New Science
Press

Science Reviews, *imprint of* Science Reviews
2000 Ltd

Science Reviews 2000 Ltd
37 Warren St, London W1T 6AD
Mailing Address: PO Box 314, St Albans, Herts
AL1 4ZG
Tel: (01727) 764601
E-mail: info@sciencereviews2000.co.uk
Web Site: www.sciencereviews2000.co.uk
Key Personnel
Mng Dir: Catherine Henchek
Publishing Manager: Christine Evans
Production Manager: Sara Nash
Production & Business Coordinator: Steve Waw-
man
Founded: 1978
Subjects: Chemistry, Chemical Engineering, En-
vironmental Studies, Medicine, Nursing, Den-
tistry, Science (General), Technology, Culture

Associate Companies: Science & Technology Let-
ters
Imprints: Science Reviews; Science & Technol-
ogy Letters; Symposium Press
Orders to: c/o MPS *Tel:* (020) 3318 3141
Fax: (020) 3318 3139; (01202) 233874
E-mail: scr@adi-mps.com

Scion Publishing Ltd
The Old Hayloft, Vantage Business Park, Blox-
ham Rd, Banbury, Oxon OX16 9UX
Tel: (01295) 258577 *Fax:* (01295) 275624
E-mail: info@scionpublishing.com
Web Site: www.scionpublishing.com
Key Personnel
Mng Dir: Dr Jonathan Ray *E-mail:* jonathan.
ray@scionpublishing.com
Sales & Marketing Dir: Simon Watkins
E-mail: simon.watkins@scionpublishing.com
Founded: 2003
Subjects: Biological Sciences, Chemistry, Chem-
ical Engineering, Disability, Special Needs,
Medicine, Nursing, Dentistry, Psychology, Psy-
chiatry, Science (General)
ISBN Prefix(es): 978-1-904842; 978-1-907904
Foreign Rep(s): Academic Marketing Services
(Michael Brightmore) (South Africa); Durnell
Marketing Ltd (Andrew Durnell) (Europe, Ire-
land, Northern Ireland, Scandinavia); Interna-
tional Publishing Services Ltd (Zoe Kaviani)
(Middle East); Palgrave Macmillan (Australia,
New Zealand); The White Partnership (Andrew
White) (Asia)
Distribution Center: NBN International, Airport
Business Centre, 10 Thornbury Rd, Plymouth,
Devon PL6 7PP *Tel:* (01752) 202 301 (UK &
Europe)
Chicago Distribution Center, 11030 S Langley
Ave, Chicago, IL 60628, United States, Cus-
tomer Service Manager: Karen Hyzy *Tel:* 773-
702-7109 *E-mail:* khyzy@pressuchicago.edu
(North & South America)

SCM Press, *imprint of* Hymns Ancient &
Modern Ltd

SCM Press+
Imprint of Hymns Ancient & Modern Ltd
Invicta House, 3rd floor, 108-114 Golden Lane,
London EC1Y 0TG
Tel: (020) 7776 7540 *Fax:* (020) 7776 7556
Web Site: www.scmpress.co.uk
Key Personnel
Group Chief Executive Officer: Dominic Vaughn
Tel: (020) 7776 7541 *E-mail:* dominic@
hymnsam.co.uk
Group Finance Dir: Sue Stapleford *Tel:* (01603)
785 908 *E-mail:* sue.stapleford@hymnsam.co.
uk
Publishing Dir: Christine Smith *Tel:* (020) 7776
7546 *E-mail:* christine@hymnsam.co.uk
Retail Sales Dir: Aude Pasquier *Tel:* (07831)
145964 *E-mail:* aude@hymnsam.co.uk
Sales & Marketing Dir: Michael Addison
Tel: (020) 7776 7551 *E-mail:* michael@
hymnsam.co.uk
Sales & Marketing Controller: Josie Gunn
Tel: (020) 7776 7555 *E-mail:* josie@hymnsam.
co.uk
Customer Services Manager: Richard Pickett
Tel: (01603) 758 907 *E-mail:* richard.pickett@
hymnsam.co.uk
Editorial Manager: Mary Matthews *Tel:* (020)
7776 7548 *E-mail:* mary@hymnsam.co.uk
Production Manager: Stephen Rogers *Tel:* (020)
7776 7543 *E-mail:* stephen@hymnsam.co.uk
Rights & Permissions Manager: Rebecca Gold-
smith *Tel:* (020) 7776 7547 *E-mail:* rebecca@
hymnsam.co.uk
Sales & Marketing Manager: Nicola Prince
Tel: (020) 7776 1072 *E-mail:* nicola@
hymnsam.co.uk

Senior Commissioning Editor: Dr Natalie K Watson *Tel:* (020) 7776 7545 *E-mail:* natalie@scmpress.co.uk
Founded: 1929
Membership(s): Publishers Association.
Subjects: Biblical Studies, Biography, Memoirs, Philosophy, Religion - Catholic, Religion - Jewish, Religion - Protestant, Religion - Other, Theology
ISBN Prefix(es): 978-0-334
Number of titles published annually: 100 Print; 6 CD-ROM; 6 Audio
Total Titles: 3,000 Print; 12 CD-ROM; 12 Audio
Associate Companies: Canterbury Press
Orders to: Norwich Books & Music, 13a Hellesdon Park Rd, Norwich, Norfolk NR6 5DR *Tel:* (01603) 785 925 *Fax:* (01603) 785 915 *E-mail:* orders@norwichbooksandmusic.co.uk *Web Site:* www.norwichbooksandmusic.co.uk

Scottish Braille Press
Division of Royal Blind School
Craigmillar Park, Edinburgh EH16 5NB
Tel: (0131) 662 4445 *Fax:* (0131) 662 1968
E-mail: enquiries.sbp@royalblind.org
Web Site: www.royalblind.org/scottishbraillepress
Key Personnel
Manager: John Donaldson
Deputy Manager: Sandra Wright
Founded: 1891
Also acts as printer.

Scottish Council for Research in Education
University of Glasgow, St Andrew's Bldg, 11 Eldon St, Glasgow G3 6NH
Tel: (0141) 330 3493
Web Site: www.gla.ac.uk/schools/education
Key Personnel
Research Officer: Kevin Lowden *E-mail:* kevin.lowden@glasgow.ac.uk
Founded: 1932
Research in the service of education, using research series, research reviews & research reports.
Subjects: Education
ISBN Prefix(es): 978-0-901116; 978-0-947833; 978-1-86003
Total Titles: 153 Print
Distributed by ACER Press (Australia)

Scottish Falcon, *imprint of* Orkney Press Ltd

Scottish Literature International, *imprint of* Association for Scottish Literary Studies

Scottish Text Society
25 Buccleuch Pl, Edinburgh EH8 9LN
Mailing Address: School of English Studies, University of Nottingham, Notts NG7 2RD
Tel: (0115) 951 5922 *Fax:* (0115) 951 5924
E-mail: editorialsecretary@scottishtextsociety.org
Web Site: www.scottishtextsociety.org
Key Personnel
President: Dr Nicola Royan *E-mail:* president@scottishtextsociety.org
Editorial Secretary: Dr Rhiannon Purdie
Founded: 1882
Learned society, publishing scholarly editions of works written in Scotland prior to 1800 & related material.
Membership(s): Publishing Scotland.
Subjects: Genealogy, History, Literature, Literary Criticism, Essays, Poetry, Religion - Protestant, Theology, Medieval Literature
ISBN Prefix(es): 978-0-9500245; 978-1-897976
Number of titles published annually: 1 Print
Total Titles: 30 Print; 1 CD-ROM
Distributed by Boydell & Brewer

SCRE Centre, see Scottish Council for Research in Education

Scribblers, *imprint of* The Salariya Book Co Ltd

Scribe UK
2 John St, London WC1N 2ES
Tel: (020) 3405 4218
Web Site: scribepublications.co.uk
Key Personnel
Publisher-at-Large: Philip Gwyn Jones
Mng Dir: Sarah Braybrooke *E-mail:* sarah@scribepub.co.uk
Editorial & Publicity Manager: Molly Slight
Digital Marketing Coordinator: Sophie Leeds
Publicist: Adam Howard
Subjects: Fiction, Nonfiction (General)
ISBN Prefix(es): 978-0-9503183
Branch Office(s)
18-20 Edward St, Brunswick, Victoria 3056, Australia *Tel:* (03) 9388 8780 *Fax:* (03) 9388 8787 *E-mail:* info@scribe.com.au *Web Site:* scribepublications.com.au
Foreign Rights: Big Apple Agency (Lily Chen) (China, Indonesia); Big Apple Agency (Chris Lin) (Taiwan); Dar Cherlin (Amelie Cherlin) (Middle East); Lora Fountain & Associates (Lora Fountain) (France); Paul & Peter Fritz AG (Christian Dittus) (Germany); Graal Literary Agency (Urszula Jedrach) (Poland); Laura Grandi & Associates (Agnese Fabbri) (Italy); The Deborah Harris Agency (Rena Rossner) (Israel); InkWell Management LLC (Catherine Drayton & George Lucas) (USA); JLM Literary Agency (Nelly Moukakou) (Greece); Katai & Bolza Literary Agency (Peter Bolza) (Hungary); Korea Copyright Center Inc (Sangeun Lee) (Korea); Mo Literary Services (Monique Oosterhof) (Netherlands, Scandinavia); Nurcihan Kesim Literary Agency (Filiz Karaman) (Turkey); Andrew Nurnberg Associates (Ludmilla Sushkova) (Russia); Andrew Nurnberg Associates (Mira Droumeva) (Bulgaria, Romania, Serbia); Kristin Olson Literary Agency (Kristin Olson) (Czechia, Slovakia); RDC Agencia Literaria SL (Beatriz Coll) (Spain); Riff Agency (Laura Riff) (Brazil, Portugal); Silkroad Publishers Agency (Jane Vejjajiva) (Thailand); Tuttle-Mori Agency (Manami Tamaoki) (Japan)
Distribution Center: Grantham Book Services *Tel:* (014) 7654 1080 *Fax:* (014) 7654 1061 *E-mail:* orders@gbs.tbs-ltd.co.uk

Scribner UK, *imprint of* Simon & Schuster UK Ltd

Charles Scribner's Sons, *imprint of* Gale

Scribo, *imprint of* The Salariya Book Co Ltd

Scripta Technica, *imprint of* John Wiley & Sons Ltd

Scriptum Editions
Imprint of Co & Bear Productions (UK) Ltd
63 Edith Grove, London SW10 0LB
E-mail: info@cobear.co.uk; sales@cobear.co.uk
Web Site: www.scriptumeditions.co.uk
Founded: 1996
Subjects: Architecture & Interior Design, Fashion, Natural History, Photography, Botanical Art, Exploration
ISBN Prefix(es): 978-0-9527665; 978-1-902686
Orders to: Thames & Hudson Distributors Ltd, 181A High Holborn, London WC1V 7QX *Tel:* (020) 7845 5000 *Fax:* (020) 7845 5055 *E-mail:* sales@thameshudson.co.uk

Scripture Union
207-209 Queensway, Bletchley, Milton Keynes, Bucks MK2 2EB
Tel: (01908) 856000 *Fax:* (01908) 856111
E-mail: info@scriptureunion.org.uk

Web Site: www.scriptureunion.org.uk
Key Personnel
Ministry Development Dir: Mr Terry Clutterham
Copyright Permissions, Overseas Rights Administration: Rosemary North *E-mail:* rosemaryn@scriptureunion.org.uk
Founded: 1867
Specialize in Bible-based resources for children, youth & adults.
Subjects: Biblical Studies, Education, Religion - Protestant, Theology
ISBN Prefix(es): 978-0-85421; 978-0-86201; 978-0-949720; 978-1-84427; 978-1-85999; 978-1-873824
Number of titles published annually: 50 Print
Total Titles: 650 Print; 2 CD-ROM; 650 Online; 2 Audio
Subsidiaries: Ligue pour la Lecture de la Bible
Branch Office(s)
157 Albertbridge Rd, Belfast BT5 4PS *Tel:* (028) 9045 4806 *Fax:* (028) 9073 9758 *E-mail:* admin@suni.co.uk *Web Site:* www.suni.co.uk
70 Milton St, Glasgow G4 0HR *Tel:* (0141) 332 1162 *Fax:* (0141) 352 7600 *E-mail:* info@suscotland.org.uk *Web Site:* www.suscotland.org.uk
87 Lower George's St, Dun Laoghaire, Co Dublin, Ireland *Tel:* (01) 280 2300 *Fax:* (01) 280 2409 *E-mail:* info@scriptureunion.ie *Web Site:* www.scriptureunion.ie
Orders to: Marston Book Services Ltd, 160 Eastern Ave, Milton Park, Abingdon, Oxon OX14 4SB *Tel:* (01235) 465579 *Fax:* (01235) 465518 *E-mail:* christian.orders@marston.co.uk *Web Site:* www.marston.co.uk
Scripture Union Mail Order, PO Box 5148, Milton Keynes MLO MK2 2YZ *Tel:* (08450) 706 006 (local call rate) *Fax:* (01908) 856020 *E-mail:* mailorder@scriptureunion.org.uk (UK)

Seaflower Books, *imprint of* Ex Libris Press

Seaforth Publishing, *imprint of* Pen & Sword Books Ltd

Search Press Ltd+
Wellwood, North Farm Rd, Tunbridge Wells, Kent TN2 3DR
Tel: (01892) 510850 *Fax:* (01892) 515903
E-mail: searchpress@searchpress.com; enquiries@searchpress.com
Web Site: www.searchpress.com
Key Personnel
Mng Dir: Martin de la Bedoyere
Head, Editorial: Katie French
Head, UK Sales: Linda Ayres *E-mail:* linda.ayres@searchpress.com
Marketing & Export Dir: Caroline de la Bedoyere
Mng Editor: Sofie Kersey
Production: Jeff Boatwright
Founded: 1970
Specialist art & craft book publishers.
Subjects: Art, Crafts, Games, Hobbies, How-to
ISBN Prefix(es): 978-0-85532; 978-1-903975; 978-1-84448; 978-1-78126; 978-1-78221
Branch Office(s)
Search Press Australia, Robertson Pl, Units 9, 10 & 11, Penrith, NSW 2750, Australia *Tel:* (02) 47323411 *Fax:* (02) 47218259 *E-mail:* sales@searchpress.com.au
U.S. Office(s): Search Press USA, 1338 Ross St, Petaluma, CA 94954-1117, United States *Tel:* 707-762-3362 *Fax:* 707-762-0335 *E-mail:* sales@searchpressusa.com
Foreign Rep(s): Angell Eurosales (Gill Angell & Stewart Siddall) (Belgium, Denmark, Finland, France, Iceland, Luxembourg, Netherlands, Norway, Sweden); David Bateman Ltd (New Zealand); Belsu Ic ve Dis Tic Ltd Sti (Turkey); Gill (Paul Neilan) (Ireland); IMA (Tony Mog-

gach) (Africa, Eastern Europe); IMA/Interme-diaamericana Ltd (David Williams) (Caribbean, Latin America); Maya Publishers Pvt Ltd (Surit Mitra) (India); Padovani Books Ltd (Cyprus, Gibraltar, Greece, Italy, Portugal, Spain); PS Publishers Services (Gabriele Kern) (Austria, Germany, Switzerland); Publishers International Marketing (Chris Ashdown) (Asia); Publishers Representatives (Tahir Lodhi) (Pakistan); Samin Far Co (Iran); Search Press Australia (Australia); Search Press USA (Robert Woodcock) (Canada, USA); Trinity Books CC (South Africa); Vijeh Nashr International Book & Journal Services (Iran); Ward International Ltd (Richard Ward) (Middle East)
Distribution Center: Penguin Random House Publisher Services, 1745 Broadway, New York, NY 10019, United States *E-mail:* distribution@randomhouse.com (North American sales)

SEDA Publications
Woburn House, 20-24 Tavistock Sq, London WC1H 9HF
Tel: (020) 7380 6767 *Fax:* (020) 7387 2655
E-mail: office@seda.ac.uk
Web Site: www.seda.ac.uk/publications.htm
Key Personnel
Events & Publications Officer: Joseph Callanan
Senior Finance Officer: Reeta Gupta
Administrator: Rosalind Grimmit
Founded: 1993
Subjects: Education, Professional Development
ISBN Prefix(es): 978-1-902435
Number of titles published annually: 3 Print
Total Titles: 38 Print

SelfMadeHero
139 Pancras Rd, London NW1 1UN
Tel: (020) 7383 5157
E-mail: info@selfmadehero.com; press@selfmadehero.com; rights@selfmadehero.com
Web Site: www.selfmadehero.com
Key Personnel
Publisher & Mng Dir: Emma Hayley
Sales & Marketing Manager: Sam Humphrey
Publishing Assistant & Digital Content Manager: Guillaume Rater
Press Officer: Paul Smith
Founded: 2007
Subjects: Biography, Memoirs, Fiction, Science Fiction, Fantasy, Crime Classics, Horror
ISBN Prefix(es): 978-0-9552856; 978-1-906838; 978-0-9558169
Foreign Rep(s): A-Z Africa Services (Anita Zih-De Haan) (Cameroon, Ethiopia, Ghana, Kenya, Malawi, Mauritius, Nigeria, Seychelles, Sierra Leone, Tanzania, Uganda, Zambia); John Fitzpatrick & Siobhan Mullet (Ireland); Peter Hyde Associates (Botswana, Lesotho, Namibia, South Africa, Swaziland); Christian & Adriana Juncu (Eastern Europe, Russia); Gabriele Kern Publishers' Services (Austria, Germany, Switzerland); Gunnar Lie & Associates Ltd (Guillaume Ferrand) (Belgium, France, South America); Padovani Books Ltd (Penny Padovani) (Greece, Italy, Portugal, Spain); Publishers International Marketing (Chris Ashdown) (North Asia, Southeast Asia); Mediehuset Rubrik (Melanie Boesen) (Denmark, Faroe Islands, Finland, Greenland, Norway, Sweden); Scotland Publishers Group UK (Midlands, Northern England, Northern Wales, Southern England, Southern Wales); Francine Siemer-Ankersmit (Netherlands); Thames & Hudson Australia Pty Ltd (Saraid Banahan) (Australia, New Zealand); Richard Ward (Middle East, Turkey)
Distribution Center: Canadian Manda Group, 165 Dufferin St, Toronto, ON M6K 3H6, Canada *Tel:* 416-516-0911 *Fax:* 416-516-0917 *E-mail:* general@mandagroup.com
Hachette Book Group USA *Toll Free Tel:* 800-759-0190 *Toll Free Fax:* 800-286-9471 (North American ordering & customer service)

Semiotext(e), *imprint of* The MIT Press

Seren+
Imprint of Poetry Wales Press Ltd
57 Nolton St, Bridgend CF31 3AE
Tel: (01656) 663018
E-mail: seren@serenbooks.com
Web Site: www.serenbooks.com
Key Personnel
Publisher: Mick Felton *E-mail:* mickfelton@serenbooks.com
Poetry Editor: Amy Wack
Founded: 1982
Subjects: Art, Biography, Memoirs, Fiction, History, Music, Dance, Photography, Poetry, Travel & Tourism, Women's Studies, Anthologies
ISBN Prefix(es): 978-0-907476; 978-1-85411; 978-1-78172
Number of titles published annually: 20 Print; 15 E-Book
Total Titles: 450 Print; 100 E-Book
Distribution Center: Welsh Books Council, Uned 15, Stad Glanyrafon, Llanbadarn, Aberystwyth SY23 3AQ *Tel:* (01970) 624455 *Fax:* (01970) 625506 *Web Site:* www.gwales.com
NBN International, 10 Thornbury Rd, Plymouth PL6 7PP, Senior Client Account Agent: Ms Karen Putt *Tel:* (01752) 202301 *E-mail:* orders@nbninternational.com *Web Site:* www.nbninternational.com
Independent Publishers Group, 814 N Franklin St, Chicago, IL 60610, United States, Vice President, Professional & Academic Markets: Paul Murphy *Tel:* 312-337-0747 *Fax:* 312-337-5985 *E-mail:* frontdesk@ipgbook.com

Serif Books+
Imprint of OR Books
47 Strahan Rd, London E3 5DA
Tel: (020) 8981 3990 *Fax:* (020) 8981 3990
E-mail: info@serifbooks.co.uk; rights@serifbooks.co.uk; press@serifbooks.co.uk
Web Site: www.serifbooks.co.uk
Founded: 1993
Subjects: Cookery, Developing Countries, Foreign Countries, Government, Political Science, History, Travel & Tourism
ISBN Prefix(es): 978-1-897959
Foreign Rep(s): Charles Gibbs Associates (Greece, Italy); Ewa Ledochowica (Central Europe, Eastern Europe); Mare Nostrum (Cristina de Lara Ruiz) (Spain); Sales East (Peter Couzens) (China, East Asia, Hong Kong, India, Japan, Pakistan, Singapore, South Asia, South Korea, Taiwan); Robert Towers (Ireland); Turnaround (UK)
Distribution Center: Central Books Ltd, One Heath Park Industrial Estate, Freshwater Rd, Dagenham RM8 1RX *Tel:* (020) 8525 8800 *Fax:* (020) 8599 2694 *E-mail:* orders@centralbooks.com *Web Site:* www.centralbooks.com (UK, Greece, Italy & International)
Wakefield Press, 16 Rose St, Mile End, Adelaide, SA 5031, Australia *Tel:* (08) 8362 8800 *Fax:* (08) 8362 7592 *E-mail:* sales@wakefieldpress.com.au *Web Site:* www.wakefieldpress.com.au (Australia & New Zealand)
Argosy Books, Unit 12 North Park, North Rd, Finglas, Dublin 11, Ireland *Tel:* (01) 823 9500 *Fax:* (01) 823 9599 *E-mail:* info@argosybooks.ie *Web Site:* www.argosybooks.ie
Stephan Phillips (Pty) Ltd, PO Box 12246, Mill St, Cape Town 8010, South Africa *Tel:* (021) 448 9839 *Fax:* (021) 447 9879 *E-mail:* info@stephanphillips.com *Web Site:* www.stephanphillips.com
Interlink Publishing, 46 Crosby St, Northampton, MA 01060, United States *Tel:* 413-582-7054 *Fax:* 413-582-6731 *E-mail:* sales@interlinkbooks.com *Web Site:* www.interlinkbooks.com (USA & Canada)

Serpent's Tail, *imprint of* Profile Books Ltd

Serpent's Tail+
Imprint of Profile Books Ltd
3 Holford Yard, Bevin Way, London WC1X 9HD
Mailing Address: 3A Exmouth House, Pine St, London EC1R 0JH
Tel: (020) 7841 6300 *Fax:* (020) 7833 3969
E-mail: info@serpentstail.com; info@profilebooks.com
Web Site: www.serpentstail.com
Key Personnel
Mng Dir: Andrew Franklin
Publisher: Hannah Westland
Editor-at-Large: Peter Ayrton
Commissioning Editor: Rebecca Gray
Rights Dir: Penny Daniel *E-mail:* penny.daniel@profilebooks.com
Sales & Marketing: Claire Beaumont *E-mail:* claire.beaumont@profilebooks.com
Founded: 1986
Subjects: African American Studies, Asian Studies, Biography, Memoirs, Ethnicity, Fiction, LGBTQ, Literature, Literary Criticism, Essays, Music, Dance, Mysteries, Suspense, Nonfiction (General), Women's Studies, High Risk/Cult
ISBN Prefix(es): 978-1-85242; 978-1-84668
Number of titles published annually: 45 Print
Total Titles: 450 Print
Foreign Rep(s): Allen & Unwin (Austria, New Zealand); APD Singapore Pte Ltd (Indonesia, Malaysia, Singapore, Thailand, Vietnam); Book Promotions (South Africa); Consortium Book Sales & Distribution (Canada, USA); Faber & Faber (Hattie Castelburg) (North Africa, Turkey); Faber & Faber (Europe, UK); Faber & Faber (Melissa Elders) (China, Hong Kong, Korea, Macau, Taiwan); Hachette India (Bangladesh, Bhutan, India, Nepal, Pakistan, Sri Lanka); InterMediaAmericana (Caribbean, Central America, South America); Profile Books (Sarah Ward) (Middle East); Repforce Ireland (Ireland)
Orders to: The Book Service Ltd, Distribution Centre, Colchester Rd, Frating Green, Colchester, Essex CO7 7DW *Tel:* (01206) 256000 *Fax:* (01206) 255715 *E-mail:* sales@tbs-ltd.co.uk *Web Site:* www.thebookservice.co.uk

Severn House Publishers Ltd, see Canongate Books

The Shabby Tatter Press, *imprint of* Raven's Quill Ltd

Shakti Communications Ltd
28a Popin Business Centre, South Way, Wembley HA9 0HF
Tel: (020) 8903 5442 *Fax:* (020) 8903 4684
Key Personnel
Contact: Mr Ravi Jain
Subjects: Fiction, Poetry
ISBN Prefix(es): 978-0-7128; 978-0-906666; 978-0-9505709

Sheep Meadow Press, *imprint of* Carcanet Press Ltd

Sheldon Press, *imprint of* The Society for Promoting Christian Knowledge (SPCK)

Sheldon Press
Imprint of The Society for Promoting Christian Knowledge (SPCK)
36 Causton St, London SW1P 4ST
Tel: (020) 7592 3900 *Fax:* (020) 7592 3939
E-mail: director@sheldonpress.co.uk; orders@sheldonpress.co.uk; sheldon@spck.org.uk
Web Site: www.sheldonpress.com

Key Personnel
Sales Dir: Alan Mordue *E-mail:* amordue@spck.
org.uk
Founded: 1973
Subjects: Health, Nutrition, Psychology, Psychia-
try, Self-Help
ISBN Prefix(es): 978-0-85969; 978-1-84709
Number of titles published annually: 30 Print
Total Titles: 250 Print
Orders to: Macmillan Distribution, Brunel Rd,
Houndmills, Basingstoke, Hants RG21 6XS
Tel: (01256) 302692 *Fax:* (01256) 812558
E-mail: orders@macmillan.co.uk

Sheldrake Press+
Imprint of Sheldrake Publications Ltd
188 Cavendish Rd, London SW12 0DA
Tel: (020) 8675 1767 *Fax:* (020) 8675 7736
E-mail: editorial@sheldrakepress.co.uk;
enquiries@sheldrakepress.co.uk; publisher@
sheldrakepress.co.uk; sales@sheldrakepress.co.
uk
Web Site: www.sheldrakepress.co.uk
Key Personnel
Contact: Mr J S Rigge
Founded: 1979
Subjects: Architecture & Interior Design, Art,
Cookery, History, House & Home, Humor,
Music, Dance, Nonfiction (General), Outdoor
Recreation, Transportation, Travel & Tourism
ISBN Prefix(es): 978-1-873329
Number of titles published annually: 2 Print
Total Titles: 30 Print
Distributed by Interlink
Distribution Center: Orca Book Services,
Fleets Corner, Unit A3, Poole BH17 0HL
Tel: (01235) 4655000 *E-mail:* orders@
orcabookservices.co.uk *Web Site:* www.
orcabookservices.co.uk
Returns: Saltway Global Ltd, 33 Hatherop,
Cirencester GL7 3NA, Mng Dir: Chris
McLaren *Tel:* (01285) 750212 *E-mail:* chris.
mclaren@saltwaypublishing.co.uk *Web
Site:* www.saltway.co.uk

Shepheard-Walwyn (Publishers) Ltd+
107, Parkway House, Sheen Lane, London SW14
8LS
Tel: (020) 8241 5927
E-mail: books@shepheard-walwyn.co.uk
Web Site: www.shepheard-walwyn.co.uk
Key Personnel
Publisher & Rights: Anthony Werner
Founded: 1972
This publisher has indicated that 50% of their
product line is author subsidized.
Subjects: Biography, Memoirs, Economics, His-
tory, Philosophy, Poetry, Body/Mind/Spirit,
Royalty, Scottish Interest
ISBN Prefix(es): 978-0-85683
Number of titles published annually: 6 Print; 5 E-
Book
Total Titles: 100 Print; 25 E-Book
Foreign Rep(s): Delphian Books (Australia, New
Zealand); Independent Publishers Group (North
America, South America)
Warehouse: Central Books Ltd, One Heath Park
Industrial Estate, Freshwater Rd, Dagenham
RM8 1RX *Tel:* (020) 8525 8800 *Fax:* (020)
8599 2694 *E-mail:* orders@centralbooks.com
Web Site: www.centralbooks.com
Distribution Center: Central Books Ltd, One
Heath Park Industrial Estate, Freshwater
Rd, Dagenham RM8 1RX *Tel:* (020) 8525
8800 *Fax:* (020) 8599 2694 *E-mail:* orders@
centralbooks.com *Web Site:* www.centralbooks.
com
Orders to: Central Books Ltd, One Heath Park
Industrial Estate, Freshwater Rd, Dagenham
RM8 1RX *Tel:* (020) 8525 8800 *Fax:* (020)
8599 2694 *E-mail:* orders@centralbooks.com
Web Site: www.centralbooks.com

Sheppard, *imprint of* Richard Joseph Publishers
Ltd

Sherwood Publishing
Subsidiary of Psychological Intelligence Ltd
Wildhill, Broadoak End, Hertford, Herts SG14
2JA
Tel: (01992) 550246 *Fax:* (01992) 525283
Web Site: www.sherwoodpublishing.com
Key Personnel
Chief Executive: Julie Hay
Founded: 1993
Books, packs, audio for organizational trainers,
consultants, HR professionals, coaches, etc &
for general public & managers.
Subjects: Behavioral Sciences, Career Develop-
ment, Education, Human Relations, Manage-
ment, Psychology, Psychiatry, Self-Help
ISBN Prefix(es): 978-0-9521964
Distributed by Gower; Open University Press

Shipping Regulations and Guidance, *imprint of*
Witherby Publishing Group

Shire Publications Ltd+
Kemp House, Chawley Park, Cumnor Hill, Bot-
ley, Oxford OX2 9PH
Tel: (01865) 811332 *Fax:* (01865) 242009
Web Site: www.bloomsbury.com
Key Personnel
Publisher & Mng Dir: Nick Wright
Mng Dir, Sales & Operations: Sarah Broadway
Rights Dir: Joanna Sharland
Founded: 1962
Subjects: Antiques, Archaeology, Architecture &
Interior Design, Biography, Memoirs, Crafts,
Games, Hobbies, Electronics, Electrical Engi-
neering, Ethnicity, Fashion, Gardening, Plants,
Genealogy, History, House & Home, Labor,
Industrial Relations, Maritime, Military Sci-
ence, Music, Dance, Natural History, Nonfic-
tion (General), Photography, Regional Interests,
Social Sciences, Sociology, Sports, Athletics,
Transportation, Travel & Tourism, Canals,
Coins & Medals, Collectibles, Costume &
Fashion Accessories, Egyptology, Furniture &
Furnishings, Glass, London, Motoring, Railway
& Steam, Scottish Heritage, Textile History,
Toys, Walking
ISBN Prefix(es): 978-0-85263; 978-0-7478; 978-
0-85994
Number of titles published annually: 30 Print
Total Titles: 500 Print
Parent Company: Osprey Publishing Ltd
Distribution Center: The Book Service Ltd, Dis-
tribution Centre, Colchester Rd, Frating Green,
Colchester, Essex CO7 7DW *Tel:* (01206)
256000 *Fax:* (01206) 255715 *E-mail:* sales@
tbs-ltd.co.uk *Web Site:* www.thebookservice.co.
uk
Random House Customer Service, 400 Hahn
Rd, Westminster, MD 21157, United States
E-mail: ecustomerservice@randomhouse.com
(USA & Canada)

Sickle Moon Books, *imprint of* Eland Publishing
Ltd

Sidgwick & Jackson, *imprint of* Pan Macmillan

Sidgwick & Jackson Ltd+
Imprint of Pan Macmillan
20 New Wharf Rd, London N1 9RR
Tel: (020) 7014 6000 *Fax:* (020) 7014 6001
E-mail: books@macmillan.co.uk; publicity@
macmillan.com; internationalsales@macmillan.
com
Web Site: www.panmacmillan.com
Key Personnel
International Dir: Jonathan Atkins *Tel:* (020) 7014
6082 *E-mail:* j.atkins@macmillan.co.uk

Publicity: Phillipa McEwan
Founded: 1908
Subjects: Archaeology, Biography, Memoirs,
Cookery, Economics, Fiction, Government,
Political Science, History, Military Science,
Music, Dance, Nonfiction (General), Sports,
Athletics, Travel & Tourism
ISBN Prefix(es): 978-0-283
Orders to: Macmillan Distribution Ltd, Brunel
Rd, Houndmills, Basingstoke, Hants RG21
6XS

Sigma Leisure, *imprint of* Sigma Press

Sigma Press, *imprint of* Stobart Davies Ltd

Sigma Press+
Imprint of Stobart Davies Ltd
c/o Stobart Davies Ltd, Stobart House, Ponty-
clerc, Penybanc Rd, Ammanford, Carmarthen-
shire SA18 3HP
Tel: (01269) 593100 *Fax:* (01269) 596116
E-mail: info@sigmapress.co.uk
Web Site: www.sigmapress.co.uk
Founded: 1980
Specialize in books on all aspects of leisure activ-
ities, particulary of the outdoors.
Membership(s): IPG.
Subjects: Crafts, Games, Hobbies, Music, Dance,
Outdoor Recreation, Regional Interests, Sports,
Athletics, Transportation, Travel & Tourism,
Cycling, Local Heritage
ISBN Prefix(es): 978-1-85058; 978-0-905104
Total Titles: 150 Print
Imprints: Sigma Leisure
Distributed by Salt Way Publishing Ltd
Foreign Rep(s): Casemate Academic (USA);
Footprint Books (Australia, New Zealand)

Silver Link Publishing Ltd+
The Trundle, Ringstead Rd, Great Addington,
Kettering, Northants NN14 4BW
Tel: (01536) 330588 *Fax:* (01536) 330588
E-mail: sales@nostalgiacollection.com
Web Site: www.nostalgiacollection.com
Key Personnel
Publisher: Peter Townsend
Company Secretary: Frances Townsend
Founded: 1985
Also acts as book packager.
Subjects: Animals, Pets, Biography, Memoirs,
Business, Crafts, Games, Hobbies, Health,
Nutrition, History, Humor, Maritime, Non-
fiction (General), Transportation, Farming,
Towns/Cities in the UK
ISBN Prefix(es): 978-0-947971; 978-1-85794
Associate Companies: Past & Present Publishing
Ltd

Simon & Schuster, *imprint of* Simon & Schuster
UK Ltd

Simon & Schuster Children's, *imprint of* Simon
& Schuster UK Ltd

Simon & Schuster UK Ltd+
Division of Simon & Schuster, Inc
222 Gray's Inn Rd, 1st floor, London WC1X
8HB
Tel: (020) 7316 1900 *Fax:* (020) 7316 0332
E-mail: uk.sales@simonandschuster.co.uk
Web Site: www.simonandschuster.co.uk
Key Personnel
Chief Executive & Publisher, UK & International:
Ian Chapman
Mng Dir, Adult Publishing Division: Suzanne
Baboneau
Mng Dir, Children's Division: Alexandra Mara-
menides
Publishing Dir, Fiction: Jo Dickinson
Publishing Dir, Nonfiction: Iain MacGregor

Adult Art Dir: Matt Johnson
Children's Art Dir, Fiction: Jenny Richards
Children's Art Dir, Picture Books & Novelty:
  Jane Buckley
Children's Editorial Dir: Jane Griffiths
Children's Marketing & Publicity Dir: Elisa Offord
Commercial Dir: Russell Evans
Editorial Dir, Children's Picture Books: Helen
  Mackenzie Smith
Finance Dir: Mark Ollard
Group Rights Dir: Stephanie Purcell
Marketing Dir, Adult: Dawn Burnett
Sales Dir: Gill Richardson
Deputy Rights Dir: Maud Sepult *E-mail:* maud.
  sepult@simonandschuster.co.uk
Head of Contracts, UK, Australia & India:
  Suzanne King
Senior Mng Editor: Jane Pizzey
Adult Mng Editor: Gail Hallet *E-mail:* gail.
  hallet@simonandschuster.co.uk
Senior Rights Manager: Amy Fletcher
Human Resources Manager: Jessica Harris
Founded: 1987
Subjects: Biography, Memoirs, Business, Cookery, Fiction, History, Nonfiction (General), Science (General), Self-Help
ISBN Prefix(es): 978-0-671; 978-0-689; 978-0-684; 978-0-7434; 978-0-7432; 978-0-7435; 978-1-4169; 978-1-4165; 978-1-84737; 978-1-84738; 978-1-84739; 978-1-84983; 978-0-85720; 978-0-85707
Number of titles published annually: 250 Print;
  50 Audio
Ultimate Parent Company: CBS Corporation, 51 W 52 St, New York, NY 10019-6188, United States
Associate Companies: Simon & Schuster (Australia) Pty Ltd, Suite 19A, Level 1, Bldg C, 450 Miller St, Camme Ray, NSW 2062, Australia *Tel:* (02) 9988 4232; Simon & Schuster Canada, 166 King St E, Suite 300, Toronto, ON M5A 1J3, Canada *Tel:* 647-427-8882 *Fax:* 647-430-9446; Simon & Schuster Publishers India, 163, 6th floor, Tower-A, The Corenthum, A-41, Sector 62, Noida, Uttar Pradesh 201 301, India
Imprints: Scribner UK; Simon & Schuster; Simon & Schuster Children's
U.S. Office(s): 1230 Avenue of the Americas, New York, NY 10020, United States
Distributor for Andrews McMeel Publishing LLC (UK, Europe & South Africa); Black Library Publishing (UK, Europe & South Africa); Inner Traditions (UK & Ireland); National Geographic (UK & Ireland); Rebellion Publishing (UK & Ireland); VIZ Media (UK & Ireland)
Foreign Rep(s): Jonathan Ball Publishers (South Africa); Gill Hess (Ireland); MPH Distributors Sdn Bhd (S&S Adult) (Malaysia, Singapore); Pansing Distribution Pte Ltd (S&S Children's) (Malaysia, Singapore); Simon & Schuster (Australia) Pty Ltd (Australia, New Zealand); Simon & Schuster Canada (Canada); Simon & Schuster India (India); Simon & Schuster USA (USA)
Shipping Address: HarperCollins Publishing Ltd, Westerhill Rd, Bishopbriggs, Glasgow G64 2QT *Tel:* (0141) 306 3100 *Fax:* (0141) 306 3767
Warehouse: HarperCollins Publishing Ltd, Westerhill Rd, Bishopbriggs, Glasgow G64 2QT *Tel:* (0141) 306 3100 *Fax:* (0141) 306 3767
Orders to: HarperCollins Publishing Ltd, Westerhill Rd, Bishopbriggs, Glasgow G64 2QT *Tel:* (0141) 306 3100 *Fax:* (0141) 306 3767
Returns: HarperCollins Publishing Ltd, Westerhill Rd, Bishopbriggs, Glasgow G64 2QT *Tel:* (0141) 306 3100 *Fax:* (0141) 306 3767

Simple Guides, *imprint of* Kuperard

Sirrocco-Parkstone International
Langdale House, 11 Marshalsea Rd, London SE1 1EN
Tel: (020) 7940 4659 *Fax:* (020) 7940 5652
Subjects: Art, History, Photography, Culture
ISBN Prefix(es): 978-1-85995; 978-1-904310; 978-1-84484; 978-1-906981; 978-1-78042; 978-1-78310

Sisters of the Love of God, see SLG Press

6th Books, *imprint of* O Books

Sleeping Bear Press, *imprint of* Gale

SLG Press
Convent of the Incarnation, Fairacres, Parker St, Oxford OX4 1TB
Tel: (01865) 241874 *Fax:* (01865) 241889
E-mail: editor@slgpress.co.uk; orders@slgpress.co.uk
Web Site: www.slgpress.co.uk
Founded: 1967
Subjects: Religion - Other, Theology
ISBN Prefix(es): 978-0-7283
Number of titles published annually: 5 Print
Total Titles: 80 Print
Parent Company: SLG Charitable Trust Ltd
Imprints: Fairacres Publications
Distributed by SCM-Canterbury Press (Australia, UK)

SLP Education+
23 West View, Chirk, Wrexham LL14 5HL
Tel: (01691) 774778 *Fax:* (01691) 774849
E-mail: sales@slpeducation.co.uk
Web Site: www.slpeducation.co.uk
Key Personnel
Contact: Phil Roberts
Founded: 1988
Specialize in educational publications for key stage 1 & key stage 2.
Subjects: Disability, Special Needs, Drama, Theater, Education, English as a Second Language, Geography, Geology, History, Humor, Mathematics, Poetry, Science (General)
ISBN Prefix(es): 978-1-86109; 978-1-871585
Distributed by Galt Educational; Hope Education; The Yorkshire Purchasing Group

Jacqui Small, *imprint of* Quarto Publishing Group UK

Jacqui Small LLP
Imprint of Quarto Publishing Group UK
74-77 White Lion St, London N1 9PF
Tel: (020) 7284 9300 *Fax:* (020) 7485 0490
E-mail: sales@jacquismallpub.com; publicity@jacquismallpub.com
Web Site: www.quartoknows.com/jacqui-small
Key Personnel
Publisher: Jacqui Small
Subjects: Architecture & Interior Design, Cookery, Crafts, Games, Hobbies, Gardening, Plants, Wine & Spirits
ISBN Prefix(es): 978-1-903221; 978-1-906417; 978-1-910254; 978-1-909342
Ultimate Parent Company: The Quarto Group Inc

small world creations
Member of Quarto International Co-Editions Group
Kingston House, 4 Oaklands Business Park, Armstrong Way, Yate BS37 5NA
Tel: (01454) 327333 *Fax:* (01454) 327666
Web Site: www.quartoknows.com/small-world-creations
Key Personnel
Mng Dir: Debbie Backhouse *E-mail:* debbie.backhouse@quarto.com

Sales Dir: Donna Webber *E-mail:* donna.webber@quarto.com
Founded: 1997
Novelty children's books for 0-5 years age range.
ISBN Prefix(es): 978-1-908078
Ultimate Parent Company: The Quarto Group Inc

Smellessence, *imprint of* Autumn Publishing Ltd

Smith-Gordon+
Division of Mimeo UK
Units 1-3, The Ermine Centre, Hurricane Close, Huntingdon, Cambs PE29 6XX
Tel: (01480) 410410 *Fax:* (01480) 311101
E-mail: publisher@smithgordon.com
Web Site: smith-gordon-publishing.co
Key Personnel
Publisher: Eldred Smith-Gordon
Founded: 1988
Subjects: Health, Nutrition, Medicine, Nursing, Dentistry, Science (General), Technology
ISBN Prefix(es): 978-1-85463
Number of titles published annually: 6 Print
Total Titles: 80 Print
Divisions: CLE Group Ltd

Smithers Pira
Member of The Smithers Group
Cleeve Rd, Leatherhead, Surrey KT22 7RU
Tel: (01372) 802000 *Fax:* (01372) 802079
Web Site: www.smitherspira.com
Key Personnel
President: Nathanial "Nat" Leonard
Global Sales Dir: Stephen Hill *Tel:* (01372) 802025 *E-mail:* shill@smithers.com
Founded: 2010
A consultancy business with major publishing & conference activities, serving the printing, publishing, packaging & paper industries.
Subjects: Publishing & Book Trade Reference, Technology
ISBN Prefix(es): 978-1-85802; 978-0-902799; 978-1-905189; 978-0-85168; 978-0-948905; 978-1-85713
U.S. Office(s): Smithers Apex, 19 Northbrook Dr, Portland, ME 04105, United States *Tel:* 207-781-9800 *Fax:* 207-781-2150
Distribution Center: US Distribution Testing Laboratory, 6539 Westland Way, Suite 24, Lansing, MI 48917, United States *Tel:* 517-322-2400

Smithers Rapra+
Member of The Smithers Group
Shawbury, Shrewsbury, Salop SY4 4NR
Tel: (01939) 250383 *Fax:* (01939) 251118
E-mail: info@smithersrapra.com
Web Site: www.smithersrapra.com
Key Personnel
Pres: Nathaniel "Nat" Leonard
Marketing Coordinator, Publishing: Claire Griffiths *E-mail:* cgriffiths@smithers.com
Founded: 1925
Produces books, reports, databases relating to all aspects of rubber & plastics processes, products & properties.
Subjects: Automotive, Chemistry, Chemical Engineering, Science (General), Technology, Polymer Science & Technology
ISBN Prefix(es): 978-1-85957; 978-1-84735; 978-0-902348
Number of titles published annually: 25 Print; 10 Online
Total Titles: 300 Print

Colin Smythe Ltd
38 Mill Lane, Gerrards Cross, Bucks SL9 8BA
Tel: (01753) 886000 *Fax:* (01753) 886469
Web Site: colinsmythe.co.uk
Key Personnel
Mng Dir & International Rights: Colin Smythe *E-mail:* cpsmythe@aol.com
Founded: 1966
Book publishers & author's agent.

Membership(s): Publishers' Association.
Subjects: Biography, Memoirs, Drama, Theater, Literature, Literary Criticism, Essays, Religion - Catholic, Folklore, Mysticism
ISBN Prefix(es): 978-0-900675; 978-0-901072; 978-0-905715; 978-0-86140; 978-0-85105
Number of titles published annually: 3 Print
Total Titles: 310 Print
Distributed by Dufour Editions (USA & Canada)
Distributor for ELT Press (Europe); Tir Eolas (Britain & Europe)

Snowbooks Ltd
Chiltern House, Thame Rd, Haddenham HP17 8BY
Tel: (01865) 600 995
E-mail: info@snowbooks.com
Web Site: snowbooks.com
Key Personnel
Mng Dir: Emma Barnes *E-mail:* emma@ snowbooks.com
Founded: 2003
Publishes intelligent yet readable, needful fiction & nonfiction. Nonfiction categories include popular science, business & society.
Membership(s): IPG.
Subjects: Biography, Memoirs, Business, Crafts, Games, Hobbies, Earth Sciences, Fiction, Government, Political Science, History, Management, Mysteries, Suspense, Nonfiction (General), Philosophy, Physics, Psychology, Psychiatry, Science (General), Science Fiction, Fantasy, Sports, Athletics, Cycling, Fitness, Historical Fiction
ISBN Prefix(es): 978-0-9545759; 978-1-905005; 978-1-906727; 978-1-907777
Number of titles published annually: 21 Print; 5 E-Book
Total Titles: 153 Print; 28 E-Book
Associate Companies: General Products Ltd
Foreign Rep(s): A&B (Susie Dunlop) (UK); Hardie Grant Publishers (Julie Pinkham) (Australia); Sales East (Peter Couzens) (Far East)
Distribution Center: Gardners Books, One Whittle Dr, Eastbourne, East Sussex BN23 6QH *Tel:* (01323) 521555 *E-mail:* sales@gardners. com

Snowflake Books Ltd
Suite 241, 266 Banbury Rd, Summerton, Oxford OX2 7DL
E-mail: info@snowflakebooks.co.uk
Web Site: www.snowflakebooks.co.uk
Founded: 2007
ISBN Prefix(es): 978-0-9565457; 978-1-908350
Foreign Rights: B K Norton Ltd (Taiwan)

SOAS, see School of Oriental & African Studies (SOAS)

Society for Endocrinology
22 Apex Court, Woodlands, Bradley Stoke, Bristol BS32 4JT
Tel: (01454) 642220 *Fax:* (01454) 642222
E-mail: info@endocrinology.org; sales@ endocrinology.org
Web Site: www.endocrinology.org
Founded: 1946
Established to promote the study of the endocrine system, publishes journals, books, conference proceedings & newsletters & offers a publication service to pharmaceutical companies.
Learned society.
ISBN Prefix(es): 978-1-898099
Total Titles: 12 Print
Imprints: Bio Scientifica
Distributed by Portland Press Ltd

The Society for Promoting Christian Knowledge (SPCK)+
36 Causton St, London SW1P 4ST

Tel: (020) 7592 3900 *Fax:* (020) 7592 3939
E-mail: spck@spck.org.uk
Web Site: www.spckpublishing.co.uk; www.spck. org.uk
Key Personnel
Chief Executive: Sam Richardson
Commercial Dir: Alexandra McDonald
E-mail: amcdonald@spck.org.uk
Sales Dir: Alan Mordue *E-mail:* amordue@spck. org.uk
Sales Representative: Raymond Witty
E-mail: raymondwitty@btinternet.com
Founded: 1698
Subjects: Biblical Studies, Biography, Memoirs, Inspirational, Spirituality, Religion - Catholic, Religion - Protestant, Religion - Other, Science (General), Self-Help, Theology, Liturgy
ISBN Prefix(es): 978-0-7459; 978-0-85969; 978-0-281; 978-1-902694
Number of titles published annually: 80 Print
Total Titles: 500 Print
Imprints: Marylebone House; Sheldon Press
Distributed by Baker & Taylor (USA & Canada); Ingram (USA & Canada)
Foreign Rep(s): Chris Ashdown (Far East); John Garratt Publishing Pty Ltd (Australia, New Zealand)
Orders to: Macmillan Distribution, Brunel Rd, Houndmills, Basingstoke, Hants RG21 6XS *Tel:* (01256) 302692

Society for Research into Higher Education, see SRHE

Sophia Books, *imprint of* Rudolf Steiner Press

Soundings, see Isis Publishing Ltd

South Street Press, *imprint of* Garnet Publishing Ltd

Southgate Publishers+
The Square, Sandford, Crediton, Devon EX17 4LW
Tel: (01363) 776888 *Fax:* (01363) 776889
E-mail: info@southgatepublishers.co.uk
Web Site: www.southgatepublishers.co.uk
Key Personnel
Mng Dir: Drummond Johnstone *E-mail:* dj@ southgatepublishers.co.uk
Founded: 1991
Specialize in resources for teachers, home learning & life-long learning.
Subjects: Art, Education, Environmental Studies, Finance, Language Arts, Linguistics, Mathematics, Music, Dance, Science (General), Technology, Family Learning, Language & Humanities, Learning, Parenting
ISBN Prefix(es): 978-1-85741
Total Titles: 120 Print
Subsidiaries: Mosaic Educational Publications
Distributed by Bacon & Hughes (Canada)

Southover Press, *imprint of* Equinox Publishing Ltd

Southwater, *imprint of* Anness Publishing Ltd

Souvenir Press Ltd+
43 Great Russell St, London WC1B 3PD
Tel: (020) 7580 9307 *Fax:* (020) 7580 5064
E-mail: souvenirpress@souvenirpress.co.uk
Web Site: www.souvenirpress.co.uk
Founded: 1951
Membership(s): Publishers' Association.
Subjects: Animals, Pets, Art, Biography, Memoirs, Business, Education, Fiction, Gardening, Plants, Government, Political Science, Health, Nutrition, History, How-to, Humor, Inspirational, Spirituality, Literature, Literary Criti-

cism, Essays, Medicine, Nursing, Dentistry, Music, Dance, Nonfiction (General), Philosophy, Poetry, Psychology, Psychiatry, Religion - Other, Self-Help, Social Sciences, Sociology, Sports, Athletics, Travel & Tourism, Mythology
ISBN Prefix(es): 978-0-285
Number of titles published annually: 55 Print
Total Titles: 700 Print
Imprints: Condor Books; Human Horizons Series; Independent Voices; The Story-Tellers
Subsidiaries: Euro-Features Ltd; Pictorial Presentations Ltd; Pop-Universal Ltd; Souvenir Press (Educational & Academic) Ltd; Souvenir Press (Films) Ltd
Distributed by Independent Publishers Group (IPG)
Foreign Rep(s): Ted Dougherty (Austria, Belgium, France, Germany, Greece, Italy, Netherlands, Switzerland); John Edgler (Caribbean, Scandinavia); Vivienne Lavery (Ireland, Northern Ireland); Rupa & Co (India); Trinity Books (South Africa); Peter Ward Book Exports (Cyprus, Malta, Middle East, North Africa)
Orders to: BookPoint Ltd, 130 Milton Park, Abingdon, Oxon OX14 4SE *Tel:* (01235) 400400 *E-mail:* export@bookpoint.co.uk

Sovereign World Ltd+
PO Box 784, Ellel, Lancaster LA1 9DA
Tel: (01524) 753805
Web Site: www.sovereignworld.com
Key Personnel
Chairman & International Dir: Peter J Horrobin
Founded: 1986
Subjects: Biography, Memoirs, Religion - Protestant, Theology
ISBN Prefix(es): 978-1-85240
Parent Company: The Christian Trust
Foreign Rep(s): Bridge-Logos Foundation (USA); Ellel Ministries (S) - Zion Healing Centre Ltd (Brunei, Cambodia, East Asia, Indonesia, Laos, Malaysia, Myanmar, Philippines, Singapore, Thailand, Vietnam); Ellel Ministries South Africa (Africa); KI Entertainment (Australia, New Zealand, Singapore); Sovereign Christian Books Inc (Canada)

Sparkling Books Ltd
59 The Avenue, Southampton, Hants SO17 1XS
Tel: (020) 3291 2471
Web Site: www.sparklingbooks.com; www. sparklingbooks.biz
Membership(s): Independent Publishers Guild.
Subjects: Fiction, Nonfiction (General)
ISBN Prefix(es): 978-1-907230
Foreign Rep(s): Geoff Bryan (Ireland, Northern Ireland)
Distribution Center: BookSource, 50 Cambuslang Rd, Cambuslang, Glasgow G32 8NB, Contact: Louise Morris *Tel:* (0845) 370 0063; (0141) 642 9192 *Fax:* (0845) 370 0064; (0141) 642 9181 *E-mail:* louise.morris@booksource.net
Silvermine International Books, 25 Perry Ave, Suite 11, Norwalk, CT 06850, United States, Mng Partner: John Atkin *Tel:* 203-451-2396 *E-mail:* info@jawilsons.com *Web Site:* jawilsons.com/pages/who-we-are (USA & Canada)

SPCK, see The Society for Promoting Christian Knowledge (SPCK)

Special Interest Model Books Ltd+
50a Willis Way, Poole, Dorset BH15 3SY
Tel: (01202) 649930 *Fax:* (01202) 649950
E-mail: orders@specialinterestmodelbooks.co.uk
Web Site: www.specialinterestmodelbooks.co.uk
Key Personnel
Contact: Chris Lloyd
Specialize in model hobby books.
Subjects: Aeronautics, Aviation, Crafts, Games, Hobbies, Electronics, Electrical Engineering,

Engineering (General), Maritime, Wine & Spirits, Modelling
ISBN Prefix(es): 978-0-85344; 978-1-85486; 978-0-85076; 978-0-85242; 978-0-900841
Total Titles: 130 Print
Imprints: Amateur Winemaker; Argus Books; Nexus Special Interests
Distribution Center: Orca Book Services, Fleets Corner Industrial Estate, Unit A3, Poole, Dorset BH17 0HL *Tel:* (01202) 465577
E-mail: orders@orcabookservices.co.uk

Speechmark Editions, *imprint of* Speechmark Publishing Ltd

Speechmark Publishing Ltd+
5 Thomas More Sq, St Katharine Docks, London E1W 1YW
Tel: (0845) 034 4610 *Fax:* (0845) 034 4649
E-mail: customer.services@speechmark.net
Web Site: www.speechmark.net
Key Personnel
Publisher: Katrina Hulme-Cross *E-mail:* katrina.hulmecross@speechmark.net
Editorial & Production Manager: Tanya Dean *E-mail:* tanya.dean@speechmark.net
Marketing Manager: Rebecca Leakey *Tel:* (020) 7954 3422 *E-mail:* rebecca.leakey@speechmark.net
Sales & Business Development: Neil Macdonald *E-mail:* neil.macdonald@speechmark.net
Founded: 1984
Practical handbooks for teachers, speech & language therapists, psychologists, occupational therapists, nursing staff & parents.
Membership(s): BESA; IPG.
Subjects: Behavioral Sciences, Child Care & Development, Crafts, Games, Hobbies, Disability, Special Needs, Drama, Theater, Education, Health, Nutrition, Language Arts, Linguistics, Medicine, Nursing, Dentistry, Psychology, Psychiatry, Social Sciences, Sociology, Autism, Early Development, Gerontology, Mental Health, Speech & Language
ISBN Prefix(es): 978-0-86388
Number of titles published annually: 30 Print
Total Titles: 300 Print; 4 CD-ROM; 7 Audio
Parent Company: Electric Word Group PLC
Imprints: ColorCards; Pocket ColorCards; Speechmark Editions
Distributed by Speechbin
Foreign Rights: John Scott Co (USA)

Spellmount+
Imprint of The History Press
The Mill, Brimscombe Port, Stroud, Glos GL5 2QG
Tel: (01453) 883300 *Fax:* (01453) 883233
E-mail: web@thehistorypress.co.uk
Web Site: www.thehistorypress.co.uk
Founded: 1983
Subjects: Biography, Memoirs, History, Military Science, Nonfiction (General)
ISBN Prefix(es): 978-0-946771; 978-1-873376; 978-1-86227
Associate Companies: National Army Museum Publications
Warehouse: Marston Book Service Ltd, 160 Eastern Ave, Milton Park, Abingdon, Oxon OX14 4SB *Tel:* (01235) 465500 *Fax:* (01235) 465555 *E-mail:* direct.enq@marston.co.uk *Web Site:* www.marston.co.uk
Orders to: Marston Book Service Ltd, 160 Eastern Ave, Milton Park, Abingdon, Oxon OX14 4SB *Tel:* (01235) 465500 *Fax:* (01235) 465555 *E-mail:* direct.orders@marston.co.uk *Web Site:* www.marston.co.uk

Sphere, *imprint of* Little, Brown Book Group

Spindlewood, *imprint of* Ragged Bears Ltd

Spitfire, *imprint of* Elliott & Thompson

Spitfire Originals, *imprint of* Elliott & Thompson

The Spokesman+
Imprint of Bertrand Russell Peace Foundation Ltd
Russell House, Bulwell Lane, Basford, Nottingham, Notts NG6 0BT
Tel: (0115) 970 8318 *Fax:* (0115) 942 0433
E-mail: elfeuro@compuserve.com
Web Site: www.spokesmanbooks.com; www.russfound.org
Key Personnel
Dir: Anthony Simpson
Founded: 1970
Subjects: Business, Economics, Environmental Studies, Government, Political Science, Labor, Industrial Relations, Philosophy, Social Sciences, Sociology, Human Rights & Peace
ISBN Prefix(es): 978-0-85124; 978-0-902917; 978-0-9500300
Associate Companies: Russell Press Ltd *E-mail:* info@russellpress.com *Web Site:* www.russellpress.com
Distribution Center: Central Books Ltd, One Heath Park Industrial Estate, Freshwater Rd, Dagenham RM8 1RX *Tel:* (020) 8525 8800 *Fax:* (020) 8599 2694 *E-mail:* orders@centralbooks.com *Web Site:* www.centralbooks.com

Sports Turf Research Institute (STRI)
St Ives Estate, Bingley, W Yorks BD16 1AU
Tel: (01274) 565131; (01274) 518918 (sales & marketing) *Fax:* (01274) 561891
E-mail: info@stri.co.uk
Web Site: www.stri.co.uk
Founded: 1929
Independent consultancy & research organization specializing in natural turf grass & sports surfaces.
Subjects: Ecology, Turfgrass Science for Sports Surfaces
ISBN Prefix(es): 978-1-873431; 978-0-9503647
Number of titles published annually: 4 Print; 1 CD-ROM
Total Titles: 18 Print; 3 CD-ROM

SportsBooks Ltd
9 St Aubyns Pl, York YO24 1EQ
Tel: (01904) 613475
E-mail: info@sportsbooks.ltd.uk
Web Site: www.sportsbooks.ltd.uk
Key Personnel
Founder: Randall Northam
Founded: 1995
Subjects: Fiction, Nonfiction (General), Sports, Athletics
ISBN Prefix(es): 978-1-899807; 978-1-907524
Imprints: BMM
Foreign Rights: Jill Hughes
Distribution Center: Turnaround Publisher Services Ltd, Unit 3, Olympia Trading Estate, Coburg Rd, London N22 6TZ *Tel:* (020) 8829 3000 *E-mail:* orders@turnaround-uk.com (UK & Europe)

The Sportsman's Press, *imprint of* Quiller Publishing Ltd

The Sportsman's Press+
Imprint of Quiller Publishing Ltd
Wykey House, Wykey, Shrewsbury, Salop SY4 1JA
Tel: (01939) 261616 *Fax:* (01939) 261606
E-mail: admin@quillerbooks.com
Web Site: www.countrybooksdirect.com
Key Personnel
Editorial & Foreign Rights: John Beaton *E-mail:* john@beaton.org.uk

Trade Sales: Matt Collis *E-mail:* matt@quillerbooks.com
Customer Services: Nicola Evans *E-mail:* nicola@quillerbooks.com
Founded: 1984
Subjects: Cookery, Humor, Sports, Athletics, Country Sports, Equestrian
ISBN Prefix(es): 978-0-948253
Distribution Center: Grantham Book Services, Trent Rd, Grantham, Lincs NG31 7XQ *Tel:* (01476) 541080 *Fax:* (01476) 541061 *E-mail:* orders@gbs.tbs-ltd.co.uk

Spring, *imprint of* Orion Publishing Group Ltd

Springer-Verlag London Ltd+
236 Gray's Inn Rd, 6th floor, London WC1X 8HB
Tel: (020) 3192 2000
Web Site: www.springer.com
Key Personnel
Editorial Dir: Beverley Ford *E-mail:* beverley.ford@springer.com
Founded: 1987
Subjects: Astronomy, Chemistry, Chemical Engineering, Computer Science, Engineering (General), Mathematics, Medicine, Nursing, Dentistry, Biomedicine, Clinical Medicine, Human Sciences, Life Sciences, Physical Sciences, Statistics
ISBN Prefix(es): 978-0-7923; 978-3-540; 978-1-85233; 978-0-85200; 978-0-7462; 978-1-4020; 978-1-84628; 978-1-84800; 978-1-84882; 978-1-84996; 978-1-4471; 978-0-85729
Parent Company: Springer Science+Business Media, Heidelberger Platz 3, 14197 Berlin, Germany
Orders to: Springer Customer Service Center GmbH, Haberstr 7, 69126 Heidelberg, Germany *Tel:* (06221) 345-4301 *Fax:* (06221) 345-4229

Spruce, *imprint of* Octopus Publishing Group Ltd

Square One Publications+
The Tudor House, 16 Church St, Worcester, Worcs WR8 0HT
Tel: (01684) 593704; (0843) 266 9124
Founded: 1988
Subjects: Biography, Memoirs, Militaria
ISBN Prefix(es): 978-1-899955; 978-1-872017
Warehouse: Upton Office Services, 18 Riverside Close, Upton upon Severn, Worcs WR8 0JN, Contact: Deidre Thompson *Tel:* (01684) 592035 *E-mail:* deidre@uptonjazz.farmcom.net

Square Peg, *imprint of* The Random House Group Ltd, a Penguin Random House Company

SRHE
73 Collier St, London N1 9BE
Tel: (020) 7427 2350 *Fax:* (020) 7278 1135
E-mail: srhe@srhe.ac.uk
Web Site: www.srhe.ac.uk
Key Personnel
Dir: Helen Perkins *E-mail:* hsperkins@srhe.ac.uk
Finance Officer: Franco Carta *E-mail:* fcarta@srhe.ac.uk
Founded: 1965
The Society is a registered charity & publishes mainly in cooperation with Open University Press.
Subjects: Education
ISBN Prefix(es): 978-0-900868

Stacey International+
19 Catherine Pl, SW1E 6DX London
Tel: (020) 7221 7166
E-mail: editorial@stacey-international.co.uk
Web Site: www.stacey-international.co.uk

Key Personnel
Sales & Marketing Manager: David Birkett
Founded: 1974
Subjects: Archaeology, Architecture & Interior Design, Art, Business, Cookery, Education, Fiction, Foreign Countries, Gardening, Plants, Genealogy, Geography, Geology, History, Natural History, Photography, Poetry, Religion - Islamic, Travel & Tourism
ISBN Prefix(es): 978-0-905743; 978-0-9503304; 978-0-948695; 978-1-900988; 978-0-9533300; 978-1-905299; 978-0-9559447
Imprints: Capuchin Classics; Gorilla Guides; Rubicon Press
Foreign Rep(s): Casemate | academic (USA); Durnell Marketing Ltd (Europe, Ireland); Signature Book Representation (UK)
Distribution Center: NBN International, 10 Thornbury Rd, Plymouth PL6 7PP *Tel:* (01752) 202301 *Fax:* (01752) 202333 *E-mail:* orders@nbninternational.com

Staff & Educational Development Association, see SEDA Publications

Stainer & Bell Ltd
Victoria House, 23 Gruneisen Rd, London N3 1DZ
Mailing Address: PO Box 110, London N3 1DZ
Tel: (020) 8343 3303 *Fax:* (020) 8343 3024
E-mail: post@stainer.co.uk
Web Site: www.stainer.co.uk
Key Personnel
Publishing Dir: Nicholas Williams
Joint Mng Dir: Carol Wakefield
Joint Mng Dir, Publicity, Rights & Permissions: Keith Wakefield *E-mail:* keith@stainer.co.uk
Founded: 1907
Subjects: Education, Music, Dance, Religion - Other
ISBN Prefix(es): 978-0-85249; 978-0-900844; 978-0-903000
Number of titles published annually: 20 Print; 1 CD-ROM
Total Titles: 2,300 Print; 1 CD-ROM; 2,000 Online
Imprints: Augener; Galliard; A Weekes; Joseph Williams

Stanborough Press Ltd
Alma Park, Grantham, Lincs NG31 9SL
Tel: (01476) 591700 *Fax:* (01476) 577144
E-mail: stanborg@aol.com
Web Site: www.stanboroughpress.co.uk
Key Personnel
Mng Dir: Paul Hammond
Founded: 1892
Publisher for the Seventh-Day Adventist Church in the UK.
Subjects: Religion - Other
ISBN Prefix(es): 978-0-904748; 978-0-900703; 978-1-899505; 978-1-904685; 978-1-907456; 978-1-909545
U.S. Office(s): Review & Herald Publishing Association, Hagerstown, MD 21740, United States

The Stationery Office, see TSO (The Stationery Office)

Rudolf Steiner Press+
Hillside House, The Square, Forest Row, East Sussex RH18 5ES
Tel: (01342) 824433 *Fax:* (01342) 826437
E-mail: office@rudolfsteinerpress.com
Web Site: www.rudolfsteinerpress.com
Key Personnel
Mng Dir: Sevak Gulbekian
Founded: 1920
Subjects: Agriculture, Art, Biography, Memoirs, Drama, Theater, Education, Health, Nutrition, Literature, Literary Criticism, Essays,

Medicine, Nursing, Dentistry, Music, Dance, Philosophy, Religion - Other, Self-Help
ISBN Prefix(es): 978-0-85440; 978-1-85584
Number of titles published annually: 15 Print
Total Titles: 400 Print; 1 Audio
Imprints: Sophia Books
Distributor for Completion Press; Mercury Arts Publications; New Knowledge Books; St George Publications; Rudolf Steiner Verlag; SteinerBooks
Foreign Rep(s): Ceres Books (New Zealand); Footprint Books Pty Ltd (Australia); Rudolf Steiner Publications (South Africa); SteinerBooks (USA); Tri-Fold Books (Canada)
Orders to: BookSource, 50 Cambuslang Rd, Glasgow G32 8NB *Tel:* (0845) 370 0063 *Fax:* (0845) 370 0064 *E-mail:* orders@booksource.net
Returns: BookSource, 50 Cambuslang Rd, Glasgow G32 8NB

Stenlake Publishing Ltd+
54-58 Mill Sq, Catrine, Ayrshire KA5 6RD
Tel: (01290) 552233 (editorial); (01290) 551122 (sales) *Fax:* (01290) 551122
E-mail: info@stenlake.co.uk; sales@stenlake.co.uk
Web Site: stenlake.co.uk
Key Personnel
Mng Dir: Richard Stenlake
Founded: 1987
Subjects: Architecture & Interior Design, Art, Cookery, Crafts, Games, Hobbies, History, Maritime, Regional Interests, Transportation, Beekeeping, Ceramics, Horticulture, Pottery
ISBN Prefix(es): 978-1-872074; 978-1-84033; 978-0-907526
Number of titles published annually: 50 Print
Total Titles: 390 Print
Imprints: Alloway Publishing Ltd; Marston House

Stobart Davies Ltd+
Stobart House Pontyclerc, Penybanc Rd, Ammanford, Carmarthenshire SA18 3HP
Tel: (01269) 593100 *Fax:* (01269) 596116
E-mail: sales@stobartdavies.com
Web Site: www.stobartdavies.com
Key Personnel
Mng Dir: Nigel Evans
Editorial Dir: Jane Evans *E-mail:* jane@stobartdavies.com
Founded: 1989
Subjects: Crafts, Games, Hobbies, How-to, Natural History, Forestry, Woodwork
ISBN Prefix(es): 978-0-85442
Number of titles published annually: 40 Print
Total Titles: 65 Print
Imprints: Sigma Press

The Story-Tellers, *imprint of* Souvenir Press Ltd

Strategic Comments, *imprint of* International Institute for Strategic Studies

Strategic Dossiers, *imprint of* International Institute for Strategic Studies

Strategic Survey, *imprint of* International Institute for Strategic Studies

Stratus Books Ltd, see House of Stratus

Strauss House Productions
Lumby Grange Cass Lane, South Milford LS25 5JA
Tel: (07850) 687321
E-mail: info@strausshouseproductions.com
Web Site: strausshouseproductions.com/publishing
Key Personnel
Owner: Hilary Robinson

Founded: 2011
ISBN Prefix(es): 978-0-9571245
Distribution Center: York Publishing, 64 Hallfield Rd, Layerthorpe, York YO31 7ZQ, Contact: Nerys Spofforth *Tel:* (01904) 431 213 *E-mail:* nspofforth@yps-publishing.co.uk *Web Site:* www.yps-publishing.co.uk
Independent Publishers Group, 814 N Franklin St, Chicago, IL 60610, United States (USA & Canada)

STRI, see Sports Turf Research Institute (STRI)

Strident Publishing
22 Strathwhillan Dr, Hairmyres, East Kilbride G75 8GT
Tel: (01355) 220588
E-mail: info@stridentpublishing.co.uk
Web Site: www.stridentpublishing.co.uk
Subjects: Fiction
ISBN Prefix(es): 978-1-905537
Distribution Center: Booksource, 50 Cambuslang Rd, Glasglow G32 8NB *Tel:* (0870) 370 0063 (customer service) *Fax:* (0845) 370 0064 *E-mail:* orders@booksource.net *Web Site:* www.booksource.net

Stripes Publishing, *imprint of* Little Tiger Press Group

Stripes Publishing
Imprint of Magi Publications
Little Tiger, One The Coda Centre, 189 Munster Rd, London SW6 6AW
Tel: (020) 7385 6333 *Fax:* (020) 7385 7333
Web Site: www.littletiger.co.uk/stripes-publishing
Key Personnel
Associate Publisher: Jane Harris
Group Sales & Marketing Dir: David Bucknor *Tel:* (07967) 672906 (cell) *E-mail:* dbucknor@littletiger.co.uk
Group UK Sales Manager: Patricia Cooper *Tel:* (07950) 410320 (cell) *E-mail:* pcooper@littletiger.co.uk
Group Export Sales: Nik Bhatia *Tel:* (07786) 333889 (cell) *E-mail:* nbhatia@littletiger.co.uk
Senior Editor: Ruth Bennett
Founded: 2006
Subjects: Fiction
ISBN Prefix(es): 978-1-84715; 978-1-84745
Foreign Rep(s): Butler Sims Ltd (Brian Blennerhassett) (Ireland)
Distribution Center: Macmillan Distribution (MDL), Customer Services Dept, Brunel Rd, Houndmills, Basingstoke, Hants RG21 6XT *Tel:* (01256) 302 692 *Fax:* (01256) 812 558 *E-mail:* orders@macmillan.co.uk *Web Site:* www.macmillandistribution.co.uk

Studio Fun International+
The Ice House, 124-126 Walcot St, Bath, Avon BA1 5BG
Tel: (01225) 4734211
Web Site: www.studiofun.com
Key Personnel
Associate Publisher: Rosanne McManus *E-mail:* rosanne.mcmanus@studiofun.com
International Dir: Jennifer Fifield *E-mail:* jennifer.fifield@studiofun.com
Sales Dir, North America: Frank Fochetta *E-mail:* frank.fochetta@studiofun.com
Founded: 1983
Subjects: Education
ISBN Prefix(es): 978-1-85724; 978-1-84088; 978-0-907874
Parent Company: The Readers Digest Association Inc
U.S. Office(s): 44 S Broadway, White Plains, NY 10601, United States
Distributed by Simon & Schuster, Inc (USA & Canada)
Foreign Rep(s): Jonathan Ball Publishers (South Africa); Simon & Schuster International (Amy

Lin) (Hong Kong, Thailand); Simon & Schuster International (Jennifer Javier) (Philippines); Simon & Schuster International (Jill Su) (Indonesia, Malaysia, Singapore, Taiwan)

Studio Press, *imprint of* Kings Road Publishing

Studymates, *imprint of* GLMP Ltd

Summersdale, *imprint of* Octopus Publishing Group Ltd

Summersdale Publishers Ltd
Imprint of Octopus Publishing Group Ltd
46 West St, Chichester, West Sussex PO19 1RP
Tel: (01243) 771107
Web Site: www.summersdale.com
Key Personnel
Mng Dir: Alastair Williams
Sales & Marketing Dir: Nicky Douglas
Rights & Digital Sales Manager: Amy Hunter
  E-mail: amy@summersdale.com
Publicity: Dean Chant *E-mail:* dean@
  summersdale.com
Founded: 1990
Subjects: Health, Nutrition, Humor, Nonfiction (General), Self-Help, Travel & Tourism, True Crime
ISBN Prefix(es): 978-1-84024; 978-1-873475; 978-1-84953
Foreign Rep(s): Bookport Associates Ltd (Joe Portelli) (Southern Europe); Michael Geoghegan (Eastern Europe, Northern Europe); InterMedia Ltd (Caribbean, South America); Maya Publishers Pvt Ltd (Surit Mitra) (India); Nationwide Book Distribution Ltd (New Zealand); Peribo (Australia); Publishers International Marketing Ltd (Chris Ashdown) (Northeast Asia, Southeast Asia); Real Books (South Africa)
Foreign Rights: Arrowsmith Agency (Nina Arrowsmith) (Germany); The Artemis Agency (Michelle Lin) (China, Taiwan); L'Autre Agence (Corinne Marotte) (France); BC Agency (Jenny Jung) (Korea); BookPack (Agata Radkiewicz) (Poland); Agenzia Servizi Editorali (Guido Lagomarsino & Anna Spadolini) (Italy); Agentia Literara Livia Stoia (Mirela Calota) (Romania); Tuttle-Mori Agency (Manami Tamaoki) (Japan)
Distribution Center: Littlehampton Book Services Ltd, Faraday Close, Durrington, Worthing, West Sussex BN13 3RB *Tel:* (01903) 828500; (01903) 828501 (customer service) *Web Site:* lbsltd.wp.hachette.co.uk

Supernova Books, *imprint of* Aurora Metro Books

Survival, *imprint of* International Institute for Strategic Studies

Sussex Academic Press
PO Box 139, Eastbourne, East Sussex BN24 9BP
Tel: (01323) 479220
E-mail: edit@sussex-academic.com
Web Site: www.sussex-academic.com
Key Personnel
Editorial Dir: Anthony V P Grahame
Sales & Marketing Dir: Anita Grahame
Founded: 1994
Subjects: Archaeology, Art, Biography, Memoirs, Drama, Theater, Economics, Education, Environmental Studies, Geography, Geology, Government, Political Science, History, Language Arts, Linguistics, Literature, Literary Criticism, Essays, Management, Philosophy, Psychology, Psychiatry, Religion - Other, Theology, Women's Studies, Cultural & Social Studies, Jewish Studies, Latin American Studies, Li-

brary Studies, Middle East Studies, Migration, Musicology, Psychotherapy
ISBN Prefix(es): 978-1-898723; 978-1-902210; 978-1-903900; 978-1-84519; 978-1-78284; 978-1-898595
Distribution Center: Gazelle Book Services, White Cross Mills, Hightown, Lancaster, Lancs LA1 4XS *Tel:* (01524) 68765 *Fax:* (01524) 63232 *E-mail:* sales@gazellebooks.co.uk *Web Site:* www.gazellebooks.co.uk (worldwide exc Asia, Canada & USA)
Independent Publishers Group (IPG), 814 N Franklin St, Chicago, IL 60610, United States *Tel:* 312-337-0747 *Fax:* 312-337-1807 *E-mail:* orders@ipgbook.com *Web Site:* www. ipgbook.com

Swan Hill Press, *imprint of* Quiller Publishing Ltd

Symposium Press, *imprint of* Science Reviews 2000 Ltd

Ta-Ha Publishers Ltd+
Unit 4, The Windsor Centre, Windsor Grove, West Norwood, London SE27 9NT
Tel: (020) 8670 1888 *Fax:* (020) 8670 1888
E-mail: sales@tahapublishers.com; enquiries@ tahapublishers.com
Web Site: www.taha.co.uk
Subjects: Religion - Islamic
ISBN Prefix(es): 978-0-907461; 978-1-897940; 978-1-84200
Number of titles published annually: 30 Print
Total Titles: 270 Print; 120 Online

Tabb House Originals, *imprint of* Tabb House Publishers

Tabb House Publishers+
7 Church St, Padstow, Cornwall PL28 8BG
Tel: (01841) 532316
Web Site: www.tabbhousebooks.com
Key Personnel
Dir: Caroline White
Founded: 1980
Subjects: Biography, Memoirs, Fiction, History, Literature, Literary Criticism, Essays, Nonfiction (General), Philosophy, Poetry, Regional Interests, Religion - Other, Children's Fiction
ISBN Prefix(es): 978-0-907018; 978-1-873951; 978-0-9534079
Number of titles published annually: 4 Print
Total Titles: 102 Print
Imprints: Tabb House Originals
Distributed by Tor Mark Press (selected titles)

The TAFT Group, *imprint of* Gale

Taigh Na Teud Music Publishers (Harpstring House Music Publishers)
13 Upper Breakish, Isle of Skye IV42 8PY
Tel: (01471) 822528 *Fax:* (01471) 822811
E-mail: info@scotlandsmusic.com
Web Site: www.scotlandsmusic.com; www. playscottishmusic.com
Key Personnel
Sales Manager: Alasdair Martin
Founded: 1985
Subjects: Music, Dance, Scottish Traditional Music
ISBN Prefix(es): 978-1-871931
Number of titles published annually: 6 Print; 2 CD-ROM
Total Titles: 60 Print; 12 CD-ROM

Tamarind, *imprint of* The Random House Group Ltd, a Penguin Random House Company

Tango Books Ltd+
Unit 121, The Lightbox, London W4 5PY
Mailing Address: PO Box 32595, London W4 5YD
Tel: (020) 8996 9970 *Fax:* (020) 8996 9977
E-mail: sales@tangobooks.co.uk; info@ tangobooks.co.uk
Web Site: www.tangobooks.co.uk
Key Personnel
Owner & Dir: David Fielder *E-mail:* david. fielder@tangobooks.co.uk
Founded: 1991
ISBN Prefix(es): 978-1-85707
Imprints: Tango Cards
Distributor for Innovative Kids; Soundprints; Van der Meer
Foreign Rep(s): Bounce Sales & Marketing (worldwide exc Australia, Canada, Japan, New Zealand, South Africa & USA)
Distribution Center: Grantham Book Services, Trent Rd, Grantham, Lincs NG31 7XQ
Tel: (01476) 541080 *Fax:* (01476) 541061
E-mail: orders@gbs.tbs-ltd.co.uk

Tango Cards, *imprint of* Tango Books Ltd

Tarquin, *imprint of* Tarquin Publications

Tarquin Publications+
17 Holywell Hill, Suite 74, St Albans, Herts AL1 1DT
Tel: (01727) 833866 *Fax:* (0845) 4566385
E-mail: info@tarquingroup.com
Web Site: www.tarquingroup.com
Founded: 1970
Membership(s): IPG.
Subjects: Education, Mathematics, Science (General)
ISBN Prefix(es): 978-0-906212; 978-1-899618
Number of titles published annually: 7 Print
Total Titles: 99 Print
Parent Company: Richard Griffin Ltd
Imprints: DIME; Tarquin

TASCHEN UK Ltd+
Subsidiary of TASCHEN GmbH
One Heathcock Court, 5th floor, 415 Strand, London WC2R 0NS
Tel: (020) 7845 8585 *Fax:* (020) 7836 3696
E-mail: contact-uk@taschen.com
Web Site: www.taschen.com
Key Personnel
Public Relations: Mallory Testa *E-mail:* m.testa@ taschen.com
Founded: 1994
Subjects: Architecture & Interior Design, Art, Fashion, Photography
ISBN Prefix(es): 978-3-8228; 978-3-8365; 978-3-89450
Associate Companies: TASCHEN France, 82, rue Mazarine, 75006 Paris, France, Public Relations: Lou Mollgaard *Tel:* 01 40 51 70 93 *Fax:* 01 43 26 73 80 *E-mail:* l.mollgaard@ taschen.com; TASCHEN Deutschland, Hohenzollernring 53, 50672 Cologne, Germany, Public Relations: Dr Christine Waiblinger *Tel:* (0221) 201 80 0 *Fax:* (0221) 201 80 865 *E-mail:* c.waiblinger@taschen.com (headquarters); TASCHEN Hong Kong, 27/F, The Workstation, 43 Lyndhurst Terrace, Central Hong Kong, Hong Kong *Tel:* 2544 8018 *Fax:* 2544 8012 *E-mail:* contact-hk@taschen. com; TASCHEN Espana, c/ Victor Hugo, 1, 2º Dcha, Madrid 28004, Spain, Public Relations: Maria Eugenia Mariam *Tel:* 91 360 50 75 *Fax:* 91 360 50 64 *E-mail:* m.mariam@ taschen.com
U.S. Office(s): TASCHEN America, 6671 Sunset Blvd, Los Angeles, CA 90028, United States *Tel:* 323-463-4441 *Fax:* 323-463-4442 *E-mail:* contact-us@taschen.com

Tate Publishing Ltd+
Division of Tate Enterprises
Millbank, London SW1P 4RG
Tel: (020) 7887 8869 *Fax:* (020) 7887 8878
E-mail: tgpl@tate.org.uk; orders@tate.org.uk
Web Site: www.tate.org.uk/publishing
Key Personnel
Founder & Chairman of the Board: Richard Tate
  E-mail: richard@tatepublishing.com
Co-Founder & Executive Creative Writer: Rita
  Tate *E-mail:* rita@tatepublishing.com
President & Chief Executive Officer: Ryan Tate
  E-mail: ryan@tatepublishing.com
Dir, Production: Curtis Winkle *E-mail:* curtis@
  tatepublishing.com
Dir of Marketing: Mark Mingle
  E-mail: mmingle@tatepublishing.com
Associate Dir of Marketing: Terry Cordingley
  E-mail: terry@tatepublishing.com
Associate Print Production Manager: Tim Kelley
  E-mail: tim@tatepublishing.com
Founded: 1932
Publishers of art books, exhibition catalogues &
  gallery guides of modern art & British art.
Subjects: Architecture & Interior Design, Art, Ed-
  ucation, Art History
ISBN Prefix(es): 978-0-900874; 978-0-905005;
  978-1-85437; 978-0-946590; 978-1-84976
Number of titles published annually: 45 Print
Total Titles: 150 Print
Ultimate Parent Company: Tate Gallery
Foreign Rep(s): Harry N Abrams Inc (Canada,
  North America); Asia Publishers Services Ltd
  (Asia, China, Hong Kong, Korea, Philippines,
  Taiwan); Exhibitions International (Austria,
  Belgium, Germany, Netherlands, Switzerland);
  Elisabeth Harder-Kreimann (Denmark, Finland,
  Iceland, Norway, Sweden); Humphrys Roberts
  Associates (Christopher Humphrys & Linda
  Hopkins) (Bermuda, Caribbean, Central Amer-
  ica, Mexico); IMA/Intermedia-Americana Ltd
  (David Williams) (South America); Interart
  Paris (France); David Krut Publishing (South
  Africa); Padovani Books Ltd (Penny Padovani)
  (Greece, Italy); Padovani Books Ltd (Jenny
  Padovani) (Portugal, Spain); Thames & Hudson
  Australia Pty Ltd (Australia); Philip Tyers (Al-
  bania, Bosnia and Herzegovina, Bulgaria, Croa-
  tia, Czechia, Eastern Europe, Estonia, Hungary,
  Latvia, Lithuania, Montenegro, Poland, Roma-
  nia, Russia, Serbia, Slovakia, Slovenia)

I B Tauris & Co Ltd
6 Salem Rd, London W2 4BU
Tel: (020) 7243 1225 *Fax:* (020) 7243 1226
E-mail: mail@ibtauris.com
Web Site: www.ibtauris.com
Key Personnel
Chairman: Iradj Bagherzade
  E-mail: ibagherzade@ibtauris.com
Mng Dir: Jonathan McDonnell
  E-mail: jmcdonnell@ibtauris.com
Production Dir: Stuart Weir *E-mail:* sweir@
  ibtauris.com
Sales & Marketing Dir: Paul Davighi
  E-mail: pdavighi@ibtauris.com
Financial Controller: Liz Stuckey
  E-mail: lstuckey@ibtauris.com
Executive Editor, Religion & Classics: Alex
  Wright *E-mail:* awright@ibtauris.com
Senior Editor, Academic: Joanna Godfrey
  E-mail: jgodfrey@ibtauris.com
Senior Editor, History: Lester Crook
  E-mail: lcrook@ibtauris.com
Senior Editor, Politics & International Relations:
  Tomasz Hoskins *E-mail:* thoskins@ibtauris.com
Senior Editor, Visual Culture: Philippa Brewster
  E-mail: pbrewster@ibtauris.com
Editor, Geography & Social Sciences: David
  Stonestreet
Editor, Tauris Parke Paperbacks: Tatiana Wilde
  E-mail: twilde@ibtauris.com

Academic Publicist: Rory Gormley
  E-mail: rgormley@ibtauris.com
Trade Publicist: Ashlee Khan *E-mail:* akhan@
  ibtauris.com
Founded: 1983
Independent publisher of both academic & general interest books.
Specialize in Middle East studies, history, politics, international relations, film, visual culture,
  religion & classics.
Subjects: Archaeology, Architecture & Interior
  Design, Art, Asian Studies, Biography, Memoirs, Cookery, Criminology, Developing Countries, Economics, Environmental Studies, Fashion, Film, Video, Geography, Geology, Government, Political Science, History, Inspirational,
  Spirituality, Military Science, Nonfiction (General), Philosophy, Religion - Buddhist, Reli-
  gion - Catholic, Religion - Hindu, Religion -
  Islamic, Religion - Jewish, Religion - Protestant, Religion - Other, Social Sciences, Sociology, Theology, Travel & Tourism, Women's
  Studies, Ancient History, Contemporary Art,
  Film Studies, International Relations, Middle
  East Studies, Visual Culture
ISBN Prefix(es): 978-1-85043; 978-1-86064; 978-
  1-84511; 978-1-84885; 978-0-85771 (ebooks);
  978-0-85772 (ebooks); 978-0-85773 (ebooks);
  978-1-78076; 978-1-78543; 978-1-78672
  (ebooks); 978-1-78673 (ebooks); 978-1-78674
  (ebooks); 978-1-78831
Number of titles published annually: 320 Print
Total Titles: 3,200 Print
Imprints: Tauris Parke; Tauris Parke Paperbacks
Subsidiaries: Philip Wilson Publishers Ltd
Distributor for American University in Cairo
  Press (worldwide exc Canada, Egypt & USA);
  Philip Wilson Publishers (worldwide)
Distribution Center: Baker & Taylor Publisher
  Services, 30 Amberwood Parkway, Ash-
  land, OH 44805, United States *Tel:* 567-215-
  0030 *E-mail:* info@btpubservices.com *Web
  Site:* www.btpubservices.com
Orders to: Macmillan Distribution Ltd, Brunel
  Rd, Houndsmill, Basingstoke, Hants RG21
  6XS

Tauris Parke, *imprint of* I B Tauris & Co Ltd

Tauris Parke Paperbacks, *imprint of* I B Tauris
  & Co Ltd

Taylor & Francis, *imprint of* Taylor & Francis
  Group, an Informa Business

**Taylor & Francis Group, an Informa
Business+**
Member of Informa PLC
2-4 Park Sq, Milton Park, Abingdon, Oxon OX14
  4RN
Tel: (020) 7017 6000
E-mail: enquiries@taylorandfrancis.com
Web Site: taylorandfrancisgroup.com
Key Personnel
Rights Manager: Adele Parker *E-mail:* adele.
  parker@tandf.co.uk
Advertising Coordinator, Journal Sales: Patrick
  Dunn *E-mail:* patrick.dunn@taylorandfrancis.
  com
Academic publisher.
Subjects: Anthropology, Archaeology, Art, Asian
  Studies, Biological Sciences, Business, Civil
  Engineering, Criminology, Economics, Educa-
  tion, Energy, Engineering (General), Environ-
  mental Studies, Finance, Geography, Geology,
  History, Language Arts, Linguistics, Law, Lit-
  erature, Literary Criticism, Essays, Medicine,
  Nursing, Dentistry, Military Science, Music,
  Dance, Philosophy, Psychology, Psychiatry, Re-
  ligion - Buddhist, Religion - Catholic, Religion
  - Hindu, Religion - Islamic, Religion - Jewish,
  Religion - Protestant, Religion - Other, Science

  (General), Social Sciences, Sociology, Sports,
  Athletics, Travel & Tourism, Veterinary Science, Women's Studies
ISBN Prefix(es): 978-0-389; 978-0-85066; 978-
  0-905273; 978-1-85000; 978-0-7484; 978-1-
  85728; 978-1-84142; 978-1-84872; 978-0-203;
  978-1-134; 978-1-136
Imprints: Cogent OA; CRC Press; Garland Science; Routledge; Taylor & Francis
Orders to: Bookpoint, 130 Milton Park, Abingdon, Oxon OX14 4SB *Tel:* (01235) 400 400
  Web Site: bookpoint.wp.hachette.co.uk (Africa,
  Asia, Australia, Europe, UK)
Taylor & Francis, 7625 Empire Dr, Florence, KY
  41042-2919, United States *E-mail:* orders@
  taylorandfrancis.com (North & South America)

Teach Yourself, *imprint of* Hodder Education
  Group

Teachers' Pocketbooks, *imprint of* Management
  Pocketbooks Ltd

Telegram Books, *imprint of* Saqi Books

Telegraph Books
Tresprison Business Park, Units 1 & 2, Helston,
  Cornwall TR13 0QD
Tel: (0844) 871 1515; (01326) 569 777 (UK)
  Fax: (020) 7931 2878
Web Site: www.telegraph.co.uk; books.telegraph.
  co.uk
Founded: 1930
Subjects: Cookery, Gardening, Plants, Health,
  Nutrition, House & Home, How-to, Humor,
  Self-Help, Military
ISBN Prefix(es): 978-0-86367; 978-0-901684
Number of titles published annually: 50 Print
Parent Company: Telegraph Media Group Ltd
Orders to: PO Box 582, Norwich NR7 0GB

Thomas Telford Ltd, see ICE Publishing

Templar Publishing, *imprint of* Kings Road
  Publishing

Templar Publishing
Imprint of Kings Road Publishing
Suite 2.08, The Plaza, 535 Kings Rd, London
  SW10 0SZ
Tel: (020) 3770 8888
E-mail: enquiries@bonnierpublishing.co.uk;
  submissions@templarco.co.uk
Web Site: www.templarco.co.uk
Key Personnel
Publisher: Rachel Williams *E-mail:* rachel.
  williams@templarco.co.uk
Mng Dir: Mike McGrath *E-mail:* mike.mcgrath@
  templarco.co.uk
Founded: 1978
ISBN Prefix(es): 978-1-84011; 978-1-870956;
  978-1-898784; 978-1-84877; 978-0-9555719;
  978-1-78370
Ultimate Parent Company: Bonnier Publishing
  Ltd
Imprints: Big Picture Press; Pippbrook Books
Foreign Rep(s): Bill Bailey Publishers Represen-
  tatives (Tessa Brown) (Europe exc Gibraltar,
  Portugal & Spain); Jonathan Ball (Eugene Ash-
  ton) (South Africa); Capricorn Link (David
  Inwood) (Australia); Kelvin Van Hasselt (East
  Africa, West Africa); Gill Hess Ltd (Eamonn
  Phelan) (Ireland); Humphrys Roberts Asso-
  ciates (Chris Humphrys) (Caribbean, Gibraltar,
  Portugal, Spain); Pansing (David Buckland)
  (Malaysia, Singapore); Publishers Interna-
  tional Marketing (Chris Ashdown) (Far East,
  Southeast Asia exc Malaysia & Singapore);
  Research Press (Ajay Parmar) (India); South
  Pacific (Liza Raybould) (New Zealand); Ward
  International (Richard Ward) (Middle East)

Orders to: Grantham Book Services (GBS), Trent Rd, Grantham, Lincs NG31 7XQ *Tel:* (01476) 541 080 *Fax:* (01476) 541 061 *E-mail:* orders@gbs.tbs-ltd.co.uk *Web Site:* www.granthambookservices.co.uk

Temple Lodge Publishing Ltd+
Hillside House, The Square, Forest Row, East Sussex RH18 5ES
Tel: (01342) 824000 *Fax:* (01342) 826437
E-mail: office@templelodge.com
Web Site: www.templelodge.com
Subjects: Biography, Memoirs, Inspirational, Spirituality, Philosophy
ISBN Prefix(es): 978-0-904693; 978-1-902636; 978-1-906999
Distributed by Ceres Books (New Zealand); Footprint Books Pty Ltd (Australia); Rudolf Steiner Publications (South Africa); SteinerBooks (USA); Tri-Fold Books (Canada)
Orders to: BookSource, 50 Cambuslang Rd, Cambuslang, Glasgow G32 8NB *Tel:* (0845) 370 0063 *Fax:* (0845) 370 0064 *E-mail:* orders@booksource.net *Web Site:* www.booksource.net
Returns: Scottish Book Source Distribution, Cowlairs Industrial Estate, 32 Finlas St, Springburn, Glasgow G22 5DU

Terra Publishing, *imprint of* Dunedin Academic Press

Textile & Art Publications Ltd+
Studio 28 Liddell Rd, London NW6 2EW
Tel: (020) 7328 4844 *Fax:* (020) 7624 1732
E-mail: post@textile-art.com
Web Site: www.textile-art.com
Founded: 1993
Subjects: Art, Asian Studies, Religion - Buddhist, Textile art
ISBN Prefix(es): 978-1-898406
Number of titles published annually: 2 Print
Total Titles: 4 Print

TFM Publishing Ltd
Castle Hill Barns, Harley, Shrewsbury, Salop SY5 6LS
Tel: (01952) 510061 *Fax:* (01952) 510192
E-mail: info@tfmpublishing.com
Web Site: www.tfmpublishing.com
Subjects: Medicine, Nursing, Dentistry, Neurology, Radiology, Surgery
ISBN Prefix(es): 978-1-910079; 978-1-903378; 978-1-9530052
Foreign Rep(s): Academic Marketing Services (Pty) Ltd (Michael Brightmore) (South Africa); Baker & Taylor Publisher Services (Canada, North America, South America); Bhalani Medical Book House (India, Sri Lanka); China Publishers Services Ltd (Edwin Chu) (China); CoInfo Book Services (Australia, New Zealand); Distribuna Editorial y Libreria Medica (Colombia); GOBO® Library Solutions (Canada, North America, South America); Igaku-Shoin Ltd (Japan); International Publishing Services Ltd (Middle East, North Africa); Libreria Ciencias Medicas (Itzchel Herrera Wackett) (Chile); Login Brothers Canada (Canada, North America, South America); Majors Education Solutions (Canada, North America, South America); Matthews Book Co (Canada, North America, South America); McBarron Book Co (Hong Kong); Nankodo Co Ltd (Japan); Probook Ltd (Israel); Rittenhouse Book Distributors (Canada, North America, South America); Topbooks Health Information Provider Inc (Southeast Asia); Unifacmanu Trading Co Ltd (Taiwan)
Distribution Center: Gazelle Book Services, Hightown, White Cross Mills, Lancaster

LA1 4XS *Tel:* (01524) 68765 *Fax:* (01524) 63232 *E-mail:* sales@gazellebooks.co.uk *Web Site:* www.gazellebooks.co.uk

TFPL Ltd
Borough House, 80 Borough High St, London SE1 1LL
Tel: (020) 7751 7104 *Fax:* (0844) 586 8702
E-mail: info@tfpl.com
Web Site: www.tfpl.com
Founded: 1987
Specialist in recruitment, advisory, research & training services company focusing on knowledge, information, library, records, web & content management.
Membership(s): Directory Publishers Association.
Subjects: Communications, Computer Science, Human Relations, Library & Information Sciences
ISBN Prefix(es): 978-1-870889
Distributor for TFPL Inc

Thames & Hudson Ltd+
181A High Holborn, London WC1V 7QX
Tel: (020) 7845 5000 *Fax:* (020) 7845 5050
E-mail: marketing@thameshudson.co.uk; press@thameshudson.co.uk; rights@thameshudson.co.uk; sales@thameshudson.co.uk
Web Site: www.thamesandhudson.com
Key Personnel
Chairman: Thomas Neurath
Publishing Dir: Sophy Thompson
Mng Dir: Jamie Camplin
Marketing Executive: Anna Bent
Founded: 1949
Subjects: Archaeology, Architecture & Interior Design, Art, Crafts, Games, Hobbies, Ethnicity, Fashion, History, Music, Dance, Philosophy, Photography, Psychology, Psychiatry, Religion - Other, Science (General), Technology, Travel & Tourism, Graphics, Popular Culture
ISBN Prefix(es): 978-0-500
Subsidiaries: Interart; Thames & Hudson (Australia) Pty Ltd; Thames & Hudson (China) Ltd; Thames & Hudson (S) Pvt Ltd
U.S. Office(s): Thames & Hudson Inc, 500 Fifth Ave, New York, NY 10110, United States *Tel:* 212-354-3763 *Fax:* 212-398-1252 *E-mail:* bookinfo@thames.wwnorton.com
Distributor for Aperture; AVA Publishing; Mark Batty Publisher; Braun Publishing AG; British Museum Press; Flammarion; Guggenheim Foundation; ILEX; Ivy Press Ltd; Laurence King; MoMA; Royal Academy of Arts; Royal Collection Publications; Skira Editore; Steidl Verlag
Foreign Rep(s): Asia Books Co Ltd (Thailand); Asia Publishers Services (Helen Lee) (Taiwan); Asia Publishers Services (Ed Summerson) (Korea); Bas van der Zee (Belgium, Luxembourg, Netherlands); Per Burrell (Armenia, Azerbaijan, Baltic States, Belarus, Kazakhstan, Kyrgyzstan, Moldova, Russia, Scandinavia, Tajikistan, Ukraine, Uzbekistan); John Edgeler (Caribbean); Peter Hyde Associates (Botswana, Lesotho, Namibia, South Africa, Swaziland); Interart Sarl (France); Michael Klein (Austria, Germany exc South Germany); Levant Distributors (Lebanon); Roli Books (Bangladesh, Bhutan, India, Nepal); Thames & Hudson (Australia) Pty Ltd (Australia, New Zealand); Thames & Hudson China Ltd (China, Hong Kong, Macau); Thames & Hudson (S) Pvt Ltd (Malaysia, Singapore, Southeast Asia)
Orders to: Littlehampton Book Services Ltd, Faraday Close, Durrington, Worthing, West Sussex BN13 3RB *Tel:* (01903) 828500; (01903) 828501 (customer service) *Web Site:* lbsltd.wp.hachette.co.uk

Thames River Press
Imprint of Wimbledon Publishing Co

75-76 Blackfriars Rd, London SE1 8HA
Tel: (020) 7401 4200 *Fax:* (020) 7401 4225
E-mail: info@thamesriverpress.com
Web Site: www.thamesriverpress.com
Key Personnel
Chairman: Kamaljit S Sood *E-mail:* ksood@wpcpress.com
Founded: 2011
Subjects: Fiction, Nonfiction (General)
ISBN Prefix(es): 978-0-85728
Associate Companies: Anthem Press; Plurus Books
Divisions: Cosmopolis Modern Writings (bilingual editions); Thames River Imaginations (fiction); Thames River Perspectives (nonfiction); Thames River World Classics (literature from the past)

Tharpa Publications
Conishead Priory, Ulverston, Cumbria LA12 9QQ
Tel: (01229) 588599
E-mail: info.uk@tharpa.com
Web Site: www.tharpa.com/uk
Founded: 1984
Subjects: Inspirational, Spirituality, Religion - Buddhist, Self-Help, Meditation
ISBN Prefix(es): 978-0-948006; 978-1-910368
Associate Companies: Tharpa Publications Australia, 25 McCarthy Rd, PO Box 63, Monbulk, Victoria 3793, Australia *Tel:* (03) 9756 7203 *E-mail:* info.au@tharpa.com *Web Site:* www.tharpa.com/au; Editora Tharpa Brasil, Rua Artur De Azevedo 1360, Sao Paulo-SP, Brazil *Tel:* (011) 3476 2330 *Fax:* (011) 3476 2329 *Web Site:* www.tharpa.com.br; Tharpa Canada Inc, 631 Crawford St, Toronto, ON M6G 3K1, Canada *Tel:* 416-762-8710 *Web Site:* www.tharpa.com/ca; Editions Tharpa France, Chateau de Segrais, 72220 Saint-Mars-d'Outille, France *Tel:* 02 43 87 71 02 *Web Site:* www.tharpa.com/fr; Tharpa Verlag Deutschland, Mehringdamm 33, 10961 Berlin, Germany *Tel:* (030) 430 55666 *E-mail:* info.de@tharpa.com *Web Site:* www.tharpa.com/de; Tharpa Asia, Bo Wah Mansion, Flat H, 4th floor, 54 Queen's Rd E, Wanchai, Hong Kong *Tel:* 2520 5137 *Fax:* 2507 2208 *Web Site:* www.tharpa.com/hk-en; Tharpa South Africa, c/o Mahasiddha Kadampa Buddhist Centre, 2 Hollings Rd, Malvern, Durban 4093, South Africa *Tel:* (031) 464 0984 *E-mail:* info.za@tharpa.com *Web Site:* www.tharpa.com/za; Editorial Tharpa Espana, C/ Manuela Malasana, 26, 28004 Madrid, Spain *Tel:* 917 557 535 *E-mail:* info.es@tharpa.com *Web Site:* www.tharpa.com/es; Tharpa Verlag AG, Mirabellenstr 1, 8048 Zurich, Switzerland *Tel:* (044) 401 02 20 *Fax:* (044) 461 36 88 *E-mail:* info.ch@tharpa.com *Web Site:* www.tharpa.com/ch
U.S. Office(s): Tharpa Publications USA, 47 Sweeney Rd, Glen Spey, NY 12737, United States *Tel:* 845-856-5102 *Fax:* 845-856-2110 *E-mail:* info.us@tharpa.com *Web Site:* www.tharpa.com/us
Foreign Rep(s): Gary Allen Pty Ltd (Australia); Motilal Banarsidass Ltd (India); MPH Distributors Pte Ltd (Malaysia, Singapore); Peaceful Living Publications (New Zealand)

Thin Red Line, *imprint of* Ashgrove Publishing

Third Millennium, *imprint of* Profile Books Ltd

Thirsty Books, *imprint of* Argyll Publishing

Thistle Publishing+
Imprint of Andrew Lownie Literary Agency Ltd
36 Great Smith St, London SW1P 3BU
Tel: (020) 7222 7574 *Fax:* (020) 7222 7576
E-mail: info@thistlepublishing.co.uk
Web Site: www.thistlepublishing.co.uk

Key Personnel
Editor: David Haviland *E-mail:* david@
thistlepublishing.co.uk
Founded: 1996
UK publisher of fiction & nonfiction.
Membership(s): Independent Publishers Guild.
Subjects: Biography, Memoirs, Economics, Edu-
cation, Fiction, History, Humor, Inspirational,
Spirituality, Journalism, Literature, Literary
Criticism, Essays, Mysteries, Suspense, Nonfic-
tion (General), Pop Culture, Romance, Science
(General), Science Fiction, Fantasy, Self-Help,
Social Sciences, Sociology, Sports, Athletics
ISBN Prefix(es): 978-1-910198; 978-1-909869;
978-1-909609; 978-1-910670; 978-1-78608
Number of titles published annually: 50 Print; 50
E-Book; 10 Audio
Total Titles: 500 Print; 500 E-Book; 50 Audio

DC Thomson & Co Ltd
80 Kingsway East, Dundee DD4 8SL
Tel: (01382) 223 131
Web Site: www.dcthomson.co.uk
Key Personnel
Dir: Andrew F Thomson; Christopher H W
Thomson; David Thomson; Richard Hall
Group Marketing Manager: Kirsty Matthews
Tel: (01382) 575 426 *E-mail:* kimatthews@
dcthomson.co.uk
Founded: 1905
Subjects: Animals, Pets, Crafts, Games, Hobbies,
Fashion, House & Home, Humor, Regional In-
terests
ISBN Prefix(es): 978-0-85116; 978-1-84535
Branch Office(s)
Lang Stracht, Mastrick, Aberdeen AB15 6DF
Tel: (01224) 690 222
2 Albert Sq, Dundee DD1 9QJ
Skypark, Suite 6, 8 Elliott Pl, Glasgow G3 8EP
Tel: (0141) 332 9933
185 Fleet St, London EC4A 2HS *Tel:* (020) 7400
1030

Thorndike Press, *imprint of* Gale

Thorsons, *imprint of* HarperCollins UK

Thoth Publications+
64 Leopold St, Loughborough, Leics LE11 5DN
Tel: (01509) 210626 *Fax:* (07092) 091129
E-mail: sales@thoth.co.uk
Web Site: www.thoth.co.uk
Key Personnel
Owner: Tom Clarke
Founded: 1988
Subjects: Esoteric, New Age
ISBN Prefix(es): 978-1-870450
Number of titles published annually: 9 Print
Total Titles: 60 Print

THP Ireland, *imprint of* The History Press Ltd

Thrass (UK) Ltd
The Willows, 18 Long Lane, Upton, Chester CH2
2PD
Tel: (01244) 323079 *Toll Free Tel:* 0872 111
4327 (UK customers only)
E-mail: office@thrass.co.uk
Web Site: www.thrass.co.uk
Key Personnel
Executive Dir: Alan Davies *E-mail:* alandavies@
thrass.co.uk
Publish educational books, charts & software,
CDs & DVDs.
Subjects: Education, Literacy Resources
ISBN Prefix(es): 978-1-904912; 978-1-906295
Total Titles: 50 Print; 4 CD-ROM

Threshold, *imprint of* Kenilworth Press Ltd

Tide Mill Press, *imprint of* Top That Publishing
Ltd

Timber Press+
6a Lonsdale Rd, London NW6 6RD
Tel: (020) 7372 4601 *Fax:* (020) 7372 4601
E-mail: info@timberpress.co.uk; orders@
timberpress.com; sales@timberpress.com;
editorial@timberpress.com
Web Site: www.timberpress.co.uk
Key Personnel
Marketing Manager (UK): Rebecca Rochester
Tel: (01395) 232166 *E-mail:* rrochester@
timberpress.com
Founded: 1978
Books for sophisticated gardeners, horticulturists,
botanists, naturalists & landscape professionals.
Subjects: Agriculture, Gardening, Plants, Natural
History, Science (General)
ISBN Prefix(es): 978-0-88192; 978-0-931340;
978-0-931146; 978-1-60469; 978-0-917304
Imprints: Amadeus Press
U.S. Office(s): 133 SW Second Ave, Suite 450,
Portland, OR 97204, United States *Fax:* 503-
227-3070 *E-mail:* info@timberpress.com
Foreign Rep(s): Thomas Allen & Sons Ltd
(Canada); Bookreps NZ Ltd (New Zealand);
Capricorn Link (Australia); Michelle Mor-
row Curreri (Asia, Middle East); Melia Pub-
lishing Services (Europe, UK); Trinity Books
CC (South Africa); Workman Publishing
Co (worldwide exc Asia, Australia, Canada,
Caribbean, Europe, Latin America, Middle
East, New Zealand, South Africa & UK);
Zimpfer Books (Caribbean, Latin America)
Orders to: Grantham Book Services, Trent Rd,
Grantham, Lincs NG31 7XQ *Tel:* (01476)
541080 *Fax:* (01476) 541061 *E-mail:* orders@
gbs.tbs-ltd.co.uk

Time Out Group Ltd+
125 Shaftsbury Ave, 4th floor, London WC2H
8AD
Tel: (020) 7813 3000 *Fax:* (020) 7813 6000
E-mail: hello@timeout.com
Web Site: www.timeout.com
Key Personnel
Founder & Chairman: Tony Elliott
Chief Executive Officer: Tim Arthur
Chief Financial Officer: Matt White
Chief Technology Officer: Dave Cook
Commercial Dir: St John Betteridge
Business Development Dir, UK: Ray Jones
Group Marketing Dir: Carolyn Sims
Group Operations Dir: Andrew Aitchison
Editor-in-Chief: Caroline McGinn
Founded: 1968
International magazine, guides & online informa-
tion media company.
Membership(s): PPA.
Subjects: Art, Communications, Drama, Theater,
Fashion, Film, Video, Journalism, LGBTQ,
Music, Dance, Poetry, Pop Culture, Radio, TV,
Sports, Athletics, Travel & Tourism
ISBN Prefix(es): 978-0-903446; 978-1-905042;
978-1-904978; 978-1-84670
Number of titles published annually: 50 Print
Divisions: Time Out Communications (online
company); Time Out Guides (guidebook pub-
lisher); Time Out International (International
Time Out magazines throughout the world);
Time Out Magazine (London weekly magazine
publisher)
U.S. Office(s): Time Out New York, 475 Tenth
Ave, 12th floor, New York, NY 10018, United
States *Tel:* 646-432-3000 *Fax:* 646-432-3001

Time Out Guides, *imprint of* Ebury Publishing

The Times Books, *imprint of* HarperCollins UK

Tindal Street Press, *imprint of* Profile Books Ltd

Tinder Press, *imprint of* Headline Publishing
Group Ltd

Titan Books Ltd+
Titan House, 144 Southwark St, London SE1
0UP
Tel: (020) 7620 0200 *Fax:* (020) 7803 1990
E-mail: rights@titanemail.com; sales@titanemail.
com
Web Site: titanbooks.com
Key Personnel
Publisher: Nick Landau
Head, Rights: Jenny Boyce *E-mail:* jenny.boyce@
titanemail.com
Founded: 1981
Subjects: Art, Biography, Memoirs, Film, Video,
Radio, TV, Science Fiction, Fantasy
ISBN Prefix(es): 978-1-85286; 978-0-907610;
978-1-84023; 978-1-900097; 978-1-84576; 978-
1-84856; 978-0-85768; 978-1-78116; 978-1-
78329
Number of titles published annually: 150 Print
Parent Company: Titan Entertainment Group,
London
Imprints: Hard Case Crime
Divisions: Titan Magazines
Bookshop(s): London; Birmingham; Cambridge;
Coventry; Croydon; Edinburgh; Glasgow; Liv-
erpool; Newcastle; Southampton
Orders to: Littlehampton Book Services (LBS),
Faraday Close, Durrington, Worthing, West
Sussex BN13 3RB *Tel:* (01903) 828500
Fax: (01903) 828801 *Web Site:* lbsltd.wp.
hachette.co.uk
New South Books, c/o TL Distribution, 15-23
Helles Ave, Moorebank, NSW 2170, Aus-
tralia *Tel:* (02) 8778 9999 *Fax:* (02) 8778
9944 *E-mail:* orders@tldistribution.com.au *Web
Site:* www.newsouthbooks.com.au (Australia &
New Zealand)
Random House of Canada, 2775 Matheson
Blvd E, Mississauga, ON L4W 4P7, Canada
E-mail: orderscanada@randomhouse.com
Random House Distribution Services, 400 Hahn
Rd, Westminster, MD 21157, United States
E-mail: csorders@randomhouse.com

Tobin Music Books, *imprint of* Tobin Music Ltd

Tobin Music Ltd
Escher House, 17b Oxford St, Wellingborough,
Northants NN8 4HY
Tel: (01933) 274472
E-mail: enquiry@tobinmusic.co.uk; sales@
tobinmusic.co.uk
Web Site: www.tobinmusic.co.uk
Key Personnel
Commercial Dir: Richard Tobin
Founded: 1973
Music education books & workbooks covering all
musical theory & simple composition for home
& school use for all ages & abilities.
A unique system of teaching using patterns &
colors, tutors on various instruments.
Specialize in classroom music teaching recorder,
classical guitar & piano.
Subjects: Education, Music, Dance, Nonfiction
(General), Tutors, Information Books
ISBN Prefix(es): 978-0-905684
Total Titles: 31 Print; 1 CD-ROM
Imprints: Tobin Music Books

Top That! Kids, *imprint of* Top That Publishing
Ltd

Top That Publishing Ltd
Marine House, Tide Mill Way, Woodbridge, Suf-
folk IP12 1AP
Tel: (01394) 386 651
E-mail: customerservice@topthatpublishing.com
Web Site: topthatpublishing.com

Key Personnel
Chairman: Barrie Henderson
Mng Dir: David Henderson
Head, Foreign Rights Sales: Odette Lusby
Creative Dir: Simon Couchman
Editorial Dir: Daniel Graham
Finance Dir: Douglas Eadie
Production Dir: Stuart Buck
Sales & Export Manager: Steve Munnings
  Tel: (01394) 386 651 ext 236 *E-mail:* steve@
  topthatpublishing.com
Founded: 1999
ISBN Prefix(es): 978-1-84229; 978-1-84510; 978-
  1-902973; 978-1-904748; 978-1-905359; 978-
  1-84666; 978-1-84956; 978-1-78244; 978-1-
  78445
Parent Company: Tide Mill Media Group
Imprints: Imagine That!; Kudos; Quest; Tide Mill
  Press; Top That! Kids
Foreign Rep(s): Peter Matthews Agencies
  (Botswana, South Africa); Steve Wallace
  (USA); Peter Ward Book Exports (Middle
  East)
Distribution Center: The Trade Counter Ltd,
  Mendlesham Industrial Estate, Norwich Rd,
  Mendlesham, Suffolk
Trafalgar Square Publishing, c/o Independent
  Publishers Group (IPG), 814 N Franklin St,
  Chicago, IL 60610, United States

Tor, *imprint of* Pan Macmillan

Torchlights, *imprint of* Moonlight Publishing Ltd

Total Politics, *imprint of* Biteback Publishing

Totally Bound Publishing, *imprint of* Totally
Entwined Group Ltd

Totally Entwined Group Ltd
Imprint of Bonnier Zaffre Ltd
Think Tank, Ruston Way, Lincoln LN6 7FL
Web Site: www.totallyentwinedgroup.com
Key Personnel
Founder & Chief Executive Officer: Claire
  Siemaszkiewicz
Founder & Technical Dir: Marek Siemaszkiewicz
Publisher: Nicki Richards *E-mail:* nicki.richards@
  totallybound.com
Subjects: Erotica, Fiction, LGBTQ, Mysteries,
  Suspense, Romance
ISBN Prefix(es): 978-0-85715; 978-1-78184; 978-
  1-906590; 978-1-907010; 978-1-907280
Imprints: Evidence Press; Finch Books; Pride
  Publishing; Totally Bound Publishing
U.S. Office(s): 853 Broadway, Suite 2014, New
  York, NY 10003, United States

Totem Books, *imprint of* Icon Books Ltd

Toucan Press Guernsey
Apartment 1, St Mary's Court, Queen's Rd, St
  Peter Port, Guernsey GY1 1PT
E-mail: toucan.guernsey@gmail.com
Web Site: www.toucanpressguernsey.com
Key Personnel
Mng Dir: Dr Gregory Stevens Cox
Founded: 1850
Subjects: History, Literature, Literary Criticism,
  Essays
ISBN Prefix(es): 978-0-85694; 978-0-900749
Total Titles: 90 Print

Tour & Trail Maps, *imprint of* Discovery
Walking Guides Ltd

TPL, *imprint of* Training Publications Ltd

Trailblazer Publications
The Old Manse, Tower Rd, Hindhead, Surrey
  GU26 6SU
Tel: (01428) 606399
E-mail: info@trailblazer-guides.com
Web Site: www.trailblazer-guides.com
Key Personnel
Owner: Bryn Thomas
Founded: 1991
Travel, walking, rail, motorbiking & cycling
  guides.
Subjects: Outdoor Recreation, Travel & Tourism
ISBN Prefix(es): 978-1-873756; 978-1-905864
Foreign Rep(s): Books International (Italy); Car-
  totheque - EGG (France); Craenen BVBA
  (Belgium, Netherlands); Faradawn cc (South
  Africa); GeoCenter Touristik Medienservice
  GmbH (Germany); Heritage Publishers (In-
  dia); mapiberia f&b SL (Spain); National Book
  Network (Canada, USA); OLF Centre de Dis-
  tribution Multi-Media (Austria, Switzerland);
  Platypus Rese & Dykboecker (Sweden); Scan-
  vik A/S (Denmark); Steinhart Katzir Publishers
  Ltd (Israel); The Travel Alliance (Ireland, UK);
  Woodslane Pty Ltd (Australia, New Zealand)

Training Publications, *imprint of* Training
Publications Ltd

Training Publications Ltd
The Orient Centre, Unit 2, Greycaine Rd, Wat-
  ford, Herts WD24 7GP
Founded: 1965
Subjects: Engineering (General)
ISBN Prefix(es): 978-1-84019
Imprints: EAL; EITB; Entra; TPL; Training Pub-
  lications

Transworld Ireland, *imprint of* Transworld
Publishers

Transworld Publishers
Division of The Random House Group Ltd, a
  Penguin Random House Company
61-63 Uxbridge Rd, London W5 5SA
Tel: (020) 8579 2652 *Fax:* (020) 8579 5479
E-mail: info@transworld-publishers.co.uk
Web Site: www.penguinrandomhouse.co.uk/
  publishers/transworld/
Key Personnel
Mng Dir: Larry Finlay
Publisher: Bill Scott-Kerr
Publishing Dir, Commercial Fiction: Sarah Adams
Publisher, Transworld Ireland: Eoin McHugh
Publishing Dir, Doubleday: Marianne Velmans
Marketing Dir: Janine Giovanni
Publicity Dir: Patsy Irwin
Rights Dir: Helen Edwards
Art Dir: Richard Ogle
Editorial Dir: Michelle Signore
Dir, Media Relations: Alison Barrow *E-mail:* a.
  barrow@transworld-publishers.co.uk
Founded: 1950
Subjects: Biography, Memoirs, Computer Sci-
  ence, Criminology, Fiction, Film, Video, Gov-
  ernment, Political Science, Health, Nutrition,
  Humor, Nonfiction (General), Science Fiction,
  Fantasy, Sports, Athletics
ISBN Prefix(es): 978-0-552
Ultimate Parent Company: Penguin Random
  House
Associate Companies: Transworld Publishers
  (Australia) Pty Ltd; Transworld Publishers
  (New Zealand) Pty
Imprints: Bantam; Bantam Press; Black Swan;
  Corgi; Doubleday; Transworld Ireland
Warehouse: PO Box 17, Wellingborough,
  Northants NN8 4BU

Trapdoor, *imprint of* Little, Brown Book Group

Trapeze, *imprint of* Orion Publishing Group Ltd

Trentham Books, *imprint of* Institute of
Education Press

Trentham Books Ltd+
Imprint of Institute of Education Press
UCL Institute of Educations, 20 Bedford Way,
  London WC1H 0AL
Tel: (020) 7911 5563
E-mail: ioepress@ioe.ac.uk
Web Site: ioepress.co.uk
Key Personnel
Dir: Dr Gillian Klein *E-mail:* g.klein@ioe.ac.uk;
  Nicky Platt
Production Manager: Jonathan Dore
Editor: Nicole Edmondson
Founded: 1981
Publisher of professional books & journals.
Membership(s): Independent Publishers Guild.
Subjects: Child Care & Development, Drama,
  Theater, Education, Ethnicity, Humor, Law,
  Psychology, Psychiatry, Social Sciences, Soci-
  ology, Technology, Women's Studies, Inclusive
  Education
ISBN Prefix(es): 978-0-948080; 978-1-85856;
  978-0-9507735; 978-1-897898; 978-1-904133
Number of titles published annually: 35 Print; 2
  Online
Total Titles: 460 Print; 2 Online
Distributor for Arts Council of England
Foreign Rep(s): Co Info Pty Ltd (Australia); Sty-
  lus Publishing LLC (USA); UBS Library Ser-
  vices PTE Ltd (Singapore)
Distribution Center: Central Books Ltd, One
  Heath Park Industrial Estate, Freshwater
  Rd, Dagenham RM8 1RX *Tel:* (020) 8525
  8800 *Fax:* (020) 8599 2694 *E-mail:* orders@
  centralbooks.com *Web Site:* www.centralbooks.
  com (UK)

Trotman, *imprint of* Crimson Publishing Ltd

TSO (The Stationery Office)+
St Crispins, Duke St, Norwich NR3 1PD
Tel: (01603) 622211; (0870) 600 5522 (orders)
E-mail: customer.services@tso.co.uk
Web Site: www.tso.co.uk
Key Personnel
Chief Executive Officer: Marco Pierleoni
Dir, Parliamentary & Official Publishing: Andrew
  Allen *Tel:* (020) 7394 4218
Head, Government Services: Jeremy Hook
Head, Business Development: Richard South
Founded: 1786
UK sales agent for most major international orga-
  nizations.
Subjects: Agriculture, Archaeology, Architecture
  & Interior Design, Business, Computer Sci-
  ence, Earth Sciences, Economics, Education,
  Energy, Environmental Studies, Finance, Gov-
  ernment, Political Science, Health, Nutrition,
  History, Law, Library & Information Sciences,
  Medicine, Nursing, Dentistry, Social Sciences,
  Sociology, Technology, Transportation
ISBN Prefix(es): 978-0-10; 978-0-11; 978-0-337
Parent Company: Williams Lea Group
Branch Office(s)
TSO Press, Mandela Way, London SE1 5SS
  Tel: (020) 7394 4200
TSO Ireland, 19a Weavers Court, Weavers
  Court Business Park, Linfield Rd, Belfast
  BT12 5GH, Ireland *Fax:* (02890) 235401
  E-mail: enquiries@tsoireland.co.uk

Tuba Press
Tunley Cottage, Tunley, near Cirencester, Glos
  GL7 6LW
E-mail: tubapoetry@icloud.com
Web Site: www.tubapress.eu

Key Personnel
Partner: Susan Clydesdale-Cotter; Peter Ellson; Charles Graham; Margaret Hannigan Popp
Founded: 1976
Specialize in poetry, chiefly unpublished authors.
Subjects: Biography, Memoirs, History, Poetry
ISBN Prefix(es): 978-0-907155; 978-0-9505956
Number of titles published annually: 1 Print
Total Titles: 58 Print

Tufton Books, *imprint of* The Church Union

Twayne Publishers, *imprint of* Gale

Twelveheads Press
2 Woodside Cottages, Chacewater, Truro, Cornwall TR4 8LP
E-mail: enquiries@twelveheads.com
Web Site: www.twelveheads.com
Key Personnel
Partner: Alan Kittridge; Michael Messenger; John Stengelhofen
Founded: 1978
Subjects: Archaeology, History, Maritime, Regional Interests, Transportation
ISBN Prefix(es): 978-0-906294
Number of titles published annually: 4 Print
Total Titles: 42 Print
Distribution Center: Tor Mark Press, United Downs Industrial Estate, St Day, Redruth TR16 5HY *Tel:* (01209) 822101 *Fax:* (01209) 822035 *E-mail:* info@tormark.co.uk *Web Site:* www.tormark.co.uk

Twenty7 Books+
Imprint of Bonnier Zaffre Ltd
80-81 Wimpole St, London W1G 9RE
Tel: (020) 7490 3875
E-mail: hello@twenty7books.co.uk
Web Site: twenty7books.co.uk
Founded: 2015
Publishing commercial debut fiction across a broad range of genres with an ebook-first strategy. Particular commercial focus on thrillers, crime & women's fiction.
Subjects: Fiction, Mysteries, Suspense
ISBN Prefix(es): 978-1-78577
Number of titles published annually: 50 Print; 50 E-Book; 12 Audio
Ultimate Parent Company: Bonnier Group AB
Foreign Rights: Tassy Barham Associates Ltd (Brazil); The English Agency of Japan (Japan); Agencja Literacka Graal (Poland); International Editors Co (Portugal, Spain); Kalem Agency (Turkey); Andrew Nurnberg Associates International Ltd (China, Taiwan); Kristin Olson Literary Agency sro (Czechia); Tuttle-Mori Agency Co Ltd (Japan); Eric Yang Agency (Korea)
Warehouse: Grantham Book Services (GBS), Trent Rd, Grantham NG31 7XQ *Tel:* (01476) 541000 *Fax:* (01476) 541060
Distribution Center: Grantham Book Services (GBS), Trent Rd, Grantham NG31 7XQ *Tel:* (01476) 541000 *Fax:* (01476) 541060

Two Roads, *imprint of* Hodder & Stoughton Ltd

UBM Information Ltd
240 Blackfriars Rd, London SE1 8BF
Tel: (020) 7921 5000
Web Site: www.ubm.com
Key Personnel
Dir, Communications: Peter Bancroft
Subjects: Advertising, Architecture & Interior Design, Business, Energy, Film, Video, Health, Nutrition, Publishing & Book Trade Reference
ISBN Prefix(es): 978-0-86213
Number of titles published annually: 12 Print; 2 CD-ROM; 5 Online

Total Titles: 12 Print; 2 CD-ROM; 5 Online
Divisions: UBM Built Environment; UBM Conferences; UBM Connect; UBM Live

UK Academy of Science, see The Royal Society

Ulster Historical Foundation+
49 Malone Rd, Belfast BT9 6RY
Tel: (028) 9066 1988
E-mail: enquiry@uhf.org.uk
Web Site: www.ancestryireland.com
Key Personnel
Executive Dir: Fintan Mullan
Research Dir: Dr William Roulston
Founded: 1956
Subjects: Education, Genealogy, History, Regional Interests, Conferences, Genealogy, Historical Publishing
ISBN Prefix(es): 978-0-901905; 978-1-903688; 978-1-908448

Ulverscroft Large Print Books Ltd+
The Green, Bradgate Rd, Anstey, Leicester, Leics LE7 7FU
Tel: (0116) 236 4325 *Fax:* (0116) 234 0205
E-mail: marketing@ulverscroft.co.uk
Web Site: www.ulverscroft.co.uk
Key Personnel
Sales Manager: Mark Merrill *E-mail:* m.merrill@ulverscroft.co.uk
Founded: 1964
Publishers of Ulverscroft Large Print Books, Charnwood Library Series, Linford Mystery Library Series, Linford Romance Library Series, Linford Western Library Series.
Subjects: Biography, Memoirs, Fiction, Literature, Literary Criticism, Essays, Mysteries, Suspense, Nonfiction (General), Romance, Travel & Tourism, Western Fiction
ISBN Prefix(es): 978-0-85456; 978-0-7089; 978-1-84395; 978-1-84617
U.S. Office(s): Ulverscroft Large Print (USA) Inc, 950A Union Rd, Suite 427, PO Box 1230, West Seneca, NY 14224-1230, United States *Tel:* 716-674-4270 *Fax:* 716-674-4195 *E-mail:* sales@ulverscroftusa.com *Web Site:* www.ulverscroft.com
Distributor for Magna Large Print (Australia, Canada, New Zealand, South Africa, USA)
Showroom(s): Prospect Business Park, Unit C, North Wing, Leadgate, Consett, Co Durham DH8 6RR, Contact: Peter Douglas *Tel:* (07767) 646 576 (cell) *E-mail:* p.douglas@ulverscroft. co.uk; 3 Maple Grove Business Centre, Ground floor, Lawrence Rd, off Green Lane, Hounslow, Middx TW4 6DR, Contact: Jim Sacre *Tel:* (07767) 646 572 (cell) *E-mail:* j.sacre@ulverscroft.co.uk; Automobile Palace, Unit 5/6, Temple Street, Lladrindod Wells LD1 5HO, Contact: Mark Merrill *Tel:* (07880) 506 505 (cell) *E-mail:* m.merrill@ulverscroft.co.uk; Magna Headquarters, Magna House, Long Preston, Nr Skipton, N Yorks BD23 4ND, Contact: Helen Bibby *Tel:* (01729) 840 225 *Fax:* (01729) 840 683 *E-mail:* helen.bibby@magnaprint.co.uk; Trecerus Industrial Estate, Padstow, Cornwall PL28 8RW, Contact: Mark Merrill *Tel:* (07880) 506 505 (cell) *E-mail:* m.merrill@ulverscroft.co.uk

Under the Maple Tree Books, *imprint of* Knox Robinson Publishing

Unicorn Press Ltd, *imprint of* Unicorn Publishing Group LLP

Unicorn Publishing Group LLP
101 Wardour St, London W1F 0UG
Tel: (07836) 633377
Web Site: www.unicornpress.org

Key Personnel
Chairman: Ian Strathcarron *E-mail:* ian@unicornpress.org
Editorial & Co-Editions Dir: Mark Eastment *E-mail:* mark@unicornpress.org
Editorial & Production Dir: Lucy Duckworth *Tel:* (01892) 871413 *E-mail:* lucy@unicornpress.org
Publishing Dir, Uniform Press: Ryan Gearing *Tel:* (07563) 201918 *E-mail:* ryan@unicornpress.org
Sales & Marketing Dir: Simon Perks *Tel:* (07775) 891738 *E-mail:* simon@unicornpress.org
Subjects: Art, History, Military Science
ISBN Prefix(es): 978-1-910065; 978-1-910500; 978-0-906290
Imprints: Unicorn Press Ltd; Uniform Press; Unity Press; Universe Press
Divisions: Unicorn Sales & Distribution US&D
Branch Office(s)
Acorn House, Tonbridge Rd, Bough Beech, Edenbridge, Kent TN8 7AU *Tel:* (01892) 871413
Distributor for Royal Armories
Foreign Rep(s): Durnell Marketing (Europe); IMA (David Williams) (Caribbean, South America); The White Partnership (Cambodia, Hong Kong, India, Japan, Laos, Malaysia, Myanmar, Philippines, Singapore, South Korea, Taiwan, Thailand, Vietnam); Woodslane Pty Ltd (Australia, Fiji, New Zealand)
Distribution Center: Marston Book Services Ltd, 160 Eastern Ave, Milton Park, Abingdon, Oxon OX14 4SB *Tel:* (01235) 465500 *Fax:* (01235) 465555 *E-mail:* trade.orders@marston.co.uk *Web Site:* www.marston.co.uk
The University of Chicago Press, 11030 S Langley Ave, Chicago, IL 60628, United States *Tel:* 773-702-7000 *Fax:* 773-702-7212 *E-mail:* sales@press.uchicago.edu *Web Site:* www.press.uchicago.edu (USA & Canada)

Uniform Press, *imprint of* Unicorn Publishing Group LLP

Unique Inspiration Ltd
Ground floor, Fort Dunlop, Fort Parkway, Birmingham B24 9FE
Tel: (0121) 698 8524 *Fax:* (0121) 270 9636
E-mail: contact@uniqueinspiration.co.uk; akuandkamu@uniqueinspiration.co.uk
Web Site: www.uniqueinspiration.co.uk; www.akuandkamu.com
Key Personnel
Founder & Publisher: Asif Bashir
Founded: 2001
Subjects: Asian Studies, Foreign Countries
ISBN Prefix(es): 978-1-907525

United Business Media Ltd, see UBM Information Ltd

United Writers Publications Ltd+
Ailsa, Castle Gate, Penzance, Cornwall TR20 8BG
Tel: (01736) 365954 *Fax:* (01736) 365954
E-mail: mail@unitedwriters.co.uk
Web Site: www.unitedwriters.co.uk
Key Personnel
Mng Dir, Editorial, Sales: Malcolm Sheppard *E-mail:* malcolm@unitedwriters.co.uk
Production: Tina Sully
Publicity: Peter Keane
Rights & Permissions: Julian Tremayne
Founded: 1962
Subjects: Biography, Memoirs, Fiction, Nonfiction (General), Sports, Athletics, Travel & Tourism
ISBN Prefix(es): 978-0-901976; 978-1-85200
Number of titles published annually: 6 Print
Total Titles: 150 Print

Unity Press, *imprint of* Unicorn Publishing Group LLP

Universe Press, *imprint of* Unicorn Publishing Group LLP

Universitas, *imprint of* Voltaire Foundation Ltd

University of Birmingham, Institute of Local Government Studies
School of Government & Society, Muirhead Tower, Edgbaston, Birmingham B15 2TT
Tel: (0121) 414 5008
Web Site: www.inlogov.bham.ac.uk
Key Personnel
Dir: Catherine Staite *Tel:* (0121) 414 4999 *E-mail:* c.staite@bham.ac.uk
Subjects: Government, Political Science, Democractic Local Governance, Strategic Public Management
ISBN Prefix(es): 978-0-7044; 978-0-85057; 978-0-903054

The University of Buckingham Press
Yeomanry House, Hunter St, Buckingham MK18 1EG
Tel: (01280) 814080; (01280) 828338
Web Site: ubpl.buckingham.ac.uk
Key Personnel
Publisher: Christopher Woodhead *E-mail:* christopher.woodhead@buckingham.ac.uk
Founded: 1983
Subjects: Biography, Memoirs, Economics, Education, Government, Political Science, History, Literature, Literary Criticism, Essays, Poetry, Religion - Other, Science (General)
ISBN Prefix(es): 978-0-9554642
Foreign Rep(s): International Publishers Marketing (IPM) (USA)

University of Exeter Press+
Reed Hall, Streatham Dr, Exeter EX4 4QR
Tel: (01392) 263066 *Fax:* (01392) 263064
E-mail: uep@exeter.ac.uk
Web Site: www.exeterpress.co.uk
Key Personnel
Publisher: Simon C Baker *E-mail:* s.c.baker@exeter.ac.uk
Founded: 1956
Academic book publishing.
Subjects: Archaeology, Drama, Theater, Education, Film, Video, History, Literature, Literary Criticism, Essays, Maritime, Poetry, Regional Interests
ISBN Prefix(es): 978-0-85989; 978-0-900771; 978-0-902414; 978-0-9501308; 978-1-904675; 978-1-905816
Number of titles published annually: 30 Print
Total Titles: 300 Print
Distributed by University of Chicago Press (Canada, Caribbean, Central America, Mexico, South America, USA)
Foreign Rep(s): Avicenna Partnership Ltd (Middle East, North Africa, Southeast Europe); Book Bird (M Anwer Iqbal) (Pakistan); Footprint Books Pty Ltd (Australia, New Zealand); Laszlo Horvath (Central Europe, Eastern Europe, Russia); Iberian Book Services (Peter Prout) (Gibraltar, Portugal, Spain); Kemper Conseil Publishing & Consultancy (Benelux); Publishers Services Pte Ltd (Tony Poh) (China, Hong Kong, Malaysia, Philippines, Singapore, Taiwan, Thailand, Vietnam); United Publishers Services Ltd (Japan, Korea); Viva Books Private Ltd (India)
Orders to: NBN International, Airport Business Centre, 10 Thornbury Rd, Plymouth PL6 7PP
Tel: (01752) 202301 *Fax:* (01752) 202333 *E-mail:* orders@nbninternational.com

University of Hertfordshire Press
University of Hertfordshire, College Lane, Hatfield AL10 9AB

Tel: (01707) 284681; (01707) 284654 (orders)
E-mail: uhpress@herts.ac.uk; uhpsales@herts.ac.uk
Web Site: www.herts.ac.uk/uhpress
Key Personnel
Publisher & Press Manager: Jane Housham
Founded: 1992
This publisher has indicated that 30% of their product line is author subsidized.
Subjects: Drama, Theater, Education, History, Literature, Literary Criticism, Essays, Local & Regional Academic History
ISBN Prefix(es): 978-1-902806; 978-0-900458
Number of titles published annually: 12 Print; 12 E-Book
Total Titles: 120 Print; 1 CD-ROM; 70 E-Book
Imprints: Hertfordshire Publications
Foreign Rep(s): IPG (Australia, Canada, USA)
Foreign Rights: Iberian Book Services (Peter Prout) (Portugal, Spain); Netwerk Academic Book Agency (Benelux)
Distribution Center: Central Books Ltd, One Heath Park Industrial Estate, Freshwater Rd, Dagenham RM8 1RX *Tel:* (020) 8525 8800 *Fax:* (020) 8599 2694 *E-mail:* info@centralbooks.com *Web Site:* www.centralbooks.com
IPG, 814 Franklin St, Chicago, IL 60610, United States *Tel:* 312-337-0747 *Fax:* 312-337-5985 *E-mail:* orders@ipgbook.com *Web Site:* www.ipgbook.com (Australia, Canada & USA)

University of Wales Press (Gwasg Prifysgol Cymru)+
10 Columbus Walk, Brigantine Pl, Cardiff CF10 4UP
Tel: (029) 2049-6899 *Fax:* (029) 2049-6108
E-mail: press@press.wales.ac.uk
Web Site: www.uwp.co.uk
Key Personnel
Dir: Helgard Krause
Production & Editorial Manager: Sian Chapman *E-mail:* s.chapman@press.wales.ac.uk
Sales & Marketing Manager: Eleri Lloyd-Cresci *E-mail:* elloyd-cresci@press.wales.ac.uk
Head, Commissioning: Sarah Lewis *E-mail:* s.lewis@press.wales.ac.uk
Founded: 1922
Subjects: Archaeology, Architecture & Interior Design, Art, Economics, Education, Geography, Geology, History, Language Arts, Linguistics, Literature, Literary Criticism, Essays, Philosophy, Social Sciences, Sociology, Theology, Women's Studies
ISBN Prefix(es): 978-0-7083; 978-0-900768; 978-1-900477
Number of titles published annually: 60 Print; 1 CD-ROM; 20 E-Book
Total Titles: 500 Print; 6 CD-ROM; 200 E-Book
Bookshop(s): 12 High St, Cardiff CF10 1AX *Tel:* (029) 2022 8205 *E-mail:* shop@wales.ac.uk
Distribution Center: Turpin Customer Services, Pegasus Dr, Stratton Business Park, Biggleswade, Beds SG18 8TQ *Tel:* (01767) 604 4951 *E-mail:* custserv@turpin-distribution.com (journals)
Welsh Books Council, Distribution Centre, Glanyrafon Enterprise Park, Llanbadarn Fawr, Aberystwyth, Ceredigion SY23 3AQ *Tel:* (01970) 624455 *Fax:* (01970) 625506 *E-mail:* distribution.centre@wbc.org.uk *Web Site:* www.gwales.com (Wales)
NBN International, Airport Business Centre, 10 Thornbury Rd, Plymouth PL6 7PP *Tel:* (01752) 202301 *Fax:* (01752) 202333 *E-mail:* orders@nbninternational.com *Web Site:* www.nbninternational.com (UK, Europe & Asia)
United Publishers Services Ltd, 1-32-5, Higashishinagawa, Shinagawa-ku, Tokyo 140-0002, Japan *Tel:* (03) 5479 7255 *Fax:* (03) 5479 7307 *E-mail:* info@ups.jp

The University of Chicago Press, Chicago Distribution Centre, 11030 S Langley, Chicago, IL 60628, United States *Tel:* 773-702-7000 *Fax:* 773-702-7212 (North & South America, Australia & New Zealand)

Urbane Publications Ltd
20 St Nicholas Gardens, Rochester, Kent ME2 3NT
Web Site: urbanepublications.com
Key Personnel
Dir: Matthew Smith *E-mail:* matthew@urbanepublications.com
Subjects: Biography, Memoirs, Business, Fiction, Humor, Science Fiction, Fantasy, Self-Help
ISBN Prefix(es): 978-1-909273

Urdd Gobaith Cymru
Swyddfa'r Urdd, Gwersyll yr Urdd, Glan-Ilyn, Llanuwcllyn y Bala LL23 7ST
Tel: (01678) 541000
E-mail: helo@urdd.org
Web Site: www.urdd.cymru
Key Personnel
Chief Executive: Sioned Hughes *Tel:* (02920) 635 690 *E-mail:* sionedhughes@urdd.org
Founded: 1922
ISBN Prefix(es): 978-0-903131; 978-0-9500535; 978-0-9572407

Usborne Publishing Ltd+
Usborne House, 83-85 Saffron Hill, London EC1N 8RT
Tel: (020) 7430 2800 *Fax:* (020) 7430 1562; (020) 7242 0974 (illustrations)
E-mail: mail@usbornebooksathome.co.uk
Web Site: www.usborne.com
Key Personnel
Founder: Peter Usborne
General Manager: Robert Jones
Senior Marketing Executive: Alesha Bonser *E-mail:* aleshab@usborne.co.uk; Hannah Reardon Steward *Tel:* (020) 7890 3174 *E-mail:* hannahr@usborne.co.uk
Marketing & Publicity Manager: Anna Howorth *Tel:* (020) 8636 3734 *E-mail:* annah@usborne.co.uk
Founded: 1973
ISBN Prefix(es): 978-0-7460; 978-0-86020; 978-0-7945; 978-1-85123; 978-1-4095
Branch Office(s)
Usborne Books at Home & School, Oasis Park, Unit 8, Stanton Harcourt Rd, Eynsham, Witney, Oxon OX29 4TU *Tel:* (01865) 883731 *Fax:* (01865) 883759 *E-mail:* mail@usbornebooksathome.co.uk
Distributed by HarperCollins Canada
Foreign Rep(s): Educational Development Corp (USA); HarperCollins Australia (Gemma Fahy) (Australia); HarperCollins Australia (Teresa Garnett) (New Zealand); HarperCollins Canada (Canada); Kel Ediciones (Rose Passero) (Argentina); Libromania (Arturo Ramirez) (Chile); LISER - Libreria y Servicios (Cesar Arechavala) (Honduras); Mosca Hnos (Estefany Calvete) (Uruguay); MPH Distributors Pte Ltd (Rahim Awang) (Singapore); MPH Distributors Sdn Bhd (Tai Kwai Meng) (Malaysia); Scholastic India Pvt Ltd (Indrajit Jash) (India); Wild Dog Press (Nicola O'Flynn Madden) (South Africa)
Distribution Center: HarperCollins Distribution Services, Westerhill Rd, Bishopbriggs, Glasgow G64 2QT *Tel:* (0141) 306 3100 *Fax:* (0141) 306 3767 *E-mail:* uk.orders@harpercollins.co.uk

UXL, *imprint of* Gale

Vacation Work, *imprint of* Crimson Publishing Ltd

Vagabond Voices
8 Ibroxholm Pl, Flat 2 1/2, Glasgow G51 2TP
Tel: (07767) 064614
E-mail: sales@vagabondvoices.co.uk
Web Site: vagabondvoices.co.uk
Founded: 2008
Subjects: Fiction, Government, Political Science
ISBN Prefix(es): 978-0-9560560; 978-1-908251
Foreign Rep(s): Dufour Editions (Canada, USA)
Foreign Rights: The St Mark's Agency (France)
Distribution Center: Marston Book Services Ltd,
    160 Eastern Ave, Milton Park, Abingdon, Oxon
    OX14 4SB *Tel:* (01235) 465500 *Fax:* (01235)
    465555 *E-mail:* direct.orders@marston.co.uk
    Web Site: www.marston.co.uk

Vallentine-Mitchell Publishers+
Middlesex House, 29/45 High St, Edgware,
    Middx HA8 7UU
Tel: (020) 8952 9526 *Fax:* (020) 8952 9242
E-mail: info@vmbooks.com
Web Site: www.vmbooks.com; www.vmbooksuk.
    com
Founded: 1950
Subjects: Cookery, Government, Political Science,
    History, Literature, Literary Criticism, Essays,
    Religion - Jewish, Theology, Holocaust, Mili-
    tary History
ISBN Prefix(es): 978-0-85303
Associate Companies: Irish Academic Press; The
    Woburn Press
Orders to: ISBS, 920 NE 58 Ave, Suite 300,
    Portland, OR 97216, United States *Fax:* 503-
    280-8832 *E-mail:* vmuk@isbs.com *Web
    Site:* www.isbs.com

ValuSource, *imprint of* John Wiley & Sons Ltd

Van Duren Publishers Ltd, see Colin Smythe
    Ltd

V&A Publishing
Victoria & Albert Museum, Cromwell Rd, Lon-
    don SW7 2RL
Tel: (020) 7942 2966
E-mail: vapubs@vam.ac.uk
Web Site: vandapublishing.com; www.vandashop.
    com
Subjects: Architecture & Interior Design, Art,
    Fashion
ISBN Prefix(es): 978-1-85177; 978-0-905209;
    978-0-901486; 978-0-948107; 978-0-9521209
Total Titles: 180 Print
Parent Company: V&A Enterprises Ltd
Distributed by Abrams (North America); Blooms-
    bury Publishing Pty Ltd (Australia & New
    Zealand); Hachette Book Group USA (North
    America)
Distribution Center: Littlehampton Book Ser-
    vices Ltd, Faraday Close, Durrington, Wor-
    thing, West Sussex BN13 3RB *Tel:* (01903)
    828500; (01903) 828501 (customer service)
    Web Site: lbsltd.wp.hachette.co.uk

Veloce Publishing Ltd+
Veloce House, Parkway Farm Business Park,
    Middle Farm Way, Poundbury, Dorchester DT1
    3AR
Tel: (01305) 260068 *Fax:* (01305) 250479
E-mail: info@veloce.co.uk; sales@veloce.co.uk
Web Site: www.veloce.co.uk; www.velocebooks.
    com
Key Personnel
Publisher & Dir: Rod Grainger
Dir: Judith Brooks
Founded: 1991
Also specialize in motorsports & workshop manu-
    als.
Subjects: Automotive, Biography, Memoirs, Me-
    chanical Engineering, Outdoor Recreation,
    Transportation

ISBN Prefix(es): 978-1-874105; 978-1-901295;
    978-1-903706; 978-1-904788; 978-1-84584
Number of titles published annually: 45 Print
Total Titles: 300 Print
Distributed by Motorbooks International Inc
    (USA)

Venton, *imprint of* Intellect Ltd

Ventura, *imprint of* Penguin Books Ltd

Venture Press Ltd
16 Kent St, Birmingham B5 6RD
Tel: (0121) 622 3911 *Fax:* (0121) 622 4860
E-mail: info@basw.co.uk
Web Site: www.basw.co.uk
Key Personnel
Publishing & Events Manager: Sue Hatton
    E-mail: s.hatton@basw.co.uk
Subjects: Social Sciences, Sociology
ISBN Prefix(es): 978-0-900102; 978-0-9501603;
    978-1-86178; 978-1-873878
Parent Company: British Association of Social
    Workers

Veritas Foundation Publication Centre+
63 Jeddo Rd, London W12 9EE
Tel: (020) 8749 4957
E-mail: orders@veritasbookshop.co.uk
Web Site: www.veritasfoundation.co.uk
Founded: 1947
Also publishes weekly newspaper.
Subjects: Education, Religion - Other
ISBN Prefix(es): 978-0-948202; 978-0-901215;
    978-0-904639

Vermilion, *imprint of* Ebury Publishing

Verso Books+
6 Meard St, London W1F 0EG
Tel: (020) 7437 3546 *Fax:* (020) 7734 0059
E-mail: enquiries@verso.co.uk
Web Site: www.versobooks.com
Key Personnel
Sales & Marketing Dir: Rowan Wilson
    E-mail: rowan@verso.co.uk
Senior Editor: Leo Hollis
Rights & Permissions: Federico Campagna
    E-mail: federico@verso.co.uk
Founded: 1971
Subjects: Economics, Ethnicity, Film, Video,
    Government, Political Science, History, Lit-
    erature, Literary Criticism, Essays, Nonfiction
    (General), Philosophy, Psychology, Psychiatry,
    Social Sciences, Sociology, Women's Studies
ISBN Prefix(es): 978-0-86091; 978-0-902308;
    978-1-85984; 978-1-84467; 978-1-78168
Number of titles published annually: 100 Print
Parent Company: New Left Review
U.S. Office(s): 20 Jay St, Suite 1010, Brooklyn,
    NY 11201, United States, Marketing Manager:
    Anne Rumberger *Tel:* 718-246-8160 *Fax:* 718-
    246-8165 *E-mail:* anne@versobooks.com
Distributed by Bloomsbury Publishing Pty Ltd
    (Australia & New Zealand); Yale University
    Press (UK)
Foreign Rep(s): APD Malaysia (Lilian Koe)
    (Malaysia); APD Singapore Ptd Ltd (Brunei,
    Singapore, Thailand); Avicenna Partnership
    Ltd (Middle East); Bloomsbury Publishing Pty
    Ltd (Australia, New Zealand); Blue Weaver
    (South Africa); Tim Burland (Japan); Durnell
    Marketing/Publishers European Sales Agency
    (Andrew Durnell) (Europe); Claire de Gruchy
    (Cyprus, Greece, Jordan, Malta, North Africa,
    Turkey); IMA (David Williams) (Caribbean,
    Latin America); Bill Kennedy (Arab Mid-
    dle East, Iran, Sudan); Maya Publishers Pvt
    Ltd (Surit Mitra) (India); Missing Link (Klaus
    Tapken) (Germany); B K Norton Ltd (Jerome
    C Su) (China, Hong Kong, Korea, Taiwan);

Random House Distribution Center (Canada,
    USA); Repforce Ireland (Ireland); Segment
    Book Distributors (India)
Foreign Rights: The English Agency (Japan) Ltd
    (Tsutomu Yawata) (Japan); Metis Yayinlari
    (Muge Gursoy Sokmen) (Turkey)
Orders to: Marston Book Services Ltd, 160 East-
    ern Ave, Milton Park, Abingdon, Oxon OX14
    4SB *Tel:* (01235) 465500 *Fax:* (01235) 465
    55 *E-mail:* direct.orders@marston.co.uk *Web
    Site:* www.marston.co.uk

Victoria & Albert Museum, see V&A
    Publishing

Vif, *imprint of* Voltaire Foundation Ltd

Viking, *imprint of* Penguin Books Ltd

Viking+
Imprint of Penguin Books Ltd
80 Strand, London WC2R 0RL
Tel: (020) 7010 3000 *Fax:* (020) 7010 6692
E-mail: customer.service@penguin.co.uk
Web Site: www.penguin.co.uk
Key Personnel
Publisher: Daniel Crewe; Joel Rickett
Mng Dir: Joanna Prior
Founded: 1969
Subjects: Art, Biography, Memoirs, Cookery, Fic-
    tion, History, Nonfiction (General), Social Sci-
    ences, Sociology, Travel & Tourism
ISBN Prefix(es): 978-0-14; 978-0-670; 978-0-
    7139; 978-1-84614
Imprints: Allen Lane; The Penguin Press
U.S. Office(s): 375 Hudson St, New York, NY
    10014, United States *E-mail:* international.
    sales@us.penguingroup.com *Web Site:* www.
    penguinputnam.com
Orders to: Penguin Books, Bath Rd, Har-
    mondsworth, Middx UB7 0DA *Tel:* (01)
    7591984

Viking Children's Books+
80 Strand, London WC2R 0RL
Tel: (020) 70103000 *Fax:* (020) 70106060
E-mail: customerservice@penguinrandomhouse.
    com
Web Site: www.penguin.co.uk; www.penguin.com/
    meet/publishers/vikingchildrensbooks
Key Personnel
Publisher: Kenneth Wright
Founded: 1933
ISBN Prefix(es): 978-0-14; 978-0-670; 978-0-
    7139; 978-1-84614
Parent Company: Penguin Books Ltd
U.S. Office(s): Viking Children's Books, 375
    Hudson St, New York, NY 10014, United
    States *Tel:* 212-366-2000
Orders to: Penguin Books, Bath Rd, Har-
    mondsworth, Middx UB7 0DA *Tel:* (01)
    7591984

Vintage, *imprint of* The Random House Group
    Ltd, a Penguin Random House Company

Vintage Children's Classics, *imprint of* The
    Random House Group Ltd, a Penguin Random
    House Company

Vintage Classics, *imprint of* The Random House
    Group Ltd, a Penguin Random House
    Company

Vintage Digital, *imprint of* The Random House
    Group Ltd, a Penguin Random House
    Company

Virago, *imprint of* Little, Brown Book Group

Virago Press+
Imprint of Little, Brown Book Group
c/o Little, Brown Book Group Ltd, Carmelite
House, 50 Victoria Embankment, London
EC4Y 0DZ
Tel: (020) 7911 8000 *Fax:* (020) 7911 8100
E-mail: virago@littlebrown.co.uk
Web Site: www.virago.co.uk
Key Personnel
Chair: Ms Lennie Goodings
Publisher: Sarah Savitt
Founded: 1973
Subjects: Biography, Memoirs, Education, Fic-
tion, Government, Political Science, Health,
Nutrition, History, Philosophy, Public Admin-
istration, Social Sciences, Sociology, Travel &
Tourism, Women's Studies
ISBN Prefix(es): 978-0-86068; 978-1-86049; 978-
1-85381; 978-1-84408

Virgin Books, *imprint of* Ebury Publishing

Vision On, *imprint of* Omnibus Press

Visit Wales
Welsh Government, QED Centre, Main Ave, Tre-
forest Industrial Estate, Treforest, Pontypridd
CF37 5YR
E-mail: info@visitwales.com
Web Site: www.visitwales.com
Subjects: Travel & Tourism
ISBN Prefix(es): 978-1-4734

Visual Editions
Panther House, Unit 319, 38 Mount Pleasant,
London WC1X 0AN
Tel: (020) 3077 2056
E-mail: hey@visual-editions.com; orders@visual-
editions.com; press@visual-editions.com
Web Site: www.visual-editions.com
Key Personnel
Co-Founder: Anna Gerber; Britt Iversen
Founded: 2010
Subjects: Fiction, Nonfiction (General), Visual
Writing
ISBN Prefix(es): 978-0-9565692
Foreign Rep(s): Publishers Group West (PGW)
(Canada, USA)

The Vital Spark, *imprint of* Neil Wilson
Publishing Ltd

Voltaire Foundation, *imprint of* Voltaire
Foundation Ltd

Voltaire Foundation Ltd+
c/o University of Oxford, 99 Banbury Rd, Oxford
OX2 6JX
Tel: (01865) 284600 *Fax:* (01865) 284610
E-mail: email@voltaire.ox.ac.uk
Web Site: www.voltaire.ox.ac.uk
Key Personnel
Dir, General Editor: Prof Nicholas Cronk
Tel: (01865) 284602 *E-mail:* nicholas.cronk@
voltaire.ox.ac.uk
Publisher: Clare Fletcher *E-mail:* clare.fletcher@
voltaire.ox.ac.uk
Deputy Publisher: Janet Godden *E-mail:* janet.
godden@voltaire.ox.ac.uk
Publishing Manager: Karen Chidwick
E-mail: karen.chidwick@voltaire.ox.ac.uk;
Pippa Faucheux *E-mail:* pippa.faucheux@
voltaire.ox.ac.uk
Senior Editor: Dr Martin Smith *E-mail:* martin.
smith@voltaire.ox.ac.uk
Founded: 1971
Publishing & seminars on the European Enlight-
enment.
Specialize in works by & about Voltaire & other
enlightenment writers.

Subjects: History, Language Arts, Linguistics, Lit-
erature, Literary Criticism, Essays, Philosophy
ISBN Prefix(es): 978-0-7294; 978-0-903588; 978-
0-9502162
Number of titles published annually: 20 Print
Total Titles: 400 Print; 1 CD-ROM; 100 Online
Parent Company: University of Oxford
Imprints: Universitas; Vif; Voltaire Foundation
Foreign Rep(s): Amalivre
Orders to: Marston Book Services, 160 Eastern
Ave, Milton Park, Abingdon, Oxon OX14 4SB
Tel: (01235) 465500 *Fax:* (01235) 465509
E-mail: trade.orders@marston.co.uk *Web
Site:* www.marston.co.uk
Amalivre, 62 Ave de Suffren, 75015 Paris, France
Tel: 01 45 67 18 38 *Fax:* 01 45 66 50 70
E-mail: anne-sophie@amalivre.fr

Walker Books Ltd+
87 Vauxhall Walk, London SE11 5HJ
Tel: (020) 7793 0909
E-mail: export@walker.co.uk; editorial@walker.
co.uk; customerservices@walker.co.uk
Web Site: www.walker.co.uk
Key Personnel
Chairman & Editorial: David Lloyd
Chief Global Development Officer, Walker Books
Group: Helen McAleer
Executive Vice President & Commercial Dir,
Group Rights & Development, Walker Group:
Julia Posen
Joint Mng Dir, Walker Group: Karen Lotz
International Sales Dir, Foreign Rights & Co-
Editions: Caroline Muir
Group Export Sales Dir: Fiona MacDonald
Group Export Sales Executive, Northern & East-
ern Europe: Amelia Vahtrick
Group Export Sales Executive, Southern Europe:
Julia Finnegan
Senior Group & Intercompany Sales Manager:
Lucy Pleydell-Pearce
Group Export Product & Sales Manager: David
McMillan
Publicity Manager: Rosi Crawley *E-mail:* rosi.
crawley@walker.co.uk
Founded: 1978
Subjects: Fiction, Nonfiction (General)
ISBN Prefix(es): 978-1-56402; 978-0-7636; 978-
0-7445; 978-1-84428; 978-1-4063
Imprints: Walker Eireann
U.S. Office(s): Candlewick Press, 99 Dover
St, Somerville, MA 02144, United States
Fax: 617-661-0565 *E-mail:* licensing@
candlewick.com *Web Site:* www.candlewick.
com

Walker Canongate, *imprint of* Canongate Books

Walker Eireann, *imprint of* Walker Books Ltd

Wallflower Press+
Imprint of Columbia University Press
4 Eastern Terrace Mews, Brighton BN2 1EP
E-mail: info@wallflowerpress.co.uk
Web Site: www.wallflowerpress.co.uk
Key Personnel
Commissioning Editor & Editorial Dir: Yoram
Allon *E-mail:* yoram@wallflowerpress.co.uk
Assistant Editor: Jodie Taylor *E-mail:* jodie@
wallflowerpress.co.uk
Production Manager: Tom Cabot *E-mail:* tom@
wallflowerpress.co.uk
Specialize in cinema & the moving image. Pub-
lish academic & popular literature in film, tele-
vision & media studies as well as related areas
of the visual arts.
Subjects: Drama, Theater, Film, Video, Visual
Arts
ISBN Prefix(es): 978-1-903364; 978-1-904764;
978-1-905674; 978-1-906660
Distribution Center: Wiley European Distribution Centre, New Era Estate, Oldlands Way,

Bognor Regis PO22 9NQ *Tel:* (01243) 843
291 *Fax:* (01243) 843 296 *E-mail:* customer@
wiley.com (UK & Europe)
Two Rivers Distribution, 210 American Dr, Jackson, TN 38301, United States (Asia, North
America & South America)

The Warburg Institute+
University of London, Woburn Sq, London
WC1H 0AB
Tel: (020) 7862 8949 *Fax:* (020) 7862 8955
E-mail: warburg@sas.ac.uk; warburg.books@sas.
ac.uk (orders)
Web Site: www.warburg.sas.ac.uk
Founded: 1921
Subjects: Art, History, Philosophy, Science (Gen-
eral)
ISBN Prefix(es): 978-0-85481
Number of titles published annually: 2 Print
Total Titles: 39 Print
Parent Company: University of London
Distributed by Nino Aragno Editore

Warc+
85 Newman St, London W1T 3EU
Tel: (020) 7467 8100 *Fax:* (020) 7467 8101
E-mail: enquiries@warc.com
Web Site: www.warc.com
Founded: 1984
Membership(s): Periodical Publishers Association
(PPA).
Subjects: Advertising, Economics, Government,
Political Science, Marketing, Radio, TV
ISBN Prefix(es): 978-1-870562; 978-1-84116;
978-1-899314
Branch Office(s)
20 A Teck Lim Rd, Singapore 088391, Singapore
Tel: 3157 6200 *E-mail:* asiapacific@warc.com
U.S. Office(s): 2233 Wisconsin Ave NW, Suite
535, Washington, DC 20007, United States
Tel: 202-778-0680 *E-mail:* americas@warc.com

Warm Island Walking Guides, *imprint of*
Discovery Walking Guides Ltd

Frederick Warne, *imprint of* Penguin Books Ltd

Frederick Warne Publishers Ltd+
80 Strand, London WC2R 0RL
Tel: (020) 7010 3000
Web Site: www.penguin.com/meet/publishers/
frederickwarne
Key Personnel
Mng Dir: Francesca Dow
Founded: 1865
Specializes in classic characters & licensed mer-
chandise programs.
ISBN Prefix(es): 978-0-7232
Parent Company: Penguin Books Ltd
U.S. Office(s): Penguin Group (USA) Inc, 375
Hudson St, New York, NY 10014, United
States *Tel:* 212-366-2000
Orders to: Penguin Books Ltd, Bath Rd, Har-
mondsworth, West Drayton, Middx UB7 0DA
Tel: (02) 208 757 4000

Watkins Publishing
Imprint of Watkins Media Ltd
359 Goswell Rd, London EC1V 7JL
Tel: (020) 3468 0102
E-mail: enquiries@watkinspublishing.com
Web Site: www.watkinspublishing.com
Key Personnel
Owner: Etan Ilfeld
Publisher: Jo Lal
Publisher-at-Large: Michael Mann
Subjects: Health, Nutrition, Inspirational, Spiritu-
ality, Science (General), Self-Help
ISBN Prefix(es): 978-1-84293; 978-1-907486;
978-1-78028; 978-1-84899

Foreign Rep(s): Hay House South Africa (South Africa); Messinter SpA (Italy); Pansing (Singapore); Research Press (Ajay Parmar) (India); S&S Australia (Australia, New Zealand)

Franklin Watts+
Imprint of Hachette Children's Books
Carmelite House, 50 Victoria Embankment, London EC4Y 0DZ
Tel: (020) 3122 6000
E-mail: ad@hachettechildrens.co.uk
Web Site: www.hachettechildrens.co.uk/homepage_franklinwatts
Key Personnel
Mng Dir: Hilary Murray Hill
Publishing Dir: Rachel Cooke *Tel:* (020) 7053 6620 *E-mail:* rachel.cooke@hachettechildrens.co.uk
Group Rights & Digital Dir: Andrew Sharp *Tel:* (020) 7873 6316 *E-mail:* andrew.sharp@hachettechildrens.co.uk
Trade Sales Dir: Paul Litherland *Tel:* (020) 7053 6670 *E-mail:* paul.litherland@hachettechildrens.co.uk
Head, Educational Sales: Peter Smith *Tel:* (020) 7053 6631 *E-mail:* peter.smith@hachettechildrens.co.uk
Head, Export: Rachel Graves *Tel:* (020) 7053 6632 *E-mail:* rachel.graves@hachettechildrens.co.uk
Senior Education Marketing Executive: Janet Aspey *Tel:* (020) 7053 6602 *E-mail:* janet.aspey@hachettechildrens.co.uk
Founded: 1969
Subjects: Fiction, Nonfiction (General)
ISBN Prefix(es): 978-0-7496; 978-0-85166; 978-0-86313; 978-1-4451
Ultimate Parent Company: Hachette UK
Orders to: Bookpoint, 130 Milton Park, Abingdon, Oxon OX14 4SE *Tel:* (01235) 400 400 *Web Site:* bookpoint.wp.hachette.co.uk
Returns: Bookpoint, 130 Milton Park, Abingdon, Oxon OX14 4SE

Waverley Books, *imprint of* Geddes & Grosset

Wayland, *imprint of* Hachette Children's Books

The Waywiser Press+
Christmas Cottage, Church Enstone, Chipping Norton, Oxon OX7 4NN
Tel: (01608) 677492
E-mail: info@waywiser-press.com
Web Site: waywiser-press.com
Key Personnel
Editor-in-Chief: Philip Hoy
Founded: 2001
Subjects: Fiction, Literature, Literary Criticism, Essays, Poetry
ISBN Prefix(es): 978-0-9532841; 978-1-903291
Number of titles published annually: 5 Print
Total Titles: 80 Print
Imprints: Between The Lines (BTL)
U.S. Office(s): PO Box 6205, Baltimore, MD 21206, United States
Foreign Rep(s): Dufour Editions Inc (North America); Inpress Ltd (UK)
Foreign Rights: The Marsh Agency (Paul Marsh) (worldwide)
Distribution Center: NBN International, 10 Thornbury Rd, Plymouth PL6 7PP *Tel:* (01752) 202301 *E-mail:* cservs@nbninternational.com
Web Site: distribution.nbni.co.uk

Weatherbys Ltd+
Sanders Rd, Wellingborough, Northants NN8 4BX
Tel: (01933) 440077
E-mail: ihelp@weatherbys.co.uk; shop@weatherbys.co.uk

Web Site: www.weatherbys.co.uk; www.weatherbysshop.co.uk (sales)
Key Personnel
Chairman: Johnny Weatherby
  E-mail: jweatherby@weatherbys.co.uk
Mng Dir: Graham Ayres *E-mail:* gayres@weatherbys.co.uk
Founded: 1926
Subjects: Animals, Pets, Sports, Athletics
ISBN Prefix(es): 978-0-900964; 978-0-902959
Subsidiaries: Weatherbys Chase Ltd; Weatherbys GSB
Branch Office(s)
Weatherbys Ireland, Tara Court, Dublin Rd, Naas, Co Kildare, Ireland *Tel:* (045) 879979 *Fax:* (045) 879691 *E-mail:* info@weatherbys.ie

Websters International Publishers Ltd+
Lancaster House, floor 2(b), 38 Southwark St, London SE1 1UN
Tel: (020) 7089 2110 *Fax:* (020) 7089 2111
E-mail: contact@websters.co.uk
Web Site: www.websters.co.uk
Key Personnel
Chairman: Adrian Webster
Mng Dir: Jean-Luc Barbanneau
Dir: David Skinner
Financial Dir: Alan Fennell
Founded: 1983
Specialize in wine information in all formats.
Subjects: Cookery, Health, Nutrition, Travel & Tourism, Wine & Spirits
ISBN Prefix(es): 978-1-870604
Number of titles published annually: 6 Print; 1 CD-ROM
Total Titles: 20 Print
Associate Companies: Adrian Webster Ltd
Subsidiaries: Websters Multimedia Inc
Distributed by Little, Brown & Co (UK) Ltd

A Weekes, *imprint of* Stainer & Bell Ltd

Weidenfeld & Nicolson, *imprint of* Orion Publishing Group Ltd

Weldon Owen Pty Ltd, *imprint of* Kings Road Publishing

Weldon Owen Pty Ltd
Imprint of Kings Road Publishing
Suite 2.08, The Plaza, 535 Kings Rd, London SW10 0SZ
Tel: (020) 3770 8888
E-mail: info@weldonowen.co.uk
Web Site: weldonowen.co.uk
Key Personnel
President: Roger Shaw
Group UK Sales & Marketing Dir: Andrew Sauerwine *Tel:* (020) 3771 4268 *E-mail:* andrew.sauerwine@bonnierpublishing.co.uk
Group Creative Dir: Helen Wicks *Tel:* (01306) 876 361 *E-mail:* helen.wicks@bonnierpublishing.co.uk
Senior Editor: Lydia Halliday *Tel:* (01306) 748 105 *E-mail:* lydia.halliday@weldonowen.co.uk
Editor: Fay Evans *Tel:* (01306) 748 138 *E-mail:* fay.evans@weldonowen.co.uk
Founded: 1984
ISBN Prefix(es): 978-1-875137; 978-1-876778; 978-1-74089; 978-1-877019; 978-1-877022; 978-1-921530; 978-1-74252
Number of titles published annually: 30 Print
Total Titles: 1,000 Print
Ultimate Parent Company: Bonnier Publishing Ltd
Imprints: Little Bee (North America); Red Lemon Press (UK & North America); Weldon Owen Publishing (UK)

U.S. Office(s): 1045 Sansome St, Suite 100, San Francisco, CA 94111, United States *Tel:* 415-291-0100 *Fax:* 415-291-8841 *Web Site:* www.weldonowen.com

Weldon Owen Publishing, *imprint of* Weldon Owen Pty Ltd

Welsh Academic Press
Imprint of Ashley Drake Publishing Ltd
PO Box 733, Cardiff CF14 7ZY
Tel: (029) 2056 0343 *Fax:* (029) 2056 1631
E-mail: post@welsh-academic-press.com; dragon@welsh-academic-press.com (orders)
Web Site: www.welsh-academic-press.com
Key Personnel
Mng Dir: Mr Ashley Drake
Founded: 1994
Specialize in the publishing of scholarly & academic books that are also accessible to the general reader. Company's mission is to be "Welsh in identity, international in outlook".
Subjects: Biography, Memoirs, Education, Government, Political Science, History, Language Arts, Linguistics, Literature, Literary Criticism, Essays, Military Science, Transportation, Baltic, Cultural, Celtic, Scandinavian Studies
ISBN Prefix(es): 978-1-86057
Number of titles published annually: 15 Print
Total Titles: 40 Print
Imprints: St David's Press
Orders to: Welsh Books Council, Uned Glanyrafon, Aberystwyth, Ceredigion SY23 5QA
NBN International, 10 Thornbury Rd, Plymouth PL6 7PP *E-mail:* orders@nbninternational.com *Web Site:* www.nbninternational.com (outside of Wales)
International Specialized Book Services (ISBS), 920 NE 58th Ave, Suite 300, Portland, OR 97213, United States *Tel:* 503-287-3093 *Fax:* 503-280-8832 *E-mail:* orders@isbs.com *Web Site:* www.isbs.com

Welsh Women's Classics, *imprint of* Honno Welsh Women's Press

Welsh Women's Press, see Honno Welsh Women's Press

Edition WELTKIOSK
5 New Street Sq, London EC4A 3TW
Tel: (079) 0486 5442 *Fax:* (087) 2115 2681
E-mail: office@weltkiosk.net; publishing@weltkiosk.net
Web Site: www.weltkiosk.net
Subjects: Government, Political Science, Journalism, International Affairs
ISBN Prefix(es): 978-3-942377
Distribution Center: Leipziger Kommissions- und Grossbuchhandelsgesellschaft mbH (LKG), An der Suedspitze 1-12, 04571 Roetha, Germany, Contact: Martina Koernig *Tel:* (034206) 65-122 *Fax:* (034206) 65-1739 *E-mail:* mkoernig@lkg-service.de *Web Site:* www.lkg-va.de (Austria & Germany)
Kaktus Verlagsauslieferung, Unterlachenstr 32, Postfach 3120, 6002 Lucerne, Switzerland *Tel:* (041) 202 1417 *Fax:* (041) 202 1418 *E-mail:* auslieferung@kaktus.net

David West Children's Books
6 Princeton Court, 55 Felsham Rd, London SW15 1AZ
Tel: (020) 8780 3836; (020) 8780 2196 *Fax:* (020) 8780 9313
E-mail: dww@btinternet.com
Web Site: www.davidwestchildrensbooks.com
Key Personnel
Owner: David West
Partner: Lynn Lockett

Foreign Rights Manager & Sales: Frederique Eti-
enney
Subjects: Archaeology, Biography, Memoirs, Biological Sciences, Film, Video, History, Science
(General), Sports, Athletics, Anatomy, Mythology
ISBN Prefix(es): 978-0-9553477; 978-1-909089

West Highland Series, *imprint of* House of
Lochar

The Westbourne Press, *imprint of* Saqi Books

WH Allen, *imprint of* Ebury Publishing

Wharncliffe Books, *imprint of* Pen & Sword
Books Ltd

Wharncliffe Publishing Ltd+
Imprint of Pen & Sword Books Ltd
47 Church St, Barnsley, S Yorks S70 2AS
Tel: (01226) 734302 (editorial); (01226) 734555
Fax: (01226) 734438
E-mail: enquiries@pen-and-sword.co.uk
Web Site: www.wharncliffepublishing.co.uk/
history
Key Personnel
Mng Dir: Michael Hewitt
Founded: 1988
Membership(s): IPG.
Subjects: History, Outdoor Recreation, Regional
Interests, Local History, Countryside Books,
Military History
ISBN Prefix(es): 978-1-871647; 978-0-9507892;
978-1-903425; 978-1-84563
Ultimate Parent Company: Acredula Group Ltd
Distributed by Casemate

Wheeler Publishing, *imprint of* Gale

White Cockade Publishing
West Fossil Farmhouse, West Fossil, Dorchester,
Dorset DT2 8DA
Tel: (01305) 852826
E-mail: mail@whitecockade.co.uk
Web Site: www.whitecockade.co.uk
Founded: 1988
Subjects: Antiques, Architecture & Interior De-
sign, Crafts, Games, Hobbies, History, Re-
gional Interests, Social Sciences, Sociology,
Women's Studies, Design History
ISBN Prefix(es): 978-0-9513124; 978-1-873487
Number of titles published annually: 1 Print
Total Titles: 12 Print

White Eagle Publishing Trust+
New Lands, Brewells Lane, Liss, Hants GU33
7HY
Tel: (01730) 893300 *Fax:* (01730) 892235
E-mail: sales@whiteagle.org
Web Site: www.whiteaglepublishing.org
Founded: 1953
Subjects: Astrology, Occult, Inspirational, Spiritu-
ality, Religion - Other
ISBN Prefix(es): 978-0-85487
Total Titles: 46 Print; 10 Audio
Parent Company: White Eagle Lodge
Distributed by De Vorss & Co Inc (North Amer-
ica)

White Ladder, *imprint of* Crimson Publishing
Ltd

Whiting & Birch Ltd+
90 Dartmouth Rd, London SE23 3HZ
Tel: (020) 8244 2421 *Fax:* (020) 7183 5996
E-mail: enquiries@whitingbirch.net
Web Site: www.whitingbirch.net

Key Personnel
Dir: David J Whiting *E-mail:* davidwhiting@
whitingbirch.net
Editor: Nigel Malin *E-mail:* nigel.malin@
sunderland.ac.uk
Founded: 1987
Publish books & journals in the fields of social
sciences & human services.
Subjects: Child Care & Development, Criminol-
ogy, Education, Ethnicity, Language Arts, Lin-
guistics, Literature, Literary Criticism, Essays,
Social Sciences, Sociology
ISBN Prefix(es): 978-1-871177; 978-1-86177
Number of titles published annually: 25 Print; 3
Online
Total Titles: 100 Print; 3 Online

Whittet Books Ltd+
One St John's Lane, Stansted, Essex CM24 8JU
Tel: (01279) 815871
E-mail: mail@whittetbooks.com
Web Site: www.whittetbooks.com
Key Personnel
Publisher/Dir: Shirley Greenall
Dir: George Papa
Founded: 1976
Subjects: Animals, Pets, Natural History, Vet-
erinary Science, Equids: Donkeys, Horses,
Livestock; Wildlife: Birds, Flowers, Mammals,
Trees
ISBN Prefix(es): 978-0-905483; 978-1-873580
Distributed by Diamond Farm Book Publishers
(Canada & USA)
Distribution Center: Book Systems Plus Ltd,
c/o GFS Ltd, 4 Hollands Rd, Haverhill, Suf-
folk CB9 8PP, Customer Services Manager:
Judith Baulcomb *Tel:* (01440) 706716 (or-
ders) *E-mail:* bsp2b@aol.com *Web Site:* www.
booksystemsplus.com (worldwide)

Whittles Publishing
Dunbeath Mill, Dunbeath, Caithness KW6 6EG
Tel: (01593) 731333 *Fax:* (01593) 731400
E-mail: info@whittlespublishing.com
Web Site: www.whittlespublishing.com
Key Personnel
Publisher & Dir: Dr Keith Whittles
Sales Manager: Sue Steven
Founded: 1986
Specialize in geomatics, civil & structural engi-
neering, geotechnical, landscape & architecture,
fuel & energy science, manufacturing & mate-
rials technology.
Membership(s): Publishing Scotland.
Subjects: Biography, Memoirs, Civil Engineering,
Earth Sciences, Maritime, Natural History, Fuel
& Energy Science, Geomatics Structural Engi-
neering, Geotechnics Materials & Manufactur-
ing Technology, Landscape, Military History,
Pharology
ISBN Prefix(es): 978-1-870325; 978-1-904445;
978-1-84995
Number of titles published annually: 25 Print
Total Titles: 160 Print
Foreign Rep(s): Asia Publishers Services Ltd
(China, Hong Kong, Korea, Taiwan); IMA/In-
termediamericana (Caribbean, Latin Amer-
ica); Edwin Makabenta (Philippines, Thai-
land); Missing Link (Germany); Netwerk Aca-
demic Book Agency (Belgium, Luxembourg,
Netherlands); The White Partnership (Indone-
sia, Japan, Malaysia, Pakistan, Singapore)
Orders to: BookSource, 50 Cambuslang
Rd, Cambuslang, Glasgow G32 8NB
Tel: (0141) 643 3961 *Fax:* (0141) 642 9182
E-mail: orders@booksource.net

WI Enterprises Ltd
104 New Kings Rd, London SW6 4LY
Tel: (020) 7371 9300
E-mail: hq@nfwi.org.uk
Web Site: www.thewi.org.uk

Key Personnel
General Secretary: Jana Osborne
Group Manager: Mark Linacre
Head, Communications: Charlotte Fiander
Founded: 1977
Subjects: Cookery, Crafts, Games, Hobbies, Eco-
nomics, Gardening, Plants, Women's Studies
ISBN Prefix(es): 978-0-947990; 978-0-900556
Parent Company: National Federation of
Women's Institutes (NFWI)
Branch Office(s)
19 Cathedral Rd, Cardiff *Tel:* (029) 2022 1712
Warehouse: WI Enterprises Ltd, Penzance TR93
OWW *Tel:* (01736) 333 333

Wide-Eyed Editions, *imprint of* Quarto
Publishing Group UK

Wide Eyed Editions
Imprint of Quarto Publishing Group UK
74-77 White Lion St, London N1 9PF
Tel: (020) 7284 9300 *Fax:* (020) 7485 0490
Web Site: www.quartoknows.com/wide-eyed-
editions
Key Personnel
Publisher: Rachel Williams *E-mail:* rachel.
williams@quarto.com
Editorial Dir: Jenny Broom *E-mail:* jenny.
broom@quarto.com
UK Marketing: Ellen John *E-mail:* ellen.john@
quarto.com
US Marketing: Michelle Bayuk *E-mail:* michelle.
bayuk@quarto.com
Founded: 2014
Subjects: Natural History, Nonfiction (General)
ISBN Prefix(es): 978-1-84780
Ultimate Parent Company: The Quarto Group Inc
U.S. Office(s): 142 W 36 St, 4th floor, New York,
NY 10018, United States *Tel:* 212-779-1809
Fax: 212-779-6058

Wild Goose Publications
Savoy House, 4th floor, 140 Sauchiehall St, Glas-
gow G2 3DH
Tel: (0141) 332 6343 *Fax:* (0141) 332 1090
E-mail: admin@ionabooks.com
Web Site: www.ionabooks.com
Key Personnel
Publishing Manager: Sandra Kramėr
Assistant Publishing Manager: Alex O'Neill
Founded: 1985
Produces books on social justice, political &
peace issues, holistic spirituality, healing &
innovative approaches to worship. Part of the
IONA community established in the Celtic
Christian tradition of Saint Columba.
Membership(s): IPG.
Subjects: Biblical Studies, Religion - Catholic,
Religion - Protestant, Theology, Celtic Chris-
tianity, Ecumenical Christianity
ISBN Prefix(es): 978-0-947988; 978-1-901557;
978-1-905010; 978-0-9501351; 978-1-84952
Number of titles published annually: 10 Print; 10
E-Book; 2 Audio
Total Titles: 150 Print; 70 E-Book; 25 Audio
Parent Company: The Iona Community
Foreign Rep(s): Novalis Bayard (Canada); Willow
Connection (Australasia)

Wildfire, *imprint of* Headline Publishing Group
Ltd

Wiley-Blackwell Ltd+
Imprint of John Wiley & Sons Ltd
9600 Garsington Rd, Oxford, Oxon OX4 2DQ
Tel: (01865) 776868 *Fax:* (01865) 714591
Web Site: www.wiley.com
Key Personnel
Chairman of the Board: Peter Booth Wiley
Founded: 1922

Subjects: Business, Computer Science, Economics, Finance, Geography, Geology, Government, Political Science, History, Labor, Industrial Relations, Language Arts, Linguistics, Law, Literature, Literary Criticism, Essays, Philosophy, Psychology, Psychiatry, Religion - Other, Social Sciences, Sociology, Women's Studies
ISBN Prefix(es): 978-0-631; 978-0-85520; 978-0-86216; 978-0-86542; 978-0-7279; 978-0-632; 978-3-89412; 978-3-8263; 978-0-85238; 978-0-905774; 978-1-85075; 978-1-84127; 978-1-4051; 978-0-913848
Imprints: Blackwell Futura; Blackwell Munksgaard; Blackwell Publishing; Blackwell Publishing Asia; BPS Blackwell (British Psychological Society)
U.S. Office(s): Wiley-Blackwell, 350 Main St, Malden, MA 02148, United States Tel: 781-388-8200 Fax: 781-388-8210
Distribution Center: John Wiley & Sons Ltd, New Era Estate, Oldlands Way, Bognor Regis, West Sussex PO22 9NQ Tel: (01243) 779777 Fax: (01243) 843274 E-mail: customer@wiley.com

Wiley-Heyden, imprint of John Wiley & Sons Ltd

Wiley-Interscience, imprint of John Wiley & Sons Ltd

John Wiley & Sons Ltd+
The Atrium, Southern Gate, Chichester, West Sussex PO19 8SQ
Tel: (01243) 779777 Fax: (01243) 775878
E-mail: customer@wiley.co.uk
Web Site: www.wiley.co.uk
Key Personnel
Chief Executive Officer & President: Stephen M Smith
Chief Marketing Officer: Clay Stobaugh
Senior Vice President, International Development & Group Sales: Reed Elfenbein
Vice President & Sales Dir, EMEA: Karen Wootton
Founded: 1960
Subjects: Accounting, Architecture & Interior Design, Biological Sciences, Business, Chemistry, Chemical Engineering, Computer Science, Cookery, Earth Sciences, Economics, Finance, Management, Marketing, Mathematics, Mechanical Engineering, Medicine, Nursing, Dentistry, Physics, Psychology, Psychiatry, Religion - Other, Technology
Total Titles: 11,000 Print; 300 E-Book
Parent Company: John Wiley & Sons Inc, 111 River St, Hoboken, NJ 07030-5774, United States
Associate Companies: John Wiley & Sons Australia Ltd, 42 McDougall St, Milton, Qld 4064, Australia Tel: (07) 3859 9755 Fax: (07) 3859 9715 E-mail: brisbane@wiley.com; John Wiley & Sons Canada Ltd, 5353 Dundas St W, Suite 400, Toronto, ON M9B 6H8, Canada Tel: 416-236-4433 Fax: 416-236-8743 E-mail: canada@wiley.com; Wiley-VCH Verlag GmbH, Boschstr 12, 69469 Weinheim, Germany Tel: (06201) 60 60 Fax: (06201) 60 63 28 E-mail: info@wiley-vch.de; John Wiley & Sons (Singapore) Pte Ltd, Solaris South Tower, No 07-01, One Fusionopolis Walk, Singapore 138628, Singapore Tel: 6643 8000 Fax: 6643 8008 E-mail: asiacart@wiley.com
Imprints: Halsted Press; Jossey-Bass; Scripta Technica; ValuSource; Wiley-Heyden; Wiley-Interscience; Wiley Liss
Distributor for Boydell & Brewer; California, Columbia & Princeton University Presses (Europe, Middle East, Africa); Harvard University Press/MIT Press Ltd & LOEB Classical Library (Europe, Middle East, Africa); Indiana

University Press (Continental Europe); Kegan Paul International Ltd (Europe); W W Norton & Co Ltd (Europe, Middle East, Africa, Asia, West Indies); O'Reilly UK Ltd (Europe, Middle East, Africa, Asia, West Indies); Research Studies Press Ltd (Europe, Middle East, Africa); Sybex International Corp (Continental Europe); The University of Chicago Press (Europe); Yale University Press (Europe, Middle East, Africa)

Wiley Liss, imprint of John Wiley & Sons Ltd

William Andrew, imprint of Elsevier Ltd

Joseph Williams, imprint of Stainer & Bell Ltd

Wilmington Publishing & Information Ltd
6-14 Underwood St, London N1 7JQ
Tel: (020) 7549 8708 Fax: (020) 7490 8238
E-mail: info@wilmingtonplc.com
Web Site: www.wilmington.co.uk; www.wlrstore.com
Key Personnel
Chief Executive Officer: Pedro Ros
E-mail: pedro.ros@wilmingtonplc.com
Subjects: Accounting, Finance, Health, Nutrition, Law, Charities, Healthcare, Media, Pensions, Surveying
ISBN Prefix(es): 978-0-9529798; 978-1-903077
Parent Company: Wilmington Group PLC

Wilmington Square Books, imprint of Bitter Lemon Press Ltd

Philip Wilson Publishers Ltd+
Subsidiary of I B Tauris & Co Ltd
6 Salem Rd, London W2 4BU
Tel: (020) 7243 1225 Fax: (020) 7243 1226
E-mail: mail@ibtauris.com
Web Site: www.philip-wilson.co.uk
Key Personnel
Mng Dir: Jonathan McDonnell
E-mail: jmcdonnell@ibtauris.com
Commissioning Editor: Anne Jackson
E-mail: ajackson@philip-wilson.co.uk
Editor: Clare Martelli E-mail: cmartelli@ibtauris.com
Founded: 1977
Subjects: Antiques, Archaeology, Architecture & Interior Design, Art, Fashion, Photography
ISBN Prefix(es): 978-0-85667; 978-0-302; 978-1-78130
Foreign Rep(s): Baker & Taylor Publisher Services (Canada, USA); Durnell Marketing Ltd (Continental Europe, Israel, Russia); Footprint (Australia, New Zealand); InterMedia Americana Ltd (Africa exc South Africa); MHM Ltd (Japan); I B Tauris & Co Ltd (Paul Davighi) (Middle East); Taylor & Francis Asia Pacific (East Asia, South Asia); Viva Books Pvt Ltd (India); Yale University Press (UK)
Distribution Center: Macmillan Distribution Ltd Tel: (01256) 329242 (UK trade & export); (01256) 302699 (direct) Fax: (01256) 812558 (UK trade); (01256) 812521 (UK trade & direct); (01256) 842084 (export) E-mail: orders@macmillan.co.uk

Windhorse Publications Ltd+
169 Mill Rd, Cambridge CB1 3AN
Tel: (01223) 213300
E-mail: info@windhorsepublications.com
Web Site: www.windhorsepublications.com
Key Personnel
Publishing Dir: Priyananda Joseph
Publishing Assistant: Hannah Atkinson
Founded: 1976
Subjects: Religion - Buddhist
ISBN Prefix(es): 978-0-904766; 978-1-899579; 978-1-907314

Number of titles published annually: 9 Print
Total Titles: 100 Print
Foreign Rep(s): Horizon Books (Brunei, Hong Kong, Indonesia, Malaysia, Singapore); Two Rivers Distribution (North America)
Distribution Center: BookSource, 50 Cambuslang Rd, Cambuslang, Glasgow G32 8NB Tel: (0845) 370 0067 E-mail: orders@booksource.net (UK & Europe)
Windhorse Books, PO Box 574, Newtown, NSW 2042, Australia Tel: (02) 9519 8826 E-mail: books@windhorse.com.au Web Site: www.windhorse.com.au (Australia & New Zealand)
Bacchus Books, Ajax House, 1st floor, Suite 7, 120 Caroline St, Brixton, Johannesburg 2092, South Africa Tel: (011) 839 0299 E-mail: baccus@telkomsa.net (Southern Africa)
Consortium Book Sales & Distribution, c/o Two Rivers Distribution, 210 American Dr, Jackson, TN 38301, United States (USA & Canada)

Windmill, imprint of The Random House Group Ltd, a Penguin Random House Company

Windmill Books Ltd+
9-17 St Albans Pl, 1st floor, London N1 0NX
Tel: (020) 7424 5640 Fax: (020) 7424 5641
Web Site: www.windmillbooks.co.uk; www.brownbearbooks.co.uk
Key Personnel
Chairman: Ashley Brown E-mail: abrown@windmillbooks.co.uk
Children's Publisher: Anne O'Daly
E-mail: aodaly@brownbearbooks.co.uk
Editorial Dir: Lindsey Lowe Tel: (020) 7424 5680 E-mail: llowe@windmillbooks.co.uk
Marketing & Rights: Sian Chueng
E-mail: schueng@windmillbooks.co.uk
Founded: 1995
Packager of books, partworks & continuity series.
Subjects: Animals, Pets, Art, Cookery, Crafts, Games, Hobbies, Geography, Geology, History, Music, Dance, Natural History, Pop Culture, Science (General), Social Sciences, Sociology, Military History
ISBN Prefix(es): 978-1-84044; 978-1-78121
Imprints: Brown Bear Books

WISE Publications, imprint of Omnibus Press

WIT Press+
Ashurst Lodge, Ashurst, Southampton SO40 7AA
Tel: (0238) 029 3223 Fax: (0238) 029 2853
E-mail: witpress@witpress.com; marketing@witpress.com
Web Site: www.witpress.com
Key Personnel
Chief Executive Officer: David S Anderson
E-mail: danderson@witpress.com
Marketing Manager: Dee Halzack
E-mail: dhalzack@witpress.com
Marketing Coordinator: Simon Ibbotson
E-mail: sibbotson@witpress.com
Sales Coordinator: Lorraine Carter
E-mail: lcarter@witpress.com
Founded: 1976
Publisher in advanced engineering subjects, including environmental engineering, engineering analysis & computational methods. Also publishes the proceedings of conferences organized by the Wessex Institute of Technology, edited/authored volumes & journals.
Subjects: Architecture & Interior Design, Automotive, Biological Sciences, Civil Engineering, Computer Science, Earth Sciences, Electronics, Electrical Engineering, Engineering (General), Environmental Studies, Maritime, Mathematics, Mechanical Engineering, Technology, Transportation, Acoustics, Air Pollution, Biomedicine, Earthquake, Ecology, Engineering, Environmental & Ecological Engineering, Fluid Mechanics, Fracture Mechanics, Heat

Transfer, Marine Engineering, Transport Engineering
ISBN Prefix(es): 978-0-931215; 978-0-945824; 978-1-56252; 978-1-85312; 978-0-905451; 978-1-84564; 978-1-78466
Number of titles published annually: 50 Print
Total Titles: 500 Print; 6 CD-ROM
Parent Company: Computational Mechanics International
U.S. Office(s): Computational Mechanics Inc, 25 Bridge St, Billerica, MA 01821, United States *Tel:* 978-667-5841 *Fax:* 978-667-7582
E-mail: salesusa@witpress.com

Witherby Insurance & Legal, *imprint of* Witherby Publishing Group

Witherby Publishing Group+
4 Dunlop Sq, Deans Estate, Livingston, Edinburgh EH54 8SB
Tel: (01506) 463 227 *Fax:* (01506) 468 999
E-mail: info@witherbys.com
Web Site: www.witherbypublishinggroup.com
Key Personnel
Chairman: Alan Witherby
Dir: Katrina Heathcote
Mng Dir: Iain Macneil
Finance Dir: Donna Tait
Information Technoloy Dir: Johan Machtelinckx
Senior Editor: Anne Martin
Sales: Alexandra Finlay *E-mail:* alex.finlay@emailws.com
Founded: 1740
Membership(s): The Booksellers Association; Independent Publishers Guild (IPG); Institute of Export.
Subjects: Business, Economics, Management, Maritime, Technology, Transportation, Insurance
ISBN Prefix(es): 978-0-900886; 978-1-85609; 978-0-948691; 978-0-907591; 978-0-906720
Number of titles published annually: 20 Print; 4 Online; 3 E-Book; 2 Audio
Total Titles: 350 Print; 3 CD-ROM; 3 E-Book; 2 Audio
Imprints: Monument Series; Shipping Regulations and Guidance; Witherby Insurance & Legal; Witherby Seamanship International; Witherby Shipping Business

Witherby Seamanship International, *imprint of* Witherby Publishing Group

Witherby Shipping Business, *imprint of* Witherby Publishing Group

WOL Books, *imprint of* Pallas Athene

Woodhead Publishing+
Imprint of Elsevier BV
80 High St, Sawston, Cambs CB22 3HJ
Tel: (01223) 499140
E-mail: wp@woodheadpublishing.com
Web Site: store.elsevier.com/woodhead-publishing
Key Personnel
Senior Marketing Manager: Neil MacLeod
Tel: (01223) 381606 *E-mail:* n.macleod@elsevier.com
Founded: 1989
Specialize in engineering, materials, welding, food science, food technology, biomedicine, textiles, energy, environment, finance & investment, mathematics.
Membership(s): IPG.
Subjects: Aeronautics, Aviation, Asian Studies, Automotive, Biological Sciences, Chemistry, Chemical Engineering, Civil Engineering, Electronics, Electrical Engineering, Energy, Engineering (General), Environmental Studies, Finance, Health, Nutrition, Library & Information

Sciences, Maritime, Mathematics, Mechanical Engineering, Technology, Transportation
ISBN Prefix(es): 978-0-08; 978-1-85573; 978-1-84569; 978-1-78242; 978-1-908818; 978-1-907568
Number of titles published annually: 175 Print; 2 CD-ROM; 175 Online; 175 E-Book
Total Titles: 1,300 Print; 4 CD-ROM; 900 Online; 900 E-Book
Ultimate Parent Company: RELX Group PLC

words & pictures
Member of Quarto International Co-Editions Group
The Old Brewery, 6 Blundell St, London N7 9BH
Tel: (020) 7800 8043 *Fax:* (020) 7700 8066
Web Site: www.quartoknows.com/words-pictures
Key Personnel
Group Publisher: Zeta Jones *E-mail:* zeta.jones@quarto.com
Publisher: Maxime Boucknooghe
E-mail: maxime.boucknooghe@quarto.com
Founded: 2012
ISBN Prefix(es): 978-1-910277
Ultimate Parent Company: The Quarto Group Inc

Wordsworth Editions, *imprint of* Wordsworth Editions Ltd

Wordsworth Editions Ltd+
8b East St, Ware, Herts SG12 9HJ
Tel: (01920) 465167 *Fax:* (01920) 462267
E-mail: enquiries@wordsworth-editions.com; sales@wordsworth-editions.com
Web Site: www.wordsworth-editions.com
Founded: 1987
Specialize in Wordsworth Editions & classics with CD-ROM, folklore, myths & legends.
Subjects: History, Literature, Literary Criticism, Essays, Mysteries, Suspense, Poetry, Supernatural
ISBN Prefix(es): 978-1-85326; 978-1-84022
Number of titles published annually: 50 Print
Total Titles: 700 Print
Imprints: Wordsworth Editions; Wordsworth Education
Foreign Rep(s): Depozitul De Carte Distributie SRL (Romania); IMA (Intermediaamericana Ltd) (David Williams) (Caribbean, Latin America); Lale Colakoglu (Turkey); L B May & Associates Inc (Wordsworth Classics) (USA); Nationwide Book Distributors Ltd; Om Books International (India); Peribo Pty Ltd (Australia); Publishers International Marketing (Chris Ashdown) (Far East); Publishers International Marketing (Ray Potts) (Middle East); Ribera Libros SL (Spain); Roberts Wholesale Books (Ireland); Top Mark Centre (Poland)
Warehouse: Wordsworth Editions, The Airfield, Mendlesham, Suffolk IP14 5NA
Orders to: Bibliophile Books, Unit 5 Datapoint, South Crescent, London E16 4TL
Tel: (020) 74 74 24 74 *Fax:* (020) 74 74 85 89 *E-mail:* orders@bibliophilebooks.com *Web Site:* www.bibliophilebooks.com

Wordsworth Education, *imprint of* Wordsworth Editions Ltd

World Microfilms Publications Ltd+
Microworld House, PO Box 67686, London NW11 1LQ
Tel: (020) 7586 4499
E-mail: microworld@ndirect.co.uk
Key Personnel
Dir: Stephen C Albert; Rosalind Albert
Founded: 1969
Microfilm collections & online subscription web sites.
Subjects: Architecture & Interior Design, Art, Drama, Theater, Economics, Film, Video, His-

tory, Music, Dance, Religion - Other, Science (General), Self-Help
ISBN Prefix(es): 978-1-85035; 978-1-86013; 978-0-905272
Number of titles published annually: 20 CD-ROM; 20 Online
Total Titles: 300 CD-ROM; 5 Online
Associate Companies: Pidgeon Digital; Sussex Publications

World of Islam Altajir Trust+
11 Elvaston Pl, London SW7 5QG
Tel: (020) 7581 3522 *Fax:* (020) 7584 1977
E-mail: awitrust@tiscali.co.uk
Web Site: www.altajirtrust.org.uk
Key Personnel
Dir: Richard Muir
Administrator: Ursula Guy
Founded: 1982
UK based charity supporting exhibitions, publications, educational activities & other programs related to Islamic culture & Muslim-Christian relations.
Subjects: Archaeology, Art, Religion - Islamic, Theology
ISBN Prefix(es): 978-0-905035; 978-1-901435

The World Today, *imprint of* Royal Institute of International Affairs

Worldlife Library, *imprint of* Colin Baxter Photography Ltd

Worth Press Ltd+
The Manse, 34 South End, Bassingbourn, Herts SG8 5NJ
Tel: (01763) 248075 *Fax:* (01763) 248155
Key Personnel
Owner: Ken Webb
Mng Dir: Rupert Webb
Founded: 1998
Also acts as a packager.
Subjects: History, Mathematics, Science (General)
ISBN Prefix(es): 978-1-903025
Distribution Center: Book Trade Services Ltd, Blaby Rd, Wigston, Leics LE18 4SE
Tel: (01162) 759 086

Writers & Their Work, *imprint of* Northcote House Publishers Ltd

Writer's Digest, *imprint of* David & Charles Ltd

Xcite Books, *imprint of* Accent Press Ltd

Ya Cafe, *imprint of* Accent Press Ltd

Yale English Monarchs, *imprint of* Yale University Press London

Yale University Press London+
47 Bedford Sq, London WC1B 3DP
Tel: (020) 7079 4900 *Fax:* (020) 7079 4901
E-mail: sales@yaleup.co.uk
Web Site: www.yalebooks.co.uk
Key Personnel
Mng Dir: Heather McCallum *E-mail:* heather.mccallum@yaleup.co.uk
Editorial Dir: Robert Baldock
UK Sales Manager: Andrew Jarmain
E-mail: andrew.jarmain@yaleup.co.uk
Head, Rights: Anne Bihan *E-mail:* anne.bihan@yaleup.co.uk
Publisher, Art & Architecture: Gillian Malpass
E-mail: gillian.malpass@yaleup.co.uk
Publicity: Katie Harris
Editor: Sally Salvesen
Founded: 1961

Subjects: Anthropology, Architecture & Interior Design, Art, Asian Studies, Biography, Memoirs, Economics, Environmental Studies, Government, Political Science, History, Language Arts, Linguistics, Law, Literature, Literary Criticism, Essays, Music, Dance, Natural History, Nonfiction (General), Philosophy, Photography, Physical Sciences, Psychology, Psychiatry, Religion - Jewish, Science (General), Social Sciences, Sociology, Theology, Women's Studies, Current Affairs
ISBN Prefix(es): 978-0-300
Parent Company: Yale University Press, 302 Temple St, PO Box 209040, New Haven, CT 06520-9040, United States
Imprints: Pelican History of Art; Pevsner Architectural Guides; Yale English Monarchs
Subsidiaries: Yale Representation Ltd
Distributor for Metropolitan Museum of Art; National Gallery Publications
Foreign Rep(s): APD Malaysia Pte Ltd (Malaysia); APD Singapore Pte Ltd (Brunei, Cambodia, Indonesia, Singapore, Thailand, Vietnam); Asia Publishers Services Ltd (Ed Summerson) (China, Hong Kong, Philippines); Avicenna Partnership Ltd (Claire de Gruchy & Bill Kennedy) (Cyprus, Greece, Malta, Middle East, North Africa, Turkey); Book Bird (Anwer Iqbal) (Pakistan); Book Marketing Services (Mr S Janakiraman) (India); Book Promotions (Southern Africa); Footprint Books Pty Ltd (Australia, New Zealand); Kelvin van Hasselt (Africa exc South Africa, Nigeria); ICK (Se-Young Jun & Min-Hwa Yoo) (Korea); Ewa Ledochowicz (Central Europe); Uwe Luedemann (Austria, France, Germany, Italy, Portugal, Spain, Switzerland); Mirjam Mayenburg (Benelux); B K Norton Ltd (Chifeng Peng) (Taiwan); Rockbook (Akiko Iwamoto & Gilles Fauveau) (Japan); Christopher Stamp (Scandinavia); Robert Towers (Ireland, Northern Ireland); Yale University Press (Canada, Central America, Mexico, South America, USA)
Orders to: John Wiley & Sons Ltd, Customer Services Dept, European Distribution Centre, New Era Estate, Oldlands Way, Bognor Regis, West Sussex PO22 9NQ *Tel:* (01243) 843 291
Toll Free Tel: 0800 243 407

Yellow Jersey Press, *imprint of* The Random House Group Ltd, a Penguin Random House Company

Yellow Kite, *imprint of* Hodder & Stoughton Ltd

York Notes, *imprint of* Pearson Education Ltd

Young Arrow, *imprint of* The Random House Group Ltd, a Penguin Random House Company

Young Spitfire, *imprint of* Elliott & Thompson

Zed Books Ltd+
The Foundry, 17 Oval Way, London SE11 5RR
Tel: (020) 3752 5841 (editorial); (020) 3752 5830 (sales)
E-mail: editorial@zedbooks.net; info@zedbooks.net; sales@zedbooks.net
Web Site: www.zedbooks.co.uk
Key Personnel
Commissioning Editor: Ken Barlow *E-mail:* ken.barlow@zedbooks.net; Kika Sroka-Miller *E-mail:* kika.sroka-miller@zedbooks.net; Kim Walker *E-mail:* k.walker@zedbooks.net
Production: Dan Och *E-mail:* dan.och@zedbooks.net
Founded: 1977
Subjects: Environmental Studies, Government, Political Science, Social Sciences, Sociology,

Women's Studies, Current Affairs, Development Studies, International Relations
ISBN Prefix(es): 978-0-905762; 978-0-86232; 978-1-85649; 978-1-84277; 978-1-84813; 978-1-78032
Number of titles published annually: 55 Print
Total Titles: 500 Print
Distributed by University of Chicago Press (Australia, South America & USA)
Foreign Rep(s): Chris Ashdown (Central Asia, East Asia); Avicenna Partnership (Claire de Gruchy) (Algeria, Cyprus, Jordan, Libya, Morocco, Palestine, Tunisia, Turkey); Geoff Bryan (Ireland); Compass Academic (UK exc Ireland); Durnell Marketing (Europe); Invergarry (Bill Kennedy) (Afghanistan, Bahrain, Egypt, Iran, Iraq, Kuwait, Lebanon, Libya, Oman, Qatar, Saudi Arabia, Sudan, Syria, United Arab Emirates, Yemen); Maya Publishers (Surit Mitra) (Bangladesh, India, South Asia, Sri Lanka); Tony Moggach (Africa, Sub-Saharan Africa exc South Africa)
Foreign Rights: AnatoliaLit Agency (Turkey); Arrowsmith Agency (Germany); The English Agency (Japan) Ltd (Tsutomu Yawata) (Japan); Korea Copyright Center Inc (Ms Jinhee Cha) (Korea); Sandrine Paccher (France); World Media Rights Agency Ltd (Nicole Ying) (China)
Distribution Center: NBN International, 10 Thornbury Rd, Plymouth, Devon PL6 7PP *Tel:* (01752) 202301 *Fax:* (01752) 202331
E-mail: orders@nbninternational.com
Brunswick Books, 20 Maud St, Suite 303, Toronto, ON M5V 2M5, Canada *Tel:* 416-703-3598 *Fax:* 416-703-6561 *E-mail:* orders@brunswickbooks.ca *Web Site:* www.brunswickbooks.ca
Blueweaver, PO Box 30370, Tokai 7966, South Africa *Tel:* (021) 701 4477 *Fax:* (021) 701 7302 *E-mail:* orders@blueweaver.co.za (Botswana, Lesotho, Namibia, South Africa & Swaziland)
Chicago Distribution Center, 11030 S Langley Ave, Chicago, IL, United States *Tel:* 773-702-7010

Zephyr, *imprint of* Ashgrove Publishing

Zephyr, *imprint of* Head of Zeus

Zero Books, *imprint of* O Books

Zomba Books, *imprint of* Omnibus Press

Zone Books, *imprint of* The MIT Press

Uruguay

General Information

Capital: Montevideo
Language: Spanish
Religion: Predominantly Roman Catholic
Population: 3.1 million
Bank Hours: 1300-1700 Monday-Friday
Shop Hours: 0900-1200, 1400-1900 Monday-Friday; 0900-1230 Saturday
Currency: 100 centesimos = 1 new Uruguayan peso
Export/Import Information: Member Southern Cone Common Market (MERCOSUR). No tariffs on books or single copies catalogues but surcharge on advertising matter. Additional surcharge on all imports, plus VAT CIF, plus

Stamp Tax of percentage of total invoice value. No import licenses. No exchange controls.
Copyright: UCC, Berne, Buenos Aires (see Copyright Conventions, pg viii)

Editorial Agropecuaria Hemisferio Sur
Buenos Aires 335, 11000 Montevideo
Mailing Address: CC 1755, 11000 Montevideo
Tel: 29164515 *Fax:* 29164520
E-mail: libreriaperi@hemisferiosur.com.uy
Web Site: www.hemisferiosur.com.uy
Key Personnel
Dir: Margarita Peri Carrere
Subjects: Agriculture, Biological Sciences, Natural History, Animal Production, Forestry
ISBN Prefix(es): 978-9974-556; 978-9974-645
Number of titles published annually: 5 Print
Total Titles: 70 Print

Ediciones de la Banda Oriental
Gaboto 1582, 11200 Montevideo
Tel: 24083206; 24010164 *Fax:* 24098138
E-mail: info@bandaoriental.com.uy
Web Site: www.bandaoriental.com.uy
Key Personnel
Dir: Heber Raviolo
Founded: 1961
Subjects: Fiction, History, Literature, Literary Criticism, Essays, Nonfiction (General)
ISBN Prefix(es): 978-9974-1

Cotidiano Mujer
San Jose 1436, 11200 Montevideo
Tel: 2901 8782; 2902 0393
E-mail: cotidian@cotidianomujer.org.uy
Web Site: www.cotidianomujer.org.uy
Key Personnel
Contact: Elena Fonseca
Founded: 1985
Subjects: Journalism, Women's Studies, Ecology, Feminism, Human Rights
ISBN Prefix(es): 978-9974-8263

Departamento de Publicaciones de la Universidad de la Republica
Av 18 de Julio 1824, 11200 Montevideo
Tel: 2408 2566; 2408 9574
E-mail: infoed@edic.edu.uy
Web Site: www.universidad.edu.uy
Subjects: Education
ISBN Prefix(es): 978-9974-0; 978-84-89277; 978-84-89252

Fundacion de Cultura Universitaria-Editorial Juridica+
25 de Mayo 583, 11000 Montevideo
Tel: 29161152 *Fax:* 29152549
E-mail: administrador@fcu.com.uy; ventas@fcu.com.uy
Web Site: www.fcu.com.uy
Founded: 1968
Subjects: Accounting, Architecture & Interior Design, Chemistry, Chemical Engineering, Communications, Criminology, Economics, Education, Finance, Government, Political Science, History, Law, Literature, Literary Criticism, Essays, Philosophy, Regional Interests, Social Sciences, Sociology, Forensic Technology

Instituto del Tercer Mundo (ITeM) (The Third World Institute)+
Avda 18 de julio 2095/301, 11200 Montevideo
Tel: 598 240 1424
E-mail: item@item.org.uy
Web Site: www.item.org.uy
Key Personnel
President: Cecilia Fernandez
Dir: Roberto Bissio
Editor: Victor Bacchetta
Founded: 1986

Membership(s): Association for Progressive Communications (APC).
Subjects: Human Relations, Civil Society
ISBN Prefix(es): 978-9974-574
U.S. Office(s): Humanities Press International Inc, 165 First Ave, Atlantic Highlands, NJ 07716, United States *Tel:* 908-872-1441 *Fax:* 908-872-0717
Distributed by Andenbuch-Romanische Buchhandlung (Germany); Arning Publications (Norway); CEDIB (Bolivia); Fondo de Cultura Economica (Peru); Hillco Media Group (Sweden); Humanities Press International Inc (USA); Ibercultura GmbH (Switzerland); IEPALA (Spain); Instituto del Tercer Mundo (Uruguay); Lamuv Verlag (Germany); Libreria Lectura SA (Venezuela); Leer Ltda (Colombia); Libri Mundi (Ecuador); MARCIAL PONS Libreros (Spain); Libreria Milnovecientos (Chile); Mellemfolkeligt Samvirke (Denmark); NCOS (Belgium); New Internationalist Aotearoa; New Internationalist Australia (Australia); New Internationalist Canada (Canada); New Internationalist Publications (UK); Novib Publications (Netherlands); Oxfam Publications (UK); Libreria De La Paz (Argentina); Sipro (Servicios Informativos Procesados AC) (Mexico); Tyron SA (Argentina)
Distributor for Social Watch
Orders to: Hersilia Fonseca/Marketing

Linardi y Risso Libreria
Juan Carlos Gomez 1435, 11000 Montevideo
Tel: 29157129
E-mail: info@linardiyrisso.com
Web Site: www.linardiyrisso.com
Founded: 1944
Specialize in Latin American books.
Subjects: Government, Political Science, History, Literature, Literary Criticism, Essays
ISBN Prefix(es): 978-9974-559

Prensa Medica Latinoamericana+
El Viejo Pancho 2410, 11300 Montevideo
Tel: 27079109 *Fax:* 27079109
E-mail: editor@prensamedica.com.uy; info@prensamedica.com.uy
Web Site: www.prensamedica.com.uy
Key Personnel
Editor: Heber Saldivia *E-mail:* hebersaldivia@prensamedica.com.uy
Founded: 1988
Subjects: Child Care & Development, Health, Nutrition, Medicine, Nursing, Dentistry, Psychology, Psychiatry
ISBN Prefix(es): 978-9974-568

Psicolibros (Waslala)
Mercedes 1673, 11203 Montevideo
Tel: 24003808; 24030332
E-mail: info@psicolibroswaslala.com
Web Site: www.psicolibroswaslala.com
Key Personnel
Dir: Lourdes Perez *E-mail:* lperez@psicolibroswaslala.com
Membership(s): Camara Uruguaya del Libro.
Subjects: Anthropology, Child Care & Development, Economics, Education, Psychology, Psychiatry, Physical Education
ISBN Prefix(es): 978-9974-7591; 978-9974-7637; 978-9974-7688; 978-9974-7813; 978-9974-7851; 978-9974-7917

Ediciones Santillana SA
Juan Manuel Blanes 1132, 11200 Montevideo
Tel: 24107342
E-mail: consultas@santillana.com.uy
Web Site: www.santillana.com.uy
Key Personnel
Dir General: Fernando Rama
Editorial Dir: Alejandra Campos

Subjects: Art, Education, Fiction, Literature, Literary Criticism, Essays
ISBN Prefix(es): 978-9974-590; 978-9974-671

Ediciones Trilce+
San Salvador 2075, 11200 Montevideo
Tel: 24127662
E-mail: trilce@trilce.com.uy; infoventas@trilce.com.uy
Web Site: www.trilce.com.uy
Key Personnel
Dir: Pablo Harari
Founded: 1985
Subjects: Anthropology, Architecture & Interior Design, Biography, Memoirs, Communications, Developing Countries, Drama, Theater, Economics, Education, Environmental Studies, Fiction, Film, Video, Government, Political Science, History, Humor, Literature, Literary Criticism, Essays, Medicine, Nursing, Dentistry, Music, Dance, Philosophy, Poetry, Psychology, Psychiatry, Regional Interests, Religion - Other, Science (General), Social Sciences, Sociology, Sports, Athletics, Technology, Women's Studies, Culture, Human Rights, Psychoanalysis
ISBN Prefix(es): 978-9974-32; 978-84-89269
Number of titles published annually: 35 Print
Total Titles: 400 Print
Distribution Center: Gussi Books, Yaro 1119, Montevideo *Tel:* 24136195 *Fax:* 24133042 *Web Site:* www.gussi.com.uy

Uzbekistan

General Information

Capital: Tashkent
Language: Uzbek
Religion: Predominantly Islamic (mostly Sunni Muslim)
Population: 21.6 million
Bank Hours: Generally open for short hours between 0930-1230 Monday-Friday
Shop Hours: Generally 0900-1800 Monday-Friday; often open weekends
Currency: 100 kopeks = 1 rubl

Uzbekistan+
ul Navoi 30, 100129 Tashkent
Tel: (871) 244-34-01; (871) 244-37-81 *Fax:* (871) 244-38-10
E-mail: info@iptd-uzbekistan.uz
Web Site: www.iptd-uzbekistan.uz
Key Personnel
Dir: Zair Tursunbaevich Isadjanov *E-mail:* isadjanov@iptd-uzbekistan.uz
First Deputy Dir: Mukhamadjon Zaytaev *Tel:* (871) 244-54-04 *E-mail:* zaytaev@iptd-uzbekistan.uz
Editor-in-Chief: Boboniyozov Azimboy Yuldashvich *Tel:* (871) 244-38-10 *E-mail:* boboniyozov.a@iptd-uzbekistan.uz
Subjects: Economics, Government, Political Science, Science (General), Social Sciences, Sociology, Politics, Technical
ISBN Prefix(es): 978-5-640

Venezuela

General Information

Capital: Caracas
Language: Spanish
Religion: Predominantly Roman Catholic
Population: 20.7 million

Bank Hours: 0830-1130, 1400-1630 Monday-Friday
Shop Hours: 0900-1300, 1500-1900 Monday-Saturday
Currency: 1 bolivar fuerte = 1,004 bolivar
Export/Import Information: Member of the Latin American Free Trade Association.
Copyright: UCC, Berne (see Copyright Conventions, pg viii)

Academia Nacional de la Historia
Palacio de las Academias, Ave Universidad, Bolsa a San Francisco, Caracas 1010
Tel: (0212) 482 67 20; (0212) 483 94 35; (0212) 481 34 13; (0212) 482 27 06 *Fax:* (0212) 482 67 20; (0212) 483 94 35
E-mail: publicaciones@anhistoria.org.ar
Web Site: www.anh.org.ar
Key Personnel
Dir: Lldefonso Leal
Founded: 1888
Subjects: History
ISBN Prefix(es): 978-980-222

Alfadil Ediciones+
Calle Las Flores con calles Pascual Navarro y Paraiso, Edif Torre Buena Ventura, Mezzanina, Sabana Grande, Caracas 1050
Mailing Address: Apdo 50304, Caracas 1050
Tel: (0212) 762-3036; (0212) 761-3576; (0212) 763-5676 *Fax:* (0212) 762-0210
Key Personnel
Dir: Ulises Milla
Deputy Dir: Carolina Saravia
Administration: Sorangel Martinez
Sales: Alberto Vera
Founded: 1978
Subjects: Astrology, Occult, Economics, Fiction, Geography, Geology, History, Journalism, Literature, Literary Criticism, Essays, Music, Dance, Nonfiction (General), Philosophy, Poetry, Self-Help, Social Sciences, Sociology
ISBN Prefix(es): 978-980-6005; 978-980-354; 978-980-6273
Parent Company: Alfa Grupo Editorial
Associate Companies: Distribuidora de Ediciones Noray, CA
Subsidiaries: Libreria Ludens
Bookshop(s): Libreria Ludens I, Edificio Torre Polar, PB, Local F, Plaza Venezuela, Caracas, Manager: Janeth Marquez *Tel:* (0212) 576 1615 *Fax:* (0212) 574 3591 *E-mail:* ludens1@editorial-alfa.com; Libreria Ludens II Merida, Av Los Proceres, CC Alto Prado, Nivel 1, Local 23, Merida, Estado Merida, Manager: Luis Ramirez *Tel:* (0274) 244 8485 *Fax:* (0274) 244 6685 *E-mail:* ludens2@editorial-alfa.com; Libreria Alejander 332 aC I, Centro Comercial Cada, ave principal de Las Mercedes, Caracas, Manager: Jonathan Bustamante *Tel:* (0212) 993 0325 *Fax:* (0212) 991 4875 *E-mail:* alejandria1@editorial-alfa.com; Libreria Alejandria 332 aC II, Centro Comercial Paseo Las Mercedes, rivel PB, Las Mercedes, Caracas, Manager: Rodnei Casares *Tel:* (0212) 991 0546 *Fax:* (0212) 993 6966 *E-mail:* alejandria2@editorial-alfa.com; Libreria Alejandria 332 aC III, Centro Comercial Chacaito, planeta principal, Chacaito, Caracas, Manager: Mario Gimenez *Tel:* (0212) 952 11 04 *Fax:* (0212) 952 10 93 *E-mail:* alejandria3@editorial-alfa.com

Amolca CA
1ra Ave Sur de Altamira, Edif Rokaje, Planta 3, Urb Altamira, Caracus
Tel: (0212) 266 61 76; (0212) 266 86 01; (0212) 264 46 08
E-mail: administracion@amolca.us; editorial@amolca.us; facturacion@amolca.com (billing)
Web Site: www.amolca.com; www.facebook.com/pages/Amolca/656326924487250
Founded: 1984

Publishers of over 100 medical & dental books, audiobooks & videos annually.
Subjects: Medicine, Nursing, Dentistry, Endodontics, Periodontics, Radiology
ISBN Prefix(es): 978-980-392; 978-980-6184; 978-980-6574

Monte Avila Editores Latinoamericana CA+
Piso 22 de la Torre Norte, Centro Simon Bolivar, Ed Silencio, Caracas 1070
Tel: (0212) 482 28 50
E-mail: produccion@monteavila.gob.ve; monteavilaeditorial1@gmail.com; administracion@monteavila.gob.ve; prensa@monteavila.gob.ve; promocionmonteavila@gmail.com
Web Site: www.monteavila.gob.ve
Key Personnel
Executive Dir: Nelci Marin *E-mail:* nelmarin1@cantv.net
Publicity Coordinator: Isabel Rivero de Armas *Tel:* (0212) 482 04 72
Founded: 1968
Subjects: Anthropology, Art, Economics, Education, Fiction, Geography, Geology, Government, Political Science, History, Literature, Literary Criticism, Essays, Music, Dance, Philosophy, Poetry, Psychology, Psychiatry, Regional Interests, Science (General), Social Sciences, Sociology
ISBN Prefix(es): 978-980-01
Foreign Rep(s): Editora y Distribuidora Azteca SA de CV (Mexico); Ideal Foreign Books Inc (USA); Ediciones de Intervencion Cultural SL (Spain); The Latin American Book Source Inc (USA); The Latin American Book Source Ltd (USA); Lectorum Publications Inc (USA); Libros Sin Fronteras (USA); Siglo del Hombre Editores (Colombia); Visor Libros (Spain); Jorge Waldhuter (Argentina)

Biblioteca Ayacucho
Ave Urdaneta, Animas a Plaza Espana, Centro Financiero Latino, Piso 12, Ofics 1, 2, 3, Caracas 1010
Mailing Address: Apdo 14413/2122, Caracas 1010
Tel: (0212) 561 6691 *Fax:* (0212) 564 5643
Web Site: www.bibliotecayacucho.gob.ve
Key Personnel
President: Humberto Mata
Executive Dir: Luis Edgar Paez
Founded: 1974
Subjects: Anthropology, Architecture & Interior Design, Art, Developing Countries, Drama, Theater, Fiction, History, Literature, Literary Criticism, Essays, Philosophy, Photography, Poetry
ISBN Prefix(es): 978-980-276

Editorial Biosfera CA+
Ave Chama, Quinta Coral, Colinas de Bello Monte, Apdo 50634, Caracas 1050
Tel: (0212) 751 9119; (0212) 753 8892
Fax: (0212) 751 9320
Web Site: www.facebook.com/EditorialBiosfera
Founded: 1978
Subjects: Art, Biological Sciences, Language Arts, Linguistics, Mathematics, Nonfiction (General), Science (General)
ISBN Prefix(es): 978-980-210
Subsidiaries: Litho-Mundo SA
Bookshop(s): Ediciones Amanecer (Libreria) Centro Polo

Camelia Ediciones
Calle el Buen Pastor, Edif Molorca, Piso 1 Boleita Norte, Caracas 1071
Tel: (0212) 2371222 *Fax:* (0212) 2349964
Key Personnel
Editorial Dir: Javier Aizpurua; Maria Angelica Barreto

Founded: 1999
Subjects: Music, Dance, Philosophy, Photography, Painting
ISBN Prefix(es): 978-980-6450

Ediciones CO-BO, see Colegial Bolivariana CA

Colegial Bolivariana CA
Av Diego Cisneros (Principal) Los Ruices, Caracas 1071-A
Tel: (0212) 2391433 *Fax:* (0212) 2396502; (0212) 2379307
E-mail: ventas@co-bo.com
Web Site: www.co-bo.com
Founded: 1961
ISBN Prefix(es): 978-980-262

Ediciones Ekare+
Av Luis Roche, Edif Banco del Libro, Altamira Sur, Caracas 1062
SAN: 001-6780
Tel: (0212) 264 76 15; (0212) 264 14 21
Fax: (0212) 263 32 91
E-mail: editorial@ekare.com.ve; comunicaciones@ekare.com.ve; ventas@ekare.com.ve
Web Site: www.ekare.com
Key Personnel
President: Carmen Diana Dearden
Editorial Dir & Foreign Rights: Maria Francisca Mayobre
Founded: 1978
Specialize in children's picture books. Publish in Spanish only.
Subjects: Fiction
ISBN Prefix(es): 978-980-257; 978-84-8351; 978-84-937212; 978-84-937767
Branch Office(s)
Ediciones Ekare Espana, C/ Sant Augusti 6, bajos, 08012 Barcelona, Spain *Tel:* 93 415 21 56 *Fax:* 93 415 21 98 *E-mail:* ekare@ekare.es
Foreign Rep(s): Grupo Amanuense SA (Guatemala); Aparicio Distributors Inc (Puerto Rico); Babel Libros SAS (Colombia); Calibroscopio Ediciones (Argentina); Colofon SA de CV (Mexico); Edumas SAC (Peru); Ediciones Ekare Sur Ltda (Chile); Garimbo, Distribuidor de Libros Infantiles (Ecuador); Ibero Librerias (Peru); Lectorum Publications Inc (North America, USA); Libruras SRL (Uruguay); Ediciones Minimas (Spain)

Fundacion Centro de Estudios Latinoamericanos Romulo Gallegos
Av Luis Roche con 3ra Transversal, Altamira, Caracas 1060, MI
Tel: (0212) 285 29 90; (0212) 285 27 21; (0212) 285 26 44
Web Site: www.celarg.gob.ve/Ingles/Presentacion.htm
Subjects: Finance, Commerce, Industry, Production
ISBN Prefix(es): 978-980-6197

Fundacion Centro Gumilla
Edificio Centro Valores, Local 2, Esquina de La Luneta-Altagracia, Caracas 1010-A
Tel: (0212) 564 9803; (0212) 564 5871
Fax: (0212) 564 7557
E-mail: centro@gumilla.org
Web Site: www.gumilla.org
Key Personnel
Dir: Jesus Maria Aguirre
Deputy Dir: Fernando Giuliani
General Manager: Lisbeth Mora
Founded: 1968
Subjects: Economics, Education, Government, Political Science, Labor, Industrial Relations, Religion - Catholic, Social Sciences, Sociology, Theology
ISBN Prefix(es): 978-980-250

Ediciones IESA
Av IESA, San Bernardino, Caracas 1010, DF
Tel: (0212) 555 4260
E-mail: ediesa@iesa.edu.ve; debates@iesa.edu.ve
Web Site: www.iesa.edu.ve
Key Personnel
Editor: Jose Malave
Administration: Yudyt Medina
ISBN Prefix(es): 978-980-217

Instituto de Estudios Superiores, see Ediciones IESA

McGraw-Hill Venezuela
Ave Francisco Solano Lopez, Entre los Jabillos y San Geronimo, Torre Solano Mezz 1 y 2, Sabana Grande, Caracas 1050
Tel: (0212) 7618181; (0212) 7625562
ISBN Prefix(es): 978-980-6168; 978-980-373
Parent Company: McGraw-Hill Financial

Editorial Planeta Venezolana SA
Member of Grupo Planeta
Av Libertador, Edificio Exa, Piso 3, Oficina 302, El Rosal, Municipio Chacao, Caracas 1060, DF
Tel: (0212) 526 6300
E-mail: info@planetadelibros.com.ve
Web Site: www.planetadelibros.com.ve
Founded: 1966
Subjects: Art, Business, Cookery, Drama, Theater, Economics, Fiction, Health, Nutrition, History, Humor, Poetry, Romance, Science Fiction, Fantasy, Travel & Tourism
ISBN Prefix(es): 978-980-271

Playco Editores CA
Zona Industrial San Vincente 2, Calle N, galpon nº 2, Maracay 2107, Aragua
Tel: (0243) 551 6070; (0243) 551 5509
Fax: (0243) 551 6528
E-mail: playco@cantv.net; playcoeditores@gmail.com
Web Site: playcoeditores.com.ve
Key Personnel
Rights: Katiuska Suarez
Founded: 1991
Subjects: Fiction, Geography, Geology, History, Science (General)
ISBN Prefix(es): 978-980-6437
Foreign Rep(s): Babel Libros EU (Colombia); Ediciones Euromexico SA de CV (Mexico); Editorial Lector (Puerto Rico); PlaycoBooks (USA); Proyectos Editoriales Borneo (Spain); Tajamar Editores (Chile)
Distribution Center: La Barca de la Luna Ediciones, Calle El Carmen, Edificio Centro dos Caminos, Piso 2, Oficina 2-D, Los Dos Caminos, Caracas 1071 *Tel:* (0212) 237 6736
Ri-ver Ediciones CA *Tel:* (0241) 838 8716 *E-mail:* river-ediciones@hotmail.com (Maracay & Valencia)

Editorial Santillana SA
Av Romulo Gallegos, Edificio Zulia, PB, Sector Monte Cristo, Boleita, Caracas 1071
Tel: (0212) 235 30 33; (0212) 280 94 00
Fax: (0212) 280 94 04
Web Site: www.santillana.com.ve
Founded: 1977
Subjects: Education
ISBN Prefix(es): 978-980-275
Parent Company: Grupo Santillana
Associate Companies: Santillana SA de Ediciones, Spain
Orders for: Urbanizacion Industrial Cloris, Ave 2, Local 84-03 Ave Norte, Guarenas, Edo, Miranda

Sociedad Fondo Editorial CENAMEC
Esquina de Salas, Piso 5 Parroquia Altagracia, Caracas 1010

Tel: (0212) 563 55 97; (0212) 563 55 91; (0212) 563 55 93 *Fax:* (0212) 564 25 28
Founded: 1981
Subjects: Biological Sciences, Chemistry, Chemical Engineering, Mathematics, Physics
ISBN Prefix(es): 978-980-218

Universidad de los Andes, Consejo de Publicaciones
Ave Andres Bello, Antiguo Cala, La Parroquia, Merida 5101
Fax: (0274) 2711955; (0274) 2713210; (0274) 2712034
E-mail: cpula@ula.ve
Web Site: www2.ula.ve/cp
Key Personnel
Executive Secretary: Jose Antonio Rivas Leone
   E-mail: rivasleone@ula.ve
Distribution & Sales: Argimiro Pineda
   E-mail: ventascpula@gmail.com
Founded: 1977
Subjects: Medicine, Nursing, Dentistry, Regional Interests, Science (General), Social Sciences, Sociology, Technology
ISBN Prefix(es): 978-980-221

Vadell Hermanos Editores CA+
Commercial Dir, Golden Bldg, Hazard Skin Eye, La Candelaria, Caracas
Tel: (0212) 5723108; (0414) 2340250 *Fax:* (0212) 5725243
E-mail: edvadell@gmail.com
Web Site: www.vadellhermanos.com
Key Personnel
General Manager: Dr Manuel M Vadell Graterol
Founded: 1973
Membership(s): Association Venezuelan Editors.
Subjects: Computer Science, Economics, Education, Geography, Geology, Law, Psychology, Psychiatry, Science (General), Social Sciences, Sociology, Technology
ISBN Prefix(es): 978-980-212

Vietnam

General Information

Capital: Hanoi
Language: Vietnamese
Religion: Predominantly Buddhist
Population: 69 million
Currency: 100 xu = 1 new dong
Export/Import Information: None available at present.
Copyright: Florence (see Copyright Conventions, pg viii)

Chinh Tri Quoc Gia Publishing House (Nha Xuat Ban Chinh Tri Quoc Gia - Su That)
12/86 DTU-Cau Giay, Hanoi
Tel: (04) 39422008 *Fax:* (04) 39410661
E-mail: suthat@nxbctqg.vn
Web Site: www.nxbctqg.org.vn
Founded: 1945
Under the Central Committee of the Communist Party of Vietnam.
Subjects: Government, Political Science, Philosophy, Social Sciences, Sociology

Nha Xuat Ban Giao duc Vietnam (Vietnam Education Publishing House)
81 Tran Hung Dao St, Hanoi
Tel: (04) 38220801 *Fax:* (04) 39422010
E-mail: vanphong@nxbgd.vn
Web Site: www.nxbgd.vn
Founded: 1957
Subjects: Education

The Gioi Publishers (World Publishers)
46 Tran Hung Dao Str, Hanoi
Tel: (04) 38253841 *Fax:* (04) 38269578
E-mail: thegioi@hn.vnn.vn
Web Site: www.thegioipublishers.vn
Key Personnel
Dir & Editor-in-Chief: Dr Tran Doan Lam
Founded: 1957
Subjects: Education, Ethnicity, Geography, Geology, Government, Political Science, History, Literature, Literary Criticism, Essays, Religion - Other, Science (General), Technology, Travel & Tourism, Culture, Globalization, Human Rights, Politics, Warfare
Branch Office(s)
7 Nguyen Thi Minh Khai Str, Dist 1, Ho Chi Minh City *Tel:* (08) 8220102
   E-mail: cnthegioi@hcm.fpt.vn

National Political Publishing House, see Chinh Tri Quoc Gia Publishing House

Science & Technology Publishing House (Nha Xuat Ban Khoa Hoc Va Ky Thuat)+
70 Tran Hung Dao St, Hanoi
Tel: (04) 38220686; (04) 39423172 *Fax:* (04) 8220658
E-mail: nxbkhkt@hn.vnn.vn
Web Site: nxbkhkt.com.vn
Key Personnel
Dir & Editor-in-Chief: Pham Ngoc Khoi *Tel:* (04) 39422443 *E-mail:* pnkhoi@most.gov.vn
Vice President: Truong Quang Hung *Tel:* (04) 39424786 *E-mail:* quanghung@most.gov.vn
Founded: 1960
Membership(s): Vietnam Publishers Association.
Subjects: Accounting, Advertising, Aeronautics, Aviation, Agriculture, Animals, Pets, Archaeology, Architecture & Interior Design, Astronomy, Automotive, Behavioral Sciences, Biological Sciences, Business, Career Development, Chemistry, Chemical Engineering, Civil Engineering, Communications, Computer Science, Computers, Crafts, Games, Hobbies, Earth Sciences, Economics, Education, Electronics, Electrical Engineering, Energy, Engineering (General), English as a Second Language, Environmental Studies, Finance, Gardening, Plants, Geography, Geology, Health, Nutrition, How-to, Management, Maritime, Marketing, Mathematics, Mechanical Engineering, Medicine, Nursing, Dentistry, Natural History, Physical Sciences, Physics, Radio, TV, Science (General), Securities, Technology, Transportation, Veterinary Science, Agricultural Science, Construction, Pharmacology, Physiology, Refrigeration
Number of titles published annually: 350 Print
Total Titles: 12,000 Print
Branch Office(s)
28 Dong Khoi St, 1st district, Ho Chi Minh City *Tel:* (08) 38225062 *Fax:* (08) 38296628
   E-mail: chinhanhkhkt@hcm.fpt.vn
Bookshop(s): 116A Nguyen Chi Tran, Tri District, Danang *Tel:* (0511) 3820129

Su That, see Chinh Tri Quoc Gia Publishing House

Zambia

General Information

Capital: Lusaka
Language: English is official language
Religion: Most follow traditional animist beliefs (70%), about 20% Christian (Protestant and Roman Catholic)

Population: 8.7 million
Bank Hours: 0815-1245 Monday, Tuesday, Wednesday, Friday; 0815-1200 Thursday; 0815-1100 Saturday
Shop Hours: Generally 0800-1700 Monday-Friday; 0800-1300 Saturday
Currency: 100 ngwee = 1 Zambian kwacha
Export/Import Information: No tariffs on books but all imports subject to sales tax. Single copies of advertising free. Import license required. Exchange controls.
Copyright: UCC, Berne (see Copyright Conventions, pg viii)

BirdWatch Zambia (BWZ)
25 Joseph Mwilwa Rd, Lusaka
Mailing Address: Box 33944, 10101 Lusaka
Tel: (021) 1239420; (097) 7485446 (cell)
E-mail: birdwatch.zambia@gmail.com
Web Site: www.birdwatchzambia.org
Bird conservation in Zambia.
Subjects: Natural History
ISBN Prefix(es): 978-9982-811

Bookworld Publishers, see Gadsden Publishers

BWZ, see BirdWatch Zambia (BWZ)

Gadsden Publishers+
Formerly Bookworld Publishers
PO Box 32581, 10101 Lusaka
Tel: (0211) 290331; (0977) 841643 (cell)
   Fax: (0211) 290326
E-mail: gadsden@zamnet.zm
Web Site: www.gadsdenpublishers.com
Founded: 1995 (as Bookworld Publishers)
Membership(s): African Books Collective, UK.
Subjects: Anthropology, Biography, Memoirs, Career Development, Developing Countries, Education, Fiction, Government, Political Science, History, Language Arts, Linguistics, Literature, Literary Criticism, Essays, Social Sciences, Sociology, Humanities
ISBN Prefix(es): 978-9982-24
Number of titles published annually: 4 Print
Total Titles: 45 Print

Macmillan Publishers (Zambia) Ltd
Plot No 9212, Lumumba Rd, South End, Private Bag RX 348X, Ridgeway, Lusaka
Tel: (021) 1286702 *Fax:* (021) 1286703
Key Personnel
General Manager: Job Lusanso
Educational publishers.
Parent Company: Macmillan Education

Times Printpak Zambia Ltd
Freedom Way, PO Box 30394, Ndola
Tel: (021) 1229076; (021) 1221695 *Fax:* (021) 1227348
E-mail: times@zamtel.zm
Web Site: www.times.co.zm
Subjects: Business, Drama, Theater, Economics, Music, Dance, Regional Interests, Sports, Athletics
ISBN Prefix(es): 978-9982-13

University of Zambia Press
PO Box 32379, 10101 Lusaka
Tel: (021) 1292269 *Fax:* (021) 1253952
E-mail: press@unza.zm; sales.unzapress@unza.zm
Web Site: www.unza.zm/l/units/up
Key Personnel
Publisher: Christopher K Siulapwa *E-mail:* chris.siulapwa@unza.zm
Acting Deputy Publisher: Christopher Bwalya
   E-mail: cbwalya@unza.zm
Editor: Brenda E M Mukata *E-mail:* brenda.mukata@unza.zm
Senior Administrative Officer: Ceaser Mwanza
   E-mail: ceaser.mwanza@unza.zm

Marketing Officer: Joseph Siwo
Founded: 1989
Membership(s): Booksellers & Publishers Association of Zambia (BPAZ).
Subjects: Education, Social Sciences, Sociology
ISBN Prefix(es): 978-9982-03

UNZA Press, see University of Zambia Press

Zambia Educational Publishing House+
Chishango Rd, 10101 Lusaka
Mailing Address: PO Box 32708, 10101 Lusaka
Tel: (021) 1222324
Web Site: www.facebook.com/
zambiaeducationalpublishinghouse
Key Personnel
Sales & Marketing Manager: Anthony Tumeo Chanda
Founded: 1966
Membership(s): Booksellers & Publishers Association of Zambia.
Subjects: Agriculture, Biography, Memoirs, Drama, Theater, Education, Ethnicity, Fiction, Government, Political Science, History, Language Arts, Linguistics, Literature, Literary Criticism, Essays, Poetry, Social Sciences, Sociology
ISBN Prefix(es): 978-9982-00; 978-9982-01
Parent Company: Ministry of Education
Distributed by Dzuka Publishing Co (Malawi); Gamsberg Publishers (Namibia)
Distributor for Longman Zambia; Macmillan Zambia; Multimedia Zambia; Printpak Ltd
Book Club(s): Read-a-Book Club

ZEPH, see Zambia Educational Publishing House

Zimbabwe

General Information

Capital: Harare
Language: English is the official language. Chishona and Sindebele are major African languages.
Religion: Majority (55%) Christian, most of the rest follow traditional beliefs
Population: 10 million
Bank Hours: 0830-1400 Monday, Tuesday, Thursday, Friday; 0830-1200 Wednesday; 0830-1100 Saturday
Shop Hours: 0800 or 0830-1700 Monday-Friday; 0800-1300 Saturday
Currency: 100 cents = 1 Zimbabwe dollar
Export/Import Information: Surcharge duty of 20% CIF to order, and 12 1/2% tax on retail sales on books. Advertising matter in bulk has duty and VAT charged. Import license is normally required for books and printed matter. Exchange controls.
Copyright: Berne (see Copyright Conventions, pg viii)

College Press Publishers (Pvt) Ltd+
Subsidiary of Macmillan Publishers Ltd
15 Douglas Rd, Workington, Harare
Mailing Address: PO Box 3041, Harare
Tel: (04) 754145; (04) 757150; (04) 757154
Fax: (04) 754256
Key Personnel
Mng Dir: Benias Benison Mugabe
Mng Editor: Shepherd Murevanhema
Founded: 1968
Primarily an educational publisher.
Membership(s): APNET; Zimbabwe Book Publishers Association.
Subjects: Accounting, Agriculture, Biblical Studies, Biography, Memoirs, Biological Sciences,

Business, Chemistry, Chemical Engineering, Child Care & Development, Cookery, Drama, Theater, Economics, English as a Second Language, Environmental Studies, Fiction, Geography, Geology, History, Mathematics, Physics, Poetry, Science (General), Teachers Education
ISBN Prefix(es): 978-0-86925; 978-1-77900
Number of titles published annually: 40 Print
Total Titles: 920 Print
Imprints: Focus Books; Ventures
Branch Office(s)
PO Box 298, Bulawayo, Contact: G Ndlovu
Tel: (09) 74174
PO Box 1239, Gweru, Contact: G K Madzime
Tel: (054) 220394
PO Box 355, Masvingo, Contact: G Muzenda
Tel: (039) 262264
PO Box 963, Mutare, Contact: S J Chikuse
Tel: (020) 64211
Distributed by Macmillan Publishers (worldwide)
Distributor for Macmillan Publishers
Foreign Rep(s): Macmillan Publishers (worldwide)

Dorothy Duncan Braille Library
119 Fife Ave, Harare
Tel: (04) 251116; (04) 797725 *Fax:* (04) 251117
Web Site: www.ddbl.org
Key Personnel
Dir: Sr Catherine Jackson
Administrator: Andrew Mutambisa
Founded: 1963
Parent Company: Dorothy Duncan Centre for the Blind & Physically Handicapped

Focus Books, *imprint of* College Press Publishers (Pvt) Ltd

Legal Resources Foundation Legal Publications Unit
16 Oxford Rd, Avondale, Harare
Tel: (04) 333707; (04) 334732 *Fax:* (04) 304928
Web Site: www.lrfzim.com/publications
Founded: 1987
Subjects: Law
ISBN Prefix(es): 978-0-908312; 978-1-77906

Mambo Press+
Senga Rd, Gweru
Mailing Address: PO Box 779, Gweru
Tel: (054) 224016; (054) 224017 *Fax:* (054) 221991
Key Personnel
Publishing Manager: Vonai Bernadette Paradza
Tel: (054) 224579 *E-mail:* vonaiparadza@gmail.com
Sales Manager: Nicholas Matemadanda *Tel:* (077) 9398259 (cell)
Accounts: Mr Juba Chekenyere
Founded: 1957
Innovative, scholarly & prestigious works in the fields of religion, missiology, fiction, history of social sciences & culture.
Subjects: Economics, Fiction, History, Language Arts, Linguistics, Literature, Literary Criticism, Essays, Natural History, Nonfiction (General), Poetry, Religion - Other, Social Sciences, Sociology, Culture, Grammar
ISBN Prefix(es): 978-0-86922
Number of titles published annually: 12 Print
Total Titles: 320 Print
Foreign Rep(s): Africa Book Centre (UK); Botswana Book Centre (Botswana, USA); Pauline Multimedia (Zambia)
Bookshop(s): Bulawayo, 127 RG Mugabe Way between 13 & 14 Ave, Bulawayo, Contact: Mrs S Kamutingondo *Tel:* (09) 61162; Speke Ave, PO Box UA 320, Harare, Contact: Mrs R Mabuza *Tel:* (04) 705899; 56 Hughes St, PO Box 1010, Masvingo, Contact: Mr H Muromo *Tel:* (039) 64566

National Archives of Zimbabwe+
Borrowdale Rd, Gunhill, Private Bag 7729, Causeway, Harare
Tel: (04) 792741; (04) 792743; (04) 792744; (04) 795695 *Fax:* (04) 792398
Web Site: www.archives.gov.zw
Key Personnel
Dir: Mr I M Murambiwa
Founded: 1935
Subjects: Ethnicity, Genealogy, History, Nonfiction (General), Social Sciences, Sociology
ISBN Prefix(es): 978-0-908302

NAZ, see National Archives of Zimbabwe

Sapes Books, see Sapes Trust Ltd

Sapes Trust Ltd (The Southern Africa Political & Economic Series (SAPES) Trust)+
4 Deary Ave, Belgravia, Harare
Mailing Address: PO Box MP 111, Mount Pleasant, Harare
Tel: (04) 252 962; (04) 252 965 *Fax:* (04) 252 964
E-mail: info@sapes.org.zw
Web Site: www.sapes.org.zw
Key Personnel
Chairperson & Trustee: Dr Ibbo Day Mandaza
Trustee: Dr Chinyamata Chipeta; Dr Gilbert Nombwana Mudenda
Founded: 1987
Research, training & publications.
Subjects: Developing Countries, Economics, Environmental Studies, Government, Political Science, Public Administration, Social Sciences, Sociology
ISBN Prefix(es): 978-1-77905
Number of titles published annually: 5 Print; 1 CD-ROM
Subsidiaries: Southern Africa Publishing & Printing Houses (SAPPHO)
Distributed by African Books Collective
Distributor for CODESRIA

SAZ, see Standards Association of Zimbabwe (SAZ)

Standards Association of Zimbabwe (SAZ)
Northend Close, Northridge Park, Borrowdale
Mailing Address: PO Box 2259, Harare
Tel: (04) 882021; (04) 885511; (04) 885512
Fax: (04) 882020
E-mail: info@saz.org.zw
Web Site: www.saz.org.zw
Key Personnel
Dir General: Mrs E C Gadzikwa
Dir, Operations: Mr C Siringwani
Founded: 1957
Subjects: Agriculture, Automotive, Chemistry, Chemical Engineering, Civil Engineering, Electronics, Electrical Engineering, Energy, Engineering (General), Mechanical Engineering
ISBN Prefix(es): 978-0-86928
Number of titles published annually: 96 Print
Total Titles: 1,173 Print
Branch Office(s)
7 Bessborough St, PO Box RY 129, Raylton, Bulawayo *Tel:* (09) 71876; (09) 70447 *Fax:* (09) 70447 *E-mail:* sazbyo@mweb.co.zw
32a Simon Mazorodze Rd, PO Box 591, Mutare *Tel:* (020) 60516; (020) 60553 *Fax:* (020) 66252 *E-mail:* sazmutare@zol.co.zw

University of Zimbabwe Publications+
PO Box MP 203, Mount Pleasant, Harare
Tel: (04) 303211-5 (ext 11194) *Fax:* (04) 333407
E-mail: uzpub@admin.uz.ac.zw
Web Site: www.uz.ac.zw
Key Personnel
Chairman, Publications Committee: Prof C F B Nhachi *E-mail:* cnhachi@gmail.com
Founded: 1969

Subjects: Agriculture, Art, Biological Sciences, Drama, Theater, Economics, Engineering (General), Finance, Geography, Geology, Health, Nutrition, History, Language Arts, Linguistics, Law, Literature, Literary Criticism, Essays, Mathematics, Medicine, Nursing, Dentistry, Religion - Other, Social Sciences, Sociology, Gender Studies, Politics, Theatre Arts
ISBN Prefix(es): 978-0-908307; 978-1-77920; 978-0-86924
Distributed by African Books Collective (UK)

Ventures, *imprint of* College Press Publishers (Pvt) Ltd

Weaver Press
38 Broadlands Rd, Emerald Hill, Harare
Mailing Address: PO Box A1922, Avondale, Harare

Tel: (04) 308330; (04) 339631
E-mail: weaver@mango.zw
Web Site: www.weaverpresszimbabwe.com
Key Personnel
Founder & Dir: Murray McCartney
Publisher: Irene Staunton
Subjects: Environmental Studies, Fiction, History, Literature, Literary Criticism, Essays, Media Issues, Political History, Southern Africa, Social History, Women & Children's Rights
ISBN Prefix(es): 978-1-77922
Distribution Center: African Books Collective, PO Box 721, Oxford OX1 9EN, United Kingdom *Fax:* (01865) 412 341 *E-mail:* orders@africanbookscollective.com

Zimbabwe Women Writers (ZWW)+
2 Harvey Brown Ave, Milton Park, Harare
Founded: 1990

Subjects: Nonfiction (General), Poetry
ISBN Prefix(es): 978-7-974200

Zimbabwe Women's Bureau+
43 Hillside Rd, Cranborne, Harare
Mailing Address: PO Box CR 120, Cranborne, Harare
Tel: (04) 747434 *Toll Free Tel:* 800-450-6935; 800-450-6940
Key Personnel
Executive Dir: Ronika Mumbire
Founded: 1978
Subjects: Agriculture, Education, Finance, Health, Nutrition, Human Relations

ZWW, see Zimbabwe Women Writers (ZWW)

Type of Publication Index

BIBLES

CHILDREN'S BOOKS

DICTIONARIES, ENCYCLOPEDIAS

FINE EDITIONS, ILLUSTRATED BOOKS

FOREIGN LANGUAGE & BILINGUAL BOOKS

JUVENILE & YOUNG ADULT BOOKS

LARGE PRINT BOOKS

MAPS, ATLASES

PAPERBACK BOOKS - MASS MARKET

PROFESSIONAL BOOKS

Subject Index

ACCOUNTING

ALTERNATIVE

ANTHROPOLOGY

ARCHITECTURE & INTERIOR DESIGN

BEHAVIORAL SCIENCES

BIOGRAPHY, MEMOIRS

BIOLOGICAL SCIENCES

CAREER DEVELOPMENT

CHEMISTRY, CHEMICAL ENGINEERING

CHILD CARE & DEVELOPMENT

CRAFTS, GAMES, HOBBIES

CRIMINOLOGY

DISABILITY, SPECIAL NEEDS

EARTH SCIENCES

ELECTRONICS, ELECTRICAL ENGINEERING

ENGINEERING (GENERAL)

ENVIRONMENTAL STUDIES

GARDENING, PLANTS

HEALTH, NUTRITION

HISTORY

HOUSE & HOME

HOW-TO

HUMAN RELATIONS

INSPIRATIONAL, SPIRITUALITY

LABOR, INDUSTRIAL RELATIONS

LANGUAGE ARTS, LINGUISTICS

LGBTQ

LITERATURE, LITERARY CRITICISM, ESSAYS

MILITARY SCIENCE

Uruguay

Venezuela

Zambia

MYSTERIES, SUSPENSE

Argentina

Australia

Austria

Belgium

Brazil

Bulgaria

Chile

Colombia

Czech Republic

Denmark

Finland

France

French Polynesia

Germany

Greece

Hong Kong

India

PHOTOGRAPHY

RELIGION - CATHOLIC

RELIGION - ISLAMIC

SCIENCE (GENERAL)

SCIENCE FICTION, FANTASY

THEOLOGY

Literary Agents

Argentina

Agencia Literaria Irene Barki
Ave Independencia 984, dto 10, C1099AAW
  Buenos Aires
Tel: (011) 4300 3514
E-mail: info@irenebarki.com
Founded: 2007
Represents literary fiction writers from Latin
  American countries, including Argentina,
  Uruguay & Colombia. Handles foreign rights
  for Argentinian publishers. No unsolicited
  manuscripts.

**Monica Herrero Representaciones y Servicios
  Editoriales**
Posadas 1463, 6° B, C1011ABI Buenos Aires
Tel: (011) 4331 5262; (011) 4342 0347
  Fax: (011) 4331 5262; (011) 4342 0347
E-mail: monica@monicaherrero.com.ar
Web Site: monicaherrero.com.ar
Founded: 2005
Specializes in translation rights between Brazil &
  the Spanish-speaking world.

IECO, see International Editors' Co

International Editors' Co
Ave Cabildo 1156, 10° A, 1426 Buenos Aires
Tel: (011) 4788-2992 *Fax:* (011) 4786-0888
E-mail: ieco@internationaleditors.com
Founded: 1939
Subsidiaries in Spain & Brazil.

Australia

Australian Licensing Corp
140 Royal St, Tuart Hill, Perth, WA 6060
Tel: (02) 9280 2220 *Fax:* (02) 9280 2223
E-mail: alc@alc-online.com
Web Site: www.alc-online.com
Key Personnel
Chief Executive Officer: Rod Hare *Tel:* (07561)
  567675 *E-mail:* rodhare@alc-online.com
Vice President, Sales: Mary Hare *Tel:* (07718)
  586425 *E-mail:* maryhare@alc-online.com
Rights Assistant: Debra Walker
Founded: 1999
Membership(s): Australian Publishers Association
  (APA).
Specializes in children's books.

Australian Literary Management
2-A Booth St, Balmain, NSW 2041
Tel: (02) 9818 8557 *Fax:* (02) 9818 8569
E-mail: alpha@austlit.com
Web Site: www.austlit.com
Key Personnel
Proprietor: Lyn Tranter
Founded: 1980
No scripts or children's books by unpublished
  authors.

The Authors' Agent
PO Box 577, Terrigal, NSW 2260
Tel: (02) 4384 4466
Web Site: www.theauthorsagent.com.au

Key Personnel
Agent: Brian Cook *E-mail:* briancook@
  theauthorsagent.com.au
Specializes in adult fiction & nonfiction, children's books.

Curtis Brown (Australia) Pty Ltd
2 Boundary St, Level 1, Paddington, Sydney,
  NSW 2021
Mailing Address: PO Box 19, Paddington, NSW
  2021
Tel: (02) 9331 5301 *Fax:* (02) 9360 3935
E-mail: info@curtisbrown.com.au
Web Site: curtisbrown.com.au
Key Personnel
Mng Dir: Fiona Inglis *E-mail:* fiona@
  curtisbrown.com.au
Founded: 1967

Cameron Creswell Agency
Level 7, 61 Marlborough St, Surry Hills, NSW
  2010
Mailing Address: Locked Bag 848, Surry Hills,
  NSW 2010
Tel: (02) 9319 7199 *Fax:* (02) 9319 6866
E-mail: info@cameronsmanagement.com.au
Web Site: camerons.dreamhosters.com
Key Personnel
Dir: Anthony Blair; Jane Cameron
Agent: Jo Butler; Needeya Islam; Alicia Johnston;
  Sue Muggleton
Specializes in nonfiction, fiction & children's.

Jenny Darling & Associates Pty Ltd
PO Box 5328, South Melbourne, Victoria 3205
Tel: (03) 9696 7750
E-mail: office@jennydarling.com.au (permissions)
Web Site: jennydarling.com.au
Key Personnel
Contact: Jenny Darling *E-mail:* jenny@
  jennydarling.com.au
Membership(s): Australian Literary Agents' Asso-
  ciation.

The Drummond Agency
PO Box 572, Woodend, Victoria 3442
Tel: (03) 5427 3644 *Fax:* (03) 5427 3655
E-mail: info@drummondagency.com.au
Web Site: www.drummondagency.com.au
Key Personnel
Dir: Sheila Drummond *E-mail:* sheilad@ozemail.
  com.au
Founded: 1997
Also offers international rights consultancy to
  publishers.
Membership(s): Australian Literary Agents' Asso-
  ciation.

Golvan Arts Management
PO Box 766, Kew, Victoria 3101
Tel: (03) 9853 5341 *Fax:* (03) 9853 8555
E-mail: golvan@ozemail.com.au
Web Site: www.golvanarts.com.au
Key Personnel
Dir: Colin Golvan
Manager: Debbie Golvan
Specializes in adult & children's fiction & nonfic-
  tion & poetry.

**HLA Management Theatrical Agency
  Australia**
87 Pitt St, Redfern, Sydney, NSW 2016

Mailing Address: PO Box 1536, Strawberry Hills,
  Sydney, NSW 2012
Tel: (02) 9549 3000 *Fax:* (02) 9310 4113
E-mail: hla@hlamgt.com.au
Web Site: www.hlamgt.com.au
Currently not accepting unsolicited material or
  solicitations. Requests for representation exclu-
  sively by referral.
Specializes in publications of the entertainment
  industry.

Margaret Kennedy Agency
Taringa, Brisbane, Qld 4068
E-mail: info@margaretkennedyagency.com
Web Site: www.margaretkennedyagency.com
Key Personnel
Owner: Margaret Kennedy
Founded: 1996
Membership(s): Australian Literary Agents Asso-
  ciation.
Specializes in general literary nonfiction, narrative
  nonfiction, literary fiction, children's picture
  book texts & young adult. No genre fiction, no
  poetry.

Margaret Kennedy Agency, see Margaret
  Kennedy Agency

The Naher Agency
104 Commonwealth St, Level 5, Surry Hills,
  NSW 2010
Tel: (04) 1462 4568 (cell)
Web Site: naher.com.au
Key Personnel
Dir: Gaby Naher *E-mail:* gaby@naher.com.au
Founded: 2008
Specializes in intelligent, ambitious adult fiction
  & narrative nonfiction.

Rick Raftos Management
59 Great Buckingham St, Suite 202, Redfern,
  NSW 2016
Mailing Address: PO Box 445, Paddington, NSW
  2021
Tel: (02) 9281 9622
E-mail: raftos@raftos.com.au
Web Site: www.rickraftosmanagement.com.au
Key Personnel
Mng Dir: Rick Raftos
Founded: 1985
Represents writers in all media.

Austria

VOGELMEDIA GmbH Literaturagentur
Korneuburger Str 21, 2102 Bisamberg
Tel: (02262) 62 800 *Fax:* (02262) 718 18-18
E-mail: lektorat@literaturagent.at
Web Site: www.literaturagent.at
Key Personnel
Mng Dir: Richard Vogel
New manuscripts are not being accepted at this
  time.

Belgium

AAA Allied Authors Agency
Kasteeldreef 44, 8930 Rekkem
Tel: (0496) 11 90 36
E-mail: info@alliedauthorsagency.be
Web Site: www.alliedauthorsagency.be
Founded: 2004
Literary & rights agents for Belgian authors &
publishers.
Specializes in fiction, nonfiction & youth litera-
ture.

Toneelfonds J Janssens
Te Boelaerlei 107, 2140 Borgerhout, Antwerp
Tel: (03) 366 44 00 *Fax:* (03) 366 45 01
E-mail: info@toneelfonds.be
Web Site: www.toneelfonds.be
Key Personnel
Dir: Jessica Janssens
Founded: 1880
Publisher of plays & literary agent for play-
wrights.
Specializes in plays.

Zeitgeist Media Group Agency
Ave de Vent Chasseur 8A, 1180 Brussels
Tel: (0479) 262843
Web Site: www.zeitgeistmediagroup.com
Key Personnel
Founding Dir & Agent: Sharon Galant
    E-mail: sharon@zeitgeistmediagroup.com
Dir: Benython Oldfield
Agent: Emma Nicholas
Founded: 2006

Brazil

**Pagina da Cultura Agencia Literaria Ideias
sobre Linhas Ltda**
Affiliate of Camara Brasileira do Livro
R Coronel Jose Eusebio, 95, Travessa Dona Paula
2, 01239-030 Sao Paulo-SP
Tel: (011) 31293900 *Fax:* (011) 31293900
Web Site: paginadacultura.com.br
Key Personnel
Contact: Marisa Moura *E-mail:* marisa.moura@
paginadacultura.com.br
Founded: 1994
Specializes in business, essays, fiction, history,
religions, self-help, children & juvenile books.

Agencia Riff (Riff Agency)
Ave Calogeras n° 6, sala 1007, 20030-070 Rio de
Janeiro-RJ
Tel: (021) 2287 6299 *Fax:* (021) 2287 6393
E-mail: agenciariff@agenciariff.com.br
Web Site: www.agenciariff.com.br
Key Personnel
Literary Agent & Executive: Lucia Riff
    E-mail: lucia@agenciariff.com.br
Founded: 1991
Agent for Brazilian authors & co-agent for for-
eign publishers & literary agencies.
Specializes in Brazilian/Portuguese language mar-
ket & Brazilian authors for Brazil & abroad.

Schindler's Literary Agency (Agencia Literaria
Schindler)
CP 19051, 04505-970 Sao Paulo-SP
Tel: (011) 5041-9177 *Fax:* (011) 5041-9077
Key Personnel
Chief Executive Officer: Suely Pedro dos Santos
    E-mail: suely@agschindler.com.br

H Katia Schumer Literary Agent
Av do Pepe, 1120/1010, 22620-171 Rio de
Janeiro-RJ
Tel: (021) 2158-6370 *Fax:* (021) 2491-9841
E-mail: hkatia@schumer.com.br
Web Site: www.hkatiaschumerliteraryagent.com
Specializes in esoteric, spiritual, self-help, fiction,
nonfiction, biographies & psychology.

VBM Literary Agency & Consultancy, see
Villas-Boas & Moss Literary Agency &
Consultancy

**Villas-Boas & Moss Literary Agency &
Consultancy**
Av Delfim Moreira 1.222/102, 22441-000 Rio de
Janeiro-RJ
Tel: (021) 3724-1046
Web Site: www.vbmlitag.com
Key Personnel
Partner & Agent: Lucinda Villas-Boas
Partner: Raymond Moss *E-mail:* raymond@
vbmlitag.com
Founded: 2012
Represents Brazilian authors & publishers in
Brazil & abroad & European & US authors
& publishers selling into Brazil. Accept unso-
licited manuscripts by e-mail (include all items
in the body of the e-mail, not as an attach-
ment). For fiction, send query letter, one-page
synopsis, brief bio & first 10-15 pages. For
nonfiction, send query letter, project overview
with chapter outline, brief bio, description of
competing books & first 10-15 pages of first
chapter.
U.S. Office(s): 3630 Peachtree Rd, Suite 1025,
Atlanta, GA 30326, United States *Tel:* 678-
381-8601 *Fax:* 815-364-0515
110 Wall St, 11th floor, New York, NY 10001,
United States *Tel:* 212-709-8043

Bulgaria

Anthea Agency Ltd
62 G M Dimitrov Blvd, Suite 20, 1172 Sofia
Tel: (02) 9863581
Web Site: anthearights.com
Key Personnel
Mng Dir: Katalina Sabeva *E-mail:* katalina@
anthearights.com
Agent: Zlatka Mironova *E-mail:* zlatka@
anthearights.com
Founded: 1992
Represents a full array of authors & genres–fiction & nonfiction of all categories, business books, children's fiction & illustrated reference, textbooks & products of book engineering. Currently, the agency cooperates with
over 50 literary agencies & publishers from the
USA, UK, Germany, Switzerland & Russia.

RT Copyright Ltd
14, Elisaveta Bagryana St, floor 8, pk 24, 1111
Sofia
Tel: (089) 9557619 *Fax:* (089) 9557619
Key Personnel
Executive Dir: Radoslav I Trenev
Specializes in translation rights.

China

Big Apple Agency Inc
3F, No 838, Zhong Shan Bei Rd, Zha-Bei District, Shanghai 200070

Tel: (021) 6658-0055 *Fax:* (021) 6658-1977
E-mail: bigapple1@bigapple-china.com
Web Site: www.bigapple1.info
Key Personnel
President: Lily Chen
Executive Dir: Dr Luc Kwanten
Vice President & US Representative: Wendy
King *Tel:* 808-258-5080 *E-mail:* wendy-king@
bigapple1-china.com
European Representative: Nina Martyn
Founded: 1987
Affiliates in all major countries. Rights & authors
agent.
Branch Office(s)
Beijing *Tel:* (010) 8831-0879 *Fax:* (010) 8831-
0879
16F, No 866-8, Zhongzheng Rd, Zhonghe Dis-
trict, New Taipei City 235, Taiwan *Tel:* (02)
8228-7211 *Fax:* (02) 8228-6741

**Chengdu Rightol Media & Advertisement Co
Ltd**
6-1-2801, 66 Ruillan Rd, Chengdu, Sichuan
610091
Tel: (028) 86183888; (028) 86183999 *Fax:* (028)
86118086
E-mail: manager@rightol.com
Web Site: www.rightol.com
Founded: 2006
Representing publishers worldwide to sell Chi-
nese translation rights.

Czech Republic

A R T Dialog
Michelska 81, 141 00 Prague 4
Tel: 241 482 808 *Fax:* 241 481 442
E-mail: artdialog@mybox.cz
Web Site: www.mybox.cz/artdialog
Key Personnel
Contact, English Literature: Rene J Tesar
    E-mail: rene.tesar@worldonline.cz
Contact, German Literature: Daniela Vranovska
Founded: 1990
Specializes in import of English & German lan-
guage literature translation rights to Czech
book market.

Dana Blatna Literary Agency
Jinacovice 3, 664 34 Kurim
Tel: 608 748 157
E-mail: blatna@dbagency.cz
Web Site: www.dbagency.cz
Key Personnel
Manager: Dana Blatna
Founded: 2006
Specializes in contemporary Czech fiction.

**DILIA (Divadelni, Literarni, Audiovizualni
Agentura o s) (Theatre, Literary &
Audiovisual Agency)**
Kratkeho 1, 190 03 Prague 9
Tel: 266 199 813 *Fax:* 283 893 599
Web Site: www.dilia.cz
Key Personnel
Head, Literary Dept: Alena Jakoubkova *Tel:* 266
199 841 *E-mail:* jakoubkova@dilia.cz
Founded: 1949
Membership(s): Society for Protection of Au-
thors' Rights.

**Divadelni, Literarni, Audiovizualni Agentura o
s**, see DILIA (Divadelni, Literarni,
Audiovizualni Agentura o s)

Kristin Olson Literary Agency sro
Klimentska 24, 110 00 Prague 1

Tel: 222 582 042 *Fax:* 222 580 048
E-mail: kristin.olson@litag.cz
Web Site: www.litag.cz
Key Personnel
Agent: Kristin Olson
Founded: 1994
Independent rights agency representing international publishers & agents in the Czech & Slovak markets.

Agency Rene Tesar Dialog, see A R T Dialog

Denmark

Bookman Literary Agency
Bastager 3, Vedbaek, 2950 Copenhagen
Tel: 4589 2520 *Fax:* 4589 2501
E-mail: ihl@bookman.dk
Web Site: www.bookman.dk
Key Personnel
Agent: Bebbe Lauritzen; Ib H Lauritzen
Founded: 1912
Acts as a literary agent in Denmark, Sweden, Norway, Finland & Iceland for foreign authors.
Specializes in general fiction & nonfiction (business books, golf & tennis), serial sales.

Copenhagen Literary Agency ApS
Frederiksholms Kanal 2, 3, 1220 Copenhagen
Tel: 33 13 25 23
E-mail: info@cphla.dk; royalty@cphla.dk
Web Site: www.cphla.dk
Key Personnel
Owner & Agent: Monica Gram *Tel:* 26 71 60 42
  E-mail: monica@cphla.dk; Lars Ringhof
  Tel: 27 11 13 13 *E-mail:* lars@cphla.dk
Literary Agent: Eva Haagerup *E-mail:* eva@
  cphla.dk; Anneli Hoier *Tel:* 51 51 50 37
  E-mail: anneli@cphla.dk; Esthi Kunz *Tel:* 31
  24 10 15 *E-mail:* esthi@cphla.dk; Ane Lauenblad *Tel:* 25 32 53 94 *E-mail:* ane@cphla.dk
Founded: 2015 (result of merger between Leonhardt & Hoier Literary Agency & Lars Ringhof Agency)

Gyldendal Group Agency
Klareboderne 3, 1001 Copenhagen K
Tel: 33 75 55 55
E-mail: info@gyldendalgroupagency.dk
Web Site: www.gyldendalgroupagency.dk
Key Personnel
Mng Dir: Jenny Thor *Tel:* 33 75 56 68
  E-mail: jenny_thor@gyldendalgroupagency.dk
Children's Book Agent: Stinne Hjortlund
  Tel: 33 75 55 17 *E-mail:* stinne_hjortlund@
  gyldendalgroupagency.dk
Coordinator: Cecilie Hojmark *Tel:* 33
  75 57 74 *E-mail:* cecilie_hojmark@
  gyldendalgroupagency.dk
Founded: 2004
Represents authors in the Gyldendal Group: Gyldendal, Host & Son, Pretty Ink, Rosinante & Samleren. Also handles film & drama rights.
Specializes in literary fiction, crime fiction, classics, narrative nonfiction, nonfiction & children's books.

Licht & Burr Literary Agency
Ny Vestergade 1, st, 1471 Copenhagen K
Mailing Address: PO Box 2142, 1015 Copenhagen K
Tel: 3333 0021
E-mail: tl@licht-burr.dk
Web Site: www.licht-burr.dk
Key Personnel
Chief Executive & Agent: Trine Licht

Representing American, Australian, British & Canadian agents & publishers in Denmark, Finland, Iceland, Norway & Sweden & representing Scandinavian authors worldwide.

PeopleGroupAgency
Vester Farimagsgade 41, 1606 Copenhagen
Tel: 2265 5368
Web Site: www.peoplegroupagency.com
Key Personnel
Rights Dir: Louise Langhoff Koch *E-mail:* lolk@
  artpeople.dk
Foreign Rights Manager: Lise Nielsen
  E-mail: lise.nielsen@artpeople.dk

Finland

Elina Ahlback Literary Agency Oy Ltd
Unioninkatu 20-22, 00130 Helsinki
Tel: (040) 0512101 (cell)
E-mail: info@ahlbackagency.com
Web Site: www.ahlbackagency.com
Key Personnel
Chief Executive Officer: Elina Ahlback *Tel:* (040)
  0548402 (cell) *E-mail:* elina.ahlback@
  ahlbackagency.com
Junior Agent: Lotta Dufva *E-mail:* lotta.dufva@
  ahlbackagency.com
Business Development Agent: Silja Niemi
  Tel: (040) 8673231 (cell) *E-mail:* silja.niemi@
  ahlbackagency.com
Founded: 2009
Agent for Finnish authors, illustrators & publishers in international markets & international publishers, agents & their authors exclusively in Scandinavian markets.

Werner Soderstrom Osakeyhtio (WSOY)
Korkeavuorenkatu 37, 00130 Helsinki
Mailing Address: PL 314, 00101 Helsinki
Tel: (010) 5060 200 *Fax:* (010) 5060 287
Web Site: www.wsoy.fi
Founded: 1878
Also publisher.
Parent Company: Bonnier AB

WSOY, see Werner Soderstrom Osakeyhtio (WSOY)

France

Alnovas Literary & Film Agency
BP 298, 06227 Vallauris Cedex
Tel: 04 93 67 51 29
Web Site: www.alnovas.fr
Key Personnel
Agent: Noelle Mouska *E-mail:* noelle.mouska@
  wanadoo.fr
Founded: 2004
Represents French & foreign authors & publishers.
Specializes in literary fiction, popular fiction, nonfiction & art books.

Astier-Pecher Literary & Film Agency
5, rue Cave, 75018 Paris
Tel: 09 52 01 39 16
E-mail: contact@pierreastier.com
Web Site: pierreastier.com
Key Personnel
Agent: Pierre Astier; Laure Pecher
  E-mail: lpecher@pierreastier.com
Founded: 2006

Represents French & foreign authors, as well as French & foreign publishers. Manuscripts should be sent by e-mail; allow two months for a reply; include self-addressed, stamped envelope for materials to be returned.
Specializes in fiction, nonfiction & crime fiction.

L'Autre Agence
45 rue Marx Dormoy, 75018 Paris
Tel: 01 80 50 28 70
E-mail: contact@lautreagence.eu
Web Site: www.lautreagence.eu
Key Personnel
Agent: Marie Lannurien; Corinne Marotte
Founded: 2009
Represents French & foreign publishers & agents in France & abroad.

Eliane Benisti Literary Agency
80 rue des Sts-Peres, 75007 Paris
Tel: 01 42 22 85 33 *Fax:* 01 45 44 18 17
E-mail: elianebenisti@hotmail.com
Key Personnel
Dir: Eliane Benisti

Lora Fountain Literary Agency
7 rue de Belfort, 75011 Paris
Tel: 01 43 56 21 96
E-mail: agence@fountlit.com
Web Site: www.lorafountainagency.com
Founded: 1985
Representing publishers & agents from Australia, Brazil, Canada, Ireland, Spain, UK & USA in France. Also selling graphic novels & children's books to Brazil, Italy, Netherlands, Portugal & Spain. No unsolicited manuscripts.
Specializes in quality adult fiction & nonfiction, children's literature, graphic novels.

Hannele & Associates
38 rue Alfred de Vigny, 33200 Bordeaux
Tel: 06 10 52 55 73
E-mail: info@hanneleandassociates.fr
Web Site: hanneleandassociates.fr
Key Personnel
Agent: Stephanie Hauray; Hannele Legras
Represents French independent & creative companies, offering quality children's books.

Anna Jarota Agency (AJA)
5, rue de Pontoise, 75005 Paris
Tel: 01 45 75 21 28
Web Site: annajarota.fr
Key Personnel
Dir & Agent: Anna Jarota *E-mail:* ajarota@ajafr.
  com
Agent: David Camus; Deborah Druba
Founded: 2008
Branch Office(s)
Rynek Starego Miasta 22/24 m 6, 00-272 Warsaw, Poland, Contact: Dominika Bojanowska
  Web Site: annajarota-poland.pl

Agence Michelle Lapautre
91 ter, rue du Cherche-Midi, 75006 Paris
Tel: 01 47 34 82 41 *Fax:* 01 47 34 00 90
E-mail: agence@lapautre.com
Key Personnel
Dir: Catherine Lapautre *E-mail:* catherine@
  lapautre.com
Specializes in representation of English language agents & publishers for French language rights.

Susanna Lea Associates
28, rue Bonaparte, 75006 Paris
Tel: 01 53 10 28 40 *Fax:* 01 53 10 28 49
E-mail: inquiries@susannalea.com
Web Site: www.susannalea.com
Key Personnel
Contact: Mark Kessler *E-mail:* mkessler@
  susannalea.com

Founded: 2000

No poetry, plays, screen plays, science fiction, educational textbooks, short stories or illustrated works. Submissions accepted via e-mail only. Send concise query letter, brief synopsis & first three chapters +/or proposal. No reading fee.

Branch Office(s)
34 Lexington St, London W1F 0LH, United Kingdom, Contact: Kerry Glencorse
Tel: (020) 7287 7757 *Fax:* (020) 7287 7775
E-mail: kglencorse@susannalea.com
U.S. Office(s): 331 W 20 St, New York, NY 10011, United States *Tel:* 646-638-1435
Fax: 646-638-1436 *E-mail:* sla.ny@susannalea.com

Mon Agent et Compagnie
6, rue Victor Hugo, 73000 Chambery
Tel: 06 24 79 50 91
E-mail: help@monagentetcompagnie.com
Web Site: www.monagentetcompagnie.com
Key Personnel
Agent: Nickie Athanassi; Emmanuel Bonnet
Founded: 2010
Representing authors & French publishers for foreign, subsidiary & audiovisual rights.

La Nouvelle Agence
7 rue Corneille, 75006 Paris
Tel: 01 43 25 85 60 *Fax:* 01 43 25 47 98
E-mail: lna@lanouvelleagence.fr
Key Personnel
Contact: Vanessa Kling

Patricia Pasqualini Literary Agency
Creative Valley Bldg, 11, rue Carnot, 94270 Le Kremlin-Bicetre
Tel: 06 65 46 79 28
Founded: 1999
Representation of authors worldwide. More than 3,000 contracts signed since 1999.

The Picture Book Agency
142 ave Parmentier, 75011 Paris
Tel: 09 73 61 64 43
Web Site: www.thepicturebookagency.com
Key Personnel
Contact: Stephanie Vernet *E-mail:* stephanie@thepicturebookagency.com
Represents French publishers abroad & foreign publishers in France.

Georgia

Amodis Natdeba Literary Agency
14, Rustaveli Ave, 0108 Tbilisi
Tel: (0790) 64-06-40
Web Site: amodis-natdeba.weebly.com
No reading fee. Accept fiction & nonfiction. Submissions (manuscripts & illustrations) welcome by e-mail with preliminary query & brief synopsis.

Germany

Antas Bindermann Listau GbR
Gneisenaustr 2a, 10961 Berlin
Tel: (030) 30341976
Web Site: antas-bindermann-listau.com
Key Personnel
Partner: Maria Antas *Tel:* (030) 30346419; Susan Bindermann; Kristine Listau

Founded: 2015

Represents German & foreign publishers, agencies & authors in German language countries, as well as German & foreign authors worldwide.

Specializes in literature & social & cultural political nonfiction.

Arrowsmith Agency
Poststr 14-16, 20354 Hamburg
Tel: (040) 85 100 295 *Fax:* (040) 85 100 296
E-mail: info@arrowsmith-agency.com; welcome@arrowsmith-agency.com
Web Site: www.arrowsmith-agency.com
Key Personnel
Agent: Nina Arrowsmith
Junior Editor: Leona Stahlmann *E-mail:* leona@arrowsmith-agency.com
Founded: 2005
Represents international authors, publishers & agencies.

Verlag der Autoren-Literaturagentur
Taunusstr 19, 60329 Frankfurt am Main
Tel: (069) 23 85 74-33 *Fax:* (069) 24 27 76 44
E-mail: literaturagentur@verlagderautoren.de
Web Site: www.verlagderautoren.de/literaturagentur
Key Personnel
Agent: Dr Sebastian Richter *E-mail:* richter@verlagderautoren.de

AVA International GmbH
Hohenzollernstr 38 Rgb, 80801 Munich
Tel: (089) 45209 220-0 *Fax:* (089) 45209 220-9
E-mail: info@ava-international.de
Web Site: www.ava-international.de
Key Personnel
President: Roman Hocke
Agent: Markus Michalek
Foreign Rights: Claudia von Hornstein
Founded: 1989
Specializes in fiction & nonfiction.

Dr Ivana Beil, Internationale Handelsvermittlung im Medien- und Verlagswesen
Schollstr 1, 69469 Weinheim
Tel: (06201) 14611 *Fax:* (06201) 16883
E-mail: dribeil@aol.com
Founded: 1984
Specializes in copyright intervention, coproductions, representation of publishing houses, authors, illustrators, children's & young readers' books (also on film & television productions), marketing.

Guenter Berg Literary Agency GmbH & Co KG
Mittelweg 117, 20149 Hamburg
Tel: (040) 45 000 996; (040) 4414 029 928
Fax: (040) 4130 8998
E-mail: info@guenterbergagency.com
Web Site: guenterbergagency.com
Key Personnel
Founder: Guenter Berg
Translation Rights: Katharina Muders
E-mail: katharina@guenterbergagency.com
Founded: 2013
Specializes in German & international fiction & nonfiction.

The Berlin Agency
Mommsenstr 2, 10629 Berlin
Tel: (030) 88 70 28 88 *Fax:* (030) 88 70 28 89
E-mail: jung-lindemann@berlinagency.de
Web Site: www.berlinagency.de
Key Personnel
Contact: Dr Frauke Jung-Lindemann
Founded: 1999
Specializes in fiction & nonfiction.

Claudia Boehme Rights & Literary Agency - Publishing Consultant
Goseriede 4 - Tiedthof (C), 30159 Hannover
Tel: (0511) 6008484 *Fax:* (0511) 6008474
E-mail: post@agency-boehme.com
Web Site: www.agency-boehme.com
Represents German, American, English, French, Dutch & Danish publishers & authors.
Specializes in fiction, books on crafts, illustrated books & screenplays.

Brentano-Gesellschaft Frankfurt/M mbh
Grosser Hirschgraben 15, 60311 Frankfurt
Tel: (069) 13377-177 *Fax:* (069) 13377-175
E-mail: info@brentano-gesellschaft.de
Web Site: www.brentano-gesellschaft.de
Key Personnel
Mng Dir: Dr Uwe Frank

Silke Bruenink Agency
Margit-Schramm-Str 12, 80639 Munich
Tel: (089) 930 947 44
E-mail: silke@silkeagency.de
Web Site: www.silkeagency.de
Founded: 2004
Specializes in nonfiction for adults & children.

Connecting Team
Lessingstr 10, 60325 Frankfurt am Main
Tel: (069) 74 74 99 90 *Fax:* (069) 74 74 99 99
Web Site: www.connectingteam.de
Key Personnel
Press & Communications: Regina Eisele
E-mail: eisele@connectingteam.de
Specializes in politics & society, economy, science & technology, history, culture, biographies, philosophy & psychology.

Copyright International Agency CorInA GmbH
Beerenstr 22A, 14163 Berlin
Tel: (030) 80902386 *Fax:* (030) 80902388
E-mail: info@corina.com
Web Site: www.corina.com
Key Personnel
President: Werner B Thiele *E-mail:* wbt@corina.com
Founded: 1998
Internet literary agency. Acts with translation rights for publishers & authors. Own publication (in Russian language): *Medical Textbooks and Learning Aids for Students.*
Specializes in literature from & for Middle & Eastern European countries.

Literarische Agentur Galina Dursthoff
Marsiliusstr 70, 50937 Cologne
Tel: (0221) 444 254
E-mail: info@dursthoff.de
Web Site: www.dursthoff.de
Key Personnel
Agent: Galina Dursthoff *E-mail:* galina@dursthoff.de
Represents Russian authors & publishers worldwide, offering fiction (literary & commercial), nonfiction, theatre & film rights.

Agentur Petra Eggers
Friedrichstr 133, 10117 Berlin
Tel: (030) 275 950 70 *Fax:* (030) 275 950 710
E-mail: info@agentur-eggers.de
Web Site: www.agentur-eggers.de
Key Personnel
Agent: Dr Petra Eggers *E-mail:* petra.eggers@agentur-eggers.de
Represents German authors.

erzaehl:perspektive
Karl-Theodor-Str 82, 80803 Munich
Tel: (089) 20 33 99 26 *Fax:* (089) 20 33 99 25

E-mail: info@erzaehlperspektive.de
Web Site: www.erzaehlperspektive.de
Key Personnel
Agent: Klaus Groener *E-mail:* klaus.groener@
erzaehlperspektive.de; Michaela Groener
E-mail: michaela.groener@erzaehlperspektive.
de
Founded: 2007
Represents German authors internationally & international book & film rights to publishing houses in Germany & abroad.
Specializes in fiction, nonfiction, children's & young reader's books.

Anoukh Foerg Literary Agency
Herzogstr 73, 80796 Munich
Tel: (089) 4521 9059; (0176) 240 175 08 (cell)
E-mail: anoukhfoerg@anoukhfoerg.com
Web Site: www.anoukhfoerg.com
Specializes in fiction, nonfiction, current affairs, young adult, crime & women's interests.

Literarische Agentur Michael Gaeb
Chodowieckistr 26, 10405 Berlin
Tel: (030) 54 71 40 02 *Fax:* (030) 54 71 40 05
E-mail: info@litagentur.com
Web Site: www.litagentur.com
Key Personnel
Proprietor: Michael Gaeb *E-mail:* gaeb@
litagentur.com
Founded: 2003
Representing German & international authors, primarily from Latin America, worldwide & French, Hispanic & Italian publishers for the German market.

Gattys Global
Jahnstr 7 rgb, 80469 Munich
Mailing Address: Postfach 14 02 29, 80452 Munich
Tel: (089) 202 554-0 *Fax:* (089) 202 554-30
E-mail: info@gattysglobal.de
Web Site: www.gattysglobal.de
Key Personnel
Agent: Christina Gattys *E-mail:* gattys@
gattysglobal.de
Founded: 1992
Represents screenwriters, film rights, fiction writers, nonfiction authors, children's & youth book authors & film production companies in the field of books on film.

Gesellschaft zur Foerderung der Literatur aus Afrika, Asien und Lateinamerika eV (Society for the Promotion of African, Asian & Latin American Literature)
Reineckstr 3, 60313 Frankfurt am Main
Mailing Address: Postfach 10 01 16, 60001 Frankfurt am Main
Tel: (069) 2102 113 *Fax:* (069) 2102 227
E-mail: litprom@book-fair.com
Web Site: www.litprom.de
Key Personnel
President: Juergen Boos
Press & Public Relations: Anita Djafari
E-mail: djafari@book-fair.com
Contact: Petra Kassler *E-mail:* kassler@book-fair.com
Founded: 1980
The Society seeks to promote German translations of creative writing from Africa, Asia & Latin America. It works as a nonprofit agency & as a consultant for German language publishers & for "Third World" publishers & authors who have German translation rights to offer. Publishes *Literaturnachrichten* (Literary News).

Agentur Gorus
Muehlestr 2, 78345 Moos
Tel: (07732) 940 75-0 *Fax:* (07732) 940 75-55
E-mail: info@gorus.de

Web Site: www.gorus.de
Key Personnel
Owner: Oliver Gorus *E-mail:* oliver.gorus@gorus.de
No unsolicited manuscripts, query first.
Specializes in nonfiction books, reference books & guides for the German book market.

Agentur Literatur Gudrun Hebel
Kurfuerstenstr 15-16, 10785 Berlin
Tel: (030) 347 077 67 *Fax:* (030) 347 077 68
E-mail: brief@agentur-literatur.de
Web Site: agentur-literatur.de
Key Personnel
Mng Dir: Gudrun Hebel
Founded: 1998
Representing foreign publishers, agencies & authors in German language speaking countries as well as German authors & publishers worldwide.
Specializes in Scandinavian literature.

Dr Saskia von Hoegen Literarische Agentur
Stolzenfelsstr 1A, 10318 Berlin
Tel: (030) 48811267
E-mail: info@saskiavonhoegen.de; svh@
saskiavonhoegen.de
Web Site: www.saskiavonhoegen.de
Representing Spanish-speaking & German authors & Spanish agencies & pubishers in German language territories & internationally.

IBA International Media & Book Agency
Torstr 43, 10119 Berlin
Tel: (030) 4437 9155 *Fax:* (030) 4437 9199
E-mail: office@iba-berlin.de
Web Site: www.iba-berlin.de
Key Personnel
President & Executive Dir: Ingo-Eric M Schmidt-Braul
Founded: 1991
Also acts as representative of authors & publishing houses.
Specializes in fiction, nonfiction & economics.

Keil & Keil Literary Agency
Schulterblatt 58, 20357 Hamburg
Tel: (040) 36 02 124-00 *Fax:* (040) 36 02 124-99
E-mail: anfragen@keil-keil.com
Web Site: www.keil-keil.com
Key Personnel
Agent: Anja Keil; Bettina Keil; Sabine Langohr; Sarah Haag
Founded: 1995
E-mail queries preferred. Have representatives in all major international markets. No unsolicited manuscripts.
Specializes in general trade fiction & nonfiction, children's & young adult, fantasy.

Ingrid Anna Kleihues Verlags und Autorenagentur
Wiesenaeckerstr 32, 70619 Stuttgart
Tel: (0711) 6788800
E-mail: info@agentur-kleihues.de
Founded: 1990
Specializes in nonfiction.

Agentur Hanne Knickmann
Roemerstr 45, 69115 Heidelberg
Tel: (06221) 67342-50 *Fax:* (06151) 67342-51
Web Site: www.hanne-knickmann.de
Key Personnel
Contact: Hanne Knickmann *E-mail:* hk@hanne-knickmann.de
Founded: 2003
Specializes in literary & cultural journals.

Agentur Susanne Koppe Auserlesen Ausgezeichnet
Lindenstr 23, 20099 Hamburg

Tel: (040) 37 17 29 *Fax:* (040) 689 900 54
E-mail: agentur@susanne-koppe.de
Web Site: www.auserlesen-ausgezeichnet.de
Founded: 2002
Represents authors & illustrators of children's literature & fiction.

Literarische Agentur Kossack GbR
Caecilienstr 14, 22301 Hamburg
Tel: (040) 27163 828 *Fax:* (040) 27163 829
E-mail: info@mp-litagency.com
Web Site: www.mp-litagency.com
Key Personnel
Mng Dir: Lars Schultze-Kossack *E-mail:* lars.schultze@mp-litagency.com
Agent: Sonja Brueckmann *E-mail:* sonja.brueckmann@mp-litagency.com; Lisbeth Koerbelin *E-mail:* lisbeth.koerbelin@mp-litagency.com; Stefanie Kruschandl *E-mail:* stefanie.kruschandl@mp-litagency.com; Annette Wolf *E-mail:* annette.wolf@mp-litagency.com
Founded: 1995
Representing German-speaking authors, publishers & agencies.
Specializes in fiction, nonfiction & children's.

Landwehr & Cie KG
Neue Schoenhauser Str 13, 10178 Berlin
Tel: (030) 55 77 90-0 *Fax:* (030) 55 77 90-100
E-mail: info@landwehr-cie.de
Web Site: www.landwehr-cie.de
Key Personnel
Agent: Marko Jacob; Matthias Landwehr
No unsolicited manuscripts.

Langenbuch & Weiss Literaturagentur GbR
Rellinger Str 16, 20257 Hamburg
Tel: (040) 33382044
E-mail: mail@langenbuch-weiss.de
Web Site: www.langenbuch-weiss.de
Key Personnel
Partner: Kristina Langenbuch *E-mail:* kristina@langenbuch-weiss.de; Gesa Weiss
E-mail: gesa@langenbuch-weiss.de
Founded: 2014

LKM (Literaturbetreuung Klaus Middendorf)
Altes Lazarett 47, 86836 Graben
Tel: (08232) 78463 *Fax:* (08232) 78468
E-mail: lkmcorp@t-online.de
Web Site: www.lkmcorp.com
Key Personnel
Owner & Agent: Klaus Middendorf
Founded: 1986
Author & publisher representation.

MCS Schabert GmbH Agentur & Verlagsproduktion
Schwanthalerstr 73, 80336 Munich
Tel: (089) 76 72 92 02 *Fax:* (089) 76 72 92 03
E-mail: info@mcs-schabert.de
Web Site: www.mcs-schabert.de
Key Personnel
Manager: Ulrike Aschenbrenner-Schabert; Werner Schabert
Founded: 1996
Also packager of illustrated nonfiction media production & merchandising agency for facsimiles.
Specializes in nonfiction for adults & children.

Medienbuero Muenchen (Media Agency Munich)
Division of Philosophia Verlag GmbH
Gundelindenstr 10, 80805 Munich
Mailing Address: Postfach 2213 62, 80503 Munich
Tel: (089) 299975 *Fax:* (089) 30767586
E-mail: info@medienbuero-muenchen.com
Web Site: www.medienbuero-muenchen.com
Key Personnel
Publisher: Ulrich Staudinger *E-mail:* ulrich.staudinger@philosophiaverlag.com

Founded: 2000
Agency for authors & publishers in print, TV, film & new media.
Specializes in fiction, nonfiction & scientific philosophy.

Michael Meller Literary Agency GmbH
Landwehrstr 17, 80336 Munich
Tel: (089) 36 63 71 *Fax:* (089) 36 63 72
E-mail: info@melleragency.com
Web Site: www.melleragency.com
Key Personnel
Agent: Michael Meller *E-mail:* m.meller@melleragency.com; Cristina Bernardi *E-mail:* c.bernardi@melleragency.com; Franziska Hoffmann *E-mail:* f.hoffmann@melleragency.com; Niclas Schmoll *E-mail:* n.schmoll@melleragency.com; Regina Seitz *E-mail:* r.seitz@melleragency.com
Founded: 1988
Specializes in fiction, nonfiction & children's books.

Dr Ray-Guede Mertin Literarische Agentur
Taunusstr 38, 60329 Frankfurt am Main
Tel: (069) 27 10 89 66 *Fax:* (069) 27 10 89 67
E-mail: info@mertin-litag.de
Web Site: www.mertin-litag.de
Key Personnel
Owner: Nicole Witt *E-mail:* n.witt@mertin-litag.de
Founded: 1982
Worldwide representation of authors from Africa, Brazil, Latin America, Portugal & Spain.
Specializes in fiction & nonfiction.

Literaturbetreuung Klaus Middendorf, see LKM (Literaturbetreuung Klaus Middendorf)

Peter Molden Literarische Agentur fuer Autoren und Verlage
Konrad Adenauer Ufer 31, 50668 Cologne
Tel: (0221) 70 90 90 05 *Fax:* (0221) 12 60 67 79
E-mail: info@agentur-molden.de
Web Site: www.agentur-molden.de
Key Personnel
Agent: Peter Molden *E-mail:* p.molden@agentur-molden.de
Founded: 2005
Specializes in representation of German language authors in Germany & abroad.

Mundt Agency
Kolhagenstr 38, 40593 Duesseldorf
Tel: (0211) 3905239 *Fax:* (0211) 47454433
E-mail: info@mundtagency.com
Web Site: www.mundtagency.com
Key Personnel
Proprietor: Anja Mundt *E-mail:* anja@mundtagency.com
Founded: 2010
Rights agency representing international children's book publishers. Handling translation rights, ebook rights, audio rights & co-editions. Does not represent authors or illustrators. Portfolio includes board books, picture books, children's & young adult fiction & nonfiction.

Nibbe & Wiedling Literary Agency
Hoehenweg 11, 82229 Seefeld
Tel: (08152) 98 18 77; (08974) 56 71 88
  Fax: (08152) 78 548
E-mail: wiedling@nibbe-wiedling.de
Web Site: www.nibbe-wiedling.de
Key Personnel
Agent: Thomas Wiedling
Sales: Bettina Nibbe *E-mail:* nibbe@nibbe-wiedling.de
Founded: 2001
Specializes in Russian book & film rights.

Partner + Propaganda Literaturagentur
Rosspl 1, 04103 Leipzig
Tel: (0341) 9939177 *Fax:* (0341) 9939178
E-mail: info@partner-propaganda.de
Web Site: www.partner-propaganda.de
Key Personnel
Agent: Christine Koschmieder
  E-mail: fraukoschmieder@partner-propaganda.de; Talina Rinke *E-mail:* fraurinke@partner-propaganda.de
Founded: 2007
Specializes in contemporary German & post-Yugoslavian fiction.

Literaturagentur Ernst Piper
Fechnerstr 23, 10717 Berlin
Tel: (030) 283 84 343 *Fax:* (030) 283 84 345
E-mail: info@ernst-piper.de
Web Site: www.ernst-piper.de
Represents German language authors. No poetry, science fiction, fantasy or children's books.

Literatur-Agentur Axel Poldner Media GmbH
Bitterfelder Weg 81, 12355 Berlin
Tel: (030) 604 908 62 *Fax:* (030) 604 908 63
E-mail: sekretariat@poldner.de
Web Site: www.poldner.de
Key Personnel
Contact: Axel Poldner *E-mail:* axel.poldner@poldner.de
Founded: 1970
Specializes in multimedia projects.

Agentur Poppenhusen (Poppenhusen Agency)
Gipsstr 8/9, 10119 Berlin
Web Site: agentur-poppenhusen.de
Key Personnel
Agent: Astrid Poppenhusen
Founded: 2003 (as part of Piper & Poppenhusen GbR, since 2014 Agentur Poppenhusen)

Verlags Agentur Prahl
Viktoriastr 1, 80803 Munich
Tel: (089) 121 631 51 *Fax:* (089) 121 631 52
E-mail: info@verlagsagentur.de
Web Site: www.verlagsagentur.de
Key Personnel
Founder & Agent: Eckhart Prahl
Founded: 1999
Specializes in children's & young adult book trade.

Literaturagentur Bettina Querfurth
Burgstr 140, 60389 Frankfurt
Tel: (069) 96866297 *Fax:* (069) 96865752
E-mail: bq@bettinaquerfurth.de
Web Site: www.bettinaquerfurth.de
Founded: 2005
Representing German & international authors in the areas of fiction & nonfiction.

rauchzeichen ag/Agentur und Lektorat
Carmerstr 17, 10623 Berlin
Tel: (030) 32 76 63 40 *Fax:* (030) 32 76 63 41
E-mail: info@rauchzeichen-agentur.de
Web Site: www.rauchzeichen-ag.de
Key Personnel
Agent: Dr Hanna Leitgeb

Literaturagentur Beate Riess
Stuehlingerstr 24, 79106 Freiburg
E-mail: info@beate-riess.de
Web Site: www.beate-riess.de
Founded: 2010
Representing German language authors.
Specializes in fiction, nonfiction & children's/young adult books.

rights & audio
Mozartstr 14, 69121 Heidelberg

Tel: (06221) 65 21 222 *Fax:* (06221) 65 21 222
E-mail: info@rights-and-audio.de
Web Site: www.rights-and-audio.de
Key Personnel
Proprietor: Charlotte Lorat
Services in the area of international licensing & audiobook production.

Elisabeth Ruge Agentur GmbH
Rosenthaler Str 34/35, 10178 Berlin
Tel: (030) 2888 406 00
E-mail: info@elisabeth-ruge-agentur.de
Web Site: elisabeth-ruge-agentur.de
Represents authors of fiction & nonfiction in all formats.

Autoren- und Projektagentur Gerd F Rumler
Jutastr 13, 80636 Munich
Tel: (089) 13928955
Web Site: www.agentur-rumler.de
Key Personnel
Proprietor: Gerd F Rumler *E-mail:* rumler@agentur-rumler.de
Founded: 2004
Specializes in adult fiction, historical novels, thrillers, humor, advice & nonfiction.

Thomas Schlueck GmbH
Hinter der Worth 12, 30827 Garbsen
Tel: (05131) 4975-60 *Fax:* (05131) 4975-89
E-mail: mail@schlueckagent.com
Web Site: www.schlueckagent.com
Key Personnel
Agent: Julia Aumueller *E-mail:* j.aumueller@schlueckagent.com; Joachim Jessen *E-mail:* j.jessen@schlueckagent.com; Bastian Schlueck *E-mail:* b.schlueck@schlueckagent.com; Franka Zastrow *E-mail:* f.zastrow@schlueckagent.com
Agent, Children/Juvenile: Friederike Biesel *E-mail:* f.biesel@schlueckagent.com; Tanja Heitmann *E-mail:* t.heitmann@schlueckagent.com
Founded: 1970
Full representation of Anglo-American, Spanish & Scandinavian authors, agents & publishers in German language areas, as well as representation of German authors. Also handles second rights of cover illustrations, Europe wide.

The Science Factory
Scheideweg 34c, 20253 Hamburg
Tel: (040) 4327 4959 (Skype); (020) 7193 7296
E-mail: info@sciencefactory.co.uk
Web Site: www.sciencefactory.co.uk
Key Personnel
Owner: Peter Tallack *E-mail:* peter@sciencefactory.co.uk
Founded: 2008
Query first via e-mail. Proposal & sample chapter may be attached.
Membership(s): Association of Authors' Agents.
Specializes in nonfiction.

Agentur Scriptzz
Kieferndamm 82, 15566 Schoeneiche
Tel: (030) 68 83 57 06 *Fax:* (030) 72 02 15 39
E-mail: info@scriptzz.de
Web Site: www.scriptzz.de
Key Personnel
Mng Dir: Anja Koeseling
Founded: 2008
Accept unsolicited manuscripts; submit expose (4-page maximum), curriculum vitae, sample 30 pages & list of publishers & agencies to which text was already available via e-mail (.doc or .pdf attachment). No screenplays, poetry, short stories, tales or picture books.
Specializes in German language fiction, crime, humor, women's interests, fantasy & children's & youth books.

Literarische Agentur Simon
Eisenacher Str 76, 10823 Berlin
Tel: (030) 31518844 *Fax:* (030) 31518855
E-mail: info@agentursimon.com
Web Site: www.agentursimon.com
Key Personnel
Founder & Agent: Alexander Simon
Agent: Gila Keplin; Bettina Kuehn; Hanne Reinhardt
Founded: 1999
Mainly represent German language writers & selected international writers in the fields of fiction & nonfiction. No poetry, straight science fiction & short stories or children's books. Send introductory letter, synopsis of the whole work & first three chapters.

Tipress Deutschland GmbH, see Tipress Dienstleistungen fuer das Verlagswesen GmbH

Tipress Dienstleistungen fuer das Verlagswesen GmbH
Obertalstr 20a, 79295 Sulzburg
Tel: (07634) 591193 *Fax:* (07634) 591192
E-mail: tipress@tipress.com
Web Site: www.tipress.com
Key Personnel
President: Roberto Toso
Founded: 1980
Also packager.
Specializes in co-editions, illustrated books, handbooks, encyclopedias, children's books, film.

UnderCover Literary Agents
Suelzguertel 22, 50937 Cologne
Tel: (0221) 972 55 72; (0221) 972 55 73
  Fax: (0221) 972 56 40
E-mail: info@undercover-koeln.de
Web Site: www.undercover-koeln.de
Founded: 1997
Represents Spanish & Latin-American fiction; trades book rights worldwide. Accept unsolicited manuscripts; submit curriculum vitae, sample chapter & one- to two-page outline with contact info via mail or fax.

UTOPROP Literary Agency/Verlagsservice
Naabstr 23, 40699 Erkrath
Tel: (02104) 390 591
Web Site: www.utoprop.de
Key Personnel
Agent: Werner Fuchs *E-mail:* fuchs@fanpro.com
Founded: 1973
Represents Anglo-American & some German authors of fiction & nonfiction.

Literarische Agentur Silke Weniger
Wuermstr 11a, 82166 Graefelfing
Tel: (089) 89 89 94 90 *Fax:* (089) 89 89 94 929
Web Site: www.litag.de
Key Personnel
Manager: Silke Weniger *E-mail:* weniger@litag.de
Agent, Children's & Young Adult Literature: Alexandra Legath *E-mail:* legath@litag.de
Represents publishers & agencies from English & French-speaking countries.
Specializes in fiction & children's & young adult literature.

The Wittmann Agency
Lutherstr 23, 06886 Lutherstadt Wittenberg
Tel: (03491) 695 1243
E-mail: contact@the-wittmann-agency.com
Web Site: www.the-wittmann-agency.com
Key Personnel
Founder: Claudia Wittmann
Specializes in nonfiction & fiction, including crime & thrillers, psychological suspense, women's fiction, romance & select fiction for children & young adults.

Ghana

Golden Baobab
Ampomah House, 3rd floor, off Obasanjo Highway, Roman Ridge, Accra
Mailing Address: PO Box KD 862, Kanda, Accra
Tel: (030) 2963639
E-mail: info@goldenbaobab.org
Web Site: www.goldenbaobab.org
Key Personnel
Executive Dir: Deborah Ahenkorah
Connects authors to a wide array of top children's publishers in Africa, the USA & the UK. Dedicated to producing enthralling literary content that inspires the imaginations of African children.

Greece

Iris Literary Agency
18, Komotinis St, Thrakomakedones Attiki 136 76
Tel: 210 24 32 473 *Fax:* 210 24 35 042
E-mail: irislit@otenet.gr
Web Site: www.irisliteraryagency.gr
Key Personnel
Owner: Catherine Fragou
Agent: Marcela Hammerly
Assistant: Ellianna Farazi
Founded: 1995
Represents Greek authors in Greece & internationally & foreign publishers in Greece.

Hong Kong

Creative Work
Winsome House, Room 2401, 24/F, 71-73 Wyndham St, Hong Kong
Tel: 2167 8887
Web Site: www.creative-work.com
Key Personnel
Dir: Duncan Jepson; Ilyas Khan; Peter Koenig
Publisher of the *Asia Literary Review*.
Specializes in general fiction & nonfiction, children's & young adult.

Hungary

Artisjus
Meszaros u 15-17, Budapest 1016
Mailing Address: PO Box 593, Budapest 1539
Tel: (01) 488 2600 *Fax:* (01) 212 1544
E-mail: info@artisjus.com
Web Site: www.artisjus.hu
Key Personnel
Dir General: Dr Andras Szinger *Tel:* (01) 488 2601; (01) 488 2602
Agency for theater & literature of the Hungarian Bureau for Copyright Protection.

Katai & Bolza Irodalmi Ugynokseg (Katai & Bolza Literary Agents)
Benczur u 11, Budapest 1068
Mailing Address: PO Box 55, Budapest 1406
Tel: (01) 456-0313 *Fax:* (01) 215-4420
Web Site: www.kataibolza.hu

Key Personnel
Agent: Peter Bolza *E-mail:* peter@kataibolza.hu; Katalin Katai *E-mail:* katalin@kataibolza.hu
Founded: 1995
Represents mainly US, British & Italian publishers & agents in the Hungarian market.

Lex Copyright Iroda
Szemere u 21, Budapest 1054
Tel: (01) 332-9340 *Fax:* (01) 331-6181
E-mail: lexcopy.bp@mail.datanet.hu
Web Site: www.lexcopyright.hu
Key Personnel
Founder: George Szanto
Founded: 1990
Specializes in Hungarian language rights.

India

Bulbul Literary Agency
Gazal-19/1557 P, Kallai Rd, Chalapuram PO, Calicut, Kerala State 673 002
Tel: 9895219697; 9496695147
E-mail: info@bulbulliterary.com; bulbulliterary@gmail.com
Web Site: www.bulbulliterary.com
Key Personnel
Dir: Mr S A Qudsi *E-mail:* saqudsi@gmail.com
Founded: 2005
Foreign rights of bestseller/award-winning Indian novels, story anthology, poems, etc. Translation projects of foreign literature undertaken.
Specializes in Indian fiction rights, translation projects from foreign countries, after sale service.

Dipak Kumar Guha
C1A 115B Janakpuri, New Delhi 110 058
Tel: (011) 25531842 *Fax:* (011) 25541258
E-mail: dkginfo@netvigator.com; dkginfo@gmail.com (Hong Kong office)
Web Site: www.dkginfosystems.com
Founded: 1986
Activities also include market evaluation, promotion & public relations, special sales, excess inventory sales. Now also covering China from Hong Kong office excluding Southeast Asia & South Asia.
Specializes in East/West rights, co-editions, English & regional languages, wire services syndication/hook-ups, magazine syndication & reprint consulting, seek multimedia rights on CDs, multimedia OEM & distribution marketing consulting service.
Parent Company: DKG Info Systems, 17H, Block 4, Parkland Villas, One Tuen On Lane, Tuen Mun, New Territories, Hong Kong

Red Ink Literary Agency
Flat No 6, Khan Market, New Delhi 110 003
E-mail: support@redinkliteraryagency.com
Web Site: www.redinkliteraryagency.com
Key Personnel
Agent: Mr Anuj Bahri

Ireland

Author Rights Agency Ltd
20 Victoria Rd, Dublin D06 DR02
Tel: (01) 49 22 112
Web Site: www.authorrightsagency.com

Key Personnel
Dir: Svetlana Pironko
Specializes in representation of Irish, British & American fiction writers to the world market.

Jonathan Williams Literary Agency
Rosney Mews, Upper Glenageary Rd, Glenageary, Co Dublin
Tel: (01) 2803482 *Fax:* (01) 2803482
Key Personnel
Dir: Jonathan Williams
Founded: 1981
International coupons, return postage appreciated.
Specializes in works by Irish writers or of Irish interest.

Israel

The Book Publishers' Association of Israel, International Promotion & Literary Rights Dept
29 Carlebach St, 67132 Tel Aviv
Mailing Address: PO Box 20123, 61201 Tel Aviv
Tel: (03) 5614121 *Fax:* (03) 5611996
E-mail: info@tbpai.co.il
Web Site: www.tbpai.co.il
Key Personnel
Chairman: Yaron Sadan
Mng Dir: Amnon Ben-Shmuel
Founded: 1939

Chesla Literature
122 Hagolan St, Apartment 8, 69271 Tel Aviv
Tel: (50) 8442703 (cell)
E-mail: mickey@cheslalit.com
Web Site: www.cheslalit.com
Key Personnel
Chief Executive Officer: Michal Chesla
Founded: 2008
Represent Israel's children's authors & illustrators to the international market as well as international children's books to the Israeli market.
Specializes in children's picture books.

The Deborah Harris Agency
9 Yael St, 93502 Jerusalem
Mailing Address: PO Box 8528, 91083 Jerusalem
Tel: (02) 6722143; (02) 6722145 *Fax:* (02) 6725797
Web Site: www.thedeborahharrisagency.com
Key Personnel
Dir: Deborah Harris *E-mail:* deborah@thedeborahharrisagency.com
Mng Editor: Ines Austern Gander *E-mail:* ines@thedeborahharrisagency.com
Foreign Rights Dir: Efrat Lev *Tel:* (02) 5633237 *Fax:* (02) 5618711 *E-mail:* efrat@thedeborahharrisagency.com
Senior Agent: George Eltman *Tel:* (02) 5633237 *Fax:* (02) 5618711 *E-mail:* george@thedeborahharrisagency.com
Agent: Sharon Katz *E-mail:* sharon@thedeborahharrisagency.com; Hadar Makov-Hasson *Tel:* (050) 8224221 *Fax:* (02) 6725797 *E-mail:* hadar@thedeborahharrisagency.com
Literary & Foreign Rights Agent: Rena Rossner *Tel:* (02) 5633237 *Fax:* (02) 5618711 *E-mail:* rena@thedeborahharrisagency.com
Founded: 1991
Represents worldwide publishing & dramatic rights of Israeli, Palestinian & international authors, writers of fiction & nonfiction, including high-profile personalities in the fields of science, business, politics & history. In addition, the agency acts as sub-agents for numerous publishers & agencies overseas for representation to Israeli publishing houses.

The Institute for the Translation of Hebrew Literature (ITHL)
23 Baruch Hirsch St, 5120217 Bnei Brak
Tel: (03) 579 6830 *Fax:* (03) 579 6832
E-mail: litscene@ithl.org.il
Web Site: www.ithl.org.il
Key Personnel
Dir: Nilli Cohen
Founded: 1962
Main activities include promotion of modern Hebrew literature & children's literature in translation; general literary agency services; subsidies to authors & publishers for translation of Hebrew literary works & their publication abroad; assistance in the preparation of anthologies of Hebrew literature.
Specializes in Hebrew literature in translation.

ITHL, see The Institute for the Translation of Hebrew Literature (ITHL)

Italy

Agenzia Letteraria Internazionale, see The Italian Literary Agency SRL (TILA)

S Allegra Literary Agency & Co
Formerly Atena SAS S Allegra Literary Agency & Co
Via Francavilla 371, 98039 Taormina ME
Tel: 3493060250 (cell) *Fax:* (0942) 620079
E-mail: s.allegra.literaryagency@gmail.com
Web Site: www.groupnuovaatena.com/old/LA
Key Personnel
Contact: Prof Stefania Allegra, PhD
Founded: 1969
Treat every aspect of developing & drafting of a manuscript: revision, editing, publishing, translations into any language, etc. Specialize in national & international law contract negotiations with publishers in Italy & abroad. Send (via Word files) a one-page synopsis, whole text ended, one-page biography, identity card or passport & resume in European format. Reading fee charged based on the current market & services requested.

Gabriella Ambrosioni SRL
Via San Giorgio 1, 40121 Bologna BO
Tel: (051) 2961096 *Fax:* (051) 2914000
E-mail: gabriella@gabriellaambrosioni.com
Web Site: www.gabriellaambrosioni.com
Founded: 2002
Agent for foreign agencies & publishers in Italy & Italian authors in Italy & abroad.
Specializes in literary & commercial fiction, children's literature, narrative nonfiction, history, biographies, business, adventure, current affairs, science & medicine.

Argosy Foreign Rights Agency
Via Trentino Alto Adige 15, 30030 Venice VE
Fax: (041) 513 1117
Web Site: argosyagency.com
Key Personnel
Agent: Sarah Katooki *E-mail:* sarahkatooki@argosyagency.com; Caterina da Lisca *E-mail:* caterinadalisca@argosyagency.com; Arantxa Martinez *E-mail:* arantxamartinez@argosyagency.com; Heber Ostroviesky *E-mail:* heber@argosyagency.com
Founded: 2012
Manages foreign rights on behalf of publishers & authors. Focus on Portuguese, Brazilian, Catalan, Latin American & Francophone literary & upmarket fiction.

Atena SAS S Allegra Literary Agency & Co, see S Allegra Literary Agency & Co

Berla & Griffini Rights Agency SRL
Via Stampa, 4, 20123 Milan MI
Tel: (02) 80504179 *Fax:* (02) 89010646
E-mail: info@bgagency.it
Web Site: www.bgagency.it
Key Personnel
Agent: Erica Berla *E-mail:* berla@bgagency.it; Barbara Griffini *E-mail:* griffini@bgagency.it
Founded: 2007
Represents Italian authors worldwide. Represents foreign publishing houses & literary agents in the Italian publishing market.
Specializes in promotion of German, English & Spanish language literature.

Luigi Bernabo Associates SRL, see The Italian Literary Agency SRL (TILA)

Il Caduceo di Marinella Magri
Via Mazzini 72/3, 16031 Bogliasco GE
Tel: (339) 2802814 (cell)
Key Personnel
Owner: Marinella Magri *E-mail:* marinella.magr@gmail.com
Founded: 2002
Represents foreign authors & agents & publishers in Italy.

Caminito SAS
Corso Roma, 24, 20811 Cesano Maderno MB
Tel: (0362) 546258 *Fax:* (02) 70030684
E-mail: agora@caminito.biz
Web Site: www.caminito.biz
Key Personnel
Mng Dir: Ivan Giovannucci
Represents foreign publishing houses & literary agents in the Italian publishing market. Also represents: Quino, Grazia Nidasio, Enzo d'Alo, Andrea Valente, Carlo Carzan & more.

Donzelli Fietta Literary Agency
Viale Abruzzi 11, 20131 Milan MI
E-mail: info@donzellifiettaagency.com
Web Site: www.donzellifiettaagency.com
Key Personnel
Owner & Agent: Silvia Donzelli *Tel:* (333) 4736284 (cell) *E-mail:* silvia@donzellifiettaagency.com; Stefania Fietta *Tel:* (339) 2541650 (cell) *E-mail:* stefania@donzellifiettaagency.com
Founded: 2013
Specializes in narrative nonfiction.

Kylee Doust Agency
via Flaminia 61, 00196 Rome RM
Tel: (06) 99345171 *Fax:* (06) 99335374
Web Site: kyleedoustagency.com
Key Personnel
Founder & Agent: Kylee Doust *E-mail:* kylee@kyleedoustagency.com
Agent & Foreign Rights: Laura Ceccacci *E-mail:* laura@kyleedoustagency.com
Agent: Francesca Mancini *E-mail:* francesca@kyleedoustagency.com
Founded: 2003
Represents Italian authors of fiction in Italy & abroad.

Eulama Literary Agencies
Via Guido de Ruggiero 28, 00142 Rome RM
Tel: (06) 5407309 *Fax:* (06) 5407309
E-mail: info@eulama.com
Web Site: www.eulama.com
Key Personnel
Chief Executive Officer & President: Pina Ocello von Prellwitz
Dir: Norbert von Prellwitz
Founded: 1962

Also translation agency.
Specializes in history, philosophy, psychology, fiction, religion, social sciences, Spanish & Latin-American literature.
Branch Office(s)
Eulama SRL, Germany

Find Out Team SRL
Corso Felice Cavallotti, 29, 28100 Novara NO
Tel: (0321) 16 44 015
E-mail: info@findout-team.com
Web Site: www.findout-team.com
Key Personnel
General Manager: Cinzia Seccamani
Art Dir: Paolo Cubadda
Rights Manager: Laura Cianolini; Yangyu Sun
Represents international publishers, authors & illustrators in children's & young adult publishing worldwide.

Grandi & Associati SRL
Via Degli Olivetani 12, 20123 Milan MI
Tel: (02) 4818962 *Fax:* (02) 48195108
E-mail: agenzia@grandieassociati.it
Web Site: www.grandieassociati.it
Key Personnel
Agent: Laura Grandi; Maria Paola Romeo; Stefano Tettamanti
Administration: Irina Focsaneanu; Mara Franchini
Foreign Rights: Agnese Fabbri *E-mail:* agnese. fabbri@grandieassociati.it
Founded: 1988
Represents writers & acts as a subagent for selected publishing houses & agencies outside Italy. Sells foreign rights & acts as a consultant for various Italian publishing houses.

The Italian Literary Agency SRL (TILA)
Via De Amicis 53, 20123 Milan MI
Tel: (02) 862445 *Fax:* (02) 876222
Web Site: www.italianliterary.com
Key Personnel
President/Chairperson: Chiara Boroli
Chief Executive Officer: Marco Vigevani
Mng Dir/Chief Operating Officer: Claire Sabatie-Garat
Founded: 2015
Specializes in general adult fiction, children's fiction, educational material, general fiction & nonfiction.

Elena Kostioukovitch Agency
via Bronzino 8, 20133 Milan MI
Tel: (02) 87236557 *Fax:* 700444601
E-mail: elkost@elkost.com
Web Site: www.elkost.com
Key Personnel
Chief Executive Officer & Agent: Elena Kostioukovitch
Founded: 2000
Worldwide agent of most famous Russian writers.
Specializes in Russian literary & commercial fiction, popular nonfiction & history.
Branch Office(s)
Moskovskaya oblast, gorod Pushkino, mkr Serebrianka, d 48, k 1, kv 118, 141202 Moscow, Russia, Contact: Natalia Tsarkova *Tel:* (915) 1974570 *E-mail:* post.nat@mail.ru
c/Londres, 78, 6-1, 08036 Barcelona, Spain, Contact: Yulia Dobrovolskaya *Tel:* 639413320; 933221232 *E-mail:* rights@elkost.com

Silvia Meucci Literary Agency
Via Pietro Colletta, 10, 20135 Milan MI
Web Site: www.meucciagency.com
Key Personnel
Proprietor: Silvia Meucci *E-mail:* silvia@ meucciagency.com
Partner: Alberto Suarez *E-mail:* alberto@ meucciagency.com

Founded: 2012
Representing Spanish authors in Italy & Italian international authors in Italy & abroad.

Nabu Agenzia Letteraria Internazionale
via San Romano 60, 50135 Florence FI
E-mail: staff@nabu.it
Web Site: www.nabu.it
Key Personnel
Founder: Silvia Brunelli
Founded: 1989
Specializes in literary fiction & geopolitical nonfiction.

Natoli Stefan & Oliva Literary Agency
Corso Plebisciti, 12, 20129 Milan MI
Key Personnel
Partner: Roberta Oliva *E-mail:* roberta.oliva@ natoli.191.it
Founded: 1962
Handles foreign publishers & agents' authors in Italy & Italian authors in Italy & worldwide.

Perroni&Morli Studio
Via Guardiola Vecchia, 36, 98039 Taormina
Tel: (0942) 23347
E-mail: info@morli.it
Web Site: www.morli.it/agenzia-letteraria.html

Piergiorgio Nicolazzini Literary Agency (PNLA)
via G B Moroni 22, 20146 Milan MI
Tel: (02) 83420192 *Fax:* (02) 83420192
E-mail: info@pnla.it
Web Site: www.pnla.it
Key Personnel
Owner: Piergiorgio Nicolazzini
E-mail: piergiorgio.nicolazzini@pnla.it
Founded: 1999
Represents publishers, agents & authors in Italy & abroad.
Specializes in fiction & nonfiction.

PNLA, see Piergiorgio Nicolazzini Literary Agency (PNLA)

RCS Libri SpA
Subsidiary of RCS MediaGroup SpA
Via Angelo Rizzoli, 8, 20132 Milan MI
Tel: (02) 25841 *Fax:* (02) 50952647 (rights)
Web Site: www.rcsmediagroup.it; www.foreign-rights.rcslibri.it
Key Personnel
Rights Dir: Giovanna Canton *E-mail:* giovanna. canton@rcs.it
Press Contact: Annamaria Guadagni *Tel:* (06) 8448 4337 *E-mail:* annamaria.guadagni@rcs.it
Also publisher & major bookseller.
Specializes in literature, fiction, essays, art & history.

Agenzia Letteraria Loredana Rotundo
Via Sant'Angelo 3, 20037 Paderno Dugnano MI
Tel: (02) 99041699 *Fax:* (02) 91089084
E-mail: info@lrliteraryagency.com
Web Site: www.lrliteraryagency.com
Representing Italian authors worldwide & foreign publishers & agencies in Italy & worldwide.

Vicki Satlow Literary Agency
Via Cenisio 16, 20154 Milan MI
Tel: (02) 48015553
E-mail: vickisatlow@tin.it
Key Personnel
President: Vicki Satlow
Founded: 1999
Sell translation rights & represents authors.
Specializes in fiction & narrative nonfiction.

Agenzia Servizi Editoriali
Via Livorno 515/c 9, 20099 Sesto San Giovanni MI
Tel: (02) 2408204
E-mail: info@serv-ed.it
Web Site: www.serv-ed.it
Key Personnel
Foreign Rights: Guido Lagomarsino
E-mail: guido@serv-ed.it
Agent for foreign publishing houses in Italy & international translation rights on behalf of several Italian & foreign publishers. No unsolicited manuscripts.
Specializes in children's, cinema, fiction, literary fiction, nonfiction, travel & young adult.

Thesis Contents Agenzia Letteraria
Via Reginaldo Giuliani 88, 50141 Florence FI
Tel: (055) 4223786 *Fax:* (055) 4223791
Web Site: www.thesis.it
Key Personnel
Agent: Tiziana Arrighi *E-mail:* tarrighi@thesis. it; Maria Cristina Guerra *E-mail:* mcguerra@ thesis.it
Representing authors in Italian & international markets.
Branch Office(s)
Via M Giuntini 62, 56023 Cascina PI *Tel:* (0339) 7594315
Via Carlo Osma 2, 20151 Milan MI *Tel:* (02) 3083913 *Fax:* (02) 38000086

Ultreya SRL
Piazza Grandi 9, 20129 Milan MI
Tel: (02) 5691460 *Fax:* (02) 56610357
E-mail: ultreya@ultreya.it
Web Site: www.ultreya.it
Specializes in art, fine photograhy & architecture.

Marco Vigevani Agenzia Letteraria, see The Italian Literary Agency SRL (TILA)

R Vivian Literary Agency
Piazzale Mazzini, 43, 35137 Padova PD
Tel: (049) 8761273
Web Site: www.rvivianliteraryagency.com
Key Personnel
Founder: Rita Vivian *E-mail:* rita.vivian@alice.it
Represents Italian authors in domestic & international markets & foreign agencies & publishers in Italy.

Susanna Zevi Agenzia Letteraria
Via Appiani, 19, 20121 Milan MI
Tel: (02) 6570863 *Fax:* (02) 6570915
E-mail: office@agenzia-zevi.it; segretaria@ agenzia-zevi.it
Web Site: www.susannazevi.com
Key Personnel
Agent: Susanna Zevi *E-mail:* susanna@szevi.it
Represents US, European & Israeli agents & publishers for Italian translation rights & individual authors worldwide.

Japan

The Asano Agency Inc
44-8-302, Sengoku, 4-chome, Bunkyo-ku, Tokyo 112-0011
Tel: (03) 39434171; (03) 39434314 *Fax:* (03) 39437637
Key Personnel
President: Kiyoshi Asano *E-mail:* kiyoshi@asano-agency.com
Founded: 1988

The English Agency (Japan) Ltd
Sakuragi Bldg 4F, 6-7-3 Minami Aoyama,
  Minato-ku, Tokyo 107-0062
Tel: (03) 3406 5385 *Fax:* (03) 3406 5387
E-mail: info@eaj.co.jp
Web Site: www.eajco.jp
Key Personnel
Dir: Junzo Sawa *E-mail:* junzo_sawa@eaj.co.jp
Representative Dir & Mng Dir: Hamish Macaskill
  E-mail: hamish@eaj.co.jp
Representative Dir: Peter Thompson
Dir & Agent, Adult Books: Atsushi Hori
  E-mail: atsushi.hori@eaj.co.jp
Agent, Adult & Academic Books: Tsutomu
  Yawata *E-mail:* tsutomu_yawata@eaj.co.jp
Agent, Adult Books: Kohei Hattori *E-mail:* kohei.
  hattori@eaj.co.jp
Agent, Business & Children's Books: Noriko
  Hasegawa *E-mail:* noriko@eaj.co.jp
Agent, Children's Books: Corinne Shioji
  E-mail: corinne@eaj.co.jp
UK Representative: Louise Allen-Jones *Tel:* (020)
  2220 2453 *E-mail:* louise@louiseallenjones.
  com
US Representative: Liz Gately *Tel:* 917-374-3864
  E-mail: liz@lizgately.com
Founded: 1979
Sales of book & ancillary rights for translation
  mainly into Japanese; author's agent for books
  with international appeal by writers living in or
  frequently visiting Japan.

Japan Foreign-Rights Centre (JFC)
Sun Mall No 3, Room 201, 1-19-10 Shinjuku,
  Shinjuku-ku, Tokyo 160-0022
Tel: (03) 3226-2711 *Fax:* (03) 3226-2714
Key Personnel
President & Chief Executive Officer: Yurika
  Yokota Yoshida
Founded: 1981 (as Kurita-Bando Literary
  Agency)
Specializes in foreign rights to Japanese books,
  co-production, packaging.

Japan UNI Agency Inc
Tokyodo-Jinbocho, No 2 Bldg, 1-27 Kanda Jinbo-
  cho, Chiyoda-ku, Tokyo 101-0051
Tel: (03) 32950301 *Fax:* (03) 32945173
E-mail: info@japanuni.co.jp
Web Site: www.japanuni.co.jp
Key Personnel
President & Executive Dir: Miko Yamanouchi
  E-mail: miko.yamanouchi@japanuni.co.jp
Dir: Miyoko Sakata; Masaru Suzuki
Founded: 1967

JFC, see Japan Foreign-Rights Centre (JFC)

Motovun Co Ltd, Tokyo
Coop Nomura Ichibancho, No 103, 15-6 Ichiban-
  cho, Chiyoda-ku, Tokyo 102-0082
Tel: (03) 3261-4002 *Fax:* (03) 3264-1443
Key Personnel
President: Mari Koga *E-mail:* koga_motovun@
  mbd.ocn.ne.jp
Dir: Norio Irie *E-mail:* irie_motovun@mbd.ocn.
  ne.jp
Founded: 1983
Firm sells rights & co-production between foreign
  publishers & Japanese publishers.

Owls Agency Inc
Ganshodo Bldg, 1-7 Kanda Jinbocho, Chiyoda-
  ku, Tokyo 101-0051
Tel: (03) 3259-0061 *Fax:* (03) 3259-0063
E-mail: info@owlsagency.com
Web Site: www.owlsagency.com
Founded: 2001
Author management & sale of domestic & for-
  eign rights.

The Sakai Agency Inc
1-58-4F Kanda-Jimbo-cho, Chiyoda-ku, Tokyo
  101-0051
Tel: (03) 32951405 *Fax:* (03) 32954366
E-mail: info@sakaiagency.com
Key Personnel
Contact: Harumi Sakai
Founded: 1952
Specializes in publishing, theatrical, audiovisual
  & merchandising rights.

Tuttle-Mori Agency Inc
Kanda Jimbocho Bldg, 4th floor, 2-17 Kanda-
  Jimbocho, Chiyoda-ku, Tokyo 101-0051
Tel: (03) 3230-4081 *Fax:* (03) 3234-5249
Web Site: www.tuttlemori.com
Key Personnel
President: Ken Mori
Executive Dir: Yoshikazu Iwasaki
Dir: Yasuko Mori; Chigusa Ogino
Specializes in book rights, serial rights, co-
  productions, motion picture, TV, radio & stage
  rights, merchandising rights.
Branch Office(s)
55 Earl's Court Sq, Flat 17, London SW5 9DG,
  United Kingdom, Contact: Nina Martyn
  Tel: (020) 7373-2018 *Fax:* (020) 7286-8629
Foreign Rep(s): Anne Martyn & Nina Martyn;
  Carol Frederick

Malaysia

**Yusof Gajah Lingard Literary Agency Sdn
Bhd**
24-2 Medan Setia 2, Plaza Damansara,
  Damansara Heights, 50490 Kuala Lumpur
Tel: (03) 2092 5626 *Fax:* (03) 2093 1241
Web Site: www.yusofgajahlingard.com
Key Personnel
Principal: Yusof Gajah
Mng Partner: Linda Tan Lingard
  E-mail: lindalingard@yusofgajahlingard.com
Dir: Zakiah Mohd Isa
Founded: 2009
Represents writers, illustrators & publishers for
  international rights.
Specializes in children & young adult books, fic-
  tion & nonfiction.

Netherlands

ILB, see Internationaal Literatuur Bureau (ILB)

IMR Agency Worldwide BV
PO Box 23454, 3001 KL Rotterdam
Tel: (065) 348 7159 *Fax:* (010) 436 6103
E-mail: info@imrights.com
Web Site: www.imrights.com
Represents English & American medical publish-
  ers.
Specializes in translation rights services.

Internationaal Literatuur Bureau (ILB)
Keizersgracht 188-hs, 1016 DW Amsterdam
Tel: (020) 3306658 *Fax:* (020) 4229210
Web Site: www.lindakohn.nl
Key Personnel
Chief Executive: Linda Kohn *E-mail:* lkohn@
  planet.nl

The Rights Company
Jekerstr 28, 6211 NT Maastricht
Tel: (06) 81 15 93 02

E-mail: books@therightscompany.nl
Web Site: www.therightscompany.nl
Key Personnel
Owner: Cecile Oomen
Founded: 2000
Represents worldwide rights of selective titles
  from German & Dutch authors.

Marianne Schoenbach Literary Agency BV
Rokin 44 III, 1012 KV Amsterdam
Tel: (020) 62 000 20 *Fax:* (020) 62 404 50
E-mail: info@schonbach.nl
Web Site: www.schonbach.nl
Key Personnel
Founder & Agent: Marianne Schoenbach
  E-mail: m.schonbach@schonbach.nl
Agent: Diana Gvozden; Ageeth Heising
  E-mail: a.heising@schonbach.nl; Neeltje Smit-
  skamp *E-mail:* n.smitskamp@schonbach.nl
Foreign Rights: Stien van Waardt *E-mail:* s.van.
  waardt@schonbach.nl
Founded: 2001
Representing Dutch publishers & authors &
  Dutch translation rights in Netherlands &
  Flemish Belgium on behalf of literary agencies
  & publishing houses in Europe & overseas.

Sebes & Bisseling Literary Agency
Herengracht 162, 1016 BP Amsterdam
Tel: (020) 6160940
E-mail: office@sebes.nl
Web Site: www.sebes.nl
Key Personnel
Founder: Paul Sebes
Agent: Willem Bisseling; Jeanine Langenberg
Agent & Contracts Manager: Lester George
  Hekking
Founded: 1998
Represents Dutch authors & acts as sub-agent for
  Anglo-Saxon authors on behalf of their original
  publishers. Also represents English-speaking
  authors on behalf of their primary agent or
  publisher, usually in the UK or USA. Accept
  unsolicited manuscripts; submit proposal &
  partial manuscript via e-mail. See web site for
  complete manuscript & proposal guidelines.
Specializes in fiction & nonfiction for the general
  adult & children's market.

Servire BV Uitgevers
Herculesplein 96, Stadionzijde, 3584 AA Utrecht
Mailing Address: Postbus 13288, 3507 LG
  Utrecht
Tel: (088) 700 2600 *Fax:* (088) 700 2999
E-mail: info@kosmosuitgevers.nl
Web Site: www.servire.nl; www.kosmosuitgevers.
  nl
Founded: 1921
Also publisher.
Specializes in psychology, health & spirituality.

Alice Toledo, see Toledo Creative Management

Toledo Creative Management
Binnenkant 20-D, 1011 BH Amsterdam
Tel: (020) 622 68 73; (06) 55 71 6123 (cell)
E-mail: toledo.alice@gmail.com
Web Site: www.toledo-cm.nl
Founded: 1991
Literary, TV & film agency. Represents Dutch
  authors.

New Zealand

Gilbert Literary & Film Agency International
Subsidiary of Hawkspurr Productions
3859 Danseys Pass Rd, RD2, Ranfurly, Otago
  9396

Tel: (03) 4449893 *Fax:* (03) 4449893
E-mail: gilbertliteraryagency@gmail.com;
  acquisitions@gilbertliteraryagency.com;
  hawkspurrproductions@gmail.com
Web Site: www.gilbertliteraryagency.com; www.
  gilbertliteraryagencyauthors.com
Key Personnel
Owner: Emerantia Antonia Parnall-Gilbert, Esq;
  E A M Parnall-Gilbert, MA; Mr M E J Parnall-
  Gilbert
Associate Partner: Miles Francis Parnall-Gilbert,
  MA; Nigel John Parnall-Gilbert
Founded: 1990
International literary & film agency based in New
  Zealand offering client representation. Welcomes submissions from international prospec-
  tive clientele based in USA, Canada, UK,
  Europe, Asia & Australia. Offers free proofreading & line editing/professional screenplay
  adaptation services; in-depth manuscript assessments covering areas such as characterization,
  plot, settings, dialogue & style.
Manuscript submissions must be accompanied by
  author's name, contact address, contact e-mail,
  synopsis, overview & completed manuscript
  (in basic Word document or RTF format as per
  attachment); CDs also accepted.
Specializes in film representation; fiction (including children's, young adult, fantasy, romance & crime, literary fiction, general fiction,
  women's popular fiction, gay & lesbian, sci-fi
  fantasy/horror & sci-fi adult/fantasy/thriller);
  nonfiction (including autobiography, life story,
  biography, short story collections & poetry volumes).

Playmarket
35 Cambridge Terrace, Suite 4, Te Aro, Welling-
  ton 6011
Mailing Address: PO Box 9767, Wellington 6141
Tel: (04) 382 8462
E-mail: info@playmarket.org.nz
Web Site: www.playmarket.org.nz
Key Personnel
Dir: Murray Lynch *Tel:* (04) 382 8464
  E-mail: director@playmarket.org.nz
Publication & Event Coordinator: Salesi Le'ota
  E-mail: sal@playmarket.org.nz
Founded: 1973
New Zealand's playwrights' agency & script ad-
  visory service.

Richards Literary Agency
PO Box 31-240, Milford, Auckland 0741
Tel: (09) 4100209 *Fax:* (09) 4100209
E-mail: rla.richards@clear.net.nz
Key Personnel
Owner & Agent: Ray Richards
Associate: Judy Bartlam
Founded: 1977
Specializes in young adult & adult: fiction, non-
  fiction, educational, academic. Rights available:
  films, television, stage, radio.

Nigeria

Kris Literary Agency
34 Oguntona Crescent, Phase 1, Gbagada Estate,
  Lagos
Tel: (0806) 7628017
Key Personnel
Chief Executive Officer: Chris Agada
Founded: 2009
No reading fee. Also copy & manuscript editing.

Norway

Aschehoug Agency
Sehestedsgate 3, 0164 Oslo
Mailing Address: Postboks 363 Sentrum, 0102
  Oslo
E-mail: epost@aschehougagency.no
Web Site: www.aschehougagency.no
Key Personnel
Rights Dir: Even Rakil *Tel:* 22 90 02 44 97
  E-mail: even.rakil@aschehougagency.no
Founded: 2004
Represents authors of Aschehoug, Forlaget Okto-
  ber, Universitetsforlaget & individual authors.
Specializes in fiction, children's & young adults'
  books, crime, biographies & nonfiction.

Hagen Agency
Ullevalsvn 55, 0171 Oslo
Tel: 22 46 52 54; 93 41 10 56
E-mail: hagency@online.no
Web Site: www.hagenagency.no
Key Personnel
Agent: Eirin Hagen
Founded: 2005
Specializes in fiction & children's books, in addi-
  tion to selected nonfiction, including academic
  literature.

Poland

Agencja Literacka Book/lab (Book/lab Literary
  Agency)
Kurhan 18/8, 02-203 Warsaw
Tel: (22) 646 58 60 *Fax:* (22) 646 58 60
E-mail: agencja@literatura.com.pl
Web Site: www.literatura.com.pl; www.facebook.
  com/booklabagency
Key Personnel
Chief Executive Officer & Agent: Aleksandra
  Lapinska
Mng Dir & Agent: Renata Paczewska
Financial Dir: Monika Zelechowska
Agent: Patrycja Swiat; Piotr Wawrzenczyk; Agata
  Zabowska
Founded: 1996

Agencja Literacka Graal (Graal Literary
  Agency)
ul Pruszkowska 29, lok 252, 02-119 Warsaw
Tel: (22) 895-2000 *Fax:* (22) 895-2001
E-mail: info@graal.com.pl
Web Site: www.graal.com.pl
Key Personnel
Owner: Maria Kanski; Zbigniew Kanski
Founded: 1993
Representing authors, publishers & literary agen-
  cies in Eastern Europe & Eastern European
  authors worldwide.

Macadamia Literary Agency
ul Kobielska 23 m 66, 04-359 Warsaw
Tel: (79) 393 03 60
E-mail: info@macadamialit.com
Web Site: macadamialit.com
Key Personnel
Literary Agent: Magda Cabajewska
  E-mail: magda@macadamialit.com; Maria Ka-
  bat *E-mail:* maria@macadamialit.com; Kamila
  Kanafa *E-mail:* kamila@macadamialit.com
Founded: 2013
Accepts manuscripts in Polish & English only.
For fiction, submit query letter (including genre
  & word count), full manuscript, complete syn-
  opsis (1-2 pages), brief note on why book was
  written & target reader, short author bio.

For nonfiction, submit query letter, full
  manuscript or book proposal with table of contents & sample chapters, brief note on why
  book was written & target reader, short author
  bio.
Do not send more than one manuscript. Accept e-
  mail queries only.

Polish Rights
ul Kochanowskiego 19/1, 31-127 Krakow
Web Site: polishrights.com
Key Personnel
Agent: Magdalena Debowska *E-mail:* debowska@
  polishrights.com
Founded: 2008
Translation rights for contemporary Polish litera-
  ture.

Romania

**Simona Kessler International Copyright
  Agency Ltd**
Str Banul Antonache 37, 011663 Bucharest
Tel: (021) 316 48 06 *Fax:* (021) 316 47 94
Key Personnel
President: Simona Kessler *E-mail:* simona@
  kessler-agency.ro
Founded: 1994
Specializes in subsidiary rights.

Livia Stoia Literary Agency
58 Garlei Str, 013724 Bucharest
Tel: (021) 2329909 *Fax:* (021) 2329909
E-mail: office@liviastoiaagency.ro
Web Site: www.liviastoiaagency.ro
Key Personnel
Mng Dir: Livia Stoia *E-mail:* livia.stoia@
  liviastoiaagency.ro
Agent: Mirela Calota *E-mail:* mirela.calota@
  liviastoiaagency.ro; Cristiana Lazareanu
  E-mail: cristiana.lazareanu@liviastoiaagency.ro
Founded: 2003
Represents (in Romania) publishers, literary agen-
  cies & authors from Australia, Canada, Den-
  mark, France, Germany, Holland, Israel, Italy,
  Latin America, Russia, Serbia, Spain & the
  UK.
Also provides market analysis on the Romanian
  publishing field.

Russia

Libright
Blvd General Karbysheva 18/3 off 58, 123154
  Moscow
Tel: (926) 255 15 36
Web Site: www.libright.ru
Key Personnel
Chief Executive Officer & Mng Partner: Nadya
  Kazakova *E-mail:* kazakova@libright.ru
Mng Partner: Tatyana Doump *E-mail:* doump@
  libright.ru
Founded: 2009
Specializes in business & nonfiction.

Limbus Press Literary Agency
Izmaylovsky pr 14, 190005 St Petersburg
Tel: (0812) 712-65-47 *Fax:* (0812) 712-67-06
E-mail: limbus.foreign.rights@gmail.com; limb@
  limbuspress.ru
Web Site: www.limbus-press.ru
Key Personnel
Dir: Olga Tublin *E-mail:* o_tublin@limbuspress.ru
Founded: 1988

Represents Russian language authors from Russian publishing houses.
Specializes in translation rights.

RAO, see Rossijskoye Avtorskoye Obshestvo

Rossijskoye Avtorskoye Obshestvo (Russian Authors' Society)
6A-1 Bolshaya Bronnaya St, GSP-3, 125993 Moscow
Tel: (495) 6973777; (495) 6973260 *Fax:* (495) 6099363
E-mail: rao@rao.ru
Web Site: www.rao.ru
Key Personnel
General Dir: Sergey S Fedotov *E-mail:* s. fedotov@rao.ru
Dir, International Relations: Ivan Zadorozhniy *E-mail:* i.zadorozhniy@rao.ru
Dir, Rights & Permissions Dept: Inna I Voznesenskaya *E-mail:* i.voznesenskaya@rao.ru
Founded: 1993
Literary & grand rights, Internet, mechanical & musical rights; licensing of TV & radio stations.
Specializes in collective management of authors' rights.

Serbia

Plima Literary Agency
Branka Copica 20, PO Box 6, 11160 Belgrade
Tel: (011) 304 6386 *Fax:* (011) 304 6386
Web Site: www.plimaliterary.rs
Key Personnel
Dir: Mila Perisic *E-mail:* mila@plimaliterary.rs
Rights Consultant: Vuk Perisic *E-mail:* vuk@plimaliterary.rs
Founded: 2004
Represents British, American, Australian, German, French, Spanish & Italian authors in Eastern Europe, with a focus on Balkan countries.

Prava i prevodi
Blvd Mihaila Pupina 10B/I, 5th floor, 11070 Belgrade
Tel: (011) 311 9880 *Fax:* (011) 311 9879
E-mail: office@pravaiprevodi.org
Web Site: www.pravaiprevodi.org
Key Personnel
Chief Executive Officer & President: Jovan Milenkovic *E-mail:* jovan@pravaiprevodi.org
Vice President: Predrag Milenkovic *E-mail:* predrag@pravaiprevodi.org
Mng Dir: Suzana Kocic
Dir, Rights: Ana Milenkovic *E-mail:* ana@pravaiprevodi.org
Rights Manager: Milena Kaplarevic *E-mail:* milena@pravaiprevodi.org
Represents authors in countries of the former Yugoslavia: Bosnia and Herzegovina, Croatia, Macedonia, Montenegro, Serbia & Slovenia.

Slovakia

LITA Autorska Spolocnost (LITA Society of Authors)
Mozartova 9, 810 01 Bratislava
Mailing Address: PO Box 28, 810 01 Bratislava
Tel: (02) 6720 9301 *Fax:* (02) 6280 2246
E-mail: lita@lita.sk
Web Site: www.lita.sk

Key Personnel
Dir: Magdalena Debnarova *Tel:* (02) 6720 9302
E-mail: debnarova@lita.sk
Founded: 1993
Collective management organization representing authors of literary, dramatic, audiovisual works, works of visual arts & photography.
Membership(s): CISAC; EVA; IFRRO; SAA.

South Korea

Imprima Korea Agency
4F, GNC Media Bldg, 156-4 Donggyo-ro, Mapo-gu, Seoul 04031
Tel: (02) 325-9155 *Fax:* (02) 334-9160
E-mail: imprima@imprima.co.kr
Web Site: www.imprima.co.kr
Key Personnel
Dir & Chief Operating Officer: Terry Kim *E-mail:* terrykim@imprima.co.kr
President: Hong Sung-Il
Founded: 1992

Duran Kim Agency
2F Taeyang Bldg, 263 Hyoryeong-ro, Seocho-gu, Seoul 06653
Tel: (02) 583-5724; (02) 583-5725 *Fax:* (02) 584-5724
E-mail: duran@durankim.com
Web Site: www.durankim.com
Key Personnel
President: Duran Kim
Founded: 2001
Represents books, films & multimedia.

Korea Copyright Center Inc
Gyonghigung-achim 3 Officetel Room 520, 34, Sajik-ro 8-gil, Jongno-gu, Seoul 110-872
Tel: (02) 725-3350 *Fax:* (02) 725-3612
E-mail: kcc@kccseoul.com
Web Site: www.kccseoul.com
Founded: 1990
Specializes in book rights, serial rights, co-productions, CD-ROM & video rights.

Orange Agency
624 Suji Charmant, B/D, 410 Poeundaero, Suji-gu, Yongin-si, Gyeonggi-do 448-170
Tel: (031) 262 8623 *Fax:* (031) 262 8624
E-mail: orangeagency@paran.com
Web Site: www.orangeagency.co.kr
Key Personnel
Chief Executive Officer: Muriel Park *E-mail:* muriel@orangeagency.co.kr
Senior Agent: K Yun *E-mail:* yun@orangeagency.co.kr
Founded: 2003
Specializes in European publications, importing books published in Europe & exporting & intermediating copyrights of Koren comics & graphic novels to European countries.

Shinwon Agency
373-3 Seogyo-dong, Mapo-gu, Seoul 121-839
Tel: (02) 335-6388 *Fax:* (02) 335-6389
E-mail: main@shinwonagency.co.kr
Web Site: www.shinwonagency.co.kr
Key Personnel
Mng Dir: Kim Soon-Eung
Rights Manager: Tae Eun Kim *E-mail:* tae2k@shinwonagency.co.kr
Founded: 1986
Literary agency & editorial production.

Time-Space Inc
3F Jijunghae Bldg, 43-3, Pildong-1ga, Jung-gu, Seoul 100-866

Tel: (02) 2272 2381 *Fax:* (02) 2273 8900
Web Site: www.timespace.co.kr
Key Personnel
Chief Executive Officer: Song-Mok Choi
Contact: Steve Lee
Founded: 1985
Specialize in stock photography & royalty free CD-ROM.
Specializes in photography, arts.

Eric Yang Agency
3F, E-Bldg 20, Seochojungang-ro 33-gil, Seocho-gu, Seoul 06593
Tel: (02) 592-3356 *Fax:* (02) 592-3359
E-mail: info@ericyangagency.co.kr
Web Site: www.ericyangagency.co.kr
Key Personnel
President: Sue Yang *E-mail:* sueyang@eyagency.com
Founded: 1995
Import & export intellectual properties.
Branch Office(s)
No 802, Kuntai B/D No 10, Chaowai Dajie, Beijing 100-020, China, Li Fei *Tel:* (010) 6522-2778; (010) 6528-7756 *E-mail:* eyabeijing@eyagency.com

Spain

ACER Agencia Literaria
Amor de Dios, 1, 28014 Madrid
Tel: 91 369 20 61 *Fax:* 91 369 20 52
E-mail: contacta@acerliteraria.com
Web Site: www.acerliteraria.com
Key Personnel
Dir: Elizabeth Atkins *Tel:* 91 369 46 75
E-mail: eatkins@acerliteraria.com
Agent: Laure Merle d'Aubigne *E-mail:* lma@acerliteraria.com
Founded: 1959

AMV Agencia Literaria
Calle de las Maldonadas, 9, 2° dcha, 28005 Madrid
Tel: 913 652 516; 913 642 925 *Fax:* 913 640 700
E-mail: info@amvagencialiteraria.com; rights@amvagencialiteraria.com
Web Site: www.amvagencialiteraria.com
Key Personnel
Partner: Anne-Marie Vallat
Dir: Eduardo Melon Vallat *E-mail:* eduardo@amvagencialiteraria.com
Rights Assistant: Giovanna Carlotta Intra
Founded: 1995
Represents French authors for publication rights & sale to Spanish & Portuguese-speaking countries, Spanish & Portuguese authors to other countries. No unsolicited manuscripts.

Agencia Literaria Carmen Balcells SA
Av Diagonal 580, 08021 Barcelona
Tel: 932 008 933
E-mail: info@agenciabalcells.com
Web Site: www.agenciabalcells.com
Key Personnel
Dir General: Lluis Miguel Palomares Balcells
Mng Dir: Javier Martin
Agent & Literary Manager: Gloria Gutierrez
Authors' Agent & Reading Dept Coordinator: Ramon Conesa
Authors' Agent: Teresa Pinto; Carina Pons
Agent, International Dept: Ivette Antoni; Anna Bofill

Silvia Bastos SL - Agencia Literaria
C/ Girona 24, 4°, 3a, 08010 Barcelona
Tel: 932 654 165 *Fax:* 932 657 610

E-mail: correo@silviabastos.com
Web Site: www.silviabastos.com
Key Personnel
Agent: Silvia Bastos Simmersbach
Spanish & Foreign Rights: Pau Centellas
Founded: 2000
Representing authors, especially Spanish & Catalan, all over the world & foreign literary agencies & publishers in Spain, Brazil & Portugal.

Bookbank SL Agencia Literaria
San Martin de Porres, 14, 28035 Madrid
Tel: 91 373 3539 *Fax:* 91 316 5591
E-mail: info@bookbank.es
Web Site: www.bookbank.es
Key Personnel
Dir: Alicia Gonzalez Sterling
Founded: 1986
Represents Spanish authors in Spain & worldwide.
Specializes in fiction for adults, children & young adults; nonfiction, from academic essays to popular science & general nonfiction.

Brandt New Agency
Calandries 5, local 1, 08034 Barcelona
Tel: 930073545 *Fax:* 666656654
E-mail: info@brandtnewagency.com
Web Site: www.brandtnewagency.com
Key Personnel
Agent: Carina Brandt
Represents authors of literary & commercial fiction worldwide. Accept unsolicited manuscripts in Swedish, Norwegian & Danish. Send synopsis & personal letter.

Sandra Bruna Agencia Literaria
Placa Gal-la Placida, 2 5° 2a, 08006 Barcelona
Tel: 932177406
E-mail: jbruna@sandrabruna.com
Web Site: www.sandrabruna.com
Key Personnel
Founder & Dir: Sandra Bruna *E-mail:* sbruna@sandrabruna.com
Founded: 2001
Represents national & international authors as well as foreign agencies & publishing houses in Spain, Brazil, Portugal & South America.

Casanovas & Lynch Literary Agency
(Casanovas & Lynch Agencia Literaria)
Mutaner, 340, 2° 1a, 08021 Barcelona
Tel: 932124791 *Fax:* 932092239
E-mail: info@casanovaslynch.com
Web Site: www.casanovaslynch.com
Key Personnel
Agent: Mercedes Casanovas *E-mail:* mercedes@casanovaslynch.com; Maria Lynch *E-mail:* maria@casanovaslynch.com; Marina Penalva
Represents Spanish & Latin American authors, foreign publishers & agents.

DOSPASSOS Agencia Literaria y Comunicacion
C/ Arlaban 7, 5°, Oficina 53, 28014 Madrid
Tel: 915 215 812
E-mail: aliteraria@dospassos.es; dospassos@dospassos.es
Web Site: www.dospassos.es
Key Personnel
Dir: Palmira Marquez
Coordinator: Mercedes Boned
Foreign Rights: Ludovic Assemat
Representing international authors.

ELKOST International Literary Agency
C/ Londres 78, 6-1, 08036 Barcelona
Tel: 639 413 320; 933 221 232
E-mail: rights@elkost.com
Web Site: www.elkost.com

Key Personnel
Agent: Yulia Dubrovolskaya; Alexander Klimin
Tel: 617 602 034
Specializes in fiction & nonfiction titles by Russian authors.
Branch Office(s)
via Bronzino 8, 20133 Milan MI, Italy, Contact: Elena Kostioukovich *Tel:* (02) 87236557; (0346) 5064334 *E-mail:* elkost@elkost.com
Pravdi str 1/2, kv 132, 125040 Moscow, Russia, Contact: Alexander Klianitskiy *Tel:* (903) 7154948; (903) 7154538 *E-mail:* aklianitskiy@mail.ru

The Foreign Office
c/ Rossello 104, Entl 2a, 08029 Barcelona
Tel: 933 214 290
E-mail: info@theforeignoffice.net
Web Site: www.theforeignoffice.net
Key Personnel
Agent: Teresa Vilarrubla *E-mail:* teresa@theforeignoffice.net; Iria Villahemosa *E-mail:* iria@theforeignoffice.net
Founded: 2009
Representing foreign publishing houses & literary agents for Spanish & Portuguese speaking countries.

Ilustrata
Espronceda 300, 4-4, 08027 Barcelona
Tel: 932 469 056 *Fax:* 932 470 118
E-mail: info@ilustrata.com
Web Site: www.ilustrata.com
Key Personnel
Dir & Agent: Angela Reynolds
Agent: Patricia Bertin
Founded: 1991
Membership(s): Association of Spanish Literary Agencies.
Specializes in children's & young adult fiction, adult fiction & nonfiction, health, self-help & personal development.

IMC Agencia Literaria
Ave de Sarria, 21, entlo 5a, 08029 Barcelona
Tel: 933 638 757 *Fax:* 933 638 758
E-mail: info@iemece.com
Web Site: www.iemece.com
Key Personnel
Dir: Isabel Marti Castro *E-mail:* isabel@iemece.com
Foreign Rights: Alba Adell Carmona *E-mail:* alba@iemece.com; Lola Esquina Munoz *E-mail:* lola@iemece.com
Specializes in children's & young adult literature.

International Editors' Co SL
Provenza 276, 1st floor, 08008 Barcelona
Tel: 932 158 812 *Fax:* 934 873 583
E-mail: ieco@internationaleditors.com
Key Personnel
Manager: Isabel Monteagudo
Branch Office(s)
International Editors' Co, Ave Cabildo 1156, 10° A, 1426 Buenos Aires, Argentina *Tel:* (011) 4788-2992 *Fax:* (011) 4786-0888 *E-mail:* info@iecobaires.com.ar

Antonia Kerrigan Literary Agency
Travesera de Gracia, 22, 1°, 2a, 08021 Barcelona
Tel: 932093820 *Fax:* 934144328
E-mail: antonia@antoniakerrigan.com
Web Site: www.antoniakerrigan.com
Key Personnel
Founder: Antonia Kerrigan
Agent: Hilde Gersen *E-mail:* hilde@antoniakerrigan.com; Lola Gulias *E-mail:* lola@antoniakerrigan.com; Victor Hurtado *E-mail:* victor@antoniakerrigan.com

Represents domestic & foreign authors around the world & agencies & foreign publishers in Spain.
Specializes in fiction & nonfiction.

Ute Koerner Literary Agent SL
Arago, 224-pral-2, 08011 Barcelona
Tel: 93 323 89 70 *Fax:* 93 451 48 69
E-mail: office@uklitag.com
Web Site: www.uklitag.com
Key Personnel
Agent: Sandra Rodericks; Guenter G Rodewald
Founded: 1984
Representing foreign publishers, authors & agents in Spanish & Portuguese-speaking countries.

Laetus Cultura
Calle el Yunque 9, nave 11A, Tres Cantos, 28760 Madrid
Tel: 657135066
E-mail: info@laetuscultura.com
Web Site: laetuscultura.com
Specializes in children's & young adult literature, including romance, fantasy & science fiction.

Agencia Literaria Virginia Lopez-Ballesteros
Avda Menendez y Pelayo 15, 28009 Madrid
Tel: 911 124 185
E-mail: virginia@vlopez-ballesteros.com
Web Site: www.vlopez-ballesteros.com
Founded: 2005
Represents mostly French & Spanish-speaking authors & some American authors. No unsolicited manuscripts. All genres accepted, except science-fiction, fantasy, poetry & theatre.

Marcombo SA
Gran Via de les Corts Catalanes 594, 08007 Barcelona
Tel: 93 318 00 79 *Fax:* 93 318 93 39
E-mail: info@marcombo.com
Web Site: www.marcombo.com
Key Personnel
Dir General: Jeroni Boixareu Pallares *E-mail:* jeroni@marcombo.com
Founded: 1945
Specializes in technical books.

MB Agencia Literaria
Ronda Sant Pere, 62, 1°-2a, 08010 Barcelona
Tel: 932659064 *Fax:* 932327221
E-mail: info@mbagencialiteraria.es
Web Site: www.mbagencialiteraria.es
Key Personnel
Founder & Agent: Monica Martin
Agent: Christian Marti-Menzel; Ines Planells; Aida Tarragona; Txell Torrent
Founded: 1997
Manages rights for Spanish authors worldwide & represents foreign agencies & publishing houses for Spain, Brazil & Portugal.

Cristina Mora Literary & Film Agency
Bailen 77, 2°2a, 08009 Barcelona
Tel: 932 312120
E-mail: info@cristinamora-litagency.com
Web Site: cristinamora-litagency.com
Founded: 2010
Represents Catalan & Spanish authors worldwide & foreign authors, publishing houses & agencies for the Catalan, Portuguese & Spanish speaking world.

Pagina Tres Agencia Literaria SL
C/ Valencia n° 268, Principal 2a, 08007 Barcelona
Tel: 930 079 121
E-mail: agencia@paginatres.es; rights@paginatres.es
Web Site: www.paginatres.es
Key Personnel
Agent: Fernando Riquelme; Piluca Vega

Foreign Rights: Victoria Sanjuan
Specializes in fiction & nonfiction for adults, young adults & children.

Pontas Agency
Seneca, 31, 08006 Barcelona
Tel: 93 218 22 12 *Fax:* 93 218 22 12
E-mail: info@pontas-agency.com
Web Site: www.pontas-agency.com
Key Personnel
Founder, Dir & Agent: Anna Soler-Pont
   E-mail: anna@pontas-agency.com
Founded: 1992

RDC Agencia Literaria
C Fernando VI, No 13-15, 28004 Madrid
Tel: 913 085 585 *Fax:* 913 085 600
E-mail: rdc@rdclitera.com
Key Personnel
Dir: Raquel de la Concha
Representing Spanish writers & foreign publishers, fiction & nonfiction.

Mercedes Ros Literary Agency
Castell 38, 08329 Teia, Barcelona
Tel: 93 540 13 53 *Fax:* 93 540 13 46
E-mail: info@mercedesros.com
Web Site: www.mercedesros.com
Key Personnel
Dir: Mercedes Ros *E-mail:* mercedes@mercedesros.com
Founded: 1996
Represents publishers, packagers & authors all over the world.
Specializes in children: fiction & nonfiction, albums, board books, games & crafts; adults: crafts, hobbies, parenting, self-help & sports.

Lennart Sane Agency AB
Calle de Eraso 36, 1a planta, 28028 Madrid
Tel: 91 579 80 46 *Fax:* 91 579 89 84
E-mail: info@lennartsaneagency.com
Web Site: www.lennartsaneagency.com
Key Personnel
President: Lennart Sane *E-mail:* lennart.sane@lennartsaneagency.com
Agent: Philip Sane *E-mail:* philip.sane@lennartsaneagency.com
Administration: Elisabeth Sane
Founded: 1969 (in Sweden. Spain office opened in 1986)
Represents authors in all markets for rights in fiction, nonfiction, children's books, films & associated rights.
No unsolicited manuscripts.
Branch Office(s)
Hollandareplan 9, 374 34 Karlshamn, Sweden
   Tel: (0454) 123 56 *Fax:* (0454) 149 20

Sant Jordi Asociados Agencia
Paseo Garcia i Faria, 73-75, Torre A, 7° 5°, 08019 Barcelona
Tel: 93 224 01 07 *Fax:* 93 356 26 96
E-mail: mail@santjordi-asociados.com
Web Site: www.santjordi-asociados.com
Key Personnel
Owner: Monica R Antunes
Founded: 1994
Specializes in Latin America authors & Spanish.

Guillermo Schavelzon & Asociados Literary Agency
Muntaner, 339 - 5°, 08021 Barcelona
Tel: 932 011 310 *Fax:* 932 006 886
E-mail: info@schavelzon.com
Web Site: www.schavelzon.com
Key Personnel
Principal: Guillermo Schavelzon
   E-mail: guillermo@schavelzon.com
Foreign Rights: Barbara Graham
   E-mail: barbaragraham@schavelzon.com

Founded: 1998
Specializes in Latin American & Spanish-speaking writers (fiction & nonfiction).

Agencia Literaria Transmit
Laforja 81 1, 08021 Barcelona
Tel: 932076028
Key Personnel
Agent: Christian Marti-Menzel *E-mail:* christian.marti@eurotransmit.com
Founded: 1984
Representation of literary authors from Central & Eastern Europe.

Julio F Yanez Agencia Literaria SL
Via Augusta 139 6° 2a, 08021 Barcelona
Tel: 932 007 107; 932 005 443 *Fax:* 932 007 656
Key Personnel
Literary Agent: Montse F Yanez
   E-mail: montse@yanezag.com
Rights Executor: Sandra Biel *E-mail:* sandra@yanezag.com
Founded: 1960
Also represents Spanish authors abroad.
Specializes in foreign language literature (fiction & nonfiction) of all genres covering all Spanish & Portuguese-speaking countries.

Zarana Agencia Literaria
Republica Argentina 90, At 2a, 08912 Badalona
Tel: 931 857 256
E-mail: info@zarana.es
Web Site: www.zarana.es
Key Personnel
Foreign Rights: Marta Sevilla *E-mail:* marta-sevilla@zarana.es
Represents Spanish & Portuguese authors internationally. Accept unsolicited manuscripts. Send proposal including contact details, brief bio, first 30 pages & synopsis plot.
Specializes in nonfiction, health, psychology, spirituality & business.

Sweden

Ahlander Agency AB
Vastmannagatan 73, 113 26 Stockholm
Tel: (08) 27 54 55
E-mail: info@ahlanderagency.com
Web Site: ahlanderagency.com
Key Personnel
Agent: Astri von Arbin Ahlander
Represents Scandinavian authors at home & abroad. Accept unsolicited manuscripts written in Scandinavian language. Include cover letter, brief synopsis & first 50 pages.

Ia Atterholm Agency/ICBS
Fersens vag 14a, 211 42 Malmo
Mailing Address: PO Box 17615, 200 10 Malmo
Tel: (040) 305883; (0709) 924866 (cell)
E-mail: ia.atterholm@telia.com
Web Site: www.iaatterholmagency.com
Key Personnel
Founder: Ia Atterholm
Founded: 2001
Represents foreign publishers & agents in Scandinavia & Scandinavian authors worldwide.

Banke, Goumen & Smirnova Literary Agency
Foreningsg 48C, 212 14 Malmo
Tel: (040) 12 22 66
Web Site: bgs-agency.com
Key Personnel
Agent: Natasha Banke *E-mail:* banke@bgs-agency.com; Julia Goumen *E-mail:* goumen@bgs-agency.com; Natalia Smirnova

Represents Russian authors internationally.
Branch Office(s)
Nauki pr 19/2, floor 293, 195220 St Petersburg, Russia

Bennet Agency
Soder Malarstrand 21, 118 20 Stockholm
Tel: (0704) 67 42 70 (cell)
Web Site: www.bennetagency.com
Key Personnel
Owner: Amelie Bennet *E-mail:* amelie.bennet@bennetagency.com
Founded: 2010
Specializes in Swedish illustrated nonfiction, gift books & books on humour to foreign publishers.

Bonnier Rights
Member of Bonnier Publishing Group
Sveavaegen 56, 111 34 Stockholm
Mailing Address: PO Box 3159, 103 63 Stockholm
Tel: (08) 696 89 10
E-mail: info@bonnierrights.se
Web Site: www.bonnierrights.se
Key Personnel
Agent: Amanda Bertolo Alderin *Tel:* (08) 696 81 31 *E-mail:* amanda.bertolo.alderin@bonnierrights.se; Elisabet Brannstrom *Tel:* (08) 696 87 07 *E-mail:* elisabet.brannstrom@bonnierrights.se; Eleonoora Kirk *E-mail:* eleonoora.kirk@bonnierrights.se
Rights Dir: Ulla Joneby *Tel:* (08) 696 86 08 *E-mail:* ulla.joneby@bonnierrights.se
Contracts Manager: Maria Montner *Tel:* (08) 696 89 15 *E-mail:* maria.montner@bonnierrights.se
Rights Manager: Mathilde Coffy *Tel:* (08) 696 80 89 *E-mail:* mathilde.coffy@bonnierrights.se
Sells foreign rights to fiction, illustrated & narrative nonfiction & children's books. Also represents film & TV rights on behalf of selected authors.

Grand Agency
Vanadisvagen 41, 113 23 Stockholm
Tel: (08) 444 47 47
Web Site: www.grandagency.se
Key Personnel
Chief Executive Officer & Mng Dir: Lena Stjernstrom *Tel:* (0709) 96 98 89 (cell) *E-mail:* lena@grandagency.se
Administrator & Contract Manager: Umberto Ghidoni *Tel:* (0702) 47 23 06 (cell) *E-mail:* umberto@grandagency.se
Agent & Marketing: Lotta Jaemtsved Millberg *Tel:* (0707) 14 70 06 (cell) *E-mail:* lotta@grandagency.se
Marketing & Finances: Peter Stjernstrom *Tel:* (0708) 93 57 59 (cell) *E-mail:* peter@grandagency.se
Agent: Jenni Brunn *Tel:* (0702) 36 70 14 (cell) *E-mail:* jenni@grandagency.se
Founded: 2007
Specializes in commercial & literary fiction - general & romantic, thrillers & crime mysteries; children, juvenile & young adult.
Parent Company: Full Tank AB

Hedlund Literary Agency
Tyska Brinken 19, 111 27 Stockholm
Mailing Address: PO Box 2262, 113 16 Stockholm
Web Site: www.hedlundagency.se
Key Personnel
Agent: Magdalena Hedlund *Tel:* (070) 6690568 *E-mail:* magdalena@hedlundagency.se; Susanne Widen *Tel:* (076) 6440648 *E-mail:* susanne@hedlundagency.se
Founded: 2011
Representing Nordic authors worldwide, general fiction, crime & thrillers along with a few selected authors of children's books.
Specializes in Swedish translation & film rights.

Kontext Agency
Kaplansbacken 4, 131 50 Saltsjo-Duvnas
Tel: (0736) 40 85 00
Web Site: www.kontextagency.com
Key Personnel
Owner: Rita G Karlsson *E-mail:* rita@
kontextagency.com
Specializes in narrative nonfiction in the areas
of investigative journalism, politics & current
affairs, history, biography, business & manage-
ment, health & psychology.

**Kerstin Kvint Literary & Co-Production
Agency**
Nyodlingsvagen 16, 167 66 Bromma
Mailing Address: Box 45164, 104 30 Stockholm
Tel: (08) 107014 *Fax:* (08) 107606
E-mail: k.kvint@telia.com
Handles foreign rights sales for individual writ-
ers & Scandinavian publishers. Co-productions
arranged for children's picture books.

Nilsson Literary Agency
Fridhemsvagen 2, 217 74 Malmo
Tel: (040) 794 00
E-mail: info@nilssonagency.com
Web Site: www.nilssonagency.com
Key Personnel
Agent: Henrik Nilsson *E-mail:* henrik@
nilssonagency.com
Representing Scandinavian authors worldwide.

Nordin Agency
Hogbergsgatan 33, 116 20 Stockholm
Mailing Address: PO Box 4022, 102 61 Stock-
holm
Tel: (08) 57168525 *Fax:* (08) 57168524
E-mail: info@nordinagency.com
Web Site: www.nordinagency.se
Key Personnel
Owner & Chief Executive Officer: Joakim Hans-
son *E-mail:* joakim@nordinagency.com
Agent & Contracts Manager: Lina Salazar
E-mail: lina@nordinagency.se
Public Relations & Marketing: Anna Osterholm
E-mail: annaosterholm@nordinagency.se
Founded: 1990 (present owner 2007)
Branch Office(s)
Grabrodersgatan 8, PO Box 4244, 203 13 Malmo
Tel: (040) 611 69 39

Norstedts Agency
Division of Norstedts Forlagsgrupp Ab
Tryckerigatan 4, 111 28 Stockholm
Mailing Address: PO Box 2052, 103 12 Stock-
holm
Tel: (08) 769 87 00 *Fax:* (08) 769 88 04
Web Site: www.norstedtsagency.se
Key Personnel
Rights Dir, Fiction & General Nonfiction: Linda
Altrov-Berg *Tel:* (08) 769 87 18 *E-mail:* linda.
altrovberg@norstedts.se; Catherine Mork
Tel: (08) 769 88 37 *E-mail:* catherine.mork@
norstedts.se
Rights Dir, Illustrated Nonfiction: Petra Ward
Tel: (08) 769 88 77 *E-mail:* petra.ward@
norstedts.se
Royalty Manager: Eva Josefsson *Tel:* (08) 769 87
31 *E-mail:* eva.josefsson@norstedts.se
Rights Coordinator: Maria Machirant *Tel:* (08)
769 88 43 *E-mail:* maria.machirant@norstedts.
se
Foreign rights division of Norstedts Publish-
ing Group, representing Norstedts, Prisma,
Nautiska, Raben & Sjogren, Tiden & Eriksson
& Lindgren.

Partners in Stories
Ferkens Grand 1, 111 30 Stockholm
E-mail: info@partnersinstories.se
Web Site: partnersinstories.se

Key Personnel
Chief Executive Officer: Henrik Lindvall
E-mail: henrik@partnersinstories.se
Agent: Maria Machirant *Tel:* (070) 4480 98 85
(cell) *E-mail:* maria@partnersinstories.se
Coordinator: Alice Stenberg *Tel:* (070) 9192 160
(cell) *E-mail:* alice@partnersinstories.se
Founded: 2013
Represents Scandinavian international translation
rights. Accepts unpublished manuscripts. Include cover letter, brief synopsis & manuscript
by e-mail or post. Submissions sent by post
will not be returned.

Salomonsson Agency
Gotgatan 27, 116 21 Stockholm
Tel: (08) 22 32 11
E-mail: info@salomonssonagency.com
Web Site: www.salomonssonagency.se
Key Personnel
Founder: Marcus Salomonsson; Niclas Salomons-
son
Founded: 2000
Represents Scandinavian authors worldwide. Ac-
cept unsolicted manuscripts written in Scandi-
navian language & sent by e-mail or post. Sub-
mit cover letter, brief synopsis & first 30 pages.
Submissions in English are not considered.
Specializes in fiction, crime fiction & narrative
nonfiction.

Lennart Sane Agency AB
Hollandareplan 9, 374 34 Karlshamn
Tel: (0454) 123 56 *Fax:* (0454) 149 20
E-mail: info@lennartsaneagency.com
Web Site: www.lennartsaneagency.com
Key Personnel
President: Lennart Sane *E-mail:* lennart.sane@
lennartsaneagency.com
Administration: Elisabeth Sane
Agent: Lina Hammarling *E-mail:* lina.
hammarling@lennartsaneagency.com; Philip
Sane *E-mail:* philip.sane@lennartsaneagency.
com
Founded: 1969
Represents authors in all markets for rights in
fiction, nonfiction, children's books, films &
associated rights.
No unsolicited manuscripts.
Branch Office(s)
Calle de Eraso 36, 1a planta, 28028 Madrid,
Spain, Contact: Philip Sane *Tel:* 91 579 80
46 *Fax:* 91 579 89 84 *E-mail:* philip.sane@
lennartsaneagency.com

Sane Toregard Agency
Hollaendareplan 9, 374 34 Karlshamn
Tel: (0454) 123 56 *Fax:* (0454) 149 20
Key Personnel
Dir: Lennart Sane; Ulf Toregard *E-mail:* ulf.
toregard@sanetoregard.se
Founded: 1995
Representing publishers & agents in Scandinavia
& Netherlands for rights in fiction & nonfic-
tion.

Stilton Literary Agency
Vargatan 1c, 126 33 Hagersten
Web Site: www.stilton.se
Key Personnel
Agent: Emma Gate *Tel:* (073) 673 09 32
E-mail: emma@stilton.se
Represents authors from Nordic countries to bring
Scandinavian literature to the attention of pub-
lishers abroad.
Branch Office(s)
Valopoiju 2 A 18, 02320 Espoo, Finland, Contact:
Tiina Kristoffersson *Tel:* (040) 0815912 (cell)
E-mail: tiina@stilton.fi
Fougners vei 14B, 0571 Oslo, Norway, Con-
tact: Hans Petter Bakketeig *Tel:* (047) 674759
E-mail: hanspetter@stilton.no

Switzerland

Paul und Peter Fritz AG Literary Agency
Seefeldstr 303, 8008 Zurich
Tel: (044) 388 41 40
E-mail: info@fritzagency.com
Web Site: www.fritzagency.com
Key Personnel
Mng Dir: Peter S Fritz *Tel:* (044) 388 41 41
E-mail: pfritz@fritzagency.com
Agent: Christian Dittus *Tel:* (044) 388 41 42
E-mail: cdittus@fritzagency.com; Antonia
Fritz *Tel:* (044) 388 41 43 *E-mail:* afritz@
fritzagency.com
Founded: 1962
Representation of American, Australian & British
authors, agents & publishers in German lan-
guage areas, German language authors world-
wide, also in conjunction with Doerthe Binkert
Autorenagentur, Literatur Agentur Ernst Piper,
Agentur Poppenhusen & Agentur Barbara Wen-
ner. Representing literary estates such as the
works of C G Jung.

Hagenbach & Bender GmbH
Hofenstr 17, 3032 Bern
Mailing Address: PO Box 377, 3032 Bern
Tel: (031) 3816666 *Fax:* (031) 3816677
E-mail: rights@hagenbach-bender.com
Web Site: www.hagenbach-bender.com
Key Personnel
Mng Dir: Hans-Joachim Bender
Founded: 2001
Represents world rights for German & selected
international authors.

Liepman Agency AG
Englischviertelstr 59, 8032 Zurich
Tel: (043) 268 23 80 *Fax:* (043) 268 23 81
E-mail: info@liepmanagency.com
Web Site: www.liepmanagency.com
Key Personnel
Dir: Marc Koralnik
Founded: 1949
Represent authors, publishers & agents for the
German language publication rights & authors
from manuscript on throughout the world.

MOHRBOOKS AG Literary Agency
Klosbachstr 110, 8032 Zurich
Tel: (043) 244 86 26 *Fax:* (043) 244 86 27
E-mail: info@mohrbooks.com
Web Site: www.mohrbooks.de
Key Personnel
Owner & Head, Agency: Sebastian Ritscher
E-mail: sebastian.ritscher@mohrbooks.com
Mng Dir & Head of Finance: Marlis Gaemperli
E-mail: marlis.gaemperli@mohrbooks.com
Contracts Manager: Barbara Brachwitz
E-mail: barbara.brachwitz@mohrbooks.com;
Bettina Kaufmann *E-mail:* bettina.kaufmann@
mohrbooks.com
Agent: Annelie Geissler *E-mail:* annelie.
geissler@mohrbooks.com; Annina Meyerhans
E-mail: annina.meyerhans@mohrbooks.com

Taiwan

Bardon-Chinese Media Agency
3F, No 150, Roosevelt Rd, Sec 2, Taipei
Tel: (02) 2364-4995 *Fax:* (02) 2364-1967
Web Site: www.bardonchinese.com
Key Personnel
Mng Partner: Phillip C Chen; Jian-mei Wang

Founded: 1988
Literary & rights agency covering Taiwan, China, Hong Kong & Singapore.
Specializes in Chinese language, simplified & complex.
Branch Office(s)
Room 2-702, Bldg 2 RongHua Shijia, No 29, Xiao Ying Bei Lu, Chaoyang District, Beijing, China *Tel:* (010) 8223 5383 *Fax:* (010) 8223 5362

Chan's Agency
No 66, Gongyequ 1st Rd, Xitun District, 12F-1, Taichung City 407
Tel: (09) 34138688
Key Personnel
Owner: Martin Chan *E-mail:* martinchan2000@gmail.com
Founded: 2015
Accept unsolicited manuscripts. Submit sample chapter (first 20 pages), outline synopsis & author's biography. No reading fee.

The Grayhawk Agency
5F, 109-7, Sec 3, Xinyi Rd, Taipei 10658
Tel: (02) 27059231 *Fax:* (02) 27059610
E-mail: info@grayhawk-agency.com
Web Site: www.grayhawk-agency.com
Key Personnel
President: Gray Tan
Senior Agent: Nicholas Wu
Agent: Gloria Cheng
Founded: 2008
Represents foreign publishers & agencies in the Chinese markets (both China & Taiwan).

Thailand

Silkroad Publishers Agency Co Ltd
32/3 Sukhumvit 31 Rd (Sawasdee), North Klongton, Wattana, Bangkok 10110
Tel: (02) 258 4798; (02) 258 8266 *Fax:* (02) 662 0553
E-mail: info@silkroadagency.com
Web Site: www.silkroadagency.com
Key Personnel
Mng Dir: Jane Ngarmpun Vejjajiva
E-mail: jane@silkroadagency.com
Founded: 1996
Specializes in general trade fiction & nonfiction, juvenile.

Turkey

Akcali Copyright Agency
Bahariye Caddesi 8/9-10, 34714 Kadikoy, Istanbul
Tel: (0216) 338 87 71; (0216) 348 51 60
    Fax: (0216) 347 61 08; (0216) 414 22 65
E-mail: info@akcalicopyright.com
Web Site: www.akcalicopyright.com
Handles fiction & nonfiction adult, young adult & children's books.

AnatoliaLit Agency
Caferaga Mah, Gunesli Bahce Sok No 48, Or Ko Apartment B Blok D 4, 34710 Kadikoy, Istanbul
Tel: (0216) 700 1088 *Fax:* (0216) 700 1089
E-mail: info@anatolialit.com
Web Site: www.anatolialit.com
Key Personnel
Co-Founder: Dilek Akdemir *E-mail:* dilek@anatolialit.com; Amy Spangler *E-mail:* amy@anatolialit.com
Founded: 2005
Representation of Turkish authors to foreign publishers. Also acts as sub-agent for publishers & agencies outside of Turkey. Provides translation, editing & proofreading services.

Gamma Medya Agency
Eceler Sok, No 6/1, Florya, 34153 Istanbul
Tel: (0212) 663 96 80 *Fax:* (0212) 663 96 81
E-mail: web@gammamedya.net
Web Site: www.gammamedya.net
Key Personnel
Mng Dir: Zeynep Ataman *E-mail:* zeynep@gammamedya.net
Founded: 1991
Publishing, press & licensing agency.

Kalem Literary Agency
Tunel General Yazgan Sok no 11/2, Beyoglu, 34430 Istanbul
Tel: (0212) 245 44 06 *Fax:* (0212) 245 44 19
E-mail: info@kalemagency.com
Web Site: www.kalemagency.com
Key Personnel
Founder: Nermin Mollaoglu *E-mail:* nermin@kalemagency.com
Agent: Fatma Cihan Akkartal; Sedef Ilgic
Founded: 2005
Handles Turkish authors & literary agencies & foreign publishers in the Turkish market.
Specializes in contemporary fiction.

Nurcihan Kesim Literary Agency Inc
Esentepe Mah Milangaz Cad No 77, Dumankaya Vizyon A1 K23 D128, Kartal, Istanbul
Mailing Address: PO Box 868, Kartal, Istanbul
Tel: (0216) 511 5686 *Fax:* (0212) 526 9128
Key Personnel
Mng Dir & Executive President: Filiz Karaman
Founded: 1971
Specializes in fiction, nonfiction, art works, serials, encyclopedias, licensing, merchandising, music rights & children's books.

ONK Agency Ltd
Cumhuriyet Cad Pak Apartment No 30/9, Elmadag, 34367 Istanbul
Mailing Address: PO Box 983, Sirkeci, 34115 Istanbul
Tel: (0212) 241 77 00 *Fax:* (0212) 241 77 31
E-mail: info@onkagency.com
Web Site: www.onkagency.com
Key Personnel
Chairman of the Board: Mehmet N Karaca *E-mail:* karaca@onkagency.com
Mng Dir: Meric Gulec *E-mail:* meric@onkagency.com
Key Account Manager: Gulnaz Yildiz *E-mail:* gulnaz@onkagency.com
Drama & Stage Rights: Aslihan Gulay *E-mail:* asli@onkagency.com
Foreign Book Rights: Hatice Goek *E-mail:* hatice@onkagency.com
Turkish Authors' Rights: S Aykut Ozturk *E-mail:* aykut@onkagency.com
Founded: 1959
Representing Turkish & international writers, illustrators, playwriters, SACD (France), major foreign publishers & agents, as well as dramatic adaptation rights of the authors for cinema & TV channels.
Specializes in books (adult/young adult & children's books), serials, encyclopedias, comics & cartoons, plays, Dia Positive.

Sentries Licensing
Baran Is Merkezi Cumhuriyet Mah, Haminne Cesme Sok No 13, 34696 Uskudar, Istanbul
Tel: (0216) 524 2121 *Fax:* (0216) 520 2490
E-mail: contact@sentries.com.tr
Web Site: www.sentries.com.tr
Key Personnel
Mng Dir: Mr Hakan Tungac *Tel:* (0216) 524 2121 ext 2851 *E-mail:* ht@sentries.com.tr
Licensing Specialist: Mr A Ali Unsal *Tel:* (0216) 524 2121 ext 2838 *E-mail:* au@sentries.com.tr
Rights Specialist: Mr Alpay Karaca *Tel:* (0216) 524 2121 ext 2551 *E-mail:* ak@sentries.com.tr
Founded: 1979
Full service independent international copyright, licensing & merchandising agency representing brands, publishing houses, authors, characters, film/TV, music, video games & software. Specialize in licensing of entertainment, corporate & lifestyle properties, developing a broad range of compatible products on behalf of clients.
All submissions are by invitation only & should include a cover letter in the body of the e-mail with approximately 200 words about the book & 200 words about yourself & your writing. Subject line should include book title & your name. Attachment should be one Word or PDF document including a title page & numbered pages. No reading fee.
For fiction: Three opening chapters (double spaced) & very brief synopsis of plot (with word-count of the complete book).
For nonfiction: Proposal with book completion date, full word-count, detailed synopsis & three chapters (double spaced).
Membership(s): LIMA.
Specializes in literary rights including fiction & nonfiction, especially novel, story, coffee table, history, spiritual, popular culture, children's, education & course books.

ZNN Literary Agency
Halitaga Cad Ergener Ishani, No 24, Kat 2, Daire 9, 34714 Kadikoy, Istanbul
Tel: (0216) 348 37 78
Web Site: znnliteraryagency.com
Key Personnel
Founder: Nurgul Senefe *E-mail:* nurgul.senefe@znn.com.tr
Founded: 2007
Specializes in children's books, comics, plays, business, personal development, food, amine, manga, culture, history & biographies.

United Kingdom

A & B Personal Management Ltd
Linden Hall, Suite 330, 162-168 Regent St, London W1B 5TD
Tel: (020) 7434 4262 *Fax:* (020) 7038 3699
Key Personnel
Dir: R W Ellis *E-mail:* billellis@aandb.co.uk
Founded: 1982
Full-length manuscripts for TV, theatre, cinema; also fiction, nonfiction & performance rights. No unsolicited manuscripts. Send letter first with return postage. No reading fee for synopsis, plays or screenplays, but fee charged for full-length manuscripts.

The Agency (London) Ltd
24 Pottery Lane, Holland Park, London W11 4LZ
Tel: (020) 7727 1346 *Fax:* (020) 7727 9037
E-mail: info@theagency.co.uk
Web Site: www.theagency.co.uk
Key Personnel
Founder: Stephen Durbridge *E-mail:* sd-office@theagency.co.uk

Co-Dir: Hilary Delamere *E-mail:* hd-office@
theagency.co.uk; Katie Haines *E-mail:* kh-
office@theagency.co.uk
Founded: 1995
Represents screenwriters, directors, playwrights,
composers & children's authors & illustrators.
No unsolicited manuscripts.
Specializes in theater, film, TV, radio, novels,
children's fiction.

The Agency of Four Freedom Publishing
Division of Four Freedom Publishing LP
35 High St, Ballyhalbert, Co Down
Tel: (07375) 083513 (cell)
E-mail: fourfreedompublishing@gmail.com
Web Site: fourfreedom.wixsite.com/literaryagency
Key Personnel
Chief Financial Officer: Patricia Gregory
President: Hubert O'Hearn
Associate Agent: Christie Parry
Office Manager: Carol Coney
Founded: 2014
Full service literary agency offering personalized
service to an elite group of international writers. Edit & develop book-length manuscripts
alongside the author, then market the completed book to major & mid-major publishers in Europe & North America. Additional
services include contract negotiation, personal
finance planning, marketing & negotiation of
media rights. Book length projects only. Subject specialties include literary, genre fiction,
nonfiction academic studies, children's, drama
& poetry.
Accept unsolicited manuscripts. Provide short biography, including previous publishing history
(although brand new authors are considered).
Include web site (if available), contact information & brief 100-250 word description of
book. Attach maximum 25 pages/6,000 words
of manuscript. All documents should be in unlocked Word format, or unlocked PDF files
that will allow for editing & notes. Negotiable
limited deposit, refundable against future commissions.

Aitken Alexander Associates Ltd
291 Gray's Inn Rd, Kings Cross, London WC1X
8QJ
Tel: (020) 7373 8672 *Fax:* (020) 7373 6002
E-mail: reception@aitkenalexander.co.uk
Web Site: www.aitkenalexander.co.uk
Key Personnel
Mng Dir: Lesley Thorne
Agent: Matthew Hamilton; Ayesha Karim; Gillie
Russell; Chris Wellbelove
Founded: 1976
Handles fiction, nonfiction, commercial & chil-
dren's. No illustrated books, plays or scripts.
Send preliminary letter with half page synopsis,
first 30 pages & return postage. No reading fee.
Commission: Home 15%; US 20%; Translation
20%.
U.S. Office(s): 30 Vandam St, Suite 5A, New
York, NY 10013, United States

The Ampersand Agency Ltd
Ryman's Cottages, Little Tew, Chipping Norton,
Oxon OX7 4JJ
Tel: (01608) 683677; (01608) 683898
Fax: (01608) 683449
Web Site: www.theampersandagency.co.uk
Key Personnel
Mng Dir: Peter Buckman *E-mail:* peter@
theampersandagency.co.uk
Editorial: Jamie Cowen *E-mail:* jamie@
theampersandagency.co.uk
Founded: 2003
Membership(s): Association of Authors' Agents.
Specializes in literary & commercial fiction &
nonfiction.

Darley Anderson Literary TV & Film Agency
Estelle House, 11 Eustace Rd, London SW6 1JB
Tel: (020) 7385 6652 *Fax:* (020) 7386 5571
Web Site: www.darleyanderson.com
Key Personnel
President & Agent, Thrillers: Darley Anderson
Agent, Crime, Thrillers & General Fiction:
Camilla Wray *E-mail:* camilla@darleyanderson.
com
Rights Manager: Clare Wallace *E-mail:* clare@
darleyanderson.com
Founded: 1988
Handles commercial fiction & nonfiction, children's fiction & selected scripts for film &
TV. Send cover letter, one-page synopsis &
first three chapters. Include self-addressed,
stamped envelope if you wish submission to
be returned. Commission: Home 15%; USA
20%; Translation 20-25%; TV/Film/Radio 20%.
Specializes in fiction: American & Irish novels, crime/mystery, humor, thrillers, women's
& male fiction; childrens; nonfiction: animals, beauty, biographies, celebrity autobiographies, cookery, diet, fashions, gardening,
health, history, humor/cartoons, inspirational,
popular psychology, religion, science, self-
improvement.

Asia Literary Agency
Bedford Sq, 6 Bayley St, London WC1B 3HE
E-mail: admin@asialiteraryagency.org
Web Site: www.asialiteraryagency.org
Key Personnel
Founder: Kelly Falconer
Founded: 2013
Represents Asian fiction & nonfiction writers, ex-
perts on Asia & writers living in Asia. Handle
foreign rights for Hong Kong-based publisher
Typhoon Media. Currently closed for submis-
sions.

Author Literary Agents
53 Talbot Rd, Highgate, London N6 4QX
Tel: (020) 8341 0442 *Fax:* (020) 8341 0442
E-mail: agile@authors.co.uk
Key Personnel
Principal/Agent: John Ridley Havergal
Founded: 1997
To receive a free opinion, e-mail a one-page out-
line plus opening chapter writing sample. Self-
addressed envelope is a must with postal sub-
missions. No reading fee.
Specializes in taut thrillers, transformational
epics, awesome epiphanies, transcendental dis-
coveries.
Parent Company: Acclaim Marketing UK

Bell Lomax Moreton Agency Ltd
131 Queensway, Suite C, Pets Wood, Kent BR5
1DG
Tel: (020) 7930 4447 *Fax:* (020) 7839 2667
E-mail: agency@bell-lomax.co.uk
Web Site: belllomaxmoreton.co.uk
Key Personnel
Agent: Eddie Bell; June Bell; Pat Lomax; Paul
Moreton; Josephine Hayes; Helen Mackenzie
Smith
Founded: 2000
Specializes in adult fiction & nonfiction, chil-
dren's books.
Foreign Rights: Valerie Hoskins Associates; Inter-
continental Literary Agency (ILA)

Lorella Belli Literary Agency
54 Hartford House, 35 Tavistock Crescent, Not-
ting Hill, London W11 1AY
Tel: (020) 7727 8547 *Fax:* (0870) 787 4194
E-mail: info@lorellabelliagency.com
Web Site: www.lorellabelliagency.com
Founded: 2002
Specializes in full-length adult & young adult fic-
tion & general nonfiction.

The Blair Partnership
Middlesex House, 4th floor, 34-42 Cleveland St,
London W1T 4JE
Tel: (020) 7504 2520 *Fax:* (020) 7504 2521
E-mail: info@theblairpartnership.com
Web Site: www.theblairpartnership.com
Key Personnel
Agent: Neil Blair
Representing new & established writers across a
wide variety of genres.

**Blake Friedmann Literary, Film & TV Agency
Ltd**
Selous House, 1st floor, 5-12 Mandela St, London
NW1 0DU
Tel: (020) 7387 0842
E-mail: info@blakefriedmann.co.uk
Web Site: www.blakefriedmann.co.uk
Key Personnel
Chairman: Julian Friedmann *E-mail:* julian@
blakefriedmann.co.uk
Dir: Isobel Dixon *E-mail:* isobel@
blakefriedmann.co.uk
Contracts Manager: Resham Naqvi
E-mail: resham@blakefriedmann.co.uk
Foreign Rights, Digital & Audio Manager: Louise
Brice *E-mail:* louise@blakefriedmann.co.uk
Book Agent: Hattie Grunewald *E-mail:* hattie@
blakefriedmann.co.uk; Juliet Pickering
E-mail: juliet@blakefriedmann.co.uk; Tom Wit-
comb *E-mail:* tom@blakefriedmann.co.uk
Head, Media Dept: Conrad Williams
E-mail: conrad@blakefriedmann.co.uk
Founded: 1976
Handles fiction & nonfiction, scripts for TV, radio
& film. No poetry or short stories. Send initial
e-mail with synopsis & first two chapters after
reading submission guidelines on web site. No
reading fee. Commission: Home 15%; US &
Translation 20%; Radio/TV/Film 15%.
Specializes in commercial women's fiction, liter-
ary fiction, thrillers, up-market nonfiction.

Booklink
42 Reigate Rd, Ewell, Epsom, Surrey KT17 1PX
Tel: (020) 8394 1578
E-mail: info@booklink.co.uk
Web Site: www.booklink.co.uk
Key Personnel
President: Evelyne Duval *Tel:* 04 88 00 04 46
E-mail: evelyne@booklink.co.uk
Agent: Maria White *Tel:* (020) 8394 1578
E-mail: maria@booklink.co.uk
Founded: 1978
International rights agency.
Specializes in foreign rights, co-editions.

The Bright Literary Agency (BLA)
The Bright Agency, Studio 102, 250 York Rd,
Battersea, London SW11 3SJ
Tel: (020) 7326 9140
E-mail: literarysubmissions@
brightgroupinternational.com
Web Site: www.brightliteraryagency.com
Key Personnel
Mng Dir: Vicki Willden-Lebrecht *E-mail:* vicki@
brightgroupinternational.com
Senior Agent: Arabella Stein
Children's Literary Agent: Lauren Holowaty
Boutique children's literary agency. Submissions
accepted via e-mail only. Fiction: First 3 chap-
ters & synopsis, .doc or .pdf format with short
cover letter. Picture Books: Up to 3 stories with
few line synopsis of each, .doc or .pdf format
with short cover letter. Authors/Illustrators: E-
mail .jpg or .pdf with text & images.
Specializes in all genres of children's publishing,
including novelty, picture books & fiction.
Parent Company: Bright Group International

Brotherstone Creative Management
6 Bayley St, Bloomsbury, London WC1B 3HE
Tel: (07908) 542 866; (020) 7502 5037
E-mail: info@bcm-agency.com; submissions@
  bcm-agency.com
Web Site: bcm-agency.com
Key Personnel
Owner: Charlie Brotherstone
Founded: 2017
For fiction, include first 3 chapters or 50 pages,
  1-2 page synopsis & short covering letter. For
  nonfiction, send detailed outline, sample chap-
  ter & covering note. Do not accept scripts for
  theatre, film or television.
Foreign Rights: United Agents (Georgina Le
  Grice)

Jenny Brown Associates
33, Argyle Pl, Edinburgh EH9 1JT
Tel: (0131) 229 5334
E-mail: info@jennybrownassociates.com
Web Site: www.jennybrownassociates.com
Key Personnel
Agent: Jenny Brown *E-mail:* jenny@
  jennybrownassociates.com; Allan Guthrie
  E-mail: allan@jennybrownassociates.com; Lucy
  Juckes *E-mail:* lucy@jennybrownassociates.
  com; Bob McDevitt; Mark Stanton
  E-mail: stan@jennybrownassociates.com
Rights Manager: Kevin Pocklington
  E-mail: kevin@jennybrownassociates.com
Founded: 2002
Membership(s): Association of Authors' Agents.

Felicity Bryan Associates
2a North Parade Ave, Banbury Rd, Oxford, Oxon
  OX2 6LX
Tel: (01865) 513816 *Fax:* (01865) 310055
E-mail: agency@felicitybryan.com
Web Site: www.felicitybryan.com
Key Personnel
Chairman of the Board: Felicity Bryan
Mng Dir: Catherine Clarke
Dir: Caroline Wood
Agent: Carrie Plitt
Associate Agent: Sally Holloway
Accounts Manager: Carole Robinson
Founded: 1988
Handles fiction & nonfiction with emphasis on
  history, biography, science & current affairs.
  No scripts for TV, radio or theatre; no crafts,
  how-to, science fiction or light romance. No
  unsolicited manuscripts. No reading fee. Com-
  mission: Home 10%; USA & Translation 20%.

The Buckman Agency
Ryman's Cottage, Little Tew, Oxford, Oxon OX7
  4JJ
Tel: (01608) 683677 *Fax:* (01608) 683449
Key Personnel
Contact: Rosemarie Buckman *E-mail:* r.
  buckman@talk21.com; Jessica Buckman
  Tel: (01444) 455 801 *E-mail:* j.buckman@
  talk21.com
Representing American & UK publishers &
  agents for the handling of all translation rights.
Specializes in translation rights.

Georgina Capel Associates Ltd
29 Wardour St, London W1D 6PS
Tel: (020) 7734 2414 *Fax:* (020) 7734 8101
Web Site: www.georginacapel.com
Key Personnel
Dir: Georgina Capel *E-mail:* georgina@
  georginacapel.com
Agent: Philippa Brewster
  E-mail: philippabrewster@gmail.com; Rachel
  Conway *E-mail:* rachel@georginacapel.com
Literary & Foreign Rights: Valeria Huerta
  E-mail: valeria@georginacapel.com
Founded: 2000

Represents authors in international markets. Submit by post cover letter with outline of writing
  history, synopsis of work (approximately 500
  words), first three chapters, e-mail address +/or
  telephone number.

Caroline Sheldon Literary Agency Ltd
71 Hillgate Pl, London W8 7SS
Tel: (020) 7727 9102
Web Site: www.carolinesheldon.co.uk
Key Personnel
Literary Agent & Proprietor: Caroline Sheldon
  E-mail: carolinesheldon@carolinesheldon.co.uk
Literary Agent: Felicity Trew
  E-mail: felicitytrew@carolinesheldon.co.uk
Founded: 1985
Handles adult fiction, in particular women's (both
  commercial & literary) & human interest non-
  fiction. Also full-length children's fiction,
  younger children's fiction, picture books & pic-
  ture book artists. No TV/Film scripts unless by
  book-writing clients. Commission: Home 15%;
  USA & Translation 20%. Submissions preferred via e-mail, including information about
  yourself & first 3 chapters of work.
Membership(s): Association of Authors' Agents.
Specializes in fiction, human-interest nonfiction,
  children's books of all types including illustrations.

Casarotto Ramsay & Associates Ltd
Waverly House, 7-12 Noel St, London W1F 8GQ
Tel: (020) 7287 4450 *Fax:* (020) 7287 9128
E-mail: info@casarotto.co.uk
Web Site: www.casarotto.co.uk
Key Personnel
Owner: Jenne Casarotto *E-mail:* jenne@casarotto.
  co.uk
Mng Dir & Senior Agent: Rachel Holroyd
  E-mail: rachel@casarotto.co.uk
Senior Agent (Film & TV): Jodi Shields
  E-mail: jodi@casarotto.co.uk
Agent (Film & TV): Elinor Burns
  E-mail: elinor@casarotto.co.uk
Agent (Film & TV), Dublin: Charlotte Kelly
  Tel: (01) 498 3627 *E-mail:* charlotte@
  casarotto.co.uk
Agent (Theatre): Tom Erhardt *E-mail:* tom@
  casarotto.co.uk; Mel Kenyon *E-mail:* mel@
  casarotto.co.uk
Founded: 1989
Also represent writers, producers, directors & key
  technical staff in film, TV & theater.

Teresa Chris Literary Agency Ltd
43 Musard Rd, London W6 8NR
Tel: (020) 7386 0633
E-mail: teresachris@litagency.co.uk
Web Site: www.teresachrisliteraryagency.co.uk
Key Personnel
Owner: Teresa Chris
Commercial & literary fiction. Also represents
  nonfiction, including biography, cookery, crafts,
  gardening, history & lifestyle. For fiction, submit first three chapters, one-page synopsis &
  cover letter with contact details. For nonfiction,
  submit overview & two sample chapters. Include self-addressed, stamped envelope for re-
  sponse. Send submissions to Charles Brudenell-
  Bruce.
Membership(s): Association of Authors' Agents.
Specializes in crime & women's commercial fiction.

Jonathan Clowes Ltd
10 Iron Bridge House, Bridge Approach, London
  NW1 8BD
Tel: (020) 7722 7674 *Fax:* (020) 7722 7677
E-mail: admin@jonathanclowes.co.uk
Web Site: www.jonathanclowes.co.uk
Key Personnel
Dir: Ann Evans

Agent: Olivia Guest *E-mail:* olivia@
  jonathanclowes.co.uk; Nemonie Craven Roderick *E-mail:* nemonie@jonathanclowes.co.uk
Founded: 1960
No science fiction, poetry, short stories or academic writing. Send synopsis & three chapters (or an equivalent sample) via e-mail only
  to Olivia or Nemonie. Commission: Home &
  USA 15%; Translation 19%.
Membership(s): Association of Authors' Agents.
Specializes in film & TV rights, situation comedy.

Rosica Colin Ltd
One Clareville Grove Mews, London SW7 5AH
Tel: (020) 7370 1080 *Fax:* (020) 7244 6441
Key Personnel
Dir: Joanna Marston; Sylvie Marston
Founded: 1949
Handles full-length manuscripts, plus theatre,
  film, TV & radio. Preliminary letter with return
  postage essential. No reading fee. Commission:
  Home 10%; USA 15%; Translation 20%.

Collier International
19 White Lodge Court, Staines Rd E, Sunbury-
  on-Thames, Middx TW16 5GA
Tel: (01932) 770123 *Fax:* (01932) 770123
E-mail: rights@collier-international.co.uk
Web Site: www.collier-international.co.uk
Key Personnel
Owner: Christopher Collier
Foreign Rights: Manuela Kerkhoff *E-mail:* mk@
  manuela-kerkhoff.de
Founded: 2004
Represents publishers in book & digital formats.
Specializes in general nonfiction, reference & il-
  lustrated books.

Conville & Walsh Ltd
Haymarket House, 28-29 Haymarket, London
  SW1Y 4SP
Tel: (02) 7393 4200
Web Site: www.cwagency.co.uk
Key Personnel
Co-Founder & Agent: Clare Conville
Mng Dir: Jake Smith-Bosanquet
Agent: Sue Armstrong; Carrie Kania; Lucy Luck
Founded: 2000
Representation of novelists, scientists, historians,
  travel writers, biographers & children's authors.

Jane Conway-Gordon Ltd
38 Cromwell Grove, London W6 7RG
Tel: (020) 7371 6939
E-mail: jane@conway-gordon.co.uk
Web Site: www.janeconwaygordon.com
Key Personnel
Mng Dir: Jane Conway-Gordon
Founded: 1982
No poetry or science fiction. Unsolicited
  manuscripts welcome; preliminary letter & re-
  turn postage essential. No reading fee. Com-
  mission: Home 15%; USA & Translation 20%.
Specializes in fiction, general nonfiction.
Foreign Rep(s): McIntosh & Otis, Inc

Rupert Crew Ltd
6 Windsor Rd, London N3 3SS
Tel: (020) 8346 3000 *Fax:* (020) 8346 3009
E-mail: info@rupertcrew.co.uk
Web Site: www.rupertcrew.co.uk
Key Personnel
Mng Dir: Caroline Montgomery
Founded: 1927
International representation, handling volume &
  subsidiary rights in fiction & nonfiction. No
  plays, poetry, journalism or short stories. No
  unsolicited manuscripts, please see web site for
  current submissions policy. Commission: Home
  15%; Elsewhere 20%.
Specializes in fiction, nonfiction & major book
  projects with international appeal.

Curtis Brown Group Ltd
Haymarket House, 28-29 Haymarket, London
SW1Y 4SP
Tel: (020) 7393 4400 *Fax:* (020) 7393 4401
E-mail: cb@curtisbrown.co.uk
Web Site: www.curtisbrown.co.uk
Key Personnel
Chairman: Jonathan Lloyd
Joint Chief Executive Officer: Jonny Geller; Ben
  Hall
Mng Dir, Media Division: Nick Marston
  E-mail: nick@curtisbrown.co.uk
Dir: Jacquie Drewe; Sarah Spear
Head, Book Contracts & Agent: Anna Davis
Agent: Cathryn Summerhayes
Book-to-Film Agent: Luke Speed
Founded: 1899
Representation of directors, writers, designers,
  presenters & actors in theater, film & televi-
  sion & a wide range of authors of fiction &
  nonfiction. Commission: Home 15%; US &
  Translation 20%.

The Cutting Edge
Archery House, 33 Archery Sq, Walmer Deal,
  Kent CT14 7JA
Tel: (01304) 371721
Web Site: www.thecuttingedge.biz
Key Personnel
Contact: Jon Thurley *E-mail:* jmthurley@aol.com;
  Patricia Preece
Founded: 1976
Specializes in literary & commercial fiction &
  nonfiction.

David Godwin Associates
55 Monmouth St, London WC2H 9DG
Tel: (020) 7240 9992 *Fax:* (020) 7395 6110
E-mail: assistant@davidgodwinassociates.co.uk
Web Site: www.davidgodwinassociates.com
Key Personnel
Film & TV Rights: Kirsty McLachlan
  E-mail: kirsty@davidgodwinassociates.co.uk
Founded: 1995
Small literary agency representing one hundred
  authors.
Specializes in fiction & general nonfiction.

Diamond Kahn & Woods Literary Agency Ltd
66 Onslow Gardens, Top floor, London N10 3JX
Tel: (020) 3514 6544
E-mail: info@dkwlitagency.co.uk
Web Site: dkwlitagency.co.uk
Key Personnel
Founder & Agent: Ella Diamond Kahn
  E-mail: submissions.ella@dkwlitagency.co.uk;
  Bryony Woods *E-mail:* submissions.bryony@
  dkwlitagency.co.uk
Founded: 2012
Accept unsolicited manuscripts. E-mail first three
  chapters, synopsis & cover letter to either Bry-
  ony or Ella. No reading fee.

Elise Dillsworth Agency
9 Grosvenor Rd, London N10 2DR
E-mail: submissions@elisedillsworthagency.com
Web Site: elisedillsworthagency.com
Key Personnel
Agent: Elise Dillsworth
Founded: 2012
Represents literary & commercial fiction & nonfiction. No science fiction, fantasy or children's
  books. For fiction, send covering letter, first
  three chapters (approximately 50 pages) &
  synopsis. For nonfiction, send full outline &
  covering letter. To submit via e-mail, be sure
  attachments are in Microsoft Word or PDF format.

Drake Educational Associates Ltd
St Fagans Rd, Fairwater, Cardiff CF5 3AE
Tel: (029) 2056 0333 *Fax:* (029) 2055 4909
E-mail: enquiries@drakeed.com
Web Site: www.drakegroup.co.uk; www.drakeed.
  com
Key Personnel
Mng Dir: Mr R G Drake
Specializes in education, children's.

Durnell Marketing Ltd
2 Linden Close, Turnbridge Wells, Kent TN4
  8HH
Tel: (01892) 544272 *Fax:* (01892) 5111152
E-mail: admin@durnell.co.uk; orders@durnell.co.
  uk
Web Site: www.durnell.co.uk

Eccles Fisher Associates
11 Wells Mews, London W1T 3HD
Tel: (020) 7494 4609
E-mail: info@ecclesfisher.com
Web Site: www.ecclesfisher.com
Key Personnel
Publisher's Scout: Catherine Eccles
Literary Scout: Rosie Welsh
Founded: 1982
Literary scout representing Doubleday & Nan
  Talese in the US; Random House, Knopf,
  Doubleday & Bond Street in Canada; Edi-
  tions Robert Laffont in France; C Bertelsmann,
  Knaus, Blanvalet, DVA, Siedler & C Bertels-
  mann Jugenbuch in Germany; Arnoldo Mon-
  dadori Editore, Oscar & Mondadori Ragazzi
  in Italy; Albert Bonniers in Sweden; Oc-
  tava in Finland; Gyldendal Norsk in Norway;
  Gyldendal in Denmark; Singel Group including
  Athenaeum, Arbeiderspers, Querido, Q Nijgh
  & Van Ditmar in Holland; Penguin Random
  House including Plaza & Janes, Grijalbo, Ran-
  dom House, Lumen, Debate, Alfaguara, Suma,
  Aguilar & Montena in Spain; Companhia das
  Letras & Objetiva in Brazil; Objectiva in Portu-
  gal; Libri in Hungary; Yapi Kred in Turkey,
  Patakis in Greece, W Literackie in Poland,
  CITIC in China & Heyday Film Co.

Edwards Fuglewicz Literary Agency
49 Great Ormond St, London WC1N 3HZ
Tel: (020) 7405 6725 *Fax:* (020) 7405 6726
Key Personnel
Partner: Ros Edwards *E-mail:* ros@efla.co.uk;
  Helenka Fuglewicz
Founded: 1996
Represent literary & commercial fiction & non-
  fiction (no science fiction, horror or fantasy).
  No unsolicited manuscripts. No e-mail submis-
  sions.
Membership(s): Association of Authors' Agents
  (AAA).

Faith Evans Associates
27 Park Ave North, London N8 7RU
Tel: (020) 8340 9920 *Fax:* (020) 8340 9410
Key Personnel
Contact: Faith Evans
Founded: 1987
No unsolicated submissions please. Only accept
  calls or submissions by recommendations.
  Commission: Home 15%; US & Translation
  20%.

FRA
91 St Leonards Rd, London SW14 7BL
Tel: (020) 8255 7755 *Fax:* (020) 8286 4860
E-mail: enquiries@futermanrose.co.uk
Web Site: www.futermanrose.co.uk
Key Personnel
Principal: Guy Rose *E-mail:* guy@futermanrose.
  co.uk
Founded: 1984
Specializes in commercial & literary fiction, aca-
  demic nonfiction, biography & autobiography,
  TV film & theatre scripts.

Furniss Lawton
94 Strand on the Green, Chiswick, London W4
  3NN
Tel: (020) 8987 6804 *Fax:* (020) 8742 4951
E-mail: info@furnisslawton.co.uk
Web Site: www.jamesgrant.com/furniss-lawton/
Key Personnel
Agent: Eugenie Furniss; Rowan Lawton; Rory
  Scarfe
Electronic submissions only. Accept unsolicited
  manuscripts. Submit up to 10,000 words of
  your manuscript, or the first 3 chapters, as either a Word document or PDF along with a
  1-page synopsis. Include the word 'submission'
  on the subject line. Attachments are to include
  the title of your work & your name. Screenwriters for film or television not represented.
Specializes in fiction (adult & children's), memoirs & narrative nonfiction.
Parent Company: James Grant Group Ltd

Eric Glass Ltd
25 Ladbroke Crescent, Notting Hill, London W11
  1PS
Tel: (020) 7229 9500 *Fax:* (020) 7229 6220
E-mail: eglassltd@aol.com
Key Personnel
Dir: Janet Glass
Founded: 1934
Handles fiction, nonfiction & scripts for publi-
  cation or production in all media. No poetry,
  short stories, or children's works. No unso-
  licited manuscripts. No reading fee. Commis-
  sion: Home 10%; USA & Translation 20%.
Represents Societe des Auteurs et Compositeurs
  Dramatiques (SACD), Paris.

Global Book Marketing Ltd
99B Wallis Rd, London E9 5LN
Web Site: www.globalbookmarketing.co.uk
Key Personnel
Contact: Arlene Hanson *Tel:* (014) 5230 5494
  E-mail: arlene@globalbookmarketing.co.uk;
  Anthony Zurbrugg *Tel:* (020) 8533 5800
  E-mail: tz@globalbookmarketing.co.uk
Provides representation & marketing services to
  publishers.

Annette Green Authors' Agency
5 Henwoods Mount, Pembury, Tunbridge Wells,
  Kent TN4 9AD
Tel: (01892) 263252
Web Site: www.annettegreenagency.co.uk
Key Personnel
Founder & Agent: Annette Green
  E-mail: annette@annettegreenagency.co.uk
Agent: David Smith *E-mail:* david@
  annettegreenagency.co.uk
Founded: 1998
No poetry or dramatic scripts. Send or e-mail
  short cover letter, brief synopsis & 5,000-
  10,000 words from book. If sending hard copy,
  include stamped, self-addressed envelope. Com-
  mission: UK Sales 15%; US Sales 20%; Trans-
  lation Rights 20%; Film & TV Rights 20%.
  Commission attracts VAT at the full rate. No
  reading fee.
Membership(s): Association of Authors' Agents.
Specializes in literary fiction, general & mass
  market fiction, serious nonfiction, popular culture, memoir, biography & older children's &
  teenage fiction.

Christine Green Authors' Agent
PO Box 70098, London SE15 5AU
E-mail: info@christinegreen.co.uk
Web Site: www.christinegreen.co.uk
Key Personnel
Contact: Christine Green
Founded: 1984

Fiction (adult & young adult) & narrative non-fiction only. No scripts, poetry or children's. Initial letter & synopsis preferred by e-mail. No reading fee but return postage essential. Commission: Home 15%; USA & Translation 20%.
Specializes in general fiction, general nonfiction, young adult & literary fiction.

Louise Greenberg Books Ltd
The End House, Church Crescent, London N3 1BG
Tel: (020) 8349 1179 *Fax:* (020) 8343 4559
E-mail: louisegreenberg@btinternet.com
Web Site: louisegreenbergbooks.co.uk
Key Personnel
Contact: Louise Greenberg
Founded: 1997
Specializes in literary fiction & serious nonfiction only.

Greene & Heaton Ltd
37 Goldhawk Rd, London W12 8QQ
Tel: (020) 8749 0315 *Fax:* (020) 8749 0318
E-mail: info@greeneheaton.co.uk
Web Site: www.greeneheaton.co.uk
Key Personnel
Mng Dir: Antony Topping
Chmn: Carol Heaton
Agent: Judith Murray
Agent, Children's: Linda Davis
Founded: 1963
Handles all types of fiction & nonfiction. No children's picture books or original scripts for theatre, film or TV. Commission: Home 15%; US & Translation 20%.

David Grossman Literary Agency Ltd
118B Holland Park Ave, London W11 4UA
Tel: (020) 7221 2770 *Fax:* (020) 7221 1445
Founded: 1976
Handles full-length fiction & general nonfiction. No verse or technical books for students. No original screenplays or teleplays. Approach by preliminary letter giving full description of the work &, in the case of fiction, with the first 50 pages. All material must by accompanied by return postage. No approaches or submissions by fax or e-mail. No unsolicited manuscripts. No reading fee. Material should be addressed to the Submissions Dept. Commission rates vary for different markets. Overseas associates throughout Europe, Asia, Brazil & the USA.
Membership(s): Association of Authors' Agents.

The Hanbury Agency Ltd
28 Moreton St, London SW1Y 2PE
Tel: (020) 7630 6768
E-mail: enquiries@hanburyagency.com
Web Site: www.hanburyagency.com
Key Personnel
Agent: Maggie Hanbury
Media Manager: Henry de Rougemont
Founded: 1983
Represents general fiction & nonfiction. See web site for submission guidelines. Expanded in 2011 to support media campaigns for authors, including George Alagiah, Tom Bergin, Simon Callow, Anna Caltabiano, Jimmy Connors, Luke Dormehl, Jane Glover, Imran Khan, Roman Krznaric, Judith Lennox, Paul McMahon, Katie Price, Jerry White & Mitch Winehouse. The agency has a strong stable of ghostwriters.
Membership(s): The Association of Authors Agents.
Specializes in popular culture, current affairs & celebrity memoirs.

Hardman & Swainson
4 Kelmscott Rd, London SW11 6QY
Tel: (020) 7223 5176
E-mail: submissions@hardmanswainson.com
Web Site: www.hardmanswainson.com
Key Personnel
Agent: Caroline Hardman *E-mail:* caroline@hardmanswainson.com; Joanna Swainson *E-mail:* joanna@hardmanswainson.com
Rights Dir: Therese Coen
Currently accepting e-mail submissions only. For fiction, send cover letter, one-page synopsis & first three chapters. For nonfiction, send cover letter, proposal or outline, plus sample chapter.

A M Heath & Co Ltd
6 Warwick Court, Holborn, London WC1R 5DJ
Tel: (020) 7242 2811 *Fax:* (020) 7242 2711
E-mail: enquiries@amheath.com
Web Site: www.amheath.com
Key Personnel
Mng Dir: William Hamilton
Dir: Victoria Hobbs
Dir, Foreign Rights: Alexandra McNicoll
Agent: Julia Churchill; Zoe King; Oliver Munson; Euan Thorneycroft
Founded: 1919
No dramatic scripts, poetry or short stories. Preliminary letter, synopsis & first three chapters essential. No reading fee. Commission: Home 10-15%; US & Translation 20%; Film & TV 15%. Overseas associates in Europe, Far East, Japan, South America & USA.
Specializes in fiction, general nonfiction & children's.

Rupert Heath Literary Agency
50 Albemarle St, London W1S 4BD
E-mail: emailagency@rupertheath.com
Web Site: www.rupertheath.com
Key Personnel
Agent: Rupert Heath
Founded: 2001
Represents writers of both fiction & nonfiction. Accepts unsolicited manuscripts by e-mail.
Membership(s): Association of Authors' Agents.
Foreign Rights: Marsh Agency (Camilla Ferrier); Natoli Stefan & Oliva (Roberta Oliva)

Sophie Hicks Agency
60 Gray's Inn Rd, London WC1X 8AQ
Tel: (0203) 735 8870
E-mail: info@sophiehicksagency.com
Web Site: www.sophiehicksagency.com
Key Personnel
Founder: Sophie Hicks *E-mail:* sophie@sophiehicksagency.com
Agent: Sarah Williams *E-mail:* sarah@sophiehicksagency.com
Foreign Rights Dir: Morag O'Brien *E-mail:* morag@sophiehicksagency.com
Founded: 2014
Represent authors of fiction & nonfiction, both adult & children.

David Higham Associates Ltd
5-8 Lower John St, Golden Sq, London W1F 9HA
Tel: (020) 7434 5900 *Fax:* (020) 7437 1072
E-mail: dha@davidhigham.co.uk
Web Site: www.davidhigham.co.uk
Key Personnel
Mng Dir: Anthony Goff *E-mail:* anthonygoff@davidhigham.co.uk
Agent, Books: Veronique Baxter; Jemima Forrester; Georgia Glover; Andrew Gordon; Lizzy Kremer; Caroline Walsh; Alice Williams; Jessica Woollard
Agent, Scripts: Nicky Lund; Georgina Ruffhead
Founded: 1935
Handles fiction, nonfiction (biography, history, current affairs), children's books & scripts. See web site for submissions policy. No reading fee. Commission: Home 15%; US & Translation 20%.

Holroyde Cartey
9 Bickells Yard, 151-153 Bermondsey St, London SE1 3HA
Web Site: www.holroydecartey.com
Key Personnel
Founder: Claire Cartey *E-mail:* claire@holroydecartey.com; Penny Holroyde *E-mail:* penny@holroydecartey.com
Welcomes submissions from debut & established authors & illustrators via e-mail only.

Vanessa Holt Ltd
59 Crescent Rd, Leigh-on-Sea, Essex SS9 2PF
Tel: (01702) 473787
E-mail: v.holt791@btinternet.com
Key Personnel
Contact: Vanessa Holt
Founded: 1989
No unsolicited material. Handles general fiction, nonfiction & non-illustrated children's books. Commission: Home 15%; US & Translation 20%; Radio/TV/Film 15%.
Specializes in commercial & literary fiction, crime fiction & books with potential for international sales.

Kate Hordern Literary Agency
18 Mortimer Rd, Clifton, Bristol BS8 4EY
Tel: (0117) 923 9368
E-mail: katehordern@blueyonder.co.uk
Web Site: www.katehordern.co.uk
Key Personnel
Founder: Kate Hordern
Agent: Anne Williams *E-mail:* annewilliamskhla@googlemail.com
Founded: 1999
General fiction, including crime, thrillers, historical, saga, literary, commercial women's & general nonfiction. Submissions via e-mail only from authors resident in the UK. Send pitch, outline or synopsis & first three chapters. Commission: Home 15%; US & Translation 20%.

Tanja Howarth Literary Agency
19 New Row, London WC2N 4LA
Tel: (020) 7240 5553 *Fax:* (020) 7379 0969
E-mail: tanja.howarth@btinternet.com
Key Personnel
Contact: Tanja Howarth
Founded: 1970
No children's books, plays or poetry. No unsolicited manuscripts. Preliminary letter preferred. No reading fee. Established agent for foreign literature, particularly from the German language. Commission: Home 15%; Translation 20%.
Specializes in fiction & nonfiction from British authors.

Jill Hughes Foreign Rights
Hop Hill Cottage, Auburn, Lincoln LN5 9DZ
Tel: (01522) 788 110 *Fax:* (01522) 788 199
E-mail: contact@jhforeignrights.co.uk
Web Site: www.jhforeignrights.co.uk
Key Personnel
Agent: Jill Hughes
No English language rights or submissions from authors seeking an agent; no foreign books for UK publication.
Specializes in translation rights for fiction, nonfiction & children's books for authors, independent publishers & literary agencies from the UK & USA.

Intercontinental Literary Agency
5 New Concordia Wharf, Mill St, London SE1 2BB
Tel: (020) 7379 6611
E-mail: ila@ila-agency.co.uk
Web Site: www.ila-agency.co.uk

Key Personnel
Mng Dir: Nicki Kennedy *E-mail:* nicki.kennedy@
ila-agency.co.uk
Agent: Sam Edenborough *E-mail:* sam.
edenborough@ila-agency.co.uk; Clementine
Gaisman *E-mail:* clementine.gaisman@ila-
agency.co.uk; Jenny Robson *E-mail:* jenny.
robson@ila-agency.co.uk; Katherine West
E-mail: katherine.west@ila-agency.co.uk
Founded: 1965
Translation rights only.

Janklow & Nesbit (UK) Ltd
13a Hillgate St, London W8 7SP
Tel: (020) 7243 2975 *Fax:* (020) 7243 4339
E-mail: queries@janklow.co.uk
Web Site: www.janklowandnesbit.co.uk
Key Personnel
Agent: Jessie Botterill; Rebecca Carter; Will
Francis; Tim Glister; Hellie Ogden; Claire Pa-
terson Conrad
Chief Financial Officer: Kirsty Gordon
Head of Rights: Rebecca Folland
Founded: 1973
For fiction submissions, send informative cover
letter, first three chapters (approximately 50
pages) & brief synopsis. For nonfiction submis-
sions, send full outline & cover letter. Include
e-mail address on cover letter & return enve-
lope with sufficient postage if material is to be
returned.
U.S. Office(s): Janklow & Nesbit Associates, 445
Park Ave, New York, NY 10022-2606, United
States *Tel:* 212-421-1700 *Fax:* 212-980-3671
E-mail: info@janklow.com *Web Site:* www.
janklowandnesbit.com

Johnson & Alcock Ltd
Clerkenwell House, 45-47 Clerkenwell Green,
London EC1R 0HT
Tel: (020) 7251 0125 *Fax:* (020) 7251 2172
Web Site: www.johnsonandalcock.co.uk
Key Personnel
Agent: Michael Alcock; Andrew Hewson; Anna
Power; Edward Wilson
Associate Agent: Becky Thomas
Founded: 1956
Specializes in general fiction & nonfiction.

Jane Judd Literary Agency
18 Belitha Villas, London N1 1PD
Tel: (020) 7607 0273 *Fax:* (020) 7607 0623
Web Site: www.janejudd.com
Key Personnel
Contact: Jane Judd
Founded: 1986
Handles general fiction & nonfiction. Also repre-
sents USA companies Avon Books & Mercury
House & USA agents Marian Young & Pen-
guin Canada. No scripts, academic, gardening
or do-it-yourself. Approach with letter, includ-
ing synopsis, first chapter & return postage.
Initial telephone call helpful in the case of
nonfiction. Commission: Home 10%, USA &
Translation 20%.
Specializes in biography, crime, health, humor, in-
vestigative journalism, literary, thrillers, travel,
women's interests.

The Frances Kelly Agency
111 Clifton Rd, Kingston upon Thames, Surrey
KT2 6PL
Tel: (020) 8549 7830 *Fax:* (020) 8547 0051
Founded: 1978
No unsolicited manuscripts. Send letter with brief
synopsis, cover & return postage. Commission:
Home 10%; USA & Translation 20%.
Specializes in nonfiction, including illustrated bi-
ography, history, art, self-help, food & wine,
complementary medicine & therapies, finance
& business; trade, reference, academic.

Ki Agency
Studio 315, Screenworks, 22 Highbury Grove,
London N5 2ER
Tel: (020) 3214 8287
Web Site: www.ki-agency.co.uk
Key Personnel
Owner & Agent: Meg Davis *E-mail:* meg@ki-
agency.co.uk
Agent: Ruth Needham *E-mail:* ruth@ki-agency.
co.uk
Founded: 2011
Screenplays: E-mail to Meg as PDF. Books: E-
mail full synopsis & first 3 chapters to appro-
priate agent (see web site for areas of represen-
tation).

Knight Features
20 Crescent Grove, London SW4 7AH
Tel: (020) 7622 1467 *Fax:* (020) 7622 1522
E-mail: info@knightfeatures.co.uk
Web Site: www.knightfeatures.com
Key Personnel
Dir & Proprietor: Peter Knight *E-mail:* peter@
knightfeatures.co.uk
Associate: Samantha Ferris *E-mail:* sam@
knightfeatures.co.uk; Andrew Knight; Gaby
Martin *E-mail:* gaby@knightfeatures.co.uk
Founded: 1985
No poetry, science fiction or cookery. Send by
post letter of introduction, self-addressed,
stamped envelope & CV. Commission depen-
dent upon authors & territories.
Specializes in strip cartoons, major features, se-
rializations, autobiography/memoirs/letters,
biography, astrology, business & economics,
history, humour, formula one racing, puzzles.
Branch Office(s)
Peter Knight Book Associates
Foreign Rep(s): United Media

LAW (Lucas Alexander Whitley Ltd)
14 Vernon St, London W14 0RJ
Tel: (020) 7471 7900 *Fax:* (020) 7471 7910
Web Site: www.lawagency.co.uk
Key Personnel
Mng Dir: Philippa Milnes-Smith
E-mail: philippa@lawagency.co.uk
Dir: Sophie Laurimore
Agent: Julian Alexander; Mark Lucas; Alice
Saunders; Araminta Whitley
Founded: 1996
Handles full-length commercial & literary fiction,
nonfiction & children's books. No plays, po-
etry, textbooks or fantasy. Film & TV scripts
handled for established clients only. Unsolicited
manuscripts considered; send brief covering let-
ter, short synopsis & first three chapters. Self-
addressed, stamped envelope required. No e-
mailed submissions. Commission: Home 15%;
USA & Translation 20%. Overseas associates
worldwide.

LBA Books
91 Great Russell St, London WC1B 3PS
Tel: (020) 7637 1234
E-mail: info@lbabooks.com
Web Site: www.lbabooks.com
Key Personnel
Owner & Agent: Luigi Bonomi
Agent: Louise Lamont; Amanda Preston
Junior Agent: Danielle Zigner
Founded: 2005
Unsolicited manuscripts accepted. No poetry, film
scripts or short stories.

Lenz-Mulligan Rights & Co-Editions
15 Sandbourne Ave, Merton Park, London SW19
3EW
Tel: (077759) 48300 (cell)
E-mail: lenzmulligan@btinternet.com
Key Personnel
Proprietor: Gundhild Lenz-Mulligan

Founded: 1998
Specializes in children's books.

Barbara Levy Literary Agency
64 Greenhill, Hampstead High St, London NW3
5TZ
Tel: (020) 7435 9046 *Fax:* (020) 7431 2063
Key Personnel
Dir: Barbara Levy
Associate: John F Selby
Founded: 1986
Handles fiction, nonfiction & TV presenters. No
unsolicited manuscripts. Send detailed prelim-
inary letter. Commission: Home 15%; USA
20%.

Gunnar Lie & Associates Ltd
3 Linkside, New Malden, Surrey KT3 4LA
Tel: (020) 8605 1097
E-mail: gunnar@gunnarlie.com
Key Personnel
Mng Dir: Gunnar Lie *E-mail:* gunnar@gunnarlie.
com
Export Manager: John Edgeler *E-mail:* john@
gunnarlie.com; Guillaume Ferrand
E-mail: guillaume@gunnarlie.com
Export Sales & Marketing Administrator:
Matthew Walsh *E-mail:* matthew@gunnarlie.
com
Founded: 1995
Export sales & marketing.
Specializes in international sales & marketing for
illustrated adult & children's books.

Limelight Celebrity Management Ltd
10 Filmer Mews, 75 Filmer Rd, London SW6 7JF
Tel: (020) 7384 9950 *Fax:* (020) 7384 9955
E-mail: mail@limelightmanagement.com
Web Site: www.limelightmanagement.com
Key Personnel
Mng Dir: Fiona Lindsay *E-mail:* fiona@
limelightmanagement.com
TV & literary agency with celebrity management.
No poetry, scripts or screenplays. Send preliminary letter, brief synopsis & the first 3 chapters
by e-mail.
Specializes in literary fiction, especially crime,
thrillers, historical, biography, autobiography &
women's commercial fiction; nonfiction, especially cookery, self-improvement, health, diet,
animals, parenting, lifestyle, memoir & TV tie-
ins.

Litopia Corp Ltd, see Redhammer Management
Ltd

Litro Represents
1-15 Cremer St, Studio 213, London E2 8HD
Tel: (020) 3371 9971
E-mail: info@litro.co.uk
Web Site: www.litro.co.uk/litro-represents
Represents handpicked writers published in *Litro
Magazine.* Not currently open to submissions
from authors seeking representation.

Christopher Little Literary Agency
10 Eel Brook Studios, 125 Moore Park Rd, Lon-
don SW6 4PS
Tel: (020) 7736 4455 *Fax:* (020) 7736 4490
E-mail: info@christopherlittle.net
Web Site: www.christopherlittle.net
Key Personnel
Proprietor: Christopher J Little
E-mail: christopher@christopherlittle.net
Senior Agent: Zoe King
Founded: 1979
No unsolicited manuscripts.
Foreign Rights: Curtis Brown Group Ltd

Andrew Lownie Literary Agency Ltd
36 Great Smith St, London SW1P 3BU

Tel: (020) 7222 7574 *Fax:* (020) 7222 7576
E-mail: andrew@andrewlownie.co.uk
Web Site: www.andrewlownie.co.uk
Key Personnel
Chief Executive: Andrew Lownie
Founded: 1988
Specializes in general nonfiction (especially history, biography & current affairs) & fiction (especially crime, historical literary & thrillers).

Lucas Alexander Whitley Ltd, see LAW (Lucas Alexander Whitley Ltd)

Jennifer Luithlen Agency
88 Holmfield Rd, Leicester LE2 1SB
Tel: (0116) 2738863
Web Site: luithlenagency.com
Key Personnel
Proprietor: Jennifer Luithlen *E-mail:* jennifer@luithlenagency.co.uk
Founded: 1986
Specializes in high quality children's fiction.

Lutyens & Rubinstein
21 Kensington Park Rd, London W11 2EU
Tel: (020) 7792 4855 *Fax:* (020) 7792 4855
E-mail: info@lutyensrubinstein.co.uk
Web Site: www.lutyensrubinstein.co.uk
Key Personnel
Partner: Jane Finigan; Sarah Lutyens; Felicity Rubinstein
Foreign Rights: Anna Steadman *E-mail:* anna@lutyensrubinstein.co.uk
Founded: 1993
No TV, film radio or theatre scripts. Unsolicited manuscripts accepted; send material via e-mail only (submissions@lutyensrubinstein.co.uk). No reading fee. Commission: Home 15%; USA & Translation 20%.
Membership(s): Association of Authors' Agents.
Specializes in adult fiction & nonfiction.

Marjacq Scripts Ltd
19/21 Crawford St, Box 412, London W1H 1PJ
Tel: (020) 7935 9499 *Fax:* (020) 7935 9115
E-mail: enquiries@marjacq.com
Web Site: www.marjacq.com
Key Personnel
Dir: Guy Herbert *E-mail:* guy@marjacq.com
Literary Agent: Diana Beaumont
  E-mail: diana@marjacq.com; Philip Patterson
  E-mail: philip@marjacq.com; Imogen Pelham
  E-mail: imogen@marjacq.com
Literary Agent & Foreign Rights Manager: Sandra Sawicka *E-mail:* sandra@marjacq.com
Film & TV Agent: Leah Middleton
  E-mail: leah@marjacq.com
Associate Agent: Catherine Pellegrino
  E-mail: catherine@marjacq.com
Founded: 1974 (as TV script agency by George Markstein & Jacqui Lyons)
General literary agency, with broad experience in other entertainment rights licensing.
Specializes in literary & commercial fiction & nonfiction, crime, thrillers, women's fiction, children's, sci-fi, horror, history, biography, sport, travel & health.
Parent Company: Marjacq Micro Ltd

The Marsh Agency Ltd
50 Albemarle St, London W1S 4BD
Tel: (020) 7493 4361
E-mail: hello@marsh-agency.co.uk
Web Site: www.marsh-agency.co.uk
Key Personnel
Chief Executive Officer: Susie Nicklin
Mng Dir: Camilla Ferrier
Founded: 1994
Specializes in international rights, literary & commercial fiction & nonfiction.

J P Marshall Literary Agency
Affiliate of A M Heath & Co Ltd
c/o A M Heath & Co Ltd, 6 Warwick Court, Holborn, London WC1R 5DJ
Key Personnel
Owner & Agent: Jaime Marshall *E-mail:* jaime@jpmarshall.co.uk
Specializes in upmarket nonfiction in the areas of popular economics, psychology & business.

MBA Literary Agents Ltd
62 Grafton Way, London W1T 5DW
Tel: (020) 7387 2076 *Fax:* (020) 7387 2042
E-mail: agent@mbalit.co.uk
Web Site: www.mbalit.co.uk
Key Personnel
Mng Dir: Laura Longrigg *E-mail:* laura@mbalit.co.uk; Diana Tyler *E-mail:* diana@mbalit.co.uk
Dir: David Riding *E-mail:* david@mbalit.co.uk; Susan Smith *E-mail:* susan@mbalit.co.uk
Agent: Sophie Gorell Barnes *E-mail:* sophie@mbalit.co.uk
Founded: 1971
Handles fiction & nonfiction, TV, film radio & theatre scripts. No poetry. Works in conjunction with agents in most countries. No unsolicited manuscripts. Commission: Home 15%, Overseas 20%; Theatre/TV Radio 10%; Film 10-20%.
Foreign Rep(s): JABberwocky Literary Agency; Donald Maass Literary Agency; Writers House LLC

Duncan McAra
3 Viewfield Ave, Bishopbriggs, Glasgow G64 2AG
Tel: (0141) 772 1067
E-mail: duncanmcara@mac.com
Founded: 1988
Also editorial consultancy.
Specializes in archaeology, architecture, art, biography, history, literary fiction, literature, military & Scottish.

Madeleine Milburn Literary, TV & Film Agency
10 Shepherd Market, Mayfair, London W1J 7QF
Tel: (020) 7499 7550
E-mail: submissions@madeleinemilburn.com
Web Site: madeleinemilburn.com
Key Personnel
Dir & Agent: Madeleine Milburn
Financial Dir: Giles Milburn
Agent & Editor: Anna Hogarty
Rights Agent: Alice Sutherland-Hawes
Membership(s): Association of Authors' Agents (AAA).
Specializes in fiction including literary, Richard & Judy selections, crime, thrillers, psychological suspense, horror, women's, romantic comedy, children's, young adult, crossover & general. Also looking for nonfiction including historical, memoirs, popular psychology & self-help.

Cathy Miller Foreign Rights Agency
29A The Quadrangle, 49 Atalanta St, London SW6 6TU
Tel: (020) 7386 5473 *Fax:* (020) 7385 1774
Key Personnel
Mng Dir: Cathy Miller *E-mail:* cathy@millerrightsagency.com
Founded: 1981
Consultants to publishers worldwide in the field of translation rights, worldwide market research for publishers interested in European potential, help with negotiating rights contracts & representation.
Specializes in foreign rights.

William Morris Agency (UK) Ltd
100 New Oxford St, London WC1A 1HB

Tel: (020) 7534 6800
E-mail: ldnofficeasst1@wmeentertainment.com
Web Site: www.wmeauthors.co.uk; www.wma.com
Key Personnel
Agent: Simon Trewin
Founded: 1965
Worldwide theatrical & literary agency with offices in New York, Beverly Hills & Nashville & associates in Sydney. Handles TV scripts, fiction & general nonfiction. No unsolicited film, TV or stage material at all. Manuscripts for books with preliminary letter. No reading fee. Commission: TV 10%; UK Books 15%; USA Books & Translation 20%.

Mulcahy Associates Ltd
The Old Truman Brewery, 91 Brick Lane, London E1 6QL
E-mail: enquiries@ma-agency.com; submissions@mmbcreative.com
Web Site: www.mmbcreative.com
Key Personnel
Owner & Agent: Ivan Mulcahy
Agent: Sallyanne Sweeney
Accept unsolicited manuscripts by e-mail only. Send covering letter, synopsis & first 3 chapters to submissions@mmbcreative.com. No reading fee.

Toby Mundy Associates Ltd
6 Bayley St, Bedford Sq, London WC1B 3HE
Tel: (020) 3713 0067
E-mail: submissions@tma-agency.com
Web Site: tma-agency.com
Key Personnel
Founder & Agent: Toby Mundy
Founded: 2014
Creative management company that represents authors & speakers & helps brands to publish. Send brief synopsis, first chapter (cut & pasted into body of e-mail) & note about yourself via e-mail only. No hard copies accepted.

Northbank Talent Management
Acre House, 11-15 William Rd, London NW1 3ER
E-mail: info@northbanktalent.com
Web Site: www.northbanktalent.com
Key Personnel
Founder & Chief Executive: Diane Banks
Executive Dir & Agent, Nonfiction: Martin Redfern
Agent, Children's & Young Adult, Sci-Fi & Fantasy: Chloe Seager
Agent, Fiction: Kate Burke
Broadcast & Brand Licensing Agent: James Carroll
Operations Assistant: Ciara Corrigan
Full service literary & talent agency welcoming all submissions from debut or established talent. Send background information about yourself, synopsis & first 3 chapters by e-mail to fiction@northbanktalent.com, nonfiction@northbanktalent.com or childrens@northbanktalent.com. No hard copy submissions; no poetry, plays, scripts, academic books or short stories.

Andrew Nurnberg Associates International Ltd
20-23 Greville St, London EC1N 8SS
Tel: (020) 3327 0400 *Fax:* (020) 7430 0801
E-mail: info@nurnberg.co.uk
Web Site: www.andrewnurnberg.com
Key Personnel
Mng Dir: Andrew Nurnberg
Deputy Mng Dir (Italy, Latin America, Portugal, Spain): Sarah Nundy
Dir, Support Operations: Vicky Mark
Financial Dir: Helen Dudley
Founded: 1977
Represent fiction, nonfiction & children's fiction. No children's picture books, poetry or scripts

for film, TV, radio or theatre. No reading fee. See web site for submission guidelines. Commission: Home 15%; USA & Translation 20%. Specializes in foreign rights.
Branch Office(s)
Andrew Nurnberg Associates Sofia, jk Yavorov Blvd, 56-B, Apartment 9, 1111 Sofia, Bulgaria, Contact: Anna Droumeva *Tel:* (02) 9862819 *Fax:* (02) 9862819 *E-mail:* anna@anas-bg.com (covers Albania, Bosnia, Bulgaria, Macedonia, Montenegro, Romania, Serbia)
Room 1705, Culture Sq, No 59 Jia, Zhongguancun St, Haidian District, Beijing 100872, China, Contact: Jackie Huang *Tel:* (010) 825-04106; (010) 888-10959 *Fax:* (010) 825-04200 *E-mail:* jhuang@nurnberg.com.cn *Web Site:* www.nurnberg.com.cn
Andrew Nurnberg Associates Prague, Jugoslavskych Partyzanu 17, 160 00 Prague 6, Czech Republic, Contact: Petra Tobiskova *Tel:* 222 782 041 *Fax:* 222 782 041 *E-mail:* tobiskova@nurnberg.cz (covers Czech Republic, Slovak Republic, Slovenia)
Andrew Nurnberg Associates Budapest, Gyori ut 20, Budapest 1123, Hungary, Contact: Judit Hermann *Tel:* (01) 3026451; (01) 3113948 *Fax:* (01) 5500080 *E-mail:* j.hermann@nurnberg.hu *Web Site:* www.nurnberg.hu (covers Croatia, Hungary)
Andrew Nurnberg Associates Baltic, PO Box 77, Riga LV-1011, Latvia, Contact: Tatjana Zoldnere *Tel:* 67506495 *Fax:* 67506494 *E-mail:* zoldnere@anab.apollo.lv (covers Estonia, Latvia, Lithuania, Ukraine)
Andrew Nurnberg Associates Warsaw, Moldawska 9, 6th floor, 02-127 Warsaw, Poland, Contact: Marcin Biegaj *E-mail:* marcin.biegaj@nurnberg.pl
Andrew Nurnberg Literary Agency, Flat 72, Stroenie 6, 21 Tsvetnoy Blvd, 127051 Moscow, Russia, Contact: Ludmilla Sushkova *Tel:* (495) 625 8188 *Fax:* (495) 625 8188 *E-mail:* sushkova@awax.ru
Andrew Nurnberg Associates Taiwan, 9F, No 164, Sec 4, Nan-King East Rd, Taipei 10553, Taiwan, Contact: Whitney Hsu *Tel:* (02) 2579 8251 *Fax:* (02) 2579 8564 *E-mail:* whsu@nurnberg.com.tw *Web Site:* www.nurnberg.com.tw

Clare Painter Associates Ltd
122 Caldecott Rd, Abingdon, Oxon OX14 5EP
Tel: (01235) 528432
Web Site: www.clarepainterassociates.com
Key Personnel
Founder & Dir: Clare Painter *E-mail:* clare@clarepainterassociates.com
Founded: 2009 (includes digital licensing agency originally founded in 2002 as Attwooll Associates Ltd)
Digital licensing agency & digital rights consultancy.
Specializes in digital licensing representing publishers for institutional, educational & corporate markets; copyright audits; rights research, assessment & clearances for digital use (for archives, ebooks, web sites, e-learning etc).

Peake Associates
PO Box 66726, London NW5 9FE
Tel: (020) 7681 4307
E-mail: tony@tonypeake.com
Web Site: www.tonypeake.com/agency/index.htm
Key Personnel
Proprietor: Tony Peake
Currently not accepting new clients.
Specializes in fiction & nonfiction.

Maggie Pearlstine Associates Ltd
31 Ashley Gardens, Ambrosden Ave, London SW1P 1QE
Tel: (020) 7828 4212 *Fax:* (020) 7834 5546

Key Personnel
Dir: Maggie Pearlstine *E-mail:* maggie@pearlstine.co.uk
Founded: 1989
Small, selective agency. UK based authors only. Handles general nonfiction & fiction. No children's poetry, horror, science fiction short stories or scripts. Commission: Home 12.5% (fiction), 10% (nonfiction); US & Translation 20%; TV, Film & Journalism 20%.
Specializes in biography, current affairs, health & history.

Jonathan Pegg Literary Agency
32 Batoum Gardens, London W6 7QD
Tel: (020) 7603 6830 *Fax:* (020) 7348 0629
E-mail: info@jonathanpegg.com; submissions@jonathanpegg.com
Web Site: www.jonathanpegg.com
Key Personnel
Owner: Jonathan Pegg
Unsolicited manuscripts accepted. See web site for full submission guidelines.
Membership(s): Association of Authors' Agents.
Specializes in fiction (literary fiction, thrillers & quality commercial); nonfiction (current affairs, memoir & biography, history, popular science, nature, arts & culture, lifestyle & popular psychology).

Peters Fraser + Dunlop
Drury House, Books Division, 34-43 Russell St, London WC2B 5HA
Tel: (020) 7344 1000 *Fax:* (020) 7836 9539
E-mail: info@pfd.co.uk
Web Site: www.petersfraserdunlop.com
Key Personnel
Chief Executive Officer: Caroline Michel
Executive Dir, Books Dept & Senior Agent: Elizabeth Sheinkman
International Rights Dir: Alexandra Cliff
Head, Books: Tim Bates
Senior Agent: Annabel Merullo
Agent: Rowan Lawton
Rights Agent: Rebecca Wearmouth
Founded: 1988
Handles adult fiction & nonfiction. Send hard copy of first three chapters along with synopsis & brief CV. No reading fee. Commission: Home 10%; US & Translation 20%.
Specializes in literary, film & actors agency.

PEW Literary Agency Ltd
46 Lexington St, London W1F 0LP
Tel: (020) 7734 4464
E-mail: assistant@pewliterary.com; submissions@pewliterary.com
Web Site: www.pewliterary.com
Key Personnel
Founder & Agent: Patrick Walsh
Foreign Rights: Margaret Halton
Assistant: John Ash *E-mail:* john@pewliterary.com
Submissions accepted by post & e-mail. Do not send SASE. For fiction, submit cover letter, opening 3 chapters (or 50 pages) & synopsis. Nonfiction proposals should include cover letter, be approximately 30 pages & address what the book is about, who you are, summary of the market for the book, chapter of sample text & outline of chapters. See web site for full details.

The Piquant Agency
4 Thornton Rd, Carlisle CA3 9HZ
Mailing Address: PO Box 83, Carlisle CA3 9GR
Tel: (01228) 525075
E-mail: info@piquant.net
Key Personnel
Contact: Pieter J Kwant *E-mail:* pieter@piquant.net

Founded: 2000
Specializes in theology, Christian missions & life stories.

Redhammer Management Ltd
186 Bickenhall Mansions, Bickenhall St, London W1U 6BX
Tel: (020) 7486 3465 *Fax:* (020) 7000 1249
E-mail: info@redhammer.info
Web Site: www.redhammer.info
Key Personnel
Chief Executive Officer: Peter Cox *E-mail:* peter@redhammer.info
Founded: 1993
Require all submissions to follow the guidelines on web site. Commission by negotiation.
Specializes in general, no children's or poetry.

Rights People
Division of Working Partners Ltd
Stanley House, St Chad's Pl, London WC1X 9HH
Tel: (020) 7841 3950
E-mail: info@rightspeople.com
Web Site: www.rightspeople.com
Key Personnel
Dir: Alexandra Devlin *E-mail:* alexandradevlin@rightspeople.com; Allison Hellegers *E-mail:* allisonh@rightspeople.com
Rights Dir: Rachel Richardson *E-mail:* rachelr@rightspeople.com; Harim Yim *E-mail:* harimy@rightspeople.com
Founded: 2006
Specializes in children's fiction.

Rogers, Coleridge & White Ltd
20 Powis Mews, London W11 1JN
Tel: (020) 7221 3717 *Fax:* (020) 7229 9084
E-mail: info@rcwlitagency.com
Web Site: www.rcwlitagency.com
Key Personnel
Chair: Gill Coleridge
Dir: Natasha Fairweather; Peter Straus
Dir, USA: Patricia White
Agent: Georgia Garrett
Foreign Rights: Stephen Edwards; Laurence Laluyaux
Founded: 1967
No scripts for theatre, film or television. Fiction submissions by post only including cover letter & first three chapters. Nonfiction submissions should include proposal up to 20 pages. Include stamped, self-addressed envelope for return of material. Young adult & children's fiction should be submitted via e-mail to clairewilson@rcwlitagency.com. Commission: Home 10%; USA 15%; Translation 20%.
Specializes in fiction, nonfiction & children's.
Foreign Rep(s): ICM

Elizabeth Roy Literary Agency
White Cottage, Greatford, Near Stamford, Lincs PE9 4PR
Tel: (01778) 560672
Web Site: www.elizabethroy.co.uk
Key Personnel
Contact: Elizabeth Roy
Founded: 1991
Send preliminary letter, synopsis, sample chapters, names of previous publishers & agents & return postage. No reading fee. Commission: Home 10-15%; Overseas 20%.
Specializes in children's books (fiction & nonfiction), children's books illustrators.

The Sayle Literary Agency
One Petersfield, Cambridge CB1 1BB
Tel: (01223) 303035
E-mail: info@sayleliteraryagency.com
Web Site: www.sayleliteraryagency.com
Key Personnel
Proprietor: Rachel Calder
Founded: 1896

Send first three chapters & outline of the remainder plus biographical details. No reading fee.
Specializes in literary & crime fiction, biography, history, current affairs, popular science, travel, music & general nonfiction.

Sheil Land Associates Ltd
52 Doughty St, London WC1N 2LS
Tel: (020) 7405 9351 *Fax:* (020) 7831 2127
E-mail: info@sheilland.co.uk
Web Site: www.sheilland.co.uk
Key Personnel
Chief Executive: Sonia Land
Book Agent: Piers Blofeld; Ian Drury; Vivien Green
Foreign Agent: Virginia Ascione; Gaia Banks
Film & TV: Lucy Fawcett; Holly Hawkins
Founded: 1962
Literary, Theatre & Film Agents. Submission by post only. Include typed cover letter, synopsis of work, short CV & first three chapters. No reading fee. Commission: Home 15%; US & Translation 20%.
Specializes in commercial & literary fiction & nonfiction, including politics, history, military history, thrillers, crime, romance, fantasy, drama, biography, travel, cookery, humor, science fiction & fantasy.
U.S. Office(s): Sheil Land Associates in association with George Borchart Inc, 136 E 57 St, New York, NY 10022, United States *Tel:* 212-753-5785
Foreign Rep(s): APA; Georges Borchardt, Inc; CAA; Farrar, Straus & Giroux, Inc

Dorie Simmonds Agency Ltd
Riverside Quarter, One Eastfields Ave, Unit 5, London SW18 1FQ
Tel: (020) 7736 0002
E-mail: info@doriesimmonds.com
Key Personnel
Proprietor: Dorie Simmonds
Handles a wide range of subjects including general nonfiction & commercial fiction as well as children's books (particularly young adult fiction) & associated rights.
Outline required for nonfiction, short synopsis for fiction with 2-3 sample chapters, writing experience & publishing history explained. Include self-addressed, stamped envelope if return requested.
Specializes in commercial fiction & nonfiction including thrillers, women's fiction, self-help, contemporary & historical biographies, cookbooks, young adult fiction.

Jeffrey Simmons
15 Penn House, Mallory St, London NW8 8SX
Tel: (020) 7224 8917
E-mail: jasimmons@unicombox.co.uk
Key Personnel
Contact: Jeffrey Simmons
Founded: 1978
No science fiction/fantasy, children's books, cookery, crafts, hobbies or gardening. Film scripts handled only if by book-writing clients. Commission: Home 10-15%; US & Foreign 15%.
Specializes in biography & autobiography, cinema & theatre, history, law & crime, politics & world affairs, parapsychology & sport.

Abner Stein Agency
10 Roland Gardens, London SW7 3PH
Tel: (020) 7373 0456 *Fax:* (020) 7370 6316
Key Personnel
Co-Dir: Caspian Dennis *E-mail:* caspian@abnerstein.co.uk; Sandy Violette
Founded: 1971
No scientific, technical. Commission: Home 10%; US & Translation 20%.
Specializes in children's books, fiction, nonfiction.

Micheline Steinberg Associates
Studio 315 ScreenWorks, 22 Highbury Grove, London N5 2ER
Tel: (020) 3214 8292
E-mail: info@steinplays.com
Web Site: www.steinplays.com
Key Personnel
Dir: Micheline Steinberg
Founded: 1985
Dramatic associate for Laurence Pollinger Ltd.
E-mail CV & brief outline of work to submissions@steinplays.com. Commission: Home 10%; Elsewhere 15%.
Specializes in plays for stage, TV, radio & film.

Rochelle Stevens & Co
2 Terretts Pl, Upper St, London N1 1QZ
Tel: (020) 7359 3900
E-mail: info@rochellestevens.com; books@rochellestevens.com (book submissions)
Web Site: www.rochellestevens.com
Key Personnel
Owner & Agent: Rochelle Stevens
Agent: Frances Arnold; Elinor Cooper
Founded: 1984
Represents writers, directors & designers for film, TV, theatre, radio & books. Unsolicited book submissions for fiction, nonfiction or children's books should include a letter about yourself & what has brought you to your current work as well as a synopsis of no more than 1 page & the first 3 chapters.

Miles Stott Children's Literary Agency
East Hook Farm, Lower Quay Rd, Hook, Haverfordwest, Pembrokeshire SA62 4LR
Tel: (01437) 890570
Web Site: www.milesstottagency.co.uk
Key Personnel
Agent: Victoria Birkett *Tel:* (01789) 488142 *E-mail:* victoriabirkett@tiscali.co.uk; Nancy Miles *E-mail:* nancy@milesstottagency.co.uk
Associate Agent: Mandy Suhr *Tel:* (07753) 988143 *E-mail:* mandy@thestoryworks.me.uk
Founded: 2003
Membership(s): Association of Authors' Agents.
Specializes in children's books.

The Susijn Agency Ltd
820 Harrow Rd, London NW10 5JU
Tel: (020) 8968 7435 *Fax:* (020) 8968 7435
E-mail: info@thesusijnagency.com
Web Site: www.thesusijnagency.com
Key Personnel
Founder: Laura Susijn
Founded: 1998
Specializes in fiction & nonfiction in any language, selling worldwide.

Tassy Barham Associates
231 Westbourne Park Rd, London W11 1EB
Tel: (020) 7221 8551
E-mail: tassy@tassybarham.com
Key Personnel
Proprietor: Tassy Barham
Founded: 1999
Specializes in representation of European & American authors, literary agents & publishers in Brazil & Portugal. Also represents Brazilian authors worldwide.

Tibor Jones & Associates
2-6 Atlantic Rd, 2nd floor, Suite A, London SW9 8HY
Tel: (020) 7733 0555
E-mail: enquiries@tiborjones.com
Web Site: tiborjones.com
Key Personnel
Dir: Landa Acevedo-Scott
Creative Dir: Kevin Conroy Scott

Agent: Laura Macdougall *E-mail:* laura@tiborjones.com
Founded: 2007
Submit via e-mail a cover letter, one-page synopsis & first five pages of novel or proposal.
Specializes in fiction & nonfiction.

TMA, see Toby Mundy Associates Ltd

Lavinia Trevor Literary Agency
29 Addison Pl, London W11 4RJ
Tel: (020) 7603 0895
E-mail: info@laviniatrevor.co.uk
Web Site: www.laviniatrevor.co.uk
Key Personnel
Contact: Lavinia Trevor
Founded: 1993
No unsolicited manuscripts.
Specializes in general fiction & nonfiction, including popular science.

Turnaround Publisher Services Ltd
Unit 3, Olympia Trading Estate, Coburg Rd, Wood Green, London N22 6TZ
Tel: (020) 8829 3000; (020) 8829 3002 *Fax:* (020) 8881 5088
E-mail: customercare@turnaround-uk.com
Web Site: www.turnaround-uk.com
Key Personnel
Mng Dir: Bill Godber
Finance Dir: Sue Gregg
Marketing Dir: Claire Thompson *Tel:* (020) 8829 3009 *E-mail:* claire.thompson@turnaround-uk.com
Sales Dir: Ian West *Tel:* (020) 8829 3012 *E-mail:* ian.west@turnaround-uk.com
Customer Service Manager: Julie Thelot *Tel:* (020) 8829 3002 *E-mail:* julie.thelot@turnaround-uk.com
Founded: 1984
Sales agent & distributor to the UK & continental European book trade for a wide variety of quality US & UK publishers.
Specializes in black interest, gay interest, American imports, fiction, music, social & political issues, arts.

Jane Turnbull
58 Elgin Crescent, London W11 2JJ
Mailing Address: Barn Cottage, Veryan, Truro TR2 5QA
Tel: (020) 7727 9409; (01872) 501317
Web Site: www.janeturnbull.co.uk
Key Personnel
Contact: Jane Turnbull *E-mail:* jane@janeturnbull.co.uk
Founded: 1986
No science fiction, sagas or romantic fiction. No unsolicited manuscripts or reading fee. Approach with letter in the first instance. Translation rights handled by Gillon Aitken Associates Ltd. Commission: Home 15%; USA & foreign 20%.
Specializes in biography, history, current affairs, health & diet, fiction & nonfiction & high quality.

United Agents
12-26 Lexington St, London W1F 0LE
Tel: (020) 3214 0800 *Fax:* (020) 3214 0801
E-mail: info@unitedagents.co.uk
Web Site: unitedagents.co.uk
Key Personnel
Dir & Agent: Robert Kirby
Partner: Caradoc King
Joint Head, Foreign Rights: Linda Shaughnessy
Associate Agent: Ariella Feiner; Katy Jones; Wendy Millyard
Agent: Caroline Dawnay; Jon Elek; Jodie Marsh; Charlotte Robertson; Zoe Ross
Founded: 2007

Jo Unwin Literary Agency
c/o Rogers, Coleridge & White Ltd, 20 Powis
    Mews, London W11 1JN
Tel: (020) 7221 3717
E-mail: jo@jounwin.co.uk
Web Site: www.jounwin.co.uk
Key Personnel
Owner & Agent: Jo Unwin
Accept unsolicited manuscripts.

VeroK Agency
29 Strathearn Rd, Sutton, Surrey SM1 2RS
Tel: (020) 8395 6916
E-mail: info@verokagency.com
Web Site: www.verokagency.com
Key Personnel
Founder: Veronique Kirchhoff
Founded: 2008
Specializes in children's & young adult publish-
    ing.

Vertigo Communications LLP
37 Eton Ave, London N12 0BDA
Tel: (020) 7100 2523
E-mail: info@vertigocommunications.co.uk
Web Site: www.vertigocommunications.co.uk
Key Personnel
Founder: Jenny Boyce *E-mail:* jenny@
    vertigocommunications.co.uk
Founded: 2007
Specializes in popular culture, fiction, music, il-
    lustrated & licensed entertainment.

The Viney Agency
23 Erlanger Rd, Telegraph Hill, London SE14
    5TF
Tel: (020) 7732 3331
Web Site: www.thevineyagency.com
Key Personnel
Owner & Agent: Charlie Viney *E-mail:* charlie@
    thevineyagency.com
Agent: Kate Shaw
Editorial Dir, Children's: Pippa Le Quesne
Founded: 2008
Acts for published authors across many genres in-
    cluding adult & children's fiction writers, biog-
    raphers & historians. Sells world English rights

for its authors directly to UK, Australasia &
    North America. No reading fee.
Membership(s): Association of Authors' Agents.

Peter Ward Book Exports
One Adams Mews, London SW17 7RD
Tel: (020) 8672 1171
Key Personnel
Owner: Richard Ward *E-mail:* richard@
    pwbookex.com
Founded: 1974
Publishers' commission representatives.
Specializes in Arab world, Cyprus, Greece, Iran,
    Israel, Malta & Turkey.

Watson, Little Ltd
48-56 Bayham Pl, London NW1 0EU
Tel: (020) 7388 7529 *Fax:* (020) 7388 8501
E-mail: office@watsonlittle.com
Web Site: www.watsonlittle.com
Key Personnel
Mng Dir: Mandy Little *E-mail:* al@watsonlittle.
    com
Dir: James Wills *E-mail:* jw@watsonlittle.com
Agent: Laetitia Rutherford; Donald Winchester
Handles fiction & nonfiction. No scripts. Send
    preliminary letter with synopsis. Commission:
    Home 15%; US 20%; Translation 20%.
Specializes in business, history, popular science,
    psychology & self-help, literary & commer-
    cial fiction, serious nonfiction, popular culture,
    celebrity, health, children's sport, humor.

Josef Weinberger Ltd
12-14 Mortimer St, London W1T 3JJ
Tel: (020) 7580 2827 *Fax:* (020) 7436 9616
E-mail: general.info@jwmail.co.uk
Web Site: www.josef-weinberger.com
Key Personnel
Manager: Michael Callahan
Founded: 1885
No unsolicited manuscripts; introductory letter
    essential. No reading fee.
Agent & publisher of scripts for the theatre.

Eve White Literary Agency Ltd
54 Gloucester St, London SW1V 4EG
Tel: (020) 7630 1155
Web Site: www.evewhite.co.uk
Key Personnel
Agent: Eve White
Founded: 2003
Please see the web site before submitting. E-mail
    submissions accepted for adult fiction, nonfic-
    tion & children's fiction; include sample in one
    e-mail & one attachment. Include title page &
    numbered pages, first three chapters (double-
    spaced) & very brief synopsis. Nonfiction sub-
    missions must include proposal.
Does not accept poetry, short stories or screen-
    plays & are not reading science fiction or fan-
    tasy for adults, picture books or books for chil-
    dren under 7. No American or Australian au-
    thors.
Specializes in fiction & nonfiction for adults &
    children ages 7 & up.

Dinah Wiener Ltd
12 Cornwall Grove, London W4 2LB
Tel: (020) 8994 6011 *Fax:* (020) 8994 6044
E-mail: dinah@dwla.co.uk
Key Personnel
Dir: Dinah Wiener
Associate: Marianna Wiener
Founded: 1985
Handles fiction & general nonfiction. No scripts,
    children's or poetry. Manuscripts submitted
    must include self-addressed envelope & be
    typed in double-spacing. Commission: Home
    15%; USA & Translation 20%.
Specializes in autobiography, cookery, popular
    science.

Zeno Agency Ltd
Primrose Hill Business Centre, 110 Gloucester
    Ave, London NW1 3LH
Tel: (020) 7096 0927
E-mail: info@zenoagency.com
Web Site: zenoagency.com
Key Personnel
Dir: John Berlyne
Founded: 2008
Specializes in fantasy & science fiction.

Translation Agencies & Associations

Austria

Interessengemeinschaft von Uebersetzerinnen und Uebersetzern literarischer und wissenschaftlicher Werke (Association of Literary & Scientific Translators)
Seidengasse 13, 1070 Vienna
Tel: (01) 5262044-18; (01) 5262044-51; (01) 5262044-52 *Fax:* (01) 5262044-30
E-mail: info@literturhaus.at; ueg@literturhaus.at
Web Site: www.literaturhaus.at
Key Personnel
Mng Dir: Brigitte Rapp *E-mail:* br@literaturhaus.at
Translator: Nadja Groessing; Claudia Zecher
Founded: 1981

UNIVERSITAS Austria, Berufsverband fuer Dolmetschen und Uebersetzen (UNIVERSITAS Austria, Professional Association for Interpretation & Translation)
Gymnasiumstr 50, 1190 Vienna
Tel: (01) 368 60 60 *Fax:* (01) 368 60 60
E-mail: info@universitas.org
Web Site: www.universitas.org
Key Personnel
President: Alexandra Jantscher-Karlhuber *E-mail:* jantscher.alexandra@universitas.org
Vice President: Edith Vanghelof *E-mail:* edith.vanghelof@universitas.org
Secretary General: Dagmar Sanjath *E-mail:* dagmar.sanjath@universitas.org
Deputy Secretary General: Bianca Schoenhofer *E-mail:* bianca.schoenhofer@universitas.org
Treasurer: Karin Tippelt *E-mail:* karin.tippelt@universitas.org
Founded: 1954

Bulgaria

Bulgarian Translator's Union
29 Slavyanska St, No 4, 6th floor, Room 609, 1000 Sofia
Tel: (02) 986 45 00; (02) 989 45 43 *Fax:* (02) 981 09 60
E-mail: office@bgtranslators.org; prevodi_spb@mail.orbitel.bg
Web Site: www.bgtranslators.org
Key Personnel
Chairman: Emilia Staicheva
Founded: 1974
Also publishes.
Membership(s): European Council of Associations of Literary Translators; International Federation of Translators.
Publication(s): *Panorama* (magazine)

China

Polyglot Ltd
New World Times Center, 904 S Tower, 2191 Guangyuan Rd E, Guangzhou 510500
Tel: (020) 8764 1878 *Fax:* (020) 8764 2003
E-mail: info@polyglot.biz
Web Site: www.polyglot.biz

Provides translation, interpretation & simultaneous meeting interpretation in all fields. Also provides localization of web sites into Chinese, writing articles in multi-languages, foreign languages recording, proofreading, interpreters/translators recommending, web site designing & making, etc. Provides translating services in more than 30 languages such as Arabic, Bengalese, Bulgarian, Burmese, Cambodian, Czech, Dutch, English, Finnish, French, German, Hungarian, Indic, Indonesian, Italian, Japanese, Korean, Laotian, Malay, Mongolian, Nepali, Polish, Portuguese, Romanian, Russian, Slovak, Spanish, Swedish, Tamil, Thai, Turkish & Vietnamese.

TAC, see Translators Association of China

Translators Association of China
24 Baiwanzhuang St, Xicheng District, Beijing 100037
Tel: (010) 68997177
E-mail: info@tac-online.org.cn; taccn@tac-online.org.cn
Web Site: www.tac-online.org.cn
Key Personnel
President: Zhou Mingwei
Executive Vice President: Wang Gangyi
Founded: 1982
Publication(s): *Chinese Translators Journal (CTJ)*

Czech Republic

Jednota Tlumocniku a Prekladatelu (JTP) (Union of Interpreters & Translators)
Senovazne nam 23, 110 00 Prague 1
Tel: 224 142 517 *Fax:* 224 142 312
E-mail: jtp@jtpunion.org
Web Site: www.jtpunion.org
Founded: 1990
Glossaries, dictionaries, terminology, proceedings of specialised conferences.
Membership(s): International Federation of Translators (FIT).
Publication(s): *ToP* (quarterly, bulletin)

JTP, see Jednota Tlumocniku a Prekladatelu (JTP)

Obec Prekladatelu (Czech Literary Translators' Guild)
Pod Nuselskymi schody 3, 120 00 Prague 2
Tel: 222 564 082 *Fax:* 222 564 082
E-mail: info@obecprekladatelu.cz
Web Site: www.obecprekladatelu.cz
Key Personnel
President: Hana Linhartova
Vice President: Alena Lhotova
Secretary: Jarmila Zelenkova
A voluntary association of Czech translators of belles lettres as well as translation theorists, critics, historians & scholars.
Publication(s): *The Unmentionables: Banned Translators 1948-1989*

France

Societe Francaise des Traducteurs (French Society of Translators)
109, rue de Faubourg Saint-Honore, 75008 Paris
Tel: 03 29 46 46 34
E-mail: secretariat@sft.fr
Web Site: www.sft.fr
Key Personnel
President: Bjorn Bratteby
Associate Vice President: Laurence Cuzzolin
Secretary General: Pauline Joustra
Treasurer: Dominique Durand-Fleischer
Editor-in-Chief: Daniele Laruelle
Founded: 1947
Publication(s): *Traduire* (biannually, journal)

Germany

AS Translations Uebersetzungs- und Dolmetscherdienst
Vogesenstr 23, 63456 Hanau
Tel: (06181) 65221 *Fax:* (06181) 3692888
Key Personnel
Contact: Annerose Scheidel *E-mail:* annerose.scheidel@as-translations.de
Membership(s): Bundesverbandes der Dolmetscher und Uebersetzer eV (BDUE).

BDUE, see Bundesverband der Dolmetscher und Uebersetzer eV (BDUE)

Bundesverband der Dolmetscher und Uebersetzer eV (BDUE) (Federal Association of Interpreters & Translators)
Uhlandstr 4-5, 10623 Berlin
Tel: (030) 88712830 *Fax:* (030) 88712840
E-mail: info@bdue.de
Web Site: www.bdue.de
Key Personnel
President: Andre Lindemann
Publication(s): *Mitteilung fuer Dolmetscher und Uebersetzer - MDUE* (6 times/yr, journal)

Deutscher Uebersetzerfonds
c/o Literary Colloquium Berlin, Am Sandwerder 5, 14109 Berlin
Tel: (030) 80 49 08 56 *Fax:* (030) 80 49 08 57
E-mail: mail@uebersetzerfonds.de
Web Site: www.uebersetzerfonds.de
Key Personnel
Chairman: Thomas Brovot
Deputy Chairman: Ulrich Blumenbach
Mng Dir: Juergen Jakob Becker *Tel:* (030) 81 69 96 25
Founded: 1997

VDU, see Verband deutschsprachiger Uebersetzer literarischer und wissenschaftlicher Werke eV (VDUe)

Verband deutschsprachiger Uebersetzer literarischer und wissenschaftlicher Werke eV (VDUe) (Association of German-speaking Translators of Literary & Scientific Works)
Paula-Thiede-Ufer 10, 10179 Berlin
Tel: (030) 6956-2327 *Fax:* (030) 6956-3656

Web Site: www.literaturuebersetzer.de
Key Personnel
First Chairman: Hinrich Schmidt-Henkel
   E-mail: hinrich.schmidt-henkel@
   literaturuebersetzer.de
Second Chairman: Luis Ruby *E-mail:* luis.ruby@
   literaturuebersetzer.de
Secretary: Martina Tuchy *E-mail:* martina.tuchy@
   literaturuebersetzer.de
Treasurer: Josef Winiger *E-mail:* josef.winiger@
   literaturuebersetzer.de
Founded: 1954

Ghana

Bureau of Ghana Languages
Division of National Commission on Culture
PO Box 1851, Accra
Tel: (021) 760551; (021) 772151
Web Site: www.ghanaculture.gov.gh
Founded: 1951
Also publisher.

Hong Kong

KAMS Information & Publishing Ltd
Ho King Coml Centre, Mong Kok, Kowloon
Tel: 8101 0108
Founded: 1989
Specializes in editing, translation & publishing
   services in more than 20 languages.

India

**CSIR-National Institute of Science
Communication & Information Resources
(CSIR-NISCAIR)**
Dr K S Krishanan Marg, Pusa Campus, New
   Delhi 110 012
Tel: (011) 25846301; (011) 25846304; (011)
   25846305; (011) 25846306; (011) 25846307
   Fax: (011) 25847062
E-mail: director@niscair.res.in
Web Site: www.niscair.res.in
Key Personnel
Dir & Editor-in-Chief: Dr Manoj Kumar Patairiya
   Tel: (011) 25847062
Head, Sales & Marketing: Mr L K Chopra
   E-mail: lkc@niscair.res.in
Founded: 2002
Membership(s): FID.
Specializes in publication of research journals,
   popular science magazines, encyclopedias,
   science & technology books, translation of
   Japanese into English, library automation, com-
   puter networking & database design.
Publication(s): *Annals of Library & Information
   Studies* (journal); *Bharat ki Sampada (Hindi)*
   (journal); *Bhartiya Vaigyanik evam Audyogik
   Anusandhan Patrika (Hindi)* (journal); *CSIR
   News* (newsletter); *CSIR Samachar* (newsletter); *Directory of Scientific Research Institutions in India; Encyclopaedias; Indian Journal
   of Biochemistry & Biophysics; Indian Journal
   of Biotechnology; Indian Journal of Chemical
   Technology; Indian Journal of Chemistry, Section A; Indian Journal of Chemistry, Section B;
   Indian Journal of Engineering & Materials Sciences; Indian Journal of Experimental Biology;
   Indian Journal of Fibre & Textile Research;*

*Indian Journal of Geo-Marine Sciences; In-
   dian Journal of Natural Products & Resources;
   Indian Journal of Pure & Applied Physics; In-
   dian Journal of Radio & Space Physics; Indian
   Journal of Traditional Knowledge; Indian Sci-
   ence Abstracts; Journal of Intellectual Property
   Rights; Journal of Scientific & Industrial Re-
   search; Medicinal & Aromatic Plants Abstracts;
   National Union Catalogue of Scientific Serials
   in India (NUCSSI); Science ki Duniya (Urdu);
   Science Reporter (English); Vigyan Pragati
   (Hindu); The Wealth of India English*
Parent Company: Council of Scientific & Indus-
   trial Research (CSIR)
Branch Office(s)
Spl Institutional Area, 14 Satsang Vihar Marg,
   New Delhi 110 067 *Tel:* (011) 26560141
   Fax: (011) 26862228

**National Institute of Science Communication &
Information Resources**, see CSIR-National
Institute of Science Communication &
Information Resources (CSIR-NISCAIR)

NISCAIR, see CSIR-National Institute of Science
Communication & Information Resources
(CSIR-NISCAIR)

Ireland

**Cumann Aistritheoiri agus Teangairi na
hEireann**, see Irish Translators' & Interpreters'
Association (ITIA)

**Irish Translators' & Interpreters' Association
(ITIA)**
c/o Irish Writers' Centre, 19 Parnell Sq, Dublin 1
Tel: (087) 673 83 86
E-mail: info@translatorsassociation.ie; secretary@
   translatorsassociation.ie
Web Site: www.translatorsassociation.ie
Key Personnel
Chairperson: Mary Phelan
Honorary Secretary: Miriam Watchorn
Honorary Treasurer: Graziano Ciulli
Founded: 1986
Membership(s): European Board of Literary
   Translators Associations (CEATL); Interna-
   tional Federation of Translators (FIT).
Publication(s): *ITIA Bulletin* (monthly, ezine);
   Translation Ireland (journal)

ITIA, see Irish Translators' & Interpreters'
Association (ITIA)

Literature Ireland
Trinity College Dublin, Centre for Literary Trans-
   lation, 36 Fenian St, Dublin 2
Tel: (01) 896 4184
E-mail: info@irelandliterature.com
Web Site: www.irelandliterature.com
Key Personnel
Acting Dir: Rita McCann *E-mail:* rita@
   literatureireland.com
Communications Manager: Florence McDonald
   E-mail: florence@literatureireland.com
Project Manager: Aoife Coughlan *E-mail:* aoife@
   literatureireland.com
Founded: 1994
Not-for-profit organization founded to fund trans-
   lations of literature from Ireland into foreign
   languages & foreign literature into English &
   Irish.
Publication(s): *The Irish Literary Tradition & the
   Contemporary Irish Novel; Literary Treasures
   from Ireland* (catalog); *New Writing from Ire-
   land* (annually, catalog)

Israel

**The Institute for the Translation of Hebrew
Literature (ITHL)**
23 Baruch Hirsch St, 5120217 Bnei Brak
Tel: (03) 579 6830 *Fax:* (03) 579 6832
E-mail: litscene@ithl.org.il
Web Site: www.ithl.org.il
Key Personnel
Dir: Nilli Cohen
Founded: 1962
Main activities include promotion of modern
   Hebrew literature & children's literature in
   translation & serves as literary agent for a
   large number of Israeli writers & assists in the
   preparation of anthologies of Hebrew literature.
Specializes in Hebrew literature in translation.
Publication(s): *Modern Hebrew Literature* (annu-
   ally)

Israel Translators' Association
PO Box 16115, 6116002 Tel Aviv
Tel: (054) 5680398
Web Site: www.ita.org.il
Key Personnel
Chair: Danit Ben-Kiki
Deputy Chair: Yael Cahane-Shadmi
Secretary: Arie Gus
Treasurer: Sarita Krause
Founded: 1987
Association of some 500 translators, mostly free-
   lance. Detailed database of members, with lan-
   guages & specialties.
Publication(s): *Targima*

ITHL, see The Institute for the Translation of
Hebrew Literature (ITHL)

Italy

**AITI (Associazione Italiana Traduttori e
Interpreti)** (Italian Association of Translators
& Interpreters)
c/o Studio Budriesi, Via Camillo Ronzani, 3/9,
   40033 Casalecchio di Reno BO
Tel: (0340) 697 90 89 *Fax:* (06) 233 295 502
Web Site: www.aiti.org
Key Personnel
President: Sandra Bertolini *E-mail:* presidenza@
   aiti.org
Vice President: Orietta Olivetti
   E-mail: vicepresidenza@aiti.org
Secretary: Eleonora Sacchi *E-mail:* segreteria@
   aiti.org
Treasurer: Sylvie Huet *E-mail:* tesoreria@aiti.org
Founded: 1950
Membership(s): Federation Internationale des Tra-
   ducteurs (FIT).
Publication(s): *Guida all'acquisto del servizi di
   traduzione* (handbook); *Guida Interpretazione*
   (handbook); *Il traduttore nuovo* (biannually,
   periodical); *Il Vademecum Fiscale* (handbook)

Associazione Italiana Traduttori e Interpreti,
see AITI (Associazione Italiana Traduttori e
Interpreti)

Lebanon

Ecole de Traducteurs et d'Interpretes de Beyrouth (ETIB)
Rue de Damas, BP 17-5208, Mar Mikhael, Beirut 1104 2020
Tel: (01) 421522 *Fax:* (01) 421060
E-mail: etib@usj.edu.lb
Web Site: www.etib.usj.edu.lb
Key Personnel
Dir: Gina Abou Fadel Saad *E-mail:* gina. aboufadel@usj.edu.lb
Head, Interpretation & Translation: Elaine Farhat Ghanem *E-mail:* elaine.farhatghanem@usj.edu. lb
Head, Translation: Mary Yazbeck *E-mail:* mary. yazbeck@usj.edu.lb
Founded: 1980

ETIB, see Ecole de Traducteurs et d'Interpretes de Beyrouth (ETIB)

Malaysia

Institut Terjemahan & Buku Malaysia (ITBM)
Wisma ITBM, No 2, Jl 2/27E, Seksyen 10, Wangsa Maju, 53300 Kuala Lumpur
Tel: (03) 4145 1800 *Fax:* (03) 4149 1535
E-mail: info@itbm.com.my
Web Site: www.itbm.com.my
Key Personnel
Chief Executive Officer & Mng Dir: Mohd Khair Ngadiron *E-mail:* mkhair@itbm.com.my
General Manager: Sakri Abdullah *E-mail:* sakri@ itbm.com.my
Head, Communications, Sales & Marketing: Mohd Khairulanuar Anshor *E-mail:* anuar@ itbm.com.my
Head, Dept of Translation & Training: Siti Rafiah Sulaiman *E-mail:* s.rafiah@itbm.com.my
Founded: 1993
Translation, editing, subtitling, interpreting, training & support services.

ITBM, see Institut Terjemahan & Buku Malaysia (ITBM)

Norway

Aschehoug Agency
Postboks 363 Sentrum, 0102 Oslo
Tel: 22 40 04 00 *Fax:* 22 20 63 95
E-mail: epost@aschehougagency.no
Web Site: www.aschehougagency.no; www. aschehoug.no
Key Personnel
Rights Dir: Even Rakil *Tel:* 22 90 02 44 97
E-mail: even.rakil@aschehougagency.no
Rights Manager: Henrik Francke *Tel:* 22 91 35 39 22 *E-mail:* henrik.francke@aschehougagency.no
Rights & Contracts Manager: Terje Ekrene Vik *Tel:* 22 91 12 44 85 *E-mail:* terje.ekrene.vik@ aschehougagency.no
Founded: 2004

Norsk Oversetterforening (The Norwegian Association of Literary Translators)
Forfatternes House, Radhusgata 7, 0151 Oslo
Mailing Address: Postboks 579 Sentrum, 0105 Oslo
Tel: 22 47 80 90

E-mail: post@translators.no
Web Site: oversetterforeningen.no
Key Personnel
Chief Executive Officer: Hilde Sveinsson *Tel:* 22 47 80 91 *E-mail:* hilde.sveinsson@translators. no
Founded: 1948
Member organisation.
Specializes in fiction literature.

Poland

Stowarzyszenie Tlumaczy Polskich (Association of Polish Translators & Interpreters)
ul Grazyny 13, 02-548 Warsaw
Tel: (22) 621 56 78
E-mail: stp@stp.org.pl
Web Site: www.stp.org.pl
Key Personnel
President: Monika Ordon-Krzak
Vice President: Maria Janssen
Vice President & Treasurer: Leszek Krol
Secretary: Magdalena Macinska
Founded: 1981

STP, see Stowarzyszenie Tlumaczy Polskich

Slovakia

LIC, see Literarne Informacne Centrum

Literarne Informacne Centrum (The Centre for Information on Literature)
Nam SNP 12, 812 24 Bratislava
Tel: (02) 2047 3506 *Fax:* (02) 5296 4563
E-mail: lic@litcentrum.sk
Web Site: www.litcentrum.sk
Key Personnel
Dir: Miroslava Vallova *Tel:* (02) 2047 3505
E-mail: miroslava.vallova@litcentrum.sk
Publication(s): *Knizna Revue* (11 issues/yr, magazine); *Slniecko* (monthly, magazine); *Slovak Literary Review* (2 issues/yr, magazine)

South Korea

Seoul Selection
6, Samcheong-ro, 2nd floor, Jongno-gu, Seoul 110-190
Tel: (070) 5038-5034; (070) 4060-5064 (direct)
Fax: (070) 8668-1090
E-mail: atoz@seoulselection.com
Web Site: www.seoulselection.com
Founded: 2008
English to Korean/Korean to English.

Spain

Editorial Demipage
C/Pez, 12, 28004 Madrid
Tel: 91 563 88 67 *Fax:* 91 563 00 38
E-mail: madrid@demipage.com
Web Site: www.demipage.com

Key Personnel
Editor: David Villanueva
Founded: 2003

Euro Transmit SL
Grumet 47, 17220 Sant Feliu de Guixols
Tel: 972 32 51 42 *Fax:* 972 32 51 67
E-mail: info@eurotransmit.com
Web Site: www.eurotransmit.com
Key Personnel
Founder: Roswitha Menzel
Founded: 1984
Translation services available in Spanish, German, English, French, Italian, Portuguese & Russian.
Specializes in economic, legal, advertising, scientific & industrial technology texts.

Sweden

Exportradet Swedish Trade Council
World Trade Center, Klarabergsviadukten 70, 101 24 Stockholm
Mailing Address: Box 240, 101 24 Stockholm
Tel: (08) 588 660 00 *Fax:* (08) 588 661 90
E-mail: info@business-sweden.se
Web Site: www.business-sweden.se/export/ exporthjalp
Key Personnel
Chief Executive Officer: Ylva Berg
Chief Financial Officer: Lena Arnelind
Vice President, Sales & Marketing: Charlotte Rylme
Dir, Public Affairs & Corporate Communications: Kristina Windrup Olander
Founded: 1972
Translating & interpreting service of the Swedish Trade Council.

FAT, see Foreningen Auktoriserade Translatorer (FAT)

Foreningen Auktoriserade Translatorer (FAT) (Federation of Authorized Translators)
Blekingegatan 59, 116 62 Stockholm
E-mail: info@aukttranslator.se
Web Site: www.aukttranslator.se
Key Personnel
Chairman: Nadja Chekhov *Tel:* (08) 642 61 24
E-mail: ordforande@aukttranslator.se
Secretary: Donald Hughes *Tel:* (08) 651 59 01
E-mail: sekreterare@aukttranslator.se
Treasurer: Johan Sor *Tel:* (073) 656 18 80 (cell)
E-mail: ekonomi@aukttranslator.se
Founded: 1932
Membership(s): Federation Internationale des Traducteur (FIT).
Publication(s): *FATaburen* (in Swedish, quarterly)

Switzerland

Association Suisse des Traducteurs, Terminologues et Interpretes (ASTTI) (Swiss Association of Translators & Interpreters)
Altenbergstr 29, 3013 Bern
Mailing Address: CP 686, 3000 Bern
Tel: (031) 313 88 10 *Fax:* (031) 313 88 99
E-mail: astti@astti.ch
Web Site: new.astti.ch
Key Personnel
President: Christoph Ruegger *E-mail:* c.ruegger@ astti.ch
General Secretary: Sabine Nonhebel *E-mail:* s. nonhebel@astti.ch

Marketing & Public Relations: Marina Graham
  E-mail: grahammar@astti.ch
Founded: 1966
Promotes the professional, legal, economic & so-
  cial needs of its members, encourages their
  continuing education & seeks continuous im-
  provement of their professional qualifications.
Publication(s): *Hieronymus* (quarterly, newsletter)

ASTTI, see Association Suisse des Traducteurs,
  Terminologues et Interpretes (ASTTI)

Tanzania

BAKITA, see Baraza la Kiswahili la Taifa
  (BAKITA)

Baraza la Kiswahili la Taifa (BAKITA)
  (National Swahili Council)
PO Box 4766, Kijitonyama, Dar es Salaam
Tel: (022) 2762243; (022) 2762213
E-mail: bakari@habari.go.tz; bakita201067@
  yahoo.com
Web Site: www.bakita.go.tz
Founded: 1983
Translations in English, Kiswahili, Arabic,
  French, Portuguese & Spanish.

Turkey

AnatoliaLit Agency
Caferaga Mah, Gunesli Bahce Sok No 48, Or Ko
  Apartment B Blok D 4, 34710 Kadikoy, Istan-
  bul
Tel: (0216) 700 1088 *Fax:* (0216) 700 1089
E-mail: info@anatolialit.com
Web Site: www.anatolialit.com
Key Personnel
Co-Founder: Dilek Akdemir *E-mail:* dilek@
  anatolialit.com; Amy Spangler *E-mail:* amy@
  anatolialit.com
Founded: 2005
Translation services available in English, Turkish,
  French, German, Kurdish, Russian & Spanish.
  Also provides editing & proofreading services
  for English & Turkish.

United
Kingdom

Accurate Translations Ltd
Member of Comtec Translations
Burgon House, 2 Burgon St, London EC4V 5DR
Tel: (020) 7248 9266 *Fax:* (020) 7248 9267
E-mail: info@accuratetranslations.co.uk
Web Site: www.accuratetranslations.co.uk
Founded: 1988
Translating, proofreading, transcription, interpret-
  ing & voice-over services.
Membership(s): Association of Translation Com-
  panies (ATC); European Union of Associations
  of Translation Companies (EUATC).
Specializes in legal, financial, commercial, diplo-
  matic, pharmaceutical & medical translation.

**Deborah Adlam MA Hons Classic, Latin
  Translator**
41 W Savile Terrace, Edinburgh EH9 3DP

Tel: (0131) 667 6048
E-mail: d.adlam@academiclatinandgreek.co.uk
Web Site: www.academiclatinandgreek.co.uk
Founded: 1987
Translation into English from Latin, Russian,
  French & Classical Greek. Academic, literary,
  medical, legal & theological texts. Research
  work also translated.
Specializes in 12th through 19th century Latin
  legal documents, Classical Greek & Latin texts.

Aradco VSI Ltd
Aradco House, 128-134 Cleveland St, London
  W1T 6AB
Tel: (020) 7692 7700 *Fax:* (020) 7692 7711
E-mail: info@aradco.com
Web Site: www.aradco.com
Key Personnel
Founder & Chairman: N J Dawood
Founded: 1958
Translation, interpreting, desktop publishing,
  copywriting & web site localization.
Specializes in Arabic.

Asian Absolute
Beaufort House, 11th floor, 15 St Botolph St,
  London EC3A 7DT
Tel: (020) 7456 1058 *Fax:* (0870) 762 7568
E-mail: info@asianabsolute.co.uk
Web Site: www.asianabsolute.co.uk
Key Personnel
Founder & Mng Dir: Henry Clough
Operations Dir: Julie Giguere
General Manager: Justin Wang
Founded: 2000
Translation interpreters, localisation & marketing
  for China, Japan & the Asia Pacific region.
Membership(s): Association of Translation Com-
  panies (ATC).
Specializes in Chinese, Japanese, Korean & Ara-
  bic.
Branch Office(s)
8 Canterbury St, Moonee Ponds, Victo-
  ria 3039, Australia *Tel:* (03) 9005 8295
    E-mail: melbourne@asianabsolute.com
Alexander Dyakovich Str 45, 9000 Varna, Bul-
  garia *Tel:* (052) 94 0541 *E-mail:* varna@
  asianabsolute.com
Asian Absolute Beijing, ZhuBang 2000, 100
  Balizhuang Xili, Room 602, Bldg 1, Tower
  A, Beijing 100025, China *Tel:* (010) 6550
  2681 *Fax:* (010) 6550 1807 *E-mail:* info@
  asianabsolute.com.cn
Av Peru, Edificio Business Point, Oficina Buenos
  Aires, Frente a la Clinica Bella Vista, Panama
  City, Panama
27/F Prudential Tower, 30 Cecil St, Singa-
  pore 049712, Singapore *Tel:* 3158 9987
    E-mail: singapore@asianabsolute.com
No 20, Lane 268, Beigang Rd Section 2, Mayu-
  liao, Taibao, Chiayi, Taiwan *Tel:* (0932) 344
  657 *E-mail:* chiayi@asianabsolute.com
U.S. Office(s): 641 Lexington Ave, 15th floor,
  New York, NY, United States *Tel:* 347-918-
  3994 *E-mail:* newyork@asianabsolute.com

AT&T Group Ltd
Alexander House, 64 Robin Hood Lane, Hall
  Green, Birmingham B28 0JT
Tel: (0121) 603 6344; (0845) 528 1888
E-mail: info@att-group.com
Web Site: www.att-group.com
Key Personnel
Mng Dir: Mr Sikander Ahmed
Founded: 1971
Supplies a full range of language-related services
  to organizations operating in foreign markets or
  approaching ethnic minority citizens in the UK.
Specializes in translation & typesetting into most
  European languages (& vice versa), plus Ara-
  bic, Bengali, Chinese (Cantonese, Hakka &
  Mandarin) Farsi (Persian), Greek, Hindi, Pun-

jabi, Polish, Russian, Somali, Turkish, Urdu,
  Vietnamese & Welsh. Also typesetting of European, Russian, Vietnamese, Chinese & various
  Indian languages. Provide translation services
  of multilingual technical translation, documentation, computer manuals, reports, promotional
  literature, brochures, packaging & books.

CBA Translations
Straightaway Head, Whimple, Exeter EX5 2QT
Tel: (01404) 822284; (01404) 823136
Toll Free Tel: 0800 169 2496
Key Personnel
Proprietor: Gerd Ziemer
Founded: 1979

Chartered Institute of Linguists
Dunstan House, 14a St Cross St, London EC1N
  8XA
Tel: (020) 7940 3100
E-mail: info@ciol.org.uk
Web Site: www.ciol.org.uk
Key Personnel
Chair: Keith Moffitt
Chief Executive: Ann Carlisle
Deputy Chief Executive Officer & Operations
  Dir: Adam Ladbury
President: Nicholas Bowen
Business Development Manager: Matthias Postel
Communications & Marketing Manager: Debbie
  Butler
Founded: 1910
Membership organization promoting proficiency
  in modern languages worldwide among pro-
  fessional linguists, including translators, in-
  terpreters & educationalists, as well as those
  in the public & private sectors. Also acts as a
  respected language assessment & accredited
  awarding body.
Publication(s): *Bilingual in Britain*; *Glossary of
  Social Services Terms*; *Languages & Your Career*; *The Linguist* (bimonthly, journal)

Chinese Marketing & Communications (CMC)
Wuhan House, 16 Nicholas St, Manchester M1
  4EJ
Tel: (07971) 888 080
E-mail: info@chinese-marketing.com
Web Site: www.chinese-marketing.com
Founded: 1986
Marketing materials in Chinese language. Market
  research & advertising agency.

CIG, see Conference Interpreters Group (CIG)

CMC, see Chinese Marketing & Communications
  (CMC)

Conference Interpreters Group (CIG)
50 Ellington St, London N7 8PL
Tel: (07733) 887765
E-mail: info@cig-interpreters.com
Web Site: www.cig-interpreters.com
Key Personnel
Executive Secretary: Sally Sadler
Founded: 1978
Professional conference interpreters providing
  clients with language consultancy & interpreta-
  tion services.
Membership(s): International Association of Con-
  ference Interpreters.

Creative Translation Ltd
The Lightbox, 111 Power Rd, London W4 5PY
Tel: (020) 7294 7710
E-mail: info@creativetranslation.com
Web Site: creativetranslation.com
Key Personnel
Contact: Luke Innes
Founded: 1991

Dutch Connection
Lamb Howe, 196 Prestbury Rd, Upton, Maccles-
field, Cheshire SK10 3BS
Tel: (01625) 610613

Eastword
16 Pines Close, Northwood, Middx HA6 3SJ
Tel: (01923) 836 326 *Fax:* (01923) 827 823
Oriental language translation including Chinese,
Japanese, Korean, Thai & Vietnamese.

First Edition Translations Ltd
8 Wellington Mews, Wellington St, Cambridge,
Cambs CB1 1HW
Tel: (01223) 356733
E-mail: enquiries@firstedit.co.uk
Web Site: www.firstedit.co.uk
Key Personnel
Mng Dir: Jerry Froggett
General Manager: Sheila Waller
Commercial Translation Manager: Ana Grilo
Founded: 1981
Services include copy-editing, proofreading, in-
dexing, interpreting, voice-overs, typesetting.
Specializes in translations of all material for pub-
lication.

Michael Fulton Partnership
The Chase, Behoes Lane, Woodcote, Reading,
Berks RG8 0PP
Tel: (01491) 680042
Web Site: www.thamestranslators.co.uk/
fultonmichael.htm
Key Personnel
Senior Partner: Michael Fulton, PhD *Tel:* (07950)
037766 (cell) *E-mail:* mike@mike-fulton.co.uk
Founded: 1968
Translations from Spanish, Galician & Portuguese
(technical, engineering, scientific, commercial
& patents subject matter); Spanish interpreting.
Some limited French to English translation.
Membership(s): Institute of Linguists; Institute of
Translation & Interpreting.

Global Language Services Ltd
Craig House, 60-64 Darnley St, Glasgow G41
2SE
Tel: (0141) 429 3429
E-mail: mail@globallanguageservices.co.uk
Web Site: www.globallanguageservices.co.uk
Founded: 1983
Provides translations into most languages cov-
ering a vast range of subject areas including
commercial, technical, medical & legal.
Branch Office(s)
Belgrave Business Centre, 45 Frederick St,
Edinburgh EH2 1EP *Tel:* (0131) 220 0115
Fax: (0131) 624 1166 *E-mail:* mail@
globaledinburgh.com
Fairways House, Fairways Business Park, Cas-
tle Heather, Inverness IV2 6AA *Tel:* (01463)
258839 *Fax:* (01463) 258851 *E-mail:* mail@
globalinverness.com

The Greek Institute
29 Onslow Gardens, Grange Park, London N21
1DY
Tel: (020) 8360 7968 *Fax:* (020) 8360 7968
E-mail: info@greekinstitute.co.uk
Web Site: www.greekinstitute.co.uk
Key Personnel
Dir: Dr Kypros Tofallis
Founded: 1969
Publication(s): *A History of Cypriot Literature
(in Greek); A History of Cyprus; A History of
Cyprus- From the Ancient Times to the Present
(in English); A History of Modern Cyprus-
From British Rule (1878) to the Present (in
Greek); A History of Modern Greek Litera-
ture (in Greek); A Textbook of Modern Greek;
Anglo-Greek Review; English-Greek Transla-
tion; Modern Greek Translation*

Institute of Translation & Interpreting (ITI)
Milton Keynes Business Centre, Foxhunter Dr,
Linford Wood, Suite 165, Milton Keynes,
Bucks MK14 6GD
Tel: (01908) 325250
E-mail: info@iti.org.uk
Web Site: www.iti.org.uk
Key Personnel
Chief Executive: Paul Wilson
Operations Manager: Caroline Wells
Membership Officer: Parveen Mann *Tel:* (01908)
325251 *E-mail:* membership@iti.org.uk
Professional Development Officer: Ann Brooks
E-mail: professionaldevelopment@iti.org.uk
Founded: 1986
Publication(s): *ITI Bulletin* (bimonthly)

International Translations Ltd (ITL)
9 Queensway, Heswall, Wirral CH60 3SL
Tel: (0151) 342 7044
E-mail: admin@itltranslations.com
Web Site: www.itltranslations.com
Key Personnel
Dir: Merula Smith
Founded: 1919
Translations in over 30 languages; literary, com-
mercial, financial, medical, technical & legal
topics.
Membership(s): Association of Translation Com-
panies (ATC).
Specializes in translation, interpreting, proofread-
ing, typesetting & voice-overs.

Intonation Ltd
21-23 East St, Fareham, Hamps PO16 0BZ
Tel: (01329) 828438 *Fax:* (01329) 823543
E-mail: info@intonation.co.uk
Web Site: www.intonation.co.uk
Key Personnel
Mng Dir: Rebecca Rubio
Commercial Dir: Dan Peachy
Document translation in a wide variety of techni-
cal & specialist areas, from manuals, patents &
brochures to marketing material, medical docu-
ments & catalogues. Offer translations in over
100 languages.
Membership(s): Association of Translation Com-
panies.

ITI, see Institute of Translation & Interpreting
(ITI)

ITL, see International Translations Ltd (ITL)

Lexus Translations Ltd
60 Brook St, Glasgow G40 2AB
Tel: (0141) 556 0440 *Fax:* (0141) 556 2202
E-mail: translations@lexusforlanguages.co.uk
Web Site: www.lexusforlanguages.co.uk
Key Personnel
Mng Dir: Peter Terrell *E-mail:* peterterrell@
lexusforlanguages.co.uk
Contact: Elfreda Crehan *Tel:* (0845) 270 2552
Fax: (0845) 272 2552 *E-mail:* elfredacrehan@
lexusforlanguages.co.uk
Founded: 1980
Translation of a broad range of subjects both
technical & non-technical from & into English.
Also publisher & packager.
Specializes in bilingual dictionaries.

Newcom Translations
Newcom House, Unit 2, 125 Poplar High St,
London E14 0AE
Tel: (020) 7517 1270; (020) 7193 8952
Fax: (020) 7517 1271
E-mail: newcom@newcomgroup.com
Web Site: www.newcomgroup.com
Membership(s): Association of Translation Com-
panies; Institute of Translation & Interpreting.

Specializes in European translation & interpretation.
Parent Company: Newcom (UK) Ltd

Peak Translations
Ringstones Industrial Estate, Bridgemont, Whaley
Bridge, Derbys SK23 7PD
Tel: (01663) 732074 *Fax:* (01663) 735499
E-mail: enquiries@peak-translations.co.uk
Web Site: www.peak-translations.co.uk
Key Personnel
Mng Dir: Helen Provart *E-mail:* helen.provart@
peak-translations.co.uk
Marketing & Administrative Assistant: Shannon
Bennett
Founded: 1978
Experts available in all fields. Also supply soft-
ware translation tools for professional transla-
tors.
Membership(s): Association of Translation Com-
panies (ATC).
Specializes in translation, interpreting, proofread-
ing, typesetting/DTP & subtitling.

Sally Walker Language Services
Bank House, One Burlington Rd, Bristol BS6 6TJ
Tel: (0117) 973 4742
E-mail: translations@sallywalker.co.uk
Web Site: www.sallywalker.co.uk
Key Personnel
Dir: Jonathon Baker
Translations Manager: Lucia Clements; Mike
Downey; Anna Lopes
Marketing: Emily Armstrong
Founded: 1969
Translation & interpreting service.
Membership(s): Institute of Translation & Inter-
preting (ITI).
Specializes in 80 languages, all subjects.

Satrap Publishing & Translation
55-57 Shoot Up Hill, 13 Princes Court, London
NW2 3PX
Tel: (020) 8748 9397
E-mail: info@satraptranslation.co.uk; satrap@
btconnect.com
Web Site: www.satrap.co.uk; www.
satraptranslation.co.uk
Key Personnel
Mng Dir: Ahmed Vahdat Khah
Founded: 1989
A single source for translation, typesetting, pub-
lishing, marketing & advertising literature in
major languages of the world.
Specializes in Middle & Far Eastern, East & West
European languages.

SDL
Globe House, Clivemont Rd, Maidenhead, Berks
SL6 7DY
Tel: (01628) 410100 *Fax:* (01628) 410150
Web Site: www.sdl.com
Key Personnel
Executive Chairman: David Clayton
Chief Executive Officer: Adolfo Hernandez
Chief Financial Officer: Dominic Lavelle
Chief Marketing Officer: Peggy Chen
Chief Tranformation Officer: Azad Ootam
Services include foreign language publishing,
translating & interpreting.
Publication(s): *Share Club*
Branch Office(s)
5700 Granite Parkway, Suite 900, Plano, TX
75024, United States *Tel:* 720-304-4950

SEL, see Services for Export & Language (SEL)

SELTA, see The Swedish-English Literary
Translators' Association (SELTA)

Services for Export & Language (SEL)
Joule House, University of Salford The Crescent,
Salford, Manchester M5 4WT
Tel: (0161) 295 5491
E-mail: seluk.translation@gmail.com
Web Site: www.sel-uk.com
Key Personnel
Translations Manager: Patrick Murphy
Founded: 1986
Services include translation, interpreting, language
training & language assessments.

**The Swedish-English Literary Translators'
Association (SELTA)**
c/o Norvik Press, Dept Scandinavian Studies,
University College London, Gower St, London
WC1E 6BT
E-mail: seltasecretary@gmail.com
Web Site: www.selta.org.uk; www.
swedishbookreview.com
Key Personnel
Chair: Ruth Urbom
Honorary Secretary: Saskia Vogel *E-mail:* saskia.
vogel@gmail.com
Treasurer: Ian Giles
Swedish Book Review Editor: Deborah Bragan-
Turner
Founded: 1982
SELTA aims to promote the publication of
Swedish & Finnish-Swedish literature in En-
glish & to represent the interests of those in-
volved in its translation.
Publication(s): *Swedish Book Review* (2 issues/yr)

thebigword Group Ltd
Link Up House, Ring Rd, Lower Wortley, Leeds
LS12 6AB
Tel: (0870) 748 8000
E-mail: info@thebigword.com
Web Site: en-gb.thebigword.com
Key Personnel
Chief Executive Officer: Laurence J Gould
Deputy Chief Executive Officer: Diane Cheese-
brough

Chief Commercial Officer: Josh Gould
Financial Dir: Marcus Mills
Operations Dir: Mark Daley
Dir, Technology: Mark Clayton
Founded: 1980
Branch Office(s)
thebigword London, Well Court, 14-16 Farringdon Lane, London EC1R 3AU *Tel:* (020) 7012
6293
thebigword Sao Paulo, Top Center Bldg, 10th
floor, Paulista Ave, 854 Bela Vista, Sao Paulo,
Brazil *Tel:* (011) 2186 0453
thebigword Beijing, 1209 Huapu International
Plaza, 19 ChaoyangmenWai Ave, Beijing
100020, China *Tel:* (010) 65802501
thebigword Helsinki, Luna House, Mannerheim-
intie 12 B, Helsinki 00100, Finland *Tel:* (09)
2516 6303
thebigword Germany, Koenigsallee 61, 40215
Duesseldorf, Germany *Tel:* (0211) 42471 135
thebigword Italy, Galleria Vittorio Emanuele,
Via Mengoni 4, 20121 Milan, Italy *Tel:* (02)
30315324
thebigword Tokyo, Hamamatsucho General Bldg
2F, 2-2-15 Hamamatsucho, Minato-Ku, Tokyo
105-0013, Japan *Tel:* (03) 4550 6551
thebigword The Hague, Koningin Juliana, 11th
floor, Plein 10, 2595 AA Den Haag, Netherlands *Tel:* (070) 891 8461
thebigword New York, 250 W 57 St, Suite 420,
New York, NY 10019, United States *Tel:* 646-
770-8000

TransAction Translators Ltd
Redlands, 3/5 Tapton House Rd, Broomhill,
Sheffield S10 5BY
Mailing Address: PO Box 4376, Sheffield S10
9DP
Tel: (0114) 266 1103 *Fax:* (0114) 263 1959
E-mail: transaction@transaction.co.uk
Web Site: www.transaction.co.uk
Key Personnel
Dir: Maryline Tergella
Projects & Marketing Manager: Richard Furlong
Founded: 1983

Translation, interpreting & web site translation &
localization services.
Membership(s): Association of Translation Companies (ATC).
Publication(s): *TransAction Translators' Newsletter*

Translators Association
The Society of Authors, 84 Drayton Gardens,
London SW10 9SB
Tel: (020) 7373 6642 *Fax:* (020) 7373 5768
E-mail: info@societyofauthors.org
Web Site: www.societyofauthors.org/translators-
association
Key Personnel
Chair: David Donachie
Chief Executive: Nicola Soloman
E-mail: nsoloman@societyofauthors.org
Contracts Advisor: Sarah Burton
E-mail: sburton@societyofauthors.org
Founded: 1958
Specialist group within The Society of Authors.
Publication(s): *In Other Words* (journal)

Wessex Translations Ltd
Barn 500, The Grange, Romsey Rd, Michelmersh,
Romsey, Hants SO51 0AE
Tel: (0870) 1669 300 *Fax:* (0870) 1669 299
E-mail: sales@wt-lm.com
Web Site: www.wt-lm.com/index.html
Key Personnel
Dir: Paul Stewart
Founded: 1972
Complete language service.
Membership(s): Association of Translation Com-
panies; Institute of Translations & Interpreters.
Specializes in translations, face-to-face & tele-
phone interpreting, software localisation, lan-
guage training, transcription, typesetting, tele-
marketing, editing & proofreading, voice-overs,
copywriting, web page translation.

WT Language Management, see Wessex
Translations Ltd

Manufacturing

Complete Book Manufacturing

This section includes companies throughout the world that offer complete book manufacturing services. Those U.S. and Canadian companies with 10% or more of their business done outside North America are also included.

Austria

ADEVA (Akademische Druck-u Verlagsanstalt)
(Academic Printing & Publishing House)
St Peter Hauptstr 98, 8042 Graz
Mailing Address: Postfach 598, 8011 Graz
Tel: (0316) 46 3003 *Fax:* (0316) 46 3003-24
E-mail: info@adeva.com
Web Site: www.adeva.com
Key Personnel
Chief Executive Officer & Dir, Marketing & Sales: Dr Paul Struzl *E-mail:* pstruzl@adeva. com
President: Dr Michael Struzl *E-mail:* struzl@ adeva.com
Founded: 1949
Print Runs: 300 min - 10,000 max
Business from Other Countries: 80%

Akademische Druck- u Verlagsanstalt, see ADEVA (Akademische Druck-u Verlagsanstalt)

Dr Paul Struzl GmbH, see ADEVA (Akademische Druck-u Verlagsanstalt)

Bahrain

Al Waraqoon Co WLL
Budaiya Highway, Jannusan
Mailing Address: PO Box 30143, Manama
Tel: 17 592 598 *Fax:* 17 592 597
E-mail: info@alwaraqoon.com
Web Site: alwaraqoon.com
Key Personnel
Owner: Maysa Mohammed Jaber al Ansari
Mng Dir: Mohammed Bu Hassan

Belgium

Drukkerij Lannoo NV (Lannoo Printers NV)
Plantinstr 6, 8700 Tielt
Tel: (051) 42 42 11; (051) 42 43 08 *Fax:* (051) 40 70 70
E-mail: info@lannooprint.be; lannoo@ lannooprint.be
Web Site: www.lannoo-print.be
Founded: 1909
Turnaround: 10 Workdays
Print Runs: 100 min - 1,000,000 max
Business from Other Countries: 30%

Brunei

Brunei Press Sdn Bhd
Lot 8 & 11, Perindustrian Beribi II, Gadong BE 1118
Tel: 2451460; 2451468 *Fax:* 2451460
E-mail: brupress@bruneipress.com.bn; marketing@bruneipress.com.bn
Branch Office(s)
Unit 8B, Supasave Panaga, Lorong 14 Barat, Seria KB 4533 *Tel:* 3334344; 3334345 *Fax:* 3334346
Sales Office(s): Brunei Press Sales (M) Sdn Bhd, No 8-1-6, 1st floor, Menara Mutiara Bangsar, Jl Liku Off Jl Bangsar, 59100 Kuala Lumpur, Malaysia *Tel:* (03) 22876623 *Fax:* (03) 22870093 *E-mail:* brupress@tm.net.my
Brunei Press Sales (S) Pte Ltd, Pico Creative Centre, 20 Kallang Ave, No 03-00, Singapore 339411, Singapore *Tel:* 6297 9622 *Fax:* 6297 9633 *E-mail:* brupress@singnet.com.sg

Canada

Cenveo McLaren Morris & Todd Co
3270 American Dr, Mississauga, ON L4V 1B5
Tel: 905-677-3592 *Fax:* 905-677-3675
E-mail: sales@mmt.ca
Web Site: www.mmt.ca
Key Personnel
Pres & CEO: Tony Sgro
Cont: Nancy Marquis
Founded: 1956
Turnaround: 15 Workdays
Print Runs: 5,000 min - 1,000,000 max
Business from Other Countries: 10%

Friesens Corp
One Printers Way, Altona, MB R0G 0B0
Tel: 204-324-6401 *Fax:* 204-324-1333
E-mail: book_info@friesens.com
Web Site: www.friesens.com; www.books.friesens. com
Key Personnel
Pres & COO: Chad Friesen
Gen Sales Mgr: Doug Symington *E-mail:* dougs@friesens.com
Founded: 1907
Turnaround: 3-4 Weeks
Print Runs: 250 min - 250,000 max
Business from Other Countries: 30%
Membership(s): BMI

Mad Dog Design Connection Inc
11328 Redbud Place, North Saanich, BC V8L 5J9
Tel: 250-655-1657; 250-655-3757 *Fax:* 250-655-3757
E-mail: maddogs9@shaw.ca
Key Personnel
Owner & Designer: Linda Pellowe
Founded: 1998
Turnaround: As needed to meet deadline
Business from Other Countries: 10%

Maracle Press Ltd
1156 King St E, Oshawa, ON L1H 1H8
Tel: 905-723-3438 *Toll Free Tel:* 800-558-8604 *Fax:* 905-723-1759
E-mail: info@maraclepress.com
Web Site: www.maraclepress.com
Key Personnel
Pres & Gen Mgr: George Sittlinger *Tel:* 905-723-3438 ext 236
Acct Mgr: Ronald G Taylor *E-mail:* rtaylor@ maraclepress.com
Founded: 1920
Turnaround: 10 Workdays
Print Runs: 500 min - 500,000 max
Business from Other Countries: 25%
Membership(s): BMI; Ontario Printing & Imaging Association; Printing Industries of America

PrintWest
1111 Eighth Ave, Regina, SK S4R 1C9
Tel: 306-525-2304 *Toll Free Tel:* 800-236-6438 *Fax:* 306-757-2439
E-mail: general@printwest.com
Web Site: www.printwest.com
Key Personnel
CEO: Corie Triffo
VP, Sales: Ken Benson
Founded: 1992
Turnaround: 15 Workdays
Print Runs: 1,000 min - 100,000 max
Business from Other Countries: 15%

Webcom Inc
3480 Pharmacy Ave, Toronto, ON M1W 2S7
Tel: 416-496-1000 *Toll Free Tel:* 800-665-9322 *Fax:* 416-496-1537
E-mail: webcom@webcomlink.com
Web Site: www.webcomlink.com
Key Personnel
CEO & Pres: Mike Collinge
Founded: 1975
Turnaround: 15 Workdays
Print Runs: 10 min - 100,000 max
Business from Other Countries: 40%
Sales Office(s): 65 Spring Valley Ave, River Edge, NJ 07661, United States, Sales: Susan Ginch *Tel:* 201-262-4301 *Fax:* 201-262-6375 *E-mail:* susan.ginch@webcomlink.com

Croatia

Radin repro i roto doo
Gospodarska 9, 10431 Sveta Nedelja
Tel: (01) 7772 300 *Fax:* (01) 7772 399
E-mail: prodaja@radin.hr
Web Site: www.radin.hr
Key Personnel
Chief Executive Officer: Sanja Pusec Mukavec
Chief Financial Officer: Goran Ledinscak
Founded: 1995

Vjesnik dd
Slavonska Avenija 4, 10000 Zagreb
Tel: (01) 6161 700; (01) 6161 453 (sales)
   Fax: (01) 6161 606; (01) 6161 486 (sales)
E-mail: uprava@vjesnik.hr; prodaja@vjesnik.hr
Web Site: vjesnik.hr; www.vjesnik.com
Founded: 1999 (created through merger of
   Vjesknik Publishing Co & Hrvatska tishava
   dd)
Print Runs: 25,000 min - 55,000 max
Business from Other Countries: 1%

Denmark

PRAXIS-Nyt Teknisk Forlag (Danish Technical
   Press)
Munkehatten 28, 5220 Odense
Tel: 6315 1700 *Fax:* 6315 1733
E-mail: info@praxis.dk
Web Site: ntf.praxis.dk
Key Personnel
Editor: Thomas Rump

Finland

Bookwell Oy
Teollisuustie 4, 06150 Porvoo
Tel: (019) 219 41
Web Site: www.bookwell.fi
Key Personnel
President & Chief Executive Officer: Vesa
   Junkkarinen *Tel:* (040) 569 2999 *E-mail:* vesa.
   junkkarinen@bookwell.fi
Sales Dir: Markus Ruohonen *E-mail:* markus.
   ruohonen@bookwell.fi
Export Manager: Kjell Karlsson *Tel:* (040) 518
   0948 *E-mail:* kjell.karlsson@bookwell.fi
Production Manager: Juha Harmonen
   E-mail: juha.harmonen@bookwell.fi
Founded: 1860
Parent Company: Sanoma
Branch Office(s)
Tenhusentie 3, 51900 Juva
Sales Office(s): Hulvejen 52, 9530 Stovring, Den-
   mark, Representative: Steffen Janum *Tel:* 5092
   5555 *E-mail:* steffen.janum@bookwell.fi
Raiffeisenstr 5, 63939 Woerth am Main, Ger-
   many, Representative: Frank Hohmann
   Tel: (09372) 94810811 *E-mail:* frank.
   hohmann@bookwell.fi
Manor House, Church St, Brassington, Derbys
   DE4 4HJ, United Kingdom, Representative: Pe-
   ter Everest *Tel:* (01629) 540 934 *Fax:* (01629)
   540 938 *E-mail:* petereverest@bookwell.co.uk

France

Plein Chant
35, route de Conde, 16120 Bassac, Charente
Tel: 05 45 81 93 26 *Fax:* 05 45 81 92 83
E-mail: pleinchant@wanadoo.fr
Web Site: www.pleinchant.fr
Key Personnel
Contact: Edmond Thomas
Founded: 1970
Print Runs: 300 min - 1,000 max
Business from Other Countries: 5%

Germany

Druckerei C H Beck
Bergerstr 3-5, 86720 Noerdlingen
Tel: (09081) 85-0 *Fax:* (09081) 85-206
E-mail: info@becksche.de
Web Site: www.becksche.de
Key Personnel
Mng Dir: Christian Matthiesen *Tel:* (09081) 85-
   101 *E-mail:* matthiesen.christian@becksche.de
Commercial Dir: Ernest Zoller *Tel:* (09081) 85-
   111 *E-mail:* zoller.ernest@becksche.de
Head, Inside Sales: Roland Schroeppel
   Tel: (09081) 85-195 *E-mail:* schroeppel.
   roland@becksche.de
Head, Sales: Andre Sommer *Tel:* (09081) 85-123
   E-mail: sommer.andre@becksche.de
Founded: 1763
Parent Company: Verlag C H Beck oHG
Branch Office(s)
Augsburgerstr 67, 86720 Noerdlingen

Bertelsmann Printing Group
Division of Bertelsmann SE & Co KGaA
Carl-Bertelsmann-Str 161M, 33311 Guetersloh
Tel: (05241) 80-0
E-mail: contact@bertelsmann-printing-group.com
Web Site: www.bertelsmann-printing-group.com
Key Personnel
Co-Chief Executive Officer: Axel Hentrei; Dr
   Bertram Stausberg
Chief Financial Officer: Ulrich Cordes
Corporate Communications: Matthias Wulff
   E-mail: matthias.wulff@bertelsmann.de
Founded: 2016

Bertelsmann SE & Co KGaA
Carl-Bertelsmann-Str 270, 33311 Guetersloh
Tel: (05241) 80-0 *Fax:* (05241) 80-62321
E-mail: info@bertelsmann.de
Web Site: www.bertelsmann.com
Key Personnel
Chief Executive Officer: Thomas Rabe
Chief Financial Officer: Bernd Hirsch
Executive Vice President, Corporate Commu-
   nications: Karin Schlautman *E-mail:* karin.
   schlautman@bertelsmann.de
Executive Vice President, Digital Business Devel-
   opment & Partnerships: Marcel Reichart
Founded: 1835

**Druck- und Verlagshaus FROMM GmbH &
   Co KG**
Breiter Gang 10-16, 49074 Osnabrueck
Tel: (0541) 310-333 *Fax:* (0541) 310-411
E-mail: druckhaus@fromm-os.de
Web Site: www.druckhaus-fromm.de
Key Personnel
Chief Executive Officer: Georg Landvogt
   Tel: (0541) 310-325 *E-mail:* g.landvogt@
   fromm-os.de; Laurence Mehl

Head, Sales: Claus Vierkoetter *Tel:* (0541) 310-
   421 *E-mail:* c.vierkoetter@fromm-os.de
Founded: 1868

GGP Media GmbH
Member of Bertelsmann Printing Group
Karl-Marx-Str 24, 07381 Poessneck
Tel: (03647) 430-0 *Fax:* (03647) 430-390
E-mail: ggp.poessneck@bertelsmann.de
Web Site: www.ggp-media.de
Key Personnel
Mng Dir: Axel Hentrei; Christof Ludwig
Sales Dir: Christine Bergmann *Tel:* (03647) 430-
   225 *Fax:* (03647) 430-230 *E-mail:* christine.
   bergmann@bertelsmann.de
Customer Service Manager & International
   Sales: Cindy Girbert *Tel:* (03647) 430-415
   Fax: (03647) 430-66415 *E-mail:* cindy.
   girbert@bertelsmann.de
Founded: 1891
Ultimate Parent Company: Bertelsmann SE & Co
   KGaA

Druckhaus Gummersbach PP GmbH
Stauweiher 4, 51645 Gummersbach
Tel: (02261) 9572-0 *Fax:* (02261) 56338
E-mail: info@druckhaus-gummersbach.de
Web Site: www.druckhaus-gummersbach.de
Key Personnel
General Manager: Benita Kramer; Ulrich Kramer
Founded: 1845

Interconcept Medienagentur
Lindwurmstr 64, 80337 Munich
Tel: (089) 72 98 95 02
E-mail: info@interconceptmedien.de
Web Site: interconceptmedien.de
Key Personnel
Dir: Frank Ferschen
Founded: 1998

Kessler Druck + Medien GmbH & Co KG
Michael Schaeffer-Str 1, 86399 Bobingen
Tel: (0908) 2349-619-0 *Fax:* (0908) 2349-619-19
E-mail: info@kesslerdruck.de
Web Site: kesslerdruck.de
Key Personnel
Mng Dir: Caspar Kessler

Media-Print Informationstechnologie GmbH
Unit of Media-Print Group GmbH
Eggertstr 30, 33100 Paderborn
Tel: (05251) 5408-0 *Fax:* (05251) 5408-144
E-mail: group@mediaprint.de
Web Site: www.mediaprint.de
Key Personnel
Mng Dir: Dr Otto W Drosihn; Rainer Rings; Ulf
   Stornebel
Founded: 1993
Turnaround: 5-10 Workdays
Print Runs: 100 min - 30,000 max
Business from Other Countries: 10%

Mohn Media Mohndruck GmbH
Member of Bertelsmann Printing Group
Carl-Bertelsmann-Str 161M, 33311 Guetersloh
Tel: (05241) 80-40410 *Fax:* (05241) 80-65288
E-mail: mohnmedia@bertelsmann.de
Web Site: www.mohnmedia.de
Key Personnel
Mng Dir: Axel Hentrei; Wilfried Velte
Sales Dir: Alasdair Gibson
Founded: 1824
Business from Other Countries: 25%
Ultimate Parent Company: Bertelsmann SE & Co
   KGaA

Priese GmbH
Saatwinkler Damm 42A, 13627 Berlin
Tel: (030) 8263024 *Fax:* (030) 8266024

Druckhaus Schuetze GmbH
Fiete-Schulze-Str 13a, 06116 Halle (Saale)
Tel: (0345) 56666-0 *Fax:* (0345) 56666-66
E-mail: info@dhs-halle.de; vertrieb@dhs-halle.de
Web Site: www.dhs-halle.de
Key Personnel
Mng Dir: Stephan Probst; Florian Schaefer
Founded: 1990
Print Runs: 105 min - 1,020 max

Strobel Verlag GmbH & Co KG
Zur Feldmuehle 9-11, 59821 Arnsberg
Mailing Address: Postfach 5654, 59806 Arnsberg
Tel: (02931) 8900-0 *Fax:* (02931) 8900-38
E-mail: leserservice@strobel-verlag.de
Web Site: www.ikz.de; www.strobel-verlag.de
Key Personnel
Mng Dir: Christopher Strobel
Editor-in-Chief: Markus Sironi *E-mail:* m.sironi@strobel-verlag.de
Head, Online Media: Stefan Schuette *E-mail:* s.schuette@strobel-verlag.de
Sales Manager: Uwe Derr *E-mail:* u.derr@strobel-verlag.de
Corporate Communications & Marketing: Peter Hallmann *E-mail:* p.hallmann@strobel-verlag.de
Founded: 1872
Print Runs: 2,500 min - 90,000 max

Greece

Motibo Publishing SA
2 Plapouta & Kallidromiou St, 114 73 Athens
Tel: 2108222835 *Fax:* 2108222684
E-mail: info@motibo.com
Web Site: www.motibo.com
Founded: 2004

Hong Kong

C & C Offset Printing Co Ltd
Subsidiary of C & C Joint Printing Co (HK) Ltd
14/F, C & C Bldg, 36 Ting Lai Rd, Tai Po, New Territories
Tel: 2666 4988 *Fax:* 2666 4938
E-mail: offsetprinting@candcprinting.com
Web Site: www.ccoffset.com; www.candcprinting.com
Key Personnel
Chief Executive Officer, C & C Joint Printing Co (HK) Ltd: Jackson Leung
Founded: 1980
Turnaround: 30-42 Workdays for printing, binding & book finishing
Print Runs: 2,000 min - 3,000,000 max
Business from Other Countries: 60%
Ultimate Parent Company: Sino United Publishing (Holdings) Ltd
Branch Office(s)
3-7 Permas Way, Truganina, Victoria 3029, Australia, Contact: Lena Frew *Tel:* (03) 6264 3751 *Fax:* (03) 6264 3752 *E-mail:* lena.frew@candcprinting.com
Room 301, No 29, 165 lane, DongZhuAnBang Rd (C), Shanghai 200050, China, Contact: Ms Zhang Zhi Ying *Tel:* (021) 6240 1305 *Fax:* (021) 5922 6111 *E-mail:* zhang.zhi.ying@candcprinting.com
3, rue Chabanais, 75002 Paris, France, Contact: Michele Olson Niel *Tel:* 01 71 70 39 00 *Fax:* 01 70 71 92 85 *E-mail:* info@candcoffset.fr (Continental Europe off)

C & C Printing Japan Co Ltd, Jewel Ginza 301, 7-17-18 Ginza, Chuo-ku, Tokyo 104-0061, Japan, Contact: Mr Masaaki Yamamoto *Tel:* (03) 6264 3751 *Fax:* (03) 6264 3752 *E-mail:* yamamoto@candcprinting.co.jp *Web Site:* www.candcprinting.co.jp
C & C Offset Printing Co (UK) Ltd, Tudor House, 4th floor, 35 Grasse St, London W1T 1QY, United Kingdom, Contact: Helena Coryndon *Tel:* (020) 7637 5033 *Fax:* (020) 7637 5044 *E-mail:* helena@candcoffset.co.uk
U.S. Office(s): C & C Offset Printing Co (Chicago) Inc, PO Box 4678, Naperville, IL 60567, United States, Contact: Ernest Li *Tel:* 630-390-5617 *E-mail:* ernest.li@ccoffset.com
C & C Offset Printing Co (NY) Inc, 70 W 36 St, Unit 10C, New York, NY 10018, United States, Contact: Simon Chan *Tel:* 212-431-4210 *E-mail:* schan@ccoffset.com

CA Design
16/F, China Hong Kong Tower, 8-12 Hennessy Rd, Wan Chai
Tel: 2865 6787
E-mail: cadesign@pacific.net.hk
Web Site: www.cadesign.com.hk
Key Personnel
Dir: Rosanne Chan
Founded: 1982
Print Runs: 500 min
Business from Other Countries: 50%

Caritas Printing Training Centre
Caritas House, 2 Caine Rd, Hong Kong
Tel: 2843 4734; 2524 2071 *Fax:* 2523 0438
E-mail: info@caritas.org.hk
Web Site: www.caritas.org.hk
Founded: 1953
Print Runs: 1,000 min - 100,000 max
Business from Other Countries: 50%
Parent Company: Caritas Hong Kong

Colorprint Offset
Unit 1808-9, 18/F, 8 Commercial Tower, 8 Sun Yip St, Chai Wan
Tel: 2896 7777 *Fax:* 2869 6666
E-mail: info@cpo.com.hk
Web Site: www.cpo.com.hk
Key Personnel
General Manager: Rachel Lai
Founded: 1989
Turnaround: Standard 2 week turnaround
Print Runs: 3,000 min - 100,000 max
Business from Other Countries: 80%
Branch Office(s)
Zone E1, Tangtou Industrial Estate, Shiyan, Shenzhen 518018, China *Tel:* (0755) 29680000 *Fax:* (0755) 29680203
Untergassli 7, 2502 Biel/Bienne, Switzerland *Tel:* (032) 322 05 08 *Fax:* (032) 322 05 08
St Niklaus Str 12, 6005 Lucerne, Switzerland *Tel:* (041) 340 3192 *Fax:* (041) 340 1237
Sales Office(s): Niederwaldstr 40, 76532 Baden-Baden, Germany *Tel:* (07221) 60582 *Fax:* (07221) 3759747

Communication Art Design & Printing Ltd,
see CA Design

The Elite Printing Hong Kong Co Ltd
1401-8, 1413 & 1414, Hong Man Industrial Center, 2 Hong Man St, Chai Wan
Tel: 2558 0119 *Fax:* 2897 2675
E-mail: sales@elite.com.hk
Web Site: www.elite.com.hk
Founded: 1979
Turnaround: 7-15 Workdays
Print Runs: 2,000 min - 50,000 max
Business from Other Countries: 30%
Parent Company: Elite Printing Group

Branch Office(s)
The Elite Printing Guangzhou Co Ltd, West Area, Block 1, Sui Dong St, Nan Ji Industrial Zone, Huang Pu District, Guangzhou 510760, China *Tel:* (020) 8222 1839; (020) 8221 4172 *Fax:* (020) 8221 4175 *E-mail:* elite.gz@elitegroup.cn
The Elite Digital Printing Shanghai Co Ltd, Shop 103, 51 Cao Bao Rd, Xu Hui District, Shanghai 200233, China *Tel:* (021) 6470 5990 *Fax:* (021) 5448 1512
The Elite Packaging Shanghai Co Ltd, Wei Xiang Rd (South), Rong Bei Industrial Zone, Song Jiang District, Shanghai 201613, China *Tel:* (021) 5778 1289; (021) 5778-2843 *Fax:* (021) 5778 2597
The Elite Printing Shanghai Co Ltd, Hu Song Expressway, Guang Ming Station, Song Jiang District, Shanghai 200233, China *Tel:* (021) 5778 0459; (021) 5778 0086 *Fax:* (021) 5778 1703
Sales Office(s): Elite Shanghai Sales Office, 506 Qin Zhou Rd, Xu Hui District, Shanghai 200233, China *Tel:* (021) 6451 1411; (021) 6451 1821 *Fax:* (021) 6451 2410 *E-mail:* xubin@eliteprinting-sh.com
U.S. Office(s): The Elite Printing International Co Ltd, 606 Monterey Pass Rd, No 106, Monterey Park, CA 91754, United States *Tel:* 626-282-1898 *Fax:* 626-282-1126 *E-mail:* eliteprinter@cs.com

Empire Printing & Production Specialist Ltd
Room 1202, 12/F, Wan Chai Commercial Centre, 194 Johnston Rd, Wan Chai
Tel: 2555 1881 *Fax:* 2104 2345
E-mail: info@empireprinting.com.hk
Web Site: empireprinting.com.hk
Founded: 1978
Turnaround: 2 Workdays
Print Runs: 2,500 min - 500,000 max
Business from Other Countries: 15%

Everbest Printing Co Ltd
10/F, Block C, Seaview Estate, 2-8 Watson Rd, North Point, Hong Kong
Tel: 2727 4433 *Fax:* 2772 7687
E-mail: sales@everbest.com.hk
Web Site: www.everbest.com
Founded: 1954
Turnaround: 28 Workdays
Print Runs: 1,000 min - 1,000,000 max
Business from Other Countries: 90%
Branch Office(s)
Everbest (Guangzhou) Printing Co Ltd, 334 Huanshi Rd S, Nansha, Panyu, Guangdong 511458, China *Tel:* (020) 8498 1812 (manufacturing plant)
Sales Office(s): C5, 10/F, Ko Fai Industrial Bldg, 7 Ko Fai Rd, Yau Tong *Tel:* 2727 4433 *Fax:* 2772 7687 (Australia, Europe & New Zealand)
313 30 St, Toronto, ON M8W 3E4, Canada, Contact: Doris Chung *Tel:* 416-286-2525 *Fax:* 416-804-8930 *E-mail:* doris@everbestcanada.ca
Origo Ediciones, Padre Alonso de Ovalle 748, 8330169 Santiago, Chile, Contact: Hernan Maino *Tel:* (02) 480 9800 *E-mail:* hernan.maino@origo.cl *Web Site:* www.origo.cl (Chile & South America)
Nostra Ediciones SA de CV, Av Revolucion 1181 piso 7, Col Merced Gomez, Del Benito Juarez, 03930 Mexico, DF, Mexico, Contact: Mauricio Volpi *Tel:* (0155) 5554 7030 *E-mail:* impresion@nostraediciones.com
31 Palatine Rd, London N16 8SY, United Kingdom, Contact: Nicky Bowden *Tel:* (020) 7249 9483 *Fax:* (020) 7241 3460 *E-mail:* nickybowden@everbest.co.uk
Todd Communications, 611 E 12 Ave, Anchorage, AK 99501, United States, Contact: Flip Todd *Tel:* 907-274-8633 *Fax:* 907-929-5550

E-mail: flip@toddcom.com *Web Site:* www. toddcom.com

Four Colour Imports Ltd, 2410 Frankfort Ave, Louisville, KY 40206, United States, Contact: George Dick *Tel:* 502-896-9644 *Fax:* 502-896-9594 *E-mail:* sales@fourcolour.com

Golden Cup Printing Co Ltd
6/F, 177 Hoi Bun Rd, Kwun Tong, Kowloon
Tel: 2343 4254 *Fax:* 2341 5426
E-mail: sales@goldencup.com.hk
Web Site: www.goldencup.com.hk
Key Personnel
Chairman: Kam Kai Yeung
Founded: 1971
Turnaround: 25 Workdays
Print Runs: 5,000 min - 200,000 max
Business from Other Countries: 80%
Sales Office(s): Tutang Industrial Area, Jin Bei Rd, Changping, Dongguan, Guangdong, China *Tel:* (0769) 8339 4888 *Fax:* (0769) 8339 4999
Qilin Industrial Estate, Guanlan, Shenzhen, Guangdong, China *Tel:* (0755) 2805 6279 *Fax:* (0755) 2805 6086
Jinma Town, Guandu District, Kunming, Yunnan, China *Tel:* (0871) 316 1226 *Fax:* (0871) 316 1226
Terley House, Cadbury, Exeter EX5 5JZ, United Kingdom *Tel:* (01884) 855736 *E-mail:* info@gcpservices.com
Spectrum Books Inc, 2455 Bennett Valley Rd, Suite C-116, Santa Rosa, CA 95404-5671, United States *Tel:* 707-542-6044 *Fax:* 707-542-6045

Great Wall Printing Co Ltd
Member of Prosperous Printing Group
3/F, Yip Cheung Centre, 10 Fung Yip St, Chai Wan
Tel: 2897 1083 *Fax:* 2558 1473
E-mail: books@gwp.com.hk
Web Site: www.gwp.com.hk
Key Personnel
Mng Dir: Franky Ho; George Lo
Founded: 1984
Print Runs: 3,000 min - 500,000 max
Business from Other Countries: 80%
Branch Office(s)
Haverdreef 39, 7006 LH Doetinchen, Netherlands, Contact: Buro Doral *Tel:* (0314) 35 40 40 *Fax:* (0314) 35 46 00 *E-mail:* info@ssip-holland.nl *Web Site:* www.ssip-holland.nl
The High Barn, Snailing Lane, Hawkley GU33 6NJ, United Kingdom, Contact: Myles Wells *Tel:* (01) 730 827 326 *Fax:* (01) 730 827 537 *E-mail:* members@eastwest.fsworld.co.uk

Hung Hing Off-Set Printing Co Ltd
Subsidiary of Hung Hing Printing Group Ltd
Tai Po Industrial Estate, 17-19 Dai Hei St, New Territories
Tel: 2664 8682 *Fax:* 2664 2070
E-mail: info@hunghingprinting.com
Web Site: www.hhop.com.hk
Key Personnel
Executive Chairman: Matthew Yum Chak Ming
Executive Dir: Spencer Sung Chee Keung
Chief Information Officer: Yee Y Yu
Founded: 1950
Turnaround: 20-30 Workdays
Print Runs: 5,000 min - 1,000,000 max
Business from Other Countries: 15%
Sales Office(s): Santiago del Estero 454, Piso 1, Oficina 5 y 6, C1075AAJ Buenos Aires, Argentina, Contact: Leonardo Adami *Tel:* (011) 4-179-2178 *E-mail:* enquiry@sa.hunghingprinting.com (South America)
Vilvordevej 35, 2920 Charlottenlund, Denmark, Contact: Jesper Frederiksen *Tel:* 40 26 40 57 *Fax:* 39 90 40 58 *E-mail:* jf@sc.hunghingprinting.com (Scandinavia)

33, Avenue du Maine, 75755 Paris, France, Contact: Florent Verlet *Tel:* 01 44 10 40 85 *E-mail:* florent@fr.hunghingprinting.com
PI Print Innovations GmbH, Untere Haupstr 13, 85354 Freising, Germany, Contact: Birgit von der Gathen *Tel:* (08161) 88717-0 *Fax:* (08161) 887717-10 *E-mail:* birgit@de.hunghingprinting.com *Web Site:* www.hunghing.de (Central Europe & Germany)
IPP Printers, Emmastr 2-D, 4811 AG Breda, Netherlands, Dir & Sales: Peter Jonkers *Tel:* (076) 521 7025; (0473) 561 565 *Fax:* (076) 520 7281 *E-mail:* peter@bn.hunghingprinting.com *Web Site:* www.ippprinters.com (Benelux)
Hung Hing UK, 49 Leigh Rd, Eastleigh, Hants SO50 9DF, United Kingdom, Sales Dir: Karen Giles *Tel:* (023) 8062 5858 *Fax:* (023) 8062 9366 *E-mail:* enquiries@hunghing.co.uk *Web Site:* www.hunghing.co.uk
U.S. Office(s): 29 Arden Rd, East Rockaway, NY 11518, United States, Contact: Jeff Tollin *Tel:* 516-593-0030 *Fax:* 516-593-7024 *E-mail:* hunghingusa@aol.com *Web Site:* www.hunghing-usa.com

Icicle Production Co Ltd
7/F, Cheung Wah Industrial Bldg, 10-12 Shipyard Lane, Quarry Bay, Hong Kong
Tel: 2235 2880
E-mail: info@iciclegroup.com
Web Site: www.iciclegroup.com
Key Personnel
Founding Chairman: Alex Chan *Tel:* 2235 2818 *E-mail:* alex.chan@iciclegroup.com
Chief Executive Officer: Bonnie Chan *Tel:* 2235 2888 *E-mail:* bonnie.chan@iciclegroup.com
Senior Partner: Josephine Cheung *Tel:* 2235 2800
Founded: 1998
Turnaround: 28-56 Workdays
Print Runs: 1,000 min - 200,000 max
Business from Other Countries: 100%
Parent Company: Icicle Group
Branch Office(s)
Room 1215, 12/F, Silver Tower, No 2 North Dong Sanhuan Rd, Chaoyang District, Beijing 100027, China *Tel:* (010) 6410 9926 *E-mail:* china@iciclegroup.com
6 F/E Wenxin Press Bldg, 755 Weihai Rd, Shanghai 200041, China *Tel:* (010) 6410 9926
Unit 16-0 Burgundy Corporate Tower, 252 Gil Puyat Ave, Makati City, Metro Manila, Philippines
19 Carpenter St, 04-01, Singapore 059908, Singapore *Tel:* 8438 5601 *E-mail:* singapore@iciclegroup.com
2F, 1, No 37, Sec 3, Minquan E Rd, Taipei, Taiwan *Tel:* (020) 7702 1168 *E-mail:* taiwan@iciclegroup.com
Garden Studios, DL10, 71-75 Shelton St, Covent Garden, London WC2H 9JQ, United Kingdom *Tel:* (020) 8123 1868 *E-mail:* london@iciclegroup.com

Imago Services (HK) Ltd
Tung Chong Factory Bldg, 6th floor, Flat B, 653-659 Kings Rd, North Point
Tel: 2811 3316 *Fax:* 2597 5256
E-mail: enquiries@imago.com.hk
Web Site: www.imago.com.hk
Branch Office(s)
Room 1806-07, Block B, TaiPing Yang Commercial & Trade Bldg, No 4028, Jiabin Rd, Luoho District, Shenzhen 518001, China *Tel:* (0755) 8304 8899 *Fax:* (0755) 8251 4073
Sales Office(s): Imago Australia, North Tower, Suite 5a, Level 2, 1-5 Railway St, Chatswood, NSW 2067, Australia *Tel:* (02) 9415 2713 *Fax:* (02) 9415 2714 *E-mail:* sales@imagoaus.com
Imago France, 23 rue Lavoisier, 75008 Paris, France *Tel:* 01 45 26 47 74 *Fax:* 01 78 94 14 44 *E-mail:* sales@imagogroup.com

Imago Productions (Malaysia) Pte Ltd, BBT One Blvd Lebuh Batu, Nilam 2, Bandar Bukit Tinggi, 41200 Klang, Selangor Darul Ehsan, Malaysia *Tel:* (03) 3318 1715 *Fax:* (03) 3325 1431
Imago Publishing Ltd, Albury Court, Albury, Thame, Oxon 0X9 2LP, United Kingdom *Tel:* (01844) 337000 *Fax:* (01844) 339935 *E-mail:* sales@imago.co.uk
U.S. Office(s): Imago Sales (USA) Inc, 23412 Moulton Parkway, Suite 250, Laguna Hills, CA 92653, United States *Tel:* 949-367-1635 *Fax:* 949-367-1639 *E-mail:* sales@imagousa.com
Imago Sales (USA) Inc, 110 W 40 St, 26th floor, New York, NY 10018, United States *Tel:* 212-921-4411 *Fax:* 212-921-8226 *E-mail:* sales@imagousa.com

Leo Paper Products Ltd
Subsidiary of Leo Paper Group
Level 9, Telford House, 16 Wang Hoi Rd, Kowloon Bay, Kowloon
Tel: 2884 1374 *Fax:* 2513 0698
E-mail: info@leo.com.hk
Web Site: www.leo.com.hk
Key Personnel
Sales Dir: Mr Kelly Fok *E-mail:* kelly@leo.com.uk
Founded: 1982
Turnaround: 15-30 Workdays
Print Runs: 5,000 min
Parent Company: Leo Paper Group
Sales Office(s): Leo Paper Products (Europe) BVBA, Korte Leemstr 3, 2018 Antwerp, Belgium *Tel:* (03) 609 6810 *Fax:* (03) 609 6830 *E-mail:* leo@leo-europe.com
Heshan Astros Printing Ltd, Industrial Development Area, Xijiang River, Gulao Town, Heshan City, Guangdong, China *Tel:* (0750) 8766-115 *Fax:* (0750) 8766-369
Heshan Leo Packaging & Printing Ltd, Sanlian Industrial City, Gulao Town, Heshan City, Guangdong, China *Tel:* (0750) 8861-888 *Fax:* (0750) 8861-500
Heshan Leo United Paper Products Ltd, 023 Industrial Zone 1, Hecheng Town, Heshan City, Guangdong 529727, China *Tel:* (0750) 8383-300 *Fax:* (0750) 8383-301
JiangXi HuaAo Printing Co Ltd, Changdong Industrial District, Middle Dong Tai Rd, Nanchang, Jiangxi 330012, China
Leo Creative (Shanghai) Trading Co Ltd, HuaJing Bldg, 3rd floor, 678 HuaShang Rd, Shanghai 200040, China *Tel:* (021) 6211-8799 *Fax:* (021) 6289-6226 *E-mail:* info@leo-creative.com
Shanghai Tophand Business Printing Co Ltd, 1F Bldg 10, No 189 Jinglian Rd, Minhang District, Shanghai 201108, China
Leo Paper Products (Europe) BVBA, Via Galliera, Unit 24, 40121 Bologna, Italy *Tel:* (051) 0922610 *Fax:* (051) 0922630 *E-mail:* leo@leo-europe.com
Leo Paper Products (UK) Ltd, The Oast House, 10 Brewery Court, Theale, Reading RG7 5AJ, United Kingdom *Tel:* (0118) 9165450 *E-mail:* info@leouk.com
U.S. Office(s): Leo Paper USA, 27 W 24 St, Suite 601, New York, NY 10010-3204, United States *Tel:* 917-305-0708 *Fax:* 917-305-0709 *E-mail:* info@leousanewyork.com
Leo Paper USA, 1180 NW Maple St, Suite 102, Issaquah, WA 98027, United States *Tel:* 425-646-8801 *Fax:* 425-646-8805 *E-mail:* info@leousa.com

Mei Ka Printing & Publishing Enterprise Ltd
23/F, Hong Kong Plaza, Rooms 2312A-B, 188 Connaught Rd W, Hong Kong
Tel: 2540 1131 *Fax:* 2559 8718; 2559 7137
E-mail: info@meika-printing.com; mkpp@netvigator.com
Web Site: www.meika-printing.com

Founded: 1982
Branch Office(s)
No 106 Changhong, 2nd Industrial Areas, June
St, Baiyun District, Guangzhou, China

Midas International Holdings Ltd
25/F, Alexandra House, 18 Chater Rd, Central
Hong Kong
Tel: 2407 6888 *Fax:* 2408 0611
E-mail: info@midasprinting.com; marketing@
midasprinting.com
Web Site: www.midasprinting.com
Key Personnel
Chairman & Group Mng Dir: Richard Hung Ting
Ho
Deputy Group Mng Dir: Geoffrey Chuang Ka
Kam
Founded: 1990
Turnaround: 10 Workdays for paperback; 15
Workdays for casebound
Print Runs: 3,000 min
Business from Other Countries: 85%
Branch Office(s)
88 Kingsway, Holborn, London WC2B 6AA,
United Kingdom, Sales Manager: Christos Ple-
gas *E-mail:* christos_plegas@midasprinting.com

New Island Printing Co Ltd
Billion Plaza, Room 1701, 17/F, 8 Cheung Yue
St, Cheung Sha Wan, Kowloon
Tel: 2442 8282 *Fax:* 2443 9882
E-mail: info@newisland.com
Web Site: www.newisland.com
Key Personnel
Chairman & Executive Dir: Mr Meng Guang Bao
Chief Executive Officer & Executive Dir: Mr Wu
Jiwei
Deputy Chief Executive Officer & Executive Dir:
Mr Guo Song
Founded: 1964
Branch Office(s)
Dongguan News Island Printing Co Ltd, Da Ling
Shan Science & Industrial Park, Dongguan,
China *Tel:* (0769) 8562 5222 *Fax:* (0769) 8561
6131
Shanghai New Island Packaging Printing Co Ltd,
1550 E Rongle Rd, Songjiang, Shanghai, China
Tel: (021) 5774 2828 *Fax:* (021) 5774 2288
U.S. Office(s): New Island Printing (US) Inc,
115 E 57 St, 1st floor, Suite 1104, New York,
NY 10022, United States *Tel:* 646-435-9415
Fax: 646-435-9414

Paper Art Product Ltd
Sung Fung Centre, Room 819, Block B, 88 Kwok
Shui Rd, Kwai Chung, New Territories
Tel: 2481 2929 *Fax:* 2489 2255
E-mail: paperart@netvigator.com
Founded: 1988
Turnaround: 2-4 Weeks
Print Runs: 2,000 min - 100,000 max
Business from Other Countries: 80%

Papercom Ltd, see Icicle Production Co Ltd

Paramount Printing Co Ltd
Member of Next Media Group
3 Chun Kwong St, T K O Industrial Estate W,
Tseung Kwan O, New Territories
Tel: 2896 8688 *Fax:* 2897 8942
E-mail: paramountcs@paramount.com.hk
Web Site: www.paramount.com.hk
Founded: 1968
Turnaround: 30-45 Workdays
Print Runs: 1,000 min - 1,000,000 max
Business from Other Countries: 60%
Branch Office(s)
Book Art Inc, 2800 John St, Unit 13, Markham,
ON L3R 0E2, Canada *Tel:* 905-940-8282
Fax: 905-470-1800 *E-mail:* enquires@
bookartinc.com

Sing Cheong Printing Co Ltd
Tung Chong Factory Bldg, G/F, 655 Kings Rd,
North Point
Tel: 2561 8801 *Fax:* 2565 9467
Key Personnel
Dir & Manager: Karen Shen Fishel
Founded: 1965
Business from Other Countries: 96%

South China Printing Co Ltd
Subsidiary of RR Donnelley Asia Printing Solu-
tions Ltd
Unit 2010-11, 20/F, C-Bons International Center,
108 Wai Yip St, Kwun Tong, Kowloon
Tel: 2637 3611 *Fax:* 2637 4221
Founded: 1988
Turnaround: 20 Workdays
Print Runs: 2,000 min - 150,000 max
Business from Other Countries: 98%
Branch Office(s)
Heath & Reach, Beds, United Kingdom, Contact:
Alan Lynch *Tel:* (0152) 523-7455 *Fax:* (0152)
523-7756 *E-mail:* alan.lynch@lineone.net
U.S. Office(s): Los Angeles, CA, United States,
Contact: Mr Moon Chuen Lo *Tel:* 626-291-
7398 *Fax:* 626-285-2870 *E-mail:* moonclo@
earthlink.com
New York, NY, United States, Contact: Peter
Lawrence *Tel:* 212-570-9010 *Fax:* 212-628-
0137 *E-mail:* scpco@aol.com

Speedflex Asia Ltd
1/F Hua Qin International Bldg, 340 Queen's Rd
Central, Hong Kong
Tel: 2542 2780 *Fax:* 2542 3733
E-mail: info@speedflex.com.hk
Web Site: www.speedflex.com.hk
Founded: 1981
Turnaround: 1 Workday
Print Runs: 1 min
Business from Other Countries: 20%

Sunshine Press Ltd
Room 4, 5, 11-12, 21/F, Fullagar Industrial Bldg,
234 Aberdeen Main Rd, Aberdeen
Tel: 2553 0228 *Fax:* 2873 2930
E-mail: spl@sunshinepress.com.hk
Key Personnel
Dir: Raymond Wong
Administration Manager: Joney Chan
Founded: 1976
Turnaround: 21-28 Workdays
Print Runs: 3,000 min - 500,000 max
Business from Other Countries: 25%

Toppan Lefung (Hong Kong) Ltd
Subsidiary of Toppan Leefung Pte Ltd
169 Electric Rd, 20th floor, at Convoy, North
Point
Tel: 2810 6801 *Fax:* 2810 5530
E-mail: enquiries@toppanleefung.com
Web Site: www.toppanleefung.com
Key Personnel
President & Chief Executive Officer: Yeo Chee
Tong
Mng Dir, China Division: Yuan Fu Yin
Founded: 1960

Wing King Tong Group
Leader Industrial Centre, Block I, 3/F, 188-202
Texaco Rd, Tsuen Wan, New Territories
Tel: 2407 3287 *Fax:* 2408 7939
E-mail: marketing@wktco.com
Web Site: www.wkt.cc
Key Personnel
Mng Dir: Alex Yan Tak Chung
Founded: 1944
Turnaround: 15 Workdays
Print Runs: 1,000 min - 100,000 max
Business from Other Countries: 95%

Branch Office(s)
No 67, Li Xin Lu, Dan Zhu Tou Community,
Nan Wan St, Longgang District, Shenzhen,
Guangdong 518114, China *Tel:* (0755) 8473
6801; (0755) 8473 6802; (0755) 8473 6803
Fax: (0755) 8473 6303 *E-mail:* szwktsales@
wkt.cc

Hungary

Interpress Kuelkereskedelmi Kft
Becsi ut 67, Budapest 1037
Tel: (01) 250-8263; (01) 250-8266 *Fax:* (01) 250-
8262
E-mail: interpress@interpress.eu
Web Site: www.interpress.eu
Key Personnel
Sales: Zsuzsa Cserna *Tel:* (01) 430 0860
E-mail: zsuzsa.cserna@interpress.eu
Contact: Katalin Multas *E-mail:* katalin.multas@
interpress.eu
Founded: 1991

India

Repro India Ltd
Sun Paradise Business Plaza, 11th floor, B Wing,
Senapati Bapat Marg, Lower Parel, Mumbai
400 013
Tel: (022) 7191 4000 *Fax:* (022) 7191 4001
E-mail: info@reproindialtd.com
Web Site: www.reproindialtd.com
Founded: 1984
Branch Office(s)
Plot No 50/2, TTC MIDC Industrial Area, Ma-
hape, Navi Mumbai 400 710 *Tel:* (022) 7178
5000 *Fax:* (022) 7178 5011 (plant)
Repro Innovative Digiprint Pvt Ltd, No 146,
East Coast Rd, Vettuvankeni, Chennai 600 115
(plant)
Plot No 90-93, 165 Surat Special Economic
Zone, Rd No 11, GIDC, Sachin, Surat 394
230 *Tel:* (0261) 3107396; (0261) 3107397
Fax: (0261) 2398030 (plant)
Sales Office(s): 1211, South City, Pinnacle, 11/1,
Salt Lake City, Block EP, Sector 5, Kolkata
700 091 *Tel:* 9650003189 (cell)
Unit No 205, 2nd floor, DLF Tower-A, Jasola
District Centre, Jasola, New Delhi 110 076
Tel: (011) 41323212 *Fax:* (011) 41323214
11 Whitman St, Hastings-on-Hudson, NY 10706-
1605, United States

Indonesia

PT Victory Offset Prima
JL Aria Santika No 8, Desa Pasir Bolang-
Tigaraksa, Tangerang 15610
Tel: (021) 5940-5343 *Fax:* (021) 5940-5345
E-mail: info@victoryoffset.com
Web Site: www.victoryoffset.com
Key Personnel
General Manager: S Wilson Pinady
Founded: 1971
Turnaround: 14 Workdays
Print Runs: 5,000 min
Business from Other Countries: 10%

Ireland

Tower Books
Iniscarra View Estate, 13 Hawthorn Ave,
Ballincollig, Co Cork
Tel: (021) 4872294
E-mail: towerbooks@eircom.net
Web Site: towerbooks.ie
Key Personnel
Contact: Patricia Deasy
Founded: 1974
Turnaround: 7-30 Workdays
Print Runs: 300 min - 2,000 max

Israel

The Government Printer
One Kaplan St, 9195015 Jerusalem
Mailing Address: PO Box 3100, 9195015
Jerusalem
Tel: (02) 5317215 *Fax:* (02) 5695347
Web Site: mof.gov.il/gp
Founded: 1948

Har-El Printers & Publishers
PO Box 8053, 6108402 Jaffa
Tel: (03) 6816834 *Fax:* (03) 6813563
Web Site: www.harelart.com
Key Personnel
Owner & Dir: Monique L Har-El
E-mail: mharel@harelart.co.il
Manager: Jaacov Har-El
Founded: 1974
Turnaround: 60-90 Workdays
Print Runs: 30 min - 5,000 max
Business from Other Countries: 70%

Italy

G Canale & C SpA
Via Liguria, 24, 10071 Borgaro Turin TO
Tel: (011) 40 78 511 *Fax:* (011) 40 78 607
E-mail: sales@canale.it
Web Site: www.gcanale.it
Founded: 1915
Turnaround: 30 Workdays
Print Runs: 3,000 min
Business from Other Countries: 65%
Branch Office(s)
SOS Cernica, 47, Pantellimon Jud ILFOV,
Bucharest, Romania *Tel:* (021) 351 72 55
Fax: (021) 351 72 57 *E-mail:* office@canale-
bucarest.ro

Creabooks Packagers
Via Martiri della Liberazione 14, 16043 Chiavari
GE
Tel: (0185) 1873688 *Fax:* (0185) 1898316
E-mail: info@abooks.it
Web Site: www.creabooks.it
Key Personnel
Art Dir: Donatella Bergamino *E-mail:* d.
bergamino@abooks.it
Foreign Rights Manager: Giorgio Bergamino
E-mail: g.bergamino@abooks.it
Editorial: Laura Aceti *E-mail:* l.aceti@abooks.it

Dedalo Litostampa SRL
Viale Luigi Jacobini, 5, 70123 Bari BA
Tel: (080) 531 14 13 *Fax:* (080) 531 14 14
E-mail: info@dedalolitostampa.it
Web Site: www.dedalolitostampa.it

Founded: 1961
Print Runs: 2,000 min - 10,000 max

Istituto Poligrafico e Zecca dello Stato SpA
(Government Printing Office & Mint SpA)
Via Salaria, 1027, 00138 Rome
Tel: (06) 85081; (06) 85082147 (bookshop)
Toll Free Tel: 800 864035 *Fax:* (06) 85082517
E-mail: informazioni@ipzs.it; ufficiostampa@
ipzs.it
Web Site: www.ipzs.it
Key Personnel
Chief Executive Officer: Dr Ferruccio Ferranti
Dir, Communications: Manuela Bravi
Founded: 1928

Legatoria Editoriale Giovanni Olivotto SpA,
see LEGO SpA

LEGO SpA
Via dell'Industria, 2, 36100 Vicenza
Tel: (0444) 564622 *Fax:* (0444) 564929
E-mail: lego@legogroup.com
Web Site: www.legogroup.com
Key Personnel
Mng Dir: Giulio Olivotto
Founded: 1900

Stamperia Valdonega
Member of SIZ Group
Viale Copernico n 11, 37059 Campagnola di Ze-
vio VR
Tel: (045) 8730411 *Fax:* (045) 8731522
Web Site: www.stamperiavaldonega.it
Key Personnel
Chief Executive Officer: Simioni Nicola
Founded: 1948
Print Runs: 1,000 min
Business from Other Countries: 70%

Lithuania

Spindulio Spaustuve (Spindulys Printing House)
B Brazdzionio g 23, LT-48184 Kaunas
Tel: (037) 200744 *Fax:* (037) 204970
E-mail: info@spindulys.lt
Web Site: www.spindulys.lt
Key Personnel
Sales & Marketing Manager: Sigita Varniene
E-mail: sigita@spindulys.lt
Project Manager: Kristina Petruskeviciute
E-mail: kristina@spindulys.lt
Founded: 1928
Print Runs: 500 min - 100,000 max
Business from Other Countries: 6%

Madagascar

Imprimerie Catholique
129 Ave Lenine Vladimir, Antanimena, 101 Antananarivo
Tel: 22 223 04

Malawi

Likuni Press & Publishing
PO Box 133, Lilongwe
Tel: 766122; 766095
E-mail: likuni.press@gmail.com

Web Site: likunipress.wordpress.com
Founded: 1949
Print Runs: 12,000 min - 15,000 max
Business from Other Countries: 5%

Netherlands

Hoonte Bosch & Keuning
Zeehaenkade 30, 3526 LC Utrecht
Tel: (030) 287 91 00 *Fax:* (030) 287 91 01

New Zealand

Bookprint Consultants Ltd
1104, One Market Lane, Wellington 6011
Tel: (04) 381 3070
Web Site: www.granthamhouse.co.nz
Key Personnel
Chief Executive: Graham C Stewart
E-mail: graham@ghbil.com
Founded: 1982
Print Runs: 2,000 min - 7,500 max
Business from Other Countries: 10%
Branch Office(s)
Bookprint International Ltd, New Trend Cen-
tre, 104 King Fuk St, Sanpokong, Kowloon,
Hong Kong *Tel:* 2327 0101 *Fax:* 2350 0325
E-mail: bil@kingstime.com.hk

Caxton
2 Stark Dr, Wigram, Christchurch 8042
Mailing Address: PO Box 36411, Merivale,
Christchurch 8146
Tel: (03) 366 8516 *Fax:* (03) 365 7840
Web Site: www.caxton.co.nz
Key Personnel
Mng Dir: Bruce Bascand *E-mail:* bruce@caxton.
co.nz
Dir: Dave Bascand *E-mail:* dave@caxton.
co.nz; Peter Watson *Tel:* (03) 353 0734
E-mail: peter@caxton.co.nz
Dir/Sales Manager: Bridget Batchelor *Tel:* (03)
353 0730 *E-mail:* bridget@caxton.co.nz
Artroom Manager: Janice Page *Tel:* (03) 353
0735 *E-mail:* janice@caxton.co.nz
Founded: 1935

Philippines

Cacho Hermanos Inc
Pines Corner, Union Sts, 1550 Mandaluyong,
Metro Manila
Tel: (02) 631 8361; (02) 631 8362; (02) 631
8363; (02) 631 8364; (02) 631 8365 *Fax:* (02)
631 5244
Founded: 1880
Turnaround: 7-120 Workdays
Print Runs: 500 min - 50,000 max
Parent Company: National Book Store

Portugal

Edicoes Silabo Lda
Rua Cidade de Manchester, 2, 1170-100 Lisbon
Tel: 218130345 *Fax:* 218166719
E-mail: silabo@silabo.pt

Web Site: www.silabo.pt
Key Personnel
Marketing Dir & Editor: Manuel Robalo
   E-mail: manuel.robalo@silabo.pt
Founded: 1983
Turnaround: 5 Workdays

Romania

Editura Paideia
Piata Unirii, Nr 1, 030119 Bucharest
Tel: (021) 316 82 10
E-mail: comenzi@paideia.ro
Web Site: www.paideia.ro
Founded: 1990
Turnaround: 3-20 Workdays
Business from Other Countries: 10%

Singapore

Chong Moh Offset Printing Pte Ltd
19 Joo Koon Rd, Singapore 628978
Tel: 6862 2701 *Fax:* 6862 4335
Founded: 1946
Turnaround: 10-14 Workdays
Print Runs: 1,000 min
Business from Other Countries: 35%

HB Media Holdings Pte Ltd
119 Genting Lane, No 04-08, Singapore 349570
Tel: 6296 4289
Founded: 1980
Turnaround: 5 Workdays
Business from Other Countries: 97%

Ho Printing Singapore Pte Ltd
31 Changi South St One, Changi South Industrial
   Estate, Singapore 486769
Tel: 6542 9322 *Fax:* 6542 8322
E-mail: sales@hoprinting.com.sg
Web Site: www.hoprinting.com
Founded: 1951
Turnaround: 35-50 Workdays
Print Runs: 5,000 min - 50,000 max
Business from Other Countries: 30%

Kim Hup Lee Printing Co Pte Ltd
16 King George's Ave, Singapore 208558
Tel: 6298 6911 *Fax:* 6298 6415
Web Site: www.khlprint.com.sg
Key Personnel
Dir: Mr Lim Geok Khoon
Parent Company: Kim Hup Lee Group

Magenta Lithographic Consultants Pte Ltd
1093 Lower Delta Rd, No 04-01, Singapore
   169240
Tel: 6274 6288 *Fax:* 6274 6795
Founded: 1975
Turnaround: 2-3 Workdays
Business from Other Countries: 30%

Markono Print Media Pte Ltd
Subsidiary of Markono Holdings Pte Ltd
21 Neythal Rd, Singapore 628586
Tel: 6281 1118
E-mail: enquiry@markono.com; sales@markono.
   com
Web Site: www.markono.com
Key Personnel
Chairman: Bob Lee
Mng Dir: Edwin Ng

Sales & Marketing Dir: Max Lee
Founded: 1967
Turnaround: 14 Workdays
Print Runs: 1,000 min - 100,000 max
Business from Other Countries: 20%
Branch Office(s)
Markono Logistics, 4 Toh Tuck Link, Singapore
   596226 *Tel:* 6465 1498 *E-mail:* ml.sales@
   markono.com
Markono Digital Solutions (M) Sdn Bhd, 7
   Lorong Jelawat 4, 13700 Seberang Jaya,
   Penang, Malaysia *Tel:* (04) 397-8700
   E-mail: mdsm.sales@markono.com

Saik Wah Print Media Pte Ltd
171 Kallang Way, No 03-08, Singapore 349250
Tel: 6292 8759 *Fax:* 6296 0638
E-mail: sales@saikwah.com.sg
Web Site: www.saikwah.com.sg
Founded: 1973
Turnaround: 20 Workdays
Print Runs: 1,000 min - 100,000 max
Business from Other Countries: 70%
Parent Company: Winson Press Co

Stamford Press Pte Ltd
209 Kallang Bahru, Singapore 339344
Tel: 6294 7227 *Fax:* 6294 4396; 6294 3319
E-mail: info@stamford.com.sg
Web Site: www.stamford.com.sg
Key Personnel
Dir, Sales & Marketing: Mr V Balu
   E-mail: balu@stamford.com.sg
Founded: 1963 (as Stamford College Press)
Turnaround: 3-4 Workdays for small jobs; 3-4
   Weeks for big jobs
Print Runs: 1,500 min - 50,000 max
Business from Other Countries: 20%
Parent Company: Stamford Media International
   Pte Ltd
Branch Office(s)
Stamford Aus-Trade & Press Pty Ltd, 32 Ada
   Ave, Strathfield, NSW 2135, Australia *Tel:* (02)
   9758 7715 *Fax:* (02) 9758 7716
Raffles-Stamford Press (India) Pvt Ltd, No 1
   Survey No 16/1, Singasandra Village, Begur
   Hobli, Hosur Main Rd, Bangalore 560 068,
   India *Tel:* (080) 573 0717; (080) 573 0718
   Fax: (080) 573 3992
Stamford Lake Pvt Ltd, 366, High Level Rd, Pan-
   nipitiya, Sri Lanka *Tel:* (01) 846 002; (074)
   208 134 *Fax:* (01) 846 002; (074) 208 134
No 61, Tryfan Close Redbridge, Ilford, Es-
   sex IG4 5JY, United Kingdom *Tel:* (01223)
   504754; (020) 8262 6515 *Fax:* (01223)
   574538; (020) 8262 6514

Times Printers Pte Ltd
Subsidiary of Times Publishing Ltd
16 Tuas Ave 5, Singapore 639340
Tel: 6311 2888; 6295 3211; 6295 2138; 6311
   2872 (customer service); 6311 2780 (sales &
   marketing) *Fax:* 6862 1313; 6311 2872 (cus-
   tomer service)
E-mail: marketing@timesprinters.com
Web Site: www.timesprinters.com.sg
Key Personnel
Deputy General Manager, Group Sales & Market-
   ing: Patsy Tan
Operations Manager: Alex Tang
Assistant General Manager: Phan Ming Ruey
Founded: 1968
Turnaround: 5-25 Workdays
Print Runs: 3,000 min - 300,000 max
Business from Other Countries: 75%
Branch Office(s)
Times Offset (Malaysia) Sdn Bhd, Lot 46, Sub-
   ang Hi-Tech Industrial Park, Batu Tiga, 40000
   Selangor Darul Ehsan, Malaysia *Tel:* (03) 5628
   6888 *Fax:* (03) 5628 6899
Sales Office(s): Everbest Printing Co Ltd, 25
   The Palisade, Umina Beach, NSW 2257, Aus-

tralia *Tel:* (02) 4342 3563 *Fax:* (02) 4342 1564
   E-mail: adam@everbestprinting.com.au
Everbest Printing Co Ltd, Ko Fai Industrial
   Bldg, C5 10th floor, 7 Ko Fai Rd, Yau
   Tong, Kowloon, Hong Kong *Tel:* 2727 4433
   Fax: 2772 7687 *E-mail:* sales@everbest.com.hk
13 Nthombeni Way Noordhoek, 7979 Cape
   Town, South Africa, Contact: Arlene Gippert
   Tel: (021) 789 2865 *E-mail:* arlenegippert@tpg.
   com.my
Everbest UK, 31 Palatine Rd, London N16 8SY,
   United Kingdom, Contact: Nicky Bowden
   Tel: (020) 7249 9483 *Fax:* (020) 7241 3460
   E-mail: nickybowden@everbest.co.uk
3240 Vicente St, Apartment 3, San Fran-
   cisco, CA 94116, United States, Contact:
   Brian Olshansky-Lucero *Tel:* 646-847-9874
   E-mail: brian.olshansky-lucero@tpg.com.my

Toppan Security Printing Pte Ltd
97 Ubi Ave 4, Singapore 408754
Tel: 6741 2500 *Fax:* 6744 7098
Web Site: www.toppanleefung.com/toppansecurity.
   aspx
Key Personnel
President & Chief Executive Officer: Yeo Chee
   Tong
General Manager & Digital Printing: David
   Ng *Tel:* 6846 3518 *E-mail:* davidng@
   toppanleefung.com
Deputy Sales Dir, Security Printing: Rick
   Ang *Tel:* 6846 3912 *E-mail:* rickang@
   toppanleefung.com
Founded: 1994
Turnaround: 30 Workdays
Print Runs: 2,000 min - 200,000 max
Business from Other Countries: 35%
Parent Company: Toppan Printing Co Ltd, One
   Kanda Izumi-cho, Chiyoda-ku, Toyko 101-
   0024, Japan

Viva Lithographers Pte Ltd
221 Henderson Bldg, No 02-12, Singapore
   159557
Tel: 6272 1880 *Fax:* 6273 5425
E-mail: vivasing@singnet.com.sg
Web Site: www.vivalitho.com
Key Personnel
Executive Dir: Kris Chua *Tel:* 9172 9199
Mng Dir: Michael Oh *Tel:* 9171 9919
General Manager: Abdul Rahman *Tel:* 9152 9919
Business Manager: Jerry Chen *Tel:* 9618 9919
Marketing Manager: Dominic Ng *Tel:* 9155 9919
Production Manager: Karen Chau *Tel:* 9785 9919
Founded: 1980

Slovakia

Neografia AS
ul Sucianska 39 A, 038 61 Martin-Priekopa
Tel: (043) 4201 241 *Fax:* (043) 4201 704
E-mail: info@neografia.sk
Web Site: www.neografia.sk
Key Personnel
General Dir: Patrick Schwab *E-mail:* patrick.
   schwab@neografia.sk
Production Dir: Milos Lukac *Tel:* (043) 4201 300
   E-mail: milos.lukac@neografia.sk
Commercial Dir: Helena Magvasiova *Tel:* (043)
   4201 240 *E-mail:* helena.magvasiova@
   neografia.sk
Financial Dir: Peter Budisky *Tel:* (043) 4201 400
   E-mail: peter.budisky@neografia.sk
Founded: 1869

Slovenia

Gorenjski Tisk Storitve doo
Ul Mirka Vadnova 6, SI-4000 Kranj
Tel: (04) 20 16 300 *Fax:* (04) 20 16 301
E-mail: info@go-tisk.si
Web Site: www.go-tisk.si
Key Personnel
Mng Dir: Goran Celesnik *Tel:* (04) 20 16 330
  E-mail: goran.celesnik@go-tisk.si
Dir, Sales & Marketing: Dr Andrej Krope, PhD
  Tel: (04) 20 16 326 *E-mail:* andrej.krope@go-
  tisk.si
Production Manager: Dusan Kuljic *Tel:* (04) 20
  16 451 *E-mail:* dusan.kuljic@go-tisk.si
Founded: 1888
Turnaround: 30 Workdays
Print Runs: 3,000 min - 15,000 max
Business from Other Countries: 50%

South Korea

Mirae N Co Ltd
321 Sinbanpo-ro, Seocho-gu, Seoul 137-905
Fax: (02) 541-8158
Web Site: www.mirae-n.com
Key Personnel
President: Kim Young-jin
Manager: Ji Young Park *Tel:* (02) 3475-3870
  E-mail: park.jiyoung@mirae-n.com
Founded: 1948

Spain

Edelvives, see Editorial Luis Vives (Edelvives)

Graficas Santa Maria
Av Blas Infante, s/n, 41100 Coria del Rio, Seville
Tel: 954 771 091
Web Site: graficassantamaria.com
Founded: 1960
Turnaround: 1 Workday
Print Runs: 500 min - 150,000 max
Business from Other Countries: 15%

Offo Artes Graficas SL
Calle Rio Guadalimar, 7, 28906 Getafe (Madrid)
Tel: 91 691 82 40 *Fax:* 91 691 92 26

Editorial Luis Vives (Edelvives)
Xaudaro, 25, 28034 Madrid
Tel: 913 344 884
E-mail: info@edelvives.es
Web Site: www.edelvives.com
Founded: 1889
Turnaround: 1 Workday
Business from Other Countries: 25%
Parent Company: Grupo Editorial Luis Vives
Branch Office(s)
Ctra de Madrid, km 315,700, 50012 Zaragoza
  Tel: 976 304 030

Sri Lanka

Sarvodaya Vishva Lekha
Unit of Sarvodaya
No 98, Rawatawatta Rd, Moratwa 10400
Tel: (011) 264-7159 *Fax:* (011) 2656-512
Web Site: www.sarvodaya.org
Founded: 1985
Print Runs: 500 min
Business from Other Countries: 5%

Sumathi Printers (Pvt) Ltd
Subsidiary of Sumathi Global Consolidated (Pvt)
  Ltd
445/1, Sirimavo Bandaranaike Mawatha, Colombo
  14
Tel: (011) 2330673; (011) 2330674 *Fax:* (011)
  2399924
E-mail: spb@sumathi.lk
Web Site: www.sumathi.lk/xampp/printing.html
Founded: 1980
Business from Other Countries: 75%

Switzerland

Autorinnen und Autoren der Schweiz AdS
  (Association of Swiss Authors)
Konradstr 61, 8031 Zurich
Tel: (044) 350 04 60 *Fax:* (044) 350 04 61
E-mail: sekretariat@a-d-s.ch
Web Site: www.a-d-s.ch
Key Personnel
Mng Dir: Nicole Pfister Fetz *E-mail:* npfister@a-
  d-s.ch
Founded: 2002

Autrices et Auteurs de Suisse, see Autorinnen
  und Autoren der Schweiz AdS

Autrici ed Autori della Svizzera AdS, see
  Autorinnen und Autoren der Schweiz AdS

hep verlag AG
Gutenbergstr 31, 3001 Bern
Tel: (031) 310 29 29 *Fax:* (031) 318 31 35
E-mail: info@hep-verlag.ch
Web Site: www.hep-verlag.ch
Key Personnel
Publishing Dir & Chairman: Peter Egger
  Tel: (031) 310 29 20 *E-mail:* peter.egger@hep-
  verlag.ch
Vice President: Dr Men Haupt *E-mail:* men.
  haupt@hep-verlag.ch
Marketing: Gisela Fluehmann *Tel:* (031) 310 29
  17 *E-mail:* gisela.fluehmann@hep-verlag.ch
Marketing & Sales: Rahel Wenger *Tel:* (031) 310
  29 21 *E-mail:* rahel.wenger@hep-verlag.ch
Founded: 2000

IBBY, see International Board on Books for
  Young People (IBBY)

**International Board on Books for Young
  People (IBBY)**
Nonnenweg 12, Postfach, 4009 Basel
Tel: (061) 272 29 17 *Fax:* (061) 272 27 57
E-mail: ibby@ibby.org
Web Site: www.ibby.org
Key Personnel
President: Wally De Doncker *E-mail:* wally.de.
  doncker@telenet.de
Vice President: Akoss Ofori-Mensah
  E-mail: saharanp@africaonline.gh; Azucena
  Galindo Ortega *E-mail:* agalindo@ibbymexico.
  org.mx
Executive Dir: Elizabeth Page *E-mail:* liz.page@
  ibby.org
Founded: 1953

Tanzania

Peramiho Printing Press
PO Box 41, Songea, Ruvuma
Tel: (025) 260 2299
Founded: 1937
Print Runs: 4,000 min - 6,000 max

Thailand

Amarin Printing & Publishing Public Co Ltd
378 Chaiyaphruk Rd, Taling Chan, Bangkok
  10170
Tel: (02) 882-1010; (02) 422-9000 *Fax:* (02) 433-
  2742; (02) 434-1385
Web Site: www.amarin.co.th
Key Personnel
President: Mrs Metta Utakapan
Administrative Dir: Bussapakes Wongchaoum
Sales Dir: Jutamas Smitanon
Founded: 1976

J Film Process Co Ltd
440/7 Soi Ratchawithi 3, Ratchawithi Rd, Ra-
  jchatha, Bangkok 10400
Tel: (02) 248-6888; (02) 248-6887 *Fax:* (02) 246-
  4719
Founded: 1970
Turnaround: 6 Workdays
Print Runs: 25,000 min - 65,000 max
Business from Other Countries: 45%

Phongwarin Printing Ltd
299-299/1 Moo 10, Sukhumvit 107, Sumrongnue,
  Ampur Muang, Samutprakarn 10270
Tel: (02) 7498934-45; (02) 7498275-79; (02)
  3994525-31 *Fax:* (02) 3994524; (02) 3994255;
  (02) 3931028
E-mail: intemarketing@phongwarin.co.th
Web Site: www.phongwarin.co.th
Key Personnel
Mng Dir: Mr Somphong Charnsirisaksakul
Founded: 1983
Turnaround: 7 Workdays
Print Runs: 1,000 min - 500,000 max
Business from Other Countries: 5%

United Kingdom

Bell & Bain Ltd
303 Burnfield Rd, Thornliebank, Glasgow G46
  7UQ
Tel: (0141) 649 5697 *Fax:* (0141) 632 8733
Web Site: www.bell-bain.com
Key Personnel
Co-Owner & Mng Dir: Stephen Docherty
  E-mail: sd@bell-bain.co.uk
Co-Owner & Sales Dir: Tony Campbell
  E-mail: tcampbell@bell-bain.co.uk
Sales Dir Designate: Derek Kenney
  E-mail: dkenney@bell-bain.co.uk
Operations Dir: Karen Baillie *E-mail:* kbaillie@
  bell-bain.co.uk
Customer Services Manager: Tracey Mallon
  E-mail: tmallon@bell-bain.co.uk
Information Technology Manager: Gordon Rogers
  E-mail: grogers@bell-bain.co.uk
Founded: 1831
Turnaround: 7-10 Workdays
Print Runs: 100 min - 100,000 max
Business from Other Countries: 25%

Book Production Consultants Ltd
Affiliate of Granta Editions
25-27 High St, Chesterton, Cambridge, Cambs
 CB4 1ND
Tel: (01223) 352790; (01223) 841748
 Fax: (01223) 460718
E-mail: enquiries@bpccam.co.uk
Web Site: www.bpccam.co.uk
Key Personnel
Mng Dir: Colin Walsh
Founded: 1973
Turnaround: 50 Workdays
Business from Other Countries: 25%

Clays Ltd
Subsidiary of St Ives PLC
One Tudor St, London EC4Y 0AH
Tel: (020) 7928 8844
E-mail: sales@clays.co.uk
Web Site: www.clays.co.uk
Key Personnel
Mng Dir: Paul Hulley
Account Dir: Andrew Cochrane; Vicky Ellis
Customer Service Dir: Anne Perrin
Digital Sales Dir: Andrew Copley
Finance Dir: Andrew Spring
Manufacturing Dir: Ian Smith
Strategic Dir: Kate McFarlan
Self-Publishing Account Manager: Rebecca
 Souster
Founded: 1817
Turnaround: 15 Workdays
Print Runs: 1,000 min - 1,000,000 max
Business from Other Countries: 15%
Branch Office(s)
Popson St, Bungay, Suffolk NR35 1ED
 Tel: (01986) 893 211

William Clowes Ltd, see CPI William Clowes
 Ltd

CPI Antony Rowe
Bumper's Farm, Chippenham, Wilts SN14 6LH
Tel: (01249) 659705 *Fax:* (01249) 443103
Web Site: www.cpi-print.co.uk
Key Personnel
General Manager: Martin Collyer
Sales Manager: Geoff Fisher
Divisional Mng Dir: Alison Kaye
Founded: 1983
Turnaround: 20 Workdays
Print Runs: 50 min - 2,000 max
Business from Other Countries: 2%
Parent Company: CPI Group UK Ltd
Branch Office(s)
48-50 Birch Close, Eastbourne, East Sussex
 BN23 6PE *Tel:* (01323) 434700

CPI William Clowes Ltd
Copland Way, Ellough, Beccles, Suffolk NR34
 7TL
Tel: (01502) 712884
E-mail: williamclowes@cpibooks.co.uk
Key Personnel
Divisional Mng Dir: Alison Kaye
Head, Sales: Jonathan Huddart
Founded: 1803
Turnaround: 10 Workdays
Print Runs: 2,000 min
Business from Other Countries: 1%
Parent Company: CPI Group UK Ltd

Garden House Editions Ltd
15 Grafton Sq, London SW4 0DQ
Tel: (020) 7622 1720 *Fax:* (020) 7720 9114

Gee & Son (Denbigh) Ltd
Uned 7, Felin Fawr, Bethesda, Gwynedd LL57
 4YY

Key Personnel
Dir: Emlyn Evans
Founded: 1808

Intype Libra Ltd
3/4 Elm Grove Industrial Estate, Elm Grove,
 Wimbledon, London SW19 4HE
Tel: (020) 8947 7863 *Fax:* (020) 8947 3652
E-mail: hello@intypelibra.co.uk
Web Site: www.intypelibra.co.uk
Key Personnel
Owner & Mng Dir: Tony Chapman
Owner: David Greenwood
Founded: 1974
Turnaround: 1-6 Workdays
Print Runs: 1 min - 2,500 max
Business from Other Countries: 5%

Gerald Judd Sales Ltd
Paper House, 47-51 Gillingham St, London
 SW1V 1HS
Tel: (020) 7828 8821
E-mail: enquiries@geraldjudd.co.uk
Web Site: www.geraldjudd.com
Key Personnel
Mng Dir: Jonathan Addy *E-mail:* jonathanaddy@
 geraldjudd.co.uk
Sales Dir: Robert Thompstone
 E-mail: robertthompstone@geraldjudd.co.uk
Customer Services Manager: Ben Caulfield
 E-mail: bencaulfield@geraldjudd.co.uk
Sales Manager: Jonathan Clay
 E-mail: jonathanclay@geraldjudd.co.uk
Founded: 1936

Lavenham Press Ltd
Arbons House, 47 Water St, Lavenham, Suffolk
 CO10 9RN
Tel: (01787) 247436 *Fax:* (01787) 248267
E-mail: enquiries@lavenhamgroup.co.uk
Web Site: www.lavenhampress.com
Key Personnel
Mng Dir: Terence Dalton
Founded: 1953
Business from Other Countries: 1%
Parent Company: Lavenham Group

Librios Ltd
20 Lochaline St, London W6 9SH
Tel: (020) 3355 0200
E-mail: info@librios.com
Web Site: www.librios.com
Key Personnel
Software Development Dir: David Wilcockson
 E-mail: david@librios.com
System Administrator: Neville Mooney
Project Developer: Chris Lewis *E-mail:* chris.
 lewis@librios.com
Founded: 1997
Business from Other Countries: 30%

Masons Design & Print
Viscount House, River Lane, Saltney, Chester,
 Cheshire CH4 8RH
Tel: (01244) 674433 *Fax:* (01244) 674274
Founded: 1908
Turnaround: 5-10 Workdays
Print Runs: 500 min - 500,000 max

Page Bros (Norwich) Ltd
Subsidiary of Milex Ltd
Mile Cross Lane, Norwich, Norfolk NR6 6SA
Tel: (01603) 778800 *Fax:* (01603) 778801
E-mail: info@pagebros.co.uk
Web Site: www.pagebros.co.uk
Key Personnel
Mng Dir: Craig Eastaugh *E-mail:* c.eastaugh@
 pagebros.co.uk
Sales & Commercial Dir: Andrew Spelman
 E-mail: a.spelman@pagebros.co.uk
Founded: 1750

Turnaround: 10 Workdays
Print Runs: 100 min - 30,000 max
Business from Other Countries: 20%

Precision Publishing Paper
St Stephens House, 2nd floor, Dogflud Way, Farn-
 ham, Surrey GU9 7RX
Tel: (01252) 719 461 *Fax:* (01252) 719 487
Web Site: www.hspg.com
Key Personnel
Dir: Mariusz Siwak
Parent Company: Howard Smith Paper Group Ltd

F J Ratchford Ltd
Kennedy Way, Green Lane, Stockport, Cheshire
 SK4 2JX
Tel: (0161) 480 8484 *Fax:* (0161) 480 3679
E-mail: enquiries@ratchford.co.uk; info@
 ratchford.co.uk; sales@ratchford.co.uk
Web Site: www.ratchford.co.uk
Key Personnel
Dir: J P Ratchford
Mng Dir: Jonathan Ratchford
Founded: 1889

Scottish Braille Press
Division of Royal Blind School
Craigmillar Park, Edinburgh EH16 5NB
Tel: (0131) 662 4445 *Fax:* (0131) 662 1968
E-mail: enquiries.sbp@royalblind.org
Web Site: www.royalblind.org/scottishbraillepress
Key Personnel
Manager: John Donaldson
Deputy Manager: Sandra Wright
Founded: 1891
Turnaround: 15-20 Workdays

TJ International Ltd
Trecerus Industrial Estate, Padstow, Cornwall
 PL28 8RW
Tel: (01841) 532691 *Fax:* (01841) 532862
E-mail: sales@tjinternational.ltd.uk
Web Site: www.tjinternational.ltd.uk
Key Personnel
Chief Executive Officer: Angus Clark
Deputy Chief Executive Officer: Andy Vosper
Sales & Marketing Manager: Neil Clarke
Founded: 1970
Turnaround: 10 Workdays
Print Runs: 10 min
Business from Other Countries: 5%

Toppan Europe GmbH-London Branch
Subsidiary of Toppan Group
15 Basinghall St, 5th floor, London EC2V 5BR
Tel: (020) 7213 0500
E-mail: info@toppan.co.uk
Web Site: www.toppan.co.uk
Key Personnel
Mng Dir: Hideo Yoshikawa
Founded: 1900

The Word Factory Ltd
2 Chartwell Ave, Ruddington, Nottingham NG11
 6DJ
Tel: (0115) 914 5654
Web Site: www.thewordfactory.co.uk
Key Personnel
Owner: Rory Baxter *Tel:* (07970) 415153 (cell)
 E-mail: roryb@thewordfactory.co.uk
Founded: 1992

United States

A-R Editions Inc
1600 Aspen Commons, Suite 100, Middleton, WI
 53562

Tel: 608-836-9000 *Fax:* 608-831-8200
E-mail: info@areditions.com
Web Site: www.areditions.com
Key Personnel
Pres & CEO: Patrick Wall *Tel:* 608-203-2575
   E-mail: patrick.wall@areditions.com
Dir, Spec Projs: James Zychowicz *Tel:* 608-203-
   2580 *E-mail:* james.zychowicz@areditions.com
Founded: 1962
Business from Other Countries: 10%
Membership(s): American Musicological Soci-
   ety; Audio Engineering Society; Music Library
   Association; Music Publishers Association

ADR Inc
2012 E Northern St, Wichita, KS 67216
Tel: 316-522-5599 *Toll Free Tel:* 800-767-6066
   Fax: 316-522-5445
E-mail: info@adr.biz
Web Site: www.adr.biz
Key Personnel
CEO: Patrick Tuttle *E-mail:* ptuttle@adr.biz
Pres: Jim Rishel
Founded: 1978
Print Runs: 1 min - 25,000 max
Business from Other Countries: 10%
Membership(s): Print Services & Distribution As-
   sociation; Printing Industries of America

Arbor Books
244 Madison Ave, Box 254, New York, NY
   10016-2834
Tel: 212-956-0950 *Toll Free Tel:* 877-822-2500
   Fax: 914-737-3639
E-mail: info@arborbooks.com; editorial@
   arborbooks.net
Web Site: www.arborbooks.com
Key Personnel
Owner: Joel Hochman *Tel:* 877-822-
   2502 *E-mail:* arborbooksjoel@aol.com;
   Larry Leichman *Tel:* 877-822-2504
   E-mail: arborbookslarry@aol.com
Mktg Dir: Olga Vladi
Founded: 1992
Turnaround: 21 Workdays; 1-7 Workdays for art
Print Runs: 1 min - 1,000,000 max
Business from Other Countries: 15%

Asia Pacific Offset Inc
1312 "Q" St NW, Suite B, Washington, DC
   20009
Tel: 202-462-5436 *Toll Free Tel:* 800-756-4344
   Fax: 202-986-4030
Web Site: www.asiapacificoffset.com
Key Personnel
Pres: Andrew Clarke *E-mail:* andrew@
   asiapacificoffset.com
Founded: 1997
Turnaround: 104 Workdays including color sepa-
   ration & shipping
Print Runs: 2,000 min
Business from Other Countries: 100%
Sales Office(s): 870 Market St, Suite 801, San
   Francisco, CA 94102, Dir, Sales: Amy Arm-
   strong *Tel:* 415-433-3488 *Fax:* 415-433-3489
   E-mail: amy@asiapacificoffset.com
62 Rivington St, Suite 2-B, New York, NY
   10002, Dir, Sales: Simona Jansons *Tel:* 212-
   941-8300 *Fax:* 212-941-9810 *E-mail:* simona@
   asiapacificoffset.com

C & C Offset Printing Co USA Inc
Subsidiary of C & C Joint Printing Co (HK) Ltd
70 W 36 St, Unit 10C, New York, NY 10018
Web Site: www.ccoffset.com
Key Personnel
Dir & EVP, C & C Offset Printing Co (USA)
   Inc, Portland, OR & C & C Offset Printing
   Co (NYC) Inc, New York, NY: Simon Chan
   E-mail: schan@ccoffset.com

VP, C & C Offset Printing Co (Chicago) Inc,
   Chicago, IL: Ernest Li *E-mail:* ernest.li@
   ccoffset.com
Sales Mgr, C & C Offset Printing Co (NYC)
   Inc, New York, NY: Frances Harkness
   E-mail: fharkness@ccoffset.com; Timothy Mc-
   Nulty
CEO, C & C Joint Printing Co (HK) Ltd, Hong
   Kong: Jackson Leung
Mng Dir, Hong Kong Head Off: Ken Lee
Deputy Gen Mgr, Hong Kong Head Off: Kit
   Wong
Sr Sales Mgr (Spec Projs), Hong Kong Head Off:
   Francis Ho
Dir, C & C Offset Printing Co (France) Ltd:
   Michele Olson Niel *E-mail:* michele@
   candcoffset.fr
Pres, C & C Printing Japan Co Ltd, Tokyo,
   Japan: Yamamoto Masaaki
Dir, C & C Offset Printing Co (UK) Ltd: Tracy
   Broderick *E-mail:* tracy@candcoffset.co.uk
Sales Rep, Australian Off: Lena Frew
   E-mail: lena.frew@candcprinting.com
Founded: 1980
Turnaround: Varies
Print Runs: 2,000 min - 3,000,000 max
Business from Other Countries: 70%
Branch Office(s)
C & C Offset Printing (Chicago) Inc, 800 W
   Fifth Ave, Suite 100D, Naperville, IL 60563
   Tel: 630-737-0820; 630-390-5617 *Fax:* 630-
   737-1997
C & C Offset Printing Co Ltd (Australia Off),
   Lithocraft Graphics, 3-7 Permas Way, Trugan-
   ina, Victoria 3029, Australia *Tel:* (0613) 8366
   0200 *Fax:* (0613) 8366 0299
C & C Joint Printing Co (Beijing) Ltd, Beijing
   Economic & Technological Development Area
   (BDA), Donghuan North Rd, No 3, Beijing
   100176, China *Tel:* (010) 6787 6655 *Fax:* (010)
   6787 8255 *E-mail:* ccbj@candcprinting.cn
   (plant)
C & C Joint Printing Co (Guangdong) Ltd, Hua
   Xin Bldg E Block, Rm 1511, 2 Shuiyin Rd,
   Huanshi East, Guangzhou 510075, China
   Tel: (020) 3760 0979; (020) 3760 0980
   Fax: (020) 3760 0977 *E-mail:* guangzhou@
   candcprinting.com
C & C Joint Printing (Shanghai) Co Ltd, 3333
   Cao Ying Rd, Qingpu Industrial Zone, Shang-
   hai 201712, China *Tel:* (021) 5922 6000
   Fax: (021) 5922 6111 *E-mail:* shanghai@
   candcprinting.com *Web Site:* www.
   candcprinting.com (plant)
C & C Joint Printing Co (Guangdong)
   Ltd, Chunhu Industrial Estate, Pinghu,
   Long Gang, Shenzhen 518111, China
   Tel: (0755) 3360 9988 *Fax:* (0755) 3360 9998
   E-mail: guangdong@candcprinting.com *Web
   Site:* www.candcprinting.com (plant)
C & C Offset Printing Co (France) Ltd, 15, rue
   d'Aboukir, 75002 Paris, France *Tel:* 01 40 26
   21 07 *Fax:* 01 44 76 08 96
C & C Offset Printing Co Ltd, C & C Bldg,
   36 Ting Lai Rd, Tai Po, New Territories,
   Hong Kong *Tel:* 2666 4988 *Fax:* 2666
   4938 *E-mail:* info@candcprinting.com *Web
   Site:* www.candcprinting.com (corp headquar-
   ters)
C & C Printing Japan Co Ltd, Tozaido Bldg, 3F,
   2-6-12 Hitotsubashi, Chiyoda-ku, Tokyo 101-
   0003, Japan *Tel:* (03) 5216 4580 *Fax:* (03)
   5216 4610 *E-mail:* mail@candcprinting.co.jp
   Web Site: www.candcprinting.co.jp
C & C Offset Printing Co (UK) Ltd, 7-9 Charlotte St, 2nd fl, London W1T 1RG, United
   Kingdom *Tel:* (020) 7637 5033 *Fax:* (020)
   7637 5044

Codra Enterprises Inc
17821 Mitchell N, Irvine, CA 92614
Tel: 949-756-8400 *Toll Free Tel:* 888-992-6372
   Fax: 949-756-8484

E-mail: codra@codra.com; sales@codra.com
Web Site: www.codra.com
Key Personnel
Pres: Gary Kim
Sales: Chris Scotti *Tel:* 949-322-5639
   E-mail: chris@codra.com
Founded: 1985
Turnaround: 4-6 Weeks
Print Runs: 5,000 min
Business from Other Countries: 10%
Membership(s): Independent Publishers Associ-
   ation; Pacific Northwest Booksellers Associa-
   tion; Publishers Association of the West

Consolidated Printers Inc
2630 Eighth St, Berkeley, CA 94710
Tel: 510-843-8524 (sales); 510-843-8565 (admin)
   Fax: 510-486-0580
E-mail: cpi@consoprinters.com; sales@
   consoprinters.com
Web Site: www.consoprinters.com
Key Personnel
CEO: Lawrence A Hawkins
Founded: 1952
Turnaround: 2-20 Workdays
Print Runs: 2,000 min - 500,000 max
Business from Other Countries: 15%

DNP America LLC
Subsidiary of Dai Nippon Printing Co Ltd
335 Madison Ave, 3rd fl, New York, NY 10017
Tel: 212-503-1060 *Fax:* 212-286-1501
Web Site: www.dnpamerica.com
Key Personnel
Gen Mgr: Seiichi Suzuki
Founded: 1974
Print Runs: 1,000 min
Business from Other Countries: 54%
Branch Office(s)
3235 Kifer Rd, Suite 100, Santa Clara, CA 95051
   Tel: 408-735-8880
3858 Carson St, Suite 300, Torrance, CA 90503
   Tel: 310-540-5123 *Fax:* 310-543-3260

Ecological Fibers Inc
40 Pioneer Dr, Lunenburg, MA 01462
Tel: 978-537-0003 *Fax:* 978-537-2238
E-mail: info@ecofibers.com
Web Site: www.ecofibers.com
Key Personnel
Pres: John A Quill
VP, Sales: Dave Robbins *E-mail:* drobbins@
   ecofibers.com
Dir, Busn Opers: Joyce Hardell *E-mail:* joyce@
   ecofibers.com
Book Group Mgr: Jim McCafferty
   E-mail: jmccafferty@ecofibers.com
Founded: 1972
Business from Other Countries: 35%
Branch Office(s)
730 York Ave, Pawtucket, RI 02861 *Tel:* 401-725-
   9700 *Fax:* 401-724-4970
Membership(s): BMI; Book Industry Guild of
   New York; Bookbuilders of Boston; Publishing
   Professionals Network

Imago
110 W 40 St, New York, NY 10018
Tel: 212-921-4411 *Fax:* 212-921-8226
E-mail: sales@imagousa.com
Web Site: www.imagousa.com
Key Personnel
Pres/CEO: Howard Musk *E-mail:* hmusk@
   imagousa.com
Founded: 1985
Turnaround: 5-10 Workdays for color separations;
   4-6 Weeks for printing & binding
Print Runs: 3,000 min
Business from Other Countries: 100%
Branch Office(s)
Imago West Coast, 23412 Moulton Pkwy, La-

guna Hills, CA 92653, Contact: Tammy Simms
Tel: 949-367-1635 *Fax:* 949-367-1639

Imago Services (HK) Ltd, Unit 16, 2F, Metro
Center Phase 1, 32 Lam Heng St, Kowloon
Bay, Hong Kong, Contact: Kendrick Cheung
Tel: 2811 3316 *Fax:* 2597 5256

Imago Shenzhen, Rm 2511-2512, Block A,
United Plaza No 5022, Bin He Rd, Fu Tian
Centre District, Shenzhen 518033, China, Contact: Kendrick Cheung *Tel:* (0755) 8304 8899
Fax: (0755) 8251 4073

Imago (UK/Europe) Publishing Ltd, Albury Ct,
Albury Thame, Oxon OX9 2LP, United Kingdom, Contact: Simon Rosenheim *Tel:* (01844)
337000 *Fax:* (01844) 339935 *E-mail:* sales@
imago.co.uk *Web Site:* www.imago.co.uk

King Printing
181 Industrial Ave E, Lowell, MA 01852-5147
Tel: 978-458-2345 *Fax:* 978-458-1441
E-mail: inquiries@kingprinting.com
Web Site: www.kingprinting.com; www.adibooks.
com
Founded: 1978
Print Runs: 1 min - 10,000 max
Business from Other Countries: 10%
Membership(s): The Association of Publishers for
Special Sales; Epicomm; Printing Industries of
New England

Leo Paper USA
Division of Leo Paper Group
1180 NW Maple St, Suite 102, Issaquah, WA
98027
Tel: 425-646-8801 *Fax:* 425-646-8805
E-mail: info@leousa.com
Web Site: www.leopaper.com
Key Personnel
SVP, Sales: John DiMasi *E-mail:* john@leousa.
com
Founded: 1982
Turnaround: 30-40 Workdays
Print Runs: 3,500 min - 2,000,000 max
Business from Other Countries: 20%
Branch Office(s)
27 W 24 St, Suite 601, New York, NY 10010
Tel: 917-305-0708 *Fax:* 917-305-0709
E-mail: info@leousanewyork.com

Marrakech Express Inc
720 Wesley Ave, No 10, Tarpon Springs, FL
34689
Tel: 727-942-2218 *Toll Free Tel:* 800-940-6566
Fax: 727-937-4758
E-mail: print@marrak.com
Web Site: www.marrak.com
Key Personnel
CEO: Peter Henzell
Prodn Mgr: Steen Sigmund
Sales/Estimator: Shirley Copperman
Founded: 1976

Turnaround: 7-10 Workdays
Print Runs: 500 min - 1,000,000 max
Business from Other Countries: 15%

Oddi Printing Corp
118 Heacock Lane, Wyncote, PA 19095
Tel: 215-885-5210
Web Site: www.oddi.com
Key Personnel
Dir: Charles B Gershwin *E-mail:* cbgershwin@
comcast.net
Founded: 1943 (parent co opened in Iceland)
Turnaround: 15-20 Workdays
Business from Other Countries: 20%

OGM USA
4141 44 St, Suite 3F, Sunnyside, NY 11104
Tel: 212-964-2430 *Fax:* 212-964-2497
Web Site: www.ogm.it
Key Personnel
Chmn, CEO & Sales Rep: Rino Varrasso
E-mail: rvarrasso@ogm-usa.com
Founded: 1998
Turnaround: 30 Workdays
Print Runs: 1,000 min - 3,000,000 max
Business from Other Countries: 75%

Overseas Printing Corporation
Division of InnerWorkings Inc
655 Montgomery St, Suite 1710, San Francisco,
CA 94111
Tel: 415-835-9999 *Fax:* 415-835-9899
Web Site: www.overseasprinting.com
Key Personnel
Contact: Hal Belmont *E-mail:* hbelmont@inwk.
com
Founded: 1972
Turnaround: 8-12 Weeks, or shorter depending on
job requirements
Business from Other Countries: 10%

Palace Printing & Design (PPD)
PO Box 12023, San Rafael, CA 94912
Tel: 415-526-1378
Key Personnel
Sales Dir: Sreedharan Vijayarangam *Tel:* 415-
307-6065 (cell) *E-mail:* sreed@palacepress.com
Founded: 1984
Turnaround: 90 Workdays
Print Runs: 3,000 min - 1,000,000 max
Business from Other Countries: 20%

Printing Corp of the Americas Inc
620 SW 12 Ave, Fort Lauderdale, FL 33069
Tel: 954-781-8100 *Toll Free Tel:* 866-721-1PCA
(721-1722) *Fax:* 954-781-8421
Web Site: www.commercialprintingflorida.com
Key Personnel
Pres: Jan Tuchman
Founded: 1979

Turnaround: 5-10 Workdays
Print Runs: 500 min - 100,000 max
Business from Other Countries: 10%

Publishers' Graphics LLC
140 Della Ct, Carol Stream, IL 60188
Tel: 630-221-1850 *Toll Free Tel:* 888-404-3769
Fax: 630-221-1870
E-mail: contactpg@pubgraphics.com
Web Site: pubgraphics.com; www.
pubgraphicsdirect.com
Key Personnel
Pres: Nick A Lewis *E-mail:* nlewis@pubgraphics.
com
VP: Kathleen Lewis
Founded: 1996
Turnaround: 5-10 Workdays
Print Runs: 1 min - 20,000 max
Business from Other Countries: 60%
Branch Office(s)
3777 Rider Trail S, St Louis, MO 63045
Tel: 314-739-3777 *Fax:* 314-739-1436
Sales Office(s): New York, NY, Contact: Anthony
Ferrigno *Tel:* 908-672-5685

Taylor Specialty Books
Division of Balfour/Taylor
1550 W Mockingbird Lane, Dallas, TX 75235
Tel: 214-819-8588 (cust serv) *Fax:* 214-819-5051
(cust serv) *Toll Free Fax:* 800-203-9778
E-mail: rfq@taylorpub.com (estimates)
Web Site: www.taylorspecialtybooks.com
Key Personnel
VP, Sales & Mktg, Specialty Books: Rick Parra
Tel: 214-819-5027 *E-mail:* rick.parra@balfour.
com
Sales Rep: Kim Hawley *E-mail:* khawley@
taylorpub.com; George Levesque
E-mail: glevesque@taylorpub.com; Mark Mc-
Combs *E-mail:* mmcombs@taylorpub.com
Founded: 1939
Turnaround: 25-30 Workdays
Print Runs: 250 min - 25,000 max
Business from Other Countries: 10%

Vicks Inc
5166 Commercial Dr, Yorkville, NY 13495
Mailing Address: PO Box 270, Yorkville, NY
13495-0270
Tel: 315-736-9344 *Fax:* 315-736-1901
Web Site: www.vicks.biz
Key Personnel
Chmn: Dwight E "Duke" Vicks, Jr
Regl Sales Mgr: Michael J Notar *Tel:* 315-723-
1176 *E-mail:* mnotar@vicks.biz
Founded: 1918
Turnaround: 10 Workdays
Print Runs: 1 min - 100,000 max
Business from Other Countries: 10%
Membership(s): BMI; Printing Industries of
America

COMPUTERIZED TYPESETTING

DATA PROCESSING SERVICES

FOREIGN LANGUAGE COMPOSITION

INDEXING

MATHEMATICS & CHEMISTRY COMPOSITION

MUSIC COMPOSITION

NON-ROMAN ALPHABETS

PRODUCTION SERVICES

SCIENTIFIC COMPOSITION

UPC & BAR CODE SERVICES

WORD PROCESSING INTERFACE

Prepress Services

This section includes companies throughout the world that offer a variety of prepress services. Those U.S. and Canadian companies with 10% or more of their business done outside North America are also included. Immediately preceding this section is an index classifying companies by services offered.

Argentina

Editorial Dunken
Ayacucho 357, C1025AAG Buenos Aires
Tel: (011) 4954 7700; (011) 4954 7300
E-mail: info@dunken.com.ar
Web Site: www.dunken.com.ar
Key Personnel
Dir: Guillermo A de Urquiza
Founded: 1988

Proietto & Lamarque SA
Jose Marmol 2131, C1255ABW Buenos Aires
Tel: (011) 4925-0111; (011) 4921-1689; (011) 4924-1812
E-mail: info@lamarquenet.com; ventas@lamarquenet.com; administracion@lamarquenet.com
Web Site: proiettoylamarque.com.ar
Founded: 1951

Armenia

Antares Ltd
50a/1 Mashtots Ave, 0009 Yerevan
Tel: (010) 58 76 69; (010) 58 10 59; (010) 58 09 59; (010) 56 15 26 *Fax:* (010) 58 76 69
E-mail: antares@antares.am
Web Site: antares.am
Founded: 1992
Parent Company: Antares Media Holding

Tigran Mets Publishing House
2 Arshakunyats Ave, 0023 Yerevan
Tel: (060) 62 32 06 *Fax:* (010) 52 22 48
E-mail: info@tigran-mets.am
Web Site: tigran-mets.am
Key Personnel
General Dir: Vrezh Markosyan

Australia

Ligare Pty Ltd
138-152 Bonds Rd, Riverwood, NSW 2210
Tel: (02) 9533 2555 *Fax:* (02) 9534 6320; (02) 9533 3719 (sales)
E-mail: info@ligare.com.au
Web Site: www.ligare.com.au
Founded: 1979

MAPG, see Modern Art Production Group (MAPG)

Modern Art Production Group (MAPG)
27 Izett St, Studio 8, Prahran, Victoria 3181
Mailing Address: PO Box 2067, Prahran, Victoria 3181
Tel: (03) 9525 2005 *Fax:* (03) 9525 2151
E-mail: enquiry@mapg.com.au
Web Site: www.mapg.com.au

Austria

partner4media Management & Marketing Systembertung Gesellschaft mbH
Jakobgasse 3, 3400 Klosterneuburg
Tel: (02243) 22010 0 *Fax:* (02243) 22010 40
E-mail: office@partner4media.com
Web Site: www.partner4media.com
Key Personnel
Mng Dir: Peter R Herzog; Dr Wolfgang Vitovec
Founded: 1990

Belgium

Crius Group
Industriepark 20, 2235 Hulshout
Tel: (015) 750 750 *Fax:* (015) 750 751
E-mail: info@crius-group.com
Web Site: www.crius-group.com
Founded: 1989

Cultura bvba
Hoenderstr 22, 9230 Wetteren
Tel: (09) 369 15 95 *Fax:* (09) 369 59 25
E-mail: info@cultura.be; cultura@cultura-net.com
Web Site: www.cultura.be
Key Personnel
Dir: Jan De Meester
Founded: 1893

INNI Print NV
Industrielaan 5, 8501 Heule
Tel: (056) 36 32 11
E-mail: info@inniprint.com
Web Site: print.innigroup.com
Key Personnel
Mng Dir: Tom Deschildre *Tel:* (056) 36 32 25
  E-mail: tom.deschildre@innigroup.com
Finance Dir: Nico Declerck *Tel:* (056) 36 32 37
  E-mail: nico.declerck@innigroup.com
Operations Dir: David Strobbe *Tel:* (056) 36 19 99 *E-mail:* david.strobbe@innigroup.com
General Manager: David Tielemans *Tel:* (056) 36 32 03 *E-mail:* david.tielemans@innigroup.com
Founded: 1948
Parent Company: INNI Group NV

Drukkerij Lannoo NV (Lannoo Printers NV)
Plantinstr 6, 8700 Tielt
Tel: (051) 42 42 11; (051) 42 43 08 *Fax:* (051) 40 70 70
E-mail: info@lannooprint.be; lannoo@lannooprint.be
Web Site: www.lannoo-print.be
Founded: 1909
Turnaround: 10 Workdays
Business from Other Countries: 30%

Proost NV
Everdongenlaan 23, 2300 Turnhout
Tel: (014) 40 08 11 *Fax:* (014) 42 87 94
E-mail: proost@proost.be
Web Site: www.proost.be
Founded: 1913

Brunei

Brunei Press Sdn Bhd
Lot 8 & 11, Perindustrian Beribi II, Gadong BE 1118
Tel: 2451468; 2451460 *Fax:* 2451460
E-mail: brupress@bruneipress.com.bn; marketing@bruneipress.com.bn
Branch Office(s)
Unit 8B, Supasave Panaga, Lorong 14 Barat, Seria KB 4533 *Tel:* 3334344; 3334345 *Fax:* 3334346
Sales Office(s): Brunei Press Sales (M) Sdn Bhd, No 8-1-6, 1st floor, Menara Mutiara Bangsar, Jl Liku Off Jl Bangsar, 59100 Kuala Lumpur, Malaysia *Tel:* (03) 22876623 *Fax:* (03) 22870093 *E-mail:* brupress@tm.net.my
Brunei Press Sales (S) Pte Ltd, Pico Creative Centre, 20 Kallang Ave, No 03-00, Singapore 339411, Singapore *Tel:* 6297 9622 *Fax:* 6297 9633 *E-mail:* brupress@singnet.com.sg

Bulgaria

Abagar JSC
98 Nikola Gabrovski Str, 5000 Veliko Tarnovo
Tel: (062) 643936; (062) 647814 *Fax:* (062) 646993
E-mail: abagar@dir.bg
Web Site: www.abagar.net
Key Personnel
Executive Dir: Marian Kenarov
Founded: 1991

Janet-45 Print & Publishing
Blvd Al Stambolijski 9, 4004 Plovdiv
Tel: (032) 609090 *Fax:* (032) 677723
E-mail: mail@janet45.com; books@janet45.com
Web Site: printing.janet45.com; books.janet45.com
Key Personnel
Chief Executive Officer: Bozhana Apostolova
Mng Partner: Manol Peykov
Founded: 1992

Canada

Barcode Graphics Inc
25 Brodie Dr, Unit 5, Richmond Hill, ON L4B 3K7
Tel: 905-770-1154 *Toll Free Tel:* 800-263-3669 (orders) *Fax:* 905-787-1575
E-mail: info@barcodegraphics.com
Web Site: www.barcodegraphics.com
Key Personnel
Pres: John Herzig *E-mail:* jherzig@barcodegraphics.com
Founded: 1982
Business from Other Countries: 10%

CANADA

David Berman Communications
340 Selby Ave, Ottawa, ON K2A 3X6
Tel: 613-728-6777 *Toll Free Tel:* 800-665-1809
Fax: 613-728-4777
E-mail: info@davidberman.com
Web Site: www.davidberman.com
Key Personnel
Pres: David Berman
Founded: 1984
Business from Other Countries: 50%
Branch Office(s)
182 Pearson Ave, Toronto, ON *Fax:* 416-532-
 7786
969 Second St SE, Charlottesville, VA 22902,
 United States
6 Jl 14/7, Petaling Jaya Selangor, 46100 Kuala
 Lumpur, Malaysia

Leanne Franson
4 Poplar Ave, Martensville, SK S0K 2T0
Mailing Address: PO Box 1327, Martensville, SK
 S0K 2T0
Tel: 306-382-1696
E-mail: leanne@leannefranson.com
Web Site: www.leannefranson.com
Founded: 1991
Turnaround: 3-7+ Workdays
Business from Other Countries: 50%
Membership(s): Communication-Jeunesse; Illus-
 tration Quebec; Picture Book Artists Associa-
 tion

Celia Godkin
Mod 6, Comp 12, 10 James St, Frankville, ON
 K0E 1H0
Tel: 613-275-7204 *Fax:* 613-275-7204
E-mail: celia@godkin.ca
Web Site: www.celiagodkin.com; www.
 celiagodkin.ca
Founded: 1983
Business from Other Countries: 10%
Membership(s): The Botanical Artists of Canada;
 Canadian Society of Children's Authors Illus-
 trators & Performers; Southern Ontario Nature
 and Science Illustrators; The Writers' Union of
 Canada

Maracle Press Ltd
1156 King St E, Oshawa, ON L1H 1H8
Tel: 905-723-3438 *Toll Free Tel:* 800-558-8604
Fax: 905-723-1759
E-mail: info@maraclepress.com
Web Site: www.maraclepress.com
Key Personnel
Pres & Gen Mgr: George Sittlinger *Tel:* 905-723-
 3438 ext 236
Acct Mgr: Ronald G Taylor *E-mail:* rtaylor@
 maraclepress.com
Founded: 1920
Turnaround: 10 Workdays
Business from Other Countries: 25%
Membership(s): BMI

PrintWest
1111 Eighth Ave, Regina, SK S4R 1C9
Tel: 306-525-2304 *Toll Free Tel:* 800-236-6438
Fax: 306-757-2439
E-mail: general@printwest.com
Web Site: www.printwest.com
Key Personnel
CEO: Corie Triffo
VP, Sales: Ken Benson
Founded: 1992
Turnaround: 15 Workdays
Business from Other Countries: 15%

Barbara Spurll Illustration
160 Browning Ave, Toronto, ON M4K 1W5
Tel: 416-594-6594
Web Site: www.barbaraspurll.com

Key Personnel
Prop: Barbara Spurll *E-mail:* barbara@
 barbaraspurll.com
Founded: 1975
Business from Other Countries: 50%
Membership(s): Canadian Association of Profes-
 sional Image Creators; Canadian Society of
 Children's Authors Illustrators & Performers;
 Picture Book Artists Association

China

Artron Art (Group) Co Ltd
Artron Art Center Shenzhen, No 19 Shenyun Rd,
 Nanshan District, Shenzhen 518053
Tel: (0755) 8336 6138 *Fax:* (0755) 8321 9630
E-mail: info@artron.net
Web Site: artron.com.cn
Founded: 1993
Branch Office(s)
Unit 603, 6/F, Delta House, 3 On Yiu St, Shatin,
 Hong Kong *Tel:* 2312 2193 *Fax:* 2312 2820

Beijing Allied Fortune International Trade Ltd
Room 1501, Bldg No 5, Ronghua International,
 No 10, Rong Hua South Rd, BDA, Beijing
 100176
Tel: (010) 67817768 *Fax:* (010) 67817758
E-mail: daniel@af-print.com
Web Site: www.af-print.com

Guangzhou Zhongtian Colour Printing Co Ltd
No 38A, Xinguang Rd, Panyu District,
 Guangzhou 511436
Tel: (020) 6685 3808 *Fax:* (020) 3472 9257
Web Site: www.zt-online.cn
Key Personnel
Contact: Hylix Wu *E-mail:* hylix.wu@
 zhongtiancp.com
Founded: 1993
Branch Office(s)
Unit 601-605 6/F, Prosperity Pl, No 6, Shing
 Yip St, Kwun Tong, Kowloon, Hong Kong
 Tel: 3150 6435; 3150 6452 *Fax:* 3914 7664
PO Box 11398, Papamoa Beach 3151, New
 Zealand, Contact: David Reid *Tel:* (07) 985
 6137 *Fax:* (07) 985 6138 *E-mail:* dave@
 realmedia.net.nz

Hengyuan Printing Co Ltd
Gaopu Rd, Tianhe Software Park, Guangshan
 er Lu, Gaotangshi, Yangmeiling 3, Tianhe,
 Guangzhou 510520
Tel: (020) 66834591; (020) 66834568 *Fax:* (020)
 66834595
E-mail: sales@hyprint.cn
Web Site: www.hyprint.cn
Founded: 1993

Reliance Printing (Shenzhen) Co Ltd
25 Longshan Industrial Zone, Longgang District,
 Shenzhen 518019
Tel: (0755) 25802197 *Fax:* (0755) 25802199
E-mail: jessie@relianceprinting.com
Web Site: www.relianceprinting.com
Founded: 1994
Parent Company: Reliance (Hong Kong) Corp

**Shenzhen Huaxin Colour-Printing &
 Platemaking Co Ltd**
Bldg 5, Lijincheng Tech & Industrial Park, Indus-
 trial Rd E, Longhua, Shenzhen 518129
Tel: (0755) 8242 8168 *Fax:* (0755) 8170 4065
E-mail: info@huaxinprinting.com
Web Site: www.huaxinprinting.com
Founded: 1988

Costa Rica

Litografia e Imprenta LIL SA
Apdo 75, 1100 San Jose
Tel: 2235-0011 *Fax:* 2240-7814
E-mail: info@lilcr.com; ventas.editoriales@lilcr.
 com (editorial sales)
Web Site: www.lilprinting.com
Founded: 1896

Czech Republic

Tiskarny Havlickuv Brod AS
Husova ul 1881, 580 01 Havlickuv Brod
Tel: 569 664 110 *Fax:* 569 664 111
E-mail: thb@thb.cz
Web Site: www.thb.cz
Key Personnel
Dir: Ludmila Dockalova *Tel:* 569 664 140
 E-mail: dockalova@thb.cz
Head, Sales: Premysl Moravec *Tel:* 569 664 145
 E-mail: moravec@thb.cz
Commercial Pruduction Assistant: Miloslav Henzl
 Tel: 569 664 129 *E-mail:* henzl@thb.cz
Founded: 1992
Branch Office(s)
Pujmanove 1221/4, 140 00 Prague 4

Librix.eu
Subsidiary of Tribun EU sro
Cejl 892/32, 602 00 Brno
Tel: 543 210 089 *Fax:* 530 332 374; 543 210 089
E-mail: librix@librix.eu; sales@librix.eu
Web Site: www.librix.eu
Key Personnel
Chief Manager for Western Europe: Jaroslav
 Janosek, PhD *E-mail:* janosek@librix.eu
Mng Dir: Jan Homola *E-mail:* jan.homola@librix.
 eu
Founded: 1970

Tesinska tiskarna AS
Stefanikova ul 1828/2, 737 36 Cesky Tesin
Tel: 558 761 311 *Fax:* 558 711 536
E-mail: info@tesinskatiskarna.cz
Web Site: www.tesinskatiskarna.cz
Founded: 1806

Typos, tiskarske zavody sro
Podnikatelska 1160/14, 320 56 Plzen
Tel: 377 193 353 *Fax:* 377 193 354
E-mail: klik@typos.cz
Web Site: www.typos.cz
Key Personnel
Mng Dir: Jiri Fricek *Tel:* 377 193 315 *Fax:* 377
 193 217 *E-mail:* fricek@typos.cz
Founded: 1998
Branch Office(s)
Prodejna Uslavska 2, 326 00 Plzen *Tel:* 377 249
 294 *E-mail:* prodejna@typos.cz
Nadrazni 473/3, 339 01 Klatovy *Tel:* 376 375 711
 Fax: 376 375 713 *E-mail:* klatovy@typos.cz
Sazecska 560/8, 108 25 Prague 10 *Tel:* 266 021
 364; 266 021 156 *E-mail:* obchod.vivas@typos.
 cz

Egypt

Sahara Printing Co
Nasr City, Free Zone, Cairo
Tel: (02) 2274 4056 *Fax:* (02) 2274 1907

E-mail: info@saharaprinting.com; sales@
saharaprinting.com
Web Site: www.saharaprinting.com
Key Personnel
Chairman & Chief Executive Officer: Nadim
Elias
Sales & Marketing Manager: Dahlia Sobhy
Founded: 1995
Business from Other Countries: 60%

Germany

abavo GmbH
Nebelhornstr 8, 86807 Buchloe
Tel: (08241) 9686-0 Fax: (08241) 9686-26
E-mail: info@abavo.de
Web Site: www.abavo.de
Key Personnel
Mng Dir: Stefan Bachfischer; Stefan Schmitz
Founded: 2006
Branch Office(s)
Geisenbrunner Str 69, 81475 Munich

APPL Firmengruppe
Senefelderstr 3-11, 86650 Wemding
Mailing Address: Postfach 11 63, 86648 Wemd-
ing
Tel: (09092) 999-0; (09092) 999-111
Fax: (09092) 999-209
E-mail: info@appl.de
Web Site: www.appl.de
Key Personnel
Mng Dir: Markus Appl E-mail: m.appl@appl.de;
Monika Stimpfle E-mail: m.stimpfle@appl.de;
Thomas Zinn E-mail: t.zinn@appl.de

AZ Druck und Datentechnik GmbH
Heisinger Str 16, 87437 Kempten
Tel: (0831) 206-311 Fax: (0831) 206-246
E-mail: kempten@az-druck.de
Web Site: www.az-druck.de
Key Personnel
Mng Dir: Guenther Hartmann
Founded: 1945
Branch Office(s)
Landfliegerstr 11, 12487 Berlin Tel: (030)
639959-0 E-mail: berlin@az-druck.de

The Bear Press - Dr Wolfram Benda
Schleiermacherstr 7, 95447 Bayreuth
Tel: (0921) 81418 Fax: (0921) 1503478
E-mail: info@thebearpress.de
Web Site: www.thebearpress.de
Key Personnel
Owner: Dr Wolfram Benda
Founded: 1979

Druckerei C H Beck
Bergerstr 3-5, 86720 Noerdlingen
Tel: (09081) 85-0 Fax: (09081) 85-206
E-mail: info@becksche.de
Web Site: www.becksche.de
Key Personnel
Mng Dir: Christian Matthiesen Tel: (09081) 85-
101 E-mail: matthiesen.christian@becksche.de
Commercial Dir: Ernest Zoller Tel: (09081) 85-
111 E-mail: zoller.ernest@becksche.de
Head, Inside Sales: Roland Schroeppel
Tel: (09081) 85-195 E-mail: schroeppel.
roland@becksche.de
Head, Sales: Andre Sommer Tel: (09081) 85-123
E-mail: sommer.andre@becksche.de
Founded: 1763
Parent Company: Verlag C H Beck oHG
Branch Office(s)
Augsburgerstr 67, 86720 Noerdlingen

Beltz Grafische Betriebe
Neustaedter Str 1-4, 99947 Bad Langensalza
Mailing Address: Postfach 1151, 99947 Bad Lan-
gensalza
Tel: (03603) 399-0 Fax: (03603) 399-109
E-mail: info-bbl@beltz.de
Web Site: www.beltz-grafische-betriebe.de
Key Personnel
General Manager: Christian Gaidies Tel: (03603)
399-100 E-mail: c.gaidies@beltz.de
Manager, Business Development, Beltz Me-
dia: Chris Felgner Tel: (03603) 399-372
E-mail: c.felgner@beltz.de
Prepress Manager: Bernhard Beier Tel: (03603)
399-200 E-mail: b.beier@beltz.de
Production Manager: Karsten Stolze Tel: (03603)
399-400 E-mail: k.stolze@beltz.de
Marketing: Juliane Schilde Tel: (03603) 399-559
E-mail: j.schilde@beltz.de
Founded: 1841
Branch Office(s)
Am Fliegerhorst 8, 99947 Bad Langensalza (pro-
duction)

Bertelsmann Printing Group
Division of Bertelsmann SE & Co KGaA
Carl-Bertelsmann-Str 161M, 33311 Guetersloh
Tel: (05241) 80-0
E-mail: contact@bertelsmann-printing-group.com
Web Site: www.bertelsmann-printing-group.com
Key Personnel
Co-Chief Executive Officer: Axel Hentrei; Dr
Bertram Stausberg
Chief Financial Officer: Ulrich Cordes
Corporate Communications: Matthias Wulff
E-mail: matthias.wulff@bertelsmann.de
Founded: 2016

Clausen & Bosse
Birkstr 10, 25917 Leck
Tel: (04662) 83-0
E-mail: info@cpibooks.de
Web Site: cpibooks.com/de
Parent Company: CPI Group

CMS-Cross Media Solutions GmbH
Alfred-Nobel-Str 33, 97080 Wuerzburg
Tel: (09) 31 3 85-252 Fax: (09) 31 3 85-275
E-mail: info@crossmediasolutions.de
Web Site: www.crossmediasolutions.de
Key Personnel
Mng Dir: Konstantin Amrehn E-mail: konstantin.
amrehn@crossmediasolutions.de;
Rudolf Krieger E-mail: rudolf.krieger@
crossmediasolutions.de; Sylvia Soosaar
E-mail: sylvia.soosaar@crossmediasolutions.de

Cross Media Solutions, see CMS-Cross Media
Solutions GmbH

Einhand Press
Burghofgasse 4, 76829 Landau in der Pfalz
Tel: (06341) 89349
Web Site: www.einhandpress.de
Key Personnel
Owner: Reinhold Nasshan E-mail: r.nasshan@
web.de
Founded: 1987

Euro-Druckservice GmbH
Medienstr 5b, 94036 Passau
Tel: (0851) 851 600-0 Fax: (0851) 851 600-60
E-mail: office@edsgroup.de
Web Site: www.edsgroup.de
Key Personnel
Chief Executive Officer & Mng Dir: Christian
Senff
Chief Financial Officer & Mng Dir: Peter
Neubacher
Chief Operating Officer & Mng Dir: Kai-Uwe
Gross

GGP Media GmbH
Member of Bertelsmann Printing Group
Karl-Marx-Str 24, 07381 Poessneck
Tel: (03647) 430-0 Fax: (03647) 430-390
E-mail: ggp.poessneck@bertelsmann.de
Web Site: www.ggp-media.de
Key Personnel
Mng Dir: Axel Hentrei; Christof Ludwig
Sales Dir: Christine Bergmann Tel: (03647) 430-
225 Fax: (03647) 430-230 E-mail: christine.
bergmann@bertelsmann.de
Customer Service Manager & International
Sales: Cindy Girbert Tel: (03647) 430-415
Fax: (03647) 430-66415 E-mail: cindy.
girbert@bertelsmann.de
Founded: 1891
Ultimate Parent Company: Bertelsmann SE & Co
KGaA

Griebsch & Rochol Druck GmbH & Co KG
Gabelsbergerstr 1, 59069 Hamm
Mailing Address: Postfach 7145, 59029 Hamm
Tel: (02385) 931 0 Fax: (02385) 931 213
E-mail: info@grd.de
Web Site: www.grd.de
Key Personnel
Mng Partner: Rainer Grobe Tel: (02385) 931 200
E-mail: grob@grd.de; Marc von Kiedrowsky
Tel: (02385) 931 201 E-mail: mvk@grd.de
Chief Executive Officer: Mark Wiethoff
Tel: (02385) 931 271 E-mail: wiethoff@grd.de
Sales Dir: Michael Knubbe Tel: (02385) 931 207
E-mail: knubbe@grd.de

Druckhaus Gummersbach PP GmbH
Stauweiher 4, 51645 Gummersbach
Tel: (02261) 9572-0 Fax: (02261) 56338
E-mail: info@druckhaus-gummersbach.de
Web Site: www.druckhaus-gummersbach.de
Key Personnel
General Manager: Benita Kramer; Ulrich Kramer
Founded: 1845

Anja Harms Ateliers
Erlenbachweg 6, 61440 Oberursel
Tel: (06171) 268240
E-mail: mail@anja-harms.de
Web Site: www.anja-harms.de
Key Personnel
Owner: Anja Harms
Founded: 2005

**Holzer Druck und Medien Druckerei und
Zeitungsverlag GmbH & Co KG**
Fridolin-Holzer-Str 22 & 24, 88171 Weiler im
Allgaeu
Tel: (08387) 399-0 Fax: (08387) 399-33
E-mail: info@druckerei-holzer.de
Web Site: www.druckerei-holzer.de
Key Personnel
Manager: Klaus Huber Tel: (08387) 399-38
E-mail: k.huber@druckerei-holzer.de
Production Manager: Uwe Dittman Tel: (08387)
399-30 E-mail: u.dittman@druckerei-holzer.de
Sales Manager: Jochen Hole Tel: (08387) 399-59
E-mail: j.hole@druckerei-holzer.de
Technical Manager: Robert Schaefer Tel: (08387)
399-24 E-mail: robert.schaefer@druckerei-
holzer.de

Druckverlag Kettler GmbH
Robert-Bosch-Str 14, 59199 Boenen, Westfalen
Tel: (02383) 91013-0 Fax: (02383) 91013-40
E-mail: info@druckverlag-kettler.de
Web Site: www.druckverlag-kettler.com
Key Personnel
Mng Dir: Gunnar Kettler Tel: (02383) 91013-13
E-mail: g.kettler@druckverlag-kettler.de

le-tex publishing services GmbH
Weissenfelser Str 84, 04229 Leipzig
Tel: (0341) 355356 0 *Fax:* (0341) 355356 950
E-mail: info@le-tex.de
Web Site: www.le-tex.de
Key Personnel
Head, Administration: Dr Reinhard Voeckler
 Tel: (0341) 355356 123 *Fax:* (0341) 355356
 523 *E-mail:* reinhard.voeckler@le-tex.de
Mng Dir: Gerrit Imsieke *Tel:* (0341) 355356
 110 *Fax:* (0341) 355356 510 *E-mail:* gerrit.
 imsieke@le-tex.de
Production Manager: Svea Jelonek *Tel:* (0341)
 355356 122 *Fax:* (0341) 355356 522
 E-mail: svea.jelonek@le-tex.de
Founded: 1999

C Maurer Druck und Verlag GmbH & Co KG
Schubartstr 21, 73312 Geislingen/Steige
Tel: (07331) 930-0 *Fax:* (07331) 930-190
E-mail: info@maurer-online.de
Web Site: www.maurer-online.de
Key Personnel
Mng Dir: Carl Otto Maurer
Founded: 1856

Media-Print Informationstechnologie GmbH
Unit of Media-Print Group GmbH
Eggertstr 30, 33100 Paderborn
Tel: (05251) 5408-0 *Fax:* (05251) 5408-144
E-mail: group@mediaprint.de
Web Site: www.mediaprint.de
Key Personnel
Mng Dir: Dr Otto W Drosihn; Rainer Rings; Ulf
 Stornebel
Founded: 1993
Turnaround: 5-10 Workdays
Business from Other Countries: 25%

mediaTEXT Jena GmbH
Richard-Sorge-Str 6a/b, 07747 Jena
Tel: (03641) 30 800-0 *Fax:* (03641) 30 800-29
E-mail: info@mediatext.de
Web Site: www.mediatext.de
Key Personnel
Management: Stefan Gassmann; Steffen Kaiser
Founded: 1995

MK-MediaSolutions GmbH
Raiffeisenallee 10, 82041 Oberhaching
Tel: (089) 61387113 *Fax:* (089) 61387126
E-mail: info@mk-mediasolutions.com
Web Site: www.mk-mediasolutions.com
Key Personnel
Chief Executive Officer: Johannes Moskon

Mohn Media Mohndruck GmbH
Member of Bertelsmann Printing Group
Carl-Bertelsmann-Str 161M, 33311 Guetersloh
Tel: (05241) 80-40410 *Fax:* (05241) 80-65288
E-mail: mohnmedia@bertelsmann.de
Web Site: www.mohnmedia.de
Key Personnel
Mng Dir: Axel Hentrei; Wilfried Velte
Sales Dir: Alasdair Gibson
Head, Prepress: Friedel Kathoefer *Tel:* (05241)
 80-3650 *E-mail:* friedel.kathoefer@
 bertelsmann.de
Founded: 1824
Business from Other Countries: 25%
Ultimate Parent Company: Bertelsmann SE & Co
 KGaA

Monarda Publishing House Ltd
Grosse Brauhausstr 8, 06108 Halle
Tel: (0345) 470 13 78 *Fax:* (0345) 470 09 49
E-mail: info@monarda.eu
Web Site: www.monarda.eu

optimal media GmbH
Glienholzweg 7, 17207 Roebel/Mueritz

Tel: (039931) 56 500 *Fax:* (039931) 56 555
E-mail: info@optimal-media.com
Web Site: www.optimal-media.com
Key Personnel
Mng Dir: Joerg Hahn *Tel:* (039931) 56 516
 E-mail: joerg.hahn@optimal-media.com
Dir, Finance: Rainer Hake *E-mail:* rainer.hake@
 optimal-media.com
Dir, Operations: Dr Peter Runge *E-mail:* peter.
 runge@optimal-media.com
Dir, Sales & Marketing: Grit Schreiber
 Tel: (039931) 56 525 *E-mail:* grit.schreiber@
 optimal-media.com
Head, Accounting & Licensing: Anke Mauerhoff
 Tel: (039931) 56 641
Head, International Sales & Executive Manager:
 Rufus Kalex *E-mail:* rufus.kalex@optimal-
 media.com
Executive Assistant/Public Relations: Petra Funk
 Tel: (039931) 56 516 *E-mail:* petra.funk@
 optimal-media.com
Branch Office(s)
Str der Pariser Kommune 38, 10243 Berlin
 Tel: (030) 28883790 *Fax:* (030) 2888379 11
Neumuehlen 17, 22763 Hamburg *Tel:* (040)
 29812050 *Fax:* (040) 2981205 13
Idungatan 8, 113 45 Stockholm, Sweden, Con-
 tact: Carl-Marcus Gidloef *Tel:* (08) 704 581412
 E-mail: carl-marcus.gidloef@optimal-media.
 com
optimal media UK Ltd, Coppergate House, 16
 Brune St, London E1 7NJ, United Kingdom,
 Contact: Julia Voelkel *E-mail:* julia.voelkel@
 optimal-media.com

Pagina GmbH
Herrenberger Str 51, Tuebingen 72070
Tel: (07071) 9876-0 *Fax:* (07071) 9876-22
Web Site: www.pagina-online.de
Key Personnel
Mng Dir: Tobias Ott *Tel:* (07071) 9876-50
 E-mail: tobias.ott@pagina-tuebingen.de
Product Manager: Tobias Fischer *Tel:* (07071)
 9876-44 *E-mail:* tobias.fischer@pagina-
 tuebingen.de
Accounting: Sabine Ott *E-mail:* sabine.ott@
 pagina-tuebingen.de

Christine Paxmann Text Konzept Grafik
Linprunstr 42 (Rgb), 80335 Munich
Tel: (089) 288 05 89-20 *Fax:* (089) 288 05 89-23
E-mail: cp@christinepaxmann.de; paxmann@
 eselsohr-leseabenteuer.de
Web Site: www.christinepaxmann.de

Priese GmbH
Saatwinkler Damm 42A, 13627 Berlin
Tel: (030) 8263024 *Fax:* (030) 8266024

Printsystem GmbH
Schafwaesche 1-3, 71296 Heimsheim
Tel: (07033) 3825 *Fax:* (07033) 3827
E-mail: info@printsystem.de
Web Site: www.printsystem.de
Key Personnel
Mng Dir: Harmut Harfensteller
Manager: Gero Hausmann
Founded: 1979

LN Schaffrath GmbH & Co KG DruckMedien
Markweg 42-50, 47608 Geldern
Tel: (028) 31396-0 *Fax:* (028) 31396-110
E-mail: info@schaffrath.de
Web Site: www.schaffrath.de; www.schaffrath-
 print.de
Key Personnel
General Manager: Dirk Alten *Tel:* (028) 31396-
 132 *E-mail:* dirk.alten@schaffrath.de; Dirk
 Devers *Tel:* (028) 31396-121 *E-mail:* dirk.
 devers@schaffrath.de

Management, Bookbinding: Hans-Josef Schmetter
 Tel: (028) 31396-178 *E-mail:* hans.schmetter@
 schaffrath.de
Technical Dir: Martin Sellmann *Tel:* (028) 31396-
 216 *E-mail:* martin.sellmann@schaffrath.de
Parent Company: Schaffrath Medien

Druckhaus Schuetze GmbH
Fiete-Schulze-Str 13a, 06116 Halle (Saale)
Tel: (0345) 56666-0 *Fax:* (0345) 56666-66
E-mail: info@dhs-halle.de; vertrieb@dhs-halle.de
Web Site: www.dhs-halle.de
Key Personnel
Mng Dir: Stephan Probst; Florian Schaefer
Founded: 1990

SDK Systemdruck Koeln GmbH & Co KG
Member of Rudolf Mueller Group
Maarweg 233, 50825 Cologne
Tel: (0221) 949868-0 *Fax:* (0221) 949868-19
E-mail: info@sdk-koeln.de
Web Site: www.sdk-koeln.de
Key Personnel
Management: Dr Christoph Mueller *Tel:* (0221)
 5497-236 *E-mail:* gf@rudolf-mueller.de; Nicole
 Royar *Tel:* (0221) 949868-16 *Fax:* (0221)
 949868-39 *E-mail:* n.royar@sdk-koeln.de

THEMA media GmbH & Co KG
Zepplinstr 43, 81669 Munich
Tel: (089) 45 87 34-0 *Fax:* (089) 45 87 34-15
E-mail: info@themamedia.com
Web Site: www.themamedia.com
Key Personnel
Mng Dir: Claus Hilschmann; Felix Hilschmann

Thiekoetter Druck GmbH & Co KG
An der Kleimannbruecke 32, 48157 Muenster
Tel: (0251) 14 14 60 *Fax:* (0251) 14 14 666
E-mail: info@thiekoetter-druck.de
Web Site: www.thiekoetter-druck.de
Key Personnel
Mng Dir: Bernd Thiekoetter
Founded: 1879

TOPICMedia Service
Alte Landstr 21, 85521 Ottobrunn
Tel: (089) 66000774
E-mail: office@topicmedia.com
Web Site: www.topicmedia.com
Key Personnel
Mng Dir: Juergen Lindenburger

twinbooks
Division of Thomas Martin Verlagsgesellschaft
 mbH & Co KG
Schwanthalerstr 81, 80336 Munich
Tel: (089) 20 23 86 03 *Fax:* (089) 20 23 86 04
E-mail: info@twinbooks.com
Web Site: www.twinbooks.com
Key Personnel
Mng Dir: Thomas Martin *E-mail:* thomas.
 martin@twinbooks.com
Founded: 1997

Vier-Tuerme-GmbH, Benedict Press
Schweinfurter Str 40, 97359 Muensterschwarzach
 Abtei
Tel: (09324) 20214 *Fax:* (09324) 20444
E-mail: druckerei@vier-tuerme.de
Web Site: www.druckerei.abtei-
 muensterschwarzach.de
Key Personnel
Mng Dir: Fr Christoph Gerhard
Prepress: Michael Blass *Tel:* (09324) 20440
 E-mail: m.blass@vier-tuerme.de
Founded: 1923
Turnaround: 8-16 Workdays
Business from Other Countries: 5%

Vogel Druck und Medienservice GmbH
Member of Bertelsmann Printing Group

Leibnizstr 5, 97204 Hoechberg
Tel: (0931) 4600-02 *Fax:* (0931) 4600-2145
E-mail: info@vogel-druck.de
Web Site: www.vogel-druck.de
Key Personnel
Mng Dir: Rolf Lenertz *E-mail:* rolf.lenertz@
vogel-druck.de; Axel Hentrei
Assistant Mng Dir: Sonja Endres *E-mail:* sonja.
endres@vogel-druck.de
Head, Marketing: Beatrice Rieck *E-mail:* beatrice.
rieck@vogel-druck.de
Head, Sales: Dietmar Fuchs *E-mail:* dietmar.
fuchs@vogel-druck.de
Prepress: Harald Lochner *E-mail:* harald.
lochner@vogel-druck.de
Ultimate Parent Company: Bertelsmann SE & Co
KGaA

Greece

Grivas Publications
3 Irodotou St, 193 00 Aspropyrgos, Attiki
Mailing Address: PO Box 72, 193 00 Aspropyr-
gos, Attiki
Tel: 2105573470 *Fax:* 2105574086
E-mail: info@grivas.gr; grivasbooks@yahoo.gr
Web Site: www.grivas.gr
Branch Office(s)
4 Moustakli & Doridos St, 122 43 Attiki

Hong Kong

Anpak Printing Ltd
9/F, Eastern Center, 1065 King's Rd, Hong Kong
Tel: 2811 4118; 2563 4133 *Fax:* 2565 7710; 2811
3501
E-mail: info@anpak.com
Web Site: www.anpak.com
Founded: 1971
Branch Office(s)
Anpak Printing (Shenzhen) Ltd, 36 Tangxiayong
Gongye Ave, Songgang Town, Baoan District,
Shenzhen, China
Songan Printing (Shenzhen) Co Ltd, 2 Langhui
Rd, Songgang Town, Baoan District, Shenzhen,
China

AOP, see Asia One Printing (AOP)

Asia One Printing (AOP)
Division of Asia One Communications Group
13/F, Asia One Tower, 8 Fung Yip St, Chai Wan
Tel: 2889 2320 *Fax:* 2889 3837
E-mail: enquiry@asiaone.com.hk
Web Site: www.asiaone.com.hk
Key Personnel
Business Development Dir: Evan Cheung
Tel: 2889 8189 *E-mail:* evanccp@asiaone.com.
hk
Sales Dir: Andy Chan *Tel:* 2889 2406
E-mail: andy@asiaone.com.hk
Production Dir: Alan Tam *Tel:* 2889 8520
E-mail: alantam@asiaone.com.hk
Founded: 1997

Bookbuilders Ltd
Unit A-B, 7th floor, Yeung Yiu Chung No 8 In-
dustrial Bldg, 20 Wang Hoi Rd, Kowloon Bay
Tel: 2796 8123 *Fax:* 2796 8690
Key Personnel
General Manager: Kevin Wan

Bright Arts (HK) Ltd
11/F, Block D, Tung Chong Factory Bldg, 659
King's Rd, North Point
Tel: 2562 0119 *Fax:* 2565 7031
E-mail: tinokwok@brightartshk.com.hk
Web Site: www.brightartshk.com.hk
Key Personnel
Mng Dir: Sunny Shum
Dir, China Operations: Jimmy Wong
Founded: 1975
Branch Office(s)
5/F 172 Shen Sha Rd, Sha Tou Jiao, Shenzhen,
China *Tel:* (0755) 2555 4743 *Fax:* (0755) 2555
7125

C & C Offset Printing Co Ltd
Subsidiary of C & C Joint Printing Co (HK) Ltd
14/F, C & C Bldg, 36 Ting Lai Rd, Tai Po, New
Territories
Tel: 2666 4988 *Fax:* 2666 4938
E-mail: offsetprinting@candcprinting.com
Web Site: www.ccoffset.com; www.candcprinting.
com
Key Personnel
Chief Executive Officer, C & C Joint Printing Co
(HK) Ltd: Jackson Leung
Founded: 1980
Turnaround: 30-42 Workdays for printing, binding
& book finishing
Business from Other Countries: 60%
Ultimate Parent Company: Sino United Publish-
ing (Holdings) Ltd
Branch Office(s)
3-7 Permas Way, Truganina, Victoria 3029, Aus-
tralia, Contact: Lena Frew *Tel:* (03) 8366
0200 *Fax:* (03) 8366 0299 *E-mail:* lena.frew@
candcprinting.com
Room 301, No 29, 165 lane, DongZhuAnBang
Rd (C), Shanghai 200050, China, Contact:
Ms Zhang Zhi Ying *Tel:* (021) 6249 1305
Fax: (021) 5922 6111 *E-mail:* zhang.zhi.ying@
candcprinting.com
3, rue Chabanais, 75002 Paris, France, Contact: Michele Olson Niel *Tel:* 01 71 70 39 00
Fax: 01 70 71 92 85 *E-mail:* info@candcoffset.
fr (Continental Europe off)
C & C Printing Japan Co Ltd, Jewel Ginza
301, 7-17-18 Ginza, Chuo-ku, Tokyo 104-
0061, Japan, Contact: Mr Masaaki Yamamoto
Tel: (03) 6264 3751 *Fax:* (03) 6264 3752
E-mail: yamamoto@candcprinting.co.jp *Web
Site:* www.candcprinting.co.jp
C & C Offset Printing Co (UK) Ltd, Tudor
House, 4th floor, 35 Grasse St, London W1T
1QY, United Kingdom, Contact: Helena Coryn-
don *Tel:* (020) 7637 5033 *Fax:* (020) 7637
5044 *E-mail:* helena@candcoffset.co.uk
U.S. Office(s): C & C Offset Printing Co
(Chicago) Inc, PO Box 4678, Naperville,
IL 60567, United States, Contact: Ernest Li
Tel: 630-390-5617 *E-mail:* ernest.li@ccoffset.
com
C & C Offset Printing Co (NY) Inc, 70 W 36
St, Unit 10C, New York, NY 10018, United
States, Contact: Simon Chan *Tel:* 212-431-4210
E-mail: schan@ccoffset.com

Caritas Printing Training Centre
Caritas House, 2 Caine Rd, Hong Kong
Tel: 2843 4734; 2524 2071 *Fax:* 2523 0438
E-mail: info@caritas.org.hk
Web Site: www.caritas.org.hk
Founded: 1953
Business from Other Countries: 50%
Parent Company: Caritas Hong Kong

Colorprint Offset
Unit 1808-9, 18/F, 8 Commercial Tower, 8 Sun
Yip St, Chai Wan
Tel: 2896 7777 *Fax:* 2869 6666
E-mail: info@cpo.com.hk
Web Site: www.cpo.com.hk

Key Personnel
General Manager: Rachel Lai
Founded: 1989
Turnaround: 30-40 Workdays
Business from Other Countries: 80%
Branch Office(s)
Zone E1, Tangtou Industrial Estate, Shiyan, Shen-
zhen 518018, China *Tel:* (0755) 29680000
Fax: (0755) 29680203
Untergassli 7, 2502 Biel/Bienne, Switzerland
Tel: (032) 322 05 08 *Fax:* (032) 322 05 08
St Niklaus Str 12, 6005 Lucerne, Switzerland
Tel: (041) 340 3192 *Fax:* (041) 340 1237
Sales Office(s): Niederwaldstr 40, 76532
Baden-Baden, Germany *Tel:* (07221) 60582
Fax: (07221) 3759747

Cristy's Atelier
37 Jervois St, Sheung Wan
Tel: 2541 8609
Key Personnel
Contact: Cristina Lee
Founded: 1982

Elegance Finance Printing Services Ltd
Subsidiary of Elegance Printing Co Ltd
2402 China Merchants Tower, Shun Tak Centre,
168-200 Connaught Rd Central, Central Hong
Kong
Tel: 2283 2222 *Fax:* 2283 2283
E-mail: csr@eleganceholdings.com
Web Site: www.eleganceholdings.com
Founded: 1980
Business from Other Countries: 2%

Everbest Printing Co Ltd
10/F, Block C, Seaview Estate, 2-8 Watson Rd,
North Point, Hong Kong
Tel: 2727 4433 *Fax:* 2772 7687
E-mail: sales@everbest.com.hk
Web Site: www.everbest.com
Founded: 1954
Turnaround: 28 Workdays
Business from Other Countries: 90%
Branch Office(s)
Everbest (Guangzhou) Printing Co Ltd, 334
Huanshi Rd S, Nansha, Panyu, Guangdong
511458, China *Tel:* (020) 8498 1812 (manu-
facturing plant)
Sales Office(s): C5, 10/F, Ko Fai Industrial
Bldg, 7 Ko Fai Rd, Yau Tong *Tel:* 2727 4433
Fax: 2772 7687 (Australia, Europe & New
Zealand)
313 30 St, Toronto, ON M8W 3E4, Canada, Con-
tact: Doris Chung *Tel:* 416-286-2525 *Fax:* 416-
804-8930 *E-mail:* doris@everbestcanada.ca
Origo Ediciones, Padre Alonso de Ovalle 748,
8330169 Santiago, Chile, Contact: Hernan
Maino *Tel:* (02) 480 9800 *E-mail:* hernan.
maino@origo.cl *Web Site:* www.origo.cl (Chile
& South America)
Nostra Ediciones SA de CV, Av Revolucion
1181 piso 7, Col Merced Gomez, Del Ben-
ito Juarez, 03930 Mexico, DF, Mexico, Con-
tact: Mauricio Volpi *Tel:* (0155) 5554 7030
E-mail: impresion@nostraediciones.com
31 Palatine Rd, London N16 8SY, United
Kingdom, Contact: Nicky Bowden
Tel: (020) 7249 9483 *Fax:* (020) 7241 3460
E-mail: nickybowden@everbest.co.uk
Todd Communications, 611 E 12 Ave, Anchor-
age, AK 99501, United States, Contact: Flip
Todd *Tel:* 907-274-8633 *Fax:* 907-929-5550
E-mail: flip@toddcom.com *Web Site:* www.
toddcom.com
Four Colour Imports Ltd, 2410 Frankfort Ave,
Louisville, KY 40206, United States, Contact:
George Dick *Tel:* 502-896-9644 *Fax:* 502-896-
9594 *E-mail:* sales@fourcolour.com

Golden Cup Printing Co Ltd
6/F, 177 Hoi Bun Rd, Kwun Tong, Kowloon

Tel: 2343 4254 *Fax:* 2341 5426
E-mail: sales@goldencup.com.hk
Web Site: www.goldencup.com.hk
Key Personnel
Chairman: Kam Kai Yeung
Founded: 1971
Turnaround: 25 Workdays
Business from Other Countries: 80%
Sales Office(s): Tutang Industrial Area, Jin Bei
Rd, Changping, Dongguan, Guangdong, China
Tel: (0769) 8339 4888 *Fax:* (0769) 8339 4999
Qilin Industrial Estate, Guanlan, Shenzhen,
Guangdong, China *Tel:* (0755) 2805 6279
Fax: (0755) 2805 6086
Jinma Town, Guandu District, Kunming, Yunnan,
China *Tel:* (0871) 316 1226 *Fax:* (0871) 316
1226
Terley House, Cadbury, Exeter EX5 5JZ, United
Kingdom *Tel:* (01884) 855736 *E-mail:* info@
gcpservices.com
Spectrum Books Inc, 2455 Bennett Valley Rd,
Suite C-116, Santa Rosa, CA 95404-5671,
United States *Tel:* 707-542-6044 *Fax:* 707-542-
6045

Great Wall Printing Co Ltd
Member of Prosperous Printing Group
3/F, Yip Cheung Centre, 10 Fung Yip St, Chai
Wan
Tel: 2897 1083 *Fax:* 2558 1473
E-mail: books@gwp.com.hk
Web Site: www.gwp.com.hk
Key Personnel
Mng Dir: George Lo; Franky Ho
Founded: 1984
Business from Other Countries: 80%
Branch Office(s)
Haverdreef 39, 7006 LH Doetinchen, Nether-
lands, Contact: Buro Doral *Tel:* (0314) 35 40
40 *Fax:* (0314) 35 46 00 *E-mail:* info@ssip-
holland.nl *Web Site:* www.ssip-holland.nl
The High Barn, Snailing Lane, Hawkley GU33
6NJ, United Kingdom, Contact: Myles Wells
Tel: (01) 730 827 326 *Fax:* (01) 730 827 537
E-mail: members@eastwest.fsworld.co.uk

The Green Pagoda Press Ltd
13/F, Block A, Tung Chong Factory Bldg, 633-
655 King's Rd, North Point, Hong Kong
Tel: 2561 1924 *Fax:* 2811 0946
E-mail: gpinfo@gpp.com.hk
Web Site: www.greenpagoda.com
Key Personnel
Mng Dir: Yip Yu Bun
Founded: 1957
Turnaround: 1-14 days
Business from Other Countries: 30%

HK Scanner Arts International Ltd
Block B1, 6/F Fortune Factory Bldg, 40 Lee
Chung St, Chai Wan
Tel: 2976 0289 *Fax:* 2976 0292
E-mail: info@hksagp.net
Web Site: www.hksagp.net
Key Personnel
Chief Executive Dir: Wayne C Ling
Branch Office(s)
Beijing, China *Tel:* (010) 8361 9840 *Fax:* (010)
8361 0416
390 Fuzhou Ru, Shanghai, China
Zhejiang HK Graphics & Printing Ltd, Qian Long
Ki Kai Fa Qu, Deqing County, Huzhou, Zhe-
jiang, China *Tel:* (0572) 8422 550 *Fax:* (0572)
8422 005
68 Bathurst Rd, Winnersh, Workingham, Berks
RG41 5JF, United Kingdom *Tel:* (0118) 961
9155 *Fax:* (0118) 901 8359
U.S. Office(s): 34-27 Cresent St, Astoria, NY
11106, United States *Tel:* 718-361-8164
Fax: 718-361-2002

Hung Hing Off-Set Printing Co Ltd
Subsidiary of Hung Hing Printing Group Ltd
Tai Po Industrial Estate, 17-19 Dai Hei St, New
Territories
Tel: 2664 8682 *Fax:* 2664 2070
E-mail: info@hunghingprinting.com
Web Site: www.hhop.com.hk
Key Personnel
Executive Chairman: Matthew Yum Chak Ming
Executive Dir: Spencer Sung Chee Keung
Chief Information Officer: Yee Y Yu
Founded: 1950
Turnaround: 20-30 Workdays
Business from Other Countries: 15%
Sales Office(s): Santiago del Estero 454,
Piso 1, Oficina 5 y 6, C1075AAJ Buenos
Aires, Argentina, Contact: Leonardo Adami
Tel: (011) 4-179-2178 *E-mail:* enquiry@sa.
hunghingprinting.com (South America)
Vilvordevej 35, 2920 Charlottenlund, Den-
mark, Contact: Jesper Frederiksen *Tel:* 40
26 40 57 *Fax:* 39 90 40 58 *E-mail:* jf@sc.
hunghingprinting.com (Scandinavia)
33, Avenue du Maine, 75755 Paris, France,
Contact: Florent Verlet *Tel:* 01 44 10 40 85
E-mail: florent@fr.hunghingprinting.com
PI Print Innovations GmbH, Untere Haupstr 13,
85354 Freising, Germany, Contact: Birgit von
der Gathen *Tel:* (08161) 88717-0 *Fax:* (08161)
88717-10 *E-mail:* birgit@de.hunghingprinting.
com *Web Site:* www.hunghing.de (Central Eu-
rope & Germany)
IPP Printers, Emmastr 2-D, 4811 AG Breda,
Netherlands, Dir & Sales: Peter Jonkers
Tel: (076) 521 7025; (0473) 561 565
Fax: (076) 520 7281 *E-mail:* peter@bn.
hunghingprinting.com *Web Site:* www.
ippprinters.com (Benelux)
Hung Hing UK, 49 Leigh Rd, Eastleigh, Hants
SO50 9DF, United Kingdom, Sales Dir: Karen
Giles *Tel:* (023) 8062 5858 *Fax:* (023) 8062
9366 *E-mail:* enquiries@hunghing.co.uk *Web
Site:* www.hunghing.co.uk
U.S. Office(s): 29 Arden Rd, East Rockaway,
NY 11518, United States, Contact: Jeff
Tollin *Tel:* 516-593-0030 *Fax:* 516-593-7024
E-mail: hunghingusa@aol.com *Web Site:* www.
hunghing-usa.com

Icicle Production Co Ltd
7/F, Cheung Wah Industrial Bldg, 10-12 Shipyard
Lane, Quarry Bay, Hong Kong
Tel: 2235 2880
E-mail: info@iciclegroup.com
Web Site: www.iciclegroup.com
Key Personnel
Founding Chairman: Alex Chan *Tel:* 2235 2818
E-mail: alex.chan@iciclegroup.com
Chief Executive Officer: Bonnie Chan *Tel:* 2235
2888 *E-mail:* bonnie.chan@iciclegroup.com
Senior Partner: Josephine Cheung *Tel:* 2235 2800
Founded: 1998
BISAC compatible software
Turnaround: 28-56 Workdays
Business from Other Countries: 90%
Parent Company: Icicle Group
Branch Office(s)
Room 1215, 12/F, Silver Tower, No 2 North
Dong Sanhuan Rd, Chaoyang District, Bei-
jing 100027, China *Tel:* (010) 6410 9926
E-mail: china@iciclegroup.com
6 F/E Wenxin Press Bldg, 755 Weihai Rd, Shang-
hai 200041, China *Tel:* (010) 6410 9926
Unit 16-0 Burgundy Corporate Tower, 252 Gil
Puyat Ave, Makati City, Metro Manila, Philip-
pines
19 Carpenter St, 04-01, Singapore 059908, Singapore *Tel:* 8438 5601 *E-mail:* singapore@
iciclegroup.com
2F, 1, No 37, Sec 3, Minquan E Rd, Taipei, Taiwan *Tel:* (020) 7702 1168 *E-mail:* taiwan@
iciclegroup.com

Garden Studios, DL10, 71-75 Shelton St, Covent
Garden, London WC2H 9JQ, United Kingdom *Tel:* (020) 8123 1868 *E-mail:* london@
iciclegroup.com

Leo Paper Products Ltd
Subsidiary of Leo Paper Group
Level 9, Telford House, 16 Wang Hoi Rd,
Kowloon Bay, Kowloon
Tel: 2884 1374 *Fax:* 2513 0698
E-mail: info@leo.com.hk
Web Site: www.leo.com.hk
Key Personnel
Sales Dir: Mr Kelly Fok *E-mail:* kelly@leo.com.
uk
Founded: 1982
Turnaround: 15-30 Workdays
Parent Company: Leo Paper Group
Sales Office(s): Leo Paper Products (Europe)
BVBA, Korte Leemstr 3, 2018 Antwerp, Bel-
gium *Tel:* (03) 609 6810 *Fax:* (03) 609 6830
E-mail: leo@leo-europe.com
Heshan Astros Printing Ltd, Industrial Develop-
ment Area, Xijiang River, Gulao Town, Heshan
City, Guangdong, China *Tel:* (0750) 8766-115
Fax: (0750) 8766-369
Heshan Leo Packaging & Printing Ltd, San-
lian Industrial City, Gulao Town, Heshan
City, Guangdong, China *Tel:* (0750) 8861-888
Fax: (0750) 8861-500
Heshan Leo United Paper Products Ltd, 023 In-
dustrial Zone 1, Hecheng Town, Heshan City,
Guangdong 529727, China *Tel:* (0750) 8383-
300 *Fax:* (0750) 8383-301
JiangXi HuaAo Printing Co Ltd, Changdong In-
dustrial District, Middle Dong Tai Rd, Nan-
chang, Jiangxi 330012, China
Leo Creative (Shanghai) Trading Co Ltd, HuaJing
Bldg, 3rd floor, 678 HuaShang Rd, Shanghai
200040, China *Tel:* (021) 6211-8799 *Fax:* (021)
6289-6226 *E-mail:* info@leo-creative.com
Shanghai Tophand Business Printing Co Ltd, 1F
Bldg 10, No 189 Jinglian Rd, Minhang Dis-
trict, Shanghai 201108, China
Leo Paper Products (Europe) BVBA, Via Gal-
liera, Unit 24, 40121 Bologna, Italy *Tel:* (051)
0922610 *Fax:* (051) 0922630 *E-mail:* leo@leo-
europe.com
Leo Paper Products (UK) Ltd, The Oast House,
10 Brewery Court, Theale, Reading RG7
5AJ, United Kingdom *Tel:* (0118) 9165450
E-mail: info@leouk.com
U.S. Office(s): Leo Paper USA, 27 W 24 St,
Suite 601, New York, NY 10010-3204, United
States *Tel:* 917-305-0780 *Fax:* 917-305-0709
E-mail: info@leousanewyork.com
Leo Paper USA, 1180 NW Maple St, Suite 102,
Issaquah, WA 98027, United States *Tel:* 425-
646-8801 *Fax:* 425-646-8805 *E-mail:* info@
leousa.com

Mei Ka Printing & Publishing Enterprise Ltd
23/F, Hong Kong Plaza, Rooms 2312A-B, 188
Connaught Rd W, Hong Kong
Tel: 2540 1131 *Fax:* 2559 8718; 2559 7137
E-mail: info@meika-printing.com; mkpp@
netvigator.com
Web Site: www.meika-printing.com
Founded: 1982
Branch Office(s)
No 106 Changhong, 2nd Industrial Areas, June
St, Baiyun District, Guangzhou, China

Midas International Holdings Ltd
25/F, Alexandra House, 18 Chater Rd, Central
Hong Kong
Tel: 2407 6888 *Fax:* 2408 0611
E-mail: info@midasprinting.com; marketing@
midasprinting.com
Web Site: www.midasprinting.com

SERVICES (continued)

Key Personnel
Chairman & Group Mng Dir: Richard Hung Ting Ho
Deputy Group Mng Dir: Geoffrey Chuang Ka Kam
Founded: 1990
Business from Other Countries: 85%
Branch Office(s)
88 Kingsway, Holborn, London WC2B 6AA, United Kingdom, Sales Manager: Christos Plegas *E-mail:* christos_plegas@midasprinting.com

New Arts Graphic Reproduction Co Ltd
Lok's Industrial Bldg, 4/F, 204 Tsat Tsz Mui Rd, North Point
Tel: 2564 1323 *Fax:* 2565 8262
E-mail: sales@newartsgraphic.com
Web Site: www.newartsgraphic.com
Key Personnel
Mng Dir: Andrew Choy
Founded: 1970
Business from Other Countries: 50%

Papercom Ltd, see Icicle Production Co Ltd

Paramount Printing Co Ltd
Member of Next Media Group
3 Chun Kwong St, T K O Industrial Estate W, Tseung Kwan O, New Territories
Tel: 2896 8688 *Fax:* 2897 8942
E-mail: paramountcs@paramount.com.hk
Web Site: www.paramount.com.hk
Branch Office(s)
Book Art Inc, 2800 John St, Unit 13, Markham, ON L3R 0E2, Canada *Tel:* 905-940-8282 *Fax:* 905-470-1800 *E-mail:* enquires@bookartinc.com

Sunshine Press Ltd
Room 4, 5, 11-12, 21/F, Fullagar Industrial Bldg, 234 Aberdeen Main Rd, Aberdeen
Tel: 2553 0228 *Fax:* 2873 2930
E-mail: spl@sunshinepress.com.hk
Key Personnel
Dir: Raymond Wong
Administration Manager: Joney Chan
Founded: 1976
Turnaround: 21-28 Workdays
Business from Other Countries: 25%

Toppan Best-Set Premedia Ltd
Subsidiary of Toppan Leefung (Hong Kong) Ltd
20/F @ Convoy, 169 Electric Rd, North Point
Tel: 2897 6033 *Fax:* 2897 5170
E-mail: bestset@toppanleefung.com
Web Site: www.toppanbestset.com
Key Personnel
Mng Dir: Johnson Yeung *E-mail:* johnsonyeung@toppanleefung.com
Contact: Cynthia Hui *E-mail:* cynthiahui@toppanleefung.com
Founded: 1986
Turnaround: 5 workdays
Business from Other Countries: 98%
Ultimate Parent Company: Toppan Leefung Pte Ltd
Branch Office(s)
No 3, Da Song Gang, Jiang Nan Main Ave C, Guangzhou 510240, China, Contact: Patrick Au *Tel:* (020) 8441-5873
Sales Office(s): 33 Alpin Way, Isleworth, Middx TW7 4RJ, United Kingdom, Contact: Keith Harrocks *Tel:* (07515) 775 299 *E-mail:* keithharrocks@toppanleefung.com
50 S Buckhout St, Suite 208, Irvington, NY 10533, United States, Contact: Wai Man Yeung *Fax:* 914-674-5923 *E-mail:* waimanyeung@toppanleefung.com

Toppan Printing Co (HK) Ltd
Division of Toppan Printing Co Ltd

Yuen Long Industrial Estate, One Fuk Wang St, Yuen Long, New Territories
Tel: 2561 0101 *Fax:* 2475 4321
E-mail: info.e@toppan.co.jp
Web Site: www.toppan.co.jp
Founded: 1963
Turnaround: 30 Workdays
Business from Other Countries: 25%

Wing King Tong Group
Leader Industrial Centre, Block I, 3/F, 188-202 Texaco Rd, Tsuen Wan, New Territories
Tel: 2407 3287 *Fax:* 2408 7939
E-mail: marketing@wktco.com
Web Site: www.wkt.cc
Key Personnel
Mng Dir: Alex Yan Tak Chung
Founded: 1944
Turnaround: 15 Workdays
Business from Other Countries: 95%
Branch Office(s)
No 67, Li Xin Lu, Dan Zhu Tou Community, Nan Wan St, Longgang District, Shenzhen, Guangdong 518114, China *Tel:* (0755) 8473 6801; (0755) 8473 6802; (0755) 8473 6803 *Fax:* (0755) 8473 6303 *E-mail:* szwktsales@wkt.cc

Hungary

Realszistema Dabas Printing House
Vasut u 105, Dabas 2373
Tel: (029) 567-501
E-mail: export@dabasinyomda.hu; info@dabasinyomda.hu
Web Site: www.dabasprint.hu
Key Personnel
General Manager: Magdolna Vago
   E-mail: vagom@dabasinyomda.hu
Dir, Sales & Marketing: Zoltan Csondes
   E-mail: csondesz@dabasinyomda.hu
Financial Dir: Erzsebet Tarjanyine Kirtak
   E-mail: tarjanyie@dabasinyomda.hu
Production Dir: Irme Ujvari *E-mail:* ujvarii@dabasinyomda.hu
Founded: 1972

Iceland

Oddi Printing Ltd
Hofdabakka 7, 110 Reykjavik
Tel: 515 5000 *Fax:* 515 5001
E-mail: oddi@oddi.is
Web Site: www.oddi.is
Key Personnel
Chief Executive Officer: Gunnar Sverrisson
   Tel: 515 5005 *E-mail:* gs@oddi.is
Mng Dir: Baldur Thorgeirsson *Tel:* 893 6533
   E-mail: baldur@oddi.is
Dir, Production: Runar Mar Jonatansson *Tel:* 545 2911 *E-mail:* runar@oddi.is
Marketing & Human Resource Manager: Stefan Hrafn Hagalin *Tel:* 515 5019 *E-mail:* hagalin@oddi.is
U.S. Office(s): 118 Heacock Lane, Wyncote, PA 19095, United States, Contact: Charles B Gershwin *Tel:* 215-885-5210 *Fax:* 215-885-6364 *E-mail:* chuck@oddi.com

India

AEL Data Services LLP
Block 7, DLF 1T SEZ, Manapakkam, Chennai 600 089
Tel: (044) 2252 3680; (044) 2252 3690
E-mail: info@aeldata.com; sales@aeldata.com
Web Site: www.aeldata.com
Branch Office(s)
Menara Keck Seng, 203 Jl Bukit Bintang, 55100 Kuala Lumpur, Malaysia *Tel:* (03) 21165862
Communication House, 26 York St, London W1U 6PZ, United Kingdom *Tel:* (020) 7873 2354

DiTech Process Solutions
Solaris 1, F-Wing, 6th floor, Opposite to L & T Gate No 6, Saki Vihar Rd, Powai, Andheri, Mumbai 400 072
Tel: (022) 4066-3600 *Fax:* (022) 4066-3601
E-mail: sales@ditechps.com
Web Site: www.ditechps.com
Key Personnel
Founder & Chief Executive Officer: Nizam Ahmed
Founded: 2004
Business from Other Countries: 100%
U.S. Office(s): 15252 N 100 St, Unit 2162, Scottsdale, AZ 85260, United States *Tel:* 602-410-1317 *Fax:* 480-248-3183
19 W 34 St, Suite 1018, New York, NY 10001, United States *Tel:* 917-464-3518; 646-383-8014

Exeter Premedia Services
Ascendas International Tech Park, Unit 3, Level 1, Pinnacle, CSIR Rd, Taramani, Chennai 600 113
Tel: (044) 23452922
E-mail: sales@exeterpremedia.com
Web Site: www.exeterpremedia.com
Founded: 2004

International Print-o-Pac Ltd
C-4 to C-11, Hosiery Complex, Phase-II Ext, Noida, Uttar Pradesh 201 305
Tel: (0120) 4192 100 *Fax:* (0120) 4192 199
E-mail: ippnoida@ippindia.com
Web Site: www.ippindia.com
Key Personnel
Chairman: Ravindra Singhvi
Mng Dir: Amila Singhvi
Executive Dir: Rishabh Singhvi
Branch Office(s)
404, Commercial Point, 79 Lenin Sarani, Kolkata 700 013 *Tel:* 9331294305 (cell)
   E-mail: malvu2007@yahoo.com
306, Shiv Smriti, 49A Dr Annie Besant Rd, Worli, Mumbai 400 018 *Tel:* (022) 6610 1966
   E-mail: ippmumbai2@yahoo.com (marketing)
B-206, Okhla Industrial Area, Phase-I, New Delhi 110 020 *Tel:* (011) 4077 7000 *Fax:* (011) 4077 7157 *E-mail:* csfm@ippindia.com

Manipal Technologies Ltd
Udayavani Bldg, Press Corner, Manipal 576 104
Tel: (0820) 2571151 *Fax:* (0820) 2570131
E-mail: info@manipaltechnologies.com
Web Site: www.manipaltechnologies.com
Parent Company: The Manipal Group

MPS Ltd
HMG Ambassador, 137 Residency Rd, Bangalore 560 025
Tel: (080) 4178 4242 *Fax:* (080) 4178 4222
E-mail: marketing@adi-mps.com
Web Site: www.adi-mps.com
Branch Office(s)
RR Towers, Super A, 16/17 TVK Industrial Estate, Guindy, Chennai 600 032 *Tel:* (044) 4916 2222 *Fax:* (044) 4916 2225

340 Udyog Vihar, Phase IV, Gurgaon 122 016
  Tel: (0124) 476 0000 *Fax:* (0124) 428 7310
33 IT Park, Sahastradhara Rd, Dehradun 248 001
  Tel: (0135) 6677 926
C35, Sector 62, Noida 201 307 *Tel:* (0120)
  4599750 *Fax:* (0120) 4021280
U.S. Office(s): 1717 NE 42 Ave, Suite 2101, Portland, OR 97213, United States *Tel:* 503-221-
  9911 *Fax:* 212-981-2983

Newstech Publishing Inc
E-2 Greater Kailash Part 2, New Delhi 110 048
Tel: (011) 41435648
E-mail: kb@newstechglobal.com
Web Site: www.newstechglobal.com/books.html
Key Personnel
Chief Executive Officer: Kul Bhusan
Founded: 1988

Nutech Print Services
B-240 Okhla Industrial Area, Phase 1, New Delhi
  110 020
Tel: (011) 40564949; (011) 45459550 *Fax:* (011)
  41609146
E-mail: info@nutech.in; sales@nutechprint.com
Web Site: www.nutechprint.com
Founded: 1970

Paragon Prepress Inc
N-31, Kalkaji, New Delhi 110 019
Tel: (011) 4160 4999 *Fax:* (011) 4160 4999
E-mail: info@paragonprepress.com
Web Site: www.paragonprepress.com
Key Personnel
Chief Executive Officer: Shailander Mal-
  hotra *Tel:* (011) 93128 41420 (cell)
  E-mail: shailander@paragonprepress.com
Chief Business Development & Operations: Van-
  dana Malhotra *Tel:* (011) 95559 97155 (cell)
  E-mail: vandana@paragonprepress.com
Founded: 1991

Replika Press Pvt Ltd
310-311 & 444-445 EPIP, Kundli Industrial Park,
  Sonipat, Haryana 131 028
Tel: (0130) 2219044; (0130) 2219045; (0130)
  2219046 *Fax:* (0130) 2219042
E-mail: info@replikapress.com
Web Site: www.replikapress.com
Key Personnel
Mng Dir: Bhuvnesh Seth *Tel:* (0130) 2217863
  E-mail: bhuvnesh@replikapress.com
Dir, Business Promotion: Jagdish Seth *Tel:* (0130)
  2219041 *E-mail:* jagdishseth@replikapress.com
Dir, Marketing: Sanandan Seth *Tel:* 9810254636
  (cell) *E-mail:* sanandan@replikapress.com
Dir, Production: Vikaran Seth *Tel:* 9899930999
  (cell) *E-mail:* vikaran@replikapress.com
Founded: 1998

Repro India Ltd
Sun Paradise Business Plaza, 11th floor, B Wing,
  Senapati Bapat Marg, Lower Parel, Mumbai
  400 013
Tel: (022) 7191 4000 *Fax:* (022) 7191 4001
E-mail: info@reproindialtd.com
Web Site: www.reproindialtd.com
Founded: 1984
Branch Office(s)
Plot No 50/2, TTC MIDC Industrial Area, Ma-
  hape, Navi Mumbai 400 710 *Tel:* (022) 7178
  5000 *Fax:* (022) 7178 5011 (plant)
Repro Innovative Digiprint Pvt Ltd, No 146,
  East Coast Rd, Vettuvankeni, Chennai 600 115
  (plant)
Plot No 90-93, 165 Surat Special Economic
  Zone, Rd No 11, GIDC, Sachin, Surat 394
  230 *Tel:* (0261) 3107 396; (0261) 3107 397
  Fax: (0261) 2398 030 (plant)
Sales Office(s): 1211, South City, Pinnacle, 11/1,
  Salt Lake City, Block EP, Sector 5, Kolkata
  700 091 *Tel:* 9650003189 (cell)

Unit No 205, 2nd floor, DLF Tower-A, Jasola
  District Centre, Jasola, New Delhi 110 076
  Tel: (011) 41323212 *Fax:* (011) 41323214
11 Whitman St, Hastings-on-Hudson, NY 10706-
  1605, United States

S4Carlisle Publishing Services
No 141, Prakash Towers, 1st floor, Rajiv Gandhi
  Salai (OMR), Kottivakkam, Chennai 600 041
Tel: (044) 24545411; (044) 24545412 *Fax:* (044)
  24545413
E-mail: sales@s4carlisle.com
Web Site: www.s4carlisle.com
Key Personnel
Founder & Chief Executive Officer: Kris Srinaath
Chief Operating Officer: Nandakumar Ramachan-
  dran
Founded: 2000 (as S4Ind Software Pvt Ltd)
Branch Office(s)
S4Carlisle Publishing Services Pte Ltd, 3, Shen-
  ton Way, No 13-09A, Shenton House, Singa-
  pore 068805, Singapore *Tel:* 233-2610
U.S. Office(s): 2436 Meinen Ct, Dubuque, IA
  52002, United States *Tel:* 563-557-1500
  Fax: 563-557-1376

Srinivas Fine Arts (P) Ltd
340/3, Keelathiruthangal, Sivakasi 626 130
Tel: (04562) 226588; (04562) 232589
  Fax: (04562) 230038; (04562) 232662
E-mail: sales@sfa.co.in
Web Site: www.srinivasfinearts.com
Key Personnel
General Manager: Mr P Nandakumar
National Sales Manager: B Venkatesan
  E-mail: venkatesan@sfa.co.in
Founded: 1964
Branch Office(s)
Rain Tree Pl, 1st floor, 7, McNichols Rd, Chet-
  pet, Chennai 600 031 *Tel:* (044) 2836 3014
  Fax: (044) 4284 9804 *E-mail:* customer@sfa.
  co.in

Thomson Digital
Division of Thomson Press (India) Ltd
A-5/6, Noida Special Economic Zone, Noida 201
  305
Tel: (0120) 3085000 *Fax:* (0120) 3085062
E-mail: contact@thomsondigital.com
Web Site: www.thomsondigital.com
Key Personnel
Chairman: Aroon Purie
Executive Dir: Vinay Kumar Singh
Group Executive & Finance Dir: Anil Kumar
  Mehra
Mng Dir: Ankoor Purie
Founded: 1988
Branch Office(s)
129, Noida Special Economic Zone, Noida 201
  301 *Tel:* (0120) 4511500 *Fax:* (0120) 4511501
No 12-A, (SP), 5th floor, Kamak Towers, Thiru
  Vika Industrial Estate, Chennai 600 032
  Tel: (044) 2225 1140 *Fax:* (044) 2225 1151
08A4, 8th floor, Cyber Tower, Ebene Cyber City,
  Mauritius *Tel:* 4667-421
U.S. Office(s): 4 Mahland Pl, Oceanside, NY
  11572, United States, Business Development
  Manager: Joseph Varghese *Tel:* 516-665-2641
  E-mail: joseph.v@thomsondigital.com

Indonesia

Ichtiar Baru van Hoeve
Jl Raya Pasar Jumat 38 D-E, Pondok Pinang,
  Jakarta 12310
Tel: (021) 7511856; (021) 7511901 *Fax:* (021)
  7511855
E-mail: redaksi@ibvh.com

Web Site: www.ibvh.com
Founded: 1980
Turnaround: 6 Workdays

PT Victory Offset Prima
JL Aria Santika No 8, Desa Pasir Bolang-
  Tigaraksa, Tangerang 15610
Tel: (021) 5940-5343 *Fax:* (021) 5940-5345
E-mail: info@victoryoffset.com
Web Site: www.victoryoffset.com
Key Personnel
General Manager: S Wilson Pinady
Founded: 1971
Turnaround: 14 Workdays
Business from Other Countries: 10%

Israel

Har-El Printers & Publishers
PO Box 8053, 6108402 Jaffa
Tel: (03) 6816834 *Fax:* (03) 6813563
Web Site: www.harelart.com
Key Personnel
Owner & Dir: Monique L Har-El
  E-mail: mharel@harelart.co.il
Manager: Jaacov Har-El
Founded: 1974
Turnaround: 60-90 Workdays
Business from Other Countries: 70%

Italy

Artigrafiche Boccia SpA
Via Tiberio Claudio Felice, 7, 84131 Salerno SA
Tel: (089) 303311 *Fax:* (089) 771017
E-mail: info@artigraficheboccia.com
Web Site: artigraficheboccia.com
Founded: 1950
Branch Office(s)
Via Tevere, 44, 00198 Rome RM *Tel:* (06)
  68801898 *Fax:* (06) 68802416
Via Andrea Verga, n 12, 20144 Milan MI
  Tel: (02) 7532750 *Fax:* (02) 7532750

Vincenzo Bona SpA
Str Settimo, 370/30, 10156 Turin TO
Tel: (011) 273 77 77 *Fax:* (011) 273 77 00
E-mail: info@vincenzobona.com
Web Site: www.vincenzobona.com
Founded: 1777

G Canale & C SpA
Via Liguria, 24, 10071 Borgaro Turin TO
Tel: (011) 40 78 511 *Fax:* (011) 40 78 607
E-mail: prepress@canaleprepress.com; sales@
  canale.it
Web Site: www.gcanale.it
Founded: 1915
Turnaround: 30 Workdays
Business from Other Countries: 65%
Branch Office(s)
SOS Cernica, 47, Pantellimon Jud ILFOV,
  Bucharest, Romania *Tel:* (021) 351 72 55
  Fax: (021) 351 72 57 *E-mail:* office@canale-
  bucarest.ro

Creabooks Packagers
Via Martiri della Liberazione 14, 16043 Chiavari
  GE
Tel: (0185) 1873688 *Fax:* (0185) 1898316
E-mail: info@abooks.it
Web Site: www.creabooks.it

Key Personnel
Art Dir: Donatella Bergamino *E-mail:* d.
bergamino@abooks.it
Foreign Rights Manager: Giorgio Bergamino
E-mail: g.bergamino@abooks.it

Dedalo Litostampa SRL
Viale Luigi Jacobini, 5, 70123 Bari BA
Tel: (080) 531 14 13 *Fax:* (080) 531 14 14
E-mail: info@dedalolitostampa.it
Web Site: www.dedalolitostampa.it
Founded: 1961

Elcograf SpA
Via Mondadori 15, 37131 Verona VR
Tel: (045) 934111 *Fax:* (045) 934763
E-mail: info.printing@verona.pozzoni.it
Web Site: www.elcograf.com
Key Personnel
Contact: Alberto Gibellini
Founded: 1907

Grafiche Damiani SRL
Via Zanardi, 376, 40131 Bologna BO
Tel: (051) 6356811 *Fax:* (051) 6347188
E-mail: info@grafichedamiani.it
Web Site: www.grafichedamiani.it

Graphicom SRL
Viale dell'Industria, 67, 36100 Vicenza VI
Tel: (0444) 189900 *Fax:* (0444) 189990; (0444)
189991; (0444) 189992
E-mail: info@graphicom.it
Web Site: www.graphicom.it
Founded: 1986

Legatoria Editoriale Giovanni Olivotto SpA,
see LEGO SpA

LEGO SpA
Via dell'Industria, 2, 36100 Vicenza
Tel: (0444) 564622 *Fax:* (0444) 564929
E-mail: lego@legogroup.com
Web Site: www.legogroup.com
Key Personnel
Mng Dir: Giulio Olivotto
Founded: 1900

Marchesi Grafiche Editoriali SpA
Via Flaminia 995/997, 00189 Rome RM
Tel: (06) 33216 1 *Fax:* (06) 33216 333
E-mail: info@marchesigrafiche.it
Web Site: www.marchesigrafiche.it
Founded: 1927

Milanostampa SpA
Corso PEG Ferrero 5, 12060 Farigliano CN
Tel: (0173) 746111 *Fax:* (0173) 746248
Founded: 1965
Turnaround: 15 Workdays
Business from Other Countries: 65%
U.S. Office(s): Milanostampa USA, 141 Berkeley
Pl, No 2, Brooklyn, NY 11217-3971, United
States *Tel:* 212-964-2430 (North American
sales & production off)

Musumeci SpA
Loc Amerique, 97, 11020 Quart, Valle d'Aosta
AO
Tel: (0165) 76 11 11 *Fax:* (0165) 76 11 12
E-mail: info@musumecispa.it
Web Site: www.musumecispa.it

NIIAG SpA, see Nuovo Istituto Italiano d'Arti
Grafiche SpA

Nuovo Istituto Italiano d'Arti Grafiche SpA
Via Zanica 92, 24126 Bergamo BG
Web Site: www.arti-group.eu

Founded: 1873
Turnaround: 10 Workdays
Business from Other Countries: 30%
Parent Company: Bavaria Industries Group AG

OGM SpA
Via 1a Str, 87, 35129 Padova PD
Tel: (049) 8076266 *Fax:* (049) 8076212
E-mail: ogm@ogm.it
Web Site: ogm.it
Key Personnel
Owner: Guido Muzzio; Marco Schiavon; Flavia
Vezzani
Founded: 1962

Printer Trento SRL
Via alle Roste, 12, 38121 Trento TN
Tel: (0461) 957 200
Web Site: www.printertrento.it
Key Personnel
Owner & General Manager: Dario Martelli
Co-Owner: Gianni Girardi
Sales: Susanna Geier *Tel:* (0461) 957 219
E-mail: susanna.geier@printertrento.it
Founded: 1980
Sales Office(s): Regentesselaan 187, 2562 CX
The Hague, Netherlands, Contact: Janneke
Verdonk *Tel:* (070) 7850 922 *E-mail:* janneke.
verdonk@gmail.com
Printer Trento UK Ltd, United Kingdom, Con-
tact: Jo Clark *Tel:* (01845) 577221 *E-mail:* jo.
clark@printertrento.co.uk

Promedia SRL
Division of Vincenzo Bona SpA
Str Settimo, 370/30, 10156 Turin TO
Tel: (011) 273 77 20 *Fax:* (011) 273 77 04
E-mail: info@promediasolutions.it; marketing@
promediasolutions.it
Web Site: www.promediasolutions.it
Founded: 2005

Puntoweb SRL
Industrial Zone, Via Nettunense, 00040 Ariccia
RM
Tel: (06) 9349721 *Fax:* (06) 934972242
E-mail: info@puntowebsrl.it; commerciale@
puntowebsrl.it (sales)
Web Site: www.puntowebsrl.it

Societa Editoriale Grafiche AZ SRL
viale del Lavoro, 8, 37036 San Martino Albergo
VR
Tel: (045) 99 44 33 *Fax:* (045) 99 50 16
Web Site: www.graficheaz.it
Key Personnel
Marketing & Communications: Leonardo
Aldegheri
Production: Daniele Armano
Sales: Lisanna Andreis; Eva Blum
Technical Production: Roberto Girlanda

Spadamedia SRL
Viale del Lavoro 31, 00043 Ciampino RM
Tel: (06) 96846542 *Fax:* (06) 96847295
Web Site: www.spadamedia.it
Key Personnel
Sales Dir: Dr Marco Marziale
Administrative Executive: Paolo Ruberta

Gruppo Editoriale Zanardi SRL
via Venezia, 3, 35127 Padua PD
Tel: (049) 8069511 *Fax:* (049) 8069510
E-mail: info@zanardi.it
Web Site: www.zanardi.it
Branch Office(s)
Via Alessandro Volta, 22, 20094 Corsico MI
Tel: (02) 48620286 *Fax:* (02) 45864967

U.S. Office(s): 41-41 44 St, Suite 3F, Sunnyside,
NY 11104, United States *Tel:* 212-964-2430
Fax: 212-964-2497 *E-mail:* rvarrasso@zanardi-
usa.com

Latvia

Tipografija Lapa
Raina Str 6, Valmiera LV-4201
Tel: 261854845
E-mail: info@lapaprint.com
Web Site: www.lapaprint.com
Key Personnel
Contact: Arnis Skuja *E-mail:* arnis.skuja@
lapaprint.com
Founded: 1973
Sales Office(s): Brivibas Str 99/2-13, Riga LV-
1001, Contact: Ingars Klavins *E-mail:* ingars.
klavins@lapaprint.lv

Veiters Korporacija
Brivibas gatve 437, Riga LV-1024
Tel: 67994419; 67545174 (sales) *Fax:* 67994419
E-mail: veiters@veiters.lv
Web Site: www.veiters.lv
Key Personnel
Commercial Dir: Diana Novicka *E-mail:* diana@
veiters.lv

Lithuania

Druka Spaustuve (Druka Printing House)
Mainu St 5, LT-94101 Klaipeda
Tel: (046) 380458 *Fax:* (046) 380459
E-mail: info@druka.lt
Web Site: www.druka.lt
Key Personnel
Mng Dir: Algirdas Apulskis
Head, Sales: Lina Sniukiene
Sales Manager: Kristina Rimke

Lietuvos Rytas Spaustuve UAB
12A Gedimino Ave, LT-01103 Vilnius
Tel: (05) 274 3743 *Fax:* (05) 274 3728
E-mail: print@lrytas.lt; spaustuve@lrytas.lt
Web Site: print.lrytas.lt
Key Personnel
General Dir: Nerijus Baura
Founded: 1994
Business from Other Countries: 60%
Branch Office(s)
83 Sodu St, LT-13274 Skaidiskes
51 Kauno St, LT-21371 Vievis

Reprodukcija
Chemijos g 29, LT-51333 Kaunas
Tel: (037) 408866 *Fax:* (037) 408867
E-mail: repro@repro.lt
Web Site: www.repro.lt
Branch Office(s)
Riovoniu g 33A, LT-03154 Vilnius
Tel: (05) 2335689 *Fax:* (05) 2388951
E-mail: reprovilnius@repro.lt

Sapnu Sala Spaustuve
Moniuskos g 21, LT-08121 Vilnius
Tel: (05) 278 05 80 *Fax:* (05) 278 05 90

Spindulio Spaustuve (Spindulys Printing House)
B Brazdzionio g 23, LT-48184 Kaunas
Tel: (037) 200744 *Fax:* (037) 204970
E-mail: info@spindulys.lt
Web Site: www.spindulys.lt

Key Personnel
Sales & Marketing Manager: Sigita Varniene
  E-mail: sigita@spindulys.lt
Project Manager: Kristina Petruskeviciute
  E-mail: kristina@spindulys.lt
Founded: 1928
Business from Other Countries: 6%

Malaysia

Abadi Ilmu Sdn Bhd
14, Jl SS4D/14, 47301 Petaling Jaya, Selangor
  Darul Ehsan
Tel: (03) 7804 4588; (03) 7804 4157; (03) 7804
  3967 *Fax:* (03) 7804 4152
E-mail: abadi_ilmu@time.net.my; abadiilmu@
  gmail.com; abadi_ilmu@yahoo.com
Web Site: www.abadilmu.com
Founded: 1997

BHS Book Printing Sdn Bhd
Lot 17-22 to 17-25, Jl CJ 1/1, Bersatu Industrial
  Park, Chera Jaya, 43200 Selangor Darul Ehsan
Tel: (03) 9074 7558; (03) 9074 7018 *Fax:* (03)
  9074 7573
E-mail: bhsprint@tm.net.my
Web Site: www.bhs.my
Key Personnel
Executive Dir: Koo Thiam Yoong
Mng Dir: Dato Lim Thiam Huat
Founded: 1980
Parent Company: BHS Industries Berhad

Malta

Print It
Division of Salander Group Co Ltd
KW3, Corradino Industrial Estate, Paola
Tel: 2189 4446; 2189 4447 *Fax:* 2189 4448
E-mail: info@printit.com.mt
Web Site: www.printit.com.mt

Progress Press Co Ltd
Member of Allied Group
Zona Industrijali, Triq l-Intornjatur, Mriehel BKR
  3000
Tel: 22764400 *Fax:* 25594115
E-mail: info@progresspress.com.mt
Web Site: www.progresspress.com.mt
Key Personnel
Chief Operations Officer: Noel Galea
Mng Dir: Michel Rizzo
Founded: 1922

Mexico

Solar, Servicios Editoriales SA de CV
Calle 2, No 21, Colonia San Pedro de los Pinos,
  Delegacion Benito Juarez, 03800 Mexico,
  CDMX
Tel: (0155) 5515-1657
E-mail: solar@solareditores.com
Web Site: www.solareditores.com
Key Personnel
Dir General: Alejandro Zenker *E-mail:* alejandro.
  zenker@solareditores.com
Production Manager: Beatriz Hernandez
  E-mail: beatriz.hernandez@solareditores.com
Founded: 1985

Netherlands

Uitgeven Duurzaam
Bakhuis 6, 3262 CB Oud-Beijerland
Tel: (06) 5495 6704
E-mail: info@duurzaamuitgeven.nl
Web Site: www.duurzaamuitgeven.nl
Key Personnel
Mng Dir: Pieter Kers

Eurasia
JP Thijsseweg 1E, 2408 ER Alphen aan den Rijn
Tel: (0172) 200 088
Web Site: www.eurasiainternational.com
Key Personnel
Mng Dir: Ka Lok Man *Tel:* (0651) 491 065
  E-mail: kalok.man@eurasiainternational.com
Founded: 2004

Roto Smeets
Hunneperkade 4, 7418 BT Deventer
Mailing Address: Postbus 825, 7400 AV Deventer
Tel: (0570) 69 48 50 *Fax:* (0570) 69 41 08
E-mail: info@rotosmeets.com
Web Site: www.rotosmeets.nl
Key Personnel
Dir, International Sales: Rene van Werkhoven
  Tel: (0570) 69 48 64 *E-mail:* rene.van.
  werkhoven@rotosmeets.com
Branch Office(s)
Parallelweg 5, 4878 AH Etten Leur *Tel:* (076)
  508 40 00 *Fax:* (076) 501 43 75
Roto Smeets GrafiServices, Kanaalweg 30, 3526
  KM Utrecht, Dir: Michiel Hack *Tel:* (030) 282
  28 22 *Fax:* (030) 282 28 44 *E-mail:* michiel.
  hack@grafiservices.nl *Web Site:* www.
  grafiservices.nl
Molenveldstr 100, 6001 HL Weert *Tel:* (0495) 57
  09 11 *Fax:* (0495) 54 29 05

New Zealand

Craigs Design & Print Ltd
122 Yarrow St, Invercargill 9840
Mailing Address: PO Box 99, Invercargill 9840
Tel: (03) 211-0393; (03) 211-8618 (showroom)
  Fax: (03) 214-9930
E-mail: info@craigprint.co.nz
Web Site: www.craigprint.co.nz
Key Personnel
Chief Executive & Dir: Tony Wills *Tel:* (027)
  672-7147 (cell) *E-mail:* tony@craigprint.co.nz
Dir & Administration: Eleanor Wills *Tel:* (027)
  284-6524 (cell) *E-mail:* eleanor@craigprint.co.
  nz
Dir & Promotional/Digital Manager:
  Richard Wills *Tel:* (021) 264-2772 (cell)
  E-mail: richard@craigprint.co.nz
Dir & Sales Manager: Rodger Wills *Tel:* (027)
  434-2757 (cell) *E-mail:* rodger@craigprint.co.
  nz
Print Services Manager: Alan Shirley *Tel:* (027)
  681-5240 (cell) *E-mail:* alan@craigprint.co.nz
Production Manager: Brent Hollingworth
  Tel: (027) 221-2083 (cell) *E-mail:* brent@
  craigprint.co.nz
Founded: 1876

Poland

Drukarnia Wydawnictwo Bernardinum Sp z oo
ul Bpa Dominika 11, 83-130 Pelplin

Tel: (58) 536-43-76; (58) 536-17-57 *Fax:* (58)
  536-43-76
E-mail: drukarnia@bernardinum.pl;
  biuroobslugi@bernardinum.com.pl
Web Site: www.drukarnia.bernardinum.com.pl
Key Personnel
Printing Dir: Radoslaw Jaszewski
  E-mail: radoslaw.jaszewski@bernardinum.com.
  pl
Sales Executive: Mr Miroslaw Chyla
  E-mail: miroslaw.chyla@bernardinum.com.pl
Founded: 1830

Eurodruk Poznan Sp z oo
ul Wiezbowa 17/19, 62-080 Tarnowo Podgorne
Tel: (61) 816 40 10 *Fax:* (61) 816 40 11
E-mail: edp@eurodruk.com.pl
Web Site: www.eurodruk.com.pl
Key Personnel
Sales & Marketing Dir: Mariusz Majewski
  Tel: (61) 816 40 07 *Fax:* (61) 814 76 81
  E-mail: m.majewski@eurodruk.com.pl
Sales & Marketing Manager: Agnieszka Rybak-
  Burzynska *E-mail:* a.rybak@eurodruk.com.pl
Client Service Manager: Marek Karwat
  E-mail: m.karwat@eurodruk.com.pl
Founded: 1997
Parent Company: Euro Druckservice AG (EDS)

LCL Dystrybucja Sp z oo
ul Dabrowskiego 247/249, 93-231 Lodz
Tel: (42) 250 83 00 *Fax:* (42) 250 83 00
E-mail: sekretariat@lcldystrybucja.pl
Web Site: www.lcldystrybucja.pl
Key Personnel
Prepress: Dariusz Szlauderbach
  E-mail: dszlauderbach@lcldystrybucja.pl
Sales: Maciej Lewy *E-mail:* mlewy@
  lcldystrybucja.pl; Robert Sacharczuk
  E-mail: rsacharczuk@lcldystrybucja.pl
Founded: 1988

Drukarnia im Karola Miarki (Karol Miarka
  Printing House)
ul Zwirki i Wigury 1, 43-190 Mikolow
Tel: (32) 326 20 96 *Fax:* (32) 326 20 99
E-mail: export@tolek.com.pl
Web Site: www.tolek.com.pl
Key Personnel
Owner: Adolf Janczyk *E-mail:* adolf.janczyk@
  tolek.com.pl
Contact: Aleksandra Janczyk *E-mail:* aleksandra.
  janczyk@tolek.com.pl

101 Studio DTP Tomasz Tegi i Spolka Sp z oo
ul Ekonomiczna 30/36, 93-426 Lodz
Tel: (42) 250 70 92; (42) 250 70 93; (42) 250 70
  94 *Fax:* (42) 250 70 95
E-mail: ac@poczta.101studio.com.pl
Web Site: www.101studio.com.pl
Key Personnel
DTP Manager: Janusz Majerowski *Tel:* (42) 250
  70 92 ext 19 *Fax:* (42) 250 70 959
Sales & Marketing Manager: Jaroslaw
  Soltyszewski *Tel:* (42) 250 70 92 ext 21
  E-mail: j.soltyszewski@101studio.com.pl
Founded: 1990

Opolgraf SA
ul Niedzialkowskiego 8-12, 45-085 Opole
Tel: (77) 454-52-44; (77) 454-52-46 *Fax:* (77)
  454-53-13
Web Site: www.opolgraf.com.pl
Key Personnel
President: Miroslaw Szewczyk *Tel:* (77) 454-54-
  48 *E-mail:* szewczyk@opolgraf.com.pl
Vice President: Bartosz Mazurkiewicz *Tel:* (77)
  454-54-48 *E-mail:* mazurkiewicz@opolgraf.
  com.pl

Prepress Manager: Wojciech Starczewski *Tel:* (77) 454-52-44 ext 21 *E-mail:* ctp@opolgraf.com.pl
Production Manager: Henryk Gonschior *Tel:* (77) 454-52-44 ext 48 *E-mail:* szefprodukcji@opolgraf.com.pl
Sales Manager: Joanna Tolpa *Tel:* (77) 454-52-44 ext 45 *E-mail:* joanna.tolpa@opolgraf.com.pl

WEMA Wydawnictwo-Poligrafia Sp z oo
ul Rolna 191/193, 02-729 Warsaw
Tel: (22) 827 21 17 *Fax:* (22) 828 57 79
Web Site: www.wp-wema.pl

Portugal

Edicoes Silabo Lda
Rua Cidade de Manchester, 2, 1170-100 Lisbon
Tel: 218130345 *Fax:* 218166719
E-mail: silabo@silabo.pt
Web Site: www.silabo.pt
Key Personnel
Marketing Dir & Editor: Manuel Robalo
   E-mail: manuel.robalo@silabo.pt
Founded: 1983
Turnaround: 5 Workdays

Puerto Rico

Publishing Resources Inc
425 Carr 693, PMB 160, Dorado 00646-4802
Tel: (787) 626-0607; (787) 647-9342 (cell)
E-mail: pri@chevako.net
Web Site: www.publishingresources.net
Key Personnel
President: Ronald J Chevako
Executive Vice President & Editor: Anne W Chevako
Production: Jay A Chevako
Founded: 1982
Business from Other Countries: 5%

Singapore

Chong Moh Offset Printing Pte Ltd
19 Joo Koon Rd, Singapore 628978
Tel: 6862 2701 *Fax:* 6862 4335
Founded: 1946
Turnaround: 10-14 Workdays
Business from Other Countries: 35%

Ho Printing Singapore Pte Ltd
31 Changi South St One, Changi South Industrial Estate, Singapore 486769
Tel: 6542 9322 *Fax:* 6542 8322
E-mail: sales@hoprinting.com.sg
Web Site: www.hoprinting.com
Founded: 1951
Turnaround: 35-50 Workdays
Business from Other Countries: 30%

International Press Softcom Ltd (IPS)
26, Kallang Ave, Singapore 339417
Tel: 6298 3800 *Fax:* 6297 1668
E-mail: biz@ipsoftcom.com
Web Site: www.ipsoftcom.com
Key Personnel
Chief Executive Officer & Mng Dir: Low Ka Choon Kevin
General Manager, China Region: Chan Yee Liang

General Manager, Malaysia, Australia & Vietnam: Ng Ching Beng Alvin
Founded: 1968
Branch Office(s)
Unit 22, 6-20 Braidwood St, South Strathfield, NSW 2136, Australia *Tel:* (02) 9642 2924 *Fax:* (02) 9642 0228
No 1 Bldg, No 402, No 1299 Xin Jinqiao Rd, Pudong, Shanghai 201206, China *Tel:* (021) 5032 2228 *Fax:* (021) 5032 2229
5F, No 13, Hongfa Industrial Estate, Jingtang Rd, Shiyan St, Baoan District, Shenzhen, Guangdong 518108, China *Tel:* (0755) 2733 5200 *Fax:* (0755) 2733 5207
IP Media Xiamen, No 1 Bldg, No 285, Weng Jiao Rd, Hai Cang District, Xiamen, Fujian 361022, China *Tel:* (0592) 6806555 *Fax:* (0592) 6806556
9 Beratina Agrahara, Hosur Rd, Bangalore 560 100, India
Scantrans Chennai, No 18 & 19, Mahalakshmi Nagar Extn, Numbal Village, Thiruverkadu Post, Chennai 600 077, India *Tel:* (044) 2649 5056 *Fax:* (044) 2649 4056
IP Rudrapur, 6 KM Stone Kichha Rd, Village Shimla Pistor, Rudrapur, Uttarakhand 263 153, India *Tel:* (059) 4428 0552 *Fax:* (044) 2476 4813
IP Softcom Malaysia Sdn Bhd, Plot 46, Bayan Lepas Industrial Estate, Phase IV, SWD, 11900 Penang, Malaysia *Tel:* (04) 644 3555 *Fax:* (04) 646 2868
IPS Vietnam, Lot B54/1, Rd No 2E, Vinch Loc A Industrial Park, Binch Chanh District, Ho Chi Minh City, Vietnam *Tel:* (08) 376 56252 *Fax:* (08) 376 56251

IPS, see International Press Softcom Ltd (IPS)

Markono Print Media Pte Ltd
Subsidiary of Markono Holdings Pte Ltd
21 Neythal Rd, Singapore 628586
Tel: 6281 1118
E-mail: enquiry@markono.com; sales@markono.com
Web Site: www.markono.com
Key Personnel
Chairman: Bob Lee
Mng Dir: Edwin Ng
Sales & Marketing Dir: Max Lee
Founded: 1967
Turnaround: 14 Workdays
Business from Other Countries: 20%
Branch Office(s)
Markono Logistics, 4 Toh Tuck Link, Singapore 596226 *Tel:* 6465 1498 *E-mail:* ml.sales@markono.com
Markono Digital Solutions (M) Sdn Bhd, 7 Lorong Jelawat 4, 13700 Seberang Jaya, Penang, Malaysia *Tel:* (04) 397-8700 *E-mail:* mdsm.sales@markono.com

Pica Digital Pte Ltd
55 Ayer Rajah Crescent, No 02-25, Singapore 139949
Tel: 6776 1311 *Fax:* 6779 3055
Key Personnel
Mng Dir: Thomas Ling
Founded: 1977
Turnaround: 4 Workdays
Business from Other Countries: 60%

SC (Sang Choy) International Pte Ltd
9 Harrison Rd, No 02-01, Harrison Industrial Bldg, Singapore 369651
Tel: 6289 0829 *Fax:* 6282 1819
E-mail: marketing@sc-international.com.sg
Web Site: www.sc-international.com.sg
Key Personnel
Dir, Operations: Almond Ko *E-mail:* almond@sc-international.com.sg
Founded: 1992

Branch Office(s)
Room 521, No 2, Ten Fe Yi St, Ten Fei Yuan, Jiu Long Rd, Huangpu District, Guangzhou 510555, China *Tel:* (020) 8252 6087
Unit A, 22/F, Full Win Commercial Centre, 573 Nathan Rd, Kowloon, Hong Kong *Tel:* 5804 3265
26 York St, London W1U 6PZ, United Kingdom *Tel:* (020) 7666 3116

Stamford Press Pte Ltd
209 Kallang Bahru, Singapore 339344
Tel: 6294 7227 *Fax:* 6294 4396; 6294 3319
E-mail: info@stamford.com.sg
Web Site: www.stamford.com.sg
Key Personnel
Dir, Sales & Marketing: Mr V Balu
   E-mail: balu@stamford.com.sg
Founded: 1963 (as Stamford College Press)
Business from Other Countries: 45%
Parent Company: Stamford Media International Pte Ltd
Branch Office(s)
Stamford Aus-Trade & Press Pty Ltd, 32 Ada Ave, Strathfield, NSW 2135, Australia *Tel:* (02) 9758 7715 *Fax:* (02) 9758 7716
Raffles-Stamford Press (India) Pvt Ltd, No 1 Survey No 16/1, Singasandra Village, Begur Hobli, Hosur Main Rd, Bangalore 560 068, India *Tel:* (080) 573 0717; (080) 573 1718 *Fax:* (080) 573 3992
Stamford Lake Pvt Ltd, 366, High Level Rd, Pannipitiya, Sri Lanka *Tel:* (01) 846 002; (074) 208 134 *Fax:* (01) 846 002; (074) 208 134
No 61, Tryfan Close Redbridge, Ilford, Essex 1G4 5JY, United Kingdom *Tel:* (01223) 504754; (020) 8262 6515 *Fax:* (01223) 574538; (020) 8262 6514

Times Printers Pte Ltd
Subsidiary of Times Publishing Ltd
16 Tuas Ave 5, Singapore 639340
Tel: 6311 2888; 6295 3211; 6295 2138; 6311 2872 (customer service); 6311 2780 (sales & marketing) *Fax:* 6862 1313; 6311 2872 (customer service)
E-mail: marketing@timesprinters.com
Web Site: www.timesprinters.com.sg
Key Personnel
Deputy General Manager, Group Sales & Marketing: Patsy Tan
Operations Manager: Alex Tang
Assistant General Manager: Phan Ming Ruey
Founded: 1968
Turnaround: 5-25 Workdays
Business from Other Countries: 75%
Branch Office(s)
Times Offset (Malaysia) Sdn Bhd, Lot 46, Subang Hi-Tech Industrial Park, Batu Tiga, 40000 Selangor Darul Ehsan, Malaysia *Tel:* (03) 5628 6888 *Fax:* (03) 5628 6899
Sales Office(s): Everbest Printing Co Ltd, 25 The Palisade, Umina Beach, NSW 2257, Australia *Tel:* (02) 4342 3563 *Fax:* (02) 4342 1564 *E-mail:* adam@everbestprinting.com.au
Everbest Printing Co Ltd, Ko Fai Industrial Bldg, C5 10th floor, 7 Ko Fai Rd, Yau Tong, Kowloon, Hong Kong *Tel:* 2727 4433 *Fax:* 2772 7687 *E-mail:* sales@everbest.com.hk
13 Nthombeni Way Noordhoek, 7979 Cape Town, South Africa, Contact: Arlene Gippert *Tel:* (021) 789 2865 *E-mail:* arlenegippert@tpg.com.my
Everbest UK, 31 Palatine Rd, London N16 8SY, United Kingdom, Contact: Nicky Bowden *Tel:* (020) 7249 9483 *Fax:* (020) 7241 3460 *E-mail:* nickybowden@everbest.co.uk
3240 Vicente St, Apartment 3, San Francisco, CA 94116, United States, Contact: Brian Olshansky-Lucero *Tel:* 646-847-9874 *E-mail:* brian.olshansky-lucero@tpg.com.my

Toppan Security Printing Pte Ltd
97 Ubi Ave 4, Singapore 408754
Tel: 6741 2500 *Fax:* 6744 7098
Web Site: www.toppanleefung.com/toppansecurity.
   aspx
Key Personnel
President & Chief Executive Officer: Yeo Chee
   Tong
General Manager & Digital Printing: David
   Ng *Tel:* 6846 3518 *E-mail:* davidng@
   toppanleefung.com
Deputy Sales Dir, Security Printing: Rick
   Ang *Tel:* 6846 3912 *E-mail:* rickang@
   toppanleefung.com
Turnaround: 30 Workdays
Business from Other Countries: 40%
Parent Company: Toppan Printing Co Ltd, One
   Kanda Izumi-cho, Chiyoda-ku, Toyko 101-
   0024, Japan

Slovakia

Neografia AS
ul Sucianska 39 A, 038 61 Martin-Priekopa
Tel: (043) 4201 241 *Fax:* (043) 4201 704
E-mail: info@neografia.sk
Web Site: www.neografia.sk
Key Personnel
General Dir: Patrick Schwab *E-mail:* patrick.
   schwab@neografia.sk
Production Dir: Milos Lukac *Tel:* (043) 4201 300
   E-mail: milos.lukac@neografia.sk
Commercial Dir: Helena Magvasiova *Tel:* (043)
   4201 240 *E-mail:* helena.magvasiova@
   neografia.sk
Financial Dir: Peter Budisky *Tel:* (043) 4201 400
   E-mail: peter.budisky@neografia.sk
Founded: 1869

Polygraf Print spol sro
Capajevova 44, 080 01 Presov
Tel: (051) 77 13 285; (051) 74 60 111 *Fax:* (051)
   77 13 270; (051) 77 13 271
E-mail: polygrafprint@polygrafprint.sk
Web Site: www.polygrafprint.sk
Key Personnel
General Dir: Stanislav Potocnak *Tel:* (051) 77 13
   272 *E-mail:* potocnak@polygrafprint.sk
Assistant General Dir: Vladimir Kirchnerova
   Tel: (051) 77 13 272-3
Commercial Dir: Drahos Kvasna *Tel:* (051) 74 60
   113 *E-mail:* kvasna@polygrafprint.sk
Founded: 1996
Parent Company: Grafobal Group AS

Slovenia

DZS Grafik doo
Ul Jozeta Jame 12, SI-1210 Ljubljana-Sentvid
Tel: (01) 586 72 00 *Fax:* (01) 586 72 15
E-mail: info@dzs-grafik.si
Web Site: www.dzs-grafik.si
Key Personnel
Dir: Marko Tomazevic *E-mail:* marko.
   tomazevic@dzs-grafik.si
Dir, Graphic Services: Ksenija Blazevic
   E-mail: blazevic@dzs-grafik.si
Dir, Paper Sector: Bojan Forjan *E-mail:* bojan.
   forjan@dzs-grafik.si
Parent Company: DZS dd

Gorenjski Tisk Storitve doo
Ul Mirka Vadnova 6, SI-4000 Kranj
Tel: (04) 20 16 300 *Fax:* (04) 20 16 301

E-mail: info@go-tisk.si
Web Site: www.go-tisk.si
Key Personnel
Mng Dir: Goran Celesnik *Tel:* (04) 20 16 330
   E-mail: goran.celesnik@go-tisk.si
Dir, Sales & Marketing: Dr Andrej Krope, PhD
   Tel: (04) 20 16 326 *E-mail:* andrej.krope@go-
   tisk.si
Production Manager: Dusan Kuljic *Tel:* (04) 20
   16 451 *E-mail:* dusan.kuljic@go-tisk.si
Founded: 1888
Turnaround: 30 Workdays
Business from Other Countries: 50%

South Africa

CTP Printers Cape Town
Division of Caxton & CTP Publishers & Printers
   Ltd
12-14 Boompies St, Parow, Cape Town 7501
Tel: (021) 929 6200 *Fax:* (021) 939 1559
E-mail: ctp@ctpprinters.co.za; info@ctpprinters.
   co.za
Web Site: www.ctpprinters.co.za
Key Personnel
Chief Executive Officer: Caroline Sturgeon
Dir: Vaughn Glover *E-mail:* vaughng@
   ctpprinters.co.za; Wayne Julies
   E-mail: waynej@ctpprinters.co.za
Operations Dir: Colin Sturgeon
Sales Dir: Paul Snowdon

South Korea

KK Printing Co Ltd, see Kum-Kang Printing Co
   Ltd

Kum-Kang Printing Co Ltd
356 Jikji-gil, Paju Book-City, Kyunggi-do 413-
   120
Tel: (031) 943 0082 *Fax:* (031) 943 0046
E-mail: trade@kkprint.co.kr
Web Site: www.kkprint.co.kr
Key Personnel
Chief Executive Officer: Chang-Kyu Song

Mirae N Co Ltd
321 Sinbanpo-ro, Seocho-gu, Seoul 137-905
Fax: (02) 541-8158
Web Site: www.mirae-n.com
Key Personnel
President: Kim Young-jin
Manager: Ji Young Park *Tel:* (02) 3475-3870
   E-mail: park.jiyoung@mirae-n.com
Founded: 1948

Pacom Korea Inc
8F, Jellone Tower II 159-4, Jeongja-dong,
   Bundang-gu, Seongnam-si, Gyeonggi-do 463-
   834
Tel: (031) 718 3666 *Fax:* (031) 718 5857
E-mail: info@gopacom.com
Web Site: www.gopacom.com; pacomprinting.com
   (English)
Key Personnel
Chief Executive Officer: Kyong Su Kim
General Manager: J S Kook
Prepress Manager: Sang Yong Jo
Founded: 1999
Branch Office(s)
7-12 Rd 59, Nongsim-ro, Gunpo-si, Gyeonggi-do
   435-831 *Fax:* (031) 452 7519
Sales Office(s): Printmodel, Paris, France, Con-
   tact: Frederic Dahan *Tel:* 09 52 35 69 58

Freerun Co Ltd, Chuo-ku, Tokyo, Japan, Contact:
   Hidetake Imai *Tel:* (03) 5651-3011
Benicia, CA, United States, Contact: Jerry Jee
   Tel: 707-746-1670 *Fax:* 707-746-0670
Los Angeles, CA, United States, Contact: Sabra
   Chili *Tel:* 310-993-0058; 310-425-8258
Framingham, MA, United States, Contact: Sung S
   Yun *Tel:* 508-651-8851 *Fax:* 508-651-9187
Waxhaw, NC, United States, Contact: Petrice
   Beard *Tel:* 704-906-6642; 704-243-7205
Flower Mound, TX, United States, Contact:
   Lawrence Dagadu *Tel:* 972-724-0120 *Fax:* 972-
   539-5597

Samhwa Printing Co Ltd
237-10, Kuro-dong, Kuro-ku, Seoul 08382
Fax: (02) 8500-777
Web Site: www.samhwaprinting.com
Key Personnel
Founder & Chairman: Mr Ki-jung Ryu
President: Mr Sung-keun Ryu
Senior Manager: Henry Park *Tel:* (02) 8500-775
   E-mail: henry@samhwaprinting.com
Founded: 1954

Tara TPS Co Ltd
245 Sangjiseok-gil, Paju-si, Kyunggi-do 413-140
Tel: (031) 945 1080 *Fax:* (031) 942 9547
Web Site: www.taratps.com
Key Personnel
President & Chief Executive Officer: Jae-Soo Lee
Dir: Winston Park *Tel:* (031) 939 2040
   E-mail: winston@taratps.com
General Manager: Chris Kim *Tel:* (031) 939 2077
   E-mail: chris@taratps.com; I W Lee *Tel:* (031)
   939 2125 *E-mail:* julee@taratps.com
Founded: 1989

Spain

Artes Graficas Palermo SL
Ave de la Tecnica, 7, 28522 Rivas, Madrid
Tel: 91 499 01 30
E-mail: palermo@agpalermo.es
Web Site: www.agpalermo.es

Graficas Estella SL
Crta Estella-Tafalla km 2, 31132 Villatuerta-
   Estella, Navarra
Tel: 948 54 84 00
Web Site: estellaprint.com
Key Personnel
President & Chief Executive Officer: Francisco
   Gonzalez Cudeiro
General Manager & Commercial Dir: Jesus
   Uranga
Export Dir: Sonia Luqui *Tel:* 948 54 84 66
   E-mail: s.luqui@graficasestella.com
Founded: 1968
Parent Company: Lantero Group
Branch Office(s)
C/ Carme Galceran Nº4, Molins de Rei, 08750
   Barcelona *Tel:* 936 68 55 21
C/ Ave del Sol, 1, Torrejon de Ardoz, 28850
   Madrid *Tel:* 916 75 60 00

Graficas Santa Maria
Av Blas Infante, s/n, 41100 Coria del Rio, Seville
Tel: 954 771 091
Web Site: graficassantamaria.com
Founded: 1960
Turnaround: 1 Workday
Business from Other Countries: 15%

Sri Lanka

M D Gunasena & Co Ltd
No 217, Olcott Mawatha, Colombo 11
Tel: (011) 2323981; (011) 2323982; (011)
2323983; (011) 2323984 *Fax:* (011) 2323336
E-mail: headoffice@mdgunasena.com; info@
mdgunasena.com
Web Site: www.mdgunasena.com

Sarvodaya Vishva Lekha
Unit of Sarvodaya
No 98, Rawatawatta Rd, Moratwa 10400
Tel: (011) 264-7159 *Fax:* (011) 2656-512
Web Site: www.sarvodaya.org
Founded: 1985

Sumathi Printers (Pvt) Ltd
Subsidiary of Sumathi Global Consolidated (Pvt)
Ltd
445/1, Sirimavo Bandaranaike Mawatha, Colombo
14
Tel: (011) 2330673; (011) 2330674 *Fax:* (011)
2399924
E-mail: spb@sumathi.lk
Web Site: www.sumathi.lk/xampp/printing.html
Founded: 1980
Business from Other Countries: 75%

Switzerland

Canisius Druck & Grafik
Beauregard 3, 1700 Fribourg
Tel: (026) 425 51 61
E-mail: info@canisius.ch
Web Site: www.canisius.ch
Key Personnel
Dir: Beat Schultheiss
Founded: 1898

EMB-Service fuer Verleger
Talrain 6, 6043 Adligenswil Lucerne
Tel: (041) 410 50 68
E-mail: info@embservice.ch
Web Site: www.embservice.ch

Imprimerie Messeiller SA
Route des Falaises 94, 2000 Neuchatel
Tel: (032) 725 12 96 *Fax:* (032) 724 19 37
E-mail: admin@messeiller.ch
Web Site: www.messeiller.ch
Key Personnel
Dir: Raphael Gambarini *E-mail:* raphael@
messeiller.ch

Manufacture of Art
Seestr 105, 9326 Horn
Tel: (071) 888 6663 *Fax:* (071) 888 6664
E-mail: info@manufacture-of-art.com
Web Site: www.manufacture-of-art.com
Key Personnel
Mng Dir: Sabine Irion
Founded: 2009

Photolitho AG
Industriestr 12, 8625 Gossau
Tel: (043) 833 70 20
E-mail: info@photolitho.ch
Web Site: www.photolitho.ch
Key Personnel
Mng Dir: Michael von Eicke *E-mail:* voneicke@
photolitho.ch
Client Advisor: Juergen Luedicke
E-mail: luedicke@photolitho.ch

Founded: 1965
Business from Other Countries: 50%

Taiwan

Red & Blue Color Printing Co Ltd
9, Lane 327, Sect 2, Zhongshan Rd, Zhonghe
District, New Taipei City 23547
Tel: (02) 2240-1141 *Fax:* (02) 2240-7087
E-mail: webmaster@redblue.com.tw
Web Site: www.redblue.com.tw
Founded: 1965

Tanzania

Peramiho Printing Press
PO Box 41, Songea, Ruvuma
Tel: (025) 260 2299
Founded: 1937

Thailand

Amarin Printing & Publishing Public Co Ltd
378 Chaiyaphruk Rd, Taling Chan, Bangkok
10170
Tel: (02) 882-1010; (02) 422-9000 *Fax:* (02) 433-
2742; (02) 434-1385
Web Site: www.amarin.co.th
Key Personnel
President: Mrs Metta Utakapan
Administrative Dir: Bussapakes Wongchaoum
Sales Dir: Jutamas Smitanon
Founded: 1976

Cyberprint Group
959 Soi Suthiporn, Prachasongkroh Rd, Ding-
daeng, Bangkok 10400
Tel: (02) 641-9135-8 *Fax:* (02) 641-9139
E-mail: info@cyberprint.co.th; digital@
cyberprint.th
Web Site: www.cyberprint.co.th

Phongwarin Printing Ltd
299-299/1 Moo 10, Sukhumvit 107, Sumrongnue,
Ampur Muang, Samutprakarn 10270
Tel: (02) 7498934-45; (02) 7498275-79; (02)
3994525-31 *Fax:* (02) 3994524; (02) 3994255;
(02) 3931028
E-mail: intemarketing@phongwarin.co.th
Web Site: www.phongwarin.co.th
Key Personnel
Mng Dir: Mr Somphong Charnsirisaksakul
Founded: 1983
Turnaround: 7 Workdays
Business from Other Countries: 5%

Siam Offset Co Ltd
9/1 Soi Sri Ak-Sorn, Tungmahamek, Sathorn,
Bangkok 10120
Tel: (02) 249-1575; (02) 249-1576; (02) 249-
5419; (02) 249-5420 *Fax:* (02) 249-5415
E-mail: info@siamoffset.com
Web Site: www.siamoffset.com
Founded: 1950

Sirivatana Interprint PLC
125 Soi Chan 32, Chan Rd, Thungwatdon,
Sathorn, Bangkok 10120
Tel: (02) 6755600 *Fax:* (02) 6755623

Web Site: www.sirivatana.co.th
Key Personnel
Mng Dir: Tavinee Samatiyadekul
E-mail: tavinee@sirivatana.co.th
Founded: 1976
Branch Office(s)
14/8 Moo 12, Bangna-Trad Km 46 Rd, Bang-
pakong, Chachoengsao 24130 *Tel:* (038)
532000 *Fax:* (038) 830716

Turkey

Bilnet Baski Sistemleri AS
Dudullu Organize Sanayi Bolgesi, One Cadde No
16, 34775 Umraniye, Istanbul
Tel: (0216) 444 44 03 *Fax:* (0216) 365 99 07-08
E-mail: info@bilnet.net.tr
Web Site: www.bilnet.net.tr
Founded: 2007
Parent Company: Bilfen Group

EGE Basim
Esatpasa Mah Ziyapasa Cad No 4, 34704 Atase-
hir, Istanbul
Tel: (0216) 470 4470 *Fax:* (0216) 472 8405
E-mail: ege@egebasim.com.tr
Web Site: www.egebasim.com.tr

Elma Basim Yayin ve Iletisim
Halkali Cad, No 162/7 Sefakoy Kucukcekmece,
34295 Istanbul
Tel: (0212) 697 30 30 *Fax:* (0212) 697 70 70
E-mail: elma@elmabasim.com
Web Site: www.elmabasim.com
Key Personnel
Partner: Cafer Ihsan Elhan; Mehmet Karagoz

Imak Ofset Basim Yayin
Merkez Mah Ataturk Cd Gol Sk No 1, 34192
Yenibosna, Istanbul
Tel: (0212) 656 49 97 *Fax:* (0212) 656 29 26
E-mail: info@imakofset.com.tr
Web Site: www.imakofset.com.tr
Founded: 1997

Karakter Color AS
Mas/Sit No 200, 34560 Bagcilar, Istanbul
Tel: (0212) 4323001 *Fax:* (0212) 6289565
E-mail: info@karaktercolor.com.tr
Web Site: www.karaktercolor.com
Founded: 1959

Mega Basim Yayin San ve Tic AS
Guvercin Cad, No 3/1 Baha Is Merkezi, 34310
Haramidere, Istanbul
Tel: (0212) 412 1700 *Fax:* (0212) 422 1151
E-mail: info@mega.com.tr
Web Site: www.mega.com.tr
Founded: 1991

Ofset Yapimevi
Sair Sokak 4, 34410 Kagithane, Istanbul
Tel: (0212) 295 86 01 *Fax:* (0212) 295 64 55
E-mail: sales@ofset.com
Web Site: www.ofset.com
Key Personnel
Dir, Business Development & Fine Art: Ferah
Perker *E-mail:* ferah.perker@ofset.com
International Business Development & Export
Dir: Sandra Kohen Filizer
Founded: 1982

Olusur Basim Hizmetleri Sanayi Ticaret AS
Vuzyil Mah Mas-Sit Matbaacilar Sitesi, 4 Cad No
52-53, 34204 Bagcilar, Istanbul
Tel: (0212) 6290606 *Fax:* (0212) 6290594

E-mail: info@olusur.com.tr
Web Site: olusur.com
Key Personnel
Chairman & Chief Executive Officer: Sadettin
    Kasikirik
Chief Financial Officer: Ali Atmacaoglu
Chief Operating Officer: Erhan Dohuman
Business Development Manager: Kerem At-
    macaoglu
Marketing Manager: Baris Kasikirik

Pasifik Ofset Ltd Sti
Guvercin Cad No 3/1, Baha Is Merkezi Blok A,
    34310 Haramidere, Istanbul
Tel: (0212) 412 17 77 *Fax:* (0212) 422 11 51
E-mail: info@pasifikofset.com.tr
Web Site: www.pasifikofset.com.tr

Ukraine

Unisoft Book Factory
Morozova Str 136, Kharkov 61036
Tel: 57 730-17-13; 57 730-17-09 (prepress)
E-mail: info@ttornado.com.ua
Web Site: ttornado.com.ua
Founded: 1994

United Arab Emirates

United Printing & Publishing (UPP)
PO Box 39955, Abu Dhabi
Tel: (02) 5039 998; (02) 5039 999 *Fax:* (02) 5039
    990
E-mail: info@upp.ae
Web Site: www.upp.ae

UPP, see United Printing & Publishing (UPP)

United Kingdom

Aradco VSI Ltd
Aradco House, 128-134 Cleveland St, London
    W1T 6AB
Tel: (020) 7692 7700 *Fax:* (020) 7692 7711
E-mail: info@aradco.com
Web Site: www.aradco.com
Key Personnel
Chairman: N J Dawood
Founded: 1958
Business from Other Countries: 20%

AT&T Group Ltd
Alexander House, 64 Robin Hood Lane, Hall
    Green, Birmingham B28 0JT
Tel: (0121) 603 6344
E-mail: info@att-group.com
Web Site: www.att-group.com
Key Personnel
Mng Dir: Mr Sikander Ahmed
Founded: 1971
Business from Other Countries: 50%

Axicon Innovations Ltd
Church Rd, Weston on the Green, Oxon OX25
    3QP

Tel: (01869) 351155 *Fax:* (01869) 352404
E-mail: info@axicon.com; sales@axicon.com
Web Site: www.axicon.com
Key Personnel
Mng Dir: Peter Hicks
Founded: 1978
Turnaround: 1-2 Workdays
Business from Other Countries: 30%
Branch Office(s)
Axicon China, Ying Qi Tiao Ma Jing, Xiang
    Xing Lou B2, No 68 Qian Tou Rd, Dong-
    guan, Guangdong 523106, China *Tel:* (0136)
    00 285 982 *E-mail:* hhy228229@126.com *Web
    Site:* www.axicon.cn
Axicon France, 11 rue Perdonnet, 75010 Paris,
    France *Tel:* 01 55 06 19 77 *Fax:* 01 73 72 98
    44 *E-mail:* info@axicon.fr *Web Site:* www.
    axicon.fr
Axicon Netherlands, Wilhelminapassage 12, 5831
    GX Boxmeer, Netherlands *Tel:* (044) 79124
    78060 *E-mail:* wvb@axicon.com
Axicon South Africa, 9 Lavenham Rd, Ron-
    debosch, Weston Cape 7700, South Africa
    Tel: (021) 6891124 *Fax:* (021) 6896314
Axicon Espana, Torres Trade, Gran Via de Car-
    los III, 84, 08028 Barcelona, Spain *Tel:* 93 492
    3407 *Fax:* 93 496 5701 *E-mail:* info@axicon.es
    Web Site: www.axicon.es
U.S. Office(s): Axicon Auto ID LLC, 3262
    Hardisty Ave, Cincinnati, OH 45208-3007,
    United States *Tel:* 513-871-6657 *Fax:* 513-672-
    9679 *Web Site:* www.axicon.us

W&G Baird Ltd
Greystone Press, Caulside Dr, Antrim BT41 2RS
Tel: (028) 9446 3911 *Fax:* (028) 9446 6250
E-mail: wgbaird@wgbaird.com
Web Site: www.wgbaird.com
Key Personnel
Owner: David Hinds
Mng Dir: Patrick Moffett
Commercial Dir: Ian McCurry
Business Development Manager: Amanda Stewart
Founded: 1862
Business from Other Countries: 45%
Sales Office(s): 8 Braefell Close, West Bridg-
    ford, Nottingham, Notts NG2 6SS *Tel:* (07918)
    742161
Broomfield House, Malahide, Dublin, Ireland
    Tel: (0872) 585 273

Baseline Creative Ltd
25 Oakwood Rd, Henleaze, Bristol BS9 4NP
Tel: (0117) 962 0006
Web Site: www.baseline.co
Key Personnel
Owner: John Buchmueller
Founded: 1984
Turnaround: 30 Workdays

Bell & Bain Ltd
303 Burnfield Rd, Thornliebank, Glasgow G46
    7UQ
Tel: (0141) 649 5697 *Fax:* (0141) 632 8733
Web Site: www.bell-bain.com
Key Personnel
Co-Owner & Mng Dir: Stephen Docherty
    E-mail: sd@bell-bain.co.uk
Co-Owner & Sales Dir: Tony Campbell
    E-mail: tcampbell@bell-bain.co.uk
Operations Dir: Karen Baillie *E-mail:* kbaillie@
    bell-bain.co.uk
Sales Dir Designate: Derek Kenney
    E-mail: dkenney@bell-bain.co.uk
Customer Services Manager: Tracey Mallon
    E-mail: tmallon@bell-bain.co.uk
Information Technology Manager: Gordon Rogers
    E-mail: grogers@bell-bain.co.uk
Prepress Supervisor: Paul McCormack
    E-mail: pmccormack@bell-bain.co.uk
Founded: 1831

Turnaround: 7-10 Workdays
Business from Other Countries: 25%

Blackmore Ltd
Longmead, Shaftesbury, Dorset SP7 8PX
Tel: (01747) 853034 *Fax:* (01747) 854500
E-mail: sales@blackmore.co.uk
Web Site: www.blackmore.co.uk
Key Personnel
Mng Dir: Peter Smith
Parent Company: TH Brickell Group

Book Production Consultants Ltd
Affiliate of Granta Editions
25-27 High St, Chesterton, Cambridge, Cambs
    CB4 1ND
Tel: (01223) 352790; (01223) 841748
    Fax: (01223) 460718
E-mail: enquiries@bpccam.co.uk
Web Site: www.bpccam.co.uk
Key Personnel
Mng Dir: Colin Walsh
Founded: 1973
Business from Other Countries: 25%

Cambridge University Press - Printing Division
Division of Cambridge University Press
University Printing House, Shaftesbury Rd, Cam-
    bridge, Cambs CB2 8BS
Tel: (01223) 358331
E-mail: information@cambridge.org
Web Site: www.cambridge.org/us/information/
    about.htm
Founded: 1534

Charlesworth Press
Flanshaw Way, Flanshaw Lane, Wakefield WF2
    9LP
Tel: (01924) 204 830 *Fax:* (01924) 332 637
E-mail: info@charlesworth-group.com; cw.sales@
    charlesworth.com
Web Site: www.charlesworth.com
Key Personnel
Mng Dir: David Boothman
Commercial Dir: Sue Sheldon *Tel:* (07870) 239
    480 *E-mail:* sue.sheldon@charlesworth.com
Sales Manager: Nick Crowther *Tel:* (07775) 503
    476 *E-mail:* nick.crowther@charlesworth.com
Founded: 1928
Turnaround: 1 to 10 Workdays
Business from Other Countries: 30%
Parent Company: Charlesworth Group

William Clowes Ltd, see CPI William Clowes
    Ltd

CPI Antony Rowe
Bumper's Farm, Chippenham, Wilts SN14 6LH
Tel: (01249) 659705 *Fax:* (01249) 443103
Web Site: www.cpi-print.co.uk
Key Personnel
General Manager: Martin Collyer
Sales Manager: Geoff Fisher
Divisional Mng Dir: Alison Kaye
Founded: 1983
Turnaround: 10 Workdays
Business from Other Countries: 10%
Parent Company: CPI Group UK Ltd
Branch Office(s)
48-50 Birch Close, Eastbourne, East Sussex
    BN23 6PE *Tel:* (01323) 434 700

CPI William Clowes Ltd
Copland Way, Ellough, Beccles, Suffolk NR34
    7TL
Tel: (01502) 712884
E-mail: williamclowes@cpibooks.co.uk
Key Personnel
Divisional Mng Dir: Alison Kaye
Head, Sales: Jonathan Huddart
Founded: 1803
Turnaround: 10 Workdays

Business from Other Countries: 1%
Parent Company: CPI Group UK Ltd
Ultimate Parent Company: CPI Group

Diagram Visual Information Ltd
34 Elaine Grove, London NW5 4QH
Tel: (020) 7485 5941 *Fax:* (020) 7485 5941
E-mail: info@diagramgroup.com
Web Site: www.diagramgroup.com
Key Personnel
Mng Dir: Bruce Robertson
  E-mail: brucerobertson@diagramgroup.com
Administration: Eva Flores *E-mail:* evaflores@
  diagramgroup.com
Founded: 1960
Business from Other Countries: 80%

Headley Brothers Ltd
The Invicta Press, Queens Rd, Ashford, Kent
  TN24 8HH
Tel: (01233) 623131 *Fax:* (01233) 612345
E-mail: printing@headley.co.uk; sales@headley.
  co.uk
Web Site: www.headley.co.uk
Key Personnel
Chief Executive Officer: Roger Pitt *E-mail:* roger.
  pitt@headley.co.uk
Commercial Dir: Jon Pitt *E-mail:* jon.pitt@
  headley.co.uk
Sales Dir: Paul Palmer *E-mail:* paul.palmer@
  headley.co.uk
Founded: 1881
Business from Other Countries: 3%

Hobbs The Printers Ltd
Brunel Rd, Totton, Hants SO40 3WX
Tel: (023) 8066 4800 *Fax:* (023) 8066 4801
E-mail: info@hobbs.uk.com
Web Site: www.hobbstheprinters.co.uk; www.
  hobbs.uk.com
Key Personnel
Mng Dir: David Hobbs *E-mail:* d.a.hobbs@hobbs.
  uk.com
Deputy Mng & Operations Dir: Graham Bromley
  E-mail: g.bromley@hobbs.uk.com
Commercial Dir: Terry Ozanne *E-mail:* t.
  ozanne@hobbs.uk.com
Customer Services Manager: Colin Richardson
  E-mail: c.richardson@hobbs.uk.com
Founded: 1884
Turnaround: 5-10 days litho; up to 5 days digital
Business from Other Countries: 4%

Holbrook Design Oxford Ltd
Holbrook House, 105 Rose Hill, Oxford OX4
  4HT
Tel: (01865) 459000 *Fax:* (01865) 459006
Web Site: www.holbrook-design.co.uk
Key Personnel
Mng Dir: Peter Tucker
Founded: 1974
Business from Other Countries: 20%

Intype Libra Ltd
3/4 Elm Grove Industrial Estate, Elm Grove,
  Wimbledon, London SW19 4HE
Tel: (020) 8947 7863 *Fax:* (020) 8947 3652
E-mail: hello@intypelibra.co.uk
Web Site: www.intypelibra.co.uk
Key Personnel
Owner & Mng Dir: Tony Chapman
Owner: David Greenwood
Founded: 1974
Turnaround: 10-15 Workdays for proofs; 5-10
  Workdays for books
Business from Other Countries: 5%

Keytec Typesetting Ltd
Hounsell Bldgs, North Mills, Bridport, Dorset
  DT6 3BE
Tel: (01308) 427580

E-mail: info@keytectype.co.uk
Web Site: www.keytectype.co.uk
Key Personnel
Mng Dir: Mark Riddington
Founded: 1983

Lavenham Press Ltd
Arbons House, 47 Water St, Lavenham, Suffolk
  CO10 9RN
Tel: (01787) 247436 *Fax:* (01787) 248267
E-mail: enquiries@lavenhamgroup.co.uk
Web Site: www.lavenhampress.com
Key Personnel
Mng Dir: Terence Dalton
Founded: 1953
Parent Company: Lavenham Group

Librios Ltd
20 Lochaline St, London W6 9SH
Tel: (020) 3355 0200
E-mail: info@librios.com
Web Site: www.librios.com
Key Personnel
Software Development Dir: David Wilcockson
  E-mail: david@librios.com
System Administrator: Neville Mooney
Project Developer: Chris Lewis *E-mail:* chris.
  lewis@librios.com
Founded: 1997
Business from Other Countries: 30%

Linden Artists Ltd
41 Battersea Business Centre, 103 Lavender Hill,
  London SW11 5QL
Tel: (020) 7738 2505 *Fax:* (020) 7738 2513
E-mail: lindenartists@aol.com
Web Site: www.lindenartists.co.uk
Key Personnel
Dir: Martin J Gibbs; Sheila Wall
Founded: 1962
Business from Other Countries: 30%

Lowfield Printing Co Ltd
9 Kennet Rd, Dartford, Kent DA1 4QN
Tel: (01322) 522216 *Fax:* (01322) 555362
E-mail: info@lowfieldprinting.co.uk
Web Site: www.lowfieldprinting.co.uk
Key Personnel
Mng Dir: James Dow
Dir: Nigel Starkey *E-mail:* nigel@
  lowfieldprinting.co.uk
Founded: 1964

Market House Books Ltd
Elsinore House, Suite B, 43 Buckingham St,
  Aylesbury, Bucks HP20 2NQ
Tel: (01296) 484911
E-mail: books@mhbref.com
Web Site: www.markethousebooks.com
Key Personnel
Dir: Anne Kerr
Editorial Dir: Jonathan Law
Mng Editor: Elizabeth Martin
Founded: 1970

Page Bros (Norwich) Ltd
Subsidiary of Milex Ltd
Mile Cross Lane, Norwich, Norfolk NR6 6SA
Tel: (01603) 778800 *Fax:* (01603) 778801
E-mail: info@pagebros.co.uk
Web Site: www.pagebros.co.uk
Key Personnel
Mng Dir: Craig Eastaugh *E-mail:* c.eastaugh@
  pagebros.co.uk
Sales & Commercial Dir: Andrew Spelman
  E-mail: a.spelman@pagebros.co.uk
Founded: 1750
Turnaround: 10 Workdays
Business from Other Countries: 20%

Pindar Scarborough Ltd
Thornburgh Rd, Eastfield, Scarborough, N Yorks
  YO11 3UY
Tel: (01723) 581581 *Fax:* (01723) 583086
E-mail: pindarestimates@pindar.com
Web Site: www.pindar.com
Key Personnel
Group Sales Dir: Norman Revill *Tel:* (07725)
  219763 *E-mail:* n.revill@pindar.com
Commercial Manager: David Stephenson
  Tel: (01723) 502387 *E-mail:* d.stephenson@
  pindar.com

Playne Books Ltd
25 Melbourne Close, Stonehouse, Glos GL10
  2PY
Tel: (01453) 826094
Key Personnel
Design & Production Dir: David Playne
Founded: 1996

Shore Books & Design
Castle House, E Winch Rd, Blackborough End,
  King's Lynn, Norfolk PE32 1SF
Tel: (01553) 842477; (07896) 844867 (cell)
E-mail: enquiries@shore-books.co.uk
Web Site: www.shore-books.co.uk
Key Personnel
Owner: Nigel Mitchell

Smith Settle
Gateway Dr, Yeadon, W Yorks LS19 7XY
Tel: (0113) 250 9201 *Fax:* (0113) 250 9223
Web Site: www.smithsettle.com
Key Personnel
Mng Dir: Don Walters *E-mail:* dwalters@
  smithsettle.com
Financial Dir: Tracey Thorne *E-mail:* tthorne@
  smithsettle.com
Founded: 1981

University of London Central Printing Services
University of London, Senate House, Malet St,
  London WC1E 7HU
Tel: (020) 7862 8000; (020) 7862 8163
E-mail: print.services@london.ac.uk
Web Site: w01.uoldev.wf.ulcc.ac.uk/printing.html

Gavin Watson Printers
79-109 Glasgow Rd, Glasgow G72 0LY
Tel: (01698) 826000 *Fax:* (01698) 824944
Web Site: www.gavinwatson.co.uk
Key Personnel
Chief Executive Officer: Tom Brown
  E-mail: tbrown@gavinwatson.co.uk
Founded: 1863
Turnaround: 7 days
Business from Other Countries: 5%

United States

A-R Editions Inc
1600 Aspen Commons, Suite 100, Middleton, WI
  53562
Tel: 608-836-9000 *Fax:* 608-831-8200
E-mail: info@areditions.com
Web Site: www.areditions.com
Key Personnel
Pres & CEO: Patrick Wall *Tel:* 608-203-2575
  E-mail: patrick.wall@areditions.com
Dir, Publg Servs: Lance Ottman *E-mail:* lance.
  ottman@areditions.com
Dir, Spec Projs: James Zychowicz *Tel:* 608-203-
  2580 *E-mail:* james.zychowicz@areditions.com
Founded: 1962
Business from Other Countries: 10%

ADR Inc
2012 E Northern St, Wichita, KS 67216
Tel: 316-522-5599 *Toll Free Tel:* 800-767-6066
Fax: 316-522-5445
E-mail: info@adr.biz
Web Site: www.adr.biz
Key Personnel
CEO: Patrick Tuttle *E-mail:* ptuttle@adr.biz
Pres: Jim Rishel
Founded: 1978
Turnaround: 1-5 days
Business from Other Countries: 10%
Membership(s): Print Services & Distribution Association; Printing Industries of America

Arbor Books
244 Madison Ave, Box 254, New York, NY 10016-2834
Tel: 212-956-0950 *Toll Free Tel:* 877-822-2500
Fax: 914-737-3639
E-mail: info@arborbooks.com; editorial@ arborbooks.net
Web Site: www.arborbooks.com
Key Personnel
Owner: Joel Hochman *Tel:* 877-822-2502 *E-mail:* arborbooksjoel@aol.com; Larry Leichman *Tel:* 877-822-2504 *E-mail:* arborbookslarry@aol.com
Mktg Dir: Olga Vladi
Founded: 1992
BISAC compatible software
Turnaround: 21 Workdays; 1-7 for art
Business from Other Countries: 15%

Asia Pacific Offset Inc
1312 "Q" St NW, Suite B, Washington, DC 20009
Tel: 202-462-5436 *Toll Free Tel:* 800-756-4344
Fax: 202-986-4030
Web Site: www.asiapacificoffset.com
Key Personnel
Pres: Andrew Clarke *E-mail:* andrew@ asiapacificoffset.com
Founded: 1997
Turnaround: 105 Workdays including color separation & shipping
Business from Other Countries: 100%
Sales Office(s): 870 Market St, Suite 801, San Francisco, CA 94102, Dir, Sales: Amy Armstrong *Tel:* 415-433-3488 *Fax:* 415-433-3489 *E-mail:* amy@asiapacificoffset.com
62 Rivington St, Suite 2-B, New York, NY 10002, Dir, Sales: Simona Jansons *Tel:* 212-941-8300 *Fax:* 212-941-9810 *E-mail:* simona@ asiapacificoffset.com

Bang Printing Co Inc
3323 Oak St, Brainerd, MN 56401
Tel: 218-829-2877 *Toll Free Tel:* 800-328-0450
Fax: 218-829-7145
E-mail: info@bangprinting.com
Web Site: www.bangprinting.com
Key Personnel
CEO: Chris Kurtzman
EVP, Sales: Todd Vanek *Tel:* 218-822-2124 *E-mail:* toddv@bangprinting.com
SVP, Fin & Opers: Tom Campion
Founded: 1899
Turnaround: 10-25 Workdays
Business from Other Countries: 50%

C & C Offset Printing Co USA Inc
Subsidiary of C & C Joint Printing Co (HK) Ltd
70 W 36 St, Unit 10C, New York, NY 10018
Web Site: www.ccoffset.com
Key Personnel
Dir & EVP, C & C Offset Printing Co (USA) Inc, Portland, OR & C & C Offset Printing Co (NYC) Inc, New York, NY: Simon Chan *E-mail:* schan@ccoffset.com

VP, C & C Offset Printing Co (Chicago) Inc, Chicago, IL: Ernest Li *E-mail:* ernest.li@ ccoffset.com
Sales Mgr, C & C Offset Printing Co (NYC) Inc, New York, NY: Frances Harkness *E-mail:* fharkness@ccoffset.com; Timothy McNulty
CEO, C & C Joint Printing Co (HK) Ltd, Hong Kong: Jackson Leung
Mng Dir, Hong Kong Head Off: Ken Lee
Deputy Gen Mgr, Hong Kong Head Off: Kit Wong
Sr Sales Mgr (Spec Projs), Hong Kong Head Off: Francis Ho
Dir, C & C Offset Printing Co (France) Ltd: Michele Olson Niel *E-mail:* michele@ candcoffset.fr
Pres, C & C Printing Japan Co Ltd, Tokyo, Japan: Yamamoto Masaaki
Dir, C & C Offset Printing Co (UK) Ltd: Tracy Broderick *E-mail:* tracy@candcoffset.co.uk
Sales Rep, Australian Off: Lena Frew *E-mail:* lena.frew@candcprinting.com
Founded: 1980
Turnaround: Varies
Business from Other Countries: 70%
Branch Office(s)
C & C Offset Printing (Chicago) Inc, 800 W Fifth Ave, Suite 100D, Naperville, IL 60563 *Tel:* 630-737-0820; 630-390-5617 *Fax:* 630-737-1997
C & C Offset Printing Co Ltd (Australia Off), Lithocraft Graphics, 3-7 Permas Way, Trugania, Victoria 3029, Australia *Tel:* (613) 8366 0200 *Fax:* (613) 8366 0299
C & C Joint Printing Co (Beijing) Ltd, Beijing Economic & Technological Development Area (BDA), Donghuan North Rd, No 3, Beijing 100176, China *Tel:* (010) 6787 6655 *Fax:* (010) 6787 8255 *E-mail:* ccbj@candcprinting.cn (plant)
C & C Joint Printing Co (Guangdong) Ltd, Hua Xin Bldg E Block, Rm 1511, 2 Shuiyin Rd, Huanshi East, Guangzhou 510075, China *Tel:* (020) 3760 0979; (020) 3760 0980 *Fax:* (020) 3760 0977 *E-mail:* guangzhou@ candcprinting.com
C & C Joint Printing (Shanghai) Co Ltd, 3333 Cao Ying Rd, Qingpu Industrial Zone, Shanghai 201712, China *Tel:* (021) 5922 6000 *Fax:* (021) 5922 6111 *E-mail:* shanghai@ candcprinting.com *Web Site:* www. candcprinting.com (plant)
C & C Joint Printing Co (Guangdong) Ltd, Chunhu Industrial Estate, Pinghu, Long Gang, Shenzhen 518111, China *Tel:* (0755) 3360 9988 *Fax:* (0755) 3360 9998 *E-mail:* guangdong@candcprinting.com *Web Site:* www.candcprinting.com (plant)
C & C Offset Printing Co (France) Ltd, 15, rue d'Aboukir, 75002 Paris, France *Tel:* 01 40 26 21 07 *Fax:* 01 44 76 08 96
C & C Offset Printing Co Ltd, C & C Bldg, 36 Ting Lai Rd, Tai Po, New Territories, Hong Kong *Tel:* 2666 4988 *Fax:* 2666 4938 *E-mail:* info@candcprinting.com *Web Site:* www.candcprinting.com (corp headquarters)
C & C Printing Japan Co Ltd, Tozaido Bldg, 3F, 2-6-12 Hitotsubashi, Chiyoda-ku, Tokyo 101-0003, Japan *Tel:* (03) 5216 4580 *Fax:* (03) 5216 4610 *E-mail:* mail@candcprinting.co.jp *Web Site:* www.candcprinting.co.jp
C & C Offset Printing Co (UK) Ltd, 7-9 Charlotte St, 2nd fl, London W1T 1RG, United Kingdom *Tel:* (020) 7637 5033 *Fax:* (020) 7637 5044

Custom Studios
Subsidiary of Nationwide Custom Services Inc
77 Main St, Tappan, NY 10983
Tel: 845-365-0414 *Toll Free Tel:* 800-631-1362
Fax: 845-365-0864

E-mail: customusa@aol.com
Web Site: customstudios.com
Key Personnel
Owner & Pres: Norman Shaifer
VP: Helen Newman; Harry Title
Founded: 1960
Business from Other Countries: 15%

Desktop Miracles Inc
112 S Main St, Suite 294, Stowe, VT 05672
Tel: 802-253-7900 *Toll Free Fax:* 888-293-2676
Web Site: www.desktopmiracles.com
Key Personnel
CEO & Pres: Barry T Kerrigan *E-mail:* barry@ desktopmiracles.com
Founded: 1994
Turnaround: 10-15 Workdays
Business from Other Countries: 10%

DNP America LLC
Subsidiary of Dai Nippon Printing Co Ltd
335 Madison Ave, 3rd fl, New York, NY 10017
Tel: 212-503-1060 *Fax:* 212-286-1501
Web Site: www.dnpamerica.com
Key Personnel
Gen Mgr: Seiichi Suzuki
Founded: 1974
Turnaround: 30-60 Workdays
Business from Other Countries: 54%
Branch Office(s)
3235 Kifer Rd, Suite 100, Santa Clara, CA 95051 *Tel:* 408-735-8880
3858 Carson St, Suite 300, Torrance, CA 90503 *Tel:* 310-540-5123 *Fax:* 310-543-3260

Fairfield Marketing Group Inc
Subsidiary of FMG Inc
The Direct Mail Ctr, 830 Sport Hill Rd, Easton, CT 06112-1241
Tel: 203-261-5585; 203-261-5568 *Fax:* 203-261-0884
E-mail: info@fairfieldmarketing.com
Web Site: www.fairfieldmarketing.com
Key Personnel
CEO & Pres: Edward P Washchilla, Jr
VP, Cust Serv: Mike Lozada *Tel:* 203-261-5585 ext 204
VP, Fin: Pamela L Washchilla
VP, Fulfillment: Jason Paul Miller *Tel:* 203-261-5585 ext 203 *E-mail:* jason@fairfieldmarketing. com
Founded: 1987
Turnaround: 5-10 Workdays
Business from Other Countries: 10%
Membership(s): AAP PreK-12 Learning Group; ABA; Data & Marketing Association; Direct Marketing Club of New York; Education Market Association; Hudson Valley Direct Marketing Association; International Literacy Association; United States Chamber of Commerce

The Font Bureau Inc
Affiliate of Type Network
179 South St, 7th fl, Boston, MA 02111
Tel: 617-423-8770
E-mail: info@fontbureau.com
Web Site: fontbureau.typenetwork.com
Key Personnel
Founder: David Berlow; Roger Black
Founded: 1989
Turnaround: 1 Workday
Business from Other Countries: 20%

Goose River Press
3400 Friendship Rd, Waldoboro, ME 04572-6337
Tel: 207-832-6665
E-mail: gooseriverpress@roadrunner.com
Web Site: gooseriverpress.com
Key Personnel
Owner & Ed: Deborah J Benner
Founded: 1999

Turnaround: 20-40 Workdays
Business from Other Countries: 15%
Membership(s): Maine Writers & Publishers Alliance; Waldoboro Business Association

Innodata Inc
55 Challenger Rd, Suite 202, Ridgefield Park, NJ 07660
Tel: 201-371-8000 *Toll Free Tel:* 877-454-8400
E-mail: info@innodata.com; marketing@innodata.com
Web Site: www.innodata.com
Key Personnel
Pres & CEO: Jack S Abuhoff
EVP & COO: Ashok Kumar Mishra
SVP & CFO: O'Neil Nalavadi
Founded: 1988
Turnaround: As little as 12 hours
Business from Other Countries: 51%
Membership(s): AAP Professional & Scholarly Publishing Division; The Association for Work Process Improvement; Center for Information Development & Content Management Strategies; International Association of Outsourcing Professionals; National Federation of Abstracting and Information Services; Society for Technical Communication; Society of Knowledge Based Publishers; Software & Information Industry Association

K1 Creative
271 W First St, Eureka, MO 63025
Tel: 636-940-9146
Web Site: k1create.com
Key Personnel
Pres & Owner: Wayne Kissel *E-mail:* wkissel@k1create.com
Founded: 1989
Business from Other Countries: 20%

Leo Paper USA
Division of Leo Paper Group
1180 NW Maple St, Suite 102, Issaquah, WA 98027
Tel: 425-646-8801 *Fax:* 425-646-8805
E-mail: info@leousa.com
Web Site: www.leopaper.com
Key Personnel
SVP, Sales: John DiMasi *E-mail:* john@leousa.com
Founded: 1982
Turnaround: 30-40 Workdays
Business from Other Countries: 20%
Branch Office(s)
27 W 24 St, Suite 601, New York, NY 10010
Tel: 917-305-0708 *Fax:* 917-305-0709
E-mail: info@leousanewyork.com

MPS North America LLC
Subsidiary of MPS Ltd
5750 Major Blvd, Suite 100, Orlando, FL 32819
Tel: 407-472-1280 *Fax:* 212-981-2983
E-mail: marketing@adi-mps.com
Web Site: adi-mps.com
Key Personnel
CEO: Rahul Arora *E-mail:* rahul.arora@adi-mps.com
Founded: 1973
Business from Other Countries: 10%
Membership(s): Publishing Professionals Network

OGM USA
4141 44 St, Suite 3F, Sunnyside, NY 11104
Tel: 212-964-2430 *Fax:* 212-964-2497
Web Site: www.ogm.it
Key Personnel
Chmn, CEO & Sales Rep: Rino Varrasso *E-mail:* rvarrasso@ogm-usa.com

Founded: 1974
Turnaround: 30 Workdays
Business from Other Countries: 75%

Palace Printing & Design (PPD)
PO Box 12023, San Rafael, CA 94912
Tel: 415-526-1378
Key Personnel
Sales Dir: Sreedharan Vijayarangam *Tel:* 415-307-6065 (cell) *E-mail:* sreed@palacepress.com
Founded: 1984
Turnaround: 90 Workdays
Business from Other Countries: 20%

Printing Corp of the Americas Inc
620 SW 12 Ave, Fort Lauderdale, FL 33069
Tel: 954-781-8100 *Toll Free Tel:* 866-721-1PCA (721-1722) *Fax:* 954-781-8421
Web Site: www.commercialprintingflorida.com
Key Personnel
Pres: Jan Tuchman
Founded: 1979
Turnaround: 5-10 Workdays
Business from Other Countries: 15%

SENCOR International
445 Park Ave, 9th fl, New York, NY 10022
Tel: 212-980-6726
Web Site: www.sencorinternational.com
Key Personnel
CEO: George Martel *E-mail:* georgemartel@sencorinternational.com
Founded: 1984
BISAC compatible software
Turnaround: 5 Workdays
Business from Other Countries: 10%
Branch Office(s)
6781 Ayala Ave, 9th & 10th fl, 1226 Makati City, Philippines, EVP & Gen Mgr: Michael Martel *Tel:* (02) 817-1500 *Fax:* (02) 817-1504 *E-mail:* sales@sencor.net *Web Site:* www.sencor.net
377 Senator Gil Puyat Ave, 3rd & 4th fl, 1226 Makati City, Philippines *Tel:* (02) 817-1500 *Fax:* (02) 817-1504 *E-mail:* sales@sencor.net *Web Site:* www.sencor.net

Square Two Design Inc
2325 Third St, Suite 213, San Francisco, CA 94107
Tel: 415-437-3888
E-mail: info@square2.com
Web Site: www.square2.com
Key Personnel
Pres & Creative Dir: Eddie Lee *Tel:* 415-437-3888 ext 101
Founded: 1991
Business from Other Countries: 10%
Branch Office(s)
No 8 Hua Jia Di Nan Jie, Chao Yang District, Beijing 100102, China, Principal: Min Wang *Tel:* (01350) 1084-543 *E-mail:* mwang@square2.com

Studio 31 Inc
2740 SW Martin Downs Blvd, Suite 358, Palm City, FL 34990
Tel: 772-781-7195 *Fax:* 772-781-6044
Web Site: www.studio31.com
Key Personnel
Founder & Pres: James Wasserman *E-mail:* jim@studio31.com
Partner: Bill Corsa
Founded: 1977
Business from Other Countries: 10%

Taylor Specialty Books
Division of Balfour/Taylor

1550 W Mockingbird Lane, Dallas, TX 75235
Tel: 214-819-8588 (cust serv) *Fax:* 214-819-5051 (cust serv) *Toll Free Tel:* 800-203-9778
E-mail: rfq@taylorpub.com (estimates)
Web Site: www.taylorspecialtybooks.com
Key Personnel
VP, Sales & Mktg, Specialty Books: Rick Parra *Tel:* 214-819-5027 *E-mail:* rick.parra@balfour.com
Sales Rep: Kim Hawley *E-mail:* khawley@taylorpub.com; George Levesque *E-mail:* glevesque@taylorpub.com; Mark McCombs *E-mail:* mmcombs@taylorpub.com
Founded: 1939
Turnaround: 25-30 Workdays
Business from Other Countries: 10%

Toppan Best-Set Premedia Ltd
Subsidiary of Toppan Leefung (HK) Ltd
50 S Buckhout St, Suite 208, Irvington, NY 10533
Tel: 914-693-1565 *Toll Free Tel:* 866-888-8767 *Fax:* 914-674-5923
Web Site: www.toppanbestset.com
Key Personnel
Mng Dir (Hong Kong): Johnson Yeung *E-mail:* johnsonyeung@toppanleefung.com
Sales Rep: Wai Man Yeung *E-mail:* waimanyeung@toppanleefung.com
Founded: 1986
Turnaround: 10 Workdays
Business from Other Countries: 98%
Branch Office(s)
No 3, Da Song Gang, Jiang Nan Main Ave C, Guangzhou 510240, China, Contact: Patrick Au *Tel:* (020) 8441-5873 *E-mail:* bestset@toppanleefung.com (main prodn)
20/F Manulife Tower, 169 Electric Rd, North Point, Hong Kong, Contact: Cynthia Hui *Tel:* 2897 6033 *Fax:* 2897 5170 *E-mail:* cynthiahui@toppanleefung.com (headquarters)
33 Alpin Way, Isleworth, Middx TW7 4RJ, United Kingdom, Contact: Keith Harrocks *Tel:* (07515) 775 299 *E-mail:* keithharrocks@toppanleefung.com

Fred Weidner & Daughter Printers
99 Hudson St, 5th fl, New York, NY 10013
Tel: 646-706-5180
E-mail: info@fwdprinters.com
Web Site: www.fwdprinters.com
Key Personnel
Pres: Cynthia Weidner *E-mail:* cynthia@fwdprinters.com
Creative Dir: Carol Mittelsdorf *E-mail:* carol@fwdprinters.com
Founded: 1860
Turnaround: 5-10 Workdays
Business from Other Countries: 25%

Uzbekistan

Uzbekistan
ul Navoi 30, 100129 Tashkent
Tel: (871) 244-34-01; (871) 244-37-81 *Fax:* (871) 244-38-10
E-mail: info@iptd-uzbekistan.uz
Web Site: www.iptd-uzbekistan.uz
Key Personnel
Dir: Zair Tursunbaevich Isadjanov *E-mail:* isadjanov@iptd-uzbekistan.uz
First Deputy Dir: Mukhamadjon Zaytaev *Tel:* (871) 244-54-04 *E-mail:* zaytaev@iptd-uzbekistan.uz

Printing, Binding & Book Finishing Index

BOOK PRINTING - HARDBOUND

EDITION (HARDCOVER) BINDING

OFFSET PRINTING - WEB

Printing, Binding & Book Finishing

This section includes companies throughout the world that offer printing, binding and/or book finishing services. Those U.S. and Canadian companies with 10% or more of their business done outside North America are also included here. Immediately preceding this section is an index classifying companies by services offered.

Argentina

Editorial Dunken
Ayacucho 357, C1025AAG Buenos Aires
Tel: (011) 4954 7700; (011) 4954 7300
E-mail: info@dunken.com.ar
Web Site: www.dunken.com.ar
Key Personnel
Dir: Guillermo A de Urquiza
Founded: 1988

Proietto & Lamarque SA
Jose Marmol 2131, C1255ABW Buenos Aires
Tel: (011) 4925-0111; (011) 4921-1689; (011) 4924-1812
E-mail: info@lamarquenet.com; ventas@ lamarquenet.com; administracion@lamarquenet. com
Web Site: proiettoylamarque.com.ar
Founded: 1951

Armenia

Antares Ltd
50a/1 Mashtots Ave, 0009 Yerevan
Tel: (010) 58 76 69; (010) 58 10 59; (010) 58 09 59; (010) 56 15 26 *Fax:* (010) 58 76 69
E-mail: antares@antares.am
Web Site: antares.am
Founded: 1992
Parent Company: Antares Media Holding

Tigran Mets Publishing House
2 Arshakunyats Ave, 0023 Yerevan
Tel: (060) 62 32 06 *Fax:* (010) 52 22 48
E-mail: info@tigran-mets.am
Web Site: tigran-mets.am
Key Personnel
General Dir: Vrezh Markosyan

Australia

Ligare Pty Ltd
138-152 Bonds Rd, Riverwood, NSW 2210
Tel: (02) 9533 2555 *Fax:* (02) 9534 6320; (02) 9533 3719 (sales)
E-mail: info@ligare.com.au
Web Site: www.ligare.com.au
Founded: 1979
Business from Other Countries: 1%

Openbook Howden Design & Print
2-14 Paul St, St Marys, SA 5042
Tel: (08) 8124 0000 *Fax:* (08) 8277 2354
E-mail: sales@openbookhowden.com.au
Web Site: www.openbookhowden.com.au
Founded: 1913
Branch Office(s)
Melbourne, Victoria, Contact: Brendan Rodway *Tel:* (04) 1861 1579 *E-mail:* brendan@ openbookhowden.com.au

Austria

Bucher Druck GmbH
Diepoldsauer Str 41, 6845 Hohenems
Tel: (05576) 7118-0 *Fax:* (05576) 7118-44
E-mail: office@quintessence.at
Web Site: www.bucherverlag.com/druckerei
Key Personnel
Contact: Reinhard Schwaerzler *Tel:* (05576) 7118-23 *E-mail:* schwaerzler@quintessence.at
Founded: 1966

Herold Druck und Verlag AG
Faradaygasse 6, 1030 Vienna
Tel: (01) 79594-0 *Fax:* (01) 79594-550
E-mail: herold@herold.cc
Web Site: www.herold.cc
Key Personnel
Chief Executive: Leopold Kurz *Tel:* (01) 79594-525 *E-mail:* kurz@herold.cc

Belarus

Printcorp
40 F Skoriny St, 220141 Minsk
Tel: 17 267 7513; 17 267 0109 *Fax:* 17 265 90 98
E-mail: office@printcorp.biz
Web Site: printcorp.biz
Key Personnel
Dir: Olga Yushkevich
Deputy Dir, Marketing/Sales: Alex Zhuk *E-mail:* alex@printcorp.biz
Deputy Dir, Production: Alexander Sadovsky
Head, Production: Andrey Lebedka

Belgium

Crius Group
Industriepark 20, 2235 Hulshout
Tel: (015) 750 750 *Fax:* (015) 750 751
E-mail: info@crius-group.com
Web Site: www.crius-group.com
Founded: 1989

Cultura bvba
Hoenderstr 22, 9230 Wetteren
Tel: (09) 369 15 95 *Fax:* (09) 369 59 25
E-mail: info@cultura.be; cultura@cultura-net.com
Web Site: www.cultura.be
Key Personnel
Dir: Jan De Meester
Founded: 1893

Delabie SA
ZI La Martinoire, Blvd de l'Eurozone 9, 7700 Mouscron
Tel: (056) 84 10 00 *Fax:* (056) 84 09 62
E-mail: info@delabie.be
Web Site: www.delabie.be

Founded: 1964
Turnaround: 8 Workdays
Print Runs: 100,000 min - 1,000,000 max
Business from Other Countries: 60%

De Duurzame Drukker
Subsidiary of Graphius NV
Eekhoutdriesstr 67, 9041 Gent
Tel: (09) 218 08 41
E-mail: info@deduurzamedrukker.be
Web Site: www.deduurzamedrukker.be
Founded: 1898

Drukkerij Geers Offset
Subsidiary of Graphius NV
Eekhoutdriesstr 67, 9041 Gent
Tel: (09) 218 08 41
E-mail: info@geersoffset.be
Web Site: www.geersoffset.be
Founded: 1928

INNI Print NV
Industrielaan 5, 8501 Heule
Tel: (056) 36 32 11
E-mail: info@inniprint.com
Web Site: print.innigroup.com
Key Personnel
Mng Dir: Tom Deschildre *Tel:* (056) 36 32 25 *E-mail:* tom.deschildre@innigroup.com
Finance Dir: Nico Declerck *Tel:* (056) 36 32 37 *E-mail:* nico.declerck@innigroup.com
Operations Dir: David Strobbe *Tel:* (056) 36 19 99 *E-mail:* david.strobbe@innigroup.com
General Manager: David Tielemans *Tel:* (056) 36 32 03 *E-mail:* david.tielemans@innigroup.com
Founded: 1948
Parent Company: INNI Group NV

Drukkerij Lannoo NV (Lannoo Printers NV)
Plantinstr 6, 8700 Tielt
Tel: (051) 42 42 11 *Fax:* (051) 40 70 70
E-mail: info@lannooprint.be; lannoo@ lannooprint.be
Web Site: www.lannoo-print.be
Founded: 1909
Turnaround: 10 Workdays
Print Runs: 100 min - 1,000,000 max
Business from Other Countries: 30%

Drukkerij New Goff
Subsidiary of Graphius NV
Eekhoutdriesstr 67, 9041 Gent
Tel: (09) 218 08 41
E-mail: info@newgoff.be
Web Site: www.newgoff.be
Founded: 1976

Proost NV
Everdongenlaan 23, 2300 Turnhout
Tel: (014) 40 08 11 *Fax:* (014) 42 87 94
E-mail: proost@proost.be
Web Site: www.proost.be
Founded: 1913

Brunei

Brunei Press Sdn Bhd
Lot 8 & 11, Perindustrian Beribi II, Gadong BE
 1118
Tel: 2451468; 2451460 *Fax:* 2451460
E-mail: brupress@bruneipress.com.bn;
 marketing@bruneipress.com.bn
Branch Office(s)
Unit 8B, Supasave Panaga, Lorong 14 Barat,
 Seria KB 4533 *Tel:* 3334344; 3334345
 Fax: 3334346
Sales Office(s): Brunei Press Sales (M) Sdn Bhd,
 No 8-1-6, 1st floor, Menara Mutiara Bangsar, Jl
 Liku Off Jl Bangsar, 59100 Kuala Lumpur,
 Malaysia *Tel:* (03) 22876623 *Fax:* (03)
 22870093 *E-mail:* brupress@tm.net.my
Brunei Press Sales (S) Pte Ltd, Pico Creative
 Centre, 20 Kallang Ave, No 03-00, Singapore
 339411, Singapore *Tel:* 6297 9622 *Fax:* 6297
 9633 *E-mail:* brupress@singnet.com.sg

Bulgaria

Abagar JSC
98 Nikola Gabrovski Str, 5000 Veliko Tarnovo
Tel: (062) 643936; (062) 647814 *Fax:* (062)
 646993
E-mail: abagar@dir.bg
Web Site: www.abagar.net
Key Personnel
Executive Dir: Marian Kenarov
Founded: 1991

EA
ul San Stefano 43, 5800 Pleven
Tel: (064) 822827; (064) 846774 *Fax:* (064)
 822528
E-mail: ea@eapleven.com
Web Site: eapleven.com

Janet-45 Print & Publishing
Blvd Al Stambolijski 9, 4004 Plovdiv
Tel: (032) 609090 *Fax:* (032) 677723
E-mail: mail@janet45.com; books@janet45.com
Web Site: printing.janet45.com; books.janet45.
 com
Key Personnel
Chief Executive Officer: Bozhana Apostolova
Mng Partner: Manol Peykov
Founded: 1992

Canada

Blitzprint Inc
1235 64 Ave SE, Suite 1, Calgary, AB T2H 2J7
Toll Free Tel: 866-479-3248 *Fax:* 403-253-5642
E-mail: books@blitzprint.com
Web Site: www.blitzprint.com
Key Personnel
Pres: Kevin Lanuke
Founded: 1999
Turnaround: 15-20 business days
Print Runs: 25 min - 1,000 max
Business from Other Countries: 50%
Membership(s): Association of Book Publishers
 of British Columbia; Canadian Booksellers As-
 sociation

Cenveo McLaren Morris & Todd Co
3270 American Dr, Mississauga, ON L4V 1B5
Tel: 905-677-3592 *Fax:* 905-677-3675

E-mail: sales@mmt.ca
Web Site: www.mmt.ca
Key Personnel
Pres & CEO: Tony Sgro
Cont: Nancy Marquis
Founded: 1956
Turnaround: 15 Workdays
Print Runs: 5,000 min - 1,000,000 max
Business from Other Countries: 10%

Coach House Printing
80 bpNichol Lane, Toronto, ON M5S 3J4
Tel: 416-979-2217 *Toll Free Tel:* 800-367-6360
 (outside Toronto) *Fax:* 416-977-1158
E-mail: mail@chbooks.com
Web Site: www.chbooks.com
Key Personnel
Publr: Stan Bevington *E-mail:* stan@chbooks.com
Edit Dir: Alana Wilcox *E-mail:* alana@chbooks.
 com
Prodn Mgr: John De Jesus *E-mail:* john@
 chbooks.com
Founded: 1965
Turnaround: 14 Workdays
Print Runs: 200 min - 2,000 max
Business from Other Countries: 10%

Maracle Press Ltd
1156 King St E, Oshawa, ON L1H 1H8
Tel: 905-723-3438 *Toll Free Tel:* 800-558-8604
 Fax: 905-723-1759
E-mail: info@maraclepress.com
Web Site: www.maraclepress.com
Key Personnel
Pres & Gen Mgr: George Sittlinger *Tel:* 905-723-
 3438 ext 236
Acct Mgr: Ronald G Taylor *E-mail:* rtaylor@
 maraclepress.com
Founded: 1920
Turnaround: 10 Workdays
Print Runs: 500 min - 500,000 max
Business from Other Countries: 25%
Membership(s): BMI; Canadian Book Manufac-
 turer Association; Ontario Printing & Imaging
 Association; Printing Industries of America

Marquis Book Printing Inc
350, rue des Entrepreneurs, Montmagny, QC G5V
 4T1
Toll Free Tel: 855-566-1937 *Fax:* 418-241-1768
Web Site: www.marquislivre.com
Key Personnel
Pres: Serge Loubier
VP, Oper: Pierre Frechette
Founded: 1937
Turnaround: 5-10 Workdays
Print Runs: 1 min - 1,000,000 max
Business from Other Countries: 39%
Sales Office(s): 2700 rue Rachel, Montreal, QC
 H2H 1S7 *Tel:* 514-954-1131 *Fax:* 514-954-
 0004

Webcom Inc
3480 Pharmacy Ave, Toronto, ON M1W 2S7
Tel: 416-496-1000 *Toll Free Tel:* 800-665-9322
 Fax: 416-496-1537
E-mail: webcom@webcomlink.com
Web Site: www.webcomlink.com
Key Personnel
CEO & Pres: Mike Collinge
Founded: 1975
Turnaround: 15 Workdays
Print Runs: 10 min - 100,000 max
Business from Other Countries: 40%
Sales Office(s): 65 Spring Valley Ave, River
 Edge, NJ 07661, United States, Contact: Susan
 Ginch *Tel:* 201-262-4301 *Fax:* 201-262-6375
 E-mail: susan.ginch@webcomlink.com
Membership(s): BMI; Canadian Book & Periodi-
 cal Council; Printing Industries of America

China

Amity Printing Co Ltd
No 99, Mo Zhou Zhong Lu, Dong Shan Qiao,
 Jiangning District, Nanjing 211153
Tel: (025) 57928000 *Fax:* (025) 57928001
E-mail: sales@amityprinting.com
Web Site: www.amityprinting.com
Founded: 1988

Artron Art (Group) Co Ltd
Artron Art Center Shenzhen, No 19 Shenyun Rd,
 Nanshan District, Shenzhen 518053
Tel: (0755) 8336 6138 *Fax:* (0755) 8321 9630
E-mail: info@artron.net
Web Site: artron.com.cn
Founded: 1993
Branch Office(s)
Unit 603, 6/F, Delta House, 3 On Yiu St, Shatin,
 Hong Kong *Tel:* 2312 2193 *Fax:* 2312 2820

Beijing Allied Fortune International Trade Ltd
Room 1501, Bldg No 5, Ronghua International,
 No 10, Rong Hua South Rd, BDA, Beijing
 100176
Tel: (010) 67817768 *Fax:* (010) 67817758
E-mail: daniel@af-print.com
Web Site: www.af-print.com

Beijing Shengtong Printing Co Ltd
11 Xingsheng St, Economic & Technological De-
 velopment Zone, Beijing 100176
Tel: (010) 67869712; (010) 67887676 *Fax:* (010)
 67884903
E-mail: xiawei@shengtongprint.com; ir@
 shengtongprint.com
Web Site: www.shengtongprint.com
Key Personnel
Contact: Eric Hsu
Founded: 2000

Call 2 Print
1205, Tower 2, The Third Space, 926 Zhenhua
 Rd, Baoshan District, Shanghai 200442
Tel: (021) 6129 9228 *Fax:* (021) 5436 0956
E-mail: callus@call2print.com
Web Site: www.call2print.com
Key Personnel
Vice President: Apollo Wang *E-mail:* apollo@
 call2print.com
Print Runs: 1 min - 1,000,000 max

Chenxi Printing, see Shanghai Chenxi Printing
 Co Ltd

Fuzhou QianFan Printing Co Ltd
Xiandian Bldg, Jincheng Investment Zone, No 86,
 E Nanping Rd, Fuzhou 350012
Tel: (0591) 62036808 *Fax:* (0591) 62036811

Guangdong Xinyuan Color Printing Co Ltd
Dongxing Industrial Park, Nancun, Panyu District,
 Guangzhou 511442
Tel: (020) 31035544 *Fax:* (020) 31035538
Web Site: childrens-bookprinting.btrworlds.com
Founded: 1996

Guangzhou Haohan Printing Co Ltd
Datong Industry Zone, Dongyong Town, Panyu
 District, Guangzhou City 511475
Tel: (020) 84910009 *Fax:* (020) 22935784
E-mail: haohan@haohanprint.com
Web Site: www.haohanprint.com
Founded: 1991

Guangzhou Xin Yi Printing Co Ltd
No 3 Kangmei Rd, Fuling Industry Park, Tang-
mei, Xintang Town, Zengcheng, Guangzhou
Tel: (020) 32052716; (020) 32050514 *Fax:* (020)
32052712
E-mail: sales@xinyiprint.com
Web Site: www.xinyiprint.com; www.gzxinyiprint.
com
Key Personnel
Sales Manager: Leo Xiao *Tel:* (020) 32051515
Fax: (020) 32052820 *E-mail:* leo@xinyiprint.
com
Founded: 1998

Guangzhou XY Printing Co Ltd
7th floor, A5 Bldg, Kehui Jingu, Science Ave,
Science City, Luogang District, Guangzhou
510530
Tel: (020) 32096688 *Fax:* (020) 32096161
E-mail: market@xyprinting.com
Web Site: www.xyprinting.cn
Founded: 1992
Turnaround: 7-14 Workdays
Branch Office(s)
Postplatz 5, 35781 Weilburg, Germany, Contact:
Ruixi Zhang *Tel:* (06471) 380865 *Fax:* (06471)
429643 *E-mail:* germany@xyprinting.cn

Guangzhou Zhongtian Colour Printing Co Ltd
No 38A, Xinguang Rd, Panyu District,
Guangzhou 511436
Tel: (020) 6685 3808 *Fax:* (020) 3472 9257
Web Site: www.zt-online.cn
Key Personnel
Contact: Hylix Wu *E-mail:* hylix.wu@
zhongtiancp.com
Founded: 1993
Branch Office(s)
Unit 601-605 6/F, Prosperity Pl, No 6, Shing
Yip St, Kwun Tong, Kowloon, Hong Kong
Tel: 3150 6435; 3150 6452 *Fax:* 3914 7664
PO Box 11398, Papamoa Beach 3151, New
Zealand, Contact: David Reid *Tel:* (07) 985
6137 *Fax:* (07) 985 6138 *E-mail:* dave@
realmedia.net.nz

Hangzhou Lihe Digital Technology Co Ltd
Greentown, Zijin Plaza, Room B 802, 701 Gudun
Rd, Hangzhou 310030
Tel: (0571) 87755663; (0571) 87755818; (0571)
86625528 *Fax:* (0571) 87755816
E-mail: lihe@lihehz.com
Web Site: www.lihehz.com

Hengyuan Printing Co Ltd
Gaopu Rd, Tianhe Software Park, Guangshan
er Lu, Gaotangshi, Yangmeiling 3, Tianhe,
Guangzhou 510520
Tel: (020) 66834591; (020) 66834568 *Fax:* (020)
66834595
E-mail: sales@hyprint.cn
Web Site: www.hyprint.cn
Founded: 1993

Hunan Tianwen Xinhua Printing Co Ltd
Hunan Publishing Technological Park, No 8,
Yinxing Rd, Leifeng St, Changsa 410219
Tel: (0731) 88387575; (0731) 84442356 (market-
ing) *Fax:* (0731) 88387676
Web Site: www.hntwprinting.com

Shanghai KS Printing Co Ltd
Bldg 7, No 1800, Longwu Rd, Xuhui District,
Shanghai 20031
Tel: (021) 51718508 (ext 807)
E-mail: sales@ksprinting.net
Web Site: www.ksprinting.net
Branch Office(s)
Room 1501, 15/F, SPA Center, 53-55 Lockhart
Rd, Wanchai, Hong Kong

Million Printing Co Ltd
No 32, Changhong Rd, Fengxiang Industrial Park,
Daliang, Shunde District, Foshan City 528300
Tel: (0757) 22218989 *Fax:* (0757) 22385266
E-mail: sales1@million-printing.com; smartkan@
vip.163.com
Web Site: www.million-printing.com
Key Personnel
Contact: Simon Kan *E-mail:* kan@million-
printing.com
Founded: 1995

**Ningbo Newspapering Printing & Development
Co Ltd**
No 558 Chengxin Rd, Business & Investment
Center, Yinzhou District, Ningbo 315104
Tel: (0574) 87685512
E-mail: office@ningboprint.com
Web Site: www.ningboprint.com

RACTR Printing Co Ltd
25F Bldg C, Yitai Center, 1006 Dongmen Rd,
Shenzhen 518003
Tel: (0755) 25191692 (sales) *Fax:* (0755)
25191276
E-mail: ractr@ractr.com
Web Site: www.ractr.com
Founded: 1999
U.S. Office(s): 7702 S 94 East Ave, Tulsa, OK
74133, United States

Reliance Printing (Shenzhen) Co Ltd
25 Longshan Industrial Zone, Longgang District,
Shenzhen 518019
Tel: (0755) 25802197 *Fax:* (0755) 25802199
E-mail: jessie@relianceprinting.com
Web Site: www.relianceprinting.com
Founded: 1994
Parent Company: Reliance (Hong Kong) Corp

Shanghai Chenxi Printing Co Ltd
5553 Hutai Rd, Suite 3, Shanghai 201907
Tel: (021) 56021684 *Fax:* (021) 56021913
E-mail: info@chenxish.com
Web Site: www.chenxish.com
Key Personnel
Marketing Dir: Shannon Niu *E-mail:* niuxiuqin@
chenxish.com
Founded: 1999

Shanghai iPrinting Co Ltd
No 28, Alley 23, Yingao Rd, Shanghai 200439
Tel: (021) 65918300 *Fax:* (021) 65918322
E-mail: wuxm@tuyu.cn
Web Site: www.tuyu.cn
Key Personnel
Marketing Manager: Maggie Qin
Parent Company: Shanghai New Press Technol-
ogy Group

Shenzhen Boeye Technology Co Ltd
401, No 3, Bldg C, Kexing Scientific Park, Nan-
shan District, Shenzhen 518057
Tel: (0755) 8635 8666 *Fax:* (0755) 8607 9111
E-mail: sales@szboeye.com
Web Site: www.szboeye.com

**Shenzhen Huaxin Colour-Printing &
Platemaking Co Ltd**
Bldg 5, Lijincheng Tech & Industrial Park, Indus-
trial Rd E, Longhua, Shenzhen 518129
Tel: (0755) 8242 8168 *Fax:* (0755) 8170 4065
E-mail: info@huaxinprinting.com
Web Site: www.huaxinprinting.com
Founded: 1988

Shenzhen Jinhao Color Printing Co Ltd
Jianjin Industrial Estate, 3rd floor, Bldg E, Dong-
guan 2 Rd, Longhua District, Shenzhen,
Guangdong 518129

Tel: (0755) 84161089 *Fax:* (0755) 84192325
E-mail: admin@lzjhy.com
Web Site: www.lzjhy.com
Key Personnel
General Manager: Ms Rose Liu *Tel:* (0755)
29529811 *Fax:* (0755) 29529811

Shenzhen Xinlian Artistic Printing Co Ltd
Jinbolong Industrial Park, floor 1-2, Bldg A,
Qingquan Rd, Longhua, Baoan District, Shen-
zhen, Guangdong 518109
Tel: (0755) 28071282; (0755) 83238313
Fax: (0755) 28071032
Key Personnel
Chief Executive Officer, Dir & General Manager:
Guo Liang Wu
Founded: 1993

Voion Printing Group (International) Co Ltd
Voion Industrial Zone, Yangtian Rd, 72 Area,
Bao'an District, Shenzhen 518000
Tel: (0755) 61155888 *Fax:* (0755) 61155566
E-mail: voion@voion.com
Web Site: www.voion.com
Key Personnel
Mng Dir: Mr Li Xiaoping

XY Printing, see Guangzhou XY Printing Co
Ltd

**Yinbo Printing Technology Development Co
Ltd**
86 Zhangxingzhuang Rd, Hebei District, Tianjin
300412
Tel: (022) 86331268 *Fax:* (022) 86331978
Founded: 2001

Colombia

Carvajal Soluciones de Comunicacion (Carvajal
Communication Solutions)
Member of Grupo Carvajal SA
Calle 17, No 69-95, Bogota
Tel: (01) 4104977
Web Site: www.cargraphics.com/cscweb
Founded: 1904
Branch Office(s)
Calle 15, No 23-234, Acopi-Yumbo, Cali
Tel: (02) 6618150
Carrera 42, No 85a-95 Itagui, Medellin *Tel:* (04)
3845600

Panamericana Formas e Impresos SA
Calle 65, No 95-28, Bogota
Mailing Address: AA 095557, Bogota
Tel: (01) 430-2110; (01) 430-0355 *Fax:* (01) 252-
8354; (01) 276-1500
E-mail: atencionalcliente@panamericana.com.co
Web Site: www.panamericanafei.com.co
Key Personnel
International Sales Manager: Fabio Caicedo
Gomez
Founded: 1987

Printer Colombiana SA
Calle 64G, No 88A-30, Bogota
Tel: (01) 294 2930 *Fax:* (01) 223 3154
E-mail: printer@printercol.com
Web Site: www.printercol.com
Key Personnel
Contact: Hernando Estrada *E-mail:* hestrada@
printercol.com
Founded: 1976

Costa Rica

Litografia e Imprenta LIL SA
Apdo 75, 1100 San Jose
Tel: 2235-0011 *Fax:* 2240-7814
E-mail: info@lilcr.com; ventas.editoriales@lilcr.
  com (editorial sales)
Web Site: www.lilprinting.com
Founded: 1896

Czech Republic

CPI Moravia Books sro
Affiliate of CPI Group
Brnenska 1024, 691 23 Pohorelice
Tel: 519 440 111 *Fax:* 519 440 107
E-mail: moravia@cpibooks.de
Web Site: www.cpibooks.cz
Key Personnel
Mng Dir: Juergen Heisters *Tel:* 519 440 106
  E-mail: juergen.heisters@cpibooks.de
Dir, Sales: Pawel Slawatycki *Tel:* 519 440 160
  E-mail: pawel.slawatycki@cpibooks.de
Founded: 1996

Europrint AS
Pod Kotlarkou 3, 150 00 Prague 5
Tel: 225 347 111
E-mail: europrint@europrint.cz
Web Site: www.europrint.cz
Key Personnel
Chief Executive: Petr Litvan
Chief Operating Officer: Petr Valda
Chief Financial Officer: Karel Prochazka
Dir, Production: Vaclav Benda
Commercial Manager: Vladimir Dostal
Founded: 2003

FINIDR sro
Lipova cp 1965, 737 01 Cesky Tesin
Tel: 558 772 111 *Fax:* 558 772 221
E-mail: tiskarna@finidr.cz
Web Site: www.finidr.cz
Key Personnel
Owner & Mng Dir: Jaroslav Drahos
Sales & Financial Dir: Miroslav Klos
Founded: 1994
Print Runs: 300 min - 100,000 max
Business from Other Countries: 80%

GRASPO CZ AS - Druckerei und
  Buchbinderei (Graspo CZ AS - Printing &
  Bookbinding House)
Pod Sternberkem 324, 763 02 Zlin
Tel: 577 606 112; 577 606 247 (sales) *Fax:* 577
  104 052 (sales); 577 606 251
E-mail: graspo@graspo.com; marketing@graspo.
  com; sales@graspo.com
Web Site: www.graspo.com
Key Personnel
Sales Dir: Michal Dostalek *Tel:* 577 606 201
  E-mail: michal.dostalek@graspo.com; Andrea
  Krystkova *Tel:* 577 606 213 *E-mail:* andrea.
  krystek@graspo.com
Production Manager: Stepan Mudrik
Founded: 1995
Print Runs: 1,000 min
Business from Other Countries: 60%
Sales Office(s): U Bakalare 552, Prague 9,
  Contact: Ivo Neumann *Tel:* 281 912 257
  E-mail: graspoprag@graspo.com
Bahnhofstr 23, 67596 Dittelsheim/Hessloch, Ger-
  many, Contact: Pavla Protzen *Tel:* (06244) 91
  80 81 *E-mail:* pavla.protzen@graspo.com

Racianska 109/b, 831 02 Bratislava, Slovakia,
  Contact: Miro Kandar *Tel:* 905 806 072
  E-mail: mirokan@ba.psg.sk
ul M Burdychovych 256, 549 41 Cerveny Kost-
  elec, Slovakia, Contact: Zdenek Hanus *Tel:* 491
  462 037 *E-mail:* hanus.zdenek@centrum.cz

Tiskarny Havlickuv Brod AS
Husova ul 1881, 580 01 Havlickuv Brod
Tel: 569 664 110 *Fax:* 569 664 111
E-mail: thb@thb.cz
Web Site: www.thb.cz
Key Personnel
Dir: Ludmila Dockalova *Tel:* 569 664 140
  E-mail: dockalova@thb.cz
Head, Sales: Premysl Moravec *Tel:* 569 664 145
  E-mail: moravec@thb.cz
Commercial Pruduction Assistant: Miloslav Henzl
  Tel: 569 664 129 *E-mail:* henzl@thb.cz
Founded: 1992
Branch Office(s)
Pujmanove 1221/4, 140 00 Prague 4

Librix.eu
Subsidiary of Tribun EU sro
Cejl 892/32, 602 00 Brno
Tel: 543 210 089 *Fax:* 530 332 374; 543 210 089
E-mail: librix@librix.eu; sales@librix.eu
Web Site: www.librix.eu
Key Personnel
Chief Manager for Western Europe: Jaroslav
  Janosek, PhD *E-mail:* janosek@librix.eu
Mng Dir: Jan Homola *E-mail:* jan.homola@librix.
  eu
Founded: 2007

Tesinska tiskarna AS
Stefanikova ul 1828/2, 737 36 Cesky Tesin
Tel: 558 761 311 *Fax:* 558 711 536
E-mail: info@tesinskatiskarna.cz
Web Site: www.tesinskatiskarna.cz
Founded: 1806

Typos, tiskarske zavody sro
Podnikatelska 1160/14, 320 56 Plzen
Tel: 377 193 370; 377 193 300 *Fax:* 377 193 216
E-mail: typos@typos.cz
Web Site: www.typos.cz
Key Personnel
Mng Dir: Jiri Fricek *Tel:* 377 193 315 *Fax:* 377
  193 217 *E-mail:* fricek@typos.cz
Founded: 1998
Branch Office(s)
Prodejna Uslavska 2, 326 00 Plzen *Tel:* 377 249
  294 *E-mail:* prodejna@typos.cz
Nadrazni 473/3, 339 01 Klatovy *Tel:* 376 375 711
  Fax: 376 375 713 *E-mail:* klatovy@typos.cz
Sazecska 560/8, 108 25 Prague 10 *Tel:* 266 021
  364; 266 021 156 *E-mail:* obchod.vivas@typos.
  cz

Univerzita Palackeho v Olomouci Vydavatelstvi
Krizkovskeho 8, 771 47 Olomouc
Tel: 585 631 111 *Fax:* 585 631 012
Web Site: www.upol.cz/vup
Key Personnel
Dir: Hana Dzikova *Tel:* 585 631 704
  E-mail: hana.dzikova@upol.cz
Assistant Dir: Radka Voborska *Tel:* 585 631 710
  E-mail: radka.voborska@upol.cz
Head, Printing Center: Monika Reichlova
  Tel: 585 631 725 *E-mail:* monika.reichlova@
  upol.cz

Egypt

Sahara Printing Co
Nasr City, Free Zone, Cairo
Tel: (02) 2274 4056 *Fax:* (02) 2274 1907
E-mail: info@saharaprinting.com; sales@
  saharaprinting.com
Web Site: www.saharaprinting.com
Key Personnel
Chairman & Chief Executive Officer: Nadim
  Elias
Sales & Marketing Manager: Dahlia Sobhy
Founded: 1995
Business from Other Countries: 60%

Estonia

Tallinna Raamatutrukikoja OU (Tallinn Book
  Printers)
Laki 26, 12915 Tallinn
Tel: 6509990 *Fax:* 6509999
E-mail: trt@trt.ee
Web Site: www.trt.ee
Key Personnel
Sales Manager: Aivar Altkula *Tel:* 6509988
  E-mail: aivar@trt.ee; Krista Kolk *Tel:* 6509992
  E-mail: krista@trt.ee; Urmas Muur
  Tel: 6509987 *E-mail:* urmas@trt.ee; Tiina
  Poldaru *Tel:* 6509991 *E-mail:* tiina.poldaru@trt.
  ee; Ole Salo *Tel:* 6509951 *E-mail:* salo@trt.ee
Founded: 1985

Finland

Bookwell Oy
Teollisuustie 4, 06150 Porvoo
Tel: (019) 219 41
Web Site: www.bookwell.fi
Key Personnel
President & Chief Executive Officer: Vesa
  Junkkarinen *Tel:* (040) 569 2999 *E-mail:* vesa.
  junkkarinen@bookwell.fi
Sales Dir: Markus Ruohonen *E-mail:* markus.
  ruohonen@bookwell.fi
Export Manager: Kjell Karlsson *Tel:* (040) 518
  0948 *E-mail:* kjell.karlsson@bookwell.fi
Production Manager: Juha Harmonen
  E-mail: juha.harmonen@bookwell.fi
Founded: 1860
Business from Other Countries: 50%
Parent Company: Sanoma
Branch Office(s)
Tenhusentie 3, 51900 Juva
Sales Office(s): Hulvejen 52, 9530 Stovring, Den-
  mark, Representative: Steffen Janum *Tel:* 5092
  5555 *E-mail:* steffen.janum@bookwell.fi
Raiffeisenstr 5, 63939 Woerth am Main, Ger-
  many, Representative: Frank Hohmann
  Tel: (09372) 94810811 *E-mail:* frank.
  hohmann@bookwell.fi
Manor House, Church St, Brassington, Derbys
  DE4 4HJ, United Kingdom, Representative: Pe-
  ter Everest *Tel:* (01629) 540 934 *Fax:* (01629)
  540 938 *E-mail:* petereverest@bookwell.co.uk

St Michel Print Oy
Teollisuuskatu 2-6, 50130 Mikkeli
Mailing Address: PL 193, 50101 Mikkeli
Tel: (015) 3501 *Fax:* (015) 350 3295
E-mail: info@stmichelprint.fi
Web Site: www.stmichelprint.fi

Key Personnel
Mng Dir: Heikki Suomala *Tel:* (044) 035 02 68 (cell) *E-mail:* heikki.suomala@stmichelprint.fi
Production Manager: Harri Pasonen *Tel:* (044) 035 02 66 (cell) *E-mail:* harri.pasonen@stmichelprint.fi
Sales Manager: Olli Kivijarvi *Tel:* (044) 035 02 69 (cell) *E-mail:* olli.kivijarvi@stmichelprint.fi; Elisa Vesanen *Tel:* (044) 035 02 64 (cell) *E-mail:* elisa.vesanen@stmichelprint.fi
Founded: 1980
Parent Company: Lansi-Savo Group

France

Holinail France SAS
16, rue de la Pierre Levee, 75011 Paris
Tel: 01 48 05 12 21
E-mail: info@holinail.com
Web Site: www.holinail.com
Branch Office(s)
Holinail Edition, 4, rue Massilian, 34000 Montpellier *Tel:* 04 67 12 85 70 *E-mail:* info.edition@holinail.com
Shenzhen Holinail Asia Ltd, Room 1006, 10/F, Coastal City East Tower, Hai De San Dao, Hou Hai Bin Rd, Nanshan District, Shenzhen 518054, China *Tel:* (0755) 8886 6571

Jouve
11, bd de Sebastopol, 75001 Paris Cedex 01
Tel: 01 44 76 54 40 *Fax:* 01 44 76 86 39
Web Site: www.jouve.com
Branch Office(s)
Jouve Germany GmbH & Co KG, Landshuter Allee 8-10, 80637 Munich, Germany *Tel:* (08954) 55 81 45 *Fax:* (06989) 54 83 99
Jouve UK Ltd, c/o Mazars LLP, The Pinnacle, 160 Midsummer Blvd, Milton Keynes, Bucks MK9 1FF, United Kingdom *Tel:* (07554) 000288
U.S. Office(s): Jouve North America, 70 Landmark Hill Dr, Brattleboro, VT 05301, United States *Tel:* 802-254-6073

Plein Chant
35, route de Conde, 16120 Bassac, Charente
Tel: 05 45 81 93 26 *Fax:* 05 45 81 92 83
E-mail: pleinchant@wanadoo.fr
Web Site: www.pleinchant.fr
Key Personnel
Contact: Edmond Thomas
Founded: 1970
Print Runs: 300 min - 1,000 max
Business from Other Countries: 5%

Germany

Achilles Gruppe
Burgstr 4-10, 29221 Celle
Tel: (05141) 753-0 *Fax:* (05141) 753-186
E-mail: celle@achilles.de; zentrale@achilles.de
Web Site: www.achilles.de
Key Personnel
Chief Executive Officer: Thorsten Drews
Mng Dir: Stefan Hoernicke; Frank Jahrand
Manager: Thomas Theunissen *Tel:* (05141) 753-137 *E-mail:* thomas.theunissen@achilles.de
Founded: 1990

APPL Firmengruppe
Senefelderstr 3-11, 86650 Wemding
Mailing Address: Postfach 11 63, 86648 Wemding
Tel: (09092) 999-0; (09092) 999-111 *Fax:* (09092) 999-209
E-mail: info@appl.de
Web Site: www.appl.de
Key Personnel
Mng Dir: Markus Appl *E-mail:* m.appl@appl.de; Monika Stimpfle *E-mail:* m.stimpfle@appl.de; Thomas Zinn *E-mail:* t.zinn@appl.de

Atelierhof Scholen 53
Scholen 53, 27251 Scholen
Tel: (04245) 267 *Fax:* (04245) 1384
E-mail: atelierhof@scholen53.de
Web Site: www.scholen53.de
Key Personnel
Bookbinder: Sabine Rasper *E-mail:* sabine.rasper@scholen53.de
Founded: 1997

AZ Druck und Datentechnik GmbH
Heisinger Str 16, 87437 Kempten
Tel: (0831) 206-311 *Fax:* (0831) 206-246
E-mail: kempten@az-druck.de
Web Site: www.az-druck.de
Key Personnel
Mng Dir: Guenther Hartmann
Founded: 1945
Branch Office(s)
Landfliegerstr 11, 12487 Berlin *Tel:* (030) 639959-0 *E-mail:* berlin@az-druck.de

The Bear Press - Dr Wolfram Benda
Schleiermacherstr 7, 95447 Bayreuth
Tel: (0921) 81418 *Fax:* (0921) 1503478
E-mail: info@thebearpress.de
Web Site: www.thebearpress.de
Key Personnel
Owner: Dr Wolfram Benda
Founded: 1979

Druckerei C H Beck
Bergerstr 3-5, 86720 Noerdlingen
Tel: (09081) 85-0 *Fax:* (09081) 85-206
E-mail: info@becksche.de
Web Site: www.becksche.de
Key Personnel
Mng Dir: Christian Matthiesen *Tel:* (09081) 85-101 *E-mail:* matthiesen.christian@becksche.de
Commercial Dir: Ernest Zoller *Tel:* (09081) 85-111 *E-mail:* zoller.ernest@becksche.de
Head, Inside Sales: Roland Schroeppel *Tel:* (09081) 85-195 *E-mail:* schroeppel.roland@becksche.de
Head, Sales: Andre Sommer *Tel:* (09081) 85-123 *E-mail:* sommer.andre@becksche.de
Founded: 1763
Parent Company: Verlag C H Beck oHG
Branch Office(s)
Augsburgerstr 67, 86720 Noerdlingen

Beltz Grafische Betriebe
Neustaedter Str 1-4, 99947 Bad Langensalza
Mailing Address: Postfach 1151, 99947 Bad Langensalza
Tel: (03603) 399-0 *Fax:* (03603) 399-109
E-mail: info-bbl@beltz.de
Web Site: www.beltz-grafische-betriebe.de
Key Personnel
General Manager: Christian Gaidies *Tel:* (03603) 399-100 *E-mail:* c.gaidies@beltz.de
Manager, Business Development, Beltz Media: Chris Felgner *Tel:* (03603) 399-372 *E-mail:* c.felgner@beltz.de
Prepress Manager: Bernhard Beier *Tel:* (03603) 399-200 *E-mail:* b.beier@beltz.de
Production Manager: Karsten Stolze *Tel:* (03603) 399-400 *E-mail:* k.stolze@beltz.de
Marketing: Juliane Schilde *Tel:* (03603) 399-559 *E-mail:* j.schilde@beltz.de

Founded: 1841
Branch Office(s)
Am Fliegerhorst 8, 99947 Bad Langensalza (production)

Bertelsmann Printing Group
Division of Bertelsmann SE & Co KGaA
Carl-Bertelsmann-Str 161M, 33311 Guetersloh
Tel: (05241) 80-0
E-mail: contact@bertelsmann-printing-group.com
Web Site: www.bertelsmann-printing-group.com
Key Personnel
Co-Chief Executive Officer: Axel Hentrei; Dr Bertram Stausberg
Chief Financial Officer: Ulrich Cordes
Corporate Communications: Matthias Wulff *E-mail:* matthias.wulff@bertelsmann.de
Founded: 2016

Books on Demand GmbH
In de Tarpen 42, 22848 Norderstedt
Tel: (040) 53 43 35-11 *Fax:* (040) 53 43 35-84
E-mail: info@bod.de
Web Site: www.bod.de
Key Personnel
Mng Dir: Dr Gerd Robertz; Yogesh Torani
Editor: Iris Kirberg
Founded: 2001

Buch Buecher.de GmbH
Affiliate of CPI Group
Zum Alten Berg 24, 96158 Frensdorf/Birkach
Tel: (09502) 92094-0 *Fax:* (09502) 92094-20
E-mail: info.birkach@cpibooks.de; info@cpibooks.de
Web Site: cpibooks.com/de

Buch-Einband-Kunst
Reutebachgasse 26, 79108 Freiburg
Tel: (0178) 2810833
E-mail: buch-einband-kunst@gmx.de
Web Site: buch-einband-kunst.de; www.bookdesign.de
Key Personnel
Mng Dir: Ulrich Widmann

Dr Cantz'sche Druckerei Medien GmbH (Dr Cantz'sche Printing & Media Company)
Member of Wurzel Mediengruppe
Zeppelinstr 29-31, 73760 Ostfildern
Tel: (0711) 4405-0 *Fax:* (0711) 4405-111
E-mail: info@cantz.de
Web Site: w-mg.com
Key Personnel
Mng Dir: Heinz Wurzel *E-mail:* h.wurzel@cantz.de
Executive Dir, Media Management: Harri Christ *E-mail:* h.christ@cantz.de
Executive Dir, Sales: Thomas Uehling *E-mail:* t.uehling@cantz.de
Founded: 1933

Clausen & Bosse
Birkstr 10, 25917 Leck
Tel: (04662) 83-0
E-mail: info@cpibooks.de
Web Site: cpibooks.com/de
Print Runs: 1 min - 1,000,000 max
Parent Company: CPI Group

Digital Print Group O Schimek GmbH
Neuwieder Str 17, 90411 Nuremberg
Tel: (0911) 239846-3 *Fax:* (0911) 239846-66
E-mail: buchhaltung@digital-print-group.de; webkatalog@digital-print-group.de (marketing); kundenbetreuung@digital-print-group.de
Web Site: www.digital-print-group.de
Key Personnel
Mng Dir: Oliver Schimek

Digitale Buch manufaktur (DiBuMa) GmbH
Taubenweg 5, 93149 Nittenau
Tel: (09436) 30100-0 *Fax:* (09436) 30100-500
E-mail: info@dibuma.eu
Web Site: www.dibuma.eu
Key Personnel
Mng Dir: Daniel Schieb *E-mail:* daniel.schieb@
dibuma.eu
Customer Service: Maria Schmidkonz
E-mail: maria.schmidkonz@dibuma.eu
Founded: 1987

Ebner & Spiegel GmbH
Eberhard-Finckh-Str 61, 89075 Ulm
Tel: (0731) 2056-0
E-mail: info@cpibooks.de
Web Site: www.cpibooks.com
Founded: 2002
Parent Company: CPI Group

Einhand Press
Burghofgasse 4, 76829 Landau in der Pfalz
Tel: (06341) 89349
Web Site: www.einhandpress.de
Key Personnel
Owner: Reinhold Nasshan *E-mail:* r.nasshan@
web.de
Founded: 1987

Euro-Druckservice GmbH
Medienstr 5b, 94036 Passau
Tel: (0851) 851 600-0 *Fax:* (0851) 851 600-60
E-mail: office@edsgroup.de
Web Site: www.edsgroup.de
Key Personnel
Chief Executive Officer & Mng Dir: Christian
Senff
Chief Financial Officer & Mng Dir: Peter
Neubacher
Chief Operating Officer & Mng Dir: Kai-Uwe
Gross

Fines Mundi GmbH
An den Ziegelhuetten 1-3, 66127 Saarbruecken
Tel: (06898) 3097740 *Fax:* (06898) 3097742
E-mail: info@fines-mundi.de
Web Site: www.fines-mundi.de
Key Personnel
Mng Dir: Rolf Kittler

GGP Media GmbH
Member of Bertelsmann Printing Group
Karl-Marx-Str 24, 07381 Poessneck
Tel: (03647) 430-0 *Fax:* (03647) 430-390
E-mail: ggp.poessneck@bertelsmann.de
Web Site: www.ggp-media.de
Key Personnel
Mng Dir: Axel Hentrei; Christof Ludwig
Sales Dir: Christine Bergmann *Tel:* (03647) 430-
225 *Fax:* (03647) 430-230 *E-mail:* christine.
bergmann@bertelsmann.de
Customer Service Manager & International
Sales: Cindy Girbert *Tel:* (03647) 430-415
Fax: (03647) 430-66415 *E-mail:* cindy.
girbert@bertelsmann.de
Founded: 1891
Ultimate Parent Company: Bertelsmann SE & Co
KGaA

Griebsch & Rochol Druck GmbH & Co KG
Gabelsbergerstr 1, 59069 Hamm
Mailing Address: Postfach 7145, 59029 Hamm
Tel: (02385) 931 0 *Fax:* (02385) 931 213
E-mail: info@grd.de
Web Site: www.grd.de
Key Personnel
Mng Partner: Rainer Grobe *Tel:* (02385) 931 200
E-mail: grob@grd.de; Marc von Kiedrowsky
Tel: (02385) 931 201 *E-mail:* mvk@grd.de

Chief Executive Officer: Mark Wiethoff
Tel: (02385) 931 271 *E-mail:* wiethoff@grd.de
Sales Dir: Michael Knubbe *Tel:* (02385) 931 207
E-mail: knubbe@grd.de

Druckhaus Gummersbach PP GmbH
Stauweiher 4, 51645 Gummersbach
Tel: (02261) 9572-0 *Fax:* (02261) 56338
E-mail: info@druckhaus-gummersbach.de
Web Site: www.druckhaus-gummersbach.de
Key Personnel
General Manager: Benita Kramer; Ulrich Kramer
Founded: 1845

**Anna Helm Atelier fuer Buchkunst und
Gestaltung**
Muehlweg 22, 06114 Halle
Tel: (0176) 7684 7831 *Fax:* (0345) 20 32 362
Web Site: www.annahelm.de
Key Personnel
Owner: Anna Helm *E-mail:* annahelm@thaja.de

**Holzer Druck und Medien Druckerei und
Zeitungsverlag GmbH & Co KG**
Fridolin-Holzer-Str 22 & 24, 88171 Weiler im
Allgaeu
Tel: (08387) 399-0 *Fax:* (08387) 399-33
E-mail: info@druckerei-holzer.de
Web Site: www.druckerei-holzer.de
Key Personnel
Manager: Klaus Huber *Tel:* (08387) 399-38
E-mail: k.huber@druckerei-holzer.de
Production Manager: Uwe Dittman *Tel:* (08387)
399-30 *E-mail:* u.dittman@druckerei-holzer.de
Sales Manager: Jochen Hole *Tel:* (08387) 399-59
E-mail: j.hole@druckerei-holzer.de

Holzmann Druck GmbH & Co KG
Gewerbestr 2, 86825 Bad Woerishofen
Tel: (08247) 9 93-0 *Fax:* (08247) 9 93-208
E-mail: contact@holzmann-druck.de
Web Site: www.holzmann-druck.de
Key Personnel
Manager: Tobias Schneider *E-mail:* tobias.
schneider@holzmann-druck.de; Peter
Strohmeier *E-mail:* peter.strohmeier@
holzmann-druck.de
Sales: Andreas Kopf *E-mail:* andreas.kopf@
holzmann-druck.de; Anton Niedermayer
E-mail: anton.niedermayer@holzmann-druck.de

Kartonagenwerkstatt
Dorfstr 49, 09306 Koenigshain-Wiederau
Tel: (037202) 2583 *Fax:* (037202) 89024
E-mail: info@kartonagenwerkstatt.de
Web Site: www.kartonagenwerkstatt.de
Key Personnel
Owner: Eckhart Trommer
Founded: 1992

Druckverlag Kettler GmbH
Robert-Bosch-Str 14, 59199 Boenen, Westfalen
Tel: (02383) 91013-0 *Fax:* (02383) 91013-40
E-mail: info@druckverlag-kettler.de
Web Site: www.druckverlag-kettler.com
Key Personnel
Mng Dir: Gunnar Kettler *Tel:* (02383) 91013-13
E-mail: g.kettler@druckverlag-kettler.de

LASERLINE
Scheringstr 1, 13355 Berlin-Mitte
Tel: (030) 46 70 96-0 *Fax:* (030) 46 70 96-66
E-mail: info@laser-line.de
Web Site: www.laser-line.de
Key Personnel
Executive Partner: Tomislav Bucec
E-mail: bucec@laser-line.de
Technical Dir: Rolf Henkel *E-mail:* rolf.henkel@
laser-line.de
Commercial Manager: Christian Luther
E-mail: christian.luther@laser-line.de

Sales & Marketing Manager: Steffen Setzer
E-mail: steffen.setzer@laser-line.de
Branch Office(s)
Doventorstr 6, 28195 Bremen *Tel:* (0421) 222 33-
0 *E-mail:* bremen@laser-line.de

**Makrolog Content Management
Aktiengesellschaft**
Patrickstr 43, 65191 Wiesbaden
Tel: (0611) 95782-0 *Fax:* (0611) 95782-28
E-mail: postmaster@makrolog.ag
Web Site: www.makrolog.ag
Key Personnel
Management: Andreas Herberger
Founded: 1980

C Maurer Druck und Verlag GmbH & Co KG
Schubartstr 21, 73312 Geislingen/Steige
Tel: (07331) 930-0 *Fax:* (07331) 930-190
E-mail: info@maurer-online.de
Web Site: www.maurer-online.de
Key Personnel
Mng Dir: Carl Otto Maurer
Founded: 1856

Mayr Miesbach GmbH
Am Windfeld 15, 83714 Miesbach
Tel: (08025) 294-0 *Fax:* (08025) 294-235
E-mail: info@mayrmiesbach.de
Web Site: www.mayrmiesbach.de
Key Personnel
Mng Dir: Ulrich Herzog; Siegfried Kaspar
Founded: 1874

Media-Print Informationstechnologie GmbH
Unit of Media-Print Group GmbH
Eggertstr 30, 33100 Paderborn
Tel: (05251) 5408-0 *Fax:* (05251) 5408-144
E-mail: group@mediaprint.de
Web Site: www.mediaprint.de
Key Personnel
Mng Dir: Dr Otto W Drosihn; Rainer Rings; Ulf
Stornebel
Founded: 1993
Turnaround: 5-10 Workdays
Print Runs: 100 min - 300,000 max
Business from Other Countries: 10%

Mohn Media Mohndruck GmbH
Member of Bertelsmann Printing Group
Carl-Bertelsmann-Str 161M, 33311 Guetersloh
Tel: (05241) 80-40410 *Fax:* (05241) 80-65288
E-mail: mohnmedia@bertelsmann.de
Web Site: www.mohnmedia.de
Key Personnel
Mng Dir: Axel Hentrei; Wilfried Velte
Sales Dir: Alasdair Gibson
Founded: 1824
Business from Other Countries: 25%
Ultimate Parent Company: Bertelsmann SE & Co
KGaA

MXM Digital Service GmbH
Alpenstr 12a, 81541 Munich
Tel: (089) 69364680 *Fax:* (089) 69373939
E-mail: info@mxm.de
Web Site: www.mxm.de
Key Personnel
Mng Dir: Marion Moeller; Rita Moeller

optimal media GmbH
Glienholzweg 7, 17207 Roebel/Mueritz
Tel: (039931) 56 500 *Fax:* (039931) 56 555
E-mail: info@optimal-media.de
Web Site: www.optimal-media.com
Key Personnel
Mng Dir: Joerg Hahn *Tel:* (039931) 56 516
E-mail: joerg.hahn@optimal-media.com
Dir, Finance: Rainer Hake *E-mail:* rainer.hake@
optimal-media.com
Dir, Operations: Dr Peter Runge *E-mail:* peter.
runge@optimal-media.com

Dir, Sales & Marketing: Grit Schreiber
Tel: (039931) 56 525 *E-mail:* grit.schreiber@
optimal-media.com
Head, International Sales & Executive Manager:
Rufus Kalex *E-mail:* rufus.kalex@optimal-
media.com
Executive Assistant/Public Relations: Petra Funk
Tel: (039931) 56 516 *E-mail:* petra.funk@
optimal-media.com
Branch Office(s)
Str der Pariser Kommune 38, 10243 Berlin
Tel: (030) 28883790 *Fax:* (030) 2888379 11
Neumuehlen 17, 22763 Hamburg *Tel:* (040)
29812050 *Fax:* (040) 2981205 13
Idungatan 8, 113 45 Stockholm, Sweden, Con-
tact: Carl-Marcus Gidloef *Tel:* (08) 704 581412
E-mail: carl-marcus.gidloef@optimal-media.
com
optimal media UK Ltd, Coppergate House, 16
Brune St, London E1 7NJ, United Kingdom,
Contact: Julia Voelkel *E-mail:* julia.voelkel@
optimal-media.com

Peyer Graphic GmbH
Mollenbachstr 33-35, 71229 Leonberg
Tel: (07152) 608591 *Fax:* (07152) 608510
E-mail: cover@peyergraphic.de
Web Site: www.peyergraphic.de
Key Personnel
Chief Executive Officer: Oliver Schibli
E-mail: oliver.schibli@peyergraphic.de
Chief Financial Officer: Daniel Erne
E-mail: daniel.erne@peyergraphic.de
Mng Dir: Andreas Lenz *Tel:* (01752) 608511
E-mail: andreas.lenz@peyergraphic.de
Sales Manager: Frank Balzereit *E-mail:* frank.
balzereit@peyergraphic.de
Branch Office(s)
Peyer Graphic AG, Weststr 10, 5426 Lengnau,
Switzerland *Tel:* (056) 266 5151 *Fax:* (056)
266 5152 *E-mail:* info@peyergraphic.ch

Phoenix Print GmbH
Alfred-Nobel-Str 33, 97080 Wuerzburg
Tel: (0931) 385-0 *Fax:* (0931) 385-200
E-mail: info@phoenixprint.de
Web Site: www.phoenixprint.de
Key Personnel
Mng Dir: Ramona Weiss Weber

Priese GmbH
Saatwinkler Damm 42A, 13627 Berlin
Tel: (030) 8263024 *Fax:* (030) 8266024

Prinovis GmbH & Co KG
Member of Bertelsmann Printing Group
Gasstr 18, 22761 Hamburg
Tel: (040) 570130-0 *Toll Free Tel:* 0800
77466847 (sales)
E-mail: kontakt@prinovis.com; sales@prinovis.
com
Web Site: www.prinovis.com
Key Personnel
Chief Executive Officer: Dr Bertram Stausberg
Executive Dir: Dr Ulrich Cordes
Corporate Communications: Mathias Wulff
Tel: (040) 570130-9150 *E-mail:* mathias.
wulff@prinovis.com
Ultimate Parent Company: Bertelsmann SE & Co
KGaA
Branch Office(s)
Alter Postweg 6, 22926 Ahrensburg *Tel:* (04102)
71-1270
Meinholdstr 2, 01129 Dresden *Tel:* (0351) 8545-0
Breslauer Str 300, 90471 Nuremberg *Tel:* (0911)
8003-0
93, Avenue Charles de Gaulle, 92521 Neuilly-sur-
Seine Cedex, France *Tel:* 01 76 21 85 07
Prinovis UK Ltd, Liverpool International Business
Park, 4 Dakota Dr, Speke, Liverpool L24 8RJ,
United Kingdom *Tel:* (0151) 4945200

Printsystem GmbH
Schafwaesche 1-3, 71296 Heimsheim
Tel: (07033) 3825 *Fax:* (07033) 3827
E-mail: info@printsystem.de
Web Site: www.printsystem.de
Key Personnel
Mng Dir: Harmut Harfensteller
Manager: Gero Hausmann
Founded: 1979

Sachsendruck Plauen GmbH
Paul-Schneider-Str 12, 08525 Plauen
Tel: (03741) 213 180 *Fax:* (03741) 213 117
E-mail: dialog@sachsendruck.de
Web Site: www.sachsendruck.de
Key Personnel
Chief Executive Officer: Andreas Moessner
Mng Partner: Stephan Treuleben *Tel:* (03741) 213
0 *E-mail:* stephan.treuleben@sachsendruck.de
International Sales: Alexander Treuleben
E-mail: alexander.treuleben@sachsendruck.de

LN Schaffrath GmbH & Co KG DruckMedien
Markweg 42-50, 47608 Geldern
Tel: (028) 31396-0 *Fax:* (028) 31396-110
E-mail: info@schaffrath.de
Web Site: www.schaffrath.de; www.schaffrath-
print.de
Key Personnel
General Manager: Dirk Alten *Tel:* (028) 31396-
132 *E-mail:* dirk.alten@schaffrath.de; Dirk
Devers *Tel:* (028) 31396-121 *E-mail:* dirk.
devers@schaffrath.de
Management, Bookbinding: Hans-Josef Schmetter
Tel: (028) 31396-178 *E-mail:* hans.schmetter@
schaffrath.de
Technical Dir: Martin Sellmann *Tel:* (028) 31396-
216 *E-mail:* martin.sellmann@schaffrath.de
Parent Company: Schaffrath Medien

Buchbinderei Schaumann GmbH
Staudingerstr 4, 64293 Darmstadt
Tel: (06151) 86060-0 *Fax:* (06151) 86060-29
E-mail: buchbinderei_schaumann@bbsm.de
Web Site: www.buchbinderei-schaumann.de
Key Personnel
Mng Dir: Juergen Blitz; Reiner Vettermann; Ul-
rike Vettermann
Founded: 1963

Druckerei Schroeder
Schuppertsgasse 2, 35083 Wetter
Tel: (06423) 921-33 *Fax:* (06423) 921-35
E-mail: info@druckerei-schroeder.de
Web Site: www.druckerei-schroeder.de
Key Personnel
Mng Dir: Bernard Schroeder

Druckhaus Schuetze GmbH
Fiete-Schulze-Str 13a, 06116 Halle (Saale)
Tel: (0345) 56666-0 *Fax:* (0345) 56666-66
E-mail: info@dhs-halle.de; vertrieb@dhs-halle.de
Web Site: www.dhs-halle.de
Key Personnel
Mng Dir: Stephan Probst; Florian Schaefer
Founded: 1990

SDK Systemdruck Koeln GmbH & Co KG
Member of Rudolf Mueller Group
Maarweg 233, 50825 Cologne
Tel: (0221) 949868-0 *Fax:* (0221) 949868-19
E-mail: info@sdk-koeln.de
Web Site: www.sdk-koeln.de
Key Personnel
Management: Dr Christoph Mueller *Tel:* (0221)
5497-236 *E-mail:* gf@rudolf-mueller.de; Nicole
Royar *Tel:* (0221) 949868-16 *Fax:* (0221)
949868-39 *E-mail:* n.royar@sdk-koeln.de

Tabor Presse Berlin GbR
Taborstr 22, 10997 Berlin

Tel: (030) 6116096
E-mail: mail@taborpresse.de
Web Site: www.taborpresse.de; www.taboerlin.de
Key Personnel
Owner: Klaus Buescher *E-mail:* kb@taboerlin.de;
Paul Kloes; Jan Pelkofer
Founded: 1983

Thiekoetter Druck GmbH & Co KG
An der Kleimannbruecke 32, 48157 Muenster
Tel: (0251) 14 14 60 *Fax:* (0251) 14 14 666
E-mail: info@thiekoetter-druck.de
Web Site: www.thiekoetter-druck.de
Key Personnel
Mng Dir: Bernd Thiekoetter
Founded: 1879

Vier-Tuerme-GmbH, Benedict Press
Schweinfurter Str 40, 97359 Muensterschwarzach
Abtei
Tel: (09324) 20214 *Fax:* (09324) 20444
E-mail: druckerei@vier-tuerme.de
Web Site: www.druckerei.abtei-
muensterschwarzach.de
Key Personnel
Mng Dir: Fr Christoph Gerhard
Dir: Br Alfred Engert
Technical Dir: Reinhold Doering *Tel:* (09324)
20442
Founded: 1923
Turnaround: 8-16 Workdays
Print Runs: 300 min - 20,000 max
Business from Other Countries: 5%

Vogel Druck und Medienservice GmbH
Member of Bertelsmann Printing Group
Leibnizstr 5, 97204 Hoechberg
Tel: (0931) 4600-02 *Fax:* (0931) 4600-2145
E-mail: info@vogel-druck.de
Web Site: www.vogel-druck.de
Key Personnel
Mng Dir: Rolf Lenertz *E-mail:* rolf.lenertz@
vogel-druck.de; Axel Hentrei
Assistant Mng Dir: Sonja Endres *E-mail:* sonja.
endres@vogel-druck.de
Head, Marketing: Beatrice Rieck *E-mail:* beatrice.
rieck@vogel-druck.de
Head, Sales: Dietmar Fuchs *E-mail:* dietmar.
fuchs@vogel-druck.de
Ultimate Parent Company: Bertelsmann SE & Co
KGaA

**Wanderer Werbedruck Horst Wanderer
GmbH**
Lagenfeldstr 8, 30952 Ronnenberg
Tel: (0511) 13 22 11 50 *Fax:* (0511) 13 22 11 55
E-mail: offizin@wanderer-druck.de
Web Site: www.wanderer-druckerei.de
Key Personnel
Mng Dir: Jochen Wanderer *Tel:* (0511) 13 22 11
99 *E-mail:* wanderer@wanderer-druck.de

Edition Winterwork
Carl-Zeiss-Str 3, 04451 Borsdorf
Tel: (034291) 3172-0 *Fax:* (034291) 3172-16
E-mail: mail@edition-winterwork.de
Web Site: www.edition-winterwork.de
Key Personnel
Contact: Mike Winter *Tel:* (034291) 3172-18
E-mail: mike.winter@winterwork.de

Hong Kong

Anpak Printing Ltd
9/F, Eastern Center, 1065 King's Rd, Hong Kong
Tel: 2811 4118; 2563 4133 *Fax:* 2565 7710; 2811
3501

E-mail: info@anpak.com
Web Site: www.anpak.com
Founded: 1971
Branch Office(s)
Anpak Printing (Shenzhen) Ltd, 36 Tangxiayong Gongye Ave, Songgang Town, Baoan District, Shenzhen, China
Songan Printing (Shenzhen) Co Ltd, 2 Langhui Rd, Songgang Town, Baoan District, Shenzhen, China

AOP, see Asia One Printing (AOP)

Asia One Printing (AOP)
Division of Asia One Communications Group
13/F, Asia One Tower, 8 Fung Yip St, Chai Wan
Tel: 2889 2320 *Fax:* 2889 3837
E-mail: enquiry@asiaone.com.hk
Web Site: www.asiaone.com.hk
Key Personnel
Business Development Dir: Evan Cheung
   Tel: 2889 8189 *E-mail:* evanccp@asiaone.com.hk
Sales Dir: Andy Chan *Tel:* 2889 2406
   E-mail: andy@asiaone.com.hk
Production Dir: Alan Tam *Tel:* 2889 8520
   E-mail: alantam@asiaone.com.hk
Founded: 1997

Bookbuilders Ltd
Unit A-B, 7th floor, Yeung Yiu Chung No 8 Industrial Bldg, 20 Wang Hoi Rd, Kowloon Bay
Tel: 2796 8123 *Fax:* 2796 8690
Key Personnel
General Manager: Kevin Wan

C & C Offset Printing Co Ltd
Subsidiary of C & C Joint Printing Co (HK) Ltd
14/F, C & C Bldg, 36 Ting Lai Rd, Tai Po, New Territories
Tel: 2666 4988 *Fax:* 2666 4938
E-mail: offsetprinting@candcprinting.com
Web Site: www.ccoffset.com; www.candcprinting.com
Key Personnel
Chief Executive Officer, C & C Joint Printing Co (HK) Ltd: Jackson Leung
Founded: 1980
Turnaround: 30-42 Workdays
Print Runs: 2,000 min - 1,000,000 max
Business from Other Countries: 60%
Ultimate Parent Company: Sino United Publishing (Holdings) Ltd
Branch Office(s)
3-7 Permas Way, Truganina, Victoria 3029, Australia, Contact: Ms Lena Frew *Tel:* (03) 8366 0200 *Fax:* (03) 8366 0299 *E-mail:* lena.frew@candcprinting.com
Room 301, No 29, 165 lane, DongZhuAnBang Rd (C), Shanghai 200050, China, Contact: Ms Zhang Zhi Ying *Tel:* (021) 6240 1305 *Fax:* (021) 5922 6111 *E-mail:* zhang.zhi.ying@candcprinting.com
3, rue Chabanais, 75002 Paris, France, Contact: Michele Olson Niel *Tel:* 01 71 70 39 00 *Fax:* 01 70 71 92 85 *E-mail:* info@candcoffset.fr (Continental Europe off)
C & C Printing Japan Co Ltd, Jewel Ginza 301, 7-17-18 Ginza, Chuo-ku, Tokyo 104-0061, Japan, Contact: Mr Masaaki Yamamoto *Tel:* (03) 6264 3751 *Fax:* (03) 6264 3752 *E-mail:* yamamoto@candcprinting.co.jp *Web Site:* www.candcprinting.co.jp
C & C Offset Printing Co (UK) Ltd, Tudor House, 4th floor, 35 Grasse St, London W1T 1QY, United Kingdom, Contact: Helena Coryndon *Tel:* (020) 7637 5033 *Fax:* (020) 7637 5044 *E-mail:* helena@candcoffset.co.uk
U.S. Office(s): C & C Offset Printing Co (Chicago) Inc, PO Box 4678, Naperville, IL 60567, United States, Contact: Mr Ernest Li

Tel: 630-390-5617 *E-mail:* ernest.li@ccoffset.com
C & C Offset Printing Co (NY) Inc, 70 W 36 St, Unit 10C, New York, NY 10018, United States, Contact: Simon Chan *Tel:* 212-431-4210 *E-mail:* schan@ccoffset.com

Caritas Printing Training Centre
Caritas House, 2 Caine Rd, Hong Kong
Tel: 2843 4734; 2524 2071 *Fax:* 2523 0438
E-mail: info@caritas.org.hk
Web Site: www.caritas.org.hk
Founded: 1953
Print Runs: 1,000 min - 100,000 max
Business from Other Countries: 50%
Parent Company: Caritas Hong Kong

Colorprint Offset
Unit 1808-9, 18/F, 8 Commercial Tower, 8 Sun Yip St, Chai Wan
Tel: 2896 7777 *Fax:* 2869 6666
E-mail: info@cpo.com.hk
Web Site: www.cpo.com.hk
Key Personnel
General Manager: Rachel Lai
Founded: 1989
Turnaround: Standard 2 week turnaround
Print Runs: 3,000 min - 100,000 max
Business from Other Countries: 80%
Branch Office(s)
Zone E1, Tangtou Industrial Estate, Shiyan, Shenzhen 518018, China *Tel:* (0755) 29680000 *Fax:* (0755) 29680203
Untergassli 7, 2502 Biel/Bienne, Switzerland *Tel:* (032) 322 05 08 *Fax:* (032) 322 05 08
St Niklaus Str 12, 6005 Lucerne, Switzerland *Tel:* (041) 340 3192 *Fax:* (041) 340 1237
Sales Office(s): Niederwaldstr 40, 76532 Baden-Baden, Germany *Tel:* (07221) 60582 *Fax:* (07221) 3759747

Everbest Printing Co Ltd
10/F, Block C, Seaview Estate, 2-8 Watson Rd, North Point, Hong Kong
Tel: 2727 4433 *Fax:* 2772 7687
E-mail: sales@everbest.com.hk
Web Site: www.everbest.com
Founded: 1954
Turnaround: 21-28 Workdays
Print Runs: 1,000 min - 1,000,000 max
Business from Other Countries: 90%
Branch Office(s)
Everbest (Guangzhou) Printing Co Ltd, 334 Huanshi Rd S, Nansha, Panyu, Guangdong 511458, China *Tel:* (020) 8498 1812 (manufacturing plant)
Sales Office(s): C5, 10/F, Ko Fai Industrial Bldg, 7 Ko Fai Rd, Yau Tong *Tel:* 2727 4433 *Fax:* 2772 7687 (Australia, Europe & New Zealand)
313 30 St, Toronto, ON M8W 3E4, Canada, Contact: Doris Chung *Tel:* 416-286-2525 *Fax:* 416-804-8930 *E-mail:* doris@everbestcanada.ca
Origo Ediciones, Padre Alonso de Ovalle 748, 8330169 Santiago, Chile, Contact: Hernan Maino *Tel:* (02) 480 9800 *E-mail:* hernan.maino@origo.cl *Web Site:* www.origo.cl (Chile & South America)
Nostra Ediciones SA de CV, Av Revolucion 1181 piso 7, Col Merced Gomez, Del Benito Juarez, 03930 Mexico, DF, Mexico, Contact: Mauricio Volpi *Tel:* (0155) 5554 7030 *E-mail:* impresion@nostraediciones.com
31 Palatine Rd, London N16 8SY, United Kingdom, Contact: Nicky Bowden *Tel:* (020) 7249 9483 *Fax:* (020) 7241 3460 *E-mail:* nickybowden@everbest.co.uk
Todd Communications, 611 E 12 Ave, Anchorage, AK 99501, United States, Contact: Flip Todd *Tel:* 907-5274-8633 *Fax:* 907-929-5550 *E-mail:* flip@toddcom.com *Web Site:* www.toddcom.com

Four Colour Imports Ltd, 2410 Frankfort Ave, Louisville, KY 40206, United States, Contact: George Dick *Tel:* 502-896-9644 *Fax:* 502-896-9594 *E-mail:* sales@fourcolour.com

Golden Cup Printing Co Ltd
6/F, 177 Hoi Bun Rd, Kwun Tong, Kowloon
Tel: 2343 4254 *Fax:* 2341 5426
E-mail: sales@goldencup.com.hk
Web Site: www.goldencup.com.hk
Key Personnel
Chairman: Kam Kai Yeung
Founded: 1971
Turnaround: 25 Workdays
Print Runs: 5,000 min - 200,000 max
Business from Other Countries: 80%
Sales Office(s): Tutang Industrial Area, Jin Bei Rd, Changping, Dongguan, Guangdong, China *Tel:* (0769) 8339 4888 *Fax:* (0769) 8339 4999
Qilin Industrial Estate, Guanlan, Shenzhen, Guangdong, China *Tel:* (0755) 2805 6279 *Fax:* (0755) 2805 6086
Jinma Town, Guandu District, Kunming, Yunnan, China *Tel:* (0871) 316 1226 *Fax:* (0871) 316 1226
Terley House, Cadbury, Exeter EX5 5JZ, United Kingdom *Tel:* (01884) 855736 *E-mail:* info@gcpservices.com
Spectrum Books Inc, 2455 Bennett Valley Rd, Suite C-116, Santa Rosa, CA 95404-5671, United States *Tel:* 707-542-6044 *Fax:* 707-542-6045

Great Wall Printing Co Ltd
Member of Prosperous Printing Group
3/F, Yip Cheung Centre, 10 Fung Yip St, Chai Wan
Tel: 2897 1083 *Fax:* 2558 1473
E-mail: books@gwp.com.hk
Web Site: www.gwp.com.hk
Key Personnel
Mng Dir: George Lo; Franky Ho
Founded: 1984
Print Runs: 3,000 min - 500,000 max
Business from Other Countries: 80%
Branch Office(s)
Haverdreef 39, 7006 LH Doetinchen, Netherlands, Contact: Buro Doral *Tel:* (0314) 35 40 40 *Fax:* (0314) 35 46 00 *E-mail:* info@ssip-holland.nl *Web Site:* www.ssip-holland.nl
The High Barn, Snailing Lane, Hawkley GU33 6NJ, United Kingdom, Contact: Myles Wells *Tel:* (01) 730 827 326 *Fax:* (01) 730 827 537 *E-mail:* members@eastwest.fsworld.co.uk

The Green Pagoda Press Ltd
13/F, Block A, Tung Chong Factory Bldg, 633-655 King's Rd, North Point, Hong Kong
Tel: 2561 1924 *Fax:* 2811 0946
E-mail: gpinfo@gpp.com.hk
Web Site: www.gpp.com.hk
Key Personnel
Mng Dir: Yip Yu Bun
Founded: 1957
Turnaround: 1-14 days
Print Runs: 10 min - 500,000 max
Business from Other Countries: 30%

Hing Yip Printing Co Ltd
Block C&D, 6/F, Sing Teck Factory Bldg 44, Wong Chuk Hang Rd, Aberdeen
Tel: 2870 2379 *Fax:* 2873 5317
E-mail: info@hyprint.com.hk; sales@hyprint.com.hk
Web Site: www.hyprint.com.hk
Key Personnel
Sales Manager: Edward Lee
Founded: 1962
Print Runs: 1,000 min - 100,000 max
Business from Other Countries: 95%

Hua Yang Printing Holdings Co Ltd
Tai Ping Industrial Centre, Unit B, 25/F, Block 1, 57 Ting Kok Rd, Tai Po, New Territories
Tel: 2416 7591 *Fax:* 2411 0235
Key Personnel
Founder: C M Chan
Chief Operating Officer & Chief Financial Officer: Feather S Fok
Vice President, International Marketing: Tony Brooks
Founded: 1935

Hung Hing Off-Set Printing Co Ltd
Subsidiary of Hung Hing Printing Group Ltd
Tai Po Industrial Estate, 17-19 Dai Hei St, New Territories
Tel: 2664 8682 *Fax:* 2664 2070
E-mail: info@hunghingprinting.com
Web Site: www.hhop.com.hk
Key Personnel
Executive Chairman: Matthew Yum Chak Ming
Executive Dir: Spencer Sung Chee Keung
Chief Information Officer: Yee Y Yu
Founded: 1950
Turnaround: 20-30 Workdays
Print Runs: 5,000 min - 1,000,000 max
Business from Other Countries: 15%
Sales Office(s): Santiago del Estero 454, Piso 1, Oficina 5 y 6, C1075AAJ Buenos Aires, Argentina, Contact: Leonardo Adami *Tel:* (011) 4-179-2178 *E-mail:* enquiry@sa. hunghingprinting.com (South America)
Vilvordevej 35, 2920 Charlottenlund, Denmark, Contact: Jesper Frederiksen *Tel:* 40 26 40 57 *Fax:* 39 90 40 58 *E-mail:* jf@sc. hunghingprinting.com (Scandinavia)
33, Avenue du Maine, 75755 Paris, France, Contact: Florent Verlet *Tel:* 01 44 10 40 85 *E-mail:* florent@fr.hunghingprinting.com
PI Print Innovations GmbH, Untere Haupstr 13, 85354 Freising, Germany, Contact: Birgit von der Gathen *Tel:* (08161) 887717-0 *Fax:* (08161) 88717-10 *E-mail:* birgit@de.hunghingprinting. com *Web Site:* www.hunghing.de (Central Europe & Germany)
IPP Printers, Emmastr 2-D, 4811 AG Breda, Netherlands, Dir & Sales: Peter Jonkers *Tel:* (076) 521 7025; (0473) 561 565 *Fax:* (076) 520 7281 *E-mail:* peter@bn. hunghingprinting.com *Web Site:* www. ippprinters.com (Benelux)
Hung Hing UK, 49 Leigh Rd, Eastleigh, Hants SO50 9DF, United Kingdom, Sales Dir: Karen Giles *Tel:* (023) 8062 5858 *Fax:* (023) 8062 9366 *E-mail:* enquiries@hunghing.co.uk *Web Site:* www.hunghing.co.uk
U.S. Office(s): 29 Arden Rd, East Rockaway, NY 11518, United States, Contact: Jeff Tollin *Tel:* 516-593-0030 *Fax:* 516-593-7024 *E-mail:* hunghingusa@aol.com *Web Site:* www. hunghing-usa.com

Icicle Production Co Ltd
7/F, Cheung Wah Industrial Bldg, 10-12 Shipyard Lane, Quarry Bay, Hong Kong
Tel: 2235 2880
E-mail: info@iciclegroup.com
Web Site: www.iciclegroup.com
Key Personnel
Founding Chairman: Alex Chan *Tel:* 2235 2818 *E-mail:* alex.chan@iciclegroup.com
Chief Executive Officer: Bonnie Chan *Tel:* 2235 2888 *E-mail:* bonnie.chan@iciclegroup.com
Senior Partner: Josephine Cheung *Tel:* 2235 2800
Founded: 1998
Turnaround: 28-56 Workdays
Print Runs: 1,000 min - 100,000 max
Business from Other Countries: 10%
Parent Company: Icicle Group
Branch Office(s)
Room 1215, 12/F, Silver Tower, No 2 North Dong Sanhuan Rd, Chaoyang District, Beijing 100027, China *Tel:* (010) 6410 9926 *E-mail:* china@iciclegroup.com
6 F/E Wenxin Press Bldg, 755 Weihai Rd, Shanghai 200041, China *Tel:* (010) 6410 9926
Unit 16-0 Burgundy Corporate Tower, 252 Gil Puyat Ave, Makati City, Metro Manila, Philippines
19 Carpenter St, 04-01, Singapore 059908, Singapore *Tel:* 8438 5601 *E-mail:* singapore@ iciclegroup.com
2F, 1, No 37, Sec 3, Minquan E Rd, Taipei, Taiwan *Tel:* (02) 7702 1168 *E-mail:* taiwan@ iciclegroup.com
Garden Studios, DL10, 71-75 Shelton St, Covent Garden, London WC2H 9JQ, United Kingdom *Tel:* (020) 8123 1868 *E-mail:* london@ iciclegroup.com

Lammar Offset Printing Ltd
12/F, Prince Industrial Bldg, 5 Sun Yip St, Chai Wan
Tel: 2597 6800 *Fax:* 2811 3375
Web Site: www.lammar.com.hk
Key Personnel
Marketing Manager: Alice Woo *E-mail:* awoo@ lammar.com.hk
Founded: 1970

Leo Paper Products Ltd
Level 9, Telford House, 16 Wang Hoi Rd, Kowloon Bay, Kowloon
Tel: 2884 1374 *Fax:* 2513 0698
E-mail: info@leo.com.hk
Web Site: www.leo.com.hk
Key Personnel
Sales Dir: Mr Kelly Fok *E-mail:* kelly@leo.com. uk
Founded: 1982
Turnaround: 15-30 Workdays
Print Runs: 5,000 min
Parent Company: Leo Paper Group
Sales Office(s): Leo Paper Products (Europe) BVBA, Korte Leemstr 3, 2018 Antwerp, Belgium *Tel:* (03) 609-6810 *Fax:* (03) 609-6830 *E-mail:* leo@leo-europe.com
Heshan Astros Printing Ltd, Industrial Development Area, Xijiang River, Gulao Town, Heshan City, Guangdong, China *Tel:* (0750) 8766-115 *Fax:* (0750) 8766-369
Heshan Leo Packaging & Printing Ltd, Sanlian Industrial City, Gulao Town, Heshan City, Guangdong, China *Tel:* (0750) 8861-888 *Fax:* (0750) 8861-500
Heshan Leo United Paper Products Ltd, 023 Industrial Zone 1, Hecheng Town, Heshan City, Guangdong 529727, China *Tel:* (0750) 8383-300 *Fax:* (0750) 8383-301
JiangXi HuaAo Printing Co Ltd, Changdong Industrial District, Middle Dong Tai Rd, Nanchang, Jiangxi 330012, China
Leo Creative (Shanghai) Trading Co Ltd, HuaJing Bldg, 3rd floor, 678 HuaShang Rd, Shanghai 200040, China *Tel:* (021) 6211-8799 *Fax:* (021) 6289-6226 *E-mail:* info@leo-creative.com
Shanghai Tophand Business Printing Co Ltd, 1F Bldg 10, No 189 Jinglian Rd, Minhang District, Shanghai 201108, China
Leo Paper Products (Europe) BVBA, Via Galliera, Unit 24, 40121 Bologna, Italy *Tel:* (051) 0922610 *Fax:* (051) 0922630 *E-mail:* leo@leo-europe.com
Leo Paper Products (UK) Ltd, The Oast House, 10 Brewery Court, Theale, Reading RG7 5AJ, United Kingdom *Tel:* (0118) 9165450 *E-mail:* info@leouk.com
U.S. Office(s): Leo Paper USA, 27 W 24 St, Suite 601, New York, NY 10010-3204, United States *Tel:* 917-305-0708 *Fax:* 917-305-0709 *E-mail:* info@leousanewyork.com
Leo Paper USA, 1180 NW Maple St, Suite 102, Issaquah, WA 98027, United States *Tel:* 425-646-8801 *Fax:* 425-646-8805 *E-mail:* info@ leousa.com

Lion Rock Group
Formerly 1010 Printing Group Ltd
26/F, 625 King's Rd, North Point
Tel: 8226 1010 *Fax:* 2202 3298
E-mail: investor@lionrockgrouphk.com
Web Site: www.lionrockgrouphk.com
Key Personnel
Deputy General Manager: Regan Su
Founded: 2005
Branch Office(s)
1010 Printing Australia, 75/283 Given Terrace, Paddington, Qld 4064, Australia, Sales Dir: Tiffany Johnson *Tel:* (07) 3367 2047 *Fax:* (07) 3367 2087
1010 Ave, Xia Nan Industrial District, Yuan Zhou Town, Bo Luo County, Hui Zhou, Guang Dong Province 516123, China *Tel:* (0752) 618 1010 *Fax:* (0752) 611 1010
1010 Printing UK Ltd, 4 Crescent Stables, 139 Upper Richmond Rd, London SW15 2TN, United Kingdom, Sales Dir: Andrew Law *Tel:* (020) 8780 7000 *Fax:* (020) 8788 9362
U.S. Office(s): Ocean Graphic International Inc, 105 Main St, 1st floor, Hackensack, NJ 07601, United States, Dir, US Sales: Dean Sherman *Tel:* 201-883-1816 *Fax:* 201-883-1826

Macmillan Production (Asia) Ltd
Subsidiary of Macmillan Publishers Ltd
Suite 811, 8F, Exchange Tower, 33 Wangchiu Rd, Kowloon Bay
Tel: 2811 8781 *Fax:* 2811 0743
E-mail: mpa.enquiry@macmillan.com.hk
Web Site: www.macmillan.com.hk; www. macmillanproductionasia.com
Key Personnel
Mng Dir: Colin Bond
Distribution Dir: Trevor Sanger
Production Dir: Tony Chan
General Manager: Andrew Lam
Founded: 1976
Turnaround: 20-40 Workdays
Print Runs: 1,000 min
Business from Other Countries: 100%
Branch Office(s)
3/F, Lot 25 Rawang Integrated Industrial Park, Mukim Rawang, Jl Batu Arang, 48000 Rawang, Selangor Darul Ehsan, Malaysia, Production Dir: Rieza Adriano *Tel:* (03) 6092 3808 *Fax:* (03) 6092 3230 *E-mail:* rieza. adriano@mpalmalaysia.com
Wave Place Bldg, Unit 3, 9th floor, Wireless Rd, Lumpini, Pathumwan, Bangkok 10330, Thailand, Production Dir: Tony Chan *Tel:* (02) 655 4064 *Fax:* (02) 655 4065 *E-mail:* tony@ mpalthailand.com
Sales Office(s): Weidestr 122a, 22083 Hamburg, Germany, Contact: Diana Cheung *Tel:* (040) 84 00 08-171 *Fax:* (040) 84 00 08-22 *E-mail:* diana.cheung@hgv-online.de
33 Irving Pl, 10th floor, New York, NY 10003, United States, Contact: Anthony Campanella *Tel:* 212-375-7107 *Fax:* 212-614-1885 *E-mail:* anthonyatmpa@gmail.com

Midas International Holdings Ltd
25/F, Alexandra House, 18 Chater Rd, Central Hong Kong
Tel: 2407 6888 *Fax:* 2408 0611
E-mail: info@midasprinting.com; marketing@ midasprinting.com
Web Site: www.midasprinting.com
Key Personnel
Chairman & Group Mng Dir: Richard Hung Ting Ho
Deputy Group Mng Dir: Geoffrey Chuang Ka Kam
Founded: 1990
Turnaround: 10 Workdays for paperback; 15 Workdays for casebound
Print Runs: 3,000 min
Business from Other Countries: 85%

Branch Office(s)
88 Kingsway, Holborn, London WC2B 6AA, United Kingdom, Sales Manager: Christos Plegas *E-mail:* christos_plegas@midasprinting.com

Nordica Printing Co Ltd
Unit B, 17th floor, Chang Pao Ching Bldg, 427-429 Hennessy Rd, Wanchai
Tel: 2564 8444 *Fax:* 2565 6445
E-mail: sales@nordicaprint.com
Web Site: www.nordicaprint.com
Founded: 1994
Parent Company: Nordica International Ltd
Branch Office(s)
No 349 Caixin Rd, Man Sang Industrial Area, Lanhe Town, Panyu, Guangzhou 511480, China
Tel: (020) 8492844 *Fax:* (020) 84928122

Paper Art Product Ltd
Sung Fung Centre, Room 819, Block B, 88 Kwok Shui Rd, Kwai Chung, New Territories
Tel: 2481 2929 *Fax:* 2489 2255
E-mail: paperart@netvigator.com
Founded: 1988
Turnaround: 4-8 Weeks
Print Runs: 3,000 min - 1,000,000 max
Business from Other Countries: 80%

Papercom Ltd, see Icicle Production Co Ltd

Paramount Printing Co Ltd
Member of Next Media Group
3 Chun Kwong St, T K O Industrial Estate W, Tseung Kwan O, New Territories
Tel: 2896 8688 *Fax:* 2897 8942
E-mail: paramountcs@paramount.com.hk
Web Site: www.paramount.com.hk
Founded: 1968
Turnaround: 30-45 Workdays
Print Runs: 1,000 min - 1,000,000 max
Business from Other Countries: 60%
Branch Office(s)
Book Art Inc, 2800 John St, Unit 13, Markham, ON L3R 0E2, Canada *Tel:* 905-940-8282 *Fax:* 905-470-1800 *E-mail:* enquires@bookartinc.com

Regent Publishing Services Ltd
Units B & C, 7/F, Genesis, No 33-35 Wong Chuk Hang Rd, Shau Kei Wan
Tel: 2897 7803 *Fax:* 2558 7209
Web Site: www.regent-hk.com.hk
Key Personnel
Mng Dir: George Tai *E-mail:* gtai@regent-hk.com.hk
Marketing Manager: Francis Tong
E-mail: francist@regent-hk.com.hk
Founded: 1985
Print Runs: 1,000 min - 300,000 max
Branch Office(s)
Gumpendorfer Str 41, 1060 Vienna, Austria, Sales Manager: Gabriela Scolik *Tel:* (01) 544 23 33 12 *Fax:* (01) 544 23 33 16 *E-mail:* office@printcompany.co.at
Ricorico 11c, 1-32-23 Asahi-cho, Fuchu-shi, Tokyo 183-0003, Japan, Contact: Rico Komanoya *Tel:* (042) 208-0337 *Fax:* (042) 208-0338 *E-mail:* ricoricorico@mac.com
4 Wavecrest Ave, Strandfontein, Mitchells Plain, Cape Town 7735, South Africa, Sales Manager: Paul Jones *Tel:* (082) 346 2437 *Fax:* (086) 6175 731 *E-mail:* pauljoregentsa@vodamail.co.za
U.S. Office(s): 9276 Scranton Rd, Suite 120, San Diego, CA 92121, United States, US Sales Dir: Valerie Harwell *Tel:* 858-455-5600 *Fax:* 858-455-5601 *E-mail:* valerie@regentpublishingservices.com
5105 Twin Lakes Court, Fairfield, CA 94534, United States, Sales Manager: Domini

Schmid *Tel:* 707-939-7401 *Fax:* 707-402-6489 *E-mail:* domini@regentpublishingservices.com
142 W 36 St, 4th floor, New York, NY 10018, United States, Sales Manager: Kate Brady *Tel:* 212-779-3347 *Fax:* 212-779-0150 *E-mail:* kate@regentpublishingservices.com

Sheck Wah Tong Printing Press Ltd
653-659 Kings Rd 1/F, North Point
Tel: 2562 8293 *Fax:* 2565 5431
Web Site: www.sheckwahtong.com
Founded: 1911
Turnaround: 20 Workdays
Print Runs: 3,000 min - 200,000 max

Sing Cheong Printing Co Ltd
Tung Chong Factory Bldg, G/F, 655 Kings Rd, North Point
Tel: 2561 8801 *Fax:* 2565 9467
Key Personnel
Dir & Manager: Karen Shen Fishel
Founded: 1965
Business from Other Countries: 96%

Speedflex Asia Ltd
1/F Hua Qin International Bldg, 340 Queen's Rd Central, Hong Kong
Tel: 2542 2780 *Fax:* 2542 3733
E-mail: info@speedflex.com.hk
Web Site: www.speedflex.com.hk
Founded: 1981
Turnaround: 1 Workday
Print Runs: 1 min
Business from Other Countries: 20%

Sunny Printing (Hong Kong) Co Ltd
Room 9, 8/F, Block A, Ming Pao Industrial Center, 18 Ka Yip St, Chai Wan
Tel: 2557 8663 *Fax:* 2889 8070
Web Site: www.sunnyprinting.com.hk
Founded: 1991

Sunshine Press Ltd
Room 4, 5, 11-12, 21/F, Fullagar Industrial Bldg, 234 Aberdeen Main Rd, Aberdeen
Tel: 2553 0228 *Fax:* 2873 2930
E-mail: spl@sunshinepress.com.hk
Key Personnel
Dir: Raymond Wong
Administration Manager: Joney Chan
Founded: 1976
Turnaround: 21-28 Workdays
Print Runs: 3,000 min - 500,000 max
Business from Other Countries: 25%

1010 Printing Group Ltd, see Lion Rock Group

Toppan Best-Set Premedia Ltd
Subsidiary of Toppan Leefung (Hong Kong) Ltd
20/F @ Convoy, 169 Electric Rd, North Point
Tel: 2897 6033 *Fax:* 2897 5170
E-mail: bestset@toppanleefung.com
Web Site: www.toppanbestset.com
Key Personnel
Mng Dir: Johnson Yeung *E-mail:* johnsonyeung@toppanleefung.com
Contact: Cynthia Hui *E-mail:* cynthiahui@toppanleefung.com
Founded: 1986
Turnaround: 14 workdays
Print Runs: 500 min - 5,000,000 max
Business from Other Countries: 99%
Ultimate Parent Company: Toppan Leefung Pte Ltd
Branch Office(s)
No 3, Da Song Gang, Jiang Nan Main Ave C, Guangzhou 510240, China, Contact: Patrick Au *Tel:* (020) 8441-5873
Sales Office(s): 33 Alpin Way, Isleworth, Middx TW7 4RJ, United Kingdom, Con-

tact: Keith Harrocks *Tel:* (07515) 775 299 *E-mail:* keithharrocks@toppanleefung.com
50 S Buckhout St, Suite 208, Irvington, NY 10533, United States, Contact: Wai Man Yeung *Fax:* 914-674-5923 *E-mail:* waimanyeung@toppanleefung.com

Toppan Printing Co (HK) Ltd
Division of Toppan Printing Co Ltd
Yuen Long Industrial Estate, One Fuk Wang St, Yuen Long, New Territories
Tel: 2561 0101 *Fax:* 2475 4321
E-mail: info.e@toppan.co.jp
Web Site: www.toppan.co.jp
Founded: 1963
Turnaround: 30 Workdays
Business from Other Countries: 25%

Wing King Tong Group
Leader Industrial Centre, Block I, 3/F, 188-202 Texaco Rd, Tsuen Wan, New Territories
Tel: 2407 3287 *Fax:* 2408 7939
E-mail: marketing@wktco.com
Web Site: www.wkt.cc
Key Personnel
Mng Dir: Alex Yan Tak Chung
Founded: 1944
Turnaround: 15 Workdays
Print Runs: 1,000 min - 100,000 max
Business from Other Countries: 95%
Branch Office(s)
No 67, Li Xin Lu, Dan Zhu Tou Community, Nan Wan St, Longgang District, Shenzhen, Guangdong 518114, China *Tel:* (0755) 8473 6801; (0755) 8473 6802; (0755) 8473 6803 *Fax:* (0755) 8473 6303 *E-mail:* szwktsales@wkt.cc

Hungary

Alfoldi Nyomda Zrt
Boszormenyi ut 6, Debrecen 4027
Tel: (052) 515715 *Fax:* (052) 325227
E-mail: info@anyrt.hu
Web Site: www.anyrt.hu
Key Personnel
President & General Manager: Geza Gyorgy
Financial Dir: Lajos Pataki
Technical Dir: Tamas Loos
Founded: 1561

Interpress Kuelkereskedelmi Kft
Becsi ut 67, Budapest 1037
Tel: (01) 250-8263; (01) 250-8266 *Fax:* (01) 250-8262
E-mail: interpress@interpress.eu
Web Site: www.interpress.eu
Key Personnel
Sales: Zsuzsa Cserna *Tel:* (01) 430 0860
E-mail: zsuzsa.cserna@interpress.eu
Contact: Katalin Multas *E-mail:* katalin.multas@interpress.eu
Founded: 1991

Realszistema Dabas Printing House
Vasut u 105, Dabas 2373
Tel: (029) 567-501
E-mail: export@dabasinyomda.hu; info@dabasinyomda.hu
Web Site: www.dabasprint.hu
Key Personnel
General Manager: Magdolna Vago
E-mail: vagom@dabasinyomda.hu
Dir, Sales & Marketing: Zoltan Csondes
E-mail: csondesz@dabasinyomda.hu
Financial Dir: Erzsebet Tarjanyine Kirtak
E-mail: tarjanyie@dabasinyomda.hu

Production Dir: Irme Ujvari *E-mail:* ujvarii@
dabasinyomda.hu
Founded: 1972

Iceland

Isafoldar Prentsmidja hf
Sudurhraun 1, 210 Gardabae
Tel: 59 50 300 *Fax:* 59 50 310
Web Site: www.isafold.is
Key Personnel
Manager: Kristpor Gunnarsson *Tel:* 595 0301
E-mail: kristthor@isafold.is
Administrator: Gudmundur Jonsson *Tel:* 595 0333
E-mail: gudmundur@isafold.is
Sales & Marketing: Haraldur Jonsson *Tel:* 664
0312 *E-mail:* halli@isafold.is
Founded: 1913

Oddi Printing Ltd
Hofdabakka 7, 110 Reykjavik
Tel: 515 5000 *Fax:* 515 5001
E-mail: oddi@oddi.is
Web Site: www.oddi.is
Key Personnel
Chief Executive Officer: Gunnar Sverrisson
Tel: 515 5005 *E-mail:* gs@oddi.is
Mng Dir: Baldur Thorgeirsson *Tel:* 893 6533
E-mail: baldur@oddi.is
Dir, Production: Runar Mar Jonatansson *Tel:* 545
2911 *E-mail:* runar@oddi.is
Marketing & Human Resource Manager: Stefan
Hrafn Hagalin *Tel:* 515 5019 *E-mail:* hagalin@
oddi.is
U.S. Office(s): 118 Heacock Lane, Wyncote,
PA 19095, United States, Contact: Charles B
Gershwin *Tel:* 215-885-5210 *Fax:* 215-885-
6364 *E-mail:* chuck@oddi.com

India

Aadarsh Pvt Ltd
Shikhar Varta 4, Press Complex, MP Nagar, Zone
1, Bhopal 462 011
Tel: (0755) 2555442; (0755) 4270555 *Fax:* (0755)
2555449
E-mail: info@aadarsh.com
Web Site: aadarsh.com
Founded: 1989

AEL Data Services LLP
Block 7, DLF 1T SEZ, Manapakkam, Chennai
600 089
Tel: (044) 2252 3680; (044) 2252 3690
E-mail: info@aeldata.com; sales@aeldata.com
Web Site: www.aeldata.com
Branch Office(s)
Menara Keck Seng, 203 Jl Bukit Bintang, 55100
Kuala Lumpur, Malaysia *Tel:* (03) 21165862
Communication House, 26 York St, London W1U
6PZ, United Kingdom *Tel:* (020) 7873 2354

E-Edit Infotech Pvt Ltd
No 45, College Rd, Chona Centre, Nungam-
bakkam, Tamil Nadu, Chennai 600 006
Tel: (044) 42 13 29 73
E-mail: hrm@editinfotech.in
Web Site: www.editinfotech.in
Key Personnel
President: Mr Pankaj Kumar Jhunjhunwala

Gopsons Papers Ltd
T-2, Akarshan Bhawan, 4754/23 Ansari Rd, 4th
floor, Darya Ganj, New Delhi 110 002

Tel: (011) 23281450; (011) 23289616; (011)
23289626 *Fax:* (011) 23276360
E-mail: information@gopsons.com
Web Site: www.gopsons.com
Founded: 1950
Branch Office(s)
A-14, Sector 60, Noida 201 301 *Tel:* (0120)
2580395; (0120) 2580424; (0120) 2580160
A-2 & 3, Sector 64, Noida 201 301 *Tel:* (0120)
4930100 *Fax:* (0120) 4930174
Urbanstr 64, 10967 Berlin, Germany, Con-
tact: Patrick Clayton *Tel:* (030) 555770390
E-mail: post@gopsons.de *Web Site:* www.
gopsons.de
U.S. Office(s): 675 Fifteen Mile Dr, Roseville,
CA 95678-5965, United States, Contact: Mr
Iqbal Lodhia *Tel:* 916-786-7373 *Fax:* 916-786-
7393 *E-mail:* iqbal@gopsons.com

International Print-o-Pac Ltd
C-4 to C-11, Hosiery Complex, Phase-II Ext,
Noida, Uttar Pradesh 201 305
Tel: (0120) 4192 100 *Fax:* (0120) 4192 199
E-mail: ippnoida@ippindia.com
Web Site: www.ippindia.com
Key Personnel
Chairman: Ravindra Singhvi
Mng Dir: Amila Singhvi
Executive Dir: Rishabh Singhvi
Branch Office(s)
404, Commercial Point, 79 Lenin Sarani,
Kolkata 700 013 *Tel:* 9331294305 (cell)
E-mail: malvu2007@yahoo.com
306, Shiv Smriti, 49A Dr Annie Besant Rd,
Worli, Mumbai 400 018 *Tel:* (022) 6610 1966
E-mail: ippmumbai2@yahoo.com (marketing)
B-206, Okhla Industrial Area, Phase-I, New Delhi
110 020 *Tel:* (011) 4077 7000 *Fax:* (011) 4077
7157 *E-mail:* csfm@ippindia.com

JAK Printers Pvt Ltd
JAK Compound, Dadoji Konddeo Cross Lane,
Byculla (East), Mumbai 400 027
Tel: (022) 6734 3131 *Fax:* (022) 2377 1212
E-mail: mail@jakprinters.com
Web Site: www.jakprinters.com
Founded: 1984

Jayant Printery
352/54 JSS Rd, Murlidhar Temple Compound,
Near Thakurdwar PO, Mumbai 400 002
Tel: (022) 4366 7171 *Fax:* (022) 2205 9515
E-mail: jayantprintery@gmail.com; export@
jayantprintery.com
Web Site: jayantprintery.com
Founded: 1968

Manipal Technologies Ltd
Udayavani Bldg, Press Corner, Manipal 576 104
Tel: (0820) 2571151 *Fax:* (0820) 2570131
E-mail: info@manipaltechnologies.com
Web Site: www.manipaltechnologies.com
Founded: 1941
Parent Company: The Manipal Group

Newstech Publishing Inc
E-2 Greater Kailash Part 2, New Delhi 110 048
Tel: (011) 41435648
E-mail: kb@newstechglobal.com
Web Site: www.newstechglobal.com/books.html
Key Personnel
Chief Executive Officer: Kul Bhusan
Founded: 1988

Nutech Print Services
B-240 Okhla Industrial Area, Phase 1, New Delhi
110 020
Tel: (011) 40564949; (011) 45459550 *Fax:* (011)
41609146
E-mail: info@nutech.in; sales@nutechprint.com

Web Site: www.nutechprint.com
Founded: 1970

Parksons Graphics
12 Todi Estate, Sun Mill Compound, Lower
Parel, Mumbai 400 013
Tel: (022) 2498 1721 *Fax:* (022) 2498 3124
E-mail: info@parksonsgraphics.com
Web Site: parksonsgraphics.com
Founded: 1954
Branch Office(s)
15 Shah Industrial Estate, Off Veera Desai Rd,
Andheri (West), Mumbai 400 053 *Tel:* (022)
6692 4611 *Fax:* (022) 2673 0851
Survey No 57/1 (15), Village Dunetha, Near
Bhenslore Check-post, Nani Daman, Daman
396 210 *Tel:* (0260) 2263787 *Fax:* (0260)
2263789
Plot No E 20, Taloja MIDC, Raigad 410 608
Tel: (022) 6527 1203

Replika Press Pvt Ltd
310-311 & 444-445 EPIP, Kundli Industrial Park,
Sonipat, Haryana 131 028
Tel: (0130) 2219044; (0130) 2219045; (0130)
2219046 *Fax:* (0130) 2219042
E-mail: info@replikapress.com
Web Site: www.replikapress.com
Key Personnel
Mng Dir: Bhuvnesh Seth *Tel:* (0130) 2217863
E-mail: bhuvnesh@replikapress.com
Dir, Business Promotion: Jagdish Seth *Tel:* (0130)
2219041 *E-mail:* jagdishseth@replikapress.com
Dir, Marketing: Sanandan Seth *Tel:* 9810254636
(cell) *E-mail:* sanandan@replikapress.com
Dir, Production: Vikaran Seth *Tel:* 9899930999
(cell) *E-mail:* vikaran@replikapress.com
Founded: 1998

Repro India Ltd
Sun Paradise Business Plaza, 11th floor, B Wing,
Senapati Bapat Marg, Lower Parel, Mumbai
400 013
Tel: (022) 7191 4000 *Fax:* (022) 7191 4001
E-mail: info@reproindialtd.com
Web Site: www.reproindialtd.com
Founded: 1984
Branch Office(s)
Plot No 50/2, TTC MIDC Industrial Area, Ma-
hape, Navi Mumbai 400 710 *Tel:* (022) 7178
5000 *Fax:* (022) 7178 5011 (plant)
Repro Innovative Digiprint Pvt Ltd, No 146,
East Coast Rd, Vettuvankeni, Chennai 600 115
(plant)
Plot No 90-93, 165 Surat Special Economic
Zone, Rd No 11, GIDC, Sachin, Surat 394
230 *Tel:* (0261) 3107 396; (0261) 3107 397
Fax: (0261) 2398 030 (plant)
Sales Office(s): 1211, South City, Pinnacle, 11/1,
Salt Lake City, Block EP, Sector 5, Kolkata
700 091 *Tel:* 9650003189 (cell)
Unit No 205, 2nd floor, DLF Tower-A, Jasola
District Centre, Jasola, New Delhi 110 076
Tel: (011) 41323212 *Fax:* (011) 41323214
11 Whitman St, Hastings-on-Hudson, NY 10706-
1605, United States

Srinivas Fine Arts (P) Ltd
340/3, Keelathiruthangal, Sivakasi 626 130
Tel: (04562) 226588; (04562) 232589
Fax: (04562) 230038; (04562) 232662
E-mail: sales@sfa.co.in
Web Site: www.srinivasfinearts.com
Key Personnel
General Manager: Mr P Nandakumar
National Sales Manager: B Venkatesan
E-mail: venkatesan@sfa.co.in
Branch Office(s)
Rain Tree Pl, 1st floor, 7, McNichols Rd, Chet-
pet, Chennai 600 031 *Tel:* (044) 2836 3014
Fax: (044) 4284 9804 *E-mail:* customer@sfa.
co.in

XACT Studio International
2, Modi Complex, Commercial Complex, Ashok
Vihar, Phase II, Delhi 110 052
Tel: (011) 9810563212
E-mail: mohinder.xact@gmail.com
Web Site: www.xactbook.com
Key Personnel
Chief Executive Officer & Dir: Rahul Singhal
E-mail: rahul.xact@gmail.com

Indonesia

Gramedia Printing
Unit of Kompas Gramedia Group
Jl Palmerah Selatan 22-28, Jakarta 10270
Tel: (021) 548 3008 *Fax:* (021) 532 3662
E-mail: marketing@gramediaprinting.com
Web Site: www.gramediaprinting.com
Founded: 1972

Ichtiar Baru van Hoeve
Jl Raya Pasar Jumat 38 D-E, Pondok Pinang,
Jakarta 12310
Tel: (021) 7511856; (021) 7511901 *Fax:* (021)
7511855
E-mail: redaksi@ibvh.com
Web Site: www.ibvh.com
Founded: 1980
Turnaround: 6 Workdays
Print Runs: 500 min - 18,000 max

PT Victory Offset Prima
JL Aria Santika No 8, Desa Pasir Bolang-
Tigaraksa, Tangerang 15610
Tel: (021) 5940-5343 *Fax:* (021) 5940-5345
E-mail: info@victoryoffset.com
Web Site: www.victoryoffset.com
Key Personnel
General Manager: S Wilson Pinady
Founded: 1971
Turnaround: 14 Workdays
Print Runs: 5,000 min
Business from Other Countries: 20%

Israel

Har-El Printers & Publishers
PO Box 8053, 6108402 Jaffa
Tel: (03) 6816834 *Fax:* (03) 6813563
Web Site: www.harelart.com
Key Personnel
Owner & Dir: Monique L Har-El
E-mail: mharel@harelart.co.il
Founded: 1974
Turnaround: 60-90 Workdays
Print Runs: 30 min - 5,000 max
Business from Other Countries: 70%

Italy

Artigrafiche Boccia SpA
Via Tiberio Claudio Felice, 7, 84131 Salerno SA
Tel: (089) 303311 *Fax:* (089) 771017
E-mail: info@artigraficheboccia.com
Web Site: artigraficheboccia.com
Founded: 1950

Branch Office(s)
Via Tevere, 44, 00198 Rome RM *Tel:* (06)
68801898 *Fax:* (06) 68892416
Via Andrea Verga, n 12, 20144 Milan MI
Tel: (02) 7532750 *Fax:* (02) 7532750

L'Artistica Savigliano SRL
Via Togliatti 44, 12038 Savigliano CN
Tel: (0172) 22361 *Fax:* (0172) 21601
E-mail: info@lartisavi.it
Web Site: www.lartisavi.it
Founded: 1969
Parent Company: L'Artistica Savigliano Gruppo
Grafico

Vincenzo Bona SpA
Str Settimo, 370/30, 10156 Turin TO
Tel: (011) 273 77 77 *Fax:* (011) 273 77 00
E-mail: info@vincenzobona.com
Web Site: www.vincenzobona.com
Founded: 1777

G Canale & C SpA
Via Liguria, 24, 10071 Borgaro Turin TO
Tel: (011) 40 78 511 *Fax:* (011) 40 78 607
E-mail: sales@canale.it
Web Site: www.gcanale.it
Founded: 1915
Turnaround: 30 Workdays
Print Runs: 3,000 min
Business from Other Countries: 65%
Branch Office(s)
SOS Cernica, 47, Pantelimon Jud ILFOV,
Bucharest, Romania *Tel:* (021) 351 72 55
Fax: (021) 351 72 57 *E-mail:* office@canale-
bucarest.ro

Dedalo Litostampa SRL
Viale Luigi Jacobini, 5, 70123 Bari BA
Tel: (080) 531 14 13 *Fax:* (080) 531 14 14
E-mail: info@edizionidedalo.it; info@
dedalolitostampa.it
Web Site: www.dedalolitostampa.it
Founded: 1961
Print Runs: 2,000 min - 15,000 max

Elcograf SpA
Via Mondadori 15, 37131 Verona VR
Tel: (045) 934111 *Fax:* (045) 934763
E-mail: info.printing@verona.pozzoni.it
Web Site: www.elcograf.com
Key Personnel
Contact: Alberto Gibellini
Founded: 1907

Eurocrom 4
via Edison A Thomas 21/7, 31050 Villorba TV
Tel: (0422) 608200 *Fax:* (0422) 608322
E-mail: info@eurocrom4.com
Web Site: www.eurocrom4.com

Grafiche Damiani SRL
Via Zanardi, 376, 40131 Bologna BO
Tel: (051) 6356811 *Fax:* (051) 6347188
E-mail: info@grafichedamiani.it
Web Site: www.grafichedamiani.it

Graphicom SRL
Viale dell'Industria, 67, 36100 Vicenza VI
Tel: (0444) 189900 *Fax:* (0444) 189990; (0444)
189991; (0444) 189992
E-mail: info@graphicom.it
Web Site: www.graphicom.it
Founded: 1986

Legatoria Editoriale Giovanni Olivotto SpA,
see LEGO SpA

LEGO SpA
Via dell'Industria, 2, 36100 Vicenza
Tel: (0444) 564622 *Fax:* (0444) 564929
E-mail: lego@legogroup.com
Web Site: www.legogroup.com
Key Personnel
Mng Dir: Giulio Olivotto
Founded: 1900

Marchesi Grafiche Editoriali SpA
Via Flaminia 995/997, 00189 Rome RM
Tel: (06) 33216 1 *Fax:* (06) 33216 333
E-mail: info@marchesigrafiche.it
Web Site: www.marchesigrafiche.it
Founded: 1927

Marcovalerio Edizioni
Imprint of Associazione Culturale Centro Studi
Silvio Pellico
Via Vittorio Emanuele 29, 10060 Cercenasco TO
E-mail: marcovalerio@marcovalerio.com
Web Site: www.marcovalerio.com
Founded: 2000

Milanostampa SpA
Corso PEG Ferrero 5, 12060 Farigliano CN
Tel: (0173) 746111 *Fax:* (0173) 746248
Founded: 1965
Turnaround: 15 Workdays
Print Runs: 3,000 min - 80,000 max
Business from Other Countries: 65%
U.S. Office(s): Milanostampa USA, 141 Berkeley
Pl, No 2, Brooklyn, NY 11217-3971, United
States *Tel:* 212-964-2430 (North American
sales & production off)

Musumeci SpA
Loc Amerique, 97, 11020 Quart, Valle d'Aosta
AO
Tel: (0165) 76 11 11 *Fax:* (0165) 76 11 12
E-mail: info@musumecispa.it
Web Site: www.musumecispa.it

NIIAG SpA, see Nuovo Istituto Italiano d'Arti
Grafiche SpA

Nuovo Istituto Italiano d'Arti Grafiche SpA
Via Zanica 92, 24126 Bergamo BG
Web Site: www.arti-group.eu
Founded: 1873
Turnaround: 10 Workdays
Business from Other Countries: 30%
Parent Company: Bavaria Industries Group AG

Pigini Group Printing Division
Via Brecce, 60025 Loreto AN
Tel: (071) 9747511 *Fax:* (071) 7500092
E-mail: info@piginigroup.com
Web Site: www.piginigroup.com
Key Personnel
President: Lamberto Pigini

Printer Trento SRL
Via alle Roste, 12, 38121 Trento TN
Tel: (0461) 957 200
Web Site: www.printertrento.it
Key Personnel
Owner & General Manager: Dario Martelli
Co-Owner: Gianni Girardi
Sales: Susanna Geier *Tel:* (0461) 957 219
E-mail: susanna.geier@printertrento.it
Founded: 1980
Sales Office(s): Regentesselaan 187, 2562 CX
The Hague, Netherlands, Contact: Janneke
Verdonk *Tel:* (070) 7850 922 *E-mail:* janneke.
verdonk@gmail.com
Printer Trento UK Ltd, United Kingdom, Con-
tact: Jo Clark *Tel:* (01845) 577221 *E-mail:* jo.
clark@printertrento.co.uk

Promedia SRL
Division of Vincenzo Bona SpA
Str Settimo, 370/30, 10156 Turin TO
Tel: (011) 273 77 20 *Fax:* (011) 273 77 04
E-mail: info@promediasolutions.it; marketing@
  promediasolutions.it
Web Site: www.promediasolutions.it
Founded: 2005

Puntoweb SRL
Industrial Zone, Via Nettunense, 00040 Ariccia
  RM
Tel: (06) 9349721 *Fax:* (06) 934972242
E-mail: info@puntowebsrl.it; commerciale@
  puntowebsrl.it (sales)
Web Site: www.puntowebsrl.it

Rotopress International SRL
Subsidiary of Pigini Group Printing Division
Via Brecce, 60025 Loreto AN
Tel: (071) 7500739 *Fax:* (071) 7500570
E-mail: info@rotoin.it
Web Site: www.rotoin.it
Key Personnel
Chief Executive Officer: Guiseppe Casali
President: Lamberto Pigini
Dir General: Flavio Zuin
Production Manager: Paolo Piermartiri
Sales Manager: Paolo Dameno

Societa Editoriale Grafiche AZ SRL
viale del Lavoro, 8, 37036 San Martino Albergo
  VR
Tel: (045) 99 44 33 *Fax:* (045) 99 50 16
Web Site: www.graficheaz.it
Key Personnel
Marketing & Communications: Leonardo
  Aldegheri
Production: Daniele Armano
Sales: Lisanna Andreis; Eva Blum
Technical Production: Roberto Girlanda

Societa Torinese Industrie Grafiche Editoriali
Via Pescarito 110, 10099 San Mauro Torinese TO
Tel: (011) 22 30 101 *Fax:* (011) 09 23 924
E-mail: stige@stige.it
Web Site: www.stige.it
Key Personnel
General Dir: Giorgio Martano *Tel:* (011) 22 30
  108 *E-mail:* martano@stige.it
Sales Dir: Florance Roussange *Tel:* (011) 22 30
  189 *E-mail:* roussange@stige.it
Sheet Press: Giampiero Abbiento *Tel:* (011) 22 30
  154 *E-mail:* abbiento@stige.it
Web Press: Piero Popolo *Tel:* (011) 22 30 168
  E-mail: popolo@stige.it
Founded: 1927

Spadamedia SRL
Viale del Lavoro 31, 00043 Ciampino RM
Tel: (06) 96846542 *Fax:* (06) 96847295
Web Site: www.spadamedia.it
Key Personnel
Sales Dir: Dr Marco Marziale
Administrative Executive: Paolo Ruberta

STIGE, see Societa Torinese Industrie Grafiche
  Editoriali

Gruppo Editoriale Zanardi SRL
via Venezuela, 3, 35127 Padua PD
Tel: (049) 8069511 *Fax:* (049) 8069510
E-mail: info@zanardi.it
Web Site: www.zanardi.it
Branch Office(s)
Via Alessandro Volta, 22, 20094 Corsico MI
  Tel: (02) 48620286 *Fax:* (02) 45864967
U.S. Office(s): 41-41 44 St, Suite 3F, Sunnyside,
  NY 11104, United States *Tel:* 212-964-2430
  Fax: 212-964-2497 *E-mail:* rvarrasso@zanardi-
  usa.com

Japan

Dai Nippon Printing Co Ltd
1-1-1, Ichigaya Kagacho, Shinjuku-ku, Tokyo
162-8001
Tel: (03) 3266-2111
Web Site: www.dnp.co.jp
Key Personnel
President: Yoshitoshi Kitajima
Executive Vice President: Yoshinari Kitajima;
  Koichi Takanami; Masayoshi Yamada
Senior Mng Dir: Mitsuhiko Hakii; Tokuji Kanda;
  Tetsuji Morino; Masahiko Wada
Founded: 1876
Print Runs: 5,000 min - 200,000 max
Business from Other Countries: 85%
Branch Office(s)
DNP Denmark A/S, Skruegangen 2, 2690 Karl-
  slunde, Denmark
PT DNP Indonesia, Jl Pulogadung No 16-18, Kav
  II H2 dan II H3, Kawasan Industri Pulogadung,
  Jakarta 13930, Indonesia *Tel:* (021) 4605790
  Fax: (021) 4605795 *E-mail:* sales@dnpi.co.id
  Web Site: www.dnpi.co.id
DNP Photomask Europe SpA, Via C Olivetti, 2/
  A, 20041 Agrate Brianza, Italy
DNP Imagingcomm Asia Sdn Bhd, No 19, Jl
  Thamby Abdullah Satu, Brickfiejds, 50470
  Kuala Lumpur, Malaysia
DNP Imagingcomm Europe BV, Oudeweg 42,
  2031 CC Haarlem, Netherlands *Tel:* (023)
  5533080 *Fax:* (023) 5515232 *E-mail:* sales@
  dnp.imgcomm.eu
Tien Wah Press (Pte) Ltd, 4 Pandan Crescent,
  Singapore 128475, Singapore *Tel:* 6466 6222
  Fax: 6469 3894
DNP Photomask Technology Taiwan Co Ltd, No
  6, Li-Hsin Rd, Science Based Industrial Park,
  Hsin-chu City, Taiwan
DNP Vietnam Co Ltd, Lot B_3A4_CN, My
  Phuoc Industrial Park 3, Ben Cat District, Binh
  Duong Province, Vietnam
Sales Office(s): Dai Nippon Printing Co (Aus-
  tralia) Pty Ltd, St Martins Tower, Suite 1002,
  Level 10, 31 Market St, Sydney, NSW 2000,
  Australia
DNP Business Consulting (Shanghai) Co Ltd,
  1376 Nanjing Xi Lu, Suite 602, Shanghai,
  China
DNP International Trading (Shanghai) Co Ltd,
  1376 Nanjing Xi Lu, Suite 603B, Shanghai,
  China
DNP Photo Imaging Europe SAS, ZI Paris Nord
  II 22, Avenue des Nations, BP 51077, 95948
  Roissy CDG Cedex, France
DNP Europa GmbH, Berliner Allee 26, 40212
  Duesseldorf, Germany
DNP Imagingcomm Europe BV, Oudeweg 42,
  2031 CC Haarlem, Netherlands *Tel:* (023)
  5533080 *Fax:* (023) 5515232 *E-mail:* sales@
  dnp.imgcomm.eu
DNP Singapore Pte Ltd, 4, Pandan Crescent, Sin-
  gapore 128475, Singapore
DNP Korea Co Ltd, No 1501, Trade Tower,
  World Trade Center, Samseong-dong,
  Gangnam-gu, Seoul 135-729, South Korea
DNP Taiwan Co Ltd, RM D, 6FL, 44 Chung-
  Shan N Rd Sec 2, Taipei 104, Taiwan
U.S. Office(s): DNP Electronics America LLC,
  2391 Fenton St, Chula Vista, CA 91914,
  United States
DNP Holding USA Corp, 1209 Orange St, Wilm-
  ington, DE 19801, United States
DNP America LLC, 335 Madison Ave, 3rd floor,
  New York, NY 10017, United States *Tel:* 212-
  503-1060
DNP Imagingcomm America Corp, 4524 En-
  terprise Dr NW, Concord, NC 28027, United
  States *Fax:* 704-784-7196
DNP Imagingcomm America Corp, 1001 Tech-
  nology Dr, Mount Pleasant, PA 15666-1766,
  United States

DNP, see Dai Nippon Printing Co Ltd

Nissha Printing Co Ltd
3 Mibu Hanai-cho, Nakagyo-ku, Kyoto 604-8551
Tel: (075) 811 8111 *Fax:* (075) 801 8250
Web Site: www.nissha.co.jp
Key Personnel
President & Chief Executive Officer: Junya
  Suzuki
Founded: 1929

Latvia

Jelgavas Tipografija Ltd (Jelgavas Printing
  House)
Langervaldes iela 1A, Jelgava LV-3002
Tel: 630 24 501 *Fax:* 630 22 927
E-mail: jt@jt.lv
Web Site: www.jt.lv
Key Personnel
Chairman of the Board: Juris Silis
Sales Dir: Girts Karlsons *E-mail:* girts@jt.lv;
  Maris Matrevics *Tel:* 670 27 331 *Fax:* 670 27
  231 *E-mail:* maris@jt.lv
Technical Dir: Margers Zagata *E-mail:* margers@
  jt.lv
Export Manager: Liene Skrupska *Tel:* 630 25 764
  Fax: 630 07 465 *E-mail:* liene.skrupska@jt.lv
Founded: 1996

Tipografija Lapa
Raina Str 6, Valmiera LV-4201
Tel: 261854845
E-mail: info@lapaprint.com
Web Site: www.lapaprint.com
Key Personnel
Contact: Arnis Skuja *E-mail:* arnis.skuja@
  lapaprint.com
Founded: 1973
Sales Office(s): Brivibas Str 99/2-13, Riga LV-
  1001, Contact: Ingars Klavins *E-mail:* ingars.
  klavins@lapaprint.lv

Livonia Print Ltd
Ventspils 50, Riga LV-1002
Tel: 6744 2831 *Fax:* 6744 2832
E-mail: info@livoniaprint.lv
Web Site: www.livoniaprint.lv
Key Personnel
Mng Dir: Trond Erik Isaksen *E-mail:* trond@
  livoniaprint.lv
Sales Dir: Janina Bluma *E-mail:* janina@
  livoniaprint.lv
Turnaround: 21-28 workdays

NIMS SIA
Pernavas iela 47B, 2 stavs, Riga LV-1009
Tel: 67 311 424 *Fax:* 67 311 126
E-mail: nims@nims.lv
Web Site: www.nims.lv

Veiters Korporacija
Brivibas gatve 437, Riga LV-1024
Tel: 67994419; 67545174 (sales) *Fax:* 67994419
E-mail: veiters@veiters.lv
Web Site: www.veiters.lv
Key Personnel
Commercial Dir: Diana Novicka *E-mail:* diana@
  veiters.lv

Lithuania

AJSP Printing Services
Mokslininku Str 39, LT-12187 Vilnius
Tel: (05) 2780311 *Fax:* (05) 2780312
E-mail: info@ajsp.lt
Web Site: www.ajsp.lt
Key Personnel
Manager: Gintare Relyte *E-mail:* gintare@ajsp.lt

Druka Spaustuve (Druka Printing House)
Mainu St 5, LT-94101 Klaipeda
Tel: (046) 380458 *Fax:* (046) 380459
E-mail: info@druka.lt
Web Site: www.druka.lt
Key Personnel
Mng Dir: Algirdas Apulskis
Head, Sales: Lina Sniukiene
Sales Manager: Kristina Rimke

Grafija UAB
Savanoriu Ave 219A, LT-02300 Vilnius
Tel: (05) 263 6472 *Fax:* (05) 263 6912
E-mail: grafija@grafija.lt
Web Site: www.grafija.lt
Key Personnel
Sales Manager: Renatas Andriunas *Tel:* 698 57
924 *E-mail:* renatas@grafija.lt; Donatas Jace-
vicius *Tel:* 614 25 942 *E-mail:* donatas@
grafija.lt; Marius Jogela *Tel:* 614 25 943
E-mail: marius@grafija.lt; Valentina Krochmal
Tel: 616 09 525 *E-mail:* valentina@grafija.
lt; Edvardas Sudnius *Tel:* 698 70 131
E-mail: edvardas@grafija.lt
Founded: 1996

Lietuvos Rytas Spaustuve UAB
12A Gedimino Ave, LT-01103 Vilnius
Tel: (05) 274 3743 *Fax:* (05) 274 3728
E-mail: print@lrytas.lt; spaustuve@lrytas.lt
Web Site: print.lrytas.lt
Key Personnel
General Dir: Nerijus Baura
Founded: 1994
Business from Other Countries: 60%
Branch Office(s)
83 Sodu St, LT-13274 Skaidiskes
51 Kauno St, LT-21371 Vievis

Reprodukcija
Chemijos g 29, LT-51333 Kaunas
Tel: (037) 408866 *Fax:* (037) 408867
E-mail: repro@repro.lt; spauda@repro.lt; flekso@
repro.lt
Web Site: www.repro.lt
Branch Office(s)
Riovoniu g 33A, LT-03154 Vilnius
Tel: (05) 2335689 *Fax:* (05) 2388951
E-mail: reprovilnius@repro.lt

Sapnu Sala Spaustuve
Moniuskos g 21, LT-08121 Vilnius
Tel: (05) 278 05 80 *Fax:* (05) 278 05 90

Spindulio Spaustuve (Spindulys Printing House)
B Brazdzionio g 23, LT-48184 Kaunas
Tel: (037) 200744 *Fax:* (037) 204970
E-mail: info@spindulys.lt
Web Site: www.spindulys.lt
Key Personnel
Sales & Marketing Manager: Sigita Varniene
E-mail: sigita@spindulys.lt
Project Manager: Kristina Petruskeviciute
E-mail: kristina@spindulys.lt
Founded: 1928
Print Runs: 500 min - 100,000 max
Business from Other Countries: 6%

Malaysia

Abadi Ilmu Sdn Bhd
14, Jl SS4D/14, 47301 Petaling Jaya, Selangor
Darul Ehsan
Tel: (03) 7804 4588; (03) 7804 4157; (03) 7804
3967 *Fax:* (03) 7804 4152
E-mail: abadi_ilmu@time.net.my; abadiilmu@
gmail.com; abadi_ilmu@yahoo.com
Web Site: www.abadilmu.com
Founded: 1997

AG Grafik Sdn Bhd
No 35, Jl Apollo U5/198, 40150 Shah Alam, Se-
langor
Tel: (03) 78591060 *Fax:* (03) 51924669
Key Personnel
Owner: Azrin Abdol Ghapar

BHS Book Printing Sdn Bhd
Lot 17-22 to 17-25, Jl CJ 1/1, Bersatu Industrial
Park, Chera Jaya, 43200 Selangor Darul Ehsan
Tel: (03) 9074 7558; (03) 9074 7018 *Fax:* (03)
9074 7573
E-mail: bhsprint@tm.net.my
Web Site: www.bhs.my
Key Personnel
Executive Dir: Koo Thiam Yoong
Mng Dir: Dato Lim Thiam Huat
Founded: 1980
Parent Company: BHS Industries Berhad

Percetakan Surya Sdn Bhd
Plot 29, Jl IKS Bk 2, Taman IKS Bukit Katil,
75450 Melaka
Tel: (06) 2324475; (06) 2324479 *Fax:* (06)
2324960
Key Personnel
Chairman: Hj Sebdin Osman
Founded: 1974

Maldives

Novelty Printers & Publishers Pvt Ltd
M Utility, Male 20340
Tel: 3318844 *Fax:* 3327039
Web Site: printers.novelty.com.mv
Key Personnel
Chairman: Ali Hussain
Founded: 1965
Parent Company: Novelty Group

Malta

Print It
Division of Salander Group Co Ltd
KW3, Corradino Industrial Estate, Paola
Tel: 2189 4446; 2189 4447 *Fax:* 2189 4448
E-mail: info@printit.com.mt
Web Site: www.printit.com.mt

Progress Press Co Ltd
Member of Allied Group
Zona Industrijali, Triq l-Intornjatur, Mriehel BKR
3000
Tel: 22764400 *Fax:* 25594115
E-mail: info@progresspress.com.mt
Web Site: www.progresspress.com.mt
Key Personnel
Chief Operations Officer: Noel Galea

Mng Dir: Michel Rizzo
Founded: 1922

Mexico

Solar, Servicios Editoriales SA de CV
Calle 2, No 21, Colonia San Pedro de los Pinos,
Delegacion Benito Juarez, 03800 Mexico,
CDMX
Tel: (0155) 5515-1657
E-mail: solar@solareditores.com
Web Site: www.solareditores.com
Key Personnel
Dir General: Alejandro Zenker *E-mail:* alejandro.
zenker@solareditores.com
Production Manager: Beatriz Hernandez
E-mail: beatriz.hernandez@solareditores.com
Founded: 1985

Netherlands

Bariet Ten Brink
Formerly Ten Brink Offset BV
Eekhorstweg 1, 7942 JC Meppel
Mailing Address: Postbus 41, 7940 AA Meppel
Tel: (088) 1105 400
E-mail: info@bariet-tenbrink.nl
Web Site: www.barriet-tenbrink.nl
Key Personnel
Mng Dir: Frank van Zijl *E-mail:* fvanzijl@wilco.
nl
Head, Administration: Erik Lukassen
E-mail: elukassen@wilco.nl
Founded: 2009
Parent Company: Wilco BV

Uitgeven Duurzaam
Bakhuis 6, 3262 CB Oud-Beijerland
Tel: (06) 5495 6704
E-mail: info@duurzaamuitgeven.nl
Web Site: www.duurzaamuitgeven.nl
Key Personnel
Mng Dir: Pieter Kers

Printforce
Anthonie van Leeuwenhoekweg 56A, 2408 AN
Alphen aan den Rijn
Mailing Address: Postbus 111, 2400 AC Alphen
aan den Rijn
Tel: (0172) 466 200 *Fax:* (0172) 466 222
E-mail: info@printforce.nl
Web Site: www.printforce.nl
Key Personnel
Mng Partner: Rombout Eikelenboom; Jan Prins

Roto Smeets
Hunneperkade 4, 7418 BT Deventer
Mailing Address: Postbus 825, 7400 AV Deventer
Tel: (0570) 69 48 50 *Fax:* (0570) 69 41 08
E-mail: info@rotosmeets.nl
Web Site: www.rotosmeets.nl
Key Personnel
Dir, International Sales: Rene van Werkhoven
Tel: (0570) 69 48 64 *E-mail:* rene.van.
werkhoven@rotosmeets.com
Sales Manager: Antal Beck *E-mail:* antal.beck@
rotosmeets.com
Branch Office(s)
Parallelweg 5, 4878 AH Etten Leur *Tel:* (076)
508 40 00 *Fax:* (076) 501 43 75
Roto Smeets GrafiServices, Kanaalweg 30, 3526
KM Utrecht, Dir: Michiel Hack *Tel:* (030) 282
28 22 *Fax:* (030) 282 28 44 *E-mail:* michiel.

hack@grafiservices.nl *Web Site:* www.
grafiservices.nl
Molenveldstr 100, 6001 HL Weert *Tel:* (0495) 57
09 11 *Fax:* (0495) 54 29 05

Ten Brink Offset BV, see Bariet Ten Brink

Wilco BV
Vanadiumweg 9, 3812 PX Amersfoort
Mailing Address: Postbus 1477, 3800 BL Amers-
foort
Tel: (088) 1105 500
E-mail: info@wilco.nl
Web Site: www.wilco.nl
Key Personnel
Dir: Robert Jan de Rooij *E-mail:* rjderooij@
wilco.nl; Frank van Zijl *E-mail:* fvanzijl@
wilco.nl
Deputy Dir: William Schuring
E-mail: wschuring@wilco.nl

Koninklijke Wohrmann BV
Estlandsestr 1, 7202 CP Zutphen
Mailing Address: Postbus 92, 7200 AB Zutphen
Tel: (0575) 58 21 21 *Fax:* (0575) 58 21 28
E-mail: secretariat@wohrmann.nl
Web Site: cpibooks.com/nl
Key Personnel
Mng Dir: P T M Paardekooper
Head, Financial Administration: G de Jager
Head, Production: Mr J E Boers
Head, Sales: R Bosch
Sales: Mrs J A M Derksen-Geuijen
Parent Company: CPI Group

New Zealand

Bookprint Consultants Ltd
1104, One Market Lane, Wellington 6011
Tel: (04) 381 3070
Web Site: www.granthamhouse.co.nz
Key Personnel
Chief Executive: Graham C Stewart
E-mail: graham@ghbil.com
Founded: 1982
Print Runs: 2,000 min - 7,500 max
Business from Other Countries: 10%
Branch Office(s)
Bookprint International Ltd, New Trend Cen-
tre, 104 King Fuk St, Sanpokong, Kowloon,
Hong Kong *Tel:* 2327 0101 *Fax:* 2350 0315
E-mail: bil@kingstime.com.hk

Craigs Design & Print Ltd
122 Yarrow St, Invercargill 9840
Mailing Address: PO Box 99, Invercargill 9840
Tel: (03) 211-0393; (03) 211-8618 (showroom)
Fax: (03) 214-9930
E-mail: info@craigprint.co.nz
Web Site: www.craigprint.co.nz
Key Personnel
Chief Executive & Dir: Tony Wills *Tel:* (027)
672-7147 (cell) *E-mail:* tony@craigprint.co.nz
Dir & Administration: Eleanor Wills *Tel:* (027)
284-6524 (cell) *E-mail:* eleanor@craigprint.co.
nz
Dir & Promotional/Digital Manager:
Richard Wills *Tel:* (021) 264-2772 (cell)
E-mail: richard@craigprint.co.nz
Dir & Sales Manager: Rodger Wills *Tel:* (027)
434-2757 (cell) *E-mail:* rodger@craigprint.co.
nz
Print Services Manager: Alan Shirley *Tel:* (027)
681-5240 (cell) *E-mail:* alan@craigprint.co.nz
Production Manager: Brent Hollingworth
Tel: (027) 221-2083 (cell) *E-mail:* brent@
craigprint.co.nz
Founded: 1876

Philippines

Cacho Hermanos Inc
Pines Corner, Union Sts, 1550 Mandaluyong,
Metro Manila
Tel: (02) 631 8361; (02) 631 8362; (02) 631
8363; (02) 631 8364; (02) 631 8365 *Fax:* (02)
631 5244
Founded: 1880
Turnaround: 7-120 Workdays
Print Runs: 500 min - 50,000 max
Parent Company: National Book Store

JF Printhaus
Maharlika Highway, Barangay Francisco, 4000
San Pablo City
Tel: (049) 562-0916
Key Personnel
Production Manager: Melojean Javier
Founded: 1982
Parent Company: JF Corp

Philippine Graphic Arts Inc
163 Tandang Sora St, Samson Rd, 1400 Caloocan
City
Tel: (02) 364-4591; (02) 361-9733 *Fax:* (02) 361-
9733
Key Personnel
President & General Manager: Igmedio R Silverio
Founded: 1957

Poland

Apostolicum Drukarnia Ksiezy Pallotynow
ul Wilcza 8, 05-091 Zabki
Tel: (22) 771 52 30; (22) 771 52 14 *Fax:* (22)
771 52 07
E-mail: sekretariat@apostolicum.pl
Web Site: www.apostolicum.pl
Key Personnel
Dir: Jozef Nowak
Deputy Dir: Arkadiusz Grzeszczyk *Tel:* (22) 771
52 64 *E-mail:* ap@apostolicum.pl

Drukarnia Wydawnictwo Bernardinum Sp z oo
ul Bpa Dominika 11, 83-130 Pelplin
Tel: (58) 536-43-76; (58) 536-17-57 *Fax:* (58)
536-43-76
E-mail: drukarnia@bernardinum.pl;
biuroobslugi@bernardinum.com.pl
Web Site: www.drukarnia.bernardinum.com.pl
Key Personnel
Printing Dir: Radoslaw Jaszewski
E-mail: radoslaw.jaszewski@bernardinum.com.
pl
Sales Executive: Mr Miroslaw Chyla
E-mail: miroslaw.chyla@bernardinum.com.pl
Founded: 1830

Drukarnia Dimograf Sp z oo
ul Legionow 83, 43-300 Bielsko-Biala
Tel: (33) 811 81 61; (33) 815 08 98; (33) 496 21
00 *Fax:* (33) 816 80 16
E-mail: info@dimograf.com
Web Site: www.dimograf.com
Key Personnel
President: Dariusz Mrzyglod
Vice President: Krzysztof Kantyka
Sales: Mariusz Kolodziejczyk *Tel:* (33) 811 81 61
ext 118 *E-mail:* mariusz@dimograf.com
Founded: 1989

Druk-Intro SA
ul Swietokryska 32, 88-100 Inowroclaw
Tel: (52) 354 94 50 *Fax:* (52) 354 94 51

E-mail: sekretariat@druk-intro.pl
Web Site: web.druk-intro.pl
Key Personnel
Sales Dir: Agnieszka Szczypecka *Tel:* (51) 527
53 62 *E-mail:* a.szczypecka@druk-intro.pl
Founded: 1994

Eurodruk Poznan Sp z oo
ul Wiezbowa 17/19, 62-080 Tarnowo Podgorne
Tel: (61) 816 40 10 *Fax:* (61) 816 40 11
E-mail: edp@eurodruk.com.pl
Web Site: www.eurodruk.com.pl
Key Personnel
Sales & Marketing Dir: Mariusz Majewski
Tel: (61) 816 40 07 *Fax:* (61) 814 76 81
E-mail: m.majewski@eurodruk.com.pl
Sales & Marketing Manager: Agnieszka Rybak-
Burzynska *E-mail:* a.rybak@eurodruk.com.pl
Client Service Manager: Marek Karwat
E-mail: m.karwat@eurodruk.com.pl
Founded: 1997
Parent Company: Euro Druckservice AG (EDS)

Gryf Warszawa Sp Z oo
ul Plochocinska 19, 03-191 Warsaw
Tel: (22) 510 63 11 *Fax:* (22) 510 63 12
Web Site: www.gryfwarszawa.pl
Founded: 2000

LCL Dystrybucja Sp z oo
ul Dabrowskiego 247/249, 93-231 Lodz
Tel: (42) 250 83 00 *Fax:* (42) 250 83 00
E-mail: sekretariat@lcldystrybucja.pl
Web Site: www.lcldystrybucja.pl
Key Personnel
Sales: Maciej Lewy *E-mail:* mlewy@
lcldystrybucja.pl; Robert Sacharczuk
E-mail: rsacharczuk@lcldystrybucja.pl
Founded: 1988

Drukarnia im Karola Miarki (Karol Miarka
Printing House)
ul Zwirki i Wigury 1, 43-190 Mikolow
Tel: (32) 326 20 96 *Fax:* (32) 326 20 99
E-mail: export@tolek.com.pl
Web Site: www.tolek.com.pl
Key Personnel
Owner: Adolf Janczyk *E-mail:* adolf.janczyk@
tolek.com.pl
Contact: Aleksandra Janczyk *E-mail:* aleksandra.
janczyk@tolek.com.pl

101 Studio DTP Tomasz Tegi i Spolka Sp z oo
ul Ekonomiczna 30/36, 93-426 Lodz
Tel: (42) 250 70 92; (42) 250 70 93; (42) 250 70
94 *Fax:* (42) 250 70 95
E-mail: ac@poczta.101studio.com.pl
Web Site: www.101studio.com.pl
Key Personnel
DTP Manager: Janusz Majerowski *Tel:* (42) 250
70 92 ext 19 *Fax:* (42) 250 70 959
Sales & Marketing Manager: Jaroslaw
Soltyszewski *Tel:* (42) 250 70 92 ext 21
E-mail: j.soltyszewski@101studio.com.pl
Founded: 1990

Opolgraf SA
ul Niedzialkowskiego 8-12, 45-085 Opole
Tel: (77) 454-52-44; (77) 454-52-46 *Fax:* (77)
454-53-13
Web Site: www.opolgraf.com.pl
Key Personnel
President: Miroslaw Szewczyk *Tel:* (77) 454-54-
48 *E-mail:* szewczyk@opolgraf.com.pl
Vice President: Bartosz Mazurkiewicz *Tel:* (77)
454-54-48 *E-mail:* mazurkiewicz@opolgraf.
com.pl

Production Manager: Henryk Gonschior *Tel:* (77) 454-52-44 ext 48 *E-mail:* szefprodukcji@opolgraf.com.pl
Sales Manager: Joanna Tolpa *Tel:* (77) 454-52-44 ext 45 *E-mail:* joanna.tolpa@opolgraf.com.pl

OZGraf Olsztynskie Zaklady Graficzne SA
ul Towarowa 2, 10-417 Olsztyn
Tel: (89) 533 43 80 *Fax:* (89) 533 12 08
E-mail: ozgraf@ozgraf.com.pl
Web Site: www.ozgraf.com.pl
Key Personnel
Chief Executive Officer: Peter Ciosk
Production Dir: Miroslaw Jachemek
Founded: 1997
Sales Office(s): ul Grzybowska 77, p237, 00-844 Warsaw *E-mail:* pmichalak@ozgraf.dwb.pl

Drukarnia POZKAL Spolka z oo Spolka komandytowa
ul Cegielna 10/12, 88-100 Inowroclaw
Tel: (52) 354 27 00 *Fax:* (52) 354 27 05
E-mail: sekretariat@pozkal.pl
Web Site: www.pozkal.pl
Key Personnel
President: Artur Chesy
Commercial Dir: Agnieszka Osiecka-Chesy
    E-mail: agnieszka@pozkal.pl
Production Manager: Michal Palacz
    E-mail: michal@pozkal.pl
Founded: 1986

WEMA Wydawnictwo-Poligrafia Sp z oo
ul Rolna 191/193, 02-729 Warsaw
Tel: (22) 827 21 17 *Fax:* (22) 828 57 79
Web Site: www.wp-wema.pl

Portugal

Edicoes Silabo Lda
Rua Cidade de Manchester, 2, 1170-100 Lisbon
Tel: 218130345 *Fax:* 218166719
E-mail: silabo@silabo.pt
Web Site: www.silabo.pt
Key Personnel
Marketing Dir & Editor: Manuel Robalo
    E-mail: manuel.robalo@silabo.pt
Founded: 1983
Turnaround: 5 Workdays

Romania

Dinasty Books ProEditura si Typografie SRL
(PRO Publishing & Printing)
Str Baiculesti nr 1, Sector 1, 013187 Bucharest
Tel: (0723) 61 41 83 *Fax:* (0723) 61 41 83
E-mail: marketing@proeditura.ro
Web Site: dinastybooks.ro

Tipografia Fed Print SA
Bd Tudor Vladimirescu nr 31, Sector 5, 050881 Bucharest
Tel: (021) 4110055; (021) 4114776 *Fax:* (021) 4119196
E-mail: office@fedprint.ro; comercial@fedprint.ro; productie@fedprint.ro
Web Site: www.fedprint.ro
Founded: 1996

Saudi Arabia

Obeikan Commercial Printing
Subsidiary of Obeikan Group
PO Box 355023, Riyadh 11383
Tel: (011) 283 9400 *Fax:* (011) 265 3668
E-mail: commercial.printing@obeikan.com.sa
Web Site: www.obeikan.com.sa
Key Personnel
Chief Executive Officer: Abdallah Al Obeikan
Chief Financial Officer: Andreas Boy
General Manager: Moqbel M Al-Enezi
    E-mail: moqbel@obeikan.com.sa
Production Manager: Abdulsalam Al-Arify
    E-mail: aalarify@obeikan.com.sa
Founded: 1983

Singapore

Chong Moh Offset Printing Pte Ltd
19 Joo Koon Rd, Singapore 628978
Tel: 6862 2701 *Fax:* 6862 4335
Founded: 1946
Turnaround: 10-14 Workdays
Print Runs: 1,000 min
Business from Other Countries: 35%

Ho Printing Singapore Pte Ltd
31 Changi South St One, Changi South Industrial Estate, Singapore 486769
Tel: 6542 9322 *Fax:* 6542 8322
E-mail: sales@hoprinting.com.sg
Web Site: www.hoprinting.com
Founded: 1951
Turnaround: 35-50 Workdays
Print Runs: 5,000 min - 50,000 max
Business from Other Countries: 30%

International Press Softcom Ltd (IPS)
26, Kallang Ave, Singapore 339417
Tel: 6298 3800 *Fax:* 6297 1668
E-mail: biz@ipsoftcom.com
Web Site: www.ipsoftcom.com
Key Personnel
Chief Executive Officer & Mng Dir: Low Ka Choon Kevin
General Manager, China Region: Chan Yee Liang
General Manager, Malaysia, Australia & Vietnam: Ng Ching Beng Alvin
General Manager, Singapore & India: Srihari Raghavan
Founded: 1968
Print Runs: 3,000 min - 50,000 max
Business from Other Countries: 60%
Branch Office(s)
Unit 22, 6-20 Braidwood St, South Strathfield, NSW 2136, Australia *Tel:* (02) 9642 2924 *Fax:* (02) 9642 0228
No 1 Bldg, No 402, No 1299 Xin Jinqiao Rd, Pudong, Shanghai 201206, China *Tel:* (021) 5032 2228 *Fax:* (021) 5032 2229
5F, No 13, Hongfa Industrial Estate, Jingtang Rd, Shiyan St, Baoan District, Shenzhen, Guangdong 518108, China *Tel:* (0755) 2733 5200 *Fax:* (0755) 2733 5207
IP Media Xiamen, No 1 Bldg, No 285, Weng Jiao Rd, Hai Cang District, Xiamen, Fujian 361022, China *Tel:* (0592) 6806555 *Fax:* (0592) 6806556
IP Rudrapur, 6 KM Stone Kichha Rd, Village Shimla Pistor, Rudrapur, Uttarakhand 263 153, India *Tel:* (059) 4428 0552 *Fax:* (044) 2476 4813
Scantrans Chennai, No 18 & 19, Mahalakshmi Nagar Extn, Numbal Village, Thiruverkadu Post, Chennai 600 077, India *Tel:* (044) 2649 5056 *Fax:* (044) 2649 4056
IP Softcom Malaysia Sdn Bhd, Plot 46, Bayan Lepas Industrial Estate, Phase IV, SWD, 11900 Penang, Malaysia *Tel:* (04) 644 3555 *Fax:* (04) 646 2868
IPS Vietnam, Lot B54/1, Rd No 2E, Vinch Loc A Industrial Park, Binch Chanh District, Ho Chi Minh City, Vietnam *Tel:* (08) 376 56252 *Fax:* (08) 376 56251

IPS, see International Press Softcom Ltd (IPS)

Markono Print Media Pte Ltd
Subsidiary of Markono Holdings Pte Ltd
21 Neythal Rd, Singapore 628586
Tel: 6281 1118
E-mail: enquiry@markono.com; sales@markono.com
Web Site: www.markono.com
Key Personnel
Chairman: Bob Lee
Mng Dir: Edwin Ng
Sales & Marketing Dir: Max Lee
Founded: 1967
Turnaround: 7 Workdays
Print Runs: 500 min - 150,000 max
Business from Other Countries: 20%
Branch Office(s)
Markono Logistics, 4 Toh Tuck Link, Singapore 596226 *Tel:* 6465 1498 *E-mail:* ml.sales@markono.com
Markono Digital Solutions (M) Sdn Bhd, 7 Lorong Jelawat 4, 13700 Seberang Jaya, Penang, Malaysia *Tel:* (04) 397-8700 *E-mail:* mdsm.sales@markono.com

PacPress Media Pte Ltd
1200 Depot Rd, No 07-21, Singapore 109675
Tel: 6276 8090 *Fax:* 6276 9884

SC (Sang Choy) International Pte Ltd
9 Harrison Rd, No 02-01, Harrison Industrial Bldg, Singapore 369651
Tel: 6289 0829 *Fax:* 6282 1819
E-mail: marketing@sc-international.com.sg
Web Site: www.sc-international.com.sg
Key Personnel
Dir, Operations: Almond Ko *E-mail:* almond@sc-international.com.sg
Founded: 1992
Branch Office(s)
Room 521, No 2, Ten Fe Yi St, Ten Fei Yuan, Jiu Long Rd, Huangpu District, Guangzhou 510555, China *Tel:* (020) 8252 6087
Unit A, 22/F, Full Win Commercial Centre, 573 Nathan Rd, Kowloon, Hong Kong *Tel:* 5804 3265
26 York St, London W1U 6PZ, United Kingdom *Tel:* (020) 7666 3116

Stamford Press Pte Ltd
209 Kallang Bahru, Singapore 339344
Tel: 6294 7227 *Fax:* 6294 4396; 6294 3319
E-mail: info@stamford.com.sg
Web Site: www.stamford.com.sg
Key Personnel
Dir, Sales & Marketing: Mr V Balu
    E-mail: balu@stamford.com.sg
Founded: 1963 (as Stamford College Press)
Turnaround: 3-4 Workdays for small jobs; 3-4 Weeks for big jobs
Print Runs: 1,500 min - 50,000 max
Business from Other Countries: 20%
Parent Company: Stamford Media International Pte Ltd
Branch Office(s)
Stamford Aus-Trade & Press Pty Ltd, 32 Ada Ave, Strathfield, NSW 2135, Australia *Tel:* (02) 9758 7715 *Fax:* (02) 9758 7716

Raffles-Stamford Press (India) Pvt Ltd, No 1 Survey No 16/1, Singasandra Village, Begur Hobli, Hosur Main Rd, Bangalore 560 068, India *Tel:* (080) 573 0717; (080) 573 0718 *Fax:* (080) 573 3992

Stamford Lake Pvt Ltd, 366, High Level Rd, Pannipitiya, Sri Lanka *Tel:* (01) 846 002; (074) 208 134 *Fax:* (01) 846 002; (074) 208 134

No 61, Tryfan Close Redbridge, Ilford, Essex 1G4 5JY, United Kingdom *Tel:* (01223) 504754; (020) 8262 6515 *Fax:* (01223) 574538; (020) 8262 6514

Tien Wah Press (Pte) Ltd
Member of Dai Nippon Printing (DNP) Group
4 Pandan Crescent, Singapore 128475
Tel: 6466 6222 *Fax:* 6469 3894
E-mail: enquiry@twpsin.com
Web Site: www.twp-global.com
Key Personnel
Sales: Jimmy Lim *E-mail:* jimmylim@twpsin.com
Founded: 1935
Business from Other Countries: 90%
Branch Office(s)
TWP (Johor) Sdn Bhd, Penawar, Lot 1215 Kawasan Perindustrian, Bandar Penawar, Fasa 1, Bandar Penawar, 81900 Kota Tinggi, Johor Bahru, Malaysia *Tel:* (07) 822 2015 *Fax:* (07) 822 2016
TWP Sdn Bhd, Tampoi, No 89 Jl Tampoi, Kawasan Perindustrian Tampoi, 80350 Johor Bahru, Malaysia *Tel:* (07) 231 3000 *Fax:* (07) 236 3148
Sales Office(s): Tien Wah Press Australia Pte Ltd, PO Box 2244, Carlingford Court, NSW 2118, Australia, Sales: Ruth Garratt *Tel:* (04) 2102 3387 *E-mail:* rgarratt@twpsin.com
Tien Wah Press (Pte) Ltd, 15/17, rue Mechain, 75014 Paris, France, Sales: Cornelia Lombard *Tel:* 01 42 79 07 00 *Fax:* 01 42 79 80 90 *E-mail:* clombard@twpsin.com
Tien Wah Press (UK) Ltd, Unit 16, The Ivories, 6-8 Northampton St, London N12 HY, United Kingdom, Sales: Farhat Khan *Tel:* (020) 7354 3323 *Fax:* (020) 7359 8777 *E-mail:* farhat@twpuk.com
U.S. Office(s): TWP America Inc, 303 Twin Dolphin Dr, 6th floor, Redwood City, CA 94065, United States *Tel:* 415-615-0900 *Fax:* 415-615-0798
TWP America Inc, 299 Broadway, Suite 720, New York, NY 10007, United States, Sales: Regina Ang *Tel:* 212-274-8090 *E-mail:* rang@twpny.com
TWP America Inc, 1615 E Branch Rd, State College, PA 16801, United States *Tel:* 814-234-1816

Times Printers Pte Ltd
Subsidiary of Times Publishing Ltd
16 Tuas Ave 5, Singapore 639340
Tel: 6311 2888; 6295 3211; 6295 2138; 6311 2872 (customer service); 6311 2780 (sales & marketing) *Fax:* 6862 1313; 6311 2872 (customer service)
E-mail: marketing@timesprinters.com
Web Site: www.timesprinters.com.sg
Key Personnel
Deputy General Manager, Group Sales & Marketing: Patsy Tan
Operations Manager: Alex Tang
Assistant General Manager: Phan Ming Ruey
Founded: 1968
Turnaround: 5-25 Workdays
Print Runs: 3,000 min - 300,000 max
Business from Other Countries: 75%
Branch Office(s)
Times Offset (Malaysia) Sdn Bhd, Lot 46, Subang Hi-Tech Industrial Park, Batu Tiga, 40000 Selangor Darul Ehsan, Malaysia *Tel:* (03) 5628 6888 *Fax:* (03) 5628 6899

Sales Office(s): Everbest Printing Co Ltd, 25 The Palisade, Umina Beach, NSW 2257, Australia *Tel:* (02) 4342 3563 *Fax:* (02) 4342 1564 *E-mail:* adam@everbestprinting.com.au
Everbest Printing Co Ltd, Ko Fai Industrial Bldg, C5 10th floor, 7 Ko Fai Rd, Yau Tong, Kowloon, Hong Kong *Tel:* 2727 4433 *Fax:* 2772 7687 *E-mail:* sales@everbest.com.hk
13 Nthombeni Way Noordhoek, 7979 Cape Town, South Africa, Contact: Arlene Gippert *Tel:* (021) 789 2865 *E-mail:* arlenegippert@tpg.com.my
Everbest UK, 31 Palatine Rd, London N16 8SY, United Kingdom, Contact: Nicky Bowden *Tel:* (020) 7249 9483 *Fax:* (020) 7241 3460 *E-mail:* nickybowden@everbest.co.uk
3240 Vicente St, Apartment 3, San Francisco, CA 94116, United States, Contact: Brian Olshansky-Lucero *Tel:* 646-847-9874 *E-mail:* brian.olshansky-lucero@tpg.com.my

Toppan Security Printing Pte Ltd
97 Ubi Ave 4, Singapore 408754
Tel: 6741 2500 *Fax:* 6744 7098
Web Site: www.toppanleefung.com/toppansecurity.aspx
Key Personnel
President & Chief Executive Officer: Yeo Chee Tong
Production Dir: Jeffrey Yeo
General Manager & Digital Printing: David Ng *Tel:* 6846 3518 *E-mail:* davidng@toppanleefung.com
Deputy Sales Dir, Security Printing: Rick Ang *Tel:* 6846 3912 *E-mail:* rickang@toppanleefung.com
Turnaround: 30 Workdays
Print Runs: 2,000 min - 200,000 max
Business from Other Countries: 40%
Parent Company: Toppan Printing Co Ltd, One Kanda Izumi-cho, Chiyoda-ku, Toyko 101-0024, Japan

WMG Pte Ltd
Subsidiary of World Marketing Group (WMG)
World Publications Bldg, 45 Ubi Rd 1, No 03-03A, Singapore 408696
Tel: 6744 9888 *Fax:* 6745 8285
E-mail: business@worldmarketing-group.com
Web Site: www.wmg-group.com
Founded: 1982
Turnaround: 7-14 Workdays
Print Runs: 1 min - 70,000 max
Business from Other Countries: 80%
Branch Office(s)
WMG Beijing Ltd, Haocheng Tower, Room 1402, No 6 Zuojiazhuang Middle St, Chaoyang District, Beijing 100028, China *Tel:* (02) 8221 2788 ext 185 *Fax:* (02) 8221 2789
WMG Shanghai Ltd, Jiahua Business Centre, Suite A8412, 808 Hongqiao Rd, Xuhui District, Shanghai 200030, China *Tel:* (021) 6448 3980 *Fax:* (021) 6448 1975
World Marketing Group (HKG) Ltd, Blk D, 8F, Victorious Factory Bldg, 35 Tseuk Luk St, San Po Kong, Kowloon, Hong Kong *Tel:* 2750 8978 *Fax:* 2756 8271
WMG Marketing Malaysia Sdn Bhd, No 5, Jl Mega 1/8, Taman Perindustrian Nusa Cemerlang, 79200 Nusajaya, Johor, Malaysia *Tel:* (07) 509 9014 *Fax:* (07) 509 0913
WMG Taiwan Ltd, 5F, No 661A, Bannan Rd, Zhonghe District, New Taipei City 235, Taiwan *Tel:* (010) 6491 4011 *Fax:* (010) 8460 6685
World Marketing Group (Thailand) Co Ltd, 204/11 Suriwongse Rd, Siphaya Bangrak, Bangkok 10500, Thailand *Tel:* (02) 631 5414 *Fax:* (02) 631 5419
U.S. Office(s): WMG USA Inc, 84 Business Park Dr, Suite 113, Armonk, NY 10504-1734, United States *Tel:* 732-873-0088 *Fax:* 646-219-6899

Slovakia

Neografia AS
ul Sucianska 39 A, 038 61 Martin-Priekopa
Tel: (043) 4201 241 *Fax:* (043) 4201 704
E-mail: info@neografia.sk
Web Site: www.neografia.sk
Key Personnel
General Dir: Patrick Schwab *E-mail:* patrick.schwab@neografia.sk
Production Dir: Milos Lukac *Tel:* (043) 4201 300 *E-mail:* milos.lukac@neografia.sk
Commercial Dir: Helena Magvasiova *Tel:* (043) 4201 240 *E-mail:* helena.magvasiova@neografia.sk
Financial Dir: Peter Budisky *Tel:* (043) 4201 400 *E-mail:* peter.budisky@neografia.sk
Founded: 1869

Polygraf Print spol sro
Capajevova 44, 080 01 Presov
Tel: (051) 77 13 285; (051) 74 60 111 *Fax:* (051) 77 13 270; (051) 77 13 271
E-mail: polygrafprint@polygrafprint.sk
Web Site: www.polygrafprint.sk
Key Personnel
General Dir: Stanislav Potocnak *Tel:* (051) 77 13 272 *E-mail:* potocnak@polygrafprint.sk
Assistant General Dir: Vladimir Kirchnerova *Tel:* (051) 77 13 272-3
Commercial Dir: Drahos Kvasna *Tel:* (051) 74 60 113 *E-mail:* kvasna@polygrafprint.sk
Founded: 1996
Parent Company: Grafobal Group AS

TBB AS
Partizanska cesta 59, 974 01 Banska Bystrica
Tel: (048) 4307 111 *Fax:* (048) 4307 107
E-mail: info@tbb.sk
Web Site: www.tbb.sk
Key Personnel
General Dir: Stefan Kristel
Commercial Dir: Dusan Zelinka
Financial Dir: Martin Cajko
Production Dir: Mirko Breznan
Technical Dir: Ivan Kamas
Foreign Trade Manager: Daniel Simko *E-mail:* simko@tbb.sk

Slovenia

DZS Grafik doo
Ul Jozeta Jame 12, SI-1210 Ljubljana-Sentvid
Tel: (01) 586 72 00 *Fax:* (01) 586 72 15
E-mail: info@dzs-grafik.si
Web Site: www.dzs-grafik.si
Key Personnel
Dir: Marko Tomazevic *E-mail:* marko.tomazevic@dzs-grafik.si
Dir, Graphic Services: Ksenija Blazevic *E-mail:* blazevic@dzs-grafik.si
Dir, Paper Sector: Bojan Forjan *E-mail:* bojan.forjan@dzs-grafik.si
Turnaround: 10 Workdays (paperback), 15 Workdays (hardback)
Print Runs: 500 min - 500,000 max
Parent Company: DZS dd

Gorenjski Tisk Storitve doo
Ul Mirka Vadnova 6, SI-4000 Kranj
Tel: (04) 20 16 300 *Fax:* (04) 20 16 301
E-mail: info@go-tisk.si
Web Site: www.go-tisk.si

Key Personnel

Mng Dir: Goran Celesnik *Tel:* (04) 20 16 330
  E-mail: goran.celesnik@go-tisk.si
Dir, Sales & Marketing: Dr Andrej Krope, PhD
  Tel: (04) 20 16 326 *E-mail:* andrej.krope@go-
  tisk.si
Production Manager: Dusan Kuljic *Tel:* (04) 20
  16 451 *E-mail:* dusan.kuljic@go-tisk.si
Founded: 1888
Turnaround: 30 Workdays
Print Runs: 3,000 min - 15,000 max
Business from Other Countries: 50%

Korotan Ljubljana doo
Brnciceva ul 31, SI-1231 Ljubljana-Crnuce
Tel: (059) 250 658
E-mail: info@korotan.si
Web Site: www.korotan.si
Key Personnel
General Manager: Spela Mazovec
Sales & Marketing: Zdravko Mlakar
Parent Company: Krater Group

South Africa

CTP Printers Cape Town
Division of Caxton & CTP Publishers & Printers
  Ltd
12-14 Boompies St, Parow, Cape Town 7501
Tel: (021) 929 6200 *Fax:* (021) 939 1559
E-mail: ctp@ctpprinters.co.za
Web Site: www.ctpprinters.co.za
Key Personnel
Chief Executive Officer: Caroline Sturgeon
Dir: Vaughn Glover *E-mail:* vaughng@
  ctpprinters.co.za; Wayne Julies
  E-mail: waynej@ctpprinters.co.za
Operations Dir: Colin Sturgeon
Sales Dir: Paul Snowdon
Founded: 1947

South Korea

Asia Korea Printing Inc
Misung Off Bldg 2, Suite 604, 26 Ori-ro 876
  beon-gil, Gwangmyeong-si, Gyeonggi-do 423-
  836
Tel: (070) 8672 2750 *Fax:* (070) 8277 2510
Web Site: www.asiakoreaprinting.com
Key Personnel
Head Dir: Minsoo Chung *Tel:* (010) 6363 2656
  E-mail: minsoochung@asia-chinaprinting.com
Product Manager: Koon Yoon *Tel:* (010) 7788
  6992 *E-mail:* koon@asia-chinaprinting.com
Marketing Manager: Autumn Jung *Tel:* (010)
  3778 2656 *E-mail:* autumnjung@asia-
  chinaprinting.com

Asia Printing Co Ltd
King's Garden 3, Suite 720, 72 Naesu-dong,
  Jongro-gu, Seoul 110-872
Tel: (02) 7250790
Web Site: www.koreanprinting.com
Branch Office(s)
2127 Jingxin Plaza, East 3rd King North Rd,
  Chaoyang District, Beijing 100027, China

Chong-A Printing
544 Janghang-dong, Ilsan-gu, Koyang-City,
  Gjonggi-do 410-835
Tel: (031) 908 8671 *Fax:* (031) 908 8674
E-mail: chongapt@chongaprinting.com
Web Site: www.chongaprinting.com

Key Personnel

Chief Executive Officer: Namsoo Kim
Founded: 1985

KK Printing Co Ltd, see Kum-Kang Printing Co
  Ltd

Kum-Kang Printing Co Ltd
356 Jikji-gil, Paju Book-City, Kyunggi-do 413-
  120
Tel: (031) 943 0082 *Fax:* (031) 943 0046
E-mail: trade@kkprint.co.kr
Web Site: www.kkprint.co.kr
Key Personnel
Chief Executive Officer: Chang-Kyu Song

Mirae N Co Ltd
321 Sinbanpo-ro, Seocho-gu, Seoul 137-905
Fax: (02) 541-8158
Web Site: www.mirae-n.com
Key Personnel
President: Kim Young-jin
Manager: Ji Young Park *Tel:* (02) 3475-3870
  E-mail: park.jiyoung@mirae-n.com
Founded: 1948

Pacom Korea Inc
8F, Jellone Tower II 159-4, Jeongja-dong,
  Bundang-gu, Seongnam-si, Gyeonggi-do 463-
  834
Tel: (031) 718 3666 *Fax:* (031) 718 5857
E-mail: info@gopacom.com
Web Site: www.gopacom.com; pacomprinting.com
  (English)
Key Personnel
Chief Executive Officer: Kyong Su Kim
General Manager: J S Kook
Founded: 1999
Branch Office(s)
7-12 Rd 59, Nongsim-ro, Gunpo-si, Gyeonggi-do
  435-831 *Tel:* (031) 452 7519
Sales Office(s): Printmodel, Paris, France, Con-
  tact: Frederic Dahan *Tel:* 09 52 35 69 58
Freerun Co Ltd, Chuo-ku, Tokyo, Japan, Contact:
  Hidetake Imai *Tel:* (03) 5651-3011
Benicia, CA, United States, Contact: Jerry Jee
  Tel: 707-746-1670 *Fax:* 707-746-0670
Los Angeles, CA, United States, Contact: Sabra
  Chili *Tel:* 310-993-0058; 310-425-8258
Framingham, MA, United States, Contact: Sung S
  Yun *Tel:* 508-651-8851 *Fax:* 508-651-9187
Waxhaw, NC, United States, Contact: Petrice
  Beard *Tel:* 704-906-6642; 704-243-7205
Flower Mound, TX, United States, Contact:
  Lawrence Dagadu *Tel:* 972-724-0120 *Fax:* 972-
  539-5597

PoChinChai Printing Co Ltd
250, Jikji-gil, Paju-si, Gyeonggi-do 10881
Tel: (031) 955-1114; (031) 955-1130 *Fax:* (031)
  696-6324
Web Site: www.pochinchai.co.kr
Key Personnel
Chairman: Kim Joon-Ki
President: Kim Jung-Sun
Founded: 1912

Samhwa Printing Co Ltd
237-10, Kuro-dong, Kuro-ku, Seoul 08382
Fax: (02) 8500-777
Web Site: www.samhwaprinting.com
Key Personnel
Founder & Chairman: Mr Ki-jung Ryu
President: Mr Sung-keun Ryu
Senior Manager: Henry Park *Tel:* (02) 8500-775
  E-mail: henry@samhwaprinting.com
Founded: 1954

Tara TPS Co Ltd
245 Sangjiseok-gil, Paju-si, Kyunggi-do 413-140
Tel: (031) 945 1080 *Fax:* (031) 942 9547

Web Site: www.taratps.com
Key Personnel
President & Chief Executive Officer: Jae-Soo Lee
Dir: Winston Park *Tel:* (031) 939 2040
  E-mail: winston@taratps.com
General Manager: Chris Kim *Tel:* (031) 939 2077
  E-mail: chris@taratps.com; I W Lee *Tel:* (031)
  939 2125 *E-mail:* julee@taratps.com
Founded: 1989

Spain

Artes Graficas Palermo SL
Ave de la Tecnica, 7, 28522 Rivas, Madrid
Tel: 91 499 01 30
E-mail: palermo@agpalermo.es
Web Site: www.agpalermo.es

Brizzolis SA
Calle de las Marismas 5, Area Empresarial
  Andalucia-Sector 1, 28320 Pinto, Madrid
Tel: 91 691 91 30 *Fax:* 91 691 91 16
E-mail: arteengraficas@brizzolis.com;
  preimpresion@brizzolis.com
Web Site: www.brizzolis.com
Key Personnel
Commercial Dir: Juan Carlos Lozano
  E-mail: juancarloslozano@brizzolis.com
Administration & Accounting: Jose Perea
Prepress: Julian Munoz
Production: Claudia Fernandez
  E-mail: claudiafernandez@brizzolis.com; An-
  tonio Lozano *E-mail:* antoniolozano@brizzolis.
  com
Founded: 1992

Edelvives, see Editorial Luis Vives (Edelvives)

Eurohueco SA
Division of Arvato Print Iberica
C/ Cobalt, 1-5, Area Industrial del Llobregat,
  08755 Castellbisbal/Barcelona
Tel: 93 773 07 00 *Fax:* 93 653 22 05
E-mail: contact@rotocobrhi.eurohueco.es
Web Site: www.eurohueco.es
Key Personnel
Export Sales: Xavier Conigliano *E-mail:* xavier.
  conigliano@rotocobrhi.eurohueco.es
Sales, Spain: Javier Padierna *E-mail:* javier.
  padierna@rotocobrhi.eurohueco.es
Founded: 1986
Print Runs: 200,000 min - 15,000,000 max
Business from Other Countries: 17%
Ultimate Parent Company: Bertelsmann Group

Graficas Estella SL
Crta Estella-Tafalla km 2, 31132 Villatuerta-
  Estella, Navarra
Tel: 948 54 84 00
Web Site: estellaprint.com
Key Personnel
President & Chief Executive Officer: Francisco
  Gonzalez Cudeiro
General Manager & Commercial Dir: Jesus
  Uranga
Export Dir: Sonia Luqui *Tel:* 948 54 84 66
  E-mail: s.luqui@graficasestella.com
Founded: 1968
Parent Company: Lantero Group
Branch Office(s)
C/ Carme Galceran Nº4, Molins de Rei, 08750
  Barcelona *Tel:* 936 68 55 21
C/ Ave del Sol, 1, Torrejon de Ardoz, 28850
  Madrid *Tel:* 916 75 60 00

Graficas Santa Maria
Av Blas Infante, s/n, 41100 Coria del Rio, Seville
Tel: 954 771 091

Web Site: graficassantamaria.com
Founded: 1960
Turnaround: 1 Workday
Print Runs: 500 min - 150,000 max
Business from Other Countries: 15%

Grafos SA
Zona Franca, Sector C, Calle D n° 36, 08040
  Barcelona
Tel: 93 2618750 *Fax:* 93 2631004
E-mail: info@grafos.com
Web Site: www.grafos.com
Key Personnel
Domestic Division Manager: Orencio Sales
  Tel: 93 2618751 *E-mail:* orencio@grafos.com
Exports Division Manager: Jose M Caballe
  Tel: 93 2618764 *E-mail:* jose@grafos.com
Packaging Division Manager: Elisabeth Sanahuja
  Tel: 93 2618754 *E-mail:* elisabeth@grafos.com
Founded: 1934
Turnaround: 30 Workdays
Print Runs: 3,000 min - 60,000 max
Business from Other Countries: 45%

Publicaciones Digitales SA
Calle Merka 4, Nave 16, Poligono Empresarial
  Merka, 41500 Alcala de Guadaira, Seville
Tel: 902 405 500; 954 583 425 *Fax:* 954 583 205
E-mail: info@publidisa.com
Web Site: www.publidisa.com
Key Personnel
Chairman & Founder: Luis Abril Mula
Mng Dir: Luis Francisco Rodriquez
Financial Manager: Ignacio Martin
Marketing Manager: Lucia Fournier
Operations Manager: Antonio Martin
Founded: 2000
Branch Office(s)
Bibliografika, Bucarelli 1160, C1427BDF
  Buenos Aires, Argentina *Tel:* (011) 4523-3388
  Fax: (011) 4523-3388
Publidisa Colombiana, Calle 24 A No 43-22,
  Quinta Parede, Bogota, Colombia *Tel:* (01)
  481-0505 ext 113
Chabacano, 69, Colonia Asturias, 06850 Mexico,
  DF, Mexico *Tel:* (0155) 5740 9040 *Fax:* (0155)
  5741 4959

Publidisa SA, see Publicaciones Digitales SA

Editorial Luis Vives (Edelvives)
Xaudaro, 25, 28034 Madrid
Tel: 913 344 884
E-mail: info@edelvives.es
Web Site: www.edelvives.com
Founded: 1889
Turnaround: 1 Workday
Business from Other Countries: 25%
Parent Company: Grupo Editorial Luis Vives
Branch Office(s)
Ctra de Madrid, km 315,700, 50012 Zaragoza
  Tel: 976 304 030

Sri Lanka

M D Gunasena & Co Ltd
No 217, Olcott Mawatha, Colombo 11
Tel: (011) 2323981; (011) 2323982; (011)
  2323983; (011) 2323984 *Fax:* (011) 2323336
E-mail: headoffice@mdgunasena.com; info@
  mdgunasena.com
Web Site: www.mdgunasena.com

Sarvodaya Vishva Lekha
Unit of Sarvodaya
No 98, Rawatawatta Rd, Moratwa 10400
Tel: (011) 264-7159 *Fax:* (011) 2656-512

Web Site: www.sarvodaya.org
Founded: 1985

Sumathi Printers (Pvt) Ltd
Subsidiary of Sumathi Global Consolidated (Pvt)
  Ltd
445/1, Sirimavo Bandaranaike Mawatha, Colombo
  14
Tel: (011) 2330673; (011) 2330674 *Fax:* (011)
  2399924
E-mail: spb@sumathi.lk
Web Site: www.sumathi.lk/xampp/printing.html
Founded: 1980
Business from Other Countries: 75%

Sweden

Forlagshuset Nordens Grafiska AB
Nobelvagen 135, 212 15 Malmo
Mailing Address: Box 5, 201 20 Malmo
Tel: (040) 28 61 00 *Fax:* (040) 28 61 19
E-mail: kundservice@fng.se
Web Site: www.fng.se/fng
Key Personnel
Owner: Ann-Kristin Ohlsson; Max Ohlsson
  Tel: (040) 28 61 01 *E-mail:* max.ohlsson@fng.
  se
Founded: 1974

Switzerland

Canisius Druck & Grafik
Beauregard 3, 1700 Fribourg
Tel: (026) 425 51 61
E-mail: info@canisius.ch
Web Site: www.canisius.ch
Key Personnel
Dir: Beat Schultheiss
Founded: 1898

Imprimerie Messeiller SA
Route des Falaises 94, 2000 Neuchatel
Tel: (032) 725 12 96 *Fax:* (032) 724 19 37
E-mail: admin@messeiller.ch
Web Site: www.messeiller.ch
Key Personnel
Dir: Raphael Gambarini *E-mail:* raphael@
  messeiller.ch

Handwerkliche Buchbinderei Roland Meuter
Hoechistr 39, 6353 Weggis
Tel: (041) 390 02 63
E-mail: info@rmeuter.ch
Web Site: www.rmeuter.ch
Key Personnel
Owner: Roland Meuter

Photolitho AG
Industriestr 12, 8625 Gossau
Tel: (043) 833 70 20
E-mail: info@photolitho.ch
Web Site: www.photolitho.ch
Key Personnel
Mng Dir: Michael von Eicke *E-mail:* voneicke@
  photolitho.ch
Client Advisor: Juergen Luedicke
  E-mail: luedicke@photolitho.ch
Founded: 1965
Business from Other Countries: 50%

J E Wolfensberger AG
Stallikonerstr 79, 8903 Birmensdorf
Mailing Address: Postfach 474, 8903 Birmensdorf

Tel: (044) 285 78 78
E-mail: office@wolfensberger-ag.ch
Web Site: www.wolfensberger-ag.ch
Key Personnel
General Manager: Benni Wolfensberger *Tel:* (044)
  285 78 00 *E-mail:* benni.wolfensberger@
  wolfensberger-ag.ch
Lithography & Publishing: Thomi Wolfensberger
  E-mail: thomi.wolfensberger@wolfensberger-
  ag.ch
Founded: 1902

Taiwan

Red & Blue Color Printing Co Ltd
9, Lane 327, Sect 2, Zhongshan Rd, Zhonghe
  District, New Taipei City 23547
Tel: (02) 2240-1141 *Fax:* (02) 2240-7087
E-mail: webmaster@redblue.com.tw
Web Site: www.redblue.com.tw
Founded: 1965

Tanzania

Peramiho Printing Press
PO Box 41, Songea, Ruvuma
Tel: (025) 260 2299
Founded: 1937
Print Runs: 4,000 min - 6,000 max

Thailand

Amarin Printing & Publishing Public Co Ltd
378 Chaiyaphruk Rd, Taling Chan, Bangkok
  10170
Tel: (02) 882-1010; (02) 422-9000 *Fax:* (02) 433-
  2742; (02) 434-1385
Web Site: www.amarin.co.th
Key Personnel
Deputy Chief Executive Officer & Mng Dir,
  Printing Business Division: Cheewapat Natha-
  lang
President: Mrs Metta Utakapan
Administrative Dir: Bussapakes Wongchaoum
Sales Dir: Jutamas Smitanon
Founded: 1976

Cyberprint Group
959 Soi Suthiporn, Prachasongkroh Rd, Ding-
  daeng, Bangkok 10400
Tel: (02) 641-9135-8 *Fax:* (02) 641-9139
E-mail: info@cyberprint.co.th; digital@
  cyberprint.th
Web Site: www.cyberprint.co.th

J Film Process Co Ltd
440/7 Soi Ratchawithi 3, Ratchawithi Rd, Ra-
  jchatha, Bangkok 10400
Tel: (02) 248-6888; (02) 248-6887 *Fax:* (02) 246-
  4719
Founded: 1980
Turnaround: 6 Workdays
Print Runs: 25,000 min - 65,000 max
Business from Other Countries: 45%

Phongwarin Printing Ltd
299-299/1 Moo 10, Sukhumvit 107, Sumrongnue,
  Ampur Muang, Samutprakarn 10270
Tel: (02) 7498934-45; (02) 7498275-79; (02)
  3994525-31 *Fax:* (02) 3994524; (02) 3994255;
  (02) 3931028

E-mail: intemarketing@phongwarin.co.th
Web Site: www.phongwarin.co.th
Key Personnel
Mng Dir: Mr Somphong Charnsirisaksakul
Founded: 1983
Turnaround: 7 Workdays
Print Runs: 1,000 min - 500,000 max
Business from Other Countries: 5%

Siam Offset Co Ltd
9/1 Soi Sri Ak-Sorn, Tungmahamek, Sathorn,
Bangkok 10120
Tel: (02) 249-1575; (02) 249-1576; (02) 249-
5419; (02) 249-5420 *Fax:* (02) 249-5415
E-mail: info@siamoffset.com
Web Site: www.siamoffset.com
Founded: 1950

Sirivatana Interprint PLC
125 Soi Chan 32, Chan Rd, Thungwatdon,
Sathorn, Bangkok 10120
Tel: (02) 6755600 *Fax:* (02) 6755623
Web Site: www.sirivatana.co.th
Key Personnel
Mng Dir: Tavinee Samatiyadekul
E-mail: tavinee@sirivatana.co.th
Founded: 1976
Branch Office(s)
14/8 Moo 12, Bangna-Trad Km 46 Rd, Bang-
pakong, Chachoengsao 24130 *Tel:* (038)
532000 *Fax:* (038) 830716

Turkey

Bilnet Baski Sistemleri AS
Dudullu Organize Sanayi Bolgesi, One Cadde No
16, 34775 Umraniye, Istanbul
Tel: (0216) 444 44 03 *Fax:* (0216) 365 99 07-08
E-mail: info@bilnet.net.tr
Web Site: www.bilnet.net.tr
Founded: 2007
Parent Company: Bilfen Group

EGE Basim
Esatpasa Mah Ziyapasa Cad No 4, 34704 Atase-
hir, Istanbul
Tel: (0216) 470 4470 *Fax:* (0216) 472 8405
E-mail: ege@egebasim.com.tr
Web Site: www.egebasim.com.tr

Elma Basim Yayin ve Iletisim
Halkali Cad, No 162/7 Sefakoy Kucukcekmece,
34295 Istanbul
Tel: (0212) 697 30 30 *Fax:* (0212) 697 70 70
E-mail: elma@elmabasim.com
Web Site: www.elmabasim.com
Key Personnel
Partner: Cafer Ihsan Elhan; Mehmet Karagoz

ER-AY Basim Hizmetleri Ltd
100, Yil Mah Mas-Sit 1, Cad No 191-1, 34560
Bagcilar, Istanbul
Tel: (0212) 6290640 *Fax:* (0212) 4290647
E-mail: sales@eraybasim.com
Web Site: www.eraybasim.com

Imak Ofset Basim Yayin
Merkez Mah Ataturk Cd Gol Sk No 1, 34192
Yenibosna, Istanbul
Tel: (0212) 656 49 97 *Fax:* (0212) 656 29 26
E-mail: info@imakofset.com.tr
Web Site: www.imakofset.com.tr
Founded: 1997

Karakter Color AS
Mas/Sit No 200, 34560 Bagcilar, Istanbul

Tel: (0212) 4323001 *Fax:* (0212) 6289565
E-mail: info@karaktercolor.com.tr
Web Site: www.karaktercolor.com
Founded: 1959

Levent Ofset Basim ve Ambalaj San AS
Tekstil Merkezi Fatih Cad Karadal Sok No 13,
34169 Merter, Istanbul
Tel: (0212) 6371530 *Fax:* (0212) 6371985
E-mail: info@leventofset.com
Web Site: www.leventofset.com.tr
Founded: 1954

Mega Basim Yayin San ve Tic AS
Guvercin Cad, No 3/1 Baha Is Merkezi, 34310
Haramidere, Istanbul
Tel: (0212) 412 1700 *Fax:* (0212) 422 1151
E-mail: info@mega.com.tr; export@mega.com.tr
Web Site: www.mega.com.tr
Founded: 1991

Ofset Yapimevi
Sair Sokak 4, 34410 Kagithane, Istanbul
Tel: (0212) 295 86 01 *Fax:* (0212) 295 64 55
E-mail: sales@ofset.com
Web Site: www.ofset.com
Key Personnel
Dir, Business Development & Fine Art: Ferah
Perker *E-mail:* ferah.perker@ofset.com
International Business Development & Export
Dir: Sandra Kohen Filizer
Founded: 1982

Olusur Basim Hizmetleri Sanayi Ticaret AS
Vuzyil Mah Mas-Sit Matbaacilar Sitesi, 4 Cad No
52-53, 34204 Bagcilar, Istanbul
Tel: (0212) 6290606 *Fax:* (0212) 6290594
E-mail: info@olusur.com.tr
Web Site: olusur.com
Key Personnel
Chairman & Chief Executive Officer: Sadettin
Kasikirik
Chief Financial Officer: Ali Atmacaoglu
Chief Operating Officer: Erhan Dohuman
Business Development Manager: Kerem At-
macaoglu
Marketing Manager: Baris Kasikirik

Omur Printing & Binding Co
Haramidere Beysan Sanayi Sitesi, Birlik Cad No
20, 34524 Buyukcekmece, Istanbul
Tel: (0212) 422 76 00 *Fax:* (0212) 422 46 00
Web Site: www.omurprint.com
Founded: 1980

Pasifik Ofset Ltd Sti
Guvercin Cad No 3/1, Baha Is Merkezi Blok A,
34310 Haramidere, Istanbul
Tel: (0212) 412 17 77 *Fax:* (0212) 422 11 51
E-mail: info@pasifikofset.com.tr
Web Site: www.pasifikofset.com.tr

Promat Basim Yayin San ve Tic AS
Orhangazi Mah 1673 Sok No 34, 34517 Esenyurt,
Istanbul
Tel: (0212) 6226363 *Fax:* (0212) 6050798
E-mail: info@promat.com.tr
Web Site: www.promat.com.tr
Founded: 1991

**Sena Ofset Ambalaj Matbaacilik Sana yi ve
Ticaret Ltd Sti**
Litros Yolu 2, Matbaacilar Sitesi E Blok 6, Kat
4NE 20, 34010 Zeytinburnu, Istanbul
Tel: (0212) 6133846 *Fax:* (0212) 6130321
E-mail: info@senaofset.com.tr
Web Site: senaofset.com.tr
Key Personnel
Founder: Sureyya Balkac
Founded: 1985

Ukraine

Factor Druk Printing House
Saratovskaya 51, Kharkiv 61030
Tel: (057) 717-51-85; (057) 717-53-55 (market-
ing)
E-mail: klient@druk.factor.ua
Web Site: www.factor-druk.com.ua
Key Personnel
Chief Executive Officer: Olga Shapoval
President: Sergey Politychiy
Manufacturing Dir: Vladimir Kopylov
Head, Prepress: Aleksey Sobol *Tel:* (057) 717-50-
13

Unisoft Book Factory
Morozova Str 136, Kharkov 61036
Tel: 57 730-17-13; 57 730-17-09 (prepress)
E-mail: info@ttornado.com.ua
Web Site: ttornado.com.ua
Founded: 1994

United Arab Emirates

Al-Futtaim Printers & Publishers
PO Box 799, Dubai
Tel: (04) 2222222; (04) 3477777 *Fax:* (04)
2217878; (04) 3477776
Key Personnel
Group Chairman: Othman Al Futtaim
Founded: 1992

Al Madeena Printing Press
PO Box 86910, Dubai
Tel: (04) 2678333 *Fax:* (04) 2678383

Emirates Printing Press LLC
Member of Al Shirawi Group
PO Box 5106, Dubai
Tel: (04) 3475550 *Fax:* (04) 3475959
E-mail: epp@eppdubai.com
Web Site: www.eppdubai.com
Key Personnel
Chief Executive Officer: Mohamed Abdulla Al
Shirawi
Founded: 1975
Sales Office(s): Emirates Printing Press (UK) Ltd,
4 High St, Burnham, Bucks SL1 7JH, United
Kingdom *Tel:* (01628) 668884 *Fax:* (01628)
660703 *E-mail:* epp@eppeurope.com (Europe
& USA)

United Printing & Publishing (UPP)
PO Box 39955, Abu Dhabi
Tel: (02) 5039 998; (02) 5039 999 *Fax:* (02) 5039
990
E-mail: info@upp.ae
Web Site: www.upp.ae

UPP, see United Printing & Publishing (UPP)

United Kingdom

W&G Baird Ltd
Greystone Press, Caulside Dr, Antrim BT41 2RS
Tel: (028) 9446 3911 *Fax:* (028) 9446 6250
E-mail: wgbaird@wgbaird.com
Web Site: www.wgbaird.com
Key Personnel
Owner: David Hinds
Mng Dir: Patrick Moffett
Commercial Dir: Ian McCurry
Business Development Manager: Amanda Stewart
Founded: 1862
Print Runs: 500 min - 100,000 max
Business from Other Countries: 45%
Sales Office(s): 8 Braefell Close, West Bridg-
ford, Nottingham, Notts NG2 6SS *Tel:* (07918)
742161
Broomfield House, Malahide, Dublin, Ireland
Tel: (0872) 585 273

Bell & Bain Ltd
303 Burnfield Rd, Thornliebank, Glasgow G46
7UQ
Tel: (0141) 649 5697 *Fax:* (0141) 632 8733
Web Site: www.bell-bain.com
Key Personnel
Co-Owner & Mng Dir: Stephen Docherty
E-mail: sd@bell-bain.co.uk
Co-Owner & Sales Dir: Tony Campbell
E-mail: tcampbell@bell-bain.co.uk
Sales Dir Designate: Derek Kenney
E-mail: dkenney@bell-bain.co.uk
Operations Dir: Karen Baillie *E-mail:* kbaillie@
bell-bain.co.uk
Bindery Manager: Alistair Clowes
E-mail: aclowes@bell-bain.co.uk
Customer Services Manager: Tracey Mallon
E-mail: tmallon@bell-bain.co.uk
Print Manager: Scott Hill *E-mail:* shill@bell-bain.
co.uk
Information Technology Manager: Gordon Rogers
E-mail: grogers@bell-bain.co.uk
Founded: 1831
Turnaround: 5-10 Workdays
Print Runs: 100 min - 100,000 max
Business from Other Countries: 25%

Biddles Books Ltd
Castle House, East Winch Rd, Blackborough End,
King's Lynn, Norfolk PE32 1SF
Tel: (01553) 842477
E-mail: enquiries@biddles.co.uk
Web Site: www.biddles.co.uk
Key Personnel
Owner: Nigel Mitchell; Rod Willett
Founded: 2013
Print Runs: 10 min - 5,000 max

Blackmore Ltd
Longmead, Shaftesbury, Dorset SP7 8PX
Tel: (01747) 853034 *Fax:* (01747) 854500
E-mail: sales@blackmore.co.uk
Web Site: www.blackmore.co.uk
Key Personnel
Mng Dir: Peter Smith
Parent Company: TH Brickell Group

Blockfoil Group Ltd
Ransomes Park Industrial Estate, Foxtail Rd, Ip-
swich IP3 9RT
Tel: (01473) 721701 *Fax:* (01473) 718220
E-mail: ipswich@blockfoil.com
Web Site: www.blockfoil.com
Key Personnel
Group Mng Dir: Barry Corbett *Tel:* (01473)
707203 *E-mail:* barrycorbett@blockfoil.com

Dir: Peter Starling *Tel:* (01473) 707200
E-mail: peterstarling@blockfoil.com
Marketing Executive: Matt Ash *Tel:* (01473)
707226 *E-mail:* matthewash@blockfoil.com
Factory Manager: Ben Hazelton *Tel:* (01473)
707208 *E-mail:* benhazelton@blockfoil.com
Sales Manager: Chris Mulcock *Tel:* (07788)
278003 *E-mail:* chrismulcock@blockfoil.com
Founded: 1981
Branch Office(s)
Chadderton Industrial Estate, Greenside Way,
Middleton, Manchester M24 1SW, General
Manager: Paul Makin *Tel:* (0161) 655 3842
Fax: (0161) 655 3843 *E-mail:* manchester@
blockfoil.com
Unit 4, Benneworth Close, Watnall Rd, Hucknall,
Nottingham, Notts NG15 6EL, General Man-
ager: Kevin Bloomfield *Tel:* (0115) 964 2707
Fax: (0115) 964 2727 *E-mail:* nottingham@
blockfoil.com

Cambridge University Press - Printing Division
Division of Cambridge University Press
University Printing House, Shaftesbury Rd, Cam-
bridge, Cambs CB2 8BS
Tel: (01223) 358331
E-mail: information@cambridge.org
Web Site: www.cambridge.org/us/information/
about.htm
Founded: 1534
Print Runs: 1 min

Charlesworth Press
Flanshaw Way, Flanshaw Lane, Wakefield WF2
9LP
Tel: (01924) 204 830 *Fax:* (01924) 332 637
E-mail: info@charlesworth-group.com; cw.sales@
charlesworth.com
Web Site: www.charlesworth.com
Key Personnel
Mng Dir: David Boothman
Commercial Dir: Sue Sheldon *Tel:* (07870) 239
480 *E-mail:* sue.sheldon@charlesworth.com
Sales Manager: Nick Crowther *Tel:* (07775) 503
476 *E-mail:* nick.crowther@charlesworth.com
Founded: 1928
Turnaround: 1-10 Workdays
Print Runs: 1 min - 10,000 max
Business from Other Countries: 30%
Parent Company: Charlesworth Group

Clays Ltd
Subsidiary of St Ives PLC
One Tudor St, London EC4Y 0AH
Tel: (020) 7928 8844
E-mail: sales@clays.co.uk
Web Site: www.clays.co.uk
Key Personnel
Mng Dir: Paul Hulley
Account Dir: Andrew Cochrane; Vicky Ellis
Customer Service Dir: Anne Perrin
Digital Sales Dir: Andrew Copley
Finance Dir: Andrew Spring
Manufacturing Dir: Ian Smith
Strategic Dir: Kate McFarlan
Self-Publishing Account Manager: Rebecca
Souster
Founded: 1817
Turnaround: 15 Workdays
Print Runs: 1,000 min - 1,000,000 max
Business from Other Countries: 15%
Branch Office(s)
Popson St, Bungay, Suffolk NR35 1ED
Tel: (01986) 893 211

William Clowes Ltd, see CPI William Clowes
Ltd

CPI Antony Rowe
Bumper's Farm, Chippenham, Wilts SN14 6LH
Tel: (01249) 659705 *Fax:* (01249) 443103

Web Site: www.cpi-print.co.uk
Key Personnel
General Manager: Martin Collyer
Sales Manager: Geoff Fisher
Divisional Mng Dir: Alison Kaye
Founded: 1983
Turnaround: 20 Workdays
Print Runs: 50 min - 2,000 max
Business from Other Countries: 2%
Parent Company: CPI Group UK Ltd
Branch Office(s)
48-50 Birch Close, Eastbourne, East Sussex
BN23 6PE *Tel:* (01323) 434700

CPI William Clowes Ltd
Copland Way, Ellough, Beccles, Suffolk NR34
7TL
Tel: (01502) 712884
E-mail: williamclowes@cpibooks.co.uk
Key Personnel
Divisional Mng Dir: Alison Kaye
Head, Sales: Jonathan Huddart
Founded: 1803
Turnaround: 10 Workdays
Print Runs: 2,000 min
Business from Other Countries: 1%
Parent Company: CPI Group UK Ltd
Ultimate Parent Company: CPI Group

Furnival Press
Unit 1, Kennington Enterprise Centre, 32 Bra-
ganza St, London SE17 3RJ
Tel: (020) 7924 9398
Web Site: www.furnivalpress.co.uk
Key Personnel
Owner: Johnny Gumb *E-mail:* johnny@
furnivalpress.co.uk
Dir: David Peach *E-mail:* david@furnivalpress.co.
uk
Founded: 1861

Green Street Bindery
Horspath Trading Centre, Pony Rd, Oxford, Oxon
OX4 2RD
Tel: (01865) 747459 *Fax:* (01865) 749827
E-mail: greenstbindery@aol.com
Web Site: www.maltbysbookbinders.com
Key Personnel
Mng Dir: Tony Tanner
Turnaround: 10-15 Workdays
Print Runs: 1 min - 10,000 max
Business from Other Countries: 5%
Parent Company: Kemp Hall Bindery Group

Hammond Bindery Ltd
Subsidiary of The Charlesworth Group
Flanshaw Way, Flanshaw Lane, Wakefield WF2
9LP
Tel: (01924) 204830 *Fax:* (01924) 332637
E-mail: sales@hammond-bindery.co.uk;
hammonds.sales@hammond-bindery.co.uk
Web Site: www.hammond-bindery.co.uk
Key Personnel
Mng Dir: David Boothman
Commercial Dir: Sue Sheldon *Tel:* (01924)
204850
Customer Service & Estimator: Rhonda Mof-
fat *Tel:* (01924) 204852 *E-mail:* rhonda@
hammond-bindery.co.uk
Founded: 1974
Turnaround: 3-10 Workdays
Print Runs: 5 min - 100,000 max

Headley Brothers Ltd
The Invicta Press, Queens Rd, Ashford, Kent
TN24 8HH
Tel: (01233) 623131 *Fax:* (01233) 612345
E-mail: printing@headley.co.uk; sales@headley.
co.uk
Web Site: www.headley.co.uk
Key Personnel
Chief Executive Officer: Roger Pitt *E-mail:* roger.
pitt@headley.co.uk

Commercial Dir: Jon Pitt *E-mail:* jon.pitt@
  headley.co.uk
Sales Dir: Paul Palmer *E-mail:* paul.palmer@
  headley.co.uk
Founded: 1881
Print Runs: 1,000 min - 200,000 max
Business from Other Countries: 5%

Hobbs The Printers Ltd
Brunel Rd, Totton, Hants SO40 3WX
Tel: (023) 8066 4800 *Fax:* (023) 8066 4801
E-mail: info@hobbs.uk.com
Web Site: www.hobbs.uk.com; www.
  hobbstheprinters.co.uk
Key Personnel
Mng Dir: David Hobbs *E-mail:* d.a.hobbs@hobbs.
  uk.com
Deputy Mng & Operations Dir: Graham Bromley
  E-mail: g.bromley@hobbs.uk.com
Commercial Dir: Terry Ozanne *E-mail:* t.
  ozanne@hobbs.uk.com
Customer Services Manager: Colin Richardson
  E-mail: c.richardson@hobbs.uk.com
Founded: 1884
Turnaround: 5-10 days litho; up to 5 days digital
Print Runs: 10 min - 50,000 max
Business from Other Countries: 4%

Intype Libra Ltd
3/4 Elm Grove Industrial Estate, Elm Grove,
  Wimbledon, London SW19 4HE
Tel: (020) 8947 7863 *Fax:* (020) 8947 3652
E-mail: hello@intypelibra.co.uk
Web Site: www.intypelibra.co.uk
Key Personnel
Owner & Mng Dir: Tony Chapman
Owner: David Greenwood
Founded: 1974
Turnaround: 1-2 Workdays for digital prints; 5-8
  Workdays for books
Print Runs: 25 min - 1,000 max
Business from Other Countries: 5%

J W B Finishers Ltd
PO Box 20, Pountney St, Wolverhampton WV2
  4HY
Tel: (01902) 452209 *Fax:* (01902) 352918;
  (01902) 452209
Key Personnel
Operations Manager: Mr T Cattel
Founded: 1901

Lavenham Press Ltd
Arbons House, 47 Water St, Lavenham, Suffolk
  CO10 9RN
Tel: (01787) 247436 *Fax:* (01787) 248267
E-mail: enquiries@lavenhamgroup.co.uk
Web Site: www.lavenhampress.com
Key Personnel
Mng Dir: Terence Dalton
Founded: 1953
Business from Other Countries: 1%
Parent Company: Lavenham Group

Librios Ltd
20 Lochaline St, London W6 9SH
Tel: (020) 3355 0200
E-mail: info@librios.com
Web Site: www.librios.com
Key Personnel
Software Development Dir: David Wilcockson
  E-mail: david@librios.com
System Administrator: Neville Mooney
Project Developer: Chris Lewis *E-mail:* chris.
  lewis@librios.com
Founded: 1997
Business from Other Countries: 30%

Lightning Source UK Ltd
Chapter House, Pitfield, Kiln Farm, Milton
  Keynes MK11 3LW

Tel: (0845) 121 4567; (01908) 829517; (0845)
  121 4555 (sales) *Fax:* (0845) 121 4591
E-mail: enquiries@lightningsource.co.uk
Web Site: www.lightningsource.com
Key Personnel
Senior Vice President, Content Acquisition & In-
  ternational: David Taylor
Mng Dir: Dave Piper
Dir, Operations: Terry Gridley
Finance Dir: Frank Devine
Business Development Manager: Philippa Mal-
  icka
Key Account Sales Manager: Marcelo Suarez
  Melgarejo
Founded: 1997
Parent Company: Ingram Content Group
U.S. Office(s): Lightning Source Inc, 1246 Heil
  Quaker Blvd, La Vergne, TN 37086, United
  States *Tel:* 615-213-5815 *Fax:* 615-213-4725
  E-mail: inquiry@lightningsource.com

Lowfield Printing Co Ltd
9 Kennet Rd, Dartford, Kent DA1 4QN
Tel: (01322) 522216 *Fax:* (01322) 555362
E-mail: info@lowfieldprinting.co.uk
Web Site: www.lowfieldprinting.co.uk
Key Personnel
Mng Dir: James Dow
Dir: Nigel Starkey *E-mail:* nigel@
  lowfieldprinting.co.uk
Founded: 1964
Print Runs: 500 min - 20,000 max

George Over Ltd
20 Somers Rd, Rugby, Warwicks CV22 7DG
Tel: (01788) 573621

Page Bros (Norwich) Ltd
Subsidiary of Milex Ltd
Mile Cross Lane, Norwich, Norfolk NR6 6SA
Tel: (01603) 778800 *Fax:* (01603) 778801
E-mail: info@pagebros.co.uk
Web Site: www.pagebros.co.uk
Key Personnel
Mng Dir: Craig Eastaugh *E-mail:* c.eastaugh@
  pagebros.co.uk
Sales & Commercial Dir: Andrew Spelman
  E-mail: a.spelman@pagebros.co.uk
Founded: 1750
Turnaround: 10 Workdays
Print Runs: 100 min - 30,000 max
Business from Other Countries: 20%

Pindar Scarborough Ltd
Thornburgh Rd, Eastfield, Scarborough, N Yorks
  YO11 3UY
Tel: (01723) 581581 *Fax:* (01723) 583086
E-mail: pindarestimates@pindar.com
Web Site: www.pindar.com
Key Personnel
Group Sales Dir: Norman Revill *Tel:* (07725)
  219763 *E-mail:* n.revill@pindar.com
Commercial Manager: David Stephenson
  Tel: (01723) 502387 *E-mail:* d.stephenson@
  pindar.com

Quercus Eight
133 Houndsditch, London EC3A 7DB
Tel: (020) 8366 4473
E-mail: hello@quercuseight.co.uk
Web Site: www.quercuseight.co.uk
Key Personnel
Mng Dir: David Douglas *E-mail:* david@
  quercuseight.co.uk
New Business Manager: Jane Jones
  E-mail: jane@quercuseight.co.uk
Editor: Liz Turner *E-mail:* liz@quercuseight.co.uk
Founded: 1946

Riley Dunn & Wilson Ltd
Almond Court, Falkirk, Stirlingshire FK2 9HT

Tel: (01324) 621591 *Fax:* (01324) 611508
E-mail: enquiry@rdw.co.uk; customer.services@
  rdw.co.uk
Web Site: www.rdw.co.uk
Key Personnel
Mng Dir: Charles Dunn *E-mail:* charles.dunn@
  rdw.co.uk
Dir, Strategy & Finance: Jeremy Mills
  E-mail: jeremy.mills@rdw.co.uk
Senior Manager, Heritage & Presentation Ser-
  vices: Brian Lynch *Tel:* (07973) 364095
  E-mail: brian.lynch@rdw.co.uk
Senior Manager, Operations & Resources: Colin
  McArthur *E-mail:* colin.mcarthur@rdw.co.uk
Branch Office(s)
Red Doles Lane, Huddersfield, W Yorks HD2
  1YE *Tel:* (01484) 534323 *Fax:* (01484) 435048
  E-mail: info@rdw.co.uk

Smith Settle
Gateway Dr, Yeadon, W Yorks LS19 7XY
Tel: (0113) 250 9201 *Fax:* (0113) 250 9223
Web Site: www.smithsettle.com
Key Personnel
Mng Dir: Don Walters *E-mail:* dwalters@
  smithsettle.com
Financial Dir: Tracey Thorne *E-mail:* tthorne@
  smithsettle.com
Founded: 1981

TJ International Ltd
Trecerus Industrial Estate, Padstow, Cornwall
  PL28 8RW
Tel: (01841) 532691 *Fax:* (01841) 532862
E-mail: sales@tjinternational.ltd.uk
Web Site: www.tjinternational.ltd.uk
Key Personnel
Chief Executive Officer: Angus Clark
Deputy Chief Executive Officer: Andy Vosper
Sales & Marketing Manager: Neil Clarke
Founded: 1970
Turnaround: 15 Workdays
Business from Other Countries: 5%

University of London Central Printing Services
University of London, Senate House, Malet St,
  London WC1E 7HU
Tel: (020) 7862 8000; (020) 7862 8163
E-mail: print.services@london.ac.uk
Web Site: w01.uoldev.wf.ulcc.ac.uk/printing.html

Gavin Watson Printers
79-109 Glasgow Rd, Glasgow G72 0LY
Tel: (01698) 826000 *Fax:* (01698) 824944
Web Site: www.gavinwatson.co.uk
Key Personnel
Chief Executive Officer: Tom Brown
  E-mail: tbrown@gavinwatson.co.uk
Founded: 1863
Business from Other Countries: 1%

WH Trade Binders Ltd
South March, Long March Industrial Estate, Dav-
  entry, Northants NN11 4PH
Tel: (01327) 704911 *Fax:* (01327) 872588
Key Personnel
Mng Dir: Roger Westrop
Founded: 1981
Print Runs: 10,000 min
Business from Other Countries: 1%

United States

ADR Inc
2012 E Northern St, Wichita, KS 67216
Tel: 316-522-5599 *Toll Free Tel:* 800-767-6066
  Fax: 316-522-5445
E-mail: info@adr.biz

Web Site: www.adr.biz
Key Personnel
CEO: Patrick Tuttle *E-mail:* ptuttle@adr.biz
Pres: Jim Rishel
Founded: 1978
Print Runs: 1 min - 25,000 max
Business from Other Countries: 10%
Membership(s): Print Services & Distribution Association; Printing Industries of America

Arbor Books
244 Madison Ave, Box 254, New York, NY 10016-2834
Tel: 212-956-0950 *Toll Free Tel:* 877-822-2500
Fax: 914-737-3639
E-mail: info@arborbooks.com; editorial@arborbooks.net
Web Site: www.arborbooks.com
Key Personnel
Owner: Joel Hochman *Tel:* 877-822-2502 *E-mail:* arborbooksjoel@aol.com; Larry Leichman *Tel:* 877-822-2504 *E-mail:* arborbookslarry@aol.com
Mktg Dir: Olga Vladi
Founded: 1992
Turnaround: 21 Workdays; 1-7 for art
Print Runs: 1 min - 1,000,000 max
Business from Other Countries: 15%

Asia Pacific Offset Inc
1312 "Q" St NW, Suite B, Washington, DC 20009
Tel: 202-462-5436 *Toll Free Tel:* 800-756-4344
Fax: 202-986-4030
Web Site: www.asiapacificoffset.com
Key Personnel
Pres: Andrew Clarke *E-mail:* andrew@asiapacificoffset.com
Founded: 1997
Turnaround: 105 Workdays including color separation & shipping
Print Runs: 2,000 min
Business from Other Countries: 100%
Sales Office(s): 870 Market St, Suite 801, San Francisco, CA 94102, Dir, Sales: Amy Armstrong *Tel:* 415-433-3488 *Fax:* 415-433-3489 *E-mail:* amy@asiapacificoffset.com
62 Rivington St, Suite 2-B, New York, NY 10002, Dir, Sales: Simona Jansons *Tel:* 212-941-8300 *Fax:* 212-941-9810 *E-mail:* simona@asiapacificoffset.com

BookFactory
2302 S Edwin C Moses Blvd, Dayton, OH 45417
Tel: 937-226-7100 *Toll Free Tel:* 877-431-2665
Fax: 614-388-5635
E-mail: sales@bookfactory.com
Web Site: www.bookfactory.com
Key Personnel
Founder & Pres: Andrew Gilmore *E-mail:* andrew.gilmore@bookfactory.com
Sales Mgr: Tessin Farmer
Founded: 2002
Turnaround: 20 Workdays after approval
Print Runs: 50 min - 3,000 max
Business from Other Countries: 23%
Membership(s): OMA

C & C Offset Printing Co USA Inc
Subsidiary of C & C Joint Printing Co (HK) Ltd
70 W 36 St, Unit 10C, New York, NY 10018
Tel: 212-431-4210 *Toll Free Fax:* 866-540-4134
Web Site: www.ccoffset.com
Key Personnel
Dir & EVP, C & C Offset Printing Co (USA) Inc, Portland, OR & C & C Offset Printing Co (NYC) Inc, New York, NY: Simon Chan *E-mail:* schan@ccoffset.com
VP, C & C Offset Printing Co (Chicago) Inc, Chicago, IL: Ernest Li *E-mail:* ernest.li@ccoffset.com

Sales Mgr, C & C Offset Printing Co (NYC) Inc, New York, NY: Frances Harkness *E-mail:* fharkness@ccoffset.com; Timothy McNulty
CEO, C & C Joint Printing Co (HK) Ltd, Hong Kong: Jackson Leung
Mng Dir, Hong Kong Head Off: Ken Lee
Deputy Gen Mgr, Hong Kong Head Off: Kit Wong
Sr Sales Mgr (Spec Projs), Hong Kong Head Off: Francis Ho
Dir, C & C Offset Printing Co (France) Ltd: Michele Olson Niel *E-mail:* michele@candcoffset.fr
Pres, C & C Printing Japan Co Ltd, Tokyo, Japan: Yamamoto Masaaki
Dir, C & C Offset Printing Co (UK) Ltd: Tracy Broderick *E-mail:* tracy@candcoffset.co.uk
Sales Rep, Australian Off: Lena Frew *E-mail:* lena.frew@candcprinting.com
Founded: 1980
Turnaround: Varies
Print Runs: 2,000 min - 3,000,000 max
Business from Other Countries: 70%
Branch Office(s)
C & C Offset Printing (Chicago) Inc, 800 W Fifth Ave, Suite 100D, Naperville, IL 60563 *Tel:* 630-737-0820; 630-390-5617 *Fax:* 630-737-1997
C & C Offset Printing Co Ltd (Australia Off), Lithocraft Graphics, 3-7 Permas Way, Truganina, Victoria 3029, Australia *Tel:* (0613) 8366 0200 *Fax:* (0613) 8366 0299
C & C Joint Printing Co (Beijing) Ltd, Beijing Economic & Technological Development Area (BDA), Donghuan North Rd, No 3, Beijing 100176, China *Tel:* (010) 6787 6655 *Fax:* (010) 6787 8255 *E-mail:* ccbj@candcprinting.cn (plant)
C & C Joint Printing Co (Guangdong) Ltd, Hua Xin Bldg E Block, Rm 1511, 2 Shuiyin Rd, Huanshi East, Guangzhou 510075, China *Tel:* (020) 3760 0979; (020) 3760 0980 *Fax:* (020) 3760 0977 *E-mail:* guangzhou@candcprinting.com
C & C Joint Printing (Shanghai) Co Ltd, 3333 Cao Ying Rd, Qingpu Industrial Zone, Shanghai 201712, China *Tel:* (021) 5922 6000 *Fax:* (021) 5922 6111 *E-mail:* shanghai@candcprinting.com *Web Site:* www.candcprinting.com (plant)
C & C Joint Printing Co (Guangdong) Ltd, Chunhu Industrial Estate, Pinghu, Long Gang, Shenzhen 518111, China *Tel:* (0755) 3360 9988 *Fax:* (0755) 3360 9998 *E-mail:* guangdong@candcprinting.com *Web Site:* www.candcprinting.com (plant)
C & C Offset Printing Co (France) Ltd, 15, rue d'Aboukir, 75002 Paris, France *Tel:* 01 40 26 21 07 *Fax:* 01 44 76 08 96
C & C Offset Printing Co Ltd, C & C Bldg, 36 Ting Lai Rd, Tai Po, New Territories, Hong Kong *Tel:* 2666 4988 *Fax:* 2666 4938 *E-mail:* info@candcprinting.com *Web Site:* www.candcprinting.com (corp headquarters)
C & C Printing Japan Co Ltd, Tozaido Bldg, 3F, 2-6-12 Hitotsubashi, Chiyoda-ku, Tokyo 101-0003, Japan *Tel:* (03) 5216 4580 *Fax:* (03) 5216 4610 *E-mail:* mail@candcprinting.co.jp *Web Site:* www.candcprinting.co.jp
C & C Offset Printing Co (UK) Ltd, 7-9 Charlotte St, 2nd fl, London W1T 1RG, United Kingdom *Tel:* (020) 7637 5033 *Fax:* (020) 7637 5044

Consolidated Printers Inc
2630 Eighth St, Berkeley, CA 94710
Tel: 510-843-8524 (sales); 510-843-8565 (admin) *Fax:* 510-486-0580
E-mail: cpi@consoprinters.com; sales@consoprinters.com
Web Site: www.consoprinters.com

Key Personnel
CEO: Lawrence A Hawkins
Founded: 1952
Turnaround: 2-20 Workdays
Print Runs: 2,000 min - 500,000 max
Business from Other Countries: 15%

D & K Group Inc
1795 Commerce Dr, Elk Grove Village, IL 60007
Tel: 847-956-0160 *Toll Free Tel:* 800-632-2314
Fax: 847-956-8214
E-mail: info@dkgroup.net
Web Site: www.dkgroup.com
Key Personnel
Pres: Karl Singer
VP, Sales & Mktg: Tom Pidgeon *E-mail:* tom.pidgeon@dkgroup.net
Mktg Communs Specialist: Brian Biegel *E-mail:* brian.biegel@dkgroup.net
Founded: 1979
Business from Other Countries: 15%

dix! Digital Prepress Inc
8462 Wayfarer Dr, Cicero, NY 13039
Tel: 315-288-5888 *Fax:* 315-288-5898
E-mail: info@dixtype.com
Web Site: www.dixtype.com
Key Personnel
Pres: Scott Wenger *E-mail:* swenger@dixtype.com
Acct Exec, Sales & Mktg: Kelly Farley *E-mail:* kfarley@dixtype.com
Founded: 1923
Turnaround: 2-10 Workdays
Business from Other Countries: 30%

DNP America LLC
Subsidiary of Dai Nippon Printing Co Ltd
335 Madison Ave, 3rd fl, New York, NY 10017
Tel: 212-503-1060 *Fax:* 212-286-1501
Web Site: www.dnpamerica.com
Key Personnel
Gen Mgr: Seiichi Suzuki
Founded: 1974
Turnaround: 30-60 Workdays
Business from Other Countries: 54%
Branch Office(s)
3235 Kifer Rd, Suite 100, Santa Clara, CA 95051 *Tel:* 408-735-8880
3858 Carson St, Suite 300, Torrance, CA 90503 *Tel:* 310-540-5123 *Fax:* 310-543-3260

Docunet Corp
2435 Xenium Lane N, Plymouth, MN 55441
Tel: 763-475-9600 *Toll Free Tel:* 800-936-2863
Fax: 763-475-1516
Web Site: www.docunetworks.com
Key Personnel
Partner: Wendy Morical *E-mail:* wnm@docunetworks.com; Brant Nelson
Founded: 1991
Print Runs: 1 min - 5,000 max
Business from Other Countries: 10%
Membership(s): Print Industry of Minnesota; Women's Business Enterprise Network

EP Graphics
Division of Dynamic Resource Group
169 S Jefferson St, Berne, IN 46711
Tel: 260-589-2145 *Toll Free Tel:* 877-589-2145
Fax: 260-589-2810
Web Site: www.epgraphics.com
Key Personnel
CEO: Tyler Kitt
Founded: 1925
Turnaround: 15 Workdays
Print Runs: 25,000 min - 500,000 max
Business from Other Countries: 80%

Fairfield Marketing Group Inc
Subsidiary of FMG Inc

The Direct Mail Ctr, 830 Sport Hill Rd, Easton, CT 06112-1241
Tel: 203-261-5585; 203-261-5568 *Fax:* 203-261-0884
E-mail: info@fairfieldmarketing.com
Web Site: www.fairfieldmarketing.com
Key Personnel
CEO & Pres: Edward P Washchilla, Jr
VP, Cust Serv: Mike Lozada *Tel:* 203-261-5585 ext 204
VP, Fin: Pamela L Washchilla
VP, Fulfillment: Jason Paul Miller *Tel:* 203-261-5585 ext 203 *E-mail:* jason@fairfieldmarketing.com
Founded: 1987
Turnaround: 1-7 Workdays
Print Runs: 2,500 min - 10,000,000 max
Business from Other Countries: 10%
Membership(s): AAP PreK-12 Learning Group; ABA; Data & Marketing Association; Direct Marketing Club of New York; Education Market Association; Hudson Valley Direct Marketing Association; International Literacy Association; United States Chamber of Commerce

Global Interprint Inc
800 Warrington Rd, Santa Rosa, CA 95403
Tel: 707-545-1220 *Fax:* 707-545-1210
E-mail: info@globalinterprint.com
Web Site: www.globalinterprint.com
Key Personnel
Pres: Ken Coburn *E-mail:* ken@globalinterprint.com
Gen Mgr: Augusta Cobar *E-mail:* augusta@globalinterprint.com
Founded: 1979
Business from Other Countries: 85%

Goose River Press
3400 Friendship Rd, Waldoboro, ME 04572-6337
Tel: 207-832-6665
E-mail: gooseriverpress@roadrunner.com
Web Site: gooseriverpress.com
Key Personnel
Owner & Ed: Deborah J Benner
Founded: 1999
Turnaround: 7-28 Workdays
Print Runs: 50 min - 10,000 max
Business from Other Countries: 15%
Membership(s): Maine Writers & Publishers Alliance; Waldoboro Business Association

Imago
110 W 40 St, New York, NY 10018
Tel: 212-921-4411 *Fax:* 212-921-8226
E-mail: sales@imagousa.com
Web Site: www.imagousa.com
Key Personnel
Pres/CEO: Howard Musk *E-mail:* hmusk@imagousa.com
Founded: 1985
Turnaround: 5-10 Workdays for color separations; 4-6 Weeks for printing & binding
Print Runs: 3,000 min
Business from Other Countries: 100%
Branch Office(s)
Imago West Coast, 23412 Moulton Pkwy, Laguna Hills, CA 92653, Contact: Tammy Simms *Tel:* 949-367-1635 *Fax:* 949-367-1639
Imago Services (HK) Ltd, Unit 16, 2F, Metro Center Phase 1, 32 Lam Heng St, Kowloon Bay, Hong Kong, Contact: Kendrick Cheung *Tel:* 2811 3316 *Fax:* 2597 5256
Imago Shenzhen, Rm 2511-2512, Block A, United Plaza No 5022, Bin He Rd, Fu Tian Centre District, Shenzhen 518033, China, Contact: Kendrick Cheung *Tel:* (0755) 8304 8899 *Fax:* (0755) 8251 4073
Imago (UK/Europe) Publishing Ltd, Albury Ct, Albury Thame, Oxon OX9 2LP, United King-dom, Contact: Simon Rosenheim *Tel:* (01844) 337000 *Fax:* (01844) 339935 *E-mail:* sales@imago.co.uk *Web Site:* www.imago.co.uk

Leo Paper USA
Division of Leo Paper Group
1180 NW Maple St, Suite 102, Issaquah, WA 98027
Tel: 425-646-8801 *Fax:* 425-646-8805
E-mail: info@leousa.com
Web Site: www.leopaper.com
Key Personnel
SVP, Sales: John DiMasi *E-mail:* john@leousa.com
Founded: 1982
Turnaround: 40 Workdays
Print Runs: 3,500 min - 2,000,000 max
Business from Other Countries: 20%
Branch Office(s)
27 W 24 St, Suite 601, New York, NY 10010 *Tel:* 917-305-0708 *Fax:* 917-305-0709 *E-mail:* info@leousanewyork.com

Maps.com
120 Cremona Dr, Suite H, Santa Barbara, CA 93117
Tel: 805-685-3100 *Toll Free Tel:* 800-430-7532 *Fax:* 805-699-7550
E-mail: info@maps.com
Web Site: www.maps.com
Key Personnel
Chmn: John Glanville
Dir, Busn Devt: Bennett Moe
Dir, Opers: Kimberly Herriman
Founded: 1991
Print Runs: 1,000 min
Business from Other Countries: 10%
Membership(s): AAP PreK-12 Learning Group; Association of Directory Publishers; Better Business Bureau; International Map Industry Association; National Council for the Social Studies; News Media Alliance; North American Cartography Information Society; Yellow Pages Publishers Association

Marrakech Express Inc
720 Wesley Ave, No 10, Tarpon Springs, FL 34689
Tel: 727-942-2218 *Toll Free Tel:* 800-940-6566 *Fax:* 727-937-4758
E-mail: print@marrak.com
Web Site: www.marrak.com
Key Personnel
CEO: Peter Henzell
Prodn Mgr: Steen Sigmund
Sales/Estimator: Shirley Copperman
Founded: 1976
Turnaround: 7-10 Workdays
Print Runs: 500 min - 1,000,000 max
Business from Other Countries: 10%

OGM USA
4141 44 St, Suite 3F, Sunnyside, NY 11104
Tel: 212-964-2430 *Fax:* 212-964-2497
Web Site: www.ogm.it
Key Personnel
Chmn, CEO & Sales Rep: Rino Varrasso *E-mail:* rvarrasso@ogm-usa.com
Founded: 1974
Turnaround: 30 Workdays
Print Runs: 750 min - 300,000 max
Business from Other Countries: 75%

Outskirts Press Inc
10940 S Parker Rd, Suite 515, Parker, CO 80134
Toll Free Tel: 888-OP-BOOKS (672-6657) *Toll Free Fax:* 888-208-8601
E-mail: info@outskirtspress.com
Web Site: www.outskirtspress.com
Key Personnel
CEO: Jeanine Sampson
Pres & Chief Mktg Offr: Brent Sampson
CFO & CTO: Lynn Sampson
EVP: Kelly Schuknecht
Founded: 2003
Turnaround: 35 Workdays
Print Runs: 1 min
Business from Other Countries: 20%

Palace Printing & Design (PPD)
PO Box 12023, San Rafael, CA 94912
Tel: 415-526-1378
Key Personnel
Sales Dir: Sreedharan Vijayarangam *Tel:* 415-307-6065 (cell) *E-mail:* sreed@palacepress.com
Founded: 1984
Turnaround: 90 Workdays
Print Runs: 3,000 min - 1,000,000 max
Business from Other Countries: 20%

Pint Size Productions LLC
5745 Main St, Amherst, NY 14221
Tel: 716-204-3353 *Fax:* 716-853-3353
E-mail: sales@pintsizeproductions.com
Web Site: pintsizeproductions.com
Key Personnel
Pres & Creative Dir: Terry Ortolani *E-mail:* tortolani@pintsizeproductions.com
Founded: 2002
Print Runs: 2,500 min
Business from Other Countries: 10%

Printing Corp of the Americas Inc
620 SW 12 Ave, Fort Lauderdale, FL 33069
Tel: 954-781-8100 *Toll Free Tel:* 866-721-1PCA (721-1722) *Fax:* 954-781-8421
Web Site: www.commercialprintingflorida.com
Key Personnel
Pres: Jan Tuchman
Founded: 1979
Turnaround: 5-10 Workdays
Print Runs: 500 min - 100,000 max
Business from Other Countries: 15%

Publishers' Graphics LLC
140 Della Ct, Carol Stream, IL 60188
Tel: 630-221-1850 *Toll Free Tel:* 888-404-3769 *Fax:* 630-221-1870
E-mail: contactpg@pubgraphics.com
Web Site: pubgraphics.com; www.pubgraphicsdirect.com
Key Personnel
Pres: Nick A Lewis *E-mail:* nlewis@pubgraphics.com
VP: Kathleen Lewis
Founded: 1996
Turnaround: 5-10 Workdays
Print Runs: 1 min - 20,000 max
Business from Other Countries: 60%
Branch Office(s)
3777 Rider Trail S, St Louis, MO 63045 *Tel:* 314-739-3777 *Fax:* 314-739-1436
Sales Office(s): New York, NY, Contact: Anthony Ferrigno *Tel:* 908-672-5685

Taylor Specialty Books
Division of Balfour/Taylor
1550 W Mockingbird Lane, Dallas, TX 75235
Tel: 214-819-8588 (cust serv) *Fax:* 214-819-5051 (cust serv) *Toll Free Fax:* 800-203-9778
E-mail: rfq@taylorpub.com (estimates)
Web Site: www.taylorspecialtybooks.com
Key Personnel
VP, Sales & Mktg, Specialty Books: Rick Parra *Tel:* 214-819-5027 *E-mail:* rick.parra@balfour.com
Sales Rep: Kim Hawley *E-mail:* khawley@taylorpub.com; George Levesque *E-mail:* glevesque@taylorpub.com; Mark McCombs *E-mail:* mmcombs@taylorpub.com
Founded: 1939
Turnaround: 25-30 Workdays
Print Runs: 250 min - 25,000 max
Business from Other Countries: 10%

Vicks Inc
5166 Commercial Dr, Yorkville, NY 13495
Mailing Address: PO Box 270, Yorkville, NY
  13495-0270
Tel: 315-736-9344 *Fax:* 315-736-1901
Web Site: www.vicks.biz
Key Personnel
Chmn: Dwight E "Duke" Vicks, Jr
Regl Sales Mgr: Michael J Notar *Tel:* 315-723-
  1176 *E-mail:* mnotar@vicks.biz
Founded: 1918
Turnaround: 10 Workdays
Print Runs: 1 min - 100,000 max
Business from Other Countries: 10%
Membership(s): BMI; Printing Industries of
  America

Fred Weidner & Daughter Printers
99 Hudson St, 5th fl, New York, NY 10013
Tel: 646-706-5180
E-mail: info@fwdprinters.com
Web Site: www.fwdprinters.com
Key Personnel
Pres: Cynthia Weidner *E-mail:* cynthia@
  fwdprinters.com
Creative Dir: Carol Mittelsdorf *E-mail:* carol@
  fwdprinters.com
Founded: 1860
Turnaround: 5-10 Workdays
Print Runs: 1,000 min - 500,000 max
Business from Other Countries: 25%

Uzbekistan

Uzbekistan
ul Navoi 30, 100129 Tashkent
Tel: (871) 244-34-01; (871) 244-37-81; (871)
  244-38-15 *Fax:* (871) 244-38-10
E-mail: info@iptd-uzbekistan.uz
Web Site: www.iptd-uzbekistan.uz
Key Personnel
Dir: Zair Tursunbaevich Isadjanov
  E-mail: isadjanov@iptd-uzbekistan.uz
First Deputy Dir: Mukhamadjon Zaytaev
  Tel: (871) 244-54-04 *E-mail:* zaytaev@iptd-
  uzbekistan.uz

Manufacturing Materials Index

MANUFACTURING MATERIALS INDEX

Germany

Cordier Spezialpapier GmbH, pg 1346

Papierfabrik Scheufelen GmbH & Co KG, pg 1346

Italy

Cartiere del Garda SpA, pg 1347

Spain

Guarro Casas SA, pg 1348

United States

Ecological Fibers Inc, pg 1349

Gould Paper Corp, pg 1349

Monadnock Paper Mills Inc, pg 1349

Newark Recycled Paperboard Solutions, pg 1350

Palace Printing & Design (PPD), pg 1350

StoraEnso North American Sales Inc, pg 1350

Manufacturing Materials

This section includes companies throughout the world involved in the production of book manufacturing materials such as paper and book cover material. Those U.S. and Canadian companies with 10% or more of their business done outside North America are also included here. Immediately preceding this section is an index classifying companies by materials manufactured.

Belgium

Imprimerie Bietlot SA
185, rue du Rond-point, 6060 Gilly
Tel: (071) 283 611 *Fax:* (071) 283 620
E-mail: info@bietlot.be
Web Site: www.bietlot.com
Key Personnel
Mng Dir: Eric Guillaume *E-mail:* eric.
   guillaume@bietlot.be
Dir, Production: Bernard Guilmin *Tel:* (071) 283
   645 *E-mail:* bernard.guilmin@bietlot.be
Commercial Dir: Philippe Thomas
   E-mail: philippe.thomas@bietlot.be
Production: Anne Bombecke *Tel:* (071) 283 667;
   Alain Salme *Tel:* (071) 283 677
Founded: 1988
Business from Other Countries: 35%

Sappi Europe SA, see Sappi Fine Paper Europe

Sappi Fine Paper Europe
Subsidiary of Sappi Ltd
166 Chausee de la Hulpe, 1170 Brussels
Tel: (02) 676 9700
Web Site: www.sappi.com
Key Personnel
Chief Executive Officer: Berry Wiersum
Manufacturing, Research & Development Dir:
   Mat Quaedvlieg
Marketing & Sales Dir: Marco Eikelenboom
Manager, Corporate Communications: Marjolein
   Vile *Tel:* (02) 676 9786 *E-mail:* marjolein.
   vile@sappi.com
Founded: 1993

Canada

Cenveo McLaren Morris & Todd Co
3270 American Dr, Mississauga, ON L4V 1B5
Tel: 905-677-3592 *Fax:* 905-677-3675
E-mail: sales@mmt.ca
Web Site: www.mmt.ca
Key Personnel
Pres & CEO: Tony Sgro
Cont: Nancy Marquis
Founded: 1956
Business from Other Countries: 10%

PrintWest
1111 Eighth Ave, Regina, SK S4R 1C9
Tel: 306-525-2304 *Toll Free Tel:* 800-236-6438
   Fax: 306-757-2439
E-mail: general@printwest.com
Web Site: www.printwest.com
Key Personnel
CEO: Corie Triffo
VP, Sales: Ken Benson
Founded: 1992
Business from Other Countries: 15%

St Armand Paper Mill
3700 St Patrick, Montreal, QC H4E 1A2
Tel: 514-931-8338 *Fax:* 514-931-5953
Web Site: www.st-armand.com
Key Personnel
Prop: David Carruthers
VP: Denise Lapointe
Founded: 1979
Business from Other Countries: 40%
Cover Line(s) Milled: Canal Paper; Old Masters;
   St Armand Colours
Membership(s): Alcuin Society; Canadian Book-
   binders & Book Artists Guild; NAMTA; Pulp
   & Paper Technical Association of Canada

Tembec Paperboard Group
Division of Tembec
800 Rene Levesque Blvd W, Suite 1050, Mon-
   treal, QC H3B 1X9
Tel: 514-871-0137 *Toll Free Tel:* 800-411-7011
   Fax: 514-397-0896
Web Site: www.tembec.com; www.kallimapaper.
   com
Key Personnel
Pres: Chris Black
VP, Sales & Mktg: Renee Yardley *Tel:* 514-397-
   3926 *E-mail:* renee.yardley@tembec.com
Mktg Mgr: Anton Deinekin
Founded: 1990
Business from Other Countries: 90%
Cover Line(s) Milled: Kallima® Coated Cover
   C1S; Kallima® Coated Cover C1S Plus;
   Kallima® Coated Cover C2S
Cover Line(s) Sold: Kallima® Coated Cover C1S;
   Kallima® Coated Cover C2S

Colombia

Carvajal Pulpa y Papel (Carvajal Pulp & Paper)
Member of Grupo Carvajal SA
Km 6 carretera antigua, Cali-Yumbo
Tel: (02) 6512000
E-mail: cpphabeasdata@propal.com.co
Web Site: www.carvajalpulpaypapel.com

Finland

Bookwell Oy
Teollisuustie 4, 06150 Porvoo
Tel: (019) 219 41
Web Site: www.bookwell.fi
Key Personnel
President & Chief Executive Officer: Vesa
   Junkkarinen *Tel:* (040) 569 2999 *E-mail:* vesa.
   junkkarinen@bookwell.fi
Sales Dir: Markus Ruohonen *E-mail:* markus.
   ruohonen@bookwell.fi
Export Manager: Kjell Karlsson *Tel:* (040) 518
   0948 *E-mail:* kjell.karlsson@bookwell.fi
Production Manager: Juha Harmonen
   E-mail: juha.harmonen@bookwell.fi
Founded: 1860
Business from Other Countries: 70%
Parent Company: Sanoma

Branch Office(s)
Tenhusentie 3, 51900 Juva
Sales Office(s): Hulvejen 52, 9530 Stovring, Denmark, Representative: Steffen Janum *Tel:* 5092
   5555 *E-mail:* steffen.janum@bookwell.fi
Raiffeisenstr 5, 63939 Woerth am Main, Germany, Representative: Frank Hohmann
   Tel: (09372) 94810811 *E-mail:* frank.
   hohmann@bookwell.fi
Manor House, Church St, Brassington, Derbys
   DE4 4HJ, United Kingdom, Representative: Peter Everest *Tel:* (01629) 540 934 *Fax:* (01629)
   540 938 *E-mail:* petereverest@bookwell.co.uk

Stora Enso Oyj
Kanavaranta 1, 00101 Helsinki
Mailing Address: PL 309, 00101 Helsinki
Tel: (09) 20 46 131 *Fax:* (09) 20 46 213 02
Web Site: www.storaenso.com
Key Personnel
Chairman: Gunnar Brock
Chief Executive Officer: Karl Henrick Sundstrom
Chief Financial Officer, Deputy to the Chief Ex-
   ecutive Officer: Seppo Parvi
Executive Vice President, Global Communica-
   tions Group: Ulrika Lilija *E-mail:* ulrika.lilija@
   storaenso.com
Branch Office(s)
Stora Enso AB, World Trade Center,
   Klarabergsviadukten 70, C4, PO Box 70395,
   107 24 Stockholm, Sweden *Tel:* (01046) 46
   000 *Fax:* (08) 10 60 20

UPM
Subsidiary of UPM-Kymmene Group
Alvar Aallon Katu 1, 00101 Helsinki
Mailing Address: PL 380, 00101 Helsinki
Tel: (0204) 15 111 *Fax:* (0204) 15 110
E-mail: info@upm.com; paperinfo@upm.com
Web Site: www.upm.com
Key Personnel
President & Chief Executive Officer: Jussi Peso-
   nen
Dir, Stakeholder Relations, Pulp Business: Sari
   Horkko
Founded: 1995

France

Arjobex
32, Ave Pierre Grenier, 92517 Boulogne Billan-
   court Cedex
Tel: 01 57 75 93 13 *Fax:* 01 57 75 93 73
Web Site: www.polyart.com
Founded: 1975
Parent Company: Arjowiggins SAS
Branch Office(s)
Arjobex Hong Kong, 23/F Siu On Centre,
   188 Lockhart Rd, Wan Chai, Hong Kong
   Tel: (0852) 2265 9003
U.S. Office(s): Arjobex America Inc, 10901 West-
   lake Dr, Charlotte, NC 28273, United States
   Tel: 704-587-3000 *Fax:* 704-587-1174

Germany

Cordier Spezialpapier GmbH
Jaegerthal 6, 67098 Bad Duerkheim
Tel: (063) 22 93 9-0 *Fax:* (063) 22 93 9-168;
(063) 22 61 70 2
E-mail: info@cordier-paper.de
Web Site: www.cordier-paper.de
Key Personnel
Dir, Sales: Robert Lamberty *Tel:* (063) 22 60 08-
12 *E-mail:* robert.lamberty@cordier-paper.de
Sales: Uwe Glas *Tel:* (063) 22 60 08-46
E-mail: uwe.glas@cordier-paper.de;
Oeznur Hazir *Tel:* (063) 22 60 08-44
E-mail: oeznur.hazir@cordier-paper.de; Mar-
tina Laubscher *Tel:* (063) 22 60 08-47
E-mail: martina.laubscher@cordier-paper.de;
Christine Ruppenthal *Tel:* (063) 22 60 08-45
E-mail: christine.ruppenthal@cordier-paper.de
Founded: 1836
Sales Office(s): Optenhoegel GmbH Paper Agen-
cies, Siebenmorgen 13-15, 51427 Bergisch
Gladbach *Tel:* (02204) 76 70 1-0 *Fax:* (02204)
76 70 160 *E-mail:* info@optenhoegel.de
Palmer Premium Paper & Packaging ApS,
Syvhojvaenge 120, 2625 Vallensbaek, Den-
mark *Tel:* 43 64 05 10 *Fax:* 43 64 05 30
E-mail: palmer@p-ppp.dk (Denmark & Swe-
den)
260 chemin des Oliviers, 84440 Robion, France
Tel: 06 78 93 64 59 *E-mail:* marilyn.gsell94@
orange.fr
Intercart SRL Unipersonale, Via Giuseppe
Mangili, 36, 00197 Rome RM, Italy *Tel:* (06)
32 08 128; (06) 32 24 171 *Fax:* (06) 32 24 078
E-mail: antonio.capelli@intercart.it
Mitsa (S) Pte Ltd, 150 Orchard Rd, No 08-
10, Orchard Plaza, Singapore 238841, Sin-
gapore *Tel:* 6732 3488 *Fax:* 6732 8321
E-mail: mitsa@mbox4.singnet.com.sg
Paul McDermott Paper Sales, 13 Blackthorne Rd,
Lichfield, Staffs WS14 9YJ, United Kingdom
Tel: (01543) 41 85 93 *Fax:* (01543) 41 89 89
E-mail: paul_mcdermott@talk21.com

Eratex
c/o Gustav Ernstmeier GmbH & Co KG, Bulow-
str 20, 32049 Herford
Tel: (05221) 984-0 *Fax:* (05221) 984-377
E-mail: info@ernstmeier.de
Web Site: www.ernstmeier.de
Key Personnel
Chief Executive Officer & Mng Dir: Oliver Jackl
Founded: 1867

Mohn Media Mohndruck GmbH
Member of Bertelsmann Printing Group
Carl-Bertelsmann-Str 161M, 33311 Guetersloh
Tel: (05241) 80-40410 *Fax:* (05241) 80-65288
E-mail: mohnmedia@bertelsmann.de
Web Site: www.mohnmedia.de
Key Personnel
Mng Dir: Axel Hentrei; Wilfried Velte
Sales Dir: Alasdair Gibson
Founded: 1824
Business from Other Countries: 25%
Ultimate Parent Company: Bertelsmann SE & Co
KGaA

Priese GmbH
Saatwinkler Damm 42A, 13627 Berlin
Tel: (030) 8263024 *Fax:* (030) 8266024

Papierfabrik Scheufelen GmbH & Co KG
Adolf-Scheufelen-Str 26, 73252 Lenningen
Tel: (07026) 66-0; (07026) 66-22 88 (customer
service) *Fax:* (07026) 66-32 701; (07026) 66-
32 952 (customer service)
E-mail: service@scheufelen.de
Web Site: www.scheufelen.com

Key Personnel
Mng Dir: Peter H Wardhana
Founded: 1855

**Smurfit Kappa C D Haupt Papier- und
Pappenfabrik GmbH**
Subsidiary of Smurfit Kappa Group PLC
Orpethaler Str 50, 34474 Diemelstadt-Wrexen
Tel: (05642) 79 0
Web Site: www.smurfitkappa.com
Key Personnel
Group Chief Executive Officer: Tony Smurfit

Hong Kong

Caritas Printing Training Centre
Caritas House, 2 Caine Rd, Hong Kong
Tel: 2843 4734; 2524 2071 *Fax:* 2523 0438
E-mail: info@caritas.org.hk
Web Site: www.caritas.org.hk
Founded: 1953
Business from Other Countries: 50%
Parent Company: Caritas Hong Kong

Everbest Printing Co Ltd
10/F, Block C, Seaview Estate, 2-8 Watson Rd,
North Point, Hong Kong
Tel: 2727 4433 *Fax:* 2772 7687
E-mail: sales@everbest.com.hk
Web Site: www.everbest.com
Founded: 1954
Business from Other Countries: 90%
Branch Office(s)
Everbest (Guangzhou) Printing Co Ltd, 334
Huanshi Rd S, Nansha, Panyu, Guangdong
511458, China *Tel:* (020) 8498 1812 (manu-
facturing plant)
Sales Office(s): C5, 10/F, Ko Fai Industrial
Bldg, 7 Ko Fai Rd, Yau Tong *Tel:* 2727 4433
Fax: 2772 7687 (Australia, Europe & New
Zealand)
313 30 St, Toronto, ON M8W 3E4, Canada, Con-
tact: Doris Chung *Tel:* 416-286-2525 *Fax:* 416-
804-8930 *E-mail:* doris@everbestcanada.ca
Origo Ediciones, Padre Alonso de Ovalle 748,
8330169 Santiago, Chile, Contact: Hernan
Maino *Tel:* (02) 480 9800 *E-mail:* hernan.
maino@origo.cl *Web Site:* www.origo.cl (Chile
& South America)
Nostra Ediciones SA de CV, Av Revolucion
1181 piso 7, Col Merced Gomez, Del Ben-
ito Juarez, 03930 Mexico, DF, Mexico, Con-
tact: Mauricio Volpi *Tel:* (0155) 5554 7030
E-mail: impresion@nostraediciones.com
31 Palatine Rd, London N16 8SY, United
Kingdom, Contact: Nicky Bowden
Tel: (020) 7249 9483 *Fax:* (020) 7241 3460
E-mail: nickybowden@everbest.co.uk
Todd Communications, 611 E 12 Ave, Anchor-
age, AK 99501, United States, Contact: Flip
Todd *Tel:* 907-274-8633 *Fax:* 907-929-5550
E-mail: flip@toddcom.com *Web Site:* www.
toddcom.com
Four Colour Imports Ltd, 2410 Frankfort Ave,
Louisville, KY 40206, United States, Contact:
George Dick *Tel:* 502-896-9644 *Fax:* 502-896-
9594 *E-mail:* sales@fourcolour.com

Golden Cup Printing Co Ltd
6/F, 177 Hoi Bun Rd, Kwun Tong, Kowloon
Tel: 2343 4254 *Fax:* 2341 5426
E-mail: sales@goldencup.com.hk
Web Site: www.goldencup.com.hk
Key Personnel
Chairman: Kam Kai Yeung
Founded: 1969
Business from Other Countries: 80%

Sales Office(s): Tutang Industrial Area, Jin Bei
Rd, Changping, Dongguan, Guangdong, China
Tel: (0769) 8339 4888 *Fax:* (0769) 8339 4999
Qilin Industrial Estate, Guanlan, Shenzhen,
Guangdong, China *Tel:* (0755) 2805 6279
Fax: (0755) 2805 6086
Jinma Town, Guandu District, Kunming, Yunnan,
China *Tel:* (0871) 316 1226 *Fax:* (0871) 316
1226
Terley House, Cadbury, Exeter EX5 5JZ, United
Kingdom *Tel:* (01884) 855736 *E-mail:* info@
gcpservices.com
Spectrum Books Inc, 2455 Bennett Valley Rd,
Suite C-116, Santa Rosa, CA 95404-5671,
United States *Tel:* 707-542-6044 *Fax:* 707-542-
6045

The Green Pagoda Press Ltd
13/F, Block A, Tung Chong Factory Bldg, 633-
655 King's Rd, North Point, Hong Kong
Tel: 2561 1924 *Fax:* 2811 0946
E-mail: gpinfo@gpp.com.hk
Web Site: www.greenpagoda.com
Key Personnel
Mng Dir: Yip Yu Bun
Founded: 1957
Business from Other Countries: 30%

Mei Ka Printing & Publishing Enterprise Ltd
23/F, Hong Kong Plaza, Rooms 2312A-B, 188
Connaught Rd W, Hong Kong
Tel: 2540 1131 *Fax:* 2559 8718; 2559 7137
E-mail: info@meika-printing.com; mkpp@
netvigator.com
Web Site: www.meika-printing.com
Founded: 1982
Branch Office(s)
No 106 Changhong, 2nd Industrial Areas, June
St, Baiyun District, Guangzhou, China

Speedflex Asia Ltd
1/F Hua Qin International Bldg, 340 Queen's Rd
Central, Hong Kong
Tel: 2542 2780 *Fax:* 2542 3733
E-mail: info@speedflex.com.hk
Web Site: www.speedflex.com.hk
Founded: 1981
Business from Other Countries: 20%

Wing King Tong Group
Leader Industrial Centre, Block I, 3/F, 188-202
Texaco Rd, Tsuen Wan, New Territories
Tel: 2407 3287 *Fax:* 2408 7939
E-mail: marketing@wktco.com
Web Site: www.wkt.cc
Key Personnel
Mng Dir: Alex Yan Tak Chung
Founded: 1944
Business from Other Countries: 95%
Branch Office(s)
No 67, Li Xin Lu, Dan Zhu Tou Community,
Nan Wan St, Longgang District, Shenzhen,
Guangdong 518114, China *Tel:* (0755) 8473
6801; (0755) 8473 6802; (0755) 8473 6803
Fax: (0755) 8473 6303 *E-mail:* szwktsales@
wkt.cc

Hungary

Interpress Kuelkereskedelmi Kft
Becsi ut 67, Budapest 1037
Tel: (01) 250-8263; (01) 250-8266 *Fax:* (01) 250-
8262
E-mail: interpress@interpress.eu
Web Site: www.interpress.eu
Key Personnel
Sales: Zsuzsa Cserna *Tel:* (01) 430 0860
E-mail: zsuzsa.cserna@interpress.eu

Contact: Katalin Multas *E-mail:* katalin.multas@
  interpress.eu
Founded: 1991

Iceland

Oddi Printing Ltd
Hofdabakka 7, 110 Reykjavik
Tel: 515 5000 *Fax:* 515 5001
E-mail: oddi@oddi.is
Web Site: www.oddi.is
Key Personnel
Chief Executive Officer: Gunnar Sverrisson
  Tel: 515 5005 *E-mail:* gs@oddi.is
Mng Dir: Baldur Thorgeirsson *Tel:* 893 6533
  E-mail: baldur@oddi.is
Dir, Production: Runar Mar Jonatansson *Tel:* 545
  2911 *E-mail:* runar@oddi.is
Marketing & Human Resource Manager: Stefan
  Hrafn Hagalin *Tel:* 515 5019 *E-mail:* hagalin@
  oddi.is
U.S. Office(s): 118 Heacock Lane, Wyncote,
  PA 19095, United States, Contact: Charles B
  Gershwin *Tel:* 215-885-5210 *Fax:* 215-885-
  6364 *E-mail:* chuck@oddi.com

Indonesia

Ichtiar Baru van Hoeve
Jl Raya Pasar Jumat 38 D-E, Pondok Pinang,
  Jakarta 12310
Tel: (021) 7511856; (021) 7511901 *Fax:* (021)
  7511855
E-mail: redaksi@ibvh.com
Web Site: www.ibvh.com
Founded: 1980

PT Victory Offset Prima
JL Aria Santika No 8, Desa Pasir Bolang-
  Tigaraksa, Tangerang 15610
Tel: (021) 5940-5343 *Fax:* (021) 5940-5345
E-mail: info@victoryoffset.com
Web Site: www.victoryoffset.com
Key Personnel
General Manager: S Wilson Pinady
Founded: 1971
Business from Other Countries: 10%

Italy

Cartiere del Garda SpA
Viale Rovereto 15, 38066 Riva del Garda TN
Tel: (0464) 579111 *Fax:* (0464) 579685
E-mail: info.garda@lecta.com; mktg.garda@lecta.
  com
Web Site: www.gardacartiere.it
Key Personnel
Chief Executive Officer & President: Andrea
  Minguzzi
Commercial General Dir: Giovanni Lo Presti
Financial Dir: Michele Ferrari
Production Dir: Antonio di Blas
Export Sales Dir: Alessandro Nardelli
Sales Dir: Nicola Tisi
Founded: 1956
Parent Company: Lecta Group

Dedalo Litostampa SRL
Viale Luigi Jacobini, 5, 70123 Bari BA
Tel: (080) 531 14 13 *Fax:* (080) 531 14 14

E-mail: info@dedalolitostampa.it
Web Site: www.dedalolitostampa.it
Founded: 1961

Milanostampa SpA
Corso PEG Ferrero 5, 12060 Farigliano CN
Tel: (0173) 746111 *Fax:* (0173) 746248
Founded: 1965
Business from Other Countries: 65%
U.S. Office(s): Milanostampa USA, 141 Berkeley
  Pl, No 2, Brooklyn, NY 11217-3971, United
  States *Tel:* 212-964-2430 (North American
  sales & production off)

Netherlands

BN International BV
Rokerijweg 5, 1271 AH Huizen
Tel: (035) 5248400 *Fax:* (035) 5256004
E-mail: wallcovering@bnint.nl
Web Site: www.bnint.com
Founded: 1938
Business from Other Countries: 95%
Branch Office(s)
BN International UK, Unit 38, The Metro Cen-
  tre, Tolpits Lane, Watford, Herts WD18
  9YD, United Kingdom *Tel:* (01923) 219132
  Fax: (01923) 219134

New Zealand

Bookprint Consultants Ltd
1104, One Market Lane, Wellington 6011
Tel: (04) 381 3070
Web Site: www.granthamhouse.co.nz
Key Personnel
Chief Executive: Graham C Stewart
  E-mail: graham@ghbil.com
Founded: 1982
Business from Other Countries: 10%
Branch Office(s)
Bookprint International Ltd, New Trend Cen-
  tre, 104 King Fuk St, Sanpokong, Kowloon,
  Hong Kong *Tel:* 2327 0101 *Fax:* 2350 0315
  E-mail: bil@kingstime.com.hk

Singapore

Ho Printing Singapore Pte Ltd
31 Changi South St One, Changi South Industrial
  Estate, Singapore 486769
Tel: 6542 9322 *Fax:* 6542 8322
E-mail: sales@hoprinting.com.sg
Web Site: www.hoprinting.com
Founded: 1951
Business from Other Countries: 30%

Markono Print Media Pte Ltd
Subsidiary of Markono Holdings Pte Ltd
21 Neythal Rd, Singapore 628586
Tel: 6281 1118
E-mail: enquiry@markono.com; sales@markono.
  com
Web Site: www.markono.com
Key Personnel
Chairman: Bob Lee
Mng Dir: Edwin Ng
Sales & Marketing Dir: Max Lee
Founded: 1967

Business from Other Countries: 20%
Branch Office(s)
Markono Logistics, 4 Toh Tuck Link, Singapore
  596226 *Tel:* 6465 1498 *E-mail:* ml.sales@
  markono.com
Markono Digital Solutions (M) Sdn Bhd, 7
  Lorong Jelawat 4, 13700 Seberang Jaya,
  Penang, Malaysia *Tel:* (04) 397-8700
  E-mail: mdsm.sales@markono.com

Toppan Security Printing Pte Ltd
97 Ubi Ave 4, Singapore 408754
Tel: 6741 2500 *Fax:* 6744 7098
Web Site: www.toppanleefung.com/toppansecurity.
  aspx
Key Personnel
President & Chief Executive Officer: Yeo Chee
  Tong
General Manager & Digital Printing: David
  Ng *Tel:* 6846 3518 *E-mail:* davidng@
  toppanleefung.com
Deputy Sales Dir, Security Printing: Rick
  Ang *Tel:* 6846 3912 *E-mail:* rickang@
  toppanleefung.com
Business from Other Countries: 40%
Parent Company: Toppan Printing Co Ltd, One
  Kanda Izumi-cho, Chiyoda-ku, Toyko 101-
  0024, Japan

Slovenia

DZS Grafik doo
Ul Jozeta Jame 12, SI-1210 Ljubljana-Sentvid
Tel: (01) 586 72 00 *Fax:* (01) 586 72 15
E-mail: info@dzs-grafik.si
Web Site: www.dzs-grafik.si
Key Personnel
Dir: Marko Tomazevic *E-mail:* marko.
  tomazevic@dzs-grafik.si
Dir, Graphic Services: Ksenija Blazevic
  E-mail: blazevic@dzs-grafik.si
Dir, Paper Sector: Bojan Forjan *E-mail:* bojan.
  forjan@dzs-grafik.si
Parent Company: DZS dd

Gorenjski Tisk Storitve doo
Ul Mirka Vadnova 6, SI-4000 Kranj
Tel: (04) 20 16 300 *Fax:* (04) 20 16 301
E-mail: info@go-tisk.si
Web Site: www.go-tisk.si
Key Personnel
Mng Dir: Goran Celesnik *Tel:* (04) 20 16 330
  E-mail: goran.celesnik@go-tisk.si
Dir, Sales & Marketing: Dr Andrej Krope, PhD
  Tel: (04) 20 16 326 *E-mail:* andrej.krope@go-
  tisk.si
Production Manager: Dusan Kuljic *Tel:* (04) 20
  16 451 *E-mail:* dusan.kuljic@go-tisk.si
Founded: 1888
Business from Other Countries: 50%

South Korea

Mirae N Co Ltd
321 Sinbanpo-ro, Seocho-gu, Seoul 137-905
Fax: (02) 541-8158
Web Site: www.mirae-n.com
Key Personnel
President: Kim Young-jin
Manager: Ji Young Park *Tel:* (02) 3475-3870
  E-mail: park.jiyoung@mirae-n.com
Founded: 1948

Spain

Guarro Casas SA
Subsidiary of ArjoWiggins
Can Guarro s/n, 08790 Gelida (Barcelona)
Tel: 93 776 76 76 *Fax:* 93 776 76 30
E-mail: atencion.cliente@guarrocasas.com
Web Site: www.guarrocasas.com
Key Personnel
Marketing & Commercial Dir: Manuel Freijomil
Founded: 1698
Business from Other Countries: 60%

United Kingdom

Bell & Bain Ltd
303 Burnfield Rd, Thornliebank, Glasgow G46 7UQ
Tel: (0141) 649 5697 *Fax:* (0141) 632 8733
Web Site: www.bell-bain.com
Key Personnel
Co-Owner & Mng Dir: Stephen Docherty
E-mail: sd@bell-bain.co.uk
Co-Owner & Sales Dir: Tony Campbell
E-mail: tcampbell@bell-bain.co.uk
Operations Dir: Karen Baillie *E-mail:* kbaillie@bell-bain.co.uk
Sales Dir Designate: Derek Kenney
E-mail: dkenney@bell-bain.co.uk
Customer Services Manager: Tracey Mallon
E-mail: tmallon@bell-bain.co.uk
Information Technology Manager: Gordon Rogers
E-mail: grogers@bell-bain.co.uk
Founded: 1831
Business from Other Countries: 25%

Clays Ltd
Subsidiary of St Ives PLC
One Tudor St, London EC4Y 0AH
Tel: (020) 7928 8844
E-mail: sales@clays.co.uk
Web Site: www.clays.co.uk
Key Personnel
Mng Dir: Paul Hulley
Account Dir: Andrew Cochrane; Vicky Ellis
Customer Service Dir: Anne Perrin
Digital Sales Dir: Andrew Copley
Finance Dir: Andrew Spring
Manufacturing Dir: Ian Smith
Strategic Dir: Kate McFarlan
Self-Publishing Account Manager: Rebecca Souster
Founded: 1817
Business from Other Countries: 15%
Branch Office(s)
Popson St, Bungay, Suffolk NR35 1ED
Tel: (01986) 893 211

William Clowes Ltd, see CPI William Clowes Ltd

CPI Antony Rowe
Bumper's Farm, Chippenham, Wilts SN14 6LH
Tel: (01249) 659705 *Fax:* (01249) 443103
Web Site: www.cpi-print.co.uk
Key Personnel
General Manager: Martin Collyer
Sales Manager: Geoff Fisher
Divisional Mng Dir: Alison Kaye
Founded: 1983
Business from Other Countries: 2%

Parent Company: CPI Group UK Ltd
Branch Office(s)
48-50 Birch Close, Eastbourne, East Sussex
BN23 6PE *Tel:* (01323) 434700

CPI William Clowes Ltd
Copland Way, Ellough, Beccles, Suffolk NR34 7TL
Tel: (01502) 712884
E-mail: williamclowes@cpibooks.co.uk
Key Personnel
Divisional Mng Dir: Alison Kaye
Head, Sales: Jonathan Huddart
Founded: 1803
Business from Other Countries: 1%
Parent Company: CPI Group UK Ltd
Ultimate Parent Company: CPI Group

FiberMark Red Bridge International Ltd
Ainsworth, Bolton BL2 5PD
Tel: (01204) 556900
E-mail: sales@redbridge.co.uk; info@fibermark.com; redbridge@fibermark.com
Web Site: www.redbridge.co.uk
Key Personnel
President & Chief Executive Officer: Anthony MacLaurin
Mng Dir: Jonathan Robson
Finance Dir: Brian Bateman
Business Development Manager: David Ives
Export Sales: Debbie Jones; Andrea Ross; Judith Wade
Office Manager: Catherine Tebbatt
Founded: 1927
Business from Other Countries: 35%
Parent Company: Rexam
U.S. Office(s): FiberMark North America Inc, 70 Front St, West Springfield, MA 01089, United States *Tel:* 413-533-0338 *Fax:* 413-532-4810
E-mail: info@fibermark.com

Furnival Press
Unit 1, Kennington Enterprise Centre, 32 Braganza St, London SE17 3RJ
Tel: (020) 7924 9398
Web Site: www.furnivalpress.co.uk
Key Personnel
Owner: Johnny Gumb *E-mail:* johnny@furnivalpress.co.uk
Dir: David Peach *E-mail:* david@furnivalpress.co.uk
Founded: 1861

Hammond Bindery Ltd
Subsidiary of The Charlesworth Group
Flanshaw Way, Flanshaw Lane, Wakefield WF2 9LP
Tel: (01924) 204830 *Fax:* (01924) 339107
E-mail: sales@hammond-bindery.co.uk; hammonds.sales@hammond-bindery.co.uk
Web Site: www.hammond-bindery.co.uk
Key Personnel
Mng Dir: David Boothman
Commercial Dir: Sue Sheldon *Tel:* (01924) 204850
Customer Service & Estimator: Rhonda Moffat *Tel:* (01924) 204852 *E-mail:* rhonda@hammond-bindery.co.uk
Founded: 1972

Headley Brothers Ltd
The Invicta Press, Queens Rd, Ashford, Kent TN24 8HH
Tel: (01233) 623131 *Fax:* (01233) 612345
E-mail: printing@headley.co.uk; sales@headley.co.uk
Web Site: www.headley.co.uk
Key Personnel
Chief Executive Officer: Roger Pitt *E-mail:* roger.pitt@headley.co.uk

Commercial Dir: Jon Pitt *E-mail:* jon.pitt@headley.co.uk
Sales Dir: Paul Palmer *E-mail:* paul.palmer@headley.co.uk
Founded: 1881

Hobbs The Printers Ltd
Brunel Rd, Totton, Hants SO40 3WX
Tel: (023) 8066 4800 *Fax:* (023) 8066 4801
E-mail: info@hobbs.uk.com
Web Site: www.hobbs.uk.com; www.hobbstheprinters.co.uk
Key Personnel
Mng Dir: David Hobbs *E-mail:* d.a.hobbs@hobbs.uk.com
Deputy Mng & Operations Dir: Graham Bromley *E-mail:* g.bromley@hobbs.uk.com
Commercial Dir: Terry Ozanne *E-mail:* t.ozanne@hobbs.uk.com
Customer Services Manager: Colin Richardson *E-mail:* c.richardson@hobbs.uk.com
Founded: 1884
Business from Other Countries: 4%

Intype Libra Ltd
3/4 Elm Grove Industrial Estate, Elm Grove, Wimbledon, London SW19 4HE
Tel: (020) 8947 7863 *Fax:* (020) 8947 3652
E-mail: hello@intypelibra.co.uk
Web Site: www.intypelibra.co.uk
Key Personnel
Owner & Mng Dir: Tony Chapman
Owner: David Greenwood
Founded: 1974
Business from Other Countries: 5%

Librios Ltd
20 Lochaline St, London W6 9SH
Tel: (020) 3355 0200
E-mail: info@librios.com
Web Site: www.librios.com
Key Personnel
Software Development Dir: David Wilcockson *E-mail:* david@librios.com
System Administrator: Neville Mooney
Project Developer: Chris Lewis *E-mail:* chris.lewis@librios.com
Founded: 1997
Business from Other Countries: 30%

Page Bros (Norwich) Ltd
Subsidiary of Milex Ltd
Mile Cross Lane, Norwich, Norfolk NR6 6SA
Tel: (01603) 778800 *Fax:* (01603) 778801
E-mail: info@pagebros.co.uk
Web Site: www.pagebros.co.uk
Key Personnel
Mng Dir: Craig Eastaugh *E-mail:* c.eastaugh@pagebros.co.uk
Sales & Commercial Dir: Andrew Spelman *E-mail:* a.spelman@pagebros.co.uk
Founded: 1750
Business from Other Countries: 20%

Watkiss Automation Ltd
Subsidiary of The Watkiss Group
Watkiss House, Blaydon Rd, Middlefield Industrial Estate, Sandy, Beds SG19 1RZ
Tel: (01767) 685700; (01767) 685710 (sales) *Fax:* (01767) 689900
E-mail: info@watkiss.com; sales@watkiss.com
Web Site: www.watkiss.com
Key Personnel
Communications Dir: Jo Watkiss *E-mail:* jowatkiss@watkiss.com
Technical Dir: Mike Watkiss
Founded: 1959
Business from Other Countries: 5%

Gavin Watson Printers
79-109 Glasgow Rd, Glasgow G72 0LY

Tel: (01698) 826000 *Fax:* (01698) 824944
Web Site: www.gavinwatson.co.uk
Key Personnel
Chief Executive Officer: Tom Brown
  E-mail: tbrown@gavinwatson.co.uk
Founded: 1863

Winter&Company UK Ltd
Stonehill-Stukeley, Mead Industrial Estate, Huntingdon, Cambs PE29 6ED
Tel: (01480) 377177 *Fax:* (01480) 377166
E-mail: sales@winteruk.com
Web Site: www.winter-company.com
Key Personnel
Financial Dir: Tim Edwards
Founded: 1892

United States

Bang Printing Co Inc
3323 Oak St, Brainerd, MN 56401
Tel: 218-829-2877 *Toll Free Tel:* 800-328-0450
  Fax: 218-829-7145
E-mail: info@bangprinting.com
Web Site: www.bangprinting.com
Key Personnel
CEO: Chris Kurtzman
EVP, Sales: Todd Vanek *Tel:* 218-822-2124
  E-mail: toddv@bangprinting.com
SVP, Fin & Opers: Tom Campion
Founded: 1899
Business from Other Countries: 50%

Conservation Resources International LLC
5532 Port Royal Rd, Springfield, VA 22151
Tel: 703-321-7730 *Toll Free Tel:* 800-634-6932
  Fax: 703-321-0629
E-mail: sales@conservationresources.com
Web Site: www.conservationresources.com
Key Personnel
Pres: William K Hollinger, Jr
VP: Lavonia Hollinger
Business from Other Countries: 30%
Membership(s): AIC

D & K Group Inc
1795 Commerce Dr, Elk Grove Village, IL 60007
Tel: 847-956-0160 *Toll Free Tel:* 800-632-2314
  Fax: 847-956-8214
E-mail: info@dkgroup.net
Web Site: www.dkgroup.com
Key Personnel
Pres: Karl Singer
VP, Sales & Mktg: Tom Pidgeon *E-mail:* tom.
  pidgeon@dkgroup.net
Mktg Communs Specialist: Brian Biegel
  E-mail: brian.biegel@dkgroup.net
Founded: 1979
Business from Other Countries: 15%

Desktop Miracles Inc
112 S Main St, Suite 294, Stowe, VT 05672
Tel: 802-253-7900 *Toll Free Fax:* 888-293-2676
Web Site: www.desktopmiracles.com
Key Personnel
CEO & Pres: Barry T Kerrigan *E-mail:* barry@
  desktopmiracles.com
VP: Virginia Kerrigan *E-mail:* virginia@
  desktopmiracles.com
Founded: 1994
Business from Other Countries: 10%

DNP America LLC
Subsidiary of Dai Nippon Printing Co Ltd
335 Madison Ave, 3rd fl, New York, NY 10017
Tel: 212-503-1060 *Fax:* 212-286-1501
Web Site: www.dnpamerica.com

Key Personnel
Gen Mgr: Seiichi Suzuki
Founded: 1974
Business from Other Countries: 54%
Branch Office(s)
3235 Kifer Rd, Suite 100, Santa Clara, CA 95051
  Tel: 408-735-8880
3858 Carson St, Suite 300, Torrance, CA 90503
  Tel: 310-540-5123 *Fax:* 310-543-3260

Ecological Fibers Inc
40 Pioneer Dr, Lunenburg, MA 01462
Tel: 978-537-0003 *Fax:* 978-537-2238
E-mail: info@ecofibers.com
Web Site: www.ecofibers.com
Key Personnel
Pres: John A Quill
VP, Sales: Dave Robbins *E-mail:* drobbins@
  ecofibers.com
Dir, Busn Opers: Joyce Hardell *E-mail:* joyce@
  ecofibers.com
Book Group Mgr: Jim McCafferty
  E-mail: jmccafferty@ecofibers.com
Founded: 1972
Business from Other Countries: 35%
Cover Line(s) Milled: Rainbow® 80 & 100 lb
  cream & white endleaf; Rainbow® 80 NASTA
  spec colored endleaf, side & spine material;
  Rainbow® 70 lb colored endleaf & side mate-
  rial; Arizona; Corona; Lumina Silver Pearles-
  cent; Mirage; Mirage 325 gsm; Prestige; Rain-
  bow® 17; Rainbow® 3; Rainbow® 9 Type
  II coated cover; Rainbow® Eco-Cover; Rain-
  bow® Excel; Rainbow® LX; Ultima; Ultima-7
Cover Line(s) Sold: Rainbow® 80 & 100 lb
  cream & white endleaf; Rainbow® 80 NASTA
  spec colored endleaf, side & spine material;
  Rainbow® 70 lb colored endleaf & side material
Branch Office(s)
730 York Ave, Pawtucket, RI 02861 *Tel:* 401-725-
  9700 *Fax:* 401-724-4970
Membership(s): BMI; Book Industry Guild of
  New York; Bookbuilders of Boston; Publishing
  Professionals Network

Flesher Corp
2930 N El Paso St, Colorado Springs, CO 80907
Tel: 719-633-1111 *Fax:* 719-633-8780
E-mail: sales@flesher.net
Web Site: www.flesher.net
Key Personnel
Pres: Ian Flesher *E-mail:* ian@flesher.net
VP, Sales: Richard Bruce *E-mail:* dick@flesher.
  net
Mgr: Tiffany Wismer *E-mail:* tiffany@flesher.net
Founded: 1975
Business from Other Countries: 35%
Membership(s): BMI; Foil & Specialty Effects
  Association; Library Binding Industries

Gould Paper Corp
99 Park Ave, 10th fl, New York, NY 10016
Tel: 212-301-0000 *Toll Free Tel:* 800-221-3043
  Fax: 212-481-0067
E-mail: info@gouldpaper.com
Web Site: www.gouldpaper.com
Key Personnel
Pres & CEO: David H Berkowitz
Founded: 1924
Business from Other Countries: 30%
Cover Line(s) Sold: A B Massa; Abitibi; Ap-
  pleton Papers; Beveridge; Cascade; Domtar
  Inc; Evergreen Packaging; Finch Paper LLC;
  Fraser; Georgia-Pacific; Hazen; Kruger Inc;
  Lincoln; Manistique; Mohawk Paper; Potlatch;
  St Mary's; Smart Papers; Stora Enso; Tem-
  board; Wausau Paper; Whiting
Paper Type(s) Sold: Uncoated Groundwood
Branch Office(s)
Japan Pulp & Paper (USA), 5928 S Malt Ave,

Los Angeles, CA 90040 *Tel:* 323-889-7750
  Fax: 323-889-7740 *Web Site:* www.jpusa.com
Gould Paper South, 10400 NW 21 St, Suite 104,
  Doral, FL 33172 *Tel:* 305-470-0003 *Fax:* 305-
  470-0088 *Web Site:* www.southernpaperllc.com
Gould Paper North America, 25 East St, Winch-
  ester, MD 01890 *Tel:* 781-729-2059 *Fax:* 781-
  721-1986
Western BRW Paper, 6200 Saint John Ave,
  Kansas City, MO 64123 *Web Site:* www.
  westernbrw.com
Gould Paper Corp (Metro), 100 Executive Ave,
  Edison, NJ 08817 *Tel:* 732-248-7800 *Fax:* 732-
  248-5981
Bosworth Papers (Austin), 6301 E Stassney Lane,
  Bldg 9, Suite 200, Austin, TX 78744 *Tel:* 512-
  339-9987 *Fax:* 512-339-1917 *Web Site:* www.
  bosworthpapers.com
Western BRW Paper, 1800 Kelly Blvd, Carroll-
  ton, TX 75006 *Tel:* 469-568-5000 *Fax:* 469-
  568-5016 *Web Site:* www.westernbrw.com
Membership(s): National Paper Trade Association

Holliston LLC
Subsidiary of Holliston Mills
905 Holliston Mills Rd, Church Hill, TN 37642
Tel: 423-357-6141 *Toll Free Tel:* 800-251-0451
  Fax: 423-357-8840 *Toll Free Fax:* 800-325-
  0351
Web Site: holliston.com
Key Personnel
Mktg/Sales Analyst: Jennifer Anderson
Founded: 1895
Business from Other Countries: 10%
Cover Line(s) Milled: Arrestox; Kennett; Lumi-
  naire; Pearl Linen; RoxiteC; Sturdite
Membership(s): BMI; Publishers Association of
  the West

ICG Holliston, see Holliston LLC

Imago
110 W 40 St, New York, NY 10018
Tel: 212-921-4411 *Fax:* 212-921-8226
E-mail: sales@imagousa.com
Web Site: www.imagousa.com
Key Personnel
Pres/CEO: Howard Musk *E-mail:* hmusk@
  imagousa.com
Founded: 1985
Business from Other Countries: 100%
Branch Office(s)
Imago West Coast, 23412 Moulton Pkwy, La-
  guna Hills, CA 92653, Contact: Tammy Simms
  Tel: 949-367-1635 *Fax:* 949-367-1639
Imago Services (HK) Ltd, Unit 16, 2F, Metro
  Center Phase 1, 32 Lam Heng St, Kowloon
  Bay, Hong Kong, Contact: Kendrick Cheung
  Tel: 2811 3316 *Fax:* 2597 5256
Imago Shenzhen, Rm 2511-2512, Block A,
  United Plaza No 5022, Bin He Rd, Fu Tian
  Centre District, Shenzhen 518033, China, Con-
  tact: Kendrick Cheung *Tel:* (0755) 8304 8899
  Fax: (0755) 8251 4073
Imago (UK/Europe) Publishing Ltd, Albury Ct,
  Albury Thame, Oxon OX9 2LP, United King-
  dom, Contact: Simon Rosenheim *Tel:* (01844)
  337000 *Fax:* (01844) 339935 *E-mail:* sales@
  imago.co.uk *Web Site:* www.imago.co.uk

Monadnock Paper Mills Inc
117 Antrim Rd, Bennington, NH 03442-4205
Tel: 603-588-3311 *Fax:* 603-588-3158
E-mail: info@mpm.com
Web Site: www.mpm.com
Key Personnel
Dir, Mktg: Lisa Berghaum
Business from Other Countries: 30%

Cover Line(s) Sold: Astrolite; Astrolite PC100; Caress; Dulcet®; Astrolite; Astrolite PC100; Caress; Dulcet®; Duraprint™
Membership(s): American Forest & Paper Association; University & College Designers Association

Newark Recycled Paperboard Solutions
20 Jackson Dr, Cranford, NJ 07016
Tel: 908-276-4000 *Fax:* 908-276-0575
Web Site: www.newarkgroup.com
Key Personnel
Pres & CEO: Frank Papa
VP & CFO: Gregg Kam
Founded: 1912
Business from Other Countries: 15%
Cover Line(s) Milled: ForTex Specification Board; NewEx Graphicboard
Membership(s): Binding Industries Association; BMI; Library Binding Industries; Technical Association of the Pulp & Paper Industry

OGM USA
4141 44 St, Suite 3F, Sunnyside, NY 11104
Tel: 212-964-2430 *Fax:* 212-964-2497
Web Site: www.ogm.it
Key Personnel
Chmn, CEO & Sales Rep: Rino Varrasso
  E-mail: rvarrasso@ogm-usa.com
Founded: 1974
Business from Other Countries: 75%

Omniafiltra
9567 Main St, Beaver Falls, NY 13305
Mailing Address: PO Box 410, Beaver Falls, NY 13305
Tel: 315-346-7300 *Fax:* 315-346-7301
E-mail: info@omniafiltra.com
Web Site: www.omniafiltra.com
Key Personnel
Gen Mgr: Scott Sauer
Busn Devt & Sales Mgr: Peter Gendreau
  E-mail: petergendreau@omniafiltra.com
Founded: 1955
Business from Other Countries: 20%

Palace Printing & Design (PPD)
PO Box 12023, San Rafael, CA 94912
Tel: 415-526-1378
Key Personnel
Sales Dir: Sreedharan Vijayarangam *Tel:* 415-307-6065 (cell) *E-mail:* sreed@palacepress.com
Founded: 1984
Business from Other Countries: 20%

Printing Corp of the Americas Inc
620 SW 12 Ave, Fort Lauderdale, FL 33069
Tel: 954-781-8100 *Toll Free Tel:* 866-721-1PCA (721-1722) *Fax:* 954-781-8421
Web Site: www.commercialprintingflorida.com
Key Personnel
Pres: Jan Tuchman

Founded: 1979
Business from Other Countries: 15%

StoraEnso North American Sales Inc
Canterbury Green, 201 Broad St, Stamford, CT 06901
Tel: 203-541-5100 *Fax:* 203-353-1143
Web Site: www.storaenso.com
Key Personnel
Pres: Peter Mersmann
Business from Other Countries: 100%
Cover Line(s) Milled: Belle; Bulky; Classic; Creamy; Lux; Lux Cream; Novel 80; Novel 76; LumiArt; LumiSilk; Novapress

Taylor Specialty Books
Division of Balfour/Taylor
1550 W Mockingbird Lane, Dallas, TX 75235
Tel: 214-819-8588 (cust serv) *Fax:* 214-819-5051 (cust serv) *Toll Free Fax:* 800-203-9778
E-mail: rfq@taylorpub.com (estimates)
Web Site: www.taylorspecialtybooks.com
Key Personnel
VP, Sales & Mktg, Specialty Books: Rick Parra
  Tel: 214-819-5027 *E-mail:* rick.parra@balfour.com
Sales Rep: Kim Hawley *E-mail:* khawley@taylorpub.com; George Levesque
  E-mail: glevesque@taylorpub.com; Mark McCombs *E-mail:* mmcombs@taylorpub.com
Founded: 1939
Business from Other Countries: 10%

Manufacturing Services & Equipment Index

Manufacturing Services & Equipment

This section includes companies throughout the world that offer manufacturing services & equipment. Those U.S. and Canadian companies with 10% or more of their business done outside North America are also included here. Immediately preceding this section is an index classifying companies by services offered.

Canada

Master Flo Technology Inc
625A Rue Todd, Lachute, QC J8H 4L3
Tel: 450-562-0303 *Fax:* 450-562-9708
E-mail: info@mflo.com
Web Site: www.mflo.com
Key Personnel
VP, Opers: Tim Duffy
Founded: 1984
Business from Other Countries: 75%

PrintWest
1111 Eighth Ave, Regina, SK S4R 1C9
Tel: 306-525-2304 *Toll Free Tel:* 800-236-6438
  Fax: 306-757-2439
E-mail: general@printwest.com
Web Site: www.printwest.com
Key Personnel
CEO: Corie Triffo
VP, Sales: Ken Benson
Founded: 1992
Business from Other Countries: 15%

Webcom Inc
3480 Pharmacy Ave, Toronto, ON M1W 2S7
Tel: 416-496-1000 *Toll Free Tel:* 800-665-9322
  Fax: 416-496-1537
E-mail: webcom@webcomlink.com
Web Site: www.webcomlink.com
Key Personnel
CEO & Pres: Mike Collinge
Founded: 1975
Business from Other Countries: 40%
Sales Office(s): 65 Spring Valley Ave, River
  Edge, NJ 07661, United States, Contact: Susan
  Ginch *Tel:* 201-262-4301 *Fax:* 201-262-6375
  E-mail: susan.ginch@webcomlink.com
Membership(s): BMI; Canadian Book & Periodical Council; Printing Industries of America

China

**China National Publishing Industry Trading
  Corp (CNPITC)**
Subsidiary of China National Publications Import
  & Export (Group) Corp
504 Anhuali, Andingmenwai, Beijing 100011
Tel: (010) 64210403 *Fax:* (010) 64214540
Web Site: www.cnpitc.com.cn
Founded: 1980

Germany

Priese GmbH
Saatwinkler Damm 42A, 13627 Berlin
Tel: (030) 8263024 *Fax:* (030) 8266024

Greece

Grivas Publications
3 Irodotou St, 193 00 Aspropyrgos, Attiki
Mailing Address: PO Box 72, 193 00 Aspropyrgos, Attiki
Tel: 2105573470 *Fax:* 2105574086
E-mail: info@grivas.gr; grivasbooks@yahoo.gr
Web Site: www.grivas.gr
Branch Office(s)
4 Moustakli & Doridos St, 122 43 Attiki

Hong Kong

Co-Fine Promotions
1407 & Mezz floor, Shiu Fat Bldg, 139-141 Wai
  Yip St, Kwun Tong, Kowloon
Tel: 2518 0383 *Fax:* 2518 0361
Founded: 1988
Business from Other Countries: 30%

Colorcraft Ltd
Kodak House Phase II, Unit 8-9, 16th floor, 321
  Java Rd, North Point
Tel: 2590 9033 *Fax:* 2590 9005
E-mail: enquiries@colorcraft.com.hk
Web Site: www.colorcraft.com.hk
Key Personnel
Owner & Chief Executive Officer: Fraser McFadzean
Senior Production Manager: Peggy Ng
Founded: 1970
Business from Other Countries: 100%

Elegance Finance Printing Services Ltd
Subsidiary of Elegance Printing Co Ltd
2402 China Merchants Tower, Shun Tak Centre,
  168-200 Connaught Rd Central, Central Hong
  Kong
Tel: 2283 2222 *Fax:* 2283 2283
E-mail: csr@eleganceholdings.com
Web Site: www.eleganceholdings.com
Founded: 1980
Business from Other Countries: 2%

Golden Cup Printing Co Ltd
6/F, 177 Hoi Bun Rd, Kwun Tong, Kowloon
Tel: 2343 4254 *Fax:* 2341 5426
E-mail: sales@goldencup.com.hk
Web Site: www.goldencup.com.hk
Key Personnel
Chairman: Kam Kai Yeung
Founded: 1969
Business from Other Countries: 80%
Sales Office(s): Tutang Industrial Area, Jin Bei
  Rd, Changping, Dongguan, Guangdong, China
  Tel: (0769) 8339 4888 *Fax:* (0769) 8339 4999
Qilin Industrial Estate, Guanlan, Shenzhen,
  Guangdong, China *Tel:* (0755) 2805 6279
  Fax: (0755) 2805 6086
Jinma Town, Guandu District, Kunming, Yunnan,
  China *Tel:* (0871) 316 1226 *Fax:* (0871) 316
  1226

Terley House, Cadbury, Exeter EX5 5JZ, United
  Kingdom *Tel:* (01884) 855736 *E-mail:* info@
  gcpservices.com
Spectrum Books Inc, 2455 Bennett Valley Rd,
  Suite C-116, Santa Rosa, CA 95404-5671,
  United States *Tel:* 707-542-6044 *Fax:* 707-542-
  6045

Italy

Grafiche Damiani SRL
Via Zanardi, 376, 40131 Bologna BO
Tel: (051) 6356811 *Fax:* (051) 6347188
E-mail: info@grafichedamiani.it
Web Site: www.grafichedamiani.it

Zechini Gra.For srl
Via Giuseppe Di Vittorio, 2, 20090 Vimodrone
  MI
Tel: (02) 2650713 *Fax:* (02) 2650684
Web Site: www.zechini.com
Key Personnel
Sales Manager, Africa, Near & Middle East: Giovanni Peralta
Sales Manager, Eastern Europe: Elena Kulaha
Sales Manager, Europe: Dejan Mamula
Founded: 1952

Netherlands

TopPak Fulfilment Services
Kaagschip 14, 3991 CS Houten
Tel: (030) 6660211 *Fax:* (030) 6662674
Web Site: www.postnl.nl
Key Personnel
Chief Executive Officer: Herna Verhagen
Chief Financial Officer: Jan Bos

New Zealand

Bookprint Consultants Ltd
1104, One Market Lane, Wellington 6011
Tel: (04) 381 3070
Web Site: www.granthamhouse.co.nz
Key Personnel
Chief Executive: Graham C Stewart
  E-mail: graham@ghbil.com
Founded: 1982
Business from Other Countries: 10%
Branch Office(s)
Bookprint International Ltd, New Trend Centre, 104 King Fuk St, Sanpokong, Kowloon,
  Hong Kong *Tel:* 2327 0101 *Fax:* 2350 0315
  E-mail: bil@kingstime.co.hk

Portugal

Edicoes Silabo Lda
Rua Cidade de Manchester, 2, 1170-100 Lisbon
Tel: 218130345 *Fax:* 218166719
E-mail: silabo@silabo.pt
Web Site: www.silabo.pt
Key Personnel
Marketing Dir & Editor: Manuel Robalo
   E-mail: manuel.robalo@silabo.pt
Founded: 1983

Singapore

Ho Printing Singapore Pte Ltd
31 Changi South St One, Changi South Industrial
   Estate, Singapore 486769
Tel: 6542 9322 *Fax:* 6542 8322
E-mail: sales@hoprinting.com.sg
Web Site: www.hoprinting.com
Founded: 1951
Business from Other Countries: 30%

Markono Print Media Pte Ltd
Subsidiary of Markono Holdings Pte Ltd
21 Neythal Rd, Singapore 628586
Tel: 6281 1118
E-mail: enquiry@markono.com; sales@markono.
   com
Web Site: www.markono.com
Key Personnel
Chairman: Bob Lee
Mng Dir: Edwin Ng
Sales & Marketing Dir: Max Lee
Founded: 1967
Business from Other Countries: 20%
Branch Office(s)
Markono Logistics, 4 Toh Tuck Link, Singapore
   596226 *Tel:* 6465 1498 *E-mail:* ml.sales@
   markono.com
Markono Digital Solutions (M) Sdn Bhd, 7
   Lorong Jelawat 4, 13700 Seberang Jaya,
   Penang, Malaysia *Tel:* (04) 397-8700
   E-mail: mdsm.sales@markono.com

Times Printers Pte Ltd
Subsidiary of Times Publishing Ltd
16 Tuas Ave 5, Singapore 639340
Tel: 6311 2888; 6295 3211; 6295 2138; 6311
   2872 (customer service); 6311 2780 (sales &
   marketing) *Fax:* 6862 1313; 6311 2872 (cus-
   tomer service)
E-mail: marketing@timesprinters.com
Web Site: www.timesprinters.com.sg
Key Personnel
Deputy General Manager, Group Sales & Market-
   ing: Patsy Tan
Operations Manager: Alex Tang
Assistant General Manager: Phan Ming Ruey
Founded: 1968
Business from Other Countries: 75%
Branch Office(s)
Times Offset (Malaysia) Sdn Bhd, Lot 46, Sub-
   ang Hi-Tech Industrial Park, Batu Tiga, 40000
   Selangor Darul Ehsan, Malaysia *Tel:* (03) 5628
   6888 *Fax:* (03) 5628 6899
Sales Office(s): Everbest Printing Co Ltd, 25
   The Palisade, Umina Beach, NSW 2257, Aus-
   tralia *Tel:* (02) 4342 3563 *Fax:* (02) 4342 1564
   E-mail: adam@everbestprinting.com.au
Everbest Printing Co Ltd, Ko Fai Industrial
   Bldg, C5 10th floor, 7 Ko Fai Rd, Yau
   Tong, Kowloon, Hong Kong *Tel:* 2727 4433
   Fax: 2772 7687 *E-mail:* sales@everbest.com.hk
13 Nthombeni Way Noordhoek, 7979 Cape
   Town, South Africa, Contact: Arlene Gippert

Tel: (021) 789 2865 *E-mail:* arlenegippert@tpg.
   com.my
Everbest UK, 31 Palatine Rd, London N16 8SY,
   United Kingdom, Contact: Nicky Bowden
   Tel: (020) 7249 9483 *Fax:* (020) 7241 3460
   E-mail: nickybowden@everbest.co.uk
3240 Vicente St, Apartment 3, San Fran-
   cisco, CA 94116, United States, Contact:
   Brian Olshansky-Lucero *Tel:* 646-847-9874
   E-mail: brian.olshansky-lucero@tpg.com.my

Toppan Security Printing Pte Ltd
97 Ubi Ave 4, Singapore 408754
Tel: 6741 2500 *Fax:* 6744 7098
Web Site: www.toppanleefung.com/toppansecurity.
   aspx
Key Personnel
President & Chief Executive Officer: Yeo Chee
   Tong
General Manager & Digital Printing: David
   Ng *Tel:* 6846 3518 *E-mail:* davidng@
   toppanleefung.com
Deputy Sales Dir, Security Printing: Rick
   Ang *Tel:* 6846 3912 *E-mail:* rickang@
   toppanleefung.com
Business from Other Countries: 40%
Parent Company: Toppan Printing Co Ltd, One
   Kanda Izumi-cho, Chiyoda-ku, Toyko 101-
   0024, Japan

Slovenia

Gorenjski Tisk Storitve doo
Ul Mirka Vadnova 6, SI-4000 Kranj
Tel: (04) 20 16 300 *Fax:* (04) 20 16 301
E-mail: info@go-tisk.si
Web Site: www.go-tisk.si
Key Personnel
Mng Dir: Goran Celesnik *Tel:* (04) 20 16 330
   E-mail: goran.celesnik@go-tisk.si
Dir, Sales & Marketing: Dr Andrej Krope, PhD
   Tel: (04) 20 16 326 *E-mail:* andrej.krope@go-
   tisk.si
Production Manager: Dusan Kuljic *Tel:* (04) 20
   16 451 *E-mail:* dusan.kuljic@go-tisk.si
Founded: 1888
Business from Other Countries: 50%

Spain

Edelvives, see Editorial Luis Vives (Edelvives)

Editorial Luis Vives (Edelvives)
Xaudaro, 25, 28034 Madrid
Tel: 913 344 884
E-mail: info@edelvives.es
Web Site: www.edelvives.com
Founded: 1889
Business from Other Countries: 25%
Parent Company: Grupo Editorial Luis Vives
Branch Office(s)
Ctra de Madrid, km 315,700, 50012 Zaragoza
   Tel: 976 304 030

Switzerland

Buchzentrum AG (BZ)
Industriestr Ost 10, 4614 Haegendorf

Tel: (062) 209 25 25; (062) 209 26 26 (customer
   service) *Fax:* (062) 209 26 27
E-mail: kundendienst@buchzentrum.ch; info@
   buchzentrum.ch
Web Site: www.buchzentrum.ch
Key Personnel
Chief Executive Officer: Hanspeter Buechler
   E-mail: buechler@buchzentrum.ch
Head, Purchasing & Sales: David Ryf *Tel:* (062)
   209 25 05 *E-mail:* ryf@buchzentrum.ch
Founded: 1882

Canisius Druck & Grafik
Beauregard 3, 1700 Fribourg
Tel: (026) 425 51 61
E-mail: info@canisius.ch
Web Site: www.canisius.ch
Key Personnel
Dir: Beat Schultheiss
Founded: 1898

Imprimerie Messeiller SA
Route des Falaises 94, 2000 Neuchatel
Tel: (032) 725 12 96 *Fax:* (032) 724 19 37
E-mail: admin@messeiller.ch
Web Site: www.messeiller.ch
Key Personnel
Dir: Raphael Gambarini *E-mail:* raphael@
   messeiller.ch

Centre Suisse du Livre, see Buchzentrum AG
   (BZ)

Centro Svizzero del Libro, see Buchzentrum AG
   (BZ)

Swiss Book Centre, see Buchzentrum AG (BZ)

WIFAG-Polytype Holding AG
26, route de la Glane, 1700 Fribourg
Mailing Address: PO Box 1184, 1701 Fribourg
Tel: (026) 426 11 11 *Fax:* (026) 426 11 12
E-mail: info@wifag-polytype.com
Web Site: www.wifag-polytype.com
Key Personnel
Head, Marketing: Nicole Wicht *Tel:* (026) 426 12
   40 *E-mail:* nicole.wicht@polytype.com

Tanzania

Peramiho Printing Press
PO Box 41, Songea, Ruvuma
Tel: (025) 260 2299
Founded: 1937

Thailand

J Film Process Co Ltd
440/7 Soi Ratchawithi 3, Ratchawithi Rd, Ra-
   jchatha, Bangkok 10400
Tel: (02) 248-6888; (02) 248-6887 *Fax:* (02) 246-
   4719
Founded: 1970
Business from Other Countries: 45%

United Arab Emirates

Al-Futtaim Printers & Publishers
PO Box 799, Dubai
Tel: (04) 2222222; (04) 3477777 *Fax:* (04) 2217878; (04) 3477776
Key Personnel
Group Chairman: Othman Al Futtaim
Founded: 1992

United Kingdom

ADPS, see Anno Domini Publishing

Anno Domini Publishing
Book House, Orchard Mews, 18B High St, Tring, Herts HP23 5AH
Tel: (0845) 868 1333
E-mail: info@ad-publishing.co.uk
Web Site: www.ad-publishing.com
Key Personnel
Publishing Dir: Annette Reynolds

Blackmore Ltd
Longmead, Shaftesbury, Dorset SP7 8PX
Tel: (01747) 853034 *Fax:* (01747) 854500
E-mail: sales@blackmore.co.uk
Web Site: www.blackmore.co.uk
Key Personnel
Mng Dir: Peter Smith
Parent Company: TH Brickell Group

Book Production Consultants Ltd
Affiliate of Granta Editions
25-27 High St, Chesterton, Cambridge, Cambs CB4 1ND
Tel: (01223) 352790; (01223) 841748
    Fax: (01223) 460718
E-mail: enquiries@bpccam.co.uk
Web Site: www.bpccam.co.uk
Key Personnel
Mng Dir: Colin Walsh
Founded: 1973
Business from Other Countries: 25%

Cambridge University Press - Printing Division
Division of Cambridge University Press
University Printing House, Shaftesbury Rd, Cambridge, Cambs CB2 8BS
Tel: (01223) 358331
E-mail: information@cambridge.org
Web Site: www.cambridge.org/us/information/about.htm
Founded: 1534

Clays Ltd
Subsidiary of St Ives PLC
One Tudor St, London EC4Y 0AH
Tel: (020) 7928 8844
E-mail: sales@clays.co.uk
Web Site: www.clays.co.uk
Key Personnel
Mng Dir: Paul Hulley
Account Dir: Andrew Cochrane; Vicky Ellis
Customer Service Dir: Anne Perrin
Digital Sales Dir: Andrew Copley
Finance Dir: Andrew Spring
Manufacturing Dir: Ian Smith
Strategic Dir: Kate McFarlan

Self-Publishing Account Manager: Rebecca Souster
Founded: 1817
Business from Other Countries: 15%
Branch Office(s)
Popson St, Bungay, Suffolk NR35 1ED
    Tel: (01986) 893 211

William Clowes Ltd, see CPI William Clowes Ltd

CPI Antony Rowe
Bumper's Farm, Chippenham, Wilts SN14 6LH
Tel: (01249) 659705 *Fax:* (01249) 443103
Web Site: www.cpi-print.co.uk
Key Personnel
General Manager: Martin Collyer
Sales Manager: Geoff Fisher
Divisional Mng Dir: Alison Kaye
Founded: 1983
Business from Other Countries: 10%
Parent Company: CPI Group UK Ltd
Branch Office(s)
48-50 Birch Close, Eastbourne, East Sussex BN23 6PE *Tel:* (01323) 434700

CPI William Clowes Ltd
Copland Way, Ellough, Beccles, Suffolk NR34 7TL
Tel: (01502) 712884
E-mail: williamclowes@cpibooks.co.uk
Key Personnel
Divisional Mng Dir: Alison Kaye
Head, Sales: Jonathan Huddart
Founded: 1803
Business from Other Countries: 1%
Parent Company: CPI Group UK Ltd
Ultimate Parent Company: CPI Group

Hammond Bindery Ltd
Subsidiary of The Charlesworth Group
Flanshaw Way, Flanshaw Lane, Wakefield WF2 9LP
Tel: (01924) 204830 *Fax:* (01924) 332637
E-mail: sales@hammond-bindery.co.uk; hammonds.sales@hammond-bindery.co.uk
Web Site: www.hammond-bindery.co.uk
Key Personnel
Mng Dir: David Boothman
Commercial Dir: Sue Sheldon *Tel:* (01924) 204850
Customer Service & Estimator: Rhonda Moffat *Tel:* (01924) 204852 *E-mail:* rhonda@hammond-bindery.co.uk
Founded: 1972

Headley Brothers Ltd
The Invicta Press, Queens Rd, Ashford, Kent TN24 8HH
Tel: (01233) 623131 *Fax:* (01233) 612345
E-mail: printing@headley.co.uk; sales@headley.co.uk
Web Site: www.headley.co.uk
Key Personnel
Chief Executive Officer: Roger Pitt *E-mail:* roger.pitt@headley.co.uk
Commercial Dir: Jon Pitt *E-mail:* jon.pitt@headley.co.uk
Sales Dir: Paul Palmer *E-mail:* paul.palmer@headley.co.uk
Founded: 1881
Business from Other Countries: 5%

Hobbs The Printers Ltd
Brunel Rd, Totton, Hants SO40 3WX
Tel: (023) 8066 4800 *Fax:* (023) 8066 4801
E-mail: info@hobbs.uk.com
Web Site: www.hobbs.uk.com; www.hobbstheprinters.co.uk

Key Personnel
Mng Dir: David Hobbs *E-mail:* d.a.hobbs@hobbs.uk.com
Deputy Mng & Operations Dir: Graham Bromley *E-mail:* g.bromley@hobbs.uk.com
Commercial Dir: Terry Ozanne *E-mail:* t.ozanne@hobbs.uk.com
Customer Services Manager: Colin Richardson *E-mail:* c.richardson@hobbs.uk.com
Founded: 1884
Business from Other Countries: 4%

Page Bros (Norwich) Ltd
Subsidiary of Milex Ltd
Mile Cross Lane, Norwich, Norfolk NR6 6SA
Tel: (01603) 778800 *Fax:* (01603) 778801
E-mail: info@pagebros.co.uk
Web Site: www.pagebros.co.uk
Key Personnel
Mng Dir: Craig Eastaugh *E-mail:* c.eastaugh@pagebros.co.uk
Sales & Commercial Dir: Andrew Spelman *E-mail:* a.spelman@pagebros.co.uk
Founded: 1750
Business from Other Countries: 20%

Turnaround Publisher Services Ltd
Unit 3, Olympia Trading Estate, Coburg Rd, Wood Green, London N22 6TZ
Tel: (020) 8829 3000; (020) 8829 3002
    Fax: (020) 8881 5088
E-mail: customercare@turnaround-uk.com; orders@turnaround-uk.com
Web Site: www.turnaround-uk.com
Key Personnel
Mng Dir: Bill Godber
Finance Dir: Sue Gregg
Marketing Dir: Claire Thompson *Tel:* (020) 8829 3009 *E-mail:* claire.thompson@turnaround-uk.com
Sales Dir: Ian West *Tel:* (020) 8829 3012 *E-mail:* ian.west@turnaround-uk.com
Field Sales Manager: Jim Crawley *Tel:* (07725) 203734 *E-mail:* jim.crawley@turnaround-uk.com
Founded: 1984
Business from Other Countries: 50%

Watkiss Automation Ltd
Subsidiary of The Watkiss Group
Watkiss House, Blaydon Rd, Middlefield Industrial Estate, Sandy, Beds SG19 1RZ
Tel: (01767) 685700; (01767) 685710 (sales)
    Fax: (01767) 689900
E-mail: info@watkiss.com; sales@watkiss.com
Web Site: www.watkiss.com
Key Personnel
Communications Dir: Jo Watkiss *E-mail:* jowatkiss@watkiss.com
Technical Dir: Mike Watkiss
Founded: 1959
Business from Other Countries: 5%

United States

A-R Editions Inc
1600 Aspen Commons, Suite 100, Middleton, WI 53562
Tel: 608-836-9000 *Fax:* 608-831-8200
E-mail: info@areditions.com
Web Site: www.areditions.com
Key Personnel
Pres & CEO: Patrick Wall *Tel:* 608-203-2575 *E-mail:* patrick.wall@areditions.com
Dir, Spec Projs: James Zychowicz *Tel:* 608-203-2580 *E-mail:* james.zychowicz@areditions.com
Founded: 1962
Business from Other Countries: 15%

AWT World Trade Inc
Subsidiary of AWT World Trade Group
4321 N Knox Ave, Chicago, IL 60641-1906
Tel: 773-777-7100 *Fax:* 773-777-0909
E-mail: sales@awt-gpi.com
Web Site: www.awt-gpi.com
Key Personnel
Pres: Michael Green
Business from Other Countries: 25%
Branch Office(s)
Graphic Parts International (GPI), 4321 N Knox
Ave, Chicago, IL 60641-1906 *Tel:* 773-725-
4900 *Fax:* 773-777-0909 *E-mail:* sales@
gpiparts.com *Web Site:* www.gpiparts.com (div)
American M&M Screen Printing Equip-
ment Company, 105 Washington St, Suite
116, Oshkosh, WI 54901 *Tel:* 920-230-
7100 *Fax:* 920-231-8166 *E-mail:* sales@
screenprintmachinery.com *Web Site:* www.
screenprintmachinery.com (div)

Challenge Machinery Co
6125 Norton Center Dr, Norton Shores, MI 49441
Tel: 231-799-8484 *Fax:* 231-798-1275
E-mail: info@challengemachinery.com
Web Site: www.challengemachinery.com
Key Personnel
CEO & Pres: Larry J Ritsema
Dir, Sales & Mktg: Britt Cary *E-mail:* bcary@
challengemachinery.com
Founded: 1870
Business from Other Countries: 10%

The Cleveland Vibrator Co
2828 Clinton Ave, Cleveland, OH 44113
Tel: 216-241-7157 *Toll Free Tel:* 800-221-3298
Fax: 216-241-3480
E-mail: sales@clevelandvibrator.com
Web Site: www.clevelandvibrator.com
Key Personnel
Pres: Glen Roberts *E-mail:* groberts@
clevelandvibrator.com
Gen Sales Mgr: Jack Steinbuch
Sales: Randy Hilaszek *E-mail:* rhilaszek@
clevelandvibrator.com; David Strong
E-mail: dstrong@clevelandvibrator.com
Founded: 1923
Business from Other Countries: 12%

D & K Group Inc
1795 Commerce Dr, Elk Grove Village, IL 60007
Tel: 847-956-0160 *Toll Free Tel:* 800-632-2314
Fax: 847-956-8214
E-mail: info@dkgroup.net
Web Site: www.dkgroup.com
Key Personnel
Pres: Karl Singer
VP, Sales & Mktg: Tom Pidgeon *E-mail:* tom.
pidgeon@dkgroup.net
Mktg Communs Specialist: Brian Biegel
E-mail: brian.biegel@dkgroup.net
Founded: 1979
Business from Other Countries: 15%

Desktop Miracles Inc
112 S Main St, Suite 294, Stowe, VT 05672
Tel: 802-253-7900 *Toll Free Fax:* 888-293-2676
Web Site: www.desktopmiracles.com
Key Personnel
CEO & Pres: Barry T Kerrigan *E-mail:* barry@
desktopmiracles.com
VP: Virginia Kerrigan *E-mail:* virginia@
desktopmiracles.com
Founded: 1994
Business from Other Countries: 10%

Fairfield Marketing Group Inc
Subsidiary of FMG Inc
The Direct Mail Ctr, 830 Sport Hill Rd, Easton,
CT 06112-1241

Tel: 203-261-5585; 203-261-5568 *Fax:* 203-261-
0884
E-mail: info@fairfieldmarketing.com
Web Site: www.fairfieldmarketing.com
Key Personnel
CEO & Pres: Edward P Washchilla, Jr
VP, Cust Serv: Mike Lozada *Tel:* 203-261-5585
ext 204
VP, Fin: Pamela L Washchilla
VP, Fulfillment: Jason Paul Miller *Tel:* 203-261-
5585 ext 203 *E-mail:* jason@fairfieldmarketing.
com
Founded: 1987
Business from Other Countries: 10%
Membership(s): AAP PreK-12 Learning Group;
ABA; Data & Marketing Association; Direct
Marketing Club of New York; Education Mar-
ket Association; Hudson Valley Direct Market-
ing Association; International Literacy Associa-
tion; United States Chamber of Commerce

Fife, see Maxcess International

Imago
110 W 40 St, New York, NY 10018
Tel: 212-921-4411 *Fax:* 212-921-8226
E-mail: sales@imagousa.com
Web Site: www.imagousa.com
Key Personnel
Pres/CEO: Howard Musk *E-mail:* hmusk@
imagousa.com
Founded: 1985
Business from Other Countries: 100%
Branch Office(s)
Imago West Coast, 23412 Moulton Pkwy, La-
guna Hills, CA 92653, Contact: Tammy Simms
Tel: 949-367-1635 *Fax:* 949-367-1639
Imago Services (HK) Ltd, Unit 16, 2F, Metro
Center Phase 1, 32 Lam Heng St, Kowloon
Bay, Hong Kong, Contact: Kendrick Cheung
Tel: 2811 3316 *Fax:* 2597 5256
Imago Shenzhen, Rm 2511-2512, Block A,
United Plaza No 5022, Bin He Rd, Fu Tian
Centre District, Shenzhen 518033, China, Con-
tact: Kendrick Cheung *Tel:* (0755) 8304 8899
Fax: (0755) 8251 4073
Imago (UK/Europe) Publishing Ltd, Albury Ct,
Albury Thame, Oxon OX9 2LP, United King-
dom, Contact: Simon Rosenheim *Tel:* (01844)
337000 *Fax:* (01844) 339935 *E-mail:* sales@
imago.co.uk *Web Site:* www.imago.co.uk

MAGPOWR®, see Maxcess International

Marrakech Express Inc
720 Wesley Ave, No 10, Tarpon Springs, FL
34689
Tel: 727-942-2218 *Toll Free Tel:* 800-940-6566
Fax: 727-937-4758
E-mail: print@marrak.com
Web Site: www.marrak.com
Key Personnel
CEO: Peter Henzell
Prodn Mgr: Steen Sigmund
Sales/Estimator: Shirley Copperman
Founded: 1976
Business from Other Countries: 10%

Maxcess International
222 W Memorial Rd, Oklahoma City, OK 73114
Mailing Address: PO Box 26508, Oklahoma City,
OK 73126
Tel: 405-755-1600 *Toll Free Tel:* 800-639-3433
Fax: 405-755-8425
E-mail: sales@maxcessintl.com
Web Site: www.maxcessintl.com
Key Personnel
VP, Sales: Tony Jungels
Dir, Mktg: Stephanie Millman
Brand Mgr: Ben Bowlware *E-mail:* bbowlware@
maxcessintl.com

Business from Other Countries: 35%
Membership(s): Paper Industry Machine Asso-
ciation; Technical Association of the Pulp &
Paper Industry

Palace Printing & Design (PPD)
PO Box 12023, San Rafael, CA 94912
Tel: 415-526-1378
Key Personnel
Sales Dir: Sreedharan Vijayarangam *Tel:* 415-
307-6065 (cell) *E-mail:* sreed@palacepress.com
Founded: 1984
Business from Other Countries: 20%

Publishers' Graphics LLC
140 Della Ct, Carol Stream, IL 60188
Tel: 630-221-1850 *Toll Free Tel:* 888-404-3769
Fax: 630-221-1870
E-mail: contactpg@pubgraphics.com
Web Site: pubgraphics.com; www.
pubgraphicsdirect.com
Key Personnel
Pres: Nick A Lewis *E-mail:* nlewis@pubgraphics.
com
VP: Kathleen Lewis
Founded: 1996
Business from Other Countries: 60%
Branch Office(s)
3777 Rider Trail S, St Louis, MO 63045
Tel: 314-739-3777 *Fax:* 314-739-1436
Sales Office(s): New York, NY, Contact: Anthony
Ferrigno *Tel:* 908-672-5685

Spraymation Inc
5320 NW 35 Ave, Fort Lauderdale, FL 33309-
6314
Tel: 954-484-9700 *Toll Free Tel:* 800-327-4985
Fax: 954-484-9778
E-mail: orders@spraymation.com
Web Site: www.spraymation.com
Key Personnel
VP & Gen Mgr: Richard A Griffin
Founded: 1958
Business from Other Countries: 20%

Tidland, see Maxcess International

Tobias Associates Inc
50 Industrial Dr, Ivyland, PA 18974
Mailing Address: PO Box 2699, Ivyland, PA
18974
Tel: 215-322-1500 *Toll Free Tel:* 800-877-3367
Fax: 215-322-1504
E-mail: sales@tobiasinc.com
Web Site: www.densitometer.com
Key Personnel
VP: Eric Tobias
Founded: 1959
Business from Other Countries: 10%

Valley Roller, see Maxcess International

Videojet Technologies Inc
Subsidiary of Danaher Corp
1500 Mittel Blvd, Wood Dale, IL 60191-1073
Tel: 630-860-7300 *Toll Free Tel:* 800-843-3610
Toll Free Fax: 800-582-1343
E-mail: info@videojet.com
Web Site: www.videojet.com
Key Personnel
Sr Mktg Communs Specialist: Theresa DiCanio
E-mail: theresa.dicanio@videojet.com
Founded: 1980
Business from Other Countries: 50%

Webex, see Maxcess International

Fred Weidner & Daughter Printers
99 Hudson St, 5th fl, New York, NY 10013
Tel: 646-706-5180
E-mail: info@fwdprinters.com
Web Site: www.fwdprinters.com

Key Personnel
Pres: Cynthia Weidner *E-mail:* cynthia@
 fwdprinters.com
Creative Dir: Carol Mittelsdorf *E-mail:* carol@
 fwdprinters.com
Founded: 1860
Business from Other Countries: 25%

Western Printing Machinery Co (WPM)
9229 Ivanhoe St, Schiller Park, IL 60176
Tel: 847-678-1740 *Fax:* 847-678-6176
E-mail: info@wpm.com
Web Site: www.wpm.com

Key Personnel
Pres & CEO: Paul Kapolnek
CFO: Kelvin O'Meara
Dir, Cust Servs: Renee Reckamp *Tel:* 847-994-
 8662
Founded: 1933
Business from Other Countries: 15%
Membership(s): International Association of
 Diecutting & Diemaking

Yurchak Printing Inc
920 Links Ave, Landisville, PA 17538
Tel: 717-399-0209

E-mail: ypi.info@yurchak.com
Web Site: www.yurchak.com
Key Personnel
Founder & CEO: John Yurchak, Jr *E-mail:* john.
 yurchak.jr@yurchak.com
Pres: John W Yurchak
VP, Sales: Randy Boyer *E-mail:* randy.boyer@
 yurchak.com
Founded: 1998
Business from Other Countries: 10%
Membership(s): International Printers' Network

Book Trade Information

Book Clubs

Included below are a variety of book clubs. Letters in parenthesis indicate the type of club.

(A)–Adult　　　　　(J)–Juvenile　　　　　(A-J)–Adult & Juvenile

Austria

Donauland (A-J)
Postfach 4, 6965 Wolfurt-Bahnhof
Tel: (0820) 203 062 *Fax:* (0820) 203 063
E-mail: donauland@donauland.at
Web Site: www.donauland.at
Established: 1950
Number of Members: 320,000

Colombia

Circulo de Lectores SA (A-J)
Calle 73, No 7-60, Bogota
Tel: (01) 321 0808 (ext 719)
E-mail: csecli@circulo.com.co
Web Site: www.circulodelectores.com.co
Established: 1970
Number of Members: 650,000
Owned by: Bertelsmann

Czech Republic

Knizni Klub (A-J)
Nadrazni 896/30, 150 00 Prague 5
Tel: 296 536 662; 296 536 660 (orders) *Fax:* 296 536 966
E-mail: soc.site@euromedia.cz
Web Site: www.bux.cz/knizni-klub
Key Personnel
Program Dir: Helena Cudova
Established: 1953
Subjects: Art, Fiction
Number of Members: 250,000
Owned by: Euromedia Group ks

Denmark

Gyldendals Bogklub (A)
Postbox 176, 1005 Copenhagen K
Tel: 70 11 00 33
E-mail: gbk-otrs@gyldendal.dk
Web Site: www.gyldendals-bogklub.dk
Key Personnel
Editor: Anne Kirstine Dam-Christensen

Subjects: Fiction, Nonfiction (General)
Owned by: Gyldendal Group

Gyldendals Bornebogklub (J)
Postbox 176, 1005 Copenhagen K
Tel: 70 11 00 33
E-mail: bbk-otrs@gyldendal.dk
Web Site: www.gyldendals-boernebogklub.dk
Owned by: Gyldendal Group

Samlerens Bogklub (A)
Postbox 176, 1005 Copenhagen K
Tel: 70 11 00 33
E-mail: sbk-otrs@gyldendal.dk
Web Site: www.samlerens-bogklub.dk
Key Personnel
Editor: Anna Johansen
Subjects: Fiction, Government, Political Science, Nonfiction (General)
Number of Members: 20,000
Owned by: Gyldendal Group

Finland

Suuri Suomalainen Kirjakerho Oy (Great Finnish Book Club Ltd) (A-J)
Maistraatinportti 1, 00015 Otavamedia
Tel: (09) 1566 308 *Fax:* (09) 145 510
E-mail: palaute@sskk.fi
Web Site: www.sskk.fi/etusivu
Established: 1968
Number of Members: 280,000
Owned by: Otava Kustannusosakeyhtioe Oy, Uudenmaankatu 10, Helsinki 00120

Germany

Buechergilde Gutenberg (A-J)
Stuttgarter Str 25-29, 60329 Frankfurt am Main
Mailing Address: Postfach 160 165, 60064 Frankfurt am Main
Tel: (069) 27 39 08-90 *Fax:* (069) 27 39 08-25; (069) 27 39 08-26
E-mail: service@buechergilde.de
Web Site: www.buechergilde.de
Key Personnel
Mng Dir & Press: Mario Frueh *Tel:* (069) 27 39 08 20 *Fax:* (069) 27 39 08-76 20
E-mail: frueh@buechergilde.de

Marketing: Kai Splittgerber *Tel:* (069) 27 39 08-73 *Fax:* (069) 27 39 08-76 27
E-mail: splittgerber@buechergilde.de
Established: 1924
Owned by: Buechergilde Gutenberg Verlagsgesellschaft mbH

WBG (Wissenschaftliche Buchgesellschaft) (Scientific Book Society) (A)
Hindenburgstr 40, 64295 Darmstadt
Tel: (06151) 33 08-0; (06151) 33 08-330 *Fax:* (06151) 31 41 28
E-mail: service@wbg-wissenverbindet.de
Web Site: www.wbg-wissenverbindet.de
Key Personnel
Mng Dir: Dr Beate Varnhorn *E-mail:* varnhorn@wbg-wissenverbindet.de
Marketing Dir: Dr Holger Wochnowski *E-mail:* wochnowski@wbg-wissenverbindet.de
Foreign Rights: Isabella Erb *Tel:* (06151) 33 08-159 *Fax:* (06151) 33 08-212 *E-mail:* erb@wbg-wissenverbindet.de
Press: Christina Herborg *Tel:* (06151) 33 08-161 *Fax:* (06151) 33 08-208 *E-mail:* herborg@wbg-wissenverbindet.de
Established: 1949
Number of Members: 120,000

Wissenschaftliche Buchgesellschaft, see WBG (Wissenschaftliche Buchgesellschaft)

Iceland

Lestrarhesturinn (J)
Skajaldborg -bokautafa ehf, Grensasvegi 14, 108 Reykjavik
Tel: 588 2400 *Fax:* 588 8994
E-mail: skjaldborg@skjaldborg.is
Web Site: www.skolatorg.is/vefur/efni/lestrarh.asp
Owned by: Skjaldborg Ltd

India

DC Book Club (A-J)
Good Shepherd St, Kottayam, Kerala 686 001
Tel: (0481) 2563114; (0481) 2301614
E-mail: customercare@dcbooks.com; sales@dcbooks.com
Web Site: www.dcbooks.com
Established: 1974

Number of Members: 2,500
Owned by: DC Books

Italy

Isper Club (A)
Corso Dante, 124/A, 10126 Turin
Tel: (011) 66 47 803 *Fax:* (011) 66 70 829
E-mail: isper@isper.org
Web Site: www.isper.org
Key Personnel
Dir: Laura Actis Grosso *Tel:* (011) 66 47 803 ext
   201 *E-mail:* laura.actisgrosso@isper.org
Administrator: Marco Actis Grosso
   E-mail: marco.actisgrosso@isper.org
Foreign Relations: Lorena Donadonibus
   Tel: (011) 66 47 803 ext 203 *E-mail:* lorena.
   donadonibus@isper.org
Established: 1965
Number of Members: 300
Owned by: ISPER

Netherlands

Boekenclub ECI (A-J)
Papiermolen 14-24, 3994 DK Houten
Web Site: www.eci.nl
Established: 1967

Norway

De norske Bokklubbene AS (A-J)
Gullhaug Torg 1, 0484 Oslo
Mailing Address: Postboks 4300, 0402 Nydalen
Tel: 02299
Web Site: www.bokklubben.no
Established: 1961
Subjects: Fiction, Nonfiction (General)
Book Club(s): Bokklubbens Barn; Bokklubben
   Fakta; Bokklubben Krim og Spenning;
   Bokklubben Lydboker; Bokklubben Nye Boker;
   Bokklubben Ungdom; Bokklubben Villmark-
   sliv; Den norske Bokklubben
Number of Members: 550,000
Owned by: H Aschehoug & Co; Gyldendal Norsk
   Forlag A/S; Pax Forlag AS

Energica (A)
Postboks 1900 Sentrum, 0055 Oslo
Tel: 81 55 92 00 (orders)
E-mail: kundeservice@tanumbokklubber.no
Web Site: www.energica.no; www.
   tanumbokklubber.no
Key Personnel
Editor: Nina Normann Ferguson
Books for the mind, body & spirt.
Owned by: Cappelen Damm AS

Hobbyklubben (A)
Postboks 1900 Sentrum, 0055 Oslo
Tel: 81 55 92 00 (orders)
E-mail: hobbyklubben@cappelendamm.no
Web Site: www.hobbyklubben.no; www.
   tanumbokklubber.no
Established: 1997
Craft book club.
Owned by: Cappelen Damm AS

Tanum Energica, see Energica

Tanum Hobbyklubben, see Hobbyklubben

Portugal

Circulo de Leitores (A-J)
Rua Prof Jorge da Silva Horta, 1, 1500-499 Lis-
bon
Tel: 21 762 60 00 *Fax:* 21 760 71 49
E-mail: correio@circuloleitores.pt
Web Site: www.circuloleitores.pt
Key Personnel
Head, Sales & Marketing: Sonia Campos
Editor: Ana Lucia Duarte; Jorge Garcia
Established: 1971
Subjects: Biography, Memoirs, Fiction, History,
   Nonfiction (General), Science (General), En-
   cyclopedias, Juvenile, Magazines, Special Edi-
   tions
Number of Members: 500,000
Owned by: Grupo Bertrand Circulo

Slovakia

Klub mladych citatelov (Club of Young
   Readers) (J)
Sasinkova 5, 811 08 Bratislava
Tel: (02) 50 22 72 17; (02) 50 22 72 25
E-mail: kmc@mlade-leta.sk; spn@spn.sk
Web Site: www.mladeleta.sk
Established: 1963
Subjects: Anthologies, Critiques, Fairy Tales,
   Original Slovak Literature, Poetry, Prose, Sci-
   entific Literature, Translations of World Litera-
   ture
Number of Members: 55,000
Owned by: Mlade leta sro

Spain

Biblos Clube de Lectores (A-J)
Quinta Nº 8, Mandaio, 15391 Cesuras, A Coruna
Tel: 981 777 207 *Fax:* 981 790 039
E-mail: subscritores@biblosclube.com
Web Site: www.biblosclube.com
Key Personnel
Dir: Carmela Gonzalez
Editorial Dir: Tucho Calvo

Circulo de Lectores SA (A-J)
Travessera de Gracia, 47-49, 08021 Barcelona
Tel: 902 22 33 55
E-mail: atencion-socios@circulo.es
Web Site: www.circulo.es
Key Personnel
Dir General: Carlos Lugo Ortiz
Established: 1962
Number of Members: 1,540,000
Owned by: Bertelsmann AG, Germany; Grupo
   Planeta

Sweden

Allt om Hobby Publishing Co (A)
Jarnvagsgatan 36, 131 54 Nacka
Tel: (08) 999 333
E-mail: order@hobby.se
Web Site: www.hobby.se
Key Personnel
Editor-in-Chief: Maria Orrung *E-mail:* maria.
   orrung@hobby.se
Publishing Manager: Mattias Stenbom
Publication(s): *Allt om Hobby* (magazine); *Allt om
   Modelltag* (annually); *I Luften* (annually)
Owned by: Allt om Hobby AB

Barnens Bokklubb (J)
Hantverkargatan 5 C, 11221 Stockholm
Mailing Address: Box 30104, 10425 Stockholm
Tel: (08) 737 86 90; (08) 441 34 34 (orders)
E-mail: kundservice@barnensbokklubb.se
Web Site: www.barnensbokklubb.se
Key Personnel
Chief Executive Officer: Maria Capor
   Tel: (070) 781 55 55 *E-mail:* maria.capor@
   barnensbokklubb.se
Mng Editor: Lisa Sorgenfrei
Editor: Johanna Stenius
Marketing: Ulrica Arnbom *Tel:* (08) 266 87 17
Established: 1977
Subjects: Children's Books
Number of Members: 150,000
Publication(s): *Barn Posten*; *Laese Posten*
Owned by: PA Nordstedt & Soner; Bokforlaget
   Opal

Bonniers Bokklubb (A)
Sveavagen 56, 111 34 Stockholm
Mailing Address: Box 613, 831 27 Ostersund
Tel: (08) 696 87 80
E-mail: kundservice@bbk.bonnier.se
Web Site: www.bonniersbokklubb.se
Key Personnel
Book Club Manager: Marie Bratani Olsson
   E-mail: mbo@bonnierforlagen.se
Editorial Manager: Sophie Kameus
Sales Manager: Johanna Ljungsten
   E-mail: johanna.ljungsten@bonnierforlagen.se
Established: 1970
Publication(s): *Bokspegeln* (The Book Mirror, 10
   times/yr, magazine)
Owned by: Bonnier AB

Bokklubben LivsEnergi (A)
c/o Publishing System, Box 30104, 104 25 Stock-
   holm
Tel: (08) 737 86 92
E-mail: livsenergi@fsys.se
Web Site: www.livsenergi.se
Mind-Body-Spirit books, music & multimedia.
Subjects: Inspirational, Spirituality, Music, Dance
Owned by: Massolit Forlagsgrupp AB

Lyssnarklubben (Listening Club) (A-J)
Box 613, 831 27 Ostersund
Tel: (08) 696 87 50
E-mail: kundservice@lyssnarklubben.se
Web Site: www.lyssnarklubben.se
Key Personnel
Sales Manager: Viktoria Ohlsson
Audio books & CDs.
Subjects: Biography, Memoirs, Health, Nutrition,
   History, Literature, Literary Criticism, Essays,
   Mysteries, Suspense, Beauty, Swedish & For-
   eign Literature
Owned by: Bonnier AB

Manadens Bok (The Book of the Month) (A)
Sveavagen 56, 111 34 Stockholm
Mailing Address: Box 613, 831 27 Ostersund
Tel: (08) 696 85 50

E-mail: kundservice@manadensbok.se
Web Site: www.manadensbok.se
Key Personnel
Book Club Manager: Marie Bratani Olsson
  E-mail: mbo@bonnierforlagen.se
Editorial Manager: Helena Gustafsson
Sales Manager: Viktoria Ohlsson
Established: 1973
Target audience over the age of 40.
Owned by: Bonnier AB

Spanningszonen (Voltage Zone) (A)
Box 613, 831 27 Ostersund
Tel: (08) 696 88 50
E-mail: kundservice@sz.bonnier.se
Web Site: www.spanningszonen.se
Key Personnel
Sales Manager: Johanna Ljungsten
  E-mail: johanna.ljungsten@bonnierforlagen.se
Established: 1975
Book club geared toward a male audience with
  focus on action, detective stories & thrillers.
Subjects: Animals, Pets, Cookery, Fiction, Gar-
  dening, Plants, Health, Nutrition, History, Hu-
  mor, Mysteries, Suspense, Sports, Athletics,
  Birds, Entertainment
Owned by: Bonnier AB

Bokklubben Svalan (A)
Sveavagen 56, 111 34 Stockholm
Mailing Address: Box 613, 831 27 Ostersund
Tel: (08) 696 88 00
E-mail: kundservice@svalan.bonnier.se
Web Site: svalan.se
Key Personnel
Book Club Manager: Marie Bratani Olsson
  E-mail: mbo@bonnierforlagen.se
Editor: Marita Sjogren *Tel:* (08) 696 82 87
  E-mail: marita.sjogren@bonnierforlagen.se
Sales Manager: Annette Vedsmand *Tel:* (08)
  696 88 99 *E-mail:* annette.vedsmand@
  bonnierforlagen.se
Established: 1942
Subjects: Swedish & Foreign Literature
Owned by: Bonnier AB

Ukraine

Family Leisure Club (A-J)
Gagarina Ave 20-A, Kharkiv 61140

Mailing Address: PO Box 84, Kharkiv 61001
Toll Free Tel: 0800 30 10 90
E-mail: supports@bookclub.ua
Web Site: www.bookclub.ua; catalog.ksd.ua
Established: 2009
Subjects: Cookery, Health, Nutrition, History,
  How-to, Inspirational, Spirituality, Literature,
  Literary Criticism, Essays, Mysteries, Suspense,
  Psychology, Psychiatry, Romance, Science Fic-
  tion, Fantasy

United Kingdom

Bibliophile Ltd (A)
31 Riverside, Trinity Buoy Wharf, London E14
  0FP
Tel: (020) 7474 2474 *Fax:* (020) 7474 8589
E-mail: customercare@bibliophilebooks.com;
  orders@bibliophilebooks.com
Web Site: www.bibliophilebooks.com
Key Personnel
Owner & Dir: Annie Quigley
Established: 1978
Mail order booksellers of bargain books & re-
  mainders.
Publication(s): *Bibliophile*

The Folio Society (A)
44 Eagle St, London WC1R 4FS
Tel: (020) 7400 4200 *Toll Free Tel:* 866-255-8280
E-mail: customerservice@foliosociety.com
Web Site: www.foliosociety.com
Key Personnel
Production Dir: Joe Whitlock Blundell
Marketing Manager: Samaris Huntington-Thresher
Established: 1947
Subjects: Biography, Children's, Fiction, History,
  Limited Editions, Poetry, Religion, Science

ISBC, see Scholastic International School Book
  Club

Letterbox Library (J)
Unit 151 Stratford Workshops, Burford Rd, Strat-
  ford, London E15 2SP
Tel: (020) 8534 7502 *Fax:* (020) 8555 7880

E-mail: info@letterboxlibrary.com
Web Site: www.letterboxlibrary.com
Key Personnel
Dir: Kerry Mason
Established: 1983
Inclusive, nonsexist multicultural children's
  books.

The Poetry Book Society Ltd (A)
Unit G07 Screenworks, 22 Highbury Grove, Lon-
  don N5 2EF
Tel: (020) 7831 7468 *Fax:* (020) 7831 6967
E-mail: info@poetrybooks.co.uk
Web Site: www.poetrybooks.co.uk; www.
  poetrybookshoponline.com
Key Personnel
Dir: Chris Holifield
Established: 1953
Membership organization that promotes selected
  poetry at discounted prices & runs poetry
  projects & prizes such as the T S Eliot Prize
  for Poetry.
Subjects: Poetry
Number of Members: 2,200
Publication(s): *The Bulletin* (quarterly)

Red House Books (J)
Catteshall Manor, Catteshall Lane, Godalming,
  Surrey GU7 1UU
Tel: (0345) 602 4040 *Fax:* (0345) 606 4242
E-mail: tbpsales@thebookpeople.co.uk
Web Site: www.thebookpeople.co.uk
Established: 1979
Number of Members: 350,000
Parent Company: The Book People Ltd

Scholastic International School Book Club (J)
FREEPOST RRGT-TRTJ-CHTR, Windrush Park,
  Range Rd, Witney, Oxon OX29 0YZ
Tel: (01993) 893475 *Fax:* (01993) 893412
E-mail: bookclubs@scholastic.co.uk; enquiries@
  scholastic.co.uk
Web Site: scholastic.co.uk/scholastic_international;
  world-shop.scholastic.co.uk/bookclubs
Book Club(s): mini (ages 0-6); XD (ages 7-11);
  Teen (ages 11-up)
Owned by: Scholastic Ltd

Book Trade Organizations

The organizations listed below include publisher and bookseller associations and ISBN agencies as well as book trade and allied organizations. Listings appear under the country in which they are physically located. Some of the organizations are specific to a particular country; others are international in nature.

† indicates those organizations that are international in scope.

‡ indicates United Nations agencies with publishing activities.

◇ indicates other international organizations with publishing activities.

Additional book trade associations can be found in the sections **Literary Associations & Societies** and **Library Associations**.

Albania

Shoqata e Botuesve Shqiptare (Albanian
    Publishers Association)
Frederik Shiroka Nr 31, Tirana
Mailing Address: PO Box 1441, 1023 Tirana
Tel: (04) 22 51 344; (04) 22 36 635
Web Site: www.shbsh.al
Key Personnel
Chairman: Mr Petrit Ymeri
Founded: 1992

Algeria

Agence Algerienne de l'ISBN
Bibliotheque Nationale d'Algerie, BP 127, El
    Hamma, 16000 Algiers
Tel: (021) 67 43 95 *Fax:* (021) 67 18 67
Web Site: www.biblionat.dz
Key Personnel
Contact: Sabiha Touati *E-mail:* sabihatouati@
    yahoo.fr

Standard Book Numbering Agency, see Agence
    Algerienne de l'ISBN

Andorra

Andorran Standard Book Numbering Agency
Bibloteca National d'Andorra, Casa Bauro, Plac-
    eta Sant Esteve s/n, AD500 Andorra la Vella
Tel: 826445 *Fax:* 829445
E-mail: bncultura.gov@andorra.ad
Web Site: www.cultura.ad/biblioteca-nacional
Key Personnel
Contact: Julia Fernandez
Founded: 1987

Angola

UEA, see Uniao dos Escritores Angolanos (UEA)

Uniao dos Escritores Angolanos (UEA) (Union
    of Angolan Writers)
Av Ho-chi-min, Largo das Escolas, 1° de Maio,
    Luanda
Mailing Address: CP 2767, Luanda

Tel: (022) 2322421 *Fax:* (022) 2323205
E-mail: contacto@ueangola.com
Web Site: www.ueangola.com

Argentina

Agencia Argentina ISBN, see Camara Argentina
    del Libro

Argentine Society of Authors, see Sociedad
    General de Autores de la Argentina (SGAA)

Camara Argentina de Publicaciones
Lavalle 437 5° Oficina A, C1047AAI Buenos
    Aires
Tel: (011) 5218-9707
E-mail: info@publicaciones.org.ar
Web Site: www.publicaciones.org.ar
Founded: 1970

Camara Argentina del Libro (Argentine Book
    Chamber)
Av Belgrano 1580 - Piso 4°, C1093AAQ Buenos
    Aires
Tel: (011) 4381-8383; (011) 5353-1263; (011)
    5353-1265 *Fax:* (011) 5353-1270
E-mail: cal@editores.org.ar; registrolibros@
    editores.org.ar
Web Site: www.editores.org.ar
Key Personnel
President: Graciela Rosenberg
First Vice President: Martin Gremmelspacher
Second Vice President: Luis Quevedo
Secretary: Maria Teresa Carbano
Treasurer: Juan Pampin
Founded: 1938
Publication(s): *LEA*

Fundacion El Libro
Hipolito Yrigoyen 1628, 5° Piso, C1089AAF
    Buenos Aires
Tel: (011) 4370-0600 *Fax:* (011) 4370-0607
E-mail: fundacion@el-libro.org.ar
Web Site: www.el-libro.org.ar
Key Personnel
President: Graciela Rosenberg
Vice President: Martin Gremmelspacher; Luis
    Quevedo
Secretary: Maria Teresa Carbano
Administrative Manager: Daniel Monzo
Founded: 1974

SGAA, see Sociedad General de Autores de la
    Argentina (SGAA)

**Sociedad General de Autores de la Argentina
    (SGAA)**
Pacheco de Melo 1820, C1126AAB Buenos Aires
Tel: (011) 4811-2582 *Fax:* (011) 2150-1700
E-mail: info@argentores.org.ar
Web Site: www.argentores.org.ar
Key Personnel
President: Miguel Angel Splendiani
    E-mail: madiani@argentores.org.ar
First Vice President: Bernardo Carey
    E-mail: bcarey@argentores.org.ar
Second Vice President: Ricardo Talesnik
    E-mail: rtalesnik@argentores.org.ar
Secretary: Guillermo Hardwick
    E-mail: secretario@argentores.org.ar
Treasurer: Nora Massi *E-mail:* nmassi@
    argentores.org.ar
Founded: 1910

Armenia

National Book Chamber of Armenia
G Kochar St 21, 375 009 Yerevan
Tel: (010) 52 75 95; (010) 52 98 14
E-mail: grapalat@arminco.com; info@book-
    chamber.am
Web Site: www.book-chamber.am
Key Personnel
Dir: Gevorg Harutiunyan
Deputy Dir: Hasmik Safaryan
Founded: 1922

National Publishers Association of Armenia
24g Baghramyan Ave, 0019 Yerevan
Tel: (010) 56 39 02; (010) 22 34 34; (091) 40 93
    25
E-mail: armnpa@netsys.am
Web Site: bookpublishers.am
Key Personnel
Chairman: Mr Mkrtich Karapetyan
Executive Dir: Mr Vahan Khachatryan

Australia

ABA, see Australian Booksellers Association Inc
    (ABA)

ANZAAB, see The Australian & New Zealand
    Association of Antiquarian Booksellers
    (ANZAAB) Ltd

ANZSI, see Australian & New Zealand Society
    of Indexers Inc (ANZSI)

APA, see Australian Publishers Association (APA)

ASA, see Australian Society of Authors

Australia Council Literature Board
372 Elizabeth St (corner of Cooper St), Surry Hills, NSW 2010
Mailing Address: PO Box 788, Strawberry Hills, NSW 2012
Tel: (02) 9215 9000 *Toll Free Tel:* 1800 226 912
Web Site: www.australiacouncil.gov.au
Support & promotion of Australian literature. Provides direct financial support to outstanding literary creators & grants to organizations that offer infrastructure support to the literature sector & income-generating opportunities for writers. Profesional development opportunities for individual writers, including Australian & overseas residencies, are also supported.
Publication(s): *Australia Council Support for the Arts Handbook* (1997)

The Australian & New Zealand Association of Antiquarian Booksellers (ANZAAB) Ltd
122 Raglan St, Apartment 1, Mosman, NSW 2088
Tel: (02) 6251 5191
E-mail: admin@anzaab.com
Web Site: www.anzaab.com
Key Personnel
President: Jonathan Burdon
Vice President: Roz Greenwood
Secretary: Rachel Robarts
Treasurer: Michael Sprod
Founded: 1977
Membership(s): International League of Antiquarian Booksellers (ILAB).

Australian & New Zealand Society of Indexers Inc (ANZSI)
PO Box 43, Lawson, NSW 2783
Tel: (02) 4739 8199
E-mail: info@anzsi.org
Web Site: www.anzsi.org
Key Personnel
President: Mary Coe *E-mail:* president@anzsi.org
Vice President: Daphne Lawless
    E-mail: vicepresident@anzsi.org
Treasurer: Michael Wyatt *E-mail:* treasurer@anzsi.org
Secretary: Kerry Anderson *E-mail:* secretary@anzsi.org
Affiliated with indexing societies in Britain, Canada, China, South Africa & USA.
Publication(s): *ANZSI Index Series* (ISSN: 1449-8820); *ANZSI Newsletter* (ISSN: 0314-3767, print; 1326-2718, online)
Associate Companies: American Society of Indexers; Association for Southern African Indexers & Bibliographers (ASAIB); China Society of Indexers (CSI); Indexing & Abstracting Society of Canada; Society of Indexers, United Kingdom

Australian Booksellers Association Inc (ABA)
828 High St, Unit 9, Kew East, Victoria 3102
Tel: (03) 9859 7322 *Fax:* (03) 9859 7344
E-mail: mail@aba.org.au
Web Site: booksellers.org.au
Key Personnel
Chief Executive Officer: Joel Becker
    E-mail: jbecker@aba.org.au
President: Patricia Genat
Vice President: Tim White
Treasurer: Rolf Wilkens
Communications Manager: Robyn Huppert
    E-mail: rhuppert@aba.org.au

Federal association with branches in every state & represents booksellers' interests to government bodies, publishers & other organizations.
Publication(s): *News on Bookselling* (quarterly, journal)

Australian Copyright Council
3/245 Chalmers St, Redfern, NSW 2016
Mailing Address: PO Box 1986, Strawberry Hills, NSW 2012
Tel: (02) 9101 2377 *Fax:* (02) 8815 9799
E-mail: info@copyright.org.au
Web Site: www.copyright.org.au
Key Personnel
Chairman: Prof Michael Fraser
Executive Dir: Fiona Phillips
Office & Events Manager: Sarah Hilyard
Founded: 1968
To advance the arts & the creative industries in Australia by promoting the value of copyright.

Australian Press Council
309 Kent St, Suite 2, Level 6, Sydney, NSW 2000
Tel: (02) 9261 1930 *Toll Free Tel:* 1800 02 5712
    Fax: (02) 9267 6826
E-mail: media@presscouncil.org.au
Web Site: www.presscouncil.org.au
Key Personnel
Executive Dir: John Pender
Deputy Executive Dir: Georgina Dridan
Founded: 1976
Established to help preserve the traditional freedom of the press within Australia & ensure that the free press acts responsibly & ethically.

Australian Publishers Association (APA)
60/89 Jones St, Ultimo, NSW 2007
Tel: (02) 9281 9788 *Fax:* (02) 9281 1073
E-mail: office@publishers.asn.au
Web Site: www.publishers.asn.au
Key Personnel
Chief Executive Officer: Michael Gordon Smith
President: Lee Walker
Marketing & Operations Manager: Cat Smith
    E-mail: cat.smith@publishers.asn.au
Founded: 1948
Trade association representing Australian book, journal & electronic publishers.
Publication(s): *Directory of Members* (available in print, online or as an Excel spreadsheet)

Australian Society of Authors
22-36 Mountain St, Suite C1.06, Ultimo, NSW 2007
Tel: (02) 9211 1004 *Fax:* (02) 9211 0125
E-mail: asa@asauthors.org
Web Site: www.asauthors.org
Key Personnel
Chief Executive Officer: Juliet Rogers
Program Manager: Jane Coulcher
Membership & Administration Officer: Lauren Anderson
Founded: 1963
Publication(s): *Australian Author* (2 issues/yr, magazine, for writers, readers & people who love books); *Australian Book Contracts* (step-by-step guide to publishing contracts for authors); *Between the Lines* (legal guide for writers & illustrators)

CAL, see Copyright Agency Ltd (CAL)

CBAA, see Christian Bookselling Association of Australia (CBAA)

Christian Bookselling Association of Australia (CBAA)
17 Bransby Pl, Mount Annan, NSW 2567
E-mail: info@cbaa.com.au
Web Site: www.cbaa.com.au

Key Personnel
President: Judy Hetherington
Secretary: Christine Kollaris
Treasurer: Albert Abel
Publication(s): *CBAA News*

Copyright Agency Ltd (CAL)
Level 11, 66 Goulburn St, Sydney, NSW 2000
Tel: (02) 9394 7600 *Toll Free Tel:* 1800 066 844 (Australia only) *Fax:* (02) 9394 7601
E-mail: info@copyright.com.au
Web Site: copyright.com.au
Key Personnel
Chief Executive: Adam Suckling

Educational Lending Right
GPO Box 3241, Canberra, ACT 2601
Tel: (02) 6271 1000 *Toll Free Tel:* 1800 672 842 (Australia only) *Fax:* (02) 6210 2907
E-mail: lendingrights@arts.gov.au
Web Site: www.arts.gov.au/literature/lending_rights

International Standard Book Numbering Agency, see ISBN Agency Australia

ISBN Agency Australia
Division of Thorpe-Bowker
Level One, 607 St Kilda Rd, Melbourne, Victoria 3004
Mailing Address: PO Box 6509, St Kilda Rd, Central, Victoria 8008
Tel: (03) 8517 8349; (03) 8517 8333 *Fax:* (03) 8517 8368; (03) 8517 8399
E-mail: customer.service@thorpe.com.au; isbn@thorpe.com.au
Web Site: www.thorpe.com.au; www.myidentifiers.com.au
Key Personnel
ISBN Agency Coordinator: Maria Watt
Publication(s): *Australian Books In Print*

Mardev
Tower 2, 475 Victoria Ave, Chatswood, NSW 2067
Tel: (02) 9422 2644 *Fax:* (02) 9422 2633
E-mail: mardevlists@reedbusiness.com.au
Web Site: www.mardevdm2.com
Global business-to-business marketing data & services.
Branch Office(s)
Plaza 8 @ CBP, One Changi Business Park Crescent, Tower A, No 06-01, Singapore 486025, Singapore *Tel:* 6780 4842 *Fax:* 6588 3866
    E-mail: infoasia@mardevdm2.com
Quadrant House, The Quadrant, Sutton, Surrey SM2 5AS, United Kingdom *Tel:* (020) 8652 4525 *Fax:* (020) 8652 4597 *E-mail:* enquiries@mardevdm2.com
U.S. Office(s): 2000 Clearwater Dr, Oak Brook, IL 60523, United States *Fax:* 303-265-5457
    E-mail: info@mardevm2.com
360 Park Ave S, New York, NY 10010-1710, United States *Tel:* 212-584-9370 *Fax:* 212-584-9371 *E-mail:* sales@mardevdm2.com

Public Lending Right
GPO Box 3241, Canberra, ACT 2601
Tel: (02) 6271 1000 *Toll Free Tel:* 1800 672 842 (Australia only) *Fax:* (02) 6210 2907
E-mail: lendingrights@arts.gov.au
Web Site: www.arts.gov.au/literature/lending_rights

UNILINC Ltd
Level 9, 210 Clarence St, Sydney, NSW 2000
Tel: (02) 9283 1488 *Fax:* (02) 9267 9247
E-mail: info@unilinc.edu.au
Web Site: www.unilinc.edu.au

Austria

Key Personnel
Executive Dir & Chief Executive Officer: Rona Wade *E-mail:* rona.wade@unilinc.edu.au
Associate Dir: Tony Cargnelutti *E-mail:* tony.cargnelutti@unilinc.edu.au
Founded: 1978

Austria

†**CIE (International Commission on Illumination Central Bureau)**
Babenbergerstr 9/9A, 1010 Vienna
Tel: (01) 714 31 87
E-mail: ciecb@cie.co.at
Web Site: www.cie.co.at
Key Personnel
President: Yoshihiro Ohno
Secretary: Teresa Goodman
Treasurer: Richard Distl
Founded: 1913
Exchange of information relating to the science & art of light & lighting, colour & vision, photobiology & image technology.
ISBN Prefix(es): 978-3-901906; 978-3-900734
Number of titles published annually: 15 Print
Total Titles: 200 Print

Fachverband der Buch- und Medienwirtschaft
Wiedner Hauptstr 57, 1040 Vienna
Tel: (05) 90 900-0 *Fax:* (05) 90 900-3043
E-mail: buchwirtschaft@wko.at
Web Site: www.buchwirtschaft.at

Hauptverband des Oesterreichischen Buchhandels (HVB) (Austrian Publishers' & Booksellers' Association)
Gruenangergasse 4, 1010 Vienna
Tel: (01) 512 15 35 *Fax:* (01) 512 84 82
E-mail: sekretariat@hvb.at
Web Site: www.buecher.at
Key Personnel
President: Benedict Foeger *Tel:* (01) 403 35 63 *Fax:* (01) 403 35 63-15 *E-mail:* foeger@czernin-verlag.com
Manager: Dr Inge Kralupper *Tel:* (01) 512 15 35-26 *E-mail:* kralupper@hvb.at
Founded: 1859
Represents the interests of booksellers, publishers, bookshops, wholesalers & publishers' representatives.
Publication(s): *Adressbuch des oesterreichischen Buchhandels* (Directory of Austrian Book Trade); *Anzeiger des oesterreichischen Buchhandels* (Austrian Book Trade Gazette, bimonthly)
Associate Companies: Oesterreichischer Buchhaendlerverband; Oesterreichischer Verlegerverband; Standard Book Numbering Agency; Verband der Antiquare Oesterreichs; Verband der oesterreichischen Buch- und Presse-Grossisten und der Werbenden Zeitschriftenhaendler; Verband von selbstaendigen Verlagsvertretern Oesterreichs

HVB, see Hauptverband des Oesterreichischen Buchhandels (HVB)

†‡**Institut fuer Jugendliteratur**
Mayerhofgasse 6, 1040 Vienna
Tel: (01) 505 03 59 *Fax:* (01) 505 03 59 17
E-mail: office@jugendliteratur.net
Web Site: www.jugendliteratur.net
Key Personnel
Dir: Karin Haller *Tel:* (01) 505 03 59 14
E-mail: karin.haller@jugendliteratur.net
Founded: 1965

Subjects: Children & Youth Literature, Research
Publication(s): *Bookbird* (quarterly, journal); *1000 und 1 Buch* (quarterly, magazine)

International Commission on Illumination Central Bureau, see CIE (International Commission on Illumination Central Bureau)

†◇**International Federation for Information Processing (IFIP)**
Hofstr 3, 2361 Laxenburg
Tel: (02236) 73616 *Fax:* (02236) 73616 9
E-mail: ifip@ifip.org
Web Site: www.ifip.org
Key Personnel
President: Leon Strous
Founded: 1960
Number of titles published annually: 60 Print

Literar-Mechana, Wahrnehmungsgesellschaft fuer Urheberrechte Gesmbh
Linke Wienzeile 18, 1060 Vienna
Tel: (01) 587 21 61 *Fax:* (01) 587 21 61-9
E-mail: office@literar.at
Web Site: www.literar.at
Key Personnel
Management: Dr Sandra Csillag *E-mail:* csillag@literar.at
Consultant: Franz Leo Popp *E-mail:* popp@literar.at
Founded: 1959
Organization for copyright protection.

Standard Book Numbering Agency
c/o Hauptverband des Oesterreichischen Buchhandels (HVB), Gruenangergasse 4, 1010 Vienna
Tel: (01) 512 15 35-14 *Fax:* (01) 512 84 82
E-mail: office@hvb.at
Web Site: www.buecher.at
Key Personnel
Contact: Ulrike Huetter *E-mail:* huetter@hvb.at
ISBN Prefix(es): 978-3-85103

Verband der Antiquare Oesterreichs (Antiquarian Booksellers Association of Austria)
Gruenangergasse 4, 1010 Vienna
Tel: (01) 512 15 35-14 *Fax:* (01) 512 84 82
E-mail: sekretariat@hvb.at
Web Site: www.antiquare.at
Key Personnel
President: Michael Steinbach *E-mail:* michael.steinbach@antiquariat-steinbach.com
Vice President: Dr Paul Kainbacher
Founded: 1949
Membership(s): International League of Antiquarian Booksellers.
Publication(s): *Anzeiger des Verbandes der Antiquare Oesterreichs* (Austrian Antiquarian Booksellers' Association Gazette)

Bangladesh

National Library of Bangladesh, Directorate of Archives & Libraries
32, Justice S M Murshed Sarani, Agargaon, Dhaka 1207
Tel: (02) 9129992 *Fax:* (02) 9135709
Web Site: www.nanl.gov.bd
Key Personnel
Dir: Wadudul Bari Chowdhury
E-mail: nanldirector@gmail.com
Chief Bibliographer & Deputy Dir, Library: Shahab Uddin Khan *Tel:* (02) 9127142
E-mail: ddnlbd@gmail.com

Deputy Dir, Archives: Haris Sarker *Tel:* (02) 9138053 *E-mail:* dd@nab.gov.bd
Founded: 1972

Standard Book Numbering Agency, see National Library of Bangladesh, Directorate of Archives & Libraries

Belarus

National Book Chamber of Belarus
31a, V Khoruzhei str, Room 707, 220002 Minsk
Tel: (017) 288-67-15; (017) 334-78-40 *Fax:* (017) 283-29-60
E-mail: palata@natbook.org.by
Web Site: natbook.org.by
Key Personnel
Dir: Elena V Ivanova *Tel:* (017) 283-19-14
E-mail: elvit@natbook.org.by
Deputy Dir: Alena I Yarmolich *Tel:* (017) 334-78-47 *E-mail:* ermolich@natbook.org.by
Founded: 1924

Standard Book Numbering Agency, see National Book Chamber of Belarus

Belgium

ADEB, see Association des Editeurs Belges (ADEB)

Association des Editeurs Belges (ADEB) (Belgian Publishers' Association)
Av R Vandendriessche 18 boite 19, 1150 Brussels
Tel: (02) 241 65 80 *Fax:* (02) 216 71 31
E-mail: adeb@adeb.be
Web Site: www.adeb.be
Key Personnel
Dir: Bernard Gerard
Publication(s): *Statistiques de Production du Livre Belge de Langue Francaise*

Boek.be
Te Boelaerlei 37, 2140 Borgerhout
Tel: (03) 230 89 23 *Fax:* (03) 281 22 40
E-mail: info@boek.be
Web Site: www.boek.be
Key Personnel
Chairman: Karel De Boeck
Mng Dir: Andre Vandorpe
Marketing Manager: Annemie Speybrouck
Founded: 1929
Trade association of Flemish booksellers, publishers & distributors.
Association for the promotion of Dutch language books & books from Flanders.

†‡**The Centre for European Policy Studies (CEPS)**
One Pl du Congres, 1000 Brussels
Tel: (02) 229 39 11 *Fax:* (02) 706 56 26
E-mail: info@ceps.eu
Web Site: www.ceps.eu
Key Personnel
Chief Executive Officer: Karel Lannoo *Tel:* (02) 229 39 82 *E-mail:* karel.lannoo@ceps.eu
Dir: Daniel Gros *Tel:* (02) 229 39 38
E-mail: danielg@ceps.eu
Dir, Communications, Corporate & External Relations: Kerstin Born-Sirkel *Tel:* (02) 229 39 10
E-mail: kerstin.born@ceps.eu

Head, Communications: Marco Incorti *Tel:* (02) 229 39 70 *E-mail:* marco.incorti@ceps.eu
Head, Finances & Administration: Sally Scott *Tel:* (02) 229 39 54 *E-mail:* sally.scott@ceps.eu
Editor: Anne Harrington *Tel:* (02) 229 39 59 *E-mail:* anne.harrington@ceps.eu; Jackie West *Tel:* (02) 229 39 29 *E-mail:* jackie.west@ceps.eu
Founded: 1983
Subjects: Business, Economics, Politics

CEPS, see The Centre for European Policy Studies (CEPS)

EIBF, see European & International Booksellers Federation (EIBF)

†◇European & International Booksellers Federation (EIBF)
Rue de la Science 10, 1000 Brussels
Tel: (02) 223 49 40
E-mail: info@europeanbooksellers.eu; info@eibf-booksellers.org
Web Site: www.europeanbooksellers.eu
Key Personnel
Co-President: Fabian Paagman *E-mail:* fabian.paagman@europeanbooksellers.eu; Jean Luc Treutenaere *E-mail:* jl.treutenaere@europeanbooksellers.eu
Treasurer: Juancho Pons *E-mail:* juancho@libreriapons-zaragoza.com
Dir: Fran Dubruille *E-mail:* fran@europeanbooksellers.eu

†◇Federation of European Publishers (FEP) (Federation des Editeurs Europeens)
31 rue Montoyer Box 8, 1000 Brussels
Tel: (02) 770 11 10 *Fax:* (02) 771 20 71
E-mail: info@fep-fee.eu
Web Site: www.fep-fee.eu
Key Personnel
President: Pierre Dutilleul
Vice President: Henrique Mota
Treasurer: Rudy Vanschoonbeek
Dir General: Anne Bergman-Tahon *E-mail:* abergman@fep-fee.eu
Deputy Dir: Enrico Turrin *E-mail:* eturrin@fep-fee.eu
Founded: 1967
The Federation consists of the book associations of the European Communities & European Economic Area (EEA) & aims at representing jointly the interests of the European publishers for all matters arising from the Treaty of Rome, Maastricht & Amsterdam & Nice (or the Treaties).

FEP, see Federation of European Publishers (FEP)

†◇FIAF (International Federation of Film Archives) (Federation Internationale des Archives du Film)
Rue Blanche 42, 1060 Brussels
Tel: (02) 538 3065 *Fax:* (02) 534 4774
E-mail: info@fiafnet.org
Web Site: www.fiafnet.org
Key Personnel
President: Eric Le Roy *E-mail:* president@fiafnet.org
Secretary General: Michael Loebenstein
Treasurer: Jon Wengstrom
Senior Administrator: Christophe Dupin *E-mail:* c.dupin@fiafnet.org
Founded: 1938
Dedicated to the rescue, collection, preservation & screening of moving images.
Publication(s): *Bibliography of National Filmographies*; *Glossary of Filmographic Terms, Version II*; *Handbook for Film Archives*; *Handling, Storage & Transport of Cellulose Nitrate Film*;

International Film Archive Database; *The International Index to Film Periodicals*; *Journal of Film Preservation*; *Moving Image Cataloguing Manual*; *Preservation & Restoration of Moving Images & Sound*; *Technical Manual of the FIAF Preservation Commission*

IFRRO, see International Federation of Reproduction Rights Organisations (IFRRO)

International Federation of Film Archives, see FIAF (International Federation of Film Archives)

†◇International Federation of Reproduction Rights Organisations (IFRRO)
Rue du Prince Royal 85, 1050 Brussels
Tel: (02) 234 62 60 *Fax:* (02) 234 62 69
E-mail: secretariat@ifrro.org
Web Site: www.ifrro.org
Key Personnel
President: Rainer Just
Vice President: Yngve Slettholm; Jim Alexander
Chief Executive & Secretary General: Olav Stokkmo *E-mail:* olav.stokkmo@ifrro.be
Communications & Information Officer: Veraliah Bueno *E-mail:* veraliah.bueno@ifrro.be
IFRRO links together all national Reproduction Rights Organizations (RROs) & national & international associations of rightsholders. RROs are organizations engaged in the conveyance of photocopying authorizations & royalties between rightsholders & users. IFRRO's purposes are to foster the creation of RROs worldwide; to facilitate the development of formal agreements & informal relationships between, among & on behalf of its members; & to increase public awareness of copyright & the need for effective mechanisms for conveying rights & royalties between rightsholders & users.

Ministere de la Communaute Francaise - Service de la Promotion des Lettres
Blvd Leopold II, 44, 1080 Brussels
Tel: (02) 413 23 21 *Fax:* (02) 413 28 94
E-mail: secretariat.promolettres@cfwb.be
Web Site: www.promotiondeslettres.cfwb.be
Key Personnel
Dir: Nadine Van Welkenhuyzen *E-mail:* nadine.vanwelkenhuyzen@cfwb.be
Secretary: Anne Pirson *Tel:* (02) 413 21 95 *E-mail:* anne.pirson@cfwb.be
Assists in the creation, editing & dissemination of French literature in Belgium.

†‡SIGNIS-World Catholic Association for Communication (L'Association Catholique Mondiale pour la Communication)
310, rue Royale, 1210 Brussels
Tel: (02) 7349708 *Fax:* (02) 7347018
E-mail: sg@signis.net
Web Site: www.signis.net
Key Personnel
President: Gustavo Andujar
Vice President: Frank Frost; Lawrence John Sinniah
Acting Secretary General: Ricardo Yanez
Dir, Communication: Guido Convents
Founded: 1928
Subjects: African Cinema, Cinema & Religion, Video & Religion, World Cinema
Publication(s): *SIGNIS Media* (6 issues/yr, magazine)
ISBN Prefix(es): 978-92-9080

†‡Tantalum-Niobium International Study Center (TIC)
Chaussee de Louvain 490, 1380 Lasne
Tel: (02) 649 51 58 *Fax:* (02) 649 64 47
Web Site: www.tanb.org

Founded: 1974
Subjects: Metals
ISBN Prefix(es): 978-92-9093

TIC, see Tantalum-Niobium International Study Center (TIC)

Vlaams Fonds voor de Letteren (Flemish Literature Fund)
Generaal van Merlenstr 30, 2600 Berchem
Tel: (03) 270 31 61 *Fax:* (03) 270 31 60
E-mail: info@vfl.be
Web Site: www.vfl.be
Key Personnel
Dir: Koen Van Bockstal *E-mail:* koen.vanbockstal@vfl.be
Administrator: Koen De Smedt *E-mail:* koen.desmedt@vfl.be
Founded: 1999
Supports Dutch literature & translation abroad.
Publication(s): *Alle poezie dateert van vandaag*; *Buiten de lijntjes gekleurd - het boek*; *Letteren in de wereld van vandaag en morgen - Aanzetten tot een meerjarenplan 2011-2015*; *Omzien en vooruitblikken - meerjarenplan 2005-2009*; *Overigens schitterend vertaald*; *Pizza Peperkoek & andere geheimen*; *De smaak van het geluid van het hart*; *Dat spreekt boekdelen - 10 jaar Vlaams Fonds voor de Letteren*; *Verwondingen (Paul Bogaert)*; *Zin in letteren*

Vlaamse Uitgevers Vereniging (VUV) (Flemish Publishers Association)
Huis van het Boek, Te Boelaerlei 37, 2140 Borgerhout
Tel: (03) 230 89 23
Web Site: www.boekenvak.be/voor-uitgevers/vlaamse-uitgeversvereniging
Key Personnel
Chief Executive Officer: Geert Van den Bossche *Tel:* (03) 287 66 91 *E-mail:* geert.vandenbossche@boek.be

VUV, see Vlaamse Uitgevers Vereniging (VUV)

Benin

Afrilivres
09 BP 92, Cotonou
Tel: 64 41 79 65
E-mail: contact@afrilivres.net
Web Site: www.afrilivres.net
Key Personnel
President: Marie Michele Razafintsalana
Secretary: Phocas Ekouedjin
Founded: 2002

Bolivia

Agencia Boliviana del ISBN
Camara Boliviana del Libro, Calle Capitan Ravelo 2116, 682 La Paz
Tel: (02) 2113264 *Fax:* (02) 2444077
E-mail: isbn@camaralibrolapaz.org.bo
Web Site: www.cabolib.org.bo
Key Personnel
Contact: L Marlene Perez S *E-mail:* lperez@camaralibrolapaz.org.bo

Camara Boliviana del Libro (Bolivian Book Association)
Calle Capitan Ravelo 2116, 682 La Paz
Tel: (02) 2113264

E-mail: litexsa@entelnet.com.bo
Web Site: www.cabolib.org.bo
Key Personnel
President: Carla Maria Berdegue
General Manager: Ana Patricia Navarro
Founded: 1945

Standard Book Numbering Agency, see
Agencia Boliviana del ISBN

Botswana

Botswana National Library Service
National Reference Library, Private Bag 0036,
Gaborone
Tel: 3704555; 3704546 *Fax:* 3901149
Web Site: www.gov.bw
Key Personnel
Contact: Ms Neo Mosweu

Standard Book Numbering Agency, see
Botswana National Library Service

Brazil

ABEU, see Associacao Brasileira dar Editoras
Universitarias (ABEU)

Agencia Brasileira do ISBN
Rua Debret, 23 sala 803 Centro, 20030-080 Rio
de Janeiro-RJ
Tel: (021) 2220-1683; (021) 2220-1707; (021)
2220-1981 *Fax:* (021) 2220-1702
E-mail: isbn@bn.gov.br
Web Site: www.isbn.bn.br

**Associacao Brasileira dar Editoras
Universitarias (ABEU)** (Brazilian Association
of University Publishers)
Rua Av Fagundes Filho, 77-Sala 24, Vila Monte
Alegre, 04304-010 Sao Paulo-SP
Tel: (011) 5078-8826
E-mail: abeu@abeu.org.br
Web Site: www.abeu.org.br
Key Personnel
President: Marcelo Martins Luciano Di Renzo
Tel: (013) 3228-1236 *E-mail:* mdirenzo@
unisantos.br
Vice President: Nair Maria Di Oliveira *Tel:* (062)
3946-1814 *E-mail:* editora@pucgoias.edu.br
Executive Secretary: Anibal Francisco
Alves Braganca *Tel:* (021) 2629-5287
E-mail: anibalbraganca@id.uff.br
Founded: 1987
Publication(s): *Catalogo unificado da ABEU; Tit-
ulos Da Colecao Nordestina; Revista VERBO*

Camara Brasileira do Livro (CBL) (Brazilian
Book Association)
Rua Cristiano Viana, 91, Jardim Paulista, 05411-
000 Sao Paulo-SP
Tel: (011) 3069-1300 *Fax:* (011) 3069-1300
E-mail: cbl@cbl.org.br
Web Site: www.cbl.org.br
Key Personnel
President: Luis Antonio Torelli
Vice President, Communication: Luciano Mon-
teiro
Administrative Vice President, Financial: Vitor
Tavares da Silva Filho
Founded: 1946

Meet the larger goals of its members & expand
the book market through the democratization of
access to books & promoting efforts to disseminate & encourage reading.

CBL, see Camara Brasileira do Livro (CBL)

**Fundacao Nacional do Livro Infantil e Juvenil
(FNLIJ)**
Rua de Impresa, 16/1212 a 1215, 20030-120 Rio
de Janeiro-RJ
Tel: (021) 2262-9130 *Fax:* (021) 2240-6649
E-mail: informacao@fnlij.org.br
Web Site: www.fnlij.org.br
Founded: 1968
Promotion of quality books for children & young
people, defending the right of reading for all
through school, public & community libraries.
Brazilian section of IBBY.

**Sindicato Nacional dos Editores de Livros
(SNEL)** (National Association of Book
Publishers)
Rua da Ajuda, 35 - 18° andar, 20040-000 Rio de
Janeiro-RJ
Tel: (021) 2533-0399 *Fax:* (021) 2533-0422
E-mail: snel@snel.org.br
Web Site: www.snel.org.br
Key Personnel
President: Marcos Da Veiga Pereira *Tel:* (021)
2538-4104 *Fax:* (021) 2286-9422
Vice President, Administrative: Mariana Za-
har Ribeiro *Tel:* (021) 99415-2181 (cell)
E-mail: mariana@zahar.com.br
Vice President, Technical: Mauro Koogan Lorch
Tel: (021) 3543-0770 *Fax:* (021) 2252-2732
E-mail: mlorch@grupogen.com.br
Mng Secretary: Eduardo Salomao *Tel:* (021)
99996-3205 (cell) *E-mail:* eduardo@
imagoeditora.com.br
Dir, Communications: Martha Ribas de Faria
Tel: (021) 2222-3167 *E-mail:* martha@
casadapalavra.com.br
Founded: 1941
Publication(s): *Informativo Bibliografico* (annu-
ally); *Jornal do SNEL* (bimonthly); *Producao
Editorial Brasileira* (Brazilian Publishing Out-
put, annually)
Branch Office(s)
Ave Angelica, 2530-Conjunto 43, 01228-200
Higienopolis, Sao Paulo-SP *Tel:* (011) 5051-
5424 *Fax:* (011) 5052-9582 *E-mail:* snelsp@
snel.org.br

SNEL, see Sindicato Nacional dos Editores de
Livros (SNEL)

Standard Book Numbering Agency, see
Agencia Brasileira do ISBN

Brunei

**Pusat Kebangsaan ISBN, Literature Bureau
Library Section**
Perpustakaan, Dewan Bahasa Dan Pustaka, Jl
Elizabeth II, Bandar Seri Begawan, Negara BS
8711
Tel: 2222135; 2235501 *Fax:* 2224763
E-mail: isbn.brunei@hotmail.com
Web Site: www.dpplibrary.gov.bn
Key Personnel
Contact: Hajah Masdiana

Standard Book Numbering Agency, see Pusat
Kebangsaan ISBN, Literature Bureau Library
Section

Bulgaria

Bulgarian National ISSN Centre
c/o Saints Cyril & Methodius National Library,
88 Vassil Levski Blvd, 1037 Sofia
Tel: (02) 918 32 18 *Fax:* (02) 843 54 95
E-mail: issn@nationallibrary.bg
Web Site: www.nationallibrary.bg
Key Personnel
Contact: Radoslava Stefanova
Founded: 1972

National ISBN Agency
c/o Saints Cyril & Methodius National Library,
88 Vassil Levski Blvd, 1037 Sofia
Tel: (02) 946 11 43; (02) 918 32 19 *Fax:* (02)
843 54 95
E-mail: isbn@nationallibrary.bg
Web Site: www.nationallibrary.bg
Key Personnel
Contact: Polina Simova
Founded: 1991
Publication(s): *Spravocnik na izdatelstva, redakcii
i pecatnici v Baelgariji* (annually, directory)

Standard Book Numbering Agency, see
National ISBN Agency

Union of Publishers in Bulgaria
Blvd G M Dimitrov 36, 1797 Sofia
Tel: (089) 9910374 (cell)
E-mail: office@sib.bg
Web Site: sib.bg
Membership(s): European Newspaper Publishers'
Association; World Association of Newspapers.

Cameroon

IFORD, see Institut de Formation et de
Recherche Demographiques (IFORD)

**†‡Institut de Formation et de Recherche
Demographiques (IFORD)** (Institute for
Demographic Training & Research)
BP 1556, Yaounde
Tel: 222 23 29 47; 222 03 44 12 *Fax:* 222 22 68
93
E-mail: iford@iford-cm.org
Web Site: www.iford-cm.org
Key Personnel
Executive Dir: Prof Evina Akam
Founded: 1971
Provides training in population sciences, research
on population issues & technical support to
member countries & partners.
ISBN Prefix(es): 978-2-905327

PAID-WA, see Pan African Institute for
Development-West Africa (PAID-WA)

**†Pan African Institute for Development-West
Africa (PAID-WA)** (Institut Panafricain pour le
Development)
PO Box 133, Buea
Tel: 6750 905 12; 2333 234 15
E-mail: info.wa@paidafrica.org; paidwaorg@
hotmail.com
Web Site: www.paidwa.org
Key Personnel
Regional Dir: Uwem Essia, PhD *E-mail:* essia.
uwem@paidafrica.org
Founded: 1964
Subjects: Rural Development
Publication(s): *An Integrated Approach to Rural
Development* (IRD); *Leadership for Sustain-*

able Health Service Delivery in the Context of HIV & AIDS; PAID-WA Institutional Policy on HIV/AIDS; PAID-WA Prospectus; The Rationale for Training & Development in Contemporary Organizations; Sustainable Development Strategies

Chile

Agencia Chilena ISBN
c/o Camara Chilena del Libro AG, Av Alameda del Libertador Bernardo O'Higgins 1370, Oficina 502, Santiago
Tel: (02) 672 0348 *Fax:* (02) 687 4271
E-mail: isbnchile@tie.cl
Web Site: camaradellibro.cl; www.isbnchile.cl
Publication(s): *Catalogo ISBN Libros Chilenos (Ultima Publicacion 1996)*

Camara Chilena del Libro AG
Av Libertador Bernardo O'Higgins 1370, Oficina 501, Santiago
Tel: (02) 672 0348 *Fax:* (02) 687 4271
E-mail: camaralibrochile@camaradellibro.cl
Web Site: camaradellibro.cl
Key Personnel
President: Alejandro Melo
Vice President: Eduardo Albers
Secretary: Ricardo Bernasconi
Treasurer: Norgia Nino
Founded: 1950
Chilean Association of Publishers, Distributors & Booksellers. Also acts as Standard Book Numbering Agency.

CELADE - Division de Poblacion - CEPAL, see Centro Latinoamericano y Caribeno de Demografia CELADE - Division de Poblacion - CEPAL - Naciones Unidas

†‡Centro Latinoamericano y Caribeno de Demografia CELADE - Division de Poblacion - CEPAL - Naciones Unidas (Latin American & Caribbean Demographic Center CELADE - Population Divison - CEPAL - United Nations)
Casilla 179 D, Santiago
Tel: (02) 210 2726 *Fax:* (02) 208 0252
E-mail: celade@cepal.org
Web Site: www.cepal.org
Key Personnel
Dir: Dirk Jaspers-Faijer
Founded: 1967
Subjects: Demography, Periodicals, Population Information & Data Processing, Sociology, Statistics
Publication(s): *Boletin Demografico* (biennially); *Notas de Poblacion* (biennially)

Prolibro SA, see Camara Chilena del Libro AG

Standard Book Numbering Agency, see Agencia Chilena ISBN

China

China ISBN Agency
10 Xianxiao Hutong, Room 305, Dongcheng District, Beijing 100005
Tel: (010) 58689857 *Fax:* (010) 58689995
E-mail: chinaisbn@163.com
Web Site: www.capub.cn

SPPA, see State Press & Publication Administration (SPPA)

Standard Book Numbering Agency, see China ISBN Agency

State Press & Publication Administration (SPPA)
85 Dongsi Nandajie, Dongcheng District, Beijing 100703
Tel: (010) 6512-4433 (ext 2708) *Fax:* (010) 6528-0038
Key Personnel
Dir: Yu Youxian
Dir, Foreign Affairs: Meng Chuanliang

Colombia

Agencia Colombiana del ISBN (Colombian ISBN Agency)
c/o Camara Colombiana del Libro, Calle 35 N 5A-05, Bogota
Tel: (01) 323 0111 (ext 116); (01) 323 0111 (ext 108) *Fax:* (01) 285 1082
E-mail: agenciaisbn@camlibro.com.co
Web Site: www.camlibro.com.co
Key Personnel
ISBN Agency Coordinator: Marcela Borbon Bolivar *E-mail:* mborbon@camlibro.com.co
Publication(s): *Libros Registrados En Colombia; Periodico Tinta Fresca*

Camara Colombiana del Libro (Colombian Book Association)
Calle 35 N 5A-05, Bogota
Tel: (01) 323 0111 *Fax:* (01) 285 1082
E-mail: camlibro@camlibro.com.co
Web Site: www.camlibro.com.co
Key Personnel
President: Enrique Gonzalez Villa
Secretary General: Manuel Jose Sarmient Ramirez
Administrative & Financial Coordinator: Omar Castro *E-mail:* ocastro@camlibro.com.co
Founded: 1951
Associate Companies: Agencia Colombiana del ISBN
Branch Office(s)
Camara Colombiana del Libro Seccional Occidente

†◇Centro Regional para el Fomento del Libro en America Latina y el Caribe (CERLALC) (Regional Center for the Promotion of Books in Latin America & the Caribbean)
Calle 70 No 9-52, Bogota
Tel: (01) 540 20 71 *Fax:* (01) 541 63 98
E-mail: libro@cerlalc.org
Web Site: cerlalc.org/es
Key Personnel
Dir: Marianne Ponsford *E-mail:* mponsford@cerlalc.org
Dir, Publications: Jose Diego Gonzalez *E-mail:* jgonzalez@cerlalc.org
Founded: 1971
Promotion of production & circulation of books, promoting reading & writing & the encouragement & protection of intellectual creation.
ISBN Prefix(es): 978-92-9057; 978-958-671

CERLALC, see Centro Regional para el Fomento del Libro en America Latina y el Caribe (CERLALC)

Standard Book Numbering Agency, see Agencia Colombiana del ISBN

Costa Rica

Biblioteca Nacion Miguel Abregon Lizano
Calles 15 y 17 Ave, 3 y 3B, 1000 San Jose
Fax: 2233-17-06
E-mail: isbn@sinabi.go.cr
Web Site: www.sinabi.go.cr
Key Personnel
ISBN Coordinator: Susan Coronado Zamora

IICA, see Instituto Interamericano de Cooperacion para la Agricultura (IICA)

†‡Instituto Interamericano de Cooperacion para la Agricultura (IICA) (Inter-American Institute for Cooperation on Agriculture)
600 m Norte del Cruce Ipís-Coronado, 2200 San Isidro de Coronado, San Jose
Mailing Address: Apdo 55, 2200 San Isidro de Coronado, San Jose
Tel: 2216-0222 *Fax:* 2216-0233
E-mail: iicahq@iica.int
Web Site: www.iica.int
Key Personnel
Dir General: Dr Victor M Villalobos
Founded: 1942
ISBN Prefix(es): 978-92-9039

Standard Book Numbering Agency, see Biblioteca Nacion Miguel Abregon Lizano

Croatia

†Croatian ISBN Agency (Hrvatski ured za ISBN)
c/o Nacionalna i sveucilisna knjiznica u Zagrebu, Hrvatske bratske zajednice 4, 10000 Zagreb
Tel: (01) 616 4288 *Fax:* (01) 616 4186
E-mail: isbn@nsk.hr
Web Site: www.nsk.hr/isbn
Key Personnel
Contact: Danijela Getliher *E-mail:* dgetliher@nsk.hr; Linda Karas; Jelena Pauric *E-mail:* jpauric@nsk.hr
Founded: 1992

Standard Book Numbering Agency, see Croatian ISBN Agency

Cuba

Agencia Cubana del ISBN
Camara Cubana del Libro, Calle 15, no 602, esq C, CP 10400 El Vedado, Havana
Tel: (07) 832 9526; (07) 832 9527; (07) 832 9528; (07) 832 9529; (07) 832 8829 *Fax:* (07) 833 3441
E-mail: isbn@cubarte.cult.cu; isbn@ccl.cult.cu
Web Site: www.isbncuba.cult.cu
Key Personnel
Contact: Ms Wally Thompson
Founded: 1991

Standard Book Numbering Agency, see Agencia Cubana del ISBN

UNEAC, see Union de Escritores y Artistas de Cuba (UNEAC)

Union de Escritores y Artistas de Cuba
   (UNEAC) (Union of Writers & Artists of
   Cuba)
Calle 17 No 354, entre G y H, El Vedado, CP
   10400 Havana
Tel: (07) 8324551
E-mail: escritores@uneac.co.cu
Web Site: www.uneac.org.cu
Key Personnel
President: Miguel Barnet Lanza
Senior Vice President: Luis Morlote Rivas
Founded: 1961
Publication(s): *La Gaceta de Cuba* (bimonthly,
   magazine)

Curacao

Bureau for Intellectual Property
Berg Carmelweg 10-A, Willemstad
Tel: (09) 465 7800 *Fax:* (09) 465 7815
E-mail: director@bureau-intellectual-property.cw;
   info@bip.cw
Web Site: www.bip.cw
Founded: 1893
Trademarks, copyright & patent registration.
Number of titles published annually: 161 Print
Total Titles: 296 Print

Cyprus

Cyprus Registration Center
c/o The Cyprus Library, Eleftheria Sq, 1011
   Nicosia
Tel: 22818431; 22818429 *Fax:* 22304532
E-mail: isbncentre48@yahoo.gr
Web Site: www.cypruslibrary.gov.cy
Key Personnel
Contact: Eleni Ioannou
Founded: 1987
Membership(s): International Federation of Li-
   brary Associations & Institutions (IFLA).

Standard Book Numbering Agency, see Cyprus
   Registration Center

Czech Republic

ACBP, see Svaz ceskych knihkupcu a nakladatelu
   (SCKN)

Ceske Narodni Stredisko ISSN (Czech ISSN
   National Center)
National Technical Library, Technicka 6/2710,
   160 80 Prague 6
Mailing Address: PO Box 79, 160 00 Prague 6
Tel: 232 002 440; 232 002 470
E-mail: issn@techlib.cz
Web Site: www.issn.cz
Key Personnel
Contact: Jaroslava Trckova *E-mail:* jaroslava.
   trckova@techlib.cz

Ministry of Culture of the Czech Republic,
   Literature & Libraries Division
Maltezske nam 1, 118 11 Prague 1
Tel: 257 085 111 *Fax:* 224 318 155
E-mail: epodatelna@mkcr.cz
Web Site: www.mkcr.cz

Key Personnel
Dir & Manager: Milan Nemecek, PhD *Tel:* 257
   085 214
Publication(s): *Books in Czech Republic*

Narodni agentura ISBN v CR
Narodni Knihovna Ceske Republiky, Kle-
   mentinum 190, 110 00 Prague 1
Tel: 221 663 306
E-mail: isbn@nkp.cz
Web Site: www.nkp.cz
Key Personnel
ISBN Administrator: Mr Antonin Jerabek
   E-mail: antonin.jerabek@nkp.cz

SCKN, see Svaz ceskych knihkupcu a
   nakladatelu (SCKN)

Standard Book Numbering Agency, see
   Narodni agentura ISBN v CR

Svaz ceskych knihkupcu a nakladatelu (SCKN)
   (Association of Czech Booksellers &
   Publishers (ACBP))
Drtinova 557/10, 150 00 Prague 5
Tel: 227 018 335
E-mail: sckn@sckn.cz
Web Site: www.sckn.cz
Key Personnel
Executive Secretary: Marcela Tureckova
   E-mail: tureckova@sckn.cz
Founded: 1879 (renewed 1990)
Membership(s): European Bookshops Federa-
   tion (EBF); Federation of European Publishers
   (FEP); IPA.
Publication(s): *Bookseller & Publisher* (Knihku-
   pec a nakladatel, monthly); *Czech Books In
   Print (Katalog kladovanych Knih)* (annually)
ISBN Prefix(es): 978-80-902495
Associate Companies: Svet knihy S R O (Book
   World Ltd), Fugnerovo nam 3, 120 00 Prague,
   Executive Dir: Dana Kalinova *Tel:* 224
   498 236; 224 498 464 *Fax:* 224 498 754
   E-mail: info@svetknihy.cz *Web Site:* www.
   svetknihy.cz

Denmark

Boghandlerforeningen (The Danish Booksellers
   Association)
Slotsholmsgade 1B, 1216 Copenhagen K
Mailing Address: Borsen, 1217 Copenhagen K
Tel: 3254 2255
E-mail: ddb@bogpost.dk; redaktionen@bogpost.
   dk
Web Site: www.boghandlerforeningen.dk
Key Personnel
Dir: Bo Dybkaer *E-mail:* bo@bogpost.dk
Membership(s): European Booksellers Federation
   (EBF); International Booksellers Federation
   (IBF).

Danish Arts Foundation
H C Andersens Blvd 2, 1553 Copenhagen V
Tel: 33 95 42 00; 33 73 33 73
E-mail: post@slks.dk
Web Site: www.kunst.dk
Key Personnel
Literature: Lars Sidenius *Tel:* 33 74 50 68
   E-mail: lsi@kulturstyrelsen.dk
To support collaboration between Danish & inter-
   national artists & art institutions.

Dansk ISBN - Kontor (the Danish ISBN
   Agency)
Dansk Biblioteks Center, Tempovej 7-11, 2750
   Ballerup

Tel: 44 86 77 79 *Fax:* 44 86 76 93
E-mail: isbn@dbc.dk
Web Site: www.isbn.dk
Key Personnel
Contact: Inga Jensen *E-mail:* ij@dbc.dk

Danske Forlag (Danish Publishers)
Borsen, 1217 Copenhagen K
Tel: 33 15 66 88
E-mail: info@danskeforlag.dk; info@
   danishpublishers.dk
Web Site: www.danskeforlag.dk
Key Personnel
Dir: Christine Bodtcher-Hansen *E-mail:* cbh@
   danskeforlag.dk
Founded: 1837
Publication(s): *Det Danske Bogmarked* (The Dan-
   ish Book Market with Den Danske Boghan-
   dlerforening); *Fortegnelse over Samhandels
   berettigede Boghandlere MV* (Register of Li-
   censed Booksellers, etc)

Forening for Boghaandvaerk (Association of
   Book Crafts)
c/o Det Kongelige Bibliotek Diamantinformatio-
   nen, Soren Kierkegaard Plads 1, 1219 Copen-
   hagen K
Mailing Address: Postboks 2149, 1016 Copen-
   hagen K
Tel: 91 324 546
Web Site: www.boghaandvaerk.dk
Key Personnel
Chairman: Erland Kolding Nielsen
Secretary: Mads Brunsgaard *E-mail:* mad@kb.dk
Founded: 1888
Publication(s): *Bogvennen* (The Book Lover, year-
   book)

Standard Book Numbering Agency, see Dansk
   ISBN - Kontor (the Danish ISBN Agency)

Dominican Republic

Sociedad Dominicana de Bibliofilos Inc
   (Dominican Bibliophile Society)
Calle Las Damas No 106, Zona Colonial, Santo
   Domingo
Tel: (809) 687-6655; (809) 687-6644 *Fax:* (809)
   221-5568
E-mail: info@bibliofilos.org.do
Web Site: bibliofilos.org/do
To promote & preserve Dominican culture
   through the preservation & dissemination of
   books & other publications.

Ecuador

Agencia Ecuatoriana del ISBN, see Camara
   Ecuatoriana del Libro

Camara Ecuatoriana del Libro
Av Eloy Alfaro N29-61 e Inglaterra, Edf Eloy
   Alfaro, 9 no piso, Quito
Tel: (02) 2553311; (02) 2553314 *Fax:* (02)
   2222150
E-mail: celnp@uio.satnet.net; isbn@celibro.org.ec
Web Site: www.celibro.org.ec
Key Personnel
President: Fabian Luzuriaga *E-mail:* fabianluzu@
   gmail.com
Vice President: Oswaldo Almeida
   E-mail: oswaldo_a@oceano.com.ec

Secretary: Vicente Velasquez
Treasurer: Milton Ordonez
Founded: 1978

Standard Book Numbering Agency, see Camara
Ecuatoriana del Libro

Egypt

Arab Publishers' Association
Saridar Tower, 2nd floor, 92 Tahrir St, Dokki,
Giza
Tel: (02) 37622058 *Fax:* (02) 37622058
E-mail: nmahmoud@arab-pa.org
Web Site: www.arab-pa.org
Key Personnel
President: Mohammed Rashad *Tel:* (02) 23910250
Fax: (02) 23909618 *E-mail:* president@arab-
pa.org
General Secretary: Mohamed Ali Abd-Elhafiz
Baydoun *Tel:* (01) 5804810-1 *Fax:* (01)
5804813 *E-mail:* mabaydoun@arab-pa.org
Founded: 1995

GEBO, see General Egyptian Book Organization
(GEBO)

General Egyptian Book Organization (GEBO)
1193 Cornich el Nil, Boulaq, Cairo 11511
Mailing Address: PO Box 235, Cairo 11794
Tel: (02) 25775646; (02) 25775109; (02)
25775371; (02) 25775228 *Fax:* (02) 25789316;
(02) 25754213
E-mail: info@gebo.gov.eg
Web Site: www.gebo.gov.eg
Key Personnel
Chairman: Dr Haytham El Hajaly
Founded: 1961
Also publisher.
ISBN Prefix(es): 978-977-01

Estonia

Eesti Lastekirjanduse Keskus (Estonian
Children's Literature Centre)
Pikk 73, 10133 Tallinn
Tel: 6177236
E-mail: elk@elk.ee
Web Site: www.elk.ee
Key Personnel
Dir: Triin Soone *Tel:* 6177230 *E-mail:* triin.
soone@elk.ee
Associate Dir: Krista Ruuse *Tel:* 6177231
Founded: 1933
Information, training & research center of chil-
dren's literature.

Estonian ISBN Agency
Eesti Rahvusraamatukogu, National Library of
Estonia, Tonismagi 2, 15189 Tallinn
Tel: 630 7372 *Fax:* 631 1200
E-mail: isbn@nlib.ee
Web Site: www.nlib.ee/isbn
Key Personnel
Contact: Mai Valtna *Tel:* 630 7374 *E-mail:* mai.
valtna@nlib.ee
Founded: 1992

Estonian Publishers Association (Eesti
Kirjastuste Liit)
Roosikrantsi 6, 10119 Tallinn
Tel: 644 9866

E-mail: kirjastusteliit@eki.ee
Web Site: estbook.com
Key Personnel
Mng Dir: Kaidi Urmet
Founded: 1991
Membership(s): Federation of European Publish-
ers; IBBY, Estonian section.

Standard Book Numbering Agency, see
Estonian ISBN Agency

Ethiopia

†‡**United Nations Economic Commission for
Africa, ECA**
Menelik II Ave, Addis Ababa
Mailing Address: PO Box 3001, Addis Ababa
Tel: (011) 544-3336; (011) 544-5000 *Fax:* (011)
551-4416
E-mail: ecainfo@uneca.org
Web Site: www.uneca.org
Key Personnel
Executive Secretary: Dr Carlos Lopes
Founded: 1958

Faroe Islands

Farlit
Bokamiosolan a Hjalla 7B, FO100 Torshavn
E-mail: farlit@farlit.fo
Web Site: farlit.fo
Key Personnel
Literary Coordinator: Urd Johannesen
Promotes contemporary Faroese literature on the
international book market.

Foroya Landsbokasavn (National Library of the
Faroe Islands)
J C Svabosgotu 16, FO110 Torshavn
Mailing Address: PO Box 61, FO110 Torshavn
Tel: 34 05 25 *Fax:* 34 05 27
E-mail: savn@savn.fo
Web Site: savn.fo/00008/00045
Key Personnel
National Deputy Librarian: Laura Vinther *Tel:* 34
05 16 *E-mail:* laurav@savn.fo
Founded: 1828

Standard Book Numbering Agency, see Foroya
Landsbokasavn

Fiji

Regional ISBN Agency for the South Pacific
The University of the South Pacific Library, Lau-
cala Campus, Suva
Tel: 323 2286; 323 2402; 323 2050 *Fax:* 323
1528
E-mail: library@usp.ac.fj; catalogue@usp.ac.fj
Web Site: www.usp.ac.fj
Key Personnel
University Librarian: S Joan Yee *Tel:* 323 2282
E-mail: yee_s@usp.ac.fj

Standard Book Numbering Agency, see
Regional ISBN Agency for the South Pacific

Finland

FILI
Ritarikatu 1, 00170 Helsinki
Mailing Address: PO Box 259, 00171 Helsinki
E-mail: fili@finlit.fi
Web Site: www.finlit.fi/fili
Key Personnel
Dir: Leena Majander-Reenpaa *Tel:* (050) 529
2906 *E-mail:* leena.majander@finlit.fi
Communications Manager: Silja Hakulinen
Tel: (040) 534 7526 *E-mail:* silja.hakulinen@
finlit.fi
Coordinator: Merja Aho *Tel:* (040) 534 7834
E-mail: merja.aho@finlit.fi
Promotes the export of literature from Finland.

The Finnish Book Publishers Association, see
Suomen Kustannusyhdistys

Finnish ISBN Agency
National Library of Finland, PO Box 15, 00014
Helsinki
Tel: (09) 2941 44329 *Fax:* (09) 191 44341
E-mail: isbn-keskus@helsinki.fi
Web Site: www.kansalliskirjasto.fi
Key Personnel
ISBN Administrator: Maarit Huttunen
E-mail: maarit.huttunen@helsinki.fi
The Finnish ISSN Center is located at the same
address.

Finnish Literature Exchange, see FILI

Kirjakauppaliitto Ry (The Booksellers'
Association of Finland)
Etelaranta 10, 00130 Helsinki
Tel: (040) 6899 112; (050) 3717 177
E-mail: toimisto@kirjakauppaliitto.fi
Web Site: www.kirjakauppaliitto.fi
Key Personnel
President: Mikko Parviainen *Tel:* (050) 3367 528
E-mail: mikko.parviainen@info.fi
Vice President: Timo Kopra *Tel:* (09) 852 751
E-mail: timo.kopra@suomalainenkk.com; Sari
Laurikko *Tel:* (09) 135 1292 *E-mail:* sari.
laurikko@kipa.fi
Dir: Katriina Jaakkola *Tel:* (050) 3717 177
E-mail: katriina.jaakkola@kirjakauppaliitto.fi
Membership(s): European Booksellers Federation;
International Booksellers Federation.
Publication(s): *Kirja-ja Paperialan kalenteri*
(Book & Paper Industry Register); *Kirjakaup-
paliitto* (magazine)
Parent Company: Kirjakauppalehden Julkaisu Oy
Associate Companies: Suomen Kirjakaupan Saa-
tio

Standard Book Numbering Agency, see Finnish
ISBN Agency

Suomen Kirjailijaliitto (Union of Finnish
Writers)
Runeberginkatu 32 C 28, 00100 Helsinki
Tel: (09) 445 392
E-mail: info@kirjailijaliitto.fi
Web Site: www.kirjailijaliitto.fi
Key Personnel
Executive Dir: Suvi Oinonen *Tel:* (09) 449 752
E-mail: suvi.oinonen@kirjailijaliitto.fi
Founded: 1897
Publication(s): *Suomen Runotar*

Suomen Kustannusyhdistys
Unioninkatu 11, 00130 Helsinki
Tel: (09) 228 77 252
Web Site: www.kustantajat.fi; www.publishers.fi

Key Personnel
Dir: Sakari Laiho *Tel:* (09) 228 77 258
    E-mail: sakair.laiho@kustantajat.fi
Founded: 1858
Membership(s): Federation of European Publishers; International Publishers Association.
Publication(s): *Vuoden Kirjat* (List of books published in Finland)

France

ADAGP (Societe des Auteurs dans les Arts Graphiques et Plastiques)
11 rue Berryer, 75008 Paris
Tel: 01 43 59 09 79 *Fax:* 01 43 59 61 48; 01 45 63 44 89
E-mail: adagp@adagp.fr
Web Site: www.adagp.fr
Key Personnel
General Manager: Marie-Anne Ferry-Fall
    E-mail: ferry-fall@adagp.fr
Administrative Dir, Finance: Yann Leroux
    E-mail: yann.leroux@adagp.fr
Founded: 1953
To administer & protect the rights of visual artists (painters, sculptors, engravers, architects, graphists, photographers, illustrators) in matters of copyright in France.
Membership(s): Confederation Internationale des Societes d'Auteurs et Compositeurs (CISAC); Conseil Superieur de la Propriete Litteraire et Artistique (CSPLA); Groupement Europeen des Societes d'Auteurs et Compositeurs (GESAC).

AFNIL, see Agence Francophone pour la Numerotation Internationale du Livre (AFNIL)

Agence Francophone pour la Numerotation Internationale du Livre (AFNIL)
(Francophone Agency for International Book Numbering)
35 rue Gregoire de Tours, 75279 Paris Cedex 06
Tel: 01 44 41 29 19 *Fax:* 01 44 41 29 03
E-mail: afnil@electre.com
Web Site: www.afnil.org; www.afnil.com
Key Personnel
Manager: Joelle Aernoudt
Founded: 1972

AIEF, see Association Internationale des Etudes Francaises (AIEF)

ASFORED (Association Nationale pour la Formation et le Perfectionnement Professionnels dans les Metiers de l'Edition)
21, rue Charles-Fourier, 75013 Paris
Tel: 01 45 88 39 81 *Fax:* 01 45 81 54 92
E-mail: info@asfored.org
Web Site: www.asfored.org
Key Personnel
President: Francois de Waresquiel
Dir: Aida Diab
Founded: 1972

†◇Association Internationale des Etudes Francaises (AIEF) (International Association of French Studies)
29 rue Helene-Boucher, 91300 Massy
Web Site: www.aief.fr
Key Personnel
President: Antoine Compagnon
Treasurer: Jean-Baptiste Amadieu
    E-mail: jbamadieu@yahoo.fr
Secretary-General: Emmanuel Bury
    E-mail: emmanuel.bury@uvsq.fr
Founded: 1949
Publication(s): *Cahiers de l'AIEF* (annually)

ISBN Prefix(es): 978-2-913718
Number of titles published annually: 1 Print
Bookshop(s): Les Belles Lettres, 95 Blvd Raspail, 75006 Paris

Association Nationale pour la Formation et le Perfectionnement Professionnels dans les Metiers de l'Edition, see ASFORED (Association Nationale pour la Formation et le Perfectionnement Professionnels dans les Metiers de l'Edition)

Cercle de la Librairie
35, rue Gregoire de Tours, 75006 Paris
Tel: 01 44 41 28 00 *Fax:* 01 44 41 28 65
E-mail: commercial@electre.com
Web Site: www.electre.com; www.electrelaboutique.com
Founded: 1874
Associate Companies: Booksellers' Circle Association of Book Trades & Industries

†◇CISAC (International Confederation of Societies of Authors & Composers)
20-26 Blvd du Parc, 92200 Neuilly-sur-Seine
Tel: 01 55 62 08 50
E-mail: communications@cisac.org
Web Site: www.cisac.org
Key Personnel
President: Jean Michel Jarre
Dir, Communications: Cecile Roy
Founded: 1926
Works towards increased recognition & protection of creators' rights.

CITL, see College International des Traducteurs Litteraires (CITL)

College International des Traducteurs Litteraires (CITL) (International College of Literary Translators)
Espace Van Gogh, 13200 Arles
Tel: 04 90 52 05 50 *Fax:* 04 90 93 43 21
E-mail: citl@atlas-citl.org
Web Site: www.atlas-citl.org
Key Personnel
Dir: Jorn Cambreleng
Founded: 1987
Publication(s): *Actes des Assises de la Traduction Litteraire* (annually)

Confederation Francaise de l'Industri des Papiers, Cartons & Celluloses (COPACEL)
(Confederation of the Paper, Board & Pulp Industry)
23-25, rue d'Aumale, 75009 Paris
Tel: 01 53 89 24 00 *Fax:* 01 53 89 24 01
E-mail: contacts@copacel.fr
Web Site: www.copacel.fr
Key Personnel
Vice Chairman: Jean-Marc Louvet
President: Agnes Roger
Mng Dir: Isabelle Charruaz-Roux
Dir, Publications: Paul Antoine Lacour
French manufacturer of Pocket Editions Group.

Confederation Internationale des Societes d'Auteurs et de Compositeurs, see CISAC

Editions du Conseil de l'Europe, see Council of Europe Publishing

Conseil Permanent des Ecrivains, see CPE (Conseil Permanent des Ecrivains)

COPACEL, see Confederation Francaise de l'Industri des Papiers, Cartons & Celluloses (COPACEL)

†Council of Europe Publishing
Division of Council of Europe
Palais de l'Europe, 67075 Strasbourg Cedex
Tel: 03 88 41 25 81 *Fax:* 03 88 41 39 10
E-mail: publishing@coe.int
Web Site: book.coe.int
Key Personnel
Deputy Dir: Edith Lejard-Boutsavath
Communications Dir: Charalambos Papadopoulos
    Tel: 03 88 41 29 52 *E-mail:* charalambos.papadopoulos@coe.int
Communications Officer: Sophie Lobey *Tel:* 03 88 41 22 63 *E-mail:* sophie.lobey@coe.int
Founded: 1949
Official publisher of the Council of Europe & reflects many different aspects of the Council's work, addressing the main challenges facing European society & the world today. Catalogue of over 1,200 titles in French & English includes topics ranging from international law, human rights, ethical & moral issues, society, environment, health, education & culture.
Subjects: Consumer Protection, Criminology, Culture, Education, Human Rights, Law, Local Authorities, Nature, Public Health, Social Security, Sociology, Sports, Youth
ISBN Prefix(es): 978-92-871

CPE (Conseil Permanent des Ecrivains)
c/o SNAC, 80, rue Taitbout, 75009 Paris
Tel: 01 48 74 96 30
E-mail: contact@conseilpermanentdesecrivains.org; info@conseilpermanentdesecrivains.org
Web Site: www.conseilpermanentdesecrivains.org
Key Personnel
President: Valentine Goby
Vice President: Cecile Deniard; Marie-Anne Ferry-Fall; Herve Rony
General Secretary: Geoffroy Pelletier
Treasurer: Emmanuel de Rengerve
Assistant Treasurer: Pierre-Jean Douillard
Founded: 1971

Dilicom
60, rue St Andre des Arts, 75006 Paris
Tel: 01 43 25 43 35 *Fax:* 01 43 29 76 88
E-mail: contact@dilicom.fr; service-clients@dilicom.fr
Web Site: dilicom-prod.centprod.com
Key Personnel
Dir General: Vincent Marty
Founded: 1989
Specialize in electronic data interchange (EDI) between booksellers & publishers.

Editeurs du Sud
Hotel de ville, Place de Hotel-de-ville, 04100 Manosque
Tel: 04 92 73 35 84
E-mail: info@editeursdusud.com
Web Site: www.editeursdusud.com
Key Personnel
Contact: Isabelle Cote
International promotion of publishers based in Provence-Alpes-Cote d'Azur.

†◇Federation Internationale des Traducteurs (FIT) (International Federation of Translators)
c/o REGUS, 57 rue d'Amsterdam, 75008 Paris
Tel: 01 53 32 17 55 *Fax:* 01 53 32 17 32
E-mail: secretariat@fit-ift.org
Web Site: www.fit-ift.org
Key Personnel
President: Henry Liu *E-mail:* president@fit-ift.org
Vice President: Reiner Heard *E-mail:* reiner.heard@gmx.de; Silvana Marchetti
    E-mail: savmarch@datamarkets.com.ar; Terence Oliver *E-mail:* olitrans@aol.com
Executive Dir: Jeanette Orsted
Secretary General: Sabine Colombe
    E-mail: sabine@colombetrad.com
Treasurer: Reina de Bettendorf
    E-mail: treasurer@fit-ift.org

Founded: 1953
Publication(s): *Babel* (quarterly, international journal of translation); *FIT Info* (monthly, newsletter); *Translatio* (quarterly, newsletter)

Federation Nationale de la Presse d'Information Specialisee, see FNPS (Federation Nationale de la Presse d'Information Specialisee)

FIT, see Federation Internationale des Traducteurs (FIT)

FNPS (Federation Nationale de la Presse d'Information Specialisee) (National Federation of Special Interest Press)
17, rue Castagnary, 75015 Paris
Tel: 01 44 90 43 60 *Fax:* 01 44 90 43 72
E-mail: contact@fnps.fr
Web Site: www.fnps.fr
Key Personnel
President: Christian Bruneau *E-mail:* cbruneau@fnps.fr
Deputy Dir: Catherine Chagniot
E-mail: cchagniot@fnps.fr
Founded: 1974

ICA, see International Council on Archives

IIEP, see International Institute for Educational Planning (IIEP)

Intergovernmental Copyright Committee, see UNESCO (United Nations Educational, Scientific & Cultural Organization)

†**International Association of Universities**
UNESCO House, One, rue Miollis, 75732 Paris Cedex 15
Tel: 01 45 68 48 00 *Fax:* 01 47 34 76 05
E-mail: iau@iau-aiu.net
Web Site: www.iau-aiu.net
Key Personnel
Secretary General & Executive Dir: Eva Egron-Polak *E-mail:* e.egronpolak@iau-aiu.net
President: Dzulkifli Abdul Razak
Librarian: Amanda Sudic *E-mail:* a.sudic@iau-aiu.net
Founded: 1950
Publication(s): *Guide to Higher Education in Africa*; *Higher Education Policy* (quarterly, journal); *International Handbook of Universities* (annually)

†◇**International Council on Archives** (Conseil International des Archives)
60 rue des Francs-Bourgeois, 75003 Paris
Tel: 01 40 27 63 06 *Fax:* 01 42 72 20 65
E-mail: ica@ica.org
Web Site: www.ica.org
Key Personnel
Secretary General: David A Leitch
E-mail: leitch@ica.org
Senior Publications Officer: Stephen O'Connor
Founded: 1948
Promotes the preservation & use of archives around the world.
Publication(s): *Archivum* (annually, Archival review); *Comma* (2 times/yr, journal); *Flash* (2 times/yr, newsletter); *Janus* (2 times/yr)

†‡**International Institute for Educational Planning (IIEP)**
7-9, rue Eugene-Delacroix, 75116 Paris
Tel: 01 45 03 77 00 *Fax:* 01 40 72 83 66
E-mail: info@iiep.unesco.org
Web Site: www.unesco.org/iiep; www.iiep.unesco.org
Key Personnel
Chairperson: Dr Nicholas Burnett

Chief, Communication & Publications: Estelle Zadra *Tel:* 01 45 03 77 76 *E-mail:* e.zadra@iiep.unesco.org
Founded: 1963
Established by UNESCO, IIEP is an international center for advanced training & research in educational planning. The Institute's aim is to contribute to the development of education by expanding both knowledge & the supply of competent professionals in the field of educational planning. In this endeavor the Institute cooperates with interested training & research institutions throughout the world. IIEP is financed by UNESCO & by voluntary contributions from individual member states. The program & budget of the Institute are approved by its own governing board. A catalogue of publications is available on request.
Subjects: Educational Planning (Administration & Management, Methologies, Manpower & Employment, School Locations, Nonformal, Adult & Rural Education & Literacy)
ISBN Prefix(es): 978-92-803
Branch Office(s)
Aguero 2071, C1425EHS Buenos Aires, Argentina *Tel:* (011) 4806-9366; (011) 4807-5446 *Fax:* (011) 4806-9458 *E-mail:* info@iipe-buenosaires.org.ar *Web Site:* www.buenosaires.iipe.unesco.org
Route de Ngor, Enceinte Hotel Ngor Diarama, BP 3311 Dakar, Senegal *Tel:* 33 859 77 30 *E-mail:* contact@iipe-poledakar.org *Web Site:* www.iipe-poledakar.org

†**ISSN International Centre**
45 rue de Turbigo, 75003 Paris
Tel: 01 44 88 22 20 *Fax:* 01 40 26 32 43
E-mail: issnic@issn.org; secretariat@issn.org
Web Site: www.issn.org
Key Personnel
Dir: Gaelle Bequet
Founded: 1976
International bibliographic database regarding serial publications.
Publication(s): *ISSN Register* (quarterly, CD-ROM: ISSN compact or frequently on the web: ISSN online); *List of Serial Title Word Abbreviations-Cumulated Edition* (1998)

Ministere des Affaires Etrangeres et Europeennes (Ministry of Foreign & European Affairs)
37, Quai d'Orsay, 75351 Paris
Tel: 01 43 17 53 53
Web Site: www.diplomatie.gouv.fr

le MOTif
6, villa Marcel Lods, Passage de l'Atlas, 75019 Paris
Tel: 01 53 38 60 61 *Fax:* 01 53 38 60 70
E-mail: contact@lemotif.fr
Web Site: www.lemotif.fr
Key Personnel
President: Serge Guerin
Dir: Louis Philippe-Coudray

SACEM (Societe des Auteurs Copositeurs et Editeurs de Musique)
225 ave Charles de Gaulle, 92528 Neuilly-sur-Seine Cedex
Tel: 01 47 15 47 15
E-mail: communication@sacem.fr
Web Site: www.sacem.fr
Key Personnel
President: Laurent Petitgirard
Vice President: Remy Grumbach; Jean-Claude Petit; Nelly Querol
Secretary General: Arlette Tabart
Treasurer: Thierry Communal
Mng Editor: Jean-Noel Tronc
Founded: 1851

SIBMAS, see Societe Internationale des Bibliotheques et des Musees des Arts du Spectacle (SIBMAS)

SLAM, see Syndicat National de la Librairie Ancienne et Moderne (SLAM)

SLF, see Syndicat de la Librairie Francaise (SLF)

SNE, see Syndicat National de l'Edition (SNE)

Societe des Auteurs Compositeurs et Editeurs de Musique, see SACEM (Societe des Auteurs Copositeurs et Editeurs de Musique)

Societe des Auteurs dans les Arts Graphiques et Plastiques, see ADAGP (Societe des Auteurs dans les Arts Graphiques et Plastiques)

†◇**Societe Internationale des Bibliotheques et des Musees des Arts du Spectacle (SIBMAS)** (International Association of Libraries & Museums of the Performing Arts)
c/o Bibliotheque Nationale de France, Dept des Arts du Spectacle, 5, rue Vivienne, 75002 Paris
E-mail: info@sibmas.org
Web Site: www.sibmas.org
Key Personnel
President: Jan Van Goetham *E-mail:* j.vangoetham@lamonnaie.be
First Vice President: Veronique Meunier
E-mail: veronique.meunier@bnf.fr
Second Vice President: Alan R Jones *E-mail:* a.jones@rcs.ac.uk
Secretary General: Veerle Wallebroek
E-mail: veerle@hetfirmament.be
Treasurer: Anne Zendali *E-mail:* a.zendali@geneveopera.ch
Founded: 1954
Subjects: Worldwide Performing Arts Collections
Publication(s): *Conference Proceedings* (2 times/yr)

Standard Book Numbering Agency, see Agence Francophone pour la Numerotation Internationale du Livre (AFNIL)

Syndicat de la Librairie Francaise (SLF)
Hotel de Massa, 38, rue du Faubourg Saint-Jacques, 75014 Paris
Tel: 01 53 62 23 10 *Fax:* 01 53 62 10 45
E-mail: contact@syndicat-librairie.fr
Web Site: www.syndicat-librairie.fr
Key Personnel
Delegate General: Guillaume Husson *E-mail:* g.husson@syndicat-librairie.fr
Administration: Anne Criulanscy *E-mail:* a.criulanscy@syndicat-librairie.fr
Founded: 1999 (by the merger of Union des Libraires de France & Syndicat National de la Librairie Francaise)
Publication(s): *Accueillir le numerique?*; *Les Cahiers de la Librairie*; *Dans les ombres blanches* (In the white shadows); *La Lettre du SLF*; *La librairie et le numerique: Vade-mecum a l'usage des libraires*; *La librairie, Guide 2010*; *Propos Sur Le Metier De Libraire-Conversations Sur Le Commerce De Livres* (About the Bookselling Profession-Conversations on Trade in Books)

Syndicat des Libraires Universitaires et Techniques
40, rue Gregoire de Tours, 75006 Paris
Tel: 01 43 29 88 79

Syndicat National de la Librairie Ancienne et Moderne (SLAM) (National Association of Antiquarian & Modern Booksellers)
4, rue Git-le-Coeur, 75006 Paris
Tel: 01 43 29 46 38 *Fax:* 01 43 25 41 63
E-mail: slam-livre@wanadoo.fr
Web Site: www.slam-livre.fr
Key Personnel
President: Henri Vignes
Vice President: Herve Valentin
General Secretary: Chloe Ozanne
Treasurer: Michel Saporta
Founded: 1914
Publication(s): *Guide du Livre Ancien et des libraires membres du Syndicat national de la Librairie Ancienne et Moderne*

Syndicat National de l'Edition (SNE) (National Union of Publishers)
115 blvd St-Germain, 75006 Paris
Tel: 01 44 41 40 50 *Fax:* 01 44 41 40 77
E-mail: sne.mission@sne.fr
Web Site: www.sne.fr
Key Personnel
Dir General: Pierre Dutilleul
President: Vincent Montagne
Vice President: Sylvie Marce
Treasurer: Dominique Illien
Membership(s): Federation of European Publishers (FEP); International Publishers Association (IPA).
Publication(s): *L'edition de livres en France* (annually, statistics); *Plaquette de representation de l'edition francaise* (annually)
ISBN Prefix(es): 978-2-909677

†◇UNESCO (United Nations Educational, Scientific & Cultural Organization)
7, Place de Fontenoy, 75352 Paris 07
Tel: 01 45 68 10 00 *Fax:* 01 45 67 16 90
E-mail: bpi@unesco.org; publishing.promotion@unesco.org
Web Site: publishing.unesco.org; en.unesco.org
Key Personnel
Dir-General: Irina Bokova
Founded: 1945
To date, UNESCO books have been translated into more than eighty languages. UNESCO acts as Standard Book Numbering Agency, administering ISBNs for UN publications. It also maintains responsibility, within its Copyright Division, for the Intergovernmental Copyright Committee.
Subjects: Art, Communications, Culture, Education, Human Rights, Science, Social Science, Technology
Publication(s): *The UNESCO Courier* (online, magazine); *World Heritage* (quarterly, periodical)
ISBN Prefix(es): 978-92-3
Number of titles published annually: 50 Print
Total Titles: 10,000 Print

UNIC, see Union Nationale de l'Imprimerie et de la Communication (UNIC)

Union Nationale de l'Imprimerie et de la Communication (UNIC) (National Union of Printing & Communication)
68, blvd St Marcel, 75005 Paris
Tel: 01 44 08 64 46 *Fax:* 01 43 36 09 51
Web Site: www.unic-rhonealpes.com/pages/ficg.html
Key Personnel
President: Jacques Chirat
Mng Dir: Pascal Bovero

United Nations Educational, Scientific & Cultural Organization, see UNESCO (United Nations Educational, Scientific & Cultural Organization)

The Gambia

Gambia ISBN Agency
Gambia National Library (DL-371), Reg Pye Lane, PMB 552, Banjul
Tel: 422 6491; 422 8312 *Fax:* 422 3776
E-mail: national.library@qanet.gm
Key Personnel
Contact: Matilda Johnson
Founded: 1946

Standard Book Numbering Agency, see Gambia ISBN Agency

Georgia

Georgian National Book Center
4 Sanapiro St, 0105 Tbilisi
Tel: (032) 931174
E-mail: info@book.gov.ge
Web Site: book.gov.ge
Key Personnel
Dir: Dr Medea Metreveli *E-mail:* metreveli@book.gov.ge
Deputy Dir: Maia Danelia *E-mail:* danelia@book.gov.ge
Public Relations Coordinator: Dodo Gugava *E-mail:* pr@book.gov.ge
Promotes Georgian literature abroad. Supports the process of translation of Georgian & foreign literature.

Georgian Publishers & Booksellers Association
Kostava Str 68, 4th floor, Room N10, 0154 Tbilisi
Tel: (032) 2332677
E-mail: info@gpba.ge
Web Site: www.gpba.ge
Key Personnel
Executive Dir: Tinatin Beriashvili
Public Relations Manager: Natia Pavliashvili
Founded: 1996

GPBA, see Georgian Publishers & Booksellers Association

Germany

Akademie der Deutschen Medien GmbH
Salvatorplatz 1, 80333 Munich
Tel: (089) 29 19 53-0 *Fax:* (089) 29 19 53-69
E-mail: info@medien-akademie.de
Web Site: www.medien-akademie.de
Key Personnel
Mng Dir: Bernd Zanetti *Tel:* (089) 29 19 53-61 *E-mail:* bernd.zanetti@medien-akademie.de
Head, Public Relations & Program Manager: Rachel Lied *Tel:* (089) 29 19 53-65 *E-mail:* rachel.lied@medien-akademie.de
Founded: 1993
Membership(s): Association of Bookseller & Publisher Training Organisations in Europe (ABP-TOE).

Arbeitsgemeinschaft von Jugendbuchverlagen eV (Alliance of Publishers of Children's Books)
Braubachstr 16, 60311 Frankfurt am Main
Tel: (069) 1306-248 *Fax:* (069) 1306-403
E-mail: info@avj-online.de
Web Site: www.avj-online.de

Key Personnel
Chairman: Renate Reichstein *E-mail:* renate.reichstein@avj-online.de
Manager: Margit Mueller *E-mail:* margit.mueller@avj-online.de
Founded: 1950
Publication(s): *Kinder und Jugendbuchverlage A-Z*

Arbeitskreis fuer Jugendliteratur eV (Working Group for Youth Literature)
Metzstr 14c, 81667 Munich
Tel: (089) 45 80 806 *Fax:* (089) 45 80 80 88
E-mail: info@jugendliteratur.org
Web Site: www.jugendliteratur.org
Key Personnel
Mng Dir: Doris Breitmoser *E-mail:* breitmoser@jugendliteratur.org
Project Manager: Linda Duetsch *Tel:* (089) 45 80 80 82 *E-mail:* duetsch@jugendliteratur.org; Kristina Bernd *E-mail:* bernd@jugendliteratur.org
Sales & Accounting: Petra Dostal *E-mail:* bestellung@jugendliteratur.org
Founded: 1955
Youth Literature Committee (Section of IBBY).
Publication(s): *Das Blaubuch*; *Das Bilderbuch* (2008); *Deutschen Jugendliteraturpreis Nominierungsliste* (German Youth Literature Prize Nomination List, annually)

Boersenverein de Deutschen Buchhandels-Nord eV (Association of German Publishers & Booksellers-North)
Schwanenwik 38, 22087 Hamburg
Tel: (040) 5247673-0 *Fax:* (040) 229 85 14
E-mail: info@boersenverein-nord.de
Web Site: www.boersenverein.de/de/norddeutschland
Key Personnel
Mng Dir: Carola Markwa *Tel:* (040) 5247673-21 *E-mail:* c.markwa@boersenverein-nord.de
Branch Office(s)
Fernroder Str 9, 30161 Hannover *Tel:* (0511) 33 65 29-0 *Fax:* (0511) 33 65 29-29

Boersenverein des Deutschen Buchhandels eV (German Publishers & Booksellers Association)
Braubachstr 16, 60311 Frankfurt am Main
Tel: (069) 1306 0 *Fax:* (069) 1306 201
E-mail: info@boev.de
Web Site: www.boersenverein.de
Key Personnel
President: Heinrich Riethmueller
Chief Executive Officer: Alexander Skipis *E-mail:* skipis@boev.de
Dir, Press & Information: Claudia Paul *Tel:* (069) 1306 293 *E-mail:* paul@boev.de
Public Relations: Thomas Koch *Tel:* (069) 1306 292 *Fax:* (069) 1306 17 292 *E-mail:* t.koch@boev.de
Founded: 1825
Publication(s): *Boersenblatt fuer den Deutschen Buchhandel* (German Book Trade Journal); *Buch und Buchhandel in Zahlen* (Books & the Book Trade in Figures)
Branch Office(s)
Schiffbauerdamm 5, 10117 Berlin *Tel:* (030) 28 00 783-0 *Fax:* (030) 28 00 783-50
E-mail: berlinerbuero@boev.de

Boersenverein des Deutschen Buchhandels eV-Regionalgeschaeftsstelle NRW (Association of German Publishers & Booksellers-Regional Office NRW)
Kaiserstr 42a, 40479 Duesseldorf
Tel: (0211) 86445-0 *Fax:* (0211) 86445-99
E-mail: info@buchnrw.de

Web Site: www.buchnrw.de; www.boersenverein. de/de/nordrhein_westfalen/index.html
Key Personnel
Mng Dir: Gabrielle Schink *Tel:* (0211) 86445-11 *E-mail:* schink@buchnrw.de

Boersenverein des Deutschen Buchhandels, Landesverband Baden-Wuerttemberg eV
(Association of Publishers & Booksellers in Baden-Wuerttemberg eV)
Paulinenstr 53, 70178 Stuttgart
Tel: (0711) 61941-0 *Fax:* (0711) 61941-44
E-mail: post@buchhandelsverband.de
Web Site: www.buchhandelsverband.de
Key Personnel
Chairman: Thomas Lindemann
Vice Chairman: Katrin Schmidt
Chief Executive Officer: Reinhilde Roesch
   Tel: (0711) 61941-22 *E-mail:* roesch@
   buchhandelsverband.de
Press & Public Relations: Andrea Baumann
   Tel: (0711) 61941-28 *E-mail:* baumann@
   buchhandelsverband.de

Boersenverein des Deutschen Buchhandels - Landesverband Bayern eV
Salvatorplatz 1, Literaturhaus, 80333 Munich
Tel: (089) 29 19 42-0 *Fax:* (089) 29 19 42-49
E-mail: info@buchhandel-bayern.de
Web Site: www.buchhandel-bayern.de
Key Personnel
Mng Dir: Dr Klaus Beckschulte *Tel:* (089) 29 19
   42-40 *E-mail:* beckschulte@buchhandel-bayern.
   de
Press & Public Relations: Barbara Voit *Tel:* (089)
   29 19 42-41 *E-mail:* voit@buchhandel-bayern.
   de
Membership: Rebecca Kloeber *Tel:* (089) 29 19
   42-42 *E-mail:* kloeber@buchhandel-bayern.de
Founded: 1879

Boersenverein des Deutschen Buchhandels Landesverband Berlin-Brandenburg eV
(Association of Publishers & Booksellers of Berlin-Brandenburg)
Danckelmannstr 9, 14059 Berlin
Tel: (030) 26 39 18-0 *Fax:* (030) 26 39 18-18
E-mail: verband@berlinerbuchhandel.de
Web Site: www.berlinerbuchhandel.de
Key Personnel
Mng Dir: Detlef Bluhm *Tel:* (030) 26 39 18-15
   E-mail: bluhm@berlinerbuchhandel.de; Johanna
   Hahn *Tel:* (030) 26 39 18-14 *E-mail:* hahn@
   berlinerbuchhandel.de
Founded: 1825

Boersenverein des Deutschen Buchhandels Landesverband Hessen, Rheinland-Pfalz und Saarland eV (Rhineland-Palatinate Provincial Federation of Publishers & Booksellers)
Literaturhaus Villa Clementine, Frankfurter Str 1, 65189 Wiesbaden
Tel: (0611) 166 60-0 *Fax:* (0611) 166 60-59
E-mail: briefe@boersenverein-hrs.de
Web Site: www.boersenverein-saarland.de
Key Personnel
Mng Dir: Klaus Feld *E-mail:* klaus.feld@
   boersenverein-hrs.de
Press & Public Relations: Kathrin Bucher
   Tel: (0611) 166 60-21 *E-mail:* kathrin.bucher@
   boersenverein-hrs.de
Founded: 2002

Boersenverein des Deutschen Buchhandels - Landesverband, Sachsen, Sachsen-Anhalt und Thueringen eV
Gerichtsweg 28, 04103 Leipzig
Tel: (0341) 9954 220 *Fax:* (0341) 9954 223
E-mail: landesverband@boersenverein-sasathue.de
Web Site: www.boersenverein-sasathue.de

Key Personnel
Mng Dir: Nora Milenkovic
Founded: 1990

Borro Medien GmbH
Wittelsbacherring 7-9, 53115 Bonn
Tel: (0228) 7258-0 *Fax:* (0228) 7258-189
E-mail: info@borromedien.de
Web Site: www.borromedien.de
Key Personnel
Mng Dir: Rolf Pitsch *E-mail:* pitsch@
   borromedien.de
Head, Customer Service: Martina Ackermann
   Tel: (0228) 7258-127 *E-mail:* ackermann@
   borromedien.de
Marketing: Susanne Fanz *Tel:* (0228) 7258-118
   E-mail: fanz@borromedien.de

BuchDruckKunst eV Gesellschaft zur Foerderung zeitgenoessischer Buchkunst
Koernerstr 24, 22301 Hamburg
Tel: (040) 27 80 86 95
E-mail: info@buchdruckkunst.de
Web Site: www.buchdruckkunst.de
Key Personnel
Chairperson: Wibke Bartkowiak; Erika Drapatz
Founded: 1998

Geschaeftsstelle BuecherFrauen eV
c/o Seehausen + Sandberg, Merseburger Str 5, 10823 Berlin
Tel: (030) 78 71 55 98 *Fax:* (030) 78 71 17 53
E-mail: info@buecherfrauen.de
Web Site: www.buecherfrauen.de
Key Personnel
First Chairman: Stephanie Hanel *Tel:* (07244) 72
   04 86 *E-mail:* sh@wegholz.de
Second Chairman: Jana Steel *Tel:* (06221) 72 91
   038 *E-mail:* 2.vorsitzende@buecherfrauen.de
Finance: Katrin Schroth *Tel:* (0157) 72 51 08 85
Press: Imke Folkerts *Tel:* (0871) 965 94 64
   E-mail: imke.folkerts@gmx.de
Founded: 1990
Bringing together the interests of women publishers, booksellers, translators & agents.

Bundesverband Deutscher Galerien und Kunsthaendler eV (Association of German Galleries & Art Dealers Association)
Dessauer Str 32, 10963 Berlin
Tel: (030) 263 922 980 *Fax:* (030) 263 922 985
E-mail: post@bvdg.de
Web Site: www.bvdg.de
Key Personnel
Chairman: Kristian Jarmuschek *E-mail:* mail@
   jarmuschek.de
Vice Chairman: Marcus Kurt Deschler *Tel:* (030)
   2833288 *Fax:* (030) 2833289 *E-mail:* info@
   deschler-berlin.de
Dir: Birgit Maria Sturm *E-mail:* sturm@bvdg.de
Treasurer: Thole Rotermund *Tel:* (040) 68876988
   Fax: (040) 68876989 *E-mail:* info@rotermund-
   kunsthandel.de
Founded: 1989

BVDG, see Bundesverband Deutscher Galerien und Kunsthaendler eV

EEPG, see European Educational Publishers Group (EEPG)

EMVD, see Evangelischer Medienverband in Deutschland (EMVD)

European Educational Publishers Group (EEPG)
Wielandstr 33, 10629 Berlin
Tel: (0171) 275 63 23

Web Site: www.eepg.org
Key Personnel
Dir: Helga Holtkamp *E-mail:* helga.holtkamp@
   eepg.org

Evangelischer Medienverband in Deutschland (EMVD) (Media Federation of Protestant Germany)
Postfach 50 05 50, 60394 Frankfurt am Main
Tel: (0580) 98 260 *Fax:* (0580) 98 300
E-mail: emvd@gep.de
Web Site: www.emvd.de
Key Personnel
Mng Dir: Christoph Stottele
Founded: 2005

IASA, see International Association of Sound & Audiovisual Archives

Illustratoren Organisation eV (IO)
Martin-Luther Str 7, 60316 Frankfurt am Main
Tel: (069) 97 69 16 16 *Fax:* (069) 97 69 16 14
E-mail: info@illustratoren-organisation.de
Web Site: www.io-home.org
Key Personnel
Mng Dir: Stefanie Weiffenbach

†International Association of Sound & Audiovisual Archives
c/o Deutsche Natiionalbibliothek, Digital Services, Adickesallee 1, 60322 Frankfurt am Main
Tel: (069) 1525-2500
Web Site: www.iasa-online.de
Key Personnel
Chairman: Pio Pellizzari *Tel:* (091) 961-6400
   E-mail: pellizzari@fonoteca.ch
Deputy Chairman: Claus Peter Gallen-
   miller *Tel:* (0831) 697 1842 *E-mail:* cpg-
   schallarchiv@gmx.de; Mary-Ellen Kitchens
   Tel: (089) 5900-2257 *E-mail:* mary-ellen.
   kitchens@brnet.de; Jochen Rupp *Tel:* (069)
   1525-1018 *E-mail:* j.rupp@dnb.de
Treasurer: Anke Leenings
Founded: 1969
Non-governmental UNESCO-affiliated organization established to function as a medium for international cooperation between archives that preserve recorded sound & audiovisual documents.
Publication(s): *Schall & Rauch* (annually, journal, ISSN: 1436-2619)
ISBN Prefix(es): 978-0-946475

†International ISMN Agency
Schlossstr 50, 12165 Berlin
Tel: (030) 7974 5002
E-mail: ismn@ismn-international.org
Web Site: ismn-international.org
Key Personnel
Chairman: Dr Hartmut Walravens
Vice Chairman: Dr Joachim Jaenecke
Executive Dir: Carolin Unger
Treasurer: Dr Bettina von Seyfried
Founded: 1994
Agency for the standard numbering of sheet music.
Publication(s): *ISMN Newsletter* (annually); *ISMN Users' Manual* (2009)

†◇Internationale Gutenberg-Gesellschaft in Mainz eV
Liebfrauenplatz 5, 55116 Mainz
Tel: (06131) 22 64 20 *Fax:* (06131) 23 35 30
E-mail: info@gutenberg-gesellschaft.de
Web Site: www.gutenberg-gesellschaft.de
Key Personnel
President: Michael Ebling
Vice President: Guenther Knoedler
Secretary: Dr Stephan Fuessel
Treasurer: Hans-Guenter Mann

Mng Dir: Dr Franz Stephan Pelgen
Founded: 1901
International association for past & present history of the art of printing.
Publication(s): *Festschriften und Sonder-Veroeffentlichungen*; *Gutenberg-Jahrbuch* (annually); *Kleine Drucke*
ISBN Prefix(es): 978-3-7755

†◇Internationale Jugendbibliothek
(International Youth Library)
Schloss Blutenburg, 81247 Munich
Tel: (089) 89 12 11-0 *Fax:* (089) 89 12 11-38
E-mail: info@ijb.de
Web Site: www.ijb.de
Key Personnel
Dir: Dr Christiane Raabe *Tel:* (089) 89 12 11 42
  E-mail: direktion@ijb.de
Press & Public Relations: Carola Gaede
  Tel: (089) 89 12 11 30 *E-mail:* carolagaede@ijb.de
Founded: 1949
Publication(s): *Buecherschloss* (annually); *Die Kinderbuch-brucke* (A Bridge of Children's Books, 1999); *The White Ravens* (annually, selection of international children's & youth literature)

IO, see Illustratoren Organisation eV (IO)

ISBN-Agentur fuer die Bundesrepublik Deutschland
c/o MVB Marketing-und Verlagsservice des Buchhandels GmbH, Agentur fuer Buchmarkstandards, Braubachstr 16, 60311 Frankfurt am Main
Mailing Address: Postfach 100442, 60004 Frankfurt am Main
Tel: (069) 1306-387 *Fax:* (069) 1306-258
E-mail: isbn@mvb-online.de; info@mvb-online.de
Web Site: www.german-isbn.org
Key Personnel
Mng Dir: Ronald Schild *Tel:* (069) 1306-234
  E-mail: r.schild@mvb-online.de
Founded: 1947

ISMN, see International ISMN Agency

KM katholischermedienverband eV (Catholic Media Association)
Landsberger Str 314, 80687 Munich
Tel: (089) 51 70 10-36 *Fax:* (089) 51 70 10-38
E-mail: info@katholischer-medienverband.de
Web Site: www.katholischer-medienverband.de
Key Personnel
Chairman: Ulrich Peters

Leistungsgemeinschaft Buchhandel eG
Marsstr 14b, 80335 Munich
Tel: (089) 54 34 31 80 *Fax:* (089) 54 34 31 81
E-mail: info@lg-buch.de
Web Site: www.lg-buch.de
Key Personnel
Chief Executive Officer: Dr Michael Fuertjes
  E-mail: fuertjes@lg-buch.de
Founded: 1990

LG Buch eG, see Leistungsgemeinschaft Buchhandel eG

Presse-Grosso, see Presse-Grosso-Bundesverband Deutscher Buch-, Zeitungs- und Zeitschriften-Grossisten eV

Presse-Grosso-Bundesverband Deutscher Buch-, Zeitungs- und Zeitschriften-Grossisten eV (Federation of German Wholesalers of Books, Newspapers & Periodicals)

Haendelstr 25-29, 50674 Cologne
Tel: (0221) 921337-0 *Fax:* (0221) 921337-44
E-mail: bvpg@bvpg.de
Web Site: www.pressegrosso.de
Key Personnel
Chairman: Frank Nolte
Mng Dir: Kai-Christian Albrecht *E-mail:* ka@bvpg.de
Founded: 1950

Standard Book Numbering Agency, see ISBN-Agentur fuer die Bundesrepublik Deutschland

Stiftung Lesen (German Reading Foundation)
Roemerwall 40, 55131 Mainz
Tel: (06131) 28890-0 *Fax:* (06131) 230 333
E-mail: mail@stiftunglesen.de
Web Site: www.stiftunglesen.de
Key Personnel
Chairman: Dr Jeorg Pfuhl
Vice Chairman: Barbara Schleihagen
General Manager: Dr Jeorg F Maas
Founded: 1988

UIL, see UNESCO Institute for Lifelong Learning (UIL)

†◇UNESCO Institute for Lifelong Learning (UIL)
Feldbrunnenstr 58, 20148 Hamburg
Tel: (040) 448 04 10 *Fax:* (040) 410 77 23
E-mail: uil@unesco.org
Web Site: www.unesco.org/uil; uil.unesco.org
Key Personnel
Dir: Arne Carlsen *E-mail:* uil-dir@unesco.org
Founded: 1952
Nonprofit international research, training, information, documentation & publishing centre on literacy, nonformal education, adult & lifelong learning.
Subjects: Adult Education, Basic Education, Continuing Education, Functional Illiteracy in Industrialized Countries, Lifelong Learning, Literacy, Non-Formal Education
ISBN Prefix(es): 978-92-820
Parent Company: UNESCO, Paris, France

vdav, see Verband Deutscher Auskunfts- und Verzichnismedien eV (vdav)

Verband Bildungsmedien eV (Educational Media Association)
Zeppelinallee 33, 60325 Frankfurt am Main
Tel: (069) 9866976-0 *Fax:* (069) 9866976-20
E-mail: verband@bildungsmedien.de
Web Site: www.bildungsmedien.de
Key Personnel
Chairman: Wilmar Diepgrond
Mng Dir: Andreas Baer *E-mail:* baer@bildungsmedien.de; Christoph Bornhorn
  E-mail: bornhorn@bildungsmedien.de
Press & Public Relations: Dr Dagny Lade
  E-mail: lade@bildungsmedien.de
Founded: 1957

Verband Deutscher Antiquare eV (German Antiquarian Booksellers' Association)
Seeblick 1, 56459 Elbingen
Tel: (06435) 90 91 47 *Fax:* (06435) 90 91 48
E-mail: buch@antiquare.de; info@antiquare.de
Web Site: www.antiquare.de
Key Personnel
Chairman: Sibylle Wieduwilt *E-mail:* s.wieduwilt@antiquare.de
Deputy Chairman: Christian Hesse
  E-mail: hesse@antiquare.de
Treasurer: Meinhard Knigge *E-mail:* knigge@antiquare.de
Press & Public Relations: Irene Ferchl
  E-mail: info@literaturblatt.de

Founded: 1952
Publication(s): *Katalog zur Stuttgarter Antiquariatsmesse* (annually); *Mitgliederverzeichnis* (2 times/yr)

Verband Deutscher Auskunfts- und Verzichnismedien eV (vdav) (Association of German Information & Directory Media)
Jakob Krebs Str 126a, 47877 Willich
Mailing Address: Postfach 2027, 47861 Willich
Tel: (02156) 774385-6 *Fax:* (02156) 774385-5
E-mail: info@vdav.org
Web Site: www.vdav.de
Key Personnel
President: Olaf H Tonner
Vice President: Ansgar Heise
Mng Dir: Rhett-Christian Grammatik
Treasurer: Werner Oehring
Founded: 1920

Vereinigung Evangelischer Buchhaendler und Verleger eV (Association of Evangelical Booksellers & Publishers)
Waldstr 24, 33739 Bielefeld
Tel: (06) 91 63 667 *Fax:* (06) 91 63 855
E-mail: mail@veb-medien.de
Web Site: www.veb-medien.de
Key Personnel
Chairman: Detlef Holtgrefe
Vice Chairman: Helmut Matthies
Mng Dir: Renate Nolte
Founded: 1925

Verwertungsgesellschaft WORT (Collecting Society Word)
Untere Weidenstr 5, 81543 Munich
Tel: (089) 514 12-0 *Fax:* (089) 514 12-58
E-mail: vgw@vgwort.de
Web Site: www.vgwort.de
Key Personnel
Executive Chairman: Rainer Just
Mng Dir: Dr Robert Staats
Press Office: Angelika Schindel *Tel:* (089) 514 12-92 *E-mail:* angelika.schindel@vgwort.de
Founded: 1958
Copyright society representing authors & publishers of literary & scientific works.
Branch Office(s)
Koethener Str 44, 10963 Berlin *Tel:* (030) 261 38 45; (030) 261 27 51 *Fax:* (030) 23 00 36 29

VG WORT, see Verwertungsgesellschaft WORT

World Sport Publishers' Association (WSPA)
Von Coels Str 390, 52080 Aachen
Tel: (02) 41 958 10-32 *Fax:* (02) 41 958 10-33
E-mail: info@w-s-p-a.org
Web Site: www.w-s-p-a.org
Key Personnel
President: Hans Juergen Meyer
Secretary: Nicole Massin
Founded: 1990
International organization of publishers in the field of sports, fitness & physical education.

WSPA, see World Sport Publishers' Association (WSPA)

Ghana

AAU, see Association of African Universities (AAU)

†African Publishers Network (APNET)
Kawukudi Junction, Accra
Tel: (030) 291 2764

E-mail: info.africanpublishers@gmail.com
Founded: 1992
Pan-African, nonprofit organization promoting indigenous publishing in Africa.
Publication(s): *African Publishing Review* (6 times/yr, published in English & French); *African "Rights" Indaba: proceedings of the conference on rights held in Harare 1994*; *Agricultura Books Published in Africa: A Catalogue*; *APNET Children's Books Catalogue*; *APNET Rights Catalogue*; *Development Directory of Indigenous Publishing*; *The Story of APNET: a study of the origins, structure, activities and policy of the APNET*; *Towards an African Publishing Institute: An investigaton of existing publishing training, a survey of training needs and a proposed five-year plan for an African Publishing Institute*

APNET, see African Publishers Network (APNET)

†Association of African Universities (AAU)
(Association des Universites Africaines)
African Universities House, 11 Aviation Rd Ext, Airport Residential Area, Accra
Mailing Address: PO Box AN5744, Accra-North
Tel: (0302) 774495; (0302) 761588 *Fax:* (0302) 774821
E-mail: info@aau.org
Web Site: www.aau.org
Key Personnel
President: Olusola Oyewole
Secretary-General: Prof Etienne Ehouan
Founded: 1967
Subjects: Higher Education in Africa

Ghana ISBN Agency, see Standard Book Numbering Agency

Golden Baobab
Ampomah House, 3rd floor, off Obasanjo Highway, Roman Ridge, Accra
Mailing Address: PO Box KD 862, Kanda, Accra
Tel: (030) 2963639
E-mail: info@goldenbaobab.org
Web Site: www.goldenbaobab.org
Key Personnel
Executive Dir: Deborah Ahenkorah
Aims to fuel the global imagination through African children's literature by inspiring the creation, ensuring the production & facilitating the distribution of enthralling, high quality, culturally relevant literary content by African writers & illustrators for African children. Organizes programs & workshops, develops talent & provides resources to writers & illustrators.

Standard Book Numbering Agency
c/o George Padmore Research Library on African Affairs, PO Box GP 2970, Accra
Tel: (030) 228402; (030) 247768 *Fax:* (030) 247768
E-mail: padmoreresearch@ghla.org.gh
Key Personnel
Contact: Rebecca Akita; Robert Aryee
Founded: 1961
Membership(s): International Federation of Library Associations & Institutions (IFLA).
Publication(s): *Ghana National Bibliography*
Parent Company: Ghana Library Authority
Ultimate Parent Company: Ministry of Education, Ghana

Greece

Association of Greek Publishers & Booksellers
Zalongou 9, 2nd floor, 106 78 Athens

Tel: 210 38 01 630
E-mail: info@enelvi.org
Web Site: www.enelvi.org
Key Personnel
President: John Konstantaropoulos
Vice President: Helen Pataki
Secretary: Constantinos Govostis
Treasurer: Argiris Nikolaos
Deputy Secretary General: Eva-Maria Karaitidi
Training & certification programs for employees in the book industry; intervention in matters such as ebook copyright & rights issues, organization & enrichment of libraries.

Hellenic Federation of Publishers & Booksellers
73 Themistokleous St, 106 83 Athens
Tel: 2103300924; 2103804760; 2103806801
   Fax: 2103301617
Founded: 1961
Membership(s): International Association of Publishers; Federation of European Publishing; Federation of European Booksellers.
Publication(s): *Catalogue of the Greek Children's Books*; *General Catalogue of Greek Publishers*

Panhellenic Association of Translators
Komninon 17, 546 24 Thessaloniki
Tel: 310 266 308 *Fax:* 310 266 018
E-mail: info@pem.gr
Web Site: www.pem.gr
Key Personnel
President: Fotios Fotopoulos *E-mail:* president@pem.gr
Vice President: Angelos Kaklamanis
General Secretary: Marijana Milunovic
   E-mail: gsecretary@pem.gr
Treasurer: Raina Diamantieva
Founded: 1963
To promote the best possible working conditions for translators & interpreters & protect their professional interests; to defend its members' intellectual, moral & professional rights; to pursue & foster communication & cooperation with similar professional organizations & educational institutions; to keep members abreast of translation-related activities.
Membership(s): International Federation of Translators (FIT).

Standard Book Numbering Agency
National Library of Greece, Leof Kavalas 31-33 & Spyrou Patsi 12, 104 47 Athens
Tel: 2103470330; 2103608149 *Fax:* 2103608141
E-mail: isbn@nlg.gr
Web Site: www.nlg.gr
Key Personnel
Contact: Stauroula Verveniotou
   E-mail: verveniotou@nlg.gr

Syllogos Ekdoton Bibliou Athinon (Book Publishers' Association of Athens)
Stournaras 5, 106 83 Athens
Tel: 210 38 30 029; 210 33 03 268 *Fax:* 210 38 23 222
E-mail: seva@otenet.gr
Web Site: www.seva.gr
Founded: 1945
Membership(s): Hellenic Federation of Publishers & Booksellers.

Guatemala

Comite Gremial de Editores de Guatemala
Ruta 6, 9-21, zona 4, nivel 8, Edificio Camara de Industria, Guatemala City
Tel: 2380 9000 (ext 338) *Fax:* 2380 9110

E-mail: asistencia@filgua.com; comunicacion@filgua.com
Web Site: www.filgua.com
Key Personnel
Dir: Lucrecia Ardon *E-mail:* direccionejecutiva@guatemalaedita.com

Guyana

CARICOM, see Regional ISBN Agency (CARICOM)

Regional ISBN Agency (CARICOM)
Caribbean Community Secretariat, Turkeyen, PO Box 10827, Georgetown
Tel: 222 0001 75 *Fax:* 222 0171
E-mail: registry@caricom.org; doccentre@caricom.org
Web Site: www.caricom.org; cms2.caricom.org/secretariat/isbn-agency
Key Personnel
Deputy Secretary General: Manorma Soeknandan
Publication(s): *Aging in the Commonwealth Caribbean* (1997); *Analysis of census data in CARICOM countries from a gender perspective* (1997); *Annual report of the Secretary-General of the Caribbean community*; *Balance of payments of CARICOM member states 1990-1999* (2001); *Caribbean development to the year 2000: challenges, prospects and policies* (1988); *Caribbean trade and investment report 2000: dynamic interface of regionalism and globalization* (2000); *Caribbean trade and investment report 2005: corporate integration and cross-border development* (2006); *CARICOM environment in figures 2004* (2009); *CARICOM environment in figures 2002* (2003); *CARICOM model legislation on citzenship; Domestic violence; Equality for women in employment; Equal pay; Inheritance; Maintenance and maintenance orders: Sexual harassment and Sexual offences* (1997); *CARICOM: our Caribbean Community: an introduction* (2005); *CARICOM perspective* (annually); *CARICOM view* (occasionally); *CARICOM'S trade in selected agriculture commodities: 2000-2003* (2007, CD-ROM); *CARICOM's intra-regional trade, volume 1: 1990-2000* (2001, CD-ROM); *CARICOM's intra-regional trade, volume 2 - top twenty commodities: 1998-2001* (2003, CD-ROM); *CARICOM's selected economic indicators 1990, 1998-2002: a statistical profile of the CARICOM Single Market & Economy* (2006, CD-ROM); *CARICOM's trade: a quick reference to some summary data: 1996-2001* (2005, 4th ed, CD-ROM); *CARICOM's trade in services: 1990-2000* (2002, CD-ROM); *CCS Current Awareness Service: new additions* (monthly, electronic only); *Directory of Caribbean Publishers* (2010, 8th ed, CD-ROM); *Employment problem in CARICOM countries: the role of education and training in its existence and its solution* (1997); *External public debt and balance of payments of CARICOM member states 1980-1996* (1998, print & CD-ROM); *External public debt of CARICOM member states 1990-2000* (2002, CD-ROM); *Financing Culture* (1994); *Gender equality in the Caribbean: reality or illusion* (2003); *Gender issues in Caribbean education: a module for teacher education* (2000); *International Standard Book Number (ISBN) users' manual - Caribbean* (2009, 7th ed); *National Accounts Digest 2003-2006* (2009, CD-ROM); *Pan Caribbean Partnership Against HIV and Aids eNews* (2003, electronic only); *Regional monograph: intraregional and extraregional mobility: the new Caribbean migration* (1997); *Report on a comprehensive review of the pro-*

grammes, institutions and organizations of the Caribbean community (1990); Revised Common External Tariff of the Caribbean Community: based on the Harmonised Commodity Description and Coding System (HS) 2007 (2006); Revised Treaty of Chaguarams establishing the Caribbean Community including the CARICOM Single Market & Economy, 5th July 2001 (2002); Socio-economic conditions of children and youth in CARICOM countries: a situational analysis (1997); State news and views (2 issues/yr, electronic only); Towards equity in development: a report on the status of women in sixteen Commonwealth Caribbean Countries (1995); Treaty establishing the Caribbean Community, Chaguaramas, 4th July 1973 (1987); Volume of basic tables for sixteen CARICOM countries (1997); Women and men in CARICOM member states, labor force statistics, volume 1: data series for 1980, 1990 and 2000 round of censuses; volume 2: methodological guide 1980-2002 (2006, CD-ROM); Women and men in CARICOM member states: 1980, 1990 and 2000 rounds of population census (2002, CD-ROM); Women and men in CARICOM member states-power and decision making: 1980-2002 (2003, CD-ROM); Women and men in the Caribbean community: facts and figures 1980-2001 (2003); Women and Men in the Caribbean: facts and figures 1998-2005 (2008, electronic only)

Standard Book Numbering Agency, see Regional ISBN Agency (CARICOM)

Hong Kong

Books Registration Office
Hong Kong Public Libraries, Leisure & Cultural Services Dept, Room 805, Lai Chi Kok Government Off, 19 Lai Wan Rd, Lai Chi Kok, Kowloon
Tel: 2180 9145; 2180 9146; 2742 8981 *Fax:* 2180 9841
E-mail: enquires@lcsd.gov.hk; bro@lcsd.gov.hk
Web Site: www.lcsd.gov.hk; www.hkpl.gov.hk

Information Services Department
Room 219, 2/F, Harbour Bldg, 38 Pier Rd, Central Hong Kong
Tel: 2842 8777; 2842 8847 *Fax:* 2530 2426; 2905 1572
E-mail: internet@isd.gov.hk
Web Site: www.isd.gov.hk
Key Personnel
Dir, Information Services: Patrick Nip Tak-Kuen *Tel:* 2842 8728 *E-mail:* patricknip@isd.gov.hk
Deputy Dir: Brett McEwan Free *Tel:* 2842 8626 *E-mail:* bfree@isd.gov.hk; Matthew Leung *Tel:* 2842 8786 *E-mail:* matthewleung@isd.gov.hk

Standard Book Numbering Agency, see Books Registration Office

Hungary

Magyar ISBN es ISMN Iroda
Orszagos Szechenyi Konyvtar, Budavari Palota F epulet 311, Budapest 1827
Tel: (01) 224-3753 *Fax:* (01) 487-8687
E-mail: isbn@oszk.hu; ismn@oszk.hu

Web Site: www.oszk.hu/isbn_ismn
Key Personnel
Contact: Eszter Toth *E-mail:* toth.eszter@oszk.hu

Magyar Konyvkiadok es Konyvterjesztok Egyesulese (MKKE) (Hungarian Publishers' & Booksellers' Association)
Kertesz u 41 I/4, Budapest 1073
Mailing Address: Pf 130, Budapest 1367
Tel: (01) 343-2540 *Fax:* (01) 343-2541
E-mail: mkke@mkke.hu
Web Site: www.mkke.hu
Key Personnel
President: Andras Sandor Kocsis
Dir: Keresztury Tibor
Founded: 1795
Publication(s): *Koenyvvilag*
ISBN Prefix(es): 978-963-7002; 978-963-7409

Standard Book Numbering Agency, see Magyar ISBN es ISMN Iroda

Iceland

Felag Islenskra Bokautgefenda (Icelandic Publishers' Association)
Baronsstig 5, 101 Reykjavik
Tel: 511-8020 *Fax:* 511-5020
E-mail: fibut@fibut.is
Web Site: www.fibut.is
Key Personnel
Chairman: Egill Orn Johannsson *Tel:* 575-5600 *E-mail:* egill@forlagid.is
Vice President: Heidar Ingi Svansson *Tel:* 517-7200 *E-mail:* heidar@idnu.is
Mng Dir: Benedikt Kristjansson *Tel:* 511-8021 *E-mail:* benk@fibut.is
Founded: 1889
Publication(s): *Bokatidindi* (annually)

Icelandic Literature Center (Midstod Islenskra Bokmennta)
Hverfisgata 54, 101 Reykjavik
Tel: 552 8500 *Fax:* 552 8181
E-mail: islit@islit.is
Web Site: www.islit.is
Key Personnel
Mng Dir: Hrefna Haraldsdottir *E-mail:* hrefna@islit.is
Head, Literature & Promotions: Porgerour Agla Magnusdottir *E-mail:* agla@islit.is
Supports the publication of Icelandic works of literature & the publication of literary works translated into Icelandic.

Standard Book Numbering Agency of Iceland
National & University Library of Iceland, Arngrimsgotu 3, 107 Reykjavik
Tel: 525 5600
E-mail: informa@landsbokasafn.is; isbn@landsbokasafn.is; upplys@landsbokasafn.is
Web Site: www.bok.hi.is
Key Personnel
Contact: Helga Kristen Gunnarsdottir *Tel:* 525 5755 *E-mail:* hkg@landsbokasafn.is
Founded: 1990

India

AABC, see Afro-Asian Book Council (AABC)

†◇**Afro-Asian Book Council (AABC)**
212, Shahpur Jat, New Delhi 110 049

Tel: (011) 26493326; (011) 26493327; (011) 26493328 *Fax:* (011) 41752055
E-mail: afro@aabcouncil.org; info@aabookcouncil.org
Web Site: www.aabookcouncil.org
Key Personnel
Secretary General: Ramesh Mittal *Tel:* 9810121660 (cell) *E-mail:* rkmittal@dkagencies.com
Dir: Pranav Gupta *Tel:* 9999219946 (cell) *E-mail:* pgprintsindia@gmail.com
Treasurer: Satish Malhotra *Tel:* 9810153832 (cell) *E-mail:* satishm@swanpress.com
Founded: 1990
Nonprofit, non-governmental voluntary organization, its aim is to achieve intellectual self-reliance through mutual assistance & cooperation between Africa & Asia in authorship & publishing by (a) holding exhibitions & participating in International Book Fairs where books of members are displayed, (b) holding seminars & workshops on subjects of vital interest authors & publishers, (c) through consultations & annual conferences on book-related things in Asia & Africa, facilitating flow of books & rights with a view to promote indigenous authorship & publishing.
Membership(s): African Publishers Network (APNET); Asia-Pacific Cooperative Programme for Reading Promotion & Book Development (APPREB); World Intellectual Property Organisation (WIPO).
Publication(s): *AABC Newsletter* (quarterly)
Number of titles published annually: 3 Print
Total Titles: 8 Print

Delhi State Booksellers' & Publishers' Association
4760-61, 1st floor 23, Ansari Rd, Darya Ganj, New Delhi 110 002
Tel: (011) 4350 2211 *Fax:* (011) 4350 2212
E-mail: info@dsbpa.in
Web Site: www.dsbpa.in
Key Personnel
President: Mr Ranbir S Kushvah *Tel:* (011) 4358 6946
Vice President: Mr Manish Sabharwal *Tel:* (011) 2325 0586

The Federation of Indian Publishers (FIP)
18/1C, Institutional Area, Aruna Asaf Ali Marg, Near JNU, New Delhi 110 067
Tel: (011) 26964847; (011) 26852263; (011) 26966931 *Fax:* (011) 26864054
Web Site: www.fipindia.co
Membership(s): Asian Pacific Publishers Association.

The Federation of Publishers' & Booksellers' Associations in India (FPBAI)
84, 2nd floor, Darya Ganj, New Delhi 110 002
Tel: (011) 23272845; (011) 23281227
E-mail: fpbaindia@gmail.com
Web Site: fpbai.org
Key Personnel
President: Mr S C Sethi *E-mail:* sethiindiana@gmail.com
Vice President (N): Mr S K Ghai *E-mail:* ghaisurinder@gmail.com
Vice President (S): Mr Nitin S Shah
Vice President (E): Dr Himansu Bandyopadhyay
Vice President (W): Mr A K Pandey
Honorary Secretary: Mr J L Kumar
Founded: 1955

FPBAI, see The Federation of Publishers' & Booksellers' Associations in India (FPBAI)

ICRISAT, see International Crops Research Institute for the Semi-Arid Tropics (ICRISAT)

†‡**International Crops Research Institute for
the Semi-Arid Tropics (ICRISAT)**
Patancheru 502324, Hyderabad, Telangana
Tel: (040) 30713071 *Fax:* (040) 30713071
E-mail: icrisat@cgiar.org
Web Site: www.icrisat.org
Key Personnel
Dir General: Dr David Bergvinson *E-mail:* d.
bergvinson@cgiar.org
Deputy Dir General: Dr Peter Carberry *E-mail:* p.
carberry@cgiar.org
Nonprofit, nonpolitical organization that does in-
novative agricultural research & capacity build-
ing for sustainable development with a wide
array of partners across the globe.
Subjects: Agriculture
Publication(s): *Annual reports*; *E-Newsletters*;
ICRISAT archival reports; *Journal of Semi-Arid
Tropical Agriculture Research*
ISBN Prefix(es): 978-92-9066
Branch Office(s)
CG Centers Block, NASC Complex, Dev Prakash
Shastri Marg, New Delhi 110 012 *Tel:* (011)
32472306 (liaison off)
c/o ILRI Campus, PO Box 5689, Addis Ababa,
Ethiopia *Tel:* (011) 617 2541 *Fax:* (011) 646
1252; (011) 646 4645 *E-mail:* icrisat-addis@
cgiar.org
PO Box 39063, Nairobi, Kenya *Tel:* (020)
7224550 *Fax:* (020) 7224001 *E-mail:* icrisat-
nairobi@cgiar.org
Chitedze Agricultural Research Station, PO
Box 1096, Lilongwe, Malawi *Tel:* 1707297
Fax: 1707298 *E-mail:* icrisat-malawi@cgiar.org
BP 320, Bamako, Mali *Tel:* (020) 7224550
Fax: (020) 70 92 01 *E-mail:* icrisat-w-mali@
cgiar.org
c/o IIAM, Av, das FPLM No 2698, Caxia Postal
1906, Maputo, Mozambique *Tel:* (01) 461657
Fax: (01) 461581 *E-mail:* icrisatmon@panintra.
com
BP 12404, Niamey, Niger *Tel:* 20709200;
20722725; 20722626 *Fax:* 20734329
E-mail: icrisatsc@cgiar.org
PMB 3491, Sabo Bakin Zuwo Rd, Tarauni, Kano,
Nigeria *Tel:* 7034889836
Matopos Research Station, PO Box 776, Bul-
awayo, Zimbabwe *Tel:* (09) 383 311 *Fax:* (09)
383 307 *E-mail:* icrisatzw@cgiar.org

**Raja Rammohun Roy National Agency for
ISBN**
Ministry of Human Resource Development, Dept
of Higher Education, Jeevan Deep Bldg, Room
No 13, 4th floor, Sansad Marg, New Delhi 110
001
Tel: (011) 23369668
E-mail: isbn-mhrd@gov.in
Web Site: isbn.gov.in
Key Personnel
Contact: Ms Aparna Sharma
Founded: 1985
Publication(s): *National Catalogue of ISBN Titles*

Standard Book Numbering Agency, see Raja
Rammohun Roy National Agency for ISBN

Indonesia

IKAPI, see Ikatan Penerbit Indonesia (IKAPI)

Ikatan Penerbit Indonesia (IKAPI) (Association
of Indonesian Book Publishers)
Jl Kalipasir No 32, Cikini, Jakarta 10330
Tel: (021) 3241907; (021) 31902532 *Fax:* (021)
3146050; (021) 3192614
E-mail: sekretariat@ikapi.org
Web Site: www.ikapi.org

Key Personnel
President: Rosidayati Rozalina
Secretary General: M Nurkholis Ridwan
Founded: 1950

Indonesian ISBN Agency
National Library of Indonesia, Jl Salemba Raya
28 A, Jakarta Pusat 10430
Mailing Address: PO Box 3624, Jakarta 10002
Tel: (021) 92920979 *Fax:* (021) 3927919
E-mail: isbn@perpusnas.go.id
Web Site: isbn.perpusnas.go.id
Key Personnel
Librarian: Sauliah Saleh

Standard Book Numbering Agency, see
Indonesian ISBN Agency

Iran

Standard Book Numbering Agency
Iran Book House, 1080 Palestine Crossroad, En-
ghelab Ave, Tehran 13145
Mailing Address: PO Box 13145-1455, Tehran
13145
Tel: (021) 6641 4991 *Fax:* (021) 6641 5360
E-mail: isbn@isbn.ir
Web Site: www.ketab.ir; www.isbn.ir
Key Personnel
Contact: Roholah Soltani

Ireland

CLE Teoranta, see Publishing Ireland

IEPA, see Irish Educational Publishers'
Association (IEPA)

**Irish Educational Publishers' Association
(IEPA)**
c/o Edco, Ballymount Rd, Walkinstown, Dublin
12
E-mail: info@iepa.ie
Web Site: www.iepa.ie

†◇**PEN Club-German Speaking Writers
Abroad** (PEN Zentrum deutschsprachiger
Autoren im Ausland)
c/o Michael Cronin, 54 St John's Park Ave,
Sandymount, Dublin 4
E-mail: exilpen@gmx.net
Web Site: www.exilpen.net
Key Personnel
President: Guenter Kunert
E-mail: guenterkunert@freenet.de
Secretary: Gabrielle Alioth
Treasurer: Daniel Cil Brecher
E-mail: dcbrecher@gmail.com
Mng Dir: Hubert Dammer *E-mail:* hubert.
dammer@exilpen.de
Founded: 1934

Publishing Ireland (Foilsiu Eireann)
63 Patrick St, Dun Laoghaire, Dublin
Tel: (01) 6394868
E-mail: info@publishingireland.com
Web Site: www.publishingireland.com
Key Personnel
President: Ronan Colgan
Vice President: Ivan O'Brien
Treasurer: Sharon Hannan *E-mail:* shannan@
gillmacmillan.ie

Manager: Stephanie Lawless *E-mail:* stephanie@
publishingireland.com
Founded: 1970 (as CLE-Irish Book Publishers'
Association)

Israel

The Book Publishers' Association of Israel
29 Carlebach St, 67132 Tel Aviv
Tel: (03) 5614121 *Fax:* (03) 5611996
E-mail: info@tbpai.co.il
Web Site: www.tbpai.co.il
Key Personnel
Chair: Rachel Eidelman
Mng Dir: Amnon Ben-Shmuel
Founded: 1939
The Association administers two subsidiary co-
operative associations & two joint publishing
companies - Ma'alot & Yachdav.

**The Institute for the Translation of Hebrew
Literature (ITHL)**
23 Baruch Hirsch St, 5120217 Bnei Brak
Tel: (03) 579 6830 *Fax:* (03) 579 6832
E-mail: litscene@ithl.org.il
Web Site: www.ithl.org.il
Key Personnel
Dir: Nilli Cohen
Founded: 1962
Activities of the Institute include promotion of
modern Hebrew literature in translation & co-
publishing projects, literary agency services,
subsidies to authors & publishers for transla-
tions of Hebrew literary works & their publica-
tion abroad.
Also acts as literary agent.
Publication(s): *Modern Hebrew Literature* (annu-
ally)
ISBN Prefix(es): 978-965-255

Israel ISBN Group Agency
Israeli Center for Libraries, Baruch Hirsch 22,
51131 Bnei Brak
Mailing Address: PO Box 801, 51108 Bnei Brak
Tel: (03) 6180151 *Fax:* (03) 5798048
E-mail: isbn@icl.org.il; icl@icl.org.il
Web Site: www.icl.org.il
Key Personnel
Contact: Haviva Shmueli *Tel:* (03) 6180151 ext
115
ISBN Prefix(es): 978-965-231

ITHL, see The Institute for the Translation of
Hebrew Literature (ITHL)

Standard Book Numbering Agency, see Israel
ISBN Group Agency

Italy

Agenzia ISBN per l'Area di Lingua Italiana
(ISBN Agency for the Area of Italian
Language)
c/o EDISER SRL, Corso di Porta Romana, 108,
20122 Milan MI
Tel: 0289280805 *Fax:* 0289280865
E-mail: info@isbn.it
Web Site: www.isbn.it
Key Personnel
Contact: Paola Seghi
Parent Company: Associazione Italiana Editori

AIE, see Associazione Italiana Editori

ALAI, see Associazione Librai Antiquari d'Italia

Associazione Italiana Editori (Italian Publishers Association)
Corso di Porta Romana, 108, 20122 Milan MI
Tel: (02) 89280800 *Fax:* (02) 89280860
E-mail: adozioni@aie.it; segreteria@aie.it
Web Site: www.aie.it
Key Personnel
Dir: Alfieri Lorenzon *E-mail:* alfieri.lorenzon@
aie.it
Publication(s): *Catalogo dei Libri Italiani in Commercio*; *Giornale Della Libreria*
Branch Office(s)
Via Crescenzio 19, 00193 Rome RM
Tel: (06) 95222100 *Fax:* (06) 95222101
E-mail: aieroma@aie.it

Associazione Librai Antiquari d'Italia
(Antiquarian Booksellers' Association of Italy)
Via Cassia 1020, 00189 Rome RM
Tel: (0347) 646-9147 *Fax:* (06) 9293-3756
E-mail: alai@alai.it
Web Site: www.alai.it
Founded: 1947

Associazione Orfini Numeister
Via Pignattara, 34, 06034 Foligno PG
Tel: (0742) 357541 *Fax:* (0742) 351156
E-mail: info@orfininumeister.it
Web Site: www.orfininumeister.it
Key Personnel
President: Rita Fanelli Marini
  E-mail: presidente@orfininumeister.it
Founded: 1993

Fabbrica delle Favole
via Don Minzoni 11, 62100 Macerata MC
Tel: (0733) 231740 *Fax:* (0733) 231740
E-mail: info@arsinfabula.com
Web Site: www.fabbricadellefavole.com
Key Personnel
Artistic Dir: Mauro Evangelista
  E-mail: mauroevangelista@tiscali.it
Press: Michela Avi

FAO, see Food & Agriculture Organization of the United Nations (FAO)

Federazione Italiana Editori Indipendenti
(FIDARE) (Italian Independent Publishers Alliance)
Via della Consolata 7, 10122 Turin TO
Tel: (011) 5211790 *Fax:* (011) 09652658
E-mail: info@fidare.it
Web Site: www.fidare.it
Key Personnel
President: Anita Molino *E-mail:* amolino@fidare.
  it
Vice President: Carlo Delfino *E-mail:* info@
carlodelfinoeditore.it
Founded: 2001

FIDARE, see Federazione Italiana Editori Indipendenti (FIDARE)

†‡Food & Agriculture Organization of the United Nations (FAO)
Viale delle Terme di Caracalla, 00153 Rome RM
Tel: (06) 57051
E-mail: fao-hq@fao.org
Web Site: www.fao.org
Key Personnel
Dir General: Jose Graziano de Silva
Chief, Media Relations: Mehdi Drissi *Tel:* (06)
  570 53886 *E-mail:* mehdi.drissi@fao.org
Founded: 1945
FAO publications reflect the Organization's principal aims: to increase world agriculture production; raise levels of nutrition; & improve the conditions of rural populations. Titles include books, monographs, periodicals, technical documents, annuals, yearbooks & reports of FAO conferences & meetings. Major publications are produced in the five official UN languages (Arabic, Chinese, English, French & Spanish) & all publications & documents are available on microfiche. Unsolicited manuscripts are automatically rejected. Articles of a technical nature of no more than 2,500 words on international aspects of the animal industry, food & nutrition are occasionally accepted. No payment is made.
Subjects: Agriculture, Animal Production & Health, Computerized Information Series, Economic & Social Development, Educational & Training Materials, Fisheries, Food & Nutrition, Forestry, Land & Water Development, Plant Production & Protection
ISBN Prefix(es): 978-92-5; 978-92-851; 978-92-852; 978-92-853; 978-92-854; 978-92-855

Hamelin Associazione Culturale
Via Zamboni 15, 40126 Bologna BO
Tel: (051) 233401 *Fax:* (051) 2915120
E-mail: info@hamelin.net
Web Site: hamelin.net
Founded: 1996
Promote children's literature, classic & contemporary.

†ICCROM (International Centre for the Study of the Preservation & Restoration of Cultural Property)
Via di San Michele 13, 00153 Rome RM
Tel: (06) 585-531 *Fax:* (06) 585-53349
E-mail: iccrom@iccrom.org
Web Site: www.iccrom.org
Key Personnel
Dir General: Dr Stefano De Caro
Founded: 1959
Heritage preservation & intergovernmental organization.
ISBN Prefix(es): 978-92-9077

Associazione Illustratori
Via Conchetta 9, 20136 Milan MI
Tel: (02) 36535729
E-mail: info@autoridimmagini.it
Web Site: www.associazioneillustratori.it
Key Personnel
President: Ivo Milazzo
Vice President: Benedetta Frezzotti
Dir: Andrea Bayer; Alessandra Chiarlo
Secretary: Stella Di Meo
Treasurer: Claudio Cristiani
Founded: 1980
Membership(s): European Illustrators Forum (EIF).

International Centre for the Study of the Preservation & Restoration of Cultural Property, see ICCROM (International Centre for the Study of the Preservation & Restoration of Cultural Property)

Standard Book Numbering Agency, see Agenzia ISBN per l'Area di Lingua Italiana

University Press Italiane
c/o Pisa University Press, Palazzo Vitelli, Lungarno Pacinotti 43, 56126 Pisa
Tel: (050) 2212056 *Fax:* (050) 2212945
E-mail: info@universitypressitaliane.com
Web Site: www.universitypressitaliane.com
Key Personnel
President: Claudia Napolitano *Tel:* (050) 2212053
  E-mail: napolitano.press@unipi.it

Japan

ACCU, see Asia-Pacific Cultural Centre for UNESCO (ACCU)

Antiquarian Booksellers' Association of Japan
10-10, Yotsuya Sakamachi, Shinjuku-ku, Tokyo
160-0002
Tel: (03) 3357-1417 *Fax:* (03) 3359-7790
E-mail: abaj@abaj.gr.jp
Web Site: www.abaj.gr.jp
Key Personnel
President: Atsushi Kataoka
Founded: 1964
Membership(s): International League of Antiquarian Booksellers (ILAB).

APO, see The Asian Productivity Organization (APO)

†‡Asia-Pacific Cultural Centre for UNESCO (ACCU)
Japan Publishers Bldg, 6 Fukuromachi, Shinjuku-ku, Tokyo 162-8484
Tel: (03) 3269-4435 *Fax:* (03) 3269-4510
E-mail: general@accu.or.jp; library@accu.or.jp
Web Site: www.accu.or.jp
Key Personnel
President: Fujio Cho
Dir General: Tamura Tetsuo
Founded: 1971
Asian/Pacific Copublication Programme (ACP) is a joint program of UNESCO member states in Asia & the Pacific to produce good children's books. Regional training course on book production organized annually & Noma Concours for Picture Book Illustrations biennially.
Publication(s): *Asian/Pacific Book Development (ABD)*
ISBN Prefix(es): 978-4-946438

†The Asian Productivity Organization (APO)
Leaf Sq, Hongo Bldg 2F, 1-24-1 Hongo, Bunkyo-ku, Tokyo 113-0033
Tel: (03) 3830 0411 *Fax:* (03) 5840 5322
E-mail: apo@apo-tokyo.org
Web Site: www.apo-tokyo.org
Key Personnel
Secretary General: Mari Amano
Dir, Administration & Finance Dept: Sherman Loo
Information & Public Relations Officer: Yumiko Yamashita
Founded: 1961
Subjects: Productivity Improvement in APO Member Countries
ISBN Prefix(es): 978-92-833

The Association of Japanese University Presses
1-14-13, Kudankita, Chiyoda-ku, Tokyo 102-0073
Tel: (03) 3511-2091
Web Site: www.ajup-net.com
Founded: 1963

JAIP, see Japan Association of International Publications

†◇Japan Association of International Publications
1-1-13-4F, Kanda-Jimbocho, Chiyoda-ku, Toyko
101-0051
E-mail: office@jaip.jp
Web Site: www.jaip.jp
Key Personnel
Executive Dir: Hisatoshi Aizawa
Vice Executive Dir: Steve Matsumura
Dir: Aiko Hosoya
Founded: 1941

Association of those who import & sell foreign publications, represent foreign publishers & support import of such publications.
Publication(s): *JAIP Directory*
ISBN Prefix(es): 978-4-931516

Japan Book Publishers Association (JBPA)
6 Fukuro-machi, Shinjuku-ku, Tokyo 162-0828
Tel: (03) 3268-1302; (03) 3268-1303 (research)
Fax: (03) 3268-1196
E-mail: research@jbpa.or.jp
Web Site: www.jbpa.or.jp
Key Personnel
President: Masahiro Oga
Mng Dir: Hideki Nakamachi
Founded: 1957
Publication(s): *Bulletin of Japan Book Publishers Association*; *The Catalogue of Books in the Near Future*; *Introduction to Publishing in Japan 2017-2018*; *Japanese Books in Print CD-ROM Edition*

Japan Electronic Publishing Association (JEPA)
Tsuruya Sogo Bldg 4F, 2-9-2 Misaki-cho, Chiyoda-ku, Tokyo 101-0061
Tel: (03) 3556-5224 *Fax:* (03) 3556-5259
E-mail: info@jepa.or.jp
Web Site: www.jepa.or.jp
Key Personnel
Chairman: Masao Sekido
Founded: 1986

Japan ISBN Agency
c/o Japan Library Publishers Club House, 06 2F, Fukuromachi, Shinjuku-ku, Tokyo 162-0828
Tel: (03) 3267-2301 *Fax:* (03) 3267-2304
E-mail: info@isbn-center.jp
Web Site: www.isbn-center.jp

Japanese Association of Children's Book Publishers
6, Fukuro-machi, Shinjuku-ku, Tokyo 162-0828
Tel: (03) 3267 3791 *Fax:* (03) 3267 5389
E-mail: kodomo@kodomo.gr.jp
Web Site: www.kodomo.gr.jp
Key Personnel
Chairman: Harunobu Takeshita
Founded: 1953

Japanese Board on Books for Young People (JBBY)
6 Fukuromachi, Shinjuku-ku, Tokyo 162-0828
Tel: (03) 5228-0051 *Fax:* (03) 5228-0053
E-mail: jbby-info@jbby.org
Web Site: www.jbby.org
Founded: 1974
Aims to give children access to books with high literary & artists standards; to encourage the publication & distribution of quality children's books.

JBPA, see Japan Book Publishers Association (JBPA)

JEPA, see Japan Electronic Publishing Association (JEPA)

Nihon Shoten Shogyo Kumiai Rengokai (Japan Booksellers Federation)
1-2 Surugadai Kanda, Chiyoda-ku Tokyo 101-0062
Tel: (03) 32940388 *Fax:* (03) 32957180
E-mail: info@n-shoten.jp
Web Site: www.n-shoten.jp
Publication(s): *Kodomonohon Long-seller-list* (Children's Books: A List of Best Sellers); *Zenkoku Shoten Meibo* (Address Book of Japan Booksellers); *Zenkoku Shoten Shinbun* (Bookstores Nationwide Newspaper)

Publishers Association for Cultural Exchange (PACE) Japan
1-2-1, Sarugaku-cho, Chiyoda-ku, Tokyo 101-0064
Tel: (03) 3291-5685 *Fax:* (03) 3233-3645
E-mail: culturalexchange@pace.or.jp
Web Site: www.pace.or.jp
Founded: 1953
Publication(s): *Directory of Japanese Publishers* (biennially); *Practical Guide to Publishing in Japan*

Standard Book Numbering Agency, see Japan ISBN Agency

Kazakhstan

Kazakhstan ISBN Agency
National Book Chamber of the Republic of Kazakhstan, Pushkin Str 2, Almaty 050016
Tel: 727 3976204 *Fax:* 727 3976130
E-mail: bookkz@inbox.ru
Key Personnel
Contact: Zhanat Seidumanov

Standard Book Numbering Agency, see Kazakhstan ISBN Agency

Kenya

†◇Eastern & Southern Africa Regional Branch of the International Council on Archives (ESARBICA)
PO Box 49210, Nairobi 00100
Tel: (020) 2228959
Web Site: www.esarbica.com
Key Personnel
President: Mr Francis Mwangi
  E-mail: mwangithua@gmail.com
Deputy President: Ivan Munhamo Murambiwa
  E-mail: imurambiwa@yahoo.com
Secretary-General: Richard Wato *E-mail:* rwato@yahoo.com
Founded: 1969
Preservation of Kenya's documentary heritage.
Publication(s): *ESARBICA* (annually, journal)

ESARBICA, see Eastern & Southern Africa Regional Branch of the International Council on Archives (ESARBICA)

Kenya Literature Bureau (KLB)
South C, Popo Rd Bellevue Area, off Mombasa Rd, Nairobi 00100
Mailing Address: PO Box 30022, Nairobi 00100
Tel: (020) 3541196; (020) 3541197 *Fax:* (020) 6001474
E-mail: info@klb.co.ke
Web Site: www.kenyaliteraturebureau.com; www.klb.co.ke
Key Personnel
Chairman: Serah K Ndege
Mng Dir: Eve A Obara
Publishing Manager: Mary N Khasiani
Sales & Marketing Manager: Bernard O Obura
Founded: 1980
Publish educational & general books; Government parastatal.
ISBN Prefix(es): 978-9966-44
Number of titles published annually: 20 Print
Total Titles: 700 Print

Kenya Publishers Association
Occidental Plaza, 2nd floor, Westlands, Nairobi 00100
Mailing Address: PO Box 42767, Nairobi 00100
Tel: (020) 3752344; (0724) 255848 (cell)
  Fax: (020) 3754076
E-mail: info@kenyapublishers.org
Web Site: www.kenyapublishers.org
Key Personnel
Chairperson: David Waweru
Vice Chairperson: Simon Sossion
Treasurer: John Mwazemba
Executive Officer: James Odhiambo
Founded: 1971
Membership(s): National Book Development Council of Kenya.

KLB, see Kenya Literature Bureau (KLB)

Standard Book Numbering Agency
Kenya National Library Service, PO Box 30573, Nairobi 00100
Tel: (020) 2725550; (020) 2158360 *Fax:* (020) 2721749
E-mail: knls@knls.ac.ke
Web Site: www.knls.ac.ke
Key Personnel
Dir: Richard Atuti
Librarian: Mary Kinyanjui; Philomena Mwirigi
Publication(s): *Kenya National Bibliography*

UNEP, see United Nations Environment Programme (UNEP)

†‡United Nations Environment Programme (UNEP)
PO Box 30552, Nairobi 00100
Tel: (020) 7621234
E-mail: unepinfo@unep.org
Web Site: www.unep.org
Key Personnel
Executive Dir: Achim Steiner
Deputy Executive Dir: Ibrahim Thiaw
Dir, Communications & Public Information: Naysan Sahba *Tel:* (020) 7623293 *E-mail:* dcpi.director@unep.org
Founded: 1972
Subjects: Environmental Literature
ISBN Prefix(es): 978-92-807
Number of titles published annually: 100 Print
U.S. Office(s): United Nations Environment Programme, Regional Office for North America, 900 17 St NW, Suite 506, Washington, DC 20006, United States, Information Officer: Laura Fuller *Tel:* 202-785-0465 *Fax:* 202-785-2096 *E-mail:* laura.fuller@unep.org

Kuwait

†‡Arab Centre for Medical Literature
PO Box 5225, 13053 Safat
Tel: 25338610 *Fax:* 25338618
Subjects: Arabizing Medical Literatures
Publication(s): *Atlas of Eye Diseases in the Arab Countries*; *Lecture Notes on Gynaecology*; *Teeth & Health*

Latvia

†Latvijas Gramatizdeveju Asociacija (Latvian Publishers' Association (LPA))
Baznicas iela 37-3, Riga LV-1010
Tel: 67 217 730 *Fax:* 67 217 730
E-mail: lga@gramatizdeveji.lv

Web Site: www.gramatizdeveji.lv
Key Personnel
President: Renate Punka *Tel:* 67 367 497 *Fax:* 67
  370 922 *E-mail:* renate.punka@jr.lv
Vice President: Skaidrite Naumova
Executive Dir: Dace Pugacha
Publisher: Janis Roze
Founded: 1993
Protection of rights & interests of publishers.
Membership(s): International Publishers Associa-
  tion.

Latvijas Literaturas Centrs (Latvian Literature
  Centre)
Perses iela 14-8, Riga LV-1011
Tel: 67 311021 *Fax:* 67 311024
E-mail: centre@literature.lv
Web Site: www.literature.lv
Key Personnel
Dir: Janis Oga *E-mail:* janis@literature.lv
Project Coordinator: Juta Piraga *E-mail:* juta@
  literature.lv
Founded: 2002
Established to ensure international recognition
  of & access to Latvian fiction, poetry, plays &
  children's literature.

LPA, see Latvijas Gramatizdeveju Asociacija

Standard Book Numbering Agency
c/o Latvijas Nacionala biblioteka, Mukusalas iela
  3, Riga LV-1423
Tel: 67806149
E-mail: isbn@lnb.lv; lnb@lnb.lv
Web Site: www.lnb.lv
Founded: 1993
ISBN Numbering.

Lebanon

Syndicate of Publishers Union in Lebanon
Bir Hasan-Al Chadia Bldg, 1st floor, Beirut
Mailing Address: PO Box 8843, Beirut
Tel: (03) 775638; (03) 775639 *Fax:* (03) 853712;
  (03) 853713
E-mail: info@publishersunionlb.com; magazine@
  publishersunionlb.com; publishers@
  publishersunionlb.com
Web Site: publishersunionlb.com
Key Personnel
President: Samira Assi *E-mail:* samira.assi@
  publishersunionlb.com
Vice President: Nabil Abdelhak *E-mail:* nabil.
  abdelhak@publishersunionlb.com
General Secretary: Pierre Sayegh *E-mail:* pierre.
  sayegh@publishersunionlb.com
Treasurer: Samir Baalbaky *E-mail:* samir.
  baalbaky@publishersunionlb.com
Founded: 1947

Lesotho

Standard Book Numbering Agency
National University of Lesotho Library, PO Roma
  180, Maseru
Tel: 22213 404 *Fax:* 22340 231
Web Site: library.nul.ls
Key Personnel
Contact: William Mokotjo *E-mail:* w.mokotjo@
  nul.ls
Founded: 1964
Education, humanities, law, science & technology,
  social sciences, agriculture & health sciences.

Lithuania

LALA, see Lietuvos Akademiniu Leidyklu
  Asociacija (LALA)

**Lietuvos Akademiniu Leidyklu Asociacija
  (LALA)** (Lithuanian Academic Publishers
  Association)
K Donelaicio g 73, LT-44029 Kaunas
Tel: (037) 30 00 91
E-mail: leidykla@ktu.lt
Web Site: www.akademinesleidyklos.lt; ktu.edu/lt/
  leidykla/main.php
Founded: 2005

Lietuvos Kulturos Institutas (Lithuanian Culture
  Institute)
Z Sierakausko g 15, LT-03105 Vilnius
Tel: (05) 2629115; (05) 2405624
E-mail: info@lithuanianculture.lt
Web Site: lithuanianculture.lt
Key Personnel
Head, Programs & Projects Dept: Ruta
  Statuleviciute-Kaucikiene *Tel:* (05) 2127187
  E-mail: ruta.kaucikiene@lithuanianculture.lt
Projects Manager: Kristina Agintaite
  E-mail: kristina.agintaite@lithuanianculture.
  lt; Ruta Nanartaviciute *Tel:* (05) 2405624
  E-mail: ruta.nanartaviciute@lithuanianculture.
  lt; Kotryna Pranckunaite *E-mail:* kotryna.
  pranckunaite@lithuanianculture.lt; Ruta Va-
  lentaite *Tel:* (05) 2405624 *E-mail:* ruta.
  valentaite@lithuanianculture.lt
Projects Coordinator: Ruta Melyne *E-mail:* ruta.
  melyne@lithuanianculture.lt
Founded: 1998
Promotes Lithuanian literature abroad by acting
  as a literary information centre & translation
  promoting fund.

Lietuvos Leideju Asociacija (Lithuanian
  Publishers Association)
Vokieciu g 18 A, LT-01130 Vilnius
Tel: (05) 261 77 40 *Fax:* (05) 261 77 40
E-mail: info@lla.lt
Web Site: www.lla.lt
Key Personnel
President: Remigijus Jokubauskas
Executive Dir: Aida Dobkeviciute
Founded: 1993
Represents the interests of Lithuanian publishers.
Membership(s): Federation of European Publish-
  ers (FEP); International Publishers Association
  (IPA).
ISBN Prefix(es): 978-9955-9464; 978-9955-9557

Lithuanian ISBN Agency
c/o National Library of Lithuania, Gedimino pr
  51, LT-01504 Vilnius
Tel: (05) 239 8649
E-mail: isbnltu@lnb.lt
Web Site: www.lnb.lt
Key Personnel
General Dir: Renaldas Gudauskas

Lithuanian Publishers Association, see Lietuvos
  Leideju Asociacija

Luxembourg

ISBN Agency - Luxembourg
Bibliotheque nationale de Luxembourg, Annexe
  Kirchberg, 31 Blvd Konrad Adenauer, 1115
  Luxembourg
Tel: 26 09 59-313

E-mail: agence-isbn@bnl.etat.lu
Web Site: www.bnl.lu
Key Personnel
Contact: Charles Hilger *E-mail:* charles.hilger@
  bnl.etat.lu

Letzebuerger Bicherediteuren
7 Rue Alcide de Gasperi, 1615 Luxembourg
Mailing Address: Postfach 482, 2014 Luxem-
  bourg
Tel: 439444-1
E-mail: contact@bicherediteuren.lu
Web Site: www.bicherediteuren.lu
Key Personnel
President: Manuel Schortgen
Vice President: Thomas Schoos
Secretary: Paul Bauler
Treasurer: Christiane Krecke

Editeurs de Livres Luxembourgeois, see
  Letzebuerger Bicherediteuren

Luxemburger Buchverleger, see Letzebuerger
  Bicherediteuren

**†L'Office des publications de l'Union
  europeenne** (Publications Office of the
  European Union)
2, rue Mercier, 2985 Luxembourg
Tel: 29291 *Fax:* 2929-42758
E-mail: info@publications.europa.eu; bookshop@
  publications.europa.eu; op-info-copyright@
  publications.europa.eu
Web Site: publications.europa.eu; publications.
  europa.eu/en/web/general-publications/
  publications (online bookshop)
Key Personnel
Dir General: Rudolph Strohmeier
Publications Dir: H Celms *Tel:* 2929-44969
  Fax: 2929-42758 *E-mail:* harolds.celms@
  publications.europa.eu
Founded: 1969
Subjects: Agriculture, Culture, Economy, Educa-
  tion, Employment, Energy, Enterprises & Busi-
  ness, Environment, Finance, Fishing, Foreign
  Relations, Forestry, Information, Labor, Law,
  Scientific Research & Techniques, Statistics,
  Tax
ISBN Prefix(es): 978-92-894; 978-92-79; 978-92-
  825; 978-92-826; 978-92-828; 978-92-827
Branch Office(s)
135, rue Adolphe Fischer, 1521 Luxembourg

Standard Book Numbering Agency, see ISBN
  Agency - Luxembourg

Macedonia

ISBN Agencija na Republika Makedonija
National & University Library, Blvd "Goce
  Delchev" no 6 posht fah 566, 1000 Skopje
Tel: (02) 3115 177 *Fax:* (02) 3226 846
E-mail: kliment@nubsk.edu.mk
Web Site: www.nubsk.edu.mk
Key Personnel
Contact: Olja Stojkova *Tel:* (02) 3115 177 ext
  137 *E-mail:* olja@nubsk.edu.mk

Standard Book Numbering Agency, see ISBN
  Agencija na Republika Makedonija

Malawi

Malawi National ISBN Agency
National Archives of Malawi, PO Box 62, Zomba
Tel: 01 525 240
E-mail: archivesmalawi@gmail.com
Key Personnel
Contact: Robert Mkuwira
Founded: 1991
Membership(s): ICA (International Council on Archives).

Standard Book Numbering Agency, see Malawi National ISBN Agency

Malaysia

ISBN National Centre
Pusat Bibliografi Negara, Perpusta Kaan Negara Malaysia, Aras 3, Anjung Bestari, 232 Jl Razak, 50572 Kuala Lumpur
Tel: (03) 26871700 (ext 4288); (03) 26814329
Fax: (03) 26811676
E-mail: isbn@pnm.gov.my
Web Site: www.pnm.gov.my
Key Personnel
Deputy Dir General: Mdme Maizan bt Ismail
Tel: (03) 26871902 *E-mail:* maizan@pnm.gov.my

MABOPA, see Malaysian Book Publishers' Association (MABOPA)

Malaysian Book Publishers' Association (MABOPA)
No 7-6, Block E2, Jl PJU 1/42A, Dataran Prima, 47301 Petaling Jaya, Selangor
Tel: (03) 7880 5840 *Fax:* (03) 7880 5841
E-mail: info@mabopa.com.my
Web Site: www.mabopa.com.my
Key Personnel
President: Ishak Hamzah
Deputy President: Mr Arief Hakim Sani Rahmat
Vice President: Mr Y Sahadevan; Raymond Yeo
Honorary Treasurer: Mr Kow Ching Chuan
Founded: 1969

SARBICA, see Southeast Asia Regional Branch of the International Council on Archives (SARBICA)

†◇Southeast Asia Regional Branch of the International Council on Archives (SARBICA)
c/o National Archives of Malaysia, Jl Duta, 50568 Kuala Lumpur
Tel: (03) 6201 0688 *Fax:* (03) 6201 5679
E-mail: mysarbica@arkib.gov.my
Web Site: sarbica.org.my
Key Personnel
Chairman: Mr Mustari Irawan
Vice Chairman: Mr Azemi Abdul Aziz
Secretary General: Ms Rusniza Hamdan
E-mail: rusniza@arkib.gov.my
Treasurer: Mr Afham Jauhari Aldi
E-mail: afham@arkib.gov.my
Founded: 1968
Publication(s): *SARBICA Newsletter*

Standard Book Numbering Agency, see ISBN National Centre

Maldives

Standard Book Numbering Agency
Ministry of Education, H Velaanaage, 9th floor, Ameer Ahmed Magu, Male
Tel: 3323262 *Fax:* 3321201
E-mail: admin@moe.gov.mv
Web Site: www.moe.gov.mv
Key Personnel
Contact: Dr Aishath Shiham

Malta

Standard Book Numbering Agency (Malta)
National Book Council c/o Central Public Library, Prof J Mangion St, Floriana FRN 1800
Tel: 21222654
Web Site: www.ktieb.org.mt
Key Personnel
Chairman: Mark Camilleri
E-mail: markcamilleri@autistici.org
Secretary: Joseph Debattista *E-mail:* joseph.debattista@gov.mt
ISBN Prefix(es): 978-99909-0

Mauritius

ISBN Agency
c/o Editions de l'Ocean Indien, 22B Marcel Cabon St, Stanley, Rose Hill
Tel: 464 6761 *Fax:* 464 3445
E-mail: eoipublishing@intnet.mu
Web Site: eoibooks.gov-mu.org
Key Personnel
Mng Dir: Yashvin Hassamal
Founded: 1992
ISBN Prefix(es): 978-99903-0

Standard Book Numbering Agency, see ISBN Agency

Mexico

Agencia Nacional de ISBN
Instituto Nacional del Derecho de Autor, Indautor, Puebla 143, Colonia Roma, Delegacion Cauthtemoc, 06700 Mexico, DF
Tel: (0155) 3601 8210 (ext 16)
E-mail: inava@sep.gob.mx
Web Site: www.gob.mx; www.indautor.sep.gob.mx/isbn
Key Personnel
Dir: Rogelio Rivera Lizarraga *E-mail:* rrivera@sep.gob.mx

Camara Nacional de la Industria Editorial Mexicana (National Chamber of the Mexican Publishing Industry)
Holanda No 13, Colonia San Diego Churubusco, Delegacion Coyoacan, 04120 Mexico, CDMX
Tel: (0155) 5688 2011; (0155) 5688 2221
E-mail: contacto@caniem.com; info@caniem.com
Web Site: www.caniem.org
Key Personnel
President: Carlos Anaya Rosique
E-mail: presidencia@caniem.com
Vice President: Mireya Montejo; Carlos Federico Jose Graef Sanchez
Secretary: Jose Maria Castro Mussot

Treasurer: Jesus Buenaventura Galera Lamadrid
Founded: 1964
Mexican publishers' association.
Publication(s): *Books of Mexico: How to obtain Mexican books & periodicals*

CeMPro, see Centro Mexicano de Proteccion y Fomento de los Derechos de Autor

Centro Mexicano de Proteccion y Fomento de los Derechos de Autor (Mexican Center of Protection & Promotion of Copyright)
Amsterdam 287, Piso 6, Colonia Hipodromo, Delegacion Cuauhtemoc, 06100 Mexico, CDMX
Tel: (0155) 56013528; (0155) 56012756
Fax: (0155) 56049856
E-mail: info@cempro.org.mx
Web Site: cempro.com.mx/sitio
Key Personnel
President: Clemente Merodido Lopez
General Dir: Valeria Sanchez *E-mail:* valeria.sanchez@cempro.org.mx
Membership(s): International Federation of Reproduction Rights Organization (IFRRO).

IBBY Mexico
Goya 54, Colonia Mixcoac, 03920 Mexico, CDMX
Tel: (0155) 5211-0427; (0155) 5563-1435; (0155) 5211-0492; (0155) 5211-9545
E-mail: direccion@ibbymexico.org.mx; ibbymexico@ibbymexico.org.mx
Web Site: www.ibbymexico.org.mx
Key Personnel
President: Bruno Newman Flores
Secretary: Maria Elena Castro Estrada
Treasurer: Felipe Garcia Fricke
Dir General: Azucena Galindo Ortega
E-mail: agalindo@ibbymexico.org.mx
Founded: 1979

International Board on Books for Young People, see IBBY Mexico

Standard Book Numbering Agency, see Agencia Nacional de ISBN

Moldova

Camera Nationala a Cartii din Republica Moldova, see National Book Chamber of Republic of Moldova

National Book Chamber of Republic of Moldova
Subsidiary of Ministry of Culture
bl Stefan cel Mare 180, 2004 Chisinau
Tel: (022) 295746; (022) 295916 *Fax:* (022) 295860
E-mail: bookchamber.md@gmail.com; cnc_moldova@mail.ru
Web Site: www.bookchamber.md
Key Personnel
Chief: Zabiaco Olesea
General Dir: Valentina Chitoroaga
E-mail: valentina.chitoroaga@gmail.com
Founded: 1957
ISBN Prefix(es): 978-9975-9532

Standard Book Numbering Agency, see National Book Chamber of Republic of Moldova

Morocco

Agence Marocaine de l'ISBN
c/o Bibliotheque Nationale du Royaume du
Marco, Av Ibn Khaldoun, Agdal-Rabat
Tel: 05 37 27 23 00; 05 37 27 23 14 *Fax:* 05 37
77 21 52
E-mail: depotlegal@bnrm.ma
Web Site: www.bnrm.ma/bnrm
Key Personnel
Contact: Nawfal El Moukhi *E-mail:* elmoukhi.
nawfal@gmail.com
Publication(s): *Bibliographie Nationale Maro-
caine* (online)

CAFRAD, see Centre Africain de Formation et
de Recherche Administratives pour le
Developpement, Centre de Documentation

**†◇Centre Africain de Formation et de
Recherche Administratives pour le
Developpement, Centre de Documentation**
(African Training and Research Centre in
Administration for Development,
Documentation Centre)
Bd Mohammed V, Pavillion International, 90001
Tangier
Tel: 05 39 32 27 07; 06 61 30 72 69 *Fax:* 05 39
32 57 85
E-mail: cafrad@cafrad.org
Web Site: www.cafrad.org
Key Personnel
Dir General: Dr Stephane Monney Mouandjo
Founded: 1964
Training & research center for the improvement
of public administration & governance systems
in Africa.
Publication(s): *African Administrative Studies* (2
times/yr, journal); *Directory of African Con-
sultants*; *Directory of African Training & Re-
search Institutions in Public Administration &
Management*

Standard Book Numbering Agency, see Agence
Marocaine de l'ISBN

Namibia

ISBN Agency - Namibia
National Library of Namibia, 1-7 Eugene Marais
St, Private Bag 13349, Windhoek
Tel: (061) 293 53 00 *Fax:* (061) 293 53 21
E-mail: natlib@mec.gov.na
Web Site: www.nln.gov.na/biblio.html
Key Personnel
Chief Librarian: Johan Loubser *Tel:* (061) 293 53
01
Senior Librarian Bibliographic Services: Paul
Zulu *Tel:* (061) 293 53 05
Publication(s): *Namibia National Bibliography*

Standard Book Numbering Agency, see ISBN
Agency - Namibia

Netherlands

AILC, see International Comparative Literature
Association (ICLA)

**Collectieve Propaganda van het Nederlandse
Boek (CPNB)** (Foundation for the Collective
Promotion of the Dutch Book)
Herengracht 166, 1016 BP Amsterdam
Mailing Address: Postbus 10576, 1001 EN Ams-
terdam
Tel: (020) 626 49 71 *Fax:* (020) 623 16 96
E-mail: info@cpnb.nl
Web Site: www.cpnb.nl
Key Personnel
Press: Maud Aarsen *E-mail:* m.aarsen@cpnb.nl
Founded: 1983
Publication(s): *Kinderboekenmolen, Voorleesgids*
(annually)

†‡Cour Internationale de Justice (International
Court of Justice)
Palais de la Paix, Carnegieplein 2, 2517 KJ The
Hague
Tel: (070) 302 23 23 *Fax:* (070) 364 99 28
E-mail: information@icj-cij.org
Web Site: www.icj-cij.org
Key Personnel
First Secretary of the Court & Head, Information
Dept: Andrey Poskakukhin *Tel:* (070) 302 23
36
Registrar & Contact: Philippe Couvreur
Founded: 1945

CPNB, see Collectieve Propaganda van het
Nederlandse Boek (CPNB)

CTA, see Technical Centre for Agricultural &
Rural Co-operation

†ESOMAR
Atlas Arena, Azie Bldg-5th floor, Hoogoorddreef
5, 1101 BA Amsterdam
Tel: (020) 664 2141 *Fax:* (020) 664 2922; (020)
589 7885
E-mail: info@esomar.org; customerservice@
esomar.org
Web Site: www.esomar.org
Key Personnel
President: Laurent Flores
Vice President: David Smith
Dir General: Finn Raben
Founded: 1948
Subjects: Marketing & Opinion Research

**†◇European Association for Health
Information & Libraries**
EAHIL Secretariat, PO Box 1393, 3600 BJ
Maarssen
Tel: (0346) 550 876
Web Site: eahil.eu
Key Personnel
President: Marshall Dozier *E-mail:* president@
eahil.eu
Supervisor: Suzanne Bakker *E-mail:* eahil-secr@
list.encompass.nl
Founded: 1984

**European Society for Opinion & Marketing
Research**, see ESOMAR

ICLA, see International Comparative Literature
Association (ICLA)

IEA, see International Association for the
Evaluation of Educational Achievement (IEA)

IFLA, see International Federation of Library
Associations & Institutions (IFLA)

**International Association for the Evaluation of
Educational Achievement (IEA)**
Herengracht 487, 1017 BT Amsterdam
Tel: (020) 625 3625 *Fax:* (020) 420 7136

E-mail: secretariat@iea.nl
Web Site: www.iea.nl
Key Personnel
Chairman: Anne-Berit Kavli *E-mail:* abk@udir.no
Executive Dir: Dirk Hastedt *E-mail:* d.hastedt@
iea.nl
Publications Officer: Dr Gillian Wilson *E-mail:* g.
wilson@iea.nl
Founded: 1958
Research on educational outcomes.
Subjects: Education, Student Achievement
Publication(s): *Brochures; Newsletter* (annually)
ISBN Prefix(es): 978-90-79549; 978-92-9121
Number of titles published annually: 5 Print
Total Titles: 250 Print

**†◇International Comparative Literature
Association (ICLA)** (Association Internationale
de Litterature Comparee (AILC))
c/o Utrecht University, Achter de Dom 20, 3512
JP Utrecht
E-mail: ailc-icla@gmail.com
Web Site: ailc-icla.org
Key Personnel
President: Dr Hans Bertens *E-mail:* j.w.bertens@
uu.nl
Vice President: Mark Maufort
E-mail: mmaufort@ulb.ac.be; Anders Petters-
son *E-mail:* anders.pettersson@littvet.umu.se;
Monica Spiridon *E-mail:* mspiridon@ines.ro;
Zhou Xiaoyi *E-mail:* xiaoyizhou@hotmail.com
Secretary: Miceala Symington
E-mail: msymington@club-internet.fr; John
Burt Foster *E-mail:* jfoster@gmu.edu
Treasurer: Kamaigato Ken'ichi
E-mail: kamaigato2000@yahoo.co.jp; Kathleen
Komar *E-mail:* komar@ucla.edu; Hans Joachim
Backe *E-mail:* hans-joachim.backe@rub.de
Founded: 1954
Publication(s): *ICLA Bulletin* (periodical);
Recherche Litteraire (Literary Research, peri-
odical)

**†◇International Federation of Library
Associations & Institutions (IFLA)**
(Federation internationale des associations de
bibliothecaires et des bibliotheques)
Prins Willem-Alexanderhof 5, 2595 BE The
Hague
Mailing Address: Postbus 95312, 2509 CH The
Hague
Tel: (70) 314 08 84 *Fax:* (70) 383 48 27
E-mail: ifla@ifla.org
Web Site: www.ifla.org
Key Personnel
President: Donna Scheeder
E-mail: donna_scheeder@comcast.net
Treasurer: Christine Mackenzie *E-mail:* christine.
mackenzie.au@gmail.com
Secretary General: Gerald Leitner
Founded: 1927
Represent the interests of library & information
services & their users.
Publication(s): *IFLA Annual Report; IFLA Di-
rectory* (biennially); *IFLA Journal; IFLA Pro-
fessional Reports; IFLA Publications* (series
of monographs, published by K G Saur Verlag
KG, Germany); *International Cataloguing &
Bibliographic Control* (quarterly, journal)

Bureau ISBN
c/o CB, Erasmusweg 10, 4104 AK Culemborg
Mailing Address: Postbus 360, 4100 AJ Culem-
borg
Tel: (0345) 475855
E-mail: isbn@cb.nl
Web Site: www.isbn.nl

Koninklijke Boekverkopersbond (Royal
Booksellers Association)
Prins Hendriklaan 72, 3721 AT Bilthoven
Mailing Address: Postbus 32, 3720 AA Bilthoven

Tel: (030) 22 87 956 *Fax:* (030) 22 84 566
E-mail: info@boekbond.nl
Web Site: www.boekbond.nl
Key Personnel
Chairman: Ed Nijpels
Dir: Michael van Everdingen
E-mail: everdingen@boekbond.nl
Marketing & Sales Coordinator: Marjon Lijzen
E-mail: lijzen@boekbond.nl

Koninklijke Vereniging van het Boekenvak
(The Royal Society of the Booktrade)
Hogehilweg 6, 1101 CC Amsterdam-Zuidoost
Mailing Address: Postbus 12040, 1100 AA
Amsterdam-Zuidoost
Tel: (020) 624 02 12
E-mail: info@kvb.nl
Web Site: www.kvb.nl
Key Personnel
Chairman: Wouter van Gils
Founded: 1815
Represents the common interests of Dutch pub-
lishers, booksellers, wholesalers & importers &
is committed to improving the economic, social
& cultural position of the book.

KVB, see Koninklijke Vereniging van het
Boekenvak

Nederlands Letterenfonds (Dutch Foundation for
Literature)
Nieuwe Prinsengracht 89, 1018 VR Amsterdam
Mailing Address: Postbus 16588, 1001 RB Ams-
terdam
Tel: (020) 520 73 00 *Fax:* (020) 520 73 99
E-mail: post@letterenfonds.nl
Web Site: www.letterenfonds.nl
Key Personnel
Mng Dir: Tiziano Perez *E-mail:* t.perez@
letterenfonds.nl
Founded: 1991
Supports writers & translators & promotes Dutch
literature abroad.

Nederlands Uitgeversverbond (Dutch Publishers
Association)
Hogehilweg 6, 1101 CC Amsterdam-Zuidoost
Mailing Address: Postbus 12040, 1100 AA
Amsterdam-Zuidoost
Tel: (020) 430 91 50 *Fax:* (020) 430 91 99
E-mail: info@nuv.nl
Web Site: www.nuv.nl; www.uitgeversverbond.nl
Key Personnel
Chairman: Loek Hermans
Dir: Dr Peter Stadhouders
Executive Secretary: Ria Harder
Founded: 1880
Royal Dutch publishers' association.
Publication(s): *Annual Report*; *Brochures*; *NUV
Newsletter* (bimonthly)

Nederlandsche Vereeniging van Antiquaren
(Dutch Antiquarian Booksellers' Association)
Singel 319, 1012 WJ Amsterdam
Tel: (020) 623 83 53 *Fax:* (020) 620 75 77
E-mail: info@nvva.nl
Web Site: www.nvva.nl
Key Personnel
President: Frank Rutten *E-mail:* info@
antiquariaatbrinkman.nl
Secretary: Peter Everaers
Treasurer: Simon Blok
Founded: 1935
Membership(s): International League of Antiquar-
ian Booksellers (ILAB).

Standard Book Numbering Agency, see Bureau
ISBN

Stichting Drukwerk in de Marge (Foundation of
Marginal Printers)
Kastanjestr 60, 3552 SM Utrecht
E-mail: redactie@drukwerkindemarge.org
Web Site: drukwerkindemarge.org
Key Personnel
Chairman: Roosje Keijser
Treasurer: Hans Dessens
Secretary: Mart van Duijn *E-mail:* mart@
drukwerkindemarge.org
Founded: 1975
Publication(s): *Newsletter* (quarterly)

**†Technical Centre for Agricultural & Rural
Co-operation**
Agro Business Park 2, 6708 PW Wageningen
Mailing Address: Postbus 380, 6700 AJ Wagenin-
gen
Tel: (0317) 467100 *Fax:* (0317) 460067
E-mail: info@cta.int
Web Site: www.cta.int
Key Personnel
Dir: Michael Hailu
Founded: 1983
Subjects: Information & Communication Manage-
ment, Rural Development, Tropical Agriculture
ISBN Prefix(es): 978-92-9081
Branch Office(s)
Rue Montoyer, 39, 1000 Brussels, Belgium
Tel: (02) 513 7436 *Fax:* (02) 511 3868

†‡Universala Esperanto-Asocio (Universal
Esperanto Association)
Nieuwe Binnenweg 176, 3015 BJ Rotterdam
Tel: (010) 436 1044 *Fax:* (010) 436 1751
E-mail: info@uea.org; direktoro@co.uea.org
Web Site: www.uea.org
Founded: 1908
International organization for Esperanto speakers.
Language problems & Esperanto as a possible
solution.
ISBN Prefix(es): 978-92-9017

New Zealand

**†◇Bibliographical Society of Australia & New
Zealand Inc (BSANZ)**
c/o University of Otago, Dept of English, PO Box
56, Dunedin 9054
Tel: (03) 479 8330
Web Site: www.bsanz.org
Key Personnel
President: Donald Kerr *E-mail:* donald.kerr@
otago.ac.nz
Vice President: Anthony Tedeschi
E-mail: anthony.tedeschi@gmail.com
Secretary: Dr Chris Tiffin *E-mail:* c.tiffin@uq.
edu.au
Treasurer: Janet McDonald
E-mail: bibsocanztreasurer@gmail.com
Editor: Dr Shef Rogers *E-mail:* shef.rogers@
otago.ac.nz
Founded: 1969
Publication(s): *Broadsheet* (irregularly, newslet-
ter); *Script & Print: Bulletin of the Biblio-
graphical Society of Australia & New Zealand*
(quarterly, journal)
ISBN Prefix(es): 978-0-9598271

Booksellers New Zealand
Level 13, Grand Arcade, 16-20 Willis St,
Wellington 6100
Mailing Address: Featherston St, PO Box 25033,
Wellington 6146
Tel: (04) 472 1908 *Fax:* (04) 472 1912
E-mail: info@booksellers.co.nz
Web Site: www.booksellers.co.nz

Key Personnel
Chief Executive Officer: Lincoln Gould
E-mail: lincoln.gould@booksellers.co.nz
Membership Services: Cherie Donovan
E-mail: cherie.donovan@booksellers.co.nz
Finance Manager: Fiona Stewart *E-mail:* fiona.
stewart@booksellers.co.nz
Founded: 1920

BSANZ, see Bibliographical Society of Australia
& New Zealand Inc (BSANZ)

**Christian Booksellers' Association New
Zealand**
97 Streamlands Swamp Rd, RD 1, Warkworth
0981
E-mail: info@cba.net.nz
Web Site: www.cba.net.nz
Publication(s): *Newsletters* (6 issues/yr)

**†◇International Association of Music
Libraries, Archives & Documentation
Centres (New Zealand) Inc**
c/o Massey University Library, Wellington Cam-
pus, Private Box 756, Wellington 6140
E-mail: newzealand@iaml.info
Web Site: www.iaml.info
Key Personnel
President: Marilyn Portman *E-mail:* marilyn.
portman@aucklandcity.govt.nz
Secretary: Paul Emsley *E-mail:* paul.emsley@
vuw.ac.nz
Treasurer: Phillippa McKeown-Green *E-mail:* p.
mckeown-green@auckland.ac.nz
Founded: 1970
Parent Company: IAML

**New Zealand Council for Educational
Research (NZCER)**
Education House, Level 10, West Block, 178-182
Willis St, Wellington 6011
Mailing Address: PO Box 3237, Wellington 6140
Tel: (04) 384 7939 *Fax:* (04) 384 7933
E-mail: sales@nzcer.org.nz
Web Site: www.nzcer.org.nz
Key Personnel
Dir: Graeme Cosslett *Tel:* (04) 802 1387
E-mail: graeme.cosslett@nzcer.org.nz
Publishing Manager: David Ellis *E-mail:* david.
ellis@nzcer.org.nz
General Manager, Research & Development:
Jacky Burgon *Tel:* (04) 802 1449 *E-mail:* jacky.
burgon@nzcer.org.nz
Communications Manager: Sarah Boyd *Tel:* (04)
802 1468 *E-mail:* sarah.boyd@nzcer.org.nz
Founded: 1934
Publication(s): *Assessment Matters* (annually,
journal); *Curriculum Matters* (annually, jour-
nal); *Early Childhood Folio* (2 issues/yr, jour-
nal)
ISBN Prefix(es): 978-0-908567; 978-0-908916;
978-1-877140; 978-1-877293; 978-1-877398;
978-1-877396; 978-1-927151; 978-1-927231
Number of titles published annually: 15 Print
Total Titles: 200 Print

New Zealand Press Council
79 Boulcott St, Wellington 6011
Mailing Address: PO Box 10 879, Wellington
6143
Toll Free Tel: 0800 969 357
E-mail: info@presscouncil.org.nz
Web Site: www.presscouncil.org.nz
Key Personnel
Executive Dir: Mary Major
Founded: 1972
Provides an independent forum for resolving
complaints involving the press & other news
media.

New Zealand Standard Book Numbering Agency
National Library of New Zealand, PO Box 1467, Wellington 6140
Tel: (04) 474 3074 *Fax:* (04) 474 3161
E-mail: isbn@dia.govt.nz
Web Site: www.natlib.govt.nz
Key Personnel
Contact: Linda Hall

NZCER, see New Zealand Council for Educational Research (NZCER)

NZPC, see New Zealand Press Council

PANZ, see Publishers Association of New Zealand (PANZ)

Publishers Association of New Zealand (PANZ)
B3, 72 Apollo Dr, Rosedale, Auckland 0632
Mailing Address: PO Box 102 006, North Shore, Auckland 0745
Tel: (09) 280 3212
E-mail: admin@publishers.org.nz
Web Site: www.publishers.org.nz
Key Personnel
President: Melanie Laville-Moore
 E-mail: melanie@allenandunwin.com
Vice President: Mark Sayes
Association Dir: Catriona Ferguson
Membership Services Manager: Katherine Shanks
 Tel: (09) 280 3213
Founded: 1978
Represents publishers' interests to industry & government.
Membership(s): International Publishers Association; WeCreate
Publication(s): *Directory of PANZ Members; An Introduction to New Zealand Publishing; The Publisher* (bulletin)

Nigeria

CBAN, see Christian Booksellers Association of Nigeria (CBAN)

Christian Booksellers Association of Nigeria (CBAN)
Assets-Corp Plaza, 21, Awolowo Way, Suite B64, Ikeja
Tel: (0803) 391 4873
Founded: 1980
Parent Company: Christian Booksellers Association USA, 1365 Garden of the Gods Rd, Suite 105, Colorado Springs, CO 80907, United States

NERDC, see Nigerian Educational Research & Development Council (NERDC)

Nigerian Book Fair Trust (NBFT)
94 Yaya Abatan St, Adjacent Fadare Junction, Ogba, Lagos
Mailing Address: PO Box 22362, Ikeja, Lagos State
Tel: (01) 8124705
E-mail: info@nibfng.org
Web Site: www.nibfng.org
Aims to improve the reading culture in Nigeria, create a conducive environment for authors to get published by either local or foreign publishers, establish a strong book market with economic potentials for social development using the platform of the book fairs & showcase Nigerian books in their entirety.

Nigerian Educational Research & Development Council (NERDC)
Km 135 Lokoja-Kaduna Rd, Sheda, PMB 91, Abuja
Tel: (090) 39730713; (070) 81361390
E-mail: info@nerdc.ng
Web Site: nerdc.ng
Key Personnel
Executive Secretary: Prof Ismail Junaidu
Assistant Dir: Theresa Oresanya
Founded: 1988
Branch Office(s)
Old SUBEB Bldg, Water Works Rd, Abakaliki, Ebonyi State
8 Orlu St, Area 3 Garki, Abuja (liaison off)
TTC Rd, Ikot-Ansa, Calabar, Cross River State
Yobe Government Secretariat, Opposite Government Lodge, Bukar Ibrahim, Phase 1, Damaturu, Yobe State
GP 109, State Rd, Opposite Kano State High Court, Kano, Kano State
Federal Secretariat, 3rd floor, Rooms 313-315, Minna, Niger State
3, Jibowu St, Yaba, Lagos

Nigerian ISBN Agency
National Bibliographic Control Dept, National Library of Nigeria, Plot 274 Sanusi-Dantata House, Central Business District, PMB 1, Garki, Abuja
Tel: (0703) 0617969 (cell)
E-mail: natbcdnlnig@yahoo.com
Web Site: www.nln.gov.ng
Key Personnel
Contact: Mrs Anthonia Onuoha
Publication(s): *Nigerian ISBN Manual & Directory*

Nigerian Publishers' Association (NPA)
Book House, Quarter 673, Jericho
Mailing Address: GPO Box 2541, Ibadan
Tel: (02) 7515352; (080) 37251454 (cell)
Key Personnel
President: N O Okereke
Founded: 1965
Publication(s): *Nigerian Books-in-Print* (catalog); *The Publisher* (2 times/yr, magazine)

NPA, see Nigerian Publishers' Association (NPA)

Standard Book Numbering Agency, see Nigerian ISBN Agency

Norway

Den Norske Bokhandlerforening (The Norwegian Booksellers Association)
Ovre Vollgate 15, 0158 Oslo
Tel: 22 39 68 00
E-mail: firmapost@bokhandlerforeningen.no
Web Site: www.bokhandlerforeningen.no
Key Personnel
Dir: Trine Stensen *Tel:* 950 60 117
 E-mail: trine@bokhandlerforeningen.no
Protects the interests of booksellers & works to enhance the literature & the book's place in society.
Publication(s): *Bok og Samfunn* (magazine)

†International Union of Geological Sciences (IUGS) (Union internationale des Sciences Geologiques)
Geological Survey of Norway, Leiv Eirikssons vei 39, 7040 Trondheim
Mailing Address: Postbok 6315 Sluppen, 7491 Trondheim
Tel: 73 90 40 00

E-mail: ngu@ngu.no
Web Site: www.iugs.org; www.ngu.no
Key Personnel
President: Dr Roland Oberhaensli *Tel:* (0331) 977 5870 *Fax:* (0331) 977 5700 *E-mail:* r.oberhaensli.iugs@geo.uni-postdam.de
Secretary General: Prof Jose P Calvo *Tel:* 91 394 49 02 *E-mail:* jpcalvo@ucm.es
Secretariat: Wang Wei *Tel:* (10) 6831 0893 *Fax:* (10) 6831 0894 *E-mail:* secretariat@iugs.org
Founded: 1961
Promotion & development of earth sciences.
Publication(s): *Episodes* (quarterly)

ISBN-Kontoret Norge
National Library of Norway, 8607 Mo i Rana
Tel: 75 12 11 48 *Fax:* 75 12 12 22
E-mail: isbn-kontoret@nb.no
Web Site: www.nb.no
Key Personnel
Contact: Eva Kathryn Holst

ISSN Norge (ISSN Norway)
National Library of Norway, Postboks 2674, Solli, 0203 Oslo
Tel: 23 27 61 00
E-mail: issn-norge@nb.no
Web Site: www.nb.no/sn/html/issn.html
Key Personnel
Senior Librarian: Hanna Elise Hansen
Librarian: Erik Aaslid

IUGS, see International Union of Geological Sciences (IUGS)

NMFF, see Norsk Musikkforleggerforening

Norsk Musikkforleggerforening (Norwegian Music Publishers' Association)
Kongens Gate 4, 0153 Oslo
Tel: 45 47 00 95
E-mail: mail@nmff.no
Web Site: www.nmff.no; www.musikkforleggerne.no
Key Personnel
Secretary General: Cathrine Ruud
 E-mail: cathrine@nmff.no
Founded: 1936

Den Norske Forfatterforening (Norwegian Authors' Union)
Postboks 327 Sentrum, 0103 Oslo
Tel: 23 35 76 20 *Fax:* 22 42 11 07
E-mail: post@forfatterforeningen.no
Web Site: www.forfatterforeningen.no
Key Personnel
Chairman: Sigmund Lovasen
Secretary General: Mette Moller
Founded: 1893
To protect & promote Norwegian literature & authors.

Den Norske Forleggerforening (The Norwegian Publishers Association)
Ovre Vollgate 15, 0158 Oslo
Tel: 22 00 75 80 *Fax:* 22 33 38 30
E-mail: dnf@forleggerforeningen.no
Web Site: www.forleggerforeningen.no
Key Personnel
Mng Dir: Kristen Einarsson *E-mail:* kristen.einarsson@forleggerforeningen.no
Membership(s): FEP; IPA.

Standard Book Numbering Agency, see ISBN-Kontoret Norge

Pakistan

Pakistan ISBN Agency
National Library of Pakistan, Constitution Ave, Islamabad 44000
Tel: (051) 9206436; (051) 9206440; (051) 9202544; (051) 9202549
E-mail: nlpiba@isb.paknet.com.pk
Web Site: www.nlp.gov.pk
Key Personnel
Dir General: Muhammad Nazir *Tel:* (051) 9202544 ext 237
Dir: Syed Ghyour Hussain *Tel:* (051) 9207456 ext 226 *E-mail:* ghyour_hussain@hotmail.com

Standard Book Numbering Agency, see Pakistan ISBN Agency

Urdu Science Board (USB)
299 Upper Mail, Lahore
Tel: (042) 35758475; (042) 3575874 *Fax:* (042) 35789215
E-mail: info@urduscience.org.pk
Founded: 1962
Develop & publish learning & instructional material in Urdu for science, mathematics & technical subjects.
Subjects: Mathematics, Science, Technology

USB, see Urdu Science Board (USB)

Papua New Guinea

Papua New Guinea ISBN Agency
National Library Service of PNG, PO Box 734, Waigani
Tel: 7701 4853 *Fax:* 325 4251
Key Personnel
Contact: Mr Chris Kelly Meti
  E-mail: chris_meti@education.gov.pg

Standard Book Numbering Agency, see Papua New Guinea ISBN Agency

Peru

Camara Peruana del Libro (Peruvian Publishers' Association)
Av Cuba 427, Jesus Maria Apdo 10253, Lima 11
Tel: (01) 472 9516 *Fax:* (01) 265 0735
E-mail: cp-libro@cpl.org.pe
Web Site: www.cpl.org.pe
Key Personnel
President: German Coronado Vallenas
Vice President: Ana Patricia Arevalo Majluf
Secretary: Salomon Senepo Gonzales
Treasurer: Alberto Almendres
Founded: 1946

Philippines

PEPA, see Philippine Educational Publishers Association (PEPA)

Philippine Educational Publishers Association (PEPA)
4F SEDCCO 1 bldg, Rada St, Corner of Legazpi St, Legaspi Village, Makati
Tel: (02) 843 6592; (02) 893 8501
Key Personnel
President: Jose Maria T Policarpio
Founded: 1950
Membership(s): International Trade Association; IPA.

Standard Book Numbering Agency
The National Library of the Philippines, PO Box 2926, Manila
Tel: (02) 310-5032
E-mail: isbn@nlp.gov.ph
Web Site: web.nlp.gov.ph
Key Personnel
Chief, Bibliographic Services Division, ISBN Administrator: Nina Fronda *E-mail:* bsd@nlp.gov.ph
Assistant Chief, Bibliographic Services Division: Eusebia M Accad
Founded: 1900

Poland

Instytut Ksiazki (The Book Institute)
ul Zygmunta Wroblewskiego 6, 31-148 Krakow
Tel: (12) 61 71 900 *Fax:* (12) 62 37 682
E-mail: office@bookinstitute.pl
Web Site: www.bookinstitute.pl
Key Personnel
Head: Dariusz Jaworski
Founded: 2003
Promotes Polish literature worldwide.

Krajowe Biuro ISBN
Biblioteka Narodowa, al Niepodleglosci 213, 02-086 Warsaw
Tel: (22) 608 24 10; (22) 608 24 32 *Fax:* (22) 825 52 51
E-mail: bnisbn@bn.org.pl
Web Site: www.bn.org.pl
Key Personnel
Contact: Dorota Cymer

Polska Izba Ksiazki (Polish Chamber of Books)
ul Oleandrow 8, 00-629 Warsaw
Tel: (22) 875 94 96
E-mail: biuro@pik.org.pl
Web Site: www.pik.org.pl
Key Personnel
President: Wlodzimierz Albin *E-mail:* wlodek.albin@pik.org.pl
Vice President: Barbara Jozwiak; Grzegorz Majerowicz
Founded: 1990

Polskie Towarzystwo Wydawcow Ksiazek (PTWK) (Polish Society of Book Editors)
ul Swietokrzyska 30, lok 156, 00-116 Warsaw
Tel: (22) 407 77 30; (22) 850 34 76 *Fax:* (22) 850 34 76
E-mail: ptwk@ptwk.pl
Web Site: www.wydawca.com.pl
Key Personnel
Dir: Maria Kuisz
Founded: 1921
Association of creative professionals, publishers, editors, typographers & graphic designers.

PTWK, see Polskie Towarzystwo Wydawcow Ksiazek (PTWK)

Standard Book Numbering Agency, see Krajowe Biuro ISBN

Stowarzyszenie Ksiegarzy Polskich (Association of Polish Booksellers)
ul Mazowiecka 6/8, 00-048 Warsaw
Tel: (22) 827 93 81 *Fax:* (22) 827 93 81
E-mail: skp@ksiegarze.org.pl
Web Site: www.ksiegarze.org.pl
Key Personnel
President: Tadeusz Przeslakiewicz
Vice President: Dr Andrzej Skrzypczak
Secretary: Katarzyna Balicka-Wieckowska
Treasurer: Alice Szczesna-Kania
Social organization for State book trade employees.
Publication(s): *Ksiegarz*
ISBN Prefix(es): 978-83-85020

Zarzad Targow Warszawskich SA
ul Pulawska 12A, 02-566 Warsaw
Tel: (22) 849 60 06 *Fax:* (22) 849 35 84
E-mail: ztw@ztw.pl
Web Site: www.ztw.pl
Founded: 1992
Organizer of trade fairs & exhibitions.

Zwiazek Literatow Polskich (Polish Writers' Union)
Krakowskie Przedmiescie 87/89, 00-079 Warsaw
Tel: (22) 826 57 85 *Fax:* (22) 828 39 19
E-mail: owzlp@o2.pl
Web Site: www.literatura.waw.pl
Key Personnel
President: Aldona Borowicz
Vice President: Jerzy Jandowski; Zbigniew Milewski
Secretary: Jan Cichocki
Treasurer: Ewa Zeleny
Founded: 1920
Membership(s): European Writers' Congress (EWC).

Portugal

Agencia Portuguesa de ISBN
Associacao Portuguesa de Editores e Livreiros, Av dos Estados Unidos da America, nº 97-6º esq, 1700-167 Lisbon
Tel: 21 847 35 91
E-mail: isbn@apel.pt
Web Site: www.apel.pt
Key Personnel
Contact: Ana Tristao

Associacao Portuguesa de Editores e Livreiros (Portuguese Publishers & Booksellers Association)
Av dos Estados Unidos da America, nº 97-6º esq, 1700-167 Lisbon
Tel: 21 843 51 80; 21 847 35 91 (ISBN agency)
E-mail: geral@apel.pt; isbn@apel.pt
Web Site: www.apel.pt
Key Personnel
President: Joao Amaral
Vice President: Joao Alvim
Founded: 1927
Publication(s): *Livros Disponiveis*; *Livros de Portugal, Boletim Bibliografico* (Portuguese Books in Print, monthly)

DGLAB, see Direccao Geral do Livro dos Arquivos e das Bibliotecas (DGLAB)

Direccao Geral do Livro dos Arquivos e das Bibliotecas (DGLAB) (General Directorate for Book, Archives & Libraries)
Edificio da Torre do Tombo, Alameda da Universidade, 1649 010 Lisbon

Tel: 21 003 71 00 *Fax:* 21 003 71 01
E-mail: secretariado@dglab.gov.pt
Web Site: dglab.gov.pt
Key Personnel
Dir: Silvestre Lacerda
Founded: 2012 (merger of Direccao Geral do
Livro e das Bibliotecas (DGLB) & Direcao-
Geral de Arquivos (DGARQ))

Standard Book Numbering Agency, see
Agencia Portuguesa de ISBN

Qatar

Qatar ISBN Group Agency
Qatar National Library, PO Box 5825, Doha
Tel: 4438 9888 *Fax:* 4441 2308
Key Personnel
Contact: Abdulla Nasser al-Ansari
E-mail: alansari_123@hotmail.com

Standard Book Numbering Agency, see Qatar
ISBN Group Agency

Romania

ADEPC, see Asociatia Difuzorilor si Editorilor
Patronat al Cartii (ADEPC)

AER, see Asociatia Editorilor din Romania
(AER)

**Asociatia Difuzorilor si Editorilor Patronat al
Cartii (ADEPC)**
Str Petru Maior, nr 32, Sector 1, 011264
Bucharest
Tel: (021) 2220213 *Fax:* (021) 2220213
E-mail: adepc@adepc.ro
Web Site: adepc.ro
Key Personnel
President: Lucia Ovezea
Secretary: Tamara Sandu
Founded: 1996

Asociatia Editorilor din Romania (AER)
(Publishers' Association in Romania)
Sos Nicolae Titulescu nr 18, bl 23, sc 2, et 8, ap
83, sector 1, 011142 Bucharest
Tel: (021) 3110650; (021) 3110660 *Fax:* (021)
3115941; (0378) 107299
E-mail: info@aer.ro
Web Site: www.aer.ro
Key Personnel
President: Grigore Arsene
Executive Dir: Mihai Mitrica
Founded: 1991

Centrul National ISBN-ISSN-CIP
(ISBN-ISSN-CIP National Centre)
c/o Biblioteca Nationala a Romaniei, Blvd Unirii,
nr 22, sector 3, 030833 Bucharest
Tel: (021) 3112635; (021) 3142434 (ext 1035)
Fax: (021) 3124990
E-mail: isbn@bibnat.ro; issn@bibnat.ro; cip@
bibnat.ro
Web Site: www.bibnat.ro
Key Personnel
Contact: Mihaela Laura Stanciu
Activities for a national ISBN & ISSN agency
(record all the Romanian publishers, assign
ISBN & ISSN codes, etc). In charge with the
management of Romanian Cataloguing in Pub-

lication Programme & editor of CIP National
Bibliography.
Membership(s): ISBN International Agency; ISSN
International Centre.

SER, see Societatea Editorilor din Romania
(SER)

Societatea Editorilor din Romania (SER)
(Romanian Society of Publishers)
Bd Liber tatii, nr 4, bl 117, sc 1, et 7, ap 20, sec-
tor 4, 040128 Bucharest
Tel: (021) 3102889 *Fax:* (021) 3102889
E-mail: societatea_editorilor@yahoo.com; ser@
soced.ro
Web Site: www.soced.ro
Key Personnel
President: Ioan Enescu
Vice President: Lucian Pricop
Executive Dir: Ioana Nitulescu
Founded: 2002

Societatea Ziaristilor din Romania (Journalists
Society of Romania)
Piata Presei Libere 1, 71341 Bucharest
Mailing Address: PO Box 33, 71341 Bucharest
Tel: (021) 222 83 51; (021) 222 38 71; (021) 315
24 82 *Fax:* (021) 317 97 96
E-mail: szrpress@moon.ro

Standard Book Numbering Agency, see Centrul
National ISBN-ISSN-CIP

Standard Serial Numbering Agency, see
Centrul National ISBN-ISSN-CIP

Uniunea Scriitorilor din Romania (Writers
Union of Romania)
Calea Victoriei nr 133, Sector 1, 010071
Bucharest
Tel: (021) 3165829 *Fax:* (021) 372897880
E-mail: uniunea.scriitorilor@yahoo.com
Web Site: www.uniuneascriitorilor.ro
Key Personnel
President: Nicolae Manolescu
First Vice President: Varujan Vosganian
Vice President: Gabriel Chifu
Secretary: Roxana Chioseolu
Mng Dir: Ion Pahontu
Founded: 1949
Publication(s): *Apostrof* (Apostrophe); *Convorbiri
Literare* (Literary Talk); *Euphorion*; *Helikon*;
Luceafarul (House); *Orizont* (Horizon); *Revista
Ramuri*; *Romania Literara* (Literary Romania);
Steaua (The Star); *Vatra* (Hearth); *Viata Ro-
maneasca* (Romanian Life)

Russia

†◇**International Association of Research &
Technical Libraries**
Formerly International Association of Research,
Scientific & Technical Libraries
c/o Russian National Public Library for Science
& Technology, 3rd ul Khoroshevskaya 17,
123298 Moscow
Tel: (495) 698-93-05 *Fax:* (495) 698-93-17
E-mail: gpntb@gpntb.ru
Web Site: www.gpntb.ru

**International Association of Research,
Scientific & Technical Libraries**, see
International Association of Research &
Technical Libraries

National Centre for ISSN, see Rossiiskaya
Knizhnaya Palata

PAR, see Publishers Association of Russia (PAR)

Publishers Association of Russia (PAR)
Luchnikov St 4-1, 101000 Moscow
Tel: (495) 6257520
E-mail: askibook@gmail.com
Web Site: www.aski.ru
Key Personnel
President: Chechenev Konstantin
Vice President: Oleg Filimonov
Founded: 1990
Protects the common rights & interests of Russian
publishers. Coordinates their activities to create
conditions for development & improvement of
domestic book publishing.
Membership(s): International Publishers Associa-
tion (IPA).

Rossiiskaya Knizhnaya Palata (Russian Book
Chamber)
Star Blvd, 17, Bldg 1, 129085 Moscow
Mailing Address: Kremlin Embankment, 1/9,
Bldg 8, 119019 Moscow
Fax: (495) 688-99-91; (495) 688-96-89
E-mail: info@bookchamber.ru; isbn@tass.ru
Web Site: www.bookchamber.ru
Key Personnel
Dir General: Elena Nogina
Founded: 1917
All books & publications are registered & de-
scribed.
Chamber also administers Russian National ISBN
Agency & is the National Centre for ISSN.
Publication(s): *Knizhnava Letopis'* (Book Chron-
icle, weekly bulletin & 5 indexes, journal, in-
forms about all types of books & booklets pub-
lished in Russia)

**Russian Academy of Sciences, Scientific
Publishing Council**
Leninskii ave 14, 119991 Moscow
Tel: (495) 938-0309 *Fax:* (495) 954-3320; (495)
938-1844
Web Site: www.ras.ru

Russian ISBN Agency, see Rossiiskaya
Knizhnaya Palata

Standard Book Numbering Agency, see
Rossiiskaya Knizhnaya Palata

Saudi Arabia

Standard Book Numbering Agency
King Fahd National Library, PO Box 7572,
Riyadh 11472
Tel: (011) 4186351 *Fax:* (011) 4645197
E-mail: kfnl-isn@kfnl.gov.sa
Web Site: www.kfnl.gov.sa
Key Personnel
Contact: Hassan H Al-Rewaily

Serbia

ISBN Agency for Serbia
National Library of Serbia, Skerliceva 1, 11000
Belgrade
Tel: (011) 2459 444 *Fax:* (011) 2459 444
Web Site: www.nb.rs

SERBIA

Key Personnel
Contact: Iris Djokovic *E-mail:* perunika.
djokovic@nb.rs
Founded: 1950

Publishers & Booksellers Association of Serbia
Makedonska 5, 2nd floor, 11000 Belgrade
Tel: (011) 41 21 359; (063) 398 905 (cell)
E-mail: sekretar@izdavaci.rs
Web Site: www.izdavaci.rs
Key Personnel
Chair: Dejan Papic

Standard Book Numbering Agency, see ISBN
Agency for Serbia

Udruzenje Izdavaca i Knjizara Jugoslavije
(Association of Yugoslav Publishers &
Booksellers)
Kneza Milosa 25/I, 11000 Belgrade
Tel: (011) 642-533 *Fax:* (011) 646-339
Founded: 1954
Voluntary non-governmental organization. Represents members at home, abroad & by international organizations (IPA, Geneva). Organizer of the International Book Fair in Belgrade. Publishing activities.
Membership(s): International Publishers Association (Geneva).
Publication(s): *Catalog of Yugoslav Books in Print*; *Catalogue of Book Fairs in Belgrade*; *Directory of Exhibitors at the International Book Fair in Belgrade*; *Directory of Members of the Association of Yugoslav Publishers & Booksellers* (annually)
ISBN Prefix(es): 978-86-7115

Singapore

National Library Board Singapore
National Library, 100 Victoria St, No 14-01, Singapore 188064
Tel: 6332 3255; 6332 3133 *Fax:* 6332 3233
E-mail: helpdesk@library.nlb.gov.sg
Web Site: www.nlb.gov.sg
Key Personnel
Chief Executive Officer: Elaine Ng
Deputy Chief Executive & Chief Librarian: Ms Tay Ai Cheng
Founded: 1995
Publication(s): *Singapore: National Library*; *Singapore Periodicals Index* (annually)

SBPA, see Singapore Book Publishers
Association

Singapore Book Publishers Association
20 Maxwell Rd, No 09-17 Maxwell House, Singapore 069113
Tel: 6408 9712 *Fax:* 6399 3699
E-mail: info@singaporebookpublishers.sg
Web Site: www.singaporebookpublishers.sg
Key Personnel
President: Peter Schoppert *Tel:* 6516 2382
  Fax: 6774 0652 *E-mail:* schoppert@nus.edu.sg
Vice President: Edmund Wee *Tel:* 6292
  4456 *Fax:* 6292 4414 *E-mail:* edmund@
  epigrambooks.sg
Honorary Secretary: Peh Shing Woei
  Tel: 6760 1388 ext 244 *Fax:* 6762 3247
  E-mail: shingwoei@shinglee.com.sg
Honorary Treasurer: Betty Tan *Tel:* 6225 5770
  Fax: 6377 0890 *E-mail:* betty@englishcorner.sg
Founded: 1966
Membership(s): ASEAN Book Publishers Association; Asia Pacific Publishers Association (Seoul).

Slovakia

Slovak ISBN Group Agency
Slovak National Library, Nam J C Hronskeho 1, 036 01 Martin
Tel: (043) 2451140; (043) 2451138 *Fax:* (043) 4224984
E-mail: isbn@snk.sk; snk@snk.sk
Web Site: www.snk.sk
Key Personnel
Contact: Erika Polonkova
Founded: 1989

Slovenia

Center za slovensko knjizevnost (Center for Slovenian Literature)
Metelkova 6, SI-1000 Ljubljana
Tel: (01) 505 1674 *Fax:* (01) 505 1674
E-mail: litcenter@mail.ljudmila.org
Web Site: www.ljudmila.org/litcenter
Key Personnel
Chairman: Matej Bogataj
Founded: 1999
ISBN Prefix(es): 978-961-6036

Gospodarska Zbornica Slovenije, see Zdruzenie Zaloznikov in Knjigotrzcev Slovenije
Gospodarska Zbornica Slovenije

Javna Agencija za Knjigo Republike Slovenije (Slovenian Book Agency)
Metelkova ul 2b, SI-1000 Ljubljana
Tel: (01) 369 58 20 *Fax:* (01) 369 58 30
E-mail: gp.jakrs@jakrs.si
Web Site: www.jakrs.si
Key Personnel
Dir: Ales Novak *E-mail:* ales.novak@jakrs.si
Founded: 2009
Promotes Slovenian literature & scientific journalism.

Standard Book Numbering Agency
National & University Library, Turjaska 1, p p 259, SI-1000 Ljubljana
Fax: (01) 5861-311
E-mail: isbn@nuk.uni-lj.si; cip@nuk.uni-lj.si
Web Site: www.nuk.uni-lj.si
Key Personnel
Contact: Alenka Kanic *Tel:* (01) 5861-
  333 *E-mail:* alenka.kanic@nuk.uni-lj.si;
  Metka Kramberger *Tel:* (01) 5861-330
  E-mail: margerita.kramberger@nuk.uni.lj.si

Zdruzenie Zaloznikov in Knjigotrzcev Slovenije Gospodarska Zbornica Slovenije (Association of Publishers & Booksellers of Slovenia)
Dimiceva ul 13, SI-1000 Ljubljana
Tel: (01) 5898 000 *Fax:* (01) 5898 100
E-mail: info@gzs.si
Web Site: www.gzs.si/slo
Membership(s): International Publishers Association.

South Africa

IATUL, see International Association of University Libraries (IATUL)

†**International Association of University Libraries (IATUL)**
c/o Cape Peninsula University of Technology Library, PO Box 1906, Bellville 7535
Web Site: www.iatul.org
Key Personnel
Secretary: Dr Elisha Chiware *E-mail:* chiwaree@cput.ac.za
Founded: 1955
Publication(s): *IATUL Conference Proceedings*; *IATUL News* (quarterly)

International Standard Book Numbering Agency
National Library of South Africa, 228 Proes St, Pretoria 0001
Mailing Address: National Library of South Africa, PO Box X990, Pretoria 0001
Tel: (012) 401 9718 *Fax:* (012) 325 5984
E-mail: isn.agency@nlsa.ac.za
Web Site: www.nlsa.ac.za
Key Personnel
Contact: Magret Kibido *E-mail:* magret.kibido@nlsa.ac.za

ISBN Agency, see International Standard Book Numbering Agency

PASA, see Publishers' Association of South Africa (PASA)

Publishers' Association of South Africa (PASA)
House Vincent, Wynberg Mews, Unit 104, 1st floor, Brodie Rd, Wynberg 7800
Mailing Address: PO Box 18223, Wynberg 7824
Tel: (021) 762 9083 *Fax:* (021) 762 2763
E-mail: pasa@publishsa.co.za
Web Site: www.publishsa.co.za
Key Personnel
Executive Dir: Mpuka Radinku *E-mail:* mpuka@publishsa.co.za
Operations & Office Manager: Rhulani Bila
  E-mail: rhulani@publishsa.co.za
Founded: 1992

SABA, see South African Booksellers' Association

South African Booksellers' Association
29 Golf Course Rd, Sybrand Park, Rondebosch, Cape Town 7700
Mailing Address: PO Box 870, Bellville 7535
Tel: (021) 697 1164 *Fax:* (021) 697 1410
E-mail: saba@sabooksellers.com
Web Site: sabooksellers.com
Key Personnel
President: Guru Redhi *Tel:* (032) 945 1240
  E-mail: redhi@iafrica.com
Vice President: Mohamed Kharwa *Tel:* (031) 337 2112 *E-mail:* kharwa_m@provisions.
  co.za; Riaz Hassim *Tel:* (011) 852 5903
  E-mail: info@bookexpress.co.za
Honorary Secretary: Peter Adams *Tel:* (086) 134 1341 *E-mail:* padams@adamsbooks.co.za
Founded: 1998
Membership(s): International Booksellers Federation; Pan African Booksellers Association; Publishers Association of South Africa (PASA); South African Book Development Council.

South Korea

Korea ISBN Agency
The National Library of Korea, 201 Banpo-daero, Seocho-gu, Seoul 06579

Tel: (02) 590-0700 *Fax:* (02) 590-0621
E-mail: isbn@mail.nl.go.kr
Web Site: seojl.nl.go.kr
Founded: 1991

Korean Printers Association
12, Yanghwa-Ro, 15-gil, Mapo-Gu, Seoul 121-838
Tel: (02) 335 5881 *Fax:* (02) 338 9801
E-mail: assn@print.or.kr
Web Site: www.print.or.kr
Key Personnel
Chairman: Cho Jung Seuk
Founded: 1948
Aims to protect the rights of printers & raise their status in the printing industry.

Korean Publishers Association
105-2, Sagan-Dong, Jongno-gu, Seoul 110-190
Tel: (070) 7126-4720; (070) 7126-4736 *Fax:* (02) 738-5414; (02) 735-5653
E-mail: kpa@kpa21.or.kr
Web Site: www.kpa21.or.kr
Key Personnel
Mng Dir: Sok-Ghee Baek
Founded: 1947
ISBN Prefix(es): 978-89-85231

†◇Seoul Printing Center
146-1, Sasangnim-dong, Jung-gu, Seoul 100-400
Tel: (02) 2278-3081 *Fax:* (02) 2278-3082
E-mail: webmaster@seoulprinting.com
Web Site: www.seoulprinting.com
Key Personnel
President: Jung-suk Cho
Supports printing export for developing countries overseas.

Standard Book Numbering Agency, see Korea ISBN Agency

Spain

Agencia del ISBN
Cea Bermudez, 44 2º Dcha, 28003 Madrid
Tel: 902 105 389
E-mail: agencia@agenciaisbn.es
Web Site: agenciaisbn.es
Key Personnel
Dir: Miguel Jimenez
Founded: 1972

Asociacion de Editores de Andalucia
(Publishers Association of Andalusia)
C/ Joaquin Verdugo Landi, nº1, 29007 Malaga
Tel: 952070048
E-mail: aea@aea.es
Web Site: www.aea.es
Key Personnel
Vice President: Francisco Arguelles
Founded: 1983

Asociacion de Editores en Lengua Vasca
(Basque Language Publishers' Association)
Zemoria, 25, bajo, 20013 Donostia
Tel: 943292349
Web Site: www.editoreak.eus
Key Personnel
Contact: Ana Urrestarazu
Founded: 1984
Promote & protect publication of works in the Basque language.

Asociacion de Escritores y Artistas Espanoles
(Spanish Writers' & Artists' Association)
C/ Leganitos nº 10, 1º Derecha, 28013 Madrid

Tel: 91 559 90 67 *Fax:* 91 542 44 67
E-mail: secretaria@aeae.es
Web Site: www.aeae.es
Key Personnel
President: Juan Van-Halen
Vice President: Manuel Carrion Gutiez; Evaristo Guerra
Secretary & Dir General: Jose Lopez Martinez
Treasurer: Pilar Aroca
Founded: 1871
ISBN Prefix(es): 978-84-87857

Asociacion Galega de Editores (Galician Publishers Association)
Rua do Horreo 22, 3º, 15701 Santiago de Compostela (Galicia)
Tel: 881978764
E-mail: age@editoresgalegos.org; s.tecnica@editoresgalegos.org
Web Site: www.editoresgalegos.org
Key Personnel
President: Laura Rodriguez Herrera
Vice President: Jose Aldea Moscoso
Secretary: Ana Guerra Canizo
Treasurer: Jesus Gomez Sanjurjo
The purpose of the association is to manage & protect the common interests of Galician publishers as well as the promotion & dissemination of Galician books.

Centro del Libro de Aragon
Edificio Ranillas, Av Ranillas 5D, 50071 Zaragoza
Tel: 976 71 41 80; 976 71 41 50 *Fax:* 976 71 48 08
E-mail: centrodellibro@aragon.es
Web Site: www.centrodellibrodearagon.es
Publication(s): *Letras Aragonesas* (6 times/yr)
Parent Company: El Departamento de Educacion, Cultura y Deporte del Gobierno de Aragon

Federacion de Gremios de Editores de Espana (FGEE) (Spanish Association of Publishers Guilds)
Cea Bermudez, 44-2º Dcha, 28003 Madrid
Tel: 91 534 51 95 *Fax:* 91 535 26 25
E-mail: fgee@fge.es
Web Site: www.federacioneditores.org
Key Personnel
President: Daniel Fernandez
Vice President: Rosalina Diaz
Exec Dir: Antonio Maria Avila
Treasurer: Miguel Barrero
Founded: 1978
To represent & defend the general interests of the Spanish publishing industry.

FGEE, see Federacion de Gremios de Editores de Espana (FGEE)

GECYL, see Gremio de Editores de Castilla y Leon (GECYL)

Gremi d'Editors de Catalunya (Editors Guild of Catalonia)
Valencia, 279 1r, 08009 Barcelona
Tel: 932 155 091
E-mail: info@gremieditorscat.es
Web Site: www.gremieditorscat.es

Gremio de Editores de Castilla y Leon (GECYL) (Editors Guild of Castile & Leon)
Calle Montesa nº 8, 3º A, 47011 Valladolid
Tel: 983 102 700; 670 471 707 (cell)
E-mail: secretaria@librocyl.com
Web Site: librocyl.com/gremio
Key Personnel
President: Ricardo de Luis
Founded: 1995

Gremio de Editores de Euskadi (Editors Guild of Euskadi)
Lehendakari Aguirre 11, 3º, 48014 Bilbao
Tel: 944764313 *Fax:* 944761980
E-mail: info@editores-euskadi.net
Web Site: www.editores-euskadi.com
Promotion of Euskadi book publishers.

ISBN Spanish Agency, see Agencia del ISBN

UNE, see Union de Editoriales Universitarias Espanolas (UNE)

Union de Editoriales Universitarias Espanolas (UNE) (Union of Spanish University Publishers)
Calle Vitruvio nº 8, Despacho 228, 28006 Madrid
Tel: 913600698 *Fax:* 915631383
E-mail: secretariatecnica@une.es
Web Site: www.une.es
Key Personnel
President: Lluis Pastor Perez
Vice President: Ana Isabel Gonzalez
Treasurer: Herminia Calero Egido
Secretary General: Pedro Rujula
Founded: 1987

Sri Lanka

Sri Lanka Book Publishers' Association
Maligakanda Rd, No 53, Colombo 10
Tel: (0112) 696821 *Fax:* (0112) 696821
E-mail: bookpub@sltnet.lk
Web Site: bookpublishers.lk
Key Personnel
President: H D Premasiri
Senior Vice President: Athula Jayakodi
Vice President: Janaka Inimankada
Secretary General: Upali Wanigasuriya
Treasurer: Ariyadasa Weeraman
Founded: 1984
Membership(s): Asia Pacific Publishers Association (APPA); International Publishers Association (IPA).

Sri Lanka ISBN Agency
National Library & Documentation Services Board, No 14, Independence Ave, Colombo 07
Tel: (011) 2687581; (011) 2687583 *Fax:* (011) 2685201; (011) 2687583
E-mail: isbnsrilanka@mail.natlib.lk
Web Site: www.natlib.lk
Key Personnel
Dir General: W Sunil *E-mail:* dg@mail.natlib.lk
Founded: 1990
Subjects: Computer Science, Humanities, Library & Information Science, Literature, Mass Communication (Sri Lanka), Regional Interests, Science & Technology, Social Sciences

Standard Book Numbering Agency, see Sri Lanka ISBN Agency

Suriname

Standard Book Numbering Agency
Publishers' Association Suriname, Domineestr 32 boven, Paramaribo
Mailing Address: PO Box 1841, Paramaribo
Tel: 472 545 *Fax:* 410 563
E-mail: postmaster@interfundgroup.com

Key Personnel
ISBN Administrator: Mr E Hogenboom
ISBN Prefix(es): 978-99914

Swaziland

Standard Book Numbering Agency, see
Swaziland ISBN Agency

Swaziland ISBN Agency
University of Swaziland Libraries Special Collections, Private Bag 4, Kwaluseni
Tel: 2517-0170 *Fax:* 2517-0001
Web Site: www.library.uniswa.sz
Key Personnel
Contact: Mr Abahle Thwala *E-mail:* abahle@
uniswa.sz

Sweden

Svenska Forlaggareforeningen (Swedish
Publishers' Association)
Drottninggatan 97, 113 60 Stockholm
Tel: (08) 736 19 40
E-mail: info@forlaggare.se
Web Site: www.forlaggare.se
Key Personnel
President & Dir: Kristina Ahlinder *Tel:* (08) 736
19 41 *E-mail:* kristina.ahlinder@forlaggare.se
Founded: 1843
Publication(s): *Svensk Bokhandel* (jointly with the
Swedish Booksellers' Association)

Foreningen Svenska Laromedel (FSL) (The
Swedish Association of Educational Publishers)
Norrtullsgatan 6, 6 tr, 113 29 Stockholm
Tel: (08) 588 314 00
E-mail: info@svenskalaromedel.se
Web Site: svenskalaromedel.se
Key Personnel
Chief Executive Officer & Dir: Rickard Vinde
E-mail: rickard.vinde@svenskalaromedel.se
Founded: 1974
Trade association for educational publishers.
ISBN Prefix(es): 978-91-85386; 978-91-633

Switzerland

ASDEL, see Association Suisse des Diffuseurs,
Editeurs et Libraires (ASDEL)

**Association Suisse des Diffuseurs, Editeurs et
Libraires (ASDEL)** (Swiss Association of
Broadcasters, Editors & Booksellers)
18 ave de la Gare, 1001 Lausanne
Mailing Address: Case Postal 529, 1001 Lausanne
Tel: (021) 329 02 65 *Fax:* (021) 329 02 66
E-mail: asdel@bluewin.ch
Web Site: www.asdel.ch
Key Personnel
President: Olivier Babel
Secretary General: Jacques Scherrer
Founded: 2003 (merger of ASELF, ASLLF, ASRDL & SLESR)
ISBN Prefix(es): 978-2-88303

†◇**Distripress**
Seefeldstr 35, 8008 Zurich

Tel: (044) 202 41 21 *Fax:* (044) 202 10 25
E-mail: info@distripress.net
Web Site: www.distripress.net
Key Personnel
President: Carine Nevejans *E-mail:* cnevejans@
presstalis.fr
Vice President: Detlef Sauerbier
E-mail: detlef_sauerbier@spiegel.de
Mng Dir: Tracy Jones *E-mail:* tracy.jones@
distripress.net
Founded: 1955
Association for the Promotion of the International
Circulation of the Press.
Supports promotion of the freedom of press, furthering the development of fair & efficient
trade in international press circulation & representation of interests connected with the circulation of press products & paperback books.
Membership(s): European Newspaper Publishers' Association; International Federation of the
Periodical Press; World Association of Newspapers.
Publication(s): *Gazette eEdition*; *Who's Who in
Distripress* (online only)

IBBY, see International Board on Books for
Young People (IBBY)

IILS, see International Institute for Labour
Studies (IILS)

ILAB, see International League of Antiquarian
Booksellers (ILAB)

ILO, see International Labour Organization (ILO)

†**Inter-Parliamentary Union** (Union
Interparlementaire)
5, chemin du Pommier, 1218 Le Grand Saconnex/
Geneva
Mailing Address: CP 330, 1218 Le Grand Saconnex/Geneva
Tel: (022) 919 41 50 *Fax:* (022) 919 41 60
E-mail: postbox@mail.ipu.org
Web Site: www.ipu.org
Key Personnel
President: Saber Chowdhury
Secretary General: Martin Chungong
Founded: 1889
International organization of national parliaments.
ISBN Prefix(es): 978-92-9142

†◇**International Board on Books for Young
People (IBBY)**
Nonnenweg 12, Postfach, 4009 Basel
Tel: (061) 272 29 17 *Fax:* (061) 272 27 57
E-mail: ibby@ibby.org
Web Site: www.ibby.org
Key Personnel
Executive Dir: Elizabeth Page *E-mail:* liz.page@
ibby.org
Founded: 1953
Publication(s): *Bookbird: A Journal of International Children's Literature* (quarterly); *IBBY
Honour List* (biennially)

†‡**International Commission of Jurists**
33 rue des Bains, 1211 Geneva
Mailing Address: PO Box 91, 1211 Geneva
Tel: (022) 9793800 *Fax:* (022) 9793801
E-mail: info@icj.org
Web Site: www.icj.org
Key Personnel
Secretary General: Wilder Tayler
Head, Media & Communications: Olivier van
Bogaert *Tel:* (022) 9793808 *E-mail:* olivier.
vanbogaert@icj.org
Founded: 1952
Subjects: Human Rights, International Law
ISBN Prefix(es): 978-92-9037

†‡**International Institute for Labour Studies
(IILS)**
4 route des Morillons, 1211 Geneva
Mailing Address: PO Box 6, 1211 Geneva
Tel: (022) 799 6111; (022) 799 6128 *Fax:* (022)
798 8685; (022) 799 8542
E-mail: ilo@ilo.org; inst@ilo.org
Web Site: www.ilo.org
Key Personnel
Dir: Raymond Torres *Tel:* (022) 799 7908
Founded: 1960
Publication(s): *The Bibliography Series*; *Discussion Papers*; *Organized Labour in the 21st
Century*; *The Research Series*
Parent Company: International Labour Organization (ILO)

†◇**International Labour Organization (ILO)**
4, route des Morillons, 1211 Geneva 22
Tel: (022) 799 6111 *Fax:* (022) 799 6061
E-mail: ilo@ilo.org; europe@ilo.org
Web Site: www.ilo.org
Key Personnel
Dir General: Guy Ryder
Deputy Dir General, Policy: Deborah Greenfield
Founded: 1919
From the creation of the ILO in 1919, publishing
has formed an important part of its activities.
The ILO publishes books, reports & periodicals
of international interest on major social, labor
& economic problems & trends falling within
their competence. This substantial publishing
program has over 1,300 titles in English, 827
in French & 650 in Spanish (editions in print)
which cover studies, monographs, handbooks,
training materials & periodicals.
Subjects: Equality of Rights, International Labor
Standards, Conditions of Work & Welfare Facilities, Cooperatives, Developing Countries &
Technical Cooperation, Economics, Industrial
Relations, Intermediate Technology, Employment & Development, Structural Adjustment,
Rural Development & Employment Planning,
Human Rights & Apartheid, Labor Law & Labor Administration, International Migration &
Population Questions, Multinationals, Productivity & Management Development & Training,
Occupational Safety & Health, Social Security,
Trade Unions, Vocational Guidance & Training,
Wages & Hours of Work, Vocational Rehabilitation, Workers' Education, Women's Questions, Labor Information, Statistics
ISBN Prefix(es): 978-92-2
Branch Office(s)
Av Cordoba 950, Piso 13, C1054AAV Buenos
Aires, Argentina *Tel:* (011) 4393-7076
Fax: (011) 4393-7062 *E-mail:* buenosaires@
ilo.org *Web Site:* www.ilo.org/buenosaires
Africa Hall, 6th floor, Menelik II Ave, PO Box
2788, 2532 Addis Ababa, Ethiopia *Tel:* (011)
544-4246 *Fax:* (011) 544-5573; (011) 551-3633
E-mail: addisababa@ilo.org
Core 4B, 3rd floor, India Habitat Centre, Lodhi
Rd, New Delhi 110 003, India *Tel:* (011) 4750
9200 *Fax:* (011) 2460 2111 *E-mail:* delhi@ilo.
org *Web Site:* www.ilo.org/india
UNU Headquarters Bldg, 8th floor, 53-70 Jingumae 5-chome, Shibuya-ku, Tokyo 150-0001,
Japan *Tel:* (03) 5467 2701 *Fax:* (03) 5467 2700
E-mail: ilo-tokyo@ilotokyo.jp
ARESCO Centre Justinien St-Kantari, PO
Box 11-4088, Riad Solh, Beirut 1107 2150,
Lebanon *Tel:* (01) 752400 *Fax:* (01) 752405
E-mail: beirut@ilo.org
Comte No 35 esq Thiers, Colonia Anzures, Delegacion Miguel Hidalgo, 11590 Mexico, DF,
Mexico *Tel:* (0155) 5250-3224 *Fax:* (0155)
5250-8892 *E-mail:* mexico@ilo.org *Web
Site:* www.oit.org.mx
Las Flores 275 San Isidro, PO Box 14-124,
Lince, Lima 14, Peru *Tel:* (01) 6150300
Fax: (01) 6150400 *E-mail:* lima@ilo.org

United Nations Bldg, Rajdamnem Nok Ave,
PO Box 2-349, Bangkok 10200, Thailand
Tel: (02) 288 1234 *Fax:* (02) 280 1735
E-mail: bangkok@ilo.org
U.S. Office(s): ILO Publications Center, 1808
I St, NW 9th floor, Washington, DC 20006,
United States *Tel:* 202-617-3952 *Fax:* 202-617-
3960 *E-mail:* washington@ilo.org

†◇International League of Antiquarian Booksellers (ILAB)
Rue Toepffer 5, 1206 Geneva
Mailing Address: CP 499, 1211 Geneva 12
Tel: (02) 9660 4889 *Fax:* (02) 9552 2670
E-mail: office@antiquariat-donhofer.at;
secretary@ilab.org
Web Site: www.ilab.org
Key Personnel
President: Sally Burdon *E-mail:* books@
asiabookroom.com
Treasurer: Rob Shepherd *E-mail:* rjs@
bookbinding.co.uk
Founded: 1947

†International Organization for Standardization (ISO)
Chemin de Blandonnet 8, 1214 Vernie, Geneva
Mailing Address: ISO Central Secretariat, CP
401, 1214 Vernier, Geneva
Tel: (022) 749 01 11 *Fax:* (022) 733 34 30
E-mail: central@iso.org
Web Site: www.iso.org
Key Personnel
President: Zhang Xiaogang
Vice President, Policy: John Walter
Acting Secretary General: Kevin McKinley
Treasurer: Miguel Payro
Founded: 1947
International organization of national standards
bodies with 163 members.
Development of international standards in all
fields except electrical & electronic engineer-
ing.
ISBN Prefix(es): 978-92-67

†◇International Publishers Association (IPA)
23, ave de France, 1202 Geneva
Tel: (022) 704 18 20 *Fax:* (022) 704 18 21
E-mail: info@internationalpublishers.org;
secretariat@internationalpublishers.org
Web Site: www.internationalpublishers.org
Key Personnel
President: Dr Michiel Kolman *E-mail:* president@
internationalpublishers.org
Secretary General: Jose Borghino
E-mail: borghino@internationalpublishers.org
Dir, Communications & Freedom to Pub-
lish: James Taylor *E-mail:* taylor@
internationalpublishers.org
Founded: 1896

†‡International Telecommunication Union (ITU)
Place des Nations, 1211 Geneva
Tel: (022) 730 5111 *Fax:* (022) 733 7256
E-mail: itumail@itu.int
Web Site: www.itu.int
Key Personnel
Secretary General: Houlin Zhao
Deputy Secretary General: Malcolm Johnson
The ITU was founded in 1865 as the International
Telegraphic Union. It became the International
Telecommunication Union in 1934 & a special-
ized agency of the UN in 1947. Structure: 4
permanent organizations - General Secretariat,
International Telegraph & Telephone Consulta-
tive Committee (CCITT), International Radio
Consultative Committee (CCIR) & the Inter-
national Frequency Registration Board (IFRB).
It regulates, plans, coordinates & standardizes
international telecommunications.

ISBN Prefix(es): 978-92-61; 978-92-71; 978-92-
72; 978-92-73; 978-92-74
Total Titles: 4,500 Print
Bookshop(s): ITU Publications *Web Site:* www.
itu.int/publications/default.aspx

International Union for Conservation of Nature, see IUCN (International Union for Conservation of Nature)

IPA, see International Publishers Association
(IPA)

ISBN Agentur Schweiz
c/o Schweizer Buchhaendler- und Verleger-
Verband SBVV, Limmatstr 111, Postfach, 8031
Zurich
Tel: (044) 421 36 01 *Fax:* (044) 421 36 18
E-mail: isbn@sbvv.ch
Web Site: www.sbvv.ch
Key Personnel
Contact: Beatrice Hediger *E-mail:* beatrice.
hediger@sbvv.ch
Agency for German language ISBNs.

ISO, see International Organization for
Standardization (ISO)

ITU, see International Telecommunication Union
(ITU)

†IUCN (International Union for Conservation of Nature)
Publishing Division, Rue Mauverney 28, 1196
Gland
Tel: (022) 999 0000 *Fax:* (022) 999 0002
E-mail: mail@iucn.org; press@iucn.org;
publications@iucn.org
Web Site: www.iucn.org
Key Personnel
President: Zhang Xinsheng *E-mail:* president@
iucn.org
Dir General: Inger Andersen
Deputy Dir General: Jean-Christophe Vie
Founded: 1948
Subjects: Biodiversity, Ecosystems, Environmen-
tal Education, Environmental Law & Policy,
Forests, Mountains, Poverty Development, Pro-
tected Areas, Social Policy, Sustainable De-
velopment & Threatened Species, Wetlands,
Coastal & Marine Areas
ISBN Prefix(es): 978-2-8317; 978-2-88032

SBVV, see Schweizer Buchhaendler- und
Verleger-Verband (SBVV)

Schweizer Buchhaendler- und Verleger-Verband (SBVV) (Swiss Booksellers' & Publishers' Association)
Limmatstr 111, 8005 Zurich
Tel: (044) 421 36 00 *Fax:* (044) 421 36 18
E-mail: info@sbvv.ch
Web Site: www.sbvv.ch
Key Personnel
Mng Dir: Dani Landolf *E-mail:* dani.landolf@
sbvv.ch
Publication(s): Schweizer Buchhandel

Standard Book Numbering Agency, see ISBN Agentur Schweiz

UNCTAD, see United Nations Conference on
Trade & Development (UNCTAD)

UNECE, see United Nations Economic
Commission for Europe (UNECE)

†‡United Nations Conference on Trade & Development (UNCTAD)
Palais des Nations, 8-14, Av de la Paix, 1211
Geneva 10
Tel: (022) 917 1234 *Fax:* (022) 917 0057
E-mail: unctadinfo@unctad.org
Web Site: www.unctad.org
Key Personnel
Secretary General: Mukhisa Kituyi *Tel:* (022) 917
0042 *E-mail:* sgo@unctad.org
Deputy Secretary General: Joachim Reiter
Founded: 1964
Promotes the development-friendly integration of
developing countries into the world economy.
Subjects: Trade & Development

†‡United Nations Economic Commission for Europe (UNECE)
Palais des Nations, 1211 Geneva 10
Tel: (022) 917 12 34 *Fax:* (022) 917 05 05
E-mail: info.ece@unece.org
Web Site: www.unece.org/info/ece-homepage.html
Key Personnel
Executive Secretary: Christian Friis Bach
Deputy Executive General: Andrey Vasilyev
Chief, Information: Jean Rodriguez
Founded: 1947
The commission promotes pan-European eco-
nomic integration. It provides a regional forum
for dialogue & cooperation on economic &
sectoral issues for governments from European
countries, as well as central Asia republics,
the USA, Canada & Israel. It provides analy-
sis, policy advice & assistance to governments,
gives focus to UN global mandates on eco-
nomic issues & establishes norms, standards
& conventions to facilitate international cooperation within & outside the region.
Subjects: Economic Cooperation & Integration,
Energy, Environment, Human Settlements, Population, Statistics, Timber, Trade, Transport
ISBN Prefix(es): 978-92-1
U.S. Office(s): Regional Commissions New
York Office, New York, NY 10017, United
States *Tel:* 212-963-8088 *Fax:* 212-963-1500
E-mail: rcnyo@un.org

†‡United Nations Research Institute for Social Development (UNRISD)
Palais des Nations, 1211 Geneva
Tel: (022) 917 3020 *Fax:* (022) 917 0650
E-mail: info@unrisd.org
Web Site: www.unrisd.org
Key Personnel
Dir: Paul Ladd *Tel:* (022) 917 3060
E-mail: ladd@unrisd.org
Founded: 1963
Engages in multidisciplinary research on the so-
cial dimensions of contemporary problems af-
fecting development.
Subjects: Civil Society & Social Movements,
Democracy & Human Rights, Identities, Con-
flict & Cohesion, Social Policy & Develop-
ment, Technology & Society
ISBN Prefix(es): 978-92-9085
Total Titles: 95 Print

UNRISD, see United Nations Research Institute
for Social Development (UNRISD)

VEBUKU, see Vereinigung der Buchantiquare
und Kupferstichhaendler in der Schweiz

Vereinigung der Buchantiquare und Kupferstichhaendler in der Schweiz
(Association of Swiss Antiquarian Book &
Print Dealers)
Gerechtigkeitsgasse 2, 8027 Zurich
Tel: (043) 222 48 88 *Fax:* (043) 222 48 89
E-mail: info@vebuku.ch
Web Site: www.vebuku.ch

Key Personnel
President: Peter Bichsel
Vice President: Marcus Benz
Secretary: Gerhard Becker
Treasurer: Andre Viard
Founded: 1939
Membership(s): International League of Antiquarian Booksellers (ILAB).

Weltverband der Lehrmittelfirmen, see Worlddidac Association

WIPO, see World Intellectual Property Organization (WIPO)

World Association of Publishers, Manufacturers & Distributors of Educational Materials, see Worlddidac Association

†◇World Intellectual Property Organization (WIPO)
34, chemin des Colombettes, 1211 Geneva 20
Tel: (022) 338 9111 *Fax:* (022) 733 5428
Web Site: www.wipo.int
Key Personnel
Dir General: Francis Gurry
Founded: 1967
Specialized agency of the UN dedicated to developing a balanced & accessible international intellectual property (IP) system which rewards creativity, stimulates innovation & contributes to economic development while safeguarding the public interest. It has a mandate from its 184 member states to promote the protection of intellectual property throughout the world through cooperation among states & collaboration with other stakeholders. WIPO's activities fall broadly into three areas, namely, the progressive development of international IP law, IP capacity-building programs to support the efficient use of IP, particularly in developing countries & services to industry which facilitate the process of obtaining IP rights in multiple countries & alternative dispute resolution options for private parties.

World Trade Organization, see WTO (World Trade Organization)

†◇Worlddidac Association
Bollwerk 21, 3011 Bern
Tel: (031) 311 76 82 *Fax:* (031) 312 17 44
E-mail: info@worlddidac.org
Web Site: www.worlddidac.org
Key Personnel
Dir General: Andrew Whiteley
  E-mail: whiteley@worlddidac.org
Dir, Business Development: Kateryna Schuetz
  E-mail: schuetz@worlddidac.org
Global trade association for companies providing products for education & training at all levels.

†‡WTO (World Trade Organization)
Centre William Rappard, Rue de Lausanne 154, 1211 Geneva 21
Tel: (022) 739 51 11 *Fax:* (022) 731 42 06
E-mail: enquiries@wto.org; publications@wto.org
Web Site: www.wto.org
Key Personnel
Dir General: Roberto Azevedo
Deputy Dir General: Yonov Frederick Agah; Karl Brauner; David Shark; Yi Xiaozhun
Founded: 1995
General agreement on tariffs & trade; examination & negotiations of various aspects of international trade policies & practices.
Publication(s): *Basic Instruments & Selected Documents (BISD) Series* (annually); *GATT Activities* (annually); *The International Markets for Meat* (annually); *International Trade Statistics*

(annually); *Trade Policy Review series* (about 14 countries reviewed annually); *The World Market for Dairy Products* (annually); *World Trade Report* (annually)
ISBN Prefix(es): 978-92-870

Taiwan

Standard Book Numbering Agency, see Taiwan ISBN Agency

Taiwan ISBN Agency
National Central Library (NCL) of Taiwan, 20 Chungshan S Rd, Taipei 10001
Tel: (02) 23619132 (ext 701-706) *Fax:* (02) 23115330; (02) 23316515
E-mail: isbn@ncl.edu.tw
Web Site: isbn.ncl.edu.tw/NCL_ISBNNet
Key Personnel
Contact: Mr Kun-hsien Tseng

Tanzania

Standard Book Numbering Agency, see Tanzania Library Services Board

Tanzania Library Services Board
Unit of Ministry of Education & Vocational Training
National Central Library, PO Box 9283, Dar es Salaam
Tel: (022) 2150048; (022) 2150049 *Fax:* (022) 2151100
E-mail: tlsb@africaonline.co.tz
Web Site: www.tlsb.or.tz
Key Personnel
Dir General: Dr Alli Mcharazo
Contact: Emily Meshack *E-mail:* eminayla04@gmail.com
ISBN Prefix(es): 978-9976-65

TLSB, see Tanzania Library Services Board

Thailand

PUBAT, see Publishers & Booksellers' Association of Thailand

Publishers & Booksellers' Association of Thailand
83/159 Moo Chinnakhet 2 Ngam Wong Wan Rd, Thung Song Hong, Lak Si, Bangkok 10210
Tel: (02) 9549560-4 *Fax:* (02) 9549565-6; (02) 9549566
E-mail: info@pubat.or.th
Web Site: www.pubat.or.th
Key Personnel
President: Mr Charun Homtientong
Vice President, Internal Affairs: Mrs Suchada Sahasakul
Vice President, International Affairs: Mr Prabda Yoon
Secretary: Mr Pichet Yimthin
Treasurer: Mr Nan Hongwiwat
Founded: 1960

SEAMEO RELC, see Southeast Asian Ministers of Education Organization Regional Language Centre (SEAMEO RELC)

†◇Southeast Asian Ministers of Education Organization Regional Language Centre (SEAMEO RELC)
Mom Luang Pin Malakul Centenery Bldg, 920 Sukhumvit Rd, 4th floor, Klongtoey, Prakanong, Bangkok 10110
Tel: (02) 391-0144 *Fax:* (02) 381-2587
E-mail: secretariat@seameo.org
Web Site: www.seameo.org
Key Personnel
Dir: Gatot Hari Priowirjanto
Founded: 1965
Subjects: English in Multilingual, Language Teaching & Research, Linguistics, Multicultural Situations

Standard Book Numbering Agency
National Library of Thailand, Library Resource Development Group, Samsen Rd, Dusit, Bangkok 10300
Tel: (02) 2809845; (02) 2809828-32 *Fax:* (02) 2809858
E-mail: isbn@nlt.go.th
Web Site: www.nlt.go.th
Key Personnel
Dir: Kanok-On Sakdadate *E-mail:* director@nlt.go.th
Founded: 1905

Tunisia

Agence Tunisienne de l'ISBN
Bibliotheque Nationale de Tunisie, Service de la Documentation et de l'information, Rue 9 avril 1938, 1008 Tunis
Mailing Address: 20 Ahareen Market, BP 42, 1000 Tunis
Tel: 71 57 27 06; 71 57 20 74 *Fax:* 71 57 28 87
E-mail: bibliotheque.nationale@email.ati.tn
Web Site: www.bibliotheque.nat.tn
Key Personnel
Dir: Mrs Raja bin Salama
Founded: 1988

Standard Book Numbering Agency, see Agence Tunisienne de l'ISBN

Turkey

ISBN Turkiye Ajansy
Kultur ve Turizm Bakanligi, Fevzipasa Mah, Cumhuriyet Bulvan, No 4 B Blok Kat 1, 248 Ulus, 06440 Ankara
Tel: (0312) 309 90 50 *Fax:* (0312) 309 89 99
E-mail: isbn@kultur.gov.tr
Web Site: www.ekygm.gov.tr/isbn.html
Key Personnel
Contact: Dr Mehmet Demir

Standard Book Numbering Agency, see ISBN Turkiye Ajansy

Turkiye Yayincilar Birligi (Turkish Publishers Association)
Inonu Caddesi Opera Palas Apartment No 55 D2, Gumussuyu, 34437 Beyoglu, Istanbul
Tel: (0212) 512 56 02 *Fax:* (0212) 511 77 94
E-mail: info@turkyaybir.org.tr
Web Site: www.turkyaybir.org.tr
Key Personnel
President: Metin Celal Zeynioglu
Vice President: Fahri Aral

Secretary General: Ozgur Akin
Treasurer: Arman Fikri
Founded: 1985
Membership(s): International Association of
  Broadcasters; International Publishers Asso-
  ciation (IPA).

Uganda

Uganda Publishers' Association
PO Box 7732, Kampala
Tel: (0414) 270370 *Fax:* (0414) 348224
Key Personnel
Chairman: David Kibuuka
ISBN Prefix(es): 978-9970-04

Ukraine

National ISBN Agency
Derzhavna naukova ustanova Knyzkova Palata
  Ukrainy imeni Ivana Federova, 27 Yuri Gagarin
  Ave, No 101, Kiev 02660
Tel: (044) 296-32-36 *Fax:* (044) 292-01-84
E-mail: isbn@ukrbook.net
Web Site: www.ukrbook.net
Key Personnel
Contact: Iryna Pogorelovs'ka

Standard Book Numbering Agency, see
  National ISBN Agency

United Arab Emirates

Kalima
PO Box 2380, Abu Dhabi
Fax: (02) 6 43 31 78
E-mail: info@kalima.ae
Web Site: www.kalima.ae
Key Personnel
Founder: Tahnoun Al Nahyan
Founded: 2005
Funds the translation, publication & distribution
  of high quality works of classic & contempo-
  rary writing from other languages into Arabic.

**UAE Board on Books for Young People
  (UAEBBY)**
Al Qasba, Blok D, 1st floor, Off no 40, Sharjah
Mailing Address: PO Box 1421, Sharjah
Tel: (06) 5542111 *Fax:* (06) 5542345
E-mail: info@uaebby.org.ae
Web Site: www.uaebby.org.ae
Key Personnel
Executive, International Projects: Joshua Dunning
  E-mail: joshua.d@uaebby.org.ae
Programs & Award Executive: Eman Mohamed
  E-mail: eman.m@uaebby.org.ae
General Coordinator: Meera Al Naqbi
  E-mail: meera.n@uaebby.org.ae
Aims to be the driving force for the promotion of
  a reading culture among the children & young
  people of the United Arab Emirates by facili-
  tating communication & information exchange
  among individuals & organizations concerned
  with children's literature in the UAE & abroad,
  stimulating research & scholarly studies in the
  field of children's literature, providing aspir-

ing & published authors & illustrators as well
  as publishing houses based in the UAE with
  networking, exchange & capacity building opportunities & promoting international understanding through children's books.

UAEBBY, see UAE Board on Books for Young
  People (UAEBBY)

United Kingdom

Advocate Art
The Sanctuary, 23 Oakhill Grove, Suite 7, Sur-
  biton KT6 6DU
Tel: (020) 8879 1166; (020) 8390 6293
E-mail: mail@advocate-art.com
Web Site: www.advocate-art.com
Key Personnel
Mng Dir & Chief Executive Officer: Edward
  Burns
Founded: 1992
Composed of artists & illustrators for children's
  books.
U.S. Office(s): 411 Lafayette St, New York, NY
  10003, United States *Tel:* 212-946-4792

†African Books Collective
PO Box 721, Oxford OX1 9EN
Fax: (01865) 412341
E-mail: orders@africanbookscollective.com
Web Site: www.africanbookscollective.com
Key Personnel
Chief Executive Officer: Justin Cox
  E-mail: justin.cox@africanbookscollective.com
Dir: David Brooks; Mary Jay
Founded: 1989
Donor-funded organization owned by member
  publishers. Has exclusive distribution rights of
  member publishers titles outside Africa. Schol-
  arly, literature & children's books.
ISBN Prefix(es): 978-0-9521269; 978-0-9542030;
  978-0-9545384; 978-1-904855; 978-9966-9615

ALCS, see Authors' Licensing & Collecting
  Society

ALLi (The Alliance of Independent Authors)
The Free Word Centre, 60 Farringdon Rd, Lon-
  don EC1R 3GA
E-mail: info@allianceindependentauthors.org
Web Site: allianceindependentauthors.org
Key Personnel
Founder & Dir: Orna Ross
Resources Dir: Philip Lynch
Manager, Communications & Partner Members:
  Nerys Hudson
Nonprofit professional association for author-
  publishers. Offers connection & collaboration,
  advice & education, advocacy & representation
  to writers who want to self-publish well.

The Alliance of Independent Authors, see ALLi
  (The Alliance of Independent Authors)

ALPSP, see The Association of Learned &
  Professional Society Publishers (ALPSP)

Antiquarian Booksellers' Association
6 Bell Yard, London WC2A 2JR
Tel: (020) 7421 4681 *Fax:* (020) 7421 4641
E-mail: admin@aba.org.uk
Web Site: www.aba.org.uk

Key Personnel
Events Manager: Marianne Harwood
  E-mail: marianne@aba.org.uk
Administrator: Clare Pedder *E-mail:* ped@aba.
  org.uk
Secretary: Camilla Szymanowska
  E-mail: secretary@aba.org.uk
Founded: 1906
Senior trade body for dealers in antiquarian &
  rare books, manuscripts & allied materials in
  the British Isles.
Membership(s): The International League of Anti-
  quarian Booksellers.

Association of Authors' Agents
c/o Johnson & Alcock Ltd, Clerkenwell House,
  45-47 Clerkenwell Green, London EC1R 0HT
Tel: (020) 7251 0125
Web Site: agentsassoc.co.uk
Key Personnel
President: Lizzy Kremer
Vice President: Isobel Dixon
Treasurer: Jodie Hodges
Secretary: Ed Wilson *E-mail:* ed@
  johnsonandalcock.co.uk
Trade association representing the interests of UK
  based literary agents.

**†◇The Association of Learned & Professional
  Society Publishers (ALPSP)**
Egale 1, St Albans Rd, Watford, Herts WD17
  1DL
Tel: (01245) 260571 *Fax:* (01245) 260935
E-mail: admin@alpsp.org
Web Site: www.alpsp.org
Key Personnel
Chief Executive & Company Secretary: Au-
  drey McCulloch *Tel:* (01442) 828928
  E-mail: audrey.mcculloch@alpsp.org
Marketing & Communications Executive:
  Heidi Russell-Jones *Tel:* (01727) 812777
  E-mail: heidi.russell.jones@alpsp.org
Membership Manager: Lesley Ogg *E-mail:* lesley.
  ogg@alpsp.org
Founded: 1972
Trade association for not-for-profit organizations
  that publish scholarly & professional content.
Publication(s): *ALPSP Alert* (monthly, newslet-
  ter, electronic); *Learned Publishing* (quarterly,
  journal, ISSN: 0953-1513, print; 1741-4857,
  online)
ISBN Prefix(es): 978-0-907341

Authors' Licensing & Collecting Society
Barnard's Inn, 1st floor, 86 Fetter Lane, London
  EC4A 1EN
Tel: (020) 7264 5700
E-mail: alcs@alcs.co.uk; communications@alcs.
  co.uk
Web Site: www.alcs.co.uk
Key Personnel
Executive Dir & Chief Executive: Owen Atkinson
Deputy Chief Executive: Barbara Hayes
Chief Operations Officer: Alan Smith
Head, Communications: Alison Baxter
  E-mail: alison.baxter@alcs.co.uk
Head, Finance: Mark Bispham
Head, Rights & Licensing: Richard Combes
Founded: 1977

BESA, see The British Education Suppliers
  Association

BIC, see Book Industry Communication

BMS, see Book Marketing Society

†◇Book Industry Communication
7 Ridgmount St, London WC1E 7AE
Tel: (020) 7255 0516
E-mail: info@bic.org.uk
Web Site: www.bic.org.uk

Key Personnel
Chair: Alasdair Ball
Executive Dir: Karina Luke

Book Marketing Society
c/o Nielsen Book, Endeavor House, 5th floor, 189 Shaftesbury Ave, London WC2H 8JR
Web Site: www.bookmarketingsociety.co.uk
Key Personnel
Chair: Miranda McKearney
Executive Dir: Jon Slack *E-mail:* jon.slack@nielsen.com
Mng Dir: Jo Henry *E-mail:* jo.henry@nielsen.com
Secretary: Alastair Giles
Founded: 2004
Membership organization for marketing & communications professionals in the UK book industry.
ISBN Prefix(es): 978-1-873517

Book Trade Benevolent Society, see The Book Trade Charity

The Book Trade Charity
The Foyle Centre, The Retreat, Kings Langley, Herts WD4 8LT
Tel: (01923) 263128
E-mail: info@booktradecharity.org
Web Site: www.btbs.org
Key Personnel
President: David Young
Chief Executive: David Hicks *E-mail:* david@btbs.org
Founded: 1837
Charity-Occupational Benevolent Fund.

Booksellers Association of the United Kingdom & Ireland Ltd
6 Bell Yard, London WC2A 2JR
Tel: (020) 7421 4640 *Fax:* (020) 7421 4641
E-mail: mail@booksellers.org.uk
Web Site: www.booksellers.org.uk
Key Personnel
Executive Chair, BA Group: Tim Godfray *E-mail:* tim.godfray@booksellers.org.uk
President: Nic Bottomley
Mng Dir: Meryl Halls
Dir, Strategy & Communication: Alan Staton
Head, Campaigns: Emma Bradshaw
Head, Trade & Industry: Giles Clifton *Tel:* (020) 7421 4671 *E-mail:* giles.clifton@booksellers.org.uk
Customer Relations Manager: Uzo Onuora *Tel:* (020) 7421 4654 *E-mail:* uzo.onuora@booksellers.org.uk
Database & Membership Manager: Helen Wilson *Tel:* (020) 7421 4659 *E-mail:* helen.wilson@booksellers.org.uk
Marketing & Groups Manager: Sharon Benton *Tel:* (020) 7421 4694 *E-mail:* sharon.benton@booksellers.org.uk
Membership Manager: Pippa Halpin
Founded: 1895
The Booksellers Association Group includes the BA, National Book Tokens & batch.co.uk.

Booktrust
G8 Battersea Studios, 80 Silverthorne Rd, Battersea, London SW8 3HE
Tel: (020) 7801 8800
E-mail: query@booktrust.org.uk
Web Site: www.booktrust.org.uk
Key Personnel
Chief Executive: Diana Gerald *E-mail:* chief.executive@booktrust.org.uk
Supported by Broadband Arts Council England with activities which include literary prizes such as The Orange Prize for Fiction & the Nestle Children's Book Prize. Booktrust also runs Bookstart.

BPIF, see British Printing Industries Federation (BPIF)

British Copyright Council
2 Pancras Sq, London N1C 4AG
Tel: (020) 7582 4833
E-mail: info@britishcopyright.org
Web Site: www.britishcopyright.org
Key Personnel
Dir & Chairman: Trevor Cook
Vice President: Geoffrey Adams
Chief Executive Officer & Secretary: Janet Ibbotson
Founded: 1965
National consulting & advisory body for copyright matters.

The British Education Suppliers Association
20 Beaufort Court, Admirals Way, London E14 9XL
Tel: (020) 7537 4997 *Fax:* (020) 7537 4846
E-mail: besa@besa.org.uk
Web Site: www.besa.org.uk
Key Personnel
Dir General: Dominic Savage *E-mail:* dominic@besa.org.uk
Dir: Patrick Hayes *E-mail:* patrick@besa.org.uk
International Manager: William Prieto-Parra *E-mail:* william@besa.org.uk
Membership Manager: Mark Rosser *E-mail:* mark@besa.org.uk
Public Relations Manager: Tim Edwards *E-mail:* tim@besa.org.uk

British Guild of Travel Writers
335 Lordship Rd, London N16 5HG
Tel: (020) 8144 8713
E-mail: secretariat@bgtw.org
Web Site: www.bgtw.org
Key Personnel
Chairman: Alastair McKenzie *E-mail:* chairman@bgtw.org
Vice Chairman: Roger Bray *E-mail:* vicechair@bgtw.org
Secretary: Robert Ellison; Benita Finanzio
Treasurer: Kathryn Liston
Founded: 1960
Publication(s): *Yearbook* (annually)

British Printing Industries Federation (BPIF)
Unit 2, Villiers Court, Meriden Business Park, Copse Dr, Coventry, West Midlands CV5 9RN
Tel: (0845) 250 7050 *Fax:* (01676) 526 033
E-mail: hello@bpif.org.uk
Web Site: www.britishprint.com
Key Personnel
Chief Executive: Charles Jarrold *Tel:* (01676) 526 030 *E-mail:* charles.jarrold@bpif.org.uk
Marketing Dir: Amy Hutchinson *Tel:* (020) 7915 8373 *E-mail:* amy.hutchinson@bpif.org.uk
Membership Dir: Dale Wallis *Tel:* (07736) 828 450 *E-mail:* dale.wallis@bpif.org.uk
Represents the UK print, printed packaging & graphic communication industry.
Publication(s): *Inprint* (6 issues/yr, magazine)

BSI British Standards Institution
389 Chiswick High Rd, London W4 4AL
Tel: (020) 8996 9001 *Fax:* (020) 8996 7001
E-mail: cservices@bsigroup.com
Web Site: www.bsigroup.com
Key Personnel
Chairman: Sir David Brown
Chief Executive: Howard Kerr
Founded: 1901
National standards body.
Publication(s): *Business Standards Magazine* (ezine)
U.S. Office(s): BSI Inc, 12950 Worldgate Dr, Herndon, VA 20170, United States *Fax:* 703-437-9001 *E-mail:* inquiry.msamericas@bsigroup.com *Web Site:* www.bsiamerica.com

BTBS, see The Book Trade Charity

†CAB International
Nosworthy Way, Wallingford, Oxon OX10 8DE
Tel: (01491) 832111 *Fax:* (01491) 833508
E-mail: enquiries@cabi.org; sales@cabi.org
Web Site: www.cabi.org
Key Personnel
Chief Executive Officer: Trevor Nicholls *Tel:* (01491) 829215 *E-mail:* corporate@cabi.org
Chief Information Officer: Andrea Powell *Tel:* (01491) 829302 *E-mail:* a.powell@cabi.org
Property Dir: Ian Barry *Tel:* (01491) 829220 *E-mail:* i.barry@cabi.org
Strategic Business Development Dir: Phil Abrahams *Tel:* (01491) 829374 *E-mail:* p.abrahams@cabi.org
Senior Sales Manager, Europe: Clodagh Corcoran *Tel:* (01491) 829426 *E-mail:* c.corcoran@cabi.org
Founded: 1910
Not-for-profit international organization that improves people's lives by providing information & applying scientific expertise to solve problems in agriculture & the environment.
Subjects: Agricultural Economics, Agriculture, Animal Health, Animal Science, Environmental Science, Forestry, Horticulture Health, Human Health, Nutrition, Rural Sociology
ISBN Prefix(es): 978-0-85198; 978-0-85199

†◇The Lewis Carroll Society
Flat 11 Eastfields, 24-30 Victoria Rd N, Southsea PO5 1PU
E-mail: secretary@lewiscarrollsociety.org.uk
Web Site: lewiscarrollsociety.org.uk
Key Personnel
Acting Chairman & President: Brian Sibley
Membership Secretary: Mary Lewis
Treasurer: Bob Cole
Sales Unit Manager: Edward Wakeling
Secretary: Jane Skelly
Founded: 1969
Publication(s): *Bandersnatch* (quarterly, newsletter); *Lewis Carroll Review* (3-4 times/yr, journal); *The Carrollian* (journal)

Chartered Institute of Journalists (CIOJ)
2 Dock Offices, Surrey Quays Rd, London SE16 2XU
Tel: (020) 7252 1187 *Fax:* (020) 7232 2302
E-mail: memberservices@cioj.co.uk
Web Site: cioj.co.uk
Key Personnel
President: Mark Croucher
Vice President: Janice Shillum
General Secretary: Dominic Cooper
Treasurer: Michael Hardware
Editor: Andy Smith
Founded: 1884
Professional body/independent trade union.
Subjects: Broadcasting, Journalism
Publication(s): *The Journal*

Children's Book Circle
c/o Penguin Books, 80 Strand, London WC2R 0RL
E-mail: childrensbookcircle@gmail.com
Web Site: www.childrensbookcircle.org.uk
Key Personnel
Co-Chair: Anna Barnes; Louise Grosart
Membership Secretary: Linus Alsenas
Treasurer: Helen Weir
Founded: 1962

Children's Writers & Illustrators Group
Society of Authors, 84 Drayton Gardens, London SW10 9SB
Tel: (020) 7373 6642 *Fax:* (020) 7373 5768

E-mail: info@societyofauthors.org
Web Site: www.societyofauthors.org/childrens-
writers-and-illustrators-group
Key Personnel
Chair: Nicola Morgan
Founded: 1884

CIOJ, see Chartered Institute of Journalists
(CIOJ)

†◇Circle of Wine Writers
c/o Scots Firs, 70 Joiners Lane, Chalfont St Peter,
Bucks SL9 0AU
Tel: (01753) 882320
E-mail: administrator@circleofwinewriters.org
Web Site: www.circleofwinewriters.org
Key Personnel
Chairman: Colin Hampden-White
President: Rosemary George
Vice President: Bob Campbell; Oz Clarke
Honorary Secretary: Winifred Bowman
Tel: (020) 8958 3319 *E-mail:* secretary@
circleofwinewriters.org
Honorary Treasurer: Keith Grainger
Administrator: Andrea Warren
Founded: 1960
Publication(s): *Circle Update* (quarterly, newslet-
ter, electronic)

**Comhairle nan Leabhraichean - The Gaelic
Books Council**
32 Mansfield St, Glasgow G11 5QP
Tel: (0141) 337 6211
E-mail: brath@gaelicbooks.org
Web Site: www.gaelicbooks.org
Key Personnel
Chairman: Donald Iain Brown
Dir: Rosemary Ward *E-mail:* rosemary@
gaelicbooks.org
Head, Literature & Publishing: John Storey
E-mail: john@gaelicbooks.org
Literature & Publishing Officer: Mairi MacCuish
E-mail: mairi@gaelicbooks.org
Sales & Finance Officer: John Norman MacDon-
ald *E-mail:* johnnorman@gaelicbooks.org
Retails all Gaelic & Gaelic-related titles in print.
Publication(s): *Catalog of Gaelic Books in Print*;
Gaelic Poetry Posters

†◇Copyright Licensing Agency
Barnard's Inn, 86 Fetter Lane, London EC4A
1EN
Tel: (020) 7400 3100
E-mail: cla@cla.co.uk
Web Site: www.cla.co.uk
Key Personnel
Mng Dir: Mat Pfleger *E-mail:* mat.pfleger@cla.
co.uk
Public Relations & Marketing Manager: Paul
Rollins *Tel:* (020) 7400 3140 *E-mail:* pr@cla.
co.uk
Founded: 1983
Collective administration of rights.
Membership(s): International Federation of Re-
production Rights Organizations (IFRRO).
Publication(s): *CLA Annual Review* (booklet);
Copyright and the Creative Industries (booklet)
Parent Company: Author's Licensing & Collect-
ing Society Ltd (ALCS)
Associate Companies: Publishers Licensing Soci-
ety Ltd
Branch Office(s)
CBC House, 24 Canning St, Edinburgh EH3 8EG
Tel: (0131) 272 2711 *E-mail:* clascotland@cla.
co.uk

†◇Crime Writers' Association (CWA)
Peershaws, Berewyk Hall Court, White Colne,
Colchester, Essex CO6 2QB
E-mail: director@thecwa.co.uk; secretary@
thecwa.co.uk

Web Site: thecwa.co.uk
Key Personnel
Chair: L C Tyler
Vice Chair: Martin Edwards
Founded: 1953

CWA, see Crime Writers' Association (CWA)

Cwlwm Cyhoeddwyr Cymru (Union of Welsh
Publishers & Booksellers)
Y Lolfa, Hen Swyddfa'r Heddlu, Talybont,
Ceredigion SY24 5HE
Key Personnel
Dir: Garmon Gruffudd *E-mail:* garmon@ylolfa.
com
Secretary: Myrddin ap Dafydd *E-mail:* myrddin@
carreg-gwalch.com
Founded: 2002

Cyngor Llyfrau Cymru Canolfan Dosbarthu,
see The Welsh Books Council

DACS, see Design & Artists Copyright Society
(DACS)

Design & Artists Copyright Society (DACS)
33 Old Bethnal Green Rd, London E2 6AA
Tel: (020) 7336 8811 *Fax:* (020) 7336 8822
E-mail: info@dacs.org.uk
Web Site: www.dacs.org.uk
Key Personnel
Chief Executive: Gilane Tawadros
Corporate Governance Manager & Co Sec-
retary: Helen Dutta *Tel:* (020) 7553 9079
E-mail: helen.dutta@dacs.org.uk
Chief Operating Officer: Robert Read *Tel:* (020)
7553 9089 *E-mail:* robert.read@dacs.org.uk
Head, Communications: Abby Yolda *Tel:* (020)
7553 9075 *E-mail:* abby.yolda@dacs.org.uk
Founded: 1984
Not-for-profit visual artists' rights management
organization.

EDItEUR
United House, North Rd, London N7 9DP
Tel: (020) 7503 6418 *Fax:* (020) 7503 6418
E-mail: info@editeur.org
Web Site: www.editeur.org
Key Personnel
Executive Dir: Graham Bell
Associate Dir: Stella Griffiths
Operations Manager: Nick Woods
Standards Editor: Chris Saynor
Founded: 1991
International group coordinating development of
the standards infrastructure for electronic com-
merce in the book, ebook & serials sectors.
Publication(s): *Newsletter* (6 times/yr)

Educational Writers' Group
Society of Authors, 84 Drayton Gardens, London
SW10 9SB
Tel: (020) 7373 6642 *Fax:* (020) 7373 5768
E-mail: info@societyofauthors.org
Web Site: www.societyofauthors.org/educational-
writers-group
Key Personnel
Chair: Anne Rooney

The Federation of Children's Book Groups
10 St Laurence Rd, Bradford on Avon, Wilts
BA15 1JG
Toll Free Tel: 0300 102 1559
E-mail: info@fcbg.org.uk
Web Site: www.fcbg.org.uk
Key Personnel
Secretary & Group Liaison Officer: Karen
Hellewell
Founded: 1968
Publication(s): *Newsletter* (2 issues/yr, newsletter)

FLS, see The Folklore Society (FLS)

†◇The Folklore Society (FLS)
c/o The Warburg Institute, Woburn Sq, London
WC1H 0AB
Tel: (020) 7862 8564
E-mail: thefolkloresociety@gmail.com
Web Site: www.folklore-society.com
Key Personnel
President: Prof James H Grayson
Vice President: Robert McDowall
Secretary: William Roberts
Treasurer: John Willmott
Editor, Folklore Journal: Dr Jessica Hemming
Founded: 1878
Publication(s): *FLS News* (3 times/yr, newsletter);
Folklore (3 times/yr, journal)
Number of titles published annually: 2 Print

The Gaelic Books Council, see Comhairle nan
Leabhraichean - The Gaelic Books Council

IAI, see International African Institute (IAI)

IMO, see International Maritime Organization
(IMO)

Independent Publishers Guild (IPG)
PO Box 12, Llain, Login SA34 0WU
Tel: (01437) 563335 *Fax:* (01437) 562071
E-mail: info@ipg.uk.com
Web Site: www.ipg.uk.com
Key Personnel
Chief Executive: Bridget Shine
Administrator: Angela Stanley
Events & Sponsorship Manager: Inogen Race
Head, Communications: Tom Holman
Membership(s): Federation of Small Businesses
(FSB).

†◇Index on Censorship
292 Vauxhall Bridge Rd, London SW1V 1AE
Tel: (020) 7963 7262
E-mail: info@indexoncensorship.org
Web Site: www.indexoncensorship.org
Key Personnel
Chief Executive: Jodie Ginsberg *E-mail:* jodie@
indexoncensorship.org
Events Manager: David Heinemann
E-mail: davidh@indexoncensorship.org
Finance Manager: David Sewell *E-mail:* david@
indexoncensorship.org
Associate Producer: Helen Galliano
E-mail: helen@indexoncensorship.org
Senior Advocacy Officer: Melody Patry
E-mail: melody@indexoncensorship.org
Project Officer: Hannah Machlin
E-mail: hannah@indexoncensorship.org
Founded: 1972
Information about censorship in the world today,
covering subjects such as free speech, human
rights, literature, freedom of information.
Subjects: Censorship, Current Affairs, Literature,
Politics
Publication(s): *Index on Censorship* (quarterly,
magazine)
Number of titles published annually: 4 Print

Institute of Internal Communication (IoIC)
Suite G10, Gemini House, Sunrise Parkway, Lin-
ford Wood, Milton Keynes MK14 6PW
Tel: (01908) 232168 *Fax:* (01908) 313661
E-mail: enquiries@ioic.org.uk
Web Site: www.ioic.org.uk
Key Personnel
Chief Executive: Steve Doswell
E-mail: doswell@ioic.org.uk
President: Suzanne Peck
Public Relations & Marketing Executive: Cather-
ine Park *E-mail:* catherine@ioic.org.uk

Operations & Membership Manager: Tim Beynon
E-mail: tim@ioic.org.uk
Founded: 1949
Publication(s): *InsideLine* (monthly, ezine); *Inside-eOut* (magazine, ISSN: 1741-2315)

Institute of Scientific & Technical Communicators (ISTC)
Airport House, Purley Way, Croydon, Surrey CR0 0XZ
Tel: (020) 8253 4506 *Fax:* (020) 8253 4510
E-mail: istc@istc.org.uk
Web Site: www.istc.org.uk
Key Personnel
President: Alison Peck *E-mail:* president@istc. org.uk
Commissioning Editor: Katherine Judge
Founded: 1972
Subjects: Communication, Technical
Publication(s): *Communicator* (quarterly, journal); *InfoPlus* (monthly, newsletter)

†International African Institute (IAI) (L'Institut Africain International)
School of Oriental & African Studies, Thornhaugh St, Russell Sq, London WC1H 0XG
Tel: (020) 7898 4420 *Fax:* (020) 7898 4419
E-mail: africa@internationalafricaninstitute.org; iai@soas.ac.uk
Web Site: www.internationalafricaninstitute.org
Key Personnel
Chairman: Peter Geschiere
Chair, Publications Committee & Mng Editor: Stephanie Kitchen *E-mail:* sk111@soas.ac.uk
Vice Chair: Prof Birgit Meyer
Honorary Dir: Prof Philip Burnham *E-mail:* p. burnham@ucl.ac.uk
Treasurer: Brian Johnson
Founded: 1926
Promotes the scholarly study of Africa, its history, societies & cultures, primarily by means of scholarly publishing. The Council includes representatives from Africa & elsewhere.
Subjects: Bibliography, Environmental Studies, Ethnography, History, Politics, Social Sciences
Publication(s): *Africa* (quarterly, journal, 1928); *The Africa Bibliography* (annually, 1984); *African Arguments* (2-4 titles annually, 2005, paperback); *Classics in African Anthropology Series* (annually); *International African Library Series* (2-4 titles annually, cased); *International African Seminars* (annually)
ISBN Prefix(es): 978-0-85302
Number of titles published annually: 8 Print
Total Titles: 600 Print

International Association of Scientific, Technical & Medical Publishers, see International Association of STM Publishers

†◇International Association of STM Publishers
Prama House, 267 Banbury Rd, Oxford OX2 7HT
Tel: (01865) 339 321 *Fax:* (01865) 339 325
E-mail: info@stm-assoc.org
Web Site: www.stm-assoc.org
Key Personnel
Board Chair: Eric Merkel-Sobotta
Chief Executive Officer: Michael Mabe
E-mail: mabe@stm-assoc.org
Dir, Publishing Outreach: Richard Gedye
E-mail: gedye@stm-assoc.org
International Trade Organization for STM, professional & scholarly publishers. Focus on copyright & legal issues, technology development & industry standards & library & users relations.

†◇International ISBN Agency
c/o EDItEUR, United House, North Rd, London N7 9DP
Tel: (020) 7503 6418 *Fax:* (020) 7503 6418
E-mail: info@isbn-international.org

Web Site: isbn-international.org
Key Personnel
Executive Dir: Stella Griffiths
Operations Manager: Nick Woods
Founded: 1972
This is the international ISBN office. Information on national offices included under most countries in this section.
Publication(s): *Global Register of Publishers*; *International ISBN Users' Manual*; *ISBN Newsletter*

†‡International Maritime Organization (IMO)
4, Albert Embankment, London SE1 7SR
Tel: (020) 7735 7611 *Fax:* (020) 7587 3241
E-mail: sales@imo.org (publications); info@imo. org
Web Site: www.imo.org
Key Personnel
Media & Communications Officer: Natasha Brown *Tel:* (020) 7587 3274 *E-mail:* media@ imo.org
Founded: 1959
Texts of International Maritime Treaties concluded under its auspices. Maritime technical publications.
Subjects: Maritime Safety, Oil Pollution Prevention
ISBN Prefix(es): 978-92-801

IoIC, see Institute of Internal Communication (IoIC)

IOJ, see Chartered Institute of Journalists (CIOJ)

IPG, see Independent Publishers Guild (IPG)

ISBN, see International ISBN Agency

ISSN UK Centre
British Library, Boston Spa, Wetherby, W Yorks LS23 7BQ
Tel: (01937) 546959 *Fax:* (01937) 546562
E-mail: issn-uk@bl.uk
Web Site: www.bl.uk/bibliographic/issn.html
Key Personnel
Dir: Louise Howlett
Allocates International Standard Serial Numbers (ISSNs) to serials published in UK.

ISTC, see Institute of Scientific & Technical Communicators (ISTC)

†◇Maritime Information Association (MIA)
c/o 40 Frobisher Pl, London SE15 2EQ
Web Site: www.maritime-information.net
Key Personnel
Chairman: Micheal Naxton *E-mail:* chairman@ maritime-information.net
Secretary: Roy Fenton *E-mail:* rfenton@rfenton. demon.co.uk
Treasurer & Membership Secretary: Stephen Grace *E-mail:* sgrace@iwm.org.uk
Founded: 1972
Publication(s): *Marine Information* (guide to libraries & sources of information in the UK); *MIA News* (3 times/yr)

MPA, see Music Publishers Association (MPA)

Music Publishers Association (MPA)
2 Pancras Sq, 8th floor, London N1C 4AG
Tel: (020) 3741 3800 *Fax:* (020) 3741 3810
Web Site: www.mpaonline.org.uk
Key Personnel
Chairman: Jackie Alway
Chief Executive Officer: Jane Dyball
General Manager: Claire McAuley

Press & Public Affairs Manager: Harriet Finney
E-mail: hfinney@mpaonline.org.uk
Publishing Affairs Coordinator: Jake Kirner
Founded: 1887
Trade organization for music publishers.
Publication(s): *Catalogue of Printed Music on CD-ROM*

NAG, see National Acquisitions Group (NAG)

National Acquisitions Group (NAG)
12-14 King St, Wakefield WF1 2SQ
Tel: (01924) 383010
E-mail: nag.office@nag.org.uk
Web Site: www.nag.org.uk
Key Personnel
Chair: Angela Turner
Vice Chair: Jaqui Holborn
Secretary: Gavin Phillips
Treasurer: Regina O'Brien
Publication(s): *Servicing Guidelines: Best Practice for Public Libraries* (PDF); *Supply Specification Guidelines: Best Practice for Public Libraries* (PDF); *Taking Stock* (2 times/yr, journal)

National Federation of Retail Newsagents (NFRN)
Yeoman House, Sekforde St, London EC1R 0HF
Tel: (020) 7253 4225
E-mail: service@nfrnonline.com
Web Site: www.nfrnonline.com
Key Personnel
Chief Executive: Paul Baxter *E-mail:* paul. baxter@nfrn.org.uk
Head, Operations: Margaret McCloskey
E-mail: margaret.mccloskey@nfrn.org.uk
Head, Public Affairs & Communications: Adrian Roper *E-mail:* adrian.roper@nfrn.org.uk
Head, Member Services: Theresa Neale
Communications Manager: Anne Bingham
E-mail: anne@nfrn.org.uk
Founded: 1919

National Union of Journalists (Book Branch)
Headland House, 308 Gray's Inn Rd, London WC1X 8DP
Tel: (020) 7278 7916 *Fax:* (020) 7873 8143
E-mail: info@nuj.org.uk
Web Site: www.nujbook.org
Key Personnel
Branch Vice Chair: Huw Davies *E-mail:* huw. davies@lexisnexis.co.uk
Branch Secretary: Cath Rasbash
E-mail: crasbash@acblack.com
Branch Treasurer: Andy Smith *E-mail:* andy@ nujbook.org
Founded: 1973
Trade union.
Publication(s): *Comrade Moss* (1990, biography)

NFRN, see National Federation of Retail Newsagents (NFRN)

Nielsen UK ISBN Agency, see UK ISBN Agency (UK & Ireland only)

†◇PEN Club-Writers in Exile, London Branch
10 Melfort Dr, Leighton Buzzard, Beds LU7 7XN
Key Personnel
Secretary: Robert Fearnley *E-mail:* robfearnley@ waitrose.com

†◇PEN International
Unit A, Koops Mill Mews, 162-164 Abbey St, London SE1 2AN
Tel: (020) 7405 0338 *Fax:* (020) 7405 0339
E-mail: info@pen-international.org
Web Site: www.pen-international.org

Key Personnel
International President: Jennifer Clement
Executive Dir: Carles Torner *E-mail:* carles.
torner@pen-international.org
International Secretary: Hori Takeaki
Treasurer: Jarkko Tontti
Founded: 1921
Global community of writers celebrating literature
& promotion of freedom of expression.

Picture Research Association (PRA)
10 Merrick House, Mortimer Crescent, London
NW6 5NY
Tel: (0777) 1982308
E-mail: chair@picture-research.org.uk
Web Site: www.picture-research.org.uk
Key Personnel
Chair: Veneta Bullen
Treasurer: Rosie Taylor
Founded: 1977
Professional organization for picture researchers,
picture editors, picture managers & anyone
specifically involved in the research, manage-
ment & supply of visual material to the media
industry.
Publication(s): *Montage* (quarterly, magazine)

PLA, see The Private Libraries Association
(PLA)

PLS, see Publishers Licensing Society

PPA Business Media Group
35-38 New Bridge St, London EC4V 6BW
Tel: (020) 7404 4166 *Fax:* (020) 7404 4167
E-mail: info@ppa.co.uk
Web Site: www.ppa.co.uk
Key Personnel
Chairman: James Tye
Chief Executive: Barry McIlheney
Dir, Member Services: Nicola Rowe *Tel:* (020)
7400 7527 *E-mail:* nicola.rowe@ppa.co.uk
Founded: 1970
Industry network for UK professional publishers.

PRA, see Picture Research Association (PRA)

†◇The Private Libraries Association (PLA)
29 Eden Dr, Hull HU8 8JQ
E-mail: info@plabooks.org
Web Site: www.plabooks.org
Key Personnel
President: Giles Mandelbrote
Honorary Membership Secretary: Jim Maslen
USA & South America Membership Secretary:
Prof L D Mitchell *E-mail:* numislit@yahoo.
com
Australasia Membership Secretary: Kay Kraddock
E-mail: kay@kaykraddock.com
Canadian Membership Secretary: Jim Cramton
E-mail: jcramton@shaw.ca
Founded: 1956
An international society of book collectors.
Publication(s): *Exchange List* (quarterly);
Newsletter (quarterly); *The Private Library*
(quarterly, journal); *Private Press Books* (an-
nually, bibliography)

Public Lending Right
Richard House, Sorbonne Close, Stockton-on-
Tees TS17 6DA
Tel: (01642) 604699
E-mail: corporateservices@plr.uk.com
Web Site: www.plr.uk.com
Key Personnel
Registrar: Claire Balmer
Administered by the British Library. Under the
PLR system in the UK, payments are made
from government funds to authors, illustrators

& other contributors whose books are borrowed
from public libraries.
Publication(s): *Whose Loan Is It Anyway? Essays
in Celebration of PLR's Twentieth Anniversary*
(1999); *Writers Talk* (2009, 3rd ed)

The Publishers Association Ltd
50 Southwark St, 1st floor, London SE1 1UN
Tel: (020) 7378 0504
E-mail: mail@publishers.org.uk
Web Site: www.publishers.org.uk
Key Personnel
Chief Executive: Stephen Lotinga
Deputy Chief Executive: Emma House
Dir, Operations: Mark Wharton
Dir, Policy & Communications: Susie Winter
Trade association for UK publishers of books,
journals, audio & electronic publications.

The Publishers Association Ltd, Educational, Academic & Professional Publishing
Division of The Publishers Association Ltd
50 Southwark St, 1st floor, London SE1 1UN
Tel: (020) 7378 0504
E-mail: mail@publishers.org.uk
Web Site: www.publishers.org.uk
Key Personnel
Publisher Relations Executive: Nicola Swann
E-mail: nswann@publishers.org.uk
Founded: 1977

Publishers Licensing Society
Barnard's Inn, 86 Fetter Lane, London EC4A
1EN
Tel: (020) 7079 5930
E-mail: pls@pls.org.uk
Web Site: www.pls.org.uk
Key Personnel
Chief Executive Officer: Sarah Faulder
Head, Operations: Tom West
Communications & Events Manager: Joanna Wa-
ters
Data & Distributions Manager: Pam Singh
Founded: 1981
PLS has nonexclusive mandates from publishers
to include their works in photocopying & digi-
tisation licenses negotiated by the Copyright
Licensing Agency. PLS ensures publishers re-
ceive their share of fees collected by CLA.
Associate Companies: Copyright Licensing
Agency

Publishing Connections Ltd
25 Bishops Dr, Wokingham, Berks RG40 1WA
E-mail: info@publishingconnections.co.uk
Web Site: publishingconnections.co.uk
Key Personnel
Founder & Dir: Alistair Burtenshaw
E-mail: alistair@publishingconnections.co.uk
Founded: 2012
Supports growth & development of organizations
operating in the global books & publishing sec-
tor. Provides advisory & management services.

Publishing Scotland
Scott House, 10 South St Andrews St, Edinburgh
EH2 2AZ
Tel: (0131) 228 6866
E-mail: enquiries@publishingscotland.org
Web Site: www.publishingscotland.org
Key Personnel
Chief Executive: Marion Sinclair *E-mail:* marion.
sinclair@publishingscotland.org
Book Marketing Manager: Gill Tasker
Member Services Manager: Lucy Feather
Founded: 1973
Publication(s): *Publishing Scotland Yearbook* (an-
nually)

SCOLMA, see Standing Conference on Library
Materials on Africa

Scottish Book Trust
Sandeman House, Trunk's Close, 55 High St, Ed-
inburgh EH1 1SR
Tel: (0131) 524 0160
E-mail: info@scottishbooktrust.com
Web Site: www.scottishbooktrust.com
Key Personnel
Chair: Keir Bloomer
Chief Executive Officer: Marc Lambert
E-mail: marc.lambert@scottishbooktrust.com
Dir, Marketing & Communications: Moira Find-
lay *E-mail:* moira.findlay@scottishbooktrust.
com
Promotion of literature, reading & writing in
Scotland.

The Scottish Newspaper Society
17 Polwarth Grove, Edinburgh EH11 1LY
E-mail: info@scotns.org.uk
Web Site: www.scotns.org.uk
Key Personnel
Dir: John McLellan
Founded: 2009 (from merger of the Scottish
Daily Newspaper Society & the Scottish News-
paper Publishers Association)
Trade association representing newspaper publish-
ers throughout Scotland.

The Society of Authors
84 Drayton Gardens, London SW10 9SB
Tel: (020) 7373 6642 *Fax:* (020) 7373 5768
E-mail: info@societyofauthors.org
Web Site: www.societyofauthors.org
Key Personnel
Chairman: David Donachie
Chief Executive: Nicola Solomon
E-mail: nsolomon@societyofauthors.org
Deputy Chief Executive: Kate Pool
E-mail: kpool@societyofauthors.org
Founded: 1884
Trade union for professional writers.
Publication(s): *The Author* (quarterly)

The Society of Indexers
Woodbourn Business Centre, 10 Jessell St,
Sheffield S9 3HY
Tel: (0114) 244 9561; (0845) 872 6807
Fax: (0114) 244 9563
E-mail: admin@indexers.org.uk
Web Site: www.indexers.org.uk
Key Personnel
President: Sam Leith *E-mail:* president@indexers.
org.uk
Founded: 1957
Publication(s): *The Indexer* (quarterly, journal);
SIdelights (quarterly, newsletter)
Associate Companies: American Society of In-
dexers; Association of Southern African In-
dexers & Bibliographers; Australian & New
Zealand Society of Indexers; China Society of
Indexers; Indexing Society of Canada

†◇Standing Conference on Library Materials on Africa
70 Mortlock Ave, Cambridge CB4 1TE
Web Site: scolma.org
Key Personnel
Chair: Lucy McCann *Tel:* (01865) 270908
Fax: (01865) 270911
Treasurer: Alison Metcalfe
Secretary: Terry Barringer *Tel:* (01223) 424584
SCOLMA is the UK Libraries & Archives Group
on Africa.
Membership(s): European Librarians in African
Studies.
Publication(s): *African Research & Documenta-
tion* (journal)

STM, see International Association of STM
Publishers

UK ISBN Agency (UK & Ireland only)
Midas House, 3rd floor, 62 Goldsworth Rd, Woking, Surrey GU21 6LQ
Tel: (01483) 712 215 *Fax:* (01483) 712 214
E-mail: isbn.agency@nielsen.com
Web Site: www.isbn.nielsenbook.co.uk
Key Personnel
Senior Manager, Data Development: Howard Willows
Manager, ISBN Agency: Diana Williams
Supply unique identifiers for books & publishers.

UK Serials Group, see UKSG

UKSG
Bowman & Hillier Bldg, The Old Brewery, Priory Lane, Burford, Oxon OX18 4SG
Mailing Address: PO Box 5594, Newbury, Berks RG20 0YD
Tel: (01635) 254292 *Fax:* (01635) 253826
Web Site: www.uksg.org
Key Personnel
Executive Dir: Sarah Bull
Administrator: Karen Sadler *E-mail:* karen@uksg.org
Business Manager: Alison Whitehorn
　E-mail: alison@uksg.org
Founded: 1978
Nonprofit interest group of publishers, subscription agents & librarians to encourage the exchange & promotion of ideas on printed & electronic serials.
Publication(s): *The E-Resources Management Handbook* (electronic); *Insights: the UKSG journal* (3 times/yr, e-journal ISSN: 2048-7754); *UKSG eNews* (26 issues/yr, newsletter, electronic ISSN: 2048-7746)

Union of Welsh Publishers & Booksellers, see Cwlwm Cyhoeddwyr Cymru

The Welsh Books Council (Cyngor Llyfrau Cymru)
Castell Brychan, Aberystwyth, Ceredigion SY23 2JB
Tel: (01970) 624151 *Fax:* (01970) 625385
E-mail: castellbrychan@books.wales
Web Site: www.cllc.org.uk; www.wbc.org.uk
Key Personnel
Chief Executive: Helgard Krause
Head, Sales & Marketing: Helena O'Sullivan
　E-mail: helena.osullivan@books.wales
Founded: 1963
To improve standards of book production & publication in both Welsh & English.

WGGB, see The Writers' Guild of Great Britain (WGGB)

Women in Publishing
4 Barnard Hill, London N10 2HB
E-mail: web@womeninpublishing.org.uk
Web Site: www.womeninpublishing.org.uk
Key Personnel
Treasurer: Claire Pimm
Founded: 1979
Promote the status of women within publishing & related trades.

Writers & Scholars International, see Index on Censorship

The Writers' Guild of Great Britain (WGGB)
134 Tooley St, 1st floor, London SE1 2TU
Tel: (020) 7833 0777
E-mail: admin@writersguild.org.uk
Web Site: writersguild.org.uk
Key Personnel
President: Olivia Hetreed *E-mail:* president@writersguild.org.uk
Acting General Secretary: Ellie Peers
　E-mail: ellie@writersguild.org.uk
Communications Manager: Sarah Woodley
　E-mail: sarah@writersguild.org.uk
Trade union representing professional writers in TV, film, theatre, radio, books, poetry, animation & video games.

United States

†American-Scandinavian Foundation (ASF)
58 Park Ave, New York, NY 10016
Tel: 212-779-3587
E-mail: info@amscan.org
Web Site: www.amscan.org
Key Personnel
President & Chief Executive Officer: Edward P Gallagher
Senior Advisor & Corporate Secretary: Lynn Carter
Treasurer: Bard E Bunaes
Founded: 1911
Nonprofit organization committed to promoting educational, cultural & professional exchange between the USA & the Nordic countries - Denmark, Finland, Iceland, Norway & Sweden.
Publication(s): *The Longboat* (newsletter); *Scan* (quarterly, newsletter); *Scandinavian Review* (3 times/yr, cultural/literary/political magazine)

ASF, see American-Scandinavian Foundation (ASF)

IAALD, see International Association of Agricultural Information Specialists (IAALD)

IILI, see Instituto Internacional de Literatura Iberoamericana (IILI)

†◇Instituto Internacional de Literatura Iberoamericana (IILI) (International Institute of Latin American Literature)
c/o University of Pittsburgh, 1312 Cathedral of Learning, Pittsburgh, PA 15260
Tel: 412-624-3359 *Fax:* 412-624-0829
E-mail: iili@pitt.edu; iilisus@pitt.edu
Web Site: hispanic.pitt.edu/iili/englishindex.html
Key Personnel
Dir, Publications: Mabel Morana
　E-mail: mabelmorana@yahoo.com
Secretary-Treasurer: Bobby J Chamberlain
　E-mail: chambln@pitt.edu
Founded: 1938
Publication(s): *Memorias*; *Revista Iberoamericana* (quarterly, journal, literary criticism)

†◇International Association of Agricultural Information Specialists (IAALD)
PO Box 63, Lexington, KY 40588-0063
Tel: 859-254-0752 *Fax:* 859-257-8379
E-mail: info@iaald.org
Web Site: www.iaald.org
Key Personnel
President: Frederico Sancho Guevara
　E-mail: frederico.sancho@iaald.org
President-Elect: Peter Walton *E-mail:* peter.walton@iaald.org
Secretary/Treasurer: Toni Greider *E-mail:* toni.greider@iaald.org
Founded: 1955
Publication(s): *Agricultural Information Worldwide* (2 times/yr, journal)

†◇International Literacy Association (ILA)
800 Barksdale Rd, Newark, DE 19711-3204
Mailing Address: PO Box 8139, Newark, DE 19714-8139
Tel: 302-731-1600 *Fax:* 302-731-1057
E-mail: customerservice@reading.org
Web Site: www.literacyworldwide.org; www.reading.org
Key Personnel
Executive Dir: Marcie Craig Post
　E-mail: mpost@reading.org
Associate Executive Dir: Stephen Sye
　E-mail: ssye@reading.org
Executive Assistant: Kathy Baughman
　E-mail: kbaughman@reading.org
Founded: 1956
Nonprofit global network of individuals & institutions committed to worldwide literacy.
Publication(s): *Journal of Adolescent & Adult Literacy (JAAL)* (6 times/yr); *Literacy Today* (6 times/yr, magazine, members only); *Reading Research Quarterly (RRQ)* (journal); *The Reading Teacher (RT)* (6 times/yr)

†International Monetary Fund
700 19 St NW, Washington, DC 20431
Tel: 202-623-7000 *Fax:* 202-623-4661
E-mail: publicaffairs@imf.org
Web Site: www.imf.org
Key Personnel
Mng Dir: Christine Lagarde
Founded: 1945
Subjects: Activities & Operations of the International Monetary Fund, Balance of Payments & External Adjustment Problems, Domestic Fiscal & Monetary Topics, Economics, International Finance, International Monetary & Trade Issues, International Statistics
Publication(s): *Direction of Trade Statistics* (yearbook); *Finance & Development* (quarterly, magazine); *Fiscal Monitor* (2 times/yr); *Global Financial Stability Report* (2 times/yr); *Regional Economic Reports* (2 times/yr); *World Economic Outlook* (2 times/yr)
ISBN Prefix(es): 978-0-939934; 978-1-55775; 978-1-49831

SALALM, see Seminar on the Acquisition of Latin American Library Materials (SALALM)

†◇Seminar on the Acquisition of Latin American Library Materials (SALALM)
Tulane University, Latin American Library, 422 Howard Tilton Memorial Library, 7001 Freret St, New Orleans, LA 70118-5549
Tel: 540-247-1366 *Fax:* 540-247-1367
E-mail: salalm@tulane.edu
Web Site: www.salalm.org
Key Personnel
President: Luis A Gonzalez *E-mail:* luisgonz@indiana.edu
Vice President/President-Elect: Paloma Celis Carbajal *E-mail:* pcarbajal@library.wisc.edu
Executive Dir: Hortensia Calvo *E-mail:* hcalvo@tulane.edu
Treasurer: Peter T Johnson *E-mail:* ptj4512@gmail.com
Founded: 1956
National & international forum focused exclusively on collection development & services in libraries with Latin American collections.
Publication(s): *Bibliography & Reference Series*; *Latin American Information Series*

Uruguay

Camara Uruguaya del Libro (Uruguayan Publishers' Association)
Colon 1476, ap 102, 11000 Montevideo
Tel: 29169374 *Fax:* 29167628
E-mail: info@camaradellibro.com.uy
Web Site: www.camaradellibro.com.uy

Key Personnel
President: Jorge Saracini
Vice President: Alvaro Risso
Secretary: Enrique Morrone
Treasurer: Luis Sica
Founded: 1944

IAMCR, see International Association for Media
& Communication Research (IAMCR)

**†◇International Association for Media &
Communication Research (IAMCR)**
c/o Pablo de Maria 1036, 11200 Montevideo
Web Site: www.iamcr.org
Key Personnel
President: Janet Wasko
Vice President: Graham Murdock; Aimee Vega
Secretary General: Gerard Goggin
Treasurer: Elske van de Fliert
Executive Dir: Bruce Girard
Founded: 1957
Publication(s): *IAMCR Newsletter* (3 times/yr)

Standard Book Numbering Agency
Biblioteca Nacional, 18 de Julio 1790, 11200
Montevideo
Tel: 2402 0812 (ext 216)
E-mail: isbn@bibna.gub.uy
Web Site: www.bibna.gub.uy
Key Personnel
Contact: Patricia Garcia Medina

Venezuela

Agencia Venezolana del ISBN (Venezuelan
ISBN Agency)
CENAL, Torre Norte, Piso 20, Centro Simon Bo-
livar, El Silencio, Caracas 1010

Tel: (0212) 482 2020; (0212) 482 3437
Fax: (0212) 482 2020
E-mail: cenal.isbnvenezuela@gmail.com
Web Site: www.cenal.gob.ve
Key Personnel
Contact: Angela Negrin

Camara Venezolana del Libro (Venezuelan
Publishers' Association)
Av Andres Bello, Centro Andres Bello, Torre
Oeste, Piso 11, Oficina 112-0, Caracas 1050
Tel: (0212) 793 1347 *Fax:* (0212) 793 1368
E-mail: cavelibro@gmail.com
Web Site: www.cavelibro.org.ve
Key Personnel
President: Ivan Dieguez Vazquez
Founded: 1953

Standard Book Numbering Agency, see
Agencia Venezolana del ISBN

Vietnam

**Ministry of Information & Communications of
Vietnam**
No 10 Duong Thanh St, Hanoi
Tel: (04) 38285697 *Fax:* (04) 38287738
Web Site: ppdvn.gov.vn
Key Personnel
Dir General: Chu Van Hoa *Tel:* (04) 38287737
E-mail: cvhoa@mic.gov.vn
Deputy Dir General: Nguyen Ngoc Bao *Tel:* (04)
38285698 *E-mail:* nnbao@mic.gov.vn
Guides, directs & organizes the implementation
of plans on printing, publishing & distribution.
Manages supporting activities for publishing in
conformity to the legal rules.

Zambia

**Booksellers & Publishers Association of
Zambia**
PO Box 51109, 10100 Lusaka
Key Personnel
Contact: Ms Dongo Banda *E-mail:* dongo.
banda@gmail.com

Standard Book Numbering Agency
Booksellers & Publishers Association of Zambia,
PO Box 51109, 10100 Lusaka
Tel: (0211) 253 952; (0977) 746477 (cell)
Key Personnel
Contact: Ms Dongo Banda *E-mail:* dongo.
banda@gmail.com

Zimbabwe

Standard Book Numbering Agency
National Archives of Zimbabwe, Private Bag
7729, Causeway, Harare
Tel: (04) 792 741 *Fax:* (04) 792 398
E-mail: archives@archives.gov.zw
Key Personnel
Contact: Mr Kudakwashe Tonhodzai

ZBPA, see Zimbabwe Book Publishers
Association (ZBPA)

**Zimbabwe Book Publishers Association
(ZBPA)**
PO Box 3041, Harare
Tel: (04) 773236 *Fax:* (04) 754256
Publication(s): *Making Books*

Major Book Dealers

This section contains active book dealers in one or more of the following categories: distribution, exporting, importing, major book chains, major independent booksellers, remainder dealers, online booksellers, and wholesalers.

Albania

Botimpex
Rr "Naim Frasheri" P 84, Sh 2, Ap 37, Tirana
Tel: (04) 2234 023; (068) 40 43957 (cell)
  Fax: (04) 2226 886
E-mail: info@botimpex.com
Web Site: www.botimpex.com
Founded: 1991
Publications import-export agency. Worldwide distributor of books, newspapers, magazines, journals, maps & electronic products such as CDs, DVDs & other media.
Type of Business: Distributor, Exporter, Importer

Algeria

Editions Sedia
Subsidiary of Hachette Livre
Cite les mandariniers, lot 293, 16058 Al Mohammadia-Alger
Tel: (077) 0973861 (cell) *Fax:* (02) 1210575
E-mail: sedia@sedia-dz.com
Web Site: sedia-dz.com
Key Personnel
Chief Executive Officer: Brahim Djelmami-Hani
  E-mail: bdjelmami@sedia-dz.com
Project Manager: Nacera Khiat *E-mail:* nkhiat@sedia-dz.com
Editor: Hassina Zerdaoui *E-mail:* hzerdaoui@sedia-dz.com
Founded: 2000
Type of Business: Distributor

Argentina

Alfagrama Ediciones SRL
Zapata 160, C1426AEB Buenos Aires
Tel: (011) 4772-0995
E-mail: info@alfagrama.com.ar; pedidos@alfagrama.com.ar
Web Site: alfagrama.com.ar
Key Personnel
Contact: Facundo Nunez *E-mail:* facundo@alfagrama.com.ar; Matias Nunez
Type of Business: Distributor

Cuspide Libros SA
Tacuarí 1842, C1139AAN Buenos Aires
Tel: (011) 4322 8868 *Fax:* (011) 4322 3456
E-mail: ventas@cuspide.com; info@cuspide.com
Web Site: www.cuspide.com
Key Personnel
President: Joaquin M Gil Paricio
Account Executive: Susana Fernandez
Founded: 1960
Type of Business: Distributor, Wholesaler
Bookshop(s): Ave Cabildo 1965, C1428AAB Buenos Aires *Tel:* (011) 4780-4464
  E-mail: cabildo.1965@cuspide.com; Ave Santa Fe 1818, C1123AAN Buenos Aires

Tel: (011) 4815-4606 *Fax:* (011) 4811-6325
E-mail: santafe.1818@cuspide.com; Ave Santa Fe 2077, C1123AAC Buenos Aires *Tel:* (011) 4822-8944 *E-mail:* santafe.2077@cuspide.com; Corrientes 1243, C1043AAM Buenos Aires *Tel:* (011) 4382-1865 *E-mail:* corrientes.1243@cuspide.com; Av Corrientes 1316, C1043ABN Buenos Aires *Tel:* (011) 4372-6266 *E-mail:* corrientes.1316@cuspide.com; Florida 628, C1005AAN Buenos Aires *Tel:* (011) 4328-0575 *E-mail:* florida.628@cuspide.com; Village Cines Ave Rivadavia 5045, C1424CEF Buenos Aires *Tel:* (011) 4901-6043 *E-mail:* village.caballito@cuspide.com; Village Cines Panamericana Km 50, 1629 Pilar, Buenos Aires *Tel:* (0230) 4473-228 *E-mail:* pilar@cuspide.com; Ave Gral Paz 57, 5000 Cordoba *Tel:* (0351) 424-6469 *E-mail:* cordoba@cuspide.com; Portal de Rosario Nansen 255, 2000 Rosario, Santa Fe *Tel:* (0341) 453-2212 *E-mail:* portal.rosario@cuspide.com; Village Cines Eva Peron 5856, 2000 Rosario, Santa Fe *Tel:* (0341) 457-0889 *E-mail:* rosario@cuspide.com

Gradifco SRL
Viamonte 2632, B1678DWB Caseros, Buenos Aires
Tel: (011) 4759-0286 *Fax:* (011) 4750-5688
E-mail: editorial@gradifco.com.ar
Web Site: www.gradifco.com.ar
Key Personnel
Mng Partner: Marcelo F Paolini; Sergio A Paolini
Founded: 1999
Type of Business: Distributor

Grupal Logistica y Distribucion SA
Solis 2045/49, C1134ADQ Buenos Aires
Tel: (011) 4306-2444
E-mail: ventas@grupaldistribuidora.com.ar
Web Site: www.grupaldistribuidora.com.ar
Key Personnel
Editorial Dir: Silvina Fernandez
Founded: 2004
Type of Business: Distributor, Importer

Libreria Huemul SA
Ave Santa Fe 2237, C1123AAE Buenos Aires
Tel: (011) 4822-1666 *Fax:* (011) 4825-2290
E-mail: info@libreriahuemul.com.ar
Web Site: www.libreriahuemul.com.ar
Founded: 1940
Type of Business: Major Independent Bookseller

Libreria Kier
Av Santa Fe 1260, C1059ABT Buenos Aires
Tel: (011) 4811-0507; (011) 4811-8243
E-mail: ventadirecta@kier.com.ar
Web Site: www.kier.com.ar
Founded: 1907
Type of Business: Distributor, Exporter, Importer, Major Independent Bookseller
Owned by: Editorial Kier SRL

Ediciones Nueva Vision
Tucuman 3748, C1189AAV Buenos Aires
Tel: (011) 4864-5050; (011) 4863-1461
E-mail: ventas@nuevavisionedic.com.ar; administracion@nuevavisionedic.com.ar

Web Site: www.facebook.co/Ediciones-Nueva-Vision-746426855417742
Key Personnel
President: Haydee Perez de Giacone
Vice President: Javier Ernesto Giacone

Riverside Agency SAC
Av Cordoba, 744, 5° "I", C1054AAT Buenos Aires
Tel: (011) 5353 0830 *Fax:* (011) 5353 0830
E-mail: info@riverside-agency.com.ar; prensa@riverside-agency.com.ar
Web Site: www.riversideagency.com.ar
Key Personnel
President: Jaime Rodrigue Rodrigue
Manager: Felipe Martinez
Sales Manager: Benjamin Angeloni
Press: Sebastian Lidijover
Founded: 1958
Type of Business: Distributor, Importer, Wholesaler

Libreria Santa Fe
Ave Santa Fe 2582, 1123 Buenos Aires
Tel: (011) 5254 2376 (ext 30); (011) 5254 2376 (ext 31); (011) 5219 2582 *Fax:* (011) 5254 2376 (ext 36)
E-mail: santafe2582@lsf.com.ar; asociados@lsf.com.ar
Web Site: www.lsf.com.ar
Key Personnel
Contact: Juan Pablo Aisenberg; Ruben Aisenberg
Founded: 1957
Type of Business: Importer
Branch Office(s)
Ave Santa Fe 2224, Buenos Aires *Tel:* (011) 5254-2376
Alto Palermo Shopping Local 2012, Ave Santa Fe 3253, Buenos Aires *Tel:* (011) 5219-3253; (01) 5777-8078 *E-mail:* altopalermo@lsf.com.ar
Ave Callao 335, Buenos Aires *Tel:* (011) 5246-4335 *E-mail:* callao@lsf.com.ar
Cabildo 605 esquina Gorostiaga, Buenos Aires *Tel:* (011) 4899-1916; (011) 4899-1930 *E-mail:* cabildo@lsf.com.ar

SBS Distribuidora
Benito Perez Galdos 275, C1155AGE Buenos Aires
Tel: (011) 5353-2220
Web Site: www.facebook.com/DistribuidoraSBS
Key Personnel
Sales Manager: Sebastian Garcia
Founded: 1997
Type of Business: Distributor
Parent Company: SBS Livraria Internacional

Aruba

De Wit Stores NV
L G Smith Blvd 110, Oranjestad
Tel: 582-3500
Key Personnel
General Manager: Lyanne Beaujon
Stationery, souvenirs, gifts, clothing.

Type of Business: Distributor, Importer, Major Independent Bookseller
Bookshop(s): Caya G F Betico Croes 94, Oranjestad *Tel:* 582-1573 *Fax:* 582-1573

Australia

Angus & Robertson Bookworld
Subsidiary of Booktopia Pty Ltd
c/o Booktopia Pty Ltd, 3-29 Birnie Ave, Unit E1, Lidcombe, NSW 2141
Toll Free Tel: 1800 732 701
Web Site: www.angusrobertson.com.au
Founded: 1886
Type of Business: Online Bookseller

Australian Book Group Pty Ltd (ABG)
Suite 66, 89 Jones St, Ultimo, NSW 2007
Tel: (02) 9211 3033
E-mail: inquiries@australianbookgroup.com.au
Web Site: australian-bookgroup.squarespace.com
Founded: 1992
Type of Business: Distributor

James Bennett Pty Ltd
Unit 3, Old Pittwater Rd, Brookvale, NSW 2100
Mailing Address: Locked Bag 537, Frenchs Forest, NSW 2086
Tel: (02) 8988 5000 *Fax:* (02) 8988 5031
E-mail: info@bennett.com.au
Web Site: www.bennett.com.au
Key Personnel
Mng Dir: Mr Kim Jardine *E-mail:* kjardine@bennett.com.au
Finance Dir: Nandu Mehta *E-mail:* nmehta@bennett.com.au
Production Manager: Sarah Phillpot *E-mail:* sphillpot@bennett.com.au
Sales Manager: Rod Riley *E-mail:* rriley@bennett.com.au
Founded: 1964
Library supplier.
Type of Business: Distributor, Exporter, Importer, Wholesaler
Owned by: GOBI® Library Solutions

Biramo Books Pty Ltd
5 King St, Warners Bay, NSW 2282
Tel: (02) 4954 2626
Founded: 1985
Type of Business: Distributor, Exporter, Importer, Wholesaler

Burgewood Books
PO Box 326, Warrandyte, Victoria 3113
Tel: (03) 9844 2512 *Fax:* (03) 9844 0664
Web Site: www.burgewoodbooks.com.au
Key Personnel
Owner: Doreen Burge *E-mail:* dburge@burgewoodbooks.com.au
Founded: 1997
Also book publisher. Specialize in books about sailing ships, journeys to Australia by sail & shipwrecks to remembrances of Australia in the 1920's & 1930's & of World War II.
Type of Business: Distributor, Online Bookseller

Burnet's Books
46 Bridge St, Uralla, NSW 2358
Tel: (02) 6778 4682 *Fax:* (02) 6778 4516
Key Personnel
Mng Dir & Editor: Ross Burnet
Founded: 1987
Antiquarian & secondhand bookdealer.
Type of Business: Distributor, Exporter, Importer, Major Independent Bookseller, Wholesaler

Campion Education
1/170-180 Rooks Rd, Vermont, Victoria 3131
Toll Free Tel: 1300 433 982
E-mail: elicensing@campion.com.au
Web Site: www.campion.com.au
Supplies educational print & digital resources to primary, secondary & K-12 schools across government, Catholic & independent sectors in all major Australian states.
Type of Business: Distributor, Online Bookseller
Branch Office(s)
1-5 Intrepid St, Berwick, Victoria 3806
88-92 Waterview Close, Dandenong South, Victoria 3175
8/12 Makland Dr, Derrimut, Victoria 3030
2-4 Calway St, Drouin, Victoria 3818
319-321 Pascoe Vale Rd, Essendon, Victoria 3040
36 Little Myers St, Geelong, Victoria 3220
94 McEwan Rd, Heidelberg West, Victoria 3081
232-236 Wickham Rd, Moorabbin, Victoria 3189
13 Telford Dr, Shepparton, Victoria 3630
43 Herbert St, Unit 2, Artarmon, NSW 2064
314 Montague Rd, West End, Qld 4101
46 Glynburn Rd, Hectorville, SA 5073
7 Oxleigh Dr, Malaga, WA 6090
28 Kembla Way, Willetton, WA 6155

Collins Booksellers Pty Ltd
86 Bourke St, Level 2, Melbourne, Victoria 3000
Tel: (03) 9654 7400; (03) 9662 9472 *Fax:* (03) 9654 7600
E-mail: headoffice@collinsbooks.com.au
Web Site: www.collinsbooks.com.au
Founded: 2005
Type of Business: Major Book Chain Headquarters
Bookshop(s): 80 Bridge Mall, Ballarat, Victoria 3350 *Tel:* (03) 5331 6552; 222 Sturt St, Ballarat, Victoria 3350; 130-132 Main St, Croydon, Victoria 3136 *Tel:* (03) 9723 5577; 170 Hare St, Echuca, Victoria 3564 *Tel:* (03) 5482 2902; Shop 2040, Fountain Gate Shopping Centre, Level 2, Magid Dr, Fountain Gate, Victoria 3805 *Tel:* (03) 9703 0790; 58 Langtree Mall, Mildura, Victoria 3500 *Tel:* (03) 5023 1836; 67 Puckle St, Moonee Ponds, Victoria 3039 *Tel:* (03) 9372 0585; Shop 6, Spotlight Plaza 216-228, Raymond St, Sale, Victoria 3850 *Tel:* (03) 5144 6262; 262 Maude St, Shepparton, Victoria 3630 *Tel:* (03) 5822 2679; 27 Evans St, Sunbury, Victoria 3429 *Tel:* (03) 9744 1533; 3/74 Seymour St, Traralgon, Victoria 3844 *Tel:* (03) 5176 2506; 159 Liebig St, Warrnambool, Victoria 3280, Austria *Tel:* (03) 5562 4272; Shop 15, Armidale Central, 225 Beardy St, Armidale, NSW 2350 *Tel:* (02) 6772 6000; 245 Darling St, Balmain, NSW 2041 *Tel:* (02) 9555 6055; Shop 3, 9 Lawson St, Byron Bay, NSW 2481 *Tel:* (02) 6685 7820; Shop 21, Griffin Plaza, Yambil St, Griffith, NSW 2680 *Tel:* (02) 6964 2322; Newsagency 7/33 Market St, Merimbula, NSW 2548 *Tel:* (02) 6495 1292; 230 Summer St, Orange, NSW 2800 *Tel:* (02) 6369 1333; 368 Peel St, Tamworth, NSW 2340 *Tel:* (02) 6766 4454; 75 Baylis St, Wagga Wagga, NSW 2650 *Tel:* (02) 6921 8933; 1/24 Bulcock St, Caloundra, Qld 4551 *Tel:* (07) 5438 2709; Shop 130, Smithfield Centre, Cook & Kennedy Highway, Smithfield, Qld 4878 *Tel:* (07) 4038 1786; 32 Commercial St West, Mount Gambier, SA 5290 *Tel:* (08) 8724 9068; 93 St John St, Launceston, Tas 7250 *Tel:* (03) 6334 8499; 117 Victoria St, Bunbury, WA 6230 *Tel:* (08) 9791 3755; 23 Napoleon St, Cottesloe, WA 6011 *Tel:* (08) 9284 7070; 19-21 Wilson St, Kalgoorlie, WA 6430 *Tel:* (08) 9021 7072; Shop 44-45, Southlands Shopping Centre, Burrendah Blvd, Willetton, WA 6155 *Tel:* (08) 9313 5164

Continental Bookshop
PO Box 4292, Ringwood, Victoria 3146
Tel: (03) 9015 4440 *Fax:* (03) 8820 4016

Web Site: www.continentalbookshop.com
Key Personnel
Mng Dir: Christopher Raynor
Founded: 1962
Foreign language books & language learning media.
Type of Business: Distributor, Exporter, Importer, Major Independent Bookseller

Cookery Book
54B Sailors Bay Rd, Northbridge, NSW 2063
Tel: (02) 9967 8211 *Fax:* (02) 9967 8578
E-mail: cookerybook@cookerybook.com.au
Web Site: www.cookerybook.com.au
Founded: 1985
Australia's only exclusive distributor of cookery books for the professional chef & the home cook.
Type of Business: Wholesaler

The Co-op, see University Co-operative Bookshop Ltd

O R Dolgoshein Pty Ltd
561 Foxground Rd, Foxground, NSW 2534
Tel: (02) 4234 0865
Key Personnel
Dir: Airdrie Ann Long
Founded: 1972
Type of Business: Distributor, Importer, Major Independent Bookseller, Wholesaler

Dominie Pty Ltd
8 Cross St, Brookvale, NSW 2100
Mailing Address: PO Box 7244, Brookvale, NSW 2100
Tel: (02) 9938 8686 *Fax:* (02) 9938 8690
E-mail: dominie@dominie.com.au
Web Site: www.dominie.com.au
Founded: 1951
Educational resources.
Type of Business: Major Independent Bookseller

Florilegium
65 Derwent St, Glebe, NSW 2037
Tel: (02) 9571 8222 *Fax:* (02) 8208 9938
E-mail: sales@florilegium.com.au
Web Site: www.florilegium.com.au
Founded: 1989
Subjects include Australian plants, botanical illustration, gardening & garden design/history, landscape architecture.
Type of Business: Major Independent Bookseller, Online Bookseller, Wholesaler

Footprint Books Pty Ltd
4/8 Jubilee Ave, Warriewood, NSW 2102
Tel: (02) 9997 3973 *Toll Free Tel:* 1300 260 090 *Fax:* (02) 9997 3185
E-mail: info@footprint.com.au; sales@footprint.com.au
Web Site: www.footprint.com.au
Key Personnel
Operations & Finance Dir: Simon Player
Sales & Marketing Dir: Kate O'Reilly
Founded: 1999
Subjects include ageing, art, design & photography, Asian studies, astronomy, Autism & Asperger's, business, clinical psychology, communications & media, counselling, cultural studies, dance, disabilities, economics, education, environment, health, hypnosis, language & communications, management, medical, NLP, psychiatry, psychoanalysis, psychology, psychotherapy.
Type of Business: Distributor

Foreign Language Bookshop
Division of Bookery Pty Ltd
9-11 Victoria St, Fiztroy, Victoria 3065
Tel: (03) 8417 9500 *Fax:* (03) 9416 1616

E-mail: shop@flb.com.au
Web Site: www.foreignlanguagebookshop.com.au;
www.languages.com.au
Key Personnel
Mng Dir: Jacob Miceli *E-mail:* jacob@flb.com.au
Founded: 1938
Books, language learning resources, board games
& gift items in over 125 languages.
Type of Business: Exporter, Importer, Major Independent Bookseller

Gaston Renard Pty Ltd
PO Box 1030, Ivanhoe, Melbourne, Victoria 3079
Tel: (03) 9459 5040 *Fax:* (03) 9459 6787
E-mail: books@gastonrenard.com.au
Web Site: www.gastonrenard.com.au
Key Personnel
Owner: Julien Renard
Founded: 1945
Antiquarian bookseller & limited edition publisher.
Membership(s): ANZAAB.
Type of Business: Distributor, Exporter, Importer, Major Independent Bookseller

INT Books Pty Ltd
3 Charles St, Coburg North, Victoria 3058
Tel: (03) 9354 9926 *Fax:* (03) 9326 2413
E-mail: sales@intbooks.com.au
Web Site: www.intbooks.com.au
Key Personnel
Mng Dir: Tom Danby *E-mail:* tdanby@intbooks.com.au
Type of Business: Distributor

John Reed Book Distribution
2/11 Yandala St, Tea Gardens, NSW 2324
Mailing Address: PO Box 257, Tea Gardens, NSW 2324
Tel: (02) 4497 2936 *Fax:* (02) 4997 2937
E-mail: sales@johnreedbooks.com.au
Web Site: www.johnreedbooks.com.au
Founded: 1997
Subjects include business, cooking, health, martial arts, parenting, pets, philosophy, poetry, psychology, religion, self-help, spirituality, sports, transportation.
Type of Business: Distributor

Koorong Books Pty Ltd
28 West Parade, West Ryde, NSW 2114
Tel: (02) 9857 4477 *Fax:* (02) 9857 4499
E-mail: west_ryde@koorong.com.au
Web Site: www.koorong.com
Key Personnel
Chief Executive Officer: Paul Bootes
   E-mail: pb@koorong.com.au
General Manager, Retail Operations: Rheban
   Bradley *E-mail:* rb@koorong.com.au
Marketing & Facilities Manager: Heather Lewis
   E-mail: hl@koorong.com.au
Store Manager: Sheryl Rennie *E-mail:* sr@koorong.com.au
Founded: 1978
Type of Business: Importer, Major Book Chain Headquarters
Bookshop(s): 3 Elizabeth St, Argenton,
NSW 2284, Store Manager: Joel Crichton
Tel: (02) 4941 7777 *Fax:* (02) 4941 7788
E-mail: newcastle@koorong.com.au; 120
Rusden St, Armidale, NSW 2350, Store
Manager: Warren Ward *Tel:* (02) 6772 2622
Fax: (02) 6772 7608 *E-mail:* armidale@
koorong.com.au; Unit 3b, Henry Lawson
Centre, 61-79 Henry St, Penrith, NSW 2750,
Store Manager: Warren Ward *Tel:* (02) 4724
4477 *Fax:* (02) 4724 4488 *E-mail:* penrith@
koorong.com.au; 141 Gordon St, Port Macquarie, NSW 2444, Store Manager: Martin
Camilleri *Tel:* (02) 6584 4977 *Fax:* (02) 6583
6235 *E-mail:* portmcq@koorong.com.au; 26
Maryborough St, Fyshwick, ACT 2609, Store

Manager: Costa Ligdopoulous *Tel:* (02) 6280
3477 *Fax:* (02) 6280 3488 *E-mail:* fyshwick@
koorong.com.au; 102 Brisbane Rd, Mooloolaba,
Qld 4557, Store Manager: Janie Waterhouse
Tel: (07) 5457 5677 *Fax:* (07) 5457 5688
E-mail: mooloolaba@koorong.com.au; 38
Chatswood Rd, Springwood, Qld 4127, Store
Manager: Adam Breen *Tel:* (07) 3387 4677
Fax: (07) 3387 4688 *E-mail:* springwood@
koorong.com.au; 837 Ruthven St, Toowoomba,
Qld 4350, Store Manager: Glenn Cox
Tel: (07) 4617 7177 *Fax:* (07) 4617 7188
E-mail: toowoomba@koorong.com.au; 7
Broadway St, Wooloongabba, Qld 4102, Store
Manager: David Andersen *Tel:* (07) 3896 8777
Fax: (07) 3896 8788 *E-mail:* wooloongabba@
koorong.com.au; 198 Waymouth St, Adelaide, SA 5000, Store Manager: Jo Stok
Tel: (08) 8239 6777 *Fax:* (08) 8239 6788
E-mail: adelaide@koorong.com.au; 31 Criterion St, Hobart, Tas 7000, Store Manager:
Victor Soo *Tel:* (03) 6234 0577 *Fax:* (03) 6234
0588 *E-mail:* hobart@koorong.com.au; 92 St
John St, Launceston, Tas 7250, Store Manager:
Nicole Goodwin *Tel:* (03) 6331 6759 *Fax:* (03)
6334 6013 *E-mail:* launceston@koorong.
com.au; 4-8 Vicki St, Blackburn South, Victoria 3130, Store Manager: Claire Carvosso
Tel: (03) 9262 7444 *Fax:* (03) 9262 7488
E-mail: bburn@koorong.com.au; 434 Lord
St, Mount Lawley, WA 6050, Store Manager:
Michelle Stuart-Saunders *Tel:* (08) 9427 9777
Fax: (08) 9427 9788 *E-mail:* perth@koorong.
com.au

Language Book Centre
Division of Abbey's Bookshops Pty Ltd
131 York St, Level 1, Sydney, NSW 2000
Tel: (02) 9267 1397 *Toll Free Tel:* 1800 802 432
(outside Sydney & within Australia) *Fax:* (02)
9264 8993
E-mail: language@abbeys.com.au
Web Site: www.languagebooks.com.au
Key Personnel
Manager: Melanie Macri *E-mail:* melaniem@
abbeys.com.au
Founded: 1976
Type of Business: Major Independent Bookseller

Robert Muir Old & Rare Books
17 Lindsay St, Perth, WA 6000
Tel: (08) 9228 2111
E-mail: books@muirbooks.com
Web Site: www.muirbooks.com
Key Personnel
Owner: Janet Muir *E-mail:* janetmuir@
muirbooks.com
Founded: 1973
Membership(s): ABA; Australian & New Zealand
Association of Antiquarian Booksellers (ANZAAB); International League of Antiquarian
Booksellers (ILAB).
Type of Business: Exporter, Importer, Major Independent Bookseller

Peribo Pty Ltd
58 Beaumont Rd, Mount Kuring-gai, NSW 2080
Tel: (02) 9457 0011 *Fax:* (02) 9457 0022
E-mail: info@peribo.com.au; salesdistribution@
peribo.com.au (publisher inquiry)
Web Site: www.peribo.com.au
Key Personnel
Mng Dir: Michael Edward Coffey
Founded: 1987
Sales, marketing & distribution of titles to booksellers throughout Australia & New Zealand.
Subjects include art, architecture, children's,
fashion, graphic design, interior design, military, illustrated, classic & contemporary fiction,
gift & humor, pop culture & nonfiction.
Type of Business: Distributor

Readings
309 Lygon St, Carlton, Victoria 3053
Tel: (03) 9347 6633
E-mail: customerservice@readings.com.au
Web Site: www.readings.com.au
Key Personnel
Mng Dir: Mark Rubbo *Tel:* (03) 9341 7725
   E-mail: mark.rubbo@readings.com.au
Book Division Manager: Alison Huber
   E-mail: alison@readings.com.au
Group Operations Manager: Robbie Egan
   E-mail: robbie.egan@readings.com.au
Marketing Manager: Nina Kenwood *Tel:* (03)
   9341 7726 *E-mail:* nina.kenwood@readings.
com.au
Founded: 1969
Independent retailer of books, music & film.
Type of Business: Major Book Chain Headquarters
Bookshop(s): 315 Lygon St, Carlton, Victoria
3053 *Tel:* (03) 9341 7730 *E-mail:* angela.
crocombe@readings.com.au (children's
& young adult); Westfield Doncaster, 619
Doncaster Rd, Doncaster, Victoria 3108
Tel: (03) 9810 0891 *E-mail:* doncaster@
readings.com.au; 701 Glenferrie Rd,
Hawthorn, Victoria 3122 *Tel:* (03) 9819 1917
E-mail: hawthorne@reading.com.au; 185 Glenferrie Rd, Malvern, Victoria 3144 *Tel:* (03)
9509 1952 *E-mail:* malvern@readings.com.
au; State Library Victoria, Corner La Trobe
& Swanston St, Melbourne, Victoria 3000
Tel: (03) 8664 7540 *E-mail:* slv@readings.com.
au; 112 Acland St, Saint Kilda, Victoria 3182
Tel: (03) 9525 3852 *E-mail:* stkilda@readings.
com.au

Saint Benedict Book Centre
6 Malvern St, Bayswater, Victoria 3153
Tel: (03) 9720 6499 *Fax:* (03) 9816 0899
E-mail: info@freedompublishing.com.au
Web Site: www.sbbc.com.au
Founded: 1982
Catholic book retailers/wholesalers.
Type of Business: Distributor, Major Independent Bookseller, Wholesaler

SCB Pty Ltd, see Super Cheap Books Pty Ltd

Social Club Books Pty Ltd, see Super Cheap
   Books Pty Ltd

Soundbooks
PO Box 4292, Ringwood, Victoria 3134
Tel: (03) 9015 4440 *Fax:* (03) 8820 4016
Web Site: www.soundbooks.com.au
Key Personnel
Mng Dir: Christopher Raynor
Founded: 1982
Specialize in audiobooks.
Type of Business: Distributor, Exporter, Importer, Major Independent Bookseller

Super Cheap Books Pty Ltd
Formerly Social Club Books Pty Ltd
PO Box 2937, Fitzroy, Victoria 3065
Tel: (03) 9080 7169
E-mail: preschool@scb.com.au; info@scb.com.au
Web Site: www.scb.com.au
Key Personnel
Mng Dir: Ken Finlayson
Founded: 1983
Type of Business: Distributor, Wholesaler

Michael Treloar Antiquarian Booksellers
196 North Terrace, Adelaide, SA 5000
Mailing Address: GPO Box 2289, Adelaide, SA
5001
Tel: (08) 8223 1111 *Fax:* (08) 8223 6599
E-mail: treloars@treloars.com
Web Site: www.treloars.com

Key Personnel
Owner: Michael Treloar
Founded: 1976
Membership(s): Australian & New Zealand Association of Antiquarian Book Dealers (ANZAAB); International League of Antiquarian Booksellers (ILAB).
Type of Business: Major Independent Bookseller

University Co-operative Bookshop Ltd
15 Foster St, Level 1, Surry Hills, NSW 2010
Toll Free Tel: 1300 61 71 81
E-mail: customercare@coop.com.au
Web Site: www.coop.com.au
Founded: 1958
Retailer with over 60 co-op stores located across Australia.
Type of Business: Distributor, Online Bookseller

Windhorse Books
375 King St, Newtown, NSW 2042
Mailing Address: PO Box 574, Newtown, NSW 2042
Tel: (02) 9519 8826 *Fax:* (02) 9519 8827
E-mail: books@windhorse.com.au
Web Site: www.windhorse.com.au
Founded: 1994
Specialize in Buddhism & meditation.
Type of Business: Distributor

Woodslane Pty Ltd
10 Apollo St, Warriewood, NSW 2102
Tel: (02) 8445 2300 *Fax:* (02) 9997 5850
E-mail: info@woodslane.com.au
Web Site: www.woodslane.com.au
Key Personnel
Mng Dir: David Scott
Founded: 1989
Type of Business: Distributor

Austria

Aichinger, Bernhard & Co GesmbH
Weihburggasse 16, 1010 Vienna
Tel: (01) 512 88 53 *Fax:* (01) 512 88 53 13
E-mail: office@abc-wien.at
Web Site: www.abc-wien.at
Founded: 1975
Specialize in literature, fashion, collectibles, interior design, cooking, gardening, Viennensia. Also carry old prints, postcards & items for writing.
Type of Business: Major Independent Bookseller

Robert Breuss Buchimport
Egelseestr 35, 6800 Feldkirch
Tel: (05522) 31247
Type of Business: Importer
Owned by: United Book Group B & Media GbR

Der Buchfreund Universitaets Buchhandlung & Antiquariat Walter R Schaden
Sonnenfelsgasse 4, 1010 Vienna
Tel: (01) 513 82 89; (01) 512 48 56 *Fax:* (01) 512 60 28
E-mail: info@buch-schaden.at
Web Site: www.buch-schaden.at
Key Personnel
Owner: Rainer Schaden
Founded: 1955
Second hand antiquarian books. Scientific books.
Type of Business: Importer, Major Independent Bookseller
Bookshop(s): Sonnenfelsgasse 8, 1010 Vienna, Contact: Marie Lachner *E-mail:* antiquariat@buch-schaden.at

Dr Heinrich Fuchs
Thimiggasse 82, 1180 Vienna
Tel: (01) 479 23 81
Type of Business: Major Independent Bookseller

Buchhandlung Fuerstelberger
Landstr 49, 4013 Linz
Tel: (0732) 77 31 77 *Fax:* (0732) 77 31 77 4
E-mail: buecher@fuerstelberger.at
Web Site: www.fuerstelberger.at
Key Personnel
Mng Dir: Sabine Weissensteiner *E-mail:* s.weissensteiner@fuerstelberger.at
Type of Business: Major Independent Bookseller

Hera A Hartleben GmbH
Othmargasse 25, 1200 Vienna
Tel: (01) 982 35 60 *Fax:* (01) 985 59 98
E-mail: office@hartleben.at; schulbuch@gmx.net
Web Site: www.hartleben.at
Founded: 1803
Type of Business: Distributor, Importer, Major Independent Bookseller

Buchhandlung Johannes Heyn GesmbH & Co KG
Friedensgasse 23, 9020 Klagenfurt
Tel: (0463) 33 631 *Fax:* (0463) 33 631-33
E-mail: office@verlagheyn.at
Web Site: www.verlagheyn.at
Key Personnel
Dir: Achim Zechner
Founded: 1868
Type of Business: Major Independent Bookseller

Hofbauer Buch- und Papierhandlung
Hauptplatz 31, 8430 Leibnitz
Tel: (03452) 82793 *Fax:* (03452) 71218
E-mail: buch@buchhandlunghofbauer.at
Web Site: www.members.aon.at/hofbauer.buch/page_1_1.html
Key Personnel
Co-Owner: Jutta Hofbauer; Ursula Hofbauer
Contact: Thomas Maric
Founded: 1963
Type of Business: Importer, Major Independent Bookseller

Innverlag Lehr- und Lernsystem GmbH
Egger-Lienz-Str 130, 6020 Innsbruck
Tel: (05238) 20 7000 *Fax:* (05238) 20 7000-40
E-mail: info@innverlag.at
Web Site: www.innverlag.at; www.innlibri.at
Key Personnel
Mng Dir: Roland Gatt *E-mail:* r.gatt@innverlag.at
Publishing Dir: Gerti Neuhauser *E-mail:* g.neuhauser@innverlag.at
Founded: 1947
Type of Business: Distributor, Importer, Major Independent Bookseller, Online Bookseller, Wholesaler

Antiquariat Kainbacher
Eichwaldgasse 1, 2500 Baden
Tel: (0699) 110 19 221
E-mail: kontak@antiquariat-kainbacher.at
Web Site: antiquariat-kainbacher.at
Key Personnel
Owner: Paul Kainbacher *E-mail:* paul.kainbacher@kabsi.at
Founded: 2005
Type of Business: Major Independent Bookseller

Alexander Kerbiser GmbH & Co KG
Wiener Str 17, 8680 Muerzzuschlag
Tel: (03852) 2204-0 *Fax:* (03852) 2204-22
E-mail: office@kerbiser.at
Founded: 1936
Type of Business: Major Independent Bookseller

Antiquariat Walter S Kluegel
Burggasse 72/4, 1070 Vienna
Tel: (01) 52 40 647; (0676) 55 70 126 (cell)
  Fax: (01) 52 40 647
E-mail: info@kluegel.at
Web Site: www.kluegel.at
Founded: 1921
Type of Business: Major Independent Bookseller

Antiquariat Liber Antiqua Zentraleuropa
Weinzierl 17, 3500 Krems an der Donau
Tel: (0664) 5263890 (cell); (0664) 5439879 (cell)
E-mail: liberantiqua@gmail.com
Web Site: shops.buchfreund.de
Key Personnel
Owner & Mng Dir: Guenther Ceusters
Mng Dir: Gabriele Ceusters-Ditz
Founded: 2005
Type of Business: Major Independent Bookseller

MANZ'sche Verlags- und Universitaetsbuchhandlung GmbH
Kohlmarkt 16, 1010 Vienna
Tel: (01) 531 61-0; (01) 531 61-100 (customer service) *Fax:* (01) 531 61-181
E-mail: bestellen@manz.at; vertrieb@manz.at; presse@manz.at
Web Site: www.manz.at
Key Personnel
Mng Partner: Susanne Stein-Pressl *Tel:* (01) 531 61-124 *E-mail:* susanne.stein@manz.at
Mng Dir: Peter Guggenberger *Tel:* (01) 531 61-681 *E-mail:* peter.guggenberger@manz.at
Business Development: Dr Wolfgang Pichler *Tel:* (01) 531 61-112 *E-mail:* wolfgang.pichler@manz.at
Public Relations & Media Relations: Dr Christopher Dietz *Tel:* (01) 531 61-364
Founded: 1849
Also publisher & library supplier.
Type of Business: Exporter

Mohr Morawa Buchvertrieb GmbH
Sulzengasse 2, 1230 Vienna
Mailing Address: PO Box 260, 1101 Vienna
Tel: (01) 680 14-0 *Fax:* (01) 688 71 30
E-mail: momo@mohrmorawa.at
Web Site: www.mohrmorawa.at
Key Personnel
Mng Dir: Gerald Schantin *Tel:* (01) 680 14-100 *E-mail:* gerald.schantin@mohrmorawa.at
Sales Manager: Peter Kargl *Tel:* (01) 680 14-127 *E-mail:* peter.kargl@mohrmorawa.at
Founded: 1992 (formed through merger of Mohr-ZG & Morawa)
Type of Business: Wholesaler
Parent Company: Morawa Buch und Medien-Gruppe

Versandbuchhandlung Wolfgang Neugebauer Verlag GesmbH
Duens 134, 6822 Satteins
Tel: (05524) 5199 *Fax:* (05524) 5199
E-mail: wnverlag@aon.at
Key Personnel
Contact: Wolfgang Neugebauer
Founded: 1973
Also library supplier.
Type of Business: Distributor, Exporter, Importer, Major Independent Bookseller

Osterreichische Bibelgesellschaft (Austrian Bible Society)
Bibelzentrum, Breite Gasse 4-8/1, 1070 Vienna
Tel: (01) 523 82 40 *Fax:* (01) 523 82 40-20
E-mail: bibelzentrum@bibelgesellschaft.at
Web Site: www.bibelgesellschaft.at
Key Personnel
Dir: Dr Jutta Henner *E-mail:* henner@bibelgesellschaft.at
Founded: 1970
Type of Business: Major Independent Bookseller

Rupertus Buchhandlung
Dreifaltigkeitsgasse 12, 5020 Salzburg
Tel: (0662) 878733-0 *Fax:* (0662) 871661
E-mail: info@rupertusbuch.at
Web Site: www.rupertusbuch.at; www.tyrolia.at
Key Personnel
Branch Manager: Klaus Seufer-Wasserthal
Tel: (0662) 878733-16 *E-mail:* k.seufer@
rupertusbuch.at
Also library supplier.
Type of Business: Exporter
Parent Company: Verlagsanstalt Tyrolia
Gesellschaft mbH, Exlgasse 20, 6020 Innsbruck

Buecher Stierle GesmbH
Kaigasse 1/Mozartplatz, 5010 Salzburg
Tel: (0662) 840114
E-mail: buch@buecher-stierle.at
Web Site: www.buecher-stierle.at
Key Personnel
Owner: Heinz Stierle
Founded: 1988
Type of Business: Exporter, Importer, Major Independent Bookseller

Leopold Stocker Verlag GmbH
Hofgasse 5, 8011 Graz
Mailing Address: Postfach 438, 8011 Graz
Tel: (0316) 82 16 36 *Fax:* (0316) 83 56 12
E-mail: stocker-verlag@stocker-verlag.com
Web Site: www.stocker-verlag.com
Key Personnel
Marketing & Sales: Franz Koiner *E-mail:* franz.
koiner@stocker-verlag.com
Founded: 1917
Also publisher.
Type of Business: Major Independent Bookseller
Bookshop(s): Buecherquelle Buchhandlungs GmbH, Graz, Contact: Birgit Zitz
E-mail: birgit.zitz@buecherquelle.at

J G Sydy's Buchhandlung Ludwig Schubert GmbH Nachfolge KG
Wienerstr 6, 3100 St Poelten
Tel: (02742) 35 31 89 *Fax:* (02742) 35 31 89-85
E-mail: info@buchhandlung-schubert.at
Web Site: www.buchhandlung-schubert.at
Key Personnel
Owner: Susanne Sandler
Founded: 1837
Membership(s): Hauptverband des Oesterreichischen Buchhandels.
Type of Business: Exporter, Importer, Major Independent Bookseller

Verlagsanstalt Tyrolia Gesellschaft mbH
Exlgasse 20, 6020 Innsbruck
Tel: (0512) 22 33-0 *Fax:* (0512) 22 33-501
E-mail: tyrolia@tyrolia.at
Web Site: www.tyrolia.at
Key Personnel
Mng Dir: Gottfried Kompatscher *Tel:* (0512)
22 33-202 *Fax:* (0512) 22 33-206 *E-mail:* g.
kompatscher@tyrolia.at; Christoph Schiemer
Tel: (0512) 22 33-105 *Fax:* (0512) 22 33-112
E-mail: christoph.schiemer@tyrolia.at
Branch Office(s)
Josef-Wolf-Pl 4, 6700 Bludenz, Branch Manager: Renate Sommer *Tel:* (05552) 62066
Fax: (05552) 62066-20 *E-mail:* bludenz@
tyrolia.at
Kirchplatz 21, 6632 Ehrwald, Branch Manager: Gabriele Somweber *Tel:* (05673) 2414
Fax: (05673) 2414-20 *E-mail:* ehrwald@
tyrolia.at
Dorfzentrum, 6166 Fulpmes, Branch Manager: Susanne Thaler-Prenn *Tel:* (05225) 62326
Fax: (05225) 62326-20 *E-mail:* fulpmes@
tyrolia.at
Rathausstr 1, 6460 Imst, Branch Manager: Martina Walch *Tel:* (05412) 66076 *Fax:* (05412)
66076-20 *E-mail:* imst@tyrolia.at

Kufstein Galerien, Feldgasse 1, 6330 Kufstein, Branch Manager: Maria Luise Widauer
Tel: (05372) 68326 *Fax:* (05372) 68326-20
E-mail: kufstein@tyrolia.at
Malser Str 15, 6500 Landeck, Branch Manager: Ingeborg Strobl *Tel:* (05442) 62541
Fax: (05442) 62541-20 *E-mail:* landeck@
tyrolia.at
Rosengasse 3, 9900 Lienz, Branch Manager: Carola Falkner-Lukasser *Tel:* (04852) 62127
Fax: (04852) 62127-20 *E-mail:* lienz@tyrolia.at
Hauptstr 452, 6290 Mayrhofen, Branch Manager: Susanne Mader *Tel:* (05285) 62432
Fax: (05285) 62432-20 *E-mail:* mayrhofen@
tyrolia.at
Obermarkt 22, 6600 Reutte, Branch Manager: Rebecca Berktold *Tel:* (05672) 64890
Fax: (05672) 64890-20 *E-mail:* reutte@tyrolia.
at
Rupertus Buchhandlung, Dreifaltigkeitsgasse 12, 5020 Salzburg, Branch Manager: Klaus Seufer-Wasserthal *Tel:* (0662) 878733-0 *Fax:* (0662)
871661 *E-mail:* info@rupertusbuch.at
Franz-Josef-Str 24, 6130 Schwaz, Branch Manager: Sonja Kreidl *Tel:* (05242) 63243
Fax: (05242) 63243-20 *E-mail:* schwaz@
tyrolia.at
Speckbacherstr 22, 6380 St Johann, Branch Manager: Reinhard Atzl *Tel:* (05352) 63375
Fax: (05352) 63375-20 *E-mail:* st.johann@
tyrolia.at
Rathausplatz 4, 6150 Steinach, Branch Manager: Roswitha Andres *Tel:* (05272) 6947
Fax: (05272) 6947-20 *E-mail:* steinach@
tyrolia.at
Inntalcenter, Weissenbachgasse 9, 6410 Telfs, Branch Manager: Viktoria Stoeckl *Tel:* (05262)
64390 *Fax:* (05262) 64390-20 *E-mail:* telfs@
tyrolia.at
Stephansplatz 5, 1010 Vienna, Branch Manager: Werner Riedmueller *Tel:* (01) 5124840
Fax: (01) 5124840-20 *E-mail:* wein@tyrolia.at
Kirchplatz 4, 6112 Wattens, Branch Manager: Georg Schiemer *Tel:* (05224) 52363
Fax: (05224) 52363-20 *E-mail:* wattens@
tyrolia.at
Bahnhofstr 42, 6300 Woergl, Branch Manager: Manuela Atzl *Tel:* (05332) 74580 *Fax:* (05332)
74580-20 *E-mail:* woergl@tyrolia.at

Veritas Verlags- und Handelsgesmbh & Co OG
Hafenstr 2a, 4020 Linz
Tel: (0732) 776451-0 *Fax:* (0732) 776451-2239
E-mail: kundenberatung@veritas.at
Web Site: www.veritas.at
Key Personnel
Sales, Marketing & Communications: Vera Linder
Tel: (0732) 776451-2234 *Fax:* (0732) 776451-
88 2234 *E-mail:* v.linder@veritas.at
Type of Business: Distributor
Owned by: Franz Cornelsen Bildungsgruppe

Wagner'schen Universitaetsbuchhandlung
Museumstr 4, 6020 Innsbruck
Tel: (0512) 59505-0 *Fax:* (0512) 59505-38
E-mail: office@wagnersche.at
Web Site: shop.wagnersche.at; www.wagnersche.at
Key Personnel
Mng Dir: Markus Renk
Founded: 1639
Also library supplier.
Type of Business: Exporter
Owned by: Medici Buchhandels GmbH

Kunstverlag Wolfrum
Augustinerstr 10, 1010 Vienna
Tel: (01) 512 53 98-0 *Fax:* (01) 512 53 98-57
E-mail: wolfrum@wolfrum.at
Web Site: www.wolfrum.at
Key Personnel
Mng Dir: Hubert Wolfrum
Founded: 1850

Also publisher of posters, note cards, calendars & library supplier of art books.
Type of Business: Distributor, Exporter, Importer, Major Independent Bookseller

Bangladesh

Mullick & Brothers
160-161, Dhaka New Market, Dhaka 1205
Tel: (02) 8619125; (02) 8625386 *Fax:* (02)
8610562
E-mail: mullick_161@yahoo.com
Also publisher.
Type of Business: Distributor

Barbados

Book Source
Unit C, Lot 2B, Belle Estate, St Michael
Tel: (246) 427-2800 *Fax:* (246) 436-7656
E-mail: customerservice@booksourceonline.com
Web Site: www.booksourceonline.com
Key Personnel
Dir: Beverly Smith-Hinkson
Founded: 1989
Book ordering service; college bookshop; online bookstore.
Type of Business: Importer, Major Independent Bookseller
Owned by: DataLore Inc
Bookshop(s): Campus Book Shop, Barbados Community College Campus, Howells Cross Rd, St Michael *Fax:* (246) 431-0379

Cloister Bookstore Ltd
Hicks St, Bridgetown
Tel: (246) 426-2662
E-mail: cloisterbookstore2015@gmail.com
Web Site: cloisterbookstore.com
Founded: 1958
Type of Business: Distributor, Importer, Major Independent Bookseller, Wholesaler

Belgium

Acco Boekhandel
Maria-Theresiastr 2-4, 3000 Leuven
Tel: (016) 29 11 00 *Fax:* (016) 20 73 89
E-mail: boekhandel@acco.be
Web Site: www.acco.be
Founded: 1960
Type of Business: Distributor, Exporter, Major Book Chain Headquarters, Wholesaler
Bookshop(s): Celestijnentaan 200P, 3000 Leuven *Tel:* (016) 32 78 70 *Fax:* (016) 32 78
71 *E-mail:* heverlee@acco.be; Prinsstr 21,
2000 Antwerp *Tel:* (03) 226 64 02 *Fax:* (03)
226 81 53 *E-mail:* antwerpen@acco.be; Sint-Kwintensberg 87, 9000 Gent *Tel:* (09) 235 73
00 *E-mail:* gent@acco.be; Etienne Sabbelaan
53 (Gebouw A), 8500 Kortrijk *Tel:* (056) 21 52
50 *E-mail:* kortrijk@acco.be

Agora bvba
Ninovesteenweg 24, 9320 Aalst-Erembodegem
Tel: (053) 78 87 00 *Fax:* (053) 78 26 91
E-mail: info@agorabooks.com; admin@
agorabooks.com
Web Site: www.agorabooks.com

Key Personnel
Owner & CEO: Jaki Louage *E-mail:* j.louage@
   agorabooks.com
Marketing Manager: Wouter Claes *E-mail:* w.
   claes@agorabooks.com
Founded: 1985
Type of Business: Distributor, Importer, Major
   Independent Bookseller
Owned by: Borgerhoff & Lamberigts

AMP SA
Subsidiary of Hachette Distribution Services
Rue de Lennik 451, 1070 Brussels
Tel: (02) 529 44 00
E-mail: info@ampnet.be; info.bru@ampnet.be
Web Site: www.ampnet.be
Key Personnel
Chief Executive Officer: Guilaume Beuscart
Commercial Dir: Tom Vermeirsch
Operations Dir: Rolf Vermeulin
Founded: 1885
Type of Business: Distributor, Exporter, Importer,
   Major Book Chain Headquarters, Wholesaler
Ultimate Parent Company: Lagardere Group

Ballon Media Sales
Franklin Rooseveltplaats 12, 2060 Antwerp
Tel: (03) 294-15-00 *Fax:* (03) 294-15-01
E-mail: info@ballonmedia.com
Web Site: www.ballonmedia.com
Key Personnel
Chief Executive Officer: Alexis Dragonetti
Sales Dir: Pascale Mertens *E-mail:* p.mertens@
   ballonmedia.com
Sales Manager: Herve Quillot *E-mail:* h.quillot@
   ballonmedia.com
Founded: 2008
Type of Business: Distributor, Exporter
Parent Company: Ballon Media
Branch Office(s)
Ballon Media France, 15-27 rue Moussorgski,
   75018 Paris, France *Tel:* 01 70 38 56 00
   Fax: 01 70 38 56 02

Boekhandel 't Oneindige Verhaal (The
   Neverending Story Bookshop)
Stationsstr 68, 9100 Sint-Niklaas
Tel: (03) 776 52 25 *Fax:* (03) 776 52 25
E-mail: info@oneindigeverhaal.be
Web Site: www.oneindigeverhaal.be; www.
   facebook.com/oneindigeverhaal
Founded: 1996
Type of Business: Major Independent Bookseller

Bredero
Rozenberg 15, 2400 Mol
Tel: (014) 31 84 61 *Fax:* (014) 31 84 61
Type of Business: Major Independent Bookseller

Caravelle, see SDL Caravelle SA

De Kleine Johannes Kinderboekhandel
Tiensestr 17, 3000 Leuven
Tel: (016) 23 78 45
E-mail: info@de-kleine-johannes.be
Web Site: www.de-klein-johannes.be
Key Personnel
Owner: Luc Vander Velpen
Type of Business: Distributor, Importer, Major
   Independent Bookseller

De Slegte
Wapper 5, 2000 Antwerp
Tel: (09) 225 12 52; (03) 231 66 27
E-mail: info@deslegte.be; antwerpen.wapper@
   deslegte.com
Web Site: www.deslegte.be
Type of Business: Major Book Chain Headquar-
   ters, Online Bookseller

Branch Office(s)
Kattestr 35, 9300 Aalst *Tel:* (053) 80 05 56
   E-mail: aalst@deslegte.com
Voldersstr 7, 9000 Gent *Tel:* (09) 225 59 18
   E-mail: gent@deslegte.com
Havermarkt 14, 3500 Hasselt *Tel:* (011) 22 74 00
   E-mail: hasselt@deslegte.com
Bondgenotenlaan 47, 3000 Leuven *Tel:* (016) 22
   68 81 *E-mail:* leuven@deslegte.com
Korenmarkt 9, 2800 Mechelen *Tel:* (015) 43 61
   77 *E-mail:* mechelen@deslegte.com
Breestr 73, 2311 CJ Leiden, Netherlands
   Tel: (071) 5426428 *E-mail:* leiden@deslegte.
   com

DistriMedia NV
Meulebeeksesteenweg 20, 8700 Tielt
Tel: (051) 42 38 60
E-mail: info@distrimedia.be
Web Site: www.distrimedia.be; www.lannoo.be
Founded: 1994
Type of Business: Distributor
Parent Company: Lannoo Groep

Exhibitions International NV/SA
Kol Begaultlaan 17, 3012 Leuven
Tel: (016) 296900 *Fax:* (016) 296129
E-mail: orders@exhibitionsinternational.be;
   info@exhibitionsinternational.be; accounts@
   exhibitionsinternational.be
Web Site: www.exhibitionsinternational.be
Key Personnel
Dir: Marleen Geukens *Tel:* (016)
   284540 *E-mail:* marleen.geukens@
   exhibitionsinternational.be
Accounts: Kim Janssens *Tel:* (016) 284549
Customer Services: Jill Van der Auwera
   Tel: (016) 284543; Thomas Vos *Tel:* (016)
   284544 *E-mail:* t.vos@exhibitionsinternational.
   be
Founded: 1988
Specialize in national & international distribution
   of illustrated books.
Type of Business: Distributor

Boekhandel Johannes, see De Kleine Johannes
   Kinderboekhandel

**Librairie des Presses Universitaires de
   Bruxelles**
Campus Solbosch, batiment V, ave Paul Heger 42,
   1000 Brussels
Mailing Address: CP 149, 1000 Brussels
Tel: (02) 649 97 80 *Fax:* (02) 647 79 62
E-mail: librairie@pub-ulb.be
Web Site: www.ulb.ac.be/pub
Key Personnel
President: Thomas Gillet
Dir: Patrick Willemarck *E-mail:* patrick.
   willemarck@ulb.ac.be
Founded: 1958
Scientific books & medical books.
Type of Business: Major Independent Bookseller
Owned by: Presses Universitaires de Bruxelles
   asbl (PUB)

Licap
Guimardstr One, 1040 Brussels
Tel: (02) 507 05 05 *Fax:* (02) 507 05 04
E-mail: agenda@licap.be; bestellingen@halex.be
Web Site: licap.be
Key Personnel
Dir: Toon Osaer *Tel:* (03) 210 08 23
   E-mail: toon.osaer@kerknet.be
Order Administration: Genevieve Waterkeyn
   Tel: (02) 507 05 20 *E-mail:* genevieve.
   waterkeyn@licap.be
Founded: 1972
Type of Business: Major Independent Bookseller
Bookshop(s): CDD (Centre Diocesain de Docu-
   mentation), Rue de la Liniere 14, 1060 Brus-

sels, Contact: Therese Catineau *Tel:* (02) 533
   29 40 *Fax:* (02) 533 29 41 *E-mail:* cdd@catho-
   bruxelles.be; Boekhandel De Vlaspit, Vlasfabriekstr 14, 1060 Brussels, Contact: Mia
   Roosen *Tel:* (02) 533 29 39 *Fax:* (02) 533 29
   48 *E-mail:* devlaspit@belgacom.net

De Plukvogel NV
Mechelsesteenweg 9, 1800 Vilvoorde
Tel: (02) 305-62-98
E-mail: plukvogel@telenet.be
Type of Business: Major Independent Bookseller

SDL Caravelle SA
303 Rue du Pre aux Oies, 1130 Brussels
Tel: (02) 240 93 00 *Fax:* (02) 216 35 98
E-mail: info@sdlcaravelle.com
Web Site: www.sdlcaravelle.com
Founded: 1951
Type of Business: Distributor, Wholesaler

Benin

ABM, see Au Bon Marche (ABM)

Au Bon Marche (ABM)
BP 889, Cotonou
Tel: 21 33 05 11 *Fax:* 21 33 05 11
E-mail: abmsarl@yahoo.fr
Key Personnel
Dir: Michel Goussanou
Type of Business: Distributor, Exporter, Importer,
   Wholesaler
Owned by: Maison d'Edition ABM

Bolivia

Los Amigos del Libro Ltda
Calle Espana 0-153 Edif Alba 1, Cochabamba
Tel: (04) 4256005
Key Personnel
Manager: Ingrid Guttentag
Founded: 1945
Type of Business: Distributor, Exporter, Importer,
   Major Book Chain Headquarters, Wholesaler
Branch Office(s)
Torres Sofer, Cochabamba *Tel:* (04) 4504151
Calle Ballivian 145, Santa Cruz de la Sierra
   Tel: (03) 3327937

Editorial Gisbert y Cia SA
Calle Comercio 1270, La Paz
Tel: (02) 220 2626 *Fax:* (02) 220 2911
E-mail: info@libreriagisbert.com
Web Site: libreriagisbert.com
Key Personnel
General Manager: Antonio Schulczewskila
Founded: 1907
Also publisher.
Type of Business: Distributor, Importer, Major
   Book Chain Headquarters, Online Bookseller,
   Wholesaler
Branch Office(s)
Av Ballivian 569, Cochabamba *Tel:* (04) 466
   0777 *E-mail:* cb@libreriagisbert.com
Av 6 de Marzo 335 (lado INFOCAL), El Alto
   Tel: (0232) 282 1111 *Fax:* (0232) 220 2911
   E-mail: ea@libreriagisbert.com
Calle 21 N° 8446 Edif, Santa Fe, Local 2, San
   Miguel *Tel:* (04) 277 4444 *Fax:* (04) 277 4444
   E-mail: sm@libreriagisbert.com
Calle 24 de Septiembre 245, Santa Cruz *Tel:* (03)
   335 1021 *E-mail:* sc@libreriagisbert.com

Libreria Editorial Juventud SRL
Plaza Murillo No 519, lado Joyeria Luxor (Central), La Paz
Tel: (02) 240 6248
Founded: 1948
Type of Business: Importer, Wholesaler

Bosnia and Herzegovina

Sarajevo Publishing
Obala Kulina bana 4, 71000 Sarajevo
Tel: (033) 220 809
Web Site: www.sarajevopublishing.ba
Key Personnel
Dir: Ivana Vukadin *Tel:* (033) 217 189
  E-mail: uprava@sarajevopublishing.ba
Also publisher.
Type of Business: Exporter, Importer
Bookshop(s): Titova do broja 19, 71000 Sarajevo *Tel:* (033) 207 730 *E-mail:* knjizara1@
  sarajevopublishing.ba; ul Hamze Hume
  2, 71000 Sarajevo *Tel:* (033) 665 341
  E-mail: knjizara3@sarajevopublishing.ba; ul
  Zelenih beretki 10, 71000 Sarajevo *Tel:* (033)
  216 561 *E-mail:* knjizara4@sarajevopublishing.
  ba; ul Kulovica 19, 71000 Sarajevo *Tel:* (033)
  206 469 *E-mail:* knjizara2@sarajevopublishing.
  ba

Botswana

Botswana Book Centre
Plot 1178, Main Mall, Gaborone
Mailing Address: PO Box 91, Gaborone
Tel: 395 2931; 319 1444 *Fax:* 397 4315
E-mail: bookcentre@botsnet.bw;
  bbcdistribution@botsnet.bw
Key Personnel
General Manager: Tjiyapo Mokobi-Mokhosoa
  E-mail: tjiyapo@botsnet.bw
Founded: 1826
Also publisher.
Membership(s): BOPIA.
Type of Business: Major Independent Bookseller
Bookshop(s): Barclays Mall, Lobatse *Tel:* 530
  6072 *Fax:* 530 6072; Maun *Tel:* 686 0853
Warehouse: Plot 10228, Broadhurst Industrial,
  Moporoporo Rd, Gaborone *Tel:* 395 2931
  Fax: 397 4315 *E-mail:* bookcentre@botsnet.bw

Brazil

Livraria dos Advogados Editora Ltda (LAEL)
Rua 462, No 857, Bairro Jardim Praia Mar,
  88220-000 Itapema-SC
Tel: (047) 3264 4015; (047) 3361 8322
E-mail: brasil@lael.com.br
Web Site: www.lael.com.br
Founded: 1968
Membership(s): Camara Brasileira do Livro.
Type of Business: Importer
Branch Office(s)
B1308 Art Tech-Center, 63 Haier Rd, Qingdao,
  Shandong, China *Tel:* (0532) 5557 8783

Livraria Alema Buecherstube Brooklin Ltda
Rua Bernardino de Campos, 215, Brooklin
  Paulista, 04620-001 Sao Paulo-SP

Tel: (011) 5543-3829; (011) 5044-3735 (sales)
  Fax: (011) 5041-4315
E-mail: kontakt@livrariaalema.com.br
Web Site: www.livrariaalema.com.br; www.
  lojalivrariaalema.com.br
Key Personnel
Contact: Ursula Hellner
Founded: 1961
Type of Business: Major Independent Bookseller

ASE - Associacao Sinodal de Editoracao, see
  Editora Sinodal

Livraria Brasiliense Editora SA
Rua Emilia Marengo, 216, Tatuape, 03336-000
  Sao Paulo-SP
Tel: (011) 2675-0188
Founded: 1943
Type of Business: Major Independent Bookseller

Cortez Editora
Rua Monte Alegre, 1074, Perdizes, 05014-001
  Sao Paulo-SP
Tel: (011) 3611-9616; (011) 3864-0111
E-mail: mkt@cortezeditora.com.br; sac@
  cortezeditora.com.br
Web Site: www.cortezeditora.com.br
Key Personnel
Proprietor: Jose Xavier Cortez
Founded: 1980
Membership(s): Brazilian Book Association.
Bookshop(s): Livraria Cortez, Rua Bartira, 317,
  Perdizes, 05009-000 Sao Paulo-SP *Tel:* (011)
  3873-7111

Livraria Cultura
Conjunto Nacional, Av Paulista, 2073, Bela Vista,
  01311-940 Sao Paulo-SP
Tel: (011) 3170-4033 *Fax:* (011) 3285-4457
E-mail: ventascorporativas@livrariacultura.com.br
Web Site: www.livrariacultura.com.br
Key Personnel
Chairman: Pedro Herz
Founded: 1969
Type of Business: Importer, Major Book Chain
  Headquarters, Online Bookseller
Bookshop(s): Av Dr Chucri Zaidan, 902-
  Piso 1, Loja 222, 04583-903 Sao Paulo-SP
  Tel: (011) 3474-4033 *Fax:* (011) 3474-4099;
  Av Brigadeiro Faria Lima, 2232-Piso 3, Jardim
  Paulistano, 01489-900 Sao Paulo-SP *Tel:* (011)
  3030-3310 *Fax:* (011) 3030-3319; Av Nacoes
  Unidas, 4777-Piso 2, Loja 245, Jardim Uni-
  versidade, Pinheiros, 05477-000 Sao Paulo-
  SP *Tel:* (011) 3024-3599 *Fax:* (011) 3024-
  3570; Rua Palestra Italia, 500-Piso 3, Loja
  211, 05005-030 Sao Paulo-SP *Tel:* (011) 3868-
  5100 *Fax:* (011) 3868-5122; SHIN CA4,
  Lote A-Piso Superior, Loja 101, Lago Norte,
  71503-504 Brasilia-DF *Tel:* (061) 2109-2700
  Fax: (061) 2109-2701; SGVC-Sul, Lote 22-
  Piso 2, Loja 4-A, Zona Industrial, 71215-100
  Brasilia-DF *Tel:* (061) 3410-4033 *Fax:* (061)
  3410-4099; Av Iguatemi, 777-Piso 1, Lojas
  04 e 05, Vila Brandina, 13092-902 Campinas-
  SP *Tel:* (019) 3751-4033 *Fax:* (019) 3751-
  4030; Rua Brigadeiro Franco, 2300-Piso 3,
  Loja 306, Centro, 80250-903 Curitiba-PR
  Tel: (041) 3941-0292 *Fax:* (041) 3941-0293;
  Av Dom Luis 1010-Piso 1, Loja 8, Aldeota,
  60160-230 Fortazela-CE *Tel:* (085) 4008-0800
  Fax: (085) 4008-0801; Av Tulio de Rose, 80-
  Piso 2, Loja 302, 91340-110 Porto Alegre-
  RS *Tel:* (051) 3028-4033 *Fax:* (051) 3021-
  1777; Av Republica do Libano, 251, Pina,
  51110-160 Recife-PE *Tel:* (081) 3256-7500
  Fax: (081) 3256-7518; R Madre de Deus,
  s/n, 50030-110 Recife-PE *Tel:* (081) 2102-
  4033 *Fax:* (081) 2102-4200; Av Luiz Eduardo
  de Toledo Prado, 900, Vila do Golf, 14027-
  250 Ribeirao Preto-SP *Tel:* (016) 3602-5240
  Fax: (016) 3602-5249; Estrada da Gavea, 899-

Piso 2, Loja 201, Sao Conrado, 22610-001 Rio
  de Janeiro-RJ *Tel:* (021) 3916-2630 *Fax:* (021)
  3916-2630; Rua Senador Dantas, 45, Centro, 20031-202 Rio de Janeiro-RJ *Tel:* (021)
  3916-2600 *Fax:* (021) 3916-2618; Av Tancredo
  Neves 2915-Piso 2, 41820-910 Salvador-BA
  Tel: (071) 3505-9050 *Fax:* (071) 3505-9051

Disal S/A Distribuidores Associados de Livros
Av Marginal Direita do Tiete, 800, 05118-100
  Sao Paulo-SP
Tel: (011) 3226-3111; (011) 3226-3117
  Toll Free Fax: 0800-7707106; 0800-7707105
E-mail: comercialdisal@disal.com.br
Web Site: www.disal.com.br
Key Personnel
President: Francisco S Canato
Founded: 1968
Type of Business: Distributor, Importer, Online
  Bookseller, Wholesaler
Bookshop(s): Av Dr Guilherme Dumont Vil-
  lares, 1463-Loja 1-B, Morumbi, 05640-003
  Sao Paulo-SP *Tel:* (011) 2308-8516 *Fax:* (011)
  2308-7631 *E-mail:* disalmorumbi@disal.com.
  br; Rua Biobedas, 250, 04302-010 Sao Paulo-
  SP *Tel:* (011) 5583-0264 *Fax:* (011) 2578-
  7103 *E-mail:* disalsaude@disal.com.br; Rua
  Deputado Lacerda Franco, 365, Pinheiros,
  05418-000 Sao Paulo-SP *Tel:* (011) 3816-6096;
  (011) 3813 5761 *E-mail:* disalpinheiros@disal.
  com.br; Rua Emilio Malet, 1.196, Tatuape,
  03320-001 Sao Paulo-SP *Tel:* (011) 2093-0233
  Fax: (011) 2092-4062 *E-mail:* disaltatuape@
  disal.com.br; Rua Maria Antonia, 380, Higienopolis, 01222-010 Sao Paulo-SP *Tel:* (011)
  3256-7293; (011) 3256-0264 *Fax:* (011) 3257-
  4127 *E-mail:* disalmantonia@disal.com.br; Ave
  Bias Fortes, 837 Loja 03, Lourdes, 30170-
  011 Belo Horizonte-MG *Tel:* (031) 3275-
  2098; (031) 3291-7310 *Fax:* (031) 3291-6923
  E-mail: disalbelohorizonte@disal.com.br; SEPS
  EQ Quadra 707/907 Loja 09 terreo, Asa Sul,
  70390-078 Brasilia-DF *Tel:* (061) 3244-5791
  Fax: (061) 3443-9552 *E-mail:* disalbrasiliasul@
  disal.com.br; Rua Dr Vieira Bueno, 73-
  Loja 01, Cambui, 13024-040 Campinas-
  SP *Tel:* (019) 2513-4425 *Fax:* (019) 2512-
  3775 *E-mail:* disalcampinas@disal.com.br;
  Rua Braz Cubas, 55, 07115-030 Guarulhos-
  SP *Tel:* (011) 2440-7728 *Fax:* (011) 2408-
  0571 *E-mail:* disalguarulhos@disal.com.br;
  Rua Alvaro Chaves, 270, Floresta, 90220-
  040 Porto Alegre-RS *Tel:* (051) 3311-8000;
  (051) 3311-9800 *Fax:* (051) 3311-8000; (051)
  3311-9800 *E-mail:* disalportoalegre.floresta@
  disal.com.br; Rua Mostardeiro, 333 - Loja
  114, Moinho de Vento, 90430-001 Porto
  Alegre-RS *Tel:* (051) 3346-4285 *Fax:* (051)
  3346-4285 *E-mail:* disalportoalegre@disal.
  com.br; Av Herculano Bandeira, 727, Pina,
  51110-131 Recife-PE *Tel:* (081) 3031-3101
  Fax: (081) 2126-0224 *E-mail:* disalrecife@
  disal.com.br; Rua Floriana Peixoto, 1.250,
  Jd Sumare, 14025-220 Ribeirao Preto-SP
  Tel: (016) 3610-6536 *Fax:* (016) 3931-6691
  E-mail: disalribeirao@disal.com.br; Rua Real
  Grandeza, 80, Botafogo, 22281-034 Rio de
  Janeiro-RJ *Tel:* (021) 3579-9060 *Fax:* (021)
  3579-9063 *E-mail:* disalriodejaneiro@disal.
  com.br; Alameda das Espatodias, 479, Cam-
  inho das Arvores, 41820-460 Salvador-BA
  Tel: (071) 3341-1910; (071) 3341-1971
  Fax: (071) 3341-1971 *E-mail:* disalsalvador@
  disal.com.br; Rua das Esmeraldas, 176-
  Ed Opus, Loja 4, 09090-770 Santo An-
  dre *Tel:* (011) 4903-6006 *Fax:* (011) 4903-
  6009 *E-mail:* disalsantoandre@disal.com.br;
  Rua Rafael Correa Sampaio, 1241, Santa
  Paula, 09541-250 Sao Caetano do Sul-SP
  Tel: (011) 4224-5827 *Fax:* (011) 4224-3678
  E-mail: disalsaocaetano@disal.com.br

Livraria Duas Cidades
Rua Doutor Emilio Ribas, 89, 05006-020 Sao
  Paulo-SP
Tel: (011) 3668-2160
Also publisher.
Type of Business: Major Independent Bookseller

**Ernesto Reichmann Distribuidores de Livros
Ltda**
Rua Coronel Marques, 335, Tatuape, 03440-000
  Sao Paulo-SP
Tel: (011) 2198-2122 *Fax:* (011) 2198-2122
Key Personnel
Mng Partner: Antonio Francisco Da Silva; Renato
  Reichmann
Founded: 1993
Specialize in medical & allied literature includ-
  ing health & fitness, psychology & psychiatry
  titles.
Type of Business: Distributor, Exporter, Importer,
  Wholesaler
Branch Office(s)
Livraria Cientifica Ernesto Reichmann LTDA,
  Rua Pedro de Toledo, 597, V Mariana, 04039-
  031 Sao Paulo-SP *Tel:* (011) 5082 3283
  E-mail: erdl.adsl@uol.com.br
Bookshop(s): Livraria Cientifica Ernesto Reich-
  mann LTDA, Rua Dom Jose de Barros, 168,
  Centro, 01038-000 Sao Paulo-SP

Global Editora e Distribuidora
Rua Pirapitingui, 111-Liberdade, 01508-020 Sao
  Paulo-SP
Tel: (011) 3277-7999 *Fax:* (011) 3277-8141
E-mail: global@globaleditora.com.br
Web Site: globaleditora.com.br
Key Personnel
Dir General: Luiz Alves, Jr
Founded: 1973
Type of Business: Distributor, Exporter, Importer

Livro Ibero-Americano Ltda
Rua Hermenegildo de Barros, 40, 20241-040 Rio
  de Janeiro-RJ
Tel: (021) 4105-4590 *Fax:* (021) 4105-4590
E-mail: livro-ibero@oi.com.br
Founded: 1946
Also publisher.
Type of Business: Distributor, Importer, Whole-
  saler

Livraria Kosmos Editora SA
Rua do Rosario, 155, 20050-092 Rio de Janeiro-
  RJ
Tel: (021) 2221-4582
Founded: 1935
Specialize in technical & academic books.
Type of Business: Distributor, Exporter, Importer,
  Major Book Chain Headquarters

LAEL, see Livraria dos Advogados Editora Ltda
  (LAEL)

Editora Letraviva
Rua Alagoas, 1314, 30130-160 Belo Horizonte-
  MG
Tel: (031) 3223-1509
E-mail: letraviva@letraviva.com.br
Web Site: www.letraviva.com.br
Key Personnel
Dir: Bernardo Gurbanov
Founded: 1979
Type of Business: Distributor, Exporter, Importer

Papirus Editora
R Dr Gabriel Penteado, 253, 13041-305
  Campinas-SP
Tel: (019) 3790 1300
E-mail: editora@papirus.com.br; vendas@papirus.
  com.br (sales); marketing@papirus.com.br
Web Site: www.papirus.com.br

Founded: 1976
Type of Business: Major Independent Bookseller

PTI - Publicacoes Tecnicas Internacionais Ltda
Rua Peixoto Gomide, 209, Cerqueira Cesar,
  01409-901 Sao Paulo-SP
Tel: (011) 3159-2535 *Fax:* (011) 3159-2450
E-mail: info@pti.com.br
Web Site: www.pti.com.br
Key Personnel
Owner: Pierre Grossmann
Founded: 1972
Type of Business: Distributor, Exporter, Importer

Livraria Cientifica Ernesto Reichmann Ltda
Rua Dom Jose De Barros, 158, Centro, 01038-
  000 Sao Paulo-SP
Tel: (011) 3804-1830
E-mail: livrariacientifica@ernesto.com.br
Key Personnel
Manager: Renato Reichmann
Founded: 1936
Specialize in medical & allied literature.
Type of Business: Distributor, Exporter, Importer,
  Major Book Chain Headquarters, Wholesaler

Saraiva SA Livreiros Editores
Rua Henrique Schaumann, 270, Cerqueira Cesar,
  05413-909 Sao Paulo-SP
Tel: (011) 3613-3212 *Toll Free Tel:* 0800-754-
  4000
E-mail: falecomri@saraiva.com.br
Web Site: www.saraiva.com.br; www.saraivari.
  com.br
Key Personnel
Chief Executive Officer & Investor Relations Of-
  ficer: Jorge Saraiva Neto
Chief Financial Officer: Marcus Mingoni
Chief Information Officer: Luis Claudio Correa
  Villani
Vice President, Retail: Marcelo Ubriaco
Founded: 1914
Specializes in auxiliary textbooks, administration,
  economics, legal, primary & secondary school
  books.
Type of Business: Distributor

SBS Livraria Internacional
R Alfredo Pujol 1125, Santana, 02017-011 Sao
  Paulo-SP
Tel: (011) 2238-4477; (011) 2238-4478
  Fax: (011) 2256-7151
E-mail: sbs@sbs.com.br; ventasinternet@sbs.com.
  br
Web Site: www.sbs.com.br
Founded: 1985
More than 50 bookshops throughout Brazil &
  others located in Argentina & Peru.
Type of Business: Distributor

Editora Sinodal
Rua Amadeo Rossi, 467, 93030-220 Sao
  Leopoldo-RS
Tel: (051) 3037-2366 *Fax:* (051) 3037-2366
E-mail: vendas@editorasinodal.com.br; pedidos@
  editorasinodal.com.br
Web Site: www.editorasinodal.com.br
Key Personnel
Mng Dir: Eloy Teckemeier *E-mail:* diretor@
  editorasinodal.com.br
Editorial Dir: Robson Luis Neu *E-mail:* editor@
  editorasinodal.com.br
Sales & Marketing Manager: Eliseu da Cunha
  E-mail: gerenciavendas@editorasinodal.com.br
Founded: 1927
Type of Business: Exporter, Wholesaler

Livraria Triangulo Editora Ltda
Rua Barao de Itapetininga 274, 01042-000 Sao
  Paulo-SP
Tel: (011) 3231-0362

Founded: 1985
Type of Business: Importer

Brunei

Brunei Press Sdn Bhd
Lot 8 & 11, Perindustrian Beribi II, Gadong BE
  1118
Mailing Address: Locked Bag No 2, MPC Be-
  rakas, Bandar Seri Begawan BB 3510
Tel: 2451468; 2451460 *Fax:* 2451460
E-mail: brupress@bruneipress.com.bn;
  marketing@bruneipress.com.bn
Web Site: www.bruneipress.com.bn
Founded: 1953
Printer, Publisher & Distributor.
Type of Business: Distributor
Branch Office(s)
Unit 8B, Supasave Panaga, Lorong 14 Barat,
  Seria KB 4533 *Tel:* 3334344; 3334345
  Fax: 3334346
Brunei Press Sales (M) Sdn Bhd, No 8-1-6, 1st
  floor, Menara Mutiara Bangsar, Jl Liku Off
  Jl Bangsar, 59100 Kuala Lumpur, Malaysia
  Tel: (03) 22876623 *Fax:* (03) 22870093
  E-mail: brupress@tm.net.my
Brunei Press Sales (S) Pte Ltd, Pico Creative
  Centre, 20 Kallang Ave, No 03-00, Singapore
  339411, Singapore *Tel:* 6297 9622 *Fax:* 6297
  9633 *E-mail:* brupress@singnet.com.sg

Bulgaria

Helikon PLC
Troykata Sq 4, 8000 Burgas
Tel: (02) 4604080; (02) 4604081 (online orders)
  Fax: (056) 803139
E-mail: office@helikon.bg
Web Site: www.helikon.bg
Founded: 1992
Type of Business: Distributor, Major Book Chain
  Headquarters

Burundi

Imparudi
3, Ave du 18 septembre, Bujumbura
Tel: 79 92 29 08
Type of Business: Distributor, Exporter, Importer,
  Wholesaler

Cameroon

Librairie Bilingue/The Bilingual Bookshop
Route de Melen, Yaounde
Tel: 677102021
Type of Business: Distributor, Importer, Major
  Independent Bookseller, Wholesaler

Presbook PLC
PO Box 13, Limbe, SW Province
Tel: 233 33 23 88; 677 40 56 42 *Fax:* 233 33 23
  88; 677 40 56 42
E-mail: presbook@yahoo.com
Web Site: www.pccweb.org/institutions/presbook.
  htm

Chile

Key Personnel
General Manager: James T Ako-Egbe
Founded: 1957
Also publisher & printer.
Type of Business: Distributor, Importer
Owned by: Presbyterian Church in Cameroon
Bookshop(s): Bonaberi; Buea; Deido; Ekondo
Titi; Fiango; Kumba Town; Mamfe; Mankon;
Melen; Muyuka; Ndop; Nkwen; Nlongkak;
Nso; Tiko; Wum

Libreria Eduardo Albers Ltda
Patria Vieja 358, 8441462 Santiago
Tel: (02) 29647450
E-mail: info@albers.cl
Key Personnel
Manager: Eduardo Albers *E-mail:* ealbers@albers.
cl
Founded: 1943
Type of Business: Distributor, Exporter, Importer,
Major Independent Bookseller, Wholesaler

Libreria Esoterica Karma
Merced 373, Santiago
Tel: (02) 26326376
E-mail: karmalibros@adsl.tie.cl
Founded: 1985
Type of Business: Distributor, Exporter, Importer,
Major Independent Bookseller, Wholesaler

Libreria Estudio
O'Higgins 465 Loc 38/40, Galeria Italia, Concep-
cion
Tel: (041) 2225533
Web Site: www.libreriaestudio.cl
Founded: 1962
Type of Business: Major Independent Bookseller

Feria Chilena del Libro
Huerfanos 670, Piso 27, 8320174 Santiago
Tel: (02) 2345 8316; (02) 2345 8300; (02) 2345
8317
E-mail: huerfanos@feriachilenadellibro.cl
Web Site: www.feriachilenadellibro.cl
Founded: 1952
Type of Business: Distributor, Importer, Major
Book Chain Headquarters, Online Bookseller,
Wholesaler
Branch Office(s)
Mall Espacio M, Compania N° 1214, Local 109,
Santiago *Tel:* (02) 2345 8340; (02) 2345 8341
E-mail: espaciom@feriachilenadellibro.cl
Mall Plaza el Trebol, Avda Jorge Alessandri
N° 3711 Loc 145-147-149-151, Concep-
cion *Tel:* (041) 256 3807 *E-mail:* eltrebol@
feriachilenadellibro.cl
Mall Florida Center, Av Vicuna Mackenna, N°
6100 Loc 2025, La Florida *Tel:* (02) 2345
8326; (02) 2234 8327 *E-mail:* floridacenter@
feriachilenadellibro.cl
Mall Parque Arauco, Av Presidente Kennedy, N°
5413 Loc 117, Las Condes *Tel:* (02) 2345 8378
E-mail: parque.arauco@feriachilenadellibro.cl
Mall Alt Las Condes, Av Presidente Kennedy,
N° 9001 Loc 2104, Las Condes *Tel:* (02)
2345 8372 *E-mail:* altolascondes@
feriachilenadellibro.cl
Isidora Goyenechea n° 3162, Las Condes
Tel: (02) 2345 8354 *E-mail:* isidora@
feriachilenadellibro.cl
Av Andres Bello N° 2425 Local 4142,
Cuarto Nivel, Providencia *Tel:* (02) 2345
8346; (02) 2345 8347 *E-mail:* costanera@
feriachilenadellibro.cl

Av Providencia N° 2124, Local C-D, Providencia *Tel:* (02) 2345 8344 *E-mail:* drugstore@
feriachilenadellibro.cl
Mall Paseo Costanera, Illapel 10, Loc
217, Puerto Montt *Tel:* (065) 234 1859
E-mail: puertomontt@feriachilenadellibro.cl
Portal El Belloto, Local 1089, Av Ramon Freire
2114, Quilpe *Tel:* (02) 2345 8342; (02) 2345
8343 *E-mail:* elbelloto@feriachilenadellibro.cl
Centro Nuevo Taboada, Camilo Henriquez 466
Loc 7, Valdivia *Tel:* (02) 2345 8330; (02) 2345
8331 *E-mail:* valdivia@feriachilenadellibro.cl
Galeria Pleno Centro, Calle Quinta n° 156,
Loc 14, Vina del Mar *Tel:* (032) 268 3093
E-mail: vina@feriachilenadellibro.cl
Mall Marina Arauco, Loc 108, Av Liber-
tad N° 1348, Vina del Mar *Tel:* (02) 2345
8328; (02) 2345 8329 *E-mail:* marina@
feriachilenadellibro.cl

Fondo de Cultura Economica Chile SA
Av Paseo Bulnes 152, 8330340 Santiago
Tel: (02) 594 4135; (02) 594 4140; (02) 594 4100
E-mail: libreria@fcechile.cl
Web Site: www.fcechile.cl
Key Personnel
General Manager: Julio Sau Aguayo
E-mail: julio.sau@fcechile.cl
Founded: 1934
Type of Business: Distributor, Exporter, Importer,
Online Bookseller
Branch Office(s)
Fondo de Cultura Economica de Argentina SA, El
Salvador 5665, C1414BQE Buenos Aires, Ar-
gentina, Dir General: Alejandro Archain Martin
Tel: (011) 4771 8977 *Fax:* (011) 4777 4788
E-mail: info@fce.com.ar *Web Site:* www.fce.
com.ar
Fondo de Cultura Economica Brasil Ltda,
Rua Bartira 351 Perdizes, 05009-000
Sao Paulo-SP, Brazil, General Manager:
Solange Elster *Tel:* (011) 3672-3397
E-mail: fondodeculturaeconomicabrazil@gmail.
com
Fondo de Cultura Economica de Colombia Ltda,
Calle 11 No 5-60, Bogota, Colombia, General
Manager: Alvaro Velarca Hernandez *Tel:* (01)
2832200 *Fax:* (01) 3374289 *E-mail:* avelarca@
fce.com.co *Web Site:* www.fce.com.co
Fondo de Cultura Economica del Peru SA, Calle
Berlin 38, Miraflores, Lima 18, Peru, Gen-
eral Manager: Gabriela Olivo de Alba Aven-
dano *Tel:* (01) 447-2848 *E-mail:* libreria.
blancavarela@fceperu.com.pe *Web Site:* www.
fceperu.com.pe
Fondo de Cultura Economica de Espana SA,
Calle de Fernando el Catolico, 86, 28015
Madrid, Spain, General Manager: Francisco
Ruiz Barbosa *Tel:* 91 763 2800 *Fax:* 91
763 5153 *E-mail:* libreria.juanrulfo@
fondodeculturaeconomica.es *Web Site:* www.
libreriajuanrulfo.com
Fondo de Cultura Economica de Venezuela SA,
Av Francisco Solano, Las Delicias Sabana
Grande, Caracas, Venezuela, General Manager:
Roberta Muraca de Tucat *Tel:* (0212) 762-6796
E-mail: fceven@gmail.com *Web Site:* www.
fcevenezuela.com.ve
U.S. Office(s): 2293 Verus St, San Diego, CA
92154, United States, General Manager: Do-
rina Maciel Razo Miranda *Tel:* 619-429-0455
Fax: 619-651-9684 *E-mail:* drazo@fceusa.com
Web Site: www.fceusa.com

Libreria del Fondo Gonzalo Rojas, see Fondo
de Cultura Economica Chile SA

H B Books
11 de Septiembre 2155, Torre B, Oficina 1103,
Providencia, Santiago
Tel: (02) 481 1794 *Fax:* (02) 231 7145
E-mail: info@hbbooks.cl

Web Site: hbbooks.cl
Key Personnel
Owner: Herta Berenguer Leon
Founded: 1968
Type of Business: Distributor, Exporter

Libreria Lila
Providencia 1652 Local 3, Santiago
Tel: (02) 236 1725 *Fax:* (02) 236 1725
E-mail: lilalibros@yahoo.com
Key Personnel
Owner: Jimena Pizarro
Type of Business: Major Independent Bookseller

Libreria San Pablo
Avda Libertador Bernardo O'Higgins 1626,
Casilla 3746 Correo Central, Santiago
Tel: (02) 7200300 *Fax:* (02) 6728469
Toll Free Fax: 800 202474
E-mail: alameda@sanpablochile.cl
Web Site: www.sanpablochile.cl
Founded: 1914
Also publisher.
Type of Business: Distributor, Exporter, Importer,
Online Bookseller, Wholesaler
Owned by: Ediciones San Pablo
Branch Office(s)
Avda Providencia 2343, Santiago
Tel: (02) 27200350 *Fax:* (02) 27200350
E-mail: providencia@sanpablochile.cl
Arturo Prat 470, Local 21, La Serena *Tel:* (051)
228006 *Fax:* (051) 228006 *E-mail:* laserena@
sanpablochile.cl
Colo Colo 256, Los Angeles *Tel:* (043) 2315626
Fax: (043) 2315626 *E-mail:* losangeles@
sanpablochile.cl
San Martin 230, Puerto Montt *Tel:* (065)
310154 *Fax:* (065) 310154 *E-mail:* pmontt@
sanpablochile.cl
M Montt 583, Local 3, Temuco *Tel:* (045)
210371 *Fax:* (045) 210371 *E-mail:* temuco@
sanpablochile.cl

Libreria Universitaria
Avda Bernardo O'Higgins 1050, 1° Piso, 1050
Santiago
Tel: (02) 2896 8960
E-mail: comunicaciones@universitaria.cl
Web Site: www.universitaria.cl
Key Personnel
Sales: J Guzman *E-mail:* jguzman@universitaria.
cl
Founded: 1947
Type of Business: Major Independent Bookseller
Owned by: Editorial Universitaria SA

China

**China Foreign Language Publishing &
Distribution Agency**, see China International
Book Trading Corp (CIBTC)

**China International Book Trading Corp
(CIBTC)**
Subsidiary of China International Publishing
Group
35 Chegongzhuang Xilu, Haidian District, Beijing
100048
Tel: (010) 68412045; (010) 68414284 *Fax:* (010)
68412023
E-mail: cibtc@mail.cibtc.com.cn
Web Site: www.cibtc.com.cn
Founded: 1949
Type of Business: Distributor, Exporter, Importer,
Major Independent Bookseller, Wholesaler
Branch Office(s)
Lianfa Mingge, 2F/172 Donghua Nanlu,
Guangzhou 510100 *Tel:* (020) 62728800;

(020) 62728801 *Fax:* (020) 62728800; (020)
62728801 *E-mail:* cibtcgz@21cn.com
Shanghai Cultural Mansion, 9F/355 Fuzhou Rd,
Shanghai 200001 *Tel:* (021) 53510520; (021)
63553214 *E-mail:* cibtcsh@shtel.net.cn
Xincheng Mansion, West, Room 210, 1027 Shen-
nan Zhonglu, Shenzhen 518031 *Tel:* (0755)
25986762; (0755) 25987671 *E-mail:* cibtcsz@
public.szptt.net.cn
Librairie Grande Muraille, 5 Galerie rue
de Ruysbroeck, 1000 Brussels, Belgium
Tel: (02) 512 1456 *Fax:* (02) 513 8337
E-mail: grande_muraille@swing.be
Sebunsuta Manshon Dai 2 Aobadai, Room
306, 1-29-12 Aobadai, Meguro-ku, Tokyo,
Japan *Tel:* (03) 57216536 *Fax:* (03) 57216537
E-mail: aac14940@pop17.odn.ne.jp
Cyress Book Co (UK) Ltd, Unit 13, Park Royal
Metro Centre, Britannia Way, Coronation
Rd, London NW10 7PA, United Kingdom
Tel: (020) 8453 0687 *Fax:* (020) 8453 0709
E-mail: info@cypressbooks.com
U.S. Office(s): Great Wall Books & Arts, 970 N
Broadway, No 104, Los Angeles, CA 90012,
United States *Tel:* 213-617-2817 *Fax:* 213-617-
2827 *E-mail:* info@gwbooks.com

**China National Publications Import & Export
(Group) Corp**
Member of China Publishing Group
16 Gongti East Rd, Beijing 100020
Tel: (010) 65066688
E-mail: cnpeak@cnpiec.com.cn
Web Site: www.cnpiec.com.cn
Key Personnel
President: Tan Yue
Founded: 2002
Type of Business: Distributor, Exporter, Importer,
Wholesaler
Branch Office(s)
No 15 Caiyun St, Xigang District, Dalian 116003
Tel: (0411) 82809181 *Fax:* (0411) 82819320
E-mail: ztdl_1996@126.com *Web Site:* www.
dlbook.com.cn
Xingangxilu dajiang chong 25 hao, Guang-
dong Province 510300 *Tel:* (020) 34202262
Fax: (020) 34201965 *Web Site:* www.cnpiecgb.
com
555 Guang Zhong Rd, Shanghai 200083
Tel: (021) 36357588 *Fax:* (021) 36357999
85 Bei Da Jie, Xi'an 710003, Chief Manager:
Zhang Xu *Tel:* (029) 87279743 *Fax:* (029)
87279755 *Web Site:* www.cnpiecxa.com
301 Castereagh St, Suite 23, Sydney, NSW 2000,
Australia *Tel:* (02) 9280 4068 *Fax:* (02) 9280
4018 *E-mail:* xhliu138@hotmail.com
Siemensstr 4, Postfach 1131, Egelsbach,
63329 Frankfurt am Main, Germany
Tel: (049) 6103-44812 *Fax:* (049) 6103-49378
E-mail: cnpiec_de@hotmail.com
6-24, Higashi-machi, Shinjuku-ku, Tokyo, Japan
Tel: (03) 3266-9482 *Fax:* (03) 3267-0201
E-mail: zhang@cptohan.co.jp
China Wan Da Trading Co (Moscow), ZAO PTK
Venera, St M Kalitnikovskaya, Room 106-9a,
109029 Moscow, Russia *Tel:* (495) 6700760
Fax: (495) 6700760 *E-mail:* kiepmos@rmt.ru
Unit 4, 55/57 Park Royal Rd, London NW10
7LR, United Kingdom *Tel:* (0208) 961-9283
Fax: (0208) 961-9282 *E-mail:* books@cnpiec.
co.uk
U.S. Office(s): Beijing Book Co Inc (USA), 701
E Linden Ave, Linden, NJ 07036-2495, United
States *Tel:* 908-862-0909 *Fax:* 908-862-4201
E-mail: beijingbook@cnpbbci.com

CNPIEC IT Co Ltd, see China National
Publications Import & Export (Group) Corp

Metto International Ltd
Room 203, Fuxing Bldg, Fuxing Rd, Futian,
Shenzhen 518033

Tel: (0755) 88296620; (0755) 88296612; (0755)
88355199 *Fax:* (0755) 88355199
E-mail: metto@metto.cn
Web Site: www.metto.cn
Founded: 1996
Specialize in professional publications in the
fields of achitecture & design.
Type of Business: Distributor, Exporter, Importer

Shanghai Book Traders
No 390 Fuzhou Rd, 1-2 floor, Shanghai
Tel: (021) 23204994; (021) 23204995 *Fax:* (021)
23204991; (021) 23204992; (021) 63516884
E-mail: sbt@sbt.cn
Web Site: www.sbt.com.cn
Founded: 1985
Type of Business: Major Book Chain Headquar-
ters

Xiamen International Book Co (XIBC)
No 809, South Hubin Rd, Xiamen, Fujian 361004
Tel: (0592) 8060988; (0592) 8060900 *Fax:* (0592)
8060989
E-mail: wtxmsc@xmwaitu.com
Web Site: www.xibc.com.cn
Type of Business: Distributor, Exporter, Importer,
Major Independent Bookseller, Wholesaler

XIBC, see Xiamen International Book Co
(XIBC)

Colombia

Libreria Aguirre SL
Calle Salvador de Madariaga, 1, Local 8, 27002
Lugo
Tel: 982220336 *Fax:* 982220336
E-mail: libreriaaguirre@gmail.com
Type of Business: Importer, Major Independent
Bookseller

Eurolibros Ltda, see Europea de Libros Ltda

Europea de Libros Ltda
Calle 40 No 20-27, Bogota
Tel: (01) 2886400
Key Personnel
General Dir: Carlos Roberto Jimenez
Founded: 1983
Type of Business: Distributor, Wholesaler

Editorial y Libreria Herder Ltda
Carrera 11 No 73-61, Bogota
Tel: (01) 3146935
Founded: 1925
Type of Business: Distributor, Exporter, Importer

Lemoine Editores
Carrera 23 N° 137-83, Bogota
Tel: (01) 633 24 99; (01) 633 24 31
E-mail: info@lemoineeditores.com; ventas.
librerias@lemoineeditores.com
Web Site: www.librosyeditores.com
Key Personnel
Editorial Dir & Manager: Jimena Gar-
zon Lemoine *E-mail:* jimena.lemoine@
lemoineeditores.com
National Sales Manager: Ariel Quiceno Valencia
Commercial Assistant: Magda Leonor Garcia
E-mail: magda.garcia@lemoineeditores.com
International Business Assistant: Herman David
Velasco Cardona *E-mail:* david.velasco@
lemoineeditores.com
Type of Business: Online Bookseller

Libreria Lerner
Avda Jimenez No 4-35, Bogota DC
Tel: (01) 3347826; (01) 2430567 *Fax:* (01)
3187740
E-mail: lerner-centro@librerialerner.com.co
Web Site: www.librerialerner.com.co
Founded: 1958
Type of Business: Importer, Major Independent
Bookseller
Branch Office(s)
Carrera 11, No 93A-43, Bogota *Tel:* (01)
6364284; (01) 6918832; (01) 6364261; (01)
6364295 *E-mail:* lerner-norte@librerialerner.
com.co

Libreria Nacional Ltda
Carrera 15 No 123-30, Centro Comercial Unicen-
tro Local 1-146, Bogota
Tel: (031) 2139882
E-mail: servicioalcliente@librerianacional.com
Web Site: www.librerianacional.com
Founded: 1941
Type of Business: Distributor, Major Book Chain
Headquarters, Online Bookseller

Panamericana Libreria y Papeleria SA
(Panamericana Bookshop & Stationery Shop)
Calle 12, No 34-30, Bogota
Tel: (01) 3649000
E-mail: tiendavirtual@panamericana.com.co
Web Site: www.panamericana.com.co
Key Personnel
Owner: Carlos Federico Ruiz
General Manager: Fernando Rojas Acosta
E-mail: frojas@panamericana.com.co
Founded: 1964
Type of Business: Exporter, Importer, Major
Book Chain Headquarters
Bookshop(s): Autopista Norte No 168-30, Bo-
gota *Tel:* (01) 6700161 *Fax:* (01) 6713354;
Centro Comercial Bulevar Niza, Local 279-
280, Carrera 57 No 125 A-35, Bogota *Tel:* (01)
2266366 *Fax:* (01) 2265466; Centro Comercial
Centro Mayor, Local 1-96, Carrera 38A No 34
D-50 Sur, Bogota *Tel:* (01) 7340000 *Fax:* (01)
7342999; Centro Comercia Hayuelos, Lo-
cal 101, Calle 20 No 82-52, Bogota *Tel:* (01)
3546000 *Fax:* (01) 3546007; Centro Comercial
Metopolis, Local 171-172, Av Carrera 68 No
75 A-50, Bogota *Tel:* (01) 3118088 *Fax:* (01)
2259464; Centro Comercial Plaza de las Americas, Local 2522, Carrera 71 D No 6-94 Sur,
Bogota *Tel:* (01) 4176133 *Fax:* (01) 4137592;
Centro Comercial Titan Plaza, Local 220, Car-
rera 72 No 80-94, Bogota *Tel:* (01) 7365005
Fax: (01) 7365007; Centro Comercial Buenavista 2, Local 333, Calle 99 No 52-53, Barran-
quilla *Tel:* (05) 3739977 *Fax:* (05) 3739915;
Carrera 27 No 45-05 Esquina, Bucaramanga
Tel: (07) 6979697 *Fax:* (07) 6986960; Centro
Comercial Unicentro, Local 701, Carrera 100
No 5-169, Cali *Tel:* (02) 4851100 *Fax:* (02)
4855100; Centro Comercial Caribe Plaza, Lo-
cal 226, Calle 29 D No 22-108, Cartagena
Tel: (05) 6720706 *Fax:* (05) 6720729; Centro
Comercial Ventura Plaza, Local 247, Calle 11
No 0E-94, Cucuta *Tel:* (07) 5755780 *Fax:* (07)
5755780; Carrera 5 No 60-73, Ibague *Tel:* (08)
2665155 *Fax:* (08) 2661299; Centro Comer-
cial Fundadores, Local 230, Calle 33 No 20-
03, Manizales *Tel:* (06) 8840200 *Fax:* (06)
8848080; Carrera 43 A No 6-150 S, Medellin
Tel: (04) 4480999 *Fax:* (04) 4936454; Centro
Comercial Buenavista, Local 180, Carrera 6
No 68-72, Monteria *Tel:* (04) 7894240; Centro Comercial San Pedro Plaza, Local 120-
124, Carrera 8 A No 38-42, Neiva *Tel:* (08)
8662233 *Fax:* (08) 8662266; Centro Comercial
Pereira Plaza, Local 1584, Calle 15 No 13-110,
Pereira *Tel:* (06) 3258100 *Fax:* (06) 3252501;
Centro Comercial Guatapuri, Local 254, Diagonal 10 No 6N-15, Valledupar *Tel:* (05) 5856060

Fax: (05) 5854036; Centro Comercial Villavicencio, Local 154, Calle 7 No 45-185, Villavicencio *Tel:* (08) 6684888 *Fax:* (08) 6679935

Ediciones Paulinas (Libreria San Pablo)
Calle 161A, No 15-50, Bogota
Tel: 315-3457465 (cell)
E-mail: marketing@libreriapaulinas.com
Web Site: libreriapaulinas.com
Founded: 1915
Type of Business: Distributor, Exporter, Importer,
  Major Book Chain Headquarters, Wholesaler
Bookshop(s): Carrera 9, No 12b-27/33, Bogota
  Fax: (01) 243 2782; (01) 243 5885; (01) 243
  5887 *E-mail:* centro@paulinas.org.co; Carrera
  5A, No 27-36 sur, Bogota *Tel:* (01) 361 6153;
  (01) 278 8152 *E-mail:* libreria20dejulio@
  paulinas.org.co; Calle 63A, No 10-44, Local 101, Edificio la Isla, Bogota *Tel:* (01)
  255 4632; (01) 310 0342 *Fax:* (01) 310
  0362; (01) 345 2430 *E-mail:* libreriacha@
  paulinas.org.co; Carrera 54, No 70-121, Barranquilla *Tel:* (05) 360 0200 *Fax:* (05) 356
  8943 *E-mail:* barranquillaprado@paulinas.
  org.co; Calle 34, No 42-28, Barranquilla
  Tel: (05) 351 8973; (05) 351 8971 *Fax:* (05)
  340 4792 *E-mail:* barranquilla34@paulinas.
  org.co; Calle 10, No 7-53, Cali *Tel:* (02)
  896 0929; (02) 884 2615 *Fax:* (02) 889
  1035 *E-mail:* paulinascali@paulinas.org.co;
  Calle 17, No 10-45, Centro Comerdial Santa
  Maria Local 10, Chiquinquira *Fax:* (08)
  726 1102 *E-mail:* libreriachiquinquira@
  paulinas.co; Av 5a, No 12-65, Cucuta
  Tel: (07) 571 7789 *Fax:* (07) 572 3389
  E-mail: paulinascucuta@paulinas.org.co; Carrera 23, No 25-31, Manizales *Tel:* (069) 882
  2540; (069) 505 5214 *Fax:* (069) 324 2936
  E-mail: paulinasmanizales@paulinas.org.co;
  Calle 56, No 49-51, Medellin *Tel:* (04) 511
  2046 *Fax:* (04) 293 0258 *E-mail:* paulimed@
  paulinas.org.co; Carrera 43A, No 11-71,
  Edificio El Pablo, Medellin *Fax:* (04) 311
  3291 *E-mail:* paulinaspoblado@paulinas.
  org.co; Calle 18A, No 25-31, Pasaje Cora-
  zon de Jesus, Pasto *Tel:* (02) 729 2846
  Fax: (02) 729 2848 *E-mail:* paulinaspasto@
  paulinas.org.co; Calle 21, No 7-29, Pereira
  Tel: (061) 324 2037 *Fax:* (061) 324 2037
  E-mail: paulinaspereira@paulinas.org.co;
  Alfredo Baquerizo Moreno 818-820, Entre
  Luis Urdaneta y Junin, Guayaquil, Ecuador
  Tel: (04) 256 0365 *Fax:* (04) 256 0768
  E-mail: paulinasguayaquil@paulinas.org.co;
  Selva Alegre OE1-95 y 10 de Agosto, Quito,
  Ecuador *Tel:* (02) 250 1656; (02) 254 2685
  Fax: (02) 255 6373 *E-mail:* paulinasquito@
  paulinas.org.co

Libreria Temis SA
Calle 17, No 68D-46, Bogota
Tel: (01) 4247855
E-mail: soporte@editorialtemis.com
Web Site: www.editorialtemis.com
Founded: 1951
Type of Business: Distributor, Exporter, Importer,
  Wholesaler
Parent Company: Editorial Temis SA
Bookshop(s): Av Pepe Sierra No 18B-69,
  Bogota *Tel:* (01) 6126052; (01) 6208074
  E-mail: lpepesierra@editorialtemis.com;
  Calle 12b No 6-45, Bogota *Tel:* (01) 3413225
  E-mail: lcalle13@libreriatemis.com; Calle 52
  No 42-68, Medellin *Tel:* (04) 2393747; (04)
  2399365

Libreria Universidad de los Andes
Carrera 1a No 19-27, Edificio Aulas Primer Piso,
  Bogota
Tel: (01) 33394949 (ext 2181) *Fax:* (01)
  33394949 (ext 3177)
E-mail: libreria@uniandes.edu.co

Web Site: libreria.uniandes.edu.co
Spanish & Latin American trade books; importers
  & subscription agents of academic & scientific
  publications.
Type of Business: Importer

Democratic Republic of the Congo

Librairie Paulines
c/o Filles de Saint-Paul, 76 Ave du Commerce,
  Kinshasa
Mailing Address: BP 8505, Kinshasa
Tel: (099) 8403097 (cell)
E-mail: libpaulines@paulinestamtam.org
Web Site: www.paoline.org
Founded: 1958
Type of Business: Distributor, Exporter, Importer,
  Major Independent Bookseller, Wholesaler
Owned by: Filles de Saint Paul
Branch Office(s)
Av 30 Juin 238, BP 505, Kisangani *Tel:* (099)
  8505604 *E-mail:* librairiepaulineskis@gmail.
  com
Av Lomami, 48, BP 2447, Lubumbashi *Tel:* (099)
  7238700 *E-mail:* librairiesaintpaul@gmail.com

Librairie Saint-Paul, see Librairie Paulines

Costa Rica

Carlos Federspiel & Co SA, see Libreria
  Universal-Carlos Federspiel & Co SA

Libreria Lehmann SA
Av Central, Calles 1 y 3, 10011 San Jose
Tel: 2522-4848
E-mail: sac@librerialehmann.com; servicio@
  librerialehmann.com
Web Site: www.librerialehmann.com
Founded: 1896
Also publisher.
Type of Business: Major Independent Bookseller

Libreria Universal-Carlos Federspiel & Co SA
Ave Central, Entre Calles 0 y 1, San Jose
Tel: 2222-2222; 2243-0255
E-mail: servicioalcliente@universalcr.com
Web Site: www.universalcr.com
Type of Business: Major Book Chain Headquar-
ters

Croatia

Algoritam doo
Harambasiceva 19, 10000 Zagreb
Tel: (01) 2359-333 *Fax:* (01) 2335-956
E-mail: info@algoritam.hr
Web Site: www.algoritam.hr
Distributor of foreign books, local books & text-
  books for foreign language learning. Also dis-
  tributes video games & other computer soft-
  ware for home use.
Bookshop(s): Gajeva 1, 10000 Zagreb *Tel:* (01)
  4881-555; (01) 4881-556 (orders) *Fax:* (01)

4817-497 *E-mail:* bookshop.gajeva@
algoritam.hr; Trgovacki centar King Cross
Jankomir, Velimira Skorpika 34, 10090 Zagreb *Tel:* (01) 2359-392 *Fax:* (01) 2359-392
E-mail: blagajna.kingcross@algoritam.hr; Maksimirska 77, 10000 Zagreb *Tel:* (01) 2359-388
E-mail: blagajna.maksimirska@algoritam.
hr; Trgovacki centar Avenue Mall Zagreb,
Ave Dubrovnik 16, 10000 Zagreb *Tel:* (01)
2359-359; (01) 2359-375 *E-mail:* avenue.
mall@algoritam.hr; Placa 8, 20000 Dubrovnik
Tel: (020) 322-044 *Fax:* (020) 322-043
E-mail: blagajna.dubrovnik@algoritam.hr; Trgovacki centar Avenue Mall, Ul Sv Leopolda
Mandica 50a, 31000 Osijek *Tel:* (031) 399-
526 *Fax:* (031) 399-527 *E-mail:* osijek.
avenuemall@algoritam.hr; Trg slobode 7,
31000 Osijek *Tel:* (031) 214-310 *Fax:* (031)
214-311 *E-mail:* blagajna.osijek@algoritam.hr;
Prolaz kod kazalista 1, 52000 Pula *Tel:* (052)
393-987 *Fax:* (052) 393-987 *E-mail:* blagajna.
pula@algoritam.hr; Trgovacki centar City Life,
Ante Supuka 10, 22000 Sibenik *Tel:* (022) 492-
245 *E-mail:* blagajna.sibenik@algoritam.hr;
Bajamontijeva 2, 21000 Split *Tel:* (021) 348-
030 *Fax:* (021) 321-900 *E-mail:* blagajna.
split@algoritam.hr; Trgovacki centar Roses
Fashion Outlet, Vrankovec 1, 49223 Sv Kriz
Zacretje *Tel:* (049) 228-791 *Fax:* (049) 228-
794 *E-mail:* blagajna.zacretje@algoritam.hr;
Trgovacki centar Lumini, Ul grada Lipika
15, Donji Kneginec, 42204 Turcin *Tel:* (042)
488-075 *E-mail:* blagajna.lumini@algoritam.
hr; Ivana Kukuljevica 7, 42000 Varazdin
Tel: (042) 302-422 *E-mail:* blagajna.varazdin@
algoritam.hr; Trgovacki centar City Galleria,
Murvicka 1, 23000 Zadar *Tel:* (023) 493-050
E-mail: blagajna.zadar@algoritam.hr
Warehouse: Ul Kralja Tomislava 7, 10410 Gradici
  Tel: (01) 2440-800 *Fax:* (01) 2359-381

Sveucilisna Knjizara i Antikvarijat Dominovic
Hrvatske Bratske Zajednice 4, 10001 Zagreb
Tel: (01) 6150 315 *Fax:* (01) 6130 111
E-mail: knjizara@dominovic.hr
Web Site: www.dominovic.hr
Type of Business: Major Independent Bookseller,
  Online Bookseller

Golden Marketing/Tehnicka Knjiga
Jurisiceva 10, 10000 Zagreb
Tel: (01) 4810 820 *Fax:* (01) 4810 821
E-mail: gmtk@gmtk.net
Web Site: www.gmtk.net
Key Personnel
Dir: Ana Resetar
Founded: 1992

Cuba

Ediciones Cubanas
Division of ARTEX SA
Obispo No 526 e/Bernaza y Villegas, Habana
  Vieja, CP 10300 Havana
Tel: (07) 861-3283
E-mail: libro@edicuba.artex.cu
Web Site: www.edicionescubanas.net
Key Personnel
General Manager: Niurka Eligio de la Puente
  E-mail: niurka@edicuba.artex.cu
Economics Manager: Lissette Campos
  E-mail: lissette@edicuba.artex.cu
Human Resources Manager: Ivonne Pedraza Leon
  E-mail: ivonne@edicuba.artex.cu
Image & Development Manager: Maria Elena
  Perez *E-mail:* maricusa@edicuba.artex.cu
International Commercial Sales Manager: Mar-
  garita Gomez Mozo *E-mail:* margaritaec@
  edicuba.artex.cu

National Commercial Sales Manager: Regla Esquerre Alfonso
Books, periodicals & printing material.
Type of Business: Distributor, Exporter, Importer, Major Book Chain Headquarters, Wholesaler
Bookshop(s): Aeropuerto Internacional Jose Marti, Boyeros, Havana Tel: (07) 649-7001; Calle L No 202 esquina a 27, Vedado, Havana Tel: (07) 832-9653; Palacio del Segundo Cabo, O'Reilly No 4 esquina a Tacon, Havana Tel: (07) 863-2244; Prado esquina Teniente Rey, Habana Vieja, Havana Tel: (07) 861-5849; Neptuno e/Aguila y Amistad, Central Havana Tel: (07) 860-6166; San Rafael e/Aguila y Galiano, Central Havana Tel: (07) 863-7884; Aeropuerto Varadero, Aeropuerto Internacional Juan Gualberto Gomez, Varadero Tel: (05) 28-4700; Hanoi, Calle 44 y 1ra Ave, Varadero Tel: (05) 61-2694; Centro Cultural Plaza America, Centro de Convenciones Plaza America, Varadero Tel: (05) 66-7452; Mar del Sur, 3ra Ave y calle 32, Varadero Tel: (05) 61-2865

Cyprus

The House of Cyprus & Cyprological Publications, see MAM (The House of Cyprus & Cyprological Publications)

K P Kyriakou (Books - Stationery) Ltd
Panayides Bldg, 3 Grivas Dighenis Av, 3035 Limassol
Tel: 25747555 Fax: 25747047
E-mail: kpk.info@books.com.cy
Web Site: www.facebook.com/KPKyriakou
Key Personnel
Financial Dir: Kyriakos P Kyriakou
   E-mail: kyriakospkyriakou@books.com.cy
Founded: 1978
Type of Business: Distributor, Exporter, Importer, Major Independent Bookseller, Wholesaler

MAM (The House of Cyprus & Cyprological Publications)
19 Konstantinou Palaiologou Ave, 1015 Nicosia
Mailing Address: PO Box 21722, 1512 Nicosia
Tel: 22753536 Fax: 22375802
E-mail: mam@mam.com.cy
Web Site: www.mam.com.cy
Key Personnel
Manager: Alexandros Michaelidou; Fryni Michaelidou
Founded: 1965
Specialize in all kinds of publications on Cyprus & in all publications by Cypriots. Authorized distributors of Cyprus Government publications & other Cypriot publications.
Also publisher.
Type of Business: Distributor, Exporter, Importer, Major Independent Bookseller, Wholesaler

Czech Republic

Knihkupectvi L & N - Antikvariat Galerie
Masarykova 15, 415 01 Teplice
Tel: 417 537 370
E-mail: kniha.ln@email.cz
Web Site: www.antikteplice.cz
Specialize in German & Czech books.
Type of Business: Major Independent Bookseller
Branch Office(s)
Kapelni 4, Teplice Tel: 417 538 849

Nakladatelstvi Librex
Raisova 1066/6, 709 00 Ostrava-Marianske Hory
Tel: 735 491 701
E-mail: librex.cz@gmail.com; prace.librex@gmail.com
Web Site: www.librex.eu
Key Personnel
Mng Dir: Dana Becherova Tel: 724 091 885
   E-mail: becherova.dana@gmail.com
Sales: Lenka Tvrzova E-mail: tvrzova.librex@gmail.com
Founded: 1990
Type of Business: Distributor, Exporter, Major Book Chain Headquarters

SUWECO CZ spol sro
Sestupna 153/11, 162 00 Prague 6
Tel: 242 459 204 Fax: 284 821 646
E-mail: suweco@suweco.cz; obchod@suweco.cz
Web Site: www.suweco.cz
Key Personnel
Dir: Nina Suskevicova E-mail: nina.suskevic@suweco.cz
Assistant to Dir: Jan Ferfecky Tel: 242 459 202
   E-mail: ferfecky@suweco.cz
Founded: 1993
Type of Business: Distributor, Importer

Denmark

Academic Boghandel Fond, see Academic Books

Academic Books
Solbjerg Plads 3, 2000 Fredericksberg C
Tel: 4422 3800; 4422 3890 (administration)
E-mail: academicbooks@academicbooks.dk
Web Site: academicbooks.dk
Key Personnel
Dir: Kenneth Golubov
Founded: 1967
Type of Business: Exporter, Importer, Major Independent Bookseller
Owned by: SL Fonden
Bookshop(s): Academic Books at CBS, Frederiksberg C, Sales Manager: Annette Bank Tel: 4422 3870 E-mail: cbs@academicbooks.dk; Thorvaldsensvej 40, 1871 Frederiksberg C, Sales Manager: Gry Elsborg Hayhurst Tel: 4422 3840 E-mail: ku-frb@academicbooks.dk; Oster Farimagsgade 5 A, 1353 Copenhagen K, Sales Manager: Gry Elsborg Hayhurst Tel: 4422 3835 E-mail: ku-city@academicbooks.dk; Norre Alle 20, 2200 Copenhagen N, Sales Manager: Gry Elsborg Hayhurst Tel: 4422 3845 E-mail: ku-noerre@academicbooks.dk; Karen Blixens Plads 8, 2300 Copenhagen S, Sales Manager: Morten Kjersgaard Nielsen Tel: 4422 3860 E-mail: ku-soendre@academicbooks.dk; Humletorvet 10, 1799 Copenhagen V, Sales Manager: Ronni Jorgensen Tel: 4422 3855 E-mail: ucc@academicbooks.dk; RUC, bygn 26,Universitetsvej 1 (Indgang igennem bibliotek), 4000 Roskilde, Sales Manager: Ronni Jorgensen Tel: 4422 3830 E-mail: ruc@academicbooks.dk

Bierman & Bierman ApS
Norre Torv 1, 1 sal, 7200 Grindsted
Tel: 75 32 02 88 Fax: 75 32 15 48
E-mail: mail@bierman.dk
Web Site: www.biermanaps.dk
Key Personnel
Mng Dir: Bo Lorentzen
Founded: 1968
Supplier of foreign & Danish materials to Danish libraries, educational institutions & companies.
Type of Business: Distributor, Importer

Arnold Busck A/S
Pilestr 52, 1 sal, 1112 Copenhagen K
Tel: 45 28 05 70
E-mail: info@busck.dk; web@busck.dk
Web Site: www.arnoldbusck.dk
Key Personnel
Chief Executive Officer: Helle Busck Fensvig
   E-mail: hbf@arnoldbusck.dk
Founded: 1896
Type of Business: Exporter, Major Independent Bookseller
Owned by: Ole Arnold Busck
Bookshop(s): Kobmagergade 49, 1150 Copenhagen K Tel: 33 73 35 00 Fax: 33 73 35 35 E-mail: kobmagergade@busck.dk; Kobmagergade 50, 1150 Copenhagen K Tel: 33 15 44 66 E-mail: boernenes@busck.dk; Guldbergsgade 29 D, 2200 Copenhagen N Tel: 60 37 05 00 E-mail: lab@arnoldbusck.dk; Bispensgade 10, 9000 Aalborg Tel: 98 13 21 44 E-mail: aalborgcity@busck.dk; Aalborg Storcenter 108, 9200 Aalborg SV Tel: 98 79 15 45 E-mail: aalborgstorcenter@busck.dk; Ryesgade 3, 8000 Aarhus C Tel: 60 37 04 90 E-mail: aarhus@busck.dk; Ballerupcentret, 2750 Ballerup Tel: 44 97 90 09 Fax: 44 68 23 27 E-mail: ballerup@busck.dk; Hovedgaden 37, 3460 Birkerod Tel: 45 81 01 65 E-mail: birkerod@busck.dk; Kongensgade 21, 6700 Esbjerg Tel: 75 12 11 77 Fax: 75 12 70 71 E-mail: esbjerg@busck.dk; Vester Torv 15, Espergaerde Centeret, 3060 Espergaerde Tel: 49 13 19 46 E-mail: espergaerde@busck.dk; Apotekergade 13, 6100 Haderslev Tel: 74 52 27 03 Fax: 74 53 05 82 E-mail: haderslev@busck.dk; Strandvejen 96, 2900 Hellerup Tel: 39 40 66 48 Fax: 39 40 66 49 E-mail: hellerupcity@busck.dk; Ostergade 17-19, 3200 Helsinge Tel: 48 79 40 01 E-mail: helsinge@busck.dk; Stengade 23, 3000 Helsingor Tel: 49 21 01 28 Fax: 49 21 01 11 E-mail: helsingorcity@busck.dk; Bredgade 35, 7400 Herning Tel: 97 12 07 47 E-mail: herning@busck.dk; Metropol, Ostergade 30, 22, 9800 Hjorring Tel: 98 92 80 40 E-mail: hjorring@busck.dk; Norregade 48, 7500 Holstebro Tel: 97 42 34 33 E-mail: holstebro@busck.dk; Norregade 5, 4600 Koge Tel: 56 65 02 54 Fax: 56 63 60 05 E-mail: koge@busck.dk; Kolding Storcenter 1.11, 6000 Kolding Tel: 75 50 38 34 E-mail: kolding@busck.dk; Lyngby Storcenter 54, 2800 Lyngby Tel: 45 87 04 45 Fax: 45 87 31 12 E-mail: lyngby@busck.dk; Jernbanegade 2, 4800 Nykobing F Tel: 54 85 02 55 Fax: 54 82 02 43 E-mail: nykobingfalster@busck.dk; Rosengardcentret 53, 5220 Odense Tel: 66 15 99 28 Fax: 66 15 99 44 E-mail: odensero@busck.dk; Vestergade 59-61, 5000 Odense C Tel: 66 11 40 33 E-mail: odense61@busck.dk; Raadhusstraede 2, 8900 Randers Tel: 86 42 01 13 Fax: 86 40 91 13 E-mail: randers@busck.dk; Rodovre Centrum 1C, st 116, 2610 Rodovre Tel: 36 41 04 85 Fax: 36 41 62 62 E-mail: rodovre@busck.dk; Ro's Torv 218, 4000 Roskilde Tel: 46 34 12 46 Fax: 46 34 12 80 E-mail: roskilde@busck.dk; Perlegade 21, 6400 Sonderborg Tel: 74 42 13 31 E-mail: sonderborg@busck.dk; Gerritsgade 28, 5700 Svendborg Tel: 62 17 22 90 E-mail: svendborg@busck.dk; Spinderiet 18, 2500 Valby Tel: 36 17 10 17 Fax: 36 17 10 16 E-mail: valby@busck.dk; Sonder Torv 2, 7100 Vejle Tel: 75 82 05 44 E-mail: vejle@busck.dk

Nyt Nordisk Forlag Arnold Busck A/S, Publishers, see Arnold Busck A/S

Polyteknisk Boghandel & Forlag
Anker Engelunds Vej 1, 2800 Lyngby
Tel: 77 42 43 44
E-mail: poly@polyteknisk.dk

Web Site: www.polyteknisk.dk
Key Personnel
Administrative Dir: Lise Scharff *Tel:* 77 42 43 22
  E-mail: lise@polyteknisk.dk
Founded: 1960
Type of Business: Distributor, Importer, Major
  Independent Bookseller, Wholesaler

Scanvik A/S
Provensvej 27, 2610 Rodovre
Tel: 3312 7766; 3314 2666 (Nordic dept)
  Fax: 3391 2882
E-mail: mail@scanvik.dk; nordisk@scanvik.dk
Web Site: www.scanvik.dk
Founded: 1967
Also agent.
Type of Business: Distributor, Exporter, Importer,
  Wholesaler

Studenterboghandelen ved Syddansk
  Universitet
Campusvej 55, 5230 Odense M
Tel: 6550 1700
E-mail: info@boghandel.sdu.dk
Web Site: studenterboghandel.dk
Key Personnel
Manager: Sanne Jorgensen *Tel:* 6550 1707
  E-mail: sanne@boghandel.sdu.dk
Founded: 1981
Type of Business: Importer, Major Independent
  Bookseller

Ecuador

Libreria y Papeleria Cientifica
Mejia 455 y Garcia Moreno, Quito
Tel: (02) 2281528; (02) 2281400
Web Site: www.libreriacientifica.ec
General interest, languages, stationery, profes-
  sional & school texts.
Type of Business: Distributor
Branch Office(s)
Boyaca E/Luque y Velez, Guayaquil, Guayas
  Tel: (04) 2518691
Campus Politecnica, Prosperina Facultad ICHE,
  Guayaquil, Guayas *Tel:* (04) 2856119
Edificio Universidad Catolica, Guayaquil, Guayas
  Tel: (04) 2202140
Km 2 Via Samborondon, Samborondon, Guayas
  Tel: (08) 7532464
Warehouse: Luque 223 E/Chile y Pedro Carbo,
  Guayaquil, Guayas *Tel:* (04) 2518691

Distripress Ecuatoriana Cia Ltda
10 de Agosto N29-126 y Cuero y Caicedo, Quito
Tel: (02) 2902693
Founded: 1989
Type of Business: Distributor, Importer, Whole-
  saler

Edimecien Cia Ltda
Gral Vicente Aguirre 166 y 10 de Agosto, Quito
Tel: (02) 250 2427 *Fax:* (02) 250 2429
E-mail: lexusec@lexuseditores.com
Web Site: www.lexuseditores.com
Type of Business: Distributor, Importer, Whole-
  saler
Parent Company: Lexus Editores

Egypt

ALEF
District 1, area 5, New Cairo beside Manor
  House School, Cairo 11477

E-mail: store@alefbookstores.com
Web Site: alefbookstores.com
Key Personnel
Co-Founder & General Manager: Ahmed Rahmy
Human Resources Manager: Salma Gamil
Marketing Manager: Aley Fathy
Merchandising Manager: Shaymaa Radwan
Founded: 2009
Type of Business: Major Book Chain Headquar-
  ters, Online Bookseller
Bookshop(s): City Stars Mall, 4th floor, Phase
  2, beside Burger King, Pocket Shop No
  4155, Cairo *Tel:* 01062734141 (cell); In-
  side Dandy Mall, Kilo 28, Alexandria Desert
  Rd, Cairo *Tel:* 01011377817 (cell); Mirage
  Mall, Entrance floor, behind Gate 2, Suez
  Rd, Cairo; 132 El Merghany St, Heliopo-
  lis, Cairo *Tel:* (02) 24192396; 01000224004
  (cell); The District Sheraton Heliopolis, Au-
  tostrad Rd, Wadi Degla Club, Heliopolis, Cairo
  Tel: 01151567777 (cell); 84 Rd 9, Maadi,
  Cairo *Tel:* (02) 27508661; 01000229996 (cell);
  City Center Mall (Maadi), Ring Rd, in front
  of H&M, Maadi, Cairo *Tel:* 01028077888
  (cell); 33 Geziret El Arab, Mohandeseen,
  Cairo *Tel:* (02) 33035570; 01061162238 (cell);
  City Center Mall (Nasr City), Makram Ebied,
  3rd floor, Nasr City, Cairo *Tel:* 01000250013
  (cell); Cairo Festival City Mall, beside Sky
  Court, 3rd floor, New Cairo *Tel:* 01000227007
  (cell); Kidzania, The Ring Rd, Taha Hussein
  St South of The Police Academy 5th District,
  New Cairo; Inside (Main Hall) Cairo Train
  Station, Ramsis, Cairo *Tel:* (02) 27739174;
  01000223003 (cell); Rehab Mall 2 Kiosk
  No 96, Rehab City, Cairo *Tel:* 01000228008
  (cell); Mall of Arabia, G(090b), next to CIB,
  Gates 4 & 5, 6th of October City, Cairo
  Tel: 01000229991 (cell); Mall of Arabia, ALEF
  Kiosk next to Mobaco, Gate 20, 6th of October City, Cairo *Tel:* 01020054002 (cell);
  30, Abdel Kader Ragab St, Roushdy, beside
  Roastery Roushdy Cafe, Alexandria *Tel:* (03)
  5448820; 01000229995 (cell); City Center Mall (Alexandria), Store LP 14, in front
  of Mazaya & opposite Costa Cafe, Alexandria *Tel:* 01009114033 (cell); City Center
  Mall (Alexandria), Kiosk in front of Starbucks Cafe, Alexandria *Tel:* 01026663405
  (cell); Orouba Mall, Borg El Arab, Beside
  Carrefour Gate, Alexandria *Tel:* 01099889227
  (cell); Sidi Gaber Train Station Mall, 1st floor,
  Store No F9, Alexandria *Tel:* 01020557786
  (cell); El Horria Tour, 58 El Gomhoria St,
  Assuit *Tel:* 01025000494 (cell); Al-A'sema
  Mall, 138 El Areesh St from Haram St, Giza
  Tel: 01099714714 (cell); El Mamar Sq, beside
  Super Market El Omda, 7 El Gharbia St, Is-
  mailia *Tel:* (064) 3357771; 01288803737 (cell);
  Marina Gate 4, beside Pizza Hut & Costa, Ma-
  rina *Tel:* (046) 4450013; 01099971559 (cell);
  Il-Mercato Mall, Shop 9, Bldg B12, Zone B,
  Sharm El Shekh *Tel:* 01060026070 (cell); El
  Zahraa Bldg 2, Store No 1, El Mallaha El Ga-
  dida (El Mahrousa), Suez *Tel:* 01027577137
  (cell)

Lehnert & Landrock Bookshop & Art Gallery
36 Abd-Alkhalik Sarwat, 1st floor, Cairo
Tel: (02) 2393-5324
Founded: 1904
Type of Business: Importer, Major Independent
  Bookseller, Wholesaler
Owned by: Edouard Lambelet & Co

Les Livres de France
Centre Degla, 11, rue Hassan Sabri, Zamalek,
  Cairo 11211
Tel: (02) 27360041; (02) 23935512
E-mail: farazliyvette@gmail.com

Key Personnel
Contact: Zeina Badran
Founded: 1947
Type of Business: Major Independent Bookseller
Branch Office(s)
2, rue 23 near Maadi Grand Mall, Maadi, Cairo
  11728 *Tel:* (02) 23780315

Misr Bookshop
3, Kamel Sedky St, Faggala, Cairo
Tel: (02) 25908920 *Fax:* (02) 27870051
Type of Business: Major Independent Bookseller

El Salvador

Clasicos Roxsil SA de CV
4 Ave Sur No 2-3, La Libertad, Santa Tecla
Tel: 2228-1832; 2200-5209; 2228-1212
E-mail: clasicosroxsil@yahoo.es
Web Site: ww.facebook.com/Clasicos-Roxsil-
  331476613687219/
Key Personnel
Head, Financial Division: Silvia Lopez de Barraza
  E-mail: aidabarraza@yahoo.com.mx
Founded: 1969
Type of Business: Distributor, Exporter, Importer,
  Wholesaler

Libreria UCA
Final Blvd Los Proceres, Jardines de Guadalupe,
  San Salvador
Mailing Address: Apdo (01) 168, San Salvador
Tel: 2210-6699; 2210-6659
E-mail: libreria@uca.edu.sv
Web Site: www.libreriauca.com
Key Personnel
Administrator: Claudia Annabel Arteaga Rubio
  Tel: 2210-6699 ext 288 *E-mail:* carteaga@uca.
  edu.sv
Founded: 1984
Type of Business: Major Independent Bookseller

Estonia

Apollo Raamatud
Poikmae 2, Tanassilma kula, 76406 Saku vald
  Harjumaa
Tel: 6336020 *Fax:* 6336028
E-mail: info@apollo.ee
Web Site: www.apollo.ee
Key Personnel
Sales & Marketing Manager: Eha Pank
  E-mail: eha.pank@apollo.ee
Founded: 1998
Subjects include art, astrology, biology, business,
  computers, cooking, health, history, humanities,
  law, music, reference & science.
Type of Business: Major Book Chain Headquar-
  ters
Bookshop(s): Papiniidu 8/10, 80042 Parnu; Es-
  tonia pst 9, 10143 Tallinn; Endla 45, 10615
  Tallinn; Suur-Sojamae 4, 11415 Tallinn; Ring-
  tee 75, 50501 Tartu; Riia 1, 51013 Tartu

Bookshop Krisostomus
Raekoja Plats 11, 51004 Tartu
Tel: 7440010 *Fax:* 7440011
E-mail: kriso@kriso.ee
Web Site: www.kriso.ee
Key Personnel
Sales Manager: Martin Laiapea
Accountant: Kart Vork
Founded: 1992
Subjects include architecture, art, computers,
  earth sciences, economics, home economics,

fiction, humanities, law, medicine, reference, social sciences & technology.
Type of Business: Major Independent Bookseller

Finland

Akateeminen Kirjakauppa (Academic Bookstore)
Ilmalankatu 2C, 00240 Helsinki
Tel: (02) 760 8999 (customer service)
E-mail: asiakaspalvelu@akateeminen.com (customer service)
Web Site: www.akateeminen.com
Key Personnel
Chief Executive Officer: Anne Kariniemi
E-mail: anne.kariniemi@akateeminen.com
Marketing Manager: Cia Branders *E-mail:* cia. branders@akateeminen.com
Founded: 1893
Subscriptions, CD-ROM.
Type of Business: Major Book Chain Headquarters, Wholesaler
Owned by: OY Stockmann AB
Bookshop(s): Itakatu 1, 00930 Helsinki, Store Manager: Riina Laaksonen *Tel:* (046) 876 1088; Keskuskatu 1, Pohjoisesplanadi 39, 00100 Helsinki; Lansituulentie 7, 02100 Espoo, Store Manager: Kirsi-Marja Wikman *Tel:* (046) 876 1113; Hameenkatu 4, 33100 Tampere, Store Manager: Inka Ylapelto *Tel:* (046) 876 1609; Eerikinkatu 15, 20100 Turku, Store Manager: Piia Packalen *Tel:* (046) 876 1714; Vantaanportinkatu 3, 01510 Vantaa, Store Manager: Leena Kero-Taiminen *Tel:* (046) 876 1056

Suomalainen Kirjakauppa Oy
Maistraatinportti 1, 00015 Otavamedia
Tel: (09) 156 6305; (09) 4259 9771 (customer service)
E-mail: asiakaspalvelu@suomalainenkk.fi
Web Site: www.suomalainen.com
Founded: 1999
Branch offices in Espoo (3), Forssa, Hameenlinna, Hamina, Heinola, Helsinki (7), Hyvinkka, Iisalmi, Imatra, Jarvenpaa, Joensuu, Jyvaskyla, Kajaani, Kemi, Kerava, Kokkola, Kotka (3), Kouvola, Kuopio (2), Kuusamo, Lahti, Lappeenranta, Lohja, Mikkeli, Oulu, Pori, Porvoo, Raahe, Raisio, Rauma, Riihimaaki, Rovaniemi, Salo, Savonlinni, Seinaajoki, Tampere (3), Turku (2), Vaasa, Vantaa (5), Varkaus.
Type of Business: Major Book Chain Headquarters
Owned by: Rautakirja Oy

Turun Kansallinen Kirjakauppa Oy
Turku Keskusta, Linnankatu 16, 20100 Turku
Tel: (02) 283 1000; (02) 2831 020; (02) 2831 030
E-mail: info@kansallinenkirjakauppa.fi
Web Site: www.kansallinenkirjakauppa.fi
Key Personnel
President & Chief Executive Officer: Paula Palmroth *Tel:* (050) 052 15 25 (cell) *E-mail:* paula. palmroth@kansallinenkirjakauppa.fi
Chief Financial Officer: Aila Korte *Tel:* (040) 518 8350 *E-mail:* aila.korte@ kansallinenkirjakauppa.fi
Marketing Dir: Tuula Korte *Tel:* (040) 594 5453 *E-mail:* tuula.korte@kansallinenkirjakauppa.fi
Founded: 1899
Type of Business: Major Independent Bookseller
Branch Office(s)
Hameenkatu 7, Turku *Tel:* (02) 2831 050
Lansikeskus Markulantie 150, Turku *Tel:* (02) 2831 060

France

Societe Nouvelle Rene Baudouin, see SNR Baudouin

CED-CEDIF
128 bis ave Jean Jaures, Park Mure, Ilot 4.11, 94200 Ivry sur Seine
Mailing Address: BP 40143, 94208 Ivry sur Seine
Tel: 01 46 58 38 40 *Fax:* 01 46 71 25 59
E-mail: societe@ced-cedif.com; contact@ced-cedif.com
Web Site: www.diffusion-ced-cedif.com
Key Personnel
Dir: Dorothy Perrault *Tel:* 01 77 01 88 06 *E-mail:* d-perrault@ced-cedif.com
Business Dir: Christine Jouan *Tel:* 01 46 58 38 40 *E-mail:* c-jouan@ced-cedif.com
Manager: Jean-Paul Belval
Sales Manager: Cyrill Vachon *Tel:* 01 77 01 87 94 *E-mail:* c-vachon@ced-cedif.com
Type of Business: Distributor

Critiques Livres SAS
24 rue Malmaison, 93170 Bagnolet
Tel: 01 43 60 39 10
Founded: 1976
Books in the visual arts.
Type of Business: Distributor, Exporter, Importer, Wholesaler

Dawson France
Subsidiary of Bertram Group
3, rue Galvani, 91745 Massy Cedex
Tel: 01 69 19 21 50 *Fax:* 01 69 19 21 66
E-mail: librairie@dawson.fr
Web Site: www.dawson.fr
Key Personnel
Dir: Ludovic Lautussier *E-mail:* ludovic. lautussier@dawson.fr
Founded: 1985
Type of Business: Distributor, Exporter, Importer

Dilisco
Rue du Limousin, 23220 Cheniers
Mailing Address: BP 25, 23220 Cheniers
Tel: 05 55 51 80 00 *Fax:* 05 55 62 17 39
E-mail: relation.client@dilisco.fr
Web Site: www.dilisco-diffusion-distribution.fr
Key Personnel
Manager, Customer Relations: Murielle Pinault
Founded: 1990
Type of Business: Distributor

Flammarion
6, rue Europe, 45300 Sermaises du Loiret
Tel: 01 40 51 31 00
Web Site: www.groupe-flammarion.com
Also publisher.
Branches in Bordeaux, Dijon, Grenoble, Lyon, Marseilles, Montreal (Canada) & Paris.
Type of Business: Distributor

Librairie Fnac
65 rue Carnot, 74000 Annecy
Tel: 08 25 02 00 20 *Fax:* 04 50 88 66 65
Web Site: www.fnac.com
Type of Business: Distributor

French Book Distribution
22 rue Antony Duvivier, 58000 Nevers
Tel: 03 86 61 31 46 *Fax:* 03 86 23 98 86
E-mail: info@frenchbookdistribution.com
Web Site: frenchbookdistribution.com
Key Personnel
Contact: Caroline Terrier; Regis Terrier
Type of Business: Distributor, Exporter

Interart
Subsidiary of Thames & Hudson Ltd
One rue de l'est, 75020 Paris
E-mail: commercial@interart.fr
Web Site: www.interart.fr
Key Personnel
Representative: Margot Rietsch *E-mail:* margot@ interart.fr
Founded: 1989
Sale & distribution of foreign language art books throughout France.
Type of Business: Distributor

Lavoisier Librairie
14, rue de Provigny, 94236 Cachan Cedex
Tel: 01 47 40 67 00 *Fax:* 01 47 40 67 02; 01 47 40 67 88
E-mail: livres@lavoisier.fr; info@lavoisier.fr
Web Site: www.lavoisier.fr; e.lavoisier.fr; diffusion.lavoisier.fr
Key Personnel
Chief Executive Officer: Pierre-Patrick Fenouil
Founded: 1947
French professional bookseller on scientific, technical & medical subjects.
Type of Business: Distributor, Exporter, Importer, Major Independent Bookseller
Branch Office(s)
11, rue Lavoisier, 75008 Paris *Tel:* 01 42 65 39 95 *Fax:* 01 42 65 02 46 *E-mail:* magasin@ lavoisier.fr

Librairie Mollat Bordeux
15 rue Vital-Carles, 33080 Bordeaux Cedex
Tel: 05 56 56 40 40 *Fax:* 05 56 56 40 88
E-mail: mollat@mollat.com
Web Site: www.mollat.com
Type of Business: Major Independent Bookseller

Librairie Picard
18 rue Seguier, 75006 Paris
Tel: 01 43 26 40 41
E-mail: catalogue@librairie-picard.com
Web Site: www.librairie-picard.com
Founded: 1869
Subjects include archaeology, bibliography, history, literature, philosophy & religion.
Type of Business: Distributor, Major Independent Bookseller

Librairie Sauramps Medical
11 Bd Henri IV, CS 79525, 34960 Montepellier Cedex 2
Tel: 04 67 63 68 80; 04 67 63 62 19 (orders) *Fax:* 04 67 63 68 84
E-mail: webmaster@saurampsmedical.com
Web Site: www.livres-medicaux.com
Founded: 1977
Specializes in medicine. Also publisher.
Type of Business: Importer, Major Independent Bookseller

SNR Baudouin
10, rue de Nesle, 75006 Paris
Tel: 01 43 29 00 50 *Fax:* 01 43 25 72 41
E-mail: renebaudouin@wanadoo.fr
Web Site: www.snrbaudouin.com
Founded: 1978
Subjects include antiques, architecture, art, cookery, fashion, humor, literature, music/dance, nature, photography, sports/athletics & travel/tourism.
Type of Business: Remainder Dealer, Wholesaler

Societe Internationale de Diffusion et d'Edition
1-3, ave du Bouton d'Or, 94386 Sucy-en-Brie Cedex
Tel: 01 48 84 39 34 *Fax:* 01 43 91 62 79
E-mail: france@side.fr; contact@side.fr
Web Site: www.side.fr

Founded: 1969
Type of Business: Distributor, Exporter, Wholesaler

Sodis
Subsidiary of Groupe Gallimard
128 Ave du Marechal de Lattre de Tassigny,
77400 Lagny-sur-Marne
Tel: 01 60 07 82 00 *Fax:* 01 64 30 92 22
E-mail: portail@sodis.fr
Web Site: www.servidis.fr
Key Personnel
Chief Executive Officer: Marc de La Fons
Dir, Strategy & Development: Marie-Christine
Dorel
Sales Manager: Helene de Laportaliere
Type of Business: Distributor

Librairie Le Square
2, Place Dr Leon Martin, 38000 Grenoble
Tel: 04 76 46 61 63
E-mail: librairie@librairielesquare.fr;
reservationssquare@club-internet.fr
Web Site: www.librairielesquare.fr
Key Personnel
Dir: Nicolas Trigeassou *E-mail:* nicolas.
trigeassou@librairielesquare.fr
Founded: 1964
Type of Business: Major Independent Bookseller

Les Trois Islets-Livres Rares
11, bd du tertre Gondan, 35800 Saint-Briac-sur-
Mer
Mailing Address: BP 20, 35800 Saint-Briac-sur-
Mer
Tel: 02 99 88 92 44; 06 81 35 73 35
E-mail: lib3i@orange.fr; lib-anc-trois-islets@
orange.fr
Web Site: www.librairie-trois-islets.com
Type of Business: Major Independent Bookseller

Union Distribution SA, see Flammarion

Germany

Antiquariat Aix-la-Chapelle
Pontdriesch 8A, 52062 Aachen
Tel: (0241) 30872 *Fax:* (0241) 20786
E-mail: talke@aix-rarebooks.com
Web Site: www.aix-rarebooks.com
Key Personnel
Owner: Eberhard B Talke
Founded: 1975
15th-17th century rare books.
Type of Business: Major Independent Bookseller

art book cologne GmbH & Co KG
Deutzer Freiheit 107, 50679 Cologne
Tel: (0221) 800 80 80 *Fax:* (0221) 800 80 82
E-mail: info@artbookcologne.de
Web Site: www.artbookcologne.com
Key Personnel
Founder: Bernd Detsch
Founded: 1997
Specialize in architecture, art, art theory, design,
illustrated cultural history & photography.
Type of Business: Wholesaler

Bachmann & Rybicki UG
Robert-Blum-Str 11, 01097 Dresden
Tel: (0351) 21960903
E-mail: info@dresden-antiquariat.de
Web Site: www.dresden-antiquariat.de
Key Personnel
Owner: Gregor Bachmann; Carsten Rybicki

Type of Business: Major Independent Bookseller
Bookshop(s): Hoyerswerdaer Str 1, 01936
Koenigsbrueck *Tel:* (035795) 247099

Barsortiment Koenemann Vertriebs GmbH
Pettenkoferstr 19, 58097 Hagen
Tel: (02331) 6258-0 *Fax:* (02331) 6258-222
E-mail: mail@koenemann-bs.de
Web Site: www.koenemann-bs.de
Key Personnel
Mng Dir: Stefan Koenemann *Tel:* (02331) 6258-
256 *E-mail:* s.koenemann@koenemann-bs.de;
Eckhard Suedmersen
Sales Manager: Martin Rings *Tel:* (02331) 6258-
154 *E-mail:* m.rings@koenemann-bs.de
Founded: 1987
Type of Business: Wholesaler
Parent Company: Libri GmbH

Antiquariat Bergische Buecherstube
Birkenweg 11, 51491 Overath
Tel: (02204) 769492 *Fax:* (02204) 769493
E-mail: info@bergische-buecherstube.de
Web Site: www.bergische-buecherstube.de
Key Personnel
Owner: Joerg Mewes
Founded: 1985
Subjects include architecture, art, bibliography,
ethnological studies, history, philosophy, re-
gional history & travel.
Membership(s): International Association of Anti-
quarian Booksellers (ILAB).
Type of Business: Major Independent Bookseller

BuchVertrieb Blank GmbH
Roehrmooser Str 16-20, 85256 Vierkirchen
Tel: (08139) 8 02 91-0 *Fax:* (08139) 8 02 91-20
E-mail: info@buchvertrieb-blank.de
Web Site: www.buchvertrieb-blank.de
Key Personnel
Chief Executive Officer: Ralph M Danna
E-mail: ralph.danna@buchvertrieb-blank.de
Head, Sales: Oliver Draeger *E-mail:* oliver.
draeger@buchvertrieb-blank.de
Type of Business: Remainder Dealer

Blank Media, see BuchVertrieb Blank GmbH

Antiquariat Wolfgang Braecklein
Dickhardtstr 48, 12159 Berlin
Tel: (030) 851 66 13 *Fax:* (030) 859 23 69
E-mail: info@braecklein.eu
Web Site: www.braecklein.eu
Key Personnel
Owner: Wolfgang Braecklein
Membership(s): Verband Deutscher Antiquare.
Type of Business: Major Independent Bookseller

Petersen Buchimport GmbH
Subsidiary of G Umbreit GmbH & Co KG
Weidestr 122 a, 22083 Hamburg
Tel: (040) 71003-0 *Fax:* (040) 71003-141
E-mail: vertrieb@petersen-buchimport.com
Web Site: www.petersen-buchimport.com
Key Personnel
Mng Dir: Clemens Birk *E-mail:* clemens.birk@
umbreit.de
Corporate Communications: Heiko Doerr
Tel: (07142) 596-178 *Fax:* (07142) 596-280
E-mail: heiko.doerr@umbreit.de
Sales: Alessandro di Marino *Tel:* (040) 71003-
145 *E-mail:* alessandro.dimarino@petersen-
buchimport.com
Founded: 1950
Type of Business: Importer

Fachverlag Hans Carl GmbH
Andernacher Str 33a, 90411 Nuremberg
Mailing Address: Postfach 99 01 53, 90268
Nuremberg
Tel: (0911) 95285-0 *Fax:* (0911) 95285-81 60

E-mail: info@hanscarl.com; redaktion@brauwelt.
de
Web Site: www.hanscarl.com
Key Personnel
Mng Dir: Michael Schmitt *E-mail:* m.schmitt@
hanscarl.com
Founded: 1861
Type of Business: Distributor, Major Independent
Bookseller

Dietmar Dreier Wissenschaftliche
Versandbuchhandlung GmbH
Bernhard Roecken Weg 1, 47228 Duisburg
Tel: (02065) 77 55-0 *Fax:* (02065) 77 55-33
E-mail: info@dietmardreier.de
Web Site: www.dietmardreier.de
Key Personnel
Dir: Diane Korneli-Dreier *E-mail:* diane.korneli-
dreier@dietmardreier.de
Founded: 1981
International library suppliers in all areas of sci-
ence, medicine, technology, engineering, the
humanities & social sciences.
Type of Business: Exporter, Importer

Dokumente-Verlag GmbH
Versandbuchhandlung Librairie
Hildastr 4, 77654 Offenburg
Tel: (0781) 923699-0 *Fax:* (0781) 923699-70
E-mail: info@dokumente-verlag.de
Web Site: www.dokumente-verlag.de
Key Personnel
Management: Heribert Jager *Tel:* (0781) 923699-
13 *E-mail:* hj@dokumente-verlag.de
Founded: 1945
Specialize in German & French literature.
Type of Business: Distributor, Major Independent
Bookseller

eBook.de
Friesenweg 1, 22763 Hamburg
Tel: (040) 4223 6096 *Fax:* (040) 8519 4444
E-mail: service@ebook.de
Web Site: www.ebook.de
Key Personnel
Mng Dir: Per Dalheimer; Dr Stefan Hoellermann
Founded: 1999
Type of Business: Online Bookseller
Owned by: Hugendubel Digital GmbH & Co KG

Exlibris Buchhandelsgesellschaft Hermann
Oswald & Co GmbH
Ferdinand-Dirichs-Weg 28, 60529 Frankfurt am
Main
Tel: (069) 355159 *Fax:* (069) 356099
E-mail: exlibris@exlibris.de; exlibris@t-online.de
Web Site: www.exlibris.de
Founded: 1954
Type of Business: Exporter, Importer

Werner Flach Internationale Wissenschaftliche
Buchhandlung und Zeitschriften-Agentur eK
Humboldtstr 57, 60318 Frankfurt am Main
Tel: (069) 95 91 75 0 *Fax:* (069) 95 91 75 22
E-mail: fachbuch@flachbuch.com
Web Site: www.flachbuch.com
Key Personnel
Owner: Petra Hildebrandt
Founded: 1957
Type of Business: Major Independent Bookseller

forum independent GmbH
Lindenstr 14, 50674 Cologne
Tel: (0221) 92428-230 *Fax:* (0221) 92428-232
E-mail: steinbach@forum-independent.de
Web Site: www.forum-independent.de
Key Personnel
Mng Dir: Silvia Maul *Tel:* (0221) 92428-231
E-mail: maul@forum-independent.de
Founded: 2011
Type of Business: Distributor

GeoCenter Touristik Medienservice GmbH
Schockenriedstr 44, 70565 Stuttgart
Tel: (0711) 78 19 46 10 *Fax:* (0711) 782 4375
E-mail: vertrieb@geocenter.de
Web Site: www.geocenter.de
Key Personnel
Mng Dir: Dr Klaus Hoehne *Tel:* (0711) 78 19 46 41
Mng Dir, Sales & Marketing: Hans Juergen Pfister
Sales Manager: Andreas Beermann
   E-mail: andreas.beermann@geocenter.de
Founded: 1971
Type of Business: Distributor, Wholesaler

Kai-Henning Gerlach Books & Online
Cicerostr 37, 10709 Berlin
Tel: (030) 3249441 *Fax:* (030) 3235667
E-mail: email@gerlach-books.de
Web Site: www.gerlach-books.de
Key Personnel
Owner & General Manager: Kai-Henning Gerlach
Specialize in academic books & books on Middle Eastern & Islamic studies.
Membership(s): Arbeitskreis Elektronisches Publizieren; Boersenverein des Deutschen Buchhandels eV; British Society for Middle Eastern Studies; Deutsche Arbeitsgemeinschaft Vorderer Orient eV; Deutsch-Qatarische Gesellschaft eV; European Association of Middle East Librarians; German Serials Interest Group; International Society for Islamic Legal Studies; Special Libraries Association/Arabian Gulf Chapter; Vereinigung Oesterreichischer Bibliothekarinnen und Bibliothekare.
Type of Business: Exporter, Major Independent Bookseller

Germinal Medienhandlung GmbH
Siemensstr 16, 35463 Fernwald
Mailing Address: Postfach 70, 35461 Fernwald
Tel: (0641) 41700 *Fax:* (0641) 943251
E-mail: bestellservice@germinal.de
Web Site: www.germinal.de
Key Personnel
Mng Dir: Alfred Kobel
Type of Business: Major Independent Bookseller

Buchhandlung Graff GmbH
Sack 15, 38100 Braunschweig
Tel: (0531) 480 89-0 *Fax:* (0531) 480 89-89
E-mail: infos@graff.de
Web Site: www.graff.de
Key Personnel
Mng Dir: Joachim Wrensch *E-mail:* jwrensch@graff.de; Thomas Wrensch *E-mail:* twrensch@graff.de
Founded: 1867
Type of Business: Major Independent Bookseller

Grosshandel fuer Modernes Antiquariat GmbH (GMA)
Dieckstr 71-75, 48145 Muenster
Tel: (0251) 20858080 *Fax:* (0251) 20858090
E-mail: gma@gma-muenster.de
Web Site: www.gma-muenster.de
Key Personnel
Mng Dir: K Uwe Beckmann-Denart; Jens Havelberg *Tel:* (0251) 20858083 *E-mail:* jens.havelberg@gma-muenster.de
Founded: 1993
Type of Business: Wholesaler

G Grote'sche Verlagsbuchhandlung GmbH & Co KG
Max-Planck-Str 12, 50858 Cologne
Tel: (02234) 1060
Founded: 1661
Type of Business: Distributor

Antiquariat Gerhard Gruber
Koenigsberger Str 4, 74078 Heilbronn
Tel: (07131) 45245 *Fax:* (07131) 910474
E-mail: info@antiquariat-gruber.de
Web Site: www.antiquariat-gruber.de
Key Personnel
Owner: Gerhard Gruber
Founded: 1983
Specialize in the fields of history of science, technology, medicine & their peripheries.
Membership(s): Boersenverein des Deutschen Buchhandels eV; International League of Antiquarian Booksellers; Verband Deutscher Antiquare.
Type of Business: Major Independent Bookseller

Otto Harrassowitz GmbH & Co KG
Kreuzberger Ring 7b-d, 65205 Wiesbaden
Tel: (0611) 530 0 *Fax:* (0611) 530 560
E-mail: service@harrassowitz.de
Web Site: www.harrassowitz.de
Key Personnel
Mng Partner & Dir, Sales: Friedemann Weigel
Mng Partner & Dir of Accounting: Ruth Becker-Scheicher
Mng Partner, Human Resources & Publisher Relations: Nadja Dorn-Lange
Founded: 1872
Service of books & scholarly journals to academic & research libraries. Library service agency; subscription agency.
Type of Business: Distributor, Exporter, Importer, Major Independent Bookseller

Anton Hiersemann KG Verlag
Affiliate of Dr Ernst Hauswedell & Co KG Verlag
Haldenstr 30, 70376 Stuttgart
Tel: (0711) 549971-11 *Fax:* (0711) 549971-21
E-mail: verlag@hiersemann.de
Web Site: www.hiersemann.de
Key Personnel
Chairman: Gerd Hiersemann
President & Dir, Rights & Permissions: Florian Hiersemann
Founded: 1884
Type of Business: Distributor, Online Bookseller

Antiquariat im Hufelandhaus GmbH
Affiliate of Gast & Hoyer GmbH
Hegelplatz 1, 10117 Berlin
Tel: (030) 31504196; (030) 3422011 *Fax:* (030) 3410440; (030) 31504197
E-mail: buchladen@lange-springer-antiquariat.de
Web Site: www.lange-springer-antiquariat.de
Key Personnel
Mng Dir: Dr Ekkehart Gast; Manfred Gast
Founded: 1980
Type of Business: Major Independent Bookseller

H Hugendubel GmbH & Co KG
Hilblestr 54, 80636 Munich
Tel: (089) 30 75 75 75; (089) 70 80 99 47 *Fax:* (089) 30 75 75 30
E-mail: info@hugendubel.de; service@hugendubel.de
Web Site: www.hugendubel.com; www.hugendubel.de
Key Personnel
Executive Partner: Dr Maximilian Hugendubel
Mng Partner: Nina Hugendubel
Management: Thomas Nitz
Founded: 1893
Type of Business: Major Book Chain Headquarters

Antiquariat Richard Husslein
Dompfaffweg 7, 82152 Planegg
Mailing Address: Postfach 1525, 82144 Planegg
Tel: (089) 899 795 90 *Fax:* (089) 899 795 92
E-mail: info@antiquariat-husslein.de

Web Site: www.antiquariat-husslein.de
Subjects include 20th century literature, travel, sports, history of science, law, art, medicine, photography.
Type of Business: Major Independent Bookseller

Antiquariat KaraJahn
Motzstr 25, 10777 Berlin
Tel: (030) 211 54 56 *Fax:* (030) 211 57 37
E-mail: oldbooks@karajahn.com
Web Site: www.karajahn.com
Key Personnel
Owner: Michael Jahn
Type of Business: Major Independent Bookseller

Kiefer Buch- und Kunstauktionen
Steubenstr 36, 75172 Pforzheim
Tel: (07231) 9232-0 *Fax:* (07231) 9232-16
E-mail: info@kiefer.de
Web Site: www.kiefer.de
Key Personnel
Owner & Mng Dir: Peter Kiefer
Founded: 1979
Type of Business: Major Independent Bookseller

Von Kloeden KG
Wielandstr 24, 10707 Berlin-Charlottenburg
Tel: (030) 887 125 12 *Fax:* (030) 887 125 19
E-mail: vonkloeden@web.de
Web Site: www.vonkloeden.de
Key Personnel
Mng Dir: Konrad Von Kloeden
Deputy Mng Dir: Charlotte Von Kloeden
Founded: 1967
Specialize in children's books.
Type of Business: Major Independent Bookseller

Antiquariat Knoell
Herderstr 2, 21335 Lueneburg
Tel: (04131) 323 90
Web Site: www.antiquariat-knoell.de
Key Personnel
Owner: Norbert Knoell *E-mail:* norbert.knoell@gmx.de
Type of Business: Major Independent Bookseller

Koch, Neff & Oetinger Verlagsauslieferung GmbH
Industriestr 23, 70565 Stuttgart
E-mail: kontakt@kno-va.de
Web Site: www.kno-va.de
Key Personnel
Mng Dir: Thomas Raff; Uwe Ratajczak; Oliver Voerster
Distribution: Gabriele Raff *Tel:* (0711) 7899-1124 *E-mail:* gabriele.raff@kno-va.de
Type of Business: Distributor

Koch, Neff & Volckmar GmbH (KNV)
Industriestr 23, 70565 Stuttgart
Tel: (0711) 7860-0; (0711) 7860 4755 (export) *Fax:* (0711) 7860 2800; (0711) 7860 8225 (export); (0711) 7860 2944 (sales)
E-mail: kontakt@knv.de; e-commerce@knv.de
Web Site: www.knv.de; shop.buchkatalog.de
Key Personnel
Dir: Uwe Ratajczak
Mng Dir: Oliver Voerster
Founded: 1829
Deals primarily in bibliographic titles.
Type of Business: Distributor, Exporter, Wholesaler

Antiquariat Kretzer
Alter Kirchweg 23a, 35274 Kirchhain-Stausebach
Tel: (06422) 898119 *Fax:* (06422) 8997034
E-mail: antiquariat.kretzer@gmx.de
Web Site: www.antiquariat-kretzer.de
Key Personnel
Owner: Otto W Plocher
Specialize in historical & Protestant theology.
Type of Business: Major Independent Bookseller

Leipziger Kommissions- und Grossbuchhandelsgesellschaft mbH (LKG)
An der Suedspitze 1-12, 04571 Roetha
Tel: (034206) 65-100 *Fax:* (034206) 65-110
E-mail: lkg@lkg-service.de
Web Site: www.lkg-va.de
Key Personnel
Mng Dir: Thomas Raff; Uwe Ratajczak; Oliver Voerster
Marketing/Sales: Angelica Bock; Barbara Ellendt
Head, Customer Service: Frank Waldhelm
Founded: 1946
Type of Business: Distributor

Libri GmbH
Friedensallee 273, 22763 Hamburg
Tel: (040) 853 980
E-mail: libri@libri.de; sales@libri.de
Web Site: www.libri.de
Key Personnel
Chairman: Holger Bellmann
Mng Dir: Enrico Ramminger; Eckhard Suedmersen
Sales Manager: Steffen Burmeister
E-mail: sburmeister@libri.de
Type of Business: Exporter, Importer, Wholesaler

Antiquariat Hans Lindner
Spessartweg 3, 84048 Mainburg
Tel: (08751) 5617 *Fax:* (08751) 5418
E-mail: lindner.mainburg@t-online.de
Web Site: www.antiquariat-lindner.de
Key Personnel
Owner: Hans Lindner
Founded: 1982
Specialize in children's, fine press & illustrated books as well as first editions of the 20th century.
Membership(s): International League of Antiquarian Booksellers; German Association of Antiquarian Booksellers.
Type of Business: Major Independent Bookseller

LKG, see Leipziger Kommissions- und Grossbuchhandelsgesellschaft mbH (LKG)

Antiquariat Walter Markov
Breite Str 52, 53111 Bonn - Altstadt
Tel: (0228) 96 38 565
E-mail: info@antiquariat-markov.de
Web Site: www.antiquariat-markov.de
Key Personnel
Owner: Juergen Repschlaeger
Specialize in history, philosophy, politics & social sciences.
Type of Business: Major Independent Bookseller

Massmann Internationale Buchhandlung GmbH
Luruper Chausse 125, 22761 Hamburg
Tel: (040) 767 00 40 *Fax:* (040) 767 00 410
E-mail: info@massmann.de
Web Site: www.massmann.de
Key Personnel
Mng Dir: Dorothea Massmann *Tel:* (040) 76 70 04 16 *E-mail:* dorothea.massmann@massmann.de; Kay Massmann *Tel:* (040) 76 70 04 12 *E-mail:* kay.massmann@massmann.de
Founded: 1989
Type of Business: Distributor, Importer

Mayersche Buchhandlung KG
Matthiashofstr 28-30, 52064 Aachen
Tel: (0241) 4777-345 *Fax:* (0241) 4777-475
E-mail: service@mayersche.de
Web Site: www.mayersche.de
Key Personnel
Manager: Dr Hartmut Falter; Helmut Falter; Ullrich Falter
Press & Public Relations: Simone Thelen
E-mail: s.thelen@mayersche.de

Founded: 1817
Type of Business: Distributor, Exporter, Importer, Major Independent Bookseller
Bookshop(s): Buchkremerstr 1-7, 52062 Aachen *Tel:* (0241) 4777-0 *Fax:* (0241) 4777-167 *E-mail:* info-aachenbk@mayersche.de; Hauptstr 15, 59755 Arnsberg-Neheim *Tel:* (02932) 902861-0 *Fax:* (02932) 902861-1 *E-mail:* info-neheim@mayersche.de; Berliner Platz 2, 46395 Bocholt *Tel:* (02871) 489930-0 *Fax:* (02871) 489930-1 *E-mail:* info-bocholt@mayersche.de; Kortumstr 69-71, 44787 Bochum *Tel:* (0234) 68761-0 *Fax:* (0234) 68761-110 *E-mail:* info-bochum@mayersche.de; Ruhr Park, Am Einkaufszentum, 44791 Bochum *Tel:* (0234) 68761-161 *Fax:* (0234) 6014356-1 *E-mail:* info-bochum-ruhrpark@mayersche.de; Kornmarkt 4, 46325 Borken *Tel:* (02861) 809477-0 *Fax:* (02861) 809477-1 *E-mail:* info-borken@mayersche.de; Hochstr 31a, 46236 Bottrop *Tel:* (02041) 775975-0 *Fax:* (02041) 775975-1 *E-mail:* info-bottrop@mayersche.de; Muensterstr 5, 44575 Castrop-Rauxel *Tel:* (02305) 9299330 *Fax:* (02305) 929933-1 *E-mail:* info-castrop-rauxel@mayersche.de; Neumarkt 2, 50667 Cologne *Tel:* (0221) 20307-0 *Fax:* (0221) 20307-27 *E-mail:* info-koeln-gal@mayersche.de; Wiener Platz 1, 51065 Cologne-Muelheim *Tel:* (0221) 6699343-0 *Fax:* (0221) 6699343-1 *E-mail:* info-koeln-muelheim@mayersche.de; Neusser Str 226, 50733 Cologne-Nippes *Tel:* (0221) 669 948-10 *Fax:* (0221) 669 948-11 *E-mail:* info-koeln-nippes@mayersche.de; Suelzburgstr 13, 50937 Cologne-Suelz *Tel:* (0221) 292 73 44-0 *Fax:* (0221) 292 73 44-1 *E-mail:* info-koeln-suelz@mayersche.de; Koelner Str 78, 41539 Dormagen *Tel:* (02133) 778705-0 *Fax:* (02133) 778705-1 *E-mail:* info-dormagen@mayersche.de; Westenhellweg 37-41, 44137 Dortmund *Tel:* (0231) 80905-0 *Fax:* (0231) 80905-10 *E-mail:* info-dortmund@mayersche.de; Harkortstr 61, 44225 Dortmund-Hombruch *Tel:* (0231) 7766663-0 *Fax:* (0231) 7766663-1 *E-mail:* info-hombruch@mayersche.de; Mayersche Droste GmbH & Co KG, Partner der Mayerschen, Koenigsallee 18, 40212 Duesseldorf *Tel:* (0211) 5425690-0 *Fax:* (0211) 5425690-1 *E-mail:* info-duesseldorf-droste-koe@mayersche.de; Nordstr 73, 40477 Duesseldorf *Tel:* (0211) 4163542-0 *Fax:* (0211) 4163542-1 *E-mail:* info-duesseldorf-nord@mayersche.de; Friedrichstr 19, 40217 Duesseldorf *Tel:* (0211) 7306048-0 *Fax:* (0211) 7306048-1 *E-mail:* info-duesseldorf-friedrichst@mayersche.de; Duisburg Forum, Koenigstr 48, 47051 Duisburg *Tel:* (0203) 70 900 4-00 *Fax:* (0203) 70 900 4-01 *E-mail:* info-duisburg@mayersche.de; Marienstr 2, 52249 Eschweiler *Tel:* (02403) 782911-0 *Fax:* (02403) 782911-1 *E-mail:* info-eschweiler@mayersche.de; Markt 5-6, 45127 Essen *Tel:* (0201) 36567-0 *Fax:* (0201) 36567-10 *E-mail:* info-essen@mayersche.de; Ruettenscheider Str 84, 45130 Essen *Tel:* (0201) 890 60 80-0 *Fax:* (0201) 890 60 80-1 *E-mail:* info-essen-ruettenscheid@mayersche.de; Hauptstr 120-122, 50226 Frechen *Tel:* (02234) 21919-80 *Fax:* (02234) 21919-81 *E-mail:* info-frechen@mayersche.de; Bahnhofstr 78-84, 45879 Gelsenkirchen *Tel:* (0209) 92392-3 *Fax:* (0209) 92392-10 *E-mail:* info-gelsenkirchen@mayersche.de; Hochstr 9, 45894 Gelsenkirchen-Buer *Tel:* (0209) 972000-0 *Fax:* (0209) 972000-1 *E-mail:* info-buer@mayersche.de; Hochstr 23, 45964 Gladbeck *Tel:* (02043) 375250-0 *Fax:* (02043) 375250-1 *E-mail:* info-gladbeck@mayersche.de; Koelner Str 23-25, 41515 Grevenbroich *Tel:* (02181) 22848-10 *Fax:* (02181) 22848-11 *E-mail:* info-grevenbroich@mayersche.de; Koenigstr 4, 33330 Guetersloh *Tel:* (05241) 504990-0 *Fax:* (05241) 504990-1 *E-mail:* info-guetersloh@mayersche.de; Kaiserstr 20,

51643 Gummersbach *Tel:* (02261) 92580-20 *Fax:* (02261) 92580-21 *E-mail:* info-gummersbach@mayersche.de; Obermarkt 13a, 45525 Hattingen *Tel:* (02324) 919868-0 *Fax:* (02324) 919868-1 *E-mail:* info-hattingen@mayersiche.de; Baeckerstr 24-28, 32052 Herford *Tel:* (05221) 120970-0 *Fax:* (05221) 120970-1 *E-mail:* info-herford@mayersche.de; Bahnhofstr 53, 44623 Herne *Tel:* (02323) 368910-0 *Fax:* (02323) 368910-1 *E-mail:* info-herne@mayersche.de; Weststr 75, 59174 Kamen *Tel:* (02307) 925106-0 *Fax:* (02307) 925106-1 *E-mail:* info-kamen@mayersche.de; Hindenburgstr 115-119, 41061 Moenchengladbach *Tel:* (02161) 81194-0 *Fax:* (02161) 81194-10 *E-mail:* info-moenchengladbach@mayersche.de; Stresemannstr 43, 41236 Moenchengladbach-Rheydt *Tel:* (02166) 94977-0 *Fax:* (02166) 94977-6 *E-mail:* info-rheydt@mayersche.de; Buechel 31, 41460 Neuss *Tel:* (02131) 313764-0 *Fax:* (02131) 313764-1 *E-mail:* info-neuss@mayersche.de; huma Einkaufspark, Rathausallee 16, 53757 Sankt Augustin *Tel:* (02241) 266097-0 *Fax:* (02241) 266097-1 *E-mail:* info-staugustin@mayersche.de; Bahnhofstr 28, 57072 Siegen *Tel:* (0271) 338800-00 *Fax:* (0271) 338800-11 *E-mail:* info-siegen@mayersche.de; Mayersche Interbook KG, Partner der Mayerschen, Kornmarkt 3, 54290 Trier *Tel:* (0651) 9799-0 *Fax:* (0651) 9799-300 *E-mail:* info-trier@mayersche.de; Koelner Str 13, 53840 Troisdorf *Tel:* (02241) 1239930 *Fax:* (02241) 1239931 *E-mail:* info-troisdorf@mayersche.de; Haupstr 12, 41747 Viersen *Tel:* (02162) 946914-0 *Fax:* (02162) 946914-1 *E-mail:* info-viersen@mayersche.de; Hohe Str 20-22, 46483 Wesel *Tel:* (0281) 147931-0 *Fax:* (0281) 147931-11 *E-mail:* info-wesel@mayersche.de; Bahnhofstr 30, 58452 Witten *Tel:* (02302) 28280-0 *Fax:* (02302) 28280-29 *E-mail:* info-witten@mayersche.de; Werth 54, 42275 Wuppertal Barmen *Tel:* (0202) 4304280-0 *Fax:* (0202) 4304280-1 *E-mail:* info-wuppertal-barmen@mayersche.de

Antiquariat Mertens und Pomplun
Winterfeldstr 51, 10781 Berlin
Tel: (030) 2519203
E-mail: info@mp-rarebooks.de
Web Site: www.mp-rarebooks.de
Key Personnel
Owner: Thomas Mertens; Michael Pomplun
Founded: 1989
Subjects include archaeology, art, genealogy, geography, law, literature, philosophy, politics, sports & theology.
Type of Business: Major Independent Bookseller

Minerva KG Gude Internationale Fachliteratur fuer Medizin und Naturwissenschaften Neue Medien
Bunsenstr 6, 64293 Darmstadt
Tel: (06151) 988-0 *Fax:* (06151) 988-39
E-mail: info@minerva.de
Web Site: www.minerva.de
Key Personnel
Mng Dir: Stefan Gude *E-mail:* s.gude@minerva.de
Marketing & Advertising: Gabi Reinders
Tel: (0201) 797098 *Fax:* (0201) 7988245
E-mail: g.reinders@minerva.de
Founded: 1949
Type of Business: Distributor, Major Independent Bookseller

Missing Link Versandbuchhandlung eG
Westerstr 114-116, 28199 Bremen
Tel: (0421) 504348 *Fax:* (0421) 504316
E-mail: info@missing-link.de
Web Site: www.missing-link.de

Key Personnel
Chairman: Klaus Tapken *E-mail:* klaus@missing-link.de
Founded: 1991
Specialize in English language titles.
Type of Business: Importer

Antiquariat am Moritzberg
Zierenbergstr 90, 31137 Hildesheim
Tel: (05121) 1744047 *Fax:* (05121) 1744048
E-mail: antiquariat.moritzberg@t-online.de
Web Site: www.antiquariat-hildesheim.de
Key Personnel
Owner: Dr Lothar Hennighaus
Founded: 2006
Type of Business: Major Independent Bookseller

Antiquariat Daniel Osthoff
Martinstr 19, 97070 Wuerzburg
Tel: (0931) 57 25 45 *Fax:* (0931) 35 37 9 45
E-mail: antiquariat.osthoff@t-online.de
Web Site: www.antiquariat-osthoff.de
Key Personnel
Bookseller: Daniel Osthoff; Ursula Osthoff
Founded: 1988
Type of Business: Major Independent Bookseller

Panorama Grossantiquariat und Verlag GmbH
Moehringstr 6a, 65187 Wiesbaden
Tel: (0611) 844021 *Fax:* (0611) 807984
E-mail: info@panorama-verlag.de
Web Site: panorama.juni.com
Key Personnel
Mng Dir: Dr Martin Schultheiss
Sales Dir: Hans-Dieter Meinl
Assistant: Ilsa Benesch-Zula
Type of Business: Distributor

Paulsen Buchimport
Friedrichstr 13, 79585 Hoellstein
Tel: (0762) 75 888 380 *Fax:* (0762) 75 887 449
E-mail: info@piboox.de
Web Site: www.piboox.de
Key Personnel
Contact: Hans-Juergen Paulsen
Founded: 1992
Type of Business: Importer

Antiquariat Pennartz
Amandastr 13, 13467 Berlin
Tel: (030) 32 70 28 00
E-mail: pennartz@web.de
Web Site: www.antiquariat-pennartz.de
Key Personnel
Proprietor: Karin Pennartz
Subjects include architecture, biography, ethnology, geology, law, medicine, music, philosophy, sports, travel & zoology.
Type of Business: Major Independent Bookseller

Buchhandlung Heinz Pier
Carl-Schurz-Str 98, 50374 Erftstadt
Tel: (02235) 44808; (02235) 3998 *Fax:* (02235) 41654
E-mail: buchhandlung@pier.de
Web Site: www.heinzpier.de
Key Personnel
Contact: Michaela Herrmann
Founded: 1922
Type of Business: Major Independent Bookseller

Antiquariat Thomas Rezek
Amalienstr 63, 80799 Munich
Tel: (089) 28 87 91 65 *Fax:* (089) 28 87 91 65
E-mail: arezek@web.de
Web Site: www.a-rezek.de
Type of Business: Major Independent Bookseller, Online Bookseller

Buchhandlung Sachse & Heinzelmann
Georgstr 34, 30159 Hannover
Tel: (0511) 360240 *Fax:* (0511) 324167
Type of Business: Major Independent Bookseller

Antiquariat Sander
Wachsbleichstr 22, 01067 Dresden
Tel: (0351) 796 096 07 *Fax:* (0351) 796 096 08
E-mail: info@antiquariat-sander.de
Web Site: www.antiquariat-sander.de
Key Personnel
Owner: Torsten Sander
Founded: 2013
Membership(s): International League of Antiquarian Booksellers (ILAB).
Type of Business: Major Independent Bookseller, Online Bookseller

Sandila Import-Export Handels-GmbH
Saegestr 37, 79737 Herrischried
Tel: (07764) 93 97-0 *Fax:* (07764) 93 97-39
Key Personnel
Mng Dir: Gerlinde Gloeckner
Founded: 1984
Type of Business: Distributor, Exporter, Importer, Wholesaler

Antiquariat Schaper
Dammtordamm 4, 20354 Hamburg
Tel: (040) 34 50 16
E-mail: buch@antiquariat-schaper.de
Web Site: www.antiquariat-schaper.de
Key Personnel
Owner: Brigitte Schaper; Dietrich Schaper
Founded: 1928
Membership(s): International League of Antiquarian Booksellers; Verband Deutscher Antiquare eV.
Type of Business: Major Independent Bookseller

Kurt Scholl
Steinhofweg 20, 69123 Heidelberg
Tel: (06221) 7534652; (06221) 707661
Founded: 1964
Type of Business: Major Independent Bookseller

Schweitzer Fachinformationen oHG
Elsenheimstr 41-43, 80687 Munich
Tel: (089) 55134-112 *Fax:* (089) 55134-103
Web Site: www.schweitzer-online.de
Key Personnel
Management: Philipp Neie *E-mail:* p.neie@schweitzer-online.de
Head, Marketing: Katinka Haslinger *Tel:* (089) 55134-108 *E-mail:* k.haslinger@schweitzer-online.de
Press: Susanne Teubig *Tel:* (0211) 52704-123 *E-mail:* s.teubig@schweitzer-online.de
Founded: 1868
Type of Business: Exporter, Importer, Major Book Chain Headquarters
Bookshop(s): Schweitzer Sortiment oHG, Franzoesische Str 13, 10117 Berlin, Contact: Michael Brielmaier *Tel:* (030) 25 40 83-113 *Fax:* (030) 25 40 83-103 *E-mail:* m.brielmaier@schweitzer-online.de; Kamloth & Schweitzer oHG, Ostertorstr 25-29, 28195 Bremen, Contact: Angelika Weber *Tel:* (0421) 33937-12 *Fax:* (0421) 33937-30 *E-mail:* a.weber@schweitzer-online.de; Goethe Buchhandlung Teubig GmbH, Theodor-Koerner-Platz 14, 09130 Chemnitz, Contact: Thomas Weiser *Tel:* (0371) 43 35-221 *Fax:* (0371) 43 35-299 *E-mail:* t.weiser@schweitzer-online.de; Witsch, Behrendt & Schweitzer oHG, Universitaetsstr 18, 50937 Cologne, Contact: Michael Grohe *Tel:* (0221) 4 76 97-32 *Fax:* (0221) 4 76 97-38 *E-mail:* m.grohe@schweitzer-online.de; Dreist, Kaiserstr 25, 44135 Dortmund, Contact: Christina Elbers *Tel:* (0231) 572579 *Fax:* (0231) 554263

E-mail: c.elbers@schweitzer-online.de; Goethe Buchhandlung Teubig GmbH, Schweizer Str 3b (Eingang Hohe Str), 01069 Dresden, Contact: Kathleen Wackwitz *Tel:* (0351) 217766-12 *E-mail:* k.wackwitz@schweitzer-online.de; Goethe Buchhandlung Teubig GmbH, Willstaetterstr 15, 40549 Duesseldorf, Contact: Daniela Piper *Tel:* (0211) 52704-171 *Fax:* (0211) 52704-466 *E-mail:* d.piper@schweitzer-online.de; Kerst, Tonhallenstr 11a, 47051 Duisburg, Contact: Christina Elbers *Tel:* (0231) 572579 *Fax:* (0231) 554263 *E-mail:* c.elbers@schweitzer-online.de; Kerst & Schweitzer oHG, Solmsstr 75, 60486 Frankfurt am Main, Contact: Christoph Kunz *Tel:* (069) 460934-47 *Fax:* (069) 460934-11 *E-mail:* c.kunz@schweitzer-online.de; Schweitzer am campus, Barfuesserstr 12, 06108 Halle (Saale), Contact: Sylvia Helmrich *Tel:* (0345) 501 333 *Fax:* (0345) 501 334 *E-mail:* halle@schweitzer-online.de; Fachbuchhandlung Herrmann, Volgersweg 4a, 30175 Hannover, Contact: Marion Raupach *Tel:* (0511) 343524 *Fax:* (0511) 344547 *E-mail:* m.raupach@schweitzer-online.de; Hoser & Mende KG, Karlstr 76, 76137 Karlsruhe, Contact: Constanze Koch *Tel:* (0721) 98161-29 *Fax:* (0721) 815343 *E-mail:* c.koch@schweitzer-online.de; ZNL der Goethe Buchhandlung Teubig GmbH, Universitaetsstr 20, 04109 Leipzig, Contact: Michael Palmowske *Tel:* (0351) 471 56 46 *Fax:* (0351) 471 58 37 *E-mail:* m.palmowske@schweitzer-online.de; Scherell & Mundt, Kaiser-Friedrich-Str 6, 55116 Mainz, Contact: Christoph Kunz *Tel:* (069) 460934-47 *Fax:* (069) 460934-11 *E-mail:* c.kunz@schweitzer-online.de; Zeiser & Buettner oHG, Hallplatz 3, 90402 Nuremberg, Contact: Elisabeth Konrad *Tel:* (0911) 23 68-277 *Fax:* (0911) 23 68-103 *E-mail:* e.konrad@schweitzer-online.de; Buchhandlung Thye, Schlossplatz 21-23, 26122 Oldenburg, Contact: Monika Pfeil *Tel:* (0441) 36 13 66-13 *Fax:* (0441) 36 13 66-33 *E-mail:* m.pfeil@schweitzer-online.de; Hoser & Mende KG, Wilhelmstr 12, 70182 Stuttgart, Contact: Rebecca A Guertler *Tel:* (0711) 16354-39 *Fax:* (0711) 16354-52 *E-mail:* r.guertler@schweitzer-online.de; Scherell & Mundt, Gerichtsstr 9, 65185 Wiesbaden, Contact: Christoph Kunz *Tel:* (069) 460934-47 *Fax:* (069) 460934-11 *E-mail:* c.kunz@schweitzer-online.de

Antiquariat Elvira Tasbach
Kronberger Str 20, 14193 Berlin
Tel: (030) 824 22 89 *Fax:* (030) 823 64 63
E-mail: antiquariat-tasbach@t-online.de
Web Site: www.tasbach-rare-books.com
Key Personnel
Owner: Elvira Tasbach
Founded: 1986
Subjects include early printing, economics, law, Prussian history & social sciences.
Type of Business: Major Independent Bookseller

Teo Ferrer de Mesquita Verlag-Vertrieb-Versandbuchhandlung
Grosse Seestr 47, 60486 Frankfurt am Main
Mailing Address: Postfach 10 08 39, 60008 Frankfurt am Main
Tel: (069) 282647 *Fax:* (069) 287363
E-mail: info@tfmonline.de
Web Site: www.tfmonline.de
Type of Business: Distributor

Antiquariat Trauzettel
Haumuehle 8, 52223 Stolberg
Tel: (02402) 81 54 2 *Fax:* (02402) 82 55 9
E-mail: info@antiquariat-trauzettel.de
Web Site: www.antiquariat-trauzettel.de
Key Personnel
Owner: Guenther Trauzettel
Type of Business: Major Independent Bookseller

Tresor am Roemer-Buch-und Kunstantiquariat
Braubachstr 32, 60311 Frankfurt am Main
Tel: (069) 281248 *Fax:* (069) 282160
E-mail: info@tresor-am-roemer.de
Web Site: www.tresor-am-roemer.de
Key Personnel
Proprietor: Sibylle Wieduwilt
Founded: 1977
Membership(s): Verband Deutscher Antiquare eV.
Type of Business: Major Independent Bookseller

G Umbreit GmbH & Co KG
Mundelsheimer Str 3, 74321 Bietigheim-
Bissingen
Tel: (07142) 596-0 *Fax:* (07142) 596-200
E-mail: info@umbreit.de
Web Site: www.umbreit-kg.de
Key Personnel
Mng Dir: Clemens Birk *Tel:* (07142) 596-118
Fax: (07142) 596-280 *E-mail:* clemens.birk@
umbreit.de
Founded: 1912
Type of Business: Distributor, Wholesaler

**Verlag Universitaetsbuchhandlung Blazek &
Bergmann**
Goetheplatz 11, 60313 Frankfurt am Main
Tel: (069) 138132-0; (069) 288648
Type of Business: Major Independent Bookseller
Owned by: Hunzinger Information AG

**Universitaetsbuchhandlung Bouvier
Verpachtungs GmbH**
Fuerstenstr 3, 53111 Bonn
Tel: (0228) 3 91 82 10 *Fax:* (0228) 3 91 82 21
E-mail: info@bouvier-verlag.de
Web Site: www.bouvier-verlag.de
Key Personnel
Mng Dir: Richard Feldmann
Manager: Thomas Grundmann
Type of Business: Major Independent Bookseller
Branch Office(s)
Pferdmengesstr 12, 50968 Cologne

Vice Versa Distribution GmbH
Immanuelkirchstr 12, 10405 Berlin
Tel: (030) 616 092 36 *Fax:* (030) 616 092 38
E-mail: info@vice-versa-distribution.com
Web Site: www.vice-versa-distribution.com; www.
vice-versa-select.com
Key Personnel
Mng Dir: Heike Salchli; Malte Nisch
Distribute publications from publishers, museums
& galleries with a focus on books, exhibition
catalogs, magazines & DVDs on architecture,
design, photography, art & theory.
Type of Business: Distributor

Antiquariat Dr Wolfgang Wanzke
Gartenstr 1a, 86459 Gessertshausen
Tel: (08234) 9657758
E-mail: antiquariat.wanzke@t-online.de
Web Site: antiquariat-wanzke.antiquar.de
Key Personnel
Owner: Dr Wolfgang Wanzke
Founded: 1991
Rare & out-of-print books, 16th-20th century.
Membership(s): Antiquariate im Netz; Boersen-
verein des Deutschen Buchhandels; Genossen-
schaft der Internet Antiquare eG (GIAQ); Inter-
nationale Liga der Antiquariatslouchhaendler;
Verband Deutscher Antiquare eV.
Type of Business: Major Independent Bookseller

Erich-Weinert-Universitaetsbuchhandlung
Ulrichplatz 4-6, 39104 Magdeburg
Tel: (0391) 56859-0
Founded: 1960
Type of Business: Major Independent Bookseller

**Konrad Wittwer GmbH Verlags -und
Sortimentsbuchhandlung**
Koenigstr 30, 70173 Stuttgart
Tel: (0711) 25 07 0 *Fax:* (0711) 25 07 145
E-mail: info@wittwer.de
Web Site: www.wittwer.de
Key Personnel
Mng Dir: Dr Konrad M Wittwer *E-mail:* konrad.
martin.wittwer@wittwer.de; Michael Wittwer
E-mail: rainer.bartle@wittwer.de
Founded: 1867
Type of Business: Major Independent Bookseller
Bookshop(s): Uni-book Pfaffenwald, Pfaffen-
waldring 45, Stuttgart *Tel:* (0711) 682 709
E-mail: pfaffenwald@wittwer.de; Univer-
sity of Hohenheim Bookshop, Fruwirthstr
24, 70599 Stuttgart *Tel:* (0711) 4586265
E-mail: hohenheim@wittwer.de; Buchhand-
lung Wittwer, Heinkelstr 1-11, Ludwigsburg
Tel: (07141) 22177-12; (07141) 22177-22
E-mail: ludwigsburg@wittwer.de; Buchhand-
lung Wittwer, Tilsit Rd 15, 71065 Sindelfingen
Tel: (07031) 410-34-72 *E-mail:* sindelfingen@
wittwer.de

Ghana

Ghana Publishing Co Ltd
Assembly Press, PO Box GP 124, Accra
Tel: (021) 664338; (021) 664339
E-mail: info@ghpublishingcompany.com
Web Site: www.ghpublishingcompany.com
Founded: 1965
Type of Business: Distributor

**Kwame Nkrumah University of Science &
Technology Bookshop**
PMB, University Post Office, Kumasi
Tel: (032) 2060331 *Fax:* (032) 2060137
E-mail: registrar@knust.edu.gh
Web Site: www.knust.edu.gh
Type of Business: Major Independent Bookseller

Presbyterian Book Depot Ltd
Makola, PO Box 4276, Accra
Tel: (021) 666312; (021) 660779
Founded: 1870
The organization comprises bookselling, sta-
tionery supply, printing (Presbyterian Press) &
publishing activities (see Waterville Publishing
House under Publishers). Newspapers-Christian
Messenger & The Presbyterian.
Type of Business: Distributor, Importer, Major
Book Chain Headquarters, Wholesaler
Owned by: Presbyterian Church of Ghana, PO
Box 1800, Accra
Branch Office(s)
PO Box 195, Accra *Tel:* (030) 2689971
PO Box 70, Akim Oda *Tel:* (034) 2922181
Bank Rd, Adum, Kumasi *Tel:* (032) 2028145
PO Box 16, Nkawkaw *Tel:* (034) 3122010
H/No D10 Market Sq, Tamale *Tel:* (037) 2022382

University of Ghana Bookshop
PO Box LG 1, Accra
Tel: (030) 2500398 *Fax:* (030) 2500774
E-mail: bookshop@ug.edu.gh
Founded: 1948
General books.
Type of Business: Major Independent Bookseller
Owned by: University of Ghana, PO Box LG 25,
Legon

Gibraltar

Gibraltar Bookshop
300 Main St, Gibraltar
Tel: 20071894 *Fax:* 20075554
Founded: 1973
Type of Business: Distributor, Major Independent
Bookseller

Greece

Aithra Scientific Bookstore
One Messologiou, 116 Solonos, 106 81 Athens
Tel: 2103301269; 2103302622 *Fax:* 2103302622
E-mail: aithra@otenet.gr
Web Site: www.aithra.gr
Founded: 1984
Specialize in books on mathematics, physics,
chemistry, computer science, astronomy, ge-
ology & meteorology.
Type of Business: Exporter, Importer, Major Inde-
pendent Bookseller, Wholesaler

Anastasiadis Ekdoseis
28 Oktovriou (Patision) 306, 111 41 Athens
Tel: 2102284013
Type of Business: Distributor, Wholesaler

Ekdoseis Ankyra (Publications Ankara)
271 Lamprou Katsoni & G Papandreou St, Ag
Anargiri, 135 62 Athens
Tel: 210 2693800-4 *Fax:* 210 2693806
E-mail: info@e-agyra.gr; order@e-agyra.gr
Web Site: e-agyra.gr
Key Personnel
Marketing & Editorial Rights Manager: Anna Pa-
padimitriou *E-mail:* annapap@e-agyra.gr
Sales: Dimitra Papadimitriou
E-mail: dpapadimitriou1964@gmail.com
Founded: 1890
Type of Business: Major Independent Bookseller

Ekdoseis M Bacharakis
13 Nikis Av, 546 23 Thessaloniki
Tel: 2310262411; 2310270200
E-mail: aristotelous@baharakis.gr
Web Site: www.baharakis.gr
Founded: 1967
Also publisher.
Type of Business: Distributor, Wholesaler

Giorgos Dardanos, see Typothito G Dardanos

Diavlos SA
72-74 Mavromichali Str, 106 80 Athens
Tel: 2103631169 *Fax:* 2103617473
E-mail: info@diavlos-books.gr
Web Site: www.diavlos-books.com
Key Personnel
President & Mng Dir: Emmanuel Deligiannakis
E-mail: emmanuel.deligiannakis@diavlosbooks.
gr
Founded: 1989
Specialize in scientific & technical texts in mathe-
matics, computer science, astrology, business &
marketing, translation & theatrical studies.
Type of Business: Distributor, Exporter, Major
Independent Bookseller

Ekdoseis Dion
39 Filikis Etaireias, 546 21 Thessaloniki
Tel: 2310265042 *Fax:* 2310265083
E-mail: info@psarasbooks.gr
Web Site: www.psarasbooks.gr
Founded: 1984

Bookshop & publications.
Type of Business: Distributor, Major Independent
  Bookseller, Wholesaler
Owned by: E Psaras & Co

Eleftheri Skepsis
112 Ippokratous St, 114 72 Athens
Tel: 2103614736
E-mail: info@eleftheriskepsis.gr
Web Site: www.eleftheriskepsis.gr
Founded: 1976
Type of Business: Major Independent Bookseller

G C Eleftheroudakis SA
15 Panepistimiou, 105 64 Athens
Tel: 2103258440; 2103317603 *Fax:* 2103239821
E-mail: internet@books.gr
Web Site: books.gr
Key Personnel
Executive Dir: John Sax
President: Marina Eleftheroudakis *E-mail:* m.
  eleftheroudakis@books.gr
Purchasing: George Agiovlasitis
  E-mail: agiovlasitis@books.gr
Founded: 1918
Also publisher.
Type of Business: Major Book Chain Headquar-
  ters
Bookshop(s): Nikis, Athens 105 63

Publications Enalios
Solon 136, 106 77 Athens
Tel: 2103829339 *Fax:* 2103829659
E-mail: info@enalios.gr
Web Site: www.enalios.gr
Key Personnel
Founder: Eleni Kekropoulou
Founded: 1996
Type of Business: Wholesaler

Esoptron
Armodiou 14, 105 52 Athens
Tel: 2103236852 *Fax:* 2103210472
E-mail: esoptron@otenet.gr
Web Site: www.esoptronpublications.gr
Type of Business: Wholesaler
Bookshop(s): 49 Panepistimiou Str, 106 78 Stoa
  Orfeos, Athens

Grivas Publications
3 Irodotou St, 193 00 Aspropyrgos, Attiki
Mailing Address: PO Box 72, 193 00 Aspropyr-
  gos, Attiki
Tel: 2105573470 *Fax:* 2105574086
E-mail: info@grivas.gr; grivasbooks@yahoo.gr
Web Site: www.grivas.gr
Founded: 1985
Specialize in English as a Foreign Language
  (EFL) books.
Type of Business: Distributor, Exporter, Importer
Branch Office(s)
4 Moustakli & Doridos St, 122 43 Attiki

Ekdoseis Iamvlichos
Notar 27, 106 83 Athens
Tel: 2103807828 *Fax:* 2103807435
Web Site: www.iamvlichos.gr
Founded: 1984

Ikaros Publishing Co
4 Voulis St, 105 62 Athens
Tel: 210 3225152 *Fax:* 210 3235262
E-mail: info@ikarosbooks.gr
Web Site: ikarosbooks.gr
Founded: 1943
Specialize in Greek poetry.
Owned by: Katerina & Ch Karydi

Kauffmann SA
28, Stadiou St, 105 64 Athens

Tel: 2103255321; 2103222160; 2103827844
E-mail: kauffmann.stadiou@yahoo.gr; ord@
  otenet.gr (orders)
Type of Business: Major Independent Bookseller
Bookshop(s): 60, Sina St, 106 72 Athens
  Tel: 2103643433 *Fax:* 2103633626
  E-mail: kauffmannsina@yahoo.gr; Ki-
  afas St, 106 78 Athens *Tel:* 2103818859
  Fax: 2103824786

Kritiki Publishing SA
4 Papadiamantopoulou, 115 28 Athens
Tel: 2108211811
E-mail: biblia@kritiki.gr
Web Site: kritiki.gr
Founded: 1987
Also publisher.
  Specialize in university textbooks in social sci-
  ences & humanities, economics, finance, math-
  ematics, political theory, sociology, anthropol-
  ogy & psychology.
Type of Business: Distributor, Major Independent
  Bookseller
Warehouse: Nevrokopiou 8, Athens 118 55
  Tel: 2108211470 *Fax:* 2108211487

Kyriakidis Brothers SA
Konstantinou Melenikou 5, 546 35 Thessaloniki
Tel: 2310208540 *Fax:* 2310245541
E-mail: info@kyriakidis.gr
Web Site: www.kyriakidis.gr
Founded: 1993
Type of Business: Major Independent Bookseller,
  Wholesaler

Malliaris - Pedia
Ermou 53, 546 23 Thessaloniki
Tel: 2310252888; 2310252889 *Fax:* 2310252890
E-mail: ermou@malliaris.gr
Web Site: www.malliaris.gr
Key Personnel
Head: Vaso Ziana
Sales Manager: John Papavasileiou
  E-mail: papavasileiou@malliaris.gr
Founded: 1985
Type of Business: Major Book Chain Headquar-
  ters
Bookshop(s): D Gounaris 39, 546 22
  Thessaloniki, Manager: Apostolos
  Varveris *Tel:* 2310278707; 2310277113
  Fax: 2310264856 *E-mail:* info@malliaris.gr;
  25 Maptioc, 51, 564 29 N Efkarpia, Manager:
  Efi Bakirtzi *Tel:* 2310640755; 2310640756
  Fax: 2310640757

Melissa Publishing House
58 Skoufa St, 106 80 Athens
Tel: 2103611692 *Fax:* 2103600865
E-mail: info@melissabooks.com; webmaster@
  melissabooks.com
Web Site: www.melissabooks.com
Key Personnel
Founder: George Ragias
Founded: 1954
Specialize in illustrated books on art, architecture,
  history, archaeology & Greek civilization.
Type of Business: Distributor, Major Independent
  Bookseller

Olkos Editions
56 Sina str, 106 72 Athens
Tel: 2103621379 *Fax:* 2103625576
E-mail: info@olkos.gr
Web Site: olkos.gr
Founded: 1973
Type of Business: Major Independent Bookseller

Pournaras Panagiotis
7 Panagias Dexias, 546 35 Thessaloniki
Tel: 2310270941 *Fax:* 2310228922
E-mail: info@kyriakidiseditions.gr

Web Site: www.pournarasbooks.gr
Founded: 1960
International library suppliers & publisher.
Type of Business: Distributor, Exporter, Importer,
  Major Independent Bookseller

Press Photo Publications
One Troupaki Str, 104 45 Athens
Tel: 2108541400 *Fax:* 2108541485
E-mail: info@photo.gr; eshop@photo.gr
Web Site: www.photo.gr
Founded: 1989
Type of Business: Major Independent Bookseller

Road Editions, see Travel Bookstore

Salto Publishers
21, Angelaki St, 546 21 Thessaloniki
Tel: 2310267108 *Fax:* 2310267108; 2310262854
E-mail: info@salto.gr
Web Site: www.salto.gr
Founded: 1985
Type of Business: Distributor, Major Independent
  Bookseller

Travel Bookstore
71 Solonos Str, 106 79 Athens
Tel: 2103616943 *Fax:* 2103616948
E-mail: info@travelbookstore.gr
Web Site: www.travelbookstore.gr
Retailer of maps & travel guides.
Type of Business: Exporter
Owned by: Nakas Group
Bookshop(s): 23 km Marathonos Ave, Rafina, 190
  09 Attica *Tel:* 2294032670 *Fax:* 2294079817
  E-mail: rafina@travelbookstore.gr

Typothito G Dardanos
37 Didotou, 106 80 Athens
Tel: 2103642003 *Fax:* 2103642030
E-mail: info@dardanosnet.gr
Web Site: www.dardanosnet.gr
Key Personnel
President: Giorgos Dardanos
Founded: 1993
Also publisher.
Type of Business: Distributor, Exporter, Importer,
  Major Independent Bookseller

G Vlassi Afoi OE
116 Solwnos & 2-4 Lontoy, 106 81 Athens
Tel: 2103812900 *Fax:* 2103827557
E-mail: info@vlassi.gr
Web Site: www.vlassi.gr
Key Personnel
Contact: Ioannis Vlassis; Anna Maria Vlassi-
  Galerou
Founded: 1964

Bookstore Zachariadis
Proxenou Koromila 20, 546 22 Thessaloniki
Tel: 2310276334
E-mail: info@zbooks.gr
Web Site: www.zbooks.gr
Key Personnel
Owner: Petros Zachariadis *E-mail:* petros@
  zbooks.gr
Founded: 1972
German book & information center, Greek gen-
  eral bookstore, Italian bookstore.
Type of Business: Exporter, Importer, Major Inde-
  pendent Bookseller

Guatemala

Piedra Santa Editorial & Librerias
37 Ave, 1-26, Zona 7, 01007 Guatemala City

SAN: 002-6204
Tel: 2422-7676
E-mail: info@piedrasanta.com
Web Site: www.piedrasanta.com
Key Personnel
Dir: Irene Piedra Santa
Founded: 1947
Also acts as publisher.
Type of Business: Distributor, Exporter, Importer,
    Major Book Chain Headquarters
Branch Office(s)
11° Calle 6-50, Zona 1, Guatemala City
    Tel: 2204-6600 *E-mail:* 11calle@piedrasanta.
    com
5a calle 7-55 zona 1, Guatemala City *Tel:* 2204-
    6601 *E-mail:* 5acalle@piedrasanta.com
12 calle, 1-25 zona 10, Edificio Geminis, piso 2,
    locales 202 y 203, Guatemala City *Tel:* 2204-
    6602 *E-mail:* geminis@piedrasanta.com
Km 5 Carretera al Atlantico zona 17, CC
    Metronorte, local 251, Guatemala City
    Tel: 2204-6603 *E-mail:* metronorte@
    piedrasanta.com

Libreria Universal
13 Calle 4-16 Zona 1, Guatemala City
Tel: 22328484
Type of Business: Distributor
Owned by: Distribuidora General Universal

Guyana

Austin's Book Services
190 Church St, Cummingsburg, Georgetown
Tel: (02) 227-7395 *Fax:* (02) 227-7396
E-mail: austins@guyana.net.gy
Key Personnel
Mng Dir: Lloyd F Austin
Founded: 1993
Type of Business: Distributor, Importer, Major
    Independent Bookseller
Owned by: Lloyd & Lelp Austin

Hong Kong

Hong Kong Book Centre Ltd
Affiliate of Swindon Book Co Ltd
On Lok Yuen Bldg Lower Level, 25 Des Voeux
    Rd, Central Hong Kong
Tel: 2522 7064; 2522 7065
E-mail: enquiry@hkbookcentre.com; webstore@
    hkbookcentre.com (order enquiries);
    marketing@hkbookcentre.com
Web Site: www.swindonbooks.com
Founded: 1962
Type of Business: Major Independent Bookseller
Branch Office(s)
13-15 Lock Rd, Tsimshatsui, Kowloon *Tel:* 2366
    8001

Swindon Book Co Ltd
13-15 Lock Rd, Tsimshatsui, Kowloon
Tel: 2366 8001
E-mail: webstore@hkbookcentre.com
Web Site: www.swindonbooks.com
Founded: 1918
Book & stationery retail & distribution; filofax
    agency; OECD publications.
Type of Business: Distributor, Major Independent
    Bookseller

Hungary

Foldvari Antikvarium
Henszlmann Imre u 3, Budapest 1053
Tel: (020) 4182552
E-mail: info@foldvaribooks.com
Web Site: www.foldvaribooks.com
Founded: 2007
Specialize in rare books on avant-garde, Judaica,
    literature, philosophy & art. Buy & sell first
    editions, manuscripts, original graphics, pho-
    tographs, prints & maps.
Type of Business: Major Independent Bookseller

Hungarica HB
Beethoven u 14/B, Pomaz 2013
Mailing Address: PO Box 146, 2013 Pomaz
Tel: (026) 365 967
E-mail: book@hungarica.hu
Web Site: www.hungarica.hu
Key Personnel
Owner: Hajdu Bela
Founded: 1997
Type of Business: Exporter

Librotrade Kft
Pesti ut 237, 1173 Budapest
Tel: (01) 254-0-254 *Fax:* (01) 257-74-72
E-mail: librotrade@librotrade.hu
Web Site: www.librotrade.hu
Type of Business: Importer

Talentum Konyves es Kereskedo Kft
Hrsz 062/115, Torokbalint 2045
Tel: (01) 3-541-365
Web Site: talentumkonyve-c.cegbongeszo.hu
Type of Business: Distributor, Importer, Whole-
    saler

Iceland

Bokabud Mals og menningar
Laugavegi 18, 101 Reykjavik
Tel: 580 5000
E-mail: bmm@bmm.is
Web Site: www.bmm.is
Founded: 1937
Type of Business: Distributor, Exporter, Importer,
    Wholesaler

Boksala Studenta (The University Bookstore)
Division of Felagsstofnun Studenta (Icelandic
    Student Services)
Saemundargotu 4, 101 Reykjavik
Tel: (05) 700-777 *Fax:* (05) 700-778
E-mail: boksala@boksala.is
Web Site: www.boksala.is
Key Personnel
General Manager: Valdis Elisdottir *Tel:* (05) 700-
    780 *E-mail:* valdis@boksala.is
Purchasing Manager (Computer Books):
    Reinhard Reinharsson *Tel:* (05) 700-782
    E-mail: reinhard@boksala.is
Founded: 1968
All subjects with a concentration on academic &
    professional literature, textbooks.
Type of Business: Distributor, Importer, Major
    Independent Bookseller

India

AEWP, *imprint of* Affiliated East-West Press Pvt
Ltd

Affiliated East-West Press Pvt Ltd
G-1/16, Ansari Rd, Darya Ganj, New Delhi 110
    002
Tel: (011) 23279113 *Fax:* (011) 23260538
E-mail: aewp.pub@gmail.com
Web Site: www.aewpress.com
Key Personnel
Owner: Sunny Malik
Founded: 1962
Expertise in society publications & distribution;
    publishers of undergraduate & graduate STM
    Books.
Type of Business: Distributor, Importer, Whole-
    saler
Imprints: AEWP

Allied Publishers Pvt Ltd
1/13-14 Asaf Ali Rd, New Delhi 110 002
Tel: (011) 2323 9001; (011) 2323 3002
E-mail: exports@alliedpublishers.com; delhi.
    books@alliedpublishers.com; printdiv@
    alliedpublishers.com
Web Site: www.alliedpublishers.com
Key Personnel
Dir: Mr R N Purwar *Tel:* 9810114020 (cell)
    E-mail: rnpurwar@alliedpublishers.com
Mng Dir: Mr Sunil Sachdev *Tel:* (011) 2323 5967
Dir, Allied Printing Division: Mr Ravi Sachdev
    Tel: (011) 2811 3682
Sales Dir: Mr Amit Sachdev
    E-mail: amitsachdev@alliedpublishers.com
Founded: 1934
Also a printer.
Type of Business: Distributor, Exporter, Importer,
    Wholesaler
Owned by: Allied Publishers Group
Branch Office(s)
F/1, Sun House, 1st floor, CG Rd, Ahmedabad
    380 006, Sales Manager: Mr D C Khopker
    Tel: (079) 2646 5916 *E-mail:* ahmbd.books@
    alliedpublishers.com
The Hebbar Sreevaishnava Sabha, Sudarshan
    Complex-2, No 22, Seshadri Rd, Banga-
    lore 560 009, Branch Manager: Mr P Chan-
    drashekar *Tel:* (080) 2226 2081 *E-mail:* bngl.
    books@alliedpublishers.com
751, Anna Salai, Chennai 600 002, Branch Man-
    ager: Mr S Ramdos *Tel:* (044) 2852 3938
    E-mail: chennai.books@alliedpublishers.com
3-2-844/6 & 7, Kachiguda Station Rd, Hyder-
    abad 500 027, Branch Manager: Mr L Vasan-
    thakrishnan *Tel:* (040) 2461 9079 *E-mail:* hyd.
    books@alliedpublishers.com
17, Chittaranjan Ave, Kolkata 700 072, Area Dir:
    Mr Jatinder Sachdev *Tel:* (033) 2212 9618
    E-mail: cal.books@alliedpublishers.com
87/4, Chander Nagar, Alambagh, Lucknow 226
    005, Manager: Mr Atul Srivastava *Tel:* (0522)
    4012850 *E-mail:* appltdlko9@gmail.com
15, JN Heredia Marg, Dubash House, Ballard Es-
    tate, Mumbai 400 001, Branch Manager: Mr A
    George *Tel:* (022) 4212 6969 *E-mail:* mumbai.
    books@alliedpublishers.com
Shiv Sundar Apartments, Ground floor, 60 Ba-
    jaj Nagar, Central Bazar Rd, Nagpur 440
    010, Branch Manager: Mr Pradeep Parashar
    Tel: (0712) 2234210 *E-mail:* ngp.books@
    alliedpublishers.com

Ane Books Pvt Ltd
4821 Parwana Bhawan, 24 Ansari Rd, Darya
    Ganj, New Delhi 110 002
Tel: (011) 23276843; (011) 23276844 *Fax:* (011)
    23276863
Web Site: www.anebooks.com

Key Personnel
Chief Executive Officer: Jai Raj Kapoor
  E-mail: kapoor@anebooks.com
Dir: Sunil Saxena
General Manager, South: A Rathinam
Regional Manager, West: T M Mathew
Founded: 1997
Type of Business: Distributor
Branch Office(s)
Avantika Niwas, 19, Doraiswamy Rd, 1st
  floor, T Nagar, Chennai, Tamil Nadu 600
  017 *Tel:* (044) 28141554; (044) 42127568
  E-mail: anebookschennai@gmail.com
138, Chandan Chambers, 1st floor, Off No 3,
  Modi St Fort, Mumbai, Maharashtra 400
  001 *Tel:* (022) 22622440; (022) 22622441
  E-mail: anebooksmum@gmail.com

Atma Ram & Sons
1376 Kashmere Gate, New Delhi 110 006
Tel: (011) 23973082; (011) 23946466
Also publisher.
Type of Business: Importer

Biblia Impex Pvt Ltd
2/18, Ansari Rd, New Delhi 110 002
Tel: (011) 2327 8034 *Fax:* (011) 2328 2047
E-mail: contact@bibliaimpex.com
Web Site: www.bibliaimpex.com
Key Personnel
Dir: Aditya Kumar Goel
Founded: 1963
International bookseller & subscription agent.
Type of Business: Distributor, Exporter, Major
  Independent Bookseller

Books & Periodicals Agency
WZ 241 A/1 Inder Puri, New Delhi 110 012
Tel: (085) 27000654
E-mail: web@bpagency.com
Web Site: www.bpagency.com
Key Personnel
Proprietor: Girish Gupta
Founded: 1973
Exporter of books on South Asia & Southeast
  Asia. Over 100,000 titles in 356 subjects.
Type of Business: Distributor, Exporter, Major
  Independent Bookseller

CBS Publishers & Distributors Pvt Ltd
CBS Plaza, 4819/XI, Prahlad St, 24 Ansari Rd,
  Darya Ganj, New Delhi 110 002
Tel: (011) 23289259; (011) 23266861; (011)
  23266867 *Fax:* (011) 23243014
E-mail: delhi@cbspd.com; cbspubs@airtelmail.in
Web Site: www.cbspd.com
Key Personnel
Head: Mr Satish Kumar Jain
Founded: 1972
Also publisher.
Type of Business: Distributor, Exporter
Branch Office(s)
204 Patparganj, Industrial Area, New Delhi 110
  092 *Tel:* (011) 49344934 *Fax:* (011) 49344935
  E-mail: admin@cbspd.com
Seema House, 2975, 17th Cross, K R Rd,
  Bansankari 2nd Stage, Bangalore 560 070
  Tel: (080) 26771678; (080) 26771679
  Fax: (080) 26771680 *E-mail:* bangalore@
  cbspd.com
No 7, Subbaraya St, Shenoy Nagar, Chennai 600
  030 *Tel:* (044) 26680620; (044) 26681266
  E-mail: chennai@cbspd.com
Ashana House, No 39/1904, AM Thomas
  Rd, Valanjambalam, Ernakulam, Kochi 682
  016 *Tel:* (0484) 4059061; (0484) 4059067
  E-mail: kochi@cbspd.com

Rameswar Shaw Rd, No 6/B, Ground floor,
  Kolkata 700 014 *Tel:* (033) 22891126; (033)
  22891128 *E-mail:* kolkata@cbspd.com
83-C, 1st floor, Dr E Moses Rd, Worli, Mumbai
  400 018 *Tel:* (022) 24902340; (022) 24902341
  E-mail: mumbai@cbspd.com

CTL, see Current Technical Literature Co Pvt
Ltd (CTL)

**Current Technical Literature Co Pvt Ltd
(CTL)**
Malhotra House, Opposite GPO, 1st floor, Mum-
  bai, Maharashtra 400 001
Tel: (022) 22617616; (022) 22611045 *Fax:* (022)
  22679786
E-mail: infomumbai@ctlindia.org
Web Site: www.ctlindia.org
Key Personnel
Chairman & Mng Dir: Viswanath Krishnamurthy
Book Sales: Roopa Narayan
Finance & Operations: Deepa Viswanath
Founded: 1946
Scientific, technical & medical books. Branch of-
  fices in Bangalore, Chennai, Hyderabad, Kochi
  & New Delhi.
Type of Business: Distributor

DK Agencies (P) Ltd
A/15-17, DK Ave, Mohan Garden, Najafgarh Rd,
  New Delhi 110 059
Tel: (011) 2535-7104; (011) 2535-7105
  Fax: (011) 2535-7103
E-mail: information@dkagencies.com
Web Site: www.dkagencies.com
Key Personnel
Owner: Ankur Mittal
Dir: Ramesh K Mittal
Founded: 1968
Indian books, periodicals & multimedia (audio,
  video, CDs & microfilms from India). Also
  publisher & subscription agent.
Type of Business: Distributor, Exporter, Major
  Independent Bookseller, Wholesaler

Dolphin Publications Pvt Ltd
Western India Art Litho Bldg, 1st floor Plot No
  107, Marol Co-Op Industrial Estate, off M V
  Rd, Marol, Andheri-East, Mumbai 400 057
Tel: (022) 40763000
Founded: 1986
Type of Business: Distributor

English Book Store
17-L Connaught Circus, New Delhi 110 001
Tel: (011) 2341-5031 *Fax:* (011) 2341-7731
E-mail: info@englishbookstore.net
Web Site: www.englishbookstore.net
Key Personnel
Owner: Siddharth Chowdhri
Partner: Bhupinder Chowdhri
Founded: 1936
Subjects include aviation & military.
Type of Business: Importer, Major Independent
  Bookseller

EWP, see Affiliated East-West Press Pvt Ltd

Galgotia Publications Pvt Ltd
5, Ansari Rd, Darya Ganj, New Delhi 110 002
Mailing Address: PO Box 7221, Darya Ganj,
  New Delhi 110 002
Tel: (011) 23263334; (011) 23288134; (011)
  23713227; (011) 23713228 *Fax:* (011)
  23281909
Key Personnel
Chief Executive Officer: Mr Dhruv Galgotia
Founded: 1933

Distribute children's, technical & management
  books.
Type of Business: Distributor, Importer, Major
  Independent Bookseller, Wholesaler

GBD Books, see General Book Depot

General Book Depot
I-2/16, Ansari Rd, 1st floor, Opposite Saraswati
  School, Darya Ganj, New Delhi 110 002
Tel: (011) 2326 0022
E-mail: contact@goyalbookshop.com;
  generalbookdepot@yahoo.com
Web Site: www.pigeonbooks.in
Key Personnel
Partner: Arjun Goyal *Tel:* 9871225151 (cell)
  E-mail: gbd.arjun@gmail.com; Kaushal Goyal
  Tel: 9810229648 (cell) *E-mail:* kaushalgoyal@
  yahoo.com
Founded: 1933
Type of Business: Distributor
Showroom(s): 1691, Nai Sarak, Post Box 1220,
  Delhi 110 006 *Tel:* (011) 2326 3695; (011)
  2325 0635

Giri Trading Agency Pvt Ltd
Modi Niwas Opposite Post Office, Matunga,
  Mumbai 400 019
Tel: (022) 24118107 *Fax:* (022) 24143140
E-mail: sales@giri.in
Web Site: giri.in
Key Personnel
Dir: T S Srinivasan
Founded: 1951
Producers of audio cassettes specializing in all
  (A-Z) items pertaining to Hindu Religion; also
  acts as publisher of English & all South Indian
  language books. Supplier of all items pertain-
  ing to Hindu worship.
Membership(s): Booksellers & Publishers of
  South India.
Type of Business: Distributor, Exporter, Major
  Independent Bookseller, Wholesaler
Owned by: Giri Publications; Gitaa Cassettes;
  Kaamakoti-Tamil Monthly Magazine
Bookshop(s): Mythili Co-operative Housing So-
  ciety Ltd, Rd No 2, Ground floor, Pestom
  Sagar, Chembur, Mumbai 400 089 *Tel:* (022)
  25277012; SIES Engineering & Computer
  College Complex, Anjaneyar Temple, Nerul,
  Navi, Mumbai 400 706 *Tel:* (022) 27707664;
  Seva Dham 'A' Wing, Shripal Nagar, Ra-
  jaji Path, Opposite Madrasi, Mandir, Dom-
  bivili (E) Thane District, Mumbai 421 201
  Tel: (0251) 244 9585; 2 Siddhi Vinayak
  Apartments, Bangur Nagar, Goregon (W),
  Mumbai 400 104 *Tel:* (022) 28767298; 5
  Cross Rd, 23/3 Ground floor, Sampige Rd,
  Malleswaram, Bangalore 560 003 *Tel:* (080)
  23563001; 14 Kapaleswarar Sannidhi St, My-
  lapore, Chennai 600 004 *Tel:* (044) 24640376;
  (044) 24953820; Shop A, Plot No 17, Gandhi
  Rd, Alwar Thirunagar, Opposite Chinthamani
  Vinayagar Temple, Chennai 600 087 *Tel:* (044)
  23775483; (044) 43856467; No 8, Tenth St,
  Near Anjaneyar Temple & Ragavender Temple, Nanganallur, Chennai 600 061 *Tel:* (044)
  4358889; (044) 22671335; Door No 179, Y
  Block, First St, Sixth Main Rd, Anna Nagar, Chennai 600 004 *Tel:* (044) 26203551;
  372/1, Mangadu Pattor Koot Rd, Mangadu,
  Chennai 600 122 *Tel:* (044) 66939393; No
  17/51 N Mada St, Thiruvanmiyur, Chennai
  600 041 *Tel:* (044) 42188060; New No 4, Old
  No 73, Moorthy St, West Mambalam, Chennai 600 033 *Tel:* (044) 23713347; 36, Du-
  raisamy Reddy St, West Tambaram, Chennai
  600 045 *Tel:* (044) 22262010; 372/1, Mangadu
  Pattur Koot Rd, Mangadu, Chennai 600 122
  Tel: (044) 66939393; Shop F6, T M House,
  92, Thruvenkatasami Salai West, Near Kamakshi Amman Koil, R S Puram, Coimbat-

ore 641 002 *Tel:* (0422) 2541523; No 5, Kamakshi Amman Sannadhi St, Kanchipuram 631 502 *Tel:* (04112) 224415; 15 North Tower St, Madurai 625 001 *Tel:* (0452) 2628090; Sri Subramanya Swamy Devalayam, Padmarao Nagar, Skandagiri, Secunderabad 500 061 *Tel:* (040) 27503046; D/1, First Cross, NE Extern, Near Passport Off, Thillai Nagar, Trichy 620 018 *Tel:* (0431) 2760772

Health-Harmony, *imprint of* B Jain Publishers Pvt Ltd

Higginbothams Pvt Ltd
Division of The Amalgamations Group
116 Anna Salai Rd, Opposite LIC Bldg, Mount Rd, Chennai 600 002
Tel: (044) 28513519
E-mail: higginbothams@vsnl.com
Founded: 1844
Type of Business: Importer

Hindi Book Centre
4/5 B Asaf Ali Rd, New Delhi 110 002
Tel: (011) 23286757 *Fax:* (011) 23273335; (011) 26481565
E-mail: info@hindibook.com
Web Site: www.hindibook.com
Founded: 1972
General books in Hindi.
Type of Business: Distributor
Owned by: Star Publications (Pvt) Ltd, 55 Warren St, London W1T 5NW, United Kingdom

Hindustan Book Agency
0-131, The Shopping Mall, Arjun Marg, DLF Phase 1, Gurgaon 122 002
Tel: (0124) 4307450; (0124) 4307451 *Fax:* (0124) 4307452
E-mail: info@hindbook.com
Web Site: www.hindbook.com
Key Personnel
Partner: Davendra K Jain *E-mail:* dk.jain@hindbook.com
Founded: 1947
Type of Business: Distributor

IBH, see International Book House Pvt Ltd

Impact, *imprint of* B Jain Publishers Pvt Ltd

International Book House Pvt Ltd
Indian Mercantile Mansions (Ext), Madam Cama Rd, Colaba, Mumbai 400 039
Tel: (022) 6624 2222 *Fax:* (022) 2285 1109
E-mail: info@ibhbookstore.com
Web Site: www.ibhbookstore.com
Key Personnel
Dir: Rohit Gupta *E-mail:* r.gupta@ibhbookstore.com; Sanjeev Kumar Gupta *E-mail:* s.gupta@ibhbookstore.com
Regional Manager: Liston D'souza
Regional Manager, Northern Region: Vikram Behl *E-mail:* vikram.behl@intbh.com
Manager, Marketing: Munil Kumar *E-mail:* munilkumar@rediffmail.com
Founded: 1941
Trade books, book distributors, retailers, direct mail, direct to home, magazine subscriptions.
Type of Business: Distributor, Importer
Branch Office(s)
C P Estate, Ashram Rd, Ahmedabad 380 009 *Tel:* (079) 3007 5041 *E-mail:* amd@ibhbookstore.com
97, Residency Rd, Bangalore 560 025 *Tel:* (080) 22210193 *E-mail:* veeraraghavan@intbh.in
Plot No 425, Nageswar Tangi, Lewis Rd, Jaydev Nagar, Bhubneshwar 751 002 *Tel:* (0674) 3266123 *E-mail:* bbn@ibhbokstore.com
Ground floor, Old No 12 New No 23, Damodaran St, T Nagar, Chennai 600 017 *Tel:* (044)

42070237; (044) 42070238 *E-mail:* chennai@intbh.in
D No 4-7-182, 9C Residency, Staff Quarters, Esamiah Bazaar, Koti, Hyderabad 500 027 *Tel:* (040) 24611111; (040) 24614444 *E-mail:* hyd@intbh.in
B R R A No 14, Bank Rd, Kaloor, Ernakulam, Kochi, Kerala 682 017 *Tel:* (0484) 320 8530 *E-mail:* koc@ibhbookstore.com
Shop No 5, Palace Court, One Kyd St, Kolkata 700 016 *Tel:* (033) 2229 4493 *E-mail:* ibhcal@vsnl.net
2 Yasho Gandh, East High Court Rd, Ramdas Peth, Nagpur 440 010 *Tel:* (0712) 6648353; (0712) 6648354; (0712) 6648355 *E-mail:* nag@ibhbookstore.com
2/42 2nd floor, Ansari Rd, Darya Ganj, New Delhi 110 002 *Tel:* (011) 2324 3815; (011) 2324 3816 *E-mail:* vikram.behl@intbh.com
Shakti Tower, Ground floor, 672, Narayan Peth, Pune 411 030 *Tel:* (020) 2449 7751 *E-mail:* pune@ibhbookstore.com

Jaico Publishing House
A-1, Jash Chambers Off Sir Phirozshan Mehta Rd, Opposite RBI (Amar Bldg), Fort, Mumbai 400 001
Tel: (022) 4030 67 67
E-mail: mumbai.sales@jaicobooks.com
Web Site: www.jaicobooks.com
Key Personnel
Branch Manager: Mr Randhir Patil
Founded: 1946
Type of Business: Distributor
Branch Office(s)
Shop No C-149, 1st floor, Sumel Business Park-6, Opposite Hanumanpura Brts, Dudheshwar Rd, Shahibaug, Ahmedabad 380 004, Branch Manager: Mr Sujesh Kumar *Tel:* (079) 2560 59 05; (079) 2560 59 22 *E-mail:* sujesh.kumar@jaicobooks.com
14/1, First Main Rd, 6th Cross, Gandhi Nagar, Bangalore 560 009, Branch Manager: Mr S Sreevatsa *Tel:* (080) 2226 70 16; (080) 2225 70 83 *E-mail:* bangalore.sales@jaicobooks.com
42-A Ground floor, VYAS Complex, Zone-II, M P Nagar, Bhopal 462 011, Branch Manager: Mr K S Mishra *Tel:* (0755) 422 92 45 *E-mail:* bhopal.sales@jaicobooks.com
Plot No 661/3404, Ground floor, Jayadurga Nagar, Backside of New Kalika Hotel, Bhubaneswar, Odisha 751 006, Branch Manager: Mr Shubomoy Sengupta *Tel:* (0674) 257 18 02 *E-mail:* bhubaneswar.sales@jaicobooks.com
No 48, Arya Gowder Rd, West Mambalam, Chennai 600 033, Branch Manager: Mr A R Sivaraman *Tel:* (044) 2480 30 91; (044) 2480 30 92; (044) 2480 30 93; (044) 2480 30 94 *E-mail:* chennai.sales@jaicobooks.com
3-4-512/75, (35/4RT), Opposite Lane to Raghvendra Swamy Mutt, Barkatpura, Hyderabad 500 027, Branch Manager: Mr B N Rao *Tel:* (040) 2755 19 92; (040) 2755 56 99; (040) 2755 13 29 *E-mail:* hyderabad.sales@jaicobooks.com
302, Acharya Prafulla Chandra Roy Rd, Kolkata 700 009, Branch Manager: Mr Sujit Kumar Guha *Tel:* (033) 2360 05 42; (033) 2360 05 43; (033) 2360 80 27 *E-mail:* kolkata.sales@jaicobooks.com
Hotel D/D International (Basement), 196, Gautam Budh Marg Bans Mandi Crossing, Lucknow 226 018, Branch Manager: Mr Rajnish Sinha *Tel:* (0522) 407 16 13 *E-mail:* lucknow.sales@jaicobooks.com
4736/23, G/F, Plot No 1, Ansari Rd, Darya Ganj, New Delhi 110 002, Branch Manager: Mr D K Kapoor *Tel:* (011) 4937 21 50 *E-mail:* delhi.sales@jaicobooks.com

B Jain Publishers Pvt Ltd
Member of B Jain Publishing Group
D-157, Sector-63, Noida, Uttar Pradesh 201 307

Tel: (0120) 4933333
E-mail: info@bjain.com
Web Site: www.bjain.com
Key Personnel
Dir: Nitin Jain *E-mail:* nitin@bjain.com
Founded: 1966
Books including medical, health & new age titles.
Type of Business: Distributor
Imprints: Health-Harmony; Impact; Leads Press; Pegasus

K Krishnamurthy
38, Thanikachalam Rd, Chennai, Tamil Nadu 600 017
E-mail: service@kkbooks.com; marketing@kkbooks.com
Web Site: www.kkbooks.com
Founded: 1944
Type of Business: Importer
Branch Office(s)
2 A Arulambal St, Chennai, Tamil Nadu 600 017 *Tel:* (044) 2834 4512; 9282344519 (cell)

Langers International Pvt Ltd
7/25, Mahaveer St, Ansari Rd, Darya Ganj, New Delhi 110 002
Tel: (011) 23260253; (011) 42540888
E-mail: info@langers.in
Web Site: www.langers.in
Founded: 2008
Type of Business: Distributor, Importer, Wholesaler

Leads Press, *imprint of* B Jain Publishers Pvt Ltd

MLBD, see Motilal Banarsidass Publishers Pvt Ltd

The Modern Book Depot
15A, Jawaharlal Nehru Rd, Kolkata 700 013
Tel: (033) 22493102; (033) 22490933
E-mail: modcal@vsnl.com
Key Personnel
Owner: Prem Prakash
Founded: 1949
Type of Business: Importer, Major Independent Bookseller, Wholesaler
Branch Office(s)
Station Sq, Unit 3, Bhubaneswar, Orissa 751 001 *Tel:* (0674) 2534373

Motilal Banarsidass Publishers Pvt Ltd
A-44, Naraina Industrial Area, Phase I, New Delhi 110 028
Tel: (011) 25793423; (011) 25795180; (011) 25792734 *Fax:* (011) 25797221
E-mail: web@mlbd.com; warehouse@mlbd.com
Web Site: www.mlbd.com
Key Personnel
Contact: Abhishek Jain; Varun Jain
Founded: 1903
Indological books including Indian literature, religion, philosophy, history, culture, etc. Also a publisher.
Type of Business: Distributor, Exporter, Importer, Wholesaler
Branch Office(s)
236, Ninth Main III Block, Jayanagar, Bangalore 560 011, Contact: Mr Anil Mukhi *Tel:* (080) 26542591; (080) 32711690 *E-mail:* bangalore@mlbd.com
203 Royapettah High Rd, Mylapore, Chennai 600 004, Contact: Mr V R Ravi *Tel:* (044) 24982315; (044) 43535417 *E-mail:* chennai@mlbd.com
8 Camac St, Kolkata 700 017, Contact: Mr Tapan Chatterjee *Tel:* (033) 22824872; (033) 32967029 *E-mail:* kolkata@mlbd.com
8 Mahalakshmi Chambers, Mahalaxmi Temple Lane, 22 Bhulabhai Desai Rd, Mumbai 400 026, Contact: Mr Cowsie Amra *Tel:* (022)

23516583; (022) 39222105 *E-mail:* mumbai@
mlbd.com

Ashok Rajpath, Patna 800 004, Contact: Mr S N
Yagnik *Tel:* (0612) 2671442; (0612) 3296812
E-mail: patna@mlbd.com

Chowk, Varanasi 221 001, Contact: Mr G P
Pandey *Tel:* (0542) 2412331; (0542) 3295108
E-mail: varanasi@mlbd.com

Showroom(s): 41 UA Bungalow Rd, Jawahar Nagar, Delhi 110 007, Contact: Mr R P
Jain *Tel:* (011) 23858335; (011) 23851985;
(011) 23852747; (011) 23854826 *Fax:* (011)
23850689

Munshiram Manoharlal Publishers Pvt Ltd
54 Rani Jhansi Rd, New Delhi 110 055
Mailing Address: PO Box 5715, New Delhi 110
055
Tel: (011) 23671668; (011) 23673650; (011)
23636097; (011) 23638992 *Fax:* (011)
23612745
E-mail: info@mrmlonline.com; sales@
mrmlonline.com
Web Site: www.mrmlonline.com
Key Personnel
Owner & Mng Dir: Ashok Jain
Dir: Vikram Jain
Founded: 1952
Also publisher.
Type of Business: Distributor, Exporter, Major
Independent Bookseller
Showroom(s): Sanctum Books, 68 Medical Asso-
ciation Rd, Darya Ganj, New Delhi 110 002

Narosa Book Distributors Pvt Ltd
22 Delhi Medical Association Rd, Darya Ganj,
New Delhi 110 002
Tel: (011) 23243415; (011) 23243417 *Fax:* (011)
23243225; (011) 23258934
E-mail: info@narosa.com; sales@narosa.com
Web Site: www.narosa.com/nbd
Key Personnel
Mng Dir: Sascha J Mehra
Founded: 1977
Also publisher.
Specialize in scientific, technical & medical
books.
Type of Business: Distributor
Branch Office(s)
35-36 Greams Rd, Thousand Lights, Chennai 600
006 *Tel:* (044) 28290377 *E-mail:* narosamds@
vsnl.net
2F-2G Shivam Chambers, 53 Syed Amir Ali
Ave, Kolkata 700 019 *Tel:* (033) 22902892
E-mail: narosakol@narosa.com
306 Shiv Centre, Vashi Sector 17, Mum-
bai 400 705 *Tel:* 9833070223 (cell)
E-mail: narosamum@narosa.com

Navakarnataka Publications (Pvt) Ltd
101, Embassy Centre, Crescent Rd, Kumara Park
E, Bangalore 560 001
Tel: (080) 22161900; (080) 22161901; (080)
22161902
E-mail: navakarnataka@gmail.com; nkpl.online@
gmail.com
Web Site: www.navakarnatakaonline.com
Key Personnel
Mng Dir: R S Rajaram
Founded: 1960
Subscriptions, publications & distribution.
Type of Business: Distributor, Exporter, Importer,
Major Independent Bookseller, Wholesaler
Showroom(s): Embassy Centre, 11 Crescent Rd,
Kumara Park E, PO Box 5159, Bangalore 560
001 *Tel:* (080) 22161913 *Fax:* (080) 22161914
E-mail: nkpsales@gmail.com (wholesale);
Opposite Tajmahal Hotel, 64/1, Fifth Main,
Gandhinagar, Bangalore 560 009 *Tel:* (080)
22251382 *E-mail:* nkpgnr@gmail.com; De-
vanga Tower, next to Bhumika (States) Cinema,
Opposite Adiga's Restaurant, Kempegowda

Rd, Bangalore 560 009 *Tel:* (080) 22203106;
Moquaddam Trade Centre, Station Rd, Opposite Mini Vidhana Soudha, Gulbarga 585
102 *Tel:* (08472) 224302 *E-mail:* nkpglb@
gmail.com; Modern Lodge Bldg, K S
Rao Rd, Mangalore 575 001 *Tel:* (0824)
2441016 *E-mail:* nkpmng@gmail.com; Shar-
avathi Bldg, Balmatta, Mangalore 575 001
Tel: (0824) 2425161 *E-mail:* nkpbalmatta@
gmail.com; Prestige Shopping Arcade, Ra-
maswamy Circle, Mysore 570 024 *Tel:* (0821)
2424094; (0821) 4262494; (0821) 2420383
E-mail: nkpmysuru@gmail.com

Nem Chand & Brothers
22, Civil Lines, Roorkee, UK 247 667
Tel: (01332) 272258; (01332) 272752; (01332)
264343 *Fax:* (01332) 273258
E-mail: info@nemchandbros.com; ncb_rke@
rediffmail.com
Web Site: www.nemchandbros.com
Key Personnel
Owner: Anil K Jain *Tel:* 9412071555 (cell)
E-mail: akj@nemchandbros.com
Mng Dir, Rights & Permissions: Mr N C
Jain *Tel:* 9760099779 (cell) *E-mail:* ncj@
nemchandbros.com
Founded: 1951
Also publisher.
Type of Business: Distributor, Exporter, Importer,
Major Independent Bookseller, Wholesaler

Pegasus, *imprint of* B Jain Publishers Pvt Ltd

Prints India, see Prints Publications Pvt Ltd

Prints Publications Pvt Ltd
Formerly Prints India
11, Prints House, Darya Ganj, New Delhi 110
002
Tel: (011) 45355555 *Fax:* (011) 23275542
E-mail: info@printspublications.com
Web Site: www.printspublications.com
Founded: 1966
Also publisher, subscription agent & library sup-
plier.
Type of Business: Distributor, Exporter, Major
Independent Bookseller, Wholesaler

Roorkee Press, see Nem Chand & Brothers

Rupa Publications India
161-B/4, Ground floor Gulmohar House, Yusuf
Sarai Commmunity Centre, New Delhi 110 049
Tel: (011) 49226666
E-mail: info@rupapublications.com; rupa@
rupapublications.com; sales@rupapublications.
com
Web Site: rupapublications.co.in
Founded: 1936
Also acts as publisher.
Type of Business: Distributor, Exporter, Importer,
Wholesaler

Scientific International Pvt Ltd
4850/24 Ansari Rd, Darya Ganj, New Delhi 110
002
Tel: (011) 23287580; (011) 23287584; (011)
23289263; (011) 47148284; (011) 43512984
Fax: (011) 23286096
E-mail: info@siplind.com; expo@siplind.com
Web Site: www.siplind.com
Key Personnel
Vice President: S K Chawla *Tel:* 8750855090
(cell) *E-mail:* skchawla@siplind.com; Ramesh
Wadhera
Senior Sales Head: Jijo Kuriakose
Founded: 1993
Specialize in medical sciences, engineering &
technology. Distributes books of major Amer-
ican & European publishers. Exports books

mainly to Africa, South Asia, Southeast Asia &
Middle East.
Also a publisher.
Type of Business: Distributor, Exporter, Importer,
Wholesaler
Branch Office(s)
No 1665, Ground floor (near Punyakoti Sri
Bharmagiri Manjunatheshwara Temple),
18th Main, BSK 2nd Stage, Bangalore 560
070 *Tel:* (080) 26719116; 9886285836 (cell)
E-mail: bengaluru@siplind.com
127/G, Manicktatla Main Rd, Kankurgachi,
Near Yogodyan, Kolkata 700 054, Area Man-
ager: Debashis Das *Tel:* (033) 23204041;
9433335049 (cell) *E-mail:* kolkata@siplind.
com
7, Kohinoor Flats, Lukes Lane, Ambujavi-
lasam Rd, Thiruvananthapuram 695 001
Tel: 7012268258 (cell) *E-mail:* kerala@siplind.
com

R R Sheth & Co Pvt Ltd
Dwarkesh, near Royal Apartment, Nehru Bridge
Corner, Khanpur, Ahmedabad 380 001
Tel: (079) 2550 6573 *Fax:* (079) 2550 1732
Web Site: rrsheth.com
Key Personnel
Owner: Ratnaraj Sheth
Founded: 1926
Gujarati & Hindi books.
Also publisher.
Type of Business: Wholesaler
Branch Office(s)
110-112 Princess St, Keshav Baug, Mumbai 400
002 *Tel:* (022) 2201 3441; (022) 2205 8293

Star Educational Books Distributor Pvt Ltd
4736/23, Ansari Rd, Darya Ganj, New Delhi 110
002
Tel: (011) 41562819; (011) 23264462;
9911317356 (cell) *Fax:* (011) 23264451
E-mail: sales@star-bk.com
Web Site: www.star-bk.com
Founded: 2004
Type of Business: Distributor, Exporter, Importer,
Major Independent Bookseller, Wholesaler

STAR Publications Pvt Ltd
4/5 B Asaf Ali Rd, New Delhi 110 002
Tel: (011) 2325 7220; (011) 2327 4874; (011)
2326 1696; (011) 2328 6757 *Fax:* (011) 2327
3335
E-mail: info@hindibook.com
Web Site: www.starpublic.com
Key Personnel
Chairman: Mr Amar Varma
Founded: 1957
All types of Indian Books, in all Indian languages
& English.
Also acts as publisher.
Type of Business: Distributor, Exporter
Branch Office(s)
Wembley Point, Suite 4b, floor 15, One Har-
row Rd, Wembley Middx, London HA9
6DE, United Kingdom *Tel:* (020) 8900 2640;
(020) 8900 2840 *Fax:* (020) 8900 2840
E-mail: order@foreignlanguagebooks.co.uk

Super Book House
3A Sind Chambers, Colaba, Mumbai 400 005
Tel: (022) 22020106; (022) 22830446
E-mail: superbookhouse@gmx.com
Key Personnel
Contact: M S Lehri
Type of Business: Major Independent Bookseller

TBI Publishers Distributors
46, Housing Society, South Ext Part 1, New Delhi
110 049
Tel: (011) 24690513 *Fax:* (011) 24610576
E-mail: sales@tbidelhi.com

Founded: 1985
Type of Business: Distributor, Importer, Wholesaler

UBS Publishers' Distributors Pvt Ltd
5, Ansari Rd, Darya Ganj, New Delhi 110 002
Tel: (011) 23273601; (011) 23273602; (011) 23273603; (011) 23273604 *Fax:* (011) 23276593
E-mail: ubspd@ubspd.com
Web Site: www.ubspd.com
Founded: 1963
Type of Business: Distributor, Exporter, Importer, Wholesaler
Branch Office(s)
1st floor, Shop No 133-134, Aust Laxmi, Apparel Park, Outside Dariyapur Gate, Ahmedabad 380 016 *Tel:* (079) 29092241; (079) 29092248; (079) 29092258 *E-mail:* mukesh.brahmbhatt@ubspd.com
3/2, 2nd floor, Thimmaiah, Towers First Cross, Gandhinagar, Bangalore 560 009 *Tel:* (080) 22266671; 9341621469 (cell) *Fax:* (080) 22266674 *E-mail:* er.manoharn@ubspd.com
Z-18, M P Nagar, Zone-I, Bhopal 462 011 *Tel:* (0755) 4203183; (0755) 4203193; (0755) 2555228 *Fax:* (0755) 2555285 *E-mail:* sanjay.sharma@ubspd.com
1st floor, Plot No 145, Cuttack Rd, Bhubaneshwar 751 006 *Tel:* (0674) 2314446; (0674) 2314447 *Fax:* (0674) 2314448 *E-mail:* dharmapada.tripathy@ubspb.com
Sire Manshion, 1st floor, 621 Anasalai, Chennai 600 006 *Tel:* (044) 28295057; 9566151110 (cell) *Fax:* (044) 282950754 *E-mail:* s.viswanathan@ubspb.com
2nd & 3rd floor, Sri Guru Towers, No 1-7 Sathy Rd, Cross III, Gandhipuram, Coimbatore 641 012 *Tel:* (0422) 2499916; (0422) 2499917 *Fax:* (0422) 2499914 *E-mail:* ak.sukumaran@ubspd.com
No 40/8199A, 1st floor, Public Library Bldg, Convent Rd, Ernakulam 682 035 *Tel:* (0484) 2353901; (0484) 2363905 *Fax:* (0484) 2365511 *E-mail:* vj.abraham@ubspd.com
1st floor, House No 4, Kanaklata Path, Lachit Nagar, Bharalupar, Guwahati 781 007 *Tel:* (0361) 2461982; (0361) 2461983 *Fax:* (0361) 2461984 *E-mail:* v.radhakrishnan@ubspd.com
3rd & 4th floors, Alekhya Jagadish Chambers, H No 4-1-1058, Boggulkunta, Tilak Rd, Hyderabad 500 001 *Tel:* (040) 24754473; (040) 24754474 *Fax:* (040) 24754472 *E-mail:* vinaay.kumar@ubspd.com
8/1-B, Chowringhee Lane, Kolkata 700 016 *Tel:* (033) 22529473; (033) 22521821; (033) 22522910 *Fax:* (033) 22523027 *E-mail:* tapas.ojha@ubspd.com
6, Ashok Nagar, Pratibha Press, in front of Iscon Temple, near Basmandi Chauhraha, Latush Rd, Lucknow 226 018 *Tel:* (0522) 4025124; (0522) 4025134; 9161199990 (cell) *Fax:* (0522) 4025144 *E-mail:* anand.gupta@ubspd.com
B/12, Jaywant Industrial Estate, 63 Tardeo Rd, Mumbai 400 034 *Tel:* (022) 22073477; (022) 66102069; (03) 66376922 *Fax:* (022) 66376921 *E-mail:* manoj.salvi@ubspd.com
(Janaki Sabhagruha), Plot 349/3, 159 Bajaj Nagar, Abhyankar Lay Out, Nagpur *Tel:* (0712) 6457909; (0712) 2232629 *Fax:* (0712) 2236062; (0712) 2236061 *E-mail:* niranjan.panwatkar@ubspd.com
B-3B Sector 63, Noida 201 307 *Tel:* (0120) 4205516; (0120) 2427252 *Fax:* (011) 23274261 *E-mail:* al.sharma@ubspd.com (export division)
Annapurna Complex, Ground floor, Naya Tola, Patna 800 004 *Tel:* (0612) 2672856; (0612) 2673973; (0612) 2686170 *Fax:* (0612) 2686169 *E-mail:* b.ganguly@ubspd.com
680 Budhwar Peth, 2nd floor, Near Appa Balwant Chowk, Pune 411 002 *Tel:* (020) 24461653 *Fax:* (020) 24433976 *E-mail:* pravin.indalkar@ubspd.com

UBSPD, see UBS Publishers' Distributors Pvt Ltd

Universal Book Corner
20 Civil Lines, M G Rd, Allahabad 211 001
Tel: (0532) 2623467; 9335153660 (cell)
Key Personnel
Contact: Nitin Chugh
Type of Business: Major Independent Bookseller
Owned by: Chugh Publications

Universal Book Traders
80, Gokhale Market, Opposite Tis Hazari Courts, New Delhi 110 054
Tel: (011) 23961288; (011) 23911966; (011) 23991487
E-mail: sales@ubtlawbooks.com
Founded: 1956
Membership(s): Delhi State Booksellers & Publishers Association; Federation of Publishers & Booksellers Associations in India.
Type of Business: Distributor, Exporter, Importer, Major Independent Bookseller, Wholesaler
Branch Office(s)
C-27, Connaught Pl (between Odeon & Pvr Plaza), Middle Circle, New Delhi 110 001 *Tel:* (011) 23416277; (011) 23418671

Varun Books International
Shop No 4831/24, Prahlad Gali, Ansari Rd, Darya Ganj, New Delhi 110 002
Tel: (011) 23250586
Founded: 1994
Export Indian, American & European books to developing countries.
Type of Business: Exporter

Visalaandhra Publishing House
Chandram Bldg, C R Rd, Chuttugunta, Vijayawada 520 004
Tel: (0866) 2430302; 9052101320 (cell)
E-mail: vphsales@gmail.com
Web Site: www.visalaandhrapublishinghouse.com
Founded: 1953
Publishing & marketing of general books in Telugu language.
Type of Business: Distributor, Importer, Wholesaler
Branch Office(s)
Karl Marx Rd, Vijayawada 520 004 *Tel:* (0866) 2572949; 9490952110 (cell) *E-mail:* vbhvja2012@gmail.com
College Rd, Ananthapuram 515 001 *Tel:* (08554) 220614; 9494543181 (cell) *E-mail:* vbhatp2012@gmail.com
Arundelpet, Guntur 530 002 *Tel:* (0863) 2233297; 9246464414 (cell) *E-mail:* vbhguntur2012@gmail.com
Opposite Womens College, Kadapa 523 001 *Tel:* (08562) 222970; 9908830668 (cell) *E-mail:* visalaandhrakadapa@gmail.com
Municipal Complex, Main Rd, Kakinada 533 001 *Tel:* (0884) 2378992; 9885555239 (cell) *E-mail:* vbhkakinada2012@gmail.com
Mallaih Lingam Bhavan, Eemanipales, One Town Police Station, Ongole 523 001 *Tel:* (08592) 280004; 9154139875 (cell) *E-mail:* vbhongole2012@gmail.com
Kranthi Bhavan, Rama Lakshman Junction, Srikakulam 515 001 *Tel:* (08942) 220553; 8341572855 (cell) *E-mail:* vbhsklm2012@gmail.com
Gandhi Rd, Ashok Shopping Complex, Main Rd, Tirupathi 517 501 *Tel:* (0877) 2222475; 9490271104 (cell) *E-mail:* vbhtirupathi2012@gmail.com
Main Rd, Visakhapatnam 530 002 *Tel:* (0891) 2502534; 9849257925 (cell) *E-mail:* vbhvsp2012@gmail.com
Amar Bhavan, Opposite Hotel Mayur, Vizianagaram 500 003 *Tel:* 9866359077 (cell)

Indonesia

Akademi Akuntansi Effendi Harahap Bookstore
Jl Abimanyu Raya 17-19, Banjarsari, Semarang Barat 50142
Tel: (024) 3544694; (024) 3564860 *Fax:* (024) 3564860
E-mail: irwan@effendiharahap.com

Badan Penerbit Kristen Gunung Mulia, see BPK Gunung Mulia

BPK Gunung Mulia
Jl Kwitang 22-23, Jakarta 10420
Tel: (021) 3901208 *Fax:* (021) 3901633
E-mail: jakarta@bpkgm.com; marketing@bpkgm.com; promosi@bpkgm.com; publishing@bpkgm.com
Web Site: www.bpkgm.com
Founded: 1946
Also publisher & printer.
Membership(s): CBA.
Type of Business: Distributor, Importer, Major Book Chain Headquarters
Owned by: PT BPK Gunung Mulia
Bookshop(s): Jl Dr Siwabessy No 16, Ambon 97117 *Tel:* (0911) 352648 *Fax:* (0911) 352648 *E-mail:* aguslasminpurba@gmail.com; Jl Yos Sudarso No 1, GPIB Maranatha, Komplek Pertamina Balikpapan, Balikpapan *E-mail:* aguslasminpurba@gmail.com; Jl A Nisnoni No 1B, Naikoten, Kota Raja, Kupang *Tel:* (0380) 831668 *Fax:* (0380) 831668 *E-mail:* kupang@bpkgm.com; Jl Abdullah Dg, Sirua No 68/78, Makassar 90134 *Tel:* (0411) 436078 *Fax:* (0411) 436078 *E-mail:* makassar@bpkgm.com; Jl Sam Ratulangi No 89 B Kel Titiwungen, Kec Wenea, Kota Manado, Manado 95111 *Tel:* (0852) 4072 2225 *E-mail:* manado@bpkgm.com; Jl Nibung II No 78, Komplek Medan Plaza, Medan Tuntungan 20142 *Tel:* (061) 4567973; (061) 88813672 *E-mail:* medan@bpkgm.com; Jl M T Haryono d/h Jl Mataram 517D, Semarang *Tel:* (024) 8448280 *E-mail:* semarang@bpkgm.com; Jl Genteng Besar No 28, Surabaya 60275 *Tel:* (031) 5468848 *Fax:* (031) 5342534 *E-mail:* surabaya@bpkgm.com; Jl Pasar Lama (Puskom) No 79, Paslaten Satu, Tomohon 95362 *Tel:* (0431) 351722 *Fax:* (0431) 351722 *E-mail:* manado@bpkgm.com

C V Toko Buku Tropen
Jl Hos Cokroaminoto No 29, Jakarta 10310
Tel: (021) 3140312
Key Personnel
Mng Dir: Jani Dipokusumo
Founded: 1939
Type of Business: Distributor, Exporter, Importer, Major Independent Bookseller, Wholesaler

Gramedia Bookshop
Gedung Kompas Gramedia lantai 6, Jl Palmerah Barat 29-37, Jakarta Pusat 10270
Tel: (021) 35880760; (021) 53650110
E-mail: support@gramediaonline.com
Web Site: gramediaonline.com
Founded: 1974
Type of Business: Major Book Chain Headquarters
Owned by: PT Gramedia
Branch Office(s)
Jl Merdeka 43, Bandung
Jl Melawai IV/13, Jakarta
Jl Pintu Air 72, Jakarta

Jl Jendral Sudirman 56, Jogjakarta
Jl Basuki Rachmat 95, Surabaya

Periplus
Jl Rawa Gelam IV, No 9, Kawasan Industri Pulo-
gadung, Jakarta 13930
Tel: (021) 4682 1088 *Fax:* (021) 461 0206
Key Personnel
Mng Dir: Judo Suwidji
Founded: 1999
Type of Business: Distributor, Importer
Branch Office(s)
Bali
Jakarta
Jawa Barat
Jawa Tengah
Jawa Timur
Lombok
Yogyakarta

PT Indira Ltd
Jl Borobudur 20, Jakarta, Pusat 10320
Tel: (021) 3904290; (021) 3148868; (021)
3147468; (021) 3904288
Importers of general/trade books & educa-
tional/scientific/technical books & textbooks.
Library suppliers to foreign libraries of Indone-
sian printed books. Also a publisher.
Type of Business: Distributor, Importer

Ireland

The Columba Bookservice Ltd, see Columba
Press

Columba Press
23 Merrion Sq N, Dublin 2
Tel: (01) 687 4096
E-mail: sales@columba.ie
Web Site: www.columba.ie
Key Personnel
Mng Dir: Garry O'Sullivan *E-mail:* garry@
columba.ie
Mng Editor: Mags Gargan *E-mail:* mags@
columba.ie
Founded: 1985
Type of Business: Distributor
Parent Company: Grace Communications Ltd

Connolly Books
43 E Essex St, Temple Bar, Dublin D02 XH96
Tel: (01) 6708707
E-mail: connollybooks@eircom.net
Web Site: www.connollybooks.org
Founded: 1932
Subjects include environmental issues, feminism,
Irish history, Marxist classics, philosophy, poli-
tics, progressive literature, radical periodicals &
trade union affairs.
Type of Business: Major Independent Bookseller

Dubray Books
36 Grafton St, Dublin 2
Tel: (01) 677-5568
E-mail: dublinbookshop@dubraybooks.ie
Web Site: www.dubraybooks.ie
Type of Business: Major Book Chain Headquar-
ters
Branch Office(s)
Blackrock Shopping Centre, Blackrock, Dublin
Tel: (01) 283 2193 *E-mail:* dubraybr@
dubraybooks.ie
Dun Laoghaire Shopping Centre, Dun Laoghaire,
Dublin *Tel:* (01) 280 9917 *E-mail:* dubraydl@
dubraybooks.ie

Swan Shopping Centre, Rathmines, Dublin 6
Tel: (01) 497 9722 *E-mail:* dubrayrath@
dubraybooks.ie
Stillorgan Shopping Centre, Stillorgan, Dublin
Tel: (01) 288 6341 *E-mail:* dubraystill@
dubraybooks.ie
4 Shop St, Galway *Tel:* (091) 569 070
E-mail: dubraygal@dubraybooks.ie
Market Cross Shopping Centre, Kilkenny
Tel: (056) 775 2800 *E-mail:* dubraykk@
dubraybooks.ie
10 Main St, Bray, Wicklow *Tel:* (01) 286 2786
E-mail: bray@dubraybooks.ie

ePubDirect
NSC Campus, Mahon, Cork
Tel: (021) 7304650
E-mail: info@epubdirect.com
Web Site: www.epubdirect.com
Key Personnel
Founder & Chief Executive Officer: Gareth
Cuddy
Chief Operations Officer: Aiveen Hyland
Chief Technology Officer: Joe Lennon
Financial Controller: Turlough Daly
Head, Information Technology: Mark Watkins
Sales Dir: Roger Miah
Founded: 2009
Global ebook distribution service.
Type of Business: Distributor
U.S. Office(s): 79 Madison Ave, New York, NY
10016, United States *Tel:* 646-568-7797

Gill Distribution
Hume Ave, Park West, Dublin D12 YV96
Tel: (01) 500 9500; (01) 500 9555 *Fax:* (01) 500
9599
Web Site: www.gilldistribution.ie
Key Personnel
Distribution Dir: John Manning *Tel:* (01) 500
9534 *E-mail:* jmanning@gill.ie
Warehouse Manager: Alfie Beahan *Tel:* (01) 500
9535
Type of Business: Distributor

The Library Shop
Trinity College, College St, Dublin 2
Tel: (01) 896 1000 *Fax:* (01) 608 1016
E-mail: gifts@tcd.ie
Web Site: gifts.tcd.ie
Key Personnel
Manager: Paul Corrigan *Tel:* (01) 896 1171
Type of Business: Major Independent Bookseller

O'Mahony's Booksellers Ltd
120 O'Connell St, Limerick
Tel: (061) 418155 *Fax:* (061) 414558
E-mail: info@omahonys.ie; customerservice@
omahonys.ie; websales@omahonys.ie
Web Site: www.omahonys.ie
Key Personnel
Mng Dir: Frank O'Mahony *E-mail:* frank.
omahony@omahonys.ie
General Manager: Colette Cotter *E-mail:* colette.
cotter@omahonys.ie
Founded: 1902
School & library suppliers.
Type of Business: Major Independent Bookseller
Branch Office(s)
University of Limerick Bookshop, Plassey Tech-
nological Park, Limerick, Contact: Hilary
Piert *Tel:* (061) 203048 *Fax:* (061) 335147
E-mail: university.branch@omahonys.ie
Merchant Sq, Ennis, Manager: Trish O'Grady
Tel: (065) 6828355 *E-mail:* ennis.branch@
omahonys.ie
Castle St, Tralee, Co Kerry, Manager: Bridget
Leen *Tel:* (066) 7122266 *Fax:* (066) 7129442
E-mail: tralee.branch@omahonys.ie

Veritas Co Ltd
7-8 Lower Abbey St, Dublin 1

Tel: (01) 878 8177 *Fax:* (01) 878 6507; (01) 874
4913
E-mail: sales@veritas.ie; veritas2@veritas.ie
Web Site: www.veritasbooksonline.com
Key Personnel
Dir: Aidan Chester
Sales & Operations Manager: Derek Tisdall
Marketing & Public Relations: Pamela McLough-
lin *E-mail:* pamela.mcloughlin@veritas.ie
Founded: 1928
Type of Business: Distributor, Major Book Chain
Headquarters, Wholesaler
Owned by: Irish Catholic Bishops' Conference
Branch Office(s)
Blanchardstown Centre, Unit 309,
Dublin 15, Manager: Jeff Stills
Tel: (01) 886 4030 *Fax:* (01) 886 4031
E-mail: blanchardstownshop@veritas.ie
Carey's Lane, Cork T12 AW26, Manager: Vicky
Leng *Tel:* (021) 425 1255 *Fax:* (021) 427 9165
E-mail: corkshop@veritas.ie
20 Shipquay St, Derry BT48 6DW, Manager:
Lucy Gillespie *Tel:* (028) 71266888 *Fax:* (028)
71365120 *E-mail:* derryshop@veritas.ie
83 O'Connell St, Ennis, Co Clare V95 KD34,
Manager: Geraldine Considine *Tel:* (065) 682
8696 *Fax:* (065) 682 0176 *E-mail:* ennisshop@
veritas.ie
13 Lower Main St, Letterkenny, Co Done-
gal F92 N4C8, Manager: Sheila McMacken
Tel: (074) 912 4814 *Fax:* (074) 912 2716
E-mail: letterkennyshop@veritas.ie
16-18 Park St, Monaghan, Manager: Mary Kelly
Flynn *Tel:* (047) 84077 *Fax:* (047) 84019
E-mail: monaghanshop@veritas.ie
Sallins Rd, Naas, Co Kildare W91 E3YN,
Manager: Helen Murray *Tel:* (045) 856882
Fax: (045) 856871 *E-mail:* naasshop@veritas.ie
40-41 The Mall, Newry, Co Down BT34 1AN,
Manager: Eugene McAlinden *Tel:* (028)
30250321 *E-mail:* newryshop@veritas.ie
Adelaide St, Sligo F91 AP28, Manager: Ann
O'Neill *Tel:* (071) 916 1800 *Fax:* (071) 916
0121 *E-mail:* sligoshop@veritas.ie
Warehouse: 14 Rosemount Business Park, Bally-
coolin, Dublin 11, Manager: Stephen Kearney
Tel: (01926) 451 730 *Fax:* (01926) 451 733
E-mail: warehouse@veritas.ie (Ireland & UK)

Israel

Academon Israel Ltd
45 Hareches Ave, Modiin
Tel: (08) 9147788 *Fax:* (08) 9147786
E-mail: info@academonil.co.il
Web Site: academonil.co.il
Founded: 1956
Academic & general bookstore chain serving uni-
versity & college campuses.
Type of Business: Importer, Major Book Chain
Headquarters

Librairie Francaise Alcheh
55 Nachlat Benjamin St, 65163 Tel Aviv
Mailing Address: PO Box 1550, Tel Aviv
Tel: (03) 5604173 *Fax:* (03) 5606218
E-mail: alcheh@zahav.net.il
Founded: 1939
French & English Books.
Type of Business: Major Independent Bookseller

Eric Cohen Books Ltd
27 Hata'asia St, 43654 Ra'anana
Tel: (09) 747 8000 *Fax:* (09) 747 8001
E-mail: info@ecb.co.il; orders@ecb.co.il
Web Site: www.ecb.co.il
Key Personnel
Mng Dir: Eric Cohen
Marketing Manager: Gay Bergman

Founded: 1980
Type of Business: Distributor, Importer

Dyonon
Mitchell Bldg, Tel Aviv University, 69978 Tel
Aviv
Tel: (08) 9147788 *Fax:* (08) 9147786
E-mail: info@dyonon.com
Web Site: www.dyonon.com
Founded: 1972
Type of Business: Distributor, Exporter, Importer,
Major Independent Bookseller, Wholesaler

Israbook
c/o Gefen Publishing House Ltd, 6 Hatzvi St,
94386 Jerusalem
Tel: (02) 538-0247 *Fax:* (02) 538-8423
E-mail: israbook@gefenpublishing.com; info@
gefenpublishing.com
Web Site: www.israelbooks.com
Key Personnel
Publisher: Ilan Greenfield *E-mail:* ilan@
gefenpublishing.com
Founded: 1981
Type of Business: Distributor, Importer, Whole-
saler
U.S. Office(s): Gefen Books, 600 Broadway, Lyn-
brook, NY 11563, United States, Contact:
Maury J Storch *Tel:* 516-593-1234 *Fax:* 516-
295-2739 *E-mail:* gefenny@gefenpublishing.
com

Jerusalem Books Ltd
PO Box 26190, 91261 Jerusalem
Tel: (02) 642-6653 *Fax:* (02) 643-3580
Web Site: www.jerusalembooks.co.il
Key Personnel
Owner: Jeff Cregor
Specialize in supplying libraries, universities, Ju-
daic studies collections & departments, semi-
naries, rabbis, professors, students & all those
with an interest in books from Israel.
Type of Business: Distributor, Exporter

Lonnie Kahn Ltd
Haharoshet St 31, 12380 Ashdod
Tel: (03) 9518418 *Fax:* (03) 9627976
E-mail: lk@lonibooks.co.il
Web Site: www.lonibooks.co.il
Key Personnel
General Manager: Mr Itamar Karlinski
Founded: 1943
Type of Business: Distributor, Importer, Major
Independent Bookseller, Wholesaler

Rubin Mass Ltd
7 Ha-ayin-Het St, 91009 Jerusalem
Mailing Address: PO Box 990, 91009 Jerusalem
Tel: (02) 627-7863 *Fax:* (02) 627-7864
E-mail: rmass@barak.net.il
Web Site: rubinmass.net
Key Personnel
Manager: Oren Mass
Founded: 1927
Exporter of all Israeli books & periodicals.
Also publisher.
Type of Business: Distributor, Exporter, Major
Independent Bookseller, Online Bookseller,
Wholesaler

Ludwig Mayer Jerusalem Ltd
4 Shlomzion Hamalka St, 91010 Jerusalem
Mailing Address: PO Box 1174, 91010 Jerusalem
Tel: (02) 6252628 *Fax:* (02) 6232640
E-mail: info@mayerbooks.com
Web Site: www.mayerbooks.com
Key Personnel
Owner: Marcel Marcus
Founded: 1908

Academic bookstore.
Type of Business: Exporter, Importer, Major Independent Bookseller, Online Bookseller

Michlol Ltd
Technion City, 3200003 Haifa
Tel: (04) 8322970 (ext 2) *Fax:* (04) 8322908
E-mail: michlolberman@gmail.com
Web Site: www.michlol.co.il
Type of Business: Exporter, Importer, Major Inde-
pendent Bookseller
Branch Office(s)
Faculty of Medicine at the Rambam Hospital,
One Efron St, 31096 Haifa *Tel:* (04) 8516713
Beit Berl College, 4490500 Beit Berl *Tel:* (09)
7421463
Ruppin Academic Center, 4025000 Emek Hefer
Tel: (09) 8943359
Emek Yezreel Academic College, Jezreel Valley
Tel: (072) 2650293
Ort Braude College, College of Engineering,
Snunit 51, 21982 Karmiel *Fax:* (04) 8080836
Kiryat Ono Complex, Ono Academic College
(IDF 104), Kiryat Ono *Tel:* (03) 5156335
Netanya Academic College, One HaAvudah St,
Netanya *Tel:* (09) 8872025

Mosad Harav Kook, see Rav Kook Institute

Palphot Marketing Ltd
10 Hahagana St, 43625 Herzlia
Mailing Address: PO Box 2, 46100 Herzlia
Tel: (09) 9525252 *Fax:* (09) 9525277
E-mail: palphot@palphot.com; sales@palphot.
com
Web Site: www.palphot.com
Founded: 1934
Type of Business: Distributor, Exporter, Importer,
Wholesaler

Probook Ltd
Sonol Bldg, Menachem Begin Rd, 52, 61560 Tel
Aviv
Mailing Address: PO Box 56055, 61560 Tel Aviv
Tel: (03) 5257999 *Fax:* (03) 5285397
E-mail: info@probook.co.il
Web Site: www.probook.co.il
Founded: 1989
Subscription center. Specialize in academic &
medical books.
Type of Business: Distributor, Exporter, Importer,
Major Independent Bookseller, Online Book-
seller, Wholesaler
Parent Company: Yozmot Heiliger & Dyonon Co

Rav Kook Institute
Jerusalem Rabbi Maimon 1, Jerusalem
Mailing Address: PO Box 642, 9100601
Jerusalem
Tel: (02) 6526231 *Fax:* (02) 6526968
Web Site: www.mosadharavkook.com
Key Personnel
Chairman: Yehuda Leib Rafael
Executive Dir: Yosef Elyahu Movshowitz; Natan
David Shapira
Founded: 1937
Also publisher of Judaica.
Type of Business: Exporter, Wholesaler
U.S. Office(s): 702 Ocean Parkway, Suite 1A,
Brooklyn, NY 11230, United States *Tel:* 718-
215-1197 *E-mail:* office@mosadharavkookusa.
com

Robinson Books
31 Nachlat Binyamin St, 61042 Tel Aviv
Mailing Address: PO Box 4308, 61042 Tel Aviv
Tel: (03) 560-5461
E-mail: rob_book@netvision.net.il
Web Site: www.robinson.co.il
Key Personnel
Owner: Judah Robinson

Founded: 1894
Also antiquarian bookseller.
Type of Business: Exporter

Sharbain's Bookshop Co Ltd
Salah Edin St, PO Box 19903, Jerusalem
Tel: (02) 6286775 *Fax:* (02) 6272698
Web Site: www.sharbain.com
Founded: 1963
Type of Business: Distributor, Exporter, Importer,
Major Independent Bookseller, Wholesaler
Branch Office(s)
PO Box 484, Ramallah *Tel:* (02) 2953495
Fax: (02) 2987037 *E-mail:* jsharbain@gmail.
com

Steimatzky's Agency Ltd
Jabotinsky St 61, 49517 Petach Tikva
Toll Free Tel: 1-700-70-66-00 *Fax:* (03) 579-6833
E-mail: service@steimatzky.co.il
Web Site: www.steimatzky.co.il
Key Personnel
Chief Executive Officer: Iris Barel
Founded: 1925
150 bookshops around the country. Also whole-
saler, distributor, publisher, book club & mail
order. Subjects include art, biography, fiction,
music dance, religion, social sciences & sociol-
ogy.
Type of Business: Distributor, Exporter, Importer,
Major Book Chain Headquarters, Wholesaler
Parent Company: Arledan Investments Ltd

Italy

Athesia Buch GmbH
Member of Athesia Unternehmensgruppe
Lauben 41, 39100 Bolzano BZ
Tel: (0471) 081 100 *Fax:* (0471) 081 129
E-mail: bozen.buch@athesia.it; info.shop@
athesia.it
Web Site: www.athesiabuch.it
Key Personnel
Dir: Dr Michl Ebner *Tel:* (0471) 925 201
Fax: (0471) 925 229 *E-mail:* michl.ebner@
athesia.it
Dir, Retail Sales: Patrick Pircher *Tel:* (0471) 081
101 *E-mail:* patrick.pircher@athesia.it
Sales Coordinator: Peter Stuerz *Tel:* (0471) 927
200 *Fax:* (0471) 927 009 *E-mail:* peter.stuerz@
athesia.it
Founded: 1907
Type of Business: Distributor, Importer, Major
Book Chain Headquarters, Wholesaler
Owned by: Athesiabuch GmbH
Branch Office(s)
Weissenturmgasse 1, 39042 Brixen, Branch Man-
ager: Walter Rabensteiner *Tel:* (0472) 082 150
Fax: (0472) 082 151 *E-mail:* brixen.buch@
athesia.it
Stadtgasse 4, 39031 Brunico, Branch Manager:
Evi Grunser *Tel:* (0474) 084 100 *Fax:* (0474)
084 139 *E-mail:* bruneck.buch@athesia.it
Kapuzinergasse 2, 39057 Eppan, Branch Man-
ager: Sigrid Matscher *Tel:* (0471) 081 170
Fax: (0471) 081 179 *E-mail:* eppan.buch@
athesia.it
Peter Paul Rainer Str 20/D, 39038 Innichen,
Branch Manager: Sonja Bachmann *Tel:* (0474)
084 200 *Fax:* (0474) 084 200 *E-mail:* innichen.
papier@athesia.it
Lauben 186, 39012 Meran, Branch Man-
ager: Gebhard Stuefer *Tel:* (0473) 083 140
Fax: (0473) 083 149 *E-mail:* meran.buch@
athesia.it
Hauptstr 12, 39025 Naturns, Branch Manager:
Elisabeth Mair *Tel:* (0473) 083 180 *Fax:* (0473)
083 183 *E-mail:* naturns@athesia.it

Lauben 3, 39044 Neumarkt, Branch Manager: Heidi Mayer Dipauli *Tel:* (0471) 081 180 *Fax:* (0471) 081 189 *E-mail:* neumarkt.papier@athesia.it
Hauptstr 51, 39028 Schlanders, Branch Manager: Manuel Holzknecht *Tel:* (0473) 083 100 *Fax:* (0473) 083 110 *E-mail:* schlanders.buch@athesia.it
Antoniusplatz 82, 39046 St Ulrich/Groeden, Branch Manager: Edith Rieder *Tel:* (0471) 081 190 *Fax:* (0471) 081 199 *E-mail:* groeden.buch@athesia.it
Altstadt 9, 39049 Sterzing, Branch Manager: Claudia Manferdini *Tel:* (0472) 082 100 *Fax:* (0472) 082 119 *E-mail:* sterzing.buch@athesia.it
Sonnenwiechserstr 10, 83052 Bruckmuehl, Germany, Branch Manager: Anna Pretzl *Tel:* (08062) 72 88 99 *Fax:* (08062) 72 88 98 *E-mail:* bruckmuehl@athesiabuch.de
Stadtplatz 14, 83278 Traunstein, Germany, Branch Manager: Veronika Hagenhofer *Tel:* (0861) 90 96 610 *Fax:* (0861) 90 96 616 *E-mail:* traunstein@athesiabuch.de

Libreria Bodoniana
Piazza San Domenico Maggiore 9, 80134 Naples
Tel: (081) 5802279 *Fax:* (081) 5802279
Web Site: digilander.libero.it/fmrnapoli
Key Personnel
President: Franco Maria Ricci
Founded: 1997
Type of Business: Major Independent Bookseller

Casalini Libri SpA
Via Benedetto da Maiano, 3, 50014 Fiesole FI
Mailing Address: CP 12, 50014 Fiesole FI
Tel: (055) 50 18 1 *Fax:* (055) 50 18 201
E-mail: orders@casalini.it
Web Site: www.casalini.it
Key Personnel
President: Barbara Casalini *E-mail:* barbara@casalini.it
Mng Dir: Michele Casalini *E-mail:* michele@casalini.it
Head, Sales: Patricia O'Loughlin *E-mail:* patricia.oloughlin@casalini.it
Founded: 1958
Also publisher.
Type of Business: Exporter, Importer

Libreria Commissionaria Internazionale
Via San Petronio Vecchio, 3, 40125 Bologna BO
Tel: (051) 229466
Founded: 1975
Type of Business: Importer, Major Independent Bookseller, Wholesaler

Libreria Dante di Longo
Via Armando Diaz, 39, 48121 Ravenna RA
Tel: (0544) 33500
E-mail: libreriadanteravenna@gmail.com
Web Site: www.facebook.com/LibreriaDanteRavenna
Key Personnel
Manager: Alberta Longo; Angela Longo
Founded: 1959
Specialize in books about fine arts & mosaics.
Type of Business: Exporter, Importer, Major Independent Bookseller
Owned by: Angelo Longo Editore

Librerie Feltrinelli SpA
via Tucidide 56, 20134 Milan
E-mail: comunicazione@lafeltrinelli.it; commerciale@feltrinelli.it
Web Site: www.lafeltrinelli.it
150 bookshops throughout Italy.
Type of Business: Major Book Chain Headquarters, Online Bookseller
Parent Company: Gruppo Feltrinelli SpA

Ilisso Edizioni SRL
Via Guerrazzi 6, 08100 Nuoro
Tel: (0784) 33033; (0784) 36139 *Fax:* (0784) 35413
E-mail: amministrazione@ilisso.it; info@ilisso.it; ordini@ilisso.it (orders)
Web Site: www.ilisso.it
Founded: 1985
Specialize in art books.

Libreria Internazionale Ulrico Hoepli
Via Ulrico Hoepli, 5, 20121 Milan
Tel: (02) 86487 1 *Fax:* (02) 864322
E-mail: libreria@hoepli.it; info@hoepli.it
Web Site: www.hoepli.it
Key Personnel
President: Dr Ulrico Carlo Hoepli
Founded: 1870
Type of Business: Major Independent Bookseller, Online Bookseller
Owned by: Casa Editrice Libraria Ulrico Hoepli SpA

Libro Co Italia SRL
Via Borromeo 48, San Casciano VP, 50026 Florence
Mailing Address: PO Box 23, San Casciano VP, 50026 Florence
Tel: (055) 822 94 14; (055) 822 84 61 *Fax:* (055) 829 46 03; (055) 822 84 62
E-mail: libroco@libroco.it
Web Site: www.libroco.it
Key Personnel
Mng Dir: Massimo Megli
Export Manager: Donatella Nazzi
Founded: 1992
Specialize in the research & sale of books on art & architecture in Italy & abroad.
Type of Business: Distributor

Messaggerie Libri SpA
Via G Verdi 8, 20090 Assago MI
Tel: (02) 457741 *Toll Free Tel:* 800 804 900 *Fax:* (02) 45701032
E-mail: info@meli.it; meli.dirgen@meli.it
Web Site: www.messaggerielibri.it
Type of Business: Distributor

Edizioni Minerva Medica SpA
Corso Bramante 83-85, 10126 Turin
Tel: (011) 678282 *Fax:* (011) 674502
E-mail: minervamedica@minervamedica.it; book.dept@minervamedica.it
Web Site: www.minervamedica.it
Key Personnel
Mng Editor: Dr Alberto Oliaro
Founded: 1934
Specialize in scientific literature for the medical field.
Type of Business: Distributor, Online Bookseller
Branch Office(s)
Via Spallanzani 9, 00161 Rome *Tel:* (06) 44251210 *Fax:* (06) 44291500
E-mail: minmed.rome@minervamedica.it

Pietro Missorini & Co - Libreria Commissionaria
Via Cremonese 67, 43126 Parma PR
Tel: (0521) 993919
Founded: 1972
Specialize in publications on food service & technology.
Type of Business: Major Independent Bookseller

Franco Maria Ricci Editore-Liberia, see Libreria Bodoniana

Libreria Rizzoli
Galleria Vittorio Emanuele II, 20121 Milan MI
Tel: (02) 86461071

E-mail: libreria.rizzoli@mondadori.it; rizzoligalleria@rizzolilibri.it
Web Site: www.libreriarizzoli.it
Founded: 1967
Type of Business: Major Independent Bookseller
Owned by: Mondadori Retail SpA

Sperling & Kupfer Editora SpA
Via Mondadori 1, 20090 Segrate MI
Tel: (02) 7542 2929 *Fax:* (02) 7542 3361
E-mail: info@sperling.it
Web Site: www.sperling.it
Key Personnel
Head, Press: Paola Caviggioli
Foreign Rights: Francesca Villa *E-mail:* fvilla@sperling.it
Founded: 1899
Type of Business: Distributor, Importer, Online Bookseller
Parent Company: Arnoldo Mondadori Editore SpA, Via Bianca di Savoia 12, 20122 Milan MI

Jamaica

Kingston Bookshop Ltd
74 King St, Kingston
Tel: (876) 922-7016; (876) 922 7312 *Fax:* (876) 922-0127
E-mail: info@kingstonbookshop.com
Web Site: www.kingstonbookshopjm.com
Key Personnel
Chief Executive Officer & Mng Dir: Steadman Fuller *E-mail:* sarfuller@kingstonbookshop.com
Founded: 1974
Type of Business: Major Book Chain Headquarters
Branch Office(s)
80 King St, Kingston *Tel:* (876) 948-6928 *Fax:* (876) 967-3231 *E-mail:* sales@kingstonbookshop.com (marketing & sales)

Sangster's Book Stores Ltd
33 Second St, Newport West, Kingston 13
Tel: (876) 758-6840; (876) 758-7549; (876) 758-8415; (876) 758-6612; (876) 758-8450; (876) 758-6578; (876) 758-7218 *Fax:* (876) 758-5445
E-mail: info@sangstersbooks.com
Web Site: www.sangstersbooks.com
Key Personnel
Mng Dir: Dr N Marshall
Founded: 1938
Publishing & publisher representation.
Type of Business: Major Book Chain Headquarters, Wholesaler
Bookshop(s): 93 1/2 King St, Kingston *Tel:* (876) 948-2866; (876) 922-1541 *Fax:* (876) 922-8125; 33 King St, Kingston *Tel:* (876) 967-1930; (876) 967-1931 *Fax:* (876) 967-9776; Springs Plaza, 17 Constant Spring Rd, Kingston 10 *Tel:* (876) 926-1800; (876) 960-5371 *Fax:* (876) 968-5516; 97 Harbour St, Kingston *Tel:* (876) 967-3773 *Fax:* (876) 922-3832; Mall Plaza, 20 Constant Spring Rd, Kingston 10 *Tel:* (876) 926-2271; (876) 920-6218 *Fax:* (876) 968-7155; Soverign Centre, 106 Hope Rd, Kingston 6 *Tel:* (876) 978-3518; (876) 978-3629 *Fax:* (876) 978-7825; 1-3 & 5 Old Hope Rd, Kingston 5 *Tel:* (876) 908-1876; (876) 754-2385 *Fax:* (876) 906-4728; LOJ Shopping Centre, Kingston *Tel:* (876) 960-2488; (876) 960-2489 *Fax:* (876) 960-2490; Shop G103, Baywest Shopping Centre, Harbour St, Montego Bay *Tel:* (876) 952-0319; (876) 952-1122 *Fax:* (876) 940-0182; 9 King St, Montego Bay *Tel:* (876) 979-2134; (876) 971-4844 *Fax:* (876) 971-9004; Portmore Town Centre, Portmore *Tel:* (876) 704-5450; (876)

704-5371 *Fax:* (876) 704-5459; Shop 9 &
10 Phase 3, Portmore Pines *Tel:* (876) 740-
2224; (876) 949-9127 *Fax:* (876) 989-6136;
LOJ Shopping Centre, 17 Burke Rd, Spanish
Town *Tel:* (876) 984-5003; (876) 984-0476
Fax: (876) 984-0597

Japan

Academia Scientific Book Inc
2-10-15, Kasuga, Bunkyo-ku, Tokyo 112-0003
Tel: (03) 3813-4846 *Fax:* (03) 3812-8509
E-mail: info@academia-s.com
Key Personnel
President: Satoshi Nakai
Dir, Sales & Purchase: Shunsuke Nakai
Membership(s): Japan Association of International
Publications.
Type of Business: Major Independent Bookseller,
Wholesaler

Asahiya Shoten Ltd (Booksellers)
2-12-6 Sonezaki, Kita-ku, Osaka 530-0057
Tel: 6312-0877
Web Site: www.asahiya.com
Founded: 1946
Type of Business: Major Book Chain Headquar-
ters

Bookman's & Co Ltd
2-10-13 Higashi Toyonaka, Osaka 560-0003
Tel: (06) 6850-4107 *Fax:* (06) 6850-4108
E-mail: info@bookmans.co.jp
Web Site: www.bookmans.co.jp
Key Personnel
President: Mr Mitsunobu Nakamura
Founded: 1967
Art & architecture & graphical, industrial design
photography, textile, fashion, interior design &
human science.
Type of Business: Importer
Showroom(s): Bookman's Gallery

Christian Literature Society of Japan, see
Kyobunkwan Inc (Christian Literature Society
of Japan)

France Tosho Inc
1-11-15, Shinjuku, Shinjuku-ku, Tokyo 160-0022
Tel: (03) 3226-9011 *Fax:* (03) 3226-9012
E-mail: frbooks@sepia.ocn.ne.jp
Web Site: www.francetosho.com
Key Personnel
Dir: Fumhiro Kondo
Founded: 1967
French, English, Italian & German books about
history, society & food culture. Also deal with
computer software & audiovisual software.
Type of Business: Importer, Major Independent
Bookseller, Online Bookseller, Wholesaler

Ikubundo Co Ltd
5-30-21 Hongo, Bunkyo-ku, Tokyo 113-0033
Tel: (03) 3814-5571 *Fax:* (03) 3814-5576
Web Site: www.ikubundo.com
Founded: 1899
Type of Business: Importer

**Japan Publications Trading Co Ltd (Import &
Export)**
1-2-1 Sarugaku-cho, Chiyoda-ku, Tokyo 101-0064
Tel: (03) 3292-3751 *Fax:* (03) 3292-0410
E-mail: info@jptco.co.jp
Web Site: www.jptco.co.jp
Key Personnel
President: Toyohiko Ayamori

Executive Dir: Ryuichi Kondo; Kazuhiro
Yoshizawa
Dir: Yasuhiko Hayashi; Koji Matsunami
Founded: 1942
Importer & exporter of general & academic books
& periodicals, language learning textbooks &
materials, audio/visual discs & other general
merchandise. Also deals in rental & manage-
ment of real estate.
Type of Business: Distributor, Exporter, Importer,
Wholesaler
Branch Office(s)
206 Ark Vila Yakuin, 4-5-2 Yakuin, Chuuo-
ku, Fukuoka 812-0022 *Tel:* (092) 534-2270
Fax: (092) 534-2271 *E-mail:* kyushu@jptco.co.
jp
503 Dai 5 Shin Osaka Bldg, 3-12-15 Nishi-
Nakajina, Yodogawa-ku, Osaka 532-0011
Tel: (06) 6886-7177 *Fax:* (06) 6886-7166
E-mail: osaka@jptco.co.jp
JPT Europe Ltd, 24-25 Denman St, London W1D
7HU, United Kingdom *Tel:* (020) 7287 7638
Fax: (020) 7287 0903 *E-mail:* info@jpbooks.
co.uk *Web Site:* www.jpbooks.co.uk
U.S. Office(s): JPT America Inc, 1760 Buchanan
St, Suite 1, San Francisco, CA 94115, United
States *Tel:* 415-814-2110 *Fax:* 415-814-2688
E-mail: info@jptamerica.com *Web Site:* www.
jptamerica.com

Kinokuniya Co Ltd (Japan)
3-7-10 Shimomeguro, Meguro-ku, Tokyo 153-
8504
Tel: (03) 6910-0502 *Fax:* (03) 6420-1350
E-mail: pv01@kinokuniya.co.jp
Web Site: www.kinokuniya.co.jp
Key Personnel
Exective Vice President: Tsutomu Yamamoto
President: Masashi Takai
Senior Mng Dir: Ichikawa Norhiro
Founded: 1927
Also publisher.
Type of Business: Distributor, Exporter, Importer,
Major Book Chain Headquarters, Wholesaler

**Kyobunkwan Inc (Christian Literature Society
of Japan)**
Ginza 4-5-1, Chuo-ku, Tokyo 104-0061
Tel: (03) 3561-8449 *Fax:* (03) 5250-5109; (03)
3535-5052
E-mail: fbooks@kyobunkwan.co.jp; e-shop@
kyobunkwan.co.jp; xbooks@kyobunkwan.co.jp
Web Site: www.kyobunkwan.co.jp
Key Personnel
President: Mitsuru Watabe
Deputy Manager: Kazuhiko Uejima
Founded: 1885
Branch offices in Fukuoka, Hiroshima, Kanazawa,
Kobe, Kyoto, Nagoya, Okayama, Osaka, Sap-
poro, Sendai, Singapore, Tsukuba & Yoko-
hama, London (UK) & New York (USA).
Membership(s): Japan Association of International
Publications.
Type of Business: Distributor, Importer, Major
Independent Bookseller, Online Bookseller,
Wholesaler

Maruzen-Yushodo Co Ltd
1-9-18, Kaigan, Minato-ku, Tokyo 105-0022
Mailing Address: PO Box 671, Ginza Branch,
Tokyo 100-8692
Tel: (03) 4335-9316 *Fax:* (03) 4335-9368
E-mail: e-support@maruzen.co.jp; export@
maruzen.co.jp; mg-yosho-marketing@maruzen.
co.jp
Web Site: yushodo.maruzen.co.jp
Key Personnel
President: Eisuke Matsuo
Founded: 1869
Sales of foreign & Japanese books & journals;
scientific information retrieval services; pub-
lishing.

Type of Business: Exporter, Importer, Online
Bookseller
Branch Office(s)
10-10, Yotsuyasakamachi, Shinjuku-ku, Tokyo
160-0002
U.S. Office(s): Maruzen International Co Ltd,
110B Meadowlands Pkwy, Suite 205, Secau-
cus, NJ 07094-1878, United States *Tel:* 201-
865-4400 *Fax:* 201-865-4845 *E-mail:* mic@
maruzenusa.com

Nankodo Co Ltd
3-42-6 Hongo, Bunkyo-ku, Tokyo 113-8410
Tel: (03) 3811-7140; (03) 3811-7239 (sales)
Fax: (03) 3811-7265
E-mail: nkdyosho@nankodo.co.jp
Web Site: www.nankodo.co.jp
Key Personnel
President: Kanehiko Kodachi
Founded: 1879
Also medical publishers.
Membership(s): Japan Association of International
Publications.
Type of Business: Distributor, Importer, Online
Bookseller, Wholesaler

Nellie's Ltd
Kenkyusha Fujimi Bldg 3F, 2-11-3 Fujimi,
Chiyoda-ku, Tokyo 102-0071
Tel: (03) 5275-6761 *Fax:* (03) 3556-7326
E-mail: consult@nellies.jp
Web Site: www.nellies.jp
Key Personnel
Chief Executive: Hiroyuki Yamamoto
Founded: 1989
Type of Business: Distributor, Importer

Nippan Shuppan Hanbai Inc
4-3 Kandasurugadai, Chiyoda-ku, Tokyo 101-
8710
Tel: (03) 3233-4838; (03) 3233-3829 *Fax:* (03)
3233-0486; (03) 3233-6045
E-mail: press@nippan.co.jp
Web Site: www.nippan.co.jp
Founded: 1949
Distribution of books, magazines, textbooks &
educational materials.
Type of Business: Distributor, Exporter, Importer

Osaka Oviss Inc, see OVISS Inc

**Overseas Special Technical Information
Selection Service**, see OVISS Inc

OVISS Inc
Takahashi Bldg, Higashi 6-Gokan, 7-22
Matsugae-cho, Kita-ku, Osaka 530-0037
Tel: (06) 6352 7090 *Fax:* (06) 6352 8898
E-mail: info@oviss.co.jp; import@oviss.co.jp
Web Site: www.oviss.co.jp; oviss.b-smile.jp
Key Personnel
Dir: Tadanori Oyama
Founded: 1972
Type of Business: Distributor, Importer, Major
Independent Bookseller

Sanseido Bookstore Ltd
Kanda Jinbo-cho 1-1, Chiyoda-ku, Tokyo 101-
0051
Tel: (03) 3233-3312; (03) 3295-1881 *Fax:* (03)
3291-3006
E-mail: fbook_stock3@mail.books-sanseido.co.jp
Web Site: www.books-sanseido.co.jp
Key Personnel
President: Tadao Kamei
General Manager, Sales Dept: Hideyuki Owari
Manager: Osamu Suzuki
Founded: 1881
Membership(s): Japan Association of International
Publications.
Type of Business: Importer, Major Book Chain
Headquarters, Online Bookseller

Shinko Tsusho Co Ltd
1-7-1 Wakaba, Shinjuku-ku, Tokyo 160-0011
Tel: (03) 3353-1751 *Fax:* (03) 3353-2205
Key Personnel
President: Ms Keiko Nagato
Founded: 1960
Membership(s): Japan Association of International
 Publications.
Type of Business: Distributor, Importer, Whole-
 saler

Shiseido Booksellers Ltd
55 Koyama-Minamikazusa, Kita-ku, Kyoto 603-
8149
Tel: (075) 431 2345 *Fax:* (075) 432 6588
E-mail: shiseido@jd5.so-net.ne.jp
Web Site: www.shiseido-book.co.jp
Key Personnel
Chairman & Owner: Shuko Hori
President: Hiromitsu Hori
Sales: Yoshiaki Kanda
Founded: 1947
Booksellers for scholars on the field of humani-
 ties.
Membership(s): Japan Association of International
 Publications.
Type of Business: Importer, Major Independent
 Bookseller

Tohan Corp
6-24 Higashigoken-cho, Shinjuku-ku, Tokyo 162-
8710
Tel: (03) 3269-6111
Web Site: www.tohan.jp
Key Personnel
President: Takehiko Fujii
Vice President: Toshitaka Kondo
Founded: 1949
Membership(s): Japan Association of International
 Publications.
Type of Business: Distributor, Exporter, Online
 Bookseller, Wholesaler

Tokyo Publications Service Ltd
3F, Suzuki Bldg, 10-3, Shintomi 2-chome, Chuo-
ku, Tokyo 104-0041
Tel: (03) 6228-3588 *Fax:* (03) 5543-3115
E-mail: info@tokyoyosho.com
Web Site: www.tokyoyosho.com
Key Personnel
President & Chief Executive Officer: Kensaku
 Kihara
Chairman: Kunio Kihara
Dir, Sales: Kunihiro Hirakata
Founded: 1968
Retail & wholesale. Also a subscription agency.
Membership(s): Japan Association of International
 Publications.
Type of Business: Distributor, Exporter, Importer,
 Major Independent Bookseller, Wholesaler

United Publishers Services Ltd
1-32-5 Higashi-shinagawa, Shinagawa-ku, Tokyo
140-0002
Tel: (03) 5479-7251 *Fax:* (03) 5479-7307
Founded: 1978
Membership(s): Japan Association of International
 Publications.
Type of Business: Distributor, Importer, Whole-
 saler
Owned by: Cambridge University Press, United
 Kingdom

Yushodo Co Ltd, see Maruzen-Yushodo Co Ltd

Yushodo Shuppan, see Maruzen-Yushodo Co Ltd

Jordan

ARAMEX Media
PO Box 3371, Amman 11181
Tel: (06) 5358855 *Fax:* (06) 5337733
Founded: 1982
Type of Business: Distributor, Exporter, Importer,
 Major Book Chain Headquarters, Wholesaler

Jordan Book Centre
152 Queen Rania Al Abdallah St, Amman 11941
Mailing Address: PO Box 301, Al-Jubeiha, Am-
 man 11941
Tel: (06) 5151882 *Fax:* (06) 5152016
E-mail: info@jbc.com.jo; bookshop@jbc.com.jo;
 cs@jbc.com.jo (customer service)
Web Site: www.jbc.com.jo/web
Founded: 1958
Subjects include biology, chemistry, education,
 engineering, historical fiction, history, religion,
 science, technology & theology. Also publisher.
Type of Business: Distributor, Wholesaler

**KaSha Trans Middle East International
 Distribution Co Ltd**
Jordan Trade Centre, Queen Rania Al-Abdullah
 St, Amman 11953
Mailing Address: PO Box 2376, Amman 11953
Tel: (06) 5413270 *Fax:* (06) 5411336
E-mail: info@kasha.cc; marketing@kasha.cc
Web Site: www.kashaonline.com
Distribution services of books, periodicals, En-
 glish language teaching & multimedia publi-
 cations to customers in the Middle East, North
 Africa, Turkey & Iran.
Type of Business: Distributor, Wholesaler
Branch Office(s)
Al-Thakera Bookshop, Al A'adamieh (Next to
 Indian Embassy), Baghdad, Iraq *Tel:* (01)
 4257628 *Fax:* (01) 4259987 *E-mail:* info@
 althakerabookshop.com
Al-Ahliya College School Bldg, 3rd floor, Ra-
 mallah, Palestine, Israel *Tel:* (02) 22954474
 Fax: (02) 22954474 *E-mail:* zattal@kasha.cc
Off 245, Bldg No 10, Dubai Media City, PO Box
 502122, Dubai, United Arab Emirates *Tel:* (04)
 3900965 *Fax:* (04) 3904565 *E-mail:* gulf@
 kasha.cc
4 Rickett St, London SW6 1RU, United Kingdom
 Tel: (020) 7386 0500 *Fax:* (020) 7610 3337
 E-mail: ukinfo@kasha.cc

Kenya

Book Sales (K) Ltd
Menengai House, Ronald Ngala St, Nairobi
Mailing Address: PO Box 20373, Nairobi 00200
Tel: (020) 2226543
Founded: 1976
Also a publisher.
Type of Business: Major Independent Bookseller

City Bookshop Ltd
Nkrumah Rd, Next to Kenya Cinema, Mombasa
Mailing Address: PO Box 90512, Mombasa
 80100
Tel: (041) 2313149; (041) 2225548
Founded: 1953
Fiction, nonfiction, magazines & greeting cards.
Type of Business: Distributor, Importer, Major
 Independent Bookseller, Wholesaler

Keswick Books & Gifts Ltd
Bruce House, Ground floor, Kaunda St, Nairobi
Mailing Address: PO Box 0100, Nairobi 12345

Tel: (020) 2226047; (020) 2147762
E-mail: info@keswickbook.com; keswick@
 swiftkenya.com
Web Site: www.keswickbooks.com
Founded: 1959
Specialize in Christian books.
Type of Business: Distributor, Importer, Major
 Independent Bookseller
Branch Office(s)
Sarit Centre, Ground floor, Westlands, Nairobi
 Tel: (020) 3755090
Nkurumah Rd, Mombasa *Tel:* (041) 2226520;
 (020) 2441169
Prestige Plaza, 1st floor, Ngong Rd, Ngong
 Tel: (020) 3875930

Prestige Booksellers & Stationers Ltd, see
 Prestige Bookshop

Prestige Bookshop
Prudential Bldg, Ground floor, Mama Ngina St,
 Nairobi 00100
Mailing Address: PO Box 67815, Nairobi 00200
Tel: (020) 2223515; (0707) 660-164 (cell)
E-mail: email-books@prestigebookshop.com
Web Site: prestigebookshop.com
Founded: 1972
Type of Business: Exporter, Importer, Major Inde-
 pendent Bookseller

TBC, see Text Book Centre Ltd

Text Book Centre Ltd
Sarit Centre Branch, Nairobi
Mailing Address: PO Box 47540, Nairobi 00100
Tel: (020) 708344141; (020) 725451468
E-mail: customerservice@tbc.co.ke; academic@
 tbc.co.ke
Web Site: textbookcentre.com
Key Personnel
Owner: Mr S V Shah
Founded: 1964
Type of Business: Distributor, Exporter, Importer,
 Major Independent Bookseller, Online Book-
 seller, Wholesaler
Branch Office(s)
Kijabe St, Nairobi *Tel:* (020) 722560580
 E-mail: kijaberetail@tbc.co.ke
Galleria Mall, Langata, Nairobi *Tel:* (020)
 706621623 *E-mail:* langata@tbc.co.ke
Garden City Mall, Thika Rd, Nairobi *Tel:* (020)
 718848281 *E-mail:* gardencity@tbc.co.ke
Lunga-Lunga Sq Mall, Lunga-Lunga Rd, Nairobi
 Tel: (020) 727479737 *E-mail:* lungalunga@tbc.
 co.ke
Junction Mall, Ngong Rd, Nairobi *Tel:* (020)
 716598220 *E-mail:* junctionshop@tbc.co.ke
The Hub, Dagoretti Rd, Karen, Nairobi *Tel:* (020)
 792764795 *E-mail:* thehub@tbc.co.ke
Thika Rd Mall, Thika Rd, Nairobi *Tel:* (020)
 737464081 *E-mail:* thikaroad@tbc.co.ke
Two Rivers Mall, between Northern Bypass &
 Limuru Rd, Nairobi *Tel:* (020) 799872025
 E-mail: tworivers@tbc.co.ke
Holden Mall, Kakamega *Tel:* (020) 799871808
 E-mail: kakamega@tbc.co.ke

University of Nairobi Bookshop
University of Nairobi, Gadhi Bldg, Ground floor,
 Nairobi 00100
Mailing Address: PO Box 30197, GPO, Nairobi
 00100
Tel: (020) 3318262 (ext 28353); (020) 3318262
 (ext 28111) *Fax:* (020) 3245566
E-mail: manager-bookshop@uonbi.ac.ke
Web Site: www.uonbi.ac.ke
Founded: 1974
Type of Business: Major Independent Bookseller
Owned by: University of Nairobi, University Way,
 Harry Thuku Rd, Nairobi

Kuwait

The Kuwait Book Shop Co Ltd
Al-Muthanna Complex, Fahed Al-Salem St,
13030 Safat
Mailing Address: PO Box 2942, 13030 Safat
Tel: 22424266
E-mail: kbs@ncc.moc.kw
Web Site: kuwait-bookshop-co-ltd-.kuwaitbd.com
Key Personnel
Owner: Bashir N Khatib
Type of Business: Distributor

Latvia

Janis Roze SIA
Atlasa iela 10, Riga LV-1026
Tel: 67501562 *Fax:* 67370922
E-mail: ofiss@jr.lv
Web Site: www.jr.lv
Founded: 2000
Type of Business: Wholesaler

Lebanon

Librairies Antoine SAL (Antoine Bookshops)
Akalian Bldg, Horsh Tabet, Sin el Fil
Tel: (01) 483 513; (01) 481 072
E-mail: contact@antoineonline.com
Web Site: www.antoineonline.com
Key Personnel
Chief Executive Officer: Sami Naufal
Commercial Dir: Emile Tyan
Manager: Jacqueline Kalim
Founded: 1933
Type of Business: Major Book Chain Headquarters, Online Bookseller
Bookshop(s): ABC Mall, Achrafieh, Manager: Nada Abi Kheir *Tel:* (01) 218 175; Sassine, Achrafieh, Manager: Helene Yammine *Tel:* (01) 331 811; International College, Ain Aar, Manager: George Khaled *Tel:* (04) 916 041; Faubourg Saint-Jean, Baabda, Manager: Carla Bou Karam *Tel:* (05) 952 872; American University of Beirut Campus, Beirut, Manager: Hala Halaoui *Tel:* (01) 744 808; International College, Beirut, Manager: Mirvat Saleh *Tel:* (01) 365 483; Beirut Souks, Beirut, Manager: Aida Farah *Tel:* (01) 999 650; ABC Mall, Dbayeh, Manager: Joyce Haddad *Tel:* (04) 414 296; Rue Hamra, Hamra, Manager: Arlette Matar *Tel:* (01) 341 470; NDU Bookstore, Louaize, Manager: Marc Merhej *Tel:* (09) 225 019; (09) 225 463; Metro Superstore, Maameltein, Manager: Valerie Ziadeh *Tel:* (09) 852 463; Faubourg de Tripoli, Tripoli, Manager: Suzanne Sarkis *Tel:* (06) 410 551; Centre les Dunes, Verdun, Manager: Lisa Tannous *Tel:* (01) 794 950; (01) 794 951

Librairie du Liban Publishers SAL
PO Box 11-9232, Beirut
Tel: (09) 217 944; (09) 217 945; (09) 217 946
Fax: (09) 217 734
E-mail: info@ldlp.com; sales@ldlp.com
Web Site: www.ldlp-dictionary.com
Key Personnel
Mng Dir: Habib Sayegh *E-mail:* habib.sayegh@ldlp.com; Pierre Sayegh *E-mail:* pierre.sayegh@ldlp.com
Founded: 1944
Also publisher.

Type of Business: Distributor, Exporter, Importer, Major Independent Bookseller, Wholesaler
Branch Office(s)
Rubeiz Bldg, Hamra St, Beirut *Tel:* (01) 344 070
Lazarieh Bldg, Al Amir Bashir St, Beirut *Tel:* (01) 970602; (01 970603
Esseily Bldg, Riad El Solh Sq, Beirut *Tel:* (01) 972525; (01) 966170
42, Bliss St, Ras Beirut, Beirut *Tel:* (01) 373204
Sayegh Bldg, Baabdat-Al Metn *Tel:* (04) 820 804; (04) 820 728 *Fax:* (04) 977 435 *E-mail:* ksayegh@ldlp.com
Sphinx Publishing Co, 127 Horriya St, Al Shallalat, Alexandria, Egypt *Tel:* (03) 4940539; (03) 4930356 *Fax:* (03) 4924839 *E-mail:* sphinx@internetalex.com
Sphinx Publishing Co, Higher Education Division, Cairo, Egypt *Tel:* (02) 3909169 *Fax:* (02) 3909169 *E-mail:* hesphinx@link.net
Sphinx Publishing Co, 3, Shawarby Str, Apartment 305, Cairo, Egypt *Tel:* (02) 3924616 *Fax:* (02) 3918002 *E-mail:* sphinx@intouch.com
Sphinx Publishing Co, Zahra'a St, Al Dokki, Cairo, Egypt *Tel:* (02) 7494998 *Fax:* (02) 3389595 *E-mail:* zahraasp@intouch.com
Babylon International for Educational Publishing, Shar'a Phalastin, Hay 14 Tamuz, Mahalat 510, Treet 15, Bldg 143, Baghdad, Iraq *Tel:* (07901) 338190 *Fax:* (07903) 730354 *E-mail:* b-i-e-p@hotmail.com
Petra International Publishers, H & M Bldg No 157, PO Box 6587, Amman 11118, Jordan *Tel:* (06) 5685827 *Fax:* (06) 5685819 *E-mail:* pip@go.com.jo
Librairie Sayegh, Syria, Al-Taif Str, Al-Salihiya, PO Box 704, Diab Bldg, Damascus, Syria *Tel:* (011) 4422973 *Fax:* (011) 4423236 *E-mail:* sayeghbook@net.sy
Arab Education Publishers, PO Box 52269, Jeddah 21563, Syria *Tel:* (02) 2383911 *Fax:* (02) 6622327 *E-mail:* info@aep-ksa.com
Arab Gulf Education, Al Twar Center, Al Nahda St, Al Qussais 2, PO Box 86865, Dubai, United Arab Emirates *Tel:* (04) 2617373 *Fax:* (04) 2617557 *E-mail:* agedu@emirates.net.ae

Lesotho

Morija Sesotho Book Depot
PO Box 608, Morija 190
Tel: 2232 3783 *Fax:* 2232 3783
E-mail: lec.bookdepot@ilesotho.com
Book & stationery retailer. Also publisher.
Type of Business: Major Independent Bookseller

Lithuania

Humanitas Ltd
Butrimoniu Str 9, LT-50220 Kaunas
Tel: (037) 220 333 *Fax:* (037) 423 653
E-mail: info@humanitas.lt
Web Site: www.humanitas.lt
Founded: 1994
Type of Business: Distributor, Importer, Major Book Chain Headquarters, Wholesaler
Bookshop(s): Donelaicio g 61, LT-44245 Kaunas *Tel:* (037) 202429; K Donelaicio g 52, LT-44244 Kaunas *Tel:* (037) 221530; Vilniaus g 11, LT-44282 Kaunas *Tel:* (037) 209 581; Universiteto g 4, LT-01122 Vilnius *Tel:* (05) 2661680; Dominikonu g 5, LT-01131 Vilnius *Tel:* (05) 262 11 53; Traku 5a, LT-01132 Vilnius *Tel:* (05) 2 610 416

Luxembourg

Ernster Sarl
27, rue du Fosse, 1536 Luxembourg
Tel: 22 50 77-240; 22 50 77-333 (customer service) *Fax:* 22 50 77-249
E-mail: order@ernster.com; papeterie@ernster.com
Web Site: www.ernster.com
Key Personnel
Owner & Chief Executive Officer: Fernand Ernster
Dir: Dirk Sumkotter *E-mail:* direction@ernster.com
Founded: 1889
Textbooks, supplies for schools & stationery.
Type of Business: Major Book Chain Headquarters, Online Bookseller
Bookshop(s): Ernster Erny Ernster, 4, rue de la Reine, 2418 Luxembourg *Tel:* 22 50 77-280 *E-mail:* librarie@ernster.com; Librairie Ernster City Concorde, 80, route de Longwy, 8060 Bertrange *Tel:* 22 50 77-500 *E-mail:* city.concorde@ernster.com; Librairie Ernster La Belle Etoile, 8050 Bertrange *Tel:* 22 50 77-400 *E-mail:* belle.etoile@ernster.com

LIBO SA
2, rue Christophe Plantin, 2339 Luxembourg
Tel: 40 30 30-1
E-mail: info@libo.lu; commande@libo.lu
Web Site: www.libo.lu
Founded: 1982
Type of Business: Major Book Chain Headquarters
Branch Office(s)
2-4, Rue de Brabant, 9213 Diekirch *Tel:* 40 30 30-200 *E-mail:* diekirch@libo.lu
24, Route de Treves, 6793 Grevenmacher *Tel:* 40 30 30-500
45 Grand-Rue, 9530 Wiltz *Tel:* 40 30 30-400

Librairie Promoculture Sarl
14, rue Duchscher, 1424 Luxembourg-Gare
Tel: 48 06 91 *Fax:* 40 09 50
E-mail: info@promoculture.lu
Web Site: librairiepromoculture.lu
Key Personnel
Dir: Albert P Daming
Founded: 1972
Subscription agency & technical bookshop specializing in law. Also a book publisher.
Type of Business: Major Independent Bookseller

Macedonia

Kultura Knizarnici
ul Makedonija 33, 1000 Skopje
Tel: (02) 3296-763
E-mail: ipkultura@kultura.com.mk; info@kultura.com.mk; knizarnica.kultura@gmail.com
Web Site: www.kultura.com.mk
Founded: 1945
Also publisher & stationery goods supplier.
Type of Business: Distributor, Exporter, Importer, Major Independent Bookseller, Wholesaler

Madagascar

Librairie de Madagascar
38, ave de l'Independance, Analakely, 101 Antananarivo
Mailing Address: BP 402, Analakely, 101 Antananarivo
Tel: 22 224 54
Founded: 1936
Type of Business: Major Independent Bookseller

Librairie Mixte Sarl
Analakely 17 Ave d'Andrianampoinimerina, pres Terminus Bus 134, 101 Antananarivo
Tel: 34 04 902 23 (cell)
Founded: 1940
Type of Business: Importer, Major Independent Bookseller

TPFLM, see Trano Printy Fiangonana Loterana Malagasy (TPFLM)

Trano Printy Fiangonana Loterana Malagasy (TPFLM)
9, rue General Gabriel Ramanantsoa, 101 Antananarivo
Tel: 22 245 69 *Fax:* 22 626 43
Also publisher.

Malawi

Central Bookshop
Chichiri Shopping Mall, Blantyre
Tel: 01 872 094
Founded: 1960
School supplies, books, stationery & cards, Africana.
Type of Business: Distributor, Importer, Major Independent Bookseller

CLAIM (Christian Literature Association in Malawi) Bookshop
PO Box 616, Mangochi
Tel: 01 594 350
Type of Business: Major Independent Bookseller
Owned by: Christian Literature Association in Malawi

Malaysia

Badan Cemerlang Sdn Bhd
L-3.44 Plaza Angsana, Pusat Bandar Tampoi, 81200 Johor Bahru, Johor
Tel: (07) 2359709; (07) 2360449; (07) 2360267 *Fax:* (07) 2377566
E-mail: badan@badanbookstore.com
Web Site: www.badanbookstore.com
Key Personnel
Owner: Saadon Badan
Contact: Puan Atikah *E-mail:* atikah@badanbookstore.com
Founded: 1977
Type of Business: Major Book Chain Headquarters
Branch Office(s)
Lot UG-33A, Upper Ground floor, Today's Mall, 81800 Ulu Tiram, Johor, Contact: Encik Hakim *Tel:* (07) 8634650 *Fax:* (07) 8634649 *E-mail:* badan@tm.net.my

Edukid Distributors Sdn Bhd
No 5, Jl Perusahaan Amari, Pusat Industri Amari, 68100 Batu Caves, Selangor
Tel: (03) 6178 7861 *Fax:* (03) 6178 7821
E-mail: sales@edukidbooks.com
Web Site: www.edukidbooks.com
Founded: 1989
Subjects include cookery, education, fashion & religion.
Type of Business: Distributor, Wholesaler

Flo Enterprise Sdn Bhd
24 Lorong PJS 1/2 A, Taman Perangsang, Batu 7, Jl Kelang Lama, 46000 Petaling Jaya
Tel: (03) 77833118
Type of Business: Distributor, Importer

Glad Sounds Sdn Bhd
Level 3, Luther Centre, 6, Jl Utara, 46200 Petaling Jaya, Selangor
Tel: (03) 79562901; (03) 79311512; (03) 79587188 (retail shop) *Fax:* (03) 79560528
E-mail: webstore@gladsounds.com.my; gladsounds@yahoo.com
Web Site: www.gladsounds.com.my; www.facebook.com/Glad-Sounds-642442815785963/
Founded: 1974
Type of Business: Distributor, Major Independent Bookseller, Wholesaler

IBS Buku Sdn Bhd
B3-06, P J Industrial Park, Jl Kemajuan, 46200 Petaling Jaya, Selangor Darul Ehsan
Tel: (03) 79579282; (03) 79579470 *Fax:* (03) 79576026
E-mail: hibs@tm.net.my
Founded: 1971
Specialize in academic, library & college textbooks, CD-ROMs, print & online journals.
Also publisher.
Type of Business: Distributor, Exporter, Importer, Wholesaler
U.S. Office(s): North American Division, 8152 Misty Shore Dr, West Chester, OH 45069, United States *Tel:* 513-275-4669 *Fax:* 513-942-3308 *E-mail:* masinc@gmail.com

International Book Service, see IBS Buku Sdn Bhd

Kreatif Kembara Sdn Bhd
C-516 Kelana Sq, SS7/26, Kelana Jaya, 47301 Petaling Jaya, Selangor
Tel: (03) 7494 0212
Web Site: www.facebook.com/Kreatif-Kembara-404921192896401
Founded: 1995
Type of Business: Distributor

SA Majeed & Co Sdn Bhd
7, Jl Bangsar Utama 3, 59000 Bangsar Kuala Lumpur
Tel: (03) 2283 2230 *Fax:* (03) 2282 5670
E-mail: sambooks.my@gmail.com
Web Site: www.sambooks.com.my
Key Personnel
Management: Mr Mohd Kasim
Founded: 1952
Also printer & publisher.
Type of Business: Distributor, Wholesaler

Mawaddah Enterprise Sdn Bhd
No 75, Jl Kapitan Tam Yeong, 70000 Seremban, Negeri Sembilan
Tel: (06) 7611062 *Fax:* (06) 7633062
Founded: 1977
Type of Business: Distributor, Exporter, Importer, Wholesaler

MPH Bookstores Sdn Bhd
Lot 1, 3rd floor, Bangunan TH, No 5 Jl Bersatu, Seksyen 13/4, 46200 Petaling Jaya, Selangor
Tel: (03) 7955 1090; (03) 2938 3818 (customer service) *Fax:* (03) 7955 2090
E-mail: customerservice@mph.com.my
Web Site: www.mphonline.com
Key Personnel
Chief Operating Officer: Donald Kee
Founded: 1906
Type of Business: Major Book Chain Headquarters
Owned by: MPH Group Malaysia Sdn Bhd
Bookshop(s): F319 & S319, 1st & 2nd floor, One Utama Shopping Centre, No 1, Lebuh Bandar Utama, Bandar Utama, 47800 Petaling Jaya, Selangor *Tel:* (03) 7725 9003 *Fax:* (03) 7722 4003; G 26A(1),G26B-C&G26D(1), Ground floor, Subang Parade, No 5, Jl SS16/1, Subang Jaya, 47500 Petaling Jaya, Selangor *Tel:* (03) 5633 9079 *Fax:* (03) 5637 9729; Bangi Gateway Shopping Complex, Persiaran Pekeliling, Seksyen 15, 43650 Bandar Baru Bangi, Selangor *Tel:* (03) 8912 2629 *Fax:* (03) 8920 9032; LG-10, Lower Ground floor, D'Pulze Cyberjaya Shopping Centre, Lot 47594, Mukim Dengkil, 63000 Sepang, Selangor *Tel:* (03) 8688 2573 *Fax:* (03) 8688 2572; Lot 1F-07 & IF-08, 1st floor, SACC Mall, Precincts 1.1 & 1.2, Jl Perbadanan 14/9, Seksyen 14, 40000 Shah Alam, Selangor *Tel:* (03) 5513 9677 *Fax:* (03) 5513 0776; Lot A22-A24, Giant Hypermarket Stadium Shah Alam, Lot 2, Jl Persiaran Sukan, Seksyen 13, 40100 Shah Alam, Selangor *Tel:* (03) 5511 8978 *Fax:* (03) 5511 8976; LG-41 Setia City Mall No 7 Persiaran Setia Dagang Bandar Setia Alam Seksyen U13, 40170 Shah Alam, Selangor *Tel:* (03) 3358 3017 *Fax:* (03) 3345 6802; Lot E6, Public Concourse, Aeromall Sultan Ismail International Airport, 81250 Johor Bahru, Johor *Tel:* (07) 599 0186 *Fax:* (07) 599 0286; Lot J3-10, 11, 12, Level 3, Johur Bahru City Sq, 106-108 Jl Wong Ah Fook, 80000 Johor Bahru, Johor *Tel:* (07) 228 1988 *Fax:* (07) 223 2988; UG18, Upper Ground floor, Aeon Taman Universiti Shopping Centre, Jl Pendidikan 1, Taman Universiti, 81300 Skudai, Johor *Tel:* (07) 521 1702 *Fax:* (07) 521 2702; Lot 21, 1st floor, Amanjaya Mall, Jl Jati 1, 08000 Sungai Petani, Kedah *Tel:* (04) 440 0830 *Fax:* (04) 440 0835; F 11-12, 1st floor, Alpha Angle Shopping Centre, Jl R1, Section 1, Bandar Baru Wangsa Maju, 53300 Kuala Lumpur *Tel:* (03) 4142 1246 *Fax:* (03) 4142 1245; No L2-37, UP2-01, Melawati Mall, 355 Jl Bandar Melawati, Pusat Bandar Melawati, 53100 Kuala Lumpur *Tel:* (03) 4101 9382; (03) 4101 9376 *Fax:* (03) 4101 9078; Unit G6, Blok B, Bangunan Bakti Siti Hasmah, No 6, Cangkat, Abang Haji Openg, Taman Tun Dr Ismail, 60000 Kuala Lumpur *Tel:* (03) 7724 2913 *Fax:* (03) 7724 2912; Lot F7, 1st floor, Bangsar Village Shopping Centre, No 1, Jl Telawi 1, Bangsar Baru, 59100 Kuala Lumpur *Tel:* (03) 2283 1098 *Fax:* (03) 2283 1097; Lot 2-32 & 2-33, 1018, Jl Sultan Ismail, 50250 Kuala Lumpur *Tel:* (03) 2602 2358 *Fax:* (03) 2602 2359; Lot LG-058, Lower Ground floor, Mid Valley City, 59200 Kuala Lumpur *Tel:* (03) 2938 3818 *Fax:* (03) 2938 3817; Lot 13 & 14, Level 2 Nu Sentral Mall, Jl Tun Sambanthan KL Sentral, 50470 Kuala Lumpur *Tel:* (03) 2276 2765 *Fax:* (03) 2276 4133; Lot L3-02, Level 3, MyTOWN Shopping Centre, No 6, Jl Cochrane, Seksyen 90, 55100 Kuala Lumpur *Tel:* (03) 9201 0091 *Fax:* (03) 9201 0026; Lot No Part 7B, Part 8B & 9, Level G2, Publika, Solaris Dutamas, Jl Dutamas 1, 50480 Kuala Lumpur *Tel:* (03) 6205 3226 *Fax:* (03) 6205 3204; Lot F-03, Mydin Wholesale Hypermarket, No 12, Mydin Mall MITC, Hang Tuah Jaya, Ayer Keroh, 75450 Melaka *Tel:* (06) 234 9933 *Fax:* (06) 234 9938; G73B, Ground

floor, Mahkota Parade, No 1, Jl Merdeka, 75000 Melaka *Tel:* (06) 283 3050 *Fax:* (06) 283 3003; F29, 1st floor, Aeon Seremban 2 Shopping Centre, No 112, Persiaran S2 B1, Seremban 2, 70300 Seremban, Negeri Sembilan *Tel:* (06) 601 5580 *Fax:* (06) 601 5581; Lot A1-A5, Giant Hypermarket Senawang, Lot 1571, Jl Senawang, 70450 Seremban, Negeri Sembilan *Tel:* (06) 678 0587 *Fax:* (06) 678 0617; 170-03-53A/55, 3rd floor, Gurney Plaza, Gurney Dr, 10250 Penang *Tel:* (04) 227 4202 *Fax:* (04) 227 4303; F15 & F16, 1st floor, Mydin Wholesale Hypermarket Bukit Mertajam, Lot 3424, 1619, 1611, 1511, 1186 & 850, Mukim 06, Jl Baru, Seberang Perai Tengah, 13600 Penang *Tel:* (04) 384 1440 *Fax:* (04) 384 1336; Lot No F-09, Mydin Mall Meru Raya, Lot PT 229142, Jl Meru Bestari B2, Bandar Meru Raya, Jelapang, 30020 Ipoh, Perak *Tel:* (05) 526 5740 *Fax:* (05) 526 5742; F 28 & F 29, 1st floor, Kinta City Shopping Centre, No 2, Jl Teh Lean Swee, Off Jl Sultan Azlan Shah Utara, 34100 Ipoh, Perak *Tel:* (05) 545 1452 *Fax:* (05) 545 1386; LG22-23, Lower Ground floor, Alamanda Putrajaya Shopping Centre, Jl Alamanda, Precinct 1, 62000 Putrajaya *Tel:* (03) 8889 2601 *Fax:* (03) 8889 2602; Lot 114, 1st floor, The Spring Shopping Mall, Jl Simpang Tiga, 93350 Kuching, Sarawak *Tel:* (082) 244 800 *Fax:* (082) 244 801; LG-37, Lower Ground, Plaza Merdeka, 88 Pearl St, 93000 Kuching, Sarawak *Tel:* (082) 240 230 *Fax:* (082) 241 781; Lot 2-014, Level 2, Vivacity Megamall, Jl Wan Alwi, 93350 Kuching, Sarawak *Tel:* (082) 26 3975 *Fax:* (082) 26 3977; 252 North Bridge Rd, No B1-21 Raffles City Shopping Centre, Singapore 179103, Singapore *Tel:* 6336 4232 *Fax:* 6336 4069; 80 Marine Parade Rd, No B1-83F & 83G, Parkway Parade, Singapore 449269, Singapore *Tel:* 6348 0381 *Fax:* 6345 6718

MPH Distributors Sdn Bhd
Ground Floor Warehouse, Bangunan TH, No 5, Jl Bersatu, Section 13/4, 46200 Petaling Jaya
Tel: (03) 7958 1688 *Fax:* (03) 7956 5995
E-mail: distributors@mph.com.my
Web Site: distributors.mph.com.my
Founded: 1963
Type of Business: Distributor
Owned by: MPH Group Malaysia Sdn Bhd

Pearson Malaysia Sdn Bhd
Level 1, Tower 2A, Ave 5, Bangsar South, No 8, Jl Kerinchi, 59200 Kuala Lumpur
Tel: (03) 2289 7000 *Fax:* (03) 2289 7199
E-mail: inquirymy@pearson.com
Web Site: www.pearsonapac.com
Type of Business: Distributor, Exporter
Parent Company: Pearson Education
Ultimate Parent Company: Pearson PLC

Saba Islamic Media Sdn Bhd
1-2-1 Prima Peninsula, Jl Setiawangsa 11 Taman Setiawangsa, 54200 Kuala Lumpur
Tel: (03) 42518792 *Fax:* (03) 42562030
Web Site: saba.com.my
Key Personnel
Contact: Sabariah bt Abdullah *Tel:* (019) 3500995
  E-mail: sabariah@saba.com.my
Type of Business: Major Book Chain Headquarters
Branch Office(s)
S29 & 30, 2nd floor, Maju Junction Mall, Corner of Jl Sultan Ismail/Jl Tuanku Abdul Rahman, 50250 Kuala Lumpur, Contact: Afifah bt Abu Bakar
F105, Tingkat 1, Blok A, Kuantan Centre Point, Jl Haji Abdul Rahman, 25000 Kuantan, Pahang *Tel:* (09) 5164 688 *Fax:* (09) 5082 585

Lot 393, Kompleks Pondok Antarabangsa, Jl Raja Perempuan Zainab II, 16150 Kubang Kerian, Kelantan *Tel:* (09) 7647388 *Fax:* (09) 7647389
No 173, 1st floor, PKNS Complex, 40000 Shah Alam, Selangor, Contact: Cik Noraini *Tel:* (03) 5512 4299 *Fax:* (03) 5512 4299
Pt Saba Islamic Media Indonesia, Blok D, No 1, Ruko Tol Blvd, BSD City, Tangerang, Indonesia *Tel:* (021) 5315 8066 *Fax:* (021) 5315 7931

UBSD Learning Sdn Bhd
3F-15, IOI Business Park, One Persiaran Puchong Jaya Selatan, Bandar Puchong Jaya, 47170 Puchong, Selangor
Tel: (03) 8076 3042
E-mail: enquiry@ubsd.com.my
Web Site: myknowledgeshoppe.com
Type of Business: Distributor

University of Malaya Cooperative Bookshop Ltd
University of Malaya, Rumah University, 1st floor, Peti Surat 1127, Jl Pantai Baru, 59700 Kuala Lumpur
Tel: (03) 7955 2595; (03) 7967 3414 *Fax:* (03) 7955 4424
E-mail: koopum@tm.net.my; admin-ru@streamyx.com.my
Web Site: www.um.edu.my
Type of Business: Distributor, Exporter, Importer, Major Independent Bookseller, Wholesaler

Malta

Audio Visual Centre Ltd
Shanti Ct, Flat 1 Triq Edgard Bernard, Gzira GZR 1701
Tel: 21330886 *Fax:* 21339840
E-mail: info@avc.com.mt
Key Personnel
Chairman: Simon Bonello
Sales & Marketing Dir: Steven Agius
Founded: 1971
Type of Business: Distributor

Merlin Library Ltd
Mountbatten St, Blata 1-Bajda HMR 1574
Tel: 2123 4438
E-mail: mail@merlinlibrary.com
Web Site: www.merlinlibrary.com
Founded: 1964
Type of Business: Distributor, Importer, Major Independent Bookseller, Remainder Dealer, Wholesaler

Giov Muscat & Co Ltd
31A Racecourse St, Marsa MRS 2918
Tel: 2123 2923; 2123 7668 *Fax:* 2124 0496
E-mail: info@giovmuscat.com
Web Site: www.giovmuscat.com
Key Personnel
Owner: Joseph A Muscat
Founded: 1874
Type of Business: Importer, Major Independent Bookseller

Mauritius

EOI Ltd, see Editions de l'Ocean Indien Ltd

Editions de l'Ocean Indien Ltd
22B, Rue Marcel Cabon, Stanley, Rose Hill
Tel: 464 6761 *Fax:* 465 3445

E-mail: eoimarketing@intnet.mu
Founded: 1977
Also acts as publisher.
Type of Business: Distributor, Exporter, Importer, Major Book Chain Headquarters, Wholesaler

Mexico

Libreria Acuario
Francisco Javier Mina No 793, Entre Carmen Serdan y Flores Magon, Colonia Ignacio Zaragoza, 91910 Veracruz, VER
Tel: (01229) 9316971; (01229) 9321285
Web Site: www.libreriaacuario.com.mx
Founded: 1974
Medical books. Subjects include anthropology, nursing, physiology, physiotherapy, medicine, neurology & psychology.
Type of Business: Distributor, Exporter, Importer

American Book Store SA de CV
Bolivar 23, Centro Historico, 06000 Mexico, CDMX
Tel: (0155) 5540-0047; (0155) 1203-4455
E-mail: bolivar@americanbookstore.com.mx
Web Site: www.facebook.com/American-Bookstore-131055180390207
Founded: 1928
Type of Business: Importer, Major Book Chain Headquarters
Branch Office(s)
Prado Norte 565, Lomas de Chapultepec, 11000 Mexico, CDMX *Fax:* (0155) 5540 6713
Schiller 144, Polanco, 11570 Mexico, CDMX
Tel: (0155) 5531 9447 *Fax:* (0155) 5254 4260
E-mail: abs@americanbookstore.org
Insurgentes Sur 1188, Tlacoquemecatl del Valle, 03200 Mexico, CDMX *Tel:* (0155) 5575 7969 *Fax:* (0155) 5575 7901 *E-mail:* abs@americanbookstore.org
Blvd Campestre 1305 local A, Valle del Campestre, 37150 Leon, GTO *Tel:* (01477) 636 39 00 *Fax:* (01477) 636 39 02 *E-mail:* leon@americanbookstore.org
Blvd Interlomas 5 locales U-9, Lomas Anahuac, 52760 Huixquilucan, MEX *Tel:* (01729) 5290 1414 *Fax:* (01729) 5290 3393
Circuito Medicos No 2, Ciudad Satelite, 53100 Naucalpan, MEX *Tel:* (0155) 3939815 *Fax:* (0155) 3930843
Calz del Valle Ote 400 local 34-35, Del Valle, 66220 San Pedro Garza Garcia, NL *Tel:* (01686) 8356 3845 *Fax:* (01686) 8335 7519

Asgard Distribuciones SA de CV
Av Paseo de la Reforma 42, Colonia Centro, 06010 Mexico, DF
Tel: (0155) 52939839
Type of Business: Distributor

Editora y Distribuidora Azteca SA de CV
Calle Articulo 27, 327, Colonia Nueva Santa Anita, 08210 Mexico, CDMX
Tel: (0155) 55380444
Type of Business: Distributor

Libreria Bellas Artes SA
Juarez No 18, Colonia Centro, 06010 Mexico, CDMX
Tel: (0155) 5518-3755; (0155) 5521-2105; (0155) 5510-2276
Founded: 1946
Scholarly, scientific, technical & medical books.
Type of Business: Importer

Casa de la Biblia
Calle Union No 330, Colonia Tepeyac Insurgentes, Delegacion Gustavo A Madero, 07020 Mexico, CDMX
Tel: (0155) 57501000 *Toll Free Fax:* 800 504 27 37
E-mail: info@casadelabiblia.com
Web Site: www.casadelabiblia.com
Type of Business: Distributor, Online Bookseller

Librerias de Cristal SA de CV (Crystal Bookstores)
Tehuantepec No 170, Colonia Roma Sur, 06760 Mexico, CDMX
Tel: (0155) 5564 4100; (0155) 5574 6499 *Toll Free Tel:* 01-800-849-29-86 *Fax:* (0155) 5564 4100
E-mail: ventas@libreriasdecristal.com
Key Personnel
Executive Dir: Jorge Flores; Carlos Noriega
Founded: 1939
Type of Business: Major Book Chain Headquarters
Owned by: Editorial Limusa SA de CV

Grupo Difusion Cientifica
Av Emiliano Zapata No 285, Eje 7A Sur, Colonia Santa Cruz Atoyac, 03310 Mexico, CDMX
Tel: (0155) 5090 2800; (0155) 5090 5300
E-mail: difusion@difusion.com.mx; contacto@difusion.com.mx
Web Site: www.difusion.com.mx
Key Personnel
Dir General: Victor Manuel Diaz Martinez
Founded: 1988
Type of Business: Distributor
Branch Office(s)
Av Shyris N 34-40 y Republica del Salvador, Piso 9, Off 901, Quito, Ecuador *Tel:* (02) 2433016; (02) 2241182 *E-mail:* ecuador@difusion.com.mx

Educal SA de CV
Av Ceylan 450, Colonia Euzkadi, 02660 Mexico, CDMX
Tel: (0155) 5354-4000
E-mail: express@educal.com.mx
Web Site: www.educal.gob.mx; www.educal.com.mx
Key Personnel
Dir General: Gerardo Jaramillo Herrera
Founded: 1982
Type of Business: Distributor, Online Bookseller

Librerias Gandhi SA de CV
Miguel Angel de Quevedo 121, Colonia Guadalupe Chimalistac, 01050 Mexico, CDMX
Tel: (0155) 2625-0606 *Toll Free Tel:* 01800 201 7373
E-mail: elcliente@gandhi.com.mx
Web Site: www.gandhi.com.mx
Key Personnel
President: Jose Achar
Dir General: Emilio Achar
Founded: 1971
Type of Business: Major Book Chain Headquarters
Branch Office(s)
Miguel Angel de Quevedo 121, Guadalupe Chimalistac, 01050 Mexico, CDMX
Miguel Angel de Quevedo 134, Guadalupe Chimalistac, 01050 Mexico, CDMX
Felipe Carillo Puerto 6, Coyoacan, 04000 Mexico, CDMX
Av Acoxpa 403, ExHacienda de Coapa, Centro Comercial Paseo Acoxpa, 14340 Mexico, CDMX
Av Juarez 4, Centro, 06050 Mexico, CDMX
Francisco I Madero 32, Centro, 06000 Mexico, CDMX

Av Aviacion Hangares s/n, Locales Pasues 18 y 19, Zona Federal, Aeropuerto Internacional Cd Mexico, Terminal 2, 15620 Mexico, CDMX
Av de las Palmas 840, Lomas de Chapultepec, 11000 Mexico, CDMX
Av Prolongacion, Paseo de la Reforma 880, Lomas de Santa Fe, 01210 Mexico, CDMX (dentro de la Universidad Iberoamericana)
Av Presidente Masaryk 353, Polanco, 11560 Mexico, CDMX
Centro Comercial Galerias, Aguascalientes Local No 1, Av Independencia 2351, Trojes de Alonso, 20116 Aguascalientes, AGS
Paseo Heroes 9111, Esq General M Marquez, Zona Rio, Pavilion Plaza, local 113, 22320 Tijuana, BC
Blvd Independencia 3775 Ote, Fraccionamiento El Fresno, locales 7, 8 y 9, 27018 Torreon, COAH
Blvd Campestre 1003-A, Colonia Jardines del Moral, 37160 Leon, GTO
Blvd de los Insurgentes 3356, Locales 29 y 30, San Jose de las Piletas, Leon, GTO
Lopez Cotilla 1567, Colonia Lafayette, Sector Juarez, 44140 Guadalajara, JAL
Carretera Guadalajara-Chapala Km 17.5, Local 13, Aeropuerto Internacional de Guadalajara, Tlajomulco de Zuniga, 45659 Guadalajara, JAL
Av de la Patria 2052, Santa Isabel, Zapopan, 44967 Guadalajara, JAL
El Rosario 1025, Centro Comercial Town Center Local X-5, 02430 Azcapotzalco, MEX
Circuito Medicos 5, 53100 Ciudad Satelite, MEX
Via Jose Lopez Portillo (Plaza Cosmopol) 1, Locales E-203, E-204, 55700 Coacalco de Berriozabal, MEX
Av Universidad 767, Colonia Del Valle, Coyoacan, MEX
Av Miguel Angel de Quevedo 222, Romero de Terreros, Coyaocan, MEX
Leona Vicario 936, Plaza Izar, locales 10 y 15, 52156 La Purisma, MEX
Leona Vicario 936 Poniente, La Purisima, Plaza Izar, locales 10 y 15, 52156 Metepec, MEX
Centro Comercial Gran Patio Santa Fe local SC-18, Av prolongacion paseo de la reforma 400, Colonia Santa Fe Pena Blanca Del Alvaro Obregon, 01210 Santa Fe, MEX
Av Teopanzolco 401, Reforma, 62260 Cuernavaca, MOR
Av Hidalgo 1171, Colonial Centro, 64000 Monterrey, NL
Plaza Esfera Fashion Hall, Av La Roja No 245, 64985 Monterrey, NL
Fashion Dr Av Diego Rivera 1000, Zona San Augustin, San Pedro Garza Garcia, 66260 Monterrey, NL
Av Osa Mayor 2902, Unidad Territorial Atlixcayotl, 72190 Puebla, PUE
Circuito Jardin 1 y 2, Colonia Alamos 3ra Seccion, 76160 Queretaro, QRO
Av Bonampak, Super Manzana 006, 77500 Cancun, Q ROO (Centro Comercial Malecon Americas)
Plaza Corazon Av 5 N, Centro, Playa del Carmen, Q ROO
Av Venustiano Carranza No 2301 Local 2, Colonia Las Aguilas, 78260 San Luis Potosi, SLP
Venustiano Carranza 312, 314, Centro, San Luis Potosi, SLP
Blvd Abelardo L Rodriguez 189, Cuartel Cruz Galvez, Centro, Hermosillo, SON
Calle 60, 299-A, Revolucion, Galerias Merida, Local 128, 97115 Merida, YUC

Librerias Gonvill SA de CV
8 de Julio No 825, Colonia Moderna, 44190 Guadalajara, JAL
Tel: (0133) 3837-2300
E-mail: info@gonvill.com.mx; pedidosweb@libreriasgonvill.com.mx
Web Site: www.gonvill.com.mx
Founded: 1967

Type of Business: Distributor, Exporter, Importer, Major Book Chain Headquarters, Wholesaler
Branch Office(s)
Morelos No 530, Guadalajara, JAL *Tel:* (0133) 3613-2614; (0133) 3613-5100; (0133) 3658-2884
Lopez Cotilla No 501, Esquina Donato Guerra, Guadalajara, JAL *Tel:* (0133) 3613-0123; (0133) 3658-0041
Av Juarez No 305, Esquina Av 16 de Septiembre, Guadalajara, JAL *Tel:* (0133) 3614-2856; (0133) 3614-9785
Independencia No 352, Esquina Liceo, Guadalajara, JAL *Tel:* (0133) 3613-2553; (0133) 3658-1063
Plaza Mexico Local 24 Zona A, Guadalajara, JAL *Tel:* (0133) 3813-0296; (0133) 3813-3428
Av Chapultepec Sur No 150, Esquina Lopez Cotilla, Guadalajara, JAL *Tel:* (0133) 3616-3060; (0133) 3616-3068; (0133) 3616-3069
La Gran Plaza Local 20 Zona C, Guadalajara, JAL *Tel:* (0133) 3647-7719; (0133) 3647-7727
Av Adolfo Lopez Mateos sur No 7000, Tlajomulco de Zuniga, Jalisco, JAL *Tel:* (0133) 1655-0638; (0133) 1655-1269
Centro Sur Local 17 Zona B, Tlaquepaque, JAL *Tel:* (0133) 3693-6100; (0133) 3693-6144
Plaza Revolucion Locales 12, 13 y 21 Zona A, Tlaquepaque, JAL *Tel:* (0133) 3635-7221; (0133) 3639-5985
Plaza del Sol 1 Local 4 Zona F, Zapopan, JAL *Tel:* (0133) 3122-8697; (0133) 3122-0899; (0133) 3647-4737
UAG Ciudad Universitaria, Av Patria No 1201, Bajo la explanada de rectoria, Zapopan, JAL *Tel:* (0133) 3610-0818
UAG Hospital Angel Leano, Dr Angel Leano No 500, A un lado del edificio de asuntos estudiantes, Zapopan, JAL *Tel:* (0133) 3364-1742
UAG Instituto de Ciencias Biologicas, Montevideo S/N, Explanada exterior entre el edificio I y el edificio J, Zapopan, JAL *Tel:* (0133) 3640-1501
Plaza del Sol 2 Local 7 Zona G, Zapopan, JAL *Tel:* (0133) 3647-4486; (0133) 3647-5090
Plaza Patria Locales 13 y 19 Zona B, Zapopan, JAL *Tel:* (0133) 3642-8157; (0133) 3642-8107
Plaza Universidad Locales 5 al 9 Zona B, Zapopan, JAL *Tel:* (0133) 3610-0887; (0133) 3610-0888
Plaza Andares Local UP66-114, Zapopan, JAL *Tel:* (0133) 3611-3434; (0133) 3611-1889
ITESM Campus GDL, Frente a Ciberplaza, Zapopan, JAL *Tel:* (0133) 1561-0411
Centro Comercial Altaria, Planta Baja Locales 1032 y 1033, Blvd A Zacatecas Nte 851, Fracc Troje Alonso, 20200 Aguascalientes, AGS *Tel:* (01449) 912-1523 *Fax:* (01449) 912-1521 *E-mail:* ags@gonvill.com.mx
Norte 45 No 958 Bodega 1-A, Colonia Industrial Vallejo Delegacion Azcapotzalco, 02300 Mexico, CDMX *Tel:* (0155) 5587-0127; (0155) 5368-3462 *Fax:* (0155) 5368-4175 *E-mail:* df@gonvill.com.mx
Fashion Mall, Planta Alta Locales 219-220, Periferico de la Juventud No 3501, Col Puerta de Hierro 1, 31207 Chihuahua, CHIH *Tel:* (01614) 430-0256 *Fax:* (01614) 430-0195 *E-mail:* chih@gonvill.com.mx
Centro Com Plaza Cuatro Caminos Planta Baja Local 124, Blvd Independencia Ote No 01300, Colonia Navarro, 27010 Torreon, COAH *Tel:* (01871) 722-6077 *Fax:* (01871) 718-3336 *E-mail:* torreon@gonvill.com.mx
Francisco Villa Blvd No 802 Norte, Colonia Bugambilias, 37270 Leon, GTO *Tel:* (01477) 771-4708; (01477) 711-4709; (01477) 711-5363 *Fax:* (01477) 771-4710 *E-mail:* leon@gonvill.com.mx
Plaza Mayor, Planta Baja Local, 1030 Av Las Torres No 2002, Colonia Valle del Camptestre, 37150 Leon, GTO *Tel:* (01477) 718-2187 *Fax:* (01477) 773-5283 *E-mail:* plazamayor@gonvill.com.mx

Centro Comercial Altacia Locales 1021 y 1021A, Blvd Aeropuerto No 104, Colonia Cerrito de Jerez, 37530 Leon, GTO *Tel:* (01477) 167-5529; (01477) 194-4971 *E-mail:* altacia@ gonvill.com.mx

Jose Ma Paras y Baliesteros Sur No 855, Entre Av Padre Mier y Morelos, Colonia Centro, 64000 Monterrey, NL *Tel:* (0181) 8333-7034; (0181) 8123-1018 *Fax:* (0181) 8333-6972 *E-mail:* mty@gonvill.com.mx

Av Alvaro Obregon No 1686 Norte, Esquina Blvd Dr Manuel Romero, Colonia Gabriel Leyva, 80030 Culiacan, SIN *Tel:* (01667) 712-3109; (01667) 712-3128 *Fax:* (01667) 712-2997 *E-mail:* cln@gonvill.com.mx

CC La Gran Plaza Local 1 Isla S Av Reforma S/N, Colonia Alameda, 83123 Mazatlan, SIN *Tel:* (01669) 9900-386; (01669) 9837-732 *E-mail:* mzt@gonvill.com.mx

Av Venustiano Carranza No 500, Esquina Simon Bolivar "Centro Historico", 78000 San Luis Potosi, SLP *Tel:* (01444) 812-6913; (01444) 812-6935 *Fax:* (01444) 812-7399 *E-mail:* slp@ gonvill.com.mx

Grupo Noriega Editores
Balderas 95, Colonia Centro, 06040 Mexico, CDMX
Tel: (0155) 51300700 *Toll Free Tel:* 01800 706 9100; 01800 703 7500 *Fax:* (0155) 55109415
E-mail: limusa@noriegaeditores.com; informes@ limusa.com.mx
Web Site: www.noriega.com.mx; noriegaeditores. wordpress.com
Type of Business: Distributor, Importer, Major Book Chain Headquarters, Wholesaler
Branch Office(s)
Grupo Noriega Editores de Colombia Ltda, Calle 43, No 27-20, Barrio de la Soledad, Bogota DC, Colombia *Tel:* (01) 3689036; (01) 3689067 *Fax:* (01) 3377788 *E-mail:* gerencialimusa@noriegacolombia.co
Grupo Noriega Editores CA, Av Don Diego Cisneros, Edif Colegial Bolivariana piso 4, Urbanizacion Los Ruices, Caracas, Venezuela *Tel:* (0212) 2387739; (0212) 2379047; (0212) 2376205 *Fax:* (0212) 2391262 *E-mail:* limexlc@cantv.net
Bookshop(s): Libreria Ayuntamiento, Ayuntamiento 112, Colonia Centro, 06040 Mexico, CDMX *Tel:* (0155) 51300700 ext 400; (0155) 51300700 ext 401 *Fax:* (0155) 55109415; Libreria Bellas Artes, Av Juarez 18, Colonia Centro, 06050 Mexico, CDMX *Tel:* (0155) 55120947 *Fax:* (0155) 55183755; Libreria Nori, Felix Berenguer 116, Colonia Lomas Virreyes, 11000 Mexico, CDMX *Tel:* (0155) 55206592 *Fax:* (0155) 52028793; Libreria Pasaje, Metro Zocalo - Pino Suarez, Colonia Centro, 06020 Mexico, CDMX *Tel:* (0155) 55222812; Libreria Politecnico, Av Politecnico 1848, Colonia Lindavista, 07300 Mexico, CDMX *Tel:* (0155) 55721090; Sucursal Satelite, Cto Economistas E-8 No 8, Colonia Ciudad Satelite, 53100 Mexico, CDMX *Tel:* (0155) 55626938 *Fax:* (0155) 55626939; Fco I Madero 335, Colonia Centro, 20000 Aguascalientes, AGS *Tel:* (01449) 9154507 *Fax:* (01449) 9150623; C Com Rio Tijuana L 3, Colonia Centro, 22000 Tijuana, BC *Tel:* (01664) 6341018 *Fax:* (01664) 6840151; Constitucion 195 L 1, Colonia Centro, 23000 La Paz, BCS *Tel:* (01612) 1221410 *Fax:* (01612) 1221441; Calle 12 No 157, Colonia Centro, 24000 Campeche, CAM *Tel:* (01981) 1271526 *Fax:* (01981) 8160088; Plaza Agora Baratillo L 4, Colonia Centro, 36000 Guanajuato, GTO *Tel:* (01473) 7322448 *Fax:* (01473) 7322448; Emiliano Zapata 125, Colonia Centro, 37000 Leon, GTO *Tel:* (01477) 7132656 *Fax:* (01477) 7162231; Hidalgo 204, Colonia Centro, 42000 Pachuca, HGO *Tel:* (01771) 7152130 *Fax:* (01771)

7152160; E Robles Gil 437, Colonia Americana SJ, 44290 Guadalajara, JAL *Tel:* (0133) 38269032 *Fax:* (0133) 38268899 (regional only); Av del Estado 120 Local No 7, Colonia Tecnologico, 64700 Monterrey, NL *Tel:* (0181) 83595978; (0181) 83877254; (0181) 83877691 *E-mail:* mariag@noriegaeditores.com; Av Reforma 511, Colonia Centro, 72000 Puebla, PUE *Tel:* (01222) 2425958; (0122) 2425945; Portal Hidalgo 4, Colonia Centro, 72000 Puebla, PUE *Tel:* (01222) 2460511 *Fax:* (01222) 2322649; Plaza Americas 5L 118-120, Colonia Contituyentes, 76140 Queretaro, QRO *Tel:* (01442) 2131753 *Fax:* (01442) 2131990; Venustiano Carranza 776, Colonia Zona Rosa, 78000 San Luis Potosi, SLP *Tel:* (01444) 8120665 *Fax:* (01444) 8128015; C Com Gran Plaza L 12-13-14, Colonia Alameda, 82123 Mazatlan, SIN *Tel:* (01669) 9865280 *Fax:* (01669) 9865281; Av Gregorio Mendez Magana No 717, Colonia Centro, 86000 Villa Hermosa, TAB *Tel:* (01993) 3145062 *Fax:* (01993) 3145062; Xalapenos Ilustres 35, Colonia Centro, 91000 Xalapa, VER *Tel:* (01228) 8178636 *Fax:* (01228) 8178636

Libreria Patria SA de CV
Belisario Dominguez No 53, 06010 Mexico, DF
Tel: (0155) 5518 5182
Type of Business: Major Independent Bookseller

Libreria de Porrua Hermanos y Cia SA de CV
Av Republica de Argentina No 15, Colonia Central, 06020 Mexico, CDMX
Tel: (0155) 5704 7577; (0155) 5704 7578; (0155) 5704 7585 *Toll Free Tel:* 01800 0192300
Web Site: www.porrua.mx
Founded: 1900
Type of Business: Major Book Chain Headquarters
Branch Office(s)
Presidente Masaryk No 249 Local B, Colonia Polanco IV Seccion, Delegacion Miguel Hidalgo, 11550 Mexico, CDMX *Tel:* (0155) 91309484; (0155) 91309496
Circuito Universidad No 1 Colonia Universidad Nacional Autonoma de Mexico, Ciudad Universitaria, Delegacion Coyoacan, 04510 Mexico, CDMX *Tel:* (0155) 5550 3650
Av Canal de Tezontle No 1512, Local L263-B, L263-C, Colonia Dr Alfonso Ortiz Tirado, Delegacion Iztapalapa, 09020 Mexico, CDMX *Tel:* (0155) 9129 0031; (0155) 9129 0032
Av Juarez No 16, Colonia Centro, Delegacion Cuauhtemoc, 06010 Mexico, CDMX *Tel:* (0155) 5521 2830; (0155) 5512 0175
Av Paseo de la Reforma No 135, Colonia Tabacalera, Delegacion Cuauhtemoc, 11560 Mexico, CDMX *Tel:* (0155) 5535 2915; (0155) 5535 4197
Av Ejercito Nacional No 769 Local L-104, Colonia Granada, Delegacion Miguel Hidalgo, 11520 Mexico, CDMX *Tel:* (0155) 5203 4690; (0155) 5203 4488
Bosques de Duraznos No 39, Nivel 1 Local D-07, Colonia Bosque de las Lomas, Delegacion Miguel Hidalgo, 11700 Mexico, CDMX *Tel:* (0155) 5245 1883
Camino Real a San Lorenzo Tezonco No 285, Colonia El Manto, Delegacion Iztapalapa, 09830 Mexico, CDMX *Tel:* (0155) 5804 3535; (0155) 5804 3548; (0155) 5804 3549
Av de los Poetas No 100, Colonia Tlayapaca, Delegacion Alvaro Obregon, 01389 Mexico, CDMX *Tel:* (0155) 2162 0602; (0155) 2162 0593
Av Juarez No 76 Local B2, Colonia Centro Delegacion Cuauhtemoc, 06010 Mexico, CDMX *Tel:* (0155) 5521 6075; (0155) 5521 7640; (0155) 5521 8033
Colector 13 No 280 Local SA-11A, Colonia Magdalena de las Salinas, Delegacion Gustavo

A Madero, 07760 Mexico, CDMX *Tel:* (0155) 5754 6823; (0155) 5754 0185
Calle Queretaro No 225 Local 29, Colonia Roma Norte, Delegacion Cuauhtemoc, 06700 Mexico, CDMX *Tel:* (0155) 5264 1961
Eje 1 Norte Mosqueta No 259 N2 Local 49/50/ 50A, Colonia Buenavista, Delegacion Cuauhtemoc, 06350 Mexico, CDMX *Tel:* (0155) 2630 3028; (0155) 2630 3136
Ninos Heroes No 132, Colonia Doctores, Delegacion Cuauhtemoc, 06720 Mexico, CDMX *Tel:* (0155) 5761 9430; (0155) 5588 5797
Versalles No 27, Colonia Juarez, Delegacion Cuauhtemoc, 06600 Mexico, CDMX *Tel:* (0155) 5546 3788
Av Ejercito Nacional No 843-B Local 1, Colonia Granada, Delegacion Miguel Hidalgo, 11520 Mexico, CDMX *Tel:* (0155) 5282 2977
Bahia Grutas No S/N, Colonia San Miguel Chapultepec, Delegacion Miguel Hidalgo, 11850 Mexico, CDMX *Tel:* (0155) 5212 2241; (0155) 5212 2242
Av Stim No 1358, Colonia Lomas del Chamizal, Delegacion Cuajimalpa de Morelos, 05129 Mexico, CDMX *Tel:* (0155) 5251 3351; (0155) 5251 3967; (0155) 5251 4295
Calle del Puente No 222, Colonia Ejidos Huipulco, Delegacion Tlalpan, 14380 Mexico, CDMX *Tel:* (0155) 5673 2956; (0155) 2652 3191
Av Insurgentes Sur No 357-B Local B, Colonia Hipodromo, Delegacion Cuauhtemoc, 06100 Mexico, CDMX *Tel:* (0155) 5584 8177; (0155) 5584 8397
Odontologia No 69, Colonia Copilco Universidad, Delegacion Coyoacan, 04360 Mexico, CDMX *Tel:* (0155) 5554 5918
Justo Sierra No 36, Colonia Centro, Delegacion Cuauhtemoc, 06010 Mexico, CDMX *Tel:* (0155) 5704 7568; (0155) 5704 7569; (0155) 5704 7571
Av Calzada de Guadalupe No 431 Local 17, Colonia Guadalupe Tepeyac, Delegacion Gustavo A Madero, 07840 Mexico, CDMX *Tel:* (0155) 5517 2118
Lorenzo Boturini No 258 Local SSA06, Colonia Transito, Delegacion Cuauhtemoc, 06820 Mexico, CDMX *Tel:* (0155) 5925 9460; (0155) 5925 9459
Av Revolucion No 1267 Local SC23, Colonia Los Alpes, Delegacion Alvaro Obregon, 01010 Mexico, CDMX *Tel:* (0155) 5593 1443; (0155) 5593 0286
Paseo de la Reforma No 222 Local 213B-214AB, Colonia Juarez, Delegacion Cuauhtemoc, 06600 Mexico, CDMX *Tel:* (0155) 5511 0863; (0155) 5511 0864
Seminario No 16, Colonia Centro, Delegacion Cuauhtemoc, 06000 Mexico, CDMX *Tel:* (0155) 5491 1060; (0155) 5522 3905
Pasaje Zocalo-Pino Suarez No S/N Local 11, Colonia Centro, Delegacion Cuauhtemoc, 06020 Mexico, CDMX *Tel:* (0155) 5522 5393
Pasaje Zocalo - Pino Suarez No S/N Local 24, Colonia Centro, Delegacion Cuauhtemoc, 06010 Mexico, CDMX *Tel:* (0155) 5522 1078
Av Rosario Castellanos No S/N, Colonia Centro Historico, 30098 Comitan de Dominguez, CHIS *Tel:* (01963) 101 4393; (01963) 101 4533
2da Poniente Sur No 118, Colonia Centro, 29000 Tuxtla Gutierrez, CHIS *Tel:* (01961) 612 6187; (01961) 612 6407
El Cantador No 31 Local 4-A, Colonia Centro, 36000 Guanajuato, GTO *Tel:* (01473) 688 0523; (01473) 688 0524
Blvd Adolfo Lopez Mateos No 502 Poniente, Colonia Obregon, 37320 Leon, GTO *Tel:* (01477) 716 4342; (01477) 713 8438
Av Cuauhtemoc No 211, local 1, Colonia Progreso, 39350 Acapulco, GRO *Tel:* (01744) 486 6985; (01744) 486 6995
Blvd de las Naciones No 802 Loc 38AM, 39AM y 40, Colonia Granjas del Maquex, 39760 Aca-

pulco, GRO *Tel:* (01744) 443002; (01744) 4430624

Av Revolucion No 1105, Colonia Periodistas, 42060 Pachuca, HGO *Tel:* (01771) 718 3840; (01771) 719 3755

Av 8 de Julio No 1685, Colonia Tepopote, 44910 Guadalajara, JAL *Tel:* (0133) 3812 3609; (0133) 3812 3301

Mariano Otero No 3435, Colonia Verde Valle, 44550 Guadalajara, JAL *Tel:* (0133) 3647 1936; (0133) 3647 1673

Prisciliano Sanchez No 460, Colonia Centro, 44100 Guadalajara, JAL *Tel:* (0133) 3614 4616; (0133) 3614 0858; (0133) 3614 4663; (0133) 3614 0827

Av de los Maestros No 1060, Colonia Alcalde Barranquitas, 44260 Guadalajara, JAL *Tel:* (0133) 3854 6645; (0133) 3853 5174

Av Alcalde No 1190, Colonia Miraflores, 44270 Guadalajara, JAL *Tel:* (0133) 3280 1126

Carretera Guadalajara-Morelia No Km 12.5 Local 73, Colonia Tlajomulco de Zuniga, 45640 Guadalajara, JAL *Tel:* (0133) 3188 8400; (0133) 3188 8172

Periferico Sur Manuel Gomez Morin No 8585, Colonia ITESO, 45604 Tlaquepaque, JAL *Tel:* (0133) 3694 0127

Av Tepeyac No 4800, Fracc Prados Tepeyac, 45050 Zapopan, JAL *Tel:* (0133) 3134 0800 ext 2407; (0133) 3620 7245

Prolongacion Calzada Circunvalacion Poniente No 49, Colonia Ciudad Granja, 45010 Zapopan, JAL *Tel:* (0133) 1657 0959

Av General Ramon Corona No 2514, Colonia Nuevo Mexico, 45201 Zapopan, JAL *Tel:* (0133) 5704 7513; (0133) 5704 7515

Carretera Km 3.5 Lago de Guadalupe No S/N Aula 3, Colonia Margarita Maza de Juarez, 52926 Atizapan de Zaragoza, MEX *Tel:* (0155) 5887 6960

Via Jose Lopez Portillo No 105, Colonia Bonito Coacalco, 55700 Coacalco, MEX *Tel:* (0155) 5898 5206; (0155) 5879 0914

Hacienda Sierra Vieja No 2, Lote 2, Local 802, Colonia Hacienda del Parque, 54769 Cuautitlan Izcalli, MEX *Tel:* (0155) 2075 0216; (0155) 2075 0217

Av Universidad No 46, Colonia Lomas Anahuac, 52786 Huixquilucan, MEX *Tel:* (0155) 5291 7076; (0155) 5290 3395

Vialidad de la Barranca No 6 N2-15, Colonia ExHacienda Jesus del Monte, 52763 Huixquilucan, MEX *Tel:* (0155) 5290 3115; (0155) 5290 7982

Blvd Manuel Avila Camacho No 5 2do Nivel Local L-2, Colonia Lomas de Sotelo, 53390 Naucalpan de Juarez, MEX *Tel:* (0155) 5395 1707; (0155) 5395 1388

Av Bordo de Xochiaca No 3 Local A-2, Colonia Benito Juarez, 57000 Nezahualcoyotl, MEX *Tel:* (0155) 5736 6373

Paseo Tollocan No 600, Colonia Progreso, 50150 Toluca, MEX *Tel:* (01722) 277 3593

Plaza Fray Andres de Castro No S/N Local 2, 3 y 4, Colonia Centro, 50000 Toluca, MEX *Tel:* (01722) 167 2869; (01722) 167 2853

Montana Monarca No 1000 Local 8-PB, Colonia Desarrollo Montana Monarca, 58350 Morelia, MICH *Tel:* (01443) 204 0154; (01443) 204 0097

Av Morelos No 265, Colonia Cuernavaca Centro, 62050 Cuernavaca, MOR *Tel:* (01777) 314 2802; (01777) 310 3284

Blvd Luis Donaldo Colosio No 680, Local PA16, Colonia Benito Juarez Oriente, 63175 Tepic, NAY *Tel:* (01311) 129 1600; (01311) 129 1602

Av Manuel L Barragan No 220, Loc 80, Colonia Ex Hacienda El Canada, 66054 Escobedo, NL *Tel:* (0181) 8058 9037; (0181) 8058 9038; (0181) 8058 9039

Av Hacienda Penuelas No 6771, Colonia Residencial Cumbres, 64619 Monterrey, NL *Tel:* (0181) 1095 1313; (0181) 1095 1314

Padre Mier 501-A Oriente, Colonia Zona Centro, 64000 Monterrey, NL *Tel:* (0181) 8343 4208; (0181) 8343 4210

Av Real de San Agustin No 222, Locales 14, 15 y 16, Colonia Residencial San Agustin, 66260 San Pedro Garza Garcia, NL *Tel:* (0181) 8363 2218; (0181) 8363 2365; (0181) 8363 2851

Av Reforma No 530, Colonia Centro, 72000 Puebla, PUE *Tel:* (01222) 230 5794; (01222) 230 5446

Periferico Ecologico, Arco Sur No 4000, Colonia Reserva Territorial Atlixcayotl, 72761 San Andres Cholula, PUE *Tel:* (01222) 574 8382

Recta Cholula-Puebla No S/N, Colonia Ex Hacienda Santa Catarina, 72810 San Andres Cholula, PUE *Tel:* (01222) 178 2530; (01222) 178 0133

Av Benito Juarez Norte No 38, Colonia Centro, 76000 Queretaro, QRO *Tel:* (01442) 214 3628; (01442) 214 2807

Av Coba No 3 Mz 2 Lte 3, Colonia Supermanzana 36 Delegacion Benito Juarez, Quintana Roo, 77507 Cancun, Q ROO *Tel:* (0199) 8880 9918; (0199) 8849 2769

Venustiano Carranza No 410, Colonia Centro, 78000 San Luis Potosi, SLP *Tel:* (0144) 4814 7506; (0144) 4814 7610

Av Salvador Nava Martinez No 3125 Local N1-06 B, Colonia Colinas de Parque, 78294 San Luis Potosi, SLP *Tel:* (0144) 4688 0990; (0144) 4688 0984

Blvd Cultura No Mz 21 Sub-Ancla 13, Colonia Proyecto Rio Sonora, 83280 Hermosillo, SON *Tel:* (01662) 212 2966; (01662) 212 3397

Av SS Juan Pablo II No S/N, Colonia Fracc Jardines de Virginia, 94294 Boca del Rio, VER *Tel:* (0229) 927 3190

Av Universidad No Km 8, Local PA01, Colonia El Tesoro, 96536 Coatzacoalcos, VER *Tel:* (01921) 210 4657

Universidad Veracruzana, Av Universidad No Km 7.5, Colonia Santa Isabel, 96538 Coatzacoalcos, VER *Tel:* (01921) 1218 9997

Blvd Adolfo Ruiz Cortinez No 306, Colonia Obras Sociales, 93240 Poza Rica, VER *Tel:* (01782) 119 0269

Xalapenos Ilustres No 37, Colonia Centro, 91000 Xalapa, VER *Tel:* (01228) 812 0661; (01228) 812 0844

Calle 31 No 144, Local AX40, Colonia Buenavista, 97127 Merida, YUC *Tel:* (0199) 9926 2608; (0199) 9926 2609; (0199) 9926 2611

Probooks SA de CV

Av Canal de Miramontes, No 2383, Colonia Avante, Delegacion Coyoacan, Mexico, CDMX
Tel: (0155) 5549 5660; (0155) 5549 5183
E-mail: ventas@probooks.com.mx
Web Site: www.probooks.com.mx
Type of Business: Distributor, Importer

RGS Libros SA de CV

Av Progreso No 202, Colonia Escandon, 11800 Mexico, CDMX
Tel: (0155) 5515 2922; (0155) 5515 4964; (0155) 5516 4261 *Fax:* (0155) 5277 1696
Web Site: www.rgslibros.com
Founded: 1997
Type of Business: Distributor, Importer
Parent Company: Grupo Libros & Editoriales

Sistemas Biblioinforma SA de CV

(Biblioinforma Systems)
Av Oriente 9a No 8, Colonia Isidro Fabela, Delegacion Tlalpan, 14030 Mexico, CDMX
Tel: (0155) 5528-3230 (customer service); (0155) 5665-3843
E-mail: info@biblioinforma.com
Web Site: biblioinforma.com

Key Personnel
General Manager: Marcos Vazquez
   E-mail: mvazquez@biblioinforma.com
Type of Business: Distributor, Exporter, Importer, Major Independent Bookseller

Tumbili SA de CV

Recta a Cholula 530-1B, Villa Residenciales del Puente, 72810 San Andres Cholula, PUE
Tel: (0222) 221 85 85 *Toll Free Tel:* 800 221 85 85 *Fax:* (0222) 221 85 85
E-mail: ventas@tumbili.com.mx
Web Site: www.tumbili.com.mx
Type of Business: Distributor

Libreria Vesalius

Eduardo Aguirre Pequeno 1303, Colonia Mitras Centro, 64460 Monterrey, NL
Tel: (081) 8333-3035; (081) 8123-1704
   Toll Free Tel: 01800-822-5770
E-mail: ventas@vesalius.com.mx
Web Site: www.libreriavesalius.com
Founded: 1996
Type of Business: Distributor, Major Book Chain Headquarters
Bookshop(s): Parroquia No 312-B P/A, Colonia Del Valle Sur, Delegacion Benito Juarez, 03100 Mexico, CDMX *Tel:* (0155) 5574-5797

Morocco

Librairie des Colonnes

54 blvd Pasteur, Ville Nouvelle, Tanger
Tel: 05 39 93 69 55 *Fax:* 05 39 94 29 00
E-mail: info@librairie-des-colonnes.com
Web Site: librairie-des-colonnes.com
Key Personnel
Dir: Simon-Pierre Hamelin *E-mail:* hamelin@ librairie-des-colonnes.com
Assistant Dir: Audrey Capponi *E-mail:* capponi@ librairie-des-colonnes.com
Founded: 1949
Type of Business: Importer, Major Independent Bookseller

Librairie des Ecoles

12 Ave Hassan II, 20000 Casablanca
Tel: 05 22 26 67 41; 41 67 26 22 05
E-mail: contact@librairiedesecoles.ma
Web Site: www.librairiedesecoles.ma
Key Personnel
Dir General: Hamouda Bourhaleb
Founded: 1947
Type of Business: Distributor, Exporter, Importer, Wholesaler

Librairie Internationale

2, rue de la Molouya, 10001 Rabat Agdal
Tel: 05 37 68 03 29 *Fax:* 05 37 77 09 14
Founded: 1960
Specialize in scientific books, CD-ROMs & multimedia.
Type of Business: Distributor, Exporter, Major Independent Bookseller

Librairie Livre Service

46 Ave Allal Ben Abdlelah, 20000 Rabat
Tel: 05 37 72 44 95 *Fax:* 05 37 70 19 63
E-mail: lsr@livreservice.ma
Web Site: livre-service.ma
Key Personnel
Manager: Faouzi Slaoui
Founded: 1981
Membership(s): Association Internationale des Libraires Francophones.

Type of Business: Distributor, Exporter, Importer, Major Book Chain Headquarters
Branch Office(s)
11 Rue Tata, Casablanca *Tel:* 05 22 26 20 72 *Fax:* 05 22 29 95 42

SOCHEPRESS, see Societe Cherifienne de Distribution et de Presse (SOCHEPRESS)

Societe Cherifienne de Distribution et de Presse (SOCHEPRESS)
Blvd Abou Bakr El Kadiri (Sidi Maarouf), 20280 Casablanca
Tel: 0522 58 36 33; 0522 58 33 44; 0522 58 37 66; 0522 58 38 48 *Fax:* 0522 58 46 47
E-mail: sochepress@sochepress.ma
Web Site: www.sochepress.ma
Key Personnel
Dir General: Thierry Sabouret
Type of Business: Distributor, Exporter, Importer, Wholesaler

Myanmar

Knowledge Press & Book Shop, see Pyinnyar Ahlinpya Press & Book House

Pyinnyar Ahlinpya Press & Book House
No 130, Bogyoke Aung San Rd, 9 Ward, Pazundaung, Yangon
Tel: (01) 290927; (01) 253143
Type of Business: Major Independent Bookseller

Sarpay Beikman
529-531, Merchant Rd, Yangon
Tel: (01) 283277
Founded: 1947
Type of Business: Major Independent Bookseller

SarPayLawKa
Sarpay Lawka 2, 265/264, Ground floor, Pansodan Rd (Upper Block) Kyauktadar Townshop, Yangon 11182
Tel: (097) 303 3802
Web Site: www.sarpaylawka.com
Type of Business: Major Independent Bookseller

Namibia

Swakopmunder Buchhandlung
22 Sam Nujoma Ave, PO Box 500, Swakopmund
Tel: (064) 40 2613
E-mail: christian@swakop-books.com
Founded: 1900
Type of Business: Major Independent Bookseller

Windhoeker Buchhandlung Ltd
69-73 Independence Ave, Windhoek
Mailing Address: PO Box 1327, Windhoek
Tel: (061) 225216; (061) 225036 *Fax:* (061) 225011
Web Site: www.wbuch.iway.na/book_e.htm
Founded: 1959
Type of Business: Distributor, Importer, Major Independent Bookseller

Nepal

Ratna Book Distributors (Pvt) Ltd
GPO Box 1080, Bagbazar, Kathmandu
Tel: (01) 4242077 *Fax:* (01) 4248421
E-mail: rpb@wlink.com.np; ratnapustak@gmail.com
Web Site: www.ratnabooks.com
Key Personnel
Mng Dir: Govinda P Shrestha
Founded: 1946
Type of Business: Distributor, Importer, Wholesaler
Branch Office(s)
Ratna Pustak Bhandar, GPO Box 98, Maitighar, Kathmandu *Tel:* (01) 4240850 *Fax:* (01) 4248421
Saraswati Book Centre, GPO Box 98, Pulchowk, Lalitpur, Kathmandu *Tel:* (01) 5528017; (01) 55215991 *Fax:* (01) 4248421

Netherlands

Athenaeum Boekhandel
Spui 14-16, 1012 XA Amsterdam
Tel: (020) 5141460 *Fax:* (020) 6384901
E-mail: info@athenaeum.nl
Web Site: www.athenaeum.nl
Key Personnel
Mng Dir: Maarten Asscher
Founded: 1966
Type of Business: Importer, Major Independent Bookseller, Online Bookseller
Branch Office(s)
Athenaeum Hogoeschoolboekhandel Dr Meurerlaan, Dokter Meurerlaan 8, 1067 SM Amsterdam *Tel:* (020) 5141479 *E-mail:* dml@athenaeum.nl
Athenaeum Rijksmuseumwinkel, Museumstr 1, 1071 XX Amsterdam *Tel:* (020) 6747353 *E-mail:* rma@athenaeum.nl
Athenaeum Roeterseiland, Roeterstr 41, 1018 WB Amsterdam *Tel:* (020) 5301748 *E-mail:* roeterseiland@athenaeum.nl
Athenaeum Haarlem, Gedempte Oude gracht 70, 2011 GT Haarlem *Tel:* (023) 5318755 *E-mail:* haarlem@athenaeum.nl

John Benjamins Antiquariat BV
Kelvinstr 11-13, 1446 TK Purmerend
Mailing Address: PO Box 36224, 1020 ME Amsterdam
Tel: (020) 6304747; (0299) 644951 *Fax:* (020) 6792956; (0299) 673829
E-mail: antiq@benjamins.nl; bookorder@benjamins.nl
Web Site: antiq.benjamins.com
Key Personnel
Dir: Seline Benjamins
Marketing & Publicity Manager: Karin Plijnaar
Book Orders: Eduard Jagroep
Also publisher.
Membership(s): Antiquarian Booksellers Association of the Netherlands; International League of Antiquarian Booksellers (ILAB).
Type of Business: Major Independent Bookseller

Gert Jan Bestebreurtje-Rare Books
Langendijk 8, 4132 AK Vianen
Tel: (0347) 322 548
E-mail: info@gertjanbestebreurtje.com
Web Site: www.gertjanbestebreurtje.com
Key Personnel
Owner: Gert Jan Bestebreurtje
Founded: 1981
Antiquarian bookseller & print dealer.

Membership(s): International League of Antiquarian Booksellers; Nederlandsche Vereeniging van Antiquaren (NVVA).
Type of Business: Online Bookseller

Bruna BV
Walmolen 21-23, 3994 DL Houten
Mailing Address: Postbus 439, 3990 GE Houten
E-mail: klantenservice@bruna.nl
Web Site: www.bruna.nl
Founded: 1868
Type of Business: Major Book Chain Headquarters

CB
Erasmusweg 10, 4104 AK Culemborg
Mailing Address: Postbus 125, 4100 AC Culemborg
Tel: (0345) 47 59 11; (0345) 47 57 77 (wholesale); (0345) 47 58 88 (booksellers); (0345) 47 58 85 (publishers) *Fax:* (0345) 47 53 43
E-mail: service@cb.nl
Web Site: www.cb.nl
Key Personnel
Chief Financial Officer: Marinus Ploos van Amstel
Mng Dir: Hans Willem Cortenraad
Commercial Dir: Melbert Visscher
Dir, Human Resources: Jaco Gulmans
Dir, Information Technology: Ronald Janssen
Dir, Operations: Cees Pronk
Founded: 1871
Type of Business: Wholesaler
Branch Office(s)
Baaikensstr 2/D, 9240 Zele, Belgium *Tel:* (052) 45 69 40 *Fax:* (052) 45 69 50 *E-mail:* service@cb.be

Erasmus Boekhandel BV
Veemarkt 207, 1019 CJ Amsterdam
Mailing Address: PO Box 19140, 1000 GC Amsterdam
Tel: (020) 5353433 *Fax:* (020) 6206799
E-mail: erasmus@erasmusbooks.nl
Web Site: www.erasmusbooks.nl
Key Personnel
Mng Dir: Dirk Raes *Tel:* (020) 5353435 *E-mail:* dirk.raes@erasmusbooks.nl
Operations Manager: Maarten Hepp *Tel:* (020) 5353428 *E-mail:* maarten.hepp@erasmusbooks.nl
Regional Sales Manager: Joleen McFarlane *Tel:* (020) 5353412 *E-mail:* joleen.mcfarlane@erasmusbooks.nl
Business Development: Beate A Jahnel *Tel:* (020) 5353448 *E-mail:* beate.jahnel@erasmusbooks.nl
Founded: 1934
Type of Business: Distributor
Owned by: Bertram Group

Antiquariaat FORUM BV
Tuurdijk 16, 3997 MS 't Goy-Houten
Tel: (030) 601 1955 *Fax:* (030) 601 1813
E-mail: info@forumrarebooks.com
Web Site: www.forumrarebooks.com
Key Personnel
Owner: Sebastiaan Hesselink
Founded: 1970
Rare books, manuscripts, prints, maps & drawings.
Membership(s): Dutch Association of Antiquarian Booksellers.
Type of Business: Major Independent Bookseller

ICOB BV
Leidsevaart 123, 2211 VS Noordwijkerhout
Tel: (0172) 437231 *Fax:* (0172) 416684
E-mail: algemeen@icob.nl
Web Site: www.icob.nl
Key Personnel
Owner: Peter Bomas

Founded: 1964
Also publisher.
Type of Business: Distributor, Remainder Dealer, Wholesaler

Idea Books
Nieuwe Herengracht 11, 1011 RK Amsterdam
Tel: (020) 6226154 *Fax:* (020) 6209299
Web Site: www.ideabooks.nl
Founded: 1976
Subjects include architecture, art, crafts, fashion, furniture, graphic design, literature, performing arts & textiles.
Type of Business: Distributor, Wholesaler

Antiquariaat Papyrus Oude Liefdes
Nieuwstr 29, 7411 LG Deventer
Tel: (0570) 612461
E-mail: info@papyrusboeken.nl
Web Site: www.oude-liefdes.nl/contact
Founded: 1991
Old & rare books (mostly printed before 1800).
Membership(s): Antiquarian Booksellers Association; International League of Antiquarian Booksellers (ILAB); Nederlandsche Vereeniging van Antiquaren.
Type of Business: Major Independent Bookseller, Online Bookseller

Pegasus Publishers & Booksellers
Singel 367, 1012 WL Amsterdam
Mailing Address: Postbus 11 470, 1001 GL Amsterdam
Tel: (020) 623 11 38 *Fax:* (020) 620 34 78
E-mail: pegasus@pegasusboek.nl
Web Site: www.pegasusboek.nl
Key Personnel
Dir: Susan van Oostveen
Founded: 1945
Type of Business: Exporter, Importer, Major Independent Bookseller

Antiquariaat Plantijn
Ginnekenmarkt 5, 4835 JC Breda
Tel: (076) 560 44 00 *Fax:* (03) 231 94 74
Web Site: www.plantijnmaps.com
Key Personnel
Owner: Dieter Duncker *E-mail:* dieter.d@planet.nl
Founded: 2001
Membership(s): The Brussels Map Circle; International Map Collector's Society (IMCOS); Nederlandsche Vereeniging van Antiquarian (NVvA).
Type of Business: Major Independent Bookseller

Antiquariat Die Schmiede
Brouwersgracht 4, 1013 GW Amsterdam
Tel: (020) 6250501 *Fax:* (020) 6235470
E-mail: info@dieschmiede.nl
Web Site: www.dieschmiede.nl
Key Personnel
Owner: Annemieke Leyerzapf; Gerard Leyerzapf
Subjects include biography, architecture, drama, photography, humor, law, literature, music, philosophy, politics, religion, sociology & sports.
Type of Business: Major Independent Bookseller

H de Vries Boeken
Gedempte Oude Gracht 27, 2011 GK Haarlem
Tel: (023) 5319458; (070) 3125605
E-mail: info@devriesboeken.nl; klantenservice@devriesboeken.nl
Web Site: www.devriesboeken.nl
Key Personnel
Sales Account Manager: Carla Leonhardt
Tel: (06) 49610112 *E-mail:* c.leonhardt@devriesboeken.nl
Founded: 1905
Type of Business: Major Independent Bookseller

New Zealand

David Bateman Ltd
30 Tarndale Grove, Albany, Auckland 0632
Mailing Address: North Shore Mail Centre, PO Box 100-242, Auckland 0745
Tel: (09) 415 7664 *Fax:* (09) 415 8892
E-mail: info@bateman.co.nz
Web Site: www.bateman.co.nz
Key Personnel
Mng Dir: Paul Bateman
Sales Manager: Bryce Gibson *E-mail:* bryceg@bateman.co.nz
Full book distribution, sales & marketing service.
Type of Business: Distributor

Bennetts Bookstores Ltd
Massey University Turitea Campus, One Turitea Rd, Palmerston North 4414
Tel: (06) 354 6020 *Fax:* (06) 354 6716
Toll Free Fax: 0800 118 333
E-mail: books@bennetts.co.nz; massey@bennetts.co.nz
Web Site: www.bennetts.co.nz
Key Personnel
Dir: Sean Woodward
Founded: 1889
Type of Business: Major Book Chain Headquarters
Branch Office(s)
Massey University Albany Campus, Student Central, Gate 1, East Precinct, Dairy Flat Highway (SH17), Albany, Auckland 0632 *Tel:* (09) 415 0348 *E-mail:* aku@bennetts.co.nz
Christchurch Polytechnic Institute of Technology, 130 Madras St, CSPA Bldg, C Block, Christchurch 8014 *Tel:* (03) 977 3572 *E-mail:* chp@bennetts.co.nz *Web Site:* www.cpit.ac.nz
University of Waikato, Gate 5, Hillcrest Rd, Library Bldg Level 1, Hamilton 3216 *Tel:* (07) 856 6813 *Fax:* (07) 856 2255 *E-mail:* wku@bennetts.co.nz *Web Site:* www.waikato.ac.nz
Massey University Wellington, Main Entrance-Gate A, 68 Wallace St, Mount Cook, Wellington 6021 *Tel:* (04) 384 1407 *Fax:* (04) 384 5827 *E-mail:* wgp@bennetts.co.nz *Web Site:* www.massey.ac.nz

Eton Press (Auckland) Ltd
Barry's Point Rd, Unit C 32, Takapuna 3118
Toll Free Tel: 0800 333 016 *Toll Free Fax:* 0800 333 034
E-mail: info@eton.co.nz
Web Site: www.eton.co.nz
Founded: 1968
Specialize in mathematics.
Type of Business: Importer, Major Independent Bookseller

Hedleys Booksellers
150 Queen St, Masterton
Tel: (06) 378 2875 *Fax:* (06) 378 2570
E-mail: sales@hedleysbooks.co.nz
Web Site: www.hedleysbooks.co.nz; www.booksonline.co.nz
Key Personnel
Owner & Manager: David Hedley; Jenny Hedley
Founded: 1907
Also publisher.
Specialize in new or secondhand limited edition handcrafted, leatherbound & rare books.
Type of Business: Distributor, Major Independent Bookseller, Online Bookseller

Lincoln University Bookshop
George Forbes Memorial Bldg, Corner of Ellesmere Junction Rd & Spring Rd, Lincoln University, Lincoln 7647

Mailing Address: PO Box 85084, Lincoln University, Lincoln 7647
Tel: (03) 325 3892 *Fax:* (03) 325 3615
E-mail: thelinc@lincoln.ac.nz
Web Site: bookshop.lincoln.ac.nz; shop.lincoln.ac.nz (online orders)
Located at the Waihora campus, the bookshop is open to the general public, local businesses, schools & community organisations in addition to university staff & students.
Type of Business: Major Independent Bookseller

Living Word
634 Victoria St, Hamilton 3204
Tel: (07) 839 5607
Web Site: www.livingword.net.nz
Key Personnel
Dir: Terry Hooper
Founded: 1978
Christian resources including Bibles, books, gifts, music & DVDs.
Type of Business: Distributor, Exporter, Importer, Major Independent Bookseller, Online Bookseller, Wholesaler

McLeods Booksellers Ltd
1148 Pukuatua St, Rotorua
Tel: (07) 348 5388
E-mail: shop@mcleodsbooks.co.nz
Web Site: www.mcleodsbooks.co.nz
Key Personnel
Owner: David Thorp; Lynne Thorpe
Founded: 1944
Traditional bookshop combining selection & service with latest bibliographic technology.
Type of Business: Major Independent Bookseller

Octane Books
Formerly Techbooks
Private Bag 300984, Albany, Auckland 0610
Tel: (09) 524-0138
Web Site: octanebooks.co.nz
Founded: 1983
Type of Business: Major Independent Bookseller

Page & Blackmore Booksellers Ltd
254 Trafalgar St, Nelson
Tel: (03) 548 9992 *Fax:* (03) 546 6799
E-mail: info@pageandblackmore.co.nz
Web Site: www.pageandblackmore.co.nz
Key Personnel
Owner: Tim Blackmore
Founded: 1998
Type of Business: Major Independent Bookseller

Paper Plus Taumarunui
77 Hakiaha St, Taumarunui 3920
Tel: (07) 895-7430 *Toll Free Tel:* 0800 727377
E-mail: taumarunui@paperplus.co.nz
Web Site: www.paperplus.co.nz
Type of Business: Major Independent Bookseller
Parent Company: Paper Plus Group

South Pacific Books Distributors Ltd
PO Box 303 243, North Harbour, Auckland 1330
Tel: (09) 448 1591 *Fax:* (09) 448 1592
E-mail: sales@spbooks.co.nz
Web Site: www.soupacbooks.co.nz
Key Personnel
General Manager: Liza Raybould
Office Manager: Angela Thomas
Trade Representative: Philip Anstiss *Tel:* (021) 477 307 (cell) *E-mail:* philip@spbooks.co.nz
Founded: 1984
Type of Business: Distributor, Importer, Remainder Dealer

South Sea Books
37 Hollis Ave, Christchurch 8002
Tel: (03) 3314612

E-mail: southsea46@gmail.com
Web Site: www.abebooks.com/home/southsea
Key Personnel
Owner: Glenn Haszard
Founded: 1984
Type of Business: Exporter, Importer, Major Independent Bookseller, Wholesaler

Techbooks, see Octane Books

Unity Books Ltd
57 Willis St, Wellington 6011
Tel: (04) 499 4245 Fax: (04) 499 4246
E-mail: wellington@unitybooks.co.nz
Web Site: unitybooks.nz
Key Personnel
Manager: Tilly Lloyd
Founded: 1967
Type of Business: Importer, Major Independent Bookseller
Bookshop(s): Unity Books Auckland, 19 High St, Auckland 1010 Tel: (09) 307 0731
E-mail: shop@unitybooksauckland.co.nz

University Book Shop (Otago) Ltd
378 Great King St, Dunedin 9016
Mailing Address: PO Box 6060, Dunedin 9016
Tel: (03) 477 6976 Fax: (03) 477 6571
E-mail: enquiries@unibooks.co.nz
Web Site: www.unibooks.co.nz
Key Personnel
General Manager: Phillippa Duffy Tel: (03) 474 5401 ext 888 E-mail: phillippad@unibooks.co.nz
Founded: 1945
Type of Business: Major Independent Bookseller
Owned by: Otago University Students' Association

University Bookshop (Auckland) Ltd
Student Commons Bldg, 2 Alfred St, Auckland Central 1010
Mailing Address: PO Box 90944, Victoria St W, Auckland 1142
Tel: (09) 306 2700 Fax: (09) 306 2701
E-mail: enquiries@ubsbooks.co.nz
Web Site: www.ubsbooks.co.nz
Key Personnel
Manager: Tammy Harrison Tel: (09) 306 2716
E-mail: tammy.harrison@ubsbooks.co.nz
Founded: 1966
Type of Business: Importer, Major Independent Bookseller
Bookshop(s): Bldg WC, Room 122, Hikuwai Plaza, AUT City Campus, 55 Wellesley St E, Auckland Central 1010, Manager: Cara King Tel: (09) 366 4550 Fax: (09) 366 4570 E-mail: aut.city@ubsbooks.co.nz; AUT South Campus, 640 Great South Rd, Manukau City, Auckland 2025 Tel: (09) 366 4550 E-mail: aut.manukau@ubsbooks.co.nz; Bldg AB, Room 101, AUT North Campus, 90 Akoranga Dr, Northcote, North Shore City 0627, Manager: Carla Bryant Tel: (09) 489 6105 Fax: (09) 489 7453 E-mail: aut.akoranga@ubsbooks.co.nz

University Bookshop (Canterbury) Ltd
University Dr, Ilam, Private Bag 4748, Christchurch 8140
Tel: (03) 364 2043 Toll Free Tel: 0800 827 266
E-mail: ubs@ubscan.co.nz
Web Site: www.ubscan.co.nz; www.canterbury.ac.nz
Key Personnel
Manager: Pene Whitty
Textbook Manager: Joan Shields
Founded: 1933
Type of Business: Exporter, Importer, Major Independent Bookseller

Whitcoulls
29 Union St, Level 2, Auckland 1010
Mailing Address: Auckland Mail Centre, Victoria St W, Private Bag 92098, Auckland 1142
Toll Free Tel: 0800 904 584
E-mail: customer-services@whitcoulls.co.nz
Web Site: www.whitcoulls.co.nz
Founded: 1971
56 bookshops throughout New Zealand.
Type of Business: Major Book Chain Headquarters
Owned by: James Pascoe Group (JPG)

Nicaragua

Libreria Universitaria
Universidad Nacional Autonoma de Nicaragua, Iglesia La Recoleccion 1/2 cuadra al Oeste, Leon
Mailing Address: Apdo 68, La Merced, Leon
Tel: 2311-2929
E-mail: libreria@ac.unanleon.edu.ni
Web Site: www.unanleon.edu.ni/libreria.html
Type of Business: Major Independent Bookseller

Nigeria

Ahmadu Bello University Bookshop Ltd
Ahmadu Bello University, Arewa House, No 1 Rabah Rd, PMB 2006, Zaria, Kaduna State
E-mail: kadamu@gmail.com
Web Site: www.abu.edu.ng; arewahouse.abu.edu.ng
Key Personnel
Dir, Arewa House: Prof Abdulkadir Adamu
Deputy Dir: Prof Muhammad Kabir Aliyu
Type of Business: Major Independent Bookseller

Challenge Bookshops
c/o ECWA, Omoku St, Port Harcourt
Founded: 1924
Publisher & distributor of bibles, Christian literature, music, gifts & stationery.
Membership(s): CBAN.
Type of Business: Distributor, Wholesaler
Owned by: Evangelical Church of West Africa (ECWA)
Bookshop(s): 159 Aba Rd, Port Harcourt, River State Tel: (0803) 672 8484 (cell); 10 Kano Rd, Jos, Plateau State Tel: (0802) 711 5189 (cell); 6 Ali Akilu Rd, Kaduna, Kaduna State; 27A Airport Rd, Kano, Kano State Tel: (0708) 273 4010 (cell); 271 Agege Motor Rd, Mushin, Lagos State Tel: (01) 4522199

Chosen Generation Books Ltd
13, Oyeleke St, Alausa Bus Stop, Off Kudirat Abiola Way, Alausa, Ikeja, Lagos State
Tel: (01) 474 4815; (01) 741 5540
E-mail: info@chosengenbooks.org
Web Site: www.chosengenbooks.org
Key Personnel
Sales: Mrs Wunmi Ogini E-mail: wunmi@chosengenbooks.org
Founded: 1991
Christian books, Bibles, audio visual CDs & tapes, gift items & management books.
Type of Business: Distributor, Major Independent Bookseller, Online Bookseller, Wholesaler

CSS Bookshops Ltd
Bookshop House, 4th floor, 50/52 Broad St, Lagos

Mailing Address: PO Box 174, Lagos
Tel: (01) 462 2593
E-mail: info@cssbookshopslimited.com
Web Site: www.cssbookshopslimited.com
Key Personnel
Mng Dir: Dotun Adegboyega
Founded: 1869
Specialize in the supply of Christian books & literature, educational & general books, stationery & office equipment.
Type of Business: Distributor, Importer, Major Book Chain Headquarters, Wholesaler
Branch Office(s)
10/12 Warehouse Rd, Apapa, Lagos Tel: (0815) 9490168 (cell)
Bamenda St, Beside All Saints Primary School, Opposite Abuja Shopping Mall, Zone 3, Wuse, Abuja Tel: (0815) 9490164 (cell)
Anglican Girls Grammar School, Opposite AP Filling Station, Gudu, Abuja Tel: (0815) 9490165 (cell)
26, Ahmadu Bello Way, Kaduna Tel: (0815) 9490166 (cell)
50, Hospital Rd, Opposite State Police Hq, Annepe, Port Harcourt Tel: (0815) 9490167 (cell)

Fola Abbey Educational Book Services
One, Odunlami Lane Off Kakawa St, Lagos
Tel: (01) 2636679
Suppliers of all Nigerian publications to universities, libraries & individuals.
Type of Business: Distributor, Exporter

OAU Bookshop, see Obafemi Awolowo University Bookshop

Obafemi Awolowo University Bookshop
Obafemi Awolowo University, PMB 13, Ile-Ife
Tel: (036) 230290 Fax: (036) 232401
Web Site: www.oauife.edu.org
Founded: 1964
Type of Business: Major Independent Bookseller
Branch Office(s)
Ondo
Uyo

Odusote Bookstores Ltd
68, Obafemi Awolowo Way, Oke Ado, Ibadan 200001
Mailing Address: PO Box 244, Ibadan
Tel: (02) 2316451; (02) 2315055 Fax: (02) 2318781
E-mail: odubooks@infoweb.abs.net
Founded: 1964
Type of Business: Distributor, Wholesaler
Branch Office(s)
177 Herbert Macaulay St, Yaba, Lagos Tel: (01) 8187606

Pen & Pages
Smart Bridge Plaza Shop, F08, Fingersy St, Opposite Eden Garden, Utako, Abuja
Tel: (0806) 8787631 (cell); (0803) 3201197 (cell)
E-mail: admin@penandpages.com.ng; info@penandpages.com.ng
Web Site: www.penandpages.com.ng
Founded: 2003
Knowledge resource centre.
Type of Business: Distributor, Major Independent Bookseller

University Bookshop Nigeria Ltd
University of Ibadan, Ibadan, Oyo State
Founded: 1956
Type of Business: Distributor, Exporter, Major Independent Bookseller

University of Lagos Bookshop
Bookshop Bldg, Main Campus, Akoka-Yaba, Lagos
Tel: (07) 4539984
E-mail: nfo@unilagbookshop.com

Web Site: unilagpress.com
Key Personnel
Customer Service Manager: Mr Abimbola Emmanuel
Founded: 1966
Other retail outlets located at the College of Medicine, Idi-Araba & the School of Radiography, Yaba.
Type of Business: Importer

Norway

Forlagsentralen ANS
Snipetjernveien 12, Langhus
Mailing Address: Postboks 20, 1402 Ski
Tel: 64 91 94 00 *Fax:* 64 91 94 01
E-mail: firmapost@forlagssentralen.no; ordre@forlagssentralen.no
Web Site: forlagssentralen.no
Key Personnel
Mng Dir: Einar J Einarsson *Tel:* 48 12 10 10 (cell) *E-mail:* eje@forlagssentralen.no
Dir, Administration: Tor Nygaard *Tel:* 91 54 93 11 (cell) *E-mail:* tony@forlagssentralen.no
Vice President, Operations & Marketing: Heidi Lier Wisloff *Tel:* 99 32 29 93 (cell) *E-mail:* hlw@forlagssentralen.no
Founded: 1922
Type of Business: Distributor
Owned by: H Aschehoug & Co (W Nygaard) AS; Gyldendal ASA

ARK Bokhandel AS
Sehesteds gate 4, 0164 Oslo
Mailing Address: Postboks 6693, St Olavs plass, 0129 Oslo
Tel: 22 99 07 50; 22 99 07 55
E-mail: kundeservice@arkbokhandel.no
Web Site: www.ark.no
Key Personnel
Chief Executive Officer: John Torres Thuv
Type of Business: Major Book Chain Headquarters
Owned by: Gyldendal Forlag
Bookshop(s): ARK Aker Brygge, Holmens gate 8, 0250 Oslo *Tel:* 96 91 85 84 *E-mail:* akerbrygge@ark.no; ARK Alna, Alna Senter, Stromsveien 245, 0668 Oslo *Tel:* 96 64 03 16 *E-mail:* alna@ark.no; ARK Byporten, Jernbanetorget 6, 0154 Oslo *Tel:* 96 62 56 17 *E-mail:* byporten@ark.no; ARK Egertorget, Ovre Slottsgate 23/25, 0157 Oslo *Tel:* 22 47 32 00 *E-mail:* egertorget@ark.no; ARK Grunerlokka, Thorvald Meyers gate 55, 0555 Oslo *Tel:* 96 62 56 83 *E-mail:* grunerlokka@ark.no; ARK Holmlia, Holmlia Sentervei 11, 1255 Oslo *Tel:* 96 90 32 53 *E-mail:* holmlia@ark.no; ARK Karenslyst Alle Skoyen, Karenslyst Alle 9, 0278 Oslo *Tel:* 96 62 57 32 *E-mail:* karenslyst.alle@ark.no; ARK Kiellands Hus, Waldermar Thranes gate 72, 0175 Oslo *Tel:* 96 62 56 81 *E-mail:* kiellands.hus@ark.no; ARK Klingenberggata, Olav VS gate 4, 0161 Oslo *Tel:* 96 62 56 18 *E-mail:* klingenberggata@ark.no; ARK Lambertseter Senter, Cecilie Thoresensvei 17, 1153 Oslo *Tel:* 96 62 24 42 *E-mail:* lambertseter@ark.no; ARK Linderud Senter, Eric Mogensonsvei 38, 0594 Oslo *Tel:* 96 64 02 27 *E-mail:* linderud@ark.no; ARK Manglerud Senter, Plogveien 6, 0679 Oslo *Tel:* 96 62 56 41 *E-mail:* manglerud@ark.no; ARK Oppsal, Haakon Tvetersvei 88-98, 0686 Oslo *Tel:* 96 91 80 51 *E-mail:* oppsal@ark.no; ARK Oslo Sentralstasjon, Jernbanetorget 1, 0154 Oslo *Tel:* 96 62 56 23 *E-mail:* oslo.sentralstasjon@ark.no; ARK Roa, Vaekeroveien 205, 0751 Oslo *Tel:* 96 62 56

80 *E-mail:* roa@ark.no; ARK Saeter Torg, Nordstrandveien 42, 1163 Oslo *Tel:* 47 70 26 56 *E-mail:* sater.torg@ark.no; ARK Sandaker, Sandakerveien 59, 0477 Oslo *Tel:* 96 62 56 43 *E-mail:* sandaker@ark.no; ARK Solli Plass, Henrik Ibsens gate 60c, 0255 Oslo *Tel:* 96 62 57 19 *E-mail:* solli.plass@ark.no; ARK Storgata, Storgata 33, 0184 Oslo *Tel:* 96 62 57 21 *E-mail:* storgata@ark.no; ARK Stovner Senter, Stovner Senter 3, 0985 Oslo *Tel:* 96 62 56 39 *E-mail:* stovner@ark.no; ARK Tveita, Tvetenveien 150, 0671 Oslo *Tel:* 96 62 56 40 *E-mail:* tveita@ark.no; ARK Ulleval, Sognsveien 75, 0855 Oslo *Tel:* 96 62 56 42 *E-mail:* ulleval@ark.no; ARK Amfi Moa, Moaveien 1, 6018 Alesund *Tel:* 96 64 01 38 *E-mail:* moa@ark.no; ARK Kremmergaarden Alesund, Rasmus Ronnebergs gate 6, 6002 Alesund *Tel:* 96 64 01 41 *E-mail:* kremmergaarden@ark.no; ARK Amfi Alta, Markedsgata 21-25, 9510 Alta *Tel:* 96 64 03 25 *E-mail:* alta@ark.no; ARK Arendal, Vesterveien 4, 4836 Arendal *Tel:* 96 64 01 29 *E-mail:* arendal@ark.no; ARK Arnes, Radhusgata 11, 2150 Arnes *Tel:* 96 62 56 79 *E-mail:* aarnes@ark.no; ARK Asker, Stroket 5, 1383 Asker *Tel:* 96 62 57 24 *E-mail:* asker@ark.no; ARK Bekkestua, Gml Ringeriksvei 34, 1357 Bekkestua *Tel:* 96 62 57 23 *E-mail:* bekkestua@ark.no; ARK Beyer Strandgaten, Strandgaten 4, 5013 Bergen *Tel:* 96 91 77 62 *E-mail:* beyer@ark.no; ARK City Nord Bodo, Stormyrveien 20, 8008 Bodo *Tel:* 96 64 01 44 *E-mail:* citynord@ark.no; ARK Glasshuset, Storgata 5, 8006 Bodo *Tel:* 96 64 01 43 *E-mail:* glasshuset@ark.no; ARK Odds, Storgaten 7, 8006 Bodo *Tel:* 96 64 01 42 *E-mail:* odds@ark.no; ARK Havnesenteret Bronnoysund, Storgata 58, 8900 Bronnoysund *Tel:* 96 64 12 06 *E-mail:* havnesenteret@ark.no; ARK Gulskogen-Drammen, Guldlisten 35, 3048 Drammen *Tel:* 96 62 59 48 *E-mail:* gulskogen@ark.no; ARK Stromso Senter Drammen, Bjornstjerne Bjornsonsgate 60, 3044 Drammen *Tel:* 96 90 63 54 *E-mail:* stromso@ark.no; ARK Amfi Elverum, Torggaten 3, 2408 Elverum *Tel:* 96 90 42 31 *E-mail:* elverum@ark.no; ARK Amfi Farsund, Vestersiden 1, 4550 Farsund *Tel:* 94 87 38 44 *E-mail:* amfifarsund@ark.no; ARK Amfi Fauske, Fauske, Sjogata 74, 8200 Fauske *Tel:* 96 64 01 49 *E-mail:* fauske@ark.no; ARK Amfi Finnsnes, Storgata 7, 9300 Finnsnes *Tel:* 46 82 68 19 *E-mail:* amfi.finnsnes@ark.no; ARK Amfi Flekkefjord, Jernbaneveien 12, 4400 Flekkefjord *Tel:* 96 64 01 27 *E-mail:* flekkefjord@ark.no; ARK Fornebu S, Fornebu S, Snaroyveien 55, 1364 Fornebu *Tel:* 96 91 85 85 *E-mail:* fornebu@ark.no; ARK Torvbyen, Brochsgt 7/11, 1607 Fredrikstad *Tel:* 96 64 01 30 *E-mail:* torvbyen@ark.no; ARK Oasen Senter Bergen, Folke Bernadottes vei 52, 5147 Fyllingsdalen *Tel:* 96 91 80 52 *E-mail:* oasen@ark.no; ARK CC Gjovik, Jernbanesvigen 6, 2821 Gjovik *Tel:* 96 90 78 71 *E-mail:* cc.gjovik@ark.no; ARK Halden Storsenter, Os alle 3, 1777 Halden *Tel:* 96 62 57 90 *E-mail:* halden@ark.no; ARK Tista Senter, Walkers gate 4, 1771 Halden *E-mail:* tista.senter@ark.no; ARK CC Hamar, CC Hamar, Vangsvegen 62, 2317 Hamar *Tel:* 96 90 52 68 *E-mail:* hamar@ark.no; ARK Amfi Kanebogen Harstad, Skillevegen 5, 9411 Harstad *Tel:* 46 82 62 04 *E-mail:* amfi.kanebogen@ark.no; ARK Amanda Haugesund, Longhammerveien 27, 5536 Haugesund *Tel:* 96 62 57 36 *E-mail:* amanda@ark.no; ARK Haraldsgata Haugesund, Haralds gate 159, 5527 Haugesund *Tel:* 96 90 20 01 *E-mail:* sund@ark.no; ARK Hogskolen Haugesund, Bjornsons gate 45, 5528 Haugesund *Tel:* 96 91 45 61 *E-mail:* hogskolen.haugesund@ark.no; ARK Kuben Honefoss, Kong Ringsgate 1, 3510 Honefoss *Tel:* 96 64

01 56 *E-mail:* kuben@ark.no; ARK Sjosiden Senter Horton, Teatergata 6, 3187 Horten *Tel:* 46 80 06 24 *E-mail:* sjosiden.horten@ark.no; ARK Jessheim, Furusethgata 5, 2050 Jessheim *Tel:* 96 62 56 45 *E-mail:* jessheim@ark.no; ARK Amfi Askoy, Askoy Senter, Kleppeveien 110, 5308 Kleppesto *Tel:* 96 64 03 23 *E-mail:* askoy@ark.no; ARK Romerikssenteret, Trondheimsveien 86, 2040 Klofta *Tel:* 96 62 56 47 *E-mail:* klofta@ark.no; ARK Kolsas Senter, Kolsas Senter, Rodskiferveien 1, 1352 Kolsas *Tel:* 96 91 45 53 *E-mail:* kolsas@ark.no; ARK Amfi Vagsbygd, Kirsten Flagstadsvei 32, 4621 Kristiansand *Tel:* 46 83 51 85 *E-mail:* amfi.vagsbygd@ark.no; ARK Markens, Markensgate 31, 4611 Kristiansand *Tel:* 96 64 01 26 *E-mail:* markens@ark.no; ARK Sorlandssenteret Kristians, Barstolveien 31-35, 4636 Kristiansand, India *Tel:* 96 91 45 49 *E-mail:* sorlandssenteret@ark.no; ARK Amfi Futura Kristiansund, Industriveien 17, 6517 Kristiansund *Tel:* 96 64 01 34 *E-mail:* futura@ark.no; ARK Storkaia Brygge, Arnulf Overlandsgate 2,4,8, 6509 Kristiansund *Tel:* 96 64 02 85 *E-mail:* storkaia@ark.no; ARK Nordbyen Larvik, Yttersoveien 2, 3274 Larvik *Tel:* 96 62 56 33 *E-mail:* farris@ark.no; ARK Torget Larvik, Torget 1, 3256 Larvik *Tel:* 96 62 57 29 *E-mail:* torget.larvik@ark.no; ARK Lillestrom Torv, Torvet 6, 2000 Lillestrom *Tel:* 96 62 55 63 *E-mail:* kohns@ark.no; ARK Vestkanten Storsenter, Vestkanten 2, 5171 Loddefjord *Tel:* 96 62 56 85 *E-mail:* vestkanten@ark.no; ARK Metro, Lorenskog, Bibliotekgata 30, 1473 Lorenskog *Tel:* 96 62 56 46 *E-mail:* metro@ark.no; ARK Melhus Torget, Melhustorget 7, 7224 Melhus *Tel:* 96 62 56 91 *E-mail:* melhustorget@ark.no; ARK Amfi Mo i Rana, Fridtjof Nansens gate 21, 8622 Mo i Rana *Tel:* 96 64 01 45 *E-mail:* mo@ark.no; ARK Amfi Roseby Molde, Lingedalsveienn 6-10, 6415 Molde *Tel:* 96 64 01 35 *E-mail:* roseby@ark.no; ARK Storgata Molde, Storgaten 29, 6413 Molde *Tel:* 96 64 01 39 *E-mail:* dahl@ark.no; ARK Amfi Moss, Dronningensgate 3-73-7, 1530 Moss *Tel:* 96 91 31 21 *E-mail:* amfimoss@ark.no; ARK Rygge Storsenter, Carlbergveien 2, 1526 Moss *Tel:* 96 64 01 33 *E-mail:* rygge@ark.no; ARK Namsos Storsenter, Verdtsgaten 2-4, 7800 Namsos *Tel:* 96 62 57 05 *E-mail:* namsos@ark.no; ARK Amfi Narvik, Amfisenteret, Bolagsgata 1, 8514 Narvik *Tel:* 96 64 01 46 *E-mail:* narvik@ark.no; ARK Holmen Senter, Vogellund 6, 1394 Nesbru *Tel:* 96 62 55 65 *E-mail:* holmen@ark.no; ARK Nesttun Senter, Nesttun Senter, Ostre Nesttunvei 16, 5221 Nesttun *Tel:* 55 13 07 77 *E-mail:* nesttun@ark.no; ARK Amfi Nordfjord, Sjogata 21, 6770 Nordfjordeid *Tel:* 46 94 34 11 *E-mail:* amfinordfjord@ark.no; ARK Horisont Senter, Horisont Asane, Myrdalsveien 2, 5130 Nyborg *Tel:* 96 90 52 76 *E-mail:* horisont.asane@ark.no; ARK Amfi Orkanger, 7302 Orkanger *Tel:* 96 62 56 93 *E-mail:* orkanger@ark.no; ARK Osteras, Osterassenteret, Otto Rugesvei 80, 1361 Osteras *Tel:* 96 62 53 98 *E-mail:* osteras@ark.no; ARK Down Town Porsgrunn, Kulltangvegen 70, 3921 Porsgrunn *Tel:* 96 62 56 32 *E-mail:* downtown@ark.no; ARK Storgata Porsgrunn, Storgata 154, 3915 Porsgrunn *Tel:* 96 64 01 36 *E-mail:* dyring@ark.no; ARK Amfi Eidsvoll, Gladbakkveien 1, 2070 Raholt *Tel:* 96 91 75 50 *E-mail:* eidsvoll@ark.no; ARK Ostfoldhallen, Dikeveien 28, 1661 Rolvsoy *Tel:* 96 64 01 32 *E-mail:* ostfoldhallen@ark.no; ARK Hvaltorvet, Torvet 7, 3210 Sandefjord *Tel:* 96 64 02 00 *E-mail:* hvaltorvet@ark.no; ARK Bystasjonen Sandnes, Vagsgaten 16, 4306 Sandnes *Tel:* 96 91 85 86 *E-mail:* bystasjonen@ark.no; ARK Kvadrat, Gamle Stokkavei 1, 4313 Sandnes *Tel:* 96 64 12 33 *E-mail:* kvadrat@ark.no; ARK Sand-

vika, Radmann Halmrasts Vei 12, 1337 Sandvika *Tel:* 96 62 57 22 *E-mail:* sandvika@ark.no; ARK Sandvika Storsenter, Brodtkorbsgate 7, 1338 Sandvika *Tel:* 96 91 43 11 *E-mail:* sandvika.storsenter@ark.no; ARK Selbu, Nestansringen 3, 7580 Selbu *Tel:* 96 62 57 09 *E-mail:* selbu@ark.no; ARK Ski Storsentr, Jernbanesvingen 6, 1400 Ski *Tel:* 96 62 56 26 *E-mail:* ski@ark.no; ARK Herkules Skien, Ulefossveien 32B, 3730 Skien *Tel:* 96 62 57 28 *E-mail:* herkules@ark.no; ARK Amfi Sogningen, Hovevegen 8, 6856 Sogndal *Tel:* 96 90 22 55 *E-mail:* sogningen@ark.no; ARK Brotorvet Stathelle, Gangveien 10, 3960 Stathelle *E-mail:* brotorvet@ark.no; ARK Kilden Stavanger, Prostebakken 3, 4006 Stavanger *Tel:* 96 64 92 22 *E-mail:* berge@ark.no; ARK Kilden Stavanger, Gartnerveien 15, 4016 Stavanger *Tel:* 96 64 01 15 *E-mail:* kilden@ark.no; ARK Tasta Senter Stavanger, Tastatunet 1-3, 4027 Stavanger *Tel:* 96 90 22 18 *E-mail:* tasta@ark.no; ARK Stavanger Lufthavn, Flyplassveien 230, 4055 Stavanger Lufthavn *Tel:* 96 62 56 19 *E-mail:* stavanger.lufthavn@ark.no; ARK Amfi Steinkjer, Amfi Steinkjer, Sjofartsgaten, 7714 Steinkjer *Tel:* 96 62 57 11 *E-mail:* steinkjer@ark.no; ARK Pocket Vaernes, Trondheim Lufthavn Vaernes, 7505 Stjordal *Tel:* 96 62 56 27 *E-mail:* pocket.vaernes@ark.no; ARK Stjordal, Torgkvartalet, Stokmoveien 2, 7500 Stjordal *Tel:* 96 62 56 63 *E-mail:* stjordal@ark.no; ARK Amfi Stord, Stord Amfisenter, Hamnegata 11, 5411 Stord *Tel:* 96 62 57 39 *E-mail:* stord@ark.no; ARK Heiane Storsenter, Heiane 43, 5412 Stord *Tel:* 96 62 58 18 *E-mail:* heiane@ark.no; ARK Hogskolen Stord, Hogskolen, 5414 Stord *Tel:* 96 91 45 63 *E-mail:* hogskolen.stord@ark.no; ARK Sartor Storsenter, Sartor Senter 12, 5342 Straume *Tel:* 96 62 56 87 *E-mail:* sartor@ark.no; ARK Strommen Storsenter, Stoperiveien 5, 2010 Strommen *Tel:* 96 62 56 75 *E-mail:* strommen@ark.no; ARK City Syd Trondheim, City Syd, Ostre Rosten 28, 7075 Tiller *Tel:* 96 62 57 07 *E-mail:* citysyd@ark.no; ARK Farmandstredet, Farmandstredet, Jernbanegt 1D, 3110 Tonsberg *Tel:* 96 62 56 34 *E-mail:* farmandstredet@ark.no; ARK Jekta Tromso, Karlsoyveien 2, 9015 Tromso *Tel:* 96 90 12 43 *E-mail:* jekta@ark.no; ARK Storgata Tromso, Sjogata 16, 9008 Tromso *Tel:* 96 64 01 47 *E-mail:* tromso@ark.no; ARK Tromso, Tromso Lufthavn, 9016 Tromso *Tel:* 96 64 05 55 *E-mail:* tromso.lufthavn@ark.no; ARK Brunhjornet Trondheim, Kongens gate 10, 7484 Trondheim *Tel:* 96 62 59 59 *E-mail:* brunhjornet@ark.no; ARK Sirkus Shopping Trondheim, Falkenborgvegen 9, 7044 Trondheim *Tel:* 96 90 22 19 *E-mail:* sirkus.shopping@ark.no; ARK Trondheim Torg, Trondheim Torg, Tinghusplassen, 7013 Trondheim *Tel:* 96 62 59 81 *E-mail:* trondheim.torg@ark.no; ARK Asane, Asane Senter, 5116 Ulset *Tel:* 96 62 56 86 *E-mail:* asane@ark.no; ARK Vestby Storsenter, Senterveinen 8, 1540 Vestby *Tel:* 96 90 32 08 *E-mail:* vestby@ark.no; ARK Vinterbro, Vinterbrosenteret, Sjoskogveien, 1407 Vinterbro *Tel:* 96 62 56 38 *E-mail:* vinterbro@ark.no

Biblioteksentralen SA (The Norwegian Library Bureau)
Alf Bjerckes vei 20, 0582 Oslo
Mailing Address: Postboks 24, 0614 Oslo
Tel: 22 08 34 00
E-mail: kundeservice@bibsent.no
Web Site: www.bibsent.no
Key Personnel
Administrative Dir: Borge Hofset *E-mail:* borge.hofset@bibsent.no
Sales & Marketing Dir: Jorunn Wold *Tel:* 91 64 63 43 *E-mail:* jorunn.wold@bibsent.no

Communications Manager: Kristin Lande *Tel:* 99 35 60 03 *E-mail:* krl@bibsent.no
Sales & Media Manager: Toril Anderson *Tel:* 90 19 25 68 *E-mail:* toa@bibsent.no
Founded: 1902
Bibliographic products & service. Materials, furnishings & interior architects for libraries.
Type of Business: Distributor

Lyngs Bokhandel AS
Var Frue Strete 1, 7013 Trondheim
Mailing Address: Postboks 328, 7402 Trondheim
Tel: 91806230
Founded: 1927
Type of Business: Major Independent Bookseller

Norli
Universitetsgata 20-24, 0162 Oslo
Mailing Address: Postboks 1990 Vika, 0125 Oslo
Tel: 22 00 43 00
E-mail: post@norli.no; eksport@norli.no; universitetsgata@norli.no
Web Site: www.norli.no
Founded: 1890
Specialize in medicine, education, business, computers, travel, Scandinavian literature, books in minority & immigrant languages & library supplier.
Type of Business: Distributor, Exporter, Importer, Major Independent Bookseller, Wholesaler

Notabene
Teglverksveien 100, 3057 Solbergelva
E-mail: kundeservice@notabene.no
Web Site: www.notabene.no
Over 50 bookshops throughout Norway.
Type of Business: Major Book Chain Headquarters

SentralDistribusjon AS
Alf Bjerckes vei 24 A, 0582 Oslo
Tel: 22 98 57 10; 22 98 57 00 (orders) *Fax:* 22 98 57 20
E-mail: sdinfo@sd.no
Web Site: www.sd.no
Key Personnel
Chief Financial Officer: Jan Erik Stokke
Type of Business: Distributor
Owned by: Cappelens Publishing

Tanum AS
Karl Johans gate 37-41, 0162 Oslo
Tel: 22 47 87 30; 21 89 73 00 (customer service)
E-mail: karljohaninformasjonen@tanum.no; kundeservice@tanumnettbokhandel.no
Web Site: www.tanum.no
Founded: 1928
Type of Business: Exporter, Importer, Major Book Chain Headquarters, Wholesaler
Owned by: Cappelen Damm AS
Bookshop(s): Tanum Bogstadveien, Bogstadveien 27B, 0355 Oslo *Tel:* 23 33 38 50 *E-mail:* bogstadveien@tanum.no; Tanum Bryn, Ostensjoveien 79, 0667 Oslo *Tel:* 22 76 14 20 *E-mail:* bryn@tanum.no; Tanum Byporten, Jernbanetorget 9, 0154 Oslo *Tel:* 23 16 32 80 *E-mail:* byporten@tanum.no; Tanum CC Vest, Lilleakerveien 16, 0283 Oslo *Tel:* 23 25 30 70 *E-mail:* ccvest@tanum.no; Tanum Colosseum, Sorkedalsveien 10, 0369 Oslo *Tel:* 23 68 11 30 *E-mail:* colosseum@tanum.no; Tanum Litteraturhuset, Wergelandsveien 29, 0167 Oslo *Tel:* 23 69 10 80 *E-mail:* litteraturhuset@tanum.no; Tanum Oslo City, Stenersgaten 1, 0050 Oslo *Tel:* 23 15 88 30 *E-mail:* oslocity@tanum.no; Tanum Storo, Vitaminveien 7-9, 0485 Oslo *Tel:* 23 69 17 10 *E-mail:* storo@tanum.no; Tanum Flesland, Flyplassveien 555, 5869 Bergen *Tel:* 95 40 26 10 *E-mail:* flesland@tanum.no; Tanum Kolbotn Torg, Strandliveien 6, 1410 Kolbotn *Tel:* 67 49

04 50 *E-mail:* kolbotn@tanum.no; Tanum Nordre, Nordre gate 1-3, 7011 Trondheim *Tel:* 91 52 66 81 *E-mail:* nordre@tanum.no

Tanum Karl Johan, see Tanum AS

Pakistan

Allied Book Co
Naqi Market, 75 The Mall, Lahore 54000
Tel: (042) 36306456; (042) 36310907 *Fax:* (042) 36360662
E-mail: info@alliedbook.com; alliedlhr@alliedbook.com; inquiry@alliedbook.com
Web Site: www.alliedbook.com
Key Personnel
Proprietor: Dost Mohammad *Tel:* (0307) 4444094 (cell)
Imports: Muhammad Toqeer Mobeen *Tel:* (0320) 4363256 (cell)
Subscriptions: Ali Raza *Tel:* (0321) 8831364 (cell)
Founded: 1984
Type of Business: Distributor, Exporter, Importer, Online Bookseller
Branch Office(s)
Off 18 & 19, 1st floor, Rizwan Arcade, Adamjee Rd, Saddar, Rawalpindi 46000, Manager: Mohammad Siddique *Tel:* (051) 5519620; (051) 5567711 *Fax:* (051) 5519620 *E-mail:* alliedrwp@alliedbook.com

Ferozsons
60-Shahrah-e-Quaid-e-Azam, Lahore
Tel: (042) 111-62-62-62 *Fax:* (042) 636-9204
E-mail: support@ferozsons.com.pk
Web Site: www.ferozsons.com.pk
Founded: 1894
Also publisher & printer.
Type of Business: Distributor, Exporter, Importer, Major Independent Bookseller, Wholesaler
Bookshop(s): 51-54 Gaddafi Stadium, Lahore *Tel:* (042) 571-2250; (042) 571-2276 *Fax:* (042) 571-2020; H Block, DHA, Lahore *Tel:* (042) 574-2804; (042) 574-2805; Pearl Continental Hotel Shop No 9, Lahore *Tel:* (042) 636-0210; Urdu Bazzar, Lahore *Tel:* (042) 722-7086; Z Block, DHA, Lahore *Tel:* (042) 573-5662; (042) 573-5663; Clifton, Karachi, Manager: Ms Gul Afshan *Tel:* (021) 111-62-62-62 *Fax:* (042) 582-5170; Peshawar Rd, Rawalpindi *Tel:* (042) 62-62-62 *Fax:* (051) 556-4273

Liberty Books
Shop No 3-4, Khayaban-e-Shahbaz, Phase 6, DHA, Karachi
Tel: (0311) 1444282
E-mail: query@libertybooks.com
Web Site: www.libertybooks.com
Founded: 1961
Type of Business: Distributor, Importer, Major Book Chain Headquarters, Wholesaler
Bookshop(s): Aga Khan University Hospital, Stadium Rd, Karachi *Tel:* (021) 34864586; Gloria Jeans (SMCHS), Karachi *Tel:* (021) 34534176; Dolmen Mall, Tariq Rd, Karachi *Tel:* (021) 34387085; Dolmen Mall, Clifton, Karachi *Tel:* (021) 35294276; BBQ Tonight, Karachi *Tel:* (021) 35374153; Park Towers, Karachi *Tel:* (021) 35832525 ext 125; The Forum, Karachi *Toll Free Tel:* 0300-0805927; Boulevard Mall, Hyderabad *Tel:* (022) 3413146; Emporium Mall, Lahore *Toll Free Tel:* 0333-4517737; Packages Mall, Lahore *Tel:* (042) 38914324

Multiline Books
Shop No 3, Ahmad Mansion, Regal Chowk, Mall
Rd, PO Box 1268, Lahore 54000
Tel: (042) 7210089; (042) 7353564 *Fax:* (042)
7121326
E-mail: multiline.books@gmail.com
Web Site: multilinebooks.com
Founded: 1949
Type of Business: Importer, Wholesaler
Branch Office(s)
Flat No 7, 1st floor, Plaza 2000, 1/8
Markaz, Islamabad *Tel:* (051) 4438631
E-mail: multilineisb@gmail.com

Pak American Commercial (Pvt) Ltd
60-A, Khan Chamber, Canning Rd, Saddar,
Rawalpindi
Tel: (051) 5563709 *Fax:* (051) 5565190
Type of Business: Importer, Major Independent
Bookseller, Wholesaler
Branch Office(s)
1st floor, Pak Chambers, 5 Temple Rd, Lahore

Pak Book Corp
Aziz Chambers, 21 Queen's Rd, Lahore 54000
Tel: (042) 6363222 *Fax:* (042) 6362328
E-mail: info@pakbook.com
Web Site: www.pakbook.com
Key Personnel
Chief Executive: M Iqbal Cheema
E-mail: iqbalcheema@pakbook.com
Dir: M Shahid Cheema *E-mail:* shahidcheema@
pakbook.com
Sales Coordinator: Naveeda Islam
E-mail: naveeda@pakbook.com
Sales Manager: Khalid Mahmood
E-mail: khalid@pakbook.com
Assistant Sales Manager: Ali Zaidi
E-mail: alizaidi@pakbook.com
Marketing Coordinator: Zarina Zarin
E-mail: zarina@pakbook.com
Founded: 1975
Deal with scientific books, journals & films &
CD-ROM databases.
Type of Business: Distributor, Exporter, Importer,
Major Independent Bookseller, Wholesaler
Branch Office(s)
No 222, 1st floor, Beverly Centre Blue Area,
Islamabad 44000, Manager: Zaheer A Mufti
Tel: (051) 111636636 *E-mail:* islamabad@
pakbook.com
2nd floor, Star Center, Main Tariq Rd, PECHS,
Karachi 75400, Manager: S Qamar Zaidi
Tel: (021) 34536375 *Toll Free Tel:* (0300)
8202211

Pak Company Pakistan
17-Urdu Bazar, Lahore 54000
Tel: (042) 37230555; (042) 37352427 *Fax:* (042)
37120077
E-mail: pakcompany@hotmail.com
Web Site: www.pakcompany.com.pk
Key Personnel
Dir: Syed Ahmed Shah
Founded: 1932
Also publisher.
Type of Business: Exporter, Importer, Wholesaler

Pakistan Law House
Pakistan Chowk, GPO Box 90, Karachi
Tel: (021) 32212455; (021) 32639558 *Fax:* (021)
32627549
E-mail: pak_law_house@hotmail.com
Web Site: www.pakistanlawhouse.com
Key Personnel
Owner: Kamran Noorani
Founded: 1950
Type of Business: Distributor, Exporter, Importer

Paramount Books (Pvt) Ltd
152/0 Block 2, PECHS, Karachi, Sindh 75400

Tel: (021) 34310030-2 *Fax:* (021) 34553772
E-mail: info@paramountbooks.com.pk
Web Site: www.paramountbooks.com.pk
Key Personnel
Deputy Mng Dir: Iqbal Salahuddin
Founded: 1948
Also retailer & book publisher.
Membership(s): Pakistan Publishers & Book-
sellers Association.
Type of Business: Distributor, Importer, Major
Book Chain Headquarters, Wholesaler
Branch Office(s)
The Book Tique, Alliance Francaise Karachi, St
1, Block-8, Kehkashan, Clifton, Karachi
Paramount Books, Urdu Bazar, Shop 3/A, Za-
rina Manzil G Lekhraj Rd, Karachi *Tel:* (021)
32217527
Shop No 44 Opposite Bahadur Shah Market,
Urdu Bazar, Karachi *Tel:* (021) 32217628
House No 69/8, St No 9, Habib Ullah Colony,
Abbotabad *Tel:* (0313) 6606779 (cell); (0344)
9496567 (cell)
41, 1st floor, Koh-e-Noor One, Jaranwala Rd,
Faisalabad *Tel:* (041) 8501676
Shop No 2, Ground floor, Madina Heights, Risala
Rd, Near PSO Pump, Hyderabad *Tel:* (022)
2782402
107, 1st floor, Pacific Centre, F/8 Markaz, Islamabad *Tel:* (051) 2853106; (051) 2287244
81 Block C-II, Tariq Rd, Gulberg III, Lahore
Tel: (042) 35877087
London Book Co, Arbab Rd, Saddar Cantt, Peshawar *Tel:* (091) 5272722

Royal Book Co
BG-5, Rex Centre, Fatima Jinnah Rd, Saddar,
Karachi 75530
Tel: (021) 35653418; (021) 35684244; (021)
37015471; (021) 37011123 *Fax:* (021)
37015472
E-mail: info@royalbook.com.pk;
royalbookcompany@yahoo.com; royalbook@
hotmail.com
Web Site: www.royalbook.com.pk
Founded: 1964
Also publisher.
Type of Business: Distributor, Exporter, Importer,
Major Independent Bookseller, Wholesaler

Panama

Libreria Cultural Panamena SA
Via Espana frente a Calle 1ra, Perejil, Apdo
2018, Zona 1, Panama
Tel: 223-6267; 223-5628 *Fax:* 223-7280
E-mail: lacultural@cwpanama.net
Web Site: www.libreriacultural.com
Founded: 1955
Type of Business: Distributor, Exporter, Importer,
Major Independent Bookseller, Wholesaler

Papua New Guinea

**University of Papua New Guinea Press &
Bookshop**
Division of University of Papua New Guinea
Administration Area, University of Papua New
Guinea, Waigani Campus, Port Moresby 134
NCD
Mailing Address: PO Box 413, University Post
Office 134 NCD
Tel: 3267675 *Fax:* 3267187 (university)
E-mail: upngbooks@gmail.com

Web Site: www.pngbuai.com/buybooks
Key Personnel
Manager, Bookshop & Publications: John Evans
Tel: 3267375
Founded: 1971
Unified bookselling, distribution & publishing
venture. Books on & about Papua New Guinea
in all subjects.
Type of Business: Distributor, Importer, Major
Independent Bookseller

Paraguay

Libreria Comuneros
Cerro Cora 289, Casilla de Correos no 930, 1301
Asuncion
Tel: (021) 446-176; (021) 444-667 *Fax:* (021)
444-667
Key Personnel
Proprietor: Oscar R Rolon *E-mail:* rolon@
conexion.com.py
Type of Business: Distributor, Exporter, Importer,
Major Independent Bookseller, Wholesaler

Peru

Adriatica SA
Jiron Junin 565, Trujillo
Tel: (044) 291569; (044) 294242
Founded: 1994
Type of Business: Distributor, Importer, Major
Independent Bookseller
Branch Office(s)
Av Larco 857, 2 do piso, Trujillo

CENPROLID
Universidad Nacional Mayor de San Marcos, Av
Venezuela s/n, Ciudad Universitaria, Lima 1
Tel: (01) 6197000 (ext 7633); (01) 6197000 (ext
7634); (01) 6197000 (ext 7635, sales); (01)
6197000 (ext 7637, sales)
E-mail: libreria@unmsm.edu.pe
Web Site: www.unmsm.edu.pe/cenprolid
Founded: 1996
Type of Business: Distributor, Importer

**El Centro de Produccion, Libreria y
Distribuidora**, see CENPROLID

Distribuidora Importadora Durand SA
311 Jr San Pedro Int 313, Surquillo, Lima 34
Tel: (014) 4463190
Key Personnel
General Dir: Arturo Gamero Durand Placentino
Type of Business: Distributor, Importer, Whole-
saler

Nuevas Technicas Educativas SAC (NUTESA)
Av Caminos del Inca 257-269, 2da etapa, tienda
337, Centro Comercial Caminos del Inca, San-
tiago de Surco, Lima 33
Tel: (051) 205 8642; 989010035 (cell)
E-mail: info@nutesa.com.pe
Web Site: www.nutesa.com.pe
Key Personnel
Owner: Enrique Cappelletti
Founded: 1992
Type of Business: Distributor, Importer
Branch Office(s)
Av La Marina 1602, tienda 116-117, Centro
Comercial Marina Plaza, Pueblo Libre, Lima
21 *Tel:* 989010036 (cell)

NUTESA, see Nuevas Technicas Educativas SAC (NUTESA)

SBS Special Book Services SA
Ave Angamos Oeste 301, Lima 18
Tel: (01) 206-4900 *Fax:* (01) 241-8492
E-mail: ventas@sbs.com.pe
Web Site: www.sbs.com.pe
Founded: 1996
Bookshops located in Arequipa, Chiclayo, Cusco, Huancayo, Huanuco, Iquitos, Lima, Pucallpa & Trujillo.
Type of Business: Distributor
Parent Company: SBS Livraria Internacional

Sociedad Biblica Peruana Asociacion Cultural
(Peruvian Bible Society)
Av Petit Thouars 991, Lima
Tel: (014) 433 5815; (014) 433 0077; (014) 433 0232 *Fax:* (014) 433 6389
E-mail: ventas@sbp.org.pe
Web Site: www.sbp.org.pe
Key Personnel
Executive Dir: Roberto Moises Miranda Moreno
Founded: 1947
Type of Business: Distributor, Exporter, Importer
Owned by: SBP

Ediciones Zeta SRL
Jr Pachacutec 1414, Jesus Maria, Lima
Tel: (01) 4711966
Key Personnel
Manager: Jorge Zavaleta Salvador
E-mail: jzavalet@edizeta.com.pe
Founded: 1978
Type of Business: Distributor, Importer, Major Book Chain Headquarters, Wholesaler
Bookshop(s): Zeta Bookstore SRL, Estacion Central, Lima *E-mail:* metropolitano@zetanews.pe; Zeta Bookstore SRL, Molina Plaza, La Molina, Lima *Tel:* (01) 3654016 *E-mail:* caja_molina@zetabook.com; Zeta Bookstore SRL, Av Comandante Espinar 219, Miraflores, Lima *Tel:* (01) 4465139; (01) 4449630 *E-mail:* libriosvarios@zetabook.com; Zeta Bookstore SRL, Mega Plaza, Los Olivos, Lima *Tel:* (01) 4850824 *E-mail:* megaplaza2@zetabook.com; Zeta Bookstore SRL, La Rambla, San Borja, Lima *Tel:* (01) 2268142 *E-mail:* larambla@zetabook.com; Zeta Bookstore SRL, Parque Lambramani, Arequipa; Zeta Bookstore SRL, Aeropuerto Velasco Astete, Cuzco

Philippines

The Bookmark Inc
264 Pablo Ocampo Sr Ave, San Antonio Village, 1203 Makati City
Tel: (02) 8958061 *Fax:* (02) 8970824
E-mail: bookmark1945@gmail.com; bookmark@bookmarkthefilipinobookstore.com
Web Site: www.bookmarkthefilipinobookstore.com
Key Personnel
President: Bienvenido A Tan, Jr
General Manager: Dr Anna Maria Tan-Delfin
Founded: 1945
Also publisher & retailer.
Type of Business: Exporter, Major Book Chain Headquarters, Wholesaler

Goodwill Bookstore
Goodwill Bldg, 393 Sen Gil Puyat Ave, Bel-Air Village, 1200 Makati City
Tel: (02) 895-8684 *Fax:* (02) 895-7854
E-mail: publishing@goodwillbookstore.net
Web Site: www.goodwillbookstore.com

Key Personnel
President & General Manager: Teresa Cancio-Suplico
Founded: 1938
Type of Business: Distributor, Major Book Chain Headquarters, Online Bookseller, Wholesaler
Branch Office(s)
49 P Del Rosario St at Junquera St, Cebu City
Tel: (032) 255-0825 *Fax:* (032) 255-0825
E-mail: gbscebu@goodwillbookstore.net
Saric Bldg, Door 17, Corner of Sta Ana Ave & Guerrero St, Davao City *Fax:* (082) 300-1732
University of the Philippines (Manila), Pasdre Faura St, Ermita, Manila *Fax:* (02) 536-6877
E-mail: gbsupmla@goodwillbookstore.net
Bridges Bookstore, G/F V-Mall, Greenhills Shopping Center, San Juan, Metro Manila
Tel: (02) 723-0545 *Fax:* (02) 723-6319
E-mail: bridges@goodwillbookstore.net

National Book Store Inc (NBSI)
125 Pioneer St, 1550 Mandaluyong City
Tel: (02) 631-8061 *Fax:* (02) 631-5016
E-mail: customerservice@nationalbookstore.com.ph
Web Site: www.nationalbookstore.com.ph
Key Personnel
Founder & Chairman: Mrs Socorro C Ramos
Founded: 1942
Also publisher.
Type of Business: Major Book Chain Headquarters

NBSI, see National Book Store Inc (NBSI)

Popular Bookstore
305 Tomas Morato Ave, 1100 Quezon City
Tel: (0921) 295 6429 (cell)
E-mail: pobost@yahoo.com.ph
Web Site: www.facebook.com/popularbkstore
Founded: 1946
Independent bookshop specializing in philosophy, psychology, esoteric traditions, progressive ideologies.
Type of Business: Distributor, Importer, Major Independent Bookseller, Wholesaler
Owned by: Popular Trading Corp

RBSI, see REX Book Store Inc

REX Book Store Inc
Member of The REX Group of Companies
Rex Knowledge Center, 109 Sen M Cuenco Sr, 1114 Quezon City
Tel: (02) 857-7777
E-mail: wecare@rexpublishing.com.ph; orders@rexestore.com
Web Site: www.rexpublishing.com.ph; www.rexestore.com
Key Personnel
Chief Operating Officer: Don Timothy I Buhain
President: Dominador D Buhain
E-mail: ddbuhain@rexpublishing.com.ph
Marketing Dir: Jeanne Marie Fontelera-Tordesillas
Founded: 1950
Type of Business: Major Book Chain Headquarters
Branch Office(s)
REX Book Store Cubao, Unit 10 UGF Dona Consolacion Bldg, Gen Santos Ave, Araneta Center, Cubao, Quezon City *Tel:* (02) 911-1070
REX Book Store Angeles, Unit H, JMS Bldg, McArthur Hi-way, Brgy Salapungan, Angeles City *Tel:* (045) 887-5371
REX Book Store Bacolod, No 28 Barangay-36 Purok Immaculada, Quezon Ave, Bacolod City *Tel:* (034) 707-5825
REX Hall Baguio, Upper Gen Luna cor A Bonifacio St, 2600 Baguio City *Tel:* (074) 422-0574

REX Book Store Batanes, L Lopez St, Kayvaluganan, Basco, Batanes *Tel:* (02) 681-9085; (02) 330-4937
REX Book Store, Brgy Salong, National Hi-way, Calapan City, Oriental Mindoro *Tel:* (043) 288-1650
REX Book Store Cavite, Block 4, Lot 20 Don Gregorio Heights 2 Zone, 1-A Aguinaldo Hi-way, Dasmarinas Cavite, Cavite *Tel:* (046) 416 1824
REX Book Store Cebu, 11 Sanciangko St, Cebu City *Tel:* (032) 416-9684; (032) 254-6773; (032) 505-4313
REX Book Store Davao, 156-A CM Recto St, Davao City *Tel:* (082) 300-5422; (082) 305-5772; (082) 221-0272
REX Book Store General Santos, Aparinte St, Dadiangas Heights, General Santos City *Tel:* (083) 304-8512; (083) 554-7102
REX Book Store Iloilo, No 75 Brgy San Isidro Lopez-Jaena, Jaro, Iloilo City *Tel:* (033) 329-0332; (033) 329-0336
REX Book Store Legaspi, Unit 6, 3rd floor, A Bichara Silverscreen, Legazpi City, Albay *Tel:* (052) 480-2244
REX Book Store Makati, Unit UG-2, Star Centrum Bldg, Sen Gil Puyat Ave, Makati City *Tel:* (02) 818-5363; (02) 893-3744
REX Book Store Rockwell, Ateneo Professional School, 1st floor, Rockwell Center, Bel-Air, Makati City
REX Book Store Morayta, 856 Nicanor Reyes Sr St, Sampaloc, Manila *Tel:* (02) 736-0169; (02) 736-4191; (02) 733-6746
REX Book Store Recto, 161-65 Freedom Bldg, C M Recto Ave, Sampaloc, Manila *Tel:* (02) 522-4521; (02) 522-4305; (02) 522-4107; (02) 733-8637
REX Book Store Naga, 1-1A Geronimo Bldg, Barlin St, Sta Cruz, Naga City *Tel:* (054) 811-6878
REX Book Store Ortigas, EC-02D East Tower, Ground floor, Philippine Stock Exchange Condominium (Tektite Tower) Ortigas, Pasig City
REX Book Store Tacloban, Brgy 78 Marasbaras, Tacloban City *Tel:* (053) 323-8976; (053) 523-1784
REX Book Store Tuguerarao, 10 Arellano Ext St, Barangay Ugac Sur, Tuguerarao, Cagayan *Tel:* (078) 844-8072
REX Book Store Urdaneta, Zone 6, Pinmaludpod, Urdaneta City, Pangasinan *Tel:* (075) 568-3975
REX Book Store Zamboanga, San Francisco Loop, Mayor Agan Ave, Camino Nuevo, Zamboanga City *Tel:* (088) 858-6775; (088) 309-5881

Poland

ABE-IPS Sp z oo
ul Grzybowska 37A, 00-855 Warsaw
SAN: 128-0031
Tel: (22) 654 06 75 *Toll Free Tel:* 801 777 223
Fax: (22) 652 07 67
E-mail: info@abe.pl
Web Site: www.abe.pl
Key Personnel
President: Marek Nowakowski
Dir, Online Subscription: Irena Ksiezopolska
E-mail: irena.ksiezopolska@abe.pl
Founded: 1990
Polish sole agent for K G Saur Verlag Munich; subscription services.
Type of Business: Distributor, Importer, Major Book Chain Headquarters, Online Bookseller
Branch Office(s)
ul Hoene Wronskiego 6/1, 80-210 Gdansk
Tel: (58) 550 09 36 *Fax:* (58) 550 09 36
E-mail: trojmiasto@abe.pl

Al Ignatius Daszynskiego 12, 31-534 Krakow
Tel: (12) 296 33 36 *Fax:* (12) 296 33 37
E-mail: krakow@abe.pl
ul Heweliusza 3/b, 60-281 Poznan *Tel:* (61) 856
02 79 *E-mail:* poznan@abe.pl
Kerchenska Str 7/7, 03-151 Kiev, Ukraine
Tel: (97) 318 12 10; (97) 362 28 16
E-mail: ukraine@abe.pl

Ars Polona SA
ul Obroncow 25, 03-933 Warsaw
Tel: (22) 509 86 00 *Fax:* (22) 509 86 10
E-mail: arspolona@arspolona.com.pl
Web Site: www.arspolona.com.pl
Key Personnel
President: Grzegorz Guzowski *Tel:* (22) 509 86
09 *E-mail:* grzegorz@arspolona.com.pl
Vice President: Adam Wasik *Tel:* (22) 509 86 21
E-mail: adam.wasik@arspolona.com.pl
Founded: 1953
Export & import of books & periodicals as well
as publish books. Export & import of mod-
ern art, musical instruments & philately. Orga-
nizer of Warsaw International & National Book
Fairs.
Type of Business: Distributor, Exporter, Importer,
Online Bookseller, Wholesaler

Dom Ksiazki Warszawa Sp z oo
ul Swietokrzyska 30 lok 63, 00-116 Warsaw
Tel: 533 300 978 (cell)
E-mail: ks_817@domksiazki.pl
Web Site: www.domksiazki.pl
Founded: 1996
Type of Business: Major Book Chain Headquarters, Wholesaler
Bookshop(s): ul Egipska 7, 03-977 Warsaw, Man-
ager: Elzbieta Mejsner *Tel:* 533 300 971 (cell);
(22) 612 62 84 *E-mail:* ks_800@domksiazki.pl;
ul Krola Maciusia 10, 04-526 Warsaw, Manager: Renata Siergiejuk *Tel:* 533 300 970 (cell)
E-mail: ks_801@domksiazki.pl; ul Matejki 4,
43-600 Jaworzno *Tel:* 533 300 980 (cell); (32)
616 38 67 *E-mail:* ks_815@domksiazki.pl; ul
Wyszynskiego 10, 21-400 Lukow, Manager:
Justyna Facon *Tel:* 533 300 976 (cell); (25)
798 29 43 *E-mail:* ks_808@domksiazki.pl; ul
Ryneck 11, 43-190 Mikolow, Manager: Urszula
Wojnar *Tel:* 533 300 981 (cell); (32) 226 20
62 *E-mail:* ks_816@domksiazki.pl; ul Warszawska 3, 05-100 Nowy Dwor Mazowiecki, Manager: Hanna Sobko *Tel:* 533 300 975 (cell)
E-mail: ks_802@domksiazki.pl; ul Glowack-
iego 35, 07-140 Ostroleka *Tel:* 533 300 972
(cell); (29) 760 22 69 *E-mail:* ks_805@
domksiazki.pl; ul 3 Maja 47, 07-300 Os-
trow Mazowiecka, Manager: Anna Wal-
czak *Tel:* 533 300 974 (cell); (29) 760 25 12
E-mail: ks_806@domksiazki.pl; ul Andriollego
48/50, 05-400 Otwock, Manager: Hanna Cz-
erniak *Tel:* 533 300 973 (cell); (22) 616 18 34
E-mail: ks_803@domksiazki.pl; ul Rynek 11
lok nr 10, 47-400 Raciborz, Manager: Jadwiga
Izbicka *Tel:* 533 300 982 (cell); (32) 415 44 29
E-mail: ks_814@domksiazki.pl; ul Dziewul-
skiego 21, 87-100 Torun, Manager: Agnieszka
Szczawinska *Tel:* 533 300 991 (cell); (56)
623 03 43 *E-mail:* ks_809@domksiazki.pl;
ul Kosciuski 30, 07-200 Wyszkow, Manager:
Malgorzata Tarnozek *Tel:* 533 300 977 (cell)
E-mail: ks_807@domksiazki.pl

Wydawnictwo Terra Nostra sc
ul Korotynskiego 13, 02-121 Warsaw
Mailing Address: PO Box 14, 02-105 Warsaw
Tel: (22) 6592964; (22) 6596295; (60) 5051274
(cell) *Fax:* (22) 6596295
E-mail: terra@topkart.com.pl
Web Site: www.artmap.pl
Key Personnel
Dir: Elzbieta Kuzmiuk
Sales Dir: Grzegorz Gregorczyk

Founded: 1994
Type of Business: Distributor

Portugal

Livraria Babel
Av Antonio Augusto de Aguiar, 148-6°, 1050-021
Lisbon
Tel: 213801100 *Fax:* 213865396
E-mail: babel@babel.pt
Web Site: www.babel.pt
Founded: 1899
Specialize in art-related books.
Type of Business: Major Independent Bookseller

Livraria Barata-Antonio D M Barata Lda
Ave de Roma, 11a, 1049-047 Lisbon
Tel: 218 428 350; 218 428 357
E-mail: barata@livrariabarata.pt; escolar@
livrariabarata.pt
Web Site: www.livrariabarata.pt
Founded: 1957
Type of Business: Major Independent Bookseller

Bertrand Livreiros
R Garrett, 73/75, 1200-203 Lisbon
Tel: 213476122
E-mail: chiado.livraria@bertrand.pt
Web Site: www.bertrand.pt
Founded: 1732
Type of Business: Major Book Chain Headquar-
ters
Owned by: Bertrand Editora Lda
Branch Office(s)
Amoreiras Shopping, Loja 2.108, Av Duarte
Pacheco, 1070-103 Lisbon *Tel:* 213838034
E-mail: amoreiras.livraria@bertrand.pt
Av de Roma 13B, 1000-261 Lisbon
Tel: 217969271 *E-mail:* roma.livraria@
bertrand.pt
Centro Cultural del Belem, Praca do Imperio,
1449-003 Lisbon *Tel:* 213645637 *E-mail:* ccb.
livraria@bertrand.pt
Chiado, Rua Garrett 73/75, 1200-203 Lisbon
Tel: 213476122 *E-mail:* chiado.livraria@
bertrand.pt
Colombo, Loja 0.135, 0.136, Av Lusiada, 1500-
392 Lisbon *Tel:* 217167152 *E-mail:* colombo.
livraria@bertrand.pt
Loja 117, Praca Campo Pequeno, Centro
Lazer Campo Pequeno, 1000-082 Lisbon
Tel: 217993230 *E-mail:* campopequeno.
livraria@bertrand.pt
Picoas Plaza, Loja C0.9 Rua Tomas Ribeiro
Cruzamento/Rua Viriato, 1050-225 Lisbon
Tel: 213593359 *E-mail:* picoasplaza.livraria@
bertrand.pt
Spacio Shopping, Loja 23, Rua Cidade de
Bolama, 1800-079 Lisbon *Tel:* 218551161
E-mail: olivais.livraria@bertrand.pt
Vasco da Gama, Loja 0.099, Av D Joao II,
n° 40, 1990-094 Lisbon *Tel:* 218951321
E-mail: vascodagama.livraria@bertrand.pt
Cascais Shopping, Loja 0.015/0.016, No
Rodoviaria, Estrada Nacional, 9/Estrada
Nacional, 68, 2645-543 Alcabideche
Tel: 214607092 *E-mail:* cascaisshopping.
livraria@bertrand.pt
Almada Forum, Loja 1.97, 1.101, Rua Ser-
gio Malpique, n° 2, 2810-500 Almada
Tel: 212508545 *E-mail:* almada.livraria@
bertrand.pt
Forum Aveiro, Loja 2.12 Rua Cacadores
10, 3810-064 Aviero *Tel:* 234427087
E-mail: forumaveiro.livraria@bertrand.pt
R Stara Zagora, Campo das Cardoarias, 2830-
364 Barreiro *Tel:* 212073161 *E-mail:* barreiro.
livraria@bertrand.pt

Liberdade St Fashion, Loja 8, Ave da Liber-
dade, 4710-251 Braga *Tel:* 253109976
E-mail: liberdadestreet.livraria@bertrand.pt
Vivaci Caldas da Rainha, Loja 1.05 Rua Bel-
chior de Matos, 11, 2500-234 Caldas da
Rainha *Tel:* 262880531 *E-mail:* caldasdarainha.
livraria@bertrand.pt
Ave Nuno Alvares, N° 11, Bloco D, 6000-
081 Castelo Branco *Tel:* 272092469
E-mail: castelobranco.livraria@bertrand.pt
Dolce Vita Coimbra, Rua General Hum-
berto Delgado, 207-211 Solum, Loja
209, 3030-327 Coimbra *Tel:* 239716007
E-mail: dolcevitacoimbra.livraria@bertrand.pt
Av Jose Bonifacio de Andrade e Quinta do Vale
Gemil, Planalto Santa Clara, 3040-389 Coim-
bra *Tel:* 239445324 *E-mail:* forumcoimbra.
livraria@bertrand.pt
Largo da Portagem, 9, 3000-337 Coimbra
Tel: 239823014 *E-mail:* coimbra.livraria@
bertrand.pt
Serra Shopping, Loja 0.12, Qunita do Pin-
heiro, Lote 1, Palmeira, 6200-552 Covilha
Tel: 275325035 *E-mail:* covilha.livraria@
bertrand.pt
Forum Algarve, Loja 025, Estrada Nacional
125, km 103, 8009-020 Faro *Tel:* 289865187
E-mail: forumalgarve.livraria@betrand.pt
Rua Dr Francisco Gomes 27, 8000-306 Faro
Tel: 289828147 *E-mail:* faro.livraria@bertrand.
pt
Loja 218, Rua dos Condados-Buarcos, 3080-
206 Figueira da Foz *Tel:* 233430562
E-mail: figueirafoz.livraria@bertrand.pt
Dolce Vita Funchal, Loja 117, Rua Dr Joao
Brito Camara, n° 9, 9000-039 Funchal
Tel: 291280022 *E-mail:* dolcevitafunchal.
livraria@bertrand.pt
Forum Madeira, Loja 012 Estrada Mounumen-
tal, 390, 9004-568 Funchal *Tel:* 291761693
E-mail: forummadeira.livraria@bertrand.pt
La Vieguarda, Av Bombeiros Voluntarios Egi-
tanienses 5, Loja 3.24, 6300-523 Guarda
Tel: 271237428 *E-mail:* guarda.livraria@
bertrand.pt
Leiria Shopping, Estrada Nacional n°1,
Alto do Veiro Loja 0.79, 2400-441 Leiria
Tel: 244824562 *E-mail:* leiria.livraria@
bertrand.pt
Loures Shopping, Loja 0.09, Av Das Descober-
tas, n° 90, Quinta do Infantado, 2670-457
Loures *Tel:* 219830212 *E-mail:* louresshopping.
livraria@bertrand.pt
Mar Shopping, Loja 0.16, Av Dr Oscar Lopes,
4450-337 Matosinhos *Tel:* 220164781
E-mail: marshopping.livraria@bertrand.pt
Forum Montijo, Loja 0.23, Zona Industrial do Pau
Queimado, Rua da Azinheira, 2870-100 Mon-
tijo *Tel:* 212301603 *E-mail:* montijo.livraria@
bertrand.pt
Odivelas Parque, Loja 2014, Estrada da
Paia, 2675-497 Odivelas *Tel:* 219316566
E-mail: odivelasparque.livraria@bertrand.pt
Acores, Parque Atlantico, Loja 043, Rua
da Juventude, 9500-211 Ponta Delgada
Tel: 296284553 *E-mail:* acores.livraria@
bertrand.pt
CC Portimao, Modelo Loja 105/108, Quinta
da Malata, Lote 1, 8500-510 Portimao
Tel: 282418929 *E-mail:* portimao.livraria@
bertrand.pt
Dolce Vita Porto, Rua Campeoes Europeus, 28/
198, Loja 112, 4350-414 Porto *Tel:* 225023384
E-mail: antas.livraria@bertrand.pt
Porto Gran Plaza, Rua Fernandes Tomas n°
506/508, Loja 0.18/0.19, 4000-211 Porto
Tel: 222016060 *E-mail:* portogranplaza.
livraria@bertrand.pt
Loja 115, Rua Doutor Placido da Costa, 4200-450
Porto *Tel:* 220163114 *E-mail:* campussjoao.
livraria@bertrand.pt
Loja 238, Rua Goncalo Sampaio, 350, 4150-365
Porto *Tel:* 220104882 *E-mail:* cidadedoporto.
livraria@bertrand.pt

Rua da Fabrica, nº 90, 4050-246 Porto
  Tel: 223197675 *E-mail:* ruafabrica.livraria@
  bertrand.pt
W Shopping Santarem, Loja 1.47, D Rua Pe-
  dro Santarem, nº 29, 2000-223 Santarem
  Tel: 243322828 *E-mail:* santarem.livraria@
  bertrand.pt
Av Dr Renato Araujo 1625, Loja 0022, 3700-
  346 Sao Joao da Madeira *Tel:* 256842076
  E-mail: sjmadeira.livraria@bertrand.pt
Riosul Shopping, Av Libertadores de Timor
  Lorosae, Loja 0.047, Torre da Mar-
  inha, 2840-168 Seixal *Tel:* 212226192
  E-mail: riosulshopping.livraria@bertrand.pt
Arena Shop-Loja 1.036, Casais Amiais,
  2560-586 Torres Vedras *Tel:* 261324240
  E-mail: torresvedras.livraria@bertrand.pt
Estacao Viana, Loja 1125, Av Humberto Del-
  gado nº 101, 4900-317 Viana do Castelo
  Tel: 258829726 *E-mail:* vianaestacao.livraria@
  bertrand.pt
Rua Sacadura Cabral, 32, 4900-517 Viana do
  Castelo *Tel:* 258822838 *E-mail:* viana.livraria@
  bertrand.pt
Dolce Vita Douro, Loja 218/219, Alameda de
  Grasse, 5000-703 Vila Real *Tel:* 259322670
  E-mail: vilareal.livraria@bertrand.pt
Palacio Do Gelo, Loja 014, Quinta da
  Alagoa, 3500-606 Viseu *Tel:* 232432188
  E-mail: palaciodogelo.livraria@bertrand.pt

Livraria Caravana
Rua Jose C Guerreiro Lt B-r/c-D, 8100-596 Loule
Tel: 289462879; 289422549
E-mail: livrariacaravana@mail.telepac.pt
Founded: 1996
Type of Business: Major Independent Bookseller

Cogitum Livrarias Lda
Shopping Center Massama Loja 41, 2745-000
  Queluz
Tel: 214394912
Founded: 1991
Type of Business: Major Independent Bookseller

Edicoes Destarte, *imprint of* Destarte Lda

Destarte Lda
Rua de Santo Antonio da Gloria, 90, 1250-218
  Lisbon
Tel: 213475811; 213242960 *Fax:* 213475811
E-mail: destarte@vianw.pt
Founded: 1980
Type of Business: Distributor, Importer
Imprints: Edicoes Destarte
Branch Office(s)
Livraria Linhares

Dinapress
Largo Dr Antonio de Sousa Macedo, Nº 2, 1200-
  153 Lisbon
Tel: 213955270 *Fax:* 213950390
Founded: 1989
Type of Business: Exporter, Wholesaler
Owned by: Sr Silverio Pedroso Amaro
Bookshop(s): Centro Cultural Brasi Leiro

Domingos Castro
Rua do Matadouro, Lote 42, Zona Industrial,
  2005-002 Santarem
Tel: 243 359 380 *Fax:* 243 359 389
E-mail: info@domingoscastro.com
Web Site: www.domingoscastro.com
Founded: 1984
Type of Business: Distributor, Wholesaler

EDC - Empresa de Divulgacao Cultural SA
Rua Jose Estevao, 133, 1º, 1150-201 Lisbon
Tel: 213195630 *Fax:* 213528217
Founded: 1969

Type of Business: Distributor
Owned by: Editorial Verbo SA

Electroliber Lda
Rua Vasco da Gama 4/4-A, Sacavem, 2680-165
  Fetais
Tel: 219419020
Type of Business: Distributor

Esquina Livraria
Rua Afonso Lopes Vieira, 126 (AO FOCO),
  4100-020 Porto
Tel: 226 065 314; 961 171 955
E-mail: livrariaesquina@mail.telepac.pt
Web Site: www.livrariaesquina.com
Key Personnel
Contact: Joana Barroso
Founded: 1972
Also deals in secondhand & rare books.
Type of Business: Major Independent Bookseller

Livraria Ferin Ltda
Rua Nova do Almada, 72, 1249-098 Lisbon
Tel: 213424422 *Fax:* 213471101
E-mail: livraria.ferin@ferin.pt
Web Site: www.ferin.pt
Founded: 1840
Type of Business: Exporter, Importer, Wholesaler

Livraria Manuel Ferreira Lda (Manuel Ferreira
  Bookshop)
Rua Dr Alves Veiga, 89, 4000-073 Porto
Tel: 225363237 *Fax:* 225364406
E-mail: contacto@livrariaferreira.pt
Web Site: www.livrariaferreira.pt
Founded: 1959
Antiquarian bookseller, Portuguese culture. Also
  publisher.
Membership(s): AILA; APLA; ILAB-LILA.
Type of Business: Major Independent Bookseller

Livraria Editora Figueirinhas Lda
Rua do Freixo 643, 4300-217 Porto
Tel: 225309026; 225301013 *Fax:* 225309027
E-mail: correio@liv-figueirinhas.pt
Type of Business: Distributor

Jayantilal Jamnadas Lda
Estrada Benfica 488-A/B, 1500-105 Lisbon
Tel: 217143847 *Fax:* 217159797
Founded: 1987
Type of Business: Major Independent Bookseller

Livraria Latina, see LeYa na Latina

Livraria Ler Lda
Rua Almeida e Sousa, 24-C, 1350-011 Lisbon
Tel: 213888371
Founded: 1970
Type of Business: Distributor

LeYa na Buchholz
Rua Duque de Palmela, 4, 1250-098 Lisbon
Tel: 213563212
Web Site: www.leya.com
Founded: 1943
General & academic titles in Portuguese, En-
  glish/American, French, German & Spanish
  language.
Type of Business: Exporter, Importer
Owned by: LeYa

LeYa na Latina
Formerly Livraria Latina
Rua de Santa Catarina 2/10, 4000-441 Porto
Tel: 222 001 294; 917 348 622 (cell)
E-mail: leya.latina@leya.com
Web Site: www.leya.com/pt
Founded: 1942

Also book publisher.
Type of Business: Importer, Major Independent
  Bookseller, Wholesaler
Owned by: LeYa

Martins & Coimbra Lda, see Dinapress

Livraria Multilingua Lda
Rua do Pavilhao, Edificio Canico Centrum, Bloco
  2, 7 Andar Cy, 9125-257 Canico, Madeira
Tel: 291 932235 *Fax:* 291 932288
Key Personnel
Owner: John Farrow
Founded: 1981
Specialize in exporting books worldwide & in the
  supply of Portuguese/Brazilian publications.
  Carry in stock all available books on Madeira.
Type of Business: Distributor, Exporter, Importer,
  Major Book Chain Headquarters

Publicacoes Europa America Lda
Rua Francisco Lyon de Castro, 2, Apdo 8, 2725-
  354 Mem Martins
Tel: (021) 926 77 00 *Fax:* (021) 926 77 71
E-mail: secretariado@europa-america.pt;
  livreiros@europa-america.pt
Web Site: www.europa-america.pt
Founded: 1945
Type of Business: Distributor, Major Book Chain
  Headquarters
Branch Office(s)
Rua 31 de Janeiro, 221, 4000-543 Porto *Tel:* 222
  055 658

Livraria Sa da Costa Editora
Rua Garrett, 100-102, 1200-205 Lisbon
Tel: 924 321 716
E-mail: livrariasadacosta@gmail.com
Web Site: www.facebook.com/
  LivrariaSaDaCostaEditora
Founded: 1913
Type of Business: Major Independent Bookseller

A Tavares de Carvalho
Av de Republica 46 3º, 1050-195 Lisbon
Tel: 217970377
Founded: 1959
Medium stock of old rare books in all fields, but
  mainly in Portuguese & Spanish 16th Century
  books.
Type of Business: Major Independent Bookseller

Edicoes Tecnicas e Culturais Lda, see
  Domingos Castro

Puerto Rico

Libreria Instituto de Cultura Puertorriquena
  (Institute of Puerto Rican Culture Bookstore)
Calle Beneficiencia 99, San Juan 00901
Tel: (787) 721-5105
Web Site: www.facebook.com/libreriaicp
Key Personnel
Executive Dir, Institute: Carlos Ruiz Cortes
Stock includes subjects on music, Puerto Rico,
  history, humanities, short stories, poetry & lit-
  erature. Also carry maps & sheet music. Stores
  in Ponce & Utuado.
Type of Business: Major Independent Bookseller

Qatar

Arabian Bookshop
PO Box 55000, Doha

Tel: 4436 7274; 4444 2648 *Fax:* 4444 2648
E-mail: abshop@qatar.net.qa
Type of Business: Major Independent Bookseller

Romania

Librariile Carturesti
Str Arthur Verona 13-15, Sector 1, 010312
Bucharest
Tel: (0728) 828 916; (0732) 003 040
E-mail: info@carturesti.net; librarie.verona@
carturesti.net
Web Site: carturesti.ro
Founded: 2000
Type of Business: Distributor, Major Book Chain
Headquarters, Online Bookseller
Bookshop(s): Str Edgar Quinet nr 9, Sector
1, 010017 Bucharest *Tel:* (0732) 003 004
E-mail: friends@carturesti.net; Str Lipscani,
nr 55, Centrul Istoric, Bucharest *Tel:* (072) 88
28 922 *E-mail:* carusel@carturesti.net; Pierre
de Coubertin nr 3-5, langa Arena Nationala,
Mega Mall, etajul 1, Bucharest *Tel:* (072) 88
28 923 *E-mail:* carturesti.megamall@carturesti.
net; AFI Palace Cotroceni, Blvd Vasile Milea
nr 4, Sector 6, Bucharest *Tel:* (0734) 55
44 26 *E-mail:* carturesti.afi@carturesti.net;
Baneasa Shopping City etaj 1, Ploiesti 42D,
Soseaua, Bucharest *Tel:* (0734) 55 44 45
E-mail: librarie.baneasa@carturesti.net; Prome-
nada Mall, Calea Floreasca nr 246B, Sector 1,
Bucharest *Tel:* (0734) 554 444 *E-mail:* librarie.
floreasca@carturesti.net; Park Lake Shopping Center, etajul 1, Str Liviu Rebreanu,
nr 4, Sector 3, Bucharest *Tel:* (0732) 550
898 *E-mail:* librarieparklake@carturesti.net;
Str Al Vaida-Voievod nr 53-55, Iulius Mall,
parter, 400436 Cluj *Tel:* (0732) 003 008
E-mail: librarie.cluj@carturesti.net

Centrul de Carte Straina Sitka SRL
Blvd Dacia, No 23, 010403 Bucharest
Tel: (021) 210 30 30; (021) 210 40 10; (0722)
375 477 (cell) *Fax:* (021) 210 30 30
E-mail: office@cartestraina.ro
Web Site: www.cartestraina.ro
Key Personnel
Manager: Nicolette Tabara
Founded: 1999
Type of Business: Distributor

Lamserv SRL
Str Turda 119, ap 114, Sector 1, 011322
Bucharest
Tel: (0372) 983928 *Fax:* (021) 2250616
E-mail: office@lamserv.ro
Web Site: www.lamserv.ro
Training & educational materials in English lan-
guage for personal development. Subjects in-
clude computer sciences, economics, engineer-
ing, medicine, sociology, biomedical sciences,
environmental sciences.
Type of Business: Distributor, Importer

Librarium Universitatii
Str Universitatii, Nr 1, 400091 Cluj-Napoca
Tel: (0364) 733 722
E-mail: librarium.universitatii@gmail.com
Web Site: www.facebook.com/
librariumuniversitatii
Founded: 2013
Type of Business: Major Independent Bookseller

Nautilus
Str Arhitect Ion Mincu, nr 17, Sector 1, 011356
Bucharest
Tel: (021) 2225030
Web Site: www.nautilus.ro

Founded: 1997
Type of Business: Distributor, Importer, Major
Independent Bookseller

Prior Books Distributors SRL, see Prior Media
Group SRL

Prior Media Group SRL
Str Raspantiilor 32, Sector 2, 020548 Bucharest
Tel: (021) 210 89 08; (021) 210 89 28; (0722) 51
01 33 (cell) *Fax:* (021) 212 35 61
E-mail: office@prior.ro; secretariat@prior.ro
Web Site: www.prior-books.ro; ebookshop.ro
Key Personnel
Dir General: Ion Arzoiu
Founded: 1994
Type of Business: Distributor, Importer, Online
Bookseller

Romdidac SA
Str Sfanta Vineri nr 32, sector 3, 030205
Bucharest
Tel: (021) 3212575 *Fax:* (021) 3234280
E-mail: office@romdidac.ro
Web Site: www.romdidac.ro
Founded: 1962
Type of Business: Distributor

Stand Agentie Difuzare Carte SRL
Str Petru Rares nr 15, Sector 1, 011101 Bucharest
Tel: (021) 310 78 90; (021) 260 28 56; (021) 223
26 60
Web Site: www.cartea-ta.ro
Key Personnel
Dir: Niculae Iacob
Type of Business: Distributor

Russia

Inform Systema SpA
20/3 Khersonskaya str, 117246 Moscow
Tel: (499) 789-45-55; (495) 331-1534 *Fax:* (499)
789-49-00
E-mail: info@informsystema.ru; books@
informsystema.ru
Web Site: www.informsystema.ru
Founded: 1990
Type of Business: Distributor

Informnauka Ltd
Usievich str 20, 125190 Moscow
Tel: (495) 787 38 73 *Fax:* (499) 152 54 81
E-mail: informnauka@viniti.ru
Web Site: www.informnauka.com
Key Personnel
General Dir: Leonid Alfimov, PhD
E-mail: alfimov@viniti.ru
Deputy General Dir: Nikitina Tatyana Vasilevna
E-mail: nikitina@viniti.ru
Founded: 1998
Type of Business: Distributor

MK-Periodica AG
ul Elektrodnaya, 10, 111524 Moscow
Tel: (495) 672-7012 *Fax:* (495) 306-3757
E-mail: info@periodicals.ru; export@periodicals.
ru
Web Site: www.periodicals.ru
Founded: 1923
Membership(s): Association for Periodicals Dis-
tribution (ARPP, Russia); Association for the
Promotion of the International Circulation of
Press (Distripress); International Association of
Subscription Agents & Intermediaries (ASA);
Russian Library Association.
Type of Business: Distributor, Exporter, Importer

Saudi Arabia

Al Dowaliah Bookshop
PO Box 22348, Riyadh 11495
Tel: (011) 4641851 *Fax:* (011) 4954952
Also publisher.
Type of Business: Distributor, Importer, Major
Independent Bookseller

**Dar Al-Ulum Publishers, Booksellers &
Distributors**
PO Box 1050, Riyadh 11431
Tel: (011) 4777121 *Fax:* (011) 4793446
Also publisher.
Type of Business: Distributor, Wholesaler

Tihama Bookstores
PO Box 4681, Riyadh 11412
Tel: (011) 207 9767 *Fax:* (011) 207 9604
Web Site: www.tihama.com
Type of Business: Distributor, Major Book Chain
Headquarters
Owned by: Tihama Holding Co
Bookshop(s): King Abdul Aziz Rd, Ar Rabi,
Riyadh 13315; Thimar Market, Anas Ibn Malik
Rd, Al Malqa, Riyadh 13524; Thimar Market,
6325 King Abdul Aziz Branch Rd, Al Yasmin,
Riyadh 13322 *Tel:* (011) 493 3141; Thimar
Market Al Takhassusi Branch, Ath Thumamah
Rd, As Sahafah, Riyadh 13315; Thimar Mar-
ket, Abi Mansur Alkhazraji, Al Aqiq, Riyadh
13511 *Tel:* (011) 460 7798; Thimar Market, Al
Waha 2 Dmnahour, Al Wahah, Riyadh 12443
Tel: (011) 493 3141

Senegal

Librairie Clairafrique
Clairafrique Universite, Ave Cheikh Anta, diop x
rte de l'Uniersite prolongee, BP 2005, Dakar
Tel: 33 864 44 29; 33 849 49 99 *Fax:* 33 864 58
54
E-mail: clairaf@orange.sn
Web Site: clairafrique.com
Founded: 1951
Type of Business: Distributor, Major Independent
Bookseller
Owned by: Archdiocese de Dahar
Branch Office(s)
Rue Malefant Pl de l'independance, Rue El Hadji
Mbaye Gueye, BP 2005, Dakar *Tel:* 33 822 21
69 *E-mail:* clairafinde@arc.sn
Rte nationale N° 6, Face ecole Saint Charles,
Kolda *Tel:* 33 996 19 99 *E-mail:* clairafkolda@
orange.sn
Quarter Relais Rte nationale N° 1, Mbour *Tel:* 33
957 19 99 *E-mail:* clairambour@orange.sn
116, Rue de Verdun, BP 3004, Thies *Tel:* 33 951
24 33 *Fax:* 33 952 27 84 *E-mail:* clairaottier@
orange.sn

Serbia

Evro Book doo
Formerly Evro Giunti Bookstores
Dimitrija Tucovica 41, 11000 Belgrade
Tel: (011) 34 46 618; (011) 34 46 619; (011) 34
46 620 *Fax:* (011) 24 45 926
E-mail: info@evrobook.rs; redakcija@evrobook.
com; marketing@evrobook.com

Web Site: evrobook.rs
Key Personnel
Sales Manager: Ivan Jovanovic *Tel:* (063) 104
9097 (cell) *E-mail:* ivan@evrobook.com; Ne-
manja Kotnik *Tel:* (069) 145 6408 (cell)
E-mail: nemanja@evrobook.com; Marko Maric
Tel: (063) 456 066 (cell) *E-mail:* marko@
evrobook.com
Sales Manager, Schools & Libraries, Foreign
Rights: Stefan Mijajlovic *Tel:* (069) 120 3936
(cell) *E-mail:* stefan@evrobook.com
Sales Manager, Schools & Libraries, South
Serbia: Sanja Ilic *Tel:* (063) 643 960 (cell)
E-mail: sanja.ilic@evrobook.com
Editor, Children's Editions: Sanja Durkovic
Editor, Foreign Editions: Gordana Subotic
Founded: 1989
Type of Business: Major Independent Bookseller
Bookshop(s): Dimitrija Davidovica 1, Smederevo
Tel: (026) 612 093

Evro Giunti Bookstores, see Evro Book doo

Forum Konyvkiado
Vojvode Misica 1, 21000 Novi Sad
Tel: (021) 457 216 *Fax:* (021) 456 742
E-mail: direktor@forumliber.rs
Web Site: www.forumliber.rs
Key Personnel
Dir & Editor-in-Chief: Gabor Virag
Founded: 1957
Also publisher.
Type of Business: Distributor, Exporter

Izdavacko Preduzece Vuk Karadzic
Brankova 28, 11000 Belgrade
Tel: (011) 334 2329
Also publisher.
Type of Business: Exporter, Importer

Nolit AD
Terazije 27/II, 11000 Belgrade
Tel: (011) 3245-017
Key Personnel
Dir: Slavica Sas
Type of Business: Distributor, Exporter, Importer,
Major Independent Bookseller, Wholesaler

Singapore

Alkem Co (S) Pte Ltd
One, Sunview Rd 01-27, Singapore 627615
Tel: 6265 6666 *Fax:* 6261 7875
E-mail: enquiry@alkem.com.sg
Web Site: www.alkem.com.sg
Founded: 1999
Distributor & publisher for books, training mate-
rials, digital learning, educational aids, multi-
media, research software & training kits.
Type of Business: Distributor

Alkem Distribution Center, see Alkem Co (S)
Pte Ltd

InfoHOST Pte Ltd
31 Kaki Bukit Rd 3, No 06-07 Techlink, Singa-
pore 417818
Tel: 6741 8422 *Fax:* 6741 8821
E-mail: info.sg@igroupnet.com
Web Site: www.infohost.com.sg
Key Personnel
Manager: Susan Pey *E-mail:* susanpey@
igroupnet.com
Founded: 1983
Type of Business: Distributor, Remainder Dealer
Owned by: iGroup (Asia Pacific) Ltd

MarketAsia Books Pte Ltd
Formerly MarketAsia Distributors (S) Pte Ltd
Pan-I Complex, 601 Sims Dr, No 04-05, Singa-
pore 387382
Tel: 6744 8483; 6744 8486
E-mail: service@marketasia.com.sg
Web Site: marketasiabooks.com
Key Personnel
Owner: Johnson Lee
Founded: 1987
Specialize in the publishing & distribution of
books & magazines.
Membership(s): Singapore Book Publishers Asso-
ciation.
Type of Business: Distributor

MarketAsia Distributors (S) Pte Ltd, see
MarketAsia Books Pte Ltd

Page One Publishing
20 Kaki Bukit View, Kaki Bukit Techpark II, Sin-
gapore 415956
Tel: 6742 2088 *Fax:* 6744 2088
Web Site: www.pageonegroup.com
Key Personnel
Publisher & Chief Executive Officer: Mark Tan
E-mail: mark_tan@pageonegroup.com
Founded: 1993
Type of Business: Distributor, Major Book Chain
Headquarters
Branch Office(s)
Room 303, Tower B, No 3 Bldg, North Area,
Pingguo Community, No 32, Baiziwan Rd,
Chaoyang District, Beijing 100022, China
Tel: (010) 5971 3119 *Fax:* (010) 5971 2606
E-mail: carling_chen@pageonegroup.com
Room B, 9/F, Roxy Industrial Centre, Tai Lin Pai
Rd, Kwai Chung, Hong Kong
Bookshop(s): Shop 3B201, Zone 3, China
World Mall, No 1 JianGuoMenWai Ave,
Chaoyang District, Beijing 100020, China
Tel: (010) 8535 1055 *Fax:* (010) 8535 1022
E-mail: page1_cwtc@pageonegroup.com; Shop
LG50, Indigo Mall, No 18 Jiuxianqiao Rd,
Chaoyang District, Beijing 100016, China
Tel: (010) 8426 0408 *Fax:* (010) 8426 0406
E-mail: page1_indigo@pageonegroup.com;
Units S2-14a-b, 1-2F, Taikoo Li Sanlitun, No
19 Sanlitun Rd, Chaoyang District, Beijing
100027, China *Tel:* (010) 6417 6626 *Fax:* (010)
6417 0322 *E-mail:* page1_slt@pageonegroup.
com; Units S2-14a-b, 2F, Taikoo Li Sanli-
tun, No 19 Sanlitun Rd, Chaoyang District,
Beijing 100027, China *Tel:* (010) 6417 9582
Fax: (010) 6417 5682 *E-mail:* woodhouse_slt@
pageonegroup.com; Cheng Du Interna-
tional Finance Centre IFS, Shop L510 &
L511B, IFS, No 1, Section 3, Hongxing Rd,
Jinjiang District, Chengdu 610021, China
Tel: (028) 8658 6510 *Fax:* (028) 8658 6810
E-mail: page1_cdifs@pageonegroup.com; Shop
488, 4F, MixC Mall, No 701, Fuchun Rd,
Jiangan District, Hangzhou 310020, China
Tel: (0571) 8970 5758 *Fax:* (0571) 8970 5768
E-mail: page1_hz@pageonegroup.com

PG Books Pte Ltd
402 Orchard Rd, No 05-20/21, Delfi Orchard,
Singapore 238876
Tel: 6235 2682 *Fax:* 6733 4854
E-mail: sales@pgbooks.com
Founded: 1982
Medical books.
Type of Business: Distributor
Bookshop(s): PG Lucky Plaza Medical Books

PMS Publishers Services Pte Ltd
Formerly Publishers Marketing Services Pte Ltd
10-C Jl Ampas, No 06-01, Ho Seng Lee Flatted
Warehouse, Singapore 329513
Tel: 6256 5166 *Fax:* 6253 0008
E-mail: info@pms.com.sg

Web Site: www.pms.com.sg
Key Personnel
Mng Dir: Brian Lim
Deputy Mng Dir: Raymond Lim
Founded: 1996
Type of Business: Distributor, Exporter, Importer,
Wholesaler
Branch Office(s)
509 Block E, Phileo Damansar 1, Jl 16/11, 46350
Petaling Jaya, Selangor, Malaysia, County
Manager: Karen Lim *Tel:* (03) 7955 3588
Fax: (03) 7955 3017 *E-mail:* pmsmal@pms.
com.sg

Publishers Marketing Services Pte Ltd, see
PMS Publishers Services Pte Ltd

Select Books Pte Ltd
65A, Jl Tenteram, No 02-06, St Michael's Industrial Estate, Singapore 328958
Tel: 6251 3798 *Fax:* 6251 3380
E-mail: info@selectbooks.com.sg; orders@
selectbooks.com.sg; marketing@selectbooks.
com.sg
Web Site: www.selectbooks.com.sg
Founded: 1976
Book publisher, distributor, library supplier, retail & online bookseller. Specialize in books &
journals relating to the Asia region.
Type of Business: Distributor, Exporter, Importer,
Major Independent Bookseller, Online Bookseller

Star Publishing Pte Ltd
Block 115A, Commonwealth Dr, No 05-12, Tan-
glin Halt Industrial Park, Singapore 149596
Tel: 6479 6800 *Fax:* 6474 1080
E-mail: contactus@starpub.com.sg
Web Site: www.starpub.com.sg
Founded: 2002
Publish, market & distribute educational books &
materials in Singapore, China & Asia.
Type of Business: Distributor

STM Publishers Services Pte Ltd
52 Choa Chu Kang N 6, No 12-19 Yew Mei
Green, Singapore 689575
Tel: 6468 0818 *Fax:* 6310 8258
Key Personnel
Owner & Dir: Tony Poh
Founded: 1993
Subjects: STM, laws, social science, arts, educa-
tion, agriculture & humanities.
Publishers representatives, agent for Southeast &
Northeast Asia.
Type of Business: Distributor

Tecman Holdings Pte Ltd
No 04-47/49 Bras Basah Complex, Block 231,
Bain St, Singapore 180231
Tel: 6338 6764
E-mail: tecman@tecman.com.sg
Web Site: www.tecman.com.sg
Founded: 1971
Subjects include Biblical studies, religion-
Protestant & theology.
Type of Business: Exporter, Importer, Major Inde-
pendent Bookseller, Wholesaler

Times The Bookshop Pte Ltd
438 Ang Mo Kio Industrial Park 1, No 02-01,
Ang Mo Kio Ave 10, Singapore 569619
Tel: 6459 1355 *Fax:* 6456 4832
E-mail: timesbookstores@tpl.com.sg
Web Site: www.timesbookstores.com.sg
Founded: 1978
Type of Business: Major Book Chain Headquar-
ters
Owned by: Times Publishing Group, Times
Centre, No 1, New Industrial Rd, Singapore
536196

Branch Office(s)
Centrepoint, 176 Orchard Rd, No 04-08/09/10/11, Singapore 238843 *Tel:* 6734 9022 *Fax:* 6734 9313
293 Holland Rd, No 02-16/17 Cold Storage Jelita, Singapore 278628 *Tel:* 6466 5702 *Fax:* 6465 7625
6 Raffles Blvd, No 03-149/150/151 Marina Sq, Singapore 039594 *Tel:* 6250 7528 *Fax:* 6250 7521
Plaza Singapura, 68 Orchard Rd, No 04-05, Singapore 238839 *Tel:* 6336 8861 *Fax:* 6336 1884
10 Tampines Central 1, No 03-06, Singapore 529536 *Tel:* 6782 7017 *Fax:* 6784 9950
290 Orchard Rd, Paragon No 04-41, Singapore 238859 *Tel:* 6836 6182 *Fax:* 6836 0927
83 Punggol Central, No 02-19, Singapore 828761 *Tel:* 6385 9428

Slovakia

Vydavatel'stvo Slovart spol sro
Bojnicka 10, 830 00 Bratislava 3
Mailing Address: PO Box 70, 830 00 Bratislava 3
Tel: (02) 49 20 18 00 *Fax:* (02) 49 20 18 99
E-mail: objednavky@slovart.sk
Web Site: www.slovart.sk; www.slovart.cz
Key Personnel
Dir: Juraj Heger
Assistant Dir: Kristina Nemcova
   E-mail: nemcova@slovart.sk
Export Manager: Sona Wells *Tel:* (02) 49 20 18 16 *E-mail:* wells@slovart.sk
Foreign Rights: Elena Hudakova *Tel:* (02) 49 20 18 01 *E-mail:* hudakova@slovart.sk
Marketing & Promotion: Sasa Petrasova *Tel:* (02) 49 20 18 33 *E-mail:* petrasova@slovart.sk
Founded: 1991
Type of Business: Exporter, Importer

Slovenia

Cankarjeva Zalozba-Zaloznistvo doo
Slovenska 29, SI-1000 Ljubljana
Tel: (01) 241 32 20 *Fax:* (01) 425 28 14
E-mail: info@mladinska.com
Web Site: www.mladinska.com/skupina_mk/ cankarjeva_zalozba
Key Personnel
Dir: Bojan Svigelj
Editor-in-Chief: Tatjana Cestnik
Also publisher & antiquarian bookseller.
Type of Business: Exporter, Importer
Parent Company: Mladinska knjiga Zalozba d d

South Africa

Aloe Book Agency (Pty) Ltd
28 Amalgam Pl, Amalgam, Johannesburg, Mayfair 2092
Tel: (011) 837 9142
Founded: 1968
Library suppliers & booksellers.
Type of Business: Distributor

Exclusive Books
Commerce Corner, 31 Commerce Crescent, Kramerville, Johannesburg 2090
Mailing Address: PO Box 605, Rivonia 2128

Tel: (011) 798 0111 *Toll Free Tel:* 0800 332 550 (South Africa only)
E-mail: info@exclusivebooks.co.za
Web Site: www.exclusivebooks.co.za
Key Personnel
Acting Chief Executive Officer: Frank Boner
Type of Business: Major Book Chain Headquarters
Bookshop(s): Shop DFE 02, Northern Pier, International Departures, Duty Free, O R Tambo International Airport, Johannesburg *Tel:* (011) 390 2690 *E-mail:* airportjhb@ exclusivebooks.co.za; Shop D007, Domestic Departures Terminal, O R Tambo International Airport, Johannesburg *Tel:* (011) 390 1258 *E-mail:* jhbdomestic@exclusivebooks. co.za; Shop U1A, Bedford Centre, Smith Rd, Johannesburg *Tel:* (011) 616 1183 *E-mail:* bedfordcentre@exclusivebooks.co. za; Shop 23, Dainfern Sq, Corner Broadacres Ave & William Nicol Dr, Johannesburg *Tel:* (011) 469 0514 *E-mail:* dainfern@ exclusivebooks.co.za; Shop U37, Morningside Shopping Centre, Corner Outspan Rd & Waggon Rd, Johannesburg *Tel:* (011) 798 0210 *E-mail:* morningside@exclusivebooks. co.za; Shop L113, Greenstone Shopping Centre, Corner Van Riebeeck Rd & Modderfontein Rd, Johannesburg *Tel:* (011) 553 5560 *E-mail:* greenstone@exclusivebooks.co.za; Shop U30, Hyde Park Corner, Corner Jan Smuts Ave & William Nicol Dr, Johannesburg *Tel:* (011) 325 4298 *E-mail:* hydepark@ exclusivebooks.co.za; Shop NS8, Killarney Mall, 60 Riviera Rd, Johannesburg *Tel:* (011) 646 0931 *E-mail:* killarney@ exclusivebooks.co.za; Shop U38, Nicolway Bryanston, Corner Wedgewood Link & William Nichol Dr, Johannesburg *Tel:* (011) 798 0270 *E-mail:* nicolway@exclusivebooks. co.za; Shop C331 & C332, The Mall of Rosebank, Johannesburg *Tel:* (011) 447 3028 *E-mail:* rosebankmall@exclusivebooks.co.za; Shop L10, Sandton City, Rivonia Rd, Johannesburg *Tel:* (011) 883 1010 *E-mail:* sandtoncity@ exclusivebooks.co.za; Shop F110, Mall of the South, Corner Swartkoppies Rd & Kliprivier Dr, Johannesburg *Tel:* (011) 682 3215 *E-mail:* mallofthesouth@exclusivebooks. co.za; Shop 1231, Brooklyn Mall, 338 Bronkhorst St, Pretoria *Tel:* (012) 346 5864 *E-mail:* brooklyn@exclusivebooks.co.za; Shop 118 (temp), Centurion Mall, Heuwel Ave, Pretoria *Tel:* (012) 663 3207 *E-mail:* centurion@ exclusivebooks.co.za; Shop 75C, Kolonnade Shopping Centre, Sefako Makgatho Dr, Pretoria *Tel:* (012) 548 6590 *E-mail:* kolonnade@ exclusivebooks.co.za; Shop LF51, Menlyn Park Shopping Centre, Pretoria *Tel:* (012) 361 6188 *E-mail:* menlyn@exclusivebooks.co.za; Shop 25a, Woodlands Blvd, Corner Garsfontein Rd & de Villebois Rd, Pretoria *Tel:* (012) 997 3323 *E-mail:* woodlands@exclusivebooks. co.za; Shop U28/U29, Cresta Centre, Corner DF Malan Dr & Weltevreden Rd, Randburg *Tel:* (011) 476 9390 *E-mail:* cresta@ exclusivebooks.co.za; Shop LM 138, Clearwater Mall, Corner Chistian de Wet Rd & Hendrik Potgieter Rd, Roodeport *Tel:* (011) 675 3971 *E-mail:* clearwater@exclusivebooks.co.za

Faradawn CC
PO Box 1903, Saxonwold 2132
Tel: (011) 885 1847; (011) 885 1787 *Fax:* (011) 885 1829
E-mail: faradawn@icon.co.za
Web Site: www.faradawn.co.za
Key Personnel
Contact: Belinda Stein; Lesley Thomas
Founded: 1983
Publishers representatives; book & map distributors.
Type of Business: Distributor, Importer, Wholesaler

Fogarty's Bookshop
Shop 20, Walmer Park Shopping Centre Main Rd, Walmer, Port Elizabeth 6070
Tel: (041) 368 1425
E-mail: fogartys@global.co.za
Web Site: www.fogartysbookshop.co.za
Key Personnel
Manager: Teresa Fogarty
Founded: 1946
Type of Business: Major Independent Bookseller

Logans Medical Bookshop
660 Umbilo Rd, Durban 4001
Tel: (031) 205-7279
E-mail: logansmedical@iafrica.com
Web Site: logansmedicalbookshop.yellowpages.co. za
University, medical & technical text & reference books.
Type of Business: Distributor

Logans University Bookshop (Pty) Ltd, see Logans Medical Bookshop

Maskew Miller Longman
Subsidiary of Pearson Southern Africa
Corner of Logan Way & Forest Dr, Pinelands 7405
Mailing Address: PO Box 396, Cape Town 8000
Tel: (021) 532 6000 *Fax:* (021) 531 0716; (021) 531 4049 (orders)
E-mail: customerservices@mml.co.za; orders@ mml.co.za
Web Site: www.mml.co.za
Key Personnel
Chief Executive Officer: Fathima Dada
Marketing Dir: Ginny Felps
Founded: 1893
Also publisher.
Type of Business: Importer, Wholesaler
Branch Office(s)
Off 127, Bloem Plaza, 1st floor, Corner of Maitland & East Burger Sts, Bloemfontein 9301, Contact: Donald Bojang *Tel:* (051) 448 0424 *Fax:* (051) 430 4130 *E-mail:* Donald.Bojang@ mml.co.za (Free State off)
Brackengate Business Park, 12 London Circle, Brackenfell 7560, Contact: Gaynor Higgs *Tel:* (021) 980 9500 *Fax:* (021) 555 4071 *E-mail:* Gaynor.Higgs@pearson.com (Western Cape & Northern Cape off)
Central Park, Block H, 400 16 Rd, Midrand 1685 *Tel:* (011) 347 0700 *Fax:* (011) 315 2343 (Gauteng publishing off)
Laeveldtrust, 20 Russel St, Nelspruit 1200, Contact: Gertrude Ncongwane *Tel:* (013) 752 5936 *Fax:* (013) 752 5980 *E-mail:* Gertrude. Ncongwane@pearson.com (Mpumalanga off)
Unit F102, Park Row Bldg, 4/10 School Rd, Pinetown 3620, Contact: Mbali Mkhize *Tel:* (031) 701 8813 *Fax:* (031) 702 9627 *E-mail:* Mbali.Mkhize@pearson.com (KwaZulu-Natal off)
25 Bodenstein St, Polokwane 0699, Contact: Ngaka Kekana *Tel:* (015) 295 9194 *Fax:* (015) 295 6012 *E-mail:* Ngaka.Kekana@pearson.com (Limpopo off)
61 B Boom St, Rustenburg 0299, Contact: Xoliswa Sebitlo *Tel:* (071) 602 0263 *Fax:* (018) 381 6029 *E-mail:* Xoliswa.Sebitlo@pearson. com (Northwest off)
Grayston Office Park, Bldg 5, 128 Peter Rd, Athol Ext, Sandton 2146, Contact: Rekina Makanyane *Tel:* (011) 322 8600 *Fax:* (011) 322 8611 *E-mail:* Rekina.Makanyane@pearson.com (Gauteng sales off)
4 Kings St, Southernwood 5200, Sales Assistant: Vuyokazi Nkamisa *Tel:* (043) 722 7989 *Fax:* (043) 742 5113 *E-mail:* Vuyokazi. Nkamisa@mml.co.za (King William's Town off)

Media House Publications (Pty) Ltd
161 Ninth Rd, Johannesburg 2090
Tel: (011) 882-6237 *Fax:* (011) 882-9652
Founded: 1983
Type of Business: Distributor, Exporter, Importer,
Wholesaler

Protea Boekwinkel
1067 Burnett St, Hatfield, Pretoria 0083
Tel: (012) 362 3444; (012) 362 5663 (university);
(012) 362 5683 (schools); (012) 362 6073 (the-
ology) *Fax:* (012) 362 5688
E-mail: orders@proteabooks.com; sales_online@
proteaboekwinkel.com
Web Site: www.proteaboekwinkel.com; www.
proteaboekhuis.com
Founded: 1992
Supplier of university textbooks, school books,
general books & theology books.
Type of Business: Major Book Chain Headquar-
ters, Online Bookseller
Bookshop(s): Apollo Centre, Shop 6, 210 Du
Toit St, Pretoria CBD *Tel:* (012) 320 0793
Fax: (012) 320 3472; PTA West High School
Campus, Staatsartillerie Rd, Pretoria West 0183
Tel: (012) 327 4555; University of Johannes-
burg, Shop 21, Entrance 6, 1st floor, Student
Centre, Akademie Rd, Auckland Park 2092
Tel: (011) 482 3566; (011) 482 3561; Brandwag Centre, Brandwag, Bloemfontein 9300
Tel: (051) 444 1633; (051) 444 1212 (academic); Central University of Technology,
60 Park Rd, Shop G14B, Willows, Bloemfontein 9301 *Tel:* (051) 430 2115; Rodebosch
on Main, Shop 29, 51-81 Main Rd, Cape Town
7700 *Tel:* (021) 685 9296; (021) 685 9380
(school/academic); Carlton Centre, Lower
Level, Commissioner St, Johannesburg 2001
Tel: (011) 331 5144; (011) 331 5145; (011)
331 5146; Parow Business Park, Unit 1, 2 &
3, Jean Simonis St, Parow 7500 *Tel:* (021)
911 2411; (021) 911 9549; Steve Biko St 86,
Bult, Potchefstroom 2522 *Tel:* (018) 297 1584;
Bara Mall, Shop 25, Soweto 1804 *Tel:* (011)
933 1330; Bergzicht Plaza, Andringa St, Stellenbosch 7600 *Tel:* (021) 882 9100; (021)
882 9101 (school/academic); (021) 882 9105
(school/academic); UCT Upper Campus, Steve
Biko Bldg, Chemistry Lane, University of Cape
Town 7700 *Tel:* (021) 650 2485; (021) 650
2486 (school/academic); Old Santam Bldg, 71
Church St, Worcester 6850 *Tel:* (023) 342 1141

Van Schaik Bookstore
One Old Oak Rd, 2nd floor, Delphi Arena Bldg,
Tyger Valley, Bellville 7535
Tel: (021) 918-8400; (021) 366-5400 (online or-
ders) *Fax:* (021) 914-5308; (021) 914-5309;
(012) 366-5444 (online orders)
E-mail: vsb@vanschaik.com; vsorders@
vanschaik.com
Web Site: www.vanschaik.com
Key Personnel
Mng Dir: Stephan Erasmus
Founded: 1914
Academic resource supplier.
Type of Business: Major Book Chain Headquar-
ters
Branch Office(s)
Cape Peninsula University of Technology, Student
Centre, Symphony Way (off Modderdam Rd),
Bellville 7535 *Tel:* (021) 951-4049 *Fax:* (021)
951-4149 *E-mail:* cputbell@vanschaik.com
University of Fort Hare, Henderson Hall, King
Alice Rd, Alice, East London *Tel:* (040) 653-
1366 *Fax:* (040) 552-6898 *E-mail:* vsalice@
vanschaik.com
University of Johannesburg New Student Cen-
tre, Bunting Rd, Shop 11, Auckland Park
2092 *Tel:* (011) 726-6753 *Fax:* (011) 482-4391
E-mail: vsbunting@vanschaik.com

9 Concord Rd E, Bedfordview, Gauteng 2008
Tel: (087) 288-0225 *E-mail:* bedfordview@
vanschaik.com
9 Park Rd, Willows, PO Box 20204, Bloem-
fontein 9320 *Tel:* (051) 447-6685 *Fax:* (051)
447-7837 *E-mail:* vsbloem@vanschaik.com
University of the Free State, Shop 19, Student
Centre, Bloemfontein 9300 *Tel:* (051) 444-
3048 *Fax:* (051) 444-3057 *E-mail:* qwaqwa@
vanschaik.com
Shop 10, K90 Centre, Corner Rondebult &
North Rand Rds, Boksburg, East Rand 1462
Tel: (011) 826-2045 *Fax:* (011) 826-3663
E-mail: vsboks@vanschaik.com
Cape Peninsula University of Technology, Kaiser-
gracht Rd, PO Box 2864, Cape Town 8000
Tel: (021) 465-1697 *Fax:* (021) 465-5121
E-mail: kaaptech@vanschaik.com
Shop 1, 22 Long St, Corner of Strand & Long St,
PO Box 1346, Cape Town 8000 *Tel:* (021) 418-
0202 *Fax:* (021) 418-0212 *E-mail:* capetown@
vanschaik.com
Training Room No 3, Library Bldg, Corner
Brazil Rd & R51 (Putfontein Rd), Davey-
ton *Tel:* (087) 2850-594 *Fax:* (087) 2852-186
E-mail: daveyton@vanschaik.com
70 Steve Biko Rd, Shop 1, Durban 4001
Tel: (031) 201-5652 *Fax:* (031) 201-5656
E-mail: vsdut@vanschaik.com
Shop 3, Momentum House, Corner of Stal-
wart Simelane & Bram Fischer Sts, Durban
4001 *Tel:* (031) 332-2009; (031) 332-2049
Fax: (031) 332-2029 *E-mail:* vsdurban@
vanschaik.com
Shop 4, Burleigh Court, 668 Umbilo Rd, Durban
4000 *Tel:* (031) 101-3096 *Fax:* (031) 205-0369
E-mail: durbanmed@vanschaik.com
Kaapzicht Bldg, 9 Rogers St, Tyger Val-
ley, Durbanville 7530 *Tel:* (087) 288-0224
E-mail: durbanville@vanschaik.com
Shop 31B, Caxton House, 35 Terminus St, East
London 5201 *Tel:* (043) 722-5926; (043) 722-
5934 *Fax:* (043) 722-6117 *E-mail:* vsel@
vanschaik.com
Tshwane University of Technology, Pilane St, Ga-
Rankuwa *Tel:* (012) 700-0078; (012) 700-0079
E-mail: garankuwa@vanschaik.com
NMU George Campus, Student Recreation
Centre, Shop 1, Marula House, George
Tel: (044) 801-5088 *Fax:* (086) 631-4779
E-mail: vsgeorgecampus@vanschaik.com
129 High St, Grahamstown 6139 *Tel:* (046)
622-3549 *Fax:* (046) 636-1382
E-mail: grahamstown@vanschaik.com
Walter Sisulu University, Butterworth Campus
N2, Ibiki *Tel:* (087) 285-6585 *E-mail:* ibika@
vanschaik.com
Braamfontein Centre, c/o Jorissen St & Bertha
St, Braamfontein, Johannesburg 2000
Tel: (011) 339-1711 *Fax:* (011) 339-7267
E-mail: vsbraam@vanschaik.com
Medical School, Wits University, 7 York Rd,
Parktown, Braamfontein, Johannesburg
Tel: (011) 717-2012 *Fax:* (011) 643-4318
E-mail: vsmedicas@vanschaik.com
University of Johannesburg, Student Centre, Jo-
hannesburg *Tel:* (011) 726-1698; (011) 726-
2145 *Fax:* (011) 482-1407 *E-mail:* vsrau@
vanschaik.com
Matrix Bldg, 1st floor, Wits University, East
Campus, Braamfontein, Johannesburg
Tel: (011) 339-2775 *Fax:* (011) 339-7180
E-mail: vsmatrix@vanschaik.com
Old William Pescod Room B2, 31 Scanlan St,
New Park, Kimberley *Tel:* (053) 832-7066
Fax: (053) 832-7599 *E-mail:* kimberley@
vanschaik.com
University of Zululand, KwaDlengezwa Cam-
pus, Library Bldg Basement, KwaDlengezwa
Reserve, KwaZulu-Natal *Tel:* (035) 902-
6103 *Fax:* (035) 793-4036 *E-mail:* vsunizul@
vanschaik.com
Turfloop Plaza, Shop 4B, 697 Zone A, University
St, Mankweng *Tel:* (015) 267-8279; (015) 267-

8294 *Fax:* (015) 267-8306 *E-mail:* turfloop@
vanschaik.com
University of Mpumalanga, Bldg 6, Corner R40
& D275 Rds, Mbombela 1200 *Tel:* (071) 582-
8579 *E-mail:* mbombela@vanschaik.com
Midrand Graduate Institute, 44 Alsation Rd,
Ext 3, Glen Austein, Midrand *Tel:* (087) 285-
6795 *Fax:* (087) 285-6796 *E-mail:* midrand@
vanschaik.com
Nelson Mandela University, Uitenhage Rd, Mis-
sionvale *Tel:* (041) 504-1103 *Fax:* (041) 583-
2418 *E-mail:* vsmissionvale@vanschaik.com
North West University, Student Centre Bldg,
1090 Dr Albert Lithuli Dr, Mmabatho 2735
Tel: (018) 389-2567 *Fax:* (018) 389-2321
E-mail: vsmaf@vanschaik.com
Mthatha Plaza, Shop 60, 35 Nelson Mandela Dr,
Mthatha *Tel:* (047) 531-4902 *Fax:* (047) 531-
4903 *E-mail:* mthatha@vanschaik.com
Walter Sisulu University, Zamukulungisa Cam-
pus, Room C118, Southridge Park, Mthatha
Tel: (047) 537-0010 *Fax:* (047) 537-0015
E-mail: vszamu@vanschaik.com
Walter Sisulu University, Nelson Man-
dela Dr, Mthatha *Tel:* (047) 495-0005
E-mail: mthathanmd@vanschaik.com
Shop 52, The Promenade Shopping Centre, Cor-
ner of Louis Trichardt & Henshall Sts, Nel-
spruit *Tel:* (013) 752-7623; (013) 752-7860
Fax: (013) 752-7659 *E-mail:* vsnel@vanschaik.
com
Tshwane University of Technology, General
Dan Pienaar Ave, Stand 313, Beryl, Nelspruit
1201 *Tel:* (013) 752-7623; (013) 752-7860
Fax: (013) 752-7659 *E-mail:* vsnel@vanschaik.
com
Republic Bldg, Shop 2, 78 Scott St, Newcastle *Tel:* (034) 312-6359 *Fax:* (034) 312-7298
E-mail: newcastle@vanschaik.com
Faculty of Education, Hifikepunye Pohamba Campus, Main Rd, Ongwediva *E-mail:* oshakati@
vanschaik.com
Parow Centre, Shop 120, Voortrekker Rd, Parow
7500 *Tel:* (021) 930-2480 *Fax:* (021) 939-3767
E-mail: vsparow@vanschaik.com
49B Schoeman St, Opposite Standard Bank Sq,
Polokwane 0699 *Tel:* (015) 295-9040; (015)
295-9090 *Fax:* (015) 295-9099 *E-mail:* vspol@
vanschaik.com
NMU Second Ave Campus, Summerstrand, Port
Elizabeth 6001 *Tel:* (041) 583-3171 *Fax:* (041)
583-2418 *E-mail:* vspe@vanschaik.com
Sanlam Student Village, University Way, Sum-
merstrand, Port Elizabeth *Tel:* (041) 583-3171
Fax: (041) 583-2418 *E-mail:* vspe@vanschaik.
com
Cachetpark Centre, Steve Biko Ave, Potchef-
stroom *Tel:* (018) 294-8875 *Fax:* (018) 294-
4445 *E-mail:* vspotch@vanschaik.com
Walter Sisulu University, Cafeteria Bldg,
Room D17, Potsdam *Tel:* (043) 764-8900;
(043) 764-8910 *Fax:* (043) 764-8912
E-mail: vspotsdam@vanschaik.com
Protea Hotel Bldg, Burnett St, Hatfield, Preto-
ria 0083 *Tel:* (012) 362-5701; (012) 362-5669
Fax: (012) 362-5673 *E-mail:* vshat@vanschaik.
com
Shop 1, 235 Church St, Pretoria 0001
Tel: (012) 321-2442 *Fax:* (012) 325-7832
E-mail: vskerk@vanschaik.com
22 Umgazi St, Ashlea Gardens, 0081 Preto-
ria *Tel:* (087) 288-0226 *E-mail:* menlyn@
vanschaik.com
Sefako Makgatho Health Sciences University,
Natural Science Bldg, Ground floor, Medunsa
Campus, Pretoria 0204 *Tel:* (012) 521-3882
Fax: (012) 521-4327 *E-mail:* vsmedunsa@
vanschaik.com
Tshwane University of Technology, FCM Total
Garage (Tech Pretoria), 422 Rebecca St, Preto-
ria West 0183 *Tel:* (012) 327-1945 *Fax:* (012)
327-1998 *E-mail:* vstut@vanschaik.com
Tshwane University of Technology, Bldg 4,
Room 4-G51, Staatsartillerie Rd, Pretoria

West *Tel:* (012) 327-0213; (012) 327-0215
E-mail: pretoriawest@vanschaik.com
Mandela Hall, Room 0005, UFS Qwa-Qwa Campus, Main Rd Kestell & Phuthaditjaba, Qwa-Qwa 9866 *Tel:* (058) 713-2087 *Fax:* (051) 444-3057 *E-mail:* qwaqwa@vanschaik.com
26 Main Rd, Rondebosch 7300 *Tel:* (021) 689-4112 *Fax:* (021) 686-3404 *E-mail:* vsrbosch@vanschaik.com
Monash University, 144 Peter Rd, Ruimsig, Roodepoort 1724 *Tel:* (011) 958-1349 *Fax:* (011) 958-1584 *E-mail:* vsmonash@vanschaik.com
137 Beyers Naude St, Rustenburg *Tel:* (014) 592-9915 *Fax:* (086) 551-9600 *E-mail:* rustenburg@vanschaik.com
University of KwaZulu-Natal, Sidewalk Centre, Alan Paton Ave, Scottsville 3209 *Tel:* (033) 386-9308; (033) 386-9309 *Fax:* (033) 386-9633 *E-mail:* pietermaritzburg@vanschaik.com
University of Mpumalanga, Bheki Msundi St, Siyabuswa 0472 *Tel:* (079) 714-3799 *E-mail:* siyabuswa@vanschaik.com
Shop 242 Mapoya Mall, Old Potchefstroom Rd, Klipspruit Ext 5, Soweto *Tel:* (011) 938-3460; (011) 938-3462 *Fax:* (011) 938-3486 *E-mail:* soweto@vanschaik.com
University of Johannesburg, Shop 2, Old Potch Rd, Klipspruit Ext 5, Soweto *Tel:* (011) 933-1123 *E-mail:* ujsoweto@vanschaik.com
University of Stellenbosch, Langenhoven Centre, Neelsie, Stellenbosch 7600 *Tel:* (021) 887-2830 *Fax:* (021) 886-6184 *E-mail:* vssbosch@vanschaik.com
University of Venda, Block B, Human & Social Sciences Bldg, University Rd, Thohoyandou 0950 *Tel:* (015) 962-1255; (015) 962-4654 *Fax:* (015) 962-6231 *E-mail:* univen@vanschaik.com
Venda Plaza, Shop A14, Corner Main & Casino Blvd, Thohoyandou *Tel:* (087) 285-2167; (087) 285-2169 *E-mail:* vendaplaza@vanschaik.com
University of Stellenbosch Tygerberg Medical Campus, Tygerberg Student Centre, Ground floor, Fransie van Zyl Dr, Tygerberg *Tel:* (021) 932-0203 *Fax:* (021) 932-0241 *E-mail:* tygerberg@vanschaik.com
Kwamnyandu Shopping Centre, Shop 312, 341 Griffiths Mxenge Highway, Umlazi *Tel:* (031) 906-0025; (031) 906-0027 *Fax:* (031) 906-0024 *E-mail:* vsumlazi@vanschaik.com
North West University Grounds, Bldg 4, Hendrik van Eck Blvd, Vanderbijlpark 1900 *Tel:* (016) 985-1144; (016) 985-3288 *Fax:* (016) 985-1126 *E-mail:* vsnwu@vanschaik.com
Vaal University of Technology (VUT), Andries Potgieter Blvd, Vanderbijlpark 1900 *Tel:* (016) 985-2340 *Fax:* (016) 985-1210 *E-mail:* vsvaal@vanschaik.com
Central University of Technology, 2204 Mothusi Ave, Room T2, Welkom *Tel:* (057) 355-6103 *Fax:* (057) 355-6104 *E-mail:* welkom@vanschaik.com
Walter Sisulu University, Room CB, 280 Shepstone Rd, Whittlesea *Tel:* (040) 842-1346 *Fax:* (040) 842-4924 *E-mail:* whittlesea@vanschaik.com
University of Namibia, 340 Mandume Ndemufayo Ave, Pionierspark, Windhoek, Namibia *Tel:* (061) 206-3364 *E-mail:* vsunam@vanschaik.com

South Korea

International Publications Service Inc (IPS)
Taehwa Bldg, 12th floor, 194-27, Insa-dong, Jongno-gu, Seoul 03162
Tel: (02) 2115-8800 *Fax:* (02) 2115-8866
Founded: 1983

Distributions & subscription promotions for foreign publications.
Exclusive distributor for Newsweek, Reader's Digest, National Geographic & 63 other foreign periodicals.
Type of Business: Distributor, Importer, Wholesaler

IPS Inc, see International Publications Service Inc (IPS)

Kyobo Book Centre Co Ltd
1 Jongno 1-Ga, Jongno-gu, Seoul 03154
Tel: (02) 1544 1900 *Fax:* (0502) 987 5711
E-mail: privacy@kyobobook.co.kr
Web Site: www.kyobobook.co.kr
Key Personnel
Chief Executive Officer: Lee Han-woo
Founded: 1980
Type of Business: Distributor, Exporter, Importer, Major Book Chain Headquarters, Wholesaler
Owned by: Kyobo Life Insurance Co Ltd

Panmun Book Co Ltd
CPO Box 1016, 40, Changro 1-ka, Seoul
Tel: (02) 953-2451-5 *Fax:* (02) 953-2456-7
E-mail: panmunex@unitel.co.kr
Type of Business: Exporter, Importer

Spain

Alibri Libreria SL
C/ Balmes 26, 08007 Barcelona
Tel: 933 170 578 *Fax:* 934 122 702
E-mail: alibri@alibri.es; alibri@alibri.cat
Web Site: www.alibri.es
Key Personnel
General Manager: Alejandro Lopez
Founded: 1925
Academic bookshop.
Type of Business: Exporter, Importer, Major Independent Bookseller

Libreria Bosch SL
C/ Mayor, 337 1-2, 08759 Vallirana, Barcelona
Tel: 936 831 344 *Fax:* 934 122 764
E-mail: info@libreriabosch.com
Web Site: libreriabosch.com
Founded: 1889
Technical bookstore & law publisher.
Type of Business: Distributor, Exporter, Importer, Major Independent Bookseller

Casa del Libro
Complejo Atica, Edificio 4, Via de las Dos Castillas, 33, 28224 Pozuelo de Alarcon, Madrid
Tel: 902 151 928
E-mail: atencionalcliente4@casadellibro.com
Web Site: www.casadellibro.com
Founded: 1923
46 bookshops throughout Spain.
Type of Business: Major Book Chain Headquarters
Owned by: Grupo Planeta

CELESA, see Centro de Exportacion de Libros Espanoles SA (CELESA)

Centro Andaluz del Libro SA
Destornillador Poligono Industrial Store, 3, 41008 Seville
Tel: 954357770 *Fax:* 954352166
E-mail: distribucion@centroandaluzdellibro.com
Web Site: www.centroandaluzdellibro.com
Type of Business: Distributor

Centro de Exportacion de Libros Espanoles SA (CELESA) (Spanish Books Export Center)
Calle Laurel 21, 28005 Madrid
Tel: 915 170 170 *Fax:* 915 173 481
E-mail: celesa@celesa.com; atencion@celesa.com
Web Site: www.celesa.com
Founded: 1986
Specialize in the export of any book published in Spain.
Type of Business: Distributor, Exporter
Owned by: Editoriales Espanolas y Ministerio de Educacion y Cultura de Espana

Dawson Books Espana
Subsidiary of Bertram Group
Plaza de Espana, 6-1º Off 13 & 14, 47001 Valladolid
Tel: 916 745 850
E-mail: libros@dawson.es; atencionalcliente@dawson.es
Web Site: www.dawson.es
Key Personnel
Dir: Catherine Galliot
Founded: 1995
Type of Business: Distributor, Exporter, Importer

Libreria DELSA
C/ Serrano, 80, 1º, 28006 Madrid
Tel: 91 435 74 21; 91 576 21 03 *Fax:* 91 578 28 11
E-mail: delsa@troa.es; nebli@troa.es
Web Site: www.troa.es
Founded: 1951
Type of Business: Major Book Chain Headquarters
Bookshop(s): Paseo de Tierra de Melide, 15, 28050 Madrid *Tel:* 91 750 92 00 *E-mail:* lastablas@troa.es; C/ Juan Florez, 30, 15004 A Coruna *Tel:* 98 127 31 17 *E-mail:* avir@troa.es; Via Augusta, 9, 08006 Barcelona *Tel:* 93 217 54 08 *E-mail:* garbi@troa.es; Av Pearson, 21, 08034 Barcelona *Tel:* 93 280 27 16 *E-mail:* libreriagarbi@iese.edu; C/ Inmaculada, 22, 08017 Barcelona *Tel:* 93 417 59 30 *E-mail:* uic@troa.es; C/ Colon, 19, 12001 Castellon *Tel:* 96 423 86 12 *E-mail:* castellon@troa.es; C/ Madrid, 101, 28902 Getafe *Tel:* 91 601 06 78 *E-mail:* getafe@troa.es; C/ Alvarez de Castro, 6, 17001 Girona *Tel:* 97 220 34 29 *E-mail:* empuries@troa.es; C/ Zacatin, 3, 18001 Granada *Tel:* 95 822 45 21 *E-mail:* dauro@troa.es; C/ Las Mercedes, 20, 48930 Las Arenas *Tel:* 94 423 57 55 *E-mail:* lasarenas@troa.es; Av Sancho el Fuerte, 24, 31007 Pamplona *Tel:* 94 817 02 90 *E-mail:* libreriauniversitaria@troa.es; Universidad de Navarra Nuevo Edificio Bibliotecas, 31009 Pamplona *Tel:* 94 826 72 25 *E-mail:* tiendauniversitaria@troa.es; Av Pio XII, 36, 31008 Pamplona *Tel:* 94 829 66 74 *E-mail:* cun.libuniv@troa.es; Calle Reyes Catolicos, 3, 20006 San Sebastian *Tel:* 94 342 70 08 *E-mail:* zubieta@troa.es; C/ Luis de Morales, 1, 41018 Sevilla *Tel:* 95 421 25 65 *E-mail:* tarsis@troa.es; C/ Grabador Esteve, 33, 46004 Valencia *Tel:* 96 334 83 18 *E-mail:* ideas@troa.es; C/ San Miguel, 31, 50001 Zaragoza *Tel:* 97 621 53 96 *E-mail:* fontibre@troa.es

EDHASA (Editora y Distribuidora Hispanoamericana SA)
C/ Disputacion, 262, 2a 1a, 08007 Barcelona
Tel: 934 949 720 *Fax:* 934 194 584
E-mail: info@edhasa.es; comercial@edhasa.es
Web Site: www.edhasa.es
Founded: 1946
Distributor & exporter of fine editions, illustrated books, general trade books (hardcover), juvenile & young adult books, translations, economics, fiction, history, how-to, literature, literary criticism, essays, management, maritime,

philosophy, romance, science fiction, fantasy & travel titles.
Type of Business: Distributor, Exporter

Editora y Distribuidora Hispanoamericana SA, see EDHASA (Editora y Distribuidora Hispanoamericana SA)

Libreria Hispano Americana
Gran Via de les Corts Catalanes 594, 08007 Barcelona
Tel: 93 318 05 08
E-mail: info@llibreriaha.com
Web Site: www.llibreriaha.com
Key Personnel
President: Josep M Boixareu Vilaplana
Founded: 1937
Specialize in scientific & technical books.
Type of Business: Importer, Major Independent Bookseller
Parent Company: Marcombo SA

Iberoamericana Editorial Vervuert SLU
C/ Amor de Dios, 1, 28014 Madrid
Tel: 91 429 35 22 *Fax:* 91 429 53 97
E-mail: info@iberoamericanalibros.com
Web Site: www.iberoamericana-vervuert.es
Founded: 1975
Specialize in academic books about Latin America & Spain.
Type of Business: Distributor, Exporter, Importer, Major Independent Bookseller
Bookshop(s): Libreria Iberoamericana, c/ Huertas, 40, 28014 Madrid *Tel:* 91 360 12 29 *Fax:* 91 429 53 97 *E-mail:* libreria@iberoamericanalibros.com

LEA, see Librerias Especializadas Asociadas (LEA)

LHA, see Libreria Hispano Americana

Librerias Especializadas Asociadas (LEA)
C/ Hortaleza, 34, 28004 Madrid
Tel: 915232222 *Fax:* 915231219
E-mail: info@libreriasespecializadas.com
Web Site: www.libreriasespecializadas.com
Online bookstore representing independent booksellers throughout Spain.
Type of Business: Distributor, Importer

Marcial Pons Librero SL
C/ San Sotero, 6, 28037 Madrid
Tel: 91 304 33 03 *Fax:* 91 327 23 67; 91 754 12 18
E-mail: atencion@marcialpons.es
Web Site: www.marcialpons.es
Founded: 1948
Type of Business: Distributor, Exporter, Importer, Major Independent Bookseller, Wholesaler
Branch Office(s)
Calle Provenca, 242, 08008 Barcelona *Tel:* 93 487 39 99 *Fax:* 93 488 19 40 *E-mail:* llibreter@marcialpons.es
Bookshop(s): Calle Barbara de Braganza, 11, 28004 Madrid *Tel:* 91 319 42 50 *Fax:* 91 319 43 73 *E-mail:* derecho@marcialpons.es; Plaza del Conde Valle de Suchil, 8, 28015 Madrid *Tel:* 91 448 47 97 *Fax:* 91 593 13 29 *E-mail:* humanidades@marcialpons.es

Mundi-Prensa Libros SA
Calle Velazquez no 31, 3° Derecha, 28001 Madrid
Tel: 914 463 350 *Fax:* 914 456 218
E-mail: info@paraninfo.es
Web Site: www.mundiprensa.com
Key Personnel
Editorial Dir: Jose Maria Hernandez
Commercial Dir: Ricardo Alonso
Founded: 1948

Publisher, bookseller & subscription agency.
Type of Business: Distributor, Exporter, Importer, Major Book Chain Headquarters, Wholesaler
Parent Company: Grupo Editorial Paraninfo

La Panoplia Export SL
C/ Ulises 65, 28043 Madrid
Tel: 913 004 390 *Fax:* 913 886 518
E-mail: export@panopliadelibros.com; pedidos@panopliadelibros.com
Web Site: www.panopliadelibros.com
Key Personnel
Manager: Jesus Miranda Rayo
Founded: 1985
Type of Business: Distributor, Exporter

Libreria Passim SL
Calle Floridablanca, 54-58, 08015 Barcelona
Tel: 933 250 305
Founded: 1963
Publishes catalogs of new books about Spain & Latin America published in Spain. Specialize in sales to universities & libraries.
Type of Business: Exporter, Major Independent Bookseller

Libreria Pons SL
C/ Felix Latassa, 33, 50006 Zaragoza
Mailing Address: PO Box 10348, 50006 Zaragoza
Tel: 976 554 920
E-mail: pedidos@libreriapons-zaragoza.com
Web Site: www.libreriapons-zaragoza.com
Founded: 1951
Library supplier.
Type of Business: Distributor, Importer, Major Independent Bookseller

Puvill Libros SA
C/ Estany, 13, nave D-1, 08038 Barcelona
Tel: 932 988 960 *Fax:* 932 988 961
E-mail: info@puvill.com
Web Site: www.puvill.com
Founded: 1945
Type of Business: Distributor
U.S. Office(s): Puvill Libros, Dror Faust, One E Park Dr, Paterson, NJ 07504, United States *Tel:* 973-279-9054 *Fax:* 973-278-1448 *E-mail:* dror@puvill.com
Bookshop(s): Puvill Libros Mexico SA de CV, Pennsylvania, 151 A, Desp 103, Colonia Parque San Andres, Delegacion Coyoacan, 04040 Mexico, CDMX, Mexico *Tel:* (0155) 56583100 *Fax:* (0155) 56625115 *E-mail:* puvillmexico47@yahoo.com.mx

Libreria Rodriguez
Paseo Marques de Zafra 31, 28028 Madrid
Tel: 91 725 26 80
E-mail: correo@libreriarodriguez.com
Web Site: www.libreriarodriguez.com
Key Personnel
Contact: Carlos Ballesteros Rodriguez; Maria Victoria Rodriguez Garcia
Founded: 1920
Type of Business: Major Independent Bookseller

Libreria Rubinos 1860 SA
Calle Hermosilla, 112, 28009 Madrid
Tel: 915061190; 914018500; 913092372 *Fax:* 915753272
Type of Business: Distributor, Exporter, Importer, Major Independent Bookseller, Wholesaler

Sociedad Anonima de Distribucion Edicion y Librerias, see Libreria DELSA

TROA Librerias, see Libreria DELSA

Sri Lanka

M D Gunasena & Co Ltd
No 217, Olcott Mawatha, Colombo 11
Tel: (011) 2323981; (011) 2323982; (011) 2323983; (011) 2323984 *Fax:* (011) 2323336
E-mail: headoffice@mdgunasena.com; info@mdgunasena.com
Web Site: www.mdgunasena.com
Type of Business: Major Book Chain Headquarters
Bookshop(s): No 27, Galle Rd, Colombo 04 *Tel:* (011) 2553379; (011) 2554917 *Fax:* (011) 2554917 *E-mail:* salesbp@mdgunasena.com; No 1129, Marandana Rd, Colombo 08 *Tel:* (011) 5370770 *Fax:* (011) 5370770 *E-mail:* salesbr@mdgunasena.com; 133 D, Vajira Rd, Colombo 05 *Tel:* (011) 2585666 *E-mail:* salesvi@mdgunasena.com; No 20, St Sebastian Hill, Colombo 12 *Tel:* (011) 2389802 *Fax:* (011) 2436528 *E-mail:* saleshu@mdgunasena.com; No 73, Ratnapura Rd, Avissawella *Tel:* (036) 2231106 *E-mail:* salesbr@mdgunasena.com; 239, Hill St, Dehiwala *Tel:* (011) 2718922 *E-mail:* salesde@mdgunasena.com; No 02, Matara Rd, Galle *Tel:* (091) 2222664 *E-mail:* salesgl@mdgunasena.com; No 5/1, Holy Cross Rd, Gampaha *Tel:* (033) 2228953 *E-mail:* salesgm@mdgunasena.com; No 97A, Main St, Kalutara *Tel:* (034) 2222942 *E-mail:* saleskl@mdgunasena.com; No 33, Yatinuwara Veediya, Kandy *Tel:* (081) 2223288 *E-mail:* saleskn@mdgunasena.com; No 4, Kandy Rd, Kirbathgoda *Tel:* (011) 2917394 *E-mail:* saleskb@mdgunasena.com; No 67A, Colombo Rd, Kurunegala *Tel:* (037) 2222548 *E-mail:* salesku@mdgunasena.com; No 27, Dharmapala Mw, Matara *Tel:* (041) 2222426 *E-mail:* salesma@mdgunasena.com; No 64, De Croose Rd, Negombo *Tel:* (031) 2222405 *E-mail:* salesne@mdgunasena.com; 156 B, High Level Rd, Nugegoda *Tel:* (011) 2816858 *E-mail:* salesng@mdgunasena.com; No 474/B, Arthur V Dias Mw, Panadura *Tel:* (038) 2236415 *E-mail:* salespa@mdgunasena.com

Lake House Bookshop (Pvt) Ltd
Affiliate of Stamford Press
No 100, Sir Chittampalam A, Gardiner Mawatha, Colombo 00200
Tel: (011) 4734137; (011) 4734138; (011) 4979646 *Fax:* (011) 2430582
E-mail: info@lakehousebookshop.com
Web Site: www.lakehousebookshop.com
Founded: 1941
Type of Business: Distributor, Exporter, Importer, Major Independent Bookseller, Wholesaler
Branch Office(s)
Liberty Plaza Shopping Complex, 1st floor, R A De Mel Mawatha, Colombo 00300 *Tel:* (011) 2574418 *Fax:* (011) 2574418

Sadeepa Book Shop (Pvt) Ltd
1060, Maradana Rd (Gnanartha Pradeepa Mawatha), Borella, Colombo 00800
Tel: (011) 268 6114; (011) 269 4286; (071) 223 1333 *Fax:* (011) 267 8044
E-mail: info@sadeepa.com
Web Site: www.sadeepa.com
Founded: 1987
Also printer & publisher.
Type of Business: Distributor, Importer, Major Independent Bookseller, Wholesaler

Sarasavi Bookshop Pvt Ltd
Subsidiary of Sarasavi Group of Companies
2B Samudradevi Mawatha, Nugegoda 10250
Tel: (011) 2820820 *Fax:* (011) 2814926
E-mail: info@sarasavi.lk
Web Site: www.sarasavi.lk

SRI LANKA

Key Personnel
Chairman & Mng Dir: Mr H D Premasiri
Founded: 1955
Membership(s): Book Sellers Association of Ceylon; British Booksellers Association; Sri Lanka Book Publishers' Association; Sri Lanka Book Sellers Association.
Type of Business: Importer, Major Book Chain Headquarters, Online Bookseller
Imprints: Saravasi Publishers
Branch Office(s)
1/50 YMBA Bldg, Borella *Tel:* (01) 2698886
44/9 YMBA Bldg, Colombo Fort *Tel:* (011) 2326831
24 Hill St, Dehiwala *Tel:* (011) 2722349 *Fax:* (011) 2722351
Galle Central Bus Stand, 1st floor, Galle 80000 *Tel:* (091) 2225221
87 Minuwangoda Rd, Gampaha *Tel:* (033) 2233444 *Fax:* (033) 2222376
41, Anguruwathota Rd, Horana *Tel:* (034) 2262202
86 D S Senanayake Veediya, Kandy *Tel:* (081) 2223396 *Fax:* (081) 2234036
Block 21, Level 2, Kandy City Centre *Tel:* (081) 2205344
151/1 Kandy Rd, Kiribathgoda *Tel:* (011) 2914255
147 St Michael's Rd, Kollupitiya *Tel:* (011) 2424587
56, Colombo Rd, Kurunegala 60000 *Tel:* (037) 2221397
74 High Level Rd, Maharagama *Tel:* (011) 2850340; (011) 2838848
04, Station Rd, Matara *Tel:* (041) 2234494; (041) 3492770 *Fax:* (041) 2228406
Block 47, Economic Centre, Kirimandala Mw, Narahenpita *Tel:* (011) 2369589
16, Horana Rd, Padukka *Tel:* (011) 2188388
14 Udyana Rd, Piliyandala *Tel:* (011) 2609321
No 23/1, Seneviratna Bldg, 1st floor, Colombo Rd, Ratnapura *Tel:* (045) 2230501; (045) 2230502
134A, Sunil's Bldg, Old Negombo Rd, Wattala *Tel:* (011) 2933343; (011) 2933345
Warehouse: 30, Stanley Tilakaratne Mawatha, Nugegoda *Tel:* (011) 2852519

Saravasi Publishers, *imprint of* Sarasavi Bookshop Pvt Ltd

Sudan

Khartoum Modern Bookshop
Zubeir Pasha St, Khartoum
Tel: (01) 83774425
Founded: 1956
Membership(s): The Sudan Chamber of Commerce (Khartoum).
Type of Business: Distributor, Importer, Wholesaler

The Nile Bookshop
Alamarat St 41, Khartoum
Tel: (012) 099 6505
E-mail: mohamed@thenilebookshop.com
Web Site: www.thenilebookshop.com
Type of Business: Distributor, Importer, Major Independent Bookseller

Sweden

Akademibokhandeln
Lindhagensgatan 7, 112 18 Stockholm
Mailing Address: Box 2100, 103 13 Stockholm
Tel: (010) 744 10 00; (010) 744 10 40 (customer service)
E-mail: kundservice@akademibokhandeln.se
Web Site: www.akademibokhandeln.se
Key Personnel
Chief Executive Officer: Maria Hamrefors
Sales & Operations: Maria Edsman
Founded: 1992
Type of Business: Exporter, Importer, Major Book Chain Headquarters
Owned by: Bokhandelsgruppen i Sverige AB

Bokia AB, see Akademibokhandeln

Soderbokhandeln Hansson och Bruce AB
Goetgatan 37, Stockholm
Tel: (08) 6405432
E-mail: info@soderbokhandeln.se
Web Site: soderbokhandeln.blogspot.com
Founded: 1874
Type of Business: Major Independent Bookseller

Samdistribution Logistik Sverige AB
Metallvagen 31, 195 72 Rosersberg
Mailing Address: Box 4005, 195 04 Rosersberg
Tel: (08) 696 84 10; (08) 696 84 00 *Fax:* (08) 696 84 31
E-mail: reklamation@bonnierforlagen.se
Web Site: samdistribution.se
Key Personnel
Chief Executive Officer: Bjorn Tallen *Tel:* (08) 696 84 30 *E-mail:* bjorn.tallen@samdistribution.se
Founded: 1960
Warehousing of books (book trade, book services & book club members).
Type of Business: Distributor
Owned by: Bonnierforlagen AB

Switzerland

Balmer, see Luethy + Stocker AG

Brunnen Bibel Panorama, see Fontis-Buchhandlung

Buchzentrum AG (BZ)
Industriestr Ost 10, 4614 Haegendorf
Tel: (062) 209 25 25; (062) 209 26 26 (customer service) *Fax:* (062) 209 26 27
E-mail: info@buchzentrum.ch
Web Site: www.buchzentrum.ch
Key Personnel
Chief Executive Officer: Hanspeter Buechler *E-mail:* buechler@buchzentrum.ch
Head, Purchasing & Sales: David Ryf *Tel:* (062) 209 25 05 *E-mail:* ryf@buchzentrum.ch
Communications & Marketing: Nicole Gisi *E-mail:* gisi@buchzentrum.ch
Founded: 1882
Membership(s): Swiss Booksellers & Publishers Association.
Type of Business: Distributor, Wholesaler

Fontis-Buchhandlung
Formerly Brunnen Bibel Panorama
Steinentorstr 23, 4010 Basel
Tel: (061) 295 60 03
E-mail: info@fontis.ch
Web Site: www.fontis-shop.ch
Key Personnel
Chief Operating Officer: Andre Begert *E-mail:* a.begert@fontis.ch
Specialize in Christian books, music, media & gifts.
Type of Business: Major Book Chain Headquarters
Bookshop(s): Schnabelgasse 8, 4051 Basel, Manager: Therese Peter *Tel:* (061) 263 00 15 *Fax:* (061) 263 00 16 *E-mail:* basel@fontis.ch; Bahnhofstr 76, 5000 Aarau, Manager: Elisabeth Girardier *Tel:* (062) 824 44 34 *E-mail:* aarau@fontis.ch; Zeughausgasse 35/37, 3011 Bern, Manager: Trudy Fahrni *Tel:* (031) 311 04 21 *E-mail:* bern@fontis.ch; Marktgasse 31, 8180 Buelach, Manager: Daniela Koblet *Tel:* (044) 860 06 81 *Fax:* (044) 860 12 25 *E-mail:* buelach@fontis.ch; St Gallerstr 8, 8500 Frauenfeld, Manager: Irene Haeberlin *Tel:* (052) 721 94 36 *Fax:* (052) 721 97 33 *E-mail:* frauenfeld@fontis.ch; Marktgasse 16, 3800 Interlaken, Manager: Doris Suter *Tel:* (033) 821 02 30 *E-mail:* interlaken@fontis.ch; Marktstr 16, 3550 Langnau, Manager: Susanne Utiger *Tel:* (034) 402 49 59 *Fax:* (034) 402 50 20 *E-mail:* langnau@fontis.ch; Glaernischstr 7, 8640 Rapperswil, Manager: Lucie Calderone *Tel:* (055) 210 43 23 *Fax:* (055) 211 82 33 *E-mail:* rapperswil@fontis.ch; Repfergasse, 8200 Schaffhausen, Manager: Petra Erne *Tel:* (052) 625 50 50 *E-mail:* schaffhausen@fontis.ch; Rathauspl 3, 3600 Thun, Manager: Angelina Heusser *Tel:* (033) 222 61 61 *E-mail:* thun@fontis.ch; Untere Bahnhofstr 20, 9500 Wil, Manager: Marie-Louise Kammermann *Tel:* (071) 911 31 11 *Fax:* (071) 911 31 32 *E-mail:* wil@fontis.ch; Steinberggasse 52, 8400 Winterthur, Manager: Gaby Haimann *Tel:* (052) 213 40 59 *Fax:* (052) 213 40 65 *E-mail:* winterthur@fontis.ch; Schaffhauserstr 276, 8057 Zurich, Manager: Rebekka Bollinger *Tel:* (044) 312 07 70 *Fax:* (044) 312 09 33 *E-mail:* zuerich@fontis.ch

Orell Fuessli Thalia AG
Dietzingerstr 3, 8036 Zurich
Tel: (044) 455 56 19
E-mail: geschaeftsleitung@oft.ch
Web Site: www.orellfuessli.ch; www.oft.ch
Key Personnel
Mng Dir & Chief Executive Officer: Pascal Schneebeli
Founded: 1973
Fiction & travel titles.
Type of Business: Major Book Chain Headquarters
Owned by: Orell Fuessli Buchhandlungs AG; Thalia Buecher AG
Branch Office(s)
Orell Fuessli ZH Kramhof & Bookshop, Fuesslistr 4, 8022 Zurich *Tel:* (0848) 849848 *Fax:* (044) 4555620 *E-mail:* kundenservice@orellfuessli.ch
Orell Fuessli Zurich Airport, Airport Center, 8060 Zurich *Tel:* (0848) 849848 *Fax:* (044) 4555620 *E-mail:* kundenservice@orellfuessli.ch
Orell Fuessli Zurich Bellevue, Theaterstr 8, 8001 Zurich *Tel:* (0848) 849848 *Fax:* (044) 4555620 *E-mail:* kundenservice@orellfuessli.ch
Orell Fuessli Zurich Hauptbahnhof, Shopville, Halle State Museum, 8001 Zurich *Tel:* (0848) 849848 *Fax:* (044) 4555620 *E-mail:* kundenservice@orellfuessli.ch
Orell Fuessli Zurich Oerlikon BHF, Hofwiesenstr 369, 8050 Zurich *Tel:* (0848) 849848 *Fax:* (043) 2686049 *E-mail:* kundenservice@orellfuessli.ch
Orell Fuessli Zurich Stadelhofen BHF, Stadelhoferstr 8, 8001 Zurich *Tel:* (0848) 849848 *Fax:* (044) 4555620 *E-mail:* kundenservice@orellfuessli.ch
Orell Fuessli Meissner Aarau, Bahnhofstr 41, 5000 Aarau *Tel:* (062) 8370844 *Fax:* (062) 8370845 *E-mail:* meissner@orellfuessli.ch
Orell Fuessli Wirz Aarau, Hintere Vorstadt 18, 5000 Aarau *Tel:* (062) 8323838 *Fax:* (062) 8323830 *E-mail:* wirz@orellfuessli.ch

Orell Fuessli Baden, Langhaus 4, 5400 Baden
Tel: (056) 2031997 *Fax:* (056) 2031998
E-mail: baden@orellfuessli.ch
Orell Fuessli Bahnhof SBB Basel, Gueterstr 115,
4053 Basel *Tel:* (0848) 849848 *Fax:* (044)
4555620 *E-mail:* kundenservice@orellfuessli.ch
Orell Fuessli Basel, Freie Str 17, 4001 Basel
Tel: (061) 2642626 *Fax:* (061) 2642600
E-mail: basel@orellfuessli.ch
Orell Fuessli Bahnhof SBB Bern, Bahnhofpl
10, 3011 Bern *Tel:* (0848) 849848 *Fax:* (044)
4555620 *E-mail:* kundenservice@orellfuessli.ch
Orell Fuessli Bern, Spitalgasse 47/51, 3011
Bern *Tel:* (031) 3202020 *Fax:* (031) 3202029
E-mail: loeb@orellfuessli.ch
Buchhandlung Stauffacher, Neuengasse 25-37,
3011 Bern *Tel:* (031) 3136363 *Fax:* (031)
3136339 *E-mail:* info@stauffacher.ch
ZAP* Brig, Furkastr 3, 3900 Brig *Tel:* (027)
9224800 *Fax:* (027) 9224801 *E-mail:* brig@
zap.ch
ZAP* Buero Store, Englisch-Gruss-Str 6, 3900
Brig-Glis *Tel:* (027) 9224800 *Fax:* (027)
9224801 *E-mail:* bestell@zap.ch
Orell Fuessli Brugg, Neumarktpl 12, 5200
Brugg *Tel:* (056) 4442406 *Fax:* (056) 4442407
E-mail: brugg@orellfuessli.ch
Orell Fuessli Chur-EKZ City West, Raschaerstr
35, 7000 Chur *Tel:* (0848) 849848 *Fax:* (044)
4555620 *E-mail:* kundenservice@orellfuessli.ch
Orell Fuessli Emmen Center, Emmen Center,
6020 Emmenbruecke *Tel:* (0848) 849848
Fax: (044) 4555620 *E-mail:* kundenservice@
orellfuessli.ch
Orell Fuessli Frauenfeld, Bahnhofpl 76, 8500
Frauenfeld *Tel:* (0848) 849848 *Fax:* (044)
4555626 *E-mail:* kundenservice@orellfuessli.ch
Orell Fuessli Shopping Arena, Shopping
Arena - Zuercher Str 464, 9015 St Gallen
Tel: (0848) 849848 *Fax:* (044) 4555620
E-mail: kundenservice@orellfuessli.ch
Roesslitor Buecher St Gallen, Multergasse 1-3,
9001 St Gallen *Tel:* (071) 2274747 *Fax:* (071)
2274748 *E-mail:* bestellung.roesslitor@
orellfuessli.ch
Orell Fuessli St Margrethen, Einkaufszen-
trum Rheinpark, 9430 St Margrethen
Tel: (0848) 849848 *Fax:* (044) 4555620
E-mail: kundenservice@orellfuessli.ch
Orell Fuessli Schaffhausen, Vordergasse 77, 8200
Schaffhausent *Tel:* (0848) 849848 *Fax:* (044)
4555620 *E-mail:* kundenservice@orellfuessli.ch
Orell Fuessli Shoppyland, Industriestr (im
Shoppyland) 10, 3321 Schoenbuehl
Tel: (0848) 849848 *Fax:* (044) 4555620
E-mail: kundenservice@orellfuessli.ch
ZAP* Sierre, place de la Gare 2, 3960 Sierre
Tel: (027) 4518866 *Fax:* (027) 4518868
E-mail: sierre@zap.ch
Orell Fuessli Spreitenbach, EKZ Tivoli, 8957
Spreitenbach *Tel:* (0848) 849848 *Fax:* (044)
4555620 *E-mail:* kundenservice@orellfuessli.ch
Orell Fuessli Thun, Baelliz 60, 3600 Thun
Tel: (0848) 849848 *Fax:* (044) 4555620
E-mail: kundenservice@orellfuessli.ch
ZAP* Visp, Bahnhofstr 21, 3930 Visp *Tel:* (027)
9468866 *Fax:* (027) 9468868 *E-mail:* visp@
zap.ch
Orell Fuessli EKZ Rosenberg, Schaffhauser-
str 152, 8400 Winterthur *Tel:* (0848) 849848
Fax: (044) 4555620 *E-mail:* kundenservice@
orellfuessli.ch
Orell Fuessli Winterthur, Marktgasse 41, 8400
Winterthur *Tel:* (0848) 849848 *Fax:* (044)
4555620 *E-mail:* kundenservice@orellfuessli.ch
ZAP* Zermatt, Hofmattstr 3, 3920 Zermatt
Tel: (027) 9664010 *Fax:* (027) 9664015
E-mail: zermatt@zap.ch

Luethy + Stocker AG
Weissensteinstr 81, Postfach, 4500 Solothurn
Tel: (032) 625 33 33 *Fax:* (032) 625 33 00
E-mail: luethy@buchhaus.ch

Web Site: www.buchhaus.ch
Key Personnel
Mng Dir: Simone Luethy *Tel:* (032) 625 33 89
E-mail: simone.luethy@buchhaus.ch
Branch Manager: Ralf Braunwarth *E-mail:* ralf.
braunwarth@buchhaus.ch
Founded: 1950
Type of Business: Major Book Chain Headquar-
ters
Parent Company: Luethy Balmer Stocker-Gruppe
Bookshop(s): Luethy Aarau, Bahnhofplatz
3b, 5000 Aarau *Tel:* (062) 823 18 65
E-mail: aarau@buchhaus.ch; Luethy Biel,
Nidaugasse 60, 2500 Biel *Tel:* (032) 328 12 22
E-mail: biel@buchhaus.ch; Luethy Grenchen,
Bettlachstr 8, 2540 Grenchen *Tel:* (032)
653 14 89 *E-mail:* grenchen@buchhaus.ch;
Luethy Kanisius, Bahnhofstr 6, 1700 Fri-
bourg *Tel:* (026) 322 13 45 *E-mail:* freiburg@
buchhaus.ch; Stocker Schwyz, Mythen Cen-
ter Schwyz, Mythencenterstr 18, 6438 Ibach
Tel: (041) 818 65 65 *E-mail:* mythencenter@
buchhaus.ch; Stocker Luzern, Hertensteinstr
44, Postfach 3967, 6000 Lucerne *Tel:* (041)
417 25 25 *E-mail:* stocker@buchhaus.ch;
Schoch SH, Vordergasse 72, 8200 Schaffhausen
Tel: (052) 625 43 69 *E-mail:* schaffhausen@
buchhaus.ch; Luethy Solothurn, Gurzelngasse
17, 4500 Solothurn *Tel:* (032) 625 33 15
E-mail: solothurn@buchhaus.ch; Stocker Stans,
Bitzistr 2, 6370 Stans *Tel:* (041) 610 39 10
E-mail: laenderpark@buchhaus.ch; Balmer
Zugerland, Hinterbergstr 40, 6312 Steinhausen
Tel: (041) 740 58 77 *E-mail:* zugerland@
buchhaus.ch; Luethy Zurich, EKZ Glattzen-
trum, Neue Winterthurerstr 99, 8304 Wal-
lisellen *Tel:* (044) 878 21 21 *E-mail:* glatt@
buchhaus.ch; Balmer Zug, Rigistr 3, 6300
Zug *Tel:* (041) 726 97 97 *E-mail:* citypark@
buchhaus.ch; Luethy Zurich Sihlcity, EKZ
Sihlcity, Kalanderplatz 1, 8045 Zurich
Tel: (044) 208 10 30 *E-mail:* sihlcity@
buchhaus.ch

Luethy Balmer Stocker, see Luethy + Stocker
AG

PEP + No Name Buchhandlung und
Photogalerie GmbH
Gueterstr 189, 4053 Basel
Tel: (061) 261 51 61 *Fax:* (061) 261 51 61
E-mail: info@pepnoname.ch
Web Site: www.pepnoname.ch
Founded: 1980
Specialize in photo, film, art, tattoo & Indian lit-
erature. Also photo gallery.
Type of Business: Distributor, Exporter, Importer,
Major Independent Bookseller

Servidis SA
Chemin des Chalets, 7, 1279 Chavannes-de-Bogis
Tel: (022) 960 95 10 *Fax:* (022) 776 35 44
E-mail: commercial@servidis.ch
Web Site: www.servidis.ch
Key Personnel
Dir: Raymond Filliastre *Tel:* (022) 960 95 11
E-mail: rfilliastre@servidis.ch
Founded: 1991
Type of Business: Distributor

Buchhandlung Staeheli AG, see Staeheli
Interlingua AG

Staeheli Interlingua AG
Formerly Buchhandlung Staeheli AG
Turbinenweg 6, 8866 Ziegelbruecke
Tel: (041) 726 97 21
E-mail: info@lesestoff.ch
Web Site: interlingua.lesestoff.ch
Founded: 1934
Booksellers & subscription agents.

Online bookshop. Specialize in language teaching
material.
Type of Business: Importer, Major Independent
Bookseller, Online Bookseller
Bookshop(s): Oberdorfstr 32, 8001 Zurich
Tel: (044) 209 91 11

Stocker, see Luethy + Stocker AG

Centre Suisse du Livre, see Buchzentrum AG
(BZ)

Centro Svizzero del Libro, see Buchzentrum AG
(BZ)

Swiss Book Centre, see Buchzentrum AG (BZ)

Syria

Dar Al Rowad Lil Nashr, see Pioneers
Publishing House (Dar Al Rowad Lil Nashr)

Nour E-Sham Book Centre
Bldg 2, Omar Almokhtar Ave, Opposite the Min-
istry of Education, Teliani, Damascus
Tel: (011) 4457 458; (094) 078 8002 (cell)
Fax: (011) 3324 913
E-mail: info@nouresham.org
Web Site: nouresham.org
Founded: 1980
Type of Business: Distributor
Branch Office(s)
Opposite Al Shomo'o Hotel (Candles Hotel), Hal-
boni, Demascus *Tel:* (011) 2239 644
Opposite The Safir Hotel, Al Inshaat, Homs
Tel: (031) 2124 319; (093) 511 0979 (cell)

Pioneers Publishing House (Dar Al Rowad Lil
Nashr)
Halbouni, Musallam al Baroudi St, 4943 Damas-
cus
Tel: (011) 222 8261 *Fax:* (011) 222 8261
E-mail: info@rowadpub.com
Web Site: www.rowadpub.com
Key Personnel
Dir General: Kassem Terrace *Tel:* (093) 2886087
(cell) *E-mail:* kassem@rowadpub.com
Sales Manager: Ammar Terrace *Tel:* (093)
3650977 (cell)
Founded: 1986
Type of Business: Distributor

Taiwan

Morning Star Online Bookstore
No 1, 30 Rd, Industrial District, Taichung 407
Tel: (04) 2359-5819 (ext 230); (04) 2359-5819
(ext 400) *Fax:* (04) 2359-7123
E-mail: service@morningstar.com.tw; morning@
morningstar.com.tw
Web Site: www.morningstar.com.tw
Type of Business: Online Bookseller

Tanzania

The Dar es Salaam Bookshop
Makunganya/India St, Dar es Salaam
Mailing Address: PO Box 11041, Dar es Salaam
Tel: (0755) 798124
Type of Business: Distributor

Thailand

A-Book Distribution Co Ltd
91/165/1-2 Soi Tiwanon 3 Taiwanon Rd, Tambon
Taladkwan, Mueang Nonthaburi 11000
Tel: (02) 968-9337; (02) 968-9207 *Fax:* (02) 968-
9511
E-mail: sale@thisisabook.com
Web Site: www.thisisabook.com
Founded: 2002
Type of Business: Distributor, Wholesaler

Asia Books Co Ltd
Berli Jucker House, 14th floor, 99 Soi Rubia,
Sukhumvit 42rd Pharakanong Klongtoey,
Bangkok 10110
Tel: (02) 715-9000; (02) 715-9049
E-mail: information@asiabooks.com;
ecommerce@asiabooks.com
Web Site: www.asiabooks.com
Founded: 1969
Publisher, distributor & chain of over 70 English
language bookshops throughout Thailand.
Type of Business: Distributor, Importer, Major
Book Chain Headquarters, Wholesaler
Owned by: Berli Jucker Public Co Ltd

Nibondh & Co Ltd
40-42 Chareon Krung Rd, Sikak Phaya Sri,
Bangkok 10200
Mailing Address: PO Box 402, Bangkok GPO,
Bangkok 10501
Tel: (02) 221-2611; (02) 221-1553; (02) 225-9785
Fax: (02) 224-6889
E-mail: info@nibondhbooks.com; books@
nibondhbooks.com
Web Site: www.nibondhbooks.com
Key Personnel
Export: Khun Thitiporn
Contact: Khun Saravadee
Founded: 1944
Supplier of academic books to libraries of in-
stitutes of higher learning. Subject specialties
include agriculture, food science, hospitality,
environment, science, technology & medicine.
Type of Business: Distributor, Exporter, Major
Independent Bookseller
Branch Office(s)
Books@53, 25 Soi Madee Paidee, Sukhumvit
Soi 53, Bangkok 10110 *Tel:* (02) 258-7747
Fax: (02) 258-7726 *E-mail:* books53@
nibondhbooks.com

Odeon Store
218/10-12 Siam Square Rd Soi 1, Bangkok 10330
Tel: (02) 251-4476
Key Personnel
Manager: Mrs Pornpimol Amornworanat
Founded: 1951
Membership(s): The Publishers & Booksellers
Association of Thailand.
Type of Business: Major Independent Bookseller,
Wholesaler

Suan Nguen Mee Ma Co Ltd
77, 79 Fuang Nakorn Rd, Wat Rajabopit,
Bangkok 10200
Tel: (02) 622-0955; (02) 622-0966; (02) 622-
2495; (02) 622-2496 *Fax:* (02) 622-3228
E-mail: publishers@suan-spirit.com; shopping@
suan-spirit.com
Web Site: www.suan-spirit.com
Key Personnel
Co-Owner: Hans van Willenswaard
Founded: 1992
Also library suppliers.
Type of Business: Exporter, Importer, Major Inde-
pendent Bookseller

Suriwong Book Centre Ltd
54/1-5 Sridonchai Rd, Muang, Chiang Mai 50100
Tel: (053) 281052 *Fax:* (053) 271902; (053)
449305
E-mail: cust@mailsuriwong.com
Web Site: www.suriwongbook.com
Book retailer in Thai & English.
Type of Business: Major Independent Bookseller

White Lotus Co Ltd
145/3-6 Soi Huay Yai Chin, Huay Yai Pattaya,
Banglamung, Chonburi 20150
Mailing Address: GPO Box 1141, Bangkok
10501
Tel: (038) 239-883; (038) 239-960; (038) 239-886
Fax: (038) 239-885
Web Site: thailine.com/lotus; whitelotuspress.com;
whitelotusbooks.com
Key Personnel
Chief Executive: D Ande *E-mail:* ande@loxinfo.
co.th
Founded: 1972
Distributor, antiquarian dealer, publisher of books
on Asia.
Type of Business: Distributor, Exporter, Importer,
Wholesaler

Trinidad and Tobago

Campus Corner Ltd
72 Pembroke St, Port of Spain
Tel: (868) 623-1678
Founded: 1973
Type of Business: Distributor, Importer, Major
Independent Bookseller, Wholesaler

Charran's Bookstores
53 Eastern Main Rd, Tunapuna
Tel: (868) 663-1884
Web Site: www.charranstt.com
Type of Business: Major Book Chain Headquar-
ters
Bookshop(s): Charran Bookshop St James, 8
Bournes Rd, St James, Port of Spain *Tel:* (868)
221-9402

Tunisia

Editions Ali Bouslama et Fils
15, Ave de France, 1000 Tunis
Tel: 71240056 *Fax:* 71343100
Key Personnel
Manager: Ali Bouslama
Founded: 1959
Also publisher.
Type of Business: Distributor

Turkey

Arkadas Yayinevi Ltd
Yuva Mahallesi 3702, Sokak No 4, 06105 Yen-
imahalle, Ankara
Tel: (0312) 396 0111 *Fax:* (0312) 396 0141
E-mail: info@arkadas.com.tr
Web Site: www.arkadas.com.tr
Key Personnel
Chairman & Owner: Cumhur Ozdemir

Founded: 1980
Retail trade of book stationery, music cassettes,
CD, import diskettes, poster & print. Also pub-
lisher.
Type of Business: Distributor, Importer, Major
Independent Bookseller, Wholesaler
Bookshop(s): Atlantis Alisveris Merkezi, Kent-
Koop Mahallesi Baskent Blvd, No 213 C3
Batikent Yenimahalle, Ankara *Tel:* (0312) 255
5044; Kentpark Alisveris Merkezi, Eskise-
hir Yolu 7 km No 164/2 Kat No 103 06520,
Ankara *Tel:* (0312) 219 9244 *Fax:* (0312) 219
9247; One Tower Alisveris Merkezi, Oran
Mahallesi Kudus Cad No 6 Cankaya, Ankara
Tel: (0312) 503 0062

Bilgi Dagitim
Gulbahar Mh, Gulbag Cd No 33 A-B Blok,
34387 Mecidiyekoy, Istanbul
Tel: (0212) 217 63 40; (0212) 522 52 01
Fax: (0212) 217 63 45; (0212) 527 41 19
E-mail: dagitim@bilgiyayinevi.com.tr
Web Site: www.bilgiyayinevi.com.tr
Founded: 1972
Type of Business: Distributor

Fen Kitabevi Ltd sti
Milli Mucadele Cd No:14/7, Kizilay/Ankara
Tel: (0312) 418 51 09
Founded: 1975
Type of Business: Importer, Major Independent
Bookseller, Wholesaler

Nuans Kitapcilik San Tic Ltd Sti
Selanik Cad 25/1, 06650 Kizilay, Ankara
Tel: (0312) 419 8096; (0312) 419 8492
Fax: (0312) 418 4512
E-mail: info@nuanskitabevi.com
Web Site: www.nuanskitabevi.com
Type of Business: Distributor
Bookshop(s): Camlik Mah Selcuklu Cad Mini-
point Sitesi No 26/88, 34912 Kurtkoy, Istan-
bul *Tel:* (0216) 450 1708; 858 Sokak Paykoc
Ishani No 9, Kat 2, Daire 207, Konak, Izmir
Tel: (0232) 482 0971

Redhouse, see SEV Yayincilik Egitim Ticaret AS

SEV Yayincilik Egitim Ticaret AS (SEV
Publishing Education & Trade Inc)
Nuhkuyusu Cad, No 197 Uskudar Is Merkezi, Kat
3, 34664 Baglarbasi, Uskudar, Istanbul
Tel: (0216) 474 23 41; (0216) 474 23 42; (0216)
474 23 43; (0216) 474 23 44 *Fax:* (0216) 474
23 45
E-mail: info@redhouse.com.tr
Web Site: www.redhouse.com.tr
Key Personnel
Sales Manager: Ercan Arslan
Founded: 1997
Warehouse: Muratreis Mah, Selami Ali Efendi
Cad, Muratreis Sok, Kutlu Apt No 4/2, Baglar-
basi, Uskudar, Istanbul *Tel:* (0216) 495 08 45
Fax: (0216) 495 08 46

SEV-YAY, see SEV Yayincilik Egitim Ticaret AS

Uganda

Uganda Bookshop
Plot 4, Colville St, Ebenezer House, Kampala
Tel: (0414) 343756
E-mail: ugbookshop@utonline.co.ug
Web Site: ugandabookshop.co.ug
Founded: 1927
Also printer & publisher.

Type of Business: Distributor, Importer, Major Book Chain Headquarters, Wholesaler
Owned by: Church of Uganda

Ukraine

Family Leisure Club
Gagarina Ave 20-A, Kharkiv 61140
Mailing Address: PO Box 84, Kharkiv 61001
Tel: (057) 703 44 57 *Toll Free Tel:* 0800 30 10 90 *Fax:* (057) 784 00 91
E-mail: trade@bookclub.ua
Web Site: trade.bookclub.ua
Key Personnel
Commercial Dir: Timur Kurganov
Deputy Commercial Dir: Zholob Inna
Wholesale Dept Manager: Oksana Slyunin; Oleg Volobuev
Founded: 2009
Type of Business: Distributor, Online Bookseller, Wholesaler

United Arab Emirates

Al Mutanabbi Bookshop LLC
Opposite Burjuman Shopping Centre, 4 "A" St, 116601 Dubai
Mailing Address: PO Box 56320, 116601 Dubai
Tel: (04) 396 5778; (04) 396 6518; (04) 396 7435 *Fax:* (04) 396 6177
E-mail: albatra@eim.ae; ibrahim@mutanabbi.com
Web Site: www.albatra.com
Type of Business: Major Book Chain Headquarters

United Kingdom

Abrams & Chronicle Books Ltd
161 Farringdon Rd, 3rd floor, London EC1R 3AL
Tel: (020) 7713 2060 *Fax:* (020) 7713 2061
E-mail: info@abramsandchronicle.co.uk; publicity@abramsandchronicle.co.uk; internationalsales@abramsandchronicle.co.uk
Web Site: www.abramsandchronicle.co.uk
Key Personnel
Mng Dir: Brenda Marsh
Type of Business: Distributor, Exporter

ACC Book Distribution Ltd
Division of ACC Publishing Group
Sandy Lane, Old Martlesham, Woodbridge, Suffolk IP12 4SD
Tel: (01394) 389950 *Fax:* (01394) 389999
E-mail: sales@accpublishinggroup.com
Web Site: www.accpublishinggroup.com/uk
Key Personnel
Marketing Dir: Sarah Smye *Tel:* (01394) 389966
  E-mail: sarah.smye@accpublishinggroup.com
Type of Business: Distributor
U.S. *Office(s):* ACC Distribution Ltd, 6 W 18 St, Suite 4B, New York, NY 10011, United States
  Tel: 212-645-1111 *Fax:* 212-989-3205

Africa Book Centre Ltd
22 Lakeside, Oxford OX2 8JG

Tel: (01273) 560 474
E-mail: info@africabookcentre.com
Web Site: www.africabookcentre.com
Key Personnel
Publisher: George Toby Fell Milner
Founded: 1989
Supplier of books from & about Africa.
Also publishers' agent.
Membership(s): Booksellers' Association (UK).
Type of Business: Distributor, Exporter, Importer, Major Independent Bookseller, Wholesaler

African Books Collective
PO Box 721, Oxford OX1 9EN
Fax: (01865) 412341
E-mail: orders@africanbookscollective.com
Web Site: www.africanbookscollective.com
Key Personnel
Chief Executive Officer: Justin Cox
  E-mail: justin.cox@africanbookscollective.com
Dir: David Brooks; Mary Jay
Founded: 1989
Marketing & distribution of books published in Africa by 124 publishers from 21 countries. Scholarly, literature & children's, English language titles & Swahiti children's books.
Type of Business: Distributor
Owned by: African Publishers Collective

Afterhurst Ltd
5 Howick Pl, London SW1P 1WG
Key Personnel
Dir: Simon Robert Bane; Glyn William Fullelove; Rubert John Joseph Hopley; Gareth Richard Wright
Founded: 1982
Type of Business: Distributor
Owned by: Taylor & Francis Ltd

The Anglo American Book Co Ltd
Crown Bldgs, Bancyfelin, Carmarthenshire SA33 5ND
Tel: (01267) 211880 *Fax:* (01267) 211882; (0844) 500 7211
E-mail: books@anglo-american.co.uk
Web Site: www.anglo-american.co.uk
Key Personnel
Mng Dir: David Bowman
Founded: 1992
Mail order bookseller & distributor.
Type of Business: Distributor, Exporter, Importer, Major Independent Bookseller

Art Data
12 Bell Industrial Estate, 50 Cunnington St, London W4 5HB
Tel: (020) 8747 1061 *Fax:* (020) 8742 2319
E-mail: info@artdata.co.uk; orders@artdata.co.uk
Web Site: www.artdata.co.uk
Founded: 1978
Contemporary art books.
Type of Business: Distributor, Wholesaler

Askews & Holts Library Services Ltd
218-222 North Rd, Preston PR1 1SY
Tel: (01772) 555947
E-mail: enquiries@askewsandholts.com
Web Site: askewsandholts.com
Key Personnel
Mng Dir: Kathryn Pattinson *E-mail:* kathrynp@askewsandholts.com
Customer Care Dir: Jaqui Holborn
  E-mail: jaquih@askewsandholts.com
Sales Dir: Andy Holland *E-mail:* andyh@askewsandholts.com
Founded: 2011
Provides a wide range of solutions to public, academic & school libraries & other businesses throughout the UK & overseas, including shelf ready processing, supplier selection services, bibliographic content, multimedia material,

ebooks, promotional support & market leading web technology.
Type of Business: Exporter, Major Independent Bookseller, Wholesaler
Parent Company: The Little Group Ltd

Baha'i Books UK
c/o National Spiritual Assembly of Baha'is of the UK, 27 Rutland Gate, London SW7 1PD
E-mail: books@bahai.org.uk
Web Site: www.bahaibooks.org.uk
Registered charity & an agency of the National Spiritual Assembly of the Baha'is of the United Kingdom. Importer & distributor of books of interest to the Baha'i community, mainly in the UK but also to countries in Europe & elsewhere.
Type of Business: Distributor, Exporter, Importer, Online Bookseller

B McCall Barbour
28 George IV Bridge, Edinburgh EH1 1ES
Tel: (0131) 225 4816 *Fax:* (0131) 225 4816
Founded: 1900
Also Christian publisher.
Type of Business: Distributor, Exporter, Importer, Major Independent Bookseller, Wholesaler

Bay Foreign Language Books Ltd
Unit 4, Kingsmead, Park Farm, Folkestone, Kent CT19 5EU
Fax: (01233) 721272
E-mail: sales@baylanguagebooks.co.uk
Web Site: www.baylanguagebooks.co.uk
Key Personnel
Owner: Mr Jan Barker
Founded: 1990
Bookseller, book distributor & school supplier. Over 200 languages in catalogue.
Membership(s): Bookseller's Association.
Type of Business: Distributor, Exporter, Importer, Major Independent Bookseller, Wholesaler

George Bayntun
Manvers St, Bath BA1 1JW
Tel: (01225) 466000 *Fax:* (01225) 482122
E-mail: enquiries@georgebayntun.com
Web Site: www.georgebayntun.com
Key Personnel
Proprietor & Owner: Edward Bayntun Coward
Founded: 1894
Rare books, first editions & fine bindings.
Type of Business: Major Independent Bookseller

BEBC (Bournemouth English Book Centre)
Albion Close, Parkstone, Poole, Dorset BH12 3LL
Tel: (01202) 715555; (01202) 712933 *Fax:* (0333) 800 1901
E-mail: webenquiry@bebc.co.uk
Web Site: www.bebc.co.uk
Key Personnel
Head, Sales & Marketing: Nick Edwards
  E-mail: nick.edwards@bebc.co.uk
UK Sales Manager: Melanie Behringer
  E-mail: melanie.behringer@bebc.co.uk
Marketing Specialist: Kevin Arnold
  E-mail: kevin.arnold@bebc.co.uk
Founded: 1974
Provides order fulfillment service to publishers & book clubs.
Type of Business: Distributor

Bertram Books
One Broadland Business Park, Norwich NR7 0WF
Tel: (01603) 648333; (01603) 648400 (customer service) *Fax:* (01603) 648109 (customer service)
E-mail: books@bertrams.com; sales@bertrams.com
Web Site: www.bertrams.com

1455

Key Personnel
Executive Dir: Marc Dubery *Tel:* (01603) 648065
E-mail: marc.dubery@bertrams.com
Head, Commercial Development: David Pa-
gendam *Tel:* (01603) 648278 *E-mail:* david.
pagendam@bertrams.com
Trade Marketing Manager: Nina Bueno del
Carpio *Tel:* (01603) 648346 *E-mail:* nina.
buenodelcarpio@bertrams.com
Founded: 1968
Type of Business: Distributor, Exporter, Whole-
saler
Owned by: Aurelius Equity Opportunities

Bibliophile Ltd
31 Riverside, Trinity Buoy Wharf, London E14
0FP
Tel: (020) 7474 2474 *Fax:* (020) 7474 8589
E-mail: orders@bibliophilebooks.com;
customercare@bibliophilebooks.com
Web Site: www.bibliophilebooks.com
Key Personnel
Owner & Dir: Annie Quigley
Founded: 1978
Mail order bargain books.
Membership(s): Booksellers Association of Great
Britain.
Type of Business: Major Independent Bookseller

Blackwell UK Ltd
50 Broad St, Oxford, Oxon OX1 3BQ
Tel: (01865) 333536 (online sales)
E-mail: mail.ox@blackwell.co.uk; blackwell.
online@blackwell.co.uk
Web Site: blackwells.co.uk
Key Personnel
Chief Executive Officer: David Prescott
Digital Dir: Kieron Smith
Dir, Sales & Marketing: Dean Drew
Founded: 1879
Academic, professional & specialist booksellers.
Type of Business: Exporter, Major Book Chain
Headquarters, Online Bookseller
Owned by: The Blackwell Group
Bookshop(s): 48-51 Broad St, Oxford OX1
3BQ *Tel:* (01865) 792792 *E-mail:* oxford@
blackwell.co.uk; 27 Broad St, Oxford OX1 3BS
Tel: (01865) 333641 *E-mail:* art@blackwell.
co.uk; 48-51 Broad St, Oxford OX1 3BQ
Tel: (01865) 333555 *E-mail:* rarebooks@
blackwell.co.uk; Oxford Brookes University,
Headington, Oxford OX3 0BP *Tel:* (01865)
483063 *E-mail:* brookes@blackwell.co.uk;
Westgate Oxford, 258 Queen St, Oxford OX1
1PE *Tel:* (01865) 980380 *E-mail:* westgate@
blackwells.co.uk; Aberdeen University, 99
High St, Old Aberdeen, Aberdeen AB24
3EN *Tel:* (01224) 486102 *E-mail:* aberdeen@
blackwell.co.uk; Queen's University Students'
Union, 75-79 University Rd, Belfast BT7
1NF *Tel:* (028) 9024 9523 *E-mail:* queens.
belfast@blackwell.co.uk; University of Bradford, The Richmond Bldg, Bradford BD7
1DP *Tel:* (01274) 905149 *E-mail:* bradford@
blackwell.co.uk; Briston University, The Richmond Bldg, 105 Queens Rd, Bristol BS8 1LN
Tel: (01179) 734531 *E-mail:* bristol.union@
blackwell.co.uk; Heffers, 20 Trinity St, Cambridge CB2 1TY, Manager: David Robinson
Tel: (01223) 463200 *Fax:* (01223) 463212
E-mail: heffers@heffers.co.uk; University
of Kent at Canterbury, Locke Bldg, Canterbury, Kent CT2 7UG *Tel:* (01227) 451654
E-mail: kent@blackwell.co.uk; Cardiff University Union, Senghennydd Rd, Cardiff CF24
4AZ *Tel:* (029) 20340673 *E-mail:* cardiff@
blackwell.co.uk; University of Derby, Kedle-
ston Rd, Derby DE22 1GB *Tel:* (01332)
331719 *E-mail:* derby@blackwell.co.uk; The
Royal Bank of Scotland Group, Headquarters,
Gogarburn, Edinburgh EH12 1HQ *Tel:* (0131)
626 3015 *E-mail:* rbs@blackwell.co.uk; Heriot
Watt University, Hugh Nisbet Bldg, Riccar-
ton Campus, Edinburgh EH14 4AS *Tel:* (0131)
451 5287 *E-mail:* heriotwatt@blackwell.co.
uk; 53-62 South Bridge, Edinburgh EH1 1YS
Tel: (0131) 622 8222 *E-mail:* edinburgh@
blackwell.co.uk; University of Exeter, Great
Hall Foyer, Exeter EX4 4PY *Tel:* (01392)
433992 *E-mail:* exeter@blackwell.co.uk; The
Reception, Oastler Bldg, University of Huddersfield, Huddersfield; University of Keele, Keele
ST5 5BW *Tel:* (01782) 627001 *E-mail:* keele@
blackwell.co.uk; Lancaster University, Bail-
rigg, Lancaster LA1 4YW *Tel:* (01524)
32581 *E-mail:* lancaster@blackwell.co.uk;
21 Blenheim Terrace, Woodhouse Lane,
Leeds, W Yorks LS2 9HJ *Tel:* (0113) 243
2446 *E-mail:* leeds@blackwell.co.uk; Lincoln University, Library Bldg, Brayford Pool,
Lincoln LN6 7TS *Tel:* (01522) 886 096
E-mail: lincoln@blackwell.co.uk; Liverpool
University, Block 1, Unit 2/3 Crown Pl, Peach
St, Liverpool L3 5UH *Tel:* (0151) 7098146
E-mail: liverpool@blackwell.co.uk; 183 Euston Rd, London NW1 2BE *Tel:* (020) 7611
2160 *E-mail:* wellcome@blackwell.co.uk; 50
High Holborn, London WC1V 6EP *Tel:* (020)
7292 5100 *E-mail:* orders.london@blackwells.
co.uk; Nr Arthur Lewis Bldg, Bridgeford St,
Manchester M13 9PL *Tel:* (0161) 274 3331
E-mail: manchester@blackwell.co.uk; Manch-
ester MMU Business School, Oxford Rd,
Manchester M15 6BH *E-mail:* manchester@
blackwell.co.uk; 141 Percy St, Newcastle
upon Tyne NE1 7RS *Tel:* (0191) 232 6421
E-mail: newcastle@blackwell.co.uk; Nottingham Trent University, Chaucer Bldg,
Goldsmith St, Nottingham, Notts NG1 5LT
Tel: (0115) 941 7307 *E-mail:* trent@blackwell.
co.uk; Nottingham Trent University, Clifton
Campus, Clifton Lane, Clifton, Nottingham, Notts NG11 8NS *Tel:* (0115) 984 4474
E-mail: clifton@blackwell.co.uk; University
of Nottingham, Jubilee Campus, Wollaton Rd,
Nottingham, Notts NG8 1BB *Tel:* (0115) 846
6864 *E-mail:* nottingham.jubilee@blackwell.
co.uk; University of Nottingham, Portland
Bldg, University Park, Nottingham, Notts
NG7 2RD *Tel:* (0115) 922 2630; (0115) 922
6415 *E-mail:* nottingham@blackwell.co.
uk; Portsmouth University, Cambridge Rd,
Portsmouth, Hants PO1 2EF *Tel:* (023) 9283
2813 *E-mail:* portsmouth@blackwell.co.uk;
The University of Reading, Whiteknights,
Reading RG6 6UR *Tel:* (0118) 986 7938
E-mail: reading.ub@blackwell.co.uk; Stu-
dents' Union, St Mary's Pl, St Andrews, Fife
KY16 9UZ *Tel:* (01334) 476367 *E-mail:* st.
andrews@blackwell.co.uk; Sheffield Hallam
University, Atrium Bldg, Sheffield S1 1WB
E-mail: sheffield@blackwell.co.uk; Sheffield
University, Jessop West, One Upper Hanover
St, Sheffield S3 7RA *Tel:* (0114) 278 7211
E-mail: sheffield@blackwell.co.uk

Blackwell's, see Blackwell UK Ltd

Book Trade Services Ltd
Formerly Bookmart Ltd
3 Warners Mill, Silks Way, Braintree, Essex CM7
3GB
Key Personnel
Dir: Paul Leonard Anness; Joanna Lorenz
Founded: 1989
Publish & distribute promotional books.
Type of Business: Distributor, Major Independent
Bookseller

Bookmark Remainders Ltd
7 Manaton Dr, Launceston, Cornwall PL15 9EE
Tel: (01566) 774504
E-mail: info@book-bargains.co.uk
Web Site: www.book-bargains.co.uk

Key Personnel
Mng Dir: Andrew Rattray *E-mail:* andrew.
rattray@book-bargains.co.uk
Founded: 1954
Remainder specialists.
Type of Business: Remainder Dealer

Bookmart Ltd, see Book Trade Services Ltd

Bookpoint Ltd
130 Park Dr, Milton Park, Abingdon, Oxon OX14
4SE
Tel: (01235) 400 400; (01235) 400 580 (UK
trade); (01235) 400-555 (primary educa-
tion); (01235) 827 720 (secondary education);
(01235) 827 828 (export trade); (01235) 827
702 (mail order)
Web Site: bookpoint.wp.hachette.co.uk
Key Personnel
General Manager: Paul Gibbon
Head, Operations & Logistics: Richard Bertram
Head, Customer Services: Vicky May
Head, Credit Services: Jon Swan
Head, Finance: Louise Westwood
Client Development Manager: Ray Webb
Founded: 1973
Type of Business: Distributor
Owned by: Hachette UK

Bookworld Wholesale Ltd
Unit 10, Hodfar Rd, Sandy Lane Industrial Estate,
Stourport-on-Severn, Worcs DY13 9QB
Tel: (01299) 823330 *Fax:* (01299) 829970
E-mail: info@bookworldws.co.uk
Web Site: www.bookworldws.co.uk
Key Personnel
Dir: Justin Gainham
Founded: 1986
Specialize in transport, aviation, railway, military,
maritime & modelling books.
Type of Business: Distributor, Exporter, Importer,
Wholesaler

Booth-Clibborn Editions
Studio 83, 235 Earls Court Rd, London SW5 9FE
Tel: (020) 7565 0688 *Fax:* (020) 7244 1018
E-mail: info@booth-clibborn.com
Web Site: www.booth-clibborn.com
Key Personnel
President & Publisher: Edward Booth-Clibborn
Founded: 1974
Also publisher.
Type of Business: Distributor, Exporter, Importer,
Wholesaler
Parent Company: Internos Books Ltd

Bournemouth English Book Centre, see BEBC
(Bournemouth English Book Centre)

The Bridge Book Co Ltd
Winton House, Wintonlea, Monument Way West,
Woking, Surrey GU21 5EN
Tel: (01483) 720505
Founded: 1962
Type of Business: Distributor, Exporter, Importer,
Remainder Dealer

Bridge Bookshop Ltd
Shore Rd, Port Erin, Isle of Man IM9 6HL
Tel: (01624) 833376
E-mail: mail@bridge-bookshop.com
Web Site: www.bridge-bookshop.com
Founded: 1972
Type of Business: Exporter, Major Independent
Bookseller
Branch Office(s)
62 Parliament St, Ramsey, Isle of Man IM8 1AJ
Tel: (01624) 813374

Broomfield Books Ltd
36 De La Warr Rd, East Grinstead, West Sussex
RH19 3BP

Tel: (01342) 313 237
Key Personnel
Dir: Andrea Grant-Webb; Nic Webb
Founded: 2003
Publishing consultancy & sales agency for small
& medium publishers across all genres. The
sales agency covers London, Southeast & East
of England together with UK key accounts &
the export market. Also buy & sell publisher
overstocks.
Membership(s): IPG (Independent Publishers
Guild).
Type of Business: Distributor

Bushwood Books Ltd
6 Marksbury Ave, Kew Gardens, Surrey TW9 4JF
Tel: (020) 8392 8585 *Fax:* (020) 8392 9876
Key Personnel
Dir: Richard Hansen
Secretary: Christopher Szpak
Founded: 1985
Type of Business: Distributor

CBS, see Combined Book Services Ltd

Cengage Learning (EMEA) Ltd
Cheriton House, North Way, Walworth Business
Park, Andover, Hants SP10 5BE
Tel: (01264) 332424 *Fax:* (01264) 342763
E-mail: emea.enquiries@cengage.com; emea.
customerservices@cengage.com
Web Site: edu.cengage.co.uk; www.cengage.co.uk
Key Personnel
Key Accounts Manager: Lynne Saunder-
son *Tel:* (07768) 220185 *E-mail:* lynne.
saunderson@cengage.com
UK & Europe Sales Manager: Matthew Keown
Tel: (07768) 220186 *E-mail:* matthew.keown@
cengage.com
Founded: 1988
Owned by: Cengage Learning Inc

Central Books Ltd
One Heath Park Industrial Estate, Freshwater Rd,
Dagenham RM8 1RX
Tel: (020) 8525 8800 *Fax:* (020) 8599 2694
E-mail: contactus@centralbooks.com
Web Site: www.centralbooks.com
Founded: 1939
Type of Business: Distributor, Exporter, Importer,
Major Independent Bookseller

CLC International (UK)
Unit 5, Glendale Ave, Sandycroft Industrial Es-
tate, Sandycroft, Deeside CH5 2QP
Tel: (01244) 520000 *Toll Free Tel:* 0800 373755
(orders)
E-mail: retailoffice@clcbookshops.com; sales@
clcwholesale.com
Web Site: clc.org.uk; www.clcbookshops.com;
www.clcwholesale.com
Founded: 1941
Distributor of Evangelical literature.
Type of Business: Distributor, Importer, Major
Book Chain Headquarters, Wholesaler
Bookshop(s): Unit 14, The Academy, Belmont St,
Aberdeen AB10 1LB *Tel:* (01224) 641620; 7
Carrs Lane, Birmingham B4 7SX *Tel:* (0121)
6432991; 45 Abingdon St, Blackpool FY1
1DH *Tel:* (01253) 624160; 129 Deansgate,
Bolton BL1 1HA *Tel:* (01204) 532384; 88a
Regent St, Cambridge CB2 1DP *Tel:* (01223)
352727; 112 Nethergate, Dundee DD1 4EH
Tel: (01382) 226859; 23 Castle St, Inver-
ness IV2 3EP *Tel:* (01463) 238876; 16 St
Matthews St, Ipswich IP1 3EU *Tel:* (01473)
255346; 10 Bishop St, Leicester LE1 6AF
Tel: (0116) 2558481; 3-4 Ave Maria Lane
(off Ludgate Hill), London EC4M 7AQ
Tel: (020) 7248 2356; Higham Pl, Newcastle
NE1 8AF *Tel:* (0191) 2325301; 103/105 West

St, Sheffield S1 4EQ *Tel:* (0114) 2724663; 5
Lower Hillgate, Stockport SK1 1JQ *Tel:* (0161)
4801467; 23 The Broadway, Tolworth, Sur-
biton, Surrey, Tolworth KT6 7DJ *Tel:* (020)
8390 5400; 9 Quarry Hill Parade, Tonbridge
TN9 2HR *Tel:* (01732) 364897; 13 Upper
Wickham Lane, Welling DA16 3AA *Tel:* (020)
8301 4641

Combined Academic Publishers Ltd
Windsor House, Cornwall Rd, Harrogate, N Yorks
HG1 2PW
Tel: (01494) 526350
E-mail: enquiries@combinedacademic.co.uk
Web Site: www.combinedacademic.co.uk
Key Personnel
Marketing Dir: Julia Monk *E-mail:* juliamonk@
combinedacademic.co.uk
Sales Dir: David Pickering
E-mail: davidpickering@combinedacademic.
co.uk
Founded: 1997
Specialize in academic sales, marketing & distri-
bution covering Asia Pacific, Europe, Middle
East & Africa.
Type of Business: Distributor

Combined Book Services Ltd
Unit D, Paddock Wood Distribution Center, Pad-
dock Wood, Tonbridge, Kent TN12 6UU
Tel: (01892) 839819; (01892) 837171
Fax: (01892) 837272
E-mail: info@combook.co.uk; orders@combook.
co.uk
Web Site: www.combook.co.uk
Key Personnel
Joint Mng Dir: Keith Neale; Allan Smith
Founded: 1988
Mail order book distribution.
Type of Business: Distributor, Exporter, Importer,
Wholesaler

Compass DSA, see Compass Independent
Publishing Services Ltd

Compass Independent Publishing Services Ltd
Great West House, Great West Rd, Brentford
TW8 9DF
Tel: (020) 8326 5696
Web Site: www.compass-ips.london
Key Personnel
Chairman: Alan Leitch *Tel:* (07901) 916152 (cell)
E-mail: al@compass-academic.co.uk
Dir: Alan Jessop *E-mail:* alan@compass-ips.
london
Sales Dir: Lee Morgan *Tel:* (07901) 916158 (cell)
E-mail: lm@compass-academic.co.uk
Marketing Manager: Catherine Jessop
E-mail: jessopsforever@gmail.com
Operations Manager: Nuala O'Neill
E-mail: nuala@compass-ips.london
Founded: 1998
Act as independent sales & marketing agents on
behalf of client publishers.
Type of Business: Distributor

Cordee Ltd
Dodwells Bridge Industrial Estate, 11 Jacknell
Rd, Hinckley LE10 3BS
Tel: (01455) 611 185 *Fax:* (01455) 635 687
E-mail: sales@cordee.co.uk; info@cordee.co.uk
Web Site: www.cordee.co.uk
Key Personnel
Co-Owner & Dir: Chris Balic; Jim Wilson
Founded: 1973
Specialize in outdoor recreation & travel.
Type of Business: Distributor, Wholesaler

Cyngor Llyfrau Cymru Canolfan Dosbarthu,
see The Welsh Books Council

Dawson Books Ltd
Broadland Business Park, Cranley Rd, Norwich
NR7 0WF
Tel: (01603) 648137
E-mail: enquiries@dawsonbooks.co.uk;
marketing@dawsonbooks.co.uk
Web Site: dawsonbooks.co.uk
Key Personnel
Executive Dir: Jane Johnson *E-mail:* jane.
johnson@dawsonbooks.co.uk
Head, Digital & Marketing: Helen Stratford
E-mail: helen.stratford@dawsonbooks.co.uk
Head, Library Program Management: Heather
Sherman *E-mail:* heather.sherman@
dawsonbooks.co.uk
Head, Library Support: Louise Harvey
E-mail: louise.harvey@dawsonbooks.co.uk
Senior Technical Sales Manager: Sally Barber
Founded: 1809
Academic & professional library supplier.
Type of Business: Distributor, Exporter, Importer
Owned by: Aurelius Equity Opportunities

deep books Ltd
Goose Green Trading Estate, 47 E Dulwich Rd,
East Dulwich, London SE22 9BN
Tel: (020) 8693 0234 *Fax:* (020) 8693 1400
E-mail: sales@deep-books.co.uk
Web Site: www.deep-books.co.uk
Founded: 1992
UK supplier of MBS books. Subjects include al-
ternative health, art & design, children's health,
mysticism, occult, philosophy, psychology, reli-
gion, self-help & tarot cards/books.
Type of Business: Distributor

Sophie Dupre Autographs & Manuscripts
Horsebrook House, XV The Green, Calne, Wilts
SN11 8DQ
Tel: (01249) 821121
Web Site: sophiedupreautographs.com
Key Personnel
Contact: Sophie Dupre *Tel:* (07739) 589911 (cell)
E-mail: sophie@sophiedupreautographs.com
Founded: 1981
Autograph letters, signed photos, signed books,
photography in all fields especially royalty &
literature.
Membership(s): ABA (Antiquarian Booksellers
Association); ILAB (International League of
Antiquarian Booksellers); PADA (Professional
Autograph Dealers Association).
Type of Business: Major Independent Bookseller

Elstead Maps (UK) Ltd
Jesters, Wiltown, Curry Rivel, Somerset TA10
0JF
Tel: (01458) 251572
E-mail: sales@elstead.co.uk
Web Site: www.elstead.co.uk
Key Personnel
Proprietor: Stephen Colebrooke
Founded: 1981
Mail order retailers.
Type of Business: Major Independent Bookseller

ESB, see European Schoolbooks Ltd (ESB)

European Schoolbooks Ltd (ESB)
The Runnings, Cheltenham GL51 9PQ
Tel: (01242) 245252 *Fax:* (01242) 224137
E-mail: direct@esb.co.uk
Web Site: www.eurobooks.co.uk
Key Personnel
Mng Dir: Frank A Preiss
Founded: 1964
Specialists in major European languages other
than English.
Type of Business: Distributor, Importer, Online
Bookseller, Wholesaler
Parent Company: ESB Group

Bookshop(s): The European Bookshop & Young Europeans Bookstore, 5 Warwick St, London W1B 5LU *Tel:* (020) 7734 5259 *Fax:* (020) 7287 1720 *E-mail:* mrg@esb.co.uk; The Italian Bookshop, 123 Gloucester Rd, London SW7 4TE *Tel:* (020) 7240 1634 *Fax:* (020) 7370 3129 *E-mail:* italian@esb.co.uk

Eurospan Ltd
Gray's Inn House, 127 Clerkenwell Rd, London EC1R 5DB
Tel: (020) 3286 2420
E-mail: info@eurospangroup.com; info@eurospanbookstore.com
Web Site: www.eurospangroup.com; www.eurospanbookstore.com
Key Personnel
Executive Chairman: Michael Geelan
Dir, Operations: Kate Fraser *E-mail:* kate.fraser@eurospangroup.com
Sales Manager, UK & Republic of Ireland: Phil Prestianni *Tel:* (020) 7240 0856 *E-mail:* phil.prestianni@eurospangroup.com
Founded: 1969
Worldwide marketing, sales representation & distribution for academic & professional publishers.
Type of Business: Distributor, Major Independent Bookseller

Fanshaw Books Ltd
Old Station House, 7a Coppetts Rd, Muswell Hill, London N10 1NN
Tel: (020) 7281 9387 *Fax:* (020) 8883 8513
E-mail: info@fanshawbooks.co.uk
Web Site: www.fanshawbooks.co.uk
Key Personnel
Owner & Dir: Adam Bloom *E-mail:* adamb@fanshawbooks.co.uk
Sales Dir: Paul White *E-mail:* paulw@fanshawbooks.co.uk
Founded: 1969
Specialize in publishers' overstocks & remainders.
Type of Business: Remainder Dealer, Wholesaler

Foyles
107 Charing Cross Rd, London WC2H 0DT
Tel: (020) 7440 1557 *Fax:* (020) 7434 1574
E-mail: customerservices@foyles.co.uk; orders@foyles.co.uk; marketingteam@foyles.co.uk
Web Site: www.foyles.co.uk
Key Personnel
Chief Executive Officer: Paul Currie
Founded: 1903
Type of Business: Major Book Chain Headquarters, Online Bookseller
Bookshop(s): Unit 22, Lower Concourse, London Waterloo Station, London SE1 8SW *Tel:* (020) 3206 2680 *E-mail:* waterloo@foyles.co.uk; Southbank Centre, Riverside, London SE1 8XX *Tel:* (020) 7440 3212 *Fax:* (020) 7981 9739 *E-mail:* rfh@foyles.co.uk; 74-75 Lower Ground floor, The Arcade, Westfield Stratford City, London E20 1EH *Tel:* (020) 3206 2671 *E-mail:* stratford@foyles.co.uk; Unit 2A, Grand Central, Birmingham B2 4BF *Tel:* (020) 3206 2690 *E-mail:* birmingham@foyles.co.uk; SU21, Brigstowe St, Cabot Circus, Bristol BS1 3BH *Tel:* (020) 3206 2660 *E-mail:* cabotcircus@foyles.co.uk; 86 Bond St, Chelmsford, Essex CM1 1GH *Tel:* (020) 3206 2685 *E-mail:* chelmsford@foyles.co.uk

Gardners Books
One Whittle Dr, Eastbourne, East Sussex BN23 6QH
Tel: (01323) 521777 *Fax:* (01323) 521666
E-mail: sales@gardners.com; custcare@gardners.com; advertising@gardners.com
Web Site: www.gardners.com

Key Personnel
International Sales Manager: Christine Cawley *Tel:* (01323) 525664 *E-mail:* christine.cawley@gardners.com
Regional Sales Manager: Alison Blake *Tel:* (07787) 168220 (cell) *E-mail:* alison.blake@gardners.com; Ruth Gardner *Tel:* (07771) 708063 (cell) *Fax:* (01324) 831961 *E-mail:* ruth.gardner@gardners.com; Jim Youell *Tel:* (07768) 394829 (cell) *E-mail:* jim.youell@gardners.com
UK Field Sales Manager: Roy Jones *E-mail:* roy.jones@gardners.com
International book wholesalers.
Type of Business: Exporter, Wholesaler

Gazelle Book Services Ltd
White Cross Mills, High Town, Lancaster, Lancs LA1 4XS
Tel: (01524) 528500 *Fax:* (01524) 528510
E-mail: sales@gazellebooks.co.uk
Web Site: www.gazellebookservices.co.uk
Key Personnel
Dir: Marvin Blagden; Kevin Dixon; Paul Knight
Founded: 1988
Type of Business: Distributor

Gracewing Ltd
2 Southern Ave, Leominster, Herefordshire HR6 0QF
Tel: (01568) 616835 *Fax:* (01568) 613289
E-mail: gracewingx@aol.com
Web Site: www.gracewing.co.uk
Key Personnel
Mng Dir: Tom Longford
Founded: 1958
Also publisher.
Type of Business: Distributor

Grange Books Ltd
PO Box 700, Rochester, Kent ME1 9LX
Tel: (01634) 255502
Web Site: www.grangebooks.co.uk
Key Personnel
Consultant, Greenwich Book Co Ltd: Stephen Ash *E-mail:* stephen.ash@greenwichbooks.co.uk
Administrative Dir: Heather Staples *E-mail:* heather.staples@greenwichbooks.co.uk
Sales Coordinator: Gill Levick *E-mail:* gill.levick@greenwichbooks.co.uk
Founded: 1972
Specialize in illustrated adult nonfiction, children's, promotional, reprint & remainder books; publisher of promotional books & co-editions. Umbrella organization for Greenwich Book Co Ltd & Greenvale Books Ltd.
Type of Business: Distributor, Remainder Dealer, Wholesaler

Grant & Cutler at Foyles
107 Charing Cross Rd, London WC2H 0DT
Tel: (020) 7440 3248 *Fax:* (020) 7434 1574
E-mail: grantandcutler@foyles.co.uk
Web Site: www.grantandcutler.com
Founded: 1936
Specialize in bookselling & library supplies in Western European languages as well as Critical Guides to French, Spanish & German texts.
Type of Business: Major Independent Bookseller

Grantham Book Services Ltd
Trent Rd, Grantham, Lincs NG31 7XQ
Tel: (01476) 541000; (01206) 255678 (orders) *Fax:* (01476) 541060
E-mail: sales@tbs-ltd.co.uk
Web Site: www.thebookservice.co.uk
Key Personnel
Client Services Manager: Colleen McMorran
Founded: 1975
Contract distribution (publishing).

Type of Business: Distributor
Owned by: Penguin Random House UK

Haigh & Hochland Medical Book Shop
Horniman House, 399-401 Oxford Rd, Manchester M13 9BL
Tel: (0161) 273 6799
Founded: 1951
Type of Business: Distributor, Exporter, Importer, Major Independent Bookseller

Hatchards Ltd
187 Piccadilly, London W1J 9LE
Tel: (020) 7439 9921 *Fax:* (020) 7494 1313
E-mail: books@hatchards.co.uk
Web Site: www.hatchards.co.uk
Key Personnel
General Manager: Gavin Pilgrim
Founded: 1797
Type of Business: Major Independent Bookseller, Online Bookseller
Owned by: Waterstone's Booksellers Ltd
Bookshop(s): St Pancras International, London N1C 4QP *Tel:* (020) 7278 1238 *Fax:* (084) 3290 8154 *E-mail:* stpancras@hatchards.co.uk

The Hellenic Bookservice
89 Fortess Rd, London NW5 1AG
Tel: (020) 7267 9499 *Fax:* (020) 7267 9498
E-mail: enquiries@hellenicbookservice.com
Web Site: www.hellenicbookservice.com
Key Personnel
Owner: Stelios Jackson
Founded: 1966
Classics & modern Greek books.
Type of Business: Major Independent Bookseller

Thomas Heneage Art Books
42 Duke St, St James's, London SW1Y 6DJ
Tel: (020) 7930 9223
E-mail: artbooks@heneage.com
Web Site: www.heneage.com
Key Personnel
Proprietor: Thomas Heneage
Founded: 1977
Sells art books reference, catalogue raisonnes, monographs & exhibition catalogues.
Type of Business: Major Independent Bookseller
Parent Company: Thomas Heneage & Co Ltd

JS Group, see John Smith & Son Group Ltd

Kuperard Publishers & Distributors
59 Hutton Grove, London N12 8DS
Tel: (020) 8446 2440 *Fax:* (020) 8446 2441
E-mail: office@kuperard.co.uk
Web Site: www.kuperard.co.uk
Key Personnel
Owner: Joshua Kuperard
Permissions & Copyright: Jonathan Williams *E-mail:* jonathan@kuperard.co.uk
Sales & Marketing: Martin Kaye *E-mail:* martin@kuperard.co.uk; Linda Tenenbaum *E-mail:* linda@kuperard.co.uk
Founded: 1986
Publisher.
Type of Business: Distributor, Exporter, Importer

Lavis Marketing
73 Lime Walk, Headington, Oxford, Oxon OX3 7AD
Tel: (01865) 767575 *Fax:* (01865) 750079
Founded: 1982
Type of Business: Distributor

LBS Ltd, see Littlehampton Book Services Ltd

Lexicon Bookshop
63 Strand St, Douglas, Isle of Man IM1 2RL
Tel: (01624) 673004 *Fax:* (01624) 661959
E-mail: lexicon@manx.net
Web Site: www.lexiconbookshop.co.im

Key Personnel
Proprietor: D W Ashworth
Founded: 1936
Specialize in Manx books.
Membership(s): Booksellers Association.
Type of Business: Major Independent Bookseller, Online Bookseller

Littlehampton Book Services Ltd
Faraday Close, Durrington, Worthing, West Sussex BN13 3RB
Tel: (01903) 828500; (01903) 828501 (customer service) *Fax:* (01903) 828801 (orders)
E-mail: enquiries@lbsltd.co.uk; mailorders@lbsltd.co.uk
Web Site: lbsltd.wp.hachette.co.uk
Key Personnel
General Manager: Jo Westbrook
Head, Operations: Marc Travers
Head, Customer Service: Pauline Wilson
Founded: 1992
Type of Business: Distributor
Owned by: Hachette Livre UK

Chris Lloyd Sales & Marketing Services
50a Willis Way, Poole, Dorset BH15 3SY
Tel: (01202) 649930 *Fax:* (01202) 649950
E-mail: chrlloyd@globalnet.co.uk
Web Site: www.chrislloydsales.co.uk
Founded: 1987
Type of Business: Distributor, Importer

Lomond Books Ltd
13-14 Freskyn Pl, East Mains Industrial Estate, Broxburn, West Lothian EH52 5NF
Tel: (01506) 855955 *Fax:* (01506) 855965
E-mail: getintouch@lomondbooks.com; sales@lomondbooks.co.uk; orders@lomondbooks.co.uk
Web Site: www.lomondbooks.com
Key Personnel
Sales (Central Area): Duncan Baxter *Tel:* (07903) 889710 (cell) *E-mail:* duncanb@lomondbooks.co.uk
Sales (Eastern Area): Colin Valentine *Tel:* (07554) 887307 *E-mail:* colinv@lomondbooks.co.uk
Sales (Northern Area): Bryan Sutherland *Tel:* (07793) 213691 (cell) *E-mail:* bryans@lomondbooks.co.uk
Sales (Southern Area): Ali Begg *Tel:* (07976) 369154 (cell) *E-mail:* alib@lomondbooks.co.uk
Founded: 1984
Specialize in the publication & sale of Scottish interest books.
Type of Business: Distributor, Remainder Dealer, Wholesaler

Macmillan Distribution (MDL)
Brunel Rd, Houndmills, Basingstoke, Hants RG21 6XS
Tel: (01256) 329242
E-mail: mdlqueries@macmillan.co.uk
Web Site: www.macmillandistribution.co.uk
Fulfillment service to over 40 publishers. 340,000 sq ft warehouse facility.
Type of Business: Distributor, Exporter
Warehouse: Lye Industrial Estate, Units 5-8, Pontardulais SA4 8QD

Mallory International Ltd
Aylesbeare Common Business Park, Exmouth Rd, Aylesbeare, Devon EX5 2DG
Tel: (01395) 239199 *Fax:* (01395) 239168
E-mail: enquiries@malloryint.co.uk; info@malloryint.co.uk
Web Site: www.malloryint.co.uk
Key Personnel
Chairman & Chief Executive: Julian Hardinge *E-mail:* julian@malloryint.co.uk

Dir: Ulrike Hardinge *E-mail:* ulrike@malloryint.co.uk
Founded: 1984
International booksellers.
Type of Business: Distributor, Exporter, Importer, Major Independent Bookseller, Online Bookseller

Marston Book Services Ltd
Affiliate of PubEasy
160 Eastern Ave, Milton Park, Abingdon, Oxon OX14 4SB
Tel: (01235) 465500; (01235) 465579 (Christian orders) *Fax:* (01235) 465509 (general enquiries); (01235) 465555; (01235) 465518 (Christian orders)
E-mail: direct.enq@marston.co.uk (enquiries); direct.orders@marston.co.uk (direct sales dept); christian.orders@marston.co.uk (Christian orders); trade.orders@marston.co.uk (trade orders); trade.enq@marston.co.uk (trade enquiries); pubeasy.enquiry@marston.co.uk; returns@marston.co.uk (trade returns)
Web Site: www.marston.co.uk; pubeasy.books.marston.co.uk
Key Personnel
Chairman: John Holloran *Tel:* (01235) 465505 *E-mail:* john.holloran@marston.co.uk
Mng Dir: Ross Clayton *Tel:* (01235) 465506 *E-mail:* ross.clayton@marston.co.uk
Dir of Print & Mailing: Simon Clayton *Tel:* (01235) 465680 *E-mail:* simon.clayton@marston.co.uk
Client Development & Services Manager: Monica Harding *E-mail:* monica.harding@marston.co.uk
Customer Services Manager: Melanie Khosla *E-mail:* melanie.khosla@marston.co.uk
Operations Manager: Peter James *E-mail:* peter.james@marston.co.uk
Warehouse Manager: Tony Whymark *E-mail:* tony.whymark@marston.co.uk
Type of Business: Distributor

Melia Publishing Services Ltd
One St Peter's Rd, Maidenhead, Berks SL6 7QU
Tel: (01628) 633673 *Fax:* (01628) 635562
E-mail: melia@melia.co.uk
Web Site: www.melia.co.uk
Founded: 1992
Sales & distribution services to English language publishers, both British & American.
Type of Business: Distributor

Motilal (UK) Books of India
367 High St, London Colney, St Albans, Herts AL2 1EA
Tel: (01727) 761 677 *Fax:* (01727) 761 357
Web Site: www.motilalbooks.com
Key Personnel
Owner & Mng Dir: Ray McLennan *E-mail:* ray@motilalbooks.com
Founded: 1982
Import, export & distribution agency for all books published in India, by all publishers.
Type of Business: Distributor, Exporter, Importer

NBN International
10 Thornbury Rd, Plymouth, Devon PL6 7PP
Tel: (01752) 202301
E-mail: cservs@nbninternational.com
Web Site: distribution.nbni.co.uk
Key Personnel
Chairman: Oliver Gadsby
Mng Dir: David Taylor *E-mail:* david.taylor@ingramcontent.com
Head, Operations: Ian Wordsworth *E-mail:* iwordsworth@nbninternational.com
Client & Customer Services Manager: Juliette Teague *E-mail:* jteague@nbninternational.com

Digital Services & Information Technology Manager: David Eagle *E-mail:* deagle@nbninternational.com
Finance Manager: Tony Woodley *E-mail:* twoodley@nbninternational.com
Warehouse Manager: Neil Talliss *E-mail:* ntalliss@nbninternational.com
Founded: 1976
Type of Business: Distributor
Owned by: Ingram Publishers Services LLC

Northern Map Distributors
9 Orgreave Close, Sheffield, S Yorks S13 9NP
Tel: (0114) 288 9522 *Fax:* (0114) 269 1499
Founded: 1975
Map & guide wholesaler.
Type of Business: Wholesaler

Orca Book Services Ltd
Affiliate of PubEasy
Unit A3, Fleets Corner Industrial Estate, off Nuffield Rd, Fleetsbridge, Poole, Dorset BH17 0HL
Tel: (01235) 465500
E-mail: orders@orcabookservices.co.uk
Web Site: www.orcabookservices.co.uk
Key Personnel
Commercial Dir: Martyn Chapman *Tel:* (01235) 465634 *E-mail:* martyn.chapman@orcabookservices.co.uk
Operations Manager: Matthew Groves *Tel:* (01235) 465637 *E-mail:* matthew.groves@orcabookservices.co.uk
Publisher Accounts Manager: Mary Coyne *Tel:* (01235) 465643 *E-mail:* mary.coyne@orcabookservices.co.uk
Publisher Services Manager: Trish Clapp *Tel:* (01235) 465642 *E-mail:* trish.clapp@orcabookservices.co.uk
Founded: 1976 (incorporated in 1999)
Distribution services to over 50 UK & overseas general, academic & specialist publishers. Mainly general nonfiction books.
Type of Business: Distributor
Branch Office(s)
160 Eastern Ave, Milton Park, Abingdon, Oxon OX14 4SB *E-mail:* tradeorders@orcabookservices.co.uk (customer service)

Oxbow Books
The Old Music Hall, 106-108 Cowley Rd, Oxford, Oxon OX4 1JE
Tel: (01865) 241249 *Fax:* (01865) 794449
E-mail: orders@oxbowbooks.com; trade@oxbowbooks.com
Web Site: www.oxbowbooks.com
Founded: 1983
Type of Business: Distributor, Major Independent Bookseller
Owned by: Casemate | publishers

Parfitt Books & Toys
32 High St, Warminster, Wilts BA12 9AF
Tel: (01985) 214418
Type of Business: Distributor, Exporter, Importer, Major Independent Bookseller, Wholesaler

PGUK, see Publishers Group UK

Postscript Books
6 Battle Rd, Heathfield, Newton Abbot, Devon TQ12 6RY
Tel: (01626) 897100 (orders); (01626) 897123 (customer service) *Fax:* (01626) 897129
E-mail: help@psbooks.co.uk; enquiries@psbooks.co.uk
Web Site: www.psbooks.co.uk
Founded: 1987
Specialize in publishers' overstocks & backlist titles.
Type of Business: Remainder Dealer, Wholesaler

PR Books Ltd
Mealbank Industrial Estate, Kendal Cumbria LA8
9DL
Tel: (01539) 733332
Web Site: www.prbooks.co.uk
Type of Business: Remainder Dealer, Wholesaler

Publishers Group UK
63-66 Hatton Garden, London EC1N 8LE
Tel: (020) 7405 1105 *Fax:* (020) 7242 3725
E-mail: info@pguk.co.uk; orders@pguk.co.uk;
sales@pguk.co.uk; publicity@pguk.co.uk
Web Site: www.pguk.co.uk
Key Personnel
Owner: Medwyn Hughes
Founded: 1979
Type of Business: Distributor

Pumpkin Wholesale Ltd
Grove Farms, Milton Hill Rd, Abingdon, Oxon
OX14 4DP
Tel: (01235) 833 450 *Fax:* (01235) 833 490
E-mail: info@pumpkinwholesale.com
Web Site: www.pumpkinwholesale.com
Type of Business: Wholesaler

Ragged Bears Ltd
79 Acreman St, Sherborne, Dorset DT9 3PH
Tel: (01935) 816933
E-mail: books@ragged-bears.co.uk
Web Site: ragged-bears.com
Type of Business: Distributor, Online Bookseller

Richmond Publishing Co Ltd
The Cottage, Allerds Rd, Slough, Berks SL2 3TJ
Tel: (01753) 643104
E-mail: rpc@richmond.co.uk
Web Site: richmond.co.uk
Founded: 1970
Type of Business: Distributor, Exporter, Importer,
Major Independent Bookseller, Wholesaler

RICS Books
Parliament Sq, 12 Great George St, London
SW1P 3AD
Tel: (0870) 333 1600; (024) 7686 8555
Fax: (020) 7334 3811
E-mail: contactrics@rics.org; mailorder@rics.org
Web Site: www.rics.org
Key Personnel
Chief Executive Officer: Sean Tompkins
Executive Dir, Corporate Services & Chief Finan-
cial Officer: Violetta Parylo
Mng Dir, EMEA: Mark Walley
Founded: 1981
Also publisher.
Type of Business: Distributor, Major Independent
Bookseller

Roundhouse Group
18 Marine Gardens, Unit B, Brighton BN2 1AH
Tel: (01273) 603 717 *Fax:* (01273) 697 494
E-mail: sandy@roundhousegroup.co.uk
Web Site: www.roundhousegroup.co.uk
Key Personnel
Mng Dir: Alan Goodworth *E-mail:* alan@
roundhousegroup.co.uk
Dir, Sales & Marketing: Matt Goodworth
E-mail: matthew@roundhousegroup.co.uk
Founded: 1991
Representation & distribution of publisher's lists
in the UK & Europe.
Type of Business: Distributor, Exporter, Importer,
Wholesaler
Parent Company: Roundhouse Publishing Ltd

Royal Institution of Chartered Surveyors, see
RICS Books

Sandpiper Books Ltd, see Postscript Books

Shogun International Ltd
87 Gayford Rd, London W12 9BY
Tel: (020) 8749 2022 *Fax:* (020) 8740 1086
E-mail: info@shoguninternational.com
Web Site: www.shoguninternational.com
Key Personnel
Dir: Clifford James Nash
Founded: 1974
Manufacturer & supplier of martial arts equip-
ment, clothing & books (on martial arts only).
Type of Business: Distributor, Exporter, Importer,
Wholesaler

66 Books Ltd
66 Wood Lane End, Hemel Hempstead, Herts
HP2 4RF
Tel: (01442) 239 402
E-mail: lorna@66books.co.uk
Web Site: www.66books.co.uk
Founded: 2008
Specialize in clearance, remainders & reprints.
Type of Business: Remainder Dealer, Wholesaler

John Smith & Son Group Ltd
Ash House, Headlands Business Park, Salisbury
Rd, Ringwood, Hants BH24 3PB
Tel: (01425) 485910 *Fax:* (01273) 485920
E-mail: orders.js@johnsmith.co.uk
Web Site: www.johnsmith.co.uk
Key Personnel
Chairman: Peter Gray
Business Development Dir: Peter Lake
Founded: 1751
Type of Business: Major Book Chain Headquar-
ters
Bookshop(s): University Centre (R23), Univer-
sity of Birmingham, Edgbaston, Birming-
ham B15 2TT, Manager: Richard Dhillon
Tel: (0121) 471 2701 *E-mail:* birmingham@
johnsmith.co.uk; University of Sussex, The
Library, Falmer, Brighton BN1 9QL, Man-
ager: Christian Ritter *Tel:* (01273) 678333
E-mail: sussex@johnsmith.co.uk; Anglia
Ruskin University, The Helmore Bldg, East
Rd, Cambridge CB1 1PT, Retail Manager: Ter-
rie Rogers *Tel:* (01223) 315203 *Fax:* (01223)
315204 *E-mail:* arucambridge@johnsmith.co.
uk; Anglia Ruskin University, Unit 1 River-
mead Gate, Rectory Lane, Chelmsford, Essex CM1 1RF, Retail Manager: Lilian Fox
Tel: (01245) 356851 *Fax:* (01245) 358815
E-mail: aruchelmsford@johnsmith.co.uk; University of Chester, Parkgate Rd, Chester CH1
4BJ, Manager: Nikki Gosling *Tel:* (01244)
383689 *E-mail:* chester@johnsmith.co.uk;
University of West London, St Mary's Rd,
Ealing W5 5RF, Manager: Martin Marshall
Tel: (020) 8840 7394 *Fax:* (020) 8840 6453
E-mail: uwl@johnsmith.co.uk; Glasgow Caledonian University, 70 Cowcaddens Rd, Glasgow G4 0BA, Manager: Chris McLaughlin *Tel:* (0141) 332 8778 *Fax:* (0141) 332
5717 *E-mail:* caledonian@johnsmith.co.uk;
University of Glasgow, The Frazer Bldg,
65 Hillhead St, Glasgow G12 8QF, Manager: Linda Leggett *Tel:* (0141) 342 5986;
(0141) 334 8515 *Fax:* (0141) 334 4862
E-mail: glasgow@johnsmith.co.uk; University of Strathclyde, Curran Bldg, 100 Cathedral St, Glasgow G4 0RD, Manager: Ian Merry
Tel: (0141) 552 3377 *Fax:* (0141) 552 7454
E-mail: strathclyde@johnsmith.co.uk; Avery
Hill Campus, University of Greenwich, Mansion Site, Bexley Rd, Eltham, London SE9
2PQ, Regional Manager: Samantha Bailey
Tel: (020) 8331 7584 *Fax:* (020) 8331 7584
E-mail: averyhill@johnsmith.co.uk; Queen
Mary University of London, 329 Mile End
Rd, London E1 4NT, Manager: Jenni Mor-
ton *Tel:* (020) 8981 7942 *Fax:* (020) 8981
8165 *E-mail:* queenmary@johnsmith.co.uk;
University of East London, Docklands Cam-
pus, The Atrium, East Wing, 4-6 Univer-

sity Way, London E16 2RD *Tel:* (020) 8223
7193 *E-mail:* ueldocklands@johnsmith.co.
uk; University of East London, Stratford
Campus, Conference & Computer Centre,
Water Lane, Stratford, London E15 4LZ,
Manager: Gill Isbell *Tel:* (020) 8223 4602
E-mail: uelstratford@johnsmith.co.uk; University of Greenwich, Mews Bldg, College Way,
Old Royal Naval College, Greenwich, London
SE10 9NN, Retail Manager: David Kingston
Tel: (020) 8465 5740 *Fax:* (020) 8465 5741
E-mail: greenwich@johnsmith.co.uk; Univer-
sity of Bedfordshire, Unit 7/9 The Mall, Luton,
Beds LU1 2TD, Retail Manager: Simla Cow-
ley *Tel:* (01582) 457174 *E-mail:* bedfordshire@
johnsmith.co.uk; University of Southampton,
112 Burgess Rd, Southampton SO17 1TW, Re-
tail Manager: Hayley Bunn *Tel:* (023) 8058
6725 *E-mail:* southampton@johnsmith.co.
uk; University of Stirling, Andrew Miller
Bldg, Stirling FK9 4LF, Manager: John Gray
Tel: (01786) 473891 *Fax:* (01786) 447696
E-mail: stirling@johnsmith.co.uk

WH Smith PLC
Victoria House, 4th floor, 37-63 Southampton
Row, Bloomsbury Sq, London WC1B 4DA
Tel: (01793) 616161
E-mail: customer.relations@whsmith.co.uk; press.
office@whsmith.co.uk
Web Site: www.whsmith.co.uk; www.whsmithplc.
co.uk
Key Personnel
Chairman: Henry Staunton
Chief Executive Officer: Stephen Clarke
Chief Financial Officer & Chief Operating Offi-
cer: Robert Moorhead
Business Dir, Books: Frankie Adams
Founded: 1792
There are over 600 WH Smith High Street stores
& over 600 stores at airports, train stations,
hospitals & motorway services throughout the
UK.
Type of Business: Distributor, Major Independent
Bookseller

Snazal
Unit 5, Vulcan House Business Centre, Vulcan
Rd, Leicester, Leics LE5 3EF
Tel: (0116) 251 91 23
E-mail: pcsbooks@gmail.com; snazalwholesale@
gmail.com
Web Site: www.snazal.com
Founded: 2005
Type of Business: Distributor, Online Bookseller,
Wholesaler

The Speaking Tree
5 High St, Glastonbury, Somerset BA6 9DP
Tel: (01458) 831 800; (01458) 834 188 (ware-
house)
E-mail: office@speakingtree.co.uk
Web Site: www.speakingtree.co.uk
Specialize in mind, body, spirit & related titles.
Type of Business: Wholesaler

Star Books
Freetrade House, Unit 6, Lowther Rd, Stanmore
HA7 1EP
Tel: (020) 8900 2640 *Fax:* (020) 8933 0350
E-mail: sv@starbooksuk.com; info@starbooksuk.
com; order@foreignlanguagebooks.co.uk
Web Site: www.starbooksuk.com; www.
foreignlanguagebooks.co.uk
Supplier of foreign language material to UK &
overseas public libraries.
Type of Business: Distributor

The Stationery Office, see TSO (The Stationery
Office)

Thornton's Bookshop
The Old Barn, Walnut Court, Faringdon, Oxon
SN7 7JH
Tel: (01367) 240056 *Fax:* (01367) 241544
E-mail: thorntons@booknews.demon.co.uk
Web Site: www.thorntonsbooks.co.uk
Key Personnel
Partner: Willem A Meeuws
Founded: 1835
Also publisher.
Membership(s): ABA; BA; International League
of Antiquarian Booksellers (ILAB).
Type of Business: Distributor, Exporter, Importer,
Major Independent Bookseller

Transatlantic Publishers Group Ltd
97 Greenham Rd, London N10 1LN
Tel: (020) 8815 5994
E-mail: mark.chaloner@tpgltd.co.uk
Web Site: www.transatlanticpublishers.com
Founded: 2002
Provides marketing, sales representation & fulfill-
ment in Europe & the Middle East of Ameri-
can technical publications.
Type of Business: Distributor, Importer

John Trotter Books
80 East End Rd, London N3 2SY
Tel: (020) 8349 9484
E-mail: johntrotterbooks@googlemail.com
Founded: 1973
Specialize in academic Jewish & Middle East
books, rare, secondhand & new.
Type of Business: Online Bookseller

TSO (The Stationery Office)
St Crispins, Duke St, Norwich NR3 1PD
Tel: (0333) 202 5070; (01603) 622211; (0870)
600 5522 (orders)
E-mail: customer.services@tso.co.uk
Web Site: www.tso.co.uk; www.tsoshop.co.uk
Key Personnel
Chief Executive Officer: Marco Pierleoni
Head, Business Development: Richard South
Head, Government Services: Jeremy Hook
Founded: 1996
Publishes regulatory material for UK government
departments & a wide variety of public bod-
ies on subjects covering academic & general
interests. Also UK distributor for international
organizations including UN, UNESCO, FAO,
WHO, OECD, EU & IMF.
Type of Business: Distributor, Exporter
Parent Company: Williams Lea Group
Branch Office(s)
TSO Press, Mandela Way, London SE1 5SS
Tel: (020) 7394 4200
TSO Ireland, 19a Weavers Court, Weavers
Court Business Park, Linfield Rd, Belfast
BT12 5GH, Ireland *Fax:* (02890) 235401
E-mail: enquiries@tsoireland.co.uk

Turnaround Publisher Services Ltd
Unit 3, Olympia Trading Estate, Coburg Rd,
Wood Green, London N22 6TZ
Tel: (020) 8829 3000; (020) 8829 3002
Fax: (020) 8881 5088
E-mail: orders@turnaround-uk.com;
customercare@turnaround-uk.com
Web Site: www.turnaround-uk.com
Key Personnel
Mng Dir: Bill Godber
Finance Dir: Sue Gregg
Marketing Dir: Claire Thompson *Tel:* (020) 8829
3009 *E-mail:* claire.thompson@turnaround-uk.
com
Sales Dir: Ian West *Tel:* (020) 8829 3012
E-mail: ian.west@turnaround-uk.com
Field Sales Manager: Jim Crawley *Tel:* (07725)
203734 *E-mail:* jim.crawley@turnaround-uk.
com
Founded: 1984

Book distributor of a wide range of US, UK &
Irish based publishers to the UK & continental
Europe.
Membership(s): Booksellers Association (UK).
Type of Business: Distributor, Exporter, Importer,
Wholesaler
Warehouse: Hertford DC, John Tate Rd, Foxholes
Business Park, Hertford SG13 7DT

Turpin Distribution
Stratton Business Park, Pegasus Dr, Biggleswade,
Beds SG18 8TQ
Tel: (01767) 604800 *Fax:* (01767) 601640
E-mail: custserv@turpin-distribution.com
Web Site: www.turpin-distribution.com
Key Personnel
Mng Dir: Lorna Summers
Commercial Dir: Neil Castle
Dir, Operations & Human Resources: Julie
Barnes
Head, Information Technology: Alan Medd
Founded: 1968
International fulfilment & distribution company
providing services to the academic, scholarly &
professional publishing industry.
Membership(s): Book Industry Communication;
The Association of Learned & Professional So-
ciety Publishers; The Independent Publishers
Guild; The International Committee on ED for
Serials; The Society for Scholarly Publishing;
UK Serials Group (UKSG).
Type of Business: Distributor
U.S. Office(s): Turpin Distribution Inc, The
Bleachery, 143 West St, New Milford, CT
06776, United States, Vice President, Publisher
Relations: Robert Rooney *Tel:* 860-350-0041
Fax: 860-350-0039 *E-mail:* turpinna@turpin-
distribution.com

Unicorn Sales & Distribution US&D
Division of Unicorn Publishing Group LLP
101 Wardour St, London W1F 0UG
Tel: (07836) 633377
Web Site: www.unicornpress.org/page/sales-
distribution
Key Personnel
Chairman: Ian Strathcarron *E-mail:* ian@
unicornpress.org
Sales & Marketing Dir: Simon Perks *Tel:* (07775)
891738 *E-mail:* simon@unicornpress.org
Type of Business: Distributor

Vine House Distribution Ltd
The Old Mill House, Mill Lane, Uckfield, East
Sussex TN22 5AA
Tel: (01825) 767 396 *Fax:* (01825) 765 649
E-mail: sales@vinehouseuk.co.uk
Web Site: vinehouseuk.co.uk
Key Personnel
Mng Dir: Sarah Squibb *E-mail:* sarah@
vinehouseuk.co.uk
Client & Customer Services Manager: Pauline
Gosden *E-mail:* pauline@vinehouseuk.co.uk
Research & Marketing Manger: Tara Horwood
E-mail: tara@vinehouseuk.co.uk
Sales & Marketing Manager: Julie McCarron
E-mail: julie@vinehouseuk.co.uk
Founded: 1987
International book distributors, including repre-
sentation & marketing, warehousing, order pro-
cessing, cash collecting, publicity & promotion,
accounting, book trade mailings & mail order
fulfilment.
Membership(s): Independent Publishers Guild.
Type of Business: Distributor, Exporter, Importer

Waterstones Booksellers Ltd
203/206 Piccadilly, London W1J 9HD
Tel: (020) 8045 1001 *Toll Free Tel:* (0808) 118
8787
E-mail: support@waterstones.com
Web Site: www.waterstones.com

Key Personnel
Mng Dir: James Daunt
Founded: 1982
More than 300 bookstores in the UK, Repub-
lic of Ireland, Continental Europe (Brussels &
Amsterdam), Isle of Man, Jersey & the Isle of
Wight.
Type of Business: Major Book Chain Headquar-
ters

Waterstones Economists' Bookshop, see
Waterstones Booksellers Ltd

The Welsh Books Council (Cyngor Llyfrau
Cymru)
Castell Brychan, Aberystwyth, Ceredigion SY23
2JB
Tel: (01970) 624151 *Fax:* (01970) 625385
E-mail: castellbrychan@books.wales
Web Site: www.cllc.org.uk; www.wbc.org.uk
Key Personnel
Chief Executive: Helgard Krause
Head, Distribution Centre: Arwel Evans
E-mail: arwel.evans@books.wales
Head, Sales & Marketing: Helena O'Sullivan
E-mail: helena.osullivan@books.wales
Founded: 1963
Type of Business: Distributor, Wholesaler

Worldwide Book Services Ltd
Dollymans Farm, Doublegate Lane, Rawreth,
Wickford, Essex SS11 8UD
Tel: (01268) 574110 *Fax:* (01268) 574123
E-mail: info@worldwidebookservices.com
Web Site: www.worldwidebookservices.com
Key Personnel
Dir: Marvin Blagden
Mng Dir: Paul Knight *E-mail:* paul.knight@
worldwidebookservices.com
Dir, Accounts & General Enquiries: Simon Taylor
E-mail: simon.taylor@worldwidebookservices.
com
Dir, Sales, Promotions & Operations: David
Burnham *E-mail:* david.burnham@
worldwidebookservices.com
Founded: 2003
Type of Business: Distributor, Exporter, Importer

Roy Yates Books
Smallfields Cottage, Cox Green, Rudgwick, Hor-
sham, West Sussex RH12 3DE
Tel: (01403) 822 299
Key Personnel
Proprietor: Roy Yates *E-mail:* royyatesbooks@
btconnect.com
Founded: 1987
Type of Business: Distributor, Exporter, Importer,
Major Independent Bookseller, Wholesaler

Uruguay

Libreria America Latina
Av Dieciocho de Julio 2089, 11200 Montevideo
Tel: 24015127
E-mail: libreria@libreriaamericalatina.com
Web Site: libreriaamericalatina.com
Founded: 1962
Type of Business: Distributor, Importer, Major
Independent Bookseller, Wholesaler

Feria del Libro
Affiliate of Camara Uruguaya del Libro
Av 18 de Julio 1308, 11100 Montevideo
Tel: 29004248 *Fax:* 29002070
Web Site: www.feriadellibro.com.uy
Founded: 1933

Membership(s): Camara Uruguaya del Libro.
Type of Business: Distributor, Importer, Major
  Book Chain Headquarters, Wholesaler

Libreria Amalio M Fernandez SRL
25 de Mayo 589, 11000 Montevideo
Tel: 29151782
E-mail: amflibrosjuridicos@adinet.com.uy
Founded: 1951
Type of Business: Distributor, Exporter, Importer,
  Major Independent Bookseller, Wholesaler

Libreria Linardi y Risso
Juan Carlos Gomez 1435, 11000 Montevideo
Tel: 29157129
E-mail: info@linardiyrisso.com
Web Site: www.linardiyrisso.com
Key Personnel
Partner: Andres Linardi; Alvaro J Risso
Founded: 1944
Antiquarian bookseller; Latin American books.
Type of Business: Distributor, Exporter, Major
  Independent Bookseller

Mosca Hnos SA
Av 18 de Julio 1578 esquina Carlos Roxlo, 11100
  Montevideo
SAN: 004-2757
Tel: 24093141; 24011111 *Fax:* 24011111
E-mail: sac@mosca.com.uy
Web Site: www.mosca.com.uy
Founded: 1888
Type of Business: Importer, Major Independent
  Bookseller
Bookshop(s): Av Arocena 1576 esquina Gabriel
  Otero, Montevideo; Sarandi 500 esquina
  Treinta y Tres, Ciudad Vieja, Montevideo;
  Montevideo Shopping, Luis A De Herrera
  1380, Local 333, Montevideo; Nuevo Centro
  Shopping, Luis A Herrera esquina Bvar Arti-
  gas, Local 201, Montevideo; Portones Shop-
  ping, Av Italia 5775, Local 244, Montevideo;
  Punta Carretas Shopping, Ellauri 350, Local
  T1 N10, Montevideo; Tres Cruces Shopping,
  Bvar Artigas 1825, Local 2, Montevideo; Avda
  8 de Octubre 3813 esquina Miro, Montevideo;
  Costa Urbana Shopping, Av Giannattassio Km
  21, Local 282, Ciudad de la Costa, Canelones;
  Colonia Shopping, Avda Roosevelt 458, Lo-
  cales 19/20, Colonia; Las Piedras Shopping,
  Av Bicentenario 318, Local 111, Las Piedras;
  Punta Shopping, Av Roosevelt y Parada, Local
  381, Punta del Este

Palacio del Libro
25 De Mayo 577, 11000 Montevideo
Tel: (02) 9157543
Editorial graphic bindery workshop.
Type of Business: Distributor, Exporter, Importer,
  Major Independent Bookseller, Wholesaler

Retta Libros
Paysandu 1838, 11200 Montevideo
Tel: (02) 403 00 27
E-mail: contacto@rettalibros.com
Web Site: www.rettalibros.com
Founded: 1975
Type of Business: Distributor, Online Bookseller

Venezuela

OBE, see Organizacion de Bienestar Estudiantil
(OBE)

Organizacion de Bienestar Estudiantil (OBE)
Universidad Central de Venezuela Ciudad Univer-
  sitaria de Caracas, Los Chaguaramos Caracas,
  Caracas 1050
Web Site: www.ucv.ve
Key Personnel
Dir: Aurimer Meza *Tel:* (0212) 6054751
  E-mail: aurimerobe@gmail.com
Assistant Dir: Hellen Yerena *Tel:* (0212) 6054744
  E-mail: helleryere@hotmail.com
Founded: 1943
Distribution & sale of university textbooks.
Type of Business: Distributor

Librerias del Sur
Ave La Guairita, con Calle Hipica, Las Mercedes,
  Caracas 1060
Tel: (0212) 9926534; (0212) 9920546; (0212)
  9926619
This is the distribution side of the Instituto Au-
  tonomo Biblioteca Nacional y de Servicios
  de Bibliotecas, specializing in publications by
  Venezuelan official, cultural & university orga-
  nizations. There are 61 bookstores throughout
  Venezuela.
Type of Business: Distributor

Libreria Tecnica Vega
Plaza Las Tres Gracias, Edificio Odeon, Los Cha-
  gauramos, Caracas 1010
Tel: (0212) 6622848; (0212) 6622702
E-mail: tecnicavega@cantv.net
Type of Business: Major Independent Bookseller

Vietnam

Xunhasaba Corp
32, Hai Ba Trung, Hoan Kiem District, Hanoi
Tel: (04) 3936 1795; (04) 3826 2989 *Fax:* (04)
  3825 2860
E-mail: xunhasaba@hn.vnn.vn
Web Site: www.xunhasaba.com.vn
Type of Business: Distributor, Exporter, Importer

Zambia

Bookworld Ltd
Plot 10552, Light Industrial Area, off Lumumba
  Rd, 10101 Lusaka
Tel: (0211) 230 606 *Fax:* (0211) 230 614
E-mail: info@bookworldzambia.com
Web Site: www.bookworldzambia.com
Founded: 1991
Membership(s): Booksellers Association of Zam-
  bia (BAZA).

Type of Business: Major Book Chain Headquarters
Bookshop(s): Makeni Shopping Center, Kafue
  Rd, Lusaka *Tel:* (0211) 274 591 *Fax:* (0211)
  274 591; Shop No 22845, Crossroads Shop-
  ping Mall, Leopards Hill, Lusaka *Tel:* (0211)
  268 329 *Fax:* (0211) 268 359; Manda Hill
  Shopping Center, Lusaka *Tel:* (0211) 255
  470 *Fax:* (0211) 255 516; UNZA Campus,
  Great East Rd, Lusaka *Tel:* (0211) 293 376
  Fax: (0211) 294 690; Kulima Tower, Katunjila
  Rd, Lusaka *Tel:* (0211) 237 051 *Fax:* (0211)
  237 051; Nationalist Rd, Ridgeway, Lusaka
  Tel: (0211) 256 183 *Fax:* (0211) 256 183;
  Plot No 6022, Shop No 2, Kabengele Rd,
  Kitwe *Tel:* (0212) 228 575 *Fax:* (0212) 228
  575; Town Centre, Mazabuka *Tel:* (0213) 231
  093; Rekays Shopping Mall, Off President Ave,
  Ndola *Tel:* (0950) 464 719; Solwezi City Mall,
  Solwezi *Tel:* (0950) 597 950

Zambia Catholic Bookshop
Mission Press, Franciscan Centre, Chifubu Rd,
  Ndola
Mailing Address: PO Box 71581, Ndola
Tel: (021) 2680456 *Fax:* (021) 2680484
E-mail: info@missionpress.org; sales@
  missionpress.org
Web Site: www.missionpress.org
Type of Business: Distributor, Exporter, Importer,
  Wholesaler

Zimbabwe

Kingstons Ltd
Kingstons House, 4th floor, 34 Kwame Nkrumah
  Ave, Harare
Tel: (04) 750547; (04) 750548; (04) 750549
  Fax: (04) 775533; (04) 775535
Web Site: www.kingstons.co.zw
Type of Business: Wholesaler

Mambo Bookshop
Mutual House, Speke Ave, Harare
Mailing Address: PO Box UA320, Harare
Tel: (04) 705899
E-mail: mamboacc@gmail.com
Type of Business: Distributor, Exporter, Importer,
  Major Independent Bookseller, Wholesaler
Owned by: Mambo Press
Bookshop(s): 106 Main St, PO Box FM87, Fa-
  mona, Bulawayo *Tel:* (09) 61162; Seventh
  St, PO Box 779, Gweru *Tel:* (054) 22370; 56
  Hughes St, PO Box 1010, Masvingo *Tel:* (039)
  64566

Textbook Sales (Pvt) Ltd
Executive Chambers, George Silundika Ave,
  Harare
Mailing Address: PO Box 3799, Harare
Tel: (04) 75-8381 *Fax:* (04) 77-2486
Founded: 1956
Type of Business: Distributor, Importer, Major
  Book Chain Headquarters, Wholesaler

Book Trade Reference Books & Journals

Featuring publications for and about the book trade and book publishing industries, titles listed may be relative to one specific country or may be of international relevance. Titles are arranged alphabetically by the country where the publisher is located or the country to which the title relates.

ƒ indicates those publications of international scope.

The type of publication appears in parentheses after the title:

(B) - Book   (J) - Journal   (P) - Periodical

For library-related publications see **Library Reference Books & Journals**.

Albania

Bibliografia Kombetare e Librit qe botohet ne Republiken e Shqiperise (National Bibliography of Books Published in the Republic of Albania) (J)
Published by National Library of Albania
Sheshi Skenderbe, Tirana
Tel: (042) 223 843 *Fax:* (042) 223 843
E-mail: sekretaria@bksh.al
Web Site: www.bksh.al
First published 1959.
Quarterly.
ISSN: 1025-8876

Argentina

Boletin de la Academia Argentina de Letras (Bulletin of the Argentine Academy of Letters) (P)
Published by Academia Argentina de Letras (Argentine Academy of Letters)
Sanchez de Bustamante 2663, Boedo, C1425DVA Buenos Aires
Tel: (011) 4802-3814; (011) 4802-7509 (ext 5) *Fax:* (011) 4802-3814 (ext 9); (011) 4802-7509 (ext 9)
E-mail: publicaciones@aal.edu.ar; biblioteca@aal.edu.ar
Web Site: www.aal.edu.ar
Key Personnel
President: Jose Luis Moure *Tel:* (011) 4802-3814 ext 6 *E-mail:* presidencia@aal.edu.ar
Contains articles of literary analysis & notes about trips of the Academia Argentina de Letras & academicians to the Argentine provinces, speeches in the receipt of new academicians, speeches during public & private meetings of the academicians, speeches in honor of Spanish or Latin writers, public presentations in Argentina of books like those of the Real Academia Espanola, agreements about the language, record of the Argentine words, etc.
First published 1933.
ISSN: 0001-3757

Criterio (P)
Published by Fundacion Criterio
Tucuman 1438, PB 3, C1050AAD Buenos Aires
Tel: (011) 4371-6759 *Fax:* (011) 4371-6889
E-mail: comunicacion@revistacriterio.com.ar
Web Site: www.revistacriterio.com.ar
Key Personnel
Dir: Jose Maria Poirier
Text in Spanish.

First published 1928.
Monthly.
260 USD

Australia

ANZSI Newsletter (J)
Published by Australian & New Zealand Society of Indexers Inc (ANZSI)
PO Box 43, Lawson, NSW 2783
E-mail: info@anzsi.org
Web Site: www.anzsi.org
Key Personnel
Editor: Elisabeth Thomas *E-mail:* editor@anzsi.org
Also available in electronic format (ISSN: 1326-2718).
6 times/yr.
80 AUD (nonmembers)
ISSN: 1832-3855

APA Directory of Members (B)
Published by Australian Publishers Association (APA)
60/89 Jones St, Ultimo, NSW 2007
Tel: (02) 9281 9788 *Fax:* (02) 9281 1073
E-mail: office@publishers.asn.au
Web Site: www.publishers.asn.au
Key Personnel
Chief Executive Officer: Michael Gordon Smith
President: Lee Walker
Marketing & Operations Manager: Cat Smith *E-mail:* cat.smith@publishers.asn.au
Contains details, key personnel, local & overseas distributors, imprints, ISBN's, affiliates & agencies. Available in print, online or as an Excel spreadsheet.
First published 1948.
Annually.
193 pp, Print: 15 AUD members, 39.95 AUD nonmembers, 80 AUD overseas; Online: 15 AUD members, 39.95 AUD nonmembers; Excel spreadsheet: 1,000 AUD flat rate
ISBN(s): 978-0-980328929-2

The Australian Author (P)
Published by Australian Society of Authors
22-36 Mountain St, Suite C1.06, Ultimo, NSW 2007
Tel: (02) 9211 1004 *Fax:* (02) 9211 0125
E-mail: asa@asauthors.org
Web Site: www.asauthors.org
Writers share their thoughts on what inspires, concerns & sustains them. Also contains publishing industry gossip & keeps up with issues affecting authors.
Quarterly.

Individuals: 32.20 AUD (domestic), 50 AUD (foreign); Institutions: 47 AUD (domestic), 67 AUD (foreign)
ISSN: 0045-026X

Australian Book Review (J)
Published by Australian Book Review Inc
207 City Rd, Studio 2, Southbank, Victoria 3006
Tel: (03) 9699 8822 *Fax:* (03) 9699 8803
E-mail: abr@australianbookreview.com.au
Web Site: www.australianbookreview.com.au
Key Personnel
Editor: Peter Rose *E-mail:* editor@australianbookreview.com.au
Deputy Editor: Amy Baillieu
Publishes reviews, essays, commentary & creative writing. Also presents a range of prizes, programs & events. Journal is also available online.
First published 1961.
10 times/yr.
Individuals: 90 AUD (domestic), 145 AUD (Asia & New Zealand), 160 AUD (elsewhere); Institutions: 120 AUD (domestic), 175 AUD (Asia & New Zealand), 205 AUD (elsewhere)
ISSN: 0155-2864

Australian Literary Studies (P)
School of Literature, Languages & Linguistics, 14 Ellery Crescent, Acton, ACT 2601
Web Site: www.australianliterarystudies.com.au
Key Personnel
Editor: Dr Julieanne Lamond *E-mail:* editor@australianliterarystudies.com.au
Manager: Jayne Regan *E-mail:* manager@australianliterarystudies.com.au
Academic/scholarly publication. Publishes critical essays & reviews of significance to scholars & readers of Australian literature. Online only.
First published 1963.
24 AUD (individuals); 75 AUD (schools); 450 AUD (universities & other institutions)
ISSN: 0004-9697

Books+Publishing (P)
Published by Books and Publishing Pty Ltd
Level 1, 607 St Kilda Rd, Melbourne, Victoria 3004
Web Site: www.booksandpublishing.com.au
Key Personnel
Editor-in-Chief: Andrew Wrathall
Contains in-depth features, author interviews, opinion & pre-publication reviews of forthcoming Australian & New Zealand titles.
First published 1921.
Quarterly.
69 AUD or 93 AUD (international) print only; 175 AUD online only; 214.50 AUD or 230 AUD (international) print & online
ISSN: 1833-5403

Island (P)
Published by Island Magazine Inc
4 Grace St, Sandy Bay, Tas 7005
Mailing Address: PO Box 210, Sandy Bay, Tas 7006
Tel: (03) 6226 2325
E-mail: island.magazine@utas.edu.au
Web Site: www.islandmag.com
Key Personnel
Editor: Dale Campisi
Literary magazine.
First published 1979.
Quarterly.
144 pp, Individuals: 60 AUD (domestic), 85 AUD (foreign); Institutions: 90 AUD (domestic), 115 AUD (foreign)
ISSN: 1035-3127

The Journal of Language, Literature & Culture (JLLC) (P)
Published by Australasian Universities Language & Literature Association
School of Letter Arts & Media, University of Sydney, John Woolley Bldg, Sydney, NSW 2006
E-mail: subscriptions@aulla.com.au
Web Site: aulla.com.au/AUMLA.html
Key Personnel
Mng Editor: Emily Finlay
Editor: Peter Goodall
Journal of literary criticism, language & cultural studies; published in English with occasional articles in French & German.
Also available online (ISSN: 2051-2864).
First published 1951.
3 times/yr.
60 AUD individuals
ISSN: 2051-2856

Overland (P)
Published by O L Society Ltd
9 David St, Footscray, Victoria 3011
Mailing Address: PO Box 14428, Melbourne, Victoria 8001
Tel: (03) 9689 6910 *Fax:* (03) 9687 7614
E-mail: overland@vu.edu.au
Web Site: overland.org.au
Key Personnel
Editor: Jeff Sparrow
Literary/cultural magazine features fiction, poetry, reviews, comment, artwork & opinion pieces.
First published 1954.
Quarterly.
54 AUD (individuals); 70 AUD (institutions); 40 AUD (students); 96 AUD (foreign)
ISSN: 0030-7416

Quadrant (P)
Published by Quadrant Magazine Ltd
Suite 2/5 Rosebery Pl, Balmain, NSW 2041
Mailing Address: PO Box 82, Balmain, NSW 2041
Tel: (02) 9818 1155 *Fax:* (02) 8580 4664; (02) 9818 1422 (subscriptions)
Web Site: www.quadrant.org.au
Key Personnel
Editor-in-Chief: Keith Windschuttle
E-mail: keithwindschuttle@quadrant.org.au
Independent review of controversy, ideas, literature, poetry & the arts.
First published 1956.
10 times/yr.
84 AUD (domestic); 95 AUD (New Zealand); 120 AUD (Eastern Asia Pacific Islands); 150 AUD (rest of world)
ISSN: 0033-5002

Reading Time Online (J)
Published by The Children's Book Council of Australia
PO Box 216, Kallangur LPO, Qld 4503
E-mail: readingtimeonline@gmail.com

Web Site: cbca.org.au/reading-time; readingtime.com.au
Key Personnel
Features Editor: Trisha Buckley
Reviews Editor: Tina Cavanough
Reviews, interviews, reports, booklists, articles on topics of interest to the children's book world, guest blog posts & more. Online only.
Free

Southerly (P)
Published by English Association, Sydney Branch
English Dept, A-20, University of Sydney, Sydney, NSW 2006
Tel: (02) 9351 5398
E-mail: admin@southerlyjournal.com.au
Web Site: southerlyjournal.com.au
Key Personnel
Editor: David Brooks *E-mail:* david.brooks@sydney.edu.au; Elizabeth McMahon
Poetry Editor: Kate Lilley
Reviews Editor, Poetry: A J Carruthers; Amelia Dale
Reviews Editor, Prose: Liliana Zavaglia
Editorial Assistant: Tessa Lunney
New Australian fiction & poetry, articles & essays relating to Australian literature & reviews of new Australian books.
First published 1939.
3 times/yr.
Individuals: 75 AUD (domestic), 124 AUD (overseas), 45 AUD (digital); Institutions: 90 AUD (domestic), 132 AUD (overseas), 66 (digital)
ISSN: 0038-3732

Sydney Studies in English (B)
Published by University of Sydney, Dept of English
Dept of English Room N423, John Woolley Bldg, A20, University of Sydney, NSW 2006
Tel: (02) 9351 2349 *Fax:* (02) 9351 2434
Web Site: openjournals.library.sydney.edu.au/index.php/sse/index
Key Personnel
Editor: Dr David Kelly *Tel:* (02) 9351 2214
E-mail: david.kelly@arts.usyd.edu.au
Devoted to criticism & scholarship in English literature, drama & film.
Also available online (ISSN: 1835-8071).
First published 1975.
Annually.
25 AUD
ISSN: 0156-5419

Weekly Book Newsletter (WBN) (P)
Published by Thorpe-Bowker
Level 1, 607 St Kilda Rd, Melbourne, Victoria 3004
Mailing Address: PO Box 6509, Central Victoria 8008
Tel: (03) 8517 8333 *Fax:* (03) 8517 8399
E-mail: subscriptions@thorpe.com.au
Web Site: www.booksandpublishing.com.au
Key Personnel
Editor: Jackie Tang *Tel:* (03) 8517 8353
E-mail: jackie.tang@thorpe.com.au
Provides latest Australian book industry news.
First published 1972.
Weekly (49 times/yr).
214.50 AUD (subscription includes additional publications)
ISSN: 0812-7042

Westerly (P)
Published by The Westerly Centre
University of Western Australia, Westerly Centre M202, 35 Stirling Hwy, Crawley, WA 6009
Tel: (08) 6488 3403 *Fax:* (08) 6488 1030
E-mail: westerly@uwa.edu.au
Web Site: westerlymag.com.au
Key Personnel
Editor: Catherine Noske

Administrative Officer: Lucy Dougan
E-mail: lucy.dougan@uwa.edu.au
Also available online (ISSN: 2207-8959).
First published 1956.
2 times/yr (July & December), online issues (April & October).
300 pp, 50 AUD (domestic); 55 AUD (foreign); 40 AUD (students)
ISSN: 0043-324X

Austria

Anzeiger: Das Magazin fuer die oesterreichische Buchbranche (J)
Published by Hauptverband des Oesterreichischen Buchhandels (HVB) (Austrian Publishers' & Booksellers' Association)
Gruenangergasse 4, 1010 Vienna
Tel: (01) 512 15 35 *Fax:* (01) 512 84 82
E-mail: sekretariat@hvb.at
Web Site: www.buecher.at
Key Personnel
Editor: Bettina Fuehrer *Tel:* (01) 512 15 35 11
E-mail: fuehrer@hvb.at; Silke Rabus *Tel:* (01) 512 15 35 23 *E-mail:* rabus@hvb.at
Text in German.
First published 1866.
Monthly.
54 EUR/yr (members); 109 EUR/yr (nonmembers)
ISSN: 0003-6277

Autorensolidaritaet (Solidarity of Authors) (P)
Published by IG Autorinnen Autoren (Austrian Author's Association)
im Literaturhaus, Seidengasse 13, 1070 Vienna
Tel: (01) 526 20 44-13 *Fax:* (01) 526 20 44-55
E-mail: ig@literaturhaus.at
Web Site: www.literaturhaus.at
Key Personnel
President: Renate Welsh
Vice President: Anna Mitgutsch; Peter Turrini
Mng Dir: Gerhard Ruiss *Tel:* (01) 526 20 44-35
E-mail: gr@literaturhaus.at
Text in German.
Quarterly.
15 EUR (domestic); 21 EUR (foreign)

Journal of Austrian Studies (J)
Published by University of Nebraska Press/Austrian Studies Association
c/o University of Nebraska Press, 1111 Lincoln Mall, Lincoln, NE 68588-0630, United States
E-mail: journalofaustrianstudies@gmail.com
Web Site: journalofaustrianstudies.com
Key Personnel
Editor: Hillary Hope Herzog; Todd Herzog
Text & summaries in English & German. Focuses on Austrian studies across languages, disciplines & historical periods & with a broad definition of "Austria".
First published 2012.
Quarterly.
200 pp, Individuals: 40 USD (USA), 50 USD (Canada), 60 USD (elsewhere); Institutions: 70 USD (USA), 80 (Canada), 90 USD (elsewhere)
ISSN: 0026-7503

Die Literatur der oesterreichischen Kunst-, Kultur- und Autorenverlage (Austrian Publishing in Arts, Culture & Literature) (B)
Published by IG Autorinnen Autoren (Austrian Author's Association)
im Literaturhaus, Seidengasse 13, 1070 Vienna
Tel: (01) 526 20 44-13 *Fax:* (01) 526 20 44-55
E-mail: ig@literaturhaus.at
Web Site: www.literaturhaus.at

Key Personnel
Mng Dir: Gerhard Ruiss *Tel:* (01) 526 20 44-35
  E-mail: gr@literaturhaus.at
Annually.
3.60 EUR
ISBN(s): 978-3-900419-41-7

Literatur und Kritik (Literature & Criticism) (P)
Published by Otto Mueller Verlag
Ernest-Thun-Str 11, 5020 Salzburg
Tel: (0662) 881974-0 *Fax:* (0662) 872387
E-mail: info@omvs.at
Web Site: www.omvs.at
Key Personnel
Editor: Karl Markus Gauss
Reviews German language literature & literary
  criticism.
First published 1966.
5 times/yr.
112 pp, 39 EUR; 10 EUR/issue
ISSN: 0024-466X

Manuskripte: Zeitschrift fuer Literatur
  (Manuscripts) (P)
Published by Alfred Kolleritsch Manuskripte
Sackstr 17, 8010 Graz
Tel: (0316) 82 56 08 *Fax:* (0316) 82 56 05
E-mail: lz@manuskripte.at
Web Site: www.manuskripte.at
Key Personnel
Publisher & Editor: Alfred Kolleritsch
Publisher: Guenter Waldorf
Journal for literature, art & criticism.
First published 1960.
Quarterly.
27 EUR (domestic); 32 EUR (foreign)
ISSN: 0025-2638

Die Rampe (P)
Published by StifterHaus-Zentrum fuer Literatur
  und Sprache
Adalbert-Stifter-Platz 1, 4020 Linz
Tel: (0732) 77 20-112 94; (0732) 7720-112 98
  Fax: (0732) 77 20-117 80
E-mail: office@stifter-haus.at
Web Site: www.stifter-haus.at
First published 1975.
Quarterly.
24.80 EUR
ISSN: 1562-8272

§**SPRACHKUNST. Beitraege zur**
  Literaturwissenschaft (Art of Language,
  Contributions to the Study of Literature) (P)
Published by Verlag der Oesterreichischen
  Akademie der Wissenschaften (Austrian
  Academy of Sciences Press)
Postgasse 7/1/1, 1010 Vienna
Tel: (01) 51581-3324 *Fax:* (01) 51581-3322
E-mail: verlag@oeaw.ac.at
Web Site: www.oeaw.ac.at/sprachkunst
Key Personnel
Mng Editor: Christoph Leitgeb *E-mail:* christoph.
  leitgeb@oeaw.ac.at
Editor: Hans Hoeller; Michael Roessner
Publication of articles particularly on poetical
  works, on literary history & poetics, reviews in
  addition. Accepted languages for publication
  are German, English or French.
Also available online (ISSN: 1727-6993).
First published 1970.
2 times/yr.
200 pp, 29.90 EUR
ISSN: 0038-8483

Stueckeboersekatalog (J)
Published by IG Autorinnen Autoren (Austrian
  Author's Association)
im Literaturhaus, Seidengasse 13, 1070 Vienna
Tel: (01) 526 20 44-13 *Fax:* (01) 526 20 44-55
E-mail: ig@literaturhaus.at

Web Site: www.literaturhaus.at
Key Personnel
Mng Dir: Gerhard Ruiss *Tel:* (01) 526 20 44-35
  E-mail: gr@literaturhaus.at
Catalogue of unpublished & published Austrian
  dramatic works.
First published 2004.
148 pp, 3.60 EUR
ISBN(s): 978-3-900419-33-2

Wespennest: Zeitschrift fuer brauchbare Texte
  und Bilder (P)
Published by Verein Gruppe Wespennest
Rembrandtstr 31/4, 1020 Vienna
Tel: (01) 332 66 91 *Fax:* (01) 333 29 70
E-mail: office@wespennest.at
Web Site: www.wespennest.at
Key Personnel
Mng Dir: Andrea Zederbauer
Literary essayistic cultural magazine publishing
  texts by noted authors as well as interesting
  newcomers. Each number includes a focus on
  a literary, essayistic, art-theoretical or politi-
  cal topic. The 'portraits' compile articles about
  persons in the international cultural scene. In
  addition: literary reportage, polemics, inter-
  views & reviews.
First published 1969.
Semiannually.
112 pp, 12 EUR
ISSN: 1012-7313

Bangladesh

Bangladesh National Bibliography (J)
Published by National Archives & National Li-
  brary of Bangladesh
32, Justice S M Murshed Sarani, Agargaon, Sher-
  e-Bangla Nagar, Dhaka 1207
Tel: (02) 9129992 *Fax:* (02) 9135709
Web Site: www.nanl.gov.bd
Key Personnel
Dir: Mozibor Rahman Al-Mamun
  E-mail: nanldirector@gmail.com
Deputy Dir, Archives: Tahmina Akter
  E-mail: tani.nlb@gmail.com
Deputy Dir, Library: Shahab Uddin Khan
  E-mail: ddnlbd@gmail.com
Librarian: Gulam Mustofa
Text in Bengali & English.
First published 1974.
Annually.

Belarus

Neman (P)
Published by Ministerstvo Informatsii Respubliki
  Belarus (Ministry of Information of the Repub-
  lic of Belarus)
ul Zakharova, 19, 220034 Minsk
E-mail: neman-lim@mail.ru
Web Site: www.neman.lim.by
Key Personnel
Chief Editor: Aleksey Ivanovich Cherota
Literary works, literary criticism & social fiction.
  Text in Russian.
First published 1952.
Monthly.
ISSN: 0130-7517

Belgium

Belgische Bibliografie (J)
Published by Koninklijke Bibliotheek van Belgie
  (Royal Library of Belgium)
Keizerslaan 4, 4 Blvd de l'Empereur, 1000 Brus-
  sels
Tel: (02) 519 53 11
E-mail: belbib@kbr.be; info@kbr.be
Web Site: www.kbr.be
Key Personnel
Interim Dir: Sara Lammens
Published electronically.
Monthly.

De Gulden Passer (The Golden Compass) (P)
Published by Vereniging Van Antwerpse Bib-
  liofielen (Association of Antwerp Bibliophiles)
c/o Museum Plantin-Moretus, Vrijdagmarkt 22,
  2000 Antwerp
Tel: (03) 221 14 67 *Fax:* (03) 221 14 71
Web Site: www.boekgeschiedenis.be
Key Personnel
Publication Chairperson: Maartje De Wilde
Secretary: Pierre Meulepas *E-mail:* pierre.
  meulepas@stad.antwerpen.be
Text in Dutch, English, French & German.
First published 1878.
2 times/yr.
40 EUR (membership)
ISSN: 0777-5067

Le Livre et l'Estampe (The Book & The Print)
  (P)
Published by Societe Royale des Bibliophiles et
  Iconophiles de Belgique
4, blvd de l'Empereur, 1000 Brussels
E-mail: info@bibliobel.be
Web Site: www.bibliobel.be
Key Personnel
President: M Jan De Graeve
Text in French.
First published 1954.
2 times/yr.
50 EUR
ISSN: 0024-533X

La Revue generale (General Review) (P)
Published by Revue Generale (General Review)
Chaussee de Louvain, 41, 1320 Hamme-Mille
Tel: (010) 86 66 29 *Fax:* (010) 86 66 91
E-mail: la.revue.generale@live.be; revue.
  generale@skynet.be
Web Site: www.revuegenerale.be
Key Personnel
President: Francis Delperee
Dir: Vincent Dujardin
Editor-in-Chief: France Bastia
Publication includes general information on Bel-
  gian politics, economics, literature, etc.
First published 1865.
6 times/yr.
96 pp, Individuals: 99 EUR (Belgium), 109 EUR
  (European Union), 128 EUR (elsewhere); Insti-
  tutions: 119 EUR (Belgium), 130 EUR (Euro-
  pean Union), 139 EUR (elsewhere); Students:
  74 EUR (Belgium)
ISSN: 0770-8602

Streven (P)
Prinsstr 15, 2000 Antwerp
Tel: (03) 201 60 94
E-mail: streventijdschrift@gmail.com
Web Site: www.streventijdschrift.be
Key Personnel
Editor-in-Chief: Herman Simissen
Magazine on culture & society.
First published 1933.
Monthly (except Aug).
96 pp, 66 EUR (Belgium); 69 EUR (Netherlands)
ISSN: 0039-2324

Bolivia

Bibliografia Boliviana (Bolivian Bibliography)
(P)
Published by Archivo y Biblioteca Nacionales de
Bolivia
Calle Dalence N° 4, Casilla Postal 793, Sucre
Tel: (04) 6451481; (04) 6452246 *Fax:* (04)
6461208
E-mail: abnb@entelnet.bo
Web Site: www.archivoybibliotecanacionales.org.
bo
Key Personnel
Dir: Ana Maria Lema Garret
Text in Spanish.
First published 1962.
Annually.
ISSN: 1814-9464

Bosnia and Herzegovina

Novi Izraz (P)
Published by PEN Centar Bosne i Hercegovine
Vrazova 1, 71000 Sarajevo
Tel: (033) 200 155 *Fax:* (033) 217 854
E-mail: pencentar@bih.net.ba
Web Site: www.penbih.ba
Key Personnel
Head Editor: Hanifa Kapidzic-Ozmanagic
Journal of literary & artistic criticism. Text in
Serbo-Croatian.
First published 1957.
Quarterly.
ISSN: 1512-5335

Brazil

Veritas (P)
Published by Editora da Universitaria PUCRS
Av Ipiranga, 6681, Predio 5 sala 407.16, 90619-
900 Porto Alegre-RS
Mailing Address: CP 1429, 90619-900 Porto
Alegre-RS
Tel: (051) 3320 3711
E-mail: veritas@pucrs.br
Web Site: revistaseletronicas.pucrs.br/ojs/index.
php/veritas
Key Personnel
Editor: Nythamar de Oliveira *Tel:* (051) 3320
3555 *Fax:* (051) 3320 3602
Education, Human Sciences, Philosophy. Text in
Portuguese.
Also available online (ISSN: 1984-6746).
First published 1955.
Quarterly.
ISSN: 0042-3955

Bulgaria

Literaturna Misal (Literary Thought) (P)
Published by Bulgarian Academy of Sciences, Institute of Literature (Bulgarska Akademiya na
Naukite, Institut za Literatura)
52, Blvd Shipchenski Prohod, Bldg 17, 7th & 8th
floors, 1113 Sofia
Tel: (02) 9717056 *Fax:* (02) 9717056

E-mail: literaturnamisal@gmail.com; naretov@
yahoo.com
Web Site: www.ilit.bas.bg (Institute of Literature)
Key Personnel
Dir: Elka Traykova, PhD *E-mail:* director@ilit.
bas.bg
Editor-in-Chief: Dr Radosvet Kolarov
Text in Bulgarian. Contents page in English &
French.
First published 1957.
2 times/yr.
ISSN: 0324-0495

Chile

Bibliografia chilena (Chilean Bibliographies) (J)
Published by Biblioteca Nacional de Chile
Av Libertador Bernardo O'Higgins 651, Santiago
Tel: (02) 3605272
E-mail: oirs@dibam.cl
Web Site: www.dibam.cl
Key Personnel
Dir: Angel Cabeza Monteira *E-mail:* direccion@
dibam.cl
Online resource allowing access to Chile's biblio-
graphic production since 1900.

Mapocho (P)
Published by Biblioteca Nacional de Chile
Av Libertador Bernardo O'Higgins 651, Santiago
Tel: (02) 3605272
E-mail: oirs@dibam.cl
Web Site: www.dibam.cl
Key Personnel
Dir: Angel Cabeza Monteira *E-mail:* direccion@
dibam.cl
First published 1963.
Irregularly.
ISSN: 0716-2510

Revista Chilena de Literatura (Chilean Review
of Literature) (P)
Published by Universidad de Chile, Facultad de
Filosofia y Humanidades, Departamento de Lit-
eratura
Ignacio Carrera Pinto 1025, Nunoa, Santiago
Tel: (02) 9787022 *Fax:* (02) 9787184
E-mail: rchilite@gmail.com
Web Site: www.revistaliteratura.uchile.cl
Key Personnel
Dir, Services & Information: Christian Calabrano
Torres *Tel:* (02) 9782334 *E-mail:* ccalabrano@
uchile.cl
Editorial Secretary: Bernarda Urrejola
Literary magazine.
Also available electronically (ISSN: 0718-2295).
First published 1970.
2 times/yr.
32,000 CLP (domestic); 90 USD (foreign)
ISSN: 0048-7651

China

China Today (P)
Published by China International Publishing
Group
24 Baiwanzhuang St, Beijing 100037
Tel: (010) 68996376; (010) 68998311 (distribu-
tion); (010) 68996362 (advertising) *Fax:* (010)
68328338
E-mail: chinatodaynews@yahoo.com.cn
Web Site: www.chinatoday.com.cn
Published in English, Spanish, French, Arabic &
Chinese, with digital versions in Chinese, En-

glish, French, German, Spanish & Arabic on
the Internet.
First published 1952.
Monthly.

Colombia

**Directorio de Editoriales, Distribuidoras y
Librerias de America Latina (DEDL)** (B)
Published by Centro Regional para el Fomento
del Libro en America Latina y el Caribe (CER-
LALC) (Regional Center for the Promotion of
Books in Latin America & the Caribbean)
Calle 70 No 9-52, Bogota
Tel: (01) 540 20 71 *Fax:* (01) 541 63 98
E-mail: libro@cerlalc.org
Web Site: cerlalc.org/es; www.cerlalc.org/dedl2/
index.php
Key Personnel
Dir: Marianne Ponsford *E-mail:* mponsford@
cerlalc.org
Dir, Publications: Jose Diego Gonzalez
E-mail: jgonzalez@cerlalc.org
Online database.

Costa Rica

Bibliografia Nacional Costarricense (J)
Published by Biblioteca Nacional Miguel Obre-
gon Lizano (Costa Rican Bibliography)
Calles 15 y 17 Ave, 3 y 3B, San Jose
Tel: 2223-1303 *Fax:* 2223-5510
E-mail: dibinacr@racsa.co.cr
Text in Spanish.
First published 1956.
Irregularly.
ISSN: 2215-423X

Croatia

Forum (J)
Published by Hrvatska Akademija Zhanosti i Um-
jetnosti, Razred Za Suvremenu knjizevnost
(Croatian Academy of Sciences & Arts)
Zrinski trg 11, 10000 Zagreb
Tel: (01) 48 95 111 *Fax:* (01) 48 19 979
E-mail: kabpred@hazu.hr; forum@hazu.hr
Web Site: www.hazu.hr
Key Personnel
Editor-in-Chief: Kresimir Nemec
Journal of the Section for Contemporary Litera-
ture of the Croatian Academy of Sciences &
Arts. Text in Croatian.
First published 1962.
Quarterly (triple issue).
ISSN: 0015-8446

Cuba

Union (P)
Published by Ediciones Union, Union Nacional
de Escritores y Artistas de Cuba
Calle 17 No 351 e/GyH, Plaza, Plaza de la Rev-
olucion, CP 10400 Havana
Tel: (07) 8324551; (07) 8324571
E-mail: union@uneac.co.cu
Web Site: www.uneac.org.cu

First published 1962.
96 pp, 21 USD (North America & Latin America); 25 USD (Europe); 31 USD (rest of world)

Czech Republic

∮Casopis Narodniho muzea Rada historicka
(Journal of the National Museum Series:
History) (P)
Published by Narodni Muzeum (National Museum)
Vaclavske nam 68, 115 79 Prague 1
Tel: 224 497 111; 224 497 159 (publications)
 Fax: 224 226 488
E-mail: nm@nm.cz; publikace@nm.cz
Web Site: www.nm.cz
Key Personnel
Editor: Klara Woitschova
Summaries in English, French & German.
First published 1827.
2 times/yr.
160 pp, 333 CZK
ISSN: 1214-0627

∮Muzeum: Muzejni a Vlastivedna Prace (P)
Published by Narodni Muzeum (National Museum)
Vaclavske nam 68, 115 79 Prague 1
Tel: 224 497 111; 224 497 159 (publications)
 Fax: 224 226 488
E-mail: nm@nm.cz; publikace@nm.cz
Web Site: www.nm.cz
Key Personnel
Editor-in-Chief: Pavel Dousa
 E-mail: pavel_dousa@nm.cz
Summaries in English.
First published 1963.
2 times/yr.
64 pp, 333 CZK
ISSN: 1803-0386

Numismaticke listy (Numismatics Journal) (P)
Published by Narodni Muzeum (National Museum)
Vaclavske nam 68, 115 79 Prague 1
Tel: 224 497 111; 224 497 159 (publications)
 Fax: 224 226 488
E-mail: nm@nm.cz; publikace@nm.cz
Web Site: www.nm.cz
Key Personnel
Editor-in-Chief: Lubos Polansky
 E-mail: lubos_polansky@nm.cz
Summaries in English, French, German & Russian.
First published 1945.
6 times/yr.
434 CZK
ISSN: 0029-6074

**∮Sbornik Narodniho muzea v Praze, Rada A:
 Historie** (Collection of the National Museum
of Prague, Series A: History) (P)
Published by Narodni Muzeum (National Museum)
Vaclavske nam 68, 115 79 Prague 1
Tel: 224 497 111; 224 497 159 (publications)
 Fax: 224 226 488
E-mail: nm@nm.cz; publikace@nm.cz
Web Site: www.nm.cz
Key Personnel
Editor-in-Chief: Lubomir Srsen
 E-mail: lubomir_srsen@nm.cz
Summaries in English, French, German & Russian.
2 times/yr.
112 pp, 333 CZK
ISSN: 0036-5335

**∮Sbornik Narodniho muzea v Praze, Rada B:
 Prirodni vedy** (P)
Published by Narodni Muzeum (National Museum)
Vaclavske nam 68, 115 79 Prague 1
Tel: 224 497 111; 224 497 159 (publications)
 Fax: 224 226 488
E-mail: nm@nm.cz; publikace@nm.cz
Web Site: www.nm.cz
Key Personnel
Editor: Dr Jiri Kvacek *E-mail:* jiri.kvacek@nm.cz
Also available online (ISSN: 1804-6479).
Quarterly.
140 pp, 333 CZK
ISSN: 0036-5343

**∮Sbornik Narodniho muzea v Praze, Rada C:
 Literarni historie** (Collection of the National
Museum of Prague, Series C: Literary History)
(P)
Published by Narodni Muzeum (National Museum)
Vaclavske nam 68, 115 79 Prague 1
Tel: 224 497 111; 224 497 159 (publications)
 Fax: 224 226 488
E-mail: nm@nm.cz; publikace@nm.cz
Web Site: www.nm.cz
Key Personnel
Editor-in-Chief: Katerina Spurna
 E-mail: katerina_spurna@nm.cz
Original scientific works from the fields of literary history & historical bibliography. Summaries in English & German.
Also available online (ISSN: 2533-5677).
First published 1956.
2 times/yr (double issue No 1-2 & 3-4).
50 pp, 252 CZK
ISSN: 0036-5351

Denmark

Born og Boger (Children & Books) (P)
Published by Kommunernes Forening for Paedagogiske Laeringscentre (KFPLC)
Farvergade 27 D, 2 sal, 1463 Copenhagen K
Tel: 33 11 13 91
E-mail: kfplc@kfplc.dk
Web Site: www.kfplc.dk
English Summary. Periodical concerning books
& other cultural values for children & young
adults.
8 times/yr.
693.50 DKK

Danish Literary Magazine (P)
Published by The Danish Arts Council
H C Andersens Blvd 2, 1553 Copenhagen V
Tel: 3374 5065 *Fax:* 3374 4545
E-mail: literature@danish-arts.dk
Web Site: www.danishliterarymagazine.dk
Key Personnel
Editor-in-Chief & Dir: Annette Bach *Tel:* 3374
 5074 *E-mail:* annbac@kunst.dk
Editor: Soren Beltoft *Tel:* 3374 5073
 E-mail: sorbel@kunst.dk
Excerpts from new Danish books, in addition to
news about Danish books being published in
other countries. Online only.
2 times/yr.
40 pp

Dansk Bogfortegnelse (Danish National
Bibliography, Books) (P)
Published by Danish Bibliographic Centre
Tempovej 7-11, 2750 Ballerup
Tel: 44 86 77 77
E-mail: dbc@dbc.dk
Web Site: www.dbc.dk

Key Personnel
Chief Executive Officer: Heddi Mortensen
Online database.

Hvedekorn (P)
Published by Rosinante & Co
Kobmagergade 62, 1150 Copenhagen K
Mailing Address: Postboks 2252, 1919 Copenhagen K
Tel: 3341 1800 *Fax:* 3341 1801
E-mail: hvedekorn@live.dk; kunst@hvedekorn.dk
Web Site: www.hvedekorn.dk
Key Personnel
Editor: Lars Bukdahl
Magazine for poetry & graphics.
Quarterly.
500 DKK
ISSN: 0018-8093

Nordisk Exlibris Tidsskrift (Scandinavian
Bookplate Periodical) (P)
Published by Dansk Exlibris Selskab (Danish
Bookplate Society)
c/o Frederikshavn Kunstmuseum, Parallelvej 14,
9900 Frederikshavn
Mailing Address: Postboks 47, 9900 Frederikshavn
Tel: 98459080
Web Site: danskexlibrisselskab.dk
Key Personnel
Editor: Klaus Roedel *Tel:* 98461127
Text in Danish, English & German.
First published 1946.
Quarterly.
300 DKK
ISSN: 1604-8202

**∮Orbis Litterarum: International Review of
 Literary Studies** (P)
Published by Wiley-Blackwell Ltd
University of Southern Denmark, Campusvej 55,
5230 Odense M
Tel: 6550 2125
E-mail: orbis@litcul.sdu.dk
Web Site: www.blackwellpublishing.com/journals/
oli
Key Personnel
General & English Editor: Dr Lars Ole Sauerberg
Germanic Editor: Christian Benne
Reviews Editor: Svend Erik Larsen
Romance Editor: Morten Nojgaard
Text mainly in English, occasionally in French &
German.
Also available online (ISSN: 1600-0730).
First published 1943.
6 times/yr.
90 pp, Institutional-print & online: 723 USD (The
Americas), 432 GBP (UK), 548 EUR (Europe),
846 USD (rest of world); Institutional-online
or print: 628 USD (The Americas), 375 GBP
(UK), 476 EUR (Europe), 735 USD (rest of
world)
ISSN: 0105-7510

Finland

The Finnish National Bibliography (P)
Published by Kansallis Kirjasto (The National
Library of Finland)
University of Helsinki, Unioninkatu 36, 00014
Helsinki
Mailing Address: University of Helsinki, PB 15,
00014 Helsinki
Tel: (09) 191 23196 *Fax:* (09) 191 22719
E-mail: fennica-posti@helsinki.fi
Web Site: www.kansalliskirjasto.fi; www.
nationalbiblioteket.fi; fennica.linneanet.fi

Online database containing information about monographs, serials, maps, audiovisual materials & electronic publications printed or produced in Finland.

Horisont (P)
Published by Svenska Osterbottens Litteraturforening
Wolffskavagen 36/F11, Vasa
Web Site: www.horisont.fi; www.litteratur.fi
Key Personnel
Executive Dir: Christian Lang *E-mail:* christian@horisont.fi
Executive Editor: Camilla Lindberg
  E-mail: camilla@horisont.fi
Mng Editor: Anna Remmets Askman
  E-mail: anna@horisont.fi
Literary magazine.
First published 1954.
Quarterly.
38 EUR (Finland), 27 EUR (students); 45 EUR (Nordic Countries); 450 SEK (Sweden); 52 EUR (elsewhere); Single issues 10 EUR or 120 SEK
ISSN: 0439-5530

Parnasso (P)
Published by Otavamedia Oy
Maistraatinportti 1, 00015 Helsinki
Tel: (09) 15 661; (09) 156 665 (customer service)
E-mail: asiakaspalvelu@otavamedia.fi
Web Site: otavamedia.fi/tuotteet/parnasso; plaza.fi/kategoria/parnasso
Key Personnel
Editor-in-Chief: Ville Pernaa *E-mail:* ville.pernaa@otavamedia.fi
Text in Finnish.
First published 1951.
6 times/yr.
61.20 EUR
ISSN: 0031-2320
Branch Office(s)
Esterinportti 1, 00015 Helsinki

Skrifter Utgivna av Svenska Litteratursaellskapet i Finland (P)
Published by Svenska Litteratursaellskapet i Finland (Society of Swedish Literature in Finland)
Ritarikatu 5, 00170 Helsinki
Tel: (09) 618 777
E-mail: info@sls.fi
Web Site: www.sls.fi
Scholarly publications in history, literature, ethnology, Scandinavian languages, social & political sciences.
First published 1886.
Irregularly.
ISSN: 0039-6842

Virittaejae (The Kinder) (J)
Published by Society for the Study of Finnish (Kotikielen Seura)
University of Helsinki, Castrenianum, PL 3, 00014 Helsinki
Tel: (09) 19124342 *Fax:* (09) 19123329
E-mail: virittaja@kotikielenseura.fi; seura@kotikielenseura.fi
Web Site: www.kotikielenseura.fi
Key Personnel
Editor: Anne Mantynen *E-mail:* anne.mantynen@helsinki.fi
Linguistic journal with summaries in English, French & German.
First published 1897.
Quarterly.
51 EUR (domestic); 58 EUR (abroad); 47 EUR (members); 24.50 EUR (students)
ISSN: 0042-6806

France

⊕**Bulletin du Bibliophile** (J)
Published by Electre - Editions du Cercle de la Librairie
35 rue Gregoire de Tours, 75006 Paris
Tel: 01 44 41 28 00; 01 44 41 28 05 (orders)
  Fax: 01 44 41 28 65; 01 44 41 28 19 (orders)
E-mail: abonnement@electre.com; commercial@electre.com
Web Site: www.editionsducercledelalibrairie.com
Published in English, French & German.
First published 1834.
2 times/yr (June & December).
61 EUR
ISSN: 0399-9742

Critique (P)
Published by Les Editions de Minuit SA
7, rue Bernard-Palissy, 75006 Paris
Tel: 01 44 39 39 20 *Fax:* 01 44 39 39 23
E-mail: contact@leseditionsdeminuit.fr; revues@leseditionsdeminuit.fr
Web Site: www.leseditionsdeminuit.fr
Key Personnel
Dir: Philippe Roger
General review of publications in France & abroad.
First published 1946.
9 times/yr.

⊕**Index Translationum, World Bibliography of Translations** (B)
Published by UNESCO (United Nations Educational, Scientific & Cultural Organization)
7, Place de Fontenoy, 75352 Paris 07
Tel: 01 45 68 10 00 *Fax:* 01 45 67 16 90
E-mail: index@unesco.org
Web Site: www.unesco.org/xtrans
Online database.
First published 1932.

Litterature (P)
Published by Armand Colin
11 rue Paul Bert, CS 30024, 92247 Malakoff Cedex
Fax: 01 41 23 67 35
E-mail: infos@armand-colin.fr; revues@armand-colin.com; infos@dunod.com
Web Site: www.armand-colin.com; www.revues.armand-colin.com
Text in French.
First published 1971.
Quarterly.
65 EUR (domestic individuals); 80 EUR (foreign individuals); 145 EUR (domestic institutions); 190 EUR (foreign institutions)
ISSN: 0047-4800

Livres Hebdo (Weekly Books) (J)
Published by Electre, Éditions du Cercle de la Librairie
35, rue Gregoire de Tours, 75006 Paris Cedex
Tel: 01 44 41 28 00 *Fax:* 01 43 29 77 85; 01 44 41 28 65
E-mail: livreshebdo@electre.com; commercial@electre.com
Web Site: www.electre.com; livreshebdo.fr
Key Personnel
Dir: Philippe Beauvillard
Editor-in-Chief: Christine Ferrand
Book market trade journal.
44 times/yr.
390 EUR
ISSN: 0294-0000

Le Magazine litteraire (Literary Magazine) (P)
Published by Sophia Publications
8 rue d'Aboukir, 75002 Paris
Tel: 01 70 98 19 67; 01 70 98 19 19

E-mail: courrier@magazine-litteraire.com
Web Site: www.magazine-litteraire.com
Key Personnel
Dir: Claude Perdriel
First published 1966.
Monthly.
108 pp, 54 EUR (print); 38 EUR (online)
ISSN: 0024-9807

La Nouvelle Revue francaise (P)
Published by Editions Gallimard
5, rue Gaston-Gallimard, 75328 Paris Cedex 07
Tel: 01 49 54 42 00 *Fax:* 01 45 44 94 03
E-mail: contact-nrf@gallimard.fr; catalogue@gallimard.fr
Web Site: www.gallimard.fr; www.centenaire-nrf.fr
Key Personnel
Editor: Michel Braudeau
Management: Michel Crepu
First published 1908.
Quarterly.
352 pp, 58.50 EUR (domestic); 65.50 EUR (foreign)
ISSN: 0029-4802

Quinzaine litteraire (Literary Fortnightly) (P)
Published by Selis la Quinzaine Litteraire
135, rue St-Martin, 75194 Paris Cedex 04
Tel: 01 48 87 48 58 *Fax:* 01 48 87 13 01
E-mail: quinzainelitteraire@gmail.com
Web Site: www.quinzaine-litteraire.net
Key Personnel
Dir: Maurice Nadeau
Reviews & summaries of recently published books.
First published 1966.
6 times/yr.
30 pp, 86 EUR (domestic); 114 EUR (foreign); 65 EUR (students)
ISSN: 0048-6493

Revue de Litterature comparee (Review of Comparative Literature) (J)
Published by Editions Klincksieck
95, blvd Raspail, 75006 Paris
Tel: 01 43 54 47 57 *Fax:* 01 45 44 92 88
E-mail: courrier@klincksieck.com
Web Site: www.klincksieck.com/revues/rlc
Key Personnel
Board of Directors: Pierre Brunel; Veronique Gely; Daniel-Henri Pageaux
Written in French & English. Reviews, critical studies & documentary essays of comparative literature in France.
First published 1921.
Quarterly.
75 EUR (domestic); 95 EUR (foreign)
ISSN: 0035-1466

La Revue des Livres pour Enfants (Children's Books Review Magazine) (P)
Published by La Joie par les Livres
Quai Francois Mauriac, 750706 Paris Cedex 13
Tel: 01 53 79 53 79 *Fax:* 01 53 79 41 80
E-mail: cnlj-jpl.contact@bnf.fr
Web Site: lajoieparleslivres.bnf.fr
Key Personnel
Editor-in-Chief: Maire Lallouet *E-mail:* marie.lallouet@bnf.fr
Editor: Brigitt Andrieux *E-mail:* brigitt.andrieux@bnf.fr; Manuela Barcilon
  E-mail: manuela.barcilon@bnf.fr
6 times/yr.
Individuals: 62 EUR (France), 67 EUR (Europe), 77 EUR (elsewhere); Libraries: 52 EUR (France), 57 EUR (Europe), 65 EUR (elsewhere)
ISSN: 0398-8384

Germany

ƒ**Adressbuch fuer den deutschsprachigen Buchhandel** (Directory of the German Language Book Trade) (B)
Published by MVB Marketing- und Verlagsservice des Buchhandels GmbH
Braubachstr 16, 60311 Frankfurt am Main
Mailing Address: Postfach 10 04 42, 60004 Frankfurt am Main
Tel: (069) 1306-550 (customer service) *Fax:* (069) 1306-255 (customer service)
E-mail: adressbuch@mvb-online.de; serviceline@mvb-online.de; info@mvb-online.de
Web Site: www.adb-online.de/adbwas; www.mvb-online.de
Key Personnel
Head, Marketing & Sales: Katrin Willwater
   Tel: (069) 1306-456 *E-mail:* k.willwater@mvb-online.de
Editor: Sebastian Mai *Tel:* (069) 1306-221
   Fax: (069) 1306-258 *E-mail:* s.mai@mvb-online.de
Provides access to 24,000 publishers & 7,500 bookshops in Germany, Austria & Switzerland. Online only.
First published 1839.

ƒ**The African Book Publishing Record (ABPR)** (J)
Published by De Gruyter Saur
Genthiner Str 13, 10785 Berlin
Tel: (030) 260 05-0 *Fax:* (030) 260 05-251
E-mail: africanbookpublishingrecord@gmail.com; service@degruyter.com
Web Site: www.degruyter.com/view/j/abpr
Key Personnel
Editor: Cecile Lomer
Bibliographical tool which offers systematic & comprehensive coverage of new & forthcoming African publications in a single source, providing full bibliographic & acquisitions data. Also includes an extensive book review section & features news, reports & articles about African book trade activities & developments.
Also available online (ISSN: 1865-8717).
Quarterly.
384 pp, 412 EUR/yr (print or online only); 475 EUR/yr (print & online); 114 EUR (single issue)
ISSN: 0306-0322

ƒ**African Books in Print/Livres Africains Desponibles** (B)
Published by De Gruyter Saur
Genthiner Str 13, 10785 Berlin
Tel: (030) 260 05-0 *Fax:* (030) 260 05-251
E-mail: service@degruyter.com
Web Site: www.degruyter.com
Key Personnel
Editor: Cecile Lomer
Major reference work containing full bibliographic details on 31,684 books, published in 45 African countries by 893 publishers & research institutions with publishing programs.
Irregularly.
6th ed, 2006: 1,629 pp, 929 EUR or 1,301 USD
ISBN(s): 978-3-598-11746-6
ISSN: 0306-9516

Akzente (J)
Published by Carl Hanser Verlag GmbH & Co KG
Kolbergerstr 22, 81679 Munich
Mailing Address: Postfach 86 04 20, 81631 Munich
Tel: (089) 9 98 30 0 *Fax:* (089) 98 48 09
E-mail: info@hanser.de
Web Site: www.hanser.de

Key Personnel
Editor: Jo Lendle et al
Journal for literature.
First published 1954.
Quarterly.
96 pp, 43 EUR/yr; 34 EUR (students); 9.60 EUR (single issues)
ISSN: 0002-3957

Amsterdamer Publikationen zur Sprache und Literatur (Amsterdam Publications on Language and Literature) (P)
Published by Weidler Buchverlag Berlin GbR
Luebecker Str 8, 10559 Berlin
Mailing Address: Postfach 21 03 15, 10503 Berlin
Tel: (030) 394 86 68 *Fax:* (030) 394 86 98
E-mail: weidler_verlag@yahoo.de
Web Site: www.weidler-verlag.de
Key Personnel
Mng Dir: Joachim Weidler
Editor: Norbert Otto Eke; Bodo Plachta
Germanic languages & literature. Text in German.
Vol 174, 2016
ISSN: 0169-0221

Boersenblatt (J)
Published by MVB Marketing- und Verlagsservice des Buchhandels GmbH
Braubachstr 16, 60311 Frankfurt am Main
Mailing Address: Postfach 10 04 42, 60004 Frankfurt am Main
Tel: (069) 1306-550 (customer service) *Fax:* (069) 1306-255 (customer service)
E-mail: info@mvb-online.de; boersenblatt@mvb-online.de
Web Site: www.boersenblatt.net; www.mvb-online.de
Key Personnel
Chief Editor: Torsten Casimir *E-mail:* t.casimir@mvb-online.de
First published 1834.
Weekly.
450 EUR (domestic)
ISSN: 1611-4280

Buch und Buchhandel in Zahlen (BuBiZ) (Books & the Book Trade in Figures) (B)
Published by MVB Marketing- und Verlagsservice des Buchhandels GmbH
Subsidiary of Boersenverein des Deutschen Buchhandels eV
Braubachstr 16, 60311 Frankfurt am Main
Mailing Address: Postfach 10 04 42, 60004 Frankfurt am Main
Tel: (069) 1306-550 (customer service) *Fax:* (069) 1306-255 (customer service)
E-mail: serviceline@mvb-online.de
Web Site: www.mvb-online.de
Key Personnel
Head, Marketing & Sales: Katrin Willwater
   Tel: (069) 1306-456 *E-mail:* k.willwater@mvb-online.de
2018, 39.50 EUR

BuchJournal (J)
Published by MVB Marketing- und Verlagsservice des Buchhandels GmbH
Braubachstr 16, 60311 Frankfurt am Main
Mailing Address: Postfach 10 04 42, 60004 Frankfurt am Main
Tel: (069) 1306-550 (customer service) *Fax:* (069) 1306-255 (customer service); (069) 1306-424
E-mail: mail@buchjournal.de
Web Site: www.mvb-online.de; www.buchjournal.de
Key Personnel
Editorial Dir: Eckart Baier *E-mail:* e.baier@buchjournal.de
General magazine for booksellers' customers.
6 times/yr.

30 EUR (domestic); 40.50 EUR (foreign)
ISSN: 0178-7241

BuchMarkt (Book Market) (J)
Published by Verlag K Werner GmbH
Sperberweg 4a, 40668 Meerbusch
Tel: (02150) 9191-0 *Fax:* (02150) 919191
E-mail: redaktion@buchmarkt.de
Web Site: www.buchmarkt.de
Key Personnel
Publisher, Mng Dir & Editor-in-Chief: Christian von Zittwitz *E-mail:* cvz@buchmarkt.de
Journal for the book trade in German-speaking areas.
Monthly.
246 EUR; 89 EUR (students)

Buchreport (Book Report) (J)
Published by Harenberg Kommunikation Verlags-und Medien-GmbH & Co KG
Koenigswall 21, 44137 Dortmund
Tel: (0231) 9056-0 *Fax:* (0231) 9056-110; (0231) 9056-111
E-mail: post@buchreport.de; info@buchreport.de
Web Site: www.buchreport.de
Key Personnel
Editor-in-Chief: Dr Thomas Wilking *Tel:* (0231) 9056-200 *E-mail:* wilking@buchreport.de
Deputy Editor-in-Chief: Rainer Uelbelhoede
   Tel: (0231) 9056-202
Magazine for booksellers in German-speaking areas.
First published 1970.
Monthly.
120 EUR/yr

Buchreport-Express (J)
Published by Harenberg Kommunikation Verlags-und Medien-GmbH & Co KG
Koenigswall 21, 44137 Dortmund
Tel: (0231) 9056-0 *Fax:* (0231) 9056-110; (0231) 9056-111
E-mail: post@buchreport.de; info@buchreport.de
Web Site: www.buchreport.de
Key Personnel
Editor-in-Chief: Dr Thomas Wilking *Tel:* (0231) 9056-200 *E-mail:* wilking@buchreport.de
Deputy Editor-in-Chief: Rainer Uelbelhoede
   Tel: (0231) 9056-202
Magazine for booksellers in German-speaking areas.
Weekly.
ISSN: 1615-0732

Deutsche Nationalbibliografie (German National Bibliography) (J)
Published by Deutsche Nationalbibliothek (German National Library)
Adickesallee 1, 60322 Frankfurt am Main
Tel: (069) 1525-1630 *Fax:* (069) 1525-1010
E-mail: datendienste@dnb.de
Web Site: www.dnb.de
Key Personnel
National Bibliographic Services: Claudia Werner
   E-mail: c.werner@d-nb.de
Series of online journals.

ƒ**Frankfurter Buchmesse Katalog** (Frankfurt Book Fair Catalogue) (B)
Published by Frankfurter Buchmesse GmbH
Braubachstr 16, 60311 Frankfurt am Main
Tel: (069) 2102-0 *Fax:* (069) 2102-227; (069) 2102-277
E-mail: info@book-fair.com
Web Site: www.buchmesse.de
Key Personnel
Mng Dir: Juergen Boos
Press Officer: Thomas Minkus
Vice President, Exhibition: Gabriele Rauch-Kneer
Directory of all exhibitors with a presence at the Frankfurt Book Fair. Also available online to registered users.

Annually.
25 EUR

ƒGuide to Microforms & Digital Resources (B)
Published by De Gruyter Saur
Genthiner Str 13, 10785 Berlin
Tel: (030) 260 05-0 *Fax:* (030) 260 05-251
E-mail: service@degruyter.com
Web Site: www.degruyter.com
Annually.
ISBN(s): 978-3-11-023533-3

Hebbel-Jahrbuch (Hebbel Year Book) (P)
Published by Boyens Buchverlag GmbH & Co
    KG
Wulf-Isebrand-Platz 1-3, 25746 Heide
Tel: (0481) 6886-650 *Fax:* (0481) 6886-90650
E-mail: buchverlag@boyens-medien.de
Web Site: buchverlag.boyens-medien.de
Key Personnel
Mng Dir: Inken Boyens; Soenke Boyens
Annually.
24 EUR; free to members of Hebbel-Gesellschaft
ISSN: 0073-1560

Die Horen (P)
Published by Wallstein Verlag GmbH
Geiststr 11, 37073 Goettingen
Tel: (0551) 548 98-0 *Fax:* (0551) 548 98-33
E-mail: diehoren@gmx.de; info@wallstein-verlag.
    de
Web Site: www.die-horen.de; www.wallstein-
    verlag.de
Key Personnel
Editor: Juergen Kraetzer
Library journal introducing less known or almost
    forgotten authors often by focusing on one spe-
    cial country per issue.
First published 1955.
Quarterly.
40 EUR + postage/yr
ISSN: 0018-4942

Imprimatur (J)
Published by Gesellschaft der Bibliophilen eV
    (Society of Bibliophiles)
c/o RA Michael Then, Rindermarkt 17, 80331
    Munich
Tel: (089) 545 04 210 *Fax:* (089) 545 04 219
E-mail: info@bibliophilie.de; verlag@
    harrassowitz.de
Web Site: www.bibliophilie.de; www.harrassowitz-
    verlag.de
Bibliophilia, history of books, printers, bookmind-
    edness.
First published 1937.
Biennially.
25th ed, 2017
ISBN(s): 978-3-447-10841-6
ISSN: 0073-5620

ƒInternational African Bibliography (J)
Published by De Gruyter Saur
Genthiner Str 13, 10785 Berlin
Tel: (030) 260 05-0 *Fax:* (030) 260 05-251
E-mail: service@degruyter.com
Web Site: www.degruyter.com/view/j/iabi
Key Personnel
Editor: David Hall
Indexes the latest books, articles & papers pub-
    lished internationally on Africa.
Quarterly.
392 pp, 384 EUR (print or online); 443 EUR
    (print & online); 106 EUR (single issue)
ISSN: 0020-5877

ƒJahrbuch der Auktionspreise fuer Buecher,
    Handschriften und Autographen (European
    Book Prices Current) (B)
Published by Dr Ernst Hauswedell & Co KG Ver-
    lag

Haldenstr 30, 70334 Stuttgart
Tel: (0711) 54 99 71-11 *Fax:* (0711) 54 99 71-21
E-mail: verlag@hauswedell.de
Web Site: www.hauswedell.de
Key Personnel
Contact: Gerd Hiersemann
Publication contains book auction prices in
    Germany, Austria, Belgium, Netherlands &
    Switzerland. Also avaliable on CD-ROM.
Annually.
396 EUR
ISSN: 0075-2193

ƒKritikon Litterarum (P)
Published by Walter de Gruyter GmbH & Co KG
Genthiner Str 13, 10785 Berlin
Tel: (030) 260 05-0 *Fax:* (030) 260 05-251
E-mail: info@degruyter.de
Web Site: www.degruyter.de/journals/kritikon
Key Personnel
Editor: Kirby Farrell; Gerhard Giesemann; Alain
    Niderst; Manfred Puetz
Text in English, French & Russian.
Also available online (ISSN: 1865-7249).
First published 1972.
2 times/yr.
110 pp, 188 EUR (print or online only), 216 EUR
    (print & online)
ISSN: 0340-9767

ƒLettre International (International Letter) (J)
Published by Lettre International Verlags GmbH
Erkelenzdamm 59/61, Elisabethhof Portal 3b,
    10999 Berlin
Tel: (030) 30 87 04 52; (030) 30 87 04 62 (sales)
    Fax: (030) 283 31 28
E-mail: lettre@lettre.de; redaktion@lettre.de;
    vertrieb@lettre.de
Web Site: www.lettre.de
Key Personnel
Mng Dir & Editor: Frank Berberich
Published in 9 languages.
First published 1984.
Quarterly.
49 EUR

ƒMicroform & Digitization Review (J)
Published by De Gruyter Saur
Genthiner Str 13, 10785 Berlin
Tel: (030) 260 05-0 *Fax:* (030) 260 05-251
E-mail: service@degruyter.com
Web Site: www.degruyter.com/view/j/mfir
Key Personnel
Editorial Dir: Dr Alice Keller
Editor-in-Chief: Ken Middleton
Reports on projects & technical developments in
    document conservation in libraries & archives.
Also available online (ISSN: 2190-541X).
First published 1972.
Quarterly.
176 pp, 263 EUR (print or online); 302 EUR
    (print & online); 73 EUR (single issue)
ISSN: 2190-0752

Neue Rundschau (New Review) (P)
Published by S Fischer Verlag GmbH
Hedderichstr 114, 60596 Frankfurt am Main
Mailing Address: Postfach 700 355, 60553 Frank-
    furt am Main
Tel: (069) 6062-0; (069) 6062-222 (sales)
    Fax: (069) 6062-214 (sales)
Web Site: www.fischerverlage.de
Key Personnel
Chairman: Monika Schoeller
President & Publisher: Joerg Bong
Mng Dir: Michael Justus
General Manager, Marketing/Sales: Dr Uwe
    Rosenfeld
First published 1890.
Quarterly.

15 EUR (single); 43 EUR (domestic subscrip-
    tion); 48 EUR (Europe); 56 EUR (elsewhere)
ISSN: 0028-3347

ƒPublishers' International ISBN Directory (B)
Published by De Gruyter Saur
Genthiner Str 13, 10785 Berlin
Tel: (030) 260 05-0 *Fax:* (030) 260 05-251
E-mail: service@degruyter.com; orders@
    degruyter.com
Web Site: www.degruyter.com
Includes more than 1,100,000 ISBN prefixes from
    2221 countries & territories. *Geographical Sec-
    tion* (volumes 1-5) contains information about
    1,000,000 active publishing houses arranged
    geographically. *Numerical ISBN Section* (vol-
    umes 6-7) is arranged by ISBN prefix. Sold as
    7 volume set. Text in English. Also available
    electronically.
41st ed, 2015: 9,217 pp, 1690 EUR, 2366 USD,
    1536.50 GBP (hardcover/7 volume set); 1599
    EUR, 2329 USD, 1453 GBP (ebook)
ISBN(s): 978-3-11-033619-1 (hardcover/7 volume
    set); 978-3-11-033735-8 (ebookPLUS); 978-3-
    11-033736-5 (print & ebook)
ISSN: 0939-1975

Quickborn: Zeitschrift fuer plattdeutsche
    Sprache und Dichtung (P)
Published by Quickborn, Vereinigung fuer
    Niederdeutsche Sprache und Literatur eV
Kielmannseggstr 92, 22043 Hamburg
Tel: (040) 70 38 36 91
E-mail: info@quickborn-vereinigung.de
Web Site: www.quickborn-vereinigung.de
Key Personnel
Editor: Dirk Roemmer
Magazine for low-German language & literature,
    theatre & radio. Text in German.
First published 1907.
Quarterly.
21 EUR (individuals); 55 EUR (corporate); 40
    EUR (students)
ISSN: 0170-7558

Schriften und Zeugnisse zur Buchgeschichte
    (Writings & Documents on Book History) (B)
Published by Harrassowitz Verlag
Kreuzberger Ring 7b-d, 65205 Wiesbaden
Tel: (0611) 530-905 *Fax:* (0611) 530-999
E-mail: verlag@harrassowitz.de
Web Site: www.harrassowitz-verlag.de
Key Personnel
Dir: Dr Barbara Krauss *E-mail:* bkrauss@
    harrassowitz.de
Sales: Robert Gietz *Tel:* (0611) 530-901
    E-mail: rgietz@harrassowitz.de
History of books, the book trade, publishers &
    printers. Text in German.
First published 1992.
Irregularly.
21st ed, 2013
ISBN(s): 978-3-447-06570-2
ISSN: 0942-4709

Sinn und Form (P)
Published by Akademie der Kuenste
Hanseatenweg 10, 10557 Berlin
Mailing Address: Postfach 21 02 50, 10502
    Berlin
Tel: (030) 20057-2220; (030) 20057-2221; (030)
    20057-2222 *Fax:* (030) 20057-2223
E-mail: sinnform@adk.de
Web Site: www.sinn-und-form.de
Key Personnel
Chief Editor: Sebastian Kleinschmidt
Contributions to literature. Articles on literature
    & humanities.
First published 1949.
6 times/yr.

144 pp, Single issue: 9 EUR; Subscription: 39.90
EUR (domestic), 50 EUR (abroad), 30 EUR
(students)
ISSN: 0037-5756

Uebersetzen (Translate/Translation) (J)
Published by Verband Deutschsprachiger Ue-
bersetzer Literarischer und Wissenschaftlicher
Werke eV (VDU)
Paula-Thiede-Ufer 10, 10179 Berlin
Tel: (030) 6956-2327 *Fax:* (030) 6956-3656
E-mail: vs@verdi.de
Web Site: www.literaturuebersetzer.de
Key Personnel
Editor: Dr Sabine Baumann *E-mail:* baumasa@
aol.com
Text in German.
First published 1964.
2 times/yr.
32 pp, Free to members
ISSN: 1868-6583

Wolfenbuetteler Notizen zur Buchgeschichte
(Wolfenbuetteler Notes on the History of
Books) (J)
Published by Harrassowitz Verlag
Kreuzberger Ring 7b-d, 65205 Wiesbaden
Tel: (0611) 530-905 *Fax:* (0611) 530-999
E-mail: verlag@harrassowitz.de
Web Site: www.harrassowitz-verlag.de
Key Personnel
Dir: Dr Barbara Krauss *E-mail:* bkrauss@
harrassowitz.de
Sales: Robert Gietz *Tel:* (0611) 530-901
E-mail: rgietz@harrassowitz.de
First published 1976.
2 times/yr.
49 EUR
ISSN: 0341-2253

Ghana

∮**African Publishing Review** (J)
Published by African Publishers Network (AP-
NET)
Kawukudi Junction, Accra
Tel: (030) 291 2764
E-mail: info.africanpublishers@gmail.com
Newsletter containing news, analysis & in-depth
perspectives of African publishing.
First published 1992.
6 issues/yr.
20 pp, 30 USD (Africa); 50 USD (outside Africa)
ISSN: 1019-5823

Asemka (J)
Published by University of Cape Coast
Faculty of Arts, One University of Cape Coast,
Cape Coast
Tel: (03321) 34073; (03321) 30946
E-mail: arts@ucc.edu.gh
Web Site: www.ucc.edu.gh
Publishes studies in literature (mostly African) &
languages.
First published 1974.
Quarterly.
ISSN: 0855-000X

Ghana National Bibliography (J)
Published by George Padmore Research Library
on African Affairs
Thorpe Rd, off High St, Accra
Mailing Address: PO Box 663, Accra
E-mail: padmorelibrary@gmail.com
First published 1967.
Annually.
ISSN: 0855-0093

Greece

Nea Hestia (P)
Published by Hestia Publishers & Booksellers
Euripides 84, 105 53 Athens
Tel: 2103213907; 2103213030 (subscriptions)
Fax: 2103214610
E-mail: info@hestia.gr
Web Site: www.hestia.gr
Key Personnel
Editor: Nikos Karapidakis
Text in Greek.
First published 1927.
Quarterly.
40 EUR (domestic); 70 EUR (foreign)
ISSN: 0028-1735

Hungary

∮**Helikon Irodalomtudomanyi Szemle** (Helikon
Review of General & Comparative Literature)
(J)
Published by Magyar Tudomanyos Akademia
Bolcseszettudomanyi Kutatokozpont Irodalom-
tudomanyi Intezet (Hungarian Academy of Sci-
ences, Institute of Literary Studies, Humanities
Research Center)
Menesi ut 11-13, Budapest 1118
Tel: (01) 279 2760; (01) 279 2762 *Fax:* (01) 385
3876
E-mail: iti@iti.mta.hu; helikon@t-online.hu
Web Site: www.iti.mta.hu/helikon.html
Key Personnel
Editor-in-Chief: Laszlo Varga *E-mail:* varglasz@t-
online.hu
Summaries published in English, Italian, French,
Russian & German.
First published 1955.
Quarterly.
ISSN: 0017-999X

The Hungarian Quarterly (P)
Published by The Hungarian Quarterly Society
Balassi Institute, Somloi u 51, Budapest 1016
Tel: (020) 5965339 (cell)
E-mail: editor@thehungarianquarterly.com
Text in English.
Also available online (ISSN: 1585-2350).
Quarterly.
160 pp, 50 EUR
ISSN: 1217-2545

Literatura (J)
Published by Magyar Tudomanyos Akademia
Bolcseszettudonanyi Kutatokozpont Irodalom-
tudomanyi Intezet (Hungarian Academy of Sci-
ences, Institute of Literary Studies, Humanities
Research Center)
Menesi ut 11-13, Budapest 1118
Tel: (01) 279 2760 *Fax:* (01) 385 3876
E-mail: iti@btk.mta.hu
Web Site: iti.btk.mta.hu/hu/szerkesztosegek/
literatura
Key Personnel
Editor-in-Chief: Gabor Bezeczky
E-mail: bezecz@gmail.com
Focused mainly on the study of literary moder-
nity.
First published 1974.
140 pp, 2,400 HUF
ISSN: 0133-2368

Iceland

**Skirnir: Journal of the Icelandic Literary
Society** (J)
Published by Hid Islenzka Bokmenntafelag (Ice-
landic Literary Society)
Skeifan 3b, 128 Reykjavik
Tel: 588 90 60 *Fax:* 581 40 88
E-mail: hib@hib.is
Web Site: hib.is/skirnir
Icelandic cultural studies.
First published 1827.
2 times/yr.
5,000 ISK
ISSN: 0256-8446

India

Creative Forum (J)
Published by Bahri Publications
1749 A/5, 1st floor, Gobindpuri Ext, Kalkaji, New
Delhi 110 019
Tel: 9811204673 (cell); 9212794543 (cell)
E-mail: bahripublications@yahoo.com; bahrius@
vsnl.com
Web Site: www.bahripublications.co.in
Key Personnel
Editor: Deepinder Singh Bahri; Harpreet Kaur
Bahri
A journal of current literary practices.
First published 1988.
2 times/yr.
2,099 INR (domestic); 199 USD (foreign)
ISSN: 0975-6396

Indian Book Industry (J)
Published by The Federation of Indian Publishers
(FIP)
18/1C, Institutional Area, Aruna Asaf Ali Marg,
Near JNU, New Delhi 110 067
Tel: (011) 26964847; (011) 26852263; (011)
26966931 *Fax:* (011) 26864054
Web Site: www.fipindia.co
Publication devoted to production, promotion &
distribution of books. Each issue focuses on a
particular subject.
6 times/yr.

Indian Horizons (J)
Published by Indian Council for Cultural Rela-
tions
Azad Bhavan, Indraprastha Estate, New Delhi 110
002
Tel: (011) 23370594 (publications); (011)
23369309; (011) 23379310 *Fax:* (011)
23378639; (011) 23378647
E-mail: icr@vsnl.com
Web Site: www.iccr.gov.in/journals
Key Personnel
Editor: Subhra Mazumdar
A journal in English on Indian Culture & the arts
& of cultural relations past & present between
India & the world. Contents include articles,
fiction & review.
First published 1952.
Quarterly.
ISSN: 0378-2964

Indian Journal of Applied Linguistics (J)
Published by Bahri Publications
1749 A/5, 1st floor, Gobindpuri Ext, Kalkaji, New
Delhi 110 019
Tel: 9811204673 (cell); 9212794543 (cell)
E-mail: bahripublications@yahoo.com; bahrius@
vsnl.com
Web Site: www.bahripublications.co.in

Key Personnel
Editor: Deepinder Singh Bahri; Harpreet Kaur Bahri
New theoretical & methodologist ideas & research from several disciplines engaged in applied linguistics.
First published 1975.
2 times/yr.
2,099 INR (domestic); 199 USD (foreign)
ISSN: 0379-0037

Indian Literature (J)
Published by National Academy of Letters: Sahitya Akademi
Rabindra Bhavan, 35, Ferozeshah Rd, New Delhi 110 001
Tel: (011) 23386626; (011) 23386627; (011) 23386628 *Fax:* (011) 23382428
E-mail: secy@ndb.vsnl.net.in
Web Site: sahitya-akademi.gov.in
Key Personnel
Editor: A J Thomas
Text in English.
First published 1957.
6 times/yr.
250 pp, 501 INR
ISSN: 0019-5804

Indian National Bibliography (J)
Published by Central Reference Library
Dept of Culture, Belvedere, Kolkata 700 027
Tel: (033) 24791721; (033) 24791722; (033) 24481529; (033) 24499562 *Fax:* (033) 24791722
E-mail: inb0708@bsnl.in; centralreferencelibrary@gmail.com
Web Site: www.crlindia.gov.in
Key Personnel
Librarian: K K Kochukoshy
Index Indiana: journal for Indian language periodicals, published quarterly in Roman script.
First published 1958.
Monthly with annual cumulation.

The Indian PEN (P)
Published by PEN All-India Centre
Theosophy Hall, 40 New Marine Lines, Mumbai 400 020
Tel: (022) 22039024
E-mail: india.pen@gmail.com
Key Personnel
President: Dr Dauji Gupta
Text in English.
First published 1934.
ISSN: 0019-6053

International Journal of Communication (P)
Published by Bahri Publications
1749 A/5, 1st floor, Gobindpuri Ext, Kalkaji, New Delhi 110 019
Tel: 9811204673 (cell); 9212794543 (cell)
E-mail: bahripublications@yahoo.com; bahrius@vsnl.com
Web Site: www.bahripublications.co.in
Key Personnel
Editor: Deepinder Singh Bahri; Harpreet Kaur Bahri
First published 1991.
2 times/yr.
2,099 INR (domestic); 199 USD (foreign)
ISSN: 0975-640X

International Journal of Translation (P)
Published by Bahri Publications
1749 A/5, 1st floor, Gobindpuri Ext, Kalkaji, New Delhi 110 019
Tel: 9811204673 (cell); 9212794543 (cell)
E-mail: bahrius@vsnl.com; bahripublications@yahoo.com
Web Site: www.bahripublications.co.in; bahripublications.co.in/journal.php?cat_id=27

Key Personnel
Editor: Deepinder Singh Bahri; Harpreet Kaur Bahri
A review of translation studies.
First published 1989.
2 times/yr.
160 pp, 2,099 INR (domestic) ; 199 USD (foreign)
ISSN: 0970-9819

Language Forum (J)
Published by Bahri Publications
1749 A/5, 1st floor, Gobindpuri Ext, Kalkaji, New Delhi 110 019
Tel: 9811204673 (cell); 9212794543 (cell)
E-mail: bahripublications@yahoo.com; bahrius@vsnl.com
Web Site: www.bahripublications.co.in
Key Personnel
Editor: Deepinder Singh Bahri; Harpreet Kaur Bahri
Journal of language & literature. Publishes papers on curriculum planning, linguistic analyses of Indian languages & dialects, comparative literature & linguistics & literature in general.
First published 1975.
2 times/yr.
2,095 INR (domestic); 199 USD (foreign)
ISSN: 0253-9071

Literary Criterion (J)
Published by Center for Indian Studies
Subsidiary of Dhvanyaloka Academy Foundation Pvt Ltd
124, Bhogadi Rd, Mysore, Karnataka 570 006
Tel: (0821) 2344866; (0821) 2344826; (0821) 2344827
E-mail: info@dcismysore.org
Web Site: www.dcismysore.org/The-Literary-Criterion
Key Personnel
Editor: C N Srinath *E-mail:* srinathcn@rediffmail.com
Associate Editor: Ragini Ramachandra
Text in English.
First published 1952.
Quarterly.
500 INR (individuals); 800 INR (institutions); 40 USD (foreign individuals or institutions)
ISSN: 0024-452X

∮**Marg** (P)
Published by Marg Foundation
Army & Navy Bldg, 3rd floor, 148 Mahatma Gandhi Rd, Mumbai 400 001
Tel: (022) 22842520; (022) 22821151; (022) 22045947 *Fax:* (022) 22047102
E-mail: margfound@vsnl.net
Web Site: marg-art.org
Key Personnel
Editor: Naman P Ahuja; Jyotindra Jain
Publication on Indian art, culture & related civilizations.
First published 1946.
Quarterly.
1,380 INR (India) or 79 USD (overseas)
ISSN: 0972-1444

MIWA: Major Indian Works Annual (J)
Published by D K Agencies (P) Ltd
Mohan Garden, A/15-17, D K Ave, Najafgarh Rd, New Delhi 110 059
Tel: (011) 2535-7104; (011) 2535-7105
Fax: (011) 2535-7103; (011) 2564 8053 (orders)
E-mail: information@dkagencies.com; ordproc@dkagencies.com (orders)
Web Site: www.dkagencies.com
A bibliography of significant English language works from India.
Annually.
ISSN: 0971-4669

Iran

Directory of Iranian Periodicals & Newspapers (B)
Published by National Library & Archives of the Islamic Republic of Iran
National Library Local Access Rd, Mirdamad Underground Sta, Shahid Haghani Highway, Tehran
Tel: (021) 88644080 *Fax:* (021) 88644082
E-mail: nli@nlai.ir
Web Site: www.nlai.ir
First published 1974.
Annually.
ISSN: 1028-7035

The Iranian National Bibliography (P)
Published by National Library & Archives of the Islamic Republic of Iran
National Library Local Access Rd, Mirdamad Underground Sta, Shahid Haghani Highway, Tehran
Mailing Address: PO Box 19395-69573, Tehran 1537614111
Tel: (021) 88644080 *Fax:* (021) 88644082
E-mail: nli@nlai.ir
Web Site: www.nlai.ir
First published 1963.
ISSN: 0075-0522

Ireland

Books Ireland (J)
Published by Jeremy Addis
11 Newgrove Ave, Dublin 4
Tel: (01) 269 2185
E-mail: booksi@eircom.net
Web Site: www.islandireland.com/booksireland
Listing & review medium for Irish publishing.
First published 1976.
9 times/yr.
288 pp, 33 GBP, 35 EUR, 50 USD, 53 CAD or 60 AUD/yr
ISSN: 0376-6039

Comhar (Cooperation) (P)
47 Harrington St, Dublin 8
Tel: (01) 675 1922
E-mail: gno@comhar.ie
Web Site: www.comhar.ie
Key Personnel
Editor: Sean Tadhg O Gairbhi
Literary Editor: Tristan Rosenstock
Text in Irish, covering current affairs, the arts & literature.
First published 1942.
Monthly.
70 EUR (domestic); 90 EUR (foreign); 40 EUR (students)
ISSN: 0010-2369

Israel

The Jerusalem Report (P)
Editorial Off & Administration, The Jerusalem Post Bldg, 91000 Jerusalem
Mailing Address: PO Box 81, 91000 Jerusalem
Tel: (02) 531-5666 *Toll Free Tel:* 800-574-574
Fax: (02) 538-9527
E-mail: subs@jpost.com (subscriptions)
Web Site: www.jpost.com/jerusalem-report

Key Personnel
Editor-in-Chief: Steve Linde
Original journalism from Israel, the Middle East & the Jewish world. Also available online.
First published 1990.
26 issues/yr.
4.50 USD/issue, 27 USD/6 mos, 50 USD/yr
ISSN: 0792-6049

Modern Hebrew Literature (B)
Published by The Institute for the Translation of Hebrew Literature (ITHL)
23 Baruch Hirsch St, 5120217 Bnei Brak
Tel: (03) 579 6830 *Fax:* (03) 579 6832
E-mail: litscene@ithl.org.il
Web Site: www.ithl.org.il
Key Personnel
Dir: Nilli Cohen
English language journal of contemporary Hebrew literature.
Annually.
245 pp, 12.95 USD, 7.99 GBP or 17.95 CAD
ISBN(s): 978-1-59264-264-9

Italy

Andersen-Il Mondo dell'Infanzia (Andersen-The Newspaper of Books for Boys) (J)
Published by Feguagiskia' Studios
Via Crosa di Vergagni, 3 R, 16124 Genoa GE
Tel: (010) 2510829 *Fax:* (010) 2510838
E-mail: editor@andersen,it; subscription@andersen.it
Web Site: www.andersen.it
Text in Italian. Contains articles on CYL, teaching, theatre & film as well as literary competitions. Includes reviews & news.
First published 1982.
Monthly.
69 EUR (Italy); 99 EUR (Europe); 120 EUR (elsewhere)

La Bibliofilia (P)
Published by Casa Editrice Leo S Olschki
Viuzzo del Pozzetto, 8, 50126 Florence FI
Tel: (055) 6530684 *Fax:* (055) 6530214
E-mail: periodici@olschki.it
Web Site: www.olschki.it
Key Personnel
Dir: Edoardo Barbieri *E-mail:* edoardo.barbieri@unicatt.it
Editorial Dir: Daniele Olschki *E-mail:* daniele@olschki.it
Editor: Giancarlo Petrella
Periodicals: Elisabetta Calusi
Text in English, French, German & Italian. Bibliophily, History of Printing.
First published 1899.
110 pp, Individuals: 120 EUR (domestic), 145 EUR (foreign), 108 EUR (online)
ISSN: 0006-0941

Bibliografia Nazionale Italiana (Italian National Bibliography) (J)
Published by Biblioteca Nazionale Centrale di Firenze (National Central Library of Florence)
Piazza dei Cavalleggeri, 1, 50122 Florence FI
Tel: (055) 24919 1; (055) 24919 314
E-mail: bnc-fi.bni@beniculturali.it; bnc-fi.info@beniculturali.it
Web Site: www.bncf.firenze.sbn.it
Key Personnel
Dir: Dr Luca Bellingeri
Head, Publication: Maria Chiara Giunti
E-mail: mariachiara.giunti@beniculturali.it
Available online & PDF.

First published 1958.
1,490 EUR (DVD or online); 2,000 EUR (DVD & online)

Giornale della Libreria (Book Trade Journal) (J)
Published by Associazione Italiana Editori (Italian Publishers Association)
Corso di Porta Romana, 108, 20122 Milan MI
Tel: (02) 89280802 *Fax:* (02) 89280860
E-mail: redazione@giornaledellalibreria.it; abbonamenti@giornaledellalibreria.it
Web Site: www.giornaledellalibreria.it; www.aie.it
Key Personnel
President: Marco Polillo
First published 1888.
6 times/yr.
25 EUR (digital); 30 EUR (print & digital)
ISSN: 1124-9137

Giornale Storico della Letteratura Italiana (Historical Journal of Italian Literature) (P)
Published by Loescher Editore SRL
Via Vittorio Amedeo II, 18, 10121 Turin
Tel: (011) 56 54 111 *Fax:* (011) 56 25 822; (011) 56 54 200
E-mail: mail@loescher.it
Web Site: www.loescher.it/riviste/giornale-storico-della-letteratura-italiana
First published 1883.
Quarterly.
97.50 EUR (domestic), 131.50 EUR (foreign)

Lettere Italiane (P)
Published by Casa Editrice Leo S Olschki
Viuzzo del Pozzetto, 8, 50126 Florence FI
Tel: (055) 6530684 *Fax:* (055) 6530214
E-mail: periodici@olschki.it
Web Site: www.olschki.it
Key Personnel
Dir: Carlo Delcorno; Carlo Ossola
Editorial Dir: Daniele Olschki *E-mail:* daniele@olschki.it
Periodicals: Elisabetta Calusi
History of Italian literature.
Also available online (ISSN: 0023-8503).
First published 1949.
Quarterly.
170 pp, Individuals: 110 EUR (domestic), 148 EUR (foreign), 99 EUR (online)
ISSN: 0024-1334

Libri e Riviste d'Itali (J)
Published by Centro per il libro e la lettura
Via Pasquale Stanislao Mancini, 20, 00196 Rome RM
Tel: (06) 32389301 *Fax:* (06) 32389326
E-mail: c-ll@beniculturali.it
Web Site: www.cepell.it/it/libri-e-riviste-ditalia
Available online only.
First published 1950.
Quarterly.
Parent Company: Ministero per i Beni e le Attivita Culturali

Nuova Corrente (New Current) (J)
Published by Interlinea Edizioni SRL
via Enrico Mattei 21, 28100 Novara
Tel: (0321) 612571; (0321) 1992282 *Fax:* (0321) 612636
E-mail: ordini@interlinea.com
Web Site: www.interlinea.com
Key Personnel
Editorial Dir: Stefano Verdino
Literary & philosophical criticism. Also available in digital format.
First published 1954.
2 times/yr.
40 EUR; 70 EUR (international)
ISSN: 0029-6155

Paideia (P)
Published by Editrice Stilgraf
Viale Angeloni, 407, 47521 Cesena FC
Tel: (0547) 610201 *Fax:* (0547) 367147
E-mail: info@stilgrafcesena.com
Web Site: www.stilgrafcesena.com/paideia/editrice.htm
Key Personnel
Editor: Mariella Bonvicini *E-mail:* mariella.bonvicini@unipr.it
Literary review with bibliographical information. Text in English, French, German & Italian.
First published 1946.
Annually.
58.90 EUR (domestic); 78.90 EUR (foreign)
ISSN: 0030-9435

La Rassegna della Letteratura Italiana (Italian Literature Review) (P)
Published by Casa Editrice Le Lettere
Via Duca di Calabria 1/1, 50125 Florence
Tel: (055) 2342710; (055) 2466911 *Fax:* (055) 2346010
E-mail: staff@lelettere.it
Web Site: www.lelettere.it
Key Personnel
Editorial Dir: Nicoletta Gentile Pescarolo *E-mail:* n.pescarolo@lelettere.it
Mng Editor: Tiziana Battisti *E-mail:* redazione@lelettere.it
Dir & Editor: Enrico Ghidetti
First published 1883.
2 times/yr.
Print: 150 EUR (domestic), 180 EUR (foreign); Print & Online: 180 EUR (domestic), 225 EUR (foreign)
ISSN: 0033-9423

Rivista di Letterature Moderne e Comparate (Review of Modern & Comparative Literature) (J)
Published by Pacini Editore SpA
via Gherardesca, 1, 56121 Ospedaletto, Pisa PI
Tel: (050) 313011 *Fax:* (050) 3130300
E-mail: info@pacinieditore.it
Web Site: www.pacinieditore.it
Key Personnel
Dir: Giovanni Angeli; Patrizio Collini; Claudio Pizzorusso
Text in English, French, German & Italian.
First published 1947.
Quarterly.
120 pp, Single issue: 30 EUR; Subscription: 70 EUR (domestic), 85 EUR (foreign)
ISSN: 0391-2108

Jamaica

ƒ**Caribbean Quarterly** (J)
Published by University of the West Indies Press
UWI Mona Campus, PO Box 130, Kingston 7
Tel: (876) 970-3261 *Fax:* (876) 970-3261
E-mail: cq@uwimona.edu.jm; cquarterlyedit@gmail.com
Web Site: www.uwi.edu/cq/default.aspx
Key Personnel
Editor: Dr Kim Robinson-Walcott
E-mail: kimberly.robinson@uwimona.edu.jm
Also available online (ISSN: 2470-6302).
First published 1949.
Quarterly.
120 pp, Individuals: 110 USD (print only); Institutions: 434 USD (online only), 496 USD (print & online)
ISSN: 0008-6495

Japan

Biblia (J)
Published by Tenri University Press
Tenri Central Library, 1050 Soma-no-uchi, Tenri, Nara 632-8577
Tel: (0743) 63-9200 *Fax:* (0743) 63-7728
E-mail: info@tcl.gr.jp
Web Site: www.tcl.gr.jp
Text in Japanese.
First published 1949.
2 times/yr.
ISSN: 0006-0860

Bulletin of Japan Book Publishers Association (P)
Published by Japan Book Publishers Association (JBPA)
6 Fukuro-machi, Shinjuku-ku, Tokyo 162-0828
Tel: (03) 3268-1302; (03) 3268-1303 (research)
Fax: (03) 3268-1196
E-mail: research@jbpa.or.jp
Web Site: www.jbpa.or.jp
Key Personnel
President: Masahiro Oga
Monthly.
ISSN: 0913-3631

Doitsu Bungaku (P)
Published by Nippon Dokubungakkai
Minamiotsuka 3-34-6-501, Toshima-ku, Tokyo 170-0005
Tel: (03) 5950-1147 *Fax:* (03) 5950-1147
Web Site: www.jgg.jp
German Literature. Text in Japanese.
First published 1947.
Quarterly.
ISSN: 0387-2831

Doshisha Literature (J)
Published by Doshisha University, English Literary Society
Karasuma-Imadegawa, Kamikyo-ku, Kyoto 602-8580
Tel: (075) 251 3120 *Fax:* (075) 251 3080
E-mail: ji-koho@mail.doshisha.ac.jp
Web Site: els.doshisha.ac.jp
Journal of English & American literature, English linguistics, applied linguistics & comparison of English with other languages (especially Japanese). Text in English.
Annually.
ISSN: 0046-063X

Eibungaku Kenkyu (Studies in English Literature) (P)
Published by Nihon Eibungakkai (English Literary Society of Japan)
Kenkyusha Eigo Centre Bldg, 1-2 Kagurazaka, Shinjuku-ku, Tokyo 162-0825
Tel: (03) 5261-1922 *Fax:* (03) 5261-1922
E-mail: ejimu@elsj.org
Web Site: www.elsj.org
Text in Japanese.
Also available in English (ISSN: 0387-3439) & online (ISSN: 2424-2136).
Annually (Japanese ed - Nov; English ed - March).
3,500 JPY
ISSN: 0039-3649

An Introduction to Publishing in Japan (B)
Published by Japan Book Publishers Association (JBPA)
6 Fukuro-machi, Shinjuku-ku, Tokyo 162-0828
Tel: (03) 3268-1302; (03) 3268-1303 (research)
Fax: (03) 3268-1196
E-mail: research@jbpa.or.jp
Web Site: www.jbpa.or.jp

Key Personnel
President: Masahiro Oga
A summary & introduction to the Japanese publishing world. Text in English.
Biennially.
93 pp
ISBN(s): 978-4-89003-143-6

Japan Directory of Professional Associations (P)
Published by Japan Publications Guide Service
5-5-13 Matsushiro, Tsukubashi, Ibarakiken 305-0035
Tel: (047) 434-1592 *Fax:* (047) 434-1592
E-mail: senden@jpgsonline.com
Key Personnel
Editor: Warren E Ball
Online database which lists Japanese associations, societies, institutes, centers, laboratories & similar organizations in Japan.
500 USD

Korekara deru Hon (P)
Published by Japan Book Publishers Association (JBPA)
6 Fukuro-machi, Shinjuku-ku, Tokyo 162-0828
Tel: (03) 3268-1302; (03) 3268-1303 (research)
Fax: (03) 3268-1196
E-mail: research@jbpa.or.jp
Web Site: www.jbpa.or.jp
Key Personnel
President: Masahiro Oga
24 times/yr.
Free
ISSN: 0385-1710

Practical Guide to Publishing in Japan (B)
Published by Publishers Association for Cultural Exchange (PACE) Japan
1-2-1, Sarugaku-cho, Chiyoda-ku, Tokyo 101-0064
Tel: (03) 3291-5685 *Fax:* (03) 3233-3645
E-mail: culturalexchange@pace.or.jp
Web Site: www.pace.or.jp
Key Personnel
Editor: Chitose Kajihara
Text in English.
First published 1990.
2015

Shokyo, see Bulletin of Japan Book Publishers Association

Shuppan Nyusu (Publishers' News) (J)
Published by Shuppan News Co Ltd
2-40-7, Kanda Jinbo-cho, Chiyoda-ku, Tokyo
Tel: (03) 3262-2076 *Fax:* (03) 3261-6817
E-mail: snews@snews.net
Web Site: www.snews.net
Text in Japanese.
3 issues/month.
18,000 JPY/yr
ISSN: 0386-2003

Kazakhstan

Prostor (The Expanse) (P)
Published by Writers' Union of Kazakhstan (Soyuz Pisatelei Kazakhstana)
Ablai Khan Ave, 105, 3rd floor, Off 49-50, Almaty 050000
Tel: (8727) 2728774; (8727) 2728606
E-mail: prstr@mail.ru; bks-prostor@mail.ru
Web Site: zhurnal-prostor.kz
Key Personnel
Editor-in-Chief: K S Bakbergenov
Deputy Editor-in-Chief: L K Shashkova

Literary, artistic, socio-political magazine. Text & summaries in Russian.
First published 1933.
Monthly.
ISSN: 0131-5587

Kenya

Kenya National Bibliography (B)
Published by Kenya National Library Service (KNLS)
PO Box 30573, Nairobi 00100
Tel: (020) 2725550; (020) 2158352; (020) 2158360 *Fax:* (020) 2721749
E-mail: knls@knls.ac.ke; nld@knls.ac.ke
Web Site: www.knls.ac.ke
Key Personnel
Dir: R M Atuti
Records bibliographic data of all books, annual reports, yearbooks, etc. Text in English.
First published 1980.
Annually.
450 KES (Kenya); 25 USD (rest of Africa); 30 USD (rest of world)

Luxembourg

Bibliographie Nationale Luxembourgeoise (Luxembourg Bibliography) (J)
Published by Bibliotheque Nationale de Luxembourg
37, Blvd F D Roosevelt, 2450 Luxembourg
Tel: 22 97 55-1 *Fax:* 47 56 72
E-mail: info@bnl.etat.lu
Web Site: www.bnl.public.lu
Online only.
First published 1946.

Malaysia

Malay Literature (J)
Published by Dewan Bahasa dan Pustaka (Institute of Language & Literature)
PO Box 10803, 50926 Kuala Lumpur
Tel: (03) 2147 9449; (03) 2147 9257 *Fax:* (03) 2147 9617
Web Site: malayliterature.dbp.my
Key Personnel
Mng Editor: Azmi Ibrahim *E-mail:* azmi@dbp.gov.my
Deputy Mng Editor: Salahuddin Mohamed *E-mail:* al-fatih@dbp.gov.my
Editor: Zaiton Darois *E-mail:* zaiton6@dbp.gov.my
First published 1967.
2 times/yr.
ISSN: 0128-1186

Mexico

Bibliografia Mexicana (Mexican Bibliography) (B)
Published by Biblioteca Nacional de Mexico
Centro Cultural Universitario, CU, Delegacion Coyoacan, 04510 Mexico, CDMX

Tel: (0155) 5622-6820; (0155) 5622-6850
E-mail: bnmex@iib.unam.mx
Web Site: bnm.unam.mx
Key Personnel
Head, Cataloging: Evelia Santana Chavarria
    E-mail: santanae@iib.unam.mx
Coordinator: Silvia Monica Salgado Ruelas
    E-mail: silsal@iib.unam.mx
Online database. Text in English.
First published 1967.
Annually.

Boletin (Bulletin of the Institute of Bibliographic
    Research) (J)
Published by Instituto de Investigaciones Bibli-
    ograficas (Institute of Bibliographic Research)
Editorial Dept, Centro Cultural, Ciudad Universi-
    taria, 04510 Mexico, DF
Tel: (0155) 5622 6807
E-mail: libros@iib.unam.mx; editorial@iib.unam.
    mx
Web Site: www.iib.unam.mx
Key Personnel
Editorial Dir: Hilda Leticia Dominguez Marquez
    Tel: (0155) 5622 6807 ext 48654
Sales & Distribution: Elsa Almela *Tel:* (0155)
    5622 6807 ext 48713
Book review & historic articles on Mexico &
    Latin America.
First published 1969.
2 times/yr.
250 MXN or 80 USD
ISSN: 0006-1719

Boletin Bibliografico Mexicano (Mexican
    Bibliographical Bulletin) (J)
Published by Libreria de Porrua Hermanos y Cia
    SA de CV
Av Republica de Argentina No 15, Colonia Cen-
    tral, 06020 Mexico, CDMX
Mailing Address: PO Box M-99, 06020 Mexico,
    CDMX
Tel: (0155) 5704 7500 *Fax:* (0155) 5704 7501
Web Site: www.porrua.mx
Key Personnel
Chief Executive Officer: Jose Antonio Perez Por-
    rua
Text in Spanish.
6 times/yr.
ISSN: 0185-2027

Cuadernos Americanos (American Notebooks)
    (J)
Published by Universidad Nacional Autonoma de
    Mexico (UNAM)
Torre II de Humanidades, Piso 1, Ciudad Univer-
    sitaria, 04510 Mexico, DF
Tel: (0155) 5623-0211; (0155) 5623-0212
    Fax: (0155) 5616-2515
E-mail: cuadamer@servidor.unam.mx;
    cuadamer@yahoo.com.mx
Web Site: www.cialc.unam.mx/cuadamer.html
Key Personnel
Editor: Maria Elena Rodriguez Ozan
Our America, Monograph; Our America, perma-
    nent collection; 500 Years After, commemora-
    tive collection of the 500 years of the arrival of
    Columbus to America; Annual Latin America,
    permanent collection.
First published 1942.
Quarterly.
200 USD/yr
ISSN: 0011-2356

Libros de Mexico (Books of Mexico) (J)
Published by Camara Nacional de la Industria
    Editorial Mexicana (National Chamber of the
    Mexican Publishing Industry)
Holanda No 13, Colonia San Diego Churubusco,
    Delegacion Coyoacan, 04120 Mexico, CDMX
Tel: (0155) 5688 2011

E-mail: difusion@caniem.com; contacto@caniem.
    com
Web Site: www.caniem.org
Review of book trade.
First published 1985.
2 times/yr.
150 MXN/yr (Mexico); 50 USD/yr (Americas);
    60 USD/yr (Africa, Asia & Europe)
ISSN: 0186-2243

Nepal

Nepalese National Bibliography (B)
Published by Tribhuvan University Central Li-
    brary
Kirtipur, Kathmandu
Tel: (01) 4330834; (01) 4331317
E-mail: tucl@tucl.org.np
Web Site: www.tucl.org.np
Key Personnel
Chief Librarian: Indra Prasad Adhikari
    E-mail: adhikariip@gmail.com
History or description of writings & publications
    which reveals the heritage of a country in the
    form of culture, society, history & literature of
    a nation.
First published 1981.
Annually.
500 NPR

Netherlands

ɟ**Babel (International Journal of Translation)**
    (J)
Published by John Benjamins Publishing Co
Klaprozenweg 75G, 1033 NN Amsterdam
Mailing Address: PO Box 36224, 1020 ME Ams-
    terdam
Tel: (020) 6304747 *Fax:* (020) 6739773 (publish-
    ing)
E-mail: info@benjamins.nl; subscriptions@
    benjamins.nl
Web Site: www.benjamins.com
Key Personnel
Dir, Publishing: Jan Reijer Groesbeek *E-mail:* jr.
    groesbeek@benjamins.nl
Editor-in-Chief: Frans De Laet
Journal Subscriptions: Heleen Groesbeek
Customer Service & Marketing: Karin Plijnaar
Scholarly journal concerned with current issues &
    events in the field of translation. Published for
    the Federation of Translators (FIT).
Also available online (ISSN: 1569-9668).
Quarterly.
80 EUR (individual)
ISSN: 0521-9744

ɟ**Bibliotheca Orientalis** (J)
Published by Nederlands Instituut voor Het
    Nabije Oosten (Netherlands Institute for the
    Near East)
Witte Singel 25, 2311 BG Leiden
Mailing Address: Postbus 9515, 2300 RA Leiden
Tel: (071) 527 20 36
E-mail: ninopublications@hum.leidenuniv.nl
Web Site: www.nino-leiden.nl
Key Personnel
General Dir & Editor: J Eidem
Publications Officer: C H van Zoest
Editor: L Limme; R E Kon; A van der Kooij; D J
    W Meijer; M Stol; W J I Waal
International bibliographical & reviewing jour-
    nal for Near Eastern & Mediterranean studies.

Published in English, French & German. Also
    available online.
3 times/yr.
350 pp, 150.50 EUR/yr
ISSN: 0006-1913

Boekblad (J)
Published by Veldhuis Media
Fruitweg 70, 3981 PA Bunnik
Tel: (030) 763 1260; (030) 763 1264 (editorial)
E-mail: redactie@boekblad.nl; klantenservice@
    pubmedia.nl
Web Site: boekblad.nl
Key Personnel
Publisher: Ruth Bisschop *E-mail:* ruth@
    pubmedia.nl
Editor-in-Chief: Lucie Th Vermij *E-mail:* lucie@
    boekblad.nl
Newssheet for the book trade.
11 times/yr.
21.75 EUR/mo (print & online); 16.75 EUR/mo
    (online only)
ISSN: 1568-2897

Brinkman's Cumulatieve Catalogus
    (Brinkman's Cumulative Book Catalog) (B)
Published by De Gruyter Saur
Mies-van-der-Rohe-Str 1, 80807 Munich, Ger-
    many
Tel: (030) 260 05-0 *Fax:* (030) 260 05-251
E-mail: info@degruyter.com; service@degruyter.
    com
Web Site: www.degruyter.com
Dutch national bibliography on DVD. Edited by
    Koninklijke Bibliotheck, National Library of
    the Netherlands.
First published 1981.
Quarterly.
1,835 EUR/yr; 2,753 USD (Canada, Mexico,
    USA)
ISSN: 1384-6027

Hollands Maandblad (Holland Monthly) (P)
Published by Stichting Hollands Maandblad
Willem Fenengastr 2A, 1096 BN Amsterdam
Tel: (020) 4213830
E-mail: info-hm@uitgeverijpodium.nl
Web Site: www.hollandsmaandblad.nl
Key Personnel
Editor: Bastiaan Bommelje
First published 1959.
Monthly.
79.50 EUR (domestic); 109.50 EUR (foreign)
ISSN: 0018-3601

ɟ**LIBER Quarterly: The Journal of the
    Association of European Research Libraries**
    (J)
Published by The Association of European Re-
    search Libraries
Prins Willem-Alexanderhof 5, 2595 BE The
    Hague
Mailing Address: c/o Koninklijke Bibliotheek, PO
    Box 90407, 2509 LK The Hague
Tel: (070) 314 0767 *Fax:* (070) 314 0197
E-mail: liber@kb.nl; uopen-journals@uu.nl
Web Site: www.liberquarterly.eu; www.
    libereurope.eu
Key Personnel
Mng Editor: Raf Dekeyser *E-mail:* r.dekeyser@
    kuleuven.be
Promotes cooperation among European research
    libraries. Mainly in English.
Also available online (ISSN: 2213-056X).
First published 1991.
Digital version open access (free); printed version
    (POD) 75 EUR (members); 450 EUR (non-
    members) per volume
ISSN: 1435-5205

ɟ**LOGOS** (J)
Published by Brill

Plantijnstr 2, 2321 JC Leiden
Mailing Address: Postbus 9000, 2300 PA Leiden
Tel: (071) 53 53 500 *Fax:* (071) 53 17 532
E-mail: marketing@brill.com
Web Site: www.brill.com
Key Personnel
Editor: Angus Phillips
Also available online (ISSN: 1878-4712).
First published 1990.
Quarterly.
Institutions: 300 EUR or 379 USD (online only),
330 EUR or 417 USD (print only), 360 EUR
or 455 USD (print & online); Individuals: 125
USD (print & online)
ISSN: 0957-9656

Neerlandia (P)
Published by Algemeen-Nederlands Verbond
Binckhorstlaan 36/M3.11, 2516 BE The Hague
Tel: (070) 324 55 14
E-mail: info@anv.nl
Web Site: www.anv.nl
Key Personnel
Editor-in-Chief: Peter Debrabandere
    E-mail: peter.debrabandere@scarlet.be
Editorial Secretary: Jenny Bleijenberg
Quarterly.
52 pp, 37.50 EUR
ISSN: 0028-2383

De Negentiende Eeuw (The Nineteenth Century)
    (P)
Published by Uitgeverij Verloren (Verloren Pub-
    lishers)
Torenlaan 25, 1211 JA Hilversum
Tel: (035) 6859856 *Fax:* (035) 6836557
E-mail: info@verloren.nl
Web Site: www.negentiende-eeuw.nl
Key Personnel
Editorial Secretary: Saskia Pieterse *E-mail:* s.a.
    pieterse@uu.nl
Interdisciplinary studies of the Dutch nineteenth
    century, including history, science, art & litera-
    ture. Text in Dutch.
First published 1977.
Quarterly.
275 pp, 30 EUR (individuals); 43 EUR (institu-
    tions); 28 EUR (students)
ISSN: 1381-8546

ƒ**Quaerendo** (P)
Published by Brill
Plantijnstr 2, 2321 JC Leiden
Mailing Address: Postbus 9000, 2300 PA Leiden
Tel: (071) 53 53 500 *Fax:* (071) 53 17 532
E-mail: marketing@brill.com
Web Site: www.brill.com
Key Personnel
Editor: Dr Lisa Kuitert
Journal from the Low Countries devoted to
    manuscripts & printed books; text mainly in
    English, occasionally in French & German.
Also available online (ISSN: 1570-0690).
First published 1971.
Quarterly.
500 pp, 73 EUR or 102 USD (individuals); 248
    EUR or 347 USD (institutions); 270 EUR or
    378 USD (institutions-print & online); 225
    EUR or 315 USD (institutions-online only)
ISSN: 0014-9527

De Revisor (The Auditor) (P)
Published by Uitgeverij De Bezige Bij BV
Van Miereveldstr 1, 1071 DW Amsterdam
Tel: (020) 55 18 732 (subscriptions) *Fax:* (020)
    62 31 870
E-mail: info@revisor.nl
Web Site: www.revisor.nl
Key Personnel
Editor: Jan van Mersbergen; Daan Stoffelsen;
    Thomas Heerma van Voss; Bernke Klein Zand-
    voort

First published 1974.
Quarterly.
40 EUR

New Zealand

ƒ**Script & Print: Bulletin of the
    Bibliographical Society of Australia & New
    Zealand** (J)
Published by Bibliographical Society of Australia
    & New Zealand Inc (BSANZ)
c/o University of Otago, Dept of English, PO Box
    56, Dunedin 9054
Tel: (03) 479 8892 *Fax:* (03) 479 8558
E-mail: scriptandprint@gmail.com
Web Site: scriptandprint.blogspot.com
Key Personnel
Editor: Dr Shef Rogers *E-mail:* shef.rogers@
    otago.ac.nz
First published 1970.
Quarterly.
64 pp, Free to members
ISSN: 1834-9013

Te Rarangi Pukapuka Matua o Aotearoa (New
    Zealand National Bibliography) (J)
Published by National Library of New Zealand
    (Te Puna Matauranga o Aotearoa)
Corner of Molesworth & Aitken Sts, Pipitea,
    Wellington 6011
Mailing Address: PO Box 1467, Wellington 6140
Tel: (04) 474 3000 *Fax:* (04) 474 3063
E-mail: tepuna@dia.govt.nz; information@natlib.
    govt.nz
Web Site: natlib.govt.nz
Contains descriptions of books, periodicals, films,
    music & other material published in New
    Zealand, or with a significant New Zealand
    content. Online only.
First published 1961.
Monthly.
Free for international clients
ISSN: 1177-4703

Nigeria

National Bibliography of Nigeria (J)
Published by National Library of Nigeria
Sanusi Dantata House, Plot 274, Central Business
    District, PMB 1, Garki, Abuja
Tel: (09) 2346773
E-mail: info@nln.gov.ng
Web Site: www.nln.gov.ng
Text in English.
First published 1951.
Monthly.
ISSN: 0331-0019

Norway

Bok & Samfunn (J)
Published by BOK365
Arbins Gate 1, 0253 Oslo
E-mail: redaksjon@bok365.no
Web Site: bok365.no
Key Personnel
Chief Editor: Vebjørn Rogne *E-mail:* vebjorn@
    bok365.no
Editor: Atle Nielsen *E-mail:* atle@bok365.no

Trade journal for the Norwegian book trade.
8 times/yr.
995 NOK/yr

Edda (P)
Published by Scandinavian University Press
Universitetsforlaget AS, Sehesteds gate 3, 0164
    Oslo
Mailing Address: Postboks 508 Sentrum, 0105
    Oslo
Tel: 24 14 75 00
E-mail: post@universitetsforlaget.no; post@idunn.
    no
Web Site: www.universitetsforlaget.no; www.
    idunn.no/edda
Key Personnel
Sales & Marketing: Jelena Doublinskaia
Scandinavian journal for literary research. Text in
    Danish, Norwegian, Swedish & English.
Also available online (ISSN: 1500-1989).
First published 1914.
Quarterly.
ISSN: 0013-0818

Samtiden (J)
Published by H Aschehoug & Co (W Nygaard)
Sehestedsgt 3, Oslo
Mailing Address: Postboks 363, Sentrum, 0102
    Oslo
E-mail: samtiden@aschehoug.no
Web Site: www.samtiden.no
Key Personnel
Editor: Christian Kjelstrup *E-mail:* christian.
    kjelstrup@aschehoug.no
Journal for politics, literature & other social ques-
    tions.
First published 1890.
Quarterly.
599 NOK (individuals), 899 NOK (institutions),
    399 NOK (students)
ISSN: 0036-3928

Syn og Segn (Vision & Tradition) (P)
Published by Det Norske Samlaget
Postboks 4672 Sofienberg, 0506 Oslo
Tel: 22 70 78 00 *Fax:* 22 68 75 02
E-mail: syn.og.segn@samlaget.no
Web Site: www.samlaget.no; www.synogsegn.no
Key Personnel
Editor: Bente Riise *E-mail:* bente.riise@
    synogsegn.no
Major Norwegian review on political & cultural
    affairs.
Quarterly.
410 NOK (individuals); 500 NOK (institutions);
    350 NOK (students)
ISSN: 0039-7717

Vinduet (The Window) (J)
Published by Gyldendal Norsk Forlag
Postboks 6860, St Olavs plass, 0130 Oslo
Tel: 22034337
E-mail: vinduet@vinduet.no
Web Site: www.vinduet.no
Key Personnel
Editor: Maria Horvei
Text in Norwegian.
First published 1947.
Quarterly.
Individuals: 500 NOK, 595 NOK (foreign); Stu-
    dents: 450 NOK; Institutions: 600 NOK, 670
    NOK (foreign)
ISSN: 0042-6288

Pakistan

Pakistan Journal of Information Management & Libraries (PJIM&L) (J)
Published by Department of Information Management, University of the Punjab
Quaid-e-Azam Campus, Lahore 54590
Tel: (042) 9923124
E-mail: pjiml.im@pu.edu.pk
Web Site: journals.pu.edu.pk
Key Personnel
Chief Editor: Kanwal Ameen
First published 2000.
2 times/yr.
ISSN: 2409-7462

Pakistan National Bibliography (Qaumi Kitabiaat-E-Pakistan) (J)
Published by Department of Libraries, National Library of Pakistan
Constitution Ave, Islamabad 44000
Tel: (051) 9214523
First published 1962.
Annually.
ISSN: 0078-8341

Philippines

Philippine Studies: Historical & Ethnographic Viewpoints (J)
Published by Ateneo de Manila University Press
Bellarmine Hall, Ground floor, Loyola Heights, 1108 Quezon City
Mailing Address: PO Box 154, 1099 Manila
Tel: (02) 4265984 *Fax:* (02) 4265909
E-mail: info@philippinestudies.net; unipress@admu.edu.ph
Web Site: www.ateneo.edu/ateneopress; www.philippinestudies.net
Key Personnel
Editor: Filomeno V Aguilar, Jr *Tel:* (02) 4266001 ext 4619
Associate Editor: Michael D Pante
Journal Off Manager & Manuscript Editor: Angelli F Tugado, PhD
Publishes articles, notes & reviews in the humanities, literature, history, social sciences, philosophy & Philippine arts.
Also available online (ISSN: 2244-1638).
First published 1953.
Quarterly.
160 pp, Institutions: 2,000 PHP (domestic print & online), 190 USD (foreign, print & online), 180 USD (foreign, print or online); Individuals: 1,500 PHP (domestic print & online), 150 USD (foreign print & online), 140 USD (foreign print or online)
ISSN: 2244-1093

Poland

Pamietnik Teatralny (Theathre Diary) (P)
Published by Institute of Art of the Polish Academy of Sciences
ul Dluga 26/28, 00-950 Warsaw
Tel: (22) 50 48 242; (22) 50 48 274 *Fax:* (22) 50 48 292
E-mail: iswydawnictwo@ispan.pl
Web Site: www.ispan.pl
Key Personnel
Editor-in-Chief: Jaroslaw Komorowski
E-mail: jaroslaw.komorowski@ispan.pl
History of Polish theatre.

First published 1952.
Quarterly.
ISSN: 0031-0522

Ruch Wydawniczy w Liczbach (Polish Publishing in Figures) (B)
Published by Biblioteka Narodowa w Warszawie (National Library of Poland)
al Niepodleglosci 213, 02-086 Warsaw
Tel: (22) 608 26 39; (22) 608 29 99
E-mail: kontakt@bn.org.pl
Web Site: www.bn.org.pl
Key Personnel
Contact: Olga Dawidowicz-Chymkowska
E-mail: olgadawidowicz@gazeta.pl
Also available online (ISSN: 2083-6953).
First published 1955.
Annually.
124 pp
ISSN: 0511-1196

Portugal

Livros Portugueses (B)
Published by Associacao Portuguesa de Editores e Livreiros
Av dos Estados Unidos da America, nº 97-6º esq, 1700-167 Lisbon
Tel: 21 843 51 80
E-mail: geral@apel.pt
Web Site: www.apel.pt
Portuguese Books in Print (online).
Annually.

Puerto Rico

Atenea (J)
Published by University of Puerto Rico at Mayaguez, College of Arts & Sciences
Dept of English, Chardon 323, Mayaguez 00680
Mailing Address: Dept of English, Box 9000, Mayaguez 00681
Tel: (787) 832-4040 (ext 3076); (787) 265-3847
E-mail: atenea@uprm.edu
Web Site: ece.uprm.edu/artsciences/atenea/atenea.htm
Key Personnel
Editor: Nandita Batra *E-mail:* nandita.batra@upr.edu
Text in Spanish & English. Features essays & book reviews on the humanities & social sciences, as well as some poetry & short fiction.
2 times/yr.
14 USD (Puerto Rico & USA); 26 USD (other countries)
ISSN: 0885-6079

Romania

Bibliografia Nationala Romaniei (Romanian National Bibliography) (J)
Published by Biblioteca Nationala a Romaniei (National Library of Romania)
Bd Unirii nr 22, sector 3, 030833 Bucharest
Tel: (021) 314 24 34; (021) 314 10 02 *Fax:* (021) 312 33 81
E-mail: biblioteca@bibnat.ro
Web Site: www.bibnat.ro
Key Personnel
Manager: Ioan Marius Eppel

Editor-in-Chief: Florin Nistor *E-mail:* florin.nistor@bibnat.ro
Publications Coordinator: Letitia Constantin
E-mail: letitia.constantin@bibnat.ro
First published 1952.
6 times/yr.
156 pp
ISSN: 1221-9126

Convorbiri Literare (Literary Conversations) (P)
Published by Uniunea Scriitorilor din Romania (Writers Union of Romania)
Str I C Bratianu nr 22, etaj 1, 700037 Cluj-Napoca
Tel: (0232) 260390
E-mail: convlit95@yahoo.com
Web Site: convorbiri-literare.ro
Key Personnel
Dir: Cassian Maria Spiridon
Editor-in-Chief: Mircea Platon
Deputy Editor: Dan Manuca
First published 1867.
Monthly.
160 RON
ISSN: 1841-7434

Euresis - Cahiers Roumains d'Etudes Litteraires et Culturelles (P)
Published by Institutul Cultural Roman
Aleea Alexandru nr 38, 011824 Bucharest
Tel: (031) 71 00 627; (031) 71 00 606 *Fax:* (031) 71 00 607
E-mail: icr@icr.ro
Web Site: icr.ro; euresisonline.wordpress.com
Key Personnel
Editor: Mircea Martin
Text in French & English, occasionally in German, Russian, Spanish & Italian.
First published 1973.
Quarterly.
ISSN: 1223-1193

Manuscriptum (Manuscript) (P)
Published by Muzeul National al Literaturii Romane
Blvd Dacia nr 12, Sector 1, 010402 Bucharest
Tel: (021) 212 96 54 *Fax:* (021) 212 58 46; (021) 212 96 54
E-mail: relatiipublice@mnlr.ro
Web Site: www.mnlr.ro
Manuscripts, literary documents in Romanian, or bilingual, if necessary. Summaries in French, English, German & Russian.
First published 1970.
Quarterly.
200 pp
ISSN: 1010-5492

Revista de Istorie si Teorie Literara (Review of Literary History & Theory) (P)
Published by Editura Academiei Romane
Calea 13 Septembrie nr 13, Sector 5, 050711 Bucharest
Tel: (021) 3188146 *Fax:* (021) 3182444
E-mail: edacad@ear.ro
Web Site: www.ear.ro
Summaries in French, Russian, English & German. Text in Romanian.
First published 1952.
Quarterly.
412 pp, 90 ROL
ISSN: 0034-8392

Romania Literara (Literary Romania) (P)
Published by Fundatia Romania Literara
Calea Victoriei 133, Sector 1, 010071 Bucharest
Tel: (021) 2127986 *Fax:* (021) 2127981
E-mail: revistaromanialiterara@gmail.com; romania_literara@yahoo.com
Web Site: www.romlit.ro
Key Personnel
Dir General: Nicolae Manolescu

Mng Dir: Dragos Ursache
General Secretary of Editorial: Ionela Streche
First published 1954.
Weekly.
140 ROL/yr (Romania); 230 EUR or 300 USD/yr (abroad)
ISSN: 1584-9465

ƒSecolul 21 (21st Century) (P)
Published by Fundatia Culturala Secolul 21
61 Sfintii Voievozi, 010965 Bucharest
Tel: (021) 2129774; (021) 2129773; (0723) 638243 (cell) *Fax:* (021) 2129773
E-mail: secolul_21@yahoo.com
Web Site: www.secolul21.ro
Key Personnel
Dir: Alina Ledeanu
Editor-in-Chief: Livia Szasz
Also available online.
First published 1961.
Quarterly.
300 pp, 150 ROL, 90 EUR or 185 USD
ISSN: 1582-4802

Steaua (P)
Published by Uniunea Scriitorilor din Romania (Writers Union of Romania)
Str Universitatii nr 1, 400091 Cluj
Tel: (0264) 594 382
E-mail: steauacj@gmail.com
Web Site: www.revisteaua.ro
Key Personnel
Editor-in-Chief: Adrian Popescu
First published 1953.
Monthly.
ISSN: 0039-0852

Russia

Bibliografiya (Bibliography) (J)
Published by Rossiiskaya Knizhnaya Palata (Russian Book Chamber)
Star Blvd, 17, Bldg 1, 129085 Moscow
Mailing Address: Kremlin Embankment, 1/9, Bldg 8, 119019 Moscow
Tel: (495) 766 00 85; (495) 688 98 00; (495) 688 92 15 (inquiries)
E-mail: info@bookchamber.ru; a-bibliograf@mail.ru
Web Site: www.bookchamber.ru
Scientific journal containing articles on history, theory, methods & organization of bibliography, book publishing & book trade national standards & statistical data, as well as interesting experience of bibliographical work in libraries. Helps in work with catalogues, bibliographical aids & documents.
First published 1929.
6 times/yr.
160 pp
ISSN: 0869-6020

Druzhba Narodov (People's Friendship) (P)
Published by Izvestija Sovetov Narodnych Deputatov SSSR
ul Krzhizhanovskogo, 13, 117218 Moscow
Tel: (499) 519-02-12 *Fax:* (499) 519-02-12
E-mail: dn52@mail.ru
Web Site: magazines.russ.ru/druzhba
Key Personnel
Editor-in-Chief: Sergey Nadeev
Literary, artistic, socio-political magazine.
First published 1939.
Monthly.
5,795 RUB
ISSN: 0012-6756

Knizhnaya Letopis' (Book Chronicle) (J)
Published by Rossiiskaya Knizhnaya Palata (Russian Book Chamber)
Star Blvd, 17, Bldg 1, 129085 Moscow
Mailing Address: Kremlin Embankment, 1/9, Bldg 8, 119019 Moscow
Tel: (495) 688 98 00; (495) 688 92 15 (inquiries)
E-mail: info@bookchamber.ru
Web Site: www.bookchamber.ru
Book Annals; published by Book Chamber International.
First published 1907.
Weekly.
160 pp
ISSN: 0869-5962

Knizhnoe Obozrenie (J)
Published by Federalno Agentstvo po Pechati i Massovym Kommunikatsiiam (Federal Agency for Print & Mass Communications)
Suschevsky Val, 49, Suite 6, 115054 Moscow
Tel: (495) 955-79-70
E-mail: all@knigoboz.ru
Web Site: www.knigoboz.ru
Key Personnel
Chief Executive Officer & Editor-in-Chief: Alexander Nabokov *E-mail:* nabokov@knigoboz.ru
Book Reviews. Text in Russian.
First published 1966.
Weekly.
704 RUB (individual); 1,056 RUB (institutional)
ISSN: 0023-2378

Letopis' Periodicheskikh i Prodolzhaiushchikhsya Izdanii (Chronicle of Periodical & Continual Editions) (J)
Published by Rossiiskaya Knizhnaya Palata (Russian Book Chamber)
Star Blvd, 17, Bldg 1, 129085 Moscow
Mailing Address: Kremlin Embankment, 1/9, Bldg 8, 119019 Moscow
Tel: (495) 688 98 00; (495) 688 92 15 (inquiries)
E-mail: info@bookchamber.ru
Web Site: www.bookchamber.ru
Contains information about magazines & newspapers which have changed their name or which have ceased publication in Russia, in addition to other changes in periodicals.
First published 1933.
Annually.
145 pp
ISSN: 0201-6265

Literaturnaya Rossiya (Literary Russia) (P)
Tsvetnoi Blvd, Bldg 32, p 3, 127051 Moscow
Tel: (495) 694-03-65; (495) 694-24-67 (advertising) *Fax:* (495) 694-50-10
E-mail: litrossia@litrossia.ru
Web Site: www.litrossia.ru
Key Personnel
Editor-in-Chief: Eugene Bogachkov; Vyacheslav Ogryzko
First published 1958.
Weekly.
16 pp
ISSN: 1560-6856

Molodaya Gvardiya (The Young Guards) (P)
Suschevskaya ul, 21, 127005 Moscow
Tel: (495) 767-63-85 *Fax:* (499) 978-12-86
E-mail: info@gvardiya.ru
Web Site: gvardiya.ru
Key Personnel
Dir & Editor-in-Chief: Andrei V Petrov
E-mail: petrov@gvardiya.ru
Literary, artistic, socio-political magazine.
First published 1922.
Monthly.
ISSN: 0131-2251

Nash Sovremennik (Our Contemporary) (P)
Tsvetnoi Blvd, 32, p 2, 127051 Moscow
Tel: (495) 621-48-71 *Fax:* (495) 625-01-71
E-mail: mail@nash-sovremennik.ru
Web Site: www.nash-sovremennik.ru
Key Personnel
Editor-in-Chief: Stanislav Kunyaev
Deputy Editor-in-Chief: Alexander Ivanovich Zatintsev
Literary, artistic, socio-political magazine.
First published 1956.
Monthly.
ISSN: 0027-8238

Neva (P)
Published by NEVA Magazin Ltd
Nevskii prospekt, 3, 191186 St Petersburg
Mailing Address: PO Box 9, 191186 St Petersburg
Tel: (812) 314-50-52; (812) 314-92-63 *Fax:* (812) 314-49-23
E-mail: officeneva@mail.ru; nevaredaction@mail.ru
Web Site: nevajournal.ru
Literary, artistic, socio-political illustrated magazine, black & white photos.
First published 1955.
Monthly.
ISSN: 0130-741X

Novyi Mir (New World) (P)
Maly Putinkovsky per, 1/2, k 6, 127994 Moscow
Tel: (495) 694-08-29
E-mail: nmir2007@list.ru; novi-mir@mtu-net.ru (foreign subscriptions)
Web Site: www.nm1925.ru
Key Personnel
Chief Editor: Andrei V Vasilevsky *Tel:* (495) 650-57-02
Deputy Editor: Mikhail Butov *Tel:* (495) 650-91-81
Literary, artistic & socio-political illustrated journal.
First published 1925.
Monthly.
ISSN: 0130-7673

Russkaya Literatura (Russian Literature) (P)
Published by Rossiiskaya Akademiya Nauk, Institut Russkoi Literatury (Pushkinskij Dom)
Nab Makarova, 4, 199034 St Petersburg
Tel: (812) 328-19-01 *Fax:* (812) 328-11-40
E-mail: irliran@mail.ru
Web Site: www.pushkinskijdom.ru
Key Personnel
Dir: Vsevolod Yevgenjevich Bagno
Historical & literary journal.
First published 1958.
Quarterly.
ISSN: 0131-6095

Voprosy Literatury (Questions of Literature) (P)
Published by Redaktsiia Zhurnala Voprosy Literatury
B Gnezdnikovskii per, 10, 129005 Moscow
Tel: (495) 629-49-77 *Fax:* (495) 629-64-71
E-mail: vopli@arion.ru
Web Site: magazines.russ.ru/voplit
Key Personnel
Editor-in-Chief: I O Shaitanov
First published 1957.
6 times/yr.
512 pp
ISSN: 0042-8795

Znamya (The Banner) (P)
Bolshaya Sadovaya St, 2/46, 123001 Moscow
Tel: (495) 699-5238; (495) 699-5283
E-mail: info@znamlit.ru
Web Site: znamlit.ru
Key Personnel
Chief Editor: Sergey Chuprinin
E-mail: chuprinin@znamlit.ru

First Deputy Editor-in-Chief: Natalia Ivanova
Tel: (495) 699-3960
Mng Editor: Marina Sotnikova
Literary, artistic, socio-political magazine. Contains short stories, archives, memoirs, fiction, documentaries & criticism.
First published 1931.
Monthly.
ISSN: 0130-1616

Zvezda (Star) (P)
Mokhovaya ul, d 20, 191028 St Petersburg
Tel: (812) 272-71-38 *Fax:* (812) 273-52-56
E-mail: mail@zvezdaspb.ru
Web Site: zvezdaspb.ru
Key Personnel
Editor: Andrei Yurevich Aryev; Yakov Gordin
Literary, artistic, socio-political magazine.
First published 1924.
Monthly.
272 pp
ISSN: 0321-1878

Senegal

Bibliographie du Senegal (Bibliographies of Senegal) (J)
Published by Archives Nationales du Senegal
2 eme etage, Immeuble Central Park, Ave Malick Sy X Autoroute, Dakar
Tel: 33 823 56 80
E-mail: pmarchi@primature.sn
Web Site: www.archivesdusenegal.gouv.sn
Key Personnel
Dir, Archives: Fatoumata Cisse Diarra
Also available online.
First published 1962.
Irregularly.
ISSN: 0378-9942

Singapore

Book Council Bulletin (P)
Published by National Book Development Council of Singapore
Singapore Writers Center, c/o Geylang East Public Library, 50 Geylang East Ave 1, Singapore 389777
Tel: 6848 8290 *Fax:* 6742 9466
E-mail: info@bookcouncil.sg
Web Site: www.bookcouncil.sg
Online newsletter.
First published 1981.
Irregularly.

Books About Singapore: A Select Bibliography (B)
Published by Lee Kong Chian Reference Library
100 Victoria St, Singapore 188064
Tel: 6332 3255
E-mail: ref@nlb.gov.sg
Web Site: www.nlb.gov.sg
Key Personnel
Senior Librarian: Jane Wee *E-mail:* jane_wee@nlb.gov.sg
Also available online.
Irregularly.
2014
ISSN: 0068-0176

Singapore National Bibliography (SNB) (P)
Published by National Library Board Singapore
100 Victoria St, No 14-01, Singapore 188064

Tel: 6332 3155; 6332 3233 *Fax:* 6332 3395
E-mail: nlb_cip@nlb.gov.sg
Web Site: www.nlb.gov.sg; snb.nl.sg/catindex/index.html
CD-ROM, issues 1 & 2. Each update is cumulative & replaces previous disk.
First published 1969.
2 times/yr.
137 SGD (outside Singapore); 121 SGD (within Singapore)
ISSN: 0218-6454

Slovakia

Kniha (The Book) (P)
Published by Slovenska Narodna Kniznica, Martin (Slovak National Library, Martin)
Nam J C Hronskeho 1, 036 01 Martin
Tel: (043) 2451 125
E-mail: snk@snk.sk; sluzby@snk.sk
Web Site: www.snk.sk
First published 1974.
Annually.
ISSN: 1336-5436

Slovenska Literatura (Slovak Literature) (J)
Published by Institute of Slovak Literature of the Slovak Academy of Sciences
Konventna 13, 813 64 Bratislava
Tel: (07) 54413391; (07) 54412701 *Fax:* (07) 54416025
E-mail: usllred@savba.sk
Web Site: www.uslit.sav.sk/casopis.html
Key Personnel
Chief Editor: Karol Csiba
Mng Editor: Adelaida Mezeiova
Editor: Lenka Macsaliova
Contents page & summaries in German & Russian.
6 times/yr.
16.20 EUR/yr; 2.70 EUR/issue
ISSN: 0037-6973

Slovenske pohlady na literaturu, umenie a vedu (Slovak Perspectives on Literature, Art & Life) (P)
Published by Matica Slovenska
Grosslingova 23, 812 51 Bratislava
Tel: (02) 38128001 *Fax:* (02) 54434090
E-mail: slovenskepohladyba@matica.sk; periodika@matica.sk
Web Site: matica.sk/informacne-pracoviska/slovenske-pohlady
Key Personnel
Editor-in-Chief: Bystrik Sikula
First published 1846.
Monthly.
15.60 EUR, 40 EUR (Europe), 74 USD (rest of world)
ISSN: 1335-7786

Slovenia

Slovenska Bibliografija (Slovene Bibliography) (J)
Published by Narodna in Univerzitetna Knjiznica, Ljubljana (National & University Library)
Turjaska 1, SI-1000 Ljubljana
Tel: (01) 2001 115; (01) 2001 169 *Fax:* (01) 2513-052
E-mail: info@nuk.uni-lj.si
Web Site: sb.nuk.uni-lj.si
Key Personnel
Head: Boris Rifl *E-mail:* boris.rifl@nuk.uni-lj.si

Bibliography. Online only.
Quarterly.
ISSN: 0353-1716

South Africa

ƒ**Acta Classica** (P)
Published by Classical Association of South Africa (CASA)
c/o School of Religion, Philosophy & Classics, University of KwaZulu-Natal, Memorial Tower Bldg, G109, Durban 4041
Tel: (021) 650 2319 *Fax:* (021) 685 5530
Web Site: www.casa-kvsa.org.za/acta_classica.htm
Key Personnel
Editor: J L Hilton *E-mail:* jlhilton@webafrica.org.za
Annually.
50 ZAR (domestic individuals); 25 USD (foreign individuals); 100 ZAR (domestic institutions); 45 USD (foreign institutions); free to full CASA members
ISSN: 0065-1141

Akroterion (J)
Published by Stellenbosch University Department of Ancient Studies
Private Bag X1, Matieland 7602
Tel: (021) 808 3137 *Fax:* (021) 808-3840
Web Site: akroterion.journals.ac.za/pub
Key Personnel
Editor: Dr J C Thom *E-mail:* jct@sun.ac.za
Publishes articles in English or Afrikaans aimed at the non-specialist, covering all aspects of ancient Greek & Roman civilization, but focusing especially on the influence & reception of the Classics.
Also available online (ISSN: 2079-2883).
First published 1956.
Annually.
75 ZAR (South Africa); 95 ZAR (foreign); 12 USD, 9 GBP (UK) or 10 EUR (elsewhere)
ISSN: 0303-1896

English in Africa (P)
Published by Institute for the Study of English in Africa, Rhodes University
St Peter's Bldg (off Somerset St), Grahamstown 6140
Mailing Address: PO Box 94, Grahamstown 6140
Tel: (046) 603 8565 *Fax:* (046) 603 8566
E-mail: isea@ru.ac.za
Web Site: www.ru.ac.za/isea/publications/journals/englishinafrica
Key Personnel
Dir: Prof Laurence Wright *E-mail:* l.wright@ru.ac.za
Editor: Jane Starfield *E-mail:* jstarfield@uj.ac.za
Publications Officer: Beverley Cummings
Primary source material: critical articles & book reviews on all aspects of African literature written in English.
First published 1974.
3 times/yr.
230 ZAR (individuals); 252 ZAR (institutions); 42 GBP or 70 USD (elsewhere, individuals & institutions)
ISSN: 0376-8902

New Coin Poetry (P)
Published by Institute for the Study of English in Africa, Rhodes University
St Peter's Bldg (off Somerset St), Grahamstown 6140
Mailing Address: PO Box 94, Grahamstown 6140
Tel: (046) 603 8565 *Fax:* (046) 603 8566
E-mail: isea@ru.ac.za
Web Site: www.ru.ac.za/isea/publications/journals/newcoinpoetry

Key Personnel
Dir: Prof Laurence Wright *E-mail:* l.wright@ru.
ac.za
Editor: Crystal Warren *E-mail:* c.warren@ru.ac.za
Publications Officer: Beverley Cummings
Collection of South African poetry, reviews &
interviews.
First published 1964.
2 times/yr (June & December).
90 pp, 150 ZAR (Africa); 29 GBP or 53 USD
(elsewhere)
ISSN: 0028-4459

ʃ**Shakespeare in Southern Africa** (P)
Published by Shakespeare Society of Southern
Africa
c/o ISEA, Rhodes University, St Peter's Bldg (off
Somerset St), Grahamstown 6140
Mailing Address: PO Box 94, Grahamstown 6140
Tel: (046) 603 7288; (046) 622 6063 *Fax:* (046)
603 8566
E-mail: shakespeare@ru.ac.za
Web Site: www.ru.ac.za/shakespeare
Key Personnel
Dir: Prof L S Wright *E-mail:* l.wright@ru.ac.za
Mng Editor: Chris Thurman *E-mail:* christopher.
thurman@wits.ac.za
Secretary: Prof E E Baart *E-mail:* e.baart@ru.ac.
za
Articles, commentary & reviews on all aspects of
Shakespearean studies & performance, with a
particular emphasis on the response to Shake-
speare in Southern Africa.
First published 1987.
Annually.
100 pp, 100 ZAR (Southern Africa); 30 USD or
22 GBP (elsewhere)
ISSN: 1011-582X

ʃ**South African Journal of African Languages**
(J)
Published by African Language Association of
Southern Africa (ALASA)
Dept of African Languages, UNISA, PO Box
392, Pretoria 0003
Tel: (012) 429 8232
Web Site: www.alasa.org.za
Key Personnel
Editor: Prof Inge Kosch *E-mail:* koschim@unisa.
ac.za
Peer-reviewed research journal devoted to the ad-
vancement of African (Bantu) & Khoe-San
language & literature.
Also available online (ISSN: 2305-1159).
First published 1981.
2 times/yr.
200 pp, 80 ZAR/yr (members); subscribers 70
USD (internationally), 200 ZAR (locally)
ISSN: 0257-2117

South Korea

Korean National Bibliography (J)
Published by The National Library of Korea
664 Banpo-Ro, Seocho-gu, Seoul 137-702
Tel: (02) 535-4142 *Fax:* (02) 590-0530
Web Site: www.nl.go.kr
Available only on DVD.
First published 1965.
Annually.

Korean Publication Yearbook (B)
Published by Korean Publishers Association
105-2, Sagan-Dong, Jongno-gu, Seoul 110-190
Tel: (070) 7126-4720; (070) 7126-4736 *Fax:* (02)
738-5414; (02) 735-5653
E-mail: webmaster@kpa21.or.kr
Web Site: www.kpa21.or.kr

Text in Korean.
Annually.

Spain

Litoral (P)
Published by Ediciones Litoral
Urb La Roca, Local 8, 29620 Torremolinos,
Malaga
Tel: 952 388 257
E-mail: litoral@edicioneslitoral.com
Web Site: www.edicioneslitoral.com
Key Personnel
Dir: Lorenzo Saval *E-mail:* lorenzo.saval@gmail.
com
Deputy Dir: Maria Jose Amado
Poetry review: Magazine of Poetry, Art &
Thought.
First published 1926.
2 times/yr.
56 EUR (domestic); 60 EUR (Europe); 95 EUR
(rest of world)
ISSN: 0212-4378

Nuestro Tiempo (Our Time) (P)
Published by Servicio de Publicaciones de la Uni-
versidad de Navarra SA
Edificio de Ciencias Sociales, 31009 Pamplona
Tel: 948 425 600 (ext 80 2590) *Fax:* 948 425 664
E-mail: nuestrot@unav.es
Web Site: www.unav.es/nuestrotiempo
Key Personnel
Dir: Nacho Uria
Editor: Lucia Martinez Alcalde; Ana Eva Fraile
Secretary: Palmira Velazquez
E-mail: pvelazquez@unav.es
First published 1954.
Quarterly.
35 EUR (Spain); 45 EUR (Europe); 55 EUR (rest
of world)
ISSN: 0029-5795

Razon y Fe (Reason & Faith) (P)
Published by Centro Loyola de Estudios y Comu-
nicacion Social
Pablo Aranda, 3, 28006 Madrid
Tel: 915 624 930 *Fax:* 915 634 073
E-mail: ryf@jesuitas.es
Web Site: www.razonyfe.org
Key Personnel
Dir: Alfredo Verdoy Herranz
Editor-in-Chief: Daniel Izuzquiza Regalado
Spanish-American review.
First published 1901.
Monthly.
100 pp, 60 EUR (domestic); 90 EUR (Europe);
95 EUR (elsewhere)
ISSN: 0034-0235
Parent Company: Compania de Jesus Espana

Revista de Libros. Segunda Epoca (P)
Published by Fundacion Amigos Revista de Li-
bros
C/ Principe de Vergara 80, 30B, 28006 Madrid
E-mail: ediciondigital@revistadelibros.com
Web Site: www.revistadelibros.com
Key Personnel
Dir: Alvaro Delgado-Gal
Editor: Luis Gago
Associate Editor: Martin Schifino
Digital only.

Revista de Occidente (Journal of the West) (P)
Published by Fundacion Jose Ortega y Gasset
C/Fortuny, 53, 28010 Madrid
Tel: 917 003 533 *Fax:* 917 003 530
E-mail: revistaoccidente.coordinacion@fogm.es

Web Site: www.ortegaygasset.edu
Key Personnel
Dir: Jose Varela Ortega
First published 1923.
11 times/yr.
80 EUR (Spain); 132 EUR (Europe); 200 USD or
143 EUR (Americas, Africa & Middle East);
225 USD or 162 EUR (Asia & Oceania)
ISSN: 0034-8635

Serra d'Or (P)
Published by Publicacions de l'Abadia de
Montserrat SA
Carrer Ausias Marc, 92-98, 08013 Barcelona
Tel: 932 450 303 *Fax:* 932 473 594
E-mail: serrador@pamsa.cat
Web Site: www.pamsa.cat
Key Personnel
Dir: Josep Massot i Muntaner
First published 1955.
Monthly.
80 pp, 59 EUR (domestic); 79 EUR (Europe);
125 USD (rest of world)
ISSN: 0037-2501

Sri Lanka

Sri Lanka National Bibliography (J)
Published by National Library & Documentation
Services Board
No 14, Independence Ave, Colombo 07
Tel: (011) 2698847; (011) 2685197 *Fax:* (011)
2685201
E-mail: nldsb@mail.natlib.lk; info@mail.natlib.lk
Web Site: www.natlib.lk
Key Personnel
Dir General: Mr W Sunil *Tel:* (011) 2687581
E-mail: dg@mail.natlib.lk
Text in English, Sinhala & Tamil. Contains infor-
mation of the latest publications in Sri Lanka,
publications on Sri Lanka published in for-
eign countries & publications written by Sri
Lankans & published in foreign countries.
First published 1962.
Monthly.
1,800 LKR (domestic)
ISSN: 0253-8229

Sweden

Biblis (J)
Published by Kungliga biblioteket-Sveriges na-
tionalbibliotek (Royal Library-National Library
of Sweden)
Humlegardsgatan 26, Humlegarden, 114 46
Stockholm
Mailing Address: Box 5039, 102 41 Stockholm
Tel: (010) 709 30 00 *Fax:* (010) 709 39 25
E-mail: kungl.biblioteket@kb.se
Web Site: www.kb.se/aktuellt/butik-och-
publikationer/tidskriften-biblis; biblis.se
Key Personnel
Publisher: Jonas Modig
Editor: Ulf Jacobsen *Tel:* (072) 204 00 75
E-mail: ulf.jacobsen@telia.com; Ingrid Svens-
son *Tel:* (010) 709 33 41 *E-mail:* ingrid.
svensson@kb.se
First published 1997.
Quarterly.
400 SEK/yr; 200 SEK/yr (students)
ISSN: 1403-3313

Svensk Bokhandel (Swedish Book Trade) (J)
Published by Tidnings AB Svensk Bokhandel
Birkagatan 16 C, 113 86 Stockholm

Mailing Address: PO Box 68 88, 113 86 Stock-holm
Tel: (08) 545 417 70 *Fax:* (08) 545 417 75
E-mail: redaktion@svb.se
Web Site: www.svb.se
Key Personnel
Publisher & Editor-in-Chief: Tove Leffler
   Tel: (08) 545 417 73 *E-mail:* tove@svb.se
Mng Editor: Carina Jonsson *Tel:* (08) 545 417 77
   E-mail: carina@svb.se
Published jointly with Swedish Booksellers' As-sociation & Swedish Publishers Association.
21 times/yr.
650 SEK (digital); 840 SEK (print & digital)

Switzerland

Bookbird: A Journal of International Children's Literature (J)
Published by International Board on Books for Young People (IBBY)
Nonnenweg 12, Postfach, 4009 Basel
Tel: (061) 272 29 17 *Fax:* (061) 272 27 57
E-mail: ibby@ibby.org
Web Site: www.ibby.org
Key Personnel
Executive Dir: Elizabeth Page *E-mail:* liz.page@ibby.org
Editor: Dr Roxanne Harde *E-mail:* rharde@austana.ca
Covers many facets of international children's literature & includes news from IBBY & the IBBY National Sections.
Also available online (ISSN: 1918-6983).
Quarterly.
Individuals: 50 USD (United States), 60.20 USD (Mexico), 62.70 USD (Canada), 64.60 USD (rest of world); Institutions: 100 USD (United States), 110.20 USD (Mexico), 115.20 USD (Canada), 114.60 USD (rest of world)
ISSN: 0006-7377

Buch und Maus (J)
Published by Schweizerisches Institut fuer Kinder- und Jugendmedien (SIKJM) (Swiss Federation for Youth Literature)
Georgengasse 6, 8006 Zurich
Tel: (043) 268 39 00
E-mail: info@sikjm.ch
Web Site: www.sikjm.ch/publikationen/buchundmaus
Key Personnel
Editor & Design: Elisabeth Eggenberger
   Tel: (043) 268 39 05 *E-mail:* elisabeth.eggenberger@sikjm.ch
Advertising: Silvan Heuberger *Tel:* (043) 268 23 17 *E-mail:* silvan.heuberger@sikjm.ch
First published 1975.
3 times/yr.
36 pp, 40 CHF (domestic); 35 EUR (foreign)
ISSN: 1660-7066

Cenobio (J)
Published by Edizioni Cenobio
Via alle Cascine 32, 6517 Arbedo
Tel: (091) 935 75 75 *Fax:* (091) 935 75 76
E-mail: info@cenobio.ch
Web Site: www.cenobio.ch
Key Personnel
Dir: Pietro Montorfani *E-mail:* pietro.montorfani@gmail.com
Text in French & Italian.
Quarterly.
44 CHF (domestic); 28 EUR (Italy); 58 CHF (elsewhere)
ISSN: 0008-896X

Revue Etudes de Lettres (Literary Studies) (P)
Published by Universite de Lausanne
Faculte des Lettres, Universite de Lausanne, Bati-ment Anthropole, Bureau 4116, 1015 Lausanne
Tel: (021) 692 29 07; (021) 692 29 09 *Fax:* (021) 692 29 05
E-mail: redaction.edl@unil.ch
Web Site: www.unil.ch/edl
Key Personnel
Manager: Florence Bertholet *E-mail:* florence.bertholet@unil.ch; Catherine Chene
   E-mail: catherine.chene@unil.ch
Approximately 170-400 pages.
First published 1926.
Quarterly.
60 CHF/yr (individuals); 45 CHF/yr (students)
ISSN: 0014-2026

orte (places) (P)
Published by orte Verlag (places Publisher)
Urdorferstr 59, 8953 Dietikon
E-mail: redaktion@orteverlag.ch
Web Site: appenzellerverlag.ch
Key Personnel
Editor: Annekatrin Ranft-Rehfeldt
Literary magazine for new poetry, prose & es-says. Text in German.
First published 1974.
5 times/yr.
80 CHF (domestic); 92 CHF (overseas)
ISSN: 1016-7803

Pruefen & Handeln (P)
Published by Memopress Verlag
Postfach, 8215 Hallau
Tel: (052) 681 34 85 *Fax:* (052) 687 37 39
E-mail: emil.rahm@bluewin.ch
Web Site: www.emil-rahm.ch; www.memopress.ch
Journalism & literature; text in German. Short information on politics, economics & religion with commentary. Summary in French.
Parent Company: Aktion Volk und Parlament

Schweizer Buch (The Swiss Book) (J)
Published by Das Schweizerische Nationalbiblio-thek (Swiss National Library)
Hallwylstr 15, 3003 Bern
Tel: (031) 322 89 35 (information) *Fax:* (031) 322 84 08
E-mail: info@nb.admin.ch
Web Site: www.nb.admin.ch
Key Personnel
Dir: Marie-Christine Doffey *Tel:* (031) 322 89 01
   Fax: (031) 322 64 83 *E-mail:* marie-christine.doffey@nb.admin.ch
Online bibliographical bulletin (Swiss National Bibliography): www.nb.admin.ch/sb-pdf.
First published 1943.
25 times/yr.
ISSN: 1661-8211

Schweizer Buchhandel (The Swiss Book Trade) (J)
Published by Schweizer Buchhaendler- und Verleger-Verband (SBVV) (Swiss Booksellers' & Publishers' Association)
Limmatstr 111, 8005 Zurich
Tel: (044) 421 36 16 *Fax:* (044) 421 36 18
E-mail: info@sbvv.ch; redaktion@sbvv.ch
Web Site: www.sbvv.ch
Key Personnel
Editorial Dir: Raphaela Sabel *E-mail:* raphaela.sabel@sbvv.ch
Editor: Pascale Blatter *E-mail:* pascale.blatter@sbvv.ch
10 times/yr.
190 CHF (domestic); 260 CHF (foreign); 158 CHF (electronic)
ISSN: 0036-7338

Schweizer Monatshefte (Swiss Monthly Magazine) (P)
Published by SMH Verlag AG
Rotbuchstr 46, 8037 Zurich
Tel: (044) 361 26 06 *Fax:* (044) 363 70 05
E-mail: info@schweizermonatshefte.ch
Web Site: www.schweizermonatshefte.ch
Key Personnel
Publishing Dir: Andy Fischer *E-mail:* andy.fischer@schweizermonat.ch
Editor-in-Chief: Michael Wiederstein
   E-mail: michael.wiederstein@schweizermonat.ch
First published 1921.
10 times/yr.
195 CHF (domestic); 165 EUR (foreign)

♦WIPO Magazine (P)
Published by World Intellectual Property Organi-zation (WIPO)
34, chemin des Colombettes, 1211 Geneva 20
Mailing Address: PO Box 18, 1211 Geneva
Tel: (022) 338 9111 *Fax:* (022) 733 5428
E-mail: wipomagazine@wipo.int
Web Site: www.wipo.int
Key Personnel
Editor: Catherine Jewell
Available in English, French & Spanish.
Also available online (ISSN: 1564-7854).
6 times/yr.
Free
ISSN: 1020-7074

Taiwan

The Taipei Chinese PEN (P)
Published by Taipei Chinese PEN Centre
4th floor, 4 Lane 68 When Chou St, Taipei 10900
Tel: (02) 2369 3609 *Fax:* (02) 2369 9948
E-mail: taipen@seed.net.tw
Web Site: www.taipen.org
Key Personnel
Editor: Yan Wing Leung
Text in Chinese.
First published 1972.
Quarterly.
900 TWD/yr; 65 USD/yr + postage (overseas)

Tamkang Review (J)
Published by Tamkang University, Dept of En-glish
151, Ying-Chuan Rd, Tamsui, Taipei 25137
Tel: (02) 2621 5656 (ext 2006) *Fax:* (02) 2620 9912
E-mail: tkr@mail2.tku.edu.tw
Web Site: aspers.airiti.com/TKR
Key Personnel
Publisher: Flora Chia-I Chang
Editor-in-Chief: Mei-Hwa Sung
Devoted to literary & culture studies.
First published 1970.
2 times/yr.
ISSN: 0049-2949

Tanzania

Tanzania National Bibliography (J)
Published by Tanzania Library Services Board
National Central Library, PO Box 9283, Dar es Salaam
Tel: (022) 2150048; (022) 2150049 *Fax:* (022) 2151100
E-mail: tlsb@africaonline.co.tz
Web Site: www.tlsb.or.tz

Key Personnel
Dir General: Dr Alli Mcharazo
Text in English.
First published 1970.
Annually.
ISSN: 0856-003X

Turkey

Turkiye Bibliyografyasi (Turkish National
  Bibliography) (J)
Published by National Library of Turkey
Milli Kutuphane Baskanligi, Bahcelievler Son
  Durak, 06490 Ankara
Tel: (0312) 212 62 00 *Fax:* (0312) 223 04 51
E-mail: bilgi@mkutup.gov.tr
Web Site: www.mkutup.gov.tr
Key Personnel
Dir, Dept of Periodicals Collection:
  Nevride Bahceci *Tel:* (0312) 216 73 31
  E-mail: nevride@mkutup.gov.tr
CD-ROM format only.
First published 1939.
Monthly.
ISSN: 0041-4328

Varlik (Existence) (J)
Published by Varlik Yayinlari AS
Perpa Ticaret Merkezi, B-Blok K 5 No 484,
  34384 Sisli, Istanbul
Tel: (0212) 221 31 71 *Fax:* (0212) 320 06 46
E-mail: varlik@varlik.com.tr
Web Site: www.varlik.com.tr
Key Personnel
Editor-in-Chief: Filiz Nayir Deniztekin
Executive Editor: Enver Ercan
First published 1933.
Monthly.
80 TRL (domestic); 60 EUR (foreign)
ISSN: 1300-1728

United Kingdom

∮**African Research & Documentation** (J)
Published by Standing Conference on Library
  Materials on Africa (SCOLMA)
c/o 70 Mortlock Ave, Cambridge CB4 1TE
Tel: (01223) 424584
Web Site: scolma.org/category/ard
Key Personnel
Editor: Terry Barringer *E-mail:* tabarringe@aol.
  com
First published 1973.
2 times/yr.
45 GBP individual; 55 GBP institutions

Agenda (P)
Published by Agenda Editions
The Wheelwrights, Fletching St, Mayfield, East
  Sussex TN20 6TL
Tel: (01435) 873703
E-mail: editor@agendapoetry.co.uk; admin@
  agendapoetry.co.uk
Web Site: www.agendapoetry.co.uk
Key Personnel
Editor: Patricia McCarthy
Poetry journal. Text in English.
First published 1959.
Quarterly.
Individuals: 28 GBP (UK), 30 GBP or 44 EUR
  (Europe), 33 GBP or 65 USD (elsewhere); Li-

braries & Institutions: 35 GBP (UK), 38 GBP
  or 55 EUR (Europe), 40 GBP or 75 USD (elsewhere)
ISSN: 0002-0796

Ambit (P)
Published by Dr Martin Bax
17 Priory Gardens, London N6 5QY
Tel: (020) 8340 3566
E-mail: info@ambitmagazine.co.uk
Web Site: www.ambitmagazine.co.uk
Key Personnel
Editor: Martin Bax
Poetry, prose, short fiction, illustration & reviews.
First published 1959.
Quarterly.
96 pp, 28 GBP (UK); 32 GBP or 40 EUR (rest of
  Europe); 38 GBP or 64 USD (rest of world)
ISSN: 0002-6972

∮**ANTE: Abstracts in New Technologies &
  Engineering** (J)
Published by ProQuest LLC
The Quorum, Barnwell Rd, Cambridge, Cambs
  CB5 8SW
Tel: (01223) 215 512 *Fax:* (01223) 215 513
Web Site: www.proquest.com
An index, with abstracts, to scientific & technical
  periodicals, published in the UK & USA.
Monthly (online only).
Parent Company: Cambridge Information Group
  Inc

The Author (J)
Published by The Society of Authors
84 Drayton Gardens, London SW10 9SB
Tel: (020) 7373 6642 *Fax:* (020) 7373 5768
E-mail: info@societyofauthors.org; membership@
  societyofauthors.org
Web Site: www.societyofauthors.org
Key Personnel
Chief Executive: Nicola Solomon
  E-mail: nsolomon@societyofauthors.org
Deputy Chief Executive: Kate Pool
  E-mail: kpool@societyofauthors.org
Editor: James McConnachie
First published 1890.
Quarterly.
44 GBP (UK); 50 GBP (elsewhere); free to mem-
  bers
ISSN: 0005-0628

The Book Collector (P)
Published by The Collector Ltd
PO Box 6431, London W1A 2BJ
Tel: (020) 7297 4889 *Fax:* (020) 7297 4866
E-mail: info@thebookcollector.co.uk
Web Site: www.thebookcollector.co.uk
Key Personnel
Editor: Nicolas J Barker *Tel:* (020) 7792 3492
  E-mail: editor@thebookcollector.co.uk
Antiquarian books & bibliography.
First published 1952.
Quarterly.
152 pp, 50 GBP (UK); 73.50 EUR (Europe);
  88.50 USD (elsewhere)

∮**BookData Online** (P)
Published by Nielsen Book
Midas House, 3rd floor, 62 Goldsworth Rd, Wok-
  ing, Surrey GU21 6LQ
Tel: (01483) 712 200 *Fax:* (01483) 712 201
E-mail: customerservices.book@nielsen.com;
  sales.bookdata@nielsen.com; marketing.book@
  nielsen.com
Web Site: www.nielsenbook.co.uk
Key Personnel
Sales Dir, Nielsen Book Discovery & Commerce:
  Simon Skinner
Head, Product Leadership: Jon Windus

Online professional bibliographic search & selection tool with a choice of UK & Ireland or
  international coverage. Global: Over 27 million
  English language titles published in the UK,
  Ireland, Europe, USA, Australia, New Zealand
  & South Africa. UK: 16.4 million available
  titles published or distributed in the UK & Ireland. The service offers: coverage of book &
  other published media; content-rich data updated daily; price, sourcing & availability information; publisher & distributor details; wholesaler stock identified & flagged; selected jacket
  & book covers; subject classification; territorial
  rights; literary awards & promotional information. Service also allows you to sort results by
  BookScan chart position & track orders online.
Parent Company: Nielsen Book Services Ltd
Ultimate Parent Company: The Nielsen Company

BookData Record Supply Service, see Nielsen
BookData Record Supply Service

Books for Keeps (J)
Published by Books for Keeps Community Inter-
  est Co
c/o Unit 1 Brampton Park Rd, Wood Green N22
  6BG
Tel: (078) 0789 3369
E-mail: enquires@booksforkeeps.co.uk
Web Site: www.booksforkeeps.co.uk
Key Personnel
Editor: Rosemary Stones
Reviews of children's books.
First published 1980.
6 times/yr.
ISSN: 0143-909X

The Bookseller (P)
Published by Bookseller Media Ltd
Crowne House, 56-58 Southwark St, London SE1
  1UN
Tel: (01371) 851 879 (subscriptions & customer
  service) *Fax:* (020) 7403 4912 (editorial & ad-
  vertising)
E-mail: bookseller@escosubs.co.uk
Web Site: www.thebookseller.com
Key Personnel
Publisher & Chief Executive: Nigel Roby
  Tel: (020) 3358 0361
Editor: Philip Jones *Tel:* (020) 3358 0364
  E-mail: philip.jones@thebookseller.com
Book trade newspaper.
First published 1858.
Weekly.
50 pp, Print & digital/yr: 196 GBP (UK), 224
  GBP (EU), 264 GBP (elsewhere); Digital
  only/yr: 167 GBP
ISSN: 0006-7539

Bookselling Essentials (J)
Published by Booksellers Association of the
  United Kingdom & Ireland Ltd
6 Bell Yard, London WC2A 2JR
Tel: (020) 7421 4640 *Fax:* (020) 7421 4641
E-mail: mail@booksellers.org.uk
Web Site: www.booksellers.org.uk
Key Personnel
Editor: Meryl Halls *E-mail:* meryl.halls@
  booksellers.org.uk
Quarterly.
ISSN: 1745-3798

∮**British Humanities Index (BHI)** (J)
Published by ProQuest LLC
The Quorum, Barnwell Rd, Cambridge, Cambs
  CB5 8SW
Tel: (01223) 215 512 *Fax:* (01223) 215 513
Web Site: www.proquest.com
Indexes & abstracts a wide range of English-
  language journals & weekly magazines pro-
  viding information about humanities subjects

including archaeology, architecture, cinema, history, language, literature, theatre, philosophy & music.
Monthly (online only).
Parent Company: Cambridge Information Group Inc

British National Bibliography (J)
Published by The British Library
Boston Spa, Wetherby, W Yorks LS23 7BQ
Tel: (01937) 546060 *Fax:* (01937) 546333
E-mail: metadata@bl.uk
Web Site: www.bl.uk
British National Bibliography is available in print, online & on CD-ROM.
First published 1950.
Weekly with 2 interim cumulations for Jan-April & May-Aug; annual volume.
ISSN: 0007-1544

Carousel - The Guide to Children's Books (P)
Published by David & Jenny Blanch
The Saturn Centre, 54-76 Bissell St, Birmingham B5 7HP
Tel: (0121) 622 7458
E-mail: carousel.guide@virgin.net
Web Site: www.carouselguide.co.uk
Magazine.
3 times/yr.
11.25 GBP (UK); 16 GBP (Europe & Ireland); 19 GBP (elsewhere)

Catalan Review (J)
Published by Liverpool University Press
4 Cambridge St, Liverpool L69 7ZU
Tel: (0151) 794 2233
E-mail: lup@liv.ac.uk
Web Site: online.liverpooluniversitypress.co.uk
Key Personnel
Editor: Enric Bou
Mng Editor: William Viestenz
Head, Journals: Clare Hooper *Tel:* (0151) 794 3135 *E-mail:* clare.hooper@liv.ac.uk
Published on behalf of the North American Catalan Society.
Also available online (ISSN: 2053-339X).
Annually.
See web site for tiered pricing; free to NASC members
ISSN: 0213-5949

Chapman (P)
Published by Chapman Publishing Ltd
4 Broughton Pl, Edinburgh EH1 3RX
Tel: (0131) 557 2207
E-mail: chapman-pub@blueyonder.co.uk
Web Site: www.chapman-pub.co.uk
Key Personnel
Editor: Joy Hendry
Literary magazine.
First published 1970.
Annually.
111th ed: 200 pp, One yr-Personal: 24 GBP, 48 USD (USA), 30 GBP (overseas); Institutions: 30 GBP, 60 USD (USA), 35 GBP (overseas)
ISSN: 0308-2695

ƒ**CILIP Update** (J)
Published by Chartered Institute of Library & Information Professionals (CILIP)
7 Ridgmount St, London WC1E 7AE
Tel: (020) 7255 0500 *Fax:* (020) 7255 0501
E-mail: update@cilip.org.uk
Web Site: www.cilip.org.uk
Key Personnel
Head, Publications: Gary Allman *Tel:* (020) 7255 0552 *E-mail:* gary.allman@cilip.org.uk
Advertising Manager: Angela Krzyzanowska *Tel:* (020) 7255 0553 *E-mail:* angela.krzyzanowsk@cilip.org.uk

Mng Editor: Rachel Middleton *Tel:* (020) 7255 0585 *E-mail:* rachel.middleton@cilip.org.uk
Production & Design Editor: Richard Gibbons *Tel:* (020) 7255 0587 *E-mail:* richard.gibbons@cilip.org.uk
Industry news, comment & debate within the library & information profession.
First published 2002.
10 times/yr.
Nonmember subscription: 90 GBP (UK), 195 USD (North America), 98 GBP (outside UK)

Critical Quarterly (P)
Published by Wiley-Blackwell Ltd
9600 Garsington Rd, Oxford, Oxon OX4 2DQ
Tel: (01865) 776868 *Fax:* (01865) 714591
E-mail: cs-journals@wiley.com
Web Site: www.wiley.com
Key Personnel
Editor: Colin MacCabe
Publishing Editor: Joanna Jellinek
Deputy Editor: Matthew Taunton
Also available online (ISSN: 1467-8705).
Quarterly.
Individual (print & online): 66 USD (Americas), 60 EUR (Europe) or 40 GBP (rest of world); Institutional (print & online): 749 USD (Americas), 506 EUR (Europe), 875 USD (rest of world)
ISSN: 0011-1562

ƒ**Design & Applied Arts Index (DAAI)** (J)
Published by ProQuest LLC
The Quorum, Barnwell Rd, Cambridge, Cambs CB5 8SW
Tel: (01223) 215 512 *Fax:* (01223) 215 513
Web Site: www.proquest.com
Abstracts & bibliographic records for articles, news items & reviews published in design & applied arts periodicals from 1973 onwards.
Monthly (online only).
Parent Company: Cambridge Information Group Inc

ƒ**Dictionary of International Biography** (B)
Published by Melrose Press Ltd
St Thomas' Pl, Ely, Cambs CB7 4GG
Tel: (01353) 646600 *Fax:* (01353) 646601
E-mail: info@intbiogcentre.com; tradesales@melrosepress.co.uk
Web Site: www.internationalbiographicalcentre.com
General reference publication listing leading individuals from all fields of interest.
35th ed, 265 USD or 165 GBP
ISBN(s): 978-1-903986-35-6

Directory of Publishing: United Kingdom and The Republic of Ireland (B)
Published by Bloomsbury Publishing Plc
50 Bedford Sq, London WC1B 3DP
Tel: (020) 7631 5600 *Fax:* (020) 7631 5800
E-mail: contact@bloomsbury.com; sales@bloomsbury.com
Web Site: www.bloomsbury.com
37th ed, 2014, 194.40 USD (paperback); 155.52 USD (ebook)
ISBN(s): 978-1-4725-2191-0 (paperback); 978-1-4725-3744-7 (ebook)

ƒ**The Europa World of Learning** (B)
Published by Routledge Reference
2 Park Sq, Milton Park, Abingdon, Oxon OX14 4RN
Tel: (020) 7017 6000
E-mail: wol-admin-uk@worldoflearning.com; reference@routledge.com
Web Site: www.worldoflearning.com; www.routledge.com/reference
Key Personnel
Senior Editor: Anthony Gladman

Directory lists over 26,400 academic institutions worldwide. Also available online.
First published 1947.
Annually.
68th ed, 2018: 1,624 pp, 965 GBP
ISBN(s): 978-1-85743-897-0
ISSN: 0084-2117

ƒ**The Europa World Yearbook** (B)
Published by Routledge Reference
2 Park Sq, Milton Park, Abingdon, Oxon OX14 4RN
Tel: (020) 7017 6000 *Fax:* (020) 7017 6699
Web Site: www.europaworld.com/pub; www.routledge.com/reference
Over 5,000 pages of up-to-date statistics & directory information surveying over 250 countries & territories. Also available online.
First published 1926.
Annually.
59th ed, 2018: 5,022 pp, 1,635 GBP
ISBN(s): 978-1-85743-921-2
ISSN: 0071-2302

The Good Book Guide (P)
Published by The Good Book Guide Ltd
1A All Hallows Rd, Bispham, Blackpool FY2 0AS
Tel: (0121) 314 3539
E-mail: enquiries@thegoodbookguide.com
Web Site: www.thegoodbookguide.com
Book review magazine, subscription only.
First published 1977.
Monthly.
27 GBP/yr (UK); 33.75 GBP/yr (Europe); 38.25 GBP/yr (rest of world)

Granta (P)
Published by Granta Publications
12 Addison Ave, Holland Park, London W11 4QR
Tel: (020) 7605 1360 *Fax:* (020) 7605 1361
E-mail: info@granta.com; editorial@granta.com
Web Site: granta.com
Key Personnel
Publisher & Editor: Sigrid Rausing
Deputy Editor: Rosalind Porter
First published 1979.
Quarterly.
256 pp, Print & digital: 48 USD/yr (USA), 56 USD/yr (Canada), 68 USD/yr (Mexico & South America); Digital only: 32 USD/yr
ISSN: 0017-3231

ƒ**The Indexer** (J)
Published by The Society of Indexers
Woodbourn Business Centre, 10 Jessell St, Sheffield S9 3HY
Tel: (0114) 244 9561 *Fax:* (0114) 244 9563
E-mail: info@theindexer.org
Web Site: www.indexers.org.uk; www.theindexer.org
Key Personnel
Executive Editor: Maureen MacGlashan *E-mail:* editor@theindexer.org
International journal of indexing.
Also available online (ISSN: 1756-0632).
First published 1958.
Quarterly.
72 pp, Individuals: 40 GBP (nonmembers); Institutions: 168 GBP (online or print), 210 GBP (online & print)
ISSN: 0019-4131

ƒ**The Journal of Commonwealth Literature** (J)
Published by SAGE Publications Ltd
One Oliver's Yard, 55 City Rd, London EC1Y 1SP
E-mail: jcl@york.ac.uk; journals@sagepub.com; orders@sagepub.com
Web Site: journals.sagepub.com/home/jcl
Key Personnel
Editor: Dr Clair Chambers; Dr Rachel Gilmour

Critical & bibliographical forum in the field of Commonwealth writing. Published quarterly, the first 3 issues contain critical comment on all aspects of Commonwealth & related literatures. The 4th issue contains a comprehensive bibliography of publications in the field.
Also available online (ISSN: 1741-6442).
First published 1965.
Quarterly.
77 GPB/yr (individual); 368 GBP/yr (institutions)
ISSN: 0021-9894

Journal of Literary Studies (J)
Published by Routledge
2 & 4 Park Sq, Milton Park, Abingdon, Oxon OX14 4RN
Tel: (020) 7017 6000
E-mail: subscriptions@tandf.co.uk
Web Site: www.tandf.co.uk
Key Personnel
Editor: Prof Andries W Oliphant
E-mail: oliphaw@unisa.ac.za; Rory Ryan
Journal to provide a forum for the discussion of literary theory, methodology, research & related matters. It features articles, commentary, book reviews & general announcements.
Also available online (ISSN: 1753-5387).
First published 1985.
Quarterly.
Vol 34, 2018, Institutions: 414 GBP, 649 EUR or 814 USD (print & online), 362 GBP, 568 EUR or 718 USD (online only); Individuals: 57 GBP, 96 EUR or 114 USD (print only)
ISSN: 0256-4718

Learned Publishing (J)
Published by The Association of Learned & Professional Society Publishers (ALPSP)
Egale 1, St Albans Rd, Watford, Herts WD17 1DL
Tel: (01245) 260571
E-mail: admin@alpsp.org
Web Site: www.alpsp.org
Key Personnel
Chief Executive & Company Secretary: Audrey McCulloch *Tel:* (01442) 828928
E-mail: audrey.mcculloch@alpsp.org
Editor-in-Chief: Pippa Smart *E-mail:* editor@alpsp.org
North American Editor: Lettie Conrad *E-mail:* useditor@alpsp.org
Administrator: Diane French *Tel:* (01827) 709188
E-mail: diane.french@alpsp.org
Print includes electronic access.
Also available online (ISSN: 1741-4857).
First published 1977.
Quarterly.
80 pp, 233 GBP, 463 USD or 349 EUR (nonmembers)
ISSN: 0953-1513

Literary Review (J)
Published by The Literary Review & Quarto Ltd
44 Lexington St, London W1F 0LW
Tel: (020) 7437 9392
E-mail: editorial@literaryreview.co.uk; subscriptions@warnersgroup.co.uk
Web Site: www.literaryreview.co.uk
Key Personnel
Editor: Nancy Sladek
Reviews of the best newly published fiction & nonfiction.
First published 1979.
11 times/yr.
64 pp, 38 GBP (UK); 48 GBP (Europe, USA & Canada); 65 GBP (rest of world)
ISSN: 0144-4360

London Review of Books (P)
Published by LRB Ltd
28 Little Russell St, London WC1A 2HN

Tel: (020) 7209 1141; (020) 7209 1101 (editorial) *Fax:* (020) 7209 1151
E-mail: edit@lrb.co.uk
Web Site: www.lrb.co.uk
Key Personnel
Editor: Mary-Kay Wilmers
Deputy Editor: Jean McNicol
First published 1979.
24 times/yr.
83.16 GBP (UK); 107 GBP (Europe); 49.95 USD (USA); 69.95 USD (Canada)
ISSN: 0260-9592

ʄ**The Magazine** (J)
Published by PEN International
Unit A, Koops Mill Mews, 162-164 Abbey St, London SE1 2AN
Tel: (020) 7405 0338 *Fax:* (020) 7405 0339
E-mail: info@pen-international.org
Web Site: www.pen-international.org
Key Personnel
Literary Manager: James Tennant *E-mail:* james.tennant@pen-international.org
Literary review. Online only.
First published 1950.
Quarterly.

New Books in German (J)
Published by British Centre for Literary Translation
c/o Goethe-Institut, 50 Princes Gate, Exhibition Rd, London SW7 2PH
Tel: (020) 7596 4000
E-mail: nbg@london.goethe.org
Web Site: www.new-books-in-german.com
Key Personnel
Editor: Charlotte Ryland
Reviews German language literature (Austrian, German & Swiss) in English to promote sales into the British & USA markets.
2 times/yr.

ʄ**New Review of Academic Librarianship** (J)
Published by Routledge
2 & 4 Park Sq, Milton Park, Abingdon, Oxon OX14 4RN
Tel: (020) 7017 6000
E-mail: subscriptions@tandf.co.uk
Web Site: www.tandf.co.uk
Key Personnel
Editor-in-Chief: Graham Walton, PhD *E-mail:* j.g.walton@lboro.ac.uk
Also available online (ISSN: 1740-7834).
First published 1995.
Quarterly.
Vol 24, 2018, Institutions: 345 GBP, 488 EUR or 615 USD (print & online), 302 GBP, 427 EUR or 538 USD (online only); Individuals: 67 GBP, 92 EUR or 111 USD (print only)
ISSN: 1361-4533

ʄ**New Review of Children's Literature and Librarianship** (J)
Published by Routledge
2 & 4 Park Sq, Milton Park, Abingdon, Oxon OX14 4RN
Tel: (020) 7017 6000
E-mail: subscriptions@tandf.co.uk
Web Site: www.tandf.co.uk
Key Personnel
Editor: Dr Sally Maynard *E-mail:* s.e.maynard@lboro.ac.uk
Also available online (ISSN: 1740-7885).
First published 1995.
2 times/yr.
Vol 24, 2018, Institutions: 248 GBP, 350 EUR or 439 USD (print & online), 217 GBP, 306 EUR or 384 USD (online only); Individuals: 51 GBP, 70 EUR or 87 USD (print only)
ISSN: 1361-4541

ʄ**New Review of Hypermedia and Multimedia** (J)
Published by Taylor & Francis
2 & 4 Park Sq, Milton Park, Abingdon, Oxon OX14 4RN
Tel: (020) 7017 6000
E-mail: subscriptions@tandf.co.uk
Web Site: www.tandf.co.uk
Key Personnel
Editor: Daniel Cunliffe; Yeliz Yesilada; Douglas Tudhope
Also available online (ISSN: 1740-7842).
First published 1995.
Quarterly.
Vol 23, 2017, Institutions: 457 GBP, 607 EUR or 758 USD (print & online), 400 GBP, 531 EUR or 663 USD (online only); Individuals: 271 GBP, 353 EUR or 443 USD (print only)
ISSN: 1361-4568

ʄ**New Review of Information Networking** (J)
Published by Routledge
2 & 4 Park Sq, Milton Park, Abingdon, Oxon OX14 4RN
Tel: (020) 7017 6000
E-mail: subscriptions@tandf.co.uk
Web Site: www.tandf.co.uk
Key Personnel
Editor-in-Chief: David Anderson
Associate Editor: Milena Dobreva
Also available online (ISSN: 1740-7869).
First published 1995.
2 times/yr.
Vol 22, 2017, Institutions: 241 GBP, 338 EUR or 425 USD (print & online), 211 GBP, 296 EUR or 372 USD (online only); Individuals: 50 GBP, 67 EUR or 83 USD (print only)
ISSN: 1361-4576

The New Walford Guide to Reference Resources (B)
Published by Facet Publishing
7 Ridgmount St, London WC1E 7AE
Tel: (020) 7255 0590 *Fax:* (020) 7255 0591
E-mail: info@facetpublishing.co.uk
Web Site: www.facetpublishing.co.uk
Key Personnel
Publishing Dir: Helen Carley *Tel:* (020) 7255 0592 *E-mail:* helen.carley@facetpublishing.co.uk
Production & Editorial Manager: Natalie Jones *Tel:* (020) 7255 0595 *E-mail:* natalie.jones@facetpublishing.co.uk
First published 2005.
Irregularly.
249.95 GBP (Vol 1 or 2)
ISBN(s): 978-1-85604-495-0 (Vol 1: Science, Technology & Medicine); 978-1-85604-498-1 (Vol 2: The Social Sciences); 978-1-85604-919-1 (Vol 1: Science, Technology & Medicine ebook); 978-1-85604-920-7 (Vol 2: The Social Sciences ebook)

Nielsen BookData Record Supply Service (P)
Published by Nielsen Book
Midas House, 3rd floor, 62 Goldsworth Rd, Woking, Surrey GU21 6LQ
Tel: (01483) 712 200
E-mail: sales.bookdata@nielsen.com
Web Site: www.nielsenbook.co.uk
Key Personnel
Sales Dir, Nielsen Book Discovery & Commerce: Simon Skinner
Head, Product Leadership: Jon Windus
Online resource that enables clients to enrich their web sites & internal systems supplies with enriched bibliographic data. The data is supplied in a tailored format according to the clients requirements from a source of up to 19.2 million jacket/cover images & over 27 million title records including descriptions & tables of contents for UK, US, in-print, forthcoming &

out-of-print titles. Clients can stipulate the data set & collect as a daily or weekly update, in a wide variety of formats including CSV, XML & ONIX.
Parent Company: Nielsen Book Services Ltd
Ultimate Parent Company: The Nielsen Company

Nielsen PubEasy (P)
Published by Nielsen Book
Midas House, 3rd floor, 62 Goldsworth Rd, Woking, Surrey GU21 6LQ
Tel: (01483) 712 200
Web Site: beta.pubeasy.com/static/pubeasy/index.html
Key Personnel
Sales Dir, Nielsen Book Discovery & Commerce: Simon Skinner
Business Development Dir: David Walter
Head, Product Leadership: Jon Windus
Online resource used globally by thousands of booksellers to quickly & efficiently place orders, check price & title availability, check order status & track orders online with participating publishers, distributors & wholesalers.
Parent Company: Nielsen Book Services Ltd
Ultimate Parent Company: The Nielsen Company

Orbis (P)
17 Greenhow Ave, West Kirby, Wirral CH48 5EL
Web Site: www.orbisjournal.com
Key Personnel
Editor: Carole Baldock *E-mail:* carolebaldock@hotmail.com
Independent British literary quarterly with international connections; publishes mainly poetry, but uses some prose & letters; also features news, educational & review columns.
First published 1969.
Quarterly.
Issue Price: 5 GBP (domestic); 10 GBP, 14 EUR or 16 USD (overseas)
ISSN: 0030-4425

Planet - The Welsh Internationalist (P)
Published by Berw Cyf
PO Box 44, Aberystwyth, Ceredigion SY23 3ZZ
Tel: (01970) 611255
E-mail: submissions@planetmagazine.org.uk
Web Site: www.planetmagazine.org.uk
Key Personnel
Editor: Jasmine Donahaye
Associate Editor: Emily Trahair
First published 1970.
Quarterly.
160 pp, 22 GBP (UK); 30 GBP (Europe); 40 GBP (overseas)
ISSN: 0048-4288

ʄ**PN Review** (J)
Published by Carcanet Press Ltd
Alliance House, 4th floor, 30 Cross St, Manchester M2 7AQ
Tel: (0161) 834 8730 *Fax:* (0161) 832 0084
E-mail: info@carcanet.co.uk
Web Site: www.carcanet.co.uk; www.pnreview.co.uk
Key Personnel
Editorial & Mng Dir: Michael Schmidt
   E-mail: schmidt@carcanet.co.uk
Features poetry & literary criticism.
First published 1973.
6 times/yr.
72 pp, Prices in GBP. Individuals: Print & digital 39.50 (UK), 45 (Europe), 49 (other), Digital 35 (worldwide); Institutional: Print & digital 149 (UK), 155 (Europe), 175 (other), Digital 115 (worldwide), Print 56 (UK), 62 (Europe), 70 (other); Students: see web site for pricing
ISSN: 0144-7076

Poetry Review (P)
Published by The Poetry Society

22 Betterton St, London WC2H 9BX
Tel: (020) 7420 9880 *Fax:* (020) 7240 4818
E-mail: info@poetrysociety.org.uk
Web Site: poetrysociety.org.uk/publications-section/the-poetry-review
Key Personnel
Editor: Emily Berry
Poetry & reviews.
First published 1912.
Quarterly.
Free to members

ʄ**Private Press Books** (B)
Published by The Private Libraries Association (PLA)
Ravelston, South View Rd, Pinner, Middx HA5 3YD
Web Site: www.plabooks.org
Key Personnel
Editor, Private Press Books: Dr Paul W Nash
Editor: Margaret Lock; Asa Peavy; David Chambers
Bibliography of the work of private presses throughout the world.
Irregularly.
ISSN: 0079-5402

PubEasy, see Nielsen PubEasy

ʄ**The Rialto** (P)
PO Box 309, Aylsham, Norwich, Norfolk NR11 6LN
E-mail: info@therialto.co.uk
Web Site: www.therialto.co.uk
Key Personnel
Editor: Michael Mackmin
Poetry magazine.
First published 1984.
3 times/yr.
64 pp, 24 GBP
ISSN: 0268-5981

ʄ**The School Librarian** (J)
Published by School Library Association
One Pine Court, Kembrey Park, Swindon SN2 8AD
Tel: (01793) 530166 *Fax:* (01793) 481182
E-mail: info@sla.org.uk
Web Site: www.sla.org.uk/the-school-librarian.php
Key Personnel
Features Editor: Barbara Band *E-mail:* sleditor@sla.org.uk
Reviews Editor: Joy Court *E-mail:* joy@sla.org.uk
Articles, regular features, reviews of new books-fiction & nonfiction & reviews of apps, web sites & other media.
First published 1937.
Quarterly.
56 pp, Free to members; 115 GBP (institutional nonmembers)
ISSN: 0036-6595

Scrutiny2: Issues in English Studies in Southern Africa (P)
Published by Routledge
2 & 4 Park Sq, Milton Park, Abingdon, Oxon OX14 4RN
Tel: (020) 7017 6000
E-mail: subscriptions@tandf.co.uk
Web Site: www.tandf.co.uk
Key Personnel
Mng Editor: Deirdre Byrne; Gregory Graham-Smith
Literary articles & reviews.
Co-published with UNISA Press.
Also available online (ISSN: 1753-5409).
First published 1996.
3 times/yr.
Vol 22, 2017, Institutions: 306 GBP, 486 EUR or 607 USD (print & online), 268 GBP, 425

EUR or 531 USD (online only); Individuals: 59 GBP. 90 EUR or 113 USD (print only)
ISSN: 1812-5441

Sheppard's Book Dealers in Australia & New Zealand (B)
Published by Richard Joseph Publishers Ltd
Priory Cottage, Frithelstock, Torrington, Devon EX38 8ZJ
Mailing Address: PO Box 15, Torrington, Devon EX38 8ZJ
Tel: (01805) 625750 *Fax:* (01805) 625376
E-mail: post@sheppardsworld.co.uk; info@sheppardsworld.co.uk
Web Site: www.sheppardsworld.co.uk
Key Personnel
Advertising: Rachel Heath
Editorial: Richard Joseph
Directory of antiquarian & secondhand book dealers in Australia & New Zealand. E-mail & web sites included.
4th ed: 252 pp, 30 GBP
ISBN(s): 978-1-872699-76-9

Sheppard's Book Dealers in the British Isles (B)
Published by Richard Joseph Publishers Ltd
Priory Cottage, Frithelstock, Torrington, Devon EX38 8ZJ
Mailing Address: PO Box 15, Torrington, Devon EX38 8ZJ
Tel: (01805) 625750 *Fax:* (01805) 625376
E-mail: post@sheppardsworld.co.uk; info@sheppardsworld.co.uk
Web Site: www.sheppardsworld.co.uk
Key Personnel
Advertising: Rachel Heath
Editorial: Richard Joseph
Antiquarian & secondhand book dealers in the British Isles, The Channel Islands, The Isle of Man & the Republic of Ireland. E-mail & web sites included.
Annually.
31st ed: 556 pp, 30 GBP or 60 USD
ISBN(s): 978-1-872699-86-8

ʄ**Slavonica** (J)
Published by Routledge
2 & 4 Park Sq, Milton Park, Abingdon, Oxon OX14 4RN
Tel: (020) 7017 6000
E-mail: subscriptions@tandf.co.uk
Web Site: www.tandf.co.uk
Key Personnel
Editor: John Bates; Margaret Tejerizo; Zsuzsanna Varga
Academic publication on the languages, literature, history & culture of Russia & Central & Eastern Europe.
Also available online (ISSN: 1745-8145).
First published 1983.
2 times/yr.
Institutions: 221 GBP, 317 EUR or 407 USD (print & online), 193 GBP, 277 EUR or 356 USD (online only); Individuals: 68 GBP. 98 EUR or 122 USD (print & online), 54 GBP, 78 EUR or 97 USD (online only)
ISSN: 1361-7427

Stand Magazine (P)
School of English, University of Leeds, Leeds LS2 9JT
Tel: (0113) 343 4794 *Fax:* (0113) 343 4791
E-mail: enquiries@standmagazine.org; editors@standmagazine.org
Web Site: www.standmagazine.org
Key Personnel
Mng Editor: Jon Glover
Editor: Elaine Glover; John Whale
Associate Editor: David Latane
Literary magazine.
First published 1952.
Quarterly.

Individuals-online only: 10 GBP (UK), 12 GBP (rest of world); Individuals-personal: 27 GBP (UK), 35 GBP (Europe), 37 GBP (rest of world); Individuals-senior & student: 20 GBP (UK), 21 GBP (rest of world); Institutions: 40 GBP (UK), 47 GBP (Europe), 49 GBP (rest of world)

Swedish Book Review (P)
Published by Norvik Press
85 Ediva Rd, Meopham, Kent DA13 0ND
Tel: (020) 7679 7748 (subscriptions)
E-mail: editor@swedishbookreview.com
Web Site: www.swedishbookreview.com
Key Personnel
Editor: Sarah Death
Translation & reviews, in English of works written in Swedish, originating from Sweden or Swedish writers in Finland. Official journal of the Swedish-English Literary Translators' Assocation (SELTA).
First published 1983.
2 times/yr.
64 pp, 17 GBP, 28 USD or 200 SEK; Airmail outside Europe; 20 GBP, 33 USD or 230 SEK
ISSN: 0265-8119

ƒ**The Times Literary Supplement (TLS)** (P)
Published by The Times Literary Supplement Ltd
3 Thomas More Sq, London E98 1BS
Tel: (020) 7782 4985 *Fax:* (020) 7782 4966
Web Site: entertainment.timesonline.co.uk
Key Personnel
Mng Dir: James MacManus
Editor: Peter Stothard
Deputy Editor: Alan Jenkins
First published 1902.
Weekly.
92 GBP/yr (UK), 112 GBP/yr (Europe) or 132 GBP/yr (rest of world); 169 USD/yr (USA); 225 CAD/yr (Canada)
Parent Company: News International

ƒ**Whitaker's Almanack** (B)
Published by Bloomsbury Publishing Plc
50 Bedford Sq, London WC1B 3DP
E-mail: whitakersalmanackteam@bloomsbury. com; contact@bloomsbury.com; sales@ bloomsbury.com
Web Site: www.whitakersalmanack.com; www. bloomsbury.com
Key Personnel
Executive Editor: Ruth Northey
Project Editor: James Robinson
General reference book including information on British government. Also available online.
First published 1868.
Annually.
150th ed, 2018: 1,184 pp, 90 GBP
ISBN(s): 978-1-4729-3502-1

ƒ**Willings Press Guide** (B)
Published by Cision UK Ltd
5 Churchill Pl, Canary Wharf, E14 5HU London
Tel: (020) 7074 2560
Web Site: www.cision.co.uk
Reference guide to newspapers, news agencies, radio & television stations plus UK & Ireland business & consumer titles.
Annually.
550 GBP (2-vol set); 325 GBP (1 vol)
ISBN(s): 978-1-906035-79-2 (2-vol set); 978-1-906035-80-8 (UK & Ireland); 978-1-906035-81-5 (World News Media)

ƒ**Writers' & Artists' Yearbook** (B)
Published by Bloomsbury Publishing Plc
50 Bedford Sq, London WC1B 3DP
Tel: (020) 7631 5993
E-mail: writersandartists@bloomsbury.com
Web Site: www.writersandartists.co.uk

Key Personnel
Editor: Alysoun Owen
Expert advice on writing techniques, research & markets. Text in English.
First published 1907.
Annually in July.
106th ed, 18.99 GBP
ISBN(s): 978-1-408-15749-7
ISSN: 0084-2664

Writing Magazine (P)
Published by Warners Group Publications PLC
31-32 Park Row, 5th floor, Leeds LS1 5JD
Tel: (0113) 200 2929; (01778) 392482 (subscriptions)
Web Site: www.writers-online.co.uk
Key Personnel
Editor: Jonathan Telfer *Tel:* (0113) 200 2913
  E-mail: jtelfer@warnersgroup.co.uk
Assistant Editor: Tina Jackson *Tel:* (0113) 200 2919 *E-mail:* tjackson@warnersgroup.co.uk
Marketing Manager: Lauren Beharrell
  Tel: (0113) 200 2916 *E-mail:* lauren.beharrell@ warnersgroup.co.uk
Offers interviews with famous authors, writer profiles, how-to articles on poetry, fiction, short stories, photojournalism, technology, nonfiction writing & more competitions.
Monthly.
Print: 42 GBP (UK), 55 GBP (Europe), 60 GBP (rest of world); Digital: 38.99 GBP (worldwide)
ISSN: 0964-9166

United States

ƒ**Bookman's Price Index: A Guide to the Values of Rare and Other Out of Print Books** (P)
Published by Gale
Division of Cengage Learning
27500 Drake Rd, Farmington Hills, MI 48331-3535
SAN: 213-4373
Tel: 248-699-4253 *Toll Free Tel:* 800-877-4253
  Toll Free Fax: 800-414-5043 (orders)
E-mail: gale.customerservice@cengage.com
Web Site: www.gale.cengage.com
Provides access to reviews of books, periodicals, books on tape & electronic media representing a wide range of popular, academic & professional interests. More than 600 publications are indexed including journals & national general interest publications & newspapers. Also available online.
First published 1964.
2-3 times/yr.

ƒ**Bookman's Price Index: A Guide to the Values of Rare and Other Out of Print Books** (P)
Published by Gale
Division of Cengage Learning
27500 Drake Rd, Farmington Hills, MI 48331-3535
SAN: 213-4373
Tel: 248-699-4253 *Toll Free Tel:* 800-877-4253
  Toll Free Fax: 800-414-5043 (orders)
E-mail: gale.customerservice@cengage.com
Web Site: www.gale.cengage.com
A guide to the prices & availability of more than 25,000 rare or out-of-print antiquarian books as offered for sale in the catalogs of nearly 200 leading bookdealers in the USA, UK & Canada. Each volume lists almost 15,000 titles. Volumes do not supersede previous volumes. Each volume covers catalogs from the previous 4-6 months. Each entry includes title, author, edition, year published, physical description

(size, binding, illustrations), condition of the book & price. Arranged alphabetically by author.
First published 1964.
2-3 times/yr.

ƒ**Contemporary Authors** (B)
Published by Gale
Division of Cengage Learning
27500 Drake Rd, Farmington Hills, MI 48331-3535
SAN: 213-4373
Tel: 248-699-4253 *Toll Free Tel:* 800-877-4253
  Toll Free Fax: 800-414-5043 (orders)
E-mail: gale.customerservice@cengage.com
Web Site: www.gale.cengage.com
Each volume includes biographical information on current writers in fiction, general nonfiction, poetry, journalism, drama, motion pictures & television. Also available as ebooks.
First published 1962.
12+ vols/yr.
293 USD/vol
ISBN(s): 978-1-4144-6097-0 (Vol 315); 978-1-4144-6098-7 (Vol 316); 978-1-4144-6099-4 (Vol 317); 978-1-4144-6100-7 (Vol 318); 978-1-4144-6101-4 (Vol 319); 978-1-4144-6847-1 (Vol 320); 978-1-4144-6848-8 (Vol 321)

ƒ**Directory of Special Libraries and Information Centers** (B)
Published by Gale
Division of Cengage Learning
27500 Drake Rd, Farmington Hills, MI 48331-3535
SAN: 213-4373
Tel: 248-699-4253 *Toll Free Tel:* 800-877-4253
  Toll Free Fax: 800-414-5043 (orders)
E-mail: gale.customerservice@cengage.com
Web Site: www.gale.cengage.com
A key to the holdings, services, electronic resources & personnel of more than 34,500 special libraries & special collections, information centers, documentation centers & similar units. Also available electronically.

ƒ**The Historical Novels Review** (J)
Published by Historical Novel Society
c/o Eastern Illinois University, Booth Library, 600 Lincoln Ave, Charleston, IL 61920
Tel: 217-581-7538 *Fax:* 217-581-7534
E-mail: reviews@historicalnovelsociety.org
Web Site: historicalnovelsociety.org
Key Personnel
Publr: Richard Lee *E-mail:* richard@ historicalnovelsociety.org
Mng Editor: Bethany Latham *E-mail:* blatham@ jsu.edu
Book Review Editor: Sarah Johnson
  E-mail: sljohnson2@eiu.edu
Features Ed: Lucinda Byatt *E-mail:* textline13@ gmail.com
Reviews of currently published historical fiction from the USA & the UK.
First published 1997.
Quarterly.
64 pp, 50 USD/yr
ISSN: 1471-7492

ƒ**International Literary Market Place (ILMP)** (B)
Published by Information Today, Inc
121 Chanlon Rd, Suite G-20, New Providence, NJ 07974-2195
Tel: 908-795-3755 *Toll Free Tel:* 800-409-4929 (press 3); 800-300-9868 (cust serv)
E-mail: custserv@infotoday.com
Web Site: www.literarymarketplace.com
Directory of companies & individuals in the book publishing trade, covering over 175 countries outside the USA & Canada. Entries included for more than 9,400 publishers & 3,200 book organizations, including agents, booksellers &

library associations. The USA & Canada are covered by *Literary Market Place*. Web version, which includes *Literary Market Place*, also available.
Annually.
52nd ed, 2019: 1,876 pp, 349.50 USD (print); 439.50 USD (web)
ISBN(s): 978-1-57387-547-9
ISSN: 0074-6827

Literary Market Place (LMP) (B)
Published by Information Today, Inc
121 Chanlon Rd, Suite G-20, New Providence, NJ 07974-2195
Tel: 908-795-3755 *Toll Free Tel:* 800-409-4929 (press 3); 800-300-9868 (cust serv)
E-mail: custserv@infotoday.com
Web Site: www.literarymarketplace.com
Directory of over 25,000 companies & individuals USA & Canadian publishing. A two volume set, each containing two alphabetical names & numbers indexes, one for key companies listed & one for individuals. The rest of the world is covered by *International Literary Market Place*. Web version, which includes *International Literary Market Place*, also available.
Annually.
79th ed, 2019: 1,600 pp, 439.50 USD (print); 439.50 USD (web)
ISBN(s): 978-1-57387-549-3 (2 volume set)
ISSN: 0000-1155

ф**Scandinavian Review** (J)
Published by American-Scandinavian Foundation (ASF)
58 Park Ave, New York, NY 10016
Tel: 212-779-3587 *Fax:* 212-686-2115
E-mail: info@amscan.org; editor@amscn.org
Web Site: www.amscan.org/publications
Cultural/literary/political magazine.
First published 1913.
3 times/yr.
Free to members

ф**Ulrich's Periodicals Directory**
Published by ProQuest LLC
Subsidiary of Cambridge Information Group Inc
630 Central Ave, New Providence, NJ 07974
Tel: 908-795-3659 (editorial) *Toll Free Tel:* 800-346-6049 (Ulrich's hotline, USA only)
E-mail: ulrichs@proquest.com; core_service@ proquest.com (orders)
Web Site: www.ulrichsweb.com; www.proquest.com (publisher)
Four-volume set, arranged by subject classification, includes periodicals, newsletters, newspapers, annuals & irregular serials published worldwide. Also available online.
First published 1932.
Annual.
56th ed, 2018: 12,192 pp, 3,189 USD/4 vol set
ISBN(s): 978-1-60030-668-6 (4 vol set)
ISSN: 0000-2100

Venezuela

Bibliografia Venezolana (Venezuelan Bibliography) (B)
Published by Instituto Autonomo Biblioteca Nacional y de Servicios de Bibliotecas
Final Av Panteon, Edificio Foro Libertador, Cuerpo 2, Nivel S-1, Parroquia Altagracia, Caracas 1010
Tel: (0212) 505 91 25 *Fax:* (0212) 505 91 24
Web Site: www.bnv.gob.ve
CD-ROM. Text in Spanish.
First published 1970.
2 times/yr.
45 VEF
ISSN: 1316-6654

Zambia

National Bibliography of Zambia (B)
Published by The National Archives of Zambia (NAZ)
Government Rd, PO Box 50010, Lusaka
Tel: (021) 1254081
Bibliography. Text in English.
Annually.
ISSN: 0377-1636

Literary Associations & Prizes

Literary Associations & Societies

Listed in this section are literary associations and societies. Listings appear alphabetically under the country in which they are located. Other book trade associations and organizations can be found in the sections **Book Trade Organizations** and **Library Associations**.

Argentina

Academia Argentina de Letras (Argentine Academy of Letters)
Subsidiary of Ministerio de Ciencia, Tecnologia e Innovacion Productiva
Sanchez de Bustamante 2663, Boedo, C1425DVA Buenos Aires
Tel: (011) 4802-3814; (011) 4802-7509 (ext 5) *Fax:* (011) 4802-3814 (ext 9)
E-mail: publicaciones@aal.edu.ar; biblioteca@aal. edu.ar; administracion@aal.edu.ar
Web Site: www.aal.edu.ar
Key Personnel
President: Jose Luis Moure *Tel:* (011) 4802-3814 ext 6 *E-mail:* presidencia@aal.edu.ar
Vice President: Alicia Maria Zorrilla
Secretary General: Norma Carricaburo *E-mail:* secretaria.general@aal.edu.ar
Treasurer: Rolando Costa Picazo
Founded: 1931
Specialize in philosophy, literature & linguistics.
Membership(s): Asociacion de Academias de la Lengua Espanola.
Publication(s): *Boletin de la Academia Argentina de Letras* (Bulletin of the Argentine Academy of Letters); *Coleccion Bolsillables*; *Coleccion La Academia y la Lengua del Pueblo*; *Fuera de coleccion*; *Serie de acuerdos acerca del Idioma*; *Serie de Clasicos Angentinos*; *Serie Estudios academicos*; *Serie Estudios Linguisticos y Filologicos*; *Serie Homenajes*; *Serie Practicas y representaciones bibliograficas*

Argentinian PEN Centre
Member of PEN International
Coronel Diaz 2089, 1425 Buenos Aires
Tel: (011) 4825 8548
Key Personnel
President: Teresita Frugoni de Fritzsche *E-mail:* betrizcuria@hotmail.com
Secretary: Alicia Bermolen *E-mail:* aliber@ argentina.com
Publication(s): *Boletin*

Australia

ACT Writers Centre
Gorman House Arts Center, Ainslie Ave, Braddon, ACT 2612
Tel: (02) 6262 9191 *Fax:* (02) 6262 9192
E-mail: admin@actwriters.org.au
Web Site: www.actwriters.org.au
Key Personnel
Acting Dir: Kelli-anne Moore

Communications Officer: Kimberley Gaal
Dedicated to helping ACT region writers achieve their full potential by providing targeted services & opportunities.

ASA, see Australian Society of Authors

ASAL, see Association for the Study of Australian Literature (ASAL)

Association for the Study of Australian Literature (ASAL)
c/o Federation University Australia, University Dr, Mount Helen, Victoria 3350
Web Site: www.austlit.edu.au/ASAL
Key Personnel
President: Sue Martin *E-mail:* s.martin@latrobe. edu.au
Vice President: Brigid Rooney *E-mail:* brigid. rooney@sydney.edu.au
Treasurer: Roger Osborne *E-mail:* r.osborne@uq. edu.au
Secretary: Demelza Hall *E-mail:* d.hall@ federation.edu.au
Founded: 1899
Promotes the study, discussion & creation of Australian writing.
Publication(s): *Journal of the Association for the Study of Australian Literature (JASAL)* (annually)

Australasian Association for Lexicography (Australex)
c/o Linguistics Dept, Macquarie University, North Ryde, NSW 2109
Tel: (02) 9850 8783 *Fax:* (02) 9850 9199
Web Site: www.australex.org
Key Personnel
President & Treasurer: Adam Smith *E-mail:* adam.smith@ling.mq.edu.au
Vice President: Ghil'ad Zuckermann *E-mail:* gzuckermann@gmail.com
Secretary: Julia Miller *E-mail:* julia.miller@ adelaide.edu.au
Founded: 1990
Publication(s): *Australex* (newsletter)

Australex, see Australasian Association for Lexicography (Australex)

Australian Literature Society, see Association for the Study of Australian Literature (ASAL)

Australian Society of Authors
22-36 Mountain St, Suite C1.06, Ultimo, NSW 2007
Tel: (02) 9211 1004 *Fax:* (02) 9211 0125
E-mail: asa@asauthors.org

Web Site: www.asauthors.org
Key Personnel
Foundation President: Dal Stivens
Chair: Sophie Masson
Deputy Chair: Robyn Sheahan-Bright
Treasurer: David Day
Founded: 1963
Publication(s): *Australian Author* (quarterly, magazine)

Australian Writers' Guild Ltd
5 Blackfriars St, Chippendale, NSW 2008
Tel: (02) 9319 0339 *Fax:* (02) 9319 0141
E-mail: admin@awg.com.au
Web Site: www.awg.com.au
Key Personnel
President: Jan Sardi
Vice President: Kelly Lefever; Roger Simpson
Executive Dir: Jacqueline Woodman
Founded: 1962
Represents Australian performance writers, giving access to industry information as well as providing a wide variety of services.
Publication(s): *A Matter of Cultural Sovereignty*; *The Writers' Directory: Writers for Screen, Stage, Radio & Television in Australia*

CBCA, see The Children's Book Council of Australia

The Children's Book Council of Australia
416 Magill Rd, Kensington Gardens, SA 5068
Mailing Address: PO Box 3203, Norwood, SA 5067
Tel: (08) 8332 2845 *Toll Free Tel:* 1800 248 379 *Fax:* (08) 8333 0394
Web Site: www.cbca.org.au
Key Personnel
President: Julie Wells *E-mail:* president@cbca. org.au
Secretary: Judy Miller *E-mail:* secretary@cbca. org.au
Treasurer: Robyn Cations *E-mail:* treasurer@ cbca.org.au
Awards Coordinator: Nan Halliday; Helen Martin
Branches in New South Wales, Queensland, South Australia, Tasmania, Victoria, Western Australia, Australian Capital Territory, Northern Territory.
Publication(s): *Reading Time* (quarterly, journal)

FAW, see Fellowship of Australian Writers (Vic) Inc

Fellowship of Australian Writers (Vic) Inc
6 Davies St, Brunswick, Victoria 3056
Tel: (03) 9386 2232
E-mail: austwriter@writers.asn.au
Web Site: www.fawvic.com.au/

Key Personnel
President: Lynn Smailes *E-mail:* president@
writers.asn.au
Treasurer & Awards Coordinator: Gail Blundell
E-mail: treasurer@writers.asn.au
Founded: 1928
Publication(s): *The Australian Writer* (quarterly)

NSW Writers' Centre
PO Box 1056, Rozelle, NSW 2039
Tel: (02) 9555 9757 *Fax:* (02) 9818 1327
E-mail: info@nswwc.org.au
Web Site: www.nswwc.org.au
Key Personnel
Chair: Susanne Gervay
Deputy Chair: Diane Murray
Dir: David Ryding
Secretary: Elisabeth Storrs
Founded: 1991
Resource & information centre for emerging &
professional writers.
Publication(s): *Newsbite* (weekly, newsletter);
Newswrite (monthly)

Melbourne PEN Centre
Member of PEN International
PO Box 373, Fairfield, Victoria 3078
Tel: (04) 0204 9487
E-mail: admin@melbournepen.com.au
Web Site: www.melbournepen.com.au
Key Personnel
President: Arnold Zable
Vice President: Judith Buckrich; Judith Rodriguez
Secretary: Jackie Mansourian
Treasurer: Robert Cope
Founded to promote friendship & intellectual co-
operation among writers everywhere.
Publication(s): *PEN Melbourne Quarterly*

Sydney PEN Centre
Member of PEN International
c/o FASS, UTS, PO Box 123, Broadway, NSW
2007
Tel: (02) 9514 2755 *Toll Free Tel:* 1300 364 997
(in Australia)
E-mail: sydney@pen.org.au
Web Site: www.pen.org.au
Key Personnel
President: Prof Michael Fraser
Vice President: Dr Debra Adelaide; Sandra
Symons
Executive Officer: Amy Drewe
Founded: 1931
Advocates for & raises awareness of freedom of
expression in the Asian & Pacific region.
Publication(s): *Sydney PEN Magazine* (biannually,
magazine)

Queensland Writers Centre
Level 2, State Library of Queensland, Cultural
Centre, Stanley Pl, South Bank, Qld 4101
Mailing Address: PO Box 3488, South Brisbane,
Qld 4101
Tel: (07) 3842 9922 *Fax:* (07) 3842 9920
E-mail: qldwriters@qwc.asn.au
Web Site: www.qwc.asn.au
Key Personnel
Chief Executive Officer: Kate Eltham
Acting Program & Services Manager: Sarah Gory
Works to advance the recognition of Queensland
writers by contributing to their professional de-
velopment.
Publication(s): *WQ Magazine* (monthly exc com-
bined Dec/Jan issue)

SA Writers' Centre Inc
187 Rundle St, 2nd floor, Adelaide, SA 5000
Mailing Address: PO Box 43, Rundle Mall, Ade-
laide, SA 5000
Tel: (08) 8223 7662 *Fax:* (08) 8232 3994
E-mail: admin@sawriters.org.au

Web Site: www.sawc.org.au; sawriters.org.au
Key Personnel
Dir: Sarah Tooth
Communications Officer & Editor: Malcolm
Walker
Founded: 1985
Aims to promote & encourage writers & literature
in society by providing resources & support.
Publication(s): *Southern Write* (quarterly, newslet-
ter)

The Society of Women Writers NSW Inc
GPO Box 1388, Sydney, NSW 2001
Tel: (02) 9999 2983
E-mail: enquiries@womenwritersnsw.org
Web Site: www.womenwritersnsw.org
Key Personnel
President: Bridget McKern
Vice President: Barbara Westerway
Secretary: Edita Diamante
Treasurer: Pam Bayfield
Membership: Sandra Davis
Publicity: Dr Maria Hill
Founded: 1925
Publication(s): *Images* (quarterly, journal); *SWW-
NSW News* (monthly, newsletter)

Tasmanian Writers' Centre
Salamanca Arts Centre, 1st floor, 77 Salamance
Pl, Hobart, Tas 7004
Tel: (03) 6224 0029 *Fax:* (03) 6223 3354
E-mail: admin@tasmanianwriters.org
Web Site: www.tasmanianwriters.org
Key Personnel
Dir: Chris Gallagher
Publications & Communications Coordinator: Es-
ther Ottaway
Administration & Membership Coordinator: Mar-
ion Stoneman
Founded: 1998
Aims to connect, support & inspire writers.

Writers Victoria
Wheeler Centre, Level 3, 176 Little Lonsdale St,
Melbourne, Victoria 3000
Tel: (03) 9094 7855 *Fax:* (03) 9650 8010
Web Site: writersvictoria.org.au
Key Personnel
Dir: Roderick Poole
Marketing & Membership Coordinator: Elise
Hearst
Administration & Finance Manager: Jacquelin
Low
Program Manager: Mary Napier
Publications Manager: Anna Kelsey-Sugg
Provides information & professional development
services for aspiring & established writers.
Publication(s): *The Victoria Writer* (10 times/yr,
magazine)

Austria

**Gesellschaft fuer Interkulturelle Germanistik
eV (GIG)** (Association for Intercultural
German Studies)
Universitaet Bern, Institut fuer Germanistik,
Laenggass-Str 49, 3000 Bern 9
Tel: (031) 631 83 11 (secretary) *Fax:* (031) 631
37 88
Web Site: www.germanistik.unibe.ch/gig
Key Personnel
President: Dr Ernest W B Hess-Luettich, PhD
E-mail: hess@germ.unibe.ch

Institut fuer Oesterreichkunde (Institute for the
Knowledge of Austria)
Hanuschgasse 3/3, 1010 Vienna
Tel: (01) 512 79 32 *Fax:* (01) 512 79 32

E-mail: ioek.wirtschaftsgeschichte@univie.ac.at
Web Site: www.oesterreichkunde.ac.at
Key Personnel
Chairman & Dir: Prof Ernst Bruckmueller,
PhD *Tel:* (01) 4277 41312 *E-mail:* ernst.
bruckmueller@univie.ac.at
Secretary General: Birgit Doerfl
Founded: 1957
Publication(s): *Oesterreich Archiv* (Austria
Archive, annually, book); *Oesterreich in
Geschichte und Literatur mit Geographie*
(Austria in History & Literature, bimonthly,
journal); *Schriften des Institutes fuer Oester-
reichkunde* (Writings of the Institute for
the Knowledge of Austria, annually, book);
*Schriftenreihe Literatur des Institutes fuer
Oesterreichkunde* (Series of the Institute for
the Knowledge of Austria)

Oesterreichische Gesellschaft fuer Literatur
(Austrian Literary Society)
Herrengasse 5, 1010 Vienna
Tel: (01) 533 81 59; (01) 533 08 64 *Fax:* (01)
533 40 67
E-mail: office@ogl.at
Web Site: www.ogl.at
Key Personnel
President: Marianne Gruber
Secretary General: Dr Manfred Mueller
Founded: 1961

Austrian PEN Centre (Oesterreichischer
PEN-Club)
Member of PEN International
Hahngasse 6/25, 1090 Vienna
Tel: (01) 533 44 59 *Fax:* (01) 532 87 49
E-mail: info@penclub.at
Web Site: www.penclub.at
Key Personnel
President: Dr Wolfgang Greisenegger
General Secretary: Helmet Stefan Milletich
Publication(s): *Pen-Nachrichten* (Pen-Newsletter,
biannually)

Belgium

**Academie Royale de Langue et de Litterature
Francaises de Belgique** (Royal Academy of
French Language & Literature)
Palais des Academies, rue Ducale 1, 1000 Brus-
sels
Tel: (02) 550 22 77 *Fax:* (02) 550 22 75
E-mail: alf@cfwb.be
Web Site: www.arllfb.be
Key Personnel
Dir: Francois Emmanuel
Deputy Dir: Jacques Lemaire
Permanent Secretary: Jacques De Decker
Founded: 1920
Publication(s): *Bulletin* (biannually)

**Academie Royale des Sciences, des Lettres et
des Beaux-Arts de Belgique** (Royal Academy
of Sciences, Literature & Fine Arts of
Belgium)
Rue Ducale 1, 1000 Brussels
Tel: (02) 550 22 12 *Fax:* (02) 550 22 05
E-mail: academieroyale@cfwb.be
Web Site: www.academieroyale.be
Key Personnel
President: Pierre Bartholomee
Permanent Secretary: Herve Hasquin
E-mail: herve.hasquin@cfwb.be
Founded: 1772
Publication(s): *Bulletins* (biannually); *l'Annuaire*
(directory); *Memoires*

AEBLF, see Association des Ecrivains Belges de Langue Francaise (AEBLF)

Association des Ecrivains Belges de Langue Francaise (AEBLF) (Association of the Belgian Writers of French Language)
150 Chaussee de Wavre, 1050 Brussels
Tel: (02) 512 36 57 *Fax:* (02) 502 43 73
E-mail: a.e.b@skynet.be
Web Site: www.ecrivainsbelges.be
Key Personnel
President: Jean-Pierre Dopagne
Vice President: Dominique Aguessy; Marie Nicolai
Treasurer: Jean Pirlet
Founded: 1902
Publication(s): *Nos Lettres* (Our Letters, 10 times/yr)

Commission Belge de Bibliographie et de Bibliologie (Belgian Commission of Bibliography & Bibliology)
Royal Library of Belgium, 4 Blvd de l'Empereur, 1000 Brussels
Tel: (02) 519 53 11 *Fax:* (02) 519 55 33
E-mail: info@kbr.be
Web Site: www.kbr.be
Key Personnel
Dir General: Patrick Lefevre
Founded: 1837
Publication(s): *Coll: Bibliographia Belgica*

KANTL, see Koninklijke Academie voor Nederlandse Taal- en Letterkunde

Koninklijke Academie voor Nederlandse Taal- en Letterkunde (Royal Academy of Dutch Language & Literature)
Koningstr 18, 9000 Ghent
Tel: (09) 265 93 40 *Fax:* (09) 265 93 49
E-mail: info@kantl.be
Web Site: www.kantl.be
Key Personnel
Chairman: Frank Willaert
Vice President: Stefaan Van Den Brent
Permanent Secretary: Willy Vandeweghe *Tel:* (09) 265 93 42 *E-mail:* willy.vandeweghe@kantl.be
Founded: 1886

Koninklijke Vlaamse Academie van Belgie voor Wetenschappen en Kunsten (KVAB) (Royal Flemish Academy of Belgium for Sciences & Arts)
Paleis der Academien, Hertogsstr 1, 1000 Brussels
Tel: (02) 550 23 23 *Fax:* (02) 550 23 25
E-mail: info@kvab.be
Web Site: www.kvab.be
Key Personnel
Chairman: Ludo Gelders
Permanent Secretary: Gery Van Outryve d'Ydewalle
Dutch-speaking Royal Belgium Academy of Sciences, Letters & Fine Arts.
Publication(s): *Bilingual Notaries in Hellenistic Egypt: A Study of Greek as a Second Language*; *Collectanea Biblica et religiosa Antiqua*; *Collectanea Hellenistica*; *Collectanea Maritima*; *Corpus Catalogorum Belgii*; *Corpus Catalogorum Belgii VII: The surviving manuscripts & incunables from medival Belgian libraries* (Corpus catalogorum Belgii VII: The surviving from medieval manuscripts & incunables Belgian libraries); *Eeuwen van ambitie: De adel in laatmiddeleeuws Vlaanderen* (Centuries of ambition. The nobility in late medieval Flanders); *Filips Wielant*; *Fontes Historiae Artis Neerlandicae*; *Getekend door het lichaam: de rol van het lichaam bij de totstandkoming van persoonsidentiteit* (Signed by the body: the role of the body in the cre-

ation of personal identy); *Iuris Scripta Historica*; *Iusti Lipsi Epistolae (The Correspondence of J Lipsius)*; *Moedertalen en taalmoeders: Het vroegmoderne taalvergelijkende onderzoek in de Lage Landen* (Mother Languages and Language Mothers: The early modern comparative linguistic research in the Low Countries); *Nationaal Biografisch Woordenboek* (National Biographical Dictionary); *Studies in Belgian Economic History*; *Taal, cultuurbeleid en natievorming onder Willem I* (Language, culture & nation under William I)

Belgian PEN Centre (Dutch-Speaking) (PEN Vlaanderen)
Member of PEN International
Huis van het Boek, Boelaerlei 37, 2140 Borgerhout
E-mail: info@penvlaanderen.be
Web Site: www.penvlaanderen.be
Key Personnel
President: David Van Reybrouck
Vice President: Jeroen Theunnisen
Secretary: Guy Posson *E-mail:* secretariaat@penvlaanderen.be
Treasurer: Xavier Roelens

Belgian PEN Centre (French-Speaking)
Member of PEN International
10 Ave des Cerfs, 1950 Kraainem (Bx)
Tel: (027) 31 48 47 *Fax:* (027) 31 48 47
Key Personnel
President: Huguette de Broqueville *E-mail:* huguette.db@skynet.be
Secretary: Vincent Malacor *E-mail:* vincent.malacor@iep.be
Founded: 1922
A voice of literature worldwide, bringing together poets, novelists, essayists, historians, critics, translators, editors, journalists & screenwriters. Members are united in a common concern for the craft & art of writing & a commitment to freedom of expression through the written word.

SABAM, see Societe Belge des Auteurs, Compositeurs et Editeurs (SABAM)

SLLW, see Societe de Langue et de Litterature Wallonnes (SLLW)

Societe Belge des Auteurs, Compositeurs et Editeurs (SABAM) (Belgian Society of Authors, Composers & Publishers)
Rue d'Arlon 75, 1040 Brussels
Tel: (02) 286 82 11 *Fax:* (02) 230 05 89
E-mail: contact@sabam.be
Web Site: www.sabam.be
Key Personnel
Mng Dir & Dir, Legal & International Affairs: Carine Libert
Operations Dir: Catherine Georis
Finance Dir: Frank Verschueren
Strategy, Change & ICT Dir: Guy Brouns

Societe de Langue et de Litterature Wallonnes (SLLW) (Society for Walloon Language & Literature)
Pl du XX Aout 7, 4000 Liege
E-mail: sllw.be@skynet.be
Web Site: users.skynet.be/sllw
Key Personnel
President: Guy Fontaine *Tel:* (04) 252 06 35 *E-mail:* gfo@scarlet.be
Secretary: Marc Duysinx *Tel:* (087) 23 00 71 *E-mail:* marc.duysinx@skynet.be
Treasurer: Jean Brumioul *Tel:* (04) 252 58 64

Secretary Publications: Esther Baiwir *Tel:* (04) 366 56 42 *Fax:* ebaiwir@ulg.ac.be
Publication(s): *Chronique de la Societe de Langue et de Litterature wallonnes*; *Dialectes de Wallonie* (irregularly)

Vereniging Antwerpse Bibliofielen (Association of Antwerp Bibliophiles)
Vrijdagmarkt 22, 2000 Antwerp
Tel: (03) 221 14 67 *Fax:* (03) 221 14 71
Web Site: www.boekgeschiedenis.be/index.php?q=content/vereniging-van-antwerpse-bibliofielen
Key Personnel
President: Marcus de Schepper, PhD
Vice President: Jean-Pierre Tricot
Secretary: Pierre Meulepas *E-mail:* pierre.meulepas@stad.antwerpen.be
Treasurer: Norbert Moermans
Founded: 1877
Publication(s): *De Gulden Passer* (The Golden Compasses, biannually, journal)

Bolivia

Bolivian PEN Centre (PEN Club de Bolivia (Centro Internacional de Escritores))
Member of PEN International
Casilla Postal 5920, Cochabamba
Fax: (04) 291 070
Key Personnel
President: Melita del Carpio
Secretary: Gaby Vallejo *Fax:* (04) 721 1116 *E-mail:* gabyvall@supernet.com.bo

Brazil

AAL, see Academia Amazonense de Letras (AAL)

ABL, see Academia Brasileira de Letras

Academia Amazonense de Letras (AAL) (Amazonas Academy of Letters)
Rua Ramos Ferreira, 1009, Centro, 69010-120 Manaus-AM
Tel: (092) 3234-0584
Key Personnel
President: Arlindo Porto
Founded: 1918
Publication(s): *Revista*

Academia Brasileira de Letras (Brazilian Academy of Letters)
Av Presidente Wilson 203, Castelo, 20030-021 Rio de Janeiro-RJ
Tel: (021) 3974-2500 *Fax:* (021) 220-6695
E-mail: academia@academia.org.br
Web Site: www.academia.org.br
Key Personnel
President: Ana Maria Machado
Secretary General: Geraldo Holanda Cavalcanti
Secretary: Domicio Proenca Filho; Marco Lucchesi
Treasurer: Evanildo Bechara
Publication(s): *Afranio Peixoto Collection*; *Antonio de Morais Silva Collection*; *Austregesilo de Athayde Collection*; *Revista Brasileira* (journal)

Academia Catarinense de Letras (Santa
Catarina Academy of Letters)
Av Irineu Bornhausen 5600, Argonomica, Centro
Integrado de Cultura Prof Henrique da Silva
Fontes, 88025-202 Florianopolis-SC
Tel: (048) 333-1733
Web Site: www.aclsc.ufsc.br
Key Personnel
President: Lauro Junkes *E-mail:* laujunkes@
hotmail.com
Vice President: Norberto Ungaretti
Secretary: Joao Nicolau Carvalho
Treasurer: Silvio Coelho dos Santos
Librarian: Hoyedo de Gouvea Lins
Founded: 1896
Publication(s): *Revista* (annually)

Academia Cearense de Letras (Ceara Academy
of Letters)
Rua do Rosario, 1-Centro, 60005-590 Fortaleza-
CE
Tel: (085) 231 56 69
E-mail: acletras@accvia.com.br
Web Site: www.ceara.pro.br
Key Personnel
President: Pedro Henrique Saraiva Leao
Vice President: Jose Maria de Barros Pinho
Secretary General: Virgilio Maia
Founded: 1894
Publication(s): *Colecao Antonio Sales; Colecao
Dolor Barreira; Revista da Academia Cearense
de Letras*

Academia de Letras da Bahia (Bahia Academy
of Letters)
Av Joana Angelica 198, 40050-000 Nazare,
Salvador-BA
Tel: (071) 3321-4308 *Fax:* (071) 3321-4308
E-mail: contato@academiadeletrasdabahia.org.br
Web Site: www.academiadeletrasdabahia.org.br
Key Personnel
President: Aramis Ribeiro Costa
Founded: 1917
Publication(s): *Revista* (annually, journal)

Academia Mineira de Letras (Minas Gerais
Academy of Letters)
Rua da Bahia 1466, Lourdes, 30160-011 Belo
Horizonte-MG
Tel: (031) 3222-5764
Web Site: www.academiamineiradeletras.org.br
Key Personnel
President: Orlando de Oliveira Vaz
Vice President: Francelino Pereira dos Santos
Honorary Secretary: Oiliam Jose
Secretary General: Aloisio Teixeira Garcia
First Secretary: Fabio Doyle
Second Secretary: Elizabeth Renno
Treasurer: Marcio Garcia Vilela
First Treasurer: Jose Henrique Santos
Deputy Treasurer: Bonifacio Andrada
Founded: 1909
Publication(s): *Revista* (magazine)

Academia Paraibana de Letras (Parabia
Academy of Letters)
Rua Duque de Caxias 25/37, 58010-820 Joao
Pessoa-PB
Web Site: www.aplpb.com.br
Key Personnel
President: Antonio Juarez Farias
Founded: 1941
Publication(s): *Revista*

Academia Paulista de Letras (Sao Paulo
Academy of Letters)
Largo do Arouche, 324, 01219-010 Sao Paulo-SP
Tel: (011) 3331-7222; (011) 3331-7401; (011)
3331-1562
E-mail: acadsp@terra.com.br
Web Site: www.academiapaulistadeletras.org.br

Key Personnel
President: Antonio Penteado Mendonca
Founded: 1909
Publication(s): *Biblioteca Academia Paulista de
Letras; Revista da Academia Paulista de Letras*

Academia Pernambucana de Letras
(Pernambuco Academy of Letters)
Ave Rui Barbosa 1596, Gracas, 52050-000
Recife-PE
Tel: (081) 3268-2211
Key Personnel
President: Fatima Quintas
Founded: 1901

Academia Piauiense de Letras (APL) (Piaui
Academy of Letters)
Av Miguel Rosa, 3300 Sul Centro, 64000-000
Teresina-PI
Tel: (086) 3216-1723
Web Site: www.academiapiauiensedeletras.org.br
Key Personnel
President: Reginaldo Miranda
Founded: 1917
Publication(s): *Revista da APL*

APL, see Academia Piauiense de Letras (APL)

Brazilian PEN Centre (PEN Clube do Brasil)
Member of PEN International
Flamengo 172-11º andar, 22210-030 Rio de
Janeiro-RJ
Tel: (021) 2556 0461 *Fax:* (021) 2556 0461
E-mail: pen@penclubedobrasil.br; pen@
penclubedobrasil.org.br
Web Site: www.penclubedobrasil.org.br
Key Personnel
President: Claudio Aguiar
Vice President: Cecilia Costa; Clair de Mattos
Executive Secretary: Marcia Agrau
Treasurer: Alcmeno Bastos
Founded: 1936

Universal Association of Writers, see Brazilian
PEN Centre

Bulgaria

**Bulgarian Academy of Sciences, Institute of
Literature**
52, blvd Shipchenski prohod, Bl 17, 7th & 8th
floors, 1113 Sofia
Tel: (02) 971 70 56 *Fax:* (02) 971 70 56
E-mail: director@ilit.bas.bg
Web Site: www.ilit.bas.bg
Key Personnel
Dir: Prof Elka Traykova
Deputy Dir: Prof Anna Stoykova *Tel:* (02) 971 70
64 *E-mail:* ana_stoykova@yahoo.com
Founded: 1948
Research center for Bulgarian literature from the
Middle Ages to the present day, in its theoreti-
cal, historical, cultural & comparative aspects.
Publication(s): *Literatourna Missul* (Literary
Thought, magazine); *Scripta & e-Scripta* (jour-
nal); *Starobulgarska Literatura* (Old Bulgarian
Literature, series)

China

China PEN Centre
Member of PEN International

25 Dongtuchenglu, Chaoyang Dist, Beijing
100013
Tel: (010) 64207711 *Fax:* (010) 64221704
Key Personnel
Secretary: Chen Ligang

Colombia

ICANH, see Instituto Colombiano de
Antropologia e Historia (ICANH)

Instituto Caro y Cuervo
Calle 10 Nº 4-69, Bogota
Tel: (01) 342 2121 *Fax:* (01) 284 1284
E-mail: contactenos@caroycuervo.gov.co
Web Site: www.caroycuervo.gov.co
Key Personnel
Dir General: Genoveva Iriarte Esguerra
E-mail: direcciongeneral@caroycuervo.gov.co
Founded: 1942
Linguistics, philology & literature.

**Instituto Colombiano de Antropologia e
Historia (ICANH)**
Calle 12, No 2-41, Bogota
Tel: (01) 4440544 *Fax:* (01) 4440530
E-mail: contactenos@icanh.gov.co;
quejasyreclamos@icanh.gov.co
Web Site: www.icanh.gov.co
Key Personnel
Dir General: Carlo Emilio Piazzini *Tel:* (02)
4440544 ext 116
Secretary: Clara Chapparro *Tel:* (01) 4440544 ext
102
Publication(s): *Flora de la Real Expedicion
Botanica del Nuevo*

Colombian PEN Centre (PEN Internacional de
Colombia)
Member of PEN International
Calle 88, 11A-20, Apartment 302, Bogota
Tel: (01) 691 9627 *Fax:* (01) 332 4357
Key Personnel
President: Carlos Vasquez Zawadsky
E-mail: carlosvasquez.zawadsky@crear3000.
com
Secretary: Ruben Dario Florez
E-mail: rubendario.florezarcila@gmail.com

Czech Republic

Matice Moravska
Arna Novaka 1, 602 00 Brno
Tel: 549 493 552 *Fax:* 549 491 520
E-mail: matice@phil.muni.cz
Web Site: www.matice-moravska.cz
Key Personnel
President: Prof Jiri Malir, PhD
Vice President: Dr Bohumir Smutny
Treasurer: Dr Jirina Stouracova
Mng Dir: Dr Bronislav Chocholac, PhD
E-mail: bronek@phil.munic.cz
Publication(s): *Casopis Matice moravske* (biannu-
ally)

Czech PEN Centre
Member of PEN International
Klementinum 190/5 Patro, 110 00 Prague 1
Mailing Address: PO Box 123, 111 01 Prague 1
Tel: 224 234 343 *Fax:* 224 234 343
E-mail: centrum@pen.cz
Web Site: www.pen.cz

Key Personnel
President: Jiri Dedecek *E-mail:* jiri@dedecek.cz
Chairwoman: Libuse Ludvikova *Tel:* 605 253 238
Secretary: Dana Mojzisova *Tel:* 605 253 234
Founded: 1925

Denmark

Dansk Forfatterforening (The Danish Writers
Association)
Strandgade 6, 1401 Copenhagen K
Tel: 32 95 51 00 *Fax:* 32 54 01 15
E-mail: df@danskforfatterforening.dk
Web Site: www.danskforfatterforening.dk
Founded: 1894
Professional organization for authors, translators
& illustrators of books for children & young
people.

Det Danske Sprog - og Litteraturselskab
(Danish Language & Literature)
Christians Brygge 1, 1219 Copenhagen K
Tel: 33 13 06 60 *Fax:* 33 14 06 08
E-mail: sekretariat@dsl.dk
Web Site: dsl.dk
Key Personnel
Dir: Lasse Horne Kjaelgaard *Tel:* 50 777 451
E-mail: khk@dsl.dk
Secretary: Maria Krogh Langner *Tel:* 50 777 454
E-mail: mkl@dsl.dk
Founded: 1911

DSL, see Det Danske Sprog - og
Litteraturselskab

Det Kongelige Danske Videnskabernes Selskab
(The Royal Danish Academy of Sciences &
Letters)
H C Andersens Blvd 35, 1553 Copenhagen V
Tel: 33 43 53 00 *Fax:* 33 43 53 01
E-mail: kdvs@royalacademy.dk
Web Site: www.royalacademy.dk
Key Personnel
President: Prof Kirsten Hastrup *Tel:* 35 32 34 60
E-mail: kirsten.hastrup@anthro.ku.dk
Vice President: Prof Niels Kaergard *Tel:* 35 33 22
64 *E-mail:* nik@life.ku.dk; Hans Thybo, PhD
Tel: 35 32 24 52 *E-mail:* thybo@geol.ku.dk
General Secretary: Prof Morgens Jensen Hogh
Tel: 35 32 53 71 *E-mail:* mhjensen@nbi.dk
Founded: 1742
Publication(s): *Scientia Danica: Series B, Biolog-
ica*; *Scientia Danica: Series H, Humanistica,
8*; *Scientia Danica: Series H, Humanistica,
4*; *Scientia Danica: Series M, a Mathematica
Physica*

Nyt Dansk Literaturselskab (New Danish
Society for Literature)
Gammelsohoj 9, 2640 Hedehusene
Tel: 46 59 55 20 *Fax:* 46 59 55 21
E-mail: ndl@ndl.dk
Web Site: www.ndl.dk
Key Personnel
Chairman: Vibeke Danielsen *Tel:* 33 66 74 00
E-mail: vibeke.danielsen@gmail.com
Manager: Anne Warming
Founded: 1940
Society's goal is publication/republication of
books in short supply in libraries. Special ac-
tivity, Magnaprint (large print books for par-
tially sighted), LaeseLyst (easy reading for
adults).

Ecuador

Academia Ecuatoriana de la Lengua
Vicente Ramon Roca E9-60 y Tamayo, Quito,
Pichincha
Tel: (02) 2901-518
Web Site: academiaec.org
Key Personnel
Dir: Susana Cordero
Founded: 1874
Parent Company: Association of Academies of
the Spanish Language

**Casa de la Cultura Ecuatoriana Benjamin
Carrion**
Av 6 de Diciembre, Quito
Tel: (02) 2902272; (02) 2525679; (02) 2223392
Fax: (02) 2566070
Web Site: www.casadelacultura.gob.ec
Key Personnel
Acting President: Raul Perez Torres
Vice President: Dr Jaime Galarza Z
General Secretary: Dr Juan Merino Jaramillo
E-mail: juan.merino@cce.org.ec
Founded: 1944

Egypt

Alexandria Atelier
6 Victor Bassili St, Al Pharaana - Al Azarita,
Alexandria
Tel: (03) 486 0526 *Fax:* (03) 486 0526
E-mail: info@atelieralex.com
Web Site: www.atelieralex.com
Key Personnel
President: Mohamed Rafik Khalil
E-mail: mrafikkhalil@gmail.com
Vice President: Dr Mohamed Salem
E-mail: m_salem47@yahoo.com
Honorary Secretary: Dr Reem Hassan
E-mail: hassan.reem@gmail.com
Founded: 1935
Society of Artists & Writers.

Finland

Finlands Svenska Forfattareforening (Society
of Swedish Authors in Finland)
Uhro Kekkonens gata 8 B 14, 00100 Helsinki
Tel: (09) 446 266
E-mail: forfattarna@kaapeli.fi
Web Site: www.forfattarna.fi
Key Personnel
Chairman: Mikaela Stromberg
Founded: 1919
Membership(s): Baltic Writer's Council; European
Writer's Congress; Nordic Writer's Council;
The Three Seas Writer's & Translator's Coun-
cil.

Kirjallisuudentutkijain Seura (Finnish Literary
Research Society)
University of Helsinki, Dept of Finnish Literature,
PL 3 (Faibianinkatu 33), 00014 Helsinki
Fax: (09) 191 23008
Web Site: pro.tsv.fi/skts
Key Personnel
President: Riikka Rossi *E-mail:* riikka.rossi@
helsinki.fi
Secretary: Elise Nykanen
Founded: 1927

Membership(s): International Comparative Litera-
ture Association.
Publication(s): *Avain - Finnish Review of Literary
Studies* (quarterly, journal)

Finnish PEN Centre
Member of PEN International
PL 84, 00131 Helsinki
Web Site: pen.kaapeli.fi
Key Personnel
President: Jarkko Tontti *Tel:* (040) 0784313 (cell)
E-mail: jarkkotontti@jarkkotontti.net
Vice President: Markus Nummi
Secretary: Arla Kanerva

Suomalainen Tiedeakatemia (Finnish Academy
of Science & Letters)
Mariankatu 5, 00170 Helsinki
Tel: (09) 636800 *Fax:* (09) 660117
E-mail: acadsci@acadsci.fi
Web Site: www.acadsci.fi
Key Personnel
Chairman: Jorma Sipila
Vice Chairman: Eva-Mari Aro
Secretary General: Olli Martio *Tel:* (09) 636806
E-mail: olli.martio@acadsci.fi
Founded: 1908
Publication(s): *Annales Academiae Scientiarum
Fennicae, Geologica*; *Annales Academiae
Scientiarum Fennicae, Humaniora*; *Annales
Academiae Scientiarum Fennicae, Mathemat-
ica*; *Folklore Fellows' Communications, FFC*;
Vuosikirja (yearbook)

Suomalaisen Kirjallisuuden Seura (SKS)
(Finnish Literature Society)
Hallituskatu 1, 00170 Helsinki
Mailing Address: PL 259, 00171 Helsinki
Tel: (0201) 131 231 *Fax:* (09) 656 380
E-mail: sks@finlit.fi
Web Site: www.finlit.fi
Key Personnel
Dir & Secretary General: Tuomas M S Lehtonen
Publishing Dir: Tero Norkola *Tel:* (040) 088 2700
E-mail: tero.norkola@finlit.fi
Chief Librarian: Cecilla A F Forselks
Dir, Finnish Literature Information Centre: Iris
Schwanck
Dir, Folklore Archive: Laura Harvilanti
Dir, Literature Archive: Ulla-Maija Peltonen
Specialize in folklore, ethnology, literary research,
Finnish language, cultural history.
Publication(s): *Studia Fennica*; *Suomi*; *Tietolipas*;
Toimituksia (irregularly)

Svenska Litteratursaellskapet i Finland
(Society of Swedish Literature in Finland)
Ritarikatu 5, 00170 Helsinki
Tel: (09) 618 777 *Fax:* (09) 618 772 77
E-mail: info@sls.fi
Web Site: www.sls.fi
Key Personnel
Chairman: Prof Max Engman
Vice Chairman: Prof Fred Karlsson
Secretary: Prof Marika Tandefelt
Treasurer: Magnus Bargum
Founded: 1885
Publication(s): *Skrifter utgivna av Svenska Litter-
atursaellskapet i Finland* (writings)

France

Academie Goncourt, Societe de gens de Lettres
c/o Drouant 16-18, place Gaillon, 75002 Paris
Web Site: www.academie-goncourt.fr
Key Personnel
President: Edmonde Charles-Roux
Responsible for annual prizes-poetry scholarships,
best romance novels, biographies.

ADELF, see Association des Ecrivains de Langue
  Francaise (ADELF)

AICL, see International Association of Literary
  Critics

**Association des Ecrivains de Langue Francaise
  (ADELF)** (French Language Writers'
  Association)
22, rue Deparcieux, 75014 Paris
Tel: 01 43 21 95 99; 06 69 44 00 01
E-mail: contact@adelf.fr
Web Site: www.adelf.fr
Key Personnel
President: Jacques Chevrier
Secretary General: Simone Dreyfus
Founded: 1926
Publication(s): *Lettres et cultures de francaise
  langue* (French Language Culture & Literature,
  biannually)

**Association d'Information et de Defense des
  Auteurs**, see CALCRE, Association
  d'Information et de Defense des Auteurs

**Association Internationale des Critiques
  Litteraires (NGO)**, see International
  Association of Literary Critics

**CALCRE, Association d'Information et de
  Defense des Auteurs** (CALCRE, Association
  of Information & Protection of Author)
BP 10 016, 94404 Vitry Cedex
Tel: 01 56 30 00 66 *Fax:* 01 56 30 00 66
Web Site: www.calcre.com
Key Personnel
President: Roger Gaillard
Secretary: Claude Aubert
Treasurer: Andre Muriel
Founded: 1979
Publication(s): *Arlit - Annuaire des Revues Lit-
  teraires & Cie* (3 times/yr); *Ecrire & Editer*
  (Write & Edit, bimonthly, magazine)

Centre National du Livre (CNL) (National
  Literary Centre)
Hotel de Avejan, 53, rue de Verneuil, 75343 Paris
  Cedex 07
Tel: 01 49 54 68 68 *Fax:* 01 45 49 10 21
E-mail: secretariat@centrenationaldulivre.fr
Web Site: www.centrenationaldulivre.fr
Key Personnel
President: Jean-Francios Colosimo
Secretary General: Xavier Bredin *E-mail:* xavier.
  bredin@centrenationaldulivre.fr

CNL, see Centre National du Livre (CNL)

International Association of Literary Critics
  (Association Internationale des Critiques
  Litteraires)
Affiliate of UNESCO
Hotel de Massa, 38, rue du Faubourg, St Jacques,
  75014 Paris
Web Site: www.aicl.org
Key Personnel
President: Neria de Giovanni
Vice President: Fernando Martinho; Ichiro Saito
Secretary General: Stefan Damian
Treasurer: Salvatore Pintore
Founded: 1969
Publication(s): *L'Annee Litteraire* (biannually)

**La Maison des Ecrivains et de la litterature
  (MEL)** (The House of the Writers &
  Literature)
67, blvd de Montmorency, 75016 Paris
Tel: 01 55 47 60 90 *Fax:* 01 42 84 20 87
E-mail: courrier@maison-des-ecrivains.asso.fr
Web Site: www.m-e-l.fr

Key Personnel
President: Jean-Louis Giovannoni
Dir: Sylvie Gouttebaron *Tel:* 01 55 74 60 97
  E-mail: s.gouttebaron@maison-des-ecrivains.
  assoc.fr
Founded: 1990

French PEN Centre (PEN Club Francais)
Member of PEN International
06, rue Francois-Miron, 75004 Paris
Tel: 01 42 72 41 83 *Fax:* 01 42 72 41 83
E-mail: penfrancais@aol.com
Web Site: www.penclub.fr
Key Personnel
President: Jean-Luc Despax
Vice President: Maurice Couquiaud; Daniel
  Leuwers; Jean-Luc Moreau; Philippe Pujas
Secretary General: Jeanine Baude
Deputy Secretary General: Max Alhau
Treasurer: Sylvestre Clancier

SACD, see Societe des Auteurs et Compositeurs
  Dramatiques (SACD)

SNAC, see Syndicat National des Auteurs et
  Compositeurs

**Societe des Auteurs et Compositeurs
  Dramatiques (SACD)** (Society of Dramatic
  Authors & Composers)
9 Rue Ballu, 75009 Paris
Tel: 01 40 23 44 55 *Fax:* 01 45 26 74 28
E-mail: webmaster@sacd.fr
Web Site: www.sacd.fr
Key Personnel
President: Jacques Fansten
Vice President: Georges Werler
Dir General: Pascal Rogard
Founded: 1777
Publication(s): *SACD Authors' Journal*

Societe des Gens de Lettres (SGDL)
Hotel de Massa, 38, rue du Fbg-St-Jacques,
  75014 Paris
Tel: 01 53 10 12 00 *Fax:* 01 53 10 12 12
E-mail: sgdl@sgdl.org
Web Site: www.sgdl.org
Key Personnel
President: Jean Claude Bologne
First Vice President: Noelle Chatelet
Secretary General: Dominique Le Brun
Treasurer: Hubert Tubiana
General Manager: Geoffroy Pelletier *Tel:* 01 53
  10 12 13
Founded: 1838

Societe des Poetes Francais
16, rue Monsieur le Prince, 75006 Paris
Tel: 01 40 46 99 82 *Fax:* 01 40 46 99 11
E-mail: stepoetesfrancais@orange.fr
Web Site: www.societedespoetesfrancais.asso.fr
Key Personnel
President: Vital Heurtebize *E-mail:* vital.
  heurtebize@societedespoetesfrancais.eu
Vice President: Jacques-Francois Dussottier
  E-mail: jf.dussottier@societedespoetesfrancais.
  eu; Emmanuel Mahieu
Dir General: Claire Dutrey *E-mail:* spf.
  clairedutrey@orange.fr
Founded: 1902
To promote the poetry of the French language.
Publication(s): *L'Agora* (quarterly)

**Societe et Revue d'Histoire Litteraire de la
  France** (French Literary History Association)
112, rue Monge, 75005 Paris
Mailing Address: BP 44, 75005 Paris Cedex
Tel: 01 45 87 23 30 *Fax:* 01 45 87 23 30
E-mail: srhlf@neuf.fr; srhlf@aol.com
Web Site: srhlf.free.fr

Key Personnel
President: Marc Fumaroli
Vice President: Florence Callu; Mireille Huchon;
  Sylvain Menant
Treasurer: Luc Fraisse
Dir: Pierre-Louis Rey
Founded: 1897
Publication(s): *Revue d'Histoire litteraire de la
  France* (quarterly)

Syndicat National des Auteurs et Compositeurs
80 rue Taitbout, 75009 Paris
Tel: 01 48 74 96 30 *Fax:* 01 42 81 40 21
E-mail: snac.fr@wanadoo.fr
Web Site: www.snac.fr
Key Personnel
President: Simone Douek
Vice President: Virginie Augustin Youri
Treasurer: Serge Domenica Lecog
Publication(s): *Bulletin des Auteurs* (quarterly)

Germany

**Asociacion des Autores Latinoamericanos (en
  la Inmigracion UE)**, see Verein
  Lateinamerikanischer Autoren (in der EU
  Migration)

BDS, see Bund Deutscher Schriftsteller BDS eV

Bund Deutscher Schriftsteller BDS eV
  (Association of German Writers)
Max-Planck-Str 6, 63128 Dietzenbach
Tel: (06074) 47566 *Fax:* (06074) 47540
E-mail: info@schriftsteller-verband.de
Web Site: www.bund-deutscher-schriftsteller.de
Key Personnel
Contact: Renate Stahl
Founded: 1997
Also acts as literary agent.

**Bundesverband Alphabetisierung und
  Grundbildung eV**
Berliner Platz 8-10, 48143 Muenster
Mailing Address: Postfach 100253, 48051 Muen-
  ster
Tel: (0251) 49 09 96-0 *Fax:* (0251) 49 09 96-86
E-mail: bundesverband@alphabetisierung.de
Web Site: www.alphabetisierung.de
Key Personnel
Mng Dir: Ralf Haeder *Tel:* (0251) 49 09 96-42
  E-mail: r.haeder@alphabetisierung.de
Business Manager: Nina Grams *Tel:* (0251) 49 09
  96-52 *E-mail:* n.grams@alphabetisierung.de
Founded: 1997

**Bundesverband junger Autoren und
  Autorinnen eV** (Federal Association of Young
  Authors)
Postfach 200303, 53133 Bonn
Tel: (02225) 7889 *Fax:* (02225) 7889
E-mail: info@bvja-online.de
Web Site: www.bvja-online.de
Key Personnel
Mng Dir: Thomas Stichtenoth *E-mail:* thomas.
  stichtenoth@bvja-online.de
Founded: 1987
Publication(s): *Konzepte*; *Lima-LiteraturMagazin*

BVjA eV, see Bundesverband junger Autoren
  und Autorinnen eV

**Deutsche Akademie fuer Sprache und
  Dichtung** (German Academy for Language &
  Literature)
Glueckert-Haus, Alexandraweg 23, 64287 Darm-
  stadt

Tel: (06151) 4092-0 *Fax:* (06151) 4092-99
E-mail: sekretariat@deutscheakademie.de
Web Site: www.deutscheakademie.de
Key Personnel
President: Heinrich Detering
Vice President: Aris Fioretos
General Secretary: Dr Bernd Busch
   E-mail: bernd.busch@deutscheakademie.de
Founded: 1949
Publication(s): *Dichtung & Sprache* (irregu-
   larly); *Jahrbuch der Deutschen Akademie fuer
   Sprache & Dichtung* (annually); *Preisschriften*
   (annually)

Deutscher Literaturfonds eV (German Literature
   Fund)
Alexandraweg 23, 64287 Darmstadt
Tel: (06151) 40930 *Fax:* (06151) 409333
E-mail: info@deutscher-literaturfonds.de
Web Site: www.deutscher-literaturfonds.de
Key Personnel
Dir: Dr Bernd Busch *E-mail:* busch@deutscher-
   literaturfonds.de

FiFa-Fiction & Fantasy eV
Bernauer Str 17, 81669 Munich
Tel: (0177) 750 29 37
E-mail: fifa-verlag@t-online.de
Web Site: www.fifa-verlag.de.vu
Supports young German writers of science fic-
   tion, fantasy literature, novels, short stories &
   poems.

FiFa-Verlag, see FiFa-Fiction & Fantasy eV

**Gesellschaft zur Foerderung der Literatur aus
   Afrika, Asien und Lateinamerika eV** (Society
   for the Promotion of African, Asian & Latin
   American Literature)
Braubachstr 16, 60311 Frankfurt
Mailing Address: Postfach 10 01 16, 60001
   Frankfurt
Tel: (069) 2102 143; (069) 2102 250 *Fax:* (069)
   2102 227
E-mail: litprom@book-fair.com
Web Site: www.litprom.de
Key Personnel
President: Juergen Boos
Vice President: Monika Bilstein
Treasurer: Ruth Kumpmann
Founded: 1980
The Society seeks to promote German translations
   of creative writing from Africa, Asia & Latin
   America. It works as a nonprofit agency & as
   a consultant for German language publishers
   & Third World publishers who have transla-
   tion rights to offer. It organizes reading tours
   & special promotion campaigns & is also in
   charge of a special programme for translations
   grants into German.
Publication(s): *Literaturnachrichten* (quarterly in
   German); *Newsletter*

Goethe-Gesellschaft in Weimar eV (Goethe
   Society in Weimar)
Burgplatz 4, 99423 Weimar
Mailing Address: Postfach 2251, 99403 Weimar
Tel: (03643) 20 20 50 *Fax:* (03643) 20 20 61
E-mail: info@goethe-gesellschaft.de
Web Site: www.goethe-gesellschaft.de
Key Personnel
President (Weimar): Dr Jochen Golz
   E-mail: jochen.golz@goethe-gesellschaft.de
Contact: Cornelia Brendel
Founded: 1885
Publication(s): *Goethe-Jahrbuch (yearbook)* (an-
   nually); *Schriften der Goethe-Gesellschaft*
   (Writings of the Goethe Society)

**Peter Hammer Verein fuer Literatur und
   Dialog eV** (Peter Hammer Society for
   Literature & Dialog)
Postfach 20 09 65, 42209 Wuppertal
Tel: (0234) 520396 *Fax:* (0202) 509252
E-mail: verein@peter-hammer-verein.de
Web Site: www.peter-hammer-verein.de
Key Personnel
First Chairman: Gudrun Honke

**Internationale Gutenberg-Gesellschaft in
   Mainz eV**
Liebfrauenplatz 5, 55116 Mainz
Tel: (06131) 22 64 20 *Fax:* (06131) 23 35 30
E-mail: info@gutenberg-gesellschaft.de
Web Site: www.gutenberg-gesellschaft.de
Key Personnel
President: Michael Ebling
Vice President: Guenther Knoedler
Secretary: Dr Stephan Fuessel
Treasurer: Hans-Guenter Mann
Mng Dir: Dr Franz Stephan Pelgen
Founded: 1901
Publication(s): *Gutenberg-Jahrbuch (Gutenberg
   Yearbook): Kleine Drucke der Gutenberg-
   Gesellschaft* (annually)

Literarisches Colloquium Berlin eV
Am Sandwerder 5, 14109 Berlin
Tel: (030) 816 996-0 *Fax:* (030) 816 996-19
E-mail: mail@lcb.de
Web Site: www.lcb.de
Key Personnel
Chairman & Mng Dir: Dr Ingo Fessman
Manager: Dr Ulrich Janetzki *Tel:* (030) 816 996-
   12 *E-mail:* janetzki@lcb.de
Founded: 1963
Publication(s): *Sprache im technischen Zeitalter*
   (quarterly)

Maximilian-Gesellschaft eV (Book Collectors
   Society)
Traubenstr 59, 70176 Stuttgart
E-mail: info@maximilian-gesellschaft.de
Web Site: www.maximilian-gesellschaft.de
Key Personnel
Chairman: Dr Wulf D von Lucius
Deputy Chairman: Dr Ulrich Johannes Schneider,
   PhD
Treasurer: Reinhold Busch

German PEN Centre (PEN-Zentrum
   Deutschland)
Member of PEN International
Kasinostr 3, 64293 Darmstadt
Tel: (06151) 23120 *Fax:* (06151) 293414
E-mail: pen-germany@t-online.de
Web Site: www.pen-deutschland.de
Key Personnel
President: Johano Strasser
Vice President: Sascha Feuchert; Christa
   Schuenke
Mng Dir: Claudia C Krausse
Secretary General: Herbert Wiesner
Treasurer: Matthias Biskupek

Adalbert Stifter Verein eV (Adalbert Stifter
   Association)
Hochstr 8, 81669 Munich
Tel: (089) 622 716-30 *Fax:* (089) 48 91 148
E-mail: stifterverein@stifterverein.de
Web Site: www.stifterverein.de
Key Personnel
Chairman: Dr Ernst Erich Metzner
Deputy Chairman: Horst Loffler
Mng Dir: Dr Peter Becher
Treasurer: Anette Roller
Secretary: Jitka Scholz
Founded: 1947

Information brochure in German, Czech & English; literature, art, cultural history of Bohemia
   & Moravia.
Publication(s): *Stifter-Jahrbuch* (annually since
   1987)

**Verein Lateinamerikanischer Autoren (in der
   EU Migration)** (Association of Latin-American
   Authors)
30459 Hannover
Tel: (0176) 29737349
Web Site: www.spanischdienstleistungen.de
Key Personnel
Contact: Rosales Miranda *E-mail:* rosales-
   miranda@web.de

**VS - Verband Deutscher Schriftstellerinnen
   und Schriftsteller** (Association of German
   Writers)
Paula-Thiede-Ufer 10, 10179 Berlin
Tel: (030) 69 56-0 *Fax:* (030) 69 56-3141
E-mail: info@verdi.de
Web Site: vs.verdi.de
Founded: 1969

Hong Kong

Chinese Language Society of Hong Kong
18/F Kam Chung Bldg, 19-21 Hennessy Rd,
   Hong Kong
Tel: 2528 4853; 2529 1638 *Fax:* 2527 9273
E-mail: clshk@hkstar.com
Web Site: www.hkedcity.net/iclub_files/a/1/74/
   webpage/jfiles/chinsoc.html
Key Personnel
Chairman: Yao Dehuai

Hong Kong PEN Centre (Chinese-Speaking)
Member of PEN International
71365 Kowloon Central Post Office, Hong Kong
Key Personnel
President: Liao Su Lan *E-mail:* shulantw@yahoo.
   com.hk
Founded: 1955
Publication(s): *PEN News* (weekly in Chinese)

Hong Kong PEN Centre (English-Speaking)
Member of PEN International
26B Peak Rd, 1st floor, Cheung Chau, Hong
   Kong
Tel: 25 25 39 17 *Fax:* 25 25 39 61
Key Personnel
President: Fred S Armentrout *E-mail:* farmen@
   amcham.org.hk

Hungary

Magyar Irodalomtorteneti Tarsasag (Historical
   Society of Hungarian Literature)
Muzeum krt 4/A, III/323, Budapest 1088
Tel: (01) 2664903 *Fax:* (01) 2664903
E-mail: mit.rita@freemail.hu
Web Site: irodalomtortenet.wordpress.com
Key Personnel
President: Sipos Lajos
General Secretary: Frater Zoltan
Founded: 1912

Magyar Iroszoevetseg (Hungarian Writers'
   Association)
Bajza u 18, Budapest 1062
Mailing Address: Pf 546, Budapest 1397

Tel: (01) 322-8840 *Fax:* (01) 321-3419
E-mail: titkarsag@iroszovetseg.hu
Web Site: www.iroszovetseg.hu
Key Personnel
President: Janos Szentmartoni
Secretary: Kinga Eros *Tel:* (01) 322-8849
Founded: 1945
Publication(s): *Kortars*; *Magyar Naplo* (journal)

**Magyar Tudomanyos Akademia
  Bolcseszettudomanyi Kutatokozpont
  Irodalomtudomanyi Intezet** (Hungarian
  Academy of Sciences, Institute of Literary
  Studies, Humanities Research Center)
Menesi ut 11-13, Budapest 1118
Tel: (01) 279 2762 *Fax:* (01) 385 3876
E-mail: helikon@iti.mta.hu
Web Site: www.mta.hu; www.iti.mta.hu/helikon.
  html
Key Personnel
Dir: Laszlo Szorenyi *Tel:* (01) 279 2765
  E-mail: szorenyi@iti.mta.hu
Founded: 1956
Publication(s): *Camoenae Hungaricae* (annually);
  Helikon (quarterly); *Irodalomtoerteneti Koe-
  zlemenyek* (6 times/yr, bulletin); *Literatura*
  (quarterly, periodical); *Magyar Konyvszemle*;
  Neohelicon (biannually)

Hungarian PEN Centre
Member of PEN International
Karolyi Mihaly u 16, Budapest 1053
Tel: (01) 411 0270 *Fax:* (01) 411 0270
E-mail: hungary@penclub.t-online.hu
Key Personnel
President: Geza Szocs
Secretary: Ferenc Tolvaj

Iceland

Hid Islenzka Bokmenntafelag (Icelandic
  Literary Society)
Skeifan 3b, 128 Reykjavik
Tel: 588 90 60 *Fax:* 581 40 88
E-mail: hib@hib.is
Web Site: hib.is
Key Personnel
President: Sigurdur Lindal *E-mail:* lindal@hi.is
Secretary: Reynir Axelsson
Treasurer: Gardar Gislason
Founded: 1816
Publication(s): *Skirnir* (biannually in 2 parts)

Icelandic PEN Centre
Member of PEN International
PO Box 161, 121 Reykjavik
Tel: 820 1931
E-mail: icelandicpen@gmail.com
Key Personnel
President: Sjon Sigurdsson
Secretary: Einar Karason *E-mail:* karason@
  islandia.is

Rithofundasambandio (Writers' Union of
  Iceland)
Gunnarshusi, Dyngjuvegi 8, 104 Reykjavik
Tel: 568 3190 *Fax:* 568 3192
E-mail: rsi@rsi.is
Web Site: www.rsi.is
Key Personnel
Chairman: Kristin Steinsdottir *E-mail:* krilla@
  aknet.is
Deputy Chairman: Jon Kalman Stefansson
  E-mail: kalman@bjartur.is
Manager: Ragnheidur Tryggvadottir
Founded: 1974
Publication(s): *Frettabref* (bimonthly, newsletter)

India

National Academy of Letters, see Sahitya
  Akademi

PEN All-India Centre
Member of PEN International
Theosophy Hall, 40 New Marine Lines, Mumbai
  400 020
Tel: (022) 22039024
E-mail: india.pen@gmail.com
Key Personnel
President: Dr Dauji Gupta
Secretary: Ranjit Hoskote *E-mail:* ranjit.hoskote@
  gmail.com
Publication(s): *Asian Liturature: Poetry, Short
  Stories & Essays*; *Assamese Literature*; *Bengali
  Literature*; *Drama in Modern India & Writer's
  Responsibility in a Rapidly Changing World*;
  India Writers Meet; *Indian Literature of Today*;
  The Indian PEN (quarterly); *Indian Writers at
  Chidambaram*; *Indian Writers in Conference*;
  Indian Writers in Council; *Indo-Anglian Lit-
  erature*; *The Novel in Modern India*; *Telugu
  Literature*; *Writers in Free India*; *Writing in
  India*

Sahitya Akademi (National Academy of Letters)
Rabindra Bhavan, 35, Ferozeshah Rd, New Delhi
  110 001
Tel: (011) 23386626; (011) 23386627; (011)
  23386628 *Fax:* (011) 23382428
Web Site: sahitya-akademi.gov.in
Key Personnel
President: Sunil Gangopadhyay *Tel:* (033)
  24407302
Vice President: Dr Chandrashekhar Kambar
  Tel: (011) 23386623 *Fax:* (011) 23074168
Secretary: Dr K Sreenivasa Rao *Tel:* (011)
  23387064 *E-mail:* secretary@sahitya-akademi.
  gov.in
Founded: 1954
Regional offices in Bangalore, Chennai, Kolkata
  & Mumbai.
Publication(s): *Indian Literature* (bimonthly);
  Samkaleen Bharateeya Sahitya (bimonthly);
  Samskrita Pratibha (biannually)

Ireland

Irish PEN Centre
Member of PEN International
United Arts Club, 3 Fitzwilliam St (Upr), Dublin
  2
Tel: (087) 9660770
E-mail: info@irishpen.com
Web Site: www.irishpen.com
Key Personnel
Chair: Kay Boland
Vice Chair: Vanessa O'Loughlin
Secretary: Carol Robinson Tweed
Treasurer: Timmy Conway
Founded: 1921

Israel

**ACUM Ltd (Society of Authors, Composers &
  Music Publishers in Israel)**
9 Tuval St, Hilazon Corner, 52117 Ramat-Gan
Mailing Address: PO Box 1704, 52117 Ramat-
  Gan
Tel: (03) 6113400 *Fax:* (03) 6122629
E-mail: webmaster@acum.org.il

Web Site: www.acum.org.il
Key Personnel
Chief Executive Officer: Yorik Ben David
Deputy Chief Executive Officer: Reuven Ratson
Head, Finances: Dafna Ramchurn
Manager, Licensing Performing Rights: Daliah
  Hadar
Manager, New Media Licensing: Moshe Hany
Manager, Radio/TV Licensing & Distribution:
  Smadar Noga
Founded: 1936
Administration of authors & composers' rights
Membership(s): BIEM & CISAC.

Israeli PEN Centre
Member of PEN International
21 Ha-Sharon St, 47240 Ramat Ha-Sharon
Tel: (03) 501 9275 *Fax:* (03) 501 9276
Key Personnel
President: Efraim Bauch
Secretary: Ms Shulamit Kuriansky
  E-mail: shulamit02@bezeqint.net

Palestinian PEN Centre
Member of PEN International
Al Khaldi St No 4, Wadi Al Juz, Jerusalem
Tel: (02) 598288111 *Fax:* (02) 6264620
E-mail: palpenc@palnet.com
Key Personnel
President: Dr Hannan Awwad
Secretary: Mrs Nariman al-Far
  E-mail: ahmad134@hotmail.com

**Society of Authors, Composers & Music
  Publishers in Israel**, see ACUM Ltd (Society
  of Authors, Composers & Music Publishers in
  Israel)

Italy

**Accademia Nazionale di Scienze Lettere e Arti
  Modena** (National Academy of Sciences,
  Literatures & Arts)
Corso Vittorio Emanuele, n° 59, 41121 Modena
Tel: (059) 225566 *Fax:* (059) 225566
E-mail: info@accademiasla-mo.it
Web Site: www.accademiasla-mo.it
Key Personnel
President: Prof Ferdinando Taddei
Secretary General: Prof Francesco Barbieri
Founded: 1683
Publication(s): *Atti e Memorie* (annually)

**Accademia Nazionale Virgiliana di Scienze,
  Lettere e Arti**
Via Accademia 47, 46100 Mantova
Tel: (0376) 320314 *Fax:* (0376) 222774
E-mail: info@accademianazionalevirgiliana.org
Web Site: www.accademianazionalevirgiliana.org
Key Personnel
President: Giorgio Zamboni
Vice President: Piero Gualtierotti
Secretary: Eugenio Camerlenghi
Founded: 1863
Publication(s): *Atti e Memorie NS*

**Accademia Petrarca di Lettere, Arti e Scienze
  di Arezzo** (Petrarch Academy of Letters, Arts
  & Science)
Via dell'Orto n 28, 52100 Arezzo
Tel: (0575) 24700 *Fax:* (0575) 298846
E-mail: info@accademiapetrarca.it
Web Site: www.accademiapetrarca.it
Key Personnel
President: Prof Giulio Firpo

Vice President: Giulio Rupi
Secretary General: Prof Antonio Batinti
Founded: 1787
Publication(s): *Atti e Memorie della Accademia*

**Istituto Lombardo Accademia di Scienze e
Lettere** (Lombard School Academy of
Sciences & Arts)
Palazzo Landriani, Uffici e Biblioteca, Via Bor-
gonuovo, 25, 20121 Milan
Tel: (02) 864087 *Toll Free Tel:* (02) 86461388
E-mail: istituto.lombardo@unimi.it
Web Site: www.istitutolombardo.it
Key Personnel
President: Prof Gianpiero Sironi
Vice President: Angelo Stella
Founded: 1797

Italian PEN Centre
Member of PEN International
Via Daverio, 7, 20122 Milan
Tel: (0335) 7350966 *Fax:* (0363) 350654
E-mail: segreteria@penclub.it
Web Site: www.penclub.it
Key Personnel
Honorary President: Lucio Lami *E-mail:* l.lami@
libero.it
President: Sebastiano Grasso
Vice President & Treasurer: Carlo Montaleone
E-mail: carlo.montaleone@fastwebnet.it
Secretary General: Georgio Mannacio
Publication(s): *PEN (Poets, Essayists, Novelists)*
(magazine)

Societa Dantesca Italiana (Italian Dante Society)
Palagio dell'Arte della Lana, Via Arte della Lana
1, 50123 Florence FI
Tel: (055) 287134; (055) 2675811 *Fax:* (055)
211316
E-mail: sdi@dantesca.it; biblioteca@dantesca.it
(library)
Web Site: www.dantesca.it
Key Personnel
President: Eugenio Giani
Vice President: Marcella Antonini
Founded: 1888
Publication(s): *Edizione Nazionale delle Opere
di Dante* (National Edition of Dante's Works);
*Quaderni degli Studi Danteschi; Quaderni del
Centro Studi e Documentazione Dantesca e
Medievale; Studi Danteschi* (annually)

Japan

Japanische Gesellschaft fuer Germanistik
(Literature Society Japan & Germany)
3-34-6 Minami-Otsuka, Toshima-ku, Tokyo 170-
0005
Tel: (03) 5950-1147 *Fax:* (03) 5950-1147
Web Site: www.jgg.jp
Publication(s): *Doitsu Bungaku* (biannually)

JCLA, see Nippon Hikaku Bungakukai

Nihon Eibungakkai (English Literary Society of
Japan)
Kenkyusha Eigo Centre Bldg, 1-2 Kagurazaka,
Shinjuku-ku, Tokyo 162-0825
Tel: (03) 5261-1922 *Fax:* (03) 5261-1922
E-mail: ejimu@elsj.org
Web Site: www.elsj.org
Founded: 1917
Publication(s): *Studies in English Literature* (tri-
annually)

Nippon Hikaku Bungakukai (Japan
Comparative Literature Association)
c/o Nihon University College of Law, 2-3-1 Misa-
kicho, Chiyoda-ku, Tokyo 101-8375
Tel: (03) 5275-8730 *Fax:* (03) 3802-8535
E-mail: smorosak@law.nihon-u.ac.jp
Web Site: www.nihon-hikaku.org
Key Personnel
Executive Dir: Hitoshi Oshima
Secretary General: Shigetoshi Morosaka
Founded: 1948

Japanese PEN Centre
Member of PEN International
20-3 Kabuto-cho, Nihonbashi, Chuo-ku, Tokyo
103-0026
Tel: (03) 5614-5391 *Fax:* (03) 5695-7686
E-mail: info@japanpen.or.jp
Web Site: www.japanpen.or.jp
Key Personnel
President: Jiro Asada
Vice President: Susumu Nakanishi; Akiko Shimo-
jyu
Secretary: Kazunari Yoshizawa
E-mail: kazunari_yoshizawa@japanpen.or.jp
Mng Dir: Shinobu Yoshioka
Founded: 1935
Publication(s): *Japanese Literature Today* (annu-
ally since 1976)

Liechtenstein

Liechtenstein PEN Centre
Member of PEN International
Postfach 416, 9490 Vaduz
Tel: 232 7271 *Fax:* 232 8071
E-mail: info@pen-club.li
Web Site: www.pen-club.li
Key Personnel
President: Manfred Schlapp
Secretary: Mathias Ospelt *E-mail:* mathios@
powersurf.li
Founded: 1978
Publication(s): *Zifferblatt* (annually)

Macedonia

Macedonian PEN Centre
Member of PEN International
Dimitar Vlahov Quay bb, 1000 Skopje
Tel: (02) 313 00 54 *Fax:* (02) 313 00 54
E-mail: macedpen@unet.com.mk
Web Site: www.pen.org.mk
Key Personnel
President: Risto Lazarov
Secretary: Ivan Dzeparoski
Publication(s): *The Macedonian PEN Review* (an-
nually)

Malaysia

Dewan Bahasa dan Pustaka (Institute of
Language & Literature)
Jl Dewan Bahasa, 50460 Kuala Lumpur
Tel: (03) 2147 9000 *Fax:* (03) 2147 9619; (03)
2144 5727; (03) 2141 4109
Web Site: www.dbp.gov.my/lamandbp

Publication(s): *Dewan Bahasa; Dewan Budaya;
Dewan Masyarakat; Dewan Pelajar; Dewan
Sastera* (monthly); *Dewan Siswa* (monthly);
Tenggara (biannually)

Mexico

Mexican PEN Centre
Member of PEN International
Heriberto Frias 1452-407, Colonia Del Valle,
03100 Mexico, CDMX
Tel: (0155) 56 88 42 62 *Fax:* (0155) 55 54 55 10
E-mail: penmexico@gmail.com
Key Personnel
President: Jennifer Clement
Vice President: Aline Davidoff
E-mail: vicepresidencia@penmexico.org.mx
Secretary: Sylvia Navarette
Treasurer: Catherine Austin
Publication(s): *Directorio de Escritores* (annually)

Nepal

Nepal PEN Centre
Member of PEN International
Height House Panday's Paradise, Peace Park,
Jawalakhel, Lalitpur
Key Personnel
President: Ram Kumar Panday *Tel:* (01) 5538785
E-mail: rkpanday@ntc.net.np
Secretary: Prakash A Raj *Fax:* (01) 426 2471
E-mail: paraj85@hotmail.com
Founded: 1980
Publication(s): *Jane Eyre (in Nepali)* (with help
from the Bronte Society, translated by S Rai)

Netherlands

Maatschappij der Nederlandse Letterkunde
(Dutch Society of Literature)
p/a Universiteitsbibliotheek, Postbus 9501, 2300
RA Leiden
E-mail: mnl@library.leidenuniv.nl
Web Site: maatschappijdernederlandseletterkunde.
nl
Key Personnel
President: Peter Sigmond
Vice Chairman: Luc Devoldere
Treasurer: Aad Groos
Secretary: Berry Dongelmans *Tel:* (071) 5272109
Founded: 1766
Publication(s): *Indische Letteren* (quarterly); *Jaar-
boek der Maatschappij* (annually); *De negen-
tiende eeuw* (quarterly); *Tijdschrift voor Neder-
landse Taal- en Letterkunde* (quarterly)

Netherlands PEN Centre
Member of PEN International
Lodewijk van Deysselhuis, De Lairessestra 125,
1075 HH Amsterdam
Tel: (020) 6240803
E-mail: info@pennederland.nl
Web Site: www.pennederland.nl
Key Personnel
President: Rene Appel
Secretary: Manon Uphoff

New Zealand

Bibliographical Society of Australia & New Zealand Inc (BSANZ)
c/o University of Otago, Dept of English, PO Box 56, Dunedin 9054
Web Site: www.bsanz.org
Founded: 1969
Publication(s): *Broadsheet* (irregularly, newsletter); *Script & Print: Bulletin of the Bibliographical Society of Australia & New Zealand* (quarterly, journal)

BSANZ, see Bibliographical Society of Australia & New Zealand Inc (BSANZ)

New Zealand Book Council
Stephenson & Turner House, Level 4, 156-158 Victoria St, Te Aro, Wellington 6011
Tel: (04) 801 5546 *Fax:* (04) 801 5547
E-mail: admin@bookcouncil.org.nz
Web Site: www.bookcouncil.org.nz
Key Personnel
Communications Manager: Susanna Andrew
    E-mail: communications@bookcouncil.org.nz
Education Manager: Sarah Forster
    E-mail: education@bookcouncil.org.nz
Publication(s): *Book Notes* (quarterly, magazine)

New Zealand Council for Educational Research (NZCER)
Education House, Level 10, West Block, 178-182 Willis St, Wellington 6011
Mailing Address: PO Box 3237, Wellington 6140
Tel: (04) 384 7939 *Fax:* (04) 384 7933
Web Site: www.nzcer.org.nz
Key Personnel
Publishing Manager: David Ellis *E-mail:* david. ellis@nzcer.org.nz
Founded: 1934
Publication(s): *Curriculum* (annually, journal); *Early Childhood Folio* (annually, journal); *Research Information for Teachers* (3 times/yr, journal)

New Zealand Society of Authors (NZSA)
Duthie Whyte Bldg, Level 4, 120 Mayorial Dr, Auckland 1141
Mailing Address: PO Box 7701, Wellesley St, Auckland 1141
Tel: (09) 379 4801 *Fax:* (09) 379 4801
E-mail: office@nzauthors.org.nz
Web Site: www.authors.org.nz
Key Personnel
President: Tony Simpson *E-mail:* sugarbags@xtra. co.nz
Chief Executive Officer & Executive Dir: Maggie Tarver *E-mail:* director@nzauthors.org.nz
Founded: 1934
Publication(s): *New Zealand Author* (bimonthly)

New Zealand Writers Guild
1/243 Ponsonby Rd, Ponsonby, Auckland 1011
Mailing Address: PO Box 47 886, Ponsonby, Auckland 1144
Tel: (09) 360 1408
E-mail: info@nzwg.org.nz
Web Site: www.nzwritersguild.org.nz
Key Personnel
President: Pip Hall
Vice President: Dianne Taylor
Executive Dir: Steven Gannaway
Treasurer: Fiona Macewen
Membership Manager: Claire Ashton
Southern Region Representative: Allan Baddock
Founded: 1975
Publication(s): *The Write Stuff* (newsletter); *Write Up* (magazine)

NZCER, see New Zealand Council for Educational Research (NZCER)

NZSA, see New Zealand Society of Authors (NZSA)

PEN NZ Inc, see New Zealand Society of Authors (NZSA)

Norway

NORLA (Norwegian Literature Abroad, Fiction & Non-Fiction)
Observatoriegaten 1B, 3rd floor, 0033 Oslo
Mailing Address: Postboks 1414, 0115 Oslo
Tel: 23 08 41 00; 23 08 41 02 *Fax:* 23 08 41 01
E-mail: firmapost@norla.no
Web Site: www.norla.no
Key Personnel
Senior Executive Officer: Ingrid Overwien
Executive Officer: Mette Borja
Dir: Margit Walso
Project Coordinator: Oliver Moystad
Childrens' Literature Advisor: Dina Roll-Hansen
Fiction Advisor: Andrine Pollen
Nonfiction Advisor: Per Oystein Roland
Founded: 1978
State supported foundation offering grants to translations of Norwegian literature.

Norske Akademi for Sprog og Litteratur (Norwegian Academy for Language & Literature)
Rosenborggaten 3, 0356 Oslo
Tel: 22 60 88 59
E-mail: ordet@riksmalsforbundet.no
Web Site: www.riksmalsforbundet.no
Key Personnel
Chairman: Trond Vernegg *Tel:* 98 29 45 98
Vice Chairman: Sverre Martin Gunnerud *Tel:* 90 55 14 35; Tor Guttu
President: John Ole Askedal
Founded: 1953

Det Norske Videnskaps-Akademi (The Norwegian Academy of Science & Letters)
Drammensveien 78, 0271 Oslo
Tel: 22 12 10 90 *Fax:* 22 12 10 99
E-mail: dnva@online.no
Web Site: www.dnva.no
Key Personnel
President: Prof Nils Christian Stenseth
Vice President: Kirsti Strom Bull
Secretary General & Mng Dir: Prof Oivind Andersen
Founded: 1857
The advancement of science & scholarship in Norway. The academy consists of 219 Norwegian & 183 foreign members with a governing board of 9 officials.

Norwegian Literature Abroad, Fiction & Non-Fiction, see NORLA (Norwegian Literature Abroad, Fiction & Non-Fiction)

Norwegian PEN Centre
Member of PEN International
Wergelandsveien 29, 0167 Oslo
Tel: 22 60 74 50; 926 88 023 (cell) *Fax:* 22 60 74 51
E-mail: pen@norskpen.no
Web Site: www.norskpen.no
Key Personnel
President: Anders Heger *E-mail:* anders.heger@ cappendamn.no

Vice President: Elisabeth Eide *E-mail:* elisabeth. eide@ibi.hio.no
Secretary General: Carl Morten Iversen

Pakistan

Pakistan Writers' Guild
Guild House, One Montgomery Rd, Lahore
Tel: (042) 6367124
E-mail: info@pakwritersguild.org; secretarygenral@pakwritersguild.org; trust@ pakwritersguild.org
Web Site: www.pakwritersguild.org
Founded: 1959
Publication(s): *Khaber Narmay* (monthly)

Panama

Panamanian PEN Centre
Member of PEN International
Apdo Postal 0830, 01699 San Francisco
Tel: 269 0928 *Fax:* 269 0928
E-mail: carr@mossfon.com
Key Personnel
President: Rosa Maria Britton
Secretary: Dr Juan David Morgan *Fax:* 263 9728
    E-mail: jdmor@morimor.com

Philippines

Philippine PEN Centre
Member of PEN International
Solidaridad Bookstore, 531 Padre Faura St, 1099 Ermita, Manila
Tel: (02) 254-1068 *Fax:* (02) 254-1068
E-mail: philippinepen@yahoo.com
Web Site: philippinepen.ph
Key Personnel
Chair: Bienvenido Lumbera
Vice Chair: Elmer Ordonez
Secretary: Joselito Zulueta
Treasurer: Susie Tan
Founded: 1958

Poland

Instytut Badan Literackich Polskie Akademii Nauk (Institute of Literary Research, Polish Academy of Sciences)
ul Nowy Swiat 72, 00-330 Warsaw
Tel: (22) 826 99 45; (22) 657 28 95 *Fax:* (22) 826 99 45
E-mail: ibadlit@ibl.waw.pl
Web Site: www.ibl.waw.pl
Key Personnel
Chairman: Prof Teresa Dobrzynska-Janusz
Vice Chairperson: Dr Anna Grzeskowiak-Krwawicz; Dr Jacek Leociak
Dir: Prof Mikolaj Sokobwski
Deputy Dir: Dr Dorota Krawczynska; Dr Dorota Siwicka
Secretary: Dr Anna Sobieska
Founded: 1948
Publication(s): *Pamictnik Literacki* (quarterly, journal); *Teksty Drugie* (quarterly, journal)

Polish PEN Centre (Polski PEN Club)
Member of PEN International
ul Krakowskie Przedmiescie 87/89, 00-079 Warsaw
Tel: (22) 826 57 84; (22) 828 28 23 *Fax:* (22) 826 57 84
E-mail: penclub@penclub.com.pl
Web Site: www.penclub.com.pl
Key Personnel
Honorary President: Wladyslaw Bartoszewski
President: Adam Pomorski
Vice President: Ewa Lipska; Pawel Huelle
Secretary: Barbara Miecznicka
Treasurer: Iwona Smolka
Founded: 1925

Towarzystwo Literackie im Adama Mickiewicza (Mickiewicz Literary Society)
Palac Staszica, ul Nowy Swiat 72/14A, 00-330 Warsaw
Tel: (22) 657 28 79
E-mail: towarzystwo-literackie@wp.pl
Web Site: www.towarzystwo-literackie.org
Key Personnel
President: Dr Grazyna Borkowska
Vice President: Dr Jacek Wojcicki; Dr Anna Sobieska
Secretary: Dr Irena Szypowska
Treasurer: D Iwona Wisniewska
Founded: 1886
Publication(s): *Wiek XIX Rocznik Towarzystwa Literackiego im Adama Mickiewicza*

Portugal

Instituto Portugues da Sociedade Cientifica de Goerres (Portuguese Institute of the Goerres Research Society)
c/o Universidade Catolica Portuguesa, Palma de Cima, 1649-023 Lisbon
Tel: 217 214 000 (ext 115) *Fax:* 217 260 546
E-mail: info@reitoria.ucp.pt
Web Site: www.ucp.pt
Key Personnel
Contact: Dr Maria Eugenia Rato *E-mail:* mrato@reitoria.ucp.pt
Founded: 1962
Research in Portuguese.
Publication(s): *Portugiesische Forschungen der Goerres Gesellschaft*

PEN Clube Portugues, see Portuguese PEN Centre

Portuguese PEN Centre
Member of PEN International
Campo dos Martires da Patria, 37, 1169-016 Lisbon
E-mail: geral@penclubeportugues.org
Web Site: penclubeportugues.org
Key Personnel
President: Teresa Salema
Vice President: Maria do Sameiro Barroso
Secretary: Maria Joao Cantinho
Treasurer: Manuel de Queiroz
Founded: 1988
Writers' Association.

Sociedade Portuguesa de Autores (Portuguese Society of Authors)
Av Duque de Loule, 31, 1069-153 Lisbon, Codex
Tel: 213 594 400 *Fax:* 213 530 257
E-mail: geral@spautores.pt
Web Site: www.spautores.pt
Key Personnel
President & Chief Executive Officer: Jose Jorge Letria

Founded: 1925
A limited liability cooperative established to manage author's rights. We represent authors from all literary & artistic areas.
Publication(s): *Autores*

Puerto Rico

Ateneo Puertorriqueno (Puerto Rican Society of Writers)
Apdo 9021180, San Juan 00902-1180
Tel: (787) 722-4839; (787) 721-3877 *Fax:* (787) 725-3873
E-mail: ateneopr@caribe.net
Web Site: www.puertadetierra.info/edificios/ateneo/ateneo.htm
Founded: 1876
Depository of treasures in works of art, literature, historical documents & memorabilia. Offers literary contests, annual art competitions & short academic courses.

Puerto Rican PEN Centre (PEN Club of Puerto Rico)
Member of PEN International
6 Mariano Ramerez Bages, Apartment 4B, San Juan 00907
Tel: (787) 645-9533
Key Personnel
President: Mairym Cruz-Bernall
E-mail: mairymcb@hotmail.com
Secretary: Ana Maria Fuster *E-mail:* fusterlavin@gmail.com

Romania

Romanian PEN Centre
Member of PEN International
Calea Victoriei, No 115, Sector 1, 010071 Bucharest
Tel: (021) 316 58 29
Web Site: www.penromania.ro
Key Personnel
President: Magda Carneci *E-mail:* magda.carneci@gmail.com
Vice President: Constantin Abaluta
Secretary: Simone-Grazia Dima
E-mail: simonagraziadima@yahoo.com
Founded: 1926

Societatea de Stiinte Filologice din Romania (SSF) (Romanian Philological Sciences Society)
Str Mendeleev, Nr 21-25, Et 4, Ap Cam 417, Sector 1, 010362 Bucharest
Tel: (021) 3123148
Key Personnel
Vice President: Paul Cornea
Publication(s): *Limba si literatura* (Language & Literature, quarterly, journal); *Limba si Literatura Romana* (Romanian Language & Literature, quarterly, journal)

SSF, see Societatea de Stiinte Filologice din Romania (SSF)

Russia

Russian PEN Centre
Member of PEN International

Neglinnaya St 18/1, Bldg 2, 107031 Moscow
Tel: (495) 625 2718 *Fax:* (495) 625 3573
E-mail: penrussian@dol.ru; penrussian@gmail.ru
Web Site: www.penrussia.org
Key Personnel
President: Andrei Bitov
Secretary: Alexei Simonov *E-mail:* simonov@gdf.ru
Founded: 1921

Senegal

Senegalese PEN Centre
Member of PEN International
Rue des Ecrivains Point E, BP 21464, Dakar/Ponty
E-mail: pensenegal@yahoo.fr
Key Personnel
President: Mbaye Gana Kebe
E-mail: memgoree@sentoo.sn
Secretary: Sillarneyni Gueye
E-mail: silcarneyni@gmail.com

Serbia

Serbian PEN Centre
Member of PEN International
29/11 Terazije St, 11000 Belgrade
Tel: (011) 33 44 427 *Fax:* (011) 33 44 427
E-mail: pencentar@ptt.rs
Web Site: www.serbianpen.rs
Key Personnel
President: Vida Ognjenovic *Tel:* (011) 33 44 607
E-mail: vidao@eunet.rs
Vice President: Dr Mihajlo Pantic; Zoran Paunovic
Secretary: Neda Nikolic Bobic *Fax:* (011) 33 43 411
Publication(s): *Pismo* (quarterly, published jointly with "Jovan Popovic" Library, Zemun)

Slovakia

Spolok slovenskych spisovatel'ov (Slovak Writers' Society)
Laurinska 2, 815 84 Bratislava 1
Tel: (02) 5441 8670 *Fax:* (02) 5443 5371
E-mail: spolspis@stonline.sk
Web Site: spolok-slovenskych-spisovatelov.webnode.sk
Key Personnel
President: Dr Jan Tuzinsky, PhD
Secretary-General: Pavol Janik, PhD
Founded: 1949
Publication(s): *Literarny Tyzdhennik* (Literary Weekly)

Slovenia

Slovene PEN Centre
Member of PEN International
Tomsiceva 12, SI-1000 Ljubljana
Tel: (01) 425 48 47 *Fax:* (01) 425 48 47
E-mail: slopen@guest.arnes.si
Web Site: www.penslovenia-zdruzenje.si
Key Personnel
President: Marjan Strojan

Vice President: Tone Persak
Secretary: Ifigenija Simonovic
Founded: 1926
Publication(s): *Litterae Slovenicae*

South Korea

PEN Korean Centre
Member of PEN International
No 1105 Osung Bldg, 1305 Yeoido-Dong,
  Yongdungpo-ku, Seoul 150-970
Tel: (02) 782-1337; (02) 782-1338 *Fax:* (02) 786-
  1090
E-mail: penkon2001@yahoo.co.kr; admin@
  penkorea.or.kr
Web Site: www.penkorea.or.kr
Key Personnel
President: Gil-Won Lee *E-mail:* lee@penkorea.or.
  kr
Secretary: Hae-Rim Yang
Publication(s): *Korean Literature Today* (quar-
  terly)

Spain

Ateneo Cientifico, Literario y Artistico
  (Scientific, Literary & Artistic Athenaeum)
Calle del Prado 21, 28014 Madrid
Tel: 91 429 17 50 *Fax:* 91 429 79 01
E-mail: biblioteca@ateneodemadrid.es
Web Site: www.ateneodemadrid.com
Key Personnel
President: Carlos Paris Amador
Vice President: Pedro Lopez Arriba
General Secretary: Carlos Garcia
Founded: 1837

Ateneu Cientific, Literari i Artistico de Mao
  (Scientific, Literary & Artistic Athenaeum)
Sa Rovellada de Dalt, 25, 07703 Mao, Menorca,
  Balearic Islands
Tel: 971 36 05 53 *Fax:* 971 35 21 94
E-mail: ateneu@ateneumao.org
Web Site: www.ateneumao.org
Key Personnel
President: Jose Antonio Faya Janer
Vice President & Secretary: Margarita Orfila Pons
Vice President: Jose Fco Quadrado Quintana
Secretary: Marta Marco Barber
Founded: 1905
Publication(s): *Revista de Menorca* (quarterly)

Galician PEN Centre
Member of PEN International
Casa da Para 30, Praza da Quintana s/n, 15704
  Compostella
Tel: 981 957 119
E-mail: pengalicia@mundo-r.com
Key Personnel
President: Luis Gonzalez Tosar
  E-mail: luistosar@mundo-r.com
Dir: Xabier Castro

Real Academia Sevillana de Buenas Letras
  (Seville Royal Academy of Literature)
C/ Abades, 14, 41004 Seville
Tel: 95 422 52 00
E-mail: academia@
  academiasevillanadebuenasletras.org
Web Site: www.academiasevillanadebuenasletras.
  org
Key Personnel
Dir: Enriqueta Vila Vilar

Vice Dir: Dr Manuel Olivencia Ruiz
Secretary: Jose Antonio Gomez Marin; Rafael
  Valencia Rodriguez
Founded: 1751
Publication(s): *Boletin de Buenas Letras* (quar-
  terly)

Sweden

**Kungl Vitterhets Historie och Antikvitets
  Akademien** (The Royal Swedish Academy of
  Letters, History & Antiquities)
Villagatan 3, 114 32 Stockholm
Mailing Address: Box 5622, 114 86 Stockholm
Tel: (08) 440 42 80 *Fax:* (08) 440 42 90
E-mail: kansli@vitterhetsakad.se
Web Site: www.vitterhetsakad.se
Key Personnel
Secretary-General: Erik Norberg *Tel:* (08) 440 42
  81 *E-mail:* sekreteraren@vitterhetsakad.se
Founded: 1753
Publication(s): *Arkiv (Archives)* (irregularly); *Ars-
  bok (Yearbook)* (annually); *Fornvaennen (Jour-
  nal of Swedish Antiquarian Research)* (quar-
  terly); *Handlingar (Proceedings)* (irregularly);
  Monografier (Monographs) (irregularly)

Swedish PEN Centre (Svenska Pen)
Member of PEN International
Johannesgrand 1, 111 30 Stockholm
E-mail: info@svenskapen.se
Web Site: www.pensweden.org
Key Personnel
Chairman: Ola Larsmo *Tel:* (0708) 26 85 57
  E-mail: ola.larsmo@svenskapen.se
Vice President: Martin Kaunitz *Tel:* (0704) 32 86
  40 *E-mail:* martin.kaunitz@svenskapen.se
Secretary: Peter Karlsson *Tel:* (0707) 99 85 98
  E-mail: peter.karlsson@svenskapen.se
Treasurer: Jesper Monthan *Tel:* (0706) 39 82 18
  E-mail: jesper.monthan@svenskapen.se
Founded: 1922

Samfundet De Nio (The Academy of the Nine)
Villagatan 14, 114 32 Stockholm
Tel: (070) 573 44 08 *Fax:* (08) 611 22 03
Web Site: www.samfundetdenio.se
Key Personnel
Chairman: Inge Jonsson
Secretary & Treasurer: Anders R Oehman
Founded: 1913

Switzerland

Autorinnen und Autoren der Schweiz AdS
  (Association of Swiss Authors)
Konradstr 61, 8031 Zurich
Tel: (044) 350 04 60 *Fax:* (044) 350 04 61
E-mail: sekretariat@a-d-s.ch
Web Site: www.a-d-s.ch
Key Personnel
Secretary General: Nicole Pfister Fetz
  E-mail: npfister@a-d-s.ch
Secretary: Patricia Buettiker *E-mail:* pbuettiker@
  a-d-s.ch; Verena Roethlisberger
  E-mail: vroethlisberger@a-d-s.ch

Autrices et Auteurs de Suisse, see Autorinnen
  und Autoren der Schweiz AdS

Autrici ed Autori della Svizzera AdS, see
  Autorinnen und Autoren der Schweiz AdS

**Gesellschaft fuer deutsche Sprache und
  Literatur in Zurich** (Society for German
  Language & Literature in Zurich)
c/o Deutsches Seminar, Schoenberggasse 9, 8001
  Zurich
Tel: (044) 6342571 *Fax:* (044) 6344905
E-mail: gfdsl@ds.uzh.ch
Web Site: www.ds.uzh.ch/gfdsl
Founded: 1894

GfdSL, see Gesellschaft fuer deutsche Sprache
  und Literatur in Zurich

Suisse Romand PEN Centre (PEN Club for
  French-Speaking Switzerland)
Member of PEN International
c/o 26 Av Krieg, 1208 Geneva
Tel: (022) 348 8570
Key Personnel
President: Claude Krul *E-mail:* ckrul@bluewin.ch
Vice President: Hoang Nguyen Bao Viet; Glorice
  Weinstein
Secretary General: Zeki Ergas *E-mail:* zeki.
  ergas@netplus.ch
Treasurer: Alfred de Zayas *E-mail:* zayas@
  bluewin.ch
Founded: 1949
PEN Club for French-speaking Switzerland.
Publication(s): *PEN Club romand Newsletter*
  (biannually)

Swiss German PEN Centre (Deutschweizer PEN
  Zentrum)
Member of PEN International
Freiestr 76, 8032 Zurich
Tel: (044) 350 70 70
E-mail: office@pen-dschweiz.ch
Web Site: www.pen-dschweiz.ch
Key Personnel
President: Michael Guggenheimer
  E-mail: president@pen-dschweiz.ch
Founded: 1922
Publication(s): *PEN-Brief*

Swiss Italian & Reto-Romansh PEN Centre
  (PEN Centro della Svizzera italiana e
  retoromancia)
Member of PEN International
CP 664, 6903 Lugano
Tel: (091) 967 16 02 *Fax:* (091) 967 16 02
E-mail: info@pensvizzeraitaliana.org
Web Site: www.pensvizzeraitaliana.org
Key Personnel
President: Franca Tiberto
Vice President: Gilberto Isella; Alice Moretti
Secretary: Sergej Roic *E-mail:* s.roic@ticino.com
Treasurer: Gabriella Renella
Publication(s): *Viceversa PEN International Cen-
  tro Della Svizzera Italiana e Retoromancia,
  1997*

Taiwan

Taipei Chinese PEN Centre
Member of PEN International
4th floor, 4 Lane 68 When Chou St, Taipei 10900
Tel: (02) 2369 3609 *Fax:* (02) 2369 9948
E-mail: taipen@seed.net.tw
Web Site: www.taipen.org
Key Personnel
President: Ching-Hsi Perng
Secretary General: In-shi Wei Ou
Publication(s): *The Taipei Chinese PEN* (quar-
  terly, journal)

Thailand

Thai PEN Centre
Member of PEN International
2 Pichai Rd, Dusit, Bangkok 10300
Tel: (02) 218-7492 *Fax:* (02) 255 5160
Web Site: www.phd-lit.arts.chula.ac.th/web_pen/
pen.htm
Key Personnel
President: Dr Trisilpa Boonkhachorn
E-mail: trisilpa.b@chula.ac.th
Founded: 1958
Nonprofit literary society.
Publication(s): *Thailand PEN Journal* (journal)

The Siam Society Under Royal Patronage
131 Asoke Montri Rd, Sukhumvit 21, Bangkok
10110
Tel: (02) 661-6470-7 *Fax:* (02) 258 3491
E-mail: info@siam-society.org
Web Site: www.siam-society.org
Key Personnel
President: Mrs Bilaibhan Sampatisiri
Vice President: Dr Wissanu Kreangam; Dr Weer-
achai Nanakorn
Honorary Secretary: Eileen Deeley
General Manager: Kanitha Kasina-Ubol
E-mail: kanitha@siam-society.org
Founded: 1904
Publication(s): *Journal of the Siam Society (JSS)*
(annually); *Natural History Bulletin (NHB)* (an-
nually)

Tunisia

IBLA, see Institut des Belles Lettres Arabes
(IBLA)

Institut des Belles Lettres Arabes (IBLA)
(Arabic Institute of Literature)
12bis, Rue Jamaa El Haoua, 1008 Tunis
Tel: 71 560 133 *Fax:* 71 572 683
E-mail: ibla@gnet.tn
Web Site: www.iblatunis.org
Founded: 1937
Publication(s): *Revue IBLA* (biannually)

Union des Ecrivains Tunisiens (Tunisian
Writers' Union)
20 rue de Paris, 1000 Tunis
Tel: 257 591 *Fax:* 353 243
E-mail: contact@koutteb.tn
Web Site: www.nadiadab.edunet.tn/ittihad
Key Personnel
President: Midani Ben Salah
Vice President: Souf Abid
Secretary General: Othman Ben Taleb
Treasurer: Mohamed Elhachimi Blouza
Founded: 1971

Turkey

Turkish PEN Centre (PEN Turkiye Merkzi)
Member of PEN International
Istikal Cd Beyoglu Is Merkezi, B Blok K:2 No
143, 80050 Beyoglu, Istanbul
Tel: (0212) 2920026
Web Site: www.pen.org.tr
Key Personnel
President: Tarik Gunersel
Vice President: Halil Ibrahim Ozcan

Secretary General: Sabri Kuskonmaz
E-mail: sabri.kuskonmaz@pen.org.tr
Treasurer: Tulin Dursun

Uganda

Femrite Uganda Women Writers' Association
Plot 147 Kilra Rd, Kamwokya, Kampala
Mailing Address: PO Box 705, Kampala
Tel: (0414) 543943
E-mail: info@femrite.org
Web Site: femrite.org
Key Personnel
President: Mary Karooro Okurut
Founded: 1995

Ukraine

**Ukrainian Assoiation of Publishers &
Booksellers**
Triohsvyztytelska st 4, Room 526, Kiev 01601
Tel: (044) 279-4575 *Fax:* (044) 278-6444
E-mail: upa@aranei.com
Web Site: uabooks.info
Key Personnel
President: Oleksandr Vasilyovich Afonin
Provides charitable activities for development of
book publishing & distribution businesses in
Ukraine.

United
Kingdom

AAH, see Association of Art Historians (AAH)

Yr Academi Gymreig (The Welsh Academy)
Mount Stuart House, 3rd floor, Mount Stuart Sq,
Cardiff CF10 5FQ
Tel: (029) 2047 2266 *Fax:* (029) 2049 2930
E-mail: post@literaturewales.org
Web Site: www.literaturewales.org
Key Personnel
President: Bobi Jones
Founded: 1959
The Welsh National Literature Promotion Agency
& Society of Writers.
Publication(s): *A470* (quarterly, magazine); *New
Welsh Review* (quarterly, magazine); *Taliesin*
(quarterly, periodical)

The Alliance of Literary Societies
22 Beeches Rd, Kidderminster DY11 5HF
Tel: (01562) 748996
Web Site: www.allianceofliterarysocieties.org.uk
Key Personnel
Chair: Linda J Curry *E-mail:* l.j.curry@bham.ac.
uk
President: Jenny Uglow
Honorary Secretary: Anita Fernandez-Young
E-mail: anita.fernandez-young@nottingham.
ac.uk
Treasurer & Membership Secretary: Julie
Shorland
Founded: 1973
Publication(s): *ALSo* (annually, journal)

Arts Council of Wales
Bute Pl, Cardiff CF10 5AL
Tel: (0845) 8734 900 *Fax:* (029) 2044 1400
E-mail: info@artswales.org.uk
Web Site: www.artswales.org.uk
Key Personnel
Chief Executive: Nick Capaldi *Tel:* (029) 2044
1358 *E-mail:* nick.capaldi@artscouncilofwales.
org

**ASLIB, The Association for Information
Management**
Howard House, Wagon Lane, Bingley BD16 1WA
Tel: (01274) 777700 *Fax:* (01274) 785201
E-mail: support@aslib.com
Web Site: www.aslib.com; www.
managinginformation.com
Key Personnel
Dir: Rebecca Marsh
Relationship Manager: Holly Shukla
Founded: 1924
To serve information professionals & librarians
across all sectors.
Publication(s): *ASLIB Directory of Information
Sources in the United Kngdom* (biennially);
Managing Information (10 times/yr, magazine)

ASLS, see Association for Scottish Literary
Studies

The Association for Information Management,
see ASLIB, The Association for Information
Management

Association for Scottish Literary Studies
c/o Scottish Literature, University of Glasgow, 7
University Gardens, Glasgow G12 8QH
Tel: (0141) 330 5309 *Fax:* (0141) 330 5309
E-mail: office@asls.org.uk
Web Site: www.asls.org.uk
Key Personnel
President: Prof Alison Lumsden
Treasurer: Tom Ralph
Secretary: Dr Ronnie Young
Dir: Duncan Jones
Founded: 1970
Also publisher.
Publication(s): *ASLS Annual Volume* (book); *The
Bottle Imp* (free, ezine); *New Writing Scotland*
(7.95 GBP, annually, book); *Occasional Pa-
pers* (book); *Scotlit* (biannually, newsletter);
Scotnotes (book); *Scottish Language* (annually,
journal); *Scotttish Literary Review* (biannually,
journal)

Association of Art Historians (AAH)
70 Cowcross St, London EC1M 6EJ
Tel: (020) 7490 3211 *Fax:* (020) 7490 3277
E-mail: admin@aah.org.uk
Web Site: www.aah.org.uk
Key Personnel
Chair: Alison Yarrington *E-mail:* chair@aah.org.
uk
Chief Executive: Pontus Rosen *E-mail:* pontus@
aah.org.uk
Deputy Chief Executive & Communications Offi-
cer: Claire Davies *E-mail:* claire@aah.org.uk
Honorary Secretary: Veronica Davies
E-mail: honsec@aah.org.uk
Honorary Treasurer: Richard Simpson
E-mail: hontreas@aah.org.uk
Finance & Policy Manager: Matt Lodder
Founded: 1974
Professional arts organization which promotes the
study of art history.
Publication(s): *Art History* (5 times/yr, journal);
Bulletin (triannually, newsletter)

Association of British Science Writers
Wellcome Wolfson Bldg, 165 Queen's Gate, London SW7 5HD

Tel: (0870) 770 3361
E-mail: absw@absw.org.uk
Web Site: www.absw.org.uk
Key Personnel
Chairman: Natasha Loder
Vice Chairman: Jeremy Webb
Acting Treasurer: Martin Ince
Founded: 1947
An association to help those who write about science & technology & to improve the standard of science journalism in the UK.
Publication(s): *Science Reporter* (monthly, ezine)

Authors' Club
Blacks, 67 Dean St, London W1D 4QH
Web Site: www.authorsclub.co.uk
Key Personnel
Chairman: Chris Schuler *E-mail:* cjschuler@authorsclub.co.uk
President: John Walsh
Honorary Secretary: Margaret Barnard
Honorary Treasurer: Michael Lindsay
Founded: 1892

The Beatrix Potter Society
c/o The Lodge, Salisbury Ave, Harpenden, Herts AL5 2PS
Tel: (01582) 769755
E-mail: info@beatrixpottersociety.org.uk
Web Site: www.beatrixpottersociety.org.uk
Key Personnel
President: Brian Alderson
Founded: 1980
The Society promotes study & appreciation of Potter's life & works, holds talks, events & study conferences in the UK & the USA.
Publication(s): *Books about Beatrix Potter's Life & Work* (quarterly, newsletter); *Pottering About* (bimonthly, newsletter)

E F Benson Society
The Old Coach House, High St, Rye, East Sussex TN31 7JF
Tel: (01797) 223114
E-mail: info@efbensonsociety.org
Web Site: www.efbensonsociety.org
Key Personnel
President: Gwen Watkins
Chair: Keith Cavers
Secretary: Allan Downend
Treasurer: Chris Roby
Founded: 1984
Literary society.
Publication(s): *E F Benson & His Family & Friends*; *Mary Benson* (book); *Bensoniana 1, 2 & 3* (book); *Bensons: A Victorian Family*; *The Dodo* (annually, journal)

British Fantasy Society (BFS)
23 Mayne St, Hanford, Stoke on Trent ST4 4RF
Tel: (07845) 897760
Web Site: www.britishfantasysociety.co.uk
Key Personnel
Chair: Lee Harris *E-mail:* chair@britishfantasysociety.org
President: Ramsey Campbell
Membership Secretary: Marion Pitman
    E-mail: secretary@britishfantasysociety.org
Founded: 1971
Publication(s): *BFS Journal*

The British Science Fiction Association Ltd (BSFA Ltd)
c/o 39 Glyn Ave, New Barnet, Herts EN4 9PJ
E-mail: organisation@bsfa.co.uk
Web Site: www.bsfa.co.uk
Key Personnel
Chair: Ian Whates
Treasurer: Martin Potts *E-mail:* bsfatreasurer@gmail.com

Membership Secretary: Peter Wilkinson
    E-mail: sf@pwilkinson.cix.co.uk
Founded: 1958
A not-for-profit organization that promotes science fiction, fantasy & horror by providing magazines, events, interviews & a community of fans, authors & publishing professionals.
Publication(s): *Focus* (biannually, magazine); *Matrix* (bimonthly, ezine); *Vector* (bimonthly, magazine)

The Bronte Society
Bronte Parsonage Museum, Church St, Haworth, Keighley, W Yorks BD22 8DR
Tel: (01535) 642323 *Fax:* (01535) 647131
E-mail: bronte@bronte.org.uk; info@bronte.org.uk
Web Site: www.bronte.info
Founded: 1893
Publication(s): *Bronte Gazette* (triannually, magazine); *Bronte Studies* (triannually, journal)

BSFA Ltd, see The British Science Fiction Association Ltd (BSFA Ltd)

Cambridge Bibliographical Society
c/o Cambridge University Library, West Rd, Cambridge, Cambs CB3 9DR
Tel: (01223) 333123 *Fax:* (01223) 333160
E-mail: cbs@lib.cam.ac.uk
Web Site: www.lib.cam.ac.uk/cambibsoc
Key Personnel
President: David McKitterick
Vice President: Prof E J Kenney
Honorary Secretary: Dr Tim Eggington
Treasurer: Dr J J Hall
Editor: Dr Jill Whitelock *E-mail:* jw330@cam.ac.uk
Founded: 1949
Publication(s): *Monographs* (irregularly); *Transactions of the Cambridge Bibliographical Society* (annually)

Children's Books History Society
26 St Bernard's Close, Buckfast, South Devon TQ11 0EP
Tel: (01364) 643568
E-mail: cbhs@abcgarrett.demon.co.uk
Key Personnel
Chairman & Newsletter Co-Editor: Mrs Pat Garrett
Founded: 1969
In liaison with CILIP. British branch of the Osborne & Lilian H Smith Collections.
In 1990, a biennial Harvey Darton Award was established for a book published in English, which extends our knowledge of some aspect of British children's literature of the past.
Publication(s): *CBHS Newsletter* (triannually)

The John Clare Society
9 The Chase, Ely, Cambs CB6 3DR
Tel: (01353) 668 438
E-mail: normali@arabella.wanadoo.co.uk (memberships only)
Web Site: www.johnclare.org.uk
Key Personnel
President: Ronald Blythe
Vice President: Prof John Goodridge
    E-mail: john.goodridge@ntu.ac.uk; Rodney Lines; Peter Moyse; Prof Eric Robinson; Edward Storey; Prof Kelsey Thornton
Chairman: Linda Curry *Tel:* (0121) 475 1805
    E-mail: l.j.curry@bham.ac.uk
Vice Chairman: Ron Ingamells
Honorary Secretary & Membership Secretary: Sue Holgate *E-mail:* sueholgate@hotmail.co.uk
Honorary Treasurer: Norman Lee
    E-mail: normali@arabella.wanadoo.co.uk
Journal Editor: Simon Kovesi
Newsletter Editor: Valerie Pedlar

Archivist: Sam Ward
Founded: 1981
To promote a wider & deeper knowledge of the poet, John Clare (1793-1864).
Publication(s): *The John Clare Society Journal* (annually)

The Joseph Conrad Society (UK)
c/o The Polish Social & Cultural Asssociation (POSK), 238-246 King St, London W6 0RF
Web Site: www.josephconradsociety.org
Key Personnel
Chairman: Dr Keith Carabine *E-mail:* keith@carabine.co.uk
Treasurer: Dr Allan H Simmons
    E-mail: theconradian@aol.com
Honorary Secretary: Hugh Epstein
    E-mail: hughepstein@hotmail.co.uk
Editor: Dr Tim Middleton *E-mail:* t.middleton@bathspa.ac.uk
Founded: 1973
Literary society devoted to all aspects of the study of the works & life of Joseph Conrad (1857-1924).
Membership(s): The Alliance of Literary Societies (ALS).
Publication(s): *Conrad Studies* (series); *The Conradian* (biannually, journal)

Critics' Circle
50 Finland Rd, Brockley, London SE4 2JH
Tel: (020) 7732 9636
Web Site: criticscircle.org.uk
Key Personnel
President: Tom Sutcliffe
Vice President: Simon Tait
Honorary General Secretary: William Russell
    E-mail: williamfinland@gmail.com
Honorary Treasurer: Peter Cargin *E-mail:* peter.cargin@gmail.com
Founded: 1907
Professional association of critics of drama, music, the cinema & dance.

The Dickens Fellowship
Charles Dickens Museum, 48 Doughty St, London WC1N 2LX
Tel: (020) 7405 2127 *Fax:* (020) 7831 5175
E-mail: postbox@dickensfellowship.org (enquires)
Web Site: www.dickensfellowship.org
Key Personnel
Council Chairman: Michael Rogers
President: Prof Grahame Smith
Honorary General Secretary: Mrs Lee Ault; Mrs Joan Dicks
Honorary Treasurer: Anita Fernadez Young
Editor: Prof Malcolm Andrews
Founded: 1902
To promote knowledge of the life & works of Charles Dickens.
Affiliated with the Alliance of Literary Societies, The Birmingham & Midland Institute, 9 Margaret St, Birmingham, B 3BS.
Publication(s): *The Dickens Magazine*; *The Dickensian* (3 times/yr, journal); *The London Particular* (newsletter)

The Dorothy L Sayers Society
Gimson, King's Chase, Witham, Essex CM8 1AX
Tel: (01376) 515626 *Fax:* (01376) 515626
E-mail: info@sayers.org.uk
Web Site: www.sayers.org.uk
Key Personnel ·
President: Dr Barbara Reynolds
Treasurer: Brian Ogilvie
Acting Chairman: Seona Ford
Founded: 1976
Publication(s): *Poetry of Dorothy L Sayers*; *Sidelights on Sayers* (annually)

Early English Text Society
Lady Margaret Hall, Oxford OX2 6QA
Web Site: www.eets.org.uk
Key Personnel
Honorary Dir: Prof Anne Hudson
Executive Secretary: Prof Vincent Gillespie
    E-mail: vincent.gillespie@ell.ox.ac.uk
Editorial Secretary: Dr H L Spencer
Membership Secretary: Jane Watkinson
    E-mail: janemwatkinson@hotmail.com
Founded: 1864

Edinburgh Bibliographical Society
c/o Center for the History of the Book, Edinburgh
    University, 22A Buccleuch Pl, Edinburgh EH8
    9LJ
Tel: (0131) 651 1716
Web Site: mcs.qmuc.ac.uk/ebs
Key Personnel
President: Ian McGowan
Vice President: Prof Peter Garside; Dr Heather
    Holmes
Treasurer: Prof David Finkelstein
    E-mail: dfinkelstein@gmu.ac.uk
Secretary: Helen Vincent *E-mail:* h.vincent@nls.
    uk
Founded: 1890
Publication(s): *Edinburgh Bibliographical Society
    Transactions*; *Journal of the Edinburgh Biblio-
    graphical Society* (annually)

The George Eliot Fellowship
39 Lower Rd, Barnacle, Coventry, Warwicks CV7
    9LD
Tel: (024) 7661 9126
Web Site: www.georgeeliot.org
Key Personnel
Chairman: John Burton *E-mail:* jkburton@tiscali.
    co.uk
Vice Chairman: Vivienne Wood *Tel:* (01455)
    618044 *E-mail:* vewood55@gmail.com
Membership Secretary: Juliet Hopper *Tel:* (024)
    7634 4398 *E-mail:* juliet.hopper@googlemail.
    com
Founded: 1930
Society to honor George Eliot & promote interest
    in her life & works.
Membership(s): The Alliance of Literary Soci-
    eties.
Publication(s): *George Eliot Review* (annually);
    Pitkin Guide to George Eliot (illustrated);
    *Those Of Us Who Loved Her: The Men In
    George Eliot's Life*

The English Association
University of Leicester, University Rd, Leicester
    LE1 7RH
Tel: (0116) 229 7622 *Fax:* (0116) 229 7623
E-mail: engassoc@le.ac.uk
Web Site: www.le.ac.uk/engassoc
Key Personnel
Chief Executive: Helen Lucas
Chair of the Executive Committee: Prof Adrian
    Barlow
President: Prof Maureen Moran
Honorary Treasurer: Dr Catherine Alexander
Administrator: Julia Hughes *E-mail:* jfh6@
    leicester.ac.uk
Founded: 1906
Publication(s): *Bookmarks*; *EA Newsletter* (3
    times/yr); *English* (quarterly, journal); *The En-
    glish Association 100 Years on*; *English As-
    sociation Studies*; *English 4-11* (3 times/yr,
    journal); *Essays & Studies* (annually); *Issues
    in English* (7 times/yr, journal); *Peer English* (annually,
    journal); *The Use of English* (3 times/yr, jour-
    nal); *The Year's Work in Critical & Cultural
    Theory* (annually); *The Year's Work in English
    Studies* (annually)

The English-Speaking Union (ESU)
Dartmouth House, 37 Charles St, London W1J
    5ED
Tel: (020) 7529 1550 *Fax:* (020) 7495 6108
E-mail: esu@esu.org
Web Site: www.esu.org
Key Personnel
President: Prince Philip Duke of Edinburgh
Chairman: Dame Mary Richardson
Dir-General: Peter Kyle *E-mail:* pkdg@esu.org
Membership Administrator: Kay Dacey *Tel:* (020)
    7529 1571 *E-mail:* kay.dacey@esu.org
Founded: 1918
Branches worldwide in 52 countries.
Publication(s): *Dialogue* (magazine)

ESU, see The English-Speaking Union (ESU)

FoAM, see Friends of Arthur Machen (FoAM)

Friends of Arthur Machen (FoAM)
210 Archway Rd, London N6 5AX
Web Site: www.arthurmachen.org.uk
Key Personnel
Chair & Co-Editor, Faunus: Ray Russell
    E-mail: tartarus@pavilion.co.uk
Secretary: Mark Samuels *E-mail:* mark699@
    btinternet.com
Treasurer & Membership Secretary: Jeremy
    Cantwell *E-mail:* jcantwell@ndo.co.uk
Publication(s): *Faunus* (biannually, journal);
    Machenalia (biannually, newsletter)

The Hakluyt Society
c/o Map Library, The British Library, 96 Euston
    Rd, London NW1 2DB
Tel: (01428) 641850 *Fax:* (01428) 641933
E-mail: office@hakluyt.com
Web Site: www.hakluyt.com
Key Personnel
President: Captain Michael Barritt
Honorary Treasurer: David Darbyshire
Honorary Archivist: Dr Margaret Makepeace
Honorary Joint Series Editor: Dr Gloria Clifton;
    Prof Joyce Lorimer
Honorary Editor, Online Publications: Raymond
    John Howgego
Founded: 1846
Seeks to advance knowledge & education by the
    publication of scholarly editions of records of
    voyages, travels & other geographical material.
Publication(s): *The Journal of the Hakluyt Society*
    (ezine)

The Thomas Hardy Society
c/o Dorset County Museum, Dorchester, Dorset
    DT1 1XA
Tel: (01305) 251501 *Fax:* (01305) 251501
E-mail: info@hardysociety.org
Web Site: www.hardysociety.org
Key Personnel
Chairman: Dr Anthony Fincham
Treasurer: Malcolm Pfaff
Secretary: Mike Nixon *E-mail:* mike@nixon3730.
    freeserve.co.uk
Founded: 1968
Publication(s): *The Hardy Society Journal* (bian-
    nually); *The Thomas Hardy Journal* (annually)

International Byron Society
Byron House, 6 Gertrude St, London SW10 0JN
Tel: (020) 7352 5112
Web Site: www.internationalbyronsociety.org
Key Personnel
President: The Earl of Lytton (UK); Prof John
    Clubbe (USA); Prof Byron Raizis (Greece)
Treasurer: David McClay (Scotland); Eric Wishart
    (Scotland)
Secretary: Joan Blythe (USA); Brigitte Lohmar
    (Germany)
Publication(s): *The Byron Journal* (annually)

Jane Austen Society
9 Nicola Close, South Croydon, Surrey CR2 6NA
E-mail: hq@jasoc.org.uk
Web Site: www.janeaustensoci.freeuk.com
Key Personnel
Chairman: David Selwyn
President: Richard Knight
Honorary Secretary: Maureen Stiller
Membership Secretary: Rosemary Culley
    E-mail: rvculley@gmail.com
Founded: 1940
Publication(s): *Collected Reports of The Jane
    Austen Society*; *The Complete Poems of James
    Austen*; *Fanny Knight's Diaries: Jane Austen
    through her niece's eyes*; *Fugitive Pieces:
    the poems of James Edward Austen-Leigh,
    Jane Austen's nephew & biographer*; *God-
    mersham Park, Kent - before, during & since
    Jane Austen's day*; *Jane Austen: A Celebra-
    tion*; *Jane Austen & the North Atlantic: Essays
    from the 2005 Jane Austen Society Conference
    in Halifax, Nova Scotia, Canada*; *Jane Austen:
    Collected Poems & Verse of the Austen Fam-
    ily*; *Jane Austen in Bath*; *Jane Austen in Lyme
    Regis*; *Jane Austen's Family & Tonbridge*; *Jane
    Austen's Steventon*; *The Letters of Mrs Lefroy*;
    My Aunt Jane Austen: A Memoir; *Reminis-
    cences of Caroline Austen*

The Richard Jefferies Society
Pear Tree Cottage, Longcot, Oxon SN7 7SS
Tel: (01793) 783040
E-mail: info@richardjefferiessociety.co.uk
Web Site: www.richardjefferiessociety.co.uk
Key Personnel
Honorary Secretary: Jean Saunders
Founded: 1950
Publication(s): *The Richard Jefferies Society Jour-
    nal*

Keats-Shelley Memorial Association (KSMA)
Bedford House, 76a Bedford St, Leamington Spa,
    Warwicks CV32 5DT
Fax: (01926) 335133
E-mail: hello@keats-shelley.co.uk
Web Site: www.keats-shelley.co.uk; www.keats-
    shelley.com
Key Personnel
Chairman: Harriet Cullen
Treasurer: Charles Cary-Elwes
Secretary: David Leigh-Hunt
Founded: 1903
Publication(s): *Keats & Italy: A History of the
    Keats-Shelley House in Rome* (13.95 EUR,
    book); *The Keats-Shelley Memorial Bulletin*;
    Keats-Shelley Review (annually, journal); *KSMA
    Monographs*; *KSMA Newsletter* (biannually);
    *Spellbound by Rome: the Anglo-American
    Community in Rome (1896-1914) and the
    Founding of Keats-Shelley House* (18 EUR,
    book)

Kipling Society
6 Clifton Rd, London W9 1SS
Tel: (020) 7286 0194 *Fax:* (020) 7286 0194
Web Site: www.kipling.org.uk
Key Personnel
Honorary Secretary: Jane Keskar
    E-mail: jmkeskar@btinternet.com
Founded: 1927
Charity to celebrate the work of Rudyard Kipling.
Publication(s): *The Kipling Journal* (quarterly)

KSMA, see Keats-Shelley Memorial Association
    (KSMA)

Charles Lamb Society
BM ELIA, 20 Bloomsbury Way, London WC1N
    3XX
Tel: (020) 7332 1868; (020) 7332 1870
Web Site: www.charleslambsociety.com

Key Personnel
Chairman: Nick Powell *E-mail:* nrdpowell@
gmail.com
Editor: Stephen Burley *E-mail:* stephenburley@
hotmail.com
Membership Secretary: Cecila Powell
E-mail: cecila.powell@virgin.net
Founded: 1935
Publication(s): *The Charles Lamb Bulletin* (biannually)

Lancashire Authors' Association
Heatherslade, 5 Quakerfields, Westhoughton,
Bolton, Lancs BL5 2BJ
E-mail: laaenqs@gmail.com
Web Site: lancashireauthorsassociation.wordpress.
com
Key Personnel
President: Elizabeth B Ashworth
Secretary: Michael Finney
Membership Secretary: Beryl Holt
Founded: 1909
Publication(s): *The Record* (quarterly, journal)

Medical Writers Group
Unit of The Society of Authors
c/o The Society of Authors, 84 Drayton Gardens,
London SW10 9SB
Tel: (020) 7373 6642 *Fax:* (020) 7373 5768
E-mail: info@societyofauthors.org
Web Site: www.societyofauthors.org
Key Personnel
General Secretary: Nicola Solomon
Deputy General Secretary: Kate Pool
E-mail: kpool@societyofauthors.org
Founded: 1979

William Morris Society
Kelmscott House, 26 Upper Mall, London W6
9TA
Tel: (020) 8741 3735 *Fax:* (020) 8748 5207
E-mail: info@williammorrissociety.org
Web Site: www.williammorrissociety.org
Key Personnel
President: Jan Marsh
Editor: Patrick O'Sullivan *E-mail:* editor@
williammorrissociety.org
Secretary: Penny Lyndon
E-mail: penelopelyndon@yahoo.co.uk
Publication(s): *Journal* (biannually); *Newsletter*
(quarterly)

Oxford Bibliographical Society
c/o Bodleian Library, Oxford OX1 3BG
Tel: (01865) 277069 *Fax:* (01865) 277182
E-mail: membership@oxbibsoc.org.uk
Web Site: www.oxbibsoc.org.uk
Key Personnel
President: Dr Ronald Truman
Honorary Secretary: Dr Christina Neagu
E-mail: secretary@oxbibsoc.org.uk
Honorary Treasurer: Andrew Honey
E-mail: treasurer@oxbibsoc.org.uk
Founded: 1922

English PEN Centre
Member of PEN International
c/o Free Word Centre, 60 Farringdon Rd, London
EC1R 3GA
Tel: (020) 7324 2535 *Fax:* (020) 7490 0566
E-mail: enquiries@englishpen.org
Web Site: www.englishpen.org
Key Personnel
President: Maureen Freely
Dir: Antonia Byatt
Assistant Dir: Sarah Hesketh *E-mail:* sarah@
englishpen.org
Off & Membership Manager: Amy Oliver
E-mail: amy@englishpen.org
Founded: 1921
Publication(s): *PEN News* (biannually, newsletter)

Scottish PEN Centre
Member of PEN International
The Writers' Museum, Lady Stair's Close, Lawnmarket, Edinburgh EH1 2PA
Tel: (0131) 226 5590
E-mail: info@scottishpen.org
Web Site: www.scottishpen.org
Key Personnel
President: Andrew Campbell
Founded: 1927

The Poetry Society
22 Betterton St, London WC2H 9BX
Tel: (020) 7420 9880 *Fax:* (020) 7240 4818
E-mail: info@poetrysociety.org.uk
Web Site: www.poetrysociety.org.uk
Key Personnel
President: Roger McGough
Dir: Judith Palmer
Finance Officer: Trupti Keegan
Membership Manager: Paul McGrane
Press & Marketing Manager: Lisa Roberts
Publications Manager: Michael Sims
Founded: 1909
Publication(s): *Jumpstart: Poetry in the Secondary
Classroom* (book); *The Poetry Book for Primary Schools* (book); *Poetry News* (quarterly,
newspaper); *Poetry Review* (quarterly)

The Arthur Ransome Society Ltd (TARS)
Abbot Hall Museum, Kendal, Cumbria LA9 5AL
E-mail: tarsinfo@arthur-ransome.org
Web Site: www.arthur-ransome.org
Key Personnel
President: Gabriel Woolf
Secretary: Kath Eastman
Founded: 1990
Publication(s): *Literary Transactions*; *Mixed Moss*
(annually, journal); *The Outlaw* (triannually,
magazine); *Signals* (triannually, magazine)

RNA, see Romantic Novelists' Association
(RNA)

Romantic Novelists' Association (RNA)
Ridge Gate Farm, Bluebell Lane, Shore, Todmorden OL14 8SE
E-mail: info@romanticnovelistsassociation.org
Web Site: www.romanticnovelistsassociation.org;
www.rna-uk.org
Key Personnel
Chairman: Annie Ashurst
President: Katie Fforde
Honorary Treasurer: Jenny Haddon
E-mail: hontreas@romanticnovelistsassociation.
org
Membership: Linda Hooper
Press: Catherine Jones *Tel:* (01844) 213947
E-mail: pressofficer@rna-uk.org
Founded: 1960
Publication(s): *Romance Matters* (quarterly, magazine)

Royal Literary Fund
3 Johnson's Court, London EC4A 3EA
Tel: (020) 7353 7160
E-mail: rlitfund@btconnect.com
Web Site: www.rlf.org.uk
Key Personnel
General Secretary: Eileen Gunn *Tel:* (020) 7353
7159 *E-mail:* egunnrlf@globalnet.co.uk
Founded: 1790
Publication(s): *Archives of the Royal Literary
Fund 1790-1918*

**The Royal Society for the Encouragement of
Arts, Manufactures & Commerce (RSA)**
8 John Adam St, London WC2N 6EZ
Tel: (020) 7930 5115 *Fax:* (020) 7839 5805
E-mail: general@rsa.org.uk
Web Site: www.thersa.org

Key Personnel
Chief Executive: Matthew Taylor *Tel:* (020) 7451
6883
Chief Operating Officer: Carol Jackson *Tel:* (020)
7451 6903 *E-mail:* carol.jackson@rsa.org.uk
Encourages the development of a principled, prosperous society & the release of human potential
through a program of projects & events with
the support of influential fellows from every
field & every background.
Publication(s): *RSA Journal* (newsletter, ezine)

Royal Society of Literature
Somerset House, Strand, London WC2R 1LA
Tel: (020) 7845 4676 *Fax:* (020) 7845 4679
E-mail: info@rslit.org
Web Site: www.rslit.org
Key Personnel
President: Colin Thubron
Chair of Council: Anne Chisholm
Honorary Treasurer: Robert Binyon
Dir: Maggie Fergusson *E-mail:* maggie@rslit.org
Membership Manager: Mary Ogbeide Grillon
E-mail: mary@rslit.org
Founded: 1820
Registered charity. Administers & awards three
literary prizes & confers the honor "Companion
of Literature" on selected writers.
Publication(s): *RSL-The Royal Society of Literature Review* (annual, magazine)

RSA, see The Royal Society for the
Encouragement of Arts, Manufactures &
Commerce (RSA)

The Ruskin Society
49 Hallam St, London W1W 6JP
Tel: (020) 7580 1894
Web Site: www.theruskinsociety.com
Key Personnel
President: Prof Michael Wheeler
Vice President: Anthony Page
Membership Secretary & Treasurer: Catherine
Edwards
Chairman: Robert Whelan *E-mail:* chairman@
theruskinsociety.com
Vice Chairman: Dr Cynthia Gamble
E-mail: vicechairman@theruskinsociety.com
Founded: 1997
Meetings to promote John Ruskin's (1819-1900)
ideas.

SfEP, see Society for Editors & Proofreaders
(SfEP)

Shakespearean Authorship Trust
45 Shakespeare Rd, London SE24 0LA
Tel: (020) 7902 1403
E-mail: info@shakespeareanauthorshiptrust.org.uk
Web Site: www.shakespeareanauthorshiptrust.org.
uk
Key Personnel
Chairman: Mark Rylance
Founded: 1922
Advancement of learning with particular reference to the social, political & literary history
of England in the 16th & 17th centuries & the
authorship of the literary works that appeared
under the name of William Shakespeare.

The Shaw Society
One Buckland Court, 37 Belsize Park, London
NW3 4EB
Tel: (020) 7435 6497
E-mail: contact@shawsociety.org.uk
Web Site: www.shawsociety.org.uk
Key Personnel
Chairman: Alan Knight
President: Michael Holroyd
Secretary: Evelyn Ellis

Editor: Philip Riley
Founded: 1941

Society for Editors & Proofreaders (SfEP)
Apsley House, 176 Upper Richmond Rd, Putney,
London SW15 2SH
Tel: (020) 8785 6155
E-mail: administration@sfep.org.uk
Web Site: www.sfep.org.uk
Key Personnel
Honorary President: Judith Butcher
Honorary Vice President: David Crystal
Membership Dir: Sarah Patey
E-mail: membership@sfep.org.uk
Founded: 1988
Professional body providing training, information,
support, electronic resources & newsletters.
Publication(s): *Editing Matters* (bimonthly, maga-
zine)

Society for the Study of Medieval Languages & Literature
c/o History Faculty, George St, Oxford OX1 2RL
E-mail: ssmll@history.ox.ac.uk
Web Site: mediumaevum.modhist.ox.ac.uk
Key Personnel
President: Dr Anthony Lappin
Honorable Secretary: Dr Simon Horobin
Honorable Treasurer: Dr Helen Swift
Publication(s): *Medium Aevum* (biannually)

The Society of Women Writers & Journalists (SWWJ)
Room 2, Aileen McHugo Bldg, Westmore Green,
Tatsfield, Westerham, Kent TN16 2AG
E-mail: enquiries@swwj.co.uk
Web Site: www.swwj.co.uk; www.facebook.com/
pages/SWWJ/288593147853678
Key Personnel
President: Victoria Wood
Chair: Valerie Dunmore *E-mail:* swwjval@aol.
com
Vice Chair: Barbara Field-Holmes
E-mail: editor@swwj.co.uk
Honorary Treasurer: Benita Cullingford *E-mail:* b.
cullingford@btinternet.com

Membership Secretary: Jennie Lisney
E-mail: jennie.lisney@tiscali.co.uk
Founded: 1894
Publication(s): *The Woman Writer* (4 times/yr,
magazine)

TARS, see The Arthur Ransome Society Ltd
(TARS)

The Tolkien Society
c/o Manches & Co, 3 Worcester St, Oxford OX1
2PZ
E-mail: publicity@tolkiensociety.org
Web Site: www.tolkiensociety.org
Key Personnel
Chairman: Sally Kennett *E-mail:* chairman@
tolkiensociety.org
Secretary: Madeline Flint
Publicity Officer: Ian Collier
Founded: 1969
Publication(s): *Amon Hen* (bimonthly, bulletin);
Mallorn (annually, journal)

H G Wells Society
20 Upper Field Close, Hereford, Herefordshire
HR2 7SW
E-mail: mail@hgwellsusa.50megs.com
Web Site: www.hgwellsusa.50megs.com
Key Personnel
Publicity Officer: Dr Emelyne Godfrey
Subscription & Information Officer: Eric Fitch
Founded: 1960
An international association composed of peo-
ple interested in the life, work & thought of
the British writer Herbert George Wells (1866-
1946).
Publication(s): *H G Wells: A Comprehensive Bib-
liography*; *The Wellsian* (annually, journal)

West Country Writers' Association
Trevean, Yeolmbridge, Launceston PL15 8NJ
Tel: (01566) 773615
E-mail: admin@westcountrywriters.com
Web Site: www.westcountrywriters.com
Key Personnel
Chairman: Lyn Carnaby
President: Lady Rachel Billington

Vice President: Dr Bob Cooper; Dr John Harcup;
Geraldine Kaye; Rev David Keep; E V Thomp-
son; Joanna Trollope
Secretary: Fiona McAughey
Founded: 1951
An association of published authors in any field
of writing who live in or write about the West
Country.

Uruguay

Academia Nacional de Letras (National
Academy of Literature)
Atencion al publico: de 14 a 18, Ituziango 1255,
11000 Montevideo
Tel: 29152374 *Fax:* 29167460
E-mail: academia@montevideo.com.uy;
anlacademiadeletras@yahoo.com
Web Site: www.mec.gub.uy/academiadeletras
Key Personnel
President: Adolfo Elizaincin
Secretary: Ricardo Pallares
Founded: 1943
Publication(s): *Boletin de la Academia Nacional
de Letras*; *Revista Nacional*

Venezuela

Venezuelan PEN Centre (Centro Venezolano del
PEN Internacional)
Member of PEN International
Residencias Arbolada, Apartment 14-B, 2a Av
Santa Eduviges, Caracas 7071
Tel: (0212) 283 5053 *Fax:* (0212) 286 7987
E-mail: pen.venezuela@gmail.com
Key Personnel
President: Edda Armas
Secretary: Angelina Jaffe *E-mail:* fluxus@cantv.
net
Publication(s): *Con Textos*; *Coleccion Plural*

Literary Prizes

Prizes and awards are listed alphabetically under the country where the sponsor is located. In some instances, recipients are restricted to the country in which the prize or award is presented.

☆ indicates those prizes with no geographical restriction placed upon recipients.

Argentina

Premio Academia Nacional de la Historia
(National Academy of History Award)
Academia Nacional de la Historia de la Republica Argentina (National Academy of History)
Balcarce 139, C1064AAC Buenos Aires
Tel: (011) 4343-4416; (011) 4331-4633; (011) 4331-5147 (ext 110) *Fax:* (011) 4331-5147; (011) 4343-4416; (011) 4331-4633
E-mail: admite@an-historia.org.ar
Web Site: www.an-historia.org.ar
Presented biennially for the best work written on an issue of Argentina's history.
Award: 1st prize 10,000 USD
Closing Date: Last day of Feb

Premio Sigmar de Literatura Infantil y Juvenil
(Sigmar Prize for Juvenile & Children's Literature)
Editorial Sigmar SACI
Av Belgrano 1580, 7° piso, C1093AAQ Buenos Aires
Tel: (011) 4381-2510; (011) 4381-1715
E-mail: premiosigmar@sigmar.com.ar
Web Site: www.sigmar.com.ar
Established: 2009
Award to an author each residing in Argentina & Uruguay for their work in Spanish aimed at readers 7-13 years of age.
Award: 1st prize 19,000 ARS; 2nd prize 9,500 ARS
Presented: Feria Internacional del Libro de Buenos Aires

Australia

The Adelaide Festival Awards for Literature
Arts South Australia
110 Hindley St, Adelaide, SA 5000
Mailing Address: GPO Box 2308, Adelaide, SA 5001
Tel: (08) 8463 5444 *Fax:* (08) 8463 5420
E-mail: artssa@dpc.sa.gov.au
Web Site: www.arts.sa.gov.au
Key Personnel
Manager, IMP Program: Julia Moretti
E-mail: moretti.julia@dpc.sa.gov.au
Established: 1986
Offered biennially & announced during Adelaide Writers' Week as part of the Adelaide Festival. The seven awards offered are: (1) Premier's Award for the best overall published work; (2) Children's Literature Award for a published book, fiction or nonfiction aimed at readers up to approximately 11 years; (3) Fiction Award for a published novel or collection of short stories; (4) Innovation Award for a published work, experimental in form or media, which departs from the conventional use of genre by borrowing elements from a number of different genres; (5) John Bray Poetry Award for a published collection of poetry; (6) Nonfic-

tion Award for a published work of nonfiction demonstrating a command of the subject as well as a fluent & outstanding literary style; (7) Young Adult Fiction Award for a published book of fiction aimed at readers aged approximately 12-18 years.
Award: Premier's & Innovation Awards: 10,000 AUD; all others 15,000 AUD
Closing Date: Oct 31

The Age Book of the Year Awards
The Age
655 Collins St, Level 2, Media House, Docklands, Victoria 3008
Tel: (03) 8667 2000
Web Site: www.theage.com.au
Key Personnel
Literary Editor: Jason Steger
Three prizes will be awarded: for imaginative writing to a novel or a collection of short stories; nonfiction award will be awarded to the book considered the best biography, autobiography, the best history or the best scholarly work of social, political or topical interest; the poetry prize will be awarded to a collection of poetry by one author, including selected or collected volume, the poetry award is named in honour of the late Dinny O'Hearn. One of the award winners is chosen as 'The Age' Book of the Year.
Award: Best work in each category 10,000 AUD; one work to be named 'The Age' Book of the Year 10,000 AUD
Closing Date: June 1
Presented: Melbourne Writer's Festival

Alexander Henderson Award
Australian Institute of Genealogical Studies Inc
Unit 1, 41 Railway Rd, Blackburn, Victoria 3130
Mailing Address: PO Box 339, Blackburn, Victoria 3130
Tel: (03) 9877 3789 *Fax:* (03) 9877 9066
E-mail: info@aigs.org.au
Web Site: www.aigs.org.au
Established: 1974
Best Australian family history book, written & entered for the award.
Award: Certificate & trophy
Closing Date: Nov 30 annually
Presented: Last Fri in May

The Alice Award
The Society of Women Writers NSW Inc
GPO Box 1388, Sydney, NSW 2001
E-mail: enquiries@womenwritersnsw.org
Web Site: www.womenwritersnsw.org
Key Personnel
President: Bridget McKern
Vice President: Barbara Westerway
Secretary: Edita Diamante
Treasurer: Pam Bayfield
Publicity: Dr Maria Hill
Awarded biennially to an Australian woman writer who, by her own written work, has made a distinguished & long-term contribution to Australian literature.

APA Book Design Awards
Australian Publishers Association (APA)
60/89 Jones St, Ultimo, NSW 2007
Tel: (02) 9281 9788 *Fax:* (02) 9281 1073
Web Site: www.publishers.asn.au
Key Personnel
Export & Events Manager: Tyson MacKenzie
E-mail: tyson.mackenzie@publishers.asn.au
Established: 1952
Recognizes creativity, excellence & innovation in contemporary Australian book design. Books entered must have been designed in Australia & published for the first time during the preceding calendar year. Entries open in October & close in January.
Other Sponsor(s): Better Read Than Dead Bookshop; Books Kinokuniya; Cengage Learning; Griffin Press; Hachette Australia; HarperCollins Publishers Australia; Lamb Print; McPherson's Printing Group; Midland Typesetters; Murdoch Books; 1010 Printing International; Pearson Australia; Penguin Group (Australia); Picador; Random House Australia; Scholastic Australia; Splitting Image; Thorpe-Bowker; Xou Creative
Award: 20 award categories
Closing Date: January
Presented: Sydney Writers' Festival, Powerhouse Museum, May

Aurealis Awards
Conflux Inc
1/4 Marilyn Pl, Karabar, NSW 2620
E-mail: aajudges@gmail.com; president.conflux@gmail.com
Web Site: aurealisawards.org
Established: 1995
For works of speculative fiction by authors, editors & illustrators who are Australian citizens or permanent residents, first published in English between Jan 1 & Dec 31 of year prior to award. Seven categories: Science Fiction, Fantasy, Horror, Young Adult, Children's, Anthology & Collection, Illustrated Book or Graphic Novel. No entry fee for short fiction entries or entries in Children's category. $10 entry fee for works in all other categories.
Other Sponsor(s): Chimaera Publications

Australia Council Award for Lifetime Achievement in Literature
Australia Council Literature Board
372 Elizabeth St (corner of Cooper St), Surry Hills, NSW 2010
Mailing Address: PO Box 788, Strawberry Hills, NSW 2012
Tel: (02) 9215 9057 *Toll Free Tel:* 1800 226 912
Web Site: www.australiacouncil.gov.au
Key Personnel
Project Officer, Literature: Joanne Simpson
E-mail: j.simpson@australiacouncil.gov.au
Open to Australian writers over the age of 60 who must be nominated by other people. They must have produced a critically acclaimed body of work over a long creative life. Nominations must demonstrate the literary eminence & importance of previous work.
Award: Up to 50,000 AUD
Closing Date: Nomination May 15
Presented: Sept

Australian Book Industry Awards
Australian Publishers Association (APA)
60/89 Jones St, Ultimo, NSW 2007
Tel: (02) 9281 9788 *Fax:* (02) 9281 1073
Web Site: www.publishers.asn.au
Key Personnel
Export & Events Manager: Bella Kasmas
  E-mail: bella.kasmas@publishers.asn.au
Annual awards to celebrate the best of Australian
writing, publishing & bookselling.

Australian Literature Society Gold Medal
Association for the Study of Australian Literature
  (ASAL)
c/o Federation University Australia, University
  Dr, Mount Helen, Victoria 3350
Web Site: www.austlit.edu.au/ASAL
Key Personnel
President: Sue Martin *E-mail:* s.martin@latrobe.
  edu.au
Vice President: Brigid Rooney *E-mail:* brigid.
  rooney@sydney.edu.au
Treasurer: Roger Osborne *E-mail:* r.osborne@uq.
  edu.au
Secretary: Demelza Hall *E-mail:* d.hall@
  federation.edu.au
Award Chair: Tony Simoes da Silva
  E-mail: tonys@uow.edu.au
Awarded annually for the most outstanding Aus-
  tralian literary work, published in the preceding
  calendar year.
Award: Gold medal

Australian Publisher of the Year Award
Australian Publishers Association (APA)
60/89 Jones St, Ultimo, NSW 2007
Tel: (02) 9281 9788 *Fax:* (02) 9281 1073
Web Site: www.publishers.asn.au
Key Personnel
Export & Events Manager: Tyson MacKenzie
  E-mail: tyson.mackenzie@publishers.asn.au
Established: 1994
Peer-assessment award, acknowledging profes-
  sional performance by organizations during the
  previous calendar year.
Other Sponsor(s): Get Reading; Midland Typeset-
  ters; OHL; PacStream; Publishing Technology;
  Random House Australia; Thorpe-Bowker; Xou
  Creative
Presented: Sydney Writers' Festival, annually

The Australian/Vogel's Literary Award
Allen & Unwin
83 Alexander St, Crows Nest, NSW 2065
Mailing Address: PO Box 8500, St Leonards,
  NSW 1590
Tel: (02) 8425 0100 *Fax:* (02) 9906 2218
E-mail: vogel@allenandunwin.com
Web Site: www.allenandunwin.com
Established: 1980
Literary Award for an unpublished manuscript by
  Australian authors under 35 years of age. Entry
  fee $25.
Other Sponsor(s): The Australian Newspaper; Vo-
  gel Breads
Award: 20,000 AUD
Closing Date: May annually
Presented: Sept/Oct

The Marten Bequest Travelling Scholarships
Trust Co Ltd
20 Bond St, Level 15, GPO Box 4270, Sydney,
  NSW 2001
Tel: (02) 8295 8100 *Toll Free Tel:* 1800 622 812
  Fax: (02) 8295 8659
Web Site: www.australiacouncil.gov.au/about/the-
  marten-bequest/
Key Personnel
Scholarship & Awards Coordinator: Christina Pi-
  azza
Established: 1967

Six scholarships awarded annually for study in
  the following area(s): singing, instrumental
  music, painting, ballet, sculpture, architecture,
  prose, poetry & acting. Entrants must be born
  in Australia & between the ages of 21-35 (except in the field of ballet: ages 17-35).
Award: Each scholarship 20,000 AUD over 2
  years
Closing Date: Oct/Nov of year previous
Presented: Museum of Contemporary Art, March
  22

The Carmel Bird Award
Spineless Wonders
PO Box 220, Strawberry Hills, NSW 2012
E-mail: info@shortaustralianstories.com.au
Web Site: shortaustralianstories.com.au
Long story competition, open theme. Entry fee:
  $20.
Award: $500 (1st prize)
Closing Date: Aug 31
Presented: March

Bronze Swagman Award
Winton Business & Tourism Association Inc
PO Box 120, Winton, Qld 4735
E-mail: info@bronzeswagman.info
Web Site: www.bronzeswagman.info
Established: 1972
Annual award for Bush Verse. Entry fee 15 AUD
  (1-3 entries).
Award: Bronze statuette of the Swagman,
  sculpted by Daphne Mayo & 500 AUD; Run-
  ner up: Trophy & 200 AUD; Highly Com-
  mended: Certificate
Closing Date: April 30
Presented: Easter

The Joanne Burns Award
Spineless Wonders
PO Box 220, Strawberry Hills, NSW 2012
E-mail: info@shortaustralianstories.com.au
Web Site: shortaustralianstories.com.au
Micro-literature award, 200 words maximum. En-
  try fee: $7.
Award: $300 (1st prize)

Children's Book of the Year Awards
The Children's Book Council of Australia
416 Magill Rd, Kensington Gardens, SA 5068
Mailing Address: PO Box 3203, Norwood, SA
  5067
Tel: (08) 8332 2845 *Toll Free Tel:* 1800 248 379
  Fax: (08) 8333 0394
E-mail: office@cbca.org.au; cbca@aate.org.au
Web Site: www.cbca.org.au
Established: 1946
Awarded annually. Current categories: Early
  Childhood, Young Readers, Older Readers, Pic-
  ture Book of the Year & Eve Pownall Award
  for Information Books.
Closing Date: Dec 31

The Abbie Clancy Award
The Society of Women Writers NSW Inc
GPO Box 1388, Sydney, NSW 2001
E-mail: enquiries@womenwritersnsw.org
Web Site: womenwritersnsw.org/awards/the-abbie-
  clancy-award; www.womenwritersnsw.org
Key Personnel
President: Bridget McKern
Vice President: Barbara Westerway
Secretary: Edita Diamante
Treasurer: Pam Bayfield
Publicity: Dr Maria Hill
Awarded annually, this award is open to female
  honours & post-graduate students attending
  universities in New South Wales. Entrants for
  the Award must submit an abstract (300-500
  words) of an unpublished research paper on the
  published or unpublished work(s) of fiction or

nonfiction of an Australian woman writer or
  journalist.
Award: 1,000 AUD

Tom Collins Poetry Prize
The Fellowship of Australian Writers WA Inc
88 Wood St, Swanbourne, WA 6010
Mailing Address: PO Box 6180, Swanbourne,
  WA 6910
Tel: (08) 9384 4771
E-mail: admin@fawwa.org.au
Web Site: www.fawwa.org.au
Key Personnel
President: Trisha Kotai-Ewers
Treasurer: Nathan Hondros
Established: 1975
Annual competition in memory of Australian au-
  thor Joseph Furphy, for a poem of up to 60
  lines. Entry fee 5 AUD per poem (maximum of
  three poems per entrant).
Other Sponsor(s): J Furphy & Sons
Award: 1st prize 1,000 AUD; 2nd prize 400
  AUD; Highly Commended 150 AUD; Com-
  mended Certificate
Closing Date: Dec 15

C H Currey Memorial Fellowship
Library Council of New South Wales
State Library of New South Wales, Macquarie St,
  Sydney, NSW 2000
Tel: (02) 9273 1414 *Fax:* (02) 9273 1255
E-mail: library@sl.nsw.gov.au
Web Site: www.sl.nsw.gov.au
Key Personnel
President: Robert Thomas
Contact: Margaret Bjork *Tel:* (02) 9273 1467
  Fax: (02) 9273 1245 *E-mail:* awards@sl.nsw.
  gov.au
Established: 1974
Annual award for the writing of Australian his-
  tory from original sources.
Award: 20,000 AUD
Closing Date: Sept 5

FAW Angelo B Natoli Short Story Award
Fellowship of Australian Writers (Vic) Inc
6 Davies St, Brunswick, Victoria 3056
Tel: (03) 9386 2232
E-mail: president@writers.asn.au
Web Site: www.fawvic.com.au/
Key Personnel
Treasurer & Awards Coordinator: Gail Blundell
  E-mail: treasurer@writers.asn.au
In honour of the late Angelo B Natoli, who for
  many years served as the Honorary Solicitor
  to Fellowship of Australian Writers (Vic) Inc.
  Awarded for a short story, open theme, to a
  maximum of 3,000 words. One copy of each
  story is required. More than one entry per au-
  thor may be submitted.
Entry Fee: 10 AUD; FAW members: 5 AUD.
Other Sponsor(s): A B Natoli Pty Ltd
Award: 1st prize 600 AUD; 2nd prize 400 AUD
Closing Date: Nov 30

FAW Anne Elder Award
Fellowship of Australian Writers (Vic) Inc
6 Davies St, Brunswick, Victoria 3056
Tel: (03) 9386 2232
E-mail: president@writers.asn.au
Web Site: www.fawvic.com.au/
Key Personnel
Treasurer & Awards Coordinator: Gail Blundell
  E-mail: treasurer@writers.asn.au
For a first book of poetry first published during
  the 2 years prior to the current closing date
  & not previously published locally or overseas, containing contributions from between
  1 to 4 poets. The book must be the first published book-length collection of poetry by the
  author(s) & must contain at least 20 pages of
  text. Two copies of the book are required &
  will not be returned.

Other Sponsor(s): Anne Elder Trust, managed by
   Cathie Elder & FAW
Award: 1,000 AUD
Closing Date: Nov 30

FAW Barbara Ramsden Award
Fellowship of Australian Writers (Vic) Inc
6 Davies St, Brunswick, Victoria 3056
Tel: (03) 9386 2232
E-mail: president@writers.asn.au
Web Site: www.fawvic.com.au/
Key Personnel
Treasurer & Awards Coordinator: Gail Blundell
   E-mail: treasurer@writers.asn.au
A major literary award for a book of fiction or
   nonfiction presented to the author & editor to
   recognize the combined effort of both parties to
   produce a quality product.
Entry fee: 15 AUD.
Other Sponsor(s): Institute of Professional Editors
   (IPEd)
Award: Two specially cast bronze plaques de-
   signed by Andor Meszaros
Closing Date: Nov 30

FAW Christina Stead Award
Fellowship of Australian Writers (Vic) Inc
6 Davies St, Brunswick, Victoria 3056
Tel: (03) 9386 2232
E-mail: president@writers.asn.au
Web Site: www.fawvic.com.au/
Key Personnel
Treasurer & Awards Coordinator: Gail Blundell
   E-mail: treasurer@writers.asn.au
For a work of fiction by an Australian author,
   first published after Nov 30, 2008 & not pre-
   viously published locally or overseas. Two
   copies of the book are required & will not be
   returned.
Entry Fee: 15 AUD.
Award: 500 AUD
Closing Date: Nov 30

FAW Christopher Brennan Award
Fellowship of Australian Writers (Vic) Inc
6 Davies St, Brunswick, Victoria 3056
Tel: (03) 9386 2232
E-mail: president@writers.asn.au
Web Site: www.fawvic.com.au/
Key Personnel
Treasurer & Awards Coordinator: Gail Blundell
   E-mail: treasurer@writers.asn.au
Commendation award to honour an Australian
   poet who has written work of sustained quality
   & distinction. The recipient each year is chosen
   by judges on behalf of the FAW. No entries are
   required.
Other Sponsor(s): Sally Dugan
Award: A bronze plaque designed by Michael
   Meszaros. Prize value 300 AUD
Closing Date: Nov 30

FAW Colin Thiele Poetry Award
Fellowship of Australian Writers (Vic) Inc
6 Davies St, Brunswick, Victoria 3056
Tel: (03) 9386 2232
E-mail: president@writers.asn.au
Web Site: www.fawvic.com.au/
Key Personnel
Treasurer & Awards Coordinator: Gail Blundell
   E-mail: treasurer@writers.asn.au
Award to a young writer (17-20 years of age)
   for a poem on any theme, no word limit. One
   copy of each poem is required. Poem should
   be typed in single-spacing. More than one en-
   try per author may be submitted, but only one
   prize will be issued per individual author.
Entry Fee: 6 AUD; FAW members: 3 AUD.
Award: 1st prize 200 AUD; 2nd prize 100 AUD
Closing Date: Nov 30

FAW Community of Writers' Award
Fellowship of Australian Writers (Vic) Inc
6 Davies St, Brunswick, Victoria 3056
Tel: (03) 9386 2232
E-mail: president@writers.asn.au
Web Site: www.fawvic.com.au/
Key Personnel
Treasurer & Awards Coordinator: Gail Blundell
   E-mail: treasurer@writers.asn.au
For an anthology of short prose +/or poetry which
   has been compiled, written & edited by a
   group of community writers who meet regularly to share & workshop their writing &
   compiled after Nov 30, 2008. Contributions by
   writers from outside the group may not be included & anthologies by writers who meet in
   a tertiary education setting are ineligible. The
   maximum length of the anthology should be
   30,000 words. Each piece of writing in the anthology should not exceed 3,000 words. Entries
   must include title page, content page & ap-
   proximate word length of the anthology. Each
   group, may submit only one entry. One copy
   is required & will not be returned. Entries will
   be judged solely on the quality of their writing, not their presentation - however, for ease
   of reading by the judge they should be neatly
   presented & firmly bound in some way. If your
   anthology has already been compiled into a
   semi-professional format (eg. with illustrations,
   photos, binding, etc), this will also be acceptable.
Entry Fee: 10 AUD; FAW members: 5 AUD.
Other Sponsor(s): Fresh Start Training
Award: 500 AUD
Closing Date: Nov 30

FAW Jennifer Burbidge Short Story Award
Fellowship of Australian Writers (Vic) Inc
6 Davies St, Brunswick, Victoria 3056
Tel: (03) 9386 2232
E-mail: president@writers.asn.au
Web Site: www.fawvic.com.au/
Key Personnel
Treasurer & Awards Coordinator: Gail Blundell
   E-mail: treasurer@writers.asn.au
Awarded in honour of Jenny Burbidge for a short
   story, up to 3,000 words, that deals with any
   aspect of the lives of those who suffer some
   form of physical or mental disability +/or its
   impact on their families in the Australian situa-
   tion. One copy of each story is required. More
   than one entry per author may be submitted.
Entry Fee: 10 AUD.
Other Sponsor(s): Mary Burbidge
Award: 250 AUD
Closing Date: Nov 30

FAW Jim Hamilton Award
Fellowship of Australian Writers (Vic) Inc
6 Davies St, Brunswick, Victoria 3056
Tel: (03) 9386 2232
E-mail: president@writers.asn.au
Web Site: www.fawvic.com.au/
Key Personnel
Treasurer & Awards Coordinator: Gail Blundell
   E-mail: treasurer@writers.asn.au
Award honours the contribution Jim Hamilton OAM & his family have made to Australian writers & writing for an unpublished
   novel in any theme or genre with a minimum
   length of 30,000 words. Entries must be aimed
   at teenage or adult readers. One copy is required & will not be returned. Entries should
   be neatly presented & fastened securely in
   one corner with a large 'bulldog' clip. Do not
   spiral-bind entries or send them in plastic or
   cardboard wallets. More than one entry per author may be submitted.
Entry Fee: 10 AUD; FAW members: 5 AUD.
Other Sponsor(s): Eltham High School
Award: 1st prize 1,000 AUD
Closing Date: Nov 30

FAW John Morrison Short Story Award
Fellowship of Australian Writers (Vic) Inc
6 Davies St, Brunswick, Victoria 3056
Tel: (03) 9386 2232
E-mail: president@writers.asn.au
Web Site: www.fawvic.com.au/
Key Personnel
Treasurer & Awards Coordinator: Gail Blundell
   E-mail: treasurer@writers.asn.au
Award to a young writer (15-20 years of age) for
   a short story on any theme, maximum 3,000
   words. One copy of each story is required. Sto-
   ries should be typed in double-spacing. More
   than one entry per author may be submitted,
   but only one prize will be issued per individual
   author.
Entry Fee: 6 AUD; FAW members: 3 AUD.
Other Sponsor(s): Paul Jennings
Award: 1st prize 200 AUD; 2nd prize 100 AUD
Closing Date: Nov 30

FAW John Shaw Neilson Poetry Award
Fellowship of Australian Writers (Vic) Inc
6 Davies St, Brunswick, Victoria 3056
Tel: (03) 9386 2232
E-mail: president@writers.asn.au
Web Site: www.fawvic.com.au/
Key Personnel
Treasurer & Awards Coordinator: Gail Blundell
   E-mail: treasurer@writers.asn.au
For a poem of between 14 & 60 lines including
   epigraphs. A suite of poems linked themati-
   cally may be entered as one entry provided the
   line limit is adhered to. Poems should be typed
   in single-spacing. One copy of each poem (or
   suite) is required; more than one entry per au-
   thor may be submitted.
Entry Fee: 10 AUD; FAW members: 5 AUD.
Other Sponsor(s): Collected Works Bookshop
Award: 1st prize 600 AUD; 2nd prize 150 AUD
Closing Date: Nov 30

FAW Mary Grant Bruce Short Story Award for Children's Literature
Fellowship of Australian Writers (Vic) Inc
6 Davies St, Brunswick, Victoria 3056
Tel: (03) 9386 2232
E-mail: president@writers.asn.au
Web Site: www.fawvic.com.au/
Key Personnel
Treasurer & Awards Coordinator: Gail Blundell
   E-mail: treasurer@writers.asn.au
Award to recognize & honor the contribution by
   Mary Grant Bruce to children's literature &
   to encourage the writing of quality children's
   short stories. Stories should be aimed at young
   readers aged 10-15 years. Entries may be no
   longer than 5,000 words. One copy of each
   story is required. More than one entry per au-
   thor may be submitted. Writers living within
   the defined municipal boundaries of Gippsland
   eligible for a separate 200 AUD award.
Entry Fee: 10 AUD; FAW members: 5 AUD.
Other Sponsor(s): Wellington Shire Council
Award: 1st prize 600 AUD; 2nd prize 300 AUD
Closing Date: Nov 30

FAW Mavis Thorpe Clark Award
Fellowship of Australian Writers (Vic) Inc
6 Davies St, Brunswick, Victoria 3056
Tel: (03) 9386 2232
E-mail: president@writers.asn.au
Web Site: www.fawvic.com.au/
Key Personnel
Treasurer & Awards Coordinator: Gail Blundell
   E-mail: treasurer@writers.asn.au
Awarded for a collection of writing by a student
   or group of students attending an Australian
   secondary school. Part 1 is for an individual
   entry. The collection may contain up to 10
   pieces. All forms of writing may be included
   & collection should have a title. Entries must

be securely bound & only one entry per author may be submitted. Part 2 is for a group entry. Up to 15 pieces may be submitted, with authors' names on a separate page. All forms of writing may be included. Entries must be securely bound & have a separate title page & table of contents which does not show names. Pieces in the collection must have been written in 2008 & 2009. Previously entered anthologies are ineligible. Schools may submit more than one group entry at 10 AUD each. Only one copy of the collection is required.
Entry Fee: 6 AUD; FAW members: 3 AUD.
Other Sponsor(s): Graeme & Robyn Base
Award: Part 1 (Individual) 350 AUD; Part 2 (Group) 200 AUD
Closing Date: Nov 30

FAW Michael Dugan Short Story Award
Fellowship of Australian Writers (Vic) Inc
6 Davies St, Brunswick, Victoria 3056
Tel: (03) 9386 2232
E-mail: president@writers.asn.au
Web Site: www.fawvic.com.au/
Key Personnel
Treasurer & Awards Coordinator: Gail Blundell *E-mail:* treasurer@writers.asn.au
For a short story on any theme, maximum of 3,000 words. One copy of each story is required. Stories should be typed in double-spacing. More than one entry per author may be submitted, but only one prize will be issued per individual author. Award will be divided into two age groups: Part A entrants, ages 8-12 & Part B entrants, ages 13-16.
Entry Fee: 6 AUD; FAW members: 3 AUD.
Other Sponsor(s): Penguin Group (Australia)
Award: Part A entrants 100 AUD; Part B entrants 150 AUD
Closing Date: Nov 30

FAW Young Poet of the Year Award
Fellowship of Australian Writers (Vic) Inc
6 Davies St, Brunswick, Victoria 3056
Tel: (03) 9386 2232
E-mail: president@writers.asn.au
Web Site: www.fawvic.com.au/
Key Personnel
Treasurer & Awards Coordinator: Gail Blundell *E-mail:* treasurer@writers.asn.au
For a poem on any theme, no word limit. One copy of each poem is required. Poem should be typed in single-spacing. More than one entry per author may be submitted, but only one prize will be issued per individual author. The award will be divided into two age groups: Part A entrants, ages 8-12 & Part B entrants, ages 13-16.
Entry Fee 6 AUD; FAW members: 3 AUD.
Other Sponsor(s): Clare's Desk
Award: Part A entrants 100 AUD; Part B entrants 150 AUD
Closing Date: Nov 30

The Miles Franklin Literary Award
Trust Co Ltd
20 Bond St, Level 15, GPO Box 4270, Sydney, NSW 2001
Tel: (02) 8295 8100 *Toll Free Tel:* 1800 622 812
Fax: (02) 8295 8659
Web Site: ww.perpetual.com.au/milesfranklin
Key Personnel
Scholarship & Awards Coordinator: Jane Ryan
Established: 1954
Annual award for a published novel or play portraying Australian life in any of its phases. All entries for the award must have been published in the previous calender year.
Award: 42,000 AUD
Closing Date: Dec
Presented: State Library of NSW, June

The Mary Gilmore Award
Association for the Study of Australian Literature (ASAL)
c/o Federation University Australia, University Dr, Mount Helen, Victoria 3350
Web Site: www.austlit.edu.au/ASAL
Key Personnel
President: Sue Martin *E-mail:* s.martin@latrobe.edu.au
Vice President: Brigid Rooney *E-mail:* brigid.rooney@sydney.edu.au
Treasurer: Roger Osborne *E-mail:* r.osborne@uq.edu.au
Secretary: Demelza Hall *E-mail:* d.hall@federation.edu.au
Award Chair: Jill Jones *E-mail:* jill.jones@adelaide.edu.au
Established: 1985
Awarded annually for the best first book of Australian poetry published in the preceding two calendar years.
Presented: Annual Conference of the Association for the Study of Australian Literature

Grants for Writers (New Work-Literature)
Australia Council Literature Board
372 Elizabeth St (corner of Cooper St), Surry Hills, NSW 2010
Mailing Address: PO Box 788, Strawberry Hills, NSW 2012
Tel: (02) 9215 9057 *Toll Free Tel:* 1800 226 912
Web Site: www.australiacouncil.gov.au
Key Personnel
Project Officer, Literature: Joanne Simpson *E-mail:* j.simpson@australiacouncil.gov.au
Grants to Australian writers & picture book illustrators for a period of up to 12 months. Projects are accepted in the following areas: fiction, literary nonfiction, poetry, children's & young adult literature, writing for performance or new media, graphic novels & illustrated picture books. Minimum publication/performance requirements apply. One closing date per year.
Award: 10,000 to 40,000 AUD
Closing Date: May 15

Greater Dandenong National Writing Awards
City of Greater Dandenong
PO Box 200, Dandenong, Victoria 3175
Tel: (03) 9239 5100 *Fax:* (03) 9329 5196
E-mail: council@cgd.vic.gov.au
Web Site: www.greaterdandenong.com
Key Personnel
Cultural Development Coordinator: Rosemary Gaetjens *Tel:* (03) 9239 5134
Established: 1979
National competition with categories for open poetry, open short story, ESL encouragement, teen short story, teen poetry, junior short story & junior poetry.
Award: Over 4,500 AUD
Closing Date: April 30 annually

Grenfell Henry Lawson Festival of Arts Verse & Short Story Competitions
Henry Lawson Festival of Arts
PO Box 77, Grenfell, NSW 2810
Tel: (02) 6343 1575; (02) 6343 2855
E-mail: henry@grenfell.org.au; info@henrylawsonfestival.com.au
Web Site: www.grenfell.org.au/henrylawsonfestival
Key Personnel
Coordinator: Mary Moffitt
Awards are made in six classes for verse up to 48 lines & four classes for short story up to 2,000 words. Adult fees $10 per entry, student fees $2 per entry.
Other Sponsor(s): Dr Hilary Lindsay MBE OAM - Festival Patron; Gaynor & Garth England; The Loaded Dog Cafe; Ron & Jan Mclelland; Dani Millyn Accountancy; Kath Smith

Award: Cash statuette sculpted by Michael Mandelc. Total prize money: $3,725
Closing Date: March 30
Presented: Annually in June

Lyndall Hadow/Donald Stuart Short Story Competition
The Fellowship of Australian Writers WA Inc
88 Wood St, Swanbourne, WA 6010
Mailing Address: PO Box 6180, Swanbourne, WA 6910
Tel: (08) 9384 4771
E-mail: admin@fawwa.org.au
Web Site: www.fawwa.org.au
Key Personnel
President: Trisha Kotai-Ewers
Treasurer: Nathan Hondros
Open theme competition awarded for a short story not exceeding 3,000 words. Entry fee 10 AUD per story (maximum of three stories per author).
Award: 1st prize 400 AUD; 2nd prize 100 AUD; Highly Commended 50 AUD
Closing Date: June 1

The Indie Awards
Leading Edge Books
3 Fitzsimons Lane, Level 1, Gordon, NSW 2072
Mailing Address: PO Box 148, Pymble, NSW 2073
Tel: (02) 9497 4000 *Fax:* (02) 9988 3433
Web Site: www.indies.com.au
Award: 19,000 AUD

The Grace Leven Prize for Poetry
Perpetual Ltd
Angel Pl, Level 12, 123 Pitt St, Sydney, NSW 2001
Toll Free Tel: 1800 501 227 *Fax:* (02) 8256 1471
E-mail: philanthropy@perpetual.com.au
Web Site: www.perpetual.com/philanthropy-awards.aspx
Instituted under the will of William Baylebridge, the Australian poet, who died in 1942. This prize is offered annually for the best volume of poetry published during the twelve months immediately preceding the year in which the award is made. Competitors must be either Australian born & writing as Australians, or they must be naturalized in Australia & have lived in that country for at least ten years. The volume chosen may have been published in any country, but copies of it must be freely obtainable in Australia. Winners are recommended by a judge (entries or nominations are not accepted).

Walter McRae Russell Award
Association for the Study of Australian Literature (ASAL)
c/o Federation University Australia, University Dr, Mount Helen, Victoria 3350
Web Site: www.austlit.edu.au/ASAL
Key Personnel
President: Sue Martin *E-mail:* s.martin@latrobe.edu.au
Vice President: Brigid Rooney *E-mail:* brigid.rooney@sydney.edu.au
Treasurer: Roger Osborne *E-mail:* r.osborne@uq.edu.au
Secretary: Demelza Hall *E-mail:* d.hall@federation.edu.au
Award Chair: Fiona Morrison *E-mail:* f.morrison@unsw.edu.au
Established: 1983
Awarded annually to the best book of literary scholarship on an Australian subject published in the preceding two calendar years.
Award: 1,000 AUD
Closing Date: Dec 31

National Biography Award
The State Library of New South Wales

Macquarie St, Sydney, NSW 2000
Tel: (02) 9273 1605; (02) 9273 1582
E-mail: awards@sl.nsw.gov.au
Web Site: www.sl.nsw.gov.au
Established: 1996
Awarded to a work of the highest standard that
presents an Australian subject or a subject who
has made a significant contribution to Australia. Eligible works must be biography, autobiography, or memoir, written in English,
published in book form & consist of a minimum of 40,000 words. Works must be first
published between October 1 & September 30
of the years prior to the award year. See web
site for complete nomination guidelines.
Award: $25,000; authors of up to 6 shortlisted
works each receive $1,000
Closing Date: Annually in Feb
Presented: Annually in Aug

New South Wales Premier's Literary Awards
Arts NSW
Level 9, St James Centre, 111 Elizabeth St, Syd-
ney, NSW 2000
Mailing Address: PO Box A226, Sydney South,
NSW 1235
Tel: (02) 9228 5533; (02) 8218 2222
Toll Free Tel: 1800 358 594 (within NSW)
Fax: (02) 9228 4722
E-mail: mail.artsnsw@arts.nsw.gov.au;
artsfunding@arts.nsw.gov.au
Web Site: www.arts.nsw.gov.au
Key Personnel
Executive Dir: Mary Darwell *E-mail:* ea.
artsnsw@arts.nsw.gov.au
Acting Dir, Funding Programs: Alexandra Bowen
Tel: (02) 8218 2224 *E-mail:* alex.bowen@arts.
nsw.gov.au
Established: 1979
Presented by the New South Wales Government
to honour distinguished achievement by Australian writers. The Community Relations
Commission for a multicultural NSW Award
is offered for a work that makes a significant
contribution to Australian literature, theatre,
film, radio or television in its portrayal of the
interaction of Australia's diverse cultures &
canvasses issues arising from the Australian
immigration & migrant settlement experience. In addition, the committee judging the
book awards may propose that a special award
(usually 20,000 AUD), with or without prize
money, be made for a work not readily covered
by the existing categories, or in recognition of
a writer's achievements generally.
Award: Christina Stead Prize 40,000 AUD; Douglas Stewart Prize 40,000 AUD; Kenneth
Slessor Prize 30,000 AUD; Patricia Wright-
son Prize 30,000 AUD; Ethel Turner Prize
30,000 AUD; Play Award 30,000 AUD; Script
Writing Award 30,000 AUD; Community Relations Commission Award for Multicultural
15,000 AUD; Glenda Adams UTS Award for
New Writing 5,000 AUD; Book of the Year
additional 10,000 AUD; Special Award 20,000
AUD; The New South Wales Premier's Prize
for Literary Scholarship 30,000 AUD; The Biennial Premier's Translation Prize PEN Medallion; Peoples Choice Award
Closing Date: Oct 18
Presented: State Library of NSW, Nov

New South Wales Writer's Fellowship
Arts NSW
Level 9, St James Centre, 111 Elizabeth St, Syd-
ney, NSW 2000
Mailing Address: PO Box A226, Sydney South,
NSW 1235
Tel: (02) 9228 5533 *Toll Free Tel:* 1800 358 594
(within NSW) *Fax:* (02) 9228 4722
E-mail: artsfunding@arts.nsw.gov.au
Web Site: www.arts.nsw.gov.au

Key Personnel
Executive Dir: Mary Darwell *E-mail:* ea.
artsnsw@arts.nsw.gov.au
Awarded annually by the New South Wales Government to assist the writing of new literary
work by a writer living in New South Wales.
Applicants must demonstrate their project is
likely to result in work of significant quality
& be of lasting benefit to the applicant's experience & development as a writer or the advancement of Australian literature in general.
Award: 20,000 AUD
Closing Date: June 17

Pixie O'Harris Award
Australian Publishers Association (APA)
60/89 Jones St, Ultimo, NSW 2007
Tel: (02) 9281 9788 *Fax:* (02) 9281 1073
Web Site: www.publishers.asn.au
Annual award for distinguished & dedicated ser-
vice to the development & reputation of Aus-
tralian children's books.
Other Sponsor(s): HarperCollins Publishers Aus-
tralia
Award: $500, certificate & glass plate held by
recipient for one year

Poetry Competition
The Society of Women Writers NSW Inc
GPO Box 1388, Sydney, NSW 2001
E-mail: enquiries@womenwritersnsw.org
Web Site: www.womenwritersnsw.org
Key Personnel
President: Bridget McKern
Vice President: Barbara Westerway
Secretary: Edita Diamante
Treasurer: Pam Bayfield
Publicity: Dr Maria Hill
Annual competition which, in alternate years, is
closed to members only or open to all Aus-
tralian citizens. In years open to all, it is called
the National Poetry Competition. Members
only competitions in even-numbered years; Na-
tional competitions in odd-numbered years.
Award: 1st prize 250 AUD; 2nd prize 150 AUD;
3rd prize 100 AUD
Presented: State Library of NSW, Nov

Readings Children's Book Prize
Readings
309 Lygon St, Carlton, Victoria 3053
Tel: (03) 9347 6633
E-mail: customerservice@readings.com.au
Web Site: www.readings.com.au/the-readings-
children-s-book-prize
Key Personnel
Prize Manager: Bronte Coates *E-mail:* bronte.
coates@readings.com.au
Established: 2014
Recognizes the best new Australian books written
for children ages 5-12. Open to a published
work of fiction first published in the calendar year prior to the year of the prize. Judging panel decides on eligible titles & invites
respective publishers to submit no more than
3 reading copies of the nominated book for
consideration throughout the eligibility period. Author must be an Australian citizen or
hold permanent residency & have published no
more than 3 children's books in this category
(Junior/Middle Fiction for ages 5-12). Entries
must be published in English. Books published
in ebook form only & self-published works are
not eligible.
Award: $3,000

Readings Prize for New Australian Fiction
Readings
309 Lygon St, Carlton, Victoria 3053
Tel: (03) 9347 6633
E-mail: customerservice@readings.com.au

Web Site: www.readings.com.au/the-readings-
prize-for-new-australian-fiction
Key Personnel
Prize Manager: Bronte Coates *E-mail:* bronte.
coates@readings.com.au
Established: 2014
Supports published Australian authors working
in fiction & recognizes exciting & exceptional
new contributions to local literature. First or
second published works of fiction are eligible.
Judging panel decides on eligible titles & invites respective publishers to submit no more
than 3 reading copies of the nominated book
for consideration throughout the eligibility period. Author must be an Australian citizen or
hold permanent residency. Entries must be published in English. Books published in ebook
form only & self-published works are not eligible.
Award: $3,000
Presented: Late Oct

Readings Young Adult Book Prize
Readings
309 Lygon St, Carlton, Victoria 3053
Tel: (03) 9347 6633
E-mail: customerservice@readings.com.au
Web Site: www.readings.com.au/the-readings-
young-adult-book-prize
Key Personnel
Prize Manager: Bronte Coates *E-mail:* bronte.
coates@readings.com.au
Established: 2016
Awarded to the best new contribution to Australian young adult literature. First & second
published works of young adult fiction & memoir are eligible. Judging panel decides on eligible titles & invites respective publishers to submit no more than 3 reading copies of the nominated book for consideration throughout the
eligibility period. Author must be an Australian
citizen or hold permanent residency. Entries
must be published in English. Books published
in ebook form only & self-published works are
not eligible. For the 2019 prize, books must
have been first published between April 26,
2018 & April 24, 2019.
Award: $3,000
Closing Date: Late July

The Richell Prize for Emerging Writers
Hachette Australia
207 Kent St, Level 17, Sydney, NSW 2000
Tel: (02) 8248 0800 *Fax:* (02) 8248 0810
Web Site: www.emergingwritersfestival.org.au
Established: 2014
Prize to encourage emerging writers in Australia.
Open to unpublished writers of adult fiction
& adult narrative nonfiction. Entrants must be
Australian residents aged 18 years or older.
Books for children & young adults are not eli-
gible.
Other Sponsor(s): The Emerging Writers' Festi-
val (EWF); The Guardian Australia; Razor/Joy;
Simpson Solicitors
Award: $10,000

Colin Roderick Award
Foundation for Australian Literary Studies Ltd
(FALS)
Dept of Humanities, James Cook University,
Townsville, Qld 4811
Tel: (07) 4781 5097 *Fax:* (07) 4781 4064
Web Site: www.jcu.edu.au/sass/humanities/fals
Key Personnel
Executive Dir: Prof M Ackland, PhD *Tel:* (07)
4781 6034 *E-mail:* michael.ackland@jcu.edu.au
Chairman: Justice Kerry Cullinane
Established: 1967
Annual award to the author of the best book pub-
lished in Australia in any field of writing deal-
ing with any aspect of Australian life.

Award: 10,000 AUD & the H T Priestley Memorial Medal from the Townsville Foundation for Australian Literary Studies at the James Cook University
Closing Date: Feb 26
Presented: Annual Presentation Evening of the Foundation

Society of Women Writers Biennial Book Awards
The Society of Women Writers NSW Inc
GPO Box 1388, Sydney, NSW 2001
E-mail: enquiries@womenwritersnsw.org
Web Site: www.womenwritersnsw.org
Key Personnel
President: Bridget McKern
Vice President: Barbara Westerway
Secretary: Edita Diamante
Treasurer: Pam Bayfield
Publicity: Dr Maria Hill
Established: 1925
Every 2nd year, members are invited to submit books published over the previous 2 years. Separate awards are given for fiction, nonfiction, poetry & children's books. Two children's book awards may be given - one for a book for younger readers & one for an adolescent/young adult book.
Award: 200 AUD

The Stella Prize
The Wheeler Centre, Level 1, 176 Little Lonsdale St, Melbourne, Victoria 3000
E-mail: info@thestellaprize.com.au
Web Site: thestellaprize.com.au
Key Personnel
Manager: Megan Quinlan
Established: 2013
Annual literary award to an Australian woman for her contribution to literature. Both fiction & nonfiction books are eligible. 50 AUD entry fee.
Award: 50,000 AUD

Victorian Premier's Literary Awards
The Wheeler Centre
328 Swanston St, Melbourne, Victoria 3000
Tel: (03) 8664 7000 *Fax:* (03) 9639 4737
E-mail: pla@slv.vic.gov.au
Web Site: www.slv.vic.gov.au
Established: 1985
Inaugurated to mark the centenary of the births of Vance & Nettie Palmer. Awards include: Vance Palmer Prize for Fiction, Nettie Palmer Prize for Nonfiction, C J Dennis Prize for Poetry, Louis Esson Prize for Drama, Prize for Writing for Young Adults, Premier's Award for an Unpublished Manuscript & Biennial Award for Indigenous Writing. Winners in the five annual categories contest for the 100,000 AUD Victorian Prize for Literature.
Award: Unpublished Manuscript & Indigenous Writing 15,000 AUD; all others 25,000 AUD
Closing Date: May 24
Presented: Sept

Patrick White Literary Award
Perpetual Ltd
Angel Pl, Level 12, 123 Pitt St, Sydney, NSW 2001
Mailing Address: GPO Box 4172, Sydney, NSW 2001
Toll Free Tel: 1800 501 227 *Fax:* (02) 8256 1471
E-mail: philanthropy@perpetual.com.au
Web Site: www.perpetual.com/philanthropy-awards.aspx
Key Personnel
Chairman & Independent Dir: Peter Scott
Established: 1975
Established to advance Australian literature by encouraging the writing of novels, short stories, poetry +/or plays for publication or performance.
The Trust was founded with the prize money awarded to Patrick White when he became the first Australian to receive the Nobel Prize for Literature in 1973.
Award: 25,000 AUD
Presented: Nov

Austria

Austrian Children's & Youth Book Prize
(Oesterreichischer Kinder- und Jugendbuchpreis)
Bundesministerium fuer Unterricht, Kunst und Kultur (Federal Ministry for Education, Arts & Culture)
Minoritenplatz 5, 1014 Vienna
Tel: (01) 53120-0 *Fax:* (01) 53120-3099
E-mail: ministerium@bmukk.gv.at
Web Site: www.bmukk.gv.at
Key Personnel
Contact: Dr Robert Stocker *Tel:* (01) 53120-6850
E-mail: robert.stocker@bmukk.gv.at
Established: 1955
Award: 6,000 EUR

Ehrenpreis des oesterreichischen Buchhandels fuer Toleranz in Denken und Handeln
Hauptverband des Oesterreichischen Buchhandels (HVB)
Gruenangergasse 4, 1010 Vienna
Tel: (01) 512 15 35 *Fax:* (01) 512 84 82
E-mail: sekretariat@hvb.at
Web Site: www.buecher.at
Established: 1990
Award: 10,000 EUR

Foerderungspreis fuer Kinder- und Jugenditeratur (Promotion Award for Children's Literature)
Bundesministerium fuer Unterricht, Kunst und Kultur (Federal Ministry for Education, Arts & Culture)
Minoritenplatz 5, 1014 Vienna
Tel: (01) 53120-0 *Fax:* (01) 53120-3099
E-mail: ministerium@bmukk.gv.at
Web Site: www.bmukk.gv.at
Key Personnel
Contact: Dr Robert Stocker *Tel:* (01) 53120-6850
E-mail: robert.stocker@bmukk.gv.at
Established: 1996
Biennial award to an author, illustrator or translator in appreciation of his or her outstanding contributions to children's literature. Awarded by jury.
Award: 8,000 EUR

Foerderungspreis fuer Literatur (Promotion Award for Literature)
Bundesministerium fuer Unterricht, Kunst und Kultur (Federal Ministry for Education, Arts & Culture)
Minoritenplatz 5, 1014 Vienna
Tel: (01) 53120-0 *Fax:* (01) 53120-3099
E-mail: ministerium@bmukk.gv.at
Web Site: www.bmukk.gv.at
Key Personnel
Contact: Dr Robert Stocker *Tel:* (01) 53120-6850
E-mail: robert.stocker@bmukk.gv.at
Awarded annually by jury.
Award: 8,000 EUR

Georg-Trakl-Prize fuer Lyrik (Georg Trakl Prize for Poetry)
Salzburger Landesregierung
Franziskanergasse 5a, 5020 Salzburg
Mailing Address: Postfach 527, 5010 Salzburg
Tel: (0662) 8042-2729 *Fax:* (0662) 8042-2919
E-mail: kultur@salzburg.gv.at
Web Site: www.salzburg.gv.at/themen/kultur/foerdersparten/literatur
Key Personnel
Literary Prizes: Dr Daniela Weger
E-mail: daniela.weger@salzburg.gv.at
An irregular award to a writer of lyric poetry for his/her complete poetical works.
Award: 8,000 EUR

Grosse Literaturstipendien des Landes Tirol
Amt der Tiroler Landesregierung
Dept of Culture, Sillgasse 8, 6020 Innsbruck
E-mail: kultur@tirol.gv.at
Web Site: www.tirol.gv.at
Key Personnel
Contact: Denise Waldhart *Tel:* (0512) 508-3766
Fax: (0512) 508-3755
Literature scholarship for a maximum term of two years to give the writer an opportunity to focus on a literary project.
Award: 15,000 EUR
Closing Date: Dec 31

Grosser Oesterreichischer Staatspreis (Great Austrian State Prize)
Bundesministerium fuer Unterricht, Kunst und Kultur (Federal Ministry for Education, Arts & Culture)
Minoritenplatz 5, 1014 Vienna
Tel: (01) 53120-0 *Fax:* (01) 53120-3099
E-mail: ministerium@bmukk.gv.at
Web Site: www.bmukk.gv.at
Key Personnel
Contact: Dr Robert Stocker *Tel:* (01) 53120-6850
E-mail: robert.stocker@bmukk.gv.at
Established: 1965
This annual prize alternates between literature, music, visual arts & architecture. Awarded by Austrian Art Senate. No applications.
Award: 30,000 EUR for life's work

☆Oesterreichischer Staatpreis fuer Europaeische Literatur (Austrian State Prize for European Literature)
Bundesministerium fuer Unterricht, Kunst und Kultur (Federal Ministry for Education, Arts & Culture)
Minoritenplatz 5, 1014 Vienna
Tel: (01) 53120-0 *Fax:* (01) 53120-3099
E-mail: ministerium@bmukk.gv.at
Web Site: www.bmukk.gv.at
Key Personnel
Contact: Dr Robert Stocker *Tel:* (01) 53120-6850
E-mail: robert.stocker@bmukk.gv.at
Established: 1965
Presented annually by the Austrian Minister of Education to a European author (with the exception of an Austrian national) whose work has also been acclaimed outside his own country; this must be demonstrated by translation. No applications. The prize is awarded on the recommendation of an independent jury.
Award: 25,000 EUR & testimonial awarded annually

Oesterreichischer Staatspreis fuer Kinderlyrik (Austrian State Prize for Children's Poetry)
Bundesministerium fuer Unterricht, Kunst und Kultur (Federal Ministry for Education, Arts & Culture)
Minoritenplatz 5, 1014 Vienna
Tel: (01) 53120-0 *Fax:* (01) 53120-3099
E-mail: ministerium@bmukk.gv.at
Web Site: www.bmukk.gv.at
Key Personnel
Contact: Dr Robert Stocker *Tel:* (01) 53120-6850
E-mail: robert.stocker@bmukk.gv.at
Established: 1993
For the complete works of an author of poetry for children in German language. Awarded by jury.
Award: 8,000 EUR

Oesterreichischer Staatspreis fuer literarische Uebersetzung (Austrian State Prize for Literary Translation)
Bundesministerium fuer Unterricht, Kunst und Kultur (Federal Ministry for Education, Arts & Culture)
Minoritenplatz 5, 1014 Vienna
Tel: (01) 53120-0 *Fax:* (01) 53120-3099
E-mail: ministerium@bmukk.gv.at
Web Site: www.bmukk.gv.at
Key Personnel
Contact: Dr Robert Stocker *Tel:* (01) 53120-6850
   E-mail: robert.stocker@bmukk.gv.at
Two annual awards for outstanding translation of a comprehensive single or complete work.
Award: 8,000 EUR each

Rauriser Literature Prize (Rauriser Literaturpreis)
Salzburger Landesregierung
Franziskanergasse 5a, 5020 Salzburg
Mailing Address: Postfach 527, 5010 Salzburg
Tel: (0662) 8042-2729 *Fax:* (0662) 8042-2919
E-mail: kultur@salzburg.gv.at
Web Site: www.salzburg.gv.at/themen/kultur/foerdersparten/literatur
Key Personnel
Literary Prizes: Dr Daniela Weger
   E-mail: daniela.weger@salzburg.gv.at
For an outstanding first publication in prose, as decided by jury.
Other Sponsor(s): Salzburg Provincial Government
Award: 8,000 EUR annually

Rauriser Promotion Prize (Rauriser Foederungspreis)
Salzburger Landesregierung
Franziskanergasse 5a, 5020 Salzburg
Mailing Address: Postfach 527, 5010 Salzburg
Tel: (0662) 8042-2729 *Fax:* (0662) 8042-2919
E-mail: kultur@salzburg.gv.at
Web Site: www.salzburg.gv.at/themen/kultur/foerdersparten/literatur
Key Personnel
Literary Prizes: Dr Daniela Weger
   E-mail: daniela.weger@salzburg.gv.at
Annual literary award sponsored by the Salzburg provincial government & the village of Rauris. Awarded for a specific topic, as decided by jury.
Award: 4,000 EUR

Otto Stoessl-Preis
Otto Stoessl-Stiftung
Semmelweisgasse 9, 8010 Graz
Tel: (0316) 87 746 00 *Fax:* (0316) 87 746 33
E-mail: stlbib@stmk.gv.at
Key Personnel
Contact: Dr Christoph Binder
Established: 1982
Biennial literature prize for unpublished German stories.
Award: 4,000 EUR
Closing Date: End of year, biennially in odd years
Presented: Vienna, Biennially in even years

City of Vienna Prize
City of Vienna Magistrate
Kulturabteilung Magistratsabteilung 7, 8, Friedrich-Schmidt-Platz 5, Mezzanin Zi 327, 1080 Vienna
Tel: (01) 4000 84716 *Fax:* (01) 4000-7216 (international); (01) 4000-99-8007 (national)
E-mail: post@m07.magwien.gv.at
Web Site: www.wien.gv.at
Established: 1947
Annual award to an author for total literary output.
Award: 8,000 EUR

Closing Date: March 31
Presented: Dec

Anton Wildgans Preis der Oesterreichischen Industrie (Anton Wildgans Award of the Federation of Austrian Industries)
Vereinigung der Oesterreichischen Industrie
Schwarzenbergplatz 4, 1031 Vienna
Tel: (01) 711 35-0 *Fax:* (01) 711 35 29 10
E-mail: iv.office@iv-net.at
Web Site: www.iv-net.at
Key Personnel
Marketing & Communication: Renate Hoedl-Bernscherer *Tel:* (01) 711 35-2302 *E-mail:* r.hoedl-bernscherer@iv-net.at
Established: 1962
Awarded annually at the beginning of autumn to an Austrian lyric poet, dramatist, novelist or essayist, young or middle-aged. The author must be an Austrian citizen, writing in German, who lives either in Austria or abroad. Awarded by a committee. No applications.
Award: Maximum prize 10,000 EUR

Wuerdigungspreis fuer Kinder-und Jugendliteratur (Arts Prize for Children's Literature)
Bundesministerium fuer Unterricht, Kunst und Kultur (Federal Ministry for Education, Arts & Culture)
Minoritenplatz 5, 1014 Vienna
Tel: (01) 53120-0 *Fax:* (01) 53120-3099
E-mail: ministerium@bmukk.gv.at
Web Site: www.bmukk.gv.at
Key Personnel
Contact: Dr Robert Stocker *Tel:* (01) 53120-6850
   E-mail: robert.stocker@bmukk.gv.at
Established: 1980
Awarded biennially to an author in appreciation of his life's work. Awarded by jury.
Award: 12,000 EUR

Bangladesh

Bangla Academy Literary Awards
Bangla Academy
Burdwan House, 3, Kazi Nazrul Islam Ave, Dhaka 1000
Tel: (02) 8619577; (02) 8619583; (02) 8619752; (02) 8619580 *Fax:* (02) 8612352
E-mail: bacademy@citechco.net
Web Site: www.banglaacademy.org.bd
Annual awards for outstanding overall contributions to Bangla language & literature.
Award: 100,000 BDT

Belgium

Internationale Eugene Baie Prijs (International Eugene Baie Prize)
Province of Antwerp/Eugene Baie Foundation
Dept Cultuur, Koningin Elisabethlei 22, 2018 Antwerp
Tel: (03) 2406415 *Fax:* (03) 2406470
E-mail: cultuurloket@admin.provant.be
Web Site: www.provincieantwerpen.be
Key Personnel
Contact: Jan Michiels *Tel:* (03) 2406412
   E-mail: jan.michiels@admin.provant.be
Established: 1946
Awarded every five years for a foreign writer in his native language for a work published on the Flemish civilization, culture or art. The

committee denotes a jury, who will look for a winner.
Award: 7,500 EUR

Prix Auguste Beernaert (Auguste Beernaert Prize)
Academie Royale de Langue et de Litterature Francaises de Belgique (Royal Academy of French Language & Literature)
Palais des Academies, rue Ducale, 1, 1000 Brussels
Tel: (02) 550 22 77 *Fax:* (02) 550 22 75
E-mail: alf@cfwb.be
Web Site: www.arllfb.be
Key Personnel
Permanent Secretary: Jacques De Decker
Established: 1925
Awarded every four years for the most outstanding work of a Belgian or naturalized Belgian author who has produced the most remarkable work regardless of genre or subject.
Award: 1,000 EUR

☆**Prix Anton Bergmann** (Anton Bergmann Prize)
Academie Royale des Sciences, des Lettres et des Beaux-Arts de Belgique
Rue Ducale, 1, 1000 Brussels
Tel: (02) 550 22 12 *Fax:* (02) 550 22 05
E-mail: arb@cfwb.be; academieroyale@cfwb.be
Web Site: www.academieroyale.be
Key Personnel
President: Peter Bartholomew *E-mail:* fpbartho@skynet.be
Permanent Secretary: Herve Hasquin
   E-mail: herve.hasquin@skynet.be
Contact: Beatrice Denuit *Tel:* (02) 550 22 21
   E-mail: beatrice.denuit@cfwb.be
Established: 1875
For the author of a historical account or monograph, written in Dutch & relating to a Flemish town or community in Belgium. Awarded every five years for a work appearing in print or (provisionally) in manuscript form, during the period.
Award: 1,250 EUR
Closing Date: Dec 31

Prix Bouvier-Parvillez (Bouvier-Parvillez Prize)
Academie Royale de Langue et de Litterature Francaises de Belgique (Royal Academy of French Language & Literature)
Palais des Academies, rue Ducale, 1, 1000 Brussels
Tel: (02) 550 22 77 *Fax:* (02) 550 22 75
E-mail: alf@cfwb.be
Web Site: www.arllfb.be
Key Personnel
Permanent Secretary: Jacques De Decker
Established: 1925
Awarded every four years to a French language Belgian writer for his entire work.
Award: 850 EUR

Prix Alix Charlier-Anciaux (Alix Charlier-Anciaux Prize)
Academie Royale de Langue et de Litterature Francaises de Belgique (Royal Academy of French Language & Literature)
Palais des Academies, rue Ducale, 1, 1000 Brussels
Tel: (02) 550 22 77 *Fax:* (02) 550 22 75
E-mail: alf@cfwb.be
Web Site: www.arllfb.be
Key Personnel
Permanent Secretary: Jacques De Decker
Established: 1969
Awarded every five years to a Belgian author for all of his work in the French language.
Award: 1,000 EUR

Prix Henri Cornelus (Henri Cornelus Prize)
Academie Royale de Langue et de Litterature
  Francaises de Belgique (Royal Academy of
  French Language & Literature)
Palais des Academies, rue Ducale, 1, 1000 Brussels
Tel: (02) 550 22 77 *Fax:* (02) 550 22 75
E-mail: alf@cfwb.be
Web Site: www.arllfb.be
Key Personnel
Permanent Secretary: Jacques De Decker
Established: 1991
Awarded triennially to the author, whatever his
  age, for a collection of short stories published
  in French.
Award: 3,000 EUR

☆**Prix Albert Counson** (Albert Counson Prize)
Academie Royale de Langue et de Litterature
  Francaises de Belgique (Royal Academy of
  French Language & Literature)
Palais des Academies, rue Ducale, 1, 1000 Brussels
Tel: (02) 550 22 77 *Fax:* (02) 550 22 75
E-mail: alf@cfwb.be
Web Site: www.arllfb.be
Key Personnel
Permanent Secretary: Jacques De Decker
Established: 1940
Awarded every five years to a Belgian author of
  a book in French relating to Romance Philol-
  ogy in the broadest sense. A foreign author can
  be crowned if the test has a special interest in
  Belgium.
Award: 1,500 EUR

☆**Prix Franz Cumont** (Franz Cumont Prize)
Academie Royale des Sciences, des Lettres et des
  Beaux-Arts de Belgique
Rue Ducale, 1, 1000 Brussels
Tel: (02) 550 22 12 *Fax:* (02) 550 22 05
E-mail: academieroyale@cfwb.be; arb@cfwb.be
Web Site: www.academieroyale.be
Key Personnel
President: Peter Bartholomew *E-mail:* fpbartho@
  skynet.be
Permanent Secretary: Herve Hasquin
  E-mail: herve.hasquin@skynet.be
Contact: Beatrice Denuit *Tel:* (02) 550 22 21
  E-mail: beatrice.denuit@cfwb.be
Established: 1937
For a work by a Belgian or foreign author dealing
  with the history of religion or science in antiq-
  uity, i.e. in the Mediterranean area prior to the
  time of Mohammed. The prize cannot be di-
  vided, except where one or more authors have
  acted in collaboration. Awarded triennially.
Award: 2,500 EUR
Closing Date: Dec 31

Prix Eugene Goblet d'Alviella (Eugene Goblet
  d'Alviella Prize)
Academie Royale des Sciences, des Lettres et des
  Beaux-Arts de Belgique
Rue Ducale, 1, 1000 Brussels
Tel: (02) 550 22 12 *Fax:* (02) 550 22 05
E-mail: arb@cfwb.be; academieroyale@cfwb.be
Web Site: www.academieroyale.be
Key Personnel
President: Peter Bartholomew *E-mail:* fpbartho@
  skynet.be
Permanent Secretary: Herve Hasquin
  E-mail: herve.hasquin@skynet.be
Contact: Beatrice Denuit *Tel:* (02) 550 22 21
  E-mail: beatrice.denuit@cfwb.be
Established: 1926
Awarded every five years for a book of classical
  philology published by a Belgian author.
Award: 1,500 EUR
Closing Date: Dec 31
Presented: 2021

Prix Henri Davignon (Henri Davignon Prize)
Academie Royale de Langue et de Litterature
  Francaises de Belgique (Royal Academy of
  French Language & Literature)
Palais des Academies, rue Ducale, 1, 1000 Brussels
Tel: (02) 550 22 77 *Fax:* (02) 550 22 75
E-mail: alf@cfwb.be
Web Site: www.arllfb.be
Key Personnel
Permanent Secretary: Jacques De Decker
Established: 1965
Awarded every five years to a Belgian author of a
  work of religious inspiration.
Award: 850 EUR

Prix Felix Denayer (Felix Denayer Prize)
Academie Royale de Langue et de Litterature
  Francaises de Belgique (Royal Academy of
  French Language & Literature)
Palais des Academies, rue Ducale, 1, 1000 Brussels
Tel: (02) 550 22 77 *Fax:* (02) 550 22 75
E-mail: alf@cfwb.be
Web Site: www.arllfb.be
Key Personnel
Permanent Secretary: Jacques De Decker
Established: 1956
Awarded annually to a Belgian author for a single
  work or for lifetime achievement.
Award: 850 EUR

☆**Ernest Discailles Prize**
Academie Royale des Sciences, des Lettres et des
  Beaux-Arts de Belgique
Rue Ducale, 1, 1000 Brussels
Tel: (02) 550 22 12 *Fax:* (02) 550 22 05
E-mail: arb@cfwb.be; academieroyale@cfwb.be
Web Site: www.academieroyale.be
Key Personnel
President: Peter Bartholomew *E-mail:* fpbartho@
  skynet.be
Permanent Secretary: Herve Hasquin
  E-mail: herve.hasquin@skynet.be
Contact: Beatrice Denuit *Tel:* (02) 550 22 21
  E-mail: beatrice.denuit@cfwb.be
Established: 1907
Awarded every 5 years to an author for the best
  printed or handwritten work on the history of
  French literature or on contemporary history,
  written during the previous ten-year period.
  Only Belgians, foreign students or former stu-
  dents of the University Ghent may enter the
  competition.
Award: 1,500 EUR
Closing Date: Dec 31

Prix Jules Duculot (Jules Duculot Prize)
Academie Royale des Sciences, des Lettres et des
  Beaux-Arts de Belgique
Rue Ducale, 1, 1000 Brussels
Tel: (02) 550 22 12 *Fax:* (02) 550 22 05
E-mail: academieroyale@cfwb.be; arb@cfwb.be
Web Site: www.academieroyale.be
Key Personnel
President: Peter Bartholomew *E-mail:* fpbartho@
  skynet.be
Permanent Secretary: Herve Hasquin
  E-mail: herve.hasquin@skynet.be
Contact: Beatrice Denuit *Tel:* (02) 550 22 21
  E-mail: beatrice.denuit@cfwb.be
Established: 1965
Awarded every five years for a work in print or
  manuscript form, written in French, dealing
  with the history of philosophy. Awarded only
  to Belgians, or to foreigners holding an aca-
  demic grade granted by a Belgian university.
  Printed work must have been published in the
  five years prior to the end of the relevant pe-
  riod.
Award: 3,000 EUR
Closing Date: Dec 31

Prix Robert Duterme (Robert Duterme Prize)
Academie Royale de Langue et de Litterature
  Francaises de Belgique (Royal Academy of
  French Language & Literature)
Palais des Academies, rue Ducale, 1, 1000 Brussels
Tel: (02) 550 22 77 *Fax:* (02) 550 22 75
E-mail: alf@cfwb.be
Web Site: www.arllfb.be
Key Personnel
Permanent Secretary: Jacques De Decker
Established: 1996
Awarded every four years to a writer for a French
  language collection of stories related to fantasy.
Award: 2,500 EUR

Charles Duvivier Prize (Prix Charles Duvivier)
Academie Royale des Sciences, des Lettres et des
  Beaux-Arts de Belgique
Rue Ducale, 1, 1000 Brussels
Tel: (02) 550 22 12 *Fax:* (02) 550 22 05
E-mail: arb@cfwb.be; academieroyale@cfwb.be
Web Site: www.academieroyale.be
Key Personnel
President: Peter Bartholomew *E-mail:* fpbartho@
  skynet.be
Permanent Secretary: Herve Hasquin
  E-mail: herve.hasquin@skynet.be
Contact: Beatrice Denuit *Tel:* (02) 550 22 21
  E-mail: beatrice.denuit@cfwb.be
Established: 1905
Awarded every five years to the Belgian author of
  the best work on the history of Belgian or for-
  eign law, or on the history of Belgian political,
  judicial or administrative institutions.
Award: 1,250 EUR
Closing Date: Dec 31

Leon Elaut Prize (Leon Elautprijs)
Koninklijke Academie voor Nederlandse Taal- en
  Letterkunde (Royal Academy of Dutch Lan-
  guage & Literature)
Koningstr 18, 9000 Ghent
Tel: (09) 265 93 40 *Fax:* (09) 265 93 49
E-mail: info@kantl.be
Web Site: www.kantl.be
Key Personnel
Librarian: Marijke De Wit *Tel:* (09) 265 93 43
  E-mail: mdewit@kantl.be
Permanent Secretary: Willy Vandeweghe *Tel:* (09)
  265 93 42 *E-mail:* willy.vandeweghe@kantl.be
Established: 1981
Awarded biennially for a scientific work on the
  Flemish emancipation.
Award: 2,500 EUR

European Union Prize for Literature
European Commission
c/o FEE-FEP, Rue Montoyer, 31 - Box 8, 1000
  Brussels
Tel: (02) 770 11 10 *Fax:* (02) 771 20 71
E-mail: info@euprizeliterature.eu; info@fep-fee.
  eu
Web Site: www.euprizeliterature.eu; www.fep-fee.
  eu
Prize for a European writer of contemporary liter-
  ature (fiction).
Other Sponsor(s): European Booksellers Federa-
  tion (EBF); European Writers' Council (EWC);
  Federation of European Publishers (FEP)

Joseph Gantrelle Prize (Prix Joseph Gantrelle)
Academie Royale des Sciences, des Lettres et des
  Beaux-Arts de Belgique
Rue Ducale, 1, 1000 Brussels
Tel: (02) 550 22 12 *Fax:* (02) 550 22 05
E-mail: arb@cfwb.be; academieroyale@cfwb.be
Web Site: www.academieroyale.be
Key Personnel
President: Peter Bartholomew *E-mail:* fpbartho@
  skynet.be

Permanent Secretary: Herve Hasquin
E-mail: herve.hasquin@skynet.be
Contact: Beatrice Denuit *Tel:* (02) 550 22 21
E-mail: beatrice.denuit@cfwb.be
Established: 1890
Awarded every 5 years to Belgian authors for a
work in classical philology.
Award: 1,500 EUR
Closing Date: Dec 31

Prix George Garnir (George Garnir Prize)
Academie Royale de Langue et de Litterature
Francaises de Belgique (Royal Academy of
French Language & Literature)
Palais des Academies, rue Ducale, 1, 1000 Brussels
Tel: (02) 550 22 77 *Fax:* (02) 550 22 75
E-mail: alf@cfwb.be
Web Site: www.arllfb.be
Key Personnel
Permanent Secretary: Jacques De Decker
Established: 1945
Awarded triennially to a Belgian author, in
French, of a novel or collection of stories re-
lating to the aspects & morals of the Walloon
Provinces.
Award: 850 EUR

Prix Gaston et Mariette Heux (Gaston et
Mariette Heux Prize)
Academie Royale de Langue et de Litterature
Francaises de Belgique (Royal Academy of
French Language & Literature)
Palais des Academies, rue Ducale, 1, 1000 Brussels
Tel: (02) 550 22 77 *Fax:* (02) 550 22 75
E-mail: alf@cfwb.be
Web Site: www.arllfb.be
Key Personnel
Permanent Secretary: Jacques De Decker
Established: 1991
Awarded every four years to a writer over 40
years of age for an important work or lifetime
achievement.
Award: 1,800 EUR

Prix Nicole Houssa (Nicole Houssa Prize)
Academie Royale de Langue et de Litterature
Francaises de Belgique (Royal Academy of
French Language & Literature)
Palais des Academies, rue Ducale, 1, 1000 Brussels
Tel: (02) 550 22 77 *Fax:* (02) 550 22 75
E-mail: alf@cfwb.be
Web Site: www.arllfb.be
Key Personnel
Permanent Secretary: Jacques De Decker
Established: 1964
Awarded triennially to a poet from Wallonia for
the first volume of verse, published or not.
Award: 850 EUR

Joseph Houziaux Prix (Joseph Houziaux Prize)
Academie Royale des Sciences, des Lettres et des
Beaux-Arts de Belgique
Rue Ducale, 1, 1000 Brussels
Tel: (02) 550 22 12 *Fax:* (02) 550 22 05
E-mail: arb@cfwb.be; academieroyale@cfwb.be
Web Site: www.academieroyale.be
Key Personnel
President: Peter Bartholomew *E-mail:* fpbartho@
skynet.be
Permanent Secretary: Herve Hasquin
E-mail: herve.hasquin@skynet.be
Contact: Beatrice Denuit *Tel:* (02) 550 22 21
E-mail: beatrice.denuit@cfwb.be
Established: 1994
Awarded triennially to an author of research into
the French language & to an author of either a
literary work in dialect (Picardy dialect, Wal-
loon, Lorraine dialect or Champagne dialect),
or of a study on dialectology (the domain in

question being Wallonia in the broadest mean-
ing of the term).
Award: 1,500 EUR
Closing Date: Dec 31

Tobie Jonckheere Prize (Prix Tobie Jonckheere)
Academie Royale des Sciences, des Lettres et des
Beaux-Arts de Belgique
Rue Ducale, 1, 1000 Brussels
Tel: (02) 550 22 12 *Fax:* (02) 550 22 05
E-mail: arb@cfwb.be; academieroyale@cfwb.be
Web Site: www.academieroyale.be
Key Personnel
President: Peter Bartholomew *E-mail:* fpbartho@
skynet.be
Permanent Secretary: Herve Hasquin
E-mail: herve.hasquin@skynet.be
Contact: Beatrice Denuit *Tel:* (02) 550 22 21
E-mail: beatrice.denuit@cfwb.be
Established: 1957
Awarded every 5 years for a work, in published
or manuscript form, devoted to the educational
sciences.
Award: 1,500 EUR
Closing Date: Dec 31

Prix Jean Kobs (Jean Kobs Prize)
Academie Royale de Langue et de Litterature
Francaises de Belgique (Royal Academy of
French Language & Literature)
Palais des Academies, rue Ducale, 1, 1000 Brussels
Tel: (02) 550 22 77 *Fax:* (02) 550 22 75
E-mail: alf@cfwb.be
Web Site: www.arllfb.be
Key Personnel
Permanent Secretary: Jacques De Decker
Established: 1984
Awarded triennially to a Belgian poet over the
age of 40 years for a collection of inspired,
spiritual poems & if possible, of classical form.
Award: 1,200 EUR

Prize Henri Lavachery
Academie Royale des Sciences, des Lettres et des
Beaux-Arts de Belgique
Rue Ducale, 1, 1000 Brussels
Tel: (02) 550 22 12 *Fax:* (02) 550 22 05
E-mail: arb@cfwb.be; academieroyale@cfwb.be
Web Site: www.academieroyale.be
Key Personnel
President: Peter Bartholomew *E-mail:* fpbartho@
skynet.be
Permanent Secretary: Herve Hasquin
E-mail: herve.hasquin@skynet.be
Contact: Beatrice Denuit *Tel:* (02) 550 22 21
E-mail: beatrice.denuit@cfwb.be
Established: 1961
Awarded every 5 years to honor a work on eth-
nology. Prize confined to Belgians. This work
may take the form either in writing or a film.
Award: 1,500 EUR
Closing Date: Dec 31

Prix Lucien Malpertuis (Lucien Malpertuis
Prize)
Academie Royale de Langue et de Litterature
Francaises de Belgique (Royal Academy of
French Language & Literature)
Palais des Academies, rue Ducale, 1, 1000 Brussels
Tel: (02) 550 22 77 *Fax:* (02) 550 22 75
E-mail: alf@cfwb.be
Web Site: www.arllfb.be
Key Personnel
Permanent Secretary: Jacques De Decker
Established: 1943
Biennial award alternately for a poet, a play-
wright, a novelist (or short story) & a Belgian
essayist.
Award: 850 EUR

Joseph-Edmond Marchal Prize (Prix
Joseph-Edmond Marchal)
Academie Royale des Sciences, des Lettres et des
Beaux-Arts de Belgique
Rue Ducale, 1, 1000 Brussels
Tel: (02) 550 22 12 *Fax:* (02) 550 22 05
E-mail: arb@cfwb.be; academieroyale@cfwb.be
Web Site: www.academieroyale.be
Key Personnel
President: Peter Bartholomew *E-mail:* fpbartho@
skynet.be
Permanent Secretary: Herve Hasquin
E-mail: herve.hasquin@skynet.be
Contact: Beatrice Denuit *Tel:* (02) 550 22 21
E-mail: beatrice.denuit@cfwb.be
Established: 1918
Awarded every 5 years for the Belgian author of
the best work, in print or in manuscript form,
on national antiques or archaeology.
Award: 1,500 EUR
Closing Date: Dec 31

Fonds Arthur Merghelynck (Arthur
Merghelynck Fund)
Academie Royale des Sciences, des Lettres et des
Beaux-Arts de Belgique
Rue Ducale, 1, 1000 Brussels
Tel: (02) 550 22 11; (02) 550 22 12 *Fax:* (02)
550 22 05
E-mail: arb@cfwb.be; academieroyale@cfwb.be
Web Site: www.academieroyale.be
Key Personnel
President: Peter Bartholomew *E-mail:* fpbartho@
skynet.be
Permanent Secretary: Herve Hasquin
E-mail: herve.hasquin@skynet.be
Contact: Beatrice Denuit *Tel:* (02) 550 22 21
E-mail: beatrice.denuit@cfwb.be
Established: 1999
Awarded annually.
Award: Subsidy allotted for research or to publi-
cation of works
Closing Date: Dec 31

Prix Auguste Michot (Auguste Michot Prize)
Academie Royale de Langue et de Litterature
Francaises de Belgique (Royal Academy of
French Language & Literature)
Palais des Academies, rue Ducale, 1, 1000 Brussels
Tel: (02) 550 22 77 *Fax:* (02) 550 22 75
E-mail: alf@cfwb.be
Web Site: www.arllfb.be
Key Personnel
Permanent Secretary: Jacques De Decker
Established: 1948
Awarded biennially to a Belgian author of a liter-
ary work, in prose or verse, dedicated to cele-
brating the beauty of the land of Flanders.
Award: 850 EUR

Grand prix de poesie Albert Mockel (Albert
Mockel Grand Prize for Poetry)
Academie Royale de Langue et de Litterature
Francaises de Belgique (Royal Academy of
French Language & Literature)
Palais des Academies, rue Ducale, 1, 1000 Brussels
Tel: (02) 550 22 77 *Fax:* (02) 550 22 75
E-mail: alf@cfwb.be
Web Site: www.arllfb.be
Key Personnel
Permanent Secretary: Jacques De Decker
Established: 1953
Awarded every five years alternately for a poet
who is not a member of the academy & a poet
who is a member of the academy.
Award: 2,500 EUR

Order of the Crown (Ordre de la Couronne)
Belgium Ministry of Foreign Affairs

Service du Protocole, Service des Ordres, Rue des Petites Carmes, 15, 1000 Brussels
Tel: (02) 501 81 11
E-mail: info@diplobel.org; info@diplobel.fed.be
Web Site: diplomatie.belgium.be
One of three Belgian national Orders.

Prix Sander Pierron (Sander Pierron Prize)
Academie Royale de Langue et de Litterature Francaises de Belgique (Royal Academy of French Language & Literature)
Palais des Academies, rue Ducale, 1, 1000 Brussels
Tel: (02) 550 22 77 *Fax:* (02) 550 22 75
E-mail: alf@cfwb.be
Web Site: www.arllfb.be
Key Personnel
Permanent Secretary: Jacques De Decker
Established: 1972
Biennial award to a Belgium author of a novel or a collection of stories.
Award: 850 EUR

Prix Emile Polak (Emile Polak Prize)
Academie Royale de Langue et de Litterature Francaises de Belgique (Royal Academy of French Language & Literature)
Palais des Academies, rue Ducale, 1, 1000 Brussels
Tel: (02) 550 22 77 *Fax:* (02) 550 22 75
E-mail: alf@cfwb.be
Web Site: www.arllfb.be
Key Personnel
Permanent Secretary: Jacques De Decker
Established: 1931
Biennial award to a Belgian national poet under the age of 35.
Award: 850 EUR

Prix Andre Praga (Andre Praga Prize)
Academie Royale de Langue et de Litterature Francaises de Belgique (Royal Academy of French Language & Literature)
Palais des Academies, rue Ducale, 1, 1000 Brussels
Tel: (02) 550 22 77 *Fax:* (02) 550 22 75
E-mail: alf@cfwb.be
Web Site: www.arllfb.be
Key Personnel
Permanent Secretary: Jacques De Decker
Established: 1984
Biennial award for a Belgian author of a play created for the stage or on television.
Award: 850 EUR

Prix baron de Saint-Genois
Academie Royale des Sciences, des Lettres et des Beaux-Arts de Belgique
Rue Ducale, 1, 1000 Brussels
Tel: (02) 550 22 12 *Fax:* (02) 550 22 05
E-mail: arb@cfwb.be; academieroyale@cfwb.be
Web Site: www.academieroyale.be
Key Personnel
President: Peter Bartholomew *E-mail:* fpbartho@skynet.be
Permanent Secretary: Herve Hasquin *E-mail:* herve.hasquin@skynet.be
Contact: Beatrice Denuit *Tel:* (02) 550 22 21 *E-mail:* beatrice.denuit@cfwb.be
Established: 1867
For the author of the best historical or literary work written in Dutch. Awarded every five years.
Award: 1,250 EUR
Closing Date: Dec 31

Prix Georges Lockem (Georges Lockem Prize)
Academie Royale de Langue et de Litterature Francaises de Belgique (Royal Academy of French Language & Literature)

Palais des Academies, rue Ducale, 1, 1000 Brussels
Tel: (02) 550 22 77 *Fax:* (02) 550 22 75
E-mail: alf@cfwb.be
Web Site: www.arllfb.be
Key Personnel
Permanent Secretary: Jacques De Decker
Established: 1974
Annual award to a Belgian French language poet, age 25 years maximum, or to a manuscript or a book published during the year preceding the award year.
Award: 850 EUR

Prix international Nessim Habif
Academie Royale de Langue et de Litterature Francaises de Belgique (Royal Academy of French Language & Literature)
Palais des Academies, rue Ducale, 1, 1000 Brussels
Tel: (02) 550 22 77 *Fax:* (02) 550 22 75
E-mail: alf@cfwb.be
Web Site: www.arllfb.be
Key Personnel
Permanent Secretary: Jacques De Decker
Established: 1964
Awarded biennially to a writer whose works are written in French.
Award: 3,000 EUR

Prix Litteraire du Parlement de la Federation Wallonie-Bruxelles
Parlement de la Federation Wallonie-Bruxelles
Rue de la Loi, 6, 1000 Brussels
Tel: (02) 506 39 37
E-mail: cellule-internet@pfwb.be
Web Site: www.pfwb.be
Key Personnel
President: Jean-Charles Luperto
Communications Officer: Thierry Vanderhaege *E-mail:* vanderhaeget@pcf.be
Established: 1975
Book by an author of French expression illustrating the sensitivity of the French community of Belgium or devoted to its cultural inheritance. Literary genres following in a rotation of four years: prose fiction, poetry, drama & essay.
Award: 5,000 EUR
Closing Date: Feb 1

Prix Victor Rossel (Victor Rossel Prize)
Le Soir
Rue Royale, 100, 1000 Brussels
Tel: (02) 225 54 32 *Fax:* (02) 225 59 14; (02) 225 59 10
Web Site: www.lesoir.be
Established: 1938
Annual award for the best novel or collection of short stories published during the year, written in French by a Belgian author.
Award: 5,000 EUR

Prix Leopold Rosy (Leopold Rosy Prize)
Academie Royale de Langue et de Litterature Francaises de Belgique (Royal Academy of French Language & Literature)
Palais des Academies, rue Ducale, 1, 1000 Brussels
Tel: (02) 550 22 77 *Fax:* (02) 550 22 75
E-mail: alf@cfwb.be
Web Site: www.arllfb.be
Key Personnel
Permanent Secretary: Jacques De Decker
Established: 1942
Awarded triennially to the author of an essay in French.
Award: 750 EUR

Prix Eugene Schmits (Eugene Schmits Prize)
Academie Royale de Langue et de Litterature Francaises de Belgique (Royal Academy of French Language & Literature)

Palais des Academies, rue Ducale, 1, 1000 Brussels
Tel: (02) 550 22 77 *Fax:* (02) 550 22 75
E-mail: alf@cfwb.be
Web Site: www.arllfb.be
Key Personnel
Permanent Secretary: Jacques De Decker
Established: 1963
Awarded triennially to the author of a poetic work or not, undeniable moral significance.
Award: 850 EUR

Prix de Stassart
Academie Royale des Sciences, des Lettres et des Beaux-Arts de Belgique
Rue Ducale, 1, 1000 Brussels
Tel: (02) 550 22 12 *Fax:* (02) 550 22 05
E-mail: arb@cfwb.be; academieroyale@cfwb.be
Web Site: www.academieroyale.be
Key Personnel
President: Peter Bartholomew *E-mail:* fpbartho@skynet.be
Permanent Secretary: Herve Hasquin *E-mail:* herve.hasquin@skynet.be
Contact: Beatrice Denuit *Tel:* (02) 550 22 21 *E-mail:* beatrice.denuit@cfwb.be
Established: 1851
Awarded every 5 years. Intended for a famous Belgian or literary historian, scientist or artist.
Award: 1,250 EUR
Closing Date: Dec 31

Suzanne Tassier Prize (Prix Suzanne Tassier)
Academie Royale des Sciences, des Lettres et des Beaux-Arts de Belgique
Rue Ducale, 1, 1000 Brussels
Tel: (02) 550 22 12 *Fax:* (02) 550 22 05
E-mail: arb@cfwb.be; academieroyale@cfwb.be
Web Site: www.academieroyale.be
Key Personnel
President: Peter Bartholomew *E-mail:* fpbartho@skynet.be
Permanent Secretary: Herve Hasquin *E-mail:* herve.hasquin@skynet.be
Contact: Beatrice Denuit *Tel:* (02) 550 22 21 *E-mail:* beatrice.denuit@cfwb.be
Established: 1956
Triennial award to a Belgian woman who, following study at a Belgian university, has obtained at least a Doctorate. The prize is awarded for a major scientific work, dealing with a subject from history, law, philology or the social sciences: failing a meritorious work from one of these branches, then for a subject from the natural sciences, medicine or mathematics. Preference will be given to a work of an historical nature, in its widest sense.
Award: 1,750 EUR
Closing Date: Dec 31

Auguste Teirlinck Prize (Prix Auguste Teirlinck)
Academie Royale des Sciences, des Lettres et des Beaux-Arts de Belgique
Rue Ducale, 1, 1000 Brussels
Tel: (02) 550 22 12 *Fax:* (02) 550 22 05
E-mail: arb@cfwb.be; academieroyale@cfwb.be
Web Site: www.academieroyale.be
Key Personnel
President: Peter Bartholomew *E-mail:* fpbartho@skynet.be
Permanent Secretary: Herve Hasquin *E-mail:* herve.hasquin@skynet.be
Contact: Beatrice Denuit *Tel:* (02) 550 22 21 *E-mail:* beatrice.denuit@cfwb.be
Established: 1907
For a contribution to Flemish literature. Awarded every five years.
Award: 1,250 EUR
Closing Date: Dec 31

Prix Georges Vaxelaire (Georges Vaxelaire
Prize)
Academie Royale de Langue et de Litterature
Francaises de Belgique (Royal Academy of
French Language & Literature)
Palais des Academies, rue Ducale, 1, 1000 Brussels
Tel: (02) 550 22 77 *Fax:* (02) 550 22 75
E-mail: alf@cfwb.be
Web Site: www.arllfb.be
Key Personnel
Permanent Secretary: Jacques De Decker
Established: 1945
Biennial award to a Belgian author of a play represented in Belgium in the theatre or broadcast
by radio/TV.
Award: 850 EUR

Prix Emmanuel Vossaert (Emmanuel Vossaert
Prize)
Academie Royale de Langue et de Litterature
Francaises de Belgique (Royal Academy of
French Language & Literature)
Palais des Academies, rue Ducale, 1, 1000 Brussels
Tel: (02) 550 22 77 *Fax:* (02) 550 22 75
E-mail: alf@cfwb.be
Web Site: www.arllfb.be
Key Personnel
Permanent Secretary: Jacques De Decker
Established: 1952
Awarded biennially to a Belgium writer for a
book of prose or verse & especially for a literary essay.
Award: 850 EUR

Prix Frans de Wever (Frans de Wever Prize)
Academie Royale de Langue et de Litterature
Francaises de Belgique (Royal Academy of
French Language & Literature)
Palais des Academies, rue Ducale, 1, 1000 Brussels
Tel: (02) 550 22 77 *Fax:* (02) 550 22 75
E-mail: alf@cfwb.be
Web Site: www.arllfb.be
Key Personnel
Permanent Secretary: Jacques De Decker
Established: 1962
Annual award to a Belgian author under the age
of 40 for a collection of poems, an essay or a
collection of short stories.
Award: 850 EUR

Prix Carton de Wiart (Carton de Wiart Prize)
Academie Royale de Langue et de Litterature
Francaises de Belgique (Royal Academy of
French Language & Literature)
Palais des Academies, rue Ducale, 1, 1000 Brussels
Tel: (02) 550 22 77 *Fax:* (02) 550 22 75
E-mail: alf@cfwb.be
Web Site: www.arllfb.be
Key Personnel
Permanent Secretary: Jacques De Decker
Established: 1926
Awarded every 10 years to a Belgian French-
language writer to be highlighted in a literary
form (historical novel, stories, news, impressions, memories) episodes or aspects of the
Belgian national life in the past, even recent.
Award: 750 EUR
Presented: 2026

Bolivia

Premio Nacional de Cultura (The National
Culture Award)
Ministerio de Culturas

Palacio Chico, Calle Ayacucho esquina Potosi, La
Paz
Tel: (02) 220 0910; (02) 220 0949 *Fax:* (02) 220
0948
E-mail: administracionvc@cultura.gov.bo
Web Site: www.bolivia.com/empresas/cultura/
premios_concursos/index.asp
Established: 1969
Annual award for recognition of achievements in
literature, the arts or science.
Award: Solid gold medal & 25,000 BOB

Brazil

Jabuti Prize (Premio Jabuti)
Camara Brasileira do Livro (CBL) (Brazilian
Book Association)
Rua Cristiano Viana, 91, Jardim Paulista, 05411-
000 Sao Paulo-SP
Tel: (011) 3069-1300
E-mail: jabuti@cbl.org.br; cbl@cbl.org.br
Web Site: www.cbl.org.br; www.premiojabuti.org.
br
Established: 1958
Awarded annually for best literary composition
published in previous year.

Chile

National Prize for Literature (Premio Nacional
de Literatura)
Gobierno de Chile, Consejo Nacional de la Cultura y las Artes
Plaza Sotomayor 233, Valparaiso
Tel: (032) 2326400
Established: 1942
Awarded annually to recognize an author's sum
of work.
Award: Monetary prize

Costa Rica

Editorial Costa Rica Literary Prize
Editorial Costa Rica
Apdo 10010, 1000 San Jose
Tel: 2233-0812 *Fax:* 2233-1949
E-mail: difusion@editorialcostarica.com; ventas@
editorialcostarica.com
Web Site: www.editorialcostarica.com
Key Personnel
General Manager: Maria Isabel Brenes Alvarado
E-mail: gerenciageneral@editorialcostarica.com
Established: 1972
Annual award is to encourage creative writing
generally. The prize is rotated in order to be
open to all genres - fiction, stories, theatre, essays, short stories, poetry, biography, history.
Award: 1,000,000 CRC

Premios Nacionales Aquileo J Echeverria
Ministerio de Cultura y Juventud (Ministry of
Culture & Youth)
Centro Nacional para la Cultura (CENAC), San
Jose
Tel: 2255-3093 *Fax:* 2233-1967
E-mail: premiosnacionales@cultura.cr
Web Site: www.mcj.go.cr/convocatorias_premios/
premios.aspx
Key Personnel
Contact: Filander Alfaro *Tel:* 2221-2022

E-mail: premiosnacionalesdircultura@gmail.
com
Established: 1961
For Costa Rican citizens who have excelled in
the fields of literature (novel, short story, poetry, essay, scientific literature), history, theatre,
music, fine arts. 40,000 CRC divided between
the selected works. Total sum of awards cannot
exceed 8,000,000 CRC. Awarded annually.
Award: 8,000,000 CRC

Joven Creacion Literary Prize
Editorial Costa Rica
Apdo 10010, 1000 San Jose
Tel: 2233-0812 *Fax:* 2233-1949
E-mail: difusion@editorialcostarica.com; ventas@
editorialcostarica.com
Web Site: www.editorialcostarica.com
Key Personnel
General Manager: Maria Isabel Brenes Alvarado
E-mail: gerenciageneral@editorialcostarica.com
Established: 1976
Formed in collaboration with the Associacion de
Autores, with the aim of stimulating young
writers, 30 years of age or younger, in the
fields of poetry & narrative/stories.
Award: 500,000 CRC
Closing Date: March 27

Carmen Lyra Literary Prize (Premio Carmen
Lyra - Literatura Infantil)
Editorial Costa Rica
Apdo 10010, 1000 San Jose
Tel: 2233-0812 *Fax:* 2233-1949
E-mail: difusion@editorialcostarica.com; ventas@
editorialcostarica.com
Web Site: www.editorialcostarica.com
Key Personnel
General Manager: Maria Isabel Brenes Alvarado
E-mail: gerenciageneral@editorialcostarica.com
Established: 1974
Founded in honour of the writer Maria Isabel
Carvajal (pseudonym Carmen Lyra), this annual
award is to encourage the writing of literature
intended for children & young people.
Award: 750,000 CRC
Closing Date: March 27

Cuba

☆**Casa de las Americas Literary Award**
(Premio Literario Casa de las Americas)
Casa de las Americas
3ra y G, El Vedado, CP 10400 Havana
Tel: (07) 838-2704; (07) 838-2706 (ext 10)
Fax: (07) 834-4554
E-mail: cil@casa.cult.cu
Web Site: www.casadelasamericas.org/premios/
literario/index.php
Key Personnel
President: Roberto Fernandez Retamar
E-mail: presidencia@casa.cult.cu
Dir, Literary Research Center: Jorge Fornet
Established: 1960
Annual prize awarded to an author for unpublished work in one or other of the following
genres: novels, plays, "testimonial" books, essays on artistic & literary themes - Brazilian &
French Caribbean (or national language) works;
short stories, poetry, essays on historical & social themes, books for children & young people & Anglo-Caribbean (or national language)
works. The winning work will be published.
Award: 3,000 USD (or equivalent in national currency)
Closing Date: Oct 31

Czech Republic

Jaroslava Seiferta Prize
Charta 77 Foundation
Melantrichova 5, 110 00 Prague 1
Tel: 224 214 452; 224 230 216; 224 225 092
    Fax: 224 213 647
E-mail: nadace77@bariery.cz
Web Site: www.kontobariery.cz/projekty/ceny/
cena-jaroslava-seiferta.aspx
Key Personnel
Program Dir: Indira Bornova *E-mail:* indira.
bornova@bariery.cz
Established: 1986
For recognition of the best work in Czech & Slo-
vak poetry or fiction published in the last 3
years.
Other Sponsor(s): Pioneer Global Investments
Award: 250,000 CZK & a diploma made by one
of the well known Czechoslovak artists
Closing Date: Spring every year
Presented: Autumn

Denmark

Dansk Oversaetterforbunds Aerespris
Dansk Forfatterforening (The Danish Writers As-
sociation)
Strandgade 6, 1401 Copenhagen K
Tel: 32 95 51 00 *Fax:* 32 54 01 15
E-mail: df@danskforfatterforening.dk
Web Site: www.danskforfatterforening.dk
Established: 1945
For the outstanding translation into Danish of one
or more significant works. Awarded annually.
Award: 60,000 DKK

Soren Gyldendal Prize (Soren Gyldendal Prisen)
Gyldendal
Klareboderne 3, 1001 Copenhagen K
Tel: 33 75 55 55 *Fax:* 33 75 55 57
E-mail: gyldendal@gyldendal.dk
Web Site: www.gyldendal.dk
Key Personnel
Dir: Bjarne Ponikowski
Established: 1958
For Danish authors from any field whose work is
of great literary value - Nominations only. The
prize cannot be applied for.
Award: 200,000 DKK

Holberg Medal (Holberg-Medaljen)
Dansk Forfatterforening (The Danish Writers As-
sociation)
Strandgade 6, 1401 Copenhagen K
Tel: 32 95 51 00 *Fax:* 32 54 01 15
E-mail: df@danskforfatterforening.dk
Web Site: www.danskforfatterforening.dk
Established: 1934
For outstanding contributions to Danish literature.
Awarded annually.
Award: 60,000 DKK & medal
Presented: Dec 3

☆**Nordic Council Literature Prize**
Nordic Council, Swedish Delegation
Store Strandstr 18, 1061 Copenhagen K
Tel: 33 96 04 00 *Fax:* 33 11 18 70
E-mail: nordisk-rad@norden.org
Web Site: www.norden.org
Key Personnel
Media Contact: Jasper Schou-Knudsen *Tel:* 21 21
71 35 *E-mail:* jsk@norden.org
Established: 1962
Awarded annually for a literary work in the fic-
tion, genre, written in one of the languages of

the Nordic countries. It can be a novel, a play,
a collection - of poems, short stories or essays
- or another work which meets high literary &
artistic standards. The intention of the prize is
to increase interest in the literature of neigh-
bouring countries as well in Nordic cultural
fellowship.
Award: 350,000 DKK
Presented: Nordic Council Conference or a ses-
sion in Oct

Den Store Pris (Danish Academy Prize for
Literature)
Danish Academy (Danske Akademi)
c/o Philp Advokatfirma, Vognmagergade 7, 1120
Copenhagen
Tel: 33131112 *Fax:* 33328045
E-mail: administrator@danskeakademi.dk
Web Site: www.danskeakademi.dk
Key Personnel
Administrator: Jesper Rothe
Awarded biannually for an outstanding work of
literature.
Award: 300,000 DKK

Finland

Finlandia Junior Prize
Suomen Kirjasaatio (Finnish Book Foundation)
Lonnrotinkatu 11 A, 00121 Helsinki
Mailing Address: PL 177, 00121 Helsinki
Tel: (09) 228 77 252
Web Site: www.kustantajat.fi
Key Personnel
Dir: Sakari Laiho *Tel:* (09) 228 77 258
    E-mail: sakari.laiho@publishers.fi
Established: 1997
Annual award for the outstanding Finnish book
for children & young people of the year.
Award: 30,000 EUR

Rudolf Koivu Prize
Grafia Ry
Uudenmaankatu 11 B9, 00120 Helsinki
Tel: (09) 601 941; (09) 601 942
E-mail: grafia@grafia.fi
Web Site: www.grafia.fi
Key Personnel
Executive Dir: Marita Sandelin *E-mail:* marita.
sandelin@grafia.fi
Established: 1949
Biennial award for the illustrator of the year's
best Finnish picture-book for children.
Award: 10,000 EUR

Arvid Lydecken Prize
Suomen Nuorisokirjailijat ry
Palomaentie 13 B, 02730 Espoo
Tel: (09) 852 2176
Web Site: www.nuorisokirjailijat.fi
Key Personnel
Chairman: Mrs Tuija Lehtinen *E-mail:* tuileh@
netti.fi
Established: 1946
Annual award for the writer of the year's best
Finnish book for children.
Award: 1,700 EUR

State Prizes for Literature
Ministry of Education, Finland
Meritullinkatu 10, 00171 Helsinki
Mailing Address: PL 29, 00023 Helsinki
Tel: (09) 160 04; (09) 578 14 (switchboard)
    Fax: (09) 135 9335
E-mail: opmkirjaamo@minedu.fi
Web Site: www.minedu.fi

Key Personnel
Minister of Education & Science: Henna
Virkkunen *E-mail:* henna.virkkunen@minedu.fi
Annual prizes for the best literary works.
Award: 15,000 EUR

France

**Prix de l'Academie des Sciences Arts et Belles
Lettres de Dijon** (Dijon Academy of Sciences,
Art & Literature Prize)
Academie des Sciences Arts et Belles Lettres de
Dijon
5, rue de l'Ecole-de-Droit, 21000 Dijon
Tel: 03 80 54 22 93; 09 64 43 97 11 *Fax:* 03 80
44 94 34
E-mail: secretariat@acascia-dijon.fr
Web Site: www.acascia-dijon.fr
Key Personnel
Secretary: Sylvie Brunetiere
Established: 1741
Prize rewards a work artistic, literary or scientific
written or presented in French, new or previ-
ously presented, book, series of books, mem-
oires, work of art or works of art presented
together.
Award: Gold medal & contract for publication
Closing Date: Sept 30
Presented: Jan

Prix Guillaume Apollinaire
Hotel Claret
44, blvd de Bercy, 75012 Paris
Tel: 01 46 28 41 31 *Fax:* 01 49 28 09 29
Web Site: fr.hotel-claret.com
Key Personnel
Chief Executive Officer: Monique Pignet
Established: 1941
Poetry prize.

Francois-Joseph Audiffred Prize (Prix
Francois-Joseph Audiffred)
Academie des Sciences Morales et Politiques, In-
stitut de France
23, quai Conti, 75006 Paris
Tel: 01 44 41 43 26 *Fax:* 01 44 41 43 27
Web Site: www.institut-de-france.fr; www.asmp.fr
Key Personnel
Secretary General: Pierre Kerbrat
    E-mail: kerbrat@asmp.fr
Annual award for a published work best qualified
to inspire love of ethics & virtue & to discour-
age egoism & envy; or to stimulate knowledge
& appreciation of France.
Award: Medal

Prix Baudelaire
Societe des Gens de Lettres (SGDL)
Hotel de Massa, 38, rue du Fbg-St-Jacques,
75014 Paris
Tel: 01 53 10 12 00 *Fax:* 01 53 10 12 12
E-mail: sgdl@sgdl.org
Web Site: www.sgdl.org
Key Personnel
President: Jean Claude Bologne
First Vice President: Noelle Chatelet
Secretary General: Dominique Le Brun
Treasurer: Hubert Tubiana
Awarded each Spring to the best French transla-
tion of an English work to which the author is
native of the UK or one of the Commonwealth
countries.
Award: 2,000 EUR
Presented: Hotel de Massa, Paris

Cardinal Grente Prize (Prix du Cardinal Grente)
Academie Francaise, Institut de France
23, quai Conti, 75006 Paris

Tel: 01 44 41 43 00 *Fax:* 01 43 29 47 45
E-mail: contact@academie-francaise.fr
Web Site: www.institut-de-france.fr; www.
academie-francaise.fr
Key Personnel
Contact: Marie-Claire Chatelain
Established: 1945
Awarded biennially for the entire works of a regular or secular member of the Roman Catholic clergy.
Award: 1,000 EUR
Closing Date: Jan 31
Presented: Academie Francaise, June

Louis Castex Prize (Prix Louis Castex)
Academie Francaise, Institut de France
23, quai Conti, 75006 Paris
Tel: 01 44 41 43 00 *Fax:* 01 43 29 47 45
E-mail: contact@academie-francaise.fr
Web Site: www.institut-de-france.fr; www.
academie-francaise.fr
Key Personnel
Contact: Marie-Claire Chatelain
Established: 1969
Awarded annually for a literary work celebrating aviation history or a major voyage of exploration or archaeological or ethnological discovery. Fictional romance excluded. Awarded annually.
Award: 1,800 EUR
Closing Date: Jan 31
Presented: Academie Francaise, June

Le Prix Chateaubriand
Maison de Chateaubriand
87 rue Chateaubriand, 92290 Chatenay-Malabry
Tel: 01 55 52 13 00 *Fax:* 01 55 52 12 98
E-mail: chateaubriand@cg92.fr
Web Site: maison-de-chateaubriand.hauts-de-seine.
net
Established: 1987
Awarded annually for a work of historical or literary history.
Award: 15,000 EUR

Grand Prix Magdeleine Cluzel de la SGDL
Societe des Gens de Lettres (SGDL)
Hotel de Massa, 38, rue du Fbg-St-Jacques,
75014 Paris
Tel: 01 53 10 12 00 *Fax:* 01 53 10 12 12
E-mail: sgdl@sgdl.org
Web Site: www.sgdl.org
Key Personnel
President: Jean Claude Bologne
First Vice President: Noelle Chatelet
Secretary General: Dominique Le Brun
Treasurer: Hubert Tubiana
Established: 1970
For recognition of the total works of a writer whose value has not been recognized & whose situation has been seriously affected.
Award: 3,000 EUR

Prix Maurice-Edgar Coindreau
Societe des Gens de Lettres (SGDL)
Hotel de Massa, 38, rue du Fbg-St-Jacques,
75014 Paris
Tel: 01 53 10 12 00 *Fax:* 01 53 10 12 12
E-mail: sgdl@sgdl.org
Web Site: www.sgdl.org
Key Personnel
President: Jean Claude Bologne
First Vice President: Noelle Chatelet
Secretary General: Dominique Le Brun
Treasurer: Hubert Tubiana
Established: 1981
Rewards a literary translation for American work.
Award: 2,000 EUR

Eve Delacroix Prize (Prix Eve Delacroix)
Academie Francaise, Institut de France

23, quai Conti, 75006 Paris
Tel: 01 44 41 43 00 *Fax:* 01 43 29 47 45
E-mail: contact@academie-francaise.fr
Web Site: www.institut-de-france.fr; www.
academie-francaise.fr
Key Personnel
Contact: Marie-Claire Chatelain
Established: 1977
Annual award for a literary work, essay or novel combining literary quality, a sense of human dignity & the responsibilities of authorship.
Award: 1,500 EUR
Closing Date: Jan 31
Presented: Academie Francaise, June

Deux Magots Prize (Prix Les Deux Magots)
Cafe Les Deux Magots
6 Pl St-Germain-des-Pres, 75006 Paris
Tel: 01 45 48 55 25 *Fax:* 01 45 49 31 29
Web Site: www.lesdeuxmagots.fr
Key Personnel
Manager: Catherine Mathivat
Established: 1933
Award: 7,700 EUR
Presented: Last Tuesday of Jan, annually

Alfred Dutens Prize (Prix Alfred Dutens)
Academie des Inscriptions et Belles Lettres, Institut de France
23, quai Conti, 75006 Paris Cedex 06
Tel: 01 44 41 43 10 *Fax:* 01 44 41 43 11
Web Site: www.aibl.fr; www.institut-de-france.fr
Key Personnel
Perpetual Secretary: M Jean Leclant
E-mail: secretaireperpetuel@aibl.fr
Awarded every ten years for the most useful work on linguistics. Next award will be in 2028.

Prix Paul Feval de Litterature Populaire
Societe des Gens de Lettres (SGDL)
Hotel de Massa, 38, rue du Fbg-St-Jacques,
75014 Paris
Tel: 01 53 10 12 00 *Fax:* 01 53 10 12 12
E-mail: sgdl@sgdl.org
Web Site: www.sgdl.org
Key Personnel
President: Jean Claude Bologne
First Vice President: Noelle Chatelet
Secretary General: Dominique Le Brun
Treasurer: Hubert Tubiana
Established: 1984
Award: 2,000 EUR

Jean Finot Prize (Prix Jean Finot)
Academie des Sciences Morales et Politiques, Institut de France
23, quai Conti, 75006 Paris
Tel: 01 44 41 43 26 *Fax:* 01 44 41 43 27
Web Site: www.institut-de-france.fr; www.asmp.fr
Key Personnel
Secretary General: Pierre Kerbrat
E-mail: kerbrat@asmp.fr
Biennial award for a work of a humanitarian social trend.
Award: Medal

Marshal Foch Prize (Prix du Marechal Foch)
Academie Francaise, Institut de France
23, quai Conti, 75006 Paris
Tel: 01 44 41 43 00 *Fax:* 01 43 29 47 45
E-mail: contact@academie-francaise.fr
Web Site: www.institut-de-france.fr; www.
academie-francaise.fr
Key Personnel
Contact: Marie-Claire Chatelain
Established: 1955
Biennial award for a book on the future of the nation's defence by a French officer, engineer, scholar or philosopher.
Award: Medal

Closing Date: Jan 31
Presented: Academie Francaise, June

Gegner Prize (Prix Gegner)
Academie des Sciences Morales et Politiques, Institut de France
23, quai Conti, 75006 Paris
Tel: 01 44 41 43 26 *Fax:* 01 44 41 43 27
Web Site: www.institut-de-france.fr; www.asmp.fr
Key Personnel
Secretary General: Pierre Kerbrat
E-mail: kerbrat@asmp.fr
Awarded annually to a philosophical writer whose works contribute to the advancement of philosophical science.
Award: Medal

Giles Prize (Prix Giles)
Academie des Inscriptions et Belles Lettres, Institut de France
23, quai Conti, 75006 Paris Cedex 06
Tel: 01 44 41 43 10 *Fax:* 01 44 41 43 11
Web Site: www.aibl.fr; www.institut-de-france.fr
Key Personnel
Perpetual Secretary: M Jean Leclant
E-mail: secretaireperpetuel@aibl.fr
Biennial award to a French National for a work on China, Japan or the Far East.

Goncourt Prize (Prix Goncourt)
Academie Goncourt, Societe de gens de Lettres
c/o Drouant 16-18, place Gaillon, 75002 Paris
Web Site: www.academie-goncourt.fr
Key Personnel
Dir: Marie Dabadie *Tel:* 01 40 46 88 11 *Fax:* 01 46 33 25 24
Founded by E de Goncourt, 1914, the annual prize honors a prose work by a younger writer with originality of spirit & form. The novel is the preferred medium. The Academy also awards each year, in various French towns, prizes for short story, biography, historical novel & poetry.
Presented: Nov

☆**Grand Prix de la Francophonie**
Academie Francaise, Institut de France
23, quai Conti, 75006 Paris
Tel: 01 44 41 43 00 *Fax:* 01 43 29 47 45
E-mail: contact@academie-francaise.fr
Web Site: www.institut-de-france.fr; www.
academie-francaise.fr
Key Personnel
Contact: Marie-Claire Chatelain
Established: 1986
Annual award established by the Government of Canada in collaboration with the Academie Francaise. The Government of Canada donated 400,000 CAD as a founding sum with the expectation that other countries, organizations & groups would make further contributions. The prize is to reward the work of a French-speaking writer who has contributed in an outstanding manner to the upholding & exemplification of the French language. The prize can also be for literary or philosophical work which has assured the regeneration of the French language in the fields of science, technology or information.
Award: 22,500 EUR
Closing Date: Jan 31
Presented: Academie Francaise, June

Grand Prix de la Societe des Poetes Francais
(Grand Prize of the French Poet's Society)
Societe des Poetes Francais
16, rue Monsieur le Prince, 75006 Paris
Tel: 01 40 46 99 82 *Fax:* 01 40 46 99 11
E-mail: stepoetesfrancais@orange.fr
Web Site: www.societedespoetesfrancais.asso.fr
Key Personnel
President: Vital Heurtebize *E-mail:* vital.
heurtebize@societedespoetesfrancais.eu

Vice President: Jacques-Francois Dussottier
  E-mail: jf.dussottier@societedespoetesfrancais.
  eu; Emmanuel Mahieu
Secretary General: Jean-Pierre Bechu
Dir General: Claire Dutrey *E-mail:* spf.
  clairedutrey@orange.fr
Established: 1936
Awarded annually for the whole body of a poet's
  work, as decided by the Committee of the So-
  ciete des Poetes (no applications allowed).

Grand Prix de Litterature de la SGDL
Societe des Gens de Lettres (SGDL)
Hotel de Massa, 38, rue du Fbg-St-Jacques,
  75014 Paris
Tel: 01 53 10 12 00 *Fax:* 01 53 10 12 12
E-mail: sgdl@sgdl.org
Web Site: www.sgdl.org
Key Personnel
President: Jean Claude Bologne
First Vice President: Noelle Chatelet
Secretary General: Dominique Le Brun
Treasurer: Hubert Tubiana
Established: 1947
Award: 6,000 EUR

Grand Prix de Poesie de la SGDL
Societe des Gens de Lettres (SGDL)
Hotel de Massa, 38, rue du Fbg-St-Jacques,
  75014 Paris
Tel: 01 53 10 12 00 *Fax:* 01 53 10 12 12
E-mail: sgdl@sgdl.org
Web Site: www.sgdl.org
Key Personnel
President: Jean Claude Bologne
First Vice President: Noelle Chatelet
Secretary General: Dominique Le Brun
Treasurer: Hubert Tubiana
Established: 1983
Award: 6,000 EUR

Grand Prix SGDL de la Nouvelle
Societe des Gens de Lettres (SGDL)
Hotel de Massa, 38, rue du Fbg-St-Jacques,
  75014 Paris
Tel: 01 53 10 12 00 *Fax:* 01 53 10 12 12
E-mail: sgdl@sgdl.org
Web Site: www.sgdl.org
Key Personnel
President: Jean Claude Bologne
First Vice President: Noelle Chatelet
Secretary General: Dominique Le Brun
Treasurer: Hubert Tubiana
Award: 3,000 EUR

Grand Prix SGDL de l'Essai
Societe des Gens de Lettres (SGDL)
Hotel de Massa, 38, rue du Fbg-St-Jacques,
  75014 Paris
Tel: 01 53 10 12 00 *Fax:* 01 53 10 12 12
E-mail: sgdl@sgdl.org
Web Site: www.sgdl.org
Key Personnel
President: Jean Claude Bologne
First Vice President: Noelle Chatelet
Secretary General: Dominique Le Brun
Treasurer: Hubert Tubiana
Established: 1984
For recognition of an outstanding essay.
Award: 3,000 EUR

Grand Prix SGDL du Livre Jeunesse
Societe des Gens de Lettres (SGDL)
Hotel de Massa, 38, rue du Fbg-St-Jacques,
  75014 Paris
Tel: 01 53 10 12 00 *Fax:* 01 53 10 12 12
E-mail: sgdl@sgdl.org
Web Site: www.sgdl.org
Key Personnel
President: Jean Claude Bologne
First Vice President: Noelle Chatelet

Secretary General: Dominique Le Brun
Treasurer: Hubert Tubiana
Established: 1982
Annual award to recognize a book intended for
  young people by its qualities of invention, writing & presentation. Works written in French &
  published before March of the preceding year
  may be submitted by the author or editor.
Award: 3,000 EUR

Grand Prix SGDL du Roman
Societe des Gens de Lettres (SGDL)
Hotel de Massa, 38, rue du Fbg-St-Jacques,
  75014 Paris
Tel: 01 53 10 12 00 *Fax:* 01 53 10 12 12
E-mail: sgdl@sgdl.org
Web Site: www.sgdl.org
Key Personnel
President: Jean Claude Bologne
First Vice President: Noelle Chatelet
Secretary General: Dominique Le Brun
Treasurer: Hubert Tubiana
Established: 1947
For recognition of an outstanding novel. Works
  published within the preceding year may be
  submitted.
Award: 3,000 EUR

Grand Prize for Literature Paul Morand
  (Grand Prix de Litterature Paul Morand)
Academie Francaise, Institut de France
23, quai Conti, 75006 Paris
Tel: 01 44 41 43 00 *Fax:* 01 43 29 47 45
E-mail: contact@academie-francaise.fr
Web Site: www.institut-de-france.fr; www.
  academie-francaise.fr
Key Personnel
Contact: Marie-Claire Chatelain
Established: 1977
Biennial award to a prose-writer for one or more
  works noteworthy in form & inspiration.
Award: 15,000 EUR
Closing Date: Jan 31
Presented: Academie Francaise, June

Grand Prize for Poetry (Grand Prix de Poesie)
Academie Francaise, Institut de France
23, quai Conti, 75006 Paris
Tel: 01 44 41 43 00 *Fax:* 01 43 29 47 45
E-mail: contact@academie-francaise.fr
Web Site: www.institut-de-france.fr; www.
  academie-francaise.fr
Key Personnel
Contact: Marie-Claire Chatelain
Established: 1957
Awarded annually to an author for all of his work
  in poetry.
Award: 3,800 EUR
Closing Date: Jan 31
Presented: Academie Francaise, June

☆**Heredia Prize** (Prix Heredia)
Academie Francaise, Institut de France
23, quai Conti, 75006 Paris
Tel: 01 44 41 43 00 *Fax:* 01 43 29 47 45
E-mail: contact@academie-francaise.fr
Web Site: www.institut-de-france.fr; www.
  academie-francaise.fr
Key Personnel
Contact: Marie-Claire Chatelain
Established: 1994
Award given annually to the author of a collec-
  tion of printed sonnets or to the author of a
  classical poetry collection.
Award: Medal
Closing Date: Jan 31
Presented: Academie Francaise, June

Prix Honore Chavee
Academie des Inscriptions et Belles Lettres, Institut de France

23, quai Conti, 75006 Paris Cedex 06
Tel: 01 44 41 43 10 *Fax:* 01 44 41 43 11
Web Site: www.aibl.fr; www.institut-de-france.fr
Key Personnel
Perpetual Secretary: M Jean Leclant
  E-mail: secretaireperpetuel@aibl.fr
Established: 1821
Biennial award to encourage work in linguistics
  & in particular, research on romance languages.

Prix Interallie (Interallie Prize)
Cercle de l'Union Interallie
33 rue du Fauborg St Honore, 75008 Paris
Tel: 01 42 65 96 00 *Fax:* 01 42 65 70 34
Established: 1930
Annual French literary award for a novel written
  by a journalist.

☆**Stanislas Julien Prize** (Prix Stanislas Julien)
Academie des Inscriptions et Belles Lettres, Insti-
  tut de France
23, quai Conti, 75006 Paris Cedex 06
Tel: 01 44 41 43 10 *Fax:* 01 44 41 43 11
Web Site: www.aibl.fr; www.institut-de-france.fr
Key Personnel
Perpetual Secretary: M Jean Leclant
  E-mail: secretaireperpetuel@aibl.fr
Monetary prize, awarded annually, for the best
  work related to China.

Prix Roger Kowalski
Bibliotheque Municipale de Lyon
30 blvd Vivier-Merle, 69431 Lyon
Tel: 04 78 62 18 00 *Fax:* 04 78 62 19 49
E-mail: bm@bm-lyon.fr
Web Site: www.bm-lyon.fr
Established: 1984
Award: 7,500 EUR
Presented: March 10

Prix Valery Larbaud (Valery Larbaud Prize)
L'Association Internationale des Amis de Valery
  Larbaud
Mairie de Vichy, place de l'Hotel de Ville, 03200
  Vichy
Tel: 04 70 30 17 02; 04 70 30 55 12
Web Site: www.ville-vichy.fr/valery-larbaud.htm
Key Personnel
President: Jean-Marie Laclavetine
Established: 1967
Annual award to author of books the jurists feel
  that Larbaud would have loved.
Presented: Last weekend in May

Maison de Poesie (House of Poetry)
Emile Blemont Foundation
16, rue Monsieur-le-Prince, 75006 Paris
Tel: 06 37 51 17 09
E-mail: lamaisondepoesie@gmail.com
Web Site: www.lamaisondepoesie.fr
Established: 1928

Grand Prix Thyde Monnier de la SGDL
Societe des Gens de Lettres (SGDL)
Hotel de Massa, 38, rue du Fbg-St-Jacques,
  75014 Paris
Tel: 01 53 10 12 00 *Fax:* 01 53 10 12 12
E-mail: sgdl@sgdl.org
Web Site: www.sgdl.org
Key Personnel
President: Jean Claude Bologne
First Vice President: Noelle Chatelet
Secretary General: Dominique Le Brun
Treasurer: Hubert Tubiana
Established: 1975
Annual award in recognition of a cycle of novels
  or for a separate work (novel, essay or collec-
  tion of poems) published during the preced-
  ing two years. Writers whose talents have not
  brought them material success are eligible.
Award: 2,000 EUR

Montyon Prize (Prix Montyon)
Academie Francaise, Institut de France
23, quai Conti, 75006 Paris
Tel: 01 44 41 43 00 *Fax:* 01 43 29 47 45
E-mail: contact@academie-francaise.fr
Web Site: www.institut-de-france.fr; www.
academie-francaise.fr
Key Personnel
Contact: Marie-Claire Chatelain
Established: 1976
Annual award for any work published by a
French author showing qualities of practical
idealism.
Award: Medal
Closing Date: Jan 31
Presented: Academie Francaise, June

Prix Gerard de Nerval
Societe des Gens de Lettres (SGDL)
Hotel de Massa, 38, rue du Fbg-St-Jacques,
75014 Paris
Tel: 01 53 10 12 00 *Fax:* 01 53 10 12 12
E-mail: sgdl@sgdl.org
Web Site: www.sgdl.org
Key Personnel
President: Jean Claude Bologne
First Vice President: Noelle Chatelet
Secretary General: Dominique Le Brun
Treasurer: Hubert Tubiana
Established: 1989
For recognition of an outstanding French transla-
tion of a German work.
Award: 2,000 EUR

Prix Bordin
Academie des Sciences Morales et Politiques, In-
stitut de France
23, quai Conti, 75006 Paris
Tel: 01 44 41 43 26 *Fax:* 01 44 41 43 27
Web Site: www.institut-de-france.fr; www.asmp.fr
Key Personnel
Secretary General: Pierre Kerbrat
E-mail: kerbrat@asmp.fr
Awarded biennially to authors of books on sub-
jects relating to the public interest, the good of
mankind, scientific progress & national honor.
Award: Medal

☆**Prize for the Influence of the French
Language** (Prix du Rayonnement de la Langue
et de la Litterature Francaises)
Academie Francaise, Institut de France
23, quai Conti, 75006 Paris
Tel: 01 44 41 43 00 *Fax:* 01 43 29 47 45
E-mail: contact@academie-francaise.fr
Web Site: www.institut-de-france.fr; www.
academie-francaise.fr
Key Personnel
Contact: Marie-Claire Chatelain
Established: 1960
For work contributing to the influence of the
French language.
Award: Medals
Closing Date: Jan 31
Presented: Academie Francaise, June

☆**Lucien de Reinach Prize** (Prix Lucien de
Reinach)
Academie des Sciences Morales et Politiques, In-
stitut de France
23, quai Conti, 75006 Paris
Tel: 01 44 41 43 26 *Fax:* 01 44 41 43 27
Web Site: www.institut-de-france.fr; www.asmp.fr
Key Personnel
Secretary General: Pierre Kerbrat
E-mail: kerbrat@asmp.fr
Biennial award for the best original work written
in French in the most recent two years on an
overseas subject.
Award: Medal

Prix de Poesie Charles Vildrac
Societe des Gens de Lettres (SGDL)
Hotel de Massa, 38, rue du Fbg-St-Jacques,
75014 Paris
Tel: 01 53 10 12 00 *Fax:* 01 53 10 12 12
E-mail: sgdl@sgdl.org
Web Site: www.sgdl.org
Key Personnel
President: Jean Claude Bologne
First Vice President: Noelle Chatelet
Secretary General: Dominique Le Brun
Treasurer: Hubert Tubiana
Established: 1973
Annual award to recognize a writer of a collec-
tion of poems published during the year pre-
ceding the award. Writers under 40 years of
age are eligible.
Award: 1,500 EUR

Volney Prize (Prix Volney)
Academie des Inscriptions et Belles Lettres, Insti-
tut de France
23, quai Conti, 75006 Paris Cedex 06
Tel: 01 44 41 43 10 *Fax:* 01 44 41 43 11
Web Site: www.aibl.fr; www.institut-de-france.fr
Key Personnel
Perpetual Secretary: M Jean Leclant
E-mail: secretaireperpetuel@aibl.fr
For a work in comparative philology.

Germany

**Adelbert-von-Chamisso-Preis der Robert Bosch
Stiftung**
Robert Bosch Stiftung GmbH
Heidehofstr 31, 70184 Stuttgart
Mailing Address: Postfach 10 06 28, 70005
Stuttgart
Tel: (0711) 46084-0 *Fax:* (0711) 46084-1094
E-mail: info@bosch-stiftung.de
Web Site: www.bosch-stiftung.de
Key Personnel
Contact: Frank Albers *Tel:* (0711) 46084-51
E-mail: frank.albers@bosch-stiftung.de
Established: 1985
Annually. Literature in German written by authors
with different mother tongues.
Award: 15,000 EUR
Closing Date: April 30
Presented: Munich, March

Berlin Art Prize, see Kunstpreis Berlin -
Jubilaeumsstiftung 1848/1948

Horst Bienek Award for Poetry
(Horst-Bienek-Preis fuer Lyrik)
Bavarian Academy of Fine Arts (Bayerischen
Akademie der Schoenen Kuenste)
Max-Joseph-Platz 3, 80539 Munich
Tel: (089) 29 00 77-0 *Fax:* (089) 29 00 77-23
E-mail: info@badsk.de
Web Site: www.badsk.de
Key Personnel
Secretary General: Katja Schaefer
E-mail: schaefer@badsk.de
Awarded annually for the overall work of a poet.
Presented: Dec

☆**Bremer Literature Prize** (Bremer
Literaturpreis)
Bremen State Government
c/o Stadtbibliothek Bremen, Am Wall 201, 28195
Bremen
Tel: (0421) 361-4046; (0421) 361-4757
Fax: (0421) 361-6903
E-mail: sekretariat@stadtbibliothek.bremen.de

Web Site: www.rudolf-alexander-schroeder-
stiftung.de
Key Personnel
Mng Dir: Barbara Lison
Established: 1953
Established by Senat der Freien Hansestadt
Bremen. Foundation to encourage German-
speaking poets & writers. Awarded annually for
a single work.
Other Sponsor(s): Rudolph-Alexander Schroeder
Foundation
Award: 20,000 EUR
Presented: Bremen, Townhall, Jan

Georg-Buechner Preis
Deutsche Akademie fuer Sprache und Dichtung
(German Academy for Language & Literature)
Glueckert-Haus, Alexandraweg 23, 64287 Darm-
stadt
Tel: (06151) 4092-0 *Fax:* (06151) 4092-99
E-mail: sekretariat@deutscheakademie.de
Web Site: www.deutscheakademie.de
Key Personnel
General Secretary: Dr Bernd Busch
E-mail: bernd.busch@deutscheakademie.de
Press & Public Relations: Corinna Blattmann
Tel: (06151) 4092-16 *E-mail:* corinna.
blattmann@deutscheakademie.de
Publications & Editing: Michael Assmann
Tel: (06151) 4092-17 *E-mail:* michael.
assmann@deutscheakademie.de
Established: 1923
Award: 50,000 EUR
Presented: Autumn annually

Buxtehuder Bulle
Stadt Buxtehude
Breite Str 2, 21614 Buxtehude
Tel: (04161) 501-2324 *Fax:* (04161) 501-52399
Web Site: www.buxtehuder-bulle.de
Key Personnel
Contact: Mrs K Ernst *E-mail:* kulturbuero@stadt.
buxtehude.de
Established: 1971
Annual literary prize given to the best book
(young readers 14-17 years of age) published
in Germany during the preceding year. By in-
ternal nomination only.
Award: 5,000 EUR & steel sculpture of a bull

Christoph-Martin-Wieland-Preis
Freundeskreis zur Internationalen Foerderung Lit-
erarischer und Wissenschaftlicher Uebersetzun-
gen eV
Wincklerstr 3, 20459 Hamburg
E-mail: info@freundeskreis-literaturuebersetzer.de
Web Site: www.freundeskreis-literaturuebersetzer.
de
Key Personnel
Präsident: Susanne Hoebel *E-mail:* suh@
freundeskreis-literaturuebersetzer.de
Established: 1979
Translation prize awarded biennially.
Other Sponsor(s): Ministerium fuer Wissenschaft,
Forschung und Kunst Baden-Wuerttemberg
Award: 12,000 EUR

**Johann Friedrich von Cotta-Literatur- und
Uebersetzerpreis** (Johann Friedrich von Cotta
Literary & Translation Prize)
Landeshauptstadt Stuttgart
Kulturamt der Landeshauptstadt Stuttgart, Eichstr
9, 70173 Stuttgart
Tel: (0711) 216-2850 *Fax:* (0711) 216-7628
E-mail: poststelle.kulturamt@stuttgart.de
Web Site: www.stuttgart.de
Key Personnel
Contact: Marion Kadura *Tel:* (0711) 216-6332
E-mail: marion.kadura@stuttgart.de
Established: 1978
Triennial award for recognition of achievement in
literature or for translation. Writers & transla-
tors from German-speaking areas are eligible.

Award: 10,000 EUR Literature, 10,000 EUR
  Translators
Presented: 2019

☆DAM Architectural Book Award
Deutsches Architekturmuseum
Schaumainkai 43, 60596 Frankfurt am Main
Tel: (069) 212-38844 *Fax:* (069) 212-37721;
  (069) 212-36386
E-mail: info.dam@stadt-frankfurt.de
Web Site: www.dam-online.de
Key Personnel
Press & Public Relations: Brita Koehler
  Tel: (069) 212-31318 *Fax:* (069) 212-36386
  E-mail: brita.koehler@stadt-frankfurt.de
Established: 2009
Annual honorary award given to multiple authors.
  Categories: Architecture Monographs; Exhi-
  bition Catalogues; Anthologies; Architectural
  Photography; Cities/Urban Planning; Landscape
  Design; Art of Engineering; Architecture Edu-
  cation.

Deutscher Buchpreis (German Book Prize)
Boersenverein des Deutschen Buchhandels eV
  (German Publishers & Booksellers Association)
Grosser Hirschgraben 17-21, 60311 Frankfurt am
  Main
Tel: (069) 1306 471 *Fax:* (069) 1306 435
E-mail: info@boev.de; buchpreis@boev.de
Web Site: www.deutscher-buchpreis.de; www.
  boersenverein.de
Key Personnel
Contact: Philippe Genet *Tel:* (069) 1306 391
  Fax: (069) 1306 295 *E-mail:* genet@boev.de;
  Susanne Hilf *Tel:* (069) 1306 334 *Fax:* (069)
  1306 295 *E-mail:* hilf@boev.de
Awarded annually for the best German language
  novel.
Presented: Kaisersaal of Frankfurts Roemer, Oct 4

Deutscher Jugendliteraturpreis (German Youth
  Literature Award)
Arbeitskreis fuer Jugendliteratur eV (Working
  Group for Youth Literature)
Metzstr 14c, 81667 Munich
Tel: (089) 45 80 806 *Fax:* (089) 45 80 80 88
E-mail: info@jugendliteratur.org
Web Site: www.jugendliteratur.org
Key Personnel
Project Manager: Kristina Bernd *E-mail:* bernd@
  jugendliteratur.org
Established: 1956
Annual award for outstanding works of children's
  & youth literature in the following categories:
  picture book, children's books, books for young
  people & nonfiction.
Other Sponsor(s): Bundesministerium fuer Fami-
  lie; Frauen & Jugend; Senioren
Award: 8,000 EUR per category

Alfred Doeblin Preis
Akademie der Kuenste, Berlin
Pariser Platz 4, 10117 Berlin
Mailing Address: Postfach 210250, 10502 Berlin
Tel: (030) 200 57-0; (030) 200 57-1000
  Fax: (030) 200 57-1702
E-mail: info@adk.de
Web Site: www.adk.de
Key Personnel
President: Klaus Staeck
Established: 1983
Awarded biennially for unpublished work of an
  epic nature.
Award: Up to 12,000 EUR

Konrad-Duden-Preis
Stadt Mannheim
Bibliographisches Institut AG, Dudenverlag, Du-
  den Str 6, 68167 Mannheim
Tel: (0621) 3901-01

E-mail: kundenservice@duden.de
Web Site: www.duden.de/ueber_duden/konrad-
  duden/konrad-duden-preis
Established: 1959
Awarded biennially to personalities who have par-
  ticularly contributed to the German language.
  The award is noncompetitive.
Award: 12,500 EUR
Presented: March

**Sigmund Freud Preis Fuer Wissenschaftliche
  Prosa** (Sigmund Freud Award for Scientific
  Prose)
Deutsche Akademie fuer Sprache und Dichtung
  (German Academy for Language & Literature)
Glueckert-Haus, Alexandraweg 23, 64287 Darm-
  stadt
Tel: (06151) 4092-0 *Fax:* (06151) 4092-99
E-mail: sekretariat@deutscheakademie.de
Web Site: www.deutscheakademie.de
Key Personnel
General Secretary: Dr Bernd Busch
  E-mail: bernd.busch@deutscheakademie.de
Press & Public Relations: Corinna Blattmann
  Tel: (06151) 4092-16 *E-mail:* corinna.
  blattmann@deutscheakademie.de
Publications & Editing: Michael Assmann
  Tel: (06151) 4092-17 *E-mail:* michael.
  assmann@deutscheakademie.de
Established: 1964
Award: 12,500 EUR
Presented: Autumn annually

Friedenspreis des Deutschen Buchhandels
  (Peace Prize of the German Book Trade)
Boersenverein des Deutschen Buchhandels eV
  (German Publishers & Booksellers Association)
Geschaeftsstelle Friedenspreis des Deutschen
  Buchhandels, Schiffbauerdamm 5, 10117 Berlin
Tel: (030) 2800 783-44 *Fax:* (030) 2800 783-50
Web Site: www.friedenspreis-des-deutschen-
  buchhandels.de
Key Personnel
Chief Executive Officer: Alexander Skipis
  E-mail: skipis@boev.de
Contact: Martin Schult *E-mail:* m.schult@boev.de
Established: 1950
The prize is an amount made up exclusively of
  donations from publishers & booksellers. The
  Peace Prize is an impressive indication of the
  book trade's commitment to serve interna-
  tional understanding by its activities. Gener-
  ally awarded annually & can also be granted
  posthumously.
Award: 25,000 EUR
Presented: The Frankfurt Book Fair, Autumn

**Friedrich-Gundolf Preis fuer die Vermittlung
  Deutscher Kultur im Ausland** (Friedrich
  Gundolf Prize for the Mediation of German
  Culture Abroad)
Deutsche Akademie fuer Sprache und Dichtung
  (German Academy for Language & Literature)
Glueckert-Haus, Alexandraweg 23, 64287 Darm-
  stadt
Tel: (06151) 4092-0 *Fax:* (06151) 4092-99
E-mail: sekretariat@deutscheakademie.de
Web Site: www.deutscheakademie.de
Key Personnel
General Secretary: Dr Bernd Busch
  E-mail: bernd.busch@deutscheakademie.de
Press & Public Relations: Corinna Blattmann
  Tel: (06151) 4092-16 *E-mail:* corinna.
  blattmann@deutscheakademie.de
Publications & Editing: Michael Assmann
  Tel: (06151) 4092-17 *E-mail:* michael.
  assmann@deutscheakademie.de
Established: 1964
To reward excellence in teaching & dissemination
  of German language & literature abroad.
Award: 12,500 EUR
Presented: Spring annually

**Friedrich Gerstaecker Preis fuer
  Juegendliteratur** (Friederich Gerstacker Award
  for Youth Literature)
Stadt Braunschweig
Kulturinstitut, Schlossplatz 1, 38100 Braun-
  schweig
Fax: (0531) 4 70 48 09
E-mail: kulturinstitut@braunschweig.de
Web Site: www.braunschweig.de/friedrich-
  gerstaecker-preis
Key Personnel
Contact: Dr Annette Boldt-Stuelzebach
  Tel: (0531) 4 70 48 40 *E-mail:* annette.boldt-
  stuelzebach@braunschweig.de; Roland Tiede-
  mann *Tel:* (0531) 4 70 48 20 *E-mail:* roland.
  tiedemann@braunschweig.de
Established: 1952
Award: 6,500 EUR awarded biennially
Presented: Brunswick Old Town Hall

Global Illustration Award (GIA)
Frankfurt Book Fair
Braubachstr 16, 60311 Frankfurt am Main
Tel: (069) 2102-0 *Fax:* (069) 2102-277
E-mail: press@book-fair.com
Web Site: www.buchmesse.de; www.book-fair.
  com
Key Personnel
Press & Corporate Communications: Katja
  Boehne *Tel:* (069) 2102-138
Public Relations Manager: Kathrin Gruen
  Tel: (069) 2102-170 *E-mail:* gruen@book-
  fair.com
Established: 2015
International prize for illustrators. Open to both
  digital & print media.
Other Sponsor(s): International Information Con-
  tent Industry Association (ICIA)
Award: 30,000 EUR prize fund, 10,000 EUR top
  prize
Closing Date: June
Presented: Frankfurt Book Fair, annually

Johann-Peter-Hebel-Preis
Ministerium fuer Wissenschaft, Forschung und
  Kunst Baden-Wuerttemberg
Koenigstr 46, 70173 Stuttgart
Tel: (0711) 279-0; (0711) 279-3004 (press)
  Fax: (0711) 279-3081
E-mail: presse@mwk.bwl.de; poststelle@mwk.
  bwl.de
Web Site: www.mwk-bw.de
Established: 1936
Awarded biennially to honor writers, translators,
  essayists & journalists.
Award: 10,000 EUR
Presented: May 10

Ricarda-Huch Preis
City of Darmstadt
Kulturamt Darmstadt, Frankfurter Str 71, 64293
  Darmstadt
Tel: (06151) 13 33 37 *Fax:* (06151) 13 33 98
E-mail: info@darmstadt.de
Web Site: www.darmstadt.de
Key Personnel
Contact: Kanita Hartmann *E-mail:* kanita.
  hartmann@darmstadt.de
Established: 1978
Awarded every three years.
Award: 10,000 EUR

**Kunstpreis Berlin - Jubilaeumsstiftung
  1848/1948** (Berlin Art Prize)
Akademie der Kuenste, Berlin
Pariser Platz 4, 10117 Berlin
Mailing Address: Postfach 210250, 10502 Berlin
Tel: (030) 200 57-0; (030) 200 57-1000
  Fax: (030) 200 57-1702
E-mail: info@adk.de
Web Site: www.adk.de

Key Personnel
President: Klaus Staeck
Established: 1948
Award to honor artistic achievement & the promotion of artistic works. The award, Fontane-Preis, is made once every six years (a similar award being made in other disciplines in the intervening five years). In addition, 'encouragement' prizes of 5,000 EUR are given annually by the Akademie in each of the six disciplines, including one for literature & one for film/TV/radio work (which may be for writing).
Award: 15,000 EUR
Presented: March 18 annually

LiBeraturpreis
LiBeraturpreis eV
Steinbacher Hohl 38, 60488 Frankfurt
Tel: (0170) 4851583
Web Site: www.liberaturpreis.org
Key Personnel
Chairperson: Ingeborg Kaestner *Tel:* (069) 762116
  E-mail: ingeborg.kaestner@gmx.de
Established: 1987
Annual award exclusively to women authors from countries of the south.
Award: 500 EUR

Johann-Heinrich-Merck-Preis fuer literarische Kritik und Essay (John Heinrich Merck Award for Literary Criticism & Essay)
Deutsche Akademie fuer Sprache und Dichtung (German Academy for Language & Literature)
Glueckert-Haus, Alexandraweg 23, 64287 Darmstadt
Tel: (06151) 4092-0 *Fax:* (06151) 4092-99
E-mail: sekretariat@deutscheakademie.de
Web Site: www.deutscheakademie.de
Key Personnel
General Secretary: Dr Bernd Busch
  E-mail: bernd.busch@deutscheakademie.de
Press & Public Relations: Corinna Blattmann
  Tel: (06151) 4092-16 *E-mail:* corinna.
  blattmann@deutscheakademie.de
Publications & Editing: Michael Assmann
  Tel: (06151) 4092-17 *E-mail:* michael.
  assmann@deutscheakademie.de
Established: 1964
For promotion of individual genres (criticism & essays).
Award: 12,500 EUR
Presented: Autumn annually

Thaddaeus-Troll-Preis
Foerderkreis Deutscher Schriftsteller in Baden-Wuerttemberg eV
Neckarhalde 28, 72070 Tuebingen
E-mail: info@schriftsteller-in-bawue.de
Web Site: www.schriftsteller-in-bawue.de
Key Personnel
Contact: Vivien van Straaten
Established: 1981
Applications not accepted for this award.
Award: 10,000 EUR
Presented: Annually

Thomas-Mann-Preis der Hansestadt Luebeck und der Bayerischen Akademie der Schoenen Kuenste
Bavarian Academy of Fine Arts (Bayerischen Akademie der Schoenen Kuenste)
Max-Joseph-Platz 3, 80539 Munich
Tel: (089) 29 00 77-0 *Fax:* (089) 29 00 77-23
E-mail: info@badsk.de
Web Site: www.badsk.de
Key Personnel
Contact: Sylvia Langemann *E-mail:* langemann@badsk.de
Established: 2010
Formed from the merger of the Thomas Mann Preis of the city of Luebeck, established in

1975 & the Grosser Literaturpreis of the Bavarian Academy of Fine Arts, established in 1986.
Awarded annually.
Other Sponsor(s): Hansestadt Luebeck
Award: 25,000 EUR

Johann-Heinrich-Voss-Preis fuer Uebersetzung
(Johann Heinrich Voss Prize for Translation)
Deutsche Akademie fuer Sprache und Dichtung (German Academy for Language & Literature)
Glueckert-Haus, Alexandraweg 23, 64287 Darmstadt
Tel: (06151) 4092-0 *Fax:* (06151) 4092-99
E-mail: sekretariat@deutscheakademie.de
Web Site: www.deutscheakademie.de
Key Personnel
General Secretary: Dr Bernd Busch
  E-mail: bernd.busch@deutscheakademie.de
Press & Public Relations: Corinna Blattmann
  Tel: (06151) 4092-16 *E-mail:* corinna.
  blattmann@deutscheakademie.de
Publications & Editing: Michael Assmann
  Tel: (06151) 4092-17 *E-mail:* michael.
  assmann@deutscheakademie.de
Established: 1958
Outstanding achievements in the field of translation.
Award: 15,000 EUR
Presented: Spring annually

Walter Tiemann Prize
Hochschule fuer Grafik und Buchkunst in Leipzig (Academy of Visual Arts Leipzig)
Waechterstr 11, 04107 Leipzig
Tel: (0341) 2135-168 *Fax:* (0341) 2135-166
E-mail: wtp@hbg-leipzig.de; wtp@
  waltertiemannpreis.de
Web Site: www.hgb-leipzig.de/wtp
Key Personnel
Chairperson: Julia Blume
Established: 1992
Established in honor of Walter Tiemann, a teacher & the rector from 1920 to 1945. Awarded biennially to recognize the design achievements of typographers & illustrators.
Award: Main prize 5,000 EUR; Encouragement prize (competitors under the age of 35) 1,500 EUR
Closing Date: Nov 30
Presented: March 13

White Ravens
Internationale Jugendbibliothek (International Youth Library)
Schloss Blutenburg, 81247 Munich
Tel: (089) 89 12 11-0 *Fax:* (089) 89 12 11-38
E-mail: info@ijb.de
Web Site: www.ijb.de
Key Personnel
Dir: Dr Christiane Raabe *Tel:* (089) 89 12 11 42
  E-mail: direktion@ijb.de
Established: 1983
Awarded annually to promote high quality children's books of international interest. About 250 children's books, by authors & illustrators from all over the world, are given recognition. Children's books submitted by publishers during the year prior to the award are considered. White Ravens books are listed in the annual international selected bibliography & exhibited during the Children's Book Fair in Bologna, Italy & thereafter upon request in libraries & other institutions. Titles in over 30 languages from 50 countries.
Closing Date: Dec
Presented: Bologna Children's Book Fair, Italy, March

Kurt Wolff Stiftung
Kurt Wolff Foundation
Gerichtsweg 28, 04103 Leipzig
Tel: (0341) 962 71 87 *Fax:* (0341) 962 71 87

E-mail: info@kurt-wolff-stiftung.de
Web Site: www.kurt-wolff-stiftung.de
Key Personnel
Chairman, Executive Board: Stefan Weidle
Chairman, Board of Trustees: Joachim Kersten
Contact: Kerstin Wangemann
Awarded annually to a German or Germany-based independent publisher.
Award: 26,000 EUR
Presented: Leipzig Book Fair

Ghana

Golden Baobab Prizes for Illustrations
Golden Baobab
Ampomah House, 3rd floor, off Obasanjo Highway, Roman Ridge, Accra
Mailing Address: PO Box KD 862, Kanda, Accra
Tel: (030) 2963639
E-mail: info@goldenbaobab.org
Web Site: www.goldenbaobab.org
Key Personnel
Executive Dir: Deborah Ahenkorah
Prize Coordinator: Nanama B Acheampong
Established: 2013
Pan-African illustration prizes to find the best illustrators for African children's stories. Two prizes awarded annually: Golden Baobab Prize for Illustrators & Golden Baobab Prize for Rising Illustrators.
Award: $5,000 USD (Illustrator), including travelling exhibition; $2,500 USD (Rising Illustrator), including mentorship opportunities & travelling exhibition

Golden Baobab Prizes for Literature
Golden Baobab
Ampomah House, 3rd floor, off Obasanjo Highway, Roman Ridge, Accra
Mailing Address: PO Box KD 862, Kanda, Accra
Tel: (030) 2963639
E-mail: info@goldenbaobab.org
Web Site: www.goldenbaobab.org
Key Personnel
Executive Dir: Deborah Ahenkorah
Prize Coordinator: Nanama B Acheampong
Established: 2008
Pan-African awards to recognize & celebrate excellence in stories targeting African children. Three prizes annually: Golden Baobab Prize for Picture Book, Golden Baobab Prize for Early Chapter Book & Golden Baobab Prize for Rising Writers.
Award: $5,000 USD & publishing opportunity (Picture Book & Early Chapter Book); $2,500 USD & mentorship opportunities (Rising Writers)

Greece

Book Prizes of the Circle of the Greek Children's Book
Circle of the Greek Children's Book IBBY (Greek Section)
Bouboulinas 28, 106 82 Athens
Tel: 2108222296 *Fax:* 2108222296
E-mail: kyklos@greekibby.gr
Web Site: www.greekibby.gr
Key Personnel
President: Vagelis Iliopoulos
Vice President: Vassiliki Nika
Secretary: Maria Kourkoumeli
Treasurer: Iro Papamoschou
Established: 1970

Hong Kong (continued)

Awarded annually for various types of writing & illustrating literary books for children.
Award: 1,000 to 1,500 EUR

Hong Kong

Awards for Creative Writing in Chinese
Hong Kong Public Libraries
Leisure & Cultural Services Dept, 1-3 Pai Tau St, Sha Tin, Hong Kong
Tel: 2921 2645; 2928 4601; 2414 5555 *Fax:* 2603 4567
E-mail: enquiries@lcsd.gov.hk; hotlinelib@lcsd.gov.hk
Web Site: www.hkpl.gov.hk; www.lcsd.gov.hk
Key Personnel
Senior Librarian (Extension Activities): Sin Yiu Shun
Established: 1979
Awards for creative writing in Chinese presented biennially to residents of Hong Kong 16 years of age & over, under six categories (prose, poetry, fiction, literary criticism, children's story book & children's picture book) to cultivate interest in creative writing in Chinese.
Award: 1st prize 10,000 HKD for each category; 2nd prize 8,000 HKD for each category; 3rd prize 6,000 HKD for each category; five Merit Awards 4,000 HKD

Hong Kong Biennial Award for Chinese Literature
Hong Kong Public Libraries
Leisure & Cultural Services Dept, 1-3 Pai Tau St, Sha Tin, Hong Kong
Tel: 2921 2645; 2928 4601 *Fax:* 2881 5500
E-mail: enquiries@lcsd.gov.hk; hkcl_ref@lcsd.gov.hk
Web Site: www.hkpl.gov.hk; www.lcsd.gov.hk
Key Personnel
Senior Librarian (Extension Activities): Sin Yiu Shun
Established: 1991
Award is by open nomination to give recognition to the outstanding achievements of established Hong Kong writers to encourage them in pursuit of literary excellence & to encourage local publishers to publish quality literary books. Awards presented biennially for fiction, prose, poetry, children & young adult literature & literary criticism, published in Hong Kong in the previous two years & written in Chinese.
Award: 30,000 HKD

Hungary

Kossuth Prize
Hungarian National Assembly
Kossuth Ter 1-3, Budapest 1055
Established: 1948
An irregular award to outstanding artists, including writers.

Iceland

Icelandic Literature Prize
Felag Islenskra Bokautgefenda (Icelandic Publishers' Association)
Baronsstig 5, 101 Reykjavik

Tel: 511-8020 *Fax:* 511-5020
E-mail: fibut@fibut.is
Web Site: www.fibut.is
Key Personnel
Chairman: Egill Orn Johannsson *Tel:* 575-5600 *E-mail:* egill@forlagid.is
Vice President: Heidar Ingi Svansson *Tel:* 517-7200 *E-mail:* heidar@idnu.is
Mng Dir: Benedikt Kristjansson *Tel:* 511-8021 *E-mail:* benk@fibut.is
Annual prize awarded in 3 categories: fiction, nonfiction & children's/teen.
Presented: Jan

India

Baba Sheikh Farid Award
Haryana Punjabi Sahitya Akademi
IP 16, Sector 14, Panchkula, Chandigarh 134 113
Tel: (0172) 2583016
Key Personnel
Dir: Sukhchain Singh Bhandari
Established: 2005
Awarded annually to an Indian national domiciled in Haryana State for contributions to the development of Panjabi literature. Presented for the lifelong contribution to the Panjabi writer once in a lifetime.
Award: 100,000 INR
Closing Date: July 31

Babu Balmukund Gupt Award (Hindi Journalism)
Haryana Sahitya Akademi
Sector 14, Panchkula, Haryana 134 113
Tel: (0172) 2565521 *Fax:* (0172) 2565521
Key Personnel
Dir: Radhe Shyam Sharma *E-mail:* director_hsa@yahoo.com
Awarded annually to an Indian national domiciled in Haryana State for outstanding contribution to development of Hindi Journalism.
Award: 50,000 INR
Closing Date: July 31

Babu Balmukund Gupt Award (Hindi Literature)
Haryana Sahitya Akademi
Sector 14, Panchkula, Haryana 134 113
Tel: (0172) 2565521 *Fax:* (0172) 2565521
Key Personnel
Dir: Radhe Shyam Sharma *E-mail:* director_hsa@yahoo.com
Awarded annually to an Indian national domiciled in Haryana State for outstanding contribution to development of Hindi Literature.
Award: 50,000 INR
Closing Date: July 31

I C Chacko Award
Kerala Sahitya Akademi
Thrissur, Kerala 680 020
Tel: (0487) 2331069 *Fax:* (0487) 2331069
E-mail: keralasahityaakademi@gmail.com
Web Site: www.keralasahityaakademi.org
Awarded annually for the best book published in Malayalam during the preceding three years in the field of linguistics.
Award: 2,000 INR

DSC Prize for South Asian Literature
DSC Ltd
3rd floor, K5-K9, Sector 18, Noida 201 301
Tel: (0120) 3062336; (0120) 3062337
E-mail: admin@dscprize.com
Web Site: dscprize.com
Established: 2010

Celebrates achievements of South Asian writers & aims to raise awareness of South Asian culture around the world.
Award: 50,000 USD

Haryana Gaurav Award
Haryana Sahitya Akademi
Sector 14, Panchkula, Haryana 134 113
Tel: (0172) 2565521 *Fax:* (0172) 2565521
Key Personnel
Dir: Radhe Shyam Sharma *E-mail:* director_hsa@yahoo.com
Awarded annually to an Indian national born in Haryana & living outside of the State for outstanding contributions to development of Hindi Literature.
Award: 51,000 INR
Closing Date: July 31

Jnanpith Award
Bharatiya Jnanpith
18, Institutional Area, Lodhi Rd, New Delhi 110 003
Mailing Address: PB 3113, New Delhi 110 003
Tel: (011) 24626467; (011) 24654196; (011) 24656201; (011) 24698417 *Fax:* (011) 24654197
E-mail: jnanpith@satyam.net.in; sales@jnanpith.net
Web Site: jnanpith.net
Key Personnel
Chairman: Dr Sitakant Mahapatra
Established: 1965
Best creative literary writing by any Indian citizen in any of the languages included in the VIII schedule of the Indian constitution.

Kerala Sahitya Akademi Awards
Kerala Sahitya Akademi
Thrissur, Kerala 680 020
Tel: (0487) 2331069 *Fax:* (0487) 2331069
E-mail: keralasahityaakademi@gmail.com
Web Site: www.keralasahityaakademi.org
Annual awards for literary works in Malayalam published during the preceding three years, in the following categories: fiction; drama; poetry; short stories; novels; literary criticism; (biography; autobiography; travelogs & humor); scientific & scholarly works (including philosophy; education; sociology).
Award: 20,000, citation & plaque

C B Kumar Award
Kerala Sahitya Akademi
Thrissur, Kerala 680 020
Tel: (0487) 2331069 *Fax:* (0487) 2331069
E-mail: keralasahityaakademi@gmail.com
Web Site: www.keralasahityaakademi.org
Annual award for the best collection of essays in Malayalam.
Award: 1,500 INR

Kuttipuzha Krishnanpillai Award
Kerala Sahitya Akademi
Thrissur, Kerala 680 020
Tel: (0487) 2331069 *Fax:* (0487) 2331069
E-mail: keralasahityaakademi@gmail.com
Web Site: www.keralasahityaakademi.org
Awarded annually for the best book of criticism published in Malayalam during the preceding three years.
Award: 2,000 INR

K R Namboodiri Award
Kerala Sahitya Akademi
Thrissur, Kerala 680 020
Tel: (0487) 2331069 *Fax:* (0487) 2331069
E-mail: keralasahityaakademi@gmail.com
Web Site: www.keralasahityaakademi.org
Awarded annually for the best work on Vedic literature in Malayalam.
Award: 2,000 INR

Raagi/Dhaadi Lok Gayak Award
Haryana Punjabi Sahitya Akademi
IP 16, Sector 14, Panchkula, Chandigarh 134 113
Tel: (0172) 2583016
Key Personnel
Dir: Sukhchain Singh Bhandari
Established: 2005
Awarded annually to an Indian national domiciled
in Haryana State for contributions to the devel-
opment of Panjabi literature. Presented for the
lifelong contribution to the Panjabi writer once
in a lifetime.
Award: 21,000 INR
Closing Date: July 31

Sahitya Akademi Award
Sahitya Akademi (National Academy of Letters)
Rabindra Bhavan, 35, Ferozeshah Rd, New Delhi
110 001
Tel: (011) 23386626; (011) 23386627; (011)
23386628 *Fax:* (011) 23382428
Web Site: sahitya-akademi.gov.in
Established: 1954
For outstanding literary works written in each of
the 24 languages of India recognized by the
Indian National Academy of Letters (Sahitya
Akademi). Awarded annually to Indian nation-
als only.
Award: 100,000 INR each & a plaque
Closing Date: Dec annually
Presented: New Delhi, Feb annually

Urdu Akademi Awards
Urdu Akademi Delhi
CP Bldg, Kashmiri Gate, New Delhi 110 006
Tel: (011) 23863729 (ext 32)
E-mail: urduacademydelhi@yahoo.co.in
Key Personnel
Program Officer: Mohd Shamin
Awarded annually to Indian nationals for Urdu
literature.
Award: 50,000 INR

Iran

Children's Book Council Award (Jayeze-ye
Shora-ye Ketab-e Koodak/Ketab-e bargozideh)
Children's Book Council of Iran
PO Box 13145-133, Tehran 1417753991
Tel: (021) 66408074; (021) 66492721 *Fax:* (021)
66405878; (021) 66415878
E-mail: info@cbc.ir
Web Site: www.cbc.ir; www.cbc.ir/en (English)
Key Personnel
General Secretary: Noushine Ansari
Established: 1971
Given annually for recognition of a contribution
in the field of children's literature. Iranian writ-
ers, illustrators & translations are eligible. Es-
tablished by A Yamini Sharif.
Award: A bronze plaque is awarded annually
Presented: CBCI Annual Founding Day Celebra-
tion, Jan

Ireland

Aosdana Membership
The Arts Council/An Chomhairle Ealaion
70 Merrion Sq, Dublin D02 NY52
Tel: (01) 618 0200 *Fax:* (01) 676 1302
E-mail: aosdana@artscouncil.ie
Web Site: www.artscouncil.ie
Key Personnel
Dir: Orlaith McBride *Tel:* (01) 618 0225

Established: 1981
Special honorary affiliation of creative artists. To
be eligible for membership, the artist must have
been born in Ireland or been a resident of Ireland for five years & must have produced a
distinguished body of work. Membership is by
peer nomination & election.
Award: Annuities up to 17,120 EUR
Closing Date: Nominations on an annual basis

Fish Poetry Prize
Fish Publishing
Durrus, Bantry, Co Cork
E-mail: info@fishpublishing.com
Web Site: www.fishpublishing.com
Key Personnel
Dir: Clem Cairns; Jula Walton
Established: 2006
Prize for the best ten poems written in English.
All published in annual Fish Anthology.
Other Sponsor(s): Arts Council of Ireland
Award: 1st prize 1,000 EUR; 2nd prize week at
Anam Cara Writers' & Artists' Retreat & 300
EUR traveling expense
Closing Date: March 30
Presented: West Cork Literary Festival, July

Fish Short Story Prize
Fish Publishing
Durrus, Bantry, Co Cork
E-mail: info@fishpublishing.com
Web Site: www.fishpublishing.com
Key Personnel
Dir: Clem Cairns; Jula Walton
Established: 1995
Prize for the best short story of 5,000 words or
less written in English. Best ten stories pub-
lished in annual Fish Anthology.
Other Sponsor(s): Arts Council of Ireland
Award: 1st prize 3,000 EUR; 2nd prize week at
Anam Cara Writers' & Artists' Retreat & 300
EUR traveling expense; 3rd prize 300 EUR
Closing Date: Nov 30 annually
Presented: West Cork Literary Festival, July

International Dublin Literary Award
Dublin City Council
Dublin City Library & Archive, 138-144 Pearse
St, Dublin 2
Tel: (01) 674 4802 *Fax:* (01) 674 4879
E-mail: literaryaward@dublincity.ie
Web Site: www.dublinliteraryaward.ie
Established: 1994
Annual award open to works of fiction written in
or translated into English & published within a
specified period of time. Nominations are made
by selected libraries in capital & major cities
throughout the world. Participating libraries
can nominate up to 3 books each year for the
award. Books must meet the criteria for eligibility which are distributed to libraries each
year.
Administered by Dublin City Public Libraries.
Award: 100,000 EUR to author if book in English; 75,000 EUR to author & 25,000 EUR to
translator if book in English translation

The Frank O'Connor International Short
Story Award
Munster Literature Centre
Frank O'Connor House, 84 Douglas St, Cork
Tel: (021) 4312955
E-mail: munsterlit@eircom.net
Web Site: www.frankoconnor-shortstory-award.net
Annual award for a short story collection. Prize
is awarded to the author of the book judged
to be the best collection of stories published
in English for the first time between July 1 of
the prior year & June 30 of the current year.
Translations are eligible.
Other Sponsor(s): Cork City Council; School of
English, University College Cork

Award: 25,000 EUR
Presented: Early July

One-Page Story Prize
Fish Publishing
Durrus, Bantry, Co Cork
E-mail: info@fishpublishing.com
Web Site: www.fishpublishing.com
Key Personnel
Dir: Clem Cairns; Jula Walton
Established: 2004
Prize for the best story of 300 words or less writ-
ten in English. Best ten stories published in
annual Fish Anthology.
Other Sponsor(s): Arts Council of Ireland
Award: 1,000 EUR
Closing Date: March 20
Presented: West Cork Literary Festival, July

Israel

Award for Original Hebrew Novel
Mordechai Bernstein Literary Prizes Association
c/o The Book Publishers Association of Israel, 29
Carlebach St, 67132 Tel Aviv
Mailing Address: PO Box 20123, 61201 Tel Aviv
Tel: (03) 5614121 *Fax:* (03) 5611996
E-mail: info@tbpai.co.il; hamol@tbpai.co.il
Web Site: www.tbpai.co.il
Key Personnel
Mng Dir: Amnon Ben-Shmuel
Established: 1981
Annual award to encourage authors under the age
50 who write Hebrew novels. Established to
honor Mordechai Bernstein, an Israeli author.
Award: 50,000 NIS
Closing Date: Jan 31

Award for Original Hebrew Poetry
Mordechai Bernstein Literary Prizes Association
c/o The Book Publishers Association of Israel, 29
Carlebach St, 67132 Tel Aviv
Mailing Address: PO Box 20123, 61201 Tel Aviv
Tel: (03) 5614121 *Fax:* (03) 5611996
E-mail: info@tbpai.co.il; hamol@tbpai.co.il
Web Site: www.tbpai.co.il
Key Personnel
Mng Dir: Amnon Ben-Shmuel
Established: 1981
Biennial award to encourage Hebrew poets un-
der the age of 50. Established in honor of
Mordechai Bernstein, an Israeli author.
Award: 25,000 NIS

☆The Jerusalem Prize
Jerusalem International Book Forum
PO Box 775, 91007 Jerusalem
Tel: (02) 629 6415 *Fax:* (02) 624 0663
E-mail: jerfair@jerusalem.muni.il
Web Site: www.jerusalembookfair.com
Established: 1963
Biennial award made to a world-renowned author
whose works express the idea of the freedom
of the individual in society.
Award: 10,000 USD
Presented: Jerusalem International Book Fair

Italy

Bagutta Prize
Bagutta Restaurant
Zona Centro, via Bagutta 14, 20121 Milan MI
Tel: (02) 76000902; (02) 76002767 *Fax:* (02)
799613

E-mail: segreteria@bagutta.it; premiobagutta@
  hotmail.com
Web Site: www.bagutta.it/let; www.acena.it/
  bagutta
Established: 1927
Annual award given for several literary forms in-
  cluding fiction, nonfiction & poetry.
Award: 12,500 EUR
Presented: Jan

☆BolognaRagazzi Award
Bologna Children's Book Fair
Piazza Costituzione, 6, 40128 Bologna BO
Tel: (051) 282111
E-mail: bolognaragazziaward@bolognafiere.it
Web Site: www.bookfair.bolognafiere.it
Key Personnel
President: Antonio Faeti
Established: 1966
Prizes awarded to the best books in terms of
  graphic & editorial design. Four categories:
  Fiction, Nonfiction, New Horizons (Arab coun-
  tries, Latin America, Asia & Africa) & Opera
  Prima (artists' first works).
Closing Date: Jan 31

Isle of Elba - Raffaello Brignetti Literary Award
Premio Letterario Isola d'Elba - Raffaello
  Brignetti
Via R Manganaro, 142, 57037 Portoferraio LI
Tel: (0565) 918-316 (cell)
E-mail: premioletterarioelba@gmail.com
Web Site: www.premioletterario.org
Established: 1962
Annual award to a work of fiction, poetry or non-
  fiction. Works by European authors published
  in Italy or translated into Italian during the pre-
  vious year (Feb-March) are eligible. Formerly
  Premio Letterario Isola d'Elba. Renamed in
  1984 in honor of Raffaello Brignetti.
Award: 6,000 EUR
Closing Date: April
Presented: July 14

Premio Campiello Europe
Campiello Foundation
Via Torino 151/c, 30172 Mestre VE
Tel: (041) 2517511 *Fax:* (041) 2517576
E-mail: info@premiocampiello.org
Web Site: www.premiocampiello.org
Key Personnel
President: Andrea Tomat
Established: 2005
Award for a contemporary novel published in
  Italy & translated into the language of the host
  European country. Award given also to the pub-
  lisher & translator.

Campiello Giovani
Campiello Foundation
Via Torino 151/c, 30172 Mestre VE
Tel: (041) 2517511 *Fax:* (041) 2517576
E-mail: info@premiocampiello.org
Web Site: www.premiocampiello.org
Key Personnel
President: Andrea Tomat
Established: 1994
Literary competition for young writers 15-22
  years of age for a story on any subject in Ital-
  ian.

Premio Campiello Letteratura (Campiello Literary Prize)
Campiello Foundation
Via Torino 151/c, 30172 Mestre VE
Tel: (041) 2517511 *Fax:* (041) 2517576
E-mail: info@premiocampiello.org
Web Site: www.premiocampiello.org
Key Personnel
President: Andrea Tomat

Established: 1962
Promoted by the seven industrial association
  founder members of Fondazione Campiello.
  Annual award for a previously unpublished
  work of fiction.
Award: 8,263 EUR
Presented: Italian Institute of Culture, Feb 10

Concorso Internazionale di Poesia Castello di Duino (International Poetry Prize Castello di Duino)
Ibiskos Editrice di A Risolo
Via Matteotti 21, 34138 Trieste TS
Tel: (040) 638787
Web Site: www.castellodiduinopoesia.it
Key Personnel
Contact: Gabriella Valera Gruber
  E-mail: valeragruber@alice.it
Poetry competition for young people under 30
  years of age.
Award: 1st, 2nd & 3rd prize: 500 EUR
Closing Date: Jan 7

Castello-Sanguinetto Prize
Comune di Sanguinetto
Via Interno Castello, 2, 37058 Sanguinetto VR
Tel: (0442) 81036 *Fax:* (0442) 365150
E-mail: info@comune.sanguinetto.vr.it; cultura@
  comune.sanguinetto.vr.it
Web Site: www.comune.sanguinetto.vr.it
Established: 1951
Awarded annually to encourage the development
  of novels for young readers between 10 & 15
  years of age. The novel must be published in
  Italy before July 15 of the current year. Estab-
  lished by Prof Giulletto Accordi.
Other Sponsor(s): Cassa di Risparmio di Verona -
  Vicenza e Belluno
Award: 1st prize 2,500 EUR; 2nd prize 500 EUR
Presented: Jan 27

Certamen Capitolinum
Istituto Nazionale di Studi Romani
Piazza dei Cavalieri di Malta, 2, 00153 Rome
  RM
Tel: (06) 574 34 42 *Fax:* (06) 574 34 47
E-mail: studiromani@studiromani.it
Web Site: www.studiromani.it
Key Personnel
Dir: Letizia Lanzetta *E-mail:* lanzetta@
  studiromani.it
Established: 1954
Awarded annually to provide recognition for the
  best works on the Latin language & literature.
  Teachers, scholars & students are eligible.
Award: 1st prize 500 EUR & a silver sculpture
  of a she-wolf; 2nd prize 200 EUR & a silver
  medallion; 3rd prize 100 EUR & a diploma (to
  students); Honorable Mentions

☆Antonio Feltrinelli Prize
Accademia Nazionale dei Lincei (National Italian
  Academy of Sciences)
Palazzo Corsini, Via della Lungara, 10, 00165
  Rome RM
Tel: (06) 680271 *Fax:* (06) 6893616
E-mail: segreteria@lincei.it
Web Site: www.lincei.it
Annual prizes for accomplishment in the various
  branches of sciences, humanities & literature.
  These prizes were instituted by an Italian busi-
  nessman who died in 1942 & bequeathed his
  fortune to the academy for the purpose of "re-
  warding toil, study, intelligence...those men
  who with greater success distinguished themselves with high achievements in art & science,
  since they are the true benefactors of their own
  country as well as of all humanity". The literature award is granted every five years & the
  amount varies.
Award: 5,000 EUR

Closing Date: Mar 31
Presented: June

☆Premio Napoli
Fondazione Premio Napoli
Palazzo Reale, Piazza del Plebiscito, 80132
  Naples NA
Tel: (081) 403187; (081) 422362 *Fax:* (081)
  402023
E-mail: fondazione@premionapoli.it
Web Site: www.premionapoli.it
Key Personnel
President: Gabriele Frasca *E-mail:* frasca@
  premionapoli.it
Established: 1961
Annual award for recognition of an outstanding
  work of literature in Italian. Italian & non-
  Italian authors are eligible. The award is di-
  vided into two sections: Italian literature &
  literature.
Award: 5,000 EUR each

Premio Letterario Viareggio-Repaci
Ufficio Cultura del Comune di Viareggio
Villa Paolina Bonaparte, Via Machiavelli, 2,
  55049 Viareggo LU
Tel: (0584) 966342 *Fax:* (0584) 961076
Web Site: www.premioletterarioviareggiorepaci.it
Key Personnel
President: Simona Costa *E-mail:* scosta@
  uniroma3.it
Established: 1929
Dedicated to works written in Italian by Italian
  national authors, published in the period from
  June 1 of the previous year to May 31 of the
  year of the award. Three sections: fiction, po-
  etry & books.
Award: 12,911 EUR

Premio Strega Europeo
Fondazione Marie e Goffredo Bellonci
Via Fratelli Ruspoli, 2, 00198 Rome RM
Tel: (06) 85358119
E-mail: info@fondazionebellonci.it
Web Site: www.fondazionebellonci.it;
  premiostrega.it/PSE
Key Personnel
President: Giovanni Solimine
Dir: Stefano Petrocchi
Established: 2014
Awarded annually for the best translated work of
  contemporary fiction.
Award: 3,000 EUR; 1,500 EUR to translator

Premio Strega Giovani
Fondazione Marie e Goffredo Bellonci
Via Fratelli Ruspoli, 2, 00198 Rome RM
Tel: (06) 85358119
E-mail: info@fondazionebellonci.it
Web Site: www.fondazionebellonci.it;
  premiostrega.it/PSG
Key Personnel
President: Giovanni Solimine
Dir: Stefano Petrocchi
Established: 2014
Recognizes contemporary Italian fiction among
  young adults. Prize is awarded by a jury of stu-
  dents ages 16-18.
Presented: Palazzo Montecitorio, Rome

Premio Strega
Fondazione Marie e Goffredo Bellonci
Via Fratelli Ruspoli, 2, 00198 Rome RM
Tel: (06) 85358119
E-mail: info@fondazionebellonci.it
Web Site: www.fondazionebellonci.it; www.
  premiostrega.it
Key Personnel
President: Giovanni Solimine
Dir: Stefano Petrocchi
Established: 1947

Founded by Maria Bellonci & Guido Alberti. Awarded annually to a single book of narrative prose by an Italian, published between May 1 last year & April 30 this year.

Premio Strega Ragazze e Ragazzi
Fondazione Marie e Goffredo Bellonci
Via Fratelli Ruspoli, 2, 00198 Rome RM
Tel: (06) 85358119
E-mail: info@fondazionebellonci.it
Web Site: www.fondazionebellonci.it; www. premiostrega.it/PSR
Key Personnel
President: Giovanni Solimine
Dir: Stefano Petrocchi
Established: 2016
Awarded annually to children's fiction books published in Italy, also in translation, between April 1 of the previous year & March 31 of the current year. Two categories: books for readers 6-10 years of age & books for readers 11-15 years of age.
Closing Date: Sept
Presented: March

Japan

Kodansha Essay Award
Kodansha Ltd
2-12-21 Otowa, Bunkyo-ku, Tokyo 112-8001
Web Site: www.kodansha.co.jp
Established: 1985
Annual award for the best essay.
Award: 1,000,000 JPY

Kodansha Manga Awards
Kodansha Ltd
2-12-21 Otowa, Bunkyo-ku, Tokyo 112-8001
Web Site: www.kodansha.co.jp
Award: 1,000,000 JPY each, varying categories

Kodansha Nonfiction Award
Kodansha Ltd
2-12-21 Otowa, Bunkyo-ku, Tokyo 112-8001
Web Site: www.kodansha.co.jp
Established: 1979
Annual award for the best nonfiction work.
Award: 1,000,000 JPY

Kodansha Publishing Culture Award for Book Design
Kodansha Ltd
2-12-21 Otowa, Bunkyo-ku, Tokyo 112-8001
Web Site: www.kodansha.co.jp
Award: 1,000,000 JPY

Kodansha Publishing Culture Award for Illustrations
Kodansha Ltd
2-12-21 Otowa, Bunkyo-ku, Tokyo 112-8001
Web Site: www.kodansha.co.jp
Established: 1970
Awarded annually to the best work of illustration.
Award: 1,000,000 JPY

Kodansha Publishing Culture Award for Photography
Kodansha Ltd
2-12-21 Otowa, Bunkyo-ku, Tokyo 112-8001
Web Site: www.kodansha.co.jp
Award: 1,000,000 JPY

Kodansha Publishing Culture Award for Picture Books
Kodansha Ltd
2-12-21 Otowa, Bunkyo-ku, Tokyo 112-8001

Web Site: www.kodansha.co.jp
Established: 1970
Awarded annually for the most outstanding picture book.
Award: 1,000,000 JPY

Noma Award for the Translation of Japanese Literature
Kodansha Ltd
2-12-21 Otowa, Bunkyo-ku, Tokyo 112-8001
Web Site: www.kodansha.co.jp
Established: 1990
For the best translation of a post-1926 Japanese novel or essay.
Other Sponsor(s): Noma Cultural Foundation
Award: 10,000 USD

Noma Prize for Children's Literature
Kodansha Ltd
2-12-21 Otowa, Bunkyo-ku, Tokyo 112-8001
Web Site: www.kodansha.co.jp
Established: 1963
Annual award for the best juvenile novel.
Other Sponsor(s): Noma Cultural Foundation
Award: 2,000,000 JPY

Noma Prize for Literature
Kodansha Ltd
2-12-21 Otowa, Bunkyo-ku, Tokyo 112-8001
Web Site: www.kodansha.co.jp
Established: 1941
Annual award for the best Japanese novel of the year.
Other Sponsor(s): Noma Cultural Foundation
Award: 3,000,000 JPY

Noma Prize for New Writers
Kodansha Ltd
2-12-21 Otowa, Bunkyo-ku, Tokyo 112-8001
Web Site: www.kodansha.co.jp
Established: 1979
Annual award for the best novel by a new writer.
Other Sponsor(s): Noma Cultural Foundation
Award: 1,000,000 JPY

Oya Soichi Nonfiction Prize
The Society for the Promotion of Japanese Literature
Bungei Shunju Bldg, 3-23 Kioi-cho, Chiyoda-ku, Tokyo 102-8008
Tel: (03) 3265-1211 *Fax:* (03) 3265-2624
E-mail: i-shinko@bunshun.co.jp
Web Site: www.bunshun.co.jp/award
Key Personnel
Chief Executive Officer & President: Takahiro Hirao
Established: 1969
Annual award to encourage new nonfiction writers.
Award: 1,000,000 JPY

Yoshikawa Eiji Cultural Prize
Kodansha Ltd
2-12-21 Otowa, Bunkyo-ku, Tokyo 112-8001
Web Site: www.kodansha.co.jp
Other Sponsor(s): Yoshikawa Eiji Cultural Foundation
Award: 1,000,000 JPY

Yoshikawa Eiji Prize for Literature
Kodansha Ltd
2-12-21 Otowa, Bunkyo-ku, Tokyo 112-8001
Web Site: www.kodansha.co.jp
Established: 1967
Annual award for a popular novel.
Other Sponsor(s): Yoshikawa Eiji Cultural Foundation
Award: 3,000,000 JPY & commemorative plaque

Yoshikawa Eiji Prize for New Writers
Kodansha Ltd
2-12-21 Otowa, Bunkyo-ku, Tokyo 112-8001
Web Site: www.kodansha.co.jp
Established: 1980
Annual award to recognize the most promising work of fiction by a new writer published during the preceding year.
Other Sponsor(s): Yoshikawa Eiji Cultural Foundation
Award: 1,000,000 JPY & commemorative plaque

Kenya

Jomo Kenyatta Prize for Literature
Kenya Publishers Association
Occidental Plaza, 2nd floor, Westlands, Nairobi 00100
Mailing Address: PO Box 42767, Nairobi 00100
Tel: (020) 3752344; (0724) 255848 (cell)
Fax: (020) 3754076
E-mail: info@kenyapublishers.org
Web Site: www.kenyapublishers.org
Key Personnel
Chairperson: David Waweru
Vice Chairperson: Simon Sossion
Treasurer: John Mwazemba
Executive Officer: James Odhiambo
Established: 1974
Awarded biannually to provide recognition for an outstanding work written in the English or Swahili languages. Only Kenyan authors are eligible.
Other Sponsor(s): Text Book Centre
Award: Monetary
Closing Date: Mid-year, biannually
Presented: Nairobi International Book Fair, late Sept, biannually

Wahome Mutahi Literary Award
Kenya Publishers Association
Occidental Plaza, 2nd floor, Westlands, Nairobi 00100
Mailing Address: PO Box 42767, Nairobi 00100
Tel: (020) 3752344; (0724) 255848 (cell)
Fax: (020) 3754076
E-mail: info@kenyapublishers.org
Web Site: www.kenyapublishers.org
Key Personnel
Chairperson: David Waweru
Vice Chairperson: Simon Sossion
Treasurer: John Mwazemba
Executive Officer: James Odhiambo
Established: 2004
Biannual award to a Kenyan writer whose work is published in Kenya. Entry fee is 5,000 KES (KPA members); 10,000 KES (nonmembers).
Closing Date: April

Liechtenstein

Liechtenstein-Preis zur Foerderung junger literarischer Talente (Liechenstein Prize for the Advancement of Young Literary Talent)
Liechtenstein PEN Centre
PO Box 416, 9490 Vaduz
Tel: 232 7271 *Fax:* 232 8071
E-mail: info@pen-club.li
Web Site: www.pen-club.li
Key Personnel
President: Manfred Schlapp
Secretary: Mathias Ospelt *E-mail:* mathios@ powersurf.li
Established: 1980

For the promotion of young literary talents.
Award: 20,000 CHF

Malaysia

Anugerah Sastera Negara (National Literary
Award)
Dewan Bahasa dan Pustaka (Institute of Language
& Literature)
Jl Dewan Bahasa, 50460 Kuala Lumpur
Tel: (03) 2147 9000 *Fax:* (03) 2147 9619
Web Site: www.dbp.gov.my/lamandbp
Established: 1980
The highest governmental award to an author
writing in the national language, who has made
a major contribution to the development of the
country's literature.
Award: 60,000 MYR, publication facilities &
other benefits

Mexico

Alfonso Reyes Prize (Premio Alfonso Reyes)
El Consejo Nacional para la Cultura y las Artes,
Instituto Nacional de Bellas Artes (National
Council for Culture & the Arts, National Insti-
tute of Beautiful Arts)
Coordinacion Nacional de Literatura, Republica
de Brasil 37, Colonia Centro, 06020 Mexico,
CDMX
Tel: (0155) 26 02 19; (0155) 26 04 49
E-mail: cnl.promocion@correo.inba.gob.mx
Web Site: www.literatura.bellasartes.gob.mx
Established: 1972
Awarded by the Federal Government of Mexico
to an author of any nationality for his or her
literary output on the study of the works of Al-
fonso Reyes or on Mexico.
Award: 60,000,000 MXN

Premio de Novela Jose Ruben Romero
El Consejo Nacional para la Cultura y las Artes,
Instituto Nacional de Bellas Artes (National
Council for Culture & the Arts, National Insti-
tute of Beautiful Arts)
Coordinacion Nacional de Literatura, Republica
de Brasil 37, Colonia Centro, 06020 Mexico,
CDMX
Tel: (0155) 26 02 19; (0155) 26 04 49
E-mail: cnl.promocion@correo.inba.gob.mx
Web Site: www.literatura.bellasartes.gob.mx
Established: 1978
Annual award to recognize unpublished novels of
outstanding literary quality by authors in the
Spanish language who are residents of Mex-
ico. Works to be considered should be 80-300
pages in length. Established in memory of the
Mexican author.
Other Sponsor(s): State of Michoacan
Award: 80,000,000 MXN & certificate
Closing Date: Aug 1

Juan Rulfo First Novel Prize (Premio Juan
Rulfo Para Primera Novela)
El Consejo Nacional para la Cultura y las Artes,
Instituto Nacional de Bellas Artes (National
Council for Culture & the Arts, National Insti-
tute of Beautiful Arts)
Coordinacion Nacional de Literatura, Republica
de Brasil 37, Colonia Centro, 06020 Mexico,
CDMX
Tel: (0155) 26 02 19; (0155) 26 04 49
E-mail: cnl.promocion@correo.inba.gob.mx
Web Site: www.literatura.bellasartes.gob.mx

Established: 1980
Annual award to recognize the best first novel
by an author in the Spanish language residing
in Mexico. Works to be considered should be
120-300 pages in length. Established in memory of the Mexican author.
Other Sponsor(s): Culture of the State Government Puebla; Government of the State of Tlaxcala; National Council for Culture & the Arts;
National Institute of Fine Arts
Award: 100,000,000 MXN & certificate
Closing Date: Aug 11

**Premio Xavier Villaurrutia de Escritores para
Escritores**
El Consejo Nacional para la Cultura y las Artes,
Instituto Nacional de Bellas Artes (National
Council for Culture & the Arts, National Insti-
tute of Beautiful Arts)
Coordinacion Nacional de Literatura, Republica
de Brasil 37, Colonia Centro, 06020 Mexico,
CDMX
Tel: (0155) 26 02 19; (0155) 26 04 49
E-mail: cnl.promocion@correo.inba.gob.mx
Web Site: www.literatura.bellasartes.gob.mx
Established: 1955
Annual prizes for poetry, prose, novel, short story,
drama or essays by new or young authors.
Award: 50,000 MXN

Monaco

☆**Prix Litteraire Prince Pierre-de-Monaco**
(Prince Pierre of Monaco Literary Prize)
Prince Pierre de Monaco Foundation
4, blvd des Moulins, 98000 Monte Carlo
Tel: 98 98 85 15 *Fax:* 93 50 66 94
Web Site: www.fondationprincepierre.mc
Key Personnel
Secretary General: Jean-Charles Curau
Deputy Secretary General: Francoise Gamerdinger
  E-mail: fgamerdinger@gouv.mc
Established: 1951
Restricted to French language writers.
Award: 15,000 EUR

Netherlands

Henriette de Beaufort-prijs (Henriette de
Beaufort Prize)
Maatschappij der Nederlandse Letterkunde (Dutch
Society of Literature)
p/a Universiteitsbibliotheek, Postbus 9501, 2300
RA Leiden
Fax: (071) 5144962
E-mail: mnl@library.leidenuniv.nl
Web Site: www.
maatschappijdernederlandseletterkunde.nl
Key Personnel
Secretary: Dr Berry P M Dongelmans
Established: 1985
Awarded triennially to recognize the author of a
biographical work. Awarded alternately to a
Dutch & a Flemish author.
Award: 2,500 EUR

F Bordewijk Prize
Jan Campert Foundation
p/a Letterkundig Museum, PO Box 90515, 2509
LM The Hague
Tel: (070) 333 96 66 *Fax:* (070) 347 79 41
E-mail: info@letterkundigmuseum.nl
Web Site: www.jancampertstichting.nl

Key Personnel
Chairman: Aad Meinderts
Treasurer: Jos Joosten
Secretary: Jeanette Smit
Established: 1948
Annual award for narrative prose published in the
prior year.
Award: 5,000 EUR

Jan Campert Prize
Jan Campert Foundation
p/a Letterkundig Museum, PO Box 90515, 2509
LM The Hague
Tel: (070) 333 96 66 *Fax:* (070) 347 79 41
E-mail: info@letterkundigmuseum.nl
Web Site: www.jancampertstichting.nl
Key Personnel
Chairman: Aad Meinderts
Treasurer: Jos Joosten
Secretary: Jeanette Smit
Annual award for outstanding Dutch poetry that
was published in the previous year.
Award: 5,000 EUR

Sidney Edelstein Prize
Society for the History of Technology
c/o Eindhoven University of Technology, IPO
Bldg 231, PO Box 513, 5600 MB Eindhoven
Tel: (040) 2474641
E-mail: shot.secretariaat@tue.nl
Web Site: www.historyoftechnology.org
Key Personnel
Secretary: Jan Korsten
Established: 1968
For an outstanding scholarly book in the history
of technology published during the preceding 3
years.
Other Sponsor(s): Ruth Edelstein Barish & Fam-
ily in memory of Sidney Edelstein
Award: $3,500 & plaque
Closing Date: Annually, April 15
Presented: SHOT Annual Meeting, Annually in
Oct

Erasmus Prize
Praemium Erasmianum Foundation
Jan van Goyenkade 5, 1075 HN Amsterdam
Tel: (020) 675 27 53
Web Site: www.erasmusprijs.org
Key Personnel
Dir: Santi van Dam
Executive Secretary: Lucia Aalbers *E-mail:* l.
aalbers@erasmusprijs.org
Secretary: Maral Khajeh
Awarded annually to a person or institution that
has made an exceptional contribution to the
humanities, the social sciences or the arts, in
Europe & beyond.
Award: 150,000 EUR

Dr Wijnaendts Francken Prijs
Maatschappij der Nederlandse Letterkunde (Dutch
Society of Literature)
p/a Universiteitsbibliotheek, Postbus 9501, 2300
RA Leiden
Fax: (071) 5144962
E-mail: mnl@library.leidenuniv.nl
Web Site: www.
maatschappijdernederlandseletterkunde.nl
Key Personnel
Secretary: Dr Berry P M Dongelmans
Established: 1934
Awarded triennially for a work written in Dutch
alternately in one of following categories: (1)
essays & literary criticism, (2) cultural history.
Award: 2,500 EUR

The G H's-Gravesande Prijs
Jan Campert Foundation
p/a Letterkundig Museum, PO Box 90515, 2509
LM The Hague

Tel: (070) 333 96 66 *Fax:* (070) 347 79 41
E-mail: info@letterkundigmuseum.nl
Web Site: www.jancampertstichting.nl
Key Personnel
Chairman: Aad Meinderts
Treasurer: Jos Joosten
Secretary: Jeanette Smit
Established: 1978
For special services to literature. Awarded irregularly.
Award: 5,000 EUR

J Greshoff Prijs
Jan Campert Foundation
p/a Letterkundig Museum, PO Box 90515, 2509 LM The Hague
Tel: (070) 333 96 66 *Fax:* (070) 347 79 41
E-mail: info@letterkundigmuseum.nl
Web Site: www.jancampertstichting.nl
Key Personnel
Chairman: Aad Meinderts
Treasurer: Jos Joosten
Secretary: Jeanette Smit
Established: 1978
Biennial award for the best Dutch essay.
Award: 5,000 EUR

Nienke van Hichtum Prijs
Jan Campert Foundation
p/a Letterkundig Museum, PO Box 90515, 2509 LM The Hague
Tel: (070) 333 96 66 *Fax:* (070) 347 79 41
E-mail: info@letterkundigmuseum.nl
Web Site: www.jancampertstichting.nl
Key Personnel
Chairman: Aad Meinderts
Treasurer: Jos Joosten
Secretary: Jeanette Smit
Established: 1964
Biennial award for the best Dutch children's book.
Award: 5,000 EUR

Lucy B & C W van der Hoogt-Prijs
Maatschappij der Nederlandse Letterkunde (Dutch Society of Literature)
p/a Universiteitsbibliotheek, Postbus 9501, 2300 RA Leiden
Fax: (071) 5144962
E-mail: mnl@library.leidenuniv.nl
Web Site: www.maatschappijdernederlandseletterkunde.nl
Key Personnel
President: Peter Sigmond
Secretary: Dr Berry P M Dongelmans
Established: 1921
Awarded annually to a promising Dutch or Flemish writer.
Award: 7,500 EUR & a medal

Constantijn Huygens-prijs
Jan Campert Foundation
p/a Letterkundig Museum, PO Box 90515, 2509 LM The Hague
Tel: (070) 333 96 66 *Fax:* (070) 347 79 41
E-mail: info@letterkundigmuseum.nl
Web Site: www.jancampertstichting.nl
Key Personnel
Chairman: Aad Meinderts
Treasurer: Jos Joosten
Secretary: Jeanette Smit
Established: 1948
Annual lifetime achievement award.
Award: 10,000 EUR

ILAB Breslauer Prize for Bibliography
International League of Antiquarian Booksellers (ILAB)
c/o Distelvlinderweg 37 d, 1113 LA Diemen
Web Site: www.ilab.org; www.ilabprize.org

Key Personnel
Prize Secretary: Arnoud Gerits *Tel:* (020) 698 13 75 *Fax:* (020) 625 80 70 *E-mail:* a.gerits@inter.nl.net
Established: 1967
Awarded every four years to the author(s) of the most original & outstanding published work in the broad field of bibliography. Any aspect of bibliography (e.g. enumerative, textual, history of the book, design, binding, book trade, etc) is admitted. Certain categories are not eligible, notably catalogues of books (or exhibitions of books) intended for sale, catalogues of public libraries & translations of works appearing in another language.
Other Sponsor(s): B H Breslauer Foundation
Award: 10,000 USD

Prijs der Nederlandse Letteren
Nederlandse Taalunie (Dutch Language Union)
Lange Voorhout 19, 2514 EB The Hague
Mailing Address: Postbus 10595, 2501 HN The Hague
Tel: (070) 346 95 48 *Fax:* (070) 365 98 18
E-mail: info@taalunie.org
Web Site: www.taalunie.org; www.prijsderletteren.org
Key Personnel
General Secretary: Linde van den Bosch
Established: 1956
Triennial award to the most outstanding prose writer, essay writer, drama writer or poet writing in Dutch.
Award: 40,000 EUR

☆**Martinus Nijhoff Prijs voor Vertalingen**
(Martinus Nijhoff Prize for Translators)
Prince Bernhard Cultuurfonds
Herengracht 476, 1017 CB Amsterdam
Mailing Address: Postbus 19750, 1000 GT Amsterdam
Tel: (020) 520 6130 *Fax:* (020) 623 8499
E-mail: info@cultuurfonds.nl
Web Site: www.cultuurfonds.nl
Established: 1955
Annual award for translation of literary work into & from Dutch.
Award: 35,000 EUR

Henriette Roland Holst Prijs
Maatschappij der Nederlandse Letterkunde (Dutch Society of Literature)
p/a Universiteitsbibliotheek, Postbus 9501, 2300 RA Leiden
Fax: (071) 5144962
E-mail: mnl@library.leidenuniv.nl
Web Site: www.maatschappijdernederlandseletterkunde.nl
Key Personnel
Secretary: Dr Berry P M Dongelmans
Established: 1957
Awarded triennially for a work written in Dutch & reflecting social concerns.
Award: 2,500 EUR

☆**Jenny Smelik /IBBY Prize**
Dutch Section of the International Board on Books for Young People
Buitenzagerij 60, 1021 NR Amsterdam
Tel: (020) 8468409
E-mail: ibby-nederland@planet.nl
Web Site: duijx.net/ibby
Key Personnel
President: Helma van Lierop-Debrauwer
Secretary: Toin Duijx
Established: 1983
To recognize alternately an author & an illustrator of children's books who contribute to a better understanding of minorities. Selection is by nomination & application. Established by

Klasina Smelik in honor of the children's book author, Jenny Smelik-Kiggen.
Award: 2,000 EUR biennial by the Dutch section of IBBY

Theo Thijssen for Children's & Youth Literature
P C Hooft Prize Foundation
Postbus 90515, 2509 LM The Hague
Tel: (070) 3339666 *Fax:* (070) 3477941
E-mail: info@letterkundigmuseum.nl
Web Site: www.pchooftprijs.nl
Key Personnel
Secretary: Aad Meinderts
Established: 1947
Triennial award for lifetime achievement for children's literature.
Award: 60,000 EUR

New Zealand

Russell Clark Award
New Zealand Library Association Inc t/a LIANZA
Stephenson & Turner House, Level 4, 156-158 Victoria St, Wellington 6011
Mailing Address: PO Box 12212, Thorndon, Wellington 6144
Tel: (04) 801 5542 *Fax:* (04) 801 5543
E-mail: admin@lianza.org.nz
Web Site: www.lianza.org.nz
Key Personnel
Children's Book Awards Coordinator: Wendy Walker *E-mail:* wendy@lianza.org.nz
Established: 1975
Annual award for the most distinguished illustrations for a children's book. Illustrator must be a citizen or resident of New Zealand.
Award: Medal & 1,000 NZD

Esther Glen Award
New Zealand Library Association Inc t/a LIANZA
Stephenson & Turner House, Level 4, 156-158 Victoria St, Wellington 6011
Mailing Address: PO Box 12212, Thorndon, Wellington 6144
Tel: (04) 801 5542 *Fax:* (04) 801 5543
E-mail: admin@lianza.org.nz
Web Site: www.lianza.org.nz
Key Personnel
Children's Book Awards Coordinator: Wendy Walker *E-mail:* wendy@lianza.org.nz
Established: 1944
Annual award for the most distinguished contribution to literature for children ages 0-15 by an author who is a citizen of, or resident in, New Zealand.
Award: 1,000 NZD & Medal
Presented: Annual Conference

Elsie Locke Award
New Zealand Library Association Inc t/a LIANZA
Stephenson & Turner House, Level 4, 156-158 Victoria St, Wellington 6011
Mailing Address: PO Box 12212, Thorndon, Wellington 6144
Tel: (04) 801 5542 *Fax:* (04) 801 5543
E-mail: admin@lianza.org.nz
Web Site: www.lianza.org.nz
Key Personnel
Children's Book Awards Coordinator: Wendy Walker *E-mail:* wendy@lianza.org.nz
Established: 1986
Awarded annually for the most distinguished contribution to nonfiction writing for young peo-

ple. Author(s) must be a citizen or resident of New Zealand.
Award: 1,000 NZD & medal

Margaret Mahy Award, see Storylines Margaret Mahy Award

New Zealand Post Book Awards
Booksellers New Zealand
Level 13, Grand Arcade, 16-20 Willis St, Wellington 6100
Mailing Address: Featherston St, PO Box 25033, Wellington 6146
Tel: (04) 472 1908 *Fax:* (04) 472 1912
E-mail: awards@nzbookawards.org.nz; info@ booksellers.co.nz
Web Site: www.booksellers.co.nz
Established: 1967
For the book of the year based on: (1) quality of writing & illustrations; (2) quality of editing, design & production; (3) impact on the community. Open only to books by New Zealand authors produced by New Zealand book publishers.
Also four category awards for Fiction, Poetry, Illustrated Nonfiction & Nonfiction.
Other Sponsor(s): Creative New Zealand; New Zealand Post
Award: Book of the Year: 15,000 NZD; Category Awards: 10,000 NZD each
Presented: July

New Zealand Post Children's Book Awards
Booksellers New Zealand
Level 13, Grand Arcade, 16-20 Willis St, Wellington 6100
Mailing Address: Featherston St, PO Box 25033, Wellington 6146
Tel: (04) 472 1908 *Fax:* (04) 472 1912
E-mail: childrensawards@bookawards.org.nz; info@booksellers.co.nz
Web Site: www.booksellers.co.nz
Awarded annually to provide recognition & reward to New Zealand authors & illustrators of high-quality children's literature & are awarded in four categories: Picture Book, Nonfiction, Junior Fiction & Young Adult Fiction.
Other Sponsor(s): Creative New Zealand; New Zealand Post
Award: Book of the Year: 7,500 NZD; Picture Book Award 3,750 NZD each to author & illustrator

NZSA E H McCormick Best First Book Award for Non Fiction
Booksellers New Zealand
Level 13, Grand Arcade, 16-20 Willis St, Wellington 6100
Mailing Address: Featherston St, PO Box 25033, Wellington 6146
Tel: (04) 472 1908 *Fax:* (04) 472 1912
E-mail: awards@nzbookawards.org.nz; info@ booksellers.co.nz
Web Site: www.booksellers.co.nz
Other Sponsor(s): Book Publishers Association New Zealand; Creative New Zealand; Montana Wines; New Zealand Society of Authors
Award: 2,500 NZD

NZSA Hubert Church Best First Book Award for Fiction
Booksellers New Zealand
Level 13, Grand Arcade, 16-20 Willis St, Wellington 6100
Tel: (04) 472 1908 *Fax:* (04) 472 1912
E-mail: awards@nzbookawards.org.nz; info@ booksellers.co.nz
Web Site: www.booksellers.co.nz
Established: 1944
Annual prize for the best first book of fiction, 48 pages or more (24 pages if a work of drama),

written by a New Zealand citizen or a person resident in New Zealand for the previous five years.
Other Sponsor(s): Book Publishers Association New Zealand; Creative New Zealand; New Zealand Post; New Zealand Society of Authors
Award: 2,500 NZD

NZSA Jessie Mackay Best First Book Award for Poetry
Booksellers New Zealand
Level 13, Grand Arcade, 16-20 Willis St, Wellington 6100
Mailing Address: Featherston St, PO Box 25033, Wellington 6146
Tel: (04) 472 1908 *Fax:* (04) 472 1912
E-mail: awards@nzbookawards.org.nz; info@ booksellers.co.nz
Web Site: www.booksellers.co.nz
Established: 1940
Annual prize for the best first book of published poetry, of 24 pages or more, written by a New Zealand citizen or a person resident in New Zealand for the previous five years.
Other Sponsor(s): Book Publishers Association New Zealand; Creative New Zealand; Montana Wines; New Zealand Society of Authors
Award: 2,500 NZD

Storylines Margaret Mahy Award
Storylines Children's Literature Charitable Trust of New Zealand
PO Box 96 094, Balmoral, Auckland 1342
E-mail: childlitnz@storylines.org.nz
Web Site: www.storylines.org.nz
Key Personnel
Executive Officer: Gillian Wess *E-mail:* eo@ storylines.org.nz
Events Manager/Administrator: Vicki Cunningham
Established: 1991
Awarded annually to a person who has made a significant contribution to the broad field of children's literature & literacy. This includes writing, illustration, publishing & academic fields. Their lecture is later published in *The Inside Story* for wider dissemination.
Closing Date: Oct 31 for nominations

Norway

Bastianprisen (Bastian Prize)
Norsk Oversetterforening (The Norwegian Association of Literary Translators)
Forfatternes House, Radhusgata 7, 0151 Oslo
Mailing Address: Postboks 579 Sentrum, 0105 Oslo
Tel: 22 47 80 90
E-mail: post@translators.no
Web Site: oversetterforeningen.no
Key Personnel
Chief Executive Officer: Hilde Sveinsson *Tel:* 22 47 80 91 *E-mail:* hilde.sveinsson@translators.no
Established: 1951
Award for outstanding translation of a literary work. Awarded two prizes each year, including one for children & young people.
Award: 50,000 NOK & statuette with plaque
Closing Date: Jan 15 annually
Presented: Sept

Kultur- og kirkedepartementets priser for barne- og ungdomslitteratur (Ministry of Cultural & Church Affairs - Annual Awards on Literature for Children & Young People)
Ministry of Cultural & Church Affairs

Norsk barnebokinstitutt (NBI), Henrik Ibsens gate 110, 0255 Oslo
Mailing Address: c/o Norsk barnebokinstitutt (NBI), Postboks 2674 Solli, 0203 Oslo
Tel: 23 27 63 60 *Fax:* 23 27 63 61
E-mail: post@barnebokinstituttet.no; biblioteket@ barnebokinstituttet.no
Web Site: www.barnebokinstituttet.no
Established: 1948
Annual awards for the best books for children in the following categories: novel (ca 40,000 NOK), picture book (ca 40,000 NOK), illustrations, new-comer, translations (new Norwegian), translations (literary Norwegian), facts & comics.
Presented: National Library, Mar 12

Norske Akademis Pris Til Minne om Thorleif Dahl
Norwegian Academy for Language & Literature
Rosenborggaten 3, 0356 Oslo
Tel: 22 60 88 59
E-mail: ordet@riksmalsforbundet.no
Web Site: www.riksmalsforbundet.no
Established: 1983
Annual award in memory of Thorleif Dahl for outstanding literary or nonfiction writing in riksmal or for translations into riksmal of fiction or nonfiction literature.
Award: 100,000 NOK
Presented: Nov

Tarjei Vesaas Debutantpris
Den Norske Forfatterforening (Norwegian Authors' Union)
Postboks 327 Sentrum, 0103 Oslo
Tel: 23 35 76 20
E-mail: post@forfatterforeningen.no
Web Site: www.forfatterforeningen.no
Established: 1964
Annual award to a writer under age 35 for the best first book of prose or poetry.
Award: 30,000 NOK
Presented: Author Association's annual meeting, March/April

Pakistan

President's Award for Pride of Performance
Pakistan Ministry of Education
D-Block Ministry of Education, Islamabad
Tel: (051) 9201392; (051) 9208074 *Fax:* (051) 9203245
E-mail: minedupak@hotmail.com
Web Site: www.moe.gov.pk/adminwing2.htm
Awarded annually for notable achievements in literature, arts, sports, medicine & science.

Panama

Concurso Nacional de Literatura Ricardo Miro (Ricardo Miro National Literary Prize)
Instituto Nacional de Cultura (INAC)
Departamento de Letras, Plaza de Francia, Panama 5
Tel: 501-4952; 501-4962 *Fax:* 501-4950
E-mail: letras@inac.gob.pa
Web Site: www.inac.gob.pa
Established: 1942
Annual award in honor of Ricardo Miro to pay tribute to those who furthered the cause of learning, arts & sciences. Given in each of five sections: poetry, short story, novels, essays & theater.
Award: 3,000 PAB for each section

Closing Date: June 30
Presented: National Theater, Oct 28

Philippines

Lampara Books Children's Story Writing Contest
Lampara Publishing House Inc
83 Sgt E Rivera St, San Francisco del Monte
Brgy Manresa, 1115 Quezon City
Tel: (02) 367-6222 *Fax:* (02) 367-6222
E-mail: inquiry@lamparabooks.com.ph
Web Site: www.lamparabooks.com.ph
Key Personnel
Editorial Dept: Ms Aiko Clarizza Buduan-Salazar
Contest aims to find suitable stories for children
for publication as illustrated books. Accept en-
tries of children's stories written by Filipino
citizens of all ages. Story must be original
work, written in either Filipino/Tagalog or English, written in a way that can be divided into
14 segments, be within reading comprehension
of children ages 5-12, have significant moral
lesson & strong narrative voice. Word length
800-1,200. Theme is open & free. See ms &
submission guidelines on web site.
Award: 1st prize: 30,000 PHP; 2nd prize: 15,000
PHP; 3rd prize: 10,000 PHP
Closing Date: Dec 2
Presented: Jan 1

Lampara Books Illustrator's Prize
Lampara Publishing House Inc
83 Sgt E Rivera St, San Francisco del Monte
Brgy Manresa, 1115 Quezon City
Tel: (02) 367-6222 *Fax:* (02) 367-6222
E-mail: inquiry@lamparabooks.com.ph
Web Site: www.lamparabooks.com.ph
Key Personnel
Contact: Ms Dolor Sales
Award: 25,000 PHP
Closing Date: April 30
Presented: Announced May 12 on LPHI web site;
presentation in Sept

Don Carlos Palanca Memorial Awards for Literature
Carlos Palanca Foundation Inc
One World Sq Bldg, No 10 Upper McKinley Rd,
McKinley Town Center, 1634 Fort Bonifacio,
Taguig City
Tel: (02) 856-0808 *Fax:* (02) 856-5005
E-mail: cpawards@palancaawards.com.ph;
palancaawards@yahoo.com
Web Site: www.palancaawards.com.ph
Established: 1950
To help develop Philippine Literature by provid-
ing incentives for writers to craft their most
outstanding literary work. Open to all Filipino
citizens except current officers of the Carlos
Palanca Foundation.
Award: Cash, certificate & medals
Closing Date: April 30

Poland

Nagroda Literacka Gdynia
Miejska Biblioteka Publiczna
ul Swietojanska 141-143, 81-401 Gdynia
Tel: (58) 622 73 55 *Fax:* (58) 622 64 17
E-mail: dyrektor@mbpgdynia.pl
Web Site: www.nagrodaliterackagdynia.pl
Key Personnel
Secretary: Violetta Trella

Press Room: Cyprian Maciejewski
E-mail: nlgdynia@ambermedia.com.pl
Established: 2006
Awarded annually for authors of the best books
of the year in three categories: prose, poetry &
essays. Winner of the award may be one author
in each category.
Award: 50,000 PLN & commemorative trophy
Closing Date: Jan 31

Jan Parandowski Prize
Polish PEN Centre (Polski PEN Club)
ul Krakowskie Przedmiescie 87/89, 00-079 War-
saw
Tel: (22) 826 57 84 *Fax:* (22) 826 05 84
E-mail: penclub@penclub.com.pl
Web Site: www.penclub.com.pl/nagrody
Established: 1988
Awarded annually to commemorate Jan
Parandowski's personality & works. Every Pol-
ish author of literary merit is eligible.

☆**ZAiKS Literary Award for Translators**
Stowarzyszenie Autorow ZAiKS
ul Hipoteczna 2, 00-092 Warsaw
Tel: (22) 828 17 05 *Fax:* (22) 828 92 04
E-mail: zaiks@zaiks.org.pl; prezes@zaiks.org.pl
Web Site: www.zaiks.org.pl
Established: 1966
Awarded annually.

Portugal

Premio Literario Aquilino Ribeiro
Freguesia de Oeiras e S Juliao da Barra (Aquilino
Ribeiro Literary Prize)
Rua Marques de Pombal, 42, 2780-289 Oeiras
Tel: 214 416 464 *Fax:* 214 416 345
E-mail: geral@jf-oeiras.pt
Web Site: www.jf-oeiras.pt
Key Personnel
President: Carlos Alberto Ferreira Morgado
E-mail: presidente@jf-oeiras.pt
Biennial award to an unpublished author in one
of the following categories, as determined by
the Executive Board: Prose fiction, poetry, es-
says, short stories, or monographs.

Romania

Romanian Writers' Union Prizes
Uniunea Scriitorilor din Romania (Writers Union
of Romania)
Calea Victoriei nr 133, Sector 1, 010071
Bucharest
Tel: (021) 3165829 *Fax:* (021) 372897880
E-mail: uniunea.scriitorilor@yahoo.com
Web Site: www.uniuneascriitorilor.ro
Key Personnel
President: Nicolae Manolescu
First Vice President: Varujan Vosganian
Vice President: Gabriel Chifu
Secretary: Roxana Chioseolu
For an outstanding contribution to Romanian liter-
ature in poetry, prose, drama, literary criticism,
history of literature, literary reportage, literature
for children & youth, translations from world
literature & for a promising new literary work
by a young writer. Awarded annually (separate
prizes are awarded by Bucharest, Cluj, Jassy,
Timisoara, Craiova, Sibiu, Brasov & Tiirgu-
Mures Writers' Associations). For further information contact the appropriate Associations of
the Writers' Union of Romania.

Singapore

Epigram Books Fiction Prize
Epigram Books
1008 Toa Payoh North, 03-08, Singapore 318996
Tel: 6292 4456
E-mail: enquiry@epigrambooks.sg
Web Site: ebfp.epigrambooks.sg
Key Personnel
Publisher & Chief Executive Officer: Edmund
Wee
Established: 2015
Annual prize to promote contemporary Singapore
creative writing & to reward excellence in Sin-
gapore literature. Awarded to the Singaporean,
permanent resident or Singapore-born author
for the best manuscript of a full-length, origi-
nal & unpublished novel written in the English
language. See web site to download official en-
try form, rules, regulations & manuscript style
guidelines.
Award: $25,000 SGD for the winner, $5,000 SGD
for 3 shortlisted finalists
Closing Date: Sept 1

Singapore Literature Prize
National Book Development Council of Singa-
pore
c/o Geylang East Public Library, 50 Geylang East
Ave 1, Singapore 389777
Tel: 6848 8290 *Fax:* 6742 9466
E-mail: info@bookcouncil.sg
Web Site: www.bookcouncil.sg
Key Personnel
Executive Dir: R Ramachandran *Tel:* 6848 8291
E-mail: rama@bookcouncil.sg
Established: 1976
Awarded for outstanding works of creative &
noncreative writing by local authors in any of
the four official languages (Malay, English,
Chinese & Tamil). The awards are for fiction,
poetry, drama, nonfiction, children's & young
people's books. Up to 15 prizes awarded bien-
nially.
Award: 10,000 USD for the winner in each lan-
guage with a specially commissioned plaque

Slovenia

International Literary Award Vilenica
Slovene Writers' Association
Tomsicevi ul 12, SI-1000 Ljubljana
Tel: (01) 251 41 44 *Fax:* (01) 421 64 30
E-mail: dsp@drustvo-dsp.si
Web Site: www.drustvo-dsp.si; www.
drustvopisateljev.si
Established: 1986
Award for exceptional achievements in the field
of literature & essay writing.
Award: 1,500,000 SIT
Presented: International Literary gathering
Vilenica

South Africa

Academy Prize for Translated Work
South African Academy for Science & Arts, En-
gelenburghuis
Ziervogelstr 574, Arcadia 0083

1531

Mailing Address: Privaatsak X11, Arcadia 0007
Tel: (012) 328-5082 *Fax:* (012) 328-5091
E-mail: akademie@akademie.co.za
Web Site: www.akademie.co.za
Key Personnel
Chief Executive Officer: Prof Jacques van der
   Elst *E-mail:* jvde@akademie.co.za
Established: 1948
For translations into Afrikaans of belletristic work
   from any other language. Awarded triennially.
Award: 2,500 ZAR

Alba Bouwerprys vir Kinderliteratuur (Alba
   Bouwer Prize for Children's Literature)
South African Academy for Science & Arts, En-
   gelenburghuis
Ziervogelstr 574, Arcadia 0083
Mailing Address: Privaatsak X11, Arcadia 0007
Tel: (012) 328-5082 *Fax:* (012) 328-5091
E-mail: akademie@akademie.co.za
Web Site: www.akademie.co.za
Key Personnel
Chief Executive Officer: Prof Jacques van der
   Elst *E-mail:* jvde@akademie.co.za
Established: 1989
For recognition of Afrikaans literature for chil-
   dren 7-12 years old. A monetary prize donated
   by the Akademie is awarded triennially.

Percy FitzPatrick Prize for Youth Literature
English Academy of Southern Africa
PO Box 124, Wits 2050
Tel: (011) 717-9339 *Fax:* (011) 717-9339
E-mail: englishacademy@societies.wits.ac.za
Web Site: www.englishacademy.co.za
Key Personnel
President: Dr Barbara Basel
Awarded biennially. Recognizes achievement by
   Southern African writers publishing in southern
   Africa in the field of children's books between
   the ages of 10-14 years.
Other Sponsor(s): Media Tenor South Africa
Award: 7,000 ZAR
Closing Date: May 31

Katrine Harries Award
The Children's Literature Research Unit at
   UNISA
Dept of Information Science, University of South
   Africa, PO Box 392, Pretoria 0003
Fax: (012) 4293792
E-mail: vdwaltb@unisa.ac.za
For outstanding illustrations in South African
   children's books, regardless of language.
   Awarded biennially.

Hertzog Prize
South African Academy for Science & Arts, En-
   gelenburghuis
Ziervogelstr 574, Arcadia 0083
Mailing Address: Privaatsak X11, Arcadia 0007
Tel: (012) 328-5082 *Fax:* (012) 328-5091
E-mail: akademie@akademie.co.za
Web Site: www.akademie.co.za
Key Personnel
Chief Executive Officer: Prof Jacques van der
   Elst *E-mail:* jvde@akademie.co.za
Established: 1914
A prestige prize for Afrikaans literature. Prizes
   are awarded in rotation for poetry, drama &
   prose. Awarded annually.
Other Sponsor(s): Rapport
Award: 17,000 ZAR & 18 carat gold medal

Louis Hiemstra Prize for Nonfiction
South African Academy for Science & Arts, En-
   gelenburghuis
Ziervogelstr 574, Arcadia 0083
Mailing Address: Privaatsak X11, Arcadia 0007
Tel: (012) 328-5082 *Fax:* (012) 328-5091
E-mail: akademie@akademie.co.za

Web Site: www.akademie.co.za
Key Personnel
Chief Executive Officer: Prof Jacques van der
   Elst *E-mail:* jvde@akademie.co.za
Established: 2001
Awarded every 3 years for nonfiction work in
   Afrikaans.
Award: 20,000 ZAR

W A Hofmeyr Prize
NB Publishers
Naspers Centre, 12th floor, Heerengracht 40,
   Cape Town 8001
Mailing Address: Posbus 879, Cape Town 8001
Tel: (021) 406 3033 *Fax:* (021) 406 3812
E-mail: nb@nb.co.za
Web Site: www.nb.co.za
Established: 1954
Awarded annually for the best Afrikaans literary
   work across all genres.
Award: 5,000 ZAR & gold medallion (1 ounce
   pure gold)

Tienie Holloway Medal
South African Academy for Science & Arts, En-
   gelenburghuis
Ziervogelstr 574, Arcadia 0083
Mailing Address: Privaatsak X11, Arcadia 0007
Tel: (012) 328-5082 *Fax:* (012) 328-5091
E-mail: akademie@akademie.co.za
Web Site: www.akademie.co.za
Key Personnel
Chief Executive Officer: Prof Jacques van der
   Elst *E-mail:* jvde@akademie.co.za
Established: 1969
Established by Dr J E Holloway & awarded tri-
   ennially to a writer who has produced the best
   work in Afrikaans literature for infants.
Award: Gold medal

C J Langenhoven Prize
South African Academy for Science & Arts, En-
   gelenburghuis
Ziervogelstr 574, Arcadia 0083
Mailing Address: Privaatsak X11, Arcadia 0007
Tel: (012) 328-5082 *Fax:* (012) 328-5091
E-mail: akademie@akademie.co.za
Web Site: www.akademie.co.za
Key Personnel
Chief Executive Officer: Prof Jacques van der
   Elst *E-mail:* jvde@akademie.co.za
For outstanding work in field of Afrikaans lin-
   guistics. Awarded triennially.

H Recht Malan Prize
NB Publishers
Naspers Centre, 12th floor, Heerengracht 40,
   Cape Town 8001
Mailing Address: Posbus 879, Cape Town 8001
Tel: (021) 406 3033 *Fax:* (021) 406 3812
E-mail: nb@nb.co.za
Web Site: www.nb.co.za
Awarded annually for the best nonliterary or non-
   fiction book.
Award: 5,000 ZAR & gold medallion (1 ounce
   pure gold)

Eugene Marais Prize
South African Academy for Science & Arts, En-
   gelenburghuis
Ziervogelstr 574, Arcadia 0083
Mailing Address: Privaatsak X11, Arcadia 0007
Tel: (012) 328-5082 *Fax:* (012) 328-5091
E-mail: akademie@akademie.co.za
Web Site: www.akademie.co.za
Key Personnel
Chief Executive Officer: Prof Jacques van der
   Elst *E-mail:* jvde@akademie.co.za
Established: 1961
For a first or early work of belletristic publication
   in Afrikaans. The prize can be awarded only

once to any particular writer. Awarded annually.
Award: 11,000 ZAR

MER Prize for Youth Literature
NB Publishers
Naspers Centre, 12th floor, Heerengracht 40,
   Cape Town 8001
Mailing Address: Posbus 879, Cape Town 8001
Tel: (021) 406 3033 *Fax:* (021) 406 3812
E-mail: nb@nb.co.za
Web Site: www.nb.co.za
Awarded annually for the best children's book
   published by Nasboek publishers, including
   Tafelberg, Human & Rousseau, Kwela, Queil-
   lerie, Pharos, JL van Schaik, Sunbird, Jonathan
   Ball, Van Schaik Publishers & Nasou Via
   Afrikay.
Award: 5,000 ZAR & gold medallion (1 ounce
   pure gold)

Sol Plaatje Award for Translation
English Academy of Southern Africa
PO Box 124, Wits 2050
Tel: (011) 717-9339 *Fax:* (011) 717-9339
E-mail: englishacademy@societies.wits.ac.za
Web Site: www.englishacademy.co.za
Key Personnel
President: Dr Barbara Basel
Awarded in alternate years for translation of a
   prose passage or poetry into English from any
   of the other official languages in the South
   African Republic.

Gustav Preller Prize
South African Academy for Science & Arts, En-
   gelenburghuis
Ziervogelstr 574, Arcadia 0083
Mailing Address: Privaatsak X11, Arcadia 0007
Tel: (012) 328-5082 *Fax:* (012) 328-5091
E-mail: akademie@akademie.co.za
Web Site: www.akademie.co.za
Key Personnel
Chief Executive Officer: Prof Jacques van der
   Elst *E-mail:* jvde@akademie.co.za
For literary works in Afrikaans. Awarded trienni-
   ally.

Thomas Pringle Awards
English Academy of Southern Africa
PO Box 124, Wits 2050
Tel: (011) 717-9339 *Fax:* (011) 717-9339
E-mail: englishacademy@societies.wits.ac.za
Web Site: www.englishacademy.co.za
Key Personnel
President: Dr Barbara Basel
Awarded every year in 3 of 5 categories, includ-
   ing play, book, film & television reviews in
   newspapers & periodicals; literary articles or
   substantial book reviews in academic & other
   journals & in newspapers; articles on language
   & the teaching of English in academic, teach-
   ers' & other journals & in newspapers; short
   stories, one-act plays & poetry in periodicals.
   To recognize writers who have demonstrated
   extraordinary insight in their work.
Other Sponsor(s): National Lottery Distribution
   Trust Fund
Award: 2,000 ZAR in each category
Closing Date: May 31 annually

Scheepers Prize
South African Academy for Science & Arts, En-
   gelenburghuis
Ziervogelstr 574, Arcadia 0083
Mailing Address: Privaatsak X11, Arcadia 0007
Tel: (012) 328-5082 *Fax:* (012) 328-5091
E-mail: akademie@akademie.co.za
Web Site: www.akademie.co.za
Key Personnel
Chief Executive Officer: Prof Jacques van der
   Elst *E-mail:* jvde@akademie.co.za

Established: 1956
Awarded triennially in recognition of excellence in children's literature to authors of Afrikaans.

Olive Schreiner Prize for English Literature
English Academy of Southern Africa
PO Box 124, Wits 2050
Tel: (011) 717-9339 *Fax:* (011) 717-9339
E-mail: englishacademy@societies.wits.ac.za
Web Site: www.englishacademy.co.za
Key Personnel
President: Dr Barbara Basel
For original literary work in English by a promising South African writer & published in South Africa. Awarded annually in one of the following categories: prose, poetry, drama.
Other Sponsor(s): National Lottery Distribution Trust Fund
Award: 5,000 ZAR
Closing Date: May 31 annually

South Korea

Korea Literature Translation Award
Korea Literature Translation Institute
Samseong-dong 108-5, Gangnam-gu, Seoul 135-090
Tel: (02) 6919-7700 *Fax:* (02) 3448-4247
E-mail: info@ltikorea.net; info@klti.or.kr
Web Site: www.ltikorea.net; www.klti.or.kr
Key Personnel
Chief Executive Officer: Seong-Kon Kim
Deputy Dir: Yoon-Jin Kim *E-mail:* abieux@klti.or.kr
Translation & Publication Team: Lee Yoomi
Tel: (02) 6919-7731 *E-mail:* leeyoomi@klti.or.kr
Established: 1993
Awarded biennially as part of the Korean government's efforts to introduce & promote Korean literary works overseas through translation.

Spain

Premio de Literatura en Lengua Castellana Miguel de Cervantes (Miguel de Cervantes Literary Prize for Spanish Literature)
Ministerio de Cultura
Plaza del Rey, 1, 28004 Madrid
Tel: 91 701 70 00 *Fax:* 91 701 73 34
Web Site: www.mcu.es/libro/CE/Premios/Introduccion.html
Key Personnel
Head: Alicia Garcia Molina
Established: 1975
Annual award for the work of a writer who has made an outstanding contribution to Spanish Literature.
Award: 125,000 EUR
Presented: April 23

Premio Destino Infantil-Apel.les Mestres (Destino Children's Book Prize)
Destino Infantil & Juvenil
Avda Diagonal, 662-664, 6º, 08034 Barcelona
E-mail: infoinfantilyjuvenil@planeta.es
Web Site: www.destinojoven.com
Established: 1981
Open to all illustrated literary works which have not been published in any form & are intended for children. Works can be in Spanish, Catalan, Basque, Galician, English, French or Italian. Exists to acknowledge creative effort in the world of illustrated books.

Award: 4,500 EUR
Closing Date: Sept
Presented: Oct annually

Gourmand World Cookbook Awards
Gourmand International
Marques de Urquijo, 6, bajo A, 28008 Madrid
Web Site: www.cookbookfair.com
Key Personnel
President: Edouard Cointreau *E-mail:* edouard@gourmandbooks.com
Vice President: Bo Masser *E-mail:* bo@masser.se
Head, International Off: Pilar Gutierrez
E-mail: pilar@gourmandbooks.com
Management: Edouard Cointreau
E-mail: ecointreau@gourmandbooks.com;
Yves-Laurent Svarc *E-mail:* laurent@orange.fr
Awards to honor global cookbook & wine book publishing.

Lazarillo Prize
Organizacion Espanola para el Libro Infantil
C/ Santiago Rusinol, 8, 28040 Madrid
Tel: 915 530 821 *Fax:* 915 539 990
E-mail: oepli@oepli.org
Web Site: www.oepli.org
Established: 1982
Awarded annually for the author of narration, poetry or theater, of a children's or young adult book. Two categories: Illustrated Album & Literary Creation.
Award: 8,000 EUR each category

Premi de les Lletres Catalanes Ramon Llull
Editorial Planeta SA
Diagonal, 662-664, 08034 Barcelona
Tel: 93 492 80 00 *Fax:* 93 492 85 65
Web Site: www.planetadelibros.com
Established: 1968
Founded for the purpose of contributing to the increase & promotion of narrative in Catalan. Since 1995, it has accepted both fictional works (novels, narratives, etc) & nonfiction works (essays, memoirs, biographies, etc).
Other Sponsor(s): Fundacio Ramon Llull
Award: 90,000 EUR
Presented: Jan annually

Premios Nacionales de Literatura (National Literature Prizes)
Ministerio de Cultura
Plaza del Rey, 1, 28004 Madrid
Tel: 91 701 70 00 *Fax:* 91 701 73 34
Web Site: www.mcu.es/libro/CE/Premios/Introduccion.html
Key Personnel
Head: Alicia Garcia Molina
Established: 1984
Annual awards for literature published in the previous year in one of the official languages of Spain.
Award: 20,000 EUR each

Premio Nadal (Nadal Prize)
Ediciones Destino SA
Edificio Planeta, Diagonal, 662-664, 08034 Barcelona
Tel: 93 496 70 01 *Fax:* 93 496 70 02
E-mail: edicionesdestino@edestino.es
Web Site: www.edestino.es
Established: 1944
Oldest literary prize to be awarded to novels written in Spanish. Novels presented for this award will also be competing for the Premio Destino-Guion script award, which will be awarded to the best novel according to its potential for adaptation to a film or audiovisual script.
Award: 18,030 EUR (winner); 4,988 EUR (runner-up)
Presented: Jan annually

National Prize for Children & Young Adults Literature
Ministerio de Cultura
Plaza del Rey, 1, 28004 Madrid
Tel: 91 701 70 00 *Fax:* 91 701 73 34
Web Site: www.mcu.es/libro/CE/Premios/Introduccion.html
Key Personnel
Head: Alicia Garcia Molina
Established: 1978
Annual award for the best literary works intended for children or young people, written in any of the official languages of Spain.
Award: 20,000 EUR

National Prize for Illustration of Children's Literature
Ministerio de Cultura
Plaza del Rey, 1, 28004 Madrid
Tel: 91 701 70 00 *Fax:* 91 701 73 34
Web Site: www.mcu.es/libro/CE/Premios/Introduccion.html
Key Personnel
Head: Teresa Atienza Serna
Established: 2008
Annual award for the best illustrations in a book for children or young people. Awarded in alternate years in each category.
Award: 1st prize 12,020.24 EUR; 2nd prize 6,010.12 EUR

National Prize of Spanish Letters (Premio Nacional de las Letras Espanolas)
Ministerio de Cultura
Plaza del Rey, 1, 28004 Madrid
Tel: 91 701 70 00 *Fax:* 91 701 73 34
Web Site: www.mcu.es/libro/CE/Premios/Introduccion.html
Key Personnel
Head: Alicia Garcia Molina
Established: 1984
Awarded in recognition of a Spanish author, writing in one of the official Spanish languages, for the whole of his work.
Award: 40,000 EUR

Premi Josep Pla (Josep Pla Prize)
Ediciones Destino SA
Edificio Planeta, Diagonal, 662-664, 08034 Barcelona
Tel: 93 496 70 01 *Fax:* 93 496 70 02
E-mail: edicionesdestino@edestino.es
Web Site: www.edestino.es
Established: 1969
Awarded for prose in Catalan without limits in terms of genre (novels, short stories, accounts, travel books, memoirs or biographies).
Award: 4,988 EUR
Presented: Jan annually

☆**Premio Planeta de Novela**
Editorial Planeta SA
Av Diagonal, 662-664, 08034 Barcelona
Tel: 93 492 80 00 *Fax:* 93 492 85 65
Web Site: www.planeta.es
Key Personnel
Chairman: Jose Manuel Lara
Established: 1952
Spain: promotes Spanish authors. The award is presented annually in Oct.
Argentina: given for previously unpublished works in Spanish, continuing in its objective of promoting the production of novels. Presented annually in Oct.
Chile: awarded for the first time in 2000 for journalistic research. May be entered by journalists or writers with works referring to Chilean subject matter in any written journalistic genre: information, report, chronicle, biography, analysis or interview. Pieces may be the work of a single author or of several. Presented annually in Oct.

Colombia: prize awarded in recognition of the life & works of, alternately, a journalist & historian. Presented annually in Dec.
Award: 40,000

Sri Lanka

State Literary Awards
Ministry of Culture & the Arts
Dept of Cultural Affairs, Sethsiripaya, 8th floor, Battaramulla
Tel: (011) 2872035 *Fax:* (011) 2872035
Web Site: www.cultural.gov.lk; www.culturaldept.gov.lk
Key Personnel
Dir: Anusha Gokula Fernando
Awarded annually for the best books published in the previous year in the Sinhala language in the following categories: novels, short stories, poems, songs, youth literature, drama, science fiction, children's literature, translated novels, translated short stories & translated dramas.
Award: 5,000 LKR; Children's literature 2,000 LKR

Sweden

Carl Akermarks Stipendium
Swedish Academy
Kallargrand 4, Gamla Stan, 111 29 Stockholm
Mailing Address: PO Box 2118, 103 13 Stockholm
Tel: (08) 555 125 00 *Fax:* (08) 555 125 49
E-mail: sekretariat@svenskaakademien.se
Web Site: www.svenskaakademien.se
Awarded to deserving artists in the Swedish theater (playwrights, actors, directors & set designers). This award cannot be applied for.
Award: Four prizes of 50,000 SEK
Presented: Dec 20

Aniara Priset
Svensk Biblioteksforening Kansli (Swedish Library Association)
World Trade Center, D5, Klarabergsviadukten 70/ Kungsbron 1, Box 70380, 107 24 Stockholm
Tel: (08) 545 132 30 *Fax:* (08) 545 132 31
E-mail: info@biblioteksforeningen.org
Web Site: www.biblioteksforeningen.org
Established: 1974
Awarded annually to a Swedish language author of adult fiction.
Award: 50,000 SEK
Closing Date: April

Bellmanpriset (Bellman Prize)
City of Stockholm
Stockholms Kulturforvaltning, Kulturstrategiska avdelningen, Box 16113, 103 22 Stockholm
Tel: (08) 508 31 980 *Fax:* (08) 508 31 999
Web Site: www.stockholm.se/kulturfritid/stod/kulturpriser
Annual award for poetry. This prize cannot be applied for.
Award: 100,000 SEK
Closing Date: Feb 1
Presented: City Hall, late May

Region Blekinge Kulturpris (Blekinge Region Culture Prize)
Region Blekinge
Ronnebygatan 2, 371 32 Karlskrona
Tel: (0455) 30 50 00 *Fax:* (0455) 30 50 10
E-mail: kansli@regionblekinge.se

Web Site: www.regionblekinge.se
Key Personnel
Head, Cultural Affairs: Lolita Persson
 Tel: (0455) 30 50 08 *E-mail:* lolita.persson@regionblekinge.se
Established: 1964
Annual prize to recognize a person or organization for a valuable contribution to science, technology, literature, art, music, dance, journalism or education.
Award: 60,000 SEK
Closing Date: March 1

Nils Holgersson Plaque
Svensk Biblioteksforening Kansli (Swedish Library Association)
World Trade Center, D5, Klarabergsviadukten 70/ Kungsbron 1, Box 70380, 107 24 Stockholm
Tel: (08) 545 132 30 *Fax:* (08) 545 132 31
E-mail: info@biblioteksforeningen.org
Web Site: www.biblioteksforeningen.org
Established: 1950
Awarded annually to the author of a children's or young adult book published the previous year.
Award: Glass plaque

Kellgren Prize
Swedish Academy
Kallargrand 4, Gamla Stan, 111 29 Stockholm
Mailing Address: PO Box 2118, 103 13 Stockholm
Tel: (08) 555 125 00 *Fax:* (08) 555 125 49
E-mail: sekretariat@svenskaakademien.se
Web Site: www.svenskaakademien.se
Established: 1979
Annual award for important achievements in any of the fields of the academy. This prize cannot be applied for.
Award: 200,000 SEK

The Astrid Lindgren Memorial Award
Swedish Arts Council
Borgvagen 1-5, 115 53 Stockholm
Mailing Address: PO Box 272 15, 102 53 Stockholm
Tel: (08) 519 264 00 *Fax:* (08) 519 264 99
E-mail: literatureaward@alma.se
Web Site: www.alma.se
Key Personnel
Dir: Erik Titusson *Tel:* (08) 519 264 08
 E-mail: erik.titusson@alma.se
Information Officer: Agnes Lidbeck *Tel:* (08) 519 264 17 *E-mail:* agnes.lidbeck@alma.se
Presented annually to authors, illustrators, oral storytellers & those active in reading promotion work.
Award: 5,000,000 SEK
Closing Date: Nominations May 15
Presented: March

☆Nobel Prize for Literature
Swedish Academy
Kallargrand 4, Gamla Stan, 111 29 Stockholm
Mailing Address: PO Box 2118, 103 13 Stockholm
Tel: (08) 555 125 00 *Fax:* (08) 555 125 49
E-mail: sekretariat@svenskaakademien.se
Web Site: www.svenskaakademien.se
Established: 1901
Of all the literary prizes, the Nobel Prize for Literature is the biggest in value & in honor bestowed. It is one of the five prizes founded by Alfred Nobel (1833-1896); the other four awards are for physics, chemistry, physiology or medicine & peace. By the terms of Nobel's will, the prize for literature is to be given to the person "who shall have produced in the field of literature the most distinguished work of an idealistic tendency." No one may apply for the Nobel Prize, there is no competition. It is awarded to an author usually for their total literary output & not for any single work.

Other Sponsor(s): Nobel Foundation
Award: A gold medal, a diploma & 10,000,000 SEK
Presented: Dec 10, the anniversary of Nobel's death

Margit Pahlson Prize
Swedish Academy
Kallargrand 4, Gamla Stan, 111 29 Stockholm
Mailing Address: PO Box 2118, 103 13 Stockholm
Tel: (08) 555 125 00 *Fax:* (08) 555 125 49
E-mail: sekretariat@svenskaakademien.se
Web Site: www.svenskaakademien.se
Key Personnel
Registry Coordinator: Odd Zschiedrich *Tel:* (08) 555 125 02 *E-mail:* odd.zschiedrich@svenskaakademien.se
Annual award for achievements of particular significance for the Swedish language. This award cannot be applied for.
Award: 180,000 SEK

Swedish Academy Nordic Prize
Swedish Academy
Kallargrand 4, Gamla Stan, 111 29 Stockholm
Mailing Address: PO Box 2118, 103 13 Stockholm
Tel: (08) 555 125 00 *Fax:* (08) 555 125 49
E-mail: sekretariat@svenskaakademien.se
Web Site: www.svenskaakademien.se
Established: 1986
Annual award for important achievements in any of the fields of interest of the academy. Citizens of any of the Scandinavian countries are eligible. This award cannot be applied for.
Award: 350,000 SEK
Presented: April 5

Swedish Authors' Fund Awards
Swedish Authors' Fund
Klara Norra Kyrkogata 29, 111 81 Stockholm
Mailing Address: Box 1106, 111 81 Stockholm
Tel: (08) 440 45 50 *Fax:* (08) 440 45 65
E-mail: svff@svff.se
Web Site: www.svff.se
Key Personnel
Dir: Jesper Soderstrom
To recognize authors, translators & illustrators who have made special contributions within their own fields. Main purpose of the fund is to administer the Swedish system of library loan compensation to authors, translators & book illustrators.
Award: 20,000 SEK

Switzerland

☆Hans Christian Andersen Awards
International Board on Books for Young People (IBBY)
Nonnenweg 12, Postfach, 4009 Basel
Tel: (061) 272 29 17 *Fax:* (061) 272 27 57
E-mail: ibby@ibby.org
Web Site: www.ibby.org
Key Personnel
Executive Dir: Elizabeth Page *E-mail:* liz.page@ibby.org
Deputy Dir of Administration: Forest Zhang
 E-mail: forest.zhang@ibby.org
Established: 1956
Biennial awards to a living author & a living illustrator who, through their works, have made distinguished contributions to international children's & young adult literature. Until 1966 a prize was awarded to an author only. A jury of ten members, appointed by the Executive Committee of IBBY, makes the decision from

nominations submitted from member countries all over the world.
Other Sponsor(s): Nami Island Inc
Award: Gold medal & diploma

City of Zurich Literary Prizes
Praesidialdepartement der Stadt Zurich
Ressort Literatur, Stadthaus, Stadthausquai 17, 8022 Zurich
Tel: (044) 412 31 25 *Fax:* (044) 212 14 04
E-mail: ktr-literatur@zuerich.ch
Web Site: www.stadt-zuerich.ch
Key Personnel
Head of Dept: Roman Hess
Established: 1930
Founded by the city of Zurich to reward an author for his or her whole literary work. No applications or nominations accepted.
Award: 50,000 CHF awarded at irregular intervals

Grand Prix Ramuz
Fondation C F Ramuz
Case Postale 181, 1009 Pully
Tel: (021) 721 36 43
E-mail: info@fondation-ramuz.ch
Web Site: www.fondation-ramuz.ch
Key Personnel
President: Daniel Maggetti
Vice President: Sylviane Dupuis
Secretary: Dylan Roth Mathys
Treasurer: Philippe Jaton
Established: 1955
To recognize a writer for his entire work. Swiss authors writing in the French language are eligible.
Award: 15,000 Swiss francs every 5 years

Grosser Schillerpreis
Schweizerische Schillerstiftung, Fondation Schiller Suisse
Route de Frontenex 57, 1207 Geneva
Tel: (022) 379 71 68
E-mail: schillerstiftunginfo-lettres@unige.ch
Web Site: www.schillerstiftung.ch
Key Personnel
Foundation Secretary: Pascal Steenken
Prizes for Swiss citizens only. Awarded every 5 years.
Award: 30,000 CHF
Presented: Stadttheater Solothurn, May 13

☆IBBY-Asahi Reading Promotion Award
International Board on Books for Young People (IBBY)
Nonnenweg 12, Postfach, 4009 Basel
Tel: (061) 272 29 17 *Fax:* (061) 272 27 57
E-mail: ibby@ibby.org
Web Site: www.ibby.org
Key Personnel
Executive Dir: Elizabeth Page *E-mail:* liz.page@ibby.org
Deputy Dir of Administration: Forest Zhang *E-mail:* forest.zhang@ibby.org
Established: 1986
Presented biennially to 2 groups or institutions that are making a significant contribution to book promotion programs for children & young adults.
Other Sponsor(s): Asahi Shimbun
Award: 10,000 USD & diploma
Presented: IBBY Congress

☆IBBY Honour List
International Board on Books for Young People (IBBY)
Nonnenweg 12, Postfach, 4009 Basel
Tel: (061) 272 29 17 *Fax:* (061) 272 27 57
E-mail: ibby@ibby.org
Web Site: www.ibby.org
Key Personnel
Executive Dir: Elizabeth Page *E-mail:* liz.page@ibby.org

Deputy Dir of Administration: Forest Zhang *E-mail:* forest.zhang@ibby.org
Biennial selection of outstanding, recently published books, honoring writers, illustrators & translators from IBBY member countries. Titles are selected by the National Sections. The Honor List Diplomas are presented to the recipients at the IBBY Congresses.
Award: Diploma

International Award for the Promotion of Human Understanding
The International Organization for the Elimination of All Forms of Racial Discrimination (EAFORD)
5, Route des Morillons, 1211 Geneva 2
Mailing Address: Case Postale 2100, 1211 Geneva 2
Tel: (022) 788 62 33 *Fax:* (022) 788 62 45
E-mail: info@eaford.org
Web Site: www.eaford.org
Key Personnel
President: Mr Abdalla Sharafeddin
Secretary General: Dr Anis Al-Qasem
Executive Dir: Dr Hanan Sharfelddin *Tel:* 079 573 4050 (cell)
Established: 1978
Annual international award for outstanding published work in English, French, Arabic, Spanish or Portuguese dealing with questions of racism & racial discrimination.
Award: 5,000 USD & certificate

IPA Prix Voltaire
International Publishers Association (IPA)
23, ave de France, 1202 Geneva
Tel: (022) 704 18 20
E-mail: secretariat@internationalpublishers.org
Web Site: www.internationalpublishers.org
Key Personnel
President: Dr Michiel Kolman *E-mail:* president@internationalpublishers.org
Secy Gen: Jose Borghino *E-mail:* borghino@internationalpublishers.org
Dir, Communications & Freedom to Publish: James Taylor *E-mail:* taylor@internationalpublishers.org
Established: 2005
Awarded annually to honor a person or organization adjudged to have made a significant contribution to the defense & promotion of freedom to publish in the world. The IPA issues a call for nominations & posts a downloadable nomination form on the web site 6-8 months prior to the award.
Award: 10,000 CHF & certificate

☆Gottfried Keller Prize
Martin Bodmer-Stiftung fuer einen Gottfried Keller-Preis
Postfach 1425, 8032 Zurich
E-mail: info@gottfried-keller-preis.ch
Web Site: www.gottfried-keller-preis.ch
Key Personnel
Contact: Thomas Bodmer
Established: 1921
Founded by Martin Bodmer for Swiss & other writers who have honored the Swiss spirit. Awarded every 2 or 3 years.
Award: 25,000 CHF

Literaturpreis der Innerschweiz (Cental Swiss Literature Prize)
Central Swiss Cultural Foundation
Bildungs-und Kulturdepartement Kulturfoerderung, Bahnhofstr 18, 6002 Lucerne
Tel: (041) 228 52 05 *Fax:* (041) 210 05 73
Web Site: www.kultur.lu.ch/index/innerschweiz_kulturstiftung.htm
Key Personnel
Dir: Daniel Huber *E-mail:* daniel.huber@lu.ch
Established: 1951

Annual award for recognition of outstanding literary work. Authors living in the central part of Switzerland (Innerschweiz, cantons: Lucerne, Uri, Schwyz, Obwalden, Nidwalden & Zug) or who originate from those areas are eligible.
Award: 20,000 CHF & certificate

Prix Voltaire, see IPA Prix Voltaire

United Arab Emirates

Etisalat Award for Arabic Children's Literature
UAE Board on Books for Young People (UAEBBY)
Al Qasba, Blok D, 1st floor, Off no 40, Sharjah
Mailing Address: PO Box 1421, Sharjah
Tel: (06) 5542111 *Fax:* (06) 5542345
E-mail: info@uaebby.org.az
Web Site: www.uaebby.org.ae
Key Personnel
Executive, International Projects: Joshua Dunning *E-mail:* joshua.d@uaebby.org.ae
Programs & Award Executive: Eman Mohamed *E-mail:* eman.m@uaebby.org.ae
General Coordinator: Meera Al Naqbi *E-mail:* meera.n@uaebby.org.ae
Established: 2009
Awarded annually. The book must be written in Arabic, must be original (not translated, quoted or reproduced) & must have been published within the past 3 years. Entry is open to children's books that target the age group from 0-14 years & each publishing house is entitled to nominate a maximum of 3 titles.
Award: Best Text, Best Illustration & Best Production 100,000 AED each; Best Children's Book of the Year 300,000 AED (split between author, illustrator & publisher); Best Young Adult Book of the Year 200,000 AED (split between author & publisher); Etisalat Award Workshops for Children's Books 200,000 AED
Presented: Sharjah International Book Fair

Sheikh Zayed Book Award
Abu Dhabi Authority for Culture & Heritage
PO Box 2380, Abu Dhabi
Tel: (02) 6576286; (02) 6576075 *Fax:* (02) 6433819
E-mail: info@zayedaward.ae
Web Site: zayedaward.ae
Presented annually to outstanding Arab writers, intellectuals & publishers as well as young talent whose writings & translations of humanities have scholarly & objectively enriched Arab culture, literary & social life.
Award: 750,000 AED, gold medal & appreciation certificate
Closing Date: Nominations accepted through Sept 30
Presented: Abu Dhabi International Book Fair, March, annually

United Kingdom

BAILEYS Women's Prize for Fiction, see Women's Prize for Fiction

Ackerley Prize, see PEN/Ackerley Prize

Airey Neave Research Fellowship

The Airey Neave Trust
40 Bernard St, London WC1N 1WJ
Mailing Address: PO Box 111, Leominster, Herts
HR6 6BP
E-mail: info@aireyneavetrust.org.uk;
aireyneavetrust@gmail.com
Web Site: www.aireyneavetrust.org.uk
Key Personnel
Chairman: John Giffard
Administrator: Sophie Butler
Award: 20,000 GBP

Alexander Prize

The Royal Historical Society
University College London, Gower St, London
WC1E 6BT
Tel: (020) 7387 7532 *Fax:* (020) 7387 7532
E-mail: royalhistsoc@ucl.ac.uk
Web Site: www.royalhistoricalsociety.org
Key Personnel
Executive Secretary: Sue Carr *E-mail:* s.carr@ucl.
ac.uk
Administrative Secretary: Melanie Ransom
E-mail: m.ransom@ucl.ac.uk
Awarded for a published scholarly journal article
or an essay in a collective volume based upon
original historical research. Candidates must be
doctoral students in history in a UK institution,
or be within two years of having completed a
doctorate in history in a UK institution. The
article/essay submitted for consideration must
have been published in a journal or edited collection during the calendar year of application.
Award: 250 GBP
Closing Date: Dec 31

☆Arvon International Poetry Competition

Arvon Foundation Ltd
Free Word Centre, 60 Farringdon Rd, London
EC1R 3GA
Tel: (020) 7324 2554
E-mail: london@arvonfoundation.org
Web Site: www.arvonfoundation.org
Established: 1980
Entries for the competition must be previously
unpublished poems of any length written in En-
glish. An anthology of winning poems & those
selected by the judges for special commenda-
tion, are published by the Arvon Foundation.
Other Sponsor(s): Duncan Lawrie Ltd, Private
Bank
Award: Classic FM 1st prize 7,500 GBP; 2nd
prize 2,500 GBP; 3rd prize 1,000 GBP; 3 com-
mendation prizes 500 GBP each
Closing Date: Aug

Audible Sounds of Crime Award

CrimeFest
Basement Flat, 6 Rodney Pl, Bristol BS8 4HY
Tel: (0117) 9737829
E-mail: info@crimefest.com; audio@crimefest.
com (submissions)
Web Site: www.crimefest.com
To recognize the outstanding contribution that
crime audiobooks make in popularizing both
the genre & audio format. Eligible are any
unabridged crime audiobooks such as humour,
spy, suspense & thriller titles, first published in
the year prior to the award in the UK in both
print & unabridged audio formats. The audiobook must also be available for download from
Audible UK. Excel file preferred. See web site
for complete submission guidelines.
Other Sponsor(s): Audible UK
Award: 1,000 GBP (divided equally between winning author & reader) & Bristol Blue Glass
commemorative award
Closing Date: Annually in Dec
Presented: CrimeFest Awards Dinner, Annually in
May

Authors' Club Best First Novel Award

Authors' Club
Blacks, 67 Dean St, London W1D 4QH
Web Site: dolmanprize.wordpress.com
Key Personnel
Chairman: Chris Schuler *E-mail:* cjschuler@
authorsclub.co.uk
Annual award to the most promising debut novel
issued by a British publisher in the previous
year.
Award: 1,000 GBP
Closing Date: Oct 15
Presented: April

The Baillie Gifford Prize for Non-Fiction

Baillie Gifford
c/o Four Colman Getty, 20 St Thomas St, London
SE1 9BF
Web Site: www.thesamueljohnsonprize.co.uk
Key Personnel
Prize Submissions: Christina Neou-North
E-mail: christina.neou-north@fourcolmangetty.
com
Press: Sarah Watson *E-mail:* sarah.watson@
fourcolmangetty.com
Established: 1999
UK's premier prize for nonfiction books. Open to
authors of all nonfiction books in the areas of
current affairs, history, politics, science, sport,
travel, biography, autobiography & the arts.
Award: 25,000 GBP

Banister Fletcher Award

Authors' Club
Blacks, 67 Dean St, London W1D 4QH
Web Site: dolmanprize.wordpress.com
Key Personnel
Chairman: Chris Schuler *E-mail:* cjschuler@
authorsclub.co.uk
Established: 1954
Annual award for the best book on art or archi-
tecture.
Award: 1,000 GBP
Closing Date: End of May

BBC National Short Story Award

The British Broadcasting Corp (BBC)
Cambridge University, The London Readings
Unit, Room 8015, BBC Broadcasting House,
London W1A 1AA
Web Site: www.bbc.co.uk/nssa
Established: 2005
Annual award to promote the best of contempo-
rary British short fiction.
Other Sponsor(s): Cambridge University
Award: 15,000 GBP; 4 shortlisted authors 600
GBP each
Closing Date: March

☆Benson Medal

Royal Society of Literature
Somerset House, Strand, London WC2R 1LA
Tel: (020) 7845 4676 *Fax:* (020) 7845 4679
E-mail: info@rslit.org
Web Site: www.rslit.org
Key Personnel
Awards Administrator: Paula Johnson
E-mail: paulaj@rslit.org
Established: 1916
Founded by Dr A C Benson. For a body of meri-
torious work in poetry, fiction, history or belles
lettres given periodically at the discretion of
the Council of the Royal Society of Literature.
Applications are not invited.
Award: Silver medal

David Berry Prize

The Royal Historical Society
University College London, Gower St, London
WC1E 6BT
Tel: (020) 7387 7532 *Fax:* (020) 7387 7532
E-mail: royalhistsoc@ucl.ac.uk
Web Site: www.royalhistoricalsociety.org
Key Personnel
Executive Secretary: Sue Carr *E-mail:* s.carr@ucl.
ac.uk
Administrative Secretary: Melanie Ransom
E-mail: m.ransom@ucl.ac.uk
For an essay in English on a subject, to be selected by the candidates, dealing with Scottish
history. The essay submitted must be a genuine
work of research based on original (manuscript
or printed) materials. The essay should be between 6,000 & 10,000 words in length (excluding foot-notes & appendices). It must be
submitted in typescript. The author's name
should not appear on the typescript & should
be submitted separately. No person to whom
the prize has been awarded may enter for any
subsequent competition for the prize.
Award: 250 GBP
Closing Date: Dec 31

Best Crime Novel for Children

CrimeFest
Basement Flat, 6 Rodney Pl, Bristol BS8 4HY
Tel: (0117) 9737829
E-mail: info@crimefest.com; childfiction@
crimefest.com (submissions)
Web Site: www.crimefest.com
To recognize outstanding contribution that crime
novels make to the genre, as well
as celebrating burgeoning interest of children
in fiction as a whole. Eligible are any humorous crime, spy, suspense & thriller titles for
children ages 8-12 commercially published
in hardcover or paperback format for the first
time in the British Isles in the year prior to the
award year. Excel file preferred. See web site
for complete submission guidelines.
Award: Bristol Blue Glass commemorative award
Closing Date: Annually in Dec
Presented: CrimeFest Awards Dinner, Annually in
May

Best Crime Novel for Young Adults

CrimeFest
Basement Flat, 6 Rodney Pl, Bristol BS8 4HY
Tel: (0117) 9737829
E-mail: info@crimefest.com; ya@crimefest.com
(submissions)
Web Site: www.crimefest.com
To recognize outstanding contribution that crime
novels for young adults make to the genre, as
well as celebrating the burgeoning interest of
young adults in fiction as a whole. Eligible are
any humorous crime, spy, suspense & thriller
titles for young adults ages 12-16 commercially
published in hardcover or paperback format for
the first time in the British Isles in the year
prior to the award year. Excel file preferred.
See web site for complete submission guidelines.
Award: Bristol Blue Glass commemorative award
Closing Date: Annually in Dec
Presented: CrimeFest Awards Dinner, Annually in
May

James Tait Black Memorial Prizes

University of Edinburgh
Dept of English Literature, Room 6.05, David
Hume Tower, George Sq, Edinburgh EH8 9JX
Tel: (0131) 650 3620 *Fax:* (0131) 650 6898
E-mail: english.literature@ed.ac.uk
Web Site: www.ed.ac.uk/about/people/tait-black/
about
Key Personnel
Contact: Sheila Strathdee *Tel:* (0131) 650 3619
E-mail: s.strathdee@ed.ac.uk
Established: 1919
These literary prizes were founded by the late
Mrs Janet Coats Black in memory of her hus-
band, a partner in the publishing house of

A&C Black Ltd, London. Mrs Black set aside 11,000 GBP to be used for 2 prizes of whatever income the fund would produce after paying expenses. The prizes now amount annually to approximately 10,000 GBP each. Literary prizes are awarded to the best biography & to the best work of fiction published in the previous year.
Award: 10,000 GBP each
Closing Date: Dec 1
Presented: Edinburgh International Book Festival, Aug

Blue Peter Book Awards
Booktrust
G8 Battersea Studios, 80 Silverthorne Rd, Battersea, London SW8 3HE
Tel: (020) 7801 8800
E-mail: query@booktrust.org.uk
Web Site: www.booktrust.org.uk/books/awards-and-prizes
Established: 2000
Celebrates children's books published in the last year in 2 categories: Best Story & Best Book with Facts.

The K Blundell Trust
The Society of Authors
84 Drayton Gardens, London SW10 9SB
Tel: (020) 7373 6642 *Fax:* (020) 7373 5768
E-mail: info@societyofauthors.org
Web Site: www.societyofauthors.org
Key Personnel
Awards Secretary: Paula Johnson
E-mail: pjohnson@societyofauthors.org
Provides grants twice annually (Spring & Autumn) to published British authors under 40 years whose project is for a British publisher. The project must aim to contribute to greater understanding of existing social & economic organization & can be fiction or nonfiction.
Award: Generally 1,000-2,000 GBP (not to exceed 4,000 GBP)
Closing Date: April 30 & Sept 30

☆**Boardman Tasker Prize for Mountain Literature**
Boardman Tasker Charitable Trust
8 Bank View Rd, Darley Abbey, Derby DE22 IEJ
Web Site: www.boardmantasker.com
Key Personnel
Secretary: Stephen Dean *Tel:* (01332) 342246
Established: 1983
Established to commemorate the lives of distinguished mountaineers Peter Boardman & Joe Tasker who died in 1982 on Mount Everest. Awarded annually to an author of a published work of nonfiction or fiction, drama & poetry, written in the English language, initially or in translation, which makes an outstanding contribution to mountain literature; published between Nov 1 of previous year & Oct 31 of year of the prize.
Award: 3,000 GBP
Closing Date: Aug 18 of year in which the prize is offered
Presented: Autumn

The Bollinger Everyman Wodehouse Prize for Comic Fiction
Champagne Bollinger SA
c/o Everyman's Library, 50 Albemarle St, London W1S 4BD
Web Site: www.everymanslibrary.co.uk/wodehouse.aspx
Established: 2000
Annual award for comic literature. By invitation only.
Presented: The Guardian Hay Festival, May

The Bracken Bower Prize
Financial Times Ltd

One Southwark Bridge, London SE1 9HL
E-mail: brackenbower@ft.com
Web Site: www.ft.com; www.mckinsey.com
Established: 2014
Awarded to the best proposal for a book about the challenges & opportunities for growth, providing insight into future trends in business, economics, finance or management. Authors must be 35 years of age or under.
Other Sponsor(s): McKinsey & Co
Award: 15,000 GBP
Closing Date: Sept 30
Presented: Nov

Branford Boase Award
8 Bolderwood Close, Bishopstoke, Eastleigh, Hants SO50 8PG
Tel: (02380) 600439; (07976) 082049 (cell)
Web Site: www.branfordboaseaward.org.uk
Key Personnel
Administrator: Anne Marley *E-mail:* anne.marley@tiscali.co.uk
Awarded annually to the most promising book of 6,000 words or more for seven year-olds & upwards by a first novelist in a single calendar year. The book must be published during the prior calendar year. Publishers may submit up to 5 books. See full criteria & rules for entry on web site.
Award: 1,000 GBP & hand-crafted box, inlaid with silver
Closing Date: Dec 1
Presented: Shortlist released in May, winner announced in July

Bread & Roses Award
Alliance of Radical Booksellers
c/o Housmans Bookshop, 5 Caledonian Rd, Kings Cross, London N1 9DX
Tel: (020) 7837 4473
Web Site: www.bread-and-roses.co.uk
Key Personnel
Co-Manager, Housmans Bookshop: Nik Gorecki
E-mail: nik@housmans.com
Recognizes & celebrates excellence in the field of radical political nonfiction. Books must be submitted by agents or publishers (not individuals). The first edition of the book must have been physically published during the calendar year prior to the award year. Self-published books & works by writers under 16 years of age are not eligible. No entry fee for nominated titles, but publishers will be asked for 50 GBP per shortlisted title as a contribution to marketing costs. See web site for submission address.
Other Sponsor(s): Housmans Bookshop
Award: 500 GBP
Closing Date: Annually in Jan
Presented: ARB London Radical Bookfair, Annually in June

The Brian Way Award
Theatre Centre
Shoreditch Town Hall, 380 Old St, London EC1V 9LT
Tel: (020) 7729 3066 *Fax:* (020) 7739 9741
E-mail: admin@theatre-centre.co.uk
Web Site: theatre-centre.co.uk
Annual prize for playwrights who write for young people. Submitted plays must have been produced professionally within the past year & must be at least 45 minutes long.
Award: 6,000 GBP

The Bridport Prize
Bridport Arts Centre
PO Box 6910, Dorset DT6 9BQ
Tel: (01308) 428333
Web Site: www.bridportprize.org.uk

Key Personnel
Prize Administrator: Frances Everitt
E-mail: frances@bridportprize.org.uk
Established: 1973
Open writing competition for short stories (5,000 words maximum), poetry (42 lines maximum) & flash fiction (250 words maximum).
Entry fees: 8 GBP per story, 7 GBP per poem & 6 GBP per flash fiction.
Award: Short Story & Poetry: 1st prize 5,000 GBP, 2nd prize 1,000 GBP, 3rd prize 500 GBP, 10 supplementary prizes of 50 GBP; Flash Fiction: 1st prize 1,000 GBP, 2nd prize 500 GBP, 3rd prize 250 GBP, 3 supplementary prizes of 25 GBP
Closing Date: June 30 annually
Presented: Bridport Open Book Festival

The British Book Awards
The Bookseller
Westminster Tower, 10th floor, 3 Albert Embankment, Lambeth, London SE1 7SP
Web Site: www.thebookseller.com/british-book-awards
Key Personnel
Head, Events: Grace Harrison *Tel:* (020) 3358 0386 *E-mail:* grace.harrison@thebookseller.com
Established: 1990
Annual awards to recognize the best of the book trade.
Closing Date: Feb
Presented: Grosvenor House, Park Lane, London, May

The Caine Prize for African Writing
The Menier Gallery, Menier Chocolate Factory, 51 Southwark St, London SE1 1RU
Tel: (020) 7378 6234
E-mail: info@caineprize.com
Web Site: www.caineprize.com
Key Personnel
Contact: Lizzy Attree
Established: 2000
Awarded to a work (a short story) by an African writer published in English, whether in Africa or elsewhere. Only fictional work is eligible.
Other Sponsor(s): The Beit Trust; Bodleian Library; The Booker Prize Foundation; British Council; China Africa Resources PLC; CSL; Culture Fund; Exotix; Georgetown University; Kenya Airways; Lannan Center; The Lennox & Wyfold Foundation; Miles Morland Foundation; The Oppenheimer Memorial Trust; Sigrid Rausing & Eric Abraham; Stichting Doen; Weatherly International PLC
Award: 10,000 GBP; shortlisted candidates receive 500 GBP & travel award
Closing Date: Jan 31
Presented: July

Cardiff International Poetry Competition
Llenyddiaeth Cymru (Literature Wales)
Mount Stuart House, 3rd floor, Mount Stuart Sq, Cardiff CF10 5FQ
Tel: (029) 2047 2266 *Fax:* (029) 2049 2930
E-mail: post@llenyddiaethcymru.org; post@literaturewales.org
Web Site: www.llenyddiaethcymru.org; www.literaturewales.org
Key Personnel
Chief Executive Officer: Peter Finch
Established: 1986
Awarded annually. Unpublished poems in the English language of no more than 50 lines on any subject. Open to all nationalities.
Other Sponsor(s): Cardiff Council
Award: 1st prize 5,000 GBP; 2nd prize 500 GBP; 3rd prize 250 GBP; 5 prizes of 50 GBP
Closing Date: March
Presented: June/July

The Carey Award
The Society of Indexers

Woodbourn Business Centre, 10 Jessell St, Sheffield S9 3HY
Tel: (0114) 244 9561 *Fax:* (0114) 244 9563
E-mail: admin@indexers.org.uk
Web Site: www.indexers.org.uk
Key Personnel
Chairman: Ann Kindgom *E-mail:* chair@indexers. org.uk
Established: 1977
The award is made on an occasional basis by Council for outstanding services to indexing.
Award: Framed, illuminated parchment

Carnegie Medal
Chartered Institute of Library & Information Professionals (CILIP)
7 Ridgmount St, London WC1E 7AE
Tel: (020) 7255 0500 *Fax:* (020) 7255 0501
E-mail: ckg@cilip.org.uk
Web Site: www.carnegiegreenaway.org.uk/ carnegie; www.cilip.org.uk
Key Personnel
Corporate Marketing Manager: Kasey Butler
Tel: (020) 7255 0650 *E-mail:* kasey.butler@ cilip.org.uk
Prize Coordinator: Sue Roe
Press Officer: Rebecca Wyatt
Established: 1936
Established by The Library Association in memory of Scottish-born philanthropist, Andrew Carnegie (1835-1919). Awarded annually to the writer of an outstanding book for children.
Award: Golden medal & 500 GBP worth of books to donate to a library of their choice
Presented: BAFTA Headquarters, Piccadilly, London, June 23

The Centre for Literacy in Primary Poetry Award (CLiPPA)
The Centre for Literacy in Primary Education (CLPE)
44 Webber St, London SE1 8QW
Tel: (020) 7401 3382; (020) 7401 3383
E-mail: info@clpe.org.uk
Web Site: www.clpe.org.uk
Key Personnel
Chief Executive: Louise Johns-Shepherd
Library & Literature Development Manager: Ann Lazim *E-mail:* ann@clpe.org.uk
Marketing & Communications Manager: Fatim Kesvani
Established: 2003
Annual award to recognize excellence in published poetry for children in the UK. Presented for a book of poetry by a single poet or collection of children's poetry published in the preceding year.
Closing Date: Jan 31
Presented: Annually in June

Children's Book Award
The Federation of Children's Book Groups
10 St Laurence Rd, Bradford on Avon, Wilts BA15 1JG
Toll Free Tel: 0300 102 1559
E-mail: contact@childrensbookaward.org.uk
Web Site: childrensbookaward.org.uk
Established: 1980
National award voted for solely by children. The Children's Book Award runs throughout the year. There are 2 voting stages.
Full testing: this creates a Top 50 Pick of the Year, from which the Top Ten books are selected. Only Federation of Children's Book Group members take part in this element of the award. The entire process takes a calendar year & currently runs from January-December.
Top Ten testing: this leads to the selection of the Category Winners & Overall Winner. Any child or young person across the UK can participate in this element of the award & vote online.

This process takes approximately 3 months & currently runs from February-May.
Children & young people to the age of 18 take part across 3 age-related categories: Younger Children (Picture Books); Younger Readers (age 6-11); Older Readers (age 10-18).

☆Cholmondeley Awards
The Society of Authors
84 Drayton Gardens, London SW10 9SB
Tel: (020) 7373 6642 *Fax:* (020) 7373 5768
E-mail: info@societyofauthors.org
Web Site: www.societyofauthors.org
Key Personnel
Awards Secretary: Paula Johnson
E-mail: pjohnson@societyofauthors.org
Established: 1966
Established by the late Dowager Marchioness of Cholmondeley to recognize achievement & distinction in poetry. The noncompetitive award is for work generally, not for a specific book & submissions are not accepted. Awarded annually.
Award: Total of 8,000 GBP
Presented: Literary Awards Reception, June 18

The Arthur C Clarke Award
Serendip Foundation
One Long Row Close, Everdon, Daventry, Northants NN11 3BE
E-mail: clarkeaward@gmail.com
Web Site: www.clarkeaward.com
Key Personnel
Chairman & Dir: Tom Hunter
Established: 1986
Annual award for the best science fiction novel published in the UK in the previous calendar year.
Other Sponsor(s): Rocket Publishing
Award: Engraved bookend & GBP in an amount matching the year
Presented: Sci-Fi-London Film Festival, April 30

CLiPPA, see The Centre for Literacy in Primary Poetry Award (CLiPPA)

David Cohen Prize for Literature
Arts Council of England
2 Pear Tree Court, London EC1R 0DS
Tel: (0845) 300 6200; (0845) 300 6100
Fax: (020) 7608 4100
E-mail: enquiries@artscouncil.org.uk
Web Site: www.artscouncil.org.uk
Established: 1993
Awarded biennially to a living writer who has written in English & has contributed a significant amount to British literature. Submissions are not accepted.
Other Sponsor(s): David Cohen Family Charitable Trust; Johs S Cohen Foundation
Award: 40,000 GBP
Presented: March

Commonwealth Short Story Prize
Commonwealth Foundation
Commonwealth Writers, Marborough House, Pall Mall, London SW1Y 5HY
Tel: (020) 7747 6262 (writers); (020) 7747 6328 (prizes)
E-mail: writers@commonwealth.int
Web Site: www.commonwealthwriters.org
Annual award for unpublished short fiction. Prize covers the commonwealth regions of Africa, Asia, Canada, Europe, Caribbean & Pacific.
Award: 5,000 GBP for overall winner; 2,500 GBP for 4 regional winners
Closing Date: Nov 30

☆Duff Cooper Prize
Duff Cooper
54 St Maur Rd, Box 22, London SW6 4DP

Tel: (020) 7736 3729 *Fax:* (020) 7731 7638
E-mail: info@theduffcooperprize.org
Web Site: www.theduffcooperprize.org
Key Personnel
Prize Administrator: Ms Artemis Cooper
Established: 1956
For a literary work of history, biography, poetry or politics supported by a recognized publisher & published in English within the current year. The prize is the interest from a trust fund. Awarded annually.
Award: 5,000 GBP & copy of Duff Cooper's autobiography, Old Men Forget
Closing Date: Nov 30
Presented: Feb

Costa Book Awards
Booksellers Association of the United Kingdom & Ireland Ltd
6 Bell Yard, London WC2A 2JR
Tel: (020) 7421 4640
E-mail: info@costabookawards.com
Web Site: www.costabookawards.co.uk; www. booksellers.org.uk
Key Personnel
Contact: Naomi Gane *Tel:* (020) 7802 0802
E-mail: naomi.gane@booksellers.org.uk
Established: 1971
Six awards to celebrate & promote the best contemporary British writing. The awards are judged in 2 stages & open to 5 categories: Novel, Biography, Poetry & Children's Book of the Year. The Novel, First Novel, Biography & Poetry Awards are judged by a panel of 3 judges & the winner of each category receives an award of 5,000 GBP. One of these 5 books is selected as the overall winner of the Book of the Year & receives a further 30,000 GBP.
Other Sponsor(s): Costa Coffee
Award: Total of 55,000 GBP
Closing Date: June 29
Presented: Harrogate International Centre, May 1

☆The Rose Mary Crawshay Prize
British Academy
The British Academy, 10-11 Carlton House Terrace, London SW1Y 5AH
Tel: (020) 7969 5200 *Fax:* (020) 7969 5300
E-mail: chiefexec@britac.ac.uk
Web Site: www.britac.ac.uk
Key Personnel
Events Manager: Angela Pusey *Tel:* (020) 7969 5264 *E-mail:* a.pusey@britac.ac.uk
Established: 1888
Awarded by the Council of the British Academy to women writers of any nationality for an historical or critical work of value on any subject concerning English literature published within the preceding 3 years. Preference is given to works on Byron, Shelley or Keats. Two prizes awarded annually. Applications are not sought.
Award: 500 GBP

CWA Diamond Dagger
Crime Writers' Association (CWA)
Peershaws, Berewyk Hall Court, White Colne, Colchester, Essex CO6 2QB
E-mail: admin@cwadaggers.co.uk
Web Site: thecwa.co.uk/the-daggers; cwadaggers. co.uk/cwa-diamond-dagger
Key Personnel
Chair: L C Tyler
Vice Chair: Martin Edwards
Established: 1955
Nominees must meet 2 criteria: First, their careers must be marked by sustained excellence; second, they must have made a significant contribution to crime writing published in the English language, whether originally or in transla-

tion. The award is made purely on merit without reference to age, gender or nationality. Entry via online submission after publisher registration. Processing fee 45 GBP per title (10 GBP per individual short story).

CWA Gold Dagger
Crime Writers' Association (CWA)
Peershaws, Berewyk Hall Court, White Colne, Colchester, Essex CO6 2QB
E-mail: director@thecwa.co.uk
Web Site: thecwa.co.uk
Key Personnel
Chair: L C Tyler
Vice Chair: Martin Edwards
Established: 1955
For the best crime novel written in English.
Other Sponsor(s): Booksdirect
Award: 2,500 GBP & ornamental dagger

CWA International Dagger
Crime Writers' Association (CWA)
Peershaws, Berewyk Hall Court, White Colne, Colchester, Essex CO6 2QB
E-mail: director@thecwa.co.uk
Web Site: thecwa.co.uk
Key Personnel
Chair: L C Tyler
Vice Chair: Martin Edwards
Established: 2006
Best crime novel translated into English from another language.
Award: 1,000 GBP & ornamental dagger to winning author; 500 GBP to the translator

Dagger in the Library
Crime Writers' Association (CWA)
Peershaws, Berewyk Hall Court, White Colne, Colchester, Essex CO6 2QB
E-mail: director@thecwa.co.uk
Web Site: thecwa.co.uk
Key Personnel
Chair: L C Tyler
Vice Chair: Martin Edwards
Award for the living author of crime fiction whose body of work has given the most pleasure to library users.
Other Sponsor(s): The Random House Group
Award: 1,500 GBP, ornamental dagger & 300 GBP to participating library's reader group

Rees Davies Prize
The Royal Historical Society
University College London, Gower St, London WC1E 6BT
Tel: (020) 7387 7532 *Fax:* (020) 7387 7532
E-mail: royalhistsoc@ucl.ac.uk
Web Site: www.royalhistoricalsociety.org
Key Personnel
Executive Secretary: Sue Carr *E-mail:* s.carr@ucl.ac.uk
Administrative Secretary: Melanie Ransom *E-mail:* m.ransom@ucl.ac.uk
Graduate essay prize. Winning essay will be published in the following year's edition of the Society's journal *Transactions of the Royal Historical Society.*
Award: 100 EUR, essay publication & 3 yr RHS membership

Debut Dagger
Crime Writers' Association (CWA)
Peershaws, Berewyk Hall Court, White Colne, Colchester, Essex CO6 2QB
E-mail: director@thecwa.co.uk; debut.dagger@thecwa.co.uk
Web Site: thecwa.co.uk
Key Personnel
Chair: L C Tyler
Vice Chair: Martin Edwards
Established: 1998

Annual new writing award for unpublished authors of fiction.
Other Sponsor(s): Orion
Award: 700 GBP
Presented: Feb 6

☆Isaac & Tamara Deutscher Memorial Prize
Isaac & Tamara Deutcher Memorial Prize
Faculty of Law & Social Sciences, SOAS, University of London, Thornhaugh St, Russell Sq, London WC1H 0XG
Web Site: www.deutscherprize.org.uk
Established: 1968
Awarded annually for a book which exemplifies the best & most innovative new writing in or about the Marxist tradition.
Award: 500 GBP
Closing Date: May 1
Presented: Nov

Diagram Prize for Oddest Book Title of the Year
The Bookseller
Westminster Tower, 10th floor, 3 Albert Embankment, Lambeth, London SE1 7SP
Web Site: www.thebookseller.com/diagramprize
Humorous literary award presented annually to the book with the oddest title.

DRF Bursary, see David Miller Bursary

John Dryden Translation Competition
British Comparative Literature Association/British Centre for Literary Translation
School of Literature & Creative Writing, University of East Anglia, Norwich NR4 7TJ
Tel: (01603) 593360 *Fax:* (01603) 458553
E-mail: transcomp@uea.ac.uk
Web Site: www.bcla.org; www.uea.ac.uk
Key Personnel
BCLA Secretary: Penny Brown *E-mail:* penelope.brown@besco.net
Contact: Prof Jean Boase-Beier
Literary translation from any language into English including poetry, fiction or literary prose, from any period; maximum 25 typed pages. Entry fee of 7 GBP, 12 GBP for two & 16 GBP for three.
Award: 1st prize 350 GBP; 2nd prize 200 GBP; 3rd prize 100 GBP. Winning entries will be published in full on the web site; extracts from winning entries are eligible for publication in BCLA's journal *Comparative Critical Studies*
Closing Date: Feb annually (usually mid-month)
Presented: Announced in July on BCLA web site; presentation later in the year

EBRD Literature Prize
European Bank for Reconstruction & Development (EBRD)
One Exchange Sq, London EC2A 2JN
Tel: (020) 7338 6000
Web Site: www.ebrd.com/literature-prize
Key Personnel
Contact: Svitlana Pyrkalo *Tel:* (07802) 510751 (cell) *E-mail:* pyrkalos@ebrd.com
Established: 2017
To acknowledge a translated work of literary fiction written originally in any language from an EBRD country of operations & published by a UK publisher.
Other Sponsor(s): British Council; London Book Fair
Award: 20,000 EUR first prize equally divided between author & translator; 2 runners-up & their translators receive 1,000 EUR each
Presented: EBRD headquarters, April

Edge Hill Prize
Edge Hill University
St Helens Rd, Ormskirk, Lancs L39 4QP

Tel: (01695) 575171 *Fax:* (01695) 579997
Web Site: www.edgehill.ac.uk/shortstory
Key Personnel
Contact: Harriet Hirshman
Awarded annually for excellence in a published single author short story collection in English during the previous calendar year. Authors must be born or normally resident in the British Isles, including Ireland. Translations & self-published collections are not eligible.
Award: 10,000 GBP & specially commissioned artwork
Closing Date: March 3

eDunnit Award
CrimeFest
Basement Flat, 6 Rodney Pl, Bristol BS8 4HY
Tel: (0117) 9737829
E-mail: info@crimefest.com; ebook@crimefest.com (submissions)
Web Site: www.crimefest.com
To recognize the outstanding contribution that crime fiction ebooks make to the genre. Eligible are any crime ebooks such as humour, historical, spy, suspense & thriller commercially published in both hardcopy & epub for the first time in the British Isles in the year prior to the award year. Hybrid authors—now self-published but previously commercially/traditionally published—should contact CrimeFest about eligibility. Excel file preferred. See web site for complete submission guidelines.
Award: Bristol Blue Glass commemorative award
Closing Date: Annually in Dec
Presented: CrimeFest Awards Dinner, Annually in May

The George Eliot Fellowship Essay Prize
The George Eliot Fellowship
39 Lower Rd, Barnacle, Coventry, Warwicks CV7 9LD
Tel: (024) 7661 9126
Web Site: www.georgeeliot.org
Key Personnel
Chairman: John Burton *E-mail:* jkburton@tiscali.co.uk
Vice Chairman: Vivienne Wood *Tel:* (01455) 618044 *E-mail:* vewood55@gmail.com
Membership Secretary: Juliet Hopper *Tel:* (024) 7634 4398 *E-mail:* juliet.hopper@googlemail.com
Annual prize for a previously unpublished paper on George Eliot's life or work. Essays should not normally exceed 4,000 words & should be typed (or printed out), double-spaced, on 1 side of A4 paper, leaving margins approximately 3.5 cm. Entrants may submit 2 copies by post or submit an electronic copy to the chairman at jkburton@tiscali.co.uk.
Award: 500 GBP, publication in next year's *George Eliot Review* & honorary 2-yr Fellowship membership
Closing Date: Dec 15
Presented: March 31

The Desmond Elliott Prize
The Desmond Elliott Charitable Trust
84 Godolphin Rd, London W12 8JW
Tel: (020) 8222 6580
Web Site: www.desmondelliottprize.org
Key Personnel
Administrator: Emma Manderson *E-mail:* ema.manderson@googlemail.com
Established: 2007
Awarded annually for the best first full-length work of fiction written in English & published in book form in the UK, written by an author whose permanent place of residence is in the UK or Ireland.
Award: 10,000 GBP

Thomas Ellis Memorial Fund
c/o University of Wales, University Registry, King Edward VII Ave, Cathays Park, Cardiff CF10 3NS
Tel: (029) 2037 6999 *Fax:* (029) 2037 6980
E-mail: uniwales@wales.ac.uk
Web Site: www.wales.ac.uk
Grants to assist research into the language, literature, history & antiquities of Wales & Monmouthshire & the publication of the results of such research. Applications should be sent to the Secretary General at the University Registry.

Encore Award
The Society of Authors
84 Drayton Gardens, London SW10 9SB
Tel: (020) 7373 6642 *Fax:* (020) 7373 5768
E-mail: info@societyofauthors.org
Web Site: www.societyofauthors.org
Key Personnel
Awards Secretary: Paula Johnson
E-mail: pjohnson@societyofauthors.org
Established: 1990
Awarded biennially to a second novel (or novels) judged to be the best first published in the UK during the 2 years preceding the year in which the award is presented; publisher entry only.
Award: 10,000 GBP
Closing Date: Nov 30
Presented: Spring

☆**The Geoffrey Faber Memorial Prize**
Faber & Faber Ltd
Bloomsbury House, 74-77 Great Russell St, London WC1B 3DA
Tel: (020) 7927 3800 *Fax:* (020) 7927 3801
E-mail: webmaster@faber.co.uk
Web Site: www.faber.co.uk
Key Personnel
Publicity Dir: Rachel Alexander *Tel:* (020) 7927 3883 *E-mail:* rachel.alexander@faber.co.uk
Established: 1963
Established as a memorial to the founder & first chairman of the firm. Awarded in alternate years for a volume of verse & a volume of prose fiction of greatest literary merit first published originally in the UK during the 2 years preceding the year in which the award is given. To be eligible for the prize, the volume of verse or prose fiction must be by a writer who is not more than 40 years old at date of publication & is a citizen of the UK & colonies, any other Commonwealth state, Ireland or Republic of South Africa. Nominations accepted from editors & literary editors of newspapers & magazines that review poetry or fiction. No submissions accepted.
Award: 1,000 GBP

Ian Fleming Steel Dagger
Crime Writers' Association (CWA)
Peershaws, Berewyk Hall Court, White Colne, Colchester, Essex CO6 2QB
E-mail: director@thecwa.co.uk
Web Site: thecwa.co.uk
Key Personnel
Chair: L C Tyler
Vice Chair: Martin Edwards
Established: 2002
Award for best adventure/thriller novel in the vein of James Bond.
Other Sponsor(s): Ian Fleming (Glidrose) Publications Ltd
Award: 2,000 GBP & ornamental steel dagger

John Florio Prize
The Society of Authors
84 Drayton Gardens, London SW10 9SB
Tel: (020) 7373 6642 *Fax:* (020) 7373 5768
E-mail: info@societyofauthors.org
Web Site: www.societyofauthors.org

Key Personnel
Awards Secretary: Paula Johnson
E-mail: pjohnson@societyofauthors.org
Established: 1963
Established under the auspices of the Italian Institute & the British-Italian Society & named after John Florio. Biennial prize for the best translation into English of a 20th century Italian work of literary merit & general interest, first published in the UK during the preceding 2 years.
Award: 3,000 GBP
Closing Date: Jan 31

The Folio Prize, see Rathbones Folio Prize

Forward Prizes for Poetry
Forward Arts Foundation
c/o The Society of Literature, Somerset House, Strand, London WC2R 1LA
Tel: (020) 7845 4655
E-mail: info@forwardartsfoundation.org
Web Site: www.forwardartsfoundation.org/forward-prizes-for-poetry
Key Personnel
Executive Dir: Susannah Herbert
Forward Prizes Manager: Holly Hopkins
Prizes to celebrate excellence in poetry & increase its audience. Awarded in 3 categories: The Forward Prize for Best Collection (author of the best collection of poetry published in the UK or Republic of Ireland); The Felix Dennis Prize for Best First Collection (author of the best first collection of poetry published in the UK or Republic of Ireland); The Forward Prize for Best Single Poem (author of the best single poem published in a newspaper, periodical, or magazine in the UK or Republic of Ireland, or has been the winner of a poetry competition). See dates & full eligibility guidelines on the web site.
Other Sponsor(s): Bookmark; Felix Dennis Trust
Award: The Forward Prize for Best Collection: 10,000 GBP; The Felix Dennis Prize for Best First Collection 5,000 GBP; The Forward Prize for Best Single Poem 1,000 GBP
Closing Date: Annually in March
Presented: Annually in Sept

Fraenkel Prize in Contemporary History
The Wiener Library for the Study of the Holocaust & Genocide
29 Russel Sq, London WC1B 5DP
Tel: (020) 7636 7247 *Fax:* (020) 7436 6428
E-mail: info@wienerlibrary.co.uk
Web Site: www.wienerlibrary.co.uk
Key Personnel
Development Dir: Bridget McGing
Established: 1989
Awarded for outstanding work of 20th century history in one of the Wiener Library's field of interest. Two distinct awards are given: Category A - open to all entrants. The length, not counting references & the bibliography must not be below 50,000 words & not exceed 150,000 words. Category B - open to all entrants who have yet to publish a major monograph. The length, not counting references & the bibliography, must not be below 25,000 words & not exceed 100,000 words. The work must be written in English, French or German & be unpublished in any language at the deadline for submissions.
Other Sponsor(s): Ernst Fraenkel OBE
Award: Two awards: 6,000 USD (Category A); 4,000 USD (Category B)

FT & McKinsey Business Book of the Year Award
Financial Times Ltd
One Southwark Bridge, London SE1 9HL
Tel: (020) 7775 6060

E-mail: bookaward@ft.com
Web Site: www.ft.com/management/business-book-award
Key Personnel
Contact: Ugne Griniute
Annual award to identify the book that provides the most compelling & enjoyable insight into modern business issues.
Other Sponsor(s): McKinsey & Co
Award: 30,000 GBP; shortlisted authors receive 10,000 GBP

The Gladstone History Book Prize
The Royal Historical Society
University College London, Gower St, London WC1E 6BT
Tel: (020) 7387 7532 *Fax:* (020) 7387 7532
E-mail: royalhistsoc@ucl.ac.uk
Web Site: www.royalhistoricalsociety.org
Key Personnel
Executive Secretary: Sue Carr *E-mail:* s.carr@ucl.ac.uk
Administrative Secretary: Melanie Ransom
E-mail: m.ransom@ucl.ac.uk
Established: 1998
Based on any historical subject which is not primarily related to British history. Must be its author's first solely written history book & published in English during the calendar year by a scholar normally resident in the UK. Must be an original & scholarly work of historical research. Author or publisher should submit 3 copies (non-returnable) of an eligible book by the end of the year.
Award: 1,000 GBP
Closing Date: Dec 31 annually
Presented: Royal Historical Society Annual Reception, July

Gold Dagger for Non-Fiction
Crime Writers' Association (CWA)
Peershaws, Berewyk Hall Court, White Colne, Colchester, Essex CO6 2QB
E-mail: director@thecwa.co.uk
Web Site: thecwa.co.uk
Key Personnel
Chair: L C Tyler
Vice Chair: Martin Edwards
Established: 1978
Awarded biannually. Winner is selected by an independent panel. Submission by publishers only.
Other Sponsor(s): Owatonna Media
Award: 1,000 GBP & an ornamental dagger

The Goldsmiths Prize
Goldsmiths, University of London
c/o Dept of English & Comparative Literature, Goldsmiths, University of London, New Cross, London SE14 6NW
E-mail: goldsmithprize@gold.ac.uk
Web Site: www.gold.ac.uk
Annual award for a fiction novel published by a UK-based publisher during the prize year.
Other Sponsor(s): NewStatesman
Award: 10,000 GBP
Closing Date: July 4 for finished texts
Presented: Nov

Edgar Graham Book Prize
School of Oriental & African Studies (SOAS)
University of London, Thornhaugh St, Russell Sq, London WC1H 0XG
Tel: (020) 7637 2388 *Fax:* (020) 7898 4009
Web Site: www.soas.ac.uk
Key Personnel
Chair: Dr Subir Sinha
Prize Administrator: Jenny Higgins *E-mail:* j.higgins@soas.ac.uk
Established: 1984
Awarded annually to a work of original scholarship published in English on agricultural +/or industrial development in Asia +/or Africa.

Award: 1,000 GBP
Closing Date: Oct 1

Kate Greenaway Medal
Chartered Institute of Library & Information Professionals (CILIP)
7 Ridgmount St, London WC1E 7AE
Tel: (020) 7255 0500 *Fax:* (020) 7255 0501
E-mail: info@cilip.org.uk; ckg@cilip.org.uk
Web Site: www.carnegiegreenaway.org.uk/
greenaway; www.cilip.org.uk
Key Personnel
Corporate Marketing Manager: Kasey Butler
Tel: (020) 7255 0650 *E-mail:* kasey.butler@
cilip.org.uk
Established: 1955
Offered annually for the most distinguished work in the illustration of children's books first published in the UK or have had co-publication elsewhere within a 3 month time lapse.
Award: Golden medal, 500 GBP worth of books to donate to a library of their choice & 5,000 GBP Colin Mears Award
Presented: BAFTA Headquarters, Piccadilly, London, June 23

Eric Gregory Awards
The Society of Authors
84 Drayton Gardens, London SW10 9SB
Tel: (020) 7373 6642 *Fax:* (020) 7373 5768
E-mail: info@societyofauthors.org
Web Site: www.societyofauthors.org
Key Personnel
Awards Secretary: Paula Johnson
E-mail: pjohnson@societyofauthors.org
Established: 1960
A number of awards are made each year to encourage young British poets. Candidates for awards must be British subjects by birth, ordinarily resident in the UK & under the age of 30 on March 31 in the year of the award. Candidates must submit a published or unpublished volume of belles lettres, poetry or drama-poems.
Award: 24,000 GBP in total
Closing Date: Oct 31
Presented: Ledbury Poetry Festival, July 10

☆Guardian Children's Fiction Prize
The Guardian
Kings Pl, 90 York Way, London N1 9GU
Tel: (020) 3353 3400
E-mail: childrensfictionprize@guardian.co.uk
Web Site: www.guardian.co.uk; www.
guardiannews.com
Key Personnel
Contact: Pamela Mathews
Established: 1967
Awarded to an outstanding work of fiction (not picture books) for children written by a British or Commonwealth author, first published in the UK during the calendar year preceding the year in which the award is presented. The winner is chosen by a panel of authors & the review editor for The Guardian's children's books section. Awarded annually. Entry fee 25 GBP.
Award: 1,500 GBP
Closing Date: May 9

☆The Guardian First Book Award
The Guardian
Kings Pl, 90 York Way, London N1 9GU
Tel: (020) 3353 3400
E-mail: books.editor@guardianunlimited.co.uk
Web Site: www.guardian.co.uk; www.
guardiannews.com
Established: 1999
This award recognizes & rewards new writings by honouring an author's first book. Its aim is to reflect the breadth of coverage of all genres on The Guardian books pages & underpin the paper's commitment to new quality writing.

Award: 10,000 GBP plus an advertising package within The Guardian & Observer. Also, an endowment of 1,000 GBP worth of books will be made by The Guardian to a UK school of the author's choice
Closing Date: June 4

The Calouste Gulbenkian Prize
The Society of Authors
84 Drayton Gardens, London SW10 9SB
Tel: (020) 7373 6642 *Fax:* (020) 7373 5768
E-mail: info@societyofauthors.org
Web Site: www.societyofauthors.org
Key Personnel
Awards Secretary: Paula Johnson
E-mail: pjohnson@societyofauthors.org
Biennial prize for translations of full length Portuguese works of literary merit & general interest. The original must have been published in the last 100 years. The translation must have been first published in the UK in the 3 years up to & including the year of the entry.
Award: 3,000 GBP
Closing Date: Jan 31

Francis Head Bequest
The Society of Authors
84 Drayton Gardens, London SW10 9SB
Tel: (020) 7373 6642 *Fax:* (020) 7373 5768
E-mail: info@societyofauthors.org
Web Site: www.societyofauthors.org
Key Personnel
Awards Secretary: Paula Johnson
E-mail: pjohnson@societyofauthors.org
Provides grants to professional British authors over 35 years of age whose main source of income is from their writing & who, through accident, illness or other causes, are temporarily unable to write.

The Hellenic Foundation for Culture Translation Prize
The Society of Authors
84 Drayton Gardens, London SW10 9SB
Tel: (020) 7373 6642 *Fax:* (020) 7373 5768
E-mail: info@societyofauthors.org
Web Site: www.societyofauthors.org
Key Personnel
Awards Secretary: Paula Johnson
E-mail: pjohnson@societyofauthors.org
Established: 2002
Triennial prize for translation from modern Greek into English of full-length works of imaginative literature (prose, poetry or drama). The translation must have been first published in the 3 years up to & including final year of entry. The publisher may be based anywhere in the world but the translation must be available for purchase within the UK. Next award 2020.
Award: 1,000 GBP
Closing Date: Jan 31

Felicia Hemans Prize for Lyrical Poetry
University of Liverpool
The School of English Cypress Bldg, Chatham St, Liverpool L69 3BX
Tel: (0151) 794 2000
Web Site: www.liv.ac.uk
Annual prize is open to past & present members & students of the University of Liverpool only, is awarded to a lyrical poem, the subject of which may be chosen by the competitor. Only one poem, either published or unpublished, may be submitted.
Award: 200 GBP (one year's income from the Felicia Hemans Memorial Fund plus additional generous sponsorship from Liverpool University Press)
Closing Date: May 1

William Hill Sports Book of the Year
William Hill Organization

Greenside House, 50 Station Rd, London N22 7TP
Tel: (020) 8918 3600 *Fax:* (020) 8918 3775
Web Site: www.williamhillmedia.com
Key Personnel
Media Relations Dir: Graham Sharpe *Tel:* (0780) 323 3702 *E-mail:* gsharpe@williamhill.co.uk
Awarded annually to the best sports book published in the year preceding the year in which the prize is awarded. Publisher entry only.
Award: 23,000 GBP
Closing Date: Sept
Presented: Nov

History Scotland Prize, see Royal Historical Society/History Scotland Prize

Ted Hughes Award
The Poetry Society
22 Betterton St, London WC2H 9BX
Tel: (020) 7420 9880 *Fax:* (020) 7240 4818
E-mail: award@poetrysociety.org.uk
Web Site: www.poetrysociety.org.uk
Annual award to a UK poet, working in any form, who has made the most exciting contribution to poetry in that year.
Award: 5,000 GBP
Presented: March

The Imison Award
The Society of Authors
84 Drayton Gardens, London SW10 9SB
Tel: (020) 7373 6642 *Fax:* (020) 7373 5768
E-mail: info@societyofauthors.org
Web Site: www.societyofauthors.org
Key Personnel
Awards Secretary: Paula Johnson
E-mail: pjohnson@societyofauthors.org
Established: 1994
Awarded for the best original radio drama script by a writer new to radio.
Other Sponsor(s): Peggy Ramsay Foundation
Award: 1,500 GBP

Impress Prize for New Writers
Impress Books Ltd
Innovation Centre, University of Exeter, Rennes Dr, Devon EX4 4RN
Tel: (01392) 950910
E-mail: enquiries@impress-books.co.uk
Web Site: www.impress-books.co.uk
Established: 2007
Annual award for new, unpublished writers. Winner receives a publishing contract.
Closing Date: June 17

Independent Publishing Awards
Independent Publishers Guild (IPG)
47 Bedford Sq, London WC1B 3DP
Mailing Address: PO Box 12, Llain, Login SA34 0WU
Tel: (01437) 563335 *Fax:* (01437) 562071
E-mail: info@ipg.uk.com
Web Site: www.ipg.uk.com/independent-publishing-awards
Key Personnel
Chief Executive: Bridget Shine
Administrator: Angela Stanley
Events & Sponsorship Manager: Inogen Race
Head, Communications: Tom Holman
Established: 2007
Annual awards to celebrate independent publishing. Submissions must cover the calendar year prior to the year of the awards. One form per entry accompanied by no more than 1,000 words of supporting material & 3 books, or digital material if that is more appropriate. See web site for complete entry instructions & criteria.
Categories: Trade Publisher of the Year, Academic & Professional Publisher of the Year, Children's Publisher of the Year, Education

Publisher of the Year, Specialist Consumer Publisher of the Year, Newcomer Award, International Achievement of the Year, Digital Publishing Award, Digital Marketing Award, Diversity Award, Young Independent Publisher of the Year.

Information Services Group Reference Awards
Chartered Institute of Library & Information Professionals (CILIP)
7 Ridgmount St, London WC1E 7AE
Tel: (020) 7255 0500 *Fax:* (020) 7255 0501
Web Site: www.cilip.org.uk
Key Personnel
Awards Coordinator: Jessica Dunnicliff
    E-mail: jessicadunnicliff@stratfordhigh.org.uk
Established: 1970
For outstanding works of reference published in the UK. One for print & one for electronic formats. The judges will assess the authority, scope & coverage, arrangement & currency of the information, quality of indexing, adequacy of references, physical presentation, originality & value for money.
The awards are administered by the Information Services Group.
Award: 500 GBP & certificate
Presented: Sept

☆International Prize for Arabic Fiction (IPAF)
Booker Prize Foundation
133 Hill House, 210 Upper Richmond Rd, London SW15 6NP
Tel: (079) 1373 3150
Web Site: www.arabicfiction.org
Key Personnel
Prize Administrator: Fleur Montanaro
    E-mail: fleurmontanaro@yahoo.co.uk
Established: 2007
Awarded to the best novel of that year in Arabic. Publishers can submit up to 3 of their novels from the calendar year which ends on June 30 that year.
Other Sponsor(s): TCA Abu Dhabi (Abu Dhabi Tourism & Culture Authority)
Award: 10,000 USD shortlisted authors; 50,000 USD additional to winning author with commitment that IPAF will meet the cost of translation of the winning novel into English to help underwrite its publication for an English speaking readership
Closing Date: June 30
Presented: Gala ceremony, Abu Dhabi, Annually in Spring

Jewish Quarterly Wingate Literary Prize
Jewish Quarterly
28 St Albans Lane, London NW11 7QE
Web Site: jewishquarterly.org; www.wingatefoundation.org.uk/literary_prize.php
Established: 1977
Awarded annually to the best book, fiction or nonfiction, to translate the idea of Jewishness to the general reader.
Award: 4,000 GBP
Presented: JW3, London, Feb

JQ-Wingate Prize, see Jewish Quarterly Wingate Literary Prize

HRF Keating Award
CrimeFest
Basement Flat, 6 Rodney Pl, Bristol BS8 4HY
Tel: (0117) 9737829
E-mail: info@crimefest.com; keating@crimefest.com (submissions)
Web Site: www.crimefest.com
To recognize the outstanding contribution that biographies or critical books related to crime fiction make to the genre. Eligible are any biographies or critical books related to crime

fiction commercially published in hardcover or paperback format for the first time in the British Isles in the year prior to the award year. Excel file preferred. See web site for complete submission guidelines.
Award: Bristol Blue Glass commemorative award
Closing Date: Annually in Dec
Presented: CrimeFest Awards Dinner, Annually in May

☆Kraszna-Krausz Book Awards
Kraszna-Krausz Foundation
Colman Getty, 28 Windmill St, London W1T 2JJ
Tel: (020) 7631 2666
E-mail: awards@kraszna-krausz.org.uk; info@kraszna-krausz.org.uk
Web Site: www.kraszna-krausz.org.uk
Key Personnel
Account Manager: Chris Baker *E-mail:* chris@colmangetty.co.uk
Awards Coordinator: Kathryn del Boccio
Contact: Truda Spruyt *E-mail:* truda@colmangetty.co.uk
Established: 1985
International awards made to encourage & recognize outstanding achievements in the publishing & writing of books on the art, history, practice & technology of photography & of the moving image. The awards are made annually, with prizes for books on still photography & for books on the moving image (film, television, video). Publisher entry only.
Award: 5,000 GBP for each category winner; 1,000 GBP special commendations
Closing Date: Nov 2
Presented: Sony World Photography Awards, April

Lakeland Book of the Year Awards
Hunter Davies
c/o Cumbria Tourism, Windermere Rd, Staveley, Kendal, Cumbria LA8 9PL
Tel: (01539) 822222
Key Personnel
Awards Administrator: Chris Tomlinson
    Tel: (015395) 68342 *E-mail:* chris@chriscollier.co.uk
Established: 1984
Annual awards established by Hunter Davies & Cumbria Tourist Board. There are 6 prizes offered: The Striding Edge Productions Prize for Guides, Walks & Places; The David Winkworth Prize for Illustration & Presentation; The Saint & Co Prize for People & Business; The Bookends Prize for Arts & Literature; The Bill Rollinson Prize for Landscape & Tradition; The Hunter Davies Book of the Year (the overall winner).
Other Sponsor(s): Cumbria Community Foundation; Cumbria Tourism
Award: 100 GBP & a framed certificate
Closing Date: March
Presented: July

Lancashire Book of the Year Award
University of Central Lancashire
Library Service, East Cliff, PO Box 162, Preston PR1 3EA
Tel: (01772) 534008 *Fax:* (01772) 534880
E-mail: library@lancashire.gov.uk
Web Site: www.lancashire.gov.uk
Established: 1986
Annual award given for a work of fiction or a collection of short stories by a single author. The book should be suitable for children 11-14 years of age.
Award: 500 GBP & an engraved decanter
Presented: County Hall, Preston, May 28

Last Laugh Award
CrimeFest
Basement Flat, 6 Rodney Pl, Bristol BS8 4HY

Tel: (0117) 9737829
E-mail: info@crimefest.com; laugh@crimefest.com (submissions)
Web Site: www.crimefest.com
To recognize the outstanding contribution that humorous crime novels make to the genre. Eligible are any humorous crime, spy, suspense & thriller titles commercially published for the first time in the British Isles in the year prior to the award year. Excel file preferred. See web site for complete submission guidelines.
Award: Bristol Blue Glass commemorative award
Closing Date: Annually in Dec
Presented: CrimeFest Awards Dinner, Annually in May

The Little Rebels Children's Book Award
Alliance of Radical Booksellers
c/o Letterbox Library, Unit 151 Stratford Workshops, Burford Rd, Stratford, London E15 2SP
Tel: (020) 8534 7502
E-mail: info@letterboxlibrary.com
Web Site: littlerebels.org
Key Personnel
Co-Dir, Letterbox Library: Fen Coles
Recognizes & awards radical children's fiction. Books must be submitted by publishers (not individuals) & fall under the definition of a radical fiction book (see web site for details). Books must be targeted at ages 0-12; teen & young adult books will not be considered. The first edition of the book must have been physically published in the UK during the calendar year prior to the award year. Self-published books are not eligible. No entry fee for nominated titles, but publishers will be asked for 50 GBP per shortlisted title as a contribution to marketing costs.
Other Sponsor(s): Letterbox Library
Award: 500 GBP
Closing Date: Mid-Jan
Presented: ARB London Radical Bookfair, Annually in June

The London Book Fair International Publishing Industry Excellence Awards
Reed Exhibitions UK
Gateway House, 28 The Quadrant, Richmond, Surrey TW9 1DN
Tel: (020) 8271 2124
E-mail: lbf.helpline@reedexpo.co.uk
Web Site: www.londonbookfair.co.uk/awards
Established: 2014
Other Sponsor(s): The Publishers Association
Presented: London Book Fair at Earl's Court, Annually in April

The London Book Fair Lifetime Achievement Award
Reed Exhibitions UK
Gateway House, 28 The Quadrant, Richmond, Surrey TW9 1DN
Tel: (020) 8271 2124 *Fax:* (020) 8334 0728
E-mail: lbf.helpline@reedexpo.co.uk
Web Site: www.londonbookfair.co.uk
Established: 2005
Annual award open to all members of the publishing industry to celebrate an individual's career dedication to breaking down borders in international publishing.

Elizabeth Longford Prize for Historical Biography
The Society of Authors
84 Drayton Gardens, London SW10 9SB
Tel: (020) 7373 6642
E-mail: info@societyofauthors.org
Web Site: elhb.uk/the-prize; www.societyofauthors.org/prizes
Key Personnel
Chair: Flora Fraser
Patron: Peter Soros
Established: 2003

Awarded annually for a historical biography published in the preceding year. No unsolicited submissions accepted.
Award: 5,000 GBP
Presented: Society of Authors Awards Ceremony, June

Tony Lothian Prize
Biographers' Club
8 Plimsoll Rd, London N4 2EW
E-mail: secretary@biographers.club
Web Site: www.biographers.club/the-tony-lothian-prize
Key Personnel
Prize Administrator: Ariane Bankes *Tel:* (07985) 920341 *E-mail:* ariane.bankes@gmail.com
Awarded to the best proposal for an uncommissioned first biography. Proposals of no more than 20 pages (unbound), including synopsis, 10-page sample chapter (double-spaced, numbered pages), CV & note on the market for the book & competing literature to: Ariane Bankes, ariane.bankes@gmail.com or by post to: E6 Albany, Piccadilly, London W1J 0AR. Entry fee: 15 GBP.
Other Sponsor(s): Duchess of Buccleuch
Award: 2,000 GBP
Closing Date: July

☆Enid McLeod Literary Prize
Franco-British Society
3 Dovedale Studios, 465 Battersea Park Rd, London SW11 4LR
Tel: (020) 7924 3511
E-mail: francobritsoc@gmail.com
Web Site: www.franco-british-society.org.uk
Key Personnel
President: Rt Hon Dominic Grieve
Executive Secretary: Isabel Gault
Established: 1981
Awarded annually to a book that contributes the most to Franco-British understanding, written in English & published in the UK during the calendar year preceding the year in which the award is presented.
Award: 500 GBP
Closing Date: Dec 31

Macmillan Prize for Children's Book Illustrations
Macmillan Children's Books
20 New Wharf Rd, London N1 9RR
Tel: (020) 7014 6000 *Fax:* (020) 7014 6001
E-mail: macmillanprize@macmillan.co.uk
Web Site: www.panmacmillan.com
Established: 1985
Annual award, established in order to stimulate new work from young illustrators in British art schools. Open to all art students in higher education establishments in the UK.
Award: 1st prize 1,000 GBP; 2nd prize 500 GBP; 3rd prize 250 GBP
Closing Date: last week in April
Presented: May 4

The Man Asian Literary Prize
Man Group PLC
Riverbank House, 2 Swan Lake, London EC4R 3AD
Tel: (020) 7144 1000
Web Site: www.mangroupplc.com
Established: 2007
Annual literary award given to the best novel by an Asian writer, either written in English or translated into English & published in the previous calendar year. Longlist of 10-15 titles announced in Oct, shortlist of 5-6 titles announced in Jan.
Presented: March

The Man Booker International Prize
Man Group PLC

Riverbank House, 2 Swan Lake, London EC4R 3AD
Tel: (020) 7144 1000
Web Site: www.themanbookerprize.com; www.mangroupplc.com
Key Personnel
Press: Truda Spruyt *E-mail:* truda.spruyt@fourcolman.getty.com
Established: 2005
Awarded annually for a single work of fiction, translated into English & published in the UK. Both novels & collections of short stories are eligible.
Award: 50,000 GBP divided equally between author & translator; 1,000 GBP to each shortlisted author & translator

☆The Man Booker Prize for Fiction
Man Group PLC
Riverbank House, 2 Swan Lake, London EC4R 3AD
Tel: (020) 7144 1000 *Fax:* (020) 7144 1923
E-mail: editor@themanbookerprize.com
Web Site: www.themanbookerprize.com; www.mangroupplc.com
Key Personnel
Press: Amy Barder *E-mail:* amy.barder@fourcolmangetty.com; Katy Macmillan-Scott *E-mail:* katy.macmillan-scott@fourcolmangetty.com
Established: 1969
Annual prize for any full-length novel in print or electronic format, written originally in English & published in the UK or Ireland by an imprint formally established in the UK or Ireland. The imprint must publish a list of at least 2 literary fiction novels by different authors each year. These 2 will not include a novel by the publisher. If the publisher is a company, the 2 will not include a novel by the person who owns the majority shareholding or otherwise controls the company. The novel must be published in the UK or Ireland between October 1 & September 30. If it has previously been published outside the UK & Ireland, it will only be eligible if the original date of publication outside the UK & Ireland is within the previous 2 years.
Award: 50,000 GBP, cheque for 2,500 GBP & special bound copy of their book
Closing Date: Entry forms April 2, finished books July 2

Marsh Award for Children's Literature in Translation
The English-Speaking Union (ESU)
Dartmouth House, 37 Charles St, London W1J 5ED
Tel: (020) 7529 1550 *Fax:* (020) 7495 6108
E-mail: esu@esu.org
Web Site: www.esu.org; www.marshchristiantrust.org
Key Personnel
Education Programmes Officer: Mary Greer *Tel:* (020) 7529 1590 *E-mail:* mary.greer@esu.org
Established: 1996
Awarded biennally to the best translation of a children's book, by a British translator, from a foreign language into English & published in the UK by a British publisher. Submissions are accepted from publishers for books produced for readers from 4-16 years of age. The award is made to the translator.
Other Sponsor(s): Marsh Christian Trust
Award: 2,000 GBP
Closing Date: June 30

Marsh Biography Award
The English-Speaking Union (ESU)
Dartmouth House, 37 Charles St, London W1J 5ED

Tel: (020) 7529 1550 *Fax:* (020) 7495 6108
E-mail: esu@esu.org
Web Site: www.esu.org; www.marshchristiantrust.org
Key Personnel
Education Programmes Officer: Mary Greer *Tel:* (020) 7529 1590 *E-mail:* mary.greer@esu.org
Established: 1985
Awarded biennially to a significant biography by a British author published in the UK in the two years prior to the year in which the prize is awarded. Publisher entry only.
Other Sponsor(s): Marsh Christian Trust
Award: 5,000 GBP & silver trophy
Closing Date: April 6

McIlvanney Prize
Bloody Scotland
c/o The Mitchell Library, North St, Glasgow G3 7DN
Tel: (0141) 552 8082
E-mail: press@bloodyscotland.com
Web Site: www.bloodyscotland.com/the-mcilvanney-prize
Key Personnel
Dir: Bob McDevitt *E-mail:* bob@bloodyscotland.com
Marketing Manager: Tim Donald *E-mail:* tim.donald@bloodyscotland.com
Press & Media Manager: Fiona Brownlee *E-mail:* fiona@bloodyscotland.com
Social Media Manager: Laura Jones *E-mail:* laura@bloodyscotland.com
Annual prize awarded to the best Scottish crime book of the year. Authors must either be born in Scotland, live there or set their books there. Crime fiction, nonfiction & anthologies of short crime stories are all eligible.

The McKitterick Prize
The Society of Authors
84 Drayton Gardens, London SW10 9SB
Tel: (020) 7373 6642 *Fax:* (020) 7373 5768
E-mail: info@societyofauthors.org
Web Site: www.societyofauthors.org
Key Personnel
Awards Secretary: Paula Johnson *E-mail:* pjohnson@societyofauthors.org
Established: 1990
Awarded annually for a first novel, published or unpublished, by an author over the age of 40 at the closing date.
Award: 4,000 GBP
Closing Date: Oct 31

David Miller Bursary
Deborah Rogers Foundation (DRF)
20 Powis Mews, London W11 1JN
E-mail: info@deborahrogersfoundation.org
Web Site: www.deborahrogersfoundation.org/writers-award
Established: 2017
Bursary for a publishing professional to spend 8 weeks working in the rights departments of publishing houses & agencies around the world. Next award will be for 2018/2019.
Award: 10,000 GBP
Presented: London Book Fair, March

Scott Moncrieff Prize
The Society of Authors
84 Drayton Gardens, London SW10 9SB
Tel: (020) 7373 6642 *Fax:* (020) 7373 5768
E-mail: info@societyofauthors.org
Web Site: www.societyofauthors.org
Key Personnel
Awards Secretary: Paula Johnson *E-mail:* pjohnson@societyofauthors.org
Established: 1965
Established under the auspices of the Translators Association of the Society of Authors to be awarded annually for the best translation

published by a British publisher during the previous year. Translations of French works of literary merit & general interest published in the last 150 years will be considered. The work should be entered by the publisher.
Award: 2,000 GBP
Closing Date: Jan 31

National Poetry Competition
The Poetry Society
22 Betterton St, London WC2H 9BX
Tel: (020) 7420 9880 *Fax:* (020) 7240 4818
E-mail: award@poetrysociety.org.uk
Web Site: www.poetrysociety.org.uk
Established: 1978
Awarded annually for a previously unpublished poem written in English. Send self-addressed envelope for entry form or visit web site. Entry fee 6 GBP for first poem, 3 GBP for each subsequent entry in the same submission.
Award: 1st prize 5,000 GBP; 2nd prize 2,000 GBP; 3rd prize 1,000 GBP; 7 commendations 100 GBP
Presented: Savile Club in London's Mayfair, March

New Blood Dagger
Crime Writers' Association (CWA)
Peershaws, Berewyk Hall Court, White Colne, Colchester, Essex CO6 2QB
E-mail: director@thecwa.co.uk
Web Site: thecwa.co.uk
Key Personnel
Chair: L C Tyler
Vice Chair: Martin Edwards
Established: 1973
Award for a first book by an unpublished writer. Submission by publishers only.
Other Sponsor(s): Louise Penny & Michael Whitehead
Award: Ornamental dagger & 1,000 GBP

New Voices Award, see PEN International/New Voices Award

Nibbies, see The British Book Awards

Ondaatje Prize, see Royal Society of Literature Ondaatje Prize

The Orwell Prize
The Orwell Foundation
Institute of Advanced Studies, South Wing, Wilkins Bldg, University College London, Gower St, London WC1E 6BT
Tel: (020) 3108 1618
Web Site: www.orwellfoundation.com/the-orwell-prize
Key Personnel
Programmes Manager: Robyn Donaldson
E-mail: robyn.donaldson@orwellfoundation.com; Jeremy Wikeley *E-mail:* jeremy.wikeley@orwellfoundation.com
Established: 1994
British prize for political writing first published in the previous calendar year. Three prizes are awarded: The Book Prize; The Journalism Prize; The Prize for Exposing Britain's Social Evils. Entries may be fiction or nonfiction & must be first published in the UK or Ireland. Works in translation, poetry & self-published books are not accepted. See web site for full submission guidelines.
Other Sponsor(s): A M Heath Literary Agency; The Political Quarterly; Joseph Roundtree Foundation; University College London
Award: 3,000 GBP to winner in each category
Closing Date: Annually, mid-Jan
Presented: Annually in Summer

The Orwell Youth Prize
The Orwell Foundation
Institute of Advanced Studies, South Wing, Wilkins Bldg, University College London, Gower St, London WC1E 6BT
Tel: (020) 3108 1618
E-mail: admin@orwellyouthprize.co.uk
Web Site: www.orwellfoundation.com/the-orwell-youth-prize
Key Personnel
Chair: Elizabeth Paris
Programmes Manager: Jeremy Wikeley
E-mail: jeremy.wikeley@orwellfoundation.com
Established: 2014
Open to anyone aged 13-18 who is at a school or college, from England, Northern Ireland, Scotland or Wales. Theme changes annually. Writing can be in any form: journalism, essays, short stories, blog posts, poems & plays. Word limit is 1,000 for the junior category & 1,500 for the senior category.
Award: All George Orwell's novels & full-length nonfiction works, selection of essays & cash prize (100 GBP Senior, 60 GBP Junior)
Closing Date: Annually in April (for individual feedback on your entry), May (final entries)

Oscar's Book Prize
Oscar's Book Prize Ltd
Lower Ground floor, 111 Charterhouse St, London EC1M 6AW
E-mail: oscarsbookprize@standard.co.uk
Web Site: www.oscarsbookprize.co.uk
Key Personnel
Chairman: James Ashton
Awarded to the best book published in the UK for children aged 5 or under. Publishers may enter up to 5 books per bona fide imprint. Books must be first published in the calendar year prior to the prize year. Previously published books, self-published books, ebooks & translations are not eligible. Completed entry forms & 5 copies of each book should be sent to the London Evening Standard Editor's Office, 2 Derry St, London W8 5TT.
Other Sponsor(s): Amazon; London Evening Standard; National Literacy Trust
Award: 5,000 GBP
Closing Date: Annually in March
Presented: Annually in May

PEN/Ackerley Prize
English PEN Centre
Free Word Centre, 60 Farringdon Rd, London EC1R 3GA
Tel: (020) 7324 2535
E-mail: enquiries@englishpen.org
Web Site: www.englishpen.org/prizes/penackerley-prize
Established: 1982
Award to a literary autobiography of excellence, written by an author of British nationality & published during the preceding year.

PEN International/New Voices Award
PEN International
Unit A, Koops Mill Mews, 162-164 Abbey St, London SE1 2AN
Tel: (020) 7405 0338 *Fax:* (020) 7405 0339
E-mail: info@pen-international.org
Web Site: www.pen-international.org/pen-internationalnew-voices-award
Key Personnel
Literary Manager: James Tennant *E-mail:* james.tennant@pen-international.org
Established: 2013
Award open to unpublished writers ages 18-30 nominated by their local PEN Centre.

PEN/Pinter Prize
English PEN Centre

Free Word Centre, 60 Farringdon Rd, London EC1R 3GA
Tel: (020) 7324 2535
E-mail: enquiries@englishpen.org
Web Site: www.englishpen.org/prizes
Established: 2009
Annual award to a British writer or writer resident in Britain of outstanding literary merit. Additional 1,000 GBP awarded to an imprisoned writer of conscience selected by the winner in consultation with English PEN's Writers in Prison Committee.
Award: 1,000 GBP

Ellis Peters Historical Award
Crime Writers' Association (CWA)
Peershaws, Berewyk Hall Court, White Colne, Colchester, Essex CO6 2QB
E-mail: director@thecwa.co.uk
Web Site: thecwa.co.uk
Key Personnel
Chair: L C Tyler
Vice Chair: Martin Edwards
Established: 1999
Awarded for the best historical crime novel (set in any period up to 1970).
Other Sponsor(s): Headline Book Publishing Group; Little, Brown Book Group; The Estate of Ellis Peters
Award: 3,000 GBP & an ornamental dagger

Pinter Prize, see PEN/Pinter Prize

Rathbones Folio Prize
Formerly The Folio Prize
Rathbone Investment Management
8 Finsbury Circus, London EC2M 7AZ
Web Site: www.rathbonesfolioprize.com
Key Personnel
Executive Dir: Minna Fry *E-mail:* minna.fry@rathbonesfolioprize.com
Established: 2013
Open to all works of literature written in English & published in the UK. All genres & all forms of literature are eligible, except work written primarily for children. The format of the first publication may be print or digital.
Award: 20,000 GBP
Presented: May

Red House Children's Book Award
Red House
123 Frederick Rd, Cheam, Sutton, Surrey SM1 2HT
Web Site: www.redhousechildrensbookaward.co.uk
Established: 1980
Coordinated by The Federation of Children's Book Groups, this award is given annually in 3 categories (Books for Younger Children, Books for Younger Readers & Books for Older Readers). Chosen by children for children.
Closing Date: Nominations close June 30

☆Trevor Reese Memorial Prize
Institute of Commonwealth Studies
School of Advanced Study, University of London, 2nd floor, South Block, Senate House, Malet St, London WC1E 7HU
Tel: (020) 7862 8844 *Fax:* (020) 7862 8813
E-mail: ics@sas.ac.uk
Web Site: commonwealth.sas.ac.uk/fellowships/trevor-reese-memorial-prize
Key Personnel
Events & Marketing Officer: Chloe Pieters
Tel: (020) 7862 8853 *E-mail:* chloe.pieters@sas.ac.uk
Established: 1979
The prize was established from a memorial fund to Dr Trevor Reese, Reader in Imperial Studies at the Institute of Commonwealth Studies, who

died in 1976. The adjudicators are interested in wide-ranging publications, but the terms of the prize specifically apply to scholarly works, usually by a single author, that have a wide-ranging, innovative & scholarly contribution in the broadly defined field of Imperial & Commonwealth history. Awarded triennially. The next award will be in 2019, considering books published 2015-2017.
Award: 1,000 GBP
Closing Date: Feb

The Robinson Award
Chartered Institute of Library & Information Professionals (CILIP)
7 Ridgmount St, London WC1E 7AE
Tel: (020) 7255 0500 *Fax:* (020) 7255 0501
E-mail: info@cilip.org.uk
Web Site: www.cilip.org.uk
Key Personnel
Corporate Marketing Manager: Kasey Butler
  Tel: (020) 7255 0650 *E-mail:* kasey.butler@cilip.org.uk
Awarded biennially to recognize innovation & excellence in library administration & administrative procedures. It is aimed specifically at attracting submissions from people working at paraprofessional levels in the library & information field.
Award: Trophy, certificate & 50 GBP book token
Presented: CILIP Awards Gala Ceremony, Landmark Hotel

Deborah Rogers Writer's Award
Deborah Rogers Foundation (DRF)
20 Powis Mews, London W11 1JN
E-mail: info@deborahrogersfoundation.org
Web Site: www.deborahrogersfoundation.org/writers-award
Established: 2016
Award for a first-time writer whose work demonstrates literary talent but who needs financial support to complete their first book. This can be fiction, nonfiction & short stories but not poetry. Writers must reside within the British Commonwealth & Ireland. Work must be written in the English language. Minimum 20-30,000 words of literary merit must be submitted.
Award: 10,000 GBP
Closing Date: Jan 31
Presented: Summer

Romantic Novel Awards
Romantic Novelists' Association (RNA)
c/o 42 Lexham Gardens, Flat 2, London W8 5JE
Web Site: www.romanticnovelistsassociation.org
Key Personnel
Administrator: Edwin Osborn *E-mail:* edwin.osborn@dsl.pipex.com
Established: 1960
For the best romantic novel (modern, period or historical) first published in the UK during the year. Open to members & nonmembers.
Other Sponsor(s): Parker Pen Co
Award: 10,000 GBP & a set of Parker Duofold pens worth over 400 GBP
Closing Date: Oct 1
Presented: Awards luncheon, London, Feb

Royal Historical Society/History Scotland Prize
The Royal Historical Society
University College London, Gower St, London WC1E 6BT
Tel: (020) 7387 7532 *Fax:* (020) 7387 7532
E-mail: royalhistsoc@ucl.ac.uk
Web Site: www.royalhistoricalsociety.org
Key Personnel
Executive Secretary: Sue Carr *E-mail:* s.carr@ucl.ac.uk
Administrative Secretary: Melanie Ransom
  E-mail: m.ransom@ucl.ac.uk

Prize to reward high-quality work done by undergraduates in dissertations on any aspect of Scottish history.
Other Sponsor(s): History Scotland
Award: 250 EUR

Royal Historical Society/History Today Prize
The Royal Historical Society
University College London, Gower St, London WC1E 6BT
Tel: (020) 7387 7532 *Fax:* (020) 7387 7532
E-mail: royalhistsoc@ucl.ac.uk
Web Site: www.royalhistoricalsociety.org
Key Personnel
Executive Secretary: Sue Carr *E-mail:* s.carr@ucl.ac.uk
Administrative Secretary: Melanie Ransom
  E-mail: m.ransom@ucl.ac.uk
For the best third year undergraduate dissertation in history in a higher education institution in the UK.
Other Sponsor(s): History Today
Award: 250 GBP
Closing Date: Aug 1

Royal Society Insight Investment Book Prize
The Royal Society
6-9 Carlton House Terrace, London SW1Y 5AG
Tel: (020) 7451 2500 *Fax:* (020) 7930 2170
E-mail: sciencebooks@royalsociety.org
Web Site: royalsociety.org/sciencebooks
Established: 1988
Established to celebrate outstanding popular science books from around the world. Prize is open to authors of science books written for a non-specialist audience.
Other Sponsor(s): Insight Investment
Award: Up to 15,000 GBP awarded annually: 10,000 GBP for a book with a general readership; Up to 5 shortlisted books receive 1,000 GBP each
Closing Date: April 1

Royal Society of Literature Ondaatje Prize
Royal Society of Literature
Somerset House, Strand, London WC2R 1LA
Tel: (020) 7845 4676
Web Site: www.rslit.org/rsl-ondaatje-prize
Key Personnel
Awards Administrator: Paula Johnson
  E-mail: paulaj@rslit.org
Annual award for a distinguished work of fiction, nonfiction or poetry, evoking the spirit of a place.
Award: 10,000 GBP

The Saif Ghobash-Banipal Prize for Arabic Literary Translation
The Society of Authors
84 Drayton Gardens, London SW10 9SB
Tel: (020) 7373 6642 *Fax:* (020) 7373 5768
E-mail: info@societyofauthors.org
Web Site: www.societyofauthors.org
Key Personnel
Awards Secretary: Paula Johnson
  E-mail: pjohnson@societyofauthors.org
Annual prize for published translations of full-length works of imaginative & creative writing of literary merit & general interest, first published in the original Arabic no more than 35 years preceding its submission for the prize. Entries must first have been published in English during the year previous to the prize deadline. The publisher may be based anywhere in the world but the translation must be available for purchase in the UK.
Other Sponsor(s): Omar Saif Ghobash
Award: 3,000 GBP
Closing Date: Jan 31

Saltire History Book of the Year Award
The Saltire Society

9 Fountain Close, 22 High St, Edinburgh EH1 1TF
Tel: (0131) 556 1836 *Fax:* (0131) 557 1675
E-mail: saltire@saltiresociety.org.uk
Web Site: www.saltiresociety.org.uk
Established: 1965
In memory of Dr Agnes Mure Mackenzie, this award is given annually for a published work of Scottish Historical Research (including intellectual history & the history of science). Editions of texts are not eligible.
Award: 1,500 GBP
Closing Date: Sept
Presented: The National Library of Scotland, Nov 30

Schlegel-Tieck Prize
The Society of Authors
84 Drayton Gardens, London SW10 9SB
Tel: (020) 7373 6642 *Fax:* (020) 7373 5768
E-mail: info@societyofauthors.org
Web Site: www.societyofauthors.org
Key Personnel
Awards Secretary: Paula Johnson
  E-mail: pjohnson@societyofauthors.org
Established under the auspices of the Translators Association, a subsidiary organization of the Society of Authors, to be awarded annually for the best translation published by a British publisher during the previous year. Only translations of German works of literary merit & general interest published in the last 100 years will be considered. The work should be entered by the publisher & not the individual translator.
Award: 3,000 GBP
Closing Date: Jan 31

The Walter Scott Prize for Historical Fiction
Borders Book Festival, Harmony House, St Mary's Rd, Melrose TD6 9LJ
Tel: (0844) 357 1060
Web Site: www.bordersbookfestival.org/walter-scott-prize
Key Personnel
Contact: Rebecca Salt *Tel:* (01620) 829 800
  E-mail: rebecca@stonehillsalt.co.uk
Established: 2009
Other Sponsor(s): The Duke & Duchess of Buccleuch; Edinburgh University Press; Jura Single Malt Whisky; Lochcarron of Scotland
Award: 25,000 GBP
Presented: Brewin Dolphin Borders Book Festival, Annually in June

Scottish Book of the Year Award & Scottish First Book of the Year
The Saltire Society
9 Fountain Close, 22 High St, Edinburgh EH1 1TF
Tel: (0131) 556 1836 *Fax:* (0131) 557 1675
E-mail: saltire@saltiresociety.org.uk
Web Site: www.saltiresociety.org.uk
Established: 1982
Awarded for a book of a literary nature written by an author of Scottish descent or living in Scotland, or a book which deals with the work or life of a Scot or with a Scottish problem, event or situation.
Other Sponsor(s): Royal Mail Group
Award: Scottish Book of the Year 5,000 GBP; Scottish First Book of the Year 1,500 GBP
Closing Date: Sept 3
Presented: The National Library of Scotland, Nov 30

Scottish Research Book of the Year
The Saltire Society
9 Fountain Close, 22 High St, Edinburgh EH1 1TF
Tel: (0131) 556 1836 *Fax:* (0131) 557 1675
E-mail: saltire@saltiresociety.org.uk
Web Site: www.saltiresociety.org.uk

Established: 1989
Awarded for a book written by an author of Scottish descent or living in Scotland, or a book which deals with the work or life of a Scot or with a Scottish problem, event or situation.
Other Sponsor(s): The National Library of Scotland
Award: 1,500 GBP
Closing Date: Sept
Presented: The National Library of Scotland, Nov 30

The Bernard Shaw Prize
The Society of Authors
84 Drayton Gardens, London SW10 9SB
Tel: (020) 7373 6642 *Fax:* (020) 7373 5768
E-mail: info@societyofauthors.org
Web Site: www.societyofauthors.org
Key Personnel
Awards Secretary: Paula Johnson
 E-mail: pjohnson@societyofauthors.org
Established: 1991
Triennial prize for translations of full-length Swedish language works of literary merit & general interest. The original can be from any period. The translation must have been first published in the UK during the 3 years up to & including the year of entry.
Award: 2,000 GBP
Closing Date: Jan 31

Short Story Award
Crime Writers' Association (CWA)
Peershaws, Berewyk Hall Court, White Colne, Colchester, Essex CO6 2QB
E-mail: director@thecwa.co.uk
Web Site: thecwa.co.uk
Key Personnel
Chair: L C Tyler
Vice Chair: Martin Edwards
Established: 1955
Awarded for a short story published in a crime anthology. Submission by publishers only.
Award: 500 GBP & gold pin of the CWA's crossed daggers emblem

Andre Simon Book Awards
Andre Simon Memorial Fund
One Westbourne Gardens, Glasgow G12 9XE
Tel: (0780) 131 0973
Web Site: www.andresimon.co.uk/awards.html
Key Personnel
Secretary to the Fund: Katie Lander
 E-mail: katie@andresimon.co.uk
Awards given annually for the best book in 2 categories: Food & Wine, Drink & Beverages.
Award: 2,000 GBP, 1,000 GBP Special Commendation Award, 200 GBP for Short-Listed Book

Slightly Foxed Best First Biography Prize
Biographers' Club
8 Plimsoll Rd, London N4 2EW
E-mail: secretary@biographers.club
Web Site: www.biographers.club/best-first-biography-award
Awarded annually for the best published biography. Only entries submitted by publishers will be accepted for consideration. Literary memoirs are also eligible, but the following genres are not eligible: celebrity autobiographies & ghost-written books. To qualify, the books must have a publication date between September 1 (two years prior to the award year) & December 31 (of the year prior to the award). Proofs are acceptable. Four copies of each book should be submitted with press release to confirm publication date, entry form & 25 GBP entry fee per title. Books should be sent by post, not courier to: The Slightly Foxed Best First Biography Prize, c/o Jane Mays, 21 Marsden St, London NW5 3HE. Entry fee additionally entitles the author to a year's membership in the Biographers' Club.
Other Sponsor(s): Slightly Foxed, The Real Reader's Quarterly
Award: 2,500 GBP
Closing Date: Nov 1
Presented: March

Somerset Maugham Awards
The Society of Authors
84 Drayton Gardens, London SW10 9SB
Tel: (020) 7373 6642 *Fax:* (020) 7373 5768
E-mail: info@societyofauthors.org
Web Site: www.societyofauthors.org
Key Personnel
Awards Secretary: Paula Johnson
 E-mail: pjohnson@societyofauthors.org
Established: 1947
Founded by Somerset Maugham. Awarded to British writers under the age of 35 for a published work of fiction, nonfiction or poetry. Awards must be used for foreign travel. Entry by publisher.
Award: Total of 12,000 GBP
Closing Date: Nov 30

Specsavers National Book Awards
Agile Marketing
c/o Midas Public Relations, 10-14 Old Court Pl, Kensington, London W8 4PL
Web Site: www.galaxynationalbookawards.com
Key Personnel
Contact: Danielle Bowers *E-mail:* danielle@agile-ideas.com
Established: 1990
Honors the best books of the year from UK authors or non-British nationals who hold a British passport or who have been domiciled in Great Britain & Northern Ireland for more than 2 years.
Other Sponsor(s): Audible.co.uk; National Book Tokens; The Telegraph; Waterstones; WHSmith

Edward Stanford Travel Writing Awards
Edward Stanford Ltd
c/o Agile Ideas, Magnolia House, 172 Winsley Rd, Bradford on Avon, Wilts BA15 1NY
Web Site: www.edwardstanfordawards.com
Key Personnel
Marketing Manager: Jude Brosnan *E-mail:* jude.brosnan@stanfords.co.uk
Established: 2015
Awards to celebrate the best travel writing & travel writers in the world.
Award categories: Stanford Dolman Travel Book of the Year Award, in partnership with the Authors' Club*; Children's Travel Book of the Year*; Photography & Illustrated Travel Book of the Year*; Travel Cookery Book of the Year*; Fiction, with a Sense of Place*; Outstanding General Travel Themed Book of the Year*; Adventure Travel Book of the Year*; Edward Stanford Award for Outstanding Contribution to Travel Writing; Bradt Travel Guides New Travel Writer of the Year; Lonely Planet Pathfinders Travel Blog of the Year.
Categories marked with an asterisk will incur a levy fee of 165 GBP for each title shortlisted to cover the costs of the project management of the campaign & the design, printing & distribution of the official point of sale. There is no charge for submissions. Send 3 copies of each title submitted.
Other Sponsor(s): Authors' Club; Bradt Travel Guides; Destinations; Hayes & Jarvis; London Book Fair; Lonely Planet Pathfinders; Marco Polo; Stanfords; Wanderlust
Award: Antique globe trophy; Stanford Dolman Travel Book of the Year winner also receives 5,000 GBP
Closing Date: Sept 29 (most categories); Oct 31 for Lonely Planet Pathfinders Travel Blog of the Year; Nov 7 for Bradt Travel Guides New Writer of the Year
Presented: Gala ceremony alongside Stanfords Travel Writers Festival, Destinations Show, Olympia, London, Annually in Feb

The Sunday Times EFG Private Bank Short Story Award
The Sunday Times EFG Private Bank
c/o Booktrust, Book House, 45 East Hill, London SW18 2QZ
Tel: (020) 8516 2960
E-mail: sundaytimesefg@booktrust.org.uk
Honors the finest writers of short stories in the UK & Ireland.
Award: 1st prize 30,000 GBP; 5 shortlisted writers 1,000 GBP each
Presented: Sunday Times Oxford Literary Festival, Annually in Spring

The Sunday Times/Peters Fraser + Dunlop Young Writer of the Year Award
The Society of Authors
84 Drayton Gardens, London SW10 9SB
Tel: (020) 7373 6642 *Fax:* (020) 7373 5768
E-mail: info@societyofauthors.org
Web Site: www.societyofauthors.org
Key Personnel
Awards Secretary: Paula Johnson
 E-mail: pjohnson@societyofauthors.org
Awarded for a full-length published work of fiction, nonfiction or poetry by a British writer under the age of 35. Entry by publisher.
Award: 5,000 GBP
Closing Date: Oct 31
Presented: Oxford Literary Festival, April 5

Theakstons Old Peculier Crime Novel of the Year
Theakstons Old Peculier Crime Writing Festival
Harrogate International Festivals, 32 Cheltenham Parade, Harrogate HG1 1DB
Tel: (01423) 562303 *Fax:* (01423) 521264
E-mail: crime@harrogate-festival.org.uk
Web Site: harrogateinternationalfestivals.com/crime
Established: 2004
Celebrates the best in crime writing. Open to British & Irish authors whose novels were published in paperback over the previous 12 months.
Award: 3,000 GBP & handmade, engraved beer barrel
Presented: Annually in July

The Dylan Thomas Prize
2 Princess Way, Swansea SA1 3LW
Tel: (01792) 474051
E-mail: info@dylanthomasprize.com
Web Site: www.dylanthomasprize.com
Key Personnel
Founder & Judge: Peter Stead
Established: 2006
Prestigious annual award for young writers worldwide.
Award: 30,000 GBP
Closing Date: June
Presented: Nov

Tom-Gallon Trust Award
The Society of Authors
84 Drayton Gardens, London SW10 9SB
Tel: (020) 7373 6642 *Fax:* (020) 7373 5768
E-mail: info@societyofauthors.org
Web Site: www.societyofauthors.org
Key Personnel
Awards Secretary: Paula Johnson
 E-mail: pjohnson@societyofauthors.org
Established: 1943
Awarded biennially to short story writers of limited means. Entrants must submit a list of al-

ready published fiction, one published or un-published short story & a brief statement of their financial position & willingness to devote substantial time to writing fiction as soon as they are financially able.
Award: 1,000 GBP
Closing Date: Oct 31

☆The Betty Trask Prize & Awards
The Society of Authors
84 Drayton Gardens, London SW10 9SB
Tel: (020) 7373 6642 *Fax:* (020) 7373 5768
E-mail: info@societyofauthors.org
Web Site: www.societyofauthors.org
Key Personnel
Awards Secretary: Paula Johnson
   E-mail: pjohnson@societyofauthors.org
Established: 1983
Awards are for the benefit of authors under 35 years of age who are Commonwealth citizens & are given for a first novel (published or un-published) of a romantic or traditional nature. All winners are required to use the money for a period or periods of foreign travel with a view to increasing their experience & knowledge for future literary benefit.
Award: 20,000 GBP total value
Closing Date: Nov 30

Travelling Scholarships
The Society of Authors
84 Drayton Gardens, London SW10 9SB
Tel: (020) 7373 6642 *Fax:* (020) 7373 5768
E-mail: info@societyofauthors.org
Web Site: www.societyofauthors.org
Key Personnel
Awards Secretary: Paula Johnson
   E-mail: pjohnson@societyofauthors.org
Established: 1944
Annual awards to British writers. Honorary schol-arships are awarded for a body of work. Sub-missions are not accepted.
Award: 4,000 GBP

Premio Valle Inclan
The Society of Authors
84 Drayton Gardens, London SW10 9SB
Tel: (020) 7373 6642 *Fax:* (020) 7373 5768
E-mail: info@societyofauthors.org
Web Site: www.societyofauthors.org
Key Personnel
Awards Secretary: Paula Johnson
   E-mail: pjohnson@societyofauthors.org
Established: 1997
Annual prize for published translations of full length Spanish works of literary merit & gen-eral interest (the original must have been writ-ten in Spanish but can be from any period & from anywhere in the world). The translation must have been first published in the UK.
Award: 2,000 GBP
Closing Date: Jan 31

VER Poets Open Competition
VER Poets
181 Sandridge Rd, St Albans, Herts AL1 4AH
Tel: (01727) 762601
Web Site: www.verpoets.org.uk
Key Personnel
Competitions Secretary: Gillian Knibbs
Established: 1966
For poems on any theme of no more than 30 lines.
Entry fee: 4 GBP per poem, 3 poems for 10 GBP, 2 GBP per poem thereafter.
Award: 1st prize 600 GBP; 2nd prize 300 GBP; 3rd prize 100 GBP; Young Writers Prize 100 GBP; plus publication in anthology
Closing Date: April 30
Presented: St Albans, June

Virago/The Pool New Crime Writer Award
Virago Press
c/o Little, Brown Book Group Ltd, Carmelite House, 50 Victoria Embankment, London EC4Y 0DZ
E-mail: viragoandthepool@littlebrown.co.uk
Web Site: www.virago.co.uk/virago-pool-crime-writer-competition
Key Personnel
Chair: Ms Lennie Goodings
Publisher: Sarah Savitt
Established: 2017
Awarded to a debut writer for the most original & exciting proposal for a suspenseful, intelligent, original crime or thriller novel appropriate to the Virago list. Submit proposal consisting of 500-word synopsis of the plot of the novel & first 5,000 words of the novel. Proposal must be in English & double spaced. Competition is open to women only aged 18 or over, resi-dent in the UK & must not have had any book published previously in any format.
Other Sponsor(s): The Pool (UK) Ltd
Award: Book publication, 7,500 GBP advance & 2 hours of mentoring
Closing Date: May 21
Presented: Sept 29

Vondel Translation Prize
The Society of Authors
84 Drayton Gardens, London SW10 9SB
Tel: (020) 7373 6642 *Fax:* (020) 7373 5768
E-mail: info@societyofauthors.org
Web Site: www.societyofauthors.org
Key Personnel
Awards Secretary: Paula Johnson
   E-mail: pjohnson@societyofauthors.org
Established: 1996
Biennial prize presented in odd-numbered years for translations of works into English of Dutch & Flemish works of literary merit & general interest. The translation must have been first published in the UK or the USA during the previous 2 years.
Award: 2,000 GBP

Wainwright Golden Beer Book Prize
Wainwright Golden Beer
c/o Agile Ideas, Studio 20, Glove Factory Stu-dios, Brook Lane, Holt, Wilts BA14 6RL
Web Site: wainwrightprize.com
Key Personnel
Prize Dir: Alastair Giles *Tel:* (01225) 865776
   E-mail: alastair@agile.bookswarm.co.uk
Awarded for the best writing on the outdoors, na-ture & UK-based travel writing.
Other Sponsor(s): The National Trust
Award: 5,000 GBP
Closing Date: Mid-March
Presented: Aug

Wales Book of the Year Awards
Llenyddiaeth Cymru (Literature Wales)
Mount Stuart House, 3rd floor, Mount Stuart Sq, Cardiff CF10 5FQ
Tel: (029) 2047 2266 *Fax:* (029) 2049 2930
E-mail: post@llenyddiaethcymru.org; post@literaturewales.org
Web Site: www.llenyddiaethcymru.org; www.literaturewales.org
Key Personnel
Chief Executive Officer: Peter Finch
Established: 1992
Annual awards for the best Welsh language & English language works, published in the pre-vious calendar year, in the fields of creative writing & literary critcism.
Other Sponsor(s): Arts Council of Wales
Award: 10,000 GBP for the two winning titles & four runners-up 1,000 GBP each
Presented: June

Walford Award
Chartered Institute of Library & Information Pro-fessionals (CILIP)
7 Ridgmount St, London WC1E 7AE
Tel: (020) 7255 0500 *Fax:* (020) 7255 0501
Web Site: www.cilip.org.uk
Key Personnel
Awards Coordinator: Jessica Dunnicliff
   E-mail: jessicadunnicliff@stratfordhigh.org.uk
Established: 1970
Presented to an individual who has made a sus-tained & continual contribution to the science & art of bibliography in the UK. The nominee need not be a resident in the UK.
The awards are administered by the Information Services Group.
Award: 500 GBP & certificate

Kim Scott Walwyn Prize
The Publishing Training Centre, 6 Bell Yard, London WC2A 2JR
Tel: (020) 8874 2718
E-mail: information@kimscottwalwyn.org
Web Site: kimscottwalwyn.org
Established: 2003
Recognizes achievements of women who have worked in publishing in the UK & the Repub-lic of Ireland for up to 7 years.
Other Sponsor(s): Publishing Training Centre; Society of Young Publishers
Award: 1,000 GBP & 2-day training course at Publishing Training Centre

Waterstones Children's Book Prize
Waterstones Booksellers Ltd
203/206 Piccadilly, London W1J 9HD
Tel: (020) 8045 1001 *Toll Free Tel:* (0808) 118 8787
E-mail: support@waterstones.com
Web Site: www.waterstones.com
Established: 2005
Annual award given to a work of children's liter-ature published during the previous year. Three categories: Picture Books, Fiction 5-12 & Teen.
Award: 2,000 GBP in each category with overall winner chosen from the three getting an addi-tional 3,000 GBP

Wellcome Book Prize
Wellcome Trust
Gibbs Bldg, 215 Euston Rd, London NW1 2BE
Tel: (020) 7611 8888 *Fax:* (020) 7611 8545
E-mail: bookprize@wellcome.ac.uk
Web Site: www.wellcomebookprize.org
Key Personnel
Prize Manager: Kirty Topiwala *Tel:* (020) 7611 8771 *E-mail:* k.topiwala@wellcome.ac.uk
Annual award open to new works of fiction or nonfiction with a central theme that engages with some aspect of medicine, health or illness.
Award: 30,000 GBP
Presented: April

Wheatley Medal
The Society of Indexers
Woodbourn Business Centre, 10 Jessell St, Sheffield S9 3HY
Tel: (0114) 244 9561 *Fax:* (0114) 244 9563
E-mail: admin@indexers.org.uk
Web Site: www.indexers.org.uk
Key Personnel
Chairman: Ann Kindgom *E-mail:* chair@indexers.org.uk
Established: 1961
Presented for an outstanding printed index pub-lished in the UK.
Award: 200 GBP, certificate & gold medal
Closing Date: April 30
Presented: Keele University, Sept 3

Whitfield Book Prize
The Royal Historical Society

University College London, Gower St, London
WC1E 6BT
Tel: (020) 7387 7532 *Fax:* (020) 7387 7532
E-mail: royalhistsoc@ucl.ac.uk
Web Site: www.royalhistoricalsociety.org
Key Personnel
Executive Secretary: Sue Carr *E-mail:* s.carr@ucl.
ac.uk
Administrative Secretary: Melanie Ransom
E-mail: m.ransom@ucl.ac.uk
Established: 1976
Annual prize for a new book on British or Irish
history. To be eligible for consideration the
book must be on a subject within a field of
British or Irish history & have been published
in the UK or the Republic of Ireland during the
calendar year. It must also be its author's first
solely written book & be an original & schol-
arly work of historical research.
Award: 1,000 GBP
Closing Date: Dec 31
Presented: Royal Historical Society Annual Reception, July

John Whiting Award, see Peter Wolff Trust
Supports the John Whiting Award

**Peter Wolff Trust Supports the John Whiting
Award**
Peter Wolff Theatre Trust
12 York Gate, Camden Town, London NW1 4QS
Established: 1965
National playwriting award to give recognition to
the writer of a new play that demonstrated an
original & distinctive development in dramatic
writing.
Award: 6,000 GBP
Presented: Birmingham Repertory Theatre

Wolfson History Prize
The Wolfson Foundation
8 Queen Anne St, London W1G 9LD
Tel: (020) 7323 5730 *Fax:* (020) 7323 3241
Web Site: www.wolfson.org.uk
Key Personnel
Chief Executive: Paul Ramsbottom
Established: 1972
Up to three awards are made annually to British
authors of historical writing which is consid-
ered both scholarly & accessible to the general
reader.
Award: 15,000 GBP & 10,000 GBP

Women in Publishing Awards
Women in Publishing
4 Barnard Hill, London N10 2HB
E-mail: web@womeninpublishing.org.uk
Web Site: www.womeninpublishing.org.uk
Two categories: The Pandora Award for significant & sustained contribution to the publishing
industry; The New Venture Award for pioneer-
ing work on behalf of under-represented groups
in society.

Women's Prize for Fiction
Formerly BAILEYS Women's Prize for Fiction
c/o Paula Johnson, The Society of Book Authors,
84 Drayton Gardens, London SW10 9SB
Tel: (020) 7221 7883
E-mail: womensprizeforfiction@kallaway.com
Web Site: www.womensprizeforfiction.co.uk

Key Personnel
Prize Digital Editor: Jen Acton *E-mail:* jennifer@
womensprizeforfiction.co.uk
Established: 1996
Celebrates excellence, originality & accessibility
in women's writing from throughout the world.
Other Sponsor(s): Bailey's; Deloitte; NatWest
Award: 30,000 GBP & limited edition bronze fig-
urine

Write Now!
Macmillan Children's Books
20 New Wharf Rd, London N1 9RR
Tel: (020) 7014 6000 *Fax:* (020) 7014 6001
E-mail: childrensbooks@macmillan.co.uk
Web Site: www.panmacmillan.com
Established: 2012
For unpublished work judged by independent
booksellers & their customers.
Award: 10,000 GBP

YA Book Prize
The Bookseller
Westminster Tower, 10th floor, 3 Albert Embank-
ment, Lambeth, London SE1 7SP
Web Site: www.thebookseller.com/ya-book-prize
Key Personnel
Social Media Coordinator: Caroline Carpenter
E-mail: caroline.carpenter@thebookseller.com
Established: 2014
Awarded annually to the best young adult book
written by an author living in the UK or Ire-
land. Self-published titles, nonfiction & graphic
novels are not eligible.
Award: 2,000 GBP
Presented: Hay Festival

Young Writers Prize
Hot Key Books
Northburgh House, 10 Northburgh St, London
EC1V 0AT
E-mail: youngwritersprize@hotkeybooks.com
Web Site: www.hotkeyblog.com/young-writers-
prize
Key Personnel
Hot Key Books Publisher: Emily Thomas
Established: 2012
Unpublished new young writers, ages 18 to 25,
who write in either of two categories: for ages
9-12 or 13-19 (young adult).
E-mail submissions only.
Other Sponsor(s): Kobo
Award: Two winners (one in each category) re-
ceive editorial support & chance to be pub-
lished by Hot Key Books, with additional ex-
posure via Kobo eBookstore. 10 shortlisted
candidates will also win a Kobo device
Presented: London Book Fair

United States

☆**American-Scandinavian Foundation
Translation Prize**
American-Scandinavian Foundation (ASF)
58 Park Ave, New York, NY 10016
Tel: 212-779-3587 *Fax:* 212-686-2115
E-mail: info@amscan.org
Web Site: www.amscan.org/translation.html

Key Personnel
Fellowship & Grants Officer: Carl Fritscher
E-mail: cfritscher@amscan.org
Established: 1980
Initiated by *Scandinavian Review*, 2 prizes per
year, to bring best of contemporary Scandinavian literature to American readers. There is a
prize for poetry, fiction, drama or literary prose
in addition to publication. Awarded annually
for the best translation of work by a Scandinavian author born after 1800. For more details,
request rules.
Award: 2,000 USD, publication of an excerpt in
Scandinavian Review & commemorative bronze
medallion
Closing Date: June 1 (postmark)
Presented: Fall

☆**ILA Children's & Young Adults' Book
Awards**
International Literacy Association (ILA)
800 Barksdale Rd, Newark, DE 19711-3204
Mailing Address: PO Box 8139, Newark, DE
19714-8139
Tel: 302-731-1600 *Fax:* 302-731-1057
E-mail: committees@reading.org
Web Site: www.literacyworldwide.org; www.
reading.org
Key Personnel
Executive Dir: Marcie Craig Post
E-mail: mpost@reading.org
Associate Executive Dir: Stephen Sye
E-mail: ssye@reading.org
Executive Assistant: Kathy Baughman
E-mail: kbaughman@reading.org
Established: 1975
Awarded annually for newly published authors
who show unusual promise in the children's
& young adults' book field. Awards are given
for fiction & nonfiction in each of 3 categories:
Primary, Intermediate & Young Adult. Books
from any country & published in English for
the first time during the previous calendar year
will be considered.
Award: $800 USD per book
Closing Date: Oct 31
Presented: Annual Conference, Spring

☆**Neustadt International Prize for Literature**
University of Oklahoma
630 Parrington Oval, Suite 110, Norman, OK
73019-4033
Tel: 405-325-0311
Web Site: www.ou.edu
Established: 1969
An international prize awarded biennially for distinguished & continuing artistic achievement
in the fields of poetry, drama or fiction. A new
international jury of 12 is appointed for each
successive award by the editors in consultation
with the executive director. Each juror presents
1 candidate for the prize. A majority (7) of the
jury must be present for the deliberations &
the final voting. Representative selections of a
candidate's work must be available to the jury
in English translation. *World Literature Today*
dedicates one issue to the recipient. Prize not
open to application.
Other Sponsor(s): World Literature Today (literary journal)
Award: Certificate, replica of an eagle's feather in
silver & 50,000 USD
Presented: University of Oklahoma, Norman, Oklahoma, USA

Book Trade Calendar

Calendar of Book Trade & Promotional Events— Alphabetical Index of Sponsors

Calendar of Book Trade & Promotional Events— Alphabetical Index of Events

Calendar of Book Trade & Promotional Events

Arranged chronologically by year and month, this section lists book trade events worldwide. Preceding this section are two indexes: the Sponsor Index is an alphabetical list of event sponsors followed by the names and dates of those events they sponsor; the Event Index is an alphabetical list of events along with the dates on which the events are held.

2018

SEPTEMBER

PSA® International Conference of Photography
Sponsored by Photographic Society of America®
(PSA®)
8241 S Walker Ave, Suite 104, Oklahoma City,
OK 73139, United States
Tel: 405-843-1437 *Toll Free Tel:* 855-PSA-INFO
(772-4636) *Fax:* 405-843-1438
E-mail: conferencevp@psa-photo.org
Web Site: www.psa-photo.org
Location: Sheraton Salt Lake City Hotel, 150 W
500 S, Salt Lake City, UT, USA
Sept 30-Oct 6, 2018

OCTOBER

ACP/CMA National College Media Convention
Sponsored by Associated Collegiate Press (ACP)
Division of National Scholastic Press Association
2829 University Ave SE, Suite 720, Minneapolis,
MN 55414, United States
Tel: 612-200-9254
E-mail: info@studentpress.org
Web Site: www.studentpress.org; facebook.
com/acpress; twitter.com/acpress
Key Personnel
Exec Dir, NSPA/ACP: Laura Widmer *Tel:* 612-
200-9265
Co-sponsored by College Media Association.
Location: Galt House Hotel, Louisville, KY, USA
Oct 25-28, 2018

&THEN
Sponsored by Data & Marketing Association
(DMA)
1333 Broadway, Suite 301, New York, NY
10018, United States
SAN: 692-6487
Tel: 212-768-7277
Web Site: thedma.org
Key Personnel
Asst Conference Mgr: Jeremy A Ladson *Tel:* 212-
790-1545 *E-mail:* jladson@thedma.org
Location: MGM Grand, 3799 S Las Vegas Blvd,
Las Vegas, NV, USA
Oct 7-9, 2018

Didac India
Sponsored by Worlddidac Association
Bollwerk 21, 3011 Bern, Switzerland
Tel: (031) 311 76 82 *Fax:* (031) 312 17 44
E-mail: info@worlddidac.org
Web Site: www.worlddidac.org; www.facebook.
com/DidacIndia
Key Personnel
Proj & Communs Mgr: Kateryna Schuetz
E-mail: schuetz@worlddidac.org
International exhibition for education, training,
technology & supply.
Location: Pragati Maidan, New Delhi, India
Oct 4-6, 2018

4PrintWeek
Formerly Poligrafia
Sponsored by Poznan International Fair Ltd
ul Glogowska 14, 60-734 Poznan, Poland
Tel: (61) 869 20 00 *Fax:* (61) 869 29 99
E-mail: 4printweek@mtp.pl; info@mtp.pl
Web Site: www.4printweek.pl/en (English);
www.4printweek.pl/pl (Polish); www.mtp.
pl/en/ (English); www.mtp.pl/pl/ (Polish)
Key Personnel
Proj Mgr: Martyna Dera *Tel:* (61) 869 24 54
E-mail: martyna.dera@mtp.pl
International fair of printing machines, materials
& services.
Location: Poznan International Fair Grounds,
Poznan, Poland
Oct 1-4, 2018

Frankfurter Buchmesse (Frankfurt Book Fair)
Sponsored by Frankfurter Buchmesse GmbH
Braubachstr 16, 60311 Frankfurt am Main, Ger-
many
Mailing Address: Postfach 100116, 60001 Frank-
furt am Main, Germany
Tel: (069) 21020 *Fax:* (069) 2102 277
E-mail: info@book-fair.com
Web Site: www.book-fair.com
Key Personnel
CEO & Dir: Juergen Boos
Major international book & media fair attracting
7,300 exhibitors from over 100 countries &
278,000 visitors.
Location: Frankfurt Fairgrounds, Ludwig-Erhard-
Anlage One, Frankfurt, Germany
Oct 10-14, 2018

**Inter American Press Association General
Assembly**
Sponsored by Inter American Press Association
(IAPA)
3511 NW 91 Ave, Miami, FL 33172, United
States
Tel: 305-634-2465 *Fax:* 305-860-4264
E-mail: info@sipiapa.org
Web Site: www.sipiapa.org

Key Personnel
Exec Dir: Ricardo Trotti *E-mail:* rtrotti@sipiapa.
org
Gathering of important international figures for
workshops, seminars & other related activities, while offering networking opportunities
for those interested on press/media freedom &
freedom of expression issues.
Location: Salta, Argentina
Oct 19-22, 2018

LIBER Feria Internacional del Libro
Sponsored by Federacion de Gremios de Editores
de Espana (FGEE) (Spanish Association of
Publishers Guilds)
Cea Bermudez, 44-2° Dcha, 28003 Madrid, Spain
Tel: 91 534 51 95 *Fax:* 91 535 26 25
E-mail: fgee@fge.es
Web Site: www.federacioneditores.org
Key Personnel
Exec Dir: Antonio Maria Avila
Location: Barcelona, Spain
Oct 3-5, 2018

NAIBA Fall Conference
Sponsored by New Atlantic Independent Book-
sellers Association (NAIBA)
2667 Hyacinth St, Westbury, NY 11590, United
States
Tel: 516-333-0681 *Fax:* 516-333-0689
E-mail: naibabooksellers@gmail.com
Web Site: www.naiba.com
Key Personnel
Exec Dir: Eileen Dengler *E-mail:* naibaeileen@
gmail.com
Location: Hyatt Regency Baltimore Inner Harbor,
300 Light St, Baltimore, MD, USA
Oct 6-8, 2018

PACK EXPO International
Sponsored by PMMI: The Association for Pack-
aging and Processing Technologies
11911 Freedom Dr, Suite 600, Reston, VA 20190,
United States
Tel: 571-612-3200 *Toll Free Tel:* 888-ASK-PMMI
(275-7664) *Fax:* 703-243-8556
E-mail: expo@pmmi.org
Web Site: www.packexpointernational.com; www.
packexpo.com; www.pmmi.org
Key Personnel
VP, Meetings & Events: Patti Fee *Tel:* 571-612-
3193
Sr Dir, Expositions: Laura Thompson *Tel:* 571-
612-3217
Dir, Tradeshow Mktg: Tina Warren *Tel:* 571-612-
3203
Events Mgr: Anna Hudson *Tel:* 571-612-3198
Exhibitor Servs Sr Mgr: Merideth Newman
Tel: 571-612-3208 *E-mail:* mnewman@pmmi.
org
Exhibitor Servs & Sales Mgr: Beth Murray
Tel: 571-612-3186 *E-mail:* bmurray@pmmi.org
Biennial event held in even-numbered years.
Location: McCormick Place, 2301 S Lake Shore
Dr, Chicago, IL, USA
Oct 14-17, 2018

ScienceWriters2018
Sponsored by National Association of Science
Writers (NASW)

PO Box 7905, Berkeley, CA 94707, United States
Tel: 510-647-9500
E-mail: workshops@nasw.org
Web Site: www.nasw.org
Key Personnel
Exec Dir: Tinsley Davis *E-mail:* director@nasw.
org
Location: Washington, DC, USA
Oct 12-16, 2018

Sharjah International Book Fair (SIBF)
Sponsored by Sharjah Book Authority
PO Box 73111, Sharjah, United Arab Emirates
Tel: (06) 5123344 (Arabic); (06) 5123219 (non-Arabic) *Fax:* (06) 5123337
E-mail: sibf@sibf.com
Web Site: www.sibf.com
Location: Expo Center Sharjah, Al Taawun St, Sharjah, United Arab Emirates
Oct 31-Nov 10, 2018

TAPPI PEERS Conference
Sponsored by Technical Association of the Pulp & Paper Industry (TAPPI)
15 Technology Pkwy S, Suite 115, Peachtree Corners, GA 30092, United States
Tel: 770-446-1400 *Toll Free Tel:* 800-332-8686 (US); 800-446-9431 (CN) *Fax:* 770-446-6947
E-mail: memberconnection@tappi.org
Web Site: www.tappi.org
Key Personnel
Dir of Mktg: Simona Marcellus *Tel:* 770-209-7293 *E-mail:* smarcellus@tappi.org
Location: Hilton Portland, Portland, OR, USA
Oct 28-31, 2018

Texas Book Festival
610 Brazos, Suite 200, Austin, TX 78701, United States
Tel: 512-477-4055 *Fax:* 512-322-0722
E-mail: bookfest@texasbookfestival.org
Web Site: www.texasbookfestival.org
Key Personnel
Exec Dir: Lois Kim *E-mail:* loiskim@texasbookfestival.org
Outreach Coord: Lea Bogner *E-mail:* lea@texasbookfestival.org
Devt Mgr: Claire Burrows *E-mail:* claire@texasbookfestival.com
Literary Dir: Julie Wernersbach *E-mail:* julie@texasbookfestival.org
Literary & Communs Coord: Lydia Melby *E-mail:* lydia@texasbookfestival.org
Admin Asst: Maris Finn *E-mail:* maris@texasbookfestival.org
The festival is a statewide program that promotes reading & literacy highlighted by a 2 day festival, held annually in the fall, featuring authors from Texas & across the USA. Money raised from the festival is distributed as grants to public libraries throughout the state.
Location: State Capitol Bldg, Austin, TX, USA
Oct 27-28, 2018

Twin Cities Book Festival
Sponsored by Rain Taxi
PO Box 3840, Minneapolis, MN 55403, United States
Tel: 612-825-1528 *Fax:* 612-825-1528
E-mail: bookfest@raintaxi.com
Web Site: www.raintaxi.com/twin-cities-book-festival
Key Personnel
Dir: Eric Lorberer
Gala celebration of books, featuring large exhibition, author readings & signings, book art activities, panel discussions, used book sale & children's events.
Location: Minnesota State Fairgrounds, 1265 Snelling Ave N, St Paul, MN, USA
Oct 2018

Utah Humanities Book Festival
Sponsored by Utah Humanities Council
Affiliate of Utah Center for the Book
202 W 300 N, Salt Lake City, UT 84103, United States
Tel: 801-359-9670
Web Site: utahhumanities.org
Key Personnel
Exec Dir: Jodi Graham *E-mail:* graham@utahhumanities.org
Dir: Michael McLane *E-mail:* mclane@utahhumanities.org
Communs Dir: Deena Pyle *E-mail:* pyle@utahhumanities.org
Free literary event featuring national, regional & local authors held Oct 1-31 annually (National Book Month).
Location: Statewide, UT, USA
Oct 1-31, 2018

NOVEMBER

AMWA Annual Conference
Sponsored by American Medical Writers Association (AMWA)
30 W Gude Dr, Suite 525, Rockville, MD 20850-4357, United States
Tel: 240-238-0940 *Fax:* 301-294-9006
E-mail: amwa@amwa.org
Web Site: www.amwa.org
Key Personnel
Conference Prog Mgr & Workshop Coord: Becky Phillips *Tel:* 240-238-0940 ext 103 *E-mail:* becky@amwa.org
Location: Renaissance DC Downtown Hotel, Washington, DC, USA
Nov 1-3, 2018

ASIS&T Annual Meeting
Sponsored by Association for Information Science & Technology (ASIS&T)
8555 16 St, Suite 850, Silver Spring, MD 20910, United States
Tel: 301-495-0900 *Fax:* 301-495-0810
E-mail: asist@asist.org
Web Site: www.asist.org
Key Personnel
Dir, Meetings & Events: DeVonne Parks *E-mail:* dparks@asist.org
Location: Vancouver, BC, CN
Nov 9-15, 2018

BMI Annual Conference
Sponsored by Book Manufacturers' Institute Inc (BMI)
PO Box 731388, Ormond Beach, FL 32173, United States
Tel: 386-986-4552 *Fax:* 386-986-4553
Web Site: www.bmibook.org
Key Personnel
Exec Dir: Matt Baehr *E-mail:* mbaehr@bmibook.com
Conference Coord: Jackie Murray
Location: Hyatt Regency Coconut Point, Bonita Springs, FL, USA
Nov 4-6, 2018

Feria Internacional del Libro de Guadalajara
Av Alemania 1370, Colonia Moderna, 44190 Guadalajara, Jalisco, Mexico
Tel: (033) 3810 0331; (033) 3268 0900
E-mail: fil@fil.com.mx
Web Site: www.fil.com.mx
Key Personnel
Pres: Raul Padilla Lopez
Gen Dir: Marisol Schulz Manaut *E-mail:* marisol.schulz@fil.com.mx

Contents Mgmt: Laura Niembro Diaz *E-mail:* laura.niembro@fil.com.mx
Exhibitors Coord: Armando Montes de Santiago *E-mail:* armando.desantiago@fil.com.mx
Location: Centro de Exposiciones, Expo Guadalajara, Av Mariano Otero, 1499, Col Verde Valle, Guadalajara, Jalisco, Mexico
Nov 24-Dec 2, 2018

Istanbul Book Fair
Sponsored by Tuyap Fairs & Exhibitions Organization Inc (Tuyap Fuar ve Sergiler A S)
E-5 Karayolu Uezeri, Guerpinar Kavsagi, Bueyuekcekmece, 34500 Istanbul, Turkey
Tel: (0212) 867 11 00 *Fax:* (0212) 886 66 98
E-mail: info@tuyap.com.tr
Web Site: www.istanbulbookfair.com; www.istanbulkitapfuari.com; www.tuyap.com.tr
Annual international event organized in cooperation with the Turkish Publishers Association.
Location: International Hall, Tuyap Fair, Convention & Congress Center, Buyukcekmece/Istanbul, Turkey
Nov 10-18, 2018

Jewish Book Month
Sponsored by Jewish Book Council
520 Eighth Ave, 4th fl, New York, NY 10018, United States
Tel: 212-201-2920 *Fax:* 212-532-4952
E-mail: jbc@jewishbooks.org
Web Site: www.jewishbookcouncil.org; www.facebook.com/JewishBookCouncil; twitter.com/jewishbook
Key Personnel
Exec Dir: Naomi Firestone-Teeter
Dir: Carolyn Starman Hessel
Dedicated to the celebration of Jewish books held annually during the month leading up to Hanukkah.
Location: Nationwide throughout the USA
Nov 2-Dec 2, 2018

Karlsruher Buecherschau (Karlsruhe Book Fair)
Sponsored by Boersenverein des Deutschen Buchhandels, Landesverband Baden-Wuerttemberg eV (Association of Publishers & Booksellers in Baden-Wuerttemberg eV)
Paulinenstr 53, 70178 Stuttgart, Germany
Tel: (0711) 61941-0 *Fax:* (0711) 61941-44
E-mail: post@buchhandelsverband.de
Web Site: www.karlsruher-buecherschau.de; www.buchhandelsverband.de
Key Personnel
Contact: Carolin Schneider *Tel:* (0711) 61941-26 *E-mail:* schneider@buchhandelsverband.de
Location: Karlsruhe, Germany
Nov 16-Dec 2, 2018

Louisiana Book Festival
Sponsored by Louisiana Center for the Book
Subsidiary of State Library of Louisiana
701 N Fourth St, Baton Rouge, LA 70802, United States
Tel: 225-219-9503 *Fax:* 225-219-9840
Web Site: louisianabookfestival.org
Key Personnel
Dir: Jim Davis *Tel:* 225-342-9714 *E-mail:* jdavis@slol.lib.la.us
Asst Dir: Robert Wilson *E-mail:* rwilson@slol.lib.la.us
A free festival celebrating readers, writers & books representing a variety of genres & related events for all ages, food, music.
Location: State Library of Louisiana, Louisiana State Capitol, Capitol Park Welcome Center & nearby locations, Baton Rouge, LA, USA
Nov 10, 2018

Miami Book Fair
Sponsored by Florida Center for the Literary Arts

c/o Miami Dade College, 300 NE Second Ave, Miami, FL 33132, United States
Tel: 305-237-3258
E-mail: wbookfair@mdc.edu
Web Site: www.miamibookfair.com
Key Personnel
Dir of Opers: Delia Lopez
Exhibit Coord: Giselle Hernandez
Miami Book Fair is the largest event of its kind in the USA. First held in 1984, for more than 30 years, the fair has been held over 8 days each November. In addition to readings by more than 400 authors from all over the world & the sale of thousands of books in many languages, the fair offers book-centered fun for children, panel discussions & writing classes in English & Spanish. For up to date information, call or visit the book fair web site at www.miamibookfair.com.
Location: Miami Dade College, Wolfson Campus, Miami, FL, USA
Nov 11-18, 2018

Salon du Livre de Montreal (Montreal Book Fair)
Sponsored by Salon du Livre de Montreal
300, rue du St-Secrement, Suite 430, Montreal, QC H2Y 1X4, Canada
Tel: 514-845-2365
E-mail: info@salondulivredemontreal.com
Web Site: www.salondulivredemontreal.com
Location: Place Bonaventure, 800 de la Gauchetiere Street W, Montreal, QC, CN
Nov 14-19, 2018

Salon du Livre et de la Presse Jeunesse (SLPJ)
Sponsored by Centre de Promotion du Livre de Jeunesse (CPLJ)
3, rue Francois Debergue, 93100 Montreuil, France
Tel: 01 55 86 86 55 *Fax:* 01 48 57 04 62
E-mail: contact@slpj.fr
Web Site: www.slpjplus.fr
Key Personnel
Dir: Sylvie Vassallo
Leading publishing event dedicated to children's books.
Nov 28-Dec 3, 2018

Stuttgarter Buchwochen (Stuttgart Book Weeks)
Sponsored by Boersenverein des Deutschen Buchhandels, Landesverband Baden-Wuerttemberg eV (Association of Publishers & Booksellers in Baden-Wuerttemberg eV)
Paulinenstr 53, 70178 Stuttgart, Germany
Tel: (0711) 61941-0 *Fax:* (0711) 61941-44
E-mail: post@buchhandelsverband.de
Web Site: www.buchwochen.de; www.buchhandelsverband.de
Key Personnel
Contact: Andrea Baumann *Tel:* (0711) 61941-28
E-mail: baumann@buchhandelsverband.de
Location: Haus de Wirtschaft, Willi-Bleicher-Str 19, Stuttgart, Germany
Nov 15-Dec 2, 2018

Worlddidac / Swissdidac Bern
Sponsored by Worlddidac Association
Bollwerk 21, 3011 Bern, Switzerland
Tel: (031) 311 76 82 *Fax:* (031) 312 17 44
E-mail: info@worlddidac.org
Web Site: www.worlddidac.org
International exhibition for education, training, technology & supply. Held in conjunction with Swissdidac Bern. A biennial event held in even-numbered years.
Location: Bernexpo, Mingerstr 6, Bern, Switzerland
Nov 7-9, 2018

DECEMBER

Sofia International Book Fair
Sponsored by Bulgarian Book Association (BBA)
blvd Vitosha 64, 2nd fl, ap 4, 1463 Sofia, Bulgaria
Tel: (02) 958 15 25; (02) 958 92 11
E-mail: office@abk.bg
Web Site: www.abk.bg
Key Personnel
Event Organizer: Yancho Mihaylov
    E-mail: mihaylov@abk.bg
The first Sofia International Book fair was organized in 1968. Since then it brings together over 40,000 visitors yearly to meet with exhibiting companies from Bulgaria & abroad & offers unrivaled access to the national & international book publishing & bookseller communities.
Location: National Palace of Culture, One Bulgaria Blvd, Sofia, Bulgaria
Dec 11-16, 2018

2019

JANUARY

American Library Association Midwinter Meeting
Sponsored by The American Library Association (ALA)
50 E Huron St, Chicago, IL 60611-2795, United States
Tel: 312-944-6780 *Toll Free Tel:* 800-545-2433 (ext 3223, conference servs) *Fax:* 312-440-9374
E-mail: ala@ala.org
Web Site: www.ala.org
Key Personnel
Registration & Housing Mgr: Alicia Babcock *Tel:* 800-545-2433 ext 3229
    E-mail: ababcock@ala.org
Conference Dir: Paul Graller *Tel:* 800-545-2433 ext 3219 *E-mail:* pgraller@ala.org
Meeting Coord: Amy McGuigan *Tel:* 800-545-2433 ext 3226 *E-mail:* amcguigan@ala.org
Meetings, AV & Catering Coord: Yvonne McLean *Tel:* 800-545-2433 ext 3222
    E-mail: ymclean@ala.org
Conference Coord: Lina Zabaneh *Tel:* 800-545-2433 ext 3227 *E-mail:* lzabaneh@ala.org
Meeting Coord: Alicia (Alee) Navarro *Tel:* 800-545-2433 ext 3216 *E-mail:* anavarro@ala.org
Location: Seattle, WA, USA
Jan 25-29, 2019

APE 2019
Sponsored by digiprimo GmbH & Co KG
Lutherstr 122, 14089 Berlin, Germany
Mailing Address: PO Box 22 01 16, 14061 Berlin, Germany
Tel: (030) 36 43 01 64
E-mail: info@digiprimo.com
Web Site: www.ape2019.eu; www.digiprimo.com
Location: Berlin, Germany
Jan 14-15, 2019

Football Writers Association of America Annual Meeting
Sponsored by Football Writers Association of America (FWAA)
18652 Vista del Sol, Dallas, TX 75287, United States
Tel: 972-713-6198
Web Site: www.sportswriters.net/fwaa; twitter.com/thefwaa

Key Personnel
Exec Dir: Steve Richardson *E-mail:* tiger@fwaa.com
Location: San Jose Marriott, 300 S Market St, San Jose, CA, USA
Jan 4-7, 2019

IS&T Electronic Imaging Conference
Sponsored by Society for Imaging Science & Technology (IS&T)
7003 Kilworth Lane, Springfield, VA 22151, United States
Tel: 703-642-9090 *Fax:* 703-642-9094
E-mail: info@imaging.org
Web Site: www.imaging.org
Key Personnel
Exec Dir: Suzanne E Grinnan *E-mail:* sgrinnan@imaging.org
Conference Prog Mgr: Christine Lenihan *Tel:* 703-642-9090 ext 106 *E-mail:* clenihan@imaging.org
Exec Asst: Donna Smith *E-mail:* dsmith@imaging.org
Location: Hyatt Regency San Francisco Airport, Burlingame, CA, USA
Jan 13-17, 2019

MLA Annual Convention
Sponsored by Modern Language Association of America (MLA)
85 Broad St, Suite 500, New York, NY 10004-2434, United States
SAN: 202-6422
Tel: 646-576-5266 (convention); 646-576-5000 *Fax:* 646-458-0030
E-mail: convention@mla.org
Web Site: www.mla.org/convention
Key Personnel
Assoc Dir of Convention Progs: Karin L Bagnall *E-mail:* kbagnall@mla.org
Location: Chicago, IL, USA
Jan 3-6, 2019

Remainder & Promotional Book Fair
Sponsored by Ciana Ltd
Rockholt, Ellimore Rd, Lustleigh, Newton Abbot TQ13 9TF, United Kingdom
Tel: (01626) 897 106 *Fax:* (01626) 897 107
E-mail: enquiries@ciana.co.uk
Web Site: www.ciana.co.uk
Key Personnel
Contact: Sarah Weedon; Robert Collie
Location: ILEC Conference Centre, 47 Lillie Rd, London, UK
Jan 20-21, 2019

FEBRUARY

California International Antiquarian Book Fair
Sponsored by Antiquarian Booksellers' Association of America (ABAA)
20 W 44 St, Suite 507, New York, NY 10036, United States
Tel: 212-944-8291 *Fax:* 212-944-8293
E-mail: info@cabookfair.com
Web Site: www.cabookfair.com; www.abaa.org
Key Personnel
Exec Dir: Susan Benne *E-mail:* sbenne@abaa.org
Annual event co-sponsored by International League of Antiquarian Booksellers.
Location: Oakland Marriott City Center, 1001 Broadway, Oakland, CA, USA
Feb 8-10, 2019

CAMEX
Sponsored by National Association of College Stores (NACS)

500 E Lorain St, Oberlin, OH 44074, United States
Tel: 440-775-7777 *Toll Free Tel:* 800-622-7498
  Fax: 440-775-4769
E-mail: camex@nacs.org
Web Site: www.camex.org; www.nacs.org
Key Personnel
CEO: Bob Walton *Tel:* 800-622-7498 ext 2201
  E-mail: rwalton@nacs.org
Dir, Meetings: Jodie Wilmot *Tel:* 800-622-7498
  ext 2272 *E-mail:* jwilmot@nacs.org
Dir, Expositions: Mary Adler-Kozak *Tel:* 800-
  622-7498 ext 2265 *E-mail:* madler-kozak@
  nacs.org
Conference & trade show dedicated exclusively
  to the more than $10 billion collegiate retailing
  industry.
Location: Henry B Gonzalez Convention Center,
  San Antonio, TX, USA
Feb 22-26, 2019

PSP Annual Conference
Sponsored by Association of American Publishers
  (AAP)
455 Massachusetts Ave NW, Suite 700, Washing-
  ton, DC 20001-2777, United States
Tel: 202-347-3375 *Fax:* 202-347-3690
E-mail: info@publishers.org
Web Site: www.publishers.org
Key Personnel
Dir, Prof & Scholarly Publg: Sara Pinto *Tel:* 212-
  255-1716 *E-mail:* spinto@publishers.org
Location: Ritz-Carlton, 1150 22 St NW, Washing-
  ton, DC, USA
Feb 6-8, 2019

SCBWI Winter Conference
Sponsored by Society of Children's Book Writers
  & Illustrators (SCBWI)
4727 Wilshire Blvd, Suite 301, Los Angeles, CA
  90010, United States
Tel: 323-782-1010 *Fax:* 323-782-1892
E-mail: scbwi@scbwi.org
Web Site: www.scbwi.org
Key Personnel
Pres: Stephen Mooser *E-mail:* stephenmooser@
  scbwi.org
Exec Dir: Lin Oliver *E-mail:* linoliver@scbwi.org
Location: Grand Hyatt New York, 109 E 42 St at
  Grand Central Terminal, New York, NY, USA
Feb 8-10, 2019

**Texas Outdoor Writers Association Annual
  Conference**
Sponsored by Texas Outdoor Writers Association
  (TOWA)
PO Box 151293, Austin, TX 78715-1293, United
  States
Tel: 512-358-8000
E-mail: towa@towa.org
Web Site: www.towa.org; www.facebook.com/
  TXOWA
Key Personnel
Exec Dir: Burney Brown
Location: TX, USA
Feb 28-March 3, 2019

WestPack®
Sponsored by UBM Canon
2901 28 St, Suite 100, Santa Monica, CA 90405,
  United States
Tel: 310-445-4200
E-mail: tsoperations@ubm.com
Web Site: ubmcanon.com
Location: Anaheim Convention Center, 800 W
  Katella Ave, Anaheim, CA, USA
Feb 5-7, 2019

SPRING

BookCon
Sponsored by ReedPOP
Division of Reed Exhibitions USA
383 Main Ave, Norwalk, CT 06851, United States
Tel: 203-840-5632 (cust serv); 203-840-4800
  Toll Free Tel: 800-777-8774
E-mail: inquiry@TheBookCon.com
Web Site: www.thebookcon.com; www.reedpop.
  com
Key Personnel
Event Dir: Brien McDonald *Tel:* 203-840-5483
  E-mail: brien@reedpop.com
Event Mgr: Jenny Martin *E-mail:* jenny@
  reedpop.com
Consumer event following BookExpo.
Location: Jacob K Javits Convention Center, 655
  W 43 St, New York, NY, USA
Spring 2019

BookExpo
Sponsored by ReedPOP
Division of Reed Exhibitions USA
383 Main Ave, Norwalk, CT 06851, United States
Tel: 203-840-4800 *Toll Free Tel:* 800-840-5614
  (cust serv)
E-mail: inquiry@bookexpoamerica.com (cust
  serv)
Web Site: www.bookexpoamerica.com; www.
  reedpop.com
Key Personnel
Event Dir: Brien McDonald *Tel:* 203-840-5483
  E-mail: brien@reedpop.com
Event Mgr: Jenny Martin *E-mail:* jenny@
  reedpop.com
Produced & managed by ReedPOP, BookExpo
  is sponsored by the American Booksellers As-
  sociation (ABA), the Association of American
  Publishers Inc (AAP) & the Association of Au-
  thors' Representatives Inc (AAR).
Location: Jacob K Javits Convention Center, 655
  W 43 St, New York, NY, USA
Spring 2019

MARCH

Adelaide Festival
Sponsored by Adelaide Festival Corp
Level 9, 33 King William St, Adelaide, SA 5000,
  Australia
Mailing Address: PO Box 8221, Station Arcade,
  Adelaide, SA 5000, Australia
Tel: (08) 8216 4444 *Fax:* (08) 8216 4455
E-mail: info@adelaidefestival.com.au
Web Site: www.adelaidefestival.com.au
Key Personnel
Artistic Dir: Neil Armfield; Rachel Healy
Assoc Prodr: Kate Hillgrove
Prog Dir: Lesley Newton
Prodn Mgr: Adam Hornhardt
Annual event highlighting the arts, including lit-
  erature. Adelaide Writers' Week is one of the
  high-profile events held during the festival.
Location: Adelaide's Central Business District,
  Adelaide, SA, Australia
March 1-17, 2019

AWP Annual Conference & Bookfair
Sponsored by Association of Writers & Writing
  Programs (AWP)
University of Maryland, 5245 Greenbelt Rd, Box
  246, College Park, MD 20740, United States
Tel: 301-226-9710 *Fax:* 301-226-9797
E-mail: awp@awpwriter.org
Web Site: www.awpwriter.org/awp_conference/;
  www.awpwriter.org

Key Personnel
Dir, Conferences: Christian Teresi
Assoc Dir, Conferences: Cynthia Sherman
Location: Oregon Convention Center, Portland,
  OR, USA
March 27-30, 2019

Bologna Children's Book Fair
Sponsored by BolognaFiere SpA
Piazza Costituzione, 6, 40128 Bologna, Italy
Tel: (051) 282 111 *Fax:* (051) 637 4011
E-mail: bookfair@bolognafiere.it
Web Site: www.bolognachildrensbookfair.com;
  www.facebook.com/BolognaChildrensBookFair
Key Personnel
Exhibition Mgr: Elena Pasoli *Tel:* (051) 282 966
  E-mail: elena.pasoli@bolognafiere.it
Location: Bologna Fair Centre, Piazza Costi-
  tuzione, 6, Bologna, Italy
March 25-28, 2019

The IA Conference
Formerly The IA Summit
Sponsored by Association for Information Science
  & Technology (ASIS&T)
8555 16 St, Suite 850, Silver Spring, MD 20910,
  United States
Tel: 301-495-0900 *Fax:* 301-495-0810
E-mail: asist@asist.org
Web Site: www.asist.org; www.twitter.com/
  theiaconf?lang=en
Key Personnel
Dir, Meetings & Events: DeVonne Parks
  E-mail: dparks@asist.org
Location: Renaissance Orlando at SeaWorld, Or-
  lando, FL, USA
March 13-17, 2019

Leipzig Book Fair (Leipziger Buchmesse)
Sponsored by Leipziger Messe GmbH
Messe-Allee 1, 04356 Leipzig, Germany
Mailing Address: Postfach 10 07 20, 04007
  Leipzig, Germany
Tel: (0341) 678-8240 *Fax:* (0341) 678-8242
E-mail: info@leipziger-buchmesse.de
Web Site: www.leipziger-buchmesse.de
Key Personnel
Dir: Oliver Zille
Held annually in conjunction with The Leipzig
  Antiquarian Book Fair.
Location: Leipzig Exhibition Centre, Messe-Allee
  1, Leipzig, Germany
March 21-24, 2019

Livre Paris (Book Paris)
Sponsored by Reed Expositions France
Subsidiary of Reed Exhibition Companies
52-54 quai de Dion-Bouton, CS 80001, 92806
  Puteaux Cedex, France
Tel: 01 47 56 64 31 *Fax:* 01 47 56 64 44
E-mail: info@reedexpo.fr
Web Site: www.livreparis.com
Key Personnel
Dir, Mktg & Communs: Elisa Lheureux
  E-mail: elisa.lheureux@reedexpo.fr
Annual international publishing event for publish-
  ers, booksellers, teachers & librarians. Open to
  the trade & the public.
Location: Paris Expo, Porte de Versailles, Paris,
  France
March 15-18, 2019

The London Book Fair
Sponsored by Reed Exhibitions UK
Division of RELX Group PLC
Gateway House, 28 The Quadrant, Richmond,
  Surrey TW9 1DN, United Kingdom
Tel: (020) 8271 2124
E-mail: lbf.helpline@reedexpo.co.uk
Web Site: www.londonbookfair.co.uk
Key Personnel
Conference Mgr: Orna O'Brien *Tel:* (020) 8910
  7906 *E-mail:* orna.obrien@reedexpo.co.uk

The London Book Fair is the global marketplace for rights negotiation & the sale & distribution of content across print, audio, TV, film & digital channels. Taking place every spring in the world's premier publishing & cultural capital, it is a unique opportunity to hear from authors, enjoy the vibrant atmosphere & explore innovations shaping the publishing world of the future. The London Book Fair brings you 3 days of focused access to customers, content & emerging markets.
Location: Olympia London, Hammersmith Rd, Kensington, London, UK
March 12-14, 2019

New York Antiquarian Book Fair
Sponsored by Antiquarian Booksellers' Association of America (ABAA)
20 W 44 St, Suite 507, New York, NY 10036, United States
Tel: 212-944-8291 *Fax:* 212-944-8293
Web Site: www.nyantiquarianbookfair.com; www. abaa.org
Key Personnel
Exec Dir: Susan Benne *E-mail:* sbenne@abaa.org
Co-sponsored by International League of Antiquarian Booksellers (ILAB) & managed by Sanford L Smith & Associates Ltd.
Location: Park Avenue Armory, 643 Park Ave at 67 St, New York, NY, USA
March 7-10, 2019

Paper2019
Sponsored by American Forest & Paper Association (AF&PA)
1101 "K" St NW, Suite 700, Washington, DC 20005, United States
Tel: 202-463-2700 *Fax:* 202-463-2708
E-mail: info@afandpa.org
Web Site: www.afandpa.org
Key Personnel
Dir, Meetings: Susan Van Eaton
Sr Mgr, Meetings & Memb Servs: Kathy Smith
Co-hosted with the National Paper Trade Association (NPTA), this annual paper industry event offers participants access to decision makers from an impressive array of manufacturers, merchants, publishers, distributors of printing paper, packaging material & industrial material & supplies.
Location: Chicago, IL, USA
March 24-26, 2019

Virginia Festival of the Book
Sponsored by Virginia Foundation for the Humanities
145 Ednam Dr, Charlottesville, VA 22903, United States
Tel: 434-924-3296 *Fax:* 434-296-4714
E-mail: vabook@virginia.edu
Web Site: www.vabook.org
Key Personnel
Prog Dir: Jane Kulow *Tel:* 434-924-7548
Annual public festival for children & adults featuring authors, illustrators, publishers, publicists, agents & other book professionals in panel discussions & readings. Most events are free. Hundreds of authors invited annually.
Location: Charlottesville, VA, USA
March 20-24, 2019

APRIL

AIGA Design Conference
Sponsored by AIGA, the professional association for design
233 Broadway, Suite 1740, New York, NY 10279, United States

Tel: 212-807-1990
Web Site: www.aiga.org
Key Personnel
Prog Dir: Kathleen Budny *Tel:* 212-710-3144
Mgr, Events: Susan Augenbraum *Tel:* 212-710-3133
Annual conference.
Location: Pasadena Convention Center, 300 E Green St, Pasadena, CA, USA
April 4-6, 2019

Alberta Library Conference
Sponsored by Library Association of Alberta (LAA)
80 Baker Crescent NW, Calgary, AB T2L 1R4, Canada
Tel: 403-284-5818 *Toll Free Tel:* 877-522-5550
Fax: 403-284-5818
E-mail: info@laa.ca
Web Site: www.albertalibraryconference.com; www.laa.ca
Key Personnel
Conference Coord: Christine Sheppard
Co-hosted by Alberta Library Trustees Association (ALTA).
Location: Fairmont Jasper Park Lodge, Jasper, AB, CN
April 25-28, 2019

BMI Management Conference
Sponsored by Book Manufacturers' Institute Inc (BMI)
PO Box 731388, Ormond Beach, FL 32173, United States
Tel: 386-986-4552 *Fax:* 386-986-4553
Web Site: www.bmibook.org
Key Personnel
Exec Dir: Matt Baehr *E-mail:* mbaehr@bmibook.com
Conference Coord: Jackie Murray
Location: Omni Charlotte Hotel, 132 E Trade St, Charlotte, NC, USA
April 28-30, 2019

Children's Book Week
Sponsored by The Children's Book Council (CBC)
54 W 39 St, 14th fl, New York, NY 10018, United States
Tel: 212-966-1990
E-mail: cbc.info@cbcbooks.org
Web Site: www.cbcbooks.org; www.everychildareader.net
Key Personnel
Exec Dir: Carl Lennertz *E-mail:* carl.lennertz@cbcbooks.org
Dir, Programming: Shaina Birkhead *E-mail:* shaina.birkhead@cbcbooks.org
Location: Nationwide across the USA
April 29-May 5, 2019

EPA Annual Convention
Sponsored by Evangelical Press Association (EPA)
PO Box 1787, Queen Creek, AZ 85142, United States
Toll Free Tel: 888-311-1731
Web Site: www.evangelicalpress.com
Key Personnel
Exec Dir: Lamar Keener
Annual convention for editors, publishers, writers & other staff (print & online publications). Workshop tracks & plenary sessions, opportunities for networking & fellowship.
Location: Sheraton Oklahoma City Downtown Hotel, Oklahoma City, OK, USA
April 7-9, 2019

The Federation of Children's Book Groups Annual Conference
Sponsored by The Federation of Children's Book Groups (FCBG)

10 St Laurence Rd, Bradford on Avon BA15 1JG, United Kingdom
Tel: (0300) 102 1559
E-mail: info@fcbg.org.uk
Web Site: www.fcbg.org.uk; twitter.com/fcbgnews?lang=en; www.facebook.com/The-Federation-of-Childrens-Book-Groups-119682808115620/
Organized by one of our local children's book groups in collaboration with the national executive, this conference is an opportunity for authors, illustrators, parents, teachers, librarians & all interested children's book lovers to come together to promote their mission of bringing children & books together.
Location: Woldingham School, Marden Park, Woldingham, Surrey, UK
April 12-14, 2019

4A's Accelerate
Formerly Transformation
Sponsored by 4A's (American Association of Advertising Agencies)
1065 Avenue of the Americas, 16th fl, New York, NY 10018, United States
Tel: 212-682-2500
Web Site: www.accelerate.aaaa.org; www.aaaa.org
Key Personnel
Pres & CEO: Marla Kaplowitz *E-mail:* mkaplowitz@aaaa.org
Events Mgr: Jennifer Falik Rains *Tel:* 212-850-0733 *E-mail:* jfrains@aaaa.org
Location: InterContinental Los Angeles Downtown, 900 Wilshire Blvd, Los Angeles, CA, USA
April 1-3, 2019

International Children's Book Day
Sponsored by International Board on Books for Young People (IBBY)
Nonnenweg 12, Postfach, 4009 Basel, Switzerland
Tel: (061) 272 29 17 *Fax:* (061) 272 27 57
E-mail: ibby@ibby.org
Web Site: www.ibby.org
Key Personnel
Exec Dir: Liz Page *E-mail:* liz.page@ibby.org
Admin Asst: Luzmaria Stauffenegger *E-mail:* luzmaria.stauffenegger@ibby.org
On Hans Christian Andersen's birthday, April 2nd, International Children's Book Day (ICBD) is celebrated to inspire a love of reading & to call attention to children's books. Each year a different national section has the opportunity to be the international sponsor. It decides upon a theme & invites a prominent author to write a message to the children of the world & a well-known illustrator to design a poster. These materials are used in different ways to promote books & reading around the world.
April 2, 2019

Los Angeles Times Festival of Books
Sponsored by Los Angeles Times
Subsidiary of tronc inc
202 W First St, Los Angeles, CA 90012, United States
Tel: 213-237-5000 *Toll Free Tel:* 800-528-4637
Fax: 213-237-2335
E-mail: eventinfo@latimes.com
Web Site: events.latimes.com/festivalofbooks
Location: The University of Southern California (USC), Los Angeles, CA, USA
April 13-14, 2019

MagNet
Sponsored by Magazines Canada (MC)
425 Adelaide St W, Suite 700, Toronto, ON M5V 3C1, Canada
Tel: 416-504-0274 *Fax:* 416-504-0437
E-mail: info@magazinescanada.ca; magnet@magazinescanada.ca
Web Site: magazinescanada.ca; twitter.com/magscanada

Key Personnel
Memb Servs & Events Coord: Kiley Pole
Tel: 416-504-0274 ext 238 *E-mail:* kpole@
magazinescanada.ca
Canada's magazine conference, MagNet is jointly
sponsored by Magazines Canada (MC), Cana-
dian Society of Magazine Editors (CSME) &
Circulation Management Association of Canada
(CMC).
Location: The Courtyard Downtown Toronto, 475
Yonge St, Toronto, ON, CN
April 24-25, 2019

NAAJ Annual Meeting
Sponsored by North American Agricultural Jour-
nalists (NAAJ)
6434 Hurta Lane, Bryan, TX 77808, United
States
Tel: 979-324-4302 *Fax:* 979-862-1202
Web Site: www.naaj.net
Key Personnel
Exec Secy & Treas: Kathleen Phillips *E-mail:* ka-
phillips@tamu.edu
Annual meeting, writing awards & scholarship
benefit dance.
Location: Washington, DC, USA
April 2019

NAPIM Spring Convention
Sponsored by National Association of Printing
Ink Manufacturers (NAPIM)
15 Technology Pkwy S, Peachtree Corners, GA
30092, United States
Tel: 770-209-7289 *Fax:* 770-209-7217
Web Site: www.napim.org
Key Personnel
Exec Dir: John Copeland *Tel:* 815-979-2341
E-mail: jcopeland@napim.org
Memb Rel Mgr: Deepa George *E-mail:* dgeorge@
napim.org
Location: Biltmore Hotel, Coral Gables, FL, USA
April 5-8, 2019

National Library Week
Sponsored by The American Library Association
(ALA)
50 E Huron St, Chicago, IL 60611-2795, United
States
Tel: 312-944-6780 *Toll Free Tel:* 800-545-2433
Fax: 312-440-9374
E-mail: ala@ala.org
Web Site: www.ala.org/nlw
Location: Nationwide throughout the USA
April 7-13, 2019

The Quest for Excellence® Conference
Sponsored by National Institute of Standards and
Technology (NIST)
100 Bureau Dr, Stop 1070, Gaithersburg, MD
20899-1070, United States
Tel: 301-975-2036 *Fax:* 301-948-3716
E-mail: baldrige@nist.gov
Web Site: www.nist.gov/baldrige/qe/index.cfm
Key Personnel
Conference Chair: Barbara Fischer
E-mail: barbara.fischer@nist.gov
Official conference of the Malcolm Baldrige Na-
tional Quality Award, held in partnership with
American Society for Quality (ASQ) & Associ-
ation for Talent Development (ATD).
Location: Gaylord National Harbor, 165 Water-
front St, National Harbor, MD, USA
April 7-10, 2019

Southern Kentucky Book Fest
WKU Libraries, Cravens 106, 1906 College
Heights Blvd, Bowling Green, KY 42101-1067,
United States
Tel: 270-745-4502 *Fax:* 270-745-6422
E-mail: sokybookfest@wku.edu
Web Site: www.sokybookfest.org

Key Personnel
Mtkg Coord: Jennifer Wilson *E-mail:* jennifer.
wilson@wku.edu
The Southern Kentucky Book Fest is one of the
state's largest literary events & is presented by
WKU Libraries, Warren County Public Library
& Barnes & Noble Booksellers. Book Fest is a
fundraiser for the promotion of literacy in our
community.
Location: Knicely Conference Center, 645 Camp-
bell Lane, Bowling Green, KY, USA
April 26-27, 2019

Texas Library Association Annual Conference
Sponsored by Texas Library Association (TLA)
3355 Bee Cave Rd, Suite 401, Austin, TX 78746-
6763, United States
Tel: 512-328-1518 *Toll Free Tel:* 800-580-2852
Fax: 512-328-8852
E-mail: tla@txla.org
Web Site: www.txla.org
Key Personnel
Conference Mgr: Elise Walker *Tel:* 512-328-1518
x145 *E-mail:* elisew@txla.org
Location: Austin, TX, USA
April 15-18, 2019

UKSG Annual Conference & Exhibition
Sponsored by UKSG (United Kingdom Serials
Group)
Witney Business & Innovation Centre, Windrush
House, Windrush Industrial Park, Burford Rd,
Witney, Oxon OX29 7DX, United Kingdom
Web Site: www.uksg.org
Key Personnel
Busn Mgr: Alison Whitehorn *Tel:* (01635)
254292 *Fax:* (01635) 253826 *E-mail:* alison@
uksg.org
Events Asst: Samira Koelle *Tel:* (01993) 848234
E-mail: samira@uksg.org
Annual 3 day event open to everyone.
Location: Telford International Centre, Telford,
UK
April 8-10, 2019

MAY

**ASQ World Conference on Quality &
Improvement**
Sponsored by American Society for Quality
(ASQ)
600 N Plankinton Ave, Milwaukee, WI 53203,
United States
Mailing Address: PO Box 3005, Milwaukee, WI
53201-3005, United States
Tel: 414-272-8575 *Toll Free Tel:* 800-248-1946
(US & CN) *Fax:* 414-272-1734
E-mail: help@asq.org
Web Site: www.asq.org
Key Personnel
Conference Mgr: Michael Dzick
E-mail: mdzick@asq.org
Location: Fort Worth, TX, USA
May 20-22, 2019

PaperCon
Sponsored by Technical Association of the Pulp
& Paper Industry (TAPPI)
15 Technology Pkwy S, Suite 115, Peachtree Cor-
ners, GA 30092, United States
Tel: 770-446-1400 *Toll Free Tel:* 800-332-8686
(US); 800-446-9431 (CN) *Fax:* 770-446-6947;
770-209-7206
E-mail: memberconnection@tappi.org
Web Site: www.papercon.org; www.tappi.org
Key Personnel
Dir of Mktg: Simona Marcellus *Tel:* 770-209-
7293 *E-mail:* smarcellus@tappi.org

Location: Indiana Convention Center, Indianapolis, IN, USA
May 5-8, 2019

SSP Annual Meeting
Sponsored by Society for Scholarly Publishing
(SSP)
10200 W 44 Ave, Suite 304, Wheat Ridge, CO
80033-2840, United States
Tel: 303-422-3914 *Fax:* 720-881-6101
E-mail: info@sspnet.org
Web Site: www.sspnet.org
Key Personnel
Exec/Meetings Asst: Jennifer Lanphere
Location: Marriott Marquis San Diego Marina,
San Diego, CA, USA
May 29-May 31, 2019

JUNE

**American Library Association Annual
Conference**
Sponsored by The American Library Association
(ALA)
50 E Huron St, Chicago, IL 60611-2795, United
States
Tel: 312-944-6780 *Toll Free Tel:* 800-545-2433
(ext 3223, conference servs) *Fax:* 312-440-
9374
E-mail: ala@ala.org
Web Site: www.ala.org
Key Personnel
Registration & Housing Mgr: Alicia Bab-
cock *Tel:* 800-545-2433 ext 3229
E-mail: ababcock@ala.org
Conference Dir: Paul Graller *Tel:* 800-545-2433
ext 3219 *E-mail:* pgraller@ala.org
Meeting Coord: Amy McGuigan *Tel:* 800-545-
2433 ext 3226 *E-mail:* amcguigan@ala.org
Meetings, AV & Catering Coord: Yvonne
McLean *Tel:* 800-545-2433 ext 3222
E-mail: ymclean@ala.org
Conference Coord: Lina Zabaneh *Tel:* 800-545-
2433 ext 3227 *E-mail:* lzabaneh@ala.org
Meeting Coord: Alicia (Alee) Navarro *Tel:* 800-
545-2433 ext 3216 *E-mail:* anavarro@ala.org
Location: Washington, DC, USA
June 20-25, 2019

AUPresses Annual Meeting
Sponsored by Association of University Presses
(AUPresses)
1412 Broadway, Suite 2135, New York, NY
10018, United States
Tel: 212-989-1010 *Fax:* 212-989-0275
E-mail: annualmeeting@aaup.org; info@aaupnet.
org
Web Site: www.aupresses.org
Key Personnel
Exec Dir: Peter Berkery *Tel:* 917-288-5594
E-mail: pberkery@aaupnet.org
Dir, Mktg & Communs: Brenna McLaughlin
Tel: 917-244-2051 *E-mail:* bmclaughlin@
aaupnet.org
Busn Mgr: Kim Miller *Tel:* 917-244-1264
E-mail: kmiller@aaupnet.org
Location: Detroit Marriott at the Renaissance
Center, Detroit, MI, USA
June 11-13, 2019

Catholic Media Conference
Sponsored by Catholic Press Association of the
United States & Canada
205 W Monroe St, Suite 470, Chicago, IL 60606,
United States
Tel: 312-380-6789 *Fax:* 312-361-0256
Web Site: www.catholicpress.org

Key Personnel
Exec Dir: Timothy M Walter *E-mail:* twalter@
catholicpress.org
Location: Hilton St Petersburg Bayfront, St Petersburg, FL, USA
June 18-21, 2019

EastPack®
Sponsored by UBM Canon
2901 28 St, Suite 100, Santa Monica, CA 90405,
United States
Tel: 310-445-4200
E-mail: tsoperations@ubm.com
Web Site: ubmcanon.com
Location: Jacob K Javits Convention Center, 655
W 43 St, New York, NY, USA
June 11-13, 2019

IABC World Conference
Sponsored by International Association of Business Communicators (IABC)
155 Montgomery St, Suite 1210, San Francisco,
CA 94104, United States
Tel: 415-544-4700 *Toll Free Tel:* 800-776-4222
(US & CN) *Fax:* 415-544-4747
E-mail: conference@iabc.com
Web Site: wc.iabc.com; www.iabc.com
Key Personnel
Dir, Content: Natasha Nicholson
Location: Hyatt & Fairmont, Vancouver, BC, CN
June 9-12, 2019

Jerusalem International Book Forum
Sponsored by Ariel Municipal Co Ltd
PO Box 26280, Jerusalem 9126201, Israel
Tel: (02) 546 8171; (02) 546 8170 *Fax:* (02) 546
8170
E-mail: jerfair@jerusalem.muni.il
Web Site: www.jbookfair.com; www.jbookfair.
com/en/ (English)
Biennial event.
Location: Jerusalem International Convention
Center, Jerusalem, Israel
June 2019

**National Federation of Press Women
Communications Conference**
Sponsored by National Federation of Press
Women Inc (NFPW)
PO Box 3007, Mechanicsville, VA 23116-0026,
United States
Tel: 804-746-1033 *Fax:* 804-335-1296
E-mail: info@nfpw.org
Web Site: www.nfpw.org
Location: Baton Rouge, LA, USA
June 27-29, 2019

**Outdoor Writers Association of America
Annual Conference**
Sponsored by Outdoor Writers Association of
America (OWAA)
615 Oak St, Suite 201, Missoula, MT 59801,
United States
Tel: 406-728-7434 *Fax:* 406-728-7445
E-mail: info@owaa.org
Web Site: www.owaa.org
Key Personnel
Membership & Conference Dir: Jessica (Pollett)
Seitz *E-mail:* jseitz@owaa.org
The annual OWAA Conference is an opportunity
for outdoor communicators & outdoor groups,
businesses & agencies that are involved in the
world of outdoor communication to learn &
connect with others in the industry. It will give
attendees a chance to network with other professionals, allow them to build crucial business
outlets & help improve their skills. Attend sessions geared toward general business & newsmaker sessions, plus craft improvement in multiple genres of outdoor communication.

Location: Robinson Center, Little Rock, AR,
USA
June 22-24, 2019

SIPA Annual Conference
Sponsored by Specialized Information Publishers
Association (SIPA)
Division of Software & Information Industry Association (SIIA)
1090 Vermont Ave NW, 6th fl, Washington, DC
20005-4095, United States
Tel: 202-289-7442 *Fax:* 202-289-7097
Web Site: www.siia.net/divisions/sipa-specialized-
information-publishers-association
Key Personnel
Mng Dir: Nancy Brand *Tel:* 781-754-4771
E-mail: nbrand@siia.net
Location: Capital Hilton, Washington, DC, USA
June 3-5, 2019

SLA Annual Conference & INFO-EXPO
Sponsored by Special Libraries Association
(SLA)
7918 Jones Branch Dr, Suite 300, McLean, VA
22102, United States
Tel: 703-647-4900 *Fax:* 703-506-3266
Web Site: www.sla.org
Key Personnel
Dir, Events: Mary Katherine Bilowus
E-mail: mkbilowus@sla.org
Location: Huntington Convention Center of
Cleveland, Cleveland, OH, USA
June 13-18, 2019

JULY

Hong Kong Book Fair
Sponsored by Hong Kong Trade Development
Council
c/o Exhibition Dept, Unit 13, Expo Galleria,
Hong Kong Convention & Exhibition Centre,
Wan Chai, Hong Kong
Tel: 1830 670; 1830 668 (cust serv) *Fax:* 2824
0026; 2824 0249
E-mail: exhibitions@hktdc.org
Web Site: hkbookfair.hktdc.com; hkbookfair.hktdc.
com/en/index.html (English)
Location: Hong Kong Convention & Exhibition
Center, One Expo Dr, Wan Chai, Hong Kong
July 2019

IAML Annual Conference
Sponsored by International Association of Music
Libraries, Archives & Documentation Centres
Inc (IAML)
c/o Gothenburg University Library, Music &
Drama Library, Box 210, 412 56 Gothenburg,
Sweden
Tel: (031) 786 40 57 *Fax:* (031) 786 40 59
E-mail: contact@iaml.info
Web Site: www.iaml.info
Key Personnel
Secy Gen: Pia Shekhter *E-mail:* secretary@iaml.
info
Location: Krakow, Poland
July 14-19, 2019

Payson Book Festival
Sponsored by Arizona Professional Writers
(APW)
PO Box 1495, Payson, AZ 85547, United States
E-mail: info@paysonbookfestival.org
Web Site: www.paysonbookfestival.org; www.
facebook.com/PaysonBookFestival
Key Personnel
Dir: Connie Cockrell
Jointly presented by Majestic Rim Retirement
Living, the Payson Book Festival is held to

promote literacy & showcase Arizona authors.
Our mission is to enhance the love of reading by providing a friendly environment that
encourages personal interaction between Arizona authors & readers of all ages. Proceeds
will benefit the scholarship funds of both the
Payson High School & the Gila Community
College. Over 80 Arizona authors participate
by signing books & visiting with readers of all
ages. Some will speak about their books & the
craft of writing. There will be a full schedule
of speakers & several workshops throughout
the day.
Location: Mazatzal Hotel & Casino, Hwy 87,
Mile Marker 251, Payson, AZ, USA
July 20, 2019

PrintEx 2019
Sponsored by Visual Connections Australia Ltd
Shop 4, 123 Midson Rd, Epping, NSW 2121,
Australia
Mailing Address: PO Box 3723, Marsfield, NSW
2122, Australia
Tel: (02) 9868 1577
E-mail: exhibitions@visualconnections.org.au
Web Site: www.visualconnections.org.au
PrintEx brings the latest printing & graphic communications technologies to the industry. Presented by Visual Connections Australia Ltd &
the Printing Industries Association of Australia
(PIAA), this event is held every 4 years in Sydney, NSW, Australia.
Location: Sydney Showground, Sydney Olympic
Park, Sydney, NSW, Australia
July 10-12, 2019

**Romance Writers of America Annual
Conference**
Sponsored by Romance Writers of America®
14615 Benfer Rd, Houston, TX 77069, United
States
Tel: 832-717-5200 *Fax:* 832-717-5201
E-mail: info@rwa.org
Web Site: www.rwa.org
Key Personnel
Exec Dir: Allison Kelley *Tel:* 832-717-5200 ext
124 *E-mail:* allison.kelley@rwa.org
Location: New York Marriott Marquis, 1535
Broadway, New York, NY, USA
July 24-27, 2019

UNITE 2019, CBA's International Convention
Formerly International Christian Retail Show
(ICRS)
Sponsored by CBA: The Association for Christian
Retail
1365 Garden of the Gods Rd, Suite 105, Colorado Springs, CO 80907, United States
Tel: 719-265-9895 *Toll Free Tel:* 800-252-1950
Fax: 719-272-3510
E-mail: info@cbaonline.org
Web Site: cbaunite.com; cbaonline.org
Key Personnel
Pres: Curtis Riskey *E-mail:* criskey@cbaonline.
org
For more than 65 years, CBA's annual international convention has been the singularly most
important event for the Christian products industry, providing the forum for a dynamic time
of inspiration, training, education, fellowship,
business transactions, & future planning. As the
official trade association for Christian suppliers,
retail stores, authors, artists, & professionals,
CBA sponsors the convention for the purpose
of uniting the industry in its mission of spreading the Gospel message around the world &
impacting lives for God's kingdom through
Christian products & resources.
Location: Gaylord Opryland Resort & Convention
Center, 2800 Opryland Dr, Nashville, TN, USA
July 25-28, 2019

World Conference of Science Journalists
Sponsored by National Association of Science Writers (NASW)
PO Box 7905, Berkeley, CA 94707, United States
Tel: 510-859-7229
E-mail: info@wcsj2019.eu
Web Site: www.wcsj2019.eu; www.nasw.org
Key Personnel
Exec Dir: Tinsley Davis *E-mail:* director@nasw.org
Co-hosted by Council for the Advancement of Science Writing (CASW).
Location: Lausanne, Switzerand
July 1-5, 2019

AUGUST

Beijing International Book Fair (BIBF)
Sponsored by China National Publications Import & Export (Group) Corp (CNPIEC)
Member of China Publishing Group Corp (CPG)
16 Gongti E Rd, Beijing 100020, China
Tel: (010) 6506 3080 *Fax:* (010) 6508 9188
Web Site: www.bibf.net
Key Personnel
Dir, Sales & Mktg: Mr Yuan Jiayang
    E-mail: yuanjiyang@bibf.net
Acct Mgr, Americas & the UK: Ms Xu Ruoqing
    E-mail: xuruoqing@bibf.net
Acct Mgr, Europe & Middle East: Mr Ni Hongri
    E-mail: nihongri@bibf.net
Acct Mgr, Asia & Africa: Ms Wen Bo
    E-mail: wenbo@bibf.net
Location: China International Exhibition Center, Beijing, China
Aug 2019

The Dorothy L Sayers Society Annual Convention
Sponsored by The Dorothy L Sayers Society
Witham Library, 18 Newland St, Witham CM8 2AQ, United Kingdom
Tel: (01376) 519625
E-mail: info@sayers.org.uk
Web Site: www.sayers.org.uk
Key Personnel
Convention Admin: Simon Medd
Membership Secy: Lenelle Davis
    E-mail: membership@sayers.org.uk
Members only event.
Location: UK
Aug 2019

Edinburgh International Book Festival
5 Charlotte Sq, Edinburgh EH2 4DR, United Kingdom
Tel: (0131) 718 5666
E-mail: admin@edbookfest.co.uk
Web Site: www.edbookfest.co.uk
Each year we welcome over 800 international authors & over 200,000 visitors to the biggest book festival in the world, turning Edinburgh's Charlotte Square Gardens into a literary village for 18 days every August.
Location: Charlotte Square Gardens, Edinburgh, UK
Aug 10-26, 2019

EXPOLIT (Exposicion de Literatura Cristiana Book Fair)
Sponsored by Spanish Evangelical Publishers Association (SEPA)/Asociacion Evangelica espanola de Editores
8167 NW 84 St, Medley, FL 33166, United States
Tel: 305-503-1191 *Toll Free Tel:* 866-782-3976
Fax: 305-717-6886
E-mail: info@expolit.com

Web Site: www.expolit.com
Key Personnel
Supv: Jessica Hernandez *E-mail:* jessica@expolit.com
Media & Promo Coord: Maria De La Cruz
    E-mail: medios@expolit.com
Exhibit Coord: Angela Peralta
    E-mail: exhibitors@expolit.com
Spanish Christian literature convention. Also sponsored by Editorial Unilit.
Location: DoubleTree by Hilton Hotel Miami Airport & Convention Center, 711 NW 72 Ave, Miami, FL, USA
Aug 8-11, 2019

IFLA World Library & Information Congress
Sponsored by International Federation of Library Associations & Institutions (IFLA) (Federation internationale des associations de bibliothecaires et des bibliotheques)
Prins Willem-Alexanderhof 5, 2595 BE The Hague, Netherlands
Mailing Address: Postbus 95312, 2509 CH The Hague, Netherlands
Tel: (70) 314 08 84 *Fax:* (70) 383 48 27
E-mail: ifla@ifla.org
Web Site: www.ifla.org
Key Personnel
Secy Gen: Gerald Leitner
Mgr, Conferences & Busn Rel: Josche Ouwerkerk
    E-mail: josche.ouwerkerk@ifla.org
Held simultaneously with IFLA General Conference & Assembly.
Location: Athens, Greece
Aug 24-29, 2019

The South African Booksellers Annual General Meeting
Sponsored by South African Booksellers Association (SABA)
29 Golf Course Rd, Sybrand Park, Rondebosch, South Africa
Mailing Address: PO Box 870, Bellville 7535, South Africa
Tel: (021) 697 1164 *Fax:* (021) 697 1410
E-mail: saba@sabooksellers.com
Web Site: www.sabooksellers.com
Location: South Africa
Aug 2019

Swanwick: The Writers' Summer School
Sponsored by Writers' Summer School
2 Pearce Close, Cambridge CB3 9LY, United Kingdom
Tel: (01290) 552248
Web Site: www.swanwickwritersschool.org.uk
A weeklong residential writing school with top name speakers & tutors, plus informative panels, talks & discussion groups. Comfortable rooms with all meals & tuition included in the price. Open to everyone, from absolute beginners to published authors. Beautiful setting, licensed bar & evening entertainment. Believed to be the longest established residential writers' school in the world, Swanwick, held annually in August, is a must attend event in every writer's diary.
Location: The Hayes Conference Centre, Swanwick, Alfreton, Derbyshire, UK
Aug 10-16, 2019

AUTUMN

Louisiana Book Festival
Sponsored by Louisiana Center for the Book
Subsidiary of State Library of Louisiana
701 N Fourth St, Baton Rouge, LA 70802, United States

Tel: 225-219-9503 *Fax:* 225-219-9840
Web Site: louisianabookfestival.org
Key Personnel
Dir: Jim Davis *Tel:* 225-342-9714
    E-mail: jdavis@slol.lib.la.us
Asst Dir: Robert Wilson *E-mail:* rwilson@slol.lib.la.us
A free festival celebrating readers, writers & books representing a variety of genres & related events for all ages, food, music.
Location: State Library of Louisiana, Louisiana State Capitol, Capitol Park Welcome Center & nearby locations, Baton Rouge, LA, USA
Autumn 2019

Texas Book Festival
610 Brazos, Suite 200, Austin, TX 78701, United States
Tel: 512-477-4055 *Fax:* 512-322-0722
E-mail: bookfest@texasbookfestival.org
Web Site: www.texasbookfestival.org
Key Personnel
Exec Dir: Lois Kim *E-mail:* loiskim@texasbookfestival.org
Outreach Coord: Lea Bogner *E-mail:* lea@texasbookfestival.org
Devt Mgr: Claire Burrows *E-mail:* claire@texasbookfestival.com
Literary Dir: Julie Wernersbach *E-mail:* julie@texasbookfestival.org
Literary & Communs Coord: Lydia Melby
    E-mail: lydia@texasbookfestival.org
Admin Asst: Maris Finn *E-mail:* maris@texasbookfestival.org
The festival is a statewide program that promotes reading & literacy highlighted by a 2 day festival, held annually in the fall, featuring authors from Texas & across the USA. Money raised from the festival is distributed as grants to public libraries throughout the state.
Location: State Capitol Bldg, Austin, TX, USA
Fall 2019

Texas Teen Book Festival
Sponsored by Texas Book Festival
610 Brazos, Suite 200, Austin, TX 78701, United States
Tel: 512-477-4055 *Fax:* 512-322-0722
E-mail: ttbfinfo@texasteenbookfestival.org
Web Site: texasteenbookfestival.org
Key Personnel
Dir, TTBF: Shawn Mauser
PR Dir, TTBF: Jen Bigheart *E-mail:* ttbfmedia@texasteenbookfestival.org
Celebration of the teen reading experience. Organized in collaboration with BookPeople & a dedicated group of librarian volunteers.
Location: Austin, TX, USA
Fall 2019

SEPTEMBER

Christian Resources Retailers & Suppliers Retreat
Sponsored by Christian Resources Together
Cedar Tree, 4 Ditchingham Close, Aylesbury, Bucks HP19 7SA, United Kingdom
Tel: (01296) 489860
Web Site: www.christianresourcestogether.co.uk
Location: The Hayes Conference Centre, Swanwick, Alfreton, Derbyshire, UK
Sept 17-18, 2019

Distripress Annual Congress
Sponsored by Distripress
Postfach 8034, Zurich, Switzerland
Tel: (020) 3865 3519
E-mail: welcome@distripress.org
Web Site: www.distripress.org

Key Personnel
Mng Dir: Tracy Jones *E-mail:* tracy.jones@
distripress.org
Community Mgr: Anna Sponquiado *E-mail:* anna.
sponquiado@distripress.org
Annual event sponsored by Distripress, a non-
profit association for the promotion of interna-
tional press distribution.
Location: bcc Berlin Congress Center, Berlin,
Germany
Sept 22-25, 2019

Excellence in Journalism
Sponsored by The Society of Professional Jour-
nalists (SPJ)
Eugene S Pulliam National Journalism Ctr, 3909
N Meridian St, Indianapolis, IN 46208, United
States
Tel: 317-927-8000 *Fax:* 317-920-4789
Web Site: excellenceinjournalism.org; www.spj.
org
Key Personnel
Exec Dir: Alison Bethel McKenzie *Tel:* 317-927-
4780 *E-mail:* abmckenzie@spj.org
Events Coord: Abbi Booth *Tel:* 319-920-4791
E-mail: abooth@spj.org
Location: Grand Hyatt San Antonio, 600 E Mar-
ket St, San Antonio, TX, USA
Sept 5-7, 2019

Goeteborg Book Fair
Sponsored by Bok & Bibliotek i Norden AB
Maessans Gata 10, 412 94 Gothenburg, Sweden
Tel: (031) 708 84 00 *Fax:* (031) 20 91 03
E-mail: info@goteborg-bookfair.com; hej@
bokmassan.se
Web Site: www.bokmassan.se
Key Personnel
Proj Mgr: Anneli Jonasson *Tel:* (031) 708 84 03
E-mail: aj@bokmassan.se
Prog Coord: Henriette Andersson *Tel:* (031) 708
84 16 *E-mail:* ha@bokmassan.se
Location: Gothenburg, Sweden
Sept 26-29, 2019

GWA Annual Conference & Expo
Sponsored by GWA: The Association for Garden
Communicators
355 Lexington Ave, 15th fl, New York, NY
10017, United States
Tel: 212-297-2198 *Fax:* 212-297-2149
E-mail: info@gardenwriters.org
Web Site: www.gardenwriters.org
Location: Sheraton Salt Lake City Hotel, Salt
Lake City, UT, USA
Sept 3-6, 2019

Kerrytown BookFest
PO Box 2937, Ann Arbor, MI 48106, United
States
E-mail: ktbookfest@gmail.com
Web Site: www.kerrytownbookfest.org; www.
facebook.com/kerrytownbookfest/
A celebration of books, those who create them &
those who read them held annually in Septem-
ber.
Location: Farmers Market in the historic Kerry-
town District, downtown Ann Arbor, MI, USA
Sept 2019

PACK EXPO Las Vegas
Sponsored by PMMI: The Association for Pack-
aging and Processing Technologies
11911 Freedom Dr, Suite 600, Reston, VA 20190,
United States
Tel: 571-612-3200 *Toll Free Tel:* 888-ASK-PMMI
(275-7664) *Fax:* 703-243-8556
E-mail: expo@pmmi.org
Web Site: www.packexpolasvegas.com; www.
packexpo.com; www.pmmi.org

Key Personnel
VP, Meetings & Events: Patti Fee *Tel:* 571-612-
3193
Sr Dir, Expositions: Laura Thompson *Tel:* 571-
612-3217
Dir, Tradeshow Mktg: Tina Warren *Tel:* 571-612-
3203
Events Mgr: Anna Hudson *Tel:* 571-612-3198
Exhibitor Servs Sr Mgr: Merideth Newman
Tel: 571-612-3208 *E-mail:* mnewman@pmmi.
org
Exhibitor Servs & Sales Mgr: Beth Murray
Tel: 571-612-3186 *E-mail:* bmurray@pmmi.org
Biennial event held in odd-numbered years.
Location: Las Vegas Convention Center, 3150
Paradise Rd, Las Vegas, NV, USA
Sept 23-25, 2019

**PSA® International Conference of
Photography**
Sponsored by Photographic Society of America®
(PSA®)
8241 S Walker Ave, Suite 104, Oklahoma City,
OK 73139, United States
Tel: 405-843-1437 *Toll Free Tel:* 855-PSA-INFO
(772-4636) *Fax:* 405-843-1438
E-mail: conferencevp@psa-photo.org
Web Site: www.psa-photo.org
Location: Hotel RL by Red Lion, 303 W North
River Dr, Spokane, WA, USA
Sept 22-28, 2019

SIBA Discovery Show
Sponsored by Southern Independent Booksellers
Alliance
3806 Yale Ave, Columbia, SC 29205, United
States
Tel: 803-994-9530 *Fax:* 309-410-0211
E-mail: info@sibaweb.com
Web Site: www.sibaweb.com/trade-show; www.
sibaweb.com
Key Personnel
Exec Dir: Wanda Jewell *E-mail:* wanda@sibaweb.
com
Members only event.
Location: Spartanburg, SC, USA
Sept 23-25, 2019

OCTOBER

ACP/CMA National College Media Convention
Sponsored by Associated Collegiate Press (ACP)
Division of National Scholastic Press Association
2829 University Ave SE, Suite 720, Minneapolis,
MN 55414, United States
Tel: 612-200-9254
E-mail: info@studentpress.org
Web Site: www.studentpress.org; facebook.
com/acpress; twitter.com/acpress
Key Personnel
Exec Dir, NSPA/ACP: Laura Widmer *Tel:* 612-
200-9265
Co-sponsored by College Media Association.
Location: Grand Hyatt Washington, Washington,
DC, USA
Oct 31-Nov 3, 2019

**American Translators Association Annual
Conference**
Sponsored by American Translators Association
(ATA)
225 Reinekers Lane, Suite 590, Alexandria, VA
22314, United States
Tel: 703-683-6100 *Fax:* 703-683-6122
E-mail: ata@atanet.org
Web Site: www.atanet.org

Key Personnel
Exec Dir: Walter W Bacak, Jr *E-mail:* walter@
atanet.org
Meetings Mgr: Teresa C Kelly *Tel:* 703-683-6100
ext 3014 *E-mail:* teresak@atanet.org
Location: Palm Springs, CA, USA
Oct 23-26, 2019

ASIS&T Annual Meeting
Sponsored by Association for Information Science
& Technology (ASIS&T)
8555 16 St, Suite 850, Silver Spring, MD 20910,
United States
Tel: 301-495-0900 *Fax:* 301-495-0810
E-mail: asist@asist.org
Web Site: www.asist.org
Key Personnel
Dir, Meetings & Events: DeVonne Parks
E-mail: dparks@asist.org
Location: Melbourne, Australia
Oct 2019

BMI Annual Conference
Sponsored by Book Manufacturers' Institute Inc
(BMI)
PO Box 731388, Ormond Beach, FL 32173,
United States
Tel: 386-986-4552 *Fax:* 386-986-4553
Web Site: www.bmibook.org
Key Personnel
Exec Dir: Matt Baehr *E-mail:* mbaehr@bmibook.
com
Conference Coord: Jackie Murray
Location: Sanibel Harbour Marriott, Fort Myers,
FL, USA
Oct 27-29, 2019

Frankfurter Buchmesse (Frankfurt Book Fair)
Sponsored by Frankfurter Buchmesse GmbH
Braubachstr 16, 60311 Frankfurt am Main, Ger-
many
Mailing Address: Postfach 100116, 60001 Frank-
furt am Main, Germany
Tel: (069) 21020 *Fax:* (069) 2102 277
E-mail: info@book-fair.com
Web Site: www.book-fair.com
Key Personnel
CEO & Dir: Juergen Boos
Major international book & media fair attracting
7,300 exhibitors from over 100 countries &
278,000 visitors.
Location: Frankfurt Fairgrounds, Ludwig-Erhard-
Anlage One, Frankfurt, Germany
Oct 16-20, 2019

ILA Annual Conference
Sponsored by International Literacy Association
(ILA)
800 Barksdale Rd, Newark, DE 19711-3204,
United States
Mailing Address: PO Box 8139, Newark, DE
19714-8139, United States
Tel: 302-731-1600 *Toll Free Tel:* 800-336-7323
(US & CN) *Fax:* 302-731-1057
E-mail: customerservice@reading.org
Web Site: www.literacyworldwide.org
Key Personnel
Exec Dir: Marcie Craig Post *E-mail:* mpost@
reading.org
Location: New Orleans, LA, USA
Oct 10-13, 2019

NAIBA Fall Conference
Sponsored by New Atlantic Independent Book-
sellers Association (NAIBA)
2667 Hyacinth St, Westbury, NY 11590, United
States
Tel: 516-333-0681 *Fax:* 516-333-0689
E-mail: naibabooksellers@gmail.com
Web Site: www.naiba.com

Key Personnel
Exec Dir: Eileen Dengler *E-mail:* naibaeileen@
gmail.com
Oct 2019

**National Newspaper Association Annual
  Convention & Trade Show**
Sponsored by National Newspaper Association
900 Community Dr, Springfield, IL 62703-5180,
  United States
Tel: 217-241-1400 *Fax:* 217-241-1301
Web Site: nnaweb.org
Key Personnel
Dir, Memb Servs: Lynne Lance
Location: The Pfister Hotel, 424 E Wisconsin
  Ave, Milwaukee, WI, USA
Oct 3-5, 2019

TAPPI PEERS Conference
Sponsored by Technical Association of the Pulp
  & Paper Industry (TAPPI)
15 Technology Pkwy S, Suite 115, Peachtree Cor-
  ners, GA 30092, United States
Tel: 770-446-1400 *Toll Free Tel:* 800-332-8686
  (US); 800-446-9431 (CN) *Fax:* 770-446-6947
E-mail: memberconnection@tappi.org
Web Site: www.tappi.org
Key Personnel
Dir of Mktg: Simona Marcellus *Tel:* 770-209-
  7293 *E-mail:* smarcellus@tappi.org
Location: Hyatt Regency St Louis at The Arch, St
  Louis, MO, USA
Oct 27-30, 2019

Twin Cities Book Festival
Sponsored by Rain Taxi
PO Box 3840, Minneapolis, MN 55403, United
  States
Tel: 612-825-1528 *Fax:* 612-825-1528
E-mail: bookfest@raintaxi.com
Web Site: www.raintaxi.com/twin-cities-book-
  festival
Key Personnel
Dir: Eric Lorberer
Gala celebration of books, featuring large exhi-
  bition, author readings & signings, book art
  activities, panel discussions, used book sale &
  children's events.
Location: Minnesota State Fairgrounds, 1265
  Snelling Ave N, St Paul, MN, USA
Oct 2019

Utah Humanities Book Festival
Sponsored by Utah Humanities Council
Affiliate of Utah Center for the Book
202 W 300 N, Salt Lake City, UT 84103, United
  States
Tel: 801-359-9670
Web Site: utahhumanities.org
Key Personnel
Exec Dir: Jodi Graham *E-mail:* graham@
  utahhumanities.org
Dir: Michael McLane *E-mail:* mclane@
  utahhumanities.org
Commns Dir: Deena Pyle *E-mail:* pyle@
  utahhumanities.org
Free literary event featuring national, regional &
  local authors held Oct 1-31 annually (National
  Book Month).
Location: Statewide, UT, USA
Oct 1-31, 2019

NOVEMBER

AMWA Annual Conference
Sponsored by American Medical Writers Association (AMWA)

30 W Gude Dr, Suite 525, Rockville, MD 20850-
  4357, United States
Tel: 240-238-0940 *Fax:* 301-294-9006
E-mail: amwa@amwa.org
Web Site: www.amwa.org
Key Personnel
Conference Prog Mgr & Workshop Coord:
  Becky Phillips *Tel:* 240-238-0940 ext 103
  E-mail: becky@amwa.org
Location: Sheraton San Diego Hotel & Marina,
  San Diego, CA, USA
Nov 7-9, 2019

Jewish Book Month
Sponsored by Jewish Book Council
520 Eighth Ave, 4th fl, New York, NY 10018,
  United States
Tel: 212-201-2920 *Fax:* 212-532-4952
E-mail: jbc@jewishbooks.org
Web Site: www.jewishbookcouncil.org; www.
  facebook.com/JewishBookCouncil; twitter.
  com/jewishbook
Key Personnel
Exec Dir: Naomi Firestone-Teeter
Dir: Carolyn Starman Hessel
Dedicated to the celebration of Jewish books
  held annually during the month leading up to
  Hanukkah.
Location: Nationwide throughout the USA
Nov 22-Dec 22, 2019

2020

JANUARY

**American Library Association Midwinter
  Meeting**
Sponsored by The American Library Association
  (ALA)
50 E Huron St, Chicago, IL 60611-2795, United
  States
Tel: 312-944-6780 *Toll Free Tel:* 800-545-2433
  (ext 3223, conference servs) *Fax:* 312-440-
  9374
E-mail: ala@ala.org
Web Site: www.ala.org
Key Personnel
Registration & Housing Mgr: Alicia Bab-
  cock *Tel:* 800-545-2433 ext 3229
  E-mail: ababcock@ala.org
Conference Dir: Paul Graller *Tel:* 800-545-2433
  ext 3219 *E-mail:* pgraller@ala.org
Meeting Coord: Amy McGuigan *Tel:* 800-545-
  2433 ext 3226 *E-mail:* amcguigan@ala.org
Meetings, AV & Catering Coord: Yvonne
  McLean *Tel:* 800-545-2433 ext 3222
  E-mail: ymclean@ala.org
Conference Coord: Lina Zabaneh *Tel:* 800-545-
  2433 ext 3227 *E-mail:* lzabaneh@ala.org
Meeting Coord: Alicia (Alee) Navarro *Tel:* 800-
  545-2433 ext 3216 *E-mail:* anavarro@ala.org
Location: Philadelphia, PA, USA
Jan 24-28, 2020

IS&T Electronic Imaging Conference
Sponsored by Society for Imaging Science &
  Technology (IS&T)
7003 Kilworth Lane, Springfield, VA 22151,
  United States
Tel: 703-642-9090 *Fax:* 703-642-9094
E-mail: info@imaging.org
Web Site: www.imaging.org
Key Personnel
Exec Dir: Suzanne E Grinnan *E-mail:* sgrinnan@
  imaging.org
Conference Prog Mgr: Christine Lenihan
  Tel: 703-642-9090 ext 106 *E-mail:* clenihan@
  imaging.org

Exec Asst: Donna Smith *E-mail:* dsmith@
  imaging.org
Location: Hyatt Regency San Francisco Airport,
  Burlingame, CA, USA
Jan 27-31, 2020

MLA Annual Convention
Sponsored by Modern Language Association of
  America (MLA)
85 Broad St, Suite 500, New York, NY 10004-
  2434, United States
SAN: 202-6422
Tel: 646-576-5266 (convention); 646-576-5000
  Fax: 646-458-0030
E-mail: convention@mla.org
Web Site: www.mla.org/convention
Key Personnel
Assoc Dir of Convention Progs: Karin L Bagnall
  E-mail: kbagnall@mla.org
Location: Seattle, WA, USA
Jan 9-12, 2020

FEBRUARY

CAMEX
Sponsored by National Association of College
  Stores (NACS)
500 E Lorain St, Oberlin, OH 44074, United
  States
Tel: 440-775-7777 *Toll Free Tel:* 800-622-7498
  Fax: 440-775-4769
E-mail: camex@nacs.org
Web Site: www.camex.org; www.nacs.org
Key Personnel
CEO: Bob Walton *Tel:* 800-622-7498 ext 2201
  E-mail: rwalton@nacs.org
Dir, Meetings: Jodie Wilmot *Tel:* 800-622-7498
  ext 2272 *E-mail:* jwilmot@nacs.org
Dir, Expositions: Mary Adler-Kozak *Tel:* 800-
  622-7498 ext 2265 *E-mail:* madler-kozak@
  nacs.org
Conference & trade show dedicated exclusively
  to the more than $10 billion collegiate retailing
  industry.
Location: New Orleans, LA, USA
Feb 8-12, 2020

MARCH

AWP Annual Conference & Bookfair
Sponsored by Association of Writers & Writing
  Programs (AWP)
University of Maryland, 5245 Greenbelt Rd, Box
  246, College Park, MD 20740, United States
Tel: 301-226-9710 *Fax:* 301-226-9797
E-mail: awp@awpwriter.org
Web Site: www.awpwriter.org/awp_conference/;
  www.awpwriter.org
Key Personnel
Dir, Conferences: Christian Teresi
Assoc Dir, Conferences: Cynthia Sherman
Location: Henry B Gonzalez Convention Center,
  San Antonio, TX, USA
March 4-7, 2020

Leipzig Book Fair (Leipziger Buchmesse)
Sponsored by Leipziger Messe GmbH
Messe-Allee 1, 04356 Leipzig, Germany
Mailing Address: Postfach 10 07 20, 04007
  Leipzig, Germany
Tel: (0341) 678-8240 *Fax:* (0341) 678-8242
E-mail: info@leipziger-buchmesse.de
Web Site: www.leipziger-buchmesse.de
Key Personnel
Dir: Oliver Zille

Held annually in conjunction with The Leipzig Antiquarian Book Fair.
Location: Leipzig Exhibition Centre, Messe-Allee 1, Leipzig, Germany
March 12-15, 2020

The Quest for Excellence® Conference
Sponsored by National Institute of Standards and Technology (NIST)
100 Bureau Dr, Stop 1070, Gaithersburg, MD 20899-1070, United States
Tel: 301-975-2036 *Fax:* 301-948-3716
E-mail: baldrige@nist.gov
Web Site: www.nist.gov/baldrige/qe/index.cfm
Key Personnel
Conference Chair: Barbara Fischer
   E-mail: barbara.fischer@nist.gov
Official conference of the Malcolm Baldrige National Quality Award, held in partnership with American Society for Quality (ASQ) & Association for Talent Development (ATD).
Location: Gaylord National Harbor, 165 Waterfront St, National Harbor, MD, USA
March 24-27, 2020

Texas Library Association Annual Conference
Sponsored by Texas Library Association (TLA)
3355 Bee Cave Rd, Suite 401, Austin, TX 78746-6763, United States
Tel: 512-328-1518 *Toll Free Tel:* 800-580-2852
   Fax: 512-328-8852
E-mail: tla@txla.org
Web Site: www.txla.org
Key Personnel
Conference Mgr: Elise Walker *Tel:* 512-328-1518 x145 *E-mail:* elisew@txla.org
Location: Houston, TX, USA
March 24-27, 2020

Virginia Festival of the Book
Sponsored by Virginia Foundation for the Humanities
145 Ednam Dr, Charlottesville, VA 22903, United States
Tel: 434-924-3296 *Fax:* 434-296-4714
E-mail: vabook@virginia.edu
Web Site: www.vabook.org
Key Personnel
Prog Dir: Jane Kulow *Tel:* 434-924-7548
Annual public festival for children & adults featuring authors, illustrators, publishers, publicists, agents & other book professionals in panel discussions & readings. Most events are free. Hundreds of authors invited annually.
Location: Charlottesville, VA, USA
March 18-22, 2020

APRIL

Alberta Library Conference
Sponsored by Library Association of Alberta (LAA)
80 Baker Crescent NW, Calgary, AB T2L 1R4, Canada
Tel: 403-284-5818 *Toll Free Tel:* 877-522-5550
   Fax: 403-284-5818
E-mail: info@laa.ca
Web Site: www.albertalibraryconference.com; www.laa.ca
Key Personnel
Conference Coord: Christine Sheppard
Co-hosted by Alberta Library Trustees Association (ALTA).
Location: Fairmont Jasper Park Lodge, Jasper, AB, CN
April 30-May 3, 2020

International Children's Book Day
Sponsored by International Board on Books for Young People (IBBY)
Nonnenweg 12, Postfach, 4009 Basel, Switzerland
Tel: (061) 272 29 17 *Fax:* (061) 272 27 57
E-mail: ibby@ibby.org
Web Site: www.ibby.org
Key Personnel
Exec Dir: Liz Page *E-mail:* liz.page@ibby.org
Admin Asst: Luzmaria Stauffenegger
   E-mail: luzmaria.stauffenegger@ibby.org
On Hans Christian Andersen's birthday, April 2nd, International Children's Book Day (ICBD) is celebrated to inspire a love of reading & to call attention to children's books. Each year a different national section has the opportunity to be the international sponsor. It decides upon a theme & invites a prominent author to write a message to the children of the world & a well-known illustrator to design a poster. These materials are used in different ways to promote books & reading around the world.
April 2, 2020

NAAJ Annual Meeting
Sponsored by North American Agricultural Journalists (NAAJ)
6434 Hurta Lane, Bryan, TX 77808, United States
Tel: 979-324-4302 *Fax:* 979-862-1202
Web Site: www.naaj.net
Key Personnel
Exec Secy & Treas: Kathleen Phillips *E-mail:* kaphillips@tamu.edu
Annual meeting, writing awards & scholarship benefit dance.
Location: Washington, DC, USA
April 2020

National Library Week
Sponsored by The American Library Association (ALA)
50 E Huron St, Chicago, IL 60611-2795, United States
Tel: 312-944-6780 *Toll Free Tel:* 800-545-2433
   Fax: 312-440-9374
E-mail: ala@ala.org
Web Site: www.ala.org/nlw
Location: Nationwide throughout the USA
April 19-25, 2020

MAY

IPA Congress
Sponsored by International Publishers Association (IPA)
23, ave de France, 1202 Geneva, Switzerland
Tel: (022) 704 18 20 *Fax:* (022) 704 18 21
E-mail: secretariat@internationalpublishers.org
Web Site: www.internationalpublishers.org
Key Personnel
Secy Gen: Jose Borghino *E-mail:* borghino@internationalpublishers.org
Dir, Communs: James Taylor *E-mail:* taylor@internationalpublishers.org
Held every 2 years.
Location: Lillehammer, Norway
May 2020

SSP Annual Meeting
Sponsored by Society for Scholarly Publishing (SSP)
10200 W 44 Ave, Suite 304, Wheat Ridge, CO 80033-2840, United States
Tel: 303-422-3914 *Fax:* 720-881-6101
E-mail: info@sspnet.org
Web Site: www.sspnet.org

Key Personnel
Exec/Meetings Asst: Jennifer Lanphere
Location: Westin Waterfront, Boston, MA, USA
May 27-May 29, 2020

JUNE

American Library Association Annual Conference
Sponsored by The American Library Association (ALA)
50 E Huron St, Chicago, IL 60611-2795, United States
Tel: 312-944-6780 *Toll Free Tel:* 800-545-2433 (ext 3223, conference servs) *Fax:* 312-440-9374
E-mail: ala@ala.org
Web Site: www.ala.org
Key Personnel
Registration & Housing Mgr: Alicia Babcock *Tel:* 800-545-2433 ext 3229
   E-mail: ababcock@ala.org
Conference Dir: Paul Graller *Tel:* 800-545-2433 ext 3219 *E-mail:* pgraller@ala.org
Meeting Coord: Amy McGuigan *Tel:* 800-545-2433 ext 3226 *E-mail:* amcguigan@ala.org
Meetings, AV & Catering Coord: Yvonne McLean *Tel:* 800-545-2433 ext 3222
   E-mail: ymclean@ala.org
Conference Coord: Lina Zabaneh *Tel:* 800-545-2433 ext 3227 *E-mail:* lzabaneh@ala.org
Meeting Coord: Alicia (Alee) Navarro *Tel:* 800-545-2433 ext 3216 *E-mail:* anavarro@ala.org
Location: Chicago, IL, USA
June 25-30, 2020

AUPresses Annual Meeting
Sponsored by Association of University Presses (AUPresses)
1412 Broadway, Suite 2135, New York, NY 10018, United States
Tel: 212-989-1010 *Fax:* 212-989-0275
E-mail: annualmeeting@aaup.org; info@aaupnet.org
Web Site: www.aupresses.org
Key Personnel
Exec Dir: Peter Berkery *Tel:* 917-288-5594
   E-mail: pberkery@aaupnet.org
Dir, Mktg & Communs: Brenna McLaughlin *Tel:* 917-244-2051 *E-mail:* bmclaughlin@aaupnet.org
Busn Mgr: Kim Miller *Tel:* 917-244-1264
   E-mail: kmiller@aaupnet.org
Location: Westin Seattle, 1900 Fifth Ave, Seattle, WA, USA
June 13-15, 2020

JULY

Romance Writers of America Annual Conference
Sponsored by Romance Writers of America®
14615 Benfer Rd, Houston, TX 77069, United States
Tel: 832-717-5200 *Fax:* 832-717-5201
E-mail: info@rwa.org
Web Site: www.rwa.org
Key Personnel
Exec Dir: Allison Kelley *Tel:* 832-717-5200 ext 124 *E-mail:* allison.kelley@rwa.org
Location: San Francisco Marriott Marquis, 780 Mission St, San Francisco, CA, USA
July 29-Aug 1, 2020

AUTUMN

Beijing International Book Fair (BIBF)
Sponsored by China National Publications Import
& Export (Group) Corp (CNPIEC)
Member of China Publishing Group Corp (CPG)
16 Gongti E Rd, Beijing 100020, China
Tel: (010) 6506 3080 *Fax:* (010) 6508 9188
Web Site: www.bibf.net
Key Personnel
Dir, Sales & Mktg: Mr Yuan Jiayang
　　E-mail: yuanjiyang@bibf.net
Acct Mgr, Americas & the UK: Ms Xu Ruoqing
　　E-mail: xuruoqing@bibf.net
Acct Mgr, Europe & Middle East: Mr Ni Hongri
　　E-mail: nihongri@bibf.net
Acct Mgr, Asia & Africa: Ms Wen Bo
　　E-mail: wenbo@bibf.net
Location: China International Exhibition Center,
　　Beijing, China
Aug 2020

SEPTEMBER

Excellence in Journalism
Sponsored by The Society of Professional Jour-
nalists (SPJ)
Eugene S Pulliam National Journalism Ctr, 3909
N Meridian St, Indianapolis, IN 46208, United
States
Tel: 317-927-8000 *Fax:* 317-920-4789
Web Site: excellenceinjournalism.org; www.spj.
org
Key Personnel
Exec Dir: Alison Bethel McKenzie *Tel:* 317-927-
4780 *E-mail:* abmckenzie@spj.org
Events Coord: Abbi Booth *Tel:* 319-920-4791
　　E-mail: abooth@spj.org
Location: Washington Hilton, 1919 Connecticut
Ave NW, Washington, DC, USA
Sept 10-12, 2020

Goeteborg Book Fair
Sponsored by Bok & Bibliotek i Norden AB
Maessans Gata 10, 412 94 Gothenburg, Sweden
Tel: (031) 708 84 00 *Fax:* (031) 20 91 03
E-mail: info@goteborg-bookfair.com; hej@
bokmassan.se
Web Site: www.bokmassan.se
Key Personnel
Proj Mgr: Anneli Jonasson *Tel:* (031) 708 84 03
　　E-mail: aj@bokmassan.se
Prog Coord: Henriette Andersson *Tel:* (031) 708
84 16 *E-mail:* ha@bokmassan.se
Location: Gothenburg, Sweden
Sept 24-27, 2020

**International Board on Books for Young
　People Biennial Congress**
Sponsored by International Board on Books for
Young People (IBBY)
Nonnenweg 12, Postfach, 4009 Basel, Switzerland
Tel: (061) 272 29 17 *Fax:* (061) 272 27 57
E-mail: ibby@ibby.org
Web Site: www.ibby.org; www.ibbycongress2020.
org
Key Personnel
Exec Dir: Liz Page *E-mail:* liz.page@ibby.org
Admin Asst: Luzmaria Stauffenegger
　　E-mail: luzmaria.stauffenegger@ibby.org
IBBY's biennial congresses, hosted by differ-
ent countries, are the most important meeting
points for IBBY members & other people in-
volved in children's books & reading devel-
opment. They are wonderful opportunities to
make contacts, exchange ideas & open horizons.

Location: Moscow, Russia
Sept 5-7, 2020

TAPPI/AICC SuperCorrExpo® 2020
Sponsored by Technical Association of the Pulp
& Paper Industry (TAPPI)
15 Technology Pkwy S, Suite 115, Peachtree Cor-
ners, GA 30092, United States
Tel: 770-446-1400 *Toll Free Tel:* 800-332-8686
(US); 800-446-9431 (CN) *Fax:* 770-446-6947
E-mail: memberconnection@tappi.org
Web Site: www.tappi.org
Key Personnel
Dir of Mktg: Simona Marcellus *Tel:* 770-209-
7293 *E-mail:* smarcellus@tappi.org
Location: Orange County Convention Center, Or-
lando, FL, USA
Sept 14-17, 2020

OCTOBER

ACP/CMA National College Media Convention
Sponsored by Associated Collegiate Press (ACP)
Division of National Scholastic Press Association
2829 University Ave SE, Suite 720, Minneapolis,
MN 55414, United States
Tel: 612-200-9254
E-mail: info@studentpress.org
Web Site: www.studentpress.org; facebook.
com/acpress; twitter.com/acpress
Key Personnel
Exec Dir, NSPA/ACP: Laura Widmer *Tel:* 612-
200-9265
Co-sponsored by College Media Association.
Location: Atlanta Hyatt Regency, Atlanta, GA,
USA
Oct 21-25-2020

**American Translators Association Annual
　Conference**
Sponsored by American Translators Association
(ATA)
225 Reinekers Lane, Suite 590, Alexandria, VA
22314, United States
Tel: 703-683-6100 *Fax:* 703-683-6122
E-mail: ata@atanet.org
Web Site: www.atanet.org
Key Personnel
Exec Dir: Walter W Bacak, Jr *E-mail:* walter@
atanet.org
Meetings Mgr: Teresa C Kelly *Tel:* 703-683-6100
ext 3014 *E-mail:* teresak@atanet.org
Location: Boston, MA, USA
Oct 21-24, 2020

AMWA Annual Conference
Sponsored by American Medical Writers Associa-
tion (AMWA)
30 W Gude Dr, Suite 525, Rockville, MD 20850-
4357, United States
Tel: 240-238-0940 *Fax:* 301-294-9006
E-mail: amwa@amwa.org
Web Site: www.amwa.org
Key Personnel
Conference Prog Mgr & Workshop Coord:
Becky Phillips *Tel:* 240-238-0940 ext 103
　　E-mail: becky@amwa.org
Location: Baltimore Marriott Waterfront Hotel,
Baltimore, MD, USA
Oct 12-14, 2020

Frankfurter Buchmesse (Frankfurt Book Fair)
Sponsored by Frankfurter Buchmesse GmbH
Braubachstr 16, 60311 Frankfurt am Main, Ger-
many
Mailing Address: Postfach 100116, 60001 Frank-
furt am Main, Germany
Tel: (069) 21020 *Fax:* (069) 2102 277

E-mail: info@book-fair.com
Web Site: www.book-fair.com
Key Personnel
CEO & Dir: Juergen Boos
Major international book & media fair attracting
7,300 exhibitors from over 100 countries &
278,000 visitors.
Location: Frankfurt Fairgrounds, Ludwig-Erhard-
Anlage One, Frankfurt, Germany
Oct 14-18, 2020

Twin Cities Book Festival
Sponsored by Rain Taxi
PO Box 3840, Minneapolis, MN 55403, United
States
Tel: 612-825-1528 *Fax:* 612-825-1528
E-mail: bookfest@raintaxi.com
Web Site: www.raintaxi.com/twin-cities-book-
festival
Key Personnel
Dir: Eric Lorberer
Gala celebration of books, featuring large exhi-
bition, author readings & signings, book art
activities, panel discussions, used book sale &
children's events.
Location: Minnesota State Fairgrounds, 1265
Snelling Ave N, St Paul, MN, USA
Oct 2020

Utah Humanities Book Festival
Sponsored by Utah Humanities Council
Affiliate of Utah Center for the Book
202 W 300 N, Salt Lake City, UT 84103, United
States
Tel: 801-359-9670
Web Site: utahhumanities.org
Key Personnel
Exec Dir: Jodi Graham *E-mail:* graham@
utahhumanities.org
Dir: Michael McLane *E-mail:* mclane@
utahhumanities.org
Communs Dir: Deena Pyle *E-mail:* pyle@
utahhumanities.org
Free literary event featuring national, regional &
local authors held Oct 1-31 annually (National
Book Month).
Location: Statewide, UT, USA
Oct 1-31, 2020

NOVEMBER

Jewish Book Month
Sponsored by Jewish Book Council
520 Eighth Ave, 4th fl, New York, NY 10018,
United States
Tel: 212-201-2920 *Fax:* 212-532-4952
E-mail: jbc@jewishbooks.org
Web Site: www.jewishbookcouncil.org; www.
facebook.com/JewishBookCouncil; twitter.
com/jewishbook
Key Personnel
Exec Dir: Naomi Firestone-Teeter
Dir: Carolyn Starman Hessel
Dedicated to the celebration of Jewish books
held annually during the month leading up to
Hanukkah.
Location: Nationwide throughout the USA
Nov 10-Dec 10, 2020

PACK EXPO International
Sponsored by PMMI: The Association for Pack-
aging and Processing Technologies
11911 Freedom Dr, Suite 600, Reston, VA 20190,
United States
Tel: 571-612-3200 *Toll Free Tel:* 888-ASK-PMMI
(275-7664) *Fax:* 703-243-8556
E-mail: expo@pmmi.org
Web Site: www.packexpointernational.com; www.
packexpo.com; www.pmmi.org

Key Personnel
VP, Meetings & Events: Patti Fee *Tel:* 571-612-3193
Sr Dir, Expositions: Laura Thompson *Tel:* 571-612-3217
Dir, Tradeshow Mktg: Tina Warren *Tel:* 571-612-3203
Events Mgr: Anna Hudson *Tel:* 571-612-3198
Exhibitor Servs Sr Mgr: Merideth Newman
Tel: 571-612-3208 *E-mail:* mnewman@pmmi.org
Exhibitor Servs & Sales Mgr: Beth Murray
Tel: 571-612-3186 *E-mail:* bmurray@pmmi.org
Biennial event held in even-numbered years.
Location: McCormick Place, 2301 S Lake Shore
Dr, Chicago, IL, USA
Nov 8-11, 2020

2021

JANUARY

American Library Association Midwinter Meeting
Sponsored by The American Library Association (ALA)
50 E Huron St, Chicago, IL 60611-2795, United States
Tel: 312-944-6780 *Toll Free Tel:* 800-545-2433 (ext 3223, conference servs) *Fax:* 312-440-9374
E-mail: ala@ala.org
Web Site: www.ala.org
Key Personnel
Registration & Housing Mgr: Alicia Babcock *Tel:* 800-545-2433 ext 3229
E-mail: ababcock@ala.org
Conference Dir: Paul Graller *Tel:* 800-545-2433 ext 3219 *E-mail:* pgraller@ala.org
Meeting Coord: Amy McGuigan *Tel:* 800-545-2433 ext 3226 *E-mail:* amcguigan@ala.org
Meetings, AV & Catering Coord: Yvonne McLean *Tel:* 800-545-2433 ext 3222
E-mail: ymclean@ala.org
Conference Coord: Lina Zabaneh *Tel:* 800-545-2433 ext 3227 *E-mail:* lzabaneh@ala.org
Meeting Coord: Alicia (Alee) Navarro *Tel:* 800-545-2433 ext 3216 *E-mail:* anavarro@ala.org
Location: Indianapolis, IN, USA
Jan 22-26, 2021

MLA Annual Convention
Sponsored by Modern Language Association of America (MLA)
85 Broad St, Suite 500, New York, NY 10004-2434, United States
SAN: 202-6422
Tel: 646-576-5266 (convention); 646-576-5000 *Fax:* 646-458-0030
E-mail: convention@mla.org
Web Site: www.mla.org/convention
Key Personnel
Assoc Dir of Convention Progs: Karin L Bagnall
E-mail: kbagnall@mla.org
Location: Toronto, ON, CN
Jan 7-10, 2021

FEBRUARY

CAMEX
Sponsored by National Association of College Stores (NACS)
500 E Lorain St, Oberlin, OH 44074, United States

Tel: 440-775-7777 *Toll Free Tel:* 800-622-7498
Fax: 440-775-4769
E-mail: camex@nacs.org
Web Site: www.camex.org; www.nacs.org
Key Personnel
CEO: Bob Walton *Tel:* 800-622-7498 ext 2201
E-mail: rwalton@nacs.org
Dir, Meetings: Jodie Wilmot *Tel:* 800-622-7498 ext 2272 *E-mail:* jwilmot@nacs.org
Dir, Expositions: Mary Adler-Kozak *Tel:* 800-622-7498 ext 2265 *E-mail:* madler-kozak@nacs.org
Conference & trade show dedicated exclusively to the more than $10 billion collegiate retailing industry.
Location: Atlanta, GA, USA
Feb 18-22, 2021

MARCH

AWP Annual Conference & Bookfair
Sponsored by Association of Writers & Writing Programs (AWP)
University of Maryland, 5245 Greenbelt Rd, Box 246, College Park, MD 20740, United States
Tel: 301-226-9710 *Fax:* 301-226-9797
E-mail: awp@awpwriter.org
Web Site: www.awpwriter.org/awp_conference/; www.awpwriter.org
Key Personnel
Dir, Conferences: Christian Teresi
Assoc Dir, Conferences: Cynthia Sherman
Location: Kansas City Convention Center, Kansas City, MO, USA
March 3-6, 2021

Leipzig Book Fair (Leipziger Buchmesse)
Sponsored by Leipziger Messe GmbH
Messe-Allee 1, 04356 Leipzig, Germany
Mailing Address: Postfach 10 07 20, 04007 Leipzig, Germany
Tel: (0341) 678-8240 *Fax:* (0341) 678-8242
E-mail: info@leipziger-buchmesse.de
Web Site: www.leipziger-buchmesse.de
Key Personnel
Dir: Oliver Zille
Held annually in conjunction with The Leipzig Antiquarian Book Fair.
Location: Leipzig Exhibition Centre, Messe-Allee 1, Leipzig, Germany
March 18-21, 2021

Virginia Festival of the Book
Sponsored by Virginia Foundation for the Humanities
145 Ednam Dr, Charlottesville, VA 22903, United States
Tel: 434-924-3296 *Fax:* 434-296-4714
E-mail: vabook@virginia.edu
Web Site: www.vabook.org
Key Personnel
Prog Dir: Jane Kulow *Tel:* 434-924-7548
Annual public festival for children & adults featuring authors, illustrators, publishers, publicists, agents & other book professionals in panel discussions & readings. Most events are free. Hundreds of authors invited annually.
Location: Charlottesville, VA, USA
March 17-21, 2021

APRIL

International Children's Book Day
Sponsored by International Board on Books for Young People (IBBY)

Nonnenweg 12, Postfach, 4009 Basel, Switzerland
Tel: (061) 272 29 17 *Fax:* (061) 272 27 57
E-mail: ibby@ibby.org
Web Site: www.ibby.org
Key Personnel
Exec Dir: Liz Page *E-mail:* liz.page@ibby.org
Admin Asst: Luzmaria Stauffenegger
E-mail: luzmaria.stauffenegger@ibby.org
On Hans Christian Andersen's birthday, April 2nd, International Children's Book Day (ICBD) is celebrated to inspire a love of reading & to call attention to children's books. Each year a different national section has the opportunity to be the international sponsor. It decides upon a theme & invites a prominent author to write a message to the children of the world & a well-known illustrator to design a poster. These materials are used in different ways to promote books & reading around the world.
April 2, 2021

NAAJ Annual Meeting
Sponsored by North American Agricultural Journalists (NAAJ)
6434 Hurta Lane, Bryan, TX 77808, United States
Tel: 979-324-4302 *Fax:* 979-862-1202
Web Site: www.naaj.net
Key Personnel
Exec Secy & Treas: Kathleen Phillips *E-mail:* ka-phillips@tamu.edu
Annual meeting, writing awards & scholarship benefit dance.
Location: Washington, DC, USA
April 2021

National Library Week
Sponsored by The American Library Association (ALA)
50 E Huron St, Chicago, IL 60611-2795, United States
Tel: 312-944-6780 *Toll Free Tel:* 800-545-2433
Fax: 312-440-9374
E-mail: ala@ala.org
Web Site: www.ala.org/nlw
Location: Nationwide throughout the USA
April 5-9, 2021

The Quest for Excellence® Conference
Sponsored by National Institute of Standards and Technology (NIST)
100 Bureau Dr, Stop 1070, Gaithersburg, MD 20899-1070, United States
Tel: 301-975-2036 *Fax:* 301-948-3716
E-mail: baldrige@nist.gov
Web Site: www.nist.gov/baldrige/qe/index.cfm
Key Personnel
Conference Chair: Barbara Fischer
E-mail: barbara.fischer@nist.gov
Official conference of the Malcolm Baldrige National Quality Award, held in partnership with American Society for Quality (ASQ) & Association for Talent Development (ATD).
Location: Gaylord National Harbor, 165 Waterfront St, National Harbor, MD, USA
April 11-14, 2021

Texas Library Association Annual Conference
Sponsored by Texas Library Association (TLA)
3355 Bee Cave Rd, Suite 401, Austin, TX 78746-6763, United States
Tel: 512-328-1518 *Toll Free Tel:* 800-580-2852
Fax: 512-328-8852
E-mail: tla@txla.org
Web Site: www.txla.org
Key Personnel
Conference Mgr: Elise Walker *Tel:* 512-328-1518 x145 *E-mail:* elisew@txla.org
Location: San Antonio, TX, USA
April 20-23, 2021

MAY

PacPrint 2021
Sponsored by Visual Connections Australia Ltd
Shop 4, 123 Midson Rd, Epping, NSW 2121,
Australia
Mailing Address: PO Box 3723, Marsfield, NSW
2122, Australia
Tel: (02) 9868 1577 *Fax:* (02) 9869 0554
E-mail: exhibitions@visualconnections.org.au
Web Site: www.pacprint.com.au
Key Personnel
Gen Mgr: Peter Harper *E-mail:* peterh@
visualconnections.org.au
Event Mgr: Jenny Harris *E-mail:* jennyh@
visualconnections.org.au; Sarah Moore
E-mail: sarahm@visualconnections.org.au
Presented by Visual Connections Australia Ltd &
the Printing Industries Association of Australia
(PIAA), this event is held every 4 years.
Location: Melbourne Convention & Exhibitions
Centre (MCEC), South Wharf, Victoria, Aus-
tralia
May 2021

SSP Annual Meeting
Sponsored by Society for Scholarly Publishing
(SSP)
10200 W 44 Ave, Suite 304, Wheat Ridge, CO
80033-2840, United States
Tel: 303-422-3914 *Fax:* 720-881-6101
E-mail: info@sspnet.org
Web Site: www.sspnet.org
Key Personnel
Exec/Meetings Asst: Jennifer Lanphere
Location: Gaylord National Resort, National Har-
bor, MD, USA
May 26-May 28, 2021

JUNE

**American Library Association Annual
    Conference**
Sponsored by The American Library Association
(ALA)
50 E Huron St, Chicago, IL 60611-2795, United
States
Tel: 312-944-6780 *Toll Free Tel:* 800-545-2433
(ext 3223, conference servs) *Fax:* 312-440-
9374
E-mail: ala@ala.org
Web Site: www.ala.org
Key Personnel
Registration & Housing Mgr: Alicia Bab-
cock *Tel:* 800-545-2433 ext 3229
E-mail: ababcock@ala.org
Conference Dir: Paul Graller *Tel:* 800-545-2433
ext 3219 *E-mail:* pgraller@ala.org
Meeting Coord: Amy McGuigan *Tel:* 800-545-
2433 ext 3226 *E-mail:* amcguigan@ala.org
Meetings, AV & Catering Coord: Yvonne
McLean *Tel:* 800-545-2433 ext 3222
E-mail: ymclean@ala.org
Conference Coord: Lina Zabaneh *Tel:* 800-545-
2433 ext 3227 *E-mail:* lzabaneh@ala.org
Meeting Coord: Alicia (Alee) Navarro *Tel:* 800-
545-2433 ext 3216 *E-mail:* anavarro@ala.org
Location: Chicago, IL, USA
June 24-29, 2021

JULY

**Romance Writers of America Annual
    Conference**
Sponsored by Romance Writers of America®

14615 Benfer Rd, Houston, TX 77069, United
States
Tel: 832-717-5200 *Fax:* 832-717-5201
E-mail: info@rwa.org
Web Site: www.rwa.org
Key Personnel
Exec Dir: Allison Kelley *Tel:* 832-717-5200 ext
124 *E-mail:* allison.kelley@rwa.org
Location: Gaylord Opryland Resort & Convention
Center, 2800 Opryland Dr, Nashville, TN, USA
July 14-17, 2021

AUTUMN

PRINT®
Sponsored by Association for Print Technologies
(APTech)
1899 Preston White Dr, Reston, VA 20191,
United States
Tel: 703-264-7200 *Fax:* 703-620-0994
Web Site: www.printtechnologies.org
Key Personnel
VP, Meetings & Events: Kelly Kilga
E-mail: kkilga@aptech.org
Dir, Meetings & Events: Deedee (Diana) Tinkham
E-mail: dtinkham@aptech.org
Dir, Event Mktg: Sherry MacDonald
E-mail: smacdonald@aptech.org
Mgr, Meetings & Registration: Erin Harrison
E-mail: eharrison@aptech.org
Location: McCormick Place, South Hall, 2301 S
Lake Shore Dr, Chicago, IL,
Autumn 2021

SEPTEMBER

Goeteborg Book Fair
Sponsored by Bok & Bibliotek i Norden AB
Maessans Gata 10, 412 94 Gothenburg, Sweden
Tel: (031) 708 84 00 *Fax:* (031) 20 91 03
E-mail: info@goteborg-bookfair.com; hej@
bokmassan.se
Web Site: www.bokmassan.se
Key Personnel
Proj Mgr: Anneli Jonasson *Tel:* (031) 708 84 03
E-mail: aj@bokmassan.se
Prog Coord: Henriette Andersson *Tel:* (031) 708
84 16 *E-mail:* ha@bokmassan.se
Location: Gothenburg, Sweden
Sept 23-26, 2021

OCTOBER

**American Translators Association Annual
    Conference**
Sponsored by American Translators Association
(ATA)
225 Reinekers Lane, Suite 590, Alexandria, VA
22314, United States
Tel: 703-683-6100 *Fax:* 703-683-6122
E-mail: ata@atanet.org
Web Site: www.atanet.org
Key Personnel
Exec Dir: Walter W Bacak, Jr *E-mail:* walter@
atanet.org
Meetings Mgr: Teresa C Kelly *Tel:* 703-683-6100
ext 3014 *E-mail:* teresak@atanet.org
Location: Minneapolis, MN, USA
Oct 27-30, 2021

Frankfurter Buchmesse (Frankfurt Book Fair)
Sponsored by Frankfurter Buchmesse GmbH

Braubachstr 16, 60311 Frankfurt am Main, Ger-
many
Mailing Address: Postfach 100116, 60001 Frank-
furt am Main, Germany
Tel: (069) 21020 *Fax:* (069) 2102 277
E-mail: info@book-fair.com
Web Site: www.book-fair.com
Key Personnel
CEO & Dir: Juergen Boos
Major international book & media fair attracting
7,300 exhibitors from over 100 countries &
278,000 visitors.
Location: Frankfurt Fairgrounds, Ludwig-Erhard-
Anlage One, Frankfurt, Germany
Oct 20-24, 2021

Jewish Book Month
Sponsored by Jewish Book Council
520 Eighth Ave, 4th fl, New York, NY 10018,
United States
Tel: 212-201-2920 *Fax:* 212-532-4952
E-mail: jbc@jewishbooks.org
Web Site: www.jewishbookcouncil.org; www.
facebook.com/JewishBookCouncil; twitter.
com/jewishbook
Key Personnel
Exec Dir: Naomi Firestone-Teeter
Dir: Carolyn Starman Hessel
Dedicated to the celebration of Jewish books
held annually during the month leading up to
Hanukkah.
Location: Nationwide throughout the USA
Oct 28-Nov 28, 2021

Utah Humanities Book Festival
Sponsored by Utah Humanities Council
Affiliate of Utah Center for the Book
202 W 300 N, Salt Lake City, UT 84103, United
States
Tel: 801-359-9670
Web Site: utahhumanities.org
Key Personnel
Exec Dir: Jodi Graham *E-mail:* graham@
utahhumanities.org
Dir: Michael McLane *E-mail:* mclane@
utahhumanities.org
Commns Dir: Deena Pyle *E-mail:* pyle@
utahhumanities.org
Free literary event featuring national, regional &
local authors held Oct 1-31 annually (National
Book Month).
Location: Statewide, UT, USA
Oct 1-31, 2021

2022

JANUARY

**American Library Association Midwinter
    Meeting**
Sponsored by The American Library Association
(ALA)
50 E Huron St, Chicago, IL 60611-2795, United
States
Tel: 312-944-6780 *Toll Free Tel:* 800-545-2433
(ext 3223, conference servs) *Fax:* 312-440-
9374
E-mail: ala@ala.org
Web Site: www.ala.org
Key Personnel
Registration & Housing Mgr: Alicia Bab-
cock *Tel:* 800-545-2433 ext 3229
E-mail: ababcock@ala.org
Conference Dir: Paul Graller *Tel:* 800-545-2433
ext 3219 *E-mail:* pgraller@ala.org
Meeting Coord: Amy McGuigan *Tel:* 800-545-
2433 ext 3226 *E-mail:* amcguigan@ala.org

Meetings, AV & Catering Coord: Yvonne McLean *Tel:* 800-545-2433 ext 3222 *E-mail:* ymclean@ala.org
Conference Coord: Lina Zabaneh *Tel:* 800-545-2433 ext 3227 *E-mail:* lzabaneh@ala.org
Meeting Coord: Alicia (Alee) Navarro *Tel:* 800-545-2433 ext 3216 *E-mail:* anavarro@ala.org
Location: San Antonio, TX, USA
Jan 21-25, 2022

MARCH

AWP Annual Conference & Bookfair
Sponsored by Association of Writers & Writing Programs (AWP)
University of Maryland, 5245 Greenbelt Rd, Box 246, College Park, MD 20740, United States
Tel: 301-226-9710 *Fax:* 301-226-9797
E-mail: awp@awpwriter.org
Web Site: www.awpwriter.org/awp_conference/; www.awpwriter.org
Key Personnel
Dir, Conferences: Christian Teresi
Assoc Dir, Conferences: Cynthia Sherman
Location: Pennsylvania Convention Center, Philadelphia, PA, USA
March 23-26, 2022

Virginia Festival of the Book
Sponsored by Virginia Foundation for the Humanities
145 Ednam Dr, Charlottesville, VA 22903, United States
Tel: 434-924-3296 *Fax:* 434-296-4714
E-mail: vabook@virginia.edu
Web Site: www.vabook.org
Key Personnel
Prog Dir: Jane Kulow *Tel:* 434-924-7548
Annual public festival for children & adults featuring authors, illustrators, publishers, publicists, agents & other book professionals in panel discussions & readings. Most events are free. Hundreds of authors invited annually.
Location: Charlottesville, VA, USA
March 16-20-2022

APRIL

International Children's Book Day
Sponsored by International Board on Books for Young People (IBBY)
Nonnenweg 12, Postfach, 4009 Basel, Switzerland
Tel: (061) 272 29 17 *Fax:* (061) 272 27 57
E-mail: ibby@ibby.org
Web Site: www.ibby.org
Key Personnel
Exec Dir: Liz Page *E-mail:* liz.page@ibby.org
Admin Asst: Luzmaria Stauffenegger *E-mail:* luzmaria.stauffenegger@ibby.org
On Hans Christian Andersen's birthday, April 2nd, International Children's Book Day (ICBD) is celebrated to inspire a love of reading & to call attention to children's books. Each year a different national section has the opportunity to be the international sponsor. It decides upon a theme & invites a prominent author to write a message to the children of the world & a well-known illustrator to design a poster. These materials are used in different ways to promote books & reading around the world.
April 2, 2022

NAAJ Annual Meeting
Sponsored by North American Agricultural Journalists (NAAJ)

6434 Hurta Lane, Bryan, TX 77808, United States
Tel: 979-324-4302 *Fax:* 979-862-1202
Web Site: www.naaj.net
Key Personnel
Exec Secy & Treas: Kathleen Phillips *E-mail:* kaphillips@tamu.edu
Annual meeting, writing awards & scholarship benefit dance.
Location: Washington, DC, USA
April 2022

Texas Library Association Annual Conference
Sponsored by Texas Library Association (TLA)
3355 Bee Cave Rd, Suite 401, Austin, TX 78746-6763, United States
Tel: 512-328-1518 *Toll Free Tel:* 800-580-2852 *Fax:* 512-328-8852
E-mail: tla@txla.org
Web Site: www.txla.org
Key Personnel
Conference Mgr: Elise Walker *Tel:* 512-328-1518 x145 *E-mail:* elisew@txla.org
Location: Fort Worth, TX, USA
April 11-14, 2022

JUNE

American Library Association Annual Conference
Sponsored by The American Library Association (ALA)
50 E Huron St, Chicago, IL 60611-2795, United States
Tel: 312-944-6780 *Toll Free Tel:* 800-545-2433 (ext 3223, conference servs) *Fax:* 312-440-9374
E-mail: ala@ala.org
Web Site: www.ala.org
Key Personnel
Registration & Housing Mgr: Alicia Babcock *Tel:* 800-545-2433 ext 3229 *E-mail:* ababcock@ala.org
Conference Dir: Paul Graller *Tel:* 800-545-2433 ext 3219 *E-mail:* pgraller@ala.org
Meeting Coord: Amy McGuigan *Tel:* 800-545-2433 ext 3226 *E-mail:* amcguigan@ala.org
Meetings, AV & Catering Coord: Yvonne McLean *Tel:* 800-545-2433 ext 3222 *E-mail:* ymclean@ala.org
Conference Coord: Lina Zabaneh *Tel:* 800-545-2433 ext 3227 *E-mail:* lzabaneh@ala.org
Meeting Coord: Alicia (Alee) Navarro *Tel:* 800-545-2433 ext 3216 *E-mail:* anavarro@ala.org
Location: Washington, DC, USA
June 23-28, 2022

SSP Annual Meeting
Sponsored by Society for Scholarly Publishing (SSP)
10200 W 44 Ave, Suite 304, Wheat Ridge, CO 80033-2840, United States
Tel: 303-422-3914 *Fax:* 720-881-6101
E-mail: info@sspnet.org
Web Site: www.sspnet.org
Key Personnel
Exec/Meetings Asst: Jennifer Lanphere
Location: Sheraton Chicago Hotel & Towers, Chicago, IL, USA
June 1-June 3, 2022

SEPTEMBER

Goeteborg Book Fair
Sponsored by Bok & Bibliotek i Norden AB

Maessans Gata 10, 412 94 Gothenburg, Sweden
Tel: (031) 708 84 00 *Fax:* (031) 20 91 03
E-mail: info@goteborg-bookfair.com; hej@bokmassan.se
Web Site: www.bokmassan.se
Key Personnel
Proj Mgr: Anneli Jonasson *Tel:* (031) 708 84 03 *E-mail:* aj@bokmassan.se
Prog Coord: Henriette Andersson *Tel:* (031) 708 84 16 *E-mail:* ha@bokmassan.se
Location: Gothenburg, Sweden
Sept 22-25, 2022

International Board on Books for Young People Biennial Congress
Sponsored by International Board on Books for Young People (IBBY)
Nonnenweg 12, Postfach, 4009 Basel, Switzerland
Tel: (061) 272 29 17 *Fax:* (061) 272 27 57
E-mail: ibby@ibby.org
Web Site: www.ibby.org; www.ibbycongress2020.org
Key Personnel
Exec Dir: Liz Page *E-mail:* liz.page@ibby.org
Admin Asst: Luzmaria Stauffenegger *E-mail:* luzmaria.stauffenegger@ibby.org
IBBY's biennial congresses, hosted by different countries, are the most important meeting points for IBBY members & other people involved in children's books & reading development. They are wonderful opportunities to make contacts, exchange ideas & open horizons.
Location: Putrajaya, Malaysia
Sept 5-8, 2022

OCTOBER

American Translators Association Annual Conference
Sponsored by American Translators Association (ATA)
225 Reinekers Lane, Suite 590, Alexandria, VA 22314, United States
Tel: 703-683-6100 *Fax:* 703-683-6122
E-mail: ata@atanet.org
Web Site: www.atanet.org
Key Personnel
Exec Dir: Walter W Bacak, Jr *E-mail:* walter@atanet.org
Meetings Mgr: Teresa C Kelly *Tel:* 703-683-6100 ext 3014 *E-mail:* teresak@atanet.org
Location: Los Angeles, CA, USA
Oct 12-15, 2022

Utah Humanities Book Festival
Sponsored by Utah Humanities Council
Affiliate of Utah Center for the Book
202 W 300 N, Salt Lake City, UT 84103, United States
Tel: 801-359-9670
Web Site: utahhumanities.org
Key Personnel
Exec Dir: Jodi Graham *E-mail:* graham@utahhumanities.org
Dir: Michael McLane *E-mail:* mclane@utahhumanities.org
Commns Dir: Deena Pyle *E-mail:* pyle@utahhumanities.org
Free literary event featuring national, regional & local authors held Oct 1-31 annually (National Book Month).
Location: Statewide, UT, USA
Oct 1-31, 2022

NOVEMBER

Jewish Book Month
Sponsored by Jewish Book Council
520 Eighth Ave, 4th fl, New York, NY 10018, United States
Tel: 212-201-2920 *Fax:* 212-532-4952
E-mail: jbc@jewishbooks.org
Web Site: www.jewishbookcouncil.org; www.facebook.com/JewishBookCouncil; twitter.com/jewishbook
Key Personnel
Exec Dir: Naomi Firestone-Teeter
Dir: Carolyn Starman Hessel
Dedicated to the celebration of Jewish books held annually during the month leading up to Hanukkah.
Location: Nationwide throughout the USA
Nov 18-Dec 18, 2022

2023

JANUARY

American Library Association Midwinter Meeting
Sponsored by The American Library Association (ALA)
50 E Huron St, Chicago, IL 60611-2795, United States
Tel: 312-944-6780 *Toll Free Tel:* 800-545-2433 (ext 3223, conference servs) *Fax:* 312-440-9374
E-mail: ala@ala.org
Web Site: www.ala.org
Key Personnel
Registration & Housing Mgr: Alicia Babcock *Tel:* 800-545-2433 ext 3229
  E-mail: ababcock@ala.org
Conference Dir: Paul Graller *Tel:* 800-545-2433 ext 3219 *E-mail:* pgraller@ala.org
Meeting Coord: Amy McGuigan *Tel:* 800-545-2433 ext 3226 *E-mail:* amcguigan@ala.org
Meetings, AV & Catering Coord: Yvonne McLean *Tel:* 800-545-2433 ext 3222
  E-mail: ymclean@ala.org
Conference Coord: Lina Zabaneh *Tel:* 800-545-2433 ext 3227 *E-mail:* lzabaneh@ala.org
Meeting Coord: Alicia (Alee) Navarro *Tel:* 800-545-2433 ext 3216 *E-mail:* anavarro@ala.org
Location: New Orleans, LA, USA
Jan 27-31, 2023

APRIL

International Children's Book Day
Sponsored by International Board on Books for Young People (IBBY)

Nonnenweg 12, Postfach, 4009 Basel, Switzerland
Tel: (061) 272 29 17 *Fax:* (061) 272 27 57
E-mail: ibby@ibby.org
Web Site: www.ibby.org
Key Personnel
Exec Dir: Liz Page *E-mail:* liz.page@ibby.org
Admin Asst: Luzmaria Stauffenegger
  E-mail: luzmaria.stauffenegger@ibby.org
On Hans Christian Andersen's birthday, April 2nd, International Children's Book Day (ICBD) is celebrated to inspire a love of reading & to call attention to children's books. Each year a different national section has the opportunity to be the international sponsor. It decides upon a theme & invites a prominent author to write a message to the children of the world & a well-known illustrator to design a poster. These materials are used in different ways to promote books & reading around the world.
April 2, 2023

NAAJ Annual Meeting
Sponsored by North American Agricultural Journalists (NAAJ)
6434 Hurta Lane, Bryan, TX 77808, United States
Tel: 979-324-4302 *Fax:* 979-862-1202
Web Site: www.naaj.net
Key Personnel
Exec Secy & Treas: Kathleen Phillips *E-mail:* kaphillips@tamu.edu
Annual meeting, writing awards & scholarship benefit dance.
Location: Washington, DC, USA
April 2023

Texas Library Association Annual Conference
Sponsored by Texas Library Association (TLA)
3355 Bee Cave Rd, Suite 401, Austin, TX 78746-6763, United States
Tel: 512-328-1518 *Toll Free Tel:* 800-580-2852
  Fax: 512-328-8852
E-mail: tla@txla.org
Web Site: www.txla.org
Key Personnel
Conference Mgr: Elise Walker *Tel:* 512-328-1518 x145 *E-mail:* elisew@txla.org
Location: Austin, TX, USA
April 19-22, 2023

JUNE

American Library Association Annual Conference
Sponsored by The American Library Association (ALA)
50 E Huron St, Chicago, IL 60611-2795, United States
Tel: 312-944-6780 *Toll Free Tel:* 800-545-2433 (ext 3223, conference servs) *Fax:* 312-440-9374
E-mail: ala@ala.org
Web Site: www.ala.org

Key Personnel
Registration & Housing Mgr: Alicia Babcock *Tel:* 800-545-2433 ext 3229
  E-mail: ababcock@ala.org
Conference Dir: Paul Graller *Tel:* 800-545-2433 ext 3219 *E-mail:* pgraller@ala.org
Meeting Coord: Amy McGuigan *Tel:* 800-545-2433 ext 3226 *E-mail:* amcguigan@ala.org
Meetings, AV & Catering Coord: Yvonne McLean *Tel:* 800-545-2433 ext 3222
  E-mail: ymclean@ala.org
Conference Coord: Lina Zabaneh *Tel:* 800-545-2433 ext 3227 *E-mail:* lzabaneh@ala.org
Meeting Coord: Alicia (Alee) Navarro *Tel:* 800-545-2433 ext 3216 *E-mail:* anavarro@ala.org
Location: Chicago, IL, USA
June 22-27, 2023

SEPTEMBER

Goeteborg Book Fair
Sponsored by Bok & Bibliotek i Norden AB
Maessans Gata 10, 412 94 Gothenburg, Sweden
Tel: (031) 708 84 00 *Fax:* (031) 20 91 03
E-mail: info@goteborg-bookfair.com; hej@bokmassan.se
Web Site: www.bokmassan.se
Key Personnel
Proj Mgr: Anneli Jonasson *Tel:* (031) 708 84 03
  E-mail: aj@bokmassan.se
Prog Coord: Henriette Andersson *Tel:* (031) 708 84 16 *E-mail:* ha@bokmassan.se
Location: Gothenburg, Sweden
Sept 28-Oct 1, 2023

OCTOBER

Utah Humanities Book Festival
Sponsored by Utah Humanities Council
Affiliate of Utah Center for the Book
202 W 300 N, Salt Lake City, UT 84103, United States
Tel: 801-359-9670
Web Site: utahhumanities.org
Key Personnel
Exec Dir: Jodi Graham *E-mail:* graham@utahhumanities.org
Dir: Michael McLane *E-mail:* mclane@utahhumanities.org
Communs Dir: Deena Pyle *E-mail:* pyle@utahhumanities.org
Free literary event featuring national, regional & local authors held Oct 1-31 annually (National Book Month).
Location: Statewide, UT, USA
Oct 1-31, 2023

Library Resources

Major Libraries

The majority of the libraries and archives listed are those associated with government or educational institutions. Many are also involved in publishing activities.

Afghanistan

Kabul University Central Library
Jamal Mina, Kabul
Tel: (020) 250 0236
Web Site: ku.edu.af
Founded: 1933

Ministry of Education Library
Mohammad Jan Khan Watt, Kabul
Web Site: www.moe.gov.af

Albania

Biblioteka Kombetare e Shqiperise (National
  Library of Albania)
Sheshi Skenderbe, Tirana
Tel: (04) 2223843 *Fax:* (04) 2223843
Web Site: www.bksh.al
Key Personnel
Dir: Persida Asllani *E-mail:* persida.asllani@bksh.
  al
Deputy Dir: Etleva Domi *Tel:* (04) 2257670
  Fax: (04) 2257670 *E-mail:* etlevadomi@gmail.
  com
Founded: 1922
Publication(s): *Bibliografia Kombetare e Librit qe
  botohet ne Republiken e Shqiperise* (Albanian
  National Bibliography of Books); *Bibliografia
  Kombetare e Republikes se Shiqiperise, artikujt
  e periodikut shqiptar* (Albanian National Bibli-
  ography of Periodicals)

Algeria

Agence ISBN, see Bibliotheque Nationale
  d'Algerie

Archives Nationales d'Algerie
20 Hassan Bennamane St, Algiers
Mailing Address: BP 61, Algiers Gare
Tel: (021) 54 16 20
Web Site: www.archives-dgan.gov.dz
Key Personnel
General Manager: Chikhi Abdelmadjid

**La Bibliotheque de l'Ecole National
  Polytechnique**
Rue des Freres Oudak, Hassen Badi, 16200 Al-
  giers

Mailing Address: BP 182 El-Harrach, 16200 Al-
  giers
Tel: (023) 82 85 26
E-mail: biblio@g.enp.edu.dz
Web Site: biblio.enp.edu.dz
Key Personnel
Dir: Hafida Doura *E-mail:* hafida.doura@g.enp.
  edu.dz

La Bibliotheque de l'IPA, see Institut Pasteur
  d'Algerie, Bibliotheque

Bibliotheque de l'Universite d'Alger
02 rue Didouche Mourad, 16000 Algiers
Tel: (021) 63 71 01
E-mail: bu@univ-alger.dz
Web Site: bu.univ-alger.dz
Key Personnel
Dir: Saad Taihi *E-mail:* rachid_t@hotmail.com
Founded: 1879

Bibliotheque Nationale d'Algerie (National
  Library of Algeria)
BP 127 El Hamma, 16000 Algiers
Tel: (021) 67 57 81 *Fax:* (021) 68 23 00
E-mail: contact@biblionat.dz
Web Site: www.biblionat.dz
Founded: 1835
Total Titles: 350,000 Print
Publication(s): *Bibliographie de l'Algerie* (2
  times/yr, in Arabic & French)

Bibliotheque Universitaire Centrale (BUC)
Route d'Ain El-Bey, 25017 Constantine
Mailing Address: BP 325, 25017 Constantine
Tel: (031) 818841; (031) 818842
E-mail: contact.biblio@umc.edu.dz
Web Site: bu.umc.edu.dz
Founded: 1969
Publication(s): *Des Catalogues Thematiques*

BUC, see Bibliotheque Universitaire Centrale
  (BUC)

**Ecole Nationale Superieure Agronomique
  Bibliotheque**
Ave Hassan Badi, El Harrach, 16200 Algiers
Tel: (023) 82 85 07; (023) 82 85 12 *Fax:* (023)
  82 85 03; (023) 82 85 04
E-mail: bibliotheque@ensa.dz
Web Site: www.ensa.dz/bibliotheque
Publication(s): *Annals de l'INA*; *Theses de l'INA*

ENSA, see Ecole Nationale Superieure
  Agronomique Bibliotheque

Institut Pasteur d'Algerie, Bibliotheque
Route du petit Staoueli, Dely-Brahim, Algiers
Tel: (023) 36 75 04 *Fax:* (023) 36 75 49

Web Site: www.pasteur.dz
Key Personnel
Librarian: Fatma-Zohra Ait-Ouamar
  E-mail: faitouamar@pasteur.dz
Founded: 1909
Publication(s): *Archives de l'Institut Pasteur
  d'Algerie* (annually)

Universite d'Oran, Bibliotheque
BP 1524, El M'Naouer, 31000 Oran
Tel: (041) 58 19 41; (041) 58 19 47
E-mail: mail@univ-oran.dz
Web Site: www.univ-oran.dz
Key Personnel
Dir: Lahouaria Kehel

Angola

**Biblioteca Central da Universidade Agostinho
  Neto**
Rua do Estadio 11 de Novembro, Municipio de
  Belas, Luanda-Sul
Tel: 922 975 710 (cell)
E-mail: comunicacao@uan.ao
Web Site: www.uan.ao/servicos/biblioteca

Biblioteca Nacional de Angola (National Library
  of Angola)
Largo Antonio Jacinto s/n, Luanda
Tel: 222 326331; 222 326398; 222 326799
  Fax: 222 326299
E-mail: bnangola@gmail.com
Web Site: www.nationallibraryofangola.org
Founded: 1969
Publication(s): *Novas* (News)

Argentina

Banco Central de la Republica Argentina
  (Central Bank of the Argentine Republic)
Reconquista 250, C1003ABF Buenos Aires
Tel: (011) 4348 3772 *Fax:* (011) 4348 3771
E-mail: biblio@bcra.gov.ar
Web Site: www.bcra.gov.ar
Founded: 1935
Publication(s): *Ensayos Economicos* (irregu-
  larly, journal); *Informacion Sobre Entidades
  Financieras* (monthly); *Informe Anual del Pres-
  idente al Congreso de la Nac* (annually); *In-
  forme de Estabilidad Financiera* (2 times/yr)

Branch Office(s)
Tornquist Library, Reconquista 266, Hall San Martin, Ground floor, Off 4, C1003ABF Buenos Aires

Biblioteca Argentina Dr Juan Alvarez
Roca Pte Julio Argentino 731, 2000 Rosario
Tel: 4802538; 4802539 *Fax:* 4802561
E-mail: bib-novedades@rosario.gov.ar
Web Site: www.biblioargentina.gob.ar

Biblioteca Central, Universidad de El Salvador
Tte Gral Peron 1818, C1040AAB Buenos Aires
Tel: (011) 4371-0422
Web Site: www.ues.edu.sv/content/biblioteca-central
Key Personnel
Dir: Prof Liliana Laura Rega

Biblioteca del Congreso de la Nacion (National Library of Congress)
Hipolito Yrigoyen 1750, C1089AAH Buenos Aires
Tel: (011) 4381-0976
E-mail: coordinacion@bcn.gob.ar
Web Site: www.bcnbib.gov.ar
Key Personnel
President: Maria Teresa Garcia
Dir Coordinator General: Alejandro Lorenzo Cesar Santa
Founded: 1859

Biblioteca Mayor de la Universidad Nacional de Cordoba (Principal Library of the National University of Cordoba)
Obispo Trejo 242, Primer Piso, X5000JJD Cordoba
Tel: (0351) 433 1072 *Fax:* (0351) 433 1079
E-mail: biblio@bmayor.unc.edu.ar
Web Site: www.bmayor.unc.edu.ar
Key Personnel
Dir: Gabriela Cuozzo *E-mail:* gcuozzo@bmayor.unc.edu.ar
Founded: 1613
Collections from the 16th-18th centuries.
Publication(s): *Informativo* (irregularly)

Biblioteca Nacional de Maestros (BNM)
(National Teachers' Library)
Pizzurno 953, C1020ACA Buenos Aires
Tel: (011) 4129-1272 *Fax:* (011) 4129-1268
E-mail: bnminfo@educacion.gob.ar
Web Site: www.bnm.me.gov.ar
Key Personnel
Dir: Graciela Teresa Perrone

Biblioteca Nacional Mariano Moreno (Mariano Moreno National Library)
Aguero 2502, C1425EID Buenos Aires
Tel: (011) 4808-6000
E-mail: consultas@bn.gov.ar
Web Site: www.bn.gov.ar
Key Personnel
Dir: Alberto Manguel
Deputy Dir: Elsa Barber
Founded: 1810
Publication(s): *Bibliografica Americana* (magazine); *Rivista La Biblioteca* (magazine)

Biblioteca Publica de la Universidad Nacional de La Plata
Plaza Rocha Nº 137, 1900 La Plata
Tel: (0221) 423-6607 *Fax:* (0221) 425-5004
E-mail: secretaria@biblio.unlp.edu.ar; administracion@biblio.unlp.edu.ar
Web Site: www.biblio.unlp.edu.ar
Key Personnel
Dir: Norma Mangiaterra
Founded: 1905

BNM, see Biblioteca Nacional de Maestros (BNM)

Dr Raul Prebisch Library, see Banco Central de la Republica Argentina

SISBI, see Sistema de Bibliotecas y de Informacion (SISBI)

Sistema de Bibliotecas y de Informacion (SISBI)
Av Corrientes 2052, 2º y 3º pisos, C1045AAP Buenos Aires
Tel: (011) 5285-5589 *Fax:* (011) 5285-5588
E-mail: bib@sisbi.uba.ar; sisbi@sisbi.uba.ar
Web Site: www.sisbi.uba.ar
Key Personnel
Dir General: Elsa Elena Elizalde *E-mail:* elsa@sisbi.uba.ar
Founded: 1941
Publication(s): *Contenidos Corrientes del SISBI* (monthly, magazine)

Universidad Nacional del Litoral
Blvd Pellegrini 2750, 3º Piso, 3000 Santa Fe
Tel: (0342) 457 1110
E-mail: informes@unl.edu.ar
Web Site: www.unl.edu.ar
Founded: 1919

Aruba

Biblioteca Nacional Aruba (BNA) (Aruba National Library)
George Madurostr 13, Oranjestad
Tel: 582-1580 *Fax:* 582-5493
E-mail: info@bibliotecanacional.aw
Web Site: www.bibliotecanacional.aw
Key Personnel
Dir: Astrid J T Britten
Founded: 1949
Membership(s): Acuril; International Federation of Library Associations & Institutions (IFLA).
Branch Office(s)
Peter Stuyvesantstr z/n, San Nicolas *Tel:* 584-5277; 584-3939 *Fax:* 584-5004

BNA, see Biblioteca Nacional Aruba (BNA)

Australia

ANU Library, see The Australian National University Library

The Australian National University Library
JB Chifley Bldg, No 15, Canberra, ACT 2601
Tel: (02) 6125 4428
E-mail: library.info@anu.edu.au
Web Site: anulib.anu.edu.au
Key Personnel
Chief, Scholarly Information Services & University Librarian: Roxanne Missingham
Tel: (02) 6125 2003 *E-mail:* director.sis@anu.edu.au

Commonwealth Scientific & Industrial Research Organisation, see CSIRO

CSIRO
GPO Box 1700, Canberra, ACT 2601
Mailing Address: Private Bag 10, Clayton South, Victoria 3169
Tel: (03) 9545 2176 *Toll Free Tel:* 1300 363 400
Fax: (03) 9545 2175
E-mail: csiroenquiries@csiro.au
Web Site: www.csiro.au
Founded: 1916
Library Network Services provides cost-effective, specialized library services to CSIRO's network of 45 libraries throughout Australia & delivery of a complete range of library services to staff of the Information Services Branch.

Monash University Library
40 Exhibition Walk, Monash University, Victoria 3800
Tel: (03) 9905 5054
Web Site: www.monash.edu/library
Key Personnel
University Librarian: Bob Gerrity *E-mail:* robert.gerrity@monash.edu

New South Wales State Archives, see State Archives & Records Authority of New South Wales

State Archives & Records Authority of New South Wales
161 O'Connell St, Kingswood, NSW 2747
Mailing Address: PO Box 516, Kingswood, NSW 2747
Tel: (02) 9673 1788
E-mail: info@records.nsw.gov.au
Web Site: www.records.nsw.gov.au

The State Library of New South Wales
Macquarie St, Sydney, NSW 2000
Tel: (02) 9273 1414 *Fax:* (02) 9273 1255
E-mail: library@sl.nsw.gov.au
Web Site: www.sl.nsw.gov.au
Key Personnel
State Librarian & Chief Executive: Dr John Vallance
Executive Dir, Library & Information Services & Dixson Librarian: Louise Anemaat
Executive Dir, Public Libraries & Engagement: Lisa O'Sullivan
Dir, Digital Experience & Chief Information Officer: Robin Phua
Dir, Education & Scholarship & Mitchell Librarian: Richard Neville
Founded: 1826
Publication(s): *Hot Topics* (quarterly, series); *SL Magazine* (quarterly)

State Library of Queensland
Cultural Precinct, Stanley Pl, South Bank, Brisbane, Qld 4101
Mailing Address: PO Box 3488, South Brisbane, Qld 4101
Tel: (07) 3840 7666; (07) 3840 7810 *Fax:* (07) 3840 7795
E-mail: info@slq.qld.gov.au; osl@slq.qld.gov.au
Web Site: www.slq.qld.gov.au
Key Personnel
Chief Executive Officer & State Librarian: Vicki McDonald
Includes the John Oxley Library of Queensland History.
Publication(s): *Annual Report of the Library Board of Queensland*; *The Development of State Libraries & Their Effect on the Public Library Movement in Australia (1809-1964)*; *Directory of State & Public Library Service in Queensland* (annually); *North Queensland Towns & Districts Bibliography* (1975); *Queensland Public Libraries Statistical Bulletin*

State Library of South Australia
Corner North Terrace & Kintore Ave, Adelaide, SA 5000
Mailing Address: GPO Box 419, Adelaide, SA 5001

Tel: (08) 8207 7250 *Toll Free Tel:* 1800 182 013
(South Australia only)
E-mail: slsainfo@sa.gov.au
Web Site: www.slsa.sa.gov.au
Key Personnel
Dir: Alan Smith *Tel:* (08) 8207 7204
E-mail: alan.smith@sa.gov.au
Associate Dir: Sue Lewis
Founded: 1884

State Library of Tasmania
91 Murray St, 1st floor, Hobart, Tas 7000
Tel: (03) 6165 5597
E-mail: hobart.linc@education.tas.gov.au; linc@
education.tas.gov.au
Web Site: www.linc.tas.gov.au
Founded: 1850
State library & public library service.

State Library of Victoria
328 Swanston St, Melbourne, Victoria 3000
Tel: (03) 8664 7000 *Fax:* (03) 9639 4737
E-mail: inquiries@slv.vic.gov.au
Web Site: www.slv.vic.gov.au
Key Personnel
Chief Executive Officer: Kate Torney
Dir, Corporate Services: Hanh Chau
Dir, Library Services & Experience: Justine Hyde
Head, Collections: Jo Ritale
Head, Digital Engagement & Collection Services:
Sarah Slade
Founded: 1854
Publication(s): *La Trobe Journal* (2 times/yr)

State Library of Western Australia
Perth Cultural Centre, 25 Francis St, Perth, WA
6000
Tel: (08) 9427 3111 *Toll Free Tel:* 1800 198 107
(Western Australia only) *Fax:* (08) 9427 3256
E-mail: info@slwa.wa.gov.au
Web Site: www.slwa.wa.gov.au
Key Personnel
Chief Executive Officer & State Librarian: Mar-
garet Allen *E-mail:* margaret.allen@slwa.wa.
gov.au
Marketing & Communications Manager: Susan
Parker *Tel:* (08) 9427 3153 *E-mail:* susan.
parker@slwa.wa.gov.au
Founded: 1886
Publication(s): *Katatjin: A Guide to the Indige-
nous Records in the Battye Library* (2003)

State Records NSW, see State Archives &
Records Authority of New South Wales

UniSA, see University of South Australia Library

University of Adelaide Library
The University of Adelaide, Adelaide, SA 5005
Tel: (08) 8313 5759
E-mail: library@adelaide.edu.au
Web Site: www.adelaide.edu.au/library
Key Personnel
University Librarian: Teresa Chitty *Tel:* (08) 8313
5700 *E-mail:* teresa.chitty@adelaide.edu.au
Publication(s): *Newsline* (quarterly, periodical)

University of Melbourne Baillieu Library
University of Melbourne, Melway 571 16, Bldg
177, Melbourne, Victoria 3010
Tel: (03) 9035-5511
Web Site: www.library.unimelb.edu.au
Key Personnel
University Librarian: Philip G Kent
E-mail: pgkent@unimelb.edu.au
Founded: 1959
Library of arts, humanities & social sciences.

University of New South Wales Library
University of New South Wales, Sydney, NSW
2052
Tel: (02) 9385 2650 *Fax:* (02) 9385 8002
Web Site: www.library.unsw.edu.au
Key Personnel
University Librarian: Martin Borchert *Tel:* (02)
9385 2662 *E-mail:* m.borchert@unsw.edu.au
Dir, Information Services: Robyn Drummond
Tel: (02) 9385 8055 *E-mail:* r.drummond@
unsw.edu.au
Founded: 1948

The University of Queensland Library
Level 6, Duhig North Bldg, St Lucia, Qld 4072
Tel: (07) 3346 4312
E-mail: universitylibrarian@library.uq.edu.au
Web Site: www.library.uq.edu.au
Key Personnel
Acting University Librarian: Annette McNicol
Tel: (07) 3365 6342
Dir, Information Systems & Resource Ser-
vices: Tom Ruthven *Tel:* (07) 3346 4351
E-mail: t.ruthven@library.uq.edu.au
Dir, Learning & Research Services: Heather Todd
Tel: (07) 3346 4329 *E-mail:* heather.todd@uq.
edu.au

University of South Australia Library
GPO Box 2471, Adelaide, SA 5001
Tel: (08) 8302 6231 *Fax:* (08) 8302 2466
Web Site: www.library.unisa.edu.au
Key Personnel
Chief Information Officer, Library & Information
Technology: Paul Sherlock *Tel:* (08) 8302 3575
E-mail: paul.sherlock@unisa.edu.au
Deputy Dir, Academic Library Services: Irene
Doskatsch *Tel:* (08) 8302 3414 *E-mail:* irene.
doskatsch@unisa.edu.au
Deputy Dir, Resources & Technical Services:
Julie Hockey *Tel:* (08) 8302 6634 *E-mail:* julie.
hockey@unisa.edu.au
Business Manager, Library & Informatin Technol-
ogy: Melanie Montgomery *Tel:* (08) 8302 3186
E-mail: melanie.montgomery@unisa.edu.au
Manager, Academic Library Services, Divi-
sion of Health Sciences: Anthony Stevens
Tel: (08) 8302 2144 *E-mail:* anthony.stevens@
unisa.edu.au
Manager, Academic Library Services, Divi-
sion of Information Technology, Engineer-
ing & the Environment & Division of Educa-
tion, Arts & Social Sciences: Ann Morgan
E-mail: ann.morgan@unisa.edu.au
Manager, Academic Library Services, UniSA
Business School: Sian Woolcock *Tel:* (08) 8302
0107 *E-mail:* sian.woolcock@unisa.edu.au
Manager, Collection Management & Copyright
Services: Richard Levy *Tel:* (08) 8302 6279
E-mail: richard.levy@unisa.edu.au
Manager, Information Management Ser-
vices: Jenny Quilliam *Tel:* (08) 8302 6645
E-mail: jennifer.quilliam@unisa.edu.au
Also publisher of library science texts & confer-
ence proceedings.

University of Sydney Library
University of Sydney, NSW 2006
Tel: (02) 9351 2993
Web Site: library.usyd.edu.au
Key Personnel
University Librarian: Anne Bell *Fax:* (02) 9351
7765 *E-mail:* anne.bell@sydney.edu.au

University of Technology, Sydney Library
PO Box 123, Broadway, NSW 2007
Tel: (02) 9514 3666
Web Site: www.lib.uts.edu.au

Key Personnel
University Librarian: Mal Booth *Tel:* (02) 9514
3332 *E-mail:* mal.booth@uts.edu.au
Publication(s): *Axis Online* (2 times/yr, newsletter)

University of Western Australia Library
35 Stirling Highway, Crawley, Perth, WA 6009
Toll Free Tel: 1800 263 921 (Western Australia
only) *Fax:* (08) 6488 1012
E-mail: askuwa-lib@uwa.edu.au
Web Site: www.library.uwa.edu.au
Key Personnel
University Librarian: Jill Benn *Tel:* (08) 6488
2355 *E-mail:* jill.benn@uwa.edu.au
Associate University Librarian: Scott Nicholls
Tel: (08) 6488 2341 *E-mail:* scott.nicholls@
uwa.edu.au

UNSW Library, see University of New South
Wales Library

UQ Library, see The University of Queensland
Library

Austria

**Bibliothek des Benediktinerklosters Melk in
Niederoesterreich** (Library of the Melk
Benedictine Monastery in Lower Austria)
Abt-Berthold-Diemayr-Str 1, 3390 Melk
Tel: (02752) 555-342 *Fax:* (02752) 555-52
E-mail: bibliothek@stiftmelk.at
Web Site: www.stiftmelk.at
Key Personnel
Librarian: Dr Gottfried Glassner *E-mail:* gottfried.
glassner@kirchen.net

Bibliothek des Osterreichischen Patentamtes
(Library of the Austrian Patent Office)
Dresdner Str 87, 1200 Vienna
Mailing Address: Postfach 95, 1200 Vienna
Tel: (01) 53424 153; (01) 53424 155 *Fax:* (01)
53424 110
E-mail: bibliothek@patentamt.at
Web Site: www.patentamt.at/bibliothek
Founded: 1899
Publication(s): *Oesterreichischer Markenanzeiger;
Oesterreichischer Musteranzeiger; Osterreichis-
ches Gebrauchsmusterblatt; Oesterreichisches
Patentblatt*

**Bibliothek und Archiv Osterreichischen
Akademie der Wissenschaften** (Austrian
Academy of Sciences Library & Archives)
Dr-Ignaz-Seipel-Platz 2, 1010 Vienna
Tel: (01) 51581-1600
E-mail: bibliothek@oeaw.ac.at; archiv@oeaw.ac.at
Web Site: www.oeaw.ac.at/basis
Key Personnel
Dir: Sibylle Wentker *Tel:* (01) 51581-1610
E-mail: sibylle.wentker@oeaw.ac.at
Publication(s): *Meliouchos* (1987)

Melker Stiftsbibliothek, see Bibliothek des
Benediktinerklosters Melk in Niederoesterreich

Oberoesterreichische Landesbibliothek
(Regional Library Upper Austria)
Schillerplatz 2, 4021 Linz
Tel: (0732) 664071-0
E-mail: landesbibliothek@ooe.gv.at
Web Site: www.landesbibliothek.at
Key Personnel
Dir: Renate Ploechl *Tel:* (0732) 664071-320
E-mail: renate.ploechl@ooe.gv.at

Deputy Dir: Julian Sagmeister *Tel:* (0732) 664071-321 *E-mail:* julian.sagmeister@ooe. gv.at
Founded: 1774
Reference library.
Parent Company: Department of Cultural Affairs
Ultimate Parent Company: District Administration Upper Austria

Oesterreichische Nationalbibliothek (Austrian National Library)
Josefsplatz 1, 1015 Vienna
Mailing Address: Postfach 25, 1015 Vienna
Tel: (01) 534 10 *Fax:* (01) 534 10-280
E-mail: onb@onb.ac.at
Web Site: www.onb.ac.at
Key Personnel
Dir General: Dr Johanna Rachinger *Tel:* (01) 534 10-200 *E-mail:* johanna.rachinger@onb.ac.at
Communications & Marketing: Thomas Zauner *E-mail:* thomas.zauner@onb.ac.at
Publication(s): *Newsletter* (quarterly)

Oesterreichisches Staatsarchiv (Austrian State Archives)
Nottendorfer Gasse 2, 1030 Vienna
Tel: (01) 79540 0 *Fax:* (01) 79540 109
Web Site: www.oesta.gv.at
Key Personnel
General Dir: Dr Wolfgang Maderthaner *Tel:* (01) 79540 100 *Fax:* (01) 79540 199 *E-mail:* gd@ oesta.gv.at
Founded: 1945
Membership(s): International Council on Archives.
Publication(s): *Mitteilungen des Oesterreichischen Staatsarchivs* (annually)

Die Steiermaerkische Landesbibliothek
Kalchberggasse 2, 8010 Graz
Mailing Address: Postfach 861, 8011 Graz
Tel: (0316) 877-4600 *Fax:* (0316) 877-4633
E-mail: landesbibliothek@stmk.gv.at
Web Site: www.landesbibliothek.steiermark.at
Key Personnel
Secretary: Christine Krois *E-mail:* christine. krois@stmk.gv.at
Founded: 1811
Public scientific library.
Publication(s): *Veroeffentlichungen der Steiermaerkischen Landesbibliothek* (scientific series concerning Styrian literature history & history of culture)

United Nations Library-Vienna
PO Box 500, 1400 Vienna
Tel: (01) 26060-3210 *Fax:* (01) 26060-7-3210
E-mail: viennalibrary@un.org

Universitaet Innsbruck Univerisitaets- und Landesbibliothek Tirol
Innrain 50, 6020 Innsbruck
Tel: (0512) 507 2401 *Fax:* (0512) 507 2893
E-mail: ub-hb@uibk.ac.at
Web Site: www.uibk.ac.at/ulb
Key Personnel
Dir: Eva Ramminger *Tel:* (0512) 507 2400 *E-mail:* ulb-direktion@uibk.ac.at
Deputy Dir: Dr Klaus Niedermair *E-mail:* klaus. niedermair@uibk.ac.at
Assistant Dir: Dr Karin Assmann *Tel:* (0512) 507 8010 *E-mail:* karin.assmann@uibk.ac.at

Universitaetsbibliothek der Technischen Universitaet Wien (Vienna University of Technology Library)
Resselgasse 4, 1040 Vienna
Tel: (01) 58801 44001 *Fax:* (01) 58801 44099
E-mail: info@ub.tuwien.ac.at
Web Site: www.ub.tuwien.ac.at

Key Personnel
Dir, Library Services: Beate Guba *Tel:* (01) 58801 44079 *E-mail:* beate.guba@tuwien.ac.at
Founded: 1815
Focuses on the natural & technical sciences but also covers related subjects such as environmental technology.

Universitaetsbibliothek Graz (University Library Graz)
Universitaetsplatz 3a, 8010 Graz
Tel: (0316) 380-3100; (0316) 380-3118 *Fax:* (0316) 380-9030
E-mail: info@uni-graz.at; ub.graz@uni-graz.at; ub.auskunft@uni-graz.at
Web Site: ub.uni-graz.at
Key Personnel
Executive Manager: Dr Werner Schlacher *Tel:* (0316) 380-1419 *E-mail:* werner. schlacher@uni-graz.at
Founded: 1573
Publication(s): *eNewsletter* (monthly); *Jahresbericht* (annually, report, 1973)

Universitaetsbibliothek Salzburg
Hofstallgasse 2-4, 5020 Salzburg
Tel: (0662) 8044 77350 *Fax:* (0662) 8044 103
E-mail: info.hb@sbg.ac.at
Web Site: www.uni-salzburg.at
Key Personnel
Librarian: Dr Ursula Schachl-Raber *Tel:* (0662) 8044 77330 *E-mail:* ursula.schachl-raber@sbg. ac.at

Universitaetsbibliothek Wien (Vienna University Library)
Dr-Karl-Lueger-Ring 1, 1010 Vienna
Tel: (01) 4277 1514 0
E-mail: helpdesk.ub@univie.ac.at
Web Site: bibliothek.univie.ac.at
Key Personnel
Dir: Maria Seissl *Tel:* (01) 4277 150 01 *E-mail:* direktion.ub@univie.ac.at
Deputy Dir: Dr Wolfgang Nikolaus Rappert
Founded: 1365

The Vienna International Centre Library (VIC), see United Nations Library-Vienna

Wienbibliothek im Rathaus (Vienna City Library)
Eingang Felderstr (ab 18.00 Uhr Lichtenfelsgasse), Stiege 6 (Lift), 1.Stock, Rathaus, 1082 Vienna
Tel: (01) 4000-84920 *Fax:* (01) 4000-99-84915
E-mail: post@wienbibliothek.at; oeffentlichkeitsarbeit@wienbibliothek.at
Web Site: www.wienbibliothek.at
Key Personnel
Dir: Dr Sylvia Mattl-Wurm *Tel:* (01) 4000-84911 *E-mail:* sylvia.mattl-wurm@wienbibliothek.at
Deputy Dir: Dr Anita Eichinger *Tel:* (01) 4000-84970 *E-mail:* anita.eichinger@wienbibliothek. at
Founded: 1856

Wiener Stadt- und Landesarchiv (Vienna City & National Archives)
Guglgasse 14, 5 Stock, Top 508, 1110 Vienna
Mailing Address: Rathaus, 1082 Vienna
Tel: (01) 4000 84808 *Fax:* (01) 4000 84809
E-mail: post@ma08.wien.gv.at
Web Site: www.wien.gv.at/kultur/archiv
Key Personnel
Dir: Dr Brigitte Rigele *Tel:* (01) 4000 84811 *E-mail:* brigitte.rigele@wien.gv.at
Publication(s): *Historischer Atlas Von Wien* (Historical Atlas of Vienna); *Oesterreichischer Staedteatlas* (Austrian Historic Towns Atlas)

Azerbaijan

Azarbaycan Milli Kitabxanasi im M F Akhundov (Azerbaijan National Library)
Khagani 29, 1000 Baku
Tel: (012) 4934003 *Fax:* (012) 4980822
E-mail: contact@anl.az
Web Site: www.anl.az/tarix_e.php
Key Personnel
Dir: Dr Kerim Tahirov
Founded: 1922

The Bahamas

The College of the Bahamas Library
Oakes Field Campus, Thompson Blvd, Nassau
Mailing Address: PO Box N4912, Nassau
Tel: (242) 302-4552 *Fax:* (242) 302-4531
E-mail: library@cob.edu.bs
Web Site: www.cob.edu.bs/library
Founded: 1975
Branches in Freeport, Grand Bahama & New Providence.
Publication(s): *Bahamas Reference Collection: a Bibliography* (1980, with irregular supplements); *E-Informer* (per semester, newsletter)

Department of Archives, National Archives of the Bahamas
Mackey St, Nassau 6341
Mailing Address: PO Box SS-6341, Nassau
Tel: (242) 393-2175; (242) 393-2855 *Fax:* (242) 393-2855
E-mail: archives@batelnet.bs
Web Site: bahamasnationalarchives.bs
Key Personnel
Dir, Archives: Elaine Toote
Assistant Dir: Patrice Williams
Founded: 1971
Care & preservation of government records.
Publication(s): *Annual Reports 1977-Present*; *The First Ten Years 1969-1979: History of The Bahamian Archives*; *Guide to Records of the Bahamas*; *A Guide to Selected Sources for the History of the Seminole Settlement at Red Bays, Andros* (contains historical source on the Seminole Indians of Andros); *Preservum: Journal of The Department of Archives*; *Supplement to the Guide to the Records of the Bahamas*

Sir Charles Hayward Library
The Mall Dr, PO Box F-40040, Freeport
Tel: (242) 352-7048; (242) 352-3524
Web Site: www.charleshaywardlibrary.com
Key Personnel
Chief Librarian: Shanreikah Faustin
Library Supervisor: Sophia Simmons

Nassau Public Library & Museum
Shirley St, Nassau, New Providence
Mailing Address: PO Box N-3210, Nassau
Tel: (242) 322-4907; (242) 328-5029 *Fax:* (242) 328-5028
Key Personnel
Library Supervisor: Winifred Murphy
Founded: 1873

Bahrain

AGU Library, see Arabian Gulf University Library (AGU Library)

Arabian Gulf University Library (AGU Library)
PO Box 26671, Manama
Tel: 17239754
Web Site: www.agu.edu.bh/library
Key Personnel
Library Dir: Suad Alkhalifa *Tel:* 17239606
 Fax: 17274822 *E-mail:* suad@agu.edu.bh
Founded: 1982

University of Bahrain, Library & Information Services
PO Box 32038, Sakhir
Tel: 17 43 8808 *Fax:* 17 44 9838
E-mail: library@admin.uob.bh
Web Site: libwebserver.uob.edu.bh
Key Personnel
Dir: Hedi Talbi *E-mail:* htalbi@uob.edu.bh
Deputy Dir: Tahani Hassan Al-Khalifa *Tel:* 17 43 7888 *E-mail:* talkhalifa@uob.edu.bh
Founded: 1986
Membership(s): CILIP; SLA.
Publication(s): *Journal of Educational & Psychological Science* (quarterly); *Journal of Human Sciences*

Bangladesh

Bangladesh Institute of Development Studies Library & Documentation Centre (BIDS)
E-17 Agargaon, Sher-e-Bangla Nagar, Dhaka 1207
Mailing Address: GPO Box 3854, Dhaka 1207
Tel: (02) 8181685; (02) 9143441-8 *Fax:* (02) 8141722
E-mail: dg@bids.org.bd; info@bids.org.bd; secretary@bids.org.bd
Web Site: www.bids.org.bd
Key Personnel
Librarian: Shafiqul Islam *Tel:* (02) 9140755
 E-mail: msislam@bids.org.bd; Shahana Parveen *Tel:* (02) 9140755 *E-mail:* sparveen@bids.org.bd
Publication(s): *The Bangladesh Development Studies (BDS)* (quarterly, journal, in English)

BIDS, see Bangladesh Institute of Development Studies Library & Documentation Centre (BIDS)

British Council Library
5 Fuller Rd, Dhaka 1000
Tel: (02) 9666 773377 *Fax:* (02) 861 3375; (02) 861 3255
E-mail: bd.enquiries@britishcouncil.org
Web Site: www.britishcouncil.org.bd/en
Key Personnel
Dir: Barbara Wickham
Head, Marketing & Communications: Arshia Aziz
 E-mail: arshia.aziz@bd.britishcouncil.org

Central Public Library Dhaka
3 Liaquat Ave, Dhaka 1000
Tel: (02) 8500819
Web Site: www.centralpubliclibrarydhaka.org
Founded: 1958

Dhaka University Library
Administrative Bldg, 3rd floor, Ramna, Dhaka 1000
Tel: (02) 9661920 (ext 4262)
E-mail: librarian@du.ac.bd
Web Site: www.library.du.ac.bd
Key Personnel
Librarian: Dr S M Sabed Ahmed
 E-mail: smzahmed@du.ac.bd
Founded: 1921

National Archives & National Library of Bangladesh
Dept of Archives & Libraries, Ministry of Cultural Affairs, 32, Justice S M Murshed Sarani, Agargaon, Sher-e-Bangla Nagar, Dhaka 1207
Tel: (02) 9129992 *Fax:* (02) 9135709
Web Site: www.nanl.gov.bd
Key Personnel
Dir: Mozibor Rahman Al-Mamun
 E-mail: nanldirector@gmail.com
Deputy Dir, Archives: Tahmina Akter
 E-mail: tani.nlb@gmail.com
Deputy Dir, Library: Shahab Uddin Khan
 E-mail: ddnlbd@gmail.com
Librarian: Gulam Mustofa
Founded: 1973
Publication(s): *Bangladesh National Archives Guide Book*; *Bangladesh National Bibliography*; *National Library Guide Book*; *Newsletter* (2 times/yr)

Rajshahi University Library
Rajshahi 6205
Tel: (0721) 750666; (0721) 711064 *Fax:* (0721) 750064
E-mail: ad_rucl@ru.ac.bd
Web Site: library.ru.ac.bd
Founded: 1955

Barbados

National Library Service
Independence Sq, Fairchild St, Bridgetown, St Michael
Tel: (246) 435-0016; (246) 435-3382 *Fax:* (246) 435-5962
E-mail: natlib1@caribsurf.com
Web Site: www.gov.bb
Key Personnel
Dir: Annette Smith *E-mail:* smitha@gov.bb
Publication(s): *National Bibliography of Barbados*; *West Indian Collection*
Branch Office(s)
Oistins Branch Library, Oistins, Christ Church, Supervisor: Jennifer Yarde *Tel:* (246) 428-7666
Valley Branch Library, Valley, St George, Supervisor: Avaline Henry *Tel:* (246) 429-4029
Holetown Branch Library, Holetown, St James, Supervisor: Marva Watson *Tel:* (246) 432-1818
Gall Hill Branch Library, Gall Hill, St John, Supervisor: Carl Adamson *Tel:* (246) 433-1522
Eagle Hall Branch Library, Eagle Hall, St Michael, Supervisor: John Downes *Tel:* (246) 427-3045
Speightstown Branch Library, Speightstown, St Peter, Supervisor: Kathy-Anne Latchman *Tel:* (246) 422-2311
Six Cross Roads Branch Library, Six Cross Roads, St Philip, Supervisor: Nadine Goddard *Tel:* (246) 423-6557

University of the West Indies Library (Barbados)
Cave Hill Campus, PO Box 1334, Bridgetown
Tel: (246) 417-4444; (246) 417-4440 (circulation) *Fax:* (246) 417-4460
E-mail: smlibrary@cavehill.uwi.edu
Web Site: www.cavehill.uwi.edu
Key Personnel
Readers Services Librarian: Carlyle Best
 Tel: (0246) 417-4456 *E-mail:* carlyle.best@cavehill.uwl.edu

Belarus

National Library of Belarus
Nezavisimosti Ave, 116, 220114 Minsk
Tel: (017) 266-37-02; (017) 266 37 37 *Fax:* (017) 266-37-06
E-mail: inbox@nlb.by
Web Site: www.nlb.by
Key Personnel
Dir: Prof Roman Motulsky *Tel:* (017) 266-37-00
 E-mail: director@nlb.by
Deputy Dir, Economy: Stanislav Kasperovich *Tel:* (017) 266-37-34 *E-mail:* kasperovich@nlb.by
Deputy Dir, Information & Library Services: Elena Dolgopolova *Tel:* (017) 266-37-17
 E-mail: dolgopolova@nlb.by
Deputy Dir, Information Resources: Tatiana Kuzminich, PhD *Tel:* (017) 266-37-29
 E-mail: kuzminich@nlb.by
Deputy Dir, Research & Publishing: Aleksandr Susha *Tel:* (017) 266-37-04 *E-mail:* susha@nlb.by
Founded: 1922
Publication(s): *Chernobyl* (3 times/yr, bibliographic index); *Cultural Life of Belarus* (monthly); *Current literature on the history of Belarus & its historical science* (3 times/yr, bibliographic index); *Signal Information on Culture & Arts* (weekly); *Social Sciences* (monthly)

NLB, see National Library of Belarus

Belgium

Archives Generales du Royaume (National Archives of Belgium)
Ruisbroekstr, 2, 1000 Brussels
Tel: (02) 513 76 80 *Fax:* (02) 513 76 81
E-mail: archives.generales@arch.be; algemeen.rijksarchief@arch.be
Web Site: www.arch.be
Key Personnel
Head Archivist: Karel Velle

Bibliotheque ALPHA, see Bibliotheque d'Architecture, Lettres, Philosophie, Histoire et Arts (Universite de Liege)

Bibliotheque d'Architecture, Lettres, Philosophie, Histoire et Arts (Universite de Liege)
Pl Cockerill, 1, Bldg A3, 4000 Liege
Tel: (04) 3665233 *Fax:* (04) 3665702
E-mail: bib.alpha@ulg.ac.be
Web Site: libnet.ulg.ac.be/fr/libraries/alpha
Key Personnel
Dir: Muriel Van Ruymbeke *Tel:* (04) 3662123
 E-mail: mvanruymbeke@ulg.ac.be

Bibliotheque du Musee Royal de Mariemont
Chaussee de Mariemont, 100, 7140 Morlanwelz
Tel: (064) 21 21 93 *Fax:* (064) 26 29 24
E-mail: info@musee-mariemont.be
Web Site: www.musee-mariemont.be
Key Personnel
Librarian: Delphine Gering *E-mail:* delphine.gering@musee-mariemont.be
Founded: 1917
Publication(s): *Bulletin d'Information* (quarterly); *Cahiers de Mariemont* (annually); *Catalogues d'Expositions, Monographies, Dossiers Pedagogiques*

Bibliotheque du Parlement Federal
Rue de la presse 35, 1000 Brussels
Tel: (02) 549 9212
E-mail: bibliotheque@lachambre.be
Web Site: www.lachambre.be
Founded: 1831

Bibliotheque Fonds Quetelet
City Atrium, 2e etage, Rue de Progres, 50, 1210 Brussels
Tel: (02) 277 55 55 *Fax:* (02) 277 55 53
E-mail: quetelet@economie.fgov.be
Web Site: economie.fgov.be/fr
Founded: 1841
Scientific library.
Publication(s): *Accroissements de la Bibliotheque Fonds Quetelet* (available online only through company web site)

Bibliotheque Royale Alber Ier, see Bibliotheque Royale de Belgique

Bibliotheque Royale de Belgique (Royal Library of Belgium)
Blvd de l'Empereur 2, 1000 Brussels
Tel: (02) 519 53 11 *Fax:* (02) 519 55 33
E-mail: info@kbr.be
Web Site: www.kbr.be
Key Personnel
President: Marc Libert
Chief Editor: Dirk Leyder
Treasurer: Nathael Istasse
Secretary: Sara Lammens
Administrative Secretary: Anja Marginet
Founded: 1837
Publication(s): *Bibliographie de Belgique (Belgisch Bibliographie)* (monthly); *Bulletin de la BR (KB Bulletin)* (quarterly)

Bibliotheque Universitaire Moretus Plantin (BUMP) (Moretus Plantin University Library)
Rue Grandgagnage 19, 5000 Namur
Mailing Address: rue de Bruxelles 61, 5000 Namur
Tel: (081) 72 46 46
E-mail: public@unamur.be
Web Site: www.unamur.be/bump
Key Personnel
Dir: Chantal Berhin-Lenselaer *Tel:* (081) 72 41 60 *E-mail:* chantal.berhin@unamur.be
Academic library.

Les Bibliotheques de l'Universite Catholique de Louvain
Grand Pl, 45, boite L3.01.03, 1348 Louvain-la-Neuve
Tel: (010) 47 81 87 *Fax:* (010) 47 82 98
E-mail: contact-biul@uclouvain.be
Web Site: www.uclouvain.be/biul.html
Key Personnel
Chief Librarian: Charles-Henri Nyns *Tel:* (010) 47 82 99 *E-mail:* charles-henri.nyns@uclouvain.be

BUMP, see Bibliotheque Universitaire Moretus Plantin (BUMP)

Erfgoedbibliotheek Hendrik Conscience (Hendrik Conscience Heritage Library)
Hendrik Conscienceplein 4, 2000 Antwerp
Tel: (03) 338 87 10 *Fax:* (03) 338 87 76
E-mail: consciencebibliotheek@stad.antwerpen.be
Web Site: www.consciencebibliotheek.be
Key Personnel
Dir: An Renard *Tel:* (03) 206 87 30 *E-mail:* an.renard@stad.antwerpen.be
Founded: 1481
Reference library of the city of Antwerp concentrating on humanities.

Goethe-Institut
Ave des Arts, Kunstlaan 58, 1000 Brussels
Tel: (02) 2303970 *Fax:* (02) 2307725
E-mail: info@bruessel.goethe.org
Web Site: www.goethe.de/ins/be/bru/deindex.htm
Key Personnel
Dir: Susanne Hohn *Tel:* (02) 2381164 *E-mail:* dir@bruessel.goethe.org
Deputy Dir: Klaus Brodersen *Tel:* (02) 2345783 *E-mail:* klaus.brodersen@goethe.org
Founded: 1959

Institut Royal des Sciences Naturelles de Belgique, Bibliotheque (Royal Belgian Institute of Natural Sciences Library)
RBIN-Library & Documentation Service, Vautierstr 29, 1000 Brussels
Tel: (02) 627 42 36
E-mail: bib@naturalsciences.be
Web Site: www.sciencesnaturelles.be/science/library; www.naturalsciences.be/?science/library
Key Personnel
Head, Documentation Service: Laurent Meese *Tel:* (02) 627 42 16 *Fax:* (02) 627 41 13 *E-mail:* laurent.meese@naturalsciences.be
Founded: 1846
Publication(s): *Bulletin de L'Institut Royal des Sciences Naturelles de Belgique - Biology* (annually); *Bulletin de L Institut Royal des Sciences Naturelles de Belgique - Bulletin Van Het Koninkluk Belgisch Instituut Voor Natuurwetenschappen - Entomology* (annually); *Bulletin de L'Institut Royal des Sciences Naturelles de Belgique - Earth Sciences* (annually); *Documents de Travail de L'IR Sc N B Documents de Travail de L'IR Sc N B-Studiedocumenten Van Het KBIN*

Katholieke Universiteit Leuven
Centrale Bibliotheek, Mgr Ladeuzeplein 21, 3000 Leuven
Tel: (016) 32 40 10
E-mail: centrale.bibliotheek@bib.kuleuven.be
Web Site: bib.kuleuven.be
Key Personnel
Chief Librarian: Mel Collier *Tel:* (016) 32 46 01 *E-mail:* mel.collier@kuleuven.be
Founded: 1425
Publication(s): *Ex officina* (Newsletter of the Friends of Louvain University Library)

Letterenhuis (Literary Centre)
Minderbroedersstr 22, 2000 Antwerp
Tel: (03) 222 93 20 *Fax:* (03) 222 93 21
E-mail: letterenhuis@stad.antwerpen.be
Web Site: www.letterenhuis.be
Key Personnel
Dir: Leen Van Dijck *Tel:* (03) 222 93 29 *E-mail:* helena.vandijck@stad.antwerpen.be
Founded: 1933

Museum Plantin-Moretus/Prentenkabinet
Vrijdagmarkt 22, 2000 Antwerp
Tel: (03) 221 14 50
E-mail: museum.plantin.moretus@stad.antwerpen.be
Web Site: www.museumplantinmoretus.be
Key Personnel
Dir: Iris Kockelbergh *E-mail:* iris.kockelbergh@stad.antwerpen.be
Publication(s): *About Types, Books & Prints: Didactic brochure for the Plantin-Moretus Museum & City Prints Gallery* (1989, monograph); *The Illustration of Books Published by the Moretuses* (1996, monograph); *Plantin-Moretus Museum Antwerp (Musea Nostra)* (1995, monograph)

RBIN, see Institut Royal des Sciences Naturelles de Belgique, Bibliotheque

UCL Bibliotheques, see Les Bibliotheques de l'Universite Catholique de Louvain

l'Universite Libre de Bruxelles Archives & Bibliotheques
Ave F Roosevelt 50, 1050 Brussels
Mailing Address: CP 180, 1050 Brussels
Tel: (02) 650 23 70; (02) 650 25 22 *Fax:* (02) 650 41 86
E-mail: bibdir@ulb.ac.be
Web Site: www.bib.ulb.ac.be
Key Personnel
Dir: Jean-Pierre Devroey *Tel:* (02) 650 23 68 *E-mail:* jean-pierre.devroey@ulb.ac.be

Universiteit Antwerpen Bibliotheek (University of Antwerp Library)
Prinsstr 13, 2000 Antwerp
Tel: (03) 265 44 34
E-mail: helpdesk@library.uantwerpen.be
Web Site: www.uantwerpen.be/nl/bibliotheek
Key Personnel
Chief Librarian: Trudi Noordermeer *Tel:* (03) 265 44 40 *E-mail:* trudi.noordermeer@uantwerpen.be
Campus Librarian: Veronique Rega *Tel:* (03) 265 44 64 *E-mail:* veronique.rega@uantwerpen.be
Founded: 1852
Branch Office(s)
Bldg S, 2nd floor, Groenenborgerlaan 171, 2020 Antwerp, Campus Librarian: Anke Jacobs *Tel:* (03) 265 34 58 *E-mail:* anke.jacobs@uantwerpen.be
Middelheimlaan 1, 2020 Antwerp, Campus Librarian: Anke Jacobs *Tel:* (03) 265 37 94 *Fax:* (03) 265 36 52 *E-mail:* anke.jacobs@uantwerpen.be
Universiteitsplein 1, Bldg R, 2610 Antwerp, Campus Librarian: Anke Jacobs *Tel:* (03) 265 21 45 *E-mail:* anke.jacobs@uantwerpen.be

Universiteit Hasselt Biliotheek
Campus Diepenbeek, Agoralaan-Gebouw D, 3590 Diepenbeek
Tel: (011) 26 81 23 *Fax:* (011) 26 81 26
E-mail: bib@uhasselt.be
Web Site: bibliotheek.uhasselt.be
Key Personnel
Chief Librarian: Pieter Lernout *Tel:* (011) 26 81 28 *E-mail:* pieter.lernout@uhasselt.be

University Library of Louvain (Leuven), see Katholieke Universiteit Leuven

Vrije Universiteit Brussel Universiteitsbibliotheek
Pleinlaan 2, 1050 Brussels
Tel: (02) 629 26 09 *Fax:* (02) 629 26 93
E-mail: info@biblio.vub.ac.be
Web Site: www.vub.ac.be/BIBLIO
Key Personnel
Head Librarian: Patrick Vanouplines *Tel:* (02) 629 26 14 *E-mail:* patrick.vanouplines@vub.ac.be
Founded: 1972

VUB, see Vrije Universiteit Brussel Universiteitsbibliotheek

Belize

Belize National Library Service & Information System (BNLSIS)
Princess Margaret Dr, Belize City
Mailing Address: PO Box 287, Belize City
Tel: 223-4248; 223-4249 *Fax:* 223-4246
E-mail: nls@btl.net
Web Site: www.nlsbze.bz

Benin

Key Personnel
Chief Librarian: Lusiola Castillo
Principal Librarian: Lawrence Vernon
Librarian: Glenford Barrera
Founded: 1935
Committed to the promotion of a more informed, aware & literate society & seeks to provide universal access to information through the maintenance of a National Library & Public Library service.
Membership(s): ABINIA-AC; ACURIL; Comla; International Federation of Library Associations & Institutions (IFLA); INFOLAC.
Parent Company: Ministry of Education, Government of Belize, West Block Bldg, Belmopan

BNLSIS, see Belize National Library Service & Information System (BNLSIS)

Benin

Archives Nationales du Benin
Ouando, Face a l'Ecole Regionale de la Magistrature, Porto-Novo
Tel: 20 24 80 79; 20 24 66 07
E-mail: anbenin@gmail.com
Web Site: www.dan.ilemi.net
Founded: 1914
Membership(s): AIAF; CIA; WARBICA.
Publication(s): *Bulletin des Archives; Guide de l'usager; Memoire du Benin; Repertoire Serie E: Affaires politiques; Repertoire Serie N: Affaires Militaires; Repertoire Serie Q: Affaires Economiques*

Bibliotheque de l'Universite d'Abomey-Calavi
Campus d'Abomey-Calavi, 01 BP 526, Cotonou
Tel: 21 36 01 01
E-mail: bibliotheque@uac.bj
Web Site: www.uac.bj
Key Personnel
Dir: Pascal Gandaho
Founded: 1970

Bibliotheque nationale du Benin (National Library of Benin)
BP 401, Porto Novo
Tel: 20 24 65 45
E-mail: bn.benin@bj.refer.org
Key Personnel
Dir: Mr Francis Marie-Jose Zogo
Founded: 1975
Publication(s): *Les Numeras de la Bibliographie Nationale*

BUC, see Bibliotheque de l'Universite d'Abomey-Calavi

Bermuda

Bermuda Archives
Government Administration Bldg, 30 Parliament St, Hamilton HM 12
Tel: (441) 297-7737
Web Site: www.gov.bm/department/archives
Publication(s): *A Guide to the Records of Bermuda* (1980)

Bermuda College Library
21 Stonington Ave, 2nd floor, South Rd, Paget PG 04
Tel: (441) 239-4033 *Fax:* (441) 239-4035

E-mail: circulation@college.bm; reference@college.bm
Web Site: www.college.bm/index.php/resources/library
Key Personnel
Library Dir: Robert Masters *Tel:* (441) 236-9000 ext 4034 *E-mail:* rmasters@college.bm
User Services & Cataloging Librarian: Annette Gilbert *Tel:* (441) 236-9000 ext 4386
Founded: 1974

Bermuda National Library
Par-la-ville, 13 Queen St, Hamilton HM 11
Tel: (441) 295-2905; (441) 299-0030 (information)
E-mail: library@gov.bm
Web Site: www.bnl.bm
Key Personnel
Head Librarian: C Joanne Brangman *Tel:* (441) 299-0027 *E-mail:* jbrangman@gov.bm
Local Studies Librarian: Ellen J Hollis *Tel:* (441) 299-0028 *E-mail:* ejhollis@gov.bm
Youth Services Librarian: Marla Smith *Tel:* (441) 299-0020 *E-mail:* mlsmith@gov.bm; Tasleem Talbot *Tel:* (441) 299-0023 *E-mail:* tbtalbot@gov.bm
Founded: 1839
Publication(s): *Bermuda National Bibliography* (quarterly)
Branch Office(s)
Bermuda Youth Library, 74 Church St, Hamilton HM 12 *Tel:* (441) 295-0487 *Fax:* (441) 296-0973 *E-mail:* youthlib@gov.bm

Bolivia

Archivo y Biblioteca Nacionales de Bolivia
Calle Dalence N° 4, Sucre
Mailing Address: Cajon Postal 793, Sucre
Tel: (04) 6452246; (04) 6451481 *Fax:* (04) 6461208
E-mail: abnb@entelnet.bo
Web Site: www.archivoybibliotecanacionales.org.bo
Key Personnel
Dir: Juan Carlos Fernandez
Founded: 1836

Biblioteca y Archivo de la Asamblea Legislativa Plurinacional
Calle Ayacucho y Mercado N° 308, La Paz
Tel: (02) 2142670 *Fax:* (02) 214582; (02) 2142803
Key Personnel
Dir: Luis Oporto *E-mail:* luis.oporto@vicepresidencia.gob.bo
Founded: 1911

Universidad Autonoma Tomas Frias, Biblioteca Central
Av del Maestro, Casilla 36, Potosi
Tel: (02) 26227300 *Fax:* (02) 26226663
Web Site: www.uatf.edu.bo

Bosnia and Herzegovina

Nacionalna i Univerzitetska Biblioteka Bosne i Hercegovine (National & University Library of Bosnia and Herzegovina)
Zmaja od Bosne 8B, 71000 Sarajevo
Tel: (033) 275-312 *Fax:* (033) 214-836

E-mail: nubbih@nub.ba
Web Site: www.nub.ba
Key Personnel
Dir: Dr Ismet Ovcina *E-mail:* ured.direktora@nub.ba

Botswana

Botswana National Archives & Records Services
Government Enclave, Corner of State & Parliament Drs, Gaborone
Mailing Address: PO Box 239, Gaborone
Tel: 3911820 *Fax:* 3908545
E-mail: archives@gov.bw
Web Site: www.gov.bw
Key Personnel
Dir: Peter Choto
Founded: 1967
Provides a national archives services to preserve for posterity historically important records & data for research, education & reference.
Publication(s): *Botswana National Archives & Records Services Library Accessions List* (annually)

Botswana National Library Service
Plot 1272, Loapi House, Lithuli Rd, Gaborone
Mailing Address: National Reference Library, Private Bag 0036, Gaborone
Tel: 3704555; 3704546 *Fax:* 3901149
Web Site: www.gov.bw
Key Personnel
Contact: Ms Neo Mosweu
Founded: 1967

Geological Survey Department Library
Private Bag 0014, Lobatse
Tel: 5330327 *Fax:* 5332013
Web Site: www.gov.bw
Key Personnel
Contact: Th Ngwisanyi

Standard Book Numbering Agency, see Botswana National Library Service

University of Botswana Library
Private Bag UB 00390, Gaborone
Tel: 3552300; 3552304 (customer service)
E-mail: ublib@mopipi.ub.bw
Web Site: www.ub.bw/library
Founded: 1971

Brazil

Arquivo Nacional (National Archives)
Praca da Republica, 173, 20211-350 Rio de Janeiro-RJ
Tel: (021) 2179-1227; (021) 2179-1228
E-mail: ascom@arquivonacional.gov.br
Web Site: www.arquivonacional.gov.br
Key Personnel
General Dir: Jose Ricardo Marques *Tel:* (021) 2179-1313 *E-mail:* ricardo.marques@arquivonacional.gov.br
Founded: 1838
Publication(s): *ACERVO-Revista do Arquivo Nacional; Instrumentos de Pesquisa; Normas Tecnicas; Publicacoes ACAN; Serie de Publicacoes Historicas; Serie de Publicacoes Tecnicas; Serie Instrumentos de Trabalho; Serie Premio Arquivo Nacional de Pesquisa; Serie Publicacoes Avulsas*

Biblioteca Central da Universidade Federal do Parana
Rua General Carneiro 370, Centro, 80060-150 Curitiba, Parana-PR
Tel: (041) 3360-5237
E-mail: saubc@ufpr.br
Web Site: www.ufpr.br; www.portal.ufpr.br

Biblioteca Central do Centro de Ciencias da Saude-UFRJ (Central Library of the Center of Health Sciences-UFRJ)
Av Carlos Chagas Filho, 373, Cidade Universitaria, Bloco L, 21941-902 Rio de Janeiro-RJ
Tel: (021) 2562-6632; (021) 2562-6716; (021) 2270-1640
E-mail: ccsbib@acd.ufrj.br
Web Site: www.sibi.ufrj.br; www.bib.ccs.ufrj.br
Key Personnel
Dir: Cassia Costa R de Deus
Founded: 1971

Biblioteca do Ministerio das Relacoes Exteriores
Esplanada dos Ministerios, Bloco H, Anexo II, Terreo, 70170-900 Brasilia DF
Web Site: www.itamaraty.gov.br
Publication(s): *Referencia de Periodicos* (monthly)

Biblioteca Mario de Andrade (BMA)
Rua da Consolacao, 94, 01302-000 Sao Paulo-SP
Tel: (011) 3775-0002; (011) 3775-0003
E-mail: bma@prefeitura.sp.gov.br
Web Site: www.prefeitura.sp.gov.br
Key Personnel
Dir: Luis Armando Bagolin
Founded: 1925
Membership(s): International Federation of Library Associations & Institutions (IFLA).
Publication(s): *Revista da Biblioteca Mario de Andrade* (annually)

BMA, see Biblioteca Mario de Andrade (BMA)

CEDI, see Centro de Documentacao e Informacao da Camara dos Deputados

Centro de Documentacao e Informacao da Camara dos Deputados (House of Representatives' Centre of Documentation & Information)
Palacio do Congresso Nacional, Annex 11, 2nd floor, C, Room 45, 70160-900 Brasilia-DF
Tel: (061) 3216-5777 *Fax:* (061) 3216-5757
E-mail: informa.cedi@camara.leg.br
Web Site: www2.camara.leg.br
Key Personnel
Dir: Andre Freire da Silva *Tel:* (061) 3216-5501 *E-mail:* gabinete.cedi@camara.leg.br

Fundacao Biblioteca Nacional (National Library Foundation)
Av Rio Branco 219, 20040-008 Rio de Janeiro-RJ
Tel: (021) 2220-3040; (021) 3095-3993 (bookshop)
E-mail: livraria@bn.gov.br
Web Site: www.bn.gov.br
Publication(s): *Anais da Biblioteca Nacional; Bibliografia Brasileira; Brazilian Book Magazine; Poesia Sempre* (magazine)

SIBi/USP, see Sistema Integrado de Bibliotecas da Universidade de Sao Paulo (SIBi)

Sistema Integrado de Bibliotecas da Universidade de Sao Paulo (SIBi) (University of Sao Paulo Integrated Library System)
Rua da Biblioteca, Cidade Universitaria, 05508-050 Sao Paulo-SP

Tel: (011) 3091-4195; (011) 3091-1547
Fax: (011) 3091-1567
Web Site: www.sibi.usp.br
Key Personnel
President: Dr Carlos de Almeida Prado Bacellar
Founded: 1981
Membership(s): CRB (Brazilian Regional Librarian Council); FEBAB (Brazilian Federation of Library Associations); International Federation of Library Associations & Institutions (IFLA); OCLC.
Publication(s): *Bibliotheca Universitatis - Acervo Bibliografico da Universidade de Sao Paulo - Sec XVII* (annually, book); *Boletim Annual do Departamento do SIBi/USP* (annually, print & online serial); *Cadernos de Estudos, 9* (irregularly, book, 2009); *Dados Estatisticos do Sistema Integrado de Bibliotecas da USP* (annually, print & online serial)

UFRGS, see Universidade Federal do Rio Grande do Sul (UFRGS), Biblioteca Central

Universidade de Brasilia, Biblioteca Central
Campus Universitario Darcy Ribeiro, Gleba A, 70910-900 Brasilia-DF
Tel: (061) 3107-2676
E-mail: informacoes@bce.unb.br
Web Site: www.bce.unb.br
Key Personnel
Dir: Emir Jose Suaiden *Tel:* (061) 3107-2665 *E-mail:* direcao@bce.unb.br
Founded: 1962

Universidade Federal do Rio Grande do Sul (UFRGS), Biblioteca Central
Av Paulo Gama, 110, Terreo de Reitoria Predio 12107, 90046-900 Porto Alegre-RS
Tel: (051) 3308-3065; (051) 3308-3883
E-mail: bcentral@bc.ufrgs.br
Web Site: www.ufrgs.br/bibliotecas; www.ufrgs.br/bibliotecacentral
Key Personnel
Dir: Viviane Carrion Castanho *Tel:* (051) 3308-3057 *E-mail:* direcao@bc.ufrgs.br

Brunei

Dewan Bahasa dan Pustaka Library
Jl Elizabeth II, Bandar Seri Begawan BS3510
Tel: 2235501; 2235502; 2235503; 2235504; 2235505; 2222135; 2224764 *Fax:* 2224763; 2380472
E-mail: kb_perpustakaan@brunet.bn
Web Site: www.dbplibrary.gov.bn; www.dewanbahasadanpustakalibrary.org
Founded: 1959
National Language & Literature Bureau Library.

Bulgaria

Bulgarian Academy of Sciences, Central Library
1, 15 Noemvri Str, 1040 Sofia
Tel: (02) 987 89 66 *Fax:* (02) 986 25 00
E-mail: library@cl.bas.bg
Web Site: www.cl.bas.bg
Key Personnel
Dir: Sylvia Naydenova *E-mail:* najdenova.s@cl.bas.bg
Deputy Dir: Dr Nicholas Kazanski *Tel:* (02) 989 53 79 *E-mail:* refer2@cl.bas.bg

Founded: 1869
Publication(s): *Problemi na specialnite biblioteki* (Problems of Special Libraries, irregularly)

CAL, see Central Agricultural Library (CAL)

Central Agricultural Library (CAL)
125 Tsarigradsko Shose, Block 1, 1113 Sofia
Tel: (02) 870 60 81; (02) 870 55 88 *Fax:* (02) 870 80 78
E-mail: csb@abv.bg
Web Site: www.iae-bg.com/en/library
Key Personnel
Contact: Margarita Stamatova
Founded: 1962
Specialize in agriculture & forestry.

Central Medical Library, Medical University - Sofia
One, St G Sofiiski, 1431 Sofia
Tel: (02) 92301 (ext 498); (02) 952 31 71 *Fax:* (02) 851 82 65
E-mail: library@mu-sofia.bg; cml.mu.sofia@gmail.com
Web Site: www.medun.acad.bg
Key Personnel
Dir: Dr Lydia Tacheva *E-mail:* lydia.tacheva@gmail.com
Head, Library & Information Dept: Penka Kocilkova *E-mail:* pepaslavova@gmail.com
Founded: 1918
Publication(s): *Acta Medica Bulgarica* (2 times/yr, journal, in English); *Bulgarian Medical Journal* (3 times/yr, in Bulgarian); *General Medicine-Abstracts* (quarterly, journal, in English); *Medical Review* (6 times/yr, journal)

CRTL, see National Centre for Information & Documentation Central Research & Technical Library

General Department of Archives of the Republic of Bulgaria, see Republic of Bulgaria Archives State Agency

Nacionalna biblioteka Sv sv Kiril i Metodii (Saints Cyril & Methodius National Library)
88 Vasil Levski Blvd, 1037 Sofia
Tel: (02) 918 31 01 *Fax:* (02) 84 35 495
E-mail: nl@nationallibrary.bg
Web Site: www.nationallibrary.bg
Key Personnel
Dir: Dr Krasimira Alexandrova *Tel:* (02) 988 16 00 *E-mail:* k.alexandrova@nationallibrary.bg
Deputy Dir: Desislava Georgieva *Tel:* (02) 981 35 36 *E-mail:* d.georgieva@nationallibrary.bg
Founded: 1878
Publication(s): *Biblioteka* (6 times/yr, journal, library sciences); *Bulgarska Nacionalna Bibliografija, Ser 1-8* (Bulgarian National Bibliography); *Bulgarski Knigopis* (annually, bulletin, books, official, music, prints, maps)

National Centre for Information & Documentation Central Research & Technical Library
52A, MD GM Dimitrov Blvd, 1125 Sofia
Tel: (02) 817 38 24; (02) 817 38 40; (02) 817 38 41; (02) 817 38 42 *Fax:* (02) 971 31 20
E-mail: ctb@nacid-bg.net; nacid@nacid-bg.net
Web Site: www.nacid.bg
Founded: 1962

National Library "Ivan Vazov"
17 Avksentii Veleshki St, 4000 Plovdiv
Tel: (032) 654 912 *Fax:* (032) 654 902
E-mail: nbiv@libplovdiv.com
Web Site: www.libplovdiv.com

Key Personnel
Dir: Dimitar Minev *Tel:* (032) 654 905
  E-mail: dimin@libplovdiv.com
Deputy Dir: Antoaneta Lessenska *Tel:* (032) 654
  900 *E-mail:* lessenska@libplovdiv.com
Founded: 1879
Branch Office(s)
Children's Dept, 15 Avksentii Veleshki St,
  4000 Plovdiv, Head of Dept: Vaska Tonova
  Tel: (032) 622 043 *E-mail:* nbivdet@libplovdiv.
  com

Republic of Bulgaria Archives State Agency
Formerly General Department of Archives of the
  Republic of Bulgaria
5, Moskovska Str, 1000 Sofia
Tel: (02) 940 01 01; (02) 940 01 20; (02) 940 01
  76 *Fax:* (02) 980 14 43
E-mail: daa@archives.government.bg
Web Site: www.archives.government.bg
Key Personnel
President: Mihail Gruev *E-mail:* m.gruev@
  archives.government.bg
Vice President: Rumen Borisov *Tel:* (02) 940 02
  00 *E-mail:* r.borisov@archives.government.bg
Chief Secretary: Georgi Chernev *Tel:* (02) 940 01
  04 *E-mail:* g.chernev@archives.government.bg
Founded: 1951
Administration, coordination, control & publish-
  ing of archival records.
Publication(s): *Arhiven pregled* (Archival review,
  2 times/yr); *Arhivite govoriat* (The Archives
  are Speaking); *Izvestiya na darzhavnite arhivi*
  (Journal of the State Archives, 2 times/yr)

St Kliment Ohridski University Library
15 Tzar Osvoboditel Blvd, 1043 Sofia
Tel: (02) 8467-584; (02) 9308-554; (02) 9308-209
E-mail: lsu@libsu.uni-sofia.bg
Web Site: www.libsu.uni-sofia.bg
Key Personnel
Dir: Anna Angelova *Tel:* (02) 9308-536
  E-mail: anna@libsu.uni-sofia.bg
Deputy Dir: Biliana Yavrukova *Tel:* (02) 9308-
  539 *E-mail:* byavrukova@libsu.uni-sofia.bg
Head, Library & Information Services: Diana Ku-
  tovska *Tel:* (02) 9308-554 *E-mail:* dds@libsu.
  uni-sofia.bg
Founded: 1888

Sofia University Library, see St Kliment
  Ohridski University Library

**Technical University of Sofia Library &
  Information Complex**
Blvd Kliment Ohridski 8, 1000 Sofia
Tel: (02) 965-39-14
E-mail: library@tu-sofia.bg
Web Site: library.tu-sofia.bg; www.tu-sofia.bg
Key Personnel
Dir: Hristina Mihailova Dimitrova *Tel:* (02) 965-
  20-09 *E-mail:* hdimitrova@tu-sofia.bg
Founded: 1994

Burkina Faso

Centre National des Archives
Presidence du Faso, BP 7030, Ouagadougou 03
Tel: 50 33 61 96 *Fax:* 50 31 49 26
E-mail: info@presidence.bf
Web Site: www.presidence.bf
Key Personnel
Dir General: Hamidou Diallo
Founded: 1970

Universite de Ouagadougou
BP 7021, Ouagadougou 03

Tel: 50-30-70-64; 50-30-70-65 *Fax:* 50-30-72-42
Web Site: www.univ-ouaga.bf
Founded: 1974

Burundi

Bibliotheque Nationale du Burundi (National
  Library of Burundi)
BP 1095, Bujumbura
Tel: (02) 25051 *Fax:* (02) 26231
E-mail: biefbdi@cbinf.com
Web Site: www.nationallibraryofburundi.org
Key Personnel
National Librarian: Marie Bernadette Ntahor-
  wamiye
Founded: 1989

Universite du Burundi Bibliotheque Centrale
Avenue de l'Unesco, BP 1550, Bujumbura
Tel: 22218690 *Fax:* 22222857
E-mail: info@ub.edu.bi
Web Site: bibliotheque.ub.edu.bi; www.facebook.
  com/kwabanani?fref=nf; www.ub.edu.bi
Key Personnel
Chief Librarian: Dismas Ndihokubwayo
  E-mail: dismas.ndihokubwayo@ub.edu.bi
Founded: 1964

Cameroon

Bibliotheque Centrale de l'UYI, see Universite
  de Yaounde I Bibliotheque Centrale

Bibliotheque Nationale du Cameroun (National
  Library of Cameroon)
BP 1053, Yaounde
Key Personnel
Dir: Alim Garga
Founded: 1952

Universite de Dschang Bibliotheque Centrale
  (University of Dschang Central Library)
BP 96, Dschang
Tel: 233451381 *Fax:* 233451381
Web Site: www.univ-dschang.org
Key Personnel
Chief Librarian: Mr Valere Djidere
  E-mail: valere.djidere@univ-dschang.org

Universite de Yaounde I Bibliotheque Centrale
PO Box 1312, Yaounde
Tel: 242 06 47 28
E-mail: biblio.bibliotheque@uy1.uninet.cm;
  biblio.centrale@gmail.com
Web Site: www.biblio-uy1.uninet.cm
Key Personnel
Chief Curator: Dr Marie Jose Essi

Universite de Yaounde II Bibliotheque
BP 1365, Yaounde
Tel: 697 03 43 29
E-mail: contact@univ-yde2.cm
Web Site: www.univ-yde2.cm
Key Personnel
Head of Library: Helene Menam
Publication(s): *Etudes et Recherches en Bibliothe-
  conomie*

Central African Republic

Bibliotheque Universitaire de Bangui
Ave des Martyrs, BP 1450, Bangui
Tel: 61 20 05
Web Site: www.univ-bangui.info
Founded: 1971

Chad

**Universite de N'Djamena Bibliotheque
  Centrale**
Av Mobutu, N'Djamena
Mailing Address: BP 1117, N'Djamena
Tel: 2251 44 44; 2251 46 97 *Fax:* 2251 40 33
E-mail: runiv.rectorat@sdnted.undp.org
Web Site: www.univ-ndjamena.org/library.asp
Founded: 1972

Chile

BCN, see Biblioteca del Congreso Nacional de
  Chile (BCN)

Biblioteca Central de la Universidad de Chile
Av Diagonal Paraguay No 265, piso 13, Santiago
Tel: (02) 9782000 *Fax:* (02) 9781012
E-mail: sisib@uchile.cl
Web Site: www.uchile.cl
Key Personnel
Dir: Gabriela Ortuzar Fontt *E-mail:* gortuzar@
  uchile.cl
Founded: 1936

**Biblioteca del Congreso Nacional de Chile
  (BCN)** (Library of Congress of Chile)
Huerfanos 1117, 3° Piso, 834-0327 Santiago
Tel: (02) 270 1700
Web Site: www.bcn.cl
Key Personnel
Dir: Soledad Ferreiro Serrano *E-mail:* sferreiro@
  bcn.cl
Publication(s): *Boletin Informativo*; *Serie Es-
  tudios*; *Series Bibliografias*; *Series Informes*;
  Temas de Actualidad (quarterly)

Biblioteca Nacional de Chile
Av Libertador Bernardo O'Higgins 651, Santiago
Tel: (02) 3605272
E-mail: oirs@dibam.cl
Web Site: www.dibam.cl
Key Personnel
Dir: Angel Cabeza Monteira *E-mail:* direccion@
  dibam.cl
National Library of the Office of Libraries,
  Archives & Museums.
Publication(s): *Bibliografia chilena* (1982, for-
  merly "Anuario de la Prensa"); *Referencias
  Criticas sobre Autores Chilenos* (annually)

**Pontificia Universidad Catolica de Chile
  Sistema de Bibliotecas** (Library System of
  Pontifica Universidad Catolica de Chile
  (SIBUC))
Av Vicuna Mackenna 4860, Santiago
Tel: (02) 3544616

Web Site: bibliotecas.uc.cl
Key Personnel
Dir: Evelyn Mireya Didier Carrasco

SIBUC, see Pontificia Universidad Catolica de Chile Sistema de Bibliotecas

SIBUDEC, see Sistema de Bibliotecas de la Universidad de Concepcion (SIBUDEC)

Sistema de Biblioteca de la Pontificia Universidad Catolica de Valparaiso (Library System of the Catholic University of Valparaiso)
Av Brasil 2950, 2374631 Valparaiso
Tel: (032) 2273262
Web Site: biblioteca.ucv.cl
Key Personnel
Dir: Marisol Fernandez Jimenez *Tel:* (032) 2273260 *E-mail:* mfernand@ucv.cl

Sistema de Bibliotecas de la Universidad de Concepcion (SIBUDEC)
Universidad de Concepcion, Biblioteca Central, Concepcion
Tel: (041) 220 4403
E-mail: bibliotecas@udec.cl
Web Site: www.bib.udec.cl; www.biblioteca.udec.cl
Key Personnel
Head, Library: Yasna Catalan Chavez *Tel:* (042) 208 729
Founded: 1926

Universidad Technologica Metropolitana (UTEM), Sistema de Bibliotecas
Padre Felipe Gomez de Vidaurre 1488, Santiago
Tel: (02) 755 1787; (02) 787 7544
Web Site: www.utem.cl/investigacion/biblioteca
Key Personnel
Dir: Carlos Mallea Garrido *E-mail:* cmallea@utem.cl
Founded: 1989
Academic text in the humanities, social sciences, pure & applied sciences.

China

Chongqing Library
No 106 Fengtian St, Shaopingba, Chongqing 400037
Tel: (023) 65210833; (023) 65210822
Web Site: www.cqlib.cn
Founded: 1947

Dalian University of Technology Library
Linggong Rd 2, Ganjingzi District, Dalian City, Liaoning Province 116024
Tel: (0411) 84708629
E-mail: office@dlut.edu.cn
Web Site: www.lib.dlut.edu.cn
Key Personnel
Dir: Prof Yang Haitan
Founded: 1950
Publication(s): *Chinese Journal of Computational Mechanics* (periodical); *Journal of Dalian University of Technology* (6 times/yr, periodical, 1950); *Journal of Mathematical Research & Exposition* (quarterly, periodical, 1981)

Fudan University Library
220 Handan Rd, Yangpu District, Shanghai 20043
Tel: (021) 65643179; (021) 55664282 (reference)
E-mail: liboffice@fudan.edu.cn; libref@fudan.edu.cn (reference)
Web Site: www.library.fudan.edu.cn

Key Personnel
Library Dir: Prof Chen Sihe
Founded: 1922
Publication(s): *Mathematical Analysis* (lectures on higher mathematics)

Liaoning Provincial Library (LPL)
111 Wan Liu Tang Lu, Dong Ling Qu, Shenyang, Liaoning Province 110015
Tel: (024) 2482-2449
E-mail: wzgl@lnlib.com
Web Site: www.lnlib.com
Founded: 1948

The Library of Renmin University of China
59 Zhongguancun St, Haidian District, Beijing 100872
Tel: (010) 62511588 *Fax:* (010) 62515343
E-mail: international@ruc.edu.cn
Web Site: www.ruc.edu.cn; www.lib.ruc.edu.cn
Founded: 1937
Membership(s): International Federation of Library Associations & Institutions (IFLA).

LPL, see Liaoning Provincial Library (LPL)

Nanjing tushuguan (Nanjing Library)
189 E Zhongshan Rd, Nanjing, Jiangsu Province 210000
Tel: (025) 84356000
E-mail: gzxx@jslib.org.cn
Web Site: www.jslib.org.cn
Key Personnel
Dir: Wang Mei *Tel:* (025) 84356019
Chief Librarian: Wu Guchen *Tel:* (025) 84356015
Founded: 1907
Membership(s): International Federation of Library Associations & Institutions (IFLA); Library Society of China.
Publication(s): *Xin Shiji Tushuguan* (New Century Library, 6 times/yr, Co-sponser: Jiangsu Society for Library Science)

National Science Library, Chinese Academy of Sciences
33 Beisihuan Xilu, Zhongguancum, Haidan Dist, Beijing 100190
Tel: (010) 82626611 *Fax:* (010) 82626600
E-mail: service@mail.las.ac.cn; xkgy@mail.las.ac.cn
Web Site: www.las.ac.cn
Key Personnel
Executive Dir: Huang Xiangyang
Founded: 1950
Membership(s): International Federation of Library Associations & Institutions (IFLA).
Publication(s): *Library & Information Service* (6 issues/yr, journal)

Peking University Library
Qiuzhi Rd, Haidian District, Beijing 100871
Tel: (010) 62751051 *Fax:* (010) 62761008
E-mail: is@lib.pku.edu.cn; mediadept@lib.pku.edu.cn
Web Site: www.lib.pku.edu.cn
Key Personnel
University Librarian: Zhu Qiang
Founded: 1902
Publication(s): *Annual Reports*; *Core Journal Research*; *Newsletter of PKUL*

Qinghua daxue tushuguan (Tsinghua University Library)
Tsinghua University Library, Beijing 100084
Tel: (010) 62782137 *Fax:* (010) 62781758
E-mail: bgs@lib.tsinghua.edu.cn
Web Site: www.lib.tsinghua.edu.cn
Key Personnel
Dir: Fangyu Xue *Tel:* (010) 62771838
Associate Dir: Jieyu Chen *Tel:* (010) 62781755; Xuan Gao *Tel:* (010) 62784907; Airong Jiang

Tel: (010) 62786256; Yi Yang *Tel:* (010) 62787299; Xiong Zhao *Tel:* (010) 62784909
Founded: 1912

Shanghai Academy of Social Sciences Library
No 1610, Zhong Shan Xi Rd, Bldg 2, Shanghai 200235
Tel: (021) 6486 2266 *Fax:* (021) 6487 0024
E-mail: tsgyw@sass.org.cn
Web Site: www.sass.stc.sh.cn; shsk.mh.libsou.com/templates/shsky/default.cshtml
Founded: 1958
Branch Office(s)
No 7, Lane 622, Huaihai Middle Rd, Huangpu District, Shanghai 200020 *Tel:* (021) 53060606

Shanghai Tushuguan (Shanghai Library)
1555 Huaihai Zhong Rd, Shanghai 200031
Tel: (021) 64455555 *Fax:* (021) 64455001
E-mail: service@libnet.sh.cn
Web Site: www.library.sh.cn
Key Personnel
Dir: Jianzhong Wu
Publication(s): *Library Journal* (monthly)

Sun Yat-Sen Library of Guangdong Province
213 Wen Ming Lu, Guangzhou 510110
Tel: (020) 8382 2369 *Fax:* (020) 8116 2666
E-mail: wlb@zslib.com.cn
Web Site: www.zslib.com.cn
Founded: 1912

Xiamen University Library
No 422, Si Ming Nan Lu, Xiamen, Fujian Province 361005
Tel: (0592) 2180000
E-mail: librarian@xmu.edu.cn
Web Site: library.xmu.edu.cn; www.xmu.edu.cn
Founded: 1921
Specialize in book borrowing & reading, document, information services.

Yunnan Provincial Library
141 Cui Hu Nan Lu, Kunming, Yunnan 650031
E-mail: info@powereasy.net
Web Site: www.ynlib.cn
Key Personnel
Deputy Dir: Zhou Yuqing
Founded: 1909

Zhejiang Provincial Library
No 73 Shuguang Rd, Hangzhou City 310007
Tel: (0571) 8798 8338
E-mail: zjdh@zjlib.cn
Web Site: www.zjlib.net.cn
Founded: 1900
Branch Office(s)
Chekiang Library, Hangchow

Zhongguo guojia tushuguan (The National Library of China)
No 33 Zhongguancun Nandajie, Hai Dian District, Beijing 100081
Tel: (010) 88545426; (010) 88544114; (010) 88545022; (010) 88545360
E-mail: webmaster@nlc.gov.cn
Web Site: www.nlc.gov.cn
Key Personnel
Dir: Han Yongjin
Founded: 1916
Publication(s): *Chinese Library Classification - A System Used in Chinese Libraries*; *Documentation* (series); *Journal of The National Library of China*

Colombia

Archivo General de la Nacion de Colombia
Carrera 6a No 6-91, Bogota
Tel: (01) 3282888 *Fax:* (01) 3372019
E-mail: contacto@archivogeneral.gov.co
Web Site: www.archivogeneral.gov.co
Key Personnel
Dir: Armando Martinez Garnica
National Archives.

BAC, see Biblioteca Agropecuaria de Colombia
(BAC)

Biblioteca Agropecuaria de Colombia (BAC)
(Farming & Livestock Library of Colombia)
KM-14 via Mosquera, Cundinamarca
Tel: (01) 4227300
E-mail: atencionalcliente@corpoica.org.co; bac@
corpoica.org.co
Web Site: www.corpoica.org.co
Key Personnel
Head, Library: Diana Maria Silva Gaitan *Tel:* (01)
4227300 ext 1274 *E-mail:* dsilva@corpoica.org.
co

**Biblioteca Luis Angel Arango Banco de la
Republica - Colombia** (Luis Angel Arango
Library-Central Bank of Colombia)
Calle 11 No 4-14, Piso 2, Bogota
Tel: (01) 343 12 24 *Fax:* (01) 381 29 08
E-mail: wbiblio@banrep.gov.co; prensablaa@
banrep.gov.co
Web Site: www.banrepcultural.org/blaa
Key Personnel
Dir: Alexis De Greiff Acevedo *Tel:* (01) 343 23
96
Membership(s): ICOMON; International Feder-
ation of Library Associations & Institutions
(IFLA); SALALM.
Publication(s): *Boletin Cultural y Bibliografico*
(quarterly); *Estudios sobre Politica Economica*
(2 times/yr)

Biblioteca Nacional de Colombia (National
Library of Colombia)
Calle 24 N° 5-60, Bogota
Tel: (01) 3816464 *Fax:* (01) 3816449
E-mail: bnc@bibliotecanacional.gov.co
Web Site: www.bibliotecanacional.gov.co
Founded: 1777
Publication(s): *Ivar da Coll y la critica*; *Mu-
sica y literatura infantil colombiana*; *Triunfo
Arciniegas y la critica*; *Una Historia del Libro
Ilustrado para Ninos en Colombia*

British Council Learning Centre
Carrera 9 No 76-49 Piso 5, Bogota
Tel: (01) 325 9090 *Fax:* (01) 325 9091
E-mail: servicioalcliente@britishcouncil.org.co
Web Site: www.britishcouncil.co/en

CEDE, see Centro de Estudios sobre Desarrollo
Economico (CEDE)

**Centro de Estudios sobre Desarrollo
Economico (CEDE)** (Centre for Studies on
Economic Development)
Calle 19A No 1-37 E, Bloque W, Piso 9, Bogota
Tel: (01) 3394949 *Fax:* (01) 3324492
E-mail: infocede@uniandes.edu.co
Web Site: economia.uniandes.edu.co
Key Personnel
General Secretary: Maria Andrea Leyva *Tel:* (01)
3324494 *E-mail:* marialeyva@uniandes.edu.co
Founded: 1958

Gabriel Garcia Marquez Central Library, see
Universidad Nacional de Colombia, Biblioteca
Central

**Pontificia Universidad Javeriana, Biblioteca
General**
Carrera 7 No 41-00, Bogota
Tel: (01) 320 8320 (ext 2135); (01) 320 8320 (ext
2150) *Fax:* (01) 320 8320 (ext 2131)
E-mail: biblioteca@javeriana.edu.co
Web Site: www.javeriana.edu.co
Key Personnel
Dir: Andres Felipe Echavarria Ramirez *Tel:* (01)
320 8320 ext 2132 *E-mail:* andres.echavarria@
javeriana.edu.co

**Universidad de Antioquia, Escuela
Interamericana de Bibliotecologia**
Calle 67 No 53-108, Ciudad Universitaria, 1226
Medellin
Mailing Address: Apdo Aereo 1226, Medellin
Tel: (04) 2195151; (04) 2195941
E-mail: informacionbiblioteca@udea.edu.co
Web Site: www.udea.edu.co
Membership(s): ACURIL; AIBDA; ALA; Aso-
ciacion Latinoamericana de Archivos; FID;
International Federation of Library Associations
& Institutions (IFLA); The Library Association;
SALALM.
Publication(s): *Bibliografia Bibliotecologica*; *Bib-
liografica y de Obras de Referencia Colom-
bianas* (Bibliography of Library Science, Bibli-
ography & Colombian Works of Reference); *La
Biblioteca Publication: Una Mirada Desde su
Genesis y Desarrollo*; *BitBlios: Organo Infor-
mativo Estudiantil*; *Boletin Informativo*; *Revista
Interamericana de Bibliotecologia*

**Universidad de los Andes, Sistema de
Bibliotecas**
Carrera 1a Este N° 19A-40, Bogota
Tel: (01) 3324473 *Fax:* (01) 3324472
E-mail: sisbibli@uniandes.edu.co
Web Site: biblioteca.uniandes.edu.co

Universidad Externado de Colombia Biblioteca
Calle 12 No 1-17 Este, Bloque E, Piso 1, Bogota
Tel: (01) 3419900
E-mail: biblioteca@uexternado.edu.co
Web Site: biblioteca.uexternado.edu.co
Key Personnel
Dir: Patricia Velez De Monchaux *Tel:* (01)
341990 ext 3351

**Universidad Nacional de Colombia, Biblioteca
Central** (National University of Colombia,
Central Library)
Plaza Central Santander, Edificio 102, Bogota
Tel: (01) 3165000 (ext 17453)
E-mail: bibservicios@unal.edu.co; bibtec_bog@
unal.edu.co
Web Site: bibliotecas.unal.edu.co
Founded: 1972

Congo (Brazzaville)

Bibliotheque Nationale Populaire
PB 1489, Brazzaville
Tel: 833485 *Fax:* 832253
Key Personnel
National Librarian: Francois Onday-Akiera
Publication(s): *Repertorie bibliographique na-
tionale*

**Bibliotheque Universitaire, Universite Marien
Ngouabi**
BP 69, Brazzaville
Tel: 810141
E-mail: dcri@umng.cg
Web Site: www.umng.cg
Key Personnel
Dir: J F Olakouara
Publication(s): *Annales*

CCF, see Centre Culturel Francais, Bibliotheque

Centre Culturel Francais, Bibliotheque
BP 2141, Brazzaville
Tel: 281 19 00; 323 00 91
Web Site: ccfbrazza.org

Democratic Republic of the Congo

**Archives Nationales de la Republique
Democratique du Congo**
Gombe 42 Ave de la Justice, Kinshasa
Tel: (099) 82 36 577
Key Personnel
Dir: Antoine K Lumenga-Neso
Founded: 1953

Bibliotheque Centrale, Universite de Kinshasa
BP 190, Kinshasa 11
Tel: (012) 21361; (012) 21362 (ext 320)
E-mail: centreinfo@ic.cd
Web Site: unikin.sciences.free.fr
Publication(s): *Annales de la Bibliotheque Cen-
trile de Kinshasa*

Bibliotheques de l'Universite de Lubumbashi
BP 1825, Lubumbashi, Katanga
Web Site: www.unilu.ac.cd
Key Personnel
Dir: Dr J Jeffrey Hoover
Founded: 1955

Universite de Kisangani Bibliotheque Centrale
BP 2012, Kisangani, Haut-Zaire
Tel: 231 68 57
Web Site: www.unikin.cd
Key Personnel
University Head: Prof Daniel Ngoma Ya Nzuzi
E-mail: rectorat@unikin.ac.cd

Costa Rica

**Biblioteca Mark Twain, Centro Cultural
Costarricense-Norteamericano**
Apdo 1489, 1000 San Jose
Tel: 2207-7545
E-mail: bibmarktwain@centrocultural.cr
Web Site: www.centrocultural.cr

Biblioteca Nacional Miguel Obregon Lizano
Calles 15 y 17 Av, 3 y 3B, San Jose
Mailing Address: Apdo 10.008, 1000 San Jose
Tel: 2257-4814; 2221-2479; 2221-2436
Fax: 2223-5510; 2257-4814
E-mail: dibinacr@racsa.co.cr; sinabicr@racsa.co.
cr
Web Site: www.abinia.org/costarica
Founded: 1888

Publication(s): *Bibliografia Costarricense; Cat-
alogo ISBN; Indice de Diarios y Semanarios
de Costa Rica* (Catalog of Costa Rican Daily
& Weekly Newspapers); *Indice de Revistas de
Costa Rica* (Catalog of Magazines of Costa
Rica)

SIBDI-UCR, see Universidad de Costa Rica
Sistema de Bibliotecas, Documentacion e
Informacion (SIBDI-UCR)

**Universidad de Costa Rica Sistema de
Bibliotecas, Documentacion e Informacion
(SIBDI-UCR)**
Apdo 2060, 11501 San Jose
Tel: 2253-6152 *Fax:* 2234-2809
Web Site: sibdi.ucr.ac.cr
Key Personnel
Dir: Maria E Briceno Meza *Tel:* 2253-5316
E-mail: ma.briceno@ucr.ac.cr
Administrative Services: Ana Virginia Bonilla
Nunez *E-mail:* ana.bonillanunez@ucr.ac.cr
Founded: 1984
Publication(s): *Agronomia Costarricense* (2
times/yr); *Anuario de Estudios Centroameri-
canos* (annually); *Revista de Biologia Tropical*
(2 times/yr); *Ciencia Y Tecnologia* (2 times/yr);
Ciencias Economicas (2 times/yr); *Revistas de
Ciencias Sociales* (quarterly); *Educacion* (2
times/yr); *Escena: Revista Teatral* (2 times/yr);
Revista de Filologia y Linguistica (2 times/yr);
*Revista de Filosofia; Revista Geologica de
America Central* (annually); *Revista Herencia*
(2 times/yr); *Revista de Historia* (2 times/yr);
Ingenieria (2 times/yr); *Kanina: Revista de
Artes y Letras* (2 times/yr)

Cote d'Ivoire

**Bibliotheque Nationale de Cote d'Ivoire
(BNCI)**
BP V 180, Abidjan
Tel: 20 21 35 34 *Fax:* 20 21 02 76
E-mail: bibliographie@bnci.ci; info@bnci.ci
Web Site: www.bnci.ci
Founded: 1971
Publication(s): *Bibliographie de la Cote-d'Ivoire*

BNCI, see Bibliotheque Nationale de Cote
d'Ivoire (BNCI)

**Direction des Archives Nationales et de la
Documentation**
One rue van Vollenhoven, Abidjan
Mailing Address: BP V 123, Abidjan
Tel: 20 21 41 58; 20 21 74 20 *Fax:* 20 21 75 78
Key Personnel
Dir: Venance Bahi Gouro
E-mail: bahigourovenance@yahoo.fr
Founded: 1957

Inades Formation
Rue C 13 Booker Washington-Cocody, Abidjan
08
Mailing Address: BP 8, Abidjan 08
Tel: 22 40 02 16 *Fax:* 22 40 02 30
E-mail: ifsiege@inadesfo.net
Web Site: www.inadesfo.net
Publication(s): *COURRIER* (quarterly); *Manuels
de Bibliotheconomic* (quarterly)

**Institut Africain pour le Developpement
Economique et Social - Centre Africain de
Formation**, see Inades Formation

Croatia

Nacionalna i Sveucilisna Knjiznica Biblioteka
(National & University Library)
Ul Hrvatske bratske zajednice 4 pp 550, 10000
Zagreb
Tel: (01) 616-4040 *Fax:* (01) 616-4186
E-mail: urednistvo@nsk.hr
Web Site: www.nsk.hr
Key Personnel
Dir General: Prof Tatijana Petric, PhD *Tel:* (01)
616-4023 *E-mail:* tpetric@nsk.hr
Publication(s): *Bibliografija knjiga tiskanih u SR
Hrvatskoj; Bibliografija rasprava, clanaka i
knjizevnih radova u casopisima SR Hrvatske;
Grada za hrvatsku retrospektivnu bibliografiju*

Cuba

Archivo Nacional de la Republica de Cuba
(National Archives of the Republic of Cuba)
Calle Compostela No 906, Esquina San Isidro la
Habana Vieja, CP 10100 Havana
Tel: (07) 862 9436
E-mail: arnac@ceniai.inf.cu
Web Site: www.arnac.cu
Key Personnel
Dir: Martha Ferriol Marchena *E-mail:* direccion@
arnac.cu
Founded: 1840
Membership(s): International Council on
Archives.

**Biblioteca Central de la Universidad Central
Marta Abreu de las Villas (UCLV)** (Central
Library of Central Marta Abreu University of
Las Villas)
Carretera de Camajuani, Km 5,5, CP 54830 Santa
Clara, Villa Clara
Tel: (042) 281178 *Fax:* (042) 222113
E-mail: rector@uclv.edu.cu
Web Site: www.uclv.edu.cu
Key Personnel
Dir: Dr Andres Castro Alegria *Tel:* (042) 281682
E-mail: castroalegria@uclv.edu.cu
Founded: 1952
Subdivided into small branches for technical &
social matters regarding careers studied in the
University. Specific reference (cybernetics, eco-
nomics, etc).

Biblioteca Central Ruben Martinez Villena, see
Universidad de la Habana, Direccion de
Informacion Cientifico Tecnica

Biblioteca Historica Cubana y Americana
(Cuban & American Historical Library)
Calle Tacon num 1e, Obispo y O'Reilly, Old Ha-
vana
Tel: (07) 861-5001; (07) 864-8960
E-mail: biblioteca@patrimonio.ohch.cu

Biblioteca Nacional Jose Marti (Jose Marti
National Library)
Ave Independencia y 20 de Mayo, Plaza de la
Revolucion, Havana
Mailing Address: Apdo 6670, Havana
Tel: (07) 8555442; (07) 8555449 *Fax:* (07)
335938
E-mail: publiweb@bnjm.cu
Web Site: www.josemarti.cu
Key Personnel
Dir: Dr Eduardo Torres Cuevas
Publication(s): *Bibliografia Cubana; Bibliografias
Especializadas; Documentos Extranjeros
Adquiridos; Ediciones Especializadas sobre*

*la Cultura y el Arte; Indice General de Pub-
licaciones Periodicas Cubanas; Revista de la
Biblioteca Nacional Jose Marti*

**Centro de Informacion y Gestion Technologica
(CIGET)**
Ave 52 No 2316 e/23 y 25, CP 55100 Cienfuegos
Tel: (043) 51 9732; (043) 51 8486
Web Site: www.cienfuegos.cu/ciget
Key Personnel
Dir: Alayn A Alonso Gonzalez-Abreu
E-mail: aleman@ciget.cienfuegos.cu

CIGET, see Centro de Informacion y Gestion
Technologica (CIGET)

Instituto de Literatura y Linguistica
Av Salvador Allende No 710, CP 10300 Havana
Tel: (07) 878 64 86; (07) 878 53 77 *Fax:* (07)
873 57 18
E-mail: ill@ceniai.inf.cu
Web Site: www.ill.cu
Key Personnel
Dir: Nuria Gregori Torada
Deputy Dir: Elizabeth C Martinez Gordo

UCLV, see Biblioteca Central de la Universidad
Central Marta Abreu de las Villas (UCLV)

**Universidad de la Habana, Direccion de
Informacion Cientifico Tecnica**
San Lazaro y L, CP 10400 Havana
E-mail: dict@rect.uh.cu; cienciatecnica@rect.uh.
cu
Web Site: www.uh.cu
Key Personnel
Dir: Annia Hernandez Rodriguez; Yohanis Marti
Lahera

Curacao

Biblioteka Nashonal Korsou (National Library
of Curacao)
17 Abraham Mendez Chumaceiro Blvd, Willemstad
Tel: (09) 434 52 00
Web Site: bnkcuracao.com

Openbare Bibliotheek Curacao, see Biblioteka
Nashonal Korsou

**Universiteits-Bibliotheek, Universiteit van de
Nederlandse Antillen**, see University of
Curacao Library

**University of Curacao Dr Moises da Costa
Gomez**, see University of Curacao Library

University of Curacao Library
Formerly Universiteits-Bibliotheek, Universiteit
van de Nederlandse Antillen
Jan Noorduynweg 111, Willemstad
Tel: (09) 744-2222 *Fax:* (09) 744-2100
E-mail: uoc@uoc.cw
Web Site: www.uoc.cw/biblosite
Key Personnel
Head, Library & Research Services: Dr Margo
Groenewoud, MA
Founded: 1979

Cyprus

Archbishop Makarios III Foundation Library
Archbishop Kypriano Sq, 1505 Nicosia
Mailing Address: PO Box 21269, 1505 Nicosia
Tel: 22430008 *Fax:* 22430667
E-mail: info@makariosfoundation.org.cy
Web Site: www.makariosfoundation.org.cy
Key Personnel
Dir: Dr Maria Stavrou
Librarian: Joy Crosses

British Council Library
1-3 Aristotelous St, 1011 Nicosia
Mailing Address: PO Box 21175, 1503 Nicosia
Tel: 22585000 *Fax:* 22585129
E-mail: enquiries@cy.britishcouncil.org
Web Site: www.britishcouncil.org/cyprus
Founded: 1940

Cyprus Department of Antiquities Library
One Museum, 1516 Nicosia
Mailing Address: PO Box 22024, 1516 Nicosia
Tel: 22865888 *Fax:* 22303148
E-mail: antiquitiesdept@da.mcw.gov.cy
Web Site: www.mcw.gov.cy/da
Key Personnel
Dir: Dr Marina Solomidou-Leronymides
Founded: 1935

Cyprus Library
Eleftherias Sq, 1011 Nicosia
Tel: 22303180; 22676118 *Fax:* 22304532
E-mail: cypruslibrary@cytanet.com.cy
Web Site: www.cypruslibrary.gov.cy
Key Personnel
Dir & Librarian: Dr Antonis Maratheftis
Deputy Dir: Dimitris Nikolaou
    E-mail: demnicolaou@cytanet.com.cy
Founded: 1927
Membership(s): Conference of European National
    Librarians (CENL); International Federation of
    Library Associations & Institutions (IFLA).
Publication(s): *Cyprus Bibliography* (online)

**Library of the Pedagogic Institute Academia
    (College of Education)**
Makedonias Ave 40, 2238 Latsia
Mailing Address: PO Box 12720, 2252 Nicosia
Tel: 25305388 *Fax:* 25305291
E-mail: info@cyearn.pi.ac.cy; library@cyearn.pi.
ac.cy
Web Site: www.pi.ac.cy
Key Personnel
Assistant Librarian: Louisa Pitta *E-mail:* pitta.l@
    cyearn.pi.ac.cy
Curator: Maria Demetriou *E-mail:* demetriou.m@
    cyearn.pi.ac.cy
Publication(s): *Guides for Intercultural Educa-
    tion*; *Pedagogical Institute Newsletter*

Czech Republic

Knihovna Narodniho Muzea (The National
    Museum Library)
Vinohradska 1, 110 00 Prague 1
Tel: 224 497 111; 224 497 158
E-mail: nm@nm.cz
Web Site: www.nm.cz
Key Personnel
Dir: Martin Sekera, PhD *Tel:* 224 497 343; 224
    497 344 *E-mail:* martin_sekera@nm.cz
Founded: 1818
Publication(s): *Acta Entomologica Musei Nation-
    alis Pragae* (2 times/yr, journal, 1923, text in

English, English abstracts); *Analy Naprstkova
muzea* (Annals of the Naprstek Muzeum, annually, journal, 1962, text in English, German,
French & Spanish); *Bulletin mineralogicko-
petrologickeho oddeleni* (Bulletin of the Department of Mineralogy & Petrology of the
National Museum in Prague, annually, bulletin, 1993, text in Czech, Slovak or English,
English abstracts); *Casopis Narodniho muzea,
rada historicka* (Journal of the National Museum, History Series, 2 times/yr, journal, 1829,
text in Czech, English, English abstracts, summaries in German); *Fontes Archaeologici Pra-
genses* (annually, 1958, monographic series;
text in Czech, introduction in German); *Lynx,
nova serie* (Lynx, Series nova, annually, periodical, 1959, text in Czech & English, English
abstracts); *Musicalia, Casopis Ceskeho muzea
hudby* (Musicalia, Journal of the Czech Museum of Music, annually, journal, 2009, text in
Czech & English, English abstracts); *Muzeum:
Muzejni a vlastivedna prace* (Museum: Museum & Regional Studies, 2 times/yr, journal,
1963, text in Czech, English abstracts); *Numismaticke listy* (Numismatic Papers, periodical, 1945, text in Czech, English abstracts);
*Sbornik Narodniho muzea v Praze, rada A-
Historie* (Acta Musei Nationalis Pragae, series
A-Historia, 2 times/yr, journal, 1938, text in
Czech, English abstracts, summary in German
& English); *Sbornik Narodniho muzea v Praze,
rada B-Prirodni vedy* (Acta Musei Nationalis
Pragae, series B-Historia Naturalis, journal,
1937, text preferred in English, English abstracts); *Sbornik Narodniho Muzea v Praze.
Rada C: Literarni Historie* (Journal/Magazine
of the National Museum Prague, series C: Lit-
erary History, 2 times/yr, journal, 1956, summaries in English & German, text in Czech)

Mestska knihovna v Praze (Municipal Library
    in Prague)
Marianske Nam 1/98, 110 00 Prague 1
Tel: 222 113 555
E-mail: knihovna@mlp.cz
Web Site: www.mlp.cz
Key Personnel
Mng Dir: Tomas Rehak *Tel:* 222 113 300
    E-mail: reditel@mlp.cz
Head Librarian: Jaroslava Sterbova *Tel:* 222 113
    352 *E-mail:* jaroslava.sterbova@mlp.cz
Founded: 1891

Moravska zemska knihovna Brne (Moravian
    Library)
Kounicova 65a, 601 87 Brno
Tel: 541 646 111 *Fax:* 541 646 100
E-mail: mzk@mzk.cz
Web Site: www.mzk.cz
Key Personnel
Dir: Dr Tomas Kubicek *Tel:* 541 646 101
    E-mail: tomas.kubicek@mzk.cz
Deputy Dir: Jindra Pavelkova *Tel:* 541 646 223
    E-mail: jindra.pavelkova@mzk.cz
Founded: 1808

Narodni Knihovna Ceske republiky (National
    Library of the Czech Republic)
Klementinum 190, 110 00 Prague 1
Tel: 221 663 111 *Fax:* 221 663 261
E-mail: bohmt@nkp.cz; posta@nkp.cz
Web Site: www.nkp.cz; www.facebook.com/
    narodni.knihovna
Key Personnel
Dir General: Dr Petr Kroupa *Tel:* 221 663 262
    E-mail: petr.kroupa@nkp.cz
Founded: 1777
Publication(s): *Ceska narodni bibliografie Knihy*
    (The Czech National Bibliography-Books, an-
    nually); *Narodni bibliografie Ceske republiky,
    Hudebniny* (The National Bibliography of the

Czech Republic-Music, quarterly, Czech Music); *Narodni Knihovna* (National Library, quarterly)

Narodni technicka knihovna (National Technical
    Library)
Technicka 6/2710, 160 80 Prague 6
Tel: 232 002 111; 232 002 535
E-mail: info@techlib.cz
Web Site: www.techlib.cz
Key Personnel
Dir: Martin Svoboda *Tel:* 232 002 402
    E-mail: martin.svoboda@techlib.cz
Division Head: Dr Jan Bayer *Tel:* 232 002 480
    E-mail: jan.bayer@techlib.cz
Membership(s): ASLIB; Association of European
    Research Libraries (LIBER); IATUL; IGELU.

Pamatnik narodniho pisemnictvi (Museum of
    Czech Literature)
Strahovske nadvori 1/132, 118 38 Prague 1
Tel: 220 516 695
E-mail: post@pamatnik-np.cz
Web Site: www.pamatniknarodnihopisemnictvi.cz
Key Personnel
Dir: Zdenek Freisleben *Tel:* 220 517 285
    E-mail: freisleben@pamatnik-np.cz
Head, Library: Alena Petruzelkova *Tel:* 220 516
    653 *E-mail:* petruzelkova@pamatnik-np.cz
Curator: Magdalena Srutova *E-mail:* srutova@
    pamatnik-np.cz
Founded: 1950
Membership(s): ICOM.
Publication(s): *Literarni Archiv-Almanac* (annu-
    ally)

Parlamentni Knihovna (Parliamentary Library of
    the Czech Republic)
Division of The Office of the Chamber of
    Deputies of the Parliament of the Czech Re-
    public
Snemovni 4, 118 26 Prague 1
Tel: 257 174 513
E-mail: knihovna_vypujcky@psp.cz
Web Site: www.psp.cz
Key Personnel
Dir: Dr Andrew Tikovsky *Tel:* 257 534 409
    E-mail: tikovskyo@psp.cz
Founded: 1858
Membership(s): ECPRD; International Federation
    of Library Associations & Institutions (IFLA).

Vedecka knihovna v olomouci (Research Library
    in Olomouc)
Bezrucova st 2, 779 11 Olomouc 9
Tel: 585 223 441
E-mail: info@vkol.cz; vkol@vkol.cz
Web Site: www.vkol.cz
Key Personnel
Dir: Jitka Holaskova *Tel:* 585 205 390
    E-mail: jitka.holaskova@vkol.cz
Founded: 1566
Publication(s): *Portolanoveho Atlas*
Branch Office(s)
Bezrucova 3, 779 11 Olomouc 9

**Vysoka skola banska-Technicka univerzita
    Ostrava** (VSB-Technical University of Ostrava)
17 listopadu 15/2172, 708 33 Ostrava-Poruba
Tel: 596 994 574 (circulation desk) *Fax:* 597 324
    598
E-mail: knihovna@vsb.cz
Web Site: www.vsb.cz; knihovna.vsb.cz
Key Personnel
University Librarian: Daniela Tkacikova *Tel:* 597
    321 278 *E-mail:* daniela.tkacikova@vsb.cz
Deputy Librarian: Pavla Rygelova *Tel:* 597 325
    171 *E-mail:* pavla.rygelova@vsb.cz

Denmark

Aalborg Bibliotekerne (Aalborg Public
Libraries)
Rendsburggade 2, 9000 Aalborg
Mailing Address: PB 839, 9100 Aalborg
Tel: 99 31 43 00
E-mail: bibliotek@aalborg.dk
Web Site: www.aalborgbibliotekerne.dk
Key Personnel
Library Dir: Kirsten Boelt *Tel:* 99 31 44 25
   E-mail: kirsten.boelt@aalborg.dk
Central Library for the County of North Jutland.

Aalborg Universitetsbibliotek (Aalborg
University Library)
Langagervej 2, 9220 Aalborg
Tel: 9940 9400
E-mail: aub@aub.aau.dk
Web Site: www.aub.aau.dk
Key Personnel
Head Librarian: Niels-Henrik Gylstorff *Tel:* 9940
   9347 *E-mail:* nhg@aub.aau.dk

**Aarhus University Library, Campus Emdrup
(DPB)**
Tuborgvej 164, 2400 Copenhagen NV
Mailing Address: PO Box 840, 2400 Copenhagen
   NV
Tel: 8716 1360 *Fax:* 8716 1361
E-mail: emdrup.library@au.dk
Web Site: library.au.dk
Key Personnel
Head Librarian: Ditte Jessing *Tel:* 3058 7423
   E-mail: dije@au.dk
Founded: 1887

Arhus Kommunes Biblioteker (Arhus Public
Library)
Dokk1, Hack Kampmanns Plads 2, 8000 Aarhus
   C
Tel: 89 40 92 00
E-mail: dokk1-hovedbibliotek@aarhus.dk
Web Site: www.aakb.dk; www.dokk1.dk
Key Personnel
Library Dir: Rolf Hapel *Tel:* 8940 9300
   E-mail: hapel@aarhus.dk
Chief Librarian: Knud Schulz *Tel:* 2920 8359
   E-mail: ksc@aarhus.dk

Danmarks Statistik Biblioteket (Statistics
Denmark Library)
Sejrogade 11, 2100 Copenhagen O
Tel: 39 17 39 17; 39 17 30 30 *Fax:* 39 17 30 03;
   39 17 39 99
E-mail: dst@dst.dk; bib@dst.dk
Web Site: www.dst.dk
Key Personnel
Head, Communication & Sales: Carsten Ulrik
   Zangenberg *Tel:* 39 17 39 41 *E-mail:* cuz@dst.
   dk

**Danmarks Tekniske Informationscenter
(DTIC)** (Technical Information Center of
Denmark)
Anker Engelunds Vej 1, Bygning 101 D, 2800
   Lyngby
Tel: 4525 7200; 4525 7250 *Fax:* 4588 3040
E-mail: bibliotek@dtu.dk
Web Site: www.bibliotek.dtu.dk
Key Personnel
Dir: Jacob Fritz Hansen *Tel:* 4525 7121
   E-mail: jfha@dtu.dk
Library Dir: Gitte Bruun Jensen *Tel:* 4525 7261
   E-mail: gibj@dtu.dk
Head, Bibliometrics & Data Management: Mo-
   gens Sandfaer *Tel:* 4525 7311 *E-mail:* mosa@
   dtu.dk

DTIC, see Danmarks Tekniske Informationscenter
(DTIC)

Frederiksberg Kommunes Biblioteker
(Frederiksberg Public Library)
Hovedbiblioteket, Falkoner Plads 3, 2000 Fred-
   eriksberg
Tel: 38 21 18 00
E-mail: biblioteket@frederiksberg.dk
Web Site: www.fkb.dk
Key Personnel
Dir: Tina Pihl *Tel:* 38 21 18 25 *E-mail:* tipi01@
   frederiksberg.dk
Founded: 1887

Gentofte Bibliotekerne (Gentofte Municipal
Library)
Ahlmanns Alle 6, 2900 Hellerup
Tel: 39 98 58 00
E-mail: bibliotek@gentofte.dk
Web Site: www.genbib.dk
Key Personnel
Arts & Cultural Affairs Dir: Lone Gladbo *Tel:* 39
   98 58 01 *E-mail:* lg@gentofte.dk
Librarian: Thomas Angermann *Tel:* 39 98 58 52
   E-mail: than@gentofte.dk
Branch Office(s)
Ordrup Branch Library, Ejgardsvej 11,
   2920 Charlottenlund *Tel:* 39 98 57 50
   E-mail: ordrupbibliotek@gentofte.dk
Dyssegaard Branch Library, Dyssegardsvej
   24, 2870 Dyssegard *Tel:* 39 98 57 20
   E-mail: dyssegaardbibliotek@gentofte.dk
Gentoftegade Branch Library, Gentofte-
   gade 45, 2820 Gentofte *Tel:* 39 98 57 30
   E-mail: gentoftebibliotek@gentofte.dk
Jaegersborg Branch Library, Smakkegardsvej
   112, 2820 Gentofte *Tel:* 39 98 57 40
   E-mail: jaegersborgbibliotek@gentofte.dk
Vangede Branch Library, Vangede By-
   gade 45, 2820 Gentofte *Tel:* 39 98 57 60
   E-mail: vangedebibliotek@gentofte.dk

Kobenhavns Biblioteker (Copenhagen Public
Libraries)
Krystalgade 15, 1172 Copenhagen K
Tel: 3366 3000
E-mail: bibliotek@kff.kk.dk
Web Site: bibliotek.kk.dk
Key Personnel
Dir: Jakob Heide Petersen *E-mail:* b74s@kff.kk.
   dk
Deputy Dir: Sanne Caft *E-mail:* sannec@kff.kk.
   dk
Administration Manager: Pia Schack Pedersen
   E-mail: pischa@kff.kk.dk

Kobenhavns Stadsarkiv (City Archives of
Copenhagen)
Kobenhavns Radhus, 1599 Copenhagen V
Tel: 33 66 23 70
E-mail: stadsarkiv@kff.kk.dk
Web Site: www.ksa.kk.dk
Key Personnel
Archivist: Elisabeth Bloch *Tel:* 26 86 73 84 (cell)
   E-mail: elbloc@kff.kk.dk
Publication(s): *Historiske Meddelelser om Koben-
   havn* (historical yearbook)

Nota
Teglvaerksgade 37, 2100 Copenhagen O
Tel: 39 13 46 00
E-mail: biblioteket@nota.dk; info@nota.dk
Web Site: nota.dk
Key Personnel
Dir: Michael Wright *Tel:* 39 13 46 46
   E-mail: mwr@nota.dk
Library Dir: Lene Harder *Tel:* 39 16 46 66
   E-mail: lha@nota.dk

Odense Centralbibliotek (Odense Central
Library)
Ostre Stationsvej 15, 5000 Odense C
Tel: 6613 1372 *Fax:* 6613 7337
E-mail: adm-bib@odense.dk
Web Site: www.odensebib.dk
Key Personnel
Dir: Kent Skov Andreasen *Tel:* 6551 4416
   E-mail: ksan@odense.dk

Rigsarkivet (Danish National Archives)
Rigsdagsgarden 9, 1218 Copenhagen K
Tel: 33 92 33 10
E-mail: mailbox@ra.sa.dk
Web Site: www.sa.dk
Key Personnel
Dir General & National Archivist: Asbjorn Hel-
   lum
Publication(s): *Siden Saxo*

Roskilde Universitetsbibliotek (Roskilde
University Library)
Universitetsvej 1, 4000 Roskilde
Mailing Address: Postboks 258, 4000 Roskilde
Tel: 4674 2207
E-mail: rub@ruc.dk
Web Site: rub.ruc.dk
Key Personnel
Dir & Head, Library & Management: Claus
   Vesterager Pederson *Tel:* 4674 2239
   E-mail: cvp@ruc.dk
Head, Reader Services: Peter Sondrgaard
   Tel: 4674 2287 *E-mail:* pso@ruc.dk
Founded: 1972

Slots-og Kulturstyrelsen
HC Andersens Blvd 2, 1553 Copenhagen V
Tel: 33 95 42 00 *Fax:* 33 91 77 41
E-mail: post@slks.dk
Web Site: slks.dk
Key Personnel
Dir General: Jesper Hermansen
Press & Communications: Jakob Dahl Klausen
   Tel: 41 39 38 11 *E-mail:* jdk@slks.dk
Government agency.
Publication(s): *Bibliotek og Medier* (Libraries &
   Media, quarterly, info on library related mat-
   ters)
Parent Company: Danish Agency of Culture &
   Palaces

Statsbiblioteket (State & University Library,
Aarhus)
Victor Albecks Vej 1, 8000 Aarhus C
Tel: 8946 2022 *Fax:* 8946 2220
E-mail: sb@statsbiblioteket.dk
Web Site: www.statsbiblioteket.dk
Key Personnel
Chief Executive: Svend Larsen *Tel:* 8946 2221
   E-mail: sl@statsbiblioteket.dk
Publication(s): *Avismikrofilm i Statsbiblioteket*

Syddansk Universitetsbibliotek (University
Library of Southern Denmark)
Campusvej 55, 5230 Odense M
Tel: 6550 2611; 6550 1000 *Fax:* 6550 1090
E-mail: sdub@bib.sdu.dk
Web Site: www.sdu.dk/bibliotek.aspx
Key Personnel
Chief Librarian: Bertil Dorch *Tel:* 6550 2683
   E-mail: bfd@bib.sdu.dk

Dominican Republic

Biblioteca de la Universidad Autonoma de Santo Domingo
Ciudad Universitaria, Av Alma Mater, Santo Domingo
Tel: (809) 535-8273 *Fax:* (809) 508-7374
E-mail: info@uasd.edu.do
Web Site: www.uasd.edu.do

Biblioteca Universidad Nacional Pedro Henriquez Urena
Calle Cesar Nicolas Penson No 91, Distrito Nacional, Santo Domingo 20711
Tel: (809) 562-6601; (829) 946-2674
E-mail: info@bnphu.gob.do
Web Site: bnphu.gob.do; www.unphu.edu.do
Key Personnel
Library Dir: Eloisa Marrero Sera *Tel:* (809) 562-6601 ext 2301 *E-mail:* emarrero@unphu.edu.do
Founded: 1966
Publication(s): *Revista Aula 2da Epoca y Campus*; *Revista de Ciencias Juridicas y Politicas*

Biblioteca UNPHU, see Biblioteca Universidad Nacional Pedro Henriquez Urena

Ecuador

Archivo Nacional del Ecuador (National Archive of Ecuador)
Av 10 de Agosto N11-539 y Santa Prisca, Casilla 17-12-878, Quito
Tel: (02) 2280431 *Fax:* (02) 2280431
E-mail: archivonacionalec@andinanet.net
Web Site: www.ane.gob.ec
Key Personnel
Executive Dir: Rocio Pazmino Acuna
    E-mail: rpazmino@ane.gob.ec
Founded: 1938

Biblioteca Ecuatoriana Aurelio Espinosa Polit
Jose Nogales N69-22 y Francisco Arcos, Quito
Tel: (02) 2491 157; (02) 2491 156
E-mail: info@beaep.ec
Web Site: www.beaep.ec
Founded: 1929
Publication(s): *Diccionaris Bibliografico Ecuatoriano* (Vols I, II, III & IV)

Biblioteca General, Universidad de Guayaquil
Ciudadela Universitaria Salvador Allende, Malecon del Salado entre Av Delta y Av Kennedy, Guayaquil
Tel: 2391010 *Fax:* 2282440
Web Site: www.ug.edu.ec/biblioteca%20general
Key Personnel
Dir: Leonor Villao de Santander
Founded: 1867

Biblioteca Nacional del Ecuador Eugenio Espejo (National Library of Ecuador Eugenio Espejo)
Av 12 de Octubre 555 y Patria, Quito
Tel: (02) 222 33 91 *Fax:* (02) 256 57 21
Web Site: biblioteca.casadelacultura.gob.ec; bne.gob.ec
Key Personnel
Dir: Katia Flor *E-mail:* katia.flor@casadelacultura.gob.ec

Biblioteca Nacional Eugenio Espejo
Ave 12 de Octubre nº 555 y Av Patria, Quito
Tel: (02) 222 3391 *Fax:* (02) 256 5721
E-mail: bibliotecanacionalecuador@gmail.com
Key Personnel
Dir: Katia Flor *Tel:* (02) 222 3392 ext 334
    E-mail: gestion.biblioteca@casadelacultura.gob.ec
Secretary: Patricia Palacios *Tel:* (02) 252 5679 ext 330 *E-mail:* patricia.palacios@casadelacultura.gob.ec
Founded: 1792

Sistema Integrado de Bibliotecas de la Universidad Central de Ecuador
Av America S/N Ciudadela, Quito
Tel: (02) 2505-859; (02) 2230-757
E-mail: dcc@uce.edu.ec
Web Site: www.uce.edu.ec

Egypt

Ain Shams University Central Library
Khalifa El-Maamon St, Abbasiya Sq, Cairo 11566
Tel: (02) 26831474; (02) 26831231; (02) 26831417; (02) 26831490 *Fax:* (02) 26847824
Web Site: www.asu.edu.eg
Founded: 1950

Al-Azhar University Library
El Darb El Ahmer, Cairo
Tel: (02) 22608598; (02) 224047340 *Fax:* (02) 22608652
E-mail: library@azhar.edu.eg
Web Site: www.azhar.edu.eg
Founded: 1897

ALECSO, see Institute of Arab Research & Studies Arab League Educational, Cultural & Scientific Organization Library

Alexandria University Central Library
163 El-Horria St, El-Shatby, Alexandria
Mailing Address: PO Box 233, El-Ibrahimia, Alexandria
Tel: (03) 4282928; (03) 4282927 *Fax:* (03) 4282927
Web Site: www.alexu.edu.eg
Founded: 1985

American University in Cairo Libraries & Learning Technologies
AUC Ave, New Cairo 11835
Mailing Address: PO Box 74, New Cairo 11835
Tel: (02) 2615-1000
E-mail: ouc@aucegypt.edu
Web Site: library.aucegypt.edu
Key Personnel
Dean, Libraries & Learning Technologies: Shahira El Sawy *Tel:* (02) 2615-3642
    E-mail: selsawy@aucegypt.edu
Head, External Service: Nermine Rifaat *Tel:* (02) 2615-3501 *E-mail:* nrifaat@aucegypt.edu

Bibliotheca Alexandrina (Library of Alexandria)
PO Box 138, Chatby, Alexandria 21526
Tel: (03) 4839999 *Fax:* (03) 4820458; (03) 4820460
E-mail: secretariat@bibalex.org; infobib@bibalex.org
Web Site: www.bibalex.org
Key Personnel
Dir: Ismail Serageldin
Founded: 2002

Cairo University Central Library
Cairo University, Giza 12613
Tel: (011) 5133-0070 (cell)
E-mail: info@cl.cu.edu.eg
Web Site: www.cl.cu.edu.eg; www.cu.edu.eg
Key Personnel
Dir: Dr Amany Ahmed Refaat
Founded: 1932

Institute of Arab Research & Studies Arab League Educational, Cultural & Scientific Organization Library
One Arab Advocates Union St, Garden City, Cairo
Mailing Address: PO Box 229, Garden City, Cairo
Tel: (02) 27951648; (02) 27922679 *Fax:* (02) 27962543
E-mail: iars@iarsecs.org
Web Site: iars.net/library
Founded: 1953

Ministry of Justice Library
Magles El Shaab St, Lazoughly, Cairo
Tel: (02) 27922263 *Fax:* (02) 27958103
E-mail: mjustice@moj.gov.eg

National Information & Documentation Center (NIDOC)
Al Tahrir St, Dokki, Cairo
Tel: (02) 3371696 *Fax:* (02) 3371697
E-mail: nidoc@nrc.sci.eg
Publication(s): *Directory of Scientific & Technical Libraries*

The National Library & Archives of Egypt
Corniche El Nile, Ramlet Boulac, Cairo
Tel: (02) 35750886; (02) 35751078 *Fax:* (02) 35789547
E-mail: darkotob7@gmail.com
Web Site: www.darelkotob.gov.eg
Key Personnel
Dir, International Relations: Ms Howayda Kamel
    E-mail: hkamel100@hotmail.com
Founded: 1870

NIDOC, see National Information & Documentation Center (NIDOC)

El Salvador

Biblioteca Central de la Universidad de El Salvador
Apdo Postal 2923, San Salvador
Tel: 22 25 02 78
E-mail: sb@biblio.ues.edu.sv
Web Site: www.ues.edu.sv
Publication(s): *Boletin* (monthly); *Lista de Acquisiciones Recientes* (monthly)

Biblioteca de la Universidad Centroamericana Jose Simeon Canas
Blvd Los Proceres, Antiguo Cuscatlan, La Libertad
Tel: 2210-6600 (ext 407) *Fax:* 2210-6657
E-mail: ofi-com@uca.edu.sv
Web Site: www.uca.edu.sv
Key Personnel
Dir General: Jacqueline Morales de Colocho
    E-mail: jmorales@uca.edu.sv
Administrative Assistant: Carlos Alberto Velasquez Alvarado *Tel:* 2210-6600 ext 280
    E-mail: cvelasquez@uca.edu.sv
Founded: 1965

Biblioteca Nacional de El Salvador Francisco Gavidia
4a Calle Ote y Av Monsenor Oscar Arnulfo Romero, No 124, San Salvador
Tel: 2221-6312
E-mail: biblioteca.nacional@cultura.gob.sv
Web Site: www.binaes.gob.sv

Biblioteca P Florentino Idoate SJ, see Biblioteca de la Universidad Centroamericana Jose Simeon Canas

Estonia

Eesti Rahvusraamatukogu (National Library of Estonia)
Tonismagi 2, 15189 Tallinn
Tel: 630 7611 *Fax:* 631 1410
E-mail: nlib@nlib.ee
Web Site: www.nlib.ee
Key Personnel
Dir General: Janne Andresoo *Tel:* 630 7600
E-mail: janne.andresoo@nlib.ee
Dir, Library Services: Kristel Veimann *Tel:* 630 7416 *E-mail:* kristel.veimann@nlib.ee
Library System Manager: Riin Olonen *Tel:* 630 7189 *E-mail:* riin.olonen@nlib.ee
The National Library of Estonia is also the Parliamentary Library of Estonia. It is the central library in the field of humanities & art.
Publication(s): *Eesti Rahvusbibliograafia: Artiklid* (The Estonian National Bibliography: Articles from Serials); *Eesti Rahvusraamatukogu: Raamatud* (The Estonian National Bibliography: Books)

Tartu Ulikooli Raamatukogu (University of Tartu Library)
W Struve 1, 50091 Tartu
Tel: 7375 702 *Fax:* 7375 701
E-mail: library@utlib.ee
Web Site: www.utlib.ee
Key Personnel
Dir: Martin Hallik *Tel:* 7375 700 *E-mail:* martin.hallik@ut.ee
Marketing Manager: Ilana Smuskina *Tel:* 7375 749 *E-mail:* ilana.smuskina@ut.ee
Founded: 1802
Membership(s): Association of European Research Libraries (LIBER); Eesti Muusikakogude Uhendus; ELNET Consortium; European Association of Health Information Libraries (EAHIL); European Information Association (EIA) & its branch for Baltic & Nordic countries; International Association of Law Libraries (IALL); International Association of Music Libraries (IAML).
Publication(s): *Eksliibrised Tartu Ulikooli Raamatukogus* (Bookplates in Tartu University Library, irregularly, 1975, four publications to introduce the collection); *Publicationes Bibliothecae Universitatis Litterarum Tartuensis* (irregularly, 1973, introduces Tartu University Library collections of manuscripts); *Raamataeg-restaureerimine* (Book-Time-Restoration, irregularly, 1969); *Raamatukogu toeid* (Publications of Tartu University Library. I-XI, 1968, Papers on the library); *Tartu (Riiklik) Uelikool* (Tartu State University, The Bibliography of Works Published, irregularly, records all the works published by university faculty & students); *Tartu Uelikooli Raamatukogu vanagraafika kogu kataloogid* (Tartu University Library collections of graphic art since 15th century, irregularly, 1974, nine publications about English, German, Flemish, Dutch, Italian & French works of graphic art); *Tartu Ulikooli*

Raamatukogu aastaraamat (Tartu University Library Yearbook, 1996, contains annual report, list of donations & research articles)

Ethiopia

Addis Ababa University Library
PO Box 1176, Addis Ababa
Tel: (011) 123-9719
E-mail: library@aau.edu.et
Web Site: www.aau.edu.et/library
Key Personnel
Librarian: Mesfin Gezahegn *E-mail:* mesfin.gabera@aau.edu.et
Founded: 1969

African Union Commission Library
Roosevelt St (Old Airport Area), PO Box 3243, W21 K19 Addis Ababa
Tel: (011) 551 77 00; (011) 551 14 20 *Fax:* (011) 551 78 44
E-mail: library@africa-union.org
Web Site: pages.au.int/auclibrary
Key Personnel
Chief Librarian & Archives Unit: Sika Frepeau *E-mail:* frepeaus@africa-union.org

AUC Library, see African Union Commission Library

British Council Library
Comoros St, Addis Ababa
Mailing Address: PO Box 143, Addis Ababa
Tel: (011) 662 0388 *Fax:* (011) 662 3315
E-mail: information@et.britishcouncil.org
Web Site: ethiopia.britishcouncil.org; www.britishcouncil.org
Founded: 1943
Specialize in provision of library & information services.

ECA Library, see United Nations Economic Commission for Africa Library (ECA)

Ethiopian National Archives & Library Agency (NALA)
PO Box 717, Addis Ababa
Tel: (011) 5516532
Web Site: www.nala.gov.et
Key Personnel
Dir General: Abreham Chosha *Tel:* (011) 5515462
Public & International Relations: Endalew Adam *Tel:* (011) 5150882
Founded: 1944

Haramaya University Library
PO Box 138, Dire Dawa
Tel: (025) 5530326 *Fax:* (025) 5530325; (025) 5530331; (025) 5530354
E-mail: library@haramaya.edu.et
Web Site: www.haramaya.edu.et/resources/library
Key Personnel
Dir, Library & Document Service: Mikyas Hailu
Founded: 1952

IES, see Institute of Ethiopian Studies Library (IES)

Institute of Ethiopian Studies Library (IES)
Addis Ababa University, Sidist Kilo Campus, Addis Ababa
Tel: (011) 123 97 39
Web Site: www.aau.edu.et/ies
Founded: 1963

Jimma University College of Agriculture & Veterinary Medicine Library
PO Box 307, Jimma
Tel: (047) 1110019 *Fax:* (047) 1110934
Web Site: www.ju.edu.et/jucavm
Key Personnel
Dean: Adugna Eneyew Bekele *E-mail:* adugna.eneyew@ju.edu.et
Founded: 1952

JUCAVM, see Jimma University College of Agriculture & Veterinary Medicine Library

John F Kennedy Memorial Library, see Addis Ababa University Library

NALA, see Ethiopian National Archives & Library Agency (NALA)

United Nations Economic Commission for Africa Library (ECA)
PO Box 3001, Addis Ababa
Tel: (011) 544-3114 *Fax:* (011) 551-4416
E-mail: libservice@uneca.org
Web Site: www.uneca.org/kss
Key Personnel
Chief Librarian: Irene Onyancha *E-mail:* ionyancha@uneca.org
Chief, Knowledge Services Section: Makane Faye *Tel:* (011) 544-3563
Founded: 1958
Publication(s): *Themes sur Le Developpement En Afrique* (Africa Development Topics, 2 times/yr)

Faroe Islands

Foroya Landsbokasavn (National Library of the Faroe Islands)
J C Svabosgotu 16, FO110 Torshavn
Mailing Address: PO Box 61, FO110 Torshavn
Tel: 34 05 25 *Fax:* 34 05 27
E-mail: savn@savn.fo
Web Site: savn.fo/00008/00045
Key Personnel
National Deputy Librarian: Annika Smith *Tel:* 34 05 11 *E-mail:* annikas@savn.fo
Founded: 1828
Publication(s): *The Faroese* (book list)

Standard Book Numbering Agency, see Foroya Landsbokasavn

Fiji

Library Services of Fiji
Government Bldgs, PO Box 2526, Suva
Tel: 3315344 *Fax:* 3314994
Web Site: www.education.gov.fj
Key Personnel
Dir: Merewalesi Vueti *E-mail:* mvueti@govnet.gov.fj
Founded: 1964
Parent Company: Ministry of Education, Heritage & Arts
Branch Office(s)
Northern Regional Library, Jaduram St, Labasa
Western Regional Library, 11 Tavewa Ave, Lautokia *Tel:* 6660091
Nadi Town Council Library, Main St, Nadi, Librarian: Anita Naidu *Tel:* 6700133

Fax: 6700131; 6701202 *E-mail:* ntclibrary@
connect.com.fj
Nausori Town Council Library, PO Box 72, Nausori *Tel:* 3476389 *E-mail:* librarian.nausoritc@
yahoo.com

National Archives of Fiji
25 Carnavon St, Suva
Mailing Address: PO Box 2125, Government
Bldgs, Suva
Tel: 3304144 *Fax:* 3307006
E-mail: archives@govnet.gov.fj
Web Site: www.archives.gov.fj; www.info.gov.fj/
archives.htm
Key Personnel
Archivist: Setareki Tale *E-mail:* stale@govnet.
gov.fj
Founded: 1954

Suva City Carnegie Library
Formerly Suva City Library
Civic Administration Bldg, 196 Victoria Parade,
Suva
Mailing Address: Suva City Council, PO Box
176, Suva
Tel: 331 3433 *Fax:* 330 4419
E-mail: enquiries@scc.org.fi
Web Site: suvacity.org/library
Key Personnel
Chief Librarian: Maureen Shariff *Tel:* 331 3433
ext 240 *Fax:* 331 6657 *E-mail:* maureen@scc.
org.fj
Founded: 1909
Publication(s): *Suva City Council* (annually, report)

Suva City Library, see Suva City Carnegie
Library

University of the South Pacific Library
Private Bag, Laucala Campus, Suva
Tel: 323 1000; 323 2402; 323 2050
E-mail: library@usp.ac.fj
Web Site: www.usp.ac.fj/library
Key Personnel
University Librarian: S Joan Yee *Tel:* 323 2282
Deputy University Librarian: Elizabeth Fong
Tel: 323 2363
Founded: 1969
Coordination Unit for Pacific Islands Marine Resources Information System (PIMRIS), Regional Center for Population Information Network (POPIN).
Publication(s): *Annual Report*; *Libraries Pa-C-Fika*; *Library News*; *PIMRIS Newsletter* (quarterly)

Finland

Aalto-yliopiston Kirjasto (Aalto University
Library)
Otaniementie 9, 02150 Espoo
Mailing Address: PL 17000, 00076 Aalto
Tel: (09) 316 1011
E-mail: infolib@aalto.fi; oppimiskeskus@aalto.fi
Web Site: otalib.aalto.fi
Key Personnel
Vice Dir: Matti Raatikainen *Tel:* (09) 373 2233
E-mail: matti.raatikainen@aalto.fr

Abo Akademis bibliotek (Abo Akademi
University Library)
Tuomiokirkonkatu 2-4, 20500 Turku
Tel: (02) 215 4180
E-mail: biblioteket@abo.fi
Web Site: www.abo.fi/library

Key Personnel
Chief Librarian: Pia Sodergard *Tel:* (02) 215 4182
E-mail: pia.sodergard@abo.fi
Deputy Chief Librarian: Maria Lassen-Seger
Tel: (02) 215 3614 *E-mail:* maria.lassen-
seger@abo.fi
Financial Secretary: Anders Ekberg *Tel:* (02) 215
4190 *E-mail:* anders.ekberg@abo.fi
Publication(s): *Skrifter utgivna av Abo Akademis
bibliotek*
Branch Office(s)
Axelia Library, Piispankatu 8, 20500 Turku, Contact: Erik Lax *Tel:* (02) 215 3203 *Fax:* (02) 215
4915 *E-mail:* axlan@abo.fi
The Arken Library, Tehtaankatu 2, 20500 Turku
Tel: (02) 215 3601 *E-mail:* arkbib@abo.fi
The ASA Library, Vanrikinkatu 3 A, 20500
Turku, Contact: Eva Costiander-Hulden
Tel: (02) 215 4192 *E-mail:* asalan@abo.fi
Biocity Library, Tykistokatu 6, 20520 Turku,
Contact: Eva Hoglund *Tel:* (02) 215 4040
E-mail: biobib@abo.fi
The Economics Library, Henrikinkatu 7,
20500 Turku, Contact: Ann-Louise Gronholm *Tel:* (02) 215 4568 *E-mail:* ann-louise.
gronholm@abo.fi
The Manuscript & Picture Unit,
Tuomiokirkonkatu 2-4, 20500 Turku, Contact: Catherine Halstrom *Tel:* (02) 215 4781
E-mail: manus@abo.fi
Theology Library, Piispankatu 16, 20500 Turku,
Contact: Airi Forssell *Tel:* (02) 215 3564
Fax: (02) 215 4835 *E-mail:* tflan@abo.fi

Eduskunnan Kirjasto (Library of Parliament,
Finland)
Aurorankatu 6, 00102 Helsinki
Tel: (09) 432 3423
E-mail: kirjasto@eduskunta.fi; library@
parliament.fi
Web Site: lib.eduskunta.fi
Key Personnel
Library Dir: Sari Pajula *Tel:* (09) 432 3401
E-mail: sari.pajula@parliament.fi
Chief Archivist: Jari Suutari *Tel:* (09) 432 3460
E-mail: jari.suutari@parliament.fi
Publication(s): *Bibliographia iuridica Fennica*

**Helsingin Kaupunginkirjasto - yleisten
kirjastojen keskuskirjasto** (Helsinki City
Library - Central Library for Public Libraries)
Rautatielaisenkatu 8, 00520 Helsinki
Mailing Address: PL 4101, 00099 Helsinki
Tel: (09) 3108511
Web Site: www.lib.hel.fi
Key Personnel
Library Dir: Tuula Haavisto *Tel:* (09) 31085500
E-mail: tuula.haavisto@hel.fi
Deputy Library Dir, Content Services: Anna-
Maria Soininvaara *Tel:* (09) 31085400
E-mail: anna-maria.soininvaara@hel.fi
Deputy Library Dir, Library & Customer Services: Saara Ihamaki *Tel:* (09) 31085503
E-mail: saara.ihamaki@hel.fi
Branch Office(s)
Arabianranta Library, Hameentie 135 A, 00560
Helsinki *Tel:* (09) 3108 5056
Etela-Haaga Library, Isonnevantie 16 B, 00320
Helsinki *Tel:* (09) 3108 5032
Herttoniemi Library, Kettutie 8 C, 00800 Helsinki
Tel: (09) 3108 5080
Itakeskus Library, Turunlinnantie 1,
00900 Helsinki *Tel:* (09) 3108 5990
E-mail: itakeskuksen_kirjasto@hel.fi
Jakomaki Library, Jakomaenpolku 3, 00770
Helsinki *Tel:* (09) 3108 5077
Kallio Library, Viides linja 11, 00530 Helsinki
Tel: (09) 3108 5053 *E-mail:* kallion_kirjasto@
hel.fi
Kannelmaki Library, Klaneettitie 5, 00420
Helsinki *Tel:* (09) 3108 5942
Kapyla Library, Vainolankatu 5, 00610 Helsinki
Tel: (09) 3108 5061

Kontula Library, Ostostie 4, 00940 Helsinki
Tel: (09) 3108 5094
Laajasalo Library, Koulutanhua 2, 00840 Helsinki
Tel: (09) 3108 5084
Lauttasaari Library, Pajalahdentie 10a, 00200
Helsinki *Tel:* (09) 3108 5020
Library 10, Elielinaukio 2 G, 00100 Helsinki
Tel: (09) 3108 5000
Malmi Library, Ala-Malmin tori 1, 00700
Helsinki
Malminkartano Library, Puustellintie 6, 00410
Helsinki
Maunula Library, Suursuonlaita 6, 00630 Helsinki
Tel: (09) 3108 5063
Munkkiniemi Library, Riihitie 22, 00330 Helsinki
Tel: (09) 310 8503
Myllypuro Media Library, Kiviparintie 2, 00920
Helsinki *Tel:* (09) 3108 5092
Oulunkyla Library, Kylanvanhimmantie 27, 00640
Helsinki
Paloheina Library, Paloheinantie 22, 00670
Helsinki *Tel:* (09) 3108 5067
Pasila Library, Kellosilta 9, 00520 Helsinki
Tel: (09) 3108 5001
Pikku Huopalahti Children's Library, Tilkankatu
19, 00300 Helsinki *Tel:* (09) 3108 0377
Pitajanmaki Library, Jousipolku 1, 00370 Helsinki
Tel: (09) 3108 5037
Pohjois-Haaga Library, Kaupintie 4, 00440
Helsinki *Tel:* (09) 3108 5040
Puistola Library, Nurkkatie 2, 00760 Helsinki
Pukinmaki Library, Kenttakuja 12, 00720
Helsinki *Tel:* (09) 3108 5072
Rikhardinkatu Library, Rikhardinkatu 3, 00130
Helsinki *Tel:* (09) 3108 5913
Roihuvuori Library, Roihuvuorentie 2, 00820
Helsinki *Tel:* (09) 3108 5082
Sakarinmaki Children's Library, Knutersintie 924,
00890 Helsinki
Suomenlinna Library, Suomenlinna C 31, 00190
Helsinki *Tel:* (09) 3108 5019
Suutarila Library, Seulastentie 11,
00740 Helsinki *Tel:* (09) 3108 5074
E-mail: suutarilan_kirjasto@hel.fi
Tapanila Library, Hiidenkiventie 21, 00730
Helsinki *Tel:* (09) 3108 5073
Tapulikaupunki Library, Ajurinaukio 5, 00750
Helsinki *Tel:* (09) 3108 5075
Toolo Library, Topeliuksenkatu 6, 00250 Helsinki
Vallila Library, Paijanteentie 5, 00550 Helsinki
Tel: (09) 3108 5055
Viikki Library, Viikinkaari 11 (Viikki Info Centre), 00790 Helsinki *Tel:* (09) 3108 5571
Vuosaari Library, Mosaiikkitori 2, 00980 Helsinki

Helsinki University Library, see Meilahden
Kampuskirjasto Terkko

Harald Herlin Learning Centre, see
Aalto-yliopiston Kirjasto

Ita-Suomen Yliopisto Kirjasto (University of
Eastern Finland Library)
Yliopistokatu 4, 80101 Joensuu
Mailing Address: PO Box 107, 80101 Joensuu
Tel: (0294) 45 8397
E-mail: library@uef.fi; kirjasto@uef.fi
Web Site: www.uef.fi/kirjasto
Key Personnel
Dir: Jarmo Saarti *Tel:* (0294) 45 8010
E-mail: jarmo.saarti@uef.fi
Assistant Dir: Helena Hamynen *Tel:* (0294) 45
8111 *E-mail:* helena.hamynen@uef.fi
Branch Office(s)
Ylipistonranta 1 E, PO Box 1627, 70211 Kuopio
Tel: (0294) 45 8400
KUH Medical Library, Puijo Hospital, Puijon-
laaksontie 2, PO Box 100, 70229 Kuopio
Tel: (0294) 45 8402
Kuninkaankartanonkatu 7, PO Box 124, 57101
Savonlinna *Tel:* (0294) 45 8404

Jyvaskylan Yliopisto Kirjasto (Jyvaskyla University Library)
Seminaarinkatu 15, Bldg B, 40014 Jyvaskylan Yliopisto
Mailing Address: PL 35, 40014 Jyvaskyla Yliopisto
Tel: (014) 260 1211 *Fax:* (014) 260 1021
E-mail: jyk@library.jyu.fi; jykneuvonta@library. jyu.fi
Web Site: kirjasto.jyu.fi; www.jyu.fi
Key Personnel
Library Dir: Teemu Makkonen *Tel:* (050) 594 6587 *E-mail:* teemu.makkonen@jamk.fi
Founded: 1863

Kansallis Kirjasto (The National Library of Finland)
University of Helsinki, Unioninkatu 36, 00014 Helsinki
Mailing Address: University of Helsinki, PL 15, 00014 Helsinki
Tel: (09) 191 22750; (09) 191 23196
E-mail: kk-palvelu@helsinki.fi
Web Site: www.kansalliskirjasto.fi
Key Personnel
Chief Librarian: Kai Ekholm *Tel:* (09) 191 22721 *E-mail:* kai.ekholm@helsinki.fi
Founded: 1640
Publication(s): *Books from Finland* (quarterly, mostly in English, but also in French & German); *The Finnish National Bibliography* (CD-ROM); *Publications of the University Library at Helsinki*
Branch Office(s)
American Resource Center *Fax:* (09) 652940 *E-mail:* arc@usembassy.fi
Slavonic Library

Kansallisarkiston kirjasto (National Archives Service of Finland)
Rauhankatu 17, 00171 Helsinki
Mailing Address: PL 258, 00171 Helsinki
Tel: (029) 533 7000 *Fax:* (09) 176 302
E-mail: kirjaamo@arkisto.fi
Web Site: www.arkisto.fi
Key Personnel
Dir General: Jussi Nuorteva
Head, Communications: Marie Pelkonen *Tel:* (029) 533 7079
Communications Officer: Marko Oja *Tel:* (029) 533 7137
Founded: 1869

Library of Statistics, see Statistics Finland Library

Meilahden Kampuskirjasto Terkko (Meilahti Campus Library Terkko)
University of Helsinki, Haartmaninkatu 4, 00014 Helsinki
Mailing Address: PO Box 61, 00014 Helsinki
Tel: (09) 191 26643 *Fax:* (09) 241 0385
E-mail: kirjasto-terkko@helsinki.fi; terkko-info@helsinki.fi
Web Site: www.helsinki.fi/library/terkko
Key Personnel
Library Dir: Kimmo Tuominen *Tel:* (09) 191 40300 *E-mail:* kimmo.tuominen@helsinki.fi
Publication(s): *MEDIC* (database)

Oulun Yliopiston Kirjasto (Oulu University Library)
PL 7500, 90014 Oulun Yliopisto
Tel: (0294) 483501
E-mail: kirjasto@oulu.fi
Web Site: www.kirjasto.oulu.fi/english
Founded: 1959
Publication(s): *Acta Universitatis Ouluensis* (publications of Oulu University Library)
Branch Office(s)
Architecture Library, Aleksanterinkatu 6, PL

4100, 90014 Oulun Yliopisto *Tel:* (0294) 484920
Medical Library, Aapistie 7 A, PL 7550, 90014 Oulun Yliopisto *Tel:* (08) 537 5144
Kajaani University Consortium Library, Ketunpolku 1, PL 240, 87101 Kajaani *Tel:* (08) 6189 9505 *E-mail:* amkkirjasto@kamk.fi

Sibelius-Akatemian Kirjasto (Sibelius Academy Library)
Musiikkitalo, Toolonlahdenkatu 16 C, 00100 Helsinki
Mailing Address: PL 39, 00097 Helsinki
Tel: (040) 7104 224; (040) 7104 223
E-mail: lib.siba@uniarts.fi
Web Site: lib.uniarts.fi
Key Personnel
Chief Librarian: Irmeli Koskimies *Tel:* (050) 526 1950
Founded: 1885

Statistics Finland Library
Tyopajakatu 13, 00580 Helsinki
Tel: (09) 1734 2220
E-mail: info@stat.fi; library@stat.fi
Web Site: www.stat.fi/tk/kk/index_en.html
Key Personnel
Dir General: Marjo Bruun *E-mail:* marjo.bruun@stat.fi
Deputy Dir General: Heli Mikkela *Tel:* (029) 551 3200 *E-mail:* heli.mikkela@stat.fi
Dir, Communication & Information Services: Hannele Orjala *Tel:* (029) 551 3582 *E-mail:* hannele.orjala@stat.fi

Tampere University Library
Kalevantie 5, 33014 Tampere
Mailing Address: PL 617, 33014 Tampere
Tel: (040) 190 9696
E-mail: kirjasto@uta.fi
Web Site: www.uta.fi/kirjasto
Key Personnel
Chief Librarian: Minna Niemi-Grundstrom *Tel:* (050) 383 8769 *E-mail:* minna.niemi-grundstrom@uta.fi
Founded: 1925

TERKKO, see Meilahden Kampuskirjasto Terkko

Turun Yliopiston Kirjasto (Turku University Library)
Hallinto, 20014 Turku
Tel: (02) 333 51
E-mail: library@utu.fi
Web Site: kirjasto.utu.fi/en
Key Personnel
Library Dir: Ulla Nygren *Tel:* (02) 333 6160 *E-mail:* ulla.nygren@utu.fi
Librarian: Mikko Pennanen *Tel:* (02) 333 5870 *E-mail:* mikko.pennanen@utu.fi
Founded: 1920
Publication(s): *Annales Universitatis Turkuensis*

France

The American Library in Paris (Bibliotheque Americaine de Paris)
10, rue du General Camou, 75007 Paris
Tel: 01 53 59 12 60
E-mail: alparis@americanlibraryinparis.org
Web Site: www.americanlibraryinparis.org
Key Personnel
Dir: Charles Trueheart *Tel:* 01 53 59 12 63 *E-mail:* trueheart@americanlibraryinparis.org
Reference Librarian: Audrey Chapuis *E-mail:* chapuis@americanlibraryinparis.org
Founded: 1920

Special Collections: Gregory Usher Cookbook Collection; Marlene Dietrich Collection.
Specialize in social sciences, humanities, US history & civilization, literary criticism.
Publication(s): *Ex Libris* (quarterly, newsletter)

Archives Nationales
59, rue Guynemer, 93383 Paris Cedex 03
Tel: 01 75 47 20 02
E-mail: an-mediasociaux@culture.gouv.fr
Web Site: www.archives-nationales.culture.gouv.fr

BDIC, see Bibliotheque de Documentation Internationale Contemporaine (BDIC)

BHVP, see Bibliotheque Historique de la Ville de Paris (BHVP)

Bibliotheque Centrale du Museum National d'Histoire Naturelle
38, rue Geoffroy St-Hilaire, 75005 Paris
Tel: 01 40 79 36 27 *Fax:* 01 40 79 36 57
E-mail: bcmweb@mnhn.fr
Web Site: bibliotheques.mnhn.fr/medias
Key Personnel
Dir: Michelle Lenoir
Secretary: Corrine Guignard *Tel:* 01 40 79 36 33 *E-mail:* corrine.guignard@mnhn.fr

Bibliotheque de Bordeaux (Bordeaux Public Library)
85 Cours du Marechal Juin, 33000 Bordeaux
Tel: 05 56 10 30 00 *Fax:* 05 56 10 30 90
E-mail: bibli@mairie-bordeaux.fr; dgac.lectpub@mairie-bordeaux.fr
Web Site: bibliotheque.bordeaux.fr; www.bordeaux.fr
Key Personnel
Dir: Serge Bouffange
Founded: 1736

Bibliotheque de Documentation Internationale Contemporaine (BDIC) (International Contemporary Documentation Library)
6, Allee de l'Universite, 92001 Nanterre Cedex
Tel: 01 40 97 79 00 *Fax:* 01 40 97 79 40
E-mail: reseignements@bdic.fr
Web Site: www.bdic.fr
Key Personnel
Dir: Valerie Tesniere *Tel:* 01 40 97 79 02
Deputy Dir: Cecile Tardy *Tel:* 01 40 97 79 69
This is a Paris inter-university library.
Publication(s): *Collection des Publications de la BDIC*

Bibliotheque de Geographie
191, rue St-Jacques, 75005 Paris
Tel: 01 44 32 14 60 *Fax:* 01 44 32 14 67
E-mail: bibgeo@univ-paris1.fr
Web Site: www.univ-paris1.fr; www.univ-paris1.fr/bibliotheque/bibgeo

Bibliotheque de la Sorbonne
13 rue de la Sorbonne, 75257 Paris Cedex 05
Tel: 01 40 46 30 97
E-mail: info@bis.sorbonne.fr
Web Site: www.bibliotheque.sorbonne.fr/biu
Key Personnel
Dir: Laurence Bobis *E-mail:* laurence.bobis@bis-sorbonne.fr
Assistant Dir: Valerie Grignoux *E-mail:* valerie.grignoux@bis-sorbonne.fr
Founded: 1762
This is a Paris inter-university library.
Branch Office(s)
Lettres et Sciences humaines

Bibliotheque de l'Arsenal
One, rue Sully, 75004 Paris
Tel: 01 53 79 39 39 *Fax:* 01 53 79 39 03
E-mail: arsenal@bnf.fr
Web Site: www.bnf.fr

Key Personnel
Dir: Olivier Bosc
Founded: 1797

Bibliotheque de l'INHA
2 rue Vivienne, 75002 Paris Cedex
Tel: 01 47 03 76 29
E-mail: info-bibliotheque@inha.fr
Web Site: www.inha.fr
Key Personnel
Dir: Anne-Elisabeth Buxtorf *E-mail:* anne-elisabeth.buxtorf@inha.fr

Bibliotheque de l'Institut de France
23, quai de Conti, 75270 Paris Cedex 06
Tel: 01 44 41 44 10 *Fax:* 01 44 41 44 11
Web Site: www.bibliotheque-institutdefrance.fr
Key Personnel
Dir & Curator: Francoise Berard
 E-mail: francoise.berard@institut-de-france.fr
Founded: 1795

Bibliotheque de Rennes Metropole (Rennes
 Public Library)
46, blvd Magenta, 35012 Rennes Cedex
Mailing Address: CS 91231, 35012 Rennes
 Cedex
Tel: 02 23 40 67 00 *Fax:* 02 23 40 67 36
E-mail: contact-bibliotheque@leschampslibres.fr
Web Site: www.bibliotheque-rennesmetropole.fr
Key Personnel
Dir: Roland Thomas
Publication(s): *Paul Feval, 1816-1887* (catalog);
 L'itinerarie de Kenneth White (catalog); *Jean
 Larcher Calligraphe* (catalog); *Henri Polles
 Collectionneur*

Bibliotheque Historique de la Ville de Paris
 (BHVP) (Historical Library of Paris)
Hotel de Lamoignon, 24 rue Pavee, 75004 Paris
Tel: 01 44 59 29 40
E-mail: bhvp@paris.fr

Bibliotheque Interuniversitaire de Montpellier
Bibliotheque Interuniversitaire, 60, rue des Etats
 Generaux, 34000 Montpellier Cedex 2
Tel: 04 67 13 43 50 *Fax:* 04 67 13 43 51
E-mail: biu.secretariat@univ-montp3.fr
Web Site: www.biu-montpellier.fr
Key Personnel
Dir: Matthieu Desachy *E-mail:* matthieu.desachy@univ-montp3.fr
This is a Paris inter-university library.

Bibliotheque Interuniversitaire de Sante, see
 BIU Sante

Bibliotheque Interuniversitaire de Sante
12, rue de l'Ecole de Medecine, 75270 Paris
Tel: 01 76 53 19 51 *Fax:* 01 76 53 19 64
E-mail: info-med@biusante.parisdescartes.fr
Web Site: www.biusante.parisdescartes.fr
Key Personnel
Dir & Chief Curator: Guy Cobolet *Tel:* 01 76
 53 19 70 *E-mail:* guy.cobolet@biusante.parisdescartes.fr
This is a Paris inter-university library.
Publication(s): *Bibliotheque de l'ancienne Faculte
 de Medecine de Paris: Catalogue des Livres
 du XVIe siecle extrait du catalogue general du
 fonds ancien; Catalogue des Periodiques de la
 Bibliotheque (1976-1981)*

**Bibliotheque Interuniversitaire des Langues et
 Civilisations**
65 rue des Grands Moulins, 75013 Paris
Tel: 01 81 69 18 00
E-mail: contact@bulac.fr
Web Site: www.bulac.fr

Key Personnel
Dir: Marie-Lise Tsagouria *E-mail:* marie-lise.tsagouria@bulac.fr
Deputy Dir: Jean-Francois Chanal *E-mail:* jean-francois.chanal@bulac.fr
Founded: 1868
This is a Paris inter-university library.

Bibliotheque Mazarine
23 Quai de Conti, 75006 Paris
Tel: 01 44 41 44 06
E-mail: contact@bibliotheque-mazarine.fr;
 webmaster@bibliotheque-mazarine.fr
Web Site: www.bibliotheque-mazarine.fr
Key Personnel
Dir & Chief Librarian: Yann Sordet *Tel:* 01 44
 41 44 66 *E-mail:* yann.sordet@bibliotheque-mazarine.fr

Bibliotheque Municipale de Besancon
One, rue de la Bibliotheque, 25000 Besancon
 Cedex
Tel: 03 81 87 81 40
E-mail: bib.etude@besancon.fr; bibliotheques@
 besancon.fr
Web Site: www.besancon.fr/index.php?=243
Key Personnel
Dir: Henry Ferreira-Lopes *E-mail:* henry.ferreira-lopes@besancon.fr
Conservateur: Marie-Claire Waille *E-mail:* marie-claire.waille@besancon.fr
Founded: 1694

Bibliotheque Municipale de Grenoble
12, Blvd du Marechal Lyautey, 38021 Grenoble
 Cedex 1
Tel: 04 76 86 21 10 *Fax:* 04 76 86 21 19
E-mail: bm.etude@bm-grenoble.fr; info@bm-grenoble.fr
Web Site: www.bm-grenoble.fr
Key Personnel
Dir: Christine Biron *Tel:* 04 76 86 21 18
 E-mail: christine.biron@bm-grenoble.fr
Publication(s): *Bibliotheque municipale de Grenoble, Catalogue general auteurs des livres imprimes jusqu'a 1900* (1980, 12 vols available
 from K G Saur, Germany)

Bibliotheque Municipale de Lyon
30 blvd Vivier-Merle, 69431 Lyon Cedex 03
Tel: 04 78 62 18 00 *Fax:* 04 78 62 19 49
E-mail: bm@bm-lyon.fr
Web Site: www.bm-lyon.fr
Key Personnel
Dir: Gilles Eboli *E-mail:* geboli@bm-lyon.fr
Founded: 1972

Bibliotheque Municipale de Nancy
43 rue Stanislas, 54042 Nancy Cedex
Mailing Address: CS 64230, 54042 Nancy Cedex
Tel: 03 83 37 38 83
E-mail: bibliotheque@nancy.fr
Web Site: www1.nancy.fr; www1.nancy.fr/
 culturelle/bibliotheques-de-nancy; www.reseau-colibris.fr
Founded: 1750

Bibliotheque Nationale de France (National
 Library of France)
Quai Francois-Mauriac, 75706 Paris Cedex 13
Tel: 01 53 79 59 59 *Fax:* 01 53 79 42 60
E-mail: reproduction@bnf.fr
Web Site: www.bnf.fr
Key Personnel
President: Laurence Engel
Dir General: Jacqueline Sanson

**Bibliotheque Nationale et Universitaire de
 Strasbourg (BNU)**
5, Rue Marechal Joffre, 67070 Strasbourg Cedex

Mailing Address: BP 51029, 67070 Strasbourg
 Cedex
Tel: 03 88 25 28 00
E-mail: contact@bnu.fr
Web Site: www.bnu.fr
Key Personnel
Administrator: Alain Colas *Tel:* 03 88 25 28 11
 E-mail: administrateur@bnu.fr
Publication(s): *Bibliographie alsacienne* (2 times/
 yr, 1970); *Catalogue critique des manuscrits
 persans; Papyrus grecs de la BNUS*

Bibliotheque Sainte-Genevieve
10, place du Pantheon, 75005 Paris
Tel: 01 44 41 97 97 *Fax:* 01 44 41 97 96
E-mail: bsgmail@univ-paris3.fr; mathias@univ-paris1.fr
Web Site: www-bsg.univ-paris1.fr
Key Personnel
Dir: Yves Peyre
This is a Paris inter-university library & public
 library.

**Bibliotheque Universitaire de Droit et Sciences
 Economiques**
11, place Carnot, CS 84232, 54042 Nancy Cedex
Tel: 03 54 50 37 20
Web Site: bu.univ-lorraine.fr/bibliotheques/droit-et-sciences-economiques

**Bibliotheque Universite d'Avignon et des Pays
 du Vaucluse**
74, rue Louis Pasteur, 84029 Avignon Cedex 1
Tel: 04 90 16 27 87
E-mail: bu@univ-avignon.fr
Web Site: www.univ-avignon.fr; bu.univ-avignon.
 fr
Key Personnel
Dir: Jacky Barbe *E-mail:* bu-direction@univ-avignon.fr

BIU Sante
4, ave de l'Observatoire, 75270 Paris Cedex 06
Tel: 01 53 73 95 22 *Fax:* 01 53 73 99 05
E-mail: info-pharma@biusante.parisdescartes.fr
Web Site: www.biusante.parisdescartes.fr
Key Personnel
Dir: Guy Cobolet *Tel:* 01 76 53 19 70
 E-mail: guy.cobolet@biusante.parisdescartes.fr
This is a Paris inter-university library.

BMG, see Bibliotheque Municipale de Grenoble

BNF, see Bibliotheque Nationale de France

BNU, see Bibliotheque Nationale et Universitaire
 de Strasbourg (BNU)

La Documentation Francaise
29 Quai Voltaire, 75007 Paris
Tel: 01 40 15 71 10 (bookshop) *Fax:* 01 40 15 67
 83
E-mail: libparis@ladocumentationfrancaise.fr
Web Site: www.ladocumentationfrancaise.fr
Founded: 1945

**Ecole Nationale Superieure des Sciences de
 l'information et des bibliotheques (ENSSIB)**
17/21 blvd du 11 Novembre 1918, 69623 Villeur-banne Cedex
Tel: 04 72 44 43 43 *Fax:* 04 72 44 43 44
E-mail: enssib@enssib.fr
Web Site: www.enssib.fr
Key Personnel
Dir: Elisabeth Noel *Tel:* 04 72 44 43 17
 E-mail: elisabeth.noel@enssib.fr
Curator: Anne-Marie Bertrand *Tel:* 04 72 44 43
 08 *E-mail:* anne-marie.bertrand@enssib.fr
Founded: 1992

Publication(s): *Bulletin des bibliotheques de France*; *Monographies en sciences de l'information et des bibliotheques* (travaux d'etude et de recherche); *Presses de l'Enssib*

ENSSIB, see Ecole Nationale Superieure des Sciences de l'information et des bibliotheques (ENSSIB)

INIST, see Institut de l'Information Scientifique et Technique (INIST)

Institut de l'Information Scientifique et Technique (INIST)
2, allee du Parc de Brabois, 54519 Vandoeuvre-les-Nancy
Mailing Address: CS 10310, 54519 Vandoeuvre-les-Nancy
Tel: 03 83 50 46 00 *Fax:* 03 83 50 46 50
E-mail: contact-utilisateur@inist.fr
Web Site: www.inist.fr
Founded: 1988
INIST-CNRS, a French scientific & technical information center, is a service unit of the French National Centre for Scientific Research (CNRS). It collects basic & applied research publications in cooperation with French & international organizations. Producer of multidisciplinary & multilingual bibliographical databases - PASCAL, FRANCIS & ARTICLE@INIST - listing documents published in most areas of science & technology, medicine, the humanities, social sciences & economics. Also acts as a scientific & technical document delivery service.
Publication(s): *Articlesciences* (1990, bibliographic database); *Francis* (1972, bibliographic database, monthly updates); *Pascal* (1973, bibliographic database, weekly updates)

Service commun de la documentation de l'Universite de Lille III
Universite de Sciences et Technologies de Lille, Cite Scientifque, 59653 Villeneuve d'Ascq Cedex
Tel: 03 20 43 44 20; 03 20 33 61 11
E-mail: bu-com@univ.lille1.fr; lilliad@univ-lille1.fr
Web Site: doc.univ-lille1.fr; www.univ-lille1.fr; www.univ-lille3.fr/bibliotheques
Key Personnel
Dir: M Julien Roche *Tel:* 03 20 43 44 10 *Fax:* 03 20 33 71 04 *E-mail:* julien.roche@univ-lille1.fr

Universite de Toulouse Le Mirail Bibliotheque Universitaire Centrale
Service Commun de la Documentation, 5, allees Antonio Machado, 31106 Toulouse Cedex 1
Mailing Address: BP 40650, 31106 Toulouse Cedex 1
Tel: 05 61 50 42 13
E-mail: bumirail@univ-tlse2.fr
Web Site: bibliotheques.univ-tlse2.fr
Key Personnel
Dir: Luc Garcia *E-mail:* scd-direction@univ-tlse2.fr

French Guiana

Institut Francais de Recherche Scientifique pour le Developpement en Cooperation (French Institute for Scientific Research for Cooperative Development)
Centre IRD de Cayenne, 275 Rte de Montabo, 97323 Cayenne Cedex
Mailing Address: BP 90165, 97323 Cayenne Cedex

Tel: 299 292 *Fax:* 319 855
E-mail: guyane@ird.fr
Web Site: guyane.ird.fr
Office of Scientific & Technical Research Overseas.
Publication(s): *La Nature et l'Homme* (irregularly)

Gabon

Bibliotheque de l'Universite Omar Bongo
BP 13131, Libreville
Tel: 01 730 000
E-mail: contact@uob.ga
Web Site: www.uob.ga
Founded: 1970
Publication(s): *Inventaire du fonds documentaire, par discipline* (annually)

DGABD, see Direction Generale des Archives Nationales, de la Bibliotheque Nationale et de la Documentation Gabonaise (DGABD)

Direction Generale des Archives Nationales, de la Bibliotheque Nationale et de la Documentation Gabonaise (DGABD) (Gabon National Archives, National Library)
PO Box 1188, 21 Libreville 88
Tel: 73 25 43; 73 28 71 *Fax:* 73 02 39; 83 28 71
Key Personnel
Librarian: Jean-Michel Moudodo
E-mail: moudodojeanmichel@yahoo.fr

The Gambia

The Gambia National Library Service Authority (GNLSA)
Reg Pye Lane, PO Box 552, Banjul
Tel: 4 226 491; 4 228 312 *Fax:* 4 223 776
E-mail: national.library@qanet.gm
Key Personnel
Dir General: Matilda Johnson
Founded: 1946

GNLSA, see The Gambia National Library Service Authority (GNLSA)

Germany

Ernst Moritz Arndt Universitaet Greifswald, Universitaetsbibliothek
Felix-Hausdorff-Str 10, 17489 Greifswald
Tel: (03834) 420-1515 *Fax:* (03834) 420-1105
E-mail: ubinfo@uni-greifswald.de
Web Site: ub.uni-greifswald.de
Key Personnel
Dir: Dr Peter Wolff *Tel:* (03834) 420-1500
E-mail: wolff@uni-greifswald.de
Founded: 1604
Publication(s): *400 Jahre neue Universitaetsbibliothek Greifswald: eine illustrierte Bibliotheksgeschichte* (book); *Handbuch der historischen Buchbestaende in Deutschland, Vol 16* (handbook); *Schaetze der schwarzen Kunst: Wiegendrucke in Griefswald* (catalog)

Badische LandesBibliothek
Erbprinzenstr 15, 76133 Karlsruhe
Tel: (0721) 175-22 22 *Fax:* (0721) 175-23 33

E-mail: servicezentrum@blb-karlsruhe.de; direktion@blb-karlsruhe.de
Web Site: www.blb-karlsruhe.de
Key Personnel
Dir: Dr Julia Hiller von Gaertringen *Tel:* (0721) 175-22 01 *E-mail:* hiller@blb-karlsruhe.de
Deputy Dir: Dr Volker Wittenauer
Founded: 1500

Bayerische StaatsBibliothek (Bavarian State Library)
Ludwigstr 16, 80539 Munich, Bavaria
Tel: (089) 28638-0; (089) 28638-2322 *Fax:* (089) 28638-2200
E-mail: direktion@bsb-muenchen.de
Web Site: www.bsb-muenchen.de
Key Personnel
General Dir: Dr Klaus Ceynowa *Tel:* (089) 28638-2206
Deputy Dir General: Dr Dorothea Sommer
Founded: 1558
Publication(s): *Bayerische Staatsbibliothek (ein Selbstportrait)*; *Jahresbericht* (annually)

Bibliothek der Universitaet Konstanz, see Universitaet Konstanz-KIM (Kommunikations-, Informations-, Medienzentrum)

Bibliothek fuer Zeitgeschichte/Library of Contemporary History
Gaisburgstr 4A, 70182 Stuttgart
Mailing Address: Postfach 10 54 41, 70047 Stuttgart
Tel: (0711) 212-4493; (0711) 212-4516 *Fax:* (0711) 236-4450; (0711) 212-4517
E-mail: bfz@wlb-stuttgart.de; information@wlb-stuttgart.de
Web Site: www.wlb-stuttgart.de/sammlungen/bibliothek-fuer-zeitgeschichte
Key Personnel
Deputy Dir, Dept of Contemporary History: Dr Hans-Christian Pust *Tel:* (0711) 212-4518 *E-mail:* pust@wlb-stuttgart.de
Head, Special Collections: Irina Renz *E-mail:* renz@wlb-stuttgart.de
Founded: 1915
This library is housed in same building as the Wuerttembergische Landesbibliothek, covering library (approximately 370,000 books & approximately 450 current periodicals), archives, documentation center for grey literature, research facilities, etc.
Publication(s): *Schriften der Bibliothek fuer Zeitgeschichte - Neue Folge*; *Stuttgarter Vortraege zur Zeitgeschichte*

Bibliotheks- und Informationssystem der Universitaet Oldenburg
Carl von Ossietzky Universitaet Oldenburg, Uhlhornsweg 49-55, 26129 Oldenburg
Tel: (0441) 798-4444 *Fax:* (0441) 798-4040
E-mail: bis-info@uni-oldenburg.de
Web Site: www.bis.uni-oldenburg.de
Key Personnel
Library Dir: Heike Andermann *Tel:* (0441) 798-4610 *E-mail:* heike.andermann@uni-oldenburg.de
Founded: 1974
Research library, scientific publishing house, media centre.

BLB, see Badische LandesBibliothek

Deutsche Nationalbibliothek (German National Library)
Adickesallee 1, 60322 Frankfurt am Main
Tel: (069) 1525-0 *Fax:* (069) 1525-1010
E-mail: info-f@dnb.de; postfach@dnb.de
Web Site: www.dnb.de
Key Personnel
Dir General: Dr Elisabeth Niggemann
Founded: 1912

National Library & National Bibliographic Agency. Houses the German Music Archive.
Publication(s): *Deutsche Nationalbibliografie* (brochure)
Branch Office(s)
Deutsche Nationalbibliothek Leipzig, Deutscher Platz 1, 04103 Leipzig, Public Relations: Annett Koschnick *Tel:* (0341) 2271-223 *Fax:* (0341) 2271-444 *E-mail:* a.koschnick@dnb.de
Deutsches Musikarchiv, Deutscher Platz 1, 04103 Leipzig, Head of Dept: Dr Ulrich Taschow *Tel:* (0341) 2271-145 *Fax:* (0341) 2271-140 *E-mail:* u.taschow@dnb.de

Deutsche Zentralbuecherei fuer Blinde zu Leipzig (DZB) (German Central Library for the Blind)
Gustav-Adolf-str 7, 04105 Leipzig
Tel: (0341) 71 13-0 *Fax:* (0341) 71 13-125
E-mail: bibliothek@dzb.de; info@dzb.de
Web Site: www.dzb.de
Key Personnel
Dir: Dr Thomas Kahlisch *Tel:* (0341) 71 13-124
E-mail: thomas.kahlisch@dzb.de
Audio Library: Jana Waldt *Tel:* (0341) 71 13-116
E-mail: jana.waldt@dzb.de
Public Relations: Ronald Krause *Tel:* (0341) 71 13-239 *E-mail:* ronald.krause@dzb.de
Scientific Library: Susanne Siems *Tel:* (0341) 71 13-115 *E-mail:* susanne.siems@dzb.de
Founded: 1894
Braille books, talking books, braille music books & nonfiction literature in print about blindness & related themes.

Deutscher Bundestag Bibliothek
Platz der Republik 1, 11011 Berlin
Tel: (030) 227-32312; (030) 227-32626 (information services); (030) 227-32621 (information services) *Fax:* (030) 227-36087
E-mail: bibliothek@bundestag.de
Web Site: www.bundestag.de/dokumente/bibliothek/index.html (German); www.bundestag.de/htdocs_e/documents/library/index.html (English)
Publication(s): *Neue Bucher und Aufsatze in der Bibliothek* (New Books & Articles in the Library, monthly)

DZB, see Deutsche Zentralbuecherei fuer Blinde zu Leipzig (DZB)

Fachhochschule Dortmund Hochschulbibliothek (University of Applied Sciences & Arts Dortmund Library)
Sonnenstr 96, A207-A208, 44139 Dortmund
Tel: (0231) 9112-306 *Fax:* (0231) 9112-666
Web Site: www.fh-dortmund.de
Key Personnel
Dir: Mario Huette *E-mail:* huette@fh-dortmund.de
Deputy Dir: Edelgard Zock *E-mail:* zock@fh-dortmund.de
Founded: 1972
Branch Office(s)
Emil-Figge-Str 44, 2 u 3 OG, Nordfluegel, 44227 Dortmund *Tel:* (0231) 755-4917 *Fax:* (0231) 755-4922
Max-Ophuels-Platz 2, Erdgeschoss, Raum E40, 44139 Dortmund *Tel:* (0231) 9112-441

Fachhochschule Stuttgart Hochschule der Medien (University of Applied Sciences School of Media)
Hochschule der Medien, Nobelstr 8, 70569 Stuttgart
Tel: (0711) 8923-2510 *Fax:* (0711) 8923-2504
E-mail: bibliothek@hdm-stuttgart.de
Web Site: www.hdm-stuttgart.de/bibliothek

Key Personnel
Dir: Erik Friedling *Tel:* (0711) 8923-2501
E-mail: friedling@hdm-stuttgart.de
Deputy Dir: Raffaela Haack *Tel:* (0711) 8923-2502 *E-mail:* haack@hdm-stuttgart.de
Founded: 1942
Information material on demand.

Herzog August Bibliothek
Lessingplatz 1, 38304 Wolfenbuettel
Mailing Address: Postfach 1364, 38299 Wolfenbuettel
Tel: (05331) 808-0 *Fax:* (05331) 808-173
E-mail: auskunft@hab.de
Web Site: www.hab.de
Key Personnel
Dir: Prof Helwig Schmidt-Glintzer *Tel:* (05331) 808-101 *Fax:* (05331) 808-134 *E-mail:* schmidt-gl@hab.de

Herzogin Anna Amalia Bibliothek
Platz der Demokratie 4, 99423 Weimar
Mailing Address: Postfach 2012, 99401 Weimar
Tel: (03643) 545-205 *Fax:* (03643) 545-829
E-mail: info-haab@klassik-stiftung.de
Web Site: www.klassik-stiftung.de/haab
Key Personnel
Dir: Dr Michael Knoche *Tel:* (03643) 545-200 *E-mail:* michael.knoche@klassik-stiftung.de
Library is part of the Klassik Stiftung Weimar.

Ibero-Amerikanisches Institut Preussischer Kulturbesitz (Ibero-American Institute Prussian Cultural Heritage)
Potsdamer Str 37, 10785 Berlin
Tel: (030) 266 45 2210 *Fax:* (030) 266 35 1550
E-mail: iai@iai.spk-berlin.de; info@iai.spk-berlin.de
Web Site: www.iai.spk-berlin.de
Key Personnel
Dir: Dr Barbara Goebel *Tel:* (030) 266 45 1300 *E-mail:* goebel@iai.spk-berlin.de
Library Dir: Peter Altekrueger *Tel:* (030) 266 45 2000 *E-mail:* altekrueger@iai.spk-berlin.de
Founded: 1930
Research institute & special library for Latin America, Spain & Portugal
Membership(s): Arbeitsgemeinschaft Deutsche Lateinamerikaforshung (ADLAF); Association of European Research Libraries (LIBER); Latin American Studies Association (LASA); Reseau Europeen d'Information et de Documentation sur l'Amerique Latine (REDIAL); Seminar on the Acquisition of Latin American Library Materials (SALALM).
Publication(s): *Biblioteca Luso-Brasileira* (book); *Bibliotheca Ibero-Americana* (book); *Ibero-Analysen* (book); *Ibero-Bibliographien* (book); *Iberoamericana* (quarterly, journal); *Estudios Indiana* (annually); *Revista Internacional de Linguistica Iberoamericana (RILI)* (2 times/yr)

Internationale Jugendbibliothek (International Youth Library)
Schloss Blutenburg, 81247 Munich
Tel: (089) 89 12 11-0 *Fax:* (089) 89 12 11-38
E-mail: info@ijb.de
Web Site: www.ijb.de
Key Personnel
Dir: Dr Christiane Raabe *Tel:* (089) 89 12 11 42 *E-mail:* direktion@ijb.de
Library Services: Jutta Reusch *Tel:* (089) 89 12 11 41 *E-mail:* juttareusch@ijb.de
Press & Public Relations: Carola Gaede *Tel:* (089) 89 12 11 30 *E-mail:* carolagaede@ijb.de
Founded: 1949
International children & youth literature, posters, original illustrations, manuscripts & handwriting. 600,000 volumes in over 130 languages & 150 current magazines.
Publication(s): *Buecherschloss* (2 times/yr)

Kommunikations-, Informations-, Medienzentrum, see Universitaet Konstanz-KIM (Kommunikations-, Informations-, Medienzentrum)

Landesbibliothek Mecklenburg-Vorpommern Guenther Uecker (State Library Mecklenburg-Vorpommern Guenther Uecker)
Johannes-Stelling-Str 29, 19053 Schwerin
Tel: (0385) 588 792-20 *Fax:* (0385) 588 792-24
E-mail: lb@lbmv.de
Web Site: www.kulturwerte-mv.de/Landesbibliothek
Key Personnel
Chief Library Dir: Dr Frank Pille *Tel:* (0385) 588 792-14 *E-mail:* pille@lbmv.de
Founded: 1779
Membership(s): Deutscher Bibliotheksverband.
Publication(s): *Ditmarsche Sammlung/Schmidtsche Bibliotek* (CD-ROM); *Gedaechtnis Des Landes: 225 Jahre Landesbibliothek Mecklenburg-Vorpommern* (225 Years State Library Mecklenburg-Vorpommern, book, 2004, History of the Library); *Geschichtliche Bibliographie von Mecklenburg* (CD-ROM); *Still-Leben: Konstellationen des Abschieds* (book, 2018)

Leipziger Staedtische Bibliotheken (Leipzig Municipal Library)
Wilhelm-Leuschner-Platz 10/11, 04107 Leipzig
Mailing Address: Postfach 100 927, 04009 Leipzig
Tel: (0341) 123-5309 *Fax:* (0341) 123-5305
E-mail: stadtbib@leipzig.de
Web Site: stadtbibliothek.leipzig.de
Key Personnel
Dir: Susanne Metz

Library of Contemporary History, see Bibliothek fuer Zeitgeschichte/Library of Contemporary History

Niedersaechsische Landesbibliothek (Lower Saxony State Library)
Waterloostr 8, 30169 Hannover
Tel: (0511) 1267-0 *Fax:* (0511) 1267-202
E-mail: information@gwlb.de
Web Site: www.nlb-hannover.de
Key Personnel
Dir: Anne May *Tel:* (0511) 1267-303 *Fax:* (0511) 1267-304 *E-mail:* direktion@gwlb.de
Deputy Dir: Dr Anne-Katrin Henkel *Fax:* (0511) 1267-369 *E-mail:* katrin.henkel@gwlb.de
Founded: 1665

Niedersaechsische Staats- und Universitaetsbibliothek Goettingen (Goettingen State & University Library)
Platz der Goettinger Sieben 1, 37073 Goettingen
Tel: (0551) 39-5231 *Fax:* (0551) 39-5222
E-mail: sekretariat@sub.uni-goettingen.de
Web Site: www.sub.uni-goettingen.de
Key Personnel
Dir: Dr Wolfram Horstmann *Tel:* (0551) 39-5210 *E-mail:* horstmann@sub.uni-goettingen.de
Deputy Dir: Dr Armin Mueller-Dreier *Tel:* (0551) 39-22402 *E-mail:* mdreier@sub.uni-goettingen.de; Dr Rupert Schaab *Tel:* (0551) 39-5214 *E-mail:* schaab@sub.uni-goettingen.de
Founded: 1734

Rheinisch-Westfaelische Technische Hochschule, see RWTH Aachen Hochschulbibliotek

Ruhr-Universitaet Bochum Universitaetbibliothek
Universitaetsstr 150, 44801 Bochum
Tel: (0234) 32-26929; (0234) 32-22351
Fax: (0234) 32-14736

E-mail: direktion-ub@rub.de; ub-information@
rub.de
Web Site: www.ub.ruhr-uni-bochum.de/ub.html
Key Personnel
University Librarian: Dr Erdmute Lapp
Tel: (0234) 32-22350 *E-mail:* erda.lapp@ruhr-
uni-bochum.de

RWTH Aachen Hochschulbibliotek
Templergraben 61, 52062 Aachen
Mailing Address: Bibliothek-RWTH Aachen,
52056 Aachen
Tel: (0241) 80-94459 *Fax:* (0241) 80-92273
E-mail: iz@bth.rwth-aachen.de
Web Site: www.rwth-aachen.de; www.bth.rwth-
aachen.de
Key Personnel
Librarian: Dr Ulrike Eich *Tel:* (0241) 80-94446
E-mail: eich@bth.rwth-aachen.de
Deputy Librarian: Stefan Bastian *Tel:* (0241) 80-
94447 *E-mail:* bastian@bth.rwth-aachen.de
Founded: 1870

Saarlaendische Universitaets -und
Landesbibliothek (Saarland University & State
Library (SULB))
Gebaeude B1 1, 66123 Saarbruecken
Mailing Address: Postfach 15 11 41, 66041 Saar-
bruecken
Tel: (0681) 302-2070; (0681) 302-3076
Fax: (0681) 302-2796
E-mail: sulb@sulb.uni-saarland.de
Web Site: www.sulb.uni-saarland.de
Key Personnel
Deputy Dir: Matthias Mueller *Tel:* (0681) 302-
2074 *E-mail:* m.mueller@sulb.uni-saarland.de
Library Dir: Prof Bernd Hagenau *Tel:* (0681)
302-2510 *E-mail:* b.hagenau@sulb.uni-saarland.
de
Founded: 1950
Academic library.
Branch Office(s)
Medizinische Bibliothek, Gebaeude 34, 66424
Homburg *Tel:* (06841) 162 6008 *Fax:* (06841)
162 6033 *E-mail:* madok@sulb.uni-saarland.de

Saechsische Landesbibliothek- Staats- und
Universitaetsbibliothek Dresden
Zellescher Weg 18, 01069 Dresden
Tel: (0351) 4677-123 *Fax:* (0351) 4677-111
Web Site: www.slub-dresden.de
Key Personnel
Dir General: Dr Thomas Buerger *E-mail:* thomas.
buerger@slub-dresden.de
Deputy Dir: Dr Achim Bonte *E-mail:* achim.
bonte@slub-dresden.de; Michael Golsch
E-mail: michael.golsch@slub-dresden.de
Publication(s): *Bibliographie Geschichte der*
Technik; *Saechsische Bibliographie*; *Tradition*
und Herausforderung

Staats- und Universitaetsbibliothek Bremen
(State & University Library Bremen Germany)
Bibliothekstr, 28359 Bremen
Tel: (0421) 218 59500 *Fax:* (0421) 218 59610
E-mail: suub@suub.uni-bremen.de
Web Site: www.suub.uni-bremen.de
Key Personnel
Library Dir: Maria Elisabeth Mueller *Tel:* (0421)
218 59400 *E-mail:* direktion@suub.uni-bremen.
de

Staats- und Universitaetsbibliothek Hamburg
Carl von Ossietzky (State & University
Library)
Von-Melle-Park 3, 20146 Hamburg
Tel: (040) 42838 2233 *Fax:* (040) 42838 3352
E-mail: auskunft@sub.uni-hamburg.de
Web Site: www.sub.uni-hamburg.de
Key Personnel
Executive Dir: Prof Gabriele Beger, PhD

Tel: (040) 42838 2211 *E-mail:* gabriele.beger@
sub.uni-hamburg.de
Deputy Executive Dir: Dr Petra Bloedorn-Meyer
Tel: (040) 42838 2227 *E-mail:* petra.bloedorn@
sub.uni-hamburg.de
Founded: 1479
All areas of science. Special collections: politics
& peace research, science of administration,
Spain & Portugal, coastal & sea fishing, lan-
guage & culture of North American Indians &
Eskimos, Hamburg.

Staatsbibliothek Bamberg (Bamberg State
Library)
Neue Residenz, Domplatz 8, 96049 Bamberg
Tel: (0951) 95503-0 *Fax:* (0951) 95503-145
E-mail: info@staatsbibliothek-bamberg.de
Web Site: www.staatsbibliothek-bamberg.de
Key Personnel
Dir: Prof Werner Taegert *Tel:* (0951) 95503-112
E-mail: werner.taegert@staatsbibliothek-
bamberg.de
Deputy Dir: Dr Stefan Knoch *Tel:* (0951) 95503-
114 *E-mail:* stefan.knoch@staatsbibliothek-
bamberg.de
Founded: 1803

Staatsbibliothek zu Berlin - Preussischer
Kulturbesitz (Berlin State Library - Prussian
Cultural Heritage)
Unter den Linden 8, 10117 Berlin
Tel: (030) 266-0
Web Site: staatsbibliothek-berlin.de
Key Personnel
Dir General: Barbara Schneider-Kempf
E-mail: barbara.schneider-kempf@sbb.spk-
berlin.de
Founded: 1661
International research library.
Publication(s): *Beitraege aus der Staatsbiblio-*
thek zu Berlin - PK (irregularly); *Bibliotheks-*
Magazin (quarterly); *International ISBN Pub-*
lishers' Directory (annually); *ISBN Newsletter*
(irregularly); *ISBN Review* (annually); *ISMN*
Newsletter (irregularly); *Kartographische Be-*
standsverzeichnisse (irregularly); *Kataloge der*
Handschriftenabteilung, Reihe 1: Handschriften
& Reihe 2: Nachlaesse (irregularly); *Kata-*
loge der Musikabteilung (irregularly); *Veroef-*
fentlichungen der Osteuropa-Abteilung (irregularly)

Stadt- und Regionalbibliothek Erfurt
Domplatz 1, 99084 Erfurt
Tel: (0361) 655-1590; (0361) 655-1554; (0361)
655-1555
E-mail: bibliothek@erfurt.de
Web Site: bibliothek.erfurt.de
Key Personnel
Dir: Dr Eberhard Kusber

SULB, see Saarlaendische Universitaets -und
Landesbibliothek

Technische Informationsbibliothek -
Leibniz-Informationszentrum Technik und
Naturwissenschaften und
Universitaetsbibliothek (German National
Library of Science & Technology - Leibniz
Information Centre for Science & Technology
& University Library)
Welfengarten 1 B, 30167 Hannover
Mailing Address: Postfach 6080, 30060 Hannover
Tel: (0511) 762-2268; (0511) 762-8989
E-mail: information@tib.eu; kundenservice@tib.
eu
Web Site: www.tib.eu
Key Personnel
Interim Dir & Head, Library Operations: Irina
Sens *Tel:* (0511) 762-3426 *E-mail:* irina.sens@
tib.eu

Communication & Marketing: Philip Schrenk
Tel: (0511) 762-17301 *E-mail:* philip.schrenk@
tib.eu
Founded: 1831 (University Library of Hannover;
Technical Information Library founded in
1959)
Document delivery.

Thueringer Universitaets- und
Landesbibliothek (Thuringian University &
State Library)
Bibliotheksplatz 2, 07743 Jena
Tel: (03641) 9-40000 *Fax:* (03641) 9-40002
Web Site: www.thulb.uni-jena.de
Key Personnel
Dir: Dr Sabine Wefers
Deputy Dir: Gabor Kuhles
Founded: 1558
Publication(s): *Keine Aenderungen*; *Thueringen -*
Bibliographic (online)
Branch Office(s)
Branch Library for Law, Economics & Social Sci-
ences, Carl-Zeiss-Str 3, 07743 Jena, Librarian:
Dr Thomas Nitzsche *Fax:* (03641) 9 40 430

ThULB, see Thueringer Universitaets- und
Landesbibliothek

TIB, see Technische Informationsbibliothek -
Leibniz-Informationszentrum Technik und
Naturwissenschaften und
Universitaetsbibliothek

ULB Muenster, see Universitaets- und
Landesbibliothek Muenster (ULB Muenster)

Universitaet Bonn
Universitaets -und Landesbibliothek, Adenauer-
allee 39-41, 53113 Bonn
Mailing Address: Postfach 2460, 53014 Bonn
Tel: (0228) 73-7352; (0228) 73-7525 *Fax:* (0228)
73-7546
E-mail: information@ulb.uni-bonn.de; ulb@ulb.
uni-bonn.de
Web Site: www.ulb.uni-bonn.de
Key Personnel
Executive Dir: Dr Renate Vogt *E-mail:* renate.
vogt@ulb.uni-bonn.de
Publication(s): *Universitaets -und Landesbiblio-*
thek Bonn

Universitaet Konstanz-KIM
(Kommunikations-, Informations-,
Medienzentrum)
Formerly Bibliothek der Universitaet Konstanz
Universitaetsstr 10, 78464 Konstanz
Tel: (07531) 88-2871
E-mail: beratung.kim@uni-konstanz.de;
sekretariat.kim@uni-konstanz.de
Web Site: www.kim.uni-konstanz.de
Key Personnel
Dir: Petra Haetscher *Tel:* (07531) 88-2800
E-mail: petra.haetscher@uni-konstanz.de
Deputy Dir: Oliver Kohl-Frey *Tel:* (07531) 88-
2802 *E-mail:* oliver.kohl@uni-konstanz.de

Universitaet Ulm Kommunikations- und
Informationszentrum
Albert-Einstein-Allee 11, 89081 Ulm
Tel: (0731) 50-30300 *Fax:* (0731) 50-22471
E-mail: kiz@uni-ulm.de
Web Site: www.uni-ulm.de/einrichtungen/kiz
Key Personnel
Head: Dr H C Stefan Wesner *Tel:* (0731) 50-
22500 *E-mail:* stefan.wesner@uni-ulm.de
Deputy Head: Thomas Nau *Tel:* (0731) 50-22464
E-mail: thomas.nau@uni-ulm.de

Universitaets und Landesbibliothek Darmstadt
(University & State Library Darmstadt)
Unit of Technische Universitaet Darmstadt
Magdalenenstr 8, 64289 Darmstadt

Tel: (06151) 16-76200; (06151) 16-76210;
(06151) 16-76211 *Fax:* (06151) 16-76201
E-mail: info@ulb.tu-darmstadt.de
Web Site: www.ulb.tu-darmstadt.de
Key Personnel
Senior Library Dir: Dr Hans-Georg Nolte-Fischer
Tel: (06151) 16-76202 *E-mail:* hans-georg.
nolte-fischer@ulb.tu-darmstadt.de
Founded: 1568
Branch Office(s)
Franziska-Braun-Str 10, 64287 Darmstadt
Tel: (06151) 16-76400; (06151) 16-76401
Fax: (06151) 16-76408
Landwehrstr 54, 64293 Darmstadt *Tel:* (06151)
16-57474
Mollerbau, Karolinenplatz 3, 64289 Darmstadt
Tel: (06151) 16-76525 *Fax:* (06151) 16-76532
(University archives)
Holzhofallee 38, 64295 Darmstadt *Tel:* (06151)
16-76500 *Fax:* (06151) 16-76507 (patient infor-
mation center)

**Universitaets- und Landesbibliothek Muenster
(ULB Muenster)** (University & Regional
Library Muenster)
Krummer Timpen 3, 48143 Muenster
Mailing Address: Postfach 8029, 48043 Muenster
Tel: (0251) 83-24 040 *Fax:* (0251) 83-28 398
E-mail: info.ulb@uni-muenster.de; sekretariat.
ulb@uni-muenster.de
Web Site: www.ulb.uni-muenster.de
Key Personnel
Dir: Dr Beate Troeger *Tel:* (0251) 83-24 022
Deputy Dir: Dr Peter te Boekhorst *Tel:* (0251)
83-24 023 *E-mail:* peter.te.boekhorst@uni-
muenster.de; Joerg Lorenz *Tel:* (0251) 83-24
050 *E-mail:* joerg.lorenz@uni-muenster.de
Founded: 1588

**Universitaets- und Landesbibliothek
Sachsen-Anhalt**
August-Bebel-Str 13/50, 06108 Halle (Saale)
Tel: (0345) 55 22000; (0345) 55 22001
Fax: (0345) 55 27140
E-mail: direktion@bibliothek.uni-halle.de;
auskunft@bibliothek.uni-halle.de
Web Site: bibliothek.uni-halle.de
Key Personnel
Dir: Anke Berghaus-Sprengel *E-mail:* anke.
berghaus-sprengel@bibliothek.uni-halle.de
Founded: 1696
Membership(s): DBV; GBV; IATUL; International
Federation of Library Associations & Institu-
tions (IFLA); LIBER.
Parent Company: Martin-Luther-Universitaet
Halle-Wittenberg

Universitaets- und Stadtbibliothek Koeln
(Cologne University & City Library)
Universitaetsstr 33, 50931 Cologne
Tel: (0221) 470-2374; (0221) 470-3312
Fax: (0221) 470-5166
E-mail: online-redaktion@uni-koeln.de
Web Site: www.ub.uni-koeln.de
Key Personnel
Dir: C Linnartz
Founded: 1920

Universitaetsbibliothek Augsburg (Augsburg
University Library)
Universitaetsstr 22, 86159 Augsburg
Tel: (0821) 598-5320; (0821) 598-5306; (0821)
598-5305 *Fax:* (0821) 598-5354
E-mail: dir@bibliothek.uni-augsburg.de
Web Site: www.bibliothek.uni-augsburg.de
Key Personnel
Dir & Head, Library: Dr Ulrich Hohoff
E-mail: ulrich.hohoff@bibliothek.uni-augsburg.
de
Founded: 1970

Universitaetsbibliothek Bamberg
Feldkirchenstr 21, 96052 Bamberg
Mailing Address: Postfach 2705, 96018 Bamberg
Tel: (0951) 863-1501 *Fax:* (0951) 863-1565
E-mail: universitaetsbibliothek@uni-bamberg.de
Web Site: www.uni-bamberg.de/ub
Key Personnel
Dir: Dr Fabian Franke *Tel:* (0951) 863-1500
E-mail: fabian.franke@uni-bamberg.de

Universitaetsbibliothek Braunschweig
(Braunschweig University Library)
Pockelsstr 13, 38106 Braunschweig
Mailing Address: Postfach 33 29, 38023 Braun-
schweig
Tel: (0531) 391-5018 (information) *Fax:* (0531)
391-5836
E-mail: ub@tu-bs.de
Web Site: www.biblio.tu-bs.de
Key Personnel
Dir: Dr Dietmar Brandes *Tel:* (0531) 391-5011
E-mail: d.brandes@tu-bs.de
Publication(s): *Veroeffentlichungen der Universi-
taetsbibliothek Braunschweig*

**Universitaetsbibliothek der Freie Universitaet
Berlin** (Free University of Berlin)
Garystr 39, 14195 Berlin
Tel: (030) 838-54224; (030) 838-51111
Fax: (030) 838-454224
E-mail: auskunft@ub.fu-berlin.de
Web Site: www.ub.fu-berlin.de
Key Personnel
Dir: Jiri Kende *Tel:* (030) 838-54256
E-mail: kende@ub.fu-berlin.de
Deputy Dir: Dr Andrea Tatai *Tel:* (030) 838-
57100 *E-mail:* tatai@ub.fu-berlin.de
Founded: 1952

**Universitaetsbibliothek der
Humboldt-Universitaet zu Berlin**
Unter den Linden 6, 10099 Berlin
Tel: (030) 2093 99370; (030) 2093 99399
Fax: (030) 2093 99311
E-mail: info@ub.hu-berlin.de
Web Site: www.ub.hu-berlin.de
Key Personnel
Dir: Dr Andreas Degkwitz *Tel:* (030) 2093 99300
E-mail: andreas.degkwitz@ub.hu-berlin.de
Deputy Dir: Imma Hendrix *Tel:* (030) 2093
99200 *E-mail:* imma.hendrix@ub.hu-berlin.de
Head, Library Administration: Gudrun von Gar-
rel *Tel:* (030) 2093 99260 *E-mail:* gudrun.von.
garrel@ub.hu-berlin.de

Universitaetsbibliothek Dortmund (Dortmund
University Library)
Vogelpothsweg 76, 44227 Dortmund
Tel: (0231) 755-4030; (0231) 755-4001
Fax: (0231) 755-4007
E-mail: oeffentlichkeitsarbeit@ub.tu-dortmund.de
Web Site: www.ub.tu-dortmund.de
Key Personnel
Dir: Joachim Kreische *Tel:* (0231) 755-4029
E-mail: joachim.kreische@ub.tu-dortmund.de
Deputy Dir: Norbert Goevert *Tel:* (0231) 755-
4051 *E-mail:* norbert.goevert@ub.tu-dortmund.
de

Universitaetsbibliothek Eichstaett-Ingolstadt
Universitaetsallee 1, 85072 Eichstaett
Tel: (08421) 93-21492
E-mail: ub-benutzung@ku.de; ub-direktion@ku.
de
Web Site: www.ku-eichstaett.de/bibliothek
Key Personnel
Dir: Dr Mary Loeffler *Tel:* (08421) 93-21331
E-mail: maria.loeffler@ku.de
Founded: 1972

Universitaetsbibliothek Erlangen-Nuernberg
Universitatstr 4, 91054 Erlangen
Tel: (09131) 85-2 21 51 *Fax:* (09131) 85-2 93 09
E-mail: ub-direktion@fau.de; ub-hb-info@fau.de
Web Site: ub.fau.de
Key Personnel
Dir: Konstanze Soellner *Tel:* (09131) 85-2 21 50
E-mail: konstanze.soellner@bib.uni-erlangen.de
Founded: 1743

Universitaetsbibliothek Freiburg
Platz der Universitat 2, 79098 Freiburg im Breis-
gau
Mailing Address: Postfach 1629, 79016 Freiburg
im Breisgau
Tel: (0761) 203-3918 *Fax:* (0761) 203-3987
E-mail: info@ub.uni-freiburg.de
Web Site: www.ub.uni-freiburg.de
Key Personnel
Senior Library Dir: Dr Antje Kellersohn
Tel: (0761) 203-3900 *E-mail:* antje.
kellersohn@ub.uni-freiburg.de

Universitaetsbibliothek Georgius Agricola
Technische Universitaet Bergakademie Freiberg,
Agricolastr 10, 09599 Freiberg
Tel: (03731) 39 29 59; (03731) 39 28 16
Fax: (03731) 39 32 89
E-mail: unibib@ub.tu-freiberg.de
Web Site: tu-freiberg.de/ub
Key Personnel
Dir: Susanne Kandler *Tel:* (03731) 39 29 49
E-mail: susanne.kandler@ub.tu-freiberg.de
Deputy Dir: Sabine Albani *Tel:* (03731) 39 32 34
E-mail: sabine.albani@ub.tu-freiberg.de
Publication(s): *Veroeffentlichungen der Bibliothek
"Georgius Agricola" der TU Bergakademie
Freiberg*
Branch Office(s)
Chemical Engineering/Energy Process Engineer-
ing, Reiche Zeche, 09599 Freiberg, Sachsen,
Contact: Sybille Irmscher *Tel:* (03731) 39 45
27 *E-mail:* sybille.irmscher@ub.tu-freiberg.de
Safety, Nonnengasse 22, 09596 Freiberg
Tel: (03731) 39 2378
Language Centre, Lessingstr 45, 09599 Freiberg,
Sachsen *Tel:* (03731) 39 26 15
Media Centre, Preufurstr 6, 09599 Freiberg, Sach-
sen *Tel:* (03731) 39 27 78
Sports Centre, Chemnitzer Str 50, 09599
Freiberg, Sachsen *Tel:* (03731) 39 29 88
University Archives, Prueferstr 6, 09596 Freiberg
Tel: (03731) 39 27 38

Universitaetsbibliothek Heidelberg (University
Library of Heidelberg)
Ploeck 107-109, 69117 Heidelberg
Mailing Address: Postfach 10 57 49, 69047 Hei-
delberg
Tel: (06221) 54 2380 *Fax:* (06221) 54 2623
E-mail: ub@ub.uni-heidelberg.de; presse@
rektorat.uni-heidelberg.de
Web Site: www.ub.uni-heidelberg.de
Key Personnel
Dir: Dr Veit Probst *E-mail:* probst@ub.uni-
heidelberg.de
Publication(s): *Bibliothek-Forschung und Praxis;
Bibliothek und Wissenschaft; Heidelberger Bib-
liothehsschriften; Neuerwerbungslisten der
Sondersammelgebiete Aegyptologie, Klassis-
che Archaeologie, Mittlere und Neuere Kun-
stgeschichte; Zeitschriftenverzeichnis Aegyp-
tologie, Klassische Archaeologie und Mittlere
und Neuere Kunstgeschichte; Heidelberger
Zeitschriftenverzeichnis*
Branch Office(s)
Im Neuenheimer Feld 368, 69120 Heidelberg
Tel: (06221) 54 4272 *Fax:* (06221) 54 4204

Universitaetsbibliothek Johann Christian Senckenberg
Bockenheimer Landstr 134-138, 60325 Frankfurt am Main
Tel: (069) 798-39205
E-mail: auskunft@ub.uni-frankfurt.de
Web Site: www.ub.uni-frankfurt.de
Key Personnel
Dir: Dr Heiner Schnelling *Tel:* (069) 798-39230 *Fax:* (069) 798-39062 *E-mail:* h.schnelling@ub.uni-frankfurt.de
Deputy Dir: Dr Angela Hausinger *Tel:* (069) 798-39229 *Fax:* (069) 798-39062 *E-mail:* a.hausinger@ub.uni-frankfurt.de

Universitaetsbibliothek Kaiserslautern
(University Library of Kaiserslautern)
Paul-Ehrlich-Str, 67663 Kaiserslautern
Tel: (0631) 205 2241 *Fax:* (0631) 205 2355
E-mail: unibib@ub.uni-kl.de
Web Site: www.ub.uni-kl.de
Key Personnel
Dir: Ralf Werner Wildermuth *Tel:* (0631) 205 2242 *E-mail:* wildermuth@ub.uni-kl.de
Deputy Dir: Klaus Rauber *Tel:* (0631) 205 2916 *E-mail:* rauber@ub.uni-kl.de
Founded: 1970

Universitaetsbibliothek Leipzig
Beethovenstr 6, 04107 Leipzig
Tel: (0341) 97 30577; (0341) 97 30500 *Fax:* (0341) 97 30599
E-mail: info@ub.uni-leipzig.de; direktion@ub.uni-leipzig.de
Web Site: www.ub.uni-leipzig.de
Key Personnel
Dir: Dr Ulrich Johannes Schneider *Tel:* (0341) 97 30501 *E-mail:* schneider@ub.uni-leipzig.de
Deputy Dir: Charlotte Bauer *Tel:* (0341) 97 30512 *E-mail:* bauer@ub.uni-leipzig.de
Founded: 1543
Branch Office(s)
Bibliothek Biowissenschaften, Talstr 35, 04103 Leipzig, Head Librarian: Eva Tannert *Tel:* (0341) 97 36783 *Fax:* (0341) 97 39245 *E-mail:* zbbio@ub.uni-leipzig.de
Bibliothek Chemie/Physik, Johannisallee 29, 04103 Leipzig, Head of Library: Johanna Zander *Tel:* (0341) 97 30630 *Fax:* (0341) 97 39253 *E-mail:* zbchemphys@ub.uni-leipzig.de
Bibliothek Deutsches Literaturinstitut Leipzig, Waechterstr 34, 04107 Leipzig, Head of Library: Birgit Neumann *Tel:* (0341) 97 30312 *E-mail:* zbdll@ub.uni-leipzig.de
Bibliothek Geographie, Johannisallee 19, 04103 Leipzig, Head of Library: Ellen Hoell *Tel:* (0341) 97 38586 *Fax:* (0341) 97 39241 *E-mail:* zbgeogr@ub.uni-leipzig.de
Bibliothek Geowissenschaften, Talstr 35, 04103 Leipzig, Head of Library: Irmtraut Zetzsche *Tel:* (0341) 97 30629 *Fax:* (0341) 97 39261 *E-mail:* zbgeowi@ub.uni-leipzig.de
Bibliothek Klassische Archaeologie und Ur- und Fruehgeschichte, Ritterstr 14, 04109 Leipzig, Head of Library: Martina Zink *Tel:* (0341) 97-30707 *E-mail:* zbarch@ub.uni-leipzig.de
Bibliothek Kunst, Dittrichring 18-20, 04109 Leipzig, Head of Library: Anja Johannsen *Tel:* (0341) 97-35547 *E-mail:* zbkunst@ub.uni-leipzig.de
Bibliothek Musik, Neumarkt 9-19, Aufgang D, Staedtisches Kaufhaus, 04109 Leipzig, Head of Library: Christine Boettcher *Tel:* (0341) 97-30478 *Fax:* (0341) 97-30479 *E-mail:* zbmus@ub.uni-leipzig.de
Bibliothek Orientwissenschaften, Schillerstr 6, 04109 Leipzig, Head of Library: Ulrich Endruschat *Tel:* (0341) 97-37117 *Fax:* (0341) 97-39243 (digifax); (0341) 97-30698 *E-mail:* zborient@ub.uni-leipzig.de
Bibliothek Rechtswissenschaft, Burgstr 27, 04109 Leipzig, Head of Library: Jutta Brauner

Tel: (0341) 97-30655 *Fax:* (0341) 97-39233 *E-mail:* zbrewi@ub.uni-leipzig.de
Bibliothek Sportwissenschaft, Jahnallee 59, 04109 Leipzig, Head of Library: Martin Kuemmerling *Tel:* (0341) 97-30663 *Fax:* (0341) 97-39238 *E-mail:* zbspowi@ub.uni-leipzig.de
Bibliothek Veterinaermedizin, An den Tierkliniken 5, 04103 Leipzig, Head of Library: Katrin Schmidt *Tel:* (0341) 97-38017 *Fax:* (0341) 97-39246 *E-mail:* zbvetmed@ub.uni-leipzig.de
Campus-Bibliothek, Universitaetsstr 3, 04109 Leipzig, Head of Library: Katharina Malkawi *Tel:* (0341) 97 30811 *Fax:* (0341) 97 39239 *E-mail:* zbcb@ub.un-leipzig.de (24 hour library)
Zentralbibliothek Medizin, Johannisalle 34, Haus L, 04103 Leipzig, Head, Open Access: Dr Astrid Vieler *Tel:* (0341) 97-14012 *E-mail:* zbmed@ub.uni-leipzig.de

Universitaetsbibliothek Mannheim
Schloss Schneckenhof West, 68131 Mannheim
Tel: (0621) 181-2948 *Fax:* (0621) 181-2939
E-mail: info@bib.uni-mannheim.de
Web Site: www.bib.uni-mannheim.de
Key Personnel
University Librarian: Dr Sabine Gehrlein *Tel:* (0624) 181-2941 *E-mail:* sabine.gehrlein@bib.uni-mannheim.de
Deputy University Librarian: Dr Annette Klein *Tel:* (0621) 181-2975 *E-mail:* annette.klein@bib.uni-mannheim.de

Universitaetsbibliothek Osnabrueck (University of Osnabrueck Library)
Alte Muenze 16/Kamp, 49074 Osnabruck
Mailing Address: Postfach 4469, 49034 Osnabruck
Tel: (0541) 969-4320; (0541) 969-4488 *Fax:* (0541) 969-4482
E-mail: info@ub.uni-osnabrueck.de; sekretariat@ub.uni-osnabrueck.de
Web Site: www.uni-osnabrueck.de; www.ub.uni-osnabrueck.de
Key Personnel
Senior Library Dir: Felicitas Hundhausen *Tel:* (0541) 969-4319 *E-mail:* felicitas.hundhausen@ub.uni-osnabrueck.de
Deputy Library Dir: Friederike Dauer *Tel:* (0541) 969-6106 *E-mail:* friederike.dauer@ub.uni-osnabrueck.de
Founded: 1974
Publication(s): *Ausstellungen Kataloge*

Universitaetsbibliothek Regensburg
Universitaetsstr 31, 93053 Regensburg
Tel: (0941) 943-3990; (0941) 943-3989 *Fax:* (0941) 943-1569
E-mail: info@bibliothek.uni-regensburg.de
Web Site: www.uni-regensburg.de/bibliothek
Key Personnel
Dir: Dr Andre Schueller-Zwierlein *E-mail:* andre.schueller-zwierlein@ur.de
Deputy Dir: Dr Albert Schroeder *E-mail:* albert.schroeder@ur.de
Public Relations & Marketing: Peter Bruensteiner *E-mail:* peter.bruensteiner@ur.de
Founded: 1964

Universitaetsbibliothek Rostock (Rostock University Library)
Albert-Einstein-Str 6, 18059 Rostock
Tel: (0381) 498-8600 *Fax:* (0381) 498-8602
E-mail: direktion.ub@uni-rostock.de
Web Site: www.uni-rostock.de; www.ub.uni-rostock.de
Key Personnel
Dir: Robert Zepf
Deputy Dir: Renate Baehker *Tel:* (0381) 498-8626 *E-mail:* renate.baehker@uni-rostock.de
Founded: 1569

Universitaetsbibliothek Tuebingen (Tuebingen University Library)
Wilhelmstr 32, 72074 Tuebingen
Tel: (07071) 29-72846
E-mail: info-zentrum@ub.uni-tuebingen.de
Web Site: www.ub.uni-tuebingen.de
Key Personnel
Dir: Dr Marianne Doerr *Tel:* (07071) 29-72505 *E-mail:* marianne.doerr@ub.uni-tuebingen.de
Deputy Dir: Dr Eberhard Pietzch *Tel:* (07071) 29-72584 *E-mail:* eberhard.pietzch@ub.uni-tuebingen.de
Founded: 1477

Universitaetsbibliothek Wuerzburg (Wuerzburg University Library)
Am Hubland, 97074 Wuerzburg
Tel: (0931) 31 85906; (0931) 31 85945; (0931) 31 85943 *Fax:* (0931) 31 85970
E-mail: direktion@bibliothek.uni-wuerzburg.de; information@bibliothek.uni-wuerzburg.de
Web Site: www.bibliothek.uni-wuerzburg.de
Key Personnel
Dir: Hans-Guenter Schmidt *Tel:* (0931) 31 85942 *E-mail:* hans-guenter.schmidt@bibliothek.uni-wuerzburg.de
Publication(s): *Verzeichnis auf Anfrage*

Universitaetsbibliothek Wuppertal
Gaubstr 20, 42119 Wuppertal
Mailing Address: Postfach 10 01 27, 42001 Wuppertal
Tel: (0202) 439-2705 *Fax:* (0202) 439-2695
E-mail: information@bib.uni-wuppertal.de
Web Site: www.bib.uni-wuppertal.de
Key Personnel
Dir: Uwe Stadler *Tel:* (0202) 439-2691
Branch Office(s)
Campus Haspel, Haspeler Str 27, Gebaeude HA, 42285 Wuppertal
Campus Freudenberg, Rainer-Gruenter-Str 21, Gebaeude FBZ, 42119 Wuppertal

Walther-Schuecking-Institut fuer Internationales Recht an der Universitaet Kiel
Christian-Albrechts-Universitaet zu Kiel, Westring 400, 24118 Kiel
Tel: (0431) 880 2367; (0431) 880 2153 *Fax:* (0431) 880 1619
E-mail: fb.internat-recht@ub.uni-kiel.de; uno@internat-recht.uni.kiel.de
Web Site: www.uni-kiel.de/internat-recht
Key Personnel
Dir: Dr Thomas Giegerich *Tel:* (0431) 880 2189 *E-mail:* tgiegerich@internat-recht.uni-kiel.de
Publication(s): *German Yearbook of International Law*; *Veroeffentlichungen des Walther-Schuecking-Instituts fuer Internationales Recht* (series)

Wuerttembergische Landesbibliothek
Konrad-Adenauer-Str 8, 70173 Stuttgart
Mailing Address: Postfach 10 54 41, 70047 Stuttgart
Tel: (0711) 212-4454; (0711) 212-4468; (0711) 212-4424 *Fax:* (0711) 212-4422
E-mail: direktion@wlb-stuttgart.de; information@wlb-stuttgart.de
Web Site: www.wlb-stuttgart.de
Key Personnel
Dir: Dr Hamnsjoerg Kowark *Tel:* (0711) 212-4423 *E-mail:* kowark@wlb-stuttgart.de
Deputy Dir: Dr Martina Luell *Tel:* (0711) 212-4421 *E-mail:* luell@wlb-stuttgart.de
Founded: 1765
Regional library for the state of Baden-Wurttemberg, currently comprised of 4.65 million media items.

Publication(s): *Ausstellungs- und Bestandskata-loge*
Branch Office(s)
Gaisburgstr 4a, 70182 Stuttgart

ZBW, see ZBW - Deutsche Zentralbibliothek fuer Wirtschaftswissenschaften - Leibniz Informationszentrum Wirtschaft

ZBW - Deutsche Zentralbibliothek fuer Wirtschaftswissenschaften - Leibniz Informationszentrum Wirtschaft (German National Library of Economics - Leibniz Information Center for Economics)
Duesternbrooker Weg 120, 24105 Kiel
Tel: (0431) 8814-555 *Fax:* (0431) 8814-520
E-mail: info@zbw.eu; zbw@zbw.eu
Web Site: www.zbw.eu
Key Personnel
Dir: Dr Klaus Tochtermann *Tel:* (0431) 8814-333
    E-mail: director@zbw.eu
Founded: 1919
Worldwide economics special library. Also provides document delivery services.
Publication(s): *ECONIS* (Database of references to literature in economics & adjacent subjects); *Thesaurus der ZBW*
Branch Office(s)
Neuer Jungfernstieg 21, 20354 Hamburg
    Tel: (040) 42834-219 *Fax:* (040) 42834-450

Zentral- und Landesbibliothek Berlin (ZLB)
    (Central & Regional Library of Berlin)
Bluecherplatz 1, 10961 Berlin
Tel: (030) 90226-401
E-mail: info@zlb.de
Web Site: www.zlb.de
Key Personnel
Management Dir: Volker Heller *Tel:* (030) 90226-351 *E-mail:* board@zlb.de
Founded: 1995
Full library & information services.

ZLB, see Zentral- und Landesbibliothek Berlin (ZLB)

Ghana

Balme Library, see University of Ghana Library

British Council Library
Bank Rd, Kumasi
Mailing Address: PO Box KS 1996, Kumasi
Tel: 3220-23462; 3220-30820
E-mail: infoghana@gh.britishcouncil.org
Web Site: www.britishcouncil.org/ghana
Key Personnel
Dir: Lilliana Biglou
Founded: 1943
Branch Office(s)
11 Liberia Rd, PO Box GP771, Accra *Tel:* 3026-10090

GAINS, see Ghana Agricultural Information Network System

Geological Survey Department Library
7th Ave, West Ridge, Accra
Mailing Address: PO Box M 80, Accra
Tel: (021) 679236; (021) 679237; (021) 679239; (021) 228079; (021) 224676 *Fax:* (021) 679238; (021) 224676; (021) 228063
E-mail: ghgeosur@ghana.com; ghgeophy@hotmail.com; info@gsd.ghanamining.org

Key Personnel
Regional Dir: Solomon Anum
Founded: 1913

Ghana Agricultural Information Network System
CSIR-INSTI, PO Box M 32, Accra
Tel: (020) 7416169 *Fax:* (021) 763523
E-mail: egy28@yahoo.co.uk
Key Personnel
Dir: Joel Sam *E-mail:* jsam@workmail.com
Founded: 1991

Ghana Institute of Management & Public Administration Library
PO Box AH 50, Achimota, Accra
Tel: (021) 401681; (021) 401682; (021) 401683
    Fax: (021) 404664
E-mail: info@gimpa.edu.gh; library@gimpa.edu.gh
Web Site: www.gimpa.edu.gh

Ghana Library Authority
Formerly Ghana Library Board
Thorpe Rd off High St, Accra
Tel: (057) 138 8401
E-mail: abrahamyebuah@gmail.com
Web Site: www.facebook.com/accracentrallibrary
Founded: 1946

Ghana Library Board, see Ghana Library Authority

Ghana Statistical Service
PO Box 1098, Accra
Tel: (021) 682661; (021) 932401 *Fax:* (021) 664304
E-mail: info@statsghana.gov.gh
Web Site: www.statsghana.gov.gh
Founded: 1948
Collection, compilation, analysis, publication & dissemination of statistical information.

GIMPA, see Ghana Institute of Management & Public Administration Library

Institute of African Studies Library
University of Ghana, PO Box LG 73, Legon
Tel: (030) 2213850
E-mail: iasgen@ug.edu.gh; iasdsec@ug.edu.gh
Web Site: ias.ug.edu.gh
Key Personnel
Librarian: Olive Adjah *E-mail:* oadjah@ug.edu.gh
Founded: 1961
Publication(s): *Research Review* (magazine)

KNUST Library, see Kwame Nkrumah University of Science & Technology Library

Kwame Nkrumah University of Science & Technology Library
PMB University Post Office, Kumasi
Tel: 3220-60199 *Fax:* 3220-60358
E-mail: library@knust.edu.gh
Web Site: library.knust.edu.gh; www.knust.edu.gh
Key Personnel
University Librarian: Dr Samuel Kotei Nikoi
    Tel: 3220-60133
Founded: 1961

George Padmore Research Library on African Affairs
Thorpe Rd, off High St, Accra
Mailing Address: PO Box 663, Accra
E-mail: padmorelibrary@gmail.com
Key Personnel
Resident Librarian: James K Naabah *Tel:* (026) 8768677
Founded: 1961

Publication(s): *Ghana National Bibliography* (annually)
Parent Company: Ghana Library Authority

UCC Library, see University of Cape Coast Library

University of Cape Coast Library
University of Cape Coast, Cape Coast
Tel: (021) 32440; (021) 32480 *Fax:* (021) 32484
E-mail: info@ucclib.edu.gh
Web Site: www.ucc.edu.gh
Founded: 1962
Membership(s): Consortium of Academic & Research Libraries of Ghana (CARLIGH).

University of Ghana Library
PO Box LG 24, Legon, Accra
Tel: (021) 512407; (021) 500581 (ext 3162)
E-mail: admin@libr.ug.edu.gh; balme@ug.gn.apc.org
Web Site: balme.ug.edu.gh; library.ug.edu.gh; www.ug.edu.gh
Key Personnel
University Librarian: Prof Ellis E Badu
Founded: 1948

Gibraltar

Garrison Library, see Gibraltar Garrison Library

Gibraltar Garrison Library
2, Library Ramp, Gibraltar
Tel: 20077418
E-mail: enquiries@gibraltargarrisonlibrary.gi
Web Site: www.ggl.gi
Key Personnel
Dir: Dr Jennifer Ballantine Perera *E-mail:* j.ballantine@gibraltargarrisonlibrary.gi
Research & Collection Management: Chris Tavares *E-mail:* chris.tavares@gibraltargarrisonlibrary.gi
Founded: 1793

Gibraltar Library Service, see John Mackintosh Hall Library

John Mackintosh Hall Library
308 Main St, Gibraltar
Tel: 20078000
E-mail: jmhlibrary@culture.gov.gi
Key Personnel
Dir: Angela Bula
Librarian: Kimberley Pecino
Founded: 1964
Free lending library set up under will of late John Mackintosh, mainly adult fiction & nonfiction. Now incorporating the Gibraltar Library Service.

Greece

Academy of Athens Library
28, Panepistimiou Ave, 106 79 Athens
Tel: 210 3664790; 210 3664700 *Fax:* 210 3643067; 210 3634806
E-mail: library@academyofathens.gr
Web Site: www.academyofathens.gr
Key Personnel
President: Vasilios Ch Petrakos

Deputy Chief Dir: Eirini Tsouri *E-mail:* etsouri@
academyofathens.gr
Head Librarian: Eleni Mastrogergiou *Tel:* 210
3664795 *E-mail:* mastroge@academyofathens.
gr

Aristotle University of Thessaloniki Library
University Campus, 541 24 Thessaloniki
Tel: 2310991603; 2310995354 *Fax:* 2310995322
E-mail: libraryweb@lib.auth.gr
Web Site: www.lib.auth.gr
Key Personnel
Dir: Nasta Aikaterini *Tel:* 2310995325
  E-mail: nasta@lib.auth.gr
Founded: 1927
Contains resources for the region of Macedonia,
  from antiquity to the present, in Greek & other
  languages.
Total Titles: 150,000 Print

British Council Library & Resource Centre
17 Kolonaki Sq, 106 73 Athens
Tel: 2103692333 *Fax:* 2103630675
E-mail: customerservices@britishcouncil.gr
Web Site: www.britishcouncil.org/greece
Key Personnel
Dir: Tony Buckby
Founded: 1939
Branch Office(s)
43 Tsimiski str, 546 23 Thessaloniki
  Fax: 2310241960

**Central Library of National Technical
  University of Athens**
Zografou Campus 9 Heroon, Polytechniou Ave,
  157 73 Zografos, Athens
Tel: 2107723878; 2107722229 *Fax:* 2107721565
E-mail: library@central.ntua.gr
Web Site: www.lib.ntua.gr
Key Personnel
Deputy Dir: Kouri Stavroula *Tel:* 2107721579
  E-mail: roula@central.ntua.gr
Founded: 1836

K Th Dimaras Library, see The Science &
  Technology Library of the NHRF

Eugenides Foundation Technical Library
Syngrou 387, 175 64 Athens
Tel: 2109469600 *Fax:* 2109417372
E-mail: admin@eugenfound.edu.gr; lib@eef.edu.
  gr
Web Site: www.eugenfound.edu.gr
Key Personnel
Librarian: Hara Brindesi
Founded: 1966

Gennadius Library
61 Souidias St, 106 76 Athens
Tel: 2107210536 *Fax:* 2107237767
E-mail: gen-recep@ascsa.edu.gr
Web Site: www.ascsa.edu.gr/gennadius
Key Personnel
Dir: Maria Georgopoulou
  E-mail: mgeorgopoulou@ascsa.edu.gr
Librarian: Irini Solomonidi *E-mail:* isolomonidi@
  ascsa.edu.gr
Founded: 1926
Publication(s): *Gennadeion Monographs*; *Gen-
  nadeion News* (2 times/yr); *The New Griffon*
  (in Greek)

**Library & Information Center University of
  Crete**
University Campus, 741 00 Rethymnon, Crete
Tel: 28310 77810; 28310 77800 *Fax:* 28310
  77850
E-mail: libr@lib.uoc.gr
Web Site: www.lib.uoc.gr

Key Personnel
Dir: Emmanuel Koukourakis *Tel:* 28310 77805
  E-mail: manolis@lib.uoc.gr
Acquisitions Librarian: Kalli Karadaki *Tel:* 28310
  77808 *E-mail:* karadaki@lib.uoc.gr

Library of the Technical Chamber of Greece
23-25 Lekka Str, 105 62 Athens
Tel: 2103291701; 2103291717 *Fax:* 2103237525
E-mail: tee_lib@tee.gr
Web Site: portal.tee.gr/portal/page/portal/library
Founded: 1927

National Library of Greece (Ethnike Bibliotheke
  tes Hellados)
32 Panepistimious St, 106 79 Athens
Tel: 2103382500; 2103382600 *Fax:* 2103608246
Web Site: www.nlg.gr
Key Personnel
Dir General: Dr Philip Tsimpoglou
  Tel: 2103392092
Founded: 1828

**The Science & Technology Library of the
  NHRF**
National Hellenic Research Foundation, 48 Vas-
  sileos Constantinou Av, 116 35 Athens
Tel: 2107273710; 2107273939 *Fax:* 2107246618
E-mail: eie@eie.gr
Web Site: www.eie.gr/library-en.html
Key Personnel
Dir: Dr Evi Sahini *Tel:* 2107273902
  E-mail: easachin@ekt.gr
Founded: 1958

Guatemala

Archivo General de Centro America
4 ave 7-41 zona 1, 01001 Guatemala City
Tel: 2232-3037
E-mail: agcasecretaria@yahoo.com
Founded: 1968

**Biblioteca Central de la Universidad de San
  Carlos**
Edificio Recursos Educativos, Ciudad Universi-
  taria Zona 12, Guatemala City
Tel: 2418 7880
Web Site: www.usac.edu.gt; biblioteca.usac.edu.gt
Key Personnel
Contact: Lidey Magaly Portillo
  E-mail: jefaturabibliotecacentral@usac.edu.gt
Founded: 1967
Publication(s): *Boletin Bibliografico*; *Boletin Con-
  tenidos*

Biblioteca Nacional de Guatemala (National
  Library of Guatemala)
5 ave, 7-26, Zona 1, Guatemala City
Tel: 22322443
E-mail: bibliotecanacional@mcd.gob.gt
Web Site: mcd.gob.gt/biblioteca-nacional
Key Personnel
Dir: Ilonka Matute
Founded: 1879

Guinea

Bibliotheque Nationale de Guinee (National
  Library of Guinea)
BP 561, Conakry

Key Personnel
Dir General: Mohamed Camara
Founded: 1958

Guyana

National Library of Guyana
76/77 Church & Main Sts, Georgetown
Tel: (02) 227-4053
Founded: 1909
Publication(s): *Guyanese National Bibliography*

Haiti

**Bibliotheque Haitienne des Freres de
  l'Instruction Chretienne (BHFIC)**
Institution St Louis de Gonzague, 180, Rue du
  Centre, HT6110 Port-au-Prince
Mailing Address: BP 1758, HT6110 Port-au-
  Prince
Tel: 37 70 9642
E-mail: bhfic1912@gmail.com
Founded: 1912

Bibliotheque Nationale d'Haiti (National
  Library of Haiti)
193 rue du Centre, Port-au-Prince
Fax: 22 23 87 73
Key Personnel
Dir General: Emmanuel Menard
Founded: 1939
Membership(s): ACURIL; BIEF.

Holy See (Vatican City)

Biblioteca Apostolica Vaticana (Vatican
  Apostolic Library)
Cortile del Belvedere, 00120 Vatican City
Tel: (06) 698 79411 *Fax:* (06) 698 84795
Web Site: www.vaticanlibrary.va
Key Personnel
Librarian of the Holy Roman Church: Msgr Jean-
  Louis Brugues
Prefect: Msgr Cesare Pasini *Tel:* (06) 698 79400
  Fax: (06) 698 85327
Vice Prefect: Dr Ambrogio M Piazzoni *Tel:* (06)
  698 79481 *Fax:* (06) 698 85804
Dir, Manuscripts Dept: Dr Paolo Vian
Dir, Numismatic Dept: Dr Eleanora Giampiccolo
  Tel: (06) 698 79406
Dir, Printed Books Dept: Dr Timothy Janz
  Tel: (06) 698 79470
Founded: 1451

Honduras

Biblioteca Nacional de Honduras, see Biblioteca
  Nacional Juan Ramon Molina

Biblioteca Nacional Juan Ramon Molina
Av Miguel de Cervantes, FM1100 Tegucigalpa
Tel: 2222-8577
Founded: 1880

National Library of Honduras, see Biblioteca Nacional Juan Ramon Molina

Universidad Nacional Autonoma de Honduras Sistema Bibliotecario
Blvd Suyapa Ciudad Universitaria, FM1100 Tegucigalpa, MDC
Tel: 2232-2110
E-mail: info@unah.edu.hn
Web Site: www.unah.edu.hn
Publication(s): *Boletin del Sistema Bibliotecario*

Hong Kong

British Council Library
3 Supreme Court Rd, Admirality, Hong Kong
Tel: 2913 5100 *Fax:* 2913 5102
E-mail: enquiries@britishcouncil.org
Web Site: www.britishcouncil.hk
Key Personnel
Dir: Li Bode
Founded: 1948

Chinese University of Hong Kong Library System
Shatin, New Territories
Tel: 3943 7305; 3943 7306
E-mail: library@cuhk.edu.hk
Web Site: www.lib.cuhk.edu.hk; library.cuhk.edu.hk
Key Personnel
University Librarian: Louise Jones *Tel:* 3943 7318
E-mail: louisejones@lib.cuhk.edu.hk
Deputy University Librarian: Maria Lau
E-mail: maria@lib.cuhk.edu.hk
Founded: 1963
Branch Office(s)
Architecture Library *Tel:* 3943 6599 *E-mail:* arl@lib.cuhk.edu.hk *Web Site:* www.lib.cuhk.edu.hk/en/libraries/arl
Chung Chi College Elisabeth Luce Moore Library *Tel:* 3943 6969 *E-mail:* ccl@lib.cuhk.edu.hk *Web Site:* www.lib.cuhk.edu.hk/en/libraries/ccl
Lee Quo Wei Law Library *Tel:* 3943 8641 *E-mail:* law@lib.cuhk.edu.hk *Web Site:* www.lib.cuhk.edu.hk/en/libraries/law
Li Ping Medical Library *Tel:* 2632 2459 *E-mail:* mel@lib.cuhk.edu.hk *Web Site:* www.lib.cuhk.edu.hk/en/libraries/mel
New Asia College Chien Mu Library *Tel:* 3943 7655 *E-mail:* nal@lib.cuhk.edu.hk *Web Site:* www.lib.cuhk.edu.hk/en/libraries/nal
United College WuChung Multimedia Library *Tel:* 3943 7564 *E-mail:* ucl@lib.cuhk.edu.hk *Web Site:* www.lib.cuhk.edu.hk/en/libraries/ucl

Hong Kong Public Libraries
Leisure & Cultural Services Dept, 1-3 Pai Tau St, Sha Tin, Hong Kong
Tel: 2414 5555; 2921 0208
E-mail: enquiries@lcsd.gov.hk
Web Site: www.hkpl.gov.hk
Key Personnel
Assistant Dir: Rochelle Lau Shuk-Fan *Tel:* 2601 8945
Provide free public library services through a network of 66 static libraries & 10 mobile library vans.

Pao Yue-Kong Library
Hung Hom, Kowloon
Tel: 2766 6863
E-mail: lbinf@polyu.edu.hk
Web Site: www.polyu.edu.hk; www.lib.polyu.edu.hk

Key Personnel
Executive Officer: Pauline Lai *Tel:* 2766 6855
E-mail: lbplai@polyu.edu.hk
University Librarian: Dr Shirley C W Wong
Tel: 2766 6856 *E-mail:* shirley.cw.wong@polyu.edu.hk
Founded: 1972
Publication(s): *Hongkongiana* (index to selected Hong Kong periodicals electronic database)
Parent Company: The Hong Kong Polytechnic University

University of Hong Kong Libraries
University of Hong Kong, Main Library, Pokfulam
Tel: 3917 2203 *Fax:* 2559 5045; 2517 4615
E-mail: libis@hku.hk
Web Site: lib.hku.hk
Key Personnel
Librarian: Peter Sidorko *Tel:* 3917 2200
E-mail: peters@hku.hk
Acting Deputy Librarian: Dr Y C Wan *Tel:* 3917 8056 *E-mail:* ycwan@hku.hk
Administration: Melissa So *Tel:* 3917 2206
E-mail: melissas@hku.hk
Founded: 1912
Publication(s): *The University of Hong Kong Libraries Publications Series*

Hungary

Bibliotheca Ecclesiae Metropolitanae Strigoriensis (Library of the Esztergom Cathedral)
Pazmany Peter u 2, Esztergom 2500
Tel: (033) 510-130
E-mail: bibliotheca@bibliotheca.hu
Web Site: www.bibliotheca.hu
Key Personnel
Manager: Katalin Szalai *E-mail:* szalai.katalin@bibliotheca.hu

BME OMIKK, see Budapesti Muszaki es Guzdasagtudomanyi Egyetem Orszagos Muszaki Informacios Kozpont es Konyvtar

Budapesti Corvinus Egyetem Kozponti Konyvtar (Central Library of Corvinus University of Budapest)
Kozraktar u 4-6, Budapest 1093
Tel: (01) 482-7023 *Fax:* (01) 482-7072
E-mail: tajek@uni-corvinus.hu; kolcson@uni-corvinus.hu
Web Site: www.lib.uni-corvinus.hu
Key Personnel
Dir General: Zsuzsanna Nagy *Tel:* (01) 482-7078
E-mail: zsuzsanna.nagy@uni-corvinus.hu

Budapesti Muszaki es Guzdasagtudomanyi Egyetem Orszagos Muszaki Informacios Kozpont es Konyvtar (Budapest University of Technology & Economics, National Technical Information Centre & Library)
Budafoki u 4-6, Budapest 1111
Mailing Address: PF 91, Budapest 1518
Tel: (01) 463-3534; (01) 463-1069; (01) 463-3489
Fax: (01) 463-2440
E-mail: info@omikk.bme.hu; tajekoztatas@omikk.bme.hu
Web Site: www.omikk.bme.hu
Key Personnel
Dir General: Bela Liszkay *E-mail:* bliszkay@omikk.bme.hu
Founded: 1848

Debreceni Egyetem Egyetemi es Nemzeti Konyvtar (University & National Library, University of Debrecen)
Egyetem Sq 1, Debrecen 4032
Mailing Address: PO Box 39, Debrecen 4010
Tel: (052) 410-443 *Fax:* (052) 410-443
E-mail: info@lib.unideb.hu; office@lib.unideb.hu
Web Site: www.lib.unideb.hu
Key Personnel
Dir General: Gyongyi Karacsony
Founded: 2001

Fovarosi Szabo Ervin Konyvtar (Ervin Szabo Metropolitan Library)
Szabo Ervin ter 1, Budapest 1088
Tel: (01) 411-5000; (01) 411-5009; (01) 411-5066
E-mail: info@fszek.hu; kktitkar@fszek.hu
Web Site: www.fszek.hu
Key Personnel
Dir General: Dr Peter Fodor *Tel:* (01) 411-5001
E-mail: titkar@fszek.hu

Koezponti Statisztikai Hivatal Koenyvtar es Leveltar (Hungarian Central Statistical Office, Library & Archive)
Keleti Karoly u 5, Budapest 1024
Tel: (01) 345-6036; (01) 345-6390 *Fax:* (01) 345-6112
E-mail: konyvtar@ksh.hu; ref@ksh.hu
Web Site: www.ksh.hu; lib.ksh.hu
Key Personnel
Dir General: Fulop Agnes *Tel:* (01) 345-6104
E-mail: agnes.fulop@ksh.hu
Founded: 1867
Publication(s): *Magyarorszag toerteneti helysegnevtara 1773-1808* (Historical Gazetteer of Hungary, annually); *Statisztikai adatforrasok bibliografia* (Special Bibliographies-Sources of Statistical Data Bibliography, every 5 yrs); *Toerteneti statisztikai fuezetek* (Papers on Historical Statistics, irregularly); *Toerteneti statisztikai tanulmanyok* (Studies on Historical Statistics, irregularly)

Magyar Nemzeti Leveltar (MNL) (Hungarian National Archives)
Becsi kapu ter 2-4, Budapest 1014
Mailing Address: PO Box 3, Budapest 1250
Tel: (01) 225-2800; (01) 225-2844 *Fax:* (01) 225-2817
E-mail: info@mnl.gov.hu
Web Site: mnl.gov.hu
Founded: 1756
Publication(s): *Leveltari Kozlemenyek* (Archival Publications, 2 times/yr, 1923, academical & scholar); *Magyar Orszagos Leveltar Kiadvanyai* (Publications of National Archives of Hungary, 2 times/yr)

Magyar Tudomanyos Akademia Koenyvtara (Library of the Hungarian Academy of Sciences)
Arany Janos u 1, Budapest 1051
Mailing Address: PF 1002, Budapest 1245
Tel: (01) 411-6100 *Fax:* (01) 331-6954
E-mail: mtak@konyvtar.mta.hu
Web Site: konyvtar.mtak.hu
Key Personnel
Dir General: Istvan Monok *Tel:* (01) 411-6302
E-mail: monok.istvan@konyvtar.mta.hu
Deputy Dir General: Dora Kalydy *Tel:* (01) 411-6292 *E-mail:* kalydy.dora@konyvtar.mta.hu
Founded: 1826
Publication(s): *Budapest Oriental Reprints Ser A & Ser B* (irregularly, scientific monographs); *Catalog Collection*; *Oriental Manuscripts*; *Oriental Studies* (irregularly, scientific monographs); *Publicationes Bibliothecae Academiae*

Scientiarum Hungaricae (irregularly, scientific monographs); *Teka Series*
Branch Office(s)
Szechenyi Istvan ter 9, Budapest 1051 *Tel:* (01) 411-6143 *E-mail:* acadarchiv@kunyvtar.mta.hu

MNL, see Magyar Nemzeti Leveltar (MNL)

Orszagos Szechenyi Konyvtar (National Szechenyi Library)
Budavari Palota F epulet, Budapest 1827
Tel: (01) 224 3700; (01) 224-3845 (reference); (01) 224-3848 (reference) *Fax:* (01) 202-0804
E-mail: bibliogr@oszk.hu
Web Site: www.oszk.hu
Key Personnel
Dir General: Dr Laszlo Tuske *E-mail:* director@oszk.hu
Founded: 1802
National Center for Library Science & Methodology, Hungarian national ISBN & ISDS Center.
Publication(s): *A magyar irodalom es irodalomtudomany bibliografaja* (Bibliography of Hungarian Literature & Literary Studies); *Az Orszagos Szechenyi Konyvtar evkoenyve* (National Szechenyi Library Year Book); *Hungariaka informacio* (Hungaria Information); *Magyar nemzeti bibliografia Idoszaki kiadvanyok bibliografiaja* (Hungarian National Bibliography of Serials); *Magyar nemzeti bibliografia. Idoszaki kiadvanyok repertoriuma* (Hungarian National Bibliography. Repertory of Periodicals); *Magyar nemzeti bibliografia Konyvek bibliografiaja* (Hungarian National Bibliography of Books); *Magyar nemzeti bibliografia. Zenemuvek bibliografiaja* (Hungarian National Bibliography of Music Scores & Records); *Mikrofilmek cimjegyzeke. Idoszaki kiadvanyok* (List of Microfilm Titles. Periodical Publications); *Mikrofilmek cimjegyzeke. Szines grafikai plakatok* (List of Microfilm Titles. Colored Graphic Posters); *Mikrofilmek cimjegyzeke. Zenei gyujtemeny. Zenemukeziratok* (List of Microfilm Titles. Music Collection. Music Manuscripts)

Sarospataki Reformatus Kollegium Tudomanyos Gyujtemenyeinek Nagykonyvtara (The Scientific Collection of the Reformed College Sarospatak)
Rakoczi ut 1, Sarospatak, Borsod-Abauj-Zemplen 3950
Tel: (047) 311-057 *Fax:* (047) 311-057
E-mail: reftud@iif.hu
Web Site: www.patakarchiv.hu
Founded: 2006
Membership(s): Association of Ecclesiastical Libraries; Association of Hungarian Librarians.

Szegedi Tudomanyegyetem Klebelsberg Kuno Koenyvtar (University of Szeged Klebelsberg Library)
Ady ter 10, Szeged 6722
Tel: (062) 546-633
E-mail: info@ek.szte.hu; ref@bibl.u-szeged.hu
Web Site: ww2.bibl.u-szeged.hu; www.u-szeged.hu
Key Personnel
Administrator: Eva Balog *Tel:* (062) 546-641
E-mail: mtmt@ek.szte.hu
Publication(s): *Acta Bibliothecaria*; *Koenyvtartoerteneti Fuezetek* (History of Libraries series, with German summaries)

SZTE Klebelsberg Koenyvtar, see Szegedi Tudomanyegyetem Klebelsberg Kuno Koenyvtar

Universitats-und Nationalbibliothek der Universitat Debrecen, see Debreceni Egyetem Egyetemi es Nemzeti Konyvtar

Iceland

Bokasafn Menntavisindasvios Haskola Islands (School of Education Library, University of Iceland)
u/Stakkahlid, 105 Reykjavik
Tel: 525 5930; 525 4511 (information) *Fax:* 525 5597
E-mail: menntavisindasafn@hi.is
Web Site: bokasafn.hi.is
Key Personnel
Mng Dir: Gunnhildur Bjornsdottir *Tel:* 525 5927
E-mail: gunnh@hi.is
Founded: 1908

Borgarbokasafn Reykjavikur (Reykjavik City Library)
Tryggvagata 15, 101 Reykjavik
Tel: 411 6100 *Fax:* 411 6159
E-mail: borgarbokasafn@borgarbokasafn.is; upplysingar@borgarbokasafn.is
Web Site: www.borgarbokasafn.is
Key Personnel
Chief Librarian: Erla Kristin Jonasdottir *Tel:* 411 6130 *E-mail:* erla.kristin.jonasdottir@reykjavik.is
City Librarian: Palina Magnusdottir
E-mail: palina.magnusdottir@reykjavik.is
Founded: 1923
Branch Office(s)
Arsafn, Hraunbae 119, 110 Reykjavik *Tel:* 411 6250
Foldasafn, Grafarvogskirkju v/Fjorgny, 112 Reykjavik, Branch Manager: Brjann Birgisson *Tel:* 411 6230 *Fax:* 567 5356 *E-mail:* brjann.birgisson@reykjavik.is
Gerduberg, Gerduberg 3-5, 111 Reykjavik, Branch Manager: Solveig Arngrimsdottir *Tel:* 557 9122 *E-mail:* solveig.arngrimsdottir@reykjavik.is
Kringlusafn, v/Listabraut, 103 Reykjavik, Branch Manager: Dora Thoroddsen *Tel:* 580 6200 *E-mail:* dora.thoroddsen@reykjavik.is
Solheimarsafn, Solheimar 27, 104 Reykjavik *Tel:* 411 6160

Landsbokasafn Islands-Haskolabokasafn (National & University Library of Iceland)
Arngrimsgata 3, 107 Reykjavik
Tel: 525 5600 *Fax:* 525 5615
E-mail: upplys@landsbokasafn.is
Web Site: landsbokasafn.is
Key Personnel
National Librarian: Ingibjorg Steinunn Sverrisdottir *E-mail:* iss@landsbokasafn.is
Publication(s): *Handritasafn Landsbokasafns* (catalog of manuscripts); *Ritmennt* (annually, journal)

India

American Library
American Center, 24 Kasturba Gandhi Marg, New Delhi 110 001
Tel: (011) 2347-2000
E-mail: acsnd@state.gov
Web Site: newdelhi.usembassy.gov/americanlibrary.html
Public library.
Branch Office(s)
No 220, Anna Salai, Chennai 600 006 *Tel:* (044) 2857-4000 *E-mail:* chennairefdesk@state.gov
Web Site: chennai.usconsulate.gov
38/A Jawaharlal Nehru Rd, Kolkata 700 071 *Tel:* (033) 2288-1200 *E-mail:* kolkatapas@state.gov *Web Site:* kolkata.usconsulate.gov

The Asiatic Society of Mumbai
Town Hall, Shahid Bhagatsingh Rd, Fort, Mumbai 400 023
Tel: (022) 2660956 *Fax:* (022) 2665139
E-mail: info@asiaticsociety.org.in
Web Site: asiaticsociety.org.in
Key Personnel
President: S G Kale
Vice President: Dr Devangana Desai; Vinay Sahasrabuddhe; Dr Mangala Sirdeshpande; Dr Meena Vaishampayan
Honorary Secretary: Prof Vispi Balaporia
Founded: 1804
Publication(s): *Journal of the Asiatic Society of Mumbai*

British Council Libraries
17, Kasturba Gandhi Marg, New Delhi 110 001
Tel: (011) 42199000 *Fax:* (011) 23710717
E-mail: delhi.enquiry@in.britishcouncil.org
Web Site: www.library.britishcouncil.org.in
Key Personnel
Manager: Anu Bhardwaj
Branch Office(s)
A 503-506, 5th floor, Amrapali Lakeview Tower, Ahmedabad 380 052, Manager: Moumita Bhattacharya *Fax:* (079) 26469493 *E-mail:* mumbai.enquiry@in.britishcouncil.org
23, Prestige Takt, Kasturba Rd Cross, Bangalore 560 001, Manager: Ms Charu Sapra *Fax:* (080) 2240767 *E-mail:* chennai.enquiry@in.britishcouncil.org
C515, 5th floor. Elante Office Block, 178A Industrial & Business Park, Phase 1, Chandigarh 160 002, Manager: Bipin Kumar *E-mail:* delhi.enquiry@in.britishcouncil.org
737 Anna Salai, Chennai 600 002, Manager: V Bhuvaneswari *Fax:* (044) 42050688 *E-mail:* chennai.enquiry@in.britishcouncil.org
4th floor, St Jubilee, Plot No 1202 & 1215/A, Rd No 36, Jubilee Hills, Hyderabad 500 033, Manager: Ajay Merchant *Fax:* (040) 23483100 *E-mail:* chennai.inquiry@in.britishcouncil.org
L & T Chambers, 1st floor, 16 Camac St, Kolkata 700 017, Manager: Indrani Bhattacharyya *Fax:* (033) 22824804 *E-mail:* kolkata.customercare@in.britishcouncil.org
917/1 Ferugusson College Rd, Shivajinagar, Pune 411 004, Manager: Kajari Mitra *Fax:* (020) 41005316 *E-mail:* mumbai.enquiry@in.britishcouncil.org

Central Secretariat Library (CSL)
Dept of Culture, Govt of India, G Wing, Shastri Bhavan, New Delhi 110 001
Tel: (011) 233 84846; (011) 233 89684; (011) 233 89383 *Fax:* (011) 233 84846
E-mail: directcsl@gmail.com; mailfromcsl@gmail.com
Web Site: www.csl.nic.in
Key Personnel
Dir: Deepika Pokharna *Tel:* (011) 233 81431 ext 355 *E-mail:* deepika.pokharna@gov.in; Monali P Dhakate
Founded: 1891

CSL, see Central Secretariat Library (CSL)

Delhi Public Library
S P Mukherjee Marg, Opposite Old Delhi Railway Station, New Delhi 110 006
Tel: (011) 23962682 *Fax:* (011) 23946239
E-mail: dda@dpl.gov.in
Web Site: www.dpl.gov.in
Founded: 1951

Delhi University Library System
Central Library, New Delhi 110 007
Tel: (011) 27666428; (011) 27667185

Web Site: www.du.ac.in; crl.du.ac.in
Key Personnel
University Librarian: Dr S C Jindal
  E-mail: librarian@du.ac.in
Deputy Librarian: Dr Narender Kumar
  E-mail: narenderkumar59@yahoo.com
Founded: 1922

Gujarat Vidyapith
Near Income Tax Off, Ashram Rd, Ahmedabad
  380 014
Tel: (079) 27541148; (079) 27540746; (079)
  40016200 *Fax:* (079) 27542547
E-mail: info@gujaratvidyapith.org; registrar@
  gujaratvidyapith.org
Web Site: www.gujaratvidyapith.org
Key Personnel
Vice Chancellor: Dr Anamik Shah
  E-mail: anamik_shah@yahoo.com
Founded: 1920
Combined university, state central & public li-
  brary.

IIMA, see Indian Institute of Management
Ahmedabad (IIMA)

Indian Council of World Affairs Library
Sapru House, Barakhamba Rd, New Delhi 110
  001
Tel: (011) 2331 7246; (011) 2331 7248; (011)
  2331 7249; (011) 2331 7247 *Fax:* (011) 2331
  0638; (011) 2331 1208
Web Site: icwa.in
Key Personnel
Librarian: Mahesh Chandra Sharma *Tel:* (011)
  2335 9159 *E-mail:* librarian@icwa.in
Founded: 1955
Publication(s): *India Quarterly* (journal); *Sapru
House Papers*

**Indian Institute of Management Ahmedabad
(IIMA)**
Vikram Sarabhai Library, Vastrapur, Ahmedabad
  380 015
Tel: (079) 6632 4845; (079) 6632 4848
  Fax: (079) 2630 6896
E-mail: director@iimahd.ernet.in; librarian@
  iimahd.ernet.in
Web Site: www.iimahd.ernet.in
Key Personnel
Librarian: Dr H Anil Kumar *Tel:* (079) 6632
  4987 *E-mail:* anilkumar@iimahd.ernet.in
Founded: 1962

**Indian Institute of Technology Madras Central
Library**
Central Library, Indian Institute of Technology,
  Chennai 600 036
Tel: (044) 22574951 *Fax:* (044) 22570509
E-mail: libinfo@iitm.ac.in; librarian@iitm.ac.in
Web Site: www.cenlib.iitm.ac.in
Key Personnel
Librarian: Dr Mahendra N Jadhav
  E-mail: jadhavm@iitm.ac.in
Founded: 1959

**Institute for Social & Economic Change
Library**
Dr V K R V Rao Rd, Nagarabhavi, Bangalore
  560 072
Tel: (080) 23215468; (080) 23180507 *Fax:* (080)
  23217008
E-mail: admn@isec.ac.in; deputylibrarian@isec.
  ac.in
Web Site: www.isec.ac.in
Key Personnel
Deputy Librarian: B B Chand *Tel:* (080)
  23215468 ext 302 *E-mail:* bbchand@isec.ac.in
Founded: 1972

Madras Literary Society Library
45/16 College Rd, Nungambakkam, Chennai,
  Tamil Nadu 600 006
Tel: (044) 28279666
Founded: 1812

National Archives of India
c/o Dir General of Archives, Janpath, New Delhi
  110 001
Tel: (011) 23383436 *Fax:* (011) 23384127
E-mail: archives@nic.in
Web Site: nationalarchives.nic.in
Key Personnel
Dir General: Shri Pankaj Rag
Founded: 1891
Publication(s): *Abhilekh* (newsletter)

The National Library, India
Belvedere, Kolkata 700 027
Tel: (033) 2479 1381; (033) 2479 1384; (033)
  2479 1382; (033) 2479 1383 *Fax:* (033) 2479
  1462
E-mail: nldirector@rediffmail.com
Web Site: www.nationallibrary.gov.in
Key Personnel
Dir General: Dr Arun Kumar Chakraborty
  Tel: (033) 2479 2968
Founded: 1948
Publication(s): *India's National Library: System-
atization & Modernization*; *The National Li-
brary Newsletter*

Nehru Memorial Museum & Library (NMML)
Teen Murti Bhawan, New Delhi 110 011
Tel: (011) 23017587; (011) 23017599 *Fax:* (011)
  23793296
Web Site: www.nehrumemorial.nic.in
Key Personnel
Dir: Shri Sanjiv Mittal *Tel:* (011) 23015333 ext
  201
Research center on modern Indian history, with
  emphasis on Indian Nationalism. Large collections of newspapers, microfilms, private papers,
  institutional records, photographs & oral history recordings.

NMML, see Nehru Memorial Museum & Library
(NMML)

Pt Ravishankar Shukla University Library
Amanaka G E Rd, Raipur, Chhatisgarh 492 010
Tel: (0771) 2262540 *Fax:* (0771) 2262583
E-mail: library_prsu@rediffmail.com
Web Site: library.prsu.ac.in; www.prsu.ac.in
Key Personnel
Library & Information Services: Dr Suparna Sen-
  gupta *Tel:* (0771) 2262686
Founded: 1965

Sahitya Akademi Library (National Academy of
Letters Library)
Rabindra Bhavan, 35 Ferozeshah Rd, New Delhi
  110 001
Tel: (011) 23386626; (011) 22386627; (011)
  22386628; (011) 23387064 (secretary)
  Fax: (011) 23382428
E-mail: secretary@sahitya-akademi.gov.in
Web Site: sahitya-akademi.gov.in
Key Personnel
Librarian: Sufian Ahmad *Tel:* (011) 23387386
  E-mail: librarian@sahitya-akademi.gov.in
Assistant Librarian: S Padmanabhan *Tel:* (011)
  23386626 ext 227; Biswajit Sinha *Tel:* (011)
  23386626 ext 231
Founded: 1954

State Central Library
15-5-580 National Highway, 9 Ashok Bazar,
  Afzalgunj, Hyderabad 500 012
Tel: (040) 24600107
Founded: 1891

University of Mumbai Library
Rajabai Tower Bldg, Fort Campus, Mumbai 400
  032
Tel: (022) 22673621
Web Site: mu.ac.in/portal/services/library
Key Personnel
Assistant Librarian: Anjali Kale
Founded: 1879

Vadodara Central Library
Fatepura Rd, Bajwada, Mandvi, Vadodara 390
  006
Tel: (0265) 2415713
Membership(s): Indian Library Association, New
  Delhi.

Indonesia

ANRI, see Arsip Nasional Republik Indonesia

Arsip Nasional Republik Indonesia (National
  Archives of the Republic of Indonesia)
Jl Ampera Raya, No 7, Jakarta 12560
Tel: (021) 7805851 *Fax:* (021) 7810280; (021)
  7805812
E-mail: info@anri.go.id
Web Site: www.anri.go.id
Key Personnel
Dir General: Dr Mustari Irawan
Founded: 1892

**Pusat Dokumentasi dan Informasi
  Ilmiah-Lembaga Ilmu Pengatahuan
  Indonesia** (Center for Scientific Documentation
  & Information-Institute of Sciences of
  Indonesia)
Jl Jend Gatot Subroto, kav 10, Jakarta 12710
Tel: (021) 5733465; (021) 5251063; (021)
  5250719 (library services) *Fax:* (021) 510231;
  (021) 5733467
E-mail: sek.pdii@mail.lipi.go.id
Web Site: www.pdii.lipi.go.id
Publication(s): *Baca* (Read, 6 times/yr); *Bibli-
ografi Khusus* (Special Bibliographies, irreg-
ularly); *Direktori Perpustakaan Khusus dan
Sumber Informasi di Indonesia* (Directory of
Special Libraries and Information Sources in
Indonesia, irregularly); *Indeks Laporan Peneli-
tian dan Survei* (Index of Research & Survey
Report, annually, lists of acquisitions, books
& microfiche); *Indeks Majalah Ilmiah Indone-
sia* (Index of Indonesian Learned Periodicals, 2
times/yr)

Hasanuddin University Library
Kampus Unhas Tamalanrea, Jl Perintis Ke-
  merdekaan KM 10, Makassar, Sulawesi Selatan
  90245
Tel: (0411) 586 200; (0411) 584 200 *Fax:* (0411)
  585 188
E-mail: humas@unhas.ac.id; libraryunhas@gmail.
  com
Web Site: unhas.ac.id/perpustakaan

ICALTD, see Indonesian Center for Agricultural
Library & Technology Dissemination
(ICALTD)

**Indonesian Center for Agricultural Library &
  Technology Dissemination (ICALTD)** (Pusat
  Perpustakaan dan Penyebaran Teknalogi
  Pertanian)
Jl Ir Haji Juanda No 20, Bogor 16122
Tel: (0251) 321746 *Fax:* (0251) 326561
E-mail: pustaka@litbang.deptan.go.id
Web Site: pustaka.litbang.pertanian.go.id

Founded: 1842
Publication(s): *Indonesian Agriculture Research Abstract* (2 times/yr); *Indonesian Journal of Agricultural Science (IJAS)* (2 times/yr); *Indonesian Journal of Agriculture* (2 times/yr)

Institut Teknologi Bandung Perpustakaan Pusat (Central Library, Bandung Institute of Technology)
Jl Ganesha 10, Bandung 40132
Tel: (022) 250 0089 *Fax:* (022) 250 0089
E-mail: info@lib.itb.ac.id
Web Site: www.lib.itb.ac.id
Publication(s): *ITB Journal*

PDII-LIPI, see Pusat Dokumentasi dan Informasi Ilmiah-Lembaga Ilmu Pengatahuan Indonesia

Perpustakaan Dewan Perwakilan Rakyat Republik Indonesia (Indonesia House of Representatives Library)
Jl Jenderal Gatot Subroto, Jakarta 10270
Tel: (021) 5715350
E-mail: medsos@dpr.go.id
Web Site: www.dpr.go.id
Founded: 1945
Publication(s): *Aquisition List*

Perpustakaan Nasional Republik Indonesia (National Library of Indonesia)
Jl Medan Merdeka Selatan No 11, Jakarta 10110
Tel: (021) 3154864
E-mail: info@perpusnas.go.id
Web Site: www.perpusnas.go.id
Branch Office(s)
Jl Salemba Raya No 28A, Jakarta 10430

Perpustakaan Pendidikan Nasional (National Education Library)
Dept Pendidikan Nasional Gedung A Lantai 1, Jl Jenderal Sudirman, Jakarta 10270
Tel: (021) 570 7870 *Fax:* (021) 573 1228
Founded: 1948

Perpustakaan Yayasan Hatta (Hatta Foundation Library)
Jl Laksda Adisucipto No 155, Yogyakarta 55281
Tel: (0274) 587747

Universitas Udayana Library
Kampus Bukit Jimbaran, Bali 80361
Tel: (0361) 702772; (0361) 702765 *Fax:* (0361) 702765
E-mail: info@unud.ac.id
Web Site: e-lib.unud.ac.id
Key Personnel
Head, University Library: Dr I Putu Suhartika
   E-mail: suhardharma@yahoo.com
Publication(s): *Bibliografi*

Iran

Central Library & Documentation Centre of University of Tehran
Enghelab Sq, Tehran
Mailing Address: PO Box 6575, Tehran 1417614411
Tel: (021) 61112889; (021) 66466199 *Fax:* (021) 66495388
E-mail: libpublic@ut.ac.ir
Web Site: library.ut.ac.ir
Key Personnel
Head, Library: Ali Asghar Pourezzat
   E-mail: pourezzat@ut.ac.ir
Technical Deputy Dir: Tahereh Rashidi

Founded: 1950
Membership(s): International Federation of Library Associations & Institutions (IFLA).

IRANDOC, see Iranian Research Institute for Information Science & Technology

Iranian Research Institute for Information Science & Technology
1090 Enqelab St, Tehran
Mailing Address: PO Box 13185-1371, Tehran 1315773314
Tel: (021) 66951430; (021) 66494980 *Fax:* (021) 66462254
E-mail: info@irandoc.ac.ir
Web Site: www.irandoc.ac.ir
Key Personnel
Dir: Sirous Alidousti *Tel:* (021) 66954625
   E-mail: alidousti@irandoc.ac.ir
Founded: 1968
Engaged in information sciences fields. Main activities include production & dissemination of Iranian scientific information (Persian); research on information science; Iranian dissertion abstracts (students graduated in Iran & abroad); research projects abstracts; Iranian scientific meetings & proceedings; Iranian government reports & other topics available for free online. Researchers can access the materials via the web page, periodicals & connecting to SABA intranet, a local network. They can also apply to search documents by letter or in person to the Search Unit of the library.
Publication(s): *The Abstract of Scientific & Technical Papers* (quarterly, bibliographic data & in some cases abstracts of the sci-tech articles published in Persian language journals); *Current Research in Iranian Universities and Research Centers* (quarterly, details with abstracts of the research project carried out in Iran); *Directory of Scientific Meeting Held In Iran* (quarterly, bibliographic data on the papers & lectures in the seminars held in Iran since 1989); *Dissertion Abstracts of Iranian Graduates Abroad* (quarterly, abstract of Masters & PhD dissertations of the Iranian graduates abroad since 1994); *Index to Latin periodicals available in Iranian special libraries* (journal, electronic); *Iranian Dissertion Abstracts* (quarterly, bibliographic information & abstracts of the dissertation submitted by graduate students & PhD); *Iranian Government Report* (quarterly, reports gathered from ministries & governmental research organizations); *Iranian Scholars & Experts Database* (quarterly, name & details of selected Iranian experts holding Masters & PhDs)

The Library, Museum & Documentation Center of Iran Parliament
Baharestan Sq, Tehran
Tel: (021) 3313 0911 *Fax:* (021) 3313 0920
E-mail: international@ical.ir; irl@ical.ir
Web Site: www.ical.ir
Key Personnel
Dir: Mohammad Reza Majidi
   E-mail: mrezamajidi@yahoo.com
Founded: 1912
The Parliamentary Library of Iran consists of three main buildings - two libraries & a museum. Collections of Libraries No 1 & No 2 include: manuscripts, printed books, historical & national documents, UN documents & publications, audiovisual collection, government reports & periodicals.
The library offers various services in the area of library & information, cataloging, conservation, preservation, digitization, publishing, the Internet, e-mail, print, microfilm, photocopy, writing CD-ROM, scanning, indexing of parliamentary debates, indexes, databanks & databases, technical services, purchase, donation, evaluation,

researching, exchanges, popularizing, facilitating & encouraging, compiling Muslim & Iranians history of science, accessibility, promoting the world movement on the preservation & conservation of the manuscripts as the world cultural heritage, holding conferences & ceremonies on manuscripts & other documentary heritage.
Publication(s): *Al-Shari 'a ila Istidrak al-Zari'a* (magazine); *Armaqan-e Baharestan*; *Ganjine-ye Baharestan* (The Treasure of Baharestan); *Hadith-e Eshq*; *Name-ye Baharestan* (journal); *Noskhe Pazhuhi* (Manuscripts Research, journal); *Payam-e Baharestan* (magazine)

The Organization of Libraries, Museums & Documents Center of Astan Quds Razavi
Subsidiary of AQR Cultural Council
Imam Reza Holy Shrine, Sheikh Toosi Bast, PO Box 91735-177, Mashhad, Razavi Khorasan
Tel: (0511) 2219553
E-mail: info@aqlibrary.org
Web Site: library.aqr.ir
Key Personnel
Head: Mohammad Hadi Zahedi *Tel:* (0511) 2216555 *E-mail:* mahzyarzahedi@gmail.com
Deputy Head: Jafar Darbagh Anbaran *Tel:* (0511) 2235442 *E-mail:* jdarbagha@gmail.com
Publication(s): *Library & Information Science Quarterly* (quarterly)
Ultimate Parent Company: Astan Quds Razavi (AQR) Organization

Shiraz University Central Library & Documentation Center
Shiraz University, Shiraz Eram Campus Academic Complex, Shiraz 71944
Tel: (0711) 6260011; (0711) 6134330 *Fax:* (0711) 6287301
E-mail: dir-ctr-lib@rose.shirazu.ac.ir
Web Site: shirazu.ac.ir/centlib

Tabriz University Central Library, see University of Tabriz Central Library

University of Isfahan Library
Azadi Sq, Isfahan 8174673441
Tel: (031) 37933185 *Fax:* (031) 36689918
Web Site: www.ui.ac.ir
Key Personnel
Administrator: Dr Saeid Shafieioun
   E-mail: stolu@ltr.ui.ac.ir
Founded: 1969

University of Tabriz Central Library
Central Library & Documentation Center, University of Tabriz, Tabriz 5166876393
Tel: (0411) 33294120; (0411) 33392942; (0411) 33392951
Web Site: library.tabrizu.ac.ir
Key Personnel
Dir: Dr Rasoul Zarbaghi *Tel:* (0411) 33392941
Deputy Dir: Mansour Aghazedeh Alamdari
   Tel: (0411) 33392945

Iraq

Central Library of the University of Baghdad
PO Box 47303, Al-Jadiriya, Baghdad
Tel: (01) 778 7819
E-mail: director@clib.uobaghdad.edu.iq
Web Site: www.clib.uobaghdad.edu.iq
Founded: 1959

Iraqi National Library & Archives
Bab-el-Muaddum, Baghdad

Mailing Address: PO Box 14340, Baghdad
Tel: (01) 4141303; (01) 4141314 *Fax:* (01)
4141810
E-mail: iraqnla@googlemail.com
Web Site: www.iraqnla-iq.com
Key Personnel
Dir General: Dr Saad Eskander
Founded: 1920
Publication(s): *al-Maktaba al-Arabia Journal*;
Iraqi National Bibliography (triannually)

University of Mosul Central Library
Al-Majmoa'a St, Mosul
Web Site: libcentral.uomosul.edu.iq; www.
uomosul.edu.iq
Key Personnel
Secretary-General: Mahmoud Jarjis Mohammed
Founded: 1967

University of Salahaddin Central Library
Kerkut St, Erbil, Kurdistan Region
Tel: (066) 2261693 *Fax:* (066) 2547931
Web Site: su.edu.krd
Key Personnel
Dir, International Relations: Dr Mohammed
Azeez Saeed *E-mail:* mohammed.aziz@su.edu.
krd
Library Secretary: Mohammad Mustafa Oth-
man Dzayi *Tel:* (064) 7504611637 (cell)
E-mail: mohammad.dzayi@su.edu.krd
Founded: 1968

Ireland

The Chester Beatty Library
Dublin Castle, Dublin D02 AD92
Tel: (01) 407 0750 *Fax:* (01) 407 0760
E-mail: info@cbl.ie
Web Site: www.cbl.ie
Key Personnel
Dir & Librarian: Fionnuala Croke *Tel:* (01) 407
0768
Founded: 1969
Among items on display at the Library is material
showing the development of the written word
from 2700 BC (the date of the Library's earli-
est clay tablet) down to modern times.

Boole Library, see University College Cork,
Boole Library

Central Catholic Library
74 Merrion Sq, Dublin D02 HH99
Tel: (01) 676 1264
E-mail: catholiclibrary@imagine.ie
Key Personnel
Librarian: Teresa Whitington
Founded: 1922

Dublin City Public Libraries & Archive
Administrative Headquarters, 138-144 Pearse St,
Dublin 2
Tel: (01) 674 4999
E-mail: cityarchives@dublincity.ie;
dublinstudies@dublincity.ie
Web Site: www.dublincity.ie
Headquarters of the International IMPAC Dublin
Literary Awards.
Publication(s): *A Directory of Dublin for the Year
1738*; *Directory of Graveyards in the Dublin
Area*; *Dublin Delineated*; *Dublin in Fiction: A
Selection of Novels and Stories*; *How to Trace
Your Family History: A Brief Guide to Sources
of Genealogical Research for Beginners*; *Once
Upon A Time*

James Hardiman Library, see National
University of Ireland Galway (NUI Galway)

Leabharlann Boole, see University College
Cork, Boole Library

National Archives of Ireland
Bishop St, Dublin 8
Tel: (01) 407 2300 *Fax:* (01) 407 2333
E-mail: mail@nationalarchives.ie
Web Site: www.nationalarchives.ie
Key Personnel
Dir: John McDonough
Founded: 1988

The National Library of Ireland
Kildare St, Dublin 2
Tel: (01) 603 0200 *Fax:* (01) 661 2523
E-mail: info@nli.ie
Web Site: www.nli.ie
Key Personnel
Dir: Dr Sandra Collins *Tel:* (01) 603 0244
E-mail: scollins@nli.ie
Founded: 1877
Publishes material from its collection in the
medium of folders, facsimile documents, illus-
trated booklets & books, specialist/academic
publications, education packs, postcards,
DVDs/CD-ROMs.
Publication(s): *A Bloomsday Postcard* (book);
*A Joycean Scrapbook from the National Li-
brary of Ireland* (book); *Daniel O'Connell*; *The
Dublin Scuffle* (book); *Edward MacLysaght:
A Memoir by Charles MacLysaght* (book); *Ex
Camera, 1860-1960* (book, 1990); *Faithful De-
parted: The Dublin of James Joyce's Ulysses*
(book); *Fellowship of Freedom: The United
Irishmen & the 1798 Rebellion* (CD-ROM);
*For the Safety of All: Images and Inspections
of Irish Lighthouses* (book); *From Islandbridge
to the Custom House: Four Views of 19th Century Dublin from the Brocas collection*; *From
Trinty College to the Rotunda: Four Views of
19th Century Dublin from the Brocas collection*; *Grattan's Parliament*; *Historic Dublin
Maps*; *If Ever You Go To Dublin Town* (book);
Images of Erin in the Age of Parnell (book);
*Into the Light - An Illustrated Guide to the
Photographic Collections in the National Library of Ireland* (book); *Ireland 1860-1880
from Stereo Photographs*; *Ireland from Maps*
(booklet); *The Irish Face* (booklet, 1987); *The
Irish Famine: A Documentary History* (book,
1995); *The James Joyce/Paul Leon Papers*
(book, 1992); *The Land War 1879-1903*; *The
Landed Gentry*; *Librarians, Poets & Scholars:
A Festschrift for Donall O Luanaigh* (book);
The National Library of Ireland (booklet);
*The National Library of Ireland: One Hun-
dred and Twenty Five Years* (book); *Newsplan
- Revised Edition* (book); *Padraic MacPiarais*;
Parnell: A Documentary History (book, 1991);
The Past from the Press; *Royal Roots Repub-
lican Inheritance: The Survival of the Office
of Arms* (book); *A Selection of Postcards from
the Photographic & Prints & Drawings Collections*; *Strangers to Citizens: The Irish in Europe 1600-1800* (book); *Treasures from the National Library of Ireland* (book, 1994); *Ulysses
Unbound* (book); *Works & Days: A book to
accompany The Yeats Exhibition at the National Library of Ireland* (book); *Yeats: The
Four Films* (DVD)

**National University of Ireland Galway (NUI
Galway)**
University Rd, Galway
Tel: (091) 493399 *Fax:* (091) 522394
E-mail: library@nuigalway.ie
Web Site: www.library.nuigalway.ie

Key Personnel
Chief Librarian: John Cox *Tel:* (091) 493712
E-mail: john.cox@nuigalway.ie
Founded: 1845

RCSI Library, see Royal College of Surgeons in
Ireland Library

Representative Church Body Library
Braemor Park, Churchtown, Dublin 14
Tel: (01) 492 3979
E-mail: library@ireland.anglican.org
Web Site: www.ireland.anglican.org/about/rcb-
library
Key Personnel
Librarian & Archivist: Dr Susan Hood
E-mail: susan.hood@rcbdub.org
Founded: 1931
Publication(s): *A Handlist of Church of Ireland
Parish Registers in the Representative Church
Body Library* (2015); *A Handlist of Church
of Ireland Vestry Minute Books in the Repre-
sentative Church Body Library* (2015); *Regis-
ter of Holy Trinity Church, Cork, 1643-1668*
(1998); *Register of the Cathedral Church of St
Columb, Derry, 1732-1775* (1999); *Register of
the Cathedral of St Fin Barre, Cork, 1753-1804*
(2008); *Register of the Cathedral of St Patrick,
Dublin, 1677-1869* (2007); *Register of the
Church of St Thomas, Lisnagarvey, Co Antrim,
1637-1646* (1996); *Register of the Parish of
Lexlip, Co Kildare, 1665-1778* (2001); *Register of the Parish of St Nicholas, Galway,
1792-1840* (2004); *Register of the Parish of
St Thomas, Dublin, 1750-1791* (1994); *Register
of the Parish of Shankill, Belfast, 1745-1761*
(2006); *Registers of the Parish of St Catherine, Dublin, 1636-1715* (2003); *Registers of the
Parish of St John the Evangelist, Dublin, 1619-
1699* (2000)

Royal College of Surgeons in Ireland Library
Mercer St Lower, Dublin 2
Tel: (01) 402 2407
E-mail: library@rcsi.ie; info@rcsi.ie
Web Site: www.rcsi.ie/library
Key Personnel
Librarian: Kate Kelly *Tel:* (01) 402 2412
E-mail: katekelly@rcsi.ie
Deputy Librarian: Paul Murphy *Tel:* (01) 402
2406 *E-mail:* pauljmurphy@rcsi.ie
Branch Office(s)
Beaumont Hospital Library, Beaumont Rd, Dublin
9, Contact: Catherine Lee *Tel:* (01) 809 2531
E-mail: bhlibrary@rcsi.ie

Royal Dublin Society Library
Merrion Rd, Ballsbridge, Dublin 4
Tel: (01) 240 7254; (01) 668 0866 *Fax:* (01) 660
4014
E-mail: info@rds.ie; librarydesk@rds.ie
Web Site: www.rds.ie
Key Personnel
Chief Executive: Michael Duffy
President: Matthew Dempsey
Vice President: Ms Bernie Brennan
Founded: 1731
Private society.

Trinity College Library Dublin
College Green, Dublin 2
Tel: (01) 896 1127; (01) 896 1661 *Fax:* (01) 896
3774
E-mail: dutylibrarian@tcd.ie; libraryweb@tcd.ie
Web Site: www.tcd.ie/library
Key Personnel
Librarian & College Archivist: Helen Shenton
Tel: (01) 896 1665 *E-mail:* shentonh@tcd.ie
Deputy Librarian: Jessie Shearer Kurtz *Tel:* (01)
896 1652 *E-mail:* jessie.kurtz@tcd.ie
Founded: 1592
Academic & legal deposit library.
Publication(s): *Long Room*

UCD Library, see University College Dublin
Library

University College Cork, Boole Library
College Rd, Cork
Tel: (021) 4902292 *Fax:* (021) 4273428
E-mail: library@ucc.ie
Web Site: booleweb.ucc.ie
Key Personnel
Dir, Information Services: John FitzGerald
　Tel: (021) 4902281 *E-mail:* j.fitzgerald@ucc.ie
Dir, Library Services: Colette McKenna
　Tel: (021) 4902492 *E-mail:* cmckenna@ucc.ie
Founded: 1983

University College Dublin Library
Belfield, Dublin 4
Tel: (01) 716 7583 *Fax:* (01) 283 7068
E-mail: library@ucd.ie
Web Site: www.ucd.ie/library
Key Personnel
Deputy Head/Research Service Manager: Julia Barrett *Tel:* (01) 716 7356 *E-mail:* julia.
　barrett@ucd.ie
University Librarian: John B Howard *Tel:* (01)
　716 7067 *E-mail:* john.b.howard@ucd.ie
Education.

Israel

Aranne Library, see Ben-Gurion University of
the Negev Aranne Library

**Bar-Ilan University Libraries & Information
System**
c/o Wurzweiler Central Library, Bar-Ilan University, Box 90000, 5290002 Ramat-Gan
Tel: (03) 5317955
E-mail: hadracha.centralib@biu.ac.il; intlib@mail.
　biu.ac.il
Web Site: www.biu.ac.il/lib
Key Personnel
Dir: Rachel Kedar, PhD *Tel:* (03) 5318486
　E-mail: rochelle.kedar@biu.ac.il
Founded: 1955
Publication(s): *Hebrew Subject Headings for Use
　in Cataloging* (online); *Index to Literary Supplements of the Daily Hebrew Press* (internal
　online)

Beit Ha'am Municipal Library
11 Bezalel St, 94591 Jerusalem
Tel: (02) 6234168
E-mail: lvolga@jerusalem.muni.il
Specialize in dramatic theatre, music & music
　performance.

**Ben-Gurion University of the Negev Aranne
Library**
PO Box 653, 8410501 Beer-Sheva
Tel: (08) 6461402 *Fax:* (08) 6472940
E-mail: yaatz@bgu.ac.il
Web Site: in.bgu.ac.il/aranne
Key Personnel
Library Dir: Ilona Geller *Tel:* (08) 6461432
　E-mail: igeller@bgu.ac.il
Founded: 1965

CAHJP, see The Central Archives for the History
of the Jewish People (CAHJP)

**The Central Archives for the History of the
Jewish People (CAHJP)**
Hebrew University of Jerusalem, Edmond J Safra
Campus, Giv'at Ram, 91390 Jerusalem

Mailing Address: PO Box 39077, 91390
　Jerusalem
Tel: (02) 6586249 *Fax:* (02) 6535426
E-mail: cahjp@nli.org.il
Web Site: cahjp.huji.ac.il
Founded: 1939

**Central Library for the Blind, Visually
Impaired & Handicapped**
4, Hahistadrut St, 9423005 Netanya
Tel: (09) 8617874 *Fax:* (057) 7970997
E-mail: office@clfb.org.il
Web Site: www.clfb.org.il
Key Personnel
Chairman: Zvi Engel
Chief Executive Officer: Amos Be'er
Library Dir: Abigail Raz
Branch Office(s)
66 Moshe Dayan St, Yad-Eliyahu, Tel Aviv
　Tel: (09) 8617874 ext 2 *Fax:* (03) 6315577
　E-mail: lea@clfb.org.il

Central Library of Agricultural Science
Hebrew University of Jerusalem, PO Box 12,
76100 Rehovot
Tel: (08) 9489269 *Fax:* (08) 9361348
Web Site: www.agri.huji.ac.il
Key Personnel
Dir: Susana Gurman *Tel:* (08) 9489906
　E-mail: suzanag@savion.huji.ac.il
Branch Office(s)
Lubetzky-Americus Library of Veterinary
　Medicine *E-mail:* itay@savion.huji.ac.il

Israel State Archives
Mount Artom 14, Hozuim Mount
Mailing Address: Prime Minister's Office, Qiryat
　Ben-Gurion, 91950 Jerusalem
Tel: (02) 5680612; (02) 5680662; (02) 5680673;
　(02) 5680675; (02) 5680680 *Fax:* (02) 5680670
E-mail: research@archives.gov.il
Web Site: www.archives.gov.il
Key Personnel
State Archivist: Dr Yaakov Lazovik
Dir: Ms Ruti Avramovitz *Tel:* (02) 5680680
　E-mail: ruti@archives.gov.il
Founded: 1949
Publication(s): *Commemorative Series: The Presidents & Prime Minsters of Israel*; *Documents
　on the Foreign Policy of Israel* (series)

Knesset Library
The Knesset, Kiryat Ben-Gurion, 91950
　Jerusalem
Tel: (02) 6496043
E-mail: irena_v@mail1.knesset.gov.il
Web Site: www.knesset.gov.il/main/eng/home.asp
Founded: 1950

**Library of Agricultural, Food &
Environmental Quality Sciences**, see Central
Library of Agricultural Science

The National Library of Israel
Hebrew University of Jerusalem, Edmond J Safra
　Campus, Giv'at Ram, 91390 Jerusalem
Mailing Address: PO Box 39105, 91390
　Jerusalem
Tel: (02) 7336336 *Fax:* (02) 7336122
E-mail: archives@nli.org.il
Web Site: www.huji.ac.il; web.nli.org.il
Key Personnel
Dir: Oren Weinberg *Tel:* (02) 6584651
　E-mail: oren.weinberg@nli.org.il
Founded: 1892
Publication(s): *Kiryat Sefer* (quarterly, bibliographical); *RAMBI: The Index of Articles on
　Jewish Studies* (online)

**Younes & Soraya Nazarian Library, University
of Haifa**, see University of Haifa, The Library

Pevsner Central Library
54 Pevsner St, 31053 Haifa
Tel: (04) 8667766; (04) 8667768
E-mail: pevznerlib@haifa.muni.il
Founded: 1934

Shaar Zion Library
Beit Ariela, 25 Sderot Sha'ul HaMelech, 6436725
　Jaffa, Tel Aviv
Tel: (03) 6910141-5
E-mail: beitariela@tel-aviv.gov.il
Web Site: www.tel-aviv.gov.il/live/education/
　pages/public-libraries.aspx
Founded: 1922

Sourasky Central Library, see Tel Aviv
University Sourasky Central Library

**Technion-Israel Institute of Technology
Libraries**
Elyachar Central Library, Technion City, 3200003
　Haifa
Tel: (04) 8292507; (04) 8292513 *Fax:* (04)
　8295662
E-mail: edulib@technion.ac.il; reflib@tx.technion.
　ac.il
Web Site: library.technion.ac.il
Key Personnel
Dir: Dalia Dolev *E-mail:* ddalia@tx.technion.ac.il
Founded: 1924

Tel Aviv University Sourasky Central Library
PO Box 39040, 69978 Tel Aviv
Tel: (03) 6408423; (03) 6408745 *Fax:* (03)
　6407833
E-mail: cenloan@tauex.tau.ac.il
Web Site: www.cenlib.tau.ac.il
Key Personnel
Manager: Naama Scheftelowitz *Tel:* (03) 6406891
　E-mail: naamas@tauex.tau.ac.il
Founded: 1954
Branch Office(s)
Archaeology Library, Gilman Bldg 224, 69978
　Tel Aviv, Contact: Nirit Kedem *Tel:* (03)
　6409023 *Fax:* (03) 6407237 *E-mail:* libarc@
　tauex.tau.ac.il
David Azrieli School of Architecture Library, PO
　Box 39040, 69978 Tel Aviv, Dir: Ruth Frankl-
　Gammer *Tel:* (03) 6405535 *Fax:* (03) 6407780
　E-mail: ruthf@tauex.tau.ac.il
M Grinsten Music Library, Buchmann-Mehta
　School of Music, 69978 Tel Aviv, Dir: Anna
　Kuffler *Tel:* (03) 6408716 *E-mail:* muslib@
　post.tau.ac.il
Jaime & Joan Constantiner School of Education
　Library, 69978 Tel Aviv, Dir: Ruth Frankl-
　Gammer *Tel:* (03) 6406937 *E-mail:* ruthfr@
　post.tau.ac.il
Mehlmann Library, Goldstein-Goren Diaspora Research Center, 69978 Tel Aviv, Dir: Sofia Tels-
　Abromov *Tel:* (03) 6407917 *E-mail:* sofiat@
　tauex.tau.ac.il

University of Haifa, The Library
Abba Khoushy Blvd 199, Mount Carmel,
　3498838 Haifa
Tel: (04) 8240264 *Fax:* (04) 8257753
E-mail: libmaster@univ.haifa.ac.il
Web Site: lib.haifa.ac.il
Key Personnel
Library Dir: Pnina Erez *E-mail:* epnina@univ.
　haifa.ac.il
Deputy Dir: Naomi Greidinger *E-mail:* naomig@
　univ.haifa.ac.il
Founded: 1963
Publication(s): *Index to Hebrew Periodicals* (online)

Weitz Center for Development Studies
PO Box 12, 7610001 Rehovot
Tel: (08) 9474111 *Fax:* (08) 9475884

E-mail: info@weitz-center.org
Web Site: www.weitz-center.org
Key Personnel
Mng Dir: Adi Dishon
Head, International Programs: Shirley Ben-Dak
Founded: 1963

Weizmann Institute of Science Libraries
Leon & Gina Fromer Bldg, 234 Herzl St, 76100
  Rehovot
Tel: (08) 9343874 *Fax:* (08) 9344176
E-mail: library@weizmann.ac.il
Web Site: www.weizmann.ac.il/library
Key Personnel
Chief Librarian: Hedva Milo *Tel:* (08) 9343295
  E-mail: hedva.milo@weizmann.ac.il

Italy

Archivio Centrale dello Stato
Piazzale degli Archivi, 27, 00144 Rome RM
Tel: (06) 545481 *Fax:* (06) 5413620
E-mail: acs@beniculturali.it
Web Site: www.acs.beniculturali.it
Key Personnel
President: Eugenio Lo Sardo
Library Dir: Elisabetta Orsolini *Tel:* (06)
  54548428 *E-mail:* elisabetta.orsolini@
  beniculturali.it
National archives.
Publication(s): *Bollettino Delle Nuove Accessioni*

Biblioteca Ambrosiana
Piazza Pio, XI 2, 20123 Milan MI
Tel: (02) 80 692 1 *Fax:* (02) 80 692 215
E-mail: info@ambrosiana.it
Web Site: www.ambrosiana.eu/cms/biblioteca/1-
  biblioteca.html
Key Personnel
Dir: Federico Gallo *E-mail:* fgallo@ambrosiana.it
Founded: 1607
Publication(s): *Fontes Ambrosiani*

Biblioteca Angelica
Piazza di Sant'Agostino, 8, 00186 Rome RM
Tel: 066840801
E-mail: b-ange@beniculturali.it
Web Site: www.bibliotecaangelica.beniculturali.it
Key Personnel
Dir: Dr Fiammetta Terlizzi *Tel:* 0668408039
  E-mail: fiammetta.terlizzi@beniculturali.it
Founded: 1604
Membership(s): Ministero per i Beni e le Attivita
  Couturali.

**Biblioteca Centrale della Regione Siciliana
Alberto Bombace**
Formerly Biblioteca Nazionale di Palermo
Corso Vittorio Emanuele 429/431, 90134 Palermo
Tel: (091) 7077642 *Fax:* (091) 7077644
E-mail: bcrs@regione.sicilia.it
Web Site: mw.bibliotecacentraleregionesiciliana.it
Key Personnel
Dir: Carlo Pastena

Biblioteca Comunale dell' Archiginnasio
  (Archiginnasio Public Library)
Piazza Galvani 1, 40124 Bologna
Tel: (051) 276811 *Fax:* (051) 261160
E-mail: archiginnasio@comune.bologna.it
Web Site: www.archiginnasio.it
Key Personnel
Dir: Dr Pierangelo Bellettini
Founded: 1801
Publication(s): *L'Archiginnasio: Bollettino della
  Biblioteca Comunale di Bologna* (annually)

Biblioteca Conservatorio Santa Cecilia
Via dei Greci n 18, 00187 Rome RM
Tel: (06) 36096730
E-mail: biblioteca@conservatoriosantacecilia.it
Web Site: www.conservatoriosantacecilia.it/il-
  conservatorio/la-biblioteca-2
Key Personnel
Librarian: Prof Francesco Mauro Coviello
  E-mail: f.coviello@conservatoriosantacecilia.it
Founded: 1875

**Biblioteca dell'Archivio Storico Civico e
Biblioteca Trivulziana**
Castello Sforzesco, Piazza Castello 3, 20121 Mi-
  lan MI
Tel: (02) 88463814; (02) 88463696
E-mail: c.ascbibliotrivulziana@comune.milano.it
Web Site: trivulziana.milanocastello.it
Key Personnel
Curator: Isabella Fiorentini
Library publications are sent free by request or in
  exchange for other publications.

Biblioteca Estense Universitaria
Largo S Agostino 337, 41121 Modena
Tel: (059) 4395711 *Fax:* (059) 230196
E-mail: ga-esten@beniculturali.it
Web Site: www.bibliotecaestense.beniculturali.it
Key Personnel
Dir: Annalisa Battini *E-mail:* b-este.direzione@
  beniculturali.it
Economics, medicine, engineering & mathemat-
  ics.

Biblioteca Medicea Laurenziana
Piazza San Lorenzo n° 9, 50123 Florence FI
Tel: (055) 2937911 *Fax:* (055) 2302992
E-mail: b-mela@beniculturali.it; b-mela.urp@
  beniculturali.it
Web Site: www.bmlonline.it; www.bml.firenze.
  sbn.it
Key Personnel
Dir: Ida Giovanna Rao *E-mail:* b-mela.
  direzione@beniculturali.it
Administration: Grazia Scarafile *E-mail:* grazia.
  scarafile@beniculturali.it
Founded: 1571

Biblioteca Nazionale Braidense
Via Brera, 28, 20121 Milan MI
Tel: (02) 86460907 *Fax:* (02) 72023910
E-mail: b-brai@beniculturali.it
Web Site: www.braidense.it
Key Personnel
Dir: Dr Maria Goffredo

Biblioteca Nazionale Centrale di Firenze
  (National Central Library of Florence)
Piazza dei Cavalleggeri, 1, 50122 Florence FI
Tel: (055) 24919 1; (055) 24919 314
E-mail: bnc-fi@beniculturali.it
Web Site: www.bncf.firenze.sbn.it
Key Personnel
Dir: Dr Luca Bellingeri
Founded: 1861
Branch Office(s)
Piazza S Ambrogio, 1, 50121 Florence *Tel:* (055)
  245539 *Fax:* (055) 24919 402

Biblioteca nazionale centrale di Roma (National
  Central Library of Rome)
Viale Castro Pretorio, 105, 00185 Rome RM
Tel: (06) 49891
E-mail: bnc-rm@beniculturali.it; accoglienza@
  bnc.roma.sbn.it
Web Site: www.bncrm.beniculturali.it
Key Personnel
Dir: Andrea De Pasquale *E-mail:* andrea.
  depasquale@beniculturali.it

Founded: 1876
Publication(s): *Quaderni della Biblioteca
  nazionale centrale di Roma*

Biblioteca Nazionale di Palermo, see Biblioteca
  Centrale della Regione Siciliana Alberto
  Bombace

Biblioteca Nazionale Marciana (Marciana
  National Library)
Piazzetta San Marco n 7, 30124 Venice
Tel: (041) 2407211 *Fax:* (041) 5238803
E-mail: biblioteca@marciana.venezia.sbn.it
Web Site: marciana.venezia.sbn.it
Key Personnel
Dir: Dr Maurizio Messina *Tel:* (041) 2407240
  E-mail: direzione@marciana.venezia.sbn.it
Publication(s): *Miscellanea Marciana*

Biblioteca Nazionale Sagarriga Visconti Volpi
Via Pietro Oreste, 45, 70123 Bari
Tel: (080) 2173111
E-mail: bn-ba@beniculturali.it
Web Site: www.bibliotecanazionalebari.
  beniculturali.it
Key Personnel
Dir: Dr Eugenia Scagliarini
Founded: 1865

Biblioteca Nazionale Universitaria di Torino
  (National University Library of Turin)
Piazza Carlo Alberto, 3, 10123 Turin TO
Tel: (011) 8101111 *Fax:* (011) 8121021; (011)
  8178778
E-mail: bu-to@beniculturali.it
Web Site: www.bnto.librari.beniculturali.it
Key Personnel
Dir: Guglielmo Bartoletti

Biblioteca Nazionale Vittorio Emanuele III
Piazza del Plebiscito 1, 80132 Naples NA
Tel: (081) 7819111 *Fax:* (081) 403820
E-mail: bn-na@beniculturali.it; bn-na.
  ufficiostampa@beniculturali.it (press)
Web Site: www.bnnonline.it
Key Personnel
Dir: Francesco Mercurio
Publication(s): *I Quaderni della Biblioteca
  Nazionale de Napoli*

Biblioteca Riccardiana
Palazzo Medici Riccardi, Via Ginori, 10, 50123
  Florence FI
Tel: (055) 212586; (055) 293385 *Fax:* (055)
  211379
E-mail: b-ricc@beniculturali.it
Web Site: www.riccardiana.firenze.sbn.it
Key Personnel
Dir: Dr Fulvio Silvano Stacchetti *E-mail:* b-ricc.
  direzione@beniculturali.it

Biblioteca Universitaria Alessandrina
Universita degli Studi di Roma La Sapienza, Pi-
  azzale Aldo Moro 5, 00185 Rome RM
Tel: (06) 44740220 *Fax:* (06) 44740222
E-mail: alessandrina@librari.beniculturali.it
Web Site: www.alessandrina.librari.beniculturali.it
Key Personnel
Dir: Maria Cristina Di Martino *Tel:* (06)
  44740221
Founded: 1667
Publication(s): *Catalogo del Fondo Leopardiano;
  Inchiostri per l'Infanzia: Letteratura ed Edito-
  ria in Italia dal 1880 al 1965* (catalog); *Voci di
  Roma*

Biblioteca Universitaria di Padova (University
  Library of Padua)
Via S Biagio, 7, 35121 Padua PD
Tel: (049) 8240211 *Fax:* (049) 8762711
E-mail: bu-pd@beniculturali.it

Web Site: www.bibliotecauniversitariapadova.
beniculturali.it
Key Personnel
Dir: Stefano Frassetto *Tel:* (049) 8240241
E-mail: stefano.frassetto@beniculturali.it
Deputy Dir: Pietro Gnan *Tel:* (049) 8240246
E-mail: pietro.gnan@beniculturali.it
Mng Dir: Marina Tosato *Tel:* (049) 8240232
E-mail: marina.tosato@beniculturali.it
Founded: 1629

European University Institute Library
Via dei Roccettini 9, 50014 San Domenico di
Fiesole FI
Tel: (055) 4685 340 *Fax:* (055) 4685 283
E-mail: library@eui.eu; euiref@eui.eu
Web Site: www.eui.eu
Key Personnel
Dir: Pep Torn *Tel:* (055) 4685 393 *E-mail:* josep.
torn@eui.eu

Istituzione Biblioteca Malatestiana
Piazza Bufalini, 1, 47521 Cesena FC
Tel: (0547) 610892 *Fax:* (0547) 21237
E-mail: malatestiana@sbn.provincia.ra.it
Web Site: www.comune.cesena.fc.it/malatestiana
Key Personnel
Dir: Monica Esposito *E-mail:* esposito_m@
comune.cesena.fc.it
Manager: Elisabetta Bovero *E-mail:* bovero_e@
comune.cesena.fc.it
Founded: 1452

**Universita degli Studi di Firenze, Sistema
Bibliotecario di Ateneo**
Via Gino Capponi 7-9, 50121 Florence FI
Tel: (055) 2757703; (055) 2757706 *Fax:* (055)
2757702
E-mail: cb@unifi.it
Web Site: www.sba.unifi.it
Key Personnel
Manager, Library Systems: Dr Giulia Maraviglia
Tel: (055) 2756550 *E-mail:* giulia.maraviglia@
unifi.it

Jamaica

Jamaica Archives & Records Department
Government Records Centre, 59-63 Church St,
Kingston
Tel: (876) 922-3705; (876) 922-3706 *Fax:* (876)
922-3707
E-mail: grecords@jard.gov.jm
Web Site: www.jard.gov.jm
Key Personnel
Government Archivist: Claudette Thomas

Jamaica Library Service
2 Tom Redcam Dr, Kingston 5
Tel: (876) 926-3310; (876) 926-3312 *Fax:* (876)
926-2188
E-mail: hq@jls.org.jm
Web Site: www.jls.gov.jm
Key Personnel
Chairman: Paul Lalor
Dir General: Karen Barton
Founded: 1948

Calvin McKain Library
University of Technology, Jamaica, 237 Old Hope
Rd, Kingston 6
Tel: (876) 970-5385
E-mail: library@utech.edu.jm
Web Site: library.utech.edu.jm; www.facebook.
com/calvinmckainlibrary
Founded: 1958

National Library of Jamaica
12 East St, Kingston
Mailing Address: PO Box 823, Kingston
Tel: (876) 967-1526; (876) 967-2516; (876) 967-
2494; (876) 967-2496 *Fax:* (876) 922-5567
E-mail: nljresearch@cwjamaica.com; nlj@nlj.gov.
jm
Web Site: nlj.gov.jm
Key Personnel
National Librarian & Chief Executive Officer:
Mrs Winsome Hudson *E-mail:* winsome.
hudson@nlj.gov.jm
Founded: 1979
The library is the national reference library of
Jamaica. Its main functions are to collect &
preserve the national imprint, to serve as the
bibliographic center for Jamaica & the focal
point of the national information system.
Publication(s): *Jamaican National Bibliography*
(occasionally, bibliography series)

**The United Theological College of the West
Indies Library**
7 Golding Ave, Kingston 7
Tel: (876) 977-2868; (876) 927-1724 *Fax:* (876)
977-0812
E-mail: unitheol@cwjamaica.com
Web Site: www.utcwi.edu.jm/library
Key Personnel
Librarian: Rev Gillian Wilson
Founded: 1966
Theological Seminary.

**University of the West Indies Library
(Jamaica)**
Main Library, Mona Campus, Kingston 7
Tel: (876) 935-8294 *Fax:* (876) 927-1926
E-mail: main.library@uwimona.edu.jm
Web Site: www.mona.uwi.edu/library
Key Personnel
Campus Librarian: Paulette Kerr *Tel:* (876) 970-
6569 *E-mail:* paulette.kerr@uwimona.edu.jm
Librarian: Myrna Douglas *Tel:* (876) 935-3393
E-mail: myrna.douglas@uwimona.edu.jm
Founded: 1948
Branch Office(s)
Medical Library
Science Library

Hiram S Walters Resource Center
Northern Caribbean University, Manchester Rd,
Manchester
Tel: (876) 618-1652 *Fax:* (876) 962-0075
E-mail: library@ncu.edu.jm
Web Site: www.ncu.edu.jm/library
Key Personnel
Dir, Library Services: Nicola Palmer *Tel:* (876)
963-7075 *E-mail:* nicola.palmer@ncu.edu.jm
Branch Office(s)
Andrews School of Nursing, Kingston

Japan

Gifu Diagaku Fuzoku Toshokan (Gifu
University Library)
1-1 Yanagido, Gifu-shi 501-1193
Tel: (058) 293-2191 *Fax:* (058) 293-3299
E-mail: gjin02017@jim.gifu-u.ac.jp
Web Site: www1.gifu-u.ac.jp/~gulib/index.html
Branch Office(s)
Medical Library, 1-1 Yanagido, Gifi-shi 501-
1194 *Tel:* (058) 293-6590 *Fax:* (058) 230-6592
E-mail: gjin02023@jim.gifu-u.ac.jp

Hokkaido University Library
Kita-8, Nishi-5, Kita-ku, Sapporo 060-0808
Tel: (011) 706-3956 *Fax:* (011) 746-4595

E-mail: service@lib.hokudai.ac.jp
Web Site: www.lib.hokudai.ac.jp
Key Personnel
Dir: Dr Takahiko Nitta
Founded: 1876
Publication(s): *Yuin* (quarterly, bulletin, 1967, in
Japanese)

**International Documentation Center, The
University of Tokyo**
7-3-1 General Library, 3rd floor, Hongo, Bunkyo-
ku, Tokyo 113-0033
Tel: (03) 5841-2645 *Fax:* (03) 5841-2611
E-mail: kokusai@lib.u-tokyo.ac.jp
Web Site: www.lib.u-tokyo.ac.jp

Keio University Library
Mita Media Center, 2-15-45 Mita, Minato-ku,
Tokyo 108-8345
Tel: (03) 5427-1654 *Fax:* (03) 5427-1665
E-mail: mita-webmaster@lib.keio.ac.jp
Web Site: www.mita.lib.keio.ac.jp
Founded: 1951

Kokuritsu Kobunshokan (National Archives of
Japan)
3-2 Kitanomaru Koen, Chiyoda-ku, Tokyo 102-
0091
Tel: (03) 3214-0641
E-mail: info@archives.go.jp
Web Site: www.archives.go.jp
Key Personnel
President: Masaya Takayama
Founded: 1971
Publication(s): *Kitanomaru* (The Journal of the
National Archives of Japan)

Kyoto Sangyo University Library
Kamigamo-Motoyama, Kita-ku, Kyoto 603-8555
Tel: (075) 705-1445 *Fax:* (075) 705-1447
E-mail: lib-ref@star.kyoto-su.ac.jp
Web Site: www.kyoto-su.ac.jp/lib
Founded: 1987

Kyoto United Nations Depository Library
c/o Ritusmeikan University, Meigakukan Hall, 56-
1 Tojin Kitamachi, Kita-ku, Kyoto 603-8577
Tel: (075) 4658107 *Fax:* (075) 4658334
E-mail: kyoundl@st.ristumei.ac.jp
Web Site: www.ritsumei.ac.jp/acd/in/cger/kunl/
index.html
Founded: 1956

Kyushu University Library
6-10-1, Hakozaki, Higashi-ku, Fukuoka-shi 812-
8581
Tel: (092) 642-2337 *Fax:* (092) 642-2205
E-mail: esupport@lib.kyushu-u.ac.jp
Web Site: www.lib.kyushu-u.ac.jp
Founded: 1903

National Diet Library
1-10-1 Nagata-cho, Chiyoda-ku, Tokyo 100-8924
Tel: (03) 3581-2331; (03) 3506-3300 *Fax:* (03)
3508-2934; (03) 3506-3301
E-mail: kokusai@ndl.go.jp
Web Site: www.ndl.go.jp
Key Personnel
Librarian: Sawako Hanyu
Founded: 1948
As the only national library in Japan, provides
services for the Diet (Parliament), for the government & for the general public. As the only
depository library in Japan, the library acquires
all materials published in Japan, preserves them
as national cultural heritage, compiles catalogs
of these publications in a database or other format & with these collections provides library
services.
Publication(s): *Biburosu* (Biblos, quarterly, online at www.ndl.go.jp/jp/publication/biblos/in-

dex.html, ISSN: 1344-8412); *Books on Japan* (quarterly, online at www.ndl.go.jp/jp/publication/books_on_japan/boi_top_E.html, ISSN: 1347-7684); *Current Awareness* (quarterly, print, ISSN: 0387-8007 & online at www.current.ndl.go.jp/ca, ISSN: 1348-7450); *Current Awareness-E* (6 times/yr, online at www.current.ndl.go.jp/cae, ISSN: 1347-7315); *Kin gendai nihon seiji kankei jinbutsu bunken mokuroku* (Bibliography of Persons in Modern Japanese Politics, online at rnavi.ndl.go.jp/sciji); *Kokuritsu kokkai toshokan nenpo* (Annual Report of the National Diet Library, annually, print, ISSN: 0385-325X & online at www.ndl.go.jp/jp/publication/annual/index.html, ISSN: 1349-0621); *NDL Newsletter* (6 times/yr, online at www.ndl.go.jp/en/publication/ndl_newsletter/index.html, ISSN: 1344-7238); *Nihon kagakugijutsu kankei chikuji kankobutsu soran* (Directory of Japanese Scientific Periodicals, online at refsys.ndl.go.jp/E001_EP01.nsf/PublicE?OpenFrameset); *Nihon zenkoku shoshi* (Japanese National Bibliography, weekly, online at www.ndl.go.jp/jp/publication/jnbwl/jnb_top.html, ISSN: 1347-0000); *Refarensu* (Reference, monthly, print, ISSN: 0034-2912 & online at www.ndl.go.jp/jp/data/publication/reference_index.html, ISSN: 1349-208X); *Toshokan chosa kenkyu ripoto* (NDL Research Report, irregularly, print, ISSN: 1348-6780 & online at www.current.ndl.go.jp/report, ISSN: 1348-7442); *Toshokan Kenkyu Shirizu* (NDL Library Science Series, irregularly, print, ISSN: 0454-1960 & online at www.current.ndl.go.jp/series)

Osaka Prefectural Central Library
1-2-1, Aramoto-Kita, Higashi, Osaka-shi 577-0011
Tel: (06) 6745-0170 *Fax:* (06) 6745-0262
Web Site: www.library.pref.osaka.jp
Founded: 1996
Branch Office(s)
Osaka Prefectural Nakanoshima Library, 1-2-10 Nakanoshima Kita-ku, Osaka 530-0005
Tel: (06) 6203-0474

Osaka University Library
1-4 Machikaneyama, Toyonaka, Osaka 560-0043
Tel: (06) 6850-5067
E-mail: honkan@library.osaka-u.ac.jp
Web Site: www.library.osaka-u.ac.jp
Founded: 1931
Branch Office(s)
International Studies Library, 8-1-1, Aomatani-higashi, Minoh, Osaka 562-8558 *Tel:* (072) 730-5126 *E-mail:* ml-cir@library.osaka-u.ac.jp
Life Sciences Library, 2-3 Yamadaoka, Suita, Osaka 565-0871 *Tel:* (06) 6879-2415 *E-mail:* seimei@library.osaka-u.ac.jp
Science & Engineering Library, 2-1 Yamadaoka, Suita, Osaka 565-0871 *Tel:* (06) 6879-7187 *E-mail:* w3master-sl@library.osaka-u.ac.jp

Tenri Central Library
Tenri University, 1050 Somanouchi, Tenri, Nara 632-8577
Tel: (0743) 63-9200 *Fax:* (0743) 63-7728
E-mail: info@tcl.gr.jp
Web Site: www.tcl.gr.jp
Founded: 1925

Tohoku University Library
27-1 Kawauchi, Aoba-ku, Sendai 980-8576
Tel: (022) 795-5943; (022) 795-5935 (reference) *Fax:* (022) 795-5949
E-mail: main-counter@grp.tohoku.ac.jp
Web Site: www.library.tohoku.ac.jp
Key Personnel
Dir: Keiichi Noe
Publication(s): *Kiboko* (quarterly, bulletin); *Library Now* (irregularly, bulletin)

Tokyo Metropolitan Central Library
5-7-13 Minami-Azabu, Minato-ku, Tokyo 106-8575
Tel: (03) 3442-8451
E-mail: mailmaster@library.metro.tokyo.jp
Web Site: www.library.metro.tokyo.jp
Founded: 1973
Branch Office(s)
Tama Library, 6-3-1 Nishiki-cho, Tachikawa-shi, Tokyo 190-0022 *Tel:* (04) 2524-7186

The Toyo Bunko (Oriental Library)
2-28-21 Honkomagome, Bunkyo-ku, Tokyo 113-0021
Tel: (03) 3942-0122 *Fax:* (03) 3942-0120
Web Site: www.toyo-bunko.or.jp
Key Personnel
Chairman: Makihara Minoru
Mng Dir: Yamakawa Naoyoshi
Executive Librarian: Yoshinobu Shiba
Founded: 1917
Publication(s): *Memoirs of the Research Department of the Toyo Bunko* (annually, journal); *Toyo Bunko Research Library* (annually, journal)

University of Tokyo Library System
7-3-1, Hongo, Bunkyo-ku, Tokyo 113-0033
Tel: (03) 5841 2612; (03) 5841-2643 *Fax:* (03) 5841 2636
E-mail: kikaku@lib.u-tokyo.ac.jp; shiryo@lib.u-tokyo.ac.jp
Web Site: www.lib.u-tokyo.ac.jp

Waseda University Library
1-6-1 Nishiwaseda, Shinjuku-ku, Tokyo 169-8050
Tel: (03) 3203-5581 *Fax:* (03) 3207-9224
E-mail: info@wul.waseda.ac.jp
Web Site: www.waseda.jp/library/en
Key Personnel
Dir: Yoshiaki Fukazawa
Associate Dir: Gaye Rowley
Founded: 1882
Publication(s): *Bulletin of Waseda University Library*

Jordan

Amman Public Library
PO Box 182181, Amman 11118
Tel: (06) 4610542; (06) 4627718 *Fax:* (06) 4610542
Key Personnel
Dir: Mohammad Subeihi *E-mail:* subeihi@hotmail.com
Founded: 1960

British Council Library
Rainbow St, First Circle, Amman 11118
Tel: (06) 4603420 *Fax:* (06) 4656413
E-mail: info@britishcouncil.org.jo
Web Site: www.britishcouncil.jo
Founded: 1950

Department of the National Library
Arjan, Bldg No 9, Haroun Al-Rasheed St, Amman
Tel: (06) 5662845; (06) 5662854; (06) 5662791; (06) 5662819; (06) 5662748; (06) 5662871; (06) 5662758 *Fax:* (06) 5662867
E-mail: nl@nl.gov.jo
Web Site: www.nl.gov.jo
Key Personnel
Dir General: Mohammed Amin Younis Marzouk al Abadi

Jordan University of Science & Technology Library
PO Box 3030, Irbid 22110
Tel: (02) 7201000 (ext 27501) *Fax:* (02) 72095123
E-mail: library@just.edu.jo
Web Site: www.just.edu.jo/library
Key Personnel
Dir: Raed K Al-Zoubi *Tel:* (02) 7201000 ext 27500 *E-mail:* ralzoubi@just.edu.jo

Mutah University Library
PO Box 5, Al-Karak 61710
Tel: (03) 2372380 (ext 6095); (03) 2372399 (ext 6096) *Fax:* (03) 2375703
E-mail: libdir@mutah.edu.jo
Web Site: www.mutah.edu.jo/library
Key Personnel
Library Dir: Yousef Btoush *E-mail:* yalbtoush@yahoo.com
Founded: 1984

Alhussain Bn Talal Library, see Yarmouk University Library

University of Jordan Library
PO Box 11942, Amman 11942
Tel: (06) 5355000 *Fax:* (06) 5355570; (06) 5355099; (06) 5300805
E-mail: library@ju.edu.jo
Web Site: library.ju.edu.jo
Key Personnel
Dir: Dr Mohannad Mubaidin
Founded: 1962
Publication(s): *The Library Guide* (in English & Arabic); *Theses Directory* (2 times/yr)

Yarmouk University Library
PO Box 566, Irbid 21163
Tel: (02) 7211111 (ext 2871)
E-mail: library@yu.edu.jo
Web Site: www.yu.edu.jo; library.yu.edu.jo
Key Personnel
Dir: Dr Adnan Albesol *Tel:* (02) 7211111 ext 2870
Founded: 1976

Kazakhstan

Kazakhstan Academy of Sciences
28 Shevchenko St, Almaty 050010
Tel: (8727) 261-00-25; (8727) 272-55-61
E-mail: nanrk.mzh@mail.ru
Web Site: nauka-nanrk.kz
Key Personnel
President: Prof Murat Zhurinov
Founded: 1946

National Academy of Sciences of the Republic of Kazakhstan, see Kazakhstan Academy of Sciences

Kenya

Egerton University Library
PO Box 536, Egerton 20115
Tel: (051) 2217891; (051) 2217892; (051) 2217781
E-mail: info@egerton.ac.ke
Web Site: www.egerton.ac.ke

Key Personnel
University Librarian: Janegrace K Kinyanjui
  E-mail: jgkinyanjui@egerton.ac.ke
Founded: 1939
Publication(s): *Egerton University Journal*

KALRO Library & Information Services (LIS)
Kaptagat Rd, Loresho, Nairobi
Mailing Address: PO Box 57811, City Sq,
  Nairobi 00200
Tel: (0722) 206-986 (cell); (0733) 333-223 (cell)
E-mail: info@kalro.org
Web Site: www.kalro.org/library
Key Personnel
Dir General: Dr Eliud K Kireger
Founded: 1979

Kenya Agricultural & Livestock Research Organization, see KALRO Library & Information Services (LIS)

Kenya Agricultural Documentation Centre
Kilimo House, Cathedral Rd, Nairobi
Mailing Address: PO Box 34188, Nairobi
Tel: (020) 2718870
E-mail: info@kilimo.go.ke
Web Site: www.kilimo.go.ke
Founded: 1907
Parent Company: Republic of Kenya Ministry of
  Agriculture Livestock & Fisheries

Kenya National Archives & Documentation Service
PO Box 49210, Nairobi 00100
Tel: (020) 2228959 *Fax:* (020) 2228020
E-mail: info@archives.go.ke
Web Site: www.archives.go.ke
Founded: 1965
Publication(s): *Acquisitions Guides*

Kenya National Library Service (KNLS)
PO Box 30573, Nairobi 00100
Tel: (020) 2725550; (020) 2158352; (020)
  2158360; (020) 7786710 *Fax:* (020) 2721749
E-mail: knls@knls.ac.ke
Web Site: www.knls.ac.ke
Key Personnel
Dir: R M Atuti
Founded: 1965
Publication(s): *Kenya National Bibliography;
  Kenya Periodicals Directory*

Kenya Polytechnic University College Library
PO Box 52428, Nairobi 00200
Tel: (020) 343672; (020) 2251300 *Fax:* (020)
  2219689
E-mail: inquiries@kenpoly.ac.ke
Web Site: kpuc.tukenya.ac.ke
Founded: 1980

Kenya School of Law Library
PO Box 30369, Nairobi 00100
Tel: (020) 890044; (020) 890094 *Fax:* (020)
  891772
E-mail: library@ksl.ac.ke
Web Site: www.ksl.ac.ke
Key Personnel
Dir: Prof Kulundu Bitonye
Librarian: Roseline Kwenda *E-mail:* rkwenda@
  ksl.ac.ke
Assistant Librarian: Elphas M Ngaira
Founded: 1963

Kenya Technical Trainers College Library (KTTC)
UN Ave, Gigiri, Nairobi 00100
Mailing Address: PO Box 44600, Nairobi 00100
Tel: (020) 7120212; (020) 7120213; (020)
  7120214 *Fax:* (020) 7120088

E-mail: kttclibrary@yahoo.com; library@kttc.ac.
  ke
Web Site: www.kttc.ac.ke
Key Personnel
Librarian: Mary Mburu
Deputy Librarian: David Ondieki
Founded: 1978
Publication(s): *Mwalimu Kenya Education Sup-
  plement* (monthly); *Secondary School Library
  Facilities in Central Province, Kenya; Serials
  Literature, Exploitation & Use in Libraries;
  The Problems of Providing Library Services to
  School Children in Developing Countries*

Kenyatta University Post Modern Library
PO Box 43844, Nairobi 00100
Tel: (020) 810901-16 (ext 57153) *Fax:* (020)
  811575
E-mail: library@ku.ac.ke
Web Site: library.ku.ac.ke
Key Personnel
Chief Librarian: Dr George Gitau Njoroge
  E-mail: gitau.njoroge@ku.ac.ke
Founded: 1985
Publication(s): *Directory of Research in the Uni-
  versity; Education in Kenya: an Index* (1984);
  *Education in Kenya since Independence: a bib-
  liography* (1963-1983)

KNADS, see Kenya National Archives &
  Documentation Service

KNLS, see Kenya National Library Service
  (KNLS)

KTTC, see Kenya Technical Trainers College
  Library (KTTC)

McMillan Memorial Library
Banda St, PO Box 40791, Nairobi 00100
Founded: 1931

Mines & Geological Department Library
Mines & Geology Dept, Madini House,
  Machakos Rd, Nairobi 00100
Mailing Address: PO Box 30009, Nairobi 00100
Tel: (020) 558034 *Fax:* (020) 555796
E-mail: cmg@bidii.com
Web Site: www.environment.go.ke
Parent Company: Ministry of Environment &
  Mineral Resources

Technical University of Mombasa Library
PO Box 90420, Mombasa 80100
Tel: (041) 2492222 *Fax:* (041) 2493452
Web Site: library.tum.ac.ke
Key Personnel
University Librarian: Dr Wanyenda Chilimo
  E-mail: librarian@tum.ac.ke
Deputy University Librarian: Benard Kamanda
  E-mail: dlibrarian@tum.ac.ke
Head, Technical Services: Vitalis Ougo
  E-mail: vitalisougo@tum.ac.ke
Founded: 1972

TUM Library, see Technical University of
  Mombasa Library

University of Nairobi Library
PO Box 30197, Nairobi 00100
Tel: (020) 318262
E-mail: librarian@uonbi.ac.ke
Web Site: uonlibrary.uonbi.ac.ke
Key Personnel
University Librarian: Angela Mumo *Tel:* (020)
  318262 ext 28501 *E-mail:* angela.mumo@
  uonbi.ac.ke
Specialize in supporting study, teaching & re-
  search needs of the University of Nairobi.

Branch Office(s)
Chiromo Library, College of Biological & Physical Sciences, Chiromo, Nairobi, Librarian:
  George E G Nyalwal *Tel:* (020) 444212; (020)
  4449004; (020) 4442016 *E-mail:* cho-lib@
  uonbi.ac.ke
College of Architecture, Design & Develop-
  ment (ADD), State House Rd, Nairobi, Librarian: Evelyn Emali Anambo *E-mail:* evalyn.
  anambo@uonbi.ac.ke
Kikuyu Library, College of Education & External
  Studies, PO Box 92, Kikuyu *Tel:* (020) 32117;
  (020) 32020; (020) 32029
Mwai Kibaki Library, Lower Kabete, Nairobi,
  Librarian: Florence A Odenyo *Tel:* (020)
  4184160; (020) 4184165
Medical Library, Ngong Rd, Nairobi, Li-
  brarian: John Mwangi *Tel:* (020) 2726300
  E-mail: librarian-chs@uonbi.ac.ke
Parklands Law Library, Parklands Campus, Park-
  lands, Nairobi, Librarian: Alice N Okongo
  Tel: (020) 340859; (020) 340477
Upper Kabete Library, PO Box 29053, College
  of Agriculture & Veterinary Sciences, Kabete,
  Nairobi 00625, Librarian: Rosemary Otando
  Tel: (020) 632211 ext 27207 *E-mail:* librarian-
  cavs@uonbi.ac.ke

Kuwait

Kuwait University Libraries
PO Box 5969, 13060 Safat
Tel: 24834165; 24813182 *Fax:* 24842479;
  24816595
E-mail: libraries.dept@ku.edu.kw
Web Site: kuweb.ku.edu.kw/kulib/index.htm
Publication(s): *The Library Bulletin*

National Library of Kuwait
Arabian Gulf St, Qibla
Tel: 22929803; 22929804; 22929805
  Fax: 22415195
E-mail: library@nlk.gov.kw; nlk@nlk.gov.kw
Web Site: www.nlk.gov.kw
Founded: 1923
National Depository, ISBN, UN Depository.

National Scientific & Technical Information Center (NSTIC)
Kuwait Institute for Scientific Research (KISR),
  PO Box 24885, 13109 Safat
Tel: 24836100; 24989000 *Fax:* 24989409
E-mail: marketing@kisr.edu.kw; md@kisr.edu.kw
Web Site: www.kisr.edu.kw
Key Personnel
Dir: Dr Samira A S Omar *E-mail:* kisrdg@safat.
  kisr.edu.kw
Founded: 1967

NSTIC, see National Scientific & Technical
  Information Center (NSTIC)

Laos

Bibliotheque Nationale du Laos (National
  Library of Laos)
Corner Thanon Setthathirat/Thanon Pangkham,
  Ban Xiengyeun Thong, Muang Chanthaburi,
  Vientiane
Mailing Address: PO Box 704, Vientiane
Tel: (021) 212452 *Fax:* (021) 213029
E-mail: bailane@laotel.com
Web Site: www.nationallibraryoflaos.org
Founded: 1956

Branch Office(s)
Champassak Provincial Library, Champassak
Provincial Service of Information & Culture,
PO Box 26, Muang Pakse, Khoueng Champassak *Tel:* (031) 252882
Luang Prabang Provincial Library, Thanon Setthathirat, Ban Thongchaleun, Muang Luang
Prabang, Khoueng Luang Prabang *Tel:* (071)
213021
Khammouane Provincial Library, Khammouane
Provincial Service of Information & Culture,
Ban Laophoxay, Muang Thakhek, Khoueng
Khammouane *Tel:* (051) 212416
Savannakhet Provincial Library, Ban Thongngone,
Muang Khanthaburi, Khoueng Savannakhet
Tel: (041) 251372
Xieng Khouang Provincial Library, Ban Phonsavanh, Muang Pek, Khoueng Xieng Khouang
Tel: (061) 312385

Latvia

Latvijas Universitates Akademiska Biblioteka
(Academic Library of the University of Latvia)
Rupniecibas iela 10, Riga LV-1235
Tel: 67033951; 26373599
E-mail: acadlib@lib.acadlib.lv
Web Site: www.acadlib.lv
Key Personnel
Dir: Venta Kocere *Tel:* 67033955 *E-mail:* venta.
kocere@lu.lv
Deputy Dir: Ineta Kivle *Tel:* 22021550
E-mail: ineta.kivle@lu.lv

LNB, see National Library of Latvia

National Library of Latvia (Latvijas Nacionala
Biblioteka)
Mukusalas St 3, Riga LV-1423
Tel: 67806100 *Fax:* 67280851
E-mail: lnb@lnb.lv
Web Site: www.lnb.lv
Key Personnel
Dir: Mr Andris Vilks *E-mail:* andris.vilks@lnb.lv
Founded: 1919
The National Library of Latvia is the keeper of
all printed matter of the Republic of Latvia, the
developer of national bibliographic resources
& the center for development of a system of
state libraries. NLL, coordinating with other libraries, forms a depository of national literature
& performs the functions of an interlibrary loan
center in Latvia.
Branch Office(s)
Audiovisual Resource Reading Room, 3 K
Barona St, Riga LV-1050
Cartographic Reading Room, 6/8 Jekaba St, Riga
LV-1050
5 Anglikanu St, Riga LV-1050

NLL, see National Library of Latvia

Lebanon

American University of Beirut Libraries
Bliss St, Riyad El-Solh, Beirut 1107 2020
Mailing Address: PO Box 11-0236, Riyad El-Solh, Beirut 1107 2020
Tel: (01) 37 43 74 (ext 2600); (01) 37 43 74 (ext
2618); (01) 35 00 00; (01) 34 04 60; (01) 37
44 44 *Fax:* (01) 74 47 03
E-mail: library@aub.edu.lb
Web Site: www.aub.edu.lb/ulibraries

Key Personnel
University Librarian: Dr Lokman Meho
E-mail: lmeho@aub.edu.lb
Constituent Libraries: Jafet Memorial Library
(Central Library), Farm Library; Science &
Agriculture Library; Engineering & Architecture Library.

Beirut Arab University Libraries
PO Box 115020, Beirut 1107 2809
Tel: (01) 300110
E-mail: library@bau.edu.lb
Web Site: www.bau.edu.lb/library-home1
Key Personnel
Library Consultant: Dr Hassana Moheiddine
Tel: (01) 300110 ext 2769 *E-mail:* hassana.
m@bau.edu.lb

**Bibliotheque Archeologie de l'Institut Francais
du Proche-Orient**
Rue de Damas, BP 11, Beirut 1424
Tel: (01) 420291; (01) 420293 *Fax:* (01) 420295
E-mail: bib.beyrouth@ifporient.org
Web Site: www.ifporient.org
Key Personnel
Dir: Eberhard Kienle *E-mail:* e.kienle@ifporient.
org
Regional Manager: Gilles Sentise *E-mail:* g.
sentise@ifporient.org
Contact: Annie-France Renaudin *E-mail:* af.
renaudin@ifporient.org
Publication(s): *Bibliotheque Archeologique et Historique* (147 titles); *Syria, Revue d'art oriental
et d'archeologie* (annually, 2 vols)

**Bibliotheque des Sciences Sociales de
l'Universite Saint-Joseph**
Rue Huvelin, Achrafieh, Mar Mikhael, Beirut
1104 2020
Mailing Address: BP 17-5208, Mar Mikhael,
Beirut 1104 2020
Tel: (01) 421 000 (ext 4251); (01) 421 000 (ext
4301)
E-mail: biblio.css@usj.edu.lb
Web Site: www.biblio-css.usj.edu.lb
Key Personnel
Dir: Leila Kassatly Rizk *Tel:* (01) 421 000 ext
4428 *E-mail:* leila.rizk@usj.edu.lb
Founded: 1913
Publication(s): *Proche-Orient, Etudes Juridiques*

Bibliotheque Orientale (Oriental Library)
Rue de l'Universite St-Joseph, Beirut 1100 2150
Mailing Address: BP 16-6775 - Achrafieh, Beirut
1100 2150
Tel: (01) 421 810 *Fax:* (01) 421 081
E-mail: bo@usj.edu.lb
Web Site: www.bo.usj.edu.lb
Key Personnel
Dir: Micheline Sainte-Marie Bittar *Tel:* (01) 421
811 *E-mail:* mbittar@usj.edu.lb
Founded: 1875
University research library.
Publication(s): *Melanges de l'Universite Saint-Joseph (1906-)*

**Ecole Superieure d'Ingenieurs de Beyrouth
(ESIB) Bibliotheque des Sciences et
Technologies**
Universite St-Joseph, Campus des sciences et
technologies, BP 11-514 Riad El-Solh, Beirut
1107 2050
Tel: (04) 421306 *Fax:* (04) 532645
E-mail: biblio-cst@usj.edu.lb
Web Site: www.biblio-cst.usj.edu.lb
Key Personnel
Head Librarian: Mona Tabbah *E-mail:* mona.
tabbah@usj.edu.lb
Founded: 1913

ESIB, see Ecole Superieure d'Ingenieurs de
Beyrouth (ESIB) Bibliotheque des Sciences et
Technologies

Jafet Memorial Library, see American
University of Beirut Libraries

Near East School of Theology Library
Sourati St (off Jeanne D'Arc), Hamra, Beirut
Tel: (01) 738639; (01) 349901 *Fax:* (01) 347129
E-mail: library@theonest.edu.lb
Web Site: www.theonest.edu.lb
Key Personnel
Librarian: Martine Charbel-Eid
Founded: 1932
Publication(s): *Theological Review*

**Universite Saint-Joseph de Beyrouth,
Bibliotheque des Sciences Medicales**
Campus des Sciences Medicales, Rue de Damas,
BP 11-5076 Beirut
Tel: (01) 412000 (ext 2110)
E-mail: csm.biblio@usj.edu.lb
Web Site: www.biblio-csm.usj.edu.lb
Key Personnel
Dir: May Harfouche Samaha *Tel:* (01) 421000 ext
2211
Librarian: Sylvira Hakim; Monica Maalouly; Wissam Bou Mansour; Melissa Mefleh
Founded: 1883

Lesotho

Lesotho National Library
PO Box 13, Mafeteng 900
Tel: 2270 1384
Founded: 1976

Thomas Mofolo Library, see The National
University of Lesotho Library

The National University of Lesotho Library
PO Roma 180, Maseru 100
Tel: 22213404; 22340601 (ext 3404)
Fax: 22340231
Web Site: library.nul.ls
Key Personnel
Librarian: Prof M M Moshoeshoe-Chadzingwa
E-mail: m.moshoeshoe@nul.ls
Founded: 1954

Liberia

Cuttington University College Library
PO Box 10-0277, 1000 Suakoko 10
E-mail: info@cuttingtonuniversity.edu.lr
Web Site: cuttinguniversity.edu.lr/library.html
Key Personnel
President: Dr Herman B Browne *Tel:* (06) 532
130
Dean, College Education & Dir: Theodore V K
Brown
Founded: 1889

University of Liberia Libraries
PO Box 9020, 1000 Monrovia
Tel: 886941294 (cell)
E-mail: info@ul.edu.lr
Web Site: www.ul.edu.lr

Libya

Centre for National Archives & Historical Studies, see Libyan National Archives

Libyan National Archives
Sidi Muneider St, Tripoli
Mailing Address: PO Box 570, Tripoli
Tel: (021) 4446987; (021) 4446988 *Fax:* (021) 3331616
E-mail: clar.hs@hotmail.com
Web Site: www.libsc.org.ly/mrkaz
Founded: 1928

National Library of Libya
PO Box 9127, Benghazi
Tel: (061) 9097074; (061) 9096379 *Fax:* (051) 9097073
E-mail: nat_lib_libya@hotmail.com
Web Site: www.nllnet.net
Key Personnel
Librarian: Mohamed A Eshoweihde

University of Benghazi Library
PO Box 1308, Benghazi
Tel: (061) 2220147
E-mail: info@uob.edu.ly
Web Site: uob.edu.ly; glib.uob.edu.ly
Founded: 1955

University of Tripoli Libraries
PO Box 13275, Tripoli
Web Site: uot.edu.ly

Liechtenstein

Liechtensteinische Landesbibliothek
(Liechtenstein National Library)
Gerberweg 5, 9490 Vaduz
Mailing Address: Postfach 385, 9490 Vaduz
Tel: 236 63 63
E-mail: info@landesbibliothek.li
Web Site: www.landesbibliothek.li
Key Personnel
State Librarian: Oehry Wilfried *Tel:* 236 63 61
Deputy State Librarian: Buechel Meinrad *Tel:* 236 63 71
Founded: 1961

Lithuania

Lietuvos Nacionaline Martyno Mazvydo biblioteka (Martynas Mazvydas National Library of Lithuania)
Gedimino pr 51, LT-01504 Vilnius
Tel: (05) 249 7028 *Fax:* (05) 249 6129
E-mail: biblio@lnb.lt
Web Site: www.lnb.lt
Key Personnel
Dir General: Dr Renaldas Gudauskas *Tel:* (05) 239 7023 *E-mail:* r.gudauskas@lnb.lt
Deputy Dir General: Sandra Leknickiene *Tel:* (05) 239 8505 *E-mail:* s.leknickiene@lnb.lt; Genovaite Sablauskiene *Tel:* (05) 239 8501 *E-mail:* g.sablauskiene@lnb.lt; Aidas Sinkevicius *Tel:* (05) 239 8504 *E-mail:* a.sinkevicius@lnb.lt
Founded: 1919
Library & information services.
Publication(s): *Bibliotekininkyste Lietuvoje 1991-2000* (Library Science in Lithuania 1991-2000,

electronic); *Bibliotekininkystes naujienos* (Library Science News, quarterly, index of bibliographical information); *Depozitiniu fondu naujienos. Tarptautines atomines energetikos agenturos nauji leidinial* (Depository Fund Newsletter. New Publications of the International Atomic Energy Agency (IAEA), annually, newsletter, bibliographical index); *Depozitiniu fondu naujienos. Tarptautinio valiutos fondo nauji leidiniai* (Depository Fund Newsletter. New Publications of the International Monetary Fund, quarterly, bibliographical index); *Depozitiniu fondu naujienos. Traptautinio rekonstrukcijos ir pletros banko nauji leidiniai* (Depository Fund Newsletter. New Publications of the International Bank for Reconstruction & Development, quarterly); *Ekspresinformacija apie naujus spaudinius, isejusius Lietuvoje* (Expressinformation on the Latest Publications issued in Lithuania, weekly, bulletin); *Kompiuteriniu bibliografiniu ir autoritetiniu irasu sudarymo pagrindai* (Creation Outlines of Machine-Readable Bibliographic & Authority Records, electronic); *Lietuvos spaudos statistika* (Lithuanian Publishing Statistics, annually, bulletin); *LNB Informacijos centro naujienos* (NLL Information Centre Newsletter, newsletter, Lithuanian only); *Numatomos leisti knygos* (List of Forthcoming Books, weekly, bulletin); *Tarptautinio saugumo ir NATO nauji leidiniai* (New Publications of the International Security & NATO, irregularly, bibliographical index); *Tarptautiniu katalogavimo principu isdestymas* (electronic)

Vilniaus Universiteto Biblioteka (Vilnius University Library)
Universiteto g 3, LT-01122 Vilnius
Tel: (05) 268 7100 *Fax:* (05) 268 7104
E-mail: infostalas@mb.vu.lt
Web Site: www.mb.vu.lt
Key Personnel
General Dir: Irena Kriviene *Tel:* (05) 268 7102 *E-mail:* irena.kriviene@mb.vu.lt
Founded: 1579
Membership(s): Lithuanian Academic Libraries Association.

Luxembourg

Archives Nationales du Grand-Duche de Luxembourg (National Archives of Luxembourg)
Plateau du St-Esprit, Luxembourg
Mailing Address: BP 6, 2010 Luxembourg
Tel: 2478 6660 *Fax:* 47 46 92
E-mail: archives.nationales@an.etat.lu
Web Site: www.anlux.lu
Key Personnel
Dir: Josee Kirps *Tel:* 2478 6680 *E-mail:* josee.kirps@an.etat.lu
Publication(s): *Publications des Anlux, Plusieurs Series* (catalogs, repertoires, reprints)

Bibliotheque Municipale
26, rue Emile Mayrisch, 4240 Esch-sur-Alzette
Tel: 2754-4960
E-mail: bibliotheque@villeesch.lu
Web Site: www.esch.lu/culture/bibliotheque
Founded: 1918

Bibliotheque nationale de Luxembourg (National Library of Luxembourg)
37, Blvd F D Roosevelt, 2450 Luxembourg
Tel: 22 97 55-1 *Fax:* 47 56 72
E-mail: info@bnl.etat.lu
Web Site: www.bnl.lu

Key Personnel
Dir: Dr Monique Kieffer
Founded: 1798
Publication(s): *Bibliographie d'histoire luxembourgeoise; Bibliographie luxembourgeoise*

Macau

Biblioteca Central de Macau (Macau Central Library)
Av Conselheiro Ferreira de Almeida, Nº 89 A-B, Macau
Tel: 2856 7576; 2855 8049 *Fax:* 2831 8756
E-mail: inf.bc@icm.gov.mo
Web Site: www.library.gov.mo
Founded: 1895
Publication(s): *Boletim Bibliografico de Macau*

Macedonia

Arhiv na Makedonija (Archives of Macedonia)
Kej Dimitar Viahov No 19, 1000 Skopje
Tel: (02) 3115-783; (02) 3116-571 *Fax:* (02) 3165-944
E-mail: contact@arhiv.gov.mk
Web Site: www.arhiv.gov.mk
Key Personnel
Dir: Dr Filip Petrovski *Tel:* (02) 3115-783 ext 115 *E-mail:* filip.petrovski@arhiv.gov.mk
Deputy Dir: Muzafer Bislimi *E-mail:* muzafer.bislimi@arhiv.gov.mk
Founded: 1951

Narodna i univerzitetska biblioteka Kliment Ohridski (National & University Library "St Kliment Ohridski")
St Blvd "Goce Delcev" No 6, 1000 Skopje
Mailing Address: PO Box 566, 1000 Skopje
Tel: (02) 3115 177 *Fax:* (02) 3226 846
E-mail: kliment@nubsk.edu.mk
Web Site: www.nubsk.edu.mk
Founded: 1944
Publication(s): *Bibliografija KPJ-SKM 1919-1979; Bilten na izdanija od oblasta na samoupravuvanjeto vo Jugoslavija; Katalog na staropecateni i retki knigi vo Narodnata i Univerzitetskata Biblioteka 'Kliment Ohridski' - Skopje; Makedonska Bibliografija*

Madagascar

Archives Nationales de Madagascar
23, rue Karija Tsaralalana, 101 Antananarivo
Tel: 20 235 34
E-mail: dan_madagascar@yahoo.fr
Web Site: www.archivesnationales.gov.mg
Key Personnel
Dir: Mdme Sahondra Sylvie Andriamihamina
Founded: 1895

Bibliotheque Nationale de Madagascar
BP 257, 101 Antananarivo
Tel: 22 258 72 *Fax:* 22 294 48

Bibliotheque Universitaire Antananarivo
BP 908, 101 Antananarivo
Tel: 22 612 28; 22 612 29 *Fax:* 22 612 29
E-mail: bu@univ-antananarivo.mg
Web Site: www.univ-antananarivo.mg
Founded: 1960

Mediatheque de l'Institut Francais de Madagascar
14, ave de l'Independance, 101 Antananarivo
Mailing Address: BP 488, 101 Antananarivo
Tel: 22 236 47; 22 213 75 *Fax:* 22 213 38
E-mail: contact@institutfrancais-madagascar.com; info@institutfrancais-madagascar.com
Web Site: www.institutfrancais-madagascar.com
Key Personnel
Media Dir: Volatiana Ranaivozafy
Founded: 1964
Cooperation culturelle, artistique et universitaire.

Malawi

British Council Library
Area 40, Plot 3, Capital City, Lilongwe 3
Tel: (021) 2240199
E-mail: info@britishcouncil.org.mw
Web Site: www.britishcouncil.mw
Key Personnel
Dir: Reena Johl
Founded: 1964

Bunda College Library
PO Box 219, Lilongwe
Tel: 01 277 348; 01 277 222 *Fax:* 01 277 251; 01 277 364
E-mail: principal@bunda.sdnp.org; library@bunda.luanar.mw
Web Site: www.bunda.luanar.mw/library; buncoalumni.tripod.com/id13.html
Key Personnel
College Librarian: Geoffrey F Salanje
   E-mail: gsalanje@bunda.luanar.mw

National Archives of Malawi
PO Box 62, Zomba
Tel: 01 525 240; 01 524 148; 01 524 184 *Fax:* 01 525 362; 01 524 525
E-mail: archives@sdnp.org.mw
Web Site: www.sdnp.org.mw/ruleoflaw/archives
Key Personnel
Acting Dir: O W Ambali
Records Management Officer: J S Thaulo
Founded: 1947
Publication(s): *Malawi National Bibliography*

National Library Service of Malawi
PO Box 30314, Lilongwe 3
Tel: 01 773 700 *Fax:* 01 771 616
E-mail: nls@malawi.net
Web Site: www.nls.mw
Key Personnel
National Librarian: Mr Gray L Nyali
   E-mail: gnyali@hotmail.com
Founded: 1967

University of Malawi Libraries
PO Box 278, Zomba
Tel: 01 526 622; 01 524 282; 01 524 060; 01 526 456 *Fax:* 01 524 760; 01 524 297; 01 524 031
E-mail: registrar@unima.mw; vc@unima.mw
Web Site: www.unima.mw
Founded: 1965
Publication(s): *An Annotated Bibliography of Education in Malawi; Directory of Malawi Libraries; Library Bulletin; Report on University Libraries*
Branch Office(s)
Chancellor College Library, PO Box 280, Zomba, Librarian: D B V Phiri *Tel:* 01 524 222 *E-mail:* registrar@cc.ac.mw *Web Site:* www.chanco.unima.mw
College of Medicine Library, Private Bag 360, Chichiri, Blantyre 3, Librarian: Diston S Chiweza *Tel:* 01 871 911 *E-mail:* registrar@medcol.mw *Web Site:* www.medcol.mw/library

Polytechnic Library, PB 303, Chichiri, Blantyre 3, College Librarian: Dorothy Eneya *Tel:* 01 873 861 *Fax:* 01 870 411 *E-mail:* polylibrary@poly.ac.mw *Web Site:* www.poly.ac.mw/library
Bunda College of Agriculture Library, PO Box 219, Bunda, Lilongwe, College Librarian: Geoffrey F Salanje *Tel:* 01 277 348 *Fax:* 01 277 251 *E-mail:* library@bunda.luanar.mw *Web Site:* www.bunda.luanar.mw/library
Kamuzu College of Nursing Library, Private Bag 1, Lilongwe *Tel:* 01 751 622 *Fax:* 01 756 424 *E-mail:* malico@kcn.unima.mw *Web Site:* www.malico.mw

University of Malawi, Polytechnic Library
Private Bag 303, Chichiri, Blantyre 3
Tel: 01 870 411; 01 871 637 *Fax:* 01 870 578
E-mail: registrar@poly.ac.mw; polylibrary@poly.ac.mw
Web Site: www.poly.ac.mw
Key Personnel
College Librarian: Dorothy Eneya
Founded: 1965

Malaysia

Arkib Negara Malaysia (National Archives of Malaysia)
Jl Duta, 50568 Kuala Lumpur
Tel: (03) 6201 0600 *Fax:* (03) 6201 5679
E-mail: webmaster@arkib.gov.my
Web Site: www.arkib.gov.my
Key Personnel
Dir General: Azemi Bin Abdul Aziz *Tel:* (03) 6209 0601 *E-mail:* azemi@arkib.gov.my
Dir, Archives: Habibah Binti Ismail *Tel:* (03) 6209 0750 *E-mail:* habib@arkib.gov.my
Founded: 1957
Publication(s): *Annual Report of the National Archives*

Malaysian Rubber Board Library
RRIM, 260 Jl Ampang, 50450 Kuala Lumpur
Tel: (03) 9206 3642; (03) 9206 3643; (03) 9206 3644 *Fax:* (03) 4257 3512
E-mail: general@lgm.gov.my
Web Site: rios.lgm.gov.my/cms/index.jsp
Key Personnel
Chief Librarian: Fauziah A Rahman
   E-mail: fauziah@lgm.gov.my
Librarian: Nor Faezah Ismail *E-mail:* suhaime@lgm.gov.my; Mohd Norafendy Mohd Nordin *E-mail:* norafendy@lgm.gov.my
Founded: 1925
Publication(s): *Journal of Rubber Research* (quarterly)

Perbadanan Perpustakaan Awam Selangor (Selangor Public Library)
D/A Perpustakaan Raja Tun Uda, Jl Kelab Golf 13/6 Seksyen 13, 40100 Shah Alam, Selangor
Tel: (03) 5519 7667; (03) 5519 7682; (03) 5519 7679; (03) 5519 7685; (03) 5519 7691 *Fax:* (03) 5510 4264; (03) 5519 6045
E-mail: info@ppas.org.my; infoppas@gmail.com
Web Site: www.ppas.gov.my

Perpustakaan Negara Malaysia (National Library of Malaysia)
232, Jl Tun Razak, 50572 Kuala Lumpur
Tel: (03) 2687 1700 *Fax:* (03) 2694 2490
E-mail: webmaster@pnm.gov.my
Web Site: www.pnm.gov.my
Key Personnel
Dir General: Nafisah Ahmad *Tel:* (03) 2687 1900
   E-mail: nafisah@pnm.gov.my
Founded: 1966

Publication(s): *Bibliography of books in Bahasa Malaysia; Directory of Librarians in Malaysia; Directory of Libraries in Malaysia; Index to Malaysian Conferences* (annually); *Malaysian National Bibliography* (quarterly, annually); *Malaysian Newspaper Index* (quarterly); *Malaysian Periodicals Index* (2 times/yr)

Perpustakaan Negeri Sabah, see Sabah State Library

Perpustakaan Sultanah Zanariah
Universiti Teknologi Malaysia, UTM Skudai, 81310 Johor, Darul Takzim
Tel: (07) 5530188 *Fax:* (07) 5572555
E-mail: lib-enquiryjb@utm.my
Web Site: www.library.utm.my
Key Personnel
Chief Librarian: Kamariah Nor Mohd Desa
   Tel: (07) 5530101 *E-mail:* kamariahnor@utm.my
Deputy Chief Librarian: Noraziah Sharuddin
   Tel: (07) 5530104 *E-mail:* noraziah@utm.my; Anuar Talib *Tel:* (07) 5530102 *E-mail:* anuar@utm.my
Publication(s): *Berita Unitek, Berita Satelit; Jurnal Teknologi*
Branch Office(s)
Universiti Teknologi Malaysia, Jl Semarak, 54100 Kuala Lumpur *Tel:* (03) 26154301 *Fax:* (03) 26922186 *E-mail:* lib-enquirykl@utm.my

Perpustakaan Tun Seri Lanang (National University of Malaysia Library)
Universiti Kebangsaan Malaysia, 43600 Bangi, Selangor, DE
Tel: (03) 89213446 *Fax:* (03) 89256067
E-mail: kpustaka@ukm.edu.my; webptsl@ukm.edu.my
Web Site: www.ukm.my/ptsl
Key Personnel
Chief Librarian: Hafsah Mohd *Tel:* (03) 89214134
   E-mail: hafsahm@ukm.my
Founded: 1970
Holds Malay library collection (approximately 30,000 titles).
Publication(s): *Katalog Koleksi Melayu, Penerbit Ukm 1990*

Sabah State Library
Jl Tasik, off Jl Maktab Gaya, 88300 Kota Kinabalu
Mailing Address: Locked Bag 2023, 88999 Kota Kinabalu, Sabah
Tel: (088) 214828; (088) 231623; (088) 254493 *Fax:* (088) 230714
E-mail: hq.ssl@sabah.gov.my
Web Site: www.ssl.sabah.gov.my
Key Personnel
Dir General & Manager: Wong Vui Yin
   E-mail: vuiyin.wong@sabah.gov.my
Senior Deputy Dir: Maria Sinti *E-mail:* maria.sinti@sabah.gov.my
Founded: 1953

SEACEN, see South East Asian Central Banks (SEACEN) Research & Training Centre

South East Asian Central Banks (SEACEN) Research & Training Centre
Bank Negara Malaysia, 2 Jl Dato Onn, Level 5, Sasana Kijang, 50480 Kuala Lumpur
Tel: (03) 9195 1888 *Fax:* (03) 9195 1801; (03) 9195 1802; (03) 9195 1803
E-mail: enquiries@seacen.org
Web Site: www.seacen.org
Key Personnel
Executive Dir: Dr Hans Genberg
Founded: 1977

Perpustakaan Sultan Abdul Samad, see
Universiti Putra Malaysia Library (UPM)

Universiti Putra Malaysia Library (UPM)
UPM Serdang, 43400 Selangor Darul Ehsan
Tel: (03) 89468642 *Fax:* (03) 89483745
E-mail: lib@upm.edu.my
Web Site: www.lib.upm.edu.my
Key Personnel
Deputy Chief Librarian: Muzaffar Shah Kassim
Tel: (03) 89467941 *E-mail:* msk@lib.upm.edu.
my
Founded: 1971

University Library, Universiti Sains Malaysia
11800 Pulau Penang
Tel: (04) 6533888 *Fax:* (04) 6571526
E-mail: adminlib@usm.my; chieflib@usm.my
Web Site: www.lib.usm.my
Key Personnel
Chief Librarian: Mohammed Pisol
Ghadzali *Tel:* (04) 6533888 ext 3700
E-mail: mohdpisol@usm.my
Deputy Chief Librarian: Ali Hj Abd Rahim
Tel: (04) 6533888 ext 2885 *E-mail:* lbali@usm.
my
Founded: 1969
Publication(s): *Bibliography series* (irregularly);
Jendela (bulletin); *Midas Bulletin* (quarterly)

**University of Engineering & Technology
Malaysia Library**, see Perpustakaan Sultanah
Zanariah

University of Malaya Library
Lembah Pantai, 50603 Kuala Lumpur
Tel: (03) 7956 7800 *Fax:* (03) 7957 3661
E-mail: query_perpustakaan@um.edu.my;
umlibweb@um.edu.my
Web Site: www.umlib.um.edu.my
Key Personnel
Chief Librarian: Dr Nor Edzan Che Nasir
Tel: (03) 7967 3206 *E-mail:* edzan@um.edu.my
Senior Deputy Chief: Yusof Mahbob *Tel:* (03)
7967 3304 *E-mail:* mahbobyusof@um.edu.my
Founded: 1959
Publication(s): *Kekal Abadi* (quarterly, newsletter)

UPM, see Universiti Putra Malaysia Library
(UPM)

Mali

Bibliotheque Nationale du Mali (National
Library of Mali)
BP E4473, Hamdallaye ACI 2000, Bamako
Tel: 20 29 94 23 *Fax:* 20 29 93 96
E-mail: dnbd@afribone.net.ml
Web Site: www.bn.gouv.ml
Key Personnel
National Librarian: Mr Mamadou Demba Sissko
Founded: 1962

Ecole normale superieure
BP 241, Bamako
Tel: 20 22 21 89 *Fax:* 223 04 61
E-mail: ensup@ml.refer.org
Key Personnel
Dir: Ibrahima Camara

**Mediatheque du Centre Culturel Francais de
Bamako**
Blvd de l'independance, Bamako
Mailing Address: BP 1547, Bamako
Tel: 20 22 40 19

E-mail: dir@ccfbamako.org; relationspubliques@
institutfrancaismali.org
Web Site: www.institutfrancaisdumali.org
Key Personnel
Deputy Dir: Corinne Micaelli-Mulholland
E-mail: corinne.micaelli@institutfrancaismali.
org
Head, Media: Abdoulaye Maiga *E-mail:* media@
institutfrancaismali.org

**Universite de Bamako Bibliotheque de Faculte
de Medecine de Pharmacie et
d'Odonto-Stomatologie**
BP 1805, Bamako
Tel: 20 22 52 77 *Fax:* 20 22 96 58
E-mail: diawara@mrtcbko.org
Web Site: www.keneya.net/fmpos
Founded: 1969

Malta

Bibljoteka Nazzjonali ta' Malta (National
Library of Malta)
36 Old Treasury St, Valletta VLT 1410
Tel: 21243297; 21236585; 21232691; 21245303
E-mail: customercare.nlm@gov.mt
Web Site: www.maltalibraries.gov.mt
Founded: 1776
Publication(s): *A Bibliography of the 19th Cen-
tury Periodicals*; *Charles Frederick De Brock-
torff: Watercolours of Malta at the National
Library, Valletta*; *Facsimile of Quintinus' De-
scription of Malta, 1536*; *Giuoco D'Arme Dei
Sovrani e Degli Stati D'Europa*; *A Guide to the
National Library of Malta*; *Malta National Bib-
liography*; *National Library CD-ROM*; *Printing
in Malta*; *Mikiel A Vassalli*

Gozo Public Libraries
Triq Vajringa, St Francis Sq, Victoria, Gozo VCT
1335
Tel: 21561510
E-mail: gozolibraries.mgoz@gov.mt
Web Site: www.maltalibraries.gov.mt
Founded: 1853

University of Malta Library
Msida MSD 2080
Tel: 2340 2340; 2340 2541 *Fax:* 2340 2342
Web Site: www.um.edu.mt/library
Key Personnel
Dir, Library Services: Kevin J Ellul *Tel:* 2340
2317
Deputy Dir, Library Services: Josianne Camilleri
Vella *Tel:* 2340 2011
Founded: 1954
Branch Office(s)
Faculty of Arts Library, Msida MSD 2080
Tel: 2340 2635
Faculty of Laws & Theology Library, Msida
MSD 2080 *Tel:* 2340 3523
Health Sciences Library, Mater Dei Hospital,
Block A, Level 0, Room A110 384, Msida
MSD 2090, Senior Assistant Librarian: Rachel
Grixti *Tel:* 2340 1867
Junior College Library, Guze Debono Sq, Msida
MSD 1252, Assistant Librarian: Mark Anthony
Poulton *Tel:* 2590 7237
University Gozo Centre, Mgarr Rd, Gozo XWK
9016 *Tel:* 21564559
Valletta Campus Library, Old University Bldg, St
Paul's St, Valletta VLT 1216 *Tel:* 2340 7520

Martinique

Archives Departementales de la Martinique
19 Ave St-John-Perse, 97263 Fort de France
Cedex
Mailing Address: BP 649, 97263 Fort de France
Cedex
Tel: 05 96 55 43 43 *Fax:* 05 96 70 04 50
E-mail: archives@cg972.fr
Web Site: www2.cg972.fr/arch/html/index01.htm
Key Personnel
Head, Education & Culture: Lily Thevenard
Tel: 05 96 55 43 50 *E-mail:* thevenard@cg972.
fr
Founded: 1949
Publication(s): *Actes du colloque: Moareau de
Saint-Mery ou les ambiguietes d'un creole des
lumieres*; *Cent cinquantenaire de l'abolition
de l'esclavage - Inventaire des sources con-
servees aux Archives departementales* (1998);
*Conseil souverain de la Martinique, Tome 1
(1712-1791)* (1985); *Conseil souverain de
la Martinique, Tome 2 (1791-1820)* (1999);
*Des Constitutions a la description de Saint-
Domingue* (catalog, 2004); *Declaration des
droits de l'homme et abolition de l'esclavage*
(catalog, 1998); *L'eglise martiniquaise et la
piete populaire* (catalog, 2001); *Enfances mar-
tiniquaises: 1848-1950* (catalog, 2001); *Guide
des Archives departementales de la Martinique*
(1978); *Guide des sources de l'architecture,
d'apres les registres du Conseil prive* (1991);
*L'immigration indienne a la Martinique (1853-
1900)* (2003); *Le livre, source de l'histoire
des Antilles* (catalog, 1989); *La Martinique
au temps de la Revolution francaise: 1789-
1794* (1977); *La Martinique dans la premiere
guerre mondiale* (2004); *La Martinique de
Pierre Verger* (catalog, 2000); *1902 et apres*
(catalog, 2002); *Le pays du volcan: sources de
l'histoire de Saint-Pierre et de sa region*; *La
seconde guerre mondiale: Formes de resistance
et dissidence a la Martinique* (catalog, 1990);
*Tobago et la presence francaise: XVIIe-XIXe
siecle* (catalog)

Bibliotheque Schoelcher
One Rue de la Liberte, 97200 Fort-de-France
Mailing Address: BP 640, 97262 Fort-de-France
Cedex
Tel: 05 96 55 68 30 *Fax:* 05 96 72 45 55
E-mail: bibliotheque.schoelcher@
collectivitedemartinique.mq
Web Site: mediatheques.collectivitedemartinique.
mq/bs
Key Personnel
Dir: Lyne-Rose Beuze *Tel:* 05 96 55
68 31 *E-mail:* lyne-rose.beuze@
collectivitedemartinique.mq
Founded: 1883

**Bibliotheque Universitaire Antilles-Guyane
(BUAG)**
BP 7210, 97275 Schoelcher Cedex
Tel: 05 96 72 75 44 *Fax:* 05 96 72 75 27
E-mail: bu@martinique.univ-ag.fr
Web Site: buag.univ-ag.fr
Key Personnel
Dir: Sylvain Houdebert *E-mail:* sylvain.
houdebert@univ-ag.fr

BUAG, see Bibliotheque Universitaire
Antilles-Guyane (BUAG)

Mauritania

Bibliotheque Nationale de Mauritanie
BP 193, Nouakchott
Tel: 45222423
Key Personnel
Contact: Souleymane Ould Mohamed Bouna
  E-mail: bounamohamed_soul@yahoo.fr

Direction des Archives Nationales, Bibliotheque Publique et Centre du Documentation
Ave de l'Independance, Nouakchott
Mailing Address: BP 77, Nouakchott

Mauritius

British Council Library
Royal Rd, Rose Hill
Tel: 403 0200 *Fax:* 454 9553
E-mail: general.enquiries@mu.britishcouncil.org
Web Site: www.britishcouncil.mu

Carnegie Library
Queen Elizabeth II Ave, Curepipe
Tel: 670 6733; 670 4897; 670 4899
E-mail: curpip@intnet.mu; carnegiemcc@gmail.com
Key Personnel
Senior Librarian: Bibi Nassembee Peerbucus-Bahadoor
Librarian: Shafinaz Fazall
Founded: 1917
Large collection of material on historical background of Mauritius & original manuscripts, papers on colonization by French & British.

Leoville L'Homme Municipal Library
City Hall, Sir Jules Koenig St, Port Louis
Tel: 213 5772 *Fax:* 212 4258
E-mail: mpllib@intnet.mu; mpl.ce@intnet.mu
Web Site: www.mccpl.mu/s_lib.html
Founded: 1851
Publication(s): *Bibliography: Mauritiana in City Library; Literary Publishing & Bibliographical Control in Mauritius; Newspapers Index: Mauritius*

Mauritius Institute of Education Library
Mauritius Institute of Education, Reduit
Tel: 401 6555
Web Site: www.mie.ac.mu/home/categories/library.html
Key Personnel
Chief Librarian: Mr Khemrajh Seeburrun
  E-mail: k.seeburrun@mieonline.org
Founded: 1903

Mauritius National Archives
Development Bank of Mauritius Complex, Coromandel
Fax: 2334299
E-mail: arc@govmu.org
Web Site: nationalarchives.govmu.org
Key Personnel
Acting Dir: Mrs H Ramkalawan *Tel:* 2333848
Founded: 1815
Publication(s): *Annual Report of the Archives Department* (including a bibliographical supplement); *Quarterly Memorandum of Books Printed in Mauritius and Registered in the Archives*

MIE Library, see Mauritius Institute of Education Library

University of Mauritius Library
University of Mauritius, Reduit
Tel: 403 7915; 403 7976 *Fax:* 464 0905
E-mail: uomlibrary@uom.ac.mu; cl@uom.ac.mu
Web Site: www.uom.ac.mu
Key Personnel
Chief Librarian: Mr I Dassyne *E-mail:* idassyne@uom.ac.mu
Founded: 1979
Publication(s): *University of Mauritius Calendar; University of Mauritius Report* (annually)

Mexico

Anglo Mexican Foundation Library
Antonio Caso 127, Colonia San Rafael, 06470 Mexico, CDMX
Tel: (0155) 3067 8817; (0155) 3067 8800 (ext 8860)
E-mail: biblioteca@tamf.org.mx
Web Site: tamflibrary.org.mx
Key Personnel
Contact: Anabel Contreras *E-mail:* anabel.contreras@tamf.org.mx
Founded: 1944
Anglo-Mexican cultural institute.

Archivo General de la Nacion Mexico
Eduardo Molina 113, Colonia Penitenciaria, 15280 Mexico, CDMX
Tel: (0155) 51339900 *Fax:* (0155) 57895296
E-mail: difusion@agn.gob.mx
Web Site: www.gob.mx/agn
Key Personnel
Dir General: Mercedes de Vega
  Tel: (0155) 51339900 ext 19301
  E-mail: direcciongeneral@agn.gob.mx
Founded: 1792
Publication(s): *Boletin*

Biblioteca Benjamin Franklin (USIS)
Liverpool 31, Colonia Juarez, 06600 Mexico, CDMX
Tel: (0155) 5080-2089; (0155) 5080-2733
E-mail: perezjo@state.gov; voyalabiblioteca@state.gov
Web Site: mx.usembassy.gov/education-culture/american-spaces/ben-franklin-library
Founded: 1942
Publication(s): *Boletin de Seleccion de Adquisiciones Recientes* (quarterly)

Biblioteca Daniel Cosio Villegas El Colegio de Mexico AC (Daniel Cosio Villegas Library The College of Mexico)
Camino al Ajusco 20, Pedregal de Santa Teresa, 10740 Mexico, DF
Tel: (0155) 5449 3000 (ext 2121); (0155) 5449 3000 (ext 2122); (0155) 5449 3000 (ext 2222)
Web Site: biblioteca.colmex.mx
Key Personnel
Library Dir: Micaela Chavez Villa *Tel:* (0155) 5449 3000 ext 2909 *E-mail:* mch@colmex.mx
Founded: 1940
Graduate institution for research & education in the social sciences & the humanities.
Publication(s): *Boletin de la BDCV*

Biblioteca de la Universidad Iberoamericana
Prol Paseo de la Reforma 880, Lomas de Santa Fe, 01219 Mexico, DF
Tel: (0155) 5950-4000; (0155) 9177-4400
  Fax: (0155) 5950-4248
E-mail: buzon.biblioteca@uia.mx
Web Site: www.bib.uia.mx

Biblioteca de Mexico
Plaza de la Ciudadela No 4, Colonia Centro, 06040 Mexico, CDMX
Tel: (0155) 4155 0830
E-mail: contactomexico@conaculta.gob.mx
Web Site: www.bibliotecademexico.gob.mx
Key Personnel
General Dir: Eduardo Lizalde Chavez *Tel:* (0155) 4155 0830 ext 3850 *E-mail:* elizadec@cultura.gob.mx
Founded: 1946
Publication(s): *Biblioteca de Mexico* (magazine)

Biblioteca Francisco Xavier Clavigero, see Biblioteca de la Universidad Iberoamericana

Biblioteca Nacional de Antropologia e Historia (National Library of Anthropology & History)
Av Paseo de la Reforma y Calzada Gandhi s/n, Colonia Polanco, 11560 Mexico, CDMX
Tel: (0140) 40 53 50; (0140) 40 53 00; (0155) 53 68 65
E-mail: contacto.bnah@inah.gob.mx; servicios.bnah@inah.gob.mx
Web Site: www.bnah.inah.gob.mx
Key Personnel
Dir: Baltazar Brito Guadarrama *Tel:* (0140) 40 53 51 *E-mail:* baltazar_brito@inah.gob.mx
Founded: 1888

Biblioteca Nacional de Mexico
Centro Cultural Universitario, Ciudad Universitaria, Delegacion Coyoacan, 04510 Mexico, DF
Tel: (0155) 5622-6820; (0155) 5622-6850
E-mail: bnmex@iib.unam.mx
Web Site: bnm.unam.mx
Key Personnel
Dir: Dr Pablo Mora Perez-Tejada *Tel:* (0155) 5622-6816 *E-mail:* mora@unam.mx
Coordinator: Silvia Monica Salgado Ruelas
  E-mail: silsal@iib.unam.mx
Founded: 1867
Publication(s): *Bibliografia Mexicana; Boletin del Instituto de Investigaciones Bibliograficas* (annually)

CEDIA, see Centro de Documentacion, Informacion y Analisis (CEDIA)

Centro de Documentacion, Informacion y Analisis (CEDIA)
Av Congreso de la Union, Nº 66, Colonia El Parque Del Venustiano Carranza, 15969 Mexico, CDMX
Tel: (0155) 56 28 13 00 (ext 4706) *Fax:* (0155) 56 28 13 00 (ext 4705)
Web Site: www.diputados.gob.mx/biblioteca/bibdig/Iniciativas/index.htm
Key Personnel
Dir: Florencio Soriano Eslava *E-mail:* florencio.soriano@congreso.gob.mx

Direccion General de Bibliotecas de la Universidad Nacional Autonoma de Mexico
Edificio de la Biblioteca Central, Ciudad Universitaria, Circuito Interior, 04510 Mexico, DF
Tel: (0155) 5622 1603; (0155) 5622 1632
E-mail: subbcentral@dgb.unam.mx
Web Site: dgb.unam.mx
Key Personnel
Chairperson: Silvia Gonzalez Marin, PhD
Dir General of Libraries: Dr Aldolfo Rodriguez Gallardo
Librarian: Alberto Castro Thompson *Tel:* (0155) 5622 3969 *E-mail:* acastro@dgb.unam.mx
Founded: 1966
Publication(s): *Biblioteca Universitaria Revista de la Direccion General de Bibliotecas de la UNAM* (2 times/yr, journal, 1986, specializes in library & information science); *Directorio de Bibliotecas UNAM* (monthly, directory

for the 139 libraries in UNAM's library system); *Librunam* (database of books existing in UNAM's library system); *Seriunam* (database of journals & serial publications existing in UNAM's library system); *Tesiunam* (database of theses from UNAM & other Mexican universities)

Hemeroteca Nacional de Mexico
Centro Cultural Universitario, CU, Del Coyoacan, 04510 Mexico, DF
Tel: (0155) 5622 6818; (0155) 5622 6827
Web Site: www.hnm.unam.mx
Key Personnel
Dir: Dr Pablo Mora Perez-Tejada *Tel:* (0155) 5622 6816 *E-mail:* mora@iib.unam.mx
National Periodicals Library.

Instituto Nacional de Electricidad y Energias Limpias (INEEL)
Reforma 113, Colonia Palmira, 62490 Cuernavaca, MOR
Tel: (0777) 3623811; (0777) 3623800 *Fax:* (0777) 3623881
E-mail: difusion@iie.org.mx
Web Site: www.ineel.mx
Key Personnel
Executive Dir: Dr Jose Luis Fernandez Zayas *Tel:* (0777) 3182424 *E-mail:* joseluis.fernandez@iie.org.mx
Founded: 1975

Instituto Tecnologico y de Estudios Superiores de Monterrey Biblioteca
Ave Eugenio Garza Sada 2501 Sur, 64849 Monterrey, NL
Tel: (081) 8358-2000 (ext 4031)
Web Site: bibliotecatec21.mty.itesm.mx
Key Personnel
Dir: Yolanda Maya Ortega *E-mail:* ymaya@itesm.mx
Assistant Dir: Karla Janeth Martinez Tamez *E-mail:* karla.mtz@itesm.mx
Founded: 1949
Publication(s): *Transferencia* (monthly)

ITESM Biblioteca, see Instituto Tecnologico y de Estudios Superiores de Monterrey Biblioteca

Universidad Autonoma Chapingo Biblioteca Central
Km 38.5 Carretera Mexico-Texcoco, Texcoco, Edo de Mexico, 56230 Texcoco
Tel: (0595) 952-15-00 (ext 7111); (0595) 952-15-00 (ext 5741); (0595) 952-15-00 (ext 5440) *Fax:* (0595) 952-15-01
E-mail: biblioteca_central@correo.chapingo.mx
Web Site: www.chapingo.mx/ceres
Key Personnel
Chief Librarian: Alfonso Lopez Hernandez *E-mail:* jefatura_bibcentral@chapingo.mx
Founded: 1967

Monaco

Bibliotheque Louis Notari, see Mediatheque de Monaco

Mediatheque de Monaco
8, rue Louis-Notari, 98000 Monaco
Tel: 93 15 29 40 *Fax:* 93 15 29 41
E-mail: mediatheque@mairie.mc
Web Site: www.mediatheque.mc
Founded: 1909
Branch Office(s)
19, blvd Princesse Charlotte, 9800 Monaco

Montenegro

Centralna Narodna Biblioteka SR Crne Gore
(Central National Library of the Republic of Montenegro)
Bulevar crnogorskih junaka br 163, 81250 Cetinje
Tel: (041) 231-143; (041) 231-726 *Fax:* (041) 231-020; (041) 233-370
E-mail: info@vbcg.me
Web Site: www.cnb.me
Key Personnel
Dir: Jelena Djurovic *Tel:* (067) 311-528 (cell) *E-mail:* jelena.djurovic@cnb.me
Founded: 1946
National depository, general scientific & source library; special collection of Montenegrina, old & rare books.

Morocco

Bibliotheque Ben Youssef
Ave 11 Janvier Hay Mohamadi, Daoudiat-Marrakech
Tel: 0524301412 *Fax:* 0524291108
E-mail: youssef@hotmail.fr

Bibliotheque Generale et Archives du Tetouan
(General Library & Archives of Tetouan)
32, Ave Mohammed V, Tetouan
Tel: 05 39 96 32 58 *Fax:* 05 39 96 32 58

Bibliotheque Nationale du Royaume du Maroc
(National Library of Morocco)
Ave Ibn Khaldoun, Agdal Rabat
Tel: 05 37 27 23 00 *Fax:* 05 37 77 74 30
E-mail: bnrm@bnrm.ma
Web Site: www.bnrm.ma
Key Personnel
Dir: Abdelilah Tahani
Founded: 1924
Publication(s): *Bibliographie nationale marocaine*

Bibliotheque Quaraouiyine
Pl Seffarine, BP 790, Fes
Tel: 0535638449 *Fax:* 0539963258
E-mail: bibquaraouyine@yahoo.fr
Key Personnel
Regional Dir: Abdelfateh Boukchouf

BNRM, see Bibliotheque Nationale du Royaume du Maroc

British Council Library
11 Ave Allal Ben Abdellah, Rabat
Tel: 05 37 21 81 20
E-mail: info@britishcouncil.org.ma
Web Site: www.britishcouncil.ma.en
Key Personnel
Dir: John Mitchell
British cultural centre.
Branch Office(s)
87, Blvd Nador, Polo, Casablanca *Toll Free Tel:* 08 02 00 10 45

Centre National de Documentation
Ave Al Haj Ahmed Cherkaoui, Quartier des Ministeres Haut-Agdal, 10100 Rabat
Tel: 05 37 77 31 31 *Fax:* 05 37 77 31 34
E-mail: cndportal@yahoo.fr
Web Site: www.cnd.hcp.ma
Publication(s): *voir liste jointe*

Institut Scientifique
Service d'Edition et de Documentation, Bibliotheque Centrale, Av Ibn Batouta, BP 703 Agdal, Rabat
Tel: 05 37 77 45 48; 05 37 77 45 49; 05 37 77 45 50 *Fax:* 05 37 77 45 40
E-mail: direction@israbat.ac.ma
Web Site: www.israbat.ac.ma
Key Personnel
Dir: Mohammed Fekhaoui
Librarian: Malika Lamnini
Founded: 1921
Publication(s): *Bulletin de l'Institut Scientifique; Documents de l'Institut Scientifique; Travaux de l'Institut Scientifique*

Mozambique

AHM, see Arquivo Historico de Mocambique

Arquivo Historico de Mocambique
(Mozambique Historical Archives)
Travessa do Varieta nº 58, 2033 Maputo
Tel: (021) 32 34 28
E-mail: ahm@uem.mz
Web Site: www.ahm.uem.mz
Key Personnel
Dir: Dr Joel das Neves Tembe *E-mail:* jneves@zebra.uem.mz
Deputy Dir, Administration & Finance: Dr Ligia Zacchaeus
Founded: 1934
Specialize in administrative & colonial archives 19th & 20th centuries. Bibliographic, cartographic, photographic & poster collectives.
Publication(s): *Arquivo* (Archive, every six weeks, bulletin, 1987); *Documentos* (annually, series); *Estudos* (Studies, 7 times/yr, series)

Biblioteca Nacional de Mocambique
Av 25 Setembro 1348, Maputo
Mailing Address: PO Box 141, Maputo
Tel: (021) 311 905; (021) 311 906 *Fax:* (021) 311 906
E-mail: bcanacional@yahoo.com.br
Web Site: www.bnm.gov.mz
Founded: 1961

Direccao Nacional de Geologia (Centro de Documentacao) (National Directorate of Geology (Documentation Center))
Av Samora Machel nº 380, 4º andar, Praca 25 de Junho, Maputo
Tel: (021) 312082 *Fax:* (021) 321860
Founded: 1928
Publication(s): *Boletim Geologico* (Geological Bulletin, annually, report of activities of DNG)

Universidade Eduardo Mondlane, Direccao dos Servicos de Documentacao (DSD)
Campus Principal, Av Julius Nyerere, 1169 Maputo
Tel: (021) 485403 *Fax:* (021) 485403
Web Site: www.dsd.uem.mz
Key Personnel
Dir: Dr Horacio Francisco Zimba, PhD *E-mail:* horacio.zimba@uem.mz
Founded: 1980
Eduardo Mondlane University does not have a Central Library, but controls 15 departmental libraries; Direccao is responsible for all library & documentation services throughout the University.

Myanmar

National Library of Myanmar
85, Thirimingalar Yeiktha Lane, Kabar Aye
   Pagoda Rd, Yankin Township, Yangon
Tel: (01) 662470; (01) 660387 *Fax:* (01) 663902
E-mail: nl.myanmar@gmail.com
Web Site: www.nlm.gov.mm
Key Personnel
Head: Daw Mya Oo
Founded: 1952

University of Mandalay Library
73 St, Mandalay
Tel: (09) 797 384746 *Fax:* (02) 62129
E-mail: library@mu.edu.mm
Web Site: www.mu.edu.mm/library
Founded: 1958

University of Yangon Library
Adipati Rd, Kamaryut Township, Yangon 11041
Tel: (01) 537250
E-mail: univ.yangonlibrary@gmail.com
Web Site: uy.edu.mm/library
Key Personnel
Head Librarian: Dr Hlaing Hlaing Gyi
Founded: 1930

Namibia

National Archives of Namibia
1-7 Eugene Marais St, Windhoek
Mailing Address: Private Bag 13349, Windhoek
Tel: (061) 293 5301 *Fax:* (061) 293 5308
E-mail: info@nlas.gov.na
Web Site: www.nln.gov.na
Key Personnel
Deputy Permanent Secretary, Libraries & Archive
   Services: Veno Kauaria

National Library of Namibia
1-7 Eugene Marais St, Windhoek
Mailing Address: Private Bag 13349, Windhoek
Tel: (061) 2935300; (061) 2935304 *Fax:* (061)
   2935321
E-mail: natlib@mec.gov.na
Web Site: www.nln.gov.na
Key Personnel
Chief Librarian: Johan Loubser *Tel:* (061)
   2935301
Senior Librarian, Bibliographic Services: Paul
   Zulu *Tel:* (061) 2935305
Senior Librarian, Document Delivery: Charles
   Mlambo *Tel:* (061) 2935304
Senior Librarian, ICT Services: Bravismore Mu-
   manyi *Tel:* (061) 2935313
Librarian, Bibliographic Services: Antonia
   Lusakalalu *Tel:* (061) 2935306
Founded: 1926

Windhoek Public Library
4 Luderitz St, Windhoek
Mailing Address: Private Bag 13183, Windhoek
Tel: (061) 224163 *Fax:* (061) 258745
Founded: 1925

Nepal

British Council Library
PO Box 640, Lainchaur, Kathmandu
Tel: (01) 4410 798 *Fax:* (01) 4410 545

E-mail: general.enquiry@britishcouncil.org.np
Web Site: www.britishcouncil.org.np
Key Personnel
Dir: Brendan McSharry
Founded: 1959

Madan Puraskar Library (Madan Puraskar
   Pustakalaya)
PO Box 42, Patan Dhoka, Lalitpur
Tel: 5549948; 5005515 *Fax:* 5536390
E-mail: info@mpp.org.np
Web Site: madanpuraskar.org
Key Personnel
Chairman: Kamal Mani Dixit
Founded: 1956

Nepal National Library
Harihar Bhawan, Pulchowk, Lalitpur
Tel: (01) 5521132
E-mail: info@nnl.gov.np
Web Site: www.nnl.gov.np
Key Personnel
Chief Librarian: Upendra Prasad
   Mainali *Tel:* (098) 41143485 (cell)
   E-mail: upendraprasadmainali@gmail.com
Founded: 1957
Publication(s): *Souvenir* (2005); *Union Catalogue*

Tribhuvan University Central Library
Kirtipur, Kathmandu
Tel: (01) 4330834; (01) 4331317
E-mail: tucl@tucl.org.np
Web Site: www.tucl.org.np
Key Personnel
Chief Librarian: Indra Prasad Adhikari
   E-mail: adhikariip@gmail.com
Deputy Librarian: Radhika Maiya Bajrachaya;
   Dilip Man Sthapit *E-mail:* milandms@
   gmail.com; Lunashree Upadhyaya
   E-mail: lunaupadhyaya@yahoo.com
Founded: 1959
Serves the university, government, ministries,
   foreign diplomatic missions, local & foreign
   researchers & the general public. Also is a
   depository for 16 international organizations,
   including UN publications, since 1965. The
   library has nearly 290,000 books at present.
   There are about 450 titles of learned periodicals, newspapers & valuable manuscripts.
   Nepal ISBN Agency is located here. The library has distributed 11,377 ISBNs to Nepalese
   publications & is the national coordination
   agency for the International Networking for
   Availability of Scientific Publications. This program provides access to more than 25,000 full-
   text scholarly journals to the Nepalese scholars,
   scientists & other users free of cost. More than
   200 institutions & organizations of Nepal have
   registered to have access to PERI resources.
Publication(s): *Bibliography of non-alignment,
   1982*; *Bibliography of Population & Family Planning, 1981*; *Nepalese National Bibliography* (annually, 1993, books published
   from Nepal, all subjects); *Nepal's Foreign Affairs* (bibliographical guide to resources in the
   TUCL, 1974); *Research on Nepal, a Bibliography of PhD Thesis* (2003, submitted by research scholars engaged in various fields of
   Nepal)

TUCL, see Tribhuvan University Central Library

Netherlands

de Bibliotheek Arnhem
Kortestr 16, 6811 EP Arnhem
Mailing Address: Postbus 1168, 6801 ML Arn-
   hem

Tel: (026) 354 3111
E-mail: klantenservice@bibliotheekarnhem.nl
Web Site: www.bibliotheekarnhem.nl
Founded: 1853
Branch Office(s)
Kronenburggalerij 7, 6831 ET, Arnhem
Laan van Presikhaaf 7, 6826 HA Arnhem

Bibliotheek der Rijksuniversiteit Groningen
   (University of Groningen Library)
Broerstr 4, 9712 CP Groningen
Mailing Address: Postbus 559, 9700 AN Gronin-
   gen
Tel: (050) 3635000; (050) 3635020 (info desk)
   Fax: (050) 3634996
E-mail: bibliotheek@rug.nl
Web Site: www.rug.nl/bibliotheek
Founded: 1614

Bibliotheek Rotterdam (Rotterdam Library)
Hoogstr 110, 3011 PV Rotterdam
Mailing Address: Postbus 22140, 3003 DC, Rot-
   terdam
Tel: (010) 281 61 00
E-mail: klantenservice@bibliotheek.rotterdam.nl
Web Site: www.bibliotheek.rotterdam.nl

Bibliotheek Technische Universiteit Eindhoven
   (Eindhoven University of Technology Library)
Groene Loper 5, MetaForum Bldg, 5612 AZ
   Eindhoven
Mailing Address: Postbus 90159, 5600 RM Eind-
   hoven
Tel: (040) 247 2381 *Fax:* (040) 247 4747
E-mail: iec.helpdesk@tue.nl
Web Site: www.tue.nl/en/university/library
Key Personnel
Head Librarian: J C M Figdor *Tel:* (040) 247
   4033 *E-mail:* j.c.m.figdor@tue.nl

**Bibliotheek van de Universiteit van
   Amsterdam** (Amsterdam University Library)
Singel 425, 1012 WP Amsterdam
Mailing Address: Postbus 19185, 1000 GD Ams-
   terdam
Tel: (020) 525 2301 *Fax:* (020) 525 2390
E-mail: secr-uba@uva.nl
Web Site: www.uba.uva.nl
Key Personnel
Librarian: Dr Maria Heijne *Tel:* (020) 525 2307
   E-mail: mamheijne@uva.nl
Founded: 1578

**Bibliotheek van het Centraal Bureau voor de
   Statistiek** (Statistics Netherlands Library)
Henri Faasdreef 312, 2492 JP The Hague
Mailing Address: Postbus 24500, 2490 HA The
   Hague
Tel: (070) 337 38 00
E-mail: bibliotheek@cbs.nl
Web Site: www.cbs.nl
Branch Office(s)
CBS-Weg 11, Postbus 4481, 6401 CZ Heerlen
   Tel: (045) 570 60 00

Bibliotheek Wageningen UR (Wageningen UR
   Library)
Droevendaalsesteeg 2, Bldg 102, 6708 PB Wa-
   geningen
Mailing Address: PO Box 9100, 6700 HA Wa-
   geningen
Tel: (0317) 486666
E-mail: forum.library@wur.nl
Web Site: library.wur.nl
Key Personnel
Library Dir: Dr Hubert Krekels *Tel:* (0317)
   485710
Founded: 1873

Dienst Openbare Bibliotheek Den Haag (The Hague Public Library)
Spui 68, 2511 BT The Hague
Mailing Address: Postbus 12653, 2500 DP The Hague
Tel: (070) 353 44 55
E-mail: centralebibliotheek@bibliotheekdenhaag. nl
Web Site: www.bibliotheekdenhaag.nl

IISH, see Internationaal Instituut voor Sociale Geschiedenis

Internationaal Instituut voor Sociale Geschiedenis (International Institute of Social History)
Cruquiusweg 31, 1019 AT Amsterdam
Mailing Address: Postbus 2169, 1000 CD Amsterdam
Tel: (020) 6685866 *Fax:* (020) 6654181
E-mail: info@iisg.nl; ask@iisg.nl
Web Site: www.iisg.nl
Key Personnel
General Dir: Henk Wals *E-mail:* henk.wals@iisg. nl
Dir, Collections: Afelonne Doek *E-mail:* ado@ iisg.nl
Dir, Research: Leo Lucassen *E-mail:* leo. lucassen@iisg.nl
Founded: 1935
Documentary & research institute in the field of social history.
Publication(s): *Catalogs & Monograph Series; International Review of Social History*

Koninklijke Bibliotheek (Royal Library)
Prins Willem Alexanderhof 5, 2595 BE The Hague
Mailing Address: PO Box 90407, 2509 LK The Hague
Tel: (070) 3140911; (070) 3140310; (070) 3140402 *Fax:* (070) 3140653; (070) 3140652
E-mail: directie.secretariaat@kb.nl
Web Site: www.kb.nl
Key Personnel
Dir: Dr Lily Knibbeler *Tel:* (070) 3140558
E-mail: lily.knibbeler@kb.nl
Publication(s): *Bibliography of Translations* (from the Dutch); *Dutch Bibliography - Brinkman's Cumulatieve Catalogues*

Museum Meermanno-Westreenianum
Prinsessegracht 30, 2514 AP The Hague
Tel: (070) 3462700 *Fax:* (070) 3630350
E-mail: info@meermanno.nl; bibliotheek@ meermanno.nl
Web Site: www.meermanno.nl
Key Personnel
Dir: Maartje de Haan *E-mail:* dehaan@ meermanno.nl
Librarian: Rickey Tax *E-mail:* tax@meermanno. nl; Petra Luijkx *E-mail:* luijkx@meermanno.nl
Founded: 1848
National book museum.

Radboud Universiteitsbibliotheek Nijmegen (Radboud University Nijmegen Library)
Erasmuslaan 36, 6525 GG Nijmegen
Mailing Address: PO Box 9100, 6500 HA Nijmegen
Tel: (024) 3612417; (024) 3612428; (024) 3612437
E-mail: info@ubn.ru.nl
Web Site: www.ru.nl/ubn
Key Personnel
Dir: N Grygierczyk
Faculty Librarian: Mrs G Lamers *Tel:* (024) 3612406 *E-mail:* g.lamers@ubn.ru.nl
Founded: 1923

Rijksmuseum Research Library
Museumstr 1, 1071 XX Amsterdam
Mailing Address: Postbus 74888, 1070 DN Amsterdam
Tel: (020) 67 47 267; (020) 67 47 055
E-mail: bibliotheek@rijksmuseum.nl
Web Site: library.rijksmuseum.nl
Key Personnel
Head, Library: G J Koot
Founded: 1885
Specialize in art history.
Membership(s): International Federation of Library Associations & Institutions (IFLA).

Stichting Arnhemse Openbare en Gelderse Wetenschappelijke Bibliotheek, see de Bibliotheek Arnhem

Universiteit Wageningen, see Bibliotheek Wageningen UR

Universiteitsbibliotheek Leiden (Leiden University Library)
Witte Singel 27, 2311 BG Leiden
Mailing Address: Postbus 9501, 2300 RA Leiden
Tel: (071) 527 28 14; (071) 527 28 32
E-mail: secretariaat@library.leidenuniv.nl
Web Site: library.leiden.edu; bibliotheek. leidenuniv.nl
Key Personnel
Head, University Library: Jacquelin van der Linde *Tel:* (071) 527 14 67 *E-mail:* j.h.m.van.der. linde@library.leidenuniv.nl
University Librarian & Dir: Kurt De Belder, MA, MLIS *Tel:* (071) 527 28 31 *E-mail:* k.f.k.de. belder@library.leidenuniv.nl
Founded: 1575

Universiteitsbibliotheek Utrecht (Utrecht University Library)
Heidelberglaan 3, 3584 CS Utrecht
Mailing Address: PO Box 80124, 3508 TC Utrecht
Tel: (030) 253 6115; (030) 253 6612 (service desk & renewals)
E-mail: bibliotheek@uu.nl
Web Site: www.uu.nl/library
Key Personnel
Librarian: Dr H P A Smit *Tel:* (030) 253 6502
E-mail: h.p.a.smit@uu.nl
Founded: 1636
Publication(s): *Bijzonder Onderzoek: Een Ontdekkingsreis door de Bijzondere Collecties van de Universiteitsbibliotheek Utrecht* (Special Research: An Exploration Through the Special Collections of the Utrecht University Library, 2009, essays, printed & ebook); *Handschriften en Oude Drukken van de Utrechtse Universiteits bibliotheek* (Manuscripts & Old Books of Utrecht University Library, 1984); *Illuminated & Decorated Medieval Manuscripts in the University Library Utrecht* (catalog, 1989, illustrated); *The Utrecht Psalter, Picturing the Psalms of David* (CD-ROM); *Vier eeuwen Universiteitsbibliotheek Utrecht* (Four Centuries University Library, Utrecht: Part 1 1584-1878) (summary in English)

New Caledonia

Bibliotheque Bernheim
41 ave du Marechal Foch, BP G1, 98848 Noumea Cedex
Tel: 24 20 90 *Fax:* 27 65 88
E-mail: bernheim@bernheim.nc
Web Site: www.bernheim.nc
Key Personnel
Dir: Christophe Augean

Assistant Dir: Simei Paala *Tel:* 42 67 00
Executive Assistant: Cynthia Salip *Tel:* 24 20 93
Founded: 1905

Secretariat of the Pacific Community Library
95 Promenade Roger Laroque, Anse Vata
Mailing Address: BP D5, 98848 Noumea Cedex
Tel: 26 20 00 *Fax:* 26 38 18
Web Site: www.spc.int/library
Key Personnel
Librarian & Archivist: Eleanor Kleiber *Tel:* 26 01 37 *E-mail:* eleanork@spc.int
Founded: 1947
To support development in the Pacific via SPC programs.
Branch Office(s)
Private Mail Bag, Suva, Fiji, Assistant Librarian: Samuela Nakalevu *Tel:* 337 07 33 *Fax:* 337 00 21 *E-mail:* samuealan@spc.int

SPC Library, see Secretariat of the Pacific Community Library

New Zealand

Archives New Zealand (Te Rua Mahara o te Kawanatanga)
10 Mulgrave St, Thorndon, Wellington 6011
Mailing Address: PO Box 12-050, Wellington 6011
Tel: (04) 499 5595 *Fax:* (04) 495 6210
E-mail: library@dia.govt.nz; general.enquiries@ dia.govt.nz; research.archives@dia.govt.nz
Web Site: www.archives.govt.nz
Key Personnel
Chief Archivist & General Manager: Marilyn Little
Official guardian of the record of government; manage the Public Records Act 2005; ensure public archives are kept in a protected & secure environment, accessible now & in the future.
Parent Company: New Zealand Department of Internal Affairs
Branch Office(s)
Christchurch Regional Office, 90 Peterborough St, PO Box 642, Christchurch 8140, Regional Archivist: Chris Adam *Tel:* (03) 377 0760 *Fax:* (03) 365 2662 *E-mail:* christchurch. archives@dia.govt.nz
Dunedin Regional Offices, 556 George St, PO Box 6183, Dunedin 9016, Regional Archivist: Anne Jackman *Tel:* (03) 477 0404 *Fax:* (03) 477 0422 *E-mail:* dunedin.archives@dia.govt. nz
Auckland Regional Office, 95 Richard Pearse Dr, PO Box 201103, Manukau 2022 *Tel:* (09) 270 1100 *Fax:* (09) 276 4472 *E-mail:* auckland. archives@dia.govt.nz

Auckland City Libraries
44-46 Lorne St, Auckland 1010
Mailing Address: PO Box 4138, Auckland 1010
Tel: (09) 377 0209 *Fax:* (09) 307 7741
Web Site: www.aucklandlibraries.govt.nz
Key Personnel
Principal Development Advisor, Community Services: Allison Dobbie
Branch Office(s)
Albany Village Library, Kell Dr, Albany, Auckland 0632 *Tel:* (09) 486 8460
Avondale Library, 93 Rosebank Rd, Avondale, Auckland 1026 *Tel:* (09) 374 1310 *Fax:* (09) 828 8158
Birkenhead Library, Nell Fisher Reserve, Hinemoa St, Birkenhead, Auckland 0626 *Tel:* (09) 486 8460
Blockhouse Bay Library, 578 Blockhouse Bay Rd, Blockhouse Bay, Auckland 0600 *Tel:* (09) 374 1311 *Fax:* (09) 627 0239

Botany Library, Level 1 Sunset Terrace, Botany Town Centre, Auckland 2016 *Tel:* (09) 272 0010 *Fax:* (09) 272 1648

Devonport Library, Windsor Reserve, 2 Victoria Rd, Devonport, Auckland 0624 *Tel:* (09) 486 8460

East Coast Bays Library, Bute Rd, Browns Bay, North Shore, Auckland 0630 *Tel:* (09) 486 8460

Epsom Library, 195 Manukau Rd, Epsom, Auckland 1023 *Tel:* (09) 374 1312 *Fax:* (09) 623 3198

Glen Eden Library, 12-32 Glendale Rd, Glen Eden, Auckland 0602 *Tel:* (09) 839 2260

Glen Innes Library, 108 Line Rd, Glen Innes, Auckland 1072 *Tel:* (09) 374 1313 *Fax:* (09) 521 8045

Glenfield Library, 90 Bentley Ave, Glenfield, North Shore, Auckland 0629 *Tel:* (09) 486 8460

Grey Lynn Library, 474 Great North Rd, Grey Lynn, Auckland 1021 *Tel:* (09) 374 1314 *Fax:* (09) 360 8911

Highland Park Library, 16 Highland Park Dr, Highland Park, Auckland 2010 *Tel:* (09) 535 5935 *Fax:* (09) 537 3808

Howick Library, 25 Uxbridge Rd, Howick, Auckland 2014 *Tel:* (09) 534 5301 *Fax:* (09) 537 3350

Leys Institute Library Ponsonby, 20 St Mary's Rd, Ponsonby, Auckland 1011 *Tel:* (09) 374 1315 *Fax:* (09) 376 2738

Mangere Bridge Library, 5-7 Church Rd, Mangere Bridge, Auckland 2022 *Tel:* (09) 636 6797 *Fax:* (09) 622 2986

Mangere East Library, 370 Massey Rd, Mangere East, Auckland 2024 *Tel:* (09) 275 5420 *Fax:* (09) 275 5670

Mangere Town Centre Library, Bader Dr, Mangere Town Centre, Auckland 2022 *Tel:* (09) 275 9294 *Fax:* (09) 275 9592

Manuka Library & Research Centre, 3 Osterley Way, Manuka, Auckland 2104 *Tel:* (09) 262 5748 *Fax:* (09) 262 3701

Manurewa Library, 7 Hill Rd, Manurewa, Auckland 2102 *Tel:* (09) 262 5420 *Fax:* (09) 262 5107

Massey Library, Corner Don Buck Rd & Westgate Dr, Massey, Auckland 0614 *Tel:* (09) 839 2260 *Fax:* (09) 832 5313

Mount Albert Library, 84 St Lukes Rd, Mount Albert, Auckland 1025 *Tel:* (09) 374 1316 *Fax:* (09) 846 4390

Mount Roskill Library, 546 Mount Albert Rd, (Near Three Kings Plaza), Auckland 1042 *Tel:* (09) 374 1317 *Fax:* (09) 625 7984

New Lynn War Memorial Library, 3 Memorial Dr, New Lynn, Auckland 0600 *Tel:* (09) 839 2260 *Fax:* (09) 827 3393

Northcote Library, Norman King Sq, 2 Ernie Mays St, Northcote, Auckland 0627 *Tel:* (09) 486 8460

Onehunga Library, 85 Church St, Onehunga, Auckland 1061 *Tel:* (09) 374 1319 *Fax:* (09) 634 3459

Otahuhu Library, 28-30 Mason Ave, Otahuhu, Auckland 1062 *Tel:* (09) 374 1320 *Fax:* (09) 276 3609

Otara Library, Otara Town Centre, Otara, Auckland 2023 *Tel:* (09) 274 7936 *Fax:* (09) 274 7930

Pakuranga Library, 7 Aylesbury St, Pakuranga Plaza, Pakuranga, Auckland 2010 *Tel:* (09) 576 5269 *Fax:* (09) 576 0060

Panmure Library, 7-13 Pilkington Rd, Panmure, Auckland 1072 *Tel:* (09) 374 1318 *Fax:* (09) 570 2103

Papatoetoe War Memorial Library, 30 Wallace Rd, Papatoetoe, Auckland 2025 *Tel:* (09) 278 4392 *Fax:* (09) 278 8680

Parnell Library, Jubilee Bldg, 545 Parnell Rd, Parnell, Auckland 1052 *Tel:* (09) 374 1321 *Fax:* (09) 373 5916

Pt Chevalier Library, Corner Great North & Pt Chevalier Rds, Pt Chevalier, Auckland 1022 *Tel:* (09) 374 1322 *Fax:* (09) 846 5549

Ranui Library, Corner Swanson Rd & Armada Dr, Ranui, Auckland 0612 *Tel:* (09) 839 2260 *Fax:* (09) 832 2696

Remuera Library, 429 Remuera Rd, Remuera, Auckland 1050 *Tel:* (09) 374 1323 *Fax:* (09) 520 5128

St Heliers Library, 32 St Heliers Bay Rd, St Heliers, Auckland 1071 *Tel:* (09) 374 1324 *Fax:* (09) 575 3151

Takapuna Library, 9 The Strand, Takapuna, North Shore, Auckland 0622 *Tel:* (09) 486 8460

Te Atatu Peninsula Library, 595 Te Atatu Rd, Te Atatu Peninsula, Auckland 0610 *Tel:* (09) 839 2260 *Fax:* (09) 834 9471

Te Matariki Clendon Library, 17 Palmers Rd, Clendon, Auckland 2103 *Tel:* (09) 269 0500 *Fax:* (09) 269 0498

Titirangi Library, 500 South Titirangi Rd, Titirangi, Auckland 0604 *Tel:* (09) 839 2260 *Fax:* (09) 817 6085

Tupu Youth Library, 102R Dawson Rd, Otara, Auckland 2023 *Tel:* (09) 274 2356 *Fax:* (09) 274 2359

Waitakere Central Library, 3 Ratanui St, Henderson, Auckland 0612 *Tel:* (09) 839 2260 *Fax:* (09) 892 4981

Great Barrier Library, 75 Hector Sanderson Rd, Claris, Great Barrier Island 0991 *Tel:* (09) 429 0258 *Fax:* (09) 429 0379

Helensville Library, 49 Commercial Rd, Helensville 0800 *Tel:* (09) 420 8163 *Fax:* (09) 420 8196

Kumeu Library, 296 Main Rd, Huapai, Kumeu 0810 *Tel:* (09) 412 7995 *Fax:* (09) 427 3732

Orewa Library, 12 Moana Ave, Orewa 0931 *Tel:* (09) 426 8249 *Fax:* (09) 427 3927

Sir Edmund Hillary Library, Level 1 Library & Museum Bldg, 209 Great South Rd, Papakura 2110 *Tel:* (09) 978 2665 *Fax:* (09) 978 2666

Pukekohe Library, 12 Massey Ave, Franklin Centre, Pukekohe 2120 *Tel:* (09) 237 0040

Mahurangi East Library, 21 Hamatana Rd, Snells Beach 0920 *Tel:* (09) 425 6541 *Fax:* (09) 425 6931

Waiheke Library, 131-133 Ocean View Rd, Oneroa, Waiheke Island 1081 *Tel:* (09) 374 1325 *Fax:* (09) 372 1002

Waiuku Library, 10 King St, Waiuku 2123 *Tel:* (09) 235 5699

Warkworth Library, 2 Baxter St, Warkworth 0910 *Tel:* (09) 425 9803

Wellsford War Memorial Library, 13 Port Albert Rd, Wellsford 0900 *Tel:* (09) 423 7702 *Fax:* (09) 423 7702

Whangaparaoa Library, 9 Main St, Whangaparaoa 0932 *Tel:* (09) 427 3710

Canterbury University Library
Private Bag 4800, Christchurch 8140
Tel: (03) 364 2198
E-mail: library@canterbury.ac.nz; distance@canterbury.ac.nz; eservices@libr.canterbury.ac.nz; interloans@libr.canterbury.ac.nz
Web Site: library.canterbury.ac.nz
Key Personnel
University Librarian: Anne Scott *Tel:* (03) 369 3765 *E-mail:* anne.scott@canterbury.ac.nz
Associate Librarian: Helen Thomas *Tel:* (03) 364 2987 ext 94023 *E-mail:* helen.thomas@canterbury.ac.nz
Founded: 1879

Christchurch City Libraries
PO Box 73045, Christchurch 8154
Tel: (03) 941 7923
E-mail: library@ccc.govt.nz
Web Site: my.christchurchcitylibraries.com
Key Personnel
Unit Manager, Libraries & Information: Carolyn

Robertson *E-mail:* carolyn.robertson@ccc.govt.nz
Community Libraries Manager: Dyane Hosler; Erica Rankin
Library Content Manager: Anne Anderson
Manager, Digital Libraries Services: Cath Parr
Places & Spaces Manager: Sally Thompson
Programmes & Learning Manager: Pat Street
Founded: 1859

Dunedin Public Libraries
230 Moray Pl, Dunedin 9058
Mailing Address: PO Box 5045, Dunedin 9058
Tel: (03) 474 3690 *Fax:* (03) 474 3660
E-mail: library@dcc.govt.nz
Web Site: www.dunedinlibraries.govt.nz
Key Personnel
Library Manager: Bernie Hawke *Tel:* (03) 474-3657 *E-mail:* bhawke@dcc.govt.nz
Founded: 1908
Branch Office(s)
7 Hartstonge Ave, Mosgiel 9024 *Fax:* (03) 489 0014
20 Beach St, Port Chalmers 9023 *Fax:* (03) 472 7268
192 Main Rd, Waikouaiti 9510 *Fax:* (03) 465 9110
28 Harvey St, Waitati 9085 *Fax:* (03) 482 2445

Napier Public Libraries
22 Station St, Napier 4110
Mailing Address: PO Box 940, Napier 4110
Tel: (06) 834 4180 *Fax:* (06) 834 4138
E-mail: info@napierlibrary.co.nz; research@napierlibrary.co.nz
Web Site: www.napierlibrary.co.nz
Key Personnel
Manager: Sheryl Reed *Tel:* (06) 834 4142 *E-mail:* sherylr@napier.govt.nz
Branch Office(s)
Taradale Library, 24 White St, PO Box 7056, Taradale 4141, Team Leader: Chrissy Arnold *Tel:* (06) 845 9018 *Fax:* (06) 844 7462 *E-mail:* taradale@napierlibrary.co.nz

National Library of New Zealand (Te Puna Matauranga o Aotearoa)
Corner of Molesworth & Aitken Sts, Pipitea, Wellington 6011
Mailing Address: PO Box 1467, Wellington 6140
Tel: (04) 474 3000 *Fax:* (04) 474 3063
E-mail: information@natlib.govt.nz
Web Site: natlib.govt.nz
Key Personnel
Dir & National Librarian: Bill Macnaught
Dir, Content Services: Alison Elliott
Founded: 1965
Parent Company: New Zealand Department of Internal Affairs
Branch Office(s)
Alexander Turnbull Library, 70 Molesworth St, Thorndon, Wellington 6011, Chief Librarian: Chris Szekely *Tel:* (04) 474 3120 *Fax:* (04) 474 3063 *E-mail:* atl@natlib.govt.nz

Palmerston North City Library
4 The Square, Palmerston North
Mailing Address: PO Box 1948, Palmerston North 4440
Tel: (06) 351 4100 *Fax:* (06) 351 4102
E-mail: pncl@pncc.govt.nz
Web Site: citylibrary.pncc.govt.nz
Key Personnel
City Librarian: Debbie Duncan *E-mail:* debbie.duncan@pncc.govt.nz
Head, Information Services: Leith Haarhoff *E-mail:* leith.haarhoff@pncc.govt.nz
Founded: 1876
Branch Office(s)
Linton Community Library, Corner Bells/Puttick Rd, Linton Camp, Linton 4820 *Tel:* (06) 351 9644 *E-mail:* lintonlibrarynzdf@gmail.com

Ashhurst Library, 64 Bamfield St, Ash-
hurst, Palmerston North *Tel:* (06) 326 8646
E-mail: ashhurst@pncc.govt.nz
Awapuni Library, 96c College St, College St
Shopping Centre, Palmerston North *Tel:* (06)
356 7634
Roslyn Library, 8 Kipling St, Palmerston North
Tel: (06) 357 9287 *E-mail:* roslyn@pncc.govt.
nz
Te Patikitiki, Monrad Park, 157 Highbury
Ave, Palmerston North *Tel:* (06) 357 2108
E-mail: tepatikitiki@pncc.govt.nz

Parliamentary Library
Parliament Bldgs, Private Bag 18041, Wellington
6160
Tel: (04) 817 9999 *Fax:* (04) 817 9619
E-mail: parlinfo@parliament.govt.nz
Web Site: www.parliament.nz
Key Personnel
Library Dir: Moira Fraser
Founded: 1858

Alexander Turnbull Library
National Library of New Zealand, National Li-
brary Bldg, 70 Molesworth St, Thorndon,
Wellington 6011
Mailing Address: PO Box 12349, Wellington
6140
Tel: (04) 474 3000 *Fax:* (04) 474 3063
E-mail: information@natlib.govt.nz
Web Site: www.natlib.govt.nz/atl
Key Personnel
Chief Librarian: Chris Szekely
Founded: 1918
Research library for New Zealand & the Pacific;
John Milton's life & work; the history of the
book, rare books & fine printing.
Publication(s): *Off the Record* (annually, maga-
zine); *Turnbull Library Record* (annually, jour-
nal)

University of Auckland Library
Private Bag 92019, Auckland Mail Centre, Auck-
land 1142
Tel: (09) 373 7599 (ext 88044); (09) 373 7599
(ext 85511) *Fax:* (09) 373 7565
E-mail: lending.library@auckland.ac.nz
Web Site: www.library.auckland.ac.nz
Key Personnel
University Librarian: Sue Roberts *Tel:* (09) 373
7599 ext 87352 *E-mail:* sue.roberts@auckland.
ac.nz

University of Otago Library
65 Albany St, Dunedin
Mailing Address: PO Box 56, Dunedin 9054
Tel: (03) 479 8910 *Fax:* (03) 479 8947
E-mail: library@otago.ac.nz; ask.library@otago.
ac.nz
Web Site: www.library.otago.ac.nz
Key Personnel
University Librarian: Howard Amos *Tel:* (03) 479
8933 *E-mail:* howard.amos@otago.ac.nz
Facilities Planning Coordinator, Administration:
Mark Hughes *Tel:* (03) 479 8206 *E-mail:* mark.
hughes@otago.ac.nz
Founded: 1869

Wellington City Libraries (Te Mataphihi Ki Te
Ao Nui)
65 Victoria St, Wellington 6011
Mailing Address: PO Box 1992, Wellington 6140
Tel: (04) 801 4040 *Fax:* (04) 801 4047
E-mail: enquiries@wcl.govt.nz; feedback@wcl.
govt.nz
Web Site: www.wcl.govt.nz
Key Personnel
Manager, Libraries: Chris Hay *Tel:* (04) 803 8721
E-mail: christopher.hay@wcc.govt.nz

Branch Office(s)
Brooklyn Library, Corner of Harrison St & Cleve-
land St, Brooklyn, Wellington 6021 *Tel:* (04)
384 6814 *Fax:* (04) 384 2857
Cummings Park Library, 1a Ottawa Rd, Ngaio,
Wellington 6035 *Tel:* (04) 479 2344 *Fax:* (04)
479 4186
Ruth Gotlieb (Kilbirnie) Library, 101 Kilbirnie
Crescent, Kilbirnie, Wellington 6022 *Tel:* (04)
387 1480 *Fax:* (04) 387 1490
Island Bay Library, 167 The Parade, Island Bay,
Wellington 6023 *Tel:* (04) 383 7216 *Fax:* (04)
383 7215
Johnsonville Library, 5 Broderick Rd, John-
sonville, Wellington 6037 *Tel:* (04) 477 6151
Fax: (04) 477 6153
Karori Library, 247 Karori Rd, Karori, Wellington
6012 *Tel:* (04) 476 8413 *Fax:* (04) 476 7805
Mervyn Kemp (Tawa) Library, 158 Main Rd,
Corner of Cambridge St & Main Rd, Welling-
ton 5028 *Tel:* (04) 232-1690 *Fax:* (04) 232-
1699
Khandallah Library, 8 Ganges Rd, Wellington
6035 *Tel:* (04) 479 7535 *Fax:* (04) 479 2573
Miramar Library, 68 Miramar Ave, Miramar,
Wellington 6022 *Tel:* (04) 388 8005 *Fax:* (04)
388 4187
Newtown Library, 13 Constable St, Newtown,
Wellington 6021 *Tel:* (04) 389 2830 *Fax:* (04)
389 2827
Wadestown Library, Corner of Moorehouse
St & Lennel Rd, Wadestown, Wellington
6012 *Tel:* (04) 473 5211 *Fax:* (04) 472 5389
E-mail: wadestownlibrary@wcl.govt.nz

Nicaragua

Biblioteca Nacional Ruben Dario
Palacio Nacional de la Cultura, 3514 Managua
Tel: 2222722 *Fax:* 2222722
E-mail: b.n.rd@hotmail.com
Web Site: www.abinia.org/nicarauga; www.bnrd.
gob.ni
Key Personnel
Dir: Jimmy Alvardo Moreno *E-mail:* binanic@
tmx.com.ni
Founded: 1882

INCAE, see Instituto Centroamericano de
Administracion de Empresas (INCAE) Library

**Instituto Centroamericano de Administracion
de Empresas (INCAE) Library**
Campus Francisco de Sola Montefresco, Km 15
1/2 Carretera Sur, Managua
Mailing Address: Apdo 2485, Managua
Tel: 2248-9746 *Fax:* 2265-8617
E-mail: cfds.biblioteca@incae.edu
Web Site: www.incae.ac.cr/es/biblioteca
Key Personnel
Dir: Antonio Acevedo *E-mail:* antonio.acevedo@
incae.edu
Publication(s): *Revista INCAE*

Universidad Centroamericana Biblioteca
(Central American University Library)
Apdo 69, Managua
Tel: 22783923
E-mail: otibiblioteca@ns.uca.edu.ni
Web Site: www.uca.edu.ni
Key Personnel
Library Dir: Gloria Maria Morales Arevalo
E-mail: gmorales@uca.edu.ni
Assistant Librarian: Alicia Haydee Lopez Castillo
E-mail: lopezc@ns.uca.edu.ni
Founded: 1961

Niger

**Bibliotheque l'Ecole nationale d'administration
et de Magistrature** (National School of
Administration & Public Office)
Rue Martin Luther King Jr, Niamey
Mailing Address: BP 542, Niamey
Tel: 723183 *Fax:* 724383
E-mail: enam@primature.ne
Web Site: enam.ne
Membership(s): Agence universitaire de la Fran-
cophonie.

**Bibliotheque Universitaire Centrale de
l'Universite Abdou Moumouni**
BP 10896, Niamey
Tel: 20 31 55 31 *Fax:* 20 31 58 62
Membership(s): Agence Universitaire de la Fran-
cophone.

ENAM, see Bibliotheque l'Ecole nationale
d'administration et de Magistrature

**Institut de Recherche en Sciences Humaines
(IRSH)**
BP 318, Niamey
Tel: 73 46 03; 73 55 39 *Fax:* 73 82 58
Key Personnel
Dir: Abdou Bontianti
Deputy Dir: Hamidou Seydou Hanafiou
Founded: 1944
Publication(s): *Etudes Nigeriennes*

IRSH, see Institut de Recherche en Sciences
Humaines (IRSH)

Nigeria

Ahmadu Bello University Library, see Kashim
Ibrahim Library

Kenneth Dike Library, see University of Ibadan
Library

John Harris Library, see University of Benin
Library

Hezekiah Oluwasanmi Library
c/o Obafemi Awolowo University, Ile-Ife, Osun
State
Tel: (036) 230 291
Web Site: www.oauife.edu.ng
Key Personnel
University Librarian: Mrs Bukky Asubiojo
E-mail: femibuk@yahoo.co.uk
Founded: 1962

IAR, see Institute for Agricultural Research
(IAR) Library

Kashim Ibrahim Library
Ahmadu Bello University, Zaria
Tel: (0703) 242 8263 (cell)
E-mail: library@abu.edu.ng; librarian@abu.edu.
ng; kilreference@abu.edu.ng
Web Site: library.abu.edu.ng
Key Personnel
University Librarian: Prof Umar Ibrahim
E-mail: umarahim2003@yahoo.com
Deputy University Librarian: Mr Tsuzom Mawo
Ndakotsu *E-mail:* gobbotee@yahoo.com
Founded: 1962

Institute for Agricultural Research (IAR) Library
Ahmadu Bello University, Zaria
E-mail: directoriar@abu.edu.ng
Web Site: iar.abu.edu.ng
Key Personnel
Executive Dir: Prof I U Abubakar
  E-mail: iuabubakar@abu.edu.ng
Deputy Dir: Prof Dauda Dada Yusuf
  E-mail: ddyusuf@abu.edu.ng
Institute Librarian: Olowu Labeshi Toby
  E-mail: oltaby@abu.edu.ng
Founded: 1924

International Institute of Tropical Agriculture (IITA) Library
PMB 5320, Ibadan, Oyo State
Tel: (02) 0700800
E-mail: iita@cgiar.org
Web Site: www.iita.org
Key Personnel
Dir: Robert Asiedu *E-mail:* r.asiedu@cgiar.org
Publication(s): *IITA Annual Report*; *IITA Research*

Kaduna State Library Board
6 Bida Rd, PMB 2061, Kaduna
Tel: (062) 214417 *Fax:* (062) 214417
Publication(s): *Biographies of Governors of Former Northern Nigeria & Kaduna State, 1960-1990*; *Meet Our Friends*; *Proceedings of the First Kaduna State Book Fair*; *Proceedings of the First Northern States Book Fair*; *Proceedings of the Second Kaduna State Book Fair*

Kano State Library Board
Ahmadu Bello Way, PMB 3092, Kano
Tel: (0803) 423 4969
E-mail: nuramudi21@gmail.com
Key Personnel
Executive Secretary: Ibrahim Ahmed Bichi
Publication(s): *Library Guide*

National Archives of Nigeria
University of Ibadan, PMB 4, UI Post Office, Ibadan
Founded: 1954

National Library of Nigeria
Sanusi Dantata House, Plot 274, Central Business District, PMB 1, Garki-Abuja
Tel: (09) 2346773
E-mail: info@nln.gov.ng
Web Site: www.nln.gov.ng
Key Personnel
National Librarian: Prof Lenrie O Aina
Publication(s): *Afribiblios* (2 times/yr); *Directory of Libraries in Nigeria*; *National Bibliography of Nigeria*; *Nigerbiblios* (2 times/yr, journal); *Nigerian Books in Print*; *Nominal List of Practicing Librarians in Nigeria*; *Serials in Print in Nigeria*

University of Benin Library
PMB 1154, Benin City, Edo State 300283
Tel: (0705) 679 3008 (cell)
E-mail: johnharrislibrary@uniben.edu
Web Site: www.facebook.com/library.uniben.edu
Key Personnel
Librarian: Patience Kayoma
Founded: 1970
Publication(s): *List of Serials*

University of Ibadan Library
Ibadan 200284
E-mail: info@library.ui.edu.ng;
  kennethdikelibrary@gmail.com
Web Site: library.ui.edu.ng
Founded: 1962
Publication(s): *Library Record* (monthly)

University of Jos Library
PMB 2084, Jos, Plateau State 930001
Tel: (073) 610514; (073) 453724 *Fax:* (073) 612514
E-mail: librarian@unijos.edu.ng; library@unijos.edu.ng
Web Site: www.unijos.edu.ng/library
Key Personnel
University Librarian: Dr A Ochai
  E-mail: ochaia@unijos.edu.ng
Deputy University Librarian: S A Akintunde
  E-mail: akins@unijos.edu.ng; Mrs L I Tashi
  E-mail: tashil@unijos.edu.ng
Founded: 1972
Publication(s): *JULIA (Jos University Library Information & Accessories)* (6 times/yr); *Know Your Library: Readers' Guide to the Library*

University of Lagos Library
Akoka, Yaba, Lagos
Tel: (01) 2914557
E-mail: library@unilag.edu.ng
Web Site: library.unilag.edu.ng
Key Personnel
Principal Librarian: Dr Yetunde A Zaid
Founded: 1962

University of Nigeria Nsukka Library
Nnamdi Azikiwe Library, University of Nigeria, Nsukka, Enugu State
E-mail: librarian.unn@unn.edu.ng
Web Site: library.unn.edu.ng; www.unn.edu.ng/libraries
Key Personnel
University Librarian: Chinwe Nwogo Ezeani, PhD
  E-mail: chinwe.ezeani@unn.edu.ng
Founded: 1960
Publication(s): *Nsukka Library Notes*

North Korea

GPSH, see Grand People's Study House (GPSH), DPRK

Grand People's Study House (GPSH), DPRK
Jungsong Dong, Central District, PO Box 200, Pyongyang
Tel: (02) 3814427 *Fax:* (02) 3812100
E-mail: nsj@star-co.net.kp
Founded: 1982
National Library, Central Archive & Information Base of Science & Technology with a mission of collecting, managing, storing & distributing books, documents & data.
National Correspondence University & Centre of Social Education.
Publication(s): *Grand People's Study House* (newsletter); *Library Bulletin*

Norway

Bergen Offentlige Bibliotek (Bergen Public Library)
Stromgaten 6, 5015 Bergen
Tel: 55 56 85 00; 55 56 85 05 *Fax:* 55 56 85 85
E-mail: post@bergenbibliotek.no
Web Site: bergenbibliotek.no
Key Personnel
Library Dir: Leikny Haga Indergaard
  E-mail: leikny@bergen.folkebibl.no
Founded: 1872
Branch Office(s)
Asane Senter 40, Ulset, 5116 Bergen, Contact: Anne Merete Hegrenes *Tel:* 55 56 71 20
  E-mail: aasane@bergenbibliotek.no
Lyderhorns vei 353, Loddefjord, 5171 Bergen, Contact: Merete Greve Loberg *Tel:* 55 56 29 06 *E-mail:* loddefj@bergenbibliotek.no
Nattlandsveien 76, Postboks 3053, Landas, 5825 Bergen, Contact: Ashild Saele *Tel:* 53 03 87 98 *E-mail:* landaas@bergenbibliotek.no
Peter Jebsens vei 4, Postboks 123, Ytre Arna, 5889 Bergen, Contact: Anne Merete Hegrenes *Tel:* 53 03 95 80 *E-mail:* ytrearna@bergenbibliotek.no
Folke Bernadottes vei 52, Fyllingsdalen, 5147 Bergen, Contact: Lene Heiestad *Tel:* 55 56 54 08 *E-mail:* oasen@bergenbibliotek.no
Postboks 254 Nyborg, 5871 Bergen, Contact: Cathrine Holden *Tel:* 55 25 12 44
  E-mail: bjovin@bergenbibliotek.no
Steinestoveien 401, Postboks 230, 5109 Hylkje, Contact: Kjersti Egge *Tel:* 55 39 37 90 *Fax:* 55 39 36 50 *E-mail:* fengsel@bergenbibliotek.no
Nesttunveien 102, 5221 Nesttun, Contact: Kjersti Hatland *Tel:* 55 56 11 33 *E-mail:* fana@bergenbibliotek.no

Deichmanske Bibliotek (Oslo Public Library)
Arne Garborgs plass 4, 0179 Oslo
Mailing Address: Postboks 8924, St Olavs plass, 0130 Oslo
Tel: 23 43 29 00
E-mail: postmottak@deichmanske.zendesk.com
Web Site: www.deichman.no
Key Personnel
Library Dir: Knut Skansen
Branch Office(s)
Refstadveien 70, 0589 Oslo *Tel:* 23 43 27 00
  E-mail: deichman.bjerke@deb.oslo.kommune.no
Hagegata 22, Oslo *Tel:* 23 43 27 85
Slimeveien 17, Bjornholt, 1277 Oslo *Tel:* 91 38 24 39 *E-mail:* deichman.bjornholt@deb.oslo.kommune.no
Bolerlia 3c, Boler, 0691 Oslo *Tel:* 23 43 27 60
  E-mail: deichman.boler@kul.oslo.kommune.no
Trygve Liesplass 1, Furuset, 1051 Oslo *Tel:* 46 82 82 02 *E-mail:* fubiak@deb.oslo.kommune.no
Schouspl 10, Grunerlokka, 0552 Oslo *Tel:* 22 35 65 83 *E-mail:* deichman.grynerlokka@deb.oslo.kommune.no
Holmlia sentervei 16, Holmlia, 1255 Oslo *Tel:* 23 19 19 40 *E-mail:* deichman.holmlia@deb.oslo.kommune.no
Cec Thoresensvei 19, Lambertseter, 1153 Oslo *Tel:* 23 43 27 70 *E-mail:* deichman.lambertseter@deb.oslo.kommune.no
Harald Harfagresgt 2, Majorstuen, 0363 Oslo *Tel:* 23 36 59 50 *E-mail:* deichman.majorstuen@deb.oslo.kommune.no
Nordtvetveien 28, Nordtvet, 0952 Oslo *Tel:* 22 70 96 60 *E-mail:* deichman.nordtvet@deb.oslo.kommune.no
Nydalsveien 30 C, 0484 Oslo *Tel:* 41 69 80 32
  E-mail: deichman.nydalen@deb.oslo.kommune.no
Romsas Senter 1, Romsas, Oslo *Tel:* 22 10 45 95
  E-mail: deichman.romsas@deb.oslo.kommune.no
Karen Platousvei 31, 0988 Oslo *Tel:* 23 46 53 21
  E-mail: deichman.rommen@deb.olso.kommune.no
Tore Hals Mejdellsvei 8, Roa, 0751 Oslo *Tel:* 23 43 27 90 *E-mail:* deichman.roa@deb.oslo.kommune.no
Romsas Center 1, Nordtveien 28, 0952 Oslo *Tel:* 22 10 45 95 *E-mail:* deichman.romsas@deb.oslo.kommune.no
Konventveien 27, Smestad, 0377 Oslo *Tel:* 22 51 63 92 *E-mail:* deichman.smestad@deb.oslo.kommune.no

Stovner Senter 3, Stovner, 0985 Oslo *Tel:* 23 43
27 50 *E-mail:* deichman.stovner@deb.oslo.
kommune.no
Sandakerveien 59, Torshov, 0477 Oslo *Tel:* 22
22 29 84 *E-mail:* deichman.torshov@deb.oslo.
kommune.no

Drammensbibliotek
Gronland 58, 3045 Drammen
Tel: 32 04 54 00
E-mail: bibliotek@drmk.no
Web Site: www.drammensbiblioteket.no
Key Personnel
Librarian: Monica Nyhus *Tel:* 92 43 30 09
E-mail: monica.nyhus@drammen.kommune.no
University College of Buskerud Library; Pub-
lic Library of Drammen; County Library of
Buskerud.

Kristiansand Folkebibliotek (Kristiansand Public
Library)
Radhusgt 11, 4611 Kristiansand
Mailing Address: Postboks 476, 4664 Kris-
tiansand
Tel: 38 12 49 10
E-mail: post.folkebibliotek@kristiansand.
kommune.no
Web Site: krsbib.no
Key Personnel
Librarian: Anne Kristin Undlien *Tel:* 38 12 49
11 *E-mail:* anne.kristin.undlien@kristiansand.
kommune.no
Deputy Librarian: Siv Holt *Tel:* 38 12 49 18
E-mail: siv.holt@kristiansand.kommune.no

NMBU Universitetsbiblioteket
Chr M Falsens vei 18, Tarnbygningen, 1432 As
Mailing Address: Postboks 5003, 1432 As
Tel: 67 23 04 00 *Fax:* 67 23 06 91
E-mail: biblioteket@nmbu.no
Web Site: www.nmbu.no/om/biblioteket
Key Personnel
Dir: Ann Sogge *Tel:* 67 23 04 13 *E-mail:* ann.
sogge@nmbu.no
Head Librarian: Sissel Gronseth *Tel:* 67 23 04 05

Norges miljo- og biovitenskapelige universitet,
see NMBU Universitetsbiblioteket

Norske Nobelinstituttet Bibliotek (Norwegian
Nobel Institute)
Henrik Ibsens gate 51, 0255 Oslo
Tel: 22 12 93 20 *Fax:* 94 76 11 17
E-mail: library@nobel.no
Web Site: www.nobelpeaceprize.org/library
Founded: 1905
Library covers following fields: political history
from 1800, international law, peace & interna-
tional economics. It is also a depository library
for publications from a number of international
organizations & institutions.

**Norwegian Industrial Property Office
Information Center**, see Patentstyret - Styret
for det Industrielle Rettsvern Infosenteret

**Patentstyret - Styret for det Industrielle
Rettsvern Infosenteret** (Norwegian Patent
Office Information Center)
Sandakerveien 64, 0484 Oslo
Mailing Address: Postboks 8160 Dep, 0033 Oslo
Tel: 22 38 73 00 *Fax:* 22 38 73 01
E-mail: post@patentstyret.no
Web Site: www.patentstyret.no
Key Personnel
Dir: Per Foss *Tel:* 22 38 74 20

Riksarkivet (National Archives of Norway)
Folke Bernadottes vei 21, Oslo

Mailing Address: Postboks 4013, Ulleval Stadion,
0806 Oslo
Tel: 480 55 666
E-mail: post@arkivverket.no
Web Site: www.arkivverket.no
Key Personnel
Dir General: Inga Bolstad
Founded: 1817

**Statistisk sentralbyras bibliotek og
informasjonssenter** (Statistics Norway Library
& Information Centre)
Akersveien 26, 0177 Oslo
Mailing Address: Postboks 8131 Dep, 0033 Oslo
Tel: 21 09 46 42
E-mail: biblioteket@ssb.no; informasjon@ssb.no
Web Site: www.ssb.no/biblioteket
Key Personnel
Dir, Communications: Herborg Bryn *Tel:* 21 09
43 75 *E-mail:* herborg.bryn@ssb.no
Founded: 1917

Universitetsbiblioteket i Bergen (University of
Bergen Library)
Haakon sheteligs plass 7, 5015 Bergen
Mailing Address: PO Box 7808, 5020 Bergen
Tel: 55 58 25 32 *Fax:* 55 58 46 20
E-mail: post@ub.uib.no
Web Site: www.uib.no/ub
Key Personnel
Assistant Library Dir & Head, Library Ser-
vices: Trude Faerevaag *Tel:* 55 58 66 83
E-mail: trude.ferevaag@uib.no
Founded: 1948

Universitetsbiblioteket i Oslo (University of
Oslo Library)
Georg Sverdrups hus, 4 etasje, Moltke Moes vei
39, 0851 Oslo
Mailing Address: Postboks 1085, Blindern, 0317
Oslo
Tel: 22 84 40 50 *Fax:* 22 84 41 50
E-mail: postmottak@ub.uio.no
Web Site: www.ub.uio.no
Key Personnel
Assistant Dir: Randi Ronningen *Tel:* 22 84 42 72
E-mail: randi.ronningen@ub.uio.no
University Librarian: Eystein Gullbekk *Tel:* 22 85
49 52 *E-mail:* eystein.gullbekk@ub.uio.no
Founded: 1811
Publication(s): *Bibliografi over Norges offentlige
publikasjoner 1956-1990; Kataloger pa mikro-
film kort; Maskinlesbare data; Mikrofilmer*
(35mm Norske aviser, Norske tidsskrifter,
Norske og utenlandske boker); *Nansen bilde
data base pa CD-ROM; Nasjonalbibliografiske
data NBDATA 1962- (CD-ROM); Nordisk
samkatalog for periodika CDNOSP; Norsk
lokalhistorisk litteratur 1946-1970; Norsk
lokalhistorisk litteratur 1971-1990; Norsk pe-
riodikafortegnelse 1993-* (annually); *Norsk
samkatalog for boker CDSAM 1981; Norsk
samkatalog for boker CDSAM 1983-; Norske
tidsskriftartikler 1980-; Norske tidsskrifter
1971-1983; NOSP adresseliste* (annually);
*UBO: Brosjyrer; UBO: Diverse publikasjon-
erk; UBO: Skrifter; UBO: Veiledninger*

Pakistan

British Council Library
PO Box 1135, Islamabad 44000
Toll Free Tel: 0800 22000 (Pakistan only)
Fax: (051) 111 425 425
E-mail: info@britishcouncil.org.pk
Web Site: www.britishcouncil.pk
Founded: 1948

Branch Office(s)
PO Box 13811, Karachi *Fax:* (021) 111 425 425
(Karachi & Quetta)
PO Box 88, Lahore *Fax:* (042) 111 425 425

Ewing Memorial Library
Forman Christian College University, Establish-
ment Off, Sinclair Hall, 1st floor, Room 20,
Ferozepur Rd, Lahore 54600
Tel: (042) 99231581 *Fax:* (042) 99230703
E-mail: library@fccollege.edu.pk
Web Site: www.fccollege.edu.pk; library.fccollege.
edu.pk
Key Personnel
Chief Librarian: Bushra Almas Jaswal *Tel:* (042)
99231581 ext 424 *E-mail:* bushrajaswal@
fccollege.edu.pk
Founded: 1943

Dr Mahmud Husain Library
University of Karachi, Karachi 75270
Tel: (021) 99261352 (ext 2243) *Fax:* (021)
99281353
E-mail: librarian@uok.edu.pk
Web Site: www.uok.edu.pk/library
Key Personnel
Chief Librarian: Malahat Kareem
Founded: 1952
Publication(s): *Guide to Bibliographical Sources*
(Catalog of rare books)

Allama I I Kazi Central Library
University of Sindh, Jamshoro, Sindh 76080
Tel: (022) 9213193
E-mail: librarian@usindh.edu.pk
Web Site: usindh.edu.pk/academics/central-library
Founded: 1975

National Archives of Pakistan
Pakistan Secretariat, Block N, Islamabad 44000
Tel: (051) 9202044 *Fax:* (051) 9206349
E-mail: info@nap.gov.pk
Web Site: www.facebook.com/paknap
Founded: 1951
Storage & presentation of historical & public
records.
Membership(s): International Council on Archives
(ICA).

National Library of Engineering Sciences
University of Engineering & Technology, G T Rd,
Lahore 54890
Tel: (042) 99029243; (042) 99250223; (042)
99250222
E-mail: lib@uet.edu.pk
Web Site: library.uet.edu.pk
Key Personnel
Chief Librarian: Dr Muhammad Ijaz Mairaj
E-mail: maijaz@uet.edu.pk
Assistant Librarian: Ms Azra Parveen
E-mail: azraaqeel@uet.edu.pk
Founded: 1961
Publication(s): *Central Library Bulletin* (6 times/
yr)

National Library of Pakistan
Shahrah-e-Jamhuriat, Sector G-5, Islamabad
44000
Tel: (051) 9202549; (051) 9207456; (051)
9206436 (ext 214) *Fax:* (051) 9217286
E-mail: nationallibrary2000@yahoo.com
Web Site: www.nlp.gov.pk
Key Personnel
Dir & Head: Syed Ghyour Hussain
E-mail: director@nlp.gov.pk
Founded: 1993
Membership(s): International Federation of Li-
brary Associations & Institutions (IFLA).

Pakistan Institute of Development Economics (PIDE)
Quaid-i-Azam University Campus, PO Box 1091, Islamabad 44000
Tel: (051) 9248041; (051) 9248030 *Fax:* (051) 9248065
E-mail: library@pide.org.pk
Web Site: www.pide.org.pk
Key Personnel
Librarian: Muzzammil Ahmad *Tel:* (051) 9248062 *E-mail:* muzzammil@pide.org.pk
Founded: 1957
Research organization.
Publication(s): *Pakistan Development Review* (quarterly, journal)

Pakistan Institute of Science & Technology Library, Scientific Information Division
PO Nilore, Islamabad
Tel: 9321050
E-mail: sipr@paec.gov.pk
Web Site: www.paec.gov.pk
Founded: 1966
Central source of scientific & technical information for the Pakistan Atomic Energy Commission & for other scientific organizations & universities in the country.

Pakistan Scientific & Technological Information Centre (PASTIC)
National Centre, Quaid-I-Azam University Campus, Islamabad 44000
Tel: (051) 9248103; (051) 9248104 *Fax:* (051) 9248113
Web Site: www.pastic.gov.pk
Key Personnel
Dir General: Dr Muhammad Akram Shaikh *Tel:* (051) 9248106 *E-mail:* dg@pastic.gov.pk
Dir: Ms Nageen Ainuddin *Tel:* (051) 9248114 *E-mail:* director@pastic.gov.pk
Founded: 1974
Publication(s): *Pakistan Science Abstracts* (quarterly, journal); *PJCIS (Pakistan Journal of Computer & Information Systems)* (2 times/yr); *Technology Roundup* (6 times/yr, bulletin); *Union Catalogue & Serial Holdings of S&T Libraries of Pakistan*
Parent Company: Ministry of Science & Technology

PASTIC, see Pakistan Scientific & Technological Information Centre (PASTIC)

PIDE, see Pakistan Institute of Development Economics (PIDE)

PINSTECH Library, see Pakistan Institute of Science & Technology Library, Scientific Information Division

Punjab University Library
Quaid-e-Azam Campus, Lahore, Punjab 54590
Tel: (042) 99231126; (042) 99230863 *Fax:* (042) 99230892
Web Site: pulibrary.edu.pk
Key Personnel
Chief Librarian: Dr Muhammad Haroon Usmani *E-mail:* chieflibrarian@pu.edu.pk
Founded: 1873

UET, see National Library of Engineering Sciences

University of Balochistan Library
Sariab Rd, Quetta
Tel: (081) 9211124; (081) 9211008 *Fax:* (081) 9211277
E-mail: dit@um.uob.edu.pk
Web Site: www.uob.edu.pk/digitallibrary

Key Personnel
Chief Librarian: Syed Abdullah Agha
Deputy Librarian: Abdul Naeem
Assistant Librarian: Sobia Habib
Founded: 1970

University of Engineering & Technology, see National Library of Engineering Sciences

Panama

Biblioteca Nacional de Panama, Ernesto J Castillero R
Calle 74 E, Ciudad de Panama
Tel: 224-9466; 221-5965; 221-8360
E-mail: ocuevas@binal.ac.pa
Web Site: www.binal.ac.pa
Key Personnel
Dir General: Maria Magela Brenes
Technical Dir: Guadalupe G de Rivera
Founded: 1942

Universidad de Panama, Biblioteca Interamericana Simon Bolivar
Campus Universitaria, Estafeta Universitaria, Apdo 3366, Panama 4
Tel: 523-5360
Web Site: www.sibiup.up.ac.pa; www.facebook.com/sibiup
Key Personnel
Dir: Prof Octavio Castillo Sanchez *Tel:* 523-5350 *E-mail:* ocastillos@hotmail.com
Founded: 1978
Publication(s): *Boletin Bibliografico*

Papua New Guinea

National Library of Papua New Guinea
Office of Libraries & Archives, PO Box 734, Waigani 131 NCD
Tel: 323 7775; 722 28 073 (cell)
Founded: 1975
Publication(s): *Ola Nius (formerly National Library Nius)*; *Papua New Guinea National Bibliography*; *Selective Index to the Times of Papua New Guinea*

Michael Somare Library
University of Papua New Guinea, PO Box 320, National Capital District 134
Tel: 326 7480; 326 7280 *Fax:* 326 7541
E-mail: library@upng.ac.pg
Web Site: www.upng.ac.pg
Key Personnel
University Librarian: Leah Kalamoroh
Founded: 1966
Publication(s): *Guide to Manuscripts in the New Guinea Collection* (1980, by Nancy Lutton); *New Guinea Periodical Index* (quarterly)

Paraguay

ANA, see Archivo Nacional de Asuncion

Archivo Nacional de Asuncion (National Archive of Asuncion)
Mcal Estigarribia esquina Iturbe, Asuncion

Tel: (021) 447-311
E-mail: archivonacionaldeasuncion@gmail.com
Web Site: www.archivonacional.gov.py

Biblioteca Nacional Paraguay (National Library of Paraguay)
De la Residenta 820, Asuncion
Tel: (021) 204670
E-mail: biblioteca.nacional.py@gmail.com
Web Site: bibliotecanacional.gov.py
Key Personnel
Dir: Ruben Capdevila
Founded: 1887

Peru

ALIDE, see Asociacion Latinoamericana de Instituciones Financieras Para El Desarrollo (ALIDE)

Archivo General de la Nacion del Peru
Jr Camana N° 125, Lima
Tel: (01) 4267221; (01) 4272996; (01) 4275930
E-mail: informatica@agn.gob.pe; comunicaciones@agn.gob.pe
Web Site: agn.gob.pe
Key Personnel
Head: Dr Luisa Vetter Parodi *E-mail:* lvetter@agn.gob.pe
Founded: 1861

Asociacion Latinoamericana de Instituciones Financieras Para El Desarrollo (ALIDE)
(Latin American Association of Development Financing Institutions)
Paseo de la Republica N° 3211, San Isidro, Lima 27
Tel: (01) 442-2400 *Fax:* (01) 442-8105
Web Site: www.alidebibliotecavirtual.org
Key Personnel
Head, Documentation Centre: Cristina Castillo *E-mail:* ccastillo@alide.org
Founded: 1968
Represents institutions that finance development in Latin America & the Caribbean. Provides information & documentation related to development banking fields of interest, as well as having information on materials relative to specific economic sectors & technological aspects. Collects specialized documentation concerned with banking & financing development.
Membership(s): World Federation of Development Financing Institutions (WFDFI).
Publication(s): *Alidenoticias* (6 times/yr, newsletter); *Anales de la Asamblea General* (Annals General Assembly, annually, report, proceedings of the general assembly contains presentations on the key topic analized); *Data Bank* (annually, report, institutional & financial information on development banks); *E-Banca* (monthly); *E-News* (quarterly, newsletter); *Memoria Annual* (report); *Revista Alide* (Alide Magazine, quarterly, dedicated to the provision of articles & analytical information, in depth studies & documents of a technical & legal nature related to banking & financing development)

Biblioteca Central de la Universidad Nacional de San Agustin
Calle Santa Catalina 117, Arequipa
Tel: (054) 285 067
E-mail: convenios@unsa.edu.pe
Web Site: www.unsa.edu.pe
Key Personnel
Head, Office: Jose Luis Vargas Gutierrez
Founded: 1828

Biblioteca Central de la Universidad Nacional Mayor de San Marcos
Av German Amezaga Nº 375, Edificio Bib Central Pedro Zulen, Ciudad Universitaria, Lima 1
Tel: (01) 619-7000 (ext 7701)
E-mail: bibcent@unmsm.edu.pe
Web Site: sisbib.unmsm.edu.pe
Key Personnel
Chief Librarian: Sara Esther Aliaga Romero *Tel:* (01) 619-7000 ext 7566
   E-mail: saliagar_af@unmsm.edu.pe

Biblioteca Central Luis Jaime Cisneros, see Pontificia Universidad Catolica del Peru Biblioteca Central

Biblioteca Jorge Basadre, see Universidad del Pacifico Biblioteca

Biblioteca Nacional del Peru
Av de la Poesia 160, San Borja, Lima
Tel: (01) 513-6900
E-mail: contactobnp@bnp.gob.pe
Web Site: www.bnp.gob.pe
Key Personnel
Dir: Juan Antonio Silva Sologuren
   E-mail: jefatura@bnp.gob.pe
Technical Dir: Miguel Angel Aquino Lima
   E-mail: miguel.aquino@bnp.gob.pe
Publication(s): *Anuario Bibliografico Peruano* (Bibliographical Annual of Peru); *Bibliografia Nacional* (Peruvian monthly Bibliographical Information); *Boletin de la Biblioteca Nacional* (Bulletin of the National Library); *Gaceta Bibliotecaria* (Library Gazette, irregularly); *Revista Fenix* (Phoeniz Magazine)

CEDOM, see Asociacion Latinoamericana de Instituciones Financieras Para El Desarrollo (ALIDE)

Centro Latinoamericano de Documentacion, see Asociacion Latinoamericana de Instituciones Financieras Para El Desarrollo (ALIDE)

ESAN - Escuela de Administracion de Negocios para Graduados, Direccion de Investigacion
Alonso de Molina 1652, Monterrico, Surco, Lima
Tel: (01) 317 7200 (ext 2401) *Fax:* (01) 345-1328
E-mail: cendoc@esan.edu.pe
Web Site: www.esan.edu.pe
Key Personnel
Head, Library & Information Center: Cecilia Alegre Castro *Tel:* (01) 317 7200 ext 4269
   E-mail: calegre@esan.edu.pe
Founded: 1963

Pedro Zulen, see Biblioteca Central de la Universidad Nacional Mayor de San Marcos

Pontificia Universidad Catolica del Peru Biblioteca Central
Av Universitaria Nº 1801, San Miguel, Lima 32
Tel: (01) 626-2000 *Fax:* (01) 626-2861
E-mail: biblio@pucp.edu.pe
Web Site: biblioteca.pucp.edu.pe
Key Personnel
Dir: Kathia Hanza Bacigalupo *E-mail:* khanza@pucp.edu.pe
Deputy Dir: Mariela Del Aguila Reategui
   E-mail: mdelagu@pucp.pe
Manager: Kevin Wong Crovetto *E-mail:* kevin.wong@pucp.pe
Founded: 1960

Universidad del Pacifico Biblioteca (University of the Pacific Library)
Av Salaverry 2020, Jesus Maria, Lima 11
Tel: (01) 219-0100 (ext 2236)
E-mail: biblioteca@up.edu.pe
Web Site: www.campusvirtual.up.edu.pe/biblioteca
Key Personnel
Dir: Rosa Estela Dorival Cordova de Beteta *Tel:* (01) 219-0100 ext 2234
   E-mail: dorival_re@up.edu.pe
Founded: 1962
Publication(s): *Apuntes*; *Counterbalance Points* (monthly); *Intercampus*

Universidad Nacional de San Antonio Abad del Cusco (UNSAAC) Biblioteca Central
Av de la Cultura, Nro 733, Cusco
Mailing Address: Apdo 921, Cusco
Tel: (084) 604100; (084) 604160 *Fax:* (084) 238156
E-mail: biblioteca.central@unsaac.edu.pe
Web Site: cbiblioteca.unsaac.edu.pe; www.unsaac.edu.pe
Key Personnel
Chief Administrative Officer: Carmen Luz Diaz Vera

Philippines

Far Eastern University Library
Nicanor Reyes St, Sampaloc, 1015 Manila
Tel: (02) 735-5621
E-mail: universitylibrary@feu.edu.ph
Web Site: www.feu.edu.ph; www.facebook.com/feulibrary
Founded: 1991
Publication(s): *Far Eastern University Journal*

Manila City Library
G/F Sining ng Kayumanggi Bldg, P Burgos St, Ermita, Manila
Tel: (02) 528 0630
Web Site: www.facebook.com/manila.citylibrary
Founded: 1946

Miguel de Benavides Library, see University of Santo Tomas Library

National Library of the Philippines (NLP)
TM Kalaw St, 4th floor East Wing, Ermita, 1000 Manila
Mailing Address: PO Box 2926, 1000 Manila
Tel: (02) 310-5035; (02) 336-7200
E-mail: do@nlp.gov.ph
Web Site: web.nlp.gov.ph
Key Personnel
Dir: Cesar Gilbert Q Adriano
   E-mail: cgqadriano@nlp.gov.ph
Founded: 1901

NLP, see National Library of the Philippines (NLP)

Philippine Normal University Library
E P Dagot Hall, 1st floor, Taft Ave, Manila
Tel: (02) 310 78 72
E-mail: library@pnu.edu.ph
Web Site: www.pnu.edu.ph/library
Key Personnel
Chief Librarian: Helen A Advincula
Founded: 1952

The Philippine Women's University Library, see Ramona S Tirona Memorial Library

Rizal Library
Ateneo de Manila University, Katipunan Rd, Loyola Heights, 1108 Quezon City, Metro Manila
Tel: (02) 4266001 *Fax:* (02) 4265961
Web Site: rizal.library.ateno.edu
Key Personnel
Dir: Dr Vernon R Totanes *E-mail:* vtotanes@ateneo.edu
Founded: 1921

Dr Virgilio De Los Santos Library, see University of Manila Central Library

Science & Technology Information Institute
General Santos Ave, Upper Bicutan, Taguig, 1631 Metro Manila
Tel: (02) 837-2191 *Fax:* (02) 837-7521
E-mail: library@stii.dost.gov.ph
Web Site: library.stii.dost.gov.ph; www.dost.gov.ph
Key Personnel
Secretary, DOST: Prof Fortunato dela Pena
   E-mail: osec@dost.gov.ph
Publication(s): *Philippine Science & Technology Abstracts*; *R & D Philippines*; *SEA Abstracts*; *Series of Philippine Scientific Bibliographies*; *Union Catalogue of NISST*; *Union List of Serials of NSTA and its Agencies*
Parent Company: Department of Science & Technology, Republic of the Philippines

Silliman University Library
One Hibbard Ave, Dumaguete City, 6200 Negros Oriental
Tel: (035) 4226002
E-mail: library@su.edu.ph
Web Site: su.edu.ph
Key Personnel
President: Dr Ben S Malayang, III *E-mail:* pres@su.edu.ph
University Librarian: Isabel S Marino
Founded: 1901
Publication(s): *Convergence* (irregularly, multidisciplinary journal of the arts & sciences); *Sands & Coral* (irregularly, student literary journal); *Silliman Journal* (2 times/yr, journal on humanities, sciences & social sciences); *Silliman University Library Bulletin* (6 times/yr, newsletter, contains news about the library personnel, resources, services & facilities)

STII Library, see Science & Technology Information Institute

Ramona S Tirona Memorial Library
The Philippine Women's University, 1743 Taft Ave, 1004 Manila
Tel: (02) 526-8421 (ext 176); (02) 465-1780 *Fax:* (02) 526-6935
Web Site: www.pwu.edu.ph
Key Personnel
University Librarian: Dionisia M Angeles
Assistant University Librarian: Purita P Uson
Founded: 1919
Membership(s): PAARLNET (Philippine Association of Academic & Research Librarians Network).
Publication(s): *The Alumni Link and Philippine Women's University Forum*; *The Link*; *Philippine Educational Forum*; *PWU Bulletin/FTB Bulletin*

University of Manila Central Library
Annex Bldg, 2nd floor, 546 M V de los Santos St, Sampaloc, 1008 Manila
Tel: (02) 7355098
E-mail: admin@umnla.ph
Web Site: www.umnla.ph/academics/library
Key Personnel
Chief Librarian: Prof Imee L Resurreccion
Assistant Chief Librarian: Ms Meredes G Dizon
Founded: 1913

University of San Carlos Library System
Nasipit, Talamban, 6000 Cebu City
Tel: (032) 2300100 (ext 194); (032) 2531000 (ext 126) *Fax:* (032) 2540432
Web Site: www.library.usc.edu.ph; www.facebook.com/usclibrarysystem
Key Personnel
Dir, Libraries: Maxie Doreen Leva-Cabarron
  E-mail: mlcabarron@usc.edu.ph

University of Santo Tomas Library
Espana Blvd, 1015 Manila
Tel: (02) 731-3034 *Fax:* (02) 740-9709
E-mail: library@ust.edu.ph
Web Site: library.ust.edu.ph
Key Personnel
Prefect of Libraries: Fr Angel A Aparicio
Chief Librarian: Cecilia D Lobo
Founded: 1611

University of the East Library
2219 C M Recto Ave, 1008 Manila
Tel: (02) 735-5471 *Fax:* (02) 735-8544
E-mail: webmaster@ue.edu.ph
Web Site: www.ue.edu.ph/manila/library.html
Key Personnel
Dir: Loreto T Garcia *Tel:* (02) 735-8544 ext 400
  E-mail: loriegarcia@ue.edu.ph
Assistant Dir: Fely A Diego
Founded: 1947
Branch Office(s)
Benjamin C Chua Jr Library, Yan Yan Kee Bldg, 6th floor, Caloocan, Assistant Dir: Flordelina A Manzalay *Tel:* (02) 367-4579

University of the Philippines Diliman University Library
Gonzalez Hall, Corner of Apacible St, Diliman, 1101 Quezon City
Tel: (02) 981-8500 (ext 2852); (02) 981-8500 (ext 2856); (02) 981-8500 (ext 2851)
E-mail: lilbrary.updiliman@up.edu.ph; libraryinfo.updiliman@up.edu.ph
Web Site: www.mainlib.upd.edu.ph
Key Personnel
University Librarian: Prof Chito N Angeles
  E-mail: cnangeles@up.edu.ph
Deputy University Librarian: Elvira B Lapuz
  E-mail: eblapuz@up.edu.ph
Founded: 1922
Publication(s): Index to Philippine Periodicals (IPP) (quarterly); *Philippine Radical Papers in the University of the Philippines Diliman Main Library: A Subject Guide*; *UP Library Bulletin* (newsletter, online)

Poland

Archiwum Glowne Akt Dawnych w Warszawie
(Central Archives of Historical Records in Warsaw)
ul Dluga 7, 00-263 Warsaw
Tel: (22) 831 54 91; (22) 831 54 92; (22) 831 54 93 *Fax:* (22) 831 16 08
E-mail: sekretariat@agad.gov.pl
Web Site: www.agad.archiwa.gov.pl
Key Personnel
Dir: Dr Hubert Wajs
Founded: 1808
Publication(s): Miscellanea Historico-archivistica (irregularly, periodical, 2015)

Biblioteka Gdanska Polskiej Akademii Nauk
ul Walowa 15, 80-858 Gdansk
Tel: (58) 301 22 51; (58) 301 22 52; (58) 301 22 53; (58) 301 22 54; (58) 301 55 23 *Fax:* (58) 301 55 23
E-mail: bgpan@bgpan.gda.pl

Web Site: www.bgpan.gda.pl
Key Personnel
Dir: Dr Zofia Tylewska-Ostrowska *E-mail:* z.ostrowska@bgpan.gda.pl
Publication(s): Libri Gedanenses (annually)

Biblioteka Glowna Politechniki Warszawskiej
(Main Library of Warsaw University of Technology)
pl Politechniki 1, 00-661 Warsaw
Tel: (22) 234 74 00; (22) 621 13 70 *Fax:* (22) 621 13 70
E-mail: bgpw@bg.pw.edu.pl
Web Site: www.bg.pw.edu.pl
Key Personnel
Dir & University Librarian: Alicja Portacha
  E-mail: dyrektor.bg@pw.edu.pl

Biblioteka Glowna Uniwersytet u Szczecinskiego
ul Tarczynskiego 1, 70-387 Szczecin
Tel: (91) 444 23 61 *Fax:* (91) 444 23 62
E-mail: sekret@bg.szczecin.pl; info@bg.szczecin.pl
Web Site: bg.szczecin.pl
Founded: 1968
Publication(s): Przeglad Zachodniopomorski (quarterly)

Biblioteka Jagiellonska (Jagiellonian Library)
al Mickiewicza 22, 30-059 Krakow
Tel: (12) 663 35 55; (12) 633 09 03 *Fax:* (12) 633 09 03
E-mail: ujbj@uj.edu.pl
Web Site: www.bj.uj.edu.pl
Key Personnel
Dir: Prof Zdzislaw Pietrzyk *Tel:* (12) 663 35 54
  E-mail: zdzislaw.pietrzyk@uj.edu.pl
Deputy Dir, Administration: Aleksandra Cieslar
  Tel: (12) 663 35 61 *E-mail:* aleksandra.cieslar@uj.edu.pl
Deputy Dir, Development: Krystyna Sanetra
  Tel: (12) 663 35 59 *E-mail:* krystyna.sanetra@uj.edu.pl
Deputy Dir, Special Collections & Publishing: Jacek Partyka
Founded: 1364
Publication(s): Biuletyn Biblioteki Jagiellonskiej (The Jagiellonian Library Bulletin, annually); *Catalogus codicum manuscriptorum medii aevi Latinorum qui in Bibliotheca Jagellonica Cracoviae asservantur* (Catalogue of medieval Latin manuscripts in the Jagiellonian Library, vol 1-7); *Inwentarz rekopisow Biblioteki Jagiellonskiej* (Inventory of Manuscripts of the Jagiellonian Library); *Katalog drukow XVI Wieku ze zbiorow Biblioteki Jagiellonskiej* (Catalogue of XVI Century Publications from the Jagiellonian Library Collections); *Katalog polonikow XVI wieku Biblioteki Jagiellonskiej* (Catalogue of XVI century Polinica from the Jagiellonian Library Collections, vol 1-3)

Biblioteka Narodowa w Warszawie (National Library of Poland)
al Niepodleglosci 213, 02-086 Warsaw
Tel: (22) 608 29 99; (22) 608 23 30 (reference centre) *Fax:* (22) 825 52 51
E-mail: kontakt@bn.org.pl; biblnar@bn.org.pl
Web Site: www.bn.org.pl
Key Personnel
Dir: Dr Tomasz Makowski *Tel:* (22) 608 22 33
  E-mail: dyrektor@bn.org.pl
Manager: Krzysztof Alberski *Tel:* (22) 608 23 66
  E-mail: k.alberski@bn.org.pl
Librarian: Zofia Zurawinska
Publication(s): Biuletyn Informacyjny Biblioteki Narodowej (The National Library Information Bulletin); *Rocznik Biblioteki Narodowej* (The National Library Yearbook)

Biblioteka Politechnika Gdanska
ul Narutowicza 11/12, 80-233 Gdansk Wrzeszcz
Tel: (58) 347 25 75 *Fax:* (58) 347 27 58
E-mail: library@pg.gda.pl
Web Site: www.bg.pg.gda.pl
Key Personnel
Dir: Dr Anna Walek *E-mail:* anna.walek@pg.gda.pl
Publication(s): Bibliografia publikacji pracownikow Politechniki Gdanskiej (Bibliographic Publication of the Employees of the Technical University of Gdansk); *Raporty Wydzialow PG* (annually, Berichte der Fakultaten der TU Gdansk); *Wykaz nabytkow BG PG* (monthly, Directory of New Recruiting of the Central Library of Gdansk); *Zhistorii Politechniki Gdanskiej* (The History of the Technical University of Gdansk, quarterly)

Biblioteka Politechnika Krakowska im Tadeusza Kosciuszki (Library of Cracow University of Technology)
ul Warszawska 24, 31-155 Krakow
Tel: (12) 628 20 14; (12) 628 29 62 *Fax:* (12) 628 20 14
E-mail: listy@biblos.pk.edu.pl
Web Site: www.biblos.pk.edu.pl
Key Personnel
Dir: Marek M Gorski *E-mail:* gorski@biblos.pk.edu.pl
Deputy Dir: Dorota Buzdygan
  E-mail: buzdygan@biblos.pk.edu.pl
Founded: 1945
Membership(s): International Association of Technological University Libraries (IATUL); Ligue des Bibliotheques Europeennes de Recherche (LIBER).

Biblioteka Publiczna m st Warszawy - Biblioteka Glowna Wojewodztwa Mazowieckiego (The Warsaw Public Library-The Central Library of Masovia Province)
ul Koszykowa 26/28, 00-950 Warsaw
Tel: (22) 628 31 38
E-mail: info@koszykowa.pl
Web Site: www.koszykowa.pl
Key Personnel
Dir: Michal Strak *Tel:* (22) 621 78 52
  E-mail: michal.strak@koszykowa.pl
Founded: 1907

Biblioteka Slaska (Silesian Library)
Pl Rady Europy 1, 40-021 Katowice
Tel: (32) 208 37 00; (32) 208 37 40 *Fax:* (32) 208 37 20
E-mail: info@bs.katowice.pl
Web Site: www.bs.katowice.pl
Key Personnel
Dir: Prof Jan Malicki *Tel:* (32) 208 38 75
  E-mail: jan.malicki@bs.katowice.pl
Deputy Dir: Magdalena Skora *Tel:* (32) 208 38 75 *E-mail:* magdalena.skora@bs.katowice.pl
Founded: 1922
Research library. Main collection covering: literature, history, law, religion, social science & economy; special Silesian collection; collection of old prints & rare books.
Publication(s): Bibliografia Slaska (Bibliography of Silesia, annually)
Branch Office(s)
ul Ligonia 7, 40-036 Katowice *Tel:* (32) 251 42 21 *E-mail:* lbr@bs.katowice.pl
ul Francuska 12, 40-015 Katowice *Tel:* (32) 255 43 21 *E-mail:* domoswiatowy@bs.katowice.pl

Biblioteka Uniwersytecka w Poznaniu (Poznan University Library)
ul Ratajczaka 38/40, 61-816 Poznan
Tel: (61) 829 38 17 *Fax:* (61) 829 38 24
E-mail: library@amu.edu.pl
Web Site: lib.amu.edu.pl

Key Personnel
Dir: Dr Malgorzata Dabrowicz *Tel:* (61) 829 38
  20 *E-mail:* maldabro@amu.edu.pl
Head Librarian: Sandra Szczepanowska
  E-mail: sandraz@amu.edu.pl
Deputy Librarian: Edyta Szelejewska-Dembinska
  Tel: (61) 829 38 19
Founded: 1919
Publication(s): *Biblioteka* (annually)

Biblioteka Uniwersytecka w Toruniu
  (University Library in Torun)
ul Gagarina 13, 87-100 Torun
Tel: (56) 611 44 08; (56) 654 29 52 *Fax:* (56)
  611 22 43
E-mail: sekretariat@bu.uni.torun.pl; dyrektor.
  biblio@cm.umk.pl
Web Site: www.bu.uni.torun.pl/en
Key Personnel
Library Dir: Krzysztof Nierzwicki, PhD
  E-mail: krzysn@umk.pl
Founded: 1945

Biblioteka Uniwersytecka w Warszawie
  (Warsaw University Library)
Ul Dobra 56/66, 00-312 Warsaw
Tel: (22) 55 25 660; (22) 55 25 178; (22) 55 25
  179 *Fax:* (22) 552 56 59
E-mail: buw@uw.edu.pl; oin.buw@uw.edu.pl
  (reference desk)
Web Site: www.buw.uw.edu.pl
Key Personnel
Librarian: Ewa Kobierska-Maciuszko *Tel:* (22)
  55 25 350 *E-mail:* e.kobierska-maciuszko@uw.
  edu.pl
Founded: 1817
Membership(s): AANLA; CERL; IAML; ICAM;
  International Federation of Library Associations
  & Institutions (IFLA); LIBER.
Publication(s): *Prace Biblioteki Uniwersyteckiej
  w Warszawie - Acta Bibliothecae Universitatis
  Varsoviensis* (irregularly)

Biblioteka Uniwersytecka we Wroclawiu
  (Wroclaw University Library)
ul Fryderyka Joliot-Curie 12, 50-383 Wroclaw
Tel: (71) 375 76 24; (71) 346 31 31 *Fax:* (71)
  346 31 66
E-mail: oin.bu@uwr.edu.pl
Web Site: www.bu.uni.wroc.pl
Key Personnel
Dir: Grazyna Piotrowicz *Tel:* (71) 346 31 20
  E-mail: grazyna.piotrowicz@uwr.edu.pl
Deputy Dir, General Collections: Dr Monika
  Gorska *Tel:* (71) 346 31 61 *E-mail:* monika.
  gorska@uwr.edu.pl
Deputy Dir, Special Collections: Ewa Pitak
  Tel: (71) 346 31 20 *E-mail:* ewa.pitak@uwr.
  edu.pl
Founded: 1945
Publication(s): *Bibliothecalia Wratislaviensia* (ir-
  regularly, newspaper)

Biblioteka Uniwersytetu Gdanskiego
ul Wita Stwosza 53, 80-308 Gdansk
Tel: (58) 523 32 10; (58) 523 32 11 *Fax:* (58)
  523 32 09
E-mail: bib@bg.ug.gda.pl; infonauk@bg.ug.gda.pl
Web Site: www.bg.univ.gda.pl
Key Personnel
Dir: Grazyna Jaskowiak
Deputy Dir: Ewa Chrzan *E-mail:* ewa@bg.ug.edu.
  pl
Founded: 1970

Glowna Biblioteka Lekarska (Central Medical
  Library)
ul Chocimska 22, 00-791 Warsaw
Tel: (22) 849 74 04; (22) 849 78 51; (22) 849 78
  53 *Fax:* (22) 849 78 02
E-mail: sekretariat@gbl.waw.pl

Web Site: www.gbl.waw.pl
Key Personnel
Dir: Dr Wojciech Giermaziak
Deputy Dir: Iwona Fryzowska-Chrobot *E-mail:* i.
  chorobot@gbl.waw.pl
Founded: 1945
Central medical library.
Publication(s): *Biuletyn GBL*; *Polska Bibliografia
  Lekanska*
Branch Office(s)
ul Czaplin.ecka 123, 97-400 Belchatow, Head:
  Malgorzata Owczarek *Tel:* (44) 635 84 02
  E-mail: odzbel@gbl.waw.pl
ul Brzeska 1, 21-500 Biala Podlaska, Head:
  Slawomir Potocki *Tel:* (83) 306 86 98
  E-mail: odzbiap@gbl.waw.pl
ul Krasinskiego 28, 43-300 Bielsko-Biala, Head:
  Katarzyna Mielimonka *Tel:* (33) 822 12 11
  E-mail: odzbbia@gbl.waw.pl
ul Wojska Polskiego 51, 06-400 Ciechanow,
  Head: Maria Lipinska *Tel:* (23) 672 22 13
  Fax: (23) 672 22 13 *E-mail:* odzciech@gbl.
  waw.pl
ul PCK 1, Pawilon D Ip, 42-218 Czestochowa,
  Head: Barbara Chlewicka *Tel:* (34) 367 39
  45 *Fax:* (34) 325 72 95 *E-mail:* odzczes@gbl.
  waw.pl
ul Krolewiecka 146, 82-300 Elblag, Head:
  Janusz Przecinski *Tel:* (55) 239 56 82
  E-mail: odzelb@gbl.waw.pl
ul Estkowskiego 13, 66-400 Gorzow Wielkopol-
  ski, Head: Elzbieta Frankowska *Tel:* (95) 727
  91 02 *E-mail:* odzgorz@gbl.waw.pl
ul Grazynskiego 49 A, 40-126 Katowice,
  Head: Danuta Korzon *Tel:* (32) 258 66 05
  E-mail: odzkat@gbl.waw.pl
ul Artwinskiego 3C, skr poczt 21, 25-602 Kielce,
  Head: Anna Paszkowska *Tel:* (41) 367 41 09
  E-mail: odzkiel@gbl.waw.pl
ul Partyzantow 15 A, 75-411 Koszalin, Head:
  Joanna Przybylo *Tel:* (53) 128 07 24
  E-mail: odzkosz@gbl.waw.pl
ul Oleska 48, 45-052 Opole, Head: Re-
  nata Firkowska *Tel:* (77) 545 40 07
  E-mail: odzopol@gbl.waw.pl
ul Aleksandrowicza 5, 26-600 Radom, Head:
  Halina Bonatowska *Tel:* (48) 361 33 54
  E-mail: odzrad@gbl.waw.pl
ul Warzywna 1A, 35-959 Rzeszow, Head:
  Elzbieta Zwolinska *Tel:* (17) 851 68 67
  E-mail: odzrzesz@gbl.waw.pl
ul Jana Pawla II, 1, 76-200 Slupsk, Head:
  Teresa Augustynowicz *Tel:* (59) 846 84 96
  E-mail: odzslup@gbl.waw.pl
ul Ignacy Danielewskiego 6/9, 87-100 Torun,
  Head: Krystyna Emmerling-Rychlicka *Tel:* (56)
  622 71 93 *E-mail:* odztor@gbl.waw.pl
ul Podgorna 50, 65-246 Zielona Gora, Head:
  Maria Szymanowska-Dunajko *Tel:* (68) 380
  16 07 *E-mail:* odzzgor@gbl.waw.pl

Instytut Bibliograficzny (Bibliographical
  Institute)
Division of Biblioteka Narodowa w Warszawie
Biblioteka Narodowa, al Niepodleglosci 213, 02-
  086 Warsaw
Tel: (22) 608 29 99; (22) 452 29 99 *Fax:* (22)
  825 52 51
E-mail: biblnar@bn.org.pl
Web Site: www.bn.org.pl
Key Personnel
Dir & Librarian: Dr Tomasz Makowski *Tel:* (22)
  608 22 33 *E-mail:* dyrektor@bn.org.pl
Publication(s): *Bibliografia Bibliografii Polskich*
  (Bibliography of Polish Bibliographies, annu-
  ally); *Bibliografia Wydawnictw Ciaglych* (Bib-
  liography of Serials, quarterly); *Polonica Za-
  graniczne* (Foreign Polonica, annually); *Polska
  Bibliografia Bibliologiczna* (Polish Bibliogra-
  phy of Library Science, annually); *Przewodnik
  Bibliograficzny* (Bibliographical Guide, weekly)

Naczelna Dyrekcja Archiwow Panstwowych
  (Head Office of State Archives)
ul Rakowiecka 2D, 02-517 Warsaw
Tel: (22) 565 46 00 *Fax:* (22) 565 46 14
E-mail: ndap@archiwa.gov.pl
Web Site: www.archiwa.gov.pl
Key Personnel
General Dir: Dr Wojciech Wozniak
Publication(s): *Archeion, Teki archiwalne; Miscel-
  lanea Historico-Archivistica; Nowe Miscellanea
  Historyczne*

PISM, see Polski Instytut Spraw
  Miedzynarodowych Biblioteka

Politechnika Slaska, Biblioteka Glowna
  (Silesian University of Technology Central
  Library)
ul Kaszubska 23, 44-100 Gliwice
Tel: (32) 237 15 51; (32) 237 12 69 *Fax:* (32)
  237 15 51
E-mail: bg.sekr@polsl.pl; bg-info@polsl.pl
Web Site: www.polsl.pl/Jednostki/RJO1/Strony/
  witamy.aspx; www.bg.polsl.pl
Key Personnel
Dir: Dr Krzysztof Ziolo *E-mail:* krzysztof.ziolo@
  polsl.pl
Deputy Dir: Maria Rychlewska, MA
  E-mail: maria.rychlewska@polsl.pl
Founded: 1945

**Politechnika Wroclawska/Biblioteka Glowna i
  OINT** (Wroclaw University of
  Technology/Main Library & Scientific
  Information Centre)
Wybrzeze Wyspianskiego 27, 50-370 Wroclaw
Tel: (71) 320 23 31 *Fax:* (71) 328 32 45
E-mail: biblioteka@pwr.edu.pl
Web Site: biblioteka.pwr.edu.pl
Founded: 1946

**Polski Instytut Spraw Miedzynarodowych
  Biblioteka** (The Polish Institute of International
  Affairs Library)
ul Warecka 1a, skr poczt nr 1010, 00-950 Warsaw
Tel: (22) 556 80 44; (22) 556 80 00 *Fax:* (22)
  556 80 99
E-mail: pism@pism.pl
Web Site: biblioteka.pism.pl
Key Personnel
Head of Library: Karolina Dyl *E-mail:* dyl@
  pism.pl
Publication(s): *Polski Przeglad Dyplomatyczny*
  (6/times yr, in Polish); *The Polish Quarterly of
  International Affairs* (quarterly); *Yearbook of
  Polish Foreign Policy* (annually)

Portugal

Arquivo Nacional Torre do Tombo (National
  Archive Torre do Tombo)
Alameda da Universidade, 1649-010 Lisbon
Tel: 210 037 100 *Fax:* 210 037 101
E-mail: mail@dglab.gov.pt
Web Site: antt.dglab.gov.pt
Key Personnel
Dir General: Silvestre Lacerda *E-mail:* silvestre.
  lacerda@dglab.gov.pt

Biblioteca da Academia das Ciencias de Lisboa
  (Library of the Academy of Sciences of
  Lisbon)
R Academia das Ciencias, 19, 1249-122 Lisbon
Tel: 213 219 730
E-mail: geral@acad-ciencias.pt
Web Site: www.acad-ciencias.pt
Founded: 1779

Biblioteca da Ajuda
Palacio Nacional da Ajuda, 1349-021 Lisbon
Tel: 21 363 8592 *Fax:* 21 363 8592
E-mail: bibajuda@pnajuda.dgpc.pt
Web Site: bibliotecaajuda.bnportugal.pt;
  bibliotecadaajuda.blogspot.com
Founded: 1880

Biblioteca do Palacio Nacional de Mafra
  (Library of the National Palace of Mafra)
Terreiro Dom Joao V, 2640-492 Mafra
Tel: (0261) 817 550 *Fax:* (0261) 811 947
E-mail: geral@pnmafra.dgpc.pt
Web Site: www.palaciomafra.gov.pt
Key Personnel
Head of Library: Maria Teresa Amaral
  E-mail: teresaamaral@pnmafra.dgpc.pt

Biblioteca Geral da Universidade de Coimbra
  (University of Coimbra General Library)
Largo da Porta Ferrea, 3000-447 Coimbra
Tel: 239 859 831; 239 859 800; 239 859 900
  Fax: 239 827 135
E-mail: secretaria@bg.uc.pt; sibuc@sib.uc.pt
Web Site: www.uc.pt/bguc
Key Personnel
Dir: Jose Augusto Cardoso Bernardes
  E-mail: director@bg.uc.pt
Deputy Dir: Antonio Eugenio Maia do Amaral
  E-mail: aemaia@bg.uc.pt
Publication(s): *Acta Universitatis Conimbrigensis*;
  Biblioteca da Universidade de Coimbra; *Bib-
  lioteca Geral da Universidade de Coimbra* (an-
  nually); *Divulgacao Bibliografica*; *Revista da
  Universidade de Coimbra* (annually); *Sumarios
  das Publicacoes Periodicas Portuguesas* (10
  times/yr)

Biblioteca Nacional de Portugal (National
  Library of Portugal)
Campo Grande, 83, 1749-081 Lisbon
Tel: 21 798 20 00 *Fax:* 21 798 21 38
E-mail: bn@bnportugal.pt
Web Site: www.bn.pt
Key Personnel
Dir: Maria Ines Cordeiro *Tel:* 217982022
  E-mail: icordeiro@bn.pt
Founded: 1796
Publication(s): *Leituras: Revista da Biblioteca
  Nacional* (2 times/yr)

Biblioteca Publica de Evora (Public Library of
  Evora)
Largo Conde de Vila Flor, 7000-804 Evora
Tel: 266 769 330
E-mail: bpevora@bpe.pt
Web Site: www.bpe.pt
Key Personnel
Dir: Zelia Parreira *E-mail:* zparreira@bpe.pt
Founded: 1805
Publication(s): *Evora, BPADE, 1988*; *Isabel Cid-
  Incunabulos da Biblioteca Publica e Arquivo
  Distrital de Evora-Catalogo Abreviado*; *Isabel
  Cid-Incunabulos E Seus Possuidores, Estudo
  das marcas de posse dos incunabulos da Bib-
  lioteca Publica e Arquivo Distrital de Evora,
  Lisboa INIC, 1988*; *Isabel Cid-Lil Vicente e
  asua Epoca, Evora, 1992*
Parent Company: Instituto dos Arquivos Na-
  cionais/Torre do Tombo

Biblioteca Publica Municipal do Porto (Porto
  Municipal Public Library)
Rua de D Joao IV 17, 4049-017 Porto
Tel: 225 193 480 *Fax:* 225 193 488
E-mail: bpmp@cm-porto.pt
Web Site: bmp.cm-porto.pt/bpmp; bibliotecas.cm-
  porto.pt
Key Personnel
Dir: Sofia Alves
Founded: 1833

Branch Office(s)
Jardin do Palacio de Cristal, Rua de Entre-
  Quintas, 328, 4050-239 Porto *Tel:* 226 081 000
  Fax: 226 081 057 *E-mail:* bib.agarrett@cm-
  porto.pt

BPMP, see Biblioteca Publica Municipal do
  Porto

**Fundacao para a Ciencia e a
  Tecnologia/Servico de Informacao e
  Documentacao (SID)**
Av D Carlos I, 126, 1249-074 Lisbon
Tel: 213924300 *Fax:* 213956519
E-mail: roteiro.infract@fct.pt
Web Site: www.fct.pt
Key Personnel
Coordinator: James Saborida
Centre of Scientific & Technical Information, a
  branch of the Junta Nacional de Investigacao
  Cientifica e Tecnologia (National Council for
  Scientific & Technological Research).
Publication(s): *Guia de servicos di Documentacao
  e di Bibliotecas em Portugal*

SDUM, see Universidade do Minho Bibliotecas

**Servicos de Documentacao da Universidade do
  Minho**, see Universidade do Minho Bibliotecas

Universidade do Minho Bibliotecas (Minho
  University Libraries)
Campus de Gualtar, 4710-057 Braga
Tel: 253 604 150 *Fax:* 253 604 159
E-mail: sdum@sdum.uminho.pt
Web Site: www.uminho.pt; www.sdum.uminho.pt
Key Personnel
Dir, Documentation Services: Dr Eloy Rodrigues
Founded: 1973

Puerto Rico

Archivo General de Puerto Rico (Puerto Rican
  General Archive)
Av de la Constitucion 500, Puerta de Tierra, San
  Juan 00902
Tel: (787) 725-1060
E-mail: archivogeneral@icp.pr.gov
Web Site: www.facebook.com/
  archivogeneraldepuertorico
Key Personnel
Dir: Samuel Quinones Garcia
Founded: 1955
Parent Company: Instituto de Cultura Puertor-
  riquena

Conrado F Asenjo Library, see University of
  Puerto Rico, Medical Sciences Campus Library

Biblioteca Nacional de Puerto Rico (National
  Library of Puerto Rico)
Ave de la Constitucion, 500, Puerta de Tierra,
  San Juan 00902
Mailing Address: Apdo 9024184, San Juan
  00902-4184
Tel: (787) 725-1060
Web Site: www.facebook.com/
  bibliotecanacionalpuertorico
Founded: 1967
Parent Company: Instituto de Cultura Puertor-
  riquena

**Biblioteca Regional del Caribe y de Estudios
  Latinoamericanos** (Caribbean & Latin
  American Studies Regional Library)
Edificio Jose M Lazaro, Primer piso, Ala Oeste,
  San Juan 00931
Tel: (787) 764-0000 (ext 85855) *Fax:* (787) 763-
  5685
Web Site: biblioteca.uprrp.edu/bib-col/caribe.html
Key Personnel
Chief Librarian: Almaluces Figueroa
  E-mail: almaluces.figueroa1@upr.edu
Founded: 1946
Research collection open to the general public.

**Interamerican University of Puerto Rico
  Information Access Center** (Universidad
  Interamericana de Puerto Rico Centro de
  Acceso a la Informacion)
Carretera No 2, Km 80.4, Barrio San Daniel, Sec-
  tor Las Canelas, Arecibo 00612
Mailing Address: PO Box 4050, Arecibo 00614-
  4050
Tel: (787) 878-5475 *Fax:* (787) 880-1624
Web Site: www.arecibo.inter.edu/biblioteca
Key Personnel
Dir: Sara E Abreu *Tel:* (787) 878-5475 ext 3366
  E-mail: sabreu@arecibo.inter.edu
Librarian: Dexy Garcia *E-mail:* dgarcia@arecibo.
  inter.edu

**Universidad de Puerto Rico Recinto de Rio
  Piedras Sistema de Bibliotecas** (University of
  Puerto Rico, Rio Piedras Campus Library
  System)
PO Box 23302, San Juan 00931-3302
Tel: (787) 764-0000 (ext 85509); (787) 764-
  0000 (ext 85506); (787) 764-0000 (ext 85520)
  Fax: (787) 772-1479
Web Site: biblioteca.uprrp.edu
Key Personnel
Dir: Prof Miguel A Santiago Rivera
  E-mail: miguel.santiago16@upr.edu
Associate Dir: Prof Myra M Torres Alamo
  E-mail: myra.torres@upr.edu
Publication(s): *Al Dia, Entorno*; *Biblionotas*; *Bo-
  letines de Divulgacion*; *Lumbre*; *Perspectiva*;
  Servicio de Alerta

**University of Puerto Rico, General Library,
  Mayaguez Campus** (Universidad de Puerto
  Rico, Biblioteca General Recinto Universitario
  de Mayaguez)
Call Box 9000, Mayaguez 00681
Tel: (787) 265-3810; (787) 832-4040 (ext 3810);
  (787) 832-4040 (ext 2151); (787) 832-4040
  (ext 2155) *Fax:* (787) 265-5483
E-mail: library@uprm.edu
Web Site: www.uprm.edu/library
Key Personnel
Dir & Librarian: Prof Luis O Casiano Torres
  E-mail: luis.casiano3@upr.edu
Publication(s): *Bibliorum* (irregularly, newsletter)

**University of Puerto Rico, Medical Sciences
  Campus Library**
PO Box 365067, San Juan 00936-5067
Tel: (787) 758-2525
Web Site: library.rcm.upr.edu
Key Personnel
Dir: Carmen Santos-Corrada *Tel:* (787) 758-2525
  ext 1200 *E-mail:* carmen.santos4@upr.edu

Qatar

Qatar National Library
PO Box 5825, Doha
Tel: 4454 6039

E-mail: qnl@qnl.qa
Web Site: www.qnl.qa
Key Personnel
Executive Dir: Dr Sohair F Wastawy *Tel:* 4454
1378 *E-mail:* swastawy@qnl.qa

Qatar University Library
Library Administration, PO Box 2713, Doha
Tel: 4403-6363; 4403-4068
E-mail: library@qu.edu.qa; lib.administration@
qu.edu.qa
Web Site: library.qu.edu.qa
Founded: 1973

Reunion

**Archives Departementales de la Reunion -
Sudel Fuma**
4 rue Marcel Pagnol, Champ Fleuri, 97490
Sainte-Clotilde
Tel: 02 62 94 04 14 *Fax:* 02 62 94 04 21
E-mail: archives.departementales@cg974.fr
Web Site: www.cg974.fr/culture/archives-
departementales
Key Personnel
Dir: Damien Vaisse
Founded: 1946
State & local public archives of La Reunion &
private archives & library (history & adminis-
tration of Reunion & Indian Ocean).
Parent Company: Conseil General de la Reunion

Bibliotheque Departementale de Pret
One, place Joffre, 97400 Saint Denis
Tel: 21 03 24 *Fax:* 21 41 30
E-mail: bdp@cg974.fr

Bibliotheque municipale de Saint-Pierre, see
Mediatheque Raphael Barquissau

Mediatheque Raphael Barquissau
BP 396, 97458 Saint-Pierre Cedex
Tel: 02 62 32 62 50 *Fax:* 02 62 25 74 10
E-mail: mediasp@mediatheque-saintpierre.fr
Web Site: www.mediatheque-saintpierre.fr
Key Personnel
Contact: Linda Koo Seen Lin

SCD, see Universite de la Reunion, Service
Commun de Documentation

**Universite de la Reunion, Service Commun de
Documentation**
15, Ave Rene Cassin, CS 92003, 97744 Saint-
Denis Cedex 9
Tel: 02 62 93 83 79 *Fax:* 02 62 93 83 64
E-mail: scd@univ-reunion.fr; info-bu@support.
univ-reunion.fr
Web Site: bu.univ-reunion.fr
Key Personnel
Dir: Joelle Menant *E-mail:* joelle.menant@univ-
reunion.fr

Romania

**Academia de Studii Economice, Biblioteca
Centrala** (Academy of Economic Studies
Central Library)
Piata Romana, nr 6, Sector 1, 010374 Bucharest
Tel: (021) 319 19 00 *Fax:* (021) 319 18 99
E-mail: contact@biblioteca.ase.ro

Web Site: www.biblioteca.ase.ro
Key Personnel
Dir: Liviu Bogdan Vlad
E-mail: liviubogdanvlad@yahoo.com

Arhivele Nationale ale Romaniei (National
Archives of Romania)
Bd Regina Elisabeta nr 49, sector 5, 050013
Bucharest
Tel: (021) 303 70 80 *Fax:* (021) 312 58 41; (021)
313 18 38
E-mail: secretariat@arhivelenationale.ro
Web Site: arhivelenationale.ro
Key Personnel
Dir General: Dr Ioan Dragan *Tel:* (021) 312 67
10
Deputy Dir: Dr Alina Pavelescu *Tel:* (021) 315 25
03
Library Coordinator: Camelia Cojocaru
Membership(s): International Association of Fran-
copone Archives; International Council of
Archives.
Publication(s): *Historical Abstract & America-
History & Life* (article abstracts & index)

**Biblioteca Centrala Universitara "Carol I" din
Bucuresti** (Central University Library Carol I
of Bucharest)
Str Boteanu, nr 1, sector 1, 010027 Bucharest
Tel: (021) 313 1605; (021) 313 1606 *Fax:* (021)
312 0108
E-mail: office@bcub.ro
Web Site: www.bcub.ro
Key Personnel
General Dir: Dr Mireille Carmen Radoi *Tel:* (021)
312 0108 ext 200 *E-mail:* mireille.radoi@bcub.
ro
Publication(s): *Literatura romana; Ghid bibli-
ografic Partea I: Surse. Partea a II-a: Scri-
itori. Vol.I: A-L. Vol.II: M-Z. 1979, 1982, 1983,
Partea a III-a Scriitori romani traducatori A-Z,
2003*

**Biblioteca Centrala Universitara Mihail
Eminescu Iasi** (Mihai Eminescu Central
University Library Iasi)
Str Pacurari 4, 700511 Iasi
Tel: (0232) 264245 *Fax:* (0232) 261796
E-mail: bcuis@bcu-iasi.ro
Web Site: www.bcu-iasi.ro
Key Personnel
Dir: Peter Maleon *Tel:* (0232) 264245 ext 102
E-mail: director@bcu-iasi.ro
Founded: 1835
Parent Company: Ministry of Education & Re-
search

Biblioteca Metropolitana Bucuresti (Bucharest
Metropolitan Library)
Str Tache D Ionescu, Nr 4, Sector 1, 010354
Bucharest
Tel: (021) 316 83 00 *Fax:* (021) 316 83 04
E-mail: biblioteca@bmms.ro
Web Site: www.bibmet.ro
Key Personnel
Manager: Anca Rapeanu *E-mail:* anca.rapeanu@
bibmet.ro
Founded: 1935
Membership(s): EBLIDA; IMTAMEL; Interna-
tional Federation of Library Associations &
Institutions (IFLA).
Publication(s): *Biblioteca Bucurestilor*
(Bucharest's Library Review, monthly, cultural
& library review); *Foaia Cartierului* (Neighbor-
hood's Review, monthly, local library review)

Biblioteca Nationala a Romaniei (National
Library of Romania)
Bd Unirii nr 22, sector 3, 030833 Bucharest
Tel: (021) 314 24 34; (021) 314 10 02 *Fax:* (021)
312 33 81

E-mail: biblioteca@bibnat.ro
Web Site: www.bibnat.ro
Key Personnel
Manager: Ioan Marius Eppel
Founded: 1955

Biblioteca Universitatii Transilvania din Brasov
(Library of Transilvania University of Brasov)
Str Iuliu Maniu nr 41A, 500091 Brasov
Tel: (0268) 476050 *Fax:* (0268) 476050
E-mail: biblioteca@unitbv.ro
Web Site: www.unitbv.ro
Founded: 1948
Specialize in academic library, engineering,
forestry, wood industry, humanities, sciences,
medicine, music & economy.
Parent Company: Transilvania University of
Brasov

Biblioteca Valeriu Bologo, see Universitatea de
Medicina si Farmacie, Biblioteca Valeriu
Bologa

INID, see Institutul National de Informare si
Documentare (INID)

**Institutul National de Informare si
Documentare (INID)** (National Institute for
Information & Documentation)
Str Mendeleev D I 21-25, Sector 1, 010362
Bucharest
Tel: (021) 3158765

**Universitatea de Medicina si Farmacie,
Biblioteca Valeriu Bologa**
Calle Victor Babes, Nº 8, 400012 Cluj-Napoca
Tel: (0264) 597256 (ext 2211) *Fax:* (0264)
597257
E-mail: bibliotecaumf@umfcluj.ro
Web Site: www.umfcluj.ro
Key Personnel
Contact: Ileana Iepure
Founded: 1949
Membership(s): EAHIL (European Association
for Health Information & Libraries).

**Universitatea Politehnica Bucuresti - Biblioteca
Centrala**
Splaiul Independentei 313, corp A, Ground floor,
Bucharest
Web Site: www.library.pub.ro
Key Personnel
Dir: Cristina Albu *E-mail:* christina.albu@upb.ro
Founded: 1868

Russia

All-Russian Patent & Technical Library
Berezhkovskaya naberezhnaya, 24, G-59, GSP-3,
125993 Moscow
Tel: (499) 240-4437 *Fax:* (499) 240-4437
E-mail: vptb@rupto.ru
Web Site: www1.fips.ru
Key Personnel
Deputy Head: Olga Bakhvalova *Tel:* (495)
531-6562 *E-mail:* obahvalova@rupto.
ru; Olga Ushakova *Tel:* (499) 240-2586
E-mail: ushakova@rupto.ru

Biblioteka Akademii Nauk Rossii (Russian
Academy of Sciences Library)
Birzevaja linija 1, 199034 St Petersburg
Tel: (812) 328-3592 *Fax:* (812) 328-7436
E-mail: ban@rasl.nw.ru
Web Site: www.rasl.ru

Key Personnel
Dir: Irina Mikhailovna Belyaeva *Tel:* (812) 328-3592 ext 1119
Founded: 1714

Gosudarstvennaya publichnaya istoricheskaya biblioteka Rossii (State Public Historical Library of Russia)
Starosadskyi pereulok 9, str 1, 101990 Moscow
Tel: (495) 625 6514; (495) 628 0522 *Fax:* (495) 628 0284
E-mail: info@shpl.ru
Web Site: www.shpl.ru
Key Personnel
Dir: Mikhail Afanasyev
Deputy Dir: Elena Arturovna Yastrzhembskaya *Tel:* (495) 625 7139
Founded: 1863 (as Moscow City Chertkovsky Public Libary)

Gosudarstvennaya publichnaya nauchno-tekhnicheskaya biblioteka Rossii (Russian National Public Library for Science & Technology)
ul Khoroshevskaya 17, 123298 Moscow
Tel: (495) 698-93-05
E-mail: gpntb@gpntb.ru
Web Site: www.gpntb.ru
Key Personnel
General Dir: Yakov Leonidovich *Tel:* (495) 625-92-88
Founded: 1958
Membership(s): International Association of Technological University Libraries (IATUL); International Federation of Library Associations & Institutions (IFLA).

Gosudarstvennaya publichnaya nauchno-tekhnicheskaya biblioteka Sibirskogo otdeleniya Rossiiskoi Akademii Nauk (State Public Scientific Technological Library of the Siberian Branch of the Russian Academy of Sciences)
Voskhod Str, 15, 630200 Novosibirsk
Tel: (383) 266-25-85; (383) 266-75-71
E-mail: office@spsl.nsc.ru
Web Site: www.spsl.nsc.ru
Key Personnel
Dir: Andrey Guskov *Tel:* (383) 266-18-60
E-mail: guskov@spsl.nsc.ru
Founded: 1958

GPIB Russia, see Gosudarstvennaya publichnaya istoricheskaya biblioteka Rossii

GPNTB, see Gosudarstvennaya publichnaya nauchno-tekhnicheskaya biblioteka Rossii

INION RAS, see Institut Nauchnoy Informatsii po Obschestvennym Naukam, Rossijskoj Akademii Nauk RF

Institut Nauchnoy Informatsii po Obschestvennym Naukam, Rossijskoj Akademii Nauk RF (Institute for Scientific Information in Social Sciences of the Russian Academie of Sciences, Russian Federation)
ul Krzhizhanovskogo 15, Bldg 2, 117997 Moscow
Tel: (499) 124-3076
Web Site: www.inion.ru/library
Key Personnel
Head of Library: Lyudmila Nikolaevna Tikhonova
Head, Dept of Library & Information Services: Alfyorova Anastasia Valentinovna *Tel:* (916) 646-9729
Founded: 1969
Membership(s): International Federation of Library Associations (IFLA); Russian Library Association.

Nauchnaya biblioteka im M Gor'kogo Sankt-Peterburgskogo (Maxim Gorky Scientific Library of St Petersburg State University)
Universitetskaya nab 7/9, 199034 St Petersburg
Tel: (812) 363-67-42
Web Site: www.library.spbu.ru
Key Personnel
Dir: Marina Karpova *Tel:* (812) 328-95-46
E-mail: m.karpova@spbu.ru
Membership(s): International Federation of Library Associations & Institutions (IFLA); LIBER; Russian Library Association; St Petersburg Library Association.
Branch Office(s)
Biology Library, Universitetskaya nab 7/9, 199034 St Petersburg, Head of Library: Natalja Kozlova *Tel:* (812) 328-94-42 *E-mail:* nvkozlova@spbu.ru *Web Site:* bio.spbu.ru/library
Chemistry Library, Old Peterhof, Universitet Ave 26, 198504 St Petersburg, Head of Library: Tatiana Devyatkina *Tel:* (812) 428-40-23 *E-mail:* t.devyatkina@spbu.ru
Economy Library, ul Chaikovsky, 62, 191194 St Petersburg, Head of Library: Galina Alekseeva *Tel:* (812) 363 6493 *E-mail:* g.alekseeva@spbu.ru *Web Site:* library.econ.spbu.ru
Geography Library, Middle Ave, 41, 199178 St Petersburg, VO, Head of Library: Olga Klenova *Tel:* (812) 324-12-59 ext 1606 *E-mail:* o.klenova@spbu.ru
Geology Library, Decembrists, 16, 199155 St Petersburg, Head of Library: Svetlana Platonova *Tel:* (812) 324-12-70 ext 6561 *E-mail:* svplatonova@spbu.ru
Journalism Library, One Liniya, 26, 199053 St Petersburg, VO, Head of Library: Tatiana Trotsko *Tel:* (812) 363 6111 ext 3416 *E-mail:* t.trotsko@spbu.ru *Web Site:* jf.spbu.ru
Law Library, 22 linija, 7, 199026 St Petersburg, VO, Head of Library: Ekaterina Yatsuk *Tel:* (812) 329 2836 *E-mail:* e.yatsuk@spbu.ru *Web Site:* lib.law.spbu.ru
Liberal Arts & Sciences Library, Galernaya St, 58-60, 190000 St Petersburg, Head of Library: Anna Varustina *Tel:* (812) 324-12-70 *E-mail:* a.varustina@spbu.ru *Web Site:* artesliberales.spbu.ru
Library of the Center of Russian Language & Culture, nab Leith Schmidt, 11/2, 199034 St Petersburg, Head of Library: Anastasia Ivanova *Tel:* (812) 323 3962 *E-mail:* a.w.ivanova@spbu.ru
Library of the Faculty of International Relations & Political Science, ul Smol'nogo, 1/3, 193060 St Petersburg, Head of Library: Anna Petrushina *Tel:* (812) 363-64-11 *E-mail:* a.petrushina@spbu.ru *Web Site:* sir.spbu.ru/fakultet/library
Library of the Social Sciences, Mendeleevskaya linija, 5, 199034 St Petersburg, Head of Library: Tatyana Balymova *Tel:* (812) 328-97-07 *E-mail:* t.balimova@spbu.ru
Management Library, Petrodvortsovy Borough, St Petersburg Highway, 109, 198510 St Petersburg, Head of Library: Yulia Mulya *Tel:* (812) 323-84-43 *E-mail:* j.muleva@spbu.ru *Web Site:* gsom.spbu.ru/gsom/library
Mathematics & Mechanics Library, Old Peterhof, Universitet Ave 28, 198504 St Petersburg, Head of Library: Irina Matveeva *Tel:* (812) 428-41-73 *E-mail:* i.matveeva@spbu.ru *Web Site:* www.math.spbu.ru
Medical Library, 21 linija, 8a, 199034 St Petersburg, VO, Head of Library: Alla Rastvortseva *Tel:* (812) 326-0326 ext 5238 *E-mail:* a.rastvortceva@spbu.ru
Oriental Library, Universitetskaya nab 11, 199034 St Petersburg, Head of Library: Milan Azarkina *Tel:* (812) 328-95-49 *E-mail:* m.azarkina@spbu.ru *Web Site:* orient.spbu.ru
Philology Library, Universitetskaya nab 7/9, 199034 St Petersburg, Head of Library: Olga

Vasilieva *Tel:* (812) 328-95-64 *E-mail:* o.vasileva@spbu.ru *Web Site:* phil.spbu.ru/ucheba/biblioteka
Physics Library, Old Peterhof, St Ulyanovsk, 3, 198504 St Petersburg, Head of Library: Marina Krayukhina *Tel:* (812) 428-43-26 *E-mail:* m.kraukhina@spbu.ru *Web Site:* www.phys.spbu.ru/library
Psychology Library, nab Makarova, 6, 199034 St Petersburg, VO, Head of Library: Elena Sudnitsyna *Tel:* (812) 328-94-06 *E-mail:* e.sudnitsina@spbu.ru *Web Site:* www.psy.spbu.ru/departments/biblio
Secondary & Secondary Vocational Education Library, Izmailovsky Ave, 27, 190005 St Petersburg, Head of Library: Lilia Chelpanov *E-mail:* l.chelpanova@spbu.ru

Petrozavodskij Gosudarstvennyj Universitet (Academic Library of Petrozavodsk State University)
33, Lenin St, 185910 Petrozavodsk, Republic of Karelia
Tel: (814) 274-10-44 *Fax:* (814) 271-10-16
E-mail: lib@petrsu.ru
Web Site: library.petrsu.ru
Key Personnel
Dir: Marina P Otlivanchik *Tel:* (814) 274-28-65
E-mail: otl@psu.karelia.ru
Assistant Dir: Lidia V Kovalevskaia *Tel:* (814) 271-10-44

Rossiiskaya Nacionalnaya biblioteka (National Library of Russia)
18, Sadovaya St, 191069 St Petersburg
Tel: (812) 310-71-37; (812) 415-97-09 *Fax:* (812) 310-61-48
E-mail: office@nlr.ru
Web Site: nlr.ru
Key Personnel
Deputy Dir: Alexander Visly *Tel:* (812) 310-28-56

Russian State Historical Archives
Zanevsky Ave, 36, 195112 St Petersburg
Tel: (812) 438-55-20 *Fax:* (812) 438-55-94
E-mail: fgurgia@mail.ru; rgia@rgia.su
Web Site: www.rusarchives.ru/federal/rgia; fgurgia.ru
Key Personnel
Dir: Sergey Vladimirovich Chernyavsky

Scientific Library of St Petersburg State University, see Nauchnaya biblioteka im M Gor'kogo Sankt-Peterburgskogo

Scientific Library Voronezh State University
prospekt Revoljucii, 24, 394036 Voronezh
Tel: (473) 255-35-59 *Fax:* (473) 220-82-58
E-mail: office@lib.vsu.ru; elib@lib.vsu.ru
Web Site: lib.vsu.ru
Key Personnel
Dir: Arkady Yu Minakov *E-mail:* minakov@lib.vsu.ru
Deputy Dir: Galina Novikova *Tel:* (473) 253-11-76 *E-mail:* novikova@lib.vsu.ru
Founded: 1918

SPHL Russia, see Gosudarstvennaya publichnaya istoricheskaya biblioteka Rossii

SPSTL Russia, see Gosudarstvennaya publichnaya nauchno-tekhnicheskaya biblioteka Sibirskogo otdeleniya Rossiiskoi Akademii Nauk

State Archives of the Russian Federation
ul Bolshaya Pirogovskaya 17, 119435 Moscow
Tel: (495) 580-88-41; (495) 580-87-85
E-mail: garf@statearchive.ru

Web Site: statearchive.ru; www.rusarchives.
ru/federal/garf
Key Personnel
Dir: Larisa Alexandrovna *Tel:* (495) 580-88-42
Founded: 1992

Vserossijskaja gosudarstvennaja biblioteka inostrannoj literatury im M I Rudomino (M
I Rudomino All-Russia State Library for
Foreign Literature)
Nikoloyamskaya ul 1, 109189 Moscow
Tel: (495) 915 36 21 *Fax:* (495) 915 36 37
E-mail: vgbil@libfl.ru
Web Site: www.libfl.ru
Founded: 1922
General research & public library; an interna-
tional cultural center.
Membership(s): International Federation of Li-
brary Associations & Institutions (IFLA); Rus-
sian Library Association.

Rwanda

**Bibliotheque de l'Institut de Recherche
Scientifique et Technologique** (Institute of
Scientific & Technological Research Library)
PO Box 227, Butare
Tel: 530395 *Fax:* 530939

University of Rwanda Library Services
Main Library, PO Box 117, Huye
Tel: 250 530 920 *Fax:* 250 530 210
E-mail: universitylibrarian@ur.ac.rw; nurlibrary@
yahoo.fr
Web Site: www.library.ur.ac.rw; www.lib.nur.ac.rw
Key Personnel
University Librarian: Dr Robinah Kale-
meera Namuleme *Tel:* 789 314 164 (cell)
E-mail: namulemerobinah@gmail.com
Founded: 1964

URLS, see University of Rwanda Library
Services

Saudi Arabia

**Al-Imam Muhammad ibn Saud Islamic
University Library**
PO Box 87910, Riyadh 11652
Tel: (011) 258 1222
E-mail: imamulibraries@gmail.com; centrallib@
imamu.edu.sa; sultanlib@imamu.edu.sa
Web Site: units.imamu.edu.sa/deanships/
central_library
Key Personnel
Dean, Library Affairs: Dr Mohammed bin Saleh
Al Khulaifi *Tel:* (011) 258 1200
Founded: 1371

Institute of Public Administration Library
PO Box 205, Riyadh 11141
Tel: (011) 4768888 *Fax:* (011) 4792136
E-mail: info@ipa.edu.sa; library@ipa.edu.sa
Web Site: www.ipa.edu.sa
Key Personnel
Dir: Dr Fahd bin Mohammed Freeh
E-mail: furaihf@ipa.edu.sa
Publication(s): *Maktabat Al Idarah* (Library Ad-
ministration, quarterly)

Islamic University in Madinah Central Library
PO Box 170, Almadina Al Munawwara
Tel: (014) 8470803 *Fax:* (014) 8474471

E-mail: lib@iu.edu.sa
Web Site: www.iu.edu.sa
Key Personnel
Dean of Libraries: Dr Emad Zuhair Hafiz
E-mail: hafiz@iu.edu.sa
Founded: 1961

King Abdulaziz Public Library
PO Box 86486, Riyadh 11622
Tel: (011) 4911300 *Fax:* (011) 4911949
Web Site: www.kapl.org.sa
Key Personnel
Chairman of the Board: Abdulaziz bin Abdullah
bin Abdulazis Al Saud
Founded: 1985

King Abdulaziz University Central Library
PO Box 80213, Jeddah 21589
Fax: (012) 6400169
E-mail: library@kau.edu.sa
Web Site: library.kau.edu.sa
Key Personnel
Dean, Library Affairs: Dr Nabiel Abdul-
lah Taha Komosany *Tel:* (012) 6952559
E-mail: nkomosany@kau.edu.sa
Vice Dean, Library Affairs: Dr Ghassan Rashed
Alnwaimi *E-mail:* galnwaimi@kau.edu.sa
Dir, Financial & Administrative Affairs: Dr Fayez
Ayad Alahmadi *Tel:* (012) 6952481
A central library with 10 branches in various fac-
ulties.
Publication(s): *Annual Index of Umm Al-Qura*
(Arabic); *Catalogue of MSS in the Central Li-
brary* (Arabic); *Dissertations on Saudi Arabia*
(English)

King Fahad National Library
King Fahad Rd, PO Box 7572, Riyadh 11472
Tel: (011) 4186111 *Fax:* (011) 4186222
E-mail: portal@kfnl.gov.sa
Web Site: www.kfnl.gov.sa
Key Personnel
Chairman of the Board: Salman Bin Abdulaziz
Al-Saud
Secretary-General: Mohammed Bin Abdulaziz Al-
Rashed

King Faisal University Library
PO Box 400, Hofouf 31982
Tel: (03) 5895938 *Fax:* (03) 5899306
E-mail: library@kfu.edu.sa
Web Site: www.kfu.edu.sa/en/deans/library
Key Personnel
Dean, Library Affairs: Dr Salah Abdulaziz Al-
Shami *Tel:* (013) 5899333 *E-mail:* dean.
library@kfu.edu.sa
Dir, Administrative & Financial Affairs: Saud
Abdulaziz Al-Thanyan *Tel:* (013) 5895943
E-mail: sthanyan@kfu.edu.sa
Founded: 1975

King Saud University Library
PO Box 22480, Riyadh 11495
Tel: (011) 4676148 *Fax:* (011) 4676162
E-mail: library@ksu.edu.sa
Web Site: library.ksu.edu.sa
Key Personnel
Dean: Dr Abdullah bin Mohammed bin Abdullah
Al-Mneef
Vice Dean: Dr Abdulrahman Bin Nasser Al-Saeed
E-mail: aassaeed@ksu.edu.sa
Founded: 1979
Publication(s): *Directory of Libraries in Saudi
Arabia* (1979)

Umm al-Qura University Library
PO Box 715, Makkah 21421
Tel: (012) 5565621 *Fax:* (012) 5448979
E-mail: lib@uqu.edu.sa

Web Site: www.uqu.edu.sa/lib
Key Personnel
Dean of Library Affairs: Dr Adnan Mohammed
Faiz Al-Harthi

Senegal

Archives du Senegal (National Archives of
Senegal)
Immeuble Central Park Bldg, 2nd floor, Malick
Ave, Senghor, Dakar
Tel: 33 823 56 80
Web Site: www.archivesdusenegal.gouv.sn
Publication(s): *Bibliographie du Senegal* (annual
report); *Dictionnaire de sigles et acronymes en
usage au Senegal* (1990, monographic); *Guide
de Archives de l'AOF* (monographic); *Histoire
des institutions coloniales Francaise en Afrique
de l'ouest (1816-1960)* (1991, monographic)

EBAD/UCAD, see Ecole des Bibliothecaires,
Archivistes et Documentalistes

**Ecole des Bibliothecaires, Archivistes et
Documentalistes**
l'Universite Cheikh Anta Diop de Dakar, BP
3252, Dakar
Tel: 33 825 76 60 *Fax:* 33 824 05 42
E-mail: ebad@ebad.ucad.sn
Web Site: www.ebad.ucad.sn
Key Personnel
Dir: Mamadou Diarra
Head of Library: Khardiatou Kane
Founded: 1971

Institut Fondamental d'Afrique Noire (IFAN)
(African Institute of Basic Research)
BP 206, Dakar
Tel: 33 824 16 52 *Fax:* 33 824 49 18
E-mail: ifan@ucad.edu.sn
Web Site: ifan.ucad.sn
Key Personnel
Dir: Abdoulaye Toure *E-mail:* abdoulaye.toure@
ucad.edu.sn
Head, Documentation Service: Gora Dia
E-mail: gora.dia@ucad.edu.sn
Founded: 1936
Publication(s): *Bulletin IFAN* (2 times/yr)

IDEP Library, see Institut Africain de
Developpement Economique et de Planification
(IDEP), Bibliotheque

IFAN, see Institut Fondamental d'Afrique Noire
(IFAN)

**Institut Africain de Developpement
Economique et de Planification (IDEP),
Bibliotheque** (African Institute for Economic
Development & Planning Library)
Rue du 18 Juin, derriere l'Assemblee Nationale,
Dakar
Mailing Address: PO Box 3186, 18524 Dakar
Tel: 33 823 10 20 *Fax:* 33 822 29 64
E-mail: library@unidep.org; idep@unidep.org
Web Site: www.uneca.org/idep/pages/library
Key Personnel
Dir: Karima Bounemra Ben Soltane
E-mail: director@unidep.org
Head, Library & Documentation Services: An-
tonin Benoit Diouf
Founded: 1963
Publication(s): *Eleventh Annual Conference of
the African Econometrics Society (AES); Fixing
African Economies: Policy Research for De-
velopment; Workshop on Sector-Led Growth in
Africa & Implications for Development*

Universite Cheikh Anta Diop de Dakar, Reseau des Bibliotheques
BP 2006, Dakar
Tel: 33 824 69 81 *Fax:* 33 824 23 79
E-mail: bu@ucad.edu.sn
Web Site: www.bu.ucad.sn
Key Personnel
Dir: Arona Ndiaye *E-mail:* arona.ndiaye@ucad.
edu.sn
Founded: 1957
University library.
Publication(s): *Collective Catalogue of Memoires*;
Collective Catalogue of Periodicals; *Collective
National Catalogue of Periodical Publications*

Serbia

Biblioteka Matice Srpske (Matica Srpska
Library)
Matice Srpske 1, 21000 Novi Sad
Tel: (021) 528 747; (021) 420 199; (021) 420 198
Fax: (021) 528 574; (021) 420 271; (021) 525
859
E-mail: bms@eunet.rs
Web Site: www.bms.ns.ac.rs
Key Personnel
Dir: Selimir Radulovic *Tel:* (021) 528 910
E-mail: sradulovic@bms.ns.ac.rs
Founded: 1826

**Biblioteka Srpske Akademije Nauka i
Umetnosti** (Library of the Serbian Academy of
Sciences & Arts)
Knez Mihailova 35, 11000 Belgrade
Tel: (011) 2027-260; (011) 2027-175
Web Site: www.sanu.ac.rs/jedinice/biblioteka-sanu
Key Personnel
Dir: Miro Vuksanovic *Tel:* (011) 2637-514
E-mail: miro.vuksanovic@sanu.ac.rs
Founded: 1841

Narodna Biblioteka Srbije (National Library of
Serbia)
Skerliceva 1, 11000 Belgrade
Tel: (011) 2451 242 *Fax:* (011) 2451 289
E-mail: nbs@nb.rs
Web Site: www.nb.rs
Key Personnel
Manager: Laslo Blaskovic *Tel:* (011) 2434 091
E-mail: manager@nb.rs
Deputy Administrator & Head, Library & Infor-
mation Dept: Vladan Trijic *Tel:* (011) 2451 750
E-mail: vladan.trijic@nb.rs
Librarian: Stanislava Gardasevic
Founded: 1832

SANU Library, see Biblioteka Srpske Akademije
Nauka i Umetnosti

Arhiv Srbije (Archives of Serbia)
Karnegijeva 2, 11000 Belgrade
Tel: (011) 3370 781 *Fax:* (011) 3370 246
E-mail: office@archives.org.rs
Web Site: www.archives.org.rs
Key Personnel
Dir: Dr Miroslav Perisic *E-mail:* m.perisic@
archives.org.rs
Founded: 1900

**Univerzitet u Beogradu biblioteka 'Svetozar
Markovic'** (University Library "Svetozar
Markovic")
Bulevar kralja Aleksandra 71, 11000 Belgrade
Tel: (011) 3370-512; (011) 3370-513; (011) 3370-
506 *Fax:* (011) 3370-354
E-mail: pitajbibliotekera@unilib.bg.ac.rs;
marketing@unilib.rs

Web Site: www.unilib.rs
Key Personnel
Manager: Dr Aleksandar Jerkov *Tel:* (011) 3370-
515 *E-mail:* jerkov@unilib.bg.ac.rs
Deputy Manager: Adam Sofronijevic *Tel:* (011)
3370-511 *E-mail:* sofronijevic@unilib.bg.ac.rs

Sierra Leone

British Council Library
Tower Hill, 20 AJ Momoh St, Freetown
Mailing Address: PO Box 124, Freetown
Tel: (076) 290 111; (076) 290 115
E-mail: enquiry@sl.britishcouncil.org
Web Site: www.britishcouncil.sl
Founded: 1934

Fourah Bay College Library
University of Sierra Leone, University Secretariat
Bldg, A J Momoh St, Tower Hill, Freetown
Tel: (078) 920590 (cell)
Web Site: www.usl.edu.sl/fourah-bay-college-fbc
Key Personnel
Librarian: Oliver Harding
Founded: 1827

**Njala University Library (University of Sierra
Leone)**
Njala, Bo, Bonthe, Freetown
Tel: (022) 228 788 *Fax:* (022) 226 851
E-mail: info@njala.edu.sl
Web Site: njala.edu.sl/research/njala-campus-
library
Founded: 1964

Sierra Leone Library Board (SLLB)
Rokel St, Freetown
Mailing Address: PO Box 326, Freetown
Key Personnel
Chief Librarian: Sallieu Turay
Publication(s): *Sierra Leone Publications* (annu-
ally)

Sierra Leone National Archives
Fourah Bay College, University of Sierra Leone,
Mount Aureol, Freetown
Tel: (022) 229 471

SLLB, see Sierra Leone Library Board (SLLB)

University of Sierra Leone, see Njala University
Library (University of Sierra Leone)

Singapore

National Archives of Singapore
100 Victoria St, Level 11, Singapore 188064
Tel: 6332 7909
E-mail: nas@nlb.gov.sg
Web Site: www.nas.gov.sg
Key Personnel
Dir: Mr Pitt Kuan Wah
Founded: 1968
Membership(s): International Council on
Archives.

National University of Singapore Library
12 Kent Ridge Crescent, Singapore 119275
Tel: 6516 2028 *Fax:* 6777 3571
E-mail: askalib@nus.edu.sg
Web Site: libportal.nus.edu.sg

Key Personnel
University Librarian: Mrs Cheng Ean Lee
Tel: 6516 2069 *E-mail:* clbhead@nus.edu.sg
Publication(s): *Guide to NUS Libraries* (annu-
ally); *LINUS* (quarterly, newsletter); *NUS His-
tory Bibliography*
Branch Office(s)
Chinese Library, National University of Singa-
pore, Central Library Bldg, 6th floor, Singa-
pore 119275, Head: Amy Lin *Tel:* 6516 2872
E-mail: chlib@nus.edu.sg
Hon Sui Sen Memorial Library, One Hon Sui
Sen Dr, Singapore 117588, Head: Mr Fe-
lani Bin Md Yunos Herman *Tel:* 6516 3131
E-mail: hssmlib@nus.edu.sg
C J Koh Law Library, 469D Bukit Timah
Rd, Singapore 259773, Head: Ms Yan
Chuin Foo *Tel:* 6516 2043 *Fax:* 6468 3407
E-mail: cjkohlib@nus.edu.sg
Medical Library, Block MD6, Centre for Trans-
lational Medicine, 14 Medical Dr, No 05-01,
Singapore 117599, Head: Ms Ratnala Sukanya
Naidu *Tel:* 6516 2046 *E-mail:* mdlib@nus.edu.
sg
Music Library, Yong Siew Toh Conservatory, 3
Conservatory Dr, Singapore 117376, Head:
Lynette Lim *Tel:* 6516 8130 *E-mail:* musiclib@
nus.edu.sg
Science Library, Block S6, Level 4, 10 Sci-
ence Dr 2, Singapore 117548, Head: Jonathan
Pradubsook *Tel:* 6516 2454 *E-mail:* sclib@nus.
edu.sg

Slovakia

Centrum Vedecko-Technickych Informacii SR
(Slovak Centre of Scientific & Technical
Information (SCSTI))
Lamacska cesta 8/A, 811 04 Bratislava
Tel: (02) 69 253 102
E-mail: sekretariat@cvtisr.sk
Web Site: www.cvtisr.sk
Key Personnel
Dir: Prof Jan Turna, PhD *Tel:* (02) 69 253 101
E-mail: jan.turna@cvtisr.sk
Publication(s): *Bulletin Centra VTI SR* (Signale
informacie); *EURO-info*; *Infotrend*

SAV, see Ustredna kniznica Slovenskej akademie
vied

SCSTI, see Centrum Vedecko-Technickych
Informacii SR

Slovenska Narodna Kniznica, Martin (Slovak
National Library, Martin)
Division of The National Bibliography Institute
Nam J C Hronskeho 1, 036 01 Martin
Tel: (043) 2451 125; (043) 2451 140 (ISBN
Agency)
E-mail: snk@snk.sk
Web Site: www.snk.sk
Key Personnel
Dir General: Katarina Kristofova, PhD *Tel:* (043)
2451 131 *E-mail:* katarina.kristofova@snk.sk
Publication(s): *Hudobny archiv* (Music Archive);
Kniha (The Book); *Kniznica* (monthly, libraries
& scientific information); *Literarny archiv* (Lit-
erary Archive); *Slovenska narodna bibliografia*
(Slovak National Bibliography, monthly, print
& CD-ROM)

ULB, see Univerzitna Kniznica v Bratislave

Universzita Pavla Jozefa Safarika v Kosiciach
(Pavol Jozef Safarik University in Kosice)
Moyzesova 9, 040 01 Kosice

Tel: (055) 2341608
E-mail: kniznica@upjs.sk
Web Site: www.upjs.sk/pracoviska/univerzitna-
kniznica
Key Personnel
Dir: Dr Daniela Dzuganova *Tel:* (055) 2341606
E-mail: daniela.dzuganova@upjs.sk

Univerzitna Kniznica v Bratislave (University
Library in Bratislava)
Michalska 1, 814 17 Bratislava
Tel: (02) 59 804 100 *Fax:* (02) 54 434 246
E-mail: ukb@ulib.sk
Web Site: www.ulib.sk
Key Personnel
Dir General: Silvia Stasselova *Tel:* (02) 20 466
222 *E-mail:* silvia.stasselova@ulib.sk
Founded: 1919

Ustredna kniznica Slovenskej akademie vied
(Central Library of the Slovak Academy of
Sciences)
Klemensova 19, 814 67 Bratislava
Tel: (02) 5292 1733 *Fax:* (02) 5292 1733
Web Site: www.uk.sav.sk
Key Personnel
Dir: Andrea Doktorova *E-mail:* andrea.
doktorova@savba.sk
Publication(s): *Informacny Bulletin UK SAV* (bul-
letin)
Parent Company: Slovak Academy of Sciences

Slovenia

Arhiv Republike Slovenije (Archives of the
Republic of Slovenia)
Zvezdarska 1, SI-1102 Ljubljana
Tel: (01) 2414200 *Fax:* (01) 2414276
E-mail: ars@gov.si
Web Site: www.arhiv.gov.si
Key Personnel
Dir: Dr Bojan Cvelfar *Tel:* (01) 2414240
E-mail: bojan.cvelfar@gov.si
Deputy Dir: Dr Andrej Nared *E-mail:* andrej.
nared@gov.si
Founded: 1859
Publication(s): *Arhivi* (Archives); *Inventarji* (In-
ventories); *Katalogi* (Catalogs); *Viri* (Sources);
Vodniki (Guides)

Narodna in Univerzitetna Knjiznica, Ljubljana
(National & University Library)
Turjaska 1, SI-1000 Ljubljana
Tel: (01) 2001-209; (01) 2001-110 *Fax:* (01)
2513-052
E-mail: info@nuk.uni-lj.si
Web Site: www.nuk.uni-lj.si
Key Personnel
Dir: Martina Rozman Salobir *E-mail:* martina.
rozman-salobir@nuk.uni-lj.si
Deputy Dir, University Library System: Dr Melita
Ambrozic *Tel:* (01) 2001-185 *E-mail:* melita.
ambrozic@nuk.uni-lj.si
Publication(s): *Knjiznicarske novice* (Library
News, monthly, newsletter); *NUK Novice/NUK
Newsletter* (annually, newsletter)
Branch Office(s)
Leskoskova cesta 12, SI-1000 Ljubljana *Tel:* (01)
5861-300 *Fax:* (01) 5861-311

Somalia

Maktabadda Ummadda Soomaaliyeed (Somali
National Library)
Mogadishu
E-mail: somalinationallibrary@yahoo.com
Web Site: somalinationallibrary.so; www.
facebook.com/SomaliNationalLibrary
Key Personnel
Founder & President: Dr Badal Kariye
Founded: 1986

South Africa

Bloemfontein Public Library
CBD, Corner of Charles & West Burger Sts,
Bloemfontein 9300
Mailing Address: PO Box 1029, Bloemfontein
9300
Tel: (051) 405 8248
E-mail: bloemfonteinlibrary@mangaung.co.za

Central Library, Cape Town
Old Drill Hall, Corner of Parade & Darling Sts,
Cape Town 8001
Tel: (021) 444 0983; (021) 444 0209; (021) 444
0212
E-mail: central.library@capetown.gov.za
Web Site: www.facebook.com/
centrallibrarycapetown
Key Personnel
Contact: Ms L Ntaka

CJLIS, see City of Johannesburg Library &
Information Services (CJLIS)

**The Council for Scientific & Industrial
Research (CSIR)**, see CSIR Information
Services

CSIR Information Services
Meiring Naude Rd, Brummeria, Pretoria
Mailing Address: PO Box 395, Pretoria 0001
Tel: (012) 841 2911
E-mail: enquiries@csir.co.za
Web Site: www.csir.co.za
Founded: 1945
Scientific, technological & business information,
decision support value-added services, elec-
tronic real-time access to local & international
databases.

Department of Science & Technology
DST Bldg No 53, CSIR South Gate Entrance,
Meiring Naude Rd, Brummeria 0001
Mailing Address: Private Bag X894, Pretoria
0001
Tel: (012) 843 6300
E-mail: webmaster@dst.gov.za
Web Site: www.dst.gov.za
Key Personnel
Dir General: Dr Phil Mjwara *E-mail:* phil.
mjwara@dst.gov.za
Publication(s): *Annual Report*; *Library News*

Education Library & Information Service, see
EDULIS (Education Library & Information
Service)

**EDULIS (Education Library & Information
Service)**
Private Bag X9099, Cape Town 8000
Tel: (021) 957 9600; (021) 957 9618 *Fax:* (086)
489 2500
E-mail: edulis.edulis@westerncape.gov.za

Web Site: edulis.pgwc.gov.za
Key Personnel
Head: Aubrey Africa *Tel:* (021) 957 9628
E-mail: aubrey.africa@westerncape.gov.za
Founded: 1859
Parent Company: Western Cape Education De-
partment

eThekwini Municipal Libraries
Ethekwini Library Bldg, EML 99 Umgeni Rd,
Durban
Mailing Address: PO Box 917, Durban 4000
Tel: (031) 311 2401 *Fax:* (031) 311 2403
Web Site: www.durban.gov.za
Key Personnel
Contact: Logan Perumal *E-mail:* logan.perumal@
durban.gov.za

Free State Provincial Archives Repository
29 Badenhorst St, Bloemfontein
Mailing Address: Private Bag X20504, Bloem-
fontein 9300
Tel: (051) 522 6762 *Fax:* (051) 522 6765
E-mail: fsarch@sac.fs.gov.za
Web Site: www.national.archives.gov.za

**Free State Provincial Library & Archive
Services**
Private Bag X20606, Bloemfontein 9300
Tel: (051) 407 2800
Web Site: www.sacr.fs.gov.za
Key Personnel
Dir, Library & Archive Services: Jacomien
Schimper *E-mail:* jacomien@sacr.fs.gov.za
Founded: 1948
Publication(s): *Free State Libraries* (quarterly,
journal)
Parent Company: Department of Sports, Arts,
Culture & Recreation
Ultimate Parent Company: Free State Provincial
Government

Harold Holmes Library, see University of
Witswatersrand, Education Library

**City of Johannesburg Library & Information
Services (CJLIS)**
22 Solomon St, Braamfontein 2017
Tel: (011) 226 0953 *Fax:* (011) 222 0973
Web Site: www.joburg.org.za
Key Personnel
Deputy Dir: Atilla Lourens
Founded: 1890
Publication(s): *Local Government Library Bulletin*
(irregularly)

Kempton Park Library
Kempton Park Civic Center, Corner of C R Swart
& Pretoria Rd, Kempton Park, Gauteng 1620
Tel: (011) 921 2173 *Fax:* (011) 975 0921

**KwaZulu-Natal Archives: Pietermaritzburg
Archives Repository**
231 Pietermaritz St, Pietermaritzburg 3200
Mailing Address: Private Bag X9012, Pietermar-
itzburg 3200
Tel: (033) 342 4712 *Fax:* (033) 394 4353
E-mail: pmbarchives@kzndac.gov.za
Founded: 2001

KwaZulu-Natal Law Society Library
200 Hoosen Haffejee St, 1st floor, Pietermar-
itzburg 3201
Tel: (033) 345 1304 *Fax:* (086) 500 8555
E-mail: help@lawlibrary.co.za; librarians@
lawlibrary.co.za
Web Site: www.lawlibrary.co.za
Key Personnel
Librarian: Sindiswa Ndaba; Thembinkosi Ngcobo
Founded: 1851

South African journals, legal books & pamphlets, South African trade & commercial directories. Information produced by & about the South African government.
Publication(s): Aids Bibliography (5 vols); *Natalia* (historical journal)
Branch Office(s)
1100 Salmon Grove Chambers, 407 Anton Lembede St, Durban, Librarian: Rekha Woodhaymal *Tel:* (031) 1301 1621 *Fax:* (086) 500 6929

KwaZulu-Natal Provincial Library & Information Service
230 Prince Alfred St, Pietermaritzburg 3201
Tel: (033) 341 3000 *Fax:* (033) 341 3085
Web Site: www.kzndac.gov.za
Key Personnel
Contact: Nonhlanhla Ngesi *E-mail:* ngesinon@plho.kzntl.gov.za
Publication(s): KZN Librarian (Journal of Kwa-Zulu Natal Provincial Library Service)

Library of Parliament
Library & Information Unit, PO Box 18, Cape Town 8000
Tel: (021) 403 2140; (021) 403 2141; (021) 403 2142; (021) 403 2143; (021) 403 2144
E-mail: info@parliament.gov.za; library@parliament.gov.za
Web Site: www.parliament.gov.za/parliamentary-library
Founded: 1854

National Archives Repository Library
24 Hamilton St, Arcadia, Pretoria 0001
Mailing Address: Private Bag X236, Pretoria 0001
Tel: (012) 441 3200 *Fax:* (012) 323 5287
E-mail: archives@dac.gov.za; enquiries@dac.gov.za
Web Site: www.national.archives.gov.za
Founded: 1909
Parent Company: National Archives & Record Services

National Library of South Africa
228 Proes St, Pretoria 0001
Mailing Address: Private Bag X990, Pretoria 0001
Tel: (012) 401 9700 *Fax:* (012) 325 5702
E-mail: infodesk@nlsa.ac.za
Web Site: www.nlsa.ac.za
Key Personnel
National Librarian & Chief Executive Officer: Prof Rocky Ralebipi-Simela *Tel:* (012) 401 9717 *E-mail:* dimakatso.methula@nlsa.ac.za
Founded: 1887
Publication(s): Directory of South African Publishers; Index to South African Periodicals (ISAP); Micrographic Series Indexes; Periodicals in Southern African Libraries (PISAL); Public & Community Libraries Inventory of South Africa; SANB (South African National Bibliography)
Branch Office(s)
5 Queen Victoria St, PO Box 496, Cape Town 8000 *Tel:* (021) 424 6320 *Fax:* (021) 423 3359 *E-mail:* info@nlsa.ac.za

Nelson Mandela University Library & Information Services
Second Ave Campus, Second Ave, Summerstrand, Port Elizabeth 6001
Mailing Address: Private Bag X6058, Port Elizabeth 6000
Tel: (041) 504 3851; (041) 504 2281 *Fax:* (041) 504 3701
Web Site: library.mandela.ac.za
Key Personnel
Deputy Vice Chancellor, Research & Engagement: Prof Andrew Leitch

Founded: 2005
Publication(s): UPE Publication Series

E M Ngubane Library, see KwaZulu-Natal Law Society Library

NMMU, see Nelson Mandela University Library & Information Services

Pietermaritzburg Archives Repository, see KwaZulu-Natal Archives: Pietermaritzburg Archives Repository

Rhodes University Library
PO Box 184, Grahamstown 6140
Tel: (046) 603 8436 *Fax:* (046) 603 7310
E-mail: library@ru.ac.za
Web Site: www.ru.ac.za/library
Key Personnel
Dir, Library Services: Ms Ujala Satgoor
Tel: (046) 603 8079 *E-mail:* u.satgoor@ru.ac.za
Head Librarian, Technical Services: Wynand van der Walt *Tel:* (046) 603 8281 *E-mail:* w.vanderwalt@ru.ac.za
Head Librarian, User Services & Research Commons: Larshan Naicker *Tel:* (046) 603 8690 *E-mail:* l.naicker@ru.ac.za

Royal Society of South Africa
University of Cape Town, 6.76 P D Hahn Bldg, Rhodes Gift 7700
Tel: (021) 650 2543
E-mail: royalsociety@uct.ac.za
Web Site: www.royalsocietysa.org.za
Key Personnel
President: Prof Jan-Hendrick S Hofmeyr
Founded: 1908
Publication(s): Transactions of the Royal Society of South Africa (irregularly, journal)

SALB, see South African Library for the Blind

South African Library for the Blind
112B High St, Grahamstown, Eastern Cape 6139
Mailing Address: PO Box 115, Grahamstown, Eastern Cape 6140
Tel: (046) 6227226 *Fax:* (046) 6224645
E-mail: braillelib@salb.org.za
Web Site: www.salb.org.za
Key Personnel
Dir: Francois Hendrikz *E-mail:* director@salb.org.za
Founded: 1919

Stellenbosch University Library & Information Service
JS Gericke Library, JS Marais Sq, Corner of Victoria & Ryneveld Sts, Stellenbosch 7599
Mailing Address: Private Bag X5036, Stellenbosch 7599
Tel: (021) 808 2486; (021) 808 3315
Web Site: library.sun.ac.za
Key Personnel
Senior Dir: Ellen Tise *Tel:* (021) 808 4880 *E-mail:* etise@sun.ac.za
Central library of the US Library Service.
Publication(s): Annual Reports; Bibnuus (3 times/yr, newsletter); *Strategy/Policy Documents; Subnuns (Newsletter for Library Staff)*

TCLIS, see Tshwane Community Library & Information Service (TCLIS)

Tshwane Community Library & Information Service (TCLIS)
Sammy Marks Sq, Corner Church & Prinsloo St, Pretoria 0002
Mailing Address: PO Box 2673, Pretoria 0001

Tel: (012) 358 8954; (012) 358 8956 *Fax:* (012) 358 8955
Key Personnel
Library Manager: Johannes Magoro *Tel:* (012) 358 8841
Founded: 1964

UCT Libraries, see University of Cape Town Libraries

UNISA, see University of South Africa Library (UNISA)

University of Cape Town Libraries
Private Bag X3, Rondebosch 7701
Tel: (021) 650-3703; (021) 650-3704 *Fax:* (021) 650-2965
E-mail: libraries@uct.ac.za
Web Site: www.lib.uct.ac.za
Key Personnel
Executive Dir: Gwenda Thomas *Tel:* (021) 650 3096 *E-mail:* gwenda.thomas@uct.ac.za
Publication(s): Bibliographical series (irregularly); *Jagger Journal* (annually); *The South West Africa People's Organisation 1961-1991: a guide to archival resources & special collections in Western Cape, South Africa; UCT Libraries Update* (newsletter); *Varia series* (irregularly)

University of Pretoria Department of Library Services
Dept of Library Services, PO Box 12411, Hatfield, Pretoria, Gauteng 0028
Tel: (012) 420 2235; (012) 420 2236
Web Site: www.ais.up.ac.za
Key Personnel
Dir: Robert Moropa *Tel:* (012) 420 2241 *E-mail:* robert.moropa@up.ac.za

University of South Africa Library (UNISA)
Preller St, Muckleneuk Ridge, Pretoria 0001
Mailing Address: PO Box 392, UNISA Pretoria 0003
Tel: (012) 429 3133; (012) 429 3206 *Fax:* (012) 429 8128
E-mail: library-enquiries@unisa.ac.za
Web Site: www.unisa.ac.za/library
Key Personnel
Deputy Executive Dir: Dr Judy Henning *E-mail:* hennijc@unisa.ac.za
Publication(s): Mousaion (in collaboration with the University of South Africa's Dept of Information Science)
Branch Office(s)
Sunnyside Library, Sunnyside Campus, Walker St, Bldg 15, Pretoria 0002 *Tel:* (012) 441 5781; (012) 441 5782; (012) 441 5763
Ekurhuleni Library, Corner R51 Rd & Brazil St, Daveyton, Benoni *Tel:* (011) 845 9338; (011) 845 9339
Durban Library, 230 Stawart Simelane St, Durban 4001 *Tel:* (031) 335 1722 *Fax:* (031) 337 2457
East London Library, 10 St Lukes Rd, Southernwood, East London 5201 *Tel:* (043) 709 0431; (043) 709 0432
Florida Library, GJ Gerwel Bldg, Corner of Christiaan de Wet & Pioneer Ave, Private Bag X90, Florida 1710 *Tel:* (011) 471 3068; (011) 471 2933; (011) 471 2837
Johannesburg Library, 29 Rissik St, Johannesburg 2000 *Tel:* (011) 630 4531; (011) 630 4532; (011) 630 4533
Graduate School of Business Leadership Library, Corner Janadel & Alexandra Ave, Midrand 1686 *Tel:* (011) 652 0341; (011) 652 0342
Nelspruit Library, Standard Bank Bldg, 1st floor, 31 Brown St, Nelspruit 1201 *Tel:* (013) 755 2476 *E-mail:* nelslib@unisa.ac.za
Cape Town Library, 15 Jean Simonis St, Parrow 7500 *Tel:* (021) 936 4125; (021) 936 4126 *Fax:* (021) 936 4127 *E-mail:* ctnlib@unisa.ac.za

Pietermaritzburg Library, One Langalibalele
St, Pietermaritzburg *Tel:* (033) 355 1714
E-mail: makhans@unisa.ac.za
Polokwane Library, Provincial Center - Limpopo
Province, PO Box 2805, Polokwane 0700
Tel: (015) 290 3431; (015) 290 3433; (015)
290 3436
Rustenburg Library, Corner OR Tambo & Steen
St, Rustenburg 0300 *Tel:* (011) 670 9524; (011)
670 9525
Akaki Campus Library, Ground Level, Block 2,
Addis Ababa, Ethiopia *Tel:* (011) 435 1244

University of the Western Cape Library
Robert Sobukwe Rd, Bellville 7535
Mailing Address: Private Bag X17, Bellville 7535
Tel: (021) 959 2209 *Fax:* (021) 959 2659
E-mail: library@uwc.ac.za
Web Site: lib.uwc.ac.za
Key Personnel
Dir, University Library Services: Dr S Neerputh
Deputy Dir: Ms A Fullard *E-mail:* afullard@uwc.
ac.za
Founded: 1989

University of the Witwaterstrand Libraries
One Jan Smuts Ave, Braamfontein, Johannesburg
2000
Tel: (011) 717 1902
Web Site: www.wits.ac.za/library
Key Personnel
University Librarian: Paiki Muswazi *Tel:* (011)
717 1904 *E-mail:* paiki.muswazi@wits.ac.za
Founded: 1934
Publication(s): *Quo Vadis: Library Update*
(newsletter)

**University of Witswatersrand, Education
Library**
Education Campus, 27 St Andrews Rd, Parktown,
Johannesburg 2193
Tel: (011) 717-3242
Web Site: www.wits.ac.za/library
Key Personnel
Senior Librarian: Mark Sandham *Tel:* (011) 717-
3239 *E-mail:* mark.sandham@wits.ac.za
Librarian: Alison Chisholm *Tel:* (011) 717-3240
E-mail: alison.chisholm@wits.ac.za

Western Cape Government Library Service
c/o Chiappinni & Hospital St, Cape Town 8001
Mailing Address: PO Box 2108, Cape Town 8000
Tel: (021) 483 2273 *Fax:* (021) 419 7541
E-mail: capelib@westerncape.gov.za
Web Site: www.westerncape.gov.za/library
Key Personnel
Library Services: Cecilia Sani *Tel:* (021) 483
2273 *E-mail:* cecilia.sani@westerncape.gov.za
Publication(s): *Annual Reports*; *Cape Librarian* (6
times/yr, magazine)

South Korea

Dongguk University Library
30, Pil-dong 1-gil, Jung-gu, Seoul 100-715
Web Site: lib.dongguk.edu
Key Personnel
Dir: Sung Hyun Shin *Tel:* (02) 2260-3445
E-mail: neostellar@dongguk.edu

Ewha Womans University Library
52 Ewhayeodae-gil, Seodaemun-gu, Seoul 120-
750
Tel: (02) 3277-3396; (02) 3277-4612
E-mail: englib@ewha.ac.kr; infoserv@ewha.ac.kr;
circula2@ewha.ac.kr

Web Site: lib.ewha.ac.kr
Founded: 1923

KDI Library, see Korea Development Institute
Library

KLIN, see Korea University Library

Korea Development Institute Library
Sejong-si Namsejong 263, Central Bldg 3-5 F,
Cheongnyang, Seoul 130-868
Tel: (02) 550 4264
Web Site: lib.kdi.re.kr; www.kdi.re.kr
Key Personnel
Dir: Sungjin Choi *Tel:* (02) 550 1290
E-mail: sjchoi@kdi.re.kr
Founded: 1971
Economics research institution.

Korea University Library
Anam-dong, Seongbuk-ku, Seoul 136-701
Tel: (02) 3290-1492
E-mail: libweb@korea.ac.kr
Web Site: library.korea.ac.kr
Key Personnel
Chief Librarian: Young Min Kim *Tel:* (02) 3290-
1001 *E-mail:* mink@korea.ac.kr
Founded: 1946

**Kyungpook National University Central
Library**
1370 Sangyeok-dong, Buk-gu, Daegu 702-701
Tel: (053) 950-6528 *Fax:* (053) 950-6533
E-mail: mspark@kyungpook.ac.kr
Web Site: kudos.knu.ac.kr
Founded: 1953

National Assembly Library
One Yoido-dong, Yeongdeungpo-gu, Seoul 07233
Tel: (02) 788-4125; (02) 788-4243 (English ser-
vice available); (02) 784-4211 *Fax:* (02) 788-
4291
E-mail: intlcoop@nanet.go.kr; webw3@nanet.go.
kr
Web Site: www.nanet.go.kr
Key Personnel
Chief Librarian: Lee Eun Chul, PhD
Founded: 1952
Publication(s): *Acquisition List (in Korean)*
(6 times/yr & annually); *Index to Korean-
Language Periodicals (in Korean)* (6 times/yr
& annually); *Index to Korean Laws and
Statutes (in Korean)* (biennially); *Index to Na-
tional Assembly Debates (in Korean)* (irregu-
larly); *Index to Recent Periodical Articles of
Major Interests (in Korean)* (monthly); *Issue
Briefs (in Korean)* (irregularly); *Legislative In-
formation Analysis (in Korean)* (quarterly); *List
of Theses for Doctors' and Masters' Degrees
Awarded in Korea (in Korean)* (annually)

The National Library of Korea
664 Banpo-Ro, Seocho-gu, Seoul 137-702
Tel: (02) 535-4142; (02) 590-0513-4 *Fax:* (02)
590-0530
E-mail: nlkpc@mail.nl.go.kr
Web Site: www.nl.go.kr
Key Personnel
Chief Executive: Lim Wonsun
Founded: 1945
Publication(s): *Bibliographie Index of Korea*; *Ko-
rean National Bibliography*
Branch Office(s)
635 Yeoksam-dong, Kangnam-gu, Seoul

Seoul National University Library
One, Bldg No 62, Gwanak-gu, Seoul 151-749
Tel: (02) 880-8001; (02) 880-5325
E-mail: libhelp@snu.ac.kr
Web Site: library.snu.ac.kr

Key Personnel
Dir General: Sung Gul Hong *Tel:* (02) 880-5280
E-mail: sglhong@snu.ac.kr
Dir, Library Services: Seung Cheol Shin *Tel:* (02)
880-8074 *E-mail:* scshin@snu.ac.kr

Yonsei University Library
50 Yonsei-ro, Seodaemun-gu, Seoul 03722
Tel: (02) 2123-6347
Web Site: library.yonsei.ac.kr
Founded: 1915

Spain

AECID Library, see Biblioteca de la Agencia
Espanola de Cooperacion Internacional

Archivo de la Corona de Aragon (Royal
Archives of Aragon)
C/ Comtes 2, (Palace of the Viceroys or Llocti-
nent), 08002 Barcelona
Mailing Address: C/ Almogaveres, 77, 08018
Barcelona
Tel: 93 485 42 85 *Fax:* 93 300 12 52
E-mail: aca@mecd.es
Web Site: www.mecd.gob.es/archivos-aca/portada.
html
Key Personnel
Dir: Carlos Lopez Rodriguez

Archivo General de Indias (Archives of the
Indies)
Edificio de la Lonja, Avda de la Constitucion, 3,
41071 Seville
Mailing Address: Edificio de la Cilla, C/ Santo
Tomas, 5, 41071 Seville
Tel: 95 450 05 28 *Fax:* 95 421 94 85
Web Site: www.mecd.gob.es/cultura/areas/
archivos/mc/archivos/agi/portada.html
Key Personnel
Dir: Manuel Ravina Martin
Founded: 1785

Archivo Historico Nacional (National Historical
Archives)
C/ Serrano, 115, 28006 Madrid
Tel: 91 768 85 00 *Fax:* 91 563 11 99
E-mail: ahn@mecd.es
Web Site: www.mecd.gob.es/cultura/areas/
archivos/mc/archivos/ahn/portada.html
Key Personnel
Dir: Carmen Sierra Barcena *E-mail:* carmen.
sierra@mecd.es
Deputy Dir: Jose Luis La Torre Merino
E-mail: jluis.latorre@mecd.es
Founded: 1866
Indexed genealogical records, 15th-19th century.
Parent Company: Ministerio de Educacion, Cul-
tura y Deporte

Archivo y Biblioteca Capitulares (Archives &
Library of the Cathedral Chapter)
Catedral de Toledo, C/ Hombre de Palo, 2, 45001
Toledo
Mailing Address: Apdo 295, 45001 Toledo
Tel: 925 212 423 *Fax:* 925 212 423
E-mail: archivocapitular@catedralprimada.
es; archivocatedral@catedralprimada.es;
bibliotecacapitular@catedralprimada.es;
archivocapitulardetoledo@catedralprimada.es
Web Site: www.catedralprimada.es/es/info/archivo/
la-biblioteca-capitular
Key Personnel
Dir: Dr Angel Fernandez Collado

Biblioteca de Catalunya (National Library of
Catalonia)
Carrer de l'Hospital, 56, 08001 Barcelona

Tel: 93 270 23 00 Fax: 93 270 23 04
E-mail: bustia@bnc.cat
Web Site: www.bnc.cat
Key Personnel
Dir: Eugenia Serra Aranda Tel: 93 270 2300 ext
84013122 E-mail: eserra@bnc.cat

**Biblioteca de la Agencia Espanola de
Cooperacion Internacional** (Library of the
Spanish Agency for International Cooperation)
Ciudad Universitaria, Ave Reyes Catolicos, 4,
28040 Madrid
Tel: 915 838 175; 915 838 164
E-mail: biblioteca.hispanica@aecid.es
Web Site: www.aecid.es
Founded: 1949

Biblioteca de la Universidad Complutense
Ciudad Universitaria, Edificio Multiusos 1, Profe-
sor Aranguren s/n, 28040 Madrid
Tel: 913947985 Fax: 913947849
E-mail: bucweb@buc.ucm.es
Web Site: biblioteca.ucm.es
Key Personnel
Dir: Antonio Calderon Rehecho Tel: 913947852
E-mail: dirbuc@ucm.es

Biblioteca de la Universidad de Cantabria
Ave de Los Castros, s/n, 39005 Santander
Tel: 942 201 180 Fax: 942 201 183
E-mail: admonec@gestion.unican.es
Web Site: web.unican.es/buc/biblioteca
Key Personnel
Dir: Maria Jesus Saiz Vega E-mail: mariajesus.
saiz@unican.es
Head, Administration: Elena Barriuso Palenzuela
E-mail: elena.barriuso@unican.es

Biblioteca Nacional de Espana
Pº de Recoletos 20-22, 28071 Madrid
Tel: 91 580 78 00; 91 580 78 53; 91 580 78 05
Fax: 91 577 56 34
E-mail: bib@bne.es
Web Site: www.bne.es
Key Personnel
Dir: Ana Santos Aramburo
Founded: 1711
National depository library.
Parent Company: Ministerio de Cultura

**Biblioteca Publica Municipal de Santo
Domingo de la Calzada**
Casa de Trastamara, Calle Mayor, nº 70, 26250
Santo Domingo de la Calzada
Tel: 941 341 276
E-mail: biblioteca@santodomingodelacalzada.org
Web Site: www.bibliotecaspublicas.es/
santodomingodelacalzada/index.jsp

Biblioteca Tomas Navarro Tomas
Calle Albasanz 26-28, 28037 Madrid
Tel: 91 602 23 00 Fax: 91 602 29 71
Web Site: biblioteca.cchs.csic.es
Key Personnel
Dir: Pilar Martinez Olmo Tel: 91 602 26 49
E-mail: pilar.martinez@cchs.csic.es
Deputy Dir: Carmela Perez Montes Tel: 91 602
26 83 E-mail: carmen.perezmontes@cchs.csic.
es
Library of the Council for Scientific Research.
Publication(s): Bulletin
Parent Company: Consejo Superior de Investiga-
ciones Cientificas

Biblioteca y Casa - Museo de Menendez Pelayo
C/ Rubio 6, 39001 Santander
Tel: 942 234 534 Fax: 942 373 766
E-mail: biblioteca-mp@ayto-santander.es
Web Site: www.bibliotecademenendezpelayo.org

Publication(s): La Biblioteca de Menendez
Pelayo; Boletin de la Biblioteca de Menendez Pelayo (annually); Estudios de literatura y
pensamiento hispanicos (series)

The British Council Library
Pº General Martinez Campos 31, 28010 Madrid
Tel: 91 337 35 77 Fax: 91 337 35 86
Web Site: www.britishcouncil.es

CSIC, see Biblioteca Tomas Navarro Tomas

ESADE Library
Marques de Mulhacen, 42, Bldg 2, 1st floor,
08034 Barcelona
Tel: 93 280 61 62 (ext 4018)
E-mail: biblioteca@esade.edu
Web Site: www.esade.edu/library
Branch Office(s)
Av Torreblanca, 59, 08172 Barcelona Tel: 93 280
61 62 ext 5550 E-mail: bibliotecaborja@esade.
edu

Hemeroteca Municipal de Madrid (Madrid
Municipal Newspaper Library)
Calle Conde Duque, 9, 28015 Madrid
Tel: 91 513 31 64; 91 588 57 72; 91 588 57 73
E-mail: infohemeroteca@madrid.es
Web Site: bibliotecas.madrid.es
Key Personnel
Dir: Inmaculada Zaragoza Garcia Tel: 91 588 57
74 E-mail: zaragozagi@madrid.es
Founded: 1916

**Hospital Universitario Cruces Biblioteca de
Ciencias de la Salud** (University Hospital
Cruces Library of Health Sciences)
Plaza de Cruces 12, 48903 Barakaldo, Bizkaia
Tel: 94 6006125 Fax: 94 6006049
E-mail: biblioteca.cruces@osakidetza.net
Web Site: www.hospitalcruces.com/
universitariobiblioteca.asp?lng=es
Key Personnel
Head, Library Services: Susana Gonzalez-
Larragan E-mail: susana.gonzalezlarragan@
osakidetza.net
Service in information & scientific documentation
in health sciences.
Publication(s): Catalogo de Publicaciones y Se-
ries Periodicas de Ciencias de la Salud

Patrimonio Nacional, Real Biblioteca
Palacio Real, C Bailen, sn, 28071 Madrid
Tel: 91 454 87 00; 91 454 87 32; 91 454 87 33
Fax: 91 454 88 67
E-mail: realbiblioteca@patrimonionacional.es;
info@patrimonionacional.es
Web Site: www.patrimonionacional.es; www.
realbiblioteca.es
Key Personnel
Dir: Maria Luisa Lopez-Vidriero E-mail: luisa.
vidriero@patrimonionacional.es
Library of the Royal Palace.

Servei de Biblioteques de la UAB
Edifici N Placa Civica, 08193 Bellaterra, Cer-
danyola del Valles
Tel: 93 581 10 15
E-mail: s.biblioteques@uab.cat; bib.utp@uab.cat
Web Site: www.uab.cat/biblioteques
Key Personnel
Dir: Joan Gomez Escofet
Publication(s): Actuacions (annually); Biblioteca
Informacions (irregularly, blog); Guies de les
Biblioteques; Memoria (annually); Pla estrate-
gic

**Universidad Autonoma - Biblioteca
Universitaria**
Calle Einstein 3, Edificio del Rectorado, en-
treplanta 3, Campus de Cantoblanco, 28049
Madrid
Tel: 91 497 4653 Fax: 91 497 5058
E-mail: servicio.biblioteca@uam.es
Web Site: biblioteca.uam.es
Key Personnel
Library Dir: D Santiago Fernandez Conti Tel: 91
497 4399 E-mail: santiago.conti@uam.es

Universidad Pontificia de Salamanca Biblioteca
(Pontifical University of Salamanca Library)
C/ Compania, 5, 37002 Salamanca
Tel: 923 277 118
E-mail: biblioteca@upsa.es
Web Site: biblioteca.upsa.es
Key Personnel
Dir: Maribel Manzano Garcia Tel: 923 277 118
ext 7401 E-mail: mmanzanoga@upsa.es
Deputy Dir: Elena Square Tel: 923 277 118 ext
7405 E-mail: ecuadradode@upsa.es
Founded: 1940
Higher education.

Universitat Autonoma de Barcelona, see Servei
de Biblioteques de la UAB

**Universitat de Barcelona CRAI Biblioteca de
Belles Arts**
Baldiri i Reixac 2, 08028 Barcelona
Tel: 934 034 595
E-mail: craibellesarts@ub.edu
Web Site: crai.ub.edu/ca/coneix-el-crai/
biblioteques/biblioteca-belles-arts
Key Personnel
Contact: Monica Arenas Ortigosa
E-mail: marenas@ub.edu

Sri Lanka

British Council Information Resource Centre
49 Alfred House Gardens, Colombo 3
Tel: (011) 4521521; (011) 7521521
E-mail: info.lk@britishcouncil.org
Web Site: www.britishcouncil.lk
Key Personnel
Dir: Gill Caldicott
Deputy Dir: Anna Searle
Founded: 1949
Branch Office(s)
88/1 El Senanayake Veediya, 1st floor, Kandy
Fax: (011) 7521 521

Colombo Public Library
15 Sir Marcus Fernando Mawatha, Colombo 7
Tel: (011) 4691968
Web Site: www.colombopubliclibrary.org
Founded: 1925

Department of National Archives
No 7, Philip Gunawardena Mawatha, Colombo 7
Mailing Address: PO Box 1414, Colombo 7
Tel: (011) 2694523; (011) 2696917 Fax: (011)
2694419; (011) 2693309
E-mail: slnationalarchives@gmail.com
Web Site: www.archives.gov.lk
Key Personnel
Dir: Dr Saroja Wettasinghe Tel: (011) 2671042
Branch Office(s)
Hemamali Mawatha, Kandy Tel: (081) 2223729
Fax: (081) 2223729

**Industrial Technology Institute Information
Services Centre**
363, Bauddhaloka Mawatha, Colombo 07

Tel: (011) 2379869 *Fax:* (011) 2686567
E-mail: info@iti.lk
Web Site: iti.lk
Key Personnel
Dir General, Administration & Operation: Mr
KASP Kaluarachchi *Tel:* (011) 2797316
E-mail: ad_ao@iti.lk
Dir General, Research & Development: Dr
JKRR Samarasekera *Tel:* (011) 2797313
E-mail: ad_rd@iti.lk
Dir General, Technical Services: Mr AS Pannila
Tel: (011) 2379900 *E-mail:* ad_ts@iti.lk
Institute Secretary: Ms Renuka Jayatilleka
Tel: (011) 2397316 *E-mail:* is@iti.lk
Founded: 1955
Publication(s): *ITI Bulletin* (quarterly); *Man-
agement Thought* (quarterly); *SciTech in Brief*
(quarterly)

**National Library & Documentation Services
Board**
No 14, Independence Ave, Colombo 07
Tel: (011) 2698847; (011) 2685197 *Fax:* (011)
2685201
E-mail: info@mail.natlib.lk
Web Site: www.natlib.lk
Key Personnel
Chairman: Dr W A Abeysinghe *Tel:* (011)
2685198 *E-mail:* ch@mail.natlib.lk
Dir General: Mr W Sunil *Tel:* (011) 2687581
E-mail: dg@mail.natlib.lk
Dir, Finance & Administration: Mr K Waduge
Tel: (011) 3056211 *E-mail:* dirfinadm@mail.
natlib.lk
Dir, National Library & Documentation Cen-
ter: Mr G D Amarasiri *Tel:* (011) 2685203
E-mail: dirnatlib@mail.natlib.lk
Dir, Library Development, Standardization &
Publications: Ms Senani Bandara *Tel:* (011)
2687584 *E-mail:* dirlibserv@mail.natlib.lk
Deputy Dir, Administration: Ms D R Jayasinghe
Tel: (011) 2688926 *E-mail:* ddiradm@mail.
natlib.lk
Deputy Dir, National Library & Documentation
Center: Ms C Wadasinghe *Tel:* (011) 2685195
E-mail: ddirnatlib@mail.natlib.lk
Founded: 1990
Publication(s): *Directory of Libraries in Sri
Lanka*; *Directory of Sri Lanka Government
Publications*; *NATNEK LANKA* (2 times/yr,
newsletter); *Praleka* (quarterly, magazine); *Sri
Lanka Conference Index* (online database);
Sri Lanka National Bibliography (monthly);
Sri Lanka Newspaper Article Index (online
database); *Sri Lanka Periodical Index* (quar-
terly)

National Museum of Colombo Library
Sir Marcus Fernando Mawatha, Colombo 07
Mailing Address: PO Box 854, Colombo 07
Tel: (011) 2695366 *Fax:* (011) 2692092
E-mail: nmdep@slt.lk
Web Site: www.museum.gov.lk
Key Personnel
Dir: Marcus Fernando Mawatha
Founded: 1877
See also Department of National Museums (Pub-
lisher).
Publication(s): *Ceylon Periodiocals Directory*;
*Spolia Zeylanica: Bulletin of the National Mu-
seums of Sri Lanka*; *Sri Lanka Periodicals In-
dex*

NLDSB, see National Library & Documentation
Services Board

University of Peradeniya Library
PO Box 35, Peradeniya 20400
Tel: (081) 2392471; (081) 2388678 *Fax:* (081)
2388678
E-mail: librarian@pdn.ac.lk
Web Site: www.pdn.ac.lk

Key Personnel
Librarian: Mr R Maheswaran
Founded: 1921
Publication(s): *Ceylon Journal of Science: Biological Sciences* (irregularly, academic); *Ceylon
Journal of Science: Physical Sciences* (irregularly, academic); *Modern Sri Lanka Studies*
(irregularly, journal, academic); *Sri Lanka Journal of the Humanities* (irregularly, academic)

Sudan

ACADI, see Arab Organization for Agricultural
Development (AOAD)

Al-Neelain University
52 St, Khartoum
Tel: (092) 079 0284
E-mail: library_dean@neelain.edu.sd
Web Site: neelain.edu.sd
Founded: 1993

AOAD, see Arab Organization for Agricultural
Development (AOAD)

Arab Center for Agricultural Documentation,
see Arab Organization for Agricultural
Development (AOAD)

**Arab Organization for Agricultural
Development (AOAD)**
Amarat St 7, 11111 Khartoum
Mailing Address: PO Box 474, 11111 Khartoum
Tel: (01) 83472176; (01) 83472183 *Fax:* (01)
83471402; (01) 83471050
E-mail: info@aoad.org
Web Site: www.aoad.org
Key Personnel
Dir General: Prof Ibrahim Adam El Dukhiri
Founded: 1972

British Council Library
14 Abu Sinn St, Khartoum
Mailing Address: PO Box 1253, 11111 Khartoum
Tel: (0187) 028000 *Fax:* (0183) 774935
E-mail: info@sd.britishcouncil.org
Web Site: sudan.britishcouncil.org

National Archives
PO Box 1914, 11111 Khartoum
Founded: 1949

National Records Office, see National Archives

Omdurman Islamic University Library
PO Box 382, 14415 Omdurman
E-mail: info@oiu.edu.sd
Web Site: lib.oiu.edu.sd
Founded: 1912

University of Khartoum Library
PO Box 321, 11115 Khartoum
Tel: (011) 770022
E-mail: library@uofk.edu
Web Site: lib.uofk.edu
Key Personnel
Chief Librarian: Prof Ahmed Hassan Fahal
Founded: 1945

Suriname

**Bibliotheek van de Cultureel Centrum
Suriname** (Library of the Cultural Centre
Suriname)
Henck Arronstr 112-114, Paramaribo
Tel: 473309; 476516
E-mail: stgccs1948@gmail.com
Web Site: ccsniews.blogspot.com
Founded: 1949

CCS Bibliotheek, see Bibliotheek van de
Cultureel Centrum Suriname

Swaziland

SCOT, see Swaziland College of Technology
Library

Swaziland College of Technology Library
PO Box 69, Mbabane H100
Tel: 24042681; 24042683 *Fax:* 24044521
Key Personnel
Librarian: Ms Sibongile Zwane
Founded: 1946
Membership(s): Swaziland Library Association
(SWALA).
Parent Company: Ministry of Education

Swaziland National Library Service
Corner Mahlokohla & Zwide St, Mbabane
Mailing Address: PO Box 1461, Mbabane H100
Tel: 2404 2633 *Fax:* 2404 3863
E-mail: director_snls@gov.sz
Key Personnel
Dir: Mrs Jabu Hlophe

University of Swaziland Library (UNISWA)
Private Bag 4, Kwaluseni
Tel: 2517 0153
E-mail: library@uniswa.sz
Web Site: www.library.uniswa.sz
Key Personnel
Librarian: Z G Ngcobo *E-mail:* zngcobo@uniswa.
sz
Deputy Librarian: A T Ndzimandze

Sweden

Biblioteken vid Lunds Universitet (Lund
University Libraries)
PO Box 3, 221 00 Lund
Tel: (046) 222 00 00; (046) 222 91 90 *Fax:* (046)
222 42 43
E-mail: info@ub.lu.se
Web Site: www.ub.lu.se

Goeteborgs Universitetsbibliotek (Gothenburg
University Library)
Centralbiblioteket, Renstroemsgatan 4, 405 30
Gothenburg
Mailing Address: PO Box 222, 405 30 Gothen-
burg
Tel: (031) 786 17 45 *Fax:* (031) 786 44 11
E-mail: g.info@ub.gu.se
Web Site: www.ub.gu.se/bibliotek
Key Personnel
Library Dir: Margareta Hemmed *Tel:* (031) 786
17 60 *E-mail:* margareta.hemmed@ub.gu.se
Founded: 1860
Publication(s): *Acta Bibliothecae Universitatis
Gothoburgensis* (irregularly); *New Literature on
Women* (quarterly, electronic bibliography)

KTH Biblioteket, see Kungl Tekniska Hoegskolan Biblioteket

Kungl Tekniska Hoegskolan Biblioteket
Osquars backe 31, 100 44 Stockholm
Mailing Address: Osaquars backe 25, 100 44 Stockholm
Tel: (08) 790 70 88
E-mail: ask-kthb@kth.se
Web Site: www.kth.se/kthb
Key Personnel
Chief Librarian: Maria Haglund *Tel:* (08) 790 72 90 *E-mail:* marhagl@kth.se

Kungliga biblioteket-Sveriges nationalbibliotek (Royal Library-National Library of Sweden)
Box 5039, 102 41 Stockholm
Tel: (010) 709 30 70
E-mail: info@kb.se
Web Site: www.kb.se; www.facebook.com/Foreningenbiblis?ref=nf
Key Personnel
National Librarian: Gunilla Herdenberg *Tel:* (010) 709 36 00 *E-mail:* gunilla.herdenberg@kb.se
Publication(s): *Acta Bibliothecae Regiae Stockholmiensis*; *Kungl Bibliotekets Utstaellningskatalog*; *Suecana Extranea* (online only); *Svensk Bokfoerteckning* (online only); *Svensk Musikfoerteckning* (online only); *Svensk Periodicafoerteckning* (online only)

Malmo Stadsbibliotek (Malmo City Library)
Kung Oscars vag 11, 211 33 Malmo
Tel: (040) 660 85 00
E-mail: info.stadsbiblioteket@malmo.se; malmostad@malmo.se
Web Site: www.malmo.se/stadsbibliotek
Key Personnel
City Librarian: Torbjorn Nilsson *E-mail:* torbjorn.nilsson5@malmo.se
City library & lending centre for southern & western Sweden.
Branch Office(s)
Bergsgatan 20, 214 22 Malmo *E-mail:* stadsarkiv.bibliotek@malmo.se
Dicksons vag 12, 213 68 Malmo *Tel:* (040) 660 85 48 *E-mail:* rosengards.bibliotek@malmo.se
Kronetorpsgatan 1, 212 26 Malmo *Tel:* (040) 660 85 25 *E-mail:* kirsebergs.bibliotek@malmo.se
Lonngatan 30, 214 49 Malmo *Tel:* (040) 34 02 99 *E-mail:* garaget@malmo.se
Munkhattegatan 170, 215 74 Malmo *Tel:* (040) 660 85 53 *E-mail:* lindangenbiblioteket@malmo.se
Svansjogatan 9, 217 66 Malmo *Tel:* (040) 660 85 59 *E-mail:* bellevuegardens.bibliotek@malmo.se
Videdalsvagen 13, 212 31 Malmo *Tel:* (040) 660 85 36 *E-mail:* husie.biblioteket@malmo.se
Klagshamnsvagen 46, 218 37 Bunkeflostrand *Tel:* (040) 660 85 11 *E-mail:* bunkeflo.bibliotek@malmo.se
Odengatan 43, 216 14 Limhamn *Tel:* (040) 660 85 03 *E-mail:* limhamns.bibliotek@malmo.se
Lertegelvagen 128, 238 30 Oxie *Tel:* (040) 660 85 64 *E-mail:* oxiebiblioteket@malmo.se
Angsovagen 2A, 218 74 Tygelsjo *Tel:* (040) 34 57 70 *E-mail:* tygelsjobiblioteket@malmo.se

Riksarkivet (National Archives)
PO Box 12541, 102 29 Stockholm
Tel: (010) 476 70 00 *Fax:* (010) 476 71 20
E-mail: riksarkivet@riksarkivet.se
Web Site: riksarkivet.se
Key Personnel
Chairman: Karin Astrom Iko
Archives & Scientific Coordinator: Bjorn Asker

Stadsbiblioteket Goteborg (Gothenburg City Library)
Goetaplatsen 3, 402 29 Gothenburg

Mailing Address: PO Box 5404, 402 29 Gothenburg
Tel: (031) 368 33 00
E-mail: info.stadsbiblioteket@kultur.goteborg.se
Web Site: www.stadsbiblioteket.nu

Statlstiska Centralbyran (Statistics Sweden Library)
Karlavaegen 100, 104 51 Stockholm
Mailing Address: Box 24300, 104 51 Stockholm
Tel: (010) 479 40 00; (010) 479 40 60 *Fax:* (08) 661 5261
E-mail: scb@scb.se
Web Site: www.scb.se
Key Personnel
Dir General: Joakim Stymne *E-mail:* joakim.stymne@scb.se
Deputy Dir General: Helen Stoye *E-mail:* helen.stoye@scb.se

Stockholms Stadsbibliotek (Stockholm Public Library)
Box 8100, 163 08 Spanga
Tel: (08) 508 31 100; (08) 508 30 900 *Fax:* (08) 508 31 210
E-mail: kundtjanst.ssb@stockholm.se
Web Site: www.biblioteket.stockholm.se
Key Personnel
City Librarian: Martin Hafstrom *Tel:* (08) 508 31 141 *E-mail:* martin.hafstrom@stockholm.se

Stockholms Universitetsbibliotek (Stockholm University Library)
Universitetsvaegen 14 D, 106 91 Stockholm
Tel: (08) 16 28 00
Web Site: www.su.se/biblioteket
Key Personnel
Library Dir: Wilhelm Widmark *Tel:* (08) 16 27 33 *E-mail:* wilhelm.widmark@su.se
Deputy Library Dir: Henrik Miettinen *Tel:* (08) 16 49 67 *E-mail:* henrik.miettinen@su.se
This library incorporates the Library of the Royal Swedish Academy of Sciences (Kungliga Svenska Vetenskapsakademiens Bibliotek) covering humanities, law, social sciences, mathematics & natural sciences, psychology & education.

Svenska Barnboksinstitutet (Swedish Institute for Children's Books)
Odengatan 61, 113 22 Stockholm
Tel: (08) 54 54 20 50; (08) 54 54 20 60
E-mail: info@sbi.kb.se; biblioteket@sbi.kb.se
Web Site: www.sbi.kb.se
Key Personnel
Librarian: Sofia Gydemo *Tel:* (08) 54 54 20 63 *E-mail:* sofia.gydemo@sbi.kb.se; Karin Mossed *Tel:* (08) 54 54 20 64 *E-mail:* karin.mossed@sbi.kb.se; Henrik Wallheim *Tel:* (08) 54 54 20 62 *E-mail:* henrik.wallheim@sbi.kb.se
Systems Librarian: Kajsa Backius *Tel:* (08) 54 54 20 61 *E-mail:* kajsa.backius@sbi.kb.se
Archive Assistant: Simon Springare *Tel:* (08) 54 54 20 55 *E-mail:* simon.springare@sbi.kb.se
Founded: 1965
Publication(s): *Barnboken* (journal, e-ISSN: 2000-4389)

Sveriges Lantbruksuniversitets Biblioteken (Swedish University of Agricultural Sciences Libraries)
Almas alle 2, 756 51 Uppsala
Mailing Address: PO Box 7071, 750 07 Uppsala
Tel: (018) 67 10 00; (018) 67 11 03 *Fax:* (018) 67 20 00
E-mail: biblioteket@slu.se
Web Site: www.slu.se/bibliotek
Key Personnel
Chief Librarian: Karin Gronvall *Tel:* (018) 67 12 60 *E-mail:* karin.gronvall@slu.se
Library Operations: Malin Jenslin *Tel:* (018) 67 20 82 *E-mail:* malin.jenslin@slu.se

Branch Office(s)
Sundsvagen 6C, PO Box 51, 230 53 Alnarp
PO Box 43, 739 21 Skinnskatteberg
Skogsmarksgrand 17, 901 83 Unea

Ume Universitetsbibliotek (Umea University Library)
Samhallsvetarhuset, 901 74 Umea
Tel: (090) 786 56 93
E-mail: umub@ub.umu.se
Web Site: www.ub.umu.se
Key Personnel
Library Dir: Mikael Sjogren *Tel:* (090) 786 96 80 *E-mail:* mikael.sjogren@ub.umu.se
Founded: 1958
Branch Office(s)
Forskningsarkivet, Umea, Head of Dept: Mats Danielsson *Tel:* (090) 786 65 71 *E-mail:* forsknings.arkivet@foark.umu.se
Medicinska Biblioteket, Universitetssjukhuset, byggnad 6M, 901 85 Umea, Head of Dept: Karina Sjogren *Tel:* (090) 785 26 60 *Fax:* (090) 786 91 58 *E-mail:* medbibl@ub.umu.se
UB Konstnarligt Campus, Ostra Strandgatan 30B, 901 74 Umea, Librarian: Lenita Brodin Berggren *Tel:* (090) 786 74 40 *E-mail:* kc@ub.umu.se
UB Campus Ornskoldsvik, Lasarettsgatan 5, Box 869, 891 33 Ornskoldsvik *Tel:* (0660) 787 77 *E-mail:* studentbiblioteket@ornskoldsvik.se

Uppsala Universitetsbibliotek (Uppsala University Library)
Dag Hammarskjoelds vaeg 1, 751 20 Uppsala
Mailing Address: Box 510, 751 20 Uppsala
Tel: (018) 471 39 00 *Fax:* (018) 471 39 13
E-mail: info@ub.uu.se
Web Site: www.ub.uu.se
Key Personnel
Dir: Lars Burman *Tel:* (018) 471 39 10 *E-mail:* lars.burman@ub.uu.se

Switzerland

Archives Economiques Suisses, see Schweizerisches Wirtschaftsarchiv

Bibliotheca Bodmeriana (Bodmer Library)
19-21, route du Guignard, 1223 Geneva
Tel: (022) 707 44 36; (022) 707 44 33 (administration) *Fax:* (022) 707 44 30
E-mail: info@fondationbodmer.ch
Web Site: fondationbodmer.ch/bibliotheque
Founded: 1972

Bibliotheque Cantonale et Universitaire de Lausanne
Place de la Riponne 6, 1014 Lausanne, Dorigny
Tel: (021) 692 48 02 *Fax:* (021) 692 48 45
Web Site: www.bcu-lausanne.ch
Key Personnel
Dir: Jeannette Frey *E-mail:* jeannette.frey@bcu.unil.ch
Deputy Dir: Jean-Claude Albertin *Tel:* (021) 692 48 05 *E-mail:* jean-claude.albertin@bcu.unil.ch

Bibliotheque Cantonale et Universitaire Fribourg
Rue Joseph-Piller 2, 1701 Fribourg
Tel: (026) 305 1333 *Fax:* (026) 305 1377
E-mail: bcu@fr.ch
Web Site: www.fr.ch/bcuf
Key Personnel
Dir: Martin Good *Tel:* (026) 305 1305 *E-mail:* goodm@fr.ch

Bibliotheque de Geneve (Library of Geneva)
Promenade des Bastions 1, 1211 Geneva
Tel: (022) 418 28 00 *Fax:* (022) 418 28 01
E-mail: info.bge@ville-ge.ch
Web Site: institutions.ville-geneve.ch/fr/bge
Key Personnel
Dir: Carine Bachmann *E-mail:* direction.bge@
city-ge.ch
Head, Administration: Carole Schaulin *Tel:* (022)
418 28 83 *E-mail:* carole.schaulin@ville-ge.ch
Founded: 1562
Publication(s): *Compte rendu* (annually)

Bibliotheque nationale suisse, see Das
Schweizerische Nationalbibliothek

**Bibliotheque Publique et Universitaire
Neuchatel**
Pl Numa-Droz 3, Case postale 1916, 2000
Neuchatel
Tel: (032) 717 73 02; (032) 717 73 20 *Fax:* (032)
717 73 09
E-mail: secretariat.bpu@unine.ch
Web Site: bpun.unine.ch
Key Personnel
Dir: Thierry Chatelain *E-mail:* thierry.chatelain@
unine.ch
Assistant Dir: Anne Cherbuin *E-mail:* anne.
cherbuin@unine.ch
Founded: 1788

Fondation Martin Bodmer, see Bibliotheca
Bodmeriana

ILO Library, see International Labour
Organization Library

International Labour Organization Library
4 route des Morillons, 1211 Geneva 22
Tel: (022) 799 8682 *Fax:* (022) 799 6516
E-mail: library@ilo.org
Web Site: www.ilo.org/library
Key Personnel
Dir General: Guy Ryder
Founded: 1919
Publication(s): *ILO Thesaurus 2008: Labour,
Employment & Training Terminology* (elec-
tronic in English, French & Spanish); *Labordoc*
(database in English, French & Spanish)

St Galler Zentrum fuer das Buch
Kantonsbibliothek Vadiana, Notkerstr 22, 9000 St
Gallen
Tel: (058) 229 23 49 *Fax:* (058) 229 23 47
E-mail: kb.vadiana@sg.ch
Web Site: www.sg.ch
Founded: 2006
Specialize in book studies, communications, jour-
nalism, library & information sciences, publish-
ing & book trade reference.

Das Schweizerische Nationalbibliothek (Swiss
National Library)
Hallwylstr 15, 3003 Bern
Tel: (031) 322 89 35 (information) *Fax:* (031)
322 84 08
E-mail: info@nb.admin.ch
Web Site: www.nb.admin.ch
Key Personnel
Dir: Marie-Christine Doffey *Tel:* (031) 322 89 01
Fax: (031) 322 64 83 *E-mail:* marie-christine.
doffey@nb.admin.ch
Publication(s): *Das Schweizer Buch* (national bib-
liography); *The Swiss National Library*

Schweizerisches Bundesarchiv (Swiss Federal
Archives)
Archivstr 24, 3003 Bern
Tel: (031) 322 89 89 *Fax:* (031) 322 78 23
E-mail: bundesarchiv@bar.admin.ch

Web Site: www.bar.admin.ch
Key Personnel
Deputy Dir: Philippe Kunzler
Founded: 1798

Schweizerisches Wirtschaftsarchiv (Swiss
Economic Archives)
Peter Merian-Weg 6, Postfach, 4002 Basel
Tel: (061) 267 32 19
E-mail: info-ubw-swa@unibas.ch
Web Site: www.ub.unibas.ch/ub-wirtschaft.swa
Key Personnel
Dir: Irene Amstutz *Tel:* (061) 267 32 02
E-mail: irene.amstutz@unibas.ch
Founded: 1910

Stiftsbibliothek St Gallen (Abbey Library of St
Gall)
Klosterhof 6D, 9000 St Gallen
Tel: (071) 227 34 16 *Fax:* (071) 227 34 18
E-mail: stibi@stibi.ch
Web Site: www.stibi.ch
Key Personnel
Chief Librarian: Dr Cornel Dora *E-mail:* cornel.
dora@kk-stibi.sg.ch
Deputy Chief Librarian: Dr Philipp Lenz
E-mail: philipp.lenz@kk-stibi.sg.ch
Historical library with a unique collection of early
medieval manuscripts.

**The United Nations Office at Geneva (UNOG)
Library**
Palais des Nations, 8-14 ave de la Paix, 1211
Geneva 10
Tel: (022) 917 41 81 *Fax:* (022) 917 04 18
E-mail: library@unog.ch
Web Site: www.unog.ch/library
Founded: 1919

Universitaetsbibliothek Basel (University
Library Basel)
Schoenbeinstr 18-20, 4056 Basel
Tel: (061) 207 31 00; (061) 207 31 30 *Fax:* (061)
207 31 03
E-mail: sekretariat-ub@unibas.ch; info-ub@
unibas.ch
Web Site: www.ub.unibas.ch
Key Personnel
Dir: Elisabeth Frasnelli *Tel:* (061) 207 31 31
E-mail: elisabeth.frasnelli@unibas.ch
Deputy Dir: Felix Winter *Tel:* (061) 207 31 29
E-mail: felix.winter@unibas.ch
Founded: 1471
Publication(s): *Jahresbericht* (annual report)
Branch Office(s)
Ancient World Studies Library, Petersgraben 51,
4051 Basel
Business & Economics Library, Peter Merian-
Weg 6, 4002 Basel
Maiengasse Library, Maiengasse 51, 4056 Basel
Medicine Library, Spiegelgasse 5, 4051 Basel
Faculty of Law Library, Peter Merien-Weg 8,
4002 Basel

Universitaetsbibliothek Bern (University Library
of Bern)
Hochschulstr 6, 3012 Bern
Tel: (031) 631 92 11
E-mail: info@ub.unibe.ch
Web Site: www.unibe.ch
Key Personnel
Dir: Dr Niklaus Landolt *Tel:* (031) 631 92 01
E-mail: niklaus.landolt@ub.unibe.ch
Deputy Dir & Head, Services & Coordina-
tion: Marianne Ingold *Tel:* (031) 631 92 02
E-mail: marianne.ingold@ub.unibe.ch
Head, Public Relations: Dr Elio Pellin *Tel:* (031)
631 92 06 *E-mail:* elio.pellin@ub.unibe.ch
Head, Resources: Christian Luethi *Tel:* (031) 631
92 03 *E-mail:* christian.luethi@ub.unibe.ch
Founded: 1528

Zentralbibliothek Zuerich
Zaehringerplatz 6, 8001 Zurich
Tel: (044) 2683 100 *Fax:* (044) 2683 290
E-mail: info@zb.uzh.ch
Web Site: www.zb.uzh.ch
Key Personnel
Dir: Dr Christian Oesterheld *E-mail:* christian.
oesterheld@zb.uzh.ch
Vice-Dir: Christoph Meyer *E-mail:* christoph.
meyer@zb.uzh.ch
Head, User Services: Dr Katharina Bruns

Syria

Al Assad National Library
Malki St, Damascus
Mailing Address: PO Box 3639, Damascus
Tel: (011) 3320806 *Fax:* (011) 3320804
E-mail: anl@alassad-library.gov.sy
Web Site: www.alassad-library.gov.sy
Founded: 1984
Publication(s): *Analytical Index to Syrian Peri-
odicals; List of Syrian Dissertations; Syrian
National Bibliography*

Taiwan

**Bureau of International Exchange of
Publications,** see National Central Library

**Fu Ssu-Nien Library, Institute of History &
Philology, Academia Sinica**
No 130 Yanlu Rd, Section 2, Nangang District,
Taipei 11529
Tel: (02) 2782-9555 (ext 600) *Fax:* (02) 2783-
1892
E-mail: fsndb@asihp.net
Web Site: lib.ihp.sinica.edu.tw
Key Personnel
Contact: Lin Shengzhi *Tel:* (02) 2782-9555 ext
118 *E-mail:* chih6100@asihp.net
Founded: 1928

IHP, see Fu Ssu-Nien Library, Institute of
History & Philology, Academia Sinica

National Central Library
20 Zhung-Shan South Rd, Taipei 10001
Tel: (02) 2361-9132; (02) 2361-9132 (ext 231,
general info); (02) 2361 9132 (ext 250, refer-
ence) *Fax:* (02) 2311-0155
Web Site: www.ncl.edu.tw
Key Personnel
Dir General: Dr Tseng Shu-hsien
Founded: 1933
Publication(s): *National Central Library Gazette
Online* (online); *National Central Library
Newsletter* (quarterly, print & online); *National
Central Library Online Catalog* (online); *Na-
tional Digital Library of Theses and Disser-
tations in Taiwan* (online); *National Library
Report* (annually, online); *NBINet Union Cat-
alog* (onliine); *Synergy of Metadata Resources
in Taiwan* (online); *Taiwan Citation Index -
Humanities and Social Sciences* (online)
Branch Office(s)
Information and Computing Library, Floor 13, No
106, Section 2, Ho-ping E Rd, Taipei *Tel:* (02)
2737-7737 *E-mail:* infolib@ncl.edu.tw
NCL Arts and Audiovisual Center, No 156,
Yan-ping S Rd, Taipei *Tel:* (02) 2361-2551
E-mail: nclaac@ncl.edu.tw

National Taiwan University Library
One Sec 4, Roosevelt Rd, Taipei
Tel: (02) 3366-2286; (02) 3366-2298 *Fax:* (02) 2363-4344; (02) 2362-7383
E-mail: tul@ntu.edu.tw
Web Site: www.lib.ntu.edu.tw
Key Personnel
University Librarian: Kuang-hua Chen
  Tel: (02) 3366-2963 *Fax:* (02) 2363-2859
  E-mail: khchen@ntu.edu.tw
Founded: 1928
Publication(s): *National Taiwan University Library Newsletter* (monthly); *University Library Journal* (2 times/yr)

Dr Sun Yat-sen Memorial Library
505, Sec 4, Ren-ai Rd, Taipei 11073
Tel: (02) 27588008 *Fax:* (02) 27584847
E-mail: sun@yatsen.gov.tw
Web Site: www.yatsen.gov.tw
Key Personnel
Dir General: Lin Kuo-Chang *Tel:* (02) 27588008 ext 500

Tajikistan

Firdousi Tajik National Library, see Firdousi Tajikistan National Library

Firdousi Tajikistan National Library
5 Tehron St, 734024 Dushanbe
E-mail: info@kmt.tj
Web Site: kmt.tj
Founded: 1933

Tajikistan National Library, see Firdousi Tajikistan National Library

Tanzania

British Council Library
Samora Machel Ave/Ohio St, Dar es Salaam
Mailing Address: PO Box 9100, Dar es Salaam
Tel: (022) 2165300
E-mail: info@britishcouncil.or.tz
Web Site: www.britishcouncil.or.tz
Key Personnel
Dir: Sally Robinson

Eastern & Southern African Management Institute (ESAMI)
PO Box 3030, Arusha
Tel: (027) 297 0065; (027) 297 0068; (027) 297 0069 *Fax:* (027) 297 0066
E-mail: mbd@esami-africa.org; esamicommunication@esami-africa.org
Web Site: www.esami-africa.org
Pan African Regional Management Development Centre.
Publication(s): *African Management Development Forum (AMDF)* (2 times/yr); *ESAMI Management Review* (quarterly, newsletter)
Branch Office(s)
NIC Investment House, 3rd floor, PO Box 22290, Dar es Salaam *Tel:* (022) 211 2670 *Fax:* (022) 211 3686 *E-mail:* esami@raha.com
Pamstech House, 4th floor, Mama Ngina St, PO Box 56628-00200, Nairobi, Kenya *Tel:* (020) 241 770 *Fax:* (020) 248 814 *E-mail:* esami@esami.or.ke
Development House, 1st floor, PO Box 31127, Lilongwe 3, Malawi *Tel:* (01) 774423; (01)

770253; (01) 775385 *Fax:* (01) 770957
  E-mail: esamimw@malawi.net
Ave Julius Nyerere, No 657 2 andar, PO Box 2077, Maputo, Mozambique *Tel:* (01) 21487375 *Fax:* (01) 21487375
  E-mail: esamimozambique@esami-africa.org
Corner Nelson Mandela/Sam Nujoma, Hidas Centre, 1st floor, PO Box 1836, Windhoek 9000, Namibia *Tel:* (061) 236 965; (061) 236 966 *Fax:* (061) 249 822 *E-mail:* esamiwhk@mweb.com.na
Plot 52, Bombo Rd, PO Box 824, Kampala, Uganda *Tel:* (041) 4254222; (041) 4343397; (031) 4261203 *Fax:* (041) 232168
  E-mail: esamiug@esamiug.ac.ug
Superannuation House, Ben Bella Rd, PO Box 32132, Lusaka, Zambia *Tel:* (01) 222937 *Fax:* (01) 222968 *E-mail:* esamizambia@esami-africa.org
No 6 Bantry Rd, Alexandra Park, PO Box 2627, Harare, Zimbabwe *Tel:* (04) 2926672; (04) 2926673 *Fax:* (04) 745607 *E-mail:* esamihre@africaonline.co.zw

ESAMI, see Eastern & Southern African Management Institute (ESAMI)

Mzumbe University Directorate of Library & Technical Services
PO Box 4, Mzumbe
E-mail: dlts@mzumbe.ac.tz
Web Site: dlts.mzumbe.ac.tz
Key Personnel
Dir, Library & Technical Services: Dr Albogast Musabila
Founded: 1964
Academic library.

SNAL, see Sokoine National Agricultural Library (SNAL)

Sokoine National Agricultural Library (SNAL)
PO Box 3022, Chuo Kikuu, Morogoro
Tel: (023) 2604639 *Fax:* (023) 2604639
E-mail: snal@suanet.ac.tz
Web Site: www.lib.sua.ac.tz
Key Personnel
Dir: Alfred S Sife *E-mail:* asife@suanet.ac.tz
Deputy Dir: M J F Lwehabura, PhD
  E-mail: julwe@yahoo.com
Founded: 1991
Serves also as a university library.
Publication(s): *Bibliography of Higher Degree Theseses & Dissertations held by the Library of the Sokoine University of Agriculture*

Sokoine University of Agriculture Library, see Sokoine National Agricultural Library (SNAL)

Standard Book Numbering Agency, see Tanzania Library Services Board

Tanzania Library Services Board
Unit of Ministry of Education & Vocational Training
National Central Library, PO Box 9283, Dar es Salaam
Tel: (022) 2150048; (022) 2150049 *Fax:* (022) 2151100
E-mail: tlsb@africaonline.co.tz
Web Site: www.tlsb.or.tz
Key Personnel
Dir General: Dr Alli Mcharazo
Founded: 1963
Publication(s): *Tanzania National Bibliography*
Branch Office(s)
Uhuru/Sokoine St, PO Box 1273, Arusha *Tel:* (027) 252642
PO Box 287, Bagamoyo *Tel:* (255) 02440427
Dar es Salaam Rd, PO Box 1900, Dodoma *Tel:* (026) 2322063

Uhuru St, PO Box 172, Iringa *Tel:* (026) 2702421
PO Box 321, Kagera *Tel:* (028) 2220460
PO Box 274, Katavi
Lumumba Rd, PO Box 933, Kigoma *Tel:* (028) 2803168
PO Box 146, Kilosa *Tel:* (023) 2623047
PO Box 443, Lindi *Tel:* (023) 2202156
PO Box 61, Lupembe
PO Box 240, Lushoto
PO Box 10, Makete
Maktaba St, PO Box 842, Mbeya *Tel:* (025) 2502589
PO Box 5, Mbeya
PO Box 227, Mbozi *Tel:* (025) 2580088
Old Dar es Salaam Rd, PO Box 858, Morogoro *Tel:* (023) 2602160
Kibo Rd, PO Box 863, Moshi *Tel:* (027) 275432
Uhuru St, PO Box 37, Mtwara *Tel:* (023) 2333352
PO Box 223, Mufindi
Jamat Khana St, PO Box 874, Musoma *Tel:* (028) 2622183
Station Rd, PO Box 1363, Mwanza *Tel:* (028) 41895
PO Box 25, Ngudu
PO Box 179, Njombe *Tel:* (026) 2782135
PO Box 31, Pangani
PO Box 804, Shinyanga
Sokoine Rd, PO Box 929, Songea *Tel:* (025) 2602041
Msakila Rd, PO Box 332, Sumbawanga *Tel:* (025) 282259
Lumumba St, PO Box 432, Tabora *Tel:* (026) 6099
Uhuru St, PO Box 5000, Tanga *Tel:* (027) 2643127
PO Box 40, Tunduru

TLSB, see Tanzania Library Services Board

Tumaini University Makumira Library
PO Box 55, Usa River, Arusha
Tel: (027) 2541034; (027) 2541036 *Fax:* (027) 2541030
E-mail: library@makumira.ac.tz
Web Site: www.makumira.ac.tz
Key Personnel
Chief Librarian: Ndelilio Mbise
Founded: 1947
Theology, East Africana.
Publication(s): *African Theological Journal* (2 times/yr); *Listen! God is Calling*

University of Dar es Salaam Library
PO Box 35092, Dar es Salaam
Tel: (022) 2410241
E-mail: director@libis.udsm.ac.tz
Web Site: library.udsm.ac.tz
Key Personnel
Dir: Dr A M M Kabudi
Associate Dir: Dr E Ndenje-Sichalwe
Founded: 1961
Publication(s): *East Africana Accessions Bulletin*; *University of Dar es Salaam Library Journal*

Thailand

British Council Library
254 Chulalongkorn Soi 64, Siam Sq, Phyathi Rd, Pathumwan, Bangkok 10330
Tel: (02) 657 5678 *Fax:* (02) 253 5311; (02) 253 5312
E-mail: info@britishcouncil.or.th
Web Site: www.britishcouncil.or.th
British education information provider.

Center of Academic Resources Chulalongkorn University
Phyathai Rd, Pathumwan, Bangkok 10330

Tel: (02) 218-2918; (02) 218-2929 *Fax:* (02) 215-3617; (02) 215-2907
E-mail: webmaster@car.chula.ac.th
Web Site: www.car.chula.ac.th
Includes Central Library, Thailand Information Center, Audiovisual Center, CU-GDLN & Office of the Secretary.

Digital & Information Office of TISTR
Research & Development Bldg 1, Room 1413, 4th floor, 35 Moo 3 Technopolis, Klong, 5, Klong Luang, Pathumthani 12120
Tel: (02) 5779000 (ext 9294) *Fax:* (02) 5779084
E-mail: klc@tistr.or.th
Web Site: klc.tistr.or.th/main/index.php
Founded: 1961
Publication(s): *Abstracts of TISTR Technical Reports* (annually)
Parent Company: Thailand Institute of Scientific & Technological Research (TISTR)
Ultimate Parent Company: Ministry of Science & Technology

DIO-TISTR, see Digital & Information Office of TISTR

Kasetsart University Main Library
Phahonyothin Rd, Chatuchak, Bangkok 10903
Mailing Address: PO Box 1084, Kasetsart, Bangkok
Tel: (02) 9428616 *Fax:* (02) 9405831; (02) 9405834
E-mail: lib_services@ku.ac.th
Web Site: www.lib.ku.ac.th
Key Personnel
Dir: Dr Aree Thunkijjanukij *Tel:* (02) 9428616 ext 401 *E-mail:* libarn@ku.ac.th
Founded: 1943

Knowledge Centre (KLC), see Digital & Information Office of TISTR

National Archives of Thailand
Samsen Rd, Dusit, Bangkok 10300
Tel: (02) 281 1599 *Fax:* (02) 628 5172
E-mail: contact@nat.go.th
Web Site: www.nat.gov.th
Founded: 1916
Historical & research resources services for official agencies, scholars & the public.
Membership(s): International Council on Archives, Southeast Asia Regional Branch.

The National Library of Thailand
Samsen Dusit, Bangkok 10300
Tel: (02) 281-5212
E-mail: director@nlt.go.th
Web Site: www.nlt.go.th/th
Founded: 1905

Siriraj Medical Library
Faculty of Medicine Siriraj Hospital, Mahidol University, 2 Wang Lang Rd, Bangkoknoi, Bangkok 10700
Tel: (02) 419-7635; (02) 419-7637 *Fax:* (02) 414-1116
E-mail: silib@mahidol.ac.th; siriraj.library@gmail.com
Web Site: www.medlib.si.mahidol.ac.th
Key Personnel
Chief Librarian: Sukrita Jongsomjit
E-mail: sukrita.jon@mahidol.ac.th

Srinakharinwirot University Central Library
114 Sukhumvit 23, Klongtoey Nua, Wattana, Bangkok 10110
Tel: (02) 6495443; (02) 6495000 (ext 11977); (02) 6495000 (ext 15386) *Fax:* (02) 2604514
E-mail: library@swu.ac.th
Web Site: lib.swu.ac.th

Key Personnel
Dir: Sarocha Mullanont *E-mail:* saroch@swu.ac.th
Founded: 1954
Branch Office(s)
107, Ongkharak District, Nakhon Nayok Province 26120, Head of Library: Miss Pornpimon Sansang *Tel:* (037) 322-615 *E-mail:* oklib@swu.ac.th

Thammasat University Libraries
2 Prachan Rd, Bangkok 10200
Tel: (02) 613 3501 *Fax:* (02) 623 5171
E-mail: tulib@tu.ac.th
Web Site: library.tu.ac.th
Key Personnel
Dir: Prof Akekarin Yolrabil *E-mail:* akekarin@tu.ac.th
Associate Dir, Administration & Development: Thitima Hiranvejchayangkool *Tel:* (02) 613 3502 *E-mail:* titima@tu.ac.th
Associate Dir, Information Services & Information Literacy: Krit Pattamaroj *E-mail:* kritp@tu.ac.th
Founded: 1934

United Nations ESCAP Library
United Nations Bldg, Rajadamnern Nok Ave, Bangkok 10200
Tel: (02) 288 1360 *Fax:* (02) 288 3036
Web Site: www.unescap.org/contact/library
Founded: 1947
Specialized collection of United Nations & ESCAP official documents & publications, books, journals, multimedia & e-resources related to economic & social development in Asia & the Pacific.

Togo

Bibliotheque et des Archives Nationales du Togo
41 Ave Sarakawa, Lome
Tel: 221 6367 *Fax:* 222 0783
E-mail: mabcoul@voila.fr
Founded: 1960
Publication(s): *Bibliographie Nationale*

Trinidad and Tobago

The Alma Jordan Library, see The University of the West Indies Main Library

NALIS, see National Library & Information System Authority (NALIS)

National Archives of Trinidad and Tobago (NATT)
The Government Archivist, 105 St Vincent St, Port of Spain
Mailing Address: PO Box 763, Port of Spain
Tel: (868) 625-2689; (868) 623-2874 *Fax:* (868) 625-2689
E-mail: enquiries@archives.gov.tt
Web Site: www.natt.gov.tt
Key Personnel
Government Archivist: Avril Belfon
Founded: 1960
Preserves the documentary heritage of Trinidad and Tobago.

National Library & Information System Authority (NALIS)
Hart & Abercromby Sts, Port of Spain
Tel: (868) 623-9673; (868) 624-1130 *Fax:* (868) 625-6096
E-mail: nalis@nalis.gov.tt
Web Site: www.nalis.gov.tt
Key Personnel
Executive Dir: Catherine Romain
Deputy Executive Dir: Paula Greene
Founded: 1998

National Library of Trinidad and Tobago, see National Library & Information System Authority (NALIS)

NATT, see National Archives of Trinidad and Tobago (NATT)

Trinidad Public Library, see National Library & Information System Authority (NALIS)

The University of the West Indies Main Library
University of the West Indies, St Augustine
Tel: (868) 662-2002 (ext 82132) *Fax:* (868) 662-9238
E-mail: almajordanlibrary@sta.uwi.edu
Web Site: libraries.sta.uwi.edu/ajl
Key Personnel
Librarian: Frank Soodeen *Tel:* (868) 662-2002 ext 82008 *E-mail:* frank.soodeen@sta.uwi.edu
Publication(s): *Bulletin Humanitas* (newsletter); *OPreP Newsletter*
Branch Office(s)
The Norman Girvan Library, Institute of International Relations, St Augustine, Librarian: Cherill Farrell *Tel:* (868) 662-2002 ext 82086 *E-mail:* iir.library@sta.uwi.edu
School of Education Library, St Augustine, Librarian: Dr Simone Primus *Tel:* (868) 662-2002 ext 83718 *Fax:* (868) 662-6615 *E-mail:* soelib@sta.uwi.edu
Medical Sciences Library, Eric Williams Medical Sciences Complex, Champs Fleurs, Head: Ernesta Greenidge *Tel:* (868) 645-2640 ext 85201 *Fax:* (868) 662-1392 *E-mail:* medlib@sta.uwi.edu
Republic Bank Library, Arthur Lok Jack Graduate School of Business, Max Richards Dr, Uriah Butler Highway NW, Mount Hope, Librarian: Devika Ramsingh *Tel:* (868) 645-6700 ext 8108 *Fax:* (868) 662-1411 *E-mail:* library@gsb.tt

Tunisia

Archives nationales de Tunisie (National Archives of Tunisia)
122, Blvd 9 avril 1938, 1030 Tunis
Tel: 71 576 800; 71 576 500 *Fax:* 71 569 175
E-mail: archives.nationales@email.ati.tn
Web Site: www.archives.nat.tn
Key Personnel
General Dir: Hedi Jallab *E-mail:* hedijallab@yahoo.fr
Founded: 1874

Bibliotheque de la Faculte des Sciences de Tunis
Campus Universitaire El Manar Tunis, 2092 Tunis
Tel: 71 872 600 *Fax:* 71 871 666
Web Site: www.fst.rnu.tn
Key Personnel
Library Dir: Aida Manchoul *E-mail:* aida.manchoul@fst.rnu.tn
Founded: 1960

Bibliotheque Nationale de Tunisie (National Library of Tunisia)
Blvd du 9 avril 1938, 1008 Bab Mnara
Mailing Address: BP 42, 1000 Tunis
Tel: 71 572 706 *Fax:* 71 572 887
E-mail: bibliotheque.nationale@email.ati.tn
Web Site: www.bibliotheque.nat.tn
Key Personnel
Dir General: M Mohamed Kamel Eddin Gaha
Founded: 1910
Publication(s): *National Bibliography of Tunisia* (annually)

British Council Library
87 Ave Mohamed V, 1002 Tunis
Tel: 71 14 53 00 *Fax:* 71 89 30 66
E-mail: info@tn.britishcouncil.org
Web Site: www.britishcouncil.tn

Centre d'Expertise et de Recherches Administratives (The Center of Expertise & Administrative Research)
24 Ave Docteur Calmette, 1082 Tunis
Tel: 71848 300 *Fax:* 71794 188
E-mail: info@ena.nat.tn
Web Site: www.ena.nat.tn
Founded: 1965
Parent Company: Tunis National School of Administration

CERA, see Centre d'Expertise et de Recherches Administratives

Institut de Presse & des Sciences de l'Information (IPSI) (Institute of Press & Information Sciences)
Campus Universitaire, 2010 Manouba
Tel: 71 60 08 31 *Fax:* 71 60 04 65
E-mail: ipsi@ipsi.rnu.tn; contact@ipsi.rnu.tn; information@ipsi.rnu.tn
Web Site: www.ipsi.rnu.tn
Key Personnel
Dir: Hamida El Bour
Founded: 1967
Publication(s): *Revue Tunisienne de Communication* (Tunisian Journal of Communication, annually)

IPSI, see Institut de Presse & des Sciences de l'Information (IPSI)

Turkey

Ankara University Department of Library & Documentation
Ankara University Campus Learning Center, Dogol St 06 100, Tondon Ankara
Tel: (0312) 223 57 61 *Fax:* (0312) 213 95 32
E-mail: kutuphane@ankara.edu.tr
Web Site: kutuphane.ankara.edu.tr
Key Personnel
Head of Dept: Tuna Can *E-mail:* tcan@ankara.edu.tr
Information Services Coordinator: Dr Dogan Atilgan *E-mail:* atilgan@ankara.edu.tr
Founded: 1933

The Beyazit State Library (Beyazit Devlet Kutuphanesi)
Turan Emeksiz sok No 6, 34126 Beyazit/Eminonu/Istanbul
Tel: (0212) 522 31 67 *Fax:* (0212) 512 84 74
E-mail: kutuphane3420@kultur.gov.tr; beyazitkutup@gmail.com
Web Site: www.beyazitkutup.gov.tr
Founded: 1884

Bilkent University Library
Main Campus Library Bldg, 06800 Bilkent, Ankara
Tel: (0312) 266 4472; (0312) 290 1298
Fax: (0312) 266 4391
E-mail: library@bilkent.edu.tr
Web Site: library.bilkent.edu.tr
Key Personnel
Dir: Ebru Kaya *E-mail:* ebrukaya@bilkent.edu.tr
Founded: 1986
Membership(s): ALS; IAML; IATUL; International Federation of Library Associations & Institutions (IFLA); LA (UK); LIBER; MELA.
Branch Office(s)
Bilkent University East Campus Library, 06800 Ankara *Tel:* (0312) 290 51 34
E-mail: eastlibrary@bilkent.edu.tr

Bogazici University Library (Bogazici Universitesi Kutuphanesi)
Bebek, 34342 Istanbul
Tel: (0212) 257 50 16 *Fax:* (0212) 257 50 16
E-mail: bulib@boun.edu.tr
Web Site: www.library.boun.edu.tr
Key Personnel
Manager: Zeynep Metin *Tel:* (0212) 359 67 39
E-mail: metinzey@boun.edu.tr

General Directorate of Mineral Research & Exploration Library
Universiteler Mahallesi Bulvari N° 139, 06800 Ankara
Tel: (0312) 201 10 00 *Fax:* (0312) 287 91 88
E-mail: mta@mta.gov.tr
Web Site: www.mta.gov.tr
Key Personnel
General Dir: Cengiz Erdem
Founded: 1935
Specialize in books on mining exploration, geological investigation, earth investigations.
Publication(s): *Mineral Research & Exploration Bulletin* (2 times/yr)

The Grand National Assembly of Turkey Library & Archives Service (TBMM)
Bakanliklar, 06543 Ankara
Tel: (0312) 420 67 52 *Fax:* (0312) 420 75 48
E-mail: kutuphane@tbmm.gov.tr; arsiv@tbmm.gov.tr
Web Site: www.tbmm.gov.tr/kutuphane
Key Personnel
President: Mehmet Toprak *Tel:* (0312) 420 68 35
E-mail: m.toprak@tbmm.gov.tr
Vice President: Muaz Ayhan Isik *Tel:* (0312) 420 68 37 *E-mail:* muaz.ayhan@tbmm.gov.tr
Membership(s): APLAP; ECPRD; International Federation of Library Associations & Institutions (IFLA); LIBER.

Istanbul Technical University Library & Documentation Dept
Ayazaga Kampusu, 34469 Maslak, Istanbul
Tel: (0212) 285 35 96 *Fax:* (0212) 285 33 02
E-mail: kutuphane@itu.edu.tr
Web Site: www.library.itu.edu.tr
Founded: 1795
Branch Office(s)
Faculty of Business Library, Macka, Istanbul *Tel:* (0212) 293 13 00 ext 2024
Foreign Language School Library, Macka, Istanbul *Tel:* (0212) 293 13 00 ext 2174
Library of Music Advanced Reseach Center, Macka, Istanbul *Tel:* (0212) 247 17 33 ext 129
Turkish Music State Conservatory Ercumend Berker & Professor Sehvar Besiroglu Library Archive & Documentation Center, Macka, Istanbul *Tel:* (0212) 293 13 00 ext 2189
Faculty of Machinery Ratip Berker Library, Gumussuyu, Istanbul *Tel:* (0212) 293 13 00 ext 2163

Faculty of Architecture Library, Taksim, Istanbul *Tel:* (0212) 293 13 00 ext 2346
Maritime Faculty Library, Tuzla, Istanbul *Tel:* (0216) 395 10 64 ext 1194

Istanbul Universitesi Merkez Kutuphanesi (Istanbul University Central Library)
Ordu Cad Yahni Kapan Sokak No 1, Beyazit, Fatih, 34452 Istanbul
Tel: (0212) 455 57 83 (ext 16767) *Fax:* (0212) 455 57 84
E-mail: kutuphane@istanbul.edu.tr
Web Site: kutuphane.istanbul.edu.tr
Key Personnel
Head, Dept: Dr Pervin Dedeler Bezirci
E-mail: pervinb@istanbul.edu.tr
Branch Manager: Senay Erendor *Tel:* (0212) 455 57 00 ext 11097 *E-mail:* serendor@istanbul.edu.tr

METU Library, see Middle East Technical University Library

Middle East Technical University Library
Universiteler Mahallesi, Dumlupinar Bulvari No 1, 06800 Ankara
Tel: (0312) 210 27 79; (0312) 210 27 80
Fax: (0312) 210 27 78
E-mail: lib-hot-line@metu.edu.tr
Web Site: lib.metu.edu.tr
Key Personnel
Dir: Cevat Guven *Tel:* (0312) 210 27 82
E-mail: guvenc@metu.edu.tr
Deputy Dir: Idil Aker Gokce *Tel:* (0312) 210 27 81 *E-mail:* aker@metu.edu.tr
Membership(s): American Mathematical Society (AMS); Anadolu Universite Kutuphaneleri Konsorsiyumu (ANKOS); International Association of Technological University Libraries (IATUL); LIBER.

Milli Kutuphane (National Library of Turkey)
Baskanligi Bahcelievler Son Durak, 06490 Ankara
Tel: (0312) 212 62 00 *Fax:* (0312) 223 04 51
E-mail: bilgi@mkutup.gov.tr
Web Site: www.mkutup.gov.tr
Key Personnel
President: Zulfi Toman *Tel:* (0312) 222 38 12
E-mail: zlf.tmn@mkutup.gov.tr
Vice President: Mehmet Emin Fidan *Tel:* (0312) 222 41 48 *E-mail:* meminfidan@mkutup.gov.tr
Library Services Dept Head: Asuman Akdemir *Tel:* (0312) 222 40 53 *E-mail:* asuman.akdemir@mkutup.gov.tr
Founded: 1948
Membership(s): CDNL (Conference of Directors of National Libraries); CENL (Conference of European National Librarians); ECO (Economic Cooperation Organization Council of Directors of National Libraries); International Federation of Library Associations & Institutions (IFLA); LIBER (Association of European Research Libraries).
Publication(s): *Haci Bektas Veli Bibliyografyasi* (Bibliography of Haci Bektas Veli, electronic); *Kasgarli Mahmud Bibliyografyasi* (Bibliography of Kasgarli Mahmud, electronic); *Nazim Hikmet Bibliyografyasi* (Bibliography of Nazim Hikmet, electronic); *Turkiye Makaleler Bibliyografyasi* (Bibliography of Articles in Turkish Periodicals, electronic); *Yahya Kemal Beyatli Bibliyografyasi* (Bibliography of Yahya Kemal Beyatli, electronic)
Parent Company: Turkiye Cumhuriyeti Kultur ve Turizm Bakanligi

Mustafa Inan Library, see Istanbul Technical University Library & Documentation Dept

Suleymaniye Yazma Eser Kutuphanesi
(Suleymaniye Writing Works Library)
Ayse Kadin Hamami Sk No 27, 34116 Fatih/Istanbul
Tel: (0212) 520 64 60 *Fax:* (0212) 511 22 10
E-mail: suleymaniye@yek.gov.tr
Web Site: www.suleymaniye.yek.gov.tr
Key Personnel
Manager: Menderes Velioglu
Founded: 1927

TBMM, see The Grand National Assembly of
Turkey Library & Archives Service (TBMM)

Turkmenistan

National Library of Turkmenistan
Neutrality Sq, 744000 Ashgabat
Tel: (012) 357 489 *Fax:* (012) 353 560
Founded: 1895

Uganda

Sir Albert Cook Memorial Library
Makere University College of Health Sciences,
Upper Mulago Hill Rd, Kampala
Web Site: chs.mak.ac.ug/acook
Key Personnel
Head: Alison Annet Kinengyere
E-mail: alisonk@med.mak.ac.ug
Founded: 1924
Publication(s): *The Uganda Health Information
Digest* (3 times/yr)

**Makerere Institute of Social Research Library
(MISR)**
PO Box 16022, Kampala
Tel: (0414) 532838; (0414) 554582
E-mail: communication@misr.mak.ac.ug
Web Site: misr.mak.ac.ug/research/misr-library
Key Personnel
Head Librarian: Irene Mbawaki
Founded: 1948

Makerere University Library
PO Box 7062, Kampala
Tel: (0414) 540375
E-mail: universitylibrarian@mulib.mak.ac.ug
Web Site: mulib.mak.ac.ug
Key Personnel
Acting University Librarian: Dr Helen Bya-
mugisha *E-mail:* hbyamugisha@mulib.mak.
ac.ug
Founded: 1959

MISR, see Makerere Institute of Social Research
Library (MISR)

National Library of Uganda
Plot 50, Buganda Rd, Kampala
Mailing Address: PO Box 4262, Kampala
Tel: (0414) 254661; (0414) 233633 *Fax:* (0414)
348625
E-mail: admin@nlu.go.ug; info@nlu.go.ug
Web Site: www.nlu.go.ug
Key Personnel
Dir: Gertrude Kayaga Mulindwa
Deputy Dir: Mr Adonia Katungisa
Founded: 2003
Nationwide public library service & preservation
of national heritage.

Established by the National Library Act.
Publication(s): *Annual Report; National Bibliography of Uganda*

Ukraine

Vernadsky National Library of Ukraine
Goloseevsky Ave, Kiev 03039
Tel: (044) 525-81-04; (044) 525-81-36 *Fax:* (044)
525-56-02
E-mail: library@nbuv.org.ua
Web Site: www.nbuv.gov.ua
Key Personnel
General Dir: Lyubov Andreevna Dubrovin
E-mail: irnbuv@gmail.com
Founded: 1918
Center for information, research, culture & pub-
lishing.

United Arab Emirates

Abu Dhabi National Library
PO Box 94000, Abu Dhabi
Tel: (02) 444 0444 *Fax:* (02) 444 0400
E-mail: national-library@tcaabudhabi.ae; info@
dctabudhabi.ae
Web Site: tcaabudhabi.ae/ar/what.we.do/national.
library.aspx
Founded: 1981
Total Titles: 800,000 Print
Parent Company: Abu Dhabi Department of Cul-
ture & Tourism

National Archives
Formerly National Centre for Documentation &
Research (NCDR)
Unit of MOPA (Ministry of Presidential Affairs)
PO Box 5884, Abu Dhabi
Tel: (02) 4183333 *Fax:* (02) 4445811
Web Site: www.na.ae
Key Personnel
Chairman of the Board: Sheikh Mansour bin Za-
yed Al Nahyan
Dir General: Abdulla Al Raisi, PhD
Founded: 1968
Archival collections, documentation, translation &
research.
Publication(s): *Abu Dhabi on the Fifth Anniver-
sary of Accession of Sheikh Zayed bin Sultan
Al Nahyan* (1971, text in Arabic); *Abu Dhabi,
the Emirate Unification & the Establishment
of the Federation* (2004, text in Arabic); *Aden,
History & Civilization* (2003, text in Arabic);
Al Faraid min Aqwal (Memorable Speeches of
Zayed, 2001, text in Arabic); *Camels* (1987,
text in Arabic); *Conference on Arab Docu-
ments in International Archives* (2002, text in
Arabic & English); *The Genius of Arab Civilization, Source of Renaissance* (1978, text in
Arabic); *Mawsu'at Al-'Aiyat* (*Encyclopedia
of Horses*) (2005, text in Arabic); *Mawsu'at
Al-Ma'moura: A Comprehensive Arabic En-
cyclopedia of Camels* (2005, text in Arabic);
Popular Poetry in the UAE (1979, text in Arabic); *Qasr Al Hosn: The History of the Rulers
of Abu Dhabi, 1793-1966* (2001, text in Arabic
& English); *Le Royaume d'Ormuz au Debut du
XVIe Siecle* (*The Kingdom of Hurmuz*) (2002,
text in Arabic); *The Seizure of the Three VAE
Islands* (2001, series of educational activities,
No 9, text in Arabic); *The Sociopolitical Environment & its Impact in the Establishment of
the UAE* (2002, text in Arabic); *UAE A His-*

*torical & Geographical Study of its Emirates
and its Modern Accomplishments* (1972, text in
Arabic); *Value & Treatment of Birds* (1983, text
in Arabic); *Zayed: From Challenges to Union*
(2008, text in Arabic & English); *Vom Mit-
telmeer zum Persischen Golf* (Max Von Oben-
hym Travel *"From the Mediterranean to the
Gulf"*) (2002, text in Arabic); *Zayed & Development - Series of Educational Activities No
30* (2004, text in Arabic); *Zayed & Education
- Series of Educational Activities No 13* (2002,
text in Arabic); *Zayed & Heritage: Cultural
Roots of the Political Leadership* (2002, text in
Arabic); *Zayed Diaries* (2003, text in Arabic)

**National Centre for Documentation &
Research (NCDR)**, see National Archives

United Kingdom

Belfast Central Library
Royal Ave, Belfast BT1 1EA
Tel: (028) 9050 9150 *Fax:* (028) 9033 2819
E-mail: belfast.central@librariesni.org.uk
Key Personnel
Information & Business: Gary Patterson
Founded: 1888

Bodleian Library
Broad St, Oxford OX1 3BG
Tel: (01865) 277162 *Fax:* (01865) 277182
E-mail: reader.services@bodleian.ox.ac.uk
Web Site: www.bodleian.ox.ac.uk
Key Personnel
Dir & Librarian: Richard Ovenden
E-mail: richard.ovenden@bodleian.ox.ac.uk
Deputy Librarian: Catriona Cannon

The British Library
96 Euston Rd, London NW1 2DB
Tel: (01937) 546060 *Fax:* (01937) 546333
E-mail: customer-services@bl.uk
Web Site: www.bl.uk
Key Personnel
Chief Executive Officer: Roly Keating
E-mail: roly.keating@bl.uk
Founded: 1973
Also publisher of books of interest to the gen-
eral reader & collector, including facsimiles
of items in the collection & works of general
bibliography.
Publication(s): *British National Bibliography*
(weekly); *Serials in the British Library* (quar-
terly); *The UKMARC Exchange Record Format*
(1997); *UKMARC Manual: A Cataloguer's
Guide to the Bibliographic Format* (1996)

**British Library Asia, Pacific & Africa
Collections**
St Pancras Bldg, 96 Euston Rd, London NWI
2DB
Tel: (020) 7412 7873 *Fax:* (020) 7412 7641
E-mail: apac-enquiries@bl.uk
Web Site: www.bl.uk; indiafamily.bl.uk/ui
Key Personnel
Chief Executive Officer: Roly Keating
E-mail: roly.keating@bl.uk
Founded: 1801

**British Library of Political & Economic
Science**
10 Portugal St, London WC2A 2HD
Tel: (020) 7405 7686; (020) 7955 7229
E-mail: library.enquiries@lse-uk.libanswers.com
Web Site: www.lse.ac.uk/library

Key Personnel
Dir, Library Services: Nicola Wright *Tel:* (020) 7955 7217 *E-mail:* n.c.wright@lse.ac.uk
Deputy Dir, Library Services: Martin Reid *Tel:* (020) 7955 7616 *E-mail:* m.j.reid@lse.ac.uk
User Services Manager: Joanne Taplin-Green *Tel:* (020) 7955 7947 *E-mail:* j.taplin-green@lse.ac.uk
Founded: 1896
Not a British Library division.
Publication(s): *The International Bibliography of the Social Sciences (IBSS)*

The British Library, Science Technology & Business Collections
96 Euston Rd, London NWI 2DB
Tel: (020) 7412 7288; (020) 7412 7454
E-mail: scitech@bl.uk
Web Site: www.bl.uk
Key Personnel
Chief Executive Officer: Roly Keating *E-mail:* roly.keating@bl.uk
List of seminars & publications available upon request. The national library for science, technology, business, patents & the social sciences, is the most comprehensive reference collection in Western Europe of such literature from the whole world. Inquiries are also handled by telephone, fax & e-mail. The library has inquiry & referral services (especially in business information, the environment, industrial property, health care & the social sciences); online database search, photocopy & linguistic aid services; runs courses & seminars & provides a wide range of publications from newsletters to definitive bibliographies.

Bill Bryson Library, see Durham University Library

Cambridge University Library
West Rd, Cambridge, Cambs CB3 9DR
Tel: (01223) 333000 *Fax:* (01223) 333160
E-mail: library@lib.cam.ac.uk
Web Site: www.lib.cam.ac.uk
Key Personnel
University Librarian: Dr Jessica Gardner *Tel:* (01223) 333045 *E-mail:* universitylibrarian@lib.cam.ac.uk
Founded: 1400
List of publications available on request from the library offices or online.

Durham Cathedral Library
The College, Durham DH1 3EH
Tel: (0191) 386 2489 *Fax:* (0191) 386 4267
E-mail: library@durhamcathedral.co.uk
Web Site: www.durhamcathedral.co.uk/learning/the-cathedral-library
Key Personnel
Librarian: Rev Charlie Allen

Durham University Library
Stockton Rd, Durham DH1 3LY
Tel: (0191) 334 3042; (0191) 334 2956 (administration) *Fax:* (0191) 334 2971
E-mail: main.library@durham.ac.uk
Web Site: www.dur.ac.uk/library
Key Personnel
Dir, Library Services & University Librarian: Elizabeth Waller *Tel:* (0191) 334 2960
Deputy University Librarian: Michael Wall *Tel:* (0191) 334 2933
Branch Office(s)
Durham University Business School Library, Mill Hill Lane, Durham DH1 3LB *Tel:* (0191) 334 5213 *Fax:* (0191) 334 5201 *E-mail:* main.library@dur.ac.uk
Leazes Road Library, Leazes Rd, Durham DH1 1TA *Tel:* (0191) 334 8137 *Fax:* (0191) 324 8311 *E-mail:* educ.library@durham.ac.uk

No 5, The College, 5 The College, Durham DH1 3EQ *Tel:* (0191) 334 1210 *E-mail:* pg.library@durham.ac.uk
Palace Green Library, Palace Green, Durham DH1 3RN *Tel:* (0191) 334 2932 *E-mail:* pg.library@durham.ac.uk
Queen's Campus Library, University Blvd, Thornaby, Stockton-on-Tees TS17 6BH, Manager: Jane Hodgson *Tel:* (0191) 334 0270 *Fax:* (0191) 334 0271 *E-mail:* stockton.library@durham.ac.uk

Edinburgh City Library & Information Services
Central Lending Library, 7-9 George IV Bridge, Edinburgh EH1 1EG
Tel: (0131) 242 8000; (0131) 242 8020
E-mail: libraries@edinburgh.gov.uk; centrallibrary.lending@edinburgh.gov.uk
Web Site: www.edinburgh.gov.uk/libraries
Founded: 1890
Public library service.

Edinburgh University Library
George Sq, Edinburgh EH8 9LJ
Tel: (0131) 650 3409 *Fax:* (0131) 651 5041
E-mail: is.helpdesk@ed.ac.uk
Web Site: www.ed.ac.uk/information-services/library-museum-gallery
Key Personnel
Dir, Library & University Collections: Jeremy Upton *Tel:* (0131) 650 3383 *E-mail:* jeremy.upton@ed.ac.uk
Founded: 1580
Publication(s): *Catalogue of the Library of The Rev James Nairn* (guides, leaflets, exhibition catalogs)

Glasgow City Libraries & Archives, the Mitchell Library
North St, Glasgow G3 7DN
Tel: (0141) 287 2910 *Fax:* (0141) 287 2815
E-mail: lil@cls.glasgow.gov.uk; archives@csglasgow.org
Web Site: www.mitchelllibrary.org
Founded: 1911
Publication(s): *West of Scotland Census Returns & Old Parochial Registers* (directory of public library holdings)

Guildhall Library
Aldermanbury, London EC2V 7HH
Tel: (020) 7332 1868; (020) 7332 1870
E-mail: guildhall.library@cityoflondon.gov.uk
Web Site: www.cityoflondon.gov.uk/things-to-do/guildhall-library
Founded: 1425
Total Titles: 189,000 Print

Leeds University Library
Leeds LS2 9JT
Tel: (0113) 343 5663
E-mail: library@leeds.ac.uk
Web Site: library.leeds.ac.uk
Key Personnel
University Librarian: Stella Butler *Tel:* (0113) 343 5501 *E-mail:* s.butler@leeds.ac.uk
Founded: 1874
Publication(s): *The Brotherton Collection*; *A Catalogue of the Icelandic Collection*; *Catalogue of the Romany Collection*

Linen Hall Library
17 Donegall Sq N, Belfast BT1 5GB
Tel: (028) 9032 1707 *Fax:* (028) 9043 8586
E-mail: info@linenhall.com
Web Site: linenhall.com
Key Personnel
Dir: Julie Andrews *E-mail:* j.andrews@linenhall.com

Librarian: Samantha McCombe *E-mail:* s.mccombe@linenhall.com
Customer Services Manager: Marie Ryan *E-mail:* m.ryan@linenhall.com
Digital & Marketing Communications Specialist: Rachel Wetherall *E-mail:* r.wetherall@linenhall.com
Founded: 1788

Liverpool Libraries & Information Services
Central Library, William Brown St, Liverpool L3 8EW
Tel: (0151) 233 3069
Web Site: liverpool.gov.uk/libraries
Publication(s): *The Battle of the Atlantic* (personal memories); *Liverpool-Capital of the Slave Trade* (book, 1992); *Liverpool Women at War* (1991)

London School of Economics & Political Science Library, see British Library of Political & Economic Science

LSE Library, see British Library of Political & Economic Science

The Mitchell Library, see Glasgow City Libraries & Archives, the Mitchell Library

The National Archives
Kew, Richmond, Surrey TW9 4DU
Tel: (020) 8876 3444
E-mail: asd@nationalarchives.gov.uk; press@nationalarchives.gov.uk
Web Site: www.nationalarchives.gov.uk
Key Personnel
Chief Executive: Jeff James
Digital Dir: John Sheridan
Finance & Commercial Dir: Neil Curtis
Dir, Public Engagement: Caroline Ottaway Searle
Dir, Research & Collections: Dr Valerie Johnson
Operations Dir: Paul Davies
Founded: 1838
National archive for the records of the British courts of law & central departments of state.

National Library of Scotland
George IV Bridge, Edinburgh EH1 1EW
Tel: (0131) 623 3700 *Fax:* (0131) 623 3701
E-mail: enquiries@nls.uk
Web Site: www.nls.uk
Key Personnel
National Librarian & Chief Executive: John Scally *Tel:* (0131) 623 3700 ext 3730 *E-mail:* john.scally@nls.uk
Head, Access: John Coll *Tel:* (0131) 623 3700 ext 3816 *E-mail:* j.coll@nls.uk
Head, Collections & Interpretation: Robin Smith *Tel:* (0131) 623 3700 ext 3865 *E-mail:* r.smith@nls.uk
Head, Communications & Enterprise: Alexandra Miller *Tel:* (0131) 623 3700 ext 3760 *E-mail:* a.miller@nls.uk
Head, Finance: Anthony Gillespie *Tel:* (0131) 623 3700 ext 3750 *E-mail:* a.gillespie@nls.uk
Head, Ingest: Graeme Forbes *Tel:* (0131) 623 3700 ext 3920 *E-mail:* g.forbes@nls.uk
Head, Organisational Development: Mo Dockrell *Tel:* (0131) 623 3700 ext 3717 *E-mail:* m.dockrell@nls.uk
Head, Resources: Murat Guven *Tel:* (0131) 623 3700 ext 3704 *E-mail:* m.guven@nls.uk
Publication(s): *Special & Named Printed Collections in the National Library of Scotland* (1999)

National Library of Wales
Aberystwyth, Ceredigion SY23 3BU
Tel: (01970) 632 800 *Fax:* (01970) 615 709
E-mail: gofyn@llgc.org.uk
Web Site: www.llyfrgell.cymru; www.library.wales

Key Personnel
National Librarian: Linda Tomos *Tel:* (01970) 632
806 *E-mail:* linda.tomos@llgc.org.uk
Dir, Collections & Public Programs: Pedr ap Ll-
wyd *Tel:* (01970) 632 952 *E-mail:* pedr.ap.
llwyd@llgc.org.uk
Dir, Corporate Resources: David Michael
Tel: (01970) 632 855 *E-mail:* david.michael@
llgc.org.uk
Founded: 1916
Also publisher.
Publication(s): *Llyfryddiaeth Cymru - A Bibliog-*
raphy of Wales (no print edition, available only
as an online service on the web catalog); *The*
National Library of Wales Journal (2 times/yr,
electronic format only)

The Natural History Museum Library &
Archives
Cromwell Rd, London SW7 5BD
Tel: (020) 7942 5460; (020) 7942 5000
E-mail: library@nhm.ac.uk
Web Site: www.nhm.ac.uk
Key Personnel
Head, Library & Information Services: Graham
Higley
Founded: 1881

Oxford University, Taylor Institution Library
St Giles', Oxford, Oxon OX1 3NA
Tel: (01865) 278158
E-mail: tay-enquiries@bodleian.ox.ac.uk
Web Site: www.bodleian.ox.ac.uk/taylor
Key Personnel
Librarian: James Legg *Tel:* (01865) 278160
E-mail: james.legg@bodleian.ox.ac.uk
Administrator: Elisabet Almunia *Tel:* (01865)
278088 *E-mail:* elisabet.almunia@bodleian.
ox.ac.uk
Founded: 1845
Graduate research library & undergraduate faculty
library for modern languages.

PRONI (Public Record Office of Northern
Ireland)
2 Titanic Blvd, Belfast BT3 9HQ
Tel: (028) 9053 4800 *Fax:* (028) 9025 5999
E-mail: proni@communities-ni.gov.uk
Web Site: www.nidirect.gov.uk/proni
Founded: 1923
Official archive of Northern Ireland.

Public Record Office of Northern Ireland, see
PRONI (Public Record Office of Northern
Ireland)

RNIB National Library Service
105 Judd St, London WC1H 9NE
Mailing Address: PO Box 173, Peterborough PE2
6WS
Tel: (020) 7388 1266 *Fax:* (020) 7388 2034
E-mail: library@rnib.org.uk
Web Site: www.rnib.org.uk/library
Founded: 1868
National agency providing library services for vi-
sually impaired people & Europe's largest lend-
ing library for people who cannot read print.
Publication(s): *Big Print* (weekly, newspaper);
Insight (magazine); *NB* (monthly, magazine);
Read On (quarterly, magazine); *Vision* (6
times/yr, magazine)

Royal National Institute of Blind People, see
RNIB National Library Service

School of Oriental & African Studies Library
University of London, 10 Thornhaugh St, Russell
Sq, London WC1H 0XG
Tel: (020) 7637 2388 *Fax:* (020) 7436 4159
E-mail: libenquiry@soas.ac.uk
Web Site: www.soas.ac.uk/library

Key Personnel
Interim Dir, Library Services: Christine Wise
Tel: (020) 7898 4166 *E-mail:* cw21@soas.ac.uk
Publication(s): *Library Catalogue* (1978-1984
supplement on microfiche); *Library Guide*

Scottish Poetry Library
5 Crichton's Close, Canongate, Edinburgh EH8
8DT
Tel: (0131) 557 2876 *Fax:* (0131) 557 8393
E-mail: reception@spl.org.uk
Web Site: www.scottishpoetrylibrary.org.uk
Key Personnel
Dir: Asif Khan *E-mail:* asif.khan@spl.org.uk
Deputy Dir & Head, Operations: Aly Barr
E-mail: aly.barr@spl.org.uk
Head Librarian: Rebecca Oliva *E-mail:* rebecca.
oliva@spl.org.uk
Founded: 1984
Free lending & reference library specializing in
Scottish & international poetry of mainly 20th
century. Computer index to poetry now avail-
able online. Travelling van service provided.
Stock includes books, audio & video tapes, pe-
riodicals, news cuttings. Poetry workshop pro-
gram in schools & other cultural & arts venues
throughout Scotland.
Publication(s): *The Scottish Poetry Index*

Senate House Library University of London
Senate House, Malet St, London WC1E 7HU
Tel: (020) 7862 8500
E-mail: senatehouselibrary@london.ac.uk
Web Site: www.senatehouselibrary.ac.uk
Key Personnel
Senate House Librarian: Dr Nick Barratt
Tel: (020) 7862 8840 *E-mail:* nick.barratt@
london.ac.uk
Associate Dir, Commercial Licensing & Digitisa-
tion: Caroline Kimball *Tel:* (020) 7862 8467
E-mail: caroline.kimball@london.ac.uk
Associate Dir, Information Systems: Richard
Warren *Tel:* (020) 7862 8452 *E-mail:* richard.
warren@london.ac.uk
Head, Collections Support & Operations:
Chris Foreman *Tel:* (020) 7862 8446
E-mail: christopher.foreman@london.ac.uk
Head, Special Collections & Engagement:
Dr Maria Castrillo *Tel:* (020) 7862 8413
E-mail: maria.castrillo@london.ac.uk
Operations Manager: Leslie-Ann Campbell
Tel: (020) 7862 8441 *E-mail:* leslie-ann.
campbell@london.ac.uk
Information Systems Analyst: Steven Baker
Tel: (020) 7862 8453 *E-mail:* steven.baker@
london.ac.uk
Archivist: Richard Temple *Tel:* (020) 7862 8473
E-mail: richard.temple@london.ac.uk
Founded: 1837
Academic research library.
Publication(s): *Catalogue of Goldsmiths' Li-*
brary of Economic Literature, Vol I-V (guides,
brochures)

SOAS Library, see School of Oriental & African
Studies Library

Taylor Institution Library, see Oxford
University, Taylor Institution Library

Trinity College Library
Cambridge CB2 1TQ
Tel: (01223) 338488
E-mail: college.library@trin.cam.ac.uk; wren.
library@trin.cam.ac.uk; archives@trin.cam.ac.
uk
Web Site: www.trin.cam.ac.uk/library
Key Personnel
Librarian: Dr Nicolas Bell
Founded: 1546

ULL, see Senate House Library University of
London

University of Aberdeen Library
The University Library, Bedford Rd, Aberdeen
AB24 3AA
Tel: (01224) 273330 *Fax:* (01224) 273382
E-mail: library@abdn.ac.uk
Web Site: www.abdn.ac.uk/library
Key Personnel
University Librarian & Dir: Diane Bruxvoort
Tel: (01224) 273384 *E-mail:* dbruxvoort@abdn.
ac.uk
Publication(s): *George Washington Wilson Pho-*
tographic Series (irregularly, based on the li-
brary's archive of Victorian glass plate nega-
tives)
Branch Office(s)
Medical Library, Polwarth Bldg, Foresterhill,
Aberdeen AB25 2ZD, Site Services Man-
ager: Melanie Bickerton *Tel:* (01224) 437870
E-mail: medlib@abdn.ac.uk
Taylor Library & European Documentation
Centre, Taylor Bldg, Old Aberdeen AB24
3UB, Site Services Manager: Nicola Will
Tel: (01224) 272601 *E-mail:* lawlib@abdn.ac.
uk (law & European documentation centre)
Special Collections Centre, Bedford Rd, Old
Aberdeen AB24 3AA *Tel:* (01224) 272598
E-mail: speclib@abdn.ac.uk

University of Birmingham Library Services
University of Birmingham, Edgbaston, Birming-
ham B15 2TT
Tel: (0121) 414 5828 *Fax:* (0121) 414 3971
E-mail: library@bham.ac.uk
Web Site: www.birmingham.ac.uk/libraries
Key Personnel
Dir, Library Services: Diane Job *Tel:* (0121) 414
4740 *E-mail:* d.m.job@bham.ac.uk
Founded: 1959
Publication(s): *Birmingham Between the Wars;*
Briefing (6 times/yr); *Bygone Bartley Green;*
Directory of the Irish in Birmingham; In the
Midst of Life; Lost Railways of Birming-
ham; National Socialist Literature in Birm-
ingham Reference Library; News Review (5
times/week); *The Nine Days in Birmingham;*
Statistics & Market Research (monthly); *Strug-*
gling Manor

University of Exeter Library
Prince of Wales Rd, Exeter, Devon EX4 4SB
Tel: (01392) 723867 *Fax:* (01392) 263871
E-mail: library@exeter.ac.uk
Web Site: as.exeter.ac.uk/library

University of Glasgow Library
Hillhead St, Glasgow G12 8QE
Tel: (0141) 330 6704
E-mail: library@glasgow.ac.uk
Web Site: www.gla.ac.uk/myglasgow/library
Key Personnel
Executive Dir, Information Services & Univer-
sity Librarian: Susan Ashworth *E-mail:* susan.
ashworth@glasgow.ac.uk
Founded: 1451
Specialize in university higher education.

University of Leicester Library
University Rd, Leicester LE1 9QD
Mailing Address: PO Box 248, Leicester LE1
9QD
Tel: (0116) 252 2043 *Fax:* (0116) 252 2066
E-mail: lib.ac.uk; liboffice@le.ac.uk;
library@leicester.ac.uk
Web Site: www.le.ac.uk/library
Key Personnel
University Librarian: Caroline Taylor *Tel:* (0116)
252 2034 *E-mail:* ct219@le.ac.uk

The University of Manchester Library
Oxford Rd, Manchester M13 9PP
Tel: (0161) 275 3751
Web Site: www.library.manchester.ac.uk
Key Personnel
Dir & University Librarian: Jan Wilkinson
Tel: (0161) 275 3700 *E-mail:* jrul.director@
manchester.ac.uk
Head, Research Services & Deputy Librar-
ian: Simon Bains *Tel:* (0161) 306 4920
E-mail: simon.bains@manchester.ac.uk
Publication(s): *The Bulletin of the John Rylands
University Library*
Branch Office(s)
Art & Archaeology Library, Mansfield Cooper
Bldg, Oxford Rd, Manchester M13 9PL
Tel: (0161) 275 3657
Braddick Library, School of Physics & As-
tronomy, Oxford Rd, Manchester M13
9PL *Tel:* (0161) 275 4078 *E-mail:* uml.
joulegeneral@manchester.ac.uk
Alan Gilbert Learning Commons, Oxford Rd,
Manchester M13 9PP *Tel:* (0161) 306 4306
Ahmed Iqbal Ullah Race Relations Resource
Centre, Manchester Central Library, Lower
Ground floor, St Peter's Sq, Manchester M2
5PD *Tel:* (0161) 275 2920 *E-mail:* rrarchive@
manchester.ac.uk
Joule Library, Sackville Street Bldg, Manchester
M13 9PL *Tel:* (0161) 306 4923 *Fax:* (0161)
306 4941 *E-mail:* uml.joulegeneral@
manchester.ac.uk
Kantorowich Library, Humanities Bridgeford St,
Oxford Rd, Manchester M13 9PL *Tel:* (0161)
275 6858 *E-mail:* uml.kantorowich@
manchester.ac.uk
Lenagan Library, Martin Harris Centre for Music
& Drama, Bridgeford St, Manchester M13 9PL
Tel: (0161) 275 4985
Library Finance Zone, Dover St Bldg, Manchester
M13 9PL *Tel:* (0161) 275 6515 *E-mail:* uml.
bds@manchester.ac.uk
Precinct Library, Crawford House, Alliance
Manchester Business School, Oxford Rd,
Manchester M13 9QS *Tel:* (0161) 306 3200
E-mail: uml.precinctgeneral@manchester.ac.uk
Stopford Library, Stopford Bldg, 3rd floor, Fac-
ulty of Medical & Human Sciences, Oxford
Rd, Manchester M13 9PT *Tel:* (0161) 275 5540
E-mail: uml.joulegeneral@manchester.ac.uk

The University of Reading Library
Whiteknights, PO Box 223, Reading, Berks RG6
6AE
Tel: (0118) 378 8770
E-mail: library@reading.ac.uk
Web Site: www.reading.ac.uk/library
Key Personnel
Dir & University Librarian: Julia Munro
Tel: (0118) 378 8774 *E-mail:* j.h.munro@
reading.ac.uk
Founded: 1892
Publication(s): *Catalogue of the Collection of
Children's Books 1617-1939 in the Library of
the University of Reading* (1988); *W M Childs:
An Account of His Life & Work* (1976); *The
Cole Library of Early Medicine & Zoology,
Part 1: 1472-1800* (catalog, 1969); *The Cole
Library of Early Medicine & Zoology, Part 2,
1800 to Present Day & Supplement* (catalog,
1975); *The Finzi Book Room at the University
of Reading* (catalog, 1981); *Robert Gibbings
1889-1958* (1989); *Historical Farm Records:
A Summary Guide to Manuscripts & Other
Material Collected by the Institute of Agricultural History & Museum of English Rural Life*
(1973); *The Kingsley Read Alphabet Collection* (catalog, 1983); *Records Management in
British Universities: A Survey with Some Suggestions* (1978)

University of Sussex Library
Brighton BN1 9QL
Tel: (01273) 678163
E-mail: library@sussex.ac.uk
Web Site: www.sussex.ac.uk/library
Key Personnel
Dir, Library Services & University Librarian: Jane
Harvell *Tel:* (01273) 877831 *E-mail:* j.harvell@
sussex.ac.uk
Publication(s): *Library News* (quarterly, newslet-
ter)

Wellcome Library
183 Euston Rd, London NW1 2BE
Tel: (020) 7611 8722 *Fax:* (020) 7611 8369
E-mail: library@wellcome.ac.uk
Web Site: wellcomelibrary.org
Key Personnel
Head of Library: Dr Simon Chaplin
Provides insight & information to anyone seeking
to understand medicine & its role in society,
past & present.
Parent Company: Wellcome Trust

Westminster Abbey Library
E Cloister, London SW1P 3PA
Tel: (020) 7654 4830 *Fax:* (020) 7654 4827
E-mail: library@westminster-abbey.org
Web Site: westminster-abbey.org
Key Personnel
Head: Dr Tony Trowles

Uruguay

Biblioteca Central de Educacion Secundaria
(Central Library of Secondary Education)
Dr Eduardo Acevedo N° 1427, 1st floor, 11200
Montevideo
Tel: 24083051; 24084273 *Fax:* 24081252
E-mail: biblos@adinet.com.uy;
bibliotecacentralsecundaria@gmail.com
Web Site: bibliotecacentralsecundaria.edu.uy/edu
Key Personnel
General Dir: Marianela Falero
Founded: 1885

Biblioteca del Poder Legislativo (Library of
Legislative Power)
Legislative Palace, 2nd floor, Av de las Leyes, s/
n, 11800 Montevideo
Tel: 29246107 (ext 2425); 29246107 (ext 2378)
E-mail: bdau@parlamento.gub.uy
Web Site: biblioteca.parlamento.gob.uy/biblioteca
Key Personnel
Library Dir: Rafael Andrade *E-mail:* randrade@
parlamento.gub.uy
Library Services Dir: Monica Paz *E-mail:* mpaz@
parlamento.gub.uy
Founded: 1929

Biblioteca Nacional del Uruguay
Av 18 de Julio 1790, 11200 Montevideo
Tel: 24005385; 24096012
E-mail: bibliotecanacional@bibna.gub.uy
Web Site: www.bibna.gub.uy
Key Personnel
Dir: Esther Pailos Vazquez *Tel:* 24003740
E-mail: epailos@bibna.gub.uy
Founded: 1815

**Centro Nacional de Documentacion Cientifica,
Tecnica y Economics (CNDCTE)**
18 de Julio 1790, 11200 Montevideo
Tel: 24025971
E-mail: cndcte@bibna.gub.uy
Part of the National Library (Biblioteca National
del Uruguay).

Publication(s): *Directorio de Servicios de Informacion y Documentacion en el Uruguay; Indice de publicaciones periodicas en ciencia y
tecnologia 1981-1983*

CNDCTE, see Centro Nacional de
Documentacion Cientifica, Tecnica y
Economics (CNDCTE)

**Facultad de Humanidades y Ciencias de la
Educacion Centro de Documentacion y
Biblioteca** (Faculty of Humanities & Education
Sciences Documentation Center & Library)
Av Uruguay 1695, 11200 Montevideo
Tel: 24088185
E-mail: biblioteca@fhuce.edu.uy
Web Site: www.fhuce.edu.uy/index.php/gestion-y-
servicios/biblioteca
Key Personnel
Dir: Leonor Quintela *E-mail:* lquintela@fhuce.
edu.uy

Uzbekistan

National Library of Uzbekistan, see Alisher
Navoi National Library of Uzbekistan

Alisher Navoi National Library of Uzbekistan
Navoi str 1, 100017 Tashkent
Tel: (871) 2328392; (871) 2328394 *Fax:* (871)
239 1658
E-mail: info@natlib.uz
Web Site: www.natlib.uz
Key Personnel
Dir: Abduazizov Alisher Abdushukurovich
Deputy Dir, Information & Library Services:
Teshabaeva Umida Alimdjanovna
Founded: 1870

Venezuela

Archivo General de la Nacion de Venezuela
Final de la Ave Panteon, Foro Libertador, Edif
Archivo General de la Nacion, Altagracia,
Caracas 1010
Tel: (0212) 5095783; (0212) 5095786
E-mail: agnvenezuela@gmail.com
Web Site: agn.gob.ve
Key Personnel
Dir: Fabricio Vivas *E-mail:* agnve2015@gmail.
com

**Biblioteca Central de la Universidad Catolica
Andres Bello**
Av Teheran, Montalban, Parroquia La Vega, Cara-
cas 1020
Tel: (0212) 407 42 77; (0212) 407 42 82
E-mail: ocace@ucab.edu.ve
Web Site: biblioteca.ucab.edu.ve
Key Personnel
Dir: Emilio Piriz Perez *Tel:* (0212) 407 42 07
E-mail: epiriz@ucab.edu.ve
Founded: 1953

**Biblioteca Central de la Universidad Central
de Venezuela**
Apdo 1050, Los Chaguaramos, Caracas 1170
Tel: (0212) 605 4190 *Fax:* (0212) 605 0861
E-mail: bibcentral@sicht.ucv.ve
Web Site: www.ucv.ve/bibliotecacentral
Key Personnel
Manager: Julie Gonzalez
Founded: 1954

Biblioteca Central General Rafael Urdaneta del Sistema de Servicios Bibliotecarios y de Informacion
Ciudad Universitaria Dr Antonio Borjas Romero, Ave 16 (Goajira), Nucleo Humanistico, Maracaibo 4001
Tel: (0261) 4127943; (0261) 4127944
E-mail: serbiluz@serbi.luz.edu.ve; administrador@serbi.luz.edu.ve
Web Site: www.serbi.luz.edu.ve
Key Personnel
Dir: German Cardozo Martinez
Founded: 1949
Publication(s): *Boletin* (biennially)

Biblioteca Marcel Roche del Instituto Venezolano de Investigaciones Cientificas
(Marcel Roche Library of the Venezuelan Institute of Scientific Research)
Carretera Panamericana Km 11, Altos de Pipe, Estado Miranda, Caracas 1020, A
Mailing Address: Apdo 20632, Caracas 1020, A
Tel: (0212) 504 1236; (0212) 504 1282; (0212) 504 1237
E-mail: bibliotk@ivic.gob.ve; infoivic@ivic.gob.ve
Web Site: biblioteca.ivic.gob.ve
Key Personnel
Head of Library: Gina Palma

Biblioteca Nacional de Venezuela
Parroquia Altagracia, Final Av Panteon Foro Libertador, Edificio Sede, Caracas 1010
Tel: (0212) 505 91 25 *Fax:* (0212) 505 91 24
E-mail: atencion.alciudadano@bnv.gob.ve
Web Site: www.bnv.gob.ve
Key Personnel
Dir General: Luis Edgar Paez Perez
Founded: 1833

SAIL, see Servicio Autonomo de Informacion Legislativa

Serbiluz, see Biblioteca Central General Rafael Urdaneta del Sistema de Servicios Bibliotecarios y de Informacion

SERBIULA, see Servicios Bibliotecarios Universidad de los Andes (SERBIULA)

Servicio Autonomo de Informacion Legislativa
Esquina de Pajaritos, Edificio Jose Maria Vargas, Caracas 1010
Tel: (0212) 409-66-83; (0212) 409-66-74

Servicios Bibliotecarios Universidad de los Andes (SERBIULA)
Edif Administrativo, piso 5, Av Tulio Ferbres Cordero, Merida 5101
Tel: (0274) 2402731; (0274) 2402729
E-mail: coordinador.serbiula@ula.ve; deptinfo@ula.ve
Web Site: www.serbi.ula.ve
Key Personnel
Dir: Marlene T Bauste de Castillo *Tel:* (0274) 2403893
Founded: 1980
University library services.

Vietnam

General Sciences Library of Ho Chi Minh City
69 Ly Tu Trong, Ben Thanh Ward, District 1, Ho Chi Minh City
Tel: (028) 8 38 225 055 *Fax:* (08) 8 38 299 318
E-mail: thuvientphcm@thuvientphcm.gov.vn

Web Site: www.thuvientphcm.gov.vn
Key Personnel
Dir: Mr Bui Xuan Duc *Tel:* (028) 8 38 225 055 ext 212 *E-mail:* xuanduc@thuvientphcm.gov.vn
Founded: 1976

National Library of Vietnam
31 Trang-Thi St, Hanoi
Tel: (04) 38255397 *Fax:* (04) 38253357
E-mail: info@nlv.gov.vn
Web Site: nlv.gov.vn; www.thuvienquocgia.vn
Key Personnel
Dir: Ba Kuieu Thuy Nga
Deputy Dir: Nguyen Ngoc Anh; Nguyen Xuan Dung
Founded: 1917
Publication(s): *Cong tac Thu' vien-Thu' muc* (Journal of Library & Bibliography); *Thu' muc quoc gia Viet nam* (National Bibliography)

Social Sciences Library
N° 1 Lieu Giai St, Badinh District, Hanoi

Yemen

British Council Library
Administrative Tower, 3rd floor, Sana'a Trade Centre, Algiers St, Sana'a
Mailing Address: PO Box 2157, Sana'a
Tel: (01) 44 83 56; (01) 44 83 57; (01) 44 83 58; (01) 44 83 59 *Fax:* (01) 44 83 60
E-mail: information@ye.britishcouncil.org
Web Site: yemen.britishcouncil.org

Great Mosque of Sana'a Library
Al Jamia al Kabir, Sana'a
Founded: 1925

Zambia

CBU Library, see Copperbelt University Library

Copperbelt University Library
Jambo Dr, Riverside, Kitwe
Mailing Address: PO Box 21692, Kitwe
Tel: (0212) 290899
Web Site: www.cbu.edu.zm/library
Key Personnel
University Librarian: Agnes M Chitambo *E-mail:* agnes.chitambo@cbu.ac.zm
Founded: 1987
Membership(s): Association of African Universities.

Lusaka City Library
Plot 448 Katondo, Lusaka
Mailing Address: PO Box 31304, Lusaka
Tel: (0211) 227282
E-mail: lcclibrary@zambia.co.zm; citylibrary@lcc.gov.zm
Web Site: www.lcc.gov.zm/libraries

The National Archives of Zambia (NAZ)
Government Rd, PO Box 50010, Lusaka
Tel: (021) 1254081
Founded: 1935

National Institute of Public Administration Library
4810 Dushambe Rd, 10101 Lusaka
Mailing Address: PO Box 31990, 10101 Lusaka

Tel: (021) 1228802; (021) 1228804 *Fax:* (021) 1227213
E-mail: registrar@nipa.co.zm; executivedirector@nipa.ac.zm
Web Site: www.nipa.ac.zm

Natural Resources Development College Library
No 7132 Off Great East Rd, Private Bag CH99, Chelston, Lusaka
Tel: (0211) 282496 *Fax:* (0211) 282497
E-mail: info@nrdc.biz
Web Site: www.nrdc.biz
Founded: 1965

NAZ, see The National Archives of Zambia (NAZ)

NORTEC College Library, see Northern Technical College Library

Northern Technical College Library
PO Box 250093, Chella Rd, Kansenshi, Ndola
Tel: (021) 671699
E-mail: principal@nortec.edu.zm; info@nortec.edu.zm
Web Site: www.nortec.edu.zm

University of Zambia Library
Great East Rd Campus, PO Box 32379, 10101 Lusaka
Tel: (021) 1250845 *Fax:* (021) 1250845
E-mail: librarian@unza.zm
Web Site: library.unza.zm
Key Personnel
University Librarian: Dr Vitalicy Chifwepa
Medical Librarian: Celine M Mwafulilwa
   Tel: (021) 1250801 *E-mail:* cmwafulilwa@unza.zm
Founded: 1966

Zambia Library Service
PO Box 30802, Lusaka
Web Site: www.facebook.com/zambialibraryservice
Key Personnel
Chief Librarian: Robertson Bwato *E-mail:* r.bwato@yahoo.com
Senior Librarian: Sharon Munshya
   E-mail: sharonmunshya@yahoo.co.uk
Founded: 1962
Publication(s): *Annual Report*; *Teacher/Librarians* (2 times/yr, newsletter)

Zimbabwe

Bulawayo Public Library
100 Fort St & Eighth Ave, Bulawayo
Mailing Address: PO Box 586, Bulawayo
Tel: (09) 60966
E-mail: bpl@graffiti.net
Web Site: www.angelfire.com/ky/bpl
Key Personnel
Chief Librarian: Letshani Ndlovu
Founded: 1896
Public library & legal deposit (archive) collection.

Harare City Library
Rotten Row, Harare
Tel: (086) 441 23929
E-mail: librarian@hararecitylibrary.org
Web Site: www.hararecitylibrary.org
Founded: 1902
Branch Office(s)
Hatfield Library, Elgin Rd, Hatfield
Highlands Library, Kew Dr, Highlands
Greendale Library, Kennedy Dr, Greendale
   Tel: (086) 441 30209

Mabelreign Library, Sherwood Rd, Mabelreign
Tel: (086) 441 30210
Mt Pleasant Library, Cuba Ave, Mount Pleasant
Tel: (043) 35781

Harare Polytechnic Library
PO Box CY-407, Causeway, Harare
Tel: (04) 2918080; (04) 2918081
Web Site: www.hrepoly.ac.zw
Founded: 1924
Parent Company: Ministry of Higher & Tertiary
    Education, Science & Technology Development

National Archives of Zimbabwe
Borrowdale Rd, Gunhill, Private Bag 7729,
    Causeway, Harare
Tel: (04) 792741; (04) 792742; (04) 792743
    Fax: (04) 792398
E-mail: archives@archives.gov.zw
Web Site: www.archives.gov.zw
Founded: 1935
Publication(s): *Guides to the National Archives
    collections* (series); *Zimbabwe National Bibli-
    ography; Directory of Libraries in Zimbabwe*
    (1986)

National Free Library of Zimbabwe
PO Box 1773, Bulawayo
Tel: (09) 232359 *Fax:* (09) 257662
Founded: 1944

NAZ, see National Archives of Zimbabwe

Library of Parliament
Nelson Mandela/Third St, Box CY 298, Cause-
    way, Harare
Tel: (04) 700 181; (04) 700 189 *Fax:* (04) 252
    935
E-mail: clerk@parlzim.gov.zw
Web Site: www.parlzim.gov.zw
Key Personnel
Dir, Library Services: Isaiah Munyoro
Principal Librarian: Ronald Munatsi
Founded: 1923

Turner Memorial Library
Queensway, Civic Center, Mutare
Founded: 1936

Membership(s): United Nations Associated Li-
    braries (UNAL); Zimbabwe Library Associa-
    tion.
Branch Office(s)
Dangamvura Public Library & Sakubva Public
    Library, PO Box 448, Mutare

University of Zimbabwe Libraries
Mount Pleasant Dr, Mount Pleasant, Harare
Mailing Address: PO Box MP 45, Mount Pleas-
    ant, Harare
Tel: (04) 303211-19 *Fax:* (04) 705155
E-mail: librarian@uzlib.uz.ac.zw; uzmedlib.hre@
    healthnet.zw
Web Site: library.uz.ac.zw
Key Personnel
Librarian: Agnes Chikonzo *Tel:* (04) 303211-19
    ext 12001 *E-mail:* achikonzo@uzlib.uz.ac.zw
Chief Secretary: Annifa Machaka *Tel:* (04)
    303211-19 ext 12044 *E-mail:* amachaka@uzlib.
    uz.ac.zw

Zimbabwe Geological Survey
PO Box 210, Causeway, Harare
Tel: (04) 707749; (04) 707716
E-mail: zimgeosurvey@mines.gov.zw

Library Associations

Listed below are library or library-related associations. Other book trade associations and organizations can be found in **Literary Associations & Societies** and **Book Trade Organizations**.

Argentina

ABGRA (Asociacion de Bibliotecarios Graduados de la Republica Argentina)
(Association of Graduate Librarians of Argentina)
Parana 918 2do Piso, C1017AAT Buenos Aires
Tel: (011) 4811 0043; (011) 4816 3422
  Fax: (011) 4816 2234
E-mail: info@abgra.org.ar
Web Site: www.abgra.org.ar
Key Personnel
President: Gloria Priore
Vice President: Graciela Ayos
Secretary General: Mirta Villalba
Treasurer: Isabel Piro
Founded: 1953
Publication(s): *Referencias*

Asociacion de Bibliotecarios Graduados de la Republica Argentina, see ABGRA
(Asociacion de Bibliotecarios Graduados de la Republica Argentina)

Australia

ALIA, see Australian Library & Information Association Ltd (ALIA)

ALLA, see Australian Law Librarians' Association

ASA, see Australian Society of Archivists Inc (ASA)

Australian Law Librarians' Association
PO Box 677, Canberra, ACT 2601
Tel: (02) 9230 8675 *Fax:* (02) 9233 7952
E-mail: admin@alla.asn.au
Web Site: www.alla.asn.au
Key Personnel
President: Marisa Bendeich *E-mail:* president@alla.asn.au
Vice President: Lisa Sylvester
  E-mail: vicepresident@alla.asn.au
Secretary: Linden Fairbairn *E-mail:* secretary@alla.asn.au
Treasurer: James Butler *E-mail:* treasurer@alla.asn.au
Website Coordinator: Robin Gardner
Founded: 1969
Publication(s): *Australian Law Librarian* (quarterly, journal)

Australian Library & Information Association Ltd (ALIA)
ALIA House, 9-11 Napier Close, Deakin, ACT 2600
Mailing Address: PO Box 6335, Kingston, ACT 2604
Tel: (02) 6215 8222 *Toll Free Tel:* 1800 020 071 (members only) *Fax:* (02) 6282 2249
E-mail: enquiry@alia.org.au
Web Site: www.alia.org.au

Key Personnel
President: Vanessa Little *E-mail:* vanessa.little@act.gov.au
Vice President: Julie Rae
Executive Dir: Sue Hutley *E-mail:* sue.hutley@alia.org.au
Professional association of the library & information sector.
Publication(s): *Australian Academic & Research Libraries* (quarterly, journal); *Australian Library Journal* (quarterly); *INCITE* (monthly, magazine)

Australian Society of Archivists Inc (ASA)
Suite 2, Level 4, 360 Queen St, Brisbane, Qld 4000
Mailing Address: PO Box A623, Sydney South, NSW 1235
Tel: (07) 3221 4887 *Toll Free Tel:* 1800 622 251
  Fax: (07) 3221 6885
E-mail: office@archivists.org.au
Web Site: www.archivists.org.au
Key Personnel
President: Patricia Jackson
Vice President: Kylie Percival
Secretary/Treasurer: Dr Louise Trott
Founded: 1975
Publication(s): *Archives & Manuscripts* (biannually); *ASA Bulletin* (biweekly, e-newsletter); *Debates and Discourses: Selected Australian Writings in Archival Theory, 1951-1990; Directory of Archives in Australia*

CAVAL Ltd
4 Park Dr, Bundoora, Victoria 3083
Tel: (03) 9459 2722 *Fax:* (03) 9459 2733
E-mail: caval@caval.edu.au
Web Site: www.caval.edu.au
Key Personnel
Acting Chief Executive Officer & Chief Information Officer: Cathie Jilovsky *Tel:* (03) 9450 5501 *E-mail:* cathie.jilovsky@caval.edu.au
Manager, Administration Services: Nicole Sinclair *Tel:* (03) 9450 5528 *E-mail:* nicole.sinclair@caval.edu.au
Library & information services.
Publication(s): *CAVAL Newsletter*

National & State Libraries Australasia
State Library of Victoria, 328 Swanston St, Melbourne, Victoria 3000
Tel: (03) 8664 7512
E-mail: nsla@slv.vic.gov.au
Web Site: www.nsla.org.au
Key Personnel
Chairman: Alan Smith
Deputy Chair: Margaret Allen

National Library of Australia
Parkes Pl, Canberra, ACT 2600
Tel: (02) 6262 1111 *Fax:* (02) 6257 1703
E-mail: www@nla.gov.au
Web Site: www.nla.gov.au
Key Personnel
Dir General: Anne-Marie Schwirtlich *Tel:* (02) 6262 1262 *E-mail:* aschwirtlich@nla.gov.au
Assistant Dir General, Executive & Public Programs Division: Jasmine Cameron
  E-mail: jcameron@nla.gov.au

NSLA, see National & State Libraries Australasia

Austria

Dokumentationsstelle fuer neuere Oesterreichische Literatur (Documentation Centre for Modern Austrian Literature)
Seidengasse 13, 1070 Vienna
Tel: (01) 526 20 44-0 *Fax:* (01) 526 20 44-30
E-mail: info@literaturhaus.at
Web Site: www.literaturhaus.at
Key Personnel
Chief Executive Officer: Robert Huez
Founded: 1965
Publication(s): *Zirkular* (quarterly)

Oesterreichische Gesellschaft fuer Dokumentation und Information (OGDI)
(Austrian Society for Documentation & Information)
c/o OCG, Wollzeile 1-3, 1010 Vienna
Mailing Address: PO Box 43, 1022 Vienna
E-mail: office@oegdi.at
Web Site: www.oegdi.at
Key Personnel
Chairman: Dr Gabriele Sauberer
Secretary: Dr Carola Wala
Treasurer: Dr Herman Huemer
Founded: 1951
Membership(s): Austrian Computer Society (OCG); Bibliothek Information Schweiz (BIS); Deutsche Gesellschaft fuer Informationswissenschaft und Informationspraxis eV (DGI); International Network for Terminology (TermNet).

OGDI, see Oesterreichische Gesellschaft fuer Dokumentation und Information (OGDI)

Vereinigung Oesterreichischer Bibliothekarinnen und Bibliothekare (VOEB) (Association of Austrian Librarians)
Universitaetsbibliothek Graz, Universitaetsplatz 3, 8010 Graz
E-mail: voeb@uibk.ac.at
Web Site: www.univie.ac.at/voeb
Key Personnel
President: Dr Werner Schlacher *E-mail:* werner.schlacher@uni-graz.at
First Vice President: Eva Ramminger *E-mail:* eva.ramminger@uibk.ac.at
Secretary: Markus Lackner *E-mail:* markus.lackner@uni-graz.at
Second Vice President: Dr Gerhard Zechner
  E-mail: gerhard.zechner@voralberg.at
Founded: 1945
Publication(s): *Mitteilungen der Vereinigung Oesterreichischer Bibliothekarinnen und Bibliothekare Mitteilungen* (3 times/yr, journal, published in German)

VOEB, see Vereinigung Oesterreichischer Bibliothekarinnen und Bibliothekare (VOEB)

Bangladesh

LAB, see Library Association of Bangladesh (LAB)

Library Association of Bangladesh (LAB)
c/o Nilkhet High School Bhaban, 2nd floor,
Dhaka 1000
Tel: 01713020266
E-mail: libraryassociation.bd@gmail.com
Web Site: www.lab.org.bd
Key Personnel
President: Prof Nasir Uddin Munshi, PhD
E-mail: ramanasir@yahoo.com
Secretary General: Dr Mizanur Rahman, MD
E-mail: mizan_alif68@yahoo.com
Founded: 1956
Work for the professional development in
Bangladesh & offers training courses.
Publication(s): *The Eastern Librarian* (biannually); *Upattha* (quarterly, newsletter, text in
Bengali)

**National Archives & National Library of
Bangladesh**
Dept of Archives & Libraries, Ministry of Cultural Affairs, 32, Justice S M Murshed Sarani,
Agargaon, Sher-e-Bangla Nagar, Dhaka 1207
Tel: (02) 9129992 *Fax:* (02) 9135709
Web Site: www.nanl.gov.bd
Key Personnel
Dir: Mozibor Rahman Al-Mamun
E-mail: nanldirector@gmail.com
Deputy Dir, Archives: Tahmina Akter
E-mail: tani.nlb@gmail.com
Deputy Dir, Library: Shahab Uddin Khan
E-mail: ddnlbd@gmail.com
Librarian: Gulam Mustofa
Founded: 1972
Collection, preservation & reproduction of books
& other documents; reference & readers service. ISBN Agency of all publications. Hold
seminars, exhibitions & workshops to create
awareness of library services.
Membership(s): International Federation of Library Associations & Institutions (IFLA).
Publication(s): *Bangladesh National Archives
Guide Book*; *Bangladesh National Bibliography* (annually); *Bangladesh National Library
Guide Book*; *Newsletters of Archives & National Library* (biannually)

Barbados

LAB, see Library Association of Barbados (LAB)

Library Association of Barbados (LAB)
PO Box 827E, Bridgetown
E-mail: miton@uwichill.edu.bb
Key Personnel
President: Junior Brown
Founded: 1968
Publication(s): *Bulletin* (irregularly); *Update* (irregularly, newsletter)

Belgium

APBD, see Association Professionnelle des
Bibliothecaires et Documentalistes (APBD)

Archief- en Bibliotheekwezen in Belgie (Belgian
Association of Archivists & Librarians)
Keizerslaan 4, 1000 Brussels
Tel: (02) 519 53 93 *Fax:* (02) 519 56 10
Publication(s): *Archives et Bibliotheques de Belgique* (text in Dutch, English, French, German,
Italian, Latin & Spanish)

ASBL, see Association des Bibliothecaires Belges
d'Expression Francaise

**Association Belge de Documentation/Belgische
Vereniging Voor Documentatie** (Belgian
Association for Documentation)
4 Blvd de l'Empereur, 1000 Brussels
Tel: (02) 675 58 62 *Fax:* (02) 672 74 46
E-mail: abdbvd@abd-bvd.be
Web Site: www.abd-bvd.be
Key Personnel
President: Christopher Boon
E-mail: christopherboon@hotmail.com
Vice President: Marc Van Den Bergh
E-mail: mvdbergh@serv.be
Secretary General: Dominique Vanpee
E-mail: sec.gen@abd-bvd.be
Treasurer: Didier Haas *E-mail:* didier.haas@fanc.
fgov.be
Founded: 1947
Membership(s): EBLIDA; ECIA.
Publication(s): *Cahiers de la Documentation -
Bladen voor Documentatie* (quarterly, 1947,
text in Dutch, English & French)

Association des Archivistes et Bibliotheques,
see Archief- en Bibliotheekwezen in Belgie

**Association des Bibliothecaires Belges
d'Expression Francaise** (Belgian Association
of French-Speaking Librarians)
c/o Michel C Dagneau, rue Emile Vandevandel
39, 1470 Genappe
Tel: (067) 771477 *Fax:* (067) 771477
E-mail: abbef.be@gate71.be
Key Personnel
President: Michel Dagneau *E-mail:* dagneau.
michel@skynet.be
Founded: 1964
Publication(s): *Le Bibliothecaire: Revue
d'Information culturelle et bibliographique*

**Association Professionnelle des Bibliothecaires
et Documentalistes (APBD)** (Professional
Association of Librarians & Documentation)
Place de la Wallonie, 15, 6140 Fontaine-l'Eveque
Tel: (071) 52 31 93 *Fax:* (071) 52 23 07
Web Site: www.apbd.be
Key Personnel
President: Laurence Boulanger
Vice President: Marianne Bragard; Emmanuelle
Plumat
Secretary: Fabienne Gerard
Treasurer: Guy Tondreau

Scientific & Technical Information Service
Platinum Bldg, Av Louise 231 Louisalaan, 1050
Brussels
Tel: (02) 238 37 40 *Fax:* (02) 238 37 50
Web Site: www.stis.belspo.be
Key Personnel
Dir: Dr Jean Moulin *Tel:* (02) 238 37 45
E-mail: jean.moulin@stis.belspo.be

STIS, see Scientific & Technical Information
Service

**Vereniging van Religieus-Wetenschappelijke
Bibliothecarissen** (Association of Religious
Science Librarians)
Halvestr 14, 3000 Leuven
Founded: 1965

Membership(s): Bibliotheques Europeennes de
Theologie (BETH).
Publication(s): *VRB-Informatie* (quarterly)

**Vlaamse Vereniging voor Bibliotheek, Archief
en Documentatie VZW (VVBAD)** (Flemish
Association for Libraries, Archives &
Documentation Centres)
Statiestr 179, 2600 Berchem
Tel: (03) 281 44 57
E-mail: vvbad@vvbad.be
Web Site: www.vvbad.be
Key Personnel
Coordinator: Bruno Vermeeren *E-mail:* bruno.
vermeeren@vvbad.be
Founded: 1921
Publication(s): *Archiefkunde* (monographs); *Bibliotheek & Archiefgids* (Library & Archive
Guide, 6 times/yr); *Bibliotheekkunde* (monographs); *INFO* (monthly, membership journal);
Vlaamse Archief, Bibliotheek- en Documentatiegids (biennially, address guide to archives,
libraries & documentation centers in Dutch-speaking part of Belgium)

VRB, see Vereniging van
Religieus-Wetenschappelijke Bibliothecarissen

VVBAD, see Vlaamse Vereniging voor
Bibliotheek, Archief en Documentatie VZW
(VVBAD)

Bolivia

**Centro Nacional de Documentacion Cientifica
y Tecnologica (CNDCT)** (National Scientific
& Technological Documentation Centre)
Av Mariscal Santa Cruz N° 1175, esquina c Ayacucho, La Paz
Tel: (02) 359583 *Fax:* (02) 359586
E-mail: iiicndct@huayna.umsa.edu.bo
Web Site: www.bolivian.com/industrial/cndct

CNDCT, see Centro Nacional de Documentacion
Cientifica y Tecnologica (CNDCT)

Bosnia and
Herzegovina

Drustvo Bibliotekara Bosne i Hercegovine
(Association of Librarians of Bosnia and
Herzegovina)
Zmaja od Bosne 8B, 71000 Sarajevo
Tel: (033) 2755325 *Fax:* (033) 212435
Key Personnel
President: Nevenka Hadarovi *E-mail:* nevenka@
nub.ba
Secretary: Dijana Bilos *E-mail:* dijana@nub.ba
Founded: 1945
Publication(s): *Bibliotekarstvo* (annually, 1956)

Botswana

BLA, see Botswana Library Association

Botswana Library Association
PO Box 1310, Gaborone
Tel: 371750 *Fax:* 371748
Web Site: www.bla.org.bw

Key Personnel
President: Kgomotso Radijeing
    E-mail: kgomotsor@bnpc.bw
Vice President: Keoagile Phoi *E-mail:* kphoi@
    bidpa.bw
Secretary: Stella Naledi Madzigigwa
    E-mail: tinyktus@yahoo.com
Treasurer: Boipuso Dikgang *E-mail:* dikgangb@
    mopipi.ub.bw
Founded: 1978
Publication(s): *Botswana Library Association
    Journal*

Brazil

AAB, see Associacao dos Arquivistas Brasileiros
    (AAB)

Associacao dos Arquivistas Brasileiros (AAB)
    (Association of Brazilian Archivists)
Av Presidente Vargas, 1733 - sala 903, 20210-030
    Rio de Janeiro-RJ
Tel: (021) 2507-2239 *Fax:* (021) 3852-2541
E-mail: aab@aab.org.br
Web Site: www.aab.org.br
Key Personnel
President: Lucia Maria Velloso de Oliveira
First Vice President: Margareth da Silva
Second Vice President: Isabel Cristina Borges de
    Oliveira
Secretary General: Leila Estephanio de Moura
Treasurer: Renata Silva Borges
Publication(s): *Associacao dos Arquivistas
    Brasileiros* (Association of Brazilian Archivists,
    bulletin); *Revista Arquivo & Administracao*
    (biannually)

FEBAB, see Federacao Brasileira de Associacoes
    de Bibliotecarios, Cientistas da Informacao e
    Instituicoes - Comissao Brasileira de
    Documentacao Juridica (FEBAB/CBDJ)

**Federacao Brasileira de Associacoes de
    Bibliotecarios, Cientistas da Informacao e
    Instituicoes - Comissao Brasileira de
    Documentacao Juridica (FEBAB/CBDJ)**
    (Brazilian Federation of Library Associations,
    Information Scientists & Institutions - Brazilian
    Committee of Legal Documentation)
Rua Avanhandava, 40, ap 108/110, 01306-000
    Sao Paulo-SP
Tel: (011) 3257-9979 *Fax:* (011) 3257-9979
E-mail: febab@febab.org.br
Web Site: www.febab.org.br
Key Personnel
President: Sigrid Karin Weiss
Vice President: Adriana Cybele Ferrari
Publication(s): *Revista de Biblioteconomia e
    Documentacao-RBBD* (Journal of Librarianship
    & Documentation)

IBICT, see Instituto Brasileiro de Informacao em
    Ciencia e Tecnologia

**Instituto Brasileiro de Informacao em Ciencia
    e Tecnologia**
Setor de Autarquias Sul (SAUS), Quadra 05 Lote
    06 Bloco H, 70070-912 Brasilia-DF
Tel: (061) 3217-6360; (061) 3217-6350
    Fax: (061) 3217-6490
Web Site: www.ibict.br
Key Personnel
Dir: Emir Jose Suaiden
Publication(s): *Bibliografia Brasileira de Cien-
    cia da Informacao* (Brazilian Bibliography of
    Information Science, annually); *Boletim Quali-
    dade & Produtividade* (Quality & Productivity

Bulletin, quarterly); *Calendario de Eventos em
    C&T* (Calendar of Events in C&I, quarterly);
    Ciencia da Informacao (Information Science,
    biannually)

Brunei

BLA, see Persatuan Perpustakaan Negara Brunei
    Darussalam

**Persatuan Perpustakaan Negara Brunei
    Darussalam** (Brunei Darussalam Library
    Association)
c/o Class 64 Library, SOASC, Jl Tengah, Bandar
    Seri Begawan BS8411
Fax: 2222330
E-mail: pobox.bla@gmail.com
Web Site: www.bruneilibraryassociation.
    wordpress.com
Key Personnel
Honorary Secretary: Ms Hjh Rosnani
    E-mail: rosnaniy@hotmail.com
Founded: 1986
Publication(s): *Wadah Perpustakaan* (newsletter)

Cameroon

ABADCAM, see Association des Bibliothecaires,
    Archivistes, Documentalistes et Museographes
    du Cameroun (ABADCAM)

**Association des Bibliothecaires, Archivistes,
    Documentalistes et Museographes du
    Cameroun (ABADCAM)** (Association of
    Librarians, Archivists, Documentalists &
    Museum Curators)
BP 14077, Yaounde
Web Site: www.abadcam.sitew.com
Key Personnel
President: Jerome Ndjock *Tel:* 699 99 86 08
    E-mail: jendjock@yahoo.fr
Vice Pesident: Rosemary Tsafack *Tel:* 699 69 88
    68 *E-mail:* roshafack@yahoo.com
Deputy Secretary General: Thomas Anzanga
    Tel: 677 83 05 57 *E-mail:* andzanga@gmail.
    com
Secretary General: Charles Kiven *Tel:* 699 76 31
    25 *E-mail:* kiven_c@yahoo.com
Treasurer: Francoise Belobo *Tel:* 699 93 51 23
    E-mail: fany_belobo@yahoo.fr
Communication: Jean Hassan *Tel:* 699 83 48 11
    E-mail: jeanhas2002@yahoo.fr
Works in collaboration with the Ministry of Cul-
    ture in formulating policies for librarians,
    archivists, documentalists & museographers
    in Cameroon.
Publication(s): *Newsletter*

Chile

CBC, see Colegio de Bibliotecarios de Chile
    (CBC)

Colegio de Bibliotecarios de Chile (CBC)
    (College of Librarians of Chile)
Avda Diagonal Paraguay 383, Torre 11, Oficina
    122, 6510017 Santiago
Tel: (02) 2225652
E-mail: cbc@bibliotecarios.cl
Web Site: www.bibliotecarios.cl

Key Personnel
President: Gabriela Pradenas Bobadilla
Vice President: Viviana Garcia Corrales
Secretary General: Victor Candia Arancibia
Treasurer: Karina Herrera Silva

**Comision Nacional de Investigacion Cientifica
    y Tecnologica**, see CONICYT

CONICYT (National Commission for Science &
    Technology)
Canada 308, Providencia, Santiago
Tel: (02) 3654400 *Fax:* (02) 6551396
E-mail: info@conicyt.cl
Web Site: www.conicyt.cl
Key Personnel
President: Jose Miguel Aguilera
    E-mail: jmaguilera@conicyt.cl
Executive Dir: Mateo Budinich Diez
Secretary: Claudia Palominos; Leticia Toro Silva
Founded: 1967
Publication(s): *Serie Directorios*; *Serie Informa-
    cion y Documentacion*

China

Library Society of China
33, Zhongguancun S, Beijing 100081
Tel: (010) 8854 5283 *Fax:* (010) 6841 7815
E-mail: ztxhmsc@nlc.gov.cn
Web Site: www.nlc.gov.cn; www.lsc.org.cn
Key Personnel
Dir: Zhou Heping
Secretary General: Gensheng Tang
Founded: 1979
Publication(s): *Journal of China Library Science*

Colombia

ASCOLBI, see Asociacion Colombiana de
    Bibliotecologos y Documentalistas

**Asociacion Colombiana de Bibliotecologos y
    Documentalistas** (Colombian Association of
    Librarians & Documentalists)
Calle 21 No 6-58 Oficina 404, Bogota
Tel: (01) 2823620 *Fax:* (01) 2825487
E-mail: secretaria@ascolbi.org
Web Site: www.ascolbi.org
Key Personnel
President: Edgar Allan Delgado
Colombian Library Association.
Publication(s): *Boletin*

Democratic Republic of the Congo

ABADOM, see Association des Bibliothecaires,
    Archivistes, Documentalistes et museologues
    du Congo (ABADOM)

**Association des Bibliothecaires, Archivistes,
    Documentalistes et museologues du Congo
    (ABADOM)** (Association of Librarians,

Archivists, Documentalists & Museologists of the Congo)
BP 3148, Kinshasa-Gombe
E-mail: abadom2001@yahoo.fr
Key Personnel
President: Desire Didier Tengeneza
  E-mail: didierteng@yahoo.fr
Publication(s): *Mukanda*

Croatia

HKD, see Hrvatsko knjiznicarsko drustvo

Hrvatsko knjiznicarsko drustvo (Croatian Library Association)
c/o Nacionalna i sveucilisna Knjiznica, Hrvatske bratske zajednice 4, 10 000 Zagreb
Tel: (01) 615 93 20 *Fax:* (01) 615 93 20
E-mail: hkd@hkdrustvo.hr
Web Site: www.hkdrustvo.hr
Key Personnel
Secretary: Tina Matosevic
Founded: 1940
Membership(s): European Bureau of Library, Information & Documentation Associations (EBLIDA); International Federation of Library Associations & Institutions (IFLA); UNESCO (United Nations Educational, Scientific & Cultural Organization).
Publication(s): *HKD Novosti* (3-4 times/yr, newsletter); *Vjesnik bibliotekara Hrvatske* (biannually, scientific magazine)

Cuba

ASCUBI, see Asociacion Cubana de Bibliotecarios (ASCUBI)

Asociacion Cubana de Bibliotecarios (ASCUBI) (Library Association of Cuba)
c/o Biblioteca Nacional "Jose Marti", Ave Independencia 20 de Mayo, Plaza de la Revolucion, Havana
Mailing Address: PO Box 6670, Havana
E-mail: ascubi@bnjm.cu
Web Site: www.bnjm.cu/ascubi
Key Personnel
President: Margarita Bellas Vilarino *Tel:* (07) 881-7446
Vice President: Marta Wong Curbelo
  E-mail: mwong1987@yahoo.es; Felicia Perez Moya *E-mail:* bibliotecap@hero.cult.cu; Miguel Viciedo Valdes *E-mail:* mviciedo@bpvillena.ohc.cu
Secretary: Sara Moreno Rodriguez *Tel:* (07) 881-6584

Curacao

Curacao Public Library Foundation
Abraham M Chumaceiro Blvd 17, Willemstad
Tel: (09) 434 52 00 *Fax:* (09) 465 62 47
E-mail: publiclibrary@onenet.an
Web Site: www.curacaopubliclibrary.an
Key Personnel
Chairman: Mr Shirk-Tong Chan
Secretary: Mrs M Rojer
Treasurer: Mrs D Pimentel

Board: Mrs D Larmonie-Beaumont; Mr J Lopez Ramirez; Mrs A Provence-Koek; Mrs G Rosaria-Coffi
Founded: 1922

Czech Republic

SKIP, see Svaz knihovniku a informacnich pracovniku Ceske republiky (SKIP)

Svaz knihovniku a informacnich pracovniku Ceske republiky (SKIP) (Association of Library & Information Professionals of the Czech Republic)
National Library of the Czech Republic, Klementinum 190, 110 00 Prague 1
Tel: 221 663 379 *Fax:* 221 663 175
E-mail: skip@nkp.cz
Web Site: www.skipcr.cz
Key Personnel
Chairperson: Vit Richter *Tel:* 221 663 338
  E-mail: vit.richter@nkp.cz
Honorary President: Jarmila Burgetova *Tel:* 233 335 030 *E-mail:* jarmila.burgetova@seznam.cz
Secretary: Zlata Houskova *Tel:* 221 663 330
  E-mail: zlata.houskova@nkp.cz
Founded: 1968
Membership(s): EBLIDA; International Federation of Library Associations & Institutions (IFLA).
Publication(s): *Bulletin SKIP* (quarterly)

Denmark

Arkivforeningen (Archive Association)
c/o Rigsarkivet, Rigsdagsgarden 9, 1218 Copenhagen K
Web Site: www.arkivforeningen.dk
Key Personnel
Chairman: Lars Schreiber Pedersen *Tel:* 38 21 21 53 *E-mail:* lape02@frederiksberg.dk
Secretary: Birgitte Vedel-Troelsen
Treasurer: Michael Boel Winther *E-mail:* michael.boel.winther@egekom.dk

Danmarks Biblioteksforening (Danish Library Association)
Vartov, Farvergade 27D, 2 sal, 1463 Copenhagen K
Tel: 3325 0935 *Fax:* 3325 7900
E-mail: db@db.dk
Web Site: www.db.dk
Key Personnel
Chairman: Vagn Ytte Larsen *Tel:* 2178 9383
  E-mail: vagn@ytte.dk
Vice President: Kirsten Boelt *Tel:* 9931 4425
  E-mail: kbt-kulture@aalborg.dk; Hanne Pigonska *Tel:* 4083 7358 *E-mail:* hapi@odsherred.dk
Publication(s): *Biblioteksvejviseren* (Library Directory); *Danmarks Biblioteker* (member's magazine)

Danmarks Forskningsbiblioteksforening (Danish Research Library Association)
Statsbiblioteket, Tangen 2, 8200 Aarhus N
Tel: 89 46 22 07; 4220 2177 (cell)
E-mail: df@statsbiblioteket.dk
Web Site: www.dfdf.dk
Key Personnel
President: Michael Cotta-Schonberg
  E-mail: mcs@kb.dk
Deputy Chair: Eli Greve *E-mail:* eligr@bib.sdu.dk
Secretary: Hanne Dahl

Treasurer: Gert Poulsen *E-mail:* gp.lib@cbs.dk
Founded: 1978
Membership(s): Biblioteksparaplyen; European Bureau of Library, Information & Documentation Associations; Freedom of Access to Information & Freedom of Expression; International Federation of Library Associations & Institutions; Lique des Bibliotheques Europeennes de Recherche; Nordiske Forskningsbiblioteksforeningers Netvaerk.
Publication(s): *REVY* (6 times/yr, journal, print & online)

Dansk Musikbiblioteks Forening (DMBF) (Danish Music Library Association)
c/o Koge Library, Kirkestr 18, 4600 Koge
Tel: 56672800
E-mail: sekretariat@dmbf.nu
Web Site: www.dmbf.nu
Key Personnel
Chairman: Emilie Wieth-Knudsen *Tel:* 45973700
  E-mail: emwk@ltk.dk
Vice President: Ole Bisbjerg *Tel:* 72131480
  E-mail: obi@billund.dk
Secretary: Karin Tofte-Hansen *Tel:* 56672887
  E-mail: karin.tofte-hansen@koege.dk
Treasurer: Helene Olsen *Tel:* 82325594
  E-mail: heleno@kff.kk.dk
Membership(s): Association of Danish Music Libraries (Danish section of AIBM/IAML).
Publication(s): *MusikBIB* (Journal for Music Libraries, triannually, text in Danish)

DMBF, see Dansk Musikbiblioteks Forening (DMBF)

Kommunernes Forening for Paedagogiske Laeringscentre (KFPLC)
Farvergade 27 D, 2 sal, 1463 Copenhagen K
Tel: 33 11 13 91
E-mail: kfplc@kfplc.dk
Web Site: www.kfplc.dk
Key Personnel
President: Liselotte Hillestrom *Tel:* 30 38 32 37
  E-mail: liselotte.hillestroem@hedensted.dk
Vice President: Michael Nohr *Tel:* 41 71 95 20
  E-mail: mino@viborg.dk
Publication(s): *Arbog, Antologi om paedagogiske laeringscentre* (annually, book); *Born og Boger* (Children & Books, 8 times/yr, periodical)

Egypt

MELA, see Middle East Librarians Association (MELA)

Middle East Librarians Association (MELA)
Library of Congress, US Embassy, 8 Kamal al-Din Salah St, Garden City, Cairo
Web Site: www.mela.us
Key Personnel
President: David G Hirsch *Tel:* 310-825-2930
  Fax: 310-825-6795 *E-mail:* president@mela.us
Vice President: Christof Galli *E-mail:* vice-president@mela.us
Secretary-Treasurer: William Kopycki
  E-mail: secretary@mela.us
Editor: Marlis J Saleh *Tel:* 773-702-8425
  Fax: 773-753-0569 *E-mail:* editor@mela.us
Publication(s): *MELA Notes* (journal)

Finland

Bibliothecarii Medicinae Fenniae ry (BMF)
(Finnish Medical Librarians' Association)
Ita-Suomen yliopiston kirjasto, PL 1777, 70211
Kuopio
Tel: (04) 355 3427
Web Site: www.bmf.fi
Key Personnel
Chairman: Tuulevi Ovaska *E-mail:* tuulevi.
ovaska@kuh.fi
Vice Chairman: Minna Liikala *E-mail:* minna.
liikala@thl.fi
Founded: 1980
Membership(s): European Association for Health
Information & Libraries (EAHIL); International
Federation of Library Associations & Institu-
tions (IFLA); Nordic Association for Medical
& Health Information (NAMHI).

BMF, see Bibliothecarii Medicinae Fenniae ry
(BMF)

STKS, see Suomen Tieteellinen Kirjastoseura ry
(STKS)

Suomen Kirjastoseura (Finnish Library
Association)
Runeberginkatu 15 A 26, 00100 Helsinki
Tel: (044) 522 2941
E-mail: info@fla.fi
Web Site: www.fla.fi
Key Personnel
Executive Dir: Sinikka Sipila *Tel:* (040) 659 363
(cell) *E-mail:* sinikka.sipila@fla.fi
Founded: 1910
Publication(s): *Kirjastolehti* (6 times/yr, journal)

Suomen Tieteellinen Kirjastoseura ry (STKS)
(Finnish Research Library Association)
PL 217, Kirkkokatu 6 (Tieteiden talo), 00171
Helsinki
Web Site: www.stks.fi
Key Personnel
Chairperson: Kimmo Tuominen *Tel:* (050) 364
4908 *E-mail:* kimmo.tuominen@jyu.fi
Secretary: Iiris Karppinen *Tel:* (09) 191 221 38
E-mail: iiris.karppinen@helsinki.fi
Founded: 1929
Publication(s): *Guide to Research Libraries &
Information Services in Finland*; *Signum* (6
times/yr, magazine, text in Finnish)

France

AAF, see Association des Archivistes Francais

ABCF, see Association des Bibliotheques
Chretiennes France (ABCF)

ADBS, see L'association des professionnels de
l'information et de la documentation (ADBS)

ADEBD, see Association des Diplomes de
l'Ecole de Bibliothecaires Documentalistes

Association des Archivistes Francais
(Association of French Archivists)
8, rue Jean-Marie Jego, 75013 Paris
Tel: 01 46 06 39 44 *Fax:* 01 46 06 39 52
E-mail: secretariat@archivistes.org
Web Site: www.archivistes.org
Key Personnel
President: Xavier de la Selle

Vice President: Laurent Ducol; Isabelle Vernus
Secretary: Jean-Philippe Legois
Assistant Secretary: Marie-Edith Enderle-Naud
Treasurer: Christian Perrot
Founded: 1904
Publication(s): *La Gazette des Archives* (The
Gazette Archives)
Branch Office(s)
Centre de Formation, 9, rue Rodier, 75009 Paris

Association des Bibliothecaires de France
(Association of French Librarians)
31, rue de Chabrol, 75010 Paris
Tel: 01 55 33 10 30 *Fax:* 01 55 33 10 31
E-mail: abf@abf.asso.fr
Web Site: www.abf.asso.fr
Key Personnel
President: Pascal Wagner *E-mail:* p.wagner.34@
gmail.com
Vice President: Dominique Lahary
E-mail: domlhy@gmail.com; Valerie Moreau-
Versavel *E-mail:* valerie.moreauversavel@
agorame.fr
Secretary General: Maite Vanmarque *E-mail:* m.
vanmarque@gmail.com
Treasurer: Martine Itier-Coeur *E-mail:* m.itier-
coeur@gmail.com
Founded: 1906
Publication(s): *Bulletin d'informations de l'ABF*

**Association des Bibliotheques Chretiennes
France (ABCF)** (Association of Christian
Libraries of France)
Bibliotheque de l'Abbaye Notre-Dame de Jouarre,
6 rue Montmorin, 77640 Jouarre
E-mail: contact@abcf.fr
Web Site: www.abcf.fr
Key Personnel
President: Michele Behr
Vice President: Odile Dupont
Secretary-Treasurer: Sr Emmanuel Saint-Amand
E-mail: bibliotheque@abbayejouarre.org
Publication(s): *Bulletin de liaison de l'ABCF*
(ISSN: 1773-2565)

**Association des Diplomes de l'Ecole de
Bibliothecaires Documentalistes** (Association
of Graduates of the School of Librarians &
Documentalists)
93, bd Rodin, 92130 Issy-les-Moulineaux
E-mail: adebd@ebd.fr
Web Site: www.adebd.fr
Key Personnel
President: Maud Roure
Secretary: Mikael Couraillon
Treasurer: Sophie Cauchy

**L'association des professionnels de
l'information et de la documentation (ADBS)**
(The Association of Information &
Documentation Professionals)
25 rue Claude Tillier, 75012 Paris
Tel: 01 43 72 25 25 *Fax:* 01 43 72 30 41
E-mail: adbs@adbs.fr
Web Site: www.adbs.fr
Key Personnel
Mng Dir: Flora Lagneau *Tel:* 01 43 72 99 57
Secretariat General, Communication: Carole
LeGrand *Tel:* 01 43 72 99 80
Publication(s): *Documentaliste - Sciences de
l'Information*

FADBEN, see Federation des enseignants
documentalistes de l'Education nationale

**Federation des enseignants documentalistes de
l'Education nationale** (Teachers Federation of
National Education Librarians)
25 rue Claude Tillier, 75012 Paris
E-mail: contact@fadben.asso.fr
Web Site: www.fadben.asso.fr

Key Personnel
President: Martine Ernoult *E-mail:* martine.
ernoult@laposte.net
Vice President: Thierry Adnot *E-mail:* adnotti@
club-internet.fr; Ivana Ballarini-Santonocito
E-mail: ivana.ballarini@ac-nantes.fr
Secretary: Fabienne Faucqueur *E-mail:* fabienne.
faucqueur@ac-limoges.fr; Maria Le Normand
E-mail: lenormandmaria@hotmail.fr
Treasurer: Olivia Boneu *E-mail:* olivia.boneu@
wanadoo.fr; Nicole Cardona *E-mail:* ncardona.
fadben@gmail.com
Publication(s): *Mediadoc* (triannually)

Germany

AGMB, see Arbeitsgemeinschaft fuer
medizinisches Bibliothekswesen (AGMB) eV

AjBD, see Arbeitsgemeinschaft fuer juristisches
Bibliotheks- und Dokumentationswesen

**Arbeitsgemeinschaft der Archive und
Bibliotheken in der evangelischen Kirche**
(Joint Association of Archives & Libraries in
the Evangelical Church)
Subsidiary of Evangelische Kirche in Deutschland
Altensteinstr 53, 14195 Berlin
Tel: (030) 83001-561 *Fax:* (030) 83001-122
E-mail: archiv@diakonie.de
Web Site: www.ekd.de/archive/agab.htm
Key Personnel
Chairman: Dr Michael Haeusler
Founded: 1936
Publication(s): *Aus Evangelischen Archiven,
Neue Folge der Allgemeinen Mitteilungen der
AABevk*

Arbeitsgemeinschaft der Regionalbibliotheken
(Joint Association of Regional Libraries)
c/o Deutscher Bibliotheksverband eV, Fritschestr
27-28 (2 Hof, Aufgang A, 1 Stock rechts),
10585 Berlin
Tel: (030) 644 98 99 10 *Fax:* (030) 644 98 99 29
E-mail: dbv@bibliotheksverband.de
Web Site: www.bibliotheksverband.
de/fachgruppen/arbeitsgruppen/
regionalbibliotheken.html
Key Personnel
Chairman: Dr Irmgard Siebert *Tel:* (0211) 8 11
20 30 *Fax:* (0211) 8 11 30 54 *E-mail:* siebert@
ub.uni-duesseldorf.de
Founded: 1983
German library federation.

**Arbeitsgemeinschaft der Spezialbibliotheken
eV (ASpB)** (Association of Special Libraries)
c/o Herder-Institute Bibliothek, Gisonenweg 5-7,
35037 Marburg
Tel: (06421) 184 151 *Fax:* (06421) 184 139
E-mail: geschaeftsstelle@aspb.de
Web Site: www.aspb.de
Key Personnel
Chairman: Henning Frankenberger *Tel:* (089)
38602-462 *Fax:* (089) 38602-490
E-mail: frankenberger@mpisoc.mpg.de
First Deputy Chairman: Dr Sonja Grund
Tel: (089) 001-144 *Fax:* (089) 001-400
E-mail: sonja.grund@wiko-berlin.de
Second Deputy Chairman & Treasurer: Yvonne
Brzoska *Tel:* (0241) 80-94453 *Fax:* (0241) 80-
92100 *E-mail:* brzoska@bth.rwth-aachen.de
Contact: Jadwiga Warmbrunn
Founded: 1946

Membership(s): International Federation of Library Associations & Institutions (IFLA).
Publication(s): *Bericht ueber die Tagung elektronischer* (biennially, newsletter, conference report)

Arbeitsgemeinschaft fuer juristisches Bibliotheks- und Dokumentationswesen (Joint Association for Law Libraries & Legal Documentation)
Ismaninger Str 109, 81675 Munich
Tel: (089) 9231 358 *Fax:* (089) 9231 201
Web Site: www.ajbd.de
Key Personnel
Chairman: Sabine Lieberknecht *Tel:* (0361) 2636-1701 *Fax:* (0361) 2636-2003 *E-mail:* sabine. lieberknecht@bundesarbeitsgericht.de
Deputy Chairman: Dr Hans-Peter Ziegler *E-mail:* hans-peter.ziegler@bfh.bund.de
Secretary: Gerda Graf *Tel:* (0331) 977-3571 *Fax:* (0331) 977-3816 *E-mail:* ggraf@rz.uni-potsdam.de
Treasurer: Annette Schlag *Tel:* (030) 2025-9715 *Fax:* (030) 2025-9660 *E-mail:* kassenwartin@ajbd.de
Publication(s): *Arbeitshefte* (irregularly); *Mitteilungen der Arbeitsgemeinschaft fuer juristisches Bibliotheks- und Dokumentationswesen* (triannually)

Arbeitsgemeinschaft fuer medizinisches Bibliothekswesen (AGMB) eV (Association for Medical Librarianship)
c/o Universitaetsbibliothek Kiel, Leibnizstr 9, 24118 Kiel
Tel: (0431) 880-5404 *Fax:* (0431) 880-1596
Web Site: www.agmb.de
Key Personnel
Chairman: Dr Eike Hentschel *E-mail:* hentschel@ub.uni-kiel.de
First Deputy Chairman: Dr Stefanus Schweizer *Tel:* (06131) 175-138 *Fax:* (06131) 173-412 *E-mail:* s.schweizer@ub.uni-mainz.de
Second Deputy Chairman: Alexander Messerschmid *Tel:* (089) 4562-2360 *Fax:* (089) 4562-2440 *E-mail:* alexander.messerschmid@iak-kmo.de
Secretary: Manuela Schulz *Tel:* (0621) 383-3711 *Fax:* (0621) 383-2006 *E-mail:* manuela. schulz@medma.uni-heidelberg.de
Treasurer: Christa Giese *Tel:* (0711) 278-2830 *Fax:* (0711) 278-2839 *E-mail:* c.giese@klinikum-stuttgart.de
Founded: 1970

ASpB, see Arbeitsgemeinschaft der Spezialbibliotheken eV (ASpB)

Berufsverband Information Bibliothek eV (Professional Association Information Library)
Gartenstr 18, 72764 Reutlingen
Tel: (07121) 3491-0 *Fax:* (07121) 300433
E-mail: mail@bib-info.de
Web Site: www.bib-info.de
Key Personnel
Chairman: Kirsten Marschall *Tel:* (040) 42640-140 *E-mail:* kirsten.marschall@buecherhallen. de
Founded: 2000
Publication(s): *Bub-Forum Bibliothek und Information* (Bub-Library & Information Forum, monthly)

BIB, see Berufsverband Information Bibliothek eV

Bibliothek & Information Deutschland (BID) eV
Fritschestr 27-28, 10585 Berlin
Tel: (030) 644 98 99-20 *Fax:* (030) 644 98 99-27
E-mail: bid@bideutschland.de

Web Site: www.bideutschland.de
Key Personnel
Dir: Dr Monika Brass
Formed by the joining of the German Association for Information Science & Practice (DGI) with the Federal Union of German Library Associations (BDB).
Publication(s): *Medien- und Informationskompetenz - immer mit Bibliotheken und Informationseinrichtungen!* (Media & Information Literacy - always with libraries & information facilities!, 2011); *Portale zu Vergangenheit und Zukunft-Bibliotheken in Deutschland* (Portals to the Past & Future-Libraries in Germany, 2017); *21 gute Gruende fuer gute Bibliotheken* (21 Good Reasons for Good Libraries, 2009)

BID, see Bibliothek & Information Deutschland (BID) eV

DBV, see Deutscher Bibliotheksverband eV (DBV)

DEG, see Deutsche Exlibris-Gesellschaft eV (DEG)

Deutsche Exlibris-Gesellschaft eV (DEG) (German Bookplate Society)
Bockmuehlstr 31, 41199 Moenchengladbach
Tel: (02166) 60 55 81 *Fax:* (02166) 25 59 42
E-mail: info@exlibris-blum.de
Web Site: www.exlibris-gesellschaft.de
Key Personnel
President: Klaus Thoms *Tel:* (028) 31-35 30 *E-mail:* kuh.thoms@web.de
Vice President: Heinz Decker *Tel:* (069) 47 34 16 *E-mail:* deckerheinz@aol.com
Mng Dir: Birgit Goebel-Stiegler *Tel:* (030) 20 67 19 90 *Fax:* (030) 20 67 19 91 *E-mail:* birgit. goebel@t-online.de
Treasurer: Christian Kraetz *Tel:* (02162) 6 77 49 *E-mail:* kraetz-viersen@t-online.de
Editor: Dr Henry Tauber *Tel:* (02352) 3378988 *E-mail:* henrytauber@hotmail.com
Founded: 1891
Membership(s): FISAE (Federation International des Societes Amateurs d Exlibris).
Publication(s): *DEG-Jahrbuch: Exlibriskunst und Grafik* (annually)

Deutsche Gesellschaft fuer Informationswissenschaft und Informationspraxis eV DGI (German Society for Information Science & Practice Association)
Windmuehlstr 3, 60329 Frankfurt am Main
Tel: (069) 430313 *Fax:* (069) 4909096
E-mail: mail@dgi-info.de
Web Site: www.dgd.de; www.dgi-info.de
Key Personnel
President: Dr Stefan Gradmann *E-mail:* gradmann@dgi-info.de
Vice President: Dr Luzian Weisel *E-mail:* weisel@dgi-info.de
Treasurer: Peter Genth
Publication(s): *nfd-Information Wissenschaft und Praxis* (documentation)

Deutscher Bibliotheksverband eV (DBV) (The German Library Association)
Fritschestr 27-28, 10585 Berlin
Tel: (030) 644 98 99 10 *Fax:* (030) 644 98 99 29
E-mail: dbv@bibliotheksverband.de
Web Site: www.bibliotheksverband.de
Key Personnel
Chairman: Monika Ziller *Tel:* (07131) 56 33 63 *Fax:* (07131) 56 29 50 *E-mail:* monika.ziller@stadt-heilbronn.de

Mng Dir: Barbara Schleihagen *Tel:* (030) 644 98 99-12 *E-mail:* schleihagen@bibliotheksverband. de
Publication(s): *Annual Report*; *D B V* (newsletter, online)

Deutscher Verband Evangelischer Buechereien eV (German Association of Protestant Libraries)
Buergerstr 2a, 37073 Goettingen
Tel: (0551) 500759-0 *Fax:* (0551) 500759-19
E-mail: info@eliport.de
Web Site: www.eliport.de
Key Personnel
Chairman: Bishop Jan Janssen
Mng Dir: Gabriele Kassenbrock *E-mail:* gabriele. kassenbrock@eliport.de
Publication(s): *Der Evangelische Buchberater* (quarterly); *Handwoerterbuch der evangelischen Buechereiarbeit 1980*

GBDL, see Gesellschaft fuer Bibliothekswesen und Dokumentation des Landbaues (GBDL)

Gesellschaft fuer Bibliothekswesen und Dokumentation des Landbaues (GBDL) (Society for Library & Documentation of Agriculture)
Affiliate of Arbeitsgemeinschaft der Spezialbibliotheken eV (ASpB)
Maximus-von-Imhof-Forum 3, 85354 Freising
Mailing Address: c/o TU Muenchen, Weihenstephan, 85350 Freising
Tel: (08161) 71-4029 *Fax:* (08161) 71-5309
Web Site: hal.wzw.tum.de/gbdl
Key Personnel
President: Prof W Laux, PhD
Secretary: Dr B Schlindwein *E-mail:* schlind@weihenstephan.de
Publication(s): *Mitteilungen der Gesellschaft fuer Bibliothekswesen und Dokumentation des Landbaues*

Informationszentrum fuer Informationswissenschaft und -praxis (IZ)
Fachhochschule Potsdam, Pappelalle 8-9, 14469 Potsdam
Mailing Address: Postfach 60 06 08, 14406 Potsdam
Tel: (0331) 580-2210; (0331) 580-2230 *Fax:* (0331) 580-2229
E-mail: iz@fh-potsdam.de
Web Site: iz.fh-potsdam.de
Key Personnel
Head: Karen Falke *E-mail:* falke@fh-potsdam.de
Documentation & Information Society.

IZ, see Informationszentrum fuer Informationswissenschaft und -praxis (IZ)

NABD, see Normenausschuss Bibliotheks- und Dokumentationswesen (NABD)

Normenausschuss Bibliotheks- und Dokumentationswesen (NABD) (Information & Documentation Standards Committee)
DIN Deutsches Institut fuer Normung eV, Burggrafenstr 6, 10787 Berlin
Tel: (030) 2601-0 *Fax:* (030) 2601-1231
E-mail: presse@din.de
Web Site: www.nabd.din.de
Key Personnel
Dir: Torsten Bahke
Editor: Sibylle Gabler
Publication(s): *Annual Report*; *NABD Brochure*

VdA, see VdA - Verband deutscher Archivarinnen und Archivare eV

VdA - Verband deutscher Archivarinnen und Archivare eV (Association of German Archivists)
Woerthstra 3, 36037 Fulda
Tel: (0661) 29109-72 *Fax:* (0661) 29109-74
E-mail: info@vda.archiv.net
Web Site: www.vda.archiv.net
Key Personnel
Chairman: Dr Michael Diefenbacher
E-mail: michael.diefenbacher@stadt.nuernberg.de
Vice Chairman: Dr Clemens Rehm
E-mail: clemens.rehm@la-bw.de; Katharina Tiemann *E-mail:* katharina.tiemann@lwl.org
Mng Dir: Thilo Bauer *E-mail:* bauer@vda.archiv.net
Founded: 1946

VDB, see Verein Deutscher Bibliothekare eV (VDB)

Verein Deutscher Bibliothekare eV (VDB) (Association of German Librarians)
Universitaetsbibliothek Munchen, Geschwister-scholl-Platz 1, 80539 Munich
Tel: (089) 2180-2420
E-mail: vdb@ub.uni-muenchen.de
Web Site: www.vdb-online.org
Key Personnel
Chairman: Dr Klaus-Rainer Brintzinger *Tel:* (089) 2180-2420
Vice Chairman: Dr Ewald Brahms
Tel: (05121) 883-251 *Fax:* (05121) 883-266
E-mail: brahms@uni-hildesheim.de
Deputy Chairman: Dr Wilfried Suehl-Stronhmenger *Tel:* (0761) 203-3924
Fax: (0761) 203-3987 *E-mail:* suehl@ub.uni-freiburg.de
Secretary: Dr Anke Quast *Tel:* (030) 314-76115
E-mail: anke.quast@tu-berlin.de
Treasurer: Anke Berghaus-Sprengel *Tel:* (030) 2093-99290 *Fax:* (030) 2093-99311
E-mail: anke.berghaus-sprengel@ub.hu-berlin.de
Founded: 1900
Publication(s): *Jahrbuch der Deutschen Bibliotheken* (Yearbook of German Libraries, biennially); *VDB-Mitteilungen* (VDB Messages, biannually); *Zeitschrift fuer Bibliothekswesen und Bibliographie* (Journal of Librarianship & Bibliography)

Wuerttembergische Bibliotheksgesellschaft
Wuerttembergische Landesbibliothek, Konrad-Adenauer-Str 8, 70173 Stuttgart
Mailing Address: Postfach 10 54 41, 70047 Stuttgart
Tel: (0711) 212-4428 *Fax:* (0711) 212-4422
E-mail: wbg@wlb-stuttgart.de
Web Site: www.wlb-stuttgart.de
Key Personnel
Contact: Christine Demmler
Society of Friends of the Wuerttemberg State Library.

Ghana

Ghana Library Association
c/o INSTI, PO Box GP 4105, Accra
Tel: (0244) 174930; (0262) 464073 (cell)
E-mail: info@gla-net.org
Web Site: gla-net.org
Key Personnel
President: Valentina J A Bannerman
E-mail: valnin@yahoo.com
Founded: 1962

Membership(s): International Federation of Library Associations & Institutions (IFLA).
Publication(s): *Ghana Library Journal* (irregularly)

Guinea

Direction Nationale de Recherche Scientifique et Technique (National Research & Documentation Institute)
Bibliotheque Nationale, BP 561, Conakry
Tel: 61 34 79 72
Key Personnel
Contact: Mr Tonguino Tamba Nestor
E-mail: tambanestor@yahoo.fr
Founded: 1958

DNRST, see Direction Nationale de Recherche Scientifique et Technique

Guyana

GLA, see Guyana Library Association (GLA)

Guyana Library Association (GLA)
c/o National Library, PO Box 10240, Georgetown
Tel: 222486 *Fax:* 223596
E-mail: londonh@uog.ed.gy
Key Personnel
President: Wenda R Stephenson
Vice President: Gwyneth Browman
Secretary: Althea John
Treasurer: Indrowty Dianand

Hong Kong

Hong Kong Library Association
PO Box 10095, General Post Office, Hong Kong
E-mail: hkla@hkla.org
Web Site: www.hkla.org
Key Personnel
President: Peter Sidroko *Tel:* 2859-2200
Fax: 2858-9420 *E-mail:* peters@hkucc.hku.hk
Vice President: Mary Cheng *Tel:* 2921-1244
Fax: 2877-2641 *E-mail:* mmlcheng@lscd.gov.hk
Honorary Secretary: Thomas Hung *Tel:* 2859-7001 *Fax:* 2546-5340 *E-mail:* wphung@hku.hk
Honorary Treasurer: Mandy Ip *Tel:* 3943-7317
Fax: 2603-5467 *E-mail:* mandyip@lib.cuhk.edu.hk
Founded: 1958
Publication(s): *Directory of Medical, Health & Welfare Libraries in Hong Kong*; *Hong Kong Library Association Newsletter*; *Hong Kong Library Association Yearbook*; *Journal of the Hong Kong Library Association* (irregularly)

Hungary

Magyar Konyvtarosok Egyesulete (Association of Hungarian Librarians)
H-1054, Hold u 6, Budapest 1827
Tel: (01) 311-8634 *Fax:* (01) 311-8634

E-mail: mke@oszk.hu
Web Site: www.mke.oszk.hu
Key Personnel
President: Bakos Klara *E-mail:* bakos.klara@zmne.hu
Dir: Agnes Hajdu-Barat *E-mail:* hajdu@jgypk.u-szeged.hu; Gabor Kiss *E-mail:* kissg@dfmk.hu
Secretary General: Miklos Feher
E-mail: mfeher@oszk.hu
Founded: 1935

MKE, see Magyar Konyvtarosok Egyesulete

Iceland

Upplysing - Felag bokasafns- og upplysingafraeda (Information - The Icelandic Library & Information Science Association)
Postholf 8865, 128 Reykjavik
Tel: 864-6220
E-mail: upplysing@upplysing.is
Web Site: www.upplysing.is
Key Personnel
Vice President: Helga Halldorsdottir
Secretary: Ingibjorg Osp Ottarsdottir
Treasurer: Sigrun Guonadottir *E-mail:* sigrun3@kopavogur.is

India

Documentation Research & Training Centre (DRTC)
Indian Statistical Institute, 8th Mile Mysore Rd, RV College PO, Bangalore, Karnataka 560 059
Tel: (080) 2848 3002; (080) 2848 3003; (080) 2848 3004; (080) 2848 3005; (080) 2848 3006
Fax: (080) 2848 4265
E-mail: drtc@isibang.ac.in
Web Site: drtc.isibang.ac.in
Key Personnel
Head of Dept: Dr A R D Prasad *E-mail:* ard@drtc.isibang.ac.in
Founded: 1962
Publication(s): *Annual Seminar, DRTC* (annually); *Refresher Seminar, DRTC* (annually)

DRTC, see Documentation Research & Training Centre (DRTC)

IASLIC, see Indian Association of Special Libraries & Information Centres (IASLIC)

ILA, see Indian Library Association

Indian Association of Special Libraries & Information Centres (IASLIC)
P-291, CIT Scheme No 6M, Kankurgachi, Kolkata 700 054
Tel: (033) 2362 9651
E-mail: iaslic@vsnl.net
Web Site: www.iaslic1955.org.in
Key Personnel
President: Dr Jatindranath Satpathi
E-mail: satpathijn@rediffmail.com
Vice President (Zone 6): Prof Arjun Dasgupta
E-mail: arjundasguptakol@gmail.com
General Secretary: Sajal Kanti Goswami
E-mail: sajalgoswami_123@yahoo.co.in
Associate Editor: Prof Pijushkanti Panigrahi
E-mail: panigrahipk@yahoo.com
Publication(s): *Directory of Special & Research Libraries in India* (monthly, newsletter); *Iaslic* (bulletin); *Indian Library Science Abstracts* (quarterly)

Indian Library Association
A/40-41, Flat No 201, Ansal Bldg, Dr Mukherjee
Nagar, Delhi 110 009
Tel: (011) 27651743
E-mail: ila@ilaindia.net
Web Site: ilaindia.net
Key Personnel
President: Shabahat Husain
Senior Vice President: Dr O N Chaubey
General Secretary: Dr Pardeep Rai
Tel: 9899359373 (cell) *E-mail:* raipardeep@
gmail.com
Treasurer: Dr Praveen Kumar Choudhary
Publication(s): *ILA Newsletter; Journal of Indian
Library Association (JILA)* (quarterly)

Indonesia

**Congress of Southeast Asian Librarians
(CONSAL)**
Jl Salemba Raya 28A, Jakarta 10430
Tel: (021) 3103554
Web Site: www.consal.org
Key Personnel
Secretariat: Aristianto Hakim
Founded: 1970

CONSAL, see Congress of Southeast Asian
Librarians (CONSAL)

Ikatan Pustakawan Indonesia (Indonesian
Library Association)
Jl Merdeka Selatan No 11, Jakarta, Pusat 10110
Tel: (021) 3855729 *Fax:* (021) 3855729
Web Site: ipi.pnri.go.id
Founded: 1973
Publication(s): *Majalah Ikatan Pustakawan In-
donesia*

IPI, see Ikatan Pustakawan Indonesia

Ireland

BIALL, see British & Irish Association of Law
Librarians (BIALL)

**British & Irish Association of Law Librarians
(BIALL)**
c/o Arthur Cox, Earlsfort Centre, Earlsfort Ter-
race, Dublin D02 CK83
E-mail: contact@biall.org.uk
Web Site: www.biall.org.uk
Key Personnel
President: Karen Palmer *Tel:* (020) 7825 4601
E-mail: president@biall.org.uk
President-Elect: Sandra Smythe *Tel:* (020) 7440
7462 *E-mail:* sandra.smythe@mishcon.com
Honorary Secretary: Lillian Stevenson
E-mail: LIS@aber.ac.uk
Honorary Treasurer: Julie Ferris *Tel:* (020) 3088
2998 *E-mail:* julie.ferris@allenovery.com
Founded: 1969
Publication(s): *Academic Law Library Survey;
BIALL Law Library Salary Survey; BIALL
Newsletter* (6 times/yr); *Directory of British
& Irish Law Libraries; Handbook of Legal In-
formation Management; History of the British
& Irish Association of Law Librarians 1969-
1999; Legal Research Training Pack; Sources
of Biographical Information on Past Lawyers*

Central Catholic Library Association Inc
74 Merrion Sq, Dublin D02 HH99

Tel: (01) 676 1264 *Fax:* (01) 678 7618
E-mail: catholiclibrary@imagine.ie
Web Site: www.catholiclibrary.ie
Key Personnel
Librarian: Teresa Whitington

LAI, see The Library Association of Ireland
(LAI)

The Library Association of Ireland (LAI)
(Cumann Leabharlann na h-Eireann)
c/o 138-144 Pearse St, Dublin 2
Web Site: www.libraryassociation.ie
Key Personnel
President: Philip Cohen *E-mail:* president@
libraryassociation.ie
Vice President: Mary Stuart; Bernie Fennell
Honorary Secretary: Betty Codd
E-mail: honsecretary@libraryassociation.ie
Honorary Treasurer: Marian Higgins
E-mail: hontreasurer@libraryassociation.ie
Founded: 1928
Membership(s): EBLIDA; International Feder-
ation of Library Associations & Institutions
(IFLA).
Publication(s): *An Leabharlann* (The Irish Li-
brary, journal, published jointly with CILIP-
Northern Ireland); *The Library Association of
Ireland Annual Reports*

National Library of Ireland Society
Kildare St, Dublin 2
Tel: (01) 6030284
E-mail: nlisociety@nli.ie
Web Site: www.nli.ie/en/national-library-society.
aspx
Key Personnel
Chairman: Fr J Anthony Gaughan
Founded: 1969

Israel

ASMI, see Israel Society for Libraries &
Information Centers (ASMI)

**Israel Society for Libraries & Information
Centers (ASMI)**
Blum 8, 44253 Kfar Saba
Tel: 0772151800 *Fax:* 077434509
E-mail: agudatasmi@gmail.com
Web Site: www.asmi.org.il
Key Personnel
Chairman: Dr Shachaf Hagafni *Tel:* (04) 8590125
Fax: (04) 8590134
Founded: 1966
Membership(s): International Federation of Li-
brary Associations & Institutions (IFLA).
Publication(s): *Information & Librarianship* (ir-
regularly, 2 issues per volume)

Italy

AIB, see Associazione Italiana Biblioteche

Associazione Italiana Biblioteche (Italian
Library Association)
c/o Biblioteca Nazionale Centrale, Viale Castro
Pretorio 105, 00185 Rome RM
Mailing Address: CP 2461, 00185 Rome AD
Tel: (06) 4463532 *Fax:* (06) 4441139
E-mail: aib@legalmail.it
Web Site: www.aib.it

Key Personnel
Chief Executive Officer: Palmira Maria Barbini
E-mail: barbini@aib.it
Secretary General: Joan Frigimelica
E-mail: segr@aib.it
Publication(s): *AIB Notizie* (monthly); *Bollettino
AIB* (quarterly); *Rapporti AIB* (irregularly)

ICCU, see Istituto Centrale per il Catalogo Unico
delle Biblioteche Italiane e per le Informazioni
Bibliografiche

**Istituto Centrale per il Catalogo Unico delle
Biblioteche Italiane e per le Informazioni
Bibliografiche** (Central Institute for the Union
Catalog of Italian Libraries & Bibliographic
Information)
Viale Castro Pretorio, 105, 00185 Rome RM
Tel: (06) 49210425; (06) 4989424 *Fax:* (06) 4959
302
E-mail: ic-cu@beniculturali.it
Web Site: www.iccu.sbn.it
Key Personnel
Dir: Simonetta Butto *E-mail:* simonetta.butto@
beniculturali.it
Publication(s): *Bibliografia di Inventari e Cata-
loghi a Stampa dei Manoscritti; Bibliografia
Italiana; Catalogo Collettivo di Periodici -
Archivio ISRDS/CNR; I Emilia Romagna - Il
Friuli Venezia Giulia; Le Edizioni Italiane del
XVI sec, Guida alla Catalogazione per Au-
tori delle Stampe, Inventari Non a Stampa
di Manoscritti; Periodici Italiani 1886-1981;
Quaderno RICA; Regole Italiane di Cata-
logazione per Autori; Soggettario per i Cata-
loghi delle Biblioteche Italiane*

Il Mosaico Societa Cooperativa Sociale ONLUS
Via Lume 1905, 40027 Bubano-Mordano BO
Tel: (0542) 56512 *Fax:* (0542) 56512
E-mail: coopmosaico@yahoo.com
Web Site: www.ilmosaicocooperativa.com
Assists in the planning, organization & manage-
ment of libraries & their services to the user.
Promotion, enhancement & organization of cul-
tural projects.

Jamaica

COMLA, see The Commonwealth Library
Association (COMLA)

**The Commonwealth Library Association
(COMLA)**
PO Box 144, Mona, Kingston 7
Tel: (876) 927-0083 *Fax:* (876) 927-1926
E-mail: nkpodo@uwimona.edu.jm
Web Site: www.thecommonwealth.org
Key Personnel
Secretary General: Kamalesh Sharma
E-mail: secretary-general@commonwealth.int
Founded: 1972
Publication(s): *COMLA Bulletin* (quarterly,
newsletter); *The Commonwealth Yearbook* (an-
nually)

LIAJA, see Library & Information Association of
Jamaica (LIAJA)

**Library & Information Association of Jamaica
(LIAJA)**
PO Box 125, Kingston 5
Tel: (876) 927-1614 *Fax:* (876) 927-1614
E-mail: liajapresident@yahoo.com
Web Site: www.liaja.org.jm
Key Personnel
President: Viviene Kerr-Williams
E-mail: vskwilliams@gmail.com

First Vice President: Jollette Russell
E-mail: jrussell@gcfc.edu.jm
Second Vice President: Maureen Thompson
E-mail: maureen.thompson@jls.gov.jm
Honorary Treasurer: Nicholas Graham
E-mail: nicholas.graham@nlj.gov.jm
Honorary Secretary: Marsha-Gay Robinson
E-mail: pattigay16@gmail.com
Founded: 1949
Publication(s): *LIAJA Annual Report*; *LIAJA Bulletin* (1950); *LIAJA News*; *LIAJA Newslink*

Japan

Gakujutsu Bunken Fukyu-Kai (Association for Science Documents Information)
c/o Tokyo Institute of Technology, 2-12-1 Oh-Okayama, Meguro-ku, Tokyo 152-8550
Tel: (03) 3726-3118 *Fax:* (03) 3726-3118
E-mail: a-sdi@mx10.ttcn.ne.jp;
gakujyutubunken@mvd.biglobe.ne.jp

INFOSTA, see Joho Kagaku Gijutsu Kyokai

Joho Kagaku Gijutsu Kyokai (Information Science & Technology Association (INFOSTA))
Sasaki Bldg, 2-5-7 Koishikawa, Bunkyo-ku, Tokyo 112-0002
Tel: (03) 3813-3791 *Fax:* (03) 3813-3793
E-mail: infosta@infosta.or.jp
Web Site: www.infosta.or.jp
Key Personnel
President: Natsuo Onodera
Founded: 1950
Publication(s): *The Journal of Information Science & Technology Association* (Johono Kagaku to Gijutsu, monthly, journal)

Joho Shori Gakkai (Information Processing Society of Japan)
Kagaku-kaikan (Chemistry Hall) 4F, 1-5 Kanda-Surugadai, Chiyoda-ku, Tokyo 101-0062
Tel: (03) 3518-8374 *Fax:* (03) 3518-8375
Web Site: www.ipsj.or.jp
Key Personnel
President: Kazuo Furukawa
Vice President: Prof Hideyuki Nakashima
Founded: 1960
Publication(s): *IPSJ Transactions* (monthly);
Joho-shori (monthly, journal)

JPLA, see Nippon Yakugaku Toshokan Kyogikai

JSLIS, see Nihon Toshokan Joho Gakkai

Mita Toshokan Joho Gakkai (Mita Society for Library & Information Science)
c/o School of Library & Information Science Literature, Keio University, 2-15-45 Mita, Minato-ku, Tokyo 108-8345
Tel: (03) 3453-4511
E-mail: m-slis@slis.keio.ac.jp
Web Site: www.mslis.jp
Key Personnel
Chairman: Shunsaku Tamura
Secretary: Kishida Kazuaki; Kurata Keiko
Publication(s): *Library & Information Science* (biannually, journal)

Nihon Igaku Toshokan Kyokai (Japan Medical Library Association)
Fuzambo Bldg 6F, 1-3 Kanda-jinbo-cho, Chiyoda-ku, Tokyo 101-0051
Tel: (03) 5577-4509 *Fax:* (03) 5577-4510
E-mail: jmlajimu@sirius.ocn.ne.jp

Web Site: plaza.umin.ac.jp/~jmla; jmla.umin.jp/
Key Personnel
Secretary General: Hiroshi Kimura
Founded: 1927
Publication(s): *Igaku Toshokan* (quarterly, journal)

Nihon Toshokan Joho Gakkai (Japan Society of Library & Information Science (JSLIS))
Dept of Education, College of Education, Psychology & Human Studies, Aoyama Gakuin University, 4-4-25 Shibuya, Shibuya-ku, Tokyo 150-8366
E-mail: office@jslis.jp
Web Site: www.jslis.jp
Key Personnel
President: Akira Nemoto
Vice President: Masaru Itoga
Founded: 1953
Publication(s): *Nihon Toshokan Joho Gakkai shi* (Annals of Japan Society of Library Science, quarterly)

Nihon Toshokan Kyokai (Japan Library Association)
1-11-14, Shinkawa, Chuo-ku, Tokyo 104-0033
Tel: (03) 3523-0811 *Fax:* (03) 3523-0841
E-mail: info@jla.or.jp
Web Site: www.jla.or.jp
Key Personnel
President: Shiomi Noboru
Founded: 1892
Membership(s): International Federation of Library Associations & Institutions (IFLA).
Publication(s): *BSH Kihon Kenmei Hyomokuhyo* (Basic Subject Headings (BSH)); *Gendai No Toshokan* (Libraries Today, quarterly); *NCR Nihon Mokuroku Kisoku* (Nippon Cataloging Rules (NCR)); *NDC Nihon Jusshin Bunruiho* (Nippon Decimal Classification (NDC)); *Nihon no Sankotosho* (Guide to Japanese Reference Books); *Nihon no Toshokan* (Statistics on Libraries in Japan, annually); *Sentei Tosho Somokuroku* (Standard Catalog of Selected Books, annually, catalog); *Toshokan Handobukku* (Librarian's Handbook); *Toshokan Nenkan* (Library Yearbook, annually); *Toshokan Yogoshu* (Librarian's Glossary); *Toshokan Zasshi* (Library Journal, monthly)

Nippon Yakugaku Toshokan Kyogikai (Japan Pharmaceutical Library Association (JPLA))
Mainichi Academic Forum Inc, PalaceSide Bldg 9F, 1-1-1, Hitotsubashi, Chiyoda-ku, Tokyo 100-0003
Tel: (03) 6267-4550 *Fax:* (03) 6267-4555
E-mail: info@yakutokyo.jp
Web Site: www.yakutokyo.jp
Key Personnel
Chairman: Hisashi Nagai
Founded: 1955
Contribute to pharmaceutical education & research through the promotion of pharmaceutical library projects.
Publication(s): *Yakugaku Toshokan* (Pharmaceutical Library Bulletin, quarterly)

Senmon Toshokan Kyogikai (SENTOKYO) (Japan Special Libraries Association)
c/o Japan Library Association, Bldg F6, 1-11-14 Shinkawa, Chuo-ku, Tokyo 104-0033
Tel: (03) 3537-8335 *Fax:* (03) 3537-8336
E-mail: jsla@jsla.or.jp
Web Site: www.jsla.or.jp
Founded: 1952
Publication(s): *Hakusho: Nihon no Senmon Toshokan*; *Senmon Joho Kikan Soran* (triennially, directory); *Toshokan Senmon* (bimonthly, periodical)

SENTOKYO, see Senmon Toshokan Kyogikai (SENTOKYO)

Jordan

Jordan Library & Information Association
PO Box 6289, Amman 11118
Tel: (06) 4629412
E-mail: info@jlia.org
Web Site: www.jlia.org
Key Personnel
President: Omar Mohammad Jaradat
Vice President: Nidal Al-Ahmad
Secretary: Abdul Majid Abu Jumaa
Treasurer: Ahmed Munir Al Akhras
Founded: 1963
Publication(s): *Anglo-American Cataloguing Rules* (1983, 2nd ed, in Arabic); *Directory of Jordanian Periodicals* (1982); *Directory of Libraries & Librarians in Jordan* (1984); *Directory of Libraries in Jordan 1976*; *Introduction to Librarianship & Information Science* (1982, in Arabic); *Jordanian National Bibliography* (annually); *The Palestinian Bibliography: A List of Books Published by the Arabs in Palestine 1948-1980*; *Palestinian-Jordanian Bibliography 1900-1970 & 1971-1975*; *Rissalat al-Maktaba* (The Message of the Library, quarterly); *Technical Processing of Information* (in Arabic)

Kenya

Kenya Association of Library & Information Professionals (KLA) (Kuuliza si ujinga)
PO Box 46031, Nairobi 00100
Tel: (020) 733 732 799
Web Site: www.klas.or.ke
Key Personnel
Chair: Rosemary Gitachu *E-mail:* gitachur@yahoo.com
Founded: 1973
Publication(s): *Kelias News* (bimonthly); *Maktaba Journal* (biannually, text in English & Swahili)

KLA, see Kenya Association of Library & Information Professionals (KLA)

Latvia

Latvian Librarians Association (Latvijas Bibliotekaru Biedriba (LBB))
Terbatas iela 75, Riga LV-1001
Tel: 67312791 *Fax:* 67312791
E-mail: lbb@lnb.lv
Web Site: www.lnb.lv
Founded: 1923
Publication(s): *Es Daruta* (quarterly, journal)

LBB, see Latvian Librarians Association

LLA, see Latvian Librarians Association

Lebanon

Lebanese Library Association (LLA) (L'association des Bibliotheques Libanaises)
PO Box 13-5053, Beirut 1102 2801

Tel: (01) 786456; (01) 78646 (ext 1210)
E-mail: kjaroudy@lau.edu.lb
Web Site: www.llaweb.org
Key Personnel
President: Mr Fawz Abdallah *E-mail:* fabdalla@
lau.edu.lb
Founded: 1960

LLA, see Lebanese Library Association (LLA)

Lesotho

Lesotho Library Association (LLA)
Private Bag A26, Maseru 100
Tel: 213420 *Fax:* 340000
E-mail: s.mohai@nul.ls
Key Personnel
Contact: Makemang Ntsasa
Founded: 1978
Publication(s): *Lesotho Library Association
Newsletter* (annually)

LLA, see Lesotho Library Association (LLA)

Lithuania

LBD, see Lietuvos Bibliotekininku Draugija
(LBD)

Lietuvos Bibliotekininku Draugija (LBD)
(Lithuanian Librarians Association)
S Dariaus ir S Gireno g 12, LT-59212 Birstonas
Tel: (05) 2625570 *Fax:* (05) 2625570
E-mail: lbd.sekretore@gmail.com
Web Site: www.lbd.lt
Key Personnel
President: Irma Kleiziene *Tel:* (08) 31965760
E-mail: bmb@is.lt
Founded: 1935

Macedonia

Bibliotekarsko Drustvo na Makedonija
(Macedonian Library Association)
Blvd Gotse Delchev, 6, 1000 Skopje

Malawi

The Malawi Library Association
PO Box 429, Zomba
Tel: 01 524 265 *Fax:* 01 525 255
Key Personnel
Chairman: Geoffrey F Salanja
Secretary General: Francis F C Kachala
Publication(s): *Libraries in Malawi: Textbook for
Library Assistants*; *MALA Bulletin* (biannually);
Manual for Small Libraries

Malaysia

Persatuan Pustakawan Malaysia (Librarians
Association of Malaysia)
PO Box 12545, 50782 Kuala Lumpur
Tel: (03) 2694 7390 *Fax:* (03) 2694 7390
E-mail: ppm55@po.jaring.my; pustakawan55@
gmail.com
Web Site: ppm55.org
Key Personnel
President: Mohd Sharif Mohd Saad
E-mail: mohd.sharif@gmail.com
Vice President I: Nafisah Bt Ahmad
E-mail: nafisah@pnm.my
Vice President II: Maimunah Kadir *E-mail:* mai@
ppukm.ukm.my
Honorary Secretary: Hashimah Mohd Yusoff
E-mail: shimmyyusoff@yahoo.com.my
Assistant Honorary Secretary: Kamal Bin Sujak
E-mail: kamalsujak@gmail.com
Treasurer: Chin Loy Jyoon *E-mail:* jyoonchin@
hotmail.com
Assistant Treasurer: Azlan Mohamad Hamzah
E-mail: lanzmh@ppukm.ukm.my
Founded: 1955

Mali

AMBAD, see Association Malienne des
Bibliothecaires, Archivistes et Documentalistes
(AMBAD)

**Association Malienne des Bibliothecaires,
Archivistes et Documentalistes (AMBAD)**
BP E4473, Bamako
Tel: 20 29 94 23 *Fax:* 20 29 93 96
E-mail: dnbd@afribone.net.ml
Web Site: www.bn.gouv.ml

Malta

MaLIA, see Malta Library & Information
Association (MaLIA)

**Malta Library & Information Association
(MaLIA)**
c/o University of Malta Library, Msida MSD
2080
Tel: 21322054 *Fax:* 21249841
E-mail: info@malia-malta.org
Web Site: www.malia-malta.org
Key Personnel
Chairperson: Laurence Zerafa
Deputy Chairperson: Robert Mizzi
Secretary: Cecily Rizzo
Treasurer: Josephine Spiteri
Founded: 1969
Membership(s): Commonwealth Library Associ-
ation (COMLA); European Bureau of Library,
Information & Documentation (EBLIDA); In-
ternational Federation of Library Associations
& Institutions (IFLA).
Publication(s): *Directory of Libraries & Infor-
mation Units in Malta* (1969); *Libraries &
National Development* (1999, Proceedings of
a Conference Held in 1999. Editor, Laurence
V Zerafa); *Report on the State of Maltese Li-
braries* (2006)

Mauritania

AMBAD, see Association Mauritanienne des
Bibliothecaires, des Archivistes et des
Documentalistes (AMBAD)

**Association Mauritanienne des Bibliothecaires,
des Archivistes et des Documentalistes
(AMBAD)** (Mauritanien Association of
Librarians, Archivists & Documentalists)
c/o Bibliotheque Nationale, BP 20, Nouakchott
Tel: 525 18 62 *Fax:* 525 18 68
E-mail: bibliothequenationale@yahoo.fr

Mauritius

Mauritius Library Association (MLA)
c/o Ministry of Education Public Library, Moka
Rd, Rose Hill
Tel: 403 0200 *Fax:* 454 9553
Key Personnel
President: Abdool Fareed Soogali
Vice President: Mary Joyce Alicia Bodha
Secretary: Sattiadev Appaddo
Treasurer: James Stevens Augustin
Founded: 1973
Publication(s): *Mauritius Library Association
Newsletter* (quarterly)

MLA, see Mauritius Library Association (MLA)

Mexico

AMBAC, see Asociacion Mexicana de
Bibliotecarios AC (AMBAC)

**Asociacion Mexicana de Bibliotecarios AC
(AMBAC)**
Angel Urraza 817-A, Colonia Del Valle, 03100
Mexico, CDMX
Tel: (0155) 55 75 33 96; (0155) 55 75 11 35
Fax: (0155) 55 75 11 35
E-mail: correo@ambac.org.mx
Web Site: www.ambac.org.mx
Key Personnel
President: Saul Armendariz Sanchez
E-mail: presidente@ambac.org.mx
Vice President: Marisela Castro Moreno
E-mail: vicepresidenta@ambac.org.mx
Secretary General: Alejandra Martinez del Prado
E-mail: secretariageneral@ambac.org.mx
Treasurer: Jose Armando de Jesus Gonzalez
E-mail: tesorero@ambac.org.mx
Publication(s): *Memorias de Jornadas*; *Noticiero*
(bulletin)

ENBA, see Escuela Nacional de Biblioteconomia
y Archivonomia

**Escuela Nacional de Biblioteconomia y
Archivonomia** (National School of
Librarianship & Archives)
Calz Ticoman No 645, Colonia Santa Maria Tico-
man, Delegacion Gustavo A Madero, 07330
Mexico, CDMX
Tel: (0155) 3601-1000 (ext 64442); (0155) 3601-
1000 (ext 64443)
E-mail: buzon@sep.gob.mx
Web Site: www.enba.sep.gob.mx
Key Personnel
Dir: Dr Joaquin Flores Mendez

Founded: 1945
Publication(s): *Bibliotecas y Archivos* (irregularly); *e Gaceta, Organo Informativo de la Escuela Nacional de Biblioteconomia y Archivovomia. e-Gaceta* (monthly, print & online)

Instituto de Investigaciones Bibliograficas
(Institute of Bibliographic Research)
Centro Cultural Universitario, Ciudad Universitaria, Delagacion Coyoacan, 04510 Mexico, DF
Tel: (0155) 5622-6827
E-mail: webiib@biblional.bibliog.unam.mx; difusioncultural@biblional.bibliog.unam.mx
Web Site: www.iib.unam.mx
Key Personnel
Dir: Guadalupe Curiel Defosse *Tel:* (0155) 5622-6816
Sales & Distribution: Elsa Almela *Tel:* (0155) 5622 6807 ext 48713
Publication(s): *Bibliografia Mexicana* (Mexican Bibliography)
Parent Company: Universidad Nacional Autonoma de Mexico

Nepal

Nepal Library Association
GPO 2773, Kathmandu
E-mail: info@nla.org.np
Web Site: www.nla.org.np
Key Personnel
President: Prakash Kumar Thapa
  E-mail: kyammuntar@yahoo.com
Vice President: Suresh Kumar Yadav
  E-mail: skylib72@gmail.com
Secretary General: Bishwa Raj Gautam
  E-mail: bishwa.gautam@gmail.com
Joint Secretary: Manoj Kumar Shah
  E-mail: mksah324@gmail.com
Treasurer: Sabitri Baral *E-mail:* sabitribaral@gmail.com
Founded: 1980
Science & technology membership.
Membership(s): International Federation of Library Associations & Institutions (IFLA).
Publication(s): *Encyclopedia of Library & Information Science* (2nd ed, print & online)

Netherlands

Bureau Koninklijke Vereniging van Archivarissen in Nederland (Royal Association of Archivists in the Netherlands)
Market 1, 6811 CG Arnhem
Tel: (026) 352 16 05 *Fax:* (026) 352 16 99
E-mail: bureau@kvan.nl
Web Site: www.kvan.nl
Key Personnel
Chairman: Fred Van Kan
Secretary: Pieter Koenders
Treasurer: Roelof Braad
Publication(s): *Almanak van het Nederlands archiefwezen* (annually); *Archievenblad* (10 times/yr, journal)

Bureau KVAN, see Bureau Koninklijke Vereniging van Archivarissen in Nederland

FOBID Netherlands Library Forum
Postbus 90407, 2500 LK The Hague
Tel: (070) 3140511; (070) 3140495 *Fax:* (070) 3140651

E-mail: info@fobid.nl; fobid@debibliotheken.nl
Web Site: www.fobid.nl
Key Personnel
Dir/Secretary: Dr M Koren *Tel:* (06) 51360755
  E-mail: koren@fobid.nl
Founded: 1974
National umbrella organization for cooperation between the national library organizations.
Publication(s): *Cataloguing Rules* (parts 1-2)

IFLA, see International Federation of Library Associations & Institutions (IFLA)

International Federation of Library Associations & Institutions (IFLA)
(Federation internationale des associations de bibliothecaires et des bibliotheques)
Prins Willem-Alexanderhof 5, 2595 BE The Hague
Mailing Address: Postbus 95312, 2509 CH The Hague
Tel: (70) 314 08 84 *Fax:* (70) 383 48 27
E-mail: ifla@ifla.org
Web Site: www.ifla.org
Key Personnel
President: Donna Scheeder
  E-mail: donna_scheeder@comcast.net
Treasurer: Christine Mackenzie *E-mail:* christine.mackenzie.au@gmail.com
Secretary General: Gerald Leitner
Publication(s): *IFLA Journal* (quarterly); *IFLA Professional Reports*; *IFLA Publications Series* (6 times/yr); *IFLA Series on Bibliographic Control*

LIBER, see Ligue des Bibliotheques Europeennes de Recherche (LIBER)

Ligue des Bibliotheques Europeennes de Recherche (LIBER) (Association of European Research Libraries)
Prins Willem-Alexanderhof 5, 2595 BE The Hague
Mailing Address: c/o Koninklijke Bibliotheek, Postbus 90407, 2509 LK The Hague
Tel: (070) 314 07 67 *Fax:* (070) 314 01 97
E-mail: liber@kb.nl
Web Site: www.libereurope.eu
Key Personnel
President: Kristiina Hormia-Poutanen
  E-mail: kristiina.hormia@helsinki.fi
Vice President: Jeannette Frey *E-mail:* Jeannette.frey@bcu.unil.ch
Treasurer: Dr Matthijs van Otegem
  E-mail: vanotegem@ubib.eur.nl
Secretary-General: Dr Ann Matheson *E-mail:* a.matheson@tinyworld.co.uk
Founded: 1971
Publication(s): *Annual Reports*; *Architecture Group Publications*; *European Research Libraries Cooperation*; *LIBER in the Press*; *The Liber Quarterly*; *Library Management Group Publications*

Nederlandse Vereniging voor beroepsbeoefenaren in de bibliotheek-informatie-en kennissector (NVB) (The Dutch Association for Library Information & Knowledge Professionals)
Mariaplaats 3, 3511 LH Utrecht
Tel: (030) 233 0050 *Fax:* (030) 238 0030
E-mail: info@nvbonline.nl
Web Site: www.nvbonline.nl
Key Personnel
Chairman: Michel G Wesseling *E-mail:* m.g.wesseling@gmail.com
Secretary/Treasurer: Cynthio Korlrinke
Founded: 1912

Netherlands Library Forum, see FOBID Netherlands Library Forum

Vereniging van Openbare Bibliotheken
(Association of Public Libraries)
Grote Markstr 43, 2511 BH The Hague
Mailing Address: Postbus 16146, 2500 BC The Hague
Tel: (070) 30 90 500 *Fax:* (070) 30 90 599
E-mail: infodesk@debibliotheken.nl; vereniging@debibliotheken.nl
Web Site: www.debibliotheken.nl
Key Personnel
Dir: Ap de Vries *E-mail:* devries@debibliotheken.nl
Contact: Dr Marian Koren *Tel:* (070) 30 90 541
  E-mail: koren@debibliotheken.nl
Founded: 1972
Membership(s): EBLIDA; International Federation of Library Associations & Institutions (IFLA); National Association of Public Libraries.
Publication(s): *Bibliotheek* (biweekly, journal); *New Library Buildings in the Netherlands*

New Zealand

International Association of Music Libraries, Archives & Documentation Centres (New Zealand) Inc
c/o Massey University Library, Wellington Campus, Private Box 756, Wellington 6140
Tel: (04) 801 5799 *Fax:* (04) 801 2699
E-mail: newzealand@iaml.info
Web Site: www.iaml.info
Key Personnel
President: Marilyn Portman *E-mail:* marilyn.portman@aucklandcity.govt.nz
Secretary: Paul Emsley *E-mail:* paul.emsley@vuw.ac.nz
Treasurer: Phillippa McKeown-Green *E-mail:* p.mckeown-green@auckland.ac.nz
Founded: 1970
Publication(s): *Crescendo* (triannually, bulletin)

LIANZA (Library & Information Association of New Zealand Aotearoa), see New Zealand Library Association Inc t/a LIANZA

New Zealand Library Association Inc t/a LIANZA
Stephenson & Turner House, Level 4, 156-158 Victoria St, Wellington 6011
Mailing Address: PO Box 12212, Thorndon, Wellington 6144
Tel: (04) 801 5542 *Fax:* (04) 801 5543
E-mail: admin@lianza.org.nz
Web Site: www.lianza.org.nz
Key Personnel
Executive Dir: Alli Smith *E-mail:* alli@lianza.org.nz
Communication Manager: Lisa Crombie
  E-mail: lisa@lianza.org.nz
Membership Services: Anna O'Keeffe
  E-mail: anna@lianza.og.nz
Founded: 1910
Publication(s): *The New Zealand Library & Information Management Journal* (biannually)

Nicaragua

ANIBIPA, see Asociacion Nicaraguense de Bibliotecarios y Profesionales Afines

Asociacion Nicaraguense de Bibliotecarios y Profesionales Afines (Nicaraguan Association of Librarians & Related Professionals)
Bello Horizonte, tope Sur de la Rotonda 1/2 cuadra abajo J-11-57, Managua
Tel: 277-4159 (ext 335)
E-mail: anibipa@yahoo.com
Web Site: anibipanicaraguaentubiblioteca.blogspot. com/ (blog)
Founded: 1982

Nigeria

Nigerian Library Association
c/o National Library of Nigeria, Sanusi Dantata House, Central Business District, PMB 1, Abuja GPO 900001
Tel: (805) 5365245 *Fax:* (09) 234-6773
E-mail: info@nla-ng.org
Web Site: www.nla-ng.org
Key Personnel
President: Prof Lenrie Aina
Founded: 1962
There are also regional associations in the various states under the umbrella of the Nigerian Library Association.
Publication(s): *Nigerian Libraries* (biannually); *NLA Newsletter & Resource Central*

Nigerian School Library Association
Abadina Media Resource Centre, University of Ibadan, Ibadan, Oyo 234
Tel: (0830) 3893853 (cell)
Web Site: www.nsla.org.ng
Key Personnel
President: Virginia W Dike *Tel:* (0803) 5664021 (cell) *E-mail:* vwdike@yahoo.com
Executive Secretary: Prof D F Elaturoti *E-mail:* davidelaturoti@yahoo.com
Treasurer: Mrs H K Kolade *Tel:* (0802) 3509302 (cell)
Administrative Secretary: K A Aramide *Tel:* (0802) 3795300 (cell)
Publication(s): *Newsletter* (quarterly); *Nigerian School Library Journal* (annually)

NLA, see Nigerian Library Association

NSLA, see Nigerian School Library Association

Norway

Arkivarforeningen (The Association of Archivists)
Fredrik Glads gate 1, 0482 Oslo
Tel: 913 16 895
E-mail: imb@steria.no
Web Site: www.arkivarforeningen.no
Key Personnel
Chairman: Inge Manfred Bjorlin *E-mail:* inge. bjorlin@gmail.com
Deputy Chair: Vibeke Solbakken Lunheim
Treasurer: Ketil Zahl
Publication(s): *Norsk arkivforum*

Norsk Bibliotekforening (Norwegian Library Association)
Malerhaugveien 20, 0666 Oslo
Mailing Address: Postboks 6540, 0606 Etterstad, Oslo
Tel: 23 24 34 30 *Fax:* 22 67 23 68
E-mail: nbf@norskbibliotekforening.no

Web Site: www.norskbibliotekforening.no
Key Personnel
Editor: Ingrid Stephensen
General Secretary: Hege Newth Nouri *Tel:* 23 24 34 31 *E-mail:* hege.newth.nouri@ norskbibliotekforening.no
Founded: 1913

Pakistan

Library Promotion Bureau
Karachi University Campus, PO Box 8421, Karachi 75270
Tel: (021) 3632-1959
E-mail: lpb_pakistan_66@yahoo.com
Key Personnel
Vice Chancellor: Dr Pirzada Qasim Raza Siddiqui *E-mail:* vc@uok.edu.pk
Founded: 1966
Also publisher.
Publication(s): *Bibliographical Services Throughout Pakistan* (2nd ed); *Documents Procurement Service*; *Libraries of Pakistan*; *Pakistan Book Trade Directory*; *Pakistan Library & Information Sciences Journal* (quarterly); *Secondary School Library Resources & Services in Karachi*; *University Librarianship in Pakistan*; *Who's Who in Library & Information Science in Pakistan*

Paraguay

ABIGRAP, see Asociacion de Bibliotecarios Graduados del Paraguay (ABIGRAP)

Asociacion de Bibliotecarios Graduados del Paraguay (ABIGRAP) (Association of Graduate Librarians of Paraguay)
Facultad Politecnica, Universidad Nacional de Asuncion, 2160 San Lorenzo
Tel: (021) 585-588; (021) 585-593
E-mail: abigrap@pol.una.py
Web Site: www.pol.una.py/abigrap
Founded: 1985
Publication(s): *Documentacion Paraguaya*

Peru

ADAP, see Asociacion de Archiveros del Peru (ADAP)

Asociacion de Archiveros del Peru (ADAP) (Peruvian Association of Archivists)
Av Manco Capac Nº 1180 Dpto 201, La Victoria, Lima
Tel: (01) 472-8729 *Fax:* (01) 472-7408
E-mail: contactos@adadpperu.com
Key Personnel
Contact: Juan Manuel Serrano Valencia

Philippines

ASLP, see Association of Special Libraries of the Philippines (ASLP)

Association of Special Libraries of the Philippines (ASLP)
The National Library of the Philippines, T M Kalaw St, Room 301, 1000 Ermita, Manila
Tel: (0995) 5396299 (cell)
E-mail: aslplibrarians@gmail.com
Web Site: aslpwiki.wikispaces.com
Key Personnel
President: Randolf D Mariano
Vice President: Myzel Y Marifosque
Secretary: Eugene Jose T Espinoza
Treasurer: Maria Teresa M Cabance
Public Relations Officer: Justin Harold A Hingco
Auditor: Teresita R Casio
Founded: 1954
Publication(s): *ASLP Journal* (annually); *ASLP Newsletter* (quarterly)

Philippine Librarians Association Inc
National Library Bldg, Room 301, T M Kalaw St, 1000 Ermita, Manila
Mailing Address: PO Box 2926, 1000 Ermita, Manila
Tel: (02) 525-9401 *Fax:* (02) 525-9401
Web Site: sites.google.com/site/plainational; plainational.blogspot.com
Key Personnel
President: Thelma S Kim
Executive Vice President: Victoria Santos
Secretary: Marilou L Pasion
Treasurer: Virginia Ramos
Founded: 1923
Publication(s): *PLAI Bulletin* (annually); *PLAI Newsletter* (biannually)

PLAI, see Philippine Librarians Association Inc

Poland

Stowarzyszenie Bibliotekarzy Polskich (Polish Librarians' Association)
Al Niepodleglosci 213, 02-086 Warsaw
Tel: (22) 825 83 74 *Fax:* (22) 825 53 49
E-mail: biuro@sbp.pl; biurozgsbp@wp.pl
Web Site: www.sbp.pl
Key Personnel
Vice President: Helena Bednarska; Ewa Kobierska-Maciuszko *E-mail:* e.maciuszko@ uw.edu.pl; Krzysztof Marcinowski *E-mail:* kmarcinowski@mbp.szczecin.pl
Secretary General: Marzena Przybysz *E-mail:* m. przybysz@bn.org.pl
Treasurer: Joanna Pasztaleniec-Jarzynska
Dir: Anna Grzecznowska *E-mail:* a. grzecznowska@sbp.pl
Founded: 1917
Self-governing nonprofit organization of people who, through their professional or academic careers, are involved in librarianship & scientific information in Poland. The Association gathers librarians of various specialties, irrespective of the position the library occupies in the community, as the organization is above the community divisions. The association is a publisher or co-publisher of 5 titles of journals which record & disseminate the intellectual achievements of both Polish & foreign librarianship. The specialist publisher of the Association, Wydawnictwo SBP, prepares for print a dozen or so book titles a year. Moreover, the publisher provides libraries with leaflets, posters, calendars, etc. In an attempt to exchange expertise with others & learn about the latest achievement in librarianship, the association organizes specialist symposia & conferences, also international ones. Wydawnictwo SBP publishes & disseminates materials that were subjects of discussion at the meetings.

Membership(s): EBLIDA (European Bureau of Library, Information & Documentation Association; IAML (International Association of Music Libraries; International Federation of Library Associations & Institutions (IFLA); LIBER (Ligue des Bibliotheques Europeennes de Recherche).
Publication(s): *Bibliotekarz* (The Librarian, monthly); *Poradnik Bibliotekarza* (The Librarian's Guide, monthly); *Przeglad Biblioteczny* (Library Review, quarterly); *Zagadnienia Informacji Naukowej* (biannually)

Portugal

Associacao Portuguesa de Bibliotecarios, Arquivistas e Documentalistas (BAD) (The Portuguese Association of Librarians Archivists & Documentalists)
Rua Morais Soares, 43 C, 1° Dt° e Frte, 1900-341 Lisbon
Tel: 21 816 19 80 *Fax:* 21 815 45 08
E-mail: editorial@apbad.pt; formacao@apbad.pt; contabilidade@apbad.pt
Web Site: www.apbad.pt
Key Personnel
President: Maria Alexandra Verissimo M Silva Lourenco *E-mail:* presidente@bad.pt
Vice President: Maria Jose Sabino Moura *E-mail:* vicepresidente@bad.pt
Secretary: Pedro Miguel de Oliveira Bento Principe *E-mail:* secretario@bad.pt; Maria Dulce Rosario Correia *E-mail:* secretario@bad.pt
Treasurer: Bruno Duarte Mendes Eiras *E-mail:* tesoureiro@bad.pt
Publication(s): *Cadernos de Biblioteconomia, Arquivistica e Documentacao* (Journal of Library, Archives & Documentation, biannually)

BAD, see Associacao Portuguesa de Bibliotecarios, Arquivistas e Documentalistas (BAD)

DGLAB, see Direccao Geral do Livro dos Arquivos e das Bibliotecas (DGLAB)

Direccao Geral do Livro dos Arquivos e das Bibliotecas (DGLAB) (General Directorate for Book, Archives & Libraries)
Edificio da Torre do Tombo, Alameda da Universidade, 1649 010 Lisbon
Tel: 21 003 71 00 *Fax:* 21 003 71 01
E-mail: secretariado@dglab.gov.pt
Web Site: dglab.gov.pt
Key Personnel
Dir: Silvestre Lacerda
Founded: 2012 (merger of Direccao Geral do Livro e das Bibliotecas (DGLB) & Direcao-Geral de Arquivos (DGARQ))

Puerto Rico

ACURIL
PO Box 21609, San Juan 00931-1906
Tel: (787) 763-6199
E-mail: executivesecretariat@acuril.org
Web Site: acuril.uprrp.edu
Key Personnel
President: Francoise Beaulieu Thybulle
Vice President: Cindy Jimenez Vera
Executive Secretary: Luisa Vigo-Cepeda

Treasurer: Prof Almaluces Figueroa Ortiz
Publication(s): *ACURIL, Cybernotes; Proceedings of Annual Conference*

Association of Caribbean University, Research & Institutional Libraries, see ACURIL

Sociedad de Bibliotecarios de Puerto Rico (Society of Librarians of Puerto Rico)
Apdo 22898, San Juan 00931-2898
Tel: (787) 764-0000 (ext 5205) *Fax:* (787) 764-0000 (ext 5204)
Web Site: www.sociedadbibliotecarios.org
Key Personnel
President: Juan Vargas *Tel:* (787) 844-8181 ext 2222 *E-mail:* juan.vargas3@upr.edu
Vice President: Edwin Ramos *E-mail:* edramos@pucpr.edu
Secretary: Iris V Vera Collazo *E-mail:* veracol@gmail.com
Treasurer: Luis Casiano *Tel:* (787) 764-0000 ext 5078 *E-mail:* luis.casiano3@upr.edu
Founded: 1961
Publication(s): *ACCESO: Revista Puertorriquena de Bibliotecologia y Documentacion* (ACCESS: Puerto Rican Journal of Librarianship & Documentation)

Russia

RBA, see Russian Library Association (RLA)

RLA, see Russian Library Association (RLA)

Russian Library Association (RLA) (Rossiiskaya Bibliotechnaya Assotsiatsiya (RBA))
18, Sadovaya St, 191069 St Petersburg
Tel: 812 110 58 61 *Fax:* 812 110 58 61
E-mail: rba@nlr.ru
Web Site: www.rba.ru
Key Personnel
Executive Secretary: Elena Tikhonova
Founded: 1994
Membership(s): International Federation of Library Associations & Institutions (IFLA).
Publication(s): *RLA Information Bulletin*

Senegal

ASBAD, see Association Senegalaise des Bibliothecaires, Archivistes et Documentalistes (ASBAD)

Association Senegalaise des Bibliothecaires, Archivistes et Documentalistes (ASBAD)
S/C EBAD, Universite Cheikh Anta Diop de Dakar, Dakar
Mailing Address: BP 2006, Dakar
Tel: 77 651 00 33 *Fax:* 33 824 23 79
E-mail: asbad200@hotmail.com
Web Site: www.asbad.org
Key Personnel
President: Lawrence Gomis Baaya
Secretary General: Alassane Ndiath
Founded: 1988
Publication(s): *Bulletin Mensuel D'Information* (online, newspaper); *Channel IST* (newsletter)

Bibliotheque Lecture Developpement
rue DSM No 670, Sicap Mbao - Route de Rufisque, Dakar

Mailing Address: BP 1046, Dakar
Tel: 33 834 34 94
E-mail: bld@bldsn.org
Web Site: www.bldsn.org
Aims to promote culture & education by making libraries available to populations. Equips & trains leaders for library management.

Serbia

Jugoslovenski Bibliografsko Informacijski Institut (Yugoslav Institute for Bibliography & Information)
Terazije 26, 11000 Belgrade
Tel: (011) 2687836 *Fax:* (011) 2687760
Publication(s): *Belgrade; Universal Decimal Classification, International* (Serbocroatian version)

YUBIN, see Jugoslovenski Bibliografsko Informacijski Institut

Sierra Leone

Sierra Leone Association of Archivists, Librarians & Information Professionals (SLAALIP)
c/o Sierra Leone Library Board, Rokel St, Freetown
Tel: (022) 220-758
Founded: 1987
Publication(s): *SLAALIS Bulletin* (quarterly)

SLAALIP, see Sierra Leone Association of Archivists, Librarians & Information Professionals (SLAALIP)

Singapore

LAS, see Library Association of Singapore (LAS)

Library Association of Singapore (LAS)
c/o National Library Board, 100 Victoria St No 14-01, Singapore 188064
Tel: 6332 3255 (NLB) *Fax:* 6332 3248
E-mail: lassec@las.org.sg
Web Site: www.las.org.sg
Key Personnel
President: Mrs Judy Ng *E-mail:* president@las.org.sg
Vice President: Ms Samantha Ang Seok Hian *E-mail:* vice_president@las.org.sg
Honorary Secretary: Ms Lim Li Sa Rachel *E-mail:* lassec@las.org.sg
Honorary Treasurer: Mr Lim Junhao *E-mail:* treasurer@las.org.sg
Founded: 1955
Publication(s): *Directory of Libraries & Information Centres in Singapore* (annually); *Singapore Journal of Library & Information Management* (annually); *Singapore Libraries Bulletin* (quarterly)

Slovenia

ZBDS, see Zveza bibliotekarskih drustev Slovenije (ZBDS)

Zveza bibliotekarskih drustev Slovenije (ZBDS) (Slovenian Library Association)
Turjaska 1, SI-1000 Ljubljana
Tel: (01) 2001 176 *Fax:* (01) 4257 293
E-mail: info@zbds-zveza.si
Web Site: www.zbds-zveza.si
Key Personnel
President: Sabina Fras Popovic *Tel:* (02) 2352 100 *Fax:* (02) 2352 127 *E-mail:* sabina.fras-popovic@mb.sik.si
Vice President: Irena Sesek *Tel:* (01) 5861 309 *Fax:* (01) 5861 352 *E-mail:* irena.sesek@nuk.uni-lj.si; Spela Razpotnik *Tel:* (01) 5861 325 *Fax:* (01) 5861 352 *E-mail:* spela.razpotnik@nuk.uni-lj.si
Founded: 1947
Publication(s): *Knjiznica* (Library, magazine)

South Africa

LIASA, see Library & Information Association of South Africa (LIASA)

Library & Information Association of South Africa (LIASA)
228 Johannes Ramokhoase St, Pretoria
Mailing Address: PO Box 1598, Pretoria 0001
Tel: (012) 328 2010; (012) 323 4912 *Fax:* (012) 323 1033
E-mail: liasa@liasa.org.za
Web Site: www.liasa.org.za
Key Personnel
President: Naomi Haasbroek *E-mail:* president@liasa.org.za
National Secretary: Martha De Waal *Tel:* (012) 420 5308 *E-mail:* martha.dewaal@up.ac.za
Publication(s): *LIASA-IN-Touch* (quarterly, magazine); *South African Journal of Library & Information Science* (biannually, journal)

South Korea

KLA, see Korean Library Association (KLA)

Korean Library Association (KLA)
San 60-1, Banpo-dong, Seocho-gu, Seoul 137-702
Tel: (02) 535-4868 *Fax:* (02) 535-5616
E-mail: license@kla.kr; w3master@kla.kr
Web Site: www.kla.kr
Publication(s): *KLA Bulletin* (bimonthly, text in Korean); *Korean Cataloguing Rules*; *Korean Decimal Classification*; *The Patterns of Book Cover Design in Korea (1392-1945)*; *Statistics on Libraries in Korea* (annually)

Spain

ANABAD, see Federacion Espanola de Asociaciones de Archiveros, Bibliotecarios, Arqueologos, Museologos y Documentalistas

Federacion Espanola de Asociaciones de Archiveros, Bibliotecarios, Arqueologos, Museologos y Documentalistas (Spanish Association of Archivists, Librarians, Curators & Documentalists)
c/de las Huertas, 37, baho dcha, 28014 Madrid
Tel: 91 575 17 27 *Fax:* 91 578 16 15
E-mail: anabad@anabad.org

Web Site: www.anabad.org
Key Personnel
President: Miguel Angel Gacho Santamaria
Vice President: Jose Maria Nogales Herrera
Secretary: Veronica Mateo Ripoll
Treasurer: Ignacio Vilela Fraile
Publication(s): *Boletin* (with bibliography section); *Hoja Informativa* (bimonthly, newsletter); *Monografias*

Sri Lanka

National Library & Documentation Services Board (NLDSB)
No 14, Independence Ave, Colombo 07
Tel: (011) 2674386; (011) 2685197 *Fax:* (011) 2685201
E-mail: info@mail.natlib.lk; reader@mail.natlib.lk
Web Site: www.natlib.lk
Key Personnel
Chairman: Prof Somaratne Balasuriya
Founded: 1998
Publication(s): *Directory of Social Science Libraries, Information Centres & Databases in Sri Lanka*; *International Standard Book Numbering in Sri Lanka* (brochure); *Sri Lanka (ISBN) Publishers Directory*; *Sri Lanka National Bibliography* (monthly); *Sri Lanka Newspaper Article Index-1993* (conference index)

NLDSB, see National Library & Documentation Services Board (NLDSB)

SLLA, see Sri Lanka Library Association (SLLA)

Sri Lanka Library Association (SLLA)
Sri Lanka Professional Centre, 275/75 Stanley Wijesundara Mawatha, Colombo 07
Tel: (011) 2589103 *Fax:* (011) 2589103
E-mail: slla@sltnet.lk
Web Site: www.slla.org.lk
Founded: 1960 (established as a corporate body under Parliament Act no 20 1974)
Publication(s): *SLLA Newsletter* (quarterly); *Sri Lanka Library Review* (annually)

Swaziland

SWALA, see Swaziland Library Association

Swaziland Library Association
Elwatini Bldg, Corner of Market & Warner Sts, Mbabane
Mailing Address: PO Box 2309, Mbabane H100
Tel: 404-2633 *Fax:* 404-3863
Web Site: www.swala.sz
Founded: 1984
Publication(s): *SWALA Journal*; *SWALA Newsletter*

Sweden

SFIS, see Swedish Association for Information Specialists

Svensk Biblioteksforening Kansli (Swedish Library Association)
World Trade Center, D5, Klarabergsviadukten 70/Kungsbron 1, Box 70380, 107 24 Stockholm
Tel: (08) 545 132 30 *Fax:* (08) 545 132 31
E-mail: info@biblioteksforeningen.org
Web Site: www.biblioteksforeningen.org
Key Personnel
Secretary General: Niclas Lindberg *Tel:* (08) 545 132 33 *E-mail:* nl@biblioteksforeningen.org
Editor & Chief: Marianne Steinsaphir *E-mail:* ms@bbl.sab.se
Founded: 2000
Membership(s): International Federation of Library Associations & Institutions (IFLA); European Bureau of Library, Information & Documentation Associations (EBLIDA).
Publication(s): *Biblioteksbladet* (The Swedish Library Journal, 10 times/yr)

Svenska Arkivsamfundet (Swedish Association of Archivists)
c/o Stockholms stadsarkiv, Box 22063, 104 22 Stockholm
E-mail: info@arkivsamfundet.se
Web Site: www.arkivsamfundet.se
Publication(s): *Arkiv, Samhaelle och, Forskning (ASF)* (Archives, Society, Research, biannually)

Swedish Association for Information Specialists (Svensk Forening for Informations Specialister (SFIS))
Box 2001, 135 02 Tyreso
E-mail: kansliet@sfis.nu
Web Site: www.sfis.nu/om
Key Personnel
Chairman: Peter Almerud *E-mail:* peter.almerud@gmail.com
Vice Chairman: Charlotta Eskilson *E-mail:* charlotta.eskilson@astrazeneca.com
Founded: 1936
Publication(s): *Tidskrift foer Informationsspecialister* (quarterly)

Switzerland

Bibliothek Information Schweiz (Library Information Switzerland)
Bleichmattstr 42, 5000 Arau
Tel: (062) 823 19 38 *Fax:* (062) 823 19 39
E-mail: info@bis.info
Web Site: www.bis.info
Key Personnel
Mng Dir: Hans Ulrich Locher *Tel:* (031) 382 42 40 *E-mail:* halo.locher@bis.info

BIS, see Bibliothek Information Schweiz

Verein Schweizerischer Archivarinnen und Archivare (VSA) (Swiss Association of Archivists)
c/o Buero Pontri GmbH, Solohurnstr 13, 3322 Urtenen-Schoenbuehl
Tel: (031) 312 26 66 *Fax:* (031) 312 26 68
E-mail: info@vsa-aas.org
Web Site: www.vsa-aas.org
Key Personnel
President: Anna Pia Maissen *Tel:* (044) 266 86 46 *E-mail:* annapia.maissen@zuerich.ch
Vice President: Gregor Egloff *Tel:* (041) 228 67 64 *E-mail:* gregor.egloff@lu.ch
Secretary: Daniel Kress *Tel:* (061) 267 86 06 *E-mail:* daniel.kress@bs.ch
Treasurer: Peter Erhart *Tel:* (071) 229 38 31 *E-mail:* peter.erhart@sg.ch
Founded: 1922
Membership(s): ICA.
Publication(s): *Arbido*

VSA, see Verein Schweizerischer Archivarinnen und Archivare (VSA)

Taiwan

LAROC, see Library Association of the Republic of China (LAROC)

Library Association of the Republic of China (LAROC)
20 Zhongshan South Rd, Taipei 10001
Tel: (02) 2361-9132; (02) 2331-2475 *Fax:* (02) 2370-0899
E-mail: lac@msg.ncl.edu.tw
Web Site: www.lac.org.tw
Publication(s): *Library Association of China Bulletin* (biannually)

Tanzania

Tanzania Library Association (TLA)
PO Box 33433, Dar es Salaam
Tel: (0744) 296134
E-mail: tla_tanzania@yahoo.com
Web Site: www.tla.or.tz
Founded: 1973
Publication(s): *Matukio* (Events, biannually, newsletter); *Someni* (Read, journal)

TLA, see Tanzania Library Association (TLA)

Thailand

Thai Library Association
1346 Akhan Songkhro 5 Rd, Klongjan, Bangkapi, Bangkok 10240
Tel: (02) 734-9022; (02) 734-9023 *Fax:* (02) 734-9021
E-mail: tla2497@yahoo.com
Web Site: www.tla.or.th
Founded: 1954

Trinidad and Tobago

LATT, see Library Association of Trinidad and Tobago

Library Association of Trinidad and Tobago
PO Box 1275, Port of Spain
Tel: (868) 687-0194
E-mail: latt46@gmail.com
Web Site: latt.org.tt
Key Personnel
President: Juliet Glenn-Callender
Founded: 1960
Publication(s): *BIBLIO* (quarterly, newsletter); *Blatt* (annually, Bulletin of the Library Association of Trinidad and Tobago)

Tunisia

Association Tunisienne des Documentalistes, Bibliothecaires et Archivistes (ATDBA)
(Tunisian Association of Documentalists, Librarians and Archivists)
BP 380, 1000 Tunis, RP
Tel: 895450
Publication(s): *L'Enfant et la Lecture; RASSID*

ATDBA, see Association Tunisienne des Documentalistes, Bibliothecaires et Archivistes (ATDBA)

Turkey

TKD, see Turk Kutuphaneciler Dernegi

Turk Kutuphaneciler Dernegi (Turkish Librarians' Association)
Necatibey Cad Elgun Sok, 8/8, 06440 Kizilay, Ankara
Tel: (0312) 230 13 25 *Fax:* (0312) 232 04 53
E-mail: tkd.dernek@gmail.com
Web Site: www.kutuphaneci.org.tr
Key Personnel
President: Ali Fuat Kartal
Founded: 1949
Publication(s): *Turk Kutuphaneciligi* (Turkish Librarianship, quarterly)

United Kingdom

ABTAPL, see Association of British Theological & Philosophical Libraries (ABTAPL)

Archives & Records Association UK & Ireland
Prioryfield House, 20 Canon St, Taunton, Somerset TA1 1SW
Tel: (01823) 327030 *Fax:* (01823) 271719
E-mail: societyofarchivists@archives.org.uk; ara@archives.org.uk
Web Site: www.archives.org.uk
Key Personnel
Chair: Martin Taylor
Vice Chair: Gordon Reid
Chief Executive: John Chambers
Honorary Secretary: Beth Mercer
Membership Administrator: Lorraine Logan
    E-mail: membership@archives.org.uk
Honorary Treasurer: Sylvia James
Founded: 1947
Publication(s): *ARC* (monthly, magazine); *ARC Directory of Supplies* (annually); *Journal of Archives & Records* (biannually, newsletter)

ARLIS/UK & Ireland
The National Art Library, Victoria & Albert Museum, Cromwell Rd, South Kensington, London SW7 2RL
Tel: (020) 7942 2317
E-mail: arlis@vam.ac.uk
Web Site: www.arlis.org.uk
Key Personnel
Chair: Judith Preece
Secretary: Rachel Brockhurst *Tel:* (020) 7806 2502 *E-mail:* r_brockhurst@craftscouncil.org.uk

Treasurer: Stephanie Silvester *Tel:* (01622) 620132 *E-mail:* speak@ucreative.ac.uk
Founded: 1969
Professional body for librarians & all concerned with the documentation of virtual art.
Publication(s): *ARLIS/UK & Ireland Directory* (annually); *ARLIS/UK & Ireland News-sheet* (bimonthly); *Art Libraries Journal* (quarterly); *Art Researchers Guide to Edinburgh; Art Researchers Guide to Leeds; Displays & Exhibitions in Libraries*

Art Libraries Society/UK & Ireland, see ARLIS/UK & Ireland

ASLIB, The Association for Information Management
Howard House, Wagon Lane, Bingley BD16 1WA
Tel: (01274) 777700 *Fax:* (01274) 785201
E-mail: support@aslib.com
Web Site: www.aslib.com
Key Personnel
Dir: Rebecca Marsh
Head, Dept: Eileen Breen
Editor-in-Chief: Graham Coult *E-mail:* gcoult@aslib.com
Publications & Training Manager: Diane Heath *E-mail:* dheath@aslib.com
Relationship Manager: Holly Shukla
Customer Operations & Marketing Executive: Sue Hill
Founded: 1924
Publication(s): *Aslib Booklist* (monthly); *Aslib Proceedings* (monthly); *Current Awareness Abstracts* (monthly, journal); *Forthcoming International Scientific & Technical References* (quarterly); *Journal of Documentation* (quarterly); *Managing Information* (monthly, print & online); *Program* (quarterly)

The Association for Information Management, see ASLIB, The Association for Information Management

Association of British Theological & Philosophical Libraries (ABTAPL)
c/o The Library, Woodbrooke Quaker Study Centre, 1046 Bristol Rd, Birmingham B29 6LJ
Web Site: www.newman.ac.uk/abtapl
Key Personnel
Chairman: Alan Linfield *Tel:* (0193) 456 192
    E-mail: a.linfield@lst.ac.uk
Honorary Secretary: Carol Reekie *Tel:* (01223) 741043 *E-mail:* cr248@cam.ac.uk
Honorary Treasurer: Pat Anstis *Tel:* (0161) 249 2514 *E-mail:* library@lkh.co.uk
Publication(s): *ABTAPL Union List of Periodicals; Bulletin of ABTAPL* (triannually)

The Bibliographical Society
c/o Institute of English Studies, Malet St, Senate House, Room 238, London WC1E 7HU
Web Site: www.bibsoc.org.uk
Key Personnel
President: David Pearson
Vice President: Christine Ferdinard; Kristian Jensen; Henry Woudhuysen
Honorary Secretary: Margaret Ford
    E-mail: secretary@bibsoc.org.uk
Honorary Treasurer: Richard Linenthal
    E-mail: treasurer@bibsoc.org.uk
Founded: 1892
Publication(s): *The Library* (quarterly, journal, scholarly publication on bibliographical subjects)

Book Aid International
39-41 Coldharbour Lane, Camberwell, London SE5 9NR
Tel: (020) 7733 3577 *Fax:* (020) 7978 8006
E-mail: info@bookaid.org

Web Site: www.bookaid.org
Key Personnel
Chair: Philip Walters
Honorary Treasurer: Fergus Cass
Dir: Alison Hubert
Head, Fundraising & Communications: Jacqui
  Scott *E-mail:* jacqui.scott@bookaid.org
Head, Programs & Operations: Karen Sharkey
Increases access to books & supports literacy, education & development in sub-Saharan. It sends around 500,000 new books a year for use in libraries, schools & by development organizations.
Publication(s): *Annual Review; Booklinks; Book-Mark* (newsletter)

Career Development Group
c/o CILIP, 7 Ridgmount St, London WC1E 7AE
Tel: (020) 7255 0500 *Fax:* (020) 7255 0501
E-mail: membership@cilip.org.uk
Web Site: www.careerdevelopmentgroup.org.uk
Special interest group of CILIP, the Chartered Institute of Library & Information Professionals, which undertakes international projects in support of libraries & information professionals in the developing world. International projects are funded through donations & fundraising.
Publication(s): *Impact* (up to 4 times/yr, journal, online)

CDG, see Career Development Group

Chartered Institute of Library & Information Professionals (CILIP)
7 Ridgmount St, London WC1E 7AE
Tel: (020) 7255 0500; (020) 7255 0505 (textphone) *Fax:* (020) 7255 0501
E-mail: info@cilip.org.uk
Web Site: www.cilip.org.uk
Key Personnel
Chair: John Dolan *E-mail:* john.dolan@cilip.org.uk
Vice Chair: Emma McDonald *E-mail:* emma.mcdonald@cilip.org.uk
Chief Executive: Nick Poole *E-mail:* nick.poole@cilip.org.uk
President: Kate Arnold
Vice President: Ayub Khan
Founded: 2002
Professional body for librarians & information managers.
Publication(s): *CILIP Update* (monthly, magazine)

Chartered Institute of Library & Information Professionals/Wales
7 Ridgmount St, London WC1E 7AE
Tel: (020) 7255 0500 *Fax:* (020) 7255 0501
E-mail: info@cilip.org.uk
Web Site: www.cilip.org.uk
Key Personnel
Chair: Karen Gibbins
President: Phil Bradley *E-mail:* president@cilip.org.uk
Publication(s): *Y Ddolen* (3 times/yr, journal); *Mynegai-Y Cylchgrawn Efengylaidd 1948-1999* (Index to the Welsh Language Journal Y Cylchgrawn Efengaidd, online); *Mynegai - Y Casglwr, 1-75, March 1977-Summer 2002* (online); *Yr Enfys: The Journal of Wales International Index 1948-1998* (online)

CILIP, see Chartered Institute of Library & Information Professionals (CILIP)

Friends of the National Libraries
c/o Dept of Manuscripts, The British Library, 96 Euston Rd, London NW1 2DB
Tel: (020) 7412 7559
Web Site: www.friendsofnationallibraries.org.uk

Key Personnel
Chairman: The Lord Egremont
  E-mail: chairman@fnlmail.org.uk
Honorary Secretary: Michael Borrie
  E-mail: secretary@fnlmail.org.uk
Honorary Treasurer: Charles Sebag-Montefiore
  E-mail: treasurer@fnlmail.org.uk
Honorary Membership Secretary: Howard Fox, MA *E-mail:* membership@fnlmail.org.uk
Founded: 1931
Assists libraries in the UK to acquire books, manuscripts & archives.

IAML, see International Association of Music Libraries, Archives & Documentation Centres (UK & Ireland Branch)

International Association of Music Libraries, Archives & Documentation Centres (UK & Ireland Branch)
c/o Royal Northern College of Music Library, 124 Oxford Rd, Manchester M13 9RD
Tel: (0161) 907 5245 *Fax:* (0161) 273 7611
Web Site: www.iaml.info/iaml-uk-irl
Key Personnel
President: Peter Baxter *E-mail:* pbbaxter@hotmail.com
Secretary: Roy Stanley *E-mail:* rstanley@tcd.ie
Treasurer: Monika Pietras *E-mail:* monika.pietras@rcm.ac.uk
Founded: 1953
Publication(s): *Annual Reports; Brio* (biannually); *Fontis Artis Musicae* (quarterly, journal); *IAML (UK & IRL)* (newsletter)

Network of Government Library & Information Specialists (NGLIS)
c/o Kate Pritchard, Defra, Ergon House, 17 Smith Sq, London SW1P 3JR
Mailing Address: PO Box 68208, London SW1P 9UA
Web Site: www.nglis.org.uk
Key Personnel
Chair: Lorna Goodey *E-mail:* lorna.goodey@foodstandards.gsi.gov.uk
Vice Chair: Diane Murgatroyd *E-mail:* diane.murgatroyd@fco.gov.uk
Secretary: Kate Pritchard *E-mail:* k.pritchard@defra.gsi.gov.uk
Treasurer: William Mead *E-mail:* william.mead@homeoffice.gsi.gov.uk
Network Journal Editor: Sue Westcott
  E-mail: sue.westcott@communities.gsi.gov.uk
Business Manager: Mary Susan Barry
  E-mail: marysusan.barry@bis.gsi.gov.uk
Publicity: Mark Faulkner *Tel:* (020) 7066 1000 *Fax:* (020) 7066 1051 *E-mail:* mark.faulkner@fsa.gov.uk
Publication(s): *GKIM Matters* (2 times/yr, journal, published jointly with the CILIP Government Information Group)

NGLIS, see Network of Government Library & Information Specialists (NGLIS)

School Library Association
One Pine Court, Kembrey Park, Swindon SN2 8AD
Tel: (01793) 530166 *Fax:* (01793) 481182
E-mail: info@sla.org.uk
Web Site: www.sla.org.uk
Key Personnel
President: Kevin Crossley-Holland
Chair: Lin Smith
Vice Chair: Karen Horsfield
Exhibitions & Publications Secretary: Jane Cooper *Tel:* (01793) 401152 *E-mail:* jane.cooper@sla.org.uk
Membership & Training Secretary: Ann Adams *Tel:* (01793) 401153 *E-mail:* ann.adams@sla.org.uk

Treasurer: Susan Staniforth
Dir: Tricia Adams *Tel:* (01793) 401155
  E-mail: tricia.adams@sla.org.uk
Assistant Dir: Sally Duncan *Tel:* (01793) 401156
  E-mail: sally.duncan@sla.org.uk
Production Editor: Richard Leveridge
  Tel: (01793) 401157 *E-mail:* richard.leveridge@sla.org.uk
Founded: 1937
Promote the development of effective school libraries through advocacy, publishing & training.
Publication(s): *Riveting Reads plus; The School Librarian* (quarterly, journal); *SLA Guidelines & Case Studies*

SCONUL, see Society of College, National & University Libraries (SCONUL)

Scottish Health Information Network (SHINE)
NHS Greater Glasgow & Clyde, Royal Alexandra Hospital Library, Corsebar Rd, Paisley PA2 9PN
E-mail: info@shinelib.org.uk
Web Site: www.shinelib.org.uk
Key Personnel
Chair: Paul Manson *Tel:* (01224) 437873
  E-mail: p.manson@nhs.net
Secretary: Ruth Robinson *Tel:* (0141) 314 7178
  E-mail: ruth.robinson4@nhs.net
Treasurer: Margaret Theaker *Tel:* (01292) 513 022 *Fax:* (01292) 513 964 *E-mail:* margaret.theaker@aapct.scot.nhs.uk
Branch Office(s)
Erskine Medical Library, Hugh Robson Bldg, George Sq, Edinburgh EH8 9XE *Tel:* (031) 650-3692

Scottish Library & Information Council (SLIC)
151 West George St, Glasgow G2 2JJ
Tel: (0141) 228 4790
E-mail: slic@slainte.org.uk; cilips@slainte.org.uk
Web Site: www.slainte.org.uk/slic/slicindex.htm
Key Personnel
Chair: Fiona MacLeod
Secretary: Moira Methven
Dir: Elaine Fulton *E-mail:* e.fulton@slainte.org.uk
Assistant Dir: Rhonda Arthur *E-mail:* r.arthur@slainte.org.uk; Catherine Kearney *E-mail:* c.kearney@slainte.org.uk
Founded: 1991
Publication(s): *Annual Report*

SHINE, see Scottish Health Information Network (SHINE)

SLA, see School Library Association

SLIC, see Scottish Library & Information Council (SLIC)

Society of College, National & University Libraries (SCONUL)
94 Euston St, London NW1 2HA
Tel: (020) 7387 0317 *Fax:* (020) 7383 3197
E-mail: info@sconul.ac.uk; sconul@sconul.ac.uk
Web Site: www.sconul.ac.uk
Key Personnel
Chair: Sara Marsh
Vice Chair: Liz Jolly
Executive Dir: Ann Rossiter *Tel:* (020) 3214 8271
  E-mail: ann.rossiter@sconul.ac.uk
Treasurer: Emma Bull
Founded: 1950
Publication(s): *SCONUL Annual Review; SCONUL Focus* (annually); *SCONUL Statistics* (annually); *SCONUL Vision*

United States

IALL, see International Association of Law Libraries (IALL)

IASL, see International Association of School Librarianship (IASL)

International Association of Law Libraries (IALL) (Association Internationale des Bibliotheques de Droit)
University of Michigan Law Library, Ann Arbor, MI 48109-1210
Web Site: www.iall.org
Key Personnel
President: Petal Kinder *Tel:* (02) 6270 6922
    Fax: (02) 6273 2110 *E-mail:* pkinder@hcourt.
    gov.au
First Vice President: Jeroen Vervliet *Tel:* (070)
    302 4242 *E-mail:* j.vervliet@ppl.nl
Second Vice President: Jennefer Aston *Tel:* (01)
    4974385 *E-mail:* jennefera@gmail.com
Secretary: Barbara Garavaglia *Tel:* 734-764-9338
    Fax: 734-764-5863 *E-mail:* bvaccaro@umich.
    edu
Treasurer: Xinh Luu *E-mail:* xtl5d@virginia.edu
Founded: 1959
Promotes the law library profession & access to legal information.
Publication(s): *International Journal of Legal Information* (triannually)

International Association of School Librarianship (IASL)
65 E Wacker Pl, Suite 1900, Chicago, IL 60601-7246
Fax: 312-419-8950
E-mail: iasl@mlahq.org
Web Site: www.iasl-online.org
Key Personnel
President: Dr Diljit Singh *Fax:* (03) 7957 9249
    E-mail: diljit@um.edu.my
Vice President, Association Operations: Lourense Das *E-mail:* iasl@meles.nl
Secretary: Carla Funk
Treasurer: Katy Manck *E-mail:* katy.manck@
    gmail.com
Founded: 1971

Provides an international forum for those people interested in promoting effective school library media programs.
Publication(s): *Annual Conference Proceedings*; *IASL Newsletter* (triannually); *School Libraries Worldwide* (biannually, journal, online)

Uruguay

Agrupacion Bibliotecologica del Uruguay
(Library Science Association of Uruguay)
Cerro Largo 1666, 11200 Montevideo
Tel: 24005740
E-mail: lama@adinet.com.uy
Key Personnel
President: Luis Alberto Musso
Founded: 1964
Publication(s): *Anales del Senado del Uruguay* (Annals of the Senate of Uruguay, 1971); *Aportes para la historia de la bibliotecologia en el Uruguay* (Contributions for the History of the Library Profession in Uruguay, 1969); *Archivos del Uruguay* (Uruguay Archives, 1974); *Bibliografia bibliografica y bibliotecologica* (1964); *Bibliografia de Historia del Uruguay* (Bibliography of the History of Uruguay, 1977); *Bibliografia uruguaya sobre Brasil* (Uruguayan Bibliography on Brazil, 1973); *Colonizacion Canaria en la Banda Oriental del Uruguay* (Canary Colonization in the Eastern Band of Uruguay, 1997); *El Dia - Indice General Alfabetico* (The Day - Alphabetical General Index); *La Estrella del sur-Indice* (The Southern Star, 1968); *Fernandez Saldana, relacion de su obra bibliografica* (Fernandez Saldana Bibliography, 1989); *De Libros y lectores* (Books & Readers, 2000); *El Rio de la Plata en el Archivo de Indias* (The Silver River in the Indian Archives, 1997); *Uruguay-Brasil y sus medallas* (Uruguay Brazil Medals, 1976)

Asociacion de Bibliotecologos del Uruguay
(Uruguayan Library Association)
Eduardo V Haedo 2255, 11200 Montevideo
Tel: 2409 9989 *Fax:* 2409 9989

E-mail: abu@adinet.com.uy
Web Site: www.abu.net.uy
Key Personnel
President: Ruth Santestevan
    E-mail: rsantestevan@yahoo.es
Vice President: Isabel De Leon *E-mail:* idel@
    adinet.com.uy
Secretary: Alicia Fernandez Toricez
    E-mail: torices@gmail.com
Treasurer: Leonor Porras Segurola
    E-mail: leopo21@gmail.com
Public Relations: Carina Patron
    E-mail: carinapatron@gmail.com
Founded: 1978
Publication(s): *Panel de Noticias* (News Board, monthly, free to members only)

Vietnam

Hoi Thu-Vien Vietnam (Vietnamese Library Association)
National Library of Vietnam, 31 Trang Thi, Hanoi 10000
Tel: (04) 39366596
E-mail: info@vla.org.vn
Web Site: www.vla.org.vn
Key Personnel
Contact: Phan Thi Kim Dung
Founded: 2006
Publication(s): *Thu'-Vien Tap-san* (Library Bulletin)

Zambia

Zambia Library Association
PO Box 38636, 10101 Lusaka
Key Personnel
Chairman: Benson Njobvu
    E-mail: bensonnjobvu@hotmail.com
Publication(s): *Zambia Library Association Journal* (quarterly); *Zambia Library Association Newsletter*

Library Reference Books & Journals

The publications in this section are library related and are listed alphabetically under the country of the publisher or the country to which the title relates.

The type of publication appears in parentheses after the title:

(B) - Book   (J) - Journal   (P) - Periodical

For information on reference books, journals and periodicals relating to the book publishing industry see **Book Trade Reference Books & Journals**.

Australia

Access (J)
Published by Australian School Library Association Inc
PO Box 155, Zillmere, Qld 4034
Tel: (07) 3633 0510 *Fax:* (07) 3633 0570
E-mail: asla@asla.org.au
Web Site: www.asla.org.au
Key Personnel
Editor: Rachel Hoare *E-mail:* d.r.hoare@bigpond.com
Provides an open forum for all educators at all levels who are concerned with issues arising from information literacy.
First published 1987.
Quarterly.
100 AUD
ISSN: 1030-0155

Archives and Manuscripts (J)
Published by Australian Society of Archivists Inc (ASA)
Suite 2, Level 4, 360 Queen St, Brisbane, Qld 4000
Mailing Address: PO Box A623, Sydney South, NSW 1235
Tel: (07) 3221 4887 *Toll Free Tel:* 1800 622 251 *Fax:* (07) 3221 6885
E-mail: office@archivists.org.au
Web Site: www.archivists.org.au
Key Personnel
Editor: Sebastian Gurciullo
  E-mail: journaleditor@archivists.org.au
Provides archivists & other record keeping & information professionals with up to date material on professional issues & practice.
Also available online (ISSN: 2164-6058).
First published 1955.
3 times/yr.
165 AUD
ISSN: 0157-6895

Australian Academic & Research Libraries (J)
Published by Australian Library & Information Association Ltd (ALIA)
ALIA House, 9-11 Napier Close, Deakin, ACT 2600
Mailing Address: PO Box 6335, Kingston, ACT 2604
Tel: (02) 6215 8222 *Toll Free Tel:* 1800 020 071 (members only) *Fax:* (02) 6282 2249
E-mail: enquiry@alia.org.au
Web Site: www.alia.org.au
Key Personnel
Editor: Dr Gaby Haddow *E-mail:* aarleditor@alia.org.au; Dr Mary Anne Keenan
Quarterly.
90 AUD (member); 130 AUD (member, overseas air); 120 AUD (nonmember); 160 AUD (nonmember, overseas air)
ISSN: 0004-8623

Australian Library Journal (J)
Published by Australian Library & Information Association Ltd (ALIA)
ALIA House, 9-11 Napier Close, Deakin, ACT 2600
Mailing Address: PO Box 6335, Kingston, ACT 2604
Tel: (02) 6215 8222 *Toll Free Tel:* 1800 020 071 (members only) *Fax:* (02) 6282 2249
E-mail: enquiry@alia.org.au
Web Site: www.alia.org.au
Key Personnel
Editor: Ann Ritchie *Tel:* (04) 0111 0388
  E-mail: alj.editor@alia.org.au
Academic/scholarly publication.
First published 1951.
Quarterly.
90 AUD (member); 130 AUD (member, overseas air); 120 AUD (nonmember); 160 AUD (nonmember, overseas air)
ISSN: 0004-9670

inCite (P)
Published by Australian Library & Information Association Ltd (ALIA)
ALIA House, 9-11 Napier Close, Deakin, ACT 2600
Mailing Address: PO Box 6335, Kingston, ACT 2604
Tel: (02) 6215 8222 *Toll Free Tel:* 1800 020 071 (members only) *Fax:* (02) 6282 2249
E-mail: incite@alia.org.au; enquiry@alia.org.au
Web Site: www.alia.org.au
First published 1980.
Monthly.
116 AUD (member); 166 AUD (member, overseas air); 160 AUD (nonmember); 210 AUD (nonmember, overseas air)
ISSN: 0158-0876

La Trobe Journal (J)
Published by State Library of Victoria Foundation
328 Swanston St, Melbourne, Victoria 3000
Tel: (03) 8664 7000; (03) 8664 7280 *Fax:* (03) 9639 4737
E-mail: foundation@slv.vic.gov.au
Web Site: www.slv.vic.gov.au
Key Personnel
Editor: John Arnold *E-mail:* john.arnold@monash.edu
First published 1968.
2 times/yr.
85 AUD (membership)
ISSN: 1441-3760

Austria

Biblos (J)
Published by Phoibos Verlag
Anzengrubergasse 16, 1050 Vienna
Tel: (01) 544 03 191 *Fax:* (01) 544 03 199
E-mail: office@phoibos.at
Web Site: www.phoibos.at; www.onb.ac.at/biblos/index.htm
Key Personnel
Mng Editor: Christian Gastgeber
  E-mail: christian.gastgeber@oeaw.ac.at
Austrian journal for book & library personnel, documentation, bibliography & bibliophily; published in English & German.
First published 1952.
2 times/yr.
25 EUR (one issue); 45 EUR/yr (subscription)
ISSN: 0006-2022

Mitteilungen der Vereinigung Oesterreichischer Bibliothekarinnen und Bibliothekare Mitteilungen (Communications of the Association of Austrian Librarians) (J)
Published by Vereinigung Oesterreichischer Bibliothekarinnen und Bibliothekare (VOEB) (Association of Austrian Librarians)
Universitaetsbibliothek Graz, Universitaetsplatz 3, 8010 Graz
E-mail: voeb-mitt@uibk.ac.at
Web Site: www.univie.ac.at/voeb
Key Personnel
President: Dr Werner Schlacher *E-mail:* werner.schlacher@uni-graz.at
Head, Library & Communicatlion: Dr Josef Pauser *E-mail:* josef.pauser@univie.ac.at
Text in German.
First published 1948.
3 times/yr.
50 EUR
ISSN: 1022-2588

Scrinium (J)
Published by Verband Oesterreichischer Archivarinnen und Archivare (Association of Austrian Archivists)
Archiv der Universitat Wien, Postgasse 9, 1010 Vienna
Tel: (01) 4277-17218 *Fax:* (01) 4277-9172
E-mail: sekretariat@voea.at
Web Site: www.voea.at
Key Personnel
Editor: Thomas Just *E-mail:* thomas.just@oesta.gv.at; Thomas Maisel *E-mail:* thomas.maisel@univie.ac.at; Christine Tropper *E-mail:* christine.tropper@ktn.gv.at
Text in German.
First published 1969.
2 times/yr.
Free to members
ISSN: 1012-0327

Belgium

Archives et Bibliotheques de Belgique (Archives & Libraries of Belgium) (J)
Published by Bibliotheque Royale de Belgique (Royal Library of Belgium)
Blvd de l'Empereur 2, 1000 Brussels
E-mail: abb@kbr.be
Web Site: www.archibib.be
Key Personnel
President: Marc Libert
Chief Editor: Dirk Leyder
Treasurer: Nathael Istasse
Secretary: Sara Lammens
Administrative Secretary: Anja Marginet
First published 2008.
Annually.
30 EUR
ISSN: 0775-0722

Les Cahiers de la Documentation (J)
Published by Association Belge de Documentation/Belgische Vereniging Voor Documentatie (Belgian Association for Documentation)
4 Blvd de l'Empereur, 1000 Brussels
Tel: (02) 675 58 62 *Fax:* (02) 672 74 46
E-mail: abdbvd@abd-bvd.be; cahiers-bladen@abd-bvd.net
Web Site: www.abd-bvd.be
Key Personnel
Treasurer: Didier Haas *E-mail:* didier.haas@fanc.fgov.be
Text in Dutch, English & French.
First published 1947.
Quarterly.
50 EUR/yr (individuals); 90 EUR (institutions); 12.50 EUR (students)
ISSN: 0007-9804

META, tidjschrift voor bibliotheek & archief (J)
Published by Vlaamse Vereniging voor Bibliotheek, Archief en Documentatie VZW (VVBAD) (Flemish Association for Libraries, Archives & Documentation Centres)
Statiestr 179, 2600 Berchem
Tel: (03) 281 44 57
E-mail: vvbad@vvbad.be
Web Site: www.vvbad.be
Key Personnel
Secretary: Klaartje Brits *E-mail:* klaartje.brits@vvbad.de
Scientific journal.
First published 1922.
9 times/yr.
127 EUR; 168 EUR (International)
ISSN: 2033-639X

Bulgaria

Biblioteka: spisanie za bibliotechno delo (Library Journrnal) (J)
Published by Nacionalna biblioteka Sv sv Kiril i Metodii (Saints Cyril & Methodius National Library)
88 Vasil Levski Blvd, 1037 Sofia
Tel: (02) 91 83 101 *Fax:* (02) 84 35 495
E-mail: nl@nationallibrary.bg
Web Site: www.nationallibrary.bg
Key Personnel
Editor-in-Chief: Asen Georgiev *Tel:* (02) 91 83 220 *E-mail:* a.georgiev@nationallibrary.bg
Publishes materials about bibliographic theory & practice, including unique documents. Offers information & reviews about newly published books.

First published 1954.
6 times/yr.
54 BGN
ISSN: 0861-847X

Journal Biblioteca, see Biblioteka: spisanie za bibliotechno delo

Colombia

Boletin Cultural y Bibliografico (Cultural & Bibliographical Bulletin) (J)
Published by Biblioteca Luis Angel Arango Banco de la Republica - Colombia (Luis Angel Arango Library-Central Bank of Colombia)
Calle 11 No 4-14, Bogota 12362
Tel: (01) 3431111 (ext 2936) *Fax:* (01) 381 29 08
Web Site: www.banrepcultural.org/blaa
Key Personnel
Publishing Coordinator: Ana Maria Camargo Gomez *E-mail:* acamargo@banrep.gov.co
Presents/displays articles & bibliographical reviews in diverse subjects.
First published 1958.
2 times/yr.
188 pp, 4 USD
ISSN: 0006-6184

Croatia

Vjesnik bibliotekara Hrvatske (Croatian Librarians' Herald) (J)
Published by Hrvatsko knjiznicarsko drustvo (Croatian Library Association)
c/o Nacionalna i sveucilisna Knjiznica, Hrvatske bratske zajednice 4, 10 000 Zagreb
Tel: (01) 615 93 20 *Fax:* (01) 615 93 20
E-mail: vbh@hkdrustvo.hr; hkd@hkdrustvo.hr
Web Site: www.hkdrustvo.hr
Key Personnel
Editor-in-Chief: Kornelija Petr Balog *E-mail:* kpetr@ffos.hr
Text in Croatian, English, German; summaries in Croatian & English. Back issues available. Cumulative index every 5 years.
Also available online (ISSN: 1334-6938).
First published 1950.
1-2 times/yr.
200 pp, 300 HRK or 42 EUR
ISSN: 0507-1925

Cuba

Revista de la Biblioteca Nacional de Cuba Jose Marti (Jose Marti National Library Review) (J)
Published by Biblioteca Nacional Jose Marti (Jose Marti National Library)
Ave Independencia y 20 de Mayo, Plaza de la Revolucion, Havana
Mailing Address: Apdo 6670, Havana
Tel: (07) 8555442; (07) 8555449 *Fax:* (07) 8816264
E-mail: revista_bnjm@bnjm.cu
Web Site: revistas.bnjm.cu; www.josemarti.cu
Key Personnel
Dir: Dr Eduardo Torres Cuevas
Head, Publishing: Johan Moya Ramis
Editor: Araceli Garcia Carranza *E-mail:* araceli@bnjm.cu
Text in Spanish.

Also available online (ISSN: 1683-8939).
First published 1909.
Quarterly.
30 USD (North America); 25 USD (South America); 35 USD (Europe)
ISSN: 0006-1727

Denmark

Arbog, Antologi om paedagogiske laeringscentre (B)
Published by Kommunernes Forening for Paedagogiske Laeringscentre (KFPLC)
Farvergade 27 D, 2 sal, 1463 Copenhagen K
Tel: 33 11 13 91
E-mail: kfplc@kfplc.dk
Web Site: www.kfplc.dk
First published 2015.
Annually.
ISSN: 2445-4923

Biblioteksvejviser (Guide to Danish Libraries) (B)
Published by Danmarks Biblioteksforening (Danish Library Association)
Vartov, Farvergade 27D, 2 sal, 1463 Copenhagen K
Tel: 3325 0935 *Fax:* 3325 7900
E-mail: db@db.dk
Web Site: www.db.dk
Key Personnel
Chairman: Vagn Ytte Larsen *Tel:* 2178 9383 *E-mail:* vagn@ytte.dk
Dir: Michel Steen-Hansen
Text in Danish; index in English.
First published 1970.
Annually.
412 DKK/yr (members); 492 DKK/yr (nonmembers)
ISSN: 0420-1108

Danmarks Biblioteker (J)
Published by Danmarks Biblioteksforening (Danish Library Association)
Vartov, Farvergade 27D, 2 sal, 1463 Copenhagen K
Tel: 3325 0935 *Fax:* 3325 7900
E-mail: db@db.dk
Web Site: www.db.dk
Key Personnel
Chairman: Vagn Ytte Larsen *Tel:* 2178 9383 *E-mail:* vagn@ytte.dk
Dir: Michel Steen-Hansen
Editor: Hellen Niegaard *E-mail:* hn@db.dk
Newsletter from the Danish Library Association.
First published 1987.
8 times/yr.
650 DKK (domestic); 710 DKK (foreign)
ISSN: 1397-1026

Perspektiv (J)
Published by Bibliotekarforbundet
Peter Bangs Vej 30, 2000 Frederiksberg
Tel: 38 88 22 33 *Fax:* 38 88 32 01
E-mail: bf@bf.dk; perspektiv@bf.dk
Web Site: bf.dk/fagmagasinetperspektiv
Key Personnel
Mng Editor: Anette Lerche *Tel:* 38 38 06 37 *E-mail:* lerche@bf.dk
11 times/yr.
610 DKK (domestic); 980 DKK (foreign)
ISSN: 1904-7940

Revy (J)
Published by Danmarks Forskningsbiblioteksforening (Danish Research Library Association)
Statsbiblioteket, Tangen 2, 8200 Aarhus N
Tel: 89 46 22 07
E-mail: df@statsbiblioteket.dk

Web Site: www.dfrevy.dk; www.dfdf.dk
Key Personnel
Editor: Rene Steffensen *E-mail:* rs.lib@cbs.dk
Also available online (ISSN: 1904-1977).
First published 1978.
6 times/yr.
400 DKK
ISSN: 1904-1969

Finland

Kirjastolehti (Library Journal) (J)
Published by Suomen Kirjastoseura (Finnish Library Association)
Runeberginkatu 15 A 26, 00100 Helsinki
Tel: (044) 522 2941
E-mail: info@fla.fi; kirjastolehti@fla.fi
Web Site: kirjastolehti.fi
Key Personnel
Editor-in-Chief: Ville Vaarne *Tel:* (044) 522 2940
 E-mail: ville.vaarne@fla.fi
First published 1908.
Quarterly.
40 pp, 65 EUR; 73 EUR (foreign)
ISSN: 0023-1843

Signum (J)
Published by Suomen Tieteellinen Kirjastoseura
Ry (Finnish Research Library Association)
c/o Tieteiden talo, Kirkkokatu 6, 00170 Helsinki
Web Site: www.stks.fi
Key Personnel
Editor-in-Chief: Johanna Lahikainen *Tel:* (02941)
 23753 *E-mail:* johanna.lahikainen@helsinki.fi
First published 1968.
6 times/yr.
ISSN: 0355-0036

France

Documentaliste - Sciences de l'Information
 (Documentalist - Information Sciences) (J)
Published by L'association des professionnels de
 l'information et de la documentation (ADBS)
 (The Association of Information & Documentation Professionals)
25 rue Claude Tillier, 75012 Paris
Tel: 01 43 72 25 25 *Fax:* 01 43 72 30 41
E-mail: adbs@adbs.fr
Web Site: www.adbs.fr
Key Personnel
Secretariat General, Communication: Carole
 LeGrand *Tel:* 01 43 72 99 80
Head of Publications: Michele Battisti
French review devoted to techniques, professions,
 services & policies in the information & library
 fields & to research in information sciences,
 with particular focus on European & French-
 speaking countries. Abstracts in English.
First published 1964.
Quarterly.
80 pp, 110 EUR (domestic); 122 EUR (foreign)
ISSN: 0012-4508

InterCDI (J)
Published by Centre d'Etude de la Documentation
 et de l'Information Scolaires (CEDIS)
73, rue St Jacques, 91154 Etampes Cedex
Tel: 01 64 94 39 51 *Fax:* 01 64 94 49 35; 01 64
 94 54 99 (subscriptions)
E-mail: cedis-intercdi@wanadoo.fr
Web Site: intercdi.com
Key Personnel
Président & Editor-in-Chief: Veronique Delarue

Dir, Publications: Elena Codignola
Journal for Specialist Librarians (second level).
First published 1972.
6 times/yr.
108 pp, 69.50 EUR (France); 78.50 EUR (in Europe); 97 EUR (elsewhere)
ISSN: 0242-2999

Germany

Beitraege zum Buch-und Bibliothekswesen
 (Contributions to Book & Libraries) (B)
Published by Harrassowitz Verlag
Kreuzberger Ring 7b-d, 65205 Wiesbaden
Tel: (0611) 530-905 *Fax:* (0611) 530-999
E-mail: verlag@harrassowitz.de
Web Site: www.harrassowitz-verlag.de
Key Personnel
Dir: Dr Barbara Krauss *E-mail:* bkrauss@
 harrassowitz.de
Sales: Robert Gietz *Tel:* (0611) 530-901
 E-mail: rgietz@harrassowitz.de
This book series deals with, among other things,
 library science, bibliographies & the history of
 books, libraries & publishing houses. Text in
 German.
First published 1965.
Irregularly.
Vol 61, 2017
ISSN: 0408-8107

Bibliothek und Wissenschaft (Libraries &
 Science) (J)
Published by Harrassowitz Verlag
Kreuzberger Ring 7b-d, 65205 Wiesbaden
Tel: (0611) 530-905 *Fax:* (0611) 530-999
E-mail: verlag@harrassowitz.de
Web Site: www.harrassowitz-verlag.de
Key Personnel
Dir: Dr Barbara Krauss *E-mail:* bkrauss@
 harrassowitz.de
History of books, libraries & science.
First published 1964.
Annually.
99 EUR or 168 CHF
ISSN: 0067-8236

Buchwissenschaftliche Beitraege (Contributions
 to Book Science) (B)
Published by Harrassowitz Verlag
Kreuzberger Ring 7b-d, 65205 Wiesbaden
Tel: (0611) 530-905 *Fax:* (0611) 530-999
E-mail: verlag@harrassowitz.de
Web Site: www.harrassowitz-verlag.de
Key Personnel
Dir: Dr Barbara Krauss *E-mail:* bkrauss@
 harrassowitz.de
Editor: Christine Haug; Vincent Kaufmann; Wolf-
 gang Schmitz
Sales: Robert Gietz *Tel:* (0611) 530-901
 E-mail: rgietz@harrassowitz.de
This book series deals, among other things, with
 the history of books, libraries, literature & pub-
 lishing houses.
First published 1950.
Irregularly.
Vol 95, 2017
ISSN: 0724-7001

ƒIFLA Publications (B)
Published by De Gruyter Saur
Genthiner Str 13, 10785 Berlin
Tel: (030) 260 05-0 *Fax:* (030) 260 05-251
E-mail: service@degruyter.com
Web Site: www.degruyter.com
Key Personnel
Editor: Janine Schmidt

A series of publications edited by the Interna-
 tional Federation of Library Associations &
 Institutions. Available also as ebooks.
First published 1927.
2-3 titles/yr.
ISSN: 0344-6891

Jahrbuch der Deutschen Bibliotheken
 (Yearbook of German Libraries) (J)
Published by Harrassowitz Verlag
Kreuzberger Ring 7b-d, 65205 Wiesbaden
Tel: (0611) 530-905 *Fax:* (0611) 530-999
E-mail: verlag@harrassowitz.de
Web Site: www.harrassowitz.de
Key Personnel
Dir: Dr Barbara Krauss *E-mail:* bkrauss@
 harrassowitz.de
Information about German scientific libraries.
First published 1902.
2 times/yr.
566 pp, 89 EUR
ISBN(s): 978-3-447-10337-4
ISSN: 0075-2223

Leipziger Jahrbuch zur Buchgeschichte (The
 Leipzig Yearbook for Book History) (B)
Published by Harrassowitz Verlag
Kreuzberger Ring 7b-d, 65205 Wiesbaden
Tel: (0611) 530-905 *Fax:* (0611) 530-999
E-mail: verlag@harrassowitz.de
Web Site: www.harrassowitz-verlag.de
Key Personnel
Dir: Dr Barbara Krauss *E-mail:* bkrauss@
 harrassowitz.de
Editor: Thomas Fuchs; Christine Haug; Katrin
 Loeffler
History of books, the book trade, publishers &
 printers.
First published 1990.
Annually.
Vol 25, 2017: 290 pp, 79 EUR
ISBN(s): 978-3-447-10895-9
ISSN: 0940-1954

**Marginalien Zeitschrift fuer Buchkunst und
 Bibliophilie** (Marginal Notes - Journal for
 Book Art & Bibliophily) (J)
Published by Harrassowitz Verlag
Kreuzberger Ring 7b-d, 65205 Wiesbaden
Tel: (0611) 530-905 *Fax:* (0611) 530-999
E-mail: verlag@harrassowitz.de
Web Site: www.harrassowitz-verlag.de; www.
 pirckheimer-gesellschaft.org
Key Personnel
Dir: Dr Barbara Krauss *E-mail:* bkrauss@
 harrassowitz.de
First published 1948.
Quarterly.
74 EUR per annum
ISSN: 0025-2948

Medienprofile (J)
Published by Borromaeusverein eV
Wittelsbacherring 7-9, 53115 Bonn
Tel: (0288) 7258-400 *Fax:* (0228) 7258-412
E-mail: info@borromaeusverein.de; nuesgen@
 borromaeusverein.de
Web Site: www.borromaeusverein.de
Key Personnel
Mng Dir: Guido Schroeer *Tel:* (0228) 7258-409
 E-mail: schroeer@borromaeusverein.de
Editorial, Online & Print: Ulrike Fink *Tel:* (0228)
 7258-407 *E-mail:* fink@borromaeusverein.de
Book profile for Catholic library work.
Quarterly.
52 EUR
ISSN: 1868-3460

**Wolfenbuetteler Schriften zur Geschichte des
 Buchwesens** (Wolfenbuetteler Writings on the
 History of the Book Industry) (J)
Published by Harrassowitz Verlag
Kreuzberger Ring 7b-d, 65205 Wiesbaden

Tel: (0611) 530-905 *Fax:* (0611) 530-999
E-mail: verlag@harrassowitz.de
Web Site: www.harrassowitz-verlag.de
Key Personnel
Dir: Dr Barbara Krauss *E-mail:* bkrauss@
  harrassowitz.de
Sales: Robert Gietz *Tel:* (0611) 530-901
  E-mail: rgietz@harrassowitz.de
This journal series deals with the history of
  books, libraries & publishing houses.
First published 1977.
Irregularly.
Vol 50, 2017: 336 pp, 74 EUR
ISBN(s): 978-3-447-10720-4
ISSN: 0724-9586

*∮***World Guide to Libraries** (B)
Published by De Gruyter Saur
Imprint of Walter de Gruyter GmbH & Co KG
Genthiner Str 13, 10785 Berlin
Tel: (030) 260 05-0 *Fax:* (030) 260 05-251
E-mail: service@degruyter.com
Web Site: www.degruyter.com
Furnishes details on more than 42,500 libraries
  in over 200 countries. Covers national, general
  research, university, school, government, cor-
  porate, ecclesiastical, special & public libraries
  with over 30,000 volumes. Alphabetical index.
  Available in print & eBookPLUS.
Annually.
33rd ed, 2018, 839 EUR, 960 USD or 760 GBP
  (print); 839 EUR, 960 USD or 762.50 GBP
  (eBookPLUS)
ISBN(s): 978-3-11-057610-8 (hardcover); 978-3-
  11-058044-0 (eBookPLUS)
ISSN: 0936-0085

*∮***World Guide to Special Libraries** (B)
Published by De Gruyter Saur
Imprint of Walter de Gruyter GmbH & Co KG
Genthiner Str 13, 10785 Berlin
Tel: (030) 260 05-0 *Fax:* (030) 260 05-251
E-mail: service@degruyter.com
Web Site: www.degruyter.com
Lists approximately 35,000 libraries worldwide,
  categorized by 800 subject headings.
10th ed, 2015: 1,491 pp, 619 EUR, 867 USD or
  464.99 GBP
ISBN(s): 978-3-11-040518-7
ISSN: 0724-8717

Zeitschrift fuer Bibliothekswesen und
  Bibliographie (Journal of Library Science &
  Bibliography) (J)
Published by Vittorio Klostermann GmbH
Westerbachstr 47, 60489 Frankfurt am Main
Tel: (069) 97 08 16-0 *Fax:* (069) 70 80 38
E-mail: verlag@klostermann.de
Web Site: www.klostermann.de
Key Personnel
Editor: Ann-Katrin Colomb; Martin Hollender;
  Natalie Kromm
6 times/yr.
126 EUR plus shipping (institutions)
ISSN: 0044-2380

Hungary

Konyvtari Figyelo (Library Review) (J)
Published by Orszagos Szechenyi Konyvtar (Na-
  tional Szechenyi Library)
Budavari Palota F epulet, Budapest 1827
Tel: (01) 224-3795; (01) 224-3796 *Fax:* (01) 224-
  3875
Web Site: www.oszk.hu; ki.oszk.hu/kf
Key Personnel
Editor: Katalin Kovacs *E-mail:* kovacs@oszk.hu
Text in Hungarian. Summaries in English.

Also available online (ISSN: 1586-5193).
First published 1955.
Quarterly.
ISSN: 0023-3773

Iceland

Bokasafnid
Published by Upplysing - Felag bokasafns- og
  upplysingafraeda (Information - The Icelandic
  Library & Information Science Association)
Postholf 8865, 128 Reykjavik
Tel: 864-6220
E-mail: bokasafnid.timarit@gmail.com
Web Site: upplysing.is
Key Personnel
Editor: Sveinn Olafsson
Yearbook of library & information science.
Also available online (ISSN: 1670-0066).
First published 1974.
Annually.
ISSN: 0257-6775

India

Annals of Library & Information Studies (J)
Published by CSIR-National Institute of Sci-
  ence Communication & Information Resources
  (CSIR-NISCAIR)
Dr K S Krishanan Marg, Pusa Campus, New
  Delhi 110 012
Tel: (011) 26960465; (011) 25846301; (011)
  25846304; (011) 25846305; (011) 25846306;
  (011) 25846307 *Fax:* (011) 26519231; (011)
  25847062
E-mail: annals@niscair.res.in; sales@niscair.res.in
Web Site: www.niscair.res.in
Key Personnel
Dir & Editor-in-Chief: Dr Manoj Kumar Patairiya
  Tel: (011) 25847062
Editor: Dr G Mahesh *E-mail:* gmahesh@niscair.
  res.in
Associate Editor: Ms Swarnlata Upadhyay
Text in English. Publish original papers, survey
  reports, reviews, short communications & let-
  ters pertaining to library science, information
  science & computer applications in these fields.
Also available online (ISSN: 0975-2404).
First published 1954.
Quarterly.
1,200 INR or 140 USD
ISSN: 0972-5423

Books of the Week Bulletin (J)
Published by D K Agencies (P) Ltd
Mohan Garden, A/15-17, D K Ave, Najafgarh Rd,
  New Delhi 110 059
Tel: (011) 2535-7104; (011) 2535-7105
  Fax: (011) 2535-7103
E-mail: information@dkagencies.com
Web Site: www.dkagencies.com
Comprehensive, systematic bibliographic bulletin
  with Library of Congress subject headings cov-
  ering all publications catalogued at D K.
Weekly.

D K Newsletter (J)
Published by D K Agencies (P) Ltd
Mohan Garden, A/15-17, D K Ave, Najafgarh Rd,
  New Delhi 110 059
Tel: (011) 2535-7104; (011) 2535-7105
  Fax: (011) 2535-7103
E-mail: information@dkagencies.com
Web Site: www.dkagencies.com

News & reviews of Indian publications in En-
  glish.
First published 1975.
Quarterly.
ISSN: 0971-4448

IASLIC Bulletin (J)
Published by Indian Association of Special Li-
  braries & Information Centres (IASLIC)
P-291, CIT Scheme No 6M, Kankurgachi,
  Kolkata 700 054
Tel: (033) 2362 9651
E-mail: iaslic@vsnl.net; iaslic.journal@gmail.com
Web Site: www.iaslic1955.org.in
Key Personnel
General Secretary: Sajal Kanti Goswami
  E-mail: sajalgoswami_123@yahoo.co.in
Editor: Prof Arjun Dasgupta
  E-mail: arjundasgupta@gmail.com
Associate Editor: Prof Pijushkanti Panigrahi
  E-mail: panigrahipk@yahoo.com
Corporate author: Indian Association of Special
  Libraries & Information. Text in English.
First published 1956.
Quarterly.
1,500 INR (domestic); 120 USD (foreign)
ISSN: 0018-8441

Indian Library Science Abstract (ILSA) (J)
Published by Indian Association of Special Li-
  braries & Information Centres (IASLIC)
P-291, CIT Scheme No 6M, Kankurgachi,
  Kolkata 700 054
Tel: (033) 2362 9651
E-mail: iaslic@vsnl.net
Web Site: www.iaslic1955.org.in
Key Personnel
Editor: Prof Juran Krishna Sarkhel
  E-mail: jksarkhel@hotmail.com
First published 1967.
300 USD
ISSN: 0019-5790

Journal of Indian Library Association (JILA)
  (J)
Published by Indian Library Association
A/40-41, Flat No 201, Ansal Bldg, Dr Mukherjee
  Nagar, Delhi 110 009
Tel: (011) 27651743
E-mail: ila@ilaindia.net; jila@ilaindia.net
Web Site: ilaindia.net
Key Personnel
General Secretary: Dr Pardeep Rai
  Tel: 9899359373 (cell) *E-mail:* raipardeep@
  gmail.com
Text in English.
First published 2011.
Quarterly.
1,500 INR or 50 USD (print & online)
ISSN: 2277-5145

Journal of Library & Information Science (J)
Published by University of Delhi, Dept of Library
  & Information Science
II floor, Tutorial Bldg, Delhi 110 007
Tel: (011) 27666656 *Fax:* (011) 27666656
E-mail: jlis@libinfosci.du.ac.in
Web Site: dlis.du.ac.in/JLIS.htm
Key Personnel
Editor: Dr Shailendra Kumar
First published 1976.
2 times/yr.
600 INR, 40 GBP or 70 USD
ISSN: 0970-714X

MIWA-Major Indian Works Annual (B)
Published by D K Agencies (P) Ltd
Mohan Garden, A/15-17, D K Ave, Najafgarh Rd,
  New Delhi 110 059
Tel: (011) 2535-7104; (011) 2535-7105
  Fax: (011) 2535-7103
E-mail: information@dkagencies.com

Web Site: www.dkagencies.com
Bibliographic guide to carefully chosen, genuinely significant works of higher academic/research/general value.
Annually.
ISSN: 0971-4669

Special List (J)
Published by D K Agencies (P) Ltd
Mohan Garden, A/15-17, D K Ave, Najafgarh Rd, New Delhi 110 059
Tel: (011) 2535-7104; (011) 2535-7105
   Fax: (011) 2535-7103
E-mail: custserv@dkagencies.com; information@dkagencies.com
Web Site: www.dkagencies.com
Information by subject on books & back numbers of Indian periodicals.

Subscribers' Guide to Indian Periodicals/Serials (J)
Published by D K Agencies (P) Ltd
Mohan Garden, A/15-17, D K Ave, Najafgarh Rd, New Delhi 110 059
Tel: (011) 2535-7104; (011) 2535-7105
   Fax: (011) 2535-7103
E-mail: custserv@dkagencies.com; information@dkagencies.com
Web Site: www.dkagencies.com
Index of current academic/research journals.

Iran

Faslname-ye Ketab (J)
Published by National Library & Archives of the Islamic Republic of Iran
National Library Local Access Rd, Mirdamad Underground Sta, Shahid Haghani Highway, Tehran
Mailing Address: PO Box 19395-69573, Tehran 1537614111
Tel: (021) 88644080; (021) 86644081 *Fax:* (021) 88644082
E-mail: nli@nlai.ir
Web Site: www.nlai.ir
First published 1990.
Quarterly.
ISSN: 1022-6451

Ireland

Irish Library News (J)
Published by Libraries Development
Local Government Management Agency, 35-39 Ushers Quay, Dublin 8
Tel: (01) 6332200
E-mail: info@library.ie
Web Site: www.lgma.ie/en/libraries
Online only service (since 2009) which features news & information on libraries & librarianship in Ireland, covering the activities of the 32 Public Library Authorities; library cooperation & interlending; library development & library education & training.
First published 1977.

An Leabharlann (Irish Library) (J)
Published by The Library Association of Ireland (LAI) & CILIP-Northern Ireland
138-144 Pearse St, Dublin 2
Tel: (01) 4597834
E-mail: honsecretary@libraryassociation.ie
Web Site: www.anleabharlann.ie; www.libraryassociation.ie

Key Personnel
President: Fionnuala Hanrahan
   E-mail: president@libraryassociation.ie
Editor: Marjory Sliney
First published 1930.
2 times/yr.
ISSN: 0023-9542

Long Room (J)
Published by Friends of the Library
Trinity College Library, College St, Dublin 2
Tel: (01) 8962320 *Fax:* (01) 8962690
E-mail: bookofkells@tcd.ie
Web Site: www.tcd.ie/library/support-library/friends.php; www.tcd.ie/library/old-library
Ireland's journal for the history of the book.
First published 1970.
2 times/yr.
Free to members (30 EUR minimum)
ISSN: 0024-631X

Israel

Index to Hebrew Periodicals (P)
Published by University of Haifa, The Library
Abba Khoushy Blvd 199, Mount Carmel, 3498838 Haifa
Tel: (04) 8240264 *Fax:* (04) 8257753
E-mail: libmaster@univ.haifa.ac.il
Web Site: lib.haifa.ac.il
Key Personnel
Library Dir: Pnina Erez *E-mail:* epnina@univ.haifa.ac.il
Head, Periodicals: Neta Waisman
   E-mail: nwaisman@univ.haifa.ac.il
Available online only.
First published 1977.
Annually.
ISSN: 0334-2921

Meidaat: Journal of Information Science and Librarianship (Reader's Aid) (P)
Published by The Israeli Center for Libraries
22 Baruch Hirsch St, 51108 Bnei Brak
Tel: (03) 6180151
E-mail: icl@icl.org.il
Web Site: www.icl.org.il
Key Personnel
Editor: Orly Nathan
Israel Journal for Libraries & Archives.
First published 1946.
Annually.
ISSN: 1565-544X

Italy

Accademie e Biblioteche d'Italia (Academies & Libraries of Italy) (J)
Published by Gangemi Editore SpA
Via Giulia, 142, 00186 Rome RM
Tel: (06) 6872774 *Fax:* (06) 68806189
E-mail: info@gangemieditore.it
Web Site: www.gangemieditore.com
Key Personnel
Mng Dir: Rosanna Rummo
Deputy Dir: Angela Benintende
Editorial Dir: Angela Adriana Cavarra
Editor-in-Chief: Laura Lanza
First published 1927.
Quarterly.
100 pp, 55 EUR; 75 EUR (foreign)
ISSN: 0001-4451

AIB Studi (AIB Studies) (J)
Published by Associazione Italiana Biblioteche (Italian Library Association)
c/o Biblioteca Nazionale Centrale, Viale Castro Pretorio 105, 00185 Rome RM
Tel: (06) 4463532 *Fax:* (06) 4441139
E-mail: aibstudi@aib.it
Web Site: aibstudi.aib.it
Key Personnel
Editor: Giovanni Di Domenico
   E-mail: giodidomenico@libero.it
Editorial Off Contact: Maria Teresa Natale
   E-mail: natale@aib.it
Research & analysis in the field LIS & committed to the advancement of professional practice, experimentation & theoretical methods of inquiry.
First published 1955.
Quarterly.
100 EUR
ISSN: 2280-9112

Regole Italiane di Catalogazione (Italian Rules of Cataloging) (B)
Published by Istituto Centrale per il Catalogo Unico delle Biblioteche Italiane e per le Informazioni Bibliografiche (Central Institute for the Union Catalog of Italian Libraries & Bibliographic Information)
Viale Castro Pretorio, 105, 00185 Rome RM
Tel: (06) 49210425; (06) 4989424 *Fax:* (06) 4959 302
E-mail: ic-cu@beniculturali.it; venditapubbl@iccu.sbn.it
Web Site: www.iccu.sbn.it
Key Personnel
Dir: Simonetta Butto *E-mail:* simonetta.butto@beniculturali.it
2009, 50 EUR
ISBN(s): 978-88-7107-127-5

Jamaica

LIAJA Journal (J)
Published by Library & Information Association of Jamaica (LIAJA)
PO Box 125, Kingston 5
Tel: (876) 927-1614 *Fax:* (876) 927-1614
E-mail: liajapresident@yahoo.com
Web Site: www.liaja.org.jm
Key Personnel
President: Viviene Kerr-Williams
   E-mail: vskwilliams@gmail.com
Chair, Research & Publications: Jessica Lewis
   E-mail: jessica.lewis02@uwimona.edu.jm
First published 1950.
Annually.
500 JMD
ISSN: 0799-4117

LIAJA News (P)
Published by Library & Information Association of Jamaica (LIAJA)
PO Box 125, Kingston 5
Tel: (876) 927-1614 *Fax:* (876) 927-1614
E-mail: liajapresident@yahoo.com
Web Site: www.liaja.org.jm
Key Personnel
President: Viviene Kerr-Williams
   E-mail: vskwilliams@gmail.com
News of current events in the libraries of Jamaica.
Quarterly.

Japan

Biburosu (Biblos) (J)
Published by National Diet Library
1-10-1 Nagata-cho, Chiyoda-ku, Tokyo 100-8924
Tel: (03) 3581-2331 *Fax:* (03) 3508-2934
E-mail: webmaster@ndl.go.jp
Web Site: www.ndl.go.jp
Magazine for branch, executive, judicial & other
special libraries. Available online since 1998,
www.ndl.go.jp/jp/publication/biblos/index.html
(ISSN: 1344-8412).
First published 1950.
Quarterly.
ISSN: 0006-2030

**Bulletin of the Japan Special Libraries
Association** (Senmon Toshokan) (J)
Published by Japan Special Libraries Association
c/o Japan Library Association Bldg F6, 1-11-14
Shinkawa, Chuo-ku, Tokyo 104-0033
Tel: (03) 3537-8335 *Fax:* (03) 3537-8336
Web Site: www.jsla.or.jp
Abstracts in English.
First published 1960.
6 times/yr.
70 pp, 13,000 JPY/yr

Gendai no Toshokan (Libraries Today) (J)
Published by Japan Library Association
1-11-14, Shinkawa, Chuo-ku, Tokyo 104-0033
Tel: (03) 3523-0811 *Fax:* (03) 3523-0841
E-mail: info@jla.or.jp
Web Site: www.jla.or.jp
First published 1963.
Quarterly.
ISSN: 0016-6332

**Journal of Information Science & Technology
Association** (Joho no Kagaku to Gijutsu) (J)
Published by Information Science & Technology
Association Japan (INFOSTA)
1-11-14 Shinkawa, Chuo-ku, Tokyo 104-0033
Tel: (03) 6222-8506 *Fax:* (03) 6222-8507
E-mail: infosta@infosta.or.jp
Web Site: www.infosta.or.jp
Key Personnel
Chairman: Natsuo Onodera
Features articles which review new technologies
in the global information world.
Also available online (ISSN: 2189-8278).
Monthly.
1,792 YEN
ISSN: 0913-3801

Nihon no Sankotosho (Guide to Japanese
Reference Books) (B)
Published by Japan Library Association
1-11-14, Shinkawa, Chuo-ku, Tokyo 104-0033
Tel: (03) 3523-0811 *Fax:* (03) 3523-0841
E-mail: info@jla.or.jp
Web Site: www.jla.or.jp
First published 1962.
Irregularly.
4th ed, 2002
ISBN(s): 978-4-82-040213-8

Nihon no Toshokan (Statistics on Libraries in
Japan) (B)
Published by Japan Library Association
1-11-14, Shinkawa, Chuo-ku, Tokyo 104-0033
Tel: (03) 3523-0811 *Fax:* (03) 3523-0841
E-mail: info@jla.or.jp
Web Site: www.jla.or.jp
Statistics & directory of public & university li-
braries.
First published 1952.
Annually.

Toshokan Zasshi (Library Journal) (J)
Published by Japan Library Association
1-11-14, Shinkawa, Chuo-ku, Tokyo 104-0033
Tel: (03) 3523-0811 *Fax:* (03) 3523-0841
E-mail: info@jla.or.jp
Web Site: www.jla.or.jp
First published 1907.
Monthly.
ISSN: 0385-4000

Jordan

**Al-magallat al-urdaniyyat li-l-maktabat
wa-al-ma lumat** (P)
Published by Jordan Library & Information Asso-
ciation
PO Box 6289, Amman 11118
Tel: (06) 4629412 *Fax:* (06) 4629412
E-mail: info@jlia.org
Web Site: www.jlia.org
Quarterly.
ISSN: 2308-0981

Lebanon

LLA Newsletter (J)
Published by Lebanese Library Association
(LLA) (L'association des Bibliotheques
Libanaises)
Lebanese American University, Riyad Nassar Li-
brary, PO Box 13-5053, Chouran, Beirut 1102
2801
Tel: (01) 786456
E-mail: circulation@lau.edu.lb
Web Site: www.llaweb.org; www.
lebaneselibraryassociation.org
Key Personnel
President: Randa Chidiac *E-mail:* randachidiac@
usek.edu.lb
Senior Circulation Librarian: Nabil Badran
Tel: (01) 786456 ext 1383 *E-mail:* nabadran@
lau.edu.lb
Quarterly.

Malawi

MALA Bulletin (J)
Published by Malawi Library Association
PO Box 429, Zomba
First published 1978.
Irregularly.

Malaysia

Sumber Pustaka (J)
Published by Persatuan Pustakawan Malaysia (Li-
brarians Association of Malaysia)
c/o Perpustakaan Negara Malaysia, 232, Jl Tun
Razak, 50572 Kuala Lumpur
Mailing Address: PO Box 12545, 50782 Kuala
Lumpur
Tel: (03) 2694 7390 *Fax:* (03) 2694 7390
E-mail: pustakawan55@gmail.com
Web Site: www.ppm55.org
Malaysian Library Association official newsletter.
Text in English & Malay.

First published 1978.
6 times/yr.
25 pp, 1 MYR; 6 MYR/yr

Malta

MaLIA Newsletter (J)
Published by Malta Library & Information Asso-
ciation (MaLIA)
c/o University of Malta Library, Msida MSD
2080
E-mail: info@malia-malta.org
Web Site: www.malia-malta.org
Key Personnel
Chairperson: Ms Martes Pfeiffer Paris

Mexico

Boletin (Bulletin) (J)
Published by Instituto de Investigaciones Bibli-
ograficas (Institute of Bibliographic Research)
Editorial Dept, Centro Cultural, Ciudad Universi-
taria, 04510 Mexico, DF
Tel: (0155) 5622 6807
E-mail: libros@iib.unam.mx; editorial@iib.unam.
mx
Web Site: www.iib.unam.mx
Key Personnel
Editorial Dir: Hilda Leticia Dominguez Marquez
Tel: (0155) 5622 6807 ext 48654
Sales & Distribution: Elsa Almela *Tel:* (0155)
5622 6807 ext 48713
First published 1969.
2 times/yr.
250 MXN or 80 USD
ISSN: 0006-1719

§**Investigacion Bibliotecologica: Archivonomia,
Bibliotecologia e Informacion** (Library
Science Research: Archives, Library Science &
Information)
Published by Universidad Nacional Autonoma de
Mexico (UNAM)
Investigaciones Bibliotecologicas y de la Informa-
cion, Torre II de Humanidades, piso 12, Ciudad
Universitaria, 04510 Mexico, DF
Tel: (0155) 56 23 03 25; (0155) 56 23 03 59
Fax: (0155) 55 50 74 71; (0155) 56 23 03 26
E-mail: revista@iibi.unam.mx
Web Site: cuib.unam.mx; iibi.unam.mx/revista.
html
Key Personnel
Dir: Dr Salvador Gorbea Portal
E-mail: direvista@iibi.unam.mx
Articles of research in library science.
First published 1986.
Quarterly.
505 MXN (domestic); 62 USD (foreign)
ISSN: 0187-358X

Noticiero de la AMBAC (News of the Mexican
Association of Librarians) (J)
Published by Asociacion Mexicana de Bibliote-
carios AC (AMBAC)
Angel Urraza 817-A, Colonia Del Valle, 03100
Mexico, CDMX
Tel: (0155) 55 75 33 96 *Fax:* (0155) 55 75 11 35
E-mail: correo@ambac.org.mx; publicaciones@
ambac.org.mx
Web Site: www.ambac.org.mx
Key Personnel
President: Saul Armendariz Sanchez
E-mail: presidente@ambac.org.mx
Vice President: Marisela Castro Moreno
E-mail: vicepresidenta@ambac.org.mx

Secretary General: Alejandra Martinez del Prado
  E-mail: secretariageneral@ambac.org.mx
Treasurer: Jose Armando de Jesus Gonzalez
  E-mail: tesorero@ambac.org.mx
Quarterly.
ISSN: 0001-186X

Netherlands

Archievenblad (J)
Published by Vereniging van Archivaissen in
  Nederland
Westervoortsedijk 67-D, 6827 AT Arnhem
Tel: (026) 352 16 05
E-mail: bureau@kvan.nl; niews@archievenblad.
  nl; redactie@archievenblad.nl
Web Site: www.kvan.nl/publicaties/archievenblad
Key Personnel
Editor-in-Chief: Bernadine Ypma
  E-mail: hoofdredacteur@archievenblad.nl
Editor: Joris van Dierendonck
  E-mail: eindredacteur@archievenblad.nl
First published 1892.
10 times/yr.
76.50 EUR (domestic); 88.50 EUR (Europe); 106
  EUR (elsewhere)
ISSN: 1385-4186

Bibliotheekblad (J)
Published by Uitgeverij IP
Charlotte van Pallandtlaan 18, 2272 TR Voorburg
Mailing Address: PO Box 164, 2270 AD Voor-
  burg
Web Site: www.bibliotheekblad.nl
Key Personnel
Chief Editor: Eimer Wieldraaijer *Tel:* (06)
  51236185 *E-mail:* eimer.wieldraaijer@
  bibliotheekblad.nl
Editor: Martin de Jong *E-mail:* martin.dejong@
  bibliotheekblad.nl
Web Editor: Bart Janssen *E-mail:* bart.janssen@
  bibliotheekblad.nl
First published 1997.
9 times/yr.
195 EUR/yr
ISSN: 1573-9597

IP|vakblad voor informatieprofessionals (J)
Published by Uitgeverij IP
Charlotte Pallandtlaan 18, 2272 TR Voorburg
Tel: (06) 44091985
E-mail: redactie@informatieprofessional.nl;
  administratie@informatieprofessional.nl
Web Site: www.informatieprofessional.nl
Key Personnel
Editor: Ronald de Nijs
Professional journal for librarians, researchers,
  documentalists, archivists & experts working in
  the field of cultural heritage.
First published 1997.
9 times/yr.
40 pp, 159.95 EUR/yr
ISSN: 1385-5328

New Zealand

Library Life (J)
Published by New Zealand Library Association
  Inc t/a LIANZA
Stephenson & Turner House, Level 4, 156-158
  Victoria St, Wellington 6011
Mailing Address: PO Box 12212, Thorndon,
  Wellington 6144
Tel: (04) 801 5542 *Fax:* (04) 801 5543

E-mail: admin@lianza.org.nz
Web Site: www.lianza.org.nz
Key Personnel
Editor: Hana Whaanga *E-mail:* hana.whaanga@
  gmail.com
Monthly.
Free for members
ISSN: 1176-8088

**The New Zealand Library & Information
  Management Journal** (J)
Published by New Zealand Library Association
  Inc t/a LIANZA
Stephenson & Turner House, Level 4, 156-158
  Victoria St, Wellington 6011
Mailing Address: PO Box 12212, Thorndon,
  Wellington 6144
Tel: (04) 801 5542 *Fax:* (04) 801 5543
E-mail: admin@lianza.org.nz
Web Site: www.lianza.org.nz
Key Personnel
Editor: Brenda Chawner *E-mail:* brenda.
  chawner@vuw.ac.nz
First published 1937.
2 times/yr.
ISSN: 1177-3316

Norway

Bok og Bibliotek (Books & Libraries) (J)
Published by ABM-Media AS
Postboks 4, Sankt Olavs Pl, 0130 Oslo
Tel: 41 33 77 86
Web Site: www.bokogbibliotek.no
Key Personnel
Editor: Odd Letnes *E-mail:* odd.letnes@
  bokogbibliotek.no
Print & electronic.
First published 1933.
6 times/yr.
Domestic: 440 NOK (individuals), 630 NOK (in-
  stitutions), 250 NOK (students); Foreign: 630
  NOK

Pakistan

**Pakistan Journal of Information Management
  & Libraries (PJIM&L)** (J)
Published by Department of Information Manage-
  ment, University of the Punjab
Quaid-e-Azam Campus, Lahore 54590
Tel: (042) 9923124
E-mail: pjiml.im@pu.edu.pk
Web Site: journals.pu.edu.pk
Key Personnel
Chief Editor: Kanwal Ameen
First published 2000.
2 times/yr.
ISSN: 2409-7462

Philippines

ASLP Newsletter (J)
Published by Association of Special Libraries of
  the Philippines (ASLP)
The National Library of the Philippines, T M
  Kalaw St, Room 301, 1000 Ermita, Manila
Tel: (0995) 5396299 (cell)
E-mail: aslplibrarians@gmail.com

Web Site: aslpwiki.wikispaces.com
Text in English.
First published 1954.
Quarterly.
ISSN: 2094-8417

Index to Philippine Periodicals (IPP) (P)
Published by The University Library, University
  of the Philippines Diliman
Gonzalez Hall, Apacible St, Diliman, 1101 Que-
  zon City
Tel: (02) 981-8500 (ext 2852) *Fax:* (02) 981-8500
  (ext 2851)
E-mail: libraryinfo.updiliman@up.edu.ph
Web Site: www.mainlib.upd.edu.ph
Key Personnel
University Librarian: Prof Chito N Angeles
  E-mail: cnangeles@up.edu.ph
Also available online.
First published 1956.
Quarterly.
ISSN: 0073-599X

Journal of Philippine Librarianship (J)
Published by University of the Philippines,
  School of Library & Information Studies
3/F Gonzalez Hall, UP Main Library, UP Dili-
  man, 1101 Quezon City
Tel: (02) 981 8500 (local 2869-71)
E-mail: jpl@up.edu.ph
Web Site: journals.upd.edu.ph/index.php/jpl
Online.
Text in English.
First published 1968.
Annually.
ISSN: 0022-359X

Philippine National Bibliography (J)
Published by National Library of the Philippines
  (NLP)
Bibliographic Services Division, TNL Bldg, W
  Wing, Ground floor, T M Kalaw St, 1000 Er-
  mita, Manila
Mailing Address: PO Box 2926, 1000 Manila
Tel: (02) 336-7200
Web Site: nlpbsd.wixsite.com/nlpbsd; web.nlp.gov.
  ph/nlp
Key Personnel
Chief, Bibliographic Services Division: Nina
  Fronda
Available on CD only.
First published 1974.
Quarterly with annual cumulation.
300 PHP/issue
ISSN: 0303-190X

SLIS Newsletter (J)
Published by University of the Philippines,
  School of Library & Information Studies
3/F Gonzalez Hall, UP Main Library, UP Dili-
  man, 1101 Quezon City
Tel: (02) 981 8500 (local 2869-71)
E-mail: admin@slis.upd.edu.ph
Web Site: upslis.info
Key Personnel
Administrative Officer: Josefina C Cervas
Text in English.
First published 1966.
Quarterly.
ISSN: 0300-3612

Poland

Bibliografia Wydawnictw ciaglych
  (Bibliography of Polish Serials) (J)
Published by Biblioteka Narodowa w Warszawie
  (National Library of Poland)
al Niepodleglosci 213, 02-086 Warsaw
Tel: (22) 608 29 99 *Fax:* (22) 825 52 51

E-mail: kontakt@bn.org.pl
Web Site: www.bn.org.pl
Key Personnel
Dir: Dr Tomasz Makowski *Tel:* (22) 608 22 33
  E-mail: dyrektor@bn.org.pl
Manager: Krzysztof Alberski *Tel:* (22) 608 23 66
  E-mail: k.alberski@bn.org.pl
Librarian: Zofia Zurawinska
Available in CD-ROM or online only.
Annually.

Bibliotekarz (The Librarian) (P)
Published by Stowarzyszenie Bibliotekarzy Pols-
  kich (Polish Librarians' Association)
ul Konopczynskiego 5/7, 00-335 Warsaw
Tel: (22) 827 52 96
E-mail: wydawnictwo@sbp.pl
Web Site: www.sbp.pl
Key Personnel
Dir: Anna Grzecznowska *E-mail:* a.
  grzecznowska@sbp.pl
Publishing Dir: Marta Lach *Tel:* (22) 827 08 47
  E-mail: m.lach@sbp.pl
Editor-in-Chief: Elzbieta Stefanczyk *Tel:* 600 443
  877 (cell) *E-mail:* e.stefanczyk@sbp.pl
Deputy Editor-in-Chief: Barbara Budynska
  Tel: 507 622 572 (cell) *E-mail:* budynska@
  gmail.com
Assistant Editor: Marzena Przybysz *Tel:* 697 790
  802 (cell) *E-mail:* m.przybysz@sbp.pl
Publishing Secretary: Beata Pudelko *E-mail:* b.
  pudelko@sbp.pl
Technical Editor: Elzbieta Matusiak
Text in Polish. Summaries in English & Russian.
First published 1929.
Monthly.
15 PLN/issue
ISSN: 0208-4333

Informator Nauki Polskiej (Polish Research
  Directory) (B)
Published by Osrodek Przetwarzania Informacji
Al Niepodleglosci 188 B, 00-608 Warsaw
Tel: (22) 570 14 00 *Fax:* (22) 825 33 19
E-mail: opi@opi.org.pl
Web Site: www.opi.org.pl; www.nauka-polska.pl
Key Personnel
Dir: Dr Olaf Gajl
Available in Polish & English language versions,
  5 volumes.
2006, 150 PLN

Polska Bibliografia Bibliologiczna (Polish
  Bibliography of Library Science) (B)
Published by Biblioteka Narodowa w Warszawie
  (National Library of Poland)
al Niepodleglosci 213, 02-086 Warsaw
Tel: (22) 608 29 99 *Fax:* (22) 825 52 51
E-mail: kontakt@bn.org.pl
Web Site: www.bn.org.pl
Key Personnel
Dir: Dr Tomasz Makowski *Tel:* (22) 608 22 33
  E-mail: dyrektor@bn.org.pl
Manager: Krzysztof Alberski *Tel:* (22) 608 23 66
  E-mail: k.alberski@bn.org.pl
Mng Editor: Sylwia Breczko *E-mail:* s.breczko@
  bn.org.pl
Librarian: Zofia Zurawinska
Annually.
ISSN: 0860-6560

Poradnik Bibliotekarza (The Librarian's
  Adviser) (J)
Published by Stowarzyszenie Bibliotekarzy Pols-
  kich (Polish Librarians' Association)
ul Konopczynskiego 5/7, 00-335 Warsaw
Tel: (22) 827 52 96
E-mail: poradnikbibliotekarza@wp.pl;
  wydawnictwo@sbp.pl
Web Site: www.sbp.pl;
  www.poradnikbibliotekarza.pl

Key Personnel
Dir: Anna Grzecznowska *E-mail:* a.
  grzecznowska@sbp.pl
Publishing Dir: Marta Lach *Tel:* (22) 827 08 47
  E-mail: m.lach@sbp.pl
Editor-in-Chief: Jadwiga Chruscinska
  E-mail: jchruscinska@gmail.com
First published 1949.
Monthly.
16 PLN/issue; 192 PLN/yr
ISSN: 0032-4752

Rocznik Biblioteki Narodowej (National Library
  Yearbook) (B)
Published by Biblioteka Narodowa w Warszawie
  (National Library of Poland)
al Niepodleglosci 213, 02-086 Warsaw
Tel: (22) 608 29 99 *Fax:* (22) 825 52 51
E-mail: kontakt@bn.org.pl
Web Site: www.bn.org.pl
Key Personnel
Dir: Dr Tomasz Makowski *Tel:* (22) 608 22 33
  E-mail: dyrektor@bn.org.pl
Manager: Krzysztof Alberski *Tel:* (22) 608 23 66
  E-mail: k.alberski@bn.org.pl
Librarian: Zofia Zurawinska
Covers scientific library science.
Text in Polish with English summaries.
First published 1985.
Annually.
ISSN: 0083-7261

Stan Bibliotek w Polsce (P)
Published by Biblioteka Narodowa w Warszawie
  (National Library of Poland)
al Niepodleglosci 213, 02-086 Warsaw
Tel: (22) 608 29 99 *Fax:* (22) 825 52 51
E-mail: kontakt@bn.org.pl
Web Site: www.bn.org.pl
Key Personnel
Dir: Dr Tomasz Makowski *Tel:* (22) 608 22 33
  E-mail: dyrektor@bn.org.pl
Annually.
ISSN: 2451-0963

Portugal

Cadernos BAD (J)
Published by Associacao Portuguesa de Bibliote-
  carios, Arquivistas e Documentalistas (BAD)
  (The Portuguese Association of Librarians
  Archivists & Documentalists)
Rua Morais Soares, 43 C, 1º Dtº e Frte, 1900-341
  Lisbon
Tel: 21 816 19 80 *Fax:* 21 815 45 08
E-mail: editorial@apbad.pt
Web Site: www.apbad.pt
Key Personnel
President: Maria Alexandra Verissimo M Silva
  Lourenco *E-mail:* presidente@bad.pt
Editor: Jose Antonio Calixto
Annually.
20 EUR/yr
ISSN: 0007-9421

Romania

**ABSI - Abstracte in Bibliologie si Stiinta
  Informarii** (ABSI - Abstracts in Library &
  Information Science) (J)
Published by Biblioteca Nationala a Romaniei
  (National Library of Romania)
Bd Unirii nr 22, sector 3, 030833 Bucharest

Tel: (021) 314 24 34; (021) 314 10 02 *Fax:* (021)
  312 33 81
E-mail: biblioteca@bibnat.ro
Web Site: www.bibnat.ro
Key Personnel
Manager: Ioan Marius Eppel
Publications Coordinator: Letitia Constantin
  E-mail: letitia.constantin@bibnat.ro
Bulletin.
First published 1960.
2 times/yr.
51 pp
ISSN: 2457-8290

Russia

**Bibliotechnoe Delo i Bibliografiya
  Referativno-bibliograficheskaya Informatsiya**
  (Library Science & Theory of Bibliography,
  Bibliographic Information) (J)
Published by Russian State Library
3/5, Vozdvizhenka St, 119019 Moscow
Tel: (495) 695-57-90 *Fax:* (495) 690-60-62
E-mail: post@rsl.ru
Web Site: www.rsl.ru
Key Personnel
Acting Dir General: Vladimir Ivanovich
  Gnezdilov
First published 1974.
96 pp, 185 USD
ISSN: 0869-8007

Biblioteka (The Librarian) (J)
Published by Libereya
ul Nikulinskaya, 27 Bldg 3, 119602 Moscow
Tel: (495) 2315607
E-mail: liber@liber.ru
Web Site: www.liber.ru
Key Personnel
Dir General: Stanislav Samsonov
Co-Sponsor: Ministry of Culture.
First published 1923.
Monthly.
179 USD/yr
ISSN: 0869-4915

Bibliotekovedenie (Library Studies) (J)
Published by Russian State Library
3/5, Vozdvizhenka St, 119019 Moscow
Tel: (495) 695-57-90; (499) 557-04-70 (ext 10-
  64) *Fax:* (495) 690-60-62
E-mail: bvpress@rsl.ru
Web Site: www.rsl.ru
Key Personnel
Acting Dir General: Vladimir Ivanovich
  Gnezdilov
Editor-in-Chief: Samarin Aleksandr Yurevich
First published 1952.
6 times/yr.
136 pp
ISSN: 0869-608X

**Kul'turologiia, obshchie voprosy kul'tury i
  iskusstva: referativno-bibliograficheskaia
  informatsiia** (Aesthetic Education
  Bibliographic Information) (P)
Published by Russian State Library
3/5, Vozdvizhenka St, 119019 Moscow
Tel: (495) 695-57-90 *Fax:* (495) 690-60-62
E-mail: post@rsl.ru
Web Site: www.rsl.ru
Key Personnel
Acting Dir General: Vladimir Ivanovich
  Gnezdilov *E-mail:* nbros@rsl.ru
First published 2012.
6 times/yr.

Nauchnye i tekhnicheskie biblioteki (Scientific & Technical Libraries) (J)
Published by GPNTB Rossii
K-31, GPS-6, Kuznetskii Most 12, 107996 Moscow
Tel: (495) 6282296; (495) 6627560 (ext 5080)
E-mail: gpntb@gpntb.ru; ntb@gpntb.ru
Web Site: www.gpntb.ru
Key Personnel
Dir General & Editor-in-Chief: Yakov Shrayberg
  E-mail: shra@gpntb.ru
Dir, Publishing & Reprographic Center: Olga Shlenskaya *E-mail:* os@gpntb.ru
Professional journal on library science & the practice of regional & metropolitan libraries of all types, sci-tech information centers, LIS colleges & universities.
First published 1961.
Monthly.
140 pp
ISSN: 0130-9765

Singapore

Directory of Libraries & Information Centres in Singapore (B)
Published by Library Association of Singapore (LAS)
c/o National Library Board, 100 Victoria St No 14-01, Singapore 188064
Tel: 6332 3255 (NLB) *Fax:* 6332 3248
E-mail: lassec@las.org.sg; business@las.org.sg; publications@las.org.sg
Web Site: www.las.org.sg/lib_dir.htm
Key Personnel
Chair, Publications: Phoebe Lim Choo Lan
8th ed, 60 SGD + postage & administrative fee
ISBN(s): 978-981-05-5355-5

Singapore Journal of Library & Information Management (B)
Published by Library Association of Singapore (LAS)
c/o National Library Board, 100 Victoria St No 14-01, Singapore 188064
Tel: 6332 3255 (NLB) *Fax:* 6332 3248
E-mail: lassec@las.org.sg; sjlim@las.org.sg; publications@las.org.sg
Web Site: www.las.org.sg
Key Personnel
Chair, Publications: Phoebe Lim Choo Lan
Editor: Dianne Cmor
Online only effective 2009.
Annually.
ISSN: 2382-5634

Singapore Libraries Bulletin (P)
Published by Library Association of Singapore (LAS)
c/o National Library Board, 100 Victoria St No 14-01, Singapore 188064
Tel: 6332 3255 (NLB) *Fax:* 6332 3248
E-mail: lassec@las.org.sg; slb@las.org.sg; publications@las.org.sg
Web Site: www.las.org.sg/wp/bulletin
Key Personnel
Chair, Publications: Phoebe Lim Choo Lan
Online weblog (since 2006).
Monthly.

Slovenia

Knjiznica: Revija za Podrocje Bibliotekarstva in Informacijske Znanosti (The Library: Journal for Library & Information Science) (J)
Published by Zveza bibliotekarskih drustev Slovenije (ZBDS) (Slovenian Library Association)
Turjaska 1, SI-1000 Ljubljana
Tel: (01) 2001 131 *Fax:* (01) 4257 293
Web Site: revija-knjiznica.zbds-zveza.si
Key Personnel
President: Sabina Fras Popovic *Tel:* (02) 2352 100 *Fax:* (02) 2352 127 *E-mail:* sabina.fras-popovic@mb.sik.si
Mng Editor: Ines Vodopivec *E-mail:* ines. vodopivec@nuk.uni.lj.si
Editor-in-Chief: Alenka Kavcic Colic
  E-mail: alenka.kavcic@nuk.uni.lj.si
Text in Slovenian; summaries in English.
Also available online (ISSN: 1581-7903).
First published 1957.
Quarterly.
150 pp, 68 EUR (international); free to members of ZBDS
ISSN: 0023-2424

South Africa

Cape Librarian (P)
Published by Western Cape Government Library Service
c/o Chiappinni & Hospital St, Cape Town 8001
Mailing Address: PO Box 2108, Cape Town 8000
Tel: (021) 483 2273 *Fax:* (021) 419 7541
E-mail: capelib@westerncape.gov.za
Web Site: www.westerncape.gov.za/library
Key Personnel
Editor: Grizell Azar-Luxton *Tel:* (021) 483 2446
  E-mail: grizell@iafrica.com
Text in Afrikaans & English.
First published 1957.
6 times/yr.
ISSN: 0008-5790

Index to South African Periodicals (ISAP) (J)
Published by National Library of South Africa
228 Proes St, Pretoria 0001
Mailing Address: Private Bag X990, Pretoria 0001
Tel: (012) 401 9700 *Fax:* (012) 325 5702
E-mail: infodesk@nlsa.ac.za
Web Site: www.nlsa.ac.za
Key Personnel
National Librarian & Chief Executive Officer: Prof Rocky Ralebipi-Simela *Tel:* (012) 401 9717 *E-mail:* dimakatso.methula@nlsa.ac.za
Database containing indexed articles from more than 680 South African periodicals from 1942 to the present.
First published 1940.

KZN Librarian (J)
Published by KwaZulu Natal Provincial Public Library & Information Service
230 Prince Alfred St, Pietermaritzburg, Kwazulu-Natal 3200
Tel: (033) 3413000 *Fax:* (033) 3942237
Web Site: www.kzndac.gov.za
Key Personnel
Editor: Janet Hart *E-mail:* hartj@plho.kzntl.gov.za
First published 1971.
Quarterly.
Free to libraries in South Africa
ISSN: 1027-6920

Mousaion: South African Journal for Information Studies (J)
Published by UNISA Press
PO Box 392, Pretoria 0003
Tel: (012) 429 2953; (012) 429 8255 *Fax:* (012) 429 3449
E-mail: journalsubs@unisa.ac.za
Web Site: www.unisa.ac.za
Key Personnel
Editor: Pieter Rall *E-mail:* rallpb@unisa.ac.za; Thomas van der Walt *E-mail:* vdwaltb@unisa. ac.za
Subscription Officer: Julia Mokgohloa
Institution (print & online): 1,636/yr ZAR (local) or 436.27/yr USD (foreign); Individuals (print & online): 678.40/yr ZAR (local)
ISSN: 0027-2639

Quarterly Bulletin of the National Library of South Africa (J)
Published by National Library of South Africa
62 Queen Victoria St, Cape Town 8001
Mailing Address: PO Box 15254, Viaeberg 8018
Tel: (021) 423 2669
E-mail: infodesk@nlsa.ac.za
Web Site: www.nlsa.ac.za
Key Personnel
Executive Head: Mandlakayise Matyumza
  E-mail: mandla.matyumza@nlsa.ac.za
First published 1946.
Quarterly.
120 ZAR or 40 USD
ISSN: 1562-9392

South Korea

KLA Bulletin (J)
Published by Korean Library Association (KLA)
San 60-1, Banpo-dong, Seocho-gu, Seoul 137-702
Tel: (02) 535-4868 *Fax:* (02) 535-5616
E-mail: w3master@kla.kr
Web Site: www.kla.kr
First published 1960.
6 times/yr.
ISSN: 1225-5521

Sri Lanka

Sri Lanka Library Review (J)
Published by Sri Lanka Library Association (SLLA)
Sri Lanka Professional Centre, 275/75 Stanley Wijesundara Mawatha, Colombo 07
Tel: (011) 2589103 *Fax:* (011) 2589103
E-mail: slla@sltnet.lk
Web Site: www.slla.org.lk
Key Personnel
Publications Officer: Ms Sunethra Kariyawasam
Annually.
200 LKR (domestic); 20 USD (foreign)
ISSN: 1391-2526

Sweden

Biblioteksbladet (Library Journal) (J)
Published by Svensk Biblioteksforening Kansli (Swedish Library Association)
World Trade Center, D5, Klarabergsviadukten 70/ Kungsbron 1, Box 70380, 107 24 Stockholm
Tel: (08) 545 132 30 *Fax:* (08) 545 132 31

E-mail: bbl@a4.se; info@biblioteksforeningen.org
Web Site: biblioteksbladet.se; www.
biblioteksforeningen.se
Key Personnel
Chief Editor & Publisher: Annika Persson
Tel: (070) 373 11 60 *E-mail:* annika.persson@
a4.se
Text in Scandinavian languages with summaries
in English.
8 times/yr.
ISSN: 0006-1867

Switzerland

Arbido (J)
Published by Staempfli Verlag AG
Woelflistr 1, 3001 Bern
Tel: (031) 300 66 44 *Fax:* (031) 300 66 88
E-mail: info@abido.ch; verlag@staempfli.com
Web Site: www.arbido.ch; www.staempfli.com
Key Personnel
Editor-in-Chief: Sara Marty *E-mail:* sm@arbido.
ch
Also available online (ISSN: 1661-786X).
First published 1986.
Quarterly.
110 CHF (domestic); 130 CHF (foreign)
ISSN: 1420-102X

Taiwan

Journal of Library & Information Science (J)
Published by Graduate Institute of Library & In-
formation Studies, National Taiwan Normal
University
162 Hoping East Rd, sec 1, Taipei 10610
Tel: (02) 7734-5427 *Fax:* (02) 2351-8476
E-mail: jlis@ntnu.edu.tw; glis@deps.ntnu.edu.tw
Web Site: www.glis.ntnu.edu.tw; jlis.glis.ntnu.edu.
tw
Key Personnel
Editor-in-Chief: Mei-Mei Wu *E-mail:* meiwu@
ntnu.edu.tw
Also available online (ISSN: 2224-1574).
First published 1975.
2 times/yr.
ISSN: 0363-3640

Zhonghua minguo tushuguan Xuehui huibao
(Journal of Library & Information Science
Research) (J)
Published by Library Association of the Republic
of China (LAROC)
20 Zhongshan South Rd, Taipei 10001
Tel: (02) 2331-2475; (02) 2361-9132 *Fax:* (02)
2370-0899
E-mail: lac@msg.ncl.edu.tw
Web Site: jlisr.lac.org.tw; www.lac.org.tw
Key Personnel
Editor-in-Chief: Shan-Ju Lin Chang
First published 1954.
2 times/yr.
ISSN: 1990-9128

Tanzania

Matukio (J)
Published by Tanzania Library Association (TLA)
PO Box 33433, Dar es Salaam
Tel: (0744) 296134
E-mail: tla_tanzania@yahoo.com

Web Site: www.tla.or.tz
Key Personnel
Chairperson: Juliana Manyerere
Secretary, Research, Development & Publications
Dept: Mr Daudi Danda *E-mail:* dedanda2012@
gmail.com
Newsletter.
ISSN: 0378-3375

Thailand

TLA Bulletin (J)
Published by Thai Library Association
1346 Akhan Songkhro 5 Rd, Klongjan, Bangkapi
Bangkok 10240
Tel: (02) 734-9022; (02) 734-9023 *Fax:* (02) 734-
9021
E-mail: tla2497@yahoo.com
Web Site: www.tla.or.th
First published 1957.
Quarterly.
ISSN: 0857-0086

Trinidad and Tobago

BIBLIO (Bulletin) (J)
Published by Library Association of Trinidad and
Tobago
NALIS Bldg, 3rd floor, Corner Hart & Abre-
cromby St, Port of Spain
Mailing Address: PO Box 1275, Port of Spain
Tel: (868) 687-0194
E-mail: latt46@gmail.com
Web Site: latt.org.tt
Key Personnel
President: Juliet Glenn-Callender
First published 1964.
Quarterly.
ISSN: 0521-9590

United Kingdom

Archives (J)
Published by British Records Association
70 Cowcross St, London EC1M 6EJ
Tel: (07946) 624713
E-mail: info@britishrecordsassociation.org.uk
Web Site: www.britishrecordsassociation.org.uk
Key Personnel
Editor: Dr Ruth Paley
2 times/yr.
50 GBP (institutions); free to members
ISSN: 0003-9535

**Archives and Records: The Journal of the
Archives and Records Association** (J)
Published by Routledge
2 & 4 Park Sq, Milton Park, Abingdon, Oxon
OX14 4RN
Tel: (020) 7017 6000 *Fax:* (020) 7017 6336
E-mail: subscriptions@tandf.co.uk
Web Site: www.tandfonline.com/loi/cjsa21; www.
routledge.com

Key Personnel
Editor: Charlotte Berry; Jenny Bunn; Sarah Hig-
gins
Book Review Editor: Susan Healy
Journal for archivists, record managers & conser-
vators worldwide.
Also available online (ISSN: 2325-7989).
First published 1955.
2 times/yr.
Institutions: 335 GBP, 444 EUR or 557 USD
(print & online), 293 GBP, 389 EUR or 487
USD (online only); Individuals: 128 GBP, 176
EUR or 217 USD (print only)
ISSN: 2325-7962

Art Libraries Journal (J)
Published by ARLIS/UK & Ireland
The National Art Library, Victoria & Albert Mu-
seum, Cromwell Rd, South Kensington, Lon-
don SW7 2RL
Tel: (020) 7942 2317
E-mail: arlis@vam.ac.uk
Web Site: www.arlis.org.uk
Key Personnel
Editor: Gillian Varley *E-mail:* g.varley@arlis2.
demon.co.uk
First published 1976.
Quarterly.
68 GBP or 136 USD (annually); 28 GBP or 45
USD (individual)
ISSN: 0307-4722

**ASLIB Directory of Information Sources in the
United Kingdom** (B)
Published by Routledge
2 Park Sq, Milton Park, Abingdon, Oxon OX14
4RN
Tel: (020) 7017 6000 *Fax:* (020) 7017 6699
E-mail: subscriptions@tandf.co.uk
Web Site: www.routledge.com
Provides instant access to listings of 6,700 associations, clubs, societies, companies, educational
establishments, institutes, commissions, government bodies & other organizations which
provide information freely or on a fee-paying
basis.
First published 1928.
17th ed: 1,335 pp, 432 GBP
ISBN(s): 978-1-85743-664-8 (hardcover)

Brio (J)
Published by International Association of Music
Libraries Archives & Documentation Centres,
UK & Ireland Branch
c/o Music Collections, National Library of Scot-
land, George IV Bridge, Edinburgh EH1 1EW
Tel: (020) 7412 7529 *Fax:* (020) 7412 7751
Web Site: www.iaml.info/iaml-uk-irl
Key Personnel
President: Peter Baxter
Editor: Katharine Hogg
Articles relevant to the music library profession,
reviews of books & scores & news from music
libraries.
First published 1964.
2 times/yr (June & Dec).
ISSN: 0007-0173

GKIM Matters (J)
Published by Chartered Institute of Library & In-
formation Professionals (CILIP), Government
Information Group
7 Ridgmount St, London WC1E 7AE
Tel: (020) 7255 0500 *Fax:* (020) 7255 0501
Web Site: www.cilip.org.uk
Key Personnel
Journal Editor: Martin Newman
Published jointly with the Network of Gov-
ernment Library & Information Specialists
(NGLIS).
2 times/yr.

ɸ**Information and Learning Science** (J)
Published by Emerald Group Publishing Ltd
Howard House, Wagon Lane, Bingley, W Yorks
   BD16 1WA
Tel: (01274) 777700 *Fax:* (01274) 785201
E-mail: collections@emeraldinsight.com;
   editorial@emeraldinsight.com; emerald@
   emeraldinsight.com
Web Site: www.emeraldinsight.com/loi/ils
Key Personnel
Publisher: Eileen Breen *E-mail:* ebreen@
   emeraldgroup.com
Editor: Prof David Baker *E-mail:* d.baker152@
   btinternet.com
Full text online.
2 times/yr.
44 pp
ISSN: 2398-5348

Information Discovery and Delivery (J)
Published by Emerald Group Publishing Ltd
Howard House, Wagon Lane, Bingley, W Yorks
   BD16 1WA
Tel: (01274) 777700 *Fax:* (01274) 785201
E-mail: emerald@emeraldinsight.com
Web Site: www.emeraldinsight.com/loi/idd
Key Personnel
Publisher: Eileen Breen *E-mail:* ebreen@
   emeraldgroup.com
Editor: Dr Wu He *E-mail:* whe@odu.edu
Content Editor: Adrian Paylor *E-mail:* apaylor@
   emeraldgroup.com
Full text online.
Quarterly.
ISSN: 2398-6247

JOLIS, see Journal of Librarianship &
   Information Science (JOLIS)

ɸ**Journal of Documentation** (J)
Published by Emerald Group Publishing Ltd
Howard House, Wagon Lane, Bingley, W Yorks
   BD16 1WA
Tel: (01274) 777700 *Fax:* (01274) 785201
E-mail: collections@emeraldinsight.com;
   editorial@emeraldinsight.com; emerald@
   emeraldinsight.com
Web Site: www.emeraldgroupublishing.com/jd.
   htm
Key Personnel
Publisher: Eileen Breen *E-mail:* ebreen@
   emeraldgroup.com
Editor: Prof David Bawden *E-mail:* db@soi.city.
   ac.uk
First published 1944.
6 times/yr.
ISSN: 0022-0418

ɸ**Journal of Information Science** (J)
Published by SAGE Publications Ltd
One Oliver's Yard, 55 City Rd, London EC1Y
   1SP
Tel: (020) 7324 8500 *Fax:* (020) 7324 8600
E-mail: market@sagepub.co.uk; subscriptions@
   sagepub.co.uk
Web Site: journals.sagepub.com/home/jis; www.
   uk.sagepub.com
Key Personnel
Editor: Dr Allen Foster; Dr Pauline Rafferty
Published in association with Chartered Institute
   of Library & Information Professionals.
Also available online (ISSN: 1741-6485).
6 times/yr.
505 GBP/yr (institutional print); 515 GBP/yr (in-
   stitutional print & online); 66 GBP/yr (individual print)
ISSN: 0165-5515

ɸ**Journal of Librarianship & Information
   Science (JOLIS)** (J)
Published by SAGE Publications Ltd

One Oliver's Yard, 55 City Rd, London EC1Y
   1SP
Tel: (020) 7324 8701 (customer service)
E-mail: subscriptions@sagepub.co.uk
Web Site: journals.sagepub.com/home/lis; www.
   uk.sagepub.com
Key Personnel
Editor: Anne Goulding
Publishes original papers, review articles, view-
   points & book reviews for the information pro-
   fession.
Also available online (ISSN: 1741-6477).
Quarterly.
Institutional: 544 GBP or 1,006 USD (print & on-
   line subscription), 533 GBP or 986 USD (print
   only subscription), 147 GBP or 271 USD (sin-
   gle print issue); Individuals: 68 GBP or 126
   USD (print only subscription), 22 GBP or 41
   USD (single print issue)
ISSN: 0961-0006

ɸ**Legal Information Management**
Published by Cambridge University Press
University Printing House, Shaftesbury Rd, Cam-
   bridge CB2 8BS
Tel: (01223) 326070 (journals) *Fax:* (01223)
   325150
E-mail: journals@cambridge.org
Web Site: www.cambridge.org/core/journals/legal-
   information-management
Key Personnel
Editor: David F Wills
Published for the British & Irish Association of
   Law Libraries (BIALL).
Also available online (ISSN: 1741-2021).
First published 1970.
Quarterly.
Organizations: 121 GBP or 199 USD (online &
   print), 111 GBP or 179 USD (online only)
ISSN: 1472-6696

**Libraries and Information Services in the
   United Kingdom and the Republic of Ireland**
   (B)
Published by Facet Publishing
7 Ridgmount St, London WC1E 7AE
Tel: (020) 7255 0590 *Fax:* (020) 7255 0591
E-mail: info@facetpublishing.co.uk
Web Site: www.facetpublishing.co.uk
Listing of libraries in the UK, the Channel Is-
   lands, the Isle of Man & the Republic of Ire-
   land. Also available as an ebook (PDF).
38th ed, 2015: 464 pp, 47.95 GBP (CILIP mem-
   bers), 59.95 GBP (nonmembers)
ISBN(s): 978-1-78330-044-0 (ebook); 978-1-
   85604-801-9 (paper)

The Libraries Directory (B)
Published by James Clarke & Co Ltd
PO Box 60, Cambridge CB1 2NT
Tel: (01223) 350865 *Fax:* (01223) 366951
E-mail: publishing@jamesclarke.co.uk; libdir@
   jamesclarke.co.uk
Web Site: www.jamesclarke.co.uk/libdir
Key Personnel
Mng Dir: Adrian Brink
Editor: Iain Walker
Directory of public libraries, special libraries,
   record offices, archives & library organizations
   in the UK & Ireland. Includes CD-ROM.
First published 1890.
Biennially.
50th ed: 800 pp, Single user, reference: 252.50
   GBP or 505 USD (overseas); Single user, mar-
   keting: 386 GBP + VAT or 825 USD (over-
   seas); Network, reference: 395 GBP or 825
   USD (overseas); Network, marketing: 577.76
   GBP + VAT or 1,150 USD (overseas)
ISBN(s): 978-0-227-17248-3 (single user, refer-
   ence); 978-0-227-17249-0 (single user, market-

ing); 978-0-227-17250-6 (network, reference);
   978-0-227-17251-3 (network, marketing)
ISSN: 0961-4575

The Library (J)
Published by The Bibliographical Society
c/o Institute of English Studies, Malet St, Senate
   House, Room 238, London WC1E 7HU
Web Site: www.bibsoc.org.uk
Key Personnel
Editor: Dr Bill Bell *E-mail:* b.bell@ed.ac.uk
Scholarly journal for the history of books.
Also available online via Oxford Journals (ISSN:
   1744-8581).
Quarterly.
120 pp, 180 GBP, 270 EUR or 360 USD (institu-
   tional print & online); 165 GBP, 248 EUR or
   330 USD (institutional print); 51 GBP, 76 EUR
   or 102 USD (individual)
ISSN: 0024-2160

Library & Information Science Abstracts
   (LISA) (J)
Published by ProQuest LLC
The Quorum, Barnwell Rd, Cambridge, Cambs
   CB5 8SW
Tel: (01223) 215 512 *Fax:* (01223) 215 513
E-mail: sales@proquest.co.uk
Web Site: www.proquest.com; proquest.libguides.
   com/lisa
Web database & monthly print publication. In-
   dexes & abstracts over 440 periodicals from
   over 68 countries in over 20 languages. Current
   awareness & search service for information
   about library & information science & related
   areas including the Internet & information in-
   dustry. Also available as a CD-ROM.
First published 1969.
Monthly (print); database updated biweekly.
150 pp
ISSN: 0024-2179
Parent Company: Cambridge Information Group
   Inc

Library Review (J)
Published by Emerald Group Publishing Ltd
Howard House, Wagon Lane, Bingley, W Yorks
   BD16 1WA
Tel: (01274) 777700 *Fax:* (01274) 785201
E-mail: collections@emeraldinsight.com;
   editorial@emeraldinsight.com; emerald@
   emeraldinsight.com
Web Site: www.emeraldgroupublishing.com/lr.
   htm
Key Personnel
Publisher: Eileen Breen *E-mail:* ebreen@
   emeraldgroup.com
Editor: Judith Broady-Preston *E-mail:* jbp@aber.
   ac.uk
9 times/yr.
ISSN: 0024-2535

LISA, see Library & Information Science
   Abstracts (LISA)

Managing Information (J)
Published by ASLIB, The Association for Infor-
   mation Management
Howard House, Wagon Lane, Bingley BD16 1WA
Tel: (01274) 777700 *Fax:* (01274) 785201
E-mail: support@aslib.com
Web Site: www.aslib.com; www.
   managinginformation.com
Key Personnel
Publications & Training Manager: Diane Heath
   E-mail: dheath@aslib.com
Editor-in-Chief: Graham Coult *E-mail:* gcoult@
   aslib.com
10 times/yr.
169 GBP + VAT (UK); 189 GBP + VAT (Eu-
   rope); 199 GBP + VAT (rest of world)
ISSN: 1352-0229

The Private Library (J)
Published by The Private Libraries Association
   (PLA)
Ravelston, South View Rd, Pinner, Middx HA5
   3YD
Web Site: www.plabooks.org
Key Personnel
Editor: David Butcher; David Chambers
Concerned with book collecting. Includes
   newsletter & exchange list.
First published 1957.
Quarterly.
48 pp, 30 GBP, 40 EUR, 55 USD, 60 CAD or 70
   AUD
ISSN: 0032-8898

ƒ**Reference Reviews** (J)
Published by Emerald Group Publishing Ltd
Howard House, Wagon Lane, Bingley, W Yorks
   BD16 1WA
Tel: (01274) 777700 *Fax:* (01274) 785201
E-mail: emerald@emeraldinsight.com
Web Site: www.emeraldgrouppublishing.com/rr.
   htm
Key Personnel
Publisher: Eileen Breen *E-mail:* ebreen@
   emeraldgroup.com
Editor: Anthony Chalcraft
   E-mail: referencereviews@outlook.com
Reviews of current reference materials, electronic
   version only.
First published 1987.
8 times/yr.
ISSN: 0950-4125

Uruguay

Revista de la Biblioteca Nacional (National
   Library Review) (J)
Published by Biblioteca Nacional del Uruguay
Av 18 de Julio 1790, 11200 Montevideo
Tel: 24020812
E-mail: revista@bibna.gub.uy
Web Site: www.bibna.gub.uy
Key Personnel
Dir: Ana Ines Larre Borges
Irregularly.
ISSN: 0797-9061

Company Index

Arranged alphabetically by company/organization name, the index includes the page number(s) where the listing can be found as well as the organization's country, telephone, fax, e-mail address and web address. Companies/organizations listed in the following sections are excluded from the yellow pages: **Book Trade Reference Books and Journals; Literary Prizes; Calendar of Book Trade & Promotional Events** and **Library Reference Books & Journals.**

Sheikh Shaukat Ali & Sons (Pakistan) *Tel:* (021) 32217767; (021) 32637577 *Fax:* (021) 32637877, pg 558

Alianza Editorial Mexicana SA de CV (Mexico) *Tel:* (0155) 53 54 31 00 *Web Site:* www. alianzaeditorial.es, pg 512

Alianza Editorial SA (Spain) *Tel:* 91 393 88 88 *Fax:* 91 320 74 80 *E-mail:* alianzaeditorial@alianzaeditorial.es *Web Site:* www.alianzaeditorial.es, pg 628

Compagnia Editoriale Aliberti SRLS (Italy) *Tel:* 392 9667175; 331 7053692 *E-mail:* info@ cealiberti.it; editore@cealiberti.it *Web Site:* www. alibericompagnieditoriale.it, pg 424

Alibri Libreria SL (Spain) *Tel:* 933 170 578 *Fax:* 934 122 702 *E-mail:* alibri@alibri.es; alibri@alibri.cat *Web Site:* www.alibri.es, pg 1450

Alibri Verlag GmbH (Germany) *Tel:* (06021) 581 734 *Fax:* (03212) 119 89 72 *E-mail:* verlag@alibri.de *Web Site:* www.alibri-buecher.de; www.facebook. com/alibri.verlag, pg 204

Alicat Publishing (Australia) *Tel:* (03) 9188 3650 *E-mail:* publishing@alicat.com.au *Web Site:* www. alicat.com.au, pg 16

Alice Editions (Belgium) *Tel:* (02) 660 10 45 *E-mail:* info@alice-editions.be; communication@alice-editions.be *Web Site:* www.alice-editions.be; www. facebook.com/aliceeditions, pg 63

Edizioni Alice (Italy) *Tel:* (051) 534286 *Fax:* (051) 534286 *E-mail:* alice.edizioni@tiscali.it *Web Site:* www.edizionialice.it, pg 424

Alice-Kan (Japan) *Tel:* (03) 5976-7013; (03) 5976-7011 (sales) *Fax:* (03) 3944-1228 *E-mail:* info@alicekan. com *Web Site:* www.alicekan.com, pg 473

Alienta Editorial (Spain) *Tel:* 934926956 *E-mail:* info@ centrolibrospapf.es *Web Site:* www.planetadelibros. com, pg 628

Alinari (Italy) *Tel:* (055) 23951 *Fax:* (055) 2382857 *E-mail:* casaeditrice@alinari.it *Web Site:* www.alinari. it, pg 424

Alinea (Denmark) *Tel:* 33 69 46 66 *Fax:* 33 69 46 60 *E-mail:* info@alinea.dk *Web Site:* www.alinea.dk, pg 133

Alithia Publishing Co Ltd (Cyprus) *Tel:* 22487966, pg 124

Ediciones Aljibe SL (Spain) *Tel:* 952714395 *Fax:* 952754342 *Web Site:* www.edicionesaljibe.com, pg 628

Alkem Co (S) Pte Ltd (Singapore) *Tel:* 6265 6666 *Fax:* 6261 7875 *E-mail:* enquiry@alkem.com.sg *Web Site:* www.alkem.com.sg, pg 602, 1447

Alkim Kitapcilik Yayincilik (Turkey) *Tel:* (0216) 450 20 08 (sales), pg 718

Alkor-Edition Kassel GmbH (Germany) *Tel:* (0561) 3105-282 *Fax:* (0561) 37755 *E-mail:* info.alkor@ baerenreiter.com *Web Site:* www.alkor-edition.com, pg 204

Editura ALL (Romania) *Tel:* (021) 402 26 00; (021) 402 26 30 (sales); (021) 402 26 34 (sales) *Fax:* (021) 402 26 10 *E-mail:* info@all.ro *Web Site:* www.all.ro, pg 584

All'Insegna del Giglio (Italy) *Tel:* (055) 84 50 216 *Fax:* (055) 84 53 188 *E-mail:* info@edigiglio.it; ordini@edigiglio.it (orders); redazione@edigiglio.it (editorial) *Web Site:* www.insegnadelgiglio.it/, pg 424

All Prints Distributors & Publishers sal (Lebanon) *Tel:* (01) 75 08 72; (01) 35 07 72 (sales); (01) 35 07 22 (marketing) *Fax:* (01) 34 19 07; (01) 75 25 47 (sales) *E-mail:* tradebooks@all-prints.com; copyrights@all-prints.com; allprints@allprints.ae; marketing@all-prints.com *Web Site:* www.all-prints. com, pg 497

All-Russian Patent & Technical Library (Russia) *Tel:* (499) 240-4437 *Fax:* (499) 240-4437 *E-mail:* vptb@rupto.ru *Web Site:* www1.fips.ru, pg 1626

Ian Allan Publishing (United Kingdom) *Tel:* (01932) 266600; (0844) 245 6944 *E-mail:* info@ ianallanpublishing.co.uk; enquiries@ianallandirect. co.uk *Web Site:* www.ianallanpublishing.com; www. ianallan.com, pg 729

S Allegra Literary Agency & Co (Italy) *Tel:* 3493060250 (cell) *Fax:* (0942) 620079 *E-mail:* s.allegra. literaryagency@gmail.com *Web Site:* www. groupnuovaatena.com/old/LA, pg 1230

Allegria Verlag (Germany) *Tel:* (030) 23456-300 *Fax:* (030) 23456-303 *E-mail:* info@allegria-verlag. de *Web Site:* www.ullsteinbuchverlage.de/nc/verlage/ allegria.html, pg 204

Umberto Allemandi & C SpA (Italy) *Tel:* (011) 8199111 *Fax:* (011) 8193090 *E-mail:* allemandi@allemandi. com *Web Site:* www.allemandi.com, pg 424

Allen & Unwin (Australia) *Tel:* (02) 8425 0100 *Fax:* (02) 9906 2218 *E-mail:* internationalsales@allenandunwin. com; internationalsales@allenandunwin.com *Web Site:* www.allenandunwin.com, pg 16

Allgoodbooks Ltd (Ghana) *Tel:* (030) 2246729; (024) 3430430 (cell) *E-mail:* allgoodbooks@hotmail.com; allgoodbooksgh@yahoo.com, pg 352

ALLi (The Alliance of Independent Authors) (United Kingdom) *E-mail:* info@allianceindependentauthors. org *Web Site:* allianceindependentauthors.org, pg 1393

The Alliance of Literary Societies (United Kingdom) *Tel:* (01562) 748996 *Web Site:* www. allianceofliterarysocieties.org.uk, pg 1501

Allied Book Co (Pakistan) *Tel:* (042) 36306456; (042) 36310907 *Fax:* (042) 36360662 *E-mail:* info@ alliedbook.com; alliedlhr@alliedbook.com; inquiry@ alliedbook.com *Web Site:* www.alliedbook.com, pg 1441

Allied Publishers Pvt Ltd (India) *Tel:* (011) 2323 9001; (011) 2323 3002 *E-mail:* editorials@alliedpublishers. com; printdiv@alliedpublishers.com *Web Site:* www. alliedpublishers.com, pg 375

Allied Publishers Pvt Ltd (India) *Tel:* (011) 2323 9001; (011) 2323 3002 *E-mail:* exports@alliedpublishers. com; delhi.books@alliedpublishers.com; printdiv@ alliedpublishers.com *Web Site:* www.alliedpublishers. com, pg 1421

Alligator Publishing Ltd (United Kingdom) *Tel:* (020) 8371 6622 *Fax:* (020) 8371 6633 *E-mail:* sales@ alligatorbooks.co.uk *Web Site:* www.alligatorbooks. co.uk, pg 729

Allinti Verlag GmbH (Switzerland) *E-mail:* verlag@ allinti.ch *Web Site:* www.allinti.ch, pg 688

Allison & Busby Ltd (United Kingdom) *Tel:* (020) 7580 1080 *Fax:* (020) 7580 1180 *Web Site:* www. allisonandbusby.com, pg 729

Allt om Hobby AB (Sweden) *Tel:* (08) 999 333; (08) 999 060 *E-mail:* order@hobby.se; redaktion@hobby.se *Web Site:* www.hobby.se, pg 679

Allt om Hobby Publishing Co (Sweden) *Tel:* (08) 999 333 *E-mail:* order@hobby.se *Web Site:* www.hobby.se, pg 1360

Alma Books Ltd (United Kingdom) *Tel:* (020) 8940 6917 *Fax:* (020) 8948 5599 *E-mail:* info@almabooks. com *Web Site:* www.almabooks.com, pg 729

Editorial Alma (Spain) *Tel:* 93 238 43 43 *E-mail:* info@ editorialalma.com *Web Site:* www.editorialalma.com, pg 628

Alma Edizioni SRL (Italy) *Tel:* (055) 476644 *Fax:* (055) 473531 *E-mail:* alma@almaedizioni.it *Web Site:* www. almaedizioni.it, pg 424

Forlaget alma (Denmark) *Tel:* 48 25 54 41 *Fax:* 48 25 20 41 *E-mail:* almadk@hotmail.com *Web Site:* www. alma.dk, pg 133

Leidykla Alma Littera (Lithuania) *Tel:* (05) 263 88 77 *Fax:* (05) 272 80 26 *E-mail:* post@almalittera.lt *Web Site:* www.almalittera.lt, pg 500

Alma Talent Oy (Finland) *Tel:* (010) 665 101 *Web Site:* www.almatalent.fi, pg 148

Editorial Almadia SC (Mexico) *Tel:* (01951) 5 16 21 33; (01951) 5144854; (01951) 51600489 *E-mail:* informacion@almadia.com.mx *Web Site:* www.almadia.com.mx, pg 512

Almadraba Editorial (Spain) *Tel:* 91 616 01 92 *Fax:* 902 10 68 32; 932 15 66 80 (orders) *E-mail:* info@ almadrabainforma.com; ediciones@almadrabaeditorial. com; administracio@hermeseditora.com; pedidos@ hermeseditora.com (orders) *Web Site:* www. almadrabaeditorial.com, pg 628

Almatykitap Baspasy (Kazakhstan) *Tel:* (8727) 250 29 58; (8727) 292 92 23; (8727) 292 57 20 *Fax:* (8727) 292 81 10 *E-mail:* alkitap@intelsoft.kz; info@ almatykitap.kz *Web Site:* www.almatykitap.kz, pg 492

Editorial Almed (Spain) *Tel:* 958806005; 958291581 *Fax:* 958282435 *E-mail:* almed@almed.net *Web Site:* www.almed.net, pg 628

Edicoes Almedina SA (Portugal) *Tel:* 239 851 903 *Fax:* 239 851 901 *E-mail:* editora@grupoalmedina.net *Web Site:* www.almedina.net, pg 576

Ediciones El Almendro de Cordoba SL (Spain) *Tel:* 957 082 789; 957 274 692 *Fax:* 957 274 692 *E-mail:* ediciones@elalmendro.org *Web Site:* elalmendro.org, pg 628

Editorial Almuzara (Spain) *Tel:* 957467081 *Fax:* 957461463 *E-mail:* info@editorialalmuzara.com *Web Site:* www.editorialalmuzara.com, pg 628

Alnovas Literary & Film Agency (France) *Tel:* 04 93 67 51 29 *Web Site:* www.alnovas.fr, pg 1225

Aloe Book Agency (Pty) Ltd (South Africa) *Tel:* (011) 837 9142, pg 1448

AlohaIpo Verlag (Germany) *Tel:* (08031) 2479800 *Fax:* (08031) 2479798 *E-mail:* verlag@alohaipo. com; presse@alohaipo.de *Web Site:* www.alohaipo.de, pg 205

Forlaget alokke A/S (Denmark) *Tel:* 7567 1119 *Fax:* 7567 1074 *E-mail:* alokke@get2net.dk *Web Site:* www.alokke.dk; www.alokkedigital.com (online portal), pg 133

Alouette Verlag (Germany) *Tel:* (040) 712 23 53 *Fax:* (040) 713 41 88 *E-mail:* webmaster@alouette-verlag.de *Web Site:* www.alouette-verlag.de, pg 205

Alpen Editions (Monaco) *Tel:* 97 77 62 10 *E-mail:* contact@alpen.mc; editionalpen@gmail.com *Web Site:* www.alpen.mc, pg 525

Alpha Science International Ltd (United Kingdom) *Tel:* (01865) 481433 *Fax:* (01865) 481482 *E-mail:* info@alphasci.com; editorial@alphasci.com; rights@alphasci.com; sales@alphasci.com (orders) *Web Site:* www.alphasci.com, pg 730

Alpha Test - Sironi Editore (Italy) *Tel:* (02) 5845981 *Fax:* (02) 58459896 *E-mail:* rights@alphatest.it *Web Site:* rights.alphatest.it, pg 424

Editorial Alpina SL (Spain) *Tel:* 93 879 50 83 *E-mail:* info@editorialalpina.com *Web Site:* www. editorialalpina.com, pg 629

Editorial Alreves (Spain) *Tel:* 93 203 5258 *E-mail:* info@alreveseditorial.com; lector@ alreveseditorial.com; prensa@alreveseditorial.com *Web Site:* www.alreveseditorial.com, pg 629

ALS-Verlag GmbH (Germany) *Tel:* (06074) 82 16-0 *Fax:* (06074) 82 16-75 *E-mail:* info@als-verlag.de *Web Site:* www.als-verlag.de, pg 205

Alta Fulla Editorial (Spain) *Tel:* 934 590 708 *Fax:* 932 075 203 *E-mail:* afweb@altafulla.com *Web Site:* www. altafulla.com, pg 629

Altamira (Netherlands) *Tel:* (023) 54 111 90 *Fax:* (023) 52 744 04 *E-mail:* info@gottmer.nl *Web Site:* www. gottmer.nl/spiritueleboeken, pg 528

Verlag Alte Uni (Germany) *Tel:* (07262) 4417 *Fax:* (07262) 7942 *E-mail:* alteuni@aol.com, pg 205

Editions de L'Anabase (France) *Tel:* 01 30 41 07 47 *Fax:* 01 34 85 80 73, pg 153

Anaconda Verlag GmbH (Germany) *Tel:* (0221) 589604-0 *Fax:* (0221) 589604-29 *E-mail:* info@ anacondaverlag.de *Web Site:* www.anacondaverlag.de, pg 205

Wydawnicza Anagram Sp z oo (Poland) *Tel:* (22) 698 70 70 *Fax:* (22) 698 70 70 *E-mail:* anagram@adres.pl *Web Site:* www.anagram.com.pl, pg 567

Editorial Anagrama SA (Spain) *Tel:* 932 037 652 *Fax:* 932 037 738 *E-mail:* anagrama@anagrama-ed.es *Web Site:* www.anagrama-ed.es, pg 629

Anako Editions (France) *Tel:* 01 43 94 92 88 *Fax:* 01 43 94 02 45 *E-mail:* planete.anako@free.fr *Web Site:* www.anako.com, pg 153

Ananda Publishers Pvt Ltd (India) *Tel:* (033) 22414352; (033) 22413417 *Fax:* (033) 22193856 *E-mail:* ananda@cal3.vsnl.net.in; anandapublishers@ gmail.com, pg 375

AnankeLab (Italy) *Tel:* (011) 020 5368 *E-mail:* info@ anankelab.com *Web Site:* www.anankelab.com, pg 425

Anansi Publishers/Uitgewers (South Africa) *Tel:* (021) 976 8411 *Fax:* (021) 976 9698 *E-mail:* info@ anansibooks.co.za *Web Site:* www.anansibooks.co.za, pg 612

Anastasiadis Ekdoseis (Greece) *Tel:* 2102284013, pg 1419

AnatoliaLit Agency (Turkey) *Tel:* (0216) 700 1088 *Fax:* (0216) 700 1089 *E-mail:* info@anatolialit.com *Web Site:* www.anatolialit.com, pg 1238, 1252

Grupo Anaya SA (Spain) *Tel:* 913 938 800 *Fax:* 917 426 631 *E-mail:* administrador@anaya.es *Web Site:* www. anaya.es, pg 629

Anaya-Touring Club (Spain) *Tel:* 91 393 86 00 *Fax:* 91 320 91 29 *E-mail:* administrador@anayatouring.com *Web Site:* www.anayatouring.es, pg 629

Anchor Books Australia (Australia) *E-mail:* sales@ anchorbooksaustralia.com.au *Web Site:* www. anchorbooksaustralia.com.au, pg 16

Ancora Editrice (Italy) *Tel:* (02) 3456081 *Fax:* (02) 34560866 *E-mail:* commerciale@ancoralibri.it; editrice@ancoralibri.it; foreign.rights@ancoralibri.it; redazione@ancoralibri.it; ufficio.stampa@ancoralibri.it (press) *Web Site:* www.ancoralibri.it, pg 425

Editions l'Ancre de Marine (France) *Tel:* 02 32 25 45 97 *E-mail:* service-clients@ancre-de-marine.com *Web Site:* www.ancre-de-marine.com, pg 153

And Other Stories (United Kingdom) *Tel:* (01494) 443797 *E-mail:* info@andotherstories.org *Web Site:* www.andotherstories.org, pg 730

Andana Editorial (Spain) *Tel:* 649 539 205 *Fax:* 962 484 382 *E-mail:* andana@andana.net *Web Site:* www. andana.net, pg 629

Andersen Press Ltd (United Kingdom) *Tel:* (020) 7840 8701 *Fax:* (020) 7233 6263 *E-mail:* anderseneditorial@penguinrandomhouse.co.uk *Web Site:* www.andersenpress.co.uk, pg 730

Carit Andersens Forlag A/S (Denmark) *Tel:* 3543 6222 *E-mail:* info@caritandersen.dk *Web Site:* www. caritandersen.dk, pg 133

Darley Anderson Literary TV & Film Agency (United Kingdom) *Tel:* (020) 7385 6652 *Fax:* (020) 7386 5571 *Web Site:* www.darleyanderson.com, pg 1239

Michelle Anderson Publishing (Australia) *Tel:* (03) 9826 9028 *Fax:* (03) 9826 8552 *E-mail:* mapubl@bigpond. net.au *Web Site:* www.michelleandersonpublishing. com, pg 16

AndiPublisher (Indonesia) *Tel:* (0274) 561881 *Fax:* (0274) 588282 *Web Site:* www.andipublisher. com, pg 405

Editorial Andorra (Andorra) *Tel:* 802925; 328175 (cell) *E-mail:* editorialand@andorra.ad *Web Site:* www. editorialandorra.com, pg 1

Andorran Standard Book Numbering Agency (Andorra) *Tel:* 826445 *Fax:* 829445 *E-mail:* bncultura.gov@ andorra.ad *Web Site:* www.cultura.ad/biblioteca-nacional, pg 1363

Andrea Verlags GmbH (Germany) *Tel:* (03338) 75 29 94 *Fax:* (03338) 75 29 96 *E-mail:* info@andrea-verlag.de *Web Site:* www.andrea-verlag.de, pg 205

Andreas & Andreas Verlagsbuchhandel (Austria) *Tel:* (0664) 15 65 357 (cell) *E-mail:* office@ andreasverlag.at *Web Site:* www.andreasverlag.at, pg 45

Organizacao Andrei Editora Ltda (Brazil) *Tel:* (011) 3223-5111 *Fax:* (011) 3221-0246 *E-mail:* vendas@ editora-andrei.com.br; diretoria@editora-andrei.com.br *Web Site:* www.editora-andrei.com.br, pg 76

Andrena (Lithuania) *Tel:* (05) 270 3834 *E-mail:* leidykla. andrena@gmail.com, pg 500

Andreou Chr Publishers (Cyprus) *Tel:* 22666877 *Fax:* 22666878 *E-mail:* andreou2@cytanet.com.cy, pg 124

Chris Andrews Publications Ltd (United Kingdom) *Tel:* (01865) 723404 *E-mail:* enquiries@cap-ox.com *Web Site:* www.cap-ox.com, pg 731

Ane Books Pvt Ltd (India) *Tel:* (011) 23276843; (011) 23276844 *Fax:* (011) 23276863 *Web Site:* www. anebooks.com, pg 375, 1421

Anetta Publishers (Ukraine) *Tel:* (066) 988 40 85 (cell) *E-mail:* anetta@anetta-publishers.com *Web Site:* anetta-publishers.com, pg 725

Angkasa Group (Indonesia) *Tel:* (022) 7320373; (022) 7320383; (022) 7310984 *Fax:* (022) 7320373 *E-mail:* pemasaran_angkasa@yahoo.co.id; pemasaran_titianilmu@yahoo.co.id; pemasaran@ angkasagroup.co.id *Web Site:* www.angkasagroup.co. id, pg 405

Angkor Verlag (Germany) *E-mail:* webmaster@angkor-verlag.de *Web Site:* www.angkor-verlag.de, pg 205

Angle Editorial (Spain) *Tel:* 933630823 *Fax:* 933630824 *E-mail:* angle@angleeditorial.com *Web Site:* www. angleeditorial.com, pg 629

The Anglo American Book Co Ltd (United Kingdom) *Tel:* (01267) 211880 *Fax:* (01267) 211882; (0844) 500 7211 *E-mail:* books@anglo-american.co.uk *Web Site:* www.anglo-american.co.uk, pg 1455

Anglo Mexican Foundation Library (Mexico) *Tel:* (0155) 3067 8817; (0155) 3067 8800 (ext 8860) *E-mail:* biblioteca@tamf.org.mx *Web Site:* tamflibrary. org.mx, pg 1613

Angry Robot Ltd (United Kingdom) *Tel:* (0115) 933 8456 *E-mail:* incoming@angryrobotbooks.com *Web Site:* angryrobotbooks.com, pg 731

Angus & Robertson Bookworld (Australia) *Toll Free Tel:* 1800 732 701 *Web Site:* www.angusrobertson. com.au, pg 1402

Anhui Children's Publishing House (China) *Tel:* (0551) 3533566 *Fax:* (0551) 3533566 *Web Site:* www.ahse.cn, pg 100

Anhui People Publishing House (China) *Tel:* (0551) 63533112; (0551) 63533114, pg 100

animal learn Verlag (Germany) *Tel:* (08051) 961 71-0 *Fax:* (08051) 961 71-17 *E-mail:* animal.learn@t-online.de *Web Site:* www.animal-learn.de, pg 205

Ankara University Department of Library & Documentation (Turkey) *Tel:* (0312) 223 57 61 *Fax:* (0312) 213 95 32 *E-mail:* kutuphane@ankara. edu.tr *Web Site:* kutuphane.ankara.edu.tr, pg 1639

Uitgeverij AnkhHermes BV (Netherlands) *Tel:* (088) 700 2700 *E-mail:* info@ankh-hermes.nl *Web Site:* www. ankh-hermes.nl, pg 528

Ankur Prakashani (Bangladesh) *Tel:* (02) 9564799; (02) 7176126 *Fax:* (02) 9553635; (02) 7410986 *Web Site:* www.ankur-prakashani.com, pg 61

Ankur Publishing Co (India) *Tel:* (022) 25369907; (022) 25432817 *Fax:* (022) 543 2817, pg 375

Ekdoseis Ankyra (Greece) *Tel:* 210 2693800-4 *Fax:* 210 2693806 *E-mail:* info@e-agyra.gr; order@e-agyra.gr *Web Site:* e-agyra.gr, pg 1419

Ankyunacar Press (Armenia) *Tel:* (010) 253784 *E-mail:* info@ankyunacar.com *Web Site:* ankyunacar. com/booksfromarmenia; www.booksfromarmenia.com, pg 14

Anmol Publications Pvt Ltd (India) *Tel:* (011) 23255577; (011) 23261597; (011) 23278000 *Fax:* (011) 23280289 *E-mail:* info@anmolpublications.com; anmolpub@ gmail.com *Web Site:* www.anmolpublications.com, pg 375

Anness Publishing Ltd (United Kingdom) *E-mail:* info@ anness.com *Web Site:* www.annesspublishing.com, pg 731

Anno Domini Publishing (United Kingdom) *Tel:* (0845) 868 1333 *E-mail:* info@ad-publishing.co.uk *Web Site:* www.ad-publishing.com, pg 1355

Anpak Printing Ltd (Hong Kong) *Tel:* 2811 4118; 2563 4133 *Fax:* 2565 7710; 2811 3501 *E-mail:* info@ anpak.com *Web Site:* www.anpak.com, pg 1277, 1323

Anroart Ediciones (Spain) *Tel:* 928339021 *Fax:* 928249436 *E-mail:* anroart_ediciones@yahoo.es *Web Site:* www.anroart.com, pg 629

Forlagssentralen ANS (Norway) *Tel:* 64 91 94 00 *Fax:* 64 91 94 01 *E-mail:* firmapost@forlagssentralen.no; ordre@forlagssentralen.no *Web Site:* forlagssentralen. no, pg 1440

Ansata (Germany) *Tel:* (089) 4136-0 *Fax:* (089) 4136-3333 *E-mail:* kundenservice@randomhouse.de *Web Site:* www.randomhouse.de, pg 205

Anshan Ltd (United Kingdom) *Tel:* (01892) 557767 *E-mail:* info@anshan.co.uk; shan@anshan.co.uk *Web Site:* www.anshan.co.uk, pg 731

Antares Ltd (Armenia) *Tel:* (010) 58 10 59; (010) 58 76 69; (010) 58 09 59; (010) 56 15 26 *Fax:* (010) 58 76 69 *E-mail:* antares@antares.am *Web Site:* antares.am, pg 14

Antares Ltd (Armenia) *Tel:* (010) 58 76 69; (010) 58 10 59; (010) 58 09 59; (010) 56 15 26 *Fax:* (010) 58 76 69 *E-mail:* antares@antares.am *Web Site:* antares.am, pg 1273, 1317

Antas Bindermann Listau GbR (Germany) *Tel:* (030) 30341976 *Web Site:* antas-bindermann-listau.com, pg 1226

Antenna Edicoes Tecnicas Ltda (Brazil) *Tel:* (021) 25573960 *E-mail:* antenna@anep.com.br *Web Site:* www.anep.com.br, pg 76

Antet XX Press SRL (Romania) *Tel:* (021) 2221245 *E-mail:* comenzi@antet.ro *Web Site:* www.antet.ro, pg 584

AnTex Verlag (Germany) *Tel:* (02267) 82 85 19; (02267) 659922, pg 205

Anthea Agency Ltd (Bulgaria) *Tel:* (02) 9863581 *Web Site:* anthearights.com, pg 1224

Anthem Press (United Kingdom) *Tel:* (020) 7401 4200 *Fax:* (020) 7401 4225 *E-mail:* info@anthempress.com *Web Site:* www.anthempress.com, pg 731

Anthemis SA (Belgium) *Tel:* (010) 42 02 90 *Fax:* (010) 40 21 84 *E-mail:* info@anthemis.be *Web Site:* www. anthemis.be, pg 63

Editions Anthese (France) *Tel:* 01 46 56 06 67 *Fax:* 01 49 56 06 67 *E-mail:* editions@editions-anthese.com *Web Site:* www.anthese.fr, pg 153

Anthropos Editorial-Narino SL (Spain) *Tel:* 93 697 22 96 *E-mail:* info@anthropos-editorial.com; anthropos@ anthropos-editorial.com *Web Site:* www.anthropos-editorial.com, pg 629

Edicoes Antigona (Portugal) *Tel:* 21 324 41 70 *Fax:* 21 324 41 71 *E-mail:* info@antigona.pt *Web Site:* www. antigona.pt, pg 576

Antiqua-Verlag GmbH (Germany) *Tel:* (07746) 2260; (07746) 2273 *Fax:* (07746) 2260, pg 206

Roland Asanger Verlag GmbH (Germany) *Tel:* (08744) 7262 *Fax:* (08744) 967755 *E-mail:* verlag@asanger.de *Web Site:* www.asanger.de, pg 208

The Asano Agency Inc (Japan) *Tel:* (03) 39434171; (03) 39434314 *Fax:* (03) 39437637, pg 1231

Aschehoug Agency (Norway) *E-mail:* epost@ aschehougagency.no *Web Site:* www.aschehougagency. no, pg 1233

Aschehoug Agency (Norway) *Tel:* 22 40 04 00 *Fax:* 22 20 63 95 *E-mail:* epost@aschehougagency.no *Web Site:* www.aschehougagency.no; www.aschehoug. no, pg 1251

H Aschehoug & Co (W Nygaard) A/S (Norway) *Tel:* 22 40 04 00 *Fax:* 22 20 63 95 *E-mail:* kundeservice. litteratur@aschehoug.no *Web Site:* www.aschehoug.no, pg 554

Aschendorff Verlag GmbH & Co KG (Germany) *Tel:* (0251) 690-131 *Fax:* (0251) 690-143 *E-mail:* buchverlag@aschendorff.de *Web Site:* www. aschendorff-buchverlag.de, pg 208

Asclepios Edition Lothar Baus (Germany) *Tel:* (06841) 71863 *Web Site:* www.asclepiosedition.de, pg 208

Asempa Publishers (Ghana) *Tel:* (028) 967 2514 *Web Site:* www.asempapublishers.com, pg 352

ASFORED (Association Nationale pour la Formation et le Perfectionnement Professionnels dans les Metiers de l'Edition) (France) *Tel:* 01 45 88 39 81 *Fax:* 01 45 81 54 92 *E-mail:* info@asfored.org *Web Site:* www. asfored.org, pg 1371

Asgard Distribuciones SA de CV (Mexico) *Tel:* (0155) 52939839, pg 1433

Asgard-Verlag Dr Werner Hippe GmbH (Germany) *Tel:* (02241) 3164-0 *Fax:* (02241) 3164-36 *E-mail:* info@asgard.de *Web Site:* www.asgard.de, pg 208

Ashgrove Publishing (United Kingdom) *Tel:* (020) 7242 4820 *E-mail:* ashgrovepublishing@gmail.com *Web Site:* ashgrovebooks.vpweb.co.uk, pg 733

Ashish Publishing House (India) *Tel:* (011) 23285807; (011) 23274050 *Fax:* (011) 23274050 *E-mail:* aphbooks@vsnl.net, pg 376

Ashling Books (Australia) *Tel:* (02) 6259 1027, pg 17

Ashmolean Museum Publications (United Kingdom) *Tel:* (01865) 278010 *Fax:* (01865) 278106 *E-mail:* publications@ashmus.ox.ac.uk *Web Site:* www.ashmolean.org; www.ashmolean. org/services/publications, pg 733

Ashton & Denton Publishing Co (CI) Ltd (United Kingdom), pg 733

Asia Books Co Ltd (Thailand) *Tel:* (02) 715-9000; (02) 715-9049 *E-mail:* information@asiabooks.com; ecommerce@asiabooks.com *Web Site:* www.asiabooks. com, pg 1454

Asia Ink (United Kingdom) *Tel:* (020) 7938 4476 *E-mail:* sales@asiainkbooks.com *Web Site:* asiainkbooks.com, pg 733

Asia Korea Printing Inc (South Korea) *Tel:* (070) 8672 2750 *Fax:* (070) 8277 2510 *Web Site:* www. asiakoreaprinting.com, pg 1334

Asia Literary Agency (United Kingdom) *E-mail:* admin@asialiteraryagency.org *Web Site:* www. asialiteraryagency.org, pg 1239

Asia One Printing (AOP) (Hong Kong) *Tel:* 2889 2320 *Fax:* 2889 3837 *E-mail:* enquiry@asiaone.com.hk *Web Site:* www.asiaone.com.hk, pg 1277, 1324

Asia Pacific Business Press Inc (India) *Tel:* (011) 23843955; (011) 23845886; (011) 23845654 *Fax:* (011) 23841561 *E-mail:* npcs.india@gmail.com; apbp.books@gmail.com; info@apbp-techbooks.com *Web Site:* www.niir.org, pg 376

Asia-Pacific Cultural Centre for UNESCO (ACCU) (Japan) *Tel:* (03) 3269-4435 *Fax:* (03) 3269-4510 *E-mail:* general@accu.or.jp; library@accu.or.jp *Web Site:* www.accu.or.jp, pg 1379

Asia Pacific Offset Inc (United States) *Tel:* 202-462-5436 *Toll Free Tel:* 800-756-4344 *Fax:* 202-986-4030 *Web Site:* www.asiapacificoffset.com, pg 1264, 1288, 1339

Asia Printing Co Ltd (South Korea) *Tel:* (02) 7250790 *Web Site:* www.koreanprinting.com, pg 1334

Asian Absolute (United Kingdom) *Tel:* (020) 7456 1058 *Fax:* (0870) 762 7568 *E-mail:* info@asianabsolute.co. uk *Web Site:* www.asianabsolute.co.uk, pg 1252

Asian Culture Co Ltd (Taiwan) *Tel:* (02) 2507-2606 *Fax:* (02) 2507-4260 *E-mail:* asian.culture@msa. hinet.net; ycwh1982@gmail.com *Web Site:* www. asianculture.com.tw, pg 711

Asian Development Bank (ADB) (Philippines) *Tel:* (02) 632-4444 *Fax:* (02) 636-2649; (02) 636-2444 *E-mail:* adbpub@adb.org *Web Site:* www.adb.org/ publications, pg 564

Asian Educational Services (India) *Tel:* (011) 29992586; (011) 29994059 *Fax:* (011) 29994946 *E-mail:* aes@ aes.ind.in *Web Site:* www.aes.ind.in, pg 376

The Asian Productivity Organization (APO) (Japan) *Tel:* (03) 3830 0411 *Fax:* (03) 5840 5322 *E-mail:* apo@apo-tokyo.org *Web Site:* www.apo-tokyo. org, pg 1379

Asian Trading Corp (India) *Tel:* (080) 25487444 *Fax:* (080) 25479444 *E-mail:* info@atcbooks.in; atcbooks@gmail.com *Web Site:* www.atcbooks.in, pg 376

Asiapac Books Pte Ltd (Singapore) *Tel:* 6392 8455 *Fax:* 6392 6455 *E-mail:* info@asiapacbooks.com *Web Site:* www.asiapacbooks.com, pg 603

L'Asiatheque-Maison des langues du monde (France) *Tel:* 01 42 62 04 00 *Fax:* 01 42 62 12 34 *E-mail:* info@asiatheque.com *Web Site:* www. asiatheque.com, pg 154

The Asiatic Society of Mumbai (India) *Tel:* (022) 2660956 *Fax:* (022) 2665139 *E-mail:* info@ asiaticsociety.org.in *Web Site:* asiaticsociety.org.in, pg 1600

l'asino d'oro edizioni SRL (Italy) *Tel:* (06) 90286555 *Fax:* (06) 48906391 *E-mail:* info@lasinodoroedizioni. it *Web Site:* www.lasinodoroedizioni.it, pg 426

ASK LLC (Ukraine) *Tel:* (044) 456-84-40; (044) 455-58-94 *Fax:* (044) 456-84-40; (044) 455-58-94, pg 725

Askews & Holts Library Services Ltd (United Kingdom) *Tel:* (01772) 555947 *E-mail:* enquiries@ askewsandholts.com *Web Site:* askewsandholts.com, pg 1455

Asklepios Medical Atlas (Spain) *Tel:* 931882070; 625 562 179 (cell) *E-mail:* info@asklepiosmedicalatlas. com *Web Site:* www.asklepiosmedicalatlas.com, pg 630

ASLIB, The Association for Information Management (United Kingdom) *Tel:* (01274) 777700 *Fax:* (01274) 785201 *E-mail:* support@aslib.com *Web Site:* www. aslib.com, pg 733

ASLIB, The Association for Information Management (United Kingdom) *Tel:* (01274) 777700 *Fax:* (01274) 785201 *E-mail:* support@aslib.com *Web Site:* www. aslib.com; www.managinginformation.com, pg 1501

ASLIB, The Association for Information Management (United Kingdom) *Tel:* (01274) 777700 *Fax:* (01274) 785201 *E-mail:* support@aslib.com *Web Site:* www. aslib.com, pg 1661

Asociacion Bautista Argentina de Publicaciones (ABAP) (Argentina) *Tel:* (011) 4863-8924 *Fax:* (011) 4863-6745, pg 3

Asociacion Colombiana de Bibliotecologos y Documentalistas (Colombia) *Tel:* (01) 2823620 *Fax:* (01) 2825487 *E-mail:* secretaria@ascolbi.org *Web Site:* www.ascolbi.org, pg 1649

Asociacion Cubana de Bibliotecarios (ASCUBI) (Cuba) *E-mail:* ascubi@bnjm.cu *Web Site:* www.bnjm. cu/ascubi, pg 1650

Asociacion de Archiveros del Peru (ADAP) (Peru) *Tel:* (01) 472-8729 *Fax:* (01) 472-7408 *E-mail:* contactos@adadpperu.com, pg 1658

Asociacion de Bibliotecarios Graduados del Paraguay (ABIGRAP) (Paraguay) *Tel:* (021) 585-588; (021) 585-593 *E-mail:* abigrap@pol.una.py *Web Site:* www. pol.una.py/abigrap, pg 1658

Asociacion de Bibliotecologos del Uruguay (Uruguay) *Tel:* 2409 9989 *Fax:* 2409 9989 *E-mail:* abu@adinet. com.uy *Web Site:* www.abu.net.uy, pg 1663

Asociacion de Directores de Escena de Espana (ADE) (Spain) *Tel:* 915591246 *Fax:* 915483012 *E-mail:* asociacion@adeteatro.com *Web Site:* www. adeteatro.com, pg 630

Asociacion de Editores de Andalucia (Spain) *Tel:* 952070048 *E-mail:* aea@aea.es *Web Site:* www. aea.es, pg 1389

Asociacion de Editores en Lengua Vasca (Spain) *Tel:* 943292349 *Web Site:* www.editoreak.eus, pg 1389

Asociacion de Escritores y Artistas Espanoles (Spain) *Tel:* 91 559 90 67 *Fax:* 91 542 44 67 *E-mail:* secretaria@aeae.es *Web Site:* www.aeae.es, pg 1389

Asociacion Editorial Bruno (Peru) *Tel:* (01) 202 4747 *E-mail:* informes@editorialbruno.com.pe *Web Site:* www.editorialbruno.com.pe; www. brunoeditorial.com.pe, pg 562

Asociacion Galega de Editores (Spain) *Tel:* 881978764 *E-mail:* age@editoresgalegos.org; s.tecnica@ editoresgalegos.org *Web Site:* www.editoresgalegos. org, pg 1389

Asociacion Latinoamericana de Instituciones Financieras Para El Desarrollo (ALIDE) (Peru) *Tel:* (01) 442-2400 *Fax:* (01) 442-8105 *Web Site:* www. alidebibliotecavirtual.org, pg 1621

Asociacion Mexicana de Bibliotecarios AC (AMBAC) (Mexico) *Tel:* (0155) 55 75 33 96; (0155) 55 75 11 35 *Fax:* (0155) 55 75 11 35 *E-mail:* correo@ambac.org. mx *Web Site:* www.ambac.org.mx, pg 1656

Asociacion Nicaraguense de Bibliotecarios y Profesionales Afines (Nicaragua) *Tel:* 277-4159 (ext 335) *E-mail:* anibipa@yahoo.com *Web Site:* anibipanicaraguaentubiblioteca.blogspot. com/ (blog), pg 1658

Asociacion para el Progreso de la Direccion (APD) (Spain) *Tel:* 915237900 *E-mail:* apd@mad.apd.es *Web Site:* www.apd.es, pg 630

Asociatia Difuzorilor si Editorilor Patronat al Cartii (ADEPC) (Romania) *Tel:* (021) 2220213 *Fax:* (021) 2220213 *E-mail:* adepc@adepc.ro *Web Site:* adepc.ro, pg 1387

Asociatia Editorilor din Romania (AER) (Romania) *Tel:* (021) 3110650; (021) 3110660 *Fax:* (021) 3115941; (0378) 107299 *E-mail:* info@aer.ro *Web Site:* www.aer.ro, pg 1387

Uitgeverij Asoka (Netherlands) *Tel:* (010) 4113867 *Fax:* (010) 4113932 *E-mail:* info@milinda.nl *Web Site:* www.milinda-uitgevers.nl, pg 529

Aspect (Japan) *Tel:* (03) 5281-2550 *Fax:* (03) 5281-2552 *Web Site:* www.aspect.co.jp, pg 473

Aspect Press Ltd (Russia) *Tel:* (495) 3067801; (495) 3068371 *Web Site:* www.aspectpress.ru, pg 593

Aspekt ad (Slovakia) *Tel:* (02) 5249 1639; (0918) 479 677 *Fax:* (02) 5249 139 *E-mail:* aspekt@aspekt.sk; administrativa@aspekt.sk *Web Site:* www.aspekt.sk, pg 607

ASR/IWSL (Pakistan) *Tel:* (042) 35882617; (042) 35882618 *Fax:* (042) 35883991, pg 558

Edition Assemblage (Germany) *Tel:* (0251) 1491256 *E-mail:* info@edition-assemblage.de; presse@edition-assemblage.de *Web Site:* www.edition-assemblage.de, pg 209

Assessio Sverige AB (Sweden) *Tel:* (08) 775 09 00 *E-mail:* info@assessio.se *Web Site:* assessio.com; assessio.se, pg 679

AT&T Group Ltd (United Kingdom) *Tel:* (0121) 603 6344 *E-mail:* info@att-group.com *Web Site:* www.att-group.com, pg 1286

Atanor (Italy) *Tel:* (06) 7024595 *Fax:* (06) 7014422 *E-mail:* atanor.editrice@libero.it *Web Site:* www.atanoreditrice.it, pg 427

Ataturk Kultur, Dil ve Tarih, Yuksek Kurumu (Turkey) *Tel:* (0312) 457 52 00 *Fax:* (0312) 468 07 83 *E-mail:* bilgi@tdk.gov.tr; katki@tdk.org.tr; isaretdili@tdk.org.tr *Web Site:* www.tdk.gov.tr, pg 719

Ataturk Universitesi (Turkey) *Tel:* (0442) 231 11 11 *Fax:* (0442) 236 10 14 *E-mail:* ata@atauni.edu.tr *Web Site:* www.atauni.edu.tr, pg 719

Atebol Ltd (United Kingdom) *Tel:* (01970) 832 172 *Fax:* (01970) 832 259 *E-mail:* atebol@atebol.com *Web Site:* www.atebol.com, pg 734

Alexandria Atelier (Egypt) *Tel:* (03) 486 0526 *Fax:* (03) 486 0526 *E-mail:* info@atelieralex.com *Web Site:* www.atelieralex.com, pg 1493

Atelier Books (United Kingdom) *Tel:* (0131) 5574050 *Fax:* (0131) 5578382 *E-mail:* art@bournefineart.com *Web Site:* www.bournefineart.com/publications, pg 734

Edition Atelier (Austria) *Tel:* (01) 907 34 10 *E-mail:* office@editionatelier.at; presse@editionatelier.at *Web Site:* www.editionatelier.at, pg 45

Les Editions de l'Atelier (France) *Tel:* 01 45 15 20 20 *Fax:* 01 45 15 20 22 *E-mail:* contact@editionsatelier.com *Web Site:* www.editionsatelier.com, pg 154

Verlag Atelier im Bauernhaus (Germany) *Tel:* (04293) 491; (04293) 493; (04293) 492 (bookstore) *Fax:* (04293) 1238 *E-mail:* bestellung@atelierbauernhaus.de *Web Site:* www.atelierbauernhaus.de, pg 209

Atelier Verlag Ursula Fritzsche KG (Germany) *Tel:* (0221) 9545858 *Fax:* (0221) 9545860 *E-mail:* info@atelier-verlag.de *Web Site:* www.atelier-verlag.de, pg 209

Atelierhof Scholen 53 (Germany) *Tel:* (04245) 267 *Fax:* (04245) 1384 *E-mail:* atelierhof@scholen53.de *Web Site:* www.scholen53.de, pg 1321

Ateliers et Presses de Taize (France) *Tel:* 03 85 50 30 30 *Fax:* 03 85 50 30 15 *E-mail:* editions@taize.fr *Web Site:* www.taize.fr, pg 154

Atena Kustannus Oy (Finland) *Tel:* (010) 4214 200 *E-mail:* atena@atena.fi *Web Site:* www.atenakustannus.fi, pg 148

Ateneo Cientifico, Literario y Artistico (Spain) *Tel:* 91 429 17 50 *Fax:* 91 429 79 01 *E-mail:* biblioteca@ateneodemadrid.es *Web Site:* www.ateneodemadrid.com, pg 1500

Ateneo de Manila University Press (Philippines) *Tel:* (02) 426-5984; (02) 426-6001 (ext 4613) *Fax:* (02) 426-5909 *E-mail:* unipress@admu.edu.ph *Web Site:* www.ateneopress.org; www.ateneo.edu, pg 564

Ateneo Puertorriqueno (Puerto Rico) *Tel:* (787) 722-4839; (787) 721-3877 *Fax:* (787) 725-3873 *E-mail:* ateneopr@caribe.net *Web Site:* www.puertadetierra.info/edificios/ateneo/ateneo.htm, pg 1499

Ateneu Cientific, Literari i Artistico de Mao (Spain) *Tel:* 971 36 05 53 *Fax:* 971 35 21 94 *E-mail:* ateneu@ateneumao.org *Web Site:* www.ateneumao.org, pg 1500

ATF Press (Australia) *Tel:* (08) 8232 2093 *Fax:* (08) 8223 5643 *Web Site:* atfpress.com, pg 17

Athenaeum Boekhandel (Netherlands) *Tel:* (020) 5141460 *Fax:* (020) 6384901 *E-mail:* info@athenaeum.nl *Web Site:* www.athenaeum.nl, pg 1437

Uitgeverij Athenaeum-Polak & Van Gennep (Netherlands) *Tel:* (020) 76 07 210 *E-mail:* info@uitgeverijathenaeum.nl *Web Site:* www.singeluitgeverijen.nl/athenaeum, pg 529

Editora Atheneu Ltda (Brazil) *Tel:* (011) 6858-8750 *Toll Free Tel:* 0800-0267753 *Fax:* (011) 6858-8765 *E-mail:* seditorial@atheneu.com.br; sal@atheneu.com.br *Web Site:* www.atheneu.com.br, pg 77

Ekdotike Athenon SA (Greece) *Tel:* 2103608911 *Fax:* 2103608914 *E-mail:* info@ekdotikeathenon.gr *Web Site:* www.ekdotikeathenon.gr, pg 354

Athesia Buch GmbH (Italy) *Tel:* (0471) 081 100 *Fax:* (0471) 081 129 *E-mail:* bozen.buch@athesia.it; info.shop@athesia.it *Web Site:* www.athesiabuch.it, pg 1427

Athesia-Tappeiner Verlag (Italy) *Tel:* (0471) 081081 *Fax:* (0471) 081079 *E-mail:* buchverlag@athesia.it *Web Site:* www.athesia-tappeiner.com, pg 427

Editora Atica Ltda (Brazil) *Tel:* (011) 3990-2100 *Toll Free Tel:* 0800 115 152 *Fax:* (011) 3990-1784 *E-mail:* atendimento@atica.com.br *Web Site:* www.atica.com.br, pg 77

Atico de los Libros (Spain) *E-mail:* info@aticodeloslibros.com *Web Site:* aticodeloslibros.com, pg 630

Atlantic Books (United Kingdom) *Tel:* (020) 7269 1610; (020) 7269 1628 (sales); (020) 7269 0249 (rights) *Fax:* (020) 7430 0916 *E-mail:* enquiries@atlantic-books.co.uk; sales@atlantic-books.co.uk; rights@atlantic-books.co.uk *Web Site:* atlantic-books.co.uk, pg 734

Editions Atlantica (France) *Tel:* 05 59 52 84 00; 05 59 52 84 01 *Fax:* 05 59 52 84 01 *E-mail:* contact@atlantica.fr *Web Site:* www.atlantica.fr, pg 155

Editorial Atlantida SA (Argentina) *Tel:* (011) 4346-0100 *Fax:* (011) 4331-3272 *Web Site:* www.atlantida.com.ar, pg 3

Bokforlaget Atlantis AB (Sweden) *Tel:* (08) 545 660 70 *Fax:* (08) 545 660 71 *E-mail:* info@atlantisbok.se; folj@atlantisbok.se *Web Site:* www.atlantisbok.se, pg 679

Atlantis Musikbuch-Verlag AG (Switzerland) *Tel:* (043) 499 86 60; (043) 499 86 61 *Fax:* (043) 499 86 62 *E-mail:* info@atlantismusik.ch *Web Site:* www.atlantismusik.ch, pg 688

Atlantis Spol sro (Czech Republic) *Tel:* 542 213 221; 549 255 884 (sales) *Fax:* 542 213 221; 549 255 884 (sales) *E-mail:* atlantis-brno@volny.cz *Web Site:* www.atlantis-brno.cz, pg 125

Atlantis-Verlag AG (Switzerland) *Tel:* (044) 466 77 11 *Fax:* (044) 466 74 12 *E-mail:* info@ofv.ch *Web Site:* www.ofv.ch, pg 688

Atlantisz Kiado (Hungary) *Tel:* (01) 266 3870 *Fax:* (01) 266 3870 *E-mail:* atlantis@budapest.hu *Web Site:* www.atlantiszkiado.hu, pg 367

Atlantyca Entertainment SpA (Italy) *Tel:* (02) 43 00 10 32 *Fax:* (02) 43 00 10 20 *E-mail:* foreignrights@atlantyca.it *Web Site:* www.atlantyca.it, pg 427

Uitgeverij Atlas Contact (Netherlands) *Tel:* (020) 524 98 00 *Web Site:* www.atlascontact.nl, pg 529

Les Editions Atlas (France) *Tel:* 09 70 82 01 01 *Web Site:* www.editionsatlas.fr, pg 155

Atlas Press (United Kingdom) *Tel:* (020) 7490 8742 *Fax:* (021) 7490 8742 *E-mail:* enquiries@atlaspress.co.uk *Web Site:* www.atlaspress.co.uk, pg 734

Atlex AS (Estonia) *Tel:* 7 349 099 *Fax:* 7 348 915 *E-mail:* atlex@atlex.ee *Web Site:* www.atlex.ee, pg 144

Atma Ram & Sons (India) *Tel:* (011) 23973082; (011) 23946466, pg 376, 1422

Atrium Verlag AG (Germany) *Tel:* (040) 60 79 09-04 *Fax:* (040) 60 79 09-557 *E-mail:* info@vgo-atrium.de *Web Site:* www.atrium-verlag.com, pg 209

ATS Italia Editrice SRL (Italy) *Tel:* (06) 66415961 *Fax:* (06) 66512461 *E-mail:* atsitalia@atsitalia.it *Web Site:* www.atsitalia.it, pg 427

Ia Atterholm Agency/ICBS (Sweden) *Tel:* (040) 305883; (0709) 924866 (cell) *E-mail:* ia.atterholm@telia.com *Web Site:* www.iaatterholmagency.com, pg 1236

Attic Press (Ireland) *Tel:* (021) 490 2980 *Fax:* (021) 431 5329 *E-mail:* corkuniversitypress@ucc.ie *Web Site:* www.corkuniversitypress.com, pg 409

Au Bon Marche (ABM) (Benin) *Tel:* 21 33 05 11 *Fax:* 21 33 05 11 *E-mail:* abmsarl@yahoo.fr, pg 1406

Editions de l'Aube (France) *Tel:* 04 90 07 46 60 *E-mail:* contact@editionsdelaube.com *Web Site:* editionsdelaube.fr, pg 155

Editions Aubier (France) *Tel:* 01 40 51 31 00 *Web Site:* editions.flammarion.com, pg 155

Auckland City Libraries (New Zealand) *Tel:* (09) 377 0209 *Fax:* (09) 307 7741 *Web Site:* www.aucklandlibraries.govt.nz, pg 1616

Auckland University Press (New Zealand) *Tel:* (09) 373 7528 *Fax:* (09) 373 7465 *E-mail:* press@auckland.ac.nz; pressorders@auckland.ac.nz *Web Site:* www.press.auckland.ac.nz, pg 543

Audio Visual Centre Ltd (Malta) *Tel:* 21330886 *Fax:* 21339840 *E-mail:* info@avc.com.mt, pg 1433

Aue-Verlag GmbH (Germany) *Tel:* (06298) 1328 *Fax:* (06298) 4298 *E-mail:* info@aue-verlag.de *Web Site:* www.aue-verlag.de, pg 209

Auer Verlag GmbH (Germany) *Tel:* (0906) 73-240 *Fax:* (0906) 73-177; (0906) 73-178 (orders) *E-mail:* info@auer-verlag.de; sekretariat@auer-verlag.de *Web Site:* www.auer-verlag.de, pg 209

Aufbau Taschenbuch Verlag GmbH (Germany) *Tel:* (030) 283 94-0 *Fax:* (030) 283 94-100 *E-mail:* info@bau-verlag.de *Web Site:* www.aufbau-verlag.de, pg 209

Aufbau Verlag GmbH & Co KG (Germany) *Tel:* (030) 283 94-0 *Fax:* (030) 283 94-100 *E-mail:* info@bau-verlag.de *Web Site:* www.aufbau-verlag.de, pg 209

Aufstieg Verlag GmbH (Germany) *Tel:* (0871) 54112 *Fax:* (0871) 4710831 *E-mail:* aufstieg-verlag@gmx.de *Web Site:* www.aufstieg-verlag.de, pg 209

August Dreesbach Verlag (Germany) *Tel:* (089) 95449845 *Fax:* (089) 38989169 *E-mail:* info@augustdreesbachverlag.de *Web Site:* www.augustdreesbachverlag.de, pg 210

August Publishing Sdn Bhd (Malaysia) *Tel:* (03) 8075 9168 *Fax:* (03) 8076 3142 *E-mail:* renee.see@augustpub.com, pg 506

Verlag J J Augustin GmbH (Germany) *Tel:* (04124) 2044 *Fax:* (04124) 4709 *E-mail:* augustinverlag@t-online.de, pg 210

Aulis im Friedrich Verlag (Germany) *Tel:* (0511) 400 04-150 *Fax:* (0511) 400 04-170 *Web Site:* friedrich-verlag.de/aulis-bei-friedrich, pg 210

AULOS sro (Czech Republic) *Tel:* 732 504 098 (cell) *E-mail:* info@aulos.cz *Web Site:* www.aulos.cz, pg 125

AURA Foto Film Verlag GmbH (Switzerland) *Tel:* (041) 420 65 65 *E-mail:* info@aura.ch *Web Site:* www.aura.ch; www.aurabooks.ch, pg 689

Aureus Publishing Ltd (United Kingdom) *Tel:* (01656) 880033 *Fax:* (01656) 880033 *E-mail:* info@aureus.co.uk *Web Site:* www.aureus.co.uk, pg 734

Aurora Metro Books (United Kingdom) *Tel:* (020) 3261 0000 *Fax:* (020) 8898 0735 *E-mail:* info@aurorametro.com; submissions@aurorametro.com; orders@aurorametro.com *Web Site:* www.aurorametro.com, pg 734

Nakladatelstvi Aurora (Czech Republic) *Tel:* 224 214 326 *E-mail:* eaurora@eaurora.cz *Web Site:* www.eaurora.cz, pg 125

Aurora Production AG (Switzerland) *Tel:* (041) 7201531 *Fax:* (041) 7106745 *E-mail:* info@auroraproduction.com; aurora@auroraproduction.com *Web Site:* www.auroraproduction.com, pg 689

Aurum Press (United Kingdom) *Tel:* (020) 7284 9300 *Fax:* (020) 7485 0490 *E-mail:* publicity@aurumpress.co.uk; sales@aurumpress.co.uk *Web Site:* www.quartoknows.com/aurum-press, pg 734

Ausmed Education Pty Ltd (Australia) *Tel:* (03) 9326 8101 *Fax:* (03) 9326 8179 *E-mail:* ausmed@ausmed.com.au *Web Site:* www.ausmed.com.au, pg 17

Aussie Books (Australia) *Tel:* (07) 3345 4253 *Fax:* (07) 3344 1582 *E-mail:* sildale@yahoo.com *Web Site:* www.treasureenterprises.com, pg 17

Austed Publishing Co (Australia) *Tel:* (08) 9203 6044 *Fax:* (08) 9203 6055 *E-mail:* admin@austed.com.au *Web Site:* www.austed.com.au, pg 17

Austin's Book Services (Guyana) *Tel:* (02) 227-7395 *Fax:* (02) 227-7396 *E-mail:* austins@guyana.net.gy, pg 1421

Australasian Association for Lexicography (Australex) (Australia) *Tel:* (02) 9850 8783 *Fax:* (02) 9850 9199 *Web Site:* www.australex.org, pg 1489

Australasian Medical Publishing Co Pty Ltd (AMPCo) (Australia) *Tel:* (02) 9562 6666 *Fax:* (02) 9562 6600 *E-mail:* sales@ampco.com.au *Web Site:* www.ampco.com.au, pg 17

Australia Council Literature Board (Australia) *Tel:* (02) 9215 9000 *Toll Free Tel:* 1800 226 912 *Web Site:* www.australiacouncil.gov.au, pg 1364

Australian Academic Press (Australia) *Tel:* (07) 3257 1176 *Fax:* (07) 3252 5908 *E-mail:* aap@australianacademicpress.com.au *Web Site:* www.australianacademicpress.com.au, pg 17

Australian Academy of Science (Australia) *Tel:* (02) 6201 9400 *Fax:* (02) 6201 9494 *E-mail:* eb@science.org.au; aas@science.org.au *Web Site:* www.science.org.au, pg 17

The Australian & New Zealand Association of Antiquarian Booksellers (ANZAAB) Ltd (Australia) *Tel:* (02) 6251 5191 *E-mail:* admin@anzaab.com *Web Site:* www.anzaab.com, pg 1364

Australian & New Zealand Society of Indexers Inc (ANZSI) (Australia) *Tel:* (02) 4739 8199 *E-mail:* info@anzsi.org *Web Site:* www.anzsi.org, pg 1364

Australian Book Group Pty Ltd (ABG) (Australia) *Tel:* (02) 9211 3033 *E-mail:* inquiries@australianbookgroup.com.au *Web Site:* australianbookgroup.squarespace.com, pg 1402

Australian Booksellers Association Inc (ABA) (Australia) *Tel:* (03) 9859 7322 *Fax:* (03) 9859 7344 *E-mail:* mail@aba.org.au *Web Site:* booksellers.org.au, pg 1364

Australian Bureau of Agricultural & Resource Economics (ABARES) (Australia) *Tel:* (02) 6272 2000 *Fax:* (02) 6272 2104 *Web Site:* www.agriculture.gov.au/abares, pg 17

Australian Chart Book Pty Ltd (Australia) *Tel:* (02) 9489 4786 *Fax:* (02) 9487 2089 *Web Site:* www.austchartbook.com.au, pg 17

Australian Communications & Media Authority (ACMA) (Australia) *Tel:* (02) 9334 7700 *Fax:* (02) 9334 7799 *Web Site:* www.acma.gov.au, pg 18

Australian Copyright Council (Australia) *Tel:* (02) 9101 2377 *Fax:* (02) 8815 9799 *E-mail:* info@copyright.org.au *Web Site:* www.copyright.org.au, pg 1364

Australian Film Television & Radio School (Australia) *Tel:* (02) 9805 6611 *Toll Free Tel:* 1300 13 14 61 *Fax:* (02) 9887 1030 *E-mail:* info@aftrs.edu.au; infonsw@aftrs.edu.au *Web Site:* www.aftrs.edu.au, pg 18

Australian Institute of Criminology (Australia) *Tel:* (02) 6260 9200; (02) 6260 9221 (orders) *Fax:* (02) 6260 9201; (02) 6260 9299 (orders) *E-mail:* aicpress@aic.gov.au *Web Site:* www.aic.gov.au, pg 18

Australian Institute of Family Studies (AIFS) (Australia) *Tel:* (03) 9214 7888 *Fax:* (03) 9214 7839 *E-mail:* publications@aifs.gov.au *Web Site:* www.aifs.gov.au, pg 18

Australian Law Librarians' Association (Australia) *Tel:* (02) 9230 8675 *Fax:* (02) 9233 7952 *E-mail:* admin@alla.asn.au *Web Site:* www.alla.asn.au, pg 1647

Australian Library & Information Association Ltd (ALIA) (Australia) *Tel:* (02) 6215 8222 *Toll Free Tel:* 1800 020 071 (members only) *Fax:* (02) 6282 2249 *E-mail:* enquiry@alia.org.au *Web Site:* www.alia.org.au, pg 1647

Australian Licensing Corp (Australia) *Tel:* (02) 9280 2220 *Fax:* (02) 9280 2223 *E-mail:* alc@alc-online.com *Web Site:* www.alc-online.com, pg 1223

Australian Literary Management (Australia) *Tel:* (02) 9818 8557 *Fax:* (02) 9818 8569 *E-mail:* alpha@austlit.com *Web Site:* www.austlit.com, pg 1223

Australian Marine Conservation Society Inc (AMCS) (Australia) *Tel:* (07) 3846 6777 *Toll Free Tel:* 1800 066 299 *Fax:* (07) 3846 6788 *E-mail:* amcs@amcs.org.au *Web Site:* www.amcs.org.au, pg 18

The Australian National University Library (Australia) *Tel:* (02) 6125 4428 *E-mail:* library.info@anu.edu.au *Web Site:* anulib.anu.edu.au, pg 1574

Australian Press Council (Australia) *Tel:* (02) 9261 1930 *Toll Free Tel:* 1800 02 5712 *Fax:* (02) 9267 6826 *E-mail:* media@presscouncil.org.au *Web Site:* www.presscouncil.org.au, pg 1364

Australian Publishers Association (APA) (Australia) *Tel:* (02) 9281 9788 *Fax:* (02) 9281 1073 *E-mail:* office@publishers.asn.au *Web Site:* www.publishers.asn.au, pg 1364

Australian Scholarly Publishing Pty Ltd (ASP) (Australia) *Tel:* (03) 9329 6963 *Fax:* (03) 9329 5452 *E-mail:* enquiry@scholarly.info *Web Site:* www.scholarly.info, pg 18

Australian Society for Indigenous Languages Inc (Australia) *Tel:* (08) 8931 3133 *E-mail:* ausil@sil.org *Web Site:* www.ausil.org.au, pg 18

Australian Society of Archivists Inc (ASA) (Australia) *Tel:* (07) 3221 4887 *Toll Free Tel:* 1800 622 251 *Fax:* (07) 3221 6885 *E-mail:* office@archivists.org.au *Web Site:* www.archivists.org.au, pg 1647

Australian Society of Authors (Australia) *Tel:* (02) 9211 1004 *Fax:* (02) 9211 0125 *E-mail:* asa@asauthors.org *Web Site:* www.asauthors.org, pg 1364, 1489

Australian Writers' Guild Ltd (Australia) *Tel:* (02) 9319 0339 *Fax:* (02) 9319 0141 *E-mail:* admin@awg.com.au *Web Site:* www.awg.com.au, pg 1489

Autentica Editora (Brazil) *Tel:* (031) 3214-5700 *Toll Free Tel:* 0800 28 31 322 *E-mail:* vendas@autenticaeditora.com.br *Web Site:* grupoautentica.com.br, pg 77

Authentic Media (United Kingdom) *Tel:* (01908) 268500 *E-mail:* info@authenticmedia.co.uk; orders@authenticmedia.co.uk *Web Site:* www.authenticmedia.co.uk, pg 735

Author Literary Agents (United Kingdom) *Tel:* (020) 8341 0442 *Fax:* (020) 8341 0442 *E-mail:* agile@authors.co.uk, pg 1239

Author Rights Agency Ltd (Ireland) *Tel:* (01) 49 22 112 *Web Site:* www.authorrightsagency.com, pg 1229

The Authors' Agent (Australia) *Tel:* (02) 4384 4466 *Web Site:* www.theauthorsagent.com.au, pg 1223

Authors' Club (United Kingdom) *Web Site:* www.authorsclub.co.uk, pg 1502

Authors' Licensing & Collecting Society (United Kingdom) *Tel:* (020) 7264 5700 *E-mail:* alcs@alcs.co.uk; communications@alcs.co.uk *Web Site:* www.alcs.co.uk, pg 1393

Authorspress (India) *Tel:* 9818049852 (cell) *E-mail:* authorspress@rediffmail.com; authorspress@hotmail.com *Web Site:* www.authorspressbooks.com, pg 376

Auto Media Group Ltd (New Zealand) *Tel:* (09) 309 2444 *Fax:* (09) 309 2449 *Web Site:* autotalk.co.nz, pg 544

Verlag der Autoren GmbH & Co KG (Germany) *Tel:* (069) 23 85 74 0 *Fax:* (069) 24 27 76 44 *E-mail:* buch@verlag-der-autoren.de *Web Site:* www.verlag-der-autoren.de; www.verlagderautoren.de, pg 210

Verlag der Autoren-Literaturagentur (Germany) *Tel:* (069) 23 85 74-33 *Fax:* (069) 24 27 76 44 *E-mail:* literaturagentur@verlagderautoren.de *Web Site:* www.verlagderautoren.de/literaturagentur, pg 1226

Autorenhaus Verlag GmbH (Germany) *Tel:* (030) 40 10 30 90 *E-mail:* autoren@autorenhaus-verlag.de *Web Site:* www.autorenhaus-verlag.de, pg 210

Editora Autores Associados Ltda (Brazil) *Tel:* (019) 3289 5930 *E-mail:* coordenacao@autoresassociados.com.br *Web Site:* www.autoresassociados.com.br, pg 77

Autorinnen und Autoren der Schweiz AdS (Switzerland) *Tel:* (044) 350 04 60 *Fax:* (044) 350 04 61 *E-mail:* sekretariat@a-d-s.ch *Web Site:* www.a-d-s.ch, pg 1262, 1500

L'Autre Agence (France) *Tel:* 01 80 50 28 70 *E-mail:* contact@lautreagence.eu *Web Site:* www.lautreagence.eu, pg 1225

Editions Autrement (France) *Tel:* 01 44 73 80 00 *Fax:* 01 44 73 00 12 *E-mail:* contact@autrement.com *Web Site:* www.autrement.com, pg 155

Autumn Publishing Ltd (United Kingdom) *Tel:* (01604) 741116 *Fax:* (01604) 670495 *E-mail:* info@igloobooks.com; customerservice@igloobooks.com *Web Site:* igloobooks.com; www.facebook.com/AutPub/?ref=page_internal, pg 735

Editions Auzou (France) *Tel:* 01 40 33 84 00 *Fax:* 01 47 97 20 08 *E-mail:* editions@auzou.com *Web Site:* auzou.fr, pg 155

av edition GmbH (Germany) *Tel:* (0711) 220 22 79-0 *E-mail:* sales@avedition.de; presse@avedition.de *Web Site:* www.avedition.de, pg 210

AV Studio SRO Reklamno-vydavatelska agentura (Slovakia) *Tel:* (02) 654 262 97 *Fax:* (02) 654 262 97 *E-mail:* avstudio@avstudio.sk *Web Site:* www.avstudio.sk, pg 607

AVA International GmbH (Germany) *Tel:* (089) 45209 220-0 *Fax:* (089) 45209 220-9 *E-mail:* info@ava-international.de *Web Site:* www.ava-international.de, pg 1226

Editions l'Avant-Scene Theatre (France) *Tel:* 01 53 63 80 60 *Fax:* 01 53 63 88 75 *E-mail:* contact@avant-scene-theatre.com; commercial@avant-scene-theatre.com *Web Site:* www.avant-scene-theatre.com, pg 155

avant-verlag (Germany) *Tel:* (030) 806 147 70 *Fax:* (030) 806 147 71 *E-mail:* info@avant-verlag.de *Web Site:* www.avant-verlag.de, pg 210

Editorial Avante SA de CV (Mexico) *Tel:* (0155) 9140-6500 *E-mail:* didactips@editorialavante.com.mx *Web Site:* www.editorialavante.com.mx, pg 513

Editora Ave-Maria (Brazil) *Tel:* (011) 3823-1060 *E-mail:* vendas@avemaria.com.br *Web Site:* www.avemaria.com.br, pg 77

L'Avenc (Spain) *Tel:* 93 245 79 21 *Fax:* 93 265 44 16 *E-mail:* lavenc@lavenc.cat *Web Site:* www.lavenc.cat, pg 631

Aventinum sro (Czech Republic) *Tel:* 732 801 905 *Fax:* 272 735 387 *E-mail:* info@aventinum.cz *Web Site:* www.aventinum.cz, pg 125

Uitgeverij Averbode NV (Belgium) *Tel:* (013) 780 111 *Fax:* (013) 780 183 *E-mail:* info@verbode.be *Web Site:* www.averbode.com, pg 63

Editorial Avgvstinvs (Spain) *Tel:* 915342070 *Web Site:* www.agustinosrecoletos.com, pg 631

Aviatic Verlag GmbH (Germany) *Tel:* (089) 61 38 90-0 *Fax:* (089) 61 38 90-10 *E-mail:* aviatic@aviatic.de *Web Site:* www.aviatic.de, pg 210

Monte Avila Editores Latinoamericana CA (Venezuela) *Tel:* (0212) 482 28 50 *E-mail:* produccion@monteavila.gob.ve; monteavilaeditorial1@gmail.com; administracion@monteavila.gob.ve; prensa@monteavila.gob.ve; promocionmonteavila@gmail.com *Web Site:* www.monteavila.gob.ve, pg 850

Kirjastus Avita (Estonia) *Tel:* 6275401; 6275403 (sales) *Fax:* 6411340 *E-mail:* info@avita.ee *Web Site:* www.avita.ee, pg 144

Uitgeverij Balans (Netherlands) *Tel:* (020) 305 9810 *Fax:* (020) 305 9824 *E-mail:* balans@uitgeverijbalans. nl; klantenservice@uitgeverijbalans.nl *Web Site:* www. uitgeverijbalans.nl, pg 529

Balassi Kiado Kft (Hungary) *Tel:* (01) 483 07 50; (01) 483 07 49; (01) 235 02 04 *Fax:* (01) 266 83 43 *E-mail:* balassi@balassikiado.hu *Web Site:* www. balassikiado.hu, pg 368

Agencia Literaria Carmen Balcells SA (Spain) *Tel:* 932 008 933 *E-mail:* info@agenciabalcells.com *Web Site:* www.agenciabalcells.com, pg 1234

Edizioni del Baldo SRL (Italy) *Tel:* (045) 8960275 *E-mail:* commerciale@pizzighella.com *Web Site:* www.edizionidelbaldo.it, pg 427

Verlag Dr Thomas Balistier (Germany) *Tel:* (07071) 368018; (0172) 7321899 (cell) *Fax:* (07071) 368018 *E-mail:* @balistier.de *Web Site:* www.kreta-buch. de, pg 211

Balivernes Editions (France) *Tel:* 06 76 21 32 10 *Fax:* 04 26 29 90 34 *E-mail:* presse@balivernes.com; editions@balivernes.com *Web Site:* www.balivernes. com, pg 155

Jonathan Ball Publishers (South Africa) *Tel:* (011) 601 8000 *Fax:* (011) 601 8183 *Web Site:* www. jonathanball.co.za, pg 612

Ballinakella Press (Ireland) *Tel:* (061) 927030 *E-mail:* ballinakella@hotmail.com *Web Site:* www. ballinakellapress.com, pg 409

Ballistic Media Pty Ltd (Australia) *Tel:* (08) 8463 1866 *Fax:* (08) 8212 8255 *E-mail:* info@ballisticpublishing. com *Web Site:* www.ballisticpublishing.com, pg 18

Ballon Kids (Belgium) *Tel:* (03) 294 15 00 *Fax:* (03) 294 15 01 *E-mail:* info@ballonmedia.com *Web Site:* www.ballonmedia.com, pg 63

Ballon Media Sales (Belgium) *Tel:* (03) 294-15-00 *Fax:* (03) 294-15-01 *E-mail:* info@ballonmedia.com *Web Site:* www.ballonmedia.com, pg 1406

Baltos Lankos Leidykla (Lithuania) *Tel:* (05) 240 79 06 *Fax:* (05) 240 74 46 *E-mail:* leidykla@baltoslankos.lt *Web Site:* www.baltoslankos.lt, pg 500

Bamboo Edition (France) *Tel:* 03 85 34 99 09 *Fax:* 03 85 34 47 55 *Web Site:* www.bamboo.fr, pg 155

Bancaria Editrice SpA (Italy) *Tel:* (06) 6767561 *E-mail:* editoriale@bancariaeditrice.it *Web Site:* www. bancariaeditrice.it, pg 427

Banco Central de la Republica Argentina (Argentina) *Tel:* (011) 4348 3772 *Fax:* (011) 4348 3771 *E-mail:* biblio@bcra.gov.ar *Web Site:* www.bcra.gov.ar, pg 1573

Ediciones de la Banda Oriental (Uruguay) *Tel:* 24083206; 24010164 *Fax:* 24098138 *E-mail:* info@bandaoriental.com.uy *Web Site:* www. bandaoriental.com.uy, pg 848

Bandicoot Books (Australia) *Tel:* (03) 6267 2530 *Web Site:* www.bandicootbooks.com, pg 19

B&L MedienGesellschaft mbH & Co KG (Germany) *Tel:* (02103) 204-0 *Fax:* (02103) 204-204 *E-mail:* muc@blmedien.de; info@blmedien.de *Web Site:* www.blmedien.de, pg 211

Bang Printing Co Inc (United States) *Tel:* 218-829-2877 *Toll Free Tel:* 800-328-0450 *Fax:* 218-829-7145 *E-mail:* info@bangprinting.com *Web Site:* www. bangprinting.com, pg 1288, 1349

The Bangalore Printing & Publishing Co Ltd (India) *Tel:* (080) 26709638; (080) 26709027 *E-mail:* bangalorepress@gmail.com *Web Site:* www. bangalorepress.com, pg 376

C Bange Verlag GmbH (Germany) *Tel:* (09274) 80899-0 *Fax:* (09274) 80899-10 *E-mail:* service@bange-verlag. de *Web Site:* www.bange-verlag.de, pg 211

Bangladesh Government Press (Bangladesh) *Tel:* (02) 9117415 *Web Site:* www.dpp.gov.bd/bgpress, pg 61

Bangladesh Institute of Development Studies Library & Documentation Centre (BIDS) (Bangladesh) *Tel:* (02) 8181685; (02) 9143441-8 *Fax:* (02) 8141722 *E-mail:* dg@bids.org.bd; info@bids.org.bd; secretary@ bids.org.bd *Web Site:* www.bids.org.bd, pg 1577

Bani Mandir (India) *Tel:* (0361) 520241; (0361) 513886, pg 376

Bank-Verlag GmbH (Germany) *Tel:* (0221) 5490-0 *Fax:* (0221) 5490-120 *E-mail:* bank-verlag@bank-verlag.de *Web Site:* www.bank-verlag.de, pg 212

Banke, Goumen & Smirnova Literary Agency (Sweden) *Tel:* (040) 12 22 66 *Web Site:* bgs-agency.com, pg 1236

Banlue Publications Co Ltd (Thailand) *Tel:* (02) 6419955 *Web Site:* www.banluegroup.com, pg 715

The Banner of Truth Trust (United Kingdom) *Tel:* (0131) 337 7310 *Fax:* (0131) 346 7484 *E-mail:* info@ banneroftruth.co.uk *Web Site:* www.banneroftruth.co. uk, pg 735

The Banton Press (United Kingdom) *Tel:* (01770) 820671 *E-mail:* bantonpress@ndo.co.uk *Web Site:* www.bantonpress.ndo.co.uk, pg 735

Baobab & GplusG sro (Czech Republic) *Tel:* 737 774 538 *E-mail:* gplusg@gplusg.cz *Web Site:* www. baobab-books.net, pg 125

Baobab Books (Switzerland) *Tel:* (061) 333 27 27; (061) 333 27 25 *Fax:* (061) 333 27 26 *E-mail:* info@ baobabbooks.ch *Web Site:* www.baobabbooks.ch, pg 689

Bar-Ilan University Libraries & Information System (Israel) *Tel:* (03) 5317955 *E-mail:* hadracha.centralib@ biu.ac.il; intlib@mail.biu.ac.il *Web Site:* www.biu.ac. il/lib, pg 1604

Bar-Ilan University Press (Israel) *Tel:* (03) 5318575 *Fax:* (03) 7384064 *E-mail:* press@mail.biu.ac.il; info. press@mail.biu.ac.il *Web Site:* www.biupress.co.il, pg 416

Livraria Barata-Antonio D M Barata Lda (Portugal) *Tel:* 218 428 350; 218 428 357 *E-mail:* barata@ livrariabarata.pt; escolar@livrariabarata.pt *Web Site:* www.livrariabarata.pt, pg 1444

Ediciones Barataria (Spain) *Tel:* 622043594 *E-mail:* info@barataria-ediciones.com; administracion@barataria-ediciones.com *Web Site:* www.barataria-ediciones.com, pg 631

Baraza la Kiswahili la Taifa (BAKITA) (Tanzania) *Tel:* (022) 2762243; (022) 2762213 *E-mail:* bakari@ habari.go.tz; bakita201067@yahoo.com *Web Site:* www.bakita.go.tz, pg 1252

B McCall Barbour (United Kingdom) *Tel:* (0131) 225 4816 *Fax:* (0131) 225 4816, pg 1455

Editorial Barcanova SA (Spain) *Tel:* 932 172 054 *Fax:* 932 373 469 *E-mail:* barcanova@barcanova.cat *Web Site:* www.barcanova.es; www.barcanovadigital. cat, pg 631

Barcelona eBooks (Spain) *E-mail:* info@ barcelonaebooks.com *Web Site:* www.barcelonaebooks. com, pg 631

Editorial Barcino SA (Spain) *Tel:* 933 495 935 *E-mail:* barcino@editorialbarcino.cat *Web Site:* www. editorialbarcino.cat, pg 631

Barcode Graphics Inc (Canada) *Tel:* 905-770-1154 *Toll Free Tel:* 800-263-3669 (orders) *Fax:* 905-787-1575 *E-mail:* info@barcodegraphics.com *Web Site:* www. barcodegraphics.com, pg 1273

Bardon-Chinese Media Agency (Taiwan) *Tel:* (02) 2364-4995 *Fax:* (02) 2364-1967 *Web Site:* www. bardonchinese.com, pg 1237

Barefoot Books (United Kingdom) *Tel:* (01865) 311100 *Toll Free Tel:* 0800 328 2640 (sales) *Fax:* (01865) 51496524 *E-mail:* help@barefootbooks.com; salesupport@barefootbooks.com *Web Site:* www. barefootbooks.com/uk, pg 735

Bariet Ten Brink (Netherlands) *Tel:* (088) 1105 400 *E-mail:* info@bariet-tenbrink.nl *Web Site:* www. barriet-tenbrink.nl, pg 1330

Agencia Literaria Irene Barki (Argentina) *Tel:* (011) 4300 3514 *E-mail:* info@irenebarki.com, pg 1223

Barleu Edicoes Ltda (Brazil) *Tel:* (021) 2240-7988 *E-mail:* editora@barleu.com; barleu@globo.com; comercialfalves@gmail.com (sales) *Web Site:* www. barleu.com, pg 78

Barn Dance Publications Ltd (United Kingdom) *Tel:* (020) 8668 5714 *Fax:* (020) 8645 6923 *E-mail:* info@barndancepublications.co.uk *Web Site:* shop.barndancepublications.co.uk, pg 736

Barnens Bokklubb (Sweden) *Tel:* (08) 737 86 90; (08) 441 34 34 (orders) *E-mail:* kundservice@ barnensbokklubb.se *Web Site:* www.barnensbokklubb. se, pg 1360

Editions Le Baron Perche (France) *Fax:* 01 83 64 07 89 *E-mail:* info@editionslebaronperche.com *Web Site:* www.editionslebaronperche.com, pg 155

Baronet AS (Czech Republic) *Tel:* 222 310 115 *E-mail:* info@baronet.cz *Web Site:* www.baronet.cz, pg 125

Editions Xavier Barral (France) *Tel:* 01 48 05 73 01 *E-mail:* exb@xavierbarral.fr *Web Site:* www.exb.fr, pg 156

Barrington Stoke (United Kingdom) *Tel:* (0131) 225 4113 *E-mail:* barrington@barringtonstoke.co.uk *Web Site:* www.barringtonstoke.co.uk, pg 736

Barrister & Principal os (Czech Republic) *Tel:* 545 211 015 *E-mail:* distribuce@barrister.cz *Web Site:* www. barrister.cz, pg 126

Barsortiment Koenemann Vertriebs GmbH (Germany) *Tel:* (02331) 6258-0 *Fax:* (02331) 6258-222 *E-mail:* mail@koenemann-bs.de *Web Site:* www. koenemann-bs.de, pg 1415

La Bartavelle (France) *Tel:* 04 77 60 11 94 *Fax:* 04 77 60 11 94 *E-mail:* caruslocus@aol.com *Web Site:* www. la-bartavelle-editeur.com, pg 156

Verlag Dr Albert Bartens KG (Germany) *Tel:* (030) 803 56 78 *Fax:* (030) 804 74 74 23 *E-mail:* info@bartens. com *Web Site:* www.bartens.com, pg 212

Editions A Barthelemy (France) *Tel:* 04 90 03 60 00 *Fax:* 04 90 03 60 09 *E-mail:* editions-barthelemy.com *Web Site:* www.editions-barthelemy. com, pg 156

Bartkowiaks Forum Book Art (Germany) *Tel:* (040) 279 36 74 *Fax:* (040) 270 43 97 *Web Site:* www. forumbookart.de, pg 212

Bartleby & Co (Belgium) *Tel:* (02) 538 10 51 *Web Site:* www.bartlebybooks.eu, pg 63

Basam Books Oy (Finland) *Tel:* (09) 7579 3839 *Fax:* (09) 7579 3839 *E-mail:* info@basambooks.com *Web Site:* www.basambooks.com, pg 148

Baseball Magazine-Sha Co Ltd (Japan) *Tel:* (03) 3238-0081; (025) 780-1231 (order) *Fax:* (03) 3238-0107 *E-mail:* bbm-order@bbm-japan.com *Web Site:* www. bbm-japan.com, pg 474

Baseline Creative Ltd (United Kingdom) *Tel:* (0117) 962 0006 *Web Site:* www.baseline.co, pg 1286

Basilisken-Presse (Germany) *Tel:* (033708) 20431 *Fax:* (033708) 20433 *E-mail:* info@naturundtext.de; shop@naturundtext.de *Web Site:* www.basilisken-presse.de, pg 212

BasisDruck Verlag GmbH (Germany) *Tel:* (030) 473 083 60; (030) 473 083 61 *Fax:* (030) 473 083 62 *E-mail:* infomail@basisdruck.de; bestellung@ basisdruck.de *Web Site:* www.basisdruck.de, pg 212

Verlag Bassermann (Germany) *Tel:* (089) 4136-0 (headquarters) *Fax:* (089) 4136-3333; (089) 4136-3721 (headquarters) *E-mail:* kundenservice@randomhouse. de *Web Site:* www.randomhouse.de/bassermann, pg 212

Bastion (Romania) *Tel:* (0256) 214805; (0356) 102018 *Fax:* (0256) 214805, pg 585

Bastogi Editrice Italiana SRL (Italy) *Tel:* (0881) 725070
Fax: (0881) 728119 *E-mail:* bastogi@tiscali.it
Web Site: www.bastogi.it, pg 427

Silvia Bastos SL - Agencia Literaria (Spain) *Tel:* 932
654 165 *Fax:* 932 657 610 *E-mail:* correo@
silviabastos.com *Web Site:* www.silviabastos.com,
pg 1234

Batchelor Press (Australia) *Tel:* (08) 8939 7352
Fax: (08) 8939 7354 *E-mail:* orders@batchelorpress.
com *Web Site:* batchelorpress.com, pg 19

David Bateman Ltd (New Zealand) *Tel:* (09) 415
7664 *Fax:* (09) 415 8892 *E-mail:* bateman@
bateman.co.nz; info@bateman.co.nz *Web Site:* www.
batemanpublishing.co.nz; www.bateman.co.nz, pg 544

David Bateman Ltd (New Zealand) *Tel:* (09) 415 7664
Fax: (09) 415 8892 *E-mail:* info@bateman.co.nz
Web Site: www.bateman.co.nz, pg 1438

Battenberg Gietl Verlag GmbH (Germany) *Tel:* (09402)
93 37-0 *Fax:* (09402) 93 37-24 *E-mail:* info@gietl-
verlag.de *Web Site:* www.gietl-verlag.de, pg 212

Jorge Baudino Ediciones (Argentina) *Tel:* (011)
4632-0054 *E-mail:* info@baudinoediciones.com.ar
Web Site: www.baudinoediciones.com.ar, pg 3

Edicions Baula (Spain) *Tel:* 933 540 399 *Fax:* 933
540 489 *E-mail:* comercialbaula@baula.com
Web Site: baula.com, pg 631

Editions Paul Bauler Sarl (Luxembourg) *Tel:* 48 88 93
Fax: 40 46 22 *E-mail:* libuf@pt.lu *Web Site:* www.
libuf.lu, pg 503

N E Bauman (Moscow State Technical University
Publishers) (Russia) *Tel:* (499) 263-60-45
Fax: (495) 261-45-97 *E-mail:* info@baumanpress.
ru; bauman@bmstu.ru; press@bmstu.ru (sales)
Web Site: baumanpress.ru, pg 593

Baumhaus Verlag (Germany) *Tel:* (0221) 8200 0
E-mail: webmaster@luebbe.de *Web Site:* www.luebbe.
de, pg 212

Verlag Traugott Bautz GmbH (Germany) *Tel:* (03631)
466710 *Fax:* (03631) 466711 *E-mail:* bautz@bautz.de
Web Site: www.bautz.de, pg 212

Bauverlag BV GmbH (Germany) *Tel:* (05241) 802476
Fax: (05241) 809582 *E-mail:* info@bauverlag.de
Web Site: www.bauverlag.de, pg 212

Colin Baxter Photography Ltd (United Kingdom)
Tel: (01479) 873999 *Fax:* (01479) 873888
E-mail: sales@colinbaxter.co.uk *Web Site:* www.
colinbaxter.co.uk, pg 736

Bay Foreign Language Books Ltd (United
Kingdom) *Fax:* (01233) 721272 *E-mail:* sales@
baylanguagebooks.co.uk *Web Site:* www.
baylanguagebooks.co.uk, pg 1455

Bayard Editions (France) *Tel:* 01 74 31 60 60
E-mail: contact@editions-bayard.com; foreign.rights@
editions-bayard.com *Web Site:* www.editions-bayard.
com; www.groupebayard.com, pg 156

Bayda Books (Australia) *Tel:* (03) 9380 2988, pg 19

Bayerische Akademie der Wissenschaften (Germany)
Tel: (089) 23031-0 *Fax:* (089) 23031-1100
E-mail: info@badw.de *Web Site:* www.badw.de,
pg 212

Bayerische StaatsBibliothek (Germany) *Tel:* (089)
28638-0; (089) 28638-2322 *Fax:* (089) 28638-2200
E-mail: direktion@bsb-muenchen.de *Web Site:* www.
bsb-muenchen.de, pg 1592

Druckerei und Verlagsanstalt Bayerland GmbH
(Germany) *Tel:* (08131) 7 20 66 *Fax:* (08131) 73
53 99 *E-mail:* zentrale@bayerland-amperbote.de
Web Site: www.bayerland.de, pg 212

George Bayntun (United Kingdom) *Tel:* (01225)
466000 *Fax:* (01225) 482122 *E-mail:* enquiries@
georgebayntun.com *Web Site:* www.georgebayntun.
com, pg 1455

Bazar Forlag (Norway) *E-mail:* post@bazarforlag.com
Web Site: www.bazarforlag.no, pg 554

BBC Active English Language Learning (United
Kingdom) *Tel:* (020) 7010 2754 *Fax:* (020) 7010
6965 *E-mail:* bbcactive.languages.admin@pearson.
com *Web Site:* www.bbcactivelanguages.com; www.
bbcactiveenglish.com; www.bbcactive.com, pg 736

BBC Books (United Kingdom) *Tel:* (020) 7840 8400
Fax: (020) 7233 8791 *Web Site:* www.eburypublishing.
co.uk, pg 736

BBNC Uitgevers BV (Netherlands) *Tel:* (033)
4600339 *E-mail:* info@bbnc.nl; bestellen@bbnc.nl
Web Site: www.bbnc.nl, pg 529

BC Publications GmbH (Germany) *Tel:* (089) 318905-0
Fax: (089) 318905-86 *E-mail:* info@bc-publications.de
Web Site: bc-e-edition.de, pg 212

BCM Media Inc (South Korea) *Tel:* (02) 3482-0584
Fax: (02) 3482-0585 *E-mail:* info@bcm.co.kr
Web Site: www.spworks.co.kr; corp.bcm.co.kr, pg 620

BCS, The Chartered Institute for IT (United Kingdom)
Tel: (01739) 417417; (01793) 417440 (bookshop)
Fax: (01793) 417444 *E-mail:* bcspublishing@hq.bcs.
org.uk *Web Site:* www.bcs.org/books, pg 736

BdWi-Verlag (Germany) *Tel:* (06421) 21395
E-mail: verlag@bdwi.de *Web Site:* www.bdwi.de,
pg 213

be.bra verlag GmbH (Germany) *Tel:* (030) 440 23 810
Fax: (030) 440 23 819 *E-mail:* post@bebraverlag.de
Web Site: www.bebraverlag.de, pg 213

BE-MA editrice (Italy) *Tel:* (02) 252071 *Fax:* (02)
27000692 *E-mail:* amministrazione@bema.it;
segreteria@bema.it *Web Site:* www.bema.it, pg 427

Beacon Books (Pakistan) *Tel:* (061) 6520790;
(061) 6520791; (030) 08636091 (cell)
E-mail: beaconbooks786@gmail.com *Web Site:* www.
facebook.com/beaconbookspakistan, pg 558

The Bear Press - Dr Wolfram Benda (Germany)
Tel: (0921) 81418 *Fax:* (0921) 1503478 *E-mail:* info@
thebearpress.de *Web Site:* www.thebearpress.de,
pg 1275, 1321

Beas Ediciones SRL (Argentina) *Tel:* (011) 4923-4030;
(011) 4924-5337 *Fax:* (011) 4924-0217, pg 3

Beascoa SA
Ediciones (Spain) *Tel:* 93 366 03 00 *Fax:* 93 366 04
49 *Web Site:* penguinrandomhousegrupoeditorial.com/,
pg 631

Editions des Beatitudes (France) *Tel:* 02 54 88 21
18 *Fax:* 02 54 88 97 73 *Web Site:* www.editions-
beatitudes.com, pg 156

Beatnik Publishing (New Zealand) *Tel:* (09) 365 2223
Web Site: www.beatnikpublishing.com; www.facebook.
com/beatnikpublishing, pg 544

The Beatrix Potter Society (United Kingdom)
Tel: (01582) 769755 *E-mail:* info@
beatrixpottersociety.org.uk *Web Site:* www.
beatrixpottersociety.org.uk, pg 1502

Beatriz Viterbo Editora (Argentina) *Tel:* (0341) 4256909
Fax: (0341) 4256909 *E-mail:* info@beatrizviterbo.
com.ar *Web Site:* www.beatrizviterbo.com.ar, pg 3

The Chester Beatty Library (Ireland) *Tel:* (01) 407
0750 *Fax:* (01) 407 0760 *E-mail:* info@cbl.ie
Web Site: www.cbl.ie, pg 1603

Beauchesne Editeur (France) *Tel:* 01 53 10 08 18
Fax: 01 53 10 85 19 *Web Site:* www.editions-
beauchesne.com, pg 156

John Beaufoy Publishing Ltd (United Kingdom)
Tel: (01865) 510920 *Web Site:* www.johnbeaufoy.com,
pg 736

Mitchell Beazley (United Kingdom) *Tel:* (020)
7632 5400 *Fax:* (020) 7632 5405 *E-mail:* info@
octopusbooks.co.uk; sales@octopusbooks.co.uk
Web Site: www.octopusbooks.co.uk, pg 736

BEBC (Bournemouth English Book Centre) (United
Kingdom) *Tel:* (01202) 715555; (01202) 712933
Fax: (0333) 800 1901 *E-mail:* webenquiry@bebc.co.
uk *Web Site:* www.bebc.co.uk, pg 1455

Le Bec en l'Air Editions (France) *Tel:* 04 91 50 29 88
Fax: 09 74 53 17 90 *E-mail:* contact@becair.com;
projets@becair.com (editorial) *Web Site:* www.becair.
com, pg 156

Becht (Netherlands) *Tel:* (023) 54 111 90 *Fax:* (023)
52 744 04 *E-mail:* info@gottmer.nl *Web Site:* www.
gottmer.nl/lifestyleboeken, pg 529

Bechtle, Graphische Betriebe und Verlagsgesellschaft
GmbH & Co KG (Germany) *Tel:* (0711) 93 10 0
Fax: (0711) 93 10 400 *E-mail:* info@bechtle-online.de
Web Site: www.bechtle-online.de, pg 213

Druckerei C H Beck (Germany) *Tel:* (09081) 85-0
Fax: (09081) 85-206 *E-mail:* info@becksche.de
Web Site: www.becksche.de, pg 1256, 1275, 1321

Verlag C H Beck oHG (Germany) *Tel:* (089) 38189-0
Fax: (089) 38189-402 *E-mail:* kundenservice@beck-
shop.de; beck-online@beck.de; beck-online.de
Web Site: www.chbeck.de, pg 213

edition m beck (Germany) *Tel:* (0700) 26632325;
(06848) 72152 *E-mail:* ger@comebeck.com
Web Site: www.comebeck.com, pg 213

Verlag Hartmut Becker (Germany) *Tel:* (06427) 930455
Fax: (06427) 930457 *E-mail:* verlag-hartmut-becker@
t-online.de *Web Site:* www.verlag-hartmut-becker.de,
pg 213

Becker Joest Volk Verlag GmbH & Co KG (Germany)
Tel: (02103) 9 07 88 0 *Fax:* (02103) 9 07 88 28
E-mail: info@bjvv.de *Web Site:* bjvv.de, pg 213

Barbara Beckett Publishing Pty Ltd (Australia) *Tel:* (02)
9331 2871, pg 19

Bedford Square Books (United Kingdom) *Tel:* (020)
7304 4100 *Fax:* (020) 7304 4111 *Web Site:* www.
bedfordsquarebooks.com, pg 736

Editorial Beeme (Argentina) *Tel:* (011) 4854-4200
Fax: (011) 4854-4200, pg 3

Beerenverlag (Germany) *Tel:* (069) 610 095 51
Fax: (069) 242 491 92 *E-mail:* info@beerenverlag.
de; buchhandel@beerenverlag.de *Web Site:* www.
beerenverlag.de, pg 213

Beijing Allied Fortune International Trade Ltd
(China) *Tel:* (010) 67817768 *Fax:* (010) 67817758
E-mail: daniel@af-print.com *Web Site:* www.af-print.
com, pg 1274, 1318

Beijing Arts & Photography Publishing House (China)
Tel: (010) 58572216; (010) 58572600 *Fax:* (010)
58572220 *Web Site:* www.bph.com.cn; www.bphg.
com.cn, pg 101

Beijing Children & Juvenile Publishing House
(China) *Tel:* (010) 58572216; (010) 58572600
Fax: (010) 58572220 *E-mail:* xiongyn@bphg.com.
cn *Web Site:* www.bph.com.cn; www.bphg.com.cn,
pg 101

Beijing Education Publishing House (China) *Tel:* (010)
58572216; (010) 58572253 *Fax:* (010) 58572220
E-mail: bjkgedu@163.com *Web Site:* www.bjkgedu.
com; www.bphg.com.cn; www.bph.com.cn, pg 101

Beijing Fine Arts Publishing House (China) *Tel:* (010)
84255105; (010) 84257032 *Fax:* (010) 84255105
E-mail: gms0000@126.com *Web Site:* www.gmcbs.cn,
pg 101

Beijing Normal University Press (China) *Tel:* (010)
58808015 *Fax:* (010) 58806196; (010) 58807664
Web Site: www.bnup.com, pg 101

Beijing Publishing House (China) *Tel:* (010) 58572216;
(010) 58572600 *Fax:* (010) 58572220 *Web Site:* www.
bph.com.cn; www.bphg.com.cn, pg 101

Beijing Shengtong Printing Co Ltd (China) *Tel:* (010)
67869712; (010) 67887676 *Fax:* (010) 67884903
E-mail: xiawei@shengtongprint.com; ir@
shengtongprint.com *Web Site:* www.shengtongprint.
com, pg 1318

Beijing World Publishing Corp (BWPC) (China)
Tel: (010) 64015659; (010) 64073770; (010) 64015580
Web Site: www.wpcbj.com.cn, pg 101

Biblioteca do Palacio Nacional de Mafra (Portugal) *Tel:* (0261) 817 550 *Fax:* (0261) 811 947 *E-mail:* geral@pnmafra.dgpc.pt *Web Site:* www.palaciomafra.gov.pt, pg 1625

Biblioteca Ecuatoriana Aurelio Espinosa Polit (Ecuador) *Tel:* (02) 2491 157; (02) 2491 156 *E-mail:* info@beaep.ec *Web Site:* www.beaep.ec, pg 1587

Biblioteca Estense Universitaria (Italy) *Tel:* (059) 4395711 *Fax:* (059) 230196 *E-mail:* b-esten@beniculturali.it *Web Site:* www.bibliotecaestense.beniculturali.it, pg 1605

Edizioni Biblioteca Francescana (Italy) *Tel:* (02) 29 00 27 36 *Fax:* (02) 29 00 27 36 *E-mail:* info@bibliotecafrancescana.it *Web Site:* www.bibliotecafrancescana.it, pg 428

Biblioteca General, Universidad de Guayaquil (Ecuador) *Tel:* 2391010 *Fax:* 2282440 *Web Site:* www.ug.edu.ec/biblioteca%20general, pg 1587

Biblioteca Geral da Universidade de Coimbra (Portugal) *Tel:* 239 859 831; 239 859 800; 239 859 900 *Fax:* 239 827 135 *E-mail:* secretaria@bg.uc.pt *Web Site:* www.uc.pt/bguc, pg 577

Biblioteca Geral da Universidade de Coimbra (Portugal) *Tel:* 239 859 831; 239 859 800; 239 859 900 *Fax:* 239 827 135 *E-mail:* secretaria@bg.uc.pt; sibuc@sib.uc.pt *Web Site:* www.uc.pt/bguc, pg 1625

Biblioteca Historica Cubana y Americana (Cuba) *Tel:* (07) 861-5001; (07) 864-8960 *E-mail:* biblioteca@patrimonio.ohch.cu, pg 1584

Biblioteca Luis Angel Arango Banco de la Republica - Colombia (Colombia) *Tel:* (01) 343 12 24 *Fax:* (01) 381 29 08 *E-mail:* wbiblio@banrep.gov.co; prensablaa@banrep.gov.co *Web Site:* www.banrepcultural.org/blaa, pg 1583

Biblioteca Marcel Roche del Instituto Venezolano de Investigaciones Cientificas (Venezuela) *Tel:* (0212) 504 1236; (0212) 504 1282; (0212) 504 1237 *E-mail:* bibliotk@ivic.gob.ve; infoivic@ivic.gob.ve *Web Site:* biblioteca.ivic.gob.ve, pg 1644

Biblioteca Mario de Andrade (BMA) (Brazil) *Tel:* (011) 3775-0002; (011) 3775-0003 *E-mail:* bma@prefeitura.sp.gov.br *Web Site:* www.prefeitura.sp.gov.br, pg 1580

Biblioteca Mark Twain, Centro Cultural Costarricense-Norteamericano (Costa Rica) *Tel:* 2207-7545 *E-mail:* bibmarktwain@centrocultural.cr *Web Site:* www.centrocultural.cr, pg 1583

Biblioteca Mayor de la Universidad Nacional de Cordoba (Argentina) *Tel:* (0351) 433 1072 *Fax:* (0351) 433 1079 *E-mail:* biblio@bmayor.unc.edu.ar *Web Site:* www.bmayor.unc.edu.ar, pg 1574

Biblioteca Medicea Laurenziana (Italy) *Tel:* (055) 2937911 *Fax:* (055) 2302992 *E-mail:* b-mela@beniculturali.it; b-mela.urp@beniculturali.it *Web Site:* www.bmlonline.it; www.bml.firenze.sbn.it, pg 1605

Biblioteca Metropolitana Bucuresti (Romania) *Tel:* (021) 316 83 00 *Fax:* (021) 316 83 04 *E-mail:* biblioteca@bmms.ro *Web Site:* www.bibmet.ro, pg 1626

Biblioteca Nacion Miguel Abregon Lizano (Costa Rica) *Fax:* 2233-17-06 *E-mail:* isbn@sinabi.go.cr *Web Site:* www.sinabi.go.cr, pg 1368

Biblioteca Nacional Aruba (BNA) (Aruba) *Tel:* 582-1580 *Fax:* 582-5493 *E-mail:* info@bibliotecanacional.aw *Web Site:* www.bibliotecanacional.aw, pg 1574

Biblioteca Nacional de Angola (Angola) *Tel:* 222 326331; 222 326398; 222 326799 *Fax:* 222 326299 *E-mail:* bnangola@gmail.com *Web Site:* www.nationallibraryofangola.org, pg 1573

Biblioteca Nacional de Antropologia e Historia (Mexico) *Tel:* (0140) 40 53 50; (0140) 40 53 00; (0155) 53 68 65 *E-mail:* contacto.bnah@inah.gob.mx; servicios.bnah@inah.gob.mx *Web Site:* www.bnah.inah.gob.mx, pg 1613

Biblioteca Nacional de Chile (Chile) *Tel:* (02) 3605272 *E-mail:* oirs@dibam.cl *Web Site:* www.dibam.cl, pg 1581

Biblioteca Nacional de Colombia (Colombia) *Tel:* (01) 3816464 *Fax:* (01) 3816449 *E-mail:* bnc@bibliotecanacional.gov.co *Web Site:* www.bibliotecanacional.gov.co, pg 1583

Biblioteca Nacional de El Salvador Francisco Gavidia (El Salvador) *Tel:* 2221-6312 *E-mail:* biblioteca.nacional@cultura.gob.sv *Web Site:* www.binaes.gob.sv, pg 1588

Biblioteca Nacional de Espana (Spain) *Tel:* 91 580 78 00; 91 580 78 53; 91 580 78 05 *Fax:* 91 577 56 34 *E-mail:* bib@bne.es *Web Site:* www.bne.es, pg 1633

Biblioteca Nacional de Guatemala (Guatemala) *Tel:* 22322443 *E-mail:* bibliotecanacional@mcd.gob.gt *Web Site:* mcd.gob.gt/biblioteca-nacional, pg 1598

Biblioteca Nacional de Maestros (BNM) (Argentina) *Tel:* (011) 4129-1272 *Fax:* (011) 4129-1268 *E-mail:* bnminfo@educacion.gob.ar *Web Site:* www.bnm.me.gov.ar, pg 1574

Biblioteca Nacional de Mexico (Mexico) *Tel:* (0155) 5622-6820; (0155) 5622-6850 *E-mail:* bnmex@iib.unam.mx *Web Site:* bnm.unam.mx, pg 1613

Biblioteca Nacional de Mocambique (Mozambique) *Tel:* (021) 311 905; (021) 311 906 *Fax:* (021) 311 906 *E-mail:* bcanacional@yahoo.com.br *Web Site:* www.bnm.gov.mz, pg 1614

Biblioteca Nacional de Panama, Ernesto J Castillero R (Panama) *Tel:* 224-9466; 221-5965; 221-8360 *E-mail:* ocuevas@binal.ac.pa *Web Site:* www.binal.ac.pa, pg 1621

Biblioteca Nacional de Portugal (Portugal) *Tel:* 21 798 20 00 *Fax:* 21 798 21 38 *E-mail:* bn@bnportugal.pt *Web Site:* www.bn.pt, pg 1625

Biblioteca Nacional de Puerto Rico (Puerto Rico) *Tel:* (787) 725-1060 *Web Site:* www.facebook.com/bibliotecanacionalpuertorico, pg 1625

Biblioteca Nacional de Venezuela (Venezuela) *Tel:* (0212) 505 91 25 *Fax:* (0212) 505 91 24 *E-mail:* atencion.alciudadano@bnv.gob.ve *Web Site:* www.bnv.gob.ve, pg 1644

Biblioteca Nacional del Ecuador Eugenio Espejo (Ecuador) *Tel:* (02) 222 33 91 *Fax:* (02) 256 57 21 *Web Site:* biblioteca.casadelacultura.gob.ec; bne.gob.ec, pg 1587

Biblioteca Nacional del Peru (Peru) *Tel:* (01) 513-6900 *E-mail:* contactobnp@bnp.gob.pe *Web Site:* www.bnp.gob.pe, pg 1622

Biblioteca Nacional del Uruguay (Uruguay) *Tel:* 24005385; 24096012 *E-mail:* bibliotecanacional@bibna.gub.uy *Web Site:* www.bibna.gub.uy, pg 1643

Biblioteca Nacional Eugenio Espejo (Ecuador) *Tel:* (02) 222 3391 *Fax:* (02) 256 5721 *E-mail:* bibliotecanacionalecuador@gmail.com, pg 1587

Biblioteca Nacional Jose Marti (Cuba) *Tel:* (07) 8555427; (07) 8555449 *Fax:* (07) 335938 *E-mail:* publiweb@bnjm.cu *Web Site:* www.josemarti.cu, pg 1584

Biblioteca Nacional Juan Ramon Molina (Honduras) *Tel:* 2222-8577, pg 1598

Biblioteca Nacional Mariano Moreno (Argentina) *Tel:* (011) 4808-6000 *E-mail:* consultas@bn.gov.ar *Web Site:* www.bn.gov.ar, pg 1574

Biblioteca Nacional Miguel Obregon Lizano (Costa Rica) *Tel:* 2257-4814; 2221-2479; 2221-2436 *Fax:* 2223-5510; 2257-4814 *E-mail:* dibinacr@racsa.co.cr; sinabicr@racsa.co.cr *Web Site:* www.abinia.org/costarica, pg 1583

Biblioteca Nacional Paraguay (Paraguay) *Tel:* (021) 204670 *E-mail:* biblioteca.nacional.py@gmail.com *Web Site:* bibliotecanacional.gov.py, pg 1621

Biblioteca Nacional Ruben Dario (Nicaragua) *Tel:* 2222722 *Fax:* 2222722 *E-mail:* b.n.rd@hotmail.com *Web Site:* www.abinia.org/nicarauga; www.bnrd.gob.ni, pg 1618

Biblioteca Nationala a Romaniei (Romania) *Tel:* (021) 314 24 34; (021) 314 10 02 *Fax:* (021) 312 33 81 *E-mail:* biblioteca@bibnat.ro *Web Site:* www.bibnat.ro, pg 1626

Biblioteca Nazionale Braidense (Italy) *Tel:* (02) 86460907 *Fax:* (02) 72023910 *E-mail:* b-brai@beniculturali.it *Web Site:* www.braidense.it, pg 1605

Biblioteca Nazionale Centrale di Firenze (Italy) *Tel:* (055) 24919 1; (055) 24919 314 *E-mail:* bnc-fi@beniculturali.it *Web Site:* www.bncf.firenze.sbn.it, pg 1605

Biblioteca nazionale centrale di Roma (Italy) *Tel:* (06) 49891 *E-mail:* bnc-rm@beniculturali.it; accoglienza@bnc.roma.sbn.it *Web Site:* www.bncrm.beniculturali.it, pg 1605

Biblioteca Nazionale Marciana (Italy) *Tel:* (041) 2407211 *Fax:* (041) 5238803 *E-mail:* biblioteca@marciana.venezia.sbn.it *Web Site:* marciana.venezia.sbn.it, pg 1605

Biblioteca Nazionale Sagarriga Visconti Volpi (Italy) *Tel:* (080) 2173111 *E-mail:* bn-ba@beniculturali.it *Web Site:* www.bibliotecanazionalebari.beniculturali.it, pg 1605

Biblioteca Nazionale Universitaria di Torino (Italy) *Tel:* (011) 8101111 *Fax:* (011) 8121021; (011) 8178778 *E-mail:* bu-to@beniculturali.it *Web Site:* www.bnto.librari.beniculturali.it, pg 1605

Biblioteca Nazionale Vittorio Emanuele III (Italy) *Tel:* (081) 7819111 *Fax:* (081) 403820 *E-mail:* bn-na@beniculturali.it; bn-na.ufficiostampa@beniculturali.it (press) *Web Site:* www.bnnonline.it, pg 1605

Editorial Biblioteca Nueva SL (Spain) *Tel:* 91 310 04 36 *Fax:* 91 319 82 35 *E-mail:* editorial@bibliotecanueva.es *Web Site:* www.bibliotecanueva.es, pg 632

Biblioteca Publica de Evora (Portugal) *Tel:* 266 769 330 *E-mail:* bpevora@bpe.pt *Web Site:* www.bpe.pt, pg 1625

Biblioteca Publica de la Universidad Nacional de La Plata (Argentina) *Tel:* (0221) 423-6607 *Fax:* (0221) 425-5004 *E-mail:* secretaria@biblio.unlp.edu.ar; administracion@biblio.unlp.edu.ar *Web Site:* biblio.unlp.edu.ar, pg 1574

Biblioteca Publica Municipal de Santo Domingo de la Calzada (Spain) *Tel:* 941 341 276 *E-mail:* biblioteca@santodomingodelacalzada.org *Web Site:* www.bibliotecaspublicas.es/santodomingodelacalzada/index.jsp, pg 1633

Biblioteca Publica Municipal do Porto (Portugal) *Tel:* 225 193 480 *Fax:* 225 193 488 *E-mail:* bpmp@cm-porto.pt *Web Site:* bmp.cm-porto.pt/bpmp, pg 577

Biblioteca Publica Municipal do Porto (Portugal) *Tel:* 225 193 480 *Fax:* 225 193 488 *E-mail:* bpmp@cm-porto.pt *Web Site:* bmp.cm-porto.pt/bpmp; bibliotecas.cm-porto.pt, pg 1625

Biblioteca Regional del Caribe y de Estudios Latinoamericanos (Puerto Rico) *Tel:* (787) 764-0000 (ext 85855) *Fax:* (787) 763-5685 *Web Site:* biblioteca.uprrp.edu/bib-col/caribe.html, pg 1625

Biblioteca Riccardiana (Italy) *Tel:* (055) 212586; (055) 293385 *Fax:* (055) 211379 *E-mail:* b-ricc@beniculturali.it *Web Site:* www.riccardiana.firenze.sbn.it, pg 1605

Biblioteca Tomas Navarro Tomas (Spain) *Tel:* 91 602 23 00 *Fax:* 91 602 29 71 *Web Site:* biblioteca.cchs.csic.es, pg 1633

Biblioteca Universidad Nacional Pedro Henriquez Urena (Dominican Republic) *Tel:* (809) 562-6601; (829) 946-2674 *E-mail:* info@bnphu.gob.do *Web Site:* bnphu.gob.do; www.unphu.edu.do, pg 1587

Biblioteca Universitaria Alessandrina (Italy) *Tel:* (06) 44740220 *Fax:* (06) 44740222 *E-mail:* alessandrina@librari.beniculturali.it *Web Site:* www.alessandrina.librari.beniculturali.it, pg 1605

Biblioteca Universitaria di Padova (Italy) *Tel:* (049) 8240211 *Fax:* (049) 8762711 *E-mail:* bu-pd@beniculturali.it *Web Site:* www.bibliotecauniversitariapadova.beniculturali.it, pg 1605

Verlag BibSpider (Germany) *Tel:* (030) 401 04 354 *Fax:* (030) 401 04 407 *E-mail:* mail@bibspider.de *Web Site:* www.bibspider.de, pg 216

Biddles Books Ltd (United Kingdom) *Tel:* (01553) 842477 *E-mail:* enquiries@biddles.co.uk *Web Site:* www.biddles.co.uk, pg 1337

Joseph Biddulph Publisher (United Kingdom) *Tel:* (01443) 662559 *Web Site:* www.dickgrune. com/Biddulph, pg 737

Bideena Publishing Co Pty Ltd (Australia) *Tel:* (02) 9233 6300 *Fax:* (02) 9233 7416 *E-mail:* goannapress@bideenapublishingco.com *Web Site:* www.bideenapublishingco.com, pg 19

BIEF (Bureau International de l'Edition Francaise) (France) *Tel:* 01 44 41 13 13 *Fax:* 01 46 34 63 83 *E-mail:* info@bief.org *Web Site:* www.bief.org, pg 157

Bierman & Bierman ApS (Denmark) *Tel:* 75 32 02 88 *Fax:* 75 32 15 48 *E-mail:* mail@bierman.dk *Web Site:* www.biermanaps.dk, pg 1412

Biermann Verlag GmbH (Germany) *Tel:* (02236) 376-0 *Fax:* (02236) 376-999 *E-mail:* info@biermann.net *Web Site:* www.biermann.net, pg 216

Big Apple Agency Inc (China) *Tel:* (021) 6658-0055 *Fax:* (021) 6658-1977 *E-mail:* bigapple1@bigapple-china.com *Web Site:* www.bigapple1.info, pg 1224

Uitgeverij Big Balloon BV (Netherlands) *Tel:* (023) 517 66 20 *Fax:* (023) 517 66 40 *E-mail:* info@bigballoon. nl *Web Site:* www.bigballoon.nl, pg 530

BIGZ Publishing (Serbia) *Tel:* (011) 3691 259; (011) 3690 518 (commercial) *Fax:* (011) 3690 519; (011) 3690 512 (commercial) *E-mail:* bigz@bigz-publishing. co.rs; komercijala@bigzskolstvo.rs *Web Site:* www. bigz-publishing.co.rs, pg 601

Bihar Hindi Granth Academy (BHGA) (India) *Tel:* (0612) 2924136 *Fax:* (0612) 2660811 *E-mail:* biharhindi@gmail.com *Web Site:* www.bhga. co.in, pg 377

Erven J Bijleveld (Netherlands) *Tel:* (030) 2317008; (030) 2310800 (bookshop) *Fax:* (030) 2368675; (030) 2311774 (bookshop) *E-mail:* bijleveld.publishers@ wxs.nl *Web Site:* www.bijleveldbooks.nl, pg 530

Bijutsu Shuppan-sha Co Ltd (Japan) *Tel:* (03) 6809-0259 *Web Site:* www.bijutsu.press, pg 474

Bilal Muslim Mission of Tanzania (Tanzania) *Tel:* (022) 2120111; (022) 2112419 *E-mail:* bilaltz@ africafederation.org *Web Site:* www.bilaltz.org, pg 714

Bild & Medien Vertriebs GmbH (Germany) *Tel:* (05247) 10 25 9 *Fax:* (05247) 40 87 60 *E-mail:* info@bild-medien.com *Web Site:* www.bild-medien.com, pg 216

BILD Publications (United Kingdom) *Tel:* (0121) 415 6960 *Fax:* (0121) 415 6999 *E-mail:* enquiries@bild. org.uk *Web Site:* www.bild.org.uk, pg 737

Bild und Heimat GmbH (Germany) *Tel:* (030) 20 61 09 0 *Fax:* (030) 20 61 09-75 *E-mail:* info@bild-und-heimat.de *Web Site:* www.bild-und-heimat.de, pg 216

Bilda Forlag & Ide (Sweden) *Tel:* (08) 709 04 00; (0290) 76 76 88 (customer service) *Fax:* (08) 709 04 01 *E-mail:* info@bildaforlag. se; kundtjanst@bildaforlag.se *Web Site:* www. bildaforlag.se, pg 680

Bilden Bilgisayar (Turkey) *Tel:* (0216) 449 52 50 *Fax:* (0216) 449 52 51, pg 719

BW Bildung und Wissen Verlag und Software GmbH (Germany) *Tel:* (0911) 96 76-0 *Fax:* (0911) 96 76 189 *E-mail:* info@bwverlag.de; presse@bwverlag.de; serviceteam@bwverlag.de *Web Site:* www.bwverlag.de, pg 217

bilgerverlag GmbH (Switzerland) *Tel:* (044) 271 81 46 *Fax:* (044) 271 14 44 *E-mail:* info@bilgerverlag.ch; presse@bilgerverlag.ch *Web Site:* www.bilgerverlag.ch, pg 690

Bilgi Dagitim (Turkey) *Tel:* (0212) 217 63 40; (0212) 522 52 01 *Fax:* (0212) 217 63 45; (0212) 527 41 19 *E-mail:* dagitim@bilgiyayinevi.com.tr *Web Site:* www. bilgiyayinevi.com.tr, pg 1454

Bilgi Yayinevi (Turkey) *Tel:* (0312) 431 81 22 *Fax:* (0312) 431 77 58 *E-mail:* info@bilgiyayinevi. com.tr; rights@bilgiyayinevi.com.tr *Web Site:* www. bilgiyayinevi.com.tr, pg 719

Edition bi:libri (Germany) *Tel:* (089) 80 92 41 34 *Fax:* (089) 92 56 01 28 *E-mail:* info@edition-bilibri. de *Web Site:* www.edition-bilibri.com, pg 217

Bilkent University Library (Turkey) *Tel:* (0312) 266 4472; (0312) 290 1298 *Fax:* (0312) 266 4391 *E-mail:* library@bilkent.edu.tr *Web Site:* library. bilkent.edu.tr, pg 1639

Bilnet Baski Sistemleri AS (Turkey) *Tel:* (0216) 444 44 03 *Fax:* (0216) 365 99 07-08 *E-mail:* info@bilnet.net. tr *Web Site:* www.bilnet.net.tr, pg 1285, 1336

binooki OHG (Germany) *Tel:* (030) 61 65 08 40 *Fax:* (030) 61 64 08 44 *E-mail:* info@binooki.com *Web Site:* binooki.com, pg 217

Editions Guy Binsfeld (Luxembourg) *Tel:* 49 68 68-1 *Fax:* 40 76 09 *E-mail:* editions@binsfeld.lu *Web Site:* www.editionsguybinsfeld.lu, pg 503

Bio Concepts Pty Ltd (Australia) *Tel:* (07) 3868 0699 *Fax:* (07) 3868 0612 *E-mail:* info@bioconcepts.com. au *Web Site:* www.bioconcepts.com.au, pg 19

Editorial Biosfera CA (Venezuela) *Tel:* (0212) 751 9119; (0212) 753 8892 *Fax:* (0212) 751 9320 *Web Site:* www.facebook.com/EditorialBiosfera, pg 850

BIOZONE International Ltd (New Zealand) *Tel:* (07) 856 8104 *Fax:* (07) 856 9243 *E-mail:* info@biozone. co.nz; sales@biozone.co.nz *Web Site:* www.biozone. co.nz, pg 544

BIR Publishing Co Ltd (South Korea) *Tel:* (02) 3443-4318; (02) 3443-4319 *Fax:* (02) 3442-4661 *E-mail:* bir@bir.co.kr *Web Site:* www.bir.co.kr, pg 620

Biramo Books Pty Ltd (Australia) *Tel:* (02) 4954 2626, pg 1402

BirdWatch Zambia (BWZ) (Zambia) *Tel:* (021) 1239420; (097) 7485446 (cell) *E-mail:* birdwatch.zambia@ gmail.com *Web Site:* www.birdwatchzambia.org, pg 851

Birkhauser Verlag GmbH (Switzerland) *Toll Free Tel:* (061) 306 17 00 *Fax:* (061) 306 17 01 *E-mail:* editorial@birkhauser.ch *Web Site:* www. birkhauser.com, pg 690

Birkner GmbH & Co KG (Germany) *Tel:* (040) 800 80 1777 *Fax:* (040) 800 80 1902 *E-mail:* info@birkner.de *Web Site:* www.birkner.de, pg 217

Birlinn Ltd (United Kingdom) *Tel:* (0131) 668 4371 *Fax:* (0131) 668 4466 *E-mail:* info@birlinn.co.uk *Web Site:* www.birlinn.co.uk, pg 738

Biro Editeur (France) *Tel:* 01 49 96 43 92, pg 157

Birsen Yayinevi (Turkey) *Tel:* (0212) 527 85 78 *Fax:* (0212) 527 08 95 *E-mail:* info@birsenyayinevi. com *Web Site:* www.birsenyayinevi.com, pg 719

Editora Biruta Ltda (Brazil) *Tel:* (011) 3081-5741 (sales); (011) 3081-5739 *E-mail:* biruta@editorabiruta. com.br *Web Site:* www.editorabiruta.com.br, pg 78

BIS Edizioni (Italy) *E-mail:* ordini@gruppomacro.com (orders) *Web Site:* www.gruppomacro.com/editori/bis-edizioni, pg 428

BIS Publishers (Netherlands) *Tel:* (020) 515 02 30 *Fax:* (020) 515 02 39 *E-mail:* bis@bispublishers.nl *Web Site:* www.bispublishers.nl, pg 530

Bishen Singh Mahendra Pal Singh (India) *Tel:* (0135) 655748; (0135) 2715748 *Fax:* (0135) 650107; (0135) 2715107, pg 377

Biteback Publishing (United Kingdom) *Tel:* (020) 7091 1260 *E-mail:* info@bitebackpublishing.com *Web Site:* www.bitebackpublishing.com, pg 738

Bitter Lemon Press Ltd (United Kingdom) *Tel:* (020) 7278 3738 *E-mail:* books@bitterlemonpress.com *Web Site:* www.bitterlemonpress.com, pg 738

BIU Sante (France) *Tel:* 01 53 73 95 22 *Fax:* 01 53 73 99 05 *E-mail:* info-pharma@biusante.parisdescartes.fr *Web Site:* www.biusante.parisdescartes.fr, pg 1591

Editorial Bizancio Lda (Portugal) *Tel:* 217 550 228; 217 524 548 *Fax:* 217 520 072 *E-mail:* bizancio@ editorial-bizancio.pt *Web Site:* www.editorial-bizancio. pt, pg 577

Bjartur & Verold (Iceland) *Tel:* 414 14 50 *E-mail:* bjartur@bjartur.is *Web Site:* www.bjartur.is, pg 372

The BKL (BINOM Knowledge Laboratory) Publishers (Russia) *Tel:* (499) 157-52-72; (499) 157-79-77; (499) 157-19-02 *E-mail:* info@pilotlz.ru *Web Site:* pilotlz.ru, pg 593

BKmedia eV (Germany) *Tel:* (0941) 3996705 *Fax:* (0941) 3996704 *E-mail:* info@bkmedia.info *Web Site:* www.bkmedia.info, pg 217

BL Publishing (United Kingdom) *Tel:* (0115) 900 4069 *E-mail:* contact@blacklibrary.com *Web Site:* www. blacklibrary.com, pg 738

BL Publishing Co Ltd (Japan) *Tel:* (078) 681-3111 *Fax:* (078) 681-3155 *E-mail:* blpnew@blg.co.jp *Web Site:* www.blg.co.jp/blp, pg 474

A&C Black Publishers Ltd (United Kingdom) *Tel:* (020) 7631 5600 *Fax:* (020) 7631 5800 *E-mail:* contact@ bloomsbury.com *Web Site:* www.bloomsbury.com, pg 738

Black Ace Books (United Kingdom) *Tel:* (01821) 642 822 *Fax:* (01821) 642 101 *Web Site:* www.editor. net/blackace, pg 738

Black & White Publishing Ltd (United Kingdom) *Tel:* (0131) 625 4500 *E-mail:* mail@ blackandwhitepublishing.com *Web Site:* www. blackandwhitepublishing.com, pg 738

Black Dog Books (Australia) *Tel:* (02) 9517 9577 *Fax:* (02) 9517 9997 *E-mail:* sales@walkerbooks.com. au *Web Site:* www.walkerbooks.com.au, pg 19

Black Inc (Australia) *Tel:* (03) 9486 0288 *Fax:* (03) 9486 0244 *E-mail:* enquiries@blackincbooks.com *Web Site:* www.blackincbooks.com, pg 19

Black Spring Press Ltd (United Kingdom) *Tel:* (020) 7613 3066 *Fax:* (020) 7613 0028 *E-mail:* enquiries@ blackspringpress.co.uk; info@blackspringpress.co.uk *Web Site:* www.blackspringpress.co.uk, pg 738

Blackhall Publishing (Ireland) *Tel:* (01) 278 5090 *E-mail:* info@blackhallpublishing.com *Web Site:* www.blackhallpublishing.com, pg 409

Blackie Books (Spain) *Tel:* 934 160 959 *E-mail:* info@ blackiebooks.org *Web Site:* www.blackiebooks.org, pg 632

Blackmask Ltd (Ghana) *Tel:* (030) 2222204; (030) 8199532 (cell) *E-mail:* bmask4u@yahoo.com, pg 352

Blackmore Ltd (United Kingdom) *Tel:* (01747) 853034 *Fax:* (01747) 854500 *E-mail:* sales@blackmore.co.uk *Web Site:* www.blackmore.co.uk, pg 1286, 1337, 1355

Blacksmith Books (Hong Kong) *Tel:* 2877 7899 *E-mail:* mail@blacksmithbooks.com (submissions) *Web Site:* www.blacksmithbooks.com; www.facebook. com/BlacksmithBooks, pg 363

Blackstaff Press (United Kingdom) *Tel:* (028) 9034 7510 *E-mail:* info@blackstaffpress.com *Web Site:* www. blackstaffpress.com, pg 738

Blackwell & Ruth (New Zealand) *Tel:* (09) 300 9955 *Fax:* (09) 300 9959 *E-mail:* contact@pqblackwell.com *Web Site:* www.pqblackwell.com, pg 544

Blackwell UK Ltd (United Kingdom) *Tel:* (01865) 333536 (online sales) *E-mail:* mail.ox@blackwell. co.uk; blackwell.online@blackwell.co.uk *Web Site:* blackwells.co.uk, pg 1456

Blaetter Verlagsgesellschaft mbH (Germany) *Tel:* (030) 3088-3644; (030) 3088-3640 *Fax:* (030) 3088-3645 *E-mail:* abo@blaetter.de; info@blaetter.de; redaktion@ blaetter.de *Web Site:* www.blaetter.de, pg 217

The Blair Partnership (United Kingdom) *Tel:* (020) 7504 2520 *Fax:* (020) 7504 2521 *E-mail:* info@ theblairpartnership.com *Web Site:* www. theblairpartnership.com, pg 1239

Blake Education (Australia) *Tel:* (03) 9558 4433 *Fax:* (03) 9558 5433 *E-mail:* accounts@blake.com.au; customerservice@blake.com.au; info@blake.com.au; vip@blake.com.au (marketing) *Web Site:* www.blake. com.au, pg 19

Blake Friedmann Literary, Film & TV Agency Ltd (United Kingdom) *Tel:* (020) 7387 0842 *E-mail:* info@blakefriedmann.co.uk *Web Site:* www. blakefriedmann.co.uk, pg 1239

John Blake Publishing Ltd (United Kingdom) *Tel:* (020) 7381 0666 *E-mail:* help@johnblakebooks.com *Web Site:* johnblakebooks.com, pg 739

Editions William Blake & Co (France) *Fax:* 05 56 31 45 47 *E-mail:* editions.william.blake@wanadoo.fr *Web Site:* www.editions-william-blake-and-co.com, pg 157

Editions Albert Blanchard (France) *Tel:* 01 43 26 90 34 *Fax:* 01 43 29 90 34 *E-mail:* librairie.blanchard@ wanadoo.fr *Web Site:* www.blanchard75.fr, pg 157

BuchVertrieb Blank GmbH (Germany) *Tel:* (08139) 8 02 91-0 *Fax:* (08139) 8 02 91-20 *E-mail:* info@ buchvertrieb-blank.de *Web Site:* www.buchvertrieb-blank.de, pg 217, 1415

Blanvalet Verlag (Germany) *Tel:* (089) 4136-0 *Toll Free Tel:* (0800) 500 33 22 *Fax:* (089) 4136-3333 *E-mail:* kundenservice@randomhouse.de *Web Site:* www.randomhouse.de/blanvalet, pg 217

Dana Blatna Literary Agency (Czech Republic) *Tel:* 608 748 157 *E-mail:* blatna@dbagency.cz *Web Site:* www. dbagency.cz, pg 1224

Verlag Die Blaue Eule (Germany) *Tel:* (0201) 8 77 69 63 *Fax:* (0201) 8 77 69 64 *E-mail:* info@die-blaue-eule.de *Web Site:* www.die-blaue-eule.de, pg 217

Blaukreuz-Verlag Bern (Switzerland) *Tel:* (031) 300 58 66 *Fax:* (031) 300 58 69 *E-mail:* verlag@blaueskreuz. ch *Web Site:* www.blaukreuzverlag.ch, pg 690

Blaukreuz-Verlag und Versandbuchhandel eK (Germany) *Tel:* (02351) 4324943 *Fax:* (02351) 4324945 *E-mail:* info@blaukreuz-verlag.de *Web Site:* www. blaukreuz.de, pg 217

Blay-Foldex (France) *Tel:* 02 47 49 90 49 *Fax:* 02 47 79 91 49 *E-mail:* info@blayfoldex.com *Web Site:* www. blayfoldex.com, pg 157

Bleicher Verlag GmbH (Germany) *Tel:* (07156) 43 08-0 *Fax:* (07156) 43 08-27; (07156) 43 08-40 *E-mail:* info@bleicher-verlag.de *Web Site:* www. bleicher-verlag.de, pg 217

Karl Blessing Verlag (Germany) *Tel:* (089) 4136-0 *Toll Free Tel:* (0800) 500 33 22 *Fax:* (089) 4136-3333 *E-mail:* kundenservice@randomhouse.de *Web Site:* www.randomhouse.de/blessing, pg 217

Editions Bleu autour (France) *Tel:* 04 70 45 72 45 *Fax:* 04 70 45 72 54 *E-mail:* dialogue@bleu-autour. com *Web Site:* www.bleu-autour.com, pg 157

Blex Ideas (Spain) *Tel:* 922653401 *Fax:* 922653801 *E-mail:* info@blexideas.com *Web Site:* www.blexideas. com, pg 633

Blink Publishing (United Kingdom) *Tel:* (020) 3770 8888 *E-mail:* info@blinkpublishing.co.uk *Web Site:* www.blinkpublishing.co.uk, pg 739

Blitzprint Inc (Canada) *Toll Free Tel:* 866-479-3248 *Fax:* 403-253-5642 *E-mail:* books@blitzprint.com *Web Site:* www.blitzprint.com, pg 1318

Blockfoil Group Ltd (United Kingdom) *Tel:* (01473) 721701 *Fax:* (01473) 718220 *E-mail:* ipswich@ blockfoil.com *Web Site:* www.blockfoil.com, pg 1337

Bloemfontein Public Library (South Africa) *Tel:* (051) 405 8248 *E-mail:* bloemfonteinlibrary@mangaung.co. za, pg 1630

Bloodaxe Books Ltd (United Kingdom) *Tel:* (01434) 611 581 *Fax:* (01434) 611 586 *E-mail:* editor@ bloodaxebooks.com; publicity@bloodaxebooks.com; sales@bloodaxebooks.com; rights@bloodaxebooks. com; finance@bloodaxebooks.com *Web Site:* www. bloodaxebooks.com, pg 739

Bloomsbury Academic (United Kingdom) *Tel:* (020) 7631 5600 *Fax:* (020) 7631 5800 *E-mail:* academic@ bloomsbury.com *Web Site:* www.bloomsbury.com/uk/ academic, pg 739

Bloomsbury Professional Ltd (United Kingdom) *Tel:* (01444) 416119 *Fax:* (01444) 440426 *E-mail:* customerservices@bloomsburyprofessional. com *Web Site:* www.bloomsburyprofessional.com, pg 740

Bloomsbury Publishing India Pvt Ltd (India) *Web Site:* www.bloomsbury.com/bloomsbury-india, pg 377

Bloomsbury Publishing Plc (United Kingdom) *Tel:* (020) 7631 5600 *Fax:* (020) 7631 5800 *E-mail:* contact@bloomsbury.com; sales@bloomsbury. com *Web Site:* www.bloomsbury.com, pg 740

Blorenge Books (United Kingdom) *Tel:* (01873) 856114 *E-mail:* cbarber010@aol.com *Web Site:* blorenge-books.co.uk, pg 740

Eberhard Blottner Verlag GmbH (Germany) *Tel:* (06128) 2 36 00 *Fax:* (06128) 2 11 80 *E-mail:* blottner@ blottner.de *Web Site:* www.blottner.de, pg 218

Blu Edizioni SRL (Italy) *Tel:* (011) 74616 *Fax:* (011) 8127634 *E-mail:* info@bluedizioni.it *Web Site:* www. bluedizioni.it, pg 428

Editora Edgard Blucher Ltda (Brazil) *Tel:* (011) 3078-5366 *Fax:* (011) 3079-2707 *Web Site:* www.blucher. com.br, pg 78

Blue Angel Gallery Pty Ltd (Australia) *Tel:* (03) 9574 7776 *Fax:* (03) 9574 7772 *E-mail:* info@ blueangelonline.com *Web Site:* www.blueangelonline. com; www.tonicarminesalerno.com, pg 20

Editorial Blume/Naturart SA (Spain) *Tel:* 932054000 *Fax:* 932051441 *E-mail:* info@blume.net; export@ blume.net; rights@blume.net *Web Site:* www.blume. net, pg 633

Blumenbar (Germany) *Tel:* (030) 28394 0 *Fax:* (030) 28394-100 *E-mail:* info@aufbau-verlag.de *Web Site:* www.aufbau-verlag.de, pg 218

BLV Buchverlag GmbH & Co KG (Germany) *Tel:* (089) 12 02 12-0 *Fax:* (089) 12 02 12-120 *E-mail:* blv-verlag@blv.de *Web Site:* www.blvverlag.de, pg 218

BMI Research (United Kingdom) *Tel:* (020) 7248 0468 *Fax:* (020) 7248 0467 *E-mail:* enquiry@bmiresearch. com *Web Site:* www.bmiresearch.com, pg 740

BMJ Publishing Group Ltd (United Kingdom) *Tel:* (020) 7387 4410; (020) 7111 1105 (customer service) *E-mail:* support@bmj.com *Web Site:* group.bmj.com, pg 740

BN International BV (Netherlands) *Tel:* (035) 5248400 *Fax:* (035) 5256004 *E-mail:* wallcovering@bnint.nl *Web Site:* www.bnint.com, pg 1347

BNN Inc (Japan) *Fax:* (03) 5725-1511 *E-mail:* world_info@bnn.co.jp *Web Site:* www.bnn. co.jp, pg 474

Board of Studies NSW (Australia) *Tel:* (02) 9367 8111 *Fax:* (02) 9367 8484 *E-mail:* information@bos.nsw. edu.au; service@bos.nsw.edu.au *Web Site:* www. boardofstudies.nsw.edu.au, pg 20

Boat Books Australia (Australia) *Tel:* (02) 9439 1133 *Toll Free Tel:* 1300 2628 2665 *Fax:* (02) 9439 8517 *E-mail:* boatbooks@boatbooks-aust.com.au *Web Site:* www.boatbooks-aust.com.au, pg 20

Editions De Boccard (France) *Tel:* 01 43 26 00 37 *E-mail:* info@deboccard.com *Web Site:* www. deboccard.com, pg 157

BOCK + HERCHEN Verlag (Germany) *Tel:* (02224) 57 75 *Fax:* (02224) 7 83 10 *E-mail:* info@bock-und-herchen.de *Web Site:* www.bock-und-herchen.de, pg 218

Bocola Verlag GmbH (Germany) *Tel:* (0228) 9106174-0 *Fax:* (0228) 9106174-29 *E-mail:* info@bocola.de *Web Site:* www.bocola.de, pg 218

Theodor Boder Verlag (Switzerland) *Tel:* (079) 566 81 84 *Fax:* (079) 566 81 84 *E-mail:* info@boderverlag.ch *Web Site:* www.boderverlag.ch, pg 690

Bodleian Library (United Kingdom) *Tel:* (01865) 277162 *Fax:* (01865) 277182 *E-mail:* reader.services@ bodleian.ox.ac.uk *Web Site:* www.bodleian.ox.ac.uk, pg 1640

Bodleian Library Publishing (United Kingdom) *Tel:* (01865) 283850 *E-mail:* publishing@bodleian.ox. ac.uk; orders@bodleianshop.co.uk; customerservice@ bodleianshop.co.uk *Web Site:* www.bodleianshop.co. uk, pg 740

Libreria Bodoniana (Italy) *Tel:* (081) 5802279 *Fax:* (081) 5802279 *Web Site:* digilander.libero.it/fmrnapoli, pg 1428

De Boeck Universite (Belgium) *Tel:* (010) 48 25 11 *Fax:* (010) 48 26 93 *E-mail:* info@superieur.deboeck. com *Web Site:* superieur.deboeck.com, pg 63

Firma Boehlau Verlag GmbH & Cie (Germany) *Tel:* (0221) 91390-0 *Fax:* (0221) 91390-11 *E-mail:* info@boehlau.de; vertrieb@boehlau.de *Web Site:* www.boehlau.de; www.boehlau-verlag.com, pg 218

Claudia Boehme Rights & Literary Agency - Publishing Consultant (Germany) *Tel:* (0511) 6008484 *Fax:* (0511) 6008474 *E-mail:* post@agency-boehme. com *Web Site:* www.agency-boehme.com, pg 1226

Boek.be (Belgium) *Tel:* (03) 230 89 23 *Fax:* (03) 281 22 40 *E-mail:* info@boek.be *Web Site:* www.boek.be, pg 1365

Boekencentrum Uitgevers BV (Netherlands) *Tel:* (079) 361 54 81; (079) 362 82 82 (sales) *Fax:* (079) 361 54 89 *E-mail:* info@boekencentrum.nl; verkoop@ boekencentrum.nl *Web Site:* www.boekencentrum.nl, pg 530

Boekhandel 't Oneindige Verhaal (Belgium) *Tel:* (03) 776 52 25 *Fax:* (03) 776 52 25 *E-mail:* info@ oneindigeverhaal.be *Web Site:* www.oneindigeverhaal. be; www.facebook.com/oneindigeverhaal, pg 1406

Boekwerk & Partners (Netherlands) *Tel:* (06) 51285050, pg 530

Boer Verlag (Germany) *Tel:* (08144) 998781 *Fax:* (08144) 998782 *Web Site:* www.boerverlag.de, pg 218

Boerm Bruckmeier Verlag GmbH (Germany) *Tel:* (089) 697781-0 *Fax:* (089) 697781-28 *E-mail:* info@ media4u.com *Web Site:* www.media4u.com/de, pg 218

Boersenbuchverlag (Germany) *Tel:* (09221) 9051-304 *E-mail:* kontakt@plassen.de; buecher@plassen.de (manuscript submission) *Web Site:* www.plassen-buchverlage.de/boersenbuchverlag.htm, pg 218

Boersenverein de Deutschen Buchhandels-Nord eV (Germany) *Tel:* (040) 5247673-0 *Fax:* (040) 229 85 14 *E-mail:* info@boersenverein-nord.de *Web Site:* www. boersenverein.de/de/norddeutschland, pg 1373

Boersenverein des Deutschen Buchhandels eV (Germany) *Tel:* (069) 1306 0 *Fax:* (069) 1306 201 *E-mail:* info@boev.de *Web Site:* www.boersenverein. de, pg 1373

Boersenverein des Deutschen Buchhandels eV-Regionalgeschaeftsstelle NRW (Germany) *Tel:* (0211) 86445-0 *Fax:* (0211) 86445-99 *E-mail:* info@buchnrw. de *Web Site:* www.buchnrw.de; www.boersenverein. de/de/nordrhein_westfalen/index.html, pg 1373

Boersenverein des Deutschen Buchhandels, Landesverband Baden-Wuerttemberg eV (Germany) *Tel:* (0711) 61941-0 *Fax:* (0711) 61941-44 *E-mail:* post@buchhandelsverband.de *Web Site:* www. buchhandelsverband.de, pg 1374

Boersenverein des Deutschen Buchhandels - Landesverband Bayern eV (Germany) *Tel:* (089) 29 19 42-0 *Fax:* (089) 29 19 42-49 *E-mail:* info@ buchhandel-bayern.de *Web Site:* www.buchhandel-bayern.de, pg 1374

Editorial Boveda (Spain) *Tel:* 913 938 800 *Fax:* 917 426 631 *Web Site:* www.editorialboveda.com, pg 633

Italo Bovolenta Editore (Italy) *Tel:* (0532) 259386 *Fax:* (0532) 259387 *E-mail:* bovolenta@ bovolentaeditore.it; bovolenta@iol.it *Web Site:* multimedia.bovolentaeditore.com, pg 429

Bower Bird Books (Australia), pg 20

Bowker, an affiliate of ProQuest (United Kingdom) *Tel:* (020) 7832 1700 *E-mail:* sales@bowker.co.uk *Web Site:* www.bowker.com, pg 741

Boxer Books Ltd (United Kingdom) *Tel:* (020) 7138 3650 *E-mail:* info@boxerbooks.com; sales@ boxerbooks.com *Web Site:* www.boxerbooksltd.co.uk, pg 741

Boxtree Ltd (United Kingdom) *Tel:* (020) 7014 6000 *Fax:* (020) 7014 6001 *E-mail:* webqueries@ macmillan.co.uk *Web Site:* www.panmacmillan.com, pg 742

Boyce's Automotive Data Pty Ltd (Australia) *Tel:* (02) 9319 7484 *Fax:* (02) 9698 7346 *E-mail:* support@ boyce.com.au; sales@boyce.com.au *Web Site:* www. boyce.com.au, pg 20

Boydell & Brewer Ltd (United Kingdom) *Tel:* (01394) 610600 *Fax:* (01394) 610316 *E-mail:* editorial@ boydell.co.uk; marketing@boydell.co.uk; production@ boydell.co.uk *Web Site:* www.boydellandbrewer.com, pg 742

Boyens Buchverlag GmbH & Co KG (Germany) *Tel:* (0481) 6886-650 *Fax:* (0481) 6886-90650 *E-mail:* buchverlag@boyens-medien.de *Web Site:* buchverlag.boyens-medien.de, pg 219

Boyut Yayin Grubu (Turkey) *Tel:* (0212) 413 33 33 *Fax:* (0212) 413 33 34 *Web Site:* www.boyutstore.com, pg 719

Bozen-Bolzano University Press (Italy) *Tel:* (0471) 012300 *Fax:* (0471) 012309 *E-mail:* universitypress@ unibz.it; info@unibz.it *Web Site:* bupress.unibz.it; www.unibz.it, pg 429

BPB Publications (India) *Tel:* (011) 23254990; (011) 23254991; (011) 23272329; (011) 23250318 *Fax:* (011) 23266427 *E-mail:* orders@bpbonline.com; sales@bpbonline.com *Web Site:* www.bpbonline.com, pg 378

BPK Gunung Mulia (Indonesia) *Tel:* (021) 3901208 *Fax:* (021) 3901633 *E-mail:* jakarta@bpkgm.com; marketing@bpkgm.com; promosi@bpkgm.com; publishing@bpkgm.com *Web Site:* www.bpkgm.com, pg 1425

BPP Publishing Ltd (United Kingdom) *Tel:* (020) 8740 2222 *Fax:* (020) 8740 1111 *E-mail:* learningmedia@ bpp.com *Web Site:* www.bpp.com, pg 742

BPS Blackwell (British Psychological Society) (United Kingdom) *Tel:* (0116) 252 9568 *E-mail:* enquiries@ bps.org.uk *Web Site:* psychsource.bps.org.uk, pg 742

BR Publishing Corp (India) *Tel:* (011) 23259196; 9810441875 (cell) *E-mail:* brpc@vsnl.com, pg 378

Bra Bocker AB (Sweden) *Tel:* (040) 665 46 00 *Fax:* (040) 665 46 22 *E-mail:* stockholm@ stockholmtext.com *Web Site:* www.bbb.se, pg 680

Bradipolibri Editore SRL (Italy) *Tel:* (0125) 639428 *Fax:* (0125) 639428 *E-mail:* edizioni@bradipolibri.it *Web Site:* www.bradipolibri.it, pg 429

Bradt Travel Guides Ltd (United Kingdom) *Tel:* (01753) 893444 *Fax:* (01753) 892333 *E-mail:* info@ bradtguides.com *Web Site:* www.bradtguides.com, pg 742

Antiquariat Wolfgang Braecklein (Germany) *Tel:* (030) 851 66 13 *Fax:* (030) 859 23 69 *E-mail:* info@ braecklein.eu *Web Site:* www.braecklein.eu, pg 1415

Editions Bragelonne (France) *Tel:* 01 56 88 20 90 *Web Site:* www.bragelonne.fr, pg 157

Louis Braille Audio (Australia) *Tel:* (03) 8378 1259 *Toll Free Tel:* 1300 84 74 66 *Fax:* (03) 9747 5993 *E-mail:* library@visionaustralia.org *Web Site:* www. visionaustralia.org, pg 20

Braille Publishing Co Ltd (South Korea) *Tel:* (02) 3426-7500; (02) 3426-7511 *Fax:* (02) 3426-7502 *E-mail:* kbraille@naver.com; kbraille1@gmail.com *Web Site:* www.kbraille.net; bfbooks.koreasme.com, pg 620

Braintrust GmbH (Austria) *Tel:* (01) 40416-0 *Fax:* (01) 40416-33 *E-mail:* office@braintrust.at *Web Site:* www. braintrust.at, pg 46

Bramann-Verlag und Beratung (Germany) *Tel:* (06101) 30 78 60 *Fax:* (06101) 30 78 80 *E-mail:* info@ bramann.de *Web Site:* www.bramann.de, pg 220

Nakladatelstvi BRANA AS (Czech Republic) *Tel:* 220 191 313 *E-mail:* info@brana-knihy.cz *Web Site:* brana-knihy.cz, pg 126

BrandBooks (United Kingdom) *Tel:* (0845) 676 9254 *Fax:* (0845) 075 3702 *E-mail:* sales@brandbooks.co. uk *Web Site:* www.spellingmadeeasy.co.uk, pg 742

Editura Brandbuilders (Romania) *Tel:* (021) 3231985 *Fax:* (031) 8178779 *E-mail:* office@brandbuilders.ro *Web Site:* www.brandbuilders.ro, pg 585

Brandes & Apsel Verlag (Germany) *Tel:* (069) 272 995 17 0 *Fax:* (069) 272 995 17 10 *E-mail:* info@brandes-apsel.de; presse@brandes-apsel.de; vertrieb@brandes-apsel.de *Web Site:* www.brandes-apsel-verlag.de, pg 220

Brandl & Schlesinger Pty Ltd (Australia) *Tel:* (02) 4787 5848 *Fax:* (02) 4787 5672 *E-mail:* books@brandl. com.au (orders) *Web Site:* www.brandl.com.au, pg 20

Brandon (Ireland) *Tel:* (01) 4923333 *Fax:* (01) 4922777 *E-mail:* books@obrien.ie; sales@obrien.ie *Web Site:* www.obrien.ie/brandon, pg 409

Christian Brandstaetter Verlag GmbH & Co KG (Austria) *Tel:* (01) 512 15 43-0 *Fax:* (01) 512 15 43-231 *E-mail:* info@cbv.at *Web Site:* www.brandstaetter-verlag.at; www.cbv.at, pg 46

Oscar Brandstetter Verlag GmbH & Co KG (Germany) *Tel:* (0611) 991200 *Fax:* (0611) 9912019 *E-mail:* info@brandstetter-verlag.de *Web Site:* www. brandstetter-verlag.de, pg 220

Brandt New Agency (Spain) *Tel:* 930073545 *Fax:* 666656654 *E-mail:* info@brandtnewagency.com *Web Site:* www.brandtnewagency.com, pg 1235

Editora do Brasil SA (Brazil) *Tel:* (011) 3226-0211 *Fax:* (011) 3223-7709 *Web Site:* www.editoradobrasil. com.br, pg 78

Brasilienkunde-Verlag (Germany) *Tel:* (05452) 4598 *Fax:* (05452) 4357 *E-mail:* brasilien@t-online.de *Web Site:* www.brasilienkunde.de, pg 220

Editora Brasiliense SA (Brazil) *Tel:* (011) 3087-0000 *Fax:* (011) 3087-0000 *E-mail:* editorabrasiliense@ editorabrasiliense.com.br; editorabrasiliense@gmail. com *Web Site:* www.editorabrasiliense.com.br, pg 78

Livraria Brasiliense Editora SA (Brazil) *Tel:* (011) 2675-0188, pg 1407

Brau Edicions (Spain) *Tel:* 972 670 417 *Fax:* 972 670 417 *E-mail:* brau@brauedicions.com *Web Site:* www. brauedicions.com, pg 633

Wilhelm Braumueller Universitaets-Verlagsbuchhandlung GmbH (Austria) *Tel:* (01) 319 11 59 *Fax:* (01) 310 28 05 *E-mail:* office@braumueller.at; bestellung@ braumueller.at; presse@braumueller.at *Web Site:* www. braumueller.at, pg 46

Braun Publishing AG (Switzerland) *Tel:* (044) 586 11 97 *Fax:* (071) 664 31 32 *E-mail:* info@braun-publishing. ch *Web Site:* www.braun-publishing.ch, pg 690

Edition Braus GmbH (Germany) *Tel:* (030) 28394-234 *Fax:* (030) 28394-100 *E-mail:* information@ editionbraus.de *Web Site:* www.editionbraus.de, pg 220

Breakthrough Ltd - Breakthrough Publishers (Hong Kong) *Tel:* 2632 0000; 2632 0257 *Fax:* 2632 0388 *E-mail:* breakthrough@breakthrough.org.hk; marketing@breakthrough.org.hk; pub@breakthrough. org.hk *Web Site:* www.breakthrough.org.hk; www. btproduct.com, pg 363

Editions Breal (France) *Tel:* 01 41 06 64 99; 01 41 06 59 17 *Web Site:* www.editions-breal.fr, pg 158

Nicholas Brealey Publishing (United Kingdom) *Tel:* (020) 7239 0360 *Fax:* (020) 7239 0370 *E-mail:* sales@nicholasbrealey.com; rights@ nicholasbrealey.com; publicity@nicholasbrealey. com; translations@nicholasbrealey.com *Web Site:* nicholasbrealey.com, pg 742

Bredero (Belgium) *Tel:* (014) 31 84 61 *Fax:* (014) 31 84 61, pg 1406

Breitkopf & Hartel KG (Germany) *Tel:* (0611) 450080 *Fax:* (0611) 45008 59; (0611) 45008 60; (0611) 45008 61 *E-mail:* info@breitkopf.com; sales@breitkopf.com *Web Site:* www.breitkopf.com; www.breitkopf.de, pg 220

Verlagsbuchhandlung Julius Breitschopf GmbH & Co KG (Austria) *Tel:* (02243) 36868-0; (0664) 4502116 (cell) *Fax:* (02243) 36868-20 *E-mail:* breitschopf. verlag@utanet.at *Web Site:* www.breitschopf-verlag. com, pg 46

Les Editions Emgleo Breiz (France) *Tel:* 02 98 02 68 17 *E-mail:* emgleo.breiz@wanadoo.fr *Web Site:* www. emgleobreiz.com, pg 158

Breklumer Verlag (Germany) *Tel:* (04841) 9041800 *E-mail:* bv@breklumer.de *Web Site:* www.breklumer. de, pg 220

Editions Jacques Bremond (France) *Tel:* 04 66 57 45 61 *Fax:* 04 66 37 27 40 *E-mail:* editions-jacques-bremond@wanadoo.fr, pg 158

Joh Brendow & Sohn Verlag GmbH (Germany) *Tel:* (02841) 809 201; (02841) 809 0 *Fax:* (02841) 809 210; (02841) 809 291 *E-mail:* info-verlag@brendow. de; service@brendow-verlag.de *Web Site:* www. brendow.de; www.brendow-verlag.de, pg 220

Brenner Editore (Italy) *Tel:* (0984) 74537 *Fax:* (0984) 74537 *Web Site:* brennereditore.com, pg 429

Verlag Das Brennglas GmbH (Germany) *Tel:* (09391) 50 42 36 *Fax:* (09391) 50 42 37 *E-mail:* info@brennglas. com *Web Site:* www.brennglas.com, pg 220

Brentano-Gesellschaft Frankfurt/M mbh (Germany) *Tel:* (069) 13377-177 *Fax:* (069) 13377-175 *E-mail:* info@brentano-gesellschaft.de *Web Site:* www. brentano-gesellschaft.de, pg 220, 1226

The Brenthurst Press (Pty) Ltd (South Africa) *Tel:* (011) 544-5400 *Fax:* (011) 486-1651 *E-mail:* info@ brenthurst.org.za; orders@brenthurst.co.az *Web Site:* www.brenthurst.org.za, pg 612

Brepols Publishers NV (Belgium) *Tel:* (014) 44 80 20; (014) 44 80 30 (sales) *Fax:* (014) 42 89 19 *E-mail:* info@brepols.net; orders@brepols.net *Web Site:* www.brepols.net, pg 64

Breslich & Foss Ltd (United Kingdom) *Tel:* (020) 7819 3990 *E-mail:* sales@breslichfoss.co.uk *Web Site:* www.breslichfoss.co.uk, pg 743

Breslov Research Institute (Israel) *Tel:* (02) 582-4641 *Fax:* (02) 582-5542 *E-mail:* sales@breslov.org *Web Site:* www.breslov.org, pg 416

Giorgio Bretschneider Editore (Italy) *Tel:* (06) 6879361 *Fax:* (06) 6864543 *E-mail:* info@bretschneider.it; orders@bretschneider.it *Web Site:* www.bretschneider. it, pg 429

Robert Breuss Buchimport (Austria) *Tel:* (05522) 31247, pg 1404

Brewin Books Ltd (United Kingdom) *Tel:* (01527) 854228; (01527) 853624 *Fax:* (01527) 852746 *E-mail:* admin@brewinbooks.com *Web Site:* www. brewinbooks.com, pg 743

Editions BRGM (France) *Tel:* 02 38 64 34 34 *E-mail:* contact-brgm@brgm.fr *Web Site:* editions. brgm.fr/editions.jsp, pg 158

Bricks Education (South Korea) *Tel:* (02) 326-1182; (02) 326-1168 *Fax:* (02) 326-3173 *E-mail:* ake@ebricks. co.kr; aslee@ebricks.co.kr; jwkim@ebricks.co.kr *Web Site:* www.ebricks.co.kr, pg 620

The Bridge Book Co Ltd (United Kingdom) *Tel:* (01483) 720505, pg 1456

Bridge Books (United Kingdom) *Tel:* (01948) 770125 *E-mail:* books@bridgebooks.co.uk *Web Site:* www.bridgebooks.co.uk, pg 743

Bridge Bookshop Ltd (United Kingdom) *Tel:* (01624) 833376 *E-mail:* mail@bridge-bookshop.com *Web Site:* www.bridge-bookshop.com, pg 1456

Editorial Brief SL (Spain) *Tel:* 96 310 60 37 *Fax:* 96 362 00 77 *E-mail:* info@editorialbrief.com *Web Site:* editorialbrief.com, pg 633

Briefmarken Zumstein & Cie (Switzerland) *Tel:* (031) 312 00 55 *Fax:* (031) 312 23 26 *E-mail:* post_zumstein@briefmarken.ch *Web Site:* www.briefmarken.ch, pg 690

Brigg Verlag Franz-Josef Buechler KG (Germany) *Tel:* (0821) 78 09 46 60 *Fax:* (0821) 78 09 46 61 *E-mail:* info@brigg-verlag.de *Web Site:* www.brigg-verlag.de, pg 220

Bright Arts (HK) Ltd (Hong Kong) *Tel:* 2562 0119 *Fax:* 2565 7031 *E-mail:* tinokwok@brightartshk.com.hk *Web Site:* www.brightartshk.com.hk, pg 1277

The Bright Literary Agency (BLA) (United Kingdom) *Tel:* (020) 7326 9140 *E-mail:* literarysubmissions@brightgroupinternational.com *Web Site:* www.brightliteraryagency.com, pg 1239

Brighton Verlag (Germany) *Tel:* (0152) 531 273 16 *Fax:* (06735) 941 445 *E-mail:* info@brightonverlag.com *Web Site:* www.brightonverlag.com, pg 220

Brijbasi Printers Pvt Ltd (India) *Tel:* (011) 26841897; (011) 26314115; (011) 26314119, pg 378

Brill (Netherlands) *Tel:* (071) 53 53 500 *Fax:* (071) 53 17 532 *E-mail:* marketing@brill.com; sales-nl@brill.com *Web Site:* www.brill.com, pg 530

Brilliant Publications (United Kingdom) *Tel:* (01525) 222292 *Fax:* (01525) 222720 *E-mail:* sales@brilliantpublications.co.uk *Web Site:* www.brilliantpublications.co.uk, pg 743

Brinkmann & Bose Verlag (Germany) *Tel:* (030) 615-48-92 *E-mail:* brinkmann_bose@t-online.de *Web Site:* www.brinkmann-bose.de, pg 220

Brinque Book Editora de Livros Ltda (Brazil) *Tel:* (011) 3032-6436 *Fax:* (011) 3032-6436 *E-mail:* brinquebook@brinquebook.com.br; vendas@brinquebook.com.br; editorial@brinquebook.com.br *Web Site:* www.brinquebook.com.br, pg 78

Brio Books (Australia) *Tel:* (02) 8399 1850 *Web Site:* www.xoum.com.au, pg 20

Nakladatelstvi Brio (Czech Republic) *Tel:* 266 177 141 *Fax:* 266 177 147 *Web Site:* www.slovart.cz, pg 126

The British Academy (United Kingdom) *Tel:* (020) 7969 5200 *Fax:* (020) 7969 530 *E-mail:* pubs@britac.ac.uk *Web Site:* www.britac.ac.uk, pg 743

British & Irish Association of Law Librarians (BIALL) (Ireland) *E-mail:* contact@biall.org.uk *Web Site:* www.biall.org.uk, pg 1654

British Copyright Council (United Kingdom) *Tel:* (020) 7582 4833 *E-mail:* info@britishcopyright.org *Web Site:* www.britishcopyright.org, pg 1394

British Council Information Resource Centre (Sri Lanka) *Tel:* (011) 4521521; (011) 7521521 *E-mail:* info.lk@britishcouncil.org *Web Site:* www.britishcouncil.lk, pg 1633

British Council Learning Centre (Colombia) *Tel:* (01) 325 9090 *Fax:* (01) 325 9091 *E-mail:* servicioalcliente@britishcouncil.org.co *Web Site:* www.britishcouncil.co/en, pg 1583

British Council Libraries (India) *Tel:* (011) 42199000 *Fax:* (011) 23710717 *E-mail:* delhi.enquiry@in.britishcouncil.org *Web Site:* www.library.britishcouncil.org.in, pg 1600

British Council Library (Bangladesh) *Tel:* (02) 9666 773377 *Fax:* (02) 861 3375; (02) 861 3255 *E-mail:* bd.enquiries@britishcouncil.org *Web Site:* www.britishcouncil.org.bd/en, pg 1577

British Council Library (Cyprus) *Tel:* 22585000 *Fax:* 22585129 *E-mail:* enquiries@cy.britishcouncil.org *Web Site:* www.britishcouncil.org/cyprus, pg 1585

British Council Library (Ethiopia) *Tel:* (011) 662 0388 *Fax:* (011) 662 3315 *E-mail:* information@et.britishcouncil.org *Web Site:* ethiopia.britishcouncil.org; www.britishcouncil.org, pg 1588

British Council Library (Ghana) *Tel:* 3220-23462; 3220-30820 *E-mail:* infoghana@gh.britishcouncil.org *Web Site:* www.britishcouncil.org/ghana, pg 1597

British Council Library (Hong Kong) *Tel:* 2913 5100 *Fax:* 2913 5102 *E-mail:* enquiries@britishcouncil.org *Web Site:* www.britishcouncil.hk, pg 1599

British Council Library (Jordan) *Tel:* (06) 4603420 *Fax:* (06) 4656413 *E-mail:* info@britishcouncil.org.jo *Web Site:* www.britishcouncil.jo, pg 1607

British Council Library (Malawi) *Tel:* (021) 2240199 *E-mail:* info@britishcouncil.org.mw *Web Site:* www.britishcouncil.mw, pg 1611

British Council Library (Mauritius) *Tel:* 403 0200 *Fax:* 454 9553 *E-mail:* general.enquiries@mu.britishcouncil.org *Web Site:* www.britishcouncil.mu, pg 1613

British Council Library (Morocco) *Tel:* 05 37 21 81 20 *E-mail:* info@britishcouncil.org.ma *Web Site:* www.britishcouncil.ma.en, pg 1614

British Council Library (Nepal) *Tel:* (01) 4410 798 *Fax:* (01) 4410 545 *E-mail:* general.enquiry@britishcouncil.org.np *Web Site:* www.britishcouncil.org.np, pg 1615

British Council Library (Pakistan) *Toll Free Tel:* 0800 22000 (Pakistan only) *Fax:* (051) 111 425 425 *E-mail:* info@britishcouncil.org.pk *Web Site:* www.britishcouncil.pk, pg 1620

British Council Library (Sierra Leone) *Tel:* (076) 290 111; (076) 290 115 *E-mail:* enquiry@sl.britishcouncil.org *Web Site:* www.britishcouncil.sl, pg 1629

The British Council Library (Spain) *Tel:* 91 337 35 77 *Fax:* 91 337 35 86 *Web Site:* www.britishcouncil.es, pg 1633

British Council Library (Sudan) *Tel:* (0187) 028000 *Fax:* (0183) 774935 *E-mail:* info@sd.britishcouncil.org *Web Site:* sudan.britishcouncil.org, pg 1634

British Council Library (Tanzania) *Tel:* (022) 2165300 *E-mail:* info@britishcouncil.or.tz *Web Site:* www.britishcouncil.or.tz, pg 1637

British Council Library (Thailand) *Tel:* (02) 657 5678 *Fax:* (02) 253 5311; (02) 253 5312 *E-mail:* info@britishcouncil.or.th *Web Site:* www.britishcouncil.or.th, pg 1637

British Council Library (Tunisia) *Tel:* 71 14 53 00 *Fax:* 71 89 30 66 *E-mail:* info@tn.britishcouncil.org *Web Site:* www.britishcouncil.tn, pg 1639

British Council Library (Yemen) *Tel:* (01) 44 83 56; (01) 44 83 57; (01) 44 83 58; (01) 44 83 59 *Fax:* (01) 44 83 60 *E-mail:* information@ye.britishcouncil.org *Web Site:* yemen.britishcouncil.org, pg 1644

British Council Library & Resource Centre (Greece) *Tel:* 2103692333 *Fax:* 2103630675 *E-mail:* customerservices@britishcouncil.gr *Web Site:* www.britishcouncil.org/greece, pg 1598

The British Education Suppliers Association (United Kingdom) *Tel:* (020) 7537 4997 *Fax:* (020) 7537 4846 *E-mail:* besa@besa.org.uk *Web Site:* www.besa.org.uk, pg 1394

British Fantasy Society (BFS) (United Kingdom) *Tel:* (07845) 897760 *Web Site:* www.britishfantasysociety.co.uk, pg 1502

British Guild of Travel Writers (United Kingdom) *Tel:* (020) 8144 8713 *E-mail:* secretariat@bgtw.org *Web Site:* www.bgtw.org, pg 1394

British Institute in Eastern Africa (BIEA) (Kenya) *Tel:* (020) 434 3190; (020) 434 7195 *Fax:* (020) 434 3365 *E-mail:* office@biea.ac.uk *Web Site:* www.biea.ac.uk; www.facebook.com/BIEA.Nairobi, pg 492

British Institute of Non-Destructive Testing (BINDT) (United Kingdom) *Tel:* (01604) 89 3811 *Fax:* (01604) 89 3861 *E-mail:* info@bindt.org *Web Site:* www.bindt.org, pg 743

The British Library (United Kingdom) *Tel:* (01937) 546060 *Fax:* (01937) 546333 *E-mail:* customer-services@bl.uk *Web Site:* www.bl.uk, pg 1640

British Library Asia, Pacific & Africa Collections (United Kingdom) *Tel:* (020) 7412 7873 *Fax:* (020) 7412 7641 *E-mail:* apac-enquiries@bl.uk *Web Site:* www.bl.uk; indiafamily.bl.uk/ui, pg 1640

British Library of Political & Economic Science (United Kingdom) *Tel:* (020) 7405 7686; (020) 7955 7229 *E-mail:* library.enquiries@lse-uk.libanswers.com *Web Site:* www.lse.ac.uk/library, pg 1640

British Library Publishing (United Kingdom) *Tel:* (020) 7412 7294 (editorial & sales) *E-mail:* publishing_editorial@bl.uk; publishing_sales@bl.uk *Web Site:* bl.uk/publishing, pg 743

The British Library, Science Technology & Business Collections (United Kingdom) *Tel:* (020) 7412 7288; (020) 7412 7454 *E-mail:* scitech@bl.uk *Web Site:* www.bl.uk, pg 1641

British Museum Press (United Kingdom) *Tel:* (020) 7323 1234 *Toll Free Tel:* 0800 218 2222 (customer services) *Fax:* (020) 7436 7315 *E-mail:* reception@britishmuseum.co.uk; sales@britishmuseum.co.uk *Web Site:* www.britishmuseum.org, pg 743

British Printing Industries Federation (BPIF) (United Kingdom) *Tel:* (0845) 250 7050 *Fax:* (01676) 526 033 *E-mail:* hello@bpif.org.uk *Web Site:* www.britishprint.com, pg 1394

The British School at Rome (Italy) *Tel:* (06) 326 4939 *Fax:* (06) 322 1201 *E-mail:* info@bsrome.it *Web Site:* www.bsr.ac.uk, pg 429

The British Science Fiction Association Ltd (BSFA Ltd) (United Kingdom) *E-mail:* organisation@bsfa.co.uk *Web Site:* www.bsfa.co.uk, pg 1502

British Tourist Authority (United Kingdom) *Tel:* (020) 7578 1000 *E-mail:* industry.relations@visitbritain.org *Web Site:* www.visitbritain.org, pg 744

Briza Publications (South Africa) *Tel:* (012) 329-3896 *Fax:* (012) 329-4525 *E-mail:* books@briza.co.za *Web Site:* www.briza.co.za, pg 612

Brizzolis SA (Spain) *Tel:* 91 691 91 30 *Fax:* 91 691 91 16 *E-mail:* arteengraficas@brizzolis.com; preimpresion@brizzolis.com *Web Site:* www.brizzolis.com, pg 1334

Broad Leys Publications Ltd (United Kingdom) *Tel:* (01493) 249 160 *Web Site:* broadleys.org, pg 744

Verlag Ekkehard & Ulrich Brockhaus KG (Germany) *Tel:* (0202) 44 74 74; (0172) 2 55 59 61 (cell) *Fax:* (0202) 42 82 82 *E-mail:* mail@verlag-brockhaus.de *Web Site:* www.verlag-brockhaus.de, pg 220

Brockhaus Kommissionsgeschaeft GmbH (Germany) *Tel:* (07154) 13270 *Fax:* (07154) 132713 *E-mail:* info@brocom.de *Web Site:* www.brocom.de, pg 220

Brolga Publishing (Australia) *Tel:* (03) 9614 3209 *Web Site:* www.brolgapublishing.com.au, pg 20

Brolly Books (Australia) *Tel:* (03) 5975 5414 *Web Site:* www.brollybooks.com, pg 21

Brombergs Bokforlag AB (Sweden) *Tel:* (08) 562 620 80 *Fax:* (08) 562 620 85 *E-mail:* info@brombergs.se *Web Site:* brombergs.se, pg 680

Edicions Bromera SL (Spain) *Tel:* 962 402 254 *Fax:* 962 403 191 *E-mail:* adm@bromera.com; bromera@bromera.com; comunicacio@bromera.com; comercial@bromera.com *Web Site:* www.bromera.com, pg 633

Ediciones del Bronce (Spain) *Tel:* 93 496 70 01 *Fax:* 93 217 77 48 *E-mail:* comunicacioneditorialplaneta@planeta.es *Web Site:* www.planeta.es, pg 633

Edition Buechergilde GmbH (Germany) *Tel:* (069) 273908-0 *Fax:* (069) 273908-27 *E-mail:* info@edition-buechergilde.de; service@buechergilde.de *Web Site:* www.edition-buechergilde.de; www.buechergilde.de, pg 222

Buechergilde Gutenberg (Germany) *Tel:* (069) 27 39 08-90 *Fax:* (069) 27 39 08-25; (069) 27 39 08-26 *E-mail:* service@buechergilde.de *Web Site:* www.buechergilde.de, pg 1359

Buchergilde Gutenberg Verlagsgesellschaft mbH (Germany) *Tel:* (069) 27 39 08-0 *Fax:* (069) 27 39 08-26; (069) 27 39 08-25 *E-mail:* service@buechergilde.de *Web Site:* www.buechergilde.de, pg 222

Buechse der Pandora Verlags GmbH (Germany) *Tel:* (06441) 911312 *Fax:* (06441) 911318 *E-mail:* buechse.der.pandora.vlg@gmail.com, pg 222

Fachverlag fuer Buergerinformation (Austria) *Tel:* (0316) 686727 *Fax:* (0316) 686727-4, pg 46

Gruppo Buffetti SpA (Italy) *Tel:* (06) 2319150 *Web Site:* www.buffetti.it, pg 429

Buijten & Schipperheijn BV (Netherlands) *Tel:* (020) 524 10 10 *Fax:* (020) 524 10 11 *E-mail:* info@buijten.nl *Web Site:* www.buijten.nl, pg 531

Building & Road Research Institute (BRRI) (Ghana) *Tel:* (032) 2060064; (032) 2060065 *Fax:* (032) 2060080 *E-mail:* admin@brri.csir.org.gh; brriadmin@gmail.com *Web Site:* www.brri.org, pg 352

Bulan Bintang (Indonesia) *Tel:* (021) 3901651; (021) 3107027 *Fax:* (021) 3901652, pg 405

Bulawayo Public Library (Zimbabwe) *Tel:* (09) 60966 *E-mail:* bpl@graffiti.net *Web Site:* www.angelfire.com/ky/bpl, pg 1644

Bulbul Literary Agency (India) *Tel:* 9895219697; 9496695147 *E-mail:* info@bulbulliterary.com; bulbulliterary@gmail.com *Web Site:* www.bulbulliterary.com, pg 1229

Bulgarian Academy of Sciences, Central Library (Bulgaria) *Tel:* (02) 987 89 66 *Fax:* (02) 986 25 00 *E-mail:* library@cl.bas.bg *Web Site:* www.cl.bas.bg, pg 1580

Bulgarian Academy of Sciences, Institute of Literature (Bulgaria) *Tel:* (02) 971 70 56 *Fax:* (02) 971 70 56 *E-mail:* director@ilit.bas.bg *Web Site:* www.ilit.bas.bg, pg 1492

Bulgarian National ISSN Centre (Bulgaria) *Tel:* (02) 918 32 18 *Fax:* (02) 843 54 95 *E-mail:* issn@nationallibary.bg *Web Site:* www.nationallibrary.bg, pg 1367

Bulgarian Translator's Union (Bulgaria) *Tel:* (02) 986 45 00; (02) 989 45 43 *Fax:* (02) 981 09 60 *E-mail:* office@bgtranslators.org; prevodi_spb@mail.orbitel.bg *Web Site:* www.bgtranslators.org, pg 1249

Bulgarski Houdozhnik Publishers (Bulgaria) *Fax:* (02) 8467285, pg 94

Bulgarski Pisatel (Bulgaria) *Tel:* (02) 987-35-01 *E-mail:* izdatelstvo_bulgarskipisatel@abv.bg, pg 94

Editions Bulles de Savon (France) *Tel:* 09 86 20 31 13 *E-mail:* contact@editions-bullesdesavon.com *Web Site:* www.editions-bullesdesavon.com, pg 158

Bulvest 2000 Ltd (Bulgaria) *Tel:* (02) 8061 300; (02) 8061 301; (02) 8061 302 *Fax:* (02) 8061 313 *E-mail:* administration@bulvest2000.com; bulvest@bulvest2000.com *Web Site:* www.bulvest.com, pg 94

Bulzoni Editore SRL (Le Edizioni Universitarie d'Italia) (Italy) *Tel:* (06) 4455207 *Fax:* (06) 4450355 *E-mail:* administrazione@bulzoni.it; bulzoni@bulzoni.it *Web Site:* www.bulzoni.it, pg 429

Bumi Aksara Group (Indonesia) *Tel:* (021) 4700988 *E-mail:* info@bumiaksara.com; info@bumiaksaraonline.com *Web Site:* bumiaksara.com; bumiaksaraonline.com (orders), pg 405

Bumwoosa Co Ltd (South Korea) *Tel:* (031) 955-6900 *Fax:* (031) 955-6905 *E-mail:* bumwoosa@chol.com; bumwoosa1966@naver.com *Web Site:* www.bumwoosa.co.kr, pg 620

Bun-ichi Sogo Shuppan (Japan) *Tel:* (03) 3235-7341 (sales); (03) 3235-7342 *Fax:* (03) 3269-1402 *E-mail:* bunichi@bun-ichi.co.jp *Web Site:* www.bun-ichi.co.jp, pg 474

Bund Deutscher Schriftsteller BDS eV (Germany) *Tel:* (06074) 47566 *Fax:* (06074) 47540 *E-mail:* info@schriftsteller-verband.de *Web Site:* www.bund-deutscher-schriftsteller.de, pg 1494

Bund fuer deutsche Schrift und Sprache eV (Germany) *Tel:* (05381) 46355 *Fax:* (05381) 46355 *E-mail:* verwaltung@bfds.de *Web Site:* www.bfds.de; www.deutscheschrift.de, pg 223

Bund-Verlag GmbH (Germany) *Tel:* (069) 79 50 10-0 *Fax:* (069) 79 50 10 11 *E-mail:* kontakt@bund-verlag.de *Web Site:* www.bund-verlag.de, pg 223

Bunda College Library (Malawi) *Tel:* 01 277 348; 01 277 222 *Fax:* 01 277 251; 01 277 364 *E-mail:* principal@bunda.sdnp.org; library@bunda.luanar.mw *Web Site:* www.bunda.luanar.mw/library; buncoalumni.tripod.com/id13.html, pg 1611

Bundes-Verlag GmbH (Germany) *Tel:* (02302) 930 93 0 *Fax:* (02302) 930 93 689 *E-mail:* info@bundes-verlag.de *Web Site:* bundes-verlag.net, pg 223

Bundesamt fuer Landestopografie, Swisstopo (Switzerland) *Tel:* (058) 469 01 11 *Fax:* (058) 469 04 59 *E-mail:* info@swisstopo.ch; mapsales@swisstopo.ch *Web Site:* www.swisstopo.ch, pg 690

Bundesanzeiger Verlag GmbH (Germany) *Tel:* (0221) 9 76 68-0; (0221) 9 76 68-200 (sales) *Toll Free Tel:* 0800 1234339 *Fax:* (0221) 9 76 68-278; (0221) 9 76 68-115 (sales) *E-mail:* vertrieb@bundesanzeiger.de; service@bundesanzeiger.de *Web Site:* www.bundesanzeiger-verlag.de, pg 223

Bundesverband Alphabetisierung und Grundbildung eV (Germany) *Tel:* (0251) 49 09 96-0 *Fax:* (0251) 49 09 96-86 *E-mail:* bundesverband@alphabetisierung.de *Web Site:* www.alphabetisierung.de, pg 1494

Bundesverband der Dolmetscher und Uebersetzer eV (BDUE) (Germany) *Tel:* (030) 88712830 *Fax:* (030) 88712840 *E-mail:* info@bdue.de *Web Site:* www.bdue.de, pg 1249

Bundesverband Deutscher Galerien und Kunsthaendler eV (Germany) *Tel:* (030) 263 922 980 *Fax:* (030) 263 922 985 *E-mail:* post@bvdg.de *Web Site:* www.bvdg.de, pg 1374

Bundesverband junger Autoren und Autorinnen eV (Germany) *Tel:* (02225) 7889 *Fax:* (02225) 7889 *E-mail:* info@bvja-online.de *Web Site:* www.bvja-online.de, pg 1494

Bundeszentrale fuer Politische Bildung (Germany) *Tel:* (0228) 99515-0; (0228) 99515-115 (customer service) *Fax:* (0228) 99515-113 *E-mail:* info@bpb.de; redaktion@bpb.de *Web Site:* www.bpb.de, pg 223

Bunkasha Publishing Co Ltd (Japan) *Tel:* (03) 3222-5111 *Fax:* (03) 3222-3672 *E-mail:* general-info@bunkasha.co.jp *Web Site:* www.bunkasha.co.jp, pg 474

Bunkashobo-Hakubun-Sha (Japan) *Tel:* (03) 3947-2034 *Fax:* (03) 3947-4976 *E-mail:* bunka@mvg.biglobe.ne.jp *Web Site:* user.net-web.ne.jp/bunka, pg 474

edition buntehunde GdBR (Germany) *Tel:* (0941) 5674510 *Fax:* (0941) 5674511 *E-mail:* edition.buntehunde@t-online.de *Web Site:* www.editionbuntehunde.de, pg 223

Buntpapierverlag (Germany) *Tel:* (040) 81 77 06 *E-mail:* studio@hamburgerbuntpapier.de *Web Site:* www.hamburgerbuntpapier.de, pg 223

Bur (Italy) *E-mail:* info@rizzolilibri.it; ufficiostampa.rizzoli@rizzolilibri.it; rizzoli.rights@rizzolilibri.it *Web Site:* www.bur.eu; www.rizzolilibri.it, pg 429

Aenne Burda Verlag GmbH & Co KG (Germany) *Tel:* (089) 9250-0 *Fax:* (089) 9250-2340 *E-mail:* service@burdastyle.de *Web Site:* www.burdastyle.de, pg 223

Bureau des Longitudes (France) *Tel:* 01 43 26 59 02 *Fax:* 01 43 26 80 90 *E-mail:* renseignements@bureau-des-longitudes.fr *Web Site:* www.bureau-des-longitudes.fr, pg 158

Bureau for Intellectual Property (Curacao) *Tel:* (09) 465 7800 *Fax:* (09) 465 7815 *E-mail:* director@bureau-intellectual-property.cw; info@bip.cw *Web Site:* www.bip.cw, pg 1369

Bureau Koninklijke Vereniging van Archivarissen in Nederland (Netherlands) *Tel:* (026) 352 16 05 *Fax:* (026) 352 16 99 *E-mail:* bureau@kvan.nl *Web Site:* www.kvan.nl, pg 1657

Bureau of Ghana Languages (Ghana) *Tel:* (021) 760551; (021) 772151 *E-mail:* info@ghanaculture.gov.gh *Web Site:* www.ghanaculture.gov.gh, pg 352

Bureau of Ghana Languages (Ghana) *Tel:* (021) 760551; (021) 772151 *Web Site:* www.ghanaculture.gov.gh, pg 1250

Bureau of Standards Jamaica (Jamaica) *Tel:* (876) 926-3140; (876) 632-4275; (876) 619-1131 *Fax:* (876) 929-4736 *E-mail:* info@jbs.org.jm *Web Site:* www.jbs.org.jm, pg 472

Burg Giebichenstein Kunsthochschule Halle (Germany) *Tel:* (0345) 7751-511 *Fax:* (0345) 7751-509 *E-mail:* rektorat@burg-halle.de; presse@burg-halle.de; burgpost@burg-halle.de *Web Site:* www.burg-halle.de, pg 223

Burgart Presse (Germany) *Tel:* (03672) 41 22 14 *Fax:* (03672) 41 22 14 *Web Site:* www.burgart-presse.de, pg 223

Burgewood Books (Australia) *Tel:* (03) 9844 2512 *Fax:* (03) 9844 0664 *Web Site:* www.burgewoodbooks.com.au, pg 1402

Edmund Burke Publisher (Ireland) *Tel:* (01) 288 2159 *Fax:* (01) 283 4080 *E-mail:* deburca@indigo.ie *Web Site:* www.deburcararebooks.com/publish.htm, pg 409

Burleigh Dodds Science Publishing (United Kingdom) *Tel:* (01223) 839365 *E-mail:* info@bdspublishing.com *Web Site:* www.bdspublishing.com, pg 744

Burnet's Books (Australia) *Tel:* (02) 6778 4682 *Fax:* (02) 6778 4516, pg 1402

Busche Verlagsgesellschaft mbH (Germany) *Tel:* (0231) 44477-0 *Fax:* (0231) 44477-77 *E-mail:* info@busche.de *Web Site:* www.busche.de, pg 223

Arnold Busck A/S (Denmark) *Tel:* 45 28 05 70 *E-mail:* info@busck.dk; web@busck.dk *Web Site:* www.arnoldbusck.dk, pg 1412

Bush Press Communications Ltd (New Zealand) *Tel:* (09) 486 2667 *E-mail:* bush.press@clear.net.nz *Web Site:* www.bushpress.com, pg 544

Bushwood Books Ltd (United Kingdom) *Tel:* (020) 8392 8585 *Fax:* (020) 8392 9876, pg 1457

Uitgeverij Business Contact (Netherlands) *Tel:* (020) 524 98 00 *E-mail:* start@businesscontact.nl; verkoop@atlascontact.nl (sales) *Web Site:* www.businesscontact.nl; www.boekenwereld.com, pg 531

Helmut Buske Verlag GmbH (Germany) *Tel:* (040) 29 99 58-0; (040) 29 99 58-42 (sales) *Fax:* (040) 29 99 58-20; (040) 299 36 14 *E-mail:* info@buske.de *Web Site:* www.buske.de, pg 223

Verlag Bussert & Stadeler (Germany) *Tel:* (03641) 369061 *Fax:* (03641) 369062 *E-mail:* info@bussert-stadeler.de *Web Site:* new.bussert-stadeler.de, pg 223

Buster Nordic A/S (Denmark) *Tel:* 2844 8311 *Fax:* 3967 9096 *E-mail:* publisher@busternordic.com *Web Site:* www.busternordic.com, pg 134

Butter & Cream Verlagsgesellschaft Ltd (Germany) *Tel:* (030) 61621551 *E-mail:* butter-and-cream@gmx.de *Web Site:* www.butter-and-cream.com, pg 223

Butzon & Bercker GmbH (Germany) *Tel:* (02832) 929-0 *Fax:* (02832) 929-211 *E-mail:* service@bube.de *Web Site:* www.butzon-bercker.de, pg 223

Le Buveur D'encre (France) *Tel:* 01 43 71 34 67 *Web Site:* lebuveurdencre.fr, pg 158

Centar tehnicke kulture Rijeka (Croatia) *Tel:* (051) 327 155; (051) 327 183; (051) 320 281 *Fax:* (051) 338 531 *E-mail:* info@ctk-rijeka.hr *Web Site:* www.ctk-rijeka.hr, pg 119

Centar za politoloska istrazivanja (CPI) (Croatia) *Tel:* (01) 3863 113 *Fax:* (01) 3863 113 *E-mail:* cpi@cpi.hr *Web Site:* www.cpi.hr, pg 119

Center for Advanced Welsh & Celtic Studies (United Kingdom) *Tel:* (01970) 636543 *Web Site:* www.wales.ac.uk/en/CentreforAdvancedWelshCelticStudies, pg 748

Center for Arab Unity Studies (Lebanon) *Tel:* (01) 750084; (01) 750085; (01) 750086; (01) 750087 *Fax:* (01) 750088 *E-mail:* info@caus.org.lb *Web Site:* www.caus.org.lb; www.causlb.org, pg 497

Center of Academic Resources Chulalongkorn University (Thailand) *Tel:* (02) 218-2918; (02) 218-2929 *Fax:* (02) 215-3617; (02) 215-2907 *E-mail:* webmaster@car.chula.ac.th *Web Site:* www.car.chula.ac.th, pg 1637

Center za slovensko knjizevnost (Slovenia) *Tel:* (01) 505 1674 *Fax:* (01) 505 1674 *E-mail:* litcenter@mail.ljudmila.org *Web Site:* www.ljudmila.org/litcenter, pg 610, 1388

Central Africana Ltd (Malawi) *Tel:* 01876110 *E-mail:* centralafricana@africa-online.net *Web Site:* www.centralafricana.com, pg 506

Central Agricultural Library (CAL) (Bulgaria) *Tel:* (02) 870 60 81; (02) 870 55 88 *Fax:* (02) 870 80 78 *E-mail:* csb@abv.bg *Web Site:* www.iae-bg.com/en/library, pg 1580

The Central Archives for the History of the Jewish People (CAHJP) (Israel) *Tel:* (02) 6586249 *Fax:* (02) 6535426 *E-mail:* cahjp@nli.org.il *Web Site:* cahjp.huji.ac.il, pg 1604

Central Books Ltd (United Kingdom) *Tel:* (020) 8525 8800 *Fax:* (020) 8599 2694 *E-mail:* contactus@centralbooks.com *Web Site:* www.centralbooks.com, pg 1457

Central Bookshop (Malawi) *Tel:* 01 872 094, pg 1432

Central Catequistica Salesiana (CCS) (Spain) *Tel:* 91 725 20 00 *Fax:* 91 726 25 70 *E-mail:* sei@editorialccs.com; apedidos@editorialccs.com (national orders); apedidos2@editorialccs.com (international orders) *Web Site:* www.editorialccs.com, pg 635

Central Catholic Library (Ireland) *Tel:* (01) 676 1264 *E-mail:* catholiclibrary@imagine.ie, pg 1603

Central Catholic Library Association Inc (Ireland) *Tel:* (01) 676 1264 *Fax:* (01) 678 7618 *E-mail:* catholiclibrary@imagine.ie *Web Site:* www.catholiclibrary.ie, pg 1654

Central European University Press (Hungary) *Tel:* (01) 327-3000 *Fax:* (01) 327-3183 *E-mail:* ceupress@ceu.hu *Web Site:* www.ceupress.com, pg 368

Central Library & Documentation Centre of University of Tehran (Iran) *Tel:* (021) 61112889; (021) 66466199 *Fax:* (021) 66495388 *E-mail:* libpublic@ut.ac.ir *Web Site:* library.ut.ac.ir, pg 1602

Central Library, Cape Town (South Africa) *Tel:* (021) 444 0983; (021) 444 0209; (021) 444 0212 *E-mail:* central.library@capetown.gov.za *Web Site:* www.facebook.com/centrallibrarycapetown, pg 1630

Central Library for the Blind, Visually Impaired & Handicapped (Israel) *Tel:* (09) 8617874 *Fax:* (057) 7970997 *E-mail:* office@clfb.org.il *Web Site:* www.clfb.org.il, pg 1604

Central Library of Agricultural Science (Israel) *Tel:* (08) 9489269 *Fax:* (08) 9361348 *Web Site:* www.agri.huji.ac.il, pg 1604

Central Library of National Technical University of Athens (Greece) *Tel:* 2107723878; 2107722229 *Fax:* 2107721565 *E-mail:* library@central.ntua.gr *Web Site:* www.lib.ntua.gr, pg 1598

Central Library of the University of Baghdad (Iraq) *Tel:* (01) 778 7819 *E-mail:* director@clib.uobaghdad.edu.iq *Web Site:* www.clib.uobaghdad.edu.iq, pg 1602

Central Medical Library, Medical University - Sofia (Bulgaria) *Tel:* (02) 92301 (ext 498); (02) 952 31 71 *Fax:* (02) 851 82 65 *E-mail:* library@mu-sofia.bg; cml.mu.sofia@gmail.com *Web Site:* www.medun.acad.bg, pg 1580

Central Public Library Dhaka (Bangladesh) *Tel:* (02) 8500819 *Web Site:* www.centralpubliclibrarydhaka.org, pg 1577

Central Queensland University Press (Australia) *Tel:* (07) 4923 2520 *Fax:* (07) 4923 2525 *Web Site:* www.cqunipress.com.au, pg 21

Central Secretariat Library (CSL) (India) *Tel:* (011) 233 84846; (011) 233 89684; (011) 233 89383 *Fax:* (011) 233 84846 *E-mail:* directcsl@gmail.com; mailfromcsl@gmail.com *Web Site:* www.csl.nic.in, pg 1600

Central Tanganyika Press (Tanzania) *Tel:* (026) 232 4518 *Web Site:* www.anglicancommunion.org, pg 714

Centralna Narodna Biblioteka SR Crne Gore (Montenegro) *Tel:* (041) 231-143; (041) 231-726 *Fax:* (041) 231-020; (041) 233-370 *E-mail:* info@vbcg.me *Web Site:* www.cnb.me, pg 1614

Centre Africain de Formation et de Recherche Administratives pour le Developpement, Centre de Documentation (Morocco) *Tel:* 05 39 32 27 07; 06 61 30 72 69 *Fax:* 05 39 32 57 85 *E-mail:* cafrad@cafrad.org *Web Site:* www.cafrad.org, pg 1383

Centre Culturel Differdange (Luxembourg) *Tel:* 587045 *Fax:* 580295, pg 503

Centre Culturel Francais, Bibliotheque (Congo (Brazzaville)) *Tel:* 281 19 00; 323 00 91 *Web Site:* ccfbrazza.org, pg 1583

Centre de Linguistique Appliquee (CLAD) (Senegal) *E-mail:* clad@ucad.sn *Web Site:* clad.ucad.sn, pg 600

Centre de Publications Evangeliques (Cote d'Ivoire) *Tel:* 22 44 48 05 *Fax:* 22 44 58 17 *E-mail:* cpe@aviso.ci *Web Site:* www.editionscpe.com, pg 118

Centre d'Etudes et de Documentation Economiques, Juridiques et Sociales (CEDEJ) (Egypt) *Tel:* (02) 27 93 03 50; (02) 27 93 03 51; (02) 27 93 03 52; (02) 27 93 03 54; (02) 27 93 03 55 *Fax:* (02) 27 93 03 53 *E-mail:* cedej@cedej-eg.org *Web Site:* www.cedej-eg.org, pg 143

Centre d'Informacio i Documentacio Internacionals de Barcelona (CIDOB) (Spain) *Tel:* 93 302 64 95 *E-mail:* cidob@cidob.org *Web Site:* www.cidob.org, pg 635

Centre d'Expertise et de Recherches Administratives (Tunisia) *Tel:* 71848 300 *Fax:* 71794 188 *E-mail:* info@ena.nat.tn *Web Site:* www.ena.nat.tn, pg 1639

Centre for Alternative Technology (United Kingdom) *Tel:* (01654) 705980; (01654) 705959 (mail order); (01654) 705993 (CAT shop); (01654) 703409 (mail order) *E-mail:* info@cat.org.uk; mail.order@cat.org.uk *Web Site:* www.cat.org.uk, pg 748

Centre for Asia Private Equity Research Ltd (Hong Kong) *Tel:* 2861 0102 *Fax:* 2529 6816 *E-mail:* info@asiape.com *Web Site:* www.asiape.com, pg 363

Centre for Basic Research (Uganda) *Tel:* (0414) 342987 *Fax:* (0414) 235413 *E-mail:* cbr@cbr.ug; library@cbr.ug, pg 725

The Centre for Conflict Resolution (South Africa) *Tel:* (021) 689 1005 *Fax:* (021) 689 1003 *E-mail:* mailbox@ccr.uct.ac.za *Web Site:* www.ccr.org.za, pg 612

The Centre for Educational Technology (CET) (Israel) *Tel:* (03) 6460160 *Fax:* (03) 6422679 *Web Site:* www.cet.ac.il; www.cet.org.il, pg 417

The Centre for European Policy Studies (CEPS) (Belgium) *Tel:* (02) 229 39 11 *Fax:* (02) 706 56 26 *E-mail:* info@ceps.eu *Web Site:* www.ceps.eu, pg 1365

Centre for Information Studies (Australia) *Tel:* (02) 6933 2325 *Fax:* (02) 6933 2733 *E-mail:* cis@csu.edu.au *Web Site:* www.csu.edu.au, pg 21

Centre for South Asian Studies (Pakistan) *Web Site:* www.pu.edu.pk, pg 558

Centre for the Book (South Africa) *Tel:* (021) 423 2669 *Fax:* (021) 424 1484 *E-mail:* cbreception@nlsa.ac.za *Web Site:* www.nlsa.ac.za, pg 613

Centre International de Poesie Marseille (France) *Tel:* 04 91 91 26 45 *Fax:* 04 91 90 99 51 *E-mail:* cipm@cipmarseille.com *Web Site:* www.cipmarseille.com, pg 159

Centre National de Documentation (Morocco) *Tel:* 05 37 77 31 31 *Fax:* 05 37 77 31 34 *E-mail:* cndportal@yahoo.fr *Web Site:* www.cnd.hcp.ma, pg 1614

Centre National de Documentation Pedagogique (CNDP) (France) *Tel:* 05 49 49 78 78 *Fax:* 05 49 49 78 16 *Web Site:* www2.cndp.fr/accueil.htm, pg 159

Centre national de litterature (CNL) (Luxembourg) *Tel:* 326955 1 *Fax:* 327090 *E-mail:* info@cnl.public.lu *Web Site:* www.cnl.public.lu, pg 503

Centre National des Archives (Burkina Faso) *Tel:* 50 33 61 96 *Fax:* 50 31 49 26 *E-mail:* info@presidence.bf *Web Site:* www.presidence.bf, pg 1581

Centre National du Livre (CNL) (France) *Tel:* 01 49 54 68 68 *Fax:* 01 45 49 10 21 *E-mail:* secretariat@centrenationaldulivre.fr *Web Site:* www.centrenationaldulivre.fr, pg 1494

Centre of Legal Information (Lithuania) *Tel:* (05) 261 7529; (05) 261 1065 (bookshop) *Toll Free Tel:* 800 22 088 *Fax:* (05) 262 1523 *E-mail:* tminfo@tm.lt *Web Site:* www.teisingumas.lt, pg 501

Editions du Centre Pompidou (France) *Tel:* 01 44 78 12 33 *E-mail:* cahiers.musee@centrepompidou.fr *Web Site:* www.centrepompidou.fr/editions, pg 160

Centre Technique des Industries de la Fonderie-Service Edition (France) *Tel:* 01 41 14 63 82 *Fax:* 01 41 14 63 91 *Web Site:* www.ctif.com, pg 160

Centro Agronomico Tropical de Investigacion y Ensenanza (CATIE) (Costa Rica) *Tel:* 2558-2000 *E-mail:* comunica@catie.ac.cr; catie@catie.ac.cr *Web Site:* www.catie.ac.cr, pg 117

Centro Ambrosiano di Dialogo con le Religioni (CADR) (Italy) *Tel:* (02) 8375476 *Fax:* (02) 8375476 *E-mail:* cadr@cadr.it *Web Site:* www.cadr.it, pg 433

Centro Ambrosiano IPL (Italy) *Tel:* (02) 6713161 *Fax:* (02) 66984388 *E-mail:* itlbook@tin.it, pg 433

Centro Andaluz del Libro SA (Spain) *Tel:* 954357770 *Fax:* 954352166 *E-mail:* distribucion@centroandaluzdellibro.com *Web Site:* www.centroandaluzdellibro.com, pg 1450

Edizioni Centro Biblico (Italy) *Tel:* (081) 3340532 *Toll Free Tel:* 800 13 46 28 *Fax:* (081) 3340877, pg 433

Edizioni del Centro Camuno di Studi Preistorici (Italy) *Tel:* (0364) 42091 *Fax:* (0364) 42572 *E-mail:* info@ccsp.it *Web Site:* www.ccsp.it, pg 433

Centro de Documentacao e Informacao da Camara dos Deputados (Brazil) *Tel:* (061) 3216-5777 *Fax:* (061) 3216-5757 *E-mail:* informa.cedi@camara.leg.br *Web Site:* www2.camara.leg.br, pg 1580

Centro de Documentacion, Informacion y Analisis (CEDIA) (Mexico) *Tel:* (0155) 56 28 13 00 (ext 4706) *Fax:* (0155) 56 28 13 00 (ext 4705) *Web Site:* www.diputados.gob.mx/biblioteca/bibdig/Iniciativas/index.htm, pg 1613

Centro de Ediciones de la Diputacion de Malaga (CEDMA) (Spain) *Tel:* 952 069 207 *Fax:* 952 069 215 *E-mail:* cedma@malaga.es *Web Site:* cedma.es, pg 635

Centro de Estudios Adams-Ediciones Valbuena SA (Spain) *Tel:* 902 333 543 *Fax:* 915 774 221 *E-mail:* adams@adams.es *Web Site:* www.adams.es, pg 635

China Fortune Press (China) *Tel:* (010) 52227588; (010) 52227566 *E-mail:* zgcfcbs@126.com *Web Site:* www. cfpress.com.cn, pg 102

China Human Resources & Social Security Publishing Group Co Ltd (China) *Tel:* (010) 64929196 *Web Site:* www.class.com.cn, pg 102

China International Book Trading Corp (CIBTC) (China) *Tel:* (010) 68412045; (010) 68414284 *Fax:* (010) 68412023 *E-mail:* cibtc@mail.cibtc.com.cn *Web Site:* www.cibtc.com.cn, pg 1409

China International Culture Press Ltd (China) *Tel:* (010) 57733086; (010) 57733087; (010) 57733088 *Fax:* (010) 89506878 *E-mail:* book@bookhk. com; book9@bookhk.com; bookbj@bookhk.com *Web Site:* www.bookhk.com, pg 102

China ISBN Agency (China) *Tel:* (010) 58689857 *Fax:* (010) 58689995 *E-mail:* chinaisbn@163.com *Web Site:* www.capub.cn, pg 1368

China Knowledge Press (Singapore) *Tel:* 6235 8468 *Fax:* 6235 2374 *E-mail:* info@chinaknowledge.com *Web Site:* www.chinaknowledge.com, pg 603

China Light Industry Press (China) *Tel:* (010) 65241695; (010) 85119752; (010) 85009896 *Fax:* (010) 65128352 *E-mail:* faxing@vip.163.com *Web Site:* www.chlip. com.cn, pg 102

China Machine Press (CMP) (China) *Tel:* (010) 88361066; (010) 88379977; (010) 88379973 (overseas) *Fax:* (010) 88379345; (010) 68320405 (overseas) *Web Site:* www.cmpbook.com, pg 102

China National Publications Import & Export (Group) Corp (China) *Tel:* (010) 65066688 *E-mail:* cnpeak@ cnpiec.com.cn *Web Site:* www.cnpiec.com.cn, pg 1410

China National Publishing Industry Trading Corp (CNPITC) (China) *Tel:* (010) 64210403 *Fax:* (010) 64214540 *Web Site:* www.cnpitc.com.cn, pg 1353

China Ocean Press (China) *Tel:* (010) 62114335; (010) 62100963; (010) 62100075 *Fax:* (010) 62100074 *Web Site:* www.oceanpress.com.cn, pg 102

China Pictorial Publishing House (China) *Tel:* (010) 88417359; (010) 88417358; (010) 68469053 *Fax:* (010) 88417359 *E-mail:* cpph1985@126.com *Web Site:* www.zghbcbs.com, pg 103

China Renmin University Press Co Ltd (China) *Tel:* (010) 62510566 *Fax:* (010) 62514760 *E-mail:* club@crup.com.cn *Web Site:* www.crup. cn, pg 103

China Social Sciences Press (China) *Tel:* (010) 84029453; (010) 61294748 *Fax:* (010) 84002041 *E-mail:* duzhe_cbs@cass.org.cn *Web Site:* www.csspw. com.cn, pg 103

China Textile & Apparel Press (China) *Tel:* (010) 67004461; (010) 67004471; (010) 87155800 (rights) *Fax:* (010) 87155801 (rights) *E-mail:* zongbianshi8240@c-textilep.com (rights) *Web Site:* www.c-textilep.com, pg 103

China Tibetology Publishing House (China) *Tel:* (010) 64917618; (010) 64937991 *Fax:* (010) 64917619, pg 103

China Times Publishing Co (Taiwan) *Tel:* (02) 2304-7103; (02) 2306-6600 *Fax:* (02) 2304-6858 *E-mail:* newstudy@readingtimes.com.tw; newlife@ readingtimes.com.tw *Web Site:* www.readingtimes. com.tw, pg 711

China Translation & Publishing Corp (China) *Tel:* (010) 68359725; (010) 68005858 *Fax:* (010) 53223646, pg 103

China Water & Power Press (CWPP) (China) *Tel:* (010) 68317638; (010) 68367658 (marketing) *Fax:* (010) 68353010; (010) 68331835 (marketing) *E-mail:* info@ waterpub.com.cn; cwpp@waterpub.com.cn; sales@ waterpub.com.cn *Web Site:* www.waterpub.com.cn, pg 103

China Youth Publishing House (China) *Tel:* (010) 57350300; (010) 57350312 *Fax:* (010) 57350313 *E-mail:* cypzbs@126.com *Web Site:* www.cyp.com.cn, pg 103

Chinese Christian Literature Council Ltd (Hong Kong) *Tel:* 2367 8031 *Fax:* 2739 6030 *E-mail:* info@cclc. org.hk *Web Site:* www.cclc.org.hk, pg 363

Chinese Language Society of Hong Kong (Hong Kong) *Tel:* 2528 4853; 2529 1638 *Fax:* 2527 9273 *E-mail:* clshk@hkstar.com *Web Site:* www.hkedcity. net/iclub_files/a/1/74/webpage/jfiles/chinsoc.html, pg 1495

Chinese Marketing & Communications (CMC) (United Kingdom) *Tel:* (07971) 888 080 *E-mail:* info@ chinese-marketing.com *Web Site:* www.chinese-marketing.com, pg 1252

Chinese Theatre Publishing House (China) *Tel:* (010) 58930235; (010) 58930238 (orders) *Fax:* (010) 58930242 (orders), pg 103

Chinese University of Hong Kong Library System (Hong Kong) *Tel:* 3943 7305; 3943 7306 *E-mail:* library@ cuhk.edu.hk *Web Site:* www.lib.cuhk.edu.hk; library. cuhk.edu.hk, pg 1599

The Chinese University Press (Hong Kong) *Tel:* 3943 9800 (general office) *Fax:* 2603 7355 *E-mail:* cup@ cuhk.edu.hk *Web Site:* www.chineseupress.com, pg 363

Ching Chic Publishers (Australia) *Tel:* (07) 5575 8572 *E-mail:* chingchic@winshop.com.au *Web Site:* www. chingchic.com, pg 22

Chinh Tri Quoc Gia Publishing House (Vietnam) *Tel:* (04) 39422008 *Fax:* (04) 39410661 *E-mail:* suthat@nxbctqg.vn *Web Site:* www.nxbctqg. org.vn, pg 851

Les Editions Chiron (France) *Tel:* 01 30 48 74 50 *Fax:* 01 34 98 02 44 *E-mail:* contact@editionschiron. com *Web Site:* www.editionschiron.com, pg 161

Chiron Verlag (Germany) *Tel:* (07071) 8884150 *Fax:* (07071) 8884151 *E-mail:* info@chironverlag.com *Web Site:* www.chiron-verlag.de, pg 225

Verlag Chmielorz GmbH (Germany) *Tel:* (0611) 3 60 98-0 *Fax:* (0611) 30 13 03 *E-mail:* info@chmielorz.de *Web Site:* www.chmielorz.de, pg 225

Choc Lit Ltd (United Kingdom) *Tel:* (01276) 27492 *E-mail:* info@choc-lit.com *Web Site:* www.choc-lit. com, pg 749

Choice International (India) *Tel:* (011) 64163037; 9212013637 (cell) *E-mail:* narkambooks@gmail.com; narkambooks@yahoo.com; narkambooks@ibibo.com, pg 379

Chokechai Thewet (Thailand) *Tel:* (02) 222-666-0, pg 715

Chong-A Printing (South Korea) *Tel:* (031) 908 8671 *Fax:* (031) 908 8674 *E-mail:* chongapt@ chongaprinting.com *Web Site:* www.chongaprinting. com, pg 1334

Chong Moh Offset Printing Pte Ltd (Singapore) *Tel:* 6862 2701 *Fax:* 6862 4335, pg 1261, 1283, 1332

Chongqing Library (China) *Tel:* (023) 65210833; (023) 65210822 *Web Site:* www.cqlib.cn, pg 1582

Chongqing University Press (China) *Tel:* (023) 88617000 *Fax:* (023) 88617014 *E-mail:* office@cqup.com. cn; wangbin@cqup.com.cn; liuxj@cqup.com.cn *Web Site:* www.cqup.com.cn, pg 103

Chopsticks Cooking Centre (Hong Kong) *Tel:* 2336 8433 *Fax:* 2338 1462 *E-mail:* chopsticks1971@netvigator. com, pg 363

Chorus-Verlag fuer Kunst und Wissenschaft (Germany) *Tel:* (06131) 346 64; (0171) 420 82 80 (cell) *Fax:* (06131) 369 076 *E-mail:* info@chorus-verlag.de *Web Site:* www.chorus-verlag.de, pg 225

Chosen Generation Books Ltd (Nigeria) *Tel:* (01) 474 4815, pg 551

Chosen Generation Books Ltd (Nigeria) *Tel:* (01) 474 4815; (01) 741 5540 *E-mail:* info@chosengenbooks. org *Web Site:* www.chosengenbooks.org, pg 1439

The Chosun Ilbo Co Ltd (South Korea) *Tel:* (02) 724-5114 *E-mail:* englishnews@chosun.com *Web Site:* www.chosun.com; english.chosun.com, pg 620

Chowkhamba Sanskrit Series Office (India) *Tel:* (0542) 2333458; (0542) 2334032; (0542) 2335020 *E-mail:* cssoffice01@gmail.com *Web Site:* www. chowkhambasanskritseries.com, pg 380

Chr Belser AG fuer Verlagsgeschaefte & Co KG (Germany) *Tel:* (0711) 2191-0 *Fax:* (0711) 2191-412 *E-mail:* info@belser.de *Web Site:* www.belser-verlag. de, pg 225

Teresa Chris Literary Agency Ltd (United Kingdom) *Tel:* (020) 7386 0633 *E-mail:* teresachris@litagency. co.uk *Web Site:* www.teresachrisliteraryagency.co.uk, pg 1240

Edition Chrismon (Germany) *Tel:* (0341) 71141-15 *Fax:* (0341) 71141-40 *Web Site:* chrismon.evangelisch. de/ueber-uns/edition-chrismon; www.chrismonshop.de, pg 226

Chrissi Penna - Golden Pen Books (Greece) *Tel:* 2103805672 *Fax:* 2103825205 *E-mail:* info@ chrissipenna.com; xpenna@acci.gr *Web Site:* www. chrissipenna.com, pg 354

Christchurch City Libraries (New Zealand) *Tel:* (03) 941 7923 *E-mail:* library@ccc.govt.nz *Web Site:* my. christchurchcitylibraries.com, pg 1617

Christian Art Publishers (South Africa) *Tel:* (016) 440 7000 *Fax:* (016) 421 1748 *Web Site:* www. cumuitgewers.co.za, pg 613

Christian Booksellers' Association New Zealand (New Zealand) *E-mail:* info@cba.net.nz *Web Site:* www.cba. net.nz, pg 1384

Christian Booksellers Association of Nigeria (CBAN) (Nigeria) *Tel:* (0803) 391 4873, pg 1385

Christian Bookselling Association of Australia (CBAA) (Australia) *E-mail:* info@cbaa.com.au *Web Site:* www. cbaa.com.au, pg 1364

Christian Communications Ltd (Hong Kong) *Tel:* 2725 8558 *Fax:* 2386 1804 *E-mail:* hkccl@ccl.org.hk *Web Site:* www.ccl.org.hk, pg 363

Christian Education (United Kingdom) *Tel:* (0121) 472 4242 *Fax:* (0121) 472 7575 *E-mail:* editorial@ christianeducation.org.uk; sales@christianeducation. org.uk *Web Site:* shop.christianeducation.org.uk, pg 749

Christian Focus Publications Ltd (United Kingdom) *Tel:* (01862) 871 011 *Fax:* (01862) 871 699 *E-mail:* info@christianfocus.com *Web Site:* www. christianfocus.com, pg 750

The Christian Literature Society (India) *Tel:* (044) 25354296 *Fax:* (044) 25354297, pg 380

The Christian Literature Society of Korea (South Korea) *Tel:* (02) 553-0870 *Fax:* (02) 555-7721 *E-mail:* clsk@ clsk.org *Web Site:* www.clsk.org, pg 620

Christian Research Association (United Kingdom) *Tel:* (01793) 418388 *E-mail:* admin@christian-research.org.uk *Web Site:* www.christian-research.org. uk, pg 750

Christian Verlag GmbH (Germany) *Tel:* (089) 130699-0 *Fax:* (089) 130699-100 *E-mail:* info@verlagshaus. de; verlagsleitung@verlagshaus.de *Web Site:* www. verlagshaus24.de/christian, pg 226

Christiana (Germany) *Tel:* (07563) 92006 *Fax:* (07563) 3381 *E-mail:* info@fe-medien.de *Web Site:* www.fe-medien.de, pg 226

Christians Verlag ek (Germany) *Tel:* (040) 32 90 17 80 *Fax:* (040) 32 90 17 81 *E-mail:* verlag@christians.de; bestellung@christians.de *Web Site:* www.christians.de, pg 226

Christliche Literatur-Verbreitung eV (Germany) *Tel:* (0521) 947240 *Fax:* (0521) 9472421 *E-mail:* info@clv.de *Web Site:* www.clv.de, pg 226

Christliche Schriftenverbreitung eV Verlag und Versandbuchhandlung (Germany) *Tel:* (02192) 9210-0 *Fax:* (02192) 9210-23 *E-mail:* info@csv-verlag.de *Web Site:* www.csv-verlag.de, pg 226

Civilizacao Editora (Portugal) *Tel:* 226 050 917 *Fax:* 226 050 999 *E-mail:* info@civilizacao.pt *Web Site:* www. civilizacao.pt, pg 577

Civitas Ediciones SL (Spain) *Tel:* 902 40 40 47 *Fax:* 902 40 00 10 *E-mail:* atencionclientes@thomsonreuters. com *Web Site:* www.tienda.aranzadi.es, pg 636

CLAIM (Christian Literature Association in Malawi) Bookshop (Malawi) *Tel:* 01 594 350, pg 1432

CLAIM Mabuku (Malawi) *Tel:* 01 833 714 *Fax:* 01 824 894 *E-mail:* info@claimmabuku.org *Web Site:* www. claimmabuku.org, pg 506

Librairie Clairafrique (Senegal) *Tel:* 33 864 44 29; 33 849 49 99 *Fax:* 33 864 58 54 *E-mail:* clairaf@orange. sn *Web Site:* clairafrique.com, pg 1446

editions clandestin (Switzerland) *Tel:* (032) 377 21 31 *Fax:* (032) 377 21 32 *E-mail:* edition.clandestin@ bluewin.ch *Web Site:* www.edition-clandestin.ch, pg 691

The John Clare Society (United Kingdom) *Tel:* (01353) 668 438 *E-mail:* normali@arabella.wanadoo.co.uk (memberships only) *Web Site:* www.johnclare.org.uk, pg 1502

Editorial Claret SA (Spain) *Tel:* 93 301 08 87 *E-mail:* libreria@claret.es *Web Site:* www.claret.cat, pg 636

Claretian Communications Foundation Inc (Philippines) *Tel:* (02) 921-3984 *Fax:* (02) 921-7429 *E-mail:* ccfi@ claretianpublications.com *Web Site:* www. claretianpublications.com, pg 565

Editorial Claretiana (Argentina) *Tel:* (011) 4305-9597; (011) 4305-9510 *Fax:* (011) 4305-6552 *E-mail:* editorial@editorialclaretiana.com.ar; ventas@ editorialclaretiana.com.ar; contacto@editorialclaretiana. com.ar *Web Site:* www.editorialclaretiana.com.ar, pg 4

Publicaciones Claretianas (Spain) *Tel:* 91 540 12 65 *Fax:* 91 540 00 66 *E-mail:* publicaciones@claret.org; comercial-ventas@claret.org; edicionpcl@claret.org *Web Site:* www.publicacionesclaretianas.com, pg 636

Editorial Claridad SA (Argentina) *Tel:* (011) 4804-0472; (011) 4804-8757; (011) 4804-0119 *Fax:* (011) 4804-0472; (011) 4804-8757; (011) 4804-0119 *E-mail:* editorial@heliasta.com.ar; web@heliasta.com. ar *Web Site:* www.editorialclaridad.com.ar, pg 4

James Clarke & Co Ltd (United Kingdom) *Tel:* (01223) 350865 *Fax:* (01223) 366951 *E-mail:* publishing@ jamesclarke.co.uk *Web Site:* www.jamesclarke.co.uk, pg 751

Clarkson Research Services Ltd (United Kingdom) *Tel:* (020) 7334 3134 *Fax:* (020) 7522 0330 *E-mail:* sales.crs@clarksons.com *Web Site:* www.crsl. com; www.oilpubs.com, pg 751

Clasicos Roxsil SA de CV (El Salvador) *Tel:* 2228-1832; 2200-5209; 2228-1212 *E-mail:* clasicosroxsil@ yahoo.es *Web Site:* ww.facebook.com/Clasicos-Roxsil-331476613687219/, pg 144, 1413

Class Publishing (United Kingdom) *Tel:* (01278) 427800 *E-mail:* info@class.co.uk; post@class.co.uk *Web Site:* www.classhealth.co.uk, pg 751

Classic Publishers (Pakistan) *Tel:* (042) 7312977 *Fax:* (042) 7323963, pg 558

Classica Editora (Portugal) *E-mail:* suporte@ polytechnica.pt *Web Site:* classicaeditora.pt, pg 577

Classical Publishing Co (India) *Tel:* (011) 25465978; 9015777018 (cell), pg 380

Classicus Verlag GmbH (Germany) *Tel:* (040) 41 72 79 *Fax:* (040) 44 61 27 *Web Site:* www.classicus-verlag. de, pg 226

Classikaletet (Israel) *Tel:* (03) 5582080, pg 417

Claudiana Editrice (Italy) *Tel:* (011) 668 98 04 *Fax:* (011) 65 75 42 *E-mail:* info@claudiana.it *Web Site:* www.claudiana.it, pg 434

Claudius Verlag (Germany) *Tel:* (089) 12172-0 *Fax:* (089) 12172-138 *E-mail:* claudius@epv.de *Web Site:* www.claudius.de, pg 227

Clausen & Bosse (Germany) *Tel:* (04662) 83-0 *E-mail:* info@cpibooks.de *Web Site:* cpibooks.com/de, pg 1275, 1321

Clavis Uitgeverij BVBA (Belgium) *Tel:* (011) 28 68 68 *Fax:* (011) 28 68 69 *E-mail:* info@clavisbooks.com *Web Site:* www.clavisbooks.com, pg 65

Clays Ltd (United Kingdom) *Tel:* (020) 7928 8844 *E-mail:* sales@clays.co.uk *Web Site:* www.clays.co.uk, pg 1263, 1337, 1348, 1355

CLC International (UK) (United Kingdom) *Tel:* (01244) 520000 *Toll Free Tel:* 0800 373755 (orders) *E-mail:* retailoffice@clcbookshops.com; sales@ clcwholesale.com *Web Site:* clc.org.uk; www. clcbookshops.com; www.clcwholesale.com, pg 1457

Editions CLD (France) *Web Site:* www.editionscld.fr, pg 161

Editions CLE (Cameroon) *Tel:* 222 22 35 54 *Fax:* 222 23 27 09 *E-mail:* editionscle@yahoo.fr, pg 97

CLE International (France) *Tel:* 01 45 87 44 00; 01 72 36 30 53 *Fax:* 01 45 87 44 10 *E-mail:* info@cle-inter. com; marketing@cle-inter.com *Web Site:* www.cle-inter.com, pg 161

Clean Slate Press Ltd (New Zealand) *Tel:* (09) 6300382 *Fax:* (09) 6300387 *E-mail:* info@cleanslatepress.com *Web Site:* www.cleanslatepress.com, pg 545

Cleon Verlag (Germany) *Tel:* (08031) 9411 654 *Fax:* (08031) 9412 065 *E-mail:* mail@cleon-verlag.de *Web Site:* www.cleon-verlag.de, pg 227

Clerestory Press (New Zealand) *Tel:* (03) 355 3588 *E-mail:* young.writers@xtra.co.nz, pg 545

CLEUP (Cooperativa Libraria Editrice Universita di Padova) (Italy) *Tel:* (049) 8753496 *Fax:* (049) 650261 *E-mail:* redazione@cleup.it; info@cleup.it *Web Site:* www2.cleup.it, pg 435

The Cleveland Vibrator Co (United States) *Tel:* 216-241-7157 *Toll Free Tel:* 800-221-3298 *Fax:* 216-241-3480 *E-mail:* sales@clevelandvibrator.com *Web Site:* www. clevelandvibrator.com, pg 1356

Clever Books (South Africa) *Tel:* (011) 731 3300 *Fax:* (011) 731 3535 *E-mail:* customerservices@ macmillan.co.za *Web Site:* www.macmillan.co.za, pg 613

CLEVER Publishing (Russia) *Tel:* (495) 744 03 31 *E-mail:* info@clever-publishing.com *Web Site:* clever-publishing.com; www.clever-media.ru, pg 593

Editorial Clie (Spain) *Tel:* 93 788 4262 *Fax:* 93 780 0514 *E-mail:* clie@clie.es *Web Site:* clie.es, pg 637

Editions Climats (France) *Tel:* 01 40 51 31 00 *Web Site:* editions.flammarion.com, pg 161

Clinical Publishing (United Kingdom) *Tel:* (01865) 811116 *E-mail:* info@clinicalpublishing.co.uk *Web Site:* www.clinicalpublishing.co.uk, pg 751

Clo Iar-Chonnachta Teo (Ireland) *Tel:* (091) 593 307 *Fax:* (091) 593 362 *E-mail:* info@cic.ie; cic@iol.ie *Web Site:* www.cic.ie, pg 409

Clodhanna Teoranta (Ireland) *Tel:* (01) 475 7401 *Fax:* (01) 475 7844 *E-mail:* eolas@cnag.ie *Web Site:* cnag.ie, pg 409

Cloister Bookstore Ltd (Barbados) *Tel:* (246) 426-2662 *E-mail:* cloisterbookstore2015@gmail.com *Web Site:* cloisterbookstore.com, pg 1405

Jonathan Clowes Ltd (United Kingdom) *Tel:* (020) 7722 7674 *Fax:* (020) 7722 7677 *E-mail:* admin@ jonathanclowes.co.uk *Web Site:* www.jonathanclowes. co.uk, pg 1240

Cluaran Verlag & Handels OHG (Germany) *Fax:* (06251) 770 222 *E-mail:* info@cluaran.de *Web Site:* www.cluaran.de, pg 227

Club de Lectores (Argentina) *Tel:* (011) 4327-2253 *E-mail:* tpignataro1@hotmail.com *Web Site:* www. clubdelectores.com.ar, pg 4

Casa Editrice Clueb SRL (Italy) *Tel:* (051) 220736 *Fax:* (051) 237758 *E-mail:* clueb@clueb.com; info@ clueb.com *Web Site:* www.clueb.com, pg 435

Presa Universitara Clujeana (Romania) *Tel:* (0264) 405300; (0264) 597401; (0264) 406451 *E-mail:* editura@editura.ubbcluj.ro; comenzi@editura. ubbcluj.ro *Web Site:* www.editura.ubbcluj.ro, pg 585

Editura Clusium (Romania) *Tel:* (0264) 596940 *Fax:* (0264) 596940 *E-mail:* clusium@cluj.astral.ro, pg 585

CLUT Editrice (Italy) *Tel:* (011) 0907980; (011) 542192 *Fax:* (011) 542192 *E-mail:* clut@inrete.it *Web Site:* www.clut.it, pg 435

CMC Publishing Co Ltd (Japan) *Tel:* (03) 3293-2061 *Fax:* (03) 3293-2069 *E-mail:* info@cmcbooks.co.jp *Web Site:* www.cmcbooks.co.jp, pg 475

CMS-Cross Media Solutions GmbH (Germany) *Tel:* (09) 31 3 85-252 *Fax:* (09) 31 3 85-275 *E-mail:* info@crossmediasolutions.de *Web Site:* www. crossmediasolutions.de, pg 1275

CMS Verlagsgesellschaft mbH (Switzerland) *Tel:* (071) 669 19 56 *Fax:* (071) 669 19 54 *E-mail:* info@cms-verlag.ch *Web Site:* cms-verlag.ch, pg 691

CNR Edizioni (Italy) *Tel:* (06) 4993 2287; (06) 4993 3542 (sales); (06) 4993 3428 (sales); (06) 4993 2538 (sales) *Fax:* (06) 4461954 *E-mail:* bookshop@cnr.it *Web Site:* www.edizioni.cnr.it, pg 435

CNRS Editions (France) *Tel:* 01 53 10 27 00 *E-mail:* cnrseditions@cnrseditions.fr *Web Site:* www. cnrseditions.fr, pg 161

Co-Fine Promotions (Hong Kong) *Tel:* 2518 0383 *Fax:* 2518 0361, pg 1353

Coach House Printing (Canada) *Tel:* 416-979-2217 *Toll Free Tel:* 800-367-6360 (outside Toronto) *Fax:* 416-977-1158 *E-mail:* mail@chbooks.com *Web Site:* www. chbooks.com, pg 1318

Coachwise Ltd (United Kingdom) *Tel:* (0113) 231 1310 *Fax:* (0113) 231 9606 *E-mail:* enquiries@coachwise. ltd.uk *Web Site:* www.coachwise.ltd.uk, pg 751

La Coccinella SRL (Italy) *Tel:* (02) 4381161 *Fax:* (02) 436923 *E-mail:* trade@coccinella.com; segreteria@ coccinella.com *Web Site:* www.coccinella.com, pg 435

Edizioni Coccole e Caccole (Italy) *Tel:* (0985) 887823 *Fax:* (0985) 887823; (0985) 250456 *E-mail:* edizioni@coccolebooks.com; editor@ coccoleecaccole.it *Web Site:* www.coccoleecaccole.it, pg 435

CoCon Verlag Hanau (Germany) *Tel:* (06181) 1 77 00 *Fax:* (06181) 18 13 33 *E-mail:* cocon-verlag@t-online. de; kontakt@cocon-verlag.de *Web Site:* www.cocon-verlag.de, pg 227

Editura Codecs (Romania) *Tel:* (021) 2525182 *Fax:* (021) 2525613 *E-mail:* sales@codecs.ro *Web Site:* www.codecs.ro, pg 585

Codes Rousseau SAS (France) *Tel:* 02 51 23 11 00; 02 51 23 11 31 *Fax:* 02 51 23 11 31 *E-mail:* service. commercial@codes-rousseau.fr *Web Site:* www.codes-rousseau.fr, pg 161

Codice Edizioni SRL (Italy) *Tel:* (011) 19700579; (011) 19700580 *Fax:* (011) 19700582 *E-mail:* info@ codiceedizioni.it; press@codiceedizioni.it *Web Site:* www.codiceedizioni.it, pg 435

Codra Enterprises Inc (United States) *Tel:* 949-756-8400 *Toll Free Tel:* 888-992-6372 *Fax:* 949-756-8484 *E-mail:* codra@codra.com; sales@codra.com *Web Site:* www.codra.com, pg 1264

Cogitum Livrarias Lda (Portugal) *Tel:* 214394912, pg 1445

Eric Cohen Books Ltd (Israel) *Tel:* (09) 747 8000 *Fax:* (09) 747 8001 *E-mail:* info@ecb.co.il; orders@ ecb.co.il *Web Site:* www.ecb.co.il, pg 1426

Coimbra Editora Lda (Portugal) *Tel:* 239 85 2650 *Fax:* 239 85 2651 *E-mail:* editorial@coimbraeditora. net; comercial@coimbraeditora.net; encomendas@ coimbraeditora.net *Web Site:* www.coimbraeditora.net, pg 577

Colegial Bolivariana CA (Venezuela) *Tel:* (0212) 2391433 *Fax:* (0212) 2396502; (0212) 2379307 *E-mail:* ventas@co-bo.com *Web Site:* www.co-bo.com, pg 850

Colegio de Bibliotecarios de Chile (CBC) (Chile) *Tel:* (02) 2225652 *E-mail:* cbc@bibliotecarios.cl *Web Site:* www.bibliotecarios.cl, pg 1649

Ediciones Colegio De Espana (ECE) (Spain) *Tel:* 923 214 788 *Fax:* 923 218 791 *E-mail:* info@colegioespana.com *Web Site:* www.colegioespana.com, pg 637

El Colegio de Jalisco (Mexico) *Tel:* (0133) 3633 2616 *E-mail:* publicaciones@coljal.edu.mx *Web Site:* coljal.edu.mx, pg 514

El Colegio de la Frontera Norte (Colef) (Mexico) *Tel:* (01664) 631-6300 *E-mail:* informes@colef.mx; publica@colef.mx; libros@colef.mx *Web Site:* www.colef.mx, pg 514

El Colegio de la Frontera Sur (ECOSUR) (Mexico) *Tel:* (01967) 674-9000 *Fax:* (01976) 674-9021 *E-mail:* contacto@ecosur.mx *Web Site:* www.ecosur.mx, pg 514

El Colegio de Mexico AC (COLMEX) (Mexico) *Tel:* (0155) 5449 3000 *Fax:* (0155) 5449 3000 (ext 3157) *Web Site:* publicaciones.colmex.mx; www.colmex.mx, pg 514

El Colegio de Michoacan AC (Mexico) *Tel:* (0351) 5157100 *Fax:* (0351) 5157100 *E-mail:* publica@colmich.edu.mx *Web Site:* www.colmich.edu.mx/index.php/publicaciones; www.libreriacolmich.com, pg 514

Colegio de Postgraduados en Ciencias Agricolas (Mexico) *Tel:* (01595) 58046800 *E-mail:* contacto@colpos.mx *Web Site:* www.colpos.mx, pg 514

El Colegio de San Luis (Mexico) *Tel:* (01444) 8110101 (ext 3045) *E-mail:* publicaciones@colsan.edu.mx; difusioncolsan@gmail.com; ventaslibros@colsan.edu.mx *Web Site:* www.colsan.edu.mx, pg 514

El Colegio de Sonora (Mexico) *Tel:* (01662) 259-5300 *Fax:* (01662) 212-5021 *Web Site:* www.colson.edu.mx, pg 514

El Colegio Mexiquense AC (Mexico) *Tel:* (01722) 2799908; (01722) 2180100 *Fax:* (01722) 2799908 (ext 200) *E-mail:* public@cmq.edu.mx *Web Site:* www.cmq.edu.mx, pg 514

Charles Coleman Verlag GmbH & Co KG (Germany) *Tel:* (0221) 5497-0 *Fax:* (0221) 5497-326 *E-mail:* info@coleman-verlag.de; info@rudolf-mueller.de *Web Site:* www.coleman-verlag.de; www.rudolf-mueller.de, pg 227

Edicoes Colibri (Portugal) *Tel:* 21 796 40 38 *Fax:* 21 796 40 38 *E-mail:* colibri@edi-colibri.pt *Web Site:* www.edi-colibri.pt, pg 578

Colibri Publishing Group (Bulgaria) *Tel:* (02) 987 48 10 (off); (02) 988 87 81 *E-mail:* colibri@colibri.org *Web Site:* www.colibri.bg, pg 95

Ediciones Colihue SRL (Argentina) *Tel:* (011) 4958-4442 *Fax:* (011) 4958-5673 *E-mail:* ecolihue@colihue.com.ar *Web Site:* www.colihue.com.ar, pg 5

Armand Colin (France) *Toll Free Tel:* 0820 065 095 *Fax:* 01 41 23 67 35 *E-mail:* infos@armand-colin.fr; revues@armand-colin.com; infos@dunod.com *Web Site:* www.armand-colin.com; www.revues.armand-colin.com, pg 161

Rosica Colin Ltd (United Kingdom) *Tel:* (020) 7370 1080 *Fax:* (020) 7244 6441, pg 1240

Colision Libros (Argentina) *Tel:* (011) 4807 8611 *E-mail:* colisionlibros@gmail.com *Web Site:* www.lacolision.com.ar, pg 5

Collage Ltd (Armenia) *Tel:* (010) 520217 *Fax:* (010) 584693 *E-mail:* collageltd@gmail.com *Web Site:* collage.am, pg 14

Collectieve Propaganda van het Nederlandse Boek (CPNB) (Netherlands) *Tel:* (020) 626 49 71 *Fax:* (020) 623 16 96 *E-mail:* info@cpnb.nl *Web Site:* www.cpnb.nl, pg 1383

College International des Traducteurs Litteraires (CITL) (France) *Tel:* 04 90 52 05 50 *Fax:* 04 90 93 43 21 *E-mail:* citl@atlas-citl.org *Web Site:* www.atlas-citl.org, pg 1371

College of Law Publishing (CLP) (United Kingdom) *Tel:* (01235) 465500 (orders) *E-mail:* info@clponline.co.uk; clp@bebc.co.uk; orders@orcabookservices.co.uk (orders) *Web Site:* www.clponline.co.uk, pg 751

The College of the Bahamas Library (The Bahamas) *Tel:* (242) 302-4552 *Fax:* (242) 302-4531 *E-mail:* library@cob.edu.bs *Web Site:* www.cob.edu.bs/library, pg 1576

College Press Publishers (Pvt) Ltd (Zimbabwe) *Tel:* (04) 754145; (04) 757150; (04) 757154 *Fax:* (04) 754256, pg 852

Collier International (United Kingdom) *Tel:* (01932) 770123 *Fax:* (01932) 770123 *E-mail:* rights@collier-international.co.uk *Web Site:* www.collier-international.co.uk, pg 1240

Collins Booksellers Pty Ltd (Australia) *Tel:* (03) 9654 7400; (03) 9662 9472 *Fax:* (03) 9654 7600 *E-mail:* headoffice@collinsbooks.com.au *Web Site:* www.collinsbooks.com.au, pg 1402

The Collins Press (Ireland) *Tel:* (021) 4347717 *Fax:* (021) 4347720 *E-mail:* enquiries@collinspress.ie *Web Site:* www.collinspress.ie, pg 409

Colombo Public Library (Sri Lanka) *Tel:* (011) 4691968 *Web Site:* www.colombopubliclibrary.org, pg 1633

Librairie des Colonnes (Morocco) *Tel:* 05 39 93 69 55 *Fax:* 05 39 94 29 00 *E-mail:* info@librairie-des-colonnes.com *Web Site:* librairie-des-colonnes.com, pg 1436

Gaetano Colonnese Editore SAS (Italy) *Tel:* (081) 293900; (081) 459858 (orders) *Fax:* (081) 455420 *E-mail:* editore@colonnese.it; ordini@colonnese.it (orders); stampa@colonnese.it *Web Site:* www.colonnese.it, pg 435

Colorcraft Ltd (Hong Kong) *Tel:* 2590 9033 *Fax:* 2590 9005 *E-mail:* enquiries@colorcraft.com.hk *Web Site:* www.colorcraft.com.hk, pg 1353

Colorprint Offset (Hong Kong) *Tel:* 2896 7777 *Fax:* 2869 6666 *E-mail:* info@cpo.com.hk *Web Site:* www.cpo.com.hk, pg 1257, 1277, 1324

Colourpoint Creative Ltd (United Kingdom) *Tel:* (028) 9182 6339 *Fax:* (028) 9182 1900 *E-mail:* info@colourpoint.co.uk *Web Site:* www.colourpoint.co.uk, pg 751

The Columba Press (Ireland) *Tel:* (01) 294 2556 *Fax:* (01) 294 2564 *E-mail:* info@columba.ie *Web Site:* www.columba.ie, pg 409

Columba Press (Ireland) *Tel:* (01) 687 4096 *E-mail:* sales@columba.ie *Web Site:* www.columba.ie, pg 1426

Nakladatelstvi Columbus SRO (Czech Republic) *Tel:* 284 820 446, pg 126

Columna Edicions (Spain) *Tel:* 93 443 71 00 *Web Site:* www.grup62.cat/editorial-columna-edicions-83.html, pg 637

Editorial Comares (Spain) *Tel:* 958 465 382 *E-mail:* pedidos@comares.com *Web Site:* www.comares.com, pg 637

Combel Editorial (Spain) *Tel:* 932 449 550 *Fax:* 932 656 895 *E-mail:* combel@editorialcasals.com; rights@combeleditorial.com *Web Site:* www.combeleditorial.com, pg 637

Combined Academic Publishers Ltd (United Kingdom) *Tel:* (01494) 526350 *E-mail:* enquiries@combinedacademic.co.uk *Web Site:* www.combinedacademic.co.uk, pg 1457

Combined Book Services Ltd (United Kingdom) *Tel:* (01892) 839819; (01892) 837171 *Fax:* (01892) 837272 *E-mail:* info@combook.co.uk; orders@combook.co.uk *Web Site:* www.combook.co.uk, pg 1457

Comhairle nan Leabhraichean - The Gaelic Books Council (United Kingdom) *Tel:* (0141) 337 6211 *E-mail:* brath@gaelicbooks.org *Web Site:* www.gaelicbooks.org, pg 1395

Comision Nacional Forestal (Mexico) *Tel:* (0133) 3777 7000 *Toll Free Tel:* 01 800 7370 00 (within Mexico) *E-mail:* conafor@conafor.gob.mx *Web Site:* www.conafor.gob.mx, pg 514

Comissao Nacional de Energia Nuclear (CNEN) (Brazil) *Tel:* (021) 2173-2000; (021) 2173-2001 *Fax:* (021) 2173-2003 *Web Site:* www.cnen.gov.br, pg 79

Comissao para a Cidadania e a Igualdade de Genero (Portugal) *Tel:* 217 983 000 *Fax:* 217 983 098 *E-mail:* cig@cig.gov.pt; cid@cig.gov.pt *Web Site:* www.cig.gov.pt, pg 578

Editions du Comite des Travaux Historiques et Scientifiques (CTHS) (France) *E-mail:* ventes@cths.fr; service.presse@cths.fr; actes.congres@cths.fr *Web Site:* www.cths.fr, pg 162

Comite Gremial de Editores de Guatemala (Guatemala) *Tel:* 2380 9000 (ext 338) *Fax:* 2380 9110 *E-mail:* asistencia@filgua.com; comunicacion@filgua.com *Web Site:* www.filgua.com, pg 1376

Commentum Forlag AS (Norway) *Tel:* 51 96 12 40 *Fax:* 51 96 12 51 *E-mail:* post@commentum.no *Web Site:* www.commentum.no, pg 554

The Commercial Press (China) *Tel:* (010) 65252026 (editorial); (010) 65135899 (rights); (010) 65253913 (sales) *Fax:* (010) 65134942 *E-mail:* gaoshan@cp.com.cn *Web Site:* www.cp.com.cn, pg 104

The Commercial Press (HK) Ltd (Hong Kong) *Tel:* 2565 1371 *Fax:* 2565 1113 *E-mail:* corpcomm@commercialpress.com.hk; editorial@commercialpress.com.hk *Web Site:* www.commercialpress.com.hk; www.cp1897.com.hk (orders), pg 364

Commission Belge de Bibliographie et de Bibliologie (Belgium) *Tel:* (02) 519 53 11 *Fax:* (02) 519 55 33 *E-mail:* info@kbr.be *Web Site:* www.kbr.be, pg 1491

Libreria Commissionaria Internazionale (Italy) *Tel:* (051) 229466, pg 1428

Commonwealth Council for Educational Administration & Management (Australia) *Tel:* (02) 4751 7974 *Fax:* (02) 4751 7974 *E-mail:* admin@cceam.org *Web Site:* www.cceam.org, pg 22

The Commonwealth Library Association (COMLA) (Jamaica) *Tel:* (876) 927-0083 *Fax:* (876) 927-1926 *E-mail:* nkpodo@uwimona.edu.jm *Web Site:* www.thecommonwealth.org, pg 1654

Commonwealth Publishing Co Ltd (Taiwan) *Tel:* (02) 26620012 *Fax:* (02) 26620007 *E-mail:* service@cwgv.com.tw *Web Site:* www.bookzone.com.tw; www.cwgv.com.tw, pg 711

Commonwealth Secretariat (United Kingdom) *Tel:* (020) 7747 6342 *E-mail:* publications@commonwealth.int *Web Site:* books.thecommonwealth.org, pg 752

Communicatio Kommunikations- und Publications GmbH (Austria) *Tel:* (01) 370 33 02 *Fax:* (01) 370 59 34 *E-mail:* pr@communicatio.cc *Web Site:* www.communicatio.cc, pg 46

Compact Verlag GmbH (Germany) *Tel:* (089) 74 51 61-0 *Fax:* (089) 75 60 95 *E-mail:* info@compactverlag.de *Web Site:* www.compactverlag.de, pg 227

Editora Companhia das Letras/Editora Schwarcz Ltda (Brazil) *Tel:* (011) 3707-3500 *Fax:* (011) 3707-3501 *E-mail:* pedidos@companhiadasletras.com.br *Web Site:* www.companhiadasletras.com.br, pg 79

Compass Independent Publishing Services Ltd (United Kingdom) *Tel:* (020) 8326 5696 *Web Site:* www.compass-ips.london, pg 1457

Compass Maps Ltd (United Kingdom) *Tel:* (01225) 406440 *Fax:* (01225) 469461 *E-mail:* info@popoutmaps.com *Web Site:* www.popoutproducts.co.uk, pg 752

Compass-Verlag GmbH (Austria) *Tel:* (01) 981 16-0 *Fax:* (01) 981 16-118; (01) 981 16-148 (sales) *E-mail:* office@compass.at *Web Site:* www.compass.at, pg 46

Compendio Bildungsmedien AG (Switzerland) *Tel:* (044) 368 21 11 *Fax:* (044) 368 21 70 *E-mail:* postfach@compendio.ch *Web Site:* www.compendio.ch, pg 691

Complex Kiado Kft (Hungary) *Tel:* (01) 464-565; (01) 464-5656 *Fax:* (01) 464-5657 *E-mail:* info@complex.hu *Web Site:* www.complex.hu, pg 368

Editions Complexe (Belgium) *Tel:* (02) 538 88 46 *Fax:* (02) 538 88 42 *Web Site:* www.editionscomplexe.com, pg 65

Computer Press (Czech Republic) *Toll Free Tel:* 800 555 513 *E-mail:* eshop@cpress.cz *Web Site:* www.cpress.cz, pg 126

Libreria Comuneros (Paraguay) *Tel:* (021) 446-176; (021) 444-667 *Fax:* (021) 444-667, pg 1442

Comunicacion Social Ediciones y Publicaciones (Spain) *Tel:* 923 626 722 *E-mail:* info@comunicacionsocial.es; prensa@comunicacionsocial.es *Web Site:* www.comunicacionsocial.es, pg 637

Editura Comunicare.ro (Romania) *Tel:* (021) 3135895; (021) 3100718 *Fax:* (021) 3135895 *E-mail:* editura@comunicare.ro *Web Site:* www.editura.comunicare.ro, pg 586

Editorial Comunicarte (Argentina) *Tel:* (0351) 468 43 42 *Fax:* (0351) 468 34 60 *E-mail:* editorial@comunicarteweb.com.ar *Web Site:* www.comunicarteweb.com.ar, pg 5

Comunidad Autonoma de Madrid, Servicio de Documentacion (Spain) *Tel:* 917 027 625 *Fax:* 913 195 055 *E-mail:* centrodocumentacion.economia@madrid.org *Web Site:* www.madrid.org/next, pg 637

Edizioni di Comunita SpA (Italy) *Tel:* (0347) 6393002 *Fax:* (06) 68696193 *E-mail:* info@edizionidicomunita.it; ordini@edizionidicomunita.it *Web Site:* www.edizionidicomunita.it, pg 435

Concept Publishing Co Pvt Ltd (India) *Tel:* (011) 2535 1460; (011) 2535 1794 *Fax:* (011) 2535 7109 *E-mail:* publishing@conceptpub.com *Web Site:* www.conceptpub.com, pg 380

Concordia-BUCHhandlung (Germany) *Tel:* (0375) 21 28 50 *Fax:* (0375) 29 80 80 *E-mail:* post@concordiabuch.de *Web Site:* www.concordiabuch.de, pg 227

Editora Concordia Ltda (Brazil) *Tel:* (051) 3272-3456 *Fax:* (051) 3272-3482 *E-mail:* comercial@editoraconcordia.com.br; editora@editoraconcordia.com.br *Web Site:* www.editoraconcordia.com.br, pg 79

Nakladatelstvi Concordia (Czech Republic) *Tel:* 233 357 280 *Web Site:* www.nakladatelstviconcordia.cz, pg 126

Concraid SA (Belgium) *Tel:* (065) 221307 *Fax:* (065) 221306, pg 65

The Concrete Society (United Kingdom) *Tel:* (01276) 607140; (07004) 607777 (sales) *Fax:* (01276) 607141 *E-mail:* enquiries@concretebookshop.com *Web Site:* www.concrete.org.uk, pg 752

Editorial Conexion Grafica SA de CV (Mexico) *Tel:* (0133) 3615-7424 *E-mail:* conexiongrafica@conexiongrafica.mx *Web Site:* www.conexiongrafica.mx, pg 514

Confederacion de Cooperativas del Caribe, Centro y Suramerica (CCC-CA) (Costa Rica) *Tel:* 2240-4641 *Fax:* 2240-4284 *E-mail:* info@ccc-ca.com *Web Site:* www.ccc-ca.com, pg 117

Confederation Francaise de l'Industri des Papiers, Cartons & Celluloses (COPACEL) (France) *Tel:* 01 53 89 24 00 *Fax:* 01 53 89 24 01 *E-mail:* contacts@copacel.fr *Web Site:* www.copacel.fr, pg 1371

Conference Interpreters Group (CIG) (United Kingdom) *Tel:* (07733) 887765 *E-mail:* info@cig-interpreters.com *Web Site:* www.cig-interpreters.com, pg 1252

Congress of Southeast Asian Librarians (CONSAL) (Indonesia) *Tel:* (021) 3103554 *Web Site:* www.consal.org, pg 1654

CONICYT (Chile) *Tel:* (02) 3654400 *Fax:* (02) 6551396 *E-mail:* info@conicyt.cl *Web Site:* www.conicyt.cl, pg 1649

Connecting Team (Germany) *Tel:* (069) 74 74 99 90 *Fax:* (069) 74 74 99 99 *Web Site:* www.connectingteam.de, pg 1226

Connection AG (Germany) *Tel:* (08639) 9834-0 *Fax:* (08639) 1219 *E-mail:* seminare@connection.de *Web Site:* www.connection.de, pg 227

Connolly Books (Ireland) *Tel:* (01) 6708707 *E-mail:* connollybooks@eircom.net *Web Site:* www.connollybooks.org, pg 410, 1426

Conquista Empresa de Publicacoes Ltda (Brazil), pg 79

Conrad Editora (Brazil) *Tel:* (011) 2799-7799 *E-mail:* imprensa@conradeditora.com.br; vendas@conradeditora.com.br *Web Site:* www.lojaconrad.com.br, pg 79

The Joseph Conrad Society (UK) (United Kingdom) *Web Site:* www.josephconradsociety.org, pg 1502

Conran Octopus (United Kingdom) *Tel:* (020) 7632 5400 *Fax:* (020) 7632 5405 *E-mail:* info@octopusbooks.co.uk *Web Site:* www.octopusbooks.co.uk, pg 752

Conseil International de la Langue Francaise (France) *Tel:* 01 48 78 73 95 *Fax:* 01 48 78 49 28 *E-mail:* cilf@cilf.org *Web Site:* www.cilf.org, pg 162

Consejo Episcopal Latinoamericano (CELAM) (Colombia) *Tel:* (01) 587 97 10 (ext 307); (01) 587 97 10 (ext 562) *Fax:* (01) 587 97 12 *E-mail:* celam@celam.org *Web Site:* www.celam.org/publicaciones, pg 113

Consejo Latinoamericano de Ciencias Sociales (CLACSO) (Argentina) *Tel:* (011) 4811-2301; (011) 4811-6588 *Fax:* (011) 4812-8459 *E-mail:* biblioteca@clacso.edu.ar; clacso@clacso.edu.ar; clacsoinst@clacso.edu.ar *Web Site:* www.clacso.org.ar; www.clacso.edu.ar, pg 5

Consejo para la Cultura y las Artes de Nuevo Leon (CONARTE) (Mexico) *Tel:* (0181) 2033 8450 *E-mail:* contacto@conarte.org.mx *Web Site:* www.conarte.org.mx, pg 515

Consejo Superior de Investigaciones Cientificas (Spain) *Tel:* 915 159 670 *Fax:* 915 614 851 *E-mail:* publ@csic.es *Web Site:* editorial.csic.es; www.csic.es/publica, pg 637

Consello da Cultura Galega (CCG) (Spain) *Tel:* 981 95 72 02 *Fax:* 981 95 72 05 *E-mail:* correo@consellodacultura.org *Web Site:* www.consellodacultura.org, pg 637

Conservart (Belgium) *Tel:* (02) 332 25 38 *Fax:* (02) 375 40 40 *E-mail:* conservart@skynet.be *Web Site:* www.conservart.be, pg 65

Conservation Resources International LLC (United States) *Tel:* 703-321-7730 *Toll Free Tel:* 800-634-6932 *Fax:* 703-321-0629 *E-mail:* sales@conservationresources.com *Web Site:* www.conservationresources.com, pg 1349

Conservative Policy Forum (United Kingdom) *Tel:* (020) 7222 9000 *E-mail:* cpf@conservatives.com *Web Site:* www.conservativepolicyforum.com; www.conservativesabroad.org, pg 752

Uitgeverij Conserve (Netherlands) *Tel:* (072) 509 3693 *Fax:* (072) 509 4370 *E-mail:* info@conserve.nl *Web Site:* www.conserve.nl, pg 532

Consolidated Printers Inc (United States) *Tel:* 510-843-8524 (sales); 510-843-8565 (admin) *Fax:* 510-486-0580 *E-mail:* cpi@consoprinters.com; sales@consoprinters.com *Web Site:* www.consoprinters.com, pg 1264, 1339

Constable (United Kingdom) *Tel:* (020) 3122 7000 *E-mail:* info@littlebrown.co.uk *Web Site:* www.littlebrown.co.uk, pg 752

Constitucion y Leyes SA Editorial COLEX (Spain) *Tel:* 915 811 502 *Fax:* 911 736 870 *E-mail:* info@colex.es; colexeditor@interbook.net *Web Site:* www.colex.es, pg 637

Consultor Assessoria Planejamentos Ltda (Brazil) *Tel:* (021) 2589-3030, pg 79

Conte Editore (Italy) *Tel:* (0832) 228827 *Fax:* (0832) 220280 *E-mail:* casaeditrice@conteditore.it *Web Site:* www.conteditore.it, pg 435

Conte-Verlag GmbH (Germany) *Tel:* (06894) 166 41 63 *Fax:* (06894) 166 41 64 *E-mail:* info@conte-verlag.de *Web Site:* www.conte-verlag.de, pg 227

Editora Contexto (Editora Pinsky Ltda) (Brazil) *Tel:* (011) 3832-5838 *Fax:* (011) 3832-1043 *E-mail:* contexto@editoracontexto.com.br *Web Site:* www.editoracontexto.com.br, pg 79

Continental Bookshop (Australia) *Tel:* (03) 9015 4440 *Fax:* (03) 8820 4016 *Web Site:* www.continentalbookshop.com, pg 1402

Ediciones Continente (Argentina) *Tel:* (011) 4308-3535 *Fax:* (011) 4308-4800 *E-mail:* info@edicontinente.com.ar *Web Site:* www.edicontinente.com.ar, pg 5

Contmedia GmbH (Germany) *Tel:* (05931) 40 92-40 *Fax:* (05931) 40 92-42 *E-mail:* info@contmedia.com *Web Site:* www.contmedia.com, pg 227

Contrasto SRL (Italy) *Tel:* (06) 328281 *Fax:* (06) 32828240 *E-mail:* customer@contrastobooks.com *Web Site:* www.contrastobooks.com; www.contrasto.it, pg 435

Conville & Walsh Ltd (United Kingdom) *Tel:* (02) 7393 4200 *Web Site:* www.cwagency.co.uk, pg 1240

Jane Conway-Gordon Ltd (United Kingdom) *Tel:* (020) 7371 6939 *E-mail:* jane@conway-gordon.co.uk *Web Site:* www.janeconwaygordon.com, pg 1240

Conzett Verlag (Switzerland) *Tel:* (044) 242 76 53 *Fax:* (044) 242 76 86 *Web Site:* conzettverlag.ch, pg 692

David C Cook (United Kingdom) *Tel:* (01323) 437700 *Fax:* (01323) 411970 *E-mail:* office@kingsway.co.uk *Web Site:* www.kingsway.co.uk, pg 753

Sir Albert Cook Memorial Library (Uganda) *Web Site:* chs.mak.ac.ug/acook, pg 1640

Cookery Book (Australia) *Tel:* (02) 9967 8211 *Fax:* (02) 9967 8578 *E-mail:* cookerybook@cookerybook.com.au *Web Site:* www.cookerybook.com.au, pg 1402

Coolabah Publishing (Australia) *Tel:* (04) 2865 9693 *Fax:* (02) 4967 2336, pg 22

Leo Cooper (United Kingdom) *Tel:* (01226) 734222 *Fax:* (01226) 734438 *E-mail:* enquiries@pen-and-sword.co.uk; publicity@pen-and-sword.co.uk *Web Site:* www.pen-and-sword.co.uk, pg 753

Cooperativa de Trabajo Cultura y Educativa Cefomar Ltda (Argentina) *Tel:* (011) 4382-0312 *E-mail:* soporte@cefomar.com.ar *Web Site:* cefomar.com.ar, pg 5

Cooperative Regionale de l'Enseignement Religieux (CRER) (France) *Tel:* 02 41 68 91 40 *Fax:* 02 41 68 91 41 *E-mail:* relations.commerciales@editions-crer.fr *Web Site:* www.editions-crer.fr, pg 162

Coordination Group Publications Ltd (CGP) (United Kingdom) *Tel:* (0870) 750 1262; (0870) 750 1242 (orders) *Fax:* (0870) 750 1292 *E-mail:* customerservices@cgpbooks.co.uk *Web Site:* www.cgpbooks.co.uk, pg 753

Copenhagen Business School Press (Denmark) *Tel:* 3815 3880 *E-mail:* slforlagene@samfundslitteratur.dk *Web Site:* www.cbspress.dk, pg 135

Copenhagen Literary Agency ApS (Denmark) *Tel:* 33 13 25 23 *E-mail:* info@cphla.dk; royalty@cphla.dk *Web Site:* www.cphla.dk, pg 1225

Copenhagen Publishing House ApS (CPH) (Denmark) *Tel:* 3146 4060; 2620 4060 (cell) *E-mail:* info@copenhagenpublishing.com *Web Site:* www.copenhagenpublishing.com, pg 135

CPE (Conseil Permanent des Ecrivains) (France) *Tel:* 01 48 74 96 30 *E-mail:* contact@ conseilpermanentdesecrivains.org; info@ conseilpermanentdesecrivains.org *Web Site:* www. conseilpermanentdesecrivains.org, pg 1371

CPI Antony Rowe (United Kingdom) *Tel:* (01249) 659705 *Fax:* (01249) 443103 *Web Site:* www.cpi-print.co.uk, pg 1263, 1286, 1337, 1348, 1355

CPI Moravia Books sro (Czech Republic) *Tel:* 519 440 111 *Fax:* 519 440 107 *E-mail:* moravia@cpibooks.de *Web Site:* www.cpibooks.cz, pg 1320

CPI William Clowes Ltd (United Kingdom) *Tel:* (01502) 712884 *E-mail:* williamclowes@cpibooks.co.uk, pg 1263, 1286, 1337, 1348, 1355

Craig Potton Publishing (New Zealand) *Tel:* (03) 548 9009 *Fax:* (03) 548 9456 *E-mail:* info@cpp.co.nz *Web Site:* www.craigpotton.co.nz, pg 545

Craigs Design & Print Ltd (New Zealand) *Tel:* (03) 211-0393; (03) 211-8618 (showroom) *Fax:* (03) 214-9930 *E-mail:* info@craigprint.co.nz *Web Site:* www. craigprint.co.nz, pg 545, 1282, 1331

Otto Cramwinckel Uitgever (Netherlands) *Tel:* (020) 627 66 09 *Fax:* (020) 638 38 17 *E-mail:* info@cram.nl *Web Site:* www.cram.nl, pg 532

Crawford House Publishing Pty Ltd (Australia) *Tel:* (08) 8555 0667 *Web Site:* www.crawfordhouse.com.au, pg 22

CRC Press/Balkema (Netherlands) *Tel:* (071) 524 30 80 *E-mail:* pub.nl@taylorandfrancis.com *Web Site:* www. balkema.nl; www.crcpress.com, pg 532

Creabooks Packagers (Italy) *Tel:* (0185) 1873688 *Fax:* (0185) 1898316 *E-mail:* info@abooks.it *Web Site:* www.creabooks.it, pg 1260, 1280

Creadif (Belgium) *Tel:* (02) 512 98 45 *Fax:* (02) 511 72 02, pg 65

Creations for Children International (Belgium) *Tel:* (09) 395 04 40 *Web Site:* c4ci.assist.be, pg 65

Creative Translation Ltd (United Kingdom) *Tel:* (020) 7294 7710 *E-mail:* info@creativetranslation.com *Web Site:* creativetranslation.com, pg 1252

Creative Work (Hong Kong) *Tel:* 2167 8887 *Web Site:* www.creative-work.com, pg 1229

Crecy Publishing Ltd (United Kingdom) *Tel:* (0161) 499 0024 *Fax:* (0161) 499 0298 *E-mail:* enquiries@crecy. co.uk *Web Site:* www.crecy.co.uk, pg 754

Creotz Ediciones SL (Spain) *Tel:* 986 498 628 *E-mail:* info@creotz.com *Web Site:* www.creotz.com, pg 637

Editions Crepin-Leblond (France) *Tel:* 03 25 03 87 48 *Fax:* 03 25 03 87 40 *Web Site:* www.crepin-leblond.fr, pg 162

Editora Crescer (Brazil) *Tel:* (031) 3221-9235 *Fax:* (031) 3227-0729 *E-mail:* editoracrescer@editoracrescer.com. br *Web Site:* www.editoracrescer.com.br, pg 80

Cressrelles Publishing Co Ltd (United Kingdom) *Tel:* (01684) 540154 *Web Site:* www.cressrelles.co.uk, pg 754

Rupert Crew Ltd (United Kingdom) *Tel:* (020) 8346 3000 *Fax:* (020) 8346 3009 *E-mail:* info@rupertcrew. co.uk *Web Site:* www.rupertcrew.co.uk, pg 1240

Le Cri Edition (Belgium) *Tel:* (02) 646 65 33 *Fax:* (02) 646 66 07 *E-mail:* lecri@skynet.be *Web Site:* www. lecri.be, pg 65

Crime Writers' Association (CWA) (United Kingdom) *E-mail:* director@thecwa.co.uk; secretary@thecwa.co. uk *Web Site:* thecwa.co.uk, pg 1395

Crimson Publishing Ltd (United Kingdom) *Tel:* (020) 8334 1600 *Fax:* (020) 8334 1601 *E-mail:* info@ crimsonpublishing.co.uk *Web Site:* www. crimsonpublishing.co.uk, pg 754

Edizioni Crisalide (Italy) *Tel:* (0771) 64463 *Fax:* (0771) 639121 *E-mail:* crisalide@crisalide.com *Web Site:* www.crisalide.com, pg 436

Librerias de Cristal SA de CV (Mexico) *Tel:* (0155) 5564 4100; (0155) 5574 6499 *Toll Free Tel:* 01-800-849-29-86 *Fax:* (0155) 5564 4100 *E-mail:* ventas@ libreriasdecristal.com, pg 1434

Ediciones Cristiandad (Spain) *Tel:* 91 781 9970 *Fax:* 91 781 9977 *E-mail:* info@edicionescristiandad.es *Web Site:* www.edicionescristiandad.es, pg 638

Cristy's Atelier (Hong Kong) *Tel:* 2541 8609, pg 1277

Editorial Critica SA (Spain) *Tel:* 93 496 70 31 *E-mail:* editorial@ed-critica.es *Web Site:* www. planetadelibros.com/editorial-editorial-critica-1.html, pg 638

Critics' Circle (United Kingdom) *Tel:* (020) 7732 9636 *Web Site:* criticscircle.org.uk, pg 1502

Critiques Livres SAS (France) *Tel:* 01 43 60 39 10, pg 1414

Crius Group (Belgium) *Tel:* (015) 750 750 *Fax:* (015) 750 751 *E-mail:* info@crius-group.com *Web Site:* www.crius-group.com, pg 1273, 1317

Croatian ISBN Agency (Croatia) *Tel:* (01) 616 4288 *Fax:* (01) 616 4186 *E-mail:* isbn@nsk.hr *Web Site:* www.nsk.hr/isbn, pg 1368

Studia Croatica (Argentina) *Tel:* (011) 4771-4954 *Fax:* (011) 4771-4954 *E-mail:* studiacroatica@gmail. com *Web Site:* www.studiacroatica.org, pg 5

Editions La Croisee des Chemins (Morocco) *Tel:* 0522 279 987 *Fax:* 0565 795 454 *E-mail:* editionslacroiseedeschemins@gmail.com *Web Site:* www.lacroiseedeschemins.ma, pg 526

Comite international de la Croix-Rouge (CICR) (Switzerland) *Tel:* (022) 734 60 01 *Fax:* (022) 733 20 57 *E-mail:* shop@icrc.org (publications & films) *Web Site:* www.icrc.org, pg 692

Paul H Crompton Ltd (United Kingdom) *Tel:* (020) 8780 1063 *Fax:* (020) 8780 1063 *E-mail:* cromptonph@aol. com, pg 754

Croner (United Kingdom) *Tel:* (020) 8547 3333 *E-mail:* enquiries@croner.co.uk *Web Site:* croner.co. uk, pg 754

Editorial Croquis (Argentina) *Tel:* (011) 4393 1194 *E-mail:* info@editorialcroquis.com *Web Site:* www. editorialcroquis.com, pg 5

Cross Cult (Germany) *Tel:* (07141) 64 29 22 1 *Fax:* (07141) 64 29 22 3 *E-mail:* info@cross-cult.de; presse@cross-cult.de *Web Site:* www.cross-cult.de, pg 228

Crossing Press (Australia) *Tel:* (02) 4782 4984 *Fax:* (02) 4782 4984 *E-mail:* sales@crossingpress.com.au *Web Site:* www.crossingpress.com.au, pg 22

Crotona Verlag GmbH (Germany) *Tel:* (08075) 91 32 74 *Fax:* (08075) 91 32 75 *E-mail:* kontakt@crotona.de *Web Site:* www.crotona.de, pg 228

Crown House Publishing Ltd (United Kingdom) *Tel:* (01267) 211345 *Fax:* (0844) 500 7211 *E-mail:* books@crownhouse.co.uk *Web Site:* www. crownhouse.co.uk, pg 754

The Crowood Press Ltd (United Kingdom) *Tel:* (01672) 520320 *Fax:* (01672) 520280 *E-mail:* enquiries@ crowood.com *Web Site:* www.crowood.com; www. facebook.com/TheCrowoodPress; twitter.com/ crowoodpress, pg 754

Crucible Publishers (United Kingdom) *Tel:* (01373) 834900 *Fax:* (01373) 834900 *E-mail:* cruciblepublishers@gmail.com *Web Site:* www.cruciblepublishers.com, pg 755

Editorial Cruilla SA (Spain) *Tel:* 902 12 33 36; 932 922 172 *Fax:* 902 241 222 *E-mail:* contacte@cruilla. com *Web Site:* www.cruilla.cat; www.llegircruilla.cat, pg 638

La Crujia Ediciones (Argentina) *Tel:* (011) 4375 0376; (011) 4375 0664, pg 5

CRW Publishing Ltd (United Kingdom) *Tel:* (01367) 850448 *Web Site:* www.collectors-library.com, pg 755

Crymogea ehf (Iceland) *Tel:* 511 0910 *E-mail:* crymogea@crymogea.is *Web Site:* www. crymogea.is, pg 372

CSIR Information Services (South Africa) *Tel:* (012) 841 2911 *E-mail:* enquiries@csir.co.za *Web Site:* www.csir. co.za, pg 1630

CSIR-National Institute of Science Communication & Information Resources (CSIR-NISCAIR) (India) *Tel:* (011) 25846301; (011) 25846304; (011) 25846305; (011) 25846306; (011) 25846307 *Fax:* (011) 25847062 *E-mail:* sales@niscair.res.in *Web Site:* www.niscair.res.in, pg 380

CSIR-National Institute of Science Communication & Information Resources (CSIR-NISCAIR) (India) *Tel:* (011) 25846301; (011) 25846304; (011) 25846305; (011) 25846306; (011) 25846307 *Fax:* (011) 25847062 *E-mail:* director@niscair.res.in *Web Site:* www.niscair.res.in, pg 1250

CSIRO (Australia) *Tel:* (03) 9545 2176 *Toll Free Tel:* 1300 363 400 *Fax:* (03) 9545 2175 *E-mail:* csiroenquiries@csiro.au *Web Site:* www.csiro. au, pg 1574

CSIRO Publishing (Australia) *Tel:* (03) 9545 8400 *Fax:* (03) 9545 8555 *E-mail:* publishing@csiro.au; publishing.sales@csiro.au *Web Site:* www.publish. csiro.au, pg 22

CSS Bookshops Ltd (Nigeria) *Tel:* (01) 462 2593 *E-mail:* info@cssbookshopslimited.com *Web Site:* www.cssbookshopslimited.com, pg 1439

CSS Bookshops Ltd, Printing & Publishing Division (Nigeria) *Tel:* (01) 462 2593 *E-mail:* info@ cssbookshopslimited.com *Web Site:* www. cssbookshopslimited.com, pg 551

CTBI Publications (United Kingdom) *Tel:* (0845) 680 6851 *Fax:* (0845) 680 6852 *E-mail:* info@ctbi.org.uk *Web Site:* www.ctbi.org.uk, pg 755

C3 Publishing Co (South Korea) *Tel:* (02) 2661 2811 *Fax:* (02) 2661 2456 *E-mail:* biz@c3p.kr (distribution); editor@c3p.kr (editorial); subs@c3p.kr (subscriptions) *Web Site:* www.c3p.kr, pg 621

CTIE-Division Imprimes et Fournitures de Bureau (Luxembourg) *Tel:* 247-73000 *Fax:* 40 08 81 *E-mail:* hotline-ifb@ctie.etat.lu *Web Site:* www.ctie-ifb.etat.lu, pg 504

CTL-Presse (Germany) *Tel:* (040) 3990 2223 *Fax:* (040) 3990 2224 *E-mail:* mail@ctl-presse.de *Web Site:* www.ctl-presse.de, pg 228

CTP Printers Cape Town (South Africa) *Tel:* (021) 929 6200 *Fax:* (021) 939 1559 *E-mail:* ctp@ctpprinters.co. za; info@ctpprinters.co.za *Web Site:* www.ctpprinters. co.za, pg 1284

CTP Printers Cape Town (South Africa) *Tel:* (021) 929 6200 *Fax:* (021) 939 1559 *E-mail:* ctp@ctpprinters.co. za *Web Site:* www.ctpprinters.co.za, pg 1334

Cuadernos del Vigia (Spain) *Tel:* 958 210 444; 615 114 177 *E-mail:* editorial@cuadernosdelvigia.com *Web Site:* www.acceda.com/host/cuadernosdelvigia/ index.htm, pg 638

Editorial Cuarto Propio (Chile) *Tel:* (02) 279 265 18 *Fax:* (02) 279 265 20 *E-mail:* produccioneditorial@ tie.cl *Web Site:* www.cuartopropio.cl, pg 98

Editorial Cuatro Vientos (Chile) *Tel:* (02) 2672 9226; (02) 2695 4477 *Fax:* (02) 2673 2153 *E-mail:* editorial@cuatrovientos.cl *Web Site:* www. cuatrovientos.cl, pg 98

Ediciones Cubanas (Cuba) *Tel:* (07) 861-3283 *E-mail:* libro@edicuba.artex.cu *Web Site:* www. edicionescubanas.net, pg 1411

Cubola Productions (Belize) *Tel:* 823 2083 *Fax:* 823 2240 *E-mail:* cubolabz@btl.com; sales@cubola.com *Web Site:* www.cubola.com, pg 74

CUEC Editrice (Cooperativa Universitaria Editrice Cagliaritana) (Italy) *Tel:* 070271573 *Fax:* 070271573 *E-mail:* info@cuec.eu *Web Site:* www.cuec.eu, pg 436

Cuento de Luz (Spain) *Tel:* 913 51 01 35 *E-mail:* info@ cuentodeluz.com *Web Site:* www.cuentodeluz.com, pg 638

Editions Cujas (France) *Tel:* 01 44 24 24 36 *Fax:* 01 44 24 24 38 *Web Site:* www.cujas.fr, pg 162

Cultur Prospectiv Edition (Switzerland) *Tel:* (044) 260 69 01 *Fax:* (044) 260 69 29 *Web Site:* www. culturprospectiv.ch, pg 692

Cultura bvba (Belgium) *Tel:* (09) 369 15 95 *Fax:* (09) 369 59 25 *E-mail:* info@cultura.be; cultura@cultura-net.com *Web Site:* www.cultura.be, pg 1273, 1317

Editora Cultura Crista (Brazil) *Tel:* (011) 3207-7099 *Toll Free Tel:* 0800 014 1963 (sales) *Fax:* (011) 3209-1255 *E-mail:* cep@cep.org.br *Web Site:* www. editoraculturacrista.com.br, pg 80

Editorial Cultura (Guatemala) *Tel:* 22395000 (ext 3592) *E-mail:* editorialcultura@mcd.gob.gt *Web Site:* www. mcd.gob.gt/arte/editorial-cultura, pg 361

Livraria Cultura (Brazil) *Tel:* (011) 3170-4033 *Fax:* (011) 3285-4457 *E-mail:* ventascorporativas@ livrariacultura.com.br *Web Site:* www.livrariacultura. com.br, pg 1407

Editora Cultura Medica Ltda (Brazil) *Tel:* (021) 2567-3888 *Fax:* (021) 3259-5443 *E-mail:* cultura@ culturamedica.com.br *Web Site:* culturamedica.com. br/wp/, pg 80

Libreria Cultural Panamena SA (Panama) *Tel:* 223-6267; 223-5628 *Fax:* 223-7280 *E-mail:* lacultural@ cwpanama.net *Web Site:* www.libreriacultural.com, pg 1442

Cultural Relics Press (China) *Tel:* (010) 64029006; (010) 64027424 *Fax:* (010) 64010698 *E-mail:* club@wenwu. com (sales); honglou800@aliyun.com *Web Site:* www. wenwu.com, pg 104

Ediciones Culturales Internacionales SA de CV (ECISA) (Mexico) *Tel:* (0155) 5250-8099 *Toll Free Tel:* 01 800 024 90 86 *Fax:* (0155) 5531-5176 *E-mail:* atencionaclientes@ediciones.com.mx *Web Site:* www.ediciones.com.mx, pg 515

Edicions do Cumio (Spain) *Tel:* 986 761 045 *Fax:* 986 761 022 *E-mail:* cumio@cumio.com *Web Site:* www. cumio.com, pg 638

Ediciones La Cupula SL (Spain) *Tel:* 932 682 805 *Fax:* 932 680 765 *E-mail:* consultas@lacupula.com *Web Site:* www.lacupula.com, pg 638

Curacao Public Library Foundation (Curacao) *Tel:* (09) 434 52 00 *Fax:* (09) 465 62 47 *E-mail:* publiclibrary@onenet.an *Web Site:* www. curacaopubliclibrary.an, pg 1650

Edizioni Curci SRL (Italy) *Tel:* (02) 760361 *Fax:* (02) 76014504 *E-mail:* info@edizionicurci.it *Web Site:* www.edizionicurci.it, pg 436

Curiad (United Kingdom) *Tel:* (01286) 882166 *E-mail:* curiad@curiad.co.uk *Web Site:* www.curiad. co.uk, pg 755

Curial Edicions Catalanes SA (Spain) *Tel:* 93 760 22 87 *E-mail:* info@curial.cat *Web Site:* www.curial.cat, pg 638

Currency Press (Australia) *Tel:* (02) 9319 5877 *Fax:* (02) 9319 3649 *E-mail:* enquiries@currency.com.au; orders@currency.com.au *Web Site:* www.currency.com. au, pg 22

Current Books (India) *Tel:* (0481) 2563114; (0481) 2301614 *E-mail:* info@dcbooks.com *Web Site:* www. dcbooks.com; www.currentbooks.com, pg 380

Current Pacific Ltd (New Zealand) *Tel:* (09) 480-1388 *E-mail:* info@cplnz.com; cpl_nz@hotmail.com *Web Site:* www.cplnz.com, pg 545

Current Technical Literature Co Pvt Ltd (CTL) (India) *Tel:* (022) 22617616; (022) 22611045 *Fax:* (022) 22679786 *E-mail:* infomumbai@ctlindia.org *Web Site:* www.ctlindia.org, pg 1422

James Currey (United Kingdom) *Tel:* (01394) 610 600 *Fax:* (01394) 610 316 *E-mail:* trading@boydell.co.uk; marketing@boydell.co.uk *Web Site:* boydellandbrewer. com/james-currey, pg 755

Curriculum Press (Australia) *Tel:* (03) 9207 9600 *Toll Free Tel:* 1300 780 545 (within Australia) *Fax:* (03) 9910 9800 *E-mail:* sales@esa.edu.au *Web Site:* www. curriculumpress.edu.au, pg 22

Eleanor Curtain Publishing (Australia) *Tel:* (03) 9867 4880 *Fax:* (03) 9820 4696 *E-mail:* info@ecpublishing. com.au; orders@ecpublishing.com.au *Web Site:* www. ecpublishing.com.au, pg 23

Curtea Veche Publishing (Romania) *Tel:* (021) 260 22 87; (021) 222 57 26; (021) 222 47 65 *Fax:* (021) 223 16 88 *E-mail:* redactie@curteaveche.ro (editorial); marketing@curteaveche.ro; distributie@curteaveche. ro; pr@curteaveche.ro *Web Site:* www.curteaveche.ro, pg 586

Curtis Brown Group Ltd (United Kingdom) *Tel:* (020) 7393 4400 *Fax:* (020) 7393 4401 *E-mail:* cb@ curtisbrown.co.uk *Web Site:* www.curtisbrown.co.uk, pg 1241

Cuspide Libros SA (Argentina) *Tel:* (011) 4322 8868 *Fax:* (011) 4322 3456 *E-mail:* ventas@cuspide.com; info@cuspide.com *Web Site:* www.cuspide.com, pg 1401

Custom Studios (United States) *Tel:* 845-365-0414 *Toll Free Tel:* 800-631-1362 *Fax:* 845-365-0864 *E-mail:* customusa@aol.com *Web Site:* customstudios. com, pg 1288

Cute Ediciones (Argentina) *Tel:* (011) 4824 5694 *E-mail:* info@cuteediciones.com.ar *Web Site:* www. cuteediciones.com.ar, pg 5

The Cutting Edge (United Kingdom) *Tel:* (01304) 371721 *Web Site:* www.thecuttingedge.biz, pg 1241

Cutting Edge Press (United Kingdom) *Tel:* (020) 8731 9040 *E-mail:* info@cuttingedgepress.co.uk; sales@ cuttingedgepress.co.uk; rights@cuttingedgepress.co.uk; submissions@cuttingedgepress.co.uk *Web Site:* www. cuttingedgepress.co.uk, pg 755

Cuttington University College Library (Liberia) *E-mail:* info@cuttingtonuniversity.edu.lr *Web Site:* cuttinguniversity.edu.lr/library.html, pg 1609

Cv Publications (United Kingdom) *Tel:* (020) 8943 9697 *E-mail:* cvpub@ision.co.uk *Web Site:* www. tracksdirectory.ision.co.uk, pg 755

Cvor (Croatia) *Tel:* (043) 244 572; (043) 244 050; (043) 221 773 *Fax:* (043) 243 337 *E-mail:* cvor@cvor.hr *Web Site:* www.cvor.hr, pg 119

Cwlwm Cyhoeddwyr Cymru (United Kingdom), pg 1395

CWR (United Kingdom) *Tel:* (01252) 784 700 *Fax:* (01252) 784 734 *Web Site:* www.cwr.org.uk, pg 755

Cyberprint Group (Thailand) *Tel:* (02) 641-9135-8 *Fax:* (02) 641-9139 *E-mail:* info@cyberprint.co.th; digital@cyberprint.th *Web Site:* www.cyberprint.co.th, pg 1285, 1335

Cyhoeddiadau Barddas (United Kingdom) *Tel:* (01678) 520378 *Fax:* (01678) 521051 *Web Site:* www.barddas. com, pg 755

Cyhoeddiadau'r Gair (United Kingdom) *Tel:* (01766) 819120 *Web Site:* ysgolsul.com, pg 756

CYPI Press (United Kingdom) *Tel:* (020) 3178 7279 *Fax:* (020) 8626 7064 *E-mail:* sales@cypi.net; editor@ cypi.net *Web Site:* www.cypi.net, pg 756

Cyprus Department of Antiquities Library (Cyprus) *Tel:* 22865888 *Fax:* 22303148 *E-mail:* antiquitiesdept@da.mcw.gov.cy *Web Site:* www.mcw.gov.cy/da, pg 1585

Cyprus Library (Cyprus) *Tel:* 22303180; 22676118 *Fax:* 22304532 *E-mail:* cypruslibrary@cytanet.com.cy *Web Site:* www.cypruslibrary.gov.cy, pg 1585

Cyprus Registration Center (Cyprus) *Tel:* 22818431; 22818429 *Fax:* 22304532 *E-mail:* isbncentre48@ yahoo.gr *Web Site:* www.cypruslibrary.gov.cy, pg 1369

Wydawnictwo Czarna Owca Sp z oo (Poland) *Tel:* (22) 616 12 72 (orders); (22) 616 29 20 (editorial); (22) 616 29 36 (sales) *E-mail:* sklep@czarnaowca.pl

(orders); redakcja@czarnaowca.pl (editorial); handel@ czarnaowca.pl (sales) *Web Site:* www.czarnaowca.pl, pg 568

Wydawnictwo Czarne (Poland) *Tel:* (18) 351 00 70 *Fax:* (18) 352 04 75 *E-mail:* redakcja@czarne.com.pl *Web Site:* czarne.com.pl, pg 568

Czernin Verlags GmbH (Austria) *Tel:* (01) 403 35 63 *Fax:* (01) 403 35 63-15 *E-mail:* office@czernin-verlag. com *Web Site:* www.czernin-verlag.com, pg 46

Spoldzielnia Wydawnicza "Czytelnik" (Poland) *Tel:* (22) 58 31 400; (22) 628 14 41 *Fax:* (22) 628 31 78 *E-mail:* sekretariat@czytelnik.pl; redakcja@czytelnik. pl *Web Site:* www.czytelnik.pl, pg 568

D & K Group Inc (United States) *Tel:* 847-956-0160 *Toll Free Tel:* 800-632-2314 *Fax:* 847-956-8214 *E-mail:* info@dkgroup.net *Web Site:* www.dkgroup. com, pg 1339, 1349, 1356

Ediciones Dabar SA de CV (Mexico) *Tel:* (0155) 5594-0143; (0155) 5603-3630; (0155) 5673-8855 *Fax:* (0155) 5603-3674 *E-mail:* ventas@dabar.com.mx *Web Site:* www.dabar.com.mx, pg 515

DAC Editions (Spain) *E-mail:* art7@dac-editions.com *Web Site:* www.dac-editions.com, pg 638

Editura Dacia (Romania) *Tel:* (0364) 149 797 *Fax:* (0364) 149 797 *Web Site:* edituradacia.ro, pg 586

DACO Verlag Guenter Blaese (Germany) *Tel:* (0711) 964 210 *Fax:* (0711) 964 2110 *E-mail:* info@daco-verlag.de *Web Site:* www.daco-verlag.de, pg 228

Armando Dado Editore (Switzerland) *Tel:* (091) 751 48 02 *Fax:* (091) 752 10 26 *E-mail:* info@editore.ch *Web Site:* www.editore.ch, pg 692

Daedalus Verlag (Germany) *Tel:* (0251) 23 13 55 *Fax:* (0251) 23 26 31 *E-mail:* info@daedalus-verlag.de *Web Site:* www.daedalus-verlag.de, pg 228

Daewonsa (South Korea) *Tel:* (02) 757-6717; (02) 757-6718; (02) 757-6719; (02) 757-6711 *Fax:* (02) 775-8043 *Web Site:* daewonsa.co.kr, pg 621

Dafolo Forlag (Denmark) *Tel:* 9620 6666 *Fax:* 9842 9711 *E-mail:* lkm@dafolo.dk; dafolo@dafolo.dk *Web Site:* www.dafolo.dk, pg 135

Dagbladet Borsen A/S (Denmark) *Tel:* 33 32 01 02; 72 42 34 00 (editorial) *Fax:* 33 12 24 45 *E-mail:* redaktionen@borsen.dk *Web Site:* www. borsen.dk, pg 135

Dagmar Dreves Verlag (Germany) *Tel:* (05086) 987804; (0175) 7229819 (cell) *Fax:* (05086) 987806 *E-mail:* info@dagmar-dreves-verlag.de *Web Site:* www.dagmar-dreves-verlag.de, pg 229

Dagraja Press (Australia) *Tel:* (02) 6247 0782; (02) 6262 7533, pg 23

Dahlia Books HB (Sweden) *Tel:* (070) 897 02 17, pg 681

Dai Nippon Printing Co Ltd (Japan) *Tel:* (03) 3266-2111 *Web Site:* www.dnp.co.jp, pg 1329

Daiichi Shuppan Co Ltd (Japan) *Tel:* (03) 3291-4576; (03) 3291-4577 *Fax:* (03) 3291-4579; (03) 3291-4415 *E-mail:* daiichi-eigyo@my.email.ne.jp *Web Site:* www. daiichi-shuppan.co.jp, pg 475

Daik Press (Kazakhstan) *Tel:* (8727) 394-40-45 *Fax:* (8727) 394-42-32 *E-mail:* daikpress@mail.ru; daikpress@inbox.ru *Web Site:* www.daik-press.com, pg 492

Le Daily-Bul (Belgium) *Tel:* (064) 22 29 73 *Fax:* (064) 22 29 73 *E-mail:* dailybulandco@lalouviere.be *Web Site:* www.dailybulandco.be, pg 65

Daimon Verlag AG (Switzerland) *Tel:* (055) 412 22 66 *Fax:* (055) 412 22 31 *E-mail:* daimon@daimon.ch *Web Site:* www.daimon.ch, pg 692

Dainippon Tosho Publishing Co Ltd (Japan) *Tel:* (03) 5940-8670 (administration); (03) 5940-8675 *Fax:* (03) 5940-8682 (administration); (03) 5940-8688 *Web Site:* www.dainippon-tosho.co.jp, pg 475

Dajama Vydavatel'stvo (Slovakia) *Tel:* (02) 44631702 *Fax:* (02) 44631702 *E-mail:* info@dajama.sk *Web Site:* www.dajama.sk, pg 608

Dalian Maritime University Press LLC (China) *Tel:* (0411) 84728394; (0411) 84729665; (0411) 84723216 *Fax:* (0411) 84727996 *E-mail:* dmupress@163.com *Web Site:* www.dmupress.com, pg 104

Dalian University of Technology Library (China) *Tel:* (0411) 84708629 *E-mail:* office@dlut.edu.cn *Web Site:* www.lib.dlut.edu.cn, pg 1582

Editions Dalloz (France) *Tel:* 01 40 64 54 54 *Fax:* 01 40 64 54 97 *E-mail:* ventes@dalloz.fr *Web Site:* editions-dalloz.fr; www.dalloz.fr, pg 163

Rafael Dalmau Editor (Spain) *Tel:* 93 317 33 38 *Fax:* 93 317 33 38 *E-mail:* rafaeldalmau@rafaeldalmaueditor.cat *Web Site:* www.rafaeldalmaueditor.cat, pg 638

Ediciones Daly SL (Spain) *Tel:* 952 58 25 69 *Fax:* 952 58 36 19 *E-mail:* daly@edicionesdaly.es *Web Site:* www.edicionesdaly.es, pg 638

Damanhur (Italy) *Tel:* (0124) 512236 *Fax:* (0124) 512371 *E-mail:* welcome@damanhur.it; university@damanhur.it *Web Site:* www.damanhur.org, pg 436

Damdi Publishing Co (South Korea) *Tel:* (02) 900-0652 *Fax:* (02) 900-0657 *E-mail:* dd@damdi.co.kr; m.damdi_book@naver.com *Web Site:* www.damdi.co.kr, pg 621

Dami International (Italy) *Tel:* (02) 575471 *Fax:* (02) 57547503 *Web Site:* www.dami-int.com, pg 436

Damiani Editore (Italy) *Tel:* (051) 6356811 *Fax:* (051) 6347188 *E-mail:* info@damianieditore.com; press@damianieditore.com *Web Site:* www.damianieditore.it, pg 436

Damla Yayinevi (Turkey) *Tel:* (0212) 514 28 28 *Fax:* (0212) 514 28 34 *E-mail:* iletisim@damlayayinevi.com.tr *Web Site:* www.damlayayinevi.com.tr; www.damlapublishing.com, pg 720

Dana Verlag (Germany) *Tel:* (05468) 1813 *Fax:* (05468) 239 *E-mail:* danaverlag@t-online.de *Web Site:* www.dana-verlag.de, pg 229

Dance Books Ltd (United Kingdom) *Tel:* (01420) 525 299 *Web Site:* www.dancebooks.co.uk, pg 756

Editions Dangles (France) *Tel:* 05 61 00 09 86 *Fax:* 05 61 00 09 83 *E-mail:* contact@piktos.fr *Web Site:* editions-dangles.fr; www.piktos.fr, pg 163

Danish Arts Foundation (Denmark) *Tel:* 33 95 42 00; 33 73 33 73 *E-mail:* post@slks.dk *Web Site:* www.kunst.dk, pg 1369

Dankook University Press (South Korea) *Tel:* (031) 1899-3700 *Web Site:* www.dankook.ac.kr, pg 621

Danmarks Biblioteksforening (Denmark) *Tel:* 3325 0935 *Fax:* 3325 7900 *E-mail:* db@db.dk *Web Site:* www.db.dk, pg 1650

Danmarks Forskningsbiblioteksforening (Denmark) *Tel:* 89 46 22 07; 4220 2177 (cell) *E-mail:* df@statsbiblioteket.dk *Web Site:* www.dfdf.dk, pg 1650

Danmarks Forvaltningshojskole (Denmark) *Tel:* 38 14 52 00 *Fax:* 38 14 53 45, pg 135

Danmarks Statistik Biblioteket (Denmark) *Tel:* 39 17 39 17; 39 17 30 30 *Fax:* 39 17 30 03; 39 17 39 99 *E-mail:* dst@dst.dk; bib@dst.dk *Web Site:* www.dst.dk, pg 1586

Danmarks Tekniske Informationscenter (DTIC) (Denmark) *Tel:* 4525 7200; 4525 7250 *Fax:* 4588 3040 *E-mail:* bibliotek@dtu.dk *Web Site:* www.bibliotek.dtu.dk, pg 1586

G D'Anna Casa Editrice SpA (Italy) *Tel:* (055) 93 36 600 *Fax:* (055) 93 36 650 *E-mail:* scrivo@danna.it; proposte.editorial@danna.it; curriculum@danna.it (sales); editoriale@danna.it *Web Site:* www.danna.it, pg 437

Hristo G Danov EOOD (Bulgaria) *Tel:* (032) 632552, pg 95

Dansk Biblioteks Center A/S (DBC) (Denmark) *Tel:* 44 86 77 77 *E-mail:* dbc@dbc.dk *Web Site:* www.dbc.dk, pg 135

Dansk Forfatterforening (Denmark) *Tel:* 32 95 51 00 *Fax:* 32 54 01 15 *E-mail:* df@danskforfatterforening.dk *Web Site:* www.danskforfatterforening.dk, pg 1493

Dansk ISBN - Kontor (the Danish ISBN Agency) (Denmark) *Tel:* 44 86 77 79 *Fax:* 44 86 76 93 *E-mail:* isbn@dbc.dk *Web Site:* www.isbn.dk, pg 1369

Dansk Musikbiblioteks Forening (DMBF) (Denmark) *Tel:* 56672800 *E-mail:* sekretariat@dmbf.nu *Web Site:* www.dmbf.nu, pg 1650

Dansk Psykologisk Forlag A/S (Denmark) *Tel:* 4546 0050 *E-mail:* info@dpf.dk *Web Site:* www.dpf.dk, pg 135

Dansk Teknologisk Institut, Forlaget (Denmark) *Tel:* 72 20 20 00 *Fax:* 72 20 20 19 *E-mail:* info@teknologisk.dk *Web Site:* www.teknologisk.dk; www.dti.dk, pg 135

Danske Forlag (Denmark) *Tel:* 33 15 66 88 *E-mail:* info@danskeforlag.dk; info@danishpublishers.dk *Web Site:* www.danskeforlag.dk, pg 1369

Det Danske Sprog - og Litteraturselskab (Denmark) *Tel:* 33 13 06 60 *Fax:* 33 14 06 08 *E-mail:* sekretariat@dsl.dk *Web Site:* dsl.dk, pg 1493

Libreria Dante di Longo (Italy) *Tel:* (0544) 33500 *E-mail:* libreriadanteravenna@gmail.com *Web Site:* www.facebook.com/LibreriaDanteRavenna, pg 1428

Daphne Distributie NV (Belgium) *Tel:* (09) 221 45 91 *Fax:* (09) 220 16 12 *E-mail:* info@daphne.be *Web Site:* www.daphne.be, pg 65

Daphnis-Verlag (Switzerland) *Tel:* (044) 2025271 *Fax:* (044) 2014231, pg 692

Dar Al-Farabi (Lebanon) *Tel:* (01) 301461; (01) 301138 *Fax:* (01) 307775 *E-mail:* info@dar-alfarabi.com; sales@dar-alfarabi.com; contact@dar-alfarabi.com *Web Site:* www.dar-alfarabi.com, pg 497

Dar Al-Fikr (Syria) *Tel:* (011) 2211166 *Fax:* (011) 2239716 *E-mail:* fikr@fikr.net; mailus@fikr.net *Web Site:* www.fikr.com, pg 710

Dar Al Hadaek (Lebanon) *Tel:* (01) 840389 *Fax:* (01) 840390 *E-mail:* alhadaek@alhadaekgroup.com *Web Site:* www.alhadaekgroup.com, pg 497

Dar Al Hilal Publishing Institution (Egypt) *Tel:* (02) 3625450; (02) 3625451, pg 143

Dar Al-Kitab Al-Lubnani (Lebanon) *Tel:* (01) 735731 *Fax:* (01) 351433 *E-mail:* info@daralkitabmasri.com *Web Site:* www.daralkitabalmasri.com, pg 497

Dar Al-Kitab Al-Masri (Egypt) *Tel:* (02) 3922168 *Fax:* (02) 3924657 *E-mail:* info@daralkitabalmasri.com *Web Site:* www.daralkitabalmasri.com, pg 143

Dar Al Maaref (Egypt) *Tel:* (02) 25777077 *Fax:* (02) 25744999 *E-mail:* info@daralmaaref.com *Web Site:* www.daralmaaref.com, pg 143

Dar Al-Maaref (Lebanon) *Tel:* (01) 653852 *Fax:* (01) 653857 *E-mail:* info@daralmaaref.com; al_maaref@hotmail.com *Web Site:* www.daralmaaref.com, pg 498

Dar Al Maarifah (Syria) *Tel:* (098) 635559 *Fax:* (011) 2241615 *E-mail:* info@easyquran.com *Web Site:* www.easyquran.com, pg 710

Dar Al-Mirrikh (Saudi Arabia) *Tel:* (011) 4647531; (011) 4658523; (011) 2934096; (011) 2934091 (ext 24) *Fax:* (011) 4657939, pg 599

Dar Al Moualef Publishing House (Lebanon) *Tel:* (01) 824203 *Fax:* (01) 825815 *E-mail:* info@daralmoualef.com *Web Site:* www.daralmoualef.com, pg 498

Dar Al Muna (Sweden) *Tel:* (08) 21 05 65 *Fax:* (08) 622 61 51 *E-mail:* info@daralmuna.com *Web Site:* www.daralmuna.com, pg 681

Dar Al-Rayah for Publishing & Distribution (Saudi Arabia) *Tel:* (011) 4454746 *Fax:* (011) 4931869, pg 599

Dar Al-Ulum Publishers, Booksellers & Distributors (Saudi Arabia) *Tel:* (011) 4777121 *Fax:* (011) 4793446, pg 1446

Dar alnahda alarabia (fb) (Egypt) *Tel:* (02) 392 6931 *Fax:* (02) 395 6150 *E-mail:* info@daralnahda.com *Web Site:* www.daralnahda.com, pg 143

Editions Dar An-Nahar (Lebanon) *Tel:* (01) 747 620 *Fax:* (01) 747 623 *E-mail:* darannahar@darannahar.com; info@darannahar.com *Web Site:* www.darannahar.com; www.annahar.com, pg 498

Dar el Afaq Sarl (Algeria) *Tel:* (021) 79 16 44 *Fax:* (021) 79 16 44 *E-mail:* afaq.edition@gmail.com, pg 1

Dar El Ilm Lilmalayin (Lebanon) *Tel:* (01) 306666 *Fax:* (01) 701657 *E-mail:* info@malayin.com *Web Site:* www.malayin.com, pg 498

Dar el Maaref Edition (Tunisia) *Tel:* 73 309 235; 24 241 395 *Fax:* 73 309 472 *E-mail:* edition@darelmaaref.com.tn *Web Site:* www.darelmaaref.com/edition/fr, pg 717

Dar El Shorouk (Egypt) *Tel:* (02) 24023399 *Fax:* (02) 24037567 *E-mail:* dar@shorouk.com *Web Site:* www.shorouk.com, pg 143

The Dar es Salaam Bookshop (Tanzania) *Tel:* (0755) 798124, pg 1453

Dar es Salaam University Press Ltd (DUP) (Tanzania) *Web Site:* udsm.ac.tz, pg 714

Dar Nachr Al Maarifa (Morocco) *Tel:* 05 37 79 79 63; 05 37 79 57 02; 05 37 79 79 64; 05 37 79 69 38; 05 37 79 69 14 *Fax:* 05 37 79 03 43 *Web Site:* www.facebook.com/darnachralmaarifa, pg 526

Dar Onboz (Lebanon) *Tel:* (01) 380 533 *Fax:* (01) 380 533, pg 498

Dareschta Consulting und Handels GmbH (DarCon) (Germany) *Tel:* (0933) 3389814 *Fax:* (0933) 3389815 *Web Site:* www.darcon.de; darcon.secu.net, pg 229

Darf Publishers Ltd (United Kingdom) *Tel:* (020) 7431 7009 *Fax:* (020) 7431 7655 *E-mail:* info@darfpublishers.co.uk; orders@darfpublishers.co.uk *Web Site:* darfpublishers.co.uk, pg 756

Dargaud (France) *E-mail:* contact@dargaud.fr *Web Site:* www.dargaud.com, pg 163

Dargenis UAB (Lithuania) *Tel:* (037) 205241 *Fax:* (037) 205241, pg 501

Jenny Darling & Associates Pty Ltd (Australia) *Tel:* (03) 9696 7750 *E-mail:* office@jennydarling.com.au (permissions) *Web Site:* jennydarling.com.au, pg 1223

Darton, Longman & Todd Ltd (United Kingdom) *Tel:* (020) 8875 0155 *Fax:* (020) 8875 0133 *E-mail:* editorial@darton-longman-todd.co.uk *Web Site:* www.darton-longman-todd.co.uk; www.dltbooks.com, pg 756

Das Arsenal Verlag fuer Kultur und Politik GmbH (Germany) *Tel:* (030) 3441827; (030) 34651360 *Fax:* (030) 34651362, pg 229

Dastane Ramchandra & Co (India) *Tel:* (020) 24478193 *E-mail:* drcopune@gmail.com, pg 381

Dastin SL (Spain) *Tel:* 91 637 52 54; 91 637 36 86 *Fax:* 91 636 12 56 *E-mail:* info@dastin.es *Web Site:* www.dastin.es, pg 638

DAT Publications (Israel) *Tel:* (03) 5071239 *Fax:* (03) 5070458 *E-mail:* dat@y-dat.co.il *Web Site:* www.y-dat.co.il, pg 417

DATAKONTEXT (Germany) *Tel:* (02234) 98949-30 *Fax:* (02234) 98949-32 *E-mail:* fachverlag@datakontext.com; tagungen@datakontext.com; info@datakontext.com *Web Site:* www.datakontext.com, pg 229

DataMap Europe Ltd (Bulgaria) *Tel:* (02) 951 54 50 *Toll Free Tel:* (0888) 492 172 *Fax:* (02) 951 58 24 *E-mail:* office@datamap.bg *Web Site:* www.datamap.bg, pg 95

Libreria DELSA (Spain) *Tel:* 91 435 74 21; 91 576 21 03 *Fax:* 91 578 28 11 *E-mail:* delsa@troa.es; nebli@troa.es *Web Site:* www.troa.es, pg 1450

Delta Alpha Publishing Ltd (United Kingdom) *Tel:* (020) 7359 1822 *Fax:* (020) 7359 1822 *Web Site:* www.deltaalpha.com, pg 757

Delta Books (Pty) Ltd (South Africa) *Tel:* (011) 601 8000; (011) 601 8088 (customer services) *Fax:* (011) 622 3553; (011) 601 8183 (customer services) *E-mail:* services@jonathanball.co.za; orders@jonathanball.co.za; jonathanballreturns@jonathanball.co.za (returns) *Web Site:* www.jonathanball.co.za; jonathanball.bookslive.co.za, pg 613

Editions Delta SA (Belgium) *Tel:* (02) 217 55 55 *E-mail:* editions.delta@gmail.com *Web Site:* www.delta-europe.be, pg 66

Delta Publications (Nigeria) Ltd (Nigeria) *Tel:* (042) 256595, pg 551

Delta Publishing (United Kingdom) *Tel:* (01306) 731770 *Fax:* (01306) 731770 *E-mail:* info@deltapublishing.co.uk *Web Site:* www.deltapublishing.co.uk, pg 757

Editions Delville (France) *Tel:* 05 61 00 09 86 *Fax:* 05 61 00 09 83 *E-mail:* contact@piktos.fr *Web Site:* www.editions-delville.fr; www.piktos.fr, pg 164

Demeter Editions (Tunisia) *Tel:* 71 94 52 42; 71 94 53 15 *Fax:* 71 94 51 99 *E-mail:* demeter@planet.tn, pg 717

Editorial Demipage (Spain) *Tel:* 91 563 88 67 *Fax:* 91 563 00 38 *E-mail:* madrid@demipage.com *Web Site:* www.demipage.com, pg 638, 1251

Dienst Openbare Bibliotheek Den Haag (Netherlands) *Tel:* (070) 353 44 55 *E-mail:* centralebibliotheek@bibliotheekdenhaag.nl *Web Site:* www.bibliotheekdenhaag.nl, pg 1616

Den Norske Bokhandlerforening (Norway) *Tel:* 22 39 68 00 *E-mail:* firmapost@bokhandlerforeningen.no *Web Site:* www.bokhandlerforeningen.no, pg 1385

Editions Denoel (France) *Tel:* 01 44 39 73 73 *Fax:* 01 44 39 73 90 *E-mail:* denoel@denoel.fr; rights@denoel.fr; presse@denoel.fr *Web Site:* www.denoel.fr, pg 164

Denor Press Ltd (United Kingdom) *Tel:* (07768) 855 995 *Fax:* (020) 8446 4504 *E-mail:* denorgroup@gmail.com *Web Site:* www.denorpress.com, pg 757

Denzel-Verlag (Austria) *Tel:* (0512) 586880 *Fax:* (0512) 586880 *E-mail:* denzel-verlag@web.de; denzel.verlag@yahoo.de *Web Site:* www.denzel-verlag.de, pg 47

Editorial Depalma SRL (Argentina) *Tel:* (011) 4371-7306 *Fax:* (011) 4371-6913, pg 6

Departamento de Publicaciones de la Universidad de la Republica (Uruguay) *Tel:* 2408 2566; 2408 9574 *E-mail:* infoed@edic.edu.uy *Web Site:* www.universidad.edu.uy, pg 848

Department of Archives, National Archives of the Bahamas (The Bahamas) *Tel:* (242) 393-2175; (242) 393-2855 *Fax:* (242) 393-2855 *E-mail:* archives@batelnet.bs *Web Site:* bahamasnationalarchives.bs, pg 1576

Department of Census & Statistics (Sri Lanka) *Tel:* (011) 2694666; (011) 2147488 (sales) *Fax:* (011) 2697634 *E-mail:* publication@statistics.gov.lk; data.requests@statistics.gov.lk (sales) *Web Site:* www.statistics.gov.lk, pg 677

Department of Environment & Heritage (OEH) (Australia) *Tel:* (02) 9995 5000 *Toll Free Tel:* 1300 361 967 *Fax:* (02) 9995 5999 *E-mail:* info@environment.nsw.gov.au *Web Site:* www.environment.nsw.gov.au, pg 23

Department of National Archives (Sri Lanka) *Tel:* (011) 2694523; (011) 2696917 *Fax:* (011) 2694419; (011) 2693309 *E-mail:* slnationalarchives@gmail.com *Web Site:* www.archives.gov.lk, pg 1633

Department of National Museums (Sri Lanka) *Tel:* (011) 2695366 *Fax:* (011) 2692092 *E-mail:* nmdep@slt.lk *Web Site:* www.museum.gov.lk, pg 677

Department of Science & Technology (South Africa) *Tel:* (012) 843 6300 *E-mail:* webmaster@dst.gov.za *Web Site:* www.dst.gov.za, pg 1630

Department of the National Library (Jordan) *Tel:* (06) 5662845; (06) 5662854; (06) 5662791; (06) 5662819; (06) 5662748; (06) 5662871; (06) 5662758 *Fax:* (06) 5662867 *E-mail:* nl@nl.gov.jo *Web Site:* www.nl.gov.jo, pg 1607

Der Hoerverlag GmbH (DHV) (Germany) *Tel:* (089) 21 06 940 *Toll Free Tel:* (0800) 500 33 22 *Fax:* (089) 21 06 94 15 *E-mail:* info@hoerverlag.de; kundenservice@randomhouse.de *Web Site:* www.hoerverlag.de; www.randomhouse.de/hoerverlag, pg 229

Editoriales de Derecho Reunidas SA (EDERSA) (Spain) *Tel:* 915 210 246, pg 638

Dergah Yayinlari (Turkey) *Tel:* (0212) 518 95 78 *Fax:* (0212) 518 95 81 *E-mail:* bilgi@dergahyayinlari.com *Web Site:* www.dergahyayinlari.com, pg 720

Derouck Geocart Edition (Belgium) *Tel:* (03) 760 14 60 *Fax:* (03) 760 15 29 *E-mail:* carto@derouckgeocart.com *Web Site:* www.derouckgeocart.com, pg 66

Editions Dervy (France) *Tel:* 01 43 36 41 05 *Web Site:* www.dervy-medicis.fr, pg 164

Editions Desclee de Brouwer (France) *Tel:* 01 40 46 54 00 *Fax:* 01 58 51 10 48 *Web Site:* www.editionsddb.fr, pg 164

Editorial Desclee De Brouwer SA (Spain) *Tel:* 944 246 843 *Fax:* 944 237 594 *E-mail:* info@edesclee.com; edicion@desclee.com *Web Site:* www.edesclee.com, pg 638

Desert Research Foundation of Namibia (DRFN) (Namibia) *Tel:* (061) 377 500 *Fax:* (061) 230 172 *E-mail:* drfn@drfn.org.na *Web Site:* drfn.org.na, pg 527

Design & Artists Copyright Society (DACS) (United Kingdom) *Tel:* (020) 7336 8811 *Fax:* (020) 7336 8822 *E-mail:* info@dacs.org.uk *Web Site:* www.dacs.org.uk, pg 1395

Design Media Publishing Co Ltd (Hong Kong) *Tel:* 6950 0355 *Fax:* 2505 0311 *E-mail:* dsdesignmedia@gmail.com, pg 364

Design Pavoni® Verlag (Germany) *Tel:* (02871) 2924176; (0172) 2918775 (cell) *Fax:* (02871) 43584 *E-mail:* pavoni1@web.de *Web Site:* www.pavoni1.de; www.design-pavoni-verlag.de, pg 230

Desina Verlag GmbH (Germany) *Tel:* (0441) 30498212 *Fax:* (0441) 30498213 *E-mail:* redaktion@desinaverlag.de *Web Site:* www.desinaverlag.de, pg 230

Desktop Miracles Inc (United States) *Tel:* 802-253-7900 *Toll Free Fax:* 888-293-2676 *Web Site:* www.desktopmiracles.com, pg 1288, 1349, 1356

Ediciones Desnivel SL (Spain) *Tel:* 913 602 242 *Fax:* 913 602 264 *E-mail:* edicionesdesnivel@desnivel.es; editorial@desnivel.com *Web Site:* www.edicionesdesnivel.com; www.desnivel.com, pg 639

Dessain et Tolra SA (France) *Tel:* 01 44 39 44 00 *E-mail:* livres-larousse@larousse.fr *Web Site:* www.editions-larousse.fr/catalogue/dessain-tolra.asp, pg 164

Destarte Lda (Portugal) *Tel:* 213475811; 213242960 *Fax:* 213475811 *E-mail:* destarte@vianw.pt, pg 1445

Destek Yayinevi (Turkey) *Tel:* (0212) 252 22 42 *Fax:* (0212) 252 22 43 *E-mail:* info@destekyayinlari.com *Web Site:* www.destekdukkan.com, pg 720

Ediciones Destino SA (Spain) *Tel:* 93 492 80 04 *E-mail:* edicionesdestino@edestino.es; comunicaciondestino@edestino.es *Web Site:* www.planetadelibros.com/editorial-ediciones-destino-7.html; www.planeta.es, pg 639

Izdatelstvo Detskaya Literatura (Russia) *Tel:* (495) 601-22-68 *Fax:* (495) 601-22-68 *E-mail:* dl@detlit.ru; tk@detlit.ru *Web Site:* www.detlit.ru, pg 593

Deusto (Spain) *Tel:* 93 492 69 56 *E-mail:* info@centrolibrospapf.es *Web Site:* www.planetadelibros.com/editorial-deusto-14.html, pg 639

Deuticke Verlag (Austria) *Tel:* (01) 505 76 61-0 *Fax:* (01) 505 76 61-10 *E-mail:* info@zsolnay.at *Web Site:* www.hanser-literaturverlage.de, pg 47

Andre Deutsch (United Kingdom) *Tel:* (020) 7612 0400 *Fax:* (020) 7612 0401 *E-mail:* sales@carltonbooks.co.uk *Web Site:* www.carltonbooks.co.uk, pg 757

Wissenschaftlicher Verlag Harri Deutsch GmbH (Germany) *Tel:* (069) 77015860 *Fax:* (069) 77015869 *E-mail:* verlag@harri-deutsch.de *Web Site:* www.harri-deutsch.de/verlag, pg 230

Deutsch Wyss & Partner (Switzerland) *Tel:* (031) 381 44 25 *Fax:* (031) 381 48 21 *Web Site:* www.advobern.ch, pg 692

Deutsche Akademie fuer Sprache und Dichtung (Germany) *Tel:* (06151) 4092-0 *Fax:* (06151) 4092-99 *E-mail:* sekretariat@deutscheakademie.de *Web Site:* www.deutscheakademie.de, pg 1494

Deutsche Bibelgesellschaft (Germany) *Tel:* (0711) 7181-0 *Toll Free Tel:* 0800 242 3546 *Fax:* (0711) 7181-126 *E-mail:* zentrale@dbg.de *Web Site:* www.dbg.de, pg 230

Deutsche Blinden-Bibliothek (Germany) *Tel:* (06421) 6060 *Fax:* (06421) 606229 *E-mail:* info@blista.de *Web Site:* www.blista.de, pg 230

Deutsche Exlibris-Gesellschaft eV (DEG) (Germany) *Tel:* (02166) 60 55 81 *Fax:* (02166) 25 59 42 *E-mail:* info@exlibris-blum.de *Web Site:* www.exlibris-gesellschaft.de, pg 1652

Deutsche Gesellschaft fuer Eisenbahngeschichte eV (DGEG) (Germany) *Tel:* (02922) 8 49 70 *Fax:* (02922) 8 49 27 *E-mail:* info@dgeg.de; gst@dgeg.de *Web Site:* www.dgeg.de, pg 230

Deutsche Gesellschaft fuer Informationswissenschaft und Informationspraxis eV DGI (Germany) *Tel:* (069) 430313 *Fax:* (069) 4909096 *E-mail:* mail@dgi-info.de *Web Site:* www.dgd.de; www.dgi-info.de, pg 1652

Deutsche Gesellschaft fuer Luft-und Raumfahrt Lilienthal Oberth eV (Germany) *Tel:* (0228) 30 80 5-0 *Fax:* (0228) 30 80 5-24 *E-mail:* info@dglr.de *Web Site:* www.dglr.de, pg 230

Deutsche Landwirtschafts-Gesellschaft Verlags GmbH (Germany) *Tel:* (069) 24 788-451 *Fax:* (069) 24 788-484 *E-mail:* dlg-verlag@dlg.org *Web Site:* www.dlg-verlag.de, pg 230

Deutsche Lyrik Verlag (Germany) *Tel:* (0241) 960 90 90 *Fax:* (0241) 960 90 99 *E-mail:* info@deutscher-lyrik-verlag.de; verkauf@karin-fischer-verlag.de (sales); presse@karin-fischer-verlag.de *Web Site:* www.deutscher-lyrik-verlag.de, pg 230

Deutsche Nationalbibliothek (Germany) *Tel:* (069) 1525-0 *Fax:* (069) 1525-1010 *E-mail:* info-f@dnb.de; postfach@dnb.de *Web Site:* www.dnb.de, pg 230, 1592

Deutsche Schillergesellschaft eV (Germany) *Tel:* (07144) 848-0 *Fax:* (07144) 848-299 *E-mail:* info@dla-marbach.de; presse@dla-marbach.de *Web Site:* www.dla-marbach.de, pg 230

Deutsche Verlags-Anstalt (DVA) (Germany) *Tel:* (089) 4136-0 *Toll Free Tel:* (0800) 500 33 22 *Fax:* (089) 4136-3333 *E-mail:* kundenservice@randomhouse.de *Web Site:* www.randomhouse.de/dva, pg 230

Deutsche Zentralbuecherei fuer Blinde zu Leipzig (DZB) (Germany) *Tel:* (0341) 71 13-0 *Fax:* (0341) 71 13-125 *E-mail:* bibliothek@dzb.de; info@dzb.de *Web Site:* www.dzb.de, pg 1593

Deutscher Aerzteverlag GmbH (Germany) *Tel:* (02234) 7011-0 *Fax:* (02234) 7011-476; (02234) 7011-6508 *E-mail:* service@aerzteverlag.de; bestellung@aerzteverlag.de (orders) *Web Site:* www.aerzteverlag.de, pg 231

Deutscher Akademischer Austauschdienst eV (Germany) *Tel:* (0228) 882-0 *Fax:* (0228) 882-444 *E-mail:* postmaster@daad.de; presse@daad.de *Web Site:* www.daad.de, pg 231

Editions Donniya (Mali) *Tel:* 20 21 46 46; 20 21 45 99; 20 21 58 54 *Fax:* 20 21 90 31 *E-mail:* imprimcolor@orangemali.net *Web Site:* www.editionsdonniya.com, pg 511

Editorial Donostiarra SA (Spain) *Tel:* 943 215 737; 943 213 011 *Fax:* 943 219 521 *E-mail:* info@editorialdonostiarra.com *Web Site:* editorialdonostiarra.com, pg 640

Donzelli Editore SRL (Italy) *Tel:* (06) 4440600 *Fax:* (06) 4440607 *E-mail:* editore@donzelli.it *Web Site:* www.donzelli.it, pg 438

Donzelli Fietta Literary Agency (Italy) *E-mail:* info@donzellifiettaagency.com *Web Site:* www.donzellifiettaagency.com, pg 1230

Nakladatelstvi Doplnek (Czech Republic) *Tel:* 545 242 455; 731 507 666 (cell) *E-mail:* doplnek@doplnek.cz; objednavky@doplnek.cz (orders) *Web Site:* www.doplnek.cz, pg 127

Dorea Books & Art (Brazil) *Tel:* (011) 3062 1643 *Fax:* (011) 3088 3361 *E-mail:* dba@dbaeditora.com.br; faleconosco@dbaeditora.com.br *Web Site:* www.dbaeditora.com.br, pg 80

Dorikos A I Klados & Co (Greece) *Tel:* 2103303609 *Fax:* 2103301866, pg 354

Dorleta SA (Spain) *Tel:* 944456597 *Fax:* 944274512, pg 640

The Dorothy L Sayers Society (United Kingdom) *Tel:* (01376) 515626 *Fax:* (01376) 515626 *E-mail:* info@sayers.org.uk *Web Site:* www.sayers.org.uk, pg 1502

Dort-Hagenhausen-Verlag (Germany) *Tel:* (089) 72 94 96 25 *Fax:* (089) 72 94 96 26 *Web Site:* www.d-hverlag.de, pg 235

Doshinsha Publishing Co Ltd (Japan) *Tel:* (03) 5976-4181; (03) 5976-4402 (editorial) *Fax:* (03) 5978-1078; (03) 5978-1079 (editorial) *Web Site:* www.doshinsha.co.jp, pg 475

DOSPASSOS Agencia Literaria y Comunicacion (Spain) *Tel:* 915 215 812 *E-mail:* aliteraria@dospassos.es; dospassos@dospassos.es *Web Site:* www.dospassos.es, pg 1235

Editorial Dossat SA (Spain) *Tel:* 914 317 479, pg 640

Les Dossiers d'Aquitaine (France) *Tel:* 05 56 91 84 98 *Fax:* 05 56 91 64 92 *E-mail:* ddabordeaux@gmail.com; ddabx.info@gmail.com *Web Site:* www.ddabordeaux.com, pg 165

Dost Kitabevi Yayinlari (Turkey) *Tel:* (0312) 435 93 70; (0312) 435 79 02 *Fax:* (0312) 435 79 02 *E-mail:* bilgi@dostyayinevi.com *Web Site:* www.dostyayinevi.com, pg 720

Dou Shuppan (Japan) *Tel:* (042) 748-1240; (042) 748-2423 (sales) *Fax:* (042) 748-2421 *Web Site:* www.dou-shuppan.com, pg 475

Kylee Doust Agency (Italy) *Tel:* (06) 99345171 *Fax:* (06) 99335374 *Web Site:* kyleedoustagency.com, pg 1230

Drachen Verlag GmbH (Germany) *Tel:* (038374) 75224 *Fax:* (038374) 75223 *E-mail:* mail@drachenverlag.de *Web Site:* www.drachenverlag.de, pg 235

Der Drachenhaus Verlag (Germany) *Tel:* (0176) 24001350 *E-mail:* info@drachenhaus-verlag.com; pr@drachenhaus-verlag.com *Web Site:* www.drachenhaus-verlag.com, pg 235

Wydawnictwo Sonia Draga Sp z oo (Poland) *Tel:* (32) 782 64 77 *Fax:* (32) 253 77 28 *E-mail:* info@soniadraga.pl *Web Site:* www.soniadraga.pl, pg 569

Drake Educational Associates Ltd (United Kingdom) *Tel:* (029) 2056 0333 *E-mail:* enquiries@drakeed.com *Web Site:* www.drakeed.com, pg 758

Drake Educational Associates Ltd (United Kingdom) *Tel:* (029) 2056 0333 *Fax:* (029) 2055 4909 *E-mail:* enquiries@drakeed.com *Web Site:* www.drakegroup.co.uk; www.drakeed.com, pg 1241

Forlaget DRAMA ApS (Denmark) *Tel:* 70 25 11 41 *Fax:* 74 65 20 93 *E-mail:* drama@drama.dk *Web Site:* www.drama.dk, pg 135

Dramatic Lines Publishers (United Kingdom) *Tel:* (020) 8296 9502 *Fax:* (020) 8296 9503 *E-mail:* mail@dramaticlines.co.uk *Web Site:* www.dramaticlines.co.uk, pg 758

Drammensbibliotek (Norway) *Tel:* 32 04 54 00 *E-mail:* bibliotek@drmk.no *Web Site:* www.drammensbiblioteket.no, pg 1620

Draupadi Verlag (Germany) *Tel:* (06221) 412 990 *Fax:* (0322) 2372 2343 *E-mail:* info@draupadi-verlag.de *Web Site:* www.draupadi-verlag.de, pg 235

Drava Verlag (Austria) *Tel:* (0463) 501 099 *Fax:* (0463) 501 099-20 *E-mail:* office@drava.at *Web Site:* www.drava.at, pg 47

Dreamland Publications (India) *Tel:* (011) 25106050; (011) 25435657; (011) 25455657 *Fax:* (011) 25438283 *E-mail:* info@dreamlandpublications.com; dreamland@vsnl.com *Web Site:* www.dreamlandpublications.com, pg 381

Dreamtech Press (India) *Tel:* (011) 4355180 *E-mail:* editorial@dreamtechpress.com; marketing@dreamtechpress.com *Web Site:* www.dreamtechpress.com, pg 381

Dref Wen (United Kingdom) *Tel:* (029) 2061 7860 *E-mail:* post@drefwen.com *Web Site:* www.drefwen.com, pg 758

Drei Brunnen Verlag GmbH & Co KG (Germany) *Tel:* (07181) 8602-0 *Fax:* (07181) 8602-29 *E-mail:* mail@drei-brunnen-verlag.de *Web Site:* www.drei-brunnen-verlag.de, pg 235

Drei Eichen Verlag (Germany) *Tel:* (09732) 9142-0 *Fax:* (09732) 9142-20 *E-mail:* info@dreieichen.de *Web Site:* www.dreieichen.com, pg 235

Drei Hasen in der Abendsonne GmbH (Germany) *Tel:* (09163) 9999-0 *Fax:* (09163) 9999-5 *E-mail:* verlag@hasehasehase.de *Web Site:* www.hasehasehase.com, pg 235

Drei Ulmen Verlag GmbH (Germany) *Tel:* (089) 3087911; (089) 3088343, pg 235

Cecilie Dressler Verlag (Germany) *Tel:* (040) 607909-03 *Fax:* (040) 6072326 *E-mail:* dressler@verlagsgruppe-oetinger.de; vertrieb@verlagsgruppe-oetinger.de; marketing@verlagsgruppe-oetinger.de *Web Site:* www.cecilie-dressler.de, pg 235

Dreyers Forlag AS (Norway) *Tel:* 23 13 69 38 *Fax:* 23 13 69 39 *E-mail:* post@dreyersforlag.no *Web Site:* www.dreyersforlag.no, pg 554

Marin Drinov Academic Publishing House (Bulgaria) *Tel:* (02) 72 09 22; (02) 979 34 49 *Fax:* (02) 870 40 54 *E-mail:* baspress@abv.bg *Web Site:* m-drinov.bas.bg, pg 95

Verlagsgruppe Droemer Knaur GmbH & Co KG (Germany) *Tel:* (089) 9271-0 *Fax:* (089) 9271-168 *E-mail:* info@droemer-knaur.de; presse@droemer-knaur.de *Web Site:* www.droemer-knaur.de, pg 235

DROFA (Russia) *Tel:* (495) 795-0550; (495) 795-0551 *Toll Free:* 800-2000-550 *Fax:* (495) 795-0552 *E-mail:* info@drofa.ru; marketing@drofa.ru; sales@drofa.ru *Web Site:* www.drofa.ru, pg 594

Editions du Dromadaire (Italy) *Tel:* (041) 2412268; (041) 5299014 *Fax:* (041) 2412268 *E-mail:* info@dromadaire.it *Web Site:* www.dromadaire.it, pg 438

Literaturverlag Droschl GmbH (Austria) *Tel:* (0316) 32-64-04 *Fax:* (0316) 32-40-71 *E-mail:* literaturverlag@droschl.com *Web Site:* www.droschl.com, pg 47

Droste Verlag GmbH (Germany) *Tel:* (0211) 8 60 52 06 *Fax:* (0211) 3 23 00 98 *E-mail:* kunst@drosteverlag.de; vertrieb@drosteverlag.de *Web Site:* www.droste-verlag.de, pg 236

Librairie Droz SA (Switzerland) *Tel:* (022) 346 66 66 *Fax:* (022) 347 23 91 *E-mail:* droz@droz.org *Web Site:* www.droz.org, pg 693

Karl Elser Druck GmbH (Germany) *Tel:* (07041) 805-0; (07041) 805-41; (07041) 805-49 *Fax:* (07041) 805-50 *E-mail:* info@elserdruck.de *Web Site:* www.elserdruck.de, pg 236

Gerhard Steidl-Druckerei & Verlag GmbH & Co OHG (Germany) *Tel:* (0551) 49 60 60 *Fax:* (0551) 49 60 649 *E-mail:* mail@steidl.de *Web Site:* www.steidl.de, pg 236

Druffel & Vowinckel Verlag (Germany) *Tel:* (08105) 730560 *Fax:* (08105) 7305629 *Web Site:* www.druffel-vowinckel.eu, pg 236

Druk-Intro SA (Poland) *Tel:* (52) 354 94 50 *Fax:* (52) 354 94 51 *E-mail:* sekretariat@druk-intro.pl *Web Site:* web.druk-intro.pl, pg 1331

Druka Spaustuve (Lithuania) *Tel:* (046) 380458 *Fax:* (046) 380459 *E-mail:* info@druka.lt *Web Site:* www.druka.lt, pg 1281, 1330

The Drummond Agency (Australia) *Tel:* (03) 5427 3644 *Fax:* (03) 5427 3655 *E-mail:* info@drummondagency.com.au *Web Site:* www.drummondagency.com.au, pg 1223

Drustvo Bibliotekara Bosne i Hercegovine (Bosnia and Herzegovina) *Tel:* (033) 2755325 *Fax:* (033) 212435, pg 1648

DRW-Verlag Weinbrenner GmbH & Co KG (Germany) *Tel:* (0711) 7591-0 *Fax:* (0711) 7591-348 *E-mail:* info@drw-verlag.de *Web Site:* www.drw-verlag.de; www.weinbrenner.de, pg 236

Dryas Verlag GbR (Germany) *Tel:* (069) 95 925 488 *Fax:* (069) 95 925 489 *E-mail:* kontakt@dryas.de *Web Site:* www.dryas.de, pg 236

DSI Data Service & Information (Germany) *Tel:* (049) 2843 3220 *Fax:* (049) 2843 3230 *E-mail:* dsi@dsidata.com *Web Site:* www.dsidata.com; www.statistischedaten.de, pg 236

Editora DSOP (Brazil) *Tel:* (011) 3660-5400; (011) 3177-7800 (sales) *E-mail:* contato@editoradsop.com.br *Web Site:* www.editoradsop.com.br, pg 80

Editions Du May (France) *Tel:* 01 46 99 24 12, pg 165

Duang Kamol Co Ltd (Thailand) *Tel:* (02) 251-6335 *Fax:* (02) 250-1262, pg 715

Livraria Duas Cidades (Brazil) *Tel:* (011) 3668-2160, pg 80, 1408

Dublin City Public Libraries & Archive (Ireland) *Tel:* (01) 674 4999 *E-mail:* cityarchives@dublincity.ie; dublinstudies@dublincity.ie *Web Site:* www.dublincity.ie, pg 1603

Dublin Institute for Advanced Studies (Ireland) *Tel:* (01) 6140100 *Fax:* (01) 6680561; (01) 6140160 *Web Site:* www.dias.ie, pg 410

Editora Dublinense Ltda (Brazil) *Tel:* (051) 3024-0787 *E-mail:* editorial@dublinense.com.br *Web Site:* www.dublinense.com.br, pg 80

Duboux Editions SA (Switzerland) *Tel:* (033) 225 60 60 *Fax:* (033) 225 60 66 *E-mail:* duboux@duboux.ch *Web Site:* duboux.ch, pg 693

Dubray Books (Ireland) *Tel:* (01) 677-5568 *E-mail:* dublinbookshop@dubraybooks.ie *Web Site:* www.dubraybooks.ie, pg 1426

Lec Alain Ducasse Editions (France) *Tel:* 01 58 00 21 95 *Fax:* 01 58 00 21 96 *Web Site:* www.alain-ducasse.com, pg 165

Gerald Duckworth & Co Ltd (United Kingdom) *Tel:* (020) 7490 7300 *Fax:* (020) 7490 0080 *E-mail:* info@duckworth-publishers.co.uk *Web Site:* www.ducknet.co.uk, pg 759

Dudenverlag (Germany) *Tel:* (030) 897 85 82-30 *E-mail:* kundenservice@duden.de; shop@duden.de *Web Site:* www.duden.de, pg 237

Duesendruck Verlag (Germany) *Tel:* (07153) 558 494 *Fax:* (07153) 558 484 *E-mail:* info@duesendruck.de *Web Site:* www.duesendruck.de, pg 237

Dumjahn Verlag (Germany) *Tel:* (06131) 330810 *Fax:* (06131) 330811 *E-mail:* info@dumjahn.de; eisenbahn@dumjahn.de *Web Site:* www.dumjahn.de, pg 237

DuMont Buchverlag GmbH & Co KG (Germany) *Tel:* (0221) 224-180 *Fax:* (0221) 224-1973 *E-mail:* info@dumont-buchverlag.de *Web Site:* www.dumont-buchverlag.de, pg 237

DuMont Reiseverlag GmbH & Co KG (Germany) *Tel:* (0711) 4502-1033 *Fax:* (0711) 4502-411 *E-mail:* info@dumontreise.de *Web Site:* www.dumontreise.de, pg 237

Dun & Bradstreet Ltd (United Kingdom) *Tel:* (0808) 278 9942 *E-mail:* enquiries@dnb.com *Web Site:* www.dnb.co.uk, pg 759

Dorothy Duncan Braille Library (Zimbabwe) *Tel:* (04) 251116; (04) 797725 *Fax:* (04) 251117 *Web Site:* www.ddbl.org, pg 852

Duncker und Humblot GmbH (Germany) *Tel:* (030) 79 00 06-0 *Fax:* (030) 79 00 06-31 *E-mail:* info@duncker-humblot.de; rights@duncker-humblot.de *Web Site:* www.duncker-humblot.de, pg 237

Dunedin Academic Press (United Kingdom) *Tel:* (0131) 473 2397 *E-mail:* mail@dunedinacademicpress.co.uk *Web Site:* www.dunedinacademicpress.co.uk, pg 759

Dunedin Public Libraries (New Zealand) *Tel:* (03) 474 3690 *Fax:* (03) 474 3660 *E-mail:* library@dcc.govt.nz *Web Site:* www.dunedinlibraries.govt.nz, pg 1617

Dunia Pustaka Jaya PT (Indonesia) *Tel:* (021) 31900629; (021) 3909284 *Fax:* (021) 3909320 *Web Site:* www.twitter.com/PUSTAKA_JAYA, pg 406

Editorial Dunken (Argentina) *Tel:* (011) 4954 7700 *E-mail:* info@dunken.com.ar *Web Site:* www.dunken.com.ar, pg 6

Editorial Dunken (Argentina) *Tel:* (011) 4954 7700; (011) 4954 7300 *E-mail:* info@dunken.com.ar *Web Site:* www.dunken.com.ar, pg 1273, 1317

Dunmore Publishing Ltd (New Zealand) *Tel:* (09) 521 3121 *E-mail:* books@dunmore.co.nz *Web Site:* www.dunmore.co.nz, pg 545

Dunod Editeur (France) *Tel:* 01 40 46 35 00 *Fax:* 01 40 46 49 95 *E-mail:* infos@dunod.com *Web Site:* www.dunod.com, pg 165

Kustannus Oy Duodecim (Finland) *Tel:* (09) 618 851 *Fax:* (09) 6188 5400 *Web Site:* www.duodecim.fi, pg 148

Duomo Ediciones (Spain) *Tel:* 93 181 01 53 *E-mail:* info@duomoediciones.com *Web Site:* www.duomoediciones.com, pg 640

Verlag duotincta (Germany) *Tel:* (0157) 85526732 *E-mail:* kontakt@duotincta.de *Web Site:* www.duotincta.de, pg 237

Sophie Dupre Autographs & Manuscripts (United Kingdom) *Tel:* (01249) 821121 *Web Site:* sophiedupreautographs.com, pg 1457

Editions Dupuis SA (Belgium) *Tel:* (071) 600 500 *Fax:* (071) 600 599 *E-mail:* info@dupuis.com; dupuis@dupuis.com; licensing@dupuis.com *Web Site:* www.dupuis.com, pg 66

Dupuis France SAS (France) *Tel:* 01 70 38 56 00 *Fax:* 01 70 38 56 01 *E-mail:* infos@dupuis.com; edito@dupuis.com *Web Site:* www.dupuis.com, pg 166

Durham Cathedral Library (United Kingdom) *Tel:* (0191) 386 2489 *Fax:* (0191) 386 4267 *E-mail:* library@durhamcathedral.co.uk *Web Site:* www.durhamcathedral.co.uk/learning/the-cathedral-library, pg 1641

Durham University Library (United Kingdom) *Tel:* (0191) 334 3042; (0191) 334 2956 (administration) *Fax:* (0191) 334 2971 *E-mail:* main.library@durham.ac.uk *Web Site:* www.dur.ac.uk/library, pg 1641

Durieux doo (Croatia) *Tel:* (01) 23 00 337 *Fax:* (01) 23 00 337 *E-mail:* prodaja@durieux.hr *Web Site:* www.durieux.hr, pg 119

Durnell Marketing Ltd (United Kingdom) *Tel:* (01892) 544272 *Fax:* (01892) 5111152 *E-mail:* admin@durnell.co.uk; orders@durnell.co.uk *Web Site:* www.durnell.co.uk, pg 1241

Literarische Agentur Galina Dursthoff (Germany) *Tel:* (0221) 444 254 *E-mail:* info@dursthoff.de *Web Site:* www.dursthoff.de, pg 1226

Durvan SA de Ediciones (Spain) *Tel:* 913 842 022 (sales) *E-mail:* editorial@durvan.com *Web Site:* www.durvan.com, pg 640

Dustri-Verlag Dr Karl Feistle GmbH & Co KG (Germany) *Tel:* (089) 61 38 61-0 *Fax:* (089) 613 54 12 *E-mail:* info@dustri.de *Web Site:* www.dustri.com, pg 237

Dutch Connection (United Kingdom) *Tel:* (01625) 610613, pg 1253

Dutta Baruah Publishing Co Pvt Ltd (India) *Tel:* (0361) 2543995, pg 381

Gottlieb Duttweiler Institute (Switzerland) *Tel:* (044) 724 61 11 *Fax:* (044) 724 62 62 *E-mail:* info@gdi.ch *Web Site:* www.gdi.ch, pg 693

Uitgeven Duurzaam (Netherlands) *Tel:* (06) 5495 6704 *E-mail:* info@duurzaamuitgeven.nl *Web Site:* www.duurzaamuitgeven.nl, pg 1282, 1330

De Duurzame Drukker (Belgium) *Tel:* (09) 218 08 41 *E-mail:* info@deduurzamedrukker.be *Web Site:* www.deduurzamedrukker.be, pg 1317

DVG-Deutsche Verlagsgesellschaft mbH (Germany) *Tel:* (05742) 930444 *Fax:* (05742) 930455, pg 237

DVS Media GmbH (Germany) *Tel:* (0211) 1591-0 *Fax:* (0211) 1591-150 *E-mail:* media@dvs-hg.de *Web Site:* www.dvs-media.info; www.dvs-media.eu, pg 237

Wydawnictwo Dwie Siostry Sp z oo (Poland) *Tel:* (22) 618 25 30 *E-mail:* biuro@wydawnictwodwiesiostry.pl *Web Site:* www.wydawnictwodwiesiostry.pl, pg 569

Gwasg Dwyfor (United Kingdom) *Tel:* (01286) 881 911 *Fax:* (01286) 881 952, pg 759

Dykinson SL (Spain) *Tel:* 91 544 28 46; 91 544 28 69 *Fax:* 91 544 60 40 *E-mail:* info@dykinson.com *Web Site:* www.dykinson.com, pg 640

Dynamo House Pty Ltd (Australia) *Tel:* (03) 8892 4844 *Fax:* (03) 9429 8036 *E-mail:* customerservice@dynamoh.com.au *Web Site:* www.dynamohouse.com.au, pg 23

Dyonon (Israel) *Tel:* (08) 9147788 *Fax:* (08) 9147786 *E-mail:* info@dyonon.com *Web Site:* www.dyonon.com, pg 1427

DZS Grafik doo (Slovenia) *Tel:* (01) 586 72 00 *Fax:* (01) 586 72 15 *E-mail:* info@dzs-grafik.si *Web Site:* www.dzs-grafik.si, pg 1284, 1333, 1347

Dzuka Publishing Ltd (Malawi) *Tel:* 0888 453 185 (sales) *E-mail:* martinyewo@gmail.com *Web Site:* www.facebook.com/dzukapublishing; www.times.mw/dzuka-publishing, pg 506

E & Z Verlag (Germany) *Tel:* (0203) 93093277 *Fax:* (0203) 9408257 *E-mail:* euz-verlag@arcor.de *Web Site:* www.euz-buchwelt.de, pg 237

E-Edit Infotech Pvt Ltd (India) *Tel:* (044) 42 13 29 73 *E-mail:* hrm@editinfotech.in *Web Site:* www.editinfotech.in, pg 1327

E/O Edizioni SRL (Italy) *Tel:* (06) 3722829 *Fax:* (06) 37351096 *E-mail:* info@edizionieo.it; ufficiostampa@edizionieo.it *Web Site:* www.edizionieo.it, pg 438

EA (Bulgaria) *Tel:* (064) 822827; (064) 846774 *Fax:* (064) 822528 *E-mail:* ea@eapleven.com *Web Site:* eapleven.com, pg 1318

Eaglemoss Publishing Group Ltd (United Kingdom) *Tel:* (020) 7605 1200 *Fax:* (020) 7605 1201 *Web Site:* www.eaglemoss.com, pg 759

earBOOKS (Germany) *Tel:* (040) 890 85-0 *E-mail:* info@edel.com *Web Site:* www.earbooks.net; www.edel.de, pg 237

Early English Text Society (United Kingdom) *Web Site:* www.eets.org.uk, pg 1503

East African Educational Publishers Ltd (Kenya) *Tel:* (020) 4445260; (020) 4445261 *E-mail:* marketing@eastafricanpublishers.com *Web Site:* www.eastafricanpublishers.com, pg 492

East China Normal University Press (China) *Tel:* (021) 60821616; (021) 62869887 *Fax:* (021) 60821717 *E-mail:* ecnup@ecnupress.com.cn *Web Site:* www.ecnupress.com.cn; www.ecnup-dayu.com.cn, pg 104

East China University of Science & Technology Press (China) *Tel:* (021) 64253300; (021) 64251231 *Fax:* (021) 64252280 *E-mail:* xiaoban@ecust.edu.cn *Web Site:* www.ecust.edu.cn, pg 104

East-West Publications (UK) Ltd (United Kingdom) *Tel:* (020) 7837 5061 *Fax:* (020) 7278 4429, pg 759

Eastern Africa Publications Ltd (Tanzania) *Tel:* (057) 26708, pg 714

Eastern & Southern Africa Regional Branch of the International Council on Archives (ESARBICA) (Kenya) *Tel:* (020) 2228959 *Web Site:* www.esarbica.com, pg 1380

Eastern & Southern African Management Institute (ESAMI) (Tanzania) *Tel:* (027) 297 0065; (027) 297 0068; (027) 297 0069 *Fax:* (027) 297 0066 *E-mail:* mbd@esami-africa.org; esamicommunication@esami-africa.org *Web Site:* www.esami-africa.org, pg 1637

Eastern Book Co (India) *Tel:* (0522) 4033608; (0522) 4033619; (0522) 4033620 *Toll Free Tel:* 1800-1800-6666 *Fax:* (0522) 4033633 *E-mail:* sales@ebc.co.in *Web Site:* www.ebc.co.in, pg 382

Eastern Law House Pvt Ltd (India) *Tel:* (033) 2215-1989; (033) 2215-2301 *Fax:* (033) 2215-0491 *E-mail:* elh@cal.vsnl.net.in; elh.cal@gmail.com *Web Site:* www.easternlawhouse.com, pg 382

Eastword (United Kingdom) *Tel:* (01923) 836 326 *Fax:* (01923) 827 823, pg 1253

Easy Computing Publishing NV (Belgium) *Tel:* (02) 346 52 52 *Fax:* (02) 346 01 20 *E-mail:* info@easycomputing.com *Web Site:* www.easycomputing.com, pg 66

Edizioni EBE (Italy) *Tel:* (0766) 858878, pg 438

ebersbach & simon (Germany) *Tel:* (030) 7688 64 40 *Fax:* (030) 7688 64 41 *E-mail:* info@ebersbach-simon.de *Web Site:* www.ebersbach-simon.de, pg 238

Ebner & Spiegel GmbH (Germany) *Tel:* (0731) 2056-0 *E-mail:* info@cpibooks.de *Web Site:* www.cpibooks.com, pg 1322

eBook.de (Germany) *Tel:* (040) 4223 6096 *Fax:* (040) 8519 4444 *E-mail:* service@ebook.de *Web Site:* www.ebook.de, pg 1415

Ebury Publishing (United Kingdom) *Tel:* (020) 7840 8400 *Web Site:* www.eburypublishing.co.uk, pg 759

Ediciones ECA SA de CV (Mexico) *Tel:* (0155) 5615-4162; (0155) 5615-4187; (0155) 5615-4088; (0155) 5615-4289 *Web Site:* edicioneseca.com, pg 515

Eccles Fisher Associates (United Kingdom) *Tel:* (020) 7494 4609 *E-mail:* info@ecclesfisher.com *Web Site:* www.ecclesfisher.com, pg 1241

Echo Publishing Co Ltd (Taiwan) *Tel:* (02) 2763-1452 *Fax:* (02) 2766-8709 *E-mail:* gifts@mail.echogroup.com.tw *Web Site:* www.hanshenggifts.com, pg 711

Echo Verlag (Germany) *Tel:* (0551) 79 68 24 *Fax:* (0551) 7 40 35 *E-mail:* webmaster@echoverlag.de *Web Site:* www.echoverlag.de, pg 238

Echter Verlag GmbH (Germany) *Tel:* (0931) 66068-0 *Fax:* (0931) 66068-23 *E-mail:* info@echter.de; presse@echter.de; vertrieb@echter.de *Web Site:* www.echter.de, pg 238

Echtzeit Verlag GmbH (Switzerland) *Tel:* (061) 322 45 00 *E-mail:* info@echtzeit.ch *Web Site:* echtzeit.ch, pg 693

The Energy & Resources Institute (TERI) (India)
Tel: (011) 2468 2100; (011) 4150 4900 *Fax:* (011)
2468 2144; (011) 2468 2145 *E-mail:* mailbox@teri.
res.in; teripress@teri.res.in *Web Site:* www.teriin.org,
pg 382

Energy Information Centre (United Kingdom)
Tel: (01527) 511 700 *Fax:* (01527) 512 712
E-mail: theenergyexperts@eic.co.uk *Web Site:* www.
eic.co.uk, pg 762

Engel & Bengel Verlag (Germany) *Tel:* (06353) 8107
Fax: (06353) 507057, pg 240

Engelsdorfer Verlag (Germany) *Tel:* (0341) 27 11 87-0
Fax: (0341) 27 11 87-10 *E-mail:* info@engelsdorfer-
verlag.de *Web Site:* www.engelsdorfer-verlag.de,
pg 240

Englisch Verlag (Germany) *Tel:* (0611) 942 72-0
Fax: (0611) 942 72-40 *E-mail:* info@englisch-verlag.
de *Web Site:* www.christophorus-verlag.de, pg 240

The English Agency (Japan) Ltd (Japan) *Tel:* (03) 3406
5385 *Fax:* (03) 3406 5387 *E-mail:* info@eaj.co.jp
Web Site: www.eajco.jp, pg 1232

The English Association (United Kingdom) *Tel:* (0116)
229 7622 *Fax:* (0116) 229 7623 *E-mail:* engassoc@le.
ac.uk *Web Site:* www.le.ac.uk/engassoc, pg 1503

English Book Store (India) *Tel:* (011) 2341-5031
Fax: (011) 2341-7731 *E-mail:* info@englishbookstore.
net *Web Site:* www.englishbookstore.net, pg 1422

English Heritage (United Kingdom) *Tel:* (01793) 414700
Fax: (01793) 414707 *E-mail:* customers@english-
heritage.org.uk *Web Site:* www.english-heritage.org.uk,
pg 762

The English-Speaking Union (ESU) (United Kingdom)
Tel: (020) 7529 1550 *Fax:* (020) 7495 6108
E-mail: esu@esu.org *Web Site:* www.esu.org, pg 1503

Verlag Peter Engstler (Germany) *Tel:* (09774) 858490
Fax: (09774) 858491 *E-mail:* engstler-verlag@t-online.
de *Web Site:* www.engstler-verlag.de, pg 240

Enitharmon Press (United Kingdom) *Tel:* (020) 7430
0844 *E-mail:* info@enitharmon.co.uk *Web Site:* www.
enitharmon.co.uk, pg 762

Ennsthaler Gesellschaft mbH & Co KG (Austria)
Tel: (07252) 52053-10; (07252) 52053-50; (07252)
52053-21 (distribution) *Fax:* (07252) 52053-16;
(07252) 52053-55; (07252) 52053-22 (distribution)
E-mail: verlag@ennsthaler.at; buchhandlung@
ennsthaler.at; buero@ennsthaler.at; auslieferung@
ennsthaler.at *Web Site:* www.ennsthaler.at, pg 47

Enodare Ltd (Ireland) *E-mail:* info@enodare.com
Web Site: enodare.com, pg 410

Enrich Professional Publishing Ltd (Hong Kong)
Tel: 2793 5678 *Fax:* 2793 5030 *E-mail:* epp.info@
enrichculture.com *Web Site:* www.enrichprofessional.
com, pg 364

ENS Editions (France) *Tel:* 04 26 73 11 91; 04 26 73 11
98 *Fax:* 04 26 73 12 68 *E-mail:* editions@ens-lyon.fr
Web Site: www.ens-lyon.fr/editions/catalogue, pg 167

Editions L'Entretemps (France) *Tel:* 04 99 53 09 75
Fax: 09 58 09 15 14 *E-mail:* info@entretemps.org;
administration@entretemps.org *Web Site:* www.
entretemps.org, pg 167

Envirobook (Australia) *Tel:* (0402) 361 424 (cell)
Fax: (0402) 361 424 (cell) *E-mail:* sales@envirobook.
com.au *Web Site:* www.envirobook.com.au, pg 24

EOS Editions Sankt Ottilien (Germany) *Tel:* (08193)
71700 *Fax:* (08193) 71709 *E-mail:* mail@eos-verlag.
de *Web Site:* www.eos-verlag.de, pg 240

EOS Gabinete de Orientacion Psicologica (Spain)
Tel: 915 541 204 *E-mail:* eos@eos.es *Web Site:* www.
eos.es, pg 643

eoVision GmbH (Austria) *Tel:* (0662) 243217-0
Fax: (0662) 243217-11 *E-mail:* office@eovision.at
Web Site: www.eovision.at, pg 48

EP Graphics (United States) *Tel:* 260-589-2145 *Toll Free*
Tel: 877-589-2145 *Fax:* 260-589-2810 *Web Site:* www.
epgraphics.com, pg 1339

Editions EP&S (France) *Tel:* 01 41 74 82 82 *Fax:* 01
43 98 37 38 *E-mail:* revue@revue-eps.com
Web Site: www.revue-eps.com, pg 167

Les Editions de l'Epargne SA (France) *Tel:* 01 45 87 76
76 *Web Site:* www.editions-epargne.fr, pg 168

Epigram Books (Singapore) *Tel:* 6292 4456
E-mail: enquiry@epigrambooks.sg; rights@
epigrambooks.sg; sales@epigrambooks.sg
Web Site: www.epigrambooks.sg, pg 603

Ekdoseis Epikairotita (Greece) *Tel:* 2103607382
Fax: 2103636083 *E-mail:* epikero@yahoo.gr; info@
epikerotita.com *Web Site:* www.epikerotita.com.gr,
pg 354

EPLA-Verlag (Germany) *Tel:* (04221) 850143
Fax: (04221) 850146 *E-mail:* epla.plachetka@t-online.
de *Web Site:* www.epla-verlag.de, pg 241

Uitgeverij EPO (Belgium) *Tel:* (03) 239 68 74 *Fax:* (03)
218 46 04 *E-mail:* uitgeverij@epo.be *Web Site:* www.
epo.be, pg 66

Edition Epoca (Switzerland) *Tel:* (031) 772 10 10
Fax: (031) 772 10 11 *E-mail:* info@epoca.ch
Web Site: www.epoca.ch, pg 693

epodium Verlag (Germany) *Tel:* (089) 272 723 22
Fax: (03212) 104 03 38 *Web Site:* www.epodium.de,
pg 241

EPP Books Services (Ghana) *Tel:* (030) 2784849
Fax: (030) 2779099 *E-mail:* info@eppbookservices.
com *Web Site:* www.eppbookservices.com, pg 352

EPSILON Verlag & Versand (Germany) *Tel:* (04804)
1866 28 *Fax:* (04804) 1866 31 *E-mail:* epsilongrafix@
web.de *Web Site:* www.epsilongrafix.de, pg 241

Epsilon Yayinevi (Turkey) *Tel:* (0212) 252 38
21 *Fax:* (0212) 252 63 98 *E-mail:* epsilon@
epsilonyayinevi.com *Web Site:* www.epsilonyayinevi.
com, pg 720

EPU - Editora Pedagogica e Universitaria Ltda
(Brazil) *Tel:* (011) 3168-6077 *Fax:* (011) 3078-5803
Web Site: www.grupogen.com.br, pg 81

ePubDirect (Ireland) *Tel:* (021) 7304650 *E-mail:* info@
epubdirect.com *Web Site:* www.epubdirect.com,
pg 1426

Equilibri (Italy) *Tel:* (059) 365327 *Fax:* (059) 365327
E-mail: info@equilibri-libri.it *Web Site:* www.
equilibri-libri.it, pg 441

Equinox Publishing Ltd (United Kingdom) *Tel:* (0114)
221 0285 *Fax:* (0114) 279 6522 *Web Site:* www.
equinoxpub.com, pg 762

Editions Equinoxe/Edisud (France) *Tel:* 04 90 90
21 10 *E-mail:* contact@editions-equinoxe.com
Web Site: www.edisud.com, pg 168

Equipo Difusor del Libro SL (Spain) *Tel:* 91 616 23 11
Fax: 91 616 61 98 *E-mail:* libros@equipodifusor.
com *Web Site:* www.equipodifusor.com, pg 643

ER-AY Basim Hizmetleri Ltd (Turkey) *Tel:* (0212)
6290640 *Fax:* (0212) 4290647 *E-mail:* sales@
eraybasim.com *Web Site:* www.eraybasim.com,
pg 1336

Edizioni Era Nuova SRL (Italy) *E-mail:* info@
edizionieranuova.it *Web Site:* www.edizionieranuova.it,
pg 441

Era Publications (Australia) *Tel:* (08) 8352 4122
Fax: (08) 8219 0180 *E-mail:* service@erapublications.
com *Web Site:* www.erapublications.com, pg 24

Ediciones Era SA de CV (Mexico) *Tel:* (0155)
5528 1221 *Fax:* (0155) 5606 2904 *E-mail:* info@
edicionesera.com.mx; erapedidos@edicionesera.com.
mx; editorial@edicionesera.com.mx *Web Site:* www.
edicionesera.com.mx, pg 515

Erasmus Boekhandel BV (Netherlands) *Tel:* (020)
5353433 *Fax:* (020) 6206799 *E-mail:* erasmus@
erasmusbooks.nl *Web Site:* www.erasmusbooks.nl,
pg 1437

Erasmus Grasser-Verlag GmbH (Germany) *Tel:* (08861)
9309 742; (08861) 241 900 *Fax:* (08861) 8578;
(08861) 241 901 *E-mail:* technik@vogelsgesang.com;
info@eg-v.de *Web Site:* www.eg-v.de, pg 241

Eratex (Germany) *Tel:* (05221) 984-0 *Fax:* (05221) 984-
377 *E-mail:* info@ernstmeier.de *Web Site:* www.
ernstmeier.de, pg 1346

Editura Erc Press (Romania) *Tel:* (021) 5699011
Fax: (021) 5699012 *E-mail:* office@ercpress.ro
Web Site: www.ercpress.ro, pg 586

Erdem Yayinlari (Turkey) *Tel:* (0216) 492 55 55-15
Fax: (0216) 201 14 80 *E-mail:* bilgi@erdemyayinlari.
com *Web Site:* www.erdemyayinlari.com, pg 720

L'Ere Nouvelle (France) *Tel:* 04 93 99 30
13 *E-mail:* lerenouvelle@wanadoo.fr
Web Site: lerenouvelle.pagespro-orange.fr/pub, pg 168

Erein Argitaletxea (Spain) *Tel:* 943 21 83 00 *Fax:* 943
21 83 11 *E-mail:* erein@erein.com *Web Site:* www.
erein.com, pg 643

Eren Yayincilik Kitap, Dagitim Ltd (Turkey) *Tel:* (0212)
252 05 60; (0212) 251 28 58 *Fax:* (0212) 243 30 16
E-mail: eren@eren.com.tr *Web Site:* www.eren.com.tr,
pg 720

Eres Edition Musikverlag (Germany) *Tel:* (04298)
1676 *Fax:* (04298) 5312 *E-mail:* info@notenpost.de
Web Site: www.notenpost.de, pg 241

Editions Eres (France) *Tel:* 05 61 75 15 76 *Fax:* 05
61 73 52 89 *E-mail:* eres@editions-eres.com
Web Site: www.editions-eres.com, pg 168

Eretz Hemdah Institute for Advanced Jewish Studies
(Israel) *Tel:* (02) 537-1485 *Fax:* (02) 537-9626
E-mail: info@eretzhemdah.org *Web Site:* www.
eretzhemdah.org, pg 417

Erfgoedbibliotheek Hendrik Conscience (Belgium)
Tel: (03) 338 87 10 *Fax:* (03) 338 87 76
E-mail: consciencebibliotheek@stad.antwerpen.be
Web Site: www.consciencebibliotheek.be, pg 1578

ERGA Edizioni (Italy) *Tel:* (010) 8328441 *Fax:* (010)
8328799 *E-mail:* edizioni@erga.it *Web Site:* www.
erga.it/edizioni, pg 441

Ergon Verlag GmbH (Germany) *Tel:* (0931) 280084
Fax: (0931) 282872 *E-mail:* service@ergon-verlag.de;
orders@ergon-verlag.de; marketing@ergon-verlag.de
Web Site: www.ergon-verlag.de, pg 241

Erhvervsstyrelsen (Denmark) *Tel:* 35 29 10
00 *Fax:* 35 46 60 01 *E-mail:* erst@erst.dk
Web Site: erhvervsstyrelsen.dk, pg 136

Edizioni Centro Studi Erickson SRL (Italy) *Tel:* (0461)
950690 *Fax:* (0461) 950698 *E-mail:* info@erickson.it
Web Site: www.erickson.it, pg 441

Erkam Publishing (Turkey) *Tel:* (0212) 671 07 00
Fax: (0212) 671 07 17 *Web Site:* store.erkamyayinlari.
com, pg 720

Erlanger Verlag Fuer Mission und Oekumene
(Germany) *Tel:* (09874) 9 17 00 *Fax:* (09874) 9
33 70 *E-mail:* verlagsleitung@erlanger-verlag.de
Web Site: www.erlanger-verlag.de, pg 241

Penerbit Erlangga (Indonesia) *Tel:* (021) 8717006
Fax: (021) 87794609 *Web Site:* www.erlangga.co.id,
pg 406

L'Erma di Bretschneider SRL (Italy) *Tel:* (06) 68 74
127 *Fax:* (06) 68 74 129 *E-mail:* lerma@lerma.it;
edizioni@lerma.it *Web Site:* www.lerma.it, pg 441

Ediciones del Ermitano (Mexico) *Tel:* (0155) 5515-
1657 *E-mail:* minimalia@edicionesdelermitano.com
Web Site: www.edicionesdelermitano.com, pg 515

Ernest Press (United Kingdom) *Tel:* (0141) 637 1410
Web Site: www.ernest-press.co.uk, pg 762

Ernesto Reichmann Distribuidores de Livros Ltda
(Brazil) *Tel:* (011) 2198-2122 *Fax:* (011) 2198-2122,
pg 1408

Ernst & Young (United Kingdom) *Tel:* (020) 7951 2000
Fax: (020) 7951 1345 *Web Site:* www.ey.com/uk,
pg 762

Etas Libri (Italy) *Tel:* (02) 2584 2368 *Fax:* (02) 2584 2218 *E-mail:* etaslab@rcs.it *Web Site:* etaslab.corriere. it, pg 442

Publicaciones Etea (Spain) *Tel:* 957 222 100 *Fax:* 957 222 182 *E-mail:* comunica@etea.com; cordoba@etea. com *Web Site:* www.etea.com/web/etea/publicaciones-etea, pg 643

Eterna Cadencia Editora (Argentina) *Tel:* (011) 4774-4100 *E-mail:* info@eternacadencia.com.ar *Web Site:* www.eternacadencia.com, pg 6

eThekwini Municipal Libraries (South Africa) *Tel:* (031) 311 2401 *Fax:* (031) 311 2403 *Web Site:* www.durban. gov.za, pg 1630

Ethics International Press Ltd (United Kingdom) *Tel:* (01954) 710086 *Fax:* (01954) 710103 *E-mail:* info@ethicspress.com *Web Site:* www. ethicspress.com, pg 762

Ethiope Publishing Corp (Nigeria) *Tel:* (052) 253036, pg 551

Ethiopian National Archives & Library Agency (NALA) (Ethiopia) *Tel:* (011) 5516532 *Web Site:* www.nala. gov.et, pg 1588

The Ethnic Publishing House (China) *Tel:* (010) 64212794; (010) 58130000; (010) 58130363 *Fax:* (010) 64211734; (010) 64284284; (010) 64228007 *E-mail:* e56@e56.com.cn *Web Site:* www. e56.com.cn, pg 104

Editura Etna (Romania) *Tel:* (0727) 317 800 (cell) *Fax:* (031) 8105942 *Web Site:* www.etna.ro, pg 586

Eton Press (Auckland) Ltd (New Zealand) *Toll Free Tel:* 0800 333 016 *Toll Free Fax:* 0800 333 034 *E-mail:* info@eton.co.nz *Web Site:* www.eton.co.nz, pg 1438

ETR (Editrice Trasporti su Rotaie) (Italy) *Tel:* (03) 6541092 *Fax:* (03) 6541092 *E-mail:* etr@etreditrice. eu; direzione@etreditrice.eu *Web Site:* www.etreditrice. eu, pg 442

Institut d'Etudes Augustiniennes (IEA) (France) *Tel:* 01 43 54 80 25 *Fax:* 01 43 54 39 55 *E-mail:* etudes. augustiniennes@gmail.com *Web Site:* www.etudes-augustiniennes.paris-sorbonne.fr, pg 168

Institut d'etudes slaves (France) *Tel:* 01 42 02 27 54 *Fax:* 01 43 26 16 23 *E-mail:* ies.paris@orange.fr *Web Site:* institut-etudes-slaves.fr, pg 168

EUDEBA (Editorial Universitaria de Buenos Aires) (Argentina) *Tel:* (011) 4383-8025 *Fax:* (011) 4383-2202 *E-mail:* pedidos@eudeba.com.ar *Web Site:* www. eudeba.com.ar, pg 7

Eudora-Verlag Leipzig (Germany) *Tel:* (0341) 2288 582; (0176) 2261 7202 (cell) *Fax:* (03221) 2369 376 *E-mail:* info@eudora-verlag.de *Web Site:* www.eudora-verlag.de, pg 242

Eugenides Foundation Technical Library (Greece) *Tel:* 2109469600 *Fax:* 2109417372 *E-mail:* admin@ eugenfound.edu.gr; lib@eef.edu.gr *Web Site:* www. eugenfound.edu.gr, pg 1598

Leidykla Eugrimas (Lithuania) *Tel:* (05) 273 3955; (05) 275 4754 *Fax:* (05) 273 3955; (05) 275 4754 *E-mail:* info@eugrimas.lt *Web Site:* www.eugrimas.lt, pg 501

Eulama Literary Agencies (Italy) *Tel:* (06) 5407309 *Fax:* (06) 5407309 *E-mail:* info@eulama.com *Web Site:* www.eulama.com, pg 1230

Eulen Verlag (Germany) *Tel:* (089) 47 07 77 44 *Fax:* (08581) 91 06 68 *E-mail:* info@suedost-verlag.de *Web Site:* www.suedost-verlag.de, pg 242

Eulenspiegel Verlagsgruppe - Das Neue Berlin Verlagsgesellschaft mbH (Germany) *Tel:* (030) 23 80 91-0 *Fax:* (030) 23 80 91-23 *E-mail:* info@ eulenspiegelverlag.de *Web Site:* www.eulenspiegel-verlag.de, pg 242

Eulyoo Publishing Co Ltd (South Korea) *Tel:* (02) 7338151; (02) 7338152; (02) 7338153 *Fax:* (02) 7329154 *E-mail:* eulyoo1945@eulyoo.co.kr *Web Site:* www.eulyoo.co.kr, pg 621

Eumo Editorial (Spain) *Tel:* 93 889 28 18 *E-mail:* eumoeditorial@eumoeditorial.com *Web Site:* www.eumoeditorial.com, pg 643

EUNSA (Ediciones Universidad de Navarra SA) (Spain) *Tel:* 948 256 850 *Fax:* 948 256 854 *E-mail:* eunsa@ eunsa.es *Web Site:* www.eunsa.es, pg 643

Eurailpress-DVV Media Group GmbH (Germany) *Tel:* (040) 237 14-03 *Fax:* (040) 237 14-259 *E-mail:* info@eurailpress.de *Web Site:* www. eurailpress.de, pg 242

Eurasia (Netherlands) *Tel:* (0172) 200 088 *Web Site:* www.eurasiainternational.com, pg 1282

euregioverlag (Germany) *Tel:* (0561) 50049330 *Fax:* (0561) 50049340 *E-mail:* info@euregioverlag.de *Web Site:* www.euregioverlag.de, pg 242

Euro-Druckservice GmbH (Germany) *Tel:* (0851) 851 600-0 *Fax:* (0851) 851 600-60 *E-mail:* office@ edsgroup.de *Web Site:* www.edsgroup.de, pg 1275, 1322

Euro GeoGrafiche Mencattini SRL (EGM) (Italy) *Tel:* (0575) 900010 *Fax:* (0575) 911161 *E-mail:* info@ egm.it *Web Site:* www.egm.it, pg 442

Euro Transmit SL (Spain) *Tel:* 972 32 51 42 *Fax:* 972 32 51 67 *E-mail:* info@eurotransmit.com *Web Site:* www.eurotransmit.com, pg 1251

Eurocrom 4 (Italy) *Tel:* (0422) 608200 *Fax:* (0422) 608322 *E-mail:* info@eurocrom4.com *Web Site:* www. eurocrom4.com, pg 1328

Eurodimension Publication Advertising (Greece) *Tel:* 2108611303 *Fax:* 2108611303, pg 355

Eurodruk Poznan Sp z oo (Poland) *Tel:* (61) 816 40 10 *Fax:* (61) 816 40 11 *E-mail:* edp@eurodruk.com.pl *Web Site:* www.eurodruk.com.pl, pg 1282, 1331

Eurohueco SA (Spain) *Tel:* 93 773 07 00 *Fax:* 93 653 22 05 *E-mail:* contact@rotocobrhi.eurohueco.es *Web Site:* www.eurohueco.es, pg 1334

EuroImpala Books Lda (Portugal) *Tel:* 219238246 (orders) *Fax:* 219238463 (orders) *E-mail:* vendadireta@euroimpalabooks.com *Web Site:* www.euroimpalabooks.com, pg 578

Eurolibros Ltda (Colombia) *Tel:* (01) 2886400 *Fax:* (01) 3401811 *E-mail:* eurolibros@gmail.com, pg 113

Euromedia Group ks (EMG) (Czech Republic) *Tel:* 296 536 111 *Fax:* 296 536 935 *E-mail:* knizni.klub@ euromedia.cz *Web Site:* www.euromedia.cz, pg 127

Euromonitor International Ltd (United Kingdom) *Tel:* (020) 7251 8024 *Fax:* (020) 7608 3149 *E-mail:* info@euromonitor.com *Web Site:* www. euromonitor.com, pg 763

Publicacoes Europa-America Lda (Portugal) *Tel:* 21 926 77 00 *Fax:* 21 926 77 71 *E-mail:* secretariado@ europa-america.pt *Web Site:* www.europa-america.pt, pg 578

Europa Editions UK (United Kingdom) *E-mail:* info@ europaeditions.com *Web Site:* www.europaeditions. com, pg 763

Europa Konyvkiado Kft (Hungary) *Tel:* (01) 331-2700 *Fax:* (01) 331-4162 *E-mail:* info@europakiado.hu *Web Site:* www.europakiado.hu, pg 368

Europa Law Publishing (Netherlands) *Tel:* (050) 526 3844 *Fax:* (084) 832 5076 *E-mail:* info@ europalawpublishing.com *Web Site:* www. europalawpublishing.com, pg 533

Verlag Europa-Lehrmittel Nourney, Vollmer GmbH & Co KG (Germany) *Tel:* (02104) 6916-0 *Fax:* (02104) 6916-27 *E-mail:* info@europa-lehrmittel.de; rights@ europa-lehrmittel.de *Web Site:* www.europa-lehrmittel. de, pg 242

Europa Verlag GmbH & Co KG (Germany) *Tel:* (089) 18 94 733-0 *Fax:* (089) 18 94 733-16 *E-mail:* info@ europa-verlag.com *Web Site:* www.europa-verlag.com, pg 242

Europaeisches Burgeninstitut (Germany) *Tel:* (02627) 974156 *Fax:* (02627) 970394 *E-mail:* ebi@deutsche-burgen.org; ebi.sekretariat@deutsche-burgen.org; ebi. leiter@deutsche-burgen.org *Web Site:* www.deutsche-burgen.org, pg 243

Europea de Libros Ltda (Colombia) *Tel:* (01) 2886400, pg 1410

European & International Booksellers Federation (EIBF) (Belgium) *Tel:* (02) 223 49 40 *E-mail:* info@ europeanbooksellers.eu; info@eibf-booksellers.org *Web Site:* www.europeanbooksellers.eu, pg 1366

European Association for Health Information & Libraries (Netherlands) *Tel:* (0346) 550 876 *Web Site:* eahil.eu, pg 1383

European Educational Publishers Group (EEPG) (Germany) *Tel:* (0171) 275 63 23 *Web Site:* www. eepg.org, pg 1374

European Foundation for the Improvement of Living & Working Conditions (Ireland) *Tel:* (01) 2043100 *Fax:* (01) 2826456; (01) 2824209 *E-mail:* information@eurofound.europa.eu *Web Site:* www.eurofound.europa.eu, pg 410

European Health Management Association (EHMA) (Belgium) *Tel:* (02) 502 65 25 *Fax:* (02) 503 10 07 *E-mail:* joinehma@ehma.org *Web Site:* www.ehma.org, pg 66

European Schoolbooks Ltd (ESB) (United Kingdom) *Tel:* (01242) 245252 *Fax:* (01242) 224137 *E-mail:* direct@esb.co.uk *Web Site:* www.eurobooks. co.uk, pg 763, 1457

European University Institute Library (Italy) *Tel:* (055) 4685 340 *Fax:* (055) 4685 283 *E-mail:* library@eui. eu; euiref@eui.eu *Web Site:* www.eui.eu, pg 1606

Europress Editores e Distribuidores de Publicacoes Lda (Portugal) *Tel:* 218444340 *Fax:* 218492061 *E-mail:* geral@europress.pt; europress@mail.telepac.pt *Web Site:* www.europress.pt; www.europresseditora.pt, pg 579

Europrint AS (Czech Republic) *Tel:* 225 347 111 *E-mail:* europrint@europrint.cz *Web Site:* www. europrint.cz, pg 1320

Eurospan Ltd (United Kingdom) *Tel:* (020) 3286 2420 *E-mail:* info@eurospangroup.com; info@ eurospanbookstore.com *Web Site:* www.eurospangroup. com; www.eurospanbookstore.com, pg 1458

Euskaltzaindia-Royal Academy of the Basque Language (Spain) *Tel:* 944 15 81 55 *Fax:* 944 15 81 44 *E-mail:* info@euskaltzaindia.net *Web Site:* www. euskaltzaindia.eus, pg 644

EVA Europaeische Verlagsanstalt GmbH & Co KG (Germany) *Tel:* (040) 450194-0 *Fax:* (040) 450194-50 *E-mail:* info@europaeische-verlagsanstalt.de *Web Site:* www.europaeische-verlagsanstalt.de, pg 243

Evagean Publishing Ltd (New Zealand) *Tel:* (07) 884-8783; (07) 884-8594 *Web Site:* www.evagean.co.nz, pg 546

Evangel Publishing House, Nairobi (Kenya) *Tel:* (020) 8560839; (020) 856204 *Fax:* (020) 8562050 *E-mail:* info@evangelpublishing.org; editorial@ evangelpublishing.org; accounts@evangelpublishing. org *Web Site:* www.evangelpublishing.org, pg 493

Evangelical Press (United Kingdom) *Tel:* (0333) 772 0214 *E-mail:* sales@epbooks.org *Web Site:* www. epbooks.org, pg 763

Evangelische Buchhandlungen und Basileia Verlag GmbH (Switzerland) *Tel:* (061) 260 21 20 *Fax:* (061) 260 22 68, pg 693

Evangelische Verlagsanstalt GmbH (Germany) *Tel:* (0341) 711 41 0 *Fax:* (0341) 711 41 50 *Web Site:* www.eva-leipzig.de, pg 243

Verlag und Buchhandlung der Evangelischen Gesellschaft GmbH (Germany) *Tel:* (0711) 6 01 00-0 *Fax:* (0711) 6 01 00-76 *E-mail:* info@ evanggemeindeblatt.de *Web Site:* www.verlag-eva.de, pg 243

Faculte des Sciences Humaines et Sociales de Tunis (Tunisia) *Tel:* 71 560 840 *Fax:* 71 567 551 *E-mail:* fshst@fshst.rnu.tn *Web Site:* www.fshst.rnu.tn, pg 717

FADL's Forlag A/S (Denmark) *Tel:* 35 35 62 87 *Fax:* 35 36 62 29 *E-mail:* kundeservice@fadlsforlag.dk; redaktion@fadlsforlag.dk *Web Site:* fadlforlag.dk, pg 136

Gruppo Editorial Faenza Editrice SpA (Italy) *Tel:* (0546) 670411 *Fax:* (0546) 660440, pg 442

Fagbokforlaget AS (Norway) *Tel:* 55 38 88 00; 55 38 88 38 (orders) *Fax:* 55 38 88 01; 55 38 88 39 (orders) *E-mail:* fagbokforlaget@fagbokforlaget.no; ordre@fagbokforlaget.no; faktural@fagbokforlaget.no *Web Site:* www.fagbokforlaget.no, pg 554

Fage Editions (France) *Tel:* 04 72 07 70 98 *E-mail:* fage. editions@free.fr *Web Site:* www.fage-editions.com, pg 169

Fairfield Marketing Group Inc (United States) *Tel:* 203-261-5585; 203-261-5568 *Fax:* 203-261-0884 *E-mail:* info@fairfieldmarketing.com *Web Site:* www. fairfieldmarketing.com, pg 1288, 1339, 1356

Faksimile Verlag (Germany) *Tel:* (089) 41 36 83 61 *Fax:* (089) 41 36 54 11 *E-mail:* info@faksimile.de *Web Site:* www.faksimile.de, pg 244

Fakultet Gradevinarstva Arhitekture I Geodezue (Croatia) *Tel:* (021) 303 333 *Fax:* (021) 465 117 *Web Site:* www.gradst.hr, pg 120

Falkplan BV (Netherlands) *Tel:* (040) 26 45 104 *Fax:* (040) 26 45 115 *E-mail:* helpdesk@falk.nl; info@falk.nl; media@falk.nl; fietsplanner@falk.nl *Web Site:* www.falk.nl, pg 533

Editions de Fallois (France) *Tel:* 01 42 66 91 95 *Fax:* 01 49 24 06 37, pg 169

C J Fallon Ltd (Ireland) *Tel:* (01) 6166400; (01) 6166490 (sales) *Fax:* (01) 6166499 *E-mail:* sales@cjfallon.ie; editorial@cjfallon.ie; info@cjfallon.ie *Web Site:* www. cjfallon.ie, pg 410

Falter Verlagsgesellschaft mbH (Austria) *Tel:* (01) 536 60-0 *Fax:* (01) 536 60-935 *E-mail:* service@falter.at *Web Site:* www.falter.at, pg 48

Fama Publishers (Bulgaria) *Tel:* (02) 418 41 34; (02) 416 24 62 *E-mail:* famapublishers@famapublishers.com *Web Site:* famapublishers.com, pg 95

Famedram Publishers Ltd (United Kingdom) *Tel:* (01651) 842429 *Fax:* (01651) 842180 *E-mail:* info@famedram.com; orders@famedram.com; online@famedram.com *Web Site:* www.famedram.com; www.northernbooks.co.uk; www.artwork.co.uk, pg 764

familia Verlag (Germany) *Tel:* (0341) 231001712 *Fax:* (0341) 231001718 *E-mail:* info@familia-verlag. de *Web Site:* www.familia-verlag.de, pg 244

Family Health Publications (Australia) *Tel:* (08) 9389 8777 *Fax:* (08) 9389 8444 *Web Site:* www.calorieking. com.au, pg 24

Family Leisure Club (Ukraine) *Tel:* (057) 783 8888 *Toll Free Tel:* 0800 30 10 90 *E-mail:* publish@bookclub.ua (manuscripts) *Web Site:* www.ksd.ua, pg 726

Family Leisure Club (Ukraine) *Toll Free Tel:* 0800 30 10 90 *E-mail:* supports@bookclub.ua *Web Site:* www. bookclub.ua; catalog.ksd.ua, pg 1361

Family Leisure Club (Ukraine) *Tel:* (057) 703 44 57 *Toll Free Tel:* 0800 30 10 90 *Fax:* (057) 784 00 91 *E-mail:* trade@bookclub.ua *Web Site:* trade.bookclub. ua, pg 1455

Family Media GmbH & Co KG (Germany) *Tel:* (0761) 70 578 0 *Fax:* (0761) 70 57 86 51 *E-mail:* info@ familymedia.de *Web Site:* www.familymedia.de, pg 244

Fand Music Press (United Kingdom) *Tel:* (01730) 267341 *Fax:* (01730) 267341 *E-mail:* contact@ fandmusic.com; orders@fandmusic.com *Web Site:* www.fandmusic.com, pg 765

F&G Editores (Guatemala) *Tel:* 2439 8358; 5406 0909 *Fax:* 2439 8358 *E-mail:* informacion@fygeditores.com *Web Site:* www.fygeditores.com, pg 361

Editions Fanlac (France) *Tel:* 05 53 53 41 90 *Fax:* 05 53 08 05 85 *E-mail:* info@fanlac.com *Web Site:* www. fanlac.com, pg 169

Fanshaw Books Ltd (United Kingdom) *Tel:* (020) 7281 9387 *Fax:* (020) 8883 8513 *E-mail:* info@ fanshawbooks.co.uk *Web Site:* www.fanshawbooks. co.uk, pg 1458

Fantasi Books (Pty) Ltd (South Africa) *Tel:* (012) 804 2616 *Fax:* (012) 804 0480 *E-mail:* fantasi@ffg.net *Web Site:* fantasi.co.za, pg 613

Fanucci Editore SRL (Italy) *Tel:* (06) 39366384 *Fax:* (06) 6382998 *E-mail:* info@fanucci.it; foreign.rights@fanucci.it; info.ordini@fanucci.it; comunicazione@fanucci.it *Web Site:* www.fanucci.it, pg 442

The Far East Book Co Ltd (Taiwan) *Tel:* (02) 2311-8740 *Fax:* (02) 2311-4184 *E-mail:* service@mail.fareast. com.tw *Web Site:* www.fareast.com.tw, pg 711

Far Eastern Federal University (FEFU) (Russia) *Web Site:* www.dvfu.ru, pg 594

Far Eastern University Library (Philippines) *Tel:* (02) 735-5621 *E-mail:* universitylibrary@feu.edu.ph *Web Site:* www.feu.edu.ph; www.facebook.com/ feulibrary, pg 1622

Far Far Away Books & Media Ltd (United Kingdom) *Tel:* (020) 7400 3375 *E-mail:* office@ farfarawaybooksandmedia.co.uk *Web Site:* www. farfarawaybooks.com, pg 765

Faradawn CC (South Africa) *Tel:* (011) 885 1847; (011) 885 1787 *Fax:* (011) 885 1829 *E-mail:* faradawn@ icon.co.za *Web Site:* www.faradawn.co.za, pg 1448

Editions Farel (France) *Tel:* 01 64 68 46 44 *Fax:* 01 64 68 39 90 *E-mail:* lire@editionsfarel.com; english@ editionsfarel.com *Web Site:* www.editionsfarel.com, pg 169

Farlit (Faroe Islands) *E-mail:* farlit@farlit.fo *Web Site:* farlit.fo, pg 1370

Faroe University Press (Faroe Islands) *Tel:* 352500 *Fax:* 352501 *E-mail:* frodskapur@setur.fo; setur@ setur.fo *Web Site:* www.setur.fo/frodskapur, pg 147

Farseeing Publishing Co Ltd (Taiwan) *Tel:* (02) 2392-1167; (02) 2392-1167 (ext 722, customer service) *Fax:* (02) 2322-5455 *E-mail:* fars@ms6.hinet.net *Web Site:* www.farseeing.com.tw, pg 711

Verlag Fassbaender (Austria) *Tel:* (01) 892-35-46 *E-mail:* office@fassbaender.com *Web Site:* www. fassbaender.com, pg 48

Editions Fata Morgana (France) *Tel:* 04 67 54 40 40 *E-mail:* fatamorgana@wanadoo.fr *Web Site:* www. fatamorgana.fr, pg 169

Editorial Fata Morgana SA de CV (Mexico) *Tel:* (0155) 5280-0829 *E-mail:* editorial@fatamorgana.com.mx *Web Site:* www.fatamorgana.com.mx, pg 516

Fatatrac SRL (Italy) *Tel:* (051) 753358 *Fax:* (051) 752637 *E-mail:* info@fatatrac.com *Web Site:* www. fatatrac.com; www.edizionidelborgo.it, pg 442

Editions Faton (France) *Tel:* 03 80 40 41 00 *Fax:* 03 80 30 15 37 *E-mail:* infos@faton.fr *Web Site:* www.faton. fr; www.art-metiers-du-livre.com, pg 169

Ekkehard Faude Verlag (Switzerland) *Tel:* (04171) 688 35 55 *Fax:* (04171) 688 35 65 *E-mail:* info@libelle.ch *Web Site:* www.libelle.ch, pg 693

Edition Faust (Germany) *Tel:* (069) 56 40 25 *Fax:* (069) 56 43 21 *E-mail:* verlag@editionfaust.de *Web Site:* www.editionfaust.de, pg 244

Editions Favre SA (Switzerland) *Tel:* (021) 312 17 17 *Fax:* (021) 320 50 59 *E-mail:* lausanne@editionsfavre. com *Web Site:* www.editionsfavre.com, pg 694

Librairie Artheme Fayard (France) *Tel:* 01 45 49 82 00 *Web Site:* www.fayard.fr, pg 169

Fazi Editore (Italy) *Tel:* (06) 96 03 14 00 *Fax:* (06) 85 57 532 *E-mail:* info@fazieditore.it *Web Site:* www. fazieditore.it, pg 442

Fazlee Sons (Pvt) Ltd (Pakistan) *Tel:* (021) 32563971; (021) 32572210 *Fax:* (021) 32571688 *E-mail:* contact@fazlee.com; tfazlee@gmail.com *Web Site:* www.fazlee.com, pg 559

Maria Pacini Fazzi Editore (Italy) *Tel:* (0583) 440188 *Fax:* (0583) 464656 *E-mail:* mpf@pacinifazzi.it *Web Site:* www.pacinifazzi.it, pg 442

FBA Group (United Kingdom) *Tel:* (01970) 636400 *E-mail:* info@fbagroup.co.uk *Web Site:* fbagroup. wales, pg 765

FCA Editora de Informatica Lda (Portugal) *Tel:* 21 351 14 48 *Fax:* 21 317 32 59 *E-mail:* fca@fca.pt *Web Site:* www.fca.pt, pg 579

Federacao Brasileira de Associacoes de Bibliotecarios, Cientistas da Informacao e Instituicoes - Comissao Brasileira de Documentacao Juridica (FEBAB/CBDJ) (Brazil) *Tel:* (011) 3257-9979 *Fax:* (011) 3257-9979 *E-mail:* febab@febab.org.br *Web Site:* www.febab.org. br, pg 1649

Federacion de Gremios de Editores de Espana (FGEE) (Spain) *Tel:* 91 534 51 95 *Fax:* 91 535 26 25 *E-mail:* fgee@fge.es *Web Site:* www. federacioneditores.org, pg 1389

Federacion Espanola de Asociaciones de Archiveros, Bibliotecarios, Arqueologos, Museologos y Documentalistas (Spain) *Tel:* 91 575 17 27 *Fax:* 91 578 16 15 *E-mail:* anabad@anabad.org *Web Site:* www.anabad.org, pg 1660

Federal Publications (S) Pte Ltd (Singapore) *Tel:* 6213 9288 *Fax:* 6284 4733; 6288 1186 *E-mail:* tpl@tpl. com.sg *Web Site:* www.timespublishing.sg; www.tpl. com.sg, pg 603

Feder&Schwert GmbH (Germany) *Tel:* (0621) 720 798-0 *Fax:* (0621) 720 798-1 *E-mail:* verkauf@feder-und-schwert.com; marketing@feder-und-schwert.com *Web Site:* www.feder-und-schwert.com, pg 244

Federation des enseignants documentalistes de l'Education nationale (France) *E-mail:* contact@ fadben.asso.fr *Web Site:* www.fadben.asso.fr, pg 1651

Federation Francaise de la Randonnee Pedestre (France) *Tel:* 01 44 89 93 93; 01 44 89 93 90 *Fax:* 01 40 35 85 67 *E-mail:* info@ffrandonnee.fr; e-publicite@ffrandonnee.fr (advertising) *Web Site:* www. ffrandonnee.fr, pg 169

Federation Internationale des Traducteurs (FIT) (France) *Tel:* 01 53 32 17 55 *Fax:* 01 53 32 17 32 *E-mail:* secretariat@fit-ift.org *Web Site:* www.fit-ift. org, pg 1371

The Federation of Children's Book Groups (United Kingdom) *Toll Free Tel:* 0300 102 1559 *E-mail:* info@fcbg.org.uk *Web Site:* www.fcbg.org.uk, pg 1395

Federation of European Publishers (FEP) (Belgium) *Tel:* (02) 770 11 10 *Fax:* (02) 771 20 71 *E-mail:* info@fep-fee.eu *Web Site:* www.fep-fee.eu, pg 1366

The Federation of Indian Publishers (FIP) (India) *Tel:* (011) 26964847; (011) 26852263; (011) 26966931 *Fax:* (011) 26864054 *Web Site:* www.fipindia.co, pg 1377

The Federation of Publishers' & Booksellers' Associations in India (FPBAI) (India) *Tel:* (011) 23272845; (011) 23281227 *E-mail:* fpbaindia@gmail. com *Web Site:* fpbai.org, pg 1377

The Federation Press (Australia) *Tel:* (02) 9552 2200 *Fax:* (02) 9552 1681 *E-mail:* info@federationpress. com.au *Web Site:* www.federationpress.com.au *Web Site:* www. federationpress.com.au, pg 25

Federazione Italiana Editori Indipendenti (FIDARE) (Italy) *Tel:* (011) 5211790 *Fax:* (011) 09652658 *E-mail:* info@fidare.it *Web Site:* www.fidare.it, pg 1379

Federighi Editori (Italy) *Tel:* (0571) 664016 *Fax:* (0571) 663568 *E-mail:* info@federighieditori.it *Web Site:* www.federighieditori.it, pg 443

Feguagiskia' Studios (Italy) *Tel:* (010) 2510829 *Fax:* (010) 2510838, pg 443

Felag Islenskra Bokautgefenda (Iceland) *Tel:* 511-8020 *Fax:* 511-5020 *E-mail:* fibut@fibut.is *Web Site:* www. fibut.is, pg 1377

Fellowship of Australian Writers (Vic) Inc (Australia) *Tel:* (03) 9386 2232 *E-mail:* austwriter@writers.asn.au *Web Site:* www.fawvic.com.au/, pg 1489

Ediciones Felou (Mexico) *Tel:* (0155) 525 60 561 *Fax:* (0155) 525 62 168 *E-mail:* ventas@felou.com *Web Site:* www.felou.com, pg 516

Giangiacomo Feltrinelli Editore SRL (Italy) *Tel:* (02) 725721 *Fax:* (02) 72572500; (02) 72001064 (press) *E-mail:* commerciale@feltrinelli.it; ufficio.stampa@ feltrinelli.it *Web Site:* www.feltrinellieditore.it; www. feltrinelli.it, pg 443

Librerie Feltrinelli SpA (Italy) *E-mail:* comunicazione@ lafeltrinelli.it; commerciale@feltrinelli.it *Web Site:* www.lafeltrinelli.it, pg 1428

Feltron-Elektronik Zeissler & Co GmbH (Germany) *Tel:* (02241) 4867-0 *Fax:* (02241) 404241 *E-mail:* feltron@feltron.de *Web Site:* www.feltron-zeissler.de, pg 244

Editions des Femmes (France) *Tel:* 01 42 22 60 74; 01 42 60 93 76 *Fax:* 01 42 22 62 73; 01 58 62 20 13 *E-mail:* contact@desfemmes.fr; librairie@ desfemmes.fr *Web Site:* www.desfemmes.fr; www. alliancedesfemmes.fr, pg 169

Femrite Uganda Women Writers' Association (Uganda) *Tel:* (0414) 543943 *E-mail:* info@femrite.org *Web Site:* femrite.org, pg 1501

Fen Kitabevi Ltd sti (Turkey) *Tel:* (0312) 418 51 09, pg 1454

Fenestra-Verlag (Germany) *Tel:* (0611) 5440693 *Fax:* (0611) 9545911 *E-mail:* info@fenestra-verlag.de *Web Site:* www.fenestra-verlag.de, pg 244

Fenix-Kustannus Oy (Finland) *Tel:* (050) 0448146 *E-mail:* tilaus@fenixkustannus.fi, pg 148

Editions Le Fennec (Morocco) *Tel:* 05 22 20 93 14; 05 22 20 92 68 *Fax:* 05 22 27 77 02 *E-mail:* info@ lefennec.com *Web Site:* www.lefennec.com, pg 526

Editions Feret (France) *Tel:* 05 56 13 79 95 *Fax:* 05 56 13 79 96 *E-mail:* feret@feret.com *Web Site:* www. feret.com, pg 169

Feria Chilena del Libro (Chile) *Tel:* (02) 2345 8316; (02) 2345 8300; (02) 2345 8317 *E-mail:* huerfanos@ feriachilenadellibro.cl *Web Site:* www. feriachilenadellibro.cl, pg 1409

Feria del Libro (Uruguay) *Tel:* 29004248 *Fax:* 29002070 *Web Site:* www.feriadellibro.com.uy, pg 1461

Livraria Ferin Ltda (Portugal) *Tel:* 213424422 *Fax:* 213471101 *E-mail:* livraria.ferin@ferin.pt *Web Site:* www.ferin.pt, pg 1445

Fermoeditore (Italy) *Tel:* (0521) 977384 *Fax:* (0521) 4463726 *E-mail:* info@fermoeditore.it *Web Site:* www. fermoeditore.it, pg 443

Fern House (United Kingdom) *Tel:* (01353) 740 222 *E-mail:* info@fernhouse.com *Web Site:* www. fernhouse.com, pg 765

Libreria Amalio M Fernandez SRL (Uruguay) *Tel:* 29151782 *E-mail:* amflibrosjuridicos@adinet.com. uy, pg 1462

Fernandez Editores SA de CV (Mexico) *Tel:* (0155) 5090 7700 *Toll Free Tel:* 01 800 712 49 99; 01 800 021 50 16 *E-mail:* tecnologia.fesa@gmail.com *Web Site:* www.tareasya.com.mx, pg 516

Fernhurst Books Ltd (United Kingdom) *Tel:* (01926) 337488 *Web Site:* fernhurstbooks.com, pg 765

Fernwood Press CC (South Africa) *Tel:* (021) 786 2460 *Fax:* (021) 786 2478, pg 613

Ferozsons (Pakistan) *Tel:* (042) 111-62-62-62 *Fax:* (042) 636-9204 *E-mail:* support@ferozsons.com.pk *Web Site:* www.ferozsons.com.pk, pg 559, 1441

Livraria Manuel Ferreira Lda (Portugal) *Tel:* 225363237 *Fax:* 225364406 *E-mail:* contacto@livrariaferreira.pt *Web Site:* www.livrariaferreira.pt, pg 1445

Franz Ferzak World & Space Publications (Germany) *Tel:* (09446) 1403, pg 244

Festina Lente (Italy) *Tel:* (055) 292612, pg 443

Festland Verlag GmbH (Germany) *Tel:* (0228) 362021; (0228) 362022 (sales) *Fax:* (0228) 351771 *E-mail:* verlag@oeckl.de *Web Site:* www.oeckl.de, pg 244

Festo Didactic GmbH & Co KG (Germany) *Tel:* (0711) 346 70 *Fax:* (0711) 34 75 48 85 00 *E-mail:* did@ de.festo.com *Web Site:* www.festo-didactic.de; www. festo-didactic.com, pg 245

Edition Ralf Fetzer (Germany) *Tel:* (0621) 48179005 *E-mail:* kontakt@edition-ralf-fetzer.de *Web Site:* www. edition-ralf-fetzer.de, pg 245

Feuervogel-Verlag (Germany) *Tel:* (069) 57 42 57 *Fax:* (069) 57 42 57 *E-mail:* info@feuervogel-verlag. de *Web Site:* www.feuervogel-verlag.de, pg 245

Editora FGV (Brazil) *Tel:* (021) 3799-4426; (021) 3799-4427; (021) 3799-4228; (021) 3799-4429 *Toll Free Tel:* 0800 021 7777 *Fax:* (021) 3799-4430 *E-mail:* editora@fgv.br *Web Site:* www.editora.fgv.br; www.fgv.br, pg 81

FIAF (International Federation of Film Archives) (Belgium) *Tel:* (02) 538 3065 *Fax:* (02) 534 4774 *E-mail:* info@fiafnet.org *Web Site:* www.fiafnet.org, pg 1366

FiberMark Red Bridge International Ltd (United Kingdom) *Tel:* (01204) 556900 *E-mail:* sales@ redbridge.co.uk; info@fibermark.com; redbridge@ fibermark.com *Web Site:* www.redbridge.co.uk, pg 1348

fibre Verlag (Germany) *Tel:* (0541) 431838 *Fax:* (0541) 432786 *E-mail:* info@fibre-verlag.de *Web Site:* www. fibre-verlag.de, pg 245

David Fickling Books (United Kingdom) *Tel:* (01865) 339000 *Web Site:* www.davidficklingbooks.com, pg 765

Fidia Edizioni d'Arte (Italy) *Tel:* (02) 895 462 86 *Fax:* (02) 843 941 1 *E-mail:* info@cfs-editore.com *Web Site:* www.cfs-editore.com, pg 443

Groupe Revue Fiduciaire (France) *Tel:* 08 26 80 52 52; 01 41 83 62 58 *E-mail:* src@grouperf.com; courrier@ grouperf.com *Web Site:* corporate.grouperf.com, pg 170

FIELL Publishing Ltd (United Kingdom) *Tel:* (01386) 840882 *E-mail:* info@fiell.com *Web Site:* www.fiell. com, pg 765

Wolfgang Fietkau Verlag (Germany) *Tel:* (033203) 711 05 *Fax:* (033203) 711 09 *E-mail:* post@fietkau.de *Web Site:* www.fietkau.de, pg 245

FiFa-Fiction & Fantasy eV (Germany) *Tel:* (0177) 750 29 37 *E-mail:* fifa-verlag@t-online.de *Web Site:* www. fifa-verlag.de.vu, pg 1495

Livraria Editora Figueirinhas (Portugal) *Tel:* 223 325 300 *Fax:* 223 325 907, pg 579

Livraria Editora Figueirinhas Lda (Portugal) *Tel:* 225309026; 225301013 *Fax:* 225309027 *E-mail:* correio@liv-figueirinhas.pt, pg 1445

Fil Rouge Press (United Kingdom) *Tel:* (020) 3669 1922 *Web Site:* www.filrougepress.com, pg 765

FILI (Finland) *E-mail:* fili@finlit.fi *Web Site:* www.finlit. fi/fili, pg 1370

Filmart-Sha Co Ltd (Japan) *Tel:* (03) 5725-2001 *Fax:* (03) 5725-2626 *E-mail:* info@filmart.co.jp *Web Site:* www.filmart.co.jp, pg 476

Ekdoseis ton Filon (Greece) *Tel:* 2108547723 *E-mail:* gelbesi@hol.gr, pg 355

Filozofski Fakultet Sveucilista u Zagrebu (Croatia) *Tel:* (01) 6120-111 *Fax:* (01) 6156-879 *Web Site:* www.ffzg.unizg.hr, pg 120

Finansy i Statistika Publishing House (Russia) *Tel:* (495) 625-47-08; (495) 625-35-02; (495) 625-36-28; (495) 621-86-57 *Fax:* (495) 625-09-57 *E-mail:* mail@finstat. ru *Web Site:* www.finstat.ru, pg 594

FinanzBuch Verlag GmbH (Germany) *Tel:* (089) 651285-0 *Fax:* (089) 652096 *E-mail:* info@finanzbuchverlag. de *Web Site:* www.m-vg.de/finanzbuchverlag, pg 245

Finch Publishing (Australia) *Tel:* (02) 9418 6247 *Fax:* (02) 9418 8878 *Web Site:* finch.com.au, pg 25

Find Out Team SRL (Italy) *Tel:* (0321) 16 44 015 *E-mail:* info@findout-team.com *Web Site:* www. findout-team.com, pg 1231

Findhorn Press Ltd (United Kingdom) *Tel:* (01309) 690582 *E-mail:* info@findhornpress.com *Web Site:* www.findhornpress.com, pg 765

Fine Wine Editions (United Kingdom) *Tel:* (020) 7812 8645 *Fax:* (020) 7400 8066 *Web Site:* www. quartoknows.com/fine-wine-editions, pg 765

Fines Mundi GmbH (Germany) *Tel:* (06898) 3097740 *Fax:* (06898) 3097742 *E-mail:* info@fines-mundi.de *Web Site:* www.fines-mundi.de, pg 1322

FINIDR sro (Czech Republic) *Tel:* 558 772 111 *Fax:* 558 772 221 *E-mail:* tiskarna@finidr.cz *Web Site:* www.finidr.cz, pg 1320

Edition Fink (Switzerland) *Tel:* (044) 280 55 62 *Fax:* (044) 280 55 63 *E-mail:* verlag@editionfink.ch *Web Site:* www.editionfink.ch, pg 694

J Fink Verlag GmbH & Co KG (Germany) *Tel:* (0711) 280 40 60-0 *Fax:* (0711) 280 40 60-70 *E-mail:* kontakt@jfink-verlag.de *Web Site:* www.jfink-verlag.de, pg 245

Kunstverlag Josef Fink (Germany) *Tel:* (08381) 8 37 21 *Fax:* (08381) 8 37 49 *E-mail:* info@kunstverlag-fink.de *Web Site:* www.kunstverlag-fink.de, pg 245

Verlag Wilhelm Fink GmbH & Co Verlags-KG (Germany) *Tel:* (05251) 127-5 *Fax:* (05251) 127-860 *E-mail:* info@fink.de *Web Site:* www.fink.de, pg 245

Finken Verlag GmbH (Germany) *Tel:* (06171) 6388-0 *Fax:* (06171) 6388-44 *E-mail:* info@finken.de; kundenservice@finken.de *Web Site:* www.finken.de, pg 245

Finlands Svenska Forfattareforening (Finland) *Tel:* (09) 446 266 *E-mail:* forfattarna@kaapeli.fi *Web Site:* www.forfattarna.fi, pg 1493

Oy Finn Lectura AB (Finland) *Tel:* (09) 74151 005 *Fax:* (09) 1464 370 *E-mail:* info@finnlectura.fi *Web Site:* www.finnlectura.fi, pg 148

Finnish ISBN Agency (Finland) *Tel:* (09) 2941 44329 *Fax:* (09) 191 44341 *E-mail:* isbn-keskus@helsinki.fi *Web Site:* www.kansalliskirjasto.fi, pg 1370

Barbara Fiore Editora SL (Spain) *Tel:* 958 175 303; 958 569 833 *Web Site:* www.barbara-fiore.es, pg 644

Libreria Editrice Fiorentina (Italy) *Tel:* (055) 2399342 *Fax:* (055) 2399342 *E-mail:* editrice@lef.firenze.it *Web Site:* www.lef.firenze.it, pg 443

Firdousi Tajikistan National Library (Tajikistan) *E-mail:* info@kmt.tj *Web Site:* kmt.tj, pg 1637

Firecrest Publishing Ltd (United Kingdom) *Tel:* (01296) 613800 *E-mail:* pfirecrest@aol.com; ps@ firecrestbooks.net *Web Site:* www.firecrestbooks.net, pg 765

Firenze Libri (Italy) *Tel:* (055) 5357250 *Fax:* (055) 5609191 *E-mail:* info@firenzelibri.it *Web Site:* www. firenzelibri.net, pg 443

Firma KLM Pvt Ltd (India) *Tel:* (033) 2221 7294; (033) 2237 4391 *E-mail:* firmaklm@yahoo.com, pg 382

First & Best in Education Ltd (United Kingdom) *Tel:* (01536) 399005 *Fax:* (01536) 399012 *E-mail:* sales@firstandbest.co.uk *Web Site:* www. firstandbest.co.uk, pg 766

Editions First & First Interactive (France) *Tel:* 01 45 49 60 00 *Fax:* 01 45 49 60 01 *E-mail:* firstinfo@ efirst.com; foreign.rights@grund.fr *Web Site:* www. editionsfirst.fr, pg 170

First Edition Translations Ltd (United Kingdom) *Tel:* (01223) 356733 *E-mail:* enquiries@firstedit.co.uk *Web Site:* www.firstedit.co.uk, pg 1253

Les Editions Fischbacher (France) *Tel:* 01 44 54 55 11 *Fax:* 01 44 54 55 15 *E-mail:* info@ editionsfischbacher.com *Web Site:* www. editionsfischbacher.com, pg 170

Bokforlaget Fischer & Co (Sweden) *Tel:* (08) 643 38 46 *Fax:* (08) 643 38 98 *E-mail:* info@lindco. se *Web Site:* www.lindco.se; forlaggare.se/content/ bokforlaget-fischer-co, pg 681

Fischer & Gann Publishing (Austria) *Tel:* (07744) 200 80-0 *E-mail:* office@fischerundgann.com *Web Site:* fischerundgann.com, pg 48

Harald Fischer Verlag GmbH (Germany) *Tel:* (09131) 205620 *Fax:* (09131) 206028 *E-mail:* info@ haraldfischerverlag.de *Web Site:* www. haraldfischerverlag.de, pg 245

Verkehrs-Verlag J Fischer GmbH & Co KG (Germany) *Tel:* (0211) 9 91 93-0 *Fax:* (0211) 6 80 15 44; (0211) 9 91 93 27 *E-mail:* vvf@verkehrsverlag-fischer.de *Web Site:* www.verkehrsverlag-fischer.de, pg 246

Karin Fischer Verlag GmbH (Germany) *Tel:* (0241) 960 90 90 *Fax:* (0241) 960 90 99 *E-mail:* info@karin-fischer-verlag.de *Web Site:* www.karin-fischer-verlag. de, pg 246

Edition Michael Fischer GmbH (Germany) *Tel:* (08248) 96 91 67 *Fax:* (08248) 96 91 68 *E-mail:* info@ edition-m-fischer.de *Web Site:* www.edition-m-fischer. de, pg 246

R G Fischer Verlag GmbH (Germany) *Tel:* (069) 941 942-0; (069) 941 942-11 (orders) *Fax:* (069) 941 942-98; (069) 941 942-99 (orders) *E-mail:* info@rgfischer-verlag.de; bestellung@rgfischer-verlag.de (orders) *Web Site:* www.rgfischer-verlag.de; www.edition-fischer.com, pg 246

S Fischer Verlag GmbH (Germany) *Tel:* (069) 6062-0 *Fax:* (069) 6062-214 (sales); (069) 6062-319 *Web Site:* www.fischerverlage.de, pg 246

Fiton + (Russia) *Tel:* (499) 256-67-20; (499) 256-25-75 (wholesale) *Fax:* (499) 256-67-20 *E-mail:* fiton@ fiton-knigi.ru; sales@fiton-knigi.ru; curaren@cea.ru *Web Site:* www.phytonflowers.ru; plantarya.ru, pg 594

Fitzcarraldo Editions (United Kingdom) *Tel:* (07772) 249942 (cell) *E-mail:* info@fitzcarraldoeditions.com *Web Site:* fitzcarraldoeditions.com, pg 766

5 Continents Editions SRL (Italy) *Tel:* (02) 33 60 32 76 *Fax:* (02) 92 87 14 57 *E-mail:* info@ fivecontinentseditions.com *Web Site:* www. fivecontinentseditions.com, pg 443

Five Islands Press (Australia) *Tel:* (03) 8344 9727 *E-mail:* contact@fiveislandspress.com; orders@ fiveislandspress.com *Web Site:* fiveislandspress.com, pg 25

Izdatelstvo Fizkultura i Sport (Russia) *Tel:* (495) 2582690, pg 594

Fizmatlit Publishing Co (Russia) *Tel:* (495) 334-74-21 *Fax:* (495) 334-76-20 *E-mail:* fizmat@maik.ru *Web Site:* www.fml.ru, pg 594

Dario Flaccovio Editore SRL (Italy) *Tel:* (091) 6700686 *Fax:* (091) 525738 *E-mail:* editore@darioflaccovio. it; direzione@darioflaccovio.it *Web Site:* www. darioflaccovio.com, pg 443

Flaccovio Editore (Italy) *Tel:* (091) 589442 *Fax:* (091) 331992 *E-mail:* editore@flaccovio.com; viaruggerosettimo@flaccovio.com *Web Site:* www. flaccovio.com, pg 443

Werner Flach Internationale Wissenschaftliche Buchhandlung und Zeitschriften-Agentur eK (Germany) *Tel:* (069) 95 91 75 0 *Fax:* (069) 95 91 75 22 *E-mail:* fachbuch@flachbuch.com *Web Site:* www. flachbuch.com, pg 1415

Ediciones FLACSO Costa Rica (Costa Rica) *Tel:* 2224-8059 *Fax:* 2224-2638 *E-mail:* dalfaro@flacso.or.cr; eazofeifa@flacso.or.cr *Web Site:* www.flacso.or.cr, pg 117

Les Editions du Flamboyant (Benin) *Tel:* 21 31 02 20 *Fax:* 90 91 57 27, pg 74

Flame of the Forest Publishing Pte Ltd (Singapore) *Tel:* 6484 8887 *Fax:* 6484 2208 *E-mail:* mail@ flameoftheforest.com; editor@flameoftheforest.com; sales@flameoftheforest.com; rights@flameoftheforest. com *Web Site:* www.flameoftheforest.com, pg 603

Flame Tree Publishing (United Kingdom) *Tel:* (020) 7386 4700 *Fax:* (020) 7386 4701 *E-mail:* info@ flametreepublishing.com *Web Site:* www. flametreepublishing.com, pg 766

Flammarion (France) *Tel:* 01 40 51 31 00 *Web Site:* www.groupe-flammarion.com, pg 1414

Flammarion Groupe (France) *Tel:* 01 40 51 31 00 *Fax:* 01 43 29 21 48 *Web Site:* editions.flammarion. com, pg 170

Flechsig Verlag (Germany) *Tel:* (0931) 465 889-11 *Fax:* (0931) 465 889-29 *E-mail:* info@verlagshaus. com *Web Site:* www.verlagshaus.com, pg 246

Erich Fleischer Verlag GmbH & Co KG (Germany) *Tel:* (04202) 517-0 *Fax:* (04202) 517-41 *E-mail:* info@efv-online.de *Web Site:* www.efv-online. de, pg 246

Fleischhauer & Spohn Verlag GmbH & Co KG (Germany) *Tel:* (07071) 6885-0 *Fax:* (07071) 6885-20 *E-mail:* info@silberburg.de *Web Site:* www.silberburg. de, pg 246

Flensburger Hefte Verlag GmbH (Germany) *Tel:* (0461) 2 63 63 *Fax:* (0461) 2 69 12 *E-mail:* info@ flensburgerhefte.de *Web Site:* www.flensburgerhefte.de, pg 246

Flesher Corp (United States) *Tel:* 719-633-1111 *Fax:* 719-633-8780 *E-mail:* sales@flesher.net *Web Site:* www.flesher.net, pg 1349

Fleurus Editions (France) *E-mail:* fleuruseditions@ fleuruseditions.com; foreignrights@fleuruseditions.com *Web Site:* www.fleuruseditions.com, pg 170

Fleuve Editions (France) *Tel:* 01 44 16 05 00 *E-mail:* foreignrights@universpoche.com *Web Site:* www.fleuve-editions.fr, pg 170

Flintas Publishing House (Lithuania) *Tel:* (061) 007 362 *Fax:* (037) 224 489 *E-mail:* info@flintaspublishing. com *Web Site:* www.flintaspublishing.com, pg 501

Flo Enterprise Sdn Bhd (Malaysia) *Tel:* (03) 77833118, pg 1432

Florilegium (Australia) *Tel:* (02) 9571 8222 *Fax:* (02) 8208 9938 *E-mail:* sales@florilegium.com.au *Web Site:* www.florilegium.com.au, pg 1402

Floris Books (United Kingdom) *Tel:* (0131) 337 2372 *E-mail:* floris@florisbooks.co.uk *Web Site:* www. florisbooks.co.uk, pg 766

Flying Eye Books (United Kingdom) *Tel:* (020) 7033 4430 *E-mail:* sales@flyingeyebooks.com *Web Site:* flyingeyebooks.com, pg 766

Flyleaf Press (Ireland) *Tel:* (01) 2854658 *E-mail:* books@flyleaf.ie *Web Site:* www.flyleaf.ie, pg 411

FMG Fachverlag fuer Druck und Medien GmbH (Germany) *Tel:* (089) 332568 *Fax:* (089) 33036200, pg 246

FN-Verlag der Deutschen Reiterlichen Vereinigung GmbH (Germany) *Tel:* (02581) 63 62-115; (02581) 63 62-154 (sales) *Fax:* (02581) 63 31 46; (02581) 63 62-212 (sales) *E-mail:* vertrieb-fnverlag@fn-dorkr.de; fnverlag@fn-dorkr.de *Web Site:* www.fnverlag, pg 246

Librairie Fnac (France) *Tel:* 08 25 02 00 20 *Fax:* 04 50 88 66 65 *Web Site:* www.fnac.com, pg 1414

FNPS (Federation Nationale de la Presse d'Information Specialisee) (France) *Tel:* 01 44 90 43 60 *Fax:* 01 44 90 43 72 *E-mail:* contact@fnps.fr *Web Site:* www. fnps.fr, pg 1372

FOBID Netherlands Library Forum (Netherlands) *Tel:* (070) 3140511; (070) 3140495 *Fax:* (070) 3140651 *E-mail:* info@fobid.nl; fobid@ debibliotheken.nl *Web Site:* www.fobid.nl, pg 1657

Focus Publications (Int) SA (Panama) *Tel:* 225-6638 *Fax:* 225-0466 *E-mail:* focusint@cableonda. net; focusint507@gmail.com *Web Site:* www. focuspublicationsint.com, pg 561

Focus Publishers Ltd (Kenya) *Tel:* (020) 559296; (020) 559315; (0722) 835649 (cell) *E-mail:* focus@ africaonline.co.ke *Web Site:* www.focuspublishers.co. ke, pg 493

Focus Publishing (Israel) *Fax:* (03) 5746513 *E-mail:* shaul@focus.co.il *Web Site:* www.focus.co.il, pg 417

Anoukh Foerg Literary Agency (Germany) *Tel:* (089) 4521 9059; (0176) 240 175 08 (cell) *E-mail:* anoukhfoerg@anoukhfoerg.com *Web Site:* www.anoukhfoerg.com, pg 1227

Fovarosi Szabo Ervin Konyvtar (Hungary) *Tel:* (01) 411-5000; (01) 411-5009; (01) 411-5066 *E-mail:* info@ fszek.hu; kktitkar@fszek.hu *Web Site:* www.fszek.hu, pg 1599

Fogarty's Bookshop (South Africa) *Tel:* (041) 368 1425 *E-mail:* fogartys@global.co.za *Web Site:* www. fogartysbookshop.co.za, pg 1448

Fogola Editore (Italy) *Tel:* (011) 53 58 97 *Fax:* (011) 53 03 05 *E-mail:* info@fogola.it *Web Site:* www.fogola.it, pg 444

Fohrmann Verlag (Germany) *Tel:* (0179) 94 83 939 *E-mail:* pf@fohrmann-verlag.de *Web Site:* www. fohrmann-verlag.de, pg 247

Fola Abbey Educational Book Services (Nigeria) *Tel:* (01) 2636679, pg 1439

Foldvari Antikvarium (Hungary) *Tel:* (020) 4182552 *E-mail:* info@foldvaribooks.com *Web Site:* www. foldvaribooks.com, pg 1421

Folens Publishers (Ireland) *Tel:* (01) 4137200 *Fax:* (01) 4137282 *E-mail:* info@folens.ie; orders@folens.ie *Web Site:* www.folens.ie, pg 411

Foliant Publishing House (Kazakhstan) *Tel:* (8727) 2395459 *Fax:* (8727) 2397249 *E-mail:* foliant@foliant. kz *Web Site:* www.foliant.kz, pg 492

Editions Folies d'Encre (France) *Tel:* 01 49 20 80 00; 01 49 20 80 06 *E-mail:* folies@nerim.fr; editionsfoliesdencre@yahoo.fr *Web Site:* www. foliesdencre.com, pg 170

Editoriale Fernando Folini (Italy) *Tel:* (0131) 1826301 *Fax:* (0131) 1826301 *E-mail:* folini@edifolini.com *Web Site:* www.edifolini.com, pg 444

The Folio Society (United Kingdom) *Tel:* (020) 7400 4200 *Toll Free:* 866-255-8280 *E-mail:* customerservice@foliosociety.com *Web Site:* www.foliosociety.com, pg 1361

Folio Verlagsgesellschaft mbH (Austria) *Tel:* (01) 5813708-0 *Fax:* (01) 5813708-20 *E-mail:* office@ folioverlag.com *Web Site:* www.folioverlag.com, pg 48

Folklore Comtois Editions (France) *Tel:* 03 81 55 87 60 *E-mail:* folklore-comtois@orange.fr *Web Site:* www. folklore-comtois.fr, pg 170

The Folklore Society (FLS) (United Kingdom) *Tel:* (020) 7862 8564 *E-mail:* thefolkloresociety@gmail.com *Web Site:* www.folklore-society.com, pg 1395

Folkuniversitetets forlag (Sweden) *Tel:* (046) 14 87 20 *E-mail:* info@folkuniversitetetsforlag.se *Web Site:* www.folkuniversitetet.se, pg 681

FONA Verlag AG (Switzerland) *Tel:* (062) 886 91 91 *Fax:* (062) 886 91 99 *E-mail:* info@fona.ch *Web Site:* www.fona.ch, pg 694

Institut Fondamental d'Afrique Noire (IFAN) (Senegal) *Tel:* 33 824 16 52 *Fax:* 33 824 49 18 *E-mail:* ifan@ ucad.edu.sn *Web Site:* ifan.ucad.sn, pg 600, 1628

Fondation Presses Universitaires de Strasbourg (France) *Tel:* 03 68 85 60 15 *Fax:* 03 68 85 62 85 *E-mail:* lapierre@unistra.fr *Web Site:* www.unistra.fr, pg 170

Fondation Temimi pour la Recherche Scientifique et l'Information (Tunisia) *Tel:* 71 23 14 44; 71 75 11 64 *Fax:* 71 23 66 77 *E-mail:* fondationtemimi@gnet.tn; fondationtemimi@yahoo.fr *Web Site:* temimi.refer.org, pg 717

Fondazione Museo Storico del Trentino (Italy) *Tel:* (0461) 230482 *Fax:* (0461) 237418 *E-mail:* info@museostorico.tn.it *Web Site:* www.museostorico.tn.it, pg 444

Fondazzjoni Patrimonju Malti (Malta) *Tel:* 21231515 *E-mail:* info@patrimonju.org *Web Site:* www.patrimonju.org, pg 511

Fondo de Cultura Economica (Mexico) *Tel:* (0155) 5227-4672 *Fax:* (0155) 5227-4694 *E-mail:* foreign.rights@fondodeculturaeconomica.com *Web Site:* www.fondodeculturaeconomica.com, pg 516

Fondo de Cultura Economica Chile SA (Chile) *Tel:* (02) 594 4135; (02) 594 4140; (02) 594 4100 *E-mail:* libreria@fcechile.cl *Web Site:* www.fcechile.cl, pg 1409

Fondo de Cultura Economica de Espana SA (Spain) *Tel:* 91 763 28 00 *Fax:* 91 763 51 33 *E-mail:* info@fondodeculturaeconomica.es *Web Site:* www.fcede.es, pg 644

Fondo de Publicaciones del Gobierno de Navarra (Spain) *Tel:* 848 42 7121 *Fax:* 848 42 7123 *E-mail:* fondo.publicaciones@navarra.es *Web Site:* www.publicaciones.navarra.es, pg 644

Fondo Editorial Casa de las Americas (Cuba) *Tel:* (07) 8382706; (07) 8382707; (07) 8382708; (07) 8382709 *Web Site:* www.casa.cult.cu/editorial.php, pg 123

Fondo Editorial de la Pontificia Universidad Catolica del Peru (Peru) *Tel:* (01) 626 2650 *E-mail:* feditor@pucp.edu.pe *Web Site:* www.fondoeditorial.pucp.edu.pe; www.pucp.edu.pe, pg 562

Fondo Editorial EAFIT (Colombia) *Tel:* (04) 261 9271 *E-mail:* fonedit@eafit.edu.co *Web Site:* www.eafit.edu.co/cultura-eafit/fondo-editorial, pg 113

Fondo Editorial Universidad de Lima (Peru) *Tel:* (01) 437-6767; (01) 436-0500 *Fax:* (01) 437-8066 *E-mail:* fondoeditorial@ulima.edu.pe *Web Site:* www.ulima.edu.pe, pg 562

Fonna Forlag L/L (Norway) *Tel:* 22 69 10 10; 95 10 96 15 (cell) *E-mail:* post@fonna.no; fonna@fonna.no *Web Site:* www.fonna.no, pg 554

The Font Bureau Inc (United States) *Tel:* 617-423-8770 *E-mail:* info@fontbureau.com *Web Site:* fontbureau.typenetwork.com, pg 1288

Font Forlag (Norway) *Tel:* 90 79 50 22 *Web Site:* fontforlag.no, pg 554

Fontana Media Ab (Finland) *Tel:* (09) 612 615 30 *Fax:* (09) 278 4138 *E-mail:* redaktionen@fontanamedia.fi; info@fontanamedia.fi *Web Site:* www.fontanamedia.fi, pg 148

Uitgeverij De Fontein|Tirion (Netherlands) *Tel:* (088) 700 26 00; (030) 252 85 00 *E-mail:* info@defonteintirion.nl *Web Site:* www.defonteintirion.nl, pg 533

Fontis - Brunnen Basel (Switzerland) *Tel:* (061) 295 60 00 *Fax:* (061) 295 60 68 *E-mail:* info@fontis-verlag.ch *Web Site:* www.fontis-verlag.com, pg 694

Fontis-Buchhandlung (Switzerland) *Tel:* (061) 295 60 03 *E-mail:* info@fontis.ch *Web Site:* www.fontis-shop.ch, pg 1452

Food & Agriculture Organization of the United Nations (FAO) (Italy) *Tel:* (06) 57051 *E-mail:* fao-hq@fao.org *Web Site:* www.fao.org, pg 1379

Footprint Books Pty Ltd (Australia) *Tel:* (02) 9997 3973 *Toll Free Tel:* 1300 260 090 *Fax:* (02) 9997 3185 *E-mail:* info@footprint.com.au; sales@footprint.com.au *Web Site:* www.footprint.com.au, pg 1402

Footprint Travel Guides (United Kingdom) *Tel:* (01225) 469141 *Fax:* (01225) 469461 *E-mail:* contactus@morriscontentalliance.com *Web Site:* www.footprinttravelguides.com, pg 766

Forbes Publications Ltd (United Kingdom) *Tel:* (020) 8973 0040, pg 766

Foreign Language Bookshop (Australia) *Tel:* (03) 8417 9500 *Fax:* (03) 9416 1616 *E-mail:* shop@flb.com.au *Web Site:* www.foreignlanguagebookshop.com.au; www.languages.com.au, pg 1402

Foreign Language Teaching & Research Press (China) *Tel:* (010) 88819000; (010) 88819476 (orders) *Fax:* (010) 88819433 *E-mail:* international@fltrp.com; sales@fltrp.com; overseas@fltrp.com; service@fltrp.com *Web Site:* www.fltrp.com, pg 104

Foreign Languages Press (China) *Tel:* (010) 68320579; (010) 68326853; (010) 68996138; (010) 68997794 *Fax:* (010) 68326642; (010) 68993501 *E-mail:* flprights@yahoo.com.cn *Web Site:* www.flp.com.cn, pg 104

Foreign Languages Publishing House (North Korea), pg 553

The Foreign Office (Spain) *Tel:* 933 214 290 *E-mail:* info@theforeignoffice.net *Web Site:* www.theforeignoffice.net, pg 1235

Forening for Boghaandvaerk (Denmark) *Tel:* 91 324 546 *Web Site:* www.boghaandvaerk.dk, pg 1369

Foreningen Auktoriserade Translatorer (FAT) (Sweden) *E-mail:* info@aukttranslator.se *Web Site:* www.aukttranslator.se, pg 1251

Foreningen Svenskt naringsliv (Sweden) *Tel:* (08) 553 430 00 *Fax:* (08) 553 430 99 *Web Site:* www.svensktnaringsliv.se, pg 681

Editora Forense (Brazil) *Tel:* (021) 3543-0770; (021) 3543-0780 (sales) *E-mail:* diretoria@grupogen.com.br; vendas@grupogen.com.br *Web Site:* www.grupogen.com.br, pg 82

Forense Universitaria (Brazil) *Tel:* (021) 3543-0770; (021) 3543-0780 (sales) *E-mail:* diretoria@grupogen.com.br; vendas@grupogen.com.br *Web Site:* www.grupogen.com.br, pg 82

Forlagid (Iceland) *Tel:* 575-5600 *Fax:* 575-5601 *E-mail:* forlagid@forlagid.is *Web Site:* www.forlagid.is, pg 372

FormAsia Books Ltd (Hong Kong) *Tel:* 2525 8572 *Fax:* 2522 4234 *E-mail:* needinfo@formasiabooks.com *Web Site:* www.formasiabooks.com, pg 364

Format Publishers (Nig) Ltd (Nigeria) *Tel:* (042) 256025, pg 551

Arnaldo Forni Editore SRL (Italy) *Tel:* (051) 6814142; (051) 6814198 *Fax:* (051) 6814672 *E-mail:* info@fornieditore.com *Web Site:* www.fornieditore.com, pg 444

Foroya Landsbokasavn (Faroe Islands) *Tel:* 34 05 25 *Fax:* 34 05 27 *E-mail:* savn@savn.fo *Web Site:* savn.fo/00008/00045, pg 1370, 1588

Forth Naturalist & Historian (United Kingdom) *Tel:* (01786) 467269 *E-mail:* fnh@stir.ac.uk *Web Site:* www.fnh.natsci.stir.ac.uk, pg 766

Fortuna Libri spol sro (Czech Republic) *Tel:* 267 911 813 *E-mail:* fortuna@fortunalibri.cz *Web Site:* www.fortunaprint.cz, pg 127

Bokforlaget Forum AB (Sweden) *Tel:* (08) 696 84 40 *Fax:* (08) 696 83 58 *E-mail:* info@forum.se; kundservice@bonnierforlagen.se *Web Site:* www.forum.se, pg 681

Antiquariaat FORUM BV (Netherlands) *Tel:* (030) 601 1955 *Fax:* (030) 601 1813 *E-mail:* info@forumrarebooks.com *Web Site:* www.forumrarebooks.com, pg 1437

Forlaget Forum (Denmark) *Tel:* 3341 1800 *Fax:* 3341 1801 *E-mail:* info@rosinante-co.dk *Web Site:* www.forlagetforum.dk, pg 136

forum independent GmbH (Germany) *Tel:* (0221) 92428-230 *Fax:* (0221) 92428-232 *E-mail:* steinbach@forum-independent.de *Web Site:* www.forum-independent.de, pg 1415

Forum Konyvkiado (Serbia) *Tel:* (021) 457 216 *Fax:* (021) 456 742 *E-mail:* direktor@forumliber.rs *Web Site:* www.forumliber.rs, pg 601, 1447

Forum Verlag GmbH & Co KG (Germany) *Tel:* (0711) 76727-0 *Fax:* (0711) 76727-28, pg 247

Forum Verlag Herkert GmbH (Germany) *Tel:* (08233) 381-123 *Fax:* (08233) 381-222 *E-mail:* service@forum-verlag.com *Web Site:* www.forum-verlag.com, pg 247

Forum Verlag Leipzig Buch-Gesellschaft mbH (Germany) *Tel:* (0341) 9 80 50 08 *Fax:* (0341) 9 80 50 07 *E-mail:* info@forumverlagleipzig.de *Web Site:* www.forumverlagleipzig.de, pg 247

Fostering Network (United Kingdom) *Tel:* (020) 7620 6400 *Fax:* (020) 7620 6401 *E-mail:* info@fostering.net *Web Site:* www.fostering.net, pg 767

Fotohof Edition (Austria) *Tel:* (0662) 84 92 96 *Fax:* (0662) 84 92 96 4 *E-mail:* fotohof@fotohof.at *Web Site:* www.fotohof.at, pg 48

Les Editions Foucher (France) *Tel:* 01 41 23 65 60; 01 41 23 65 65 *Fax:* 01 41 23 65 03 *E-mail:* fouchercontact@editions-foucher.fr *Web Site:* www.editions-foucher.fr, pg 170

W Foulsham & Co Ltd (United Kingdom) *Tel:* (01628) 400 631 *Fax:* (01753) 535003 *E-mail:* sales@foulsham.com *Web Site:* www.foulsham.com, pg 767

Foundation for Mediterranean Cooperation (Greece) *Tel:* 2103810465 *Fax:* 2103805113, pg 355

Lora Fountain Literary Agency (France) *Tel:* 01 43 56 21 96 *E-mail:* agence@fountlit.com *Web Site:* www.lorafountainagency.com, pg 1225

Fountain of Fairy Tales (Ukraine) *Tel:* (044) 33 111 33 *E-mail:* info@fontan-book.com; rights@fontan-book.com *Web Site:* www.fontan-book.com, pg 726

Fountain Publishers Ltd (Uganda) *Tel:* (0414) 259163; (0414) 251112; (0414) 312 263041; (0414) 312 263042 *Fax:* (0414) 251160 *E-mail:* publishing@fountainpublishers.co.ug; sales@fountainpublishers.co.ug *Web Site:* www.fountainpublishers.net, pg 725

Four Courts Press Ltd (Ireland) *Tel:* (01) 453-4668 *Fax:* (01) 453-4672 *E-mail:* info@fourcourtspress.ie *Web Site:* www.fourcourtspress.ie, pg 411

Fourah Bay College Library (Sierra Leone) *Tel:* (078) 920590 (cell) *Web Site:* www.usl.edu.sl/fourah-bay-college-fbc, pg 1629

Les Fourmis Rouges (France) *Tel:* 01 70 24 18 38 *E-mail:* manuscrits@fourmisrouges.fr (manuscript submission) *Web Site:* editionslesfourmisrouges.com; www.facebook.com/EditionsLesFourmisRouges, pg 170

4th Estate (United Kingdom) *Tel:* (020) 8741 7070 *E-mail:* 4thestate.marketing@harpercollins.co.uk; 4thestate.publicity@harpercollins.co.uk *Web Site:* www.harpercollins.co.uk, pg 767

Foyles (United Kingdom) *Tel:* (020) 7440 1557 *Fax:* (020) 7434 1574 *E-mail:* customerservices@foyles.co.uk; orders@foyles.co.uk; marketingteam@foyles.co.uk *Web Site:* www.foyles.co.uk, pg 1458

FRA (United Kingdom) *Tel:* (020) 8255 7755 *Fax:* (020) 8286 4860 *E-mail:* enquiries@futermanrose.co.uk *Web Site:* www.futermanrose.co.uk, pg 1241

Nakladatelstvi Fragment sro (Czech Republic) *Tel:* 241 004 011 *Fax:* 241 004 071 *E-mail:* fragment@fragment.cz *Web Site:* www.fragment.cz, pg 127

Libreria Fragua (Spain) *Tel:* 91 544 22 97; 91 549 18 06 *Fax:* 91 543 17 94 *E-mail:* pedidos@fragua.es *Web Site:* www.fragua.es, pg 644

Fraktura doo (Croatia) *Tel:* (01) 335 78 63 *Fax:* (01) 335 83 20 *E-mail:* fraktura@fraktura.hr *Web Site:* www.fraktura.hr, pg 120

Garland Science (United Kingdom) *Tel:* (020) 7017 6000 *Fax:* (020) 7017 6699 *E-mail:* science@garland.com *Web Site:* www.garlandscience.com, pg 769

Garnet Publishing Ltd (United Kingdom) *Tel:* (0118) 959 7847 *Fax:* (0118) 959 7356 *E-mail:* info@ garnetpublishing.co.uk *Web Site:* www. garnetpublishing.co.uk, pg 769

Archivio Federico Garolla (Italy) *Tel:* (02) 6554548 *Web Site:* www.garolla.net, pg 445

Garratt Publishing (Australia) *Tel:* (03) 8545 2911 *Toll Free Tel:* 1300 650 878 *Fax:* (03) 8545 2922 *E-mail:* sales@garrattpublishing.com.au *Web Site:* www.garrattpublishing.com.au, pg 25

Ekdoseis Gartaganis (Greece) *Tel:* 2310201210 *Fax:* 2310209680 *E-mail:* gartaganisbooks@gmail.com *Web Site:* www.gartaganisbooks.gr, pg 355

Garuda-Verlag Eisenegger & Eisenegger (Switzerland) *Tel:* (041) 917 02 45 *Fax:* (041) 917 02 46 *E-mail:* garuda@bluewin.ch, pg 694

Garzanti Libri SRL (Italy) *Tel:* (02) 00623-201 *E-mail:* info@garzantilibri.it; redazione@garzantilibri. it; ufficiostampa@garzantilibri.it *Web Site:* www. garzantilibri.it, pg 445

Gasser Verlag (Switzerland) *Tel:* (079) 542 67 66 *E-mail:* regulagasser@gmx.ch *Web Site:* www. brunogasser.ch, pg 694

Gaston Renard Pty Ltd (Australia) *Tel:* (03) 9459 5040 *Fax:* (03) 9459 6787 *E-mail:* books@gastonrenard. com.au *Web Site:* www.gastonrenard.com.au, pg 1403

Gateway Books (United Kingdom) *Tel:* (0141) 270 6110 *Fax:* (0141) 270 6122 *E-mail:* ceg@ceg.org.uk *Web Site:* www.ceg.org.uk, pg 769

Gatidhara (Bangladesh) *Tel:* (02) 7392077 (press); (02) 7117515 (showroom); (02) 7118273 (showroom); 01552-385784 (cell); 01711-053196 (cell); 0171-1602442 (cell); 01552-337280 (cell) *Fax:* (02) 7123472 *E-mail:* info@gatidhara.com; gatidhara2008@yahoo.com; gatidhara2008@gmail.com *Web Site:* www.gatidhara.com, pg 61

Editorial GatoMalo (Colombia) *Tel:* (01) 264 2587 *Fax:* (01) 264 2587 *E-mail:* editorialgatomalo@yahoo. com *Web Site:* www.editorialgatomalo.com, pg 114

Gattys Global (Germany) *Tel:* (089) 202 554-0 *Fax:* (089) 202 554-30 *E-mail:* info@gattysglobal.de *Web Site:* www.gattysglobal.de, pg 1227

GATZANIS GmbH (Germany) *Tel:* (0711) 964 05 70 *Fax:* (0711) 964 05 72 *E-mail:* info@gatzanis.de *Web Site:* www.gatzanis.de, pg 250

Gaudeamus Oy (Finland) *Tel:* (09) 50 540 1303 *E-mail:* info@gaudeamus.fi *Web Site:* www. gaudeamus.fi, pg 148

Ediciones Gaviota (Spain) *Tel:* 91 358 01 08 *Fax:* 91 729 38 58 *E-mail:* ventas@ediciones-gaviota.com, pg 646

Gazelle Book Services Ltd (United Kingdom) *Tel:* (01524) 528500 *Fax:* (01524) 528510 *E-mail:* sales@gazellebooks.co.uk *Web Site:* www. gazellebookservices.co.uk, pg 1458

Gbabeks Publishers Ltd (Nigeria) *Tel:* (02) 2315705, pg 551

Gdanskie Wydawnictwo Psychologiczne Sp z oo (Poland) *Tel:* (58) 555 71 89; (58) 555 71 94 *Fax:* (58) 550 16 04 *E-mail:* sekretariat@gwp. pl; handel@gwp.pl (sales); redakcja@gwp.pl *Web Site:* www.wydawnictwogwp.pl; www.gwp.pl, pg 569

Gea Libris Publishing House (Bulgaria) *Tel:* (02) 9867131 *Fax:* (02) 9866900 *E-mail:* book@gealibris. com; info@gealibris.com *Web Site:* www.gealibris. com, pg 95

Gebrueder Borntraeger Verlagsbuchhandlung (Germany) *Tel:* (0711) 3514560 *Fax:* (0711) 351456-99 *E-mail:* mail@schweizerbart.de *Web Site:* www. schweizerbart.de, pg 250

Gecko Press (New Zealand) *Tel:* (04) 801 9333 *E-mail:* info@geckopress.com *Web Site:* www. geckopress.co.nz, pg 546

GECTI (Gabinete de Especializacao e Cooperacao Tecnica Internacional Lda) (Portugal) *Tel:* 217968877 *Fax:* 217963465, pg 579

Geddes & Grosset (United Kingdom) *Tel:* (0141) 375 1998 *Fax:* (0141) 427 1791 *E-mail:* info@waverley-books.co.uk *Web Site:* www.geddesandgrosset.com; www.waverley-books.co.uk, pg 769

Editorial Gedisa SA (Spain) *Tel:* 93 253 09 04 *E-mail:* informacion@gedisa.com *Web Site:* www. gedisa.com, pg 646

Gee & Son (Denbigh) Ltd (United Kingdom), pg 1263

Drukkerij Geers Offset (Belgium) *Tel:* (09) 218 08 41 *E-mail:* info@geersoffset.be *Web Site:* www. geersoffset.be, pg 1317

Geeta Prakashan (India) *Tel:* (040) 24751344 *E-mail:* geetaprakashan7@gmail.com *Web Site:* geetaprakashan.yolasite.com/, pg 383

Geetha Sdn Bhd (Malaysia) *Tel:* (03) 40417073 *Fax:* (03) 40417073, pg 507

Gefen Publishing House (Israel) *Tel:* (02) 538-0247 *Fax:* (02) 538-8423 *E-mail:* gefenny@gefenpublishing. com *Web Site:* www.gefenpublishing.com, pg 417

Geheimsprachen Verlag (Germany) *Tel:* (0251) 218869-81; (0170) 5469192 *Fax:* (0251) 289169-82 *E-mail:* geheimsprachenverlag@gmx.de *Web Site:* www.geheimsprachenverlag.de, pg 250

Gehrmans Musikforlag AB (Sweden) *Tel:* (08) 610 06 00 *Fax:* (08) 610 06 27 *E-mail:* info@gehrmans.se; order@gehrmans.se *Web Site:* www.gehrmans.se, pg 681

Verlag Junge Gemeinde E Schwinghammer GmbH & Co KG (Germany) *Tel:* (0711) 99078-0 *Fax:* (0711) 99078-25 *E-mail:* vertrieb@junge-gemeinde.de *Web Site:* www.junge-gemeinde.de, pg 250

Gemser Publications SL (Spain) *Tel:* 935 401 353 *Fax:* 935 401 346 *E-mail:* info@mercedesros.com *Web Site:* www.mercedesros.com, pg 646

General Book Depot (India) *Tel:* (011) 2326 0022 *E-mail:* contact@goyalbookshop.com; generalbookdepot@yahoo.com *Web Site:* www. pigeonbooks.in, pg 383, 1422

General Directorate of Mineral Research & Exploration Library (Turkey) *Tel:* (0312) 201 10 00 *Fax:* (0312) 287 91 88 *E-mail:* mta@mta.gov.tr *Web Site:* www. mta.gov.tr, pg 1639

General Egyptian Book Organization (GEBO) (Egypt) *Tel:* (02) 25775646; (02) 25775109; (02) 25775371; (02) 25775228 *Fax:* (02) 25789316; (02) 25754213 *E-mail:* info@gebo.gov.eg *Web Site:* www.gebo.gov. eg, pg 143, 1370

General Printers & Publishers (India) *Tel:* (022) 2387 3113; (022) 2382 6854, pg 383

General Sciences Library of Ho Chi Minh City (Vietnam) *Tel:* (028) 8 38 225 055 *Fax:* (08) 8 38 299 318 *E-mail:* thuvientphcm@thuvientphcm.gov.vn *Web Site:* www.thuvientphcm.gov.vn, pg 1644

Librairie Generale Francaise (France) *Tel:* 01 49 54 37 00 *Fax:* 01 49 54 37 01 *E-mail:* contact-ldp@ livredepoche.com *Web Site:* www.livredepoche.com, pg 172

Generalitat de Catalunya, Entitat Autonoma del Diari Oficial i de Publicacions (Spain) *Tel:* 932 925 400 *Fax:* 932 925 435 *Web Site:* www20.gencat.cat/portal/ site/portaldogc, pg 646

Genesis Forlag AS (Norway) *Tel:* 63 80 30 99 *Fax:* 63 81 69 22 *Web Site:* www.genesis.no, pg 555

Genesis Publications Ltd (United Kingdom) *Tel:* (01483) 540970 *Fax:* (01483) 304709 *E-mail:* info@genesis-publications.com; orders@genesis-publications.com *Web Site:* www.genesis-publications.com, pg 769

Genius Verlag (Germany) *Tel:* (0421) 17 66 55 86 *Fax:* (0421) 62 67 885 *E-mail:* info@genius-verlag.de *Web Site:* www.genius-verlag.de, pg 250

Genkosha (Japan) *Tel:* (03) 3263-3511; (03) 3263-3515 (sales) *Fax:* (03) 3263-3830; (03) 3263-3045 (sales) *E-mail:* gks@genkosha.co.jp *Web Site:* www.genkosha. co.jp, pg 476

Gennadius Library (Greece) *Tel:* 2107210536 *Fax:* 2107237767 *E-mail:* gen-recep@ascsa.edu.gr *Web Site:* www.ascsa.edu.gr/gennadius, pg 1598

Uitgeverij Van Gennep BV (Netherlands) *Tel:* (020) 6247033 *Fax:* (020) 6247035 *E-mail:* info@ vangennep-boeken.nl *Web Site:* www.vangennep-boeken.nl, pg 533

Genossenschaft Edition Exodus (Switzerland) *Tel:* (041) 422 04 63 *Fax:* (041) 422 04 62 *E-mail:* editionexodus@bluewin.ch, pg 694

Editora Gente Livraria e Editora Ltda (Brazil) *Tel:* (011) 3670-2500 *E-mail:* marketing@editoragente.com. br; vendas@editoragente.com.br *Web Site:* www. editoragente.com.br, pg 83

Editorial Gente Nueva (Cuba) *Tel:* (07) 624753 *Fax:* (07) 338187 *Web Site:* www.gentenueva.cult.cu, pg 124

Alfons W Gentner Verlag GmbH & Co KG (Germany) *Tel:* (0711) 63 67 2-0 *Fax:* (0711) 63 67 27 47 *E-mail:* gentner@gentner.de *Web Site:* www.gentner. de, pg 250

Gentofte Bibliotekerne (Denmark) *Tel:* 39 98 58 00 *E-mail:* bibliotek@gentofte.dk *Web Site:* www.genbib. dk, pg 1586

Geocarto International Centre Ltd (Hong Kong) *Tel:* 2546 4262 *Fax:* 2559 3419 *E-mail:* geocarto@ geocarto.com *Web Site:* www.geocarto.com, pg 364

GeoCenter Touristik Medienservice GmbH (Germany) *Tel:* (0711) 78 19 46 10 *Fax:* (0711) 782 4375 *E-mail:* vertrieb@geocenter.de *Web Site:* www. geocenter.de, pg 1416

Geographers' A-Z Map Co Ltd (United Kingdom) *Tel:* (01732) 783422 *Web Site:* www.az.co.uk; www. facebook.com/azmaps; twitter.com/azmaps, pg 769

The Geographical Association (United Kingdom) *Tel:* (0114) 296 0088 *Fax:* (0114) 296 7176 *E-mail:* info@geography.org.uk *Web Site:* www. geography.org.uk, pg 769

Geography Publications (Ireland) *Tel:* (01) 4566085 *Fax:* (01) 4566085 *E-mail:* info@ geographypublications.com *Web Site:* www. geographypublications.com, pg 411

Geological Publishing House (GPH) (China) *Tel:* (010) 82324519; (010) 82324537 *Fax:* (010) 82328538 *Web Site:* www.gph.com.cn, pg 105

Geological Society Publishing House (United Kingdom) *Tel:* (01225) 445046 *Fax:* (01225) 442836 *E-mail:* sales@geolsoc.org.uk *Web Site:* www.geolsoc. org.uk, pg 769

Geological Survey Department Library (Botswana) *Tel:* 5330327 *Fax:* 5332013 *Web Site:* www.gov.bw, pg 1579

Geological Survey Department Library (Ghana) *Tel:* (021) 679236; (021) 679237; (021) 679239; (021) 228052; (021) 224676 *Fax:* (021) 679238; (021) 224676; (021) 228063 *E-mail:* ghgeosur@ghana.com; ghgeophy@hotmail.com; info@gsd.ghanamining.org, pg 1597

Geophon (Germany) *Tel:* (030) 20 64 49 85 *E-mail:* info@geophon.de *Web Site:* geophon.de, pg 251

GEOprojects Sarl (Lebanon) *Tel:* (01) 342 110 *Fax:* (01) 342 217 *E-mail:* info@geo-publishers. com *Web Site:* www.geo-publishers.com; www.geo-cartographers.com, pg 364

Georeto-Geogidsen (Belgium) *Tel:* (011) 37 52 54 *Fax:* (011) 37 52 54 *E-mail:* info@geogidsen.be *Web Site:* www.geogidsen.be, pg 67

Georg Editeur SA (Switzerland) *Tel:* (022) 702 93 11 *Fax:* (022) 702 93 55 *E-mail:* livres@medhyg.ch *Web Site:* www.georg.ch, pg 694

1749

Ginger Fox Ltd (United Kingdom) *Tel:* (01242) 241765 *E-mail:* sales@gingerfox.co.uk *Web Site:* gingerfox.co. uk; www.millyandflynn.com, pg 770

Gingko Library (United Kingdom) *Tel:* (020) 7838 9055 *Fax:* (020) 7584 9501 *E-mail:* gingko@gingkolibrary. com *Web Site:* www.gingkolibrary.com, pg 770

Ginninderra Press (Australia) *Tel:* (08) 7005 0370 *Web Site:* www.ginninderrapress.com.au, pg 25

Il gioco di leggere Edizioni SRL (Italy) *Tel:* (02) 36 55 53 58 *Fax:* (02) 99 98 07 54 *E-mail:* edizioni@ ilgiocodileggere.it *Web Site:* www.ilgiocodileggere.it, pg 445

The Gioi Publishers (Vietnam) *Tel:* (04) 38253841 *Fax:* (04) 38269578 *E-mail:* thegioi@hn.vnn.vn *Web Site:* www.thegioipublishers.vn, pg 851

Giourdas Moschos (Greece) *Tel:* 2103630219; 2103303145 *Fax:* 2103303126 *E-mail:* edizioni@ mgiurdas.gr *Web Site:* www.mgiurdas.gr, pg 355

Bernard Giovanangeli Editeur (France) *E-mail:* bged@ wanadoo.fr *Web Site:* www.bgedition.com, pg 172

Giramondo Publishing Co (Australia) *Tel:* (02) 9772 6350 *Fax:* (02) 9419 7934 *E-mail:* books@giramondopublishing.com *Web Site:* giramondopublishing.com, pg 25

Edizioni del Girasole SRL (Italy) *Tel:* (0544) 212830; (0544) 418986 *E-mail:* edizionigirasole@libero.it; ufficiostampa.girasole@virgilio.it, pg 445

Girassol Edicoes Lda (Portugal) *Tel:* 21 915 15 40 *E-mail:* editorial@girassoledicoes.com *Web Site:* www. girassoledicoes.com, pg 579

Giri Trading Agency Pvt Ltd (India) *Tel:* (022) 24118107 *Fax:* (022) 24143140 *E-mail:* sales@giri.in *Web Site:* giri.in, pg 1422

Girotondo SNC (Italy) *Tel:* (011) 320 30 94 *Fax:* (011) 47 85 115 *E-mail:* info@girotondoedizioni.it *Web Site:* www.girotondoedizioni.it, pg 445

Editorial Gisbert y Cia SA (Bolivia) *Tel:* (02) 220 2626 *Fax:* (02) 220 2911 *E-mail:* info@libreriagisbert.com *Web Site:* libreriagisbert.com, pg 75, 1406

Editions Jean-Paul Gisserot (France) *Tel:* 01 43 31 80 04; 01 43 31 88 24 *Fax:* 01 43 31 88 15 *E-mail:* editions@editions-gisserot.com *Web Site:* www.editions-gisserot.com, pg 172

Dott A Giuffre' Editore SpA (Italy) *Tel:* (02) 380891; (02) 38089311 *Fax:* (02) 38009582; (02) 38089432 *E-mail:* service@giuffre.it; editoriale@giuffre.it *Web Site:* www.giuffre.it, pg 445

Giunti Editore SpA (Italy) *Tel:* (055) 5062 1; (02) 5754 71 (rights) *Fax:* (055) 5062 298; (02) 5754 7503 (rights) *E-mail:* info@giunti.it; ufficiostampa@giunti.it *Web Site:* www.giunti.it, pg 445

Editrice la Giuntina (Italy) *Tel:* (055) 2476781 *Fax:* (055) 2009800; (055) 2349067 *E-mail:* info@ giuntina.it *Web Site:* www.giuntina.it, pg 445

Gius Laterza e Figli SpA (Italy) *Tel:* (080) 528 12 11 *Fax:* (080) 524 34 61 *E-mail:* commerciale@laterza.it (sales); foreignrights@laterza.it *Web Site:* www.laterza. it, pg 446

Glad Sounds Sdn Bhd (Malaysia) *Tel:* (03) 79562901; (03) 79311512; (03) 79587188 (retail shop) *Fax:* (03) 79560528 *E-mail:* webstore@gladsounds.com. my; gladsounds@yahoo.com *Web Site:* www. gladsounds.com.my; www.facebook.com/Glad-Sounds-642442815785963/, pg 1432

Glare Verlag (Germany) *Tel:* (069) 52 02 83 *E-mail:* info@glareverlag.de *Web Site:* www. glareverlag.de, pg 252

Glasgow City Libraries & Archives, the Mitchell Library (United Kingdom) *Tel:* (0141) 287 2910 *Fax:* (0141) 287 2815 *E-mail:* lil@cls.glasgow.gov.uk; archives@ csglasgow.org *Web Site:* www.mitchelllibrary.org, pg 1641

Glasgow City Libraries Publications (United Kingdom) *Tel:* (0141) 287 2910 *Fax:* (0141) 287 2815 *E-mail:* archives@glasgowlife.org.uk, pg 770

Eric Glass Ltd (United Kingdom) *Tel:* (020) 7229 9500 *Fax:* (020) 7229 6220 *E-mail:* eglassltd@aol.com, pg 1241

Gleaner Co Ltd (Jamaica) *Tel:* (876) 922-3400 *Toll Free Tel:* 888-453-2637 (Jamaica only); 800-233-9540 (USA & Canada) *Fax:* (876) 922-6223 *E-mail:* feedback@jamaica-gleaner.com *Web Site:* www.jamaica-gleaner.com, pg 472

Glenat Benelux NV (Belgium) *Tel:* (02) 761 26 40 *Fax:* (02) 761 26 45 *Web Site:* www.glenat.be, pg 67

Glenat Editions SA (France) *Tel:* 04 76 88 75 75 *Fax:* 04 76 88 75 70 *Web Site:* www.glenat.com, pg 172

GLMP Ltd (United Kingdom) *Tel:* (01745) 832863 *Fax:* (01745) 826606, pg 770

Global Book Marketing Ltd (United Kingdom) *Web Site:* www.globalbookmarketing.co.uk, pg 1241

Global Book Publishing (United Kingdom) *Tel:* (01273) 716009 *Web Site:* www.quartoknows.com/global-book-publishing, pg 770

Global Editora e Distribuidora (Brazil) *Tel:* (011) 3277-7999 *Fax:* (011) 3277-8141 *E-mail:* global@ globaleditora.com.br *Web Site:* globaleditora.com.br, pg 1408

Global Editora e Distribuidora Ltda (Brazil) *Tel:* (011) 3277-7999 *Fax:* (011) 3277-8141 *E-mail:* global@ globaleditora.com.br *Web Site:* www.globaleditora. com.br, pg 83

Global Interprint Inc (United States) *Tel:* 707-545-1220 *Fax:* 707-545-1210 *E-mail:* info@globalinterprint.com *Web Site:* www.globalinterprint.com, pg 1340

Global Language Services Ltd (United Kingdom) *Tel:* (0141) 429 3429 *E-mail:* mail@ globallanguageservices.co.uk *Web Site:* www. globallanguageservices.co.uk, pg 1253

Global Oriental (Netherlands) *Tel:* (071) 53 53 500 *Fax:* (071) 53 17 532 *E-mail:* sales-nl@brill.nl; marketing@brill.nl *Web Site:* www.brill.com, pg 533

Global Professional Publishing Ltd (United Kingdom), pg 770

Forlaget Globe A/S (Denmark) *Tel:* 70151400 *Fax:* 70151410 *E-mail:* info@globe.dk *Web Site:* www.globe.dk, pg 136

Globe Law & Business (United Kingdom) *Tel:* (020) 7234 0606 *Web Site:* www.globelawandbusiness.com, pg 771

Globi Verlag AG (Switzerland) *Tel:* (044) 466 73 18 *Fax:* (044) 466 74 12 *E-mail:* info@globi.ch *Web Site:* www.globi.ch, pg 695

Editora Globo SA (Brazil) *Tel:* (011) 3767-7000 *Web Site:* editoraglobo.globo.com, pg 83

GLOOR Verlag (Germany) *Tel:* (08151) 5568180 *Fax:* (08151) 5567381 *E-mail:* info@gloorverlag.de *Web Site:* www.gloorverlag.de, pg 252

Glossa Editrice SRL (Italy) *Tel:* (02) 877609 *Fax:* (02) 72003162 *E-mail:* informazioni@glossaeditrice.it *Web Site:* www.glossaeditrice.it, pg 446

glotzi Verlag (Germany) *Tel:* (06251) 705 99 88 *Fax:* (03222) 690 559 3 *E-mail:* glotzi@glotzi-verlag. de *Web Site:* www.glotzi-verlag.de, pg 252

Glowna Biblioteka Lekarska (Poland) *Tel:* (22) 849 74 04; (22) 849 78 51; (22) 849 78 53 *Fax:* (22) 849 78 02 *E-mail:* sekretariat@gbl.waw.pl *Web Site:* www.gbl. waw.pl, pg 1624

Glowworm Books Ltd (United Kingdom) *Tel:* (01506) 857570 *Fax:* (01506) 858100 *Web Site:* www. glowwormbooks.co.uk, pg 771

Glueckschuh Verlag (Germany) *Tel:* (03322) 28 68 94 *Fax:* (03322) 240 238 *E-mail:* info@ glueckschuh-verlag.de; vertrieb@glueckschuh-verlag. de *Web Site:* www.glueckschuh-verlag.de, pg 252

GMC Publications Ltd (United Kingdom) *Tel:* (01273) 477374; (01273) 488005 (orders) *Fax:* (01273) 478606 *E-mail:* *Web Site:* www.thegmcgroup.com, pg 771

Gmeiner-Verlag GmbH (Germany) *Tel:* (07575) 2095-0 *Fax:* (07575) 2095-29 *E-mail:* info@gmeiner-verlag.de *Web Site:* www.gmeiner-verlag.de, pg 252

Gmelin-Verlag GmbH (Germany) *Tel:* (08152) 9099762, pg 252

Gnostic Press Ltd (New Zealand) *Tel:* (09) 412 7054 *Fax:* (09) 412 6476 *E-mail:* gnosticpress@ihug.co.nz *Web Site:* www.gnosticpress.co.nz, pg 546

Gobierno de Canarias - Consejeria de Cultura, Deportes, Politicas Sociales y Vivienda (Spain) *Tel:* 922 47 70 00 *Fax:* 922 47 70 56 *E-mail:* contacto. cepsv@gobiernodecanarias.org *Web Site:* www. gobiernodecanarias.org/ccdpsv, pg 646

Celia Godkin (Canada) *Tel:* 613-275-7204 *Fax:* 613-275-7204 *E-mail:* celia@godkin.ca *Web Site:* www. celiagodkin.com; www.celiagodkin.ca, pg 1274

Godsfield Press (United Kingdom) *Tel:* (020) 7632 5400 *Fax:* (020) 7632 5405 *E-mail:* info@octopus-publishing.co.uk *Web Site:* www.octopusbooks.co.uk, pg 771

Alois Goeschl & Co (Austria) *Tel:* (01) 3201080, pg 49

Goeteborgs Universitetsbibliotek (Sweden) *Tel:* (031) 786 17 45 *Fax:* (031) 786 44 11 *E-mail:* g.info@ub. gu.se *Web Site:* www.ub.gu.se/bibliotek, pg 1634

August Von Goethe Literaturverlag (Germany) *Tel:* (069) 40894-0 *Fax:* (069) 40894-194 *E-mail:* lektorat@ august-von-goethe-literaturverlag.de *Web Site:* www. august-von-goethe-literaturverlag.de, pg 252

Cornelia Goethe Literaturverlag (Germany) *Tel:* (069) 40894-0 *Fax:* (069) 40894-194 *E-mail:* lektorat@ cornelia-goethe-verlag.de *Web Site:* www.cornelia-goethe-verlag.de, pg 252

Goethe-Gesellschaft in Weimar eV (Germany) *Tel:* (03643) 20 20 50 *Fax:* (03643) 20 20 61 *E-mail:* info@goethe-gesellschaft.de *Web Site:* www. goethe-gesellschaft.de, pg 1495

Goethe-Institut (Belgium) *Tel:* (02) 2303970 *Fax:* (02) 2307725 *E-mail:* info@bruessel.goethe.org *Web Site:* www.goethe.de/ins/be/bru/deindex.htm, pg 1578

Verlag am Goetheanum (Switzerland) *Tel:* (061) 706 42 00 *Fax:* (061) 706 42 01 *E-mail:* info@vamg.ch *Web Site:* vamg.ch, pg 695

Zalozba Goga (Slovenia) *Tel:* (07) 393 08 01 *Fax:* (07) 393 08 00 *E-mail:* goga@goga.si *Web Site:* www. goga.si, pg 610

Goldegg Verlag GmbH (Austria) *Tel:* (01) 505 43 76-0 *Fax:* (01) 505 43 76-20 *E-mail:* office@goldegg-verlag.at *Web Site:* www.goldegg-verlag.at, pg 49

Golden Baobab (Ghana) *Tel:* (030) 2963639 *E-mail:* info@goldenbaobab.org *Web Site:* www. goldenbaobab.org, pg 1229, 1376

Golden Books Centre Sdn Bhd (GBC) (Malaysia) *Tel:* (03) 7727 3890; (03) 7728 3890; (03) 7727 4121; (03) 7727 4122 *Fax:* (03) 7727 3884 *E-mail:* gbc@ pc.jaring.my *Web Site:* www.goldenbookscentre.com, pg 507

Golden Cup Printing Co Ltd (Hong Kong) *Tel:* 2343 4254 *Fax:* 2341 5426 *E-mail:* sales@goldencup.com. hk *Web Site:* www.goldencup.com.hk, pg 1258, 1277, 1324, 1346, 1353

Golden Marketing/Tehnicka Knjiga (Croatia) *Tel:* (01) 4810 820 *Fax:* (01) 4810 821 *E-mail:* gmtk@gmtk.net *Web Site:* www.gmtk.net, pg 120, 1411

Das Goldene Tor Ltd (Germany) *Tel:* (06821) 8690355 *Fax:* (06821) 8690832 *E-mail:* hallo@das-goldene-tor.de *Web Site:* das-goldene-tor.de, pg 252

Goldland Business Co Ltd (Nigeria) *Tel:* (01) 5821203, pg 551

Goldmann Verlag (Germany) *Tel:* (089) 4136-0 *Toll Free Tel:* (0800) 500 33 22 *Fax:* (089) 4136-3333 *E-mail:* kundenservice@randomhouse.de *Web Site:* www.randomhouse.de/goldmann, pg 253

Goldschmidt Basel AG (Switzerland) *Tel:* (061) 261 61 91 *Fax:* (061) 261 61 23 *E-mail:* info@goldschmidt-basel.ch *Web Site:* www.victorgoldschmidt.ch, pg 695

La Goliardica Pavese SRL (Italy) *Tel:* (0382) 529570 *Fax:* (0382) 423140, pg 446

Edizioni Goliardiche SRL (Italy) *Tel:* (0432) 996332 *Fax:* (040) 566278 *E-mail:* info@edizionigoliardiche.it *Web Site:* www.edizionigoliardiche.it, pg 446

Golvan Arts Management (Australia) *Tel:* (03) 9853 5341 *Fax:* (03) 9853 8555 *E-mail:* golvan@ozemail.com.au *Web Site:* www.golvanarts.com.au, pg 1223

Gomer Press Ltd (United Kingdom) *Tel:* (01559) 363090 (publishing); (01559) 362371 (printing); (01559) 363092 (orders) *Fax:* (01559) 363758 *E-mail:* gwasg@gomer.co.uk; orders@gomer.co.uk; sales@gomer.co.uk *Web Site:* www.gomer.co.uk, pg 771

Gomez Gomez Hermanos Editores S de RL (Mexico) *Tel:* (0155) 56743548; (0155) 56727625; (0155) 55225903, pg 517

Miguel Gomez Ediciones (Spain) *Tel:* 952 602 873 *E-mail:* mge@miguelgomezediciones.com *Web Site:* miguelgomezediciones.com; miguelgomezediciones.com/editorial.php, pg 646

Gondolat Kiado (Hungary) *Tel:* (01) 486-1527 *Fax:* (01) 486-1527 *E-mail:* info@gondolatkiado.hu *Web Site:* www.gondolatkiado.hu, pg 368

Gondrom Verlag GmbH (Germany) *Tel:* (09208) 51-0 *Fax:* (09208) 51-21 *E-mail:* presse@gondrom-verlag.de *Web Site:* www.gondrom-verlag.de, pg 253

Librerias Gonvill SA de CV (Mexico) *Tel:* (0133) 3837-2300 *E-mail:* info@gonvill.com.mx; pedidosweb@libreriasgonvill.com.mx *Web Site:* www.gonvill.com.mx, pg 1434

Good Times Books Pvt Ltd (India) *Tel:* (011) 259 133 01; (011) 450 690 86 *Fax:* (011) 450 690 86 *E-mail:* info@goodtimesbooks.com *Web Site:* www.goodtimesbooks.com, pg 383

Goodwill Bookstore (Philippines) *Tel:* (02) 895-8684 *Fax:* (02) 895-7854 *E-mail:* publishing@goodwillbookstore.net *Web Site:* www.goodwillbookstore.com, pg 1443

Goodwill Publishing House (India) *Tel:* (011) 25750801; (011) 25755519; (011) 25820556 *Fax:* (011) 25763428; (011) 25764396 *E-mail:* contact@goodwillpublishinghouse.com; info@goodwillpublishinghouse.com *Web Site:* www.goodwillpublishinghouse.com, pg 383

Goodword Books (India) *Tel:* (011) 4652 1511; (011) 4182 7083; (011) 2435 5454; (011) 2435 6666 *Fax:* (011) 4565 1771 *E-mail:* info@goodwordbooks.com *Web Site:* www.goodwordbooks.com; www.goodword.net, pg 383

Van Goor (Netherlands) *Tel:* (030) 799 83 00 *Fax:* (030) 799 83 98 *E-mail:* info@unieboekspectrum.nl *Web Site:* www.unieboekspectrum.nl, pg 533

Goose River Press (United States) *Tel:* 207-832-6665 *E-mail:* gooseriverpress@roadrunner.com *Web Site:* gooseriverpress.com, pg 1288, 1340

Gopsons Papers Ltd (India) *Tel:* (011) 23281450; (011) 23289616; (011) 23289626 *Fax:* (011) 23276360 *E-mail:* information@gopsons.com *Web Site:* www.gopsons.com, pg 1327

Adam Gordon Books (United Kingdom) *Tel:* (01408) 622660 *E-mail:* adam@ahg-books.com *Web Site:* www.ahgbooks.com, pg 771

Gorenjski Tisk Storitve doo (Slovenia) *Tel:* (04) 20 16 300 *Fax:* (04) 20 16 301 *E-mail:* info@go-tisk.si *Web Site:* www.go-tisk.si, pg 1262, 1284, 1333, 1347, 1354

Agentur Gorus (Germany) *Tel:* (07732) 940 75-0 *Fax:* (07732) 940 75-55 *E-mail:* info@gorus.de *Web Site:* www.gorus.de, pg 1227

Gosudarstvennaya publichnaya istoricheskaya biblioteka Rossii (Russia) *Tel:* (495) 625 6514; (495) 628 0522 *Fax:* (495) 628 0284 *E-mail:* info@shpl.ru *Web Site:* www.shpl.ru, pg 1627

Gosudarstvennaya publichnaya nauchno-tekhnicheskaya biblioteka Rossii (Russia) *Tel:* (495) 698-93-05 *E-mail:* gpntb@gpntb.ru *Web Site:* www.gpntb.ru, pg 1627

Gosudarstvennaya publichnaya nauchno-tekhnicheskaya biblioteka Sibirskogo otdeleniya Rossiiskoi Akademii Nauk (Russia) *Tel:* (383) 266-25-85; (383) 266-75-71 *E-mail:* office@spsl.nsc.ru *Web Site:* www.spsl.nsc.ru, pg 1627

Gothia Fortbildning (Sweden) *Tel:* (08) 462 26 60; (08) 462 26 70 (orders) *Fax:* (08) 644 46 67 *E-mail:* info@gothiafortbildning.se *Web Site:* www.gothiafortbildning.se, pg 682

Gottmer Uitgevers Groep (Netherlands) *Tel:* (023) 54 111 90; (023) 54 116 09 (foreign rights) *Fax:* (023) 52 744 04 *E-mail:* info@gottmer.nl *Web Site:* www.gottmer.nl, pg 533

Gould Genealogy & History (Australia) *Tel:* (08) 8396 1110 *Fax:* (08) 8396 1163 *E-mail:* inquiries@gould.com.au; orders@gould.com.au *Web Site:* www.gould.com.au, pg 25

Gould Paper Corp (United States) *Tel:* 212-301-0000 *Toll Free Tel:* 800-221-3043 *Fax:* 212-481-0067 *E-mail:* info@gouldpaper.com *Web Site:* www.gouldpaper.com, pg 1349

Grupo Gourmets (Progourmet) (Spain) *Tel:* 915489651 *Fax:* 915487133 *E-mail:* gourmets@gourmets.net *Web Site:* www.gourmets.net, pg 647

Government of Sharjah Department of Culture (United Arab Emirates) *Tel:* (06) 5123333; (06) 5671116; (06) 5673139 *Fax:* (06) 5123303; (06) 5662126; (06) 5660535 *E-mail:* sdci@sdci.gov.ae *Web Site:* www.sdci.gov.ae/english/index1.html, pg 727

The Government Printer (Israel) *Tel:* (02) 5317215 *Fax:* (02) 5695347 *Web Site:* mof.gov.il/gp, pg 1260

Government Printer (Lesotho) *Tel:* 22313023 *Fax:* 22310452 *E-mail:* gpsec@printer.gov.ls, pg 499

Government Printer (South Africa) *Tel:* (012) 334-4500; (012) 334-4508; (012) 334-4509; (012) 334-4510 *Fax:* (012) 323-0009 *E-mail:* info@gpw.gov.za *Web Site:* www.gpwonline.co.za, pg 613

Government Printer (Imprimerie Nationale) (Malawi), pg 506

Government Printer (Imprimerie Officielle) (Morocco) *Tel:* 05 37 76 50 24 *Fax:* 05 37 76 51 79, pg 526

The Government Printer, Nairobi (Kenya) *Tel:* (020) 317840; (020) 317841, pg 493

Govi-Verlag Pharmazeutischer Verlag GmbH (Germany) *Tel:* (06196) 928-250 *Fax:* (06196) 928-259; (06196) 928-203 *E-mail:* service@govi.de *Web Site:* www.govi.de, pg 253

Govinda-Verlag GmbH (Switzerland) *Tel:* (043) 321 66 77 *Fax:* (043) 321 66 77 *E-mail:* info@govinda.ch *Web Site:* www.govinda.ch, pg 695

Govostis Publishing SA (Greece) *Tel:* 2103815433; 2103822251 *Fax:* 2103816661 *E-mail:* cotsos@govostis.gr *Web Site:* www.govostis.gr, pg 355

Gozo Public Libraries (Malta) *Tel:* 21561510 *E-mail:* gozolibraries.mgoz@gov.mt *Web Site:* www.maltalibraries.gov.mt, pg 1612

Agencja Literacka Graal (Poland) *Tel:* (22) 895-2000 *Fax:* (22) 895-2001 *E-mail:* info@graal.com.pl *Web Site:* www.graal.com.pl, pg 1233

Edicoes Graal Ltda (Brazil) *Tel:* (011) 3337-8399 *Fax:* (011) 3223-6290 *E-mail:* divulgacao@pazeterra.com.br; editorial@pazeterra.com.br *Web Site:* www.pazeterra.com.br, pg 83

Ordem do Graal na Terra (Brazil) *Tel:* (011) 4781-0006 *E-mail:* graal@graal.org.br *Web Site:* www.graal.org.br, pg 83

Grabert Verlag (Germany) *Tel:* (07071) 4070-0 *Fax:* (07071) 4070-26 *E-mail:* info@grabertverlag.de *Web Site:* www.grabert-verlag.de, pg 253

Gracewing Ltd (United Kingdom) *Tel:* (01568) 616835 *Fax:* (01568) 613289 *E-mail:* gracewingx@aol.com *Web Site:* www.gracewing.co.uk, pg 1458

Gracewing Publishing (United Kingdom) *Tel:* (01568) 616835 *Fax:* (01568) 613289 *E-mail:* gracewingx@aol.com *Web Site:* www.gracewing.co.uk, pg 771

Grada Publishing AS (Czech Republic) *Tel:* 234 264 401; 234 264 402 *Fax:* 234 264 400 *E-mail:* info@grada.cz *Web Site:* www.grada.cz, pg 127

Izadavacko Preduzece Gradevinska Knjiga (Serbia) *Tel:* (011) 32 47 662; (011) 32 33 565 *Fax:* (011) 32 33 234 *Web Site:* www.gk.izlog.org, pg 601

Editorial Gradifco (Argentina) *Tel:* (011) 4750-5688; (011) 4759-0286 *Fax:* (011) 4759-0286 *E-mail:* info@gradifco.com.ar *Web Site:* www.gradifco.com.ar, pg 7

Gradifco SRL (Argentina) *Tel:* (011) 4759-0286 *Fax:* (011) 4750-5688 *E-mail:* editorial@gradifco.com.ar *Web Site:* www.gradifco.com.ar, pg 1401

Gradiva Publicacoes SA (Portugal) *Tel:* 21 397 40 67; 21 397 40 68; 21 397 13 57; 21 395 34 70 *Fax:* 21 395 34 71 *E-mail:* geral@gradiva.mail.pt; encomendas@gradiva.mail.pt (orders); gradivapublicacoessa@gmail.com *Web Site:* www.gradiva.pt, pg 579

Graduate Institute Publications (Switzerland) *Tel:* (022) 908 43 60 *Fax:* (022) 908 62 73 *E-mail:* publications@graduateinstitute.ch *Web Site:* www.graduateinstitute.ch/publications, pg 695

Graefe und Unzer Verlag GmbH (Germany) *Tel:* (089) 4 19 81-0 *Fax:* (089) 4 19 81-250; (089) 4 19 81-113 *E-mail:* info@graefe-und-unzer.de; leserservice@graefe-und-unzer.de; rights@graefe-und-unzer.de *Web Site:* www.gu.de, pg 253

Graf Editions (Germany) *Tel:* (089) 2715957 *Fax:* (089) 2715997 *E-mail:* info@graf-editions.de *Web Site:* www.graf-editions.de, pg 253

Grafalco Ediciones SL (Spain) *Tel:* 91 620 02 03 *E-mail:* inquiry@navneet.com, pg 647

Buchhandlung Graff GmbH (Germany) *Tel:* (0531) 480 89-0 *Fax:* (0531) 480 89-89 *E-mail:* infos@graff.de *Web Site:* www.graff.de, pg 1416

Graffeg Ltd (United Kingdom) *Tel:* (01554) 824000; (01554) 823489 *E-mail:* croeso@graffeg.com *Web Site:* www.graffeg.com, pg 771

Graffiti Publications Pty Ltd (Australia) *Tel:* (03) 5472 3805; (03) 5472 3653 *E-mail:* info@graffitipub.com.au; sales@graffitipub.com.au *Web Site:* www.graffitipub.com.au, pg 25

Graffito Books Ltd (United Kingdom) *Tel:* (020) 3239 0968 *E-mail:* contact@graffitobooks.com *Web Site:* www.graffitobooks.com, pg 772

Grafica & Arte SRL (Italy) *Tel:* (035) 255014 *Fax:* (035) 250164 *E-mail:* info@graficaearte.it; ordini@graficaearte.it (orders) *Web Site:* www.graficaearte.it, pg 446

Graficas Estella SL (Spain) *Tel:* 948 54 84 00 *Web Site:* estellaprint.com, pg 1284, 1334

Graficas Santa Maria (Spain) *Tel:* 954 771 091 *Web Site:* graficassantamaria.com, pg 1262, 1284, 1334

Grafiche Calosci (Italy) *Tel:* (0575) 67 82 82 *Fax:* (0575) 67 82 82 *E-mail:* info@calosci.com *Web Site:* www.calosci.com, pg 446

Grafiche Damiani SRL (Italy) *Tel:* (051) 6356811 *Fax:* (051) 6347188 *E-mail:* info@grafichedamiani.it *Web Site:* www.grafichedamiani.it, pg 1281, 1328, 1353

Graficki zavod Hrvatske doo (Croatia) *Tel:* (01) 2499 000 *Fax:* (01) 2407 166 *E-mail:* info@gzh.hr *Web Site:* www.gzh.hr, pg 120

Grafija UAB (Lithuania) *Tel:* (05) 263 6472 *Fax:* (05) 263 6912 *E-mail:* grafija@grafija.lt *Web Site:* www.grafija.lt, pg 1330

Klaus Dieter Guhl (Germany) *Tel:* (030) 3213062 *Fax:* (030) 30823868 *E-mail:* kdguhl@t-online.de, pg 255

Guildhall Library (United Kingdom) *Tel:* (020) 7332 1868; (020) 7332 1870 *E-mail:* guildhall.library@ cityoflondon.gov.uk *Web Site:* www.cityoflondon.gov. uk/things-to-do/guildhall-library, pg 1641

Guinea Pig Education (United Kingdom) *Tel:* (01932) 336554 *E-mail:* info@guineapigeducation.co.uk *Web Site:* www.guineapigeducation.co.uk, pg 772

Guinness World Records Ltd (United Kingdom) *Tel:* (020) 7891 4567 *Fax:* (020) 7891 4501 *E-mail:* enquiries@guinnessworldrecords.com *Web Site:* www.guinnessworldrecords.com, pg 772

Guizhou Education Publishing House (China) *Tel:* (0851) 6828337, pg 105

Gujarat Vidyapith (India) *Tel:* (079) 27541148; (079) 27540746; (079) 40016200 *Fax:* (079) 27542547 *E-mail:* info@gujaratvidyapith.org; registrar@ gujaratvidyapith.org *Web Site:* www.gujaratvidyapith. org, pg 1601

Editorial Gulaab (Spain) *Tel:* 916145849 *Fax:* 916184012 *E-mail:* alfaomega@alfaomega.es *Web Site:* www.alfaomega.es, pg 648

Gulf Stream Editeur (France) *Tel:* 02 40 48 06 68 *Fax:* 02 40 48 74 69 *E-mail:* contact@gulfstream.fr *Web Site:* www.gulfstream.fr, pg 173

Druckhaus Gummersbach PP GmbH (Germany) *Tel:* (02261) 9572-0 *Fax:* (02261) 56338 *E-mail:* info@druckhaus-gummersbach.de *Web Site:* www.druckhaus-gummersbach.de, pg 1256, 1275, 1322

Gummerus Publishing Co (Finland) *Tel:* (010) 6836 200 *E-mail:* info@gummerus.fi *Web Site:* www.gummerus. fi, pg 148

M D Gunasena & Co Ltd (Sri Lanka) *Tel:* (011) 2323981; (011) 2323982; (011) 2323983; (011) 2323984 *Fax:* (011) 2323336 *E-mail:* info@ mdgunasena.com; publishinginfo@mdgunasena.com; publishingmgr@mdgunasena.com *Web Site:* www. mdgunasena.com, pg 677

M D Gunasena & Co Ltd (Sri Lanka) *Tel:* (011) 2323981; (011) 2323982; (011) 2323983; (011) 2323984 *Fax:* (011) 2323336 *E-mail:* headoffice@ mdgunasena.com; info@mdgunasena.com *Web Site:* www.mdgunasena.com, pg 1285, 1335, 1451

Gunisigi Kitapligi (Turkey) *Tel:* (0212) 212 99 73 *Fax:* (0212) 217 91 74 *E-mail:* info@ gunisigikitapligi.com; satis@gunisigikitapligi.com *Web Site:* gunisigikitapligi.com, pg 720

Gustav-Adolf-Werk eV (Germany) *Tel:* (0341) 490 62 0 *Fax:* (0341) 490 62 66; (0341) 490 62 67 *E-mail:* info@gustav-adolf-werk.de; presse@gustav-adolf-werk.de *Web Site:* www.gustav-adolf-werk.de, pg 255

Th Gut Verlag (Switzerland) *Tel:* (044) 209 91 11 *E-mail:* admin@baeschlin.ch *Web Site:* www.lesestoff. ch/verlage/gutverlag, pg 695

Das Gute Buch Verlagsanstalt (Liechtenstein) *Tel:* 390 09 03 *Fax:* 390 09 02 *E-mail:* dasgutebuch@verlag. li; www.dasgutebuch.net, pg 500

Der Gute Hirte Verlag (Germany) *Tel:* (0351) 4109969 *Fax:* (0351) 4109969 *Web Site:* www.dgh-verlag.de, pg 255

Verlag Guthmann-Peterson (Austria) *Tel:* (01) 877 04 26 *Fax:* (01) 876 40 04 *E-mail:* verlag@guthmann-peterson.de *Web Site:* www.guthmann-peterson.de, pg 49

Gutleut Verlag (Germany) *Tel:* (069) 87 87 86 58 *Fax:* (069) 25 32 69 *E-mail:* mail@gutleut-verlag.com *Web Site:* www.gutleut-verlag.com, pg 255

Guyana Library Association (GLA) (Guyana) *Tel:* 222486 *Fax:* 223596 *E-mail:* londonh@uog.ed.gy, pg 1653

Gwasg Carreg Gwalch (United Kingdom) *Tel:* (01492) 642031 *Fax:* (01492) 641502 *E-mail:* llanrwst@ carreg-gwalch.com *Web Site:* www.carreg-gwalch.co. uk, pg 773

Gyan Books Pvt Ltd (India) *Tel:* (011) 23261060; (011) 23282060 *Fax:* (011) 23285914 *E-mail:* editor@ gyanbooks.com (for authors); order@gyanbooks.com; data@gyanbooks.com (for publishers) *Web Site:* www. gyanbooks.com, pg 384

Gyldendal (Denmark) *Tel:* 33 75 55 55 *Fax:* 33 75 55 56 *E-mail:* gyldendal@gyldendal.dk; kundeservice@ gyldendal.dk *Web Site:* www.gyldendal.dk, pg 136

Gyldendal Akademisk (Norway) *Tel:* 22 03 41 00 *Fax:* 22 03 41 05 *E-mail:* akademisk@gyldendal. no; gnf@gyldendal.no *Web Site:* www.gyldendal. no/faglitteratur, pg 555

Gyldendal Group Agency (Denmark) *Tel:* 33 75 55 55 *E-mail:* info@gyldendalgroupagency.dk *Web Site:* www.gyldendalgroupagency.dk, pg 1225

Gyldendal Norsk Forlag (Norway) *Tel:* 22 03 41 00 *Fax:* 22 03 41 05 *E-mail:* gnf@gyldendal.no *Web Site:* www.gyldendal.no, pg 555

Gyldendals Bogklub (Denmark) *Tel:* 70 11 00 33 *E-mail:* gbk-otrs@gyldendal.dk *Web Site:* www. gyldendals-bogklub.dk, pg 1359

Gyldendals Bornebogklub (Denmark) *Tel:* 70 11 00 33 *E-mail:* bbk-otrs@gyldendal.dk *Web Site:* www. gyldendals-boernebogklub.dk, pg 1359

Gyosei Corp (Japan) *Tel:* (03) 6892-6342; (03) 6892-6589 *Fax:* (03) 6892-6932; (03) 6892-6925 *E-mail:* business@gyosei.co.jp *Web Site:* www.gyosei. co.jp, pg 476

H & H Publishing (Australia) *Tel:* (03) 9877 4428, pg 26

H B Books (Chile) *Tel:* (02) 481 1794 *Fax:* (02) 231 7145 *E-mail:* info@hbbooks.cl *Web Site:* hbbooks.cl, pg 1409

H Blume (Spain) *Tel:* 918 061 996 *Fax:* 918 044 028 *E-mail:* pedidos.blume@akal.com; edicion@akal.com; universidad@akal.com; educacion@akal.com; prensa@ akal.com; atencion-cliente@akal.com *Web Site:* www. akal.com, pg 648

H I Holdings Sdn Bhd (Malaysia) *Tel:* (03) 4270 1340 *Fax:* (03) 4270 1344, pg 507

Haag + Herchen Verlag GmbH (Germany) *Tel:* (06181) 520670-0 *Fax:* (06181) 520670-40 *E-mail:* verlag@ haagundherchen.de *Web Site:* www.haagundherchen.de, pg 255

C W Haarfeld GmbH (Germany) *Toll Free Tel:* 0800 88 85 440 *Toll Free Fax:* 0800 88 85 445 *E-mail:* online@cw-haarfeld.de; cwh@wolterskluwer. com *Web Site:* www.cw-haarfeld.de; www.cwh.de, pg 255

Wolfgang G Haas - Musikverlag Koeln eK (Germany) *Tel:* (02203) 98 88 3-0 *Fax:* (02203) 98 88 3-50 *E-mail:* order@haas-koeln.de *Web Site:* www.haas-koeln.de, pg 256

Haase & Sons Forlag A/S (Denmark) *Tel:* 3314 4175 *Fax:* 3311 5959 *E-mail:* haase@haase.dk *Web Site:* www.haase.dk, pg 136

Dr Rudolf Habelt GmbH (Germany) *Tel:* (0228) 9 23 83-0; (0228) 9 23 83-55 (antiquarian bookshop) *Fax:* (0228) 9 23 83-6 *E-mail:* info@habelt.de; verlag@habelt.de *Web Site:* www.habelt.de, pg 256

Habermann Institute for Literary Research (Israel) *Tel:* (08) 9234008 *Fax:* (08) 9234008, pg 418

Habib Publishers (Lebanon) *Tel:* (09) 224090 *Fax:* (09) 210037 *E-mail:* info@habibpublishers.com *Web Site:* www.habibpublishers.com, pg 498

Hachette Australia (Australia) *Tel:* (02) 8248 0800; (02) 4390 1300 (customer service) *Fax:* (02) 8248 0810 *E-mail:* auspub@hachette.com.au (Australian publishing); hsales@hachette.com.au; adscs@ alliancedist.com.au (customer service); rights@ hachette.com.au *Web Site:* www.hachette.com.au, pg 26

Hachette Book Publishing India Pvt Ltd (India) *Tel:* (0124) 4195000 *Fax:* (0124) 4148900 *E-mail:* sales@hachetteindia.com; rights@ hachetteindia.com; publicity@hachetteindia.com *Web Site:* www.hachetteindia.com, pg 384

Hachette Children's Books (United Kingdom) *Tel:* (020) 3122 6000 *E-mail:* ad@hachettechildrens.co.uk *Web Site:* www.hachettechildrens.co.uk, pg 773

Hachette Education (France) *Tel:* 01 43 92 30 00 *E-mail:* relations-enseignants.hachette-education@lpc. fr *Web Site:* www.hachette-education.com, pg 173

Hachette Francais Langue Etrangere - FLE (France) *Tel:* 01 43 92 30 00 *E-mail:* relations-enseignants. hachette-education@lpc.fr *Web Site:* www.hachettefle. com, pg 173

Hachette Jeunesse (France) *Tel:* 01 43 92 30 00 *Web Site:* www.hachette-jeunesse.com/livres-illustres/ accueil.html, pg 173

Hachette Livre (France) *Tel:* 01 43 92 30 00 *Web Site:* www.hachette.com, pg 173

Hachette Livre International (France) *Tel:* 01 55 00 11 00 *Fax:* 01 55 00 11 20 *E-mail:* hli@hachette-livre-intl.com *Web Site:* www.editions-hachette-livre-international.com; www.hachette-livre-international. com, pg 174

Hachette Pratique (France) *Tel:* 01 43 92 30 30 *Web Site:* www.hachette-pratique.com, pg 174

Hachette Romans (France) *Tel:* 01 43 92 30 00 *Fax:* 01 43 92 30 30 *Web Site:* www.lecture-academy.com; www.livredepochejeunesse.com, pg 174

Hachette UK (United Kingdom) *Tel:* (020) 3122 6000 *E-mail:* enquiries@hachette.co.uk *Web Site:* www. hachette.co.uk, pg 773

Hachmeister Verlag + Galerie (Germany) *Tel:* (0251) 51210 *Fax:* (0251) 57217, pg 256

Walter Haedecke Verlag (Germany) *Tel:* (07033) 13 80 80 *Fax:* (07033) 138 08 13 *E-mail:* info@haedecke-verlag.de *Web Site:* www.haedecke-verlag.de, pg 256

Dr Curt Haefner-Verlag GmbH (Germany) *Tel:* (0711) 7594-0 *Fax:* (0711) 7594-390 *Web Site:* www. konradin.de, pg 256

Editions Haere Po (French Polynesia) *Tel:* 58 26 36; 77 23 46 (cell); 71 85 00 (cell) *Fax:* 58 04 01 *E-mail:* haerepotahiti@mail.pf *Web Site:* www. haerepo.com, pg 201

Haeusser Media (Germany) *Tel:* (06151) 22824 *Fax:* (06151) 26854 *E-mail:* info@haeusser-media.com *Web Site:* www.haeusser-media.com, pg 256

Haffmans & Tolkemitt GmbH (Germany) *Tel:* (030) 240 472 39 *Fax:* (030) 240 474 15 *E-mail:* office@ haffmans-tolkemitt.de *Web Site:* haffmans-tolkemitt.de, pg 256

Hagemann & Partner Bildungsmedien Verlagsgesellschaft mbH (Germany) *Tel:* (0211) 17 92 70 0 *Fax:* (0211) 17 92 70 70 *E-mail:* aktuell@hagemann.de *Web Site:* www.hagemann.de, pg 256

Hagen Agency (Norway) *Tel:* 22 46 52 54; 93 41 10 56 *E-mail:* hagency@online.no *Web Site:* www. hagenagency.no, pg 1233

Hagenbach & Bender GmbH (Switzerland) *Tel:* (031) 3816666 *Fax:* (031) 3816677 *E-mail:* rights@ hagenbach-bender.com *Web Site:* www.hagenbach-bender.com, pg 1237

Hahner Verlagsgesellschaft mbH (Germany) *Tel:* (02408) 55 05 *Fax:* (02408) 58081 *E-mail:* office@hvg.de *Web Site:* www.hvg.de, pg 256

Verlag Hahnsche Buchhandlung (Germany) *Tel:* (0511) 80 71 80 40 *Fax:* (0511) 36 36 98 *E-mail:* info@ hahnsche-buchhandlung.de; order@hahnsche-buchhandlung.de *Web Site:* www.hahnsche-buchhandlung.de, pg 256

Editions Haho (Togo) *Tel:* 9046745, pg 716

Editora Harbra Ltda (Brazil) *Tel:* (011) 5084-2403; (011) 5084-2482; (011) 5571-1122; (011) 5549-2244; (011) 5571-0276 *Fax:* (011) 5575-6876; (011) 5571-9777 (sales) *E-mail:* editorial@harbra.com.br; vendas@harbra.com.br; administracao@harbra.com.br *Web Site:* www.harbra.com.br, pg 83

Harden's Ltd (United Kingdom) *Tel:* (020) 7839 4763 *E-mail:* editorial@hardens.com *Web Site:* www.hardens.com, pg 774

Hardie Grant Books (Australia) *Tel:* (03) 8520 6444 *Fax:* (03) 8520 6422 *E-mail:* info@hardiegrant.com.au *Web Site:* www.hardiegrant.com.au, pg 26

Hardie Grant Travel (Australia) *Tel:* (03) 8520 6444 *Fax:* (03) 8520 6422 *E-mail:* info@exploreaustralia.net.au *Web Site:* www.hardiegrant.com/au/travel; www.exploreaustralia.net.au, pg 26

Hardman & Swainson (United Kingdom) *Tel:* (020) 7223 5176 *E-mail:* submissions@hardmanswainson.com *Web Site:* www.hardmanswainson.com, pg 1242

Hardt & Woerner Unternehmensberatung GbR (Germany) *Tel:* (0611) 97173902 *Web Site:* www.hardt-woerner.de, pg 258

The Thomas Hardy Society (United Kingdom) *Tel:* (01305) 251501 *Fax:* (01305) 251501 *E-mail:* info@hardysociety.org *Web Site:* www.hardysociety.org, pg 1503

Hargreen Publishing Co (Australia) *Tel:* (03) 9329 9714, pg 26

Siegfried Haring Literatten-Verlag Ulm (Germany) *Tel:* (0731) 9806040 *Fax:* (0731) 9806042, pg 258

Harlenic Hellas Publishing SA (Greece) *Tel:* 2103609438; 2103629723 *Fax:* 2103614846 *E-mail:* info@harlenic.gr *Web Site:* www.harlenic.gr; www.bell.gr, pg 355

Editions Harlequin (France) *Tel:* 01 42 16 63 63; 01 45 82 47 47 (orders) *Fax:* 01 45 82 86 94 *Web Site:* www.harlequin.fr, pg 174

Harlequin Iberica SA (Spain) *Tel:* 914 358 623 *Fax:* 914 310 484 *E-mail:* atencion_al_cliente@harpercollinsiberica.com *Web Site:* www.harpercollinsiberica.com, pg 648

Harlequin Mills & Boon (United Kingdom) *Tel:* (020) 8288 2800 *Fax:* (020) 8288 2898 *E-mail:* info@millsandboon.co.uk *Web Site:* www.millsandboon.co.uk, pg 774

L'Harmattan (France) *Tel:* 01 40 46 79 22; 01 40 46 79 20 (sales) *Fax:* 01 43 25 82 03 (sales) *E-mail:* diffusion.harmattan@wanadoo.fr *Web Site:* www.editions-harmattan.fr, pg 174

Wydawnictwo Harmonia (Poland) *Tel:* (58) 348 09 50 *Fax:* (58) 348 09 00 *E-mail:* harmonia@harmonia.edu.pl *Web Site:* www.harmonia.edu.pl, pg 569

Uitgeverij De Harmonie (Netherlands) *Tel:* (020) 6245181 *Fax:* (020) 6230672 *E-mail:* info@deharmonie.nl *Web Site:* www.deharmonie.nl, pg 534

Harmonie-Verlag (Germany) *Tel:* (0761) 709667, pg 258

Anja Harms Ateliers (Germany) *Tel:* (06171) 268240 *E-mail:* mail@anja-harms.de *Web Site:* www.anja-harms.de, pg 1275

HarperCollins France (France) *Tel:* 01 42 16 63 63; 01 45 82 44 26 (customer service) *Web Site:* www.harpercollins.fr, pg 174

HarperCollins Germany GmbH (Germany) *Tel:* (040) 6366 420-0 *Fax:* (0711) 7252-399 *E-mail:* service@harpercollins.de *Web Site:* corporate.harpercollins.de, pg 258

HarperCollins Holland (Netherlands) *Tel:* (020) 662 6646 *E-mail:* info@harpercollins.nl *Web Site:* www.harpercollins.nl, pg 534

HarperCollins Hungary (Hungary) *Tel:* (01) 488-5569 *E-mail:* harpercollins@harpercollins.hu *Web Site:* www.harpercollins.hu, pg 368

HarperCollins Italia SpA (Italy) *E-mail:* ufficiostampa@harpercollins.it *Web Site:* www.harpercollins.it, pg 447

HarperCollins Japan (Japan) *Tel:* (03) 5295-8090 *Fax:* (03) 5295-8091 (sales) *Web Site:* corporate.harpercollins.co.jp; www.harlequin.co.jp, pg 477

HarperCollins Nordic AB (Sweden) *E-mail:* kundservice@harlequin.se *Web Site:* harpercollins.se, pg 682

HarperCollins Polska sp z oo (Poland) *Tel:* (22) 8565757 *E-mail:* info@harpercollins.pl *Web Site:* www.harpercollins.pl, pg 569

HarperCollins Publishers Australia (Australia) *Tel:* (02) 9952 5000 *Fax:* (02) 9952 5555 *E-mail:* publicity@harpercollins.com.au *Web Site:* www.harpercollins.com.au, pg 26

HarperCollins Publishers India Ltd (India) *Tel:* (0120) 4044800 *Web Site:* www.harpercollins.co.in, pg 384

HarperCollins Publishers New Zealand (New Zealand) *Tel:* (09) 443 9400 *Fax:* (09) 443 9403 *E-mail:* orders@harpercollins.com.au; publicity@harpercollins.co.nz; rights@harpercollins.com.au *Web Site:* www.harpercollins.co.nz, pg 546

HarperCollins UK (United Kingdom) *Tel:* (020) 8741 7070 *E-mail:* uk.orders@harpercollins.co.uk; enquiries@harpercollins.co.uk *Web Site:* www.harpercollins.co.uk, pg 774

Otto Harrassowitz GmbH & Co KG (Germany) *Tel:* (0611) 530 0 *Fax:* (0611) 530 560 *E-mail:* service@harrassowitz.de *Web Site:* www.harrassowitz.de, pg 1416

Harrassowitz Verlag (Germany) *Tel:* (0611) 530-905 *Fax:* (0611) 530-999 *E-mail:* verlag@harrassowitz.de *Web Site:* www.harrassowitz-verlag.de, pg 258

The Deborah Harris Agency (Israel) *Tel:* (02) 6722143; (02) 6722145 *Fax:* (02) 6725797 *Web Site:* www.thedeborahharrisagency.com, pg 1230

Hart Publishing Ltd (United Kingdom) *Tel:* (01865) 517530 *Fax:* (01865) 510710 *E-mail:* mail@hartpub.co.uk *Web Site:* www.hartpub.co.uk, pg 775

Hera A Hartleben GmbH (Austria) *Tel:* (01) 982 35 60 *Fax:* (01) 985 59 98 *E-mail:* office@hartleben.at; schulbuch@gmx.net *Web Site:* www.hartleben.at, pg 1404

Harvard University Press (United Kingdom) *Tel:* (020) 3463 2350 *Fax:* (020) 7831 9261 *E-mail:* info@harvardup.co.uk *Web Site:* www.hup.harvard.edu, pg 775

Denise Harvey (Publisher) (Greece) *Tel:* 2227031154 *Fax:* 2227031154 *E-mail:* dhp@dharveypublisher.gr *Web Site:* www.deniseharveypublisher.gr, pg 355

Harvey Map Services Ltd (United Kingdom) *Tel:* (01786) 841202 *Fax:* (01786) 841098 *E-mail:* winni@harveymaps.co.uk; sales@harveymaps.co.uk *Web Site:* www.harveymaps.co.uk, pg 775

Harvill Secker (United Kingdom) *Tel:* (020) 7840 8400 *Fax:* (020) 7233 8791 *E-mail:* enquiries@randomhouse.co.uk; harvillseckereditorial@randomhouse.co.uk; harvillseckerpublicity@randomhouse.co.uk *Web Site:* www.randomhouse.co.uk/harvillsecker; www.vintage-books.co.uk/about-us/harvill-secker, pg 775

Hasanuddin University Library (Indonesia) *Tel:* (0411) 586 200; (0411) 584 200 *Fax:* (0411) 585 188 *E-mail:* humas@unhas.ac.id; libraryunhas@gmail.com *Web Site:* unhas.ac.id/perpustakaan, pg 1601

Haschemi Edition Cologne Kunstverlag fuer Fotografie (Germany) *Tel:* (0221) 561007; (0221) 561008 *Fax:* (0221) 529282 *E-mail:* info@haschemi.de *Web Site:* www.haschemi.de; cms.haschemi.de, pg 258

Hasefer Publishing House (Romania) *Tel:* (021) 308 62 08 *Fax:* (021) 308 62 08 *E-mail:* difuzare@hasefer.ro *Web Site:* www.hasefer.ro, pg 587

Haseo Publishing Co (South Korea) *Tel:* (02) 2237-8161 *Fax:* (02) 2237-6575 *Web Site:* www.haseo.co.kr, pg 622

Haskolautgafan - University of Iceland Press (Iceland) *Tel:* 525-4003 *E-mail:* hu@hi.is *Web Site:* www.haskolautgafan.hi.is, pg 372

Hatchards Ltd (United Kingdom) *Tel:* (020) 7439 9921 *Fax:* (020) 7494 1313 *E-mail:* books@hatchards.co.uk *Web Site:* www.hatchards.co.uk, pg 1458

Editions Hatier SA (France) *Tel:* 01 49 91 87 67 *Fax:* 05 49 91 87 68 *E-mail:* infoprofs@editions-hatier.fr *Web Site:* www.editions-hatier.fr, pg 174

Hatier International (France) *Tel:* 01 55 00 11 00 *Fax:* 01 55 00 11 20 *E-mail:* hli@hachette-livre-intl.com *Web Site:* www.editions-hachette-livre-international.com, pg 175

Hatje Cantz Verlag GmbH (Germany) *Tel:* (030) 3464678-00 *Fax:* (030) 3289042-48 *E-mail:* contact@hatjecantz.de; berlin@hatjecantz.de; sales@hatjecantz.de; presse@hatjecantz.de *Web Site:* www.hatjecantz.de, pg 258

Hatter Kiado es Kereskedelmi Kft (Hungary) *Tel:* (01) 452 1768 *Fax:* (01) 452 1751 *E-mail:* hatterkiado@hatterkiado.hu; marketing@hatterkiado.hu *Web Site:* www.hatterkiado.hu, pg 368

Haufe-Hammonia Corporate Publishing (Germany) *Tel:* (040) 520103-0 *Fax:* (040) 520103-12 *E-mail:* info@hammonia.de *Web Site:* www.hammonia.de, pg 258

Haufe-Lexware GmbH & Co KG (Germany) *Tel:* (0761) 89 80 *Toll Free Tel:* 0800 50 50 445 *Fax:* (0761) 89 83 900 *Toll Free Fax:* 0800 50 50 446 *E-mail:* info@haufe.de; service@haufe.de *Web Site:* www.haufe.de, pg 258

Haupt Verlag AG (Switzerland) *Tel:* (031) 309 09 00 *Fax:* (031) 309 09 90 *E-mail:* info@haupt.ch; bestellung@haupt.ch *Web Site:* www.haupt.ch, pg 695

Hauptverband des Oesterreichischen Buchhandels (HVB) (Austria) *Tel:* (01) 512 15 35 *Fax:* (01) 512 84 82 *E-mail:* sekretariat@hvb.at *Web Site:* www.buecher.at, pg 1365

Haus Publishing (United Kingdom) *Tel:* (020) 7838 9055 *Fax:* (020) 7584 9501 *E-mail:* info@hauspublishing.com; sales@hauspublishing.com; publicity@hauspublishing.com *Web Site:* www.hauspublishing.com; www.bookhaus.co.uk, pg 775

Dr Ernst Hauswedell & Co KG Verlag (Germany) *Tel:* (0711) 54 99 71-11 *Fax:* (0711) 54 99 71-21 *E-mail:* verlag@hauswedell.de *Web Site:* www.hauswedell.de, pg 259

Tiskarny Havlickuv Brod AS (Czech Republic) *Tel:* 569 664 110 *Fax:* 569 664 111 *E-mail:* thb@thb.cz *Web Site:* www.thb.cz, pg 1274, 1320

Hawel Verlag (Germany) *Tel:* (09081) 27 50 26-5 *Fax:* (09081) 27 50 26-9 *E-mail:* info@hawelverlag.de *Web Site:* www.hawelverlag.de, pg 259

Hawker Brownlow Education (Australia) *Tel:* (03) 8558 2444 *Toll Free Tel:* 1800 334 603 (Australia); 0800 501 019 (New Zealand) *Fax:* (03) 8558 2400 *Toll Free Fax:* 1800 150 445 (Australia) *E-mail:* orders@hbe.com.au *Web Site:* www.hbe.com.au, pg 26

Hawker Publications Ltd (United Kingdom) *Tel:* (020) 7720 2108 *Fax:* (020) 7498 3023 *E-mail:* info@hawkerpublications.com *Web Site:* www.careinfo.org, pg 775

Hawthorn Press (United Kingdom) *Tel:* (01453) 757040 *Fax:* (01453) 751138 *E-mail:* info@hawthornpress.com *Web Site:* www.hawthornpress.com, pg 775

Hay House Australia Pty Ltd (Australia) *Tel:* (02) 9669 4299 *Fax:* (02) 9669 4299 *Web Site:* www.hayhouse.com.au, pg 26

Hay House UK Ltd (United Kingdom) *Tel:* (020) 3675 2450 *Toll Free Tel:* 0 333 240 2480 (customer service) *Fax:* (020) 3675 2451 *Web Site:* www.hayhouse.co.uk, pg 776

Hayakawa Publishing Inc (Japan) *Tel:* (03) 3252-3111 *Fax:* (03) 3254-1550 *E-mail:* customer@hayakawa-online.co.jp *Web Site:* www.hayakawa-online.co.jp, pg 477

Hayit Medien (Germany) *Tel:* (0221) 921635-0 *Fax:* (0221) 921635-24 *E-mail:* kontakt@hayit.de *Web Site:* www.hayit.de, pg 259

Haymarket Media GmbH & Co KG (Germany) *Tel:* (0531) 38 00 4-0 *Fax:* (0531) 38 00 4-25 *E-mail:* info@haymarket.de *Web Site:* www. haymarket.de, pg 259

Haymon Verlag GesmbH (Austria) *Tel:* (0512) 576300 *Fax:* (0512) 576300 14 *E-mail:* office@haymonverlag. at *Web Site:* www.haymonverlag.at, pg 49

Haynes Publishing (United Kingdom) *Tel:* (01963) 440635; (01476) 541085 (trade) *Fax:* (01476) 541063 (trade) *Web Site:* www.haynes.com, pg 776

Editions Monelle Hayot (France) *Tel:* 03 44 78 79 61 *Fax:* 03 44 78 78 59 *E-mail:* contact@editions-monelle-hayot.com *Web Site:* www.editions-monelle-hayot.com, pg 175

Hayrat Nesriyat Sanyi ve Ticaret AS (Turkey) *Tel:* (0212) 624 24 34; (0850) 333 99 66 *Fax:* (0212) 424 49 32 *E-mail:* info@hayrat.com *Web Site:* www. hayrat.com.tr, pg 721

Grakan Hayrenik CJSC (Armenia) *Tel:* (010) 528520; (010) 524496 *Fax:* (010) 528520, pg 14

Hayward Gallery Publishing (United Kingdom) *Tel:* (020) 7960 4200 *Fax:* (020) 7921 0607 *E-mail:* customer@southbankcentre.co.uk *Web Site:* www.southbankcentre.co.uk, pg 776

Sir Charles Hayward Library (The Bahamas) *Tel:* (242) 352-7048; (242) 352-3524 *Web Site:* www. charleshaywardlibrary.com, pg 1576

Editions Hazan (France) *Tel:* 01 41 23 67 44 *Fax:* 01 41 23 64 37 *Web Site:* www.editions-hazan.fr, pg 175

HB Media Holdings Pte Ltd (Singapore) *Tel:* 6296 4289, pg 1261

HB Publications (United Kingdom) *Tel:* (020) 8769 1585 *Fax:* (020) 8769 2320 *E-mail:* info@hbpublications. com *Web Site:* www.hbpublications.com, pg 776

Hea Lugu (Estonia) *Tel:* 661 3390 *Web Site:* www. healugu.ee, pg 145

Head of Zeus (United Kingdom) *Tel:* (020) 7253 5557 *E-mail:* info@headofzeus.com *Web Site:* headofzeus. com, pg 776

Headley Brothers Ltd (United Kingdom) *Tel:* (01233) 623131 *Fax:* (01233) 612345 *E-mail:* printing@ headley.co.uk; sales@headley.co.uk *Web Site:* www. headley.co.uk, pg 1287, 1337, 1348, 1355

Headline Publishing Group Ltd (United Kingdom) *Tel:* (020) 3122 7222 *E-mail:* enquiries@headline.co. uk *Web Site:* www.headline.co.uk, pg 776

A M Heath & Co Ltd (United Kingdom) *Tel:* (020) 7242 2811 *Fax:* (020) 7242 2711 *E-mail:* enquiries@ amheath.com *Web Site:* www.amheath.com, pg 1242

Rupert Heath Literary Agency (United Kingdom) *E-mail:* emailagency@rupertheath.com *Web Site:* www.rupertheath.com, pg 1242

Heavenly Lotus Publishing Co, Ltd (Taiwan) *Tel:* (02) 2873-6629 *Fax:* (02) 2873-6709, pg 712

Agentur Literatur Gudrun Hebel (Germany) *Tel:* (030) 347 077 67 *Fax:* (030) 347 077 68 *E-mail:* brief@ agentur-literatur.de *Web Site:* agentur-literatur.de, pg 1227

HEBN Publishers PLC (Nigeria) *Tel:* (02) 2410747; (02) 2410943; (02) 2413096; (02) 2412268 *Fax:* (02) 2411089; (02) 2413237 *E-mail:* info@hebnpublishers. com *Web Site:* www.hebnpublishers.com, pg 551

Heckner Druck-und Verlagsgesellschaft mbH & Co KG (Germany) *Tel:* (05331) 80 08-0 *Fax:* (05331) 80 08-16, pg 259

Hedleys Booksellers (New Zealand) *Tel:* (06) 378 2875 *Fax:* (06) 378 2570 *E-mail:* sales@hedleysbooks.co.nz *Web Site:* www.hedleysbooks.co.nz; www.booksonline. co.nz, pg 1438

Hedlund Literary Agency (Sweden) *Web Site:* www. hedlundagency.se, pg 1236

Heel Verlag GmbH (Germany) *Tel:* (02223) 9230-0; (02223) 9230-38 *Fax:* (02223) 9230-13; (02223) 9230-26 *E-mail:* info@heel-verlag.de *Web Site:* www.heel-verlag.de, pg 259

Bokforlaget Hegas AB (Sweden) *Tel:* (042) 33 03 40 *E-mail:* info@hegas.se *Web Site:* www.hegas.se, pg 682

Heibonsha Ltd Publishers (Japan) *Tel:* (03) 3230-6570; (03) 3230-6572 (sales) *Fax:* (03) 3230-6586 *E-mail:* webmaster@heibonsha.co.jp; shop@ heibonsha.co.jp; hanbai@heibonsha.co.jp (books) *Web Site:* www.heibonsha.co.jp, pg 477

Joh Heider Verlag GmbH (Germany) *Tel:* (02202) 9540-0 *Fax:* (02202) 21531 *E-mail:* info@heider-medien.de *Web Site:* www.heider-verlag.de, pg 259

Verlag Horst Heigl (Germany) *Tel:* (07552) 938754 *Fax:* (07552) 938756 *E-mail:* shop@heigl-verlag.de *Web Site:* www.heigl-verlag.de, pg 259

Heile Dich Selbst Verlag (Switzerland) *Tel:* (081) 834 21 22; (081) 834 20 03 *Fax:* (081) 834 20 04; (081) 834 21 24 *Web Site:* www.heile-dich-selbst.ch, pg 696

Heilongjiang Science & Technology Press (China) *Tel:* (0451) 58855674; (0451) 58930235 *Fax:* (0451) 53642143 *E-mail:* zbs53635613@163.com *Web Site:* science.ebook.dbw.cn, pg 105

Arnold Heinemann Publishers (India) Pvt Ltd (India) *Tel:* (044) 24936255, pg 384

Heinemann Educational Publishers Southern Africa (South Africa) *Tel:* (011) 322 8600 *Fax:* (086) 687 7822 *E-mail:* customerliaison@heinemann.co.za *Web Site:* www.heinemann.co.za, pg 613

William Heinemann (United Kingdom) *Tel:* (020) 7840 8400; (020) 7840 8707 (editorial) *Fax:* (020) 7233 6127 (editorial); (020) 7233 8791 *Web Site:* www. randomhouse.co.uk, pg 777

Verlag Otto Heinevetter Lehrmittel GmbH (Germany) *Tel:* (040) 25 90 19 *Fax:* (040) 251 2128 *E-mail:* info@heinevetter-verlag.de *Web Site:* www. heinevetter-verlag.de, pg 259

Heinrich-Boell-Stiftung eV (Germany) *Tel:* (030) 285 34-0 *Fax:* (030) 285 34-109 *E-mail:* info@boell.de *Web Site:* www.boell.de, pg 259

Heinrichshofen's Verlag GmbH & Co KG (Germany) *Tel:* (04421) 9267-0 *Fax:* (04421) 9267-99 *E-mail:* info@heinrichshofen.de *Web Site:* www. heinrichshofen.de, pg 259

Hekla Forlag (Denmark) *Tel:* 3375 5555 *Fax:* 3615 3616 *E-mail:* salg@borgen.dk; borgen_post@gyldendal.dk *Web Site:* www.borgen.dk, pg 137

Helbing Lichtenhahn Verlag (Switzerland) *Tel:* (061) 228 90 70 *Fax:* (061) 228 90 71 *E-mail:* info@helbing.ch *Web Site:* www.helbing.ch, pg 696

Helbling Languages GmbH (Austria) *Tel:* (0512) 26 23 33-0 *Fax:* (0512) 26 23 33-111 *E-mail:* e. amjad@helblinglanguages.com; office@helbling.co.at *Web Site:* www.helblinglanguages.at, pg 49

Helbling Verlag GmbH (Germany) *Tel:* (0711) 75 87 01-0 *Fax:* (0711) 75 87 01-11 *E-mail:* service@helbling. com *Web Site:* www.helbling-verlag.de, pg 259

Helbling Verlagsgesellschaft mbH (Austria) *Tel:* (0512) 26 23 33-0 *Fax:* (0512) 26 23 33-111 *E-mail:* office@ helbling.co.at *Web Site:* www.helbling.com, pg 49

Helden Verlag (Switzerland) *Tel:* (044) 240 44 70 *Fax:* (044) 240 44 41, pg 696

HelfRecht Verlag und Druck (Germany) *Tel:* (09232) 601-0 *Fax:* (09232) 601-280 *E-mail:* info@helfrecht. de *Web Site:* www.helfrecht.de, pg 259

Editorial Heliasta SRL (Argentina) *Tel:* (011) 4804-0472; (011) 4804-8757; (011) 4804-0119 *Fax:* (011) 4804-0472; (011) 4804-8757; (011) 4804-0119 *E-mail:* editorial@heliasta.com.ar *Web Site:* www. heliasta.com.ar, pg 7

Helikon Kiado Kft (Hungary) *Tel:* (01) 423-0080 *Fax:* (01) 423-0087 *E-mail:* helikon@helikon.hu *Web Site:* www.helikon.hu, pg 368

Helikon PLC (Bulgaria) *Tel:* (02) 4604080; (02) 4604081 (online orders) *Fax:* (056) 803139 *E-mail:* office@ helikon.bg *Web Site:* www.helikon.bg, pg 1408

Helion & Co Ltd (United Kingdom) *Tel:* (0121) 705 3393 *Fax:* (0121) 711 4075 *E-mail:* info@helion.co.uk *Web Site:* www.helion.co.uk, pg 777

Heliopol (Bulgaria) *Tel:* (02) 9867773 *E-mail:* heliopol@ abv.bg *Web Site:* www.heliopol.com, pg 95

Heliopolis-Verlag Ewald Katzmann (Germany) *Tel:* (07071) 760444, pg 260

Editions Helium (France) *Tel:* 01 45 87 99 15 *E-mail:* info@helium-editions.fr *Web Site:* www. helium-editions.fr, pg 175

The Hellenic Bookservice (United Kingdom) *Tel:* (020) 7267 9499 *Fax:* (020) 7267 9498 *E-mail:* enquiries@ hellenicbookservice.com *Web Site:* www. hellenicbookservice.com, pg 1458

Hellenic Federation of Publishers & Booksellers (Greece) *Tel:* 2103300924; 2103804760; 2103806801 *Fax:* 2103301617, pg 1376

Hellerau-Verlag Dresden GmbH (Germany) *Tel:* (0351) 803 52 93 *Fax:* (0351) 315 84 30 *E-mail:* info@ hellerau-verlag.de *Web Site:* www.hellerau-verlag.de, pg 260

Anna Helm Atelier fuer Buchkunst und Gestaltung (Germany) *Tel:* (0176) 7684 7831 *Fax:* (0345) 20 32 362 *Web Site:* www.annahelm.de, pg 1322

Christopher Helm (Publishers) Ltd (United Kingdom) *Tel:* (020) 7631 5600 *Fax:* (020) 7631 5800 *E-mail:* contact@bloomsbury.com *Web Site:* www. bloomsbury.com, pg 777

Helm Information (United Kingdom) *Tel:* (01424) 319685, pg 777

Ulrike Helmer Verlag (Germany) *Tel:* (06196) 2029977 *Fax:* (06196) 2029976 *E-mail:* info@ulrike-helmer-verlag.de *Web Site:* helmer.txt-web.de; helmer.txt9.de, pg 260

Helsingin Kaupunginkirjasto - yleisten kirjastojen keskuskirjasto (Finland) *Tel:* (09) 3108511 *Web Site:* www.lib.hel.fi, pg 1589

Verlag Helvetica Chimica Acta (Switzerland) *Tel:* (044) 360 24 34 *Fax:* (044) 360 24 35 *E-mail:* vhca@vhca. ch *Web Site:* www.vhca.ch, pg 696

Hema Maps Pty Ltd (Australia) *Tel:* (07) 3340 0000; (07) 3340 0075 (customer service) *Fax:* (07) 3340 0099 *E-mail:* sales.hema@clear.net.nz *Web Site:* www. hemamaps.com, pg 27

Van Hemeldonck BVBA (Belgium) *Tel:* (014) 611034, pg 67

Hemeroteca Municipal de Madrid (Spain) *Tel:* 91 513 31 64; 91 588 57 72; 91 588 57 73 *E-mail:* infohemeroteca@madrid.es *Web Site:* bibliotecas.madrid.es, pg 1633

Hemeroteca Nacional de Mexico (Mexico) *Tel:* (0155) 5622 6818; (0155) 5622 6827 *Web Site:* www.hnm. unam.mx, pg 1614

Editorial Hemisferio Sur SA (Argentina) *Tel:* (011) 4952-9825; (011) 4952-8454 *Fax:* (011) 4952-8454 *E-mail:* informe@hemisferiosur.com.ar *Web Site:* www.hemisferiosur.com.ar, pg 8

Editions Hemma (Belgium) *Tel:* (086) 43 01 01 *Fax:* (086) 43 36 40 *E-mail:* hemma@hemma.be *Web Site:* www.hemma.be, pg 67

Hemming Information Services (United Kingdom) *Tel:* (020) 7973 6400 *Fax:* (020) 7233 5056 *E-mail:* info@hgluk.com *Web Site:* www.hgluk.com, pg 777

Hemus Editora Ltda (Brazil) *Tel:* (011) 5093-7822 *Fax:* (011) 5044-6366 *E-mail:* atendimento@ leopardoeditora.com.br *Web Site:* www.hemus.com.br; www.leopardoeditora.com.br, pg 83

Hindi Book Centre (India) *Tel:* (011) 23286757 *Fax:* (011) 23273335; (011) 26481565 *E-mail:* info@ hindibook.com *Web Site:* www.hindibook.com, pg 1423

Hindi Pracharak Sansthan (India) *Tel:* (0542) 2356850; (0542) 2421741, pg 385

Hindustan Book Agency (India) *Tel:* (0124) 4307450; (0124) 4307451 *Fax:* (0124) 4307452 *E-mail:* info@ hindbook.com *Web Site:* www.hindbook.com, pg 1423

Hing Yip Printing Co Ltd (Hong Kong) *Tel:* 2870 2379 *Fax:* 2873 5317 *E-mail:* info@hyprint.com.hk; sales@hyprint.com.hk *Web Site:* www.hyprint.com.hk, pg 1324

Hinkler Books Pty Ltd (Australia) *Tel:* (03) 9552 1333 *Fax:* (03) 9558 2566 *E-mail:* enquiries@hinkler.com. au; sales@hinkler.com.au *Web Site:* www.hinkler.com. au, pg 27

Hinoki Shoten Co Ltd (Japan) *Tel:* (03) 3291-2488 *Fax:* (03) 3295-3554 *E-mail:* info@hinoki-shoten.co. jp; sales@hinoki-shoten.co.jp *Web Site:* www.hinoki-shoten.co.jp, pg 477

Hinstorff Verlag GmbH (Germany) *Tel:* (0381) 4 96 90 *Fax:* (0381) 4 96 91 03 *E-mail:* sekretariat@hinstorff. de; buchbestellung@hinstorff.de; presse@hinstorff.de *Web Site:* www.hinstorff.de, pg 261

Ediciones Hiperion SL (Spain) *Tel:* 91 577 60 15; 91 577 60 16 *Fax:* 91 435 86 90 *E-mail:* info@hiperion. com *Web Site:* www.hiperion.com, pg 648

Hippocampus Verlag eK (Germany) *Tel:* (02224) 919480 *Fax:* (02224) 919482 *E-mail:* verlag@hippocampus.de *Web Site:* www.hippocampus.de, pg 261

Hippogriff Press (South Africa) *Tel:* (011) 6464229 *Fax:* (011) 6464229, pg 614

Hippopotamus Press (United Kingdom) *Tel:* (01373) 466653 *Fax:* (01373) 466653, pg 778

Hirmer Verlag GmbH (Germany) *Tel:* (089) 12 15 16-0 *Fax:* (089) 12 15 16-10; (089) 12 15 16-16 (distribution) *E-mail:* vertrieb@hirmerverlag.de; info@hirmerverlag.de *Web Site:* www.hirmerverlag.de, pg 261

Hirokawa Publishing Co (Japan) *Tel:* (03) 3815-3651 *Fax:* (03) 5684-7030, pg 477

Antiquariat und Verlag Harro von Hirschheydt (Germany) *Tel:* (05130) 36758 *Fax:* (05130) 36799 *E-mail:* kontakt@hirschheydt-online.de *Web Site:* www.hirschheydt-online.de, pg 261

F Hirthammer Verlag GmbH (Germany) *Tel:* (089) 3233360 *Fax:* (089) 3241728 *E-mail:* info@ hirthammerverlag.de *Web Site:* www.hirthammerverlag. de, pg 262

Hiru Argitaletxea SL (Spain) *Tel:* 943641087 *E-mail:* hiru@euskalnet.net; hiru@hiru-ed.com *Web Site:* www.hiru-ed.com, pg 648

S Hirzel Verlag GmbH und Co (Germany) *Tel:* (0711) 2582 0; (0711) 2582 341 *Fax:* (0711) 2582 290; (0711) 2582 390 *E-mail:* service@hirzel.de *Web Site:* www.hirzel.de, pg 262

Hispabooks Publishing (Spain) *Tel:* 91 430 88 97; 690 21 36 73 *E-mail:* editorial@hispabooks.com *Web Site:* www.hispabooks.com, pg 648

Libreria Hispano Americana (Spain) *Tel:* 93 318 05 08 *E-mail:* info@llibreriaha.com *Web Site:* www. llibreriaha.com, pg 1451

Editorial Hispano Europea SA (Spain) *Tel:* 93 201 85 00 *Fax:* 93 414 26 35 *E-mail:* hispanoeuropea@ hispanoeuropea.com; admin@hispanoeuropea. com; export@hispanoeuropea.com; comercial@ hispanoeuropea.com *Web Site:* www.hispanoeuropea. com, pg 648

Editorial Hispanoamerica Ltda (Colombia) *Tel:* (01) 2216694; (01) 3155587; (01) 2213020 *Fax:* (01) 3155813 *E-mail:* info@hispanoamerica.com.co *Web Site:* hispanoamerica.com.co, pg 114

Histoire & Collections SA (France) *Tel:* 01 40 21 18 20 *Fax:* 01 47 00 51 11 *E-mail:* vpc@histecoll.com *Web Site:* www.histoireetcollections.com, pg 175

Historicky Ustav Akademie ved Ceske Republiky vvi (Czech Republic) *Tel:* 286 882 121 *Fax:* 286 887 513 *Web Site:* www.hiu.cas.cz, pg 127

Institutum Historicum Societatis Iesu (Italy) *Tel:* (06) 68977536 *Fax:* (06) 68977461 *E-mail:* arsi-seg@ sjcuria.org *Web Site:* www.sjweb.info, pg 447

Historische Uitgeverij (Netherlands) *Tel:* (050) 3181700 *E-mail:* info@historischeuitgeverij.nl; bestel@ historischeuitgeverij.nl (orders); international@ historischeuitgeverij.nl (international rights) *Web Site:* www.historischeuitgeverij.nl, pg 534

Historischer Verein fuer das Fuerstentum Liechtenstein (Liechtenstein) *Tel:* 392 17 47 *E-mail:* info@ historischerverein.li *Web Site:* www.historischerverein. li/, pg 500

Historiska Media (Sweden) *Tel:* (046) 33 34 50 *E-mail:* info@historiskamedia.se *Web Site:* www. historiskamedia.se, pg 682

The History Press Ltd (United Kingdom) *Tel:* (01453) 883300 *Fax:* (01453) 883233 *Web Site:* www. thehistorypress.co.uk, pg 778

Hituzi Shobo Publishing Ltd (Japan) *Tel:* (03) 5319-4916 *Fax:* (03) 5319-4917 *E-mail:* toiawase@hituzi.co.jp *Web Site:* www.hituzi.co.jp, pg 477

K Hjelm Forlag AB (Sweden) *Tel:* (018) 127888 *Fax:* (018) 135497 *E-mail:* info@hjelms.se *Web Site:* www.hjelms.com, pg 682

Forlaget Hjulet (Denmark) *Tel:* 4497 7664 *E-mail:* mail@hjulet.nu *Web Site:* www.forlagethjulet. nu, pg 137

HK Scanner Arts International Ltd (Hong Kong) *Tel:* 2976 0289 *Fax:* 2976 0292 *E-mail:* info@hksagp. net *Web Site:* www.hksagp.net, pg 1278

HLA Management Theatrical Agency Australia (Australia) *Tel:* (02) 9549 3000 *Fax:* (02) 9310 4113 *E-mail:* hla@hlamgt.com.au *Web Site:* www.hlamgt. com.au, pg 1223

Ho-Chi Book Publishing Co (Taiwan) *Tel:* (02) 8646-1828 *Fax:* (02) 8646-1866 *E-mail:* hochi@ms12.hinet. net *Web Site:* www.hochitw.com, pg 712

Ho Printing Singapore Pte Ltd (Singapore) *Tel:* 6542 9322 *Fax:* 6542 8322 *E-mail:* sales@hoprinting.com. sg *Web Site:* www.hoprinting.com, pg 1261, 1283, 1332, 1347, 1354

Hobbs The Printers Ltd (United Kingdom) *Tel:* (023) 8066 4800 *Fax:* (023) 8066 4801 *E-mail:* info@hobbs. uk.com *Web Site:* www.hobbstheprinters.co.uk; www. hobbs.uk.com, pg 1287

Hobbs The Printers Ltd (United Kingdom) *Tel:* (023) 8066 4800 *Fax:* (023) 8066 4801 *E-mail:* info@ hobbs.uk.com *Web Site:* www.hobbs.uk.com; www. hobbstheprinters.co.uk, pg 1338, 1348, 1355

Hobbyklubben (Norway) *Tel:* 81 55 92 00 (orders) *E-mail:* hobbyklubben@cappelendamm. no *Web Site:* www.hobbyklubben.no; www. tanumbokklubber.no, pg 1360

Hobsons PLC (United Kingdom) *Tel:* (020) 7250 6600 *Web Site:* www.hobsons.com, pg 778

Edition Hochfeld (Germany) *Tel:* (0821) 2431512 *Fax:* (0821) 2431518 *E-mail:* verlag@edition-hochfeld.de *Web Site:* www.edition-hochfeld.de, pg 262

Hod-Ami Publishing Ltd (Israel) *Tel:* (09) 9564716 *Fax:* (09) 9571582 *E-mail:* info@hod-ami.co.il *Web Site:* www.hod-ami.co.il, pg 418

Hodder & Stoughton Ltd (United Kingdom) *Tel:* (020) 3122 6777 *Web Site:* www.hodder.co.uk, pg 778

Hodder Education Group (United Kingdom) *Tel:* (020) 7873 6000 *Fax:* (020) 7873 6299 *E-mail:* educationenquiries@hodder.co.uk *Web Site:* www.hoddereducation.co.uk, pg 778

Editions Hoebeke (France) *Tel:* 01 42 22 83 81 *Fax:* 01 45 44 04 96 *E-mail:* contact@hoebeke.fr *Web Site:* www.hoebeke.fr, pg 175

Hoefer Verlag (Germany) *Tel:* (06074) 27550 *Fax:* (06074) 44964 *E-mail:* info@hoeferverlag.de *Web Site:* www.hoeferverlag.de, pg 262

Dr Saskia von Hoegen Literarische Agentur (Germany) *Tel:* (030) 48811267 *E-mail:* info@saskiavonhoegen. de; svh@saskiavonhoegen.de *Web Site:* www. saskiavonhoegen.de, pg 1227

Hoelker Verlag (Germany) *Tel:* (0251) 41 411-0 *Fax:* (0251) 41 411-20 *E-mail:* info@coppenrath.de *Web Site:* www.hoelker-verlag.de; www.facebook. com/HoelkerVerlag; www.coppenrath.de, pg 262

Hoell Verlag (Germany) *Tel:* (06167) 912220 *Fax:* (06167) 912221 *E-mail:* info@hoellverlag.de *Web Site:* www.hoellverlag.de; www.hoellverlag. homepage.t-online.de, pg 262

Hoerbuch Hamburg HHV GmbH (Germany) *Tel:* (040) 897 207 80 *Fax:* (040) 897 207 810 *E-mail:* info@ hoerbuch-hamburg.de *Web Site:* www.hoerbuch-hamburg.de, pg 262

HOERCOMPANY Schaack und Herzog oHG (Germany) *Tel:* (040) 8801411; (040) 8892616 *Fax:* (040) 8892618 *E-mail:* info@hoercompany.de *Web Site:* www.hoercompany.de, pg 262

Verlag Angelika Hoernig (Germany) *Tel:* (0621) 65 82 197-0; (0621) 65 82 197-15 (sales) *Fax:* (0621) 65 82 197-17 *E-mail:* info@bogenschiessen.de; shop@ bogenschiessen.de; redaktion@bogenschiessen.de *Web Site:* www.bogenschiessen.de, pg 262

Hofbauer Buch- und Papierhandlung (Austria) *Tel:* (03452) 82793 *Fax:* (03452) 71218 *E-mail:* buch@buchhandlunghofbauer.at *Web Site:* www.members.aon.at/hofbauer.buch/ page_1_1.html, pg 1404

Christoph Hofbauer, Ilija Trojanow & Berthold Klewing (Germany) *Tel:* (089) 51616151, pg 262

Edition & Galerie Hoffmann & Co oHG (Germany) *Tel:* (06031) 2443; (0172) 6602611 (cell) *Fax:* (06031) 62965 *E-mail:* hoffmann@galeriehoffmann.de *Web Site:* www.galeriehoffmann.de, pg 262

Hoffmann und Campe Verlag GmbH (Germany) *Tel:* (040) 44188-0 *Fax:* (040) 44188-202 *E-mail:* email@hoca.de *Web Site:* www.hoffmann-und-campe.de, pg 263

Hofmann-Verlag GmbH & Co KG (Germany) *Tel:* (07181) 402-0 *Fax:* (07181) 402-111 *E-mail:* info@hofmann-verlag.de *Web Site:* www. hofmann-verlag.de, pg 263

Friedrich Hofmeister Musikverlag (Germany) *Tel:* (0341) 9 60 77 50 *Fax:* (0341) 9 60 30 55 *E-mail:* info@ hofmeister-musikverlag.com *Web Site:* www. hofmeister-musikverlag.com, pg 263

Hogrefe AG (Switzerland) *Tel:* (031) 300 45 00 *Fax:* (031) 300 45 90 *E-mail:* verlag@hogrefe.ch *Web Site:* www.hogrefe.ch, pg 696

Hogrefe Verlag GmbH & Co Kg (Germany) *Tel:* (0551) 999 50-0 *Fax:* (0551) 999 50-111 *E-mail:* verlag@ hogrefe.de; press@hogrefe.de *Web Site:* www.hogrefe. de, pg 263

Grupo Editorial La Hoguera (Bolivia) *Tel:* (03) 335-4426; (03) 337-5169 *E-mail:* lahoguera@lahoguera. com *Web Site:* www.lahoguera.com, pg 75

Hohenrain Verlag GmbH (Germany) *Tel:* (07071) 4070-0 *Fax:* (07071) 4070-26 *E-mail:* info@hohenrainverlag. de *Web Site:* www.hohenrainverlag.de, pg 263

Hoi Thu-Vien Vietnam (Vietnam) *Tel:* (04) 39366596 *E-mail:* info@vla.org.vn *Web Site:* www.vla.org.vn, pg 1663

Ediciones Mil Hojas Ltda (Chile) *Tel:* (02) 22743172, pg 98

Hokkaido University Library (Japan) *Tel:* (011) 706-3956 *Fax:* (011) 746-4595 *E-mail:* service@lib.hokudai.ac.jp *Web Site:* www.lib.hokudai.ac.jp, pg 1606

Ibera Verlag (Austria) *Tel:* (01) 513 19 72 *Fax:* (01) 513 19 72-28 *E-mail:* office@ibera.at; buchhandel@ibera. at *Web Site:* www.ibera.at, pg 50

Editorial Iberia SA (Spain) *Tel:* 93 201 05 99; 93 201 38 07; 93 201 21 44 *Fax:* 93 209 73 62 *E-mail:* omega@ ediciones-omega.es *Web Site:* www.ediciones-omega. es, pg 648

Livro Ibero-Americano Ltda (Brazil) *Tel:* (021) 4105-4590 *Fax:* (021) 4105-4590 *E-mail:* livro-ibero@oi. com.br, pg 84, 1408

Ibero-Amerikanisches Institut Preussischer Kulturbesitz (Germany) *Tel:* (030) 266 45 2210 *Fax:* (030) 266 35 1550 *E-mail:* iai@iai.spk-berlin.de; info@iai.spk-berlin.de *Web Site:* www.iai.spk-berlin.de, pg 1593

Iberoamericana Editorial Vervuert SLU (Spain) *Tel:* 91 429 35 22 *Fax:* 91 429 53 97 *E-mail:* info@ iberoamericanalibros.com *Web Site:* www. iberoamericana-vervuert.es, pg 1451

ibidem-Verlag (Germany) *Tel:* (0711) 9807954 *Fax:* (0711) 8001889 *E-mail:* ibidem@ibidem-verlag. de *Web Site:* www.ibidemverlag.de, pg 265

IBIS (Denmark) *Tel:* 35 35 87 88 *Fax:* 35 35 06 96 *E-mail:* ibis@ibis.dk *Web Site:* www.ibis.dk; ibis-global.org, pg 137

Ibis (Italy) *Tel:* (031) 3371367 *Fax:* (031) 306829 *E-mail:* info@ibisedizioni.it *Web Site:* www. ibisedizioni.it, pg 447

Ibiskos - di A Ulivieri (Italy) *Tel:* (0571) 79807 *Fax:* (0571) 700633 *E-mail:* info@ibiskosulivieri.it *Web Site:* www.ibiskosulivieri.it, pg 447

Kashim Ibrahim Library (Nigeria) *Tel:* (0703) 242 8263 (cell) *E-mail:* library@abu.edu.ng; librarian@abu.edu. ng; kilreference@abu.edu.ng *Web Site:* library.abu.edu. ng, pg 1618

IBRASA (Instituicao Brasileira de Difusao Cultural Ltda) (Brazil) *Tel:* (011) 3284-8382 *Web Site:* www. ibrasa.com.br, pg 84

IBS Buku Sdn Bhd (Malaysia) *Tel:* (03) 79579282; (03) 79579470 *Fax:* (03) 79576026 *E-mail:* info@ibsbuku. com; hibs@tm.net.my *Web Site:* www.ibsbuku.com, pg 507

IBS Buku Sdn Bhd (Malaysia) *Tel:* (03) 79579282; (03) 79579470 *Fax:* (03) 79576026 *E-mail:* hibs@tm.net. my, pg 1432

IC Publications Ltd (United Kingdom) *Tel:* (020) 7841 3210 *Fax:* (020) 7841 3211 *E-mail:* editorial@ icpublications.com *Web Site:* www.africasia.com, pg 780

Icaria Editorial SA (Spain) *Tel:* 93 301 17 23; 93 301 17 26 *Fax:* 93 295 49 16 *E-mail:* icaria@ icariaeditorial.com; comandes@icariaeditorial.com (orders) *Web Site:* www.icariaeditorial.com, pg 648

ICC Services/Publications (France) *Tel:* 01 49 53 30 56 *Fax:* 01 49 53 29 02 *E-mail:* publications@iccwbo.org *Web Site:* www.iccwbo.org; www.storeiccwbo.org, pg 176

Publicaciones ICCE (Spain) *Tel:* 91 725 72 00 *Fax:* 91 361 10 52 *E-mail:* info@icceciberaula.es *Web Site:* www.icceciberaula.es, pg 649

ICCROM (International Centre for the Study of the Preservation & Restoration of Cultural Property) (Italy) *Tel:* (06) 585-531 *Fax:* (06) 585-53349 *E-mail:* iccrom@iccrom.org *Web Site:* www.iccrom. org, pg 1379

ICE Publishing (United Kingdom) *Tel:* (020) 7665 2019; (01892) 83 22 99 (orders) *E-mail:* info@icepublishing. com; orders@icepublishing.com *Web Site:* www. icevirtuallibrary.com; www.thomastelford.com, pg 780

Iceland Review (Iceland) *Tel:* 512-7575 *Fax:* 561-8646 *E-mail:* icelandreview@icelandreview.com *Web Site:* www.icelandreview.com, pg 372

Icelandic Literature Center (Iceland) *Tel:* 552 8500 *Fax:* 552 8181 *E-mail:* islit@islit.is *Web Site:* www. islit.is, pg 1377

Ichtiar Baru van Hoeve (Indonesia) *Tel:* (021) 7511856; (021) 7511901 *Fax:* (021) 7511855 *E-mail:* redaksi@ ibvh.com *Web Site:* www.ibvh.com, pg 1280, 1328, 1347

ICHverlag Haefner+Haefner (Germany) *Tel:* (0171) 364 34 51 *E-mail:* info@brothersinart.de *Web Site:* www. ichverlag.com, pg 265

Icicle Production Co Ltd (Hong Kong) *Tel:* 2235 2880 *E-mail:* info@iciclegroup.com *Web Site:* www. iciclegroup.com, pg 1258, 1278, 1325

ICOB BV (Netherlands) *Tel:* (0172) 437231 *Fax:* (0172) 416684 *E-mail:* algemeen@icob.nl *Web Site:* www. icob.nl, pg 1437

Icon Books Ltd (United Kingdom) *Tel:* (020) 7697 9695 *Fax:* (020) 7697 9501 *E-mail:* info@iconbooks.com; sales@iconbooks.com *Web Site:* www.iconbooks.com, pg 780

Icone Editora Ltda (Brazil) *Tel:* (011) 3392-7771 *E-mail:* sac@iconeeditora.com.br *Web Site:* www. iconeeditora.com.br, pg 84

Icono Editorial (Colombia) *Tel:* (01) 3178905 *Fax:* (01) 3178898 *Web Site:* www.iconoeditorial.com, pg 114

ICSA Publishing (United Kingdom) *Tel:* (020) 7612 7020 *E-mail:* publishing@icsa.org.uk; puborders@icsa. org.uk *Web Site:* www.icsa.org.uk/bookshop, pg 781

ID Verlag Tawereit-Fanizadeh GbR (Germany) *Tel:* (030) 694 77 03 *Fax:* (030) 694 78 08 *E-mail:* idverlag@t-online.de *Web Site:* www.idverlag.com, pg 265

Idara Isha'at-E-Diniyat (P) Ltd (India) *Tel:* (011) 26956832; (011) 26956834 *Fax:* (011) 26942787; (011) 66173545 *E-mail:* sales@idara.com *Web Site:* www.idara.com, pg 385

Idea Books (Italy) *Tel:* (0584) 425410 *Fax:* (178) 609 8685 *E-mail:* info@ideabooks.com *Web Site:* www. ideabooks.com, pg 447

Idea Books (Netherlands) *Tel:* (020) 6226154 *Fax:* (020) 6209299 *Web Site:* www.ideabooks.nl, pg 1438

Idea Design & Print SRL (Romania) *Tel:* (0264) 594634; (0264) 431661 *Fax:* (0264) 431603 *E-mail:* oferte@ idea.ro *Web Site:* www.idea.ro, pg 588

IDEA Verlag GmbH (Germany) *Tel:* (08142) 4107507 *Fax:* (08142) 4107507 *E-mail:* info@idea-verlag.de *Web Site:* www.idea-verlag.de, pg 265

Editorial Idearium de la Universidad de Mendoza (EDIUM) (Argentina) *Tel:* (0261) 420 2017; (0261) 420 0740 *Fax:* (0261) 420 1100 *E-mail:* rectorado@ um.edu.ar *Web Site:* www.um.edu.ar, pg 8

Ideaspropias Editorial SL (Spain) *Tel:* 902 100 938; 986 415 241 *E-mail:* comercial@ideaspropiaseditorial.com *Web Site:* www.ideaspropiaseditorial.com, pg 649

Idegraf SA (Switzerland) *Tel:* (022) 792 03 96 *Fax:* (022) 793 63 30 (orders) *E-mail:* info@formez-vous.com; sales@formez-vous.com *Web Site:* www. formez-vous.com, pg 697

Ideias de Ler (Portugal) *Tel:* 22 608 83 42 *Fax:* 22 608 83 43 *Web Site:* www.ideiasdeler.pt, pg 579

Idelson-Gnocchi Edizioni Scientifiche (Italy) *Tel:* (081) 5453443 *Fax:* (081) 5464991 *E-mail:* ordini@ idelsongnocchi.it; info@idelsongnocchi.it *Web Site:* www.idelsongnocchi.it, pg 447

Editions Ides et Calendes SA (Switzerland) *Tel:* (032) 725 38 61 *E-mail:* info@idesetcalendes.com *Web Site:* www.idesetcalendes.com, pg 697

IDNU Bokautgafa (Iceland) *Tel:* 517 7210; 517 7200 *Fax:* 562 3497; 552 6793 *E-mail:* idnu@idnu.is *Web Site:* www.idnu.is, pg 372

Idryma Meleton Chersonisou tou Aimou (Greece) *Tel:* 2310832143 *Fax:* 2310831429 *E-mail:* imxa@ imxa.gr *Web Site:* www.imxa.gr, pg 356

Idunn (Iceland) *Tel:* 575 5600 *Fax:* 575 5601 *E-mail:* forlagid@forlagid.is *Web Site:* www.forlagid. is, pg 372

IDW Verlag GmbH (Germany) *Tel:* (0211) 4561-280 *Fax:* (0211) 4561-277 *E-mail:* post@idw-verlag.de *Web Site:* www.idw-verlag.de, pg 265

Ie-No-Hikari Association (Japan) *Tel:* (03) 3266-9000; (03) 3266-9038 (sales) *Fax:* (03) 3266-9337 (sales) *Web Site:* www.ienohikari.net, pg 478

Ediciones IESA (Venezuela) *Tel:* (0212) 555 4260 *E-mail:* ediesa@iesa.edu.ve; debates@iesa.edu.ve *Web Site:* www.iesa.edu.ve, pg 850

Tianjin Ifengspace Media Co Ltd (China) *Tel:* (022) 60262226 *Fax:* (022) 60266199 *E-mail:* info@ ifengspace.cn; ifengspace@hotmail.com (international sales) *Web Site:* www.ifengspace.com, pg 106

IFIS Publishing (International Food Information Service) (United Kingdom) *Tel:* (0118) 988 3895 *Fax:* (0118) 988 5065 *E-mail:* ifis@ifis.org; sales@ifis.org; a.ball@ ifis.org *Web Site:* foodinfo.ifis.org, pg 781

IG Autorinnen Autoren (Austria) *Tel:* (01) 526 20 44-13 *Fax:* (01) 526 20 44-55 *E-mail:* ig@literaturhaus.at *Web Site:* www.literaturhaus.at, pg 50

Igaku-Shoin Ltd (Japan) *Tel:* (03) 38175600 *Fax:* (03) 38157791 *E-mail:* info@igaku-shoin.co.jp *Web Site:* www.igaku-shoin.co.jp, pg 478

Igel Verlag (Germany) *Tel:* (040) 65 59 92-29 *Fax:* (040) 65 59 92-22 *E-mail:* kontakt@igelverlag.com *Web Site:* www.igelverlag.com, pg 265

Igloo Books Ltd (United Kingdom) *Tel:* (01604) 741116 *Fax:* (01604) 670495 *E-mail:* customerservice@ igloobooks.com *Web Site:* igloobooks.com, pg 781

Iglu Editora Ltda (Brazil) *Tel:* (011) 3873-0227 *Fax:* (011) 3873-0227 *E-mail:* iglueditora@uol.com.br *Web Site:* www.iglueditora.com.br, pg 84

IHS Jane's, IHS Global Ltd (United Kingdom) *Tel:* (01344) 328 300 *Web Site:* www.janes.com, pg 781

IHT Gruppo Editoriale SRL (Italy) *Tel:* (02) 794181 *Fax:* (02) 784021, pg 447

Ikar as (Slovakia) *Tel:* (02) 49 104 33; (02) 49 104 341 *E-mail:* ikar@ikar.sk; redakcia@ikar.sk *Web Site:* www.ikar.sk, pg 608

Ikaros Ekdotiki (Greece) *Tel:* 2103225152 *Fax:* 2103235262 *E-mail:* info@ikarosbooks.gr *Web Site:* ikarosbooks.gr, pg 356

Ikaros Publishing Co (Greece) *Tel:* 210 3225152 *Fax:* 210 3235262 *E-mail:* info@ikarosbooks.gr *Web Site:* ikarosbooks.gr, pg 1420

Ikarus Verlag & Reisen (Germany) *Tel:* (0661) 9 01 63 60; (0170) 3 84 49 29 (cell) *E-mail:* info@ikarus-verlag.de *Web Site:* www.ikarus-verlag.de, pg 265

Ikatan Penerbit Indonesia (IKAPI) (Indonesia) *Tel:* (021) 3241907; (021) 31902532 *Fax:* (021) 3146050; (021) 3192614 *E-mail:* sekretariat@ikapi.org *Web Site:* www.ikapi.org, pg 1378

Ikatan Pustakawan Indonesia (Indonesia) *Tel:* (021) 3855729 *Fax:* (021) 3855729 *Web Site:* ipi.pnri.go.id, pg 1654

IkiNokta Bilisim Teknolojileri AS (Turkey) *Tel:* (0216) 575 05 05 *Fax:* (0216) 577 51 79 *E-mail:* bilgi@ ikinokta.com *Web Site:* www.ikinokta.com, pg 721

ikotes eK (Germany) *Tel:* (07223) 8 06 22 66 *Fax:* (07223) 9 12 93 06 *E-mail:* info@ikotes.de *Web Site:* www.ikotes.com, pg 265

Ikubundo Co Ltd (Japan) *Tel:* (03) 3814-5571 *Fax:* (03) 3814-5576 *Web Site:* www.ikubundo.com, pg 1429

ILCHOKAK Publishing Co Ltd (South Korea) *Tel:* (02) 7335430; (02) 7335431 *Fax:* (02) 7385857 *E-mail:* ilchokak@hanmail.net *Web Site:* www. ilchokak.co.kr, pg 622

Iletisim Yayinlari (Turkey) *Tel:* (0212) 5162260 *Fax:* (0212) 5161258 *E-mail:* iletisim@iletisim.com.tr *Web Site:* www.iletisim.com.tr, pg 721

Ilex Press (United Kingdom) *Tel:* (01273) 403 124 *Fax:* (01273) 487 441 *Web Site:* www.ilex.press, pg 781

Institut fuer Auslandsbeziehungen eV (IFA)
(Germany) *Tel:* (0711) 2225-0 *Fax:* (0711) 2264346
E-mail: info@ifa.de *Web Site:* www.ifa.de, pg 266

Institut fuer Baustoffe, Massivbau und Brandschutz/
Bibliothek (Germany) *Tel:* (0531) 391 5400
Fax: (0531) 391 5900 *E-mail:* info@ibmb.tu-bs.de
Web Site: www.ibmb.tu-bs.de, pg 266

Institut fuer Internationale Architektur-Dokumentation
GmbH & Co KG (Germany) *Tel:* (089) 38 16 20-
0 *Fax:* (089) 38 16 20-77 *E-mail:* mail@detail.de
Web Site: www.detail-online.com, pg 266

Institut fuer Jugendliteratur (Austria) *Tel:* (01) 505
03 59 *Fax:* (01) 505 03 59 17 *E-mail:* office@
jugendliteratur.net *Web Site:* www.jugendliteratur.net,
pg 1365

Institut fuer Landes- und Stadtentwicklungsforschung
GmbH (Germany) *Tel:* (0231) 9051-0 *Fax:* (0231)
9051-155 *E-mail:* poststelle@ils-forschung.de
Web Site: www.ils-forschung.de, pg 266

Institut fuer Oesterreichkunde (Austria) *Tel:* (01)
512 79 32 *Fax:* (01) 512 79 32 *E-mail:* ioek.
wirtschaftsgeschichte@univie.ac.at *Web Site:* www.
oesterreichkunde.ac.at, pg 1490

Institut National de la Statistique et des Etudes
Economiques du Grand-Duche du Luxembourg
(Luxembourg) *Tel:* 46 42 89 *Fax:* 247-84219
E-mail: info@statistiques.public.lu *Web Site:* www.
statistiques.public.lu, pg 504

Institut National de l'Information Geographique et
Forestiere (IGN) (France) *Tel:* 01 43 98 80 00
E-mail: communication@ign.fr *Web Site:* www.ign.fr,
pg 177

Institut Nauchnoy Informatsii po Obschestvennym
Naukam, Rossijskoj Akademii Nauk RF (Russia)
Tel: (499) 124-3076 *Web Site:* www.inion.ru/library,
pg 1627

Institut Pasteur d'Algerie, Bibliotheque (Algeria)
Tel: (023) 36 75 04 *Fax:* (023) 36 75 49
Web Site: www.pasteur.dz, pg 1573

Institut Royal des Sciences Naturelles de Belgique,
Bibliotheque (Belgium) *Tel:* (02) 627 42 36
E-mail: bib@naturalsciences.be *Web Site:* www.
sciencesnaturelles.be/science/library; www.
naturalsciences.be/?science/library, pg 1578

Institut Scientifique (Morocco) *Tel:* 05 37 77 45 48;
05 37 77 45 49; 05 37 77 45 50 *Fax:* 05 37 77 45
40 *E-mail:* direction@israbat.ac.ma *Web Site:* www.
israbat.ac.ma, pg 1614

Institut Teknologi Bandung Perpustakaan Pusat
(Indonesia) *Tel:* (022) 250 0089 *Fax:* (022) 250 0089
E-mail: info@lib.itb.ac.id *Web Site:* www.lib.itb.ac.id,
pg 1602

Institut Terjemahan & Buku Malaysia (ITBM)
(Malaysia) *Tel:* (03) 4145 1800 *Fax:* (03) 4149 1535
E-mail: info@itbm.com.my *Web Site:* www.itbm.com.
my, pg 507, 1251

El Institute de Trabajo Social y de Servicios Sociales
(Spain) *Tel:* 932 172 664 *Fax:* 932 373 634
E-mail: intressbar@intress.org *Web Site:* www.intress.
org, pg 649

Institute for Agricultural Research (IAR) Library
(Nigeria) *E-mail:* directoriar@abu.edu.ng *Web Site:* iar.
abu.edu.ng, pg 1619

Institute for Fiscal Studies (United Kingdom) *Tel:* (020)
7291 4800 *Fax:* (020) 7323 4780 *E-mail:* mailbox@
ifs.org.uk *Web Site:* www.ifs.org.uk, pg 782

Institute for Palestine Studies (IPS) (Lebanon) *Tel:* (01)
868387; (01) 814175; (01) 804959 *Fax:* (01) 814193;
(01) 868387 *E-mail:* ipsbeirut@palestine-studies.com;
sales@palestine-studies.org; ipsdc@palestine-studies.
org *Web Site:* www.palestine-studies.org, pg 498

Institute for Research Extension and Training in
Agriculture (IRETA) (Samoa) *Tel:* 22350; 21671
E-mail: enquiries@samoa.usp.ac.fj *Web Site:* www.
usp.ac.fj/ireta, pg 598

Institute for Social & Economic Change Library (India)
Tel: (080) 23215468; (080) 23180507 *Fax:* (080)
23217008 *E-mail:* admn@isec.ac.in; deputylibrarian@
isec.ac.in *Web Site:* www.isec.ac.in, pg 1601

The Institute for the Translation of Hebrew Literature
(ITHL) (Israel) *Tel:* (03) 579 6830 *Fax:* (03) 579 6832
E-mail: litscene@ithl.org.il *Web Site:* www.ithl.org.il,
pg 418, 1230, 1250, 1378

Institute of Advanced Technologies Kiev (Ukraine)
Tel: (044) 292-20-27 *E-mail:* iat@antex.kiev.ua
Web Site: www.iat.kiev.ua, pg 726

Institute of African Studies Library (Ghana) *Tel:* (030)
2213850 *E-mail:* iasgen@ug.edu.gh; iasdsec@ug.edu.
gh *Web Site:* ias.ug.edu.gh, pg 1597

Institute of African Studies (Nigeria) *Tel:* (0803) 548
3074 *E-mail:* ias.unn@unn.edu.ng *Web Site:* unn.edu.
ng/institutes/institute-african-studies, pg 552

Institute of Arab Research & Studies Arab League
Educational, Cultural & Scientific Organization
Library (Egypt) *Tel:* (02) 27951648; (02) 27922679
Fax: (02) 27962543 *E-mail:* iars@iarsecs.org
Web Site: iars.net/library, pg 1587

Institute of Clinical Research (United Kingdom)
Tel: (01628) 501700 *Fax:* (01628) 501709
E-mail: icrenquiries@yahoo.co.uk *Web Site:* www.icr-
global.org, pg 783

Institute of Development Studies (United Kingdom)
Tel: (01273) 606261 *E-mail:* ids@ids.ac.uk
Web Site: www.ids.ac.uk, pg 783

Institute of Economic Affairs (United Kingdom)
Tel: (020) 7799 8900 *Fax:* (020) 7799 2137
E-mail: iea@iea.org.uk *Web Site:* www.iea.org.uk,
pg 783

Institute of Education Press (United Kingdom)
Fax: (020) 7612 6126 *E-mail:* admin@ucl-ioe-press.
com *Web Site:* www.ucl-ioe-press.com, pg 783

Institute of Employment Rights (United Kingdom)
Tel: (0151) 207 5265 *Fax:* (0151) 207 5264
E-mail: office@ier.org.uk *Web Site:* www.ier.org.uk,
pg 783

Institute of Ethiopian Studies Library (IES) (Ethiopia)
Tel: (011) 123 97 39 *Web Site:* www.aau.edu.et/ies,
pg 1588

The Institute of Faculty & Actuaries (United Kingdom)
Tel: (020) 7632 2100 *Fax:* (020) 7632 2111
E-mail: education.services@actuaries.org.uk
Web Site: www.actuaries.org.uk, pg 783

Institute of Food Science & Technology (United
Kingdom) *Tel:* (020) 7603 6316 *E-mail:* info@ifst.org
Web Site: www.ifst.org, pg 783

Institute of Internal Communication (IoIC) (United
Kingdom) *Tel:* (01908) 232168 *Fax:* (01908) 313661
E-mail: enquiries@ioic.org.uk *Web Site:* www.ioic.org.
uk, pg 1395

Institute of Irish Studies, Queen's University Belfast
(United Kingdom) *Tel:* (028) 9097 3386 *Fax:* (028)
9097 3388 *E-mail:* irish.studies@qub.ac.uk
Web Site: www.qub.ac.uk/irishstudies, pg 783

Institute of Kiswahili Studies (Tanzania) *Tel:* (022)
2410757 *Fax:* (022) 2410328 *E-mail:* ikr@udsm.ac.
tz *Web Site:* www.iks.udsm.ac.tz; www.udsm.ac.tz,
pg 714

Institute of Modern Greek Studies (Manolis
Triandaphyllidis Foundation) (Greece)
Tel: 2310997128 *Fax:* 2310997212 *E-mail:* ins@phil.
auth.gr *Web Site:* ins.web.auth.gr, pg 356

Institute of Public Administration (Ireland) *Tel:* (01) 240
3600 *Fax:* (01) 668 9135 *E-mail:* information@ipa.ie
Web Site: www.ipa.ie, pg 411

Institute of Public Administration Library (Saudi Arabia)
Tel: (011) 4768888 *Fax:* (011) 4792136 *E-mail:* info@
ipa.edu.sa; library@ipa.edu.sa *Web Site:* www.ipa.edu.
sa, pg 1628

Institute of Scientific & Technical Communicators
(ISTC) (United Kingdom) *Tel:* (020) 8253 4506
Fax: (020) 8253 4510 *E-mail:* istc@istc.org.uk
Web Site: www.istc.org.uk, pg 1396

Institute of Southeast Asian Studies (Singapore)
Tel: 6870 2447 *Fax:* 6775 6259 *E-mail:* publish@
iseas.edu.sg *Web Site:* www.iseas.edu.sg; bookshop.
iseas.edu.sg, pg 604

Institute of Translation & Interpreting (ITI) (United
Kingdom) *Tel:* (01908) 325250 *E-mail:* info@iti.org.
uk *Web Site:* www.iti.org.uk, pg 1253

Instituti Editoriali e Poligrafici Internazionali (Italy)
Tel: (050) 542332 *Fax:* (050) 574888 *E-mail:* fse@
libraweb.net *Web Site:* www.libraweb.net, pg 448

Institution of Chemical Engineers (IChemE) (United
Kingdom) *Tel:* (01788) 578214 *Fax:* (01788) 560833
E-mail: customerservices@icheme.org *Web Site:* www.
icheme.org, pg 783

The Institution of Engineering & Technology (United
Kingdom) *Tel:* (01438) 313311 *Fax:* (01438) 765526
E-mail: books@theiet.org; postmaster@theiet.org;
submissions@theiet.org *Web Site:* www.theiet.org,
pg 783

Instituto Alicantino de Cultura Juan Gil-Albert (Spain)
Tel: 965 121 214; 965 121 216 *Fax:* 965 921 824
E-mail: galbert@dip-alicante.es *Web Site:* www.dip-
alicante.es/gilalbert/pub/inicio.asp, pg 649

Instituto Brasileiro de Geografia e Estatistica (IBGE)
(Brazil) *Tel:* (021) 2142-4780 *Toll Free Tel:* 0800 721
8181 *E-mail:* ibge@ibge.gov.br *Web Site:* www.ibge.
gov.br, pg 84

Instituto Brasileiro de Informacao em Ciencia e
Tecnologia (Brazil) *Tel:* (061) 3217-6360; (061) 3217-
6350 *Fax:* (061) 3217-6490 *Web Site:* www.ibict.br,
pg 84, 1649

Instituto Campineiro de Ensino Agricola (ICEA)
(Brazil) *Tel:* (019) 3258-8225; (019) 9791-6629 (cell)
Fax: (019) 3258-8225 *E-mail:* icea@icea.com.br
Web Site: www.icea.com.br, pg 84

Instituto Caro y Cuervo (Colombia) *Tel:* (01) 342
2121 *E-mail:* contactenos@caroycuervo.gov.co
Web Site: www.caroycuervo.gov.co, pg 114

Instituto Caro y Cuervo (Colombia) *Tel:* (01) 342 2121
Fax: (01) 284 1284 *E-mail:* contactenos@caroycuervo.
gov.co *Web Site:* www.caroycuervo.gov.co, pg 1492

Instituto Centroamericano de Administracion de
Empresas (INCAE) Library (Nicaragua) *Tel:* 2248-
9746 *Fax:* 2265-8617 *E-mail:* biblioteca@incae.
edu *Web Site:* www.incae.ac.cr/es/biblioteca, pg 1618

Instituto Colombiano de Antropologia e Historia
(ICANH) (Colombia) *Tel:* (01) 4440544 *Fax:* (01)
4440530 *E-mail:* contactenos@icanh.gov.co;
quejasyreclamos@icanh.gov.co *Web Site:* www.icanh.
gov.co, pg 1492

Instituto de Cultura Puertorriquena (Puerto Rico)
Tel: (787) 724-0700; (787) 724-0700 (ext 1341,
editorial); (787) 724-0700 (ext 1349, sales) *Fax:* (787)
724-8393 *E-mail:* editorial@icp.gobierno.pr
Web Site: www.icp.gobierno.pr/programas/editorial,
pg 583

Libreria Instituto de Cultura Puertorriquena (Puerto
Rico) *Tel:* (787) 721-5105 *Web Site:* www.facebook.
com/libreriaicp, pg 1445

Instituto de Ecologia AC (INECOL) (Mexico)
Tel: (0228) 842 18 00 *Fax:* (0228) 818 78 09
E-mail: vadamb@ecologia.edu.mx *Web Site:* www.
inecol.edu.mx, pg 517

Instituto de Estudios Altoaragoneses (Spain) *Tel:* 974
294 120 *Fax:* 974 294 122 *E-mail:* iea@iea.es
Web Site: www.iea.es, pg 649

Instituto de Estudios Economicos (Spain) *Tel:* 91 782
05 80 *Fax:* 91 562 36 13 *E-mail:* iee@ieemadrid.com
Web Site: www.ieemadrid.es, pg 649

Instituto de Estudios Fiscales (Spain) *Tel:* 91 339
88 00 *E-mail:* informacion.ief@ief.minhap.es
Web Site: www.ief.es, pg 650

Instituto de Estudios Peruanos (IEP) (Peru) *Tel:* (01)
3326194 *Fax:* (01) 3326173 *E-mail:* libreria@iep.org.
pe *Web Site:* www.iep.org.pe, pg 562

Intercontinental Editora SA (Paraguay) *Tel:* (021) 496 991; (021) 449 738 *Fax:* (021) 448 721 *Web Site:* www.libreriaintercontinental.com.py, pg 562

Intercontinental Literary Agency (United Kingdom) *Tel:* (020) 7379 6611 *E-mail:* ila@ila-agency.co.uk *Web Site:* www.ila-agency.co.uk, pg 1242

InterEditions (France) *Tel:* 01 40 46 35 00 *Fax:* 01 40 46 49 95 *E-mail:* infos@intereditions.com; crea@dunod. com *Web Site:* www.dunod.com, pg 177

Interessengemeinschaft von Uebersetzerinnen und Uebersetzern literarischer und wissenschaftlicher Werke (Austria) *Tel:* (01) 5262044-18; (01) 5262044-51; (01) 5262044-52 *Fax:* (01) 5262044-30 *E-mail:* info@literturhaus.at; ueg@literturhaus.at *Web Site:* www.literaturhaus.at, pg 1249

Les Editions Interferences (France) *Tel:* 01 45 67 33 56; 06 31 75 87 20; 06 14 15 18 62 *E-mail:* interferences@editions-interferences.com *Web Site:* www.editions-interferences.com, pg 177

Interlinea Edizioni SRL (Italy) *Tel:* (0321) 612571 *Fax:* (0321) 612636 *E-mail:* edizioni@interlinea. com; ufficiostampa@interlinea.com *Web Site:* www. interlinea.com, pg 448

Interlivros Edicoes Ltda (Brazil) *Tel:* (021) 3913134, pg 85

Ediciones Internacionales Universitarias SA (Spain) *Tel:* 91 577 5715 *E-mail:* teconte@edicionesteconte. com *Web Site:* edicionesteconte.com, pg 650

Internationaal Instituut voor Sociale Geschiedenis (Netherlands) *Tel:* (020) 6685866 *Fax:* (020) 6654181 *E-mail:* info@iisg.nl; ask@iisg.nl *Web Site:* www.iisg. nl, pg 1616

Internationaal Literatuur Bureau (ILB) (Netherlands) *Tel:* (020) 3306658 *Fax:* (020) 4229210 *Web Site:* www.lindakohn.nl, pg 1232

International African Institute (IAI) (United Kingdom) *Tel:* (020) 7898 4420 *Fax:* (020) 7898 4419 *E-mail:* africa@internationalafricaninstitute.org; iai@ soas.ac.uk *Web Site:* www.internationalafricaninstitute. org, pg 1396

International Association for Media & Communication Research (IAMCR) (Uruguay) *Web Site:* www.iamcr. org, pg 1399

International Association for the Evaluation of Educational Achievement (IEA) (Netherlands) *Tel:* (020) 625 3625 *Fax:* (020) 420 7136 *E-mail:* secretariat@iea.nl *Web Site:* www.iea.nl, pg 1383

International Association of Agricultural Information Specialists (IAALD) (United States) *Tel:* 859-254-0752 *Fax:* 859-257-8379 *E-mail:* info@iaald.org *Web Site:* www.iaald.org, pg 1398

International Association of Law Libraries (IALL) (United States) *Web Site:* www.iall.org, pg 1663

International Association of Literary Critics (France) *Web Site:* www.aicl.org, pg 1494

International Association of Music Libraries, Archives & Documentation Centres (UK & Ireland Branch) (United Kingdom) *Tel:* (0161) 907 5245 *Fax:* (0161) 273 7611 *Web Site:* www.iaml.info/iaml-uk-irl, pg 1662

International Association of Music Libraries, Archives & Documentation Centres (New Zealand) Inc (New Zealand) *E-mail:* newzealand@iaml.info *Web Site:* www.iaml.info, pg 1384

International Association of Music Libraries, Archives & Documentation Centres (New Zealand) Inc (New Zealand) *Tel:* (04) 801 5799 *Fax:* (04) 801 2699 *E-mail:* newzealand@iaml.info *Web Site:* www.iaml. info, pg 1657

International Association of Research & Technical Libraries (Russia) *Tel:* (495) 698-93-05 *Fax:* (495) 698-93-17 *E-mail:* gpntb@gpntb.ru *Web Site:* www. gpntb.ru, pg 1387

International Association of School Librarianship (IASL) (United States) *Fax:* 312-419-8950 *E-mail:* iasl@ mlahq.org *Web Site:* www.iasl-online.org, pg 1663

International Association of Sound & Audiovisual Archives (Germany) *Tel:* (069) 1525-2500 *Web Site:* www.iasa-online.de, pg 1374

International Association of STM Publishers (United Kingdom) *Tel:* (01865) 339 321 *Fax:* (01865) 339 325 *E-mail:* info@stm-assoc.org *Web Site:* www.stm-assoc.org, pg 1396

International Association of Universities (France) *Tel:* 01 45 68 48 00 *Fax:* 01 47 34 76 05 *E-mail:* iau@iau-aiu.net *Web Site:* www.iau-aiu.net, pg 1372

International Association of University Libraries (IATUL) (South Africa) *Web Site:* www.iatul.org, pg 1388

International Atomic Energy Agency (IAEA) (Austria) *Tel:* (01) 2600-0; (01) 2600-21273; (01) 2600-21279 *Fax:* (01) 2600-7; (01) 2600-29610 *E-mail:* official. mail@iaea.org; info@iaea.org *Web Site:* www.iaea.org, pg 50

International Bee Research Association (United Kingdom) *Tel:* (029) 2037 2409 *E-mail:* mail@ibra. org.uk *Web Site:* www.ibrabee.org.uk, pg 784

International Board on Books for Young People (IBBY) (Switzerland) *Tel:* (061) 272 29 17 *Fax:* (061) 272 27 57 *E-mail:* ibby@ibby.org *Web Site:* www.ibby.org, pg 1262, 1390

International Book House Pvt Ltd (India) *Tel:* (022) 6624 2222 *Fax:* (022) 2285 1109 *E-mail:* info@ ibhbookstore.com *Web Site:* www.ibhbookstore.com, pg 1423

International Byron Society (United Kingdom) *Tel:* (020) 7352 5112 *Web Site:* www.internationalbyronsociety. org, pg 1503

International Centre for Ethnic Studies (Sri Lanka) *Tel:* (011) 2679745; (011) 2674884 *Fax:* (011) 2688929 *Web Site:* www.ices.lk, pg 677

International Commission of Jurists (Switzerland) *Tel:* (022) 9793800 *Fax:* (022) 9793801 *E-mail:* info@ icj.org *Web Site:* www.icj.org, pg 1390

International Comparative Literature Association (ICLA) (Netherlands) *E-mail:* ailc-icla@gmail.com *Web Site:* ailc-icla.org, pg 1383

International Council on Archives (France) *Tel:* 01 40 27 63 06 *Fax:* 01 42 72 20 65 *E-mail:* ica@ica.org *Web Site:* www.ica.org, pg 1372

International Crops Research Institute for the Semi-Arid Tropics (ICRISAT) (India) *Tel:* (040) 30713071 *Fax:* (040) 30713071 *E-mail:* icrisat@cgiar.org *Web Site:* www.icrisat.org, pg 1378

Institut International de la Marionnette (France) *Tel:* 03 24 33 72 50 *Fax:* 03 24 33 72 69 *E-mail:* institut@ marionnette.com *Web Site:* www.marionnette.com, pg 177

International Documentation Center, The University of Tokyo (Japan) *Tel:* (03) 5841-2645 *Fax:* (03) 5841-2611 *E-mail:* kokusai@lib.u-tokyo.ac.jp *Web Site:* www.lib.u-tokyo.ac.jp, pg 1606

International Editors' Co (Argentina) *Tel:* (011) 4788-2992 *Fax:* (011) 4786-0888 *E-mail:* ieco@ internationaleditors.com, pg 1223

International Editors' Co SL (Spain) *Tel:* 932 158 812 *Fax:* 934 873 583 *E-mail:* ieco@internationaleditors. com, pg 1235

International Federation for Information Processing (IFIP) (Austria) *Tel:* (02236) 73616 *Fax:* (02236) 73616 9 *E-mail:* ifip@ifip.org *Web Site:* www.ifip.org, pg 1365

International Federation of Library Associations & Institutions (IFLA) (Netherlands) *Tel:* (70) 314 08 84 *Fax:* (70) 383 48 27 *E-mail:* ifla@ifla.org *Web Site:* www.ifla.org, pg 1383, 1657

International Federation of Reproduction Rights Organisations (IFRRO) (Belgium) *Tel:* (02) 234 62 60 *Fax:* (02) 234 62 69 *E-mail:* secretariat@ifrro.org *Web Site:* www.ifrro.org, pg 1366

International Institute for Applied Systems Analysis (IIASA) (Austria) *Tel:* (02236) 807 342 *Fax:* (02236) 71313 *E-mail:* publications@iiasa.ac.at *Web Site:* www.iiasa.ac.at, pg 50

International Institute for Educational Planning (IIEP) (France) *Tel:* 01 45 03 77 00 *Fax:* 01 40 72 83 66 *E-mail:* info@iiep.unesco.org *Web Site:* www.unesco. org/iiep; www.iiep.unesco.org, pg 1372

International Institute for Labour Studies (IILS) (Switzerland) *Tel:* (022) 799 6111; (022) 799 6128 *Fax:* (022) 798 8685; (022) 799 8542 *E-mail:* ilo@ilo. org; inst@ilo.org *Web Site:* www.ilo.org, pg 1390

International Institute for Strategic Studies (United Kingdom) *Tel:* (020) 7379 7676 *Fax:* (020) 7836 3108 *Web Site:* www.iiss.org, pg 784

International Institute of Islamic Thought (Pakistan) *Tel:* (051) 229-3734 *Fax:* (051) 228-0489 *Web Site:* www.iiit.org, pg 559

International Institute of Tropical Agriculture (IITA) Library (Nigeria) *Tel:* (02) 0700800 *E-mail:* iita@ cgiar.org *Web Site:* www.iita.org, pg 1619

International ISBN Agency (United Kingdom) *Tel:* (020) 7503 6418 *Fax:* (020) 7503 6418 *E-mail:* info@isbn-international.org *Web Site:* isbn-international.org, pg 1396

International ISMN Agency (Germany) *Tel:* (030) 7974 5002 *E-mail:* ismn@ismn-international.org *Web Site:* ismn-international.org, pg 1374

International Labour Organization (ILO) (Switzerland) *Tel:* (022) 799 6111 *Fax:* (022) 799 6061 *E-mail:* ilo@ilo.org; europe@ilo.org *Web Site:* www. ilo.org, pg 1390

International Labour Organization Library (Switzerland) *Tel:* (022) 799 8682 *Fax:* (022) 799 6516 *E-mail:* library@ilo.org *Web Site:* www.ilo.org/library, pg 1636

International Law Book Services (ILBS) (Malaysia) *Tel:* (03) 7727 4121; (03) 7727 4122; (03) 7727 3890; (03) 7728-3890 *Fax:* (03) 7727 3884 *E-mail:* ilbslaw@gmail.com *Web Site:* www. malaysialawbooks.com, pg 507

International League of Antiquarian Booksellers (ILAB) (Switzerland) *Tel:* (02) 9660 4889 *Fax:* (02) 9552 2670 *E-mail:* office@antiquariat-donhofer.at; secretary@ilab.org *Web Site:* www.ilab.org, pg 1391

International Literacy Association (ILA) (United States) *Tel:* 302-731-1600 *Fax:* 302-731-1057 *E-mail:* customerservice@reading.org *Web Site:* www. literacyworldwide.org; www.reading.org, pg 1398

International Map Industry Association (IMIA) (United Kingdom) *Tel:* (01993) 774519 *Fax:* (01993) 883096 *Web Site:* imiamaps.org, pg 784

International Maritime Organization (IMO) (United Kingdom) *Tel:* (020) 7735 7611 *Fax:* (020) 7587 3241 *E-mail:* sales@imo.org (publications); info@imo.org *Web Site:* www.imo.org, pg 1396

International Monetary Fund (United States) *Tel:* 202-623-7000 *Fax:* 202-623-4661 *E-mail:* publicaffairs@ imf.org *Web Site:* www.imf.org, pg 1398

International Organization for Migration (IOM) (Switzerland) *Tel:* (022) 717 9111 *Fax:* (022) 798 6150 *E-mail:* pubsales@iom.int; hq@iom.int; info@ iom.int *Web Site:* www.iom.int, pg 1399

International Organization for Standardization (ISO) (Switzerland) *Tel:* (022) 749 01 11 *Fax:* (022) 733 34 30 *E-mail:* central@iso.org *Web Site:* www.iso.org, pg 1391

International Press Softcom Ltd (IPS) (Singapore) *Tel:* 6298 3800 *Fax:* 6297 1668 *E-mail:* biz@ ipsoftcom.com *Web Site:* www.ipsoftcom.com, pg 1283, 1332

International Print-o-Pac Ltd (India) *Tel:* (0120) 4192 100 *Fax:* (0120) 4192 199 *E-mail:* ippnoida@ippindia. com *Web Site:* www.ippindia.com, pg 1279, 1327

International Publications Service Inc (IPS) (South Korea) *Tel:* (02) 2115-8800 *Fax:* (02) 2115-8866, pg 1450

International Publishers Association (IPA) (Switzerland) *Tel:* (022) 704 18 20 *Fax:* (022) 704 18 21 *E-mail:* info@internationalpublishers.org; secretariat@internationalpublishers.org *Web Site:* www.internationalpublishers.org, pg 1391

International Publishers Direct (S) Pte Ltd (IPD) (Singapore) *Tel:* 6741 6933, pg 604

International Publishing & Research Co (Nigeria) *Tel:* (080) 2317-5915 *Fax:* (01) 4937131, pg 552

International Rice Research Institute (IRRI) (Philippines) *Tel:* (02) 580 5600; (02) 845 0563 *Fax:* (02) 580 5699; (02) 845 0606 *E-mail:* info@irri.org *Web Site:* irri.org, pg 565

International Standard Book Numbering Agency (South Africa) *Tel:* (012) 401 9718 *Fax:* (012) 325 5984 *E-mail:* isn.agency@nlsa.ac.za *Web Site:* www.nlsa.ac.za, pg 1388

International Telecommunication Union (ITU) (Switzerland) *Tel:* (022) 730 5111 *Fax:* (022) 733 7256 *E-mail:* itumail@itu.int *Web Site:* www.itu.int, pg 1391

Uitgeverij International Theatre & Film Books (Netherlands) *Tel:* (020) 662 52 42 *E-mail:* info@itfb.nl *Web Site:* www.itfb.nl, pg 534

International Translations Ltd (ITL) (United Kingdom) *Tel:* (0151) 342 7044 *E-mail:* admin@itltranslations.com *Web Site:* www.itltranslations.com, pg 1253

International Union of Geological Sciences (IUGS) (Norway) *Tel:* 73 90 40 00 *E-mail:* ngu@ngu.no *Web Site:* www.iugs.org; www.ngu.no, pg 1385

Internationale Gutenberg-Gesellschaft in Mainz eV (Germany) *Tel:* (06131) 22 64 20 *Fax:* (06131) 23 35 30 *E-mail:* info@gutenberg-gesellschaft.de *Web Site:* www.gutenberg-gesellschaft.de, pg 266, 1374, 1495

Internationale Jugendbibliothek (Germany) *Tel:* (089) 89 12 11-0 *Fax:* (089) 89 12 11-38 *E-mail:* info@ijb.de *Web Site:* www.ijb.de, pg 1375, 1593

Librairie Internationale (Morocco) *Tel:* 05 37 68 03 29 *Fax:* 05 37 77 09 14, pg 1436

Edition fuer Internationale Wirtschaft Verlags- und Kommunikations GmbH (Germany) *Tel:* (069) 20515 *Fax:* (069) 289214 *E-mail:* info@edition-spanien.de *Web Site:* www.edition-spanien.de, pg 266

Interpet Publishing (United Kingdom) *Tel:* (01306) 881 033 *E-mail:* customercare@interpet.co.uk *Web Site:* www.interpet.co.uk, pg 784

Interpress Kuelkereskedelmi Kft (Hungary) *Tel:* (01) 250-8263; (01) 250-8266 *Fax:* (01) 250-8262 *E-mail:* interpress@interpress.eu *Web Site:* www.interpress.eu, pg 1259, 1326, 1346

Editora InterSaberes (Brazil) *Tel:* (041) 2106-4170 *E-mail:* contato@editoraintersaberes.com.br *Web Site:* www.intersaberes.com, pg 85

Intersentia NV (Belgium) *Tel:* (03) 680 15 50 *Fax:* (03) 658 71 21 *E-mail:* mail@intersentia.be *Web Site:* www.intersentia.be, pg 68

Intersistemas SA de CV (Mexico) *Tel:* (0155) 55202073 *E-mail:* intersistemas@intersistemas.com.mx *Web Site:* www.intersistemas.com.mx, pg 518

Interskol Forlag AB (Sweden) *Tel:* (040) 51 01 95 *Fax:* (040) 15 06 25 *E-mail:* info@interskol.se; order@interskol.se *Web Site:* www.interskol.se, pg 682

Uitgeverij Intertaal bv (Netherlands) *Tel:* (036) 547 16 40 *Fax:* (036) 547 15 82 *E-mail:* uitgeverij@intertaal.nl *Web Site:* www.intertaal.nl, pg 534

Interzona Editora (Argentina) *Tel:* (011) 4383 6262 *E-mail:* info@interzonaeditora.com; edicion@interzonaeditora.com *Web Site:* www.interzonaeditora.com, pg 8

Into Kustannus Oy (Finland) *Tel:* (040) 179 5297 *E-mail:* myynti@intokustannus.fi *Web Site:* intokustannus.fi, pg 149

Intonation Ltd (United Kingdom) *Tel:* (01329) 828438 *Fax:* (01329) 823543 *E-mail:* info@intonation.co.uk *Web Site:* www.intonation.co.uk, pg 1253

Intreprinderea Editorial-Poligrafica Stiinta (Moldova) *Tel:* (022) 73-96-16; (022) 73-97-44; (022) 73-99-30 *Fax:* (022) 73-96-27 *Web Site:* www.stiinta.asm.md, pg 525

Editora Intrinseca (Brazil) *Tel:* (021) 3206-7400 *E-mail:* contato@intrinseca.com.br *Web Site:* www.intrinseca.com.br/a-editora, pg 85

Intype Libra Ltd (United Kingdom) *Tel:* (020) 8947 7863 *Fax:* (020) 8947 3652 *E-mail:* hello@intypelibra.co.uk *Web Site:* www.intypelibra.co.uk, pg 1263, 1287, 1338, 1348

Invandrarfoerlaget (Sweden) *E-mail:* migrant@immi.se *Web Site:* www.immi.se, pg 682

El Inversionista Mexicano SA de CV (Mexico) *E-mail:* cuentas@elinversionista.com.mx; cservice@elinversionista.com.mx *Web Site:* www.elinversionista.com.mx, pg 518

Inwardpath Publishers (Australia) *Tel:* (03) 9499 3405 *Web Site:* inwardpath.com.au, pg 28

IOS Press BV (Netherlands) *Tel:* (020) 688 3355 *Fax:* (020) 687 0019 *E-mail:* info@iospress.nl *Web Site:* www.iospress.nl, pg 534

Editions Ipagine (France) *Tel:* 01 44 01 66 22 *Fax:* 08 26 42 48 57 *E-mail:* contact@ipagine.com *Web Site:* www.ipagine.com, pg 177

Iperborea SRL (Italy) *Tel:* (02) 87398098; (02) 87398099 *Fax:* (02) 798919 *E-mail:* ufficio.stampa@iperborea.com *Web Site:* www.iperborea.com, pg 448

Ipso Books (United Kingdom) *E-mail:* hello@ipsobooks.com *Web Site:* www.ipsobooks.com, pg 784

Ir Indo Edicions SA (Spain) *Tel:* 986 21 12 12 *Fax:* 986 21 11 33 *E-mail:* administracion@irindo.com *Web Site:* www.irindo.com, pg 650

Editorial Iralka SL (Spain) *Tel:* 943 32 30 14 *E-mail:* iralka@euskalnet.net *Web Site:* www.euskalnet.net/iralka, pg 651

Iranian Research Institute for Information Science & Technology (Iran) *Tel:* (021) 66951430; (021) 66494980 *Fax:* (021) 66462254 *E-mail:* info@irandoc.ac.ir *Web Site:* www.irandoc.ac.ir, pg 1602

Iraqi National Library & Archives (Iraq) *Tel:* (01) 4141303; (01) 4141314 *Fax:* (01) 4141810 *E-mail:* iraqnla@googlemail.com *Web Site:* www.iraqnla-iq.com, pg 1602

IRD Editions (France) *Tel:* 01 48 03 56 49 *Fax:* 01 48 02 79 09 *E-mail:* editions@ird.fr; diffusion@ird.fr *Web Site:* www.editions.ird.fr, pg 177

IRDES - Institut de Recherche et Documentation en Economie de la Sante (France) *Tel:* 01 53 93 43 00 *Fax:* 01 53 93 43 50 *E-mail:* presse@irdes.fr *Web Site:* www.irdes.fr, pg 177

Irfon (Tajikistan) *Tel:* (372) 333906; (372) 336254, pg 713

Iris Literary Agency (Greece) *Tel:* 210 24 32 473 *Fax:* 210 24 35 042 *E-mail:* irislit@otenet.gr *Web Site:* www.irisliteraryagency.gr, pg 1229

Irish Academic Press (Ireland) *Tel:* (045) 89 55 62 *Fax:* (045) 89 55 63 *E-mail:* info@iap.ie *Web Site:* www.iap.ie; www.irishacademicusa.com, pg 411

Irish Educational Publishers' Association (IEPA) (Ireland) *E-mail:* info@iepa.ie *Web Site:* www.iepa.ie, pg 1378

Irish Management Institute (Ireland) *Tel:* (01) 207 8400 *Fax:* (01) 295 5147 *E-mail:* info@imi.ie *Web Site:* www.imi.ie, pg 412

Irish Texts Society (Ireland) *Web Site:* www.irishtextssociety.org, pg 412

Irish Translators' & Interpreters' Association (ITIA) (Ireland) *Tel:* (087) 673 83 86 *E-mail:* info@translatorsassociation.ie; secretary@translatorsassociation.ie *Web Site:* www.translatorsassociation.ie, pg 1250

Irish YouthWork Press (Ireland) *Tel:* (01) 8584500 *Fax:* (01) 8724183 *E-mail:* info@youthworkireland.ie *Web Site:* www.youthworkireland.ie, pg 412

Irmaos Vitale SA (Brazil) *Tel:* (011) 5081-9499 *Fax:* (011) 5574-7388 *E-mail:* virtual@vitale.com.br *Web Site:* www.vitale.com.br, pg 85

IRSA (Institute for Art Historical Research) (Poland) *Tel:* (12) 421 90 30 *Fax:* (12) 421 48 07 *E-mail:* irsa@irsa.com.pl *Web Site:* irsa.com.pl, pg 570

Editorial Iru SL (Spain) *Tel:* 932 318032 *Fax:* 932 653670, pg 651

Isaberg Forlag ab (Sweden) *Tel:* (0370) 33 63 10 *Fax:* (0370) 33 63 20 *E-mail:* info@isaberg.nu *Web Site:* www.isaberg.nu, pg 682

Isafoldar Prentsmidja hf (Iceland) *Tel:* 59 50 300 *Fax:* 59 50 310 *Web Site:* www.isafold.is, pg 1327

ISAL (Istituto per la Storia dell'Arte Lombarda) (Italy) *Tel:* (0362) 528118 *Fax:* (0362) 659417 *E-mail:* info@istitutoartelombarda.org *Web Site:* www.istitutoartelombarda.org, pg 448

ISBN Agencija na Republika Makedonija (Macedonia) *Tel:* (02) 3115 177 *Fax:* (02) 3226 846 *E-mail:* kliment@nubsk.edu.mk *Web Site:* www.nubsk.edu.mk, pg 1381

ISBN Agency (Mauritius) *Tel:* 464 6761 *Fax:* 464 3445 *E-mail:* eoipublishing@intnet.mu *Web Site:* eoibooks.gov-mu.org, pg 1382

ISBN Agency Australia (Australia) *Tel:* (03) 8517 8349; (03) 8517 8333 *Fax:* (03) 8517 8368; (03) 8517 8399 *E-mail:* customer.service@thorpe.com.au; isbn@thorpe.com.au *Web Site:* www.thorpe.com.au; www.myidentifiers.com.au, pg 1364

ISBN Agency for Serbia (Serbia) *Tel:* (011) 2459 444 *Fax:* (011) 2459 444 *Web Site:* www.nb.rs, pg 1387

ISBN Agency - Luxembourg (Luxembourg) *Tel:* 26 09 59-313 *E-mail:* agence-isbn@bnl.etat.lu *Web Site:* www.bnl.lu, pg 1381

ISBN Agency - Namibia (Namibia) *Tel:* (061) 293 53 00 *Fax:* (061) 293 53 21 *E-mail:* natlib@mec.gov.na *Web Site:* www.nln.gov.na/biblio.html, pg 1383

ISBN-Agentur fuer die Bundesrepublik Deutschland (Germany) *Tel:* (069) 1306-387 *Fax:* (069) 1306-258 *E-mail:* isbn@mvb-online.de; info@mvb-online.de *Web Site:* www.german-isbn.org, pg 1375

ISBN Agentur Schweiz (Switzerland) *Tel:* (044) 421 36 01 *Fax:* (044) 421 36 18 *E-mail:* isbn@sbvv.ch *Web Site:* www.sbvv.ch, pg 1391

Bureau ISBN (Netherlands) *Tel:* (0345) 475855 *E-mail:* isbn@cb.nl *Web Site:* www.isbn.nl, pg 1383

ISBN-Kontoret Norge (Norway) *Tel:* 75 12 11 48 *Fax:* 75 12 12 22 *E-mail:* isbn-kontoret@nb.no *Web Site:* www.nb.no, pg 1385

ISBN National Centre (Malaysia) *Tel:* (03) 26871700 (ext 4288); (03) 26814329 *Fax:* (03) 26811676 *E-mail:* isbn@pnm.gov.my *Web Site:* www.pnm.gov.my, pg 1382

ISBN Turkiye Ajansy (Turkey) *Tel:* (0312) 309 90 50 *Fax:* (0312) 309 89 99 *E-mail:* isbn@kultur.gov.tr *Web Site:* www.ekygm.gov.tr/isbn.html, pg 1392

iSeek Ltd (United Kingdom) *Tel:* (01444) 462860 *Fax:* (01444) 232142 *Web Site:* www.iseekcreative.com, pg 784

Ediciones Fiscales ISEF SA (Mexico) *Tel:* (0155) 5096 5100 *E-mail:* editorial@grupoisef.com.mx *Web Site:* www.libreriaisef.com.mx, pg 518

Edition Isele (Germany) *Tel:* (07746) 91 11-6 *Fax:* (07746) 91 11-7 *E-mail:* mail@edition-isele.de *Web Site:* www.edition-isele.de, pg 267

Ishihara Publishing Co Ltd (Japan) *Tel:* (099) 239-1200 *Fax:* (099) 239-1202 *E-mail:* info@isihara-kk.co.jp *Web Site:* www.isihara-kk.co.jp, pg 478

Ishiyaku Publishers Inc (Japan) *Tel:* (03) 5395-7600; (03) 5395-7605 (sales) *Fax:* (03) 5395-7614 *E-mail:* wdomaster@ishiyaku.co.jp; copyright@ishiyaku.co.jp (publications affairs dept) *Web Site:* www.ishiyaku.co.jp, pg 478

The ISIS Press (Turkey) *Tel:* (0216) 321-3851; (0216) 321-6600 *Fax:* (0216) 321-8666 *E-mail:* isis@theisispress.org *Web Site:* www.theisispress.org, pg 721

Isis Publishing Ltd (United Kingdom) *Tel:* (01865) 250 333 *Toll Free Tel:* 0800 731 5637 (orders-UK only) *Fax:* (01865) 790 358 *E-mail:* new@isishousepub.com; sales@isis-publishing.co.uk *Web Site:* www.isis-publishing.co.uk; www.isishousepub.com, pg 784

Wydawnictwo Iskry Sp z oo (Poland) *Tel:* (22) 827 94 15 *E-mail:* iskry@iskry.com.pl; promocja@iskry.com.pl *Web Site:* www.iskry.com.pl, pg 570

Izdatelstvo Iskusstvo (Russia) *Tel:* (495) 2035872 *Fax:* (495) 2918882, pg 594

Islam International Publications Ltd (United Kingdom) *Tel:* (020) 8687 7831 *E-mail:* info@islaminternationalpublications.com *Web Site:* www.islaminternationalpublications.com, pg 785

Verlag der Islam (Germany) *Tel:* (069) 50688-651; (069) 50688-653 (sales) *Fax:* (069) 50688-655 *Web Site:* www.verlagderislam.de, pg 267

Islamic Publications (Pvt) Ltd (Pakistan) *Tel:* (042) 35417074 *Fax:* (042) 37214974, pg 559

Islamic Publishing House (India) *Tel:* (0495) 2720072; (0495) 2724618 *E-mail:* iphdir@gmail.com; iphcalicut@gmail.com *Web Site:* www.iphkerala.com, pg 387

Islamic Research Institute (IRI) (Pakistan) *Tel:* (051) 2281289; (051) 9261761-5 (ext 207 & 222); (051) 2254874 (orders) *Fax:* (051) 2250821; (051) 9260769 (orders) *Web Site:* iri.iiu.edu.pk, pg 559

The Islamic Texts Society (United Kingdom) *Tel:* (01223) 842425 *Fax:* (01223) 842425 *E-mail:* info@its.org.uk; orders@its.org.uk *Web Site:* www.its.org.uk, pg 785

Islamic University in Madinah Central Library (Saudi Arabia) *Tel:* (014) 8470803 *Fax:* (014) 8474471 *E-mail:* lib@iu.edu.sa *Web Site:* www.iu.edu.sa, pg 1628

Island Press Co-operative (Australia) *Tel:* (02) 4758 6635 *E-mail:* awphaw@bigpond.com *Web Site:* islandpress.tripod.com/ISLAND.htm, pg 28

Islands Business International (Fiji) *Tel:* 330 3108 *Fax:* 330 1423 *E-mail:* editor@ibi.com.fj *Web Site:* www.islandsbusiness.com, pg 147

Editions Isoete (France) *Tel:* 02 33 43 36 64 *Fax:* 02 33 43 37 13 *E-mail:* editions.isoete@wanadoo.fr *Web Site:* isoete.over-blog.fr, pg 177

Isper Club (Italy) *Tel:* (011) 66 47 803 *Fax:* (011) 66 70 829 *E-mail:* isper@isper.org *Web Site:* www.isper.org, pg 1360

ISPER SRL (Italy) *Tel:* (011) 66 47 803 *Fax:* (011) 66 70 829 *E-mail:* isper@isper.org; fondazione@fondazione-isper.edu *Web Site:* www.isper.org, pg 448

Israbook (Israel) *Tel:* (02) 538-0247 *Fax:* (02) 538-8423 *E-mail:* israbook@gefenpublishing.com; info@gefenpublishing.com *Web Site:* www.israelbooks.com, pg 1427

The Israel Academy of Sciences and Humanities (Israel) *Tel:* (02) 5676233 *Fax:* (02) 5666059 *Web Site:* www.academy.ac.il, pg 418

Israel Antiquities Authority (Israel) *Tel:* (02) 6204611 *Fax:* (02) 6260460 *Web Site:* www.antiquities.org.il, pg 418

Israel Exploration Society (Israel) *Tel:* (02) 6257991 *Fax:* (02) 6247772 *E-mail:* ies@vms.huji.ac.il *Web Site:* israelexplorationsociety.huji.ac.il, pg 418

Israel Institute for Occupational Safety & Hygiene (IIOSH) (Israel) *Tel:* (03) 5266444 *Fax:* (03) 5266457 *E-mail:* info@osh.org.il; publish@osh.org.il *Web Site:* www.osh.org.il, pg 418

Israel ISBN Group Agency (Israel) *Tel:* (03) 6180151 *Fax:* (03) 5798048 *E-mail:* isbn@icl.org.il; icl@icl.org.il *Web Site:* www.icl.org.il, pg 1378

The Israel Museum (Israel) *Tel:* (02) 6708811 *Fax:* (02) 6771332 *E-mail:* info@imj.org.il *Web Site:* www.imj.org.il, pg 419

Israel Music Institute (IMI) (Israel) *Tel:* (03) 624 70 95 *Fax:* (03) 561 28 26 *E-mail:* musicinst@bezeqint.net *Web Site:* www.imi.org.il, pg 419

Israel Society for Libraries & Information Centers (ASMI) (Israel) *Tel:* 0772151800 *Fax:* 077434509 *E-mail:* agudatasmi@gmail.com *Web Site:* www.asmi.org.il, pg 1654

Israel State Archives (Israel) *Tel:* (02) 5680612; (02) 5680662; (02) 5680673; (02) 5680675; (02) 5680680 *Fax:* (02) 5680670 *E-mail:* research@archives.gov.il *Web Site:* www.archives.gov.il, pg 1604

Israel Translators' Association (Israel) *Tel:* (054) 5680398 *Web Site:* www.ita.org.il, pg 1250

ISSN International Centre (France) *Tel:* 01 44 88 22 20 *Fax:* 01 40 26 32 43 *E-mail:* issnic@issn.org; secretariat@issn.org *Web Site:* www.issn.org, pg 1372

ISSN Norge (Norway) *Tel:* 23 27 61 00 *E-mail:* issn-norge@nb.no *Web Site:* www.nb.no/sn/html/issn.html, pg 1385

ISSN UK Centre (United Kingdom) *Tel:* (01937) 546959 *Fax:* (01937) 546562 *E-mail:* issn-uk@bl.uk *Web Site:* www.bl.uk/bibliographic/issn.html, pg 1396

Istanbul Bilgi Universitesi Yayinlari (Turkey) *Tel:* (0212) 311 61 47 *Fax:* (0212) 216 24 15 (sales & marketing) *E-mail:* yayin@bilgiyay.com *Web Site:* www.bilgiyay.com, pg 721

Istanbul Technical University Library & Documentation Dept (Turkey) *Tel:* (0212) 285 35 96 *Fax:* (0212) 285 33 02 *E-mail:* kutuphane@itu.edu.tr *Web Site:* www.library.itu.edu.tr, pg 1639

Istanbul Universitesi Merkez Kutuphanesi (Turkey) *Tel:* (0212) 455 57 83 (ext 16767) *Fax:* (0212) 455 57 84 *E-mail:* kutuphane@istanbul.edu.tr *Web Site:* kutuphane.istanbul.edu.tr, pg 1639

ISTE Ltd (United Kingdom) *Tel:* (020) 8879 4580 *Toll Free Tel:* 0800 902 354 (within France) *E-mail:* info@iste-editions.fr *Web Site:* www.iste.co.uk; www.iste-editions.fr, pg 785

Istituto Centrale per il Catalogo Unico delle Biblioteche Italiane e per le Informazioni Bibliografiche (Italy) *Tel:* (06) 49210425; (06) 4989424 *Fax:* (06) 4959302 *E-mail:* venditapubbl@iccu.sbn.it; ic-cu@beniculturali.it *Web Site:* www.iccu.sbn.it, pg 448

Istituto Centrale per il Catalogo Unico delle Biblioteche Italiane e per le Informazioni Bibliografiche (Italy) *Tel:* (06) 49210425; (06) 4989424 *Fax:* (06) 4959 302 *E-mail:* ic-cu@beniculturali.it *Web Site:* www.iccu.sbn.it, pg 1654

Istituto della Enciclopedia Italiana (Italy) *Tel:* (06) 68981; (06) 68982347 *Fax:* (06) 68982266; (06) 68982156 *E-mail:* infotreccani@treccani.it; ufficiostampa@treccani.it; servizioclienti@treccani.it; redazione@treccani.it *Web Site:* www.treccani.it, pg 448

Istituto Editoriale Ticinese (Switzerland) *Tel:* (091) 825 6622 *Fax:* (091) 825 1874 *E-mail:* casagrande@casagrande-online.ch *Web Site:* www.casagrande-online.ch/Edizioni/iet, pg 697

Istituto Geografico de Agostini SpA (Italy) *Tel:* (0321) 4241 *E-mail:* info@deagostini.it *Web Site:* www.deagostini.it, pg 448

Istituto Idrografico della Marina (IIM) (Italy) *Tel:* (010) 24431 *Fax:* (010) 261400 *E-mail:* iim.sre@marina.difesa.it *Web Site:* www.marina.difesa.it, pg 448

Istituto Italiano Edizioni Atlas SpA (Italy) *Tel:* (035) 249711 *E-mail:* edizioniatlas@edatlas.it *Web Site:* www.edatlas.it, pg 448

Istituto Italiano per l'Africa e l'Oriente (IsIAO) (Italy) *Tel:* (06) 32855223 *Fax:* (06) 32855217, pg 448

Istituto Lombardo Accademia di Scienze e Lettere (Italy) *Tel:* (02) 864087 *Toll Free Tel:* (02) 86461388 *E-mail:* istituto.lombardo@unimi.it *Web Site:* www.istitutolombardo.it, pg 1497

Istituto Nazionale di Studi Romani (Italy) *Tel:* (06) 574 34 42; (06) 574 34 45 *Fax:* (06) 574 34 47 *E-mail:* studiromani@studiromani.it; segreteria@studiromani.it *Web Site:* www.studiromani.it, pg 449

Istituto Poligrafico e Zecca dello Stato SpA (Italy) *Toll Free Tel:* 800 864035 *Fax:* (06) 85084117 *E-mail:* editoriale@ipzs.it; informazioni@ipzs.it *Web Site:* www.editoria.ipzs.it, pg 449

Istituto Poligrafico e Zecca dello Stato SpA (Italy) *Tel:* (06) 85081; (06) 85082147 (bookshop) *Toll Free Tel:* 800 864035 *Fax:* (06) 85082517 *E-mail:* informazioni@ipzs.it; ufficiostampa@ipzs.it *Web Site:* www.ipzs.it, pg 1260

Istituto Storico Italiano per l'Eta Moderna e Contemporanea (Italy) *Tel:* (06) 68806922 *Fax:* (06) 6875127 *E-mail:* segreteria@iststor.it, pg 449

Istituzione Biblioteca Malatestiana (Italy) *Tel:* (0547) 610892 *Fax:* (0547) 21237 *E-mail:* malatestiana@sbn.provincia.ra.it *Web Site:* www.comune.cesena.fc.it/malatestiana, pg 1606

Ediciones Istmo SA (Spain) *Tel:* 918 061 996 *Fax:* 918 044 028 *E-mail:* pedidos.blume@akal.com; edicion@akal.com; universidad@akal.com; educacion@akal.com; prensa@akal.com; atencion.cliente@akal.com *Web Site:* www.akal.com, pg 651

Istros Books (United Kingdom) *Tel:* (020) 7435 1540 *E-mail:* info@istrosbooks.com *Web Site:* istrosbooks.com, pg 785

Ita-Suomen Yliopisto Kirjasto (Finland) *Tel:* (0294) 45 8397 *E-mail:* library@uef.fi; kirjasto@uef.fi *Web Site:* www.uef.fi/kirjasto, pg 1589

Editorial Itaca (Mexico) *Tel:* (0155) 5840-5452 *E-mail:* itaca00@hotmail.com; itaca.editorial@gmail.com *Web Site:* editorialitaca.com.mx, pg 518

Editoriale Itaca (Italy) *Tel:* (02) 48009484, pg 449

Italia Shobo Ltd (Japan) *Tel:* (03) 3262-1656 *Fax:* (03) 3234-6469 *E-mail:* info@italiashobo.co.jp *Web Site:* italiashobo.com, pg 478

The Italian Literary Agency SRL (TILA) (Italy) *Tel:* (02) 862445 *Fax:* (02) 876222 *Web Site:* www.italianliterary.com, pg 1231

Penerbit ITB (Indonesia) *Tel:* (022) 2504257 *Fax:* (022) 2534155 *E-mail:* itbpress@penerbit.itb.ac.id *Web Site:* www.penerbit.itb.ac.id, pg 406

Ithemba! Publishing (South Africa) *Tel:* (011) 726 6529 *E-mail:* firechildren@icon.co.za, pg 614

IUCN (International Union for Conservation of Nature) (Switzerland) *Tel:* (022) 999 0000 *Fax:* (022) 999 0002 *E-mail:* publications@iucn.org *Web Site:* www.iucn.org/publications, pg 697

IUCN (International Union for Conservation of Nature) (Switzerland) *Tel:* (022) 999 0000 *Fax:* (022) 999 0002 *E-mail:* mail@iucn.org; press@iucn.org; publications@iucn.org *Web Site:* www.iucn.org, pg 1391

IUDICIUM Verlag GmbH (Germany) *Tel:* (089) 718747 *Fax:* (089) 7142039 *E-mail:* info@iudicium.de *Web Site:* www.iudicium.de, pg 267

Iustus Forlag AB (Sweden) *Tel:* (018) 65 03 30 *Fax:* (018) 69 30 99 *E-mail:* kundtjanst@iustus.se *Web Site:* www.iustus.se, pg 683

Wydawnictwo IUVI (Poland) *E-mail:* handlowy@iuvi.pl; redakcja@iuvi.pl *Web Site:* iuvi.pl, pg 570

Editions Ivoire-Clair (France) *Tel:* 02 51 68 58 33 *E-mail:* service.clients@ivoire-clair.com *Web Site:* www.ivoire-clair.com, pg 177

Kaitakusha Publishing Co Ltd (Japan) *Tel:* (03) 5842-8900 *Fax:* (03) 5842-5560 *E-mail:* info@kaitakusha. co.jp *Web Site:* www.kaitakusha.co.jp, pg 480

Kajima Institute Publishing Co Ltd (Japan) *Tel:* (03) 6202 5200 *Fax:* (03) 6202 5204 *E-mail:* info@kajima-publishing.co.jp *Web Site:* www.kajima-publishing.co. jp, pg 480

KaJo Verlag (Germany) *Tel:* (0931) 465 889-11 *Fax:* (0931) 465 889-29 *E-mail:* info@verlagshaus. com *Web Site:* www.verlagshaus.com, pg 269

Kaknus Yayinlari (Turkey) *Tel:* (0216) 341 08 65; (0212) 520 49 27 (orders) *Fax:* (0216) 334 61 48; (0212) 520 49 28 (orders) *E-mail:* info@kaknus.com.tr *Web Site:* www.kaknus.com.tr, pg 721

Editions Kalaama (Senegal) *Tel:* 33 864 43 37 *Fax:* 33 864 43 37 *E-mail:* ufce.senegal@gmail.com; kalaama@hotmail.com *Web Site:* www.ufce-senegal. org/kalaama, pg 600

Kalam Verlag KG (Germany) *Tel:* (0761) 45002152 *Fax:* (0761) 45002100 *E-mail:* info@kalam-verlag.de *Web Site:* www.kalam-verlag.de, pg 269

Kalandraka Editora (Spain) *Tel:* 986 86 02 76 *Fax:* 986 10 02 80 *E-mail:* editora@kalandraka.com *Web Site:* www.kalandraka.com, pg 651

Kalandraka Italia (Italy) *Tel:* (055) 38 40 340 *E-mail:* info@kalandraka.it *Web Site:* www.kalandraka. it; www.kalandraka.com/it, pg 449

Editions Kaleidoscope (France) *Tel:* 01 45 44 07 08 *Fax:* 01 45 44 53 71 *E-mail:* infos@editions-kaleidoscope.com *Web Site:* www.editions-kaleidoscope.com, pg 178

Kaleidoscope Publishers Ltd (Denmark) *Tel:* 33 75 55 55 *Fax:* 33 75 55 44, pg 137

Kalem Literary Agency (Turkey) *Tel:* (0212) 245 44 06 *Fax:* (0212) 245 44 19 *E-mail:* info@kalemagency. com *Web Site:* www.kalemagency.com, pg 1238

Kalendis Editions (Greece) *Tel:* 2109638790; 2103601551 *Fax:* 2109638791 *E-mail:* info@kalendis. gr *Web Site:* kalendis.gr, pg 356

Kalich (Czech Republic) *Tel:* 224 947 844 (editor); 224 947 505 (orders) *Fax:* 224 947 845 *E-mail:* kalich@ ekalich.cz (orders); kalichpub@ekalich.cz (editor) *Web Site:* www.ekalich.cz, pg 128

Kalima (United Arab Emirates) *Tel:* (02) 6 43 31 78 *E-mail:* info@kalima.ae *Web Site:* www.kalima.ae, pg 1393

Kalimat (United Arab Emirates) *Tel:* (06) 5566696 *Fax:* (06) 5566691 *E-mail:* info@kalimat.ae *Web Site:* www.kalimat.ae, pg 727

Kalla Kulor Forlag (Sweden) *E-mail:* info@kallakulor. com *Web Site:* kallakulor.com, pg 683

Kalligram spol sro (Slovakia) *Tel:* (02) 544-15-028 *Fax:* (02) 544-15-028 *E-mail:* kalligram@kalligram.sk; distribucia@kalligram.sk *Web Site:* www.kalligram. com, pg 608

Kallmeyer Verlag (Germany) *Tel:* (0511) 40 00 4-175 *Fax:* (0511) 40 00 4-176 *E-mail:* leserservice@ friedrich-verlag.de *Web Site:* www.friedrich-verlag.de, pg 269

KALRO Library & Information Services (LIS) (Kenya) *Tel:* (0722) 206-986 (cell); (0733) 333-223 (cell) *E-mail:* info@kalro.org *Web Site:* www.kalro.org/ library, pg 1608

Kalyani Publishers (India) *Tel:* (0161) 2760031 *Fax:* (0161) 2745872 *E-mail:* kalyanibooks@yahoo. co.in, pg 388

KAMA Publishing (United Kingdom) *Tel:* (01603) 749003; (07587) 178135 (cell) *E-mail:* kamapublishing@gmail.com *Web Site:* kamapublishing.co.uk, pg 786

Kamenyar (Ukraine) *Tel:* (0322) 35-59-49 *Fax:* (0322) 35-59-49 *E-mail:* vyd@kamenyar.com.ua *Web Site:* www.kamenyar.com.ua, pg 726

Verlag und Druckkontor Kamp GmbH (Germany) *Tel:* (0234) 51617-0 *Fax:* (0234) 51617-18 *E-mail:* mail@kamp-verlag.de *Web Site:* www.kamp-verlag.de, pg 269

J Kamphausen Verlag (Germany) *Tel:* (0521) 5 60 52-0 *Fax:* (0521) 5 60 52-29 *E-mail:* info@j-kamphausen. de, pg 269

KAMS Information & Publishing Ltd (Hong Kong) *Tel:* 8101 0108, pg 1250

Kanehara & Co Ltd (Japan) *Tel:* (03) 3811-7185; (03) 3811-7184 (sales) *Fax:* (03) 3813-0288 *E-mail:* sales@kanehara-shuppan.co.jp *Web Site:* www. kanehara-shuppan.co.jp, pg 480

Kanisa la Biblia Publishers (Tanzania) *Tel:* (075) 3656342 (cell); (071) 3609166 (cell) *E-mail:* contact@ klb-publishers.org *Web Site:* klb-publishers.org, pg 714

KANJIL Editeur (France) *Tel:* 01 44 27 01 04; 06 13 26 61 96 *E-mail:* kanjilediteur@gmail.com *Web Site:* www.kanjil.com, pg 179

Kano State Library Board (Nigeria) *Tel:* (0803) 423 4969 *E-mail:* nuramudi21@gmail.com, pg 1619

KANOON, Institute for the Intellectual Development of Children & Young Adults (Iran) *Tel:* (021) 88967392 *Fax:* (021) 88821121 *E-mail:* kanoon@ jamejam.net *Web Site:* www.kanoonparvaresh.com; kanoonnord.com; www.kanoonintl.com; www.kids. kanoonparvaresh.com, pg 408

Kansallis Kirjasto (Finland) *Tel:* (09) 191 22750; (09) 191 23196 *E-mail:* kk-palvelu@helsinki.fi *Web Site:* www.kansalliskirjasto.fi, pg 1590

Kansallisarkiston kirjasto (Finland) *Tel:* (029) 533 7000 *Fax:* (09) 176 302 *E-mail:* kirjaamo@arkisto.fi *Web Site:* www.arkisto.fi, pg 1590

Kanzelsberger AS (Czech Republic) *Tel:* 234 064 211 *E-mail:* info@kanzelsberger.cz *Web Site:* www. kanzelsberger.cz, pg 128

Kaos Edizioni SRL (Italy) *Tel:* (02) 39310296 *Fax:* (02) 39325749 *E-mail:* kaosedizioni@kaosedizioni.com *Web Site:* www.kaosedizioni.com, pg 449

Kapelusz Editora SA (Argentina) *Tel:* (011) 5236-5000 *Fax:* (011) 5236-5005 *E-mail:* contacto@ kapelusznorma.com.ar *Web Site:* www.kapelusznorma. com.ar, pg 9

Kaplan Publishing (United Kingdom) *Tel:* (0118) 912 3000; (0118) 989 0629 *Fax:* (0118) 979 7455 *E-mail:* publishing@kaplan.co.uk *Web Site:* kaplan-publishing.kaplan.co.uk, pg 786

Kapon Editions (Greece) *Tel:* 2109235098 *Fax:* 2109214089 *E-mail:* info@kaponeditions.gr *Web Site:* www.kaponeditions.gr, pg 356

edition KAPPA, Verlag fuer Kultur und Kommunikation GmbH (Germany) *Tel:* (089) 17 11 82 33 *Fax:* (089) 17 11 82 04 *E-mail:* info@editionkappa.de *Web Site:* www.editionkappa.de, pg 269

Karadi Tales Co Pvt Ltd (India) *Tel:* (044) 2442 1775; (044) 4205 4243 *Fax:* (044) 2440 3728 *E-mail:* contact@karaditales.com *Web Site:* www. karaditales.com, pg 388

Izdavacko Preduzece Vuk Karadzic (Serbia) *Tel:* (011) 3342329, pg 601

Izdavacko Preduzece Vuk Karadzic (Serbia) *Tel:* (011) 334 2329, pg 1447

Antiquariat KaraJahn (Germany) *Tel:* (030) 211 54 56 *Fax:* (030) 211 57 37 *E-mail:* oldbooks@karajahn.com *Web Site:* www.karajahn.com, pg 1416

Karakter Color AS (Turkey) *Tel:* (0212) 4323001 *Fax:* (0212) 6289565 *E-mail:* info@karaktercolor. tr *Web Site:* www.karaktercolor.com, pg 1285, 1336

Karakter Uitgevers BV (Netherlands) *Tel:* (0297) 38644 *E-mail:* info@karakteruitgevers.nl; bestelservice@ karakteruitgevers.nl *Web Site:* www.karakteruitgevers. nl, pg 535

Karas-Sana Oy (Finland) *Tel:* (0207) 681 610 *Fax:* (0420) 793 435 *E-mail:* krs@sana.fi *Web Site:* www.kansanraamattuseura.fi, pg 149

Karchkhadze Publishing (Georgia) *Tel:* (032) 2514527 *E-mail:* info@karchkhadze.ge *Web Site:* karchkhadze. ge, pg 201

Kardamitsa Publications (Greece) *Tel:* 2103615156 *E-mail:* info@kardamitsa.gr *Web Site:* www. kardamitsa.gr, pg 356

S Karger AG (Switzerland) *Tel:* (061) 306 11 11 *Fax:* (061) 306 12 34 *E-mail:* karger@karger.com; permission@karger.com *Web Site:* www.karger.com, pg 698

S Karger GmbH (Germany) *Tel:* (0761) 45 20 7-0 *Fax:* (0761) 45 20 7-14 *E-mail:* information@karger. de *Web Site:* www.karger.com, pg 269

Karisto Oy (Finland) *Tel:* (03) 63 151 *Fax:* (03) 616 1565 *E-mail:* kustannusliike@karisto.fi *Web Site:* www.karisto.fi, pg 149

Karl-May-Verlag GmbH (Germany) *Tel:* (0951) 9 82 06-0 *Fax:* (0951) 9 82 06-55 *E-mail:* info@karl-may.de *Web Site:* www.karl-may.de, pg 269

Karmelitanske Nakladatelstvi Sro (Czech Republic) *Tel:* 220 181 350; 230 233 140 (foreign rights) *Fax:* 220 181 390 *E-mail:* secretariat@kna.cz; rights@ kna.cz *Web Site:* www.kna.cz, pg 128

Karnac Books Ltd (United Kingdom) *Tel:* (020) 7431 1075 *Fax:* (020) 7435 9076 *E-mail:* shop@ karnacbooks.com *Web Site:* www.karnacbooks.com, pg 786

Karnak House (Trinidad and Tobago) *Tel:* (868) 351-3447 (Trinidad & North America); (020) 8830 8301 (UK) *E-mail:* karnakhouse@aol.com, pg 717

Karolinger Verlag (Austria) *Tel:* (01) 409 22 79 *Fax:* (01) 409 22 79 *E-mail:* verlag@karolinger.at *Web Site:* www.karolinger.at, pg 51

Karren Publishing (Germany) *Tel:* (0151) 120 598 01 *Web Site:* www.karren-publishing.com, pg 269

Les Editions Karthala (France) *Tel:* 01 43 31 15 59 *Fax:* 01 45 35 27 05 *E-mail:* karthala@orange.fr *Web Site:* www.karthala.com, pg 179

Kartografie PRAHA AS (Czech Republic) *Tel:* 221 969 446 *E-mail:* info@kartografie.cz *Web Site:* www. kartografie.cz, pg 129

Kartographischer Verlag Reinhard Ryborsch (Germany) *Tel:* (069) 85097707 *Fax:* (069) 85097708, pg 269

Kartonagenwerkstatt (Germany) *Tel:* (037202) 2583 *Fax:* (037202) 89024 *E-mail:* info@ kartonagenwerkstatt.de *Web Site:* www. kartonagenwerkstatt.de, pg 1322

Karunaratne & Sons (Pvt) Ltd (Sri Lanka) *Tel:* (0114) 887 227; (0112) 855 520 *Fax:* (0114) 440 313 *E-mail:* info@karusons.com *Web Site:* www.karusons. com, pg 677

Karunia CV (Indonesia) *Tel:* (031) 5344120; (031) 5342551 *Web Site:* karuniasby.wordpress.com, pg 406

Karusapa Business Organization (Suksapanpanit) (Thailand) *Tel:* (02) 5383033 *Fax:* (02) 5393215 *E-mail:* suksapan99@hotmail.com; suksapanpress@ hotmail.com *Web Site:* www.suksapan.or.th, pg 715

Karya Anda CV (Indonesia) *Tel:* (031) 5322580; (031) 5344215 *Fax:* (031) 5310594, pg 406

Karydaki Publishing (Greece) *Tel:* 2102717140 *E-mail:* info@karydaki-publishing.gr *Web Site:* www. karydaki-publishing.gr, pg 356

Kasetsart University Main Library (Thailand) *Tel:* (02) 9428616 *Fax:* (02) 9405831; (02) 9405834 *E-mail:* lib_services@ku.ac.th *Web Site:* www.lib.ku. ac.th, pg 1638

KaSha Trans Middle East International Distribution Co Ltd (Jordan) *Tel:* (06) 5413270 *Fax:* (06) 5411336 *E-mail:* info@kasha.cc; marketing@kasha.cc *Web Site:* www.kashaonline.com, pg 1430

Kasmir Promet doo (Croatia) *Tel:* (01) 4553805; (01) 4553806; (01) 4553807 *Fax:* (01) 4553805; (01) 4553806; (01) 4553807 *E-mail:* kasmir@kasmir-promet.hr *Web Site:* www.kasmir-promet.hr, pg 120

Kassel University Press GmbH (Germany) *Tel:* (0561) 804-2159 *Fax:* (0561) 804-3429 *E-mail:* info@upress. uni-kassel.de *Web Site:* cms.uni-kassel.de/unicms, pg 269

Kastaniotis Editions SA (Greece) *Tel:* 2103301208 *Fax:* 2103822530 *E-mail:* info@kastaniotis.com *Web Site:* www.kastaniotis.com, pg 356

Kastell Verlag GmbH (Germany) *Tel:* (089) 33 21 75 *Fax:* (089) 340 11 78 *E-mail:* info@kastell-verlag.de, pg 269

Kastrapeli doo (Croatia) *Tel:* (01) 888 9798 *E-mail:* info@kastrapeli.hr *Web Site:* kastrapeli.hr, pg 120

Katai & Bolza Irodalmi Ugynokseg (Hungary) *Tel:* (01) 456-0313 *Fax:* (01) 215-4420 *Web Site:* www. kataibolza.hu, pg 1229

Leidykla Kataliku Pasaulio Leidiniai (Lithuania) *Tel:* (05) 212 2422 *Fax:* (05) 262 6462 *E-mail:* referente@katalikuleidiniai.lt; leidykla@ katalikuleidiniai.lt; redakcija@katalikuleidiniai.lt *Web Site:* www.katalikuleidiniai.lt, pg 501

Katalis / Bina Mitra Plaosan (Indonesia) *Tel:* (021) 7501477 *Fax:* (021) 7697869 *E-mail:* katalis@cbn. net.id, pg 406

S K Kataria & Sons (India) *Tel:* (011) 3243489; (011) 23269324 *E-mail:* katariabooks@yahoo.com; katson_sanjeev@yahoo.co.in; katariabook@gmail.com *Web Site:* www.skkatariaandsons.com, pg 388

Kate'Art Edition (Belgium) *Tel:* (02) 648 68 58 *E-mail:* info@kateart.com *Web Site:* www.kateart.com, pg 68

Iris Kater Verlag & Medien GmbH (Germany) *Tel:* (02162) 1 02 68 06 *Fax:* (02162) 1 02 68 07 *E-mail:* info@kater-medien.de *Web Site:* www. katercom.de/verlag/; www.katercom.de, pg 269

Katholieke Universiteit Leuven (Belgium) *Tel:* (016) 32 40 10 *E-mail:* centrale.bibliotheek@bib.kuleuven.be *Web Site:* bib.kuleuven.be, pg 1578

Verlag Katholisches Bibelwerk GmbH (Germany) *Tel:* (0711) 61920-0 *Fax:* (0711) 61920-44 *E-mail:* info@bibelwerk.de *Web Site:* www.bibelwerk. de, pg 270

Katoptro Publications (Greece) *Tel:* 2109244827; 2109244852 *Fax:* 2109244756 *E-mail:* info@katoptro. gr; vivliopolio@katoptro.gr *Web Site:* www.katoptro. gr, pg 356

Katz Editores SA (Argentina) *Tel:* (011) 4554 6754 *E-mail:* info@katzeditores.com *Web Site:* www. katzeditores.com, pg 9

Kauffmann SA (Greece) *Tel:* 2103255321; 2103222160; 2103827844 *E-mail:* kauffmann.stadiou@yahoo.gr; ord@otenet.gr (orders), pg 1420

Verlag Ernst Kaufmann GmbH (Germany) *Tel:* (07821) 9390-0 *Fax:* (07821) 9390-11; (07821) 9390-30 *E-mail:* info@kaufmann-verlag.de; bestellung@ kaufmann-verlag.de; lektorat@kaufmann-verlag.de *Web Site:* www.kaufmann-verlag.de, pg 270

Kavaler Publishers (Belarus) *Tel:* (017) 203 80 41 *Fax:* (017) 203 80 41 *E-mail:* info@kavaler.by; kavaler-design@yandex.ru *Web Site:* www.kavaler.by, pg 62

KAW (Kresowa Agencja Wydawnicza) (Poland) *Tel:* (85) 732 43 47 *Fax:* (85) 732 43 47 *E-mail:* kaw@kaw. com.pl *Web Site:* www.kaw.com.pl, pg 570

Kawade Shobo Shinsha Publishers (Japan) *Tel:* (03) 3404-1201; (03) 3478-3251; (03) 3404-8611 (editorial) *Fax:* (03) 3404-6386 *E-mail:* info@kawade.co.jp; rights@kawade.co.jp *Web Site:* www.kawade.co.jp, pg 480

Kawohl Verlag eK (Germany) *Tel:* (0281) 9 62 99-0 *Fax:* (0281) 9 62 99-1 00 *E-mail:* verlag@kawohl.de; info@kawohl.de *Web Site:* shop.kawohl.de, pg 270

Kaynak Publishing Group (Turkey) *Tel:* (0216) 522 1144 (ext 3481); (0216) 522 1144 (ext 3402) *E-mail:* kaynak@kaynakpublishing.com *Web Site:* www.kaynakpublishing.com, pg 721

Kazakhstan Academy of Sciences (Kazakhstan) *Tel:* (8727) 261-00-25; (8727) 272-55-61 *E-mail:* nanrk.mzh@mail.ru *Web Site:* nauka-nanrk.kz, pg 1607

Kazakhstan ISBN Agency (Kazakhstan) *Tel:* 727 3976204 *Fax:* 727 3976130 *E-mail:* bookkz@inbox.ru, pg 1380

Kazamashobo Co Ltd (Japan) *Tel:* (03) 3291-5729 *Fax:* (03) 3291-5757 *E-mail:* pub@kazamashobo.co.jp *Web Site:* www.kazamashobo.co.jp, pg 480

Izdatel'stvo Kazanskogo Universiteta (Russia) *Tel:* (843) 233-71-09 *Fax:* (843) 292-44-48 *E-mail:* public.mail@ kpfu.ru *Web Site:* kpfu.ru, pg 595

Ekdoseis Kazantzaki (Greece) *Tel:* 2103642829 *Fax:* 2103642830 *E-mail:* contact@ kazantzakispublications.org *Web Site:* www. kazantzakispublications.org, pg 356

Allama I I Kazi Central Library (Pakistan) *Tel:* (022) 9213193 *E-mail:* librarian@usindh.edu.pk *Web Site:* usindh.edu.pk/academics/central-library, pg 1620

Kazi Publications (Pakistan) *Tel:* (042) 37311359 *Fax:* (042) 37350805 *E-mail:* kazip@brain.net.pk *Web Site:* www.brain.net.pk/~kazip/, pg 559

KBV Verlags-und Medien - GmbH (Germany) *Tel:* (06593) 998960 *Fax:* (06593) 99896-20 *E-mail:* info@kbv-verlag.de *Web Site:* www.kbv-verlag.de, pg 270

Keats-Shelley Memorial Association (KSMA) (United Kingdom) *Fax:* (01926) 335133 *E-mail:* hello@keats-shelley.co.uk *Web Site:* www.keats-shelley.co.uk; www. keats-shelley.com, pg 1503

Kedros Publishers (Greece) *Tel:* 2103802007; 2103809712 *Fax:* 2103302655; 2103821981 (orders) *E-mail:* books@kedros.gr *Web Site:* www.kedros.gr, pg 356

Gregory Kefalas Publishing (Australia) *Tel:* (02) 9789 6049 *Fax:* (02) 9787 6181, pg 28

Kehl Verlag (Germany) *Tel:* (06246) 9 97 81 *Fax:* (06241) 9 97 82 *E-mail:* info@kehl-verlag.de; kontakt@kehl-verlag.de *Web Site:* www.kehl-verlag.de, pg 270

Kehrer Verlag (Germany) *Tel:* (06221) 649 20- 10 *Fax:* (06221) 649 20-20 *E-mail:* contact@ kehrerverlag.com *Web Site:* www.kehrerverlag.com, pg 270

Keil & Keil Literary Agency (Germany) *Tel:* (040) 36 02 124-00 *Fax:* (040) 36 02 124-99 *E-mail:* anfragen@ keil-keil.com *Web Site:* www.keil-keil.com, pg 1227

Kein & Aber AG (Switzerland) *Tel:* (044) 297-12-33 *Fax:* (044) 297-12-30 *E-mail:* info@keinundaber.ch; presse@keinundaber.ch *Web Site:* www.keinundaber. ch, pg 698

Keio University Library (Japan) *Tel:* (03) 5427-1654 *Fax:* (03) 5427-1665 *E-mail:* mita-webmaster@lib. keio.ac.jp *Web Site:* www.mita.lib.keio.ac.jp, pg 1606

Keip & von Delft GmbH (Germany) *Tel:* (030) 401 083 22 *Fax:* (030) 401 083 21 *E-mail:* info@keip.net; buc@keip.net *Web Site:* www.keip.net, pg 270

Edition Keiper (Austria) *Tel:* (0316) 269298 *Fax:* (0316) 269299 *E-mail:* office@editionkeiper.at; office@ textzentrum.at *Web Site:* www.editionkeiper.at, pg 51

Keisuisha Co Ltd (Japan) *Tel:* (082) 246-7909 *Fax:* (082) 246-7876 *E-mail:* info@keisui.co.jp *Web Site:* www. keisui.co.jp, pg 480

Kellermann Editore (Italy) *Tel:* (0438) 940903 *Fax:* (0438) 947653 *E-mail:* info@kellermanneditore. it; ufficiostampa@kellermanneditore.it *Web Site:* www. kellermanneditore.it, pg 449

KellnerVerlag (Germany) *Tel:* (0421) 77 8 66 *Fax:* (0421) 70 40 58 *E-mail:* info@kellnerverlag. de; buchservice@kellnerverlag.de *Web Site:* www. kellnerverlag.de, pg 270

Kells Publishing Co Ltd (Ireland) *Tel:* (046) 40117 *Fax:* (046) 41522, pg 412

The Frances Kelly Agency (United Kingdom) *Tel:* (020) 8549 7830 *Fax:* (020) 8547 0051, pg 1243

Martin Kelter Verlag GmbH & Co KG (Germany) *Tel:* (040) 68 28 95-0 *Fax:* (040) 68 28 95 50 *E-mail:* info@kelter.de *Web Site:* www.kelter.de, pg 270

Kemongsa Publishing Co Ltd (South Korea) *Tel:* (02) 531-5500 *Fax:* (02) 531-5550 *E-mail:* kmcc@ kemongsa.co.kr *Web Site:* www.kemongsa.co.kr, pg 622

Kemps Publishing Ltd (United Kingdom) *Tel:* (0121) 765 4144 *Fax:* (0121) 706 3491 *E-mail:* enquiries@ kempspublishing.co.uk; sales@kempspublishing.co.uk *Web Site:* www.kempspublishing.co.uk, pg 787

Kempton Park Library (South Africa) *Tel:* (011) 921 2173 *Fax:* (011) 975 0921, pg 1630

Kenilworth Press Ltd (United Kingdom) *Tel:* (01939) 261616 *Fax:* (01939) 261606 *E-mail:* admin@ quillerbooks.com *Web Site:* www.kenilworthpress.co. uk; www.countrybooksdirect.com, pg 787

Kenkyusha Co Ltd (Japan) *Tel:* (03) 3288-7777; (03) 3288-7811 *Fax:* (03) 3288-7799; (03) 3288-7813 *E-mail:* eigyo-bu@kenkyusha.co.jp; publishing@kenkyusha.co.jp; editors@kenkyusha.co.jp *Web Site:* www.kenkyusha.co.jp, pg 480

Albertine Kennedy Publishing (Ireland) *Web Site:* albertinekennedy.com, pg 412

Margaret Kennedy Agency (Australia) *E-mail:* info@ margaretkennedyagency.com *Web Site:* www. margaretkennedyagency.com, pg 1223

Kenway Publications Ltd (Kenya) *Tel:* (020) 4444700; (020) 2324762 *Fax:* (020) 4448753 *E-mail:* info@ eastafricanpublishers.com; sales@eastafricanpublishers. com; marketing@eastafricanpublishers.com; publishing@eastafricanpublishers.com *Web Site:* www. eastafricanpublishers.com, pg 493

Kenya Agricultural Documentation Centre (Kenya) *Tel:* (020) 2718870 *E-mail:* info@kilimo.go.ke *Web Site:* www.kilimo.go.ke, pg 1608

Kenya Association of Library & Information Professionals (KLA) (Kenya) *Tel:* (020) 733 732 799 *Web Site:* www.klas.or.ke, pg 1655

Kenya Energy & Environment Organisation (KENGO) (Kenya) *Tel:* (020) 748281 *Fax:* (020) 749382, pg 493

Kenya Literature Bureau (KLB) (Kenya) *Tel:* (020) 3541196; (020) 3541197 *Fax:* (020) 6001474 *E-mail:* info@klb.co.ke *Web Site:* www. kenyaliteraturebureau.com; www.klb.co.ke, pg 493, 1380

Kenya Medical Research Institute (KEMRI) (Kenya) *Tel:* (020) 722541; (020) 2713349 *E-mail:* webmaster@kemri.org *Web Site:* www.kemri. org, pg 494

Kenya National Archives & Documentation Service (Kenya) *Tel:* (020) 2228959 *Fax:* (020) 2228020 *E-mail:* info@archives.go.ke *Web Site:* www.archives. go.ke, pg 1608

Kenya National Library Service (KNLS) (Kenya) *Tel:* (020) 2725550; (020) 2158352; (020) 2158360; (020) 7786710 *Fax:* (020) 2721749 *E-mail:* knls@ knls.ac.ke *Web Site:* www.knls.ac.ke, pg 1608

Kenya Polytechnic University College Library (Kenya) *Tel:* (020) 343672; (020) 2251300 *Fax:* (020) 2219689 *E-mail:* inquiries@kenpoly.ac.ke *Web Site:* kpuc. tukenya.ac.ke, pg 1608

Kenya Publishers Association (Kenya) *Tel:* (020) 3752344; (0724) 255848 (cell) *Fax:* (020) 3754076 *E-mail:* info@kenyapublishers.org *Web Site:* www. kenyapublishers.org, pg 1380

Kenya School of Law Library (Kenya) *Tel:* (020) 890044; (020) 890094 *Fax:* (020) 891772 *E-mail:* library@ksl.ac.ke *Web Site:* www.ksl.ac.ke, pg 1608

Kenya Technical Trainers College Library (KTTC) (Kenya) *Tel:* (020) 7120212; (020) 7120213; (020) 7120214 *Fax:* (020) 7120088 *E-mail:* kttclibrary@ yahoo.com; library@kttc.ac.ke *Web Site:* www.kttc.ac. ke, pg 1608

The Jomo Kenyatta Foundation (Kenya) *Tel:* (020) 2329987; (020) 2330002; (0723) 286993 (cell); (020) 2330003 *Fax:* (020) 6531966 *E-mail:* info@jkf.co.ke *Web Site:* www.jkf.co.ke, pg 494

Kenyatta University Post Modern Library (Kenya) *Tel:* (020) 810901-16 (ext 57153) *Fax:* (020) 811575 *E-mail:* library@ku.ac.ke *Web Site:* library.ku.ac.ke, pg 1608

Kenyon-Deane (United Kingdom) *Tel:* (01684) 540154 *Web Site:* www.cressrelles.co.uk, pg 787

Kerber Verlag (Germany) *Tel:* (0521) 95 00 810 *Fax:* (0521) 95 00 888 *E-mail:* info@kerberverlag. com; marketing@kerberverlag.com *Web Site:* www. kerberverlag.com, pg 270

Alexander Kerbiser GmbH & Co KG (Austria) *Tel:* (03852) 2204-0 *Fax:* (03852) 2204-22 *E-mail:* office@kerbiser.at, pg 1404

Verlag Kerle (Germany) *Tel:* (0761) 2717-300 *Fax:* (0761) 2717-360 *E-mail:* kundenservice@herder. de *Web Site:* www.herder.de/verlag-kerle, pg 271

Verlag Kern (Germany) *Tel:* (03677) 4656390 *Fax:* (03677) 4656391 *E-mail:* kontakt@verlag-kern. de *Web Site:* www.verlag-kern.de; www.verlag-kern. de/zum-bestellshop (bookshop), pg 271

Editions Kero (France) *Tel:* 01 53 01 01 75 *E-mail:* contact@editionskero.com; editorial@ editionskero.com *Web Site:* www.editionskero.com, pg 179

Antonia Kerrigan Literary Agency (Spain) *Tel:* 932093820 *Fax:* 934144328 *E-mail:* antonia@ antoniakerrigan.com *Web Site:* www.antoniakerrigan. com, pg 1235

Kesaint Blanc Publishng (Indonesia) *Tel:* (021) 4290 6862; (021) 4288 6726 *Fax:* (021) 4288 6725 *E-mail:* editorial@kesaintblanc.co.id; info@ kesaintblanc.co.id; marketing@kesaintblanc.co.id *Web Site:* www.kesaintblanc.co.id, pg 406

Nurcihan Kesim Literary Agency Inc (Turkey) *Tel:* (0216) 511 5686 *Fax:* (0212) 526 9128, pg 1238

Kessler Druck + Medien GmbH & Co KG (Germany) *Tel:* (0908) 2349-619-0 *Fax:* (0908) 2349-619-19 *E-mail:* info@kesslerdruck.de *Web Site:* kesslerdruck. de, pg 1256

Simona Kessler International Copyright Agency Ltd (Romania) *Tel:* (021) 316 48 06 *Fax:* (021) 316 47 94, pg 1233

Keswick Books & Gifts Ltd (Kenya) *Tel:* (020) 2226047; (020) 2147762 *E-mail:* info@keswickbook. com; keswick@swiftkenya.com *Web Site:* www. keswickbooks.com, pg 1430

Keter Books (Israel) *Tel:* (02) 6557822 *Fax:* (02) 6510339 *E-mail:* info@keter-books.co.il *Web Site:* www.keter-books.co.il, pg 419

Ketteler Verlag GmbH (Germany) *Tel:* (09972) 94 14-51 *Fax:* (09972) 94 14-55 *E-mail:* kontakt@ketteler-verlag.de *Web Site:* www.ketteler-verlag.de, pg 271

Druckverlag Kettler GmbH (Germany) *Tel:* (02383) 91013-0 *Fax:* (02383) 91013-40 *E-mail:* info@ druckverlag-kettler.de *Web Site:* www.druckverlag-kettler.com, pg 1275, 1322

Thomas Kettler Verlag (Germany) *Tel:* (040) 39 10 99 10 *Fax:* (040) 390 68 20 *E-mail:* mail@thomas-kettler-verlag.de *Web Site:* www.thomas-kettler-verlag. de, pg 271

Verlag Kettler (Germany) *Tel:* (0231) 223 999-08; (0231) 223 999-09 *Fax:* (0231) 223 998-69 *E-mail:* info@ verlag-kettler.de *Web Site:* www.verlag-kettler.de, pg 271

Editions Ketty & Alexandre (Switzerland) *Tel:* (021) 9051111, pg 698

Die Keure NV (Belgium) *Tel:* (050) 47 12 72 *Fax:* (050) 34 37 68 *E-mail:* info@diekeure.be *Web Site:* www. diekeure.be, pg 68

Kew Publishing (United Kingdom) *Tel:* (020) 8332 5715 *Fax:* (020) 8332 5646 *E-mail:* publishing@kew.org; info@kew.org; onlineshop@kew.org *Web Site:* www. kew.org; shop.kew.org/kewbooksonline, pg 787

Keytec Typesetting Ltd (United Kingdom) *Tel:* (01308) 427580 *E-mail:* info@keytectype.co.uk *Web Site:* www.keytectype.co.uk, pg 1287

Khanna Publishers (India) *Tel:* (011) 2912380; (011) 7224179 *E-mail:* khannapublishers@yahoo.in *Web Site:* www.khannapublishers.in, pg 388

Khartoum Modern Bookshop (Sudan) *Tel:* (01) 83774425, pg 1452

Khoudia (Senegal) *Tel:* 33 821 10 23, pg 600

Izdatelstvo Khudozhestvennaya Literatura (Russia) *Tel:* (499) 261 88 65; (499) 261 88 63 *Fax:* (499) 261 83 00 *E-mail:* realisihl@mail.ru; hudizdat@mail.ru; hudizdat@yandex.ru *Web Site:* hudlit.com, pg 595

Ki Agency (United Kingdom) *Tel:* (020) 3214 8287 *Web Site:* www.ki-agency.co.uk, pg 1243

Kibea Publishing Co (Bulgaria) *Tel:* (02) 980 50 63; (02) 980 01 69 *Fax:* (02) 980 46 98 *E-mail:* office@kibea. net *Web Site:* www.kibea.net, pg 95

Kiefer Buch- und Kunstauktionen (Germany) *Tel:* (07231) 9232-0 *Fax:* (07231) 9232-16 *E-mail:* info@kiefer.de *Web Site:* www.kiefer.de, pg 1416

Kiehl (Germany) *Tel:* (02323) 141-700 *Fax:* (02323) 141-123 *E-mail:* service@kiehl.de *Web Site:* www. kiehl.de, pg 271

Kiener Verlag (Germany) *Tel:* (089) 34 12 62 *Fax:* (089) 330 299 13 *E-mail:* info@kiener-verlag.de *Web Site:* www.kiener-verlag.de, pg 271

Verlag Kiepenheuer & Witsch GmbH & Co KG (Germany) *Tel:* (0221) 376 85-0 *Fax:* (0221) 376 85 11 *E-mail:* verlag@kiwi-verlag.de *Web Site:* www. kiwi-verlag.de, pg 271

Editorial Kier (Argentina) *Tel:* (011) 4811-0507 *Fax:* (011) 4811-3395 *E-mail:* ventadirecta@kier.com. ar; info@kier.com.ar *Web Site:* www.kier.com.ar, pg 9

Libreria Kier (Argentina) *Tel:* (011) 4811-0507; (011) 4811-8243 *E-mail:* ventadirecta@kier.com.ar *Web Site:* www.kier.com.ar, pg 1401

Kierdorf Verlag (Germany) *Tel:* (0221) 55405445 *Fax:* (0221) 5540545 *E-mail:* kierdorf-verlag@t-online.de; feilen@westernhorse.de (advertising sales) *Web Site:* www.western-horse.de, pg 271

Kijarat Kiado (Hungary) *Tel:* (01) 388-6312 *Fax:* (01) 388-6312 *E-mail:* kijarat@enternet.hu, pg 369

Kilda Verlag (Germany) *Tel:* (02571) 52115 *Fax:* (02571) 953269 *E-mail:* info@kildaverlag.de *Web Site:* www.kildaverlag.de; www.poelking.com, pg 271

KILLROY media (Germany) *Tel:* (07141) 260019 *Fax:* (07141) 640050 *E-mail:* jo.schoenauer@t-online. de *Web Site:* www.killroy-media.de, pg 271

Duran Kim Agency (South Korea) *Tel:* (02) 583-5724; (02) 583-5725 *Fax:* (02) 584-5724 *E-mail:* duran@ durankim.com *Web Site:* www.durankim.com, pg 1234

Kim Hup Lee Printing Co Pte Ltd (Singapore) *Tel:* 6298 6911 *Fax:* 6298 6415 *Web Site:* www.khlprint.com.sg, pg 1261

Kima Global Publishers Ltd (South Africa) *Tel:* (021) 782 4463 *Fax:* (021) 782 4982 *Web Site:* www. kimabooks.com, pg 615

Casa Editrice Kimerik (Italy) *Tel:* (0941) 21503 *Fax:* (0941) 243561 *E-mail:* redazione@kimerik.it *Web Site:* www.kimerik.it, pg 449

Kin-No-Hoshi Sha Co Ltd (Japan) *Tel:* (03) 3861-1861 *Fax:* (03) 3861-1507 *E-mail:* usagi1@kinnohoshi.co.jp *Web Site:* www.kinnohoshi.co.jp, pg 480

Kindai Kagaku Sha Co Ltd (Japan) *Tel:* (03) 3260-6161 *Fax:* (03) 3260-6059 *E-mail:* web-info@kindaikagaku. co.jp *Web Site:* www.kindaikagaku.co.jp, pg 480

Kinderbuchverlag (Germany) *Tel:* (08806) 550 *Fax:* (08806) 923029 *E-mail:* info@kinderbuchverlag. de *Web Site:* www.kinderbuchverlag.de, pg 272

Kindermann Verlag Berlin (Germany) *Tel:* (030) 89 757 111 *Fax:* (030) 89 753 653 *Web Site:* kindermannverlag.de, pg 272

Kindler Verlag AG GmbH (Germany) *Tel:* (040) 72 72-0 *Fax:* (040) 72 72-319 *E-mail:* info@rowohlt.de *Web Site:* www.rowohlt.de/verlag/kindler, pg 272

Editorial Kinesis (Colombia) *Tel:* (06) 7401584; (06) 7409155 *Fax:* (06) 7401584 *E-mail:* atencion@kinesis. com.co *Web Site:* kinesis.com.co, pg 114

King Abdulaziz Public Library (Saudi Arabia) *Tel:* (011) 4911300 *Fax:* (011) 4911949 *Web Site:* www.kapl.org. sa, pg 1628

King Abdulaziz University Central Library (Saudi Arabia) *Fax:* (012) 6400169 *E-mail:* library@kau.edu. sa *Web Site:* library.kau.edu.sa, pg 1628

King Baudouin Foundation (Belgium) *Tel:* (02) 511 18 40; (070) 233 065 *Fax:* (02) 511 52 21 *E-mail:* proj@ kbs-frb.be; info@kbs-frb.be *Web Site:* www.kbs-frb.be, pg 68

King Fahad National Library (Saudi Arabia) *Tel:* (011) 4186111 *Fax:* (011) 4186222 *E-mail:* portal@kfnl.gov. sa *Web Site:* www.kfnl.gov.sa, pg 1628

King Faisal University Library (Saudi Arabia) *Tel:* (03) 5895938 *Fax:* (03) 5899306 *E-mail:* library@kfu.edu. sa *Web Site:* www.kfu.edu.sa/en/deans/library, pg 1628

King Printing (United States) *Tel:* 978-458-2345 *Fax:* 978-458-1441 *E-mail:* inquiries@kingprinting. com *Web Site:* www.kingprinting.com; www.adibooks. com, pg 1265

King Saud University (Saudi Arabia) *Tel:* (011) 4676176 *Fax:* (011) 4676162 *E-mail:* acksupress@ksu.edu.sa *Web Site:* ksupress.ksu.edu.sa, pg 599

King Saud University Library (Saudi Arabia) *Tel:* (011) 4676148 *Fax:* (011) 4676162 *E-mail:* library@ksu. edu.sa *Web Site:* library.ksu.edu.sa, pg 1628

Kingfisher (United Kingdom) *Tel:* (020) 7014 6000 *Fax:* (020) 7014 6001 *E-mail:* childrensbooks@ macmillan.co.uk; webqueries@macmillan.com *Web Site:* www.panmacmillan.com/imprints/kingfisher, pg 787

The King's Fund (United Kingdom) *Tel:* (020) 7307 2400 *E-mail:* enquiry@kingsfund.org.uk *Web Site:* www.kingsfund.org.uk, pg 787

Kings Road Publishing (United Kingdom) *Tel:* (020) 3770 8888 *E-mail:* info@kingsroadpublishing.co.uk *Web Site:* www.kingsroadpublishing.co.uk, pg 787

Kingsclear Books (Australia) *Tel:* (02) 9557 4367 *Fax:* (02) 9557 2337 *E-mail:* kingsclearbooks@gmail. com *Web Site:* www.kingsclearbooks.com.au, pg 28

Kingston Bookshop Ltd (Jamaica) *Tel:* (876) 922-7016; (876) 922 7312 *Fax:* (876) 922-0127 *E-mail:* info@kingstonbookshop.com *Web Site:* www. kingstonbookshopjm.com, pg 1428

Kingston University Press (United Kingdom) *Tel:* (020) 8417 9000 *E-mail:* fass-kup@kingston.ac.uk *Web Site:* fass.kingston.ac.uk/kup, pg 787

Kingstons Ltd (Zimbabwe) *Tel:* (04) 750547; (04) 750548; (04) 750549 *Fax:* (04) 775533; (04) 775535 *Web Site:* www.kingstons.co.zw, pg 1462

Chris Kington Publishing (United Kingdom) *Tel:* (0845) 450 6404 *Fax:* (0845) 450 6410 *E-mail:* customer. services@optimus-education.com *Web Site:* www. teachingexpertise.com; www.optimus-education.com, pg 787

Kinokuniya Co Ltd (Publishing Dept) (Japan) *Tel:* (03) 6910-0508 *Fax:* (03) 6420-1354 *E-mail:* publish@kinokuniya.co.jp; info@kinokuniya. co.jp *Web Site:* www.kinokuniya.co.jp, pg 480

Verlag Kremayr & Scheriau KG (Austria) *Tel:* (01) 713 87 70-0 *Fax:* (01) 713 87 70-20 *E-mail:* office@kremayr-scheriau.at *Web Site:* www.kremayr-scheriau.at, pg 52

Hubert Krenn Verlag GmbH (Austria) *Tel:* (01) 585 34 72 *Fax:* (01) 585 04 83 *E-mail:* hwk@buchagentur.at *Web Site:* www.hubertkrenn.at, pg 52

Verlag Hubert Kretschmer (Germany) *Tel:* (089) 12345 30; (0172) 85 125 88 (cell) *Fax:* (089) 123 86 38 *E-mail:* mail@verlag-hubert-kretschmer.de; mail@archive-artistsbooks.de *Web Site:* www.verlag-hubert-kretschmer.de; www.artistbooks.de, pg 278

Antiquariat Kretzer (Germany) *Tel:* (06422) 898119 *Fax:* (06422) 8997034 *E-mail:* antiquariat.kretzer@gmx.de *Web Site:* www.antiquariat-kretzer.de, pg 1416

Verlag Kreuz GmbH (Germany) *Tel:* (0761) 2717-0 *Fax:* (0761) 2717-520 *E-mail:* kundenservice@herder.de (customer service) *Web Site:* www.verlag-kreuz.de, pg 278

Svet Kridel (Czech Republic) *Tel:* 604 109 456 *E-mail:* redakce@svetkridel.cz *Web Site:* www.svetkridel.cz, pg 129

Kriebel Verlag GmbH (Germany) *Tel:* (08033) 3 08 25 55; (0172) 8 50 91 40 (cell) *Fax:* (08033) 3 08 25 56 *E-mail:* info@kriebelverlag.de *Web Site:* www.kriebel-sat.de; www.kriebelverlag.de, pg 278

Kris Literary Agency (Nigeria) *Tel:* (0806) 7628017, pg 1233

Krishna Prakashan Media (P) Ltd (India) *Tel:* (0121) 4026111; (0121) 4026112; (0121) 2644766; (0121) 2642946 *Fax:* (0121) 2645855 *E-mail:* support@krishnaprakashan.com *Web Site:* www.krishnaprakashan.com, pg 388

K Krishnamurthy (India) *E-mail:* service@kkbooks.com; marketing@kkbooks.com *Web Site:* www.kkbooks.com, pg 1423

Bookshop Krisostomus (Estonia) *Tel:* 7440010 *Fax:* 7440011 *E-mail:* kriso@kriso.ee *Web Site:* www.kriso.ee, pg 1413

Kristiansand Folkebibliotek (Norway) *Tel:* 38 12 49 10 *E-mail:* post.folkebibliotek@kristiansand.kommune.no *Web Site:* krsbib.no, pg 1620

Kritiki Publishing SA (Greece) *Tel:* 2108211811; 2106842110 (sales); 2108212266 (marketing) *Fax:* 2106818561 (sales) *E-mail:* biblia@kritiki.gr; sales@kritiki.gr; marketing@kritiki.gr *Web Site:* kritiki.gr, pg 356

Kritiki Publishing SA (Greece) *Tel:* 2108211811 *E-mail:* biblia@kritiki.gr *Web Site:* kritiki.gr, pg 1420

Alfred Kroener Verlag GmbH & Co KG (Germany) *Tel:* (0711) 615 53 6-3 *Fax:* (0711) 615 53 6-46 *E-mail:* kontakt@kroener-verlag.de *Web Site:* www.kroener-verlag.de, pg 278

KRP Yayincilik Matbaacilik Ltd (Turkey) *Tel:* (0312) 213 44 04 *Fax:* (0312) 213 44 04 *E-mail:* info@krpyayincilik.com *Web Site:* krpcocuk.com, pg 722

Krscanska sadasnjost doo (Croatia) *Tel:* (01) 63 49 010; (01) 63 49 050 (editorial) *Fax:* (01) 46 66 815; (01) 48 28 227 (editorial) *E-mail:* uprava@ks.hr; ks@zg.t-com.hr *Web Site:* www.ks.hr, pg 120

Zalozba Krtina (Slovenia) *Tel:* (01) 251 5585 *Fax:* (01) 620 8713 *E-mail:* urednistvo@zalozbakrtina.si *Web Site:* www.zalozbakrtina.si, pg 610

Krueger Verlag (Germany) *Tel:* (069) 6062-0 *Fax:* (069) 6062-319; (069) 6062-214 *Web Site:* www.fischerverlage.de/page/krueger, pg 278

Verlag Krug & Schadenberg (Germany) *Tel:* (030) 61 62 57 52 *Fax:* (030) 61 62 57 51 *E-mail:* info@krugschadenberg.de *Web Site:* www.krugschadenberg.de, pg 278

Wydawnictwo Krytyka Polityczna (Poland) *Tel:* (22) 505 66 90 *Fax:* (22) 505 66 84 *E-mail:* editorial@krytykapolityczna.pl *Web Site:* www.krytykapolityczna.pl, pg 570

Shanghai KS Printing Co Ltd (China) *Tel:* (021) 51718508 (ext 807) *E-mail:* sales@ksprinting.net *Web Site:* www.ksprinting.net, pg 1319

Spoldzielnia Wydawniczo-Handlowa 'Ksiazka i Wiedza' (Poland) *Tel:* (22) 827-54-01; (22) 827-94-16; (22) 827-94-14 (sales) *Fax:* (22) 827-94-16; (22) 827-94-14 (sales), pg 570

Wydawnictwo Ksiaznica Sp z oo (Poland) *Tel:* (32) 757 2216 *Fax:* (32) 757 2217, pg 570

Kubbealti Akademisi Kultur ve Sasat Vakfi (Turkey) *Tel:* (0212) 516 23 56; (0212) 518 92 09 *Fax:* (0212) 638 02 72 *E-mail:* info@kubbealti.org.tr *Web Site:* www.kubbealti.org.tr, pg 722

Kube Publishing Ltd (United Kingdom) *Tel:* (01530) 249 230 *Fax:* (01530) 249 656 *E-mail:* info@kubepublishing.com *Web Site:* www.kubepublishing.com; www.islamic-foundation.com, pg 788

Kuebler Verlag GmbH (Germany) *Tel:* (06206) 155694 *Fax:* (06206) 155695 *E-mail:* info@kueblerverlag.de *Web Site:* www.kueblerverlag.de, pg 278

Kugler Publications (Netherlands) *Tel:* (020) 68 45 700 *Fax:* (020) 68 47 788 *E-mail:* info@kuglerpublications.com *Web Site:* www.kuglerpublications.com, pg 536

Verlag Ernst Kuhn (VEK) (Germany) *Fax:* (030) 44 24 732 *Web Site:* www.vek.de, pg 278

Kuiseb-Verlag (Namibia) *Tel:* (061) 225372 *Fax:* (061) 226846 *E-mail:* nwg@iway.na *Web Site:* www.kuiseb-verlag.com, pg 527

Wydawnictwo KUL (Poland) *Tel:* (81) 740 93 45 *Fax:* (81) 740 93 51 *E-mail:* wydawnictwo@kul.lublin.pl *Web Site:* www.kul.pl/1114.html; wydawnictwokul.lublin.pl/sklep (online bookstore), pg 570

Edition Kulapatiim World Teacher Trust eV (Germany) *Tel:* (02196) 971811 *Fax:* (02196) 91166 *E-mail:* wtt@kulapati.de *Web Site:* www.kulapati.de, pg 278

Kulleraugen-Verlag (Germany) *Tel:* (05123) 4330 *Fax:* (05123) 2015 *E-mail:* kulleraugen-verlag@gmx.de *Web Site:* www.kulleraugen-verlag.de, pg 278

Kultura (Serbia) *Tel:* (021) 780144; (021) 780156 *Fax:* (021) 780291, pg 601

Kultura Knizarnici (Macedonia) *Tel:* (02) 3296-763 *E-mail:* ipkultura@kultura.com.mk; info@kultura.com.mk; knizarnica.kultura@gmail.com *Web Site:* www.kultura.com.mk, pg 1431

Kulturbuch-Verlag GmbH (KBV) (Germany) *Tel:* (030) 661 84 84 *Fax:* (030) 661 78 28 *E-mail:* kbvinfo@kulturbuch-verlag.de *Web Site:* www.kulturbuch-verlag.de, pg 278

Kulturstiftung der deutschen Vertriebenen (Germany) *Tel:* (0228) 91512-0 *Fax:* (0228) 91512-29 *E-mail:* kulturstiftung@t-online.de *Web Site:* kulturportal-west-ost.eu/kulturstiftung, pg 278

Kum-Kang Printing Co Ltd (South Korea) *Tel:* (031) 943 0082 *Fax:* (031) 943 0046 *E-mail:* trade@kkprint.co.kr *Web Site:* www.kkprint.co.kr, pg 1284, 1334

Kumon Publishing Co Ltd (Japan) *Tel:* (03) 6836-0307 *Fax:* (03) 5421-1615 *E-mail:* info@kumonshuppan.com; international@kumonshuppan.com *Web Site:* www.kumonshuppan.com, pg 481

Kumsung Publishing Co Ltd (South Korea) *Tel:* (080) 969-1000 (customer service); (02) 2077-8145 (purchase inquiry) *E-mail:* webmaster@kumsung.co.kr *Web Site:* www.kumsung.co.kr, pg 623

Kungl IngenjorsVetenskapsAkademien (IVA) (Sweden) *Tel:* (08) 791 29 00 *Fax:* (08) 611 56 23 *E-mail:* info@iva.se *Web Site:* www.iva.se, pg 683

Kungl Tekniska Hoegskolan Biblioteket (Sweden) *Tel:* (08) 790 70 88 *E-mail:* ask-kthb@kth.se *Web Site:* www.kth.se/kthb, pg 1635

Kungl Vitterhets Historie och Antikvitets Akademien (Sweden) *Tel:* (08) 440 42 80 *Fax:* (08) 440 42 90 *E-mail:* kansli@vitterhetsakad.se *Web Site:* www.vitterhetsakad.se, pg 1500

Kungliga biblioteket-Sveriges nationalbibliotek (Sweden) *Tel:* (010) 709 30 70 *E-mail:* info@kb.se *Web Site:* www.kb.se; www.facebook.com/Foreningenbiblis?ref=nf, pg 1635

Kunlun Press (China) *Tel:* (010) 66730373 *E-mail:* conan9586@163.com *Web Site:* tp.chinamil.com.cn, pg 107

Kunnskapsforlaget (Norway) *Tel:* 22 02 22 00 *Fax:* 22 02 22 05 *E-mail:* forhandlersalg@kunnskapsforlaget.no *Web Site:* www.kunnskapsforlaget.no, pg 555

Verlag der Kunst Dresden Ingwert Paulsen Jr eK (Germany) *Tel:* (04841) 8352-0 *Fax:* (04841) 8352-10 *E-mail:* info@verlagsgruppe.de *Web Site:* www.verlagsgruppe.de, pg 278

Kirjastus Kunst (Estonia) *Tel:* 6411764 (editorial); 6411766 (sales) *E-mail:* tellimused@kirjastuskunst.ee *Web Site:* www.kirjastuskunst.ee, pg 145

Kunstanstifter Verlag e Kfr (Germany) *Tel:* (0621) 832 61 54 *Fax:* (0621) 832 61 53 *E-mail:* info@kunstanstifter.de *Web Site:* www.kunstanstifter.de, pg 279

Verlag Antje Kunstmann GmbH (Germany) *Tel:* (089) 12 11 93 0 *Fax:* (089) 12 11 93 20 *E-mail:* info@kunstmann.de *Web Site:* www.kunstmann.de, pg 279

Kunstmuseum Liechtenstein (Liechtenstein) *Tel:* 235 03 00; 232 63 00 *Fax:* 235 03 29 *E-mail:* mail@kunstmuseum.li *Web Site:* www.kunstmuseum.li, pg 500

Kunth Verlag GmbH & Co KG (Germany) *Tel:* (089) 45 80 20-0 *Fax:* (089) 45 80 20-21 *E-mail:* info@kunth-verlag.de *Web Site:* www.kunth-verlag.de, pg 279

Edition Kunzelmann GmbH (Switzerland) *Tel:* (044) 710 36 81 *Fax:* (044) 710 38 17 *E-mail:* edition@kunzelmann.ch *Web Site:* www.kunzelmann.ch, pg 699

Kuperard (United Kingdom) *Tel:* (020) 8446 2440 *Fax:* (020) 8446 2441 *E-mail:* office@kuperard.co.uk *Web Site:* www.kuperard.co.uk, pg 788

Kuperard Publishers & Distributors (United Kingdom) *Tel:* (020) 8446 2440 *Fax:* (020) 8446 2441 *E-mail:* office@kuperard.co.uk *Web Site:* www.kuperard.co.uk, pg 1458

Kurnia Esa CV (Indonesia) *Tel:* (021) 3104948, pg 406

Kurtulus & Friends GmbH (Germany) *Tel:* (0211) 26 10 26 00; (0177) 16 33 416 (cell) *E-mail:* info@kurtulus-friends.de *Web Site:* www.kurtulus-friends.de, pg 279

Kustannusosakeyhtio Tammi (Finland) *Tel:* (010) 5060 300 *Fax:* (010) 5060 399 *Web Site:* www.tammi.fi, pg 149

Kuva ja Sana Oy (Finland) *Tel:* (09) 85674999 *Fax:* (09) 85674950 *E-mail:* tilaukset@kuvajasana.fi *Web Site:* www.kuvajasana.fi, pg 149

The Kuwait Book Shop Co Ltd (Kuwait) *Tel:* 22424266 *E-mail:* kbs@ncc.moc.kw *Web Site:* kuwait-bookshop-co-ltd-.kuwaitbd.com, pg 1431

Kuwait Publishing House Co (Kuwait) *Tel:* 22449686; 22455171 *Fax:* 22436956, pg 495

Kuwait University Libraries (Kuwait) *Tel:* 24834165; 24813182 *Fax:* 24842479; 24816595 *E-mail:* libraries.dept@ku.edu.kw *Web Site:* kuweb.ku.edu.kw/kulib/index.htm, pg 1608

KV&H Verlag GmbH (Germany) *Tel:* (089) 693 378-0 *Fax:* (089) 693 378-139 *E-mail:* info@kvh-verlag.de; medienbuero@kvh-verlag.de *Web Site:* www.kvh-verlag.de, pg 279

Kerstin Kvint Literary & Co-Production Agency (Sweden) *Tel:* (08) 107014 *Fax:* (08) 107606 *E-mail:* k.kvint@telia.com, pg 1237

KVM - Der Medizinverlag (Germany) *Tel:* (030) 761 806 16 *Fax:* (030) 761 806 92 *E-mail:* info@kvm-verlag.de *Web Site:* www.kvm-verlag.de, pg 279

Lammers-Koll-Verlag (Germany) *Tel:* (07042) 815 2405 *Fax:* (07042) 815 2404 *E-mail:* verlag@lammers-koll-verlag.de *Web Site:* www.lammers-koll-verlag.de; www.yogabuecher.de, pg 280

Lampara Publishing House Inc (Philippines) *Tel:* (02) 367-6222 *Fax:* (02) 367-6222 *E-mail:* inquiry@lamparabooks.com.ph *Web Site:* www.lamparabooks.com.ph, pg 565

Lamserv SRL (Romania) *Tel:* (0372) 983928 *Fax:* (021) 2250616 *E-mail:* office@lamserv.ro *Web Site:* www.lamserv.ro, pg 1446

Lamuv Verlag GmbH (Germany) *Tel:* (0551) 44024 *Fax:* (0551) 41392 *E-mail:* bestsellung@gva-verlage.de *Web Site:* www.lamuv.de, pg 280

Editions Lamy (France) *Tel:* 08 25 08 08 00 *Fax:* 01 76 73 48 09 *E-mail:* contact@wkf.fr *Web Site:* www.wkf.fr, pg 179

Lancashire Authors' Association (United Kingdom) *E-mail:* laaenqs@gmail.com *Web Site:* lancashireauthorsassociation.wordpress.com, pg 1504

Landbuch-Verlagsgesellschaft mbH (Germany) *Tel:* (0511) 270460 *Fax:* (0511) 27046150, pg 280

Landesbibliothek Mecklenburg-Vorpommern Guenther Uecker (Germany) *Tel:* (0385) 588 792-20 *Fax:* (0385) 588 792-24 *E-mail:* lb@lbmv.de *Web Site:* www.kulturwerte-mv.de/Landesbibliothek, pg 1593

Landsbokasafn Islands-Haskolabokasafn (Iceland) *Tel:* 525 5600 *Fax:* 525 5615 *E-mail:* upplys@landsbokasafn.is *Web Site:* landsbokasafn.is, pg 1600

Landt Verlag (Germany) *Tel:* (030) 23 00 42 51 *Fax:* (030) 23 00 42 52 *E-mail:* landt@landtverlag.de *Web Site:* www.landtverlag.de, pg 280

Landwehr & Cie KG (Germany) *Tel:* (030) 55 77 90-0 *Fax:* (030) 55 77 90-100 *E-mail:* info@landwehr-cie.de *Web Site:* www.landwehr-cie.de, pg 1227

Landwirtschaftsverlag GmbH (Germany) *Tel:* (0251) 801-0 *Fax:* (0251) 801204 *E-mail:* buch@lv.de *Web Site:* www.lv.de, pg 280

Lanfranchi Editore (Italy) *Tel:* (02) 86465210 *Fax:* (02) 8056083 *E-mail:* info@lanfranchieditore.com *Web Site:* www.lanfranchieditore.com, pg 450

Peter Lang AG (Switzerland) *Tel:* (032) 376 17 17 *Fax:* (032) 376 17 27 *E-mail:* info@peterlang.com *Web Site:* www.peterlang.com, pg 699

Peter Lang GmbH Internationaler Verlag der Wissenschaften (Germany) *Tel:* (069) 78 07 05 0 *Fax:* (069) 78 07 05 50 *E-mail:* zentrale.frankfurt@peterlang.com *Web Site:* www.peterlang.de, pg 280

Lang Syne Publishers Ltd (United Kingdom) *Tel:* (0131) 344 0414 *Fax:* (0845) 0756085 *E-mail:* info@lang-syne.co.uk *Web Site:* www.langsyneshop.co.uk, pg 789

Langenbuch & Weiss Literaturagentur GbR (Germany) *Tel:* (040) 33382044 *E-mail:* mail@langenbuch-weiss.de *Web Site:* www.langenbuch-weiss.de, pg 1227

Buchverlage LangenMueller Herbig nymphenburger terra magica (Germany) *Tel:* (089) 29088-0 *Fax:* (089) 29088-144 *E-mail:* info@herbig.net *Web Site:* www.herbig.net, pg 280

Langenscheidt Fachverlag (Germany) *Tel:* (089) 36096-0; (089) 36096-333 (orders) *Fax:* (089) 36096-222; (089) 36096-258 (orders) *E-mail:* kundenservice@langenscheidt.de; presse@langenscheidt.de *Web Site:* www.langenscheidt.de, pg 280

Langenscheidt Hachette Verlag (Germany) *Tel:* (089) 360960; (089) 36096-333 (orders) *Fax:* (089) 36096-222; (089) 36096-258 (orders) *E-mail:* kundenservice@langenscheidt.de; presse@langenscheidt.de *Web Site:* www.langenscheidt.de, pg 281

Langenscheidt KG (Germany) *Tel:* (089) 36096-0; (089) 36096-333 (orders) *Fax:* (089) 36096-222; (089) 36096-258 (orders) *E-mail:* kundenservice@langenscheidt.de; presse@langenscheidt.de *Web Site:* www.langenscheidt.de, pg 281

Langenscheidt Verlagsgruppe (Germany) *Tel:* (089) 36096-0; (089) 36096-333 (orders) *Fax:* (089) 36096-222; (089) 36096-258 (orders) *E-mail:* kundenservice@langenscheidt.de; presse@langenscheidt.de *Web Site:* www.langenscheidt.de, pg 281

Langers International Pvt Ltd (India) *Tel:* (011) 23260253; (011) 42540888 *E-mail:* info@langers.in *Web Site:* www.langers.in, pg 1423

Karl Robert Langewiesche Nachfolger Hans Koester Verlagsbuchhandlung KG (Germany) *Tel:* (06174) 7333 *Fax:* (06174) 933-039 *E-mail:* info@langewiesche-verlag.de *Web Site:* www.langewiesche-verlag.de, pg 281

Language Book Centre (Australia) *Tel:* (02) 9267 1397 *Toll Free Tel:* 1800 802 432 (outside Sydney & within Australia) *Fax:* (02) 9264 8993 *E-mail:* language@abbeys.com.au *Web Site:* www.languagebooks.com.au, pg 1403

Language Publishing House (China) *Tel:* (010) 65283384 *E-mail:* fxzx2@sina.com; ywcbsywp@163.com, pg 107

Drukkerij Lannoo NV (Belgium) *Tel:* (051) 42 42 11; (051) 42 43 08 *Fax:* (051) 40 70 70 *E-mail:* info@lannooprint.be; lannoo@lannooprint.be *Web Site:* www.lannoo-print.be, pg 1255, 1273

Drukkerij Lannoo NV (Belgium) *Tel:* (051) 42 42 11 *Fax:* (051) 40 70 70 *E-mail:* info@lannooprint.be; lannoo@lannooprint.be *Web Site:* www.lannoo-print.be, pg 1317

Uitgeverij Lannoo NV (Belgium) *Tel:* (051) 42 42 11 *Fax:* (051) 40 11 52 *E-mail:* lannoo@lannoo.be *Web Site:* www.lannoo.com, pg 68

Editions Fernand Lanore (France) *Tel:* 01 43 25 66 61 *Fax:* 01 43 29 69 81 *E-mail:* contact@editionslanore.com *Web Site:* www.fernand-lanore.com, pg 179

Lansdowne Publishing Pty Ltd (Australia) *Tel:* (04) 1745 4615 *Fax:* (02) 9436 2974 *E-mail:* info@lansdownepublishing.com.au *Web Site:* www.lansdownepublishing.com.au, pg 29

Lansman Editeur (Belgium) *Tel:* (064) 23 78 40 *Fax:* (064) 23 78 49 *E-mail:* info.lansman@gmail.com *Web Site:* www.lansman.org, pg 69

Lantana Publishing (United Kingdom) *E-mail:* info@lantanapublishing.com; submissions@lantanapublishing.com; media@lantanapublishing.com *Web Site:* www.lantanapublishing.com, pg 789

Lanzhou University Press (China) *Tel:* (0931) 8912613; (0931) 8617156 *E-mail:* press@lzu.edu.cn *Web Site:* www.onbook.com.cn, pg 107

Tipografija Lapa (Latvia) *Tel:* 261854845 *E-mail:* info@lapaprint.com *Web Site:* www.lapaprint.com, pg 1281, 1329

LAPA Uitgewers (South Africa) *Tel:* (012) 401 0700 *Fax:* (086) 720 1583 *E-mail:* lapa@lapa.co.za; bestellings@lapa.co.za *Web Site:* www.lapa.co.za, pg 615

Agence Michelle Lapautre (France) *Tel:* 01 47 34 82 41 *Fax:* 01 47 34 00 90 *E-mail:* agence@lapautre.com, pg 1225

Edizioni Lapis (Italy) *Tel:* (06) 3295 935 *Fax:* (03) 3630 7062 *E-mail:* lapis@edizionilapis.it *Web Site:* www.edizionilapis.it, pg 450

Lappan Verlag GmbH (Germany) *Tel:* (0441) 980 66-0 *Fax:* (0441) 980 66-34 *E-mail:* info@lappan.de; presse@lappan.de; programm@lappan.de *Web Site:* www.lappan.de, pg 281

Editions Larcier (Belgium) *Tel:* (02) 548 07 13 *Fax:* (02) 548 07 14 *E-mail:* marketing@larciergroup.com; press@larciergroup.com; contact@larciergroup.com *Web Site:* editionslarcier.larciergroup.com, pg 69

Hans Richter Laromedel (Sweden) *Tel:* (0152) 15060 *E-mail:* post@richbook.se *Web Site:* www.richbook.se, pg 683

Ediciones Larousse Argentina SA (Argentina) *Tel:* (011) 4865-9581; (011) 4865-9582; (011) 4865-9583 *Toll Free Tel:* 0800-333-5757 *Fax:* (011) 4865-9581; (011) 4865-9582; (011) 4865-9583 *Web Site:* www.aique.com.br/catalogo/larousse, pg 9

Ediciones Larousse SA de CV (Mexico) *Tel:* (0155) 1102 1300 *E-mail:* larousse@larousse.com.mx *Web Site:* www.larousse.com.mx, pg 518

Les Editions Larousse (France) *Tel:* 01 44 39 44 00 *E-mail:* livres-larousse@larousse.fr *Web Site:* www.larousse.fr; www.editions-larousse.fr, pg 180

Larousse Editorial SL (Spain) *Tel:* 93 241 35 05 *Fax:* 93 241 35 11 *E-mail:* larousse@larousse.es *Web Site:* www.larousse.es, pg 652

Bokforlaget Robert Larson AB (Sweden) *Tel:* (08) 732 84 60 *Fax:* (08) 732 84 50 *E-mail:* info@larsonforlag.se *Web Site:* www.larsonforlag.se, pg 683

Laruffa Editore SRL (Italy) *Tel:* (0965) 814954 *Fax:* (0965) 027185 *E-mail:* segreteria@laruffaeditore.it *Web Site:* www.laruffaeditore.it, pg 450

Editrice LAS (Italy) *Tel:* (06) 87290626; (06) 87290445 *Fax:* (06) 87290629 *E-mail:* las@unisal.it *Web Site:* www.las.unisal.it, pg 450

LASERLINE (Germany) *Tel:* (030) 46 70 96-0 *Fax:* (030) 46 70 96-66 *E-mail:* info@laser-line.de *Web Site:* www.laser-line.de, pg 1322

Lasser Press Mexicana SA de CV (Mexico) *Tel:* (0155) 55112312 *Fax:* (0155) 55112576, pg 518

Verlag Michael Lassleben Druckerei und Buchbinderei (Germany) *Tel:* (09473) 20 5 *Fax:* (09473) 83 57 *E-mail:* druckerei@oberpfalzverlag-lassleben.de *Web Site:* www.oberpfalzverlag-lassleben.de, pg 281

Lasten Keskus ja Kirjapaja Oy (Finland) *Tel:* (09) 6877 450 *Fax:* (09) 6877 4545 *E-mail:* tilaukset@lastenkeskus.fi *Web Site:* www.lastenkeskus.fi, pg 149

Editori Laterza (Italy) *Tel:* (06) 454 65 311 *Fax:* (06) 322 38 53 *E-mail:* glaterza@laterza.it; foreignrights@laterza.it *Web Site:* www.laterza.it, pg 450

Edizioni Giuseppe Laterza SRL (Italy) *Tel:* (080) 5237936 *Fax:* (080) 5237360 *E-mail:* info@edizionigiuseppelaterza.it *Web Site:* www.edizionigiuseppelaterza.it, pg 450

J Latka Verlag GmbH (Germany) *Tel:* (0228) 91932-0 *Fax:* (0228) 9193217 *E-mail:* info@latka.de *Web Site:* www.latka.de, pg 281

Editions JC Lattes (France) *Tel:* 01 44 41 74 00 *Fax:* 01 43 25 30 47; 01 43 26 91 04 *Web Site:* www.editions-jclattes.fr, pg 180

Latvian Librarians Association (Latvia) *Tel:* 67312791 *Fax:* 67312791 *E-mail:* lbb@lnb.lv *Web Site:* www.lnb.lv, pg 1655

Latvijas Gramatizdeveju Asociacija (Latvia) *Tel:* 67 217 730 *Fax:* 67 217 730 *E-mail:* lga@gramatizdeveji.lv *Web Site:* www.gramatizdeveji.lv, pg 1380

Latvijas Literaturas Centrs (Latvia) *Tel:* 67 311021 *Fax:* 67 311024 *E-mail:* centre@literature.lv *Web Site:* www.literature.lv, pg 1381

Latvijas Universitates Akademiska Biblioteka (Latvia) *Tel:* 67033951; 26373599 *E-mail:* acadlib@lib.acadlib.lv *Web Site:* www.acadlib.lv, pg 496, 1609

Laumann Druck & Verlag GmbH u Co KG (Germany) *Tel:* (02594) 94 34-0 *Fax:* (02594) 94 34 70 *E-mail:* info@laumann-verlag.de *Web Site:* www.laumann-verlag.de, pg 281

Laurel Press (Australia) *Tel:* (03) 6239 1139, pg 29

Laurence King Publishing Ltd (United Kingdom) *Tel:* (020) 7841 6900 *Fax:* (020) 7841 6910 *E-mail:* enquiries@laurenceking.com; sales@laurenceking.com; rights@laurenceking.com *Web Site:* www.laurenceking.com, pg 789

Editions Le Laurier (France) *Tel:* 01 45 51 55 08 *Fax:* 01 45 51 81 83 *E-mail:* contact@editions-lelaurier.com *Web Site:* editions-lelaurier.com, pg 180

Edition Laurin (Austria) *Tel:* (0512) 507 9098 *Fax:* (0512) 507 9812 *E-mail:* office@editionlaurin.at *Web Site:* www.editionlaurin.at, pg 52

Les Editions Lavauzelle SA (France) *Tel:* 05 55 58 45 00 *E-mail:* editions@lavauzelle.com *Web Site:* www.lavauzelle.com/keops/edition, pg 180

Lavenham Press Ltd (United Kingdom) *Tel:* (01787) 247436 *Fax:* (01787) 248267 *E-mail:* enquiries@lavenhamgroup.co.uk *Web Site:* www.lavenhampress.com, pg 1263, 1287, 1338

Lavieri Edizioni (Italy) *Tel:* (0975) 352680 *Fax:* (0823) 1760173 *E-mail:* info@lavieri.it; ordini@lavieri.it; rights@lavieri.it; uff.stampa@lavieri.it *Web Site:* www.lavieri.it, pg 450

Lavis Marketing (United Kingdom) *Tel:* (01865) 767575 *Fax:* (01865) 750079, pg 1458

Editions Lavoisier (France) *Tel:* 01 47 40 67 00 *Fax:* 01 47 40 67 02 *E-mail:* editionslavoisier@lavoisier.fr *Web Site:* editions.lavoisier.fr, pg 180

Lavoisier Librairie (France) *Tel:* 01 47 40 67 00 *Fax:* 01 47 40 67 02; 01 47 40 67 88 *E-mail:* livres@lavoisier.fr; info@lavoisier.fr *Web Site:* www.lavoisier.fr; e.lavoisier.fr; diffusion.lavoisier.fr, pg 1414

Il Lavoro Editoriale (Italy) *Tel:* (071) 2072210 *Fax:* (071) 2083058 *E-mail:* redazione@lavoroeditoriale.com; ordini@lavoroeditoriale.com; info@anconauniversitypress.it *Web Site:* www.illavoroeditoriale.com, pg 450

Edizioni Lavoro SRL (Italy) *Tel:* (06) 44251174 *Fax:* (06) 44251177 *E-mail:* info@edizionilavoro.it; amministrazione@edizionilavoro.it; marketing@edizionilavoro.it *Web Site:* www.edizionilavoro.it, pg 450

LAW (Lucas Alexander Whitley Ltd) (United Kingdom) *Tel:* (020) 7471 7900 *Fax:* (020) 7471 7910 *Web Site:* www.lawagency.co.uk, pg 1243

Law Publishers (India) Pvt Ltd (India) *Tel:* (0532) 262374; (0532) 2623735; (0532) 2420733 *Fax:* (0532) 622781; (0532) 2622276 *E-mail:* sai@lawpublisherindia.com; virandra@sanchar.net.in *Web Site:* www.lawpublisherindia.com, pg 389

The Law Publishing House (China) *Tel:* (010) 63939796; (010) 63939792 *Fax:* (010) 63939622 *E-mail:* info@lawpress.com.cn *Web Site:* www.lawpress.com.cn, pg 107

Lawpack Publishing Ltd (United Kingdom) *Tel:* (020) 7394 4040 *Fax:* (020) 7394 4041 *E-mail:* enquiries@lawpack.co.uk *Web Site:* www.lawpack.co.uk, pg 789

Lawrence & Wishart Ltd (United Kingdom) *Tel:* (020) 8533 2506 *Fax:* (020) 8533 7369 *E-mail:* info@lwbooks.co.uk *Web Site:* www.lwbooks.co.uk, pg 789

Laxmi Publications Pvt Ltd (India) *Tel:* (011) 4353 2500; (011) 4353 2501 *Fax:* (011) 2325 2572; (011) 4353 2528 *E-mail:* info@laxmipublications.com; order@laxmipublications.com *Web Site:* www.laxmipublications.com, pg 389

LBA Books (United Kingdom) *Tel:* (020) 7637 1234 *E-mail:* info@lbabooks.com *Web Site:* www.lbabooks.com, pg 1243

LCD Mediation (France) *Tel:* 02 54 32 37 90 *Fax:* 02 54 32 37 90, pg 180

LCL Dystrybucja Sp z oo (Poland) *Tel:* (42) 250 83 00 *Fax:* (42) 250 83 00 *E-mail:* sekretariat@lcldystrybucja.pl *Web Site:* www.lcldystrybucja.pl, pg 1282, 1331

LDA (United Kingdom) *Tel:* (0845) 120 4776 *Toll Free Fax:* 0800 783 8648 *E-mail:* enquiries@ldalearning.com *Web Site:* www.ldalearning.com, pg 789

le-tex publishing services GmbH (Germany) *Tel:* (0341) 355356 0 *Fax:* (0341) 355356 950 *E-mail:* info@le-tex.de *Web Site:* www.le-tex.de, pg 1276

Ediciones LEA SA (Argentina) *Tel:* (011) 4846-9056 *E-mail:* info@edicioneslea.com; ventas@edicioneslea.com *Web Site:* www.edicioneslea.com, pg 9

Susanna Lea Associates (France) *Tel:* 01 53 10 28 40 *Fax:* 01 53 10 28 49 *E-mail:* inquiries@susannalea.com *Web Site:* www.susannalea.com, pg 1225

Leaping Hare Press (United Kingdom) *Tel:* (01273) 487440 *Web Site:* www.quartoknows.com/leaping-hare-press, pg 789

Learn Africa PLC (Nigeria) *Tel:* (01) 7403967; (01) 4393111; (0805) 5064737 (cell) *Fax:* (01) 4964370 *E-mail:* connect@learnafricaplc.com; marketing@learnafricaplc.com; sales@learnafricaplc.com *Web Site:* www.learnafricaplc.com, pg 552

Learners (India) *Tel:* (011) 2638 6165; (011) 2638 7070 *Fax:* (011) 2638 3788 *E-mail:* mail@sterlingpublishers.com *Web Site:* www.sterlingpublishers.com, pg 389

Learning & Work Institute (United Kingdom) *Tel:* (0116) 204 4200 *Fax:* (0116) 204 6988 *E-mail:* press@learningandwork.org.uk; enquiries@learningandwork.org.uk *Web Site:* www.learningandwork.org.uk, pg 789

Learning Matters Ltd (United Kingdom) *Tel:* (020) 7324 8500 *Fax:* (020) 7324 8600 *E-mail:* market@sagepub.co.uk; orders@sagepub.co.uk *Web Site:* www.uk.sagepub.com/learningmatters, pg 790

Learning Media (New Zealand) *Tel:* (04) 472 5522 *Toll Free Tel:* 0800 800 565 *Fax:* (04) 472 6444 *Toll Free Fax:* 0800 800 570 *E-mail:* info@learningmedia.co.nz; sales@learningmedia.co.nz *Web Site:* www.learningmedia.co.nz, pg 547

Learning Together (United Kingdom) *Tel:* (028) 9040 2086 *Fax:* (028) 9040 2086 *E-mail:* info@learningtogether.co.uk *Web Site:* www.learningtogether.co.uk, pg 790

Lebanese Library Association (LLA) (Lebanon) *Tel:* (01) 786456; (01) 78646 (ext 1210) *E-mail:* kjaroudy@lau.edu.lb *Web Site:* www.llaweb.org, pg 1655

Lebenshilfe-Verlag (Germany) *Tel:* (06421) 491-0; (06421) 491-123 (sales) *Fax:* (06421) 491-167; (06421) 491-623 (sales) *E-mail:* verlag@lebenshilfe.de; vertrieb@lebenshilfe.de *Web Site:* www.lebenshilfe.de, pg 281

Lebowski Publishers (Netherlands) *Tel:* (020) 4624300 *E-mail:* stijn.devries@lebowskipublishers.nl *Web Site:* www.lebowskipublishers.nl, pg 536

Lectio Ediciones (Spain) *Tel:* 977602591 *Fax:* 977604357 *E-mail:* lectio@lectio.es *Web Site:* www.lectio.es, pg 652

Editorial Lectorum SA de CV (Mexico) *Tel:* (0155) 5581-3202 *Fax:* (0155) 5646-6892 *E-mail:* ventas@lectorum.com.mx *Web Site:* www.lectorum.com.mx, pg 518

LED Edizioni Universitarie di Lettere Economia Diritto (Italy) *Tel:* (02) 59902055 *Fax:* (02) 55193636 *E-mail:* led@lededizioni.com *Web Site:* www.lededizioni.com, pg 450

LEDA (Las Ediciones de Arte) (Spain) *Tel:* 932 379 389 *Fax:* 932 155 273, pg 652

LEDA Verlag (Germany) *Tel:* (0491) 91 22 62 86 *Fax:* (0491) 91 22 62 87 *E-mail:* info@leda-verlag.de *Web Site:* www.leda-verlag.de, pg 282

Editions Musicales Alphonse Leduc (France) *Tel:* 01 42 96 89 11 *Fax:* 01 42 86 02 83 *E-mail:* alphonseleduc@wanadoo.fr *Web Site:* www.alphonseleduc.com, pg 180

Kochbuchverlag Olli Leeb (Germany) *Tel:* (089) 962 936 46 *E-mail:* rezept@ollileeb.com; anfragen@ollileeb.com; bestellen@ollileeb.com; willkommen@ollileeb.com *Web Site:* www.ollileeb.com, pg 282

Leeds University Library (United Kingdom) *Tel:* (0113) 343 5663 *E-mail:* library@leeds.ac.uk *Web Site:* library.leeds.ac.uk, pg 1641

Editions Francis Lefebvre (France) *Tel:* 01 41 05 22 00; 08 20 71 00 51 *Fax:* 01 41 05 22 30 *Web Site:* www.efl.fr, pg 180

Claude Lefrancq Editeur (Belgium) *Tel:* (02) 344 49 34 *Fax:* (02) 347 55 34, pg 69

Legal Action Group (LAG) (United Kingdom) *Tel:* (020) 7833 2931 *Fax:* (020) 7837 6094 *E-mail:* lag@lag.org.uk; books@lag.org.uk *Web Site:* www.lag.org.uk, pg 790

Legal Resources Foundation Legal Publications Unit (Zimbabwe) *Tel:* (04) 333707; (04) 334732 *Fax:* (04) 304928 *Web Site:* www.lrfzim.com/publications, pg 852

Ediciones Legales SA (Ecuador) *Tel:* (02) 248 0800; (02) 223 9470 *E-mail:* edicioneslegales@corpmyl.com *Web Site:* www.edicioneslegales.com.ec, pg 142

Legat-Verlag GmbH & Co KG (Germany) *Tel:* (07071) 650266 *Fax:* (07071) 650267 *E-mail:* info@legat-verlag.de *Web Site:* www.legat-verlag.de, pg 282

LEGIS - Editores SA (Colombia) *Tel:* (01) 425-5255 *E-mail:* webmaster@legis.com.co *Web Site:* www.legis.com.co, pg 114

Editions Legislatives (France) *Tel:* 01 40 92 36 36; 08 10 00 45 19 (customer service) *E-mail:* sav@convention-collective.fr *Web Site:* www.editions-legislatives.fr, pg 180

LEGO SpA (Italy) *Tel:* (0444) 564622 *Fax:* (0444) 564929 *E-mail:* lego@legogroup.com *Web Site:* www.legogroup.com, pg 1260, 1281, 1328

Legua Editorial SL (Spain) *E-mail:* comunicacion@leguaeditorial.es *Web Site:* leguaeditorial.com, pg 652

Libreria Lehmann SA (Costa Rica) *Tel:* 2522-4848 *E-mail:* sac@librerialehmann.com; servicio@librerialehmann.com *Web Site:* www.librerialehmann.com, pg 117, 1411

Lehmanns Media GmbH (Germany) *Tel:* (030) 617911-46 *Fax:* (030) 617911-60 *E-mail:* info@lehmanns.de *Web Site:* www.lehmanns.de, pg 282

Lehmstedt Verlag (Germany) *Tel:* (0341) 4927366 *E-mail:* info@lehmstedt.de; vertrieb@lehmstedt.de *Web Site:* www.lehmstedt.de, pg 282

Lehnert & Landrock Bookshop & Art Gallery (Egypt) *Tel:* (02) 2393-5324, pg 1413

Verlag fuer Lehrmittel Poessneck GmbH (Germany) *Tel:* (03647) 425018 *Fax:* (03647) 425020, pg 282

Leibniz-Buecherwarte (Germany) *Tel:* (05042) 15 28 *Fax:* (05042) 15 28 *E-mail:* leibniz-buecherwarte@kabelmail.de *Web Site:* www.leibnizbuecherwarte.com, pg 282

Leibniz Verlag (Germany) *Tel:* (09544) 987544 *Fax:* (09544) 987515 *Web Site:* www.leibniz-verlag.de, pg 282

Leinpfad Verlag (Germany) *Tel:* (06132) 83 69 *Fax:* (06132) 89 69 51 *E-mail:* info@leinpfadverlag.de *Web Site:* www.leinpfadverlag.de, pg 282

Leipziger Kommissions- und Grossbuchhandelsgesellschaft mbH (LKG) (Germany) *Tel:* (034206) 65-100 *Fax:* (034206) 65-110 *E-mail:* lkg@lkg-service.de *Web Site:* www.lkg-va.de, pg 1417

Leipziger Staedtische Bibliotheken (Germany) *Tel:* (0341) 123-5309 *Fax:* (0341) 123-5305 *E-mail:* stadtbib@leipzig.de *Web Site:* stadtbibliothek.leipzig.de, pg 1593

Leipziger Universitaetsverlag GmbH (Germany) *Tel:* (0341) 9900440 *Fax:* (0341) 9900440 *E-mail:* info@univerlag-leipzig.de *Web Site:* www.univerlag-leipzig.de, pg 282

Leipziger Verlagsgesellschaft (Germany) *Tel:* (0341) 2210229, pg 283

Leistungsgemeinschaft Buchhandel eG (Germany) *Tel:* (089) 54 34 31 80 *Fax:* (089) 54 34 31 81 *E-mail:* info@lg-buch.de *Web Site:* www.lg-buch.de, pg 1375

Anton G Leitner Verlag (Germany) *Tel:* (08153) 95 25-22 *E-mail:* service@dasgedicht.de *Web Site:* www.aglv.com, pg 283

Editora Leitura Ltda (Brazil) *Tel:* (031) 3292-8300; (031) 2519-8100; (031) 3379-0620, pg 85

Mandelbaum Verlag (Austria) *Tel:* (01) 53 53 477-0 *Fax:* (01) 53 53 477-12 *E-mail:* office@mandelbaum. at *Web Site:* www.mandelbaum.at, pg 53

Mandragora SRL (Italy) *Tel:* (055) 2654384 *Fax:* (055) 2655120 *E-mail:* info@mandragora.it; mandragora@mandragora.it; redazione@mandragora.it *Web Site:* www.mandragora.it, pg 452

Mandrake of Oxford (United Kingdom) *Tel:* (01865) 243671 *Fax:* (01865) 432929 *E-mail:* mandrake@ mandrake.uk.net *Web Site:* mandrake.uk.net, pg 796

Manesse Verlag (Germany) *Tel:* (089) 4136-0 *Toll Free:* 0800 500 33 22 *Fax:* (089) 4136-3333 *E-mail:* kundenservice@randomhouse.de *Web Site:* www.randomhouse.de/manesse, pg 288

Editions Mango (France) *E-mail:* fleuruseditions@ fleuruseditions.com; foreignrights@fleuruseditions.com *Web Site:* www.fleuruseditions.com/mango, pg 182

Mangschou Forlag (Norway) *Tel:* 55 55 10 50 *Fax:* 55 55 10 51 *E-mail:* mangschou@mangschou.no *Web Site:* www.mangschou.no, pg 556

Manhattan Verlag (Germany) *Tel:* (089) 4136-0 *Toll Free Tel:* 0800 500 33 22 *Fax:* (089) 4136-3333 *E-mail:* kundenservice@randomhouse.de *Web Site:* www.randomhouse.de/manhattan, pg 288

Manifesto Libri SRL (Italy) *Tel:* (06) 99709447 *Fax:* (06) 99709447 *E-mail:* redazione@manifestolibri. it; book@manifestolibri.it (orders); ufficiostampa@ manifestolibri.it *Web Site:* www.manifestolibri.it, pg 453

Manila City Library (Philippines) *Tel:* (02) 528 0630 *Web Site:* www.facebook.com/manila.citylibrary, pg 1622

Manipal Technologies Ltd (India) *Tel:* (0820) 2571151 *Fax:* (0820) 2570131 *E-mail:* info@ manipaltechnologies.com *Web Site:* www. manipaltechnologies.com, pg 1279, 1327

Manjul Publishing House Pvt Ltd (India) *Tel:* (0755) 4240 340 *Fax:* (0755) 4055 791 *E-mail:* manjul@ manjulindia.com *Web Site:* www.manjulindia.com, pg 390

Mankau Verlag GmbH (Germany) *Tel:* (08841) 627769-0 *Fax:* (08841) 627769-6 *E-mail:* kontakt@mankau-verlag.de *Web Site:* www.mankau-verlag.de, pg 288

Gebr Mann Verlag (Germany) *Tel:* (030) 700 13 88-0 *Fax:* (030) 700 13 88-11 *E-mail:* vertrieb-kunstverlage@reimer-verlag.de *Web Site:* www.reimer-mann-verlag.de, pg 288

Piero Manni SRL (Italy) *Tel:* (0832) 205577 *Fax:* (0832) 200373 *E-mail:* info@mannieditori.it *Web Site:* www. mannieditori.it, pg 453

Manohar Publishers & Distributors (India) *Tel:* (011) 23289100; (011) 23262796; (011) 23284848; (011) 23260774 *Fax:* (011) 23265162 *E-mail:* manbooks@ vsnl.com; sales@manoharbooks.com *Web Site:* www. manoharbooks.com, pg 390

Editora Manole Ltda (Brazil) *Tel:* (011) 4196 6000 *E-mail:* falecom@manole.zendesk.com; secretaria@ manole.com.br *Web Site:* www.manole.com.br, pg 86

Mantikore-Verlag (Germany) *Tel:* (0163) 80 58 461 (cell) *E-mail:* mantikoreverlag@aol.com *Web Site:* mantikore-verlag.de, pg 289

Editora Mantiqueira de Ciencia e Arte Ltda (Brazil) *Tel:* (012) 3662-1832 *Fax:* (012) 3662-1832 *E-mail:* editora@editoramantiqueira.com.br *Web Site:* www.editoramantiqueira.com.br, pg 86

Mantis Editores (Mexico) *Tel:* (033) 3657-7864 *E-mail:* mantiseditores@gmail.com *Web Site:* www. mantiseditores.com, pg 519

Mantra Lingua Ltd (United Kingdom) *Tel:* (020) 8445 5123 *Fax:* (020) 8446 7745 *E-mail:* info@ mantralingua; sales@mantralingua.com *Web Site:* www.mantralingua.com, pg 796

Editora Manuais Tecnicos de Seguros Ltda (Brazil) *Tel:* (011) 50835587, pg 86

Editorial El Manual Moderno SA de CV (Mexico) *Tel:* (0155) 5265 1100 *Fax:* (0155) 5265 1135 *E-mail:* info@manualmoderno.com *Web Site:* www. manualmoderno.com, pg 519

Manufacture of Art (Switzerland) *Tel:* (071) 888 6663 *Fax:* (071) 888 6664 *E-mail:* info@manufacture-of-art. com *Web Site:* www.manufacture-of-art.com, pg 700, 1285

Manus Verlag AG (Switzerland) *Tel:* (044) 920 27 27 *Fax:* (044) 920 27 40 *Web Site:* www.manus.ch, pg 700

Manutius Verlag Heidelberg (Germany) *Tel:* (06221) 163290 *Fax:* (06221) 167143 *E-mail:* manutiusverlag@t-online.de *Web Site:* www. manutius-verlag.de, pg 289

Edizioni Angolo Manzoni SRL (Italy) *Tel:* (011) 47 30 775 *Fax:* (011) 48 94 52 *E-mail:* info@ angolomanzoni.it *Web Site:* www.angolomanzoni.it, pg 453

MANZ'sche Verlags- und Universitaetsbuchhandlung GmbH (Austria) *Tel:* (01) 531 61-0 *Fax:* (01) 531 61-181 *E-mail:* verlag@manz.at *Web Site:* www.manz.at, pg 53

MANZ'sche Verlags- und Universitaetsbuchhandlung GmbH (Austria) *Tel:* (01) 531 61-0; (01) 531 61-100 (customer service) *Fax:* (01) 531 61-181 *E-mail:* bestellen@manz.at; vertrieb@manz.at; presse@manz.at *Web Site:* www.manz.at, pg 1404

MAPA-Mapping & Publishing Ltd (Israel) *Tel:* (03) 6210500 *Fax:* (03) 5257725 *E-mail:* info@mapa.co.il *Web Site:* www.mapa.co.il; www.books.mapa.co.il, pg 420

Editorial Mapfre SA (Spain) *Tel:* 91 581 53 57 *Fax:* 91 581 18 83 *E-mail:* edimap@mapfre.com *Web Site:* www.editorialmapfre.com, pg 654

Mapin Publishing Pvt Ltd (India) *Tel:* (079) 40228228 *Fax:* (079) 40228201 *E-mail:* mapin@mapinpub.com *Web Site:* www.mapinpub.com, pg 390

Maps.com (United States) *Tel:* 805-685-3100 *Toll Free Tel:* 800-430-7532 *Fax:* 805-699-7550 *E-mail:* info@ maps.com *Web Site:* www.maps.com, pg 1340

Maqbool Academy (Pakistan) *Tel:* (042) 7357058 *Fax:* (042) 7238241 *E-mail:* maqboolbooks@gmail. com *Web Site:* www.maqboolbooks.com, pg 559

Marabout (France) *Tel:* 01 43 92 30 00 *Fax:* 01 43 92 32 99 *E-mail:* contact@marabout.com; pressemarabout@ hachette-livre.fr *Web Site:* www.marabout.com, pg 182

Maracle Press Ltd (Canada) *Tel:* 905-723-3438 *Toll Free Tel:* 800-558-8604 *Fax:* 905-723-1759 *E-mail:* info@ maraclepress.com *Web Site:* www.maraclepress.com, pg 1255, 1274, 1318

Marbot Ediciones (Spain) *Tel:* 933014218 *E-mail:* marbot@marbotediciones.com *Web Site:* www. marbotediciones.com, pg 654

Marcador Editora (Portugal) *Tel:* 21 269 39 60 *E-mail:* info@marcador.pt *Web Site:* www.marcador.pt, pg 580

Marchesi Grafiche Editoriali SpA (Italy) *Tel:* (06) 33216 1 *Fax:* (06) 33216 333 *E-mail:* info@ marchesigrafiche.it *Web Site:* www.marchesigrafiche.it, pg 1281, 1328

Marcial Pons Ediciones Juridicas SA (Spain) *Tel:* 91 304 33 03 *Fax:* 91 327 23 67 *E-mail:* edicionesjuridicas@ marcialpons.es; atencion@marcialpons.es (customer service) *Web Site:* www.marcialpons.es, pg 654

Marcial Pons Librero SL (Spain) *Tel:* 91 304 33 03 *Fax:* 91 327 23 67; 91 754 12 18 *E-mail:* atencion@ marcialpons.es *Web Site:* www.marcialpons.es, pg 1451

Marcianum Press SRL (Italy) *Tel:* (041) 29 60 608; (041) 29 60 287 *Fax:* (041) 24 19 658 *E-mail:* marcianumpress@marcianum.it *Web Site:* www.marcianumpress.it, pg 453

Marco Zero (Brazil) *Tel:* (011) 3706-1466 *Web Site:* www.editoranobel.com.br, pg 86

Marcombo SA (Spain) *Tel:* 93 318 00 79 *Fax:* 93 318 93 39 *E-mail:* info@marcombo.com *Web Site:* www. marcombo.com, pg 654, 1235

Marcovalerio Edizioni (Italy) *E-mail:* marcovalerio@ marcovalerio.com *Web Site:* www.marcovalerio.com, pg 453, 1328

Editions Marcus (France) *Tel:* 01 45 77 04 04 *E-mail:* contact@guidesmarcus.com *Web Site:* www. guidesmarcus.com, pg 183

Editions Mardaga (Belgium) *Tel:* (02) 894 09 40 *Fax:* (02) 894 09 48 *E-mail:* info@editionsmardaga. com *Web Site:* www.editionsmardaga.com, pg 70

Mardev (Australia) *Tel:* (02) 9422 2644 *Fax:* (02) 9422 2633 *E-mail:* mardevlists@reedbusiness.com.au *Web Site:* www.mardevdm2.com, pg 1364

Editorial Marea SRL (Argentina) *Tel:* (011) 4703-0464 *Fax:* (011) 4703-0464 *E-mail:* marea@editorialmarea. com.ar *Web Site:* www.editorialmarea.com.ar, pg 10

Marencin PT spol sro (Slovakia) *Tel:* (02) 20 723 752 *Fax:* (02) 20 723 752 *E-mail:* marencin@marencin.sk *Web Site:* www.marencin.sk, pg 608

mareverlag GmbH & Co oHG (Germany) *Tel:* (040) 36 98 59 0 *Fax:* (040) 36 98 59 90 *E-mail:* buch@ mare.de; leserbrief@mare.de; mare@mare.de *Web Site:* www.mare.de, pg 289

Editorial Marfil SA (Spain) *Tel:* 963 186 007 *Fax:* 963 186 432 *E-mail:* info@tabarcallibres. com *Web Site:* www.editorialmarfil.com; www. tabarcallibres.com, pg 655

Marg Foundation (India) *Tel:* (022) 22821151; (022) 22045947; (022) 22842520 *Fax:* (022) 22047102 *E-mail:* margfound@vsnl.net *Web Site:* marg-art.org, pg 390

Marge Books (Spain) *Tel:* 932449130 *Fax:* 932310865 *E-mail:* marge@margebooks.com *Web Site:* www. marge.es, pg 655

Margraf Publishers und Morramusik Verlags GmbH (Germany) *Tel:* (07934) 30 71 *Fax:* (07934) 81 56 *E-mail:* info@margraf-verlag.de *Web Site:* www. margraf-publishers.eu; shop.margraf-publishers.net, pg 289

Druck- und Verlagsgesellschaft Marienberg mbH (Germany) *Tel:* (03735) 91 64-0 *Fax:* (03735) 23 48-6 *E-mail:* info@druckerei-marienberg.de *Web Site:* www. druckerei-marienberg.de, pg 289

Marietti Scuola (Italy) *Tel:* (02) 380861 *E-mail:* scrivi@ scuola.com *Web Site:* www.mariettiscuola.it, pg 453

Editorial Marin SA (Spain) *Tel:* 934536955 *Fax:* 965523496, pg 655

Maritime Information Association (MIA) (United Kingdom) *Web Site:* www.maritime-information.net, pg 1396

Librairie Maritime Outremer (France) *Tel:* 01 42 34 96 60 *E-mail:* librairieoutremer@wanadoo.fr *Web Site:* www.librairie-outremer.com, pg 183

Marix Verlag (Germany) *Tel:* (0611) 986 98 0 *Fax:* (0611) 986 98 26 *E-mail:* info@verlagshaus-roemerweg.de *Web Site:* www.verlagshaus-roemerweg. de/Marix_Verlag.html; www.verlagshaus-roemerweg. de, pg 289

Marjacq Scripts Ltd (United Kingdom) *Tel:* (020) 7935 9499 *Fax:* (020) 7935 9115 *E-mail:* enquiries@ marjacq.com *Web Site:* www.marjacq.com, pg 1244

Market House Books Ltd (United Kingdom) *Tel:* (01296) 484911 *E-mail:* books@mhbref.com *Web Site:* www. markethousebooks.com, pg 1287

The Market Research Society (MRS) (United Kingdom) *Tel:* (020) 7490 4911 *Fax:* (020) 7490 0608 *E-mail:* info@mrs.org.uk; publications@mrs.org.uk *Web Site:* www.mrs.org.uk, pg 796

MarketAsia Books Pte Ltd (Singapore) *Tel:* 6744 8483; 6744 8486 *E-mail:* service@marketasia.com.sg *Web Site:* marketasiabooks.com, pg 1447

Marketing Focus (Australia) *Tel:* (08) 9257 1777 *Fax:* (08) 9257 1888 *Web Site:* www.marketingfocus. net.au, pg 30

Markono Print Media Pte Ltd (Singapore) *Tel:* 6281 1118 *E-mail:* enquiry@markono.com; sales@markono. com *Web Site:* www.markono.com, pg 1261, 1283, 1332, 1347, 1354

Antiquariat Walter Markov (Germany) *Tel:* (0228) 96 38 565 *E-mail:* info@antiquariat-markov.de *Web Site:* www.antiquariat-markov.de, pg 1417

Marotta & Cafiero Editori (Italy) *Tel:* (081) 5758060 *Fax:* (081) 5758060, pg 453

Marova SL (Spain) *Tel:* 915 322 607 *Fax:* 915 225 123, pg 655

MaroVerlag + Druck eK (Germany) *Tel:* (0821) 416034 *Fax:* (0821) 416036 *E-mail:* info@maroverlag.de *Web Site:* www.maroverlag.de, pg 289

Marque Publishing Co Pty Ltd (Australia) *Tel:* (02) 4322 4803; (02) 4329 4637 *Fax:* (02) 4322 4803, pg 30

Marquis Book Printing Inc (Canada) *Toll Free Tel:* 855-566-1937 *Fax:* 418-241-1768 *Web Site:* www. marquislivre.com, pg 1318

Marrakech Express Inc (United States) *Tel:* 727-942-2218 *Toll Free Tel:* 800-940-6566 *Fax:* 727-937-4758 *E-mail:* print@marrak.com *Web Site:* www.marrak. com, pg 1265, 1340, 1356

Marren Publishing House Inc (Philippines) *Tel:* (02) 3728939 *Fax:* (02) 3728940, pg 565

Mars Business Associates Ltd (United Kingdom) *Tel:* (01367) 252 506 *Fax:* (01367) 252 506, pg 796

The Marsh Agency Ltd (United Kingdom) *Tel:* (020) 7493 4361 *E-mail:* hello@marsh-agency.co.uk *Web Site:* www.marsh-agency.co.uk, pg 1244

Tracy Marsh Publications Pty Ltd (Australia) *Tel:* (08) 8272 0001 *E-mail:* admin@tracymarsh.com *Web Site:* www.tracymarsh.com, pg 30

Marshall Cavendish International (Asia) Pte Ltd (Singapore) *Tel:* 6213 9300 *Fax:* 6285 4871 *E-mail:* genref@sg.marshallcavendish. com; genrefsales@sg.marshallcavendish.com *Web Site:* www.marshallcavendish.com/genref, pg 604

Marshall Cavendish International (Singapore) Pte Ltd (Singapore) *Tel:* 6213 9300 *Fax:* 6266 3677 *E-mail:* tmesales@sg.marshallcavendish.com; enquiry@sg.marshallcavendish.com *Web Site:* www. marshallcavendish.com, pg 604

Marshall Cavendish (Malaysia) Sdn Bhd (Malaysia) *Tel:* (03) 5628 6888; (03) 5635 2191 *Fax:* (03) 5635 2706 *E-mail:* bizinfo@my.marshallcavendish.com *Web Site:* www.marshallcavendish.com, pg 508

Marshall Editions (United Kingdom) *Tel:* (020) 7700 6700 *Fax:* (020) 7700 8066 *E-mail:* info@quarto.com *Web Site:* www.quartoknows.com/marshall-editions, pg 796

J P Marshall Literary Agency (United Kingdom), pg 1244

Marsilio Editori SpA (Italy) *Tel:* (041) 2406511 *Fax:* (041) 5238352 *E-mail:* info@marsilioeditori.it *Web Site:* www.marsilioeditori.it, pg 453

Marston Book Services Ltd (United Kingdom) *Tel:* (01235) 465500; (01235) 465579 (Christian orders) *Fax:* (01235) 465509 (general enquiries); (01235) 465555; (01235) 465518 (Christian orders) *E-mail:* direct.enq@marston.co.uk (enquiries); direct. orders@marston.co.uk (direct sales dept); christian. orders@marston.co.uk (Christian orders); trade. orders@marston.co.uk (trade orders); trade.enq@ marston.co.uk (trade enquiries); pubeasy.enquiry@ marston.co.uk; returns@marston.co.uk (trade returns) *Web Site:* www.marston.co.uk; pubeasy.books.marston. co.uk, pg 1459

Marsu Productions (France) *E-mail:* marsu@ marsuproductions.com *Web Site:* www.marsupro; www.marsupilami.com, pg 183

Editions Martelle (France) *Tel:* 03 22 71 54 54 *Fax:* 03 22 92 89 33 *E-mail:* serviceclients@librairiemartelle. com *Web Site:* www.librairiemartelle.com, pg 183

Marti Yayin Grubu (Turkey) *Tel:* (0212) 483 27 37 *Fax:* (0212) 483 27 38 *E-mail:* info@martiyayinlari. com *Web Site:* www.martiyayinlari.com, pg 722

Ediciones Martinez Roca SA (Spain) *Tel:* 91 423 03 14 *Fax:* 91 423 03 06 *E-mail:* info@mrediciones. es *Web Site:* www.planetadelibros.com/editorial-ediciones-martinez-roca-11.html, pg 655

Editions de la Martiniere (France) *Tel:* 01 41 48 80 00 *E-mail:* contact@lamartiniere.fr; rights@lamartiniere.fr *Web Site:* www.editionsdelamartiniere.fr, pg 183

Martins Editora Livraria Ltda (Brazil) *Tel:* (011) 3116-0000 *Fax:* (011) 3116-0000 *E-mail:* info@ emartinsfontes.com.br *Web Site:* www.emartinsfontes. com.br, pg 86

Maruzen Publishing Co Ltd (Japan) *Tel:* (03) 3512-3256 *Fax:* (03) 3512-3270 *Web Site:* pub.maruzen.co.jp, pg 482

Maruzen-Yushodo Co Ltd (Japan) *Tel:* (03) 4335-9316 *Fax:* (03) 4335-9368 *E-mail:* e-support@maruzen.co. jp; export@maruzen.co.jp; mg-yosho-marketing@ maruzen.co.jp *Web Site:* yushodo.maruzen.co.jp, pg 1429

Marval Editions (France) *Tel:* 01 44 41 19 79 *Fax:* 01 43 29 87 11 *E-mail:* contact@marval.fr *Web Site:* www. marval.fr, pg 183

Masaryk University Press (Czech Republic) *Tel:* 549 491 170; 549 491 171 *E-mail:* munipress@press.muni.cz; redakce@press.muni.cz *Web Site:* www.muni.cz/press, pg 129

Editorial La Mascara SL (Spain) *Tel:* 963 486 500 *Fax:* 963 487 440, pg 655

Izdatelstvo Mashinostroenie (Russia) *Tel:* (499) 268-38-58; (499) 269-52-98 *Fax:* (499) 269-48-97 *E-mail:* mashpubl@mashin.ru; realiz@mashin.ru (sales, marketing & advertising) *Web Site:* www. mashin.ru, pg 595

Masken-Verlag Friedrich Willmann (Germany) *Tel:* (0711) 13 27 14 *Fax:* (0711) 13 27 13 *E-mail:* info@masken-verlag.de *Web Site:* www. masken-verlag.de, pg 289

Maskew Miller Longman (South Africa) *Tel:* (021) 532 6000 *Fax:* (021) 531 0716; (021) 531 4049 (orders) *E-mail:* customerservices@mml.co.za; orders@mml. co.za *Web Site:* www.mml.co.za, pg 615, 1448

Masmedia doo (Croatia) *Tel:* (01) 45 77 400 *Toll Free Tel:* 0800 300 000 *Fax:* (01) 45 77 769 *E-mail:* info@masmedia.hr; informacije@masmedia.hr *Web Site:* www.masmedia.hr, pg 121

Editions Masoin (Belgium) *Tel:* (02) 478 37 06 *Fax:* (02) 478 64 29 *Web Site:* www.editions-masoin.be, pg 70

Masons Design & Print (United Kingdom) *Tel:* (01244) 674433 *Fax:* (01244) 674274, pg 1263

Editions du Masque (France) *Tel:* 01 44 41 74 00 *Fax:* 01 43 25 30 47; 01 43 26 91 04 *Web Site:* www. editions-jclattes.fr/le-masque, pg 183

Rubin Mass Ltd (Israel) *Tel:* (02) 627-7863 *Fax:* (02) 627-7864 *E-mail:* rmass@barak.net.il *Web Site:* rubinmass.net, pg 420, 1427

Massey University Press (New Zealand) *Tel:* (09) 212 7073 *E-mail:* editorial@masseypress.ac.nz *Web Site:* www.masseypress.ac.nz, pg 548

Editrice Massimo di Crespi Cesare & C SAS (Italy) *Tel:* (02) 55211315, pg 453

Charles Massin Editions (France) *Tel:* 02 41 32 40 91 (orders) *E-mail:* info@massin.fr *Web Site:* www. massin.fr, pg 183

Massmann Internationale Buchhandlung GmbH (Germany) *Tel:* (040) 767 00 40 *Fax:* (040) 767 00 410 *E-mail:* info@massmann.de *Web Site:* www. massmann.de, pg 1417

Massolit Forlag AB (Sweden) *Tel:* (08) 410 45 857 *E-mail:* info@massolit.se *Web Site:* www.massolit.se, pg 684

Editura MAST (Romania) *Tel:* (021) 4101945; 0723556196 (cell) *Fax:* (021) 4101945 *E-mail:* mast@ xnet.ro *Web Site:* www.edituramast.ro, pg 588

Vydavectva Mastackaja Litaratura (Belarus) *Tel:* (017) 2235809; (017) 2238664, pg 62

Master Flo Technology Inc (Canada) *Tel:* 450-562-0303 *Fax:* 450-562-9708 *E-mail:* info@mflo.com *Web Site:* www.mflo.com, pg 1353

Matar Publishing House (Israel) *Tel:* (03) 7105105 *Fax:* (03) 5660488 *E-mail:* info@matar.biz *Web Site:* www.matarbooks.co.il, pg 420

Math Paper Press (Singapore) *Tel:* 6222 9195 *E-mail:* shop@booksactually.com *Web Site:* www. booksactuallyshop.com/collections/math-paper-press, pg 604

Sri Ramakrishna Math (India) *Tel:* (044) 24621110 *Fax:* (044) 24934589 *E-mail:* mail@chennaimath.org *Web Site:* www.chennaimath.org, pg 390

Matica hrvatska (Croatia) *Tel:* (01) 4878-360; (01) 4819-318 (bookshop); (01) 4878-374 (bookshop) *Fax:* (01) 4819-319 *E-mail:* matica@matica.hr; knjizara@matica. hr (bookshop) *Web Site:* www.matica.hr, pg 121

Izdavacko Centar Matica Srpska (Serbia) *Tel:* (021) 527 855; (021) 527 622 *Fax:* (021) 528 901 *E-mail:* ms@ maticasrpska.org.rs; glasnik@maticasrpska.org.rs *Web Site:* www.maticasrpska.org.rs; www.icms.rs, pg 601

Matice Moravska (Czech Republic) *Tel:* 549 493 552 *Fax:* 549 491 520 *E-mail:* matice@phil.muni.cz *Web Site:* www.matice-moravska.cz, pg 1492

Editions Matrice (France) *Tel:* 01 69 42 13 02 *Fax:* 01 69 40 21 57 *E-mail:* edition.matrice@wanadoo.fr *Web Site:* pig.asso.free.fr/Matrice.dir/Matrice.htm, pg 183

Matrix Editora (Brazil) *Tel:* (011) 3868-2863 *E-mail:* editor@matrixeditora.com.br *Web Site:* www. matrixeditora.com.br, pg 86

Matrix Rom (Romania) *Tel:* (021) 4113617; (021) 4012438 *Fax:* (021) 4114280 *E-mail:* office@ matrixrom.ro *Web Site:* www.matrixrom.ro, pg 589

MatrixMedia Verlag GmbH (Germany) *Tel:* (0551) 45924 *Fax:* (0551) 487542 *E-mail:* hh@matrixmedia-verlag.de *Web Site:* www.matrixmedia.info, pg 289

Mattes Verlag GmbH (Germany) *Tel:* (06221) 459321 *Fax:* (06221) 459322 *E-mail:* verlag@mattes.de; bestellung@mattes.de (orders) *Web Site:* www.mattes. de, pg 289

Matthes Verlag GmbH (Germany) *Tel:* (0711) 21 33-329 *Fax:* (0711) 21 33-320 *E-mail:* buch@matthaes.de *Web Site:* www.matthaes.de, pg 289

Matthes und Seitz Berlin Verlagsgesellschaft mbH (Germany) *Tel:* (030) 44 32 74 01 *Fax:* (030) 44 32 74 02 *E-mail:* info@matthes-seitz-berlin.de *Web Site:* www.matthes-seitz-berlin.de, pg 290

Matthias Media (Australia) *Tel:* (02) 9663 1478 *Toll Free Tel:* 1800 814 360 (Australia) *Fax:* (02) 9663 3265 *E-mail:* info@matthiasmedia.com.au; sales@ matthiasmedia.com.au *Web Site:* www.matthiasmedia. com.au, pg 30

Matthiesen Verlag Ingwert Paulsen Jr (Germany) *Tel:* (04841) 8352-0 *Fax:* (04841) 8352-10 *E-mail:* info@verlagsgruppe.de *Web Site:* www. verlagsgruppe.de, pg 290

Hans K Matussek & Sohn oHG (Germany) *Tel:* (02153) 916430 *Fax:* (02153) 13363 *E-mail:* buchmatussek@t-online.de *Web Site:* www.buchhandlung-matussek.de, pg 290

Vydavatelstvo MATYS sro (Slovakia) *Tel:* (02) 556 423 97; (02) 556 423 98 *Fax:* (02) 554 102 82 *E-mail:* matys@matys.sk *Web Site:* www.matys.sk, pg 608

Editions de la Matze (Switzerland) *Tel:* (027) 327 72 34 (027) 327 72 44 *E-mail:* info@editionsmatze.ch *Web Site:* www.editionsmatze.ch, pg 700

Editions Mediaspaul ASBL (Democratic Republic of the Congo) *Tel:* (089) 8218984; (099) 9509598 (cell) *E-mail:* info@mediaspaul.cd; diffusion@mediaspaul. cd; marketing.msp@mediaspaul.cd; service.clients@ mediaspaul.cd *Web Site:* www.mediaspaul.cd, pg 116

mediaTEXT Jena GmbH (Germany) *Tel:* (03641) 30 800-0 *Fax:* (03641) 30 800-29 *E-mail:* mediatext.de *Web Site:* www.mediatext.de, pg 1276

Mediatheque de l'Institut Francais de Madagascar (Madagascar) *Tel:* 22 236 47; 22 213 75 *Fax:* 22 213 38 *E-mail:* contact@institutfrancais-madagascar.com; info@institutfrancais-madagascar.com *Web Site:* www. institutfrancais-madagascar.com, pg 1611

Mediatheque de Monaco (Monaco) *Tel:* 93 15 29 40 *Fax:* 93 15 29 41 *E-mail:* mediatheque@mairie.mc *Web Site:* www.mediatheque.mc, pg 1614

Mediatheque du Centre Culturel Francais de Bamako (Mali) *Tel:* 20 22 40 19 *E-mail:* dir@ccfbamako. org; relationspubliques@institutfrancaismali.org *Web Site:* www.institutfrancaisdumali.org, pg 1612

Mediatheque Raphael Barquissau (Reunion) *Tel:* 02 62 32 62 50 *Fax:* 02 62 25 74 10 *E-mail:* mediasp@ mediatheque-saintpierre.fr *Web Site:* www. mediatheque-saintpierre.fr, pg 1626

Editorial Medica JIMS SL (Spain) *Tel:* 649 479 445 *Fax:* 932 11 87 65 *E-mail:* jims@es.inter.net *Web Site:* www.jimsmedica.com, pg 655

Editorial Medica Panamericana SA (Spain) *Tel:* 911317800 *Fax:* 914570919 *E-mail:* info@ medicapanamericana.es *Web Site:* www. medicapanamericana.com, pg 655

Medica Publishing, Pavla Momcilova (Czech Republic) *Tel:* 272 680 919 *Fax:* 272 680 919 *E-mail:* momcilova@volny.cz *Web Site:* www. medicapublishing.cz; www.facebook.com/ medicapublishing, pg 129

Medical Sciences International Ltd (Japan) *Tel:* (03) 5804-6050; (03) 5804-6056 (sales) *Fax:* (03) 5804-6055; (03) 5804-6055 (sales) *E-mail:* info@medsi.co. jp *Web Site:* www.medsi.co.jp, pg 482

Medical Writers Group (United Kingdom) *Tel:* (020) 7373 6642 *Fax:* (020) 7373 5768 *E-mail:* info@ societyofauthors.org *Web Site:* www.societyofauthors. org, pg 1504

Editura Medicala (Romania) *Tel:* (021) 252 51 86 *Fax:* (021) 252 51 89 *E-mail:* office@ed-medicala.ro *Web Site:* www.ed-medicala.ro, pg 589

Edizioni Medicea SRL (Italy) *Tel:* (055) 416048 *Fax:* (055) 416048 *E-mail:* info@ edizionimediceafirenze.it *Web Site:* www. edizionimediceafirenze.it, pg 453

Ediciones Medici SA (Spain) *Tel:* 93 201 05 99; 93 201 38 07; 93 201 21 44 *Fax:* 93 209 73 62 *E-mail:* omega@ediciones-omega.es *Web Site:* www. ediciones-omega.es, pg 655

The Medici Society Ltd (United Kingdom) *Tel:* (020) 7713 8800 *Fax:* (020) 7837 7579 *E-mail:* info@ medici.co.uk *Web Site:* www.medici.co.uk, pg 797

Medicina AS (Estonia) *Tel:* 6567660; 6567620 *Fax:* 6567620, pg 145

Izdatelstvo Medicina (Russia) *Tel:* (499) 264-70-43 *Fax:* (499) 264-70-43 *E-mail:* imlaw@list.ru *Web Site:* www.medlit.ru, pg 595

Medicina Konyvkiado Zrt (Hungary) *Tel:* (01) 312-2650 *Fax:* (01) 312-2450 *E-mail:* medkiad@euroweb.hu *Web Site:* www.medicina-kiado.hu, pg 369

Medicinska Naklada doo (Croatia) *Tel:* (01) 3779 444 *Fax:* (01) 3907 041 *Web Site:* www. medicinskanaklada.hr, pg 121

Editions Medicis (France) *Tel:* 01 43 36 41 05 *Web Site:* www.dervy-medicis.fr, pg 184

medico international eV (Germany) *Tel:* (069) 94438-0 *Fax:* (069) 436002 *E-mail:* info@medico.de; presse@ medico.de *Web Site:* www.medico-international.de; www.medico.de, pg 291

Medien und Recht Verlags GmbH (Austria) *Tel:* (01) 505 27 66 *Fax:* (01) 505 27 66-15 *E-mail:* verlag@ medien-recht.ccom *Web Site:* www.medien-recht.com, pg 53

Medienbuero Muenchen (Germany) *Tel:* (089) 299975 *Fax:* (089) 30767586 *E-mail:* info@medienbuero-muenchen.com *Web Site:* www.medienbuero-muenchen.com, pg 1227

L'Officina di Studi Medievali (Italy) *Tel:* (091) 586314 *Fax:* (091) 333121 *E-mail:* info@ officinastudimedievali.it *Web Site:* www. officinastudimedievali.it, pg 453

Medios Publicitarios Mexicanos SA de CV (Mexico) *Tel:* (0155) 55-23-33-42; (0155) 55-23-33-46 *Fax:* (0155) 55-23-33-79 *E-mail:* suscripciones@ mpm.com.mx; administracion@mpm.com.mx *Web Site:* www.mpm.com.mx, pg 519

Medios y Medios SA de CV (Mexico) *Tel:* (0155) 56-01-85-13, pg 519

Mediserve (Italy) *Tel:* (081) 5452717 *Fax:* (081) 5462026 *E-mail:* contact@mediserve.it *Web Site:* www.mediserve.it, pg 453

MEDITEG-Gesellschaft fuer Informatik Technik und Systeme mbH (Germany) *Tel:* (06081) 5171 *Fax:* (06081) 56017, pg 291

Edizioni Mediterranee SRL (Italy) *Tel:* (06) 3235433 *Fax:* (06) 3236277 *E-mail:* info@edizionimediterranee. net; ordinipv@edizionimediterranee.net; press@ edizionimediterranee.net *Web Site:* www. edizionimediterranee.net, pg 454

Editorial Mediterraneo Ltda (Chile) *Tel:* (02) 2351 0600; (02) 2351 0606 *Fax:* (02) 2351 0644 *E-mail:* ventas@ mediterraneo.cl; contacto@mediterraneo.cl *Web Site:* www.mediterraneo.cl, pg 99

Editorial
Mediterrania SL (Spain) *Tel:* 93 218 34 58 *Fax:* 93 265 65 23 *E-mail:* editorial@editorialmediterrania.cat *Web Site:* editorialmediterrania.net, pg 655

Izdatelstvo Meditsina i Fizkultura EOOD (Bulgaria) *Tel:* (02) 987 99 75 *Fax:* (02) 987 13 08 *E-mail:* medpubl@abv.bg *Web Site:* www.medpubl. com, pg 96

Medium-Buchmarkt GmbH (Germany) *Tel:* (0251) 46000 *Fax:* (0251) 46745 *E-mail:* info@mediumbooks.com *Web Site:* www.medium-books.de, pg 291

Medousa/Selas Ekdotiki (Greece) *Tel:* 2103648323; 2103648324 *Fax:* 2103648321 *E-mail:* medusa@ otenet.gr, pg 357

MedPharm Polska Sp z oo (Poland) *Tel:* (71) 33 50 360 *Fax:* (71) 33 50 361 *E-mail:* info@medpharm.pl *Web Site:* www.medpharm.pl, pg 571

Medpharm Scientific Publishers (Germany) *Tel:* (0711) 2582-0 *Fax:* (0711) 2582-290 *E-mail:* service@ wissenschaftliche-verlagsgesellschaft.de *Web Site:* www.wissenschaftliche-verlagsgesellschaft. de, pg 291

MEDU Verlag (Germany) *Tel:* (06103) 3 12 54 71 *Fax:* (06103) 3 12 54 75 *E-mail:* info@medu-verlag. de *Web Site:* www.medu-verlag.de, pg 291

Mega Basim Yayin San ve Tic AS (Turkey) *Tel:* (0212) 412 1700 *Fax:* (0212) 422 1151 *E-mail:* info@mega. com.tr *Web Site:* www.mega.com.tr, pg 1285

Mega Basim Yayin San ve Tic AS (Turkey) *Tel:* (0212) 412 1700 *Fax:* (0212) 422 1151 *E-mail:* info@mega. com.tr; export@mega.com.tr *Web Site:* www.mega. com.tr, pg 1336

Mehring Verlag GmbH (Germany) *Tel:* (0201) 6462106 *E-mail:* vertrieb@mehring-verlag.de *Web Site:* www. mehring-verlag.de, pg 291

Mehta Publishing House (India) *Tel:* (020) 24476924; (020) 24463048 *E-mail:* info@mehtapublishinghouse. com; production@mehtapublishinghouse.com *Web Site:* www.mehtapublishinghouse.com, pg 390

Mei Ka Printing & Publishing Enterprise Ltd (Hong Kong) *Tel:* 2540 1131 *Fax:* 2559 8718; 2559 7137 *E-mail:* info@meika-printing.com; mkpp@netvigator. com *Web Site:* www.meika-printing.com, pg 1258, 1278, 1346

Verlag Meiga GbR (Germany) *Tel:* (033841) 30538 *Fax:* (03212) 1048983 *E-mail:* info@verlag-meiga.org *Web Site:* verlag-meiga.org, pg 291

Meijishoin Co Ltd (Japan) *Tel:* (03) 5292-0117; (03) 5292-0172 (orders) *Fax:* (03) 5292-6182; (03) 5292-6183 (orders) *E-mail:* info@meijishoin.co.jp *Web Site:* www.meijishoin.co.jp, pg 482

Meilahden Kampuskirjasto Terkko (Finland) *Tel:* (09) 191 26643 *Fax:* (09) 241 0385 *E-mail:* kirjasto-terkko@helsinki.fi; terkko-info@helsinki.fi *Web Site:* www.helsinki.fi/library/terkko, pg 1590

Uitgeverij Meinema (Netherlands) *Tel:* (079) 361 54 81; (079) 362 82 82 (sales) *Fax:* (079) 361 54 89 *E-mail:* info@boekencentrum.nl; verkoop@ boekencentrum.nl *Web Site:* www.uitgeverijmeinema. nl, pg 536

Felix Meiner Verlag GmbH (Germany) *Tel:* (040) 29 87 56-0; (040) 29 87 56-41 (sales) *Fax:* (040) 29 87 56-20; (040) 299 36 14 (orders) *E-mail:* info@meiner.de *Web Site:* www.meiner.de, pg 291

Meis & Maas (Netherlands) *Tel:* (020) 303 50 10 *E-mail:* info@meisenmaas.nl *Web Site:* www. meisenmaas.nl, pg 537

Meisenbach Verlag GmbH (Germany) *Tel:* (0951) 861-0 *Fax:* (0951) 861-158 *E-mail:* info@meisenbach.de *Web Site:* www.meisenbach.de, pg 291

Otto Meissners Verlag & Co (Germany) *Tel:* (030) 8249558 *Fax:* (030) 8233338 *E-mail:* meissners-verlag@hotmail.com *Web Site:* www.meissners-verlag. de, pg 291

Mejikarufurendo-sha (Japan) *Tel:* (03) 3264-6611; (03) 3263-7666 (sales); (03) 3264-6615 (editorial) *Fax:* (03) 3264-6639; (03) 3261-6602 (sales); (03) 3264-0704 (editorial) *Web Site:* www.medical-friend. co.jp, pg 482

Melanesian Institute (Papua New Guinea) *Tel:* 732 1777 *Fax:* 732 1214 *E-mail:* info@mi.org.pg; info1. emmai@gmail.com *Web Site:* www.mi.org.pg, pg 561

Melbourne University Publishing Ltd (Australia) *Tel:* (03) 9342 0300 *Fax:* (03) 9342 0399 *E-mail:* mup-info@unimelb.edu.au *Web Site:* www. mup.com.au, pg 31

Melbournestyle Books (Australia) *Tel:* (03) 9696 8445 *E-mail:* mca@melbournestyle.com.au *Web Site:* www. melbournestyle.com.au, pg 31

Editora Melhoramentos Ltda (Brazil) *Tel:* (011) 3874-0554 *Fax:* (011) 3874-0855 *Web Site:* www. melhoramentos.com.br, pg 86

Melia Publishing Services Ltd (United Kingdom) *Tel:* (01628) 633673 *Fax:* (01628) 635562 *E-mail:* melia@melia.co.uk *Web Site:* www.melia.co. uk, pg 1459

Melino Nerella Edizioni Solarino SRL (Italy) *Tel:* (0931) 922491 *Fax:* (0931) 922491, pg 454

Melissa Publishing House (Greece) *Tel:* 2103611692 *Fax:* 2103600865 *E-mail:* info@melissabooks.com; webmaster@melissabooks.com *Web Site:* www. melissabooks.com, pg 357, 1420

Michael Meller Literary Agency GmbH (Germany) *Tel:* (089) 36 63 71 *Fax:* (089) 36 63 72 *E-mail:* info@melleragency.com *Web Site:* www. melleragency.com, pg 1228

Melos Ediciones Musicales SA (Argentina) *Tel:* (011) 4371-9842; (011) 4371-9843 *Fax:* (011) 4372-3452; (011) 4372-3453 *E-mail:* info@melos.com.ar; ventas@ melos.com.ar *Web Site:* www.melos.com.ar, pg 10

Melrose Press Ltd (United Kingdom) *Tel:* (01353) 646600 *Fax:* (01353) 646601 *E-mail:* tradesales@ melrosepress.co.uk, pg 797

Meltemi Editore SRL (Italy) *Tel:* (06) 97619551 *Fax:* (06) 97619551 *Web Site:* www.meltemieditore.it, pg 454

MP Publishing Ltd (United Kingdom) *Tel:* (01624) 618672 *Fax:* (01624) 620798 *E-mail:* info@skoobestore.com *Web Site:* mppublishing.co.uk, pg 799

MPH Bookstores Sdn Bhd (Malaysia) *Tel:* (03) 7955 1090; (03) 2938 3818 (customer service) *Fax:* (03) 7955 2090 *E-mail:* customerservice@mph.com.my *Web Site:* www.mphonline.com, pg 1432

MPH Distributors Sdn Bhd (Malaysia) *Tel:* (03) 7958 1688 *Fax:* (03) 7956 5995 *E-mail:* distributors@mph.com.my *Web Site:* distributors.mph.com.my, pg 1433

MPS Ltd (India) *Tel:* (080) 4178 4242 *Fax:* (080) 4178 4222 *E-mail:* marketing@adi-mps.com *Web Site:* www.adi-mps.com, pg 1279

MPS North America LLC (United States) *Tel:* 407-472-1280 *Fax:* 212-981-2983 *E-mail:* marketing@adi-mps.com *Web Site:* adi-mps.com, pg 1289

Enrico Mucchi Editore SRL (Italy) *Tel:* (059) 37 40 94 *Fax:* (059) 28 26 28 *E-mail:* info@mucchieditore.it; ufficiostampa@mucchieditore.it *Web Site:* www.mucchieditore.it, pg 456

Anaya & Mario Muchnik (Spain) *Tel:* 913 938 800 *Fax:* 917 426 631 *E-mail:* cga@anaya.es; administrador@anaya.es *Web Site:* www.anaya.es, pg 657

Wydawnictwo Muchomor Sp z oo (Poland) *Tel:* (22) 839 49 68 *Fax:* (22) 839 49 68 *E-mail:* muchomor@muchomor.pl *Web Site:* www.muchomor.pl, pg 571

Mudrak Publishers & Distributors (India) *Tel:* (011) 6416317, pg 391

C F Mueller Verlag (Germany) *Tel:* (06221) 489-0 *Toll Free Tel:* 800-2183-333 *Fax:* (06221) 489-279 *E-mail:* info@hjr-verlag.de *Web Site:* www.hjr-verlag.de/marken/c-f-mueller, pg 296

Lars Mueller Publishers GmbH (Switzerland) *Tel:* (044) 274 37 40 *Fax:* (044) 274 37 41 *E-mail:* info@lars-muller.ch; editorial@lars-muller.ch; marketing@lars-muller.ch; sales@lars-muller.ch *Web Site:* www.lars-mueller-publishers.com, pg 701

Michael Mueller Verlag GmbH (Germany) *Tel:* (09131) 81 28 08-0 *Fax:* (09131) 81 28 08-60 *E-mail:* info@michael-mueller-verlag.de *Web Site:* www.michael-mueller-verlag.de, pg 296

Otto Mueller Verlag (Austria) *Tel:* (0662) 881974-0 *Fax:* (0662) 872387 *E-mail:* info@omvs.at; presse@omvs.at; vertrieb@omvs.at *Web Site:* www.omvs.at, pg 54

Mueller Rueschlikon Verlags AG (Germany) *Tel:* (0711) 2 10 80-0 *Fax:* (0711) 2 36 04 15 *E-mail:* ppv@motorbuch.de *Web Site:* www.mueller-rueschlikon-verlag.de, pg 296

Mueller-Speiser Wissenschaftlicher Verlag (Austria) *Tel:* (06246) 7 31 66 *Fax:* (06246) 7 31 66 *E-mail:* verlag@mueller-speiser.at *Web Site:* www.mueller-speiser.at, pg 54

Verlag Mueller und Schindler (Germany) *Tel:* (08571) 926129 *Fax:* (08571) 8533 *E-mail:* info@muellerundschindler.de *Web Site:* www.muellerundschindler.de, pg 296

Verlag Mueller und Steinicke KG (Germany) *Tel:* (089) 74 99 156 *Fax:* (089) 74 99 157 *E-mail:* info@mueller-und-steinicke.de *Web Site:* www.mueller-und-steinicke.de, pg 296

Muery Salzmann Verlag Gesellschaft mbH (Austria) *Tel:* (0662) 873721 *Fax:* (0662) 873942 *E-mail:* office@muerysalzmann.at *Web Site:* www.muerysalzmann.at, pg 54

Robert Muir Old & Rare Books (Australia) *Tel:* (08) 9228 2111 *E-mail:* books@muirbooks.com *Web Site:* www.muirbooks.com, pg 1403

A Mukherjee & Co Pvt Ltd (India) *Tel:* (033) 22417406; (033) 22418199, pg 391

Mulcahy Associates Ltd (United Kingdom) *E-mail:* enquiries@ma-agency.com; submissions@mmbcreative.com *Web Site:* www.mmbcreative.com, pg 1244

Muller Edition (France) *Web Site:* www.muller-edition.com, pg 185

Mullick & Brothers (Bangladesh) *Tel:* (02) 8619125; (02) 8625386 *Fax:* (02) 8610562 *E-mail:* mullick_161@yahoo.com, pg 61, 1405

Mult es Jovo Kiado (Hungary) *Tel:* (01) 316-70-19 *Fax:* (01) 316-70-19 *E-mail:* info@multesjovo.hu *Web Site:* www.multesjovo.hu, pg 370

Multi Media Synergy Corp Sdn Bhd (Malaysia) *Tel:* (03) 8948 9900 *Fax:* (03) 8945 8128 *E-mail:* info@mmsc.com.my; mmsc@mmsc.com.my *Web Site:* www.mmsc.com.my, pg 509

Multidisciplinary Research Centre (Namibia) *Tel:* (061) 2063052 *Fax:* (061) 2063050 *E-mail:* tgases@unam.na; apick@unam.na *Web Site:* www.unam.edu.na/multidisciplinary-research-centre, pg 527

Multiline Books (Pakistan) *Tel:* (042) 7210089; (042) 7353564 *Fax:* (042) 7121326 *E-mail:* multiline.books@gmail.com *Web Site:* multilinebooks.com, pg 1442

Livraria Multilingua Lda (Portugal) *Tel:* 291 932235 *Fax:* 291 932288, pg 1445

Multilingual Matters Ltd (United Kingdom) *Tel:* (0117) 315 8562 *Fax:* (0117) 315 8563 *E-mail:* info@channelviewpublications.com *Web Site:* www.multilingual-matters.com, pg 799

Multimedica Ediciones Veterinarias (Spain) *Tel:* 93 674 61 08 *Fax:* 93 674 72 67 *E-mail:* info@multimedica.es *Web Site:* www.multimedica.es, pg 657

Mul'timedijnyj Kompleks Aktual'nyh Iskusstv (Russia) *Tel:* (495) 637-1100; (495) 637-11-22 (ext 247) *E-mail:* books@mdf.ru *Web Site:* www.mamm-mdf.ru, pg 596

Mundi-Prensa Libros SA (Spain) *Tel:* 914 463 350 *Fax:* 914 456 218 *E-mail:* info@paraninfo.es *Web Site:* www.mundiprensa.com, pg 657, 1451

Editora Mundo Cristao (Brazil) *Tel:* (011) 2127-4147 *Fax:* (011) 2127-4128 *E-mail:* site_editorial@mundocristao.com.br *Web Site:* www.mundocristao.com.br, pg 87

Mundo Marketing GmbH (Germany) *Tel:* (0221) 92 16 35-0 *Fax:* (0221) 92 16 35-24 *E-mail:* info@mundo-marketing.de; kontakt@mundo-marketing.de *Web Site:* www.mundo-marketing.de; www.mundo-text.de; www.mundo-akademie.de; www.mundo-presse.de, pg 296

Editorial Mundo Negro (Spain) *Tel:* 914 152 412 *Fax:* 915 192 550 *Web Site:* www.combonianos.es, pg 657

Mundt Agency (Germany) *Tel:* (0211) 3905239 *Fax:* (0211) 47454433 *E-mail:* info@mundtagency.com *Web Site:* www.mundtagency.com, pg 1228

Toby Mundy Associates Ltd (United Kingdom) *Tel:* (020) 3713 0067 *E-mail:* submissions@tma-agency.com *Web Site:* tma-agency.com, pg 1244

Munhakdongne Publishing Group (South Korea) *Tel:* (031) 955 8888; (031) 955 2635 *Fax:* (031) 955 8855 *E-mail:* rights@munhak.com *Web Site:* www.munhak.com, pg 623

Munksgaard Danmark (Denmark) *Tel:* 3375 5560 *Web Site:* www.munksgaarddanmark.dk, pg 138

Munoz Moya Editores (Spain) *Tel:* 95 565 30 58 *E-mail:* editorial@mmoya.es *Web Site:* www.mmoya.es, pg 657

James Munro & Co (United Kingdom) *Tel:* (0141) 429 1234 *Fax:* (0141) 420 1694 *E-mail:* info@skipper.co.uk *Web Site:* www.skipper.co.uk, pg 800

Munshiram Manoharlal Publishers Pvt Ltd (India) *Tel:* (011) 23671668; (011) 23673650; (011) 23636097; (011) 23638992 *Fax:* (011) 23612745 *E-mail:* info@mrmlonline.com; editorial@mrmlonline.com; rightsandpermissions@mrmlonline.com; marketing@mrmlonline.com; orders@mrmlonline.com; production@mrmlonline.com; sales@mrmlonline.com *Web Site:* www.mrmlonline.com, pg 391

Munshiram Manoharlal Publishers Pvt Ltd (India) *Tel:* (011) 23671668; (011) 23673650; (011) 23636097; (011) 23638992 *Fax:* (011) 23612745 *E-mail:* info@mrmlonline.com; sales@mrmlonline.com *Web Site:* www.mrmlonline.com, pg 1424

Munundang Publishing Co (South Korea) *Tel:* (02) 762-6010 *Fax:* (02) 745-0265 *E-mail:* munun2@chol.com *Web Site:* munundang.co.kr, pg 623

Munzinger-Archiv GmbH (Germany) *Tel:* (0751) 7 69 31-0 *Fax:* (0751) 65 24 24 *E-mail:* box@munzinger.de *Web Site:* www.munzinger.de, pg 297

Editorial la Muralla SA (Spain) *Tel:* 91 415 36 87; 91 416 13 71 *Fax:* 91 413 59 07 *E-mail:* muralla@arcomuralla.com *Web Site:* www.arcomuralla.com, pg 657

Murdoch Books Pty Ltd Australia (Australia) *Tel:* (02) 8220 2000 *Fax:* (02) 8220 2558 *E-mail:* enquiries@murdochbooks.com.au *Web Site:* www.murdochbooks.com.au, pg 32

Murmann Verlag GmbH (Germany) *Tel:* (040) 398 083-0 *Fax:* (040) 398 083-10 *E-mail:* info@murmann-publishers.de *Web Site:* www.murmann-verlag.de, pg 297

Murray Books (Australia) *Web Site:* www.murraybooks.com.au, pg 32

John Murray Press (United Kingdom) *Tel:* (020) 7873 6000 *E-mail:* enquiries@johnmurrays.co.uk *Web Site:* www.hodder.co.uk, pg 800

Ugo Mursia Editore (Italy) *Tel:* (02) 67378500; (02) 67378518 (sales) *Fax:* (02) 67378605 *E-mail:* venditeonline@mursia.com; press@mursia.com; commerciale@mursia.com (sales) *Web Site:* www.mursia.com, pg 456

Musa Editora Ltda (Brazil) *Tel:* (011) 9354-3700 *Fax:* (011) 3862-6435 *E-mail:* musaeditora@uol.com.br; musacomercial@uol.com *Web Site:* www.musaeditora.com.br, pg 87

Giov Muscat & Co Ltd (Malta) *Tel:* 2123 2923; 2123 7668 *Fax:* 2124 0496 *E-mail:* info@giovmuscat.com *Web Site:* www.giovmuscat.com, pg 1433

Musee du Louvre Editions (France) *Tel:* 01 40 20 84 80; 01 40 20 53 53 (bookshop) *E-mail:* client.louvre@rmn.fr (orders) *Web Site:* editions.louvre.fr, pg 185

Editions du Musee Rodin (France) *Tel:* 01 44 18 61 10; 01 44 18 61 24 *Fax:* 01 44 18 65 65 *E-mail:* servcom@musee-rodin.fr *Web Site:* www.musee-rodin.fr, pg 185

Editions de la Reunion des Musees Nationaux-Grand Palais (France) *Tel:* 01 40 13 48 00 *Fax:* 01 40 13 44 00 *E-mail:* editions@rmn.fr *Web Site:* www.rmn.fr, pg 185

Museo Chileno de Arte Precolombino (Chile) *Tel:* (02) 2928 1500; (02) 2928 1510; (02) 2928 1522 *Fax:* (02) 2697 2779 *E-mail:* mmarin@museoprecolombino.cl *Web Site:* www.precolombino.cl, pg 99

Museo Historico Cultural Juan Santamaria (Costa Rica) *Tel:* 2441-4775; 2442-1838 *Fax:* 2441-6926 *E-mail:* info@mhcjs.go.cr; junta@mhcjs.go.cr *Web Site:* www.museojuansantamaria.go.cr, pg 117

Museu Maritimo (Macau) *Tel:* 2859 5481 *Fax:* 2851 2160 *E-mail:* museumaritimo@marine.gov.mo *Web Site:* www.museumaritimo.gov.mo, pg 505

Museum fuer Voelkerkunde Hamburg (Germany) *Tel:* (040) 42 88 79-0 *Fax:* (040) 42 88 79-242 *E-mail:* info@myhamburg.de; publikationen@myhamburg.de *Web Site:* www.voelkerkundemuseum.com, pg 296

Museum Meermanno-Westreenianum (Netherlands) *Tel:* (070) 3462700 *Fax:* (070) 3630350 *E-mail:* info@meermanno.nl; bibliotheek@meermanno.nl *Web Site:* www.meermanno.nl, pg 1616

Museum of Applied Arts & Sciences Media (Australia) *Tel:* (02) 9217 0129 *Fax:* (02) 9217 0434 *E-mail:* powerhousepublishing@maas.museum *Web Site:* maas.museum/maas-media, pg 32

National Central Library (Taiwan) *Tel:* (02) 2361-9132; (02) 2361-9132 (ext 231, general info); (02) 2361 9132 (ext 250, reference) *Fax:* (02) 2311-0155 *Web Site:* www.ncl.edu.tw, pg 1636

National Centre for Information & Documentation Central Research & Technical Library (Bulgaria) *Tel:* (02) 817 38 24; (02) 817 38 40; (02) 817 38 41; (02) 817 38 42 *Fax:* (02) 971 31 20 *E-mail:* ctb@nacid-bg.net; nacid@nacid-bg.net *Web Site:* www.nacid.bg, pg 1580

National Council for Voluntary Organisations (NCVO) (United Kingdom) *Tel:* (020) 7713 6161 *Fax:* (020) 7713 6300 *E-mail:* ncvo@ncvo.org.uk *Web Site:* www.ncvo.org.uk, pg 801

National Council of Applied Economic Research, Publications Division (India) *Tel:* (011) 23379861; (011) 23379862; (011) 23379863; (011) 23379865; (011) 23379866; (011) 23379868; (011) 23379857 *Fax:* (011) 23370164 *E-mail:* info@ncaer.org; publ@ncaer.org *Web Site:* www.ncaer.org, pg 392

National Council of Educational Research & Training, Publication Department (India) *Tel:* (011) 26560620; (011) 26864811 *Fax:* (011) 26868419 *E-mail:* cbm.ncert@nic.in *Web Site:* www.ncert.nic.in, pg 392

National Defense Industry Press (China) *Tel:* (010) 88540777; (010) 88540559 (editorial) *Fax:* (010) 88540776 *Web Site:* www.ndip.cn, pg 107

National Diet Library (Japan) *Tel:* (03) 3581-2331; (03) 3506-3300 *Fax:* (03) 3508-2934; (03) 3506-3301 *E-mail:* kokusai@ndl.go.jp *Web Site:* www.ndl.go.jp, pg 1606

Editura National (Romania) *Tel:* (021) 4500362 *Fax:* (021) 4500362 *Web Site:* www.editura-national.ro, pg 589

National Extension College (United Kingdom) *Tel:* (01223) 400 200 *Toll Free Tel:* 0800 389 2839 *E-mail:* info@nec.ac.uk *Web Site:* www.nec.ac.uk, pg 801

National Federation of Retail Newsagents (NFRN) (United Kingdom) *Tel:* (020) 7253 4225 *E-mail:* service@nfrnonline.com *Web Site:* www.nfrnonline.com, pg 1396

National Foundation for Educational Research (United Kingdom) *Tel:* (01753) 574123 *Fax:* (01753) 691632 *E-mail:* enquiries@nfer.ac.uk *Web Site:* www.nfer.ac.uk, pg 801

National Free Library of Zimbabwe (Zimbabwe) *Tel:* (09) 232359 *Fax:* (09) 257662, pg 1645

National Galleries of Scotland (United Kingdom) *Tel:* (0131) 624 6269 *Fax:* (0131) 623 7135 *E-mail:* publications@nationalgalleries.org *Web Site:* www.nationalgalleries.org/research/publishing, pg 801

National Gallery of Australia (Australia) *Tel:* (02) 6240 6438; (02) 6240 6411; (02) 6240 6420 (orders) *Fax:* (02) 6240 6628 (orders); (02) 6240 6529 *E-mail:* ecom@nga.gov.au *Web Site:* www.nga.gov.au, pg 32

National Gallery of Victoria (Australia) *Tel:* (03) 8620 2222; (03) 8620 2243 (bookshop) *Fax:* (03) 8620 2535 *E-mail:* enquiries@ngv.vic.gov.au; gallery.shop@ngv.vic.gov.au (bookshop) *Web Site:* www.ngv.vic.gov.au, pg 32

National Geographic Deutschland (Germany) *Tel:* (040) 3703-0 *E-mail:* service@nationalgeographic.de *Web Site:* www.nationalgeographic.de, pg 298

National Historical Commission of the Philippines (Philippines) *Tel:* (02) 2547482 *E-mail:* records@nhcp.gov.ph; rphd@nhcp.gov.ph *Web Site:* nhcp.gov.ph, pg 565

National History Museum Publishing (United Kingdom) *Web Site:* www.nhm.ac.uk/business-services/publishing.html; www.facebook.com/naturalhistorymuseum; twitter.com/NHM_London, pg 801

National Information & Documentation Center (NIDOC) (Egypt) *Tel:* (02) 3371696 *Fax:* (02) 3371697 *E-mail:* nidoc@nrc.sci.eg, pg 1587

National Institute for Health Care Excellence (NICE) (United Kingdom) *Tel:* (0300) 323 0140 *Fax:* (0300) 323 0148 *E-mail:* nice@nice.org.uk *Web Site:* www.nice.org.uk, pg 801

National Institute of Historical & Cultural Research, Centre of Excellence (Pakistan) *Tel:* (051) 2896153 (ext 102) *Fax:* (051) 2896152 *E-mail:* nihcr@yahoo.com *Web Site:* www.nihcr.edu.pk, pg 560

National Institute of Public Administration Library (Zambia) *Tel:* (021) 1228802; (021) 1228804 *Fax:* (021) 1227213 *E-mail:* registrar@nipa.co.zm; executivedirector@nipa.ac.zm *Web Site:* www.nipa.ac.zm, pg 1644

National ISBN Agency (Bulgaria) *Tel:* (02) 946 11 43; (02) 918 32 19 *Fax:* (02) 843 54 95 *E-mail:* isbn@nationallibrary.bg *Web Site:* www.nationallibrary.bg, pg 1367

National ISBN Agency (Ukraine) *Tel:* (044) 296-32-36 *Fax:* (044) 292-01-84 *E-mail:* isbn@ukrbook.net *Web Site:* www.ukrbook.net, pg 1393

The National Library & Archives of Egypt (Egypt) *Tel:* (02) 35750886; (02) 35751078 *Fax:* (02) 35789547 *E-mail:* darkotob7@gmail.com *Web Site:* www.darelkotob.gov.eg, pg 1587

National Library & Documentation Services Board (Sri Lanka) *Tel:* (011) 2698847; (011) 2685197; (011) 2685199 *Fax:* (011) 2685201 *E-mail:* nldsb@mail.natlib.lk; nldc@mail.natlib.lk *Web Site:* www.natlib.lk, pg 678

National Library & Documentation Services Board (Sri Lanka) *Tel:* (011) 2698847; (011) 2685197 *Fax:* (011) 2685201 *E-mail:* info@mail.natlib.lk *Web Site:* www.natlib.lk, pg 1634

National Library & Documentation Services Board (NLDSB) (Sri Lanka) *Tel:* (011) 2674386; (011) 2685197 *Fax:* (011) 2685201 *E-mail:* info@mail.natlib.lk; reader@mail.natlib.lk *Web Site:* www.natlib.lk, pg 1660

National Library & Information System Authority (NALIS) (Trinidad and Tobago) *Tel:* (868) 623-9673; (868) 624-1130 *Fax:* (868) 625-6096 *E-mail:* nalis@nalis.gov.tt *Web Site:* www.nalis.gov.tt, pg 1638

National Library Board Singapore (Singapore) *Tel:* 6332 3255; 6332 3133 *Fax:* 6332 3233 *E-mail:* helpdesk@library.nlb.gov.sg *Web Site:* www.nlb.gov.sg, pg 1388

The National Library, India (India) *Tel:* (033) 2479 1381; (033) 2479 1384; (033) 2479 1382; (033) 2479 1383 *Fax:* (033) 2479 1462 *E-mail:* nldirector@rediffmail.com *Web Site:* www.nationallibrary.gov.in, pg 1601

National Library "Ivan Vazov" (Bulgaria) *Tel:* (032) 654 912 *Fax:* (032) 654 902 *E-mail:* nbiv@libplovdiv.com *Web Site:* www.libplovdiv.com, pg 1580

National Library of Australia (Australia) *Tel:* (02) 6262 1111 *Fax:* (02) 6257 1703 *E-mail:* nlasales@nla.gov.au *Web Site:* www.nla.gov.au/publications, pg 32

National Library of Australia (Australia) *Tel:* (02) 6262 1111 *Fax:* (02) 6257 1703 *E-mail:* www@nla.gov.au *Web Site:* www.nla.gov.au, pg 1647

National Library of Bangladesh, Directorate of Archives & Libraries (Bangladesh) *Tel:* (02) 9129992 *Fax:* (02) 9135709 *Web Site:* www.nanl.gov.bd, pg 1365

National Library of Belarus (Belarus) *Tel:* (017) 266-37-02; (017) 266 37 37 *Fax:* (017) 266-37-06 *E-mail:* inbox@nlb.by *Web Site:* www.nlb.by, pg 1577

National Library of Engineering Sciences (Pakistan) *Tel:* (042) 99029243; (042) 99250223; (042) 99250222 *E-mail:* lib@uet.edu.pk *Web Site:* library.uet.edu.pk, pg 1620

National Library of Greece (Greece) *Tel:* 2103382500; 2103382600 *Fax:* 2103608246 *Web Site:* www.nlg.gr, pg 1598

National Library of Guyana (Guyana) *Tel:* (02) 227-4053, pg 1598

The National Library of Ireland (Ireland) *Tel:* (01) 603 0200 *Fax:* (01) 661 2523 *E-mail:* info@nli.ie *Web Site:* www.nli.ie, pg 413, 1603

National Library of Ireland Society (Ireland) *Tel:* (01) 6030284 *E-mail:* nlisociety@nli.ie *Web Site:* www.nli.ie/en/national-library-society.aspx, pg 1654

The National Library of Israel (Israel) *Tel:* (02) 7336336 *Fax:* (02) 7336122 *E-mail:* archives@nli.org.il *Web Site:* www.huji.ac.il; web.nli.org.il, pg 1604

National Library of Jamaica (Jamaica) *Tel:* (876) 967-1526; (876) 967-2516; (876) 967-2494; (876) 967-2496 *Fax:* (876) 922-5567 *E-mail:* nljresearch@cwjamaica.com; nlj@nlj.gov.jm *Web Site:* nlj.gov.jm, pg 1606

The National Library of Korea (South Korea) *Tel:* (02) 535-4142; (02) 590-0513-4 *Fax:* (02) 590-0530 *E-mail:* nlkpc@mail.nl.go.kr *Web Site:* www.nl.go.kr, pg 1632

National Library of Kuwait (Kuwait) *Tel:* 22929803; 22929804; 22929805 *Fax:* 22415195 *E-mail:* library@nlk.gov.kw; nlk@nlk.gov.kw *Web Site:* www.nlk.gov.kw, pg 1608

National Library of Latvia (Latvia) *Tel:* 67806100 *Fax:* 67280851 *E-mail:* lnb@lnb.lv *Web Site:* www.lnb.lv, pg 1609

National Library of Libya (Libya) *Tel:* (061) 9097074; (061) 9096379 *Fax:* (051) 9097073 *E-mail:* nat_lib_libya@hotmail.com *Web Site:* www.nllnet.net, pg 1610

National Library of Myanmar (Myanmar) *Tel:* (01) 662470; (01) 660387 *Fax:* (01) 663902 *E-mail:* nl.myanmar@gmail.com *Web Site:* www.nlm.gov.mm, pg 1615

National Library of Namibia (Namibia) *Tel:* (061) 2935300; (061) 2935304 *Fax:* (061) 2935321 *E-mail:* natlib@mec.gov.na *Web Site:* www.nln.gov.na, pg 1615

National Library of New Zealand (New Zealand) *Tel:* (04) 474 3000 *Fax:* (04) 474 3063 *E-mail:* information@natlib.govt.nz *Web Site:* natlib.govt.nz, pg 1617

National Library of Nigeria (Nigeria) *Tel:* (09) 2346773 *E-mail:* info@nln.gov.ng *Web Site:* www.nln.gov.ng, pg 1619

National Library of Pakistan (Pakistan) *Tel:* (051) 9202549; (051) 9207456; (051) 9206436 (ext 214) *Fax:* (051) 9217286 *E-mail:* nationallibrary2000@yahoo.com *Web Site:* www.nlp.gov.pk, pg 1620

National Library of Papua New Guinea (Papua New Guinea) *Tel:* 323 7775; 722 28 073 (cell), pg 1621

National Library of Scotland (United Kingdom) *Tel:* (0131) 623 3700 *Fax:* (0131) 623 3701 *E-mail:* enquiries@nls.uk *Web Site:* www.nls.uk, pg 801, 1641

National Library of South Africa (South Africa) *Tel:* (012) 401 9700 *Fax:* (012) 325 5702 *E-mail:* infodesk@nlsa.ac.za *Web Site:* www.nlsa.ac.za, pg 1631

The National Library of Thailand (Thailand) *Tel:* (02) 281-5212 *E-mail:* director@nlt.go.th *Web Site:* www.nlt.go.th/th, pg 1638

National Library of the Philippines (NLP) (Philippines) *Tel:* (02) 310-5035; (02) 336-7200 *E-mail:* do@nlp.gov.ph *Web Site:* web.nlp.gov.ph, pg 1622

National Library of Turkmenistan (Turkmenistan) *Tel:* (012) 357 489 *Fax:* (012) 353 560, pg 1640

National Library of Uganda (Uganda) *Tel:* (0414) 254661; (0414) 233633 *Fax:* (0414) 348625 *E-mail:* admin@nlu.go.ug; info@nlu.go.ug *Web Site:* www.nlu.go.ug, pg 1640

National Library of Vietnam (Vietnam) *Tel:* (04) 38255397 *Fax:* (04) 38253357 *E-mail:* info@nlv.gov.vn *Web Site:* nlv.gov.vn; www.thuvienquocgia.vn, pg 1644

New Holland Publishers (NZ) Ltd (New Zealand) *Tel:* (09) 481 0444 *E-mail:* books@nhp.co.nz *Web Site:* nz.newhollandpublishers.com, pg 548

New Holland Publishers (UK) Ltd (United Kingdom) *Tel:* (020) 7953 7565 *E-mail:* enquiries@nhpub.co.uk *Web Site:* newhollandpublishers.com/uk, pg 803

New Internationalist Publications Ltd (United Kingdom) *Tel:* (01865) 403345 *Fax:* (01865) 403346 *E-mail:* contracts@newint.org *Web Site:* newint.org, pg 803

New Island (Ireland) *Tel:* (01) 278 4225 *Web Site:* www.newisland.ie, pg 413

New Island Printing Co Ltd (Hong Kong) *Tel:* 2442 8282 *Fax:* 2443 9882 *E-mail:* info@newisland.com *Web Site:* www.newisland.com, pg 1259

New Light Publishers (India) *Tel:* (011) 25737448 *E-mail:* newlightpublishers@gmail.com, pg 393

New Magazine Edizioni (Italy) *Tel:* (335) 6597487 (cell) *E-mail:* info@newmagazine.it *Web Site:* www.newmagazine.it; www.rivistamedica.it/new_magazine.htm, pg 456

New Playwrights' Network (United Kingdom) *Tel:* (01684) 540154 *Web Site:* www.cressrelles.co.uk, pg 803

New Saraswati House (India) Pvt Ltd (India) *Tel:* (011) 43556600; (011) 23281022 *Fax:* (011) 43556688 *E-mail:* delhi@saraswatihouse.com *Web Site:* www.saraswatihouse.com, pg 393

New World Press (China) *Tel:* (010) 68995424 *Fax:* (010) 68998733, pg 107

New Zealand Book Council (New Zealand) *Tel:* (04) 801 5546 *Fax:* (04) 801 5547 *E-mail:* admin@bookcouncil.org.nz *Web Site:* www.bookcouncil.org.nz, pg 1498

New Zealand Council for Educational Research (NZCER) (New Zealand) *Tel:* (04) 384 7939 *Fax:* (04) 384 7933 *E-mail:* sales@nzcer.org.nz *Web Site:* www.nzcer.org.nz/nzcer-press, pg 548

New Zealand Council for Educational Research (NZCER) (New Zealand) *Tel:* (04) 384 7939 *Fax:* (04) 384 7933 *E-mail:* sales@nzcer.org.nz *Web Site:* www.nzcer.org.nz, pg 1384

New Zealand Council for Educational Research (NZCER) (New Zealand) *Tel:* (04) 384 7939 *Fax:* (04) 384 7933 *Web Site:* www.nzcer.org.nz, pg 1498

New Zealand Library Association Inc t/a LIANZA (New Zealand) *Tel:* (04) 801 5542 *Fax:* (04) 801 5543 *E-mail:* admin@lianza.org.nz *Web Site:* www.lianza.org.nz, pg 1657

New Zealand Press Council (New Zealand) *Toll Free Tel:* 0800 969 357 *E-mail:* info@presscouncil.org.nz *Web Site:* www.presscouncil.org.nz, pg 1384

New Zealand Society of Authors (NZSA) (New Zealand) *Tel:* (09) 379 4801 *Fax:* (09) 379 4801 *E-mail:* office@nzauthors.org.nz *Web Site:* www.authors.org.nz, pg 1498

New Zealand Standard Book Numbering Agency (New Zealand) *Tel:* (04) 474 3074 *Fax:* (04) 474 3161 *E-mail:* isbn@dia.govt.nz *Web Site:* www.natlib.govt.nz, pg 1385

New Zealand Writers Guild (New Zealand) *Tel:* (09) 360 1408 *E-mail:* info@nzwg.org.nz *Web Site:* www.nzwritersguild.org.nz, pg 1498

Newark Recycled Paperboard Solutions (United States) *Tel:* 908-276-4000 *Fax:* 908-276-0575 *Web Site:* www.newarkgroup.com, pg 1350

Newcom Translations (United Kingdom) *Tel:* (020) 7517 1270; (020) 7193 8952 *Fax:* (020) 7517 1271 *E-mail:* newcom@newcomgroup.com *Web Site:* www.newcomgroup.com, pg 1253

Newman Centre Publications (Australia) *Tel:* (02) 9637 3351, pg 33

Newscom Pte Ltd (Singapore) *Tel:* 6291 9861 *Fax:* 6293 1445, pg 605

Newstech Publishing Inc (India) *Tel:* (011) 41435648 *E-mail:* kb@newstechglobal.com *Web Site:* www.newstechglobal.com/books.html, pg 1280, 1327

Newton Compton Editori (Italy) *Tel:* (06) 65002553; (06) 65002908 *Fax:* (06) 65002892 *E-mail:* info@newtoncompton.com *Web Site:* www.newtoncompton.com, pg 457

NIAS Press (Denmark) *Tel:* 3532 9500 *Fax:* 3532 9549 *E-mail:* books@nias.ku.dk *Web Site:* www.niaspress.dk, pg 138

Nibbe & Wiedling Literary Agency (Germany) *Tel:* (08152) 98 18 77; (08974) 56 71 88 *Fax:* (08152) 78 548 *E-mail:* wiedling@nibbe-wiedling.de *Web Site:* www.nibbe-wiedling.de, pg 1228

Nibondh & Co Ltd (Thailand) *Tel:* (02) 221-2611; (02) 221-1553; (02) 225-9785 *Fax:* (02) 224-6889 *E-mail:* info@nibondhbooks.com; books@nibondhbooks.com *Web Site:* www.nibondhbooks.com, pg 1454

Nicolaische Verlagsbuchhandlung GmbH (Germany) *Tel:* (030) 25 37 38-0 *Fax:* (030) 25 37 38-39 *E-mail:* info@nicolai-verlag.de *Web Site:* www.nicolai-verlag.de, pg 300

Editura Niculescu (Romania) *Tel:* (021) 312 97 82 *Fax:* (021) 312 97 83 *E-mail:* editura@niculescu.ro; club@niculescu.ro (book club) *Web Site:* www.niculescu.ro, pg 589

Niederland Verlag (Germany) *Tel:* (089) 3541383 *Fax:* (089) 3541383 *E-mail:* niederlandverlag@aol.com *Web Site:* www.niederlandverlag.de, pg 300

Niedersaechsische Landesbibliothek (Germany) *Tel:* (0511) 1267-0 *Fax:* (0511) 1267-202 *E-mail:* information@gwlb.de *Web Site:* www.nlb-hannover.de, pg 1593

Niedersaechsische Staats- und Universitaetsbibliothek Goettingen (Germany) *Tel:* (0551) 39-5231 *Fax:* (0551) 39-5222 *E-mail:* sekretariat@sub.uni-goettingen.de *Web Site:* www.sub.uni-goettingen.de, pg 1593

Nieko rimto (Lithuania) *Tel:* (05) 212 2061 *Fax:* (05) 212 2061 *E-mail:* info@niekorimto.lt *Web Site:* www.niekorimto.lt, pg 502

Nielsen Book (United Kingdom) *Tel:* (01483) 712 200 *Fax:* (01483) 712 201 *E-mail:* sales.bookdata@nielsen.com; marketing.book@nielsen.com; customerservices.book@nielsen.com *Web Site:* www.nielsenbook.co.uk, pg 803

CW Niemeyer Buchverlage GmbH (Germany) *Tel:* (05151) 200-312 *Fax:* (05151) 200-319 *E-mail:* info@niemeyer-buch.de *Web Site:* www.niemeyer-buch.de, pg 301

Nieswand-Verlag GmbH (Germany) *Tel:* (0431) 7028 163 *Fax:* (0431) 7028 119 *E-mail:* info@nieswandverlag.de *Web Site:* www.nieswandverlag.de, pg 301

Hans-Nietsch-Verlag OHG (Germany) *Tel:* (07641) 46 88 530 *Fax:* (07641) 46 88 585 *E-mail:* info@nietsch.de *Web Site:* www.nietsch.de, pg 301

Uitgeverij Nieuw Amsterdam (Netherlands) *Tel:* (020) 5706100 *Fax:* (020) 5706199 *E-mail:* info@nieuwamsterdam.nl *Web Site:* www.nieuwamsterdam.nl, pg 538

Uitgeverij Nieuwe Stad (Netherlands) *Tel:* (073) 5113656 *E-mail:* nieuwe.stad@focolare.nl, pg 538

Nigensha Publishing Co Ltd (Japan) *Tel:* (03) 5395-2041; (03) 5395-0511 (sales) *Fax:* (03) 5395-2045; (03) 5395-0515 (sales) *E-mail:* info@nigensha.jp *Web Site:* www.nigensha.co.jp, pg 483

Nigerian Book Fair Trust (NBFT) (Nigeria) *Tel:* (01) 8124705 *E-mail:* info@nibfng.org *Web Site:* www.nibfng.org, pg 1385

Nigerian Educational Research & Development Council (NERDC) (Nigeria) *Tel:* (090) 39730713; (070) 81361390 *E-mail:* info@nerdc.ng *Web Site:* nerdc.ng, pg 1385

Nigerian Institute of Advanced Legal Studies (NIALS) (Nigeria) *Tel:* (01) 821223; (01) 821711; (01) 821109 *Fax:* (01) 4976078; (01) 825558 *E-mail:* info.nials@gmail.com *Web Site:* nials-nigeria.org, pg 552

Nigerian Institute of International Affairs (NIIA) (Nigeria) *Tel:* (01) 2615606; (01) 2615607; (01) 9500983 *Fax:* (01) 2611360 *E-mail:* director-general@niia.gov.ng; director-general1@hotmail.com; niia@servenigeria.com *Web Site:* www.niia.gov.ng, pg 552

Nigerian ISBN Agency (Nigeria) *Tel:* (0703) 0617969 (cell) *E-mail:* natbcdnlnig@yahoo.com *Web Site:* www.nln.gov.ng, pg 1385

Nigerian Library Association (Nigeria) *Tel:* (805) 5365245 *Fax:* (09) 234-6773 *E-mail:* info@nla-ng.org *Web Site:* www.nla-ng.org, pg 1658

Nigerian Publishers' Association (NPA) (Nigeria) *Tel:* (02) 7515352; (080) 37251454 (cell), pg 1385

Nigerian School Library Association (Nigeria) *Tel:* (0830) 3893853 (cell) *Web Site:* www.nsla.org.ng, pg 1658

Verlag Niggli AG (Switzerland) *Tel:* (044) 586 7968 *E-mail:* info@niggli.ch *Web Site:* www.niggli.ch, pg 701

Nihon Bunka Kagakusha Co Ltd (Japan) *Tel:* (03) 39463131 *Fax:* (03) 39463592; (03) 39463567 (sales) *Web Site:* www.nichibun.co.jp, pg 483

Nihon-Bunkyo Shuppan (Japan Educational Publishing Co Ltd) (Japan) *Tel:* (06) 6692-1261 *Fax:* (06) 6606-5171, pg 483

Nihon Eibungakkai (Japan) *Tel:* (03) 5261-1922 *Fax:* (03) 5261-1922 *E-mail:* jeimu@elsj.org *Web Site:* www.elsj.org, pg 1497

Nihon Igaku Toshokan Kyokai (Japan) *Tel:* (03) 5577-4509 *Fax:* (03) 5577-4510 *E-mail:* jmlajimu@sirius.ocn.ne.jp *Web Site:* plaza.umin.ac.jp/~jmla; jmla.umin.jp/, pg 1655

Nihon Rodo Kenkyu Kiko (Japan) *Tel:* (03) 5903-6111 *Fax:* (03) 3594-1113 *E-mail:* book@jil.go.jp *Web Site:* www.jil.go.jp, pg 483

Nihon Shoten Shogyo Kumiai Rengokai (Japan) *Tel:* (03) 32940388 *Fax:* (03) 32957180 *E-mail:* info@n-shoten.jp *Web Site:* www.n-shoten.jp, pg 1380

Nihon Tosho Center Co Ltd (Japan) *Tel:* (03) 3947-9387 *Fax:* (03) 3947-1774 *E-mail:* info@nihontosho.co.jp *Web Site:* www.nihontosho.co.jp, pg 483

Nihon Toshokan Joho Gakkai (Japan) *E-mail:* office@jslis.jp *Web Site:* www.jslis.jp, pg 1655

Nihon Toshokan Kyokai (Japan) *Tel:* (03) 3523-0811 *Fax:* (03) 3523-0841 *E-mail:* info@jla.or.jp *Web Site:* www.jla.or.jp, pg 1655

Nihon Vogue Co Ltd (Japan) *Tel:* (03) 5261-5082 *Fax:* (03) 3269-8760 *E-mail:* n-koukoku@tezukuritown.com *Web Site:* www.tezukuritown.com; www.nihonvogue.co.jp, pg 483

NIIR Project Consultancy Services (NPCS) (India) *Tel:* (011) 23843955; (011) 23845654; (011) 23845886 *Fax:* (011) 23841561 *E-mail:* npcs.india@gmail.com *Web Site:* www.niir.org, pg 393

Uitgeverij Nijgh & Van Ditmar (Netherlands) *Tel:* (020) 76 07 210 *E-mail:* info@nijghenvanditmar.nl *Web Site:* www.singeluitgeverijen.nl/nijgh-van-ditmar, pg 538

Nikas Publications (Greece) *Tel:* 2103307079 *Fax:* 2103834078 *E-mail:* info@nikasbooks.gr; rights@nikasbooks.gr *Web Site:* www.nikasbooks.gr, pg 358

Nikkagiren Shuppan-Sha (JUSE Press Ltd) (Japan) *Tel:* (03) 5379-1240 *Fax:* (03) 3356-3419 *E-mail:* sales@juse-p.co.jp *Web Site:* www.juse-p.co.jp, pg 483

The Nikkan Kogyo Shimbun Ltd (Japan) *Tel:* (03) 5644-7000 *Fax:* (03) 5644-7100 *E-mail:* info@media.nikkan.co.jp *Web Site:* www.nikkan.co.jp, pg 483

Nikkei Business Publications Inc (Japan) *Tel:* (03) 6811-8311 *Fax:* (03) 5421-9804 *Web Site:* www.nikkeibp. com, pg 484

Nikol Verlagsgesellschaft mbH & Co KG (Germany) *Tel:* (040) 611 683-0 *Fax:* (040) 611 683-22 *E-mail:* info@nikol-verlag.de *Web Site:* www.nikol-verlag.de, pg 301

S Nikolopoulos (Greece) *Tel:* 2103645779 *Fax:* 2103645779 *E-mail:* bkyriakid@otenet.gr; libreria@otenet.gr *Web Site:* www.bkyriakidis.gr, pg 358

NiL Editions (France) *Tel:* 01 53 67 14 00 *E-mail:* web@robert-laffont.fr *Web Site:* www.nil-editions.fr, pg 186

The Nile Bookshop (Sudan) *Tel:* (012) 099 6505 *E-mail:* mohamed@thenilebookshop.com *Web Site:* www.thenilebookshop.com, pg 1452

Nilsson Literary Agency (Sweden) *Tel:* (040) 794 00 *E-mail:* info@nilssonagency.com *Web Site:* www. nilssonagency.com, pg 1237

Nimbus, Kunst und Buecher AG (Switzerland) *Tel:* (044) 680 3704 *Fax:* (044) 680 3703 *E-mail:* verlag@nimbusbooks.ch; gelinek@nimbusbooks.ch *Web Site:* www.nimbusbooks.ch, pg 701

NIMS SIA (Latvia) *Tel:* 67 311 424 *Fax:* 67 311 126 *E-mail:* nims@nims.lv *Web Site:* www.nims.lv, pg 1329

Edicions de 1984 SA (Spain) *Tel:* 93 300 32 71 *Fax:* 93 485 43 75 *E-mail:* 1984@edicions1984.cat *Web Site:* www.edicions1984.cat, pg 658

99pages Verlag GmbH (Germany) *Tel:* (040) 35 70 12 40 *Fax:* (040) 35 70 12 28 *E-mail:* info@99pages.de *Web Site:* www.99pages.de, pg 301

Ningbo Newspapering Printing & Development Co Ltd (China) *Tel:* (0574) 87685512 *E-mail:* office@ningboprint.com *Web Site:* www.ningboprint.com, pg 1319

Nippan Shuppan Hanbai Inc (Japan) *Tel:* (03) 3233-4838; (03) 3233-3829 *Fax:* (03) 3233-0486; (03) 3233-6045 *E-mail:* press@nippan.co.jp *Web Site:* www.nippan.co.jp, pg 1429

Nippon Hikaku Bungakukai (Japan) *Tel:* (03) 5275-8730 *Fax:* (03) 3802-8535 *E-mail:* smorosak@law.nihon-u.ac.jp *Web Site:* www.nihon-hikaku.org, pg 1497

Nippon Jitsugyo Publishing Co Ltd (Japan) *Tel:* (03) 3814-5161; (03) 3818-9481 (sales) *Fax:* (03) 3818-2723; (03) 3818-1881 (sales) *E-mail:* koukoku@njg. co.jp *Web Site:* www.njg.co.jp, pg 484

Nippon Yakugaku Toshokan Kyogikai (Japan) *Tel:* (03) 6267-4550 *Fax:* (03) 6267-4555 *E-mail:* info@yakutokyo.jp *Web Site:* www.yakutokyo.jp, pg 1655

NISC (South Africa) *Tel:* (046) 622 9698 *Fax:* (046) 622 9550 *E-mail:* sales@nisc.co.za *Web Site:* www.nisc.co.za, pg 616

Nishimura Co Ltd (Japan) *Tel:* (025) 223-2388 *Fax:* (025) 224-7165 *E-mail:* office@nishimurashoten. co.jp; order@nishimurashoten.co.jp; tokyo@nishimurashoten.co.jp *Web Site:* www.nishimurashoten. co.jp, pg 484

Nissha Printing Co Ltd (Japan) *Tel:* (075) 811 8111 *Fax:* (075) 801 8250 *Web Site:* www.nissha.co.jp, pg 1329

Nistri-Lischi Editori (Italy) *Tel:* (050) 563371 *Fax:* (050) 562726 *E-mail:* lischi.press@unipi.it *Web Site:* www. nistri-lischi.it, pg 457

Rainar Nitzsche Verlag (Germany) *Tel:* (0631) 61305 *Fax:* (0631) 61305 *E-mail:* info@nitzscheverlag.de *Web Site:* www.nitzscheverlag.de, pg 301

Niyogi Books (India) *Tel:* (011) 26816301; (011) 49327000 *Fax:* (011) 26810483; (011) 26813830 *E-mail:* niyogibooks@gmail.com; pr@niyogibooksindia.com *Web Site:* www. niyogibooksindia.com, pg 393

Izdatel'stvo Nizhegorodskogo Gosudarstvennogo Universiteta (Russia) *Tel:* (831) 462-30-90; (831) 462-31-06 (public relations) *Fax:* (831) 462-30-85 *E-mail:* pr@unn.ru; rector@unn.ru *Web Site:* www. unn.ru, pg 596

Njala University Library (University of Sierra Leone) (Sierra Leone) *Tel:* (022) 228 788 *Fax:* (022) 226 851 *E-mail:* njala@njala.edu.sl *Web Site:* njala.edu. sl/research/njala-campus-library, pg 1629

NKI Nettstudier (Norway) *Tel:* 67 58 88 00 *Fax:* 67 58 89 94 *E-mail:* post@nki.no *Web Site:* www.nki.no, pg 556

NMBU Universitetsbiblioteket (Norway) *Tel:* 67 23 04 00 *Fax:* 67 23 06 91 *E-mail:* biblioteket@nmbu.no *Web Site:* www.nmbu.no/om/biblioteket, pg 1620

NMS Enterprises Ltd - Publishing (United Kingdom) *Tel:* (0131) 247 4026 *Fax:* (0131) 247 4012 *E-mail:* publishing@nms.ac.uk *Web Site:* www.nms. ac.uk; shop.nms.ac.uk, pg 803

Nobel (Brazil) *Tel:* (011) 3706-1466 *Web Site:* www. editoranobel.com.br, pg 88

Nobel Akademik Yayincilik Egetim Danismanlik Tic Ltd Sti (Turkey) *Tel:* (0312) 418 20 10 *Fax:* (0312) 418 30 20 *E-mail:* dagitim@nobelyayin.com *Web Site:* www. nobelyayin.com, pg 722

Ediciones Nobel SA (Spain) *Tel:* 985 27 74 83 *Fax:* 985 27 74 85 *E-mail:* nobel@edicionesnobel.com *Web Site:* www.edicionesnobel.com, pg 658

Livraria Nobel SA (Brazil) *Tel:* (011) 3706-1469; (011) 3706-1466 *Toll Free Tel:* 0800 160018 *Fax:* (011) 3706-1462 *E-mail:* sac@livrarianobel.com.br *Web Site:* www.livrarianobel.net.br, pg 88

Librairie de Nobele (France) *Tel:* 01 43 26 08 62 *Fax:* 01 40 46 85 96 *E-mail:* librairie.f.de. nobele@wanadoo.fr *Web Site:* www.denobele.fr; librairiedenobele.blogspot.com, pg 186

Nobrow Ltd (United Kingdom) *Tel:* (020) 7033 4430 *E-mail:* info@nobrow.net; sales@nobrow. net; nobrowsubs@gmail.com (submissions) *Web Site:* www.nobrow.net, pg 803

NodoLibri (Italy) *Tel:* (031) 243113 *Fax:* (031) 273163 *E-mail:* info@nodolibri.it *Web Site:* www.nodolibri.it, pg 457

Nodus Publikationen-Klaus D Dutz Wissenschaftlicher Verlag (Germany) *Tel:* (0251) 65514 *Fax:* (0251) 661692 *E-mail:* dutz.nodus@t-online.de *Web Site:* elverdissen.dyndns.org/~nodus/, pg 301

Florian Noetzel Verlage GmbH (Germany) *Tel:* (04421) 430 03 *Fax:* (04421) 429 85 *E-mail:* info@noetzel-verlag.de *Web Site:* noetzel-verlag.de, pg 301

Noguer y Caralt Editores SA (Spain) *Tel:* 93 280 13 99 *Fax:* 93 280 19 93, pg 658

NOI-Verlag (Austria) *Tel:* (0463) 224742 *Fax:* (0463) 224744, pg 54

Les Editions Noir sur Blanc (France) *Tel:* 01 44 32 05 60 *Fax:* 01 44 32 05 61 *E-mail:* informations@libella. fr; foreignrights@libellagroup.com *Web Site:* www. leseditionsnoirsurblanc.fr; www.libella.fr, pg 186

Nolit AD (Serbia) *Tel:* (011) 3245-017; (011) 3779-651; (011) 3232-420; (011) 3248-322 (editorial) *Fax:* (011) 3248-322, pg 601

Nolit AD (Serbia) *Tel:* (011) 3245-017, pg 1447

Nomada Verlag GmbH (Germany) *Tel:* (07072) 921696 *Fax:* (07072) 60856 *Web Site:* www.nomada-verlag.de, pg 301

Nomen Verlag (Germany) *Tel:* (069) 95 41 62 13 *Fax:* (069) 95 41 62 14 *E-mail:* nomen@nomen-verlag.de *Web Site:* www.nomen-verlag.de, pg 301

Nomiki Bibliothiki (Greece) *Tel:* 2103678800 *Fax:* 2103678922 *E-mail:* info@nb.org *Web Site:* www.nb.org, pg 358

Nomos Edizioni SRL (Italy) *Tel:* (0331) 382339 *Fax:* (0331) 367429 *E-mail:* info@nomosedizioni.it; editor@nomosedizioni.it; press@nomosedizioni.it *Web Site:* www.nomosedizioni.it, pg 457

Nomos Verlagsgesellschaft mbH & Co KG (Germany) *Tel:* (07221) 2104-0 *Fax:* (07221) 2104-27 *E-mail:* nomos@nomos.de *Web Site:* www.nomos.de, pg 301

Editions Non Lieu (France) *Tel:* 01 40 29 04 80 *E-mail:* edsnonlieu@yahoo.fr *Web Site:* www. editionsnonlieu.fr, pg 186

Noordhoff Uitgevers BV (Netherlands) *Tel:* (050) 52 26 922; (088) 52 26 888 *Web Site:* www. noordhoffuitgevers.nl, pg 538

Nora Verlagsgemeinschaft (Germany) *Tel:* (030) 20454990 *Fax:* (030) 20454991 *E-mail:* kontakt@nora-verlag.de *Web Site:* www.nora-verlag.de, pg 301

Norbertinum (Poland) *Tel:* (81) 744 11 58 *Fax:* (81) 744 11 48 *E-mail:* norbertinum@norbertinum.pl *Web Site:* www.norbertinum.pl, pg 571

Editrice Nord Srl (Italy) *Tel:* (02) 34597631 *Fax:* (02) 34597216 *Web Site:* www.editricenord.it; www. facebook.com/CasaEditriceNord, pg 457

Forlagshuset Nordens Grafiska AB (Sweden) *Tel:* (040) 28 61 00 *Fax:* (040) 28 61 19 *E-mail:* kundservice@fng.se *Web Site:* www.fng.se/fng, pg 1335

Nordic Council of Ministers Publications (Denmark) *Tel:* 33 96 02 00; 33 96 04 00 *E-mail:* nmr@norden. org; nordisk-rad@norden.org *Web Site:* www.norden. org, pg 139

Nordica Libros (Spain) *Tel:* 685104101 *E-mail:* info@nordicalibros.com *Web Site:* www.nordicalibros.com, pg 658

Nordica Printing Co Ltd (Hong Kong) *Tel:* 2564 8444 *Fax:* 2565 6445 *E-mail:* sales@nordicaprint.com *Web Site:* www.nordicaprint.com, pg 1326

Nordin Agency (Sweden) *Tel:* (08) 57168525 *Fax:* (08) 57168524 *E-mail:* info@nordinagency.com *Web Site:* www.nordinagency.se, pg 1237

Editions NordSud (Belgium) *Tel:* (081) 26 22 97 *E-mail:* info@editionsnordsud.com *Web Site:* www. editionsnordsud.com, pg 71

NordSud Verlag AG (Switzerland) *Tel:* (044) 936 68 68 *Fax:* (044) 936 68 00 *E-mail:* info@nord-sued.com *Web Site:* www.nord-sued.com, pg 701

Grupo Noriega Editores (Mexico) *Tel:* (0155) 51300700 *Toll Free Tel:* 01800 706 9100; 01800 703 7500 *Fax:* (0155) 55109415 *E-mail:* limusa@noriegaeditores.com; informes@limusa.com.mx *Web Site:* www.noriega.com.mx; noriegaeditores. wordpress.com, pg 1435

NORLA (Norwegian Literature Abroad, Fiction & Non-Fiction) (Norway) *Tel:* 23 08 41 00; 23 08 41 02 *Fax:* 23 08 41 01 *E-mail:* firmapost@norla.no *Web Site:* www.norla.no, pg 1498

Norli (Norway) *Tel:* 22 00 43 00 *E-mail:* post@norli. no; eksport@norli.no; universitetsgata@norli.no *Web Site:* www.norli.no, pg 1441

Ediciones Norma-Capitel (Spain) *Tel:* 91 637 74 14; 627 405 777 *Fax:* 91 637 74 14 *E-mail:* rpa@norma-capitel.com *Web Site:* www.norma-capitel.com, pg 658

Grupo Editorial Norma Chile (Chile) *Tel:* (02) 731 7500 *Fax:* (02) 632 2079 *E-mail:* servicliente@norma.com, pg 99

Editions Norma (France) *Tel:* 01 45 48 70 96 *Fax:* 01 45 48 05 84 *E-mail:* editionsnorma@wanadoo.fr *Web Site:* www.editions-norma.com, pg 186

Norma Editorial (Spain) *Tel:* 933036820 *Fax:* 933036831 *E-mail:* norma@normaeditorial.com; info@normacomics.com *Web Site:* www.normaeditorial.com, pg 658

Norma SA (Colombia) *Tel:* (01) 41004000 *E-mail:* servicliente@norma.com *Web Site:* www. norma.com; www.librerianorma.com, pg 114

Normenausschuss Bibliotheks- und Dokumentationswesen (NABD) (Germany) *Tel:* (030) 2601-0 *Fax:* (030) 2601-1231 *E-mail:* presse@din.de *Web Site:* www.nabd.din.de, pg 1652

COMPANY INDEX

Oculum-Verlag GmbH (Germany) *Tel:* (09131) 970694 *Fax:* (09131) 978596 *E-mail:* info@oculum. de; verlag@oculum.de; bestellung@oculum.de *Web Site:* www.oculum.de, pg 302

Oddi Printing Corp (United States) *Tel:* 215-885-5210 *Web Site:* www.oddi.com, pg 1265

Oddi Printing Ltd (Iceland) *Tel:* 515 5000 *Fax:* 515 5001 *E-mail:* oddi@oddi.is *Web Site:* www.oddi.is, pg 1279, 1327, 1347

Odense Centralbibliotek (Denmark) *Tel:* 6613 1372 *Fax:* 6613 7337 *E-mail:* adm-bib@odense.dk *Web Site:* www.odensebib.dk, pg 1586

Odeon Store (Thailand) *Tel:* (02) 251-4476, pg 715, 1454

Odins Forlag AB (Sweden) *Tel:* (0498) 24 93 18 *E-mail:* info@odinsforlag.se *Web Site:* www. odinsforlag.se, pg 684

Odonata Publishing Sdn Bhd (Malaysia) *Tel:* (03) 9101 1179 *Fax:* (03) 9101 7991 *E-mail:* online@ odonatabooks.com; info@odonatabooks.com *Web Site:* www.odonatabooks.com; www.odonata.com. my, pg 509

Odusote Bookstores Ltd (Nigeria) *Tel:* (02) 2316451; (02) 2315055 *Fax:* (02) 2318781 *E-mail:* odubooks@ infoweb.abs.net, pg 1439

Ekdoseis Odysseas (Greece) *Tel:* 2103624326; 2103625575 *Fax:* 2103648030 *E-mail:* info@odisseas. gr *Web Site:* www.odisseas.gr, pg 358

OECD Publishing (France) *Tel:* 01 45 24 82 00 *Fax:* 01 45 24 85 00 *E-mail:* sales@oecd.org; rights@oecd.org *Web Site:* www.oecd.org/publishing, pg 187

Nakladatelstvi Oeconomica (Czech Republic) *Tel:* 224 095 554 *Web Site:* nakladatelstvi.vse.cz, pg 130

OEKO-TEST Verlag GmbH (Germany) *Tel:* (069) 9 77 77-0 *Fax:* (069) 9 77 77-139 *E-mail:* verlag@oekotest. de; presse@oekotest.de *Web Site:* www.oekotest.de; shop.oekotest.de, pg 302

oekobuch Verlag & Versand GmbH (Germany) *Tel:* (07633) 50613 *Fax:* (07633) 50870 *E-mail:* verlag@oekobuch.de *Web Site:* www. oekobuch.de, pg 302

oekom verlag GmbH (Germany) *Tel:* (089) 54 41 84-0 *Fax:* (089) 54 41 84 49 *E-mail:* kontakt@oekom.de *Web Site:* www.oekom.de, pg 302

Oekotopia Verlag GmbH & Co KG (Germany) *Tel:* (0251) 48198-0 *Fax:* (0251) 48198-29 *E-mail:* info@oekotopia-verlag.de *Web Site:* www. oekotopia-verlag.de, pg 302

Oekumenischer Verlag Dr R-F Edel (Germany) *Tel:* (02351) 51547 *Fax:* (02351) 568908 *E-mail:* oekverlag@t-online.de *Web Site:* www.edel-verlag.de, pg 303

Hayati Oenel Verlag (Germany) *Tel:* (0221) 58 85 40 *Fax:* (0221) 58 85 48 *E-mail:* verlag@oenel.de *Web Site:* www.oenel.de, pg 303

Oertel + Spoerer Verlags-GmbH + Co KG (Germany) *Tel:* (07121) 302 552 *Fax:* (07121) 302 558 *E-mail:* info@oertel-spoerer.de *Web Site:* www.oertel-spoerer-verlag.de, pg 303

Oesch Verlag AG (Switzerland) *Tel:* (044) 305 70 60 *Fax:* (044) 242 76 86 *E-mail:* info@oeschverlag.ch *Web Site:* www.oeschverlag.ch, pg 702

Verlag Oesterreich GmbH (Austria) *Tel:* (01) 610 77-0 *Fax:* (01) 610 77-419 *E-mail:* office@ verlagoesterreich.at; office@voe.at *Web Site:* www. verlagoesterreich.at, pg 54

Oesterreichische Gesellschaft fuer Dokumentation und Information (OGDI) (Austria) *E-mail:* office@oegdi.at *Web Site:* www.oegdi.at, pg 1647

Oesterreichische Gesellschaft fuer Literatur (Austria) *Tel:* (01) 533 81 59; (01) 533 08 64 *Fax:* (01) 533 40 67 *E-mail:* office@ogl.at *Web Site:* www.ogl.at, pg 1490

Oesterreichische Nationalbibliothek (Austria) *Tel:* (01) 534 10 *Fax:* (01) 534 10-280 *E-mail:* onb@onb.ac.at *Web Site:* www.onb.ac.at, pg 1576

Verlag der Oesterreichischen Akademie der Wissenschaften (OEAW) (Austria) *Tel:* (01) 512 9050; (01) 51581-3402; (01) 51581-3406 *Fax:* (01) 51581-3400 *E-mail:* verlag@oeaw.ac.at *Web Site:* verlag. oeaw.ac.at, pg 55

Verlag des Oesterreichischen Gewerkschaftsbundes GmbH (Austria) *Tel:* (01) 662 32 96-0 *Fax:* (01) 662 32 96-39793 *E-mail:* office@oegbverlag.at *Web Site:* www.oegbverlag.at, pg 55

Oesterreichischer Agrarverlag, Druck- und Verlagsges mbH Nfg KG (Austria) *Tel:* (01) 98 177-0 *E-mail:* office@agrarverlag.at *Web Site:* www. agrarverlag.at, pg 55

Oesterreichischer Bundesverlag Schulbuch GmbH & Co KG (Austria) *Tel:* (01) 401 36-0 *Fax:* (01) 401 36-185 *E-mail:* office@oebv.at; service@oebv.at *Web Site:* www.oebv.at, pg 55

Oesterreichischer Jagd -und Fischerei-Verlag (Austria) *Tel:* (01) 405 16 36-39 *Fax:* (01) 405 16 36-59 *E-mail:* verlag@jagd.at *Web Site:* www.jagd.at, pg 55

Oesterreichischer Kunst und Kulturverlag (Austria) *Tel:* (01) 587 85 51 *Fax:* (01) 587 85 52 *E-mail:* office@kunstundkulturverlag.at *Web Site:* www.kunstundkulturverlag.at, pg 55

Oesterreichisches Katholisches Bibelwerk (Austria) *Tel:* (02243) 32938 *Fax:* (02243) 32938 (ext 39) *E-mail:* sekretariat@bibelwerk.at; auslieferung@ bibelwerk.at *Web Site:* www.bibelwerk.at, pg 55

Oesterreichisches Staatsarchiv (Austria) *Tel:* (01) 79540 0 *Fax:* (01) 79540 109 *Web Site:* www.oesta.gv.at, pg 1576

Verlag Friedrich Oetinger GmbH (Germany) *Tel:* (040) 607909-02 *Fax:* (040) 6072326 *E-mail:* oetinger@ verlagsgruppe-oetinger.de *Web Site:* www.oetinger.de, pg 303

Dr Oetker Verlag KG (Germany) *Tel:* (0521) 155-2862 *Fax:* (0521) 155-2995 *E-mail:* presse@oetker.de *Web Site:* www.oetker-gruppe.de, pg 303

Of Primary Importance (Australia) *Tel:* (03) 5382 1010 *Fax:* (03) 5382 4014 *E-mail:* opi@opi.com.au *Web Site:* www.opi.com.au, pg 33

Off the Shelf Publishing (Australia) *Tel:* (02) 4443 7555 *Fax:* (02) 4443 7666 *E-mail:* info@offtheshelf.com.au *Web Site:* www.offtheshelf.com.au, pg 33

L'Office des publications de l'Union europeenne (Luxembourg) *Tel:* 29291 *Fax:* 2929-42758 *E-mail:* info@publications.europa.eu; bookshop@ publications.europa.eu; op-info-copyright@ publications.europa.eu *Web Site:* publications.europa. eu; publications.europa.eu/en/web/general-publications/ publications (online bookshop), pg 504, 1381

Office National d'Edition de Presse et d'Imprimerie (ONEPI) (Benin) *Tel:* 21 30 11 52 *E-mail:* quotidienlanation@yahoo.fr, pg 74

Officina Ludi Pressendrucke (Germany) *Tel:* (04102) 62 521 *Fax:* (04102) 604 800 *E-mail:* officinaludi@aol. com *Web Site:* www.officinaludi.de, pg 303

Offizin-Verlag (Germany) *Tel:* (0511) 8076194 *Fax:* (0511) 624730 *E-mail:* info@offizin-verlag.de *Web Site:* www.offizin-verlag.de, pg 303

Offizin Zurich Verlag GmbH (Switzerland) *Tel:* (078) 714 14 32 *Fax:* (044) 202 08 11 *E-mail:* info@offizin. ch *Web Site:* www.offizin.ch, pg 702

Offo Artes Graficas SL (Spain) *Tel:* 91 691 82 40 *Fax:* 91 691 92 26, pg 1262

Oficina do Livro (Portugal) *Tel:* 21 427 22 00 *Fax:* 21 427 22 01 *E-mail:* info@oficinadolivro.leya.com *Web Site:* www.oficinadolivro.pt, pg 581

OFL SA (Switzerland) *Tel:* (026) 467 51 11; (0848) 653 653 (customer service) *Fax:* (026) 467 54 66 *E-mail:* information@olf.ch; serviceclients@olf.ch *Web Site:* www.olf.ch, pg 702

Ofset Yapimevi (Turkey) *Tel:* (0212) 295 86 01 *Fax:* (0212) 295 64 55 *E-mail:* sales@ofset.com *Web Site:* www.ofset.com, pg 1285, 1336

OGC Michele Broutta Editeur (France) *Tel:* 01 45 77 93 71 *Web Site:* www.galerie-broutta.com, pg 187

Oglak Yayinlari (Turkey) *Tel:* (0212) 251 71 08-09 *Fax:* (0212) 212 293 65 50 *E-mail:* oglakkitap@oglak. com; oglak@oglak.com (sales); info@oglak.com, pg 722

OGM SpA (Italy) *Tel:* (049) 8076266 *Fax:* (049) 8076212 *E-mail:* ogm@ogm.it *Web Site:* ogm.it, pg 1281

OGM USA (United States) *Tel:* 212-964-2430 *Fax:* 212-964-2497 *Web Site:* www.ogm.it, pg 1265, 1289, 1340, 1350

Oguz Yayinlari (Turkey) *Tel:* (0212) 5113418 *Fax:* (0212) 5114695, pg 722

OH ! Editions (France) *Tel:* 01 56 54 27 30 *Fax:* 01 56 54 27 38 *E-mail:* xoeditions@xoeditions.com *Web Site:* www.xoeditions.com, pg 187

Ohmsha Ltd (Japan) *Tel:* (03) 3233-0641; (03) 3233-2425; (03) 3233-0536 (sales) *Fax:* (03) 3233-2426; (03) 3233-3440 (sales) *E-mail:* kaigaika@ohmsha.co. jp *Web Site:* www.ohmsha.co.jp, pg 484

Oikos (Argentina) *Tel:* (011) 4951-9489; (011) 4951-8129, pg 10

Oikos-Tau SA Ediciones (Spain) *Tel:* 937590791 *Fax:* 937506825, pg 659

Editions Okad (Morocco) *Tel:* 05 37 79 69 70; 05 37 79 69 71 *Fax:* 05 37 79 85 56, pg 526

OKKER Zrt (Hungary) *Tel:* (01) 320-2474 *Fax:* (01) 320-2474 *E-mail:* titkarsag@okker.hu *Web Site:* www. okker.hu, pg 370

Forlaget Oktober A/S (Norway) *Tel:* 23 35 46 20 *Fax:* 23 35 46 21 *E-mail:* oktober@oktober.no *Web Site:* www.oktober.no, pg 556

Oktober Verlag (Germany) *Tel:* (0251) 620 650 814 *Fax:* (0251) 620 650 819 *E-mail:* mail@oktoberverlag. de *Web Site:* www.oktoberverlag.de, pg 303

Old Barn Books Ltd (United Kingdom) *Tel:* (01798) 865010 *E-mail:* info@oldbarnbooks.com *Web Site:* www.oldbarnbooks.com, pg 805

Old House Books (United Kingdom) *Tel:* (01865) 811332 *Fax:* (01865) 242009 *Web Site:* www. bloomsbury.com, pg 805

Old Pond Publishing Ltd (United Kingdom) *Tel:* (0114) 240 9930 *Fax:* (0114) 303 0085 *Web Site:* www. oldpond.com, pg 805

Old Street Publishing (United Kingdom) *Tel:* (01874) 731 222 *E-mail:* info@oldstreetpublishing.co.uk *Web Site:* www.oldstreetpublishing.co.uk, pg 805

Old Vicarage Publications (United Kingdom) *Tel:* (01260) 279276 *Fax:* (01260) 298649, pg 805

Oldcastle Books Ltd (United Kingdom) *Tel:* (01582) 766348 *Fax:* (01582) 766348 *E-mail:* info@noexit.co. uk *Web Site:* www.oldcastlebooks.co.uk; www.noexit. co.uk, pg 805

Oldenbourg Schulbuchverlag (Germany) *Tel:* (030) 897 85-0 *Fax:* (030) 897 85-578 *E-mail:* service@ cornelsen.de; presse@cornelsen.de *Web Site:* www. oldenbourg.de/osv, pg 303

Oldenbourg Wissenschaftsverlag (Germany) *Tel:* (030) 260 05-0 *Fax:* (030) 260 05-251 *E-mail:* info@ degruyter.com *Web Site:* www.degruyter.com, pg 303

The Oleander Press (United Kingdom) *Tel:* (01638) 500784 *E-mail:* editor@oleanderpress.com *Web Site:* oleanderpress.com, pg 806

Firma Ksiegarska Olesiejuk (Poland) *Tel:* (22) 721 30 00 *Fax:* (22) 721 30 01 *E-mail:* internet@olesiejuk.pl *Web Site:* www.olesiejuk.pl, pg 571

Olho d'Agua, Editora e Livraria (Brazil) *Tel:* (011) 3673-1287 *Fax:* (011) 3673-1287 *E-mail:* editora@ olhodagua.com.br *Web Site:* www.olhodagua.com.br, pg 88

Olika Forlag AB (Sweden) *E-mail:* info@olika.nu *Web Site:* www.olika.nu/olika-forlag, pg 684

Editoriale Olimpia SpA (Italy) *Tel:* (055) 30321 *Fax:* (055) 3032280, pg 458

Ediciones Olimpic SL (Spain) *Tel:* 977 650 885 *Fax:* 977 650 885 *E-mail:* edolimpic@yahoo.es, pg 659

Edizioni Olivares (Italy) *Tel:* (02) 76003602 *Fax:* (02) 76018474 *E-mail:* olivares@edizioniolivares.com *Web Site:* www.edizioniolivares.com, pg 458

Oliveira Rocha-Comercio e Servicos Ltda Dialetica (Brazil) *Tel:* (011) 5084-4544 *Fax:* (011) 5084-4544, pg 88

Editions de l'Olivier (France) *Tel:* 01 41 48 84 76 *E-mail:* editionsdelolivier@editionsdelolivier.fr *Web Site:* www.editionsdelolivier.fr, pg 187

El Olivo Azul (Spain) *Tel:* 957 450897; 957 452811, pg 659

Editions Olizane (Switzerland) *Tel:* (022) 328 52 52 *Fax:* (022) 328 57 96 *E-mail:* guides@olizane.ch *Web Site:* www.olizane.ch, pg 702

Olkos Editions (Greece) *Tel:* 2103621379 *Fax:* 2103625576 *E-mail:* info@olkos.gr *Web Site:* olkos.gr, pg 1420

Edition Olms AG (Switzerland) *Tel:* (043) 8449777 *Fax:* (043) 8449778 *E-mail:* info@edition-olms.com *Web Site:* www.edition-olms.com, pg 702

Georg Olms AG - Verlag (Germany) *Tel:* (05121) 1 50-10 *Fax:* (05121) 1 50-150 *E-mail:* info@olms. de; rights@olms.de; production@olms.de; public. relations@olms.de *Web Site:* www.olms.com, pg 303

Leo S Olschki (Italy) *Tel:* (055) 6530684 *Fax:* (055) 6530214 *E-mail:* orders@olschki.it; pressoffice@ olschki.it *Web Site:* www.olschki.it, pg 458

Kristin Olson Literary Agency sro (Czech Republic) *Tel:* 222 582 042 *Fax:* 222 580 048 *E-mail:* kristin. olson@litag.cz *Web Site:* www.litag.cz, pg 1224

OL3 SRL (Italy) *Tel:* (075) 5011993 *Fax:* (075) 5016791 *E-mail:* info@ol3online.it *Web Site:* www.ol3online.it, pg 458

Olusur Basim Hizmetleri Sanayi Ticaret AS (Turkey) *Tel:* (0212) 6290606 *Fax:* (0212) 6290594 *E-mail:* info@olusur.com.tr *Web Site:* olusur.com, pg 1285, 1336

Nakladatelstvi Olympia sro (Czech Republic) *Tel:* 233 089 999 *Fax:* *E-mail:* info@iolympia.cz; olysklad@volny.cz (sales) *Web Site:* www.iolympia.cz, pg 130

OLZOG Verlag GmbH (Germany) *Tel:* (089) 71 04 66 60 *Fax:* (089) 71 04 66 61 *E-mail:* mailkontakt@ olzog.de; service@olzog.de *Web Site:* www.olzog.de, pg 303

Om Books International (India) *Tel:* (0120) 477 4100 *Fax:* (0120) 422 9356 *E-mail:* editorial@ombooks.com *Web Site:* www.ombooksinternational.com, pg 393

O'Mahony's Booksellers Ltd (Ireland) *Tel:* (061) 418155 *Fax:* (061) 414558 *E-mail:* info@omahonys.ie; customerservice@omahonys.ie; websales@omahonys. ie *Web Site:* www.omahonys.ie, pg 1426

Omakoio Trikalon & Thessalonikis (Greece) *Tel:* 2431075505; 6974580768 (cell) *Fax:* 2431075505 *E-mail:* omakoio@omakoio.gr; omakoio@aias.gr *Web Site:* www.omakoio.gr, pg 358

Michael O'Mara Books Ltd (United Kingdom) *Tel:* (020) 7720 8643 *Fax:* (020) 7627 3041 (UK sales/publicity); (020) 7627 4900 (foreign sales) *E-mail:* enquiries@ mombooks.com *Web Site:* www.mombooks.com, pg 806

Omdurman Islamic University Library (Sudan) *E-mail:* info@oiu.edu.sd *Web Site:* lib.oiu.edu.sd, pg 1634

Ediciones Omega SA (Spain) *Tel:* 93 201 05 99; 93 201 38 07; 93 201 21 44 *Fax:* 93 209 73 62 *E-mail:* omega@ediciones-omega.es *Web Site:* www. ediciones-omega.es, pg 660

Omega-Verlag (Germany) *Tel:* (02687) 92 90 68; (02687) 92 80 52 (orders) *Fax:* (02687) 92 95 24 *E-mail:* info@silberschnur.de *Web Site:* www. silberschnur.de, pg 304

Omniafiltra (United States) *Tel:* 315-346-7300 *Fax:* 315-346-7301 *E-mail:* info@omniafiltra.com *Web Site:* www.omniafiltra.com, pg 1350

Omnibus Books (Australia) *Tel:* (08) 8425 8300 *Fax:* (08) 8425 8304 *E-mail:* customer_service@ scholastic.com.au *Web Site:* www.scholastic.com.au, pg 33

Editions Omnibus (France) *Tel:* 01 44 16 05 00 *E-mail:* omnibus@psb-editions.com *Web Site:* www. omnibus.tm.fr, pg 187

Omnibus Press (United Kingdom) *Tel:* (020) 7612 7400; (01284) 705050 (orders) *Fax:* (020) 7612 7545; (01284) 702595 (orders) *E-mail:* info@omnibuspress. com; orders@musicsales.co.uk *Web Site:* www. omnibuspress.com, pg 806

Omnicon SA (Spain) *Tel:* 91 740 20 81 *Fax:* 91 357 92 95 *E-mail:* revistafv@omnicon.es *Web Site:* www. omnicon.es, pg 660

Omsons Publications (India) *Tel:* (011) 23289353; (011) 23246448 *Fax:* (011) 23289353, pg 394

Omur Printing & Binding Co (Turkey) *Tel:* (0212) 422 76 00 *Fax:* (0212) 422 46 00 *Web Site:* www. omurprint.com, pg 1336

101 Studio DTP Tomasz Tegi i Spolka Sp z oo (Poland) *Tel:* (42) 250 70 92; (42) 250 70 93; (42) 250 70 94 *Fax:* (42) 250 70 95 *E-mail:* ac@poczta.101studio. com.pl *Web Site:* www.101studio.com.pl, pg 1282, 1331

Oneull Publishing Co Ltd (South Korea) *Tel:* (02) 716-2811 *Fax:* (02) 712-7392 *E-mail:* oneull@hanmail.net *Web Site:* www.on-publications.com, pg 624

Oneworld Publications (United Kingdom) *Tel:* (020) 7307 8900 *Fax:* (020) 7307 8900 *E-mail:* info@ oneworld-publications.com; editorial@oneworld-publications.com; marketing@oneworld-publications. com; sales@oneworld-publications.com; submissions@ oneworld-publications.com *Web Site:* www.oneworld-publications.com, pg 806

Ongakuno Tomo Sha Corp (Japan) *Tel:* (03) 3235-2111; (03) 3235-2116 *Fax:* (03) 3235-2110 *Web Site:* www. ongakunotomo.co.jp, pg 484

G O Onibonoje Press (Nigeria) *Tel:* (02) 2313956 *E-mail:* info@goonibonoje.com *Web Site:* www. goonibonoje.com, pg 552

ONK Agency Ltd (Turkey) *Tel:* (0212) 241 77 00 *Fax:* (0212) 241 77 31 *E-mail:* info@onkagency.com *Web Site:* www.onkagency.com, pg 1238

Onkel & Onkel (Germany) *Tel:* (030) 61 07 39 57 *Fax:* (030) 61 07 45 78 *E-mail:* info@onkelundonkel. com *Web Site:* www.onkelundonkel.com, pg 304

Onlywomen Press Ltd (United Kingdom) *Tel:* (020) 8354 0796 *Fax:* (020) 8960 2817, pg 806

Ons Erfdeel VZW (Belgium) *Tel:* (056) 411201 *Fax:* (056) 414707 *E-mail:* info@onserfdeel.be; adm@ onserfdeel.be *Web Site:* www.onserfdeel.be, pg 71

Onstream Publications Ltd (Ireland) *Tel:* (021) 4385798 *E-mail:* info@onstream.ie *Web Site:* www.onstream.ie, pg 414

Ontopsicologia Editrice (Italy) *Tel:* (0765) 45 53 47 *Fax:* (0765) 20 71 31 *E-mail:* books@psicoedit.com *Web Site:* www.psicoedit.com, pg 458

Uitgeverij Van Oorschot bv (Netherlands) *Tel:* (020) 6231484 *Fax:* (020) 6254083 *E-mail:* contact@ vanoorschot.nl *Web Site:* www.vanoorschot.nl, pg 538

Op der Lay (Luxembourg) *Tel:* 839742 *Fax:* 899350 *E-mail:* opderlay@pt.lu *Web Site:* www.opderlay.lu; www.opderlay.com (online store), pg 504

Bokforlaget Opal AB (Sweden) *Tel:* (08) 28 21 79 *E-mail:* opal@opal.se *Web Site:* www.opal.se, pg 684

Open Door Verlag (Switzerland) *Tel:* (041) 312 14 45 *Fax:* (041) 312 14 42 *E-mail:* info@opendoorverlag.ch *Web Site:* www.opendoorverlag.ch, pg 702

Open Gate Press Ltd (United Kingdom) *Tel:* (020) 7431 4391 *Fax:* (020) 7431 5129 *E-mail:* books@ opengatepress.co.uk *Web Site:* www.opengatepress.co. uk, pg 806

Open House Verlag (Germany) *Tel:* (0341) 222 873 83 *Fax:* (0321) 214 352 35 *E-mail:* kontakt@openhouse-verlag.de *Web Site:* www.openhouse-verlag.de, pg 304

Open University of Israel (Israel) *Tel:* (09) 7782222 *Fax:* (09) 7780664 *E-mail:* infodesk@openu.ac.il *Web Site:* www.openu.ac.il, pg 421

Open University Press (United Kingdom) *Tel:* (01628) 502500; (01628) 502720 (customer service) *Fax:* (01628) 635895 (customer service) *E-mail:* enquiries@openup.co.uk; emea_orders@ mcgraw-hill.com (orders); emea_queries@mcgraw-hill. com (customer service) *Web Site:* www.mheducation. com; www.mcgrawhillcreate.com/openup, pg 806

Open University Worldwide Ltd (United Kingdom) *Tel:* (01908) 274066 *Fax:* (01908) 858787 *E-mail:* general-enquiries@open.ac.uk *Web Site:* www. open.ac.uk, pg 807

Openbook Howden Design & Print (Australia) *Tel:* (08) 8124 0000 *Fax:* (08) 8277 2354 *E-mail:* sales@ openbookhowden.com.au *Web Site:* www. openbookhowden.com.au, pg 1317

Opera Ekdoseis, Georges Miressiotis (Greece) *Tel:* 2103304546 *Fax:* 2103303634 *E-mail:* info@ operabooks.gr *Web Site:* www.operabooks.gr, pg 358

Opera Tres Ediciones Musicales SL (Spain) *Tel:* 916801505 *Fax:* 916807626 *E-mail:* operatres@ operatres.com *Web Site:* www.operatres.com, pg 660

Editions Ophrys (France) *Tel:* 01 45 78 33 80 *Fax:* 01 45 75 37 11 *E-mail:* info@ophrys.fr *Web Site:* www. ophrys.fr, pg 188

Opna Publishing (Iceland) *Tel:* 578 9080 *E-mail:* opna@ opna.is *Web Site:* opna.is, pg 373

Opolgraf SA (Poland) *Tel:* (77) 454-52-44; (77) 454-52-46 *Fax:* (77) 454-53-13 *Web Site:* www.opolgraf.com. pl, pg 1282, 1331

optimal media GmbH (Germany) *Tel:* (039931) 56 500 *Fax:* (039931) 56 555 *E-mail:* info@optimal-media. com *Web Site:* www.optimal-media.com, pg 1276, 1322

Opus Book Publishing Ltd (United Kingdom) *Tel:* (01380) 871354 *Fax:* (01380) 871354 *E-mail:* opus@dmac.co.uk *Web Site:* www.opusbooks. co.uk, pg 807

Opus Press Ltd (Israel) *Tel:* (03) 6814231 *Fax:* (03) 6814230 *E-mail:* info@opus.co.il; dorit@opus.co.il (marketing & sales) *Web Site:* www.opus.co.il, pg 421

Opus Publishing Ltd (United Kingdom) *Tel:* (020) 7267 1034 *E-mail:* opuspub@btconnect.com, pg 807

OQO Editora (Spain) *Tel:* 986 109 270 *Fax:* 986 109 356 *Web Site:* www.oqo.es, pg 660

OR-TAV Music Publications (Israel) *Tel:* (03) 566-1599 *Fax:* (03) 566-1688 *E-mail:* info@ortav.com *Web Site:* www.ortav.com, pg 421

Edicoes Ora & Labora (Portugal) *Tel:* 252941176 *Fax:* 252872947, pg 581

Orange Agency (South Korea) *Tel:* (031) 262 8623 *Fax:* (031) 262 8624 *E-mail:* orangeagency@paran. com *Web Site:* www.orangeagency.co.kr, pg 1234

orange-press GmbH (Germany) *Tel:* (0761) 287 117 *Fax:* (0761) 287 118 *E-mail:* info@orange-press.com *Web Site:* www.orange-press.com, pg 304

Oratia Media Ltd (New Zealand) *Tel:* (09) 814 8993; (027) 614 8993 (cell) *Fax:* (09) 814 8997 *E-mail:* info@oratia.co.nz *Web Site:* www.oratia.co.nz, pg 548

Orca Book Services Ltd (United Kingdom) *Tel:* (01235) 465500 *E-mail:* orders@orcabookservices.co.uk *Web Site:* www.orcabookservices.co.uk, pg 1459

Ordalaget Bokforlag AB (Sweden) *Tel:* (08) 80 88 48 *Fax:* (08) 80 88 49 *E-mail:* bok@ordalaget.se *Web Site:* www.ordalaget.se, pg 685

Ordfront Forlag AB (Sweden) *Tel:* (070) 410 20 84 *E-mail:* forlaget@ordfrontforlag.se; info@ordfront.se *Web Site:* www.ordfrontforlag.se, pg 685

Ordnance Survey (United Kingdom) *Tel:* (03456) 05 05 05 *E-mail:* customerservices@os.uk *Web Site:* www.ordnancesurvey.co.uk, pg 807

orecchio acerbo editore (Italy) *Tel:* (06) 5811861; (06) 58364814 *Fax:* (06) 5811861 *E-mail:* ufficiostampa.orecchioacerbo@gmail.com; ordini.orecchioacerbo@gmail.com *Web Site:* www.orecchioacerbo.com, pg 458

Orenda Books (United Kingdom) *E-mail:* info@orendabooks.co.uk *Web Site:* orendabooks.co.uk, pg 807

Oreos Verlag eK (Germany) *Tel:* (08021) 86 68 *Fax:* (08021) 17 50 *E-mail:* oreos@oreos.de *Web Site:* www.oreos.de, pg 304

Editions d'Organisation (France) *Tel:* 01 44 41 11 11 *Fax:* 01 44 41 11 44 *E-mail:* editeurs_entreprise@eyrolles.com; foreignrights@eyrolles.com *Web Site:* www.editions-organisation.com, pg 188

Organizacion Cultural LP SA de CV (Mexico) *Tel:* (0155) 53584721; (0155) 53584761; (0155) 53570279, pg 520

Organizacion de Bienestar Estudiantil (OBE) (Venezuela) *Web Site:* www.ucv.ve, pg 1462

Organization for Social Science Research in Eastern & Southern Africa (OSSREA) (Ethiopia) *Tel:* (011) 123 94 84 *Fax:* (011) 122 39 21 *E-mail:* info@ossrea.net *Web Site:* www.ossrea.net, pg 147

The Organization of Libraries, Museums & Documents Center of Astan Quds Razavi (Iran) *Tel:* (0511) 2219553 *E-mail:* info@aqlibrary.org *Web Site:* library.aqr.ir, pg 1602

Editions Oriane (France) *Tel:* 02 40 77 34 20 *E-mail:* editions.oriane@gmail.com *Web Site:* www.editionsoriane.com, pg 188

Edition Orient (Germany) *Tel:* (030) 61 28 03 61 *Fax:* (030) 61 07 32 91 *E-mail:* info@edition-orient.de *Web Site:* www.edition-orient.de, pg 304

Orient Paperbacks (India) *Tel:* (011) 2327 8877 *Fax:* (011) 2327 8879 *E-mail:* info@orientpaperbacks.com *Web Site:* www.orientpaperbacks.com, pg 394

Oriental Press (Netherlands) *Tel:* (068) 1472742 (cell) *E-mail:* info@apa-publishers.com *Web Site:* www.apa-publishers.com, pg 538

Librairie Orientale Sal (Lebanon) *Tel:* (01) 485793 *Fax:* (01) 485796 *E-mail:* admin@librairieorientale.com.lb *Web Site:* www.librairieorientale.com.lb, pg 499

Editorial Oriente (Cuba) *Tel:* (022) 622496; (022) 628096 *E-mail:* edoriente@cultstgo.cult.cu *Web Site:* www.editorialoriente.cult.cu, pg 124

Ediciones del Oriente y del Mediterraneo (Spain) *Tel:* 918 543 428 *E-mail:* info@orienteymediterraneo.com *Web Site:* www.orienteymediterraneo.com, pg 660

Origo Ediciones (Chile) *Tel:* (02) 2480 9800 *E-mail:* info@origo.cl *Web Site:* www.origo.cl, pg 99

Orin Books (Australia) *Tel:* (03) 9534 5680, pg 33

Orion Publishing Group Ltd (United Kingdom) *Tel:* (020) 7873 6444 *Web Site:* www.orionbooks.co.uk, pg 807

Editura Orizonturi SRL (Romania) *Tel:* (021) 3177679 *Fax:* (021) 3177678 *E-mail:* orizonturi@editura-orizonturi.ro *Web Site:* www.editura-orizonturi.ro, pg 590

Orkney Press Ltd (United Kingdom) *Tel:* (01343) 540844, pg 807

Orlanda Verlag GmbH (Germany) *Tel:* (030) 216 29 60 *E-mail:* post@orlanda.de; presse@orlanda.de *Web Site:* www.orlanda.de, pg 304

Uitgeverij Orlando (Netherlands) *Tel:* (020) 6611397 *E-mail:* info@uitgeverijorlando.nl *Web Site:* www.uitgeverijorlando.nl, pg 538

Editions Heloise d'Ormesson (Eho) (France) *Tel:* 01 56 81 30 70 *Web Site:* www.editions-heloisedormesson.com, pg 188

Ormstunga (Iceland) *Tel:* 561 0055 *E-mail:* books@ormstunga.is *Web Site:* www.ormstunga.is, pg 373

Orpen Press (Ireland) *Tel:* (01) 278 5090 *E-mail:* info@orpenpress.com *Web Site:* www.orpenpress.com, pg 414

Orpheus Books Ltd (United Kingdom) *Tel:* (01993) 774949 *Fax:* (01993) 700330 *E-mail:* info@orpheusbooks.com *Web Site:* www.orpheusbooks.com, pg 808

Orszagos Szechenyi Konyvtar (Hungary) *Tel:* (01) 224 3700; (01) 224-3845 (reference); (01) 224-3848 (reference) *Fax:* (01) 202-0804 *E-mail:* bibliogr@oszk.hu *Web Site:* www.oszk.hu, pg 1600

orte-Verlag (Switzerland) *Tel:* (071) 888 15 56 *E-mail:* info@orteverlag.ch *Web Site:* www.orteverlag.ch, pg 702

Editorial Alfredo Ortells SL (Spain) *Tel:* 96 134 54 84 *Fax:* 96 134 54 85 *E-mail:* editorial@ortells.com *Web Site:* www.ortells.com, pg 660

Oruem Publishing House (South Korea) *Tel:* (02) 585-9122 *Fax:* (02) 584-7952, pg 624

Osaka Prefectural Central Library (Japan) *Tel:* (06) 6745-0170 *Fax:* (06) 6745-0262 *Web Site:* www.library.pref.osaka.jp, pg 1607

Osaka University Library (Japan) *Tel:* (06) 6850-5067 *E-mail:* honkan@library.osaka-u.ac.jp *Web Site:* www.library.osaka-u.ac.jp, pg 1607

Osanna Edizioni SRL (Italy) *Tel:* (0972) 35 952 *Fax:* (0972) 35 723 *E-mail:* osanna@osannaedizioni.it *Web Site:* www.osannaedizioni.it, pg 458

Osborne Books Ltd (United Kingdom) *Tel:* (01905) 748071 *Fax:* (01905) 748952 *E-mail:* books@osbornebooks.co.uk *Web Site:* www.osbornebooks.co.uk, pg 808

Oscar Book International (Malaysia) *Tel:* (03) 78753515 *Fax:* (03) 78762797, pg 509

Osho Verlag GmbH (Germany) *Tel:* (0221) 2780420 *Fax:* (0221) 2780466 *E-mail:* redaktion@oshotimes.de *Web Site:* www.oshotimes.de, pg 304

Osiris Kiado (Hungary) *Tel:* (01) 266-6560 *Fax:* (01) 267-0935 *E-mail:* kiado@osirismail.hu *Web Site:* www.osiriskiado.hu, pg 370

Osprey Publishing Ltd (United Kingdom) *Tel:* (01865) 727022 *Fax:* (01865) 242009 *E-mail:* info@ospreypublishing.com *Web Site:* www.ospreypublishing.com, pg 808

Ossian Publications (United Kingdom) *Tel:* (020) 7612 7400 *Fax:* (020) 7612 7545 *E-mail:* music@musicsales.co.uk *Web Site:* www.musicroom.com; www.musicsales.com/brands, pg 808

Ost-West-Verlag (Germany) *Tel:* (06802) 994 94 98 *Fax:* (06802) 910 74 *E-mail:* info@ost-west-verlag.org *Web Site:* www.ost-west-verlag.org, pg 304

Osterreichische Bibelgesellschaft (Austria) *Tel:* (01) 523 82 40 *Fax:* (01) 523 82 40-20 *E-mail:* bibelzentrum@bibelgesellschaft.at *Web Site:* www.bibelgesellschaft.at, pg 1404

Osterreichischer Wirtschaftsverlag GmbH (Austria) *Tel:* (01) 546 64-0 *Fax:* (01) 546 64-511 *E-mail:* office@wirtschaftsverlag.at *Web Site:* www.wirtschaftsverlag.at, pg 55

Ostfalia-Verlag (Germany) *Tel:* (05334) 92 59 02 *Fax:* (05334) 92 59 03 *E-mail:* info@ostfalia-verlag.de; info@ostfalen-portal.de *Web Site:* www.ostfalia-verlag.de; www.ostfalen-portal.de, pg 304

Antiquariat Daniel Osthoff (Germany) *Tel:* (0931) 57 25 45 *Fax:* (0931) 35 37 9 45 *E-mail:* antiquariat.osthoff@t-online.de *Web Site:* www.antiquariat-osthoff.de, pg 1418

Ostschweiz Druck AG (Switzerland) *Tel:* (071) 292 29 29 *Fax:* (071) 292 29 38 *E-mail:* info@ostschweizdruck.ch; sekretariat@ostschweizdruck.ch *Web Site:* www.ostschweizdruck.ch, pg 702

Osvita (Ukraine) *Tel:* (044) 456-08-35 *Fax:* (044) 456-08-37 *E-mail:* osvitapublish_ok@ukr.net *Web Site:* www.osvitapublish.gov.ua, pg 726

Otago University Press (New Zealand) *Tel:* (03) 479 8807 *Fax:* (03) 479 *E-mail:* university.press@otago.ac.nz; publicity@otago.ac.nz *Web Site:* www.otago.ac.nz/press, pg 548

Kustannusosakeyhtio Otava (Finland) *Tel:* (09) 19961 *Fax:* (09) 643 136 *Web Site:* www.otava.fi, pg 150

Otokar Kersovani doo (Croatia) *Tel:* (051) 338 558 *Fax:* (051) 331 690 *E-mail:* otokar-kersovani@ri.htnet.hr, pg 122

Otsuki Shoten Publishers (Japan) *Tel:* (03) 3813-4651 *Fax:* (03) 3813-4656 *E-mail:* info@otsukishoten.co.jp *Web Site:* www.otsukishoten.co.jp, pg 484

Otter-Barry Books Ltd (United Kingdom) *Tel:* (01432) 820972 *E-mail:* info@otterbarrybooks.com; sales@otterbarrybooks.com *Web Site:* www.otterbarrybooks.com, pg 808

Ottovo Nakladatelstvi sro (Czech Republic) *Tel:* 221 424 111 *E-mail:* info@ottovo.eu *Web Site:* www.ottovo.cz, pg 131

Otuken Nesriyat (Turkey) *Tel:* (0212) 251 0350; (0212) 293 8871 *Fax:* (0212) 251 0012 *E-mail:* otuken@otuken.com.tr *Web Site:* www.otuken.com.tr, pg 722

Wydawnictwo Otwarte Sp z oo (Poland) *Tel:* (12) 427 12 00 *E-mail:* otwarte@otwarte.eu *Web Site:* www.otwarte.eu, pg 572

Editions de l'Ouest (France) *Tel:* 02 41 55 19 62, pg 188

Editions Ouest-France (France) *Tel:* 02 99 32 58 23 *E-mail:* commercial@edilarge.fr; editorial@edilarge.fr; press@edilarge.fr *Web Site:* www.editionsouestfrance.eu, pg 188

Oulun Yliopiston Kirjasto (Finland) *Tel:* (0294) 483501 *E-mail:* kirjasto@oulu.fi *Web Site:* www.kirjasto.oulu.fi/english, pg 1590

Outdoor Press Pty Ltd (Australia) *Tel:* (03) 9852 8400 *Fax:* (03) 9852 8400, pg 33

Outras Letras Editora (Brazil) *Tel:* (021) 2267 6627 *E-mail:* contato@outrasletras.com.br *Web Site:* www.outrasletras.com.br, pg 88

Outskirts Press Inc (United States) *Toll Free Tel:* 888-OP-BOOKS (672-6657) *Toll Free Fax:* 888-208-8601 *E-mail:* info@outskirtspress.com *Web Site:* www.outskirtspress.com, pg 1340

Ekdoseis Ouvas (Greece) *Tel:* 2108822075; 2108822063 *Fax:* 2108824960 *Web Site:* www.oyba.gr, pg 358

Editorial Oveja Negra (Colombia) *Tel:* (01) 302 06 22 *E-mail:* info@editorialovejanegra.com *Web Site:* www.editorialovejanegra.com, pg 114

George Over Ltd (United Kingdom) *Tel:* (01788) 573621, pg 1338

Overamstel Uitgevers (Netherlands) *Tel:* (020) 4624 300 *E-mail:* info@overamstel.com *Web Site:* www.overamsteluitgevers.nl, pg 538

Overseas Printing Corporation (United States) *Tel:* 415-835-9999 *Fax:* 415-835-9899 *Web Site:* www.overseasprinting.com, pg 1265

OVISS Inc (Japan) *Tel:* (06) 6352 7090 *Fax:* (06) 6352 8898 *E-mail:* info@oviss.co.jp; import@oviss.co.jp *Web Site:* www.oviss.co.jp; oviss.b-smile.jp, pg 1429

Peter Owen Publishers (United Kingdom) *Tel:* (020) 8350 1775 *Fax:* (020) 8340 9488 *E-mail:* info@peterowen.com; sales@peterowen.com *Web Site:* www.peterowenpublishers.com, pg 808

Owl Publishing (Australia) *Tel:* (03) 9596 6064 *Fax:* (03) 9596 6942 *E-mail:* owlbooks@bigpond.com *Web Site:* www.owlpublishing.com.au, pg 33

Owls Agency Inc (Japan) *Tel:* (03) 3259-0061
Fax: (03) 3259-0063 *E-mail:* info@owlsagency.com
Web Site: www.owlsagency.com, pg 1232

Oxbow Books (United Kingdom) *Tel:* (01865) 241249
Fax: (01865) 794449 *E-mail:* orders@oxbowbooks.
com; trade@oxbowbooks.com *Web Site:* www.
oxbowbooks.com, pg 808, 1459

Oxfam Australia (Australia) *Tel:* (03) 9289 9444
Toll Free Tel: 1800 088 110 *Fax:* (03) 9347 1983
E-mail: enquire@oxfam.org.au *Web Site:* www.oxfam.
org.au, pg 34

Oxfam Publications (United Kingdom) *Tel:* (020) 01292
E-mail: enquiries@oxfam.org.uk *Web Site:* www.
oxfam.org.uk, pg 808

Oxford & IBH Publishing Co Pvt Ltd (India) *Tel:* (011)
41745490; (011) 41745356; (011) 41745358
Fax: (011) 41517559 *E-mail:* oxford@oxford-ibh.in
Web Site: oxford-ibh.in, pg 394

Oxford Bibliographical Society (United Kingdom)
Tel: (01865) 277069 *Fax:* (01865) 277182
E-mail: membership@oxbibsoc.org.uk *Web Site:* www.
oxbibsoc.org.uk, pg 1504

Oxford Fajar Sdn Bhd (Malaysia) *Tel:* (03) 5629 4000
Fax: (03) 5629 4006 *E-mail:* dcs@oxfordfajar.com.my
Web Site: www.oxfordfajar.com.my, pg 509

Oxford International Centre for Publishing Studies
(United Kingdom) *Tel:* (01865) 484967 *Fax:* (01865)
484082 *E-mail:* publishing@brookes.ac.uk
Web Site: www.publishing.brookes.ac.uk, pg 808

Oxford University Press (Australia) *Tel:* (03) 9934
9123 *Fax:* (03) 9934 9100 *E-mail:* cs.au@oup.com
Web Site: www.oup.com.au, pg 34

Oxford University Press (India) *Tel:* (011) 43600300
Fax: (011) 23360897 *E-mail:* customerservice.in@
oup.com *Web Site:* www.oup.co.in, pg 394

Oxford University Press (OUP) (United Kingdom)
Tel: (01865) 556767 *Fax:* (01865) 556646
E-mail: webenquiry.uk@oup.com *Web Site:* global.
oup.com, pg 809

Oxford University Press Espana SA (Spain) *Tel:* 902 876
878 *E-mail:* contactoprofesor@oupe.es; prensa@oupe.
es *Web Site:* www.oup.es, pg 660

Oxford University Press KK (Japan) *Tel:* (03) 5444-
5454 *Fax:* (03) 3454-2221 *E-mail:* elt.japan@oup.com
Web Site: www.oupjapan.co.jp, pg 484

Oxford University Press Mexico Sa de CV (Mexico)
Tel: (0155) 5592 4277; (0155) 5592 5600
Fax: (0155) 5705 3738; (0155) 5535 6820
E-mail: atencionaclientes@oup.com *Web Site:* global.
oup.com/mexico, pg 520

Oxford University Press Pakistan (Pakistan)
Tel: (021) 35071580; (021) 35071587 *Fax:* (021)
35055072 *E-mail:* central.marketing.pk@oup.com
Web Site: www.oup.com.pk, pg 560

Oxford University Press Tanzania Ltd (Tanzania)
Tel: (022) 781403 *Web Site:* global.oup.com, pg 714

Oxford University, Taylor Institution Library (United
Kingdom) *Tel:* (01865) 278158 *E-mail:* tay-
enquiries@bodleian.ox.ac.uk *Web Site:* www.bodleian.
ox.ac.uk/taylor, pg 1642

Jill Oxton Publications Pty Ltd (Australia) *Tel:* (08)
8276 2722 *E-mail:* jill@jilloxtonxstitch.com
Web Site: www.jilloxtonxstitch.com, pg 34

OZGraf Olsztynskie Zaklady Graficzne SA (Poland)
Tel: (89) 533 43 80 *Fax:* (89) 533 12 08
E-mail: ozgraf@ozgraf.com.pl *Web Site:* www.ozgraf.
com.pl, pg 1332

Pabel-Moewig Verlag GmbH (Germany) *Tel:* (07222)
13 0 *Fax:* (07222) 13 218 *E-mail:* info@vpm.de
Web Site: www.vpm.de, pg 304

Les Editions du Pacifique (France) *Tel:* 01 42 22 48 63
Fax: 01 42 22
12 69 *E-mail:* contact@leseditionsdupacifique.com
Web Site: leseditionsdupacifique.com, pg 188

Packard Publishing Ltd (United Kingdom)
Tel: (01243) 537977 *Fax:* (01243) 537977
E-mail: packardpublishing@gmail.com
Web Site: www.packardpublishing.com, pg 809

Packt Publishing Ltd (United Kingdom) *Tel:* (0121)
265 6484 *Fax:* (0121) 212 1419 *E-mail:* contact@
packtpub.com; customercare@packtpub.com; service@
packtpub.com *Web Site:* www.packtpub.com, pg 809

Pacom Korea Inc (South Korea) *Tel:* (031) 718 3666
Fax: (031) 718 5857 *E-mail:* info@gopacom.com
Web Site: www.gopacom.com; pacomprinting.com
(English), pg 1284, 1334

PacPress Media Pte Ltd (Singapore) *Tel:* 6276 8090
Fax: 6276 9884, pg 1332

Pademelon Press Pty Ltd (Australia) *Tel:* (02) 9634
4655 *Fax:* (02) 9680 4634 *E-mail:* enquiry@
pademelonpress.com.au *Web Site:* www.
pademelonpress.com.au, pg 34

George Padmore Research Library on African Affairs
(Ghana) *E-mail:* padmorelibrary@gmail.com, pg 1597

Page & Blackmore Booksellers Ltd (New Zealand)
Tel: (03) 548 9992 *Fax:* (03) 546 6799 *E-mail:* info@
pageandblackmore.co.nz *Web Site:* www.
pageandblackmore.co.nz, pg 1438

Page & Turner Verlag (Germany) *Tel:* (089) 4136-
0 *Toll Free Tel:* 0800 500 33 22 *Fax:* (089) 4136-
3333 *E-mail:* kundenservice@randomhouse.de
Web Site: www.randomhouse.de/pageundturner, pg 304

Page Bros (Norwich) Ltd (United Kingdom) *Tel:* (01603)
778800 *Fax:* (01603) 778801 *E-mail:* info@pagebros.
co.uk *Web Site:* www.pagebros.co.uk, pg 1263, 1287,
1338, 1348, 1355

Page One Publishing (Singapore) *Tel:* 6742 2088
Fax: 6744 2088 *Web Site:* www.pageonegroup.com,
pg 605, 1447

Pages Editors (Spain) *Tel:* 973 23 66 11 *Fax:* 973 24 07
95 *E-mail:* editorial@pageseditors.cat *Web Site:* www.
pageseditors.cat, pg 660

Pagijong Press (South Korea) *Tel:* (02) 922-1192; (02)
922-1193 *E-mail:* pijbook@naver.com *Web Site:* www.
pjbook.com, pg 624

Pagina da Cultura Agencia Literaria Ideias sobre
Linhas Ltda (Brazil) *Tel:* (011) 31293900 *Fax:* (011)
31293900 *Web Site:* paginadacultura.com.br, pg 1224

La Pagina Ediciones SL (Spain) *Tel:* 649 190 093,
pg 660

Pagina Forlags AB (Sweden) *Tel:* (08) 564 218 00
Fax: (08) 564 218 19 *E-mail:* info@pagina.se
Web Site: www.pagina.se, pg 685

Pagina GmbH (Germany) *Tel:* (07071) 9876-0
Fax: (07071) 9876-22 *Web Site:* www.pagina-online.
de, pg 1276

Pagina Tres Agencia Literaria SL (Spain) *Tel:* 930 079
121 *E-mail:* agencia@paginatres.es; rights@paginatres.
es *Web Site:* www.paginatres.es, pg 1235

Editorial Paginas de Espuma SL (Spain) *Tel:* 91 522
72 51; 91 522 49 48 *E-mail:* prensa@ppespuma.
com; ventas@ppespuma.com; ppespuma@arrakis.es
Web Site: paginasdeespuma.com, pg 660

Paginos Libros de Magia (Spain) *Tel:* 915 411 611
Fax: 639 472 625 *E-mail:* info@librosdemagia.com
Web Site: www.librosdemagia.com, pg 660

Pagoulatos Bros (Greece) *Tel:* 2103818780; 2103801485
Fax: 2103838028 *E-mail:* pagoulatos_publ@ath.
forthnet.gr, pg 358

Paideia Editrice Brescia (Italy) *Tel:* (030) 3582434
Fax: (030) 3582691 *E-mail:* info@paideiaeditrice.it
Web Site: www.paideiaeditrice.it, pg 458

Editura Paideia (Romania) *Tel:* (021) 316 82 10
E-mail: comenzi@paideia.ro *Web Site:* www.paideia.
ro, pg 590, 1261

Editorial Paidos SAICF (Argentina) *Tel:* (011) 4124-
9100 *Fax:* (011) 4124-9100 *E-mail:* paidos@paidos.
com, pg 10

Ediciones Paidos Iberica SA (Spain) *Tel:* 93 241 92
50 *E-mail:* paidos@paidos.com *Web Site:* www.
planetadelibros.com/editorial-ediciones-paidos-3.html,
pg 660

Editorial Paidos Mexicana (Mexico) *Tel:* (0155)
3000-6200; (0155) 3000-6202 (sales); (0155)
3000-6203 (sales); (0155) 3000-6204 (sales)
E-mail: ventaspaidos@paidos.com.mx *Web Site:* www.
paidos.com.mx, pg 520

Editorial Paidotribo (Spain) *Tel:* 93 323 33 11 *Fax:* 93
453 50 33 *E-mail:* paidotribo@paidotribo.com
Web Site: www.paidotribo.com, pg 660

Clare Painter Associates Ltd (United Kingdom)
Tel: (01235) 528432 *Web Site:* www.
clarepainterassociates.com, pg 1245

Ediciones El Pais SA (Spain) *Tel:* 91 337 82 00;
91 536 55 00 *Fax:* 91 304 87 66; 91 536 55 55
E-mail: prisabs@prisabs.com; deports@elpais.es
Web Site: elpais.com, pg 661

El Paisaje Editorial (Spain) *Tel:* 946390774, pg 661

Paiva Osakeyhtio (Finland) *E-mail:* paiva@paiva.fi
Web Site: www.paiva.fi, pg 150

Pak American Commercial (Pvt) Ltd (Pakistan)
Tel: (051) 5563709 *Fax:* (051) 5565190, pg 1442

Pak Book Corp (Pakistan) *Tel:* (042) 6363222 *Fax:* (042)
6362328 *E-mail:* info@pakbook.com *Web Site:* www.
pakbook.com, pg 1442

Pak Company Pakistan (Pakistan) *Tel:* (042)
37230555; (042) 37352427 *Fax:* (042) 37120077
E-mail: pakcompany@hotmail.com *Web Site:* www.
pakcompany.com.pk, pg 560, 1442

Pakistan Institute of Development Economics (PIDE)
(Pakistan) *Tel:* (051) 9248069 *Fax:* (051) 9248065
E-mail: publications@pide.org.pk; pide@pide.org.pk
Web Site: www.pide.org.pk, pg 560

Pakistan Institute of Development Economics (PIDE)
(Pakistan) *Tel:* (051) 9248041; (051) 9248030
Fax: (051) 9248065 *E-mail:* library@pide.org.pk
Web Site: www.pide.org.pk, pg 1621

Pakistan Institute of Science & Technology Library,
Scientific Information Division (Pakistan)
Tel: 9321050 *E-mail:* sipr@paec.gov.pk
Web Site: www.paec.gov.pk, pg 1621

Pakistan ISBN Agency (Pakistan) *Tel:* (051) 9206436;
(051) 9206440; (051) 9202544; (051) 9202549
E-mail: nlpiba@isb.paknet.com.pk *Web Site:* www.
nlp.gov.pk, pg 1386

Pakistan Law House (Pakistan) *Tel:* (021)
32212455; (021) 32639558 *Fax:* (021) 32627549
E-mail: pak_law_house@hotmail.com *Web Site:* www.
pakistanlawhouse.com, pg 560, 1442

Pakistan Publishing House (Pakistan)
Tel: (021) 35681457 *Fax:* (021) 3627549
E-mail: pak_law_house@hotmail.com, pg 560

Pakistan Scientific & Technological Information Centre
(PASTIC) (Pakistan) *Tel:* (051) 9248103; (051)
9248104 *Fax:* (051) 9248113 *Web Site:* www.pastic.
gov.pk, pg 1621

Pakistan Writers' Guild (Pakistan) *Tel:* (042) 6367124
E-mail: info@pakwritersguild.org; secretarygenral@
pakwritersguild.org; trust@pakwritersguild.org
Web Site: www.pakwritersguild.org, pg 1498

Pakyoungsa Publishing Co (South Korea) *Tel:* (031) 955-
4071 *Fax:* (031) 955-4076 *E-mail:* pys@pybook.co.kr
Web Site: www.pybook.co.kr, pg 624

PAL Verlagsgesellschaft mbH (Germany) *Tel:* (0621)
415741 *Fax:* (0621) 415101 *E-mail:* info@palverlag.
de *Web Site:* www.palverlag.de, pg 305

Pala-Verlag GmbH (Germany) *Tel:* (06151) 2 30 28
Fax: (06151) 29 27 13 *E-mail:* info@pala-verlag.de
Web Site: www.pala-verlag.de, pg 305

Ediciones Palabra SA (Spain) *Tel:* 91 350 77 39; 91 350
77 20 *Fax:* 91 359 02 30 *E-mail:* palabra@palabra.es
Web Site: www.palabra.es, pg 661

Pedrazzini Tipografia SA (Switzerland) *Tel:* (091) 751 77 34 *Fax:* (091) 751 51 18 *E-mail:* print@ pedrazzinitipografia.ch *Web Site:* pedrazzinitipografia. com, pg 703

Peepal Tree Press Ltd (United Kingdom) *Tel:* (0113) 245 1703 *E-mail:* contact@peepaltreepress.com *Web Site:* www.peepaltreepress.com, pg 811

Peeters-France (France) *Tel:* 01 40 51 89 20 *Fax:* 01 40 51 81 05 *E-mail:* peeters.publish@free.fr *Web Site:* www.peeters-leuven.be, pg 189

Uitgeverij Peeters Leuven (Belgie) (Belgium) *Tel:* (016) 23 51 70 *Fax:* (016) 22 85 00 *E-mail:* peeters@ peeters-leuven.be *Web Site:* www.peeters-leuven.be, pg 71

Pegasus Publishers & Booksellers (Netherlands) *Tel:* (020) 623 11 38 *Fax:* (020) 620 34 78 *E-mail:* pegasus@pegasusboek.nl *Web Site:* www. pegasusboek.nl, pg 1438

Pegasus Yayinlari (Turkey) *Tel:* (0212) 244 23 50 *Fax:* (0212) 244 23 46 *E-mail:* info@pegasusyayinlari. com *Web Site:* www.pegasusyayinlari.com, pg 723

Jonathan Pegg Literary Agency (United Kingdom) *Tel:* (020) 7603 6830 *Fax:* (020) 7348 0629 *E-mail:* info@jonathanpegg.com; submissions@ jonathanpegg.com *Web Site:* www.jonathanpegg.com, pg 1245

Pehuen Editores SA (Chile) *Tel:* (02) 27957133 *E-mail:* editorial@pehuen.cl *Web Site:* www.pehuen.cl, pg 99

Peirene Press Ltd (United Kingdom) *Tel:* (020) 7686 1941 *Web Site:* www.peirenepress.com, pg 811

Ediciones PEISA Sac (Peru) *Tel:* (01) 2215988; (01) 2215992 *Fax:* (01) 4425906 *E-mail:* editor@peisa. com.pe *Web Site:* www.peisa.com.pe, pg 563

Peking University Library (China) *Tel:* (010) 62751051 *Fax:* (010) 62761008 *E-mail:* is@lib.pku.edu.cn; mediadept@lib.pku.edu.cn *Web Site:* www.lib.pku.edu. cn, pg 1582

Peking University Press (China) *Tel:* (010) 62752036; (010) 62752015; (010) 62752033; (010) 62754697 *Fax:* (010) 62765015 *E-mail:* zpup@pup.cn; marketing@pup.cn; rights@pup.cn *Web Site:* www. pup.cn, pg 108

Pelanduk Publications (M) Sdn Bhd (Malaysia) *Tel:* (03) 56386573; (03) 56386885 *Fax:* (03) 56386577; (03) 56386575 *E-mail:* pelandukpub@gmail.com *Web Site:* www.pelanduk.com, pg 509

Penerbitan Pelangi Sdn Bhd (PPSB) (Malaysia) *Tel:* (07) 3316288 *Fax:* (07) 3329201 *E-mail:* info@ pelangibooks.com; pelangi@pelangibooks.com *Web Site:* www.pelangibooks.com, pg 509

Uitgeverij Pelckmans NV (Belgium) *Tel:* (03) 660 27 00 *Fax:* (03) 660 27 01 *E-mail:* uitgeverij@pelckmans.be *Web Site:* www.pelckmans.be, pg 71

Pelikan Vertriebsgesellschaft mbH & Co KG (Germany) *Tel:* (0511) 6969-0 *Fax:* (0511) 6969-212 *E-mail:* info@pelikan.com *Web Site:* www.pelikan. com, pg 306

Peliti Associati (Italy) *Tel:* (06) 5295548 *Fax:* (06) 5292351 *E-mail:* peliti@peliti.it *Web Site:* www. pelitiassociati.eu, pg 459

Luigi Pellegrini Editore (Italy) *Tel:* (0984) 795065 *Fax:* (0984) 792672 *E-mail:* info@pellegrinieditore.it *Web Site:* www.pellegrinieditore.com, pg 459

PEN All-India Centre (India) *Tel:* (022) 22039024 *E-mail:* india.pen@gmail.com, pg 1496

Pen & Pages (Nigeria) *Tel:* (0806) 8787631 (cell); (0803) 3201197 (cell) *E-mail:* admin@penandpages. com.ng; info@penandpages.com.ng *Web Site:* www. penandpages.com.ng, pg 1439

Pen & Sword Books Ltd (United Kingdom) *Tel:* (01226) 734222 *Fax:* (01226) 734438 *E-mail:* enquiries@pen-and-sword.co.uk *Web Site:* www.pen-and-sword.co.uk, pg 812

Argentinian PEN Centre (Argentina) *Tel:* (011) 4825 8548, pg 1489

Austrian PEN Centre (Austria) *Tel:* (01) 533 44 59 *Fax:* (01) 532 87 49 *E-mail:* info@penclub.at *Web Site:* www.penclub.at, pg 1490

Belgian PEN Centre (Dutch-Speaking) (Belgium) *E-mail:* info@penvlaanderen.be *Web Site:* www. penvlaanderen.be, pg 1491

Belgian PEN Centre (French-Speaking) (Belgium) *Tel:* (027) 31 48 47 *Fax:* (027) 31 48 47, pg 1491

Bolivian PEN Centre (Bolivia) *Fax:* (04) 291 070, pg 1491

Brazilian PEN Centre (Brazil) *Tel:* (021) 2556 0461 *Fax:* (021) 2556 0461 *E-mail:* pen@penclubedobrasil. br; pen@penclubedobrasil.org.br *Web Site:* www. penclubedobrasil.org.br, pg 1492

China PEN Centre (China) *Tel:* (010) 64207711 *Fax:* (010) 64221704, pg 1492

PEN Club-German Speaking Writers Abroad (Ireland) *E-mail:* exilpen@gmx.net *Web Site:* www.exilpen.net, pg 1378

PEN Club-Writers in Exile, London Branch (United Kingdom), pg 1396

Colombian PEN Centre (Colombia) *Tel:* (01) 691 9627 *Fax:* (01) 332 4357, pg 1492

Czech PEN Centre (Czech Republic) *Tel:* 224 234 343 *Fax:* 224 234 343 *E-mail:* centrum@pen.cz *Web Site:* www.pen.cz, pg 1492

English PEN Centre (United Kingdom) *Tel:* (020) 7324 2535 *Fax:* (020) 7490 0566 *E-mail:* enquiries@ englishpen.org *Web Site:* www.englishpen.org, pg 1504

Finnish PEN Centre (Finland) *Web Site:* pen.kaapeli.fi, pg 1493

French PEN Centre (France) *Tel:* 01 42 72 41 83 *Fax:* 01 42 72 41 83 *E-mail:* penfrancais@aol.com *Web Site:* www.penclub.fr, pg 1494

Galician PEN Centre (Spain) *Tel:* 981 957 119 *E-mail:* pengalicia@mundo-r.com, pg 1500

German PEN Centre (Germany) *Tel:* (06151) 23120 *Fax:* (06151) 293414 *E-mail:* pen-germany@t-online. de *Web Site:* www.pen-deutschland.de, pg 1495

Hong Kong PEN Centre (Chinese-Speaking) (Hong Kong), pg 1495

Hong Kong PEN Centre (English-Speaking) (Hong Kong) *Tel:* 25 25 39 17 *Fax:* 25 25 39 61, pg 1495

Hungarian PEN Centre (Hungary) *Tel:* (01) 411 0270 *Fax:* (01) 411 0270 *E-mail:* hungary@penclub.t-online.hu, pg 1496

Icelandic PEN Centre (Iceland) *Tel:* 820 1931 *E-mail:* icelandicpen@gmail.com, pg 1496

PEN International (United Kingdom) *Tel:* (020) 7405 0338 *Fax:* (020) 7405 0339 *E-mail:* info@pen-international.org *Web Site:* www.pen-international.org, pg 1396

Irish PEN Centre (Ireland) *Tel:* (087) 9660770 *E-mail:* info@irishpen.com *Web Site:* www.irishpen. com, pg 1496

Israeli PEN Centre (Israel) *Tel:* (03) 501 9275 *Fax:* (03) 501 9276, pg 1496

Italian PEN Centre (Italy) *Tel:* (0335) 7350966 *Fax:* (0363) 350654 *E-mail:* segreteria@penclub.it *Web Site:* www.penclub.it, pg 1497

Japanese PEN Centre (Japan) *Tel:* (03) 5614-5391 *Fax:* (03) 5695-7686 *E-mail:* info@japanpen.or.jp *Web Site:* www.japanpen.or.jp, pg 1497

PEN Korean Centre (South Korea) *Tel:* (02) 782-1337; (02) 782-1338 *Fax:* (02) 786-1090 *E-mail:* penkon2001@yahoo.co.kr; admin@penkorea. or.kr *Web Site:* www.penkorea.or.kr, pg 1500

Liechtenstein PEN Centre (Liechtenstein) *Tel:* 232 7271 *Fax:* 232 8071 *E-mail:* info@pen-club.li *Web Site:* www.pen-club.li, pg 1497

Macedonian PEN Centre (Macedonia) *Tel:* (02) 313 00 54 *Fax:* (02) 313 00 54 *E-mail:* macedpen@unet.com. mk *Web Site:* www.pen.org.mk, pg 1497

Melbourne PEN Centre (Australia) *Tel:* (04) 0204 9487 *E-mail:* admin@melbournepen.com.au *Web Site:* www. melbournepen.com.au, pg 1490

Mexican PEN Centre (Mexico) *Tel:* (0155) 56 88 42 62 *Fax:* (0155) 55 54 55 10 *E-mail:* penmexico@gmail. com, pg 1497

Nepal PEN Centre (Nepal), pg 1497

Netherlands PEN Centre (Netherlands) *Tel:* (020) 6240803 *E-mail:* info@pennederland.nl *Web Site:* www.pennederland.nl, pg 1497

Norwegian PEN Centre (Norway) *Tel:* 22 60 74 50; 926 88 023 (cell) *Fax:* 22 60 74 51 *E-mail:* pen@ norskpen.no *Web Site:* www.norskpen.no, pg 1498

Palestinian PEN Centre (Israel) *Tel:* (02) 598288111 *Fax:* (02) 6264620 *E-mail:* palpenc@palnet.com, pg 1496

Panamanian PEN Centre (Panama) *Tel:* 269 0928 *Fax:* 269 0928 *E-mail:* carr@mossfon.com, pg 1498

Philippine PEN Centre (Philippines) *Tel:* (02) 254-1068 *Fax:* (02) 254-1068 *E-mail:* philippinepen@yahoo.com *Web Site:* philippinepen.ph, pg 1498

Polish PEN Centre (Poland) *Tel:* (22) 826 57 84; (22) 828 28 23 *Fax:* (22) 826 57 84 *E-mail:* penclub@ penclub.com.pl *Web Site:* www.penclub.com.pl, pg 1499

Portuguese PEN Centre (Portugal) *E-mail:* geral@ penclubeportugues.org *Web Site:* penclubeportugues. org, pg 1499

Puerto Rican PEN Centre (Puerto Rico) *Tel:* (787) 645-9533, pg 1499

Romanian PEN Centre (Romania) *Tel:* (021) 316 58 29 *Web Site:* www.penromania.ro, pg 1499

Russian PEN Centre (Russia) *Tel:* (495) 625 2718 *Fax:* (495) 625 3573 *E-mail:* penrussian@dol.ru; penrussian@gmail.ru *Web Site:* www.penrussia.org, pg 1499

Scottish PEN Centre (United Kingdom) *Tel:* (0131) 226 5590 *E-mail:* info@scottishpen.org *Web Site:* www. scottishpen.org, pg 1504

Senegalese PEN Centre (Senegal) *E-mail:* pensenegal@ yahoo.fr, pg 1499

Serbian PEN Centre (Serbia) *Tel:* (011) 33 44 427 *Fax:* (011) 33 44 427 *E-mail:* pencentar@ptt.rs *Web Site:* www.serbianpen.rs, pg 1499

Slovene PEN Centre (Slovenia) *Tel:* (01) 425 48 47 *Fax:* (01) 425 48 47 *E-mail:* slopen@guest.arnes.si *Web Site:* www.penslovenia-zdruzenje.si, pg 1499

Suisse Romand PEN Centre (Switzerland) *Tel:* (022) 348 8570, pg 1500

Swedish PEN Centre (Sweden) *E-mail:* info@ svenskapen.se *Web Site:* www.pensweden.org, pg 1500

Swiss German PEN Centre (Switzerland) *Tel:* (044) 350 70 70 *E-mail:* office@pen-dschweiz.ch *Web Site:* www.pen-dschweiz.ch, pg 1500

Swiss Italian & Reto-Romansh PEN Centre (Switzerland) *Tel:* (091) 967 16 02 *Fax:* (091) 967 16 02 *E-mail:* info@pensvizzeraitaliana.org *Web Site:* www.pensvizzeraitaliana.org, pg 1500

Sydney PEN Centre (Australia) *Tel:* (02) 9514 2755 *Toll Free Tel:* 1300 364 997 (in Australia) *E-mail:* sydney@pen.org.au *Web Site:* www.pen.org. au, pg 1490

Taipei Chinese PEN Centre (Taiwan) *Tel:* (02) 2369 3609 *Fax:* (02) 2369 9948 *E-mail:* taipen@seed.net.tw *Web Site:* www.taipen.org, pg 1500

Thai PEN Centre (Thailand) *Tel:* (02) 218-7492 *Fax:* (02) 255 5160 *Web Site:* www.phd-lit.arts.chula. ac.th/web_pen/pen.htm, pg 1501

Principal Verlag (Germany) *Tel:* (02571) 589645 *Fax:* (02571) 589639 *E-mail:* principal.verlag@ t-online.de; verlag@principal.de *Web Site:* www. principal.de, pg 310

Principia Editora (Portugal) *Tel:* 21 467 87 10 *Fax:* 21 467 87 19 *E-mail:* principia@principia.pt *Web Site:* principia.pt, pg 582

Prinovis GmbH & Co KG (Germany) *Tel:* (040) 570130-0 *Toll Free Tel:* 0800 77466847 (sales) *E-mail:* kontakt@prinovis.com; sales@prinovis.com *Web Site:* www.prinovis.com, pg 1323

Print It (Malta) *Tel:* 2189 4446; 2189 4447 *Fax:* 2189 4448 *E-mail:* info@printit.com.mt *Web Site:* www. printit.com.mt, pg 1282, 1330

Printcorp (Belarus) *Tel:* 17 267 7513; 17 267 0109 *Fax:* 17 265 90 98 *E-mail:* office@printcorp.biz *Web Site:* printcorp.biz, pg 1317

Editions Le Printemps Ltee (ELP) (Mauritius) *Tel:* 696 1017 *Fax:* 686 7302 *E-mail:* elp@intnet.mu; elp. editorial@intnet.mu; munsoor.sales@elpmauritius.com; marketing@elpmauritius.com *Web Site:* elpmauritius. com, pg 512

Printer Colombiana SA (Colombia) *Tel:* (01) 294 2930 *Fax:* (01) 223 3154 *E-mail:* printer@printercol.com *Web Site:* www.printercol.com, pg 1319

Printer Trento SRL (Italy) *Tel:* (0461) 957 200 *Web Site:* www.printertrento.it, pg 1281, 1328

Printforce (Netherlands) *Tel:* (0172) 466 200 *Fax:* (0172) 466 222 *E-mail:* info@printforce.nl *Web Site:* www. printforce.nl, pg 1330

Printing Corp of the Americas Inc (United States) *Tel:* 954-781-8100 *Toll Free Tel:* 866-721-1PCA (721-1722) *Fax:* 954-781-8421 *Web Site:* www. commercialprintingflorida.com, pg 1265, 1289, 1340, 1350

Prints Publications Pvt Ltd (India) *Tel:* (011) 45355555 *Fax:* (011) 23275542 *E-mail:* info@printspublications. com *Web Site:* www.printspublications.com, pg 1424

Printsystem GmbH (Germany) *Tel:* (07033) 3825 *Fax:* (07033) 3827 *E-mail:* info@printsystem.de *Web Site:* www.printsystem.de, pg 1276, 1323

PrintWest (Canada) *Tel:* 306-525-2304 *Toll Free Tel:* 800-236-6438 *Fax:* 306-757-2439 *E-mail:* general@printwest.com *Web Site:* www. printwest.com, pg 1255, 1274, 1345, 1353

Printz Publishing (Sweden) *E-mail:* info@ printzpublishing.se *Web Site:* www.printzpublishing.se, pg 685

Prion (United Kingdom) *Tel:* (020) 7612 0400 *Fax:* (020) 7612 0411 *E-mail:* sales@carltonbooks. co.uk *Web Site:* www.carltonbooks.co.uk, pg 816

Prior Media Group SRL (Romania) *Tel:* (021) 210 89 08; (021) 210 89 28; (0722) 51 01 33 (cell) *Fax:* (021) 212 35 61 *E-mail:* office@prior.ro; secretariat@prior.ro *Web Site:* www.prior-books.ro; ebookshop.ro, pg 1446

Vydavateľstvo Priroda sro (Slovakia) *Tel:* (02) 55 42 51 60 *Fax:* (02) 20 74 96 33 *E-mail:* priroda@priroda.sk *Web Site:* www.priroda.sk, pg 608

Penerbit Prisma Sdn Bhd (Malaysia) *Tel:* (03) 56380541 *Fax:* (03) 56347256, pg 509

Prisme Editions (Belgium) *Tel:* (02) 346 13 19 *Fax:* (02) 346 13 03 *E-mail:* contact@prisme-editions.be *Web Site:* www.prisme-editions.be, pg 72

Prismi Editrice Politecnica (Italy) *Tel:* (081) 5752524 *Fax:* (081) 5983196 *E-mail:* info@arte-m.net *Web Site:* www.arte-m.net, pg 461

Priuli e Verlucca editori (Italy) *Tel:* (0125) 71 22 66 *Fax:* (0125) 71 28 07 *E-mail:* info@priulieverlucca.it *Web Site:* www.priulieverlucca.it, pg 461

Editions Privat SAS (France) *Tel:* 05 61 33 77 00 *Fax:* 05 34 31 64 44 *E-mail:* info@editions-privat.com *Web Site:* www.editions-privat.com, pg 192

The Private Libraries Association (PLA) (United Kingdom) *E-mail:* info@plabooks.org *Web Site:* www. plabooks.org, pg 1397

Privlacica doo (Croatia) *Tel:* (032) 306 068; (032) 306 069 *Fax:* (032) 306 070, pg 122

Pro Juventute Verlag (Switzerland) *Tel:* (044) 256 77 77 *Fax:* (044) 256 77 78 *E-mail:* info@projuventute.ch *Web Site:* www.projuventute.ch, pg 703

Verlag Pro Libro Luzern GmbH (Switzerland) *Tel:* (041) 210 24 03 *E-mail:* info@prolibro.ch; prolibro@ bluewin.ch *Web Site:* www.prolibro.ch, pg 703

Pro Natur-Verlag Andreas Probst (Germany) *Tel:* (07527) 91 59 14 *Fax:* (07527) 91 59 42 *E-mail:* info@pro-natur-verlag.de *Web Site:* www.pro-natur-verlag.de, pg 310

Edicions Proa SA (Spain) *Tel:* 93 443 71 00 *Fax:* 93 443 71 30 *E-mail:* original@grup62.com *Web Site:* www. grup62.cat/editorial-editorial-proa-69.html, pg 664

Probook Ltd (Israel) *Tel:* (03) 5257999 *Fax:* (03) 5285397 *E-mail:* info@probook.co.il *Web Site:* www. probook.co.il, pg 1427

Probooks SA de CV (Mexico) *Tel:* (0155) 5549 5660; (0155) 5549 5183 *E-mail:* ventas@probooks.com.mx *Web Site:* www.probooks.com.mx, pg 1436

PRODIG (France) *Tel:* 01 44 07 75 99 *Fax:* 01 44 07 75 63 *E-mail:* prodig@univ-paris.fr *Web Site:* www. prodig.cnrs.fr; www.univ-paris1.fr, pg 192

Prodim SPRL (Belgium) *Tel:* (02) 640 59 70 *Fax:* (02) 640 59 91 *E-mail:* prodim.books@prodim.be; prodim. editeur@prodim.be; prodim.journals@prodim.be *Web Site:* www.prodim.be, pg 72

Producciones de la Hamaca (Belize) *Tel:* 600-4710 *E-mail:* producciones.hamaca@gmail.com *Web Site:* producciones-hamaca.com, pg 74

Producciones Mawis SRL (Argentina) *Tel:* (011) 4567-0625 *Fax:* (011) 4567-0625 *E-mail:* info@ produccionesmawis.com.ar *Web Site:* www. produccionesmawis.com.ar, pg 11

Profil Klett doo (Croatia) *Tel:* (01) 4724 824 (management); (01) 4724 805 (sales); (01) 4724 803 (editorial); (01) 4724 809 (marketing) *E-mail:* uprava@profil-klett.hr; prodaja@profil-klett.hr; marketing@profil-klett.hr *Web Site:* www.profil-klett. hr, pg 122

Profile Books Ltd (United Kingdom) *Tel:* (020) 7841 6300 *Fax:* (020) 7833 3969 *E-mail:* info@ profilebooks.co.uk *Web Site:* www.profilebooks.com, pg 816

Profizdat (Russia) *Tel:* (495) 333-35-29; (499) 125-83-50; (499) 128-05-64 *Fax:* (495) 334-24-22 *E-mail:* profizdat@profizdat.ru *Web Site:* www. profizdat.ru, pg 597

Progensa Editorial (Spain) *Tel:* 954 186 200 *Fax:* 954 186 111 *E-mail:* progensa@progensa.com *Web Site:* www.progensa.es, pg 664

Progreso Editorial (Mexico) *Tel:* (0155) 1946-0620 *Toll Free Tel:* 01-800-777-0077 *Fax:* (0155) 1946-0625 *E-mail:* info@editorialprogreso.com. mx; servicioalcliente@editorialprogreso.com.mx; pedidos@editorialprogreso.com.mx *Web Site:* www. editorialprogreso.com.mx, pg 521

Progress Press Co Ltd (Malta) *Tel:* 22764400 *Fax:* 25594115 *E-mail:* info@progresspress.com.mt *Web Site:* www.progresspress.com.mt, pg 1282, 1330

Proietto & Lamarque SA (Argentina) *Tel:* (011) 4925-0111; (011) 4921-1689; (011) 4924-1812 *E-mail:* info@lamarquenet.com; ventas@ lamarquenet.com; administracion@lamarquenet.com *Web Site:* proiettoylamarque.com.ar, pg 1273, 1317

Projekte-Verlag Cornelius GmbH (Germany) *Tel:* (0345) 6 86 56 65 *Fax:* (0345) 1 20 22 38 *E-mail:* info@ projekte-verlag.de *Web Site:* www.projekte-verlag.de, pg 310

Prolog Publishing House Ltd (Israel) *Tel:* (03) 9022904; (03) 9022905 *Fax:* (03) 9022906 *E-mail:* info@prolog. co.il *Web Site:* www.prolog.co.il; www.prologhebrew. us, pg 421

Promat Basim Yayin San ve Tic AS (Turkey) *Tel:* (0212) 6226363 *Fax:* (0212) 6050798 *E-mail:* info@promat. com.tr *Web Site:* www.promat.com.tr, pg 1336

Promedia SRL (Italy) *Tel:* (011) 273 77 20 *Fax:* (011) 273 77 04 *E-mail:* info@promediasolutions.it; marketing@promediasolutions.it *Web Site:* www. promediasolutions.it, pg 1281, 1329

Promedia Verlag (Austria) *Tel:* (01) 405 27 02 *Fax:* (01) 405 27 02 22 *E-mail:* promedia@mediashop.at *Web Site:* www.mediashop.at/typolight/index.php/ home.html, pg 56

Ediciones Promesa (Costa Rica) *Tel:* 2283-3033 *Fax:* 2225-1286 *E-mail:* administracion@ promesacultural.com; editorialpromesa@gmail.com *Web Site:* www.promesacultural.com, pg 118

Ediciones Promesa SA de CV (Mexico) *Tel:* (0155) 5623174; (0155) 3938707, pg 522

Prometej Izdatelstvo (Russia) *Tel:* (495) 238-40-65; (495) 238-53-60, pg 597

Uitgeverij Prometheus/Bert Bakker (Netherlands) *Tel:* (020) 6241934 *Fax:* (020) 6225461; (020) 5210592 *E-mail:* info@pbo.nl *Web Site:* uitgeverijprometheus.nl, pg 539

PROMIC Sp z oo (Poland) *Tel:* (22) 642 50 82; (22) 651 90 54 (sales) *Fax:* (22) 651 90 55 *E-mail:* sprzedaz@ wydawnictwo.pl; sekretariat@wydawnictwo.pl *Web Site:* www.wydawnictwo.pl, pg 572

Promilla & Co Publishers (India) *Tel:* (011) 65284748; (011) 26864124 *Fax:* (011) 41829791 *E-mail:* books@ biblioasia.com *Web Site:* www.biblioasia.com, pg 396

Editions Promoculture (Luxembourg) *Tel:* 48 06 91 *Fax:* 40 09 50 *E-mail:* info@promoculture.lu *Web Site:* www.promoculture.lu, pg 504

Librairie Promoculture Sarl (Luxembourg) *Tel:* 48 06 91 *Fax:* 40 09 50 *E-mail:* info@promoculture.lu *Web Site:* librairiepromoculture.lu, pg 1431

Promoedition SA (Switzerland) *Tel:* (022) 809 94 94 *Fax:* (022) 809 94 00 *E-mail:* info@quorum-com.ch *Web Site:* www.promoedition.ch, pg 122

Ediciones Pronaos SA (Spain) *Tel:* 676808196 *E-mail:* edicionespronaos@yahoo.es; pedidos@ pronaos.net *Web Site:* pronaos.net, pg 664

PRONI (Public Record Office of Northern Ireland) (United Kingdom) *Tel:* (028) 9053 4800 *Fax:* (028) 9025 5999 *E-mail:* proni@communities-ni.gov.uk *Web Site:* www.nidirect.gov.uk/proni, pg 1642

I Prooptiki Ekdoseis (Greece) *Tel:* 2108226254 *Fax:* 2108226254, pg 359

Proost NV (Belgium) *Tel:* (014) 40 08 11 *Fax:* (014) 42 87 94 *E-mail:* proost@proost.be *Web Site:* www. proost.be, pg 1273, 1317

Propos 2 Editions (France) *Tel:* 06 07 41 17 70 (cell) *Toll Free Tel:* 0877 180 615 *E-mail:* courrier@ propos2editions.net *Web Site:* www.propos2editions. net, pg 192

Propylaeen Verlag (Germany) *Tel:* (030) 23456-300 *Fax:* (030) 23456-303 *E-mail:* info@propylaeen-verlag.de *Web Site:* www.ullsteinbuchverlage.de/ propylaen, pg 310

ProQuest LLC (United Kingdom) *Tel:* (01223) 215 512 *Fax:* (01223) 215 513 *E-mail:* customerservice@ proquest.com; orders@proquest.com *Web Site:* www. proquest.com, pg 816

Prospect Press (Trinidad and Tobago) *Tel:* (868) 622-3821; (868) 622-5813; (868) 622-6138 *Fax:* (868) 628-0639 *E-mail:* web-queries@meppublishers.com *Web Site:* www.meppublishers.com, pg 717

Prostor, nakladatelstvi sro (Czech Republic) *Tel:* 224 826 688 *E-mail:* prostor@eprostor.com *Web Site:* www. prostor-nakladatelstvi.cz, pg 131

Izdatelstvo Prosveshchenie (Russia) *Tel:* (495) 789-30-40 *Fax:* (495) 789-30-41 *E-mail:* prosv@prosv.ru; pressa@prosv.ru *Web Site:* www.prosv.ru, pg 597

Editions Prosveta SA (France) *Tel:* 04 94 19 33 33 *Fax:* 04 94 19 33 34 *E-mail:* international@prosveta. com *Web Site:* www.prosveta.fr, pg 192

Izdavacko preduzece Prosveta (Serbia) *Tel:* (011) 26 39 714 *E-mail:* redakcija.ipprosveta@eunet.rs; komercijala@prosveta.rs (sales); prosveta.redakcija@ gmail.com (returns) *Web Site:* www.prosveta.rs, pg 601

Prosveta Publishing House (Bulgaria) *Tel:* (02) 8182020 *Fax:* (02) 8182019 *E-mail:* prosveta@prosveta.bg *Web Site:* www.prosveta.bg, pg 96

Prosvetno Delo AD (Macedonia) *Tel:* (02) 3117 255 *Fax:* (02) 3220 373 *E-mail:* prodelo@mt.net.mk *Web Site:* prosvetnodelo.com.mk; prosvetnodelo-com-mk.webcentar.biz, pg 505

Prosvetno Delo Redakcija Detska Radost (Macedonia) *Tel:* (02) 3117 255 *Fax:* (02) 3220 373 *Web Site:* prosvetnodelo.com.mk, pg 505

Prosvjeta doo (Croatia) *Tel:* (01) 4872-477 *Fax:* (01) 3665-309 *E-mail:* prosvjeta@inet.hr *Web Site:* www. prosvjeta.hr, pg 122

Proszynski i S-ka SA (Poland) *Tel:* (22) 278 17 40 *Fax:* (22) 843 52 15 *E-mail:* proszynskimedia@ proszynskimedia.pl *Web Site:* www.proszynski.pl, pg 572

Protea Boekhuis (South Africa) *Tel:* (012) 343 6279 *Fax:* (012) 344 2653 *Web Site:* www.proteaboekhuis. com, pg 617

Protea Boekwinkel (South Africa) *Tel:* (012) 362 3444; (012) 362 5663 (university); (012) 362 5683 (schools); (012) 362 6073 (theology) *Fax:* (012) 362 5688 *E-mail:* orders@proteaboekwinkel.com; sales_online@proteaboekwinkel.com *Web Site:* www. proteaboekwinkel.com; www.proteaboekhuis.com, pg 1449

Protestant Publications (Australia) *Tel:* (02) 9868 4591 *E-mail:* bisden@pnc.net.au, pg 36

Proton Editora Ltda (Brazil) *Tel:* (011) 3032-3616 *Fax:* (011) 3815-9920 *E-mail:* proton@editoraproton. com.br *Web Site:* www.editoraproton.com.br; www. keppepacheco.com, pg 89

PROverbis eU (Austria) *Tel:* (01) 2763593 *Fax:* (01) 276359315 *E-mail:* office@proverbis.at; verlag@ proverbis.at *Web Site:* www.proverbis.at, pg 56

Prozoretz Ltd Publishing House (Bulgaria) *Tel:* (02) 983-04-85 *Fax:* (02) 983-04-86 *E-mail:* office@prozoretz. com *Web Site:* www.prozoretz.com, pg 96

Psichogios Publications SA (Greece) *Tel:* 2102804800 *Toll Free Tel:* 80011646464 *Fax:* 2102819550 *E-mail:* info@psichogios.gr *Web Site:* www. psichogios.gr, pg 359

Psicolibros (Waslala) (Uruguay) *Tel:* 24003808; 24030332 *E-mail:* info@psicolibroswaslala.com *Web Site:* www.psicolibroswaslala.com, pg 849

Psychiatrie-Verlag GmbH (Germany) *Tel:* (0221) 167 989-0 *Fax:* (0221) 167 989-20 *E-mail:* verlag@ psychiatrie.de *Web Site:* www.psychiatrie-verlag.de, pg 310

Psychoanalyticke Nakladatelstvi (Czech Republic) *Tel:* 233 340 305 *Web Site:* www.iapsa.cz, pg 131

Psychologie Verlags Union GmbH (Germany) *Tel:* (06201) 6007-0 *Fax:* (06201) 6007-310 *E-mail:* info@beltz.de *Web Site:* www.beltz.de, pg 310

Psychosozial-Verlag (Germany) *Tel:* (0641) 96 99 78 0 *Fax:* (0641) 96 99 78 19 *E-mail:* info@ psychosozial-verlag.de; vertrieb@psychosozial-verlag. de *Web Site:* www.psychosozial-verlag.de, pg 311

PT Indira Ltd (Indonesia) *Tel:* (021) 3904290; (021) 3148868; (021) 3147468; (021) 3904288, pg 407, 1426

Pt Ravishankar Shukla University Library (India) *Tel:* (0771) 2262540 *Fax:* (0771) 2262583 *E-mail:* library_prsu@rediffmail.com *Web Site:* library. prsu.ac.in; www.prsu.ac.in, pg 1601

PTI - Publicacoes Tecnicas Internacionais Ltda (Brazil) *Tel:* (011) 3159-2535 *Fax:* (011) 3159-2450 *E-mail:* info@pti.com.br *Web Site:* www.pti.com.br, pg 1408

PTS Media Group Sdn Bhd (Malaysia) *Tel:* (03) 6188 0316 *Fax:* (03) 6189 0316 *E-mail:* sales@pts.com. my; editorial@pts.com.my; marketing@pts.com.my *Web Site:* pts.com.my, pg 509

Public Lending Right (Australia) *Tel:* (02) 6271 1000 *Toll Free Tel:* 1800 672 842 (Australia only) *Fax:* (02) 6210 2907 *E-mail:* lendingrights@arts.gov. au *Web Site:* www.arts.gov.au/literature/lending_rights, pg 1364

Public Lending Right (United Kingdom) *Tel:* (01642) 604699 *E-mail:* corporateservices@plr.uk.com *Web Site:* www.plr.uk.com, pg 1397

Publicaciones de la Universidad de Alicante (Spain) *Tel:* 965 903 480 *E-mail:* publicaciones.web@ua.es *Web Site:* publicaciones.ua.es, pg 664

Publicaciones de la Universidad Pontificia Comillas-Madrid (Spain) *Tel:* 91 542 28 00 *Fax:* 91 559 65 69 *E-mail:* oia@oia.upcomillas.es *Web Site:* www.upco. es, pg 664

Publicaciones Digitales SA (Spain) *Tel:* 902 405 500; 954 583 425 *Fax:* 954 583 205 *E-mail:* info@ publidisa.com *Web Site:* www.publidisa.com, pg 1335

Publicaciones Lo Castillo SA (Chile) *Tel:* (02) 27514800 *E-mail:* contacto@plc.cl *Web Site:* www.plc.cl, pg 99

Publicaciones Nuevo Extremo SA (Chile) *Tel:* (02) 6979749 *E-mail:* publicacionesnextremo@tie.cl, pg 99

Publicaciones Turisticas CU SA de CV (Mexico) *Tel:* (0155) 55925022 *Web Site:* www. travelersguidemexico.com; www.boletinturistico.com, pg 522

Publicacions i Edicions de la Universitat de Barcelona (Spain) *Tel:* 93 403 54 39 *Fax:* 93 403 54 46 *E-mail:* comandes.edicions@ub.edu *Web Site:* www. publicacions.ub.es, pg 664

Publicacions Universitat Rovira i Virgili (URV) (Spain) *Tel:* 977 558 474 *Fax:* 977 558 393 *E-mail:* publicacions@urv.cat *Web Site:* www.urv. cat/publicacions, pg 664

Ediouro Publicacoes SA (Brazil) *Tel:* (021) 3882-8200 *Fax:* (021) 3882-8200 *Web Site:* www.ediouro.com.br, pg 89

Publicacoes Europa America Lda (Portugal) *Tel:* (021) 926 77 00 *Fax:* (021) 926 77 71 *E-mail:* secretariado@europa-america.pt; livreiros@ europa-america.pt *Web Site:* www.europa-america.pt, pg 1445

Publicat SA (Poland) *Tel:* (61) 6529252 *Fax:* (61) 6529200 *E-mail:* publicat@publicat.pl; office@ publicat.pl *Web Site:* publicat.pl, pg 573

Publication Bureau (India) *Tel:* (011) 23656503; (011) 23656950 *Fax:* (011) 23656950 *E-mail:* mail@ publicationbureau.com; info@publicationbureau. com; sales@publicationbureau.com *Web Site:* www. publicationbureau.com, pg 396

Publications des Archives du Palais de Princier (Monaco) *Tel:* 93 25 18 31 *E-mail:* archives@palais.mc *Web Site:* www.palais.mc, pg 525

Publications des Facultes Universitaires Saint-Louis (Belgium) *Tel:* (02) 211 78 94 *Fax:* (02) 211 79 97 *Web Site:* www.fusl.ac.be, pg 72

Publik-Forum Verlagsgesellschaft mbH (Germany) *Tel:* (06171) 7003-0 *Fax:* (06171) 7003-40 *E-mail:* redaktion@publik-forum.de; verlag@publik-forum.de *Web Site:* www.publik-forum.de, pg 311

Publishers & Booksellers Association of Serbia (Serbia) *Tel:* (011) 41 21 359; (063) 398 905 (cell) *E-mail:* sekretar@izdavaci.rs *Web Site:* www.izdavaci. rs, pg 1388

Publishers & Booksellers' Association of Thailand (Thailand) *Tel:* (02) 9549560-4 *Fax:* (02) 9549565-6; (02) 9549566 *E-mail:* info@pubat.or.th *Web Site:* www.pubat.or.th, pg 1392

Publishers Association for Cultural Exchange (PACE) Japan (Japan) *Tel:* (03) 3291-5685 *Fax:* (03) 3233-3645 *E-mail:* culturalexchange@pace.or.jp *Web Site:* www.pace.or.jp, pg 1380

The Publishers Association Ltd (United Kingdom) *Tel:* (020) 7378 0504 *E-mail:* mail@publishers.org.uk *Web Site:* www.publishers.org.uk, pg 1397

The Publishers Association Ltd, Educational, Academic & Professional Publishing (United Kingdom) *Tel:* (020) 7378 0504 *E-mail:* mail@publishers.org.uk *Web Site:* www.publishers.org.uk, pg 1397

Publishers Association of New Zealand (PANZ) (New Zealand) *Tel:* (09) 280 3212 *E-mail:* admin@ publishers.org.nz *Web Site:* www.publishers.org.nz, pg 1385

Publishers Association of Russia (PAR) (Russia) *Tel:* (495) 6257520 *E-mail:* askibook@gmail.com *Web Site:* www.aski.ru, pg 1387

Publishers' Association of South Africa (PASA) (South Africa) *Tel:* (021) 762 9083 *Fax:* (021) 762 2763 *E-mail:* pasa@publishsa.co.za *Web Site:* www. publishsa.co.za, pg 1388

Publishers' Graphics LLC (United States) *Tel:* 630-221-1850 *Toll Free Tel:* 888-404-3769 *Fax:* 630-221-1870 *E-mail:* contactpg@pubgraphics.com *Web Site:* pubgraphics.com; www.pubgraphicsdirect. com, pg 1265, 1340, 1356

Publishers Group UK (United Kingdom) *Tel:* (020) 7405 1105 *Fax:* (020) 7242 3725 *E-mail:* info@pguk.co.uk; orders@pguk.co.uk; sales@pguk.co.uk; publicity@ pguk.co.uk *Web Site:* www.pguk.co.uk, pg 1460

Publishers Licensing Society (United Kingdom) *Tel:* (020) 7079 5930 *E-mail:* pls@pls.org.uk *Web Site:* www.pls.org.uk, pg 1397

Publishing Connections Ltd (United Kingdom) *E-mail:* info@publishingconnections.co.uk *Web Site:* publishingconnections.co.uk, pg 1397

Publishing House of Electronics Industry (PHEI) (China) *Tel:* (010) 88258888; (010) 88254114 *E-mail:* duca@ phei.com.cn *Web Site:* www.phei.com.cn, pg 108

Publishing Ireland (Ireland) *Tel:* (01) 6394868 *E-mail:* info@publishingireland.com *Web Site:* www. publishingireland.com, pg 1378

Publishing Resources Inc (Puerto Rico) *Tel:* (787) 626-0607; (787) 647-9342 (cell) *E-mail:* pri@chevako.net *Web Site:* www.publishingresources.net, pg 1283

Publishing Scotland (United Kingdom) *Tel:* (0131) 228 6866 *E-mail:* enquiries@publishingscotland.org *Web Site:* www.publishingscotland.org, pg 1397

The Publishing Training Centre at Book House (United Kingdom) *Tel:* (020) 8874 2718 *E-mail:* publishing. training@bookhouse.co.uk *Web Site:* www. train4publishing.co.uk, pg 817

Editions Publisud (France) *Tel:* 01 45 85 78 50 *Fax:* 01 45 89 94 15 *E-mail:* publisud.editions@cegetel.net *Web Site:* editionspublisud.hautetfort.com, pg 193

Pudeleco Editores SA/Publicaciones de Legislacion (Ecuador) *Tel:* (02) 254 3273; (02) 252 9246 *E-mail:* principal@pudeleco.com *Web Site:* www. comercioexteriorecuador.com, pg 142

Editorial Pueblo y Educacion (PE) (Cuba) *Tel:* (07) 202 14 90; (07) 209 37 08; (07) 204 08 44 *Fax:* (07) 204 08 44; (07) 206 15 94, pg 124

Puentepalo (Spain) *Tel:* 607 949 637 *E-mail:* editorialpuentepalo@hotmail.com *Web Site:* www.puentepalo.com, pg 664

Ediciones Puerto (Puerto Rico) *Tel:* (787) 721-0844 *Fax:* (787) 725-0861 *E-mail:* puertomailing@gmail. com *Web Site:* www.edicionespuerto.com, pg 583

Les Editions du Puits Fleuri (France) *Tel:* 01 64 23 61 46 *Fax:* 01 64 23 69 42 *E-mail:* puitsfleuri@wanadoo. fr *Web Site:* www.puitsfleuri.com, pg 193

Pulp Master Frank Nowatzki Verlag GbR (Germany) *Tel:* (030) 686 8292 *E-mail:* hq@pulpmaster.de *Web Site:* www.pulpmaster.de, pg 311

Editorial Reverte SA (Spain) *Tel:* 93 419 33 36 *Fax:* 93 419 51 89 *E-mail:* reverte@reverte.com; export@ reverte.com *Web Site:* www.reverte.com, pg 665

Livraria e Editora Revinter Ltda (Brazil) *Tel:* (021) 2563-9700 *Fax:* (021) 2563-9701 *E-mail:* livraria@ revinter.com.br *Web Site:* www.revinter.com.br, pg 90

Revolver Publishing (Germany) *Tel:* (030) 616 092 36 *Fax:* (030) 616 092 38 *E-mail:* info@revolver-publishing.com *Web Site:* www.revolver-publishing. com; www.revolver-books.de (orders), pg 315

REX Book Store Inc (Philippines) *Tel:* (02) 857-7777 *E-mail:* wecare@rexpublishing.com.ph *Web Site:* www.rexpublishing.com.ph, pg 566

REX Book Store Inc (Philippines) *Tel:* (02) 857-7777 *E-mail:* wecare@rexpublishing.com.ph; orders@ rexstore.com *Web Site:* www.rexpublishing.com.ph; www.rexestore.com, pg 1443

Rex Verlag Luzern (Switzerland) *Tel:* (041) 419 47 19 *Fax:* (041) 419 47 11 *E-mail:* info@rex-verlag. ch *Web Site:* www.rex-verlag.ch; www.rex-buch.ch, pg 704

Antiquariat Thomas Rezek (Germany) *Tel:* (089) 28 87 91 65 *Fax:* (089) 28 87 91 65 *E-mail:* arezek@web.de *Web Site:* www.a-rezek.de, pg 1418

RGS Libros SA de CV (Mexico) *Tel:* (0155) 5515 2922; (0155) 5515 4964; (0155) 5516 4261 *Fax:* (0155) 5277 1696 *Web Site:* www.rgslibros.com, pg 1436

Rhein-Mosel-Verlag GmbH (Germany) *Tel:* (06542) 5151 *Fax:* (06542) 61158 *E-mail:* info@rmv-web.de; rhein-mosel-verlag@t-online.de *Web Site:* www.rmv-web.de; www.r-m-v.de, pg 316

Rheinland-Verlag-und Betriebsgesellschaft des Landschaftsverbandes Rheinland mbH (Germany) *Tel:* (02234) 98 54-263 *Fax:* (02234) 98 54-219, pg 316

Rhema - Verlag und Herstellung (Germany) *Tel:* (0251) 44088 *Fax:* (0251) 44089 *E-mail:* info@rhema-verlag. de *Web Site:* www.rhema-verlag.de, pg 316

Editora RHJ (Brazil) *Tel:* (031) 3334-1566 *Fax:* (031) 3332-5823 *E-mail:* editorarhj@editorarhj.com.br *Web Site:* www.editorarhj.com.br, pg 90

Rhodes University Library (South Africa) *Tel:* (046) 603 8436 *Fax:* (046) 603 7310 *E-mail:* library@ru.ac.za *Web Site:* www.ru.ac.za/library, pg 1631

Forlaget Rhodos A/S (Denmark) *Tel:* 32 54 30 20 *Fax:* 32 54 30 22 *E-mail:* rhodos@rhodos.dk *Web Site:* www.rhodos.dk, pg 139

Rhombus Verlag GmbH (Austria) *Tel:* (01) 52 661 52 *Fax:* (01) 52 287 18, pg 56

Ediciones Rialp SA (Spain) *Tel:* 91 326 05 04 *Fax:* 91 326 13 21 *E-mail:* ediciones@rialp.com; foreignrights@rialp.com; pedidos@rialp.com *Web Site:* www.rialp.com, pg 665

RIAS Publishing (United Kingdom) *Tel:* (0131) 229 7545 *Fax:* (0131) 228 2188 *E-mail:* info@rias.org. uk; bookshop@rias.org.uk *Web Site:* www.rias.org.uk, pg 821

RIBA Publishing (United Kingdom) *Tel:* (020) 7496 8300 *E-mail:* enquiry@ribapublishing.com; marketing@ribabookshops.com *Web Site:* www. ribapublishing.com, pg 821

RIC Publications Pty Ltd (Australia) *Tel:* (08) 9240 9888 *Fax:* (08) 9240 1513 *E-mail:* mail@ricgroup.com.au *Web Site:* www.ricgroup.com.au, pg 37

Helmut Richardi Verlag GmbH (Germany) *Tel:* (069) 97 08 33-0 *Fax:* (069) 707 84 00 *E-mail:* info@ kreditwesen.de; vertrieb@kreditwesen.de (sales) *Web Site:* www.kreditwesen.de, pg 316

Richards Literary Agency (New Zealand) *Tel:* (09) 4100209 *Fax:* (09) 4100209 *E-mail:* rla.richards@ clear.net.nz, pg 1233

Richmond Publishing Co Ltd (United Kingdom) *Tel:* (01753) 643104 *E-mail:* rpc@richmond.co.uk *Web Site:* richmond.co.uk, pg 822, 1460

Richter-Verlag (Germany) *Tel:* (04349) 1725 *Fax:* (04349) 571 *E-mail:* richter-verlag@t-online.de *Web Site:* www.richter-verlag.de, pg 316

Richter Verlag GmbH (Germany) *Tel:* (0211) 370202 *Fax:* (0211) 377099 *E-mail:* office@richterverlag.com *Web Site:* www.richterverlag.com, pg 316

Les Editions du Ricochet (France) *Tel:* 01 40 33 84 16 *Web Site:* ricochet-livres-jeunesse.fr; ricochet.over-blog.net, pg 194

RICS Books (United Kingdom) *Tel:* (0870) 333 1600; (024) 7686 8555 *Fax:* (020) 7334 3811 *E-mail:* contactrics@rics.org; mailorder@rics.org *Web Site:* www.rics.org, pg 822, 1460

Editora Rideel Ltda (Brazil) *Tel:* (011) 2238-5100 *E-mail:* sac@rideel.com.br *Web Site:* www.rideel.com. br, pg 90

RiderChail Editions SRL (Argentina) *Tel:* (011) 44 31 91 07 *E-mail:* contacto@riderchail.com *Web Site:* www. riderchail.com, pg 11

edition riedenburg (Austria) *Tel:* (0664) 12 43 193 *Fax:* (0662) 234 663 234 *E-mail:* verlag@ editionriedenburg.at *Web Site:* www.editionriedenburg. at, pg 56

Susanna Rieder Verlag (Germany) *Tel:* (089) 82 08 67 65 *Fax:* (089) 12 71 09 96 *E-mail:* info@riederbuch. de; presse@riederbuch.de; vertrieb@riederbuch.de *Web Site:* www.riederbuch.de, pg 316

Riemann Verlag (Germany) *Tel:* (089) 4136-0 *Toll Free Tel:* 0800 500 33 22 *Fax:* (089) 4136-3333 *E-mail:* kundenservice@randomhouse.de *Web Site:* www.randomhouse.de/riemann, pg 316

Forlaget Ries (Denmark) *Tel:* 3963 3205; 2424 1263 (cell) *E-mail:* mr@riesforlag.dk *Web Site:* www. riesforlag.dk, pg 139

Literaturagentur Beate Riess (Germany) *E-mail:* info@ beate-riess.de *Web Site:* www.beate-riess.de, pg 1228

Agencia Riff (Brazil) *Tel:* (021) 2287 6299 *Fax:* (021) 2287 6393 *E-mail:* agenciariff@agenciariff.com.br *Web Site:* www.agenciariff.com.br, pg 1224

rights & audio (Germany) *Tel:* (06221) 65 21 222 *Fax:* (06221) 65 21 222 *E-mail:* info@rights-and-audio.de *Web Site:* www.rights-and-audio.de, pg 1228

The Rights Company (Netherlands) *Tel:* (06) 81 15 93 02 *E-mail:* books@therightscompany.nl *Web Site:* www.therightscompany.nl, pg 1232

Rights People (United Kingdom) *Tel:* (020) 7841 3950 *E-mail:* info@rightspeople.com *Web Site:* www. rightspeople.com, pg 1245

Rigodon-Verlag Norbert Wehr (Germany) *Tel:* (0201) 77 81 11 *Fax:* (0201) 77 51 74 *E-mail:* schreibheft@ netcologne.de *Web Site:* www.schreibheft.de, pg 316

Rigsarkivet (Denmark) *Tel:* 33 92 33 10 *E-mail:* mailbox@ra.sa.dk *Web Site:* www.sa.dk, pg 1586

Rijksmuseum Research Library (Netherlands) *Tel:* (020) 67 47 267; (020) 67 47 055 *E-mail:* bibliotheek@ rijksmuseum.nl *Web Site:* library.rijksmuseum.nl, pg 1616

Riksarkivet (Norway) *Tel:* 480 55 666 *E-mail:* post@ arkivverket.no *Web Site:* www.arkivverket.no, pg 1620

Riksarkivet (Sweden) *Tel:* (010) 476 70 00 *Fax:* (010) 476 71 20 *E-mail:* riksarkivet@riksarkivet.se *Web Site:* riksarkivet.se, pg 1635

Riley Dunn & Wilson Ltd (United Kingdom) *Tel:* (01324) 621591 *Fax:* (01324) 611508 *E-mail:* enquiry@rdw.co.uk; customer.services@rdw. co.uk *Web Site:* www.rdw.co.uk, pg 1338

Rimal Publications (Cyprus) *Tel:* 25580029 *Fax:* 25580039 *E-mail:* info@rimalbooks.com; order@ rimalbooks.com *Web Site:* www.rimalbooks.com, pg 124

Rimbaud Verlagsgesellschaft mbH (Germany) *Tel:* (0241) 54 25 32 *Fax:* (0241) 51 41 17 *E-mail:* info@ rimbaud.de *Web Site:* www.rimbaud.de, pg 316

Edizioni Rinnovamento nello Spirito Santo (RnS) (Italy) *Tel:* (06) 2310577 *Fax:* (06) 2305014 *E-mail:* segreteria@edizionirns.it *Web Site:* www. edizionirns.it, pg 462

Rinsen Book Co (Japan) *Tel:* (075) 721-7111 *Fax:* (075) 781-6168 *E-mail:* kyoto@rinsen.com *Web Site:* www. rinsen.com, pg 485

Edizioni Ripostes (Italy) *Tel:* (0828) 303621 *Fax:* (0828) 303621 *E-mail:* info@libreriamistral.it *Web Site:* www. ripostesedizioni.it, pg 462

Rising Stars UK Ltd (United Kingdom) *Toll Free Tel:* 0800 091 1602 *Toll Free Fax:* 0800 091 1603 *E-mail:* custcare@risingstars-uk.com *Web Site:* www. risingstars-uk.com, pg 822

Riso-Sha (Japan) *Tel:* (047) 366-8003 *Fax:* (047) 360-7301 *E-mail:* risosha@risosha.co.jp, pg 485

John Ritchie Ltd (United Kingdom) *Tel:* (01563) 536394 *Fax:* (01563) 571191 *Web Site:* www. ritchiechristianmedia.co.uk, pg 822

Rithofundasambandio (Iceland) *Tel:* 568 3190 *Fax:* 568 3192 *E-mail:* rsi@rsi.is *Web Site:* www.rsi.is, pg 1496

Ritter Verlag KG (Austria) *Tel:* (0463) 42631 *Fax:* (0463) 42631-37 *E-mail:* office@ritterbooks.com *Web Site:* www.ritterbooks.com, pg 56

Ritterbach Verlag GmbH (Germany) *Tel:* (02234) 18 66-0 *Fax:* (02234) 18 66-90; (02234) 18 66 13 *E-mail:* verlag@ritterbach.de; service@ritterbach.de *Web Site:* www.ritterbach.de; www.kunstwelt-online. de; www.kunsthandwerk-design.de, pg 316

Editori Riuniti (Italy) *E-mail:* info@editoririuniti.it *Web Site:* www.editoririuniti.it, pg 462

riva Verlag (Germany) *Tel:* (089) 65 12 85-0 *Fax:* (089) 65 20 96 *E-mail:* info@rivaverlag.de *Web Site:* www. m-vg.de/riva, pg 316

River Books (Thailand) *Tel:* (02) 222 1290; (02) 224 6686 *Fax:* (02) 225 3861 *E-mail:* order@riverbooksbk. com *Web Site:* www.riverbooksbk.com, pg 716

River Press (New Zealand) *Tel:* (03) 573 6942 *E-mail:* riverpress@xtra.co.nz *Web Site:* riverpress. co.nz, pg 549

Riverfield Verlag (Switzerland) *E-mail:* info@riverfield-verlag.ch *Web Site:* www.riverfield-verlag.ch, pg 704

Riverside Agency SAC (Argentina) *Tel:* (011) 5353 0830 *Fax:* (011) 5353 0830 *E-mail:* info@riverside-agency.com.ar; prensa@riverside-agency.com.ar *Web Site:* www.riversideagency.com.ar, pg 1401

Edizioni Riza SpA (Italy) *Tel:* (02) 5845961 *Fax:* (02) 58318162 *E-mail:* info@riza.it *Web Site:* www.riza.it, pg 462

Rizal Library (Philippines) *Tel:* (02) 4266001 *Fax:* (02) 4265961 *Web Site:* rizal.library.ateno.edu, pg 1622

Rizzoli (Italy) *E-mail:* info@rizzolilibri.it; ufficiostampa. rizzoli@rizzolilibri.it; rizzoli.rights@rizzolilibri.it *Web Site:* www.rizzoli.eu; www.rizzolilibri.it, pg 462

Libreria Rizzoli (Italy) *Tel:* (02) 86461071 *E-mail:* libreria.rizzoli@mondadori.it; rizzoligalleria@ rizzolilibri.it *Web Site:* www.libreriarizzoli.it, pg 1428

Editorial RM SA de CV (Mexico) *Tel:* (0155) 5533 5658 *Fax:* (0155) 5514 6799 *E-mail:* info@editorialrm.com *Web Site:* www.editorialrm.com, pg 522

Wydawnictwo RM Sp z oo (Poland) *Tel:* (22) 870 60 24 *Fax:* (22) 870 05 33 *E-mail:* rm@rm.com.pl; sklep@ rm.com.pl *Web Site:* www.rm.com.pl, pg 573

RMIT Publishing (Australia) *Tel:* (03) 9925 8100; (03) 9925 8210 (sales) *Fax:* (03) 9925 8134 *E-mail:* publish@rmitpublishing.com.au; info@ rmitpublishing.com.au; sales@rmitpublishing.com.au *Web Site:* www.informit.com.au, pg 37

RNIB National Library Service (United Kingdom) *Tel:* (020) 7388 1266 *Fax:* (020) 7388 2034 *E-mail:* library@rnib.org.uk *Web Site:* www.rnib.org. uk/library, pg 1642

Roadmaster Books (United Kingdom) *Tel:* (07813) 632623 *E-mail:* roadmasterbooks@blueyonder.co.uk *Web Site:* www.roadmasterbooks.co.uk, pg 822

Roads Publishing (Ireland) *Tel:* (01) 675 5278 *E-mail:* publishing@roads.co *Web Site:* roads.co/books, pg 414

Le Robert (France) *Tel:* 01 53 55 26 25 *E-mail:* commercial.numerique@lerobert.com *Web Site:* www.lerobert.com, pg 194

Robert Gordon University (United Kingdom) *Tel:* (01224) 262000 *Fax:* (01224) 263553 *E-mail:* business@rgu.ac.uk *Web Site:* www.rgu.ac.uk, pg 822

Ediciones Robinbook SL (Spain) *Tel:* 935551411 *Fax:* 935404092 *E-mail:* contacto@robinbook.com *Web Site:* www.robinbook.com, pg 665

Robinson Books (Israel) *Tel:* (03) 560-5461 *E-mail:* rob_book@netvision.net.il *Web Site:* www.robinson.co.il, pg 1427

Robinswood Press Ltd (United Kingdom) *Tel:* (01384) 397475 *Fax:* (01384) 440443 *E-mail:* customers@robinswoodpress.com *Web Site:* www.robinswoodpress.co.uk, pg 822

The Robson Press (United Kingdom) *Tel:* (020) 7091 1260 *E-mail:* info@bitebackpublishing.com *Web Site:* www.bitebackpublishing.com, pg 822

Laurus Robuffo Edizioni (Italy) *Tel:* (06) 565 1492 *Fax:* (06) 565 1233 *E-mail:* laurus@laurus.tv; redazione@laurusrobuffo.it *Web Site:* www.laurusrobuffo.it, pg 462

Roca (Brazil) *Tel:* (011) 5080-0770 *Web Site:* www.grupogen.com.br, pg 90

Roca Editorial (Spain) *Tel:* 932 687 275 *Fax:* 932 688 591 *E-mail:* info@rocaeditorial.com *Web Site:* www.rocaeditorial.com, pg 665

Ediciones La Rocca SRL (Argentina) *Tel:* (011) 4382-8526 *Fax:* (011) 4384-5774 *Web Site:* www.edicioneslarocca.com, pg 11

Editora Rocco Ltda (Brazil) *Tel:* (021) 3525-2000 *Fax:* (021) 3525-2001 *E-mail:* rocco@rocco.com.br *Web Site:* www.rocco.com.br, pg 90

Editiones Roche (Switzerland) *Tel:* (061) 688 1111; (061) 688 8888 *Fax:* (061) 691 9391 *E-mail:* basel.webmaster@roche.com *Web Site:* www.roche.com; www.roche.ch, pg 704

Editions du Rocher (Monaco) *Tel:* 99 99 67 17 *Fax:* 93 50 73 71 *E-mail:* contact@editionsdurocher.fr *Web Site:* www.editionsdurocher.fr, pg 525

Rockbuch Verlag (Germany) *Tel:* (040) 890 85 0 *Fax:* (040) 890 85 9320 *E-mail:* rockbuch@edel.com *Web Site:* www.rockbuch.de, pg 316

Rockpool Children's Books Ltd (United Kingdom) *Tel:* (07711) 351 691 *E-mail:* rockpoolchildrensbookltd@gmail.com *Web Site:* www.rockpoolchildrensbooks.co.uk, pg 822

Rockpool Publishing (Australia) *Tel:* (01) 9327 7150; (02) 9560 1280 *Web Site:* www.rockpoolpublishing.com.au, pg 38

Verlag Rockstuhl (Germany) *Tel:* (03603) 812246 *Fax:* (03603) 812247 *E-mail:* verlag-rockstuhl@web.de *Web Site:* www.verlag-rockstuhl.de, pg 317

Rodeira (Spain) *Tel:* 981 133290; 981 133294 *Fax:* 981 133216 *E-mail:* rodeira@edebe.net *Web Site:* www.edebe.com/grupo_edebe/rodeira.asp, pg 666

Rodovid Press (Ukraine) *Tel:* (044) 279 46 12 *E-mail:* rodovid2@gmail.com *Web Site:* www.rodovid.net, pg 726

Ediciones Joaquin Rodrigo (Spain) *Tel:* 91 5552728 *Fax:* 91 5564335 *E-mail:* info@joaquin-rodrigo.com *Web Site:* www.joaquin-rodrigo.com, pg 666

Libreria Rodriguez (Spain) *Tel:* 91 725 26 80 *E-mail:* correo@libreriarodriguez.com *Web Site:* www.libreriarodriguez.com, pg 1451

Ediciones Libreria Rodriguez SA (Argentina) *Tel:* (011) 4326-1959, pg 11

Roehrig Universitaets Verlag GmbH (Germany) *Tel:* (06894) 87 957 *Fax:* (06894) 87 0330 *E-mail:* info@roehrig-verlag.de *Web Site:* www.roehrig-verlag.de, pg 317

J H Roell Verlag GmbH (Germany) *Tel:* (09324) 99770 *Fax:* (09324) 99771 *E-mail:* info@roell-verlag.de *Web Site:* www.roell-verlag.de, pg 317

Verlagshaus Roemerweg GmbH (Germany) *Tel:* (0611) 986 98 0 *Fax:* (0611) 986 98 26 *E-mail:* info@verlagshaus-roemerweg.de *Web Site:* www.verlagshaus-roemerweg.de, pg 317

Edition Roesner (Austria) *Tel:* (02236) 23 5 40; (0664) 234 44 67 (cell) *Fax:* (02236) 23 5 40 *E-mail:* office@edition-roesner.at *Web Site:* www.edition-roesner.at, pg 56

Roetzer Druck GmbH (Austria) *Tel:* (02682) 624 94 *Fax:* (02682) 624 94 4 *E-mail:* office@roetzerdruck.at *Web Site:* www.roetzerdruck.at, pg 57

Libreria Editrice Rogate (LER) (Italy) *Tel:* (06) 7023430 *Fax:* (06) 7020767 *E-mail:* info@editricerogate.it *Web Site:* www.editricerogate.it, pg 462

Rogers, Coleridge & White Ltd (United Kingdom) *Tel:* (020) 7221 3717 *Fax:* (020) 7229 9084 *E-mail:* info@rcwlitagency.com *Web Site:* www.rcwlitagency.com, pg 1245

Zalozba Rokus Klett doo (Slovenia) *Tel:* (01) 513 46 00; (01) 513 46 46 (orders) *Fax:* (01) 513 46 79 *E-mail:* rokus@rokus-klett.si; narocila@rokus-klett.si (orders) *Web Site:* www.rokus.com, pg 611

Ediciones ROL SA (Spain) *Tel:* 93 200 80 33 *Fax:* 93 200 27 62 *E-mail:* rol@e-rol.es *Web Site:* www.e-rol.es, pg 666

Roli Books Pvt Ltd (India) *Tel:* (011) 4068 2000 *Fax:* (011) 29217185 *E-mail:* info@rolibooks.com; sales@rolibooks.com; editorial@rolibooks.com *Web Site:* rolibooks.com, pg 398

Edizioni Universitarie Romane (Italy) *Tel:* (06) 44 36 13 77; (06) 49 40 658; (06) 49 15 03 *Fax:* (06) 44 53 438 *Web Site:* www.eurom.it, pg 462

Romantic Novelists' Association (RNA) (United Kingdom) *E-mail:* info@romanticnovelistsassociation.org *Web Site:* www.romanticnovelistsassociation.org; www.rna-uk.org, pg 1504

Romantik Verlag (Switzerland) *Tel:* (052) 503 98 09 *E-mail:* info@romantik-verlag.ch; info@zauberblume.ch *Web Site:* www.romantik-verlag.ch, pg 704

Rombach Verlag KG (Germany) *Tel:* (0761) 4500-2135 *Fax:* (0761) 4500-2125 *E-mail:* info@buchverlag.rombach.de *Web Site:* www.rombach-verlag.de, pg 317

Romdidac SA (Romania) *Tel:* (021) 3212575 *Fax:* (021) 3234280 *E-mail:* office@romdidac.ro *Web Site:* www.romdidac.ro, pg 1446

Romiosini Verlag (Germany) *Tel:* (0221) 510 12 88 *Fax:* (0221) 510 12 88 *E-mail:* edition.romiosini@cemog.fu-berlin.de *Web Site:* bibliothek.edition-romiosini.de, pg 317

Rondo Verlag (Switzerland) *Tel:* (055) 2463937 *Fax:* (055) 2464293, pg 704

Rooster Books Ltd (United Kingdom) *Toll Free Tel:* 0800 009 6036 *Fax:* (0844) 357 7035 *E-mail:* info@roosterbooks.co.uk *Web Site:* www.roosterbooks.co.uk, pg 822

Roraima Publishers (Guyana) *Tel:* 227-3551; 227-3553, pg 362

Mercedes Ros Literary Agency (Spain) *Tel:* 93 540 13 53 *Fax:* 93 540 13 46 *E-mail:* info@mercedesros.com *Web Site:* www.mercedesros.com, pg 1236

Rosenberg Publishing (Australia) *Tel:* (02) 9654 1502 *Fax:* (02) 9654 1338 *E-mail:* sales@rosenbergpub.com.au *Web Site:* www.rosenbergpub.com.au, pg 38

Rosenheimer Verlagshaus GmbH & Co KG (Germany) *Tel:* (08031) 28 38 0 *Fax:* (08031) 28 38 44 *E-mail:* info@rosenheimer.com; presse1@rosenheimer.com; vertrieb1@rosenheimer.com *Web Site:* www.rosenheimer.com, pg 317

Rosenkreuzer Philosophie Verlag & Buecherecke (Switzerland) *Tel:* (081) 834 20 03 *Fax:* (081) 834 20 04 *Web Site:* heile-dich-selbst.ch/index.php?id=103, pg 704

Rosikon Press (Poland) *Tel:* (22) 722-61-01; (22) 722-66-66 *Fax:* (22) 722-66-67 *E-mail:* biuro@rosikonpress.com; handel@rosikonpress.com (sales); promocja@rosikonpress.com; rights@rosikonpress.com *Web Site:* www.rosikonpress.com, pg 573

Rosinante & Co (Denmark) *Tel:* 3341 1800 *Fax:* 3341 1801 *E-mail:* info@rosinante-co.dk *Web Site:* www.rosinante-co.dk, pg 139

Roskilde Universitetsbibliotek (Denmark) *Tel:* 4674 2207 *E-mail:* rub@ruc.dk *Web Site:* rub.ruc.dk, pg 1586

Rosma LT (Lithuania) *Tel:* (05) 262 35 98; (06) 154 39 66 *Fax:* (05) 261 19 97 *E-mail:* prekyba@rosmos.leidyklos.lt *Web Site:* rosmos.leidyklos.lt, pg 502

Edizioni Gino Rossato (Italy) *Tel:* (0455) 411000 *Fax:* (0455) 411550 *E-mail:* info@edizionirossato.it *Web Site:* www.edizionirossato.it, pg 462

Ekdoseis H Rossi (Greece) *Tel:* 2102020126 *Fax:* 2102020131 *E-mail:* info@rossi.com.gr *Web Site:* www.rossi.com.gr, pg 359

Rossiiskaya Knizhnaya Palata (Russia) *Fax:* (495) 688-99-91; (495) 688-96-89 *E-mail:* info@bookchamber.ru; isbn@tass.ru *Web Site:* www.bookchamber.ru, pg 1387

Rossiiskaya Nacionalnaya biblioteka (Russia) *Tel:* (812) 310-71-37; (812) 415-97-09 *Fax:* (812) 310-61-48 *E-mail:* office@nlr.ru *Web Site:* nlr.ru, pg 1627

Rossijskoye Avtorskoye Obshestvo (Russia) *Tel:* (495) 6973777; (495) 6973260 *Fax:* (495) 6099363 *E-mail:* rao@rao.ru *Web Site:* www.rao.ru, pg 1234

Rossipaul Kommunikation GmbH (Germany) *Tel:* (089) 17 91 06-0 *Fax:* (089) 17 91 06-22 *E-mail:* info@rossipaul.de *Web Site:* www.rossipaul.de, pg 317

Rotas (Lithuania) *Tel:* (05) 212 47 60 *Fax:* (05) 261 54 87 *E-mail:* knygnas@rotas.lt; info@rotas.lt *Web Site:* www.rotas.lt, pg 502

Rotbuch Verlag (Germany) *Tel:* (030) 20 61 09-0 *Fax:* (030) 20 61 09-75 *E-mail:* info@rotbuch.de; rights@rotbuch.de *Web Site:* www.rotbuch.de, pg 317

Roter Fleck Verlag (Germany) *Tel:* (06151) 9516885 *Fax:* (06151) 3968460 *E-mail:* info@roter-fleck-verlag.de *Web Site:* www.roter-fleck-verlag.de, pg 317

Roth et Sauter SA (Switzerland) *Tel:* (021) 811 36 36 *Fax:* (021) 811 36 37 *E-mail:* info@rothsauter.ch *Web Site:* www.rothsauter.ch, pg 704

Walter Roth Museum of Anthropology (Guyana) *Tel:* 225-8486 *E-mail:* walterrothmuseum1974@gmail.com *Web Site:* www.mcys.gov.gy/walter_roth_museum.html, pg 362

Roto Smeets (Netherlands) *Tel:* (0570) 69 48 50 *Fax:* (0570) 69 41 08 *E-mail:* info@rotosmeets.com *Web Site:* www.rotosmeets.nl, pg 1282, 1330

Rotopress International SRL (Italy) *Tel:* (071) 7500739 *Fax:* (071) 7500570 *E-mail:* info@rotoin.it *Web Site:* www.rotoin.it, pg 1329

RotoVision SA (United Kingdom) *Tel:* (01273) 716000 *Web Site:* www.quartoknows.com/rotovision, pg 822

Rotpunktverlag (Switzerland) *Tel:* (044) 405 44 88 *Fax:* (044) 405 44 89 *E-mail:* info@rotpunktverlag.ch *Web Site:* www.rotpunktverlag.ch, pg 704

Rotten Verlag AG (Switzerland) *Tel:* (027) 948 30 32 *Fax:* (027) 948 30 33 *E-mail:* shop@rottenverlag.ch *Web Site:* www.1815.ch/rottenverlag, pg 705

Agenzia Letteraria Loredana Rotundo (Italy) *Tel:* (02) 99041699 *Fax:* (02) 91089084 *E-mail:* info@lrliteraryagency.com *Web Site:* www.lrliteraryagency.com, pg 1231

Sanshusha Publishing Co Ltd (Japan) *Tel:* (03) 3405-4511 (sales) *Fax:* (03) 3551-4522 (sales) *E-mail:* eigyo@sanshusha.co.jp (sales) *Web Site:* www.sanshusha.co.jp, pg 486

Sant Jordi Asociados Agencia (Spain) *Tel:* 93 224 01 07 *Fax:* 93 356 26 96 *E-mail:* mail@santjordi-asociados.com *Web Site:* www.santjordi-asociados.com, pg 1236

Libreria Santa Fe (Argentina) *Tel:* (011) 5254 2376 (ext 30); (011) 5254 2376 (ext 31); (011) 5219 2582 *Fax:* (011) 5254 2376 (ext 36) *E-mail:* santafe2582@lsf.com.ar; asociados@lsf.com.ar *Web Site:* www.lsf.com.ar, pg 1401

Editorial Santa Maria (Argentina) *Tel:* (011) 4671-0110 *E-mail:* info@editorialsantamaria.com *Web Site:* www.editorialsantamaria.com, pg 11

Santiago Arcos Editor (Argentina) *Tel:* (011) 4432-3107 *E-mail:* santiagoarcoseditor@uolsinectis.com.ar, pg 11

Enrique Santiago Rueda Editor (Argentina) *Tel:* (011) 4305-0745, pg 11

Santillana (Portugal) *Tel:* 214 246 901 *Fax:* 214 246 907 *E-mail:* apoioaoprofessor@santillana.com *Web Site:* www.santillana.pt, pg 582

Santillana Colombia (Colombia) *Tel:* (01) 705 77 77 *Web Site:* www.santillana.com.co, pg 115

Ediciones Santillana SA (Uruguay) *Tel:* 24107342 *E-mail:* consultas@santillana.com.uy *Web Site:* www.santillana.com.uy, pg 849

Editorial Santillana SA (Venezuela) *Tel:* (0212) 235 30 33; (0212) 280 94 00 *Fax:* (0212) 280 94 04 *Web Site:* www.santillana.com.ve, pg 850

Editorial Santillana SA de CV (Mexico) *Tel:* (0155) 5420-7530 *Toll Free Tel:* 01 800 001 900 *Fax:* (0155) 5604-2304 *Web Site:* www.santillana.com.mx; www.santillana.com, pg 522

Grupo Santillana de Ediciones SL (Spain) *Tel:* 917449060 *Fax:* 917449019 *E-mail:* grupo@santillana.es; comunicacion@santillana.es *Web Site:* www.gruposantillana.com, pg 666

Grupo Santillana Mexico (Mexico) *Tel:* (0155) 5420-7530 *Toll Free Tel:* 01 800 008 1900 *Fax:* (0155) 5604-2304 *Web Site:* www.santillana.com; www.santillana.com.mx, pg 522

Santos Editora (Brazil) *Tel:* (021) 3543-0770 *E-mail:* vendas@grupogen.com.br *Web Site:* www.grupogen.com.br, pg 90

Editora Santuario (Brazil) *Tel:* (012) 3104-2000 *Toll Free Tel:* 0800 16 00 04 *Fax:* (012) 3104-2036 *Web Site:* www.editorasantuario.com.br, pg 90

Sapere 2000 SRL (Italy) *Tel:* (06) 4465363 *Fax:* (06) 4465363 *Web Site:* www.sapere2000.it, pg 463

Sapes Trust Ltd (Zimbabwe) *Tel:* (04) 252 962; (04) 252 965 *Fax:* (04) 252 964 *E-mail:* info@sapes.org.zw *Web Site:* www.sapes.org.zw, pg 852

Sapnu Sala Spaustuve (Lithuania) *Tel:* (05) 278 05 80 *Fax:* (05) 278 05 90, pg 1281, 1330

Sappi Fine Paper Europe (Belgium) *Tel:* (02) 676 9700 *Web Site:* www.sappi.com, pg 1345

Saqi Books (United Kingdom) *Tel:* (020) 7221 9347 *Fax:* (020) 7229 7492 *Web Site:* www.saqibooks.com, pg 826

Saraband Ltd (United Kingdom) *Tel:* (0141) 339 5030 *Fax:* (0141) 332 1864 *E-mail:* hermes@saraband.net *Web Site:* www.saraband.net, pg 826

Saraiva SA Livreiros Editores (Brazil) *Tel:* (011) 3613-3212 *Toll Free Tel:* 0800-754-4000 *E-mail:* falecomri@saraiva.com.br *Web Site:* www.saraiva.com.br; www.saraivari.com.br, pg 90, 1408

Sarajevo Publishing (Bosnia and Herzegovina) *Tel:* (033) 220 809 *Web Site:* www.sarajevopublishing.ba, pg 75, 1407

Sarasavi Bookshop Pvt Ltd (Sri Lanka) *Tel:* (011) 2820820 *Fax:* (011) 2814926 *E-mail:* info@sarasavi.lk *Web Site:* www.sarasavi.lk, pg 1451

Editions Sarbacane (France) *Tel:* 01 42 46 24 00 *Fax:* 01 42 46 28 15 *E-mail:* contacts@sarbacane.net *Web Site:* www.editions-sarbacane.com, pg 194

Sardini Editrice SRL (Italy) *Tel:* (030) 7750430 *Fax:* (030) 7254348 *E-mail:* sardini@sardini.it *Web Site:* www.sardini.it, pg 463

M C Sarkar & Sons (P) Ltd (India) *Tel:* (033) 2241-7490; (033) 2464-0763 *E-mail:* mcsarkar@gmail.com, pg 399

Kustantajat Sarmala Oy (Finland) *Toll Free Tel:* 0400 703838, pg 150

Sarospataki Reformatus Kollegium Tudomanyos Gyujtemenyeinek Nagykonyvtara (Hungary) *Tel:* (047) 311-057 *Fax:* (047) 311-057 *E-mail:* reftud@iif.hu *Web Site:* www.patakarchiv.hu, pg 1600

Sarpay Beikman (Myanmar) *Tel:* (01) 283277, pg 1437

SarPayLawKa (Myanmar) *Tel:* (097) 303 3802 *Web Site:* www.sarpaylawka.com, pg 1437

Sarvodaya Vishva Lekha (Sri Lanka) *Tel:* (011) 264-7159 *Fax:* (011) 2656-512 *Web Site:* www.sarvodaya.org, pg 1262, 1285, 1335

Sasa Sema Publications Ltd (Kenya) *Tel:* (020) 6532579; (020) 6532580; (020) 6532581 *Fax:* (020) 6558551 *E-mail:* enquiries@longhornpublishers.com *Web Site:* www.longhornpublishers.com, pg 494

Sasavona Publishers and Booksellers (Pty) Ltd (South Africa) *Tel:* (013) 231-8494; (087) 802-6110; (082) 402-7267 (orders) *Fax:* (086) 726-5523 *E-mail:* info@sasavona.co.za *Web Site:* www.sasavona.co.za, pg 617

Sasbadi Sdn Bhd (Malaysia) *Tel:* (03) 6145 1188 *Fax:* (03) 6145 1199 *E-mail:* enquiry@sasbadi.com *Web Site:* www.sasbadi.com, pg 510

Sassafras Verlag (Germany) *Tel:* (02151) 787770 *Fax:* (02151) 771302, pg 319

Sassi Editore SRL (Italy) *Tel:* (0445) 523772 *E-mail:* info@sassieditore.it *Web Site:* www.sassieditore.it, pg 464

Sasta Sahitya Mandal (India) *Tel:* (011) 23310505; (011) 41523565 *Fax:* (011) 23310505 *E-mail:* info@sastasahityamandal.org; sales@sastasahityamandal.org *Web Site:* www.sastasahityamandal.org, pg 399

Sat Sahitya Prakashan Trust (India) *Tel:* (022) 2368 2055 *Web Site:* www.satsahitya.com, pg 399

Sathya Sai Vereinigung eV (Germany) *Tel:* (06074) 3901 *Fax:* (06074) 309785 *E-mail:* buchzentrum@sathya-sai.de *Web Site:* www.sathyasai-buchzentrum.de, pg 319

Vicki Satlow Literary Agency (Italy) *Tel:* (02) 48015553 *E-mail:* vickisatlow@tin.it, pg 1231

Satrap Publishing & Translation (United Kingdom) *Tel:* (020) 8748 9397 *E-mail:* info@satraptranslation.co.uk; satrap@btconnect.com *Web Site:* www.satrap.co.uk; www.satraptranslation.co.uk, pg 1253

Satyam Books (India) *Tel:* (011) 23242686; (011) 23245698 *Fax:* (011) 23267131; (011) 22459334 *E-mail:* customercare@satyambooks.net; satyambooks@hotmail.com *Web Site:* www.satyambooks.net, pg 399

Saudi Publishing & Distribution House (Saudi Arabia) *Tel:* (012) 6294039, pg 599

I H Sauer Verlag GmbH (Germany) *Tel:* (06221) 9060 *Fax:* (06221) 906 259, pg 319

J D Sauerlaender's Verlag (Germany) *Tel:* (06052) 3094667; (0173) 6972970 (cell) *Fax:* (06052) 3094668 *Web Site:* www.sauerlaender-verlag.com, pg 319

Sauramps Medical (France) *Tel:* 04 67 63 68 80; 04 67 63 62 19 *Fax:* 04 67 52 59 05 *Web Site:* www.sauramps-medical.com; www.livres-medicaux.com, pg 195

Librairie Sauramps Medical (France) *Tel:* 04 67 63 68 80; 04 67 63 62 19 (orders) *Fax:* 04 67 63 68 84 *E-mail:* webmaster@saurampsmedical.com *Web Site:* www.livres-medicaux.com, pg 1414

Editorial Saure SL (Spain) *Tel:* 945 465 825, pg 667

editions des sauvages (Switzerland) *Tel:* (022) 320 12 01 *Web Site:* www.editionsdessauvages.ch, pg 705

Steve Savage Publishers Ltd (United Kingdom) *Tel:* (020) 7770 6083 *E-mail:* sales@savagepublishers.com *Web Site:* www.savagepublishers.com, pg 826

Savannah Publications (United Kingdom) *Tel:* (020) 8244 4350 *Fax:* (020) 8244 2448 *Web Site:* www.savannahpublications.com, pg 826

Savez Inzenjera i Tehnicara Srbije (SITS) (Serbia) *Tel:* (011) 3230-067; (011) 3237-363 *Fax:* (011) 3230-067; (011) 3237-363 *E-mail:* office@sits.rs *Web Site:* www.sits.org.rs, pg 602

Savremena Administracija AD (Serbia) *Tel:* (011) 2663-733 *Fax:* (011) 2667-522; (011) 2667-633 *E-mail:* office@savremena-ad.com *Web Site:* www.savremena-ad.com, pg 602

Sawan Kirpal Publications Spiritual Society (India) *Tel:* (011) 27117100 *Fax:* (011) 27214040 *Web Site:* sos.org, pg 399

Alastair Sawday Publishing Co Ltd (United Kingdom) *Tel:* (01172) 047 810 *E-mail:* hello@sawdays.co.uk; press@sawdays.co.uk *Web Site:* www.sawdays.co.uk, pg 826

Sax-Verlag (Germany) *Tel:* (0341) 3 50 21 17 *Fax:* (0341) 3 50 21 16 *E-mail:* info@sax-verlag.de *Web Site:* www.sax-verlag.de, pg 319

Say Yayinlari (Turkey) *Tel:* (0212) 512 21 58; (0212) 528 17 54 *Fax:* (0212) 512 50 80 *E-mail:* satisdestek@saykitap.com *Web Site:* www.saykitap.com, pg 723

The Sayle Literary Agency (United Kingdom) *Tel:* (01223) 303035 *E-mail:* info@sayleliteraryagency.com *Web Site:* www.sayleliteraryagency.com, pg 1245

SBS Distribuidora (Argentina) *Tel:* (011) 5353-2220 *Web Site:* www.facebook.com/DistribuidoraSBS, pg 1401

SBS Livraria Internacional (Brazil) *Tel:* (011) 2238-4477; (011) 2238-4478 *Fax:* (011) 2256-7151 *E-mail:* sbs@sbs.com.br; ventasinternet@sbs.com.br *Web Site:* www.sbs.com.br, pg 1408

SBS Special Book Services SA (Peru) *Tel:* (01) 206-4900 *Fax:* (01) 241-8492 *E-mail:* ventas@sbs.com.pe *Web Site:* www.sbs.com.pe, pg 1443

SBT Professional Publications Sdn Bhd (Malaysia) *Tel:* (03) 20789828, pg 510

SC (Sang Choy) International Pte Ltd (Singapore) *Tel:* 6289 0829 *Fax:* 6282 1819 *E-mail:* marketing@sc-international.com.sg *Web Site:* www.sc-international.com.sg, pg 1283, 1332

Scala Arts & Heritage Publishers (United Kingdom) *Tel:* (020) 7808 1550 *E-mail:* info@scalapublishers.com *Web Site:* www.scalapublishers.com, pg 826

Edizioni la Scala (Italy) *Tel:* (080) 4975838 *Fax:* (080) 4975839 *E-mail:* edizionilascala@gmail.com *Web Site:* www.abbazialascala.it, pg 464

Scala Group SpA (Italy) *Tel:* (055) 6233200; (055) 6233257; (055) 6233210 *Fax:* (055) 641124 *E-mail:* firenze@scalarchives.it *Web Site:* www.scalarchives.it, pg 464

Scalpendi Editore SRL (Italy) *Tel:* (02) 8055266 *Fax:* (02) 8055266 *E-mail:* info@scalpendieditore.eu; redazione@scalpendieditore.eu *Web Site:* www.scalpendieditore.eu, pg 464

Scandinavia Publishing House (Denmark) *Tel:* 3123 3380 *Fax:* 3531 0334 *E-mail:* info@scanpublishing.dk *Web Site:* www.scanpublishing.dk, pg 140

scaneg Verlag eK (Germany) *Tel:* (089) 759 33 36 *Fax:* (089) 759 39 14 *E-mail:* verlag@scaneg.de *Web Site:* www.scaneg.de, pg 320

Scholastic New Zealand Ltd (New Zealand) *Tel:* (09) 274 8112 (customer service) *Fax:* (09) 274 8115 *E-mail:* enquiries@scholastic.co.nz *Web Site:* www. scholastic.co.nz, pg 549

Kurt Scholl (Germany) *Tel:* (06221) 7534652; (06221) 707661, pg 1418

School Library Association (United Kingdom) *Tel:* (01793) 530166 *Fax:* (01793) 481182 *E-mail:* info@sla.org.uk *Web Site:* www.sla.org.uk, pg 1662

The School of Life (United Kingdom) *Tel:* (020) 7833 1010 *E-mail:* shop@theschooloflife.com *Web Site:* www.theschooloflife.com, pg 827

School of Oriental & African Studies (SOAS) (United Kingdom) *Tel:* (020) 7637 2388 *Fax:* (020) 7898 4009 *E-mail:* marketing@soas.ac.uk *Web Site:* www.soas.ac. uk, pg 827

School of Oriental & African Studies Library (United Kingdom) *Tel:* (020) 7637 2388 *Fax:* (020) 7436 4159 *E-mail:* libenquiry@soas.ac.uk *Web Site:* www.soas.ac. uk/library, pg 1642

SchoolPlay Productions Ltd (United Kingdom) *Tel:* (01206) 540111 *Web Site:* www. schoolplayproductions.co.uk, pg 827

Editions Schortgen (Luxembourg) *Tel:* 54 64 87 *Fax:* 53 05 34 *E-mail:* editions@schortgen.lu *Web Site:* www. editions-schortgen.lu, pg 504

Eckart Schott Verlag (Germany) *Tel:* (06356) 91062 *Fax:* (06356) 919 302 *E-mail:* eschott@aol.com; bestellung@salleckpublications.de *Web Site:* www. salleck-publications.de; salleckpublications.de, pg 323

Schott Music GmbH & Co KG (Germany) *Tel:* (06131) 246-0; (020) 7534 0740 (press) *Fax:* (06131) 246-211 *E-mail:* info@schott-music.com; press@schott-music. com; foreign-rights@schott-music.com *Web Site:* de. schott-music.com; en.schott-music.com (English), pg 323

Verlag Schreiber & Leser (Germany) *Tel:* (040) 4018 9454 *E-mail:* verlag@schreiberundleser.de *Web Site:* www.schreiberundleser.de, pg 323

Verlag Silke Schreiber (Germany) *Tel:* (089) 2710180 *Fax:* (089) 2716957 *Web Site:* www.verlag-silke-schreiber.de, pg 323

Schrenk-Verlag (Germany) *Tel:* (0151) 424 603 68 *Fax:* (09831) 880 98 99 *E-mail:* schrenk@ buchhausschrenk.de *Web Site:* www.buchhausschrenk. de, pg 323

Druckerei Schroeder (Germany) *Tel:* (06423) 921-33 *Fax:* (06423) 921-35 *E-mail:* info@druckerei-schroeder.de *Web Site:* www.druckerei-schroeder.de, pg 1323

CH SCHROER GmbH (Germany) *Tel:* (02266) 478950 *Fax:* (02266) 4789525 *E-mail:* info@chsbooks.de *Web Site:* www.chsbooks.de, pg 323

Schubert & Franzke GesmbH Kartografischer Verlag (Austria) *Tel:* (02742) 785 01-0 *Fax:* (02742) 785 01-15 *E-mail:* office@schubert-franzke.com *Web Site:* www.schubert-franzke.com, pg 57

Carl Ed Schuenemann KG (Germany) *Tel:* (0421) 3 69 03-0 *Fax:* (0421) 3 69 03-39 *E-mail:* kontakt@ schuenemann-verlag.de *Web Site:* www.schuenemann-verlag.de, pg 323

Schueren Verlag GmbH (Germany) *Tel:* (06421) 6 30 84 *Fax:* (06421) 68 11 90 *E-mail:* info@schueren-verlag.de; presse@schueren-verlag.de *Web Site:* www. schueren-verlag.de, pg 323

Druckhaus Schuetze GmbH (Germany) *Tel:* (0345) 56666-0 *Fax:* (0345) 56666-66 *E-mail:* info@dhs-halle.de; vertrieb@dhs-halle.de *Web Site:* www.dhs-halle.de, pg 1257, 1276, 1323

Schulbuchverlag Anadolu GmbH (Germany) *Tel:* (02433) 4091 *Fax:* (02433) 41608 *E-mail:* info@anadolu-verlag.de; office@anadolu-verlag.de *Web Site:* www. anadolu-verlag.de, pg 324

Schulthess Juristische Medien AG (Switzerland) *Tel:* (044) 200 29 29 *Fax:* (044) 200 29 28 *E-mail:* verlag@schulthess.com *Web Site:* www. schulthess.com, pg 705

Schultz Information (Denmark) *Tel:* 72 28 28 27; 72 28 28 26 (customer service) *Fax:* 43 63 56 15 *E-mail:* schultz@schultz.dk; kundeservice@schultz.dk *Web Site:* www.schultz.dk, pg 140

Schulz-Kirchner Verlag GmbH (Germany) *Tel:* (06126) 93 20 0; (06126) 9320-13 *Fax:* (06126) 93 20 50 *E-mail:* info@schulz-kirchner.de; vertrieb@schulz-kirchner.de *Web Site:* www.schulz-kirchner.de, pg 324

Verlag R S Schulz GmbH (Germany) *Tel:* (0221) 94373-7000 *Fax:* (0221) 94373-7201 *E-mail:* info@ wolterskluwer.de; info-wkd@wolterskluwer. com; wkd@wolterskluwer.com *Web Site:* www. wolterskluwer.de, pg 324

H O Schulze KG (Germany) *Tel:* (09571) 7 80 18 *Fax:* (09571) 7 80 57 *E-mail:* verkauf@schulze-kg.de *Web Site:* www.schulze-kg.de, pg 324

Buchdruckerei und Verlag SchumacherGebler KG (Germany) *Tel:* (089) 5 99 49-0 *Fax:* (089) 5 99 49-149 *E-mail:* info@schumachergebler.com *Web Site:* www.schumachergebler.com; www. bibliothek-sg.de, pg 324

H Katia Schumer Literary Agent (Brazil) *Tel:* (021) 2158-6370 *Fax:* (021) 2491-9841 *E-mail:* hkatia@schumer.com.br *Web Site:* www. hkatiaschumerliteraryagent.com, pg 1224

Verlag Schuster Leer (Germany) *Tel:* (0491) 92 590 0 *Fax:* (0491) 92 590 59 *E-mail:* buchhandlung-schuster@t-online.de *Web Site:* www.verlag-schuster. de, pg 324

Heinrich Schwab Verlag GmbH & Co KG (Germany) *Tel:* (05575) 20101 *Fax:* (05575) 4745 *E-mail:* office@heinrichschwabverlag.de *Web Site:* www.heinrichschwabverlag.de, pg 324

Schwabe AG (Switzerland) *Tel:* (061) 278 95 65 *Fax:* (061) 272 95 66 *E-mail:* verlag@schwabe.ch *Web Site:* www.schwabe.ch, pg 705

Schwabenverlag (Germany) *Tel:* (0711) 44 06-162 *Fax:* (0711) 44 06-177 *E-mail:* buchverlag@ schwabenverlag.de *Web Site:* www.schwabenverlag-online.de, pg 324

Schwaneberger Verlag GmbH (Germany) *Tel:* (089) 323 93-02 *Fax:* (089) 323 93-248 *E-mail:* info@michel. de; presse@michel.de; vertrieb@michel.de (sales); vertriebsleitung@michel.de *Web Site:* www.michel.de; www.briefmarken.de, pg 324

Fachbuchhandlung Otto Schwartz (Germany) *Tel:* (0551) 31051 *Fax:* (0551) 372812 *E-mail:* fachbuchhandlung-schwartz@t-online.de *Web Site:* schwartzbuch. homepage.t-online.de, pg 324

Verlagsbuero Schwarzer (Austria) *Tel:* (01) 548 13 15 *Fax:* (01) 548 13 15-39 *E-mail:* verlagsbuero@ schwarzer.at *Web Site:* www.schwarzer.at, pg 57

Schwarzkopf & Schwarzkopf Verlag GmbH (Germany) *Tel:* (030) 44 33 63 00 *Fax:* (030) 44 33 63 044 *E-mail:* info@schwarzkopf-schwarzkopf.de *Web Site:* www.schwarzkopf-schwarzkopf.de, pg 325

Verlag Schweers + Wall GmbH (Germany) *Tel:* (0221) 290 27 72 *Fax:* (0221) 290 27 73 *E-mail:* mail@ schweers-wall.de *Web Site:* www.schweers-wall.de, pg 325

Schweitzer Fachinformationen oHG (Germany) *Tel:* (089) 55134-112 *Fax:* (089) 55134-103 *Web Site:* www.schweitzer-online.de, pg 1418

Schweizer Buchhaendler- und Verleger-Verband (SBVV) (Switzerland) *Tel:* (044) 421 36 00 *Fax:* (044) 421 36 18 *E-mail:* info@sbvv.ch *Web Site:* www.sbvv.ch, pg 1391

Schweizer Spiegel Verlag mit Rodana Verlag AG (Switzerland) *Tel:* (044) 2115000, pg 705

E Schweizerbart'sche Verlagsbuchhandlung (Naegele und Obermiller) (Germany) *Tel:* (0711) 351456-0 *Fax:* (0711) 351456-99 *E-mail:* mail@schweizerbart. de *Web Site:* www.schweizerbart.de, pg 325

Schweizerische Arbeitsgemeinschaft fuer die Berggebiete (SAB) (Switzerland) *Tel:* (031) 382 10 10 *Fax:* (031) 382 10 16 *E-mail:* info@sab.ch *Web Site:* www.sab.ch, pg 705

Das Schweizerische Nationalbibliothek (Switzerland) *Tel:* (031) 322 89 35 (information) *Fax:* (031) 322 84 08 *E-mail:* info@nb.admin.ch *Web Site:* www.nb. admin.ch, pg 1636

Schweizerische Stiftung fuer Alpine Forschung (Switzerland) *Tel:* (044) 253 12 00 *Fax:* (044) 253 12 01 *Web Site:* www.alpineresearch.ch; www.alpinfo.ch, pg 706

Schweizerisches Bundesarchiv (Switzerland) *Tel:* (031) 322 89 89 *Fax:* (031) 322 78 23 *E-mail:* bundesarchiv@bar.admin.ch *Web Site:* www. bar.admin.ch, pg 1636

Schweizerisches Jugendschriftenwerk (SJW) (Switzerland) *Tel:* (044) 462 49 40 *Fax:* (044) 462 69 13 *E-mail:* office@sjw.ch *Web Site:* www.sjw.ch, pg 706

Verlag Schweizerisches Katholisches Bibelwerk (Switzerland) *Tel:* (044) 205 99 60 *Fax:* (044) 205 99 60 *E-mail:* info@bibelwerk.ch *Web Site:* www. bibelwerk.ch, pg 706

Schweizerisches Wirtschaftsarchiv (Switzerland) *Tel:* (061) 267 32 19 *E-mail:* info-ubw-swa@unibas. ch *Web Site:* www.ub.unibas.ch/ub-wirtschaft.swa, pg 1636

Salvatore Sciascia Editore (Italy) *Tel:* (0934) 21946; (0934) 551509 *Fax:* (0934) 551336 *E-mail:* sciasciaeditore@virgilio.it, pg 464

Science & Technology Information Institute (Philippines) *Tel:* (02) 837-2191 *Fax:* (02) 837-7521 *E-mail:* library@stii.dost.gov.ph *Web Site:* library.stii. dost.gov.ph; www.dost.gov.ph, pg 1622

The Science & Technology Library of the NHRF (Greece) *Tel:* 2107273710; 2107273939 *Fax:* 2107246618 *E-mail:* eie@eie.gr *Web Site:* www. eie.gr/library-en.html, pg 1598

Science & Technology Publishing House (Vietnam) *Tel:* (04) 38220686; (04) 39423172 *Fax:* (04) 8220658 *E-mail:* nxbkhkt@hn.vnn.vn *Web Site:* nxbkhkt.com. vn, pg 851

The Science Factory (Germany) *Tel:* (040) 4327 4959 (Skype); (020) 7193 7296 *E-mail:* eie@ sciencefactory.co.uk *Web Site:* www.sciencefactory. co.uk, pg 1228

Science Navigation Group (United Kingdom) *Tel:* (020) 7323 0323 *Fax:* (020) 7022 1664 *E-mail:* info@ sciencenavigation.com *Web Site:* sciencenavigation. com, pg 1228

Science Press (Australia) *Tel:* (02) 9516 1122 *Toll Free Tel:* 1800 225 031 *Fax:* (02) 9550 1915 *E-mail:* sales@sciencepress.com.au *Web Site:* www. sciencepress.com.au, pg 38

Science Press (China) *Tel:* (010) 64034541; (010) 64010628 *Fax:* (010) mail@sciencep.com; webmaster@mail.sciencep.com *Web Site:* www. sciencep.com, pg 109

Science Reviews 2000 Ltd (United Kingdom) *Tel:* (01727) 764601 *E-mail:* info@ sciencereviews2000.co.uk *Web Site:* www. sciencereviews2000.co.uk, pg 827

Sciences Humaines Editions (France) *Tel:* 03 86 72 07 00 *Fax:* 03 86 52 53 26 *Web Site:* editions. scienceshumaines.com; www.scienceshumaines.com, pg 195

Scientific & Technical Information Service (Belgium) *Tel:* (02) 238 37 40 *Fax:* (02) 238 37 50 *Web Site:* www.stis.belspo.be, pg 1648

Scientific International Pvt Ltd (India) *Tel:* (011) 23287580; (011) 23287584; (011) 23289263; (011) 47148284; (011) 43512984 *Fax:* (011) 23286096 *E-mail:* info@siplind; expo@siplind.com *Web Site:* www.siplind.com, pg 1424

Seemann Henschel GmbH & Co KG (Germany) *Tel:* (0341) 98 210 10 *Fax:* (0341) 98 210 19 *E-mail:* info@seemann-henschel.de *Web Site:* www. seemann-henschel.de, pg 326

Editions Seghers (France) *Tel:* 01 53 67 14 00 *Web Site:* www.editions-seghers.tm.fr, pg 195

Edizioni Segno SAS (Italy) *Tel:* (0432) 575179 *Fax:* (0432) 575589 *E-mail:* info@edizionisegno.it; ordini@edizionisegno.it; redazione@edizionisegno.it *Web Site:* www.edizionisegno.it, pg 465

Segretariato Nazionale Apostolato della Preghiera (Italy) *Tel:* (06) 697 607 207 *Fax:* (06) 678 10 63 *E-mail:* adp@adp.it *Web Site:* www.adp.it, pg 465

Editions Seguier (France) *Tel:* 01 55 42 61 40 *Fax:* 01 55 42 61 41 *E-mail:* contact@editions-seguier.fr *Web Site:* www.editions-seguier.fr, pg 195

Seibido Publishing Co Ltd (Japan) *Tel:* (03) 3291-2261 *Fax:* (03) 3291-5490 *E-mail:* seibido@seibido.co. jp *Web Site:* www.seibido.co.jp/english/index.html, pg 486

Seibido Shuppan Co Ltd (Japan) *Tel:* (03) 5206-8151 *Fax:* (03) 5206-8159 *Web Site:* www.seibidoshuppan. co.jp, pg 486

Seibundo Publishing Co Ltd (Japan) *Tel:* (06) 6211-6265 *Fax:* (06) 6211-6492 *E-mail:* seibundo@triton.ocn.ne. jp; order@seibundo-pb.co.jp *Web Site:* www.seibundo-pb.co.jp, pg 486

Seibundo Shinkosha Publishing Co Ltd (Japan) *Tel:* (03) 5800-5780 *Fax:* (03) 5800-5781 *E-mail:* inquiry@ seibundo.com; cs@seibundo.com *Web Site:* www. seibundo-shinkosha.net, pg 486

Seibundoh (Japan) *Tel:* (03) 3203-9201; (03) 3203-4806 (sales) *Fax:* (03) 3203-9206; (03) 3203-2038 (sales) *E-mail:* eigyobu@seibundoh.co.jp; hanbaibu@ seibundoh.co.jp (sales); henshubu@seibundoh.co.jp *Web Site:* www.seibundoh.co.jp, pg 486

Seifert Verlag GmbH (Austria) *Tel:* (01) 712 79 55-0 *Fax:* (01) 712 79 55-25 *E-mail:* office@seifertverlag.at *Web Site:* www.seifertverlag.at, pg 57

Michael Seipp, Kartographie & Verlag (Germany) *Tel:* (069) 74309806 *Fax:* (069) 74309852 *E-mail:* info@hildebrands.de *Web Site:* www. hildebrands.de, pg 326

Seiryu Publishing Co Ltd (Japan) *Tel:* (03) 3288-5405 *Fax:* (03) 3288-5340 *E-mail:* seiryu1@seiryupub.co.jp *Web Site:* www.seiryupub.co.jp, pg 486

Seishin Shobo (Japan) *Tel:* (03) 3946-5666 *Fax:* (03) 3945-8880 *E-mail:* sei@seishinshobo.co.jp *Web Site:* www.seishinshobo.co.jp, pg 486

Seismo Verlag (Switzerland) *Tel:* (044) 261 10 94 *Fax:* (044) 251 11 94 *E-mail:* buch@seismoverlag.ch *Web Site:* www.seismoverlag.ch, pg 706

Seiun-sha (Japan) *Tel:* (03) 3947-1021 *Fax:* (03) 3947-1617, pg 486

Seiwa Shoten Co Ltd (Japan) *Tel:* (03) 3329-0031; (03) 3329-0033 (editorial) *Fax:* (03) 5374-7186; (03) 5374-7185 (editorial) *Web Site:* www.seiwa-pb.co.jp, pg 486

Editorial Seix Barral (Spain) *Tel:* 93 492 89 01 *E-mail:* editorial@seix-barral.es *Web Site:* www. planetadelibros.com/editorial-seix-barral-9.html, pg 667

Seizando-Shoten Publishing Co Ltd (Japan) *Tel:* (03) 3357-5861 *Fax:* (03) 3357-5867 *E-mail:* publisher@ seizando.co.jp; order@seizando.co.jp *Web Site:* www. seizando.co.jp, pg 487

Seizmoloska Opservatorija (Macedonia) *Tel:* (02) 2733001 *Fax:* (02) 2700713 *E-mail:* webmaster@ seismobsko.pmf.ukim.edu.mk *Web Site:* seismobsko. pmf.ukim.edu.mk, pg 505

Wydawnictwo Sejmowe (Poland) *Tel:* (22) 694-13-30; (22) 694-15-97 (sales) *Fax:* (22) 694-10-04 (sales) *E-mail:* wydawnictwo@sejm.gov.pl *Web Site:* wydawnictwo.sejm.gov.pl, pg 573

Sejong Taewang Kinyom Saophoe (South Korea) *Tel:* (02) 969-8851; (02) 969-8852; (02) 969-8853 *Fax:* (02) 969-8854 *E-mail:* sejong@sejongkorea.org *Web Site:* sejongkorea.org, pg 624

Sekai Bunka Publishing Inc (Japan) *Tel:* (03) 3262-5111 *Fax:* (03) 3262-5750 *E-mail:* bookcenter@sekaibunka. co.jp *Web Site:* www.sekaibunka.com, pg 487

Sekwang Music Publishing Co (South Korea) *Tel:* (02) 719-2652 *Fax:* (02) 719-2191 *E-mail:* sekwang@ sekwang.co.kr *Web Site:* www.sekwang.co.kr, pg 624

Sel Yayincilik (Turkey) *Tel:* (0212) 516 96 85 *Fax:* (0212) 516 97 26 *E-mail:* posta@selyayincilik. com *Web Site:* www.selyayincilik.com, pg 723

SELAS Publications Ltd (Cyprus) *Tel:* 22336633 *Fax:* 22337033 *E-mail:* info@selas.com.cy *Web Site:* www.selas.com.cy, pg 125

Select Books Pte Ltd (Singapore) *Tel:* 6251 3798 *Fax:* 6251 3380 *E-mail:* info@selectbooks.com.sg; orders@selectbooks.com.sg; marketing@selectbooks. com.sg *Web Site:* www.selectbooks.com.sg, pg 1447

Select Publishing Pte Ltd (Singapore) *Tel:* 6251 3798 *Fax:* 6251 3380 *E-mail:* info@selectbooks. com.sg; orders@selectbooks.com.sg; marketing@ selectbooks.com.sg; publishing@selectbooks.com.sg *Web Site:* www.selectbooks.com.sg, pg 606

Ediciones Selectas Diamante SA de CV (Mexico) *Tel:* (0155) 55650333; (0155) 55656120 *Toll Free Tel:* (800) 888-9300 *E-mail:* ventas@editorialdiamante. com *Web Site:* www.editorialdiamante.com, pg 522

Selection du Reader's Digest SA (France) *Web Site:* www.selectionclic.com, pg 195

Selector SA de CV (Mexico) *Tel:* (0155) 51 34 05 70 *Toll Free Tel:* 01800 821-7280 *Fax:* (0155) 51 34 05 91 *E-mail:* info@selector.com.mx *Web Site:* www. selector.com.mx, pg 522

SelfMadeHero (United Kingdom) *Tel:* (020) 7383 5157 *E-mail:* info@selfmadehero.com; press@selfmadehero. com; rights@selfmadehero.com *Web Site:* www. selfmadehero.com, pg 829

Selina Publishers (India) *Tel:* (011) 23280711; (011) 23947699; 9313542601 (cell) *E-mail:* selinapublishers@gmail.com, pg 399

Selinunte Editora Ltda (Brazil), pg 91

Sellerio Editore SRL (Italy) *Tel:* (091) 6254194 *Fax:* (091) 9255737 *E-mail:* info@sellerio.it; commerciale@sellerio.it (sales) *Web Site:* www. sellerio.it, pg 465

Dr Arthur L Sellier & Co KG-Walter de Gruyter GmbH & Co KG OHG (Germany) *Tel:* (089) 45 10 84 58-0 *Fax:* (089) 45 10 84 58-9 *E-mail:* info@sellier.de *Web Site:* www.sellier.de, pg 326

Editions Diane de Selliers (France) *Tel:* 01 42 68 09 00 *Fax:* 01 42 68 11 50 *E-mail:* contact@dianedeselliers. com *Web Site:* www.editionsdianedeselliers.com, pg 195

seltmann+soehne Kunst- und Fotobuchverlag GbR (Germany) *Tel:* (02351) 94 87 0 *E-mail:* info@ seltmannundsoehne.de *Web Site:* www. seltmannundsoehne.de, pg 326

SEMAR Publishers SRL (Netherlands) *Tel:* (062) 5472413 (cell) *E-mail:* info@semar.org; orders@ semar.org *Web Site:* www.semar.org, pg 540

Bokforlaget Semic AB (Sweden) *Tel:* (08) 799 30 50; (08) 696 84 10 (orders) *Fax:* (08) 799 30 64; (08) 696 83 58 (orders) *E-mail:* info@semic. se; kundenservice@bonnierforlagen.se (orders) *Web Site:* www.semic.se, pg 685

Semikolon-Verlag (Germany) *Tel:* (030) 53 79 00 75, pg 326

Seminar on the Acquisition of Latin American Library Materials (SALALM) (United States) *Tel:* 540-247-1366 *Fax:* 540-247-1367 *E-mail:* salalm@tulane.edu *Web Site:* www.salalm.org, pg 1398

Editura Semne (Romania) *Tel:* (021) 3188344 *Fax:* (021) 3188344 *E-mail:* office@semneartemis.ro *Web Site:* www.semneartemis.ro, pg 591

Sena Ofset Ambalaj Matbaacilik Sana yi ve Ticaret Ltd Sti (Turkey) *Tel:* (0212) 6133846 *Fax:* (0212) 6130321 *E-mail:* info@senaofset.com.tr *Web Site:* senaofset. com.tr, pg 1336

Editora Senac Rio (Brazil) *Tel:* (021) 2536-3900 *Fax:* (021) 2536-3933 *E-mail:* comercial.editora@rj. senac.br *Web Site:* www.rj.senac.br; www.senac.br, pg 91

Editora Senac Sao Paulo (Brazil) *Tel:* (011) 2187-4450; (011) 2187-4496 *Fax:* (011) 2187-4486 *E-mail:* editora@sp.senac.br *Web Site:* www. editorasenacsp.com.br, pg 91

Senate Books Co Ltd (Taiwan) *Tel:* (02) 23213054 *Fax:* (02) 23214041, pg 713

Senate House Library University of London (United Kingdom) *Tel:* (020) 7862 8500 *E-mail:* senatehouselibrary@london.ac.uk *Web Site:* www.senatehouselibrary.ac.uk, pg 1642

SENCOR International (United States) *Tel:* 212-980-6726 *Web Site:* www.sencorinternational.com, pg 1289

SendPoints Publishing Co Ltd (China) *Tel:* (020) 89095121 *E-mail:* zhangjuan@sendpoints.cn *Web Site:* www.sendpoints.cn, pg 109

Editions Le Seneve (France) *Tel:* 01 40 46 54 00 *Fax:* 01 58 51 10 48 *E-mail:* contact@ editionsleseneve.fr *Web Site:* www.editionsleseneve.fr, pg 195

Senmon Toshokan Kyogikai (SENTOKYO) (Japan) *Tel:* (03) 3537-8335 *Fax:* (03) 3537-8356 *E-mail:* jsla@jsla.or.jp *Web Site:* www.jsla.or.jp, pg 1655

Sensei Verlag Kernen (Germany) *Tel:* (07151) 910222 *Fax:* (07151) 46553 *E-mail:* info@sensei.de *Web Site:* www.sensei.de, pg 326

SentralDistribusjon AS (Norway) *Tel:* 22 98 57 10; 22 98 57 00 (orders) *Fax:* 22 98 57 20 *E-mail:* sdinfo@ sd.no *Web Site:* www.sd.no, pg 1441

Sentries Licensing (Turkey) *Tel:* (0216) 524 2121 *Fax:* (0216) 520 2490 *E-mail:* contact@sentries.com.tr *Web Site:* www.sentries.com.tr, pg 1238

Seogwangsa (South Korea) *Tel:* (031) 955-4331; (031) 955-4335 (editorial off) *Fax:* (031) 955-4336 *E-mail:* phil6161@chol.com *Web Site:* seokwangsa.or. kr, pg 624

Seoul National University Library (South Korea) *Tel:* (02) 880-8001; (02) 880-5325 *E-mail:* libhelp@ snu.ac.kr *Web Site:* library.snu.ac.kr, pg 1632

Seoul National University Press (South Korea) *Tel:* (02) 880-5252 *Fax:* (02) 888-4148; (02) 889-0785 *E-mail:* snubook@snu.ac.kr *Web Site:* www.snu.ac.kr; www.snupress.com, pg 624

Seoul Printing Center (South Korea) *Tel:* (02) 2278-3081 *Fax:* (02) 2278-3082 *E-mail:* webmaster@ seoulprinting.com *Web Site:* www.seoulprinting.com, pg 1389

Seoul Selection (South Korea) *Tel:* (070) 5038-5034; (070) 4060-5064 (direct) *Fax:* (070) 8668-1090 *E-mail:* atoz@seoulselection.com *Web Site:* www. seoulselection.com, pg 625, 1251

Editions Sepia (France) *Tel:* 01 43 97 22 14 *Fax:* 01 43 97 32 62 *E-mail:* sepia@editions-sepia.com *Web Site:* www.editions-sepia.com, pg 195

Septem Ediciones SL (Spain) *Tel:* 985 20 85 12 *E-mail:* info@septemediciones.com *Web Site:* www. septemediciones.com, pg 667

Septime Verlag eU (Austria) *Tel:* (01) 664 164 28 92 *E-mail:* office@septime-verlag.at *Web Site:* www. septime-verlag.at, pg 57

Vydavatelstvo Serafin (Slovakia) *Tel:* (0915) 700 581 *Fax:* (02) 544 343 42 *E-mail:* serafin@serafin.sk *Web Site:* www.serafin.sk, pg 609

Ediciones del Serbal SA (Spain) *Tel:* 93 408 08 34 *Fax:* 93 408 07 92 *E-mail:* serbal@ed-serbal.es *Web Site:* edicionesdelserbal.com, pg 667

Shanghai Scientific & Technical Publishers (China) *Tel:* (021) 64089888; (021) 64085630; (021) 64845386; (021) 64845328 *Fax:* (021) 64845082 *E-mail:* sstp@sstp.cn; english-c@sstp.cn; sstp-c@sstp.cn; zbb-c@sstp.cn; rights@sstp.cn *Web Site:* www.sstp.com.cn; www.sstp.cn; www.sstp-china.com, pg 110

Shanghai Scientific & Technological Literature Publishing House Co Ltd (China) *Tel:* (021) 54036563; (021) 54037397 *Fax:* (021) 54033023 *Web Site:* www.sstlp.com, pg 110

Shanghai Translation Publishing House (China) *Tel:* (021) 53594508; (021) 61914803 (rights) *Fax:* (021) 63914291 *E-mail:* info@yiwen.com.cn; rights@yiwen.com.cn *Web Site:* www.yiwen.com.cn, pg 110

Shanghai Tushuguan (China) *Tel:* (021) 64455555 *Fax:* (021) 64455001 *E-mail:* service@libnet.sh.cn *Web Site:* www.library.sh.cn, pg 1582

Shanghai University of Traditional Chinese Medicine Press (China) *Tel:* (021) 51322222; (021) 51322548; (021) 51322549 *Web Site:* www.shutcm.com/shutcm/zzcbs, pg 110

Sharbain's Bookshop Co Ltd (Israel) *Tel:* (02) 6286775 *Fax:* (02) 6272698 *Web Site:* www.sharbain.com, pg 1427

Sharda Prakashan (India) *Tel:* (011) 23280234; (011) 45652462 *Fax:* (011) 23280234 *E-mail:* shardaprakashan@gmail.com; info@shardaprakashan.co.in *Web Site:* www.shardaprakashan.co.in, pg 399

The Shaw Society (United Kingdom) *Tel:* (020) 7435 6497 *E-mail:* contact@shawsociety.org.uk *Web Site:* www.shawsociety.org.uk, pg 1504

Sheck Wah Tong Printing Press Ltd (Hong Kong) *Tel:* 2562 8293 *Fax:* 2565 5431 *Web Site:* www.sheckwahtong.com, pg 1326

Sheil Land Associates Ltd (United Kingdom) *Tel:* (020) 7405 9351 *Fax:* (020) 7831 2127 *E-mail:* info@sheilland.co.uk *Web Site:* www.sheilland.co.uk, pg 1246

Sheldon Press (United Kingdom) *Tel:* (020) 7592 3900 *Fax:* (020) 7592 3939 *E-mail:* director@sheldonpress.co.uk; orders@sheldonpress.co.uk; sheldon@spck.org.uk *Web Site:* www.sheldonpress.com, pg 829

Sheldrake Press (United Kingdom) *Tel:* (020) 8675 1767 *Fax:* (020) 8675 7736 *E-mail:* editorial@sheldrakepress.co.uk; enquiries@sheldrakepress.co.uk; publisher@sheldrakepress.co.uk; sales@sheldrakepress.co.uk *Web Site:* www.sheldrakepress.co.uk, pg 830

Shemetsneba (Georgia) *Tel:* (032) 21-01-54 *E-mail:* info@shemetsneba.ge *Web Site:* www.shemetsneba.ge, pg 201

Shenzhen Boeye Technology Co Ltd (China) *Tel:* (0755) 8635 8666 *Fax:* (0755) 8607 9111 *E-mail:* sales@szboeye.com *Web Site:* www.szboeye.com, pg 1319

Shenzhen Huaxin Colour-Printing & Platemaking Co Ltd (China) *Tel:* (0755) 8242 8168 *Fax:* (0755) 8170 4065 *E-mail:* info@huaxinprinting.com *Web Site:* www.huaxinprinting.com, pg 1274, 1319

Shenzhen Jinhao Color Printing Co Ltd (China) *Tel:* (0755) 84161089 *Fax:* (0755) 84192325 *E-mail:* admin@lzjhy.com *Web Site:* www.lzjhy.com, pg 1319

Shenzhen Xinlian Artistic Printing Co Ltd (China) *Tel:* (0755) 28071282; (0755) 83238313 *Fax:* (0755) 28071032, pg 1319

Shepheard-Walwyn (Publishers) Ltd (United Kingdom) *Tel:* (020) 8241 5927 *E-mail:* books@shepheard-walwyn.co.uk *Web Site:* www.shepheard-walwyn.co.uk, pg 830

Sherwood Publishing (United Kingdom) *Tel:* (01992) 550492 *Fax:* (01992) 525283 *Web Site:* www.sherwoodpublishing.com, pg 830

R R Sheth & Co Pvt Ltd (India) *Tel:* (022) 2201 34 41 *Fax:* (022) 2205 82 93 *Web Site:* rrsheth.com, pg 400

R R Sheth & Co Pvt Ltd (India) *Tel:* (079) 2550 6573 *Fax:* (079) 2550 1732 *Web Site:* rrsheth.com, pg 1424

Shibundo Publishing (Japan) *Tel:* (03) 6892-6961 *Fax:* (03) 6892-6962 *Web Site:* www.shibundo.net, pg 487

Shiko-Sha Co Ltd (Japan) *Tel:* (03) 3400-7151 *Fax:* (03) 3400-7294 *E-mail:* shikosha@gol.com *Web Site:* www.ehon-artbook.com, pg 487

Shiksha Bharti (India) *Tel:* (011) 2965483; (011) 2969812 *Fax:* (011) 2967791, pg 400

Shimizu-Shoin Co Ltd (Japan) *Tel:* (03) 5213-7151 *Fax:* (03) 5213-7160 *Web Site:* www.shimizushoin.co.jp, pg 487

Shinchosha Publishing Co Ltd (Japan) *Tel:* (03) 3266-5411 *Toll Free Tel:* 0120-468-465 *Fax:* (03) 3266-5432 *Toll Free Fax:* 0120-493-746 *Web Site:* www.shinchosha.co.jp, pg 487

Shing Lee Publishers Pte Ltd (Singapore) *Tel:* 6760 1388 *Fax:* 6762 5684 *E-mail:* info@shinglee.com.sg *Web Site:* www.shinglee.com.sg, pg 606

Shingakusha Co Ltd (Japan) *Tel:* (075) 581-6111; (075) 501-0510 *Fax:* (075) 501-0514; (075) 501-5321 *E-mail:* info@sing.co.jp *Web Site:* www.sing.co.jp, pg 487

Shinkenchiku-Sha Co Ltd (Japan) *Tel:* (03) 6205-4380 *Fax:* (03) 6205-4386 *E-mail:* ja-business@japan-architect.co.jp; editor@japlusu.com *Web Site:* www.japan-architect.co.jp; www.japlusu.com (English), pg 487

Shinko Tsusho Co Ltd (Japan) *Tel:* (03) 3353-1751 *Fax:* (03) 3353-2205, pg 1430

Shinkwang Publishing Co (South Korea) *Tel:* (02) 925 5051; (02) 925 5053 *Fax:* (02) 925 5054 *E-mail:* shkpub7@naver.com *Web Site:* www.shinkwangpub.com, pg 625

Shinwon Agency (South Korea) *Tel:* (02) 335-6388 *Fax:* (02) 335-6389 *E-mail:* main@shinwonagency.co.kr *Web Site:* www.shinwonagency.co.kr, pg 1234

Shiraz University Central Library & Documentation Center (Iran) *Tel:* (0711) 6260011; (0711) 6134330 *Fax:* (0711) 6287301 *E-mail:* dir-ctr-lib@rose.shirazu.ac.ir *Web Site:* shirazu.ac.ir/centlib, pg 1602

Shire Publications Ltd (United Kingdom) *Tel:* (01865) 811332 *Fax:* (01865) 242009 *Web Site:* www.bloomsbury.com, pg 830

Shiseido Booksellers Ltd (Japan) *Tel:* (075) 431 2345 *Fax:* (075) 432 6588 *E-mail:* shiseido@jd5.so-net.ne.jp *Web Site:* www.shiseido-book.co.jp, pg 1430

Shobunsha Publications Inc (Japan) *Tel:* (03) 3556-8153; (03) 3556-8155 *Fax:* (03) 3556-8161; (03) 3556-8881 *Web Site:* www.mapple.co.jp, pg 487

Vydavatelstvi SHOCart spol sro (Czech Republic) *Tel:* 577 105 911 *E-mail:* mapy@shocart.cz *Web Site:* www.shocart.cz, pg 131

Shogakukan Inc (Japan) *Tel:* (03) 3230-5211 *Toll Free Tel:* 0120-494-656 *Fax:* (03) 5281-1650 *E-mail:* info@shogakukan.co.jp *Web Site:* www.shogakukan.co.jp, pg 487

Shogun International Ltd (United Kingdom) *Tel:* (020) 8749 2022 *Fax:* (020) 8740 1086 *E-mail:* info@shoguninternational.com *Web Site:* www.shoguninternational.com, pg 1460

Mitsumura Suiko Shoin Publishing Co Ltd (Japan) *Tel:* (075) 251-2888 *Fax:* (075) 251-2881 *E-mail:* info@mitsumura-suiko.co.jp; hanbai@mitsumura-suiko.co.jp (orders) *Web Site:* www.mitsumura-suiko.co.jp, pg 487

Shokabo Publishing Co Ltd (Japan) *Tel:* (03) 3262-9166 *Fax:* (03) 3262-9130 *E-mail:* info@shokabo.co.jp; c-right@shokabo.co.jp *Web Site:* www.shokabo.co.jp, pg 487

Shokokusha Publishing Co Ltd (Japan) *Tel:* (03) 3359-3231; (03) 3359-3232 (sales); (03) 3353-5391 (editorial) *Fax:* (03) 3353-5391; (03) 3357-3961 (sales) *E-mail:* eigyo@shokokusha.co.jp *Web Site:* www.shokokusha.co.jp, pg 487

Shoqata e Botuesve Shqiptare (Albania) *Tel:* (04) 22 51 344; (04) 22 36 635 *Web Site:* www.shbsh.al, pg 1363

Shore Books & Design (United Kingdom) *Tel:* (01553) 842477; (07896) 844867 (cell) *E-mail:* enquiries@shore-books.co.uk *Web Site:* www.shore-books.co.uk, pg 1287

Shorin-Sha Co ltd (Japan) *Tel:* (03) 3815-4921 (editorial); (03) 5689-7377 (sales) *Fax:* (03) 5689-7577 (sales) *Web Site:* www.shorinsha.co.jp, pg 488

Shree Book Centre (India) *Tel:* (022) 24377516 *Web Site:* www.shreebookcentre.com; www.facebook.com/pages/Shree-Book-Centre/593052314056168?ref=hl, pg 400

Shueisha Publishing Co Ltd (Japan) *Tel:* (03) 3230-6314 *Web Site:* www.shueisha.co.jp, pg 488

Shufu-to-Seikatsu Sha Co Ltd (Japan) *Tel:* (03) 3563-5120 *Fax:* (03) 3563-2073 *Web Site:* www.shufu.co.jp, pg 488

Shufunotomo Co Ltd (Japan) *Tel:* (03) 5280-7500; (03) 5280-7551 (sales); (049) 259-1122 (orders) *Fax:* (03) 5280-7587; (049) 259-1188 (orders) *Web Site:* www.shufunotomo.co.jp, pg 488

Shunjusha Publishing Co (Japan) *Tel:* (03) 3255-9610; (03) 3255-9614 (editorial); (03) 3255-9611 (sales) *Fax:* (03) 3255-5418; (03) 3255-9370 (editorial); (03) 3253-1384 (sales) *E-mail:* main@shunjusha.co.jp *Web Site:* www.shunjusha.co.jp, pg 488

Shuppan News Co Ltd (Japan) *Tel:* (03) 3262-2076 *Fax:* (03) 3261-6817 *E-mail:* snews@snews.net *Web Site:* www.snews.net, pg 488

Shuter & Shooter Publishers (Pty) Ltd (South Africa) *Tel:* (033) 846 8700 *Fax:* (033) 846 8701 *Web Site:* www.shuters.com, pg 617

Shy Mau Publishing Co (Taiwan) *Tel:* (02) 2218-3277 *Fax:* (02) 2218-3239 *E-mail:* service@coolbooks.com.tw *Web Site:* www.coolbooks.com.tw, pg 713

Siam Offset Co Ltd (Thailand) *Tel:* (02) 249-1575; (02) 249-1576; (02) 249-5419; (02) 249-5420 *Fax:* (02) 249-5415 *E-mail:* info@siamoffset.com *Web Site:* www.siamoffset.com, pg 1285, 1336

The Siam Society Under Royal Patronage (Thailand) *Tel:* (02) 661-6470-7 *Fax:* (02) 258 3491 *E-mail:* info@siam-society.org *Web Site:* www.siam-society.org, pg 1501

Sibelius-Akatemian Kirjasto (Finland) *Tel:* (040) 7104 224; (040) 7104 223 *E-mail:* lib.siba@uniarts.fi *Web Site:* lib.uniarts.fi, pg 1590

Sibi Ltd (Bulgaria) *Tel:* (02) 9870141; (02) 9814598; (02) 9873609 *Fax:* (02) 9875709 *E-mail:* sibi@sibi.bg *Web Site:* www.sibi.bg, pg 96

SIBS Publishing House Inc (Philippines) *Tel:* (02) 376 4041 *Toll Free Tel:* 800-1-888-7427 *Fax:* (02) 376 4034 *Web Site:* www.sibs.com.ph, pg 566

Wydawnictwo SIC (Poland) *Tel:* (22) 840 07 53 *Fax:* (22) 840 07 53 *E-mail:* biuro@wydawnictwo-sic.com.pl; info@wydawnictwo-sic.com.pl *Web Site:* www.wydawnictwo-sic.com.pl, pg 573

Sicania (Italy) *Tel:* (090) 2936373 *Fax:* (090) 2932461 *E-mail:* info@gem.me.it; redazione@sicania.me.it *Web Site:* www.sicania.me.it; www.gem.me.it, pg 465

Sichuan Renmin Chubanshe (China) *Tel:* (028) 86250877 *Fax:* (028) 86259529 *E-mail:* scrmcbs@sina.com *Web Site:* www.scpph.com, pg 111

Sichuan University Press Co Ltd (China) *Tel:* (028) 85460736; (028) 85401107 *Fax:* (028) 85461699 *E-mail:* copyright@scupress.net; editor@scupress.net *Web Site:* www.scupress.cn; www.scupress.net, pg 111

Edizioni Librarie Siciliane (Italy) *Tel:* (091) 8570221, pg 465

Ekdoseis I Sideris (Greece) *Tel:* 2105140627 *E-mail:* contact@isideris.gr *Web Site:* www.isideris.gr, pg 359

Edition Sirius im Aisthesis Verlag (Germany) *Tel:* (0521) 17 26 04 *Fax:* (0521) 17 28 12 *E-mail:* info@edition-sirius.de *Web Site:* www.edition-sirius.de, pg 327

Equipo Sirius (Spain) *Tel:* 917 107 349, pg 668

Sirivatana Interprint PLC (Thailand) *Tel:* (02) 6755600 *Fax:* (02) 6755623 *Web Site:* www.sirivatana.co.th, pg 1285, 1336

R Sirkis Publishers Ltd (Israel) *Tel:* (03) 6428865 *Fax:* (03) 6413963 *E-mail:* info@sirkis.co.il *Web Site:* www.sirkis.co.il, pg 421

Sirrocco-Parkstone International (United Kingdom) *Tel:* (020) 7940 4659 *Fax:* (020) 7940 5652, pg 831

Siruela Ediciones SA (Spain) *Tel:* 91 355 57 20 *Fax:* 91 355 22 01 *E-mail:* siruela@siruela.com *Web Site:* www.siruela.com, pg 668

Sistem Yayincilik (Turkey) *Tel:* (0212) 2938372 *Fax:* (0212) 2936671, pg 723

Sistema de Biblioteca de la Pontificia Universidad Catolica de Valparaiso (Chile) *Tel:* (032) 2273262 *Web Site:* biblioteca.ucv.cl, pg 1582

Sistema de Bibliotecas de la Universidad de Concepcion (SIBUDEC) (Chile) *Tel:* (041) 220 4403 *E-mail:* bibliotecas@udec.cl *Web Site:* www.bib.udec.cl; www.biblioteca.udec.cl, pg 1582

Sistema de Bibliotecas y de Informacion (SISBI) (Argentina) *Tel:* (011) 5285-5589 *Fax:* (011) 5285-5588 *E-mail:* bib@sisbi.uba.ar; sisbi@sisbi.uba.ar *Web Site:* www.sisbi.uba.ar, pg 1574

Editorial Sistema (Spain) *Tel:* 91 448 73 19 *Fax:* 91 448 73 39 *Web Site:* www.fundacionsistema.com, pg 668

Sistema Integrado de Bibliotecas da Universidade de Sao Paulo (SIBi) (Brazil) *Tel:* (011) 3091-4195; (011) 3091-1547 *Fax:* (011) 3091-1567 *Web Site:* www.sibi.usp.br, pg 1580

Sistema Integrado de Bibliotecas de la Universidad Central de Ecuador (Ecuador) *Tel:* (02) 2505-859; (02) 2230-757 *E-mail:* dcc@uce.edu.ec *Web Site:* www.uce.edu.ec, pg 1587

Sistemas Biblioinforma SA de CV (Mexico) *Tel:* (0155) 5528-3230 (customer service); (0155) 5665-3843 *E-mail:* info@biblioinforma.com *Web Site:* biblioinforma.com, pg 1436

Sistemas Tecnicos de Edicion SA de CV (Mexico) *Tel:* (0155) 56559144 *Fax:* (0155) 55739412, pg 523

Sistemas Universales SA (Mexico) *Tel:* (0155) 5574-4895 *Fax:* (0155) 5574-4938, pg 523

Sisters of St Joseph (Australia) *Tel:* (02) 8741 2300 *Fax:* (02) 8741 2399 *E-mail:* communications@sosj.org.au *Web Site:* www.sosj.org.au, pg 39

Verlag Sisyphus (Austria) *Tel:* (0650) 7779122 *Fax:* (0463) 242246 *E-mail:* kontakt@sisyphus.at *Web Site:* www.sisyphus.at, pg 57

Sita Books & Periodicals Pvt Ltd (India) *Tel:* (022) 25555589; (022) 67973281; (022) 67973282; (022) 67973283; (022) 42156327 *Fax:* (022) 67973284 *E-mail:* info@sitabooks.com; enquiry@sitainfobytes.com *Web Site:* www.sitabooks.com, pg 400

66 Books Ltd (United Kingdom) *Tel:* (01442) 239 402 *E-mail:* lorna@66books.co.uk *Web Site:* www.66books.co.uk, pg 1460

Edicions 62 (Spain) *Tel:* 93 443 71 00 *Fax:* 93 443 71 30 *E-mail:* correu@grup62.com *Web Site:* www.edicions62.cat/editorial-ediciones-62-64.html, pg 668

66thand2nd (Italy) *Tel:* (06) 44254467 *E-mail:* info@66thand2nd.com *Web Site:* www.66thand2nd.com, pg 466

Sjostrands Forlag AB (Sweden) *Tel:* (08) 29 75 99, pg 686

SKAT (Swiss Resource Centre & Consultancies for Development) (Switzerland) *Tel:* (071) 228 54 54 *Fax:* (071) 228 54 55 *E-mail:* publications@skat.ch; info@skat.ch *Web Site:* www.skat.ch, pg 706

Skills Publishing (Australia) *Tel:* (02) 4759 2844 *Fax:* (02) 4759 3721 *E-mail:* administration@skillspublish.com.au *Web Site:* www.skillspublish.com.au, pg 39

Skira Editore (Italy) *Tel:* (02) 724441 *Fax:* (02) 72444211 *E-mail:* bookstore@skira.net; international@skira.net *Web Site:* www.skira.net, pg 466

Skjaldborg Ltd (Iceland) *Tel:* 588 2400 *Fax:* 588 8994, pg 373

Skolska Knjiga dd (Croatia) *Tel:* (01) 4830 491 (administration); (01) 4830 511 *Fax:* (01) 4830 506 *E-mail:* skolska@skolskaknjiga.hr; press@skolskaknjiga.hr *Web Site:* www.skolskaknjiga.hr, pg 122

Skorpion d o o (Croatia) *Tel:* (01) 4635 341 *Fax:* (01) 4635 342 *E-mail:* itp-skorpion@zg.htnet.hr; info@kupiknjigu.com *Web Site:* www.kupiknjigu.com, pg 123

Skrudda (Iceland) *Tel:* 552 8866 *Fax:* 552 8870 *E-mail:* skrudda@skrudda.is *Web Site:* www.skrudda.is, pg 373

Slask Sp Z oo (Poland) *Tel:* (32) 258 07 56; (32) 258 19 13 *Fax:* (32) 258 32 29 *E-mail:* biuro@slaskwn.com.pl; redakcja@slaskwn.com.pl *Web Site:* www.slaskwn.com.pl, pg 574

Slatkine Reprints (Switzerland) *Tel:* (022) 776 25 51 *Fax:* (022) 960 95 78 *E-mail:* slatkine@slatkine.ch *Web Site:* www.slatkine.com, pg 706

Slavena Ltd (Bulgaria) *Tel:* (052) 602 465 *Fax:* (052) 603 054 *E-mail:* books@slavena.net *Web Site:* www.slavena.net; www.nazz.bg, pg 97

Slavica Verlag (Germany) *Tel:* (089) 272 56 12 *Fax:* (089) 271 65 94 *Web Site:* www.slavica-kovac.com, pg 327

Sleepers Publishing (Australia) *Web Site:* sleeperspublishing.com, pg 39

SLG Press (United Kingdom) *Tel:* (01865) 241874 *Fax:* (01865) 241889 *E-mail:* editor@slgpress.co.uk; orders@slgpress.co.uk *Web Site:* www.slgpress.co.uk, pg 831

Slots-og Kulturstyrelsen (Denmark) *Tel:* 33 95 42 00 *Fax:* 33 91 77 41 *E-mail:* post@slks.dk *Web Site:* slks.dk, pg 1586

Slouch Hat Publications (Australia) *Tel:* (03) 5986 6437 *Fax:* (03) 5986 6312 *E-mail:* slouchhatbooks@gmail.com *Web Site:* www.slouch-hat.com.au, pg 39

Slovak ISBN Group Agency (Slovakia) *Tel:* (043) 2451140; (043) 2451138 *Fax:* (043) 4224984 *E-mail:* isbn@snk.sk; snk@snk.sk *Web Site:* www.snk.sk, pg 1388

Nakladatelstvi Slovart sro (Czech Republic) *Tel:* 266 177 141 *Fax:* 266 177 147 *E-mail:* slovart@slovart.cz *Web Site:* www.slovart.cz, pg 131

Vydavatel'stvo Slovart spol sro (Slovakia) *Tel:* (02) 49 20 18 00 *Fax:* (02) 49 20 18 99 *E-mail:* objednavky@slovart.sk *Web Site:* www.slovart.sk, pg 609

Vydavatel'stvo Slovart spol sro (Slovakia) *Tel:* (02) 49 20 18 00 *Fax:* (02) 49 20 18 99 *E-mail:* objednavky@slovart.sk *Web Site:* www.slovart.sk; www.slovart.cz, pg 1448

Slovenska matica (Slovenia) *Tel:* (01) 422 43 40 *Fax:* (01) 422 43 44 *E-mail:* slovenskamatica@siol.net *Web Site:* www.slovenska-matica.si, pg 611

Slovenska Narodna Galeria (Slovakia) *Tel:* (02) 59226113 *Fax:* (02) 54433971 *E-mail:* sng@sng.sk *Web Site:* www.sng.sk, pg 609

Slovenska Narodna Kniznica, Martin (Slovakia) *Tel:* (043) 2451 125; (043) 2451 140 (ISBN Agency) *E-mail:* snk@snk.sk *Web Site:* www.snk.sk, pg 609, 1629

Slovenske pedagogicke nakladatelstvo - Mlade leta sro (Slovakia) *Tel:* (02) 502 272 25; (02) 50 227 323 (sales) *E-mail:* spn@spn.sk; odbyt@spn.sk (sales) *Web Site:* www.mladeleta.sk, pg 609

Vydavatel'stvo Slovenskej Akademie Vied (Slovakia) *Tel:* (02) 2092 0203 *E-mail:* vedasav@savba.sk *Web Site:* veda.sav.sk, pg 609

Slovensky Spisovatel as (Slovakia) *Tel:* (02) 44 44 12 39; (02) 44 45 30 21 *Fax:* (02) 44 44 12 39 *E-mail:* slovenskyspisovatel@slovenskyspisovatel.sk *Web Site:* www.slovenskyspisovatel.sk, pg 609

Slovo Publishing House (Russia) *Tel:* (495) 911-69-04; (495) 911-61-33 *Fax:* (495) 911-61-33 *E-mail:* slovo@slovo-pub.ru *Web Site:* www.slovo-online.ru, pg 597

wydawnictwo slowo/obraz terytoria (Poland) *Tel:* (58) 345 47 07 *Fax:* (58) 520 80 63 *E-mail:* redakcja@terytoria.com.pl; slowo-obraz@terytoria.com.pl *Web Site:* terytoria.com.pl, pg 574

SLP Education (United Kingdom) *Tel:* (01691) 774778 *Fax:* (01691) 774849 *E-mail:* sales@slpeducation.co.uk *Web Site:* www.slpeducation.co.uk, pg 831

Sluntse Publishing House (Bulgaria) *Tel:* (02) 988 37 97 *Fax:* (02) 987 14 05 *E-mail:* sluntse@dir.bg *Web Site:* www.sluntse.com, pg 97

Sluzbeni List (Bosnia and Herzegovina) *Tel:* (033) 722-030; (033) 722-051; (033) 722-061 (editorial) *E-mail:* info@sllist.ba; redakcija@sllist.ba *Web Site:* www.sluzbenilist.ba, pg 75

Ediciones SM (Spain) *Tel:* 902 13 12 23 *E-mail:* ayudaaldocente@grupo-sm.com *Web Site:* www.grupo-sm.com, pg 669

SM Ediciones SA de CV (Mexico) *Tel:* (0155) 1087-8400 *Fax:* (0155) 1087-8484 *Web Site:* www.ediciones-sm.com.mx, pg 523

Jacqui Small LLP (United Kingdom) *Tel:* (020) 7284 9300 *Fax:* (020) 7485 0490 *E-mail:* sales@jacquismallpub.com; publicity@jacquismallpub.com *Web Site:* www.quartoknows.com/jacqui-small, pg 831

small world creations (United Kingdom) *Tel:* (01454) 327333 *Fax:* (01454) 327666 *Web Site:* www.quartoknows.com/small-world-creations, pg 831

Smaragd Verlag GmbH (Germany) *Tel:* (02689) 922 59 10 *Fax:* (02689) 922 59 20 *E-mail:* info@smaragd-verlag.de *Web Site:* smaragd-verlag.de, pg 327

Richard Smart Publishing (Australia) *Tel:* (02) 9398 7094 *Fax:* (02) 9398 7094 *E-mail:* rsppublish@primusonline.com.au *Web Site:* richardsmartpublishing.wordpress.com, pg 39

SMC Publishing Inc (Taiwan) *Tel:* (02) 2362-0190 *Fax:* (02) 2362-3834 *E-mail:* smc@smcbook.com.tw *Web Site:* www.smcbook.com.tw, pg 713

Rudolf G Smend (Germany) *Tel:* (0221) 312 0 47 *Fax:* (0221) 932 0718 *E-mail:* smend@smend.de *Web Site:* www.smend.de, pg 327

Smink Works Books (Australia) *Tel:* (03) 9018 7732 *Fax:* (03) 9428 5101 *E-mail:* books@sminkworks.com *Web Site:* www.sminkworks.com; kids.sminkworks.com, pg 39

Smith-Gordon (United Kingdom) *Tel:* (01480) 410410 *Fax:* (01480) 311101 *E-mail:* publisher@smithgordon.com *Web Site:* smith-gordon-publishing.co, pg 831

John Smith & Son Group Ltd (United Kingdom) *Tel:* (01425) 485910 *Fax:* (01273) 485920 *E-mail:* orders.js@johnsmith.co.uk *Web Site:* www.johnsmith.co.uk, pg 1460

Smith Settle (United Kingdom) *Tel:* (0113) 250 9201 *Fax:* (0113) 250 9223 *Web Site:* www.smithsettle.com, pg 1287, 1338

WH Smith PLC (United Kingdom) *Tel:* (01793) 616161 *E-mail:* customer.relations@whsmith.co.uk; press.office@whsmith.co.uk *Web Site:* www.whsmith.co.uk; www.whsmithplc.co.uk, pg 1460

Smithers Pira (United Kingdom) *Tel:* (01372) 802000 *Fax:* (01372) 802079 *Web Site:* www.smitherspira.com, pg 831

Smithers Rapra (United Kingdom) *Tel:* (01939) 250383 *Fax:* (01939) 251118 *E-mail:* info@smithersrapra.com *Web Site:* www.smithersrapra.com, pg 831

Strident Publishing (United Kingdom) *Tel:* (01355) 220588 *E-mail:* info@stridentpublishing.co.uk *Web Site:* www.stridentpublishing.co.uk, pg 834

Stripes Publishing (United Kingdom) *Tel:* (020) 7385 6333 *Fax:* (020) 7385 7333 *Web Site:* www.littletiger. co.uk/stripes-publishing, pg 834

STRK (Macedonia) *Tel:* (02) 3080430, pg 505

Strobel Verlag GmbH & Co KG (Germany) *Tel:* (02931) 8900-0 *Fax:* (02931) 8900-38 *E-mail:* leserservice@ strobel-verlag.de *Web Site:* www.ikz.de; www.strobel-verlag.de, pg 1257

Stroemfeld Verlag GmbH (Germany) *Tel:* (069) 955 226-0; (069) 955 226-22 (sales) *Fax:* (069) 955 226-24 *E-mail:* info@stroemfeld.de *Web Site:* www. stroemfeld.de, pg 331

Stromberg Brunnhages (Sweden) *Tel:* (08) 620 19 00 *E-mail:* gunilla.segerdahl@stromberg.se *Web Site:* www.stromberg.se, pg 686

Stroyizdat (Russia) *Tel:* (495) 664-27-61 *E-mail:* podpiska@panor.ru *Web Site:* panor.ru, pg 598

Studenterboghandelen ved Syddansk Universitet (Denmark) *Tel:* 6550 1700 *E-mail:* info@boghandel. sdu.dk *Web Site:* studenterboghandel.dk, pg 1413

Studentlitteratur AB (Sweden) *Tel:* (046) 31 20 00 *Fax:* (046) 30 53 38 *E-mail:* info@studentlitteratur.se *Web Site:* www.studentlitteratur.se, pg 686

Studia HumanitatiS (Slovenia) *Tel:* (01) 4250-475 *Fax:* (01) 4251-846 *E-mail:* studia.humanitatis@guest. arnes.si *Web Site:* www.studia-humanitatis.si, pg 611

Studiecentrum Vlaamse Primitieven (Belgium) *Tel:* (02) 739 68 66 *Fax:* (02) 732 01 05 *Web Site:* xv.kikirpa. be, pg 73

StudienVerlag GesmbH (Austria) *Tel:* (0512) 395045 *Fax:* (0512) 395045 15 *E-mail:* order@studienverlag.at *Web Site:* www.studienverlag.at, pg 58

Edizioni Studio Domenicano (Italy) *Tel:* (051) 582034 *Fax:* (051) 331583 *Web Site:* www.esd-domenicani.it, pg 467

Wydawnictwo Studio EMKA (Poland) *Tel:* (22) 616 00 67 *Fax:* (22) 628 08 38 *E-mail:* wydawnictwo@ studioemka.com.pl *Web Site:* www.studioemka.com.pl, pg 574

Studio Fun International (United Kingdom) *Tel:* (01225) 4734211 *Web Site:* www.studiofun.com, pg 834

Studio Kers (Netherlands) *Tel:* (06) 5495 6704 *Web Site:* studiokers.nl, pg 540

Edizioni Studio Tesi SRL (Italy) *Tel:* (06) 3235433 *Fax:* (06) 3236277 *E-mail:* info@edizionimediterranee. net *Web Site:* www.edizionimediterranee.net, pg 467

Studio 31 Inc (United States) *Tel:* 772-781-7195 *Fax:* 772-781-6044 *Web Site:* www.studio31.com, pg 1289

Edizioni Studium SRL (Italy) *Tel:* (06) 6865846; (06) 6875456 *Fax:* (06) 6875456 *E-mail:* info@ edizionistudium.it *Web Site:* www.edizionistudium.it, pg 467

Stuenings Medien GmbH (Germany) *Tel:* (02151) 51 00-0 *Fax:* (02151) 51 00-105 *E-mail:* medien@stuenings. de *Web Site:* www.stuenings.de, pg 331

Verlagsgruppe Styria GmbH & Co KG (Austria) *Tel:* (01) 512 8808-0 *Fax:* (01) 512 8808-75 *E-mail:* office@styriabooks.at *Web Site:* www. verlagsgruppestyria.at, pg 58

SU Press & Books Ltd (Nigeria) *Tel:* (02) 8101867; (02) 8102334 *E-mail:* md.supb@sunigeria.org *Web Site:* su-international.org, pg 553

Sua Edizioak (Spain) *Tel:* 944169430 *Fax:* 944166976 *E-mail:* cliente@sua-ediciones.com; sua@sua-ediciones.com *Web Site:* www.sua.eus, pg 669

Suan Nguen Mee Ma Co Ltd (Thailand) *Tel:* (02) 622-0955; (02) 622-0966; (02) 622-2495 *Fax:* (02) 222 9540; (02) 622-3228 *E-mail:* publishers@suan-spirit. com; shopping@suan-spirit.com *Web Site:* www.suan-spirit.com, pg 716

Suan Nguen Mee Ma Co Ltd (Thailand) *Tel:* (02) 622-0955; (02) 622-0966; (02) 622-2495; (02) 622-2496 *Fax:* (02) 622-3228 *E-mail:* publishers@suan-spirit. com; shopping@suan-spirit.com *Web Site:* www.suan-spirit.com, pg 1454

Sub-Saharan Publishers (Ghana) *Tel:* (021) 23 33 71 *Fax:* (021) 23 42 51 *E-mail:* saharanp@africaonline. com.gh, pg 353

Submariner Publications P/L (Australia) *Tel:* (03) 9886 0200 *Fax:* (03) 9886 0200 *E-mail:* jlpubs@bigpond. net.au *Web Site:* www.submarinerpublications.com, pg 40

Success Publications Pte Ltd (Singapore) *Tel:* 6443 1003 *Fax:* 6445 3156 *E-mail:* succpub@singnet.com.sg, pg 606

Sud Editions (Tunisia) *Tel:* 71 785 179; 71 782 991 *Fax:* 71 848 664 *E-mail:* sud.edition@planet.tn, pg 718

Editions Sud Ouest (France) *Tel:* 05 35 31 21 35 *Fax:* 05 35 31 21 39 *E-mail:* contact@editions-sudouest.com *Web Site:* www.editions-sudouest.com, pg 197

Editorial Sudamericana SA (Argentina) *Tel:* (011) 5235-4400; (011) 5235-4450 *Fax:* (011) 5235-4468; (011) 5235-4407; (011) 5235-4451 *E-mail:* info@rhm.com. ar; aclientes@rhm.com.ar *Web Site:* www.rhm.com.ar, pg 12

Sudan Literature Centre (Kenya) *Tel:* (020) 3869685; (020) 3869688; (0722) 923203 (cell) *Fax:* (020) 3864141 *E-mail:* slc.across@gmail.com, pg 494

Leitfadenverlag Sudholt eK (Germany) *Tel:* (08177) 204725 *Fax:* (08177) 204726 *E-mail:* info@ leitfadenverlag.de *Web Site:* www.leitfadenverlag.de, pg 331

Izdatelstvo Sudostroenie (Russia) *Tel:* (812) 312 44 79 *Fax:* (812) 312 08 21, pg 598

Sueddeutsche Verlagsgesellschaft mbH (Germany) *Tel:* (0731) 94 57-0 *Fax:* (0731) 94 57-224 *E-mail:* info@suedvg.de *Web Site:* www.suedvg.de, pg 331

SuedOst Verlag (Germany) *Tel:* (09402) 93 37-0 *Fax:* (09402) 93 37-24 *E-mail:* info@gietl-verlag.de *Web Site:* www.suedost-verlag.de, pg 332

Suedverlag GmbH (Germany) *Tel:* (07531) 90 53-0 *Fax:* (07531) 90 53-98 *E-mail:* willkommen@ suedverlag.de; willkommen@uvk.de *Web Site:* www. suedverlag.de, pg 332

Suedwest Verlag GmbH & Co KG (Germany) *Tel:* (089) 4136-0 *Toll Free Tel:* 0800 500 33 22 *Fax:* (089) 4136-3333 *E-mail:* kundenservice@randomhouse. de *Web Site:* www.suedwest-verlag.de; www. randomhouse.de/suedwest, pg 332

Suedwind-Buchwelt Buchhandelsges mbH (Austria) *Tel:* (01) 405 44 34; (01) 798 83 49-0 *Fax:* (01) 798 83 75-15 *Web Site:* www.suedwind-buchwelt.at, pg 58

Sugarco Edizioni SRL (Italy) *Tel:* (02) 4078370 *Fax:* (02) 4078493 *E-mail:* info@sugarcoedizioni.it *Web Site:* www.sugarcoedizioni.it, pg 467

Suhrkamp Verlag GmbH & Co KG (Germany) *Tel:* (030) 740744-0 *Fax:* (030) 740744-199 *E-mail:* geschaeftsleitung@suhrkamp.de; sales@ suhrkamp.de *Web Site:* www.suhrkamp.de, pg 332

Sujet Verlag UG (Germany) *Tel:* (0421) 703737 *E-mail:* kontakt@sujet-verlag.de *Web Site:* www.sujet-verlag.de, pg 332

Sule Yayinlari (Turkey) *Tel:* (0212) 5282357 *Fax:* (0212) 5282589 *E-mail:* iletisim@suleyayinlari.com *Web Site:* www.suleyayinlari.com, pg 723

Suleymaniye Yazma Eser Kutuphanesi (Turkey) *Tel:* (0212) 520 64 60 *Fax:* (0212) 511 22 10 *E-mail:* suleymaniye@yek.gov.tr *Web Site:* www. suleymaniye.yek.gov.tr, pg 1640

Sultan Chand & Sons (P) Ltd (India) *Tel:* (011) 43546000; (011) 23243939 *Web Site:* www.sultan-chand.com, pg 401

Suman Prakashan Pvt Ltd (India) *Tel:* (011) 28711759, pg 401

Sumatera Utara University Press (Indonesia) *Tel:* (061) 8213737 *Fax:* (061) 8213737 *E-mail:* usupress@usu. ac.id *Web Site:* www2.usu.ac.id, pg 407

Sumathi Printers (Pvt) Ltd (Sri Lanka) *Tel:* (011) 2330673; (011) 2330674 *Fax:* (011) 2399924 *E-mail:* spb@sumathi.lk *Web Site:* www.sumathi. lk/xampp/printing.html, pg 1262, 1285, 1335

Summer Institute of Linguistics (Papua New Guinea) *Tel:* 537-4431 *Fax:* 537-3507 *E-mail:* do-dlp@sil.org. pg *Web Site:* www.pnglanguages.org, pg 561

Summersdale Publishers Ltd (United Kingdom) *Tel:* (01243) 771107 *Web Site:* www.summersdale. com, pg 835

Summus Editorial Ltda (Brazil) *Tel:* (011) 3872-3322 *Fax:* (011) 3872-7476 *E-mail:* marketing@summus. com.br; summus@summus.com.br; vendas@summus. com.br *Web Site:* www.summus.com.br; www. gruposummus.com.br/summus, pg 91

Uitgeverij SUN Architecture (Netherlands) *Tel:* (020) 5218938 *Fax:* (020) 6253327 *E-mail:* info@ uitgeverijboom.nl *Web Site:* www.uitgeverijboom. nl/boeken/architectuur, pg 540

Sun Mui Press (Hong Kong) *Tel:* 9219 5150 *E-mail:* pioneerhk2003@yahoo.com.hk *Web Site:* www.xinmiao.com.hk, pg 366

Sun Ya Publications (HK) Ltd (Hong Kong) *Tel:* 2562 0161 (sales); 2138 7998 (customer service) *Fax:* 2565 9951 (sales); 2597 4003 (customer service) *E-mail:* marketing@sunya.com.hk *Web Site:* www. sunya.com.hk, pg 366

Dr Sun Yat-sen Memorial Library (Taiwan) *Tel:* (02) 27588008 *Fax:* (02) 27584847 *E-mail:* sun@yatsen. gov.tw *Web Site:* www.yatsen.gov.tw, pg 1637

Sun Yat-Sen Library of Guangdong Province (China) *Tel:* (020) 8382 2369 *Fax:* (020) 8116 2666 *E-mail:* wlb@zslib.com.cn *Web Site:* www.zslib.com. cn, pg 1582

Sunmark Publishing Inc (Japan) *Tel:* (03) 5272-3166 *Fax:* (03) 5272-3167 *E-mail:* rights@sunmark.co.jp *Web Site:* www.sunmark.co.jp/eng, pg 488

Sunny Printing (Hong Kong) Co Ltd (Hong Kong) *Tel:* 2557 8663 *Fax:* 2889 8070 *Web Site:* www. sunnyprinting.com.hk, pg 1326

Sunshine Books International Ltd (New Zealand) *Toll Free Tel:* 0800 85 5000 *Toll Free Fax:* 0800 85 1000, pg 549

Sunshine Multimedia (Australia) Pty Ltd (Australia) *Tel:* (03) 9464 7422 *Toll Free Tel:* 1800 244 542 *Fax:* (03) 9464 2226 *Toll Free Fax:* 1800 684 528 *E-mail:* info@sunshinebooks.com.au; sales@ sunshinebooks.com.au *Web Site:* sunshinebooks.com. au, pg 40

Sunshine Press Ltd (Hong Kong) *Tel:* 2553 0228 *Fax:* 2873 2930 *E-mail:* spl@sunshinepress.com.hk, pg 1259, 1279, 1326

Suomalainen Kirjakauppa Oy (Finland) *Tel:* (09) 156 6305; (09) 4259 9771 (customer service) *E-mail:* asiakaspalvelu@suomalainenkk.fi *Web Site:* www.suomalainen.com, pg 1414

Suomalainen Tiedeakatemia (Finland) *Tel:* (09) 636800 *Fax:* (09) 660117 *E-mail:* acadsci@acadsci.fi *Web Site:* www.acadsci.fi, pg 1493

Suomalaisen Kirjallisuuden Seura (SKS) (Finland) *E-mail:* books@finlit.fi *Web Site:* www.finlit.fi, pg 151

Suomalaisen Kirjallisuuden Seura (SKS) (Finland) *Tel:* (0201) 131 231 *Fax:* (09) 656 380 *E-mail:* sks@ finlit.fi *Web Site:* www.finlit.fi, pg 1493

Suomen Kirjailijaliitto (Finland) *Tel:* (09) 445 392 *E-mail:* info@kirjailijaliitto.fi *Web Site:* www. kirjailijaliitto.fi, pg 1370

Suomen Kirjastoseura (Finland) *Tel:* (044) 522 2941 *E-mail:* info@fla.fi *Web Site:* www.fla.fi, pg 1651

United Nations Economic Commission for Europe (UNECE) (Switzerland) *Tel:* (022) 917 12 34 *Fax:* (022) 917 05 05 *E-mail:* info.ece@unece.org *Web Site:* www.unece.org/info/ece-homepage.html, pg 1391

United Nations Environment Programme (UNEP) (Kenya) *Tel:* (020) 7621234 *E-mail:* unepinfo@unep.org *Web Site:* www.unep.org, pg 1380

United Nations ESCAP Library (Thailand) *Tel:* (02) 288 1360 *Fax:* (02) 288 3036 *Web Site:* www.unescap.org/contact/library, pg 1638

United Nations Library-Vienna (Austria) *Tel:* (01) 26060-3210 *Fax:* (01) 26060-7-3210 *E-mail:* viennalibrary@un.org, pg 1576

The United Nations Office at Geneva (UNOG) (Switzerland) *Tel:* (022) 917 1234 *Fax:* (022) 917 0123 *E-mail:* webmaster@unog.ch *Web Site:* www.unog.ch, pg 708

The United Nations Office at Geneva (UNOG) Library (Switzerland) *Tel:* (022) 917 41 81 *Fax:* (022) 917 04 18 *E-mail:* library@unog.ch *Web Site:* www.unog.ch/library, pg 1636

United Nations Research Institute for Social Development (UNRISD) (Switzerland) *Tel:* (022) 917 3020 *Fax:* (022) 917 0650 *E-mail:* info@unrisd.org *Web Site:* www.unrisd.org, pg 1391

United Printing & Publishing (UPP) (United Arab Emirates) *Tel:* (02) 5039 998; (02) 5039 999 *Fax:* (02) 5039 990 *E-mail:* info@upp.ae *Web Site:* www.upp.ae, pg 1286, 1336

United Publishers Services Ltd (Japan) *Tel:* (03) 5479-7251 *Fax:* (03) 5479-7307, pg 1430

The United Theological College of the West Indies Library (Jamaica) *Tel:* (876) 977-2868; (876) 927-1724 *Fax:* (876) 977-0812 *E-mail:* unitheol@cwjamaica.com *Web Site:* www.utcwi.edu.jm/library, pg 1606

United Writers Publications Ltd (United Kingdom) *Tel:* (01736) 365954 *Fax:* (01736) 365954 *E-mail:* mail@unitedwriters.co.uk *Web Site:* www.unitedwriters.co.uk, pg 840

Unity Books Ltd (New Zealand) *Tel:* (04) 499 4245 *Fax:* (04) 499 4246 *E-mail:* wellington@unitybooks.co.nz *Web Site:* unitybooks.nz, pg 1439

Uniunea Scriitorilor din Romania (Romania) *Tel:* (021) 3165829 *Fax:* (021) 372897880 *E-mail:* uniunea.scriitorilor@yahoo.com *Web Site:* www.uniuneascriitorilor.ro, pg 1387

Editura Univers SA (Romania) *Tel:* (021) 315 33 08 *Fax:* (021) 315 33 07 *E-mail:* office@edituraunivers.ro *Web Site:* www.edituraunivers.ro, pg 592

Editura Univers Enciclopedic (Romania) *Tel:* (0318) 211100 *Fax:* (0378) 105718 *E-mail:* office@universenciclopedic.ro *Web Site:* www.universenciclopedic.ro, pg 592

Universal Book Corner (India) *Tel:* (0532) 2623467; 9335153660 (cell), pg 1425

Universal Book Traders (India) *Tel:* (011) 23961288; (011) 23911966; (011) 23991487 *E-mail:* sales@ubtlawbooks.com, pg 1425

Universal Edition AG (Austria) *Tel:* (01) 337 23-218 *Fax:* (01) 337 23-420 *E-mail:* publishing@universaledition.com; vertrieb@universaledition.com *Web Site:* www.universaledition.com, pg 59

Libreria Universal (Guatemala) *Tel:* 22328484, pg 1421

Universala Esperanto-Asocio (Netherlands) *Tel:* (010) 436 1044 *Fax:* (010) 436 1751 *E-mail:* info@uea.org; direktoro@co.uea.org *Web Site:* www.uea.org, pg 1384

Universidad Autonoma - Biblioteca Universitaria (Spain) *Tel:* 91 497 4653 *Fax:* 91 497 5058 *E-mail:* servicio.biblioteca@uam.es *Web Site:* biblioteca.uam.es, pg 1633

Universidad Autonoma Chapingo (Mexico) *Tel:* (0155) 5952 1500 *E-mail:* centrodeatencion@chapingo.mx; libroschapingo@gmail.com *Web Site:* www.chapingo.mx/cultura/publicaciones, pg 524

Universidad Autonoma Chapingo Biblioteca Central (Mexico) *Tel:* (0595) 952-15-00 (ext 7111); (0595) 952-15-00 (ext 5741); (0595) 952-15-00 (ext 5440) *Fax:* (0595) 952-15-01 *E-mail:* biblioteca_central@correo.chapingo.mx *Web Site:* www.chapingo.mx/ceres, pg 1614

Universidad Autonoma de Aguascalientes (Mexico) *Tel:* (0449) 9107400; (0449) 9107402 (publications) *E-mail:* libreria@correo.uaa.mx *Web Site:* www.uaa.mx, pg 524

Universidad Autonoma de la Ciudad de Mexico (Mexico) *Tel:* (0155) 1107-0280 *E-mail:* publicaciones@uacm.edu.mx *Web Site:* publicaciones.uacm.edu.mx; portal.uacm.edu.mx, pg 524

Universidad Autonoma de Madrid-Servicio de Publicaciones (Spain) *Tel:* 914 974 233 *Fax:* 914 975 169 *E-mail:* servicio.publicaciones@uam.es *Web Site:* www.uam.es, pg 672

Universidad Autonoma del Estado de Morelos (Mexico) *Tel:* (0777) 3297000; (0777) 3297063 (editorial); (0777) 3297009 (editorial) *E-mail:* web@uaem.mx *Web Site:* www.uaem.mx/editorial, pg 524

Universidad Autonoma del Estudo de Mexico (Mexico) *Tel:* (0722) 2262300 *E-mail:* rectoria@uaemex.mx *Web Site:* www.uaemex.mx, pg 524

Universidad Autonoma "Tomas Frias", Division de Extension Universitaria (Bolivia) *Tel:* (02) 6227300; (02) 6227301 *Fax:* (02) 6226663 *Web Site:* www.uatf.edu.bo, pg 75

Universidad Autonoma Tomas Frias, Biblioteca Central (Bolivia) *Tel:* (02) 26227300 *Fax:* (02) 26226663 *Web Site:* www.uatf.edu.bo, pg 1579

Ediciones Universidad Catolica de Chile (Chile) *Tel:* (02) 2354 2417; (02) 2345 6544 *E-mail:* editorialedicionesuc@uc.cl; edicionesuc@uc.cl *Web Site:* ediciones.uc.cl, pg 100

Universidad Centroamericana Biblioteca (Nicaragua) *Tel:* 22783923 *E-mail:* otibiblioteca@ns.uca.edu.ni *Web Site:* www.uca.edu.ni, pg 1618

Universidad Complutense de Madrid Servicio de Publicaciones (Spain) *Tel:* 913 941 127 *Fax:* 913 941 126 *E-mail:* servicio.publicaciones@rect.ucm.es *Web Site:* www.ucm.es/servicio-de-publicaciones, pg 672

Editorial Universidad de Costa Rica (Costa Rica) *Tel:* 2511-5310 *Fax:* 2511-5257 *E-mail:* direccion.siedin@ucr.ac.cr *Web Site:* www.editorial.ucr.ac.cr, pg 118

Universidad de Alcala Servicio de Publicaciones (Spain) *Tel:* 918854066; 918854106 *E-mail:* serv.publicaciones@uah.es *Web Site:* publicaciones.uah.es, pg 672

Editorial Universidad de Almeria (Spain) *Tel:* 950 015459; 950 015182 *Fax:* 950 214435 *E-mail:* publicac@ual.es *Web Site:* cms.ual.es/UAL/es/universidad/serviciosgenerales/editorial/index.htm (Spanish); cms.ual.es/UAL/en/universidad/serviciosgenerales/editorial/index.htm (English), pg 672

Universidad de los Andes, Consejo de Publicaciones (Venezuela) *Fax:* (0274) 2711955; (0274) 2713210; (0274) 2712034 *E-mail:* cpula@ula.ve *Web Site:* www2.ula.ve/cp, pg 851

Editorial Universidad de Antioquia, Division Publicaciones (Colombia) *Tel:* (04) 219 5010 *Fax:* (04) 219 5012 *E-mail:* editorial@udea.edu.co *Web Site:* www.udea.edu.co, pg 115

Universidad de Antioquia, Escuela Interamericana de Bibliotecologia (Colombia) *Tel:* (04) 2195151; (04) 2195941 *E-mail:* informacionbiblioteca@udea.edu.co *Web Site:* www.udea.edu.co, pg 1583

Universidad de Cadiz Servicio de Publicaciones (Spain) *Tel:* 956 015 268 *Fax:* 956 015 634 *E-mail:* publicaciones@uca.es *Web Site:* minerva.uca.es/publicaciones/asp/default.asp, pg 672

Ediciones de la Universidad de Castilla-La Mancha (Spain) *Tel:* 969179100 *Fax:* 969179111 *E-mail:* publicaciones@uclm.es *Web Site:* publicaciones.uclm.es, pg 672

Universidad de Colima (Mexico) *Tel:* (0312) 31 61 039 *E-mail:* publicac@ucol.mx *Web Site:* www.ucol.mx, pg 524

Universidad de Costa Rica Sistema de Bibliotecas, Documentacion e Informacion (SIBDI-UCR) (Costa Rica) *Tel:* 2253-6152 *Fax:* 2234-2809 *Web Site:* sibdi.ucr.ac.cr, pg 1584

Universidad de Deusto, Dpto de Publicaciones (Spain) *Tel:* 944139000; 944139162 *Fax:* 944456817 *E-mail:* publicaciones@deusto.es; web@deusto.es *Web Site:* www.deusto-publicaciones.es, pg 672

Universidad de Extremadura-Servicio de Publicaciones (Spain) *Tel:* 927 257 041 *Fax:* 927 257 046 *E-mail:* publicac@unex.es *Web Site:* www.unex.es/publicaciones, pg 673

Editorial Universidad de Granada (Spain) *Tel:* 958 246 220; 958 506 722 *Fax:* 958 243 931 *E-mail:* pedidos@editorialugr.com *Web Site:* www.editorialugr.com, pg 673

Universidad de Jaen, Servicio de Publicaciones (Spain) *Tel:* 953 21 23 55 *Fax:* 953 21 23 55 *E-mail:* servpub@ujaen.es *Web Site:* www10.ujaen.es/conocenos/servicias-unidades/servpub, pg 673

Ediciones Universidad de la Frontera (Chile) *Tel:* (045) 2592117 *Web Site:* www.extension.ufro.cl, pg 100

Universidad de la Habana, Direccion de Informacion Cientifico Tecnica (Cuba) *E-mail:* dict@rect.uh.cu; cienciatecnica@rect.uh.cu *Web Site:* www.uh.cu, pg 1584

Libreria Universidad de los Andes (Colombia) *Tel:* (01) 33394949 (ext 2181) *Fax:* (01) 33394949 (ext 3177) *E-mail:* libreria@uniandes.edu.co *Web Site:* libreria.uniandes.edu.co, pg 1411

Universidad de los Andes, Sistema de Bibliotecas (Colombia) *Tel:* (01) 3324473 *Fax:* (01) 3324472 *E-mail:* sisbibli@uniandes.edu.co *Web Site:* biblioteca.uniandes.edu.co, pg 1583

Universidad de Malaga (Spain) *Tel:* 952 13 10 00 *E-mail:* redessociales@uma.es *Web Site:* www.uma.es, pg 673

Universidad de Oviedo Servicio de Publicaciones (Spain) *Tel:* 985 10 95 04; 985 10 95 05 *Fax:* 985 10 95 07 *E-mail:* servipub@uniovi.es *Web Site:* www.uniovi.es/publicaciones, pg 673

Universidad de Panama, Biblioteca Interamericana Simon Bolivar (Panama) *Tel:* 523-5360 *Web Site:* www.sibiup.up.ac.pa; www.facebook.com/sibiup, pg 1621

Universidad de Puerto Rico Recinto de Rio Piedras Sistema de Bibliotecas (Puerto Rico) *Tel:* (787) 764-0000 (ext 85509); (787) 764-0000 (ext 85506); (787) 764-0000 (ext 85520) *Fax:* (787) 772-1479 *Web Site:* biblioteca.uprrp.edu, pg 1625

Ediciones Universidad de Salamanca (Spain) *Tel:* 923 294 598; 923 294 500 (ext 4598) *Fax:* 923 262 579 *E-mail:* pedidos@universitas.usal.es; eusal@usal.es; comunicacion.eusal@usal.es *Web Site:* www.eusal.es, pg 673

Universidad de San Martin de Porres (Peru) *Tel:* (01) 3620064 *E-mail:* fondoeditorial@usmp.pe *Web Site:* www.usmp.edu.pe/fondo_editorial, pg 563

Universidad de Santiago de Compostela (Spain) *Tel:* 881 812 391 *E-mail:* sepinter@usc.es *Web Site:* www.usc.es/en/servizos/publicacions, pg 673

Secretariado de Publicaciones de la Universidad de Sevilla (Spain) *Tel:* 954 487 444; 954 487 450 *Fax:* 954 48 74 43; 954 487 447 *E-mail:* secpub2@us.es *Web Site:* editorial.us.es, pg 673

Editorial de la Universidad de Tres de Febrero (EDUNTREF) (Argentina) *Tel:* (011) 4519-6010 *E-mail:* rectorado@untref.edu.ar *Web Site:* www.untref.edu.ar, pg 12

University of the West Indies Library (Barbados) (Barbados) *Tel:* (246) 417-4444; (246) 417-4440 (circulation) *Fax:* (246) 417-4460 *E-mail:* smlibrary@ cavehill.uwi.edu *Web Site:* www.cavehill.uwi.edu, pg 1577

The University of the West Indies Main Library (Trinidad and Tobago) *Tel:* (868) 662-2002 (ext 82132) *Fax:* (868) 662-9238 *E-mail:* almajordanlibrary@sta.uwi.edu *Web Site:* libraries.sta.uwi.edu/ajl, pg 1638

University of the West Indies Press (Jamaica) *Tel:* (876) 977-2659; (876) 702-4081 *Fax:* (876) 977-2660 *E-mail:* cuserv@cwjamaica.com (customer service & orders); uwipress_marketing@cwjamaica.com *Web Site:* www.uwipress.com, pg 473

University of the Western Cape Library (South Africa) *Tel:* (021) 959 2209 *Fax:* (021) 959 2659 *E-mail:* library@uwc.ac.za *Web Site:* lib.uwc.ac.za, pg 1632

University of the Witwatersrand Libraries (South Africa) *Tel:* (011) 717 1902 *Web Site:* www.wits.ac.za/library, pg 1632

University of Tokyo Library System (Japan) *Tel:* (03) 5841 2612; (03) 5841-2643 *Fax:* (03) 5841 2636 *E-mail:* kikaku@lib.u-tokyo.ac.jp; shiryo@lib.u-tokyo. ac.jp *Web Site:* www.lib.u-tokyo.ac.jp, pg 1607

University of Tokyo Press (Japan) *Tel:* (03) 3811-8814; (03) 3812-6862 (sales) *Fax:* (03) 3812-6958 *E-mail:* info@utp.or.jp; order@utp.or.jp *Web Site:* www.utp.or.jp, pg 490

University of Tripoli (Libya) *Tel:* (021) 8214627910 *Fax:* (021) 8214628839 *E-mail:* president@uot.edu.ly *Web Site:* www.uot.edu.ly, pg 499

University of Tripoli Libraries (Libya) *Web Site:* uot.edu. ly, pg 1610

University of Wales Press (United Kingdom) *Tel:* (029) 2049-6899 *Fax:* (029) 2049-6108 *E-mail:* press@ press.wales.ac.uk *Web Site:* www.uwp.co.uk, pg 841

University of Western Australia Library (Australia) *Toll Free Tel:* 1800 263 921 (Western Australia only) *Fax:* (08) 6488 1012 *E-mail:* askuwa-lib@uwa.edu.au *Web Site:* www.library.uwa.edu.au, pg 1575

University of Western Australia Publishing (Australia) *Tel:* (08) 6488 3670 *Fax:* (08) 6488 1027 *E-mail:* admin-uwap@uwa.edu.au; marketing-uwap@ uwa.edu.au *Web Site:* www.uwap.uwa.edu.au; www. facebook.com/uwapublishing, pg 42

University of Witswatersrand, Education Library (South Africa) *Tel:* (011) 717-3242 *Web Site:* www.wits.ac. za/library, pg 1632

University of Yangon Library (Myanmar) *Tel:* (01) 537250 *E-mail:* univ.yangonlibrary@gmail.com *Web Site:* uy.edu.mm/library, pg 1615

University of Zambia Library (Zambia) *Tel:* (021) 1250845 *Fax:* (021) 1250845 *E-mail:* librarian@unza. zm *Web Site:* library.unza.zm, pg 1644

University of Zambia Press (Zambia) *Tel:* (021) 1292269 *Fax:* (021) 1253952 *E-mail:* press@unza.zm; sales. unzapress@unza.zm *Web Site:* www.unza.zm/l/units/ up, pg 851

University of Zimbabwe Libraries (Zimbabwe) *Tel:* (04) 303211-19 *Fax:* (04) 705155 *E-mail:* librarian@ uzlib.uz.ac.zw; uzmedlib.hre@healthnet.zw *Web Site:* library.uz.ac.zw, pg 1645

University of Zimbabwe Publications (Zimbabwe) *Tel:* (04) 303211-5 (ext 11194) *Fax:* (04) 333407 *E-mail:* uzpub@admin.uz.ac.zw *Web Site:* www.uz. ac.zw, pg 852

University Press Italiane (Italy) *Tel:* (050) 2212056 *Fax:* (050) 2212945 *E-mail:* info@ universitypressitaliane.com *Web Site:* www. universitypressitaliane.com, pg 1379

The University Press Ltd (UPL) (Bangladesh) *Tel:* (02) 9565441; (02) 9565444 *Fax:* (02) 9565443 *E-mail:* info@uplbooks.com.bd *Web Site:* www. uplbooks.com, pg 61

University Press PLC (Nigeria) *Tel:* (02) 8738896; (070) 98823872 *E-mail:* info@universitypressplc.com *Web Site:* www.universitypressplc.com, pg 553

University Publishing Co Ltd (Nigeria) *Tel:* (046) 410013; (0803) 4041661, pg 553

University Publishing Projects Ltd (Israel) *Tel:* (09) 7459955 *Fax:* (09) 7459966 *E-mail:* upp@upp.co.il *Web Site:* www.upp.co.il, pg 422

Universo dos Livros Editora Ltda (Brazil) *Tel:* (011) 3392-3336 *E-mail:* editor@universodoslivros.com. br; relacionamento@universodoslivros.com.br; vendas@universodoslivros.com.br *Web Site:* www. universodoslivros.com.br, pg 93

Universum Verlag GmbH (Germany) *Tel:* (0611) 90 30 0 *Fax:* (0611) 90 30 183 *E-mail:* uv@universum.de *Web Site:* www.universum.de, pg 339

Universzita Pavla Jozefa Safarika v Kosiciach (Slovakia) *Tel:* (055) 2341608 *E-mail:* kniznica@upjs.sk *Web Site:* www.upjs.sk/pracoviska/univerzitna-kniznica, pg 1629

Univerza v Ljubljani Ekonomska Fakulteta (Slovenia) *Tel:* (01) 5892-400 *Fax:* (01) 5892-698 *E-mail:* info@ ef.uni-lj.si *Web Site:* www.ef.uni-lj.si, pg 611

Univerzita Karlova v Praze, Nakladatelstvi Karolinum (Czech Republic) *Tel:* 224 491 276 *Fax:* 224 212 041 *E-mail:* cupress@cuni.cz *Web Site:* www.cupress.cuni. cz, pg 132

Univerzita Palackeho v Olomouci Vydavatelstvi (Czech Republic) *Tel:* 585 631 111; 585 631 783 (bookshop) *Fax:* 585 631 012; 585 631 786 (bookshop) *E-mail:* prodejna.vup@upol.cz *Web Site:* www.upol. cz/vup, pg 132

Univerzita Palackeho v Olomouci Vydavatelstvi (Czech Republic) *Tel:* 585 631 111 *Fax:* 585 631 012 *Web Site:* www.upol.cz/vup, pg 1320

Univerzitet u Beogradu biblioteka 'Svetozar Markovic' (Serbia) *Tel:* (011) 3370-512; (011) 3370-513; (011) 3370-506 *Fax:* (011) 3370-354 *E-mail:* pitajbibliotekera@unilib.bg.ac.rs; marketing@ unilib.rs *Web Site:* www.unilib.rs, pg 1629

Univerzitna Kniznica v Bratislave (Slovakia) *Tel:* (02) 59 804 100 *Fax:* (02) 54 434 246 *E-mail:* ukb@ulib.sk *Web Site:* www.ulib.sk, pg 1630

Wydawnictwa Uniwersytetu Warszawskiego (WUW) (Poland) *Tel:* (22) 55 31 318 *E-mail:* wuw@uw.edu. pl; dz.handlowy@uw.edu.pl *Web Site:* www.wuw.pl, pg 575

Wydawnictwo Uniwersytetu Wroclawskiego Sp z oo (Poland) *Tel:* (71) 375 28 09; (71) 375 28 85 (orders) *Fax:* (71) 375 27 35 *E-mail:* biuro@wuwr.com.pl *Web Site:* www.wuwr.com.pl, pg 575

UNO-Verlag, Vertriebs-und Verlagsgessellschaft GmbH (Germany) *Tel:* (0228) 94 90 2-0 *Fax:* (0228) 94 90 2-22 *Web Site:* www.uno-verlag.de, pg 339

UNR Editora (Argentina) *Tel:* (0341) 480 2687 *E-mail:* info-editora@unr.edu.ar *Web Site:* www. unreditora.unr.edu.ar, pg 13

Unrast eV (Germany) *Tel:* (0251) 66 62 93 *Fax:* (0251) 66 61 20 *E-mail:* kontakt@unrast-verlag.de; presse@ unrast-verlag.de *Web Site:* www.unrast-verlag.de, pg 339

UNSAM EDITA (Universidad Nacional de San Martin) (Argentina) *Tel:* (011) 4512 6360 *E-mail:* unsamedita@unsam.edu.ar; prensaeditorial@unsam.edu.ar; ventas@unsam.edu.ar *Web Site:* unsamedita.unsam.edu.ar, pg 13

Unsichtbar Verlag (Germany) *Tel:* (0821) 22 848 61 *E-mail:* info@unsichtbar-verlag.de *Web Site:* www. unsichtbar-verlag.de, pg 339

Unterwegs Verlag (Germany) *Tel:* (07731) 838-0 *Fax:* (07731) 83819 *E-mail:* info@unterwegs.de *Web Site:* www.reisefuehrer.com, pg 339

Jo Unwin Literary Agency (United Kingdom) *Tel:* (020) 7221 3717 *E-mail:* jo@jounwin.co.uk *Web Site:* www. jounwin.co.uk, pg 1247

Editorial UOC (Spain) *Tel:* 93 486 39 40 *Fax:* 93 451 30 16 *E-mail:* ediuoc@uoc.edu *Web Site:* www. editorialuoc.cat, pg 674

Editrice Uomini Nuovi SRL (Italy) *Tel:* (0332) 723007 *Fax:* (0332) 998080 *E-mail:* eunitaly@eun.ch (English matters) *Web Site:* www.eun.ch, pg 469

Uovonero Edizioni SNC (Italy) *Tel:* (0373) 500 622; (349) 3772839 (cell) *Fax:* (0373) 09 08 88 *E-mail:* libri@uovonero.com *Web Site:* www.uovonero. com, pg 469

UPM (Finland) *Tel:* (0204) 15 111 *Fax:* (0204) 15 110 *E-mail:* info@upm.com; paperinfo@upm.com *Web Site:* www.upm.com, pg 1345

Upplysing - Felag bokasafns- og upplysingafraeda (Iceland) *Tel:* 864-6220 *E-mail:* upplysing@upplysing. is *Web Site:* www.upplysing.is, pg 1653

Uppsala Universitetsbibliotek (Sweden) *Tel:* (018) 471 39 00 *Fax:* (018) 471 39 13 *E-mail:* info@ub.uu.se *Web Site:* www.ub.uu.se, pg 1635

Upstart Press (New Zealand) *Tel:* (09) 280 3199 *Fax:* (09) 281 3090 *E-mail:* editor@upstartpress.co.nz *Web Site:* upstartpress.co.nz, pg 550

Verlag Urachhaus (Germany) *Tel:* (0711) 285 3200 *Fax:* (0711) 285 3210 *E-mail:* info@urachhaus.com *Web Site:* www.urachhaus.de, pg 339

Urad pro Technickou Normalizaci, Metrologii a Statni Zkusebnictvi (Czech Republic) *Tel:* 221 802 111; 221 802 802 *E-mail:* info@unmz.cz *Web Site:* www.unmz. cz, pg 132

Uradni list Republike Slovenije doo (Slovenia) *Tel:* (01) 425-14-19; (01) 200 18 21 *Fax:* (01) 425-01-99 *E-mail:* info@uradni-list.si; prodaja@uradni-list.si (orders) *Web Site:* www.uradni-list.si, pg 612

Izdatel'stvo Ural'skogo gosudarstvennogo universiteta (Russia), pg 598

Urania Verlag (Germany) *Tel:* (0761) 2717-0 *Fax:* (0761) 2717-520 *E-mail:* service@urania-verlag.de; presse@ herder.de *Web Site:* www.urania-verlag.de, pg 340

Ediciones Urano SA (Spain) *Tel:* 902 131 315 *Fax:* 934 153 796 *E-mail:* infoes@edicionesurano.com; atencion@edicionesurano.com *Web Site:* www. edicionesurano.es, pg 674

Urban & Vogel GmbH (Germany) *Tel:* (089) 20 30 43 1300 *Web Site:* www.springerfachmedien-medizin.de, pg 340

Urbane Publications Ltd (United Kingdom) *Web Site:* urbanepublications.com, pg 841

Urbaniana University Press (UUP) (Italy) *Tel:* (06) 6988 9688 *Fax:* (06) 6988 2182 *E-mail:* redazioneuup@ urbaniana.edu *Web Site:* www.urbaniana.edu/uup, pg 469

Urdd Gobaith Cymru (United Kingdom) *Tel:* (01678) 541000 *E-mail:* helo@urdd.org *Web Site:* www.urdd. cymru, pg 841

Urdu Science Board (USB) (Pakistan) *Tel:* (042) 35758475; (042) 3575874 *Fax:* (042) 35789215 *E-mail:* info@urduscience.org.pk, pg 1386

Urim Publications (Israel) *Tel:* (02) 679-7633 *Fax:* (02) 679-7634 *E-mail:* urimpublisher@gmail.com *Web Site:* www.urimpublications.com, pg 422

Urmo SA de Ediciones (Spain) *Tel:* 916702189 *Fax:* 913012939 *E-mail:* ismaroto@hotmail.com *Web Site:* www.urmo.com, pg 675

Uruk Editores SA (Costa Rica) *Tel:* 2271 4824 *E-mail:* info@urukeditores.com *Web Site:* www. urukeditores.com; www.facebook.com/Uruk.Editores/, pg 118

Usborne Publishing Ltd (United Kingdom) *Tel:* (020) 7430 2800 *Fax:* (020) 7430 1562; (020) 7242 0974 (illustrations) *E-mail:* mail@usbornebooksathome.co. uk *Web Site:* www.usborne.com, pg 841

Ediciones USTA (Colombia) *Tel:* (01) 587 8797 (ext 2991) *E-mail:* editorial@usantotomas.edu.co *Web Site:* ediciones.usta.edu.co, pg 116

VAS Verlag fuer Akademische Schriften (Germany) *Tel:* (06172) 6811-656 *Fax:* (06172) 6811-657 *E-mail:* info@vas-verlag.de, pg 341 *Web Site:* www.vas-verlag.de, pg 341

Vaso Roto Ediciones (Spain) *Tel:* 915 779 152 *E-mail:* vasoroto@vasoroto.com *Web Site:* www.vasoroto.com, pg 675

Vaso Roto Ediciones S de RL de CV (Mexico) *Tel:* (0181) 8303 4247 *E-mail:* vasoroto@vasoroto.com *Web Site:* www.vasoroto.com, pg 525

Osuuskunta Vastapaino (Finland) *Tel:* (03) 3141 3501 *Fax:* (03) 3141 3550 *E-mail:* vastapaino@vastapaino.fi *Web Site:* www.vastapaino.fi, pg 151

Libreria Editrice Vaticana (Holy See (Vatican City)) *Tel:* (06) 698 83849 *Fax:* (06) 698 84716 *Web Site:* www.libreriaeditricevaticana.va, pg 362

Musei Vaticani (Holy See (Vatican City)) *Tel:* (06) 69881398 *Fax:* (06) 69882163 *E-mail:* infoshop.musei@scv.va *Web Site:* mv.vatican.va, pg 362

VBN-Verlag Luebeck (Germany) *Tel:* (0451) 38 46 48 96 *Fax:* (0451) 38 46 48 95 *E-mail:* info@vbn-verlag.de *Web Site:* www.vbn-verlag.de, pg 341

VCTA Publishing (Australia) *Tel:* (03) 9419 9622 *Fax:* (03) 9419 1205 *E-mail:* vcta@vcta.asn.au *Web Site:* www.vcta.asn.au, pg 42

VdA - Verband deutscher Archivarinnen und Archivare eV (Germany) *Tel:* (0661) 29109-72 *Fax:* (0661) 29109-74 *E-mail:* info@vda.archiv.net *Web Site:* www.vda.archiv.net, pg 1653

VDE-Verlag GmbH (Germany) *Tel:* (030) 34 80 01 0; (030) 34 80 01-222 (orders) *Fax:* (030) 34 80 01-9088 *E-mail:* kundenservice@vde-verlag.de *Web Site:* www.vde-verlag.de, pg 341

vdf Hochschulverlag AG an der ETH Zurich (Switzerland) *Tel:* (044) 632 42 42 *Fax:* (044) 632 12 32 *E-mail:* verlag@vdf.ethz.ch *Web Site:* vdf.ch, pg 708

VDG Verlag und Datenbank fuer Geisteswissenschaften (Germany) *Tel:* (03643) 83030 *Fax:* (03643) 830313 *E-mail:* info@vdg-weimar.de; herstellung@vdg-weimar.de; presse@vdg-weimar.de *Web Site:* www.vdg-weimar.de, pg 341

VDI Verlag GmbH (Germany) *Tel:* (0211) 6188-0 *Fax:* (0211) 6188-112 *E-mail:* info@vdi-nachrichten.com; www.vdi-nachrichten.com, pg 341

Editions De Vecchi (France) *Tel:* 04 66 62 98 27; 04 66 62 98 43 *Fax:* 04 66 62 98 42 *E-mail:* contact@de-vecchi.fr *Web Site:* www.de-vecchi.fr, pg 199

Vedecka knihovna v olomouci (Czech Republic) *Tel:* 585 223 441 *E-mail:* info@vkol.cz; vkol@vkol.cz *Web Site:* www.vkol.cz, pg 1585

Veen Bosch & Keuning Uitgeversgroep BV (Netherlands) *Tel:* (088) 700 2600 *E-mail:* info@vbku.nl *Web Site:* www.vbku.nl, pg 542

Vega Forlag AS (Norway) *Tel:* 21 09 04 10 *Fax:* 22 37 15 50 *E-mail:* post@vegaforlag.no *Web Site:* www.vegaforlag.no, pg 558

Libreria Tecnica Vega (Venezuela) *Tel:* (0212) 6622848; (0212) 6622702 *E-mail:* tecnicavega@cantv.net, pg 1462

Las Vegas edizioni SAS (Italy) *Tel:* (011) 6962663 *E-mail:* info@lasvegasedizioni.com; ordini@lasvegasedizioni.com *Web Site:* www.lasvegasedizioni.com, pg 469

Vehling Medienservice und Verlag GmbH (Austria) *Tel:* (0664) 84 96 922 *E-mail:* verlag@vehling.at *Web Site:* www.vehling.at, pg 59

Veiters Korporacija (Latvia) *Tel:* 67994419; 67545174 (sales) *Fax:* 67994419 *E-mail:* veiters@veiters.lv *Web Site:* www.veiters.lv, pg 1281, 1329

Editrice Velar (Italy) *Tel:* (035) 6592811 *Fax:* (035) 6592888 *E-mail:* velar@velar.it *Web Site:* www.velar.it, pg 470

Velbrueck Wissenschaft (Germany) *Tel:* (02554) 83 603-0 *Fax:* (02554) 83 603-33 *E-mail:* info@velbrueck-wissenschaft.de *Web Site:* www.velbrueck-wissenschaft.de, pg 341

Editura Vellant SRL (Romania) *Tel:* (021) 2117741; (031) 8059825 *Fax:* (021) 2117741; (031) 8059825 *E-mail:* distributie@vellant.ro; editorial@vellant.ro; comenzi@vellant.ro *Web Site:* www.vellant.ro, pg 592

Veloce Publishing Ltd (United Kingdom) *Tel:* (01305) 260068 *Fax:* (01305) 250479 *E-mail:* info@veloce.co.uk; sales@veloce.co.uk *Web Site:* www.veloce.co.uk; www.velocebooks.com, pg 842

Veltman Uitgevers BV (Netherlands) *Tel:* (0346) 284 242 *Fax:* (0346) 284 282 *E-mail:* info@veltman-uitgevers.nl *Web Site:* www.veltman-uitgevers.nl, pg 542

Ventil Verlag KG (Germany) *Tel:* (06131) 22 60 78 *Fax:* (06131) 22 60 79 *E-mail:* mail@ventil-verlag.de; presse@ventil-verlag.de *Web Site:* www.ventil-verlag.de, pg 341

Vents d'ailleurs (France) *Tel:* 04 42 50 59 92 *Fax:* 04 42 50 58 03 *E-mail:* info@ventsdailleurs.com *Web Site:* www.ventsdailleurs.fr, pg 199

Editions Vents d'Ouest (France) *Tel:* 01 41 46 11 11 *Fax:* 01 41 46 11 00 *Web Site:* www.ventsdouest.com, pg 199

Ventura Press (Australia) *Tel:* (02) 8060 9191 *E-mail:* info@venturapress.com.au *Web Site:* www.venturapress.com.au, pg 42

Venture Press Ltd (United Kingdom) *Tel:* (0121) 622 3911 *Fax:* (0121) 622 4860 *E-mail:* info@basw.co.uk *Web Site:* www.basw.co.uk, pg 842

Verband Bildungsmedien eV (Germany) *Tel:* (069) 9866976-0 *Fax:* (069) 9866976-20 *E-mail:* verband@bildungsmedien.de *Web Site:* www.bildungsmedien.de, pg 1375

Verband der Antiquare Oesterreichs (Austria) *Tel:* (01) 512 15 35-14 *Fax:* (01) 512 84 82 *E-mail:* sekretariat@hvb.at *Web Site:* www.antiquare.at, pg 1365

Verband der Wissenschaftlichen Gesellschaften Oesterreichs (VWGOe) (Austria) *Tel:* (0650) 544 8086 (cell) *Fax:* (01) 40160 933002 *E-mail:* office@vwgoe.at *Web Site:* www.vwgoe.at, pg 59

Verband Deutscher Antiquare eV (Germany) *Tel:* (06435) 90 91 47 *Fax:* (06435) 90 91 48 *E-mail:* buch@antiquare.de; info@antiquare.de *Web Site:* www.antiquare.de, pg 1375

Verband Deutscher Auskunfts- und Verzichnismedien eV (vdav) (Germany) *Tel:* (02156) 774385-6 *Fax:* (02156) 774385-5 *E-mail:* info@vdav.org *Web Site:* www.vdav.de, pg 1375

Verband deutschsprachiger Uebersetzer literarischer und wissenschaftlicher Werke eV (VDUe) (Germany) *Tel:* (030) 6956-2327 *Fax:* (030) 6956-3656 *Web Site:* www.literaturuebersetzer.de, pg 1249

Verbinum Wydawnictwo Ksiezy Werbistow (Poland) *Tel:* (52) 330 63 03 *E-mail:* wydawnictwo@verbinum.pl *Web Site:* www.verbinum.pl, pg 575

Editorial Verbo Divino (Spain) *Tel:* 948 55 65 11 *Fax:* 948 55 45 06 *E-mail:* ventas@verbodivino.es *Web Site:* www.verbodivino.es, pg 675

Editora Verbo Ltda (Brazil) *Tel:* (011) 3228-9230, pg 93

Verbrecher Verlag (Germany) *Tel:* (030) 28 38 59 54 *Fax:* (030) 28 38 59 55 *E-mail:* info@verbrecherei.de *Web Site:* www.verbrecherei.de, pg 341

Editorial Verbum SL (Spain) *Tel:* 914 468 841 *E-mail:* gestor.ed.verbum@gmail.com; editorialverbum@gmail.com *Web Site:* www.verbumeditorial.com, pg 675

Verbum Forlag (Norway) *Tel:* 47 97 64 50 *Fax:* 47 97 64 51 *E-mail:* post@bibel.no; mcm@bibel.no *Web Site:* www.bibel.no, pg 558

Verbum Forlag AB (Sweden) *Tel:* (08) 743 65 00; (08) 743 65 10 (customer service) *Fax:* (08) 644 56 04 *E-mail:* info@verbum.se *Web Site:* webshop.verbumforlag.se, pg 686

Editions Verdier (France) *Tel:* 04 68 24 05 75; 01 43 79 20 45 *E-mail:* contact@editions-verdier.fr *Web Site:* www.editions-verdier.fr, pg 199

Verein Deutscher Bibliothekare eV (VDB) (Germany) *Tel:* (089) 2180-2420 *E-mail:* vdb@ub.uni-muenchen.de *Web Site:* www.vdb-online.org, pg 1653

Verein Lateinamerikanischer Autoren (in der EU Migration) (Germany) *Tel:* (0176) 29737349 *Web Site:* www.spanischdienstleistungen.de, pg 1495

Verein Schweizerischer Archivarinnen und Archivare (VSA) (Switzerland) *Tel:* (031) 312 26 66 *Fax:* (031) 312 26 68 *E-mail:* info@vsa-aas.org *Web Site:* www.vsa-aas.org, pg 1660

Vereinigte Fachverlage GmbH (Germany) *Tel:* (06131) 992-0 *Fax:* (06131) 992-100 *E-mail:* info@vfmz.de *Web Site:* www.vereinigte-fachverlage.info; www.cahensly-medien.de, pg 342

Vereinigung der Buchantiquare und Kupferstichhaendler in der Schweiz (Switzerland) *Tel:* (043) 222 48 88 *Fax:* (043) 222 48 89 *E-mail:* info@vebuku.ch *Web Site:* www.vebuku.ch, pg 1391

Vereinigung Evangelischer Buchhaendler und Verleger eV (Germany) *Tel:* (06) 91 63 667 *Fax:* (06) 91 63 855 *E-mail:* mail@veb-medien.de *Web Site:* www.veb-medien.de, pg 1375

Vereinigung Oesterreichischer Bibliothekarinnen und Bibliothekare (VOEB) (Austria) *E-mail:* voeb@uibk.ac.at *Web Site:* www.univie.ac.at/voeb, pg 1647

Vereinte Evangelische Mission (Germany) *Tel:* (0202) 8 90 04-0 *Fax:* (0202) 8 90 04-179 *E-mail:* info@vemission.org *Web Site:* www.vemission.org, pg 342

Vereniging Antwerpse Bibliofielen (Belgium) *Tel:* (03) 221 14 67 *Fax:* (03) 221 14 71 *Web Site:* www.boekgeschiedenis.be/index.php?q=content/vereniging-van-antwerpse-bibliofielen, pg 1491

Vereniging van Openbare Bibliotheken (Netherlands) *Tel:* (070) 30 90 500 *Fax:* (070) 30 90 599 *E-mail:* infodesk@debibliotheken.nl; vereniging@debibliotheken.nl *Web Site:* www.debibliotheken.nl, pg 1657

Vereniging van Religieus-Wetenschappelijke Bibliothecarissen (Belgium), pg 1648

Vergara (Argentina) *Tel:* (011) 4343-7510; (011) 4343-7706 *Fax:* (011) 4334-0173 *E-mail:* prensa@edicionesb.com.ar *Web Site:* www.edicionesb.com.ar; www.edicionesb-argentina.com, pg 13

Javier Vergara Editor SA de CV (Mexico) *Tel:* (0155) 5543 4802; (0155) 5682 8194 *Fax:* (0155) 5682 9511, pg 525

Veritas Co Ltd (Ireland) *Tel:* (01) 878 8177 *Fax:* (01) 878 6507; (01) 874 4913 *E-mail:* sales@veritas.ie; veritas2@veritas.ie *Web Site:* www.veritasbooksonline.com, pg 415, 1426

Veritas Foundation Publication Centre (United Kingdom) *Tel:* (020) 8749 4957 *E-mail:* orders@veritasbookshop.co.uk *Web Site:* www.veritasfoundation.co.uk, pg 842

Veritas Verlags- und Handelsgesmbh & Co OG (Austria) *Tel:* (0732) 776451-0 *Fax:* (0732) 776451-2239 *E-mail:* kundenberatung@veritas.at *Web Site:* www.veritas.at, pg 1405

Veritas Verlags- und HandelsgesmbH & Co OHG (Austria) *Tel:* (0732) 776451-0 *Fax:* (0732) 776451-2239 *E-mail:* veritas@veritas.at; kundenberatung@veritas.at *Web Site:* www.veritas.at, pg 59

Verkehrshaus der Schweiz (Switzerland) *Tel:* (041) 370 44 44 *Fax:* (041) 370 61 68 *E-mail:* mail@verkehrshaus.ch *Web Site:* www.verkehrshaus.ch, pg 708

Verlag Bau+Technik GmbH (Germany) *Tel:* (0211) 9 24 99-0 *Fax:* (0211) 9 24 99-55 *E-mail:* info@verlagbt.de *Web Site:* www.verlagbt.de, pg 342

Vinciana Editrice SAS (Italy) *Tel:* (02) 4982306 *Fax:* (02) 48003275 *E-mail:* info@vinciana.com *Web Site:* www.vinciana.com, pg 470

Vindicacion Feminista Publicaciones (Spain) *Tel:* 91 369 4488 *Fax:* 91 369 4488, pg 676

Forlaget Vindrose A/S (Denmark) *Tel:* 3375 5555 *E-mail:* borgen_post@gyldendal.dk; salg@borgen.dk *Web Site:* www.borgen.dk, pg 141

Vine House Distribution Ltd (United Kingdom) *Tel:* (01825) 767 396 *Fax:* (01825) 765 649 *E-mail:* sales@vinehouseuk.co.uk *Web Site:* vinehouseuk.co.uk, pg 1461

The Viney Agency (United Kingdom) *Tel:* (020) 7732 3331 *Web Site:* www.thevineyagency.com, pg 1247

Virago Press (United Kingdom) *Tel:* (020) 7911 8000 *Fax:* (020) 7911 8100 *E-mail:* virago@littlebrown.co.uk *Web Site:* www.virago.co.uk, pg 843

Editorial VIS-A-VIA SL (Spain) *Tel:* 931633562 *Fax:* 935393565 *E-mail:* info@vis-a-via.com *Web Site:* www.vis-a-via.com, pg 676

Visalaandhra Publishing House (India) *Tel:* (0866) 2430302; 9052101320 (cell) *E-mail:* vphsales@gmail.com *Web Site:* www.visalaandhrapublishinghouse.com, pg 1425

Edition Curt Visel (Germany) *Tel:* (08331) 2853 *Fax:* (08331) 490364 *E-mail:* info@edition-curt-visel.de *Web Site:* www.edition-curt-visel.de, pg 343

Vishv Vijay Pte Ltd (India) *Tel:* (0120) 4698888; (0120) 4129946; 9899888203 (cell) *Fax:* (0120) 4111522 *Web Site:* www.vishvbook.com, pg 403

Vision Books Pvt Ltd (India) *Tel:* (011) 23862201; (011) 23862935 *Fax:* (011) 29836490 *E-mail:* editor@visionbooksindia.com; publicity@visionbooksindia.com; rights@visionbooksindia.com; sales@visionbooksindia.com; service@visionbooksindia.com *Web Site:* www.visionbooksindia.com, pg 403

Vision Publishing Co Ltd (Hong Kong) *Tel:* 2679 8119 *Fax:* 2679 4478 *E-mail:* mail@visionhk.com.hk; pe@visionhk.com.hk *Web Site:* www.visionhk.com.hk, pg 367

Vision SRL (Italy) *Tel:* (06) 44292688 *Fax:* (06) 44292688 *E-mail:* sales@visionpubl.com; ufficiostampa@visionpubl.com *Web Site:* www.visionpubl.com, pg 470

Visionary World Ltd (Hong Kong) *Tel:* 2723 1376 *Fax:* 2723 6653 *E-mail:* info@visionary-world.com *Web Site:* www.visionary-world.com, pg 367

Visit Wales (United Kingdom) *E-mail:* info@visitwales.com *Web Site:* www.visitwales.com, pg 843

Visor Distribuciones SA (Spain) *Tel:* 915301136, pg 676

Visor Libros SL (Spain) *Tel:* 91 549 26 55 *Fax:* 91 544 86 95 *E-mail:* visor-libros@visor-libros.com *Web Site:* www.visor-libros.com, pg 676

Vista Point Verlag GmbH (Germany) *Tel:* (0221) 92 16 13-0 *Fax:* (0221) 92 16 13-14 *E-mail:* info@vistapoint.de *Web Site:* www.vistapoint.de, pg 343

Visual Editions (United Kingdom) *Tel:* (020) 3077 2056 *E-mail:* hey@visual-editions.com; orders@visual-editions.com; press@visual-editions.com *Web Site:* www.visual-editions.com, pg 843

Visual Steps BV (Netherlands) *Tel:* (0297) 386444 *E-mail:* info@visualsteps.nl *Web Site:* www.visualsteps.nl, pg 542

S Viswanathan (Printers & Publishers) Pvt Ltd (India) *Tel:* (044) 2836 2723; (044) 2836 3633 *Fax:* (044) 2836 3002, pg 403

Vita e Pensiero (Italy) *Tel:* (02) 72342335 *Fax:* (02) 72342260 *E-mail:* editrice.vp@unicatt.it; libreria.vp@unicatt.it; ufficiostampa.vp@unicatt.it *Web Site:* www.vitaepensiero.it, pg 470

Edizioni La Vita Felice (Italy) *Tel:* (02) 20520585 *Fax:* (02) 20520585 *E-mail:* info@lavitafelice.it *Web Site:* www.lavitafelice.it, pg 470

Vitalis sro (Czech Republic) *Tel:* 257 181 660 *Fax:* 257 181 670 *E-mail:* info@vitalis-verlag.com *Web Site:* www.vitalis-verlag.com, pg 132

Viva Books Pvt Ltd (India) *Tel:* (011) 42242200 *Fax:* (011) 42242240 *E-mail:* viva@vivagroupindia.net *Web Site:* www.vivagroupindia.com, pg 404

Viva Lithographers Pte Ltd (Singapore) *Tel:* 6272 1880 *Fax:* 6273 5425 *E-mail:* vivasing@singnet.com.sg *Web Site:* www.vivalitho.com, pg 1261

Vivalda Editori SRL (Italy) *Tel:* (011) 7720444 *Fax:* (011) 7732170 *E-mail:* info@vivaldaeditori.it; ordini@vivaldaeditori.it *Web Site:* www.vivaldaeditori.it, pg 470

Editura Vivaldi (Romania) *Tel:* (021) 2108897; (021) 2101013 *E-mail:* contact@edituravivaldi.ro *Web Site:* www.edituravivaldi.ro, pg 592

Vivat Publishing Ltd (Ukraine) *Tel:* (057) 714-91-73 *E-mail:* ishop@vivat.factor.ua *Web Site:* www.vivat-book.com.ua, pg 727

Vivek Prakashan (India) *Tel:* (0141) 2310111; 9829523905 (cell) *E-mail:* vivekprakashan@yahoo.com *Web Site:* vivekprakashan.com, pg 404

ars vivendi verlag GmbH & Co KG (Germany) *Tel:* (09103) 71929-0; (09103) 71929-10 *Fax:* (09103) 71929-19 *E-mail:* info@arsvivendi.com *Web Site:* www.arsvivendi.com, pg 343

Edizioni VivereIn (Italy) *Tel:* (080) 6907030 *Fax:* (080) 6907026 *E-mail:* edizioniviverein@tin.it *Web Site:* www.edizioniviverein.it, pg 470

Editorial Luis Vives (Edelvives) (Spain) *Tel:* 913 344 884 *E-mail:* info@edelvives.es *Web Site:* www.edelvives.com, pg 676, 1262, 1335, 1354

R Vivian Literary Agency (Italy) *Tel:* (049) 8761273 *Web Site:* www.rvivianliteraryagency.com, pg 1231

Viviani Editore SRL (Italy) *Tel:* (06) 6872855 *Fax:* (06) 6872856 *E-mail:* viviani@vivianieditore.com; vivianieditore@tin.it *Web Site:* www.vivianieditore.net, pg 470

Vivlia Publishers & Booksellers (Pty) Ltd (South Africa) *Tel:* (011) 472-3912 *Fax:* (011) 472-4904 *E-mail:* headoffice@vivlia.co.za *Web Site:* www.vivlia.co.za, pg 619

Vivliotechnica Hellas (Greece) *Tel:* 2103831146 *Fax:* 2109564354, pg 360

Editions Vizavi (Mauritius) *Tel:* 211 24 35 *Fax:* 211 30 47 *E-mail:* vizavi@orange.mu *Web Site:* www.tikoulou.com, pg 512

Vjesnik dd (Croatia) *Tel:* (01) 6161 700; (01) 6161 453 (sales) *Fax:* (01) 6161 606; (01) 6161 486 (sales) *E-mail:* uprava@vjesnik.hr; prodaja@vjesnik.hr *Web Site:* vjesnik.hr; www.vjesnik.com, pg 1256

VK Global Publications Pvt Ltd (India) *Tel:* (011) 23250105; (011) 23250106 *Fax:* (011) 23250141 *E-mail:* mail@vkpublications.com; sales@vkpublications.com *Web Site:* www.vkpublications.com, pg 404

Vlaams Fonds voor de Letteren (Belgium) *Tel:* (03) 270 31 61 *Fax:* (03) 270 31 60 *E-mail:* info@vfl.be *Web Site:* www.vfl.be, pg 1366

Vlaamse Esperantobond VZW (Belgium) *Tel:* (03) 234 34 00 *Fax:* (03) 233 54 33 *E-mail:* info@fel.esperanto.be *Web Site:* www.esperanto.be, pg 73

Vlaamse Uitgevers Vereniging (VUV) (Belgium) *Tel:* (03) 230 89 23 *Web Site:* www.boekenvak.be/voor-uitgevers/vlaamse-uitgeversvereniging, pg 1366

Vlaamse Vereniging voor Bibliotheek, Archief en Documentatie VZW (VVBAD) (Belgium) *Tel:* (03) 281 44 57 *E-mail:* vvbad@vvbad.be *Web Site:* www.vvbad.be, pg 1648

G Vlassi Afoi OE (Greece) *Tel:* 2103812900 *Fax:* 2103827557 *E-mail:* info@vlassi.gr *Web Site:* www.vlassi.gr, pg 360, 1420

Editions VM (France) *E-mail:* editeurs-enterprise@eyrolles.com; foreignrights@eyrolles.com *Web Site:* www.editions-vm.com, pg 200

VNR Verlag fuer die Deutsche Wirtschaft AG (Germany) *Tel:* (0228) 82 05 0 *Fax:* (0228) 36 96 480 *E-mail:* info@vnr.de *Web Site:* www.vnrag.de, pg 343

Oficyna Wydawnicza Vocatio (Poland) *Tel:* (22) 648-54-50 *Fax:* (22) 648-03-79 *E-mail:* vocatio@vocatio.com.pl; ksiegarnia@vocatio.com.pl *Web Site:* www.vocatio.com.pl, pg 575

Nakladatelstvi Vodnar (Czech Republic) *Tel:* 604 674 633 *E-mail:* naklvodnar@volny.cz *Web Site:* vodnar.eu, pg 132

Voenno Izdatelstvo (Bulgaria) *Tel:* (02) 987 80 92 *E-mail:* info@vi-books.com; vi_books@abv.bg (book store) *Web Site:* www.vi-books.com, pg 97

Voetbal International Boeken (Netherlands) *Tel:* (0182) 599377 *Web Site:* www.vi-boeken.nl, pg 542

Verlag A Vogel AG (Switzerland) *Tel:* (071) 335 66 66 *Fax:* (071) 335 66 88 *E-mail:* info@verlag-avogel.ch *Web Site:* www.avogel.ch, pg 708

Vogel Business Media GmbH & Co KG (Germany) *Tel:* (0931) 418-0 *Fax:* (0931) 418-2100 *E-mail:* info@vogel.de *Web Site:* www.vogel.de, pg 343

Vogel Druck und Medienservice GmbH (Germany) *Tel:* (0931) 4600-02 *Fax:* (0931) 4600-2145 *E-mail:* info@vogel-druck.de *Web Site:* www.vogel-druck.de, pg 1276, 1323

VOGELMEDIA GmbH Literaturagentur (Austria) *Tel:* (02262) 62 800 *Fax:* (02262) 718 18-18 *E-mail:* lektorat@literaturagent.at *Web Site:* www.literaturagent.at, pg 1223

Voggenreiter Verlag GmbH (Germany) *Tel:* (0228) 935750 *Fax:* (0228) 9357575 *E-mail:* sales@voggenreiter.de *Web Site:* www.voggenreiter.de, pg 343

Vogt Multimedia Verlag (Germany) *Tel:* (06162) 911 252 *Fax:* (06162) 911 253 *E-mail:* vogt.webdesign@t-online.de *Web Site:* www.vogt-multimedia-verlag.de, pg 343

Voion Printing Group (International) Co Ltd (China) *Tel:* (0755) 61155888 *Fax:* (0755) 61155566 *E-mail:* voion@voion.com *Web Site:* www.voion.com, pg 1319

Vojnoizdavacki Zavod Vojna Knjiga (Serbia) *Tel:* (011) 3612-390; (011) 3612-657 *Fax:* (011) 3612-506, pg 602

Verlag Voland & Quist (Germany) *Tel:* (0351) 79 54 771 *Fax:* (0351) 79 54 769 *E-mail:* vertrieb@voland-quist.de; presse@voland-quist.de; info@voland-quist.de *Web Site:* www.voland-quist.de, pg 343

Voland SRL (Italy) *Tel:* (06) 4461946 *E-mail:* redazione@voland.it; ufficiostampa@voland.it *Web Site:* www.voland.it, pg 470

Volante (Sweden) *Tel:* (08) 702 15 19 *E-mail:* info@volante.se; press@volante.se *Web Site:* volante.se, pg 687

Volk Verlag (Germany) *Tel:* (089) 420 79 69 80 *Fax:* (089) 420 79 69 86 *E-mail:* info@volkverlag.de *Web Site:* www.volkverlag.de, pg 343

Voltaire Foundation Ltd (United Kingdom) *Tel:* (01865) 284600 *Fax:* (01865) 284610 *E-mail:* email@voltaire.ox.ac.uk *Web Site:* www.voltaire.ox.ac.uk, pg 843

Volumnia Editrice (Italy) *Tel:* (075) 5724950; (075) 5733187 *Fax:* (075) 5724950 *E-mail:* volumnia@volumnia.it; volumniaeditrice@gmail.com *Web Site:* www.volumnia.it, pg 470

Editorial Voluntad SA (Colombia) *Tel:* (01) 410 63 55 *Web Site:* www.voluntad.com.co, pg 116

Volvox Globator Nakladatelstvi & vydavatelstvi (Czech Republic) *Tel:* 224 236 268 *Fax:* 224 217 721 *E-mail:* volvox@volvox.cz *Web Site:* www.volvox.cz, pg 132

Verlag Vopelius Jena (Germany) *Tel:* (03641) 219860 *Fax:* (03641) 561770 *E-mail:* verlagvopelius@email.de *Web Site:* www.verlagvopelius.de, pg 343

Vorarlberger Verlagsanstalt GmbH (Austria) *Tel:* (05572) 24697-0 *Fax:* (05572) 24697-78 *E-mail:* office@vva.at *Web Site:* www.vva.at, pg 60

Izdatel'stvo Voroneskogo Gosudarstvennogo Universiteta (Russia) *Tel:* (473) 2560481; (473) 2530481 *Fax:* (473) 2208755, pg 598

Vorwaerts Buch Verlagsgesellschaft mbH (Germany) *Tel:* (030) 255 94 520 *Fax:* (030) 255 94 190; (030) 255 94 192 *E-mail:* info@vorwaerts-buch.de *Web Site:* www.vorwaerts-buch.de, pg 343

Verlag Vorwerk 8 (Germany) *Tel:* (030) 784 61 01 *Fax:* (030) 784 06 104 *E-mail:* verlag@vorwerk8.de *Web Site:* www.vorwerk8.de, pg 343

Nikos Votsis Publications (Greece) *Tel:* 2103820646; 2103835503 *Fax:* 2103820646, pg 360

Vox (Spain) *Tel:* 93 241 35 05 *Fax:* 93 241 35 11 *E-mail:* vox@vox.es *Web Site:* www.vox.es, pg 676

Editura Vox (Romania) *Tel:* (021) 222 02 13 *Fax:* (021) 222 02 13 *E-mail:* vox@edituravox.ro *Web Site:* www. edituravox.ro, pg 592

Editora Vozes Ltda (Brazil) *Tel:* (024) 2233-9000 *Fax:* (024) 2231-4676 *E-mail:* editorial@vozes.com. br; vendas@vozes.com.br; marketing@vozes.com.br *Web Site:* www.universovozes.com.br, pg 93

Editura Vremea SRL (Romania) *Tel:* (021) 335 81 31 *Fax:* (0378) 106 497 *E-mail:* office@edituravremea.ro *Web Site:* www.edituravremea.ro, pg 592

Uitgeverij de Vries & Brouwers (Belgium) *Tel:* (03) 237 41 80 *Fax:* (03) 237 70 01 *E-mail:* dvbkantoor@ skynet.be *Web Site:* www.devries-brouwers.be, pg 74

H de Vries Boeken (Netherlands) *Tel:* (023) 5319458; (070) 3125605 *E-mail:* info@devriesboeken.nl; klantenservice@devriesboeken.nl *Web Site:* www. devriesboeken.nl, pg 1438

Uitgeverij Vrijdag NV (Belgium) *Tel:* (03) 345 60 40 *E-mail:* info@uitgeverijvrijdag.be; mail@ uitgeverijvrijdag.be *Web Site:* www.uitgeverijvrijdag. be, pg 74

Vrije Universiteit Brussel Universiteitsbibliotheek (Belgium) *Tel:* (02) 629 26 09 *Fax:* (02) 629 26 93 *E-mail:* info@biblio.vub.ac.be *Web Site:* www.vub.ac. be/BIBLIO, pg 1578

Librairie Philosophique J Vrin (France) *Tel:* 01 43 54 03 47 *Fax:* 01 43 54 48 18 *E-mail:* contact@vrin.fr *Web Site:* www.vrin.fr, pg 200

VS-BOOKS Torsten Verhuelsdonk (Germany) *Tel:* (02323) 946 252 0 *Fax:* (02323) 946 252 9 *E-mail:* vertrieb@vs-books.de (orders); info@vs-books.de *Web Site:* www.vs-books.de, pg 343

VS - Verband Deutscher Schriftstellerinnen und Schriftsteller (Germany) *Tel:* (030) 69 56-0 *Fax:* (030) 69 56-3141 *E-mail:* info@verdi.de *Web Site:* vs.verdi. de, pg 1495

VSA: Verlag Hamburg GmbH (Germany) *Tel:* (040) 28 09 52 77-0 *Fax:* (040) 28 09 52 77-50 *E-mail:* info@ vsa-verlag.de *Web Site:* www.vsa-verlag.de, pg 344

Vysoka skola banska-Technicka univerzita Ostrava (Czech Republic) *Tel:* 596 994 574 (circulation desk) *Fax:* 597 324 598 *E-mail:* knihovna@vsb.cz *Web Site:* www.vsb.cz; knihovna.vsb.cz, pg 1585

Vserossijskaja gosudarstvennaja biblioteka inostrannoj literatury im M I Rudomino (Russia) *Tel:* (495) 915 36 21 *Fax:* (495) 915 36 37 *E-mail:* vgbil@libfl.ru *Web Site:* www.libfl.ru, pg 1628

VSRW-Verlag Dr Hagen Pruehs GmbH (Germany) *Tel:* (0228) 95124-0 *Fax:* (0228) 95124-90 *E-mail:* vsrw@vsrw.de *Web Site:* www.vsrw.de, pg 344

VU Boekhandel (Netherlands) *Tel:* (020) 598 40 00 *Fax:* (020) 646 27 19 *E-mail:* info@vuboekhandel.nl *Web Site:* www.vuboekhandel.nl, pg 542

VUB Brussels University Press (Belgium) *Tel:* (02) 289 26 50 *Fax:* (02) 289 26 59 *E-mail:* info@aspeditions. be *Web Site:* www.aspeditions.be, pg 74

VUD Medien GmbH (Germany) *Tel:* (07441) 91030 *Fax:* (07441) 910333 *E-mail:* info@vud.com *Web Site:* www.vud.com, pg 344

Editorial Vuelta SA de CV (Mexico) *Tel:* (0155) 9183 7800 *Fax:* (0155) 9183 7836 *E-mail:* cartas@ letraslibres.com *Web Site:* www.letraslibres.com, pg 525

Editions Vuibert (France) *Tel:* 01 42 79 44 53 *E-mail:* relations.presse@vuibert.fr *Web Site:* www. vuibert.fr, pg 200

Vulcano Ediciones SL (Spain) *Tel:* 91 500 16 49, pg 676

Vulkan Izdavastvo doo (Serbia) *Tel:* (011) 3087-515 *Fax:* (011) 3087-614 *E-mail:* office@vulkani.rs *Web Site:* www.vulkani.rs, pg 602

Vulkan-Verlag GmbH (Germany) *Tel:* (0201) 82002-14 *Fax:* (0201) 82002-40 *E-mail:* info@oiv.de *Web Site:* www.oldenbourg-industrieverlag.de, pg 344

Uitgeverij Vuurbaak (Netherlands) *Tel:* (0342) 41 17 31 *E-mail:* info@vuurbaak.nl *Web Site:* www.vuurbaak.nl, pg 542

VWB-Verlag fuer Wissenschaft und Bildung (Germany) *Tel:* (030) 251 04 15 *Fax:* (030) 251 11 36 *E-mail:* info@vwb-verlag.com *Web Site:* www.vwb-verlag.com, pg 344

Nakladatelstvi Vysehrad spol sro (Czech Republic) *Tel:* 224 221 703 *Fax:* 224 221 703 *E-mail:* info@ ivysehrad.cz *Web Site:* www.ivysehrad.cz, pg 133

Izdatelstvo Vysshaya Shkola (Russia) *Tel:* (495) 694-0456 (reception); (495) 694-1973 (sales) *Fax:* (495) 694-04-56; (495) 694-3486 (sales) *E-mail:* secretar@ vshkola.ru; sales_vshkola@mail.ru *Web Site:* www. vshkola.ru, pg 598

Verlag die Waage (Switzerland) *E-mail:* bestellungen@ verlagdiewaage.ch *Web Site:* www.verlagdiewaage.ch, pg 708

Waanders Uitgevers (Netherlands) *Tel:* (038) 337 79 96; (038) 421 53 92 *E-mail:* info@waanders.nl *Web Site:* www.waanders.nl, pg 542

Wydawnictwo WAB (Poland) *Tel:* (22) 826 08 82; (22) 828 98 08 *Fax:* (22) 380 18 01 *E-mail:* biuro@ gwfoksal.pl *Web Site:* www.wab.com.pl, pg 575

Wachholtz Verlag GmbH (Germany) *Tel:* (04321) 25093-0 *Fax:* (04321) 250930-15 *E-mail:* info@wachholtz-verlag.de *Web Site:* www.wachholtz.de, pg 344

Verlag Klaus Wagenbach (Germany) *Tel:* (030) 23 51 51-0 *Fax:* (030) 211 61 40 *E-mail:* mail@wagenbach. de; presse@wagenbach.de *Web Site:* www.wagenbach. de, pg 344

Friedenauer Presse Katharina Wagenbach-Wolff (Germany) *Tel:* (030) 3 12 99 23 *Fax:* (030) 3 12 99 02 *E-mail:* frpresse@t-online.de *Web Site:* www. friedenauer-presse.de, pg 344

Wageningen Academic Publishers (Netherlands) *Tel:* (0317) 47 65 16; (0317) 47 65 14 (sales) *Fax:* (0317) 45 34 17 *E-mail:* info@ wageningenacademic.com *Web Site:* www. wageningenacademic.com, pg 543

Universitaetsverlag Wagner GesmbH (Austria) *Tel:* (0512) 395045-23 *Fax:* (0512) 395045-15 *E-mail:* mail@uvw.at *Web Site:* www.uvw.at, pg 60

Wagner Verlag GmbH (Germany) *Tel:* (06051) 9779900; (06051) 88381-0 *Fax:* (06051) 9779901; (06051) 88381-29 *E-mail:* info@wagner-verlag.de; buch@ wagner-verlag.de *Web Site:* www.wagner-verlag.de, pg 344

Wagner'schen Universitaetsbuchhandlung (Austria) *Tel:* (0512) 59505-0 *Fax:* (0512) 59505-38 *E-mail:* office@wagnersche.at *Web Site:* shop. wagnersche.at; www.wagnersche.at, pg 1405

Wahlstrom & Widstrand (Sweden) *Tel:* (08) 696 84 80 *Fax:* (08) 696 83 80 *E-mail:* info@wwd.se *Web Site:* www.wwd.se, pg 687

B Wahlstroms Bokforlag (Sweden) *Tel:* (08) 728 23 00 *Web Site:* www.wahlstroms.se, pg 687

Wakefield Press Pty Ltd (Australia) *Tel:* (08) 8362 8800 *Fax:* (08) 8362 7592 *E-mail:* orders@wakefieldpress. com.au *Web Site:* www.wakefieldpress.com.au, pg 43

Uitgeversmaatschappij Walburg Pers (Netherlands) *Tel:* (0575) 510522; (0575) 590336 (press) *Fax:* (0575) 542289 *E-mail:* info@walburgpers. nl; publiciteit@walburgpers.nl *Web Site:* www. walburgpers.nl, pg 543

Waldgut Verlag & Atelier Bodoni (Switzerland) *Tel:* (052) 728 89 28 *Fax:* (052) 728 89 27 *E-mail:* info@waldgut.ch; bestellung@waldgut.ch *Web Site:* www.waldgut.ch, pg 708

Waldhardt Verlag (Germany) *Tel:* (06424) 30928901 *Fax:* (06424) 30928909 *Web Site:* waldhardt.com, pg 344

Walhalla Fachverlag (Germany) *Tel:* (0941) 56 84-0 *Fax:* (0941) 56 84-111 *E-mail:* walhalla@walhalla.de *Web Site:* www.walhalla.de, pg 344

Walker Books Australia (Australia) *Tel:* (02) 9517 9577 *Fax:* (02) 9517 9997 *E-mail:* sales@walkerbooks. com.au; marketingwba@walkerbooks.com.au; permissionswba@walkerbooks.com.au *Web Site:* www. walkerbooks.com.au, pg 43

Walker Books Ltd (United Kingdom) *Tel:* (020) 7793 0909 *E-mail:* export@walker.co.uk; editorial@walker. co.uk; customerservices@walker.co.uk *Web Site:* www. walker.co.uk, pg 843

Wallflower Press (United Kingdom) *E-mail:* info@ wallflowerpress.co.uk *Web Site:* www.wallflowerpress. co.uk, pg 843

Wallstein Verlag GmbH (Germany) *Tel:* (0551) 548 98-0 *Fax:* (0551) 548 98-33 *E-mail:* info@wallstein-verlag. de *Web Site:* www.wallstein-verlag.de, pg 344

Hiram S Walters Resource Center (Jamaica) *Tel:* (876) 618-1652 *Fax:* (876) 962-0075 *E-mail:* library@ncu. edu.jm *Web Site:* www.ncu.edu.jm/library, pg 1606

Walther-Schuecking-Institut fuer Internationales Recht an der Universitaet Kiel (Germany) *Tel:* (0431) 880 2367; (0431) 880 2153 *Fax:* (0431) 880 1619 *E-mail:* fb. internat-recht@ub.uni-kiel.de; uno@internat-recht. uni.kiel.de *Web Site:* www.uni-kiel.de/internat-recht, pg 1596

Wydawnictwo WAM (Poland) *Tel:* (12) 629 32 00 *Fax:* (12) 429 50 03 *E-mail:* wam@ wydawnictwowam.pl *Web Site:* www. wydawnictwowam.pl, pg 575

Wanderer Werbedruck Horst Wanderer GmbH (Germany) *Tel:* (0511) 13 22 11 50 *Fax:* (0511) 13 22 11 55 *E-mail:* offizin@wanderer-druck.de *Web Site:* www. wanderer-druckerei.de, pg 1323

Wanger Advokaturbuero (Liechtenstein) *Tel:* 237 52 52 *Fax:* 237 52 53 *E-mail:* office@wanger.net *Web Site:* www.wanger.net, pg 500

Verlag Mag Johann Wanzenboeck (Austria) *Tel:* (01) 7148542 *Fax:* (01) 7135814, pg 60

Antiquariat Dr Wolfgang Wanzke (Germany) *Tel:* (08238) 9657758 *E-mail:* antiquariat.wanzke@t-online.de *Web Site:* antiquariat-wanzke.antiquar.de, pg 1419

The Warburg Institute (United Kingdom) *Tel:* (020) 7862 8949 *Fax:* (020) 7862 8955 *E-mail:* warburg@sas.ac. uk; warburg.books@sas.ac.uk (orders) *Web Site:* www. warburg.sas.ac.uk, pg 843

Warc (United Kingdom) *Tel:* (020) 7467 8100 *Fax:* (020) 7467 8101 *E-mail:* enquiries@warc.com *Web Site:* www.warc.com, pg 843

Peter Ward Book Exports (United Kingdom) *Tel:* (020) 8672 1171, pg 1247

Frederick Warne Publishers Ltd (United Kingdom) *Tel:* (020) 7010 3000 *Web Site:* www.penguin.com/ meet/publishers/frederickwarne, pg 843

Uwe Warnke Verlag Entwerter/Oder (Germany) *Tel:* (030) 29049903, pg 345

Windhoeker Buchhandlung Ltd (Namibia) *Tel:* (061) 225216; (061) 225036 *Fax:* (061) 225011 *Web Site:* www.wbuch.iway.na/book_e.htm, pg 1437

Windhorse Books (Australia) *Tel:* (02) 9519 8826 *Fax:* (02) 9519 8827 *E-mail:* books@windhorse.com. au *Web Site:* www.windhorse.com.au, pg 1404

Windhorse Publications Ltd (United Kingdom) *Tel:* (01223) 213300 *E-mail:* info@ windhorsepublications.com *Web Site:* www. windhorsepublications.com, pg 846

Windmill Books Ltd (United Kingdom) *Tel:* (020) 7424 5640 *Fax:* (020) 7424 5641 *Web Site:* www. windmillbooks.co.uk; www.brownbearbooks.co.uk, pg 846

Windmuehle Verlag GmbH (Germany) *Tel:* (040) 679430-0 *Fax:* (040) 67943030 *E-mail:* info@ windmuehle-verlag.de *Web Site:* www.windmuehle-verlag.de, pg 348

Windpferd Verlagsgesellschaft mbH (Germany) *Tel:* (08322) 987-1149 *Fax:* (08322) 987-1489 *E-mail:* info@windpferd.de *Web Site:* www.windpferd. de, pg 348

Windward Publications Pty Ltd (Australia) *Tel:* (02) 4464 1977 *Fax:* (02) 4464 1906 *E-mail:* sales@ windward.com.au *Web Site:* www.windward.com.au, pg 43

Windy Hollow Books (Australia) *E-mail:* info@ windyhollowbooks.com.au; sales@windyhollowbooks. com.au *Web Site:* www.windyhollowbooks.com.au, pg 43

Winetitles Media Pty Ltd (Australia) *Tel:* (08) 8369 9500 *Fax:* (08) 8369 9501 *E-mail:* info@winetitles.com.au; editorial@winetitles.com.au; orders@winetitles.com.au *Web Site:* www.winetitles.com.au; www.winebiz. au, pg 43

Wing King Tong Group (Hong Kong) *Tel:* 2407 3287 *Fax:* 2408 7939 *E-mail:* marketing@wktco.com *Web Site:* www.wkt.cc, pg 1259, 1279, 1326, 1346

Verlag Dr Dieter Winkler (Germany) *Tel:* (0234) 9650200 *Fax:* (0234) 9650201 *E-mail:* order@ winklerverlag.com *Web Site:* www.winklerverlag.com, pg 348

Winter&Company UK Ltd (United Kingdom) *Tel:* (01480) 377177 *Fax:* (01480) 377166 *E-mail:* sales@winteruk.com *Web Site:* www.winter-company.com, pg 1349

Edition Winterwork (Germany) *Tel:* (034291) 3172-0 *Fax:* (034291) 3172-16 *E-mail:* mail@edition-winterwork.de *Web Site:* www.edition-winterwork.de, pg 1323

Verlag fuer Wirtschaft und Verwaltung Hubert Wingen GmbH & Co KG (Germany) *Tel:* (0201) 22 25 41 *Fax:* (0201) 22 96 60 *E-mail:* wingenverlag@t-online. de *Web Site:* www.wingenverlag.de, pg 348

Wisby & Wilkens (Denmark) *Tel:* 64 67 08 64 *E-mail:* mail@bogshop.dk *Web Site:* www.bogshop.dk, pg 141

Wisdom Tree (India) *Tel:* (011) 23247966; (011) 23247967; (011) 23247968 *E-mail:* frontoffice@ wisdomtreeindia.com; editor@wisdomtreeindia. com; sales@wisdomtreeindia.com *Web Site:* www. wisdomtreeindia.com, pg 404

Verlag Wissen & Literatur Frido Flade GmbH (Germany) *Tel:* (089) 278 134 17 *Fax:* (089) 273 128 91 *E-mail:* info@vmw-flade.de *Web Site:* www.vmw-flade.de; vmw-flade.jimdo.com, pg 348

Verlag Wissen-Kompakt GmbH (Germany) *Tel:* (069) 9819-1682 *Fax:* (069) 9819-1681 *E-mail:* info@ wissen-kompakt.eu *Web Site:* www.wissen-kompakt.eu, pg 348

Wissenschaftliche Verlagsgesellschaft mbH (Germany) *Tel:* (0711) 2582 0; (0711) 2582 341 *Fax:* (0711) 2582 290; (0711) 2582 390 *E-mail:* service@ wissenschaftliche-verlagsgesellschaft.de *Web Site:* www.wissenschaftliche-verlagsgesellschaft. de, pg 348

Wissenschaftsrat (Germany) *Tel:* (0221) 37 76-0 *Fax:* (0221) 38 84 40 *E-mail:* post@wissenschaftsrat. de *Web Site:* www.wissenschaftsrat.de, pg 348

WIT Press (United Kingdom) *Tel:* (0238) 029 3223 *Fax:* (0238) 029 2853 *E-mail:* witpress@witpress.com; marketing@witpress.com *Web Site:* www.witpress. com, pg 846

Witherby Publishing Group (United Kingdom) *Tel:* (01506) 463 227 *Fax:* (01506) 468 999 *E-mail:* info@witherbys.com *Web Site:* www. witherbypublishinggroup.com, pg 847

Witman Publishing Co (HK) Ltd (Hong Kong) *Tel:* 2562 6279 *Fax:* 2565 5482 *E-mail:* info@witmanhk.com; sales@witmanhk.com *Web Site:* www.witmanhk.com, pg 367

Wits University Press (South Africa) *Tel:* (011) 717 8700; (011) 717 8701 *Fax:* (011) 717 8708 *E-mail:* witspress@wup.wits.ac.za *Web Site:* witspress. co.za, pg 619

Wittgenstein Verlag (Germany) *Tel:* (09092) 911570 *Fax:* (09092) 911572 *E-mail:* info@wittgenstein-verlag.de *Web Site:* www.wittgenstein-verlag.de, pg 348

Friedrich Wittig Verlag GmbH (Germany) *Tel:* (0431) 55779-206; (0431) 55779-285 (orders) *Fax:* (0431) 55779-292 *E-mail:* vertrieb@lutherische-verlag.de *Web Site:* www.evangelisches-medienwerk.de/verlage; www.kirchenshop-online.de, pg 349

The Wittmann Agency (Germany) *Tel:* (03491) 695 1243 *E-mail:* contact@the-wittmann-agency.com *Web Site:* www.the-wittmann-agency.com, pg 1229

Konrad Wittwer GmbH (Germany) *Tel:* (0711) 25 07 0 *Fax:* (0711) 25 07 145 *E-mail:* info@wittwer.de *Web Site:* www.wittwer.de, pg 349

Konrad Wittwer GmbH Verlags -und Sortimentsbuchhandlung (Germany) *Tel:* (0711) 25 07 0 *Fax:* (0711) 25 07 145 *E-mail:* info@wittwer.de *Web Site:* www.wittwer.de, pg 1419

WMG Pte Ltd (Singapore) *Tel:* 6744 9888 *Fax:* 6745 8285 *E-mail:* business@worldmarketing-group.com *Web Site:* www.wmg-group.com, pg 1333

WNT Publisher (Poland) *Tel:* (22) 240 40 20; (22) 240 40 21 *Web Site:* wnt.pl, pg 575

Wochenschau Verlag (Germany) *Tel:* (06196) 860-65 *Fax:* (06196) 860-60 *E-mail:* info@wochenschau-verlag.de *Web Site:* www.wochenschau-verlag.de, pg 349

Woeli Publishing Services (Ghana) *Fax:* (021) 777098; (021) 229294 *E-mail:* info@woelipublishing.com, pg 353

Woerterseh Verlag (Switzerland) *Tel:* (044) 368 33 68 *E-mail:* verlag@woerterseh.ch *Web Site:* www. woerterseh.ch, pg 709

Verlagshaus Wohlfarth (Germany) *Tel:* (0203) 3 0527 0 *Fax:* (0203) 3 0527 820 *E-mail:* info@wohlfarth.de *Web Site:* www.wohlfarth.de, pg 349

Koninklijke Wohrmann BV (Netherlands) *Tel:* (0575) 58 21 21 *Fax:* (0575) 58 21 28 *E-mail:* secretariaat@ wohrmann.nl *Web Site:* cpibooks.com/nl, pg 1331

Wolfau-Druck AG (Switzerland) *Tel:* (071) 622 53 53 *Fax:* (071) 622 30 04 *E-mail:* wolfau-druck@bluewin. ch, pg 709

J E Wolfensberger AG (Switzerland) *Tel:* (044) 285 78 78 *Fax:* (044) 285 78 79 *E-mail:* office@ wolfensberger-ag.ch *Web Site:* www.wolfensberger-ag.ch, pg 709

J E Wolfensberger AG (Switzerland) *Tel:* (044) 285 78 78 *E-mail:* office@wolfensberger-ag.ch *Web Site:* www.wolfensberger-ag.ch, pg 1335

Kinderbuchverlag Wolff (Germany) *Tel:* (069) 50 68 21 34 *E-mail:* info@kinderbuchverlagwolff.de *Web Site:* www.kinderbuchverlagwolff.de, pg 349

Wolff Verlag R Eberhardt (Germany) *Tel:* (0162) 2877301 *E-mail:* kontakt@wolffverlag.de *Web Site:* www.wolffverlag.de; www.roberteberhardt. com, pg 349

Johann Wolfgang Goethe-Universitaet Frankfurt am Main (Germany) *Tel:* (069) 798-0 *Fax:* (069) 798-28383 *E-mail:* praesident@uni-frankfurt.de *Web Site:* www. rz.uni-frankfurt.de; www.uni-frankfurt.de, pg 349

Wolfhound Press Ltd (Ireland), pg 415

Kunstverlag Wolfrum (Austria) *Tel:* (01) 512 53 98-0 *Fax:* (01) 512 53 98-57 *E-mail:* wolfrum@wolfrum.at *Web Site:* www.wolfrum.at, pg 60, 1405

Wolke Verlags GmbH (Germany) *Tel:* (06192) 72 43 *Fax:* (06192) 95 29 39 *E-mail:* info@wolke-verlag.de *Web Site:* www.wolke-verlag.de, pg 349

Wolters Kluwer Deutschland GmbH (Germany) *Tel:* (0221) 94373-7000 *Fax:* (0221) 94373-7201 *E-mail:* info@wolterskluwer.de *Web Site:* www. wolterskluwer.de, pg 349

Wolters Kluwer Espana SA (Spain) *Tel:* 916 020 000 *E-mail:* clientes@laley.es *Web Site:* www. wolterskluwer.es, pg 676

Wolters Kluwer SA (Poland) *Tel:* (22) 535 88 00 *E-mail:* handel@wolterskluwer.pl *Web Site:* www. wolterskluwer.pl, pg 575

Wombat Books (Australia) *Tel:* (07) 3245 1938 *E-mail:* wombat@wombatbooks.com.au *Web Site:* www.wombatbooks.com.au, pg 44

Women in Publishing (United Kingdom) *E-mail:* web@ womeninpublishing.org.uk *Web Site:* www. womeninpublishing.org.uk, pg 1398

Sam Woode Ltd, Educational Publishers (Ghana) *Tel:* (030) 2305287 *Fax:* (030) 2310482 *E-mail:* info@ samwoode.com *Web Site:* www.samwoode.com, pg 353

The Woodfield Press (Ireland) *Tel:* (01) 454 7991 *E-mail:* woodfield-press@mail.com *Web Site:* www. woodfield-press.com, pg 415

Woodhead Publishing (United Kingdom) *Tel:* (01223) 499140 *E-mail:* wp@woodheadpublishing.com *Web Site:* store.elsevier.com/woodhead-publishing, pg 847

Woodslane Pty Ltd (Australia) *Tel:* (02) 8445 2300 *Fax:* (02) 9997 5850 *E-mail:* info@woodslane.com.au *Web Site:* www.woodslane.com.au, pg 44, 1404

Woongjin ThinkBig Co Ltd (South Korea) *Tel:* (031) 956-7111; (031) 956-7365 *Fax:* (031) 956-7579 *Web Site:* www.wjthinkbig.com, pg 625

The Word Factory Ltd (United Kingdom) *Tel:* (0115) 914 5654 *Web Site:* www.thewordfactory.co.uk, pg 1263

Word of Life Press (South Korea) *Tel:* (02) 595 3545 *Fax:* (02) 591 9103 *E-mail:* int@lifebook.co.kr; shopping@lifebook.co.kr *Web Site:* www.lifebook.co. kr, pg 625

WordAlive Publishers Ltd (Kenya) *Tel:* (020) 357 2380 *Fax:* (020) 357 2382 *E-mail:* info@ wordalivepublishers.com; sales@wordalivepublishers. com *Web Site:* www.wordalivepublishers.com, pg 495

words & pictures (United Kingdom) *Tel:* (020) 7800 8043 *Fax:* (020) 7700 8066 *Web Site:* www. quartoknows.com/words-pictures, pg 847

Wordsworth Editions Ltd (United Kingdom) *Tel:* (01920) 465167 *Fax:* (01920) 462267 *E-mail:* enquiries@ wordsworth-editions.com; sales@wordsworth-editions. com *Web Site:* www.wordsworth-editions.com, pg 847

Working Title Press (Australia) *Tel:* (08) 8232 0226 *Web Site:* www.workingtitlepress.com.au, pg 44

World Agroforestry Centre (Kenya) *Tel:* (020) 722 4000 *Fax:* (020) 722 4001 *E-mail:* worldagroforestry@cgiar. org *Web Site:* www.worldagroforestry.org, pg 495

The World Book Co Ltd (Taiwan) *Tel:* (02) 2311-0183; (02) 2311-3834 *Fax:* (02) 2331-7963 *E-mail:* wbc. ltd@msa.hinet.net *Web Site:* worldbook.com.tw, pg 713

World Book Publishing (Lebanon) *Tel:* (01) 659894 *Fax:* (01) 659894 *E-mail:* info@wbpbooks.com; marketing@wbpbooks.com; rights@wbpbooks.com; editor@wbpbooks.com *Web Site:* www.wbpbooks.com; www.arabook.com, pg 499

World Council of Churches (WCC Publications) (Switzerland) *Tel:* (022) 791 6171 *Fax:* (022) 791 6346 *E-mail:* publications@wcc-coe.org *Web Site:* www.oikoumene.org; publications. oikoumene.org, pg 709

World Editions Ltd (Netherlands) *E-mail:* info@ worldeditions.org *Web Site:* www.worldeditions.org, pg 543

World Health Organization (WHO) (Switzerland) *Tel:* (022) 791 32 64 *Fax:* (022) 791 48 57 *E-mail:* bookorders@who.int; publications@who.int *Web Site:* www.who.int/bookorders, pg 709

World Intellectual Property Organization (WIPO) (Switzerland) *Tel:* (022) 338 9111 *Fax:* (022) 733 5428 *Web Site:* www.wipo.int, pg 1392

World Knowledge Publishing House (China) *Tel:* (010) 65232695 *Fax:* (010) 65233645 *E-mail:* 274271772@ qq.com; wapnet_cn@sina.com, pg 112

World Meteorological Organization (WMO) (Switzerland) *Tel:* (022) 730 81 11 *Fax:* (022) 730 81 81 *E-mail:* cpa@wmo.int *Web Site:* www.wmo.int, pg 709

World Microfilms Publications Ltd (United Kingdom) *Tel:* (020) 7586 4499 *E-mail:* microworld@ndirect.co. uk, pg 847

World of Islam Altajir Trust (United Kingdom) *Tel:* (020) 7581 3522 *Fax:* (020) 7584 1977 *E-mail:* awitrust@tiscali.co.uk *Web Site:* www. altajirtrust.org.uk, pg 847

World Scientific Publishing Co Pte Ltd (Singapore) *Tel:* 6466 5775 *Fax:* 6467 7667 *E-mail:* wspc@ wspc.com.sg; sales@wspc.com.sg; editor@wspc. com.sg; mkt@wspc.com.sg; rights@wspc.com.sg *Web Site:* www.worldscientific.com, pg 607

World Sport Publishers' Association (WSPA) (Germany) *Tel:* (02) 41 958 10-32 *Fax:* (02) 41 958 10-33 *E-mail:* info@w-s-p-a.org *Web Site:* www.w-s-p-a.org, pg 1375

World Tourism Organization (UNWTO) (Spain) *Tel:* 91 567 81 00 *Fax:* 91 571 37 33 *E-mail:* info@unwto.org *Web Site:* www.unwto.org, pg 676

Worlddidac Association (Switzerland) *Tel:* (031) 311 76 82 *Fax:* (031) 312 17 44 *E-mail:* info@worlddidac.org *Web Site:* www.worlddidac.org, pg 1392

Worldwide Book Services Ltd (United Kingdom) *Tel:* (01268) 574110 *Fax:* (01268) 574123 *E-mail:* info@worldwidebookservices.com *Web Site:* www.worldwidebookservices.com, pg 1461

Worms Verlag (Germany) *Tel:* (06241) 2000314 *Fax:* (06241) 2000399 *E-mail:* info@kvg-worms.de *Web Site:* wormsverlag.de, pg 349

Verlag DAS WORT GmbH (Germany) *Tel:* (09391) 504135 *Fax:* (09391) 504133 *E-mail:* info@das-wort.com; info@gabriele-verlag.de *Web Site:* www. universal-spirit.cc; www.gabriele-verlag.de, pg 349

WortArt (Germany) *Tel:* (0221) 99 22 77 90 *Fax:* (0221) 99 22 77 920 *E-mail:* info@wortart.de *Web Site:* wortart.de, pg 349

Worth Press Ltd (United Kingdom) *Tel:* (01763) 248075 *Fax:* (01763) 248155, pg 847

The Writers' Guild of Great Britain (WGGB) (United Kingdom) *Tel:* (020) 7833 0777 *E-mail:* admin@ writersguild.org.uk *Web Site:* writersguild.org.uk, pg 1398

The Writers Publishing House (China) *Tel:* (010) 65389156 *Fax:* (010) 65389156 *E-mail:* haozuojia@ 163.com *Web Site:* www.zuojiachubanshe.com, pg 112

Writers Victoria (Australia) *Tel:* (03) 9094 7855 *Fax:* (03) 9650 8010 *Web Site:* writersvictoria.org.au, pg 1490

WTO (World Trade Organization) (Switzerland) *Tel:* (022) 739 51 11 *Fax:* (022) 731 42 06 *E-mail:* enquiries@wto.org; publications@wto.org *Web Site:* www.wto.org, pg 1392

Wu Nan Book Co Ltd (Taiwan) *Tel:* (02) 27055066 *Fax:* (02) 27066100 *E-mail:* wunan@wunan.com.tw *Web Site:* www.wunan.com.tw, pg 713

Wuerttembergische Bibliotheksgesellschaft (Germany) *Tel:* (0711) 212-4428 *Fax:* (0711) 212-4422 *E-mail:* wbg@wlb-stuttgart.de *Web Site:* www.wlb-stuttgart.de, pg 1653

Wuerttembergische Landesbibliothek (Germany) *Tel:* (0711) 212-4454; (0711) 212-4468; (0711) 212-4424 *Fax:* (0711) 212-4422 *E-mail:* direktion@ wlb-stuttgart.de; information@wlb-stuttgart.de *Web Site:* www.wlb-stuttgart.de, pg 1596

Wuhan University Press (China) *Tel:* (027) 87215593; (027) 87215822 *Fax:* (027) 87215541 *Web Site:* www. wdp.com.cn, pg 112

Verlag Das Wunderhorn GmbH (Germany) *Tel:* (06221) 40 24 28 *Fax:* (06221) 40 24 83 *E-mail:* info@ wunderhorn.de; wunderhorn.verlag@t-online.de *Web Site:* www.wunderhorn.de, pg 349

Wunderlich Verlag (Germany) *Tel:* (040) 72 72 0 *Fax:* (040) 72 72 319 *E-mail:* info@rowohlt.de *Web Site:* www.rowohlt.de/verlag/wunderlich, pg 350

Wytwornia (Poland) *E-mail:* wytwornia@wytwornia.com *Web Site:* wytwornia.com, pg 576

XACT Books (India) *Tel:* 9810563212 (cell) *E-mail:* mohinder.xact@gmail.com *Web Site:* www. xactbook.com, pg 404

XACT Studio International (India) *Tel:* (011) 9810563212 *E-mail:* mohinder.xact@gmail.com *Web Site:* www.xactbook.com, pg 1328

Xander Uitgevers (Netherlands) *Tel:* (020) 3033950 *Web Site:* www.xanderuitgevers.nl, pg 543

Ediciones Xandro (Spain) *Tel:* 91 552 02 61 *Fax:* 91 501 41 45 *E-mail:* soespgraf@soespgraf.com *Web Site:* www.soespgraf.com, pg 676

Edition Xanthippe (Switzerland) *Tel:* (044) 251 03 02; (079) 230 84 43 (cell) *E-mail:* info@xanthippe.ch *Web Site:* www.xanthippe.ch, pg 709

Editions Xenia SA (Switzerland) *Tel:* (027) 327 53 67 *Fax:* (027) 327 53 66 *E-mail:* info@editions-xenia. com *Web Site:* www.editions-xenia.com, pg 709

Xenos Verlag (Germany) *Tel:* (040) 39 804 400 *Fax:* (040) 39 804 390; (040) 39 804 388 (sales) *E-mail:* nelson@carlsen.de *Web Site:* www.carlsen. de/xenos/, pg 350

Edicions Xerais de Galicia (Spain) *Tel:* 986 214 888; 986 214 880 *Fax:* 986 201 366 *E-mail:* xerais@xerais. es; xeraispedidos@xerais.es (orders) *Web Site:* www. xerais.es, pg 676

Xiamen International Book Co (XIBC) (China) *Tel:* (0592) 8060988; (0592) 8060900 *Fax:* (0592) 8060989 *E-mail:* wtxmsc@xmwaitu.com *Web Site:* www.xibc.com.cn, pg 1410

Xiamen University Library (China) *Tel:* (0592) 2180000 *E-mail:* librarian@xmu.edu.cn *Web Site:* library.xmu. edu.cn; www.xmu.edu.cn, pg 1582

Xiamen University Press (China) *Tel:* (0592) 2181111; (0592) 2182177 *Fax:* (0592) 2181406 *E-mail:* xmup@ xmupress.com *Web Site:* www.xmupress.com, pg 112

Xinhua Publishing House (China) *Tel:* (010) 63073021; (010) 63077116 (editorial) *Fax:* (010) 63073880 *E-mail:* xh_zb@xinhuanet.com; ra98@xinhuanet.com *Web Site:* www.xinhuapub.com, pg 112

XO Editions (France) *Tel:* 01 56 80 26 80; 01 56 80 26 81 (press) *Fax:* 01 56 80 26 72 *E-mail:* press@ xoeditions.com; edito@xoeditions.com; commercial@ xoeditions.com; foreignrights@xoeditions.com *Web Site:* www.xoeditions.com, pg 200

Xunhasaba Corp (Vietnam) *Tel:* (04) 3936 1795; (04) 3826 2989 *Fax:* (04) 3825 2860 *E-mail:* xunhasaba@ hn.vnn.vn *Web Site:* www.xunhasaba.com.vn, pg 1462

Xunta de Galicia (Spain) *Tel:* 981 54 54 00 *E-mail:* 012@xunta.es *Web Site:* www.xunta.gal/ portada, pg 676

Edition XXL GmbH (Germany) *Tel:* (06164) 50 41-0 *Fax:* (06164) 50 41-41; (06164) 50 41-42 (sales) *E-mail:* info@xxl-medien-service.de *Web Site:* www. xxl-medien-service.de, pg 350

XY.IT Editore SRL (Italy) *Tel:* (0322) 019200 *Fax:* (0322) 019209 *E-mail:* info@editorexy.it *Web Site:* www.editorexy.com, pg 471

YachayPucllayPacha (Peru) *Tel:* (02) 54 05 42 *Web Site:* yachaypucllaypacha.pe, pg 563

Yachdav United Publishers Co Ltd (Israel) *Tel:* (03) 5614121 *Fax:* (03) 5611996 *E-mail:* info@tbpai.co.il; hamol@tbpai.co.il *Web Site:* www.tbpai.co.il, pg 422

Yad Ben-Zvi Press (Israel) *Tel:* (02) 5398888 *Fax:* (02) 5638310 *E-mail:* ybz@ybz.org.il *Web Site:* ybz.org.il, pg 422

Yad Tabenkin-The Research & Document Center of the Kibbutz Movement (Israel) *Tel:* (03) 5344458 *Fax:* (03) 5346376 *E-mail:* yadtabmaz@bezeqint.net *Web Site:* www.yadtabenkin.org.il, pg 422

Yad Vashem - The Holocaust Martyrs' & Heroes' Remembrance Authority (Israel) *Tel:* (02) 6443768 *Fax:* (02) 6443509 *E-mail:* publications.marketing@ yadvashem.org.il *Web Site:* www.yadvashem.org, pg 422

Yakuji Nippo Ltd (Japan) *Tel:* (03) 3862-2141 *Fax:* (03) 3866-8408 *E-mail:* shuppan@yakuji.co.jp *Web Site:* www.yakuji.co.jp, pg 490

Yale University Press London (United Kingdom) *Tel:* (020) 7079 4900 *Fax:* (020) 7079 4901 *E-mail:* sales@yaleup.co.uk *Web Site:* www.yalebooks. co.uk, pg 847

Yama-Kei Publishers Co Ltd (Japan) *Tel:* (03) 6744-1900 *E-mail:* info@yamakei.co.jp; eigyo@yamakei.co.jp (sales) *Web Site:* www.yamakei.co.jp, pg 490

Yamaguchi-Shoten (Japan) *Tel:* (075) 781-6121 *Fax:* (075) 705-2003 *Web Site:* www.yamaguchi-shoten.co.jp, pg 490

Julio F Yanez Agencia Literaria SL (Spain) *Tel:* 932 007 107; 932 005 443 *Fax:* 932 007 656, pg 1236

Eric Yang Agency (South Korea) *Tel:* (02) 592-3356 *Fax:* (02) 592-3359 *E-mail:* info@ericyangagency.co. kr *Web Site:* www.ericyangagency.co.kr, pg 1234

Yapi-Endustri Merkezi (YEM) (Turkey) *Tel:* (0212) 266 70 70 *Fax:* (0212) 266 70 10 *E-mail:* yem@yem.net *Web Site:* www.yem.net, pg 724

Yapi Kredi Kultur Sanat ve Yayincilik AS (Turkey) *Tel:* (0212) 252 47 00 *Fax:* (0212) 293 07 23 *E-mail:* ykkultur@ykykultur.com.tr; hulya.kaya@ ykykultur.com.tr (sales) *Web Site:* www.ykykultur.com. tr, pg 724

Yaran Yayincilik Tic Ltd (Turkey) *Tel:* (0216) 449 49 09 *Fax:* (0216) 449 49 11, pg 724

Yarmouk University Library (Jordan) *Tel:* (02) 7211111 (ext 2871) *E-mail:* library@yu.edu.jo *Web Site:* www. yu.edu.jo; library.yu.edu.jo, pg 1607

Roy Yates Books (United Kingdom) *Tel:* (01403) 822 299, pg 1461

Yavneh Publishing House Ltd (Israel) *Tel:* (03) 6297856 *Fax:* (03) 6293638 *E-mail:* publishing@yavneh.co.il, pg 423

Yayasan Lontar (Indonesia) *Tel:* (021) 574-6880 *Fax:* (021) 572-0353 *E-mail:* contact@lontar.org *Web Site:* www.lontar.org, pg 407

Yayasan Obor Indonesia (Indonesia) *Tel:* (021) 31920114; (021) 31926978 *Fax:* (021) 31924488 *E-mail:* yayasan_obor@cbn.net.id *Web Site:* www. obor.or.id, pg 407

Literatur Yayincilik Ltd (Turkey) *Tel:* (0212) 292 41 20 *E-mail:* literatur@literatur.com.tr *Web Site:* www. literatur.com.tr, pg 724

Zeitgeist Media GmbH Verlag und Neue Medien (Germany) *Tel:* (0211) 556255 *Fax:* (0211) 575167 *E-mail:* info@zeitgeistmedia.de *Web Site:* www.zeitgeistmedia.de, pg 350

Zeitgeist Media Group Agency (Belgium) *Tel:* (0479) 262843 *Web Site:* www.zeitgeistmediagroup.com, pg 1224

Zeitgut Verlag GmbH (Germany) *Tel:* (030) 70 20 93 0 *Fax:* (030) 70 20 93 22 *E-mail:* info@zeitgut.com *Web Site:* www.zeitgut.com, pg 350

Zellige (France) *Tel:* 01 64 00 86 92 *Fax:* 01 64 00 86 92 *E-mail:* zellige.edition@orange.fr *Web Site:* www.zellige.eu, pg 200

Zenkoku Kyoudou Publishing Co Ltd (Japan) *Tel:* (03) 3359-4811 (sales); (03) 3359-4815 (editorial) *Fax:* (03) 3358-6174 (sales); (03) 3341-3919 (editorial) *Web Site:* www.zenkyou.com, pg 491

Zeno Agency Ltd (United Kingdom) *Tel:* (020) 7096 0927 *E-mail:* info@zenoagency.com *Web Site:* zenoagency.com, pg 1247

Zentral- und Landesbibliothek Berlin (ZLB) (Germany) *Tel:* (030) 90226-401 *E-mail:* info@zlb.de *Web Site:* www.zlb.de, pg 1597

Zentralbibliothek Zuerich (Switzerland) *Tel:* (044) 2683 100 *Fax:* (044) 2683 290 *E-mail:* info@zb.uzh.ch *Web Site:* www.zb.uzh.ch, pg 1636

Zero a Oito (Portugal) *Tel:* 213 713 130 *Fax:* 213 713 139 *E-mail:* geral@zeroaoito.pt *Web Site:* www.zeroaoito.pt, pg 583

Ediciones Zeta SRL (Peru) *Tel:* (01) 4711966, pg 1443

Editorial Zeus SRL (Argentina) *Tel:* (0341) 449 5585 *Fax:* (0341) 425 4259 *E-mail:* zeus@zeus.com.ar *Web Site:* www.zeus.com.ar, pg 13

Susanna Zevi Agenzia Letteraria (Italy) *Tel:* (02) 6570863 *Fax:* (02) 6570915 *E-mail:* office@agenzia-zevi.it; segretaria@agenzia-zevi.it *Web Site:* www.susannazevi.com, pg 1231

ZheJiang Education Publishing House (China) *Tel:* (0571) 88908755; (0571) 88909753; (0571) 88909727 *Fax:* (0571) 88909717 *E-mail:* zjjy@zjcb.com; jys@zjcb.com *Web Site:* www.zjeph.com, pg 112

Zhejiang Provincial Library (China) *Tel:* (0571) 8798 8338 *E-mail:* zjdh@zjlib.cn *Web Site:* www.zjlib.net.cn, pg 1582

Zhejiang University Press (China) *Tel:* (0571) 88215650; (0571) 88273066 *Fax:* (0571) 88215650; (0571) 88273066 *E-mail:* zupress@zju.edu.cn; zup_hr@126.com *Web Site:* www.zjupress.com, pg 112

Zhongguo guojia tushuguan (China) *Tel:* (010) 88545426; (010) 88544114; (010) 88545022; (010) 88545360 *E-mail:* webmaster@nlc.gov.cn *Web Site:* www.nlc.gov.cn, pg 1582

Zhonghua Book Co (China) *Tel:* (010) 63458236; (010) 63311241 *E-mail:* zhbc@zhbc.com.cn *Web Site:* www.zhbc.com.cn, pg 112

Verlag im Ziegelhaus (Germany) *Tel:* (0711) 46 63 63 *Fax:* (0711) 46 13 41 *Web Site:* www.verlag-im-ziegelhaus.de, pg 351

Wydawnictwo Zielona Sowa Sp z oo (Poland) *Tel:* (22) 576 25 50 *Fax:* (22) 576 25 51 *E-mail:* wydawnictwo@zielonasowa.pl *Web Site:* www.zielonasowa.pl, pg 576

Ziethen-Panorama Verlag GmbH (ZVP) (Germany) *Tel:* (030) 253-6047 *Fax:* (02) 253-6756 *E-mail:* mail@ziethen-panoramaverlag.de *Web Site:* www.ziethen-panoramaverlag.de, pg 351

Empresa Editora Zig-Zag SA (Chile) *Tel:* (02) 2810 7400 *Fax:* (02) 2810 7452 *E-mail:* contacto@zigzag.cl *Web Site:* www.zigzag.cl, pg 100

Zikrul Hakim-Bestari (Indonesia) *Tel:* 0813 2090 0052 (cell) *Fax:* (021) 4754429 *E-mail:* zikrulbestari@gmail.com *Web Site:* www.penerbitbestari.com, pg 408

Zimbabwe Book Publishers Association (ZBPA) (Zimbabwe) *Tel:* (04) 773236 *Fax:* (04) 754256, pg 1399

Zimbabwe Geological Survey (Zimbabwe) *Tel:* (04) 707749; (04) 707716 *E-mail:* zimgeosurvey@mines.gov.zw, pg 1645

Zimbabwe Women Writers (ZWW) (Zimbabwe), pg 853

Zimbabwe Women's Bureau (Zimbabwe) *Tel:* (04) 747441 *Toll Free Tel:* 800-450-6935; 800-450-6940, pg 853

Musikverlag Zimmermann GmbH & Co KG (Germany) *Tel:* (069) 978286-6 *Fax:* (069) 978286-79 *E-mail:* info@zimmermann-frankfurt.de; vertrieb@zimmermann-frankfurt.de *Web Site:* www.zimmermann-frankfurt.de, pg 351

Apgads Zinatne SIA (Latvia) *Tel:* 67212797; 67225767 (bookstore) *Fax:* 67227825 *E-mail:* zinatne@zinatne.com.lv *Web Site:* www.zinatnesgramatas.lv, pg 496

Zindermans Forlag (Sweden) *Tel:* (031) 775 04 00 *Fax:* (031) 12 06 60, pg 687

Zirkular - Verlag der Dokumentationsstelle fuer neuere oesterreichische Literatur (Austria) *Tel:* (01) 526 20 44-0 *Fax:* (01) 526 20 44-30 *E-mail:* info@literaturhaus.at *Web Site:* www.literaturhaus.at, pg 60

Znaci Vremena, Institut Za Istrazivanje Biblije (Croatia) *E-mail:* info@znaci-vremena.com *Web Site:* www.znaci-vremena.com, pg 123

Znanie Izdatelstvo (Russia) *Tel:* (495) 628-15-31; (495) 237-03-08 *Fax:* (495) 237-03-08; (495) 621-24-47, pg 598

Znanje doo (Croatia) *Tel:* (01) 3689-535 *Fax:* (01) 3689-531; (01) 3638-477 *E-mail:* znanje@znanje.hr; znanje-tiskara@znanje.hr *Web Site:* znanje.hr, pg 123

ZNN Literary Agency (Turkey) *Tel:* (0216) 348 37 78 *Web Site:* znnliteraryagency.com, pg 1238

Editions Zoe (Switzerland) *Tel:* (022) 309 36 06 *Fax:* (022) 309 36 03 *E-mail:* info@editionszoe.ch; commandes@editionszoe.ch *Web Site:* www.editionszoe.ch, pg 709

ZOOlibri (Italy) *Tel:* (0522) 330566 *Fax:* (0522) 330566 *E-mail:* info@zoolibri.com; press@zoolibri.com; rights@zoolibri.com *Web Site:* www.zoolibri.com, pg 471

Libros del Zorro Rojo (Spain) *Tel:* 933 076 850; 931 853 412 *Fax:* 931 853 412 *E-mail:* info@librosdelzorrorojo.com; rights@librosdelzorrorojo.com; export@librosdelzorrorojo.com *Web Site:* www.librosdelzorrorojo.com, pg 676

Libros del Zorzal (Argentina) *E-mail:* info@delzorzal.com.ar *Web Site:* www.delzorzal.com, pg 13

Zoshindo JukenKenkyusha Publishing Co Ltd (Japan) *Tel:* (06) 6532-1581 *Fax:* (06) 6532-1588 *Web Site:* www.zoshindo.co.jp, pg 491

Zalozba ZRC (Slovenia) *Tel:* (01) 470 64 74 *Fax:* (01) 425 77 94 *E-mail:* zalozba@zrc-sazu.si; narocanje@zrc-sazu.si *Web Site:* zalozba.zrc-sazu.si; www.zrc-sazu.si, pg 612

Zrinski (Croatia) *Tel:* (040) 37 22 22; (040) 37 22 77 (sales) *Fax:* (040) 37 22 12 *E-mail:* zrinski@zrinski.hr *Web Site:* www.zrinski.com, pg 123

Zrinyi Kiado (Hungary) *Tel:* (01) 459 5327 *Fax:* (01) 459 5382 *Web Site:* www.hmzrinyi.hu, pg 372

ZS Verlag GmbH (Germany) *Tel:* (089) 548 25 15-0 *Fax:* (089) 548 25 15-222 *E-mail:* contact@zsverlag.de; rights@zsverlag.de; vertrieb@zsverlag.de *Web Site:* www.zs-verlag.com, pg 351

Paul Zsolnay Verlag GmbH (Austria) *Tel:* (01) 505 76 61-0 *Fax:* (01) 505 76 61-10 *E-mail:* info@zsolnay.at *Web Site:* www.hanser-literaturverlage.de/verlage/zsolnay-deuticke, pg 60

Dietrich zu Klampen Verlag & Dr Rolf Johannes GbR (Germany) *Tel:* (05041) 801133 *Fax:* (05041) 801336 *E-mail:* info@zuklampen.de *Web Site:* www.zuklampen.de, pg 351

Zubaan (India) *Tel:* (011) 26494617; (011) 26494618; (011) 26494613 *E-mail:* contact@zubaanbooks.com *Web Site:* www.zubaanbooks.com, pg 404

W Zuckschwerdt Verlag GmbH fuer Medizin und Naturwissenschaften (Germany) *Tel:* (089) 894349-0 *Fax:* (089) 89434950 *E-mail:* post@zuckschwerdtverlag.de; info@zuckschwerdtverlag.de *Web Site:* www.zuckschwerdtverlag.de, pg 351

Zuercher Oberland Medien AG (Switzerland) *Tel:* (044) 933 32 54 *Fax:* (044) 933 32 58 *E-mail:* info@zo-shop.ch *Web Site:* www.zo-medien.ch; www.zo-shop.ch, pg 710

Zuidnederlandse Uitgeverij NV (Belgium) *Tel:* (03) 8704400 *Fax:* (03) 8772115, pg 74

Editions Zulma (France) *Tel:* 01 58 22 19 90 *Fax:* 01 58 22 19 99 *E-mail:* zulma@zulma.fr *Web Site:* www.zulma.fr, pg 200

Zvaigzne ABC (Latvia) *Tel:* 67324518 *E-mail:* reklama@zvaigzne.lv *Web Site:* www.zvaigzne.lv, pg 497

Zvazu Slovenskych Vedeckotechnickych Spolocnosti sro (Slovakia) *Tel:* (02) 5020 7649 *Fax:* (02) 5020 7656 *E-mail:* zsvts@zsvts.sk *Web Site:* www.zsvts.sk, pg 610

Zveza bibliotekarskih drustev Slovenije (ZBDS) (Slovenia) *Tel:* (01) 2001 176 *Fax:* (01) 4257 293 *E-mail:* info@zbds-zveza.si *Web Site:* www.zbds-zveza.si, pg 1660

edition zweihorn GmbH & Co KG (Germany) *Tel:* (08583) 2454 *Fax:* (08583) 91435 *E-mail:* edition-zweihorn@web.de *Web Site:* www.edition-zweihorn.de, pg 351

Zweitausendeins Versand-Dienst GmbH (Germany) *Tel:* (0341) 21 339 0 (editorial); (0341) 21 339 339 (orders) *Fax:* (0341) 21 339 179 *E-mail:* info@zweitausendeins.de; service@zweitausendeins.de *Web Site:* www.zweitausendeins.de, pg 351

Zwiazek Literatow Polskich (Poland) *Tel:* (22) 826 57 85 *Fax:* (22) 828 39 19 *E-mail:* owzlp@o2.pl *Web Site:* www.literatura.waw.pl, pg 1386

Uitgeverij Zwijsen (Belgium) *Tel:* (03) 205 94 94 *Toll Free Tel:* 0800 94362 *Fax:* (03) 205 94 99 *E-mail:* info@uitgeverijzwijsen.be *Web Site:* www.uitgeverijzwijsen.be, pg 74

Uitgeverij Zwijsen BV (Netherlands) *Tel:* (013) 583 88 00; (013) 583 88 88 (customer service) *Fax:* (013) 583 88 80 *E-mail:* klantenservice@zwijsen.nl; zwijsenwebshop@wpg.nl *Web Site:* www.zwijsen.nl, pg 543

Zysk i S-ka Wydawnictwo (Poland) *Tel:* (61) 853 27 51; (61) 853 27 67 *Fax:* (61) 852 63 26 *E-mail:* sekretariat@zysk.com.pl; marketing@zysk.com.pl *Web Site:* www.zysk.com.pl, pg 576

Zytglogge Verlag AG (Switzerland) *Tel:* (033) 244 00 30 *Fax:* (033) 244 00 33 *E-mail:* info@zytglogge.ch *Web Site:* www.zytglogge.ch, pg 710